Grammar codes

[C] countable; shows that a noun can be counted and has a plural form: *We planted an orange* **tree**. | *Children love to climb* **trees**.

[U] uncountable; shows that a noun cannot be counted and has no plural form: *I need some* **peace** *and quiet.* | *a glass of* **milk**

[I] intransitive; shows that a verb has no direct object: *I'm sure I can* **cope**. | *Our food supplies soon* **ran out**.

[T] transitive; shows that a verb is followed by a direct object which can be either a noun phrase or a clause: *I* **like** *swimming, playing tennis, and things like that.* | *I* **hope** *I'm not disturbing you.* | *We never* **found out** *her real name.*

[I,T] intransitive or transitive; shows that a verb may be used with or without a direct object: *Bernice was* **knitting** *as she watched TV.* | *She was* **knitting** *a sweater.*

[singular] shows that a noun is used only in the singular and has no plural form: *a* **mishmash** *of different styles* | *the distant* **hum** *of traffic*

[plural] shows that a noun is used only with a plural verb or pronoun and has no singular form: *electrical* **goods** | *They lost all their* **belongings** *in the fire.*

[linking verb] shows that a verb is followed by a noun or adjective complement which refers to the subject of the verb: *Her skin* **felt** *cold and rough.* | *We* **were** *hungry.* | *Sue's brother* **became** *a lawyer.*

[always + adv./prep.] shows that a verb must be followed by an adverb or a prepositional phrase: *She started to* **rummage** *around for a tissue.* | *Someone was* **lurking** *in the bushes.*

[not in progressive] shows that a verb is not used in the progressive form, i.e. the **-ing** form after **be**: *I* **hate** *housework* (not "*I am hating housework*"). | *Who* **knows** *the answer?*

[no comparative] shows that an adjective is not used in the comparative or superlative form, i.e. not with **-er** or **-est**, and not with **more** or **most**: *the* **key** *issues in the campaign.*

[only before noun] shows that an adjective can only be used before a noun: *the* **sheer** *size of the building* | *the* **main** *points of her speech*

[not before noun] shows that an adjective cannot be used before a noun: *Quiet! The baby is* **asleep**.

[only after noun] shows that an adjective is only used immediately after a noun: *There are prizes* **galore** *at the carnival.*

[sentence adverb] shows that an adverb modifies a whole sentence: **Apparently,** *they ran out of tickets.*

[+ adj./adv.] shows an adverb of degree which is followed by an adjective or another adverb: *She plays the violin* **remarkably** *well for a child her age.* | *It's a nice restaurant, but it's* **quite** *expensive.*

[+ **between**] [+ **about**] shows that a word is followed by a particular preposition: *I'm trying to* **decide** *between the green and the blue.* | *the growing* **concern** *about the effects of pollution*

[**propose that**] shows that a word can be followed by a clause beginning with **that**: *I* **propose that** *we meet again next week.*

[**sure (that)**] shows that a word can be followed by a clause beginning with **that**, or the word **that** can be left out: *I'm* **sure** *there's a logical explanation for all this.*

[**decide who/what/how etc.**] shows that a word can be followed by a word beginning with **wh-** (such as **where**, **why**, or **when**) or by **how**: *I can't* **decide** *what to do.* | *I'm not* **sure** *where Jim is.*

[**resolve to do sth**] shows that a word can be followed by an infinitive: *He* **resolved** *to apologize to her.* | *There's one boy who's* **certain** *to succeed!*

[**see sb/sth do sth**] shows that a verb can be followed by an infinitive verb without **to**: *Pat* **saw** *her drive off about an hour later.*

[**see sb doing sth**] shows that a verb can be followed by a present participle: *Several witnesses* **saw** *the suspect entering the building.*

[**get lost/trapped/caught etc.**] shows that a verb can be followed by a past participle: *He's* **getting** *married in September.*

[**bring sb sth**] shows that a verb can be followed by an indirect object and then a direct object: *Could you* **bring** *me that chair?* | *Let me* **buy** *you a drink.*

W9-BNY-514

LONGMAN

Advanced

AMERICAN

DICTIONARY

Longman

Pearson Education Limited
Edinburgh Gate
Harlow
Essex CM20 2JE
England
and associated companies throughout the world

Visit our web site:
http://www.longman.com/dictionaries

First published 2000
This edition published 2001
005   007   008   006   004

ISBN
0 582 31729 0 (Cased edition)
0 582 31731 2 (Flexicover edition)
0 582 31732 0 (Paperback edition)
0 582 504139 (Cased edition +CDRom)
0 582 504155 (Flexicover Edition)
0 582 504090 (Paperback edition +CDRom)

Library of Congress Cataloging-in-Publication Data
A catalog record for this book is available from the
Library of Congress.

British Library Cataloguing-in-Publication Data
A catalogue record for this book is available from the
British Library.

Set in 7/7.5 Nimrod
Printed in Spain by Cayfosa-Quebecor, Barcelona

Contents

Acknowledgments

Director
Della Summers

Editorial Director
Adam Gadsby

Managing Editor
Stephen Bullon

Associate Lexicographers
Karen Stern
Ruth Urbom

Senior Lexicographer
Karen Cleveland-Marwick

Lexicographers
Rebecca Campbell
Robert Clevenger
Mark Hamer
Stephen Handorf
Dileri Borunda Johnston

Assistant Lexicographers
Daniel Barron
Elizabeth Beizai
Korey Egge
Tammy Gales
Alex Henderson
Leslie Redick

Development Editor
Wendalyn Nichols

Consultant
Michael Rundell

TOEFL® section
Deborah Phillips

TOEIC® section
Lin Lougheed

Production Editor
Michael Brooks

Project Manager
Alan Savill

Production
Clive McKeough

Editorial Manager
Sheila Dallas

Corpus Development
Steve Crowdy
Kevin Fox
Duncan Pettigrew

Spoken Corpus Development
University of California at Santa Barbara:
Professor John du Bois
Professor Wallace Chafe
Professor Sandra Thompson

Pronunciation Editors
Rebecca Dauer
Dinah Jackson

Design
Paul Price-Smith
Alex Ingr
Tony Leonard
Rachel Mitchell

Proofreaders
Gerard Delaney
Alison Steadman
Jock Graham

Illustrators
Dave Bowyer, Chris Pavely, The Maltings Partnership, Joseph Scrofani (American Artists), John Woodcock, Paul Young (Artist Partners), Stephen Player (Artist Partners), Bob Corley (Artist Partners)

Administrative Assistants
Becky Keys
Denise Denney
Janine Trainor
Samantha James

Keyboarder
Pauline Savill

Typesetting
Peter White
Peter Wray
The Pen and Ink Book Co Ltd

Photo Acknowledgments
We are grateful to the following for permission to reproduce copyright photographs:

© Bartholomew Ltd 2000 for 1334 reproduced by permission of HarperCollins Publishers; Camera Press for 693 and 1219; Bruce Coleman Collection for 185, 549, 571 bottom right, 787, 946, 1193 and 1411; Comstock for 394; Corbis Images for 219, 391, 784, 845, 1100 and 1327; Mary Evans Picture Library for 386, 447 and 1329 bottom left; Ronald Grant Archive for 358 and 796; Robert Harding Picture Library for 1328 lower middle left, 1328 bottom middle and 1333 far top right; Hulton Getty Collection for 769, 783 top right, 825, 908, 1037, 1270, 1329 far top left, 1329 far top middle, 1329 far top right, 1329 upper middle upper left, 1329 top middle right, 1329 bottom right, 1329 bottom middle, 1330 far top left, 1330 far top right, 1330 upper middle left, 1330 bottom right, 1425, 1561 and 1567; Image Bank for 1464; Images Colour Library for 712, 873 bottom right, 873 top right, 1048, 1331 bottom right (Index Stock/Phyllis Picardi); 1333 bottom right (Index Stock/Mike Agliolo); The Kobal Collection for 680; Frank Lane Picture Agency for 974; PA News for 1330 far top lower right; Photo Edit for 404, 1333 far top left, 1333 top middle middle and 1540; Pictor International for 1332 bottom and 1332 bottom right; Pictures Colour Library for 777, 799, 1328 far top right, 1328 bottom left, 1331 upper middle middle, 1331 top right, 1332 bottom upper left and 1676; Popperfoto for 145, 571 top right, 1052, 1328 upper middle left, 1329 lower middle right, 1329 bottom middle left, 1333 upper middle left and 1333 lower middle right; Redferns for 115 bottom right, 354, 449, 679 bottom right and 1135; Rex Features for 34, 36, 63, 195, 248, 451, 457, 544, 679 top right, 775, 783 bottom right, 789, 869, 1398, 1329 upper middle middle and 1329 upper middle left; South American Pictures for 1185; Sporting Pictures for 1182 and 1332 middle upper right; Tony Stone Images for 13, 31, 227, 468, 631, 872, 907, 979, 1264, 1328 lower middle right, 1331 far top left, 1331 far top right, 1331 lower top right, 1331 lower middle right and 1331 lower middle left; The Stock Shop for 830, 1064, 1328 lower middle right, 1331 upper middle left, 1331 bottom left and 1333 bottom left; Superstock for 1328 upper middle right and 1328 far top left; Telegraph Colour Library for 96, 333, 623, 803, 1111, 1328 far top bottom, 1331 upper middle left, 1331 top left, 1332 middle left, 1332 middle lower right, 1333 upper middle right and 1333 lower middle left; Topham Picturepoint for 1330 lower top left, 1330 upper middle right, 1330 lower middle left, 1330 lower middle right, 1330 bottom left, 1331 lower top left; TRIP for 1333 bottom middle; Universal Pictorial Press and Agency for 68, 115 bottom left, 600 and 944.

"Many people don't realize the wealth of grammar information to be found in a dictionary. Indeed, I use dictionaries as my primary references when writing ELT grammar textbooks. The *Longman Dictionary of Contemporary English* has long been a principal source book for me, and its new American English counterpart, The *Longman Advanced American Dictionary*, is without doubt equally valuable to those of us seeking answers to sticky questions about English grammar."

Betty Schrampfer Azar *Author of The Azar Grammar Series*

"Another fine achievement in dictionary development by Longman! Definitions are concise and user-friendly, multiple meanings are clearly differentiated, and illustrative sentences help to establish the vernacular firmly in the user's mind. A must for every serious student of American English!"

Patricia Richard-Amato, *Professor Emeritus*
California State University, Los Angeles

"The British and American lexicographic traditions beautifully combined to produce by far the best and most useful dictionary for learners of American English."

Professor Y. Ikegami, *Professor Emeritus*
University of Tokyo, Tokyo, Japan

"We encounter lively, natural-sounding examples every time we look up a word in this dictionary. It is my hope that students in Japan communicate with English speakers around the world with the help of this Longman Advanced American Dictionary."

Kumiko Torikai, *Professor of English and Interpreting*
Rikkyo University, Japan

"A fascinating learner's dictionary with a big difference, The *Longman Advanced American Dictionary* raises the bar several notches for the art of lexicography, especially as it relates to American English as a global language. Among the features that clearly set the *LAAD* apart from the rest of the field are:

- the pithy, to-the-point, and easy-to-understand definitions,
- the gold mine of authentic, ready-to-use collocations professionally culled from a most comprehensive corpus of American English,
- the hit-the-spot notes on current American usage ranging from diction to orthography to grammar,
- the ample pragmatic and cultural information of relevance to the American lexicon, and
- the generous coverage of spoken American expressions."

Nahm-Sheik Park, *Professor of English*
Seoul National University, Seoul, Korea

"The features in this new dictionary are not only unique but practical and useful for the second language learner. I believe students will find the references to names and places in both American history and literature especially helpful. The thorough definitions and the vocabulary befitting second language learners make it one of the most comprehensive and comprehensible dictionaries developed."

Bernadette Garcia, *Director, English as a Second Language Programs*
Suffolk County Community College, New York

"In the Longman tradition, this dictionary continues its intuitive organization, easy-to-understand definitions, and clear example sentences while including a unique feature that highlights the 3000 most frequently used words essential for a student's active vocabulary.

With *LAAD*, students no longer have to sift through multiple definitions of a single entry until finding just what they need because for many entries *LAAD* introduces highly visible, concise guidewords that quickly focus a student's attention on the specific meaning sought."

Kerry S. Vrabel, *Director of Instructional Resources*
The English Language Center at La Guardia Community College, City University of New York

"*LAAD* has captured the richness of American English in an appealing and comprehensive dictionary. Usage notes, signposts, example sentences and the 2,000-word defining vocabulary work together to make the entries clear and easy to understand. The dictionary is visually impressive as well. Full-color and black-and-white illustrations enrich the definitions and help students grasp the meanings of new words. *LAAD*'s user-friendly format and comprehensive coverage make it an invaluable, one-stop resource for any student of American English."

M. Lynn Poirier, *Assistant Director*
Maryland English Institute, University of Maryland, College Park, (Maryland)

Dots show how words are divided into syllables.

af·fec·tion·ate /ə'fɛkʃənɪt/ *adj.* showing in a gentle way that you love someone: *an affectionate hug* | *a very affectionate child* —**affectionately** *adv.*

Pronunciation is shown in the International Phonetic Alphabet.

ar·got /'ɑrgət, -goʊ/ *n.* [C,U] expressions used by a particular group of people; JARGON: *A "Jim Wilson" is airline-industry argot for a dead body being shipped in cargo.*

Parts of speech – verb, noun, adjective, preposition etc. – are shown in italics.

am·ber /'æmbɚ/ *n.* [U] **1** a yellowish brown substance used to make jewelry **2** a yellowish brown color —**amber** *adj.*

Words that are spelled the same but have different parts of speech are treated as homographs and have separate entries.

a·bode[1] /ə'boʊd/ *n.* [C] FORMAL OR HUMOROUS someone's home
abode[2] *v.* a past tense of ABIDE (2)

If a word has more than one meaning, each meaning is shown by a number in dark type.

an·nu·al[1] /'ænyuəl/ *adj.* **1** happening once a year: *the annual school homecoming dance* **2** based on or calculated over a period of one year: *Her annual income is about $75,000.* —**annually** *adv.*

If a word can be spelled in two different ways, both spellings are shown.

ASAP, a.s.a.p. /,eɪ ɛs eɪ 'pi/ *n.* the abbreviation of "as soon as possible": *Call him ASAP.*

Meanings are explained in clear, simple language, using the 2000-word Longman Defining Vocabulary whenever possible.

a·bra·sive[1] /ə'breɪsɪv, -zɪv/ *adj.* **1** seeming rude or unkind in the way you behave toward people, especially because you say what you think very directly: *an abrasive personality*

Words that are not in the Defining Vocabulary are shown in small capital letters.

arch·er /'ɑrtʃɚ/ *n.* [C] someone who shoots ARROWS from a BOW

Useful, natural-sounding examples, are all based on information from the Longman Corpus Network.

appeal[2] *v.* **1** [I] to make a serious public request for help, money, information etc.: [**appeal (to sb) for sth**] *The police are appealing to the public for information.* | *The Pope appealed for an end to the violence.* | [**appeal to sb to do sth**] *The water company appealed to everyone to reduce the amount of water used.* **2** [I,T] to make a formal request to a court or someone in authority asking for a decision to be changed: *The defendant is planning to appeal.*

Derived words are shown at the end of the entry when the meaning is clear from the definition of the main form.

am·biv·a·lent /æm'bɪvələnt/ *adj.* not sure whether you want or like something or not: [+ **about**] *Many members of the parish were profoundly ambivalent about the protest.* —**ambivalence** *n.* [U] —**ambivalently** *adv.*

Phrasal verbs are listed in alphabetical order directly after the entry for their main verb.

ad·here /əd'hɪr/ *v.* [I] FORMAL to stick firmly to something
adhere to sth *phr. v.* [T] FORMAL to continue to behave according to a particular rule, agreement, or belief: *Few people adhere to the guidelines.*

Compound words are shown as headwords and their stress patterns are shown.

age lim·it /ˈ. ,../ *n.* [C] the youngest or oldest age at which you are allowed to do something: *The age limit for buying tobacco has been raised to 18.*

Grammatical information is shown in brackets.

1 **at·trib·ut·a·ble** /əˈtrɪbyəṭəbəl/ *adj.* [not before noun] FORMAL likely to be caused by something: [+ **to**] *The price increase is attributable to a rise in the cost of paper.*

2 **ap·point** /əˈpɔɪnt/ *v.* [T] **1** to choose someone for a position or a job: *Pope John Paul II appointed several new bishops.* | [**appoint (sb) as sth**] *Lisa Lore was appointed as an associate athletic director at USC.*

Phrases and idioms are shown and given their own definitions.

armchair² *adj.* **an armchair traveler/critic etc.** someone who talks or reads about being a traveler, CRITIC etc., but does not have any real experience of doing it

Collocations – words that are often used together – are shown in **bold** in an example or followed by an explanation.

ar·gu·ment /ˈɑrgyəmənt/ *n.* **1** [C] a situation in which two or more people disagree, often angrily: [+ **with**] *I broke the vase during an argument with my husband.* | *Henning told the police she and her husband **had an argument** before he left.* | *I **got into an argument** with the other driver.* | *Shelton and the woman had a **heated argument*** (=very angry argument).

Signposts in longer entries help you to to find the meaning that you need.

anchor² *v.*
1 boat [I,T] to lower the anchor on a ship or boat to hold it in one place: *Three tankers were anchored in the harbor.* | *Captain Cook anchored in Opunohu Bay in the 1760s.*
2 tv news [T] to be the person who reads the news and introduces reports on TV: *The new hour-long program is anchored by Mark McEwen.*
3 fasten [T usually passive] to fasten something firmly so that it cannot move: *The panel was firmly anchored by two large bolts.*

Labels showing the contexts or situations a word is typically used in or the speaker's attitude are shown in **bold**.

ap·pend /əˈpɛnd/ *v.* [T + **to**] FORMAL to add something to a piece of writing

ante- /æntɪ/ *prefix* coming or happening before something: *to antedate* (=exist before something else) | *the antebellum South* (=before the Civil War) —compare POST-, PRE-

References to other words and phrases, and to pictures and Usage Notes, are given.

an·te¹ /ˈænti/ *n.* **up/raise the ante** to increase your demands or try to get more things from a situation, even though this involves more risks: *Sanctions upped the ante considerably in the Middle East crisis.* —see also PENNY ANTE

Words that have unpredictable spellings in plurals, across tenses, or in the comparative and superlative are shown in **bold** after the part of speech.

a·bet /əˈbɛt/ *v.* **abetted, abetting** [T] to help someone do something wrong or illegal —see also **aid and abet** (AID² (2))

a·moe·ba /əˈmibə/ *n. plural* **amoebas** or **amoebae** /-bi/ [C] a very small creature that has only one cell and a changeable shape —**amoebic** *adj.*

Los puntos indican la división de las palabras en sílabas.

af·fec·tion·ate /əˈfɛkʃənɪt/ *adj.* showing in a gentle way that you love someone: *an affectionate hug* | *a very affectionate child* —**affectionately** *adv.*

La pronunciación sigue el Alfabeto Fonético Internacional (AFI).

ar·got /ˈɑrgət, -goʊ/ *n.* [C,U] expressions used by a particular group of people; JARGON: *A "Jim Wilson" is airline-industry argot for a dead body being shipped in cargo.*

Las funciones gramaticales –verbo, sustantivo, adjetivo, preposición, etc.– se indican en cursiva.

am·ber /ˈæmbɚ/ *n.* [U] **1** a yellowish brown substance used to make jewelry **2** a yellowish brown color —**amber** *adj.*

Las palabras que se escriben igual pero que tienen distinta función gramatical se consideran homógrafas y se incluyen por separado.

a·bode¹ /əˈboʊd/ *n.* [C] FORMAL OR HUMOROUS someone's home
abode² *v.* a past tense of ABIDE (2)

Si una palabra tiene más de un significado, a cada significado se le asigna un número en negrita.

an·nu·al¹ /ˈænyuəl/ *adj.* **1** happening once a year: *the annual school homecoming dance* **2** based on or calculated over a period of one year: *Her annual income is about $75,000.* —**annually** *adv.*

Si una palabra se puede escribir de dos maneras, se muestran ambas ortografías.

ASAP, a.s.a.p. /ˌeɪ ɛs eɪ ˈpi/ *n.* the abbreviation of "as soon as possible": *Call him ASAP.*

Los significados se explican en lenguaje claro y sencillo, usando siempre que sea posible el Longman Defining Vocabulary (Vocabulario de Definiciones Longman).

a·bra·sive¹ /əˈbreɪsɪv, -zɪv/ *adj.* **1** seeming rude or unkind in the way you behave toward people, especially because you say what you think very directly: *an abrasive personality*

Las palabras no incluidas en el Defining Vocabulary aparecen en versalitas.

arch·er /ˈɑrtʃɚ/ *n.* [C] someone who shoots ARROWS from a BOW

Ejemplos útiles, que suenan naturales, todos ellos basados en información del Longman Corpus Network (red de corpus de Longman).

appeal² *v.* **1** [I] to make a serious public request for help, money, information etc.: [**appeal (to sb) for sth**] *The police are appealing to the public for information.* | *The Pope appealed for an end to the violence.* | [**appeal to sb to do sth**] *The water company appealed to everyone to reduce the amount of water used.* **2** [I,T] to make a formal request to a court or someone in authority asking for a decision to be changed: *The defendant is planning to appeal.*

Las palabras derivadas se muestran al final de la entrada, cuando el significado está claro por la definición de la palabra principal.

am·biv·a·lent /æmˈbɪvələnt/ *adj.* not sure whether you want or like something or not: [+ **about**] *Many members of the parish were profoundly ambivalent about the protest.* —**ambivalence** *n.* [U] —**ambivalently** *adv.*

Los verbos preposicionales siguen por orden alfabético directamente después de la entrada del verbo principal.

ad·here /ədˈhɪr/ *v.* [I] FORMAL to stick firmly to something
    adhere to sth *phr. v.* [T] FORMAL to continue to behave according to a particular rule, agreement, or belief: *Few people adhere to the guidelines.*

Las palabras compuestas se muestran como cabeza de artículo, indicando las partes en las que recae el acento.

age lim·it /'. ,../ n. [C] the youngest or oldest age at which you are allowed to do something: *The age limit for buying tobacco has been raised to 18.*

1

La información gramatical aparece entre corchetes.

at·trib·ut·a·ble /ə'trɪbyəṭəbəl/ *adj.* [not before noun] FORMAL likely to be caused by something: [+ **to**] *The price increase is attributable to a rise in the cost of paper.*

2

ap·point /ə'pɔɪnt/ *v.* [T] **1** to choose someone for a position or a job: *Pope John Paul II appointed several new bishops.* | [**appoint (sb) as sth**] *Lisa Lore was appointed as an associate athletic director at USC.*

Se muestran locuciones y giros idiomáticos y se les dan sus propias definiciones.

armchair² *adj.* **an armchair traveler/critic etc.** someone who talks or reads about being a traveler, CRITIC etc., but does not have any real experience of doing it

Colocaciones – palabras que con frecuencia se emplean juntas – se indican en **negrita** en un ejemplo o seguidas de una explicación.

ar·gu·ment /'ɑrgyəmənt/ *n.* **1** [C] a situation in which two or more people disagree, often angrily: [+ **with**] *I broke the vase during an argument with my husband.* | *Henning told the police she and her husband* **had an argument** *before he left.* | *I* **got into an argument** *with the other driver.* | *Shelton and the woman had a* **heated argument** (=very angry argument).

Los indicadores en las entradas más largas ayudan a dar con el significado que se necesita.

anchor² *v.*
1 boat [I,T] to lower the anchor on a ship or boat to hold it in one place: *Three tankers were anchored in the harbor.* | *Captain Cook anchored in Opunohu Bay in the 1760s.*
2 tv news [T] to be the person who reads the news and introduces reports on TV: *The new hour-long program is anchored by Mark McEwen.*
3 fasten [T usually passive] to fasten something firmly so that it cannot move: *The panel was firmly anchored by two large bolts.*

Los indicadores de los contextos o situaciones en que normalmente se emplea una palabra, o la actitud de quien habla, se indican en **negrita**.

ap·pend /ə'pɛnd/ *v.* [T + to] FORMAL to add something to a piece of writing

Hay referencias a otras palabras y frases así como a los dibujos y notas de uso.

ante- /ænti/ *prefix* coming or happening before something: *to antedate* (=exist before something else) | *the antebellum South* (=before the Civil War) —compare POST-, PRE-

an·te¹ /'ænti/ *n.* **up/raise the ante** to increase your demands or try to get more things from a situation, even though this involves more risks: *Sanctions upped the ante considerably in the Middle East crisis.* —see also PENNY ANTE

Los plurales, formas verbales o comparativos y superlativos con ortografía que no se puede deducir aparecen en **negrita** tras la categoría de la palabra principal.

a·bet /ə'bɛt/ *v.* **abetted, abetting** [T] to help someone do something wrong or illegal —see also **aid and abet** (AID² (2))

a·moe·ba /ə'mibə/ *n. plural* **amoebas** or **amoebae** /-bi/ [C] a very small creature that has only one cell and a changeable shape —**amoebic** *adj.*

音節の切れ目は中点（・）で示した。

af·fec·tion·ate /əˈfɛkʃənɪt/ *adj.* showing in a gentle way that you love someone: *an affectionate hug | a very affectionate child* —**affectionately** *adv.*

発音は国際音標文字を用いて示した。

ar·got /ˈɑrgət, -goʊ/ *n.* [C,U] expressions used by a particular group of people; JARGON: *A "Jim Wilson" is airline-industry argot for a dead body being shipped in cargo.*

品詞——動詞、名詞、形容詞、前置詞など ——は斜字体で示した。

am·ber /ˈæmbɚ/ *n.* [U] **1** a yellowish brown substance used to make jewelry **2** a yellowish brown color —**amber** *adj.*

つづりが同じであるが品詞が異なる単語は同綴異義語として取り扱い、独立した見出し語を設けた。

a·bode[1] /əˈboʊd/ *n.* [C] FORMAL OR HUMOROUS someone's home
abode[2] *v.* a past tense of ABIDE (2)

一つ以上の語義が存在する場合、各々の語義に番号（**太字**）を付けて示した。

an·nu·al[1] /ˈænyuəl/ *adj.* **1** happening once a year: *the annual school homecoming dance* **2** based on or calculated over a period of one year: *Her annual income is about $75,000.* —**annually** *adv.*

つづり方が二つある場合、その両方を示した。

ASAP, a.s.a.p. /ˌeɪ ɛs eɪ ˈpi/ *n.* the abbreviation of "as soon as possible": *Call him ASAP.*

語義はできる限り「ロングマン定義語彙2000語」を用い明確で簡潔な言葉で説明した。

a·bra·sive[1] /əˈbreɪsɪv, -zɪv/ *adj.* **1** seeming rude or unkind in the way you behave toward people, especially because you say what you think very directly: *an abrasive personality*

「ロングマン定義語彙」に含まれない単語は小型大文字で示した。

arch·er /ˈɑrtʃɚ/ *n.* [C] someone who shoots ARROWS from a BOW

「ロングマン・コーパス・ネットワーク」の情報に基づき役に立つ自然な例文を示した。

appeal[2] *v.* **1** [I] to make a serious public request for help, money, information etc.: [appeal (to sb) for sth] *The police are appealing to the public for information.* | *The Pope appealed for an end to the violence.* | [appeal to sb to do sth] *The water company appealed to everyone to reduce the amount of water used.* **2** [I,T] to make a formal request to a court or someone in authority asking for a decision to be changed: *The defendant is planning to appeal.*

派生語は見出し語の語義から意味が明確な場合は項目の最後に示した。

am·biv·a·lent /æmˈbɪvələnt/ *adj.* not sure whether you want or like something or not: [+ about] *Many members of the parish were profoundly ambivalent about the protest.* —**ambivalence** *n.* [U] —**ambivalently** *adv.*

句動詞はアルファベット順に見出しの動詞の直後に配列した。

ad·here /ədˈhɪr/ *v.* [I] FORMAL to stick firmly to something
　adhere to sth *phr. v.* [T] FORMAL to continue to behave according to a particular rule, agreement, or belief: *Few people adhere to the guidelines.*

複合語は見出し語として示し、アクセントの位置を表示した。

age lim·it /ˈ. ˌ../ *n.* [C] the youngest or oldest age at which you are allowed to do something: *The age limit for buying tobacco has been raised to 18.*

1

文法上の説明は［　］に入れて示した。

at·trib·ut·a·ble /əˈtrɪbyətəbəl/ *adj.* [not before noun] FORMAL likely to be caused by something: [+ **to**] *The price increase is attributable to a rise in the cost of paper.*

2

ap·point /əˈpɔɪnt/ *v.* [T] **1** to choose someone for a position or a job: *Pope John Paul II appointed several new bishops.* | **[appoint (sb) as sth]** *Lisa Lore was appointed as an associate athletic director at USC.*

熟語、慣用句はその語義を示した。

armchair² *adj.* **an armchair traveler/critic etc.** someone who talks or reads about being a traveler, CRITIC etc., but does not have any real experience of doing it

連語——共に使われることが多い単語——は例文中で**太字**表示、あるいは後ろに説明を加えた。

ar·gu·ment /ˈɑrgyəmənt/ *n.* **1** [C] a situation in which two or more people disagree, often angrily: [+ **with**] *I broke the vase during an argument with my husband.* | *Henning told the police she and her husband had an argument before he left.* | *I got into an argument with the other driver.* | *Shelton and the woman had a heated argument* (=very angry argument).

anchor² *v.*

長い見出し語には「標識（signpost）」を付け、探している語義を見つけやすくした。

1 boat [I,T] to lower the anchor on a ship or boat to hold it in one place: *Three tankers were anchored in the harbor.* | *Captain Cook anchored in Opunohu Bay in the 1760s.*
2 tv news [T] to be the person who reads the news and introduces reports on TV: *The new hour-long program is anchored by Mark McEwen.*
3 fasten [T usually passive] to fasten something firmly so that it cannot move: *The panel was firmly anchored by two large bolts.*

単語が使われる典型的な文脈、情況あるいは話し手の感情を示した補助ラベルを**太字**で表示した。

ap·pend /əˈpɛnd/ *v.* [T + **to**] FORMAL to add something to a piece of writing

ante- /ˈæntɪ/ *prefix* coming or happening before something: *to antedate* (=exist before something else) | *the antebellum South* (=before the Civil War) —compare POST-, PRE-

他の単語や成句、絵、語法の説明が参照できるようにした。

an·te¹ /ˈænti/ *n.* **up/raise the ante** to increase your demands or try to get more things from a situation, even though this involves more risks: *Sanctions upped the ante considerably in the Middle East crisis.* —see also PENNY ANTE

a·bet /əˈbɛt/ *v.* **abetted, abetting** [T] to help someone do something wrong or illegal —see also **aid and abet** (AID² (2))

複数形、時制による変化形、比較級、最上級をつくるときに予測のできないつづりをする単語は品詞の後に**太字**で示した。

a·moe·ba /əˈmibə/ *n.* **plural amoebas** or **amoebae** /-bi/ [C] a very small creature that has only one cell and a changeable shape —**amoebic** *adj.*

단어의 분절은 중점으로 표시하였다.

af·fec·tion·ate /ə'fɛkʃənɪt/ *adj.* showing in a gentle way that you love someone: *an affectionate hug* | *a very affectionate child* —**affectionately** *adv.*

발음은 국제 음성 기호(International Phonetic Alphabet)에 따라 표기하였다.

ar·got /'ɑrgət, -goʊ/ *n.* [C,U] expressions used by a particular group of people; JARGON: *A "Jim Wilson" is airline-industry argot for a dead body being shipped in cargo.*

동사, 명사, 형용사, 전치사 등의 품사는 이탤릭체로 표시하였다.

am·ber /'æmbə/ *n.* [U] **1** a yellowish brown substance used to make jewelry **2** a yellowish brown color —**amber** *adj.*

철자는 같은 데 품사가 다른 단어는 동형 이의어로 취급하고 별도 표제어로 내세웠다.

a·bode¹ /ə'boʊd/ *n.* [C] FORMAL OR HUMOROUS someone's home
abode² *v.* a past tense of ABIDE (2)

뜻이 하나 이상인 단어는 굵은 고딕체 번호로 각각의 뜻을 구별하였다.

an·nu·al¹ /'ænyuəl/ *adj.* **1** happening once a year: *the annual school homecoming dance* **2** based on or calculated over a period of one year: *Her annual income is about $75,000.* —**annually** *adv.*

한 단어에 두 가지 철자가 있으면 둘 다 표기하였다.

ASAP, a.s.a.p. /ˌeɪ ɛs eɪ 'pi/ *n.* the abbreviation of "as soon as possible": *Call him ASAP.*

의미는 간결하게 설명하면서 가능한 Longman Defining Vocabulary 2000어를 사용하였다.

a·bra·sive¹ /ə'breɪsɪv, -zɪv/ *adj.* **1** seeming rude or unkind in the way you behave toward people, especially because you say what you think very directly: *an abrasive personality*

Longman Defining Vocabulary에 없는 단어는 작은 대문자로 표시하였다.

arch·er /'ɑrtʃə/ *n.* [C] someone who shoots ARROWS from a BOW

Longman Corpus Network 정보에 근거한 유용하고 자연스러운 실례를 나타내었다.

appeal² *v.* **1** [I] to make a serious public request for help, money, information etc.: [**appeal (to sb) for sth**] *The police are appealing to the public for information.* | *The Pope appealed for an end to the violence.* | [**appeal to sb to do sth**] *The water company appealed to everyone to reduce the amount of water used.* **2** [I,T] to make a formal request to a court or someone in authority asking for a decision to be changed: *The defendant is planning to appeal.*

파생어의 경우 표제어의 정의에서 그 뜻이 분명하면 해당 풀이의 끝에 표시하였다.

am·biv·a·lent /æm'bɪvələnt/ *adj.* not sure whether you want or like something or not: [+ **about**] *Many members of the parish were profoundly ambivalent about the protest.* —**ambivalence** *n.* [U] —**ambivalently** *adv.*

동사구는 주요 동사 바로 다음에 알파벳순으로 나타내었다.

ad·here /əd'hɪr/ *v.* [I] FORMAL to stick firmly to something
adhere to sth *phr. v.* [T] FORMAL to continue to behave according to a particular rule, agreement, or belief: *Few people adhere to the guidelines.*

af·ter·math /'æftəˌmæθ/ *n.* [singular] the period of time after something bad such as a war, storm, or accident has happened, when people are still dealing with the results: *Several people resigned in the aftermath of the scandal.*

high heels /ˌ '/ *n.* [plural] women's shoes with high heels —**high-heeled** *adj.*

If a noun is typically followed by a preposition or prepositions, this is shown in brackets before the example that illustrates it. A construction that typically follows a noun is also shown in brackets before an example.

hope² *n.*
2 `sth you hope for` [C] something that you hope will happen: *Your donation can fulfill the hopes and dreams of a child this Christmas.* | [+ **of**] *Grant was forced to abandon the hope of re-election.* | [**hopes of doing sth**] *I moved to the city with hopes of finding a job.* | *Tina had **high hopes** (=hopes that something will be successful) for her team at the beginning of the season.* | *The search for survivors continues, but **hopes are fading** (=people are losing hope) fast.*

4.6 *Syntax – adjectives and adverbs*

Information about how an adjective or adverb behaves is shown in brackets, and includes:

[only before noun]

ac·tu·al /'æktʃuəl, -ʃəl/ *adj.* [only before noun]
1 real, especially as compared with what is believed, expected or intended: *It's a true story, based on actual events.* | *The party took place three days before Daniel's actual birthday.*

[only after noun]

ga·lore /ɡə'lɔr/ *adj.* [only after noun] in large amounts or numbers: *At the flea market, there were quilts, furniture, and books galore.*

[not before noun]

ad·vis·a·ble /əd'vaɪzəbəl/ *adj.* [not before noun] FORMAL something that is advisable should be done in order to avoid problems or risks: *For heavy smokers, regular medical checks are advisable.* | *It is advisable to disconnect the computer before you open it up.* —**advisability** /ədˌvaɪzə'bɪləti/ *n.* [U]

[no comparative]

ef·fec·tive /ɪ'fɛktɪv/ *adj.* **1** producing the result that was wanted or intended: *The less expensive drugs were just as effective in treating arthritis.* —opposite INEFFECTIVE **2** [no comparative] if a law, agreement, or system becomes effective, it officially starts: *His resignation is effective April 8.* **3** done with skill, or having a skillful way of doing things: *The effective use of color can make a small room look much bigger.* **4** [no comparative; only before noun] real, rather than what is officially intended or generally believed: *Rapid advancements in technology have reduced the effective lifespans of computers.* —**effectiveness** *n.* [U]

The grammar information [no comparative] means that the adjective has no comparative or superlative form.

[+adj./adv.]

in·creas·ing·ly /ɪn'krisɪŋli/ *adv.* more and more all the time: [+ adj./adv.] *The rebel group's actions have become increasingly violent.* [sentence adverb] *Increasingly, humans and animals are in competition for the same land.*

[sentence adverb]

hap·pi·ly /'hæpəli/ *adv.* **1** in a happy way: *The puppy wagged its tail happily.* | *a happily married couple* **2** [sentence adverb] fortunately: *Happily, Bruce's injuries were not serious.* **3** very willingly: *I'd happily go pick up the kids for you.*

The grammar information [sentence adverb] indicates that in this sense **happily** is used to modify a whole sentence.

The prepositions or constructions that follow an adjective are shown in brackets before an example.

hope·ful¹ /'hoʊpfəl/ *adj.* **1** believing that what you hope for is likely to happen: [+ **that**] *We remain hopeful that her health will continue to improve.* | [+ **about**] *Lakeisha is hopeful about the future.*

4.7 *Very infrequent words*

Very infrequent words, that a student is not likely to need to use, are given a shorter treatment, without examples, giving just the basic grammatical information.

be² *v.* **1** [linking verb] used to show that some-one or something is the same as the subject: *Hi, it's me.* | *These are Len's dogs.* | *Christie is my girlfriend.* | *The truth is, I don't have enough money.*

Brackets may also contain restrictions on the way a verb can be used, including [not in progressive]:

pre·fer /prɪ'fɚ/ *v.* **preferred, preferring** [T not in progressive] **1** to like someone or some-thing more than someone or something else

[I always + adv./prep.]:

am·ble /'æmbəl/ *v.* [I always + adv./prep.] to walk in a slow relaxed way: [+ **along/across** etc.] *Joe ambled over to say hello.* —**amble** *n.* [singular]

This code shows that you cannot just say "he ambled" without adding something like "along" or "toward me."

[usually in passive]:

carpet² *v.* [T] **1** [usually passive] to cover a floor with carpet: *The hall was carpeted in a depressing shade of green.* **2 be carpeted with grass/flowers etc.** LITERARY to be covered with a thick layer of grass etc.

[not in passive]:

concern² *v.* [T] **1** [not in passive] if an activi-ty, situation, rule etc. concerns you, it affects you or involves you: *The tax changes will con-cern large corporations more than small busi-nesses.* **2** to make someone feel worried or upset: *The potential for abuse of these products concerns me a great deal.* | *We are deeply con-cerned by America's neglect of its youth.* **3** [not in passive] if a story, book, report etc. con-cerns someone or something, it is about them: *Many of Woody Allen's movies concern life in New York.*

If this grammar information is true when-ever a word is used, you will find it after the headword. If it is true for a particular meaning of the word, you will find it after the number that marks that meaning.

Other information about how a verb behaves is shown in the examples. A typi-cal construction is shown in brackets before the example that illustrates it.

ad·e·quate /'ædəkwɪt/ *adj.* **1** an adequate amount is enough for a particular purpose: *Hardin's campaign did not have adequate funds to broadcast any ads on television.* | [+ **for**] *The earlier electric car's range of 50 miles was not adequate for suburban driving.* **2** good enough in quality for a particular purpose or activity: *Most people eat an adequate diet.* | [**adequate to do sth**] *The safety proce-dures are adequate to protect public health.* | [+ **for**] *Parents should ask whether the school's facilities are adequate for their children's needs.*

These examples are shown in frequency order, with the most frequently used con-struction first.

4.4 Phrasal verbs

For a phrasal verb, it is important to show whether the preposition can come both before and after the object or whether it is restricted to one of these positions. This is shown in this dictionary by a double arrow.

look up *phr. v.* **1** [T **look** sth ↔ **up**] to try to find information in a book, on a computer etc.: *If you don't know the word, look it up in the dic-tionary.*

look after sb/sth *phr. v.* [T] **1** to take care of someone by helping them, giving them what they need, or keeping them safe: *Will you look after the cat while we're gone?*

The arrows in the first entry show that the phrasal verb is separable. This means that you can say "look the word up" or "look up the word." It is important to remember that you can put a pronoun between the two parts of a separable phrasal verb, but *never* after the preposition or adverb. For exam-ple, you can say "look it up," but you can-not say "look up it."

The second entry tells you that you cannot put any word between "look" and "after."

4.5 Syntax – nouns

Grammatical information enclosed in brackets shows whether a noun, or a particular sense of a noun, is countable (a pen, three pens), or uncountable (honor, daylight).

hab·i·ta·tion /ˌhæbə'teɪʃən/ *n.* FORMAL **1** [U] the act of living in a place: *What are the chances of achieving permanent habitation in space?* | *Many of the housing projects are unfit for human habitation* (=not safe or healthy for people to live in). **2** [C] LITERARY a house or place to live in

as·sault¹ /ə'sɔlt/ *n.* [C,U] **1** the crime of physi-cally attacking someone: *She served three years in prison for assault.* | *an increase in sexual assaults* **2** a military attack to take control of a place controlled by the enemy: *The Combined Fleet made plans for an assault on Midway Island.*

If a noun, or a particular meaning of one, is always singular or always plural, this is also shown in brackets.

part of speech	exam
adj. (adjective)	*a* **fast** *car*, **straight** *lines*, **amazing** *speed*, **frequent** *flights*
adv. (adverb)	*smiling* **happily**, *put it* **away**, **frankly**, *I don't care*
auxiliary verb	be, have
conjunction	and, but
determiner	this, which
interjection	hey, wow

part of speech	example
modal verb	must, can, should
n. (noun)	car, rabbit, president, dignity, excuse
number	five, ninth
phr. v. (phrasal verb)	put off, shut up, take over
possessive pron. (possessive pronoun)	yours, mine, his
possessive adj. (possessive adjective)	your, my, his
prefix	dis-, centi-
prep. (preposition)	in, after, to
pron. (pronoun)	he, they, us
quantifier	many, several
suffix	-ity, -ness
v. (verb)	go, send, indicate

4.2 *Inflections*

Inflections are the changes that are made in the form of a word according to its function in a sentence. Most words form their inflections according to regular rules. For example, most nouns add *-s* or *-es* to form the plural, and most verbs add *-ed* to form the past tense. These "regular inflections" are not shown in the dictionary, except where there is a possibility of confusion or if the regular inflection has a difficult pronunciation.

"Irregular inflections" are always shown. They come directly after the part of speeech, and they are written in **bold**, like this:

cri·sis /'kraısıs/ *n. plural* **crises** /-siz/ [C,U]

eat /it/ *v. past tense* **ate** *past participle* **eaten**

good[1] /gʊd/ *adj. comparative* **better** *superlative* **best**

Irregular inflections are also shown at their own place as headwords, referring you to the main word:

ate /eıt/ *v.* the past tense of EAT

Inflections are also shown for:

verbs which have a double letter in the past and -ing forms:

hug[1] /hʌg/ *v.* **hugged, hugging**

verbs which end in -y:

car·ry[1] /'kæri/ *v.* **carried, carrying**

adjectives which end in -y:

dirt·y[1] /'dɔti/ *adj.* **dirtier, dirtiest**

There is a full list of verbs with irregular inflections at the back of the book, starting on page 1687.

4.3 Syntax – *verbs*

Basic information about the way a verb behaves is given in brackets.

The codes [I] (intransitive) and [T] (transitive) show whether a verb has or does not have an object.

hard·en /'hardn/ *v.* **1** [I,T] to become firm or stiff, or to make something firm or stiff: *The clay needs to harden before it can be painted.* | *Harden the chocolates by putting them in the fridge.* **2** [I,T] to become or sound more strict and determined and less sympathetic, or to make someone become this way: *Opposition to the peace talks has hardened since the attack.* | *The death of a parent can harden young people, making them bitter.* **3 harden your heart** to make yourself not feel pity or sympathy for someone —opposite SOFTEN

The code [linking verb] means that a verb connects the subject of a sentence to a word or phrase that describes the subject or is the same as the subject.

3 seem [linking verb] to seem to be something, especially by having a particular appearance: *Do these jeans make me look fat?* | *When I saw him last week he didn't look very good.* | *She* **looks** *just* **like** *someone I used to work with.* | **look as if/though** *This car looks as if it could cost more.* | *With all the commotion* **it looked as if** *the circus had come to town.*

between ordinary citizens and public officials.
3 `ship` [C] the raised part of a ship from which the officers control it
4 `card game` [U] a card game for four players who play in pairs
5 `part of nose` [C usually singular] the upper part of your nose between your eyes: *He had a small cut on the bridge of his nose.*
6 `pair of glasses` [C usually singular] the part of a pair of glasses that rests on the bridge of your nose
7 `musical instrument` [C usually singular] a small piece of wood under the strings of a VIO-LIN or GUITAR, used to keep them in position
8 `for teeth` [C] a small piece of metal that keeps false teeth in place by attaching them to your real teeth

2.6 *Showing words with similar and opposite meanings*

Sometimes it is useful to show a synonym (a word that has the same meaning, or almost the same meaning, as the word that is being defined). These are shown after the definition in small capital letters, like this:

an·noy /ə'nɔɪ/ *v.* **annoys, annoyed, annoying** [T] to make someone feel slightly angry and unhappy about something:

Words with similar or related meanings or similar forms are shown with a "compare" note. Useful opposites are also shown.

i·mag·i·nar·y /ɪ'mædʒəˌnɛri/ *adj.* not real, but produced from pictures or ideas in your mind: *Many young children have imaginary play-mates.* | *The events described in the book are imaginary.* —compare IMAGINATIVE

ag·ri·cul·ture /'ægrɪˌkʌltʃɚ/ *n.* [U] the practice or science of farming —**agricultural** /ˌægrɪ'kʌltʃərəl/ *adj.* —**agriculturalist** *n.* [C] —compare HORTICULTURE

as·cent /ə'sɛnt, 'æsɛnt/ *n.* **1** [C usually singular] the act of climbing something or moving toward the top of something: *The final ascent of Kilimanjaro began at 5:00 a.m.* **2** [U] the process of becoming more important, powerful, or successful than before: *Yeltsin's ascent to the presidency of Russia* **3** [C usually singular] a path or way up to the top of something, for example a mountain: *a rugged and steep ascent* —opposite DESCENT

3 *Frequency*

You have seen that this dictionary is organized on the basis of frequency. The most frequent meanings of a word are shown first, and homographs are shown in frequency order.

All our judgments about frequency are made by analysis of corpus material. This principle of organization gives important information about the language and is helpful to the student.

The dictionary also shows which are the most frequently used words in spoken and written English, according to the computer-based analysis of all American English corpus material available to Longman. If the number 1 appears in the symbol, then the word is among the 1,000 most frequent words in Spoken or Written English. The number 2 indicates that a word ranks between 1,001 and 2,000 on the list and the number 3 shows that a word ranks between 2,001 and 3,000.

S W
1 2

indicates that a word is one of the 1,000 most frequent words in spoken English and ranks between 1,001 and 2,000 in written English.

S W
3

indicates that a word ranks between 2,001 and 3,000 in spoken English but is not one of the 3,000 most frequent words in written English.

4 *Grammar*

The dictionary contains a great deal of information about the grammar of words. It tells you the part of speech that a headword belongs to – whether it is a noun, a verb, an adjective, or some other type of word. It also gives information about the inflections of words – how their form changes when they are used in the past tense, the plural, the comparative, or in some other way. And it gives a full explanation of the word's syntax – the various patterns in which the word combines with other words to form sentences.

4.1 *Parts of speech*

The part of speech, or "word class" is shown like this:

a·brupt /ə'brʌpt/ *adj.* **1** sudden and unexpected: *There may be an abrupt change in weather patterns.* | *an abrupt end/stop/halt etc. His resignation was an abrupt end to an impressive career.* **2** seeming rude and unfriendly, especially because you do not waste time in friendly conversation; BRUSQUE: *"Change it," he says in his abrupt, no-nonsense style.* —**abruptly** *adv.* —**abruptness** *n.* [U]

This means that **abrupt** is an adjective. Derived forms are also given a part of speech label: **abruptly** is an adverb, and **abruptness** is a noun.

The parts of speech used in this dictionary are:

al·low·ance /əˈlaʊəns/ *n.* [C] **1** an amount of something that is acceptable or safe: *The baggage allowance is 75 pounds per person.* | *A glass of orange juice provides the recommended daily allowance of Vitamin C* **2** an amount of money that you are given regularly or for a special reason | **a clothing/travel/ housing etc. allowance** *Joe's salary includes a monthly clothing allowance.* **3** a small amount of money that a parent regularly gives to a child: *Mom gave us kids a weekly allowance if we kept our rooms clean.*

This dictionary is based on analysis of large corpora, or databases, of spoken and written English. We analyze how often a word or phrase is used, and how often it is used in each meaning.

A phrase that contains the word and has its own distinct meaning is shown as a separate meaning and listed in frequency order. For example:

look·out /ˈlʊk-aʊt/ *n.* **1 be on the lookout for sth** to continuously watch a place or pay attention in order to find something you want or to be ready for problems or opportunities: *You've got to be on the lookout for snakes around here.* **2 keep a lookout** to keep watching carefully for something or someone, especially for danger: *Soldiers kept a lookout for enemy planes through the night.* **3** [C] someone whose duty is to watch carefully for something, especially danger **4** [C] a place for a lookout to watch from

This shows that the most common use of **lookout** is in the phrase **be on the lookout for**.

2.2 *Definitions*

All the definitions in this dictionary are written in clear and simple language, using the The Longman American Defining Vocabulary of about 2,000 common words. The list of the words in the definitions is shown at the end of the dictionary following page 1692 which explains exactly how the words are used.

2.3 *Examples*

Most definitions in this dictionary are followed by examples that show how the word is used.

These examples may be in short phrases or whole sentences, and they are written in *italic letters*:

clear instructions | *The test questions weren't very clear.* | *I'll give you until Monday to turn in your essay. Is that clear?*

All the examples in this dictionary are based on what we find in the spoken and written corpus material in the Longman Corpus Network. Some examples are taken direct from the corpus; some have been changed slightly from the corpus to remove difficult words; and some have been written specially for the entry. In each case, the examples are carefully chosen to help show the ways in which a word or phrase is typically used.

Examples also show the way the word behaves grammatically. Grammatical patterns are shown in brackets.

| [**be clear about sth**] *Smith was very clear about the school's policies on the issue.* | [**be clear about what/when/how etc.**] *Could you be more clear about how long it will take to do the job?* | [**be clear on sth**] *The manual is clear on how to operate the software.* | [**be clear to sb**] *It is clear to me that the company will have to make further job cuts.*

2.4 *Collocations*

An important aim of this dictionary is to show very clearly the collocation of a word: the other words that are frequently and typically used with it.

Collocations are shown in **bold** in examples and are followed by a short definition in parentheses when necessary.

*Before asking for a raise, get **a clear idea** (=a good understanding) of what you plan to say.* | *We need to send kids a **crystal-clear** (=very easy to understand) message that drugs are dangerous.*

These collocations are shown in frequency order, with the most important collocations coming first.

2.5 *Finding the meaning you want – Signposts*

In entries with many definitions, we have included "Signposts" to help you find the right definition quickly. A signpost is a word or short phrase that guides you to the right meaning. It may be a synonym, a short definition, or the typical subject or object of a verb. Signposts are shown in white letters on a black background strip, before the definition, and are written using only the words in the Longman American Defining Vocabulary.

bridge¹ /brɪdʒ/ *n.*
1 over a river/road etc. [C] a structure built over a river, road etc., that allows people or vehicles to cross from one side to the other
2 connection [C] something that provides a connection or relationship between two things: [+ **between**] *His job is to serve as a kind of bridge between students and the college administration.* | *The mayor has been **building bridges** (=making a better relationship)*

1.4 *Homographs*

Homographs are words that have the same spelling but are different from each other in some other way, and are listed as separate entries in a dictionary. In this dictionary, words with different parts of speech are treated as homographs.

face[1] /feɪs/ *n.* [C,U]
1 front of your head the front part of your head, where your eyes, nose, and mouth are: *Jodi has such a pretty face.* | *One of the victims had scratches all over his face.* | *Uncle Gene had a surprised look on his face.*

face[2] *v.* [T]
1 difficult situation if you face a difficult situation or if it faces you, you must deal with it: *Weber is facing the biggest challenge of his career.* | *If found guilty, Jones could face up to 20 years in jail.* | *The city council is faced with* (=is in a situation where they have to deal with) *the task of making budget cuts.*

The order of the homographs depends on how common they are. **Face** is used more often as a noun than as a verb, so the noun entry is shown first.

Words with the same part of speech and spelling that are pronounced differently are separate headwords. For example, the nouns **bow** (boʊ) and **bow** (baʊ) are separate headwords.

If two words are spelled the same, but one starts with a capital letter and has a completely different meaning, for example the adjectives **catholic** and **Catholic**, they are separate headwords.

If a word is a plural form of a noun, but has a separate meaning, it is shown as one of the meanings of that noun.

blue[2] *n.* **1** [C,U] the color of the sky on a clear day: *I especially like the rich blues and reds of the painting.* | *Carolyn's the one dressed in blue.* **2 blues** [plural] a slow sad style of music that came from the African-American CULTURE in the southern U.S.: *a blues singer* —see also RHYTHM AND BLUES **3 the blues** [plural] INFORMAL feelings of sadness: *A lot of women get the blues after the baby is born.*

A few nouns, for example the word **belongings**, exist only in the plural form. These have their own entries.

1.5 *Other types of headwords*

Abbreviations are headwords, and so are prefixes like **dis-** and suffixes like **-able**.

Different spellings or forms are shown at the headword if they are commonly used. They also have their own entries as head-words, directing you to the main entry.

aes·thet·ic, esthetic /ɛsˈθɛtɪk, ɪs-/ *adj.* **1** relating to beauty and the study of beauty: *The town council will discuss plans for aesthetic improvements at two city parks.* | *People want wood shingles on their houses for purely aesthetic reasons.*

es·thet·ic /ɛsˈθɛtɪk/ *adj.* another spelling of AESTHETIC —**esthetically** /-kli/ *adv.*

Irregular inflections of words are shown at the main form, and also as separate headwords, directing you to the main entry.

have[1] /əv, həv; *strong* hæv/ *auxiliary verb, past tense* **had** *third person singular present tense* **has** *negative short forms* **haven't, hadn't, hasn't**

had /əd, həd; *strong* hæd/ *v.* **1** the past tense and past participle of HAVE

1.6 *Phrases and idioms*

Some words are often used in particular phrases, and an important feature of this dictionary is that we treat them as separate meanings. For example:

a·live /əˈlaɪv/ *adj.* [not before noun]
6 be alive with sth to be full of something and seem busy or exciting: *The street was alive with music.* | *wooded canyons alive with birds*
7 be alive and kicking a) to be very healthy and active: *At last report, she was still alive and kicking.* **b)** to continue to exist successfully: *Despite financial problems, the firm is alive and kicking.*
8 be alive to sth to realize that something is happening and that it is important: *Murphy is alive to the romance of his job.* —see also **skin sb alive** (SKIN[2])

Phrases and idioms are usually listed under the first important word in a phrase (that is, not at words like *the, to, something,* or *be*), so the definition of **skin sb alive** is at **skin**, not at **alive**. The cross-reference note at the end of the entry above tells you to look at **skin**, homograph 2, meaning 3.

2 *Understanding meaning*

2.1 *Words with more than one meaning*

Where a word has more than one meaning, each meaning is given a separate number, and the most frequent meaning, according to analysis of our spoken and written corpora, is shown first.

Guide to the Dictionary

Contents

1 How to find the word you are looking for

Words are listed in this dictionary in alphabetical order.

1.1 Compound words

Compound words are groups of two or more words with a fixed form and a special meaning, such as **air pump** and **air rage**. Most of these are shown as full headwords (but see section 1.6 Phrases and idioms). They are listed in alphabetical order; the space or hyphen between the two parts is ignored.

air·tight
air time
air-to-air
air traf·fic con·trol·ler
air·waves

1.2 Phrasal verbs

Multi-word verbs like **give up** or **put off**, are listed in alphabetical order directly after the entry for their main verb. For example:

face[2] *v.* [T]
    face sb ↔ **down**
    face off
    face up to

1.3 Derived words without definition

Some words do not need a definition, because they are formed from a headword by adding a suffix. For example **gracefully** and **gracefulness** are derived from **graceful**, and their meaning is equal to that of the main word plus the meaning of the suffix.

These words are shown at the end of the entry for the word that they are derived from.

> **grace·ful** /ˈgreɪsfəl/ *adj.* **1** moving in a smooth and attractive way, or having a smooth attractive shape: *a graceful dancer* | *graceful silk flowers* **2** polite and exactly right for a situation: *a graceful acceptance of defeat* —**gracefully** *adv.* —**gracefulness** *n.* [U]

In this case, **gracefully** just means "in a graceful way" and **gracefulness** just means "the quality of being graceful."

합성어는 표제어로 내세우고 악센트를 표시하였다.

age lim·it /ˈ. ˌ../ *n.* [C] the youngest or oldest age at which you are allowed to do something: *The age limit for buying tobacco has been raised to 18.*

1

문법 설명은 괄호 안에 표시하였다.

at·trib·ut·a·ble /əˈtrɪbyəṭəbəl/ *adj.* [not before noun] FORMAL likely to be caused by something: [+ to] *The price increase is attributable to a rise in the cost of paper.*

2

ap·point /əˈpɔɪnt/ *v.* [T] **1** to choose someone for a position or a job: *Pope John Paul II appointed several new bishops.* | [appoint (sb) as sth] *Lisa Lore was appointed as an associate athletic director at USC.*

관용구와 숙어는 각각의 뜻과 함께 나타내었다.

armchair² *adj.* **an armchair traveler/critic etc.** someone who talks or reads about being a traveler, CRITIC etc., but does not have any real experience of doing it

연어 즉 자주 함께 쓰이는 단어들은 풀이에 굵은 글씨로 표시하거나 설명을 나타내었다.

ar·gu·ment /ˈɑrgyəmənt/ *n.* **1** [C] a situation in which two or more people disagree, often angrily: [+ with] *I broke the vase during an argument with my husband.* | *Henning told the police she and her husband **had an argument** before he left.* | *I **got into an argument** with the other driver.* | *Shelton and the woman had a **heated argument** (=very angry argument).*

단어의 뜻이 여러 가지인 경우에는 필요한 뜻을 찾게 해 주는 길잡이(Signpost)를 표시하였다.

anchor² *v.*
1 boat [I,T] to lower the anchor on a ship or boat to hold it in one place: *Three tankers were anchored in the harbor.* | *Captain Cook anchored in Opunohu Bay in the 1760s.*
2 tv news [T] to be the person who reads the news and introduces reports on TV: *The new hour-long program is anchored by Mark McEwen.*
3 fasten [T usually passive] to fasten something firmly so that it cannot move: *The panel was firmly anchored by two large bolts.*

한 단어가 전형적으로 쓰이거나 말하는 사람의 태도가 엿보이는 문맥(또는 상황)을 나타내는 약어는 굵은 글씨로 표시하였다.

ap·pend /əˈpɛnd/ *v.* [T + to] FORMAL to add something to a piece of writing

ante- /æntɪ/ *prefix* coming or happening before something: *to antedate* (=exist before something else) | *the antebellum South* (=before the Civil War) —compare POST-, PRE-

다른 단어나 관용어, 그림과 사용법에 대한 참고 사항을 표시하였다.

an·te¹ /ˈænti/ *n.* **up/raise the ante** to increase your demands or try to get more things from a situation, even though this involves more risks: *Sanctions upped the ante considerably in the Middle East crisis.* —see also PENNY ANTE

a·bet /əˈbɛt/ *v.* **abetted, abetting** [T] to help someone do something wrong or illegal —see also **aid and abet** (AID² (2))

복수, 시제, 비교급 및 최상급의 변화형이 불규칙한 단어는 품사 다음에 굵은 글씨로 나타내었다.

a·moe·ba /əˈmibə/ *n.* *plural* **amoebas** or **amoebae** /-bi/ [C] a very small creature that has only one cell and a changeable shape —**amoebic** *adj.*

5 Information on register and usage

5.1 Indicating register

Some words and meanings have information on what type of situation or writing they are likely to be used in. Others have warning labels that tell you when to be careful about using a word and when it is better not to use it. There is a list of all the labels, including explanations, inside the front cover.

This type of information is shown in italics after the headword or after the meaning number, like this:

ar·bo·re·al /ɑrˈbɔriəl/ *adj*. TECHNICAL OR LITERARY relating to trees, or living in trees

ab·ne·ga·tion /ˌæbnɪˈgeɪʃən/ *n*. [U] FORMAL the act of not allowing yourself to have or do something that you want

air kiss /ˈ. ./ *n*. [C] HUMOROUS an act of greeting someone with a kiss near the side of their face, but without touching them, often done by famous people at parties

all-night·er /ˌ. ˈ../ *n*. [C] INFORMAL an occasion when you spend the whole night studying or doing written work in college

5.2 Spoken words and phrases

The label SPOKEN indicates a phrase that is typically used in speech, rather than in writing.

> **SPOKEN PHRASES**
>
> **10 that's life/men/politics etc.** used to say that something is typical of a particular situation, group of people etc.: *I guess I made a mistake, but hey, that's life.*

Because we have spoken as well as written material on the Longman Corpus, we were able to give a lot of attention to providing information of this kind. Some words with many spoken meanings, such as **mean**, have special "spoken phrases" boxes.

5.3 Usage notes

Notes on particular points of English usage are included in the dictionary. Each note follows the entry for the main word that it relates to. Other words dealt with in that Note have cross-references from their own places of entry.

6 Pronunciation

Each word is followed by its pronunciation, given in the International Phonetic Alphabet. Other possible pronunciations are shown after a comma. If only part of the pronunciation is different, this part is given, and its place in the word shown by a hyphen.

Most words that are derived from another word in a regular way, and are shown after it without a definition, are simply pronounced as the main word plus the suffix. In these cases, no pronunciation is shown. In other cases, the pronunciation of a derived word is shown.

For further information on pronunciation, go to pages 1701 and 1703 for explanations on American pronunciation and a full pronunciation table.

6.1 Compound words

Compound words that consist of two words with a separating space or hyphen are not usually given a full pronunciation. This is because each of the words has its own entry, where the pronunciation is given. Instead a stress pattern of the compound word is shown, with a dot representing each syllable, and the marks above and below that show primary (main) and secondary stress.

aircraft car·ri·er /ˈ.. ˌ.../ *n*. [C] a type of ship that has a large flat surface that airplanes fly from and land on

A number of compounds may have a shift in stress when they are used before some nouns. For example, the compound **plate glass** would have the pattern /ˌ. ˈ./ when spoken by itself or in a sentence like *The window was made of plate glass*. But the phrase **plate glass window** would usually have the pattern /ˌ. . ˈ../. The mark /ˏ/ shows this. For example: **plate glass** /ˌ. ˈ.ˏ/. Stress shift can also happen with some single words: **artificial** /ˌɑrtəˈfɪʃəlˏ/, **independent** /ˌɪndɪˈpɛndəntˏ/.

The
Dictionary
A–Z

A

A, a /eɪ/ *plural* **A's, a's** *n.* [C] the first letter of the English alphabet

a /ə; *strong* eɪ/ also **an** *indefinite article, determiner* **1** used before a noun that names something or someone that has not been mentioned before, or that the person you are talking to does not know about: *A new Star Trek movie is out.* | *We just bought a new sofa.* —compare THE¹ **2 a)** used before a noun that is one of a particular group or class of people or things: *She's an accountant.* **b)** used before someone's family name to show that they belong to that family: *He's a McGregor all right – look at his eyes!* **3 a)** one: *a thousand dollars* | *Do you want a piece of cake?* | *Wait a minute.* **b)** a lot/a few/a little etc. used before some words that express an amount of something: *A few people arrived late.* | *They've spent a great deal of money on the house.* **4 twice a week/ $10 a day etc.** two times each week, $10 each day etc.; per: *Time Magazine is delivered once a week.* | *The pay is $6.35 an hour.* **5** used before a noun to mean all things of that type: *A square has four sides.* (=all squares have four sides) **6** used before two nouns that are mentioned together so often that they are thought of as one thing: *a needle and thread* | *a cup and saucer* **7 a)** used before singular nouns, especially words for actions, meaning one example of that action: *Can I have a look?* **b)** used before the -ing form of verbs when they are used as nouns: *a loud screeching of brakes* **c)** used before an UNCOUNTABLE noun when other information about the noun is added by an adjective or phrase: *He was struck by a certain beauty in the scene.* | *a coarseness in his manner* **8** used before an UNCOUNTABLE noun to mean a type of it: *They brew a beer that's worth looking for in the stores.* **9** used before the name of a painter, artist etc. meaning a particular painting, SCULPTURE etc. by that person: *Is it a Monet?* **10** used before a name to mean having the same qualities as that person or thing: *He's like a modern Dickens.* **11 a)** used before someone's name when you do not know who they are: *A Mrs. Barnett is waiting for you.* **b)** used before names of days, events in the year etc. to mean a particular one: *It will certainly be a winter to remember.* **12** used after "such," "what," "rather," and "many" to emphasize what you are saying: *What a great idea!* | *She's such a sweetie.*

A¹ /eɪ/ *n.* **1** [C] the best GRADE that a student can get in a class or on a test: *an A on the test* | *He got straight A's (=all A grades) in high school.* **2** [C,U] also **a** the sixth note in the musical SCALE of C MAJOR or the musical KEY based on this note **3 an A student** someone who regularly gets the best GRADES possible for their work in school or college **4 from A to B** from one place to another: *It doesn't have to be fancy – I just need a car to get me from A to B.* **5 (from) A to Z** describing, including, or knowing everything about a subject: *The book is an A to Z of French cooking.* **6** [U] a common type of blood

A² the written abbreviation of AMP

a-¹ /ə/ *prefix* **1** in a particular condition or way: *alive* (=living) | *Read it aloud, please* (=in a voice that others can hear). **2** LITERARY OR OLD-FASHIONED used to show that someone or something is in or on something, or at a place: *abed* (=in bed) | *afar* (=far away) | *atop* (=on top of something)

a-² /eɪ, æ/ *prefix* showing the opposite or the absence of something; NOT; WITHOUT: *atypically* (=not typically) | *amoral* (=not moral)

A-1 /eɪ ˈwʌn/ *adj.* OLD-FASHIONED very good or completely healthy, sometimes used in the names of companies: *He has an A-1 credit rating.* | *A-1 Window Cleaners*

AA *n.* [C] **1** Associate of Arts; a college degree given

after two years of study, usually at a COMMUNITY COLLEGE **2** ALCOHOLICS ANONYMOUS

AAA /ˌeɪ eɪ ˈeɪ, ˌtrɪpəl ˈeɪ/ American Automobile Association; an organization for people who own cars

aah /ɑ/ *interjection* another spelling of AH

aard·vark /ˈɑrdvɑrk/ *n.* [C] a large animal from southern Africa that has a very long nose and eats small insects

aargh /ɑrg, ə/ *interjection* INFORMAL used to show that you are angry, disappointed, annoyed etc.: *Aargh, this thing is so heavy!*

Aar·on /ˈærən, ˈɛr-/**, Hank** /hæŋk/ (1934–) a U.S. baseball player famous for hitting more HOME RUNs than Babe Ruth

AARP —see AMERICAN ASSOCIATION OF RETIRED PERSONS

AB *n.* [U] a common type of blood

ABA —see AMERICAN BAR ASSOCIATION, THE

a·back /əˈbæk/ *adv.* **be taken aback** to be very surprised or shocked by something: *Shulman was taken aback by the survey results.*

ab·a·cus /ˈæbəkəs, əˈbæ-/ *n.* [C] a wooden frame with small BEADS used for COUNTing

ab·a·lo·ne /ˌæbəˈloʊni/ *n.* [C,U] a type of SHELLFISH that is used as food and whose shell contains MOTHER-OF-PEARL

a·ban·don¹ /əˈbændən/ *v.* [T] **1** to leave someone, especially someone you are responsible for: *The 9-year-old boy was abandoned by his alcoholic father.* **2** to go away from a place, vehicle etc. permanently, especially because the situation makes it impossible for you to stay: *The suspect abandoned the car at Llewellyn and Hamilton Avenues.* | *The volcano eruption forced the U.S. to abandon Clark Air Force Base.* **3** to stop doing something because there are too many problems and it is impossible to continue: *There was increased pressure on North Korea to abandon nuclear arms development.* **4** to decide that you do not believe in a particular idea or principle anymore: *Education leaders do not want to abandon California's commitment to affordable college education.* | *Rescuers abandoned all hope of finding any more survivors of the crash.* **5 abandon yourself to sth** LITERARY to feel an emotion so strongly that you let it control you completely **6 abandon ship** to leave a ship because it is sinking —**abandonment** *n.* [U]

abandon² *n.* [U] **with reckless/wild abandon** in a careless or uncontrolled way, without thinking or caring about what you are doing: *Hamilton spent the company's money with reckless abandon.*

a·ban·doned /əˈbændənd/ *adj.* **1** an abandoned building, car, boat etc. has been left completely by the people who owned it and is not used anymore: *Abandoned or stolen bikes are being sold at police auctions.* **2** someone who is abandoned has been left completely alone by the person who was taking care of them, who is not coming back: *an abused and abandoned child* **3** LITERARY behaving in a wild and uncontrolled way

a·base /əˈbeɪs/ *v.* **abase yourself** to behave in a way that shows you accept that someone has complete power over you —**abasement** *n.* [U]

a·bashed /əˈbæʃt/ *adj.* [not before noun] embarrassed or ashamed because you have done something wrong or stupid: *Both girls fixed their eyes on the ground, abashed.*

a·bate /əˈbeɪt/ *v.* [I,T] FORMAL to become less strong or decrease, or to make something do this: *Public anger does not appear to be abating.* —**abatement** *n.* [U]

ab·bess /ˈæbəs/ *n.* [C] a woman who is in charge of a CONVENT (=religious institution for women)

ab·bey /ˈæbi/ *n. plural* **abbeys** [C] a large church, especially one with buildings next to it where MONKs and NUNs live or used to live

ab·bot /ˈæbət/ *n.* [C] a man who is in charge of a MONASTERY (=place where a group of MONKs live)

A

abbr. also **abbrev.** the written abbreviation of "abbreviation"

ab·bre·vi·ate /ə'briviˌeɪt/ v. [T] to make a word or expression shorter by not including letters or by using only the first letter of each word: *Extraterrestrial is often abbreviated as E.T.*

ab·bre·vi·at·ed /ə'briviˌeɪtɪd/ adj. made shorter by not including letters or not including parts of a story, statement, event etc.: *Charro gave the speech again in an abbreviated form.*

ab·bre·vi·a·tion /əˌbrivi'eɪʃən/ n. **1** [C] a short form of a word or expression: [+ of/for] *MIT is the abbreviation for the Massachusetts Institute of Technology.* **2** [U] the act of abbreviating something

ABC n. [U] American Broadcasting Corporation; one of the national television companies in the U.S.

ABCs /ˌeɪ bi 'siz/ n. **1** [plural] the letters of the English alphabet as taught to children **2 the ABCs of sth** the basic facts about a particular subject: *the ABCs of your computer*

ab·di·cate /'æbdɪˌkeɪt/ v. [I,T] **1** to give up the position of being king or queen **2 abdicate responsibility/authority/leadership etc.** FORMAL to refuse to be responsible for something, be in control of something etc., when you should be or were before: *The federal government has largely abdicated its responsibility in dealing with housing needs.* —**abdication** /ˌæbdɪ'keɪʃən/ n. [C,U]

ab·do·men /'æbdəmən/ n. [C] **1** the part of your body between your chest and legs which contains your stomach **2** the end part of an insect's body, joined to the THORAX —**abdominal** /æb'dɑmɪnl/ adj.: *abdominal cramps* —see picture at INSECT

ab·duct /əb'dʌkt, æb-/ v. [T] to take someone away by force; KIDNAP: *Lawson was abducted from her home.* —**abduction** /əb'dʌkʃən/ n. [C,U]

ab·duc·tee /ˌæbdʌk'ti, əbˌdʌk'ti/ n. [C] someone who has been abducted

ab·duc·tor /əb'dʌktə/ n. [C] someone who abducts someone else

Ab·dul-Jab·bar /æbˌdʊl dʒə'bar/, **Ka·reem** /kə'rim/ (1947–) a U.S. basketball player, who is considered one of the best players ever

a·bed /ə'bɛd/ adj. [not before noun] OLD-FASHIONED in bed

Ab·e·lard /'æbəˌlard/, **Peter** (1079–1142) a French PHILOSOPHER and THEOLOGIAN who used the methods of ancient Greek philosophers in his study of religion

ab·er·rant /'æbərənt, ə'bɛrənt/ adj. FORMAL not usual or normal: *aberrant behavior*

ab·er·ra·tion /ˌæbə'reɪʃən/ n. [C,U] an action or event that is different from what usually happens or what someone usually does: *The losses this year are an aberration, and the company will continue to grow.* —**aberrational** adj.

a·bet /ə'bɛt/ v. **abetted, abetting** [T] to help someone do something wrong or illegal —see also **aid and abet** (AID² (2))

a·bey·ance /ə'beɪəns/ n. **in abeyance** something such as a custom, rule, or system that is in abeyance is not being used at the present time: *The law is being held in abeyance until the court makes a decision about it.*

ab·hor /əb'hɔr, æb-/ v. **abhorred** [T not in progressive] FORMAL to hate a type of behavior or way of thinking, especially because you think it is morally wrong: *I oppose and abhor discrimination of any kind.*

ab·hor·rence /əb'hɔrəns, -'har-/ n. [U] FORMAL a deep feeling of hatred toward something

ab·hor·rent /əb'hɔrənt/ adj. FORMAL something that is abhorrent is completely unacceptable because it seems morally wrong; REPUGNANT: [+ to] *The practice of terrorism is abhorrent to the civilized world.* | *Ken grew up in the South, and found racism abhorrent.*

a·bide /ə'baɪd/ v. OLD-FASHIONED **1 sb can't abide sb/sth** used to say that someone dislikes someone or something very much because they are annoying: *I can't abide the idea of them getting married.* **2** [I always + adv./prep.] *past tense also* **abode** to live somewhere

abide by sth phr. v. [T] to accept and obey a decision, rule, agreement etc., even though you may not agree with it: *Tenants must abide by the rules of the mobile home park.*

a·bid·ing /ə'baɪdɪŋ/ adj. an abiding feeling or belief continues for a long time and is not likely to change: *an abiding belief in the power of justice*

a·bil·i·ty /ə'bɪləti/ n. plural **abilities** [C,U] **1** something that you are able to do, especially because you have a particular mental or physical skill: *leadership ability* | *The loss of physical abilities that is caused by aging is normal.* | [**ability to do sth**] *The goal is to improve the company's ability to compete.* | *Linda has the ability to absorb and understand large amounts of information quickly.* **2** someone's, especially a student's, level of intelligence or skill, especially in school or college work: *Even children of above-average ability are not always ready to begin school.* | *There is a place in the band for musicians of all abilities.* **3 to the best of your ability** to do something as well as you can

---

USAGE NOTE: ABILITY

WORD CHOICE: ability, skill, talent
Use these words to talk about how well someone does something. An **ability** is what you can do with your mind or your body: *musical ability* | *her ability to solve problems.* You can lose your **ability** to do something: *Joe lost the ability to walk after his motorcycle accident.* A **skill** is something that you do very well because you have learned and practiced it: *This course will help you improve your speaking and listening skills.* **Talent** is a natural ability to do something well, that cannot be learned: *Tim has a real talent for singing.*

-ability /əbɪləti/ suffix used with adjectives that end in -ABLE to form nouns: *availability* | *probability* —see also -IBILITY

ab·ject /'æbdʒɛkt, əb'dʒɛkt/ adj. **1 abject poverty/misery/failure etc.** the state of being extremely poor, unhappy, unsuccessful etc. **2** an abject action or expression shows that you feel very ashamed: *The manager was abject in his apology.* —**abjectly** adv. —**abjection** /æb'dʒɛkʃən/ n. [U]

ab·jure /æb'dʒʊr/ v. [T] FORMAL to state publicly that you will give up a particular belief or way of behaving; RENOUNCE (2) —**abjuration** /ˌæbdʒʊ'reɪʃən/ n. [U]

a·blaze /ə'bleɪz/ adj. **1 be ablaze** to be burning with a lot of flames, often causing serious damage: *Dozens of homes were ablaze.* | *During the riot, a police car was* **set ablaze.** (=made to start burning) **2** filled with a lot of bright light or color: [+ with] *We cycled through the hills, which were ablaze with fall colors.* **3 ablaze with anger/enthusiasm/excitement etc.** very angry, excited etc. about something —see also BLAZE¹

a·ble /'eɪbəl/ adj. **1 be able to do sth a)** to have the skill, strength, knowledge etc. to do something: *Thomas is expected to be able to play again next weekend.* **b)** to have the chance to do something because the situation makes it possible for you to do it: *In 1944, we were able to return to Hawaii.* | *Ammiano still isn't able to make a living from acting.* **2** smart or good at doing something, especially at doing an important job; COMPETENT (1): *an able assistant*

-able /əbəl/ suffix [in adjectives] **1** used to form adjectives that show you can do something to a particular thing or person: *washable* (=it can be washed) | *lovable* (=easy to love) | *unbreakable* (=it cannot be broken) **2** used to show that someone or something has a particular quality or condition: *comfortable* | *knowledgeable* (=knowing a lot) —**ably** suffix [in adverbs] *unbelievably* —see also -IBLE

able-bod·ied /ˈ.. ˌ../ adj. physically strong and healthy, especially when compared with someone who is DISABLED: *Every able-bodied man should have the opportunity to work.*

a·bloom /ə'blum/ adj. [not before noun] LITERARY looking healthy and full of color: *a garden abloom with roses*

ab·lu·tions /ə'bluʃənz, æ-/ [plural] n. FORMAL OR HUMOROUS the things that you do to make yourself clean, such as washing yourself, brushing your teeth etc.

a·bly /'eɪbli/ adv. intelligently, skillfully, or well: *He was ably defended by his lawyers.*

ab·ne·ga·tion /ˌæbnɪ'geɪʃən/ n. [U] FORMAL the act of not allowing yourself to have or do something that you want

ab·nor·mal /æb'nɔrməl/ adj. very different from usual in a way that seems strange, worrying, wrong, or dangerous: *Some people suffer an abnormal fear of being in open places.* | *an abnormal heartbeat*

ab·nor·mal·i·ty /ˌæbnɔr'mæləti, -nə-/ n. [C,U] plural **abnormalities** an abnormal feature or CHARACTERISTIC, especially something that is wrong with part of someone's body: *Dyslexia may be caused by a brain abnormality involving the sense of sight.*

ab·nor·mal·ly /æb'nɔrməli/ adv. **1 abnormally high/low/slow etc.** unusually high, low etc., especially in a way that could cause problems: *Abnormally dry weather is hurting crops.* **2** in an unusual and often worrying or dangerous way: *The child was acting abnormally.*

a·board[1] /ə'bɔrd/ adv. **1** on or onto a ship, airplane, or train: *The plane crashed, killing all 200 people aboard.* | *The boat swayed as he stepped aboard.* **2 All aboard!** SPOKEN used to tell passengers of a ship, bus, or train that they must get on because it will leave soon

aboard[2] prep. on or onto a ship, airplane, or train: *Reporters were not allowed to go aboard.*

a·bode[1] /ə'boud/ n. [C] FORMAL OR HUMOROUS someone's home

abode[2] v. a past tense of ABIDE (2)

a·bol·ish /ə'bɑlɪʃ/ v. [T] to officially end a law, system etc., especially one that has existed for a long time: *Welfare programs cannot be abolished that quickly.*

ab·o·li·tion /ˌæbə'lɪʃən/ n. [U] the official end of a law, system etc., especially one that has existed for a long time: [+ of] *As a judge, Marshall worked for the abolition of the death penalty.*

ab·o·li·tion·ist /ˌæbə'lɪʃənɪst/ n. [C] someone who wants to end a system or law

A-bomb /'eɪ bɑm/ n. [C] OLD-FASHIONED an ATOMIC BOMB

a·bom·i·na·ble /ə'bɑmənəbəl/ adj. extremely bad or of very bad quality: *an abominable crime* —**abominably** adv.

abominable snow·man n. [C] /ˌ.,.... '../ a large creature like a human that is supposed to live in the Himalayas; YETI

a·bom·i·nate /ə'bɑmə,neɪt/ v. [T not in progressive] FORMAL to hate something very much; ABHOR

a·bom·i·na·tion /ə,bɑmə'neɪʃən/ n. [C] a word meaning someone or something that is extremely offensive or unacceptable, sometimes used humorously: *I never cook with that abomination called "cooking wine."*

ab·o·rig·i·nal[1] /ˌæbə'rɪdʒənəl/ adj. **1** FORMAL relating to the people or animals that have existed in a place or country from the earliest times; INDIGENOUS **2** relating to Australian aborigines

aboriginal[2] n. [C] an aborigine

ab·o·rig·i·ne /ˌæbə'rɪdʒəni/ n. [C] a member of the group of people who have lived in Australia from the earliest times

a·bort[3] /ə'bɔrt/ v. **1** [T] to stop an activity because it would be difficult or dangerous to continue it: *The rescue mission had to be aborted.* **2** [T] to deliberately end a PREGNANCY when the baby is still too young to live: *The law allows women to abort an early-stage pregnancy.* —compare MISCARRY

a·bor·tion /ə'bɔrʃən/ n. [C,U] a medical operation to end a PREGNANCY so that the baby is not born alive: *The woman's doctor advised her to have an abortion*

for medical reasons. | *Abortion has become a highly political issue.*

a·bor·tion·ist /ə'bɔrʃənɪst/ n. [C] **1** someone who does abortions, especially illegally **2** someone who supports laws that make abortion legal

a·bor·tive /ə'bɔrtɪv/ adj. an abortive action is not successful: *an abortive attempt to kill the Governor*

a·bound /ə'baʊnd/ v. [I] FORMAL to exist in very large numbers or quantities: *Tales of illegal business dealings abounded.* | [+ in] *Good restaurants abound in the area.*

abound with sth phr. v. [T] if a place, situation etc. abounds with something, it contains a very large number or quantity of that thing: *Munich abounds with museums.*

a·bout[1] /ə'baʊt/ prep. **1** on or dealing with a particular subject: *an article about the famine* | *They were talking about music.* | *Robert told her all about it* (=all the details of a particular subject). **2** in the nature or character of a person or thing: *I'm not sure what it is about her, but guys really like her.* | *What did you like best about the book?* **3 what/how about** SPOKEN **a)** used to make a suggestion: *I think I'll have dessert. How about you?* **b)** used to ask for news or information about someone or something: *What about the people who were in the bus? What happened to them?* **4** SPOKEN used to introduce a subject that you want to talk about: *About this weekend – is everyone still going?* | *We have to talk – it's about your mom.* **5 do sth about** to do something to solve a problem or stop a bad situation: *What can be done about the increase in crime?* **6** if an organization, a job, an activity etc. is about something, that is its basic purpose: *Basically, the job's all about helping people get off welfare.* **7** in many different directions within a particular place, or in different parts of a place; AROUND: *Trash and food were strewn about the room.* **8** LITERARY surrounding a person or thing: *There was death all about her* (=many people were dying near her).

about[2] adv. **1** more or less a particular number or amount; APPROXIMATELY: *Tim's about 25 years old.* | *Her music lesson is about 45 minutes long.* **2** INFORMAL almost: *She's 11 months old and just about ready to start walking.* —see also **just about** (JUST[1]) **3 that's about it/all** INFORMAL **a)** used to tell someone that you have told them everything you know: *I've seen her around a few times, but that's about it.* **b)** used to tell someone that there is nothing else available: *There's some ham in the fridge, and that's about it.*

about[3] adj. **1 be about to do sth** if someone is about to do something or if something is about to happen, they will do it or it will happen very soon: *Oh, I was just about to leave you a message.* **2 not be about to do sth** INFORMAL used to emphasize that you have no intention of doing something: *I wasn't about to let him pay for it.* —see also **out and about** (OUT[1]), **be up and about** (UP[2])

about-face /ˌ.'./ n. [C usually singular] a complete change in the way someone thinks or behaves: *Bush did an about-face on his promise of no new taxes.*

a·bove[1] /ə'bʌv/ prep. **1** in or to a higher position than something else: *He had a bruise above his eye.* | *a painting above the bed* | *the hills above the university* —see also OVER[1] —opposite BELOW[1] **2** more than a particular number, amount, or level: *It was barely above freezing.* | *Tides rose six feet above their normal level.* —opposite BELOW[1] **3 above all (else)** used to emphasize that something is more important than the other things you have already mentioned: *Above all, I want my daughter to be confident.* **4** louder or having a higher PITCH than other sounds: *You had to shout to be heard above the music.* **5 above suspicion/reproach/criticism etc.** so good that no one can doubt or criticize you: *Goodwin's work ethic is above reproach.* **6** to a greater degree than someone or something else: *Americans seem to value convenience above cost.* | *Sonsini has contributed above and beyond the ordinary call of*

A

duty. **7** in a position of more importance: *Student athletes should not place athletics above academics.* **8** higher in rank, power, or authority: *She works hard, which pleases those above her.* —opposite BELOW¹ **9 be above (doing) sth** to consider yourself so important that you do not have to do all the things that everyone else has to do: *She's not above stuffing envelopes to help out the secretarial staff.* | *No one is above the law in America.* —see also **over and above** (OVER¹)

above

a picture hanging above a fireplace

a plane flying over the mountains

s w **above²** *adv.* **1** in a higher place than something else: *The cereal goes in the cabinet above.* **2** more than a particular number, amount, or level: *Big-screen TVs are defined as 27 inches or above.* | *students of above-average ability* **3** higher in rank, power, or authority: *officers of the rank of Major and above* **4** FORMAL used in a book, article etc. to describe someone or something mentioned earlier in the same piece of writing: *See the rates listed above.* | *Christine Liddell, above, talks to Santa* (=there is a picture of Christine above the words). —opposite BELOW²

above³ *adj.* [only before noun] used in a book, article etc. to describe someone or something mentioned earlier in the same piece of writing: *City offices in the above counties will be closed Wednesday.*

above⁴ *n.* **the above** FORMAL the person or thing mentioned before in the same piece of writing: *The correct answer was C:* **none of the above** (=none of the answers listed above). | *Better tasting than* **all the above** *are the cheddar rice cakes.*

a·bove·board /ə'bʌvˌbɔrd/ *adj.* [not before noun] honest and legal: *The practice has been questioned, but tax experts say it is aboveboard.*

above-men·tioned /.'. ,../ *adj.* FORMAL **1** [only before noun] mentioned on a previous page or higher up on the same page **2** the **above-mentioned** people whose names have already been mentioned in a book, document etc.

ab·ra·ca·dab·ra /ˌæbrəkə'dæbrə/ *interjection* a word you say when you do a magic trick, which is supposed to make it successful

a·brade /ə'breɪd/ *v.* [I,T] TECHNICAL to rub something so hard that the surface becomes damaged

A·bra·ham /'eɪbrəˌhæm, -həm/ in the Bible, a religious leader who established the HEBREWS as a nation

ab·ra·sion /ə'breɪʒən/ *n.* TECHNICAL **1** [C] an area, especially on the surface of your skin, that has been damaged or injured by being rubbed too hard: *She was treated for cuts and abrasions.* **2** [U] the process of rubbing a surface very hard so that it becomes damaged or disappears

a·bra·sive /ə'breɪsɪv, -zɪv/ *adj.* **1** seeming rude or unkind in the way you behave toward people, especially because you say what you think very directly: *an abrasive personality* **2** having a rough surface,

especially one that can be used to clean other surfaces by rubbing: *a dry abrasive cleaning pad* —**abrasively** *adv.*

abrasive² *n.* [C] a rough substance that you use for cleaning other things by rubbing

a·breast /ə'brɛst/ *adv.* **1 keep/stay abreast of sth** to make sure that you know all the most recent facts or information about a particular subject or situation: *Executives keep abreast of events in the company by e-mail.* **2 walk/ride etc. abreast** to walk, ride etc. next to each other: *The training planes were flying* **four abreast** (=with four airplanes next to each other).

a·bridged /ə'brɪdʒd/ *adj.* an abridged book, play etc. has been made shorter but keeps its basic structure and meaning —**abridge** *v.* [T] —**abridgment** *n.* [C,U]

a·broad /ə'brɔd/ *adv.* **1** in or to a foreign country: *You may have to pay taxes, even if you are living and working abroad.* | *High school students may benefit from going abroad to study languages.* **2** FORMAL if a feeling, piece of news etc. is abroad, a lot of people feel it or know about it: *Corporations do not want their commercial secrets spread abroad.* **3** OLD USE outdoors

s w

3

ab·ro·gate /'æbrəˌgeɪt/ *v.* [T] FORMAL to officially end a law, legal agreement, practice etc.: *It was suggested that the mutual security treaty with Japan be abrogated.* —**abrogation** /ˌæbrə'geɪʃən/ *n.* [C,U]

a·brupt /ə'brʌpt/ *adj.* **1** sudden and unexpected: *There may be an abrupt change in weather patterns.* | **an abrupt end/stop/halt etc.** *His resignation was an abrupt end to an impressive career.* **2** seeming rude and unfriendly, especially because you do not waste time in friendly conversation; BRUSQUE: *"Change it," he says in his abrupt, no-nonsense style.* —**abruptly** *adv.* —**abruptness** *n.* [U]

ABS /ˌeɪ bi 'ɛs/ *n.* [U] the abbreviation of ANTI-LOCK BRAKING SYSTEM

abs /æbz/ [plural] INFORMAL *n.* the muscles on your ABDOMEN

ab·scess /'æbsɛs/ *n.* [C] a painful swollen place in your skin or inside your body that has become infected and contains a yellow liquid

ab·scond /əb'skɑnd, æb-/ *v.* [I] FORMAL **1** to suddenly leave the place where you work after having stolen money from it: [+ **with**] *Royson absconded with money belonging to 40 clients.* **2** to escape from a place where you are being kept

ab·sence /'æbsəns/ *n.* **1** [C,U] the state of not being in the place where people expect someone or something to be, or the time someone or something is away: *Malone's absences have made it difficult on the rest of the team.* | *The Russian flag was waving again after an absence of 74 years.* | **In** *Wilson's* **absence,** (=while he is away) *Green will manage the project.* **2** [U] the lack of something or the fact that it does not exist: [+ **of**] *There was a notable absence of confidence among the boys.* | **In the absence of** *a complete ban on smoking, employers should provide a separate place for smokers.* **3 absence makes the heart grow fonder** used to say that being away from someone makes you like them more —see also **conspicuous by your absence** (CONSPICUOUS), **leave of absence** (LEAVE²)

s v

ab·sent¹ /'æbsənt/ *adj.* **1** not at work, school, a meeting etc. because you are sick or decide not to go: [+ **from**] *Half of our students were absent from class today.* —opposite PRESENT¹ **2 an absent look/ expression etc.** a look etc. that shows you are not paying attention to or thinking about what is happening —see also ABSENTLY **3** FORMAL if something is absent, it is missing or it is not in the place where it is expected to be: [+ **from**] *Absent from the book are any examples of how to solve the puzzles.*

ab·sent² /æb'sɛnt/ *v.* [T] **absent yourself (from sth)** FORMAL to not go to a place or take part in an event where people expect you to be

ab·sen·tee /ˌæbsən'ti/ *n.* [C] someone who should be in a place or at an event but is not there

absentee bal·lot /ˌ... '../ *n.* [C] a process by which

people can vote by mail before an election because they will be away during the election

ab·sen·tee·ism /ˌæbsən'tiːɪzəm/ n. [U] regular absence from work or school, usually without a good reason

absentee land·lord /ˌ... '.../ n. [C] someone who lives a long way away from a house or apartment that they rent to other people, and who rarely or never visits it

absentee vote /ˌ... './ n. [C] a vote that you send by mail in an election because you cannot be in the place where you usually vote

ab·sen·tia /æb'sɛnʃə/ n. **in absentia** FORMAL when you are not at a court or an official meeting where a decision is made about you: *The court found Collins guilty in absentia.*

ab·sent·ly /'æbsəntˀli/ adv. in a way that shows that you are not paying attention to or thinking about what is happening: *"Thanks," she said absently.*

absent-mind·ed /ˌ... '...◂/ adj. likely to forget things, especially because you are thinking about something else: *Ron's being his normal absent-minded self.* —**absent-mindedly** adv. —**absent-mindedness** n. [U]

ab·sinthe, absinth /'æbsɪnθ/ n. [U] a bitter green very strong alcoholic drink

ˢ ᵂ **ab·so·lute¹** /'æbsəˌlut, ˌæbsə'lut/ adj. **1** [only before noun] INFORMAL used to emphasize your opinion about something or someone, especially when you think they are very bad, stupid, unsuccessful etc.: *The show was an absolute disaster the first night.* | *His office is an absolute mess.* **2** complete or total: *No one can say with absolute certainty that the oil is there.* **3** definite and not likely to change: *April 10 is the absolute deadline.* **4** absolute power or authority is complete and unlimited **5** not changing and true or correct in all situations: *an absolute standard of morality* **6 in absolute terms** measured by itself, not in comparison with other things: *In absolute terms, the experiment wasn't a complete failure.*

absolute² n. [C] something that is always true and does not change: *In business, there are very few absolutes.*

ˢ ᵂ **ab·so·lute·ly** /ˌæbsə'lutli, 'æbsəˌlutli/ adv. SPOKEN **1** completely and in every way: *The ride was absolutely amazing.* | *Are you absolutely sure?* | *It's absolutely the best museum in the country.* | *We had absolutely no warning.* | *Stacy knew absolutely nothing about the business when she started.* **2** absolutely! used to say that you completely agree with someone: *"If Beverly says so, it's probably true." "Absolutely."* **3 absolutely not!** used when saying strongly that someone must not do something or when strongly disagreeing with someone: *"Can I go to the concert?" "Absolutely not!"*

absolute ze·ro /ˌ... './ n. the lowest temperature that is possible

ab·so·lu·tion /ˌæbsə'luʃən/ n. [U] a process in the Christian religion by which someone is forgiven for the things they have done wrong

ab·so·lut·ism /'æbsəluˌtɪzəm/ n. [U] a political system in which one ruler has complete power and authority —**absolutist** n. [C]

ab·solve /əb'zɑlv, -'sɑlv/ v. [T] FORMAL **1** to say publicly that someone is not guilty or responsible for something: [absolve sb of sth] *Moving away will not absolve you of the responsibility for paying your debt.* **2** [often passive] to forgive someone for something they have done wrong

ᵂ **ab·sorb** /əb'sɔrb, -'zɔrb/ v. [T]
1 liquid/substance if something absorbs a liquid or other substance, it takes the substance into itself from the surface or space around it: *Lead that gets into your body is absorbed into the bones* | *Simmer the rice for 20 minutes until all the liquid is absorbed.* **2** interest to interest someone very much, often so that you do not notice other things happening around you: [absorb sb in sth] *You could tell he was absorbed in his conversation, and not paying much attention to the road.* **3** information to read or hear a large amount of new information and understand it: *I keep the lesson simple because small kids can't absorb that much.*

absorb   **A**

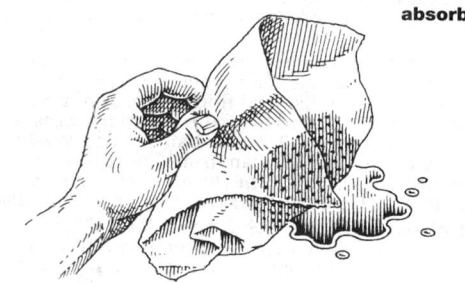

4 become part of to make a smaller country, company, or group of people become part of your country, company, or group: *In the last 10 years, California has absorbed 35% of all legal immigrants to the U.S.* | *Azerbaijan was absorbed into the Soviet Union in the 1920s.* **5** deal with bad situation to be able to deal with a problem, loss etc. without suffering too many other problems: *The university had to absorb a $14 million cut in funding.* | *Few athletic teams can successfully absorb the loss of three starting players.* **6** money/time etc. if something absorbs money, time etc. it uses a lot of it: *Defense spending absorbs almost 29% of the country's wealth.* **7** force to reduce the effect of a sudden violent movement: *The insole is designed to absorb shock and provide arch support.* **8** light/heat/energy if a substance or object absorbs light, heat, or energy, it keeps it and does not REFLECT it (=send it back): *Move the plants to a south-facing wall, where they can absorb daytime heat.*

ab·sorb·ent /əb'sɔrbənt, -'zɔr-/ adj. able to take in liquids easily: *absorbent diapers*

ab·sorb·ing /əb'sɔrbɪŋ, -'zɔr-/ adj. enjoyable and interesting and holding your attention for a long time: *It's an absorbing and engaging show.*

ab·sorp·tion /əb'sɔrpʃən, -'zɔr-/ n. [U] **1** a process in which a material or object takes in liquid, gas, or heat: *the body's absorption of iron* **2** a process in which a country or organization makes a smaller country, organization, or group of people become part of itself: *Israel asked for a loan to help with the absorption of Soviet immigrants.* **3** the fact of being very interested in something: [+ with/in] *I don't understand James' absorption with military history.*

ab·stain /əb'steɪn/ v. [I] **1** to say that you are not voting either for or against something in an election: *Three members of the committee abstained.* **2** FORMAL to not do something, especially something enjoyable, because you think it is bad for your health or morally wrong: [+ from] *Teens are being urged to abstain from sex.* —**abstainer** n. [C]

ab·ste·mi·ous /æb'stimiəs/ adj. FORMAL OR HUMOROUS careful not to have too much food, drink etc. —**abstemiously** adv. —**abstemiousness** n. [U]

ab·sten·tion /əb'stɛnʃən, æb-/ n. [C,U] a vote in an election which is neither for nor against something or someone

ab·sti·nence /'æbstənəns/ n. [U] the practice of not doing something you enjoy, especially not drinking alcohol or having sex, or the length of time you do this —**abstinent** adj.

ab·stract¹ /əb'strækt, æb-, 'æbstrækt/ adj. **1** abstract paintings, designs etc. consist of shapes and patterns that do not look like real people or things **2** existing only as an idea or quality rather than as something real that you can see or touch: *The photographs put a human face on an abstract political event.* —compare CONCRETE² **3** based on general ideas or principles rather than specific examples or real events: *By the age of about seven, children are capable of abstract thought* (=thought about complicated ideas rather than about things that are around you). | ˢ ᵂ

A

Gorbachev took the abstract idea of reform and made it a reality. —compare FIGURATIVE —see also ABSTRACT NOUN

ab·stract² /'æbstrækt, əb'strækt, æb-/ *n.* [C] **1** a painting, design etc. that contains shapes or images that do not look like real things or people **2** a short written statement of the most important ideas in a speech, article etc. **3 in the abstract** considered in a general way rather than being based on specific details and examples: *In the abstract, democracy is wonderful, but a true democracy may not be possible.*

ab·stract³ /əb'strækt, æb-, 'æbstrækt/ *v.* [T] **1** to use information from a speech, article etc. in a shorter piece of writing that contains the most important ideas **2** FORMAL to remove something from somewhere or from a place

ab·stract·ed /əb'stræktɪd, æb-, 'æbstræktɪd/ *adj.* not noticing anything around you because you are thinking carefully about something else —**abstractedly** *adv.*

ab·strac·tion /əb'strækʃən, æb-/ *n.* **1** [C] a general idea about a type of situation, thing, or person, rather than a specific example from real life: *Until now, our generation only knew war as an abstraction.* **2** [U] a state in which you do not notice what is happening around you because you are thinking carefully about something else

abstract noun /ˌ.. '. / *n.* [C] a noun that names a feeling, quality, or state rather than an object, animal, or person. For example, "hunger" and "beauty" are abstract nouns

ab·struse /əb'strus, æb-/ *adj.* FORMAL difficult to understand in a way that seems unnecessarily complicated —**abstrusely** *adv.* —**abstruseness** *n.* [U]

ab·surd /əb'sɚd, -'zɚd/ *adj.* completely stupid or unreasonable, especially in a silly way; RIDICULOUS: *a TV program with an absurd plot* | *The idea seemed absurd.* —**absurdity** *n.* [C,U]

ab·surd·ly /əb'sɚdli/ *adv.* **absurdly cheap/difficult/easy etc.** so cheap, difficult etc. that it seems surprising, unusual, or even funny: *Interest rates have risen to absurdly high levels.*

Ab·u Dha·bi /ˌɑbu 'dɑbi, ˌæ-/ **1** the largest EMIRATE of the United Arab Emirates **2** the capital city of the United Arab Emirates

A·bu·ja /ɑ'budʒə/ the capital city of Nigeria

a·bun·dance /ə'bʌndəns/ *n.* [singular,U] a large quantity of something: [+ of] *There is an abundance of fresh vegetables available.* | *Helium-3 is found in abundance on the moon.*

a·bun·dant /ə'bʌndənt/ *adj.* existing or available in large quantities so that there is more than enough; PLENTIFUL: *an abundant and cheap supply of oil*

a·bun·dant·ly /ə'bʌndəntli/ *adv.* **1** in large quantities: *Lavender will grow abundantly with little water.* **2 abundantly clear** very easy to understand, so that anyone should be able to realize it: *It's abundantly clear why he's running for governor.* | *They made it abundantly clear that they wanted to be alone.*

a·buse¹ /ə'byus/ *n.* **1** [C,U] the use of something in a way that it should not be used: [+ of] *Nixon was accused of the abuse of presidential power.* | *The environment cannot cope with our abuse of air, water, and land.* | **drug/alcohol etc. abuse** *the problem of drug abuse in our schools* | *The Medicare system is based on trust, so it is open to abuse* (=able or likely to be used in the wrong way). **2** [U] cruel or violent treatment of someone, especially by someone in a position of authority: *Women can escape domestic abuse* (=abuse by their husbands or boyfriends) *at the shelter.* | *a case of child abuse at a daycare center* | *the abuse of the elderly* **3** [U] rude or offensive things that someone says to someone else: *Worrell lost his job as coach because of his verbal abuse of players.* | **shout/scream/hurl abuse (at sb)** *People on the street were shouting abuse at the soldiers.*

a·buse² /ə'byuz/ *v.* [T] **1** to treat someone in a cruel

and violent way, especially someone that you should take care of: *She was sexually abused as a child.* | *Some nursing home patients were neglected or abused.* **2** to use alcohol, drugs etc. too much or in the wrong way: *Many of the kids are abusing drugs.* **3** to deliberately use something such as power or authority for the wrong purpose: *Most people on welfare do not abuse the system.* **4** to say rude or offensive things to someone: *Some lawyers seem to enjoy abusing witnesses.* **5** to treat something so badly that you start to destroy it: *athletes abusing their bodies with steroids* **6** OLD-FASHIONED to MASTURBATE

a·bus·er /ə'byuzɚ/ *n.* [C] **1** someone who is violent or cruel to someone else, especially someone in a position of authority or trust who hits someone: *a convicted child abuser* **2** someone who uses too much alcohol or drugs

a·bu·sive /ə'byusɪv/ *adj.* using cruel words or physical violence: *Robin left home at 16 to get away from abusive parents.* | *Vince used abusive language to her and other staff members.* —**abusively** *adv.* —**abusiveness** *n.* [U]

a·but /ə'bʌt/ also **abut on** *v.* [T] TECHNICAL if one piece of land or a building abuts another, it is next to it or touches one side of it

a·but·ment /ə'bʌt̚mənt/ *n.* [C] a structure that supports each end of a bridge

a·buzz /ə'bʌz/ *adj.* [not before noun] having a lot of noise, activity, and excitement: [+ with] *The classroom was abuzz with activity and laughter.*

a·bys·mal /ə'bɪzməl/ *adj.* very bad; TERRIBLE: *Living conditions were abysmal.* —**abysmally** *adv.*

a·byss /ə'bɪs/ *n.* [C] LITERARY **1** a very dangerous or frightening situation: *Critics accused Yeltsin of leading the country into an abyss.* | [+ of] *the abyss of war* | **fall/plunge into the abyss** *The country could plunge into the abyss of economic ruin.* **2** a deep empty space, seen from a high point such as a mountain: *Bushnell stood on the rim of the canyon, with the rocky abyss behind him.* **3** a great difference which separates two people or groups: *The economic abyss between developed and undeveloped countries is widening.*

AC 1 the abbreviation of ALTERNATING CURRENT —compare DC **2** the abbreviation of AIR CONDITIONING —see also AC/DC

a·ca·cia /ə'keɪʃə/ *n.* [C] a tree with small yellow or white flowers that grows in warm countries

ac·a·deme /'ækəˌdim, ˌækə'dim/ *n.* [U] the activities that college or university PROFESSORS are involved in, such as writing articles, teaching classes etc.: *Some of our top scientists have been pulled from the world of academe.*

ac·a·de·mi·a /ˌækə'dimiə/ *n.* [U] the area of activity and work relating to education in colleges and universities

ac·a·dem·ic¹ /ˌækə'dɛmɪk◂/ *adj.* **1** [usually before noun] relating to education, especially in a college or university: *The academic year starts September 3.* | *How is academic achievement to be measured?* | *an academic institution* **2** something that is academic is not important because it cannot happen or have any effect: *The budget meetings are not for academic discussion – some hard choices must be made.* **3** [usually before noun] relating to studying from books, as opposed to practical work: *an academic education* **4** good at studying and getting good grades at a school or college: *I'm not particularly academic, but I love to read.* —**academically** /-kli/ *adv.*

academic² *n.* **1** [C] a teacher in a college or university **2 academics** [plural] subjects that students study in school: *Not all students can excel in academics.*

ac·a·dem·i·cian /ˌækədə'mɪʃən, əˌkædə-/ *n.* [C] someone who teaches at a college or university and is well known for doing RESEARCH, writing books etc.

academic year /ˌ.... '. / *n.* [C usually singular] the period of the year during which there are school or college classes; SCHOOL YEAR

a·cad·e·my /ə'kædəmi/ *n. plural* **academies** [C] **1** a college where students are taught a particular subject or skill: *a military academy* | *the California Ballet Academy* **2** used in the names of some private schools: *St. Lawrence Academy* **3** an important official organization consisting of people interested in the development of literature, art, science etc.: *the American Academy of Arts and Letters*

Academy A·ward /.,.... .'./ *n.* [C] **1** an OSCAR: *In 1980 Redford won an Academy Award for his direction of "Ordinary People."* **2 the Academy Awards** the ceremony in which the WINNERS of the OSCARs are announced

Academy of Mo·tion Pic·ture Arts and Sci·en·ces /.,.... ,.. ,.. ,. . '.../ an organization that works to improve standards in movie making and gives the Academy Awards

a cap·pel·la /,akə'pelə, ,æ-/ *adj., adv.* sung or singing without any musical instruments: *an a cappella group*

ac·cede /æk'sid, ɪk-/ *v.*
    accede to sth *phr. v.* [T] FORMAL **1** to agree to a demand, proposal etc., especially after first disagreeing with it: *The House acceded to a request by the President to lower import taxes.* **2** to achieve a position of power or authority: *Henry IV acceded to the French throne at the end of the sixteenth century.*

ac·cel·er·an·do /æk,selə'rɑndou, ɑ,tʃɛ-/ *adj., adv.* music getting gradually faster

ac·cel·er·ant /ək'sɛlərənt, æk-/ *n.* [C] something, such as gasoline, that makes a fire begin burning more quickly

ac·cel·er·ate /ək'sɛlə,reɪt/ *v.* **1** [I,T] if a process accelerates or if something accelerates it, it happens faster than usual or sooner than you expect: *Zebtech is accelerating its cost-cutting program by cutting 2,500 jobs.* **2** [I] if a vehicle or someone who is driving it accelerates, it starts to go faster: *The Ferrari can accelerate from 0 to 60 mph in 6.3 seconds.* —opposite DECELERATE

accelerated de·pre·ci·a·tion /.,.... ...'../ *n.* [U] TECHNICAL the process of subtracting the largest amount of the cost of new machines or equipment from the profit made by a company or organization in the year in which they are bought, and smaller amounts in the following years, done in order to pay less tax

ac·cel·er·a·tion /ək,selə'reɪʃən/ *n.* **1** [singular,U] a process in which something happens more and more quickly: *a sharp acceleration in the job market* | *Looking ahead, bankers do not foresee any acceleration of loan growth.* **2** [U] the rate at which a car or other vehicle can go faster: *The Quattro offers excellent braking and acceleration after warming up.* **3** [U] TECHNICAL the rate at which the speed of an object increases: *The acceleration by Earth's gravity acts on asteroids falling through the atmosphere.*

ac·cel·er·a·tor /ək'sɛlə,reɪtɚ/ *n.* [C] **1** the part of a vehicle, especially a car, that you press to make it go faster; GAS PEDAL **2** TECHNICAL a large machine used to make extremely small pieces of matter move at extremely high speeds

ac·cent[1] /'æksɛnt/ *n.* [C] **1** the way someone pronounces the words of a language, showing which country or which part of a country they come from: *Alex spoke Portuguese with a Brazilian accent.* | *Vince has a strong New Jersey accent.* —compare DIALECT **2 an accent on sth** if there is an accent on a particular quality, idea, feeling etc., that quality or feeling is emphasized: *At the Clover Bakery, there is an accent on tradition.* | *The accent is on chunky jewelry and big, bold accessories this fall.* **3** the part of a word that you should emphasize when you say it: [+ on] *In the word "corset," the accent is on the first syllable.* —see also STRESS[1] **4** a written mark used above certain letters in some languages to show how to pronounce that letter, such as à or é

ac·cent[2] /'æksɛnt, æk'sɛnt/ *v.* [T] **1** to emphasize a part of something, especially part of a word in speech **2** to make something more noticeable so that people will pay attention to it: *Skillful use of make-up can accent your cheekbones and hide small blemishes.* | *The tables were accented by fresh flower arrangements.*

ac·cent·ed /'æksɛntɪd/ *adj.* **heavily accented** words or speech that are heavily accented are spoken with a very strong accent

ac·cen·tu·ate /ək'sɛntʃu,eɪt, æk-/ *v.* [T] to emphasize something, especially the difference between two conditions, situations etc.: *The separation between the entryway and the living room can be further accentuated by placing a screen near the doorway.* | *Albright continued to accentuate the positive, focusing on areas of agreement between the two countries.* —accentuation /ək,sɛntʃu'eɪʃən/ *n.* [C,U]

ac·cept /ək'sɛpt/ *v.*
1 gift/offer/invitation [I,T] to take something that someone offers you, or to agree to do something that someone asked you to do: *Alice accepted the job of sales manager.* | *Norton is in prison for accepting bribes.* | *The Orioles invited Taylor to sing the national anthem, and she accepted.* | **accept sth from sb** *Will you accept a collect phone call from Beverly Hillman?* | *Father Moore accepted the challenge* (=agreed to do something difficult) *to make the church more active in the community.* —opposite REFUSE[1]
2 plan/suggestion/advice [T] to decide to do what someone advises or suggests: *Yin's proposal was accepted by the committee.*
3 idea/statement/explanation [T] to agree that what someone says is right or true: *Owens refused to accept Bisonga's explanation.* | **accept that** *The jury accepted that the DNA evidence was flawed.*
4 accept blame/responsibility to admit that you were responsible for something bad that happened: *The ship's owners are refusing to accept any responsibility for the accident.*
5 think sb/sth is good enough [T] to decide that someone has the necessary skill or intelligence for a particular job, course etc., or that a piece of work is good enough: *My parents have always accepted me just as I am.* [+ to/at] *Bob's been accepted to Stanford!* | [accept sb/sth for sth] *Hsiu's article was accepted for publication in "Science" magazine.*
6 situation/problem etc. [T] to decide that there is nothing you can do to change a difficult and bad situation or fact and continue with your normal life: *Going to a new school is hard, but you have to try and accept it.* | *I find it hard to accept the fact that she's left me.*
7 become part of a group [T] to allow someone to become part of a group, society, or organization and to treat them in the same way as the other members: *The other kids gradually began to accept Shamila as one of the family.*
8 agree to take/deal with sth [T] to agree to take or deal with something that someone gives you, or say that it is appropriate or good enough: *Do you accept travelers' checks here?* | *The office does not accept applications from non-residents.* | **accept sb's apology/resignation** *The council did not accept Ms. Wilson's letter of resignation, choosing to fire her instead.*

ac·cept·a·ble /ək'sɛptəbəl/ *adj.* **1** good enough to be used for a particular purpose or to be considered satisfactory: *It's a cheap and acceptable substitute for rubber.* | [+ to] *The dispute was settled in a way that was acceptable to both sides.* | **an acceptable level/amount of sth** (=one that is not too high or too low) **2** acceptable behavior is considered to be morally or socially good enough: *Smoking is no longer considered socially acceptable by many people.* | *It is now considered acceptable for mothers to work outside the home.* —acceptably *adv.* —acceptability /ək,sɛptə'bɪləti/ *n.* [U]

ac·cept·ance /ək'sɛptəns/ *n.* **1** [U] official agreement to take something that you have been offered: [+ of] *Russia's acceptance of economic aid from Western countries will speed up recovery.* **2 gain/find acceptance** to become popular or liked: *Use of the drug has gained acceptance in the U.S.* **3** [singular,U] the act of agreeing that an idea, statement, explanation etc. is right or true: *Upper management's acceptance of the marketing plan is crucial.* **4** [U] the

A

process of allowing someone to become part of a group or a society and of treating them in the same way as the other members: *Acceptance by their peer group is important to most youngsters.* | *A part of me still longs for my father's approval and acceptance.* **5** [U] the ability to accept a bad situation which cannot be changed, without getting angry or upset about it: *By the end of the story, Nicholas has moved toward acceptance of his fate.*

ac·cept·ed /ək'sɛptɪd/ *adj.* considered right or suitable by most people: *A spokesman claimed, "Our methods are far more advanced and more accepted than ICI's."* | **generally/commonly/widely accepted** *The most widely accepted definition of artificial intelligence was developed by Alan Turing in 1950.*

sw 2 2 ac·cess¹ /'æksɛs/ *n.* [U] **1** how easy or difficult it is for people to enter a public building, reach a place, or talk to someone: [+ to] *Many are jealous of Wright's political access to the President.* | [+ for] *The hotel has rooms with access for wheelchairs.* | *Walkways allow* **easy access** *to the beach.* **2** the right to enter a place, use something, see something etc.: *Only selected employees* **have access to** *the safe.* | *All electronic mail accounts are protected by their own secret* **access code.** **3 have access to a phone/computer etc.** to have a telephone, computer etc. near you which you can use **4** the way by which you can enter a building or reach a place: [+ to] *Access to the restrooms is through the foyer.* **5 gain/get access (to sth)** to succeed in entering a place or in seeing someone or something: *The police managed to gain access through an upstairs window.*

access² *v.* [T] **1** to find information, especially on a computer: *We don't want minors accessing pornography on the Internet.* | *The library's database can be accessed via workstations in the reference room.* **2** to enter or reach a place: *The balcony is accessed by a spiral staircase from the bar.*

ac·ces·si·ble /ək'sɛsəbəl/ *adj.* **1** easy to reach or get into: *All of the ski resorts are accessible from the hotel via free public transportation.* —opposite INACCESSIBLE **2** easy to obtain or use: [+ to] *Healthcare should be made accessible to everyone.* | *The Internet makes this kind of information* **readily accessible** *to parents.* **3** someone who is accessible is easy to meet and talk to, even if they are very important or powerful: *Griffey's fans say that he is very accessible and down-to-earth.* **4** easy to understand and enjoy: *Penn's artwork has gradually become more accessible.* —accessibly *adv.* —accessibility /ək,sɛsə'bɪləti/ *n.* [U]

ac·ces·sion /ək'sɛʃən, æk-/ *n.* FORMAL **1** [U] a process in which someone becomes king, queen, president etc.: *Queen Elizabeth II's* **accession to the throne** (=the act of becoming queen) *occurred in 1952.* —compare SUCCESSION **2** [U + to] the act of agreeing to a demand **3** [C,U] an object or work of art that is added to a collection, especially in a MUSEUM

ac·ces·sor·ize /ək'sɛsə,raɪz/ *v.* [T usually passive] to add accessories to clothes, a room etc.: [+ with] *Sheila wore a skirt and a black top, accessorized with a cross.*

ac·ces·so·ry /ək'sɛsəri/ *n. plural* **accessories** [C] **1** [usually plural] something such as a bag, belt, jewelry etc. that you wear or carry because it is attractive: *The store specializes in wedding gowns and accessories.* **2** [usually plural] something such as a piece of equipment or a decoration that is not necessary, but that makes a machine, car, room etc. more useful or more attractive: *Accessories such as a carrying case and battery recharger are free with the purchase of a cellular phone.* **3** LAW someone who helps a criminal, especially by helping them hide from the police: [+ to] *Reece is charged with being an accessory to the robbery.* | **an accessory before/after the fact** (=someone who helps a criminal before or after the crime)

access road /'.. ,./ *n.* [C] a road which leads to a particular place

ac·ci·dent /'æksədənt, -,dɛnt/ *n.* [C] **1** a situation in **sw 2 2** which someone is injured or something is damaged without anyone intending them to be: *Ken* **had an accident** *at work and had to go to the hospital.* **2 by accident** in a way that is not planned or intended: *The fire started by accident.* **3** a crash involving cars, trains etc.: *Rhonda's father was in a* **car accident** *last week.* | *The highway patrol reported a* **serious** *traffic* **accident** *on Interstate 5.* **4** something, often something bad, that happens without anyone planning or intending it: *I'm really sorry about breaking your camera - it was an accident.* | *By an* **accident of history** (=an event or situation that happens without anyone planning it), *Fort Dearborn became an important trading post.* **5 have an accident** SPOKEN if someone, especially a child, has an accident, they URINATE in their clothes **6 accidents happen** SPOKEN used as an excuse for something bad that has happened: *When asked about the deaths of innocent victims, Abbas shrugged and replied, "Accidents happen."*

ac·ci·den·tal /,æksə'dɛntl/ *adj.* happening without being planned or intended: *Regulations are need to limit accidental releases of these chemicals.*

ac·ci·den·tal·ly /,æksə'dɛntl-i, -'dɛntˈli/ *adv.* **1** without intending to: *I accidentally locked myself out of the house.* **2 accidentally on purpose** HUMOROUS used to say that someone did something deliberately although they pretend they did not: *I think John lost his homework accidentally on purpose.*

accident-prone /'... ,./ *adj.* tending to get hurt or break things easily

ac·claim¹ /ə'kleɪm/ *n.* [U] praise for a person or their achievements: *Gail's artwork has* **won** *her international* **acclaim.** | *Bonet has performed several times* **to great acclaim.**

acclaim² *v.* [T] FORMAL to praise someone or something publicly: *Talen's last play was acclaimed by the critics as a masterpiece.*

ac·claimed /ə'kleɪmd/ *adj.* publicly praised by a lot of people: *Spielberg's* **highly acclaimed** *movie, "Schindler's List"* | *a* **critically acclaimed** *novel* (=praised by people who are paid to give their opinion on art, music etc.)

ac·cla·ma·tion /,æklə'meɪʃən/ *n.* [C,U] FORMAL a loud expression of approval or welcome

ac·cli·mate /'æklə,meɪt/ *also* **ac·cli·ma·tize** /ə'klaɪmə,taɪz/ *v.* [I,T] to become used to a new place, situation, or type of weather, or to make someone become used to it: [+ to] *Dogs and cats over 8 years old are often unable to acclimate to a new home.* | [**acclimate yourself**] *As Daniel was acclimating himself to his new company, the economic situation changed completely.* | *At high altitudes, it takes your body several days to* **get acclimated.** —acclimatization /ə,klaɪmətə'zeɪʃən/ *n.* [U]

ac·co·lade /'ækə,leɪd/ *n.* [C usually plural] praise for someone who is greatly admired or a prize given to them for their work: *Already, the program has won accolades for bringing investment to poor neighborhoods of Knoxville.* | *She received a Grammy Award, the highest accolade in the music business.*

ac·com·mo·date /ə'kɑmə,deɪt/ *v.* **1** [T] to have or provide enough space for a particular number of people or things: *The hotel can only accommodate 200 people.* | *If your microwave is large enough to accommodate the turkey, thaw it in a glass baking dish.* **2** [T] to accept someone's opinions or needs and try to do what they want, especially when their opinions or needs are different from yours: *We have made reasonable efforts to accommodate employees' requests for transfers.* **3** [T] to give someone a place to stay, live, or work: *Nineteen cabins on the new ship are designed to accommodate disabled passengers.* **4** [I + to, T] FORMAL to get used to a new situation, or make yourself do this: *Students can study the habits of animals that have to accommodate to changes in weather.*

ac·com·mo·dat·ing /ə'kɑmə,deɪtɪŋ/ *adj.* helpful and

willing to do what someone else wants: *Most of the hotel staff were very accommodating.*

ac·com·mo·da·tion /əˌkɑmə'deɪʃən/ *n.* **1** accommodations [plural] a room in a hotel or other place where you stay on vacation or when you are traveling: *Guest artists have to pay for their own accommodations and meals.* **2** [C,U] FORMAL an agreement or change in what is wanted or the way things are done, in order to solve a problem or end an argument: *There needs to be more accommodation by both sides.* | *Accommodations must be made for students with learning disabilities.* | *Lawmakers are working hard to reach an accommodation on the budget issue.*

ac·com·pa·ni·ment /ə'kʌmpənimənt/ *n.* **1** [C,U] music that is played in the background together with another instrument or singer that plays or sings the main tune: *Huang's wife provided accompaniment on the piano.* **2** [C] something that is provided or used with something else: [+ to] *White wine makes an excellent accompaniment to fish.* **3 to the accompaniment of sth** while another musical instrument is being played or another sound can be heard: *Guests danced to the accompaniment of pipe music and drums.* | *A huge lighted star was raised, to the accompaniment of a fireworks display.* **4** [C] FORMAL something that happens or exists at the same time as something else: [+ of] *Depression is a very common accompaniment of Parkinson's disease.*

ac·com·pa·nist /ə'kʌmpənist/ *n.* [C] someone who plays a musical instrument while another person sings or plays the main tune

S W 2 **ac·com·pa·ny** /ə'kʌmpəni/ *v.* accompanies, accompanied, accompanying [T] **1** to go somewhere with someone: *John has decided to accompany me on my trip to India.* | *Children under 10 must be accompanied by an adult.* **2** [usually passive] to happen or exist at the same time as something else: *Headaches due to viral infections may be accompanied by fever.* **3** to play a musical instrument while someone sings a song or plays the main tune: *Gary accompanied Jenna on the guitar.* **4** if a book, document etc. accompanies something, it explains what it is about or how it works: *Your completed passport application should be accompanied by two recent photographs.* | *Please read the accompanying information before taking this medication.*

ac·com·pli /ˌɑkɑm'pli, ˌæk-/ *adj.* —see FAIT ACCOMPLI

ac·com·plice /ə'kʌmplɪs/ *n.* [C] a person who helps someone such as a criminal to do something wrong

W 3 **ac·com·plish** /ə'kʌmplɪʃ/ *v.* [T] to succeed in doing something, especially after trying very hard; ACHIEVE: *Amy's very proud of what she's accomplished.*

ac·com·plished /ə'kʌmplɪʃt/ *adj.* **1** an accomplished writer, painter, singer etc. is very skillful **2 an accomplished fact** FORMAL something that is known to be true and cannot be doubted: *At first, the Soviets refused to accept Lithuania's secession as an accomplished fact.*

ac·com·plish·ment /ə'kʌmplɪʃmənt/ *n.* **1** [C] something successful or impressive that is achieved after a lot of effort and hard work; ACHIEVEMENT: *Our 15% increase in sales last year was a major accomplishment.* **2** [U] the act of finishing or achieving something good: *Setting short-term goals can help give you a sense of accomplishment.* **3** [U] skill in doing something: [+ in] *Trey's high level of accomplishment in judo is something to be admired.* **4** [C] OLD-FASHIONED an ability to do something well; SKILL: *Playing the piano is one of Joanna's many accomplishments.*

W 3 **ac·cord¹** /ə'kɔrd/ *n.* **1 of your own accord** also **on your own accord** without being asked or forced to do something: *Nunn wasn't fired. He left of his own accord.* **2** [U] FORMAL a situation in which two people, ideas, or statements agree with each other: [be in accord with sb/sth] *These results are in accord with earlier research.* | *Bouvet is in accord with Leibniz' ideas on the subject.* **3** [C] a formal agreement between countries or groups: *the Helsinki Accord on human rights* | *Cohen directed the representatives to reach an accord by Wednesday.* **4 with one accord** OLD-FASHIONED FORMAL if two or more

people do something with one accord, they do it together

accord² *v.* FORMAL **1** [T] to give someone or something special attention or a particular type of treatment: [accord sth to sb/sth] *The Japanese accord a special reverence to trees and rivers.* | *The law requires that racial minorities be accorded equal access to housing.* **2 accord with sth** to match or agree with something: *Some researchers may edit their observations to accord with their theory.*

ac·cord·ance /ə'kɔrdns/ *n.* **in accordance with sth** FORMAL according to a rule, system etc.: *The bank then invests the money in accordance with state law.* | *Warren was buried in his hometown, in accordance with his wishes* (=as he wanted).

ac·cord·ing·ly /ə'kɔrdɪŋli/ *adv.* **1** in a way that is appropriate for a particular situation or based on what someone has done or said: *Decide how much you can spend, and shop accordingly.* **2** [sentence adverb] FORMAL as a result of something; THEREFORE: *There aren't many jobs available. Accordingly, companies receive hundreds of resumés for every opening.*

according to /.'... ./ *prep.* **1** as shown by something or said by someone: *According to police, Miller was arrested at the scene of the robbery.* | *You still owe $235, according to our records.* **2** in a way that is directly affected or determined by something: *You will be paid according to the amount of work you do.* | *Everything at the dance went according to plan* (=happened as we planned it). S W 2 1

ac·cor·di·on¹ /ə'kɔrdiən/ *n.* [C] a musical instrument that you pull in and out to produce sounds while pushing buttons on one side to produce different notes —**accordionist** *n.* [C]

accordion² *adj.* [only before noun] having many folds like an accordion: *an accordion file*

ac·cost /ə'kɔst, ə'kɑst/ *v.* [T] to go toward someone you do not know and speak to them in an impolite or threatening way: *Two men accosted her in front of her apartment building.*

account¹ /ə'kaunt/ *n.* S W 2 1

1 description [C] **a)** a written or spoken description which gives details of an event: *There were several different accounts of the story in the newspapers.* | *DeJong gave an account of he incident in his book.* | *Police have an eyewitness account of the robbery* (=a description of events by someone who saw them). | *The book is a fascinating first-hand account* (=description of events by someone who saw or took part in them) *of the Chinese Cultural Revolution.* **b)** a detailed description of a process which explains how it happens and what makes it possible: [+ of] *Chomsky's account of how children learn their first language has sparked lots of debate.*

2 at a bank [C] written abbreviation **acct.** an arrangement that you have with a bank to pay in or take out money: *I'd like to deposit this check into my account.* | *My husband and I have a joint account* (=one that is shared by two people). | *You can even check your account balance* (=amount of money that is in your account) *online.* —see also BANK ACCOUNT, CHECKING ACCOUNT, DEPOSIT ACCOUNT, SAVINGS ACCOUNT

3 take account of sth also **take sth into account** to consider or include particular facts or details when making a decision or judgment about something: *These figures do not take account of changes in the rate of inflation.*

4 on account of sth because of something else, especially because of a problem or difficulty: *Games are often canceled on account of rain.*

5 accounts [plural] an exact record of the money that a company has received and the money it has spent: *The accounts for last year showed a profit of $2 million.*

6 with a store [C] an arrangement that you have with a store which allows you to buy goods and pay for them later: *We charged the sofa to our Macy's account.*

A

7 [bill] [C] a statement of money that you owe for things you have bought from a store; BILL | **pay/settle your account** | *You must settle your account within 30 days.*

8 [arrangement to sell goods] [C] an arrangement to sell goods and services to another company over a period of time: *Pheifer manages several accounts for the ad agency.*

9 by/from all accounts according to what a lot of people say: *By all accounts, Garcia was an excellent manager.*

10 on my/his etc. account if you do something on someone's account, you do it because you think they want you to: *Don't go to any trouble on my account.*

11 by your own account according to what you have said, especially when you have admitted doing something wrong: *By Dellacqua's own account, he was driving too fast.*

12 on no account also **not on any account** used when saying that someone must not, for whatever reason, do something: *On no account are members allowed to discuss meetings with outsiders.*

13 on your own account by yourself or for yourself: *Carrie decided to do a little research on her own account.*

14 on that/this account for that reason: *I would not want the program canceled on that account.*

15 bring/call sb to account FORMAL to force someone who is responsible for a mistake or a crime to explain publicly why they did it and punish them for it if necessary: *The people responsible for the accident must be brought to account.*

16 give a good/poor account of yourself FORMAL to do something or perform very well or very badly: *Cooper gave a good account of himself in the fight.*

17 put/turn sth to good account FORMAL to use something for a good purpose: *The extra time was turned to good account.*

18 of no/little account FORMAL not important: *Gelbspan's speech was of no account.*

S W **account²** *v.* [T]

account for sth *phr. v.* [T] **1** to make up a particular amount or part of something: *The value of the land accounts for 30% of the house's price.* **2** to be the reason why something happens: *Recent pressures at work may account for Steve's odd behavior.* **3** to give a satisfactory explanation of why something has happened or why you did something: *Alvarez believes racism accounts for the lack of black and Hispanic judges.* **4** to say where all the members of a group of people or things are, especially because you are worried that some of them may be lost: *All the stolen goods were later accounted for.* **5 there's no accounting for taste** FORMAL used when you find it difficult to understand why someone likes something or wants to do something

ac·count·a·ble /əˈkaʊntəbəl/ *adj.* [not before noun] responsible for the effects of your actions and willing to explain or be criticized for them: [+ **for**] *Managers must be accountable for their decisions.* | *The country will be held accountable* (=considered responsible) *for its treatment of American diplomats.* | [+ **to**] *Corporate management is accountable to the company's shareholders.* —**accountability** /əˌkaʊntəˈbɪləti/ *n.* [U] *There is strict accountability as to how the money is spent.*

ac·count·an·cy /əˈkaʊntⁿnsi/ *n.* [U] FORMAL: see ACCOUNTING

ac·count·ant /əˈkaʊntənt, əˈkaʊntⁿnt/ *n.* [C] someone whose job is to keep and check financial accounts, prepare financial reports, calculate taxes etc.

S W **ac·count·ing** /əˈkaʊntɪŋ/ *n.* [U] the profession or work of keeping or checking financial accounts, preparing financial reports, calculating taxes etc.

accounts pay·a·ble /.ˌ. ˈ.../ *n.* [U] TECHNICAL the amount of money that a company or organization owes for goods or services it has bought, or the department in a company or organization that deals with this

accounts re·ceiv·a·ble /.ˌ. .ˈ.../ *n.* [U] TECHNICAL the amount of money that a company or organization should be paid for goods or services it has sold, or the department in a company or organization that deals with this

ac·cou·ter·ments, accoutrements /əˈkutrəmənts, əˈkutə-/ *n.* [plural] FORMAL OR HUMOROUS small things, pieces of equipment etc. that you use or carry when doing a particular activity or that are related to a particular activity: *Cat furniture, cat jewelry, and all sorts of other cat accouterments will be for sale at the show.*

Ac·cra /əˈkrɑ/ the capital city of Ghana

ac·cred·i·ta·tion /əˌkrɛdəˈteɪʃən/ *n.* [U] official approval for a person or organization: *The school has gone through a lengthy accreditation process.*

ac·cred·it·ed /əˈkrɛdɪtɪd/ *adj.* **1** having official approval to do something: *an accredited teacher* **2** officially accepted as being of a satisfactory standard: *an accredited psychiatric hospital* **3 be accredited to sth** FORMAL if a government official is accredited to another country, they are sent to that country to officially represent their government there: *The Pope addressed diplomats who were accredited to the Vatican.* —**accredit** *v.* [T]

ac·cre·tion /əˈkriʃən/ *n.* **1** [C,U] TECHNICAL a layer of a substance which slowly forms on something **2** [U] FORMAL a gradual process by which new things are added and something gradually changes or gets bigger

ac·cru·al /əˈkruəl/ *n.* [C,U] TECHNICAL a gradual increase in the amount or value of something, especially money, or the process of doing this

ac·crue /əˈkru/ *v.* FORMAL **1** [I,T] if money accrues or is accrued, it gradually increases over a period of time: *The accrued interest will be paid annually.* **2** [I + **to**] if advantages accrue to you, you get those advantages over a period of time

accrued ben·e·fit /.ˌ. ˈ.../ *n.* [C usually plural] TECHNICAL money that a company owes to one of its workers, especially money that has been saved for RETIREMENT

acct. the written abbreviation of "account" or ACCOUNTANT

ac·cul·tur·ate /əˈkʌltʃəˌreɪt/ *v.* [I,T] to become part of the society of a new country or area and learn to behave in a way that is appropriate there: [+ **into**] *Younger people tend to acculturate into new surroundings more rapidly than older people.* —**acculturation** /əˌkʌltʃəˈreɪʃən/ *n.* [U]

ac·cu·mu·late /əˈkyumyəˌleɪt/ *v.* **1** [T] to gradually get more and more money, possessions, knowledge etc. over a period of time: *Martin had accumulated $80,000 in debt.* **2** [I] to gradually increase in numbers or amount until there is a large quantity in one place: *Huge snowdrifts had accumulated on the airport's runways.* —**accumulation** /əˌkyumyəˈleɪʃən/ *n.* [C,U] *a large accumulation of snow*

accumulated de·pre·ci·a·tion /.ˌ..... ...ˈ../ *n.* [U] TECHNICAL the total amount of money that a company or organization can subtract from the value of a machine or piece of equipment as it becomes older

accumulated div·i·dend /.ˌ.... ˈ.../ *n.* [C usually plural] TECHNICAL money that a company owes to someone who has bought SHARES² (4) in the company, but that has not yet been paid

accumulated prof·it /.ˌ.... ˈ../ *n.* [C] TECHNICAL the money that a company or person has earned in previous years and that they have not used or not paid to people who bought SHARES

ac·cu·mu·la·tive /əˈkyumyələtɪv, -ˌleɪtɪv/ *adj.* FORMAL gradually increasing in amount or degree over a period of time; CUMULATIVE —**accumulatively** *adv.*

ac·cu·mu·la·tor /əˈkyumyəˌleɪtə/ *n.* [C] TECHNICAL a part of a computer that calculates MATHEMATICAL problems and stores the results

ac·cu·ra·cy /ˈækyərəsi/ *n.* [U] **1** the ability to do something in an exact way without making a mistake **2** the quality of being correct or true: *There have been questions about the accuracy of the report.* —opposite INACCURACY

ac·cu·rate /'ækyərɪt/ *adj.* **1** an accurate measurement, calculation, record etc. has been done in a careful and exact way and is known to be correct: *More sophisticated equipment is needed to produce accurate results.* **2** accurate information, reports, descriptions etc. are correct because all the details are true: *Tom was able to give the police an accurate description of the gunman.* | *That's a fairly accurate assessment of the situation.* **3** a machine that is accurate is able to do something in an exact way without making a mistake: *The cutter is accurate to within 0.5 millimeter.* **4** an accurate shot, throw etc. succeeds in hitting or reaching the thing that it is intended to hit: *It was a devastatingly accurate shot by the Brazilian captain.* —**accurately** *adv.*: *It's impossible to predict the weather accurately.*

ac·cursed /ə'kɔ·st, ə'kɔ·sɪd/ *adj.* **1** [only before noun] LITERARY very annoying and causing you a lot of trouble **2** OLD-FASHIONED someone who is accursed has had a CURSE put on them

ac·cu·sa·tion /,ækyə'zeɪʃən/ *n.* [C] a statement saying that you think that someone is guilty of a crime or of doing something wrong: *Pickens has denied the bribery accusations.* | [+ of] *There are accusations of corruption within the agency.* | *Mellor has made several serious accusations against the former governor.* | *The boy's parents face accusations of* (=are accused of) *neglect and abuse.* | *The senator stated that the accusations were completely unfounded.*

ac·cu·sa·tive /ə'kyuzətɪv/ *n.* [C] TECHNICAL a form of a noun in languages such as Latin or German, which shows that the noun is the DIRECT OBJECT of a verb —**accusative** *adj.*

ac·cu·sa·to·ry /ə'kyuzə,tɔri/ *adj.* FORMAL an accusatory remark, look etc. from someone shows that they think you have done something wrong

ac·cuse /ə'kyuz/ *v.* [T] to say that you think someone is guilty of a crime or of doing something bad: [accuse sb of (doing) sth] *Are you accusing me of lying?* | *He's accused of murder.* | *The police stand accused of* (=are officially accused of) *inaction during the riots.* —**accuser** *n.* [C]

ac·cused¹ /ə'kyuzd/ *n.* **the accused** [singular or plural] the person or group of people who have been officially accused of a crime or offense in a court of law; DEFENDANT

accused² *adj.* [only before noun] **an accused murderer/rapist/bomber etc.** someone who has been officially CHARGEd with committing a crime: *The accused batterer was fined $150 for disturbing the peace in the courtroom.*

ac·cus·ing /ə'kyuzɪŋ/ *adj.* an accusing look from someone shows that they think that you have done something wrong —**accusingly** *adv.*

ac·cus·tom /ə'kʌstəm/ *v.* [T] FORMAL to make yourself or another person become used to a situation or place: *It took a while for me to accustom myself to all the new rules and regulations.*

ac·cus·tomed /ə'kʌstəmd/ *adj.* **1 be accustomed to (doing) sth** to be used to something: *I'm not accustomed to getting up so early.* | *Steph was accustomed to a regular paycheck.* | *Her eyes quickly became accustomed to the dark.* **2** [only before noun] FORMAL usual: *Mrs. Belton took her accustomed place at the head of the table.*

AC/DC /,eɪ si 'di si/ *adj.* SLANG sexually attracted to people of both sexes

ace¹ /eɪs/ *n.* [C] **1** a playing card with a single spot on it, which usually has the highest value in a game: *the ace of hearts* **2** a first shot in tennis or VOLLEYBALL which is hit so well that your opponent cannot reach the ball and you win the point **3** someone who is extremely skillful at doing something: *a World War II flying ace* | *pitching ace Doug Jones* **4 an ace in the hole** INFORMAL an advantage that you can use when you are in a difficult situation: *That fifty dollars is my ace in the hole.* **5 have an ace up your sleeve** to have a secret advantage which could help you to be successful **6 hold all the aces** to have all the advantages in a situation so that you are sure to win **7 be/come within an ace of doing sth** to almost succeed in doing

something: *The Warriors came within an ace of winning the game.*

ace² *adj.* **1 an ace pilot/pitcher/skier etc.** someone who is a very skillful pilot, player etc.: *an ace detective* **2** SLANG very good: *It'd be ace if you could come to the party.*

ace³ *v.* [T] **1** SPOKEN to do very well on a test, a piece of written work etc.: *I think I aced the history test.* **2** to hit your first shot in tennis or VOLLEYBALL so well that your opponent cannot reach the ball

a·cer·bic /ə'sɔ·bɪk/ *adj.* criticizing someone or something in an intelligent but fairly cruel way: *acerbic wit* —**acerbity** *n.* [U]

a·ce·ta·min·o·phen /ə,sitə'mɪnəfən, ,æsɪtə-/ *n.* [U] a type of medicine that helps reduce pain, similar to ASPIRIN

ac·e·tate /'æsə,teɪt/ *n.* [U] **1** a smooth SYNTHETIC cloth used to make clothes **2** TECHNICAL a chemical made from acetic acid

a·ce·tic ac·id /ə,sitɪk 'æsɪd/ *n.* [U] the acid in VINEGAR

ac·e·tone /'æsə,toun/ *n.* [U] a liquid chemical that is used to remove paint or make it thinner, or to DISSOLVE other substances

a·cet·y·lene /ə'sɛtl-ɪn, -,in/ *n.* [U] a gas which burns with a bright flame and is used in equipment for cutting and joining pieces of metal —see also OXYACETYLENE

ache¹ /eɪk/ *v.* [I] **1** if part of your body aches, you feel a continuous, but not very sharp, pain there: *Every inch of my body ached after skiing.* | *an aching back* **2 ache to do sth** also **ache for sth** to want to do or have something very much: *The children ached for attention.* **3** if your heart aches, you feel very sad, especially because someone else is in a bad situation: *The sight of those children at their mother's funeral made my heart ache.*

ache² *n.* [C] **1** a continuous pain that is not sharp, for example the pain you feel after you have used part of your body too much: *Apart from a dull ache* (=an annoying ache that is not very painful) *in his leg, Larsen has completely recovered from the crash.* | *I have a few aches and pains* (=many small pains which you feel at the same time) *but no real health problems.* **2** a strong feeling of wanting something: *Yet there remained an ache in her heart which told her she had not achieved what she wanted to.* —see also ACHY, BACKACHE, EARACHE, HEADACHE, HEARTACHE, STOMACHACHE, TOOTHACHE

a·chieve /ə'tʃiv/ *v.* **1** [T] to succeed in doing something good or getting the result you wanted, after trying hard for a long time: *Women have yet to achieve full equality in the workplace.* | *The software division expects to achieve its sales targets this year.* | *On the test drive, Segrave achieved speeds of over 200 mph.* **2** [I] to be successful in a particular kind of job or activity: *My parents constantly encouraged me to achieve.* —see Usage Notes at OBTAIN and REACH¹ —**achievable** *adj.*

a·chieve·ment /ə'tʃivmənt/ *n.* **1** [C] something important that you succeed in doing by your own efforts: *Winning three gold medals is a remarkable achievement.* | *I'm very proud of my achievements as program director.* | *All students must pass an achievement test* (=test which measures how much they have learned in school) *to move on to the next grade.* **2** [U] the act of achieving something: *We need to raise the level of academic achievement in public schools.* | *Teaching gave me a wonderful sense of achievement* (=a feeling or pride when you succeed in doing something difficult).

a·chiev·er /ə'tʃivɚ/ *n.* [C] someone who is successful because they are determined and work hard —compare OVERACHIEVER, UNDERACHIEVER

A·chil·les /ə'kɪliz/ in ancient Greek stories the greatest Greek WARRIOR in the TROJAN WAR

Achilles' heel /,.,.. './ *n.* [C] a weak part of something, especially of someone's character, which is

A

easy for other people to attack: *The team's offense is their Achilles' heel.*

Achilles ten·don /.,.. '../ *n.* [C] the part of your body that connects the muscles in the back of your foot with the muscles of your lower leg

a·choo /ə'tʃu/ *n.* [C] a word used to represent the sound you make when you SNEEZE

ach·y /'eɪki/ *adj.* if a part of your body feels achy, it is slightly painful, especially after you have used it too much: *I have an achy neck and shoulders.* —see also ACHE[1]

ac·id[1] /'æsɪd/ *n.* **1** [C,U] a substance that forms a chemical SALT when combined with a BASE[2] (12). Some acids can burn holes in things or damage your skin: *sulfuric acid* **2** [U] SLANG the illegal drug LSD

acid[2] *adj.* [only before noun] **1** having a very sour taste; ACIDIC **2 an/the acid test** a way of finding out whether something is as good as people say it is, whether it works, or whether it is true: *The acid test for the roof I fixed will be the next rainstorm.* **3 an acid remark/comment/tone etc.** an acid remark etc. uses humor in a way that is not nice, in order to criticize someone **4** TECHNICAL an acid soil does not contain enough LIME[1] (3) —**acidly** *adv.* —**acidity** /ə'sɪdəti/ *n.* [U] —see also ACID RAIN

a·cid·ic /ə'sɪdɪk/ *adj.* **1** very sour: *It tastes a little acidic.* **2** containing acid

a·cid·i·fy /ə'sɪdə,faɪ/ *v.* [I,T] TECHNICAL to become an ACID or make something become an acid

acid rain /,.. './ *n.* [U] rain that contains harmful acid which can damage the environment and is caused by smoke from factories, waste gases from cars and trucks etc.

ac·knowl·edge /ək'nɑlɪdʒ/ *v.* [T]
1 admit to admit or accept that something is true or that a situation exists: *Cooke acknowledges receiving gifts that could be seen as bribes.* | [acknowledge that] *An industry spokesman acknowledged that toxic chemicals had been released into the river.* | *It is now generally acknowledged that he was innocent.*
2 be acknowledged as sth to be thought of as being very important or very good by a large number of people: *Lasalle is widely acknowledged as the world's greatest living authority on Impressionist painting.*
3 accept sb's authority to officially accept that a government, court, leader etc. has legal or official authority: *Several Arab countries have not yet acknowledged Israel.* | [acknowledge sb as sth] *The people acknowledged Mandela as their leader.*
4 letter/message etc. to tell someone that you have received their message, letter, package etc.: *The paper never even acknowledged my letter or printed a correction.*
5 show thanks to publicly announce that you are grateful for the help that someone has given you: *The author wishes to acknowledge the assistance of the Defense Department.*
6 show you notice sb to show someone that you have seen them or heard what they have said: *Callahan waved, acknowledging his fans.*

ac·knowl·edg·ement, acknowledgment /ək'nɑlɪdʒmənt/ *n.* **1** [C,U] the act of admitting or accepting that something is true: *Simons resigned following his acknowledgment of illegal trading.* **2** [C,U] the act of publicly thanking someone for something they have done: *The award was given in acknowledgement of all Sylvia's hard work.* **3 acknowledgements** [plural] a short piece of writing at the beginning or end of a book in which the writer thanks all the people who have helped him or her **4** [C,U] a letter written to tell someone that you have received their letter, message etc.

ACLU American Civil Liberties Union; an organization that gives people advice and help about their CIVIL RIGHTS

ac·me /'ækmi/ *n.* **the acme of sth** FORMAL the best and highest level of something: *the acme of scientific knowledge*

ac·ne /'ækni/ *n.* [U] a skin problem that affects mainly young people and causes a lot of small red PIMPLES on the face and neck: *Tim had very bad acne when he was in his teens.*

ac·o·lyte /'ækə,laɪt/ *n.* [C] **1** someone who serves a leader or believes in their ideas: *Radical activists wanted to break up the estates that once belonged to the Shah and his acolytes.* **2** someone who helps a priest at a religious ceremony

a·corn /'eɪkɔrn/ *n.* [C] the nut of the OAK tree —see picture at OAK

a·cous·tic /ə'kustɪk/ *adj.* **1** relating to sound and the way people hear things **2** an acoustic GUITAR or other musical instrument does not have its sound made louder electronically —**acoustically** /-kli/ *adv.*

a·cous·tics /ə'kustɪks/ *n.* **1** [plural] the qualities of a room, such as its shape and size, which affect the way sound is heard in it: *The new auditorium has excellent acoustics.* **2** [U] the scientific study of sound

ac·quaint /ə'kweɪnt/ *v.*
acquaint sb with sth *phr. v.* [T] FORMAL **1 acquaint yourself with sth** to deliberately find out about something: *Residents should acquaint themselves with earthquake safety rules.* **2** to give someone information about something: *The guidebook acquaints the traveler with the city's history and culture.* —see also ACQUAINTED

ac·quaint·ance /ə'kweɪntⁿns/ *n.* **1** [C] someone you know, but who is not a close friend: *An acquaintance of Derek's from Texas arrived earlier in the week.* | *Erik was introduced to his future wife by a mutual acquaintance* (=someone who knows both people). **2 make sb's acquaintance** also **make the acquaintance of sb** FORMAL to meet someone for the first time: *I'm pleased to make your acquaintance.* **3** [U] FORMAL knowledge or experience of a particular subject: *John had a personal acquaintance with alcohol addiction.* **4 of your acquaintance** FORMAL a person of your acquaintance is someone that you know: *Ms. Nichols is a writer of my acquaintance.*

acquaintance rape /.'.. ,./ *n.* [C,U] an attack in which someone is forced to have sex by someone they know —compare DATE RAPE

ac·quain·tance·ship /ə'kweɪntⁿns,ʃɪp/ *n.* [U] FORMAL the fact of knowing someone socially

ac·quaint·ed /ə'kweɪntɪd/ *adj.* **1 be acquainted (with sb)** to know someone, especially because you have met them once or twice before: *I am acquainted with Tony Philips on a professional basis.* | *It was a chance for my stepdaughter and me to get better acquainted* (=learn more about someone that you have just met). **2 be acquainted with sth** FORMAL to know about something, because you have seen it, read it, used it etc.: *people who are acquainted with the problems of poverty* | *All our employees are fully acquainted with safety precautions.*

ac·qui·esce /,ækwi'ɛs/ *v.* [I] FORMAL to unwillingly agree to do what someone wants, or to let them do what they want, without arguing or complaining: [+ in/to] *City officials eventually acquiesced to the protesters' demands.*

ac·qui·es·cence /,ækwi'ɛsəns/ *n.* [U] FORMAL the quality of being too ready to agree with someone or do what they want, without arguing or complaining: [+ in] *A string of failures can create a mood of apathy and acquiescence in the status quo.* —**acquiescent** *adj.* —**acquiescently** *adv.*

ac·quire /ə'kwaɪɚ/ *v.* [T] **1** FORMAL to buy or obtain something, especially something that is expensive or difficult to get: *AC Transit recently acquired 70 new buses equipped with wheelchair lifts.* | *NTN acquired the rights to broadcast game data from football games in 1987.* **2** to learn or develop knowledge, skills etc. by your own efforts, or to become well known because of your abilities: *Research helps us acquire new insight on the causes of diseases.* | *Many inner cities have acquired reputations for violent crime.* **3 acquire a taste for sth** to begin to like something: *Americans have recently acquired a taste for gourmet coffee.* **4 an acquired taste** something that people only begin to like after they have tried, heard, seen etc. it a few times, and that some people may never begin to like: *For many people, her dry humor is an acquired taste.*

ac·qui·si·tion /ˌækwəˈzɪʃən/ *n.* **1** [U] the act of getting land, power, money etc.: *United Airlines' acquisition of the company is being investigated by the Justice Department.* **2** [C] something that you have bought or obtained, especially a valuable object or something such as a company that costs a lot of money: *Funds will be used for new museum acquisitions.* | *IBM will look at acquisitions including small service companies that complement its offerings.* | *Last year, banks reported a record $66 billion in* **mergers and acquisitions**. **3** [U] the act of getting new knowledge, skills etc.: *second language acquisition*

ac·quis·i·tive /əˈkwɪzət̬ɪv/ *adj.* FORMAL showing too much desire to get new possessions —**acquisitiveness** *n.* [U]

ac·quit /əˈkwɪt/ *v.* **acquitted, acquitting 1** [T usually passive] to give a decision in a court of law that someone is not guilty of a crime: *All the defendants were acquitted.* | **acquit sb of sth** *Bennett was acquitted of murder.* —opposite CONVICT[1] **2 acquit yourself well/honorably etc.** FORMAL to do something well, especially something difficult that you do for the first time in front of other people: *Although Perkins isn't known as a singer, he acquits himself admirably on this album.*

ac·quit·tal /əˈkwɪt̬l/ *n.* [C,U] an official statement in a court of law that someone is not guilty: *Leckie told reporters he hoped his acquittal would give hope to other people in similar situations.* —opposite CONVICTION

w
3 **a·cre** /ˈeɪkɚ/ *n.* [C] a unit for measuring areas of land, equal to 4840 square yards (4047 square meters): *They own 1500 acres of farmland.* | *a 2000-acre ranch*

a·cre·age /ˈeɪkərɪdʒ/ *n.* [U] the area of a piece of land measured in acres

ac·rid /ˈækrɪd/ *adj.* **1** an acrid smell or taste is strong and bad and stings your nose or throat: *a cloud of acrid smoke* **2** FORMAL an acrid remark, discussion etc. is very critical or angry

ac·ri·mo·ni·ous /ˌækrəˈmoʊniəs/ *adj.* FORMAL an acrimonious meeting, argument etc. is full of angry remarks because people feel very strongly about something: *an acrimonious divorce* —**acrimoniously** *adv.* —**acrimoniousness** *n.* [U]

ac·ri·mo·ny /ˈækrəˌmoʊni/ *n.* [U] FORMAL angry feelings between people

ac·ro·bat /ˈækrəˌbæt/ *n.* [C] someone who entertains people by doing difficult physical actions such as walking on their hands or balancing on a high rope, especially at a CIRCUS

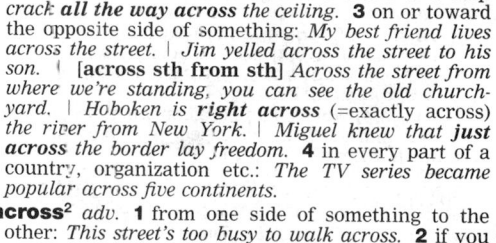

acrobat

ac·ro·bat·ic /ˌækrəˈbæt̬ɪk/ *adj.* acrobatic movements involve moving your body in a very skillful way, for example by jumping through the air or balancing on a rope: *an acrobatic catch* —**acrobatically** /-kli/ *adv.*

ac·ro·bat·ics /ˌækrəˈbæt̬ɪks/ *n.* [plural] acrobatic movements

ac·ro·nym /ˈækrəˌnɪm/ *n.* [C] a word made up from the first letters of the name of something such as an organization. For example, NASA is an acronym for the National Aeronautics and Space Administration

w
1 **a·cross¹** /əˈkrɔs/ *prep.* **1** going, looking etc. from one side of a space, area, or line to the other side: *She took a ship across the Atlantic.* | *We gazed across the valley.* | *Would you like me to* **help you across the street** (=help you to cross it)? **2** reaching or spreading from one side of an area to the other: *Slowly a smile spread across her face.* | *Do you think this shirt*

A

is too tight **across** the shoulders? | *There is a deep crack* **all the way across** *the ceiling.* **3** on or toward the opposite side of something: *My best friend lives across the street.* | *Jim yelled across the street to his son.* | **[across sth from sth]** *Across the street from where we're standing, you can see the old churchyard.* | *Hoboken is* **right across** (=exactly across) *the river from New York.* | *Miguel knew that* **just across** *the border lay freedom.* **4** in every part of a country, organization etc.: *The TV series became popular across five continents.*

across² *adv.* **1** from one side of something to the other: *This street's too busy to walk across.* **2** if you go, look shout etc. across to someone, you go, look or shout toward the other side of an area, to the place where they are: **[+ to/at]** *I looked across at the other driver.* | *I'm just taking this food across to Sarah.* **3 10 feet/10 miles etc. across** if something is 10 feet, 10 miles etc. across, that is how wide it is: *At its widest point, the river is two miles across.* **4 across from sb/sth** on the opposite side of a table, room, street, etc. from someone or something: *I looked up at the woman sitting across from me on the subway.* —see Usage Note at FRONT¹

across-the-board /ˌ.ˌ.ˈ.ˌ/ *adj.* [only before noun] affecting everyone or everything in a situation or organization: *an across-the-board pay increase* —**across the board** *adv.*

a·cros·tic /əˈkrɔstɪk, -ˈkrɑs-/ *n.* [C] a poem or piece of writing in which the first or last letter of each line can be read from top to bottom to spell a word

a·cryl·ic¹ /əˈkrɪlɪk/ *n.* **1** [U] a substance similar to plastic that is made from chemicals **2** [U] a type of cloth or YARN that is made from a particular chemical substance **3 acrylics** [plural] paints that contain a particular chemical substance

acrylic² *adj.* acrylic paints, cloth, or other materials are made from a particular chemical substance

ACT *n.* [C] TRADEMARK American College Test; an examination taken by students in order to attend some universities

act¹ /ækt/ *n.* [C]

S W
2 1

1 action [C] a particular kind of action: *a criminal act* | **[+ of]** *The attack was condemned as an act of mindless violence.* | *Garcia was given the medal of honor for his acts of bravery.* —see also SEX ACT

2 be in the act (of doing sth) to be doing something at a particular moment, especially something that you should not do: *The photo shows her in the act of raising her gun to fire.* | *The thief was* **caught in the act** (=discovered while doing something bad or illegal).

3 law [C] a law that has been officially accepted by Congress or a government: *the Civil Rights Act* | *an act of Congress*

4 get your act together INFORMAL to do something in a more organized way or use your abilities more effectively: *Angie could be an excellent photographer, if only she could get her act together.*

5 get in on the act INFORMAL to take part in an activity that someone else has started, especially in order to get a share of the advantages for yourself: *Produce stands sell exotic vegetables to Asian customers, and now even supermarkets are getting in on the act.*

6 theater [C] one of the main parts into which a stage play OPERA etc. is divided: *In Act 2, Ross and Diane get married.* | *a one-act play*

7 performance [C] **a)** one of the several short performances in a theater or CIRCUS show: *Kinison's outrageous comedy act* | *The festival will be an all-day event featuring a lot of different acts.* **b)** a performer, singer, group of musicians etc. who gives a performance: *Our next act is a young singer all the way from Dallas, Texas.*

8 an act of God an event that is caused by natural forces, such as a storm, flood, or fire, which you cannot prevent or control

9 pretending [singular] insincere behavior in which you pretend to have a particular kind of feeling: *Tony tries to be so macho, but it's just an act.* |

A

*Sally isn't just **putting on an act** (=pretending to have a particular feeling), she's really upset.*
10 balancing/juggling act the act of trying to do two or more things at once, especially when this is difficult: *For today's time-stressed parents, each day becomes a juggling act.*
11 an act of worship an occasion when people pray together and show their respect for God —see also **clean up your act** (CLEAN²)

USAGE NOTE: ACT

WORD CHOICE: act and **action**
Act is always countable, but **action** can be uncountable: *a thoughtful act | a series of quick actions | What we need now is quick action.* Use **act** in some fixed phrases when it means a particular type of action: *an act of kindness | She was caught in the act of* (NOT "in the action of") *stealing the money.*

---

s w
1 1

act² *v.*
1 do something **a)** [I] to do something to deal with an urgent problem, especially by using your official power or authority: *Congress must act soon on this vital legislation.* **b)** [I always + adv/prep] to do something in a particular way or for a particular reason: *Morganstern claims he was acting in self-defense. | I acted more out of compassion than anything else. | **Acting on** a friend's **advice** (=doing what his friend advised), Schiller bought $5,000 worth of stock. | The police were **acting on information** (=doing something because of information received) from a member of the public.*
2 behave [I always + adv./prep./adj.] to behave in a particular way or pretend to have a particular feeling or quality: *The report says the officers acted professionally and responsibly. | Larry was acting really weird. | Bill always tries to **act like** such a tough guy. | Gail **acted as if** she'd never seen me before. | For heaven's sake, Joe, **act your age** (=stop behaving like a child)!*
3 have an effect [I] **a)** to have a particular effect or use: [+ **as**] *The sugar in the fruit acts as a preservative. |* [+ **on**] *Antibiotics act on the bacteria that cause the disease.* **b)** to start to have an effect: *It takes a couple of minutes for the drug to act. | a fast-acting decongestant*
4 play/movie etc. [I,T] to perform in a play or movie: *I first started acting when I was 12 years old. | The picture has a good script and is wonderfully acted.*
5 act for sb also **act on sb's behalf** to represent someone, especially in a court of law or by doing business for them: *I'm acting on behalf of my client, Mr. Harding.*
6 act as sth to do a particular job for a short time, for example while the usual person is absent: *DeConcini acted as host at the meeting. —see also* ACTING¹

act out *phr. v.* **1** [T **act** sth ↔ **out**] if a group of people act out a real or imaginary event, they show how it happened or could happen by pretending to be the people involved in it: *"Daggerfall," the latest computer role-playing game, allows players to act out their fantasies.* **2** [I,T **act** sth ↔ **out**] to express your feelings about something through your behavior or actions, especially when you have been feeling angry or nervous: *Children who act out violently have often been abused. | Teenagers can act out their anxieties in various aggressive ways.*

act up *phr. v.* [I] INFORMAL **1** if children act up, they behave badly **2** if a machine or part of your body acts up, it does not work correctly: *The photocopier is acting up again.*

act·ing¹ /ˈæktɪŋ/ *adj.* **acting manager/director etc.** someone who does an important job while the usual person is not there, or until a new person is chosen for the job

acting² *n.* [U] the job or skill of performing in plays, movies etc.

ac·tion /ˈækʃən/ *n.*
s w
2 1

1 doing things [U] the process of doing something in order to deal with a problem or difficult situation: *Some senators are urging military action. | The police were criticized for failing to **take action** during the riots. | One possible **course of action** (=series of actions done to deal with something) would be to raise taxes on tobacco. | **swing/spring into action** (=immediately begin doing something with a lot of energy)*
2 something done [C] something that someone does: *The child could not be held responsible for his actions. | Ben's prompt action probably saved my life.*
3 in action if you see someone or something in action, you see them doing the job or activity that they are trained or designed to do: *These photos show the ski jumpers in action. | It's a chance for students to see a court in action.*
4 put/call/bring sth into action to begin to use a plan or idea that you have, and to make it work: *If we had any good ideas, we would put them into action right away.*
5 be out of action if something or someone is out of action, they are broken or injured, so that they cannot move or work: *Miller will be out of action for six weeks due to his knee injury. | The earthquake put a number of freeways out of action.*
6 court [C,U] the process of taking a case or a LAWSUIT against someone to a court of law: *Woods filed an action in the small claims court. | Payne threatened to **take legal action against** the magazine. | King decided to **bring an action against** the officers who beat him.*
7 exciting events [U] INFORMAL exciting and important things that are happening: *an action-adventure movie | If you want to be **where the action is**, come to the Grand Rapids Speedway Friday night.*
8 fighting [C,U] fighting or a battle during a war: *When the action ended, there were terrible losses on both sides. | The navy was sent **into action**. | **missing/killed in action** Their son was reported missing in action.*
9 a piece of the action INFORMAL a share of something, such as profits, a business etc.: *After five years in middle management, I'm ready for a real piece of the action.*
10 story the action the things that happen in a play or book: *In "Hamlet," the action takes place in Denmark.*
11 machinery TECHNICAL the movement of the parts of a clock, gun, piano etc.: *The clock's action needs to be adjusted.*
12 body movement [C,U] a movement of the body, especially a particular type of movement: *the action of the heart | the horse's trotting action*
13 effect [U] the way in which something such as a chemical or process has an effect on something else: *The rock had been worn away by the action of the falling water.*
14 an action group/committee/project etc. a group formed to do something specific, especially to change a social or political situation: *the AIDS Action Committee in Boston*
15 actions speak louder than words used to say that you are judged by what you do, rather than by what you say you will do
16 movies action! used by a movie DIRECTOR to tell the actors and other movie workers to begin filming —see Usage Note at ACT¹

ac·tion·a·ble /ˈækʃənəbəl/ *adj.* **1** [usually before noun] FORMAL an actionable plan, piece of information etc. is one that can be done or used **2** LAW if something you say or do is actionable, it is so serious or damaging that a LAWSUIT could be FILED against you in a court of law because of it: *The judge ruled that Newman's comments were not an actionable offense.*

action fig·ure /ˈ.. ˌ../ *n.* [C] a child's toy that looks like a small person, especially someone from a movie or television show

action-packed /ˌ.. ˈ.ˌ/ *adj.* an action-packed story, movie, or show contains a lot of exciting events

ac·ti·vate /ˈæktəˌveɪt/ *v.* [T] **1** to make something, especially an electrical system, start working: *This button actives the car's alarm system.* **2** TECHNICAL to make a chemical action or natural process happen: *The manufacture of chlorophyll in plants is activated by sunlight.* **3** TECHNICAL to make something RADIO-ACTIVE —**activation** /ˌæktəˈveɪʃən/ *n.* [U]

ac·tive¹ /ˈæktɪv/ *adj.*
1 doing things always doing things or ready to do things, especially physical activities: *Jamie's a very active little kid!* | *I'd been active all my life, and suddenly I had nothing to do.*
2 in an organization involved in an organization, activity etc. and always busy doing things to help it: *an active member of St. Mark's Episcopal Church* | *Mahke is active in the Republican Party.*
3 with continuous energy done with continuous energy and determination: *active trading on the stock market*
4 electrical system TECHNICAL operating in the way it is supposed to: *The alarm becomes active when the switch is turned on.*
5 military active duty/service **a)** a soldier etc. who is on active service is fighting in a war **b)** employment by the army etc., as opposed to being in the RESERVES² (6): *Pruitt remained an officer in the reserves after leaving active service to become a Methodist minister.*
6 volcano an active VOLCANO is likely to explode and pour out fire and LAVA (=hot liquid rock)
7 grammar TECHNICAL if a verb or sentence is active, the person or thing doing the action is the SUBJECT. In "The boy kicked the ball," the verb "kick" is active —compare PASSIVE¹
8 chemical TECHNICAL producing a reaction in a substance or with another chemical —**actively** *adv.*: *The two sides are actively engaged in discussions.*

active² *n.* **the active** also **the active voice** TECHNICAL the active form of a verb —compare PASSIVE²

ac·tiv·ist /ˈæktəvɪst/ *n.* [C] someone who works hard to achieve social or political change, especially as an active member of a political organization: *environmental activists* —**activism** *n.* [U]

ac·tiv·i·ty /ækˈtɪvəti/ *n. plural* **activities 1** [U] a situation in which a lot of things are happening or people are doing things, moving around etc.: *Residents are concerned about growing gang activity in the neighborhood.* | *The workshop was a scene of constant activity.* | —opposite INACTIVITY **2** [C] something that you do for interest or pleasure or because you want to achieve something: *leisure activities* | *the company's business activities* | *There are clubs and other extracurricular activities at the school.*

ac·tor /ˈæktə/ *n.* [C] someone who performs in a play, movie, or television program

Actors' Eq·ui·ty As·so·ci·a·tion /ˌ.. ˈ... ...ˌ..ˈ the full name of the UNION Equity

ac·tress /ˈæktrɪs/ *n.* [C] a woman who performs in a play, movie, or television program

Acts /ækts/ also **The Acts of the Apostles** a book in the New Testament of the Christian Bible

ac·tu·al /ˈæktʃuəl, -ʃəl/ *adj.* [only before noun] **1** real, especially as compared with what is believed, expected or intended: *It's a true story, based on actual events.* | *The party took place three days before Daniel's actual birthday.* **2 the actual sth** used to introduce the main part of what you are describing: *The cost is set to go up, but the actual amount is unknown.*

ac·tu·al·i·ty /ˌæktʃuˈæləti/ *n. plural* **actualities** FORMAL **1 in actuality** really; in fact: *It gives voters the impression that something is being done, but in actuality little has changed.* **2** [C usually plural] something that is real; fact: *the grim actualities of prison life* **3** [U] FORMAL the state of being real; EXISTENCE

ac·tu·al·ize /ˈæktʃuəˌlaɪz/ *v.* [T] to make something such as a dream or idea become real; REALIZE: *Sometimes mistakes are necessary steps toward actualizing your goals.* —**actualization** /ˌæktʃuələˈzeɪʃən/ *n.* [U]

ac·tu·al·ly /ˈæktʃuəli, -tʃəli/ *adv.* **1** [sentence adverb] SPOKEN used when you are giving an opinion or adding new information to what you have just said: *I don't actually remember it all that well.* | *Actually,*

A

that was the best part of the whole trip. | *Well, actually, you still owe me $200.* **2** used when you are telling or asking someone what the real and exact truth of a situation is, as opposed to what people may imagine: *He may look 30, but he's actually 45.* | *Did the guy actually attack you, or just threaten you?* | *Unemployment has actually fallen for the past two months.*

USAGE NOTE: ACTUALLY

WORD CHOICE: actually, currently, (right) now
Actually does not mean "now" or "at this time." Compare **currently** and **(right) now**: *Surprisingly, the population of Brown County actually fell during the 1980s* (=in fact). | *Currently/Right now, Steve Palmer is the assistant sales manager.*

---

ac·tu·ar·i·al /ˌæktʃuˈɛriəl/ *adj.* [only before noun] relating to CALCULATIONS of risks, especially in the insurance industry: *The organization has filed several lawsuits to prevent the use of actuarial tables in determining insurance rates.*

ac·tu·ar·y /ˈæktʃuˌɛri/ *n. plural* **actuaries** [C] someone who advises insurance companies on how much to charge for insurance, after calculating the various risks —**actuarial** *adj.*

ac·tu·ate /ˈæktʃuˌeɪt/ *v.* **1** [T] TECHNICAL to make a piece of machinery or electrical equipment start to operate: *an electrically actuated lock* **2 be actuated by sth** FORMAL to behave in a particular way because of a feeling or a quality in your character: *Gandhi was actuated by the belief that it was possible to achieve independence through nonviolence.*

a·cu·i·ty /əˈkyuəti/ *n.* FORMAL the ability to think, see, or hear quickly and clearly: *mental acuity*

a·cu·men /əˈkyumən, ˈækyəmən/ *n.* [U] the ability to think quickly and make good judgments: *Power's business acumen helped him develop a chain of successful restaurants.*

ac·u·pres·sure /ˈækyəˌprɛʃə/ *n.* [U] a method of stopping pain and curing disease by pressing on particular areas of the body

ac·u·punc·ture /ˈækyəˌpʌŋktʃə/ *n.* [U] a method of stopping pain and curing disease by putting special thin needles into particular parts of the body —**acupuncturist** *n.* [C]

a·cute /əˈkyut/ *adj.*
1 serious problem very serious or severe: *There are acute shortages of food and medical equipment.* | *The impact of the problem has been especially acute in New England.*
2 medical TECHNICAL **a)** an acute illness or disease quickly becomes dangerous: *acute tuberculosis* —compare CHRONIC **b) acute care** medical care for people with severe injuries or illnesses that need help urgently
3 pain very severe and sharp: *Patients with acute lower back pain often do well with bed rest and painkillers.*
4 intelligent quick to notice things and able to think clearly and intelligently: *Solving the problem will require acute perception and subtle communication.* | *Simmons' book is an acute analysis of Middle Eastern history.* | *De Tocqueville was an acute observer of American ways.*
5 acute hearing/an acute sense of smell etc. an ability to hear or smell things that is very sensitive, so that you are able to notice small differences
6 mathematics TECHNICAL an acute angle is one that is less than 90°
7 pronunciation mark an acute ACCENT (=a mark used to show pronunciation) is the small mark put over a letter, such as ´ in French —compare GRAVE³, CIRCUMFLEX —**acuteness** *n.* [U]

a·cute·ly /əˈkyutli/ *adv.* very strongly or painfully: *acutely ill patients* | *The President said he was acutely aware that many Americans were struggling financially.*

A

A.D. Anno Domini; used to show that a date is a particular number of years after the birth of Jesus Christ: *The Mayan civilization ended around A.D. 830.* | *The bowl was made in the sixth century A.D.* —compare B.C.

sw **ad** /æd/ *n.* [C] INFORMAL words, a picture, or a short **2 2** movie that advertises a thing or service that is available or for sale; ADVERTISEMENT: *an ad campaign* | [+ **for**] *Three hundred people responded to our ad for a secretary.* | *The best way to sell your bike is to **place an ad in** the local paper.* —see also CLASSIFIED AD, WANT AD —compare COMMERCIAL[2]

ad·age /'ædɪdʒ/ *n.* [C] a well-known phrase that says something wise about human experience; PROVERB

a·da·gio /ə'dɑdʒou, -dʒiou/ *n.* [C] a piece of music to be played or sung slowly —**adagio** *adj., adv.*

Ad·am /'ædəm/ **1** in the Bible, the first man **2 not know someone from Adam** INFORMAL to have no idea who someone is

ad·a·mant /'ædəmənt/ *adj.* FORMAL determined not to change your opinion, decision, etc.: [+ **about**] *Newman is adamant about not using pesticides on his vegetable crops.* | [+ **that**] *My mother was adamant that nothing would interfere with our education.* —**adamantly** *adv.*

Ad·ams /'ædəmz/, **An·sel** /'ænsəl/ (1902–1984) a U.S. photographer famous for his photographs of the American West

Adams, John (1735–1826) the second President of the U.S. and Vice President under George Washington

Adams, John Quin·cy /dʒɑn 'kwɪnsi/ (1767–1848) the sixth President of the U.S.

Adams, Samuel (1722–1803) an American politician and writer famous for protesting against British taxes before the American Revolution

Adam's ap·ple /'.. ,../ *n.* [C] the part at the front of a man's neck that sticks out slightly and moves up and down when you swallow

a·dapt /ə'dæpt/ *v.* **1** [T] to change something so that it can be used in a different way or for a different purpose: [**adapt sth to do sth**] *Researchers had adapted a blood test to look for early signs of the disease.* | [**adapt sth for sb/sth**] *The house has been adapted for wheelchair users.* **2** [I,T] to gradually change your behavior and ideas to fit a new situation: [**adapt to sth**] *Her children adapted quickly to living in a small town.* | *Several plants have adapted themselves to desert conditions.* **3** [T] to change a book or play so that it can be made into a movie, television program etc.: *Le Carré's latest novel is soon to be adapted for television.* —compare ADJUST

a·dapt·a·ble /ə'dæptəbəl/ *adj.* able to change in order to be appropriate or successful in new and different situations: *Red deer are hardy, adaptable animals.* | [+ **to**] *The aerobic workout is adaptable to various fitness levels.* —**adaptability** /ə,dæptə'bɪləti/ *n.* [U]

ad·ap·ta·tion /,ædæp'teɪʃən/ *n.* **1** [C] a movie or play that was first written in a different form, for example as a book **2** [U] the process by which something changes or is changed so that it can be used in a different way or in different conditions: [+ **to**] *Our company's adaptation to shifting consumer tastes has been a great success.*

a·dapt·er, adaptor /ə'dæptə/ *n.* [C] something used to connect two pieces of equipment, especially when they are of different sizes or use different levels of power

ADD *n.* [U] the abbreviation of ATTENTION DEFICIT DISORDER

sw **add** /æd/ *v.* **1 1** **1 increase/put with** [I,T] to put something with another thing or group to increase the amount, size, or cost: *Beech Co. is planning to add 500 jobs within the next 12 months.* | *Beat together the egg and sugar, then add the flour.* | [**add (sth) to sth**] *The sales tax adds 8% to the price of clothes.* | *Conforming to the new regulations will add to the cost of the project.*

2 say more [T] to say more about something you have been talking about: *That's all I have to say. Is there anything you want to add, Anita?* | *"It's Carol Flynn," she shouted. After a moment of silence, she added, "I'm a friend of Annie's."* | [**add that**] *Mike added that his father disagreed with his decision.*

3 give a quality [T] to give something a particular quality: [**add sth to sth**] *Merrill manages to add humor to a difficult role.*

4 counting [I,T] to put two numbers or amounts together and then calculate the total: *Add 6 and 6 and you get 12.* | *The calculator adds, subtracts, multiplies, and divides.* —compare SUBTRACT

5 add fuel to sth to make a bad situation even worse, especially by making someone more angry: *The report added fuel to complaints about government secrecy.* | *Threats will only **added fuel to the fire** (=made the situation worse).*

6 add insult to injury to say or do something that makes a situation even more upsetting for someone, when they have already been badly or unfairly treated: *People over age 65 who work get fewer benefits and, **to add insult to injury**, they have to pay more in taxes.*

add sth ↔ **in** *phr. v.* [T] to include something, especially in a total: *Wilson's salary is about $1.2 million when his stock options are added in.*

add sth ↔ **on** *phr. v.* **1** [T] to increase the amount or cost of something by putting something more with it: *Labor costs could add on a further 25%.* [+ **to**] *They already added the tip on to the bill.* **2** [I,T] to make a building larger by building another room: *We're thinking of adding on another bedroom.* [+ **to**] *The Lopezes recently added on to their kitchen.*

add to sth *phr. v.* [T] **1** to increase something: *The new rules only added to the problem.* **2 add to this/that** used to introduce another fact, especially one that makes a situation seem even worse: *The script was poor. Add to that the sloppy acting and you have a disaster.*

add up *phr. v.* **1** [I,T **add** sth ↔ **up**] to calculate the total of several numbers or amounts: *When you add the numbers up, you'll see how big our profit really is.* | *I can't get these figures to add up right.* **2** [I not in progressive] INFORMAL to increase by small amounts until there is a large total: *All of the small problems began to add up quickly.* | *Two or three bus passes at $15 each soon adds up.* **3 not add up** to not seem true or reasonable: *Jake's explanation **just didn't add up**.*

add up to sth *phr. v.* [T not in progressive] to have a particular result: *An increasing fear of crime has added up to a boom in the security business.*

Ad·dams /'ædəmz/, **Jane** /dʒeɪn/ (1860–1935) a U.S. social REFORMER who worked to help poor people in cities and for peace and women's rights

add·ed /'ædɪd/ *adj.* [only before noun] in addition to what is usual or expected: *We now have the added expense of having two kids in college.* | *An added bonus of holding your wedding reception at home is the lower cost.*

ad·den·dum /ə'dɛndəm/ *n. plural* **addenda** /-də/ [C] TECHNICAL something that is added to the end of a book, usually to give more information

ad·der /'ædə/ *n.* [C] **1** one of several types of snakes living in North America **2** a small poisonous snake living in northern Europe and northern Asia

ad·dict /'ædɪkt/ *n.* [C] **1** someone who is unable to stop taking drugs: *Many addicts refuse to go to treatment centers.* | **a drug/heroin etc. addict** *Kevin is a recovering cocaine addict.* **2** someone who spends too much time doing something they like, but which may not be good or healthy for them: *a television addict*

ad·dict·ed /ə'dɪktɪd/ *adj.* [not before noun] **1** unable to stop taking a harmful substance, especially a drug: [+ **to**] *One in seven people is addicted to alcohol or drugs.* **2** liking to have or do something, especially something that is not good or healthy, so much that you do not want to stop: [+ **to**] *My kids are addicted to video games.*

ad·dic·tion /ə'dɪkʃən/ *n.* [C,U] **1** the need to take a harmful drug because you are addicted to it: *drug*

addiction | [+ to] *Her addiction to alcohol ruined her life.* **2** a strong desire to have or do something regularly, when this is difficult to stop: *Some weight problems are caused by an addiction to sugar and fat.*

ad·dic·tive /ə'dɪktɪv/ *adj.* **1** a substance or drug that is addictive makes you unable to stop taking it: *Nicotine in cigarettes is an addictive drug.* | *Crack is a potent, highly addictive form of cocaine.* **2** also **addicting** INFORMAL something such as a food or an activity that is addictive is one that you want to have or do all the time, especially because you enjoy it so much: *Golf can be addictive and time-consuming.*

Ad·dis Ab·a·ba /ˌædɪs 'æbəbə/ the capital and largest city of Ethiopia

ad·di·tion /ə'dɪʃən/ *n.* **1 in addition** used in order to add information or show that something is more than what is usual or expected: *A new security system was installed. In addition, extra guards were hired.* | [+ to] *You will be paid overtime in addition to your regular salary.* | *In addition to writing, I also enjoy rock climbing.* **2** [U] the act of adding something to something else: *Despite the addition of fertilizer, flowers are still unable to grow in the soil.* **3** [C] something that is added to something else, often in order to improve it: [+ to] *A bottle of wine would make a pleasant addition to the meal.* **4** [C] a room or a part of a building that is added to the main building: *The Simpsons built a big addition onto the back of their house.* **5** [U] the process of adding numbers or amounts to make a total —compare SUBTRACTION

ad·di·tion·al /ə'dɪʃənəl/ *adj.* [usually before noun] more than what was agreed or expected; EXTRA: *Additional troops may be sent to the region.* | *Plans for the tunnel had to be revised at an additional cost of $180 million.* | *There are a number of additional factors that require consideration.*

ad·di·tion·al·ly /ə'dɪʃənəli/ *adv.* in addition; also: *Salads are not included in the price of entrees but may be ordered additionally.* | [sentence adverb] *The group may be smuggling drugs. Additionally, they're suspected of several murders.*

ad·di·tive /'ædətɪv/ *n.* [C] a substance, especially a chemical, that is added to something such as food, to preserve it, give it color, improve it etc.: *Foods sold under this label are guaranteed to be free from additives and preservatives.*

ad·dled /'ædld/ *adj.* confused and unable to think clearly —**addle** *v.* [T]

add-on /'. ./ *n.* [C] **1** something such as a piece of equipment that can be connected to a computer, car, house etc. to make it do more things or make it more useful: *Add-ons such as modems and DVD drives can easily cost you hundreds of dollars.* —compare PERIPHERAL[2] **2** something additional that is later added to a bill, plan, agreement etc.: *The Senate's add-ons to the proposed budget are likely to cause controversy.*

ad·dress[1] /ə'drɛs, 'ædrɛs/ *n.* **1** [C] the number of the building and the name of the street and town etc. where someone lives or works, especially when written on a letter or package: *Write down your name, address, and phone number.* | *Keep us informed of any change of address.* **2** /ə'drɛs/ [C] a formal speech made to a group of people who have come especially to listen to it: *President Herrera delivered the opening address* (=gave a speech). **3 a form/style/mode of address** the title or name that you use for someone when you are speaking to them: *What's the correct form of address for the governor of a state?*

address[2] *v.* [T] **1** to write on an envelope, package etc. the name and address of the person you are sending it to: [address sth to sb] *Address the letter to Dr. Joanna Miles.* | *Transcripts of the show can be obtained by sending a self-addressed, stamped envelope* (=an envelope with your own address and a stamp on it). **2** FORMAL to discuss, think about, or do something about a particular problem or question, especially with the aim of solving a problem: *The article addresses the problems of malnutrition in the state.* | *Environmental problems relating to the factory have yet to be addressed.* **3 address a meeting/crowd/conference etc.** to make a speech to a large group of people: *Dantley addressed a rally in Boston.* **4** to use a particular title or name when speaking or writing to someone: [address sb as sth] *You should address him as "Mr. President."* **5** FORMAL to speak directly to someone: *Suzanne turned to address the man asking the question.*

address book /.'. ,., '.. ,./ *n.* [C] a book in which you write the addresses of people you know

ad·dress·ee /ˌædrɛ'si, əˌdrɛs'i/ *n.* [C] the person a letter, package etc. is addressed to —compare SENDER

ad·duce /ə'dus/ *v.* [T] FORMAL to mention a fact or reason in order to prove, explain, or support what you are claiming is true

-ade /eɪd/ *suffix* [in U nouns] used in the names of drinks made from a particular fruit: *lemonade* (=drink made from lemons)

ad·e·noi·dal /ˌædn'ɔɪdl/ *adj.* an adenoidal voice sounds as if it is coming mainly through a person's nose

ad·e·noids /'ædnˌɔɪdz/ *n.* [plural] the small soft pieces of flesh at the top of your throat, behind your nose, that sometimes have to be removed because they become swollen —compare TONSIL

a·dept[1] /ə'dɛpt/ *adj.* good at doing something that needs care and skill: [+ at/in] *Holling soon became adept at sign language.* —**adeptly** *adv.*

ad·ept[2] /'ædɛpt, ə'dɛpt/ *n.* [C] someone who is very skillful at doing something

ad·e·quate /'ædəkwɪt/ *adj.* **1** an adequate amount is enough for a particular purpose: *Hardin's campaign did not have adequate funds to broadcast any ads on television.* | [+ for] *The earlier electric car's range of 50 miles was not adequate for suburban driving.* **2** good enough in quality for a particular purpose or activity: *Most people eat an adequate diet.* | [adequate to do sth] *The safety procedures are adequate to protect public health.* | [+ for] *Parents should ask whether the school's facilities are adequate for their children's needs.* **3** fairly good, but not excellent: *Redman's performance was adequate, though it lacked originality.* —**adequately** *adv.*: *She wasn't adequately insured.* —**adequacy** *n.* [U]

USAGE NOTE: ADEQUATE

WORD CHOICE: adequate, sufficient, enough, good enough, satisfactory, (will) do
Adequate and **sufficient** are both more formal than **enough**, but all three can be used to talk about quantity: *The school district does not have adequate/sufficient/enough funding for music programs.* However, **adequate** often sounds a little negative, suggesting that the amount is just barely enough: *The water supply here is adequate/sufficient.* If you want to say that the quality of something is enough, you use **good enough** or **satisfactory**: *Hanson's work simply was not good enough/not satisfactory.* **Satisfactory** is a more formal word. **Adequate** can be used to talk about both quality and quantity together, especially with uncountable nouns. For example, if you ask: *Is the food adequate?* you might be asking whether there is enough in amount or whether it is good enough. However, with a plural countable noun the meaning is more likely: *adequate resources/supplies/funds etc.* In spoken English, people often use **do**, usually with the verbs **have to**, **will**, or **should**, to talk about something being enough in either of these ways: *"Do we have enough for the guests to drink?" "Six bottles of cola should do."* (=should be enough) | *It's not very good, but it'll have to do.*

---

ad·here /əd'hɪr/ *v.* [I] FORMAL to stick firmly to something

adhere to sth *phr. v.* [T] FORMAL to continue to behave according to a particular rule, agreement, or belief: *Few people adhere to the guidelines.* | *They are a group that adheres to racist ideology.*

ad·her·ence /əd'hɪrəns/ *n.* [U] the act of behaving

according to a particular rule or belief, or supporting a particular idea, even in difficult situations: [+ to] *Principal Harris demands strict adherence to the rules.*

ad·her·ent /əd'hɪrənt/ *n.* [C] FORMAL someone who supports a particular idea, plan, political party etc.

ad·he·sion /əd'hiʒən/ *n.* TECHNICAL **1** [C] a piece of TISSUE (=flesh) that has grown around a small injury or diseased area **2** [U] the state of one thing sticking to another

ad·he·sive¹ /əd'hisɪv, -zɪv/ *n.* [C,U] a substance such as glue that can be used to make two things stick together firmly

adhesive² *adj.* adhesive material sticks firmly to surfaces: *adhesive tape*

ad hoc /ˌæd 'hɑk/ *adj.* [usually before noun] done or arranged only when the situation makes it necessary, and without any previous planning: *An ad hoc committee has been set up to deal with the problem.* | *Decisions were made on an ad hoc basis.* —**ad hoc** *adv.*

a·dieu /ə'du, ə'dyu/ *n. plural* **adieux** /ə'duz, ə'dyuz/ or **adieus** [C] LITERARY an act of saying goodbye: *He bid her a fond adieu.* —**adieu** *interjection*

ad in·fi·ni·tum /ˌæd ɪnfɪ'naɪtəm/ *adv.* FORMAL continuing or repeated for a very long time, or without ever ending: *DNA can copy itself within a cell ad infinitum.*

ad·i·os /ɑdi'ous, æ-/ *interjection* goodbye

ad·i·pose /'ædɪˌpous/ *adj.* TECHNICAL consisting of or containing animal fat: *adipose tissue*

Ad·i·ron·dacks, the /ˌædə'rɑndæks/ also **the Adirondack Moun·tains** /..'.. ..'../ a range of mountains in New York State, in the northeastern U.S.

adj. the written abbreviation of "adjective"

ad·ja·cent /ə'dʒeɪsənt/ *adj.* something that is adjacent to something else, especially a room, building, or area, is next to it: *the sale of adjacent land* | [+ to] *The fire started in the building adjacent to the library.*

ad·jec·ti·val /ˌædʒɪk'taɪvəl◂/ *adj.* **an adjectival phrase/clause etc.** TECHNICAL a phrase etc. that is used as an adjective or that consists of adjectives. For example, "fully equipped" is an adjectival phrase. —**adjectivally** *adv.*

ad·jec·tive /'ædʒɪktɪv, 'ædʒɑtɪv/ *n.* [C] a word that describes a noun or PRONOUN, such as "black" in the sentence "She wore a black hat," or "happy" in the sentence "I'll try to make you happy." —compare ADVERB

USAGE NOTE: -ed AND -ing ADJECTIVES

WORD CHOICE: bored, boring; interested in, interesting; frightened of, frightening etc.
With pairs of adjectives like this, the one ending in **-ed** describes the person who has the feeling, and the one ending in **-ing** describes the thing or person that gives them that feeling: *Two weeks later, I got bored with the job.* | *The job got really boring.* | *Judy is really interested in art.* | *Judy thinks art is really interesting.* | *Thousands are frightened of losing their jobs.* | *Losing your job is a frightening experience.*

---

ad·join /ə'dʒɔɪn/ *v.* [T] if a room, building, or piece of land adjoins another one, it is next to it and joined to it: *A luxury hotel adjoins the convention center.* —**adjoining** *adj.* [only before noun] *adjoining hotel rooms*

ad·journ /ə'dʒɚn/ *v.* **1** [I,T] if a meeting or law court adjourns, or if the person in charge adjourns it, it finishes or stops for a short time: *The chairman has the power to adjourn the meeting at any time.* | [+ for/ until] *The trial was adjourned for two weeks.* | *The committee adjourned until Tuesday.* **2 adjourn to sth** HUMOROUS to finish an activity and go somewhere: *Paula and some friends adjourned to the bar to celebrate.* —**adjournment** *n.* [C,U]

ad·judge /ə'dʒʌdʒ/ *v.* [T] FORMAL to make a judgment about something or someone: *The policy was adjudged a failure.*

ad·ju·di·cate /ə'dʒudɪˌkeɪt/ *v.* FORMAL **1** [I,T] to officially decide who is right in an argument between two groups or organizations: *An independent expert was called in to adjudicate.* | *It took over two months for our case to be adjudicated.* **2** [I] to be the judge in a competition: *Mrs. Hendricks adjudicated at all the regional music competitions.* —**adjudicator** *n.* [C] —**adjudication** /əˌdʒudɪ'keɪʃən/ *n.* [U]

ad·junct¹ /'ædʒʌŋkt/ *n.* [C] FORMAL **1** something that is added or joined to something, but is not part of it: [+ to] *Medication can be a useful adjunct to physical therapy.* **2** TECHNICAL an ADVERBIAL word or phrase that adds meaning to another part of a sentence, such as "on Sunday" in "They arrived on Sunday."

adjunct² *adj.* [only before noun] connected to something else, but not completely a part of it: *an adjunct power source* | *an adjunct professor* (=who works part-time at a college)

ad·jure /ə'dʒʊr/ *v.* [T] FORMAL to try very hard to persuade someone to do something

ad·just /ə'dʒʌst/ *v.* [I,T] **1** to make small changes to something, especially to its position, in order to improve it, make it more effective etc.: *Seat belts adjust to fit short or tall drivers.* | *Adjust the heat so that the soup doesn't boil.* **2** to gradually get used to a new situation by making small changes to the way you do things: *It's amazing how quickly kids adjust.* | [+ to] *Adjusting to the tropical heat was more difficult than I had expected.* —see also WELL-ADJUSTED

ad·just·a·ble /ə'dʒʌstəbəl/ *adj.* something that is adjustable can be changed in shape, size, or position to make it appropriate for a particular person or purpose: *an adjustable desk lamp*

ad·jus·ter /ə'dʒʌstɚ/ *n.* [C] someone who is employed by an insurance company to decide how much money to pay people who have had an accident, had something stolen etc.: *a claims adjuster*

ad·just·ment /ə'dʒʌstmənt/ *n.* [C,U] **1** a small change made to something, such as a machine, a system, or the way something looks: *We've had to make some adjustments to the schedule.* | *a slight/ minor adjustment* (=a small change) **2** a change that someone makes to the way they behave or think: *Moving to the city has been a difficult adjustment for us.* | *There will be an initial period of adjustment.*

ad·ju·tant /'ædʒətənt/ *n.* [C] an army officer responsible for office work

ad-lib /ˌæd 'lɪb/ *v.* **ad-libbed, ad-libbing** [I,T] to say something in a speech, a performance of a play etc. without preparing or planning it: *Betsy forgot her lines and had to ad-lib the rest of the scene.* —**ad-lib** *n.* [C] —**ad-lib** *adj., adv.*

ad·man /'ædmæn/ *n. plural* **admen** /-men/ [C] INFORMAL a man who works in advertising

ad·min /'ædmɪn/ *n.* [U] INFORMAL: see ADMINISTRATION (3)

ad·min·is·ter /əd'mɪnəstɚ/ *v.* [T] **1** to manage and organize the affairs of a company, government etc.: *Ms. O'Brien's office is in charge of administering welfare programs.* | *The Navajo administer their own territory within the United States.* **2** to organize the way a test or punishment is given, or to organize the way laws are used: *It was the captain's job to administer punishment on the ship.* | *The test was administered fairly and impartially.* **3** FORMAL to give someone a medicine or drug to take: *Oxygen was being administered to Mr. Ryan through a mask.*

ad·min·is·tra·tion /ədˌmɪnə'streɪʃən/ *n.* **1** [C] the government of a country at a particular time, especially the U.S. government: *the Kennedy Administration* | *The problem has been ignored by successive administrations.* **2 the administration** the people who manage a company, institution etc.: *There have been conflicts between the faculty and administration over the college's budget.* **3** [U] all the activities that are involved in managing and organizing the affairs of a company, institution etc.: *We're looking for someone with experience in administration.* | *Some hospitals spend too much on administration and not* *enough on medical care.* **4** [U] the act of administering a test, law etc.: [+ of] *the administration of justice*

s w **ad·min·is·tra·tive** /əd'mɪnə,streɪtɪv, -strə-/ *adj.*
3 relating to the work of managing or organizing a company, institution etc.: *Phil's job is mainly administrative.* —**administratively** *adv.*

administrative as·sist·ant /ˌ......ˈ..ˈ../ *n.* [C] someone who works in an office typing (TYPE[2] (2)) letters, keeping records, answering telephone calls, arranging meetings etc.

s w **ad·min·is·tra·tor** /əd'mɪnə,streɪtɚ/ *n.* [C] someone
3 whose job is related to the management and organization of a company, institution etc.: *Nadine works as a hospital administrator.*

ad·mi·ra·ble /'ædmərəbəl/ *adj.* something that is admirable has many good qualities that you respect and admire: *an admirable achievement* —**admirably** *adv.*: *The entire staff performed admirably.*

ad·mi·ral /'ædmərəl/ *n.* [C] someone with a very high rank in the Navy

ad·mi·ra·tion /ˌædmə'reɪʃən/ *n.* [U] a feeling of admiring something or someone: *Carlos has earned our respect and admiration.* | [+ for] *Ms. Wright expressed her admiration for Albright's political abilities.*

s w **ad·mire** /əd'maɪɚ/ *v.* [T not in progressive] **1** to have
3 a very high opinion of someone because of a quality they have or because of something they have done: [admire sb for sth] *Lewis was admired for his work in medieval literature.* | *Pauley says she admires the way Norville handled the controversy.* **2** to look at something and think how beautiful or impressive it is: *We stopped halfway up the hill to admire the view.* **3 admire sb from afar** OLD-FASHIONED to be attracted to someone, without telling them how you feel —**admiring** *adj.* —**admiringly** *adv.*

ad·mir·er /əd'maɪrɚ/ *n.* [C] **1** someone who admires another person, especially someone famous, or their work: *A crowd of admirers had gathered outside Dunham's door.* | [+ of] *I'm a real admirer of Robert Frost's poetry.* **2** a man who is attracted to a particular woman: *Margaret had never met a man like this, even among her admirers in the Hamptons.* | *Yesterday, I got some flowers from **a secret admirer** (=someone who likes you, but has not told you they like you).*

ad·mis·si·ble /əd'mɪsəbəl/ *adj.* FORMAL admissible reasons, facts etc. are acceptable or allowed, especially in a court of law: *admissible evidence* —**admissibility** /əd,mɪsə'bɪləti/ *n.* [U] —opposite INADMISSIBLE

w **ad·mis·sion** /əd'mɪʃən/ *n.* **1** [U] the cost of entrance
3 to a concert, sports event etc.: *Admission is only $3.50.* **2** [C] a statement in which you admit that something is true or that you have done something wrong: [+ that] *The Senator's admission that he had lied to Congress shocked many Americans.* | *The out-of-court settlement does not imply an **admission of guilt**.* | *Reese, **by his own admission**, lacks the necessary experience.* **3** [U] permission given to someone to become a member of an organization, to enter a school or building etc.: *No admission after 10 p.m.* | [+ to/into] *Karl's grades weren't good enough for admission to the university.* | *The article tells how to **gain admission to** TV show tapings.* **4 admissions** [plural] the process of allowing people to enter a college, institution, hospital etc., or the number of people who can enter: *the college's admissions policy* | *They want to limit admissions to 500 students a year.*

USAGE NOTE: ADMISSION

WORD CHOICE: admission, admittance, admissions
Admission is the usual word. **Admittance** is more formal and only used in the meaning permission to go in a building, park etc., usually given by someone in authority. On a sign you might see: *Private Road: No Admittance.* **Admissions** is the word used by official organizations about the process of entering a college, school, hospital etc.: *the admissions department*

---

ad·mit /əd'mɪt/ *v.* **admitted, admitting**
1 accept truth [I,T] to accept and agree unwillingly that something is true or that someone else is right: [admit (that)] *You may not like Joan, but you have to admit that she's good at her job.* | **I have to admit** *I was a little drunk* (=used when you are admitting something you are embarrassed about). | *Admit it. You really like those plastic reindeer on the roof at Christmas* (=used in order to try to make someone admit something). | [admit (to) doing sth] *He'd never admit to being embarrassed.* | *Dana admitted feeling hurt by what I said.* | **freely/openly admit sth** (=admit something without being ashamed)

2 sth wrong/illegal [I,T] to say that you have done something wrong, especially something illegal; CONFESS: [admit (to) doing sth] *A quarter of all workers admit to taking time off when they are not sick.* | [admit (to) sth] *After questioning, She admitted to the murder.*

3 allow to enter [T] to allow someone or something to enter a place: *In the past, some countries refused to admit travelers who had South African visas.* | [admit sb to/into sth] *Only members will be admitted to the club for tonight's performance.*

4 allow to join [T] to allow someone to join an organization, club, school etc.: [admit sb to/into sth] *Twenty-five students were admitted to the National Honor Society in a ceremony yesterday.*

5 hospital etc. [T usually passive] to take someone into the hospital, a NURSING HOME etc. for treatment and keep them there until they are well enough to leave: *Maggie asked the nurses to find a doctor who would admit Roy, but they didn't call anyone.* | [admit sb to sth] *Steve was admitted to the hospital Tuesday morning with stomach pains.*

6 admit defeat to stop trying to do something because you realize you cannot succeed: *Haskill refuses to admit defeat and sell the restaurant.*

7 an admitted alcoholic/thief etc. someone who has admitted that they are an ALCOHOLIC, thief etc.

admit of sth *phr. v.* [T] FORMAL to allow the possibility that something is correct or true: *The Chief Justice said that the law admits of no exceptions.*

ad·mit·tance /əd'mɪtns/ *n.* [U] FORMAL permission to enter a place: *Steven's grades weren't good enough to **gain admittance to** Iowa State.* —compare ADMISSION (3), —see Usage Note at ADMISSION

ad·mit·ted·ly /əd'mɪtɪdli/ *adv.* [sentence adverb] used when you are admitting that something is true: *The technique is painful, admittedly, but it benefits the patient greatly.* | *This has led to losses, though admittedly on a fairly small scale.*

ad·mix·ture /æd'mɪkstʃɚ/ *n.* [C + of] TECHNICAL a mixture, or a substance that is added to another substance in a mixture

ad·mon·ish /əd'mɑnɪʃ/ *v.* [T] **1** to tell someone very strongly what to do: [admonish sb to do sth] *Financial companies have been admonished to write documents in language the public can understand.* **2** FORMAL to tell or warn someone severely that they have done something wrong: [admonish sb for (doing) sth] *The witness was admonished for refusing to answer the question.* —**admonishment** *n.* [C]

ad·mo·ni·tion /ˌædmə'nɪʃən/ *n.* [C,U] FORMAL a warning or expression of disapproval about someone's behavior —**admonitory** /əd'mɑnə,tɔri/ *adj.* FORMAL

ad nau·se·am /æd 'nɔziəm/ *adv.* if you say or do something ad nauseam, you say or do it so often that it becomes annoying to other people: *All these old rules have been taught and repeated ad nauseam.*

a·do /ə'du/ *n.* **without further ado/with no further ado** without delaying anymore, or wasting any more time: *So without further ado, I present Professor Barbara Davies.*

a·do·be /ə'doubi/ *n.* **1** [U] earth and STRAW (1) that are made into bricks for building houses **2** [C] a house made using adobe

A

a·do·les·cence /ˌædlˈɛsəns/ n. [U] the time, usually between the ages of 12 and 18, when a young person is developing into an adult

ad·o·les·cent¹ /ˌædlˈɛsənt/ n. [C] FORMAL a young person who is developing into an adult; a TEENAGER —see Usage Note at CHILD

adolescent² adj. [usually before noun] relating to young people who are developing into adults: *adolescent girls*

s w **a·dopt** /əˈdɑpt/ v.
2 **1** child [I,T] to legally make another person's child
3 part of your family so that he or she becomes one of your own children: *David and Sheila are unable to have children, but they're hoping to adopt.* | *My mother was adopted when she was four.* —compare FOSTER¹
2 accept a suggestion [T] to formally approve a proposal, especially by voting: *Congress finally adopted the law after a two-year debate.*
3 adopt an approach/strategy/policy etc. to start to use a particular method or plan for dealing with something: *The steering committee has adopted a "wait-and-see" attitude to the proposed changes.*
4 help an organization [T] to regularly help an organization, place etc. by giving it money, working for it etc.: *PTM Co. has adopted a neighborhood school, and employees often tutor students.*
5 style/manner [T] to use a particular style of speaking, writing, or behaving, especially one that you do not usually use: *Kim adopts a southern accent when she speaks to her cousins.*
6 adopt a name/country etc. to start to use or consider something as your own: *Abdel-Rauf was known as Chris Cob before adopting the Islamic faith in 1991.*

a·dopt·ed /əˈdɑptɪd/ adj. **1** an adopted child has been legally made part of a family that he or she was not born into: *The Browns have one adopted son.* —compare ADOPTIVE **2** your adopted country, religion, name etc. is one that you have chosen to use or consider as your own

a·dop·tee /ə‚dɑpˈti/ n. [C] someone who has been adopted

a·dop·tion /əˈdɑpʃən/ n. **1** [C,U] the act or process of adopting a child **2** [U] the act of deciding to use a particular plan, method, law, way of speaking etc.: [+ of] *Adequate training is needed for the successful adoption of new technology.*

a·dop·tive /əˈdɑptɪv/ adj. [only before noun] **1** an adoptive parent/father/mother an adoptive parent, father, or mother is one who has adopted a child **2** an adoptive child a child that has been adopted

a·dor·a·ble /əˈdɔrəbəl/ adj. someone or something that is adorable is so attractive that it fills you with feelings of love: *What an adorable baby!*

ad·o·ra·tion /ˌædəˈreɪʃən/ n. [U] **1** great love and admiration: *He looked at Julia in obvious adoration.* **2** LITERARY religious worship

a·dore /əˈdɔr/ v. [T not in progressive] **1** to love someone very much and feel very proud of them: *Betty adores her grandchildren.* **2** INFORMAL to like something very much: *As a child, I adored fairy tales.*

a·dor·ing /əˈdɔrɪŋ/ adj. [only before noun] liking and admiring someone very much: *Adoring fans crowded around the stage.* —**adoringly** adv.

a·dorn /əˈdɔrn/ v. [T usually passive] FORMAL to decorate something: [adorn sth with sth] *The church walls were adorned with religious paintings.*

a·dorn·ment /əˈdɔrnmənt/ n. FORMAL **1** [C,U] something that you use to decorate something **2** [U] the act of adorning something

a·dren·a·line, adrenalin /əˈdrɛnl-ɪn/ n. [U] **1** a chemical produced by your body when you are afraid, angry, or excited, which makes your heart beat faster so that you can move quickly **2** a feeling of being full of energy and very excited: *Bungee jumping produces an incredible adrenaline rush.* | *My adrenaline was really pumping* (=I felt very excited) *before the game.* —**adrenal** /əˈdrinl/ adj.: *adrenal glands*

A·dri·at·ic, the /ˌeɪdriˈætɪk/ also **the Adriatic Sea**

/..ˈ.. ‚./ the part of the Mediterranean Sea between Italy and Slovenia, Croatia, Bosnia, Montenegro, and Albania

a·drift /əˈdrɪft/ adj., adv. [not before noun] **1** a boat that is adrift is not tied to anything or controlled by anyone | **set/cast a boat adrift** (=untie a boat) **2** someone who is adrift does not have anyone else helping them or leading them: *Too many children seem adrift in society.*

a·droit /əˈdrɔɪt/ adj. smart and skillful, especially in the way you use words and arguments: *an adroit negotiator* —**adroitly** adv. —**adroitness** n. [U]

ad·u·la·tion /ˌædʒəˈleɪʃən/ n. [U] praise and admiration for someone that is more than they really deserve: *Lewis has gained the adulation of fans around the country.* —**adulatory** /ˈædʒələ‚tɔri/ adj. —**adulate** /ˈædʒə‚leɪt/ v. [T]

a·dult¹ /əˈdʌlt, ˈædʌlt/ n. [C] **1** a fully grown person s w or animal: *Some children find it difficult to talk to* 3 *adults.* **2** someone who is old enough to be considered legally responsible, and can for example vote in elections and get married without their parents' permission: *Prosecutors are seeking to have the 15-year-old defendant tried as an adult.*

adult² adj. [only before noun] **1** fully grown or devel- s w oped: *an adult lion* | *The brothers lived most of their* 3 ***adult lives*** (=the part of their lives when they were adults) *in Vermont.* **2** typical of an adult's behavior or of the things adults do: *You need to deal with your problems in an adult way.* **3** adult movies/magazines/bookstores etc. movies, magazines etc. that relate to sex, show sexual acts etc.

adult ed·u·ca·tion /.‚.. ..ˈ../ also **adult ed** /.‚. ˈ./ SPOKEN n. [U] education provided for adults who need additional help in basic skills, usually by means of classes that are held in the evening

a·dul·ter·ate /əˈdʌltə‚reɪt/ v. [T] to make food or drinks less pure by adding another substance of lower quality to it —**adulteration** /ə‚dʌltəˈreɪʃən/ n. [C] —see also UNADULTERATED

a·dul·ter·er /əˈdʌltərə/ n. [C] OLD-FASHIONED someone who is married and has sex with someone who is not their wife or husband

a·dul·ter·ess /əˈdʌltrɪs/ n. [C] OLD-FASHIONED a married woman who has sex with a man who is not her husband

a·dul·ter·y /əˈdʌltəri/ n. [U] sex between someone who is married and someone who is not their wife or husband: *She had* ***committed adultery*** *on several occasions.* —**adulterous** adj.

a·dult·hood /əˈdʌlt‚hʊd/ n. [U] the time when you are an adult

adv. the written abbreviation of "adverb"

ad·vance¹ /ədˈvæns/ v. s
1 move [I] to move forward, especially in a slow and determined way: [+ on] *Troops advanced on* (=moved forward to attack) *the city.* | [+ across/through/toward etc.] *The army slowly advanced through the thick jungle.*
2 develop [I] if something such as technical or scientific knowledge advances, it develops and improves: *Our understanding of human genetics has advanced considerably.*
3 advance a plan/idea/proposal etc. FORMAL to suggest a plan etc. so that other people can consider it: *Hahn spend her entire career advancing the theory.*
4 advance a cause/your interests/your career etc. to do something that will help you achieve an advantage or success: *Our main goal has to be to advance the nation's economic interests.*
5 money [T] to give someone money before they have earned it: [advance sb sth] *Will they advance you some money until your get your first paycheck?*
6 price [I] TECHNICAL if the price or value of something advances, it increases: *Oil stocks advanced today in heavy trading.*
7 film/clock [T] FORMAL if you advance a film in a camera, a clock etc., you make it go forward —see also ADVANCED, ADVANCING

advance² n. s
1 in advance before something happens or is

expected to happen: *Much of the meal can be prepared in advance.* | [+ **of**] *Passport applications should be submitted well in advance of your departure.* | **days/weeks/months etc. in advance** *The tours are often booked months in advance.*
2 development/improvement [C] a change, discovery, or INVENTION that brings progress: [+ **in**] *Recent advances in biotechnology have raised serious moral questions.* | *The computer industry continues to make **major advances** every six months or so.*
3 forward movement [C] forward movement or progress: *Observers monitored the army's advance on the capital.* —opposite RETREAT[2]
4 money [C usually singular] money that is paid to someone before the usual time. [+ **on**] *The company can give you an advance on your salary to help with moving expenses.* —see also CASH ADVANCE
5 advances [plural] an attempt to start a sexual relationship with someone: *Shaffer accused her boss of **making advances** to her.*
6 increase [C] TECHNICAL an increase in the price or value of something, especially in the STOCK MARKET: *There was a big advance in the price of gold today.*

advance[3] *adj.* [only before noun] **1 advance planning/warning/notice etc.** planning etc. that is done before something else that happens. *We received no advance warning of the storm.* **2 an advance party/team** a group of people who are the first to go to a place where something will happen, in order to prepare for it

w
3
ad·vanced /ədˈvænst/ *adj.* **1** using the most modern ideas, equipment, and methods: *advanced systems* | **an advanced country/nation** (=a country or nation that has a lot of technology and industry) **2** studying or dealing with a school subject at a difficult level: *advanced students of English* | *advanced physics* **3** having reached a late point in time or development: *By this time, Greg's illness was too far advanced to be treated.*

Advanced Place·ment /.,. '../ *abbreviation* **AP** *n.* [U] TRADEMARK a type of advanced course that can be taken by students who want to earn college CREDITS while they are still in high school: *Advanced Placement history*

ad·vance·ment /ədˈvænsmənt/ *n.* [C,U] FORMAL progress or development in your job, level of knowledge etc.: *career advancement* | [+ **in**] *advancements in science*

ad·vanc·ing /ədˈvænsɪŋ/ *adj.* [only before noun] **1** moving forward: *Missile attacks had little effect on the advancing enemy. forces.* **2 advancing years/age** the time when you are becoming very old: *Chances of developing cancer increase with advancing age.*

w
2
ad·van·tage /ədˈvæntɪdʒ/ *n.*
1 sth that helps you [C,U] something that helps you to be better or more successful than others: [+ **of**] *The advantages of a college education should not be underestimated.* | *For certain types of work, wood **has advantages over** plastic.* | *The army's superior equipment definitely **gave** them an **advantage** over the enemy.* | *Amy Weeks' previous experience gives her a **big advantage** over the other applicants.* | *Government subsidies give these industries an **unfair advantage**.* | *Wagner used his strength **to** his **advantage** during the match* (=it helped him). | *Applicants with computer skills will **be at an advantage**.* | *Bush tried to use the draft issue to **gain advantage** in the 1992 elections.*
2 take advantage of sth to use a particular situation to do or get what you want: *Hundreds of people took advantage of the sale prices.*
3 take advantage of sb to treat someone unfairly to get what you want, especially someone who is generous or easily persuaded: *I felt that my friends were taking advantage of me as a free babysitter.*
4 sth good [C,U] a good or useful quality or condition that something has: [+ **of/in**] *Good restaurants are one of the many advantages of living in the city.* | *Is there really any advantage in getting there early?* | *It's **to your advantage** to be patient with your coworkers.*

5 to good advantage in a way that shows the best features of someone or something: *Professional players can use their knowledge of their opponents' weaknesses to good advantage.*
6 tennis **advantage sb** used to show that the person named has won the point after DEUCE: *Advantage Agassi.*

ad·van·taged /ədˈvæntɪdʒd/ *adj.* FORMAL having more skill, success, money etc. than someone else: **economically/culturally etc. advantaged** *She comes from a financially advantaged family.* —compare DISADVANTAGED

ad·van·ta·geous /ˌædvænˈteɪdʒəs, -vən-/ *adj.* helpful and likely to make you successful: [+ **to**] *The trade agreement is particularly advantageous to U.S. farmers.* —**advantageously** *adv.*

ad·vent /ˈædvɛnt/ *n.* **1 the advent of sth** the time when something first begins to be widely used: *Many more people died of infections before the advent of penicillin.* **2 Advent** the period of four weeks before Christmas in the Christian religion

Advent cal·en·dar /.. ,.../ *n.* [C] a picture with 25 small pictures, candies etc. hidden in it, one of which is uncovered each day in December until Christmas day

Ad·vent·ist /ədˈvɛntɪst, æd-/ *n.* [C] a member of a Christian group that believes that Jesus Christ will soon come again to Earth —**Adventist** *adj.* —see also SEVENTH-DAY ADVENTIST

s w
3
ad·ven·ture /ədˈvɛntʃə/ *n.* [C,U] an exciting experience in which dangerous or unusual things happen: *Willis was a young man looking for adventure.* | *It's a book about the author's real-life adventures in Nepal.*

ad·ven·tur·er /ədˈvɛntʃərə/ *n.* [C] **1** someone who enjoys adventure and often travels to places that are far away in order to have exciting experiences there **2** OLD-FASHIONED someone who tries to become rich or socially important using dishonest or immoral methods

ad·ven·tur·ism /ədˈvɛntʃəˌrɪzəm/ *n.* [U] involvement in risky activities that is used to gain an unfair advantage, especially in business or politics —**adventurist** *n.* [C]

ad·ven·tur·ous /ədˈvɛntʃərəs/ also **ad·ven·ture·some** /ədˈvɛntʃəsəm/ *adj.* **1** eager to go to new places and do exciting or dangerous things: *adventurous travelers* **2** not afraid of taking risks or trying new things: *Andy isn't a very adventurous cook.* —**adventurously** *adv.*

ad·verb /ˈædvəb/ *n.* [C] a word or group of words that describes or adds to the meaning of a verb, an adjective, another adverb, or a whole sentence, such as "slowly" in "He ran slowly," "very" in "It's very hot," or "naturally" in "Naturally, we want you to come." —compare ADJECTIVE

ad·ver·bi·al[1] /ædˈvəbiəl/ *adj.* TECHNICAL used as an adverb: *an adverbial phrase*

adverbial[2] *n.* [C] TECHNICAL a word or phrase used as an adverb

ad·ver·sar·i·al /ˌædvəˈsɛriəl/ *adj.* involving two sides that oppose and attack each other: *Western and Eastern Europe no longer have an adversarial relationship.* | *Reporters used extreme and adversarial methods to get their information.*

ad·ver·sar·y /ˈædvəˌsɛri/ *n. plural* **adversaries** [C] FORMAL a country or person you are fighting or competing against; OPPONENT: *Quijano wanted to ensure success against his political adversaries.*

ad·verse /ədˈvəs, æd-, ˈædvəs/ *adj.* [only before noun] **1** not favorable: *adverse publicity* | *Climate change is likely to have adverse impacts on human health.* **2 adverse conditions/effects etc.** conditions etc. that make it difficult for something to happen or exist: *We had to abandon the climb because of adverse weather conditions.* | *Scientists are still looking for a treatment with no adverse effects.* —**adversely** *adv.*

A

ad·ver·si·ty /əd'vɚsəti, æd-/ n. plural **adversities** [C,U] a situation in which you have a lot of problems that seem to be caused by bad luck: *We've been through a lot of adversity as a team.*

ad·vert /æd'vɚt/ v.
  advert to sth phr. v. [T] FORMAL to mention something

ad·ver·tise /'ædvɚˌtaɪz/ v. **1** [I,T] to make a public announcement on television, in newspapers, or magazines etc. about something that is available or an event that is going to happen, to persuade people to buy or use it, go to the event, etc.: *These companies advertise their products in magazines like Popular Electronics.* | *Billboards all over town were advertising the upcoming state fair.* | [+ **for**] *Billtech is advertising for a marketing manager.* | *In trying to attract the brightest students, colleges have found that it pays to advertise* (=advertising brings you good results). **2** [T] to show or tell something about yourself that it would be better to keep secret: *Don't advertise the fact that you're looking for another job.* —**advertiser** n. [C]

ad·ver·tise·ment /ˌædvɚ'taɪzmənt/ n. [C] **1** a picture, set of words, a short movie etc. that is used to advertise a product or service that is available, an event that is going to happen etc.: [+ **for**] *an advertisement for laundry detergent* —compare COMMERCIAL[2] **2 be an advertisement for sth** to show the advantages of something: *Ben is a walking advertisement for the benefits of regular exercise.* —see Usage Note at COMMERCIAL[2]

s w **ad·ver·tis·ing** /'ædvɚˌtaɪzɪŋ/ n. [U] the activity or business of advertising things on television, in newspapers etc.: *The pop music industry's advertising is aimed at 18- to 25-year-olds.* | *Are you interested in a career in advertising?*
  advertising a·gen·cy /'.... ,.../ also **ad agency** /'. ,.../ n. [C] a company that designs and makes advertisements for other companies

ad·ver·tor·i·al /ˌædvɚ'tɔriəl/ n. [C] an advertisement in a newspaper or magazine that is made to look like a normal article

s w **ad·vice** /əd'vaɪs/ n. [U] an opinion you give someone about what they should do: [+ **on/about**] *a booklet with advice on car problems* | *They gave me some good advice about buying a house.* | *I want to ask your advice about where to stay in Taipei.* | *Investors who followed Murphy's advice* (=did what he advised) *earned a big profit.* | *I took a friend's advice* (=did what he advised) *and tried acupuncture.* | *Let me give you a piece of advice* (=some advice). *Wear a blue or gray suit to the interview.* | *On my doctor's advice* (=because the doctor advised me), *I'm taking some time off work.* | **legal/financial etc. advice** (=advice about the law, money etc.) | **professional/expert advice** (=advice from someone who knows a lot about a subject)
  advice col·umn /.'. ,../ n. [C] part of a newspaper or magazine in which someone gives advice to readers who have written letters about their personal problems —**advice columnist** n. [C]

ad·vis·a·ble /əd'vaɪzəbəl/ adj. [not before noun] FORMAL something that is advisable should be done in order to avoid problems or risks: *For heavy smokers, regular medical checks are advisable.* | *It is advisable to disconnect the computer before you open it up.* —**advisability** /əd,vaɪzə'bɪləti/ n. [U]

s w **ad·vise** /əd'vaɪz/ v. **1** [I,T] to tell someone what you think they should do, especially when you know more than they do about something: [**advise sb to do sth**] *The doctor advised Jo to lose weight and exercise more.* | [**advise sb against doing sth**] *We were advised against getting a cat because of Joey's allergies.* | *You are strongly advised to buy medical insurance when visiting China.* | *The makers advise extreme caution* (=advise people to be careful) *when handling this material.* **2** [I,T] to be employed to give advice on a subject about which you have special knowledge or skill | **advise (sb) on sth** *Uelman*

was asked to advise on constitutional issues. | *Young advises her clients on stock investments.* **3** [T] FORMAL to inform someone about something | **advise sb of sth** *We'll advise you of any changes in the delivery dates.* | *Keep us advised* (=continue to inform us) *of the developments.* —see also ILL-ADVISED, WELL-ADVISED —see Usage Note at RECOMMEND

ad·vis·ed·ly /əd'vaɪzɪdli/ adv. after careful thought: *He behaved like a dictator, and I use the word advisedly.*

ad·vi·see /əd,vaɪ'zi/ n. [C] someone who gets advice from an adviser, especially at a school or college

ad·vise·ment /əd'vaɪzmənt/ n. **take sth under advisement** if a judge takes something under advisement, they take time outside the COURTROOM to consider something carefully: *The Appeals Court took the request under advisement.*

ad·vis·er, advisor /əd'vaɪzɚ/ n. [C] **1** someone **s w** whose job is to give advice because they know a lot about a subject, especially in business, law, or politics: *a financial adviser* **2** a teacher or PROFESSOR at a school or college who gives students advice on courses they should take, makes sure they are making good progress, and sometimes gives advice on personal problems

ad·vi·so·ry[1] /əd'vaɪzəri/ adj. having the purpose of giving advice: *the Environmental Protection Advisory Committee* | **advisory role/capacity** *The army is acting only in an advisory capacity.*

advisory[2] n. plural **advisories** [C] an official warning or notice that gives information about a dangerous situation: *The Department of State issues travel advisories to alert U.S. citizens to conditions overseas.*

ad·vo·ca·cy /'ædvəkəsi/ n. [U] public support for a group of people, process, or way of doing things

ad·vo·cate[1] /'ædvəˌkeɪt/ v. [T] to publicly support a particular way of doing things: *The extremists openly advocate violence.*

ad·vo·cate[2] /'ædvəkət, -ˌkeɪt/ n. [C] **1** someone who **s** publicly supports a particular way of doing things: [+ **of**] *She is a passionate advocate of natural childbirth.* **2** someone who acts and speaks in support of someone else: [+ **for**] *Volunteers serve as advocates for abused children.* **3** FORMAL a lawyer —see also **play/be (the) devil's advocate** (DEVIL)

adze, adz /ædz/ n. [C] a sharp tool with the blade at a right angle to the handle, used in order to shape pieces of wood

Ae·ge·an Sea, the /ɪ'dʒiən/ also **the Aegean** the part of the Mediterranean Sea between Greece and Turkey

ae·gis /'eɪdʒɪs, 'idʒɪs/ n. **under the aegis of sb/sth** FORMAL with the protection or support of a person or organization: *The refugee camp operates under the aegis of the UN.*

Ae·o·li·an /i'oʊliən/ one of the people from ancient Greece that settled on the coast of Turkey and the islands near it at the end of the twelfth century B.C.

aer·ate /'ɛreɪt/ v. [T] TECHNICAL to put a gas or air into a liquid or solid under pressure —**aeration** /ɛr'eɪʃən/ n. [U]

aer·i·al /'ɛriəl/ adj. **1** from an airplane: *an aerial attack* | *aerial photographs* **2** in or moving through the air

aer·i·al·ist /'ɛriəlɪst/ n. [C] someone who entertains people by doing difficult physical actions in the air, such as balancing on a high rope or swinging on a TRAPEZE —see also ACROBAT

aer·ie /'ɛri, 'iri/ n. [C] the NEST of a large bird, especially an EAGLE, that is usually built high up in rocks or trees

aero- /ɛroʊ, ɛrə/ prefix relating to the air or to aircraft: *aerodynamics* (=the science of how things move through air) | *aeronautics* (=the science of designing and flying planes)

aer·o·bat·ics /ˌɛrə'bætɪks/ n. [plural] tricks done in an airplane that involve making difficult or dangerous movements in the air —**aerobatic** adj.

ae·ro·bic /ə'roʊbɪk, ɛ-/ adj. **1** intended to strengthen the heart and lungs: *Examples of aerobic exercise* are running, bicycling, and swimming. **2** relating to aerobics: *aerobic shoes* (=shoes meant to be worn when doing aerobics) **3** TECHNICAL using oxygen

ae·ro·bics /əˈroubɪks, ɛ-/ n. [U] a very active type of physical exercise done to music, usually in a class

aer·o·dy·nam·ic /ˌɛroudaɪˈnæmɪk‹/ adj. **1** an aerodynamic car, design etc. uses the principles of aerodynamics to achieve high speed or low use of gasoline **2** TECHNICAL relating to or involving aerodynamics: *aerodynamic efficiency* —**aerodynamically** /-kli/ adv.

aer·o·dy·nam·ics /ˌɛroudaɪˈnæmɪks/ n. **1** [U] the scientific study of how objects move through the air **2** [plural] the qualities needed for something to move through the air, especially smoothly and quickly

aer·o·nau·tics /ˌɛrəˈnɔtɪks, -ˈnɑ-/ n. [U] the science of designing and flying airplanes —**aeronautic** adj. —**aeronautical** adj.

aer·o·plane /ˈɛrəpleɪn/ n. [C] the British spelling of airplane

aer·o·sol /ˈɛrəˌsɔl, -ˌsɑl/ n. [C] a metal can containing a liquid and a gas under pressure, from which the liquid can be SPRAYed

aer·o·space /ˈɛrouˌspeɪs/ n. [U] the industry that designs and builds airplanes and space vehicles: **aerospace companies/engineers/workers etc.** *Employment in the aerospace industry has fallen in California.*

Aes·chy·lus /ˈɛskələs, ˈis-/ (525–456 B.C.) a writer in ancient Greece, famous for his plays

Ae·sop /ˈisɑp/ (?620–?560 B.C.) a writer in ancient Greece, famous for his FABLES

aes·thete, esthete /ˈɛsθit/ n. [C] FORMAL someone who loves and understands beautiful things such as art and music

aes·thet·ic, esthetic /ɛsˈθɛtɪk, ɪs-/ adj. **1** relating to beauty and the study of beauty: *The town council will discuss plans for aesthetic improvements at two city parks.* | *People want wood shingles on their houses for purely aesthetic reasons.* **2** designed in a beautiful way: *We want to build factories that are as functional as they are aesthetic.* —**aesthetically** /-kli/ adv.: *aesthetically pleasing*

aes·the·ti·cian, esthetician /ˌɛsθəˈtɪʃən/ n. [C] someone whose job is to give people beauty treatments, especially to the face, hands, and feet

aes·thet·ics, esthetics /ɛsˈθɛtɪks/ n. [U] the study of beauty, especially beauty in art

AFAIK, afaik a written abbreviation of "as far as I know," used in EMAIL, or by people communicating in CHAT ROOMS on the Internet

a·far /əˈfɑr/ adv. from afar LITERARY from a long distance away: *I saw him from afar.*

AFC n. American Football Conference; a group of teams that is part of the NFL —see also NFC

AFDC Aid to Families with Dependent Children; a U.S. government program that gives money to poor families

af·fa·ble /ˈæfəbəl/ adj. friendly and easy to talk to: *an affable guy* —**affably** adv. —**affability** /ˌæfəˈbɪləti/ n. [U]

af·fair /əˈfɛr/ n. [C]
1 affairs [plural] **a)** public or political events and activities: *world affairs* | *They were accused of interfering in China's internal affairs.* | *Gedda has reported on foreign affairs* (=political events in other countries) *since 1968.* **b)** things relating to your personal life, your financial situation etc.: *You need to get your financial affairs in order.* —see also **a state of affairs** (STATE[1])
2 event an event or set of related events that people remember or are likely to remember, especially because it is impressive or shocking: *the Watergate affair* | *The awards celebration is an annual affair in Hollywood.*
3 relationship a secret sexual relationship between two people, when at least one of them is married to someone else: *Her husband had an affair with her best friend.* —see also LOVE AFFAIR
4 thing INFORMAL an object, machine etc. of a

particular kind: *The computer was one of those little portable affairs.*
5 be sb's affair if something is your affair, it only concerns you and you do not want anyone else to get involved in it: *What I do in my free time is my affair and nobody else's.*

af·fect[1] /əˈfɛkt/ v. [T] **1** to do something that produces an effect or change in someone or something: *The disease affects the central nervous system.* | *Emergency relief will be sent to the areas most affected by the hurricane.* | *Citizens want more control over matters which directly affect their lives.* **2** [usually passive] to make someone feel strong emotions: *We were all deeply affected by the news of Sonia's death.* **3** to pretend to have a particular feeling, way of speaking etc., especially to appear impressive to others: *It is annoying when she tries to affect a British accent.*   S W / 2 2

USAGE NOTE: AFFECT

WORD CHOICE: affect, effect
Affect is the usual verb and **effect** is the usual noun: *How do you think the changes will affect (v) you?* (NOT affect on/to/in you). *What effect (n) do you think the changes will have on you?* The verb **effect** is fairly formal and is only used in particular meanings, for example, you might **effect** changes or a plan of action (=make them happen). It does not mean the same as **affect**.

---

affect[2] n. [U] TECHNICAL emotions, feelings, and desires, which are considered separately from thoughts and actions in PSYCHOLOGY

af·fec·ta·tion /ˌæfɛkˈteɪʃən/ n. [C,U] someone's behavior, attitude, or way of speaking that is not sincere or natural, especially because they are trying to appear impressive to others: *Tim's fancy hairdo was an affectation left over from his younger days.*

af·fect·ed /əˈfɛktɪd/ adj. not sincere or natural: *I hate that stupid affected laugh of hers.*

af·fect·ing /əˈfɛktɪŋ/ adj. FORMAL producing strong emotions of sadness, pity etc.: *a deeply affecting story*

af·fec·tion /əˈfɛkʃən/ n. [C,U] **1** a gentle feeling of love and caring: [+ for] *My father didn't find it easy to express his affection for us.* | **give/show sb affection** *He finds it difficult to show affection.* **2** FORMAL a feeling of liking something very much: [+ for] *Since the age of eight, she's had an affection for music.*

af·fec·tion·ate /əˈfɛkʃənɪt/ adj. showing in a gentle way that you love someone: *an affectionate hug* | *a very affectionate child* —**affectionately** adv.

af·fec·tive /əˈfɛktɪv/ adj. TECHNICAL relating to people's feelings and emotions —see also SEASONAL AFFECTIVE DISORDER

af·fi·anced /əˈfaɪənst/ adj. OLD USE: see ENGAGED (1)

af·fi·da·vit /ˌæfəˈdeɪvɪt/ n. [C] LAW a written statement made under OATH (=after promising to tell the truth), for use as proof in a court of law

af·fil·i·ate[1] /əˈfɪliɪt, -ˌeɪt/ n. [C] a small company, organization etc. such as a television station that is related to or controlled by a larger one

af·fil·i·ate[2] /əˈfɪliˌeɪt/ v. **1 be affiliated with/to sth** if a group or organization is affiliated to a larger one, it is related to it or controlled by it: *a TV station affiliated to CBS* **2 affiliate yourself to sth** to join or become related to a larger group or organization —**affiliated** adj.: *an affiliated university*

af·fil·i·a·tion /əˌfɪliˈeɪʃən/ n. **1** [C,U] involvement with a political or religious organization: *What are her political affiliations?* **2** [U] the act of a smaller group or organization joining a larger one

af·fin·i·ty /əˈfɪnəti/ n. plural affinities **1** [C usually singular, U] a strong feeling that you like something, or that you like and understand someone because you share the same ideas or interests: [+ for/between/with] *Children have a natural affinity for mountain biking, because they have no fear.* | *Some committee members questioned Lopez's affinity for the*

A

cause. | *Morrison says he feels an affinity with Amanda.* **2** [C,U] a close similarity or relationship between two things because of qualities or features that they both have: [+ **with/between**] *There is a remarkable affinity between the two religions.* **3** [C,U] TECHNICAL a force or attraction between atoms, MOLE-CULES etc. that makes them combine: *Samples are stained with a dye that has an affinity for the proteins.*

affinity card /.'... ,./ also **affinity cred·it card** /.,... '.. ,./ *n.* [C] a CREDIT CARD that is made available by a particular company or CHARITY, so that each time it is used the charity receives money or the company gives the CREDIT CARD user a special reward

af·firm /ə'fəm/ *v.* **1** [T] FORMAL to state publicly that something is true or correct: *The Supreme Court has affirmed the lower court's ruling.* | [**affirm that**] *The general affirmed that rumors of the attack were true.* **2** [T] FORMAL to show that you support something or agree with something: *There are moral standards that we must affirm for our children.* —**affirmation** /,æfə'meɪʃən/ *n.* [C,U]

af·firm·a·tive[1] /ə'fəmətɪv/ *adj.* FORMAL a word, sign etc. that means "yes": *an affirmative nod* —**affirmatively** *adv.*

affirmative[2] *n.* **answer/reply in the affirmative** to say "yes" —opposite NEGATIVE[2]

affirmative ac·tion /.,... '../ *n.* [U] the practice of choosing people for a job, college etc. who are usually treated unfairly because of their race, sex etc.: *an affirmative action employer* —compare REVERSE DISCRIMINATION

af·fix[1] /ə'fɪks/ *v.* [T + **to**] FORMAL to fasten or stick something to something else

af·fix[2] /'æfɪks/ *n.* [C] TECHNICAL a group of letters added to the beginning or end of a word to change its meaning or use, such as "un-," "mis-," "-ness," or "-ly" —compare PREFIX[1], SUFFIX

af·flict /ə'flɪkt/ *v.* [T often passive] FORMAL to make someone have a serious illness or experience serious problems: *This type of pneumonia frequently afflicts elderly people.* | [+ **with**] *Several of Loretta's friends had been afflicted with Alzheimer's Disease.*

af·flic·tion /ə'flɪkʃən/ *n.* [C,U] FORMAL something, usually a medical condition, that causes pain or unhappiness: *Smoking is a major cause of cancer and other afflictions.*

af·flu·ent /'æfluənt/ *adj.* having plenty of money, so that you can afford to buy expensive things, live in a nice house etc., or relating to people who have plenty of money: *an affluent neighborhood* —**affluence** *n.* [U]

ᴿᵂ **af·ford** /ə'ford/ *v.* [T] **1 can afford a)** to have ₂₂ enough money to buy or pay for something: *I'm not sure I can afford $750 a month in rent.* | [**can afford to do sth**] *We can't afford to buy a new car.* **b)** to be able to do something without causing serious problems for yourself: [**can afford to do sth**] *We simply can't afford to offend such an important customer.* **c)** to have enough time to do something: *Helena doesn't feel she can afford any more time away from work.* **2** FORMAL to provide something or allow something to happen: *The window affords a beautiful view out over the city.*

af·ford·a·ble /ə'fordəbəl/ *adj.* not too expensive: *The car was affordable, and it ran pretty well, so we decided to buy it.* | *affordable housing*

af·for·es·ta·tion /ə,fɔrɪ'steɪʃən, æ-, -,far-/ *n.* [U] TECHNICAL the act of planting trees in order to make a forest —**afforest** /æ'fɔrɪst/ *v.* [T] —opposite DEFORESTATION

af·fray /ə'freɪ/ *n.* [C] LAW a noisy fight or argument in a public place

af·fri·cate /'æfrɪkɪt/ *n.* [C] TECHNICAL a CONSONANT sound consisting of a PLOSIVE such as /t/ or /d/ that is immediately followed by a FRICATIVE pronounced in the same part of the mouth, such as /ʃ/ or /ʒ/. The word "church," for example, contains the affricate /tʃ/

af·front[1] /ə'frʌnt/ *n.* [C usually singular] a remark or action that offends or insults someone: [+ **to**] *The comments were an affront to his pride.*

affront[2] *v.* [T usually passive] LITERARY to offend or insult someone, especially by not showing respect

Af·ghan /'æfgæn/ *n.* [C] **1** someone who comes from Afghanistan **2** also **Afghan hound** a tall thin dog with a pointed nose and very long silky hair —**Afghan** *adj.*

af·ghan /'æfgæn/ *n.* [C] a colorful BLANKET that is made of YARN in a pattern with many open spaces

Af·ghan·is·tan /æf'gænə,stæn/ a country in Asia that is west of Pakistan and east of Iran

a·fi·cio·na·do /ə,fɪʃə'nadoʊ/ *n. plural* **aficionados** [C] someone who is very interested in a particular activity or subject and knows a lot about it: *a movie aficionado*

a·field /ə'fild/ *adv.* **far afield** far away, especially from home: *Artists from as far afield as Paris will show their works.*

a·fire /ə'faɪə/ *adj., adv.* [not before noun] LITERARY **1** burning: *The oil tanker was afire.* **2** filled with strong emotions or excitement: [+ **with**] *The country is afire with patriotism.*

a·flame /ə'fleɪm/ *adj.* [not before noun] LITERARY **1** burning **2** very bright with color or light: [+ **with**] *The trees were aflame with autumn leaves.* **3** filled with strong emotions or excitement —**aflame** *adv.*

AFL-CIO *n.* [singular] the American Federation of Labor and Congress of Industrial Organizations; an association of American trade unions

a·float /ə'floʊt/ *adj.* [not before noun] **1** having enough money to operate or stay out of debt: *They're just hard-working people struggling to* **stay afloat.** **2** floating on water **3** LITERARY on a ship —**afloat** *adv.*

AFN *n.* Armed Forces Network; a radio station owned by the U.S. government that broadcasts American music and news all over the world

a·foot /ə'fʊt/ *adj.* [not before noun] **1** being planned or happening: *There were plans afoot for a second attack.* **2** OLD USE moving, especially walking

a·fore·men·tioned /'æfə,mɛnʃənd, ə'fɔr-/ also **a·fore·said** *adj.* **the aforementioned** [only before noun] FORMAL mentioned before in an earlier part of a document, article, book etc.: *In addition to the aforementioned film projects, Elliott has appeared in two TV comedies.* —**the aforementioned** *n.* [singular or plural]

a·fore·thought /ə'fɔrθɔt/ *adj.* —see **with malice aforethought** (MALICE)

a·foul /ə'faʊl/ *adv.* **run/fall afoul of sb/sth** FORMAL to cause problems by doing something that is against the rules or that goes against people's beliefs: *Quinn's company had run afoul of the law before.*

a·fraid /ə'freɪd/ *adj.* [not before noun]
1 **frightened** frightened because you think that someone or something may hurt you or that something bad may happen: *I could see she was afraid.* | [+ **of**] *His brother is really afraid of dogs.* | [**be afraid of doing sth**] *Luke is afraid of getting lost.* | [**be afraid to do sth**] *A lot of people are afraid to fly.*
2 **worried** very worried that something bad will happen: [**afraid (that)**] *Josh didn't say anything because he was afraid that the other kids would laugh.* | [**be afraid of doing sth**] *I didn't tell Mom because I was afraid of upsetting her.* | [+ **of**] *Businesses are afraid of a continuing recession.*
3 **afraid for sb/sth** very worried that something bad may happen to someone, or that something could be ruined: *Louise said Harry made her afraid for her personal safety around the house.*
4 I'm afraid SPOKEN used to politely tell someone something that may annoy them, upset them, or disappoint them: *I'm afraid you'll just have to wait.*
5 (I'm) afraid so SPOKEN used to say "yes" to something, especially when someone is likely to be disappointed by this: *"Do you have to work Christmas Day?" "I'm afraid so."*
6 (I'm) afraid not SPOKEN used to say "no" to

something, especially when someone is likely to be disappointed by this: *"Are there any cookies left?" "Afraid not."*

7 afraid of your own shadow INFORMAL easily frightened or always nervous

a·fresh /ə'freʃ/ *adv.* FORMAL if you do something afresh, you do it again from the beginning: **start/begin afresh** *Vinh's family escaped from Vietnam and started afresh in America.*

Af·ri·ca /'æfrɪkə/ the CONTINENT that is south of the Mediterranean Sea

Af·ri·can¹ /'æfrɪkən/ *adj.* relating to or coming from Africa

African² *n.* [C] someone from Africa

African A·mer·i·can /,... .'.../ *n.* [C] an American with dark brown skin, whose family originally came from the part of Africa south of the Sahara Desert —**African-American** *adj.*: *African-American businesses*

African-American Stud·ies /,... .,... '../ *n.* [U] a subject of study in colleges and universities which includes African-American history, politics, CULTURE etc.

Af·ri·kaans /,æfrɪ'kɑns/ *n.* [U] a language of South Africa that is similar to Dutch

Af·ri·ka·ner /,æfrɪ'kɑnə/ *n.* [C] a white South African whose family is related to the Dutch people who settled there in the 1600s

Af·ro /'æfrou/ *n. plural* **Afros** [C] a hair style popular with African Americans in the 1970s in which the hair is cut into a large round shape

Afro- /æfrou/ *prefix* relating to Africa; AFRICAN: *an Afro-American* (=an American whose family originally came from Africa) | *Afro-Cuban music* (=combining styles from Africa and Cuba)

Afro-A·mer·i·can /,... .'.../ *n.* [C] OLD-FASHIONED an AFRICAN AMERICAN —**Afro-American** *adj.*

Afr·o·cen·tric /,æfrou'sɛntrɪk◂/ *adj.* emphasizing African ideas, styles, values etc.: *NetNoir promotes and develops Afrocentric programming for the Internet.* —**Afrocentrism** *n.* [U]

AFT American Federation of Teachers; a UNION of teachers in the U.S.

aft /æft/ *adj., adv.* TECHNICAL in or toward the back part of a boat —opposite FORE²

w 1

af·ter¹ /'æftə/ *prep.*

1 when sth is finished when a particular time or event has happened or is finished: *After the dance, a few of us went out for a drink.* | *I go swimming every day after work.* | *What's on after the 6 o'clock news?* | *Do you believe in life after death?* | **a month/3 weeks/4 years etc. after sth** *A year after the fire, they rebuilt the house.* | *We leave the day after tomorrow.* | **shortly/soon etc. after sth** *Not long after the wedding, his wife got pregnant.* | *Come home right after* (=immediately after) *school.*

2 list following someone or something else on a list or in a series, piece of writing, line of people etc.: *Whose name is after yours on the list?* | *The date should be written after the address.*

3 after 10 minutes/3 hours etc. when a particular amount of time has passed: *After 25 minutes, remove the cake from the oven.* | *After a while, things started to improve.* | *After months of arguments, they decided to get a divorce.*

4 time used when telling time to say how many minutes it is past the hour: *The movie starts at a quarter after seven.*

5 day after day/year after year etc. continuously, for a very long time: *I get bored doing the same exercises day after day.*

6 go/run/chase etc. after sb to follow someone in order to catch them: *Go after him and apologize.*

7 second-best used when making a list of or naming things, to mean that you have not included a particular thing because that is the first or best one: *After dancing, going to the movies is my favorite weekend activity.*

8 because of because of something or as a result of something: *I'm not surprised he left her, after the*

A

way she treated him. | *After your letter, I didn't think I'd ever see you again.*

9 after all a) used in order to say that something is true or is a fact, in spite of something that has happened: *He wrote to say they couldn't give me a job after all.* **b)** used in order to say that something you thought was true is not true: *Rita didn't have my pictures after all – Jake did.* **c)** used in order to say that something should be remembered or considered, because it helps to explain why something else is true or is a fact: *I don't know why you're so concerned: after all, it isn't your problem.*

10 after sb when someone has left a place, when someone is finished doing something etc.: *Remember to close the door after yourself.* | *I spend all day cleaning up after the kids.*

11 be after sb to be looking for someone and trying to catch them: *The FBI is after me for fraud.*

12 be after sth INFORMAL to want to have something that belongs to someone else: *I think Chris is after my job.*

13 in spite of in spite of something: *After all the trouble I had, Reese didn't even say thank you.*

14 call/shout/gaze etc. after sb to speak to or look toward someone as they move away from you: *"You have a nice day, now!" she called after us.*

15 one after another also **one after the other** if a series of events, actions etc. happen one after another, each one happens soon after the previous one: *Ever since we moved into this house, it's been one problem after another.*

16 after you SPOKEN used to say politely that someone else can use or do something before you do: *"Do you need the copy machine?" "After you."*

17 art/music style FORMAL in the same style as a particular painter, musician etc.: *a painting after Rembrandt* —see also **a man/woman after my own heart** (HEART), **take after** (TAKE¹)

USAGE NOTE: AFTER

WORD CHOICE: after (*prep.*), **in, after** (*adv.*), **afterward, later**

You use **after** (*prep.*) to talk about something that happens at the end of a period of time that is different from something that happens within that period: *After a few weeks, Jared's strength returned* (=not until a few weeks had passed). You use **in** to talk about something that will happen in the future, often when you are speaking: *You'll feel better in a few days* (=a few days later than today). **After** (*prep.*) is more often used to talk about events in the past, and **in** about the future: *She left after an hour* (=after an hour had passed). | *She'll be leaving in an hour* (=after an hour has passed from now). With words that show a length of time, **afterward** or **later** are more usual: *She arrived three days afterward/later* (NOT usually *three days after*, though you could say *after that*). If you want to use a word with this meaning on its own, you would usually use **afterward**: *We went out to dinner and saw a movie afterward.* You would not usually begin a sentence with **after**, though: *Afterward/After that, we left* (NOT *After, we left*).

---

after² *conjunction* when a particular time or event has happened or is finished: *After you called the police, what did you do?* | *Walter changed his name after he left Germany.* | **two days/three weeks etc. after** *Ten years after I bought the painting, I discovered it was a fake.* | **shortly/soon etc. after** *Not long after we talked, I got the promotion.*

s w 1 1

after³ *adv.* later than something that has already been mentioned; AFTERWARD: *Pat arrived on Monday, and I got here the day after.* | *Not long after, I heard that Mike had gotten married.* | *Having lost the final pages, we can only guess at what might come after* (=happen after something else). —see Usage Note at AFTER¹

s w 2 3

after⁴ *adj.* [only before noun] **1 in after years** LITERARY in the years after the time that has been mentioned **2** TECHNICAL in the back part of a boat or an aircraft: *the after deck*

A

after- /ˈæftɚ/ *prefix* coming or happening after something: *aftereffects* | *the afterlife* (=life after death)

af·ter·birth /ˈæftɚˌbɚθ/ *n.* [U] NOT TECHNICAL the substance that comes out of female humans or animals just after they have had a baby; PLACENTA

af·ter·burn·er /ˈæftɚˌbɚnɚ/ *n.* [C] a piece of equipment in a JET engine that gives it more power

af·ter·ef·fect /ˈæftɚɪˌfɛkt/ *n.* [C usually plural] a bad effect that remains for a long time after the condition or event that caused it: *The town is still suffering the aftereffects of the plant closure.*

af·ter·glow /ˈæftɚˌgloʊ/ *n.* [C usually singular] **1** a good feeling that remains after a happy experience: *You could see the afterglow of the victory in his face.* **2** the light that remains in the western sky after the sun goes down

af·ter-hours /ˌ.. ˈ.ˌ/ *adj.* [only before noun] **1** an after-hours bar, club etc. is one that is legally allowed to stay open after the time the other bars etc. have to close **2** happening after the regular time when something happens or is done: *Stocks fell by 29% in after-hours trading.*

af·ter·im·age /ˈæftɚˌɪmɪdʒ/ *n.* [C] the image of something that you continue to see after you look away or close your eyes

af·ter·life /ˈæftɚˌlaɪf/ *n.* [singular] the life that some people believe people have after death

af·ter·mar·ket /ˈæftɚˌmarkɪt/ *n.* [C] TECHNICAL **1** the MARKET (=all the people who want to buy something) for products such as addition parts, services, or pieces of equipment that people want to buy after they have bought a related product: *the computing aftermarket* **2** the STOCK EXCHANGES and other places where SHARES² (4) are bought and sold —**aftermarket** *adj.*

af·ter·math /ˈæftɚˌmæθ/ *n.* [singular] the period of time after something bad such as a war, storm, or accident has happened, when people are still dealing with the results: *Several people resigned in the aftermath of the scandal.*

af·ter·noon /ˌæftɚˈnun/ *n.* [C,U] **1** the period of time between 12 p.m. and the evening: *We went swimming on Tuesday afternoon.* | *Harry went to sleep in the afternoon.* | *Do you want to go shopping tomorrow afternoon?* | *Our tickets are for the afternoon performance.* | *Could you babysit for a few hours this afternoon* (=today in the afternoon)? **2 afternoons** during the afternoon each day: *She only works afternoons.* —compare EVENING

after-school /ˈ.. ./ *adj.* [only before noun] for children and happening in the afternoon after classes are finished: *after-school programs*

af·ter·shave /ˈæftɚˌʃeɪv/ *n.* [U] a liquid with a nice smell that a man puts on his face after he SHAVES

af·ter·shock /ˈæftɚˌʃɑk/ *n.* [C] **1** a small EARTHQUAKE, usually one in a series, that happens after a larger EARTHQUAKE **2** the effects of a shocking event: *The war and its aftershocks had a profound effect on people here and abroad.*

af·ter·taste /ˈæftɚˌteɪst/ *n.* [C usually singular] **1** a taste that stays in your mouth after you eat or drink something: *The wine has a bitter aftertaste.* **2** a bad feeling that stays in your mind as a result of an event or a bad experience: *The aftertaste of that loss to Oregon State won't go away very soon.*

af·ter·thought /ˈæftɚˌθɔt/ *n.* [C usually singular] something thought of, mentioned, or added later, especially something that was not part of the original plan: *The tiles looked out of place, as if they had been an afterthought.* | *Almost as an afterthought, he said that Melanie could come too.*

af·ter·ward /ˈæftɚwɚd/ also **afterwards** *adv.* after an event or time that has already been mentioned: *The ceremony lasts half an hour and afterward there's a meal.* | **five years/six months etc. afterward** *My parents met during college but didn't marry until five years afterward.* —see Usage Note at AFTER¹

af·ter·word /ˈæftɚˌwɚd/ *n.* [C] a short piece of writing at the end of a book, which gives more information about the person who wrote it or about events that have taken place since the book was written —compare FOREWORD

a·gain /əˈgɛn/ *adv.* **1** if something happens again, or someone does something again, it happens or they do it one more time: *Can you say that again? I didn't hear you.* | *I'll never go there again.* | *If you don't succeed this time, try again.* | *Once again* (=again, after happening several times) *the Allies marched in and pushed back the enemy troops.* | *I had to ask him for advice yet again* (=again, after happening many times before). **2** at another time: *Mr. Rodriguez is in a meeting. Can you call again later?* | *Thanks for coming! Please stop by again.* **3** back to the same condition or situation that you were in before: *If Sherri gets some rest, she should feel better again soon.* | *It's great to have you home again.* **4 all over again** if you do something all over again, you repeat it from the beginning, which might make you annoyed: *There's no tape in the machine. We'll have to start the interview all over again.* **5 again and again** also **time and (time) again** or **over and over again** very often, making you or someone else annoyed: *I've told you again and again – don't play soccer near the windows.* **6** SPOKEN used when you want someone to repeat information that they have already given you: *What did you say your name was again?* **7** used when giving a fact or opinion that explains or emphasizes something you have just said: *And again, while the accident was not your fault, the damage must be paid for somehow.* —see also **but then (again)** (THEN¹) **8 half/a third etc. again as much** one and a half, one and a third etc. times the original amount: *Hulsey now earns about half again as much as he did when he started at Deltex.* —see also **now and again** (NOW¹)

a·gainst /əˈgɛnst/ *prep.*
1 disagreeing opposed to or disagreeing with an idea, belief, proposal etc.: *There were 10 votes for and 15 against the motion.* | *It's against my principles to borrow money.* | *I'm against all forms of hunting.* | *Everyone was against closing the factory.* | **against sb's wishes/will** (=when someone does not want to do something) | *You can't do that! It's against the law* (=illegal).
2 fight/compete fighting or competing with another person, team, country etc.: *He was injured in the game against the Cowboys.* | *We'll be competing against some of the best companies in Europe.* | *the fight against terrorism*
3 disadvantage in a way that has an bad effect on someone or makes them have a disadvantage: *discrimination against women* | *Your lack of experience could count against you.* | *The planning regulations tend to work against smaller companies.*
4 hit touching, hitting, or rubbing another surface: *The rain drummed against the window.* | *I hate it when the cat rubs its head against my legs.* | *The car skidded and we could hear the crunch of metal against metal.*
5 support next to and touching an upright surface, especially for support: *There was a ladder propped up against the wall.* | *The younger policeman was leaning against the desk.*
6 opposite direction in the opposite direction of something: *We had to sail against the wind.* | *It's so difficult swimming against the current.* —opposite WITH
7 be/come up against sth to have to deal with a difficult opponent or problem: *You see, this is what we're up against – the suppliers just aren't reliable.*
8 have sth against sb/sth to dislike or disapprove of someone or something: *I have nothing against people making lots of money.*
9 seen together seen or shown with something else behind or as a background: *I have trouble knowing what colors look good against each other.*
10 other events used to describe something in relation to other events that are happening at the same time: *The reforms were introduced against a background of social unrest.*
11 comparison in comparison with someone or

something: *Only 3% of blacks were registered voters against 97% of the white residents.* | *She checked the contents of the box against the list.*
12 protection providing protection from harm or damage: *Eating good food is good insurance against sickness.* | *This spray can be used against weevil and other crop pests.*

A·ga·na /ə'ganyə/ the capital city of the U.S. TERRITORY of Guam

a·gape /ə'geɪp/ *adj., adv.* [only after noun] with your mouth wide open, especially because you are surprised or shocked: *She sat there with her mouth agape, staring at the ring.*

ag·ate /'ægɪt/ *n.* [C] a hard stone with bands of different colors, used in jewelry

a·ga·ve /ə'gavi/ also **century plant** *n.* [C] a desert plant with long thin leaves at the base and a tall stem with flowers. The leaves can be used to make TEQUILA (=a type of strong alcohol)

w **age¹** /eɪdʒ/ *n.*
1 **how old** [C,U] the number of years someone has lived or something has existed: *Francis is the same age as I am.* | *Experts have given different estimates of the age of the painting.* | *Marco won the Grand Prix at the age of 19.* | *The missing girl is 9 years of age.* | *Saul entered Yale at age 14.* | *She became a mother at an early age* (=very young). | *Anne's very tall for her age* (=compared with others of the same age). | *For heaven's sake, Tony, act your age* (=behave in a way that is appropriate for someone as old as you)*.*
2 **legal age** [U] the age when you are legally old enough to do something: *What's the minimum age for getting a driver's license?* | *The clerk sold Jeff some beer, even though he was obviously under age* (=too young). | *The army wouldn't take him because he was over age* (=too old).
3 **period of life** [C,U] one of the particular periods of someone's life: *The show is sure to delight people of all ages.* | *There are very few women in the village who are of childbearing age* (=old enough but not too old to have babies). —see also MIDDLE AGE, OLD AGE, TEENAGE
4 **being old** [U] the condition or fact of being old: *The newspapers were brown with age.*
5 **period of history** [C usually singular] a particular period of history: *the Ice Age* | *We are living in the computer age.* —see also **in this day and age** (DAY), GOLDEN AGE
6 come of age a) reach the age when you are legally considered to be a responsible adult **b)** if something comes of age, it reaches a stage of development at which people accept is as being important, valuable etc.: *In the 1940s, movies really came of age as a creative art form.*
7 ages [plural] a long time: *Steve! I haven't seen you for ages!* | *It takes ages to make that recipe.*

w **age²** *v.* **1** [I,T] to start looking older or to make someone or something look older: *After his wife's death, Wilfred seemed to age quickly.* **2 age well** if something ages well, it continues to look good or be attractive as it gets older: *The wooden deck behind the house has aged well over several seasons.* **3** [I,T] if a food or alcohol ages or is aged, it is kept in controlled conditions to develop a better taste, smell etc.: *The scotch is aged for ten years in oak barrels.*

-age /ɪdʒ/ *suffix* [in nouns] **1** an activity, an action, or the result of doing something: *the passage of a bill through Congress* (=the activity of making it a law) | *I pay $49 a month for storage* (=the storing of my things in a particular place). | *Buy a larger size to allow for shrinkage* (=clothes getting smaller after they are washed). **2** a cost or amount: *Postage* (=the cost of sending something) *is extra.* | *a percentage of the profits* | *the voltage* (=how much electric power there is) *of your house wiring* **3** a particular situation or condition: *a ten-year marriage* (=the state of being married)

age brack·et /'. ,../ *n.* [C] the people between two particular ages, considered as a group: *We offer group tours for single people in the 40–50 age bracket.*

aged¹ /eɪdʒd/ *adj* **aged 5–10/16 to 18 etc.** between 5 and 10, 16 and 18 etc. years old: *The class is for*

children aged 12 and over. | *[+ between] The police are looking for a man aged between 30 and 35.*

ag·ed² /'eɪdʒɪd/ *adj.* [only before noun] very old: *my aged parents* —**the aged** *n.* [plural]

age dis·crim·i·na·tion /'. ...,./ *n.* [U] unfair treatment of old people, because of their age

age group /'. ./ *n.* [C] all the people between two particular ages, considered as a group: *The book is written for children in the 12–14 age group.*

age·ism, agism /'eɪ,dʒɪzəm/ *n.* [U] AGE DISCRIMINATION

age·less /'eɪdʒlɪs/ *adj.* **1** never looking old or old-fashioned: *her ageless blue eyes* **2** LITERARY continuing forever: *the ageless fascination of the ocean* —**agelessness** *n.* [U]

age lim·it /'. ,../ *n.* [C] the youngest or oldest age at which you are allowed to do something: *The age limit for buying tobacco has been raised to 18.*

a·gen·cy /'eɪdʒənsi/ *n. plural* **agencies** [C] **1** an organization or department, especially within a government, that does a specific job: *The UN agency is responsible for helping refugees.* **2** a business that provides information about other businesses and their products, or that provides a particular service: *a car rental agency* —see also NEWS AGENCY, TRAVEL AGENCY **3 by/through the agency of sb** FORMAL being done with or as the result of someone's help

a·gen·da /ə'dʒɛndə/ *n. plural* **agendas** [C] **1** a set of political or social beliefs that make you want to take particular actions: *The new leaders have been very aggressive in promoting their conservative agenda.* **2** a subject or problem, or several subjects or problems, that you are planning to do something about: *Health-care reform was high on the agenda* (=one of the most important things to be dealt with) *during the President's first term.* **3** a list of the subjects to be discussed at a meeting: *Does anyone have more to say about the items on the agenda?* —see also HIDDEN AGENDA

a·gent /'eɪdʒənt/ *n.* [C]
1 **business** a person or company that represents another person or company in business, in their legal problems etc.: *a travel agent* | *My meeting with the author and his agent did not go well.* | *[+ for] Watts acts as an agent for the sales department.* —see also REAL ESTATE AGENT
2 **artist/actor** someone who is paid by actors, musicians etc. to find work for them: *My agent sent me to an audition.*
3 **government/police** someone who works for a government or police department, especially someone who tries to get secret information about another country or organization: *an FBI agent* —see also SECRET AGENT, DOUBLE AGENT
4 **chemical** TECHNICAL a chemical or substance that makes other substances change: *Soap is a cleansing agent.*
5 **force** someone or something that affects or changes a situation | *an agent for/of sth Williams has been a major agent for change in the auto industry.* —see also FREE AGENT

Agent Or·ange /,. '../ *n.* [U] a chemical weapon used by U.S. soldiers during the Vietnam War to destroy forests, and which is thought to be a cause of serious health problems in people who were in the area where it was used

a·gent pro·vo·ca·teur /,aʒɑn pruʊvɑkə'tɚ, ,eɪdʒənt-/ *n.* [C] LITERARY someone who is employed to encourage people who are working against a government to do something illegal so that they can be caught

age of con·sent /,. . .'./ *n.* **the age of consent** the age when someone can legally get married or have a sexual relationship

age-old /,. '. ◂/ *adj.* [only before noun] having existed for a very long time: *The age-old hatred between the two groups has never been dealt with.*

ag·glom·er·ate /ə'glɑmərɪt/ *n.* [singular,U] TECHNICAL a type of rock formed from pieces of material from a VOLCANO that have melted together

A

ag·glom·er·a·tion /ə'glɑmə'reɪʃən/ *n.* [C,U] a large collection of things that do not seem to belong together: *an agglomeration of laws and regulations* —agglomerate /ə'glɑmə,reɪt/ *v.* [I,T] —agglomerate /ə'glɑmərɪt/ *adj.*

ag·glu·ti·na·tion /ə,glutⁿ'n'eɪʃən/ *n.* [U] TECHNICAL **1** the state of being stuck together **2** the process of making new words by combining two or more words, such as combining "ship" and "yard" to make "shipyard"

ag·gran·dize·ment /ə'grændɪzmənt, -daɪz-/ *n.* [U] FORMAL, DISAPPROVING an increase in power, size, or importance —see also SELF-AGGRANDIZEMENT

ag·gra·vate /'ægrə,veɪt/ *v.* [T] **1** to make a bad situation, an illness, or an injury worse: *Cutting down the old forests may aggravate global warming.* **2** to make someone angry or annoyed: *John claimed Susan did things just to aggravate him.* **3** LAW an aggravated offense is one in which the criminal does something that makes their original crime more serious: **aggravated assault/burglary** etc. *All three men were charged with aggravated kidnapping.* —aggravating *adj.* —aggravatingly *adv.* —aggravation /,ægrə'veɪʃən/ *n.* [C,U]

ag·gre·gate¹ /'ægrɪgɪt/ *n.* **1** [singular,U] the total after many different parts or figures have been added together: [+ of] *The company will spend an aggregate of $2 million on the product.* | *The victims got back,* **in the aggregate** (=as a group of in total), *about 75% of medical costs.* **2** [U] TECHNICAL sand or small stones that are used in making CONCRETE

aggregate² *adj.* [only before noun] TECHNICAL being the total amount of something, especially money: *aggregate income and investment*

ag·gre·gate³ /'ægrɪ,geɪt/ *v.* FORMAL **1** [linking verb] to be a particular amount when added together: *Sheila's earnings from all sources aggregated $100,000.* **2** [I,T usually passive] to put things together in a group to form a total; ASSEMBLE: *We made estimates using the aggregated data.*

ag·gres·sion /ə'grɛʃən/ *n.* [U plural] **1** angry or threatening behavior or feelings that often result in fighting: *Television violence seems to encourage aggression in children.* **2** the act of attacking a country, especially when that country has not attacked first: *Textbooks tend to ignore past military aggressions.* | *The bombing was* **an unprovoked act of aggression** *on a peaceful nation.*

ag·gres·sive /ə'grɛsɪv/ *adj.* **1** behaving in an angry, threatening way, as if you want to fight or attack someone: *When I said no, she became rude and aggressive.* | *Chris is an aggressive driver.* **2** someone who is aggressive is very determined to succeed or get what they want: *A successful businessperson has to be aggressive.* **3** an aggressive action or plan is intended to achieve the right result: *an aggressive treatment for cancer* —aggressively *adv.* —aggressiveness *n.* [U]

ag·gres·sor /ə'grɛsə/ *n.* [C] FORMAL a person or country that begins a fight or war with another person or country

ag·grieved /ə'grivd/ *adj.* **1** feeling or showing anger and unhappiness because you think you have been treated unfairly: *an aggrieved tone of voice* **2** LAW having suffered as a result of the illegal actions of someone else: *the aggrieved parties*

a·ghast /ə'gæst/ *adj., adv.* [not before noun] feeling or looking shocked by something you have seen or just found out: [+ at] *I was aghast at the violence I was witnessing.*

ag·ile /'ædʒəl, 'ædʒaɪl/ *adj.* **1** able to move quickly and easily: *Harvey is very agile and quick for a big man.* **2** someone who is mentally agile or who has an agile mind is intelligent and able to think very quickly —agility /ə'dʒɪləţi/ *n.* [U]

ag·ing¹ /'eɪdʒɪŋ/ *adj.* [only before noun] becoming old, and usually less useful, appropriate etc.: *aging movie stars* | *a fleet of aging airplanes*

aging² *n.* [U] the process of getting old: *For many, memory loss is a part of aging.*

ag·i·tate /'ædʒə,teɪt/ *v.* **1** [I] to argue strongly in public for something you want, especially a political or social change: [+ for/against] *The unions are agitating for higher pay.* **2** [T] FORMAL to make someone feel anxious, upset, and nervous **3** [T] to shake or mix a liquid quickly

ag·i·tat·ed /'ædʒə,teɪţɪd/ *adj.* so nervous or upset that you are unable to keep still or think calmly: *When her daughter didn't arrive, she became increasingly agitated.*

ag·i·ta·tion /,ædʒə'teɪʃən/ *n.* **1** [U] feeling of being so anxious, nervous, or upset that you cannot keep still or think calmly: *Perry's agitation was so great he could hardly speak.* **2** [C,U] a public argument or action for social or political change: [+ for/against] *The region's agitation for autonomy could tear the country apart.* **3** [U] the act of shaking or mixing a liquid

ag·i·ta·tor /'ædʒə,teɪţə/ *n.* [C] **1** someone who encourages people to work toward changing something in society: *a political agitator* **2** a part inside a washing machine that moves the clothes and water around

ag·it·prop /'ædʒɪt,prɑp/ *n.* [U] music, literature, or art that tries to persuade people to follow a particular set of political ideas

a·glit·ter /ə'glɪţə/ *adj.* [not before noun] LITERARY seeming to shine with flashing points of light: *Her green eyes were aglitter.*

a·glow /ə'gloʊ/ *adj.* **1** LITERARY bright and shining with warmth, light, or color: *The morning sun set the sky aglow.* **2** if someone's face or expression is aglow, they seem happy and excited: [+ with] *Linda's face was aglow with happiness.*

Ag·new /'ægnu/, **Spi·ro** /'spɪroʊ/ (1918–1996) the Vice President of the U.S. under Richard Nixon

ag·nos·tic /æg'nɑstɪk, əg-/ *n.* [C] someone who believes that people cannot know whether God exists or not —agnostic *adj.* —agnosticism /æg'nɑstɪ,sɪzəm/ *n.* [U] —compare ATHEIST

a·go /ə'goʊ/ *adv.* used to show how far back in the past something happened: *Michael left the office about half an hour ago.* | *I met Aunt Hetty once, a very long time ago.* | *I had my keys a minute ago, and now I can't find them.* | *Tom got a letter from him just a little while ago.* | *They moved to Chicago some time ago, a couple of years I think.* —compare FOR¹, SINCE² —see Usage Note at SINCE²

a·gog /ə'gɑg/ *adj., adv.* [not before noun] LITERARY very interested, excited, and surprised, especially at something you are experiencing for the first time: [+ at/over] *We stared agog at the Empire State Building.*

ag·o·nize /'ægə,naɪz/ *v.* [I] to think about a difficult decision very carefully and with a lot of effort: [+ over/about] *We agonized over whether to sell the house.* —agonizing *n.* [U]

ag·o·nized /'ægə,naɪzd/ *adj.* [only before noun] expressing very severe pain: *an agonized scream*

ag·o·niz·ing /'ægə,naɪzɪŋ/ *adj.* extremely painful or difficult: *an agonizing decision* —agonizingly *adv.*

ag·o·ny /'ægəni/ *n. plural* **agonies** [C,U] **1** very severe pain: *the agony of arthritis* | *He was lying on the floor in agony.* **2** a very sad or emotionally difficult situation: *It was agony not knowing where he was.*

ag·o·ra·pho·bi·a /,ægərə'foʊbiə/ *n.* [U] TECHNICAL the fear of crowds and open spaces —agoraphobic *n.* [C] —agoraphobic *adj.* —compare CLAUSTROPHOBIA

a·grar·i·an /ə'grɛriən/ *adj.* relating to farming or farmers: *an agrarian economy* (=an economy based on farming)

a·gree /ə'gri/ *v.*
1 `same opinion` [I,T not in progressive] to have the same opinion about something as someone else: *Teenagers and their parents rarely agree.* | [+ with] *I understand what he's saying, but I just don't agree with it.* | [agree (that)] *Most scientists agree that global warming is a serious problem.* | [+ on/about]

Mike and I certainly don't agree on everything. —opposite DISAGREE

2 `say yes` [I,T not in progressive] to say yes to an idea, plan, suggestion etc.: *I suggested we move to Chicago and she agreed.* | **[agree to do sth]** *Bryan refused at first but finally agreed to help.*

3 `decide together` [I,T not in progressive] to make a decision with someone after a discussion with them: **[agree to do sth]** *We agreed to meet again next Monday.* | **[agree that]** *The leaders agreed that missile production would be reduced.* | **[+ on]** *It's a budget that the President and Congress can agree on.* | **[+ to]** *Both sides have agreed to a ceasefire.*

4 `be the same` [I not in progressive] if two pieces of information agree, they say the same thing: **[+ with]** *Your story doesn't agree with what the police told us.*

5 agree to disagree to accept that you do not have the same opinions as someone else and agree not to argue about it

agree with sb/sth *phr. v.* [T not in passive] **1** to believe that a decision, action, or suggestion is correct or right: *I don't agree with hitting children.* **2 not agree with you** if a type of food does not agree with you, it makes you feel sick **3** TECHNICAL if an adjective, verb etc. agrees with a word, it matches that word by being plural if the subject is plural etc.

USAGE NOTE: AGREE

GRAMMAR

If you have the same opinion as someone else, you **agree** with them. You can also **agree with** (=approve of) their attitude, ideas, plans, rules etc., or an activity or principle that you approve of: *Do you agree with gun control?* You **agree** with people **about** or **on** other matters: *I agree (with you) about Tom/on politics/about this issue* (NOT *I agree this issue*). If you and others decide on something or arrange to do something after discussing it, you **agree on** it: *We finally agreed on a plan/a date/a solution/a deal.* If you accept something, especially something that was not your idea and that you may not like, you **agree to** it. *She agreed to the plan/the date/the solution/the deal* (NOT *She agreed the plan etc.*). You can also **agree to do** something: *They agreed to pay* (NOT *They accepted to pay*).

---

a·gree·a·ble /əˈgriəbəl/ *adj.* FORMAL **1** acceptable and able to be agreed on: *an agreeable solution* **2** someone who is agreeable is very nice and is liked by other people: *an agreeable young man* **3** enjoyable: *an agreeable comedy* **4 be agreeable to sth** to be willing to do something or willing to allow something to be done: *They want an outcome that is agreeable to both countries.*

a·gree·a·bly /əˈgriəbii/ *adv.* intended to be nice or enjoyable: *He smiled agreeably.*

a·greed /əˈgrid/ *adj.* **1** [only before noun] an agreed plan, price, arrangement etc. is one that people have discussed and accepted: *an agreed price for the wheat* **2 be agreed** FORMAL if people are agreed, they have discussed something and agree about what to do: **[+ on]** *All parties are now agreed on the plan.*

a·gree·ment /əˈgrimənt/ *n.* **1** [C] an arrangement or promise to do something, made by two or more companies, governments, organizations etc.: *a trade agreement* | **[+ on]** *an agreement on arms reduction* | **[+ with]** *Gardner had an agreement with Bertram to buy the farm.* | *Failure to* **reach an agreement** *will result in a strike.* | *Under the Sino-British* **agreement**, *Hong Kong came under Chinese rule in 1997.* **2** [U] a situation in which people have the same opinion as each other: **[+ that]** *There is agreement among doctors that pregnant women should not smoke.* | **[+ on]** *Is there agreement on how much aid will be sent?* | *All members of the group were* **in agreement**. **3** [C] an official document that people sign to show that they accept something: *Please read the agreement and sign it.*

agri- /ægri/ *prefix* relating to farming: *agriculture* —see also AGRO-

ag·ri·busi·ness /ˈægriˌbɪznɪs/ *n.* [C,U] the production

and sale of farm products, or a company involved in this

A

ag·ri·cul·ture /ˈægriˌkʌltʃɚ/ *n.* [U] the practice or science of farming —**agricultural** /ˌægriˈkʌltʃərəl◂/ *adj.* —**agriculturalist** *n.* [C] —compare HORTICULTURE

agro- /ægroʊ/ *prefix* relating to agriculture: *agro-industry* —see also AGRI-

a·gron·o·my /əˈgrɑnəmi/ *n.* [U] the study of plants and the soil, and how to help farmers produce better crops —**agronomist** *n.* [C]

a·ground /əˈgraʊnd/ *adv.* **run/go aground** if a ship runs aground, it becomes stuck in a place where the water is not deep enough

a·gue /ˈeɪgyu/ *n.* [C,U] OLD-FASHIONED a fever that makes you shake and feel cold

ah /ɑ/ *interjection* used in order to show your surprise, anger, pain, happiness, agreement etc.: *Ah! There you are!*

a·ha /ɑˈhɑ/ *interjection* used in order to show that you understand or realize something: *Aha! I knew you were trying to trick me!* —see also HA[1]

a·head /əˈhɛd/ *adv.*
1 `in front of sb/sth` in front of someone or something by a short distance: *The road ahead was clear.* | **[+ of]** *Tim pointed to a tree ahead of them.* | *We could see the lights of Las Vegas* **up ahead**.
2 `forward` if someone or something moves, looks ahead etc., they move or look toward a place in front of them: *Let Tom walk ahead – he knows the way.* | **[+ of]** *You can go ahead of me in the line.* | *He was just staring* **straight ahead** *in a complete daze.*
3 `before sb else` arriving, waiting, finishing etc. before other people: **[+ of]** *There were four people ahead of me at the doctor's office.*
4 `future` in the future: *You have a long trip* **ahead of you**. | *We're not sure what difficulties* **lie ahead** (=are in the future). | **plan/look ahead** *Eddie never plans ahead.* | **in the days/weeks etc. ahead** *The decisions you make in the days ahead are going to affect your whole future.*
5 `before an event` before an event happens: **[+ of]** *Stock trading was down slightly, ahead of the long holiday weekend*
6 ahead of time a) before an event happens: *Let me know ahead of time if you need a ride to the airport.* **b)** also **ahead of schedule** earlier than planned or arranged: *At this point we're ahead of schedule.*
7 `progress/success` making progress and being successful in your job, education etc.: **get/keep/ stay etc. ahead** *Getting ahead at work is the most important thing to Nita right now.*
8 `winning` winning in a competition or election: *Milligan's home run puts the Dodgers ahead by one point.*
9 go ahead SPOKEN **a)** used to tell someone they can do something: *"Can I have the sports section?" "Yeah, go ahead, I've read it."* **b)** used to say you are going to start doing something: *I'll go ahead and start the coffee.* **c)** to start doing something: *Frank will be late but we'll* **go ahead with** *the meeting anyway.* —see also GO-AHEAD[1]
10 `advanced` ideas, achievements etc. that are ahead of others, have made more progress or are more developed: **[+ of]** *VEMCO was years ahead of us in their research.* | *Her educational theories were way* **ahead of their time** (=so new that people did not like or understand them).
11 ahead of the game/curve INFORMAL in a position where you are in control of something, and more successful than your competitors: *Belmont city leaders have never been ahead of the curve in environmental matters.*

a·hem /mˈhm, əˈhɛm/ *interjection* a sound you make in your throat to attract someone's attention when you want to speak to them, warn them etc.

a·hold /əˈhoʊld/ *n.* [U] NONSTANDARD **1 get ahold of**

A

sb to find or call someone and be able to talk to them, after being unable to find them for a period of time: *I finally got ahold of Nick last night.* **2** to find something that is difficult to find, in order to buy it or own it: *I've been trying to get ahold of that album for weeks.* **3 grab/get ahold of sth** to reach for something and hold it: *Lisa grabbed ahold of my arm and wouldn't let go.* **4 get ahold of yourself** to control your emotions after being unable to control them for a period of time: *Jerry ought to get ahold of himself before it's too late.*

-aholic /əholɪk, əha-/ *suffix* [in nouns and adjectives] INFORMAL someone who wants or needs to do or use something all the time: *a chocaholic* (=someone who loves chocolate) | *a workaholic* (=someone who wants to work all the time)

a·hoy /əˈhɔɪ/ *interjection* OLD-FASHIONED used by SAILORS to get someone's attention or greet them

AI *n.* [U] the abbreviation of ARTIFICIAL INTELLIGENCE

s w aid¹ /eɪd/ *n.* **1** [U] help, such as money or food, given **3** **2** by an organization to a country or to people who are in a difficult situation: *The Red Cross is delivering aid to the refugees.* | [+ **for**] *federal disaster aid for the flood victims* —see also FINANCIAL AID **2** [C,U] something such as a machine or tool that helps someone do something, or the help it gives you: *a hearing aid* | *The star can only be seen **with the aid of** a telescope.* **3** [U] help or advice given to someone who needs it | **come/go to sb's aid** *Several people came to the man's aid after he collapsed on the sidewalk.* **4** [C] another spelling of AIDE —see also FIRST AID —see Usage Note at HELP²

aid² *v.* [I,T] FORMAL **1** to help someone or something by making their situation or what they are doing easier: *Officers were aided in the search by drug-sniffing dogs.* | [+ **in/with**] *Calcium in food aids in the development of strong bones.* | *The local community aided us with our investigation.* **2 aid and abet** LAW to help someone do something illegal

s w aide, aid /eɪd/ *n.* [C] someone whose job is to help **2** someone in an important job: *a nurse's aide* | *White House aides denied the report.*

aide-de-camp /ˌeɪd dɪ ˈkæmp/ *n. plural* **aides-de-camp** (same pronunciation) [C] a military officer who helps an officer of a higher rank to do his duties

s w AIDS /eɪdz/ *n.* [U] Acquired Immune Deficiency Syn-**3** drome; a very serious disease caused by a VIRUS (1) that makes your body unable to defend itself against infections

aid work·er /'. ˌ../ *n.* [C] someone working for an international organization who brings food and other supplies to people in danger from wars, floods etc.

Ai·ken /ˈeɪkən/**, Conrad** (1889–1973) a U.S. writer of poems and NOVELS

ail /eɪl/ *v.* **1 what ails sb/sth** the thing or things that cause difficulties for someone or something: *Bilingual education is not the answer to what ails our state's educational system.* **2** [I,T] OLD-FASHIONED to be sick, or to make someone feel sick or unhappy —see also AILING (2)

ai·le·ron /ˈeɪləˌran/ *n.* [C] TECHNICAL the back edge of the wing of an airplane which can be moved in order to keep the airplane level

Ai·ley /ˈeɪli/**, Al·vin** /ˈælvɪn/ (1931–1989) a U.S. dancer and CHOREOGRAPHER of modern dance

ail·ing /ˈeɪlɪŋ/ *adj.* [usually before noun] **1** an ailing company or ECONOMY is having a lot of problems and is not successful: *Smith transformed GM's ailing European operations in the '80s.* **2** FORMAL sick, weak, and unlikely to get better: *He's taking care of his ailing mother.*

ail·ment /ˈeɪlmənt/ *n.* [C] an illness that is not very serious

s w aim /eɪm/ *v.* **1** [I] to try or intend to achieve some-**2** thing: [**aim to do sth**] *I'm aiming to lose 10 pounds before July.* | [+ **at**] *The administration aims at reducing the federal deficit by 20%.* **2** [I,T] to do or say something to a particular group or person, in

order to influence them, annoy them etc.: [**aim sth at sb**] *Soft-drink commercials are aimed mainly at teenagers.* **3** [I,T] to choose the place, person etc. that you want to hit and carefully point your gun or another object toward them: *The man aimed his gun but did not shoot.* | [+ **at/for**] *The rebels claim they only aim at military targets.*

aim² *n.* **1** [C] something you hope to achieve by a **s v** plan, action, or activity: [+ **of**] *The aim of the tax is to raise money for education.* | *We achieved our aim of opening ten new stores within the year.* **2 take aim a)** to point a gun or weapon at someone or something you want to shoot: [+ **at**] *Alan took aim at the target.* **b) take aim at sb/sth** to choose someone or something that you want to have an effect on by means of a plan, action, or activity: *The environmental agency is taking aim at a popular but dangerous chemical used by farmers* (=they want to stop people from using it). **3** [U] someone's ability to hit what they are aiming at when they throw or shoot something: *Val's aim was very good.* | *With perfect aim, Armand struck his opponent in the throat.*

aim·less /ˈeɪmlɪs/ *adj.* without a clear purpose or reason: *an aimless, spoiled young man* —**aimlessly** *adv.* —**aimlessness** *n.* [U]

ain't /eɪnt/ *v.* SPOKEN, NONSTANDARD a short form of "am not," "is not," "are not," "has not," or "have not": *I ain't met her yet.* | *He ain't here.*

air¹ /ɛr/ *n.*
1 gas [U] the mixture of gases surrounding the **s** Earth, that we breathe: *air pollution* | *There was a* **1** *strong smell of burning in the air.* | *Let's go outside and get some fresh air.* —see also **a breath of fresh air** (BREATH)
2 space above/below the air the space above the ground or around things: *The balloon floated silently through the air.* | *She threw the ball high into the air.*
3 airplanes/flying **a) by air** traveling by or using an airplane: *It's actually less expensive to go by air to San Francisco.* **b) air travel/crash/industry etc.** involving or relating to airplanes and flying: *It was the worst air disaster in the state's history.*
4 be on/off (the) air to be broadcasting on television or the radio right now, or to stop broadcasting: *We'll be on air in about three minutes.*
5 be up in the air SPOKEN to not be decided, or not be certain to happen yet: *Our trip to Orlando is still up in the air.*
6 in the air if a particular emotion is in the air, a lot of people seem to feel it at the same time: *There was a sense of excitement in the air.*
7 appearance [singular] if something or someone has an air of confidence, mystery etc., they seem confident, mysterious etc.: [**an air of sth**] *She had an air of quiet confidence.*
8 airs [plural] a way of behaving that shows someone thinks they are more important than other people: *Monica has been putting on airs ever since she moved to Beverly Hills.*
9 air conditioning [U] AIR CONDITIONING: *Could you turn on the air?*
10 get/catch some air SLANG to jump high off the ground, especially when playing basketball, skiing, riding a SKATEBOARD
11 music [C] a simple piece of CLASSICAL music —see also **clear the air** (CLEAR²), **hot air** (HOT), ON-AIR, **thin air** (THIN¹), **be walking on air** (WALK¹)

air² *v.*
1 tv/radio [I,T] to broadcast a program on television or radio, or to be shown: *The newsconference will be aired live at 7 p.m.* | *Stahl's report is scheduled to air tonight after the news.*
2 air your views/opinions etc. to say publicly what you think about something important: *City council meetings give citizens a chance to air their complaints.*
3 clothes [I,T] also **air out** to put a piece of clothing in a place that is warm or has a lot of fresh air, especially outdoors, so that it smells clean: *I hung the blankets on the clothesline to air them out.*
4 room [I,T] also **air out** to let fresh air into a room, especially one that has been closed for a long time —see also AIRING

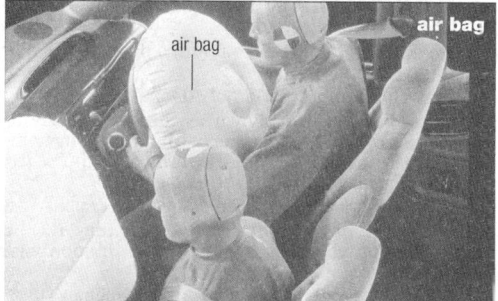
air bag

air bag, airbag /'. ./ n. [C] a bag in a car that fills with air if the car is in an accident, in order to protect the driver or passenger —see picture on page 427

air·ball, air ball /'ɛrbɔl/ n. [C] a bad SHOT in basketball that does not even touch the basket

air·base /'ɛrbeɪs/ n. [C] a place where military aircraft begin and end their flights, and where members of the military live

air·borne /'ɛrbɔrn/ adj. **1** flying or moving along through the air: As soon as the plane was airborne, the captain's voice came over the loudspeaker. | Infections can be passed around by airborne particles. **2** airborne soldiers are trained to fight in areas that they get to by jumping out of an airplane

air brake /'. ./ n. [C usually plural] a type of BRAKE that operates by using air pressure, especially in a truck

air·brush¹ /'ɛrbrʌʃ/ n. [C] a piece of equipment that uses air to put paint onto a picture smoothly

airbrush² v. [T] to use an airbrush to make a picture more attractive, to cover certain parts of it etc.
  airbrush sb/sth **out** phr. v. [T usually passive] to remove someone or something from a photograph or picture by using an airbrush: Bogart's cigarette had been airbrushed out of some of the publicity shots.

air con·di·tion·er /'. .,../ n. [C] a piece of equipment that makes the air in a building or room cooler and drier

air con·di·tion·ing /'. .,../ n. [U] a system that makes the air in a building, vehicle etc. cooler and drier —**air-conditioned** adj. —see also AC

air cov·er /'. ,./ n. [U] TECHNICAL military aircraft that fly over an area where soldiers are fighting, in order to protect them from the enemy's aircraft

air·craft /'ɛrkræft/ n. plural **aircraft** [C] an airplane or other vehicle that can fly —see also LIGHT AIRCRAFT

aircraft car·ri·er /'.. ,../ n. [C] a type of ship that has a large flat surface that airplanes fly from and land on

air crew /'. ./ n. [C] the pilot and the people who are responsible for flying an airplane and serving the passengers

air·drop /'ɛrdrɑp/ n. [C] an act of delivering supplies to people by dropping the supplies from an aircraft, when it is difficult or dangerous to use roads —**airdrop** v. [T]

air-dry /,. './ v. [I,T] to dry something or to let something dry naturally in the air, rather than by using a machine

air fare, airfare /'. ./ n. [C] the price of a trip by airplane

air·field /'ɛrfild/ n. [C] a place where airplanes can fly from, especially one used by the military

air·flow, air flow /'ɛrfloʊ/ n. [U] the smooth movement of air in a room, through a machine, through someone's nose, throat, and lungs etc.

air·foil /'ɛrfɔɪl/ n. [C] TECHNICAL a surface or structure such as an airplane wing that helps aircraft to fly and be controlled

air force /'. ./ n. [C usually singular] the part of a country's military forces that uses airplanes to fight —compare ARMY, MARINES, NAVY¹

air fresh·en·er /'. ,.../ n. [C,U] a substance or a small object used to make the air in a room or vehicle smell nice

air gui·tar /'. .,./ n. [U] if someone plays air guitar, they pretend to play a GUITAR, usually while listening to ROCK music

air gun /'. ./ n. [C] a gun that uses air pressure to shoot small round metal balls; BB GUN

air·head /'ɛr,hɛd/ n. [C] SLANG someone who is stupid and behaves in a silly way

air hock·ey /'. ,../ n. [U] a game in which two players try to hit a PUCK (=flat circular object) into a GOAL on a special table with air blowing through many very small holes in its surface, which makes the puck move more smoothly

air·i·ly /'ɛrəli/ adv. without being serious or concerned "I don't really care," he said airily.

air·ing /'ɛrɪŋ/ n. **1** [singular] an occasion when an opinion, idea etc. is discussed: The issue was **given an airing** at a public meeting. **2** [C] an occasion when a program is broadcast on television or the radio: Koslow's show got terrible ratings during its first two airings.

air kiss /'. ./ n. [C] HUMOROUS an act of greeting someone with a kiss near the side of their face, but without touching them, often done by famous people at parties

air·lane /'ɛrleɪn/ n. [C] a path through the air that is regularly used by airplanes

air·less /'ɛrlɪs/ adj. not having enough air or having air that does not move, so that it seems difficult to breathe: a hot, airless kitchen

air·lift /'ɛrlɪft/ n. [C] an act of taking people or things to an area by airplane, when it is difficult or dangerous to use roads —**airlift** v. [T]

air·line /'ɛrlaɪn/ n. [C] a business that runs a regular service to take passengers and goods to different places by airplane

air·lin·er /'ɛr,laɪnə/ n. [C] FORMAL a large passenger airplane

air·lock /'ɛrlɑk/ n. [C] a small room that connects two places that do not have the same air pressure, such as in a space vehicle or a vehicle under water

air·mail /'ɛrmeɪl/ n. [U] letters, packages etc. that are sent somewhere on an airplane, or the system of doing this

air·man /'ɛrmən/ n. [C] plural **airmen** /-mən/ a low rank in the U.S. Air Force, or someone who has this rank

air·park /'ɛrpɑrk/ n. [C] a small airport, usually near an area of business or industry

air·plane /'ɛrpleɪn/ n. [C] a vehicle that flies by using wings and one or more engines; PLANE

air·play /'ɛrpleɪ/ n. [U] the amount of time or the number of times that a particular song, music group etc. is played on the radio: "Lady of the Day" has been **getting airplay** on pop-jazz stations.

air pock·et /'. ,./ n. [C] a current of air that moves toward the ground and that makes an airplane suddenly drop down

air·port /'ɛrpɔrt/ n. [C] a place where airplanes begin and stop flying, that has buildings for passengers to wait in

air pump /'. ./ n. [C] a piece of equipment used to put air into something such as a TIRE

air rage /'. ./ n. [U] violence and angry behavior by airplane passengers toward other passengers and the people who work on the airplane

air raid /'. ./ n. [C] an attack in which a lot of bombs are dropped on a place by military airplanes

air ri·fle /'. ,./ n. [C] a gun that uses air pressure to fire a small round bullet

air·ship /'ɛr,ʃɪp/ n. [C] a large aircraft that has no wings, is filled with gas to make it float, and has an engine

air·show /'ɛrʃoʊ/ n. [C] an event at which people watch airplanes, especially military airplanes, as they fly and do tricks, such as turning over in the air or flying closely with other airplanes

A

air·sick /'ɛrsɪk/ *adj.* feeling sick because of the movement of an airplane —**airsickness** *n.* [U]

air·space /'ɛrspeɪs/ *n.* [U] the sky above a particular country, that is thought of as being controlled by that country: *Canadian airspace*

air speed /'. ./ *n.* [singular,U] the speed at which an airplane travels

air strike /'. ./ *n.* [C] an attack in which military aircraft drop bombs or shoot guns at a place

air·strip /'ɛrstrɪp/ *n.* [C] a long narrow piece of land that has been cleared so that airplanes can fly from it or land on it

air ter·mi·nal /'. ,.../ *n.* [C] a large building at an AIRPORT where passengers wait to get on airplanes; TERMINAL[2] (1)

air·tight /'ɛr,taɪt, ,ɛr'taɪt/ *adj.* **1** not allowing air to get in or out: *Store cookies in an airtight container.* **2** perfect, so that there is nothing that will cause any problems: *Security was airtight.* —compare WATERTIGHT

air time, airtime /'. ./ *n.* [U] the amount of time or the number of times that a television or radio station allows a particular song, advertisement etc. to be broadcast: *Advertisers have bought air time on the major networks.*

air-to-air /,. . '. ‹/ *adj.* **an air-to-air missile** a weapon that one airplane shoots at another airplane as they are flying

air traf·fic con·trol·ler /,. ,.. .'.., ,. '.. .,../ *n.* [C] someone at an airport who gives instructions to pilots by radio about where and when they can leave the ground or come down to the ground —**air traffic control** *n.* [U]

air·waves /'ɛrweɪvz/ *n.* INFORMAL **the airwaves** [plural] radio or television broadcasts: *The Magliozzis have been on the airwaves talking about cars since 1976.*

air·way /'ɛrweɪ/ *n.* plural **airways** [C] **1** TECHNICAL the passage in your throat that you breathe through **2** an area of the sky that is regularly used by airplanes

air·wor·thy /'ɛr,wɚði/ *adj.* an airplane that is airworthy is safe enough to fly —**airworthiness** *n.* [U]

air·y /'ɛri/ *adj.* **1** an airy room or building has plenty of fresh air because it is large or has lots of windows: *a light, airy, modern home* **2** cheerful, confident, and pleasant, even when you should be serious or concerned about something: *"Roman Holiday" is a delightfully airy romance starring Audrey Hepburn.* —see also AIRILY

aisle

an aisle in an airplane

an aisle in a store

aisle /aɪl/ *n.* [C] **1** a long passage between rows of seats in a theater, airplane, church etc. **2 go/walk**

down the aisle INFORMAL to get married —see also **be rolling in the aisles** (ROLL[1])

a·jar /ə'dʒɑr/ *adj.* [not before noun] a door that is ajar is slightly open

AK the written abbreviation of Alaska

a.k.a. /,eɪ keɪ 'eɪ/ also known as, used when giving someone's real name together with a different name they are known by: *Paul Reubens, a.k.a. Pee-wee Herman, has a bit part in the movie.*

AKDT the written abbreviation of ALASKA DAYLIGHT TIME

Akhe·na·ton /ɑk'nɑtˈn, ,ɑkə-/ (14th century B.C.) a king of Egypt who tried to start a new religion with the sun as its god

Akh·ma·to·va /,ɑkmə'touvə/, **An·na** /'ænə/ (1888–1966) a Russian poet

A·ki·hi·to /,ɑki'hitou/ (1933–) the Emperor of Japan since 1989

a·kim·bo /ə'kɪmbou/ *adj.* **(with) arms akimbo** with your hands on your HIPs so that your elbows point away from your body —see picture at ARM[1]

a·kin /ə'kɪn/ *adj.* **akin to sth** very similar to something: *The flavor is akin to chicken.*

AKST the written abbreviation of ALASKA STANDARD TIME

AKT the written abbreviation of ALASKA TIME

AL 1 the written abbreviation of Alabama **2** the abbreviation of American League

-al /əl/ *suffix* **1** [in adjectives] relating to something, or being like something: *political | emotional | industrial | a magical day* (=so good it felt like magic) —see also -IAL **2** [in nouns] the action of doing something: *her arrival* (=when she arrived) | *a refusal*

à la /'ɑlə, 'ælə, 'ɑlɑ/ *prep.* in the style of: *The band has a heavy electric sound, à la the Velvet Underground.*

Al·a·bam·a /,ælə'bæmə/ *written abbreviation* **AL** a state in the southeastern U.S.

al·a·bas·ter /'ælə,bæstɚ/ *n.* [U] a white stone, used for making STATUEs or objects used in decoration

à la carte /,ɑlə'kɑrt, ,ælə-, ,ɑlɑ-/ *adj., adv.* if food in a restaurant is à la carte, each dish has a separate price: *Dinners can be ordered à la carte or as a complete meal.*

a·lack /ə'læk/ *interjection* OLD USE used to express sorrow

a·lac·ri·ty /ə'lækrəti/ *n.* [U] FORMAL speed and eagerness: *Packages are delivered with alacrity.*

A·lad·din /ə'lædn/ in THE ARABIAN NIGHTS, a young man who finds a lamp that makes a GENIE (=a magical spirit) appear and obey him

à la mode /,ɑlə'moud, ,ælə-, ,ɑlɑ-/ *adj., adv.* **1** served with ICE CREAM: *apple pie à la mode* **2** OLD-FASHIONED according to the latest fashion

Al-A·non /'æl ə,nɑn/ an international organization for people who are related to ALCOHOLICS

a·larm[1] /ə'lɑrm/ *n.* **1** [C] something such as a bell, loud noise, or light that warns people of danger: *The bank teller pushed the alarm button.* | **a fire/burglar/security etc. alarm** *The dormitory fire alarm went off at 2 a.m.* | *Something has set the car alarm off again.* **2** [C] an alarm clock: *I set the alarm for six.* **3** [U] a feeling of fear or anxiety because something dangerous might happen: *Several oil-producing countries expressed alarm at the fall in prices.* | *It is a normal side effect of the medicine, and there is no cause for alarm.* **4 sound/raise the alarm** to warn everyone about something bad or dangerous that is already happening: [+ about] *He was one of the first scientists to sound the alarm about the destruction of the Amazon rainforest.* —see also FALSE ALARM

alarm[2] *v.* [T] to make people very worried about a possible danger: *The damage to the marsh has alarmed environmentalists.*

alarm clock /.'. ,./ *n.* [C] a clock that will make a noise at a particular time to wake you up

a·larmed /ə'lɑrmd/ *adj.* **1** frightened and worried: *She became alarmed when she could not waken her husband.* | *Alarmed storekeepers locked their doors.* [+ by/at/over] *Researchers are alarmed by an* *increase in AIDS infections among teenagers.* **2** protected by an alarm system

a·larm·ing /ə'lɑrmɪŋ/ *adj.* worrying and frightening: *An alarming number of young girls are worried about their weight.* | *Sharks are being killed at an alarming rate* (=so quickly that it makes people worried). —**alarmingly** *adv.*

a·larm·ist /ə'lɑrmɪst/ *adj.* making people unnecessarily worried about dangers that do not exist: *There has been a lot of alarmist publicity about genetically modified foods.* —**alarmist** *n.* [C]

a·las[1] /ə'læs/ *adv.* [sentence adverb] FORMAL unfortunately or sadly: *The promise, alas, was broken.*

alas[2] *interjection* LITERARY used to express sadness, shame, or fear

A·las·ka /ə'læskə/ *written abbreviation* **AK** the largest U.S. state, northwest of Canada —**Alaskan** *n., adj.*

Alaska Day·light Time /.,.. '.. ,./ *abbreviation* **AKDT** *n.* [U] the time that is used in most of Alaska for over half the year, including the summer, when clocks are one hour ahead of Alaska Standard Time

Alaska Range /.'.. ,./ a mountain RANGE in southern Alaska

Alaska Stan·dard Time /.,.. ,.. '., ,.. '.. ,./ *abbreviation* **AKST** *n.* [U] the time that is used in most of Alaska for almost half the year, including the winter —compare ALASKA DAYLIGHT TIME

Alaska Time /.'.. ,./ *abbreviation* **AKT** *n.* [U] the time that is used in most of Alaska

Al-Ateen /'æl ə,tin/ an international organization for young people who are related to ALCOHOLICS

Al·ba·ni·a /æl'beɪniə, ɔl-/ a small country in the southeast of Europe next to the Adriatic Sea —**Albanian** *n., adj.*

Al·ba·ny /'ɔlbəni/ the capital city of the U.S. state of New York

al·ba·tross /'ælbə,trɔs, -,trɑs/ *n.* [C] **1** a very large white sea bird **2 an albatross (around your neck)** something that causes problems for you and prevents you from succeeding: *The project became a financial albatross for the city.*

Al·bee /'ɔlbi, 'ælbi/, **Ed·ward** /'ɛdwəd/ (1928–) a U.S. writer of DRAMATIC plays

al·be·it /ɔl'biɪt, æl-/ *conjunction* FORMAL although; used to add information or details that are different from what you have already said: *Cather's novel has been made into a beautiful, albeit slow-paced, musical.*

Al·ber·ta /æl'bətə/ a PROVINCE in western Canada

al·bi·no /æl'baɪnoʊ/ *n. plural* **albinos** [C] a person or animal with a GENETIC condition that makes the skin and hair extremely pale or white

al·bum /'ælbəm/ *n.* [C] **1** a group of songs or pieces of music on a record, CD, TAPE: *an album of Disney songs* **2** a book in which you put photographs, stamps etc.: *a wedding album*

al·bu·men /æl'byumɪn, 'ælbyu-/ *n.* [U] TECHNICAL the white or colorless part of the inside of an egg

Al·bu·quer·que /'ælbə kəki/ a city in central New Mexico

Al·ca·traz /'ælkə,træz/ a former prison on an island in San Francisco Bay, which is now a museum

al·che·my /'ælkəmi/ *n.* [U] **1** a science studied in the Middle Ages that involved trying to change ordinary metals into gold **2** LITERARY magic: *financial alchemy* —**alchemist** *n.* [C]

al·co·hol /'ælkə,hɔl, -,hɑl/ *n.* **1** [U] drinks such as beer or wine that contain a substance that can make you drunk: *Ted doesn't drink alcohol anymore.* **2** [C,U] a chemical substance, that can be used to clean medical or industrial equipment

al·co·hol·ic[1] /,ælkə'hɔlɪk , -'hɑ-/ *n.* [C] someone who regularly drinks too much alcohol and has difficulty stopping

alcoholic[2] *adj.* **1** relating to alcohol or containing alcohol: *alcoholic beverages* **2** caused by drinking alcohol: *John lives his life in an alcoholic haze.* —**alcoholically** /-kli/ *adv.*

Alcoholics A·non·y·mous /...,.. .'.../ *abbreviation*

AA an international organization for ALCOHOLICS who want to stop drinking alcohol

al·co·hol·is·m /'ælkəhɔ,lizəm, -hɑ-/ *n.* [U] the medical condition of being an alcoholic

Al·cott /'ɔlkət, 'æl-, -kət/, **Lou·i·sa May** /lu'izə meɪ/ (1832–1888) a U.S. writer of NOVELS for children

al·cove /'ælkoʊv/ *n.* [C] a place in the wall of a room that is built further back than the rest of the wall: *A card table was set up in an alcove in the living room.*

Al·den /'ɔldən/, **John** (?1599–1687) one of the Pilgrim Fathers who came from England in the Mayflower to settle in the American colonies

al den·te /æl 'dɛnteɪ, ɑl-/ *adj.* food, especially PASTA, that is al dente is still firm after it has been cooked

al·der /'ɔldə/ *n.* [C,U] a tree that grows in northern countries, or the wood of this tree

al·der·man /'ɔldəmən/ *n.* [C] an elected member of a town or city council in the U.S.

Al·drin /'ɔldrɪn/, **Ed·win (Buzz)** /'ɛdwɪn, bʌz/ (1930–) a U.S. ASTRONAUT who was the second man to step on the moon

ale /eɪl/ *n.* [U] **1** a type of beer with a slightly bitter taste **2** OLD-FASHIONED beer

al·eck /'ælɪk/ *n.* —see SMART ALECK

ale·house /'eɪlhaʊs/ *n.* [C] OLD-FASHIONED a place where people drink beer

a·lert[1] /ə'lət/ *adj.* **1** able to think quickly and clearly: *The medicine can make it difficult to remain alert.* **2** always watching and ready to notice anything strange or unusual: *an alert driver* | *When walking alone at night,* **be alert to** *your surroundings.*

alert[2] *v.* [T] **1** to officially warn someone of a problem or danger, so that they can be ready to deal with it: *One fireman alerted the residents and helped them to safety.* **2** to make someone notice something important or dangerous: [alert sb to sth] *A large sign alerts drivers to bad road conditions.*

alert[3] *n.* [C,U] **1** a warning to be ready for possible danger: *a smog alert* | *All hospitals in the area were* **put on alert** (=given a warning) *to receive casualties.* —see also RED ALERT **2 be on the alert** to be ready to notice and deal with a situation or problem: *Teachers are on the alert for signs of drug use.* | **be on high/full alert** *Miami police were on high alert after a night of violence.*

A·leut /ə'lut/ a Native American tribe from Alaska

A·leu·tian Is·lands /ə,luʃən 'aɪləndz/ a group of islands off the southwest coast of Alaska

Al·ex·an·der the Great /ælɪg,zændə ðə 'greɪt/ (356–323 B.C.) a king of Macedonia who took control of Greece, Egypt, and most of the countries to the east of the Mediterranean Sea as far as India and established many cities including Alexandria in Egypt

al·fal·fa /æl'fælfə/ *n.* [U] a plant grown especially to feed farm animals

al·fal·fa sprout /.'.. ,./ *n.* [C] a young alfalfa plant, eaten raw in SALADS

al·fres·co /æl'frɛskoʊ/ *adj., adv.* in the open air: *alfresco dining*

al·gae /'ældʒi/ *n.* [U] a thing that looks similar to a plant without stems or leaves that grows in or near water

al·ge·bra /'ældʒəbrə/ *n.* [U] a type of mathematics that uses letters and other signs to represent numbers and values —**algebraic** /,ældʒə'breɪ-ɪk/ *adj.* —**algebraically** /-kli/ *adv.*

Al·ger /'ældʒə/, **Ho·ra·tio** /hə'reɪʃioʊ/ (1832–1899) a U.S. writer, famous for his stories about boys who become rich

Al·ge·ri·a /æl'dʒɪriə/ a country in north west Africa on the Mediterranean Sea —**Algerian** *n., adj.*

Al·giers /æl'dʒɪrz/ the capital and largest city of Algeria

A

Al·gon·quin /æl'gɑŋkwɪn/ a Native American tribe from eastern Canada

al·go·rithm /'ælgə,rɪðəm/ n. [C] TECHNICAL a set of instructions that are followed in a particular order and used for solving a mathematical problem, making a computer program etc.

A·li /ɑ'li/, **Muhammad** (1942–) a U.S. BOXER who is considered one of the greatest boxers ever

Muhammad Ali

a·li·as¹ /'eɪliəs, 'eɪlyəs/ prep. used when giving someone's real name together with another name they use: *That's a picture of Margaret Zelle, alias Mata Hari.*

alias² n. [C] a false name, usually used by a criminal: *She checked into the hotel **under an alias**.*

al·i·bi /'ælə,baɪ/ n. [C] **1** proof that someone was not where a crime happened and therefore could not have done it: [+ for] *Enstrom had an alibi for the murder.* **2** an excuse for something you have failed to do or done wrong

a·li·en¹ /'eɪliən, 'eɪlyən/ adj. **1** very different from what you are used to; STRANGE: [+ to] *New York's social problems are not alien to Californians.* **2** [only before noun] relating to creatures from another world: *an alien spaceship* **3** belonging to another country or race; FOREIGN: *Entire groups were driven from their homes to alien regions.*

alien² n. [C] **1** TECHNICAL someone who lives or works in your country, but who comes from another country: *Under the amnesty law, many **illegal aliens** were given citizenship.* **2** a creature from another world: *These people believe they were kidnapped by aliens.*

a·li·en·ate /'eɪliə,neɪt, 'eɪlyə-/ v. [T] **1** to do something that makes someone unfriendly or unwilling to support you: *Jackson's comments alienated many baseball fans.* **2** to make someone feel that they do not belong in a particular group: [+ from] *After divorce, don't alienate your child from the other parent.* **3** LAW to give the legal right to a particular piece of land, property etc. to someone else

a·li·en·at·ed /'eɪliə,neɪtɪd/ adj. feeling separated from society or the group of people around you, and often unhappy: [+ from] *Large numbers of Americans have become alienated from the political process.*

a·li·en·a·tion /,eɪliə'neɪʃən/ n. [U] **1** the feeling of not being part of society or a group: *Minority students have a sense of alienation from the mostly white teachers.* **2** separation from a person whom you used to be friendly with: *the permanent alienation of father from son*

a·light¹ /ə'laɪt/ adj. [not before noun] **1** burning: *Houses and cars were **set alight**.* **2** someone whose face or eyes are alight is excited and happy **3** bright with light or color

alight² v. past tense and past participle **alit** [I] FORMAL **1** alight on/upon sth if a bird or insect alights on something, it stops flying to stand on a surface **2** alight from sth to step out of a vehicle at the end of a trip

a·lign /ə'laɪn/ v. [T] **1** to decide to publicly support or not support a political group or country: [+ with/against] *Chavez's views are closely aligned with the board's majority.* **2** to arrange things so that they form a line or are parallel to each other: *The desks were neatly aligned in rows.*

a·lign·ment /ə'laɪnmənt/ n. **1** [U] the state of being arranged in a line or parallel to something: *Check the wheel alignment on the car.* **2** [C,U] if countries or groups form an alignment, they support

each other **3** [U] a way of arranging players in a sport to do a particular job: *The Colorado Buffaloes use a 3–4 defensive alignment.*

a·like¹ /ə'laɪk/ adj. [not before noun] very similar: *The two singers do not sound anything alike.* —see also LOOK-ALIKE

alike² adv. **1** equally: *Politicians and voters alike are too concerned with short-term problems.* **2** in a similar way: *The men in the bridal party should dress alike.*

al·i·men·ta·ry ca·nal /,ælə,mɛntri kə'næl/ n. [C] the tube in your body that takes food through your body from your mouth to your ANUS

al·i·mo·ny /'ælə,mouni/ n. [U] money that a court orders someone to pay regularly to their former wife or husband after their marriage has ended

A-line /'eɪ laɪn/ adj. an A-line dress, skirt, or coat fits close to the body at the top and is wide at the bottom

a·lit /ə'lɪt/ v. the past tense and past participle of ALIGHT²

a·live /ə'laɪv/ adj. [not before noun]
1 not dead still living and not dead: *Not knowing whether he's dead or alive is a terrible feeling.* | *They walked all night, trying to keep warm, to **stay alive**.* | *He's being **kept alive** by a feeding tube.* | *I have heard from my family, and they're **alive and well**.* (=alive and healthy)
2 still existing continuing to exist: *Blues clubs like these help keep the music alive.* | *While Payne was sick, his family helped **keep** the business **alive**.* | *Unfortunately, discrimination against black people is **alive and well**.* (=exists in many places)
3 cheerful active and happy: *I only really **feel alive** when I'm in the city.*
4 come alive a) if a situation or event comes alive, it becomes interesting and seems real: *Hodges' stories make history come alive.* **b)** if a town, city, place etc. comes alive, it becomes busy and full of activity: *The streets come alive after dark.* **c)** if a team, player etc. comes alive, they suddenly start to play well **d)** if someone comes alive, they start to be happy and interested in what is happening: *Cabral looks at the clay and her face comes alive as she begins to shape it.*
5 bring sth alive to make something interesting, busy, active etc.: *Adventureland brings alive the world of Caribbean pirates.*
6 be alive with sth to be full of something and seem busy or exciting: *The street was alive with music.* | *wooded canyons alive with birds*
7 be alive and kicking a) to be very healthy and active: *At last report, she was still alive and kicking.* **b)** to continue to exist successfully: *Despite financial problems, the firm is alive and kicking.*
8 be alive to sth to realize that something is happening and that it is important: *Murphy is alive to the romance of his job.* —see also **skin sb alive** (SKIN²)

al·ka·li /'ælkə,laɪ/ n. [C,U] a substance that forms a chemical salt when combined with an acid

al·ka·line /'ælkəlɪn, -,laɪn/ adj. containing an alkali

all¹ /ɔl/ quantifier, pron. **1** the complete amount or quantity of something; every one or every part of something: *He ate all the cake that was left.* | *Are you finished with all your chores?* | *They're all the same age.* | *I've heard it all before.* | [+ of] *Mix it together and put all of it in the big pan.* | *Bill talks about football all the time.* | **you/they/it all** *They all passed the test.* —see usage note at EACH¹ **2** used to emphasize the most basic or necessary facts or details about a situation: *Some seeds and some soil – that's all you need to start.* | *All I want is a few hours sleep.* **3 (not) at all** used in questions and negative statements to emphasize what you are saying: *Were they any help to you at all?* | *It wasn't his fault – not at all.* | *It's not at all uncommon.* | *I'm surprised the doctors said he could go at all.* | *"So you wouldn't mind if I came along?" "No, not at all!"* (=certainly not, please do) **4 all kinds of/all sorts of sth** very many different types of things, people, or places: *I met all kinds of people at the festival.* **5 for all sb knows/cares etc.** used to say that something could happen, especially something very bad or serious, and someone would not know or care about it: *Larry could be in prison for all I know.* **6 for all I know** used when you do not know anything about a subject, or when you do not know if any changes have happened to a situation: *I opened the window, and for all I know it's still open.* **7 of all people/things/places etc.** used to show surprise or annoyance when mentioning a particular person, thing, or place: *You of all people should understand exactly what I'm talking about.* **8 all in all** considering every part of a situation or thing: *It wasn't funny, but all in all it was a good movie.* **9 ...and all** SPOKEN including many other people or things that you would expect: *He has his own room, with a TV and bed and all, but it's not the same as being at home.* **10 sb was all...** SPOKEN used to report what someone said or did when telling a story: *He once drove me somewhere, and he was all, "I love this car – it's like a rocket!"* **11 for all...** in spite of a particular fact, quality, or situation: *For all his faults, he's a good father.* **12 all out** if you do something all out, you do it with a lot of energy, determination, or anger because you want to achieve something: *The Maple Leafs will have to go all out on the ice tonight.* —see also ALL-OUT **13 it's all or nothing a)** used to say that unless something is done completely or done in the exact way that you want, something else will happen, especially something bad: *The deal is all or nothing.* **b)** used to say that someone is using all their effort and energy in order to try and do something **14 it was all I could do to...** used to say that you just barely succeeded in doing something: *It was all I could do not to laugh.* **15 all innocence/smiles etc.** used to emphasize that someone or something has a particular quality of appearance: *Everyone was all smiles at the office.* —see also EACH¹, EVERY, **in all honesty** (HONESTY), **all and sundry** (SUNDRY)

USAGE NOTE: ALL

GRAMMAR
All is used with a singular verb when it comes before an uncountable noun: *All the money is gone.* It is used with a plural verb when it comes before a plural noun: *All the kids are gone.*

w **all²** *adv.* **1** [always + adj./adv./prep.] completely: *She was all alone in the house.* | *Look at the dog – he's all happy now!* | *If he can turn the company around, I'm all for it* (=I strongly support it). **2 all over a)** everywhere on an object or surface: *There are leaves all over the car.* | *She had flour and stuff all over her hands.* **b)** everywhere in a place: *People from all over the world come to visit Disneyland.* | *They're putting up new offices all over the place.* **c)** finished: *I used to travel a lot, but that's all over.* **3 all at once a)** happening all together at the same time: *Should we send the packages all at once?* **b)** suddenly and unexpectedly: *All at once, she broke into a smile.* **4 all along** INFORMAL all the time from the beginning while something was happening: *I knew all along I wanted to live in the Santa Fe area.* **5 not all that good/much/exciting etc.** SPOKEN not very good, much etc.: *It wasn't all that good a movie.* | *I don't think it matters all that much.* **6 sb/sth is not all that** SLANG to be not very attractive or desirable: *I don't know why you keep chasing her around – she's not all that.* **7 be all over sb** INFORMAL to be trying to kiss someone or touch them, especially in a sexual way: *He was all over me at the dance.* **8 be all over sb/sth** SPOKEN used humorously to emphasize that you are doing something confidently and with a lot of energy: *I was all over that history test today!* **9 one/four/ten etc. all** used when giving the points in a game in which both sides have made the same number of points: *At halftime, the teams were tied, 21 all.* **10 all of a sudden** in a very quick and surprising way: *All of a sudden I realized that the car in front of me wasn't moving.* **11 all the easier/healthier/more effectively etc.** used to emphasize how much more easy, healthy, effective etc. something is than it would normally have been:

A

She likes her job, which makes the decision to move all the more difficult. **12 all the same** SPOKEN in spite of something that you have just mentioned: *All the same, it would have been nice to go.* **13 it's all the same to sb** SPOKEN used to say that someone does not mind what decision is made, they would be pleased with any choice, or that they do not really care: *We can go out to eat if you want – it's all the same to me.* **14 all but** almost completely: *Sometimes it seems home baking is a tradition that has all but disappeared.* **15 all too** much more than is desirable: *His career as a singer was all too short.* | *All too often, making a will is put off until it's too late.* **16 all told** counting or including everyone; all together: *All told, 28 people died and 100 were wounded.* **17 (not) all there** INFORMAL someone who is not all there cannot think in a clear normal way and seems slightly crazy: *I don't think he's all there.*

all³ *n.* **give your all** LITERARY to do everything possible to try to achieve something: *Joe was the kind of guy who gave his all every moment on the job.*

all- /ɔl/ *prefix* **1** consisting of or made of only one type of thing: *an all-girl school* | *an all-wool dress* **2** during all of something: *an all-night party* (=continuing all night) | *an all-night cafe* (=staying open all night)

Al·lah /ˈælə, ˈɑlə/ *n.* the Muslim name for God

all-A·mer·i·can /ˌ. .ˈ...ˈ/ *adj.* **1** having qualities that are considered to be typically American and that American people admire, such as being healthy and working hard: *Bennett is the all-American suburban mom.* **2** belonging to a group of players who have been chosen as the best in their sport at American universities: *an all-American player from Stanford*

all-a·round /ˌ. .ˈ.ˈ/ *adj.* [only before noun] good at doing many different things, especially sports: *a good all-around athlete*

al·lay /əˈleɪ/ *v.* [T] FORMAL **allay fear/concern/suspicion etc.** to make someone feel less afraid, worried etc.: *The Secretary of State tried to allay the concerns of the Seoul government.*

all-clear /ˌ. ˈ./ *n.* **the all-clear a)** a signal such as a loud whistle that tells you that a dangerous situation has ended: *Residents ran to the bomb shelters until the all-clear sounded an hour later.* **b)** official permission to begin doing something | **get/give the all-clear** *The book was finally given the all-clear for publication.*

all com·ers /ˌ. ˈ../ *n.* [plural] anyone who wants to take part in something, especially a competition, whatever their age or experience: *The lessons are free and open to all comers.*

al·le·ga·tion /ˌæləˈgeɪʃən/ *n.* [C] a statement that s w someone has done something wrong or illegal, which has not been proved: [+ of] *allegations of sexual harassment* | [allegation that] *There was an allegation that a police officer had punched the suspect.* | *They shouldn't make allegations without knowing the facts.*

al·lege /əˈlɛdʒ/ *v.* [T] to say that something is true or that someone has done something wrong without showing proof: [allege (that)] *They alleged that Smith had failed to report $52,000 of income on his tax form.* | [be alleged to be/do sth] *He's alleged to have killed two people.*

al·leged /əˈlɛdʒd/ *adj.* [only before noun] an alleged s w fact, quality etc. is supposed to be true, but has not been proven: *an alleged conspiracy to murder President Kennedy*

al·leg·ed·ly /əˈlɛdʒɪdli/ *adv.* [sentence adverb] used when reporting something that other people say is true, although it has not been proved: *He was arrested for allegedly stabbing his former wife*

Al·le·ghe·ny Mountains, the /ˌæləˈgeɪni/ also **the Alleghenies** a range of mountains which go from Virginia to Pennsylvania in the eastern U.S. and are part of the Appalachians

A

al·le·giance /ə'lidʒəns/ n. [C,U] loyalty to a leader, country, belief etc.: [+ to] *They're successful because of their allegiance to the customer.* | *I pledge allegiance to the flag of the United States of America.*

al·le·go·ry /'ælə,gɔri/ n. [C,U] plural **allegories** a story, painting etc. in which the events and characters represent ideas or teach a moral lesson —**allegorical** /,ælə'gɔrɪkəl/ adj. —**allegorically** /-kli/ adv.

al·le·gro /ə'lɛgrou/ n. [C] a piece of music played or sung quickly —**allegro** adj., adv.

al·le·lu·ia /,ælə'luyə/ interjection HALLELUJAH

all-em·brac·ing /,. .'..◂/ adj. including everyone or everything: *an all-embracing theory*

Al·len /'ælən/, **E·than** /'iθən/ (1738–1789) an American soldier who fought against the British in the American Revolutionary War

Allen, Wood·y /'wudi/ (1935–) a U.S. movie DIRECTOR who makes humorous movies and also appears in them as an actor

Woody Allen

Allen wrench /'.. ,./ n. [C] a small tool you use to turn an Allen screw (=a type of screw with a hole that has six sides)

al·ler·gen /'ælədʒən/ n. [C] TECHNICAL a substance that causes an allergy

al·ler·gic /ə'lədʒɪk/ adj. **1** having an ailergy: [be allergic to sth] *A small number of people are allergic to nuts.* **2 an allergic reaction/rash/response** an illness or a red painful area on your skin that some people get because of an allergy **3 be allergic to sth** INFORMAL HUMOROUS to be always trying to avoid an activity or thing that you do not like

al·ler·gist /'ælədʒɪst/ n. [C] a doctor who treats people who have allergies

al·ler·gy /'ælədʒi/ n. [C,U] plural **allergies** a medical condition in which you become sick or in which your skin becomes red and painful because you have eaten particular foods, touched particular things etc.: *She gets shots for her allergies.* | [+ to] *One of my children has an allergy to cow's milk.*

al·le·vi·ate /ə'livi,eɪt/ v. [T] to make something less bad, painful, severe, or difficult: *Heavy rains in March alleviated the drought conditions.* —**alleviation** /ə,livi'eɪʃən/ n. [U]

al·ley /'æli/ n. plural **alleys** [C] **1** a narrow street between or behind buildings, that is used to get to parking areas, store GARBAGE etc., but is not used like a normal street that cars travel on: *A delivery truck blocked the alley.* **2 right up/down sb's alley** very appropriate for someone: *The job sounds right up your alley.* —see also BACK-ALLEY, BLIND ALLEY, BOWLING ALLEY, TIN PAN ALLEY

alley cat /'.. ,./ n. [C] a cat that lives on the streets and does not belong to anyone

al·ley·way /'æli,weɪ/ n. [C] an ALLEY

all-fired /,. '.◂/ adv. SPOKEN a word meaning "completely" that you use before describing a quality that you think is extreme: *Why are you so all-fired impatient?*

all fours /,. './ —see on all fours (FOUR)

all get-out /. '. ./ n. **scared/violent/nervous etc. as all get-out** SPOKEN very afraid, violent etc.

al·li·ance /ə'laɪəns/ n. [C] **1** an arrangement in which two or more countries, groups, businesses etc. agree to work together to try to change or achieve something: [+ between] *There was a brief alliance between the Communists and the Socialists.* | [+ with] *Finnair once had an alliance with Swissair.* | *The three Slavic republics formed an alliance.* **2** a group that is formed when two or more countries,

groups etc. work together: *the NATO alliance* **3 in alliance (with sb)** if two groups, countries etc. are in alliance, they work together to achieve something or protect each other: *The merchants established ports, often in alliance with local tribes.* **4** FORMAL close relationship, especially a marriage, between people —see also **unholy alliance** (UNHOLY)

al·lied /ə'laɪd, 'ælaɪd/ adj. **1 be allied to/with sth** to relate to something or be very similar: *The ideals of Alcoholics Anonymous are closely allied to Christian beliefs.* **2** joined by common political, military, or economic aims: *Information was shared between the allied governments.* **3 allied industries/organizations/trades etc.** relating to each other because of being similar to each other or dependent on each other; RELATED: *National Ocean Service also conducts research in the allied fields of radioastronomy and computer science.* **4 Allied** belonging to or relating to the countries that fought together against Germany in World War I or II, or against Iraq in the Gulf War: *the Allied navies* | *McArthur, the Allied commander in the Pacific*

Al·lies /'ælaɪz/ n. **1** the countries, including Britain, France, Russia, and the U.S., who fought together during the World War I **2** the countries, including the U.S., the U.S.S.R., and the U.K., who fought together during World War II **3** the United Nations countries who fought together against Iraq during the Gulf War

al·li·ga·tor /'ælə,geɪtə/ n. **1** [C] a large animal with a long mouth and sharp teeth that lives in the hot wet parts of the U.S. and China **2** [U] the skin of this animal used as leather: *alligator shoes*

all-in·clu·sive /,. .'..◂/ adj. including everything: *an all-inclusive vacation cruise* (=including food, entertainment, a place to sleep etc.)

al·lit·er·a·tion /ə,lɪtə'reɪʃən/ n. [U] the use of words that begin with the same sound in order to make a special effect, especially in poetry —**alliterative** /ə'lɪtərətɪv, -,reɪtɪv/ adj.

all-night /,. '.◂/ adj. **1** continuing all through the night: *an all-night negotiating session* **2** open all night: *an all-night supermarket*

all-night·er /,. '. ./ n. [C] INFORMAL an occasion when you spend the whole night studying or doing written work in college

al·lo·cate /'ælə,keɪt/ v. [T] [usually passive] to decide officially that a particular amount of money, time etc. or something such as a house or job etc. should be used for a particular purpose: *The results will depend on how each department allocates its resources.* | [allocate sth for sth] *One million dollars has been allocated for disaster relief.* | [allocate sth to sb/sth] *Most of the federal aid that was allocated to the Bay Area has already been spent.*

al·lo·ca·tion /,ælə'keɪʃən/ n. **1** [C] the amount or share of something that has been allocated to a person or organization: *Some families lie about the number of people in their household in order to get larger food stamp allocations.* **2** [U] the decision to allocate something, or the act of allocating something: *50% of the fund will be available for allocation this year.*

all-or-noth·ing /,. .'../ adj. [only before noun] **an all-or-nothing situation/strategy/approach etc.** a situation etc. in which the only possible results you consider are complete success or complete failure: *Avoid taking an all-or-nothing position – you're more likely to succeed if you can compromise.*

al·lot /ə'lɑt/ v. **allotted, allotting** [T] to decide officially to give something to someone or use something for a particular purpose: [allot sb sth] *Each speaker was allotted 30 minutes.* | [allot sth for sth] *Not enough funds are allotted for school lunches.* | [allot sth to sb/sth] *They are going to allot 30 minutes of radio time to Buck's show.*

al·lot·ment /ə'lɑtmənt/ n. [C,U] an amount or share of something such as money or time that is given to someone or something, or the process of doing this: *The budget allotment for each county is below what is needed.* | [+ of] *The allotment of scholarships to minorities has dropped.*

al·lot·ted /ə'lɑtɪd/ *adj.* [only before noun] **allotted money/time/resources etc.** allotted money, time, resources etc. have been officially given to someone for a particular purpose: *The department has spent its allotted budget for the year.* | *I couldn't finish the test in the allotted time.*

all-out /ˌ. '.◂/ *adj.* [only before noun] an all-out effort or attack involves a lot of energy, determination, or anger: *There are fears of an all-out war.* —see also **all out** (ALL¹ (12))

all-o·ver, allover /ˌ. '..◂/ *adj.* [only before noun] covering the whole surface of something: *wallpaper with an allover floral pattern* | *an all-over suntan* —see also **all over** (ALL² (2))

al·low /ə'laʊ/ *v.* [T]
1 **can do sth** to let someone do or have something or let something happen: *Our apartment complex does not allow pets.* | *We do not allow eating in the classrooms.* | [allow sb to do sth] *How could they allow the state to build a prison so close to our neighborhood?* | [allow sb in/out/up etc.] *I don't allow the cat in the bedroom.* | [be allowed (to do sth)] *"Can I smoke here?" "No, it's not allowed."* | *I'm allowed to stay out until 12 o'clock on weekends.*
2 **make sth possible** to make it possible for something to happen or for someone to do something, especially something helpful or useful: [allow sb to do sth] *A 24-hour ceasefire allowed the two armies to reach a solution to the conflict.* | [allow sb sth] *The new seatbelt allows the driver greater freedom of movement.*
3 **have enough** to be sure that you have enough time, money, food etc. available for a particular purpose: [allow sb sth] *We allowed ourselves plenty of time to get to the airport.*
4 **correct/permitted** FORMAL to accept or agree that something is correct or PERMITted by the rules or the law: *The judge allowed the evidence.*
5 **allow that** FORMAL to admit that something is true: *I allow that there may have been a mistake.*
6 **allow me!** SPOKEN used as a polite way of offering to help someone do something: *"Allow me," the waiter said, helping her with her coat.*
allow for sb/sth *phr. v.* [T] to consider all the possible facts, problems, costs etc. involved in a plan or situation and make sure that you can deal successfully with them: *Allowing for inflation, the cost of the project over ten years is $2 million.*
allow of sth *phr. v.* [T] FORMAL to show that something exists or is possible: *The facts allow of only one interpretation.*

al·low·a·ble /ə'laʊəbəl/ *adj.* acceptable according to rules or laws: *The maximum allowable dosage is two tablets a day.*

al·low·ance /ə'laʊəns/ *n.* [C] **1** an amount of something that is acceptable or safe: *The baggage allowance is 75 pounds per person.* | *A glass of orange juice provides the recommended daily allowance of Vitamin C.* **2** an amount of money that you are given regularly or for a special reason | **a clothing/travel/housing etc. allowance** *Joe's salary includes a monthly clothing allowance.* **3** a small amount of money that a parent regularly gives to a child: *Mom gave us kids a weekly allowance if we kept our rooms clean.* **4** something that you consider when making a decision, such as something unexpected that could happen: [+ for] *There is a slight allowance for error in the projected costs.* | *The budget makes allowances for additional staffing when needed.* **5 make allowances** to let someone behave in a way you would not normally approve of, because you know there are special reasons for their behavior: [+ for] *Of course, we make allowances for small children who don't know the rules.*

al·loy¹ /'ælɔɪ/ *n. plural* **alloys** [C,U] a metal that consists of two or more metals mixed together: *The pipes are made of an alloy of copper and zinc.*

al·loy² /ə'lɔɪ, 'ælɔɪ/ *v.* **alloys, alloyed, alloying** [T]
1 [+ with] TECHNICAL to mix one metal with another **2** LITERARY to lower the value or quality of something by mixing it with something else

all-pow·er·ful /ˌ. '..◂/ *adj.* having complete power

or control: *the all-powerful Senate Foreign Relations Committee*

all-pur·pose /ˌ. '..◂/ *adj.* [only before noun] able to be used in any situation: *an all-purpose cleaner*

all right /ˌ. '.◂/ *adj., adv.* [not before noun]
1 **good a)** satisfactory or acceptable, but not excellent; OK: *"What's the food like?" "Well, it's all right, but the place near campus is better."* | *"How's school going, Steve?" "Oh, all right, I guess."* **b)** good enough for a particular purpose; appropriate; correct; OK: *I'll see when Dr. Lopez is available. Is Thursday morning all right?*
2 **yes a)** used when agreeing with someone's suggestion or agreeing to do something; OK: *"Why don't we go to a movie?" "All right. Do you want to stop at Gino's for a pizza first?"* **b)** used when agreeing to do something or to allow something, even though you do not want to; OK: *"Can I play with my new computer game?" "Oh all right – as long as you don't make too much noise."*
3 **no problems** not hurt, not sick, not upset, or not having any problems; OK: *Are you all right? What happened?* | *Do you think you'll be all right by tomorrow night?* | *Katie looked really unhappy – I'd better go and make sure she's all right.* | *The kids seem to be doing all right in school.* | *Did everything go all right at the dentist?*
4 **be doing all right (for yourself)** to be successful in your job, life etc.: *Tammy's doing all right for herself – she just bought herself a new car.*
5 **it's all right/that's all right a)** used as a reply when someone thanks you: *"Thanks for all your help!" "That's all right. It's no problem."* **b)** used to tell someone that you are not angry when they say they are sorry for something: *"Sorry I'm late." "That's all right."*
6 **it's all right** used to make someone feel less afraid or worried: *It's all right. Mommy's here now.*
7 **happy** SLANG used to say you are happy about something, because you have been successful, something good has happened etc.: *"I got the job." "All right!"*
8 **is it all right if...** also **would it be all right if...** used when asking for permission do something: *Is it all right if I close the window? It's getting cold in here.*
9 **it's/that's all right by me** used to agree with someone's suggestion: *"Shall we stop there for today?" "That's all right by me."*
10 **check understanding** [sentence adverb] used to check that someone understands what you said, or to show that you understand; OK: *I'll leave the key with the neighbors, all right?* | *"Connect the positive first and then the negative." "Oh, I see, all right."*
11 **annoyed/angry** [sentence adverb] **a)** used when saying that you have heard and understood what someone has said, especially when you are annoyed: *"Krista, you have ten seconds to come downstairs." "All right! I'm coming!"* **b)** used when asking what has happened or what someone means, especially in an angry or threatening way: *All right, what have you two been doing with that knife?*
12 **introduce/change subject** [sentence adverb] used to introduce a new subject or activity: *All right, folks, I'd like to introduce our first speaker this evening.*
13 **emphasize** [sentence adverb] used to emphasize that something is definitely true, will definitely happen etc.: *Sofia is the smart one in their family, all right.*
14 **admit sth is true** [sentence adverb] used to admit that something is true, especially when saying that you also think that something else is not: *Wayne's experienced enough all right, but I don't know if he's right for this particular job.*
15 **all right already!** OLD-FASHIONED said in order to emphasize that you are annoyed by someone asking you to do something or the same question again and again: *"Cindy, come on!" "All right already! Stop rushing me!"*

all-round /ˌ. '.◂/ *adj.* ALL-AROUND

A

all·spice /ˈɔlspaɪs/ *n.* [U] a powder used in cooking to give food a special taste, made from the fruit of a tropical American tree

all-star /ˈ. ./ *adj.* [only before noun] including many famous actors or sports players: *an all-star cast*

all-ter·rain ve·hi·cle /ˌ. .. ˈ.../ *n.* [C] an ATV

all-time /ˈ. ˈ.◄/ *adj.* [only before noun] **1 all-time high/low/best etc.** the highest, lowest etc. level there has ever been: *The price of wheat reached an all-time low of 42 cents in 1932.* **2 all-time record/classic etc.** the best thing of its type ever known: *Dionne finished his career as the Kings' all-time leader in goals and assists.*

al·lude /əˈlud/ *v.*
allude to sb/sth *phr. v.* [T] FORMAL to mention something or someone in an indirect way: *In her speech, Mrs. Choo alluded to the Bible story of the three wise men.*

al·lure /əˈlʊr/ *n.* [singular, U] a mysterious, exciting, or desirable quality that is very attractive: *Fatty snacks can soon lose their allure if you have nothing else to eat.* | [the allure of sth] *the allure of foreign travel*

al·lur·ing /əˈlʊrɪŋ/ *adj.* attractive and desirable: *a low, alluring voice*

al·lu·sion /əˈluʒən/ *n.* [C,U] something that is said or written that brings attention to a particular subject in a way that is not direct: [+ to] *Eliot's poetry is full of allusions to other works of literature.* —**allusive** /əˈlusɪv/ *adj.*

al·lu·vi·al /əˈluviəl/ *adj.* TECHNICAL made of soil left by rivers, lakes, floods etc.: *an alluvial plain*

al·lu·vi·um /əˈluviəm/ *n.* [U] TECHNICAL soil left by rivers, lakes, floods etc.

all-weath·er /ˌ. ˈ..◄/ *adj.* [only before noun] made to be used in all types of weather: *an all-weather coat*

al·ly¹ /ˈælaɪ/ *n. plural* **allies** [C] **1** a country that makes an agreement to help or support another country, especially in a war: *a meeting of the European allies* —see also ALLIES **2** someone who helps and supports you in difficult situations: *The auto industry has many allies in Congress.*

al·ly² /əˈlaɪ, ˈælaɪ/ *v.* **allies, allied, allying** [I,T] to join with other people or countries to help and support each other: [ally yourself to/with sb] *Some priests and nuns openly allied themselves with the rebels.* —see also ALLIED

al·ma ma·ter /ˌælmə ˈmɑtɚ, ˌɑl-/ *n.* **1** sb's **alma mater** the school or college that you used to attend: *Mr. Inocencio regularly returns to his alma mater to encourage students to pursue their dreams.* **2** the song of a particular school or college

al·ma·nac /ˈɔlmənæk/ *n.* [C] **1** a book that gives information about the movements of the sun and moon, the times of the TIDES etc. for each day of a particular year **2** a book that gives lists of information about a particular subject or activity, especially one that is printed every year: *the 1992 World Sports Almanac*

Al·ma·ty /ɑlˈmɑti/ the capital and largest city of Kazakhstan

al·might·y /ɔlˈmaɪti/ *adj.* **1 Almighty God/Father** an expression used to talk about God when you want to emphasize his power **2 the Almighty** God **3 God/Christ Almighty** an expression used when you are angry or upset, which may be offensive to Christians: *God Almighty, what on earth will they do next?* **4 the almighty dollar** INFORMAL an expression meaning "money," used when you think money is too important to someone: *He neglects his kids while going after the almighty dollar.*

al·mond /ˈɑmənd, ˈæm-/ *n.* [C] a flat pale nut with a slightly sweet taste, or the tree that produces these nuts

al·most /ˈɔlmoʊst, ɔlˈmoʊst/ *adv.* very nearly but not completely: *I'm almost finished.* | *Are we almost there?* | *We stayed at Grandma's for almost a week.* | *It's an almost impossible task.* | *The wines are almost as expensive as champagne.* | *They sold almost everything.* | *Almost all the children here speak two languages.* | *The cause is almost certainly a virus.*

USAGE NOTE: ALMOST

WORD CHOICE: almost, nearly, hardly, scarcely, very, extremely
Both **almost** and **nearly** can be used before words like *all, every,* and *everybody*: *Almost/nearly all (of) my friends came to the party* (NOT *Almost of my friends came...* or *Almost my friends came...*). or **Almost** can also be used before negative verbs: *I almost/nearly didn't get up in time.* However, you do not use **not** with *hardly* or *scarcely*: *They hardly have enough money to pay their bills.* **Almost** (NOT **nearly**) can be used before *any* and negative words like *no, nobody, never,* and *nothing*: *Almost no one came to the party* (NOT *Nearly no one...*). | *They can make almost any color of paint you want.* You can use **not** before **nearly**, but not before **almost**: *She's not nearly as pretty as her sister* (NOT *She's not almost as pretty...*). Both **nearly** and **almost** can be used with adjectives that have an extreme or absolute meaning: *nearly/almost perfect/frozen/dead/impossible.* However, they are not usually used with other, less extreme, adjectives. In these cases you are more likely to use **very** or **extremely**: *The schools are extremely good there* (NOT *nearly good*). | *The coast was very rocky* (NOT *almost rocky*).

---

alms /ɑmz/ *n.* [plural] OLD-FASHIONED money, food, clothes etc. that are given to poor people

al·oe ver·a /ˌæloʊ ˈvɛrə/ also **aloe** *n.* [U] **1** a type of plant that has long thick pointed leaves **2** the juice from the leaves of an aloe plant used for making skin creams, medicine, etc.

a·loft /əˈlɔft/ *adv.* [not before noun] FORMAL high up in the air: *The national flag was flying aloft.*

a·lo·ha /əˈloʊhɑ/ *interjection* used as a greeting or to say goodbye in Hawaii

a·lone /əˈloʊn/ *adj., adv.* [not before noun] **1 no other people** without any other people: *Dorothy lives alone.* | *Suddenly they found themselves alone together* (=the only people there) *in the room.* | *Get a babysitter – you need some time alone with your husband* (=with only him and no other people)*!* **2 no friends** without any friends or people who you know: *Kim traveled alone through Europe.* | *Josie was all alone in a strange city.* **3 leave sb alone** to stop annoying or interrupting someone: *Go away and leave me alone.* **4 leave sth alone** to stop touching an object or changing something: *Leave that alone – you'll break it!* **5 unhappy** feeling very unhappy and lonely: *He felt terribly alone when June left.* **6 emphasize** [only after noun] **a)** used to emphasize that one particular thing or person is very important or has an effect on a situation: *The price alone was enough to make me change my mind.* **b)** used to say that someone or something is the only thing or person involved: *It's an expensive place – lunch alone was $20.* | *Stevenson alone is to blame.* **7 be alone in (doing) sth** be the only person to do something: *You're not alone in wondering what's happening here.* **8 go it alone** to start working or living on your own, especially after working or living with other people: *After years of working for a big company, I decided to go it alone.* **9 stand alone** if an object or building stands alone, it is not near other buildings or objects: *The house stood alone at the end of the road.*

USAGE NOTE: ALONE

WORD CHOICE: alone, on your own, by yourself, lonely, lonesome, lone, solitary
If you are **alone**, or less formally, **on your own/by yourself**, it just means that no one else is with you, and is neither good nor bad: *I spent the afternoon at home*

alone/by myself. With verbs of action, **on your own** and **by yourself** often suggest that no one is helping you: *I want to swim alone* (=with no one else there). | *I want to swim on my own/by myself* (=either with nobody else there, or with other people there but not helping). If you are **lonely** or **lonesome**, you are unhappy because you are alone: *I felt lonely living away from my family.* | *a lonely old man.* Places can be **lonely** or **lonesome** if they make people feel lonely: *a lonesome farmhouse.* Things that you do can also be **lonely**: *a lonely drive/job/life etc.* **Lonely** is never an adverb but **alone** often is: *She traveled alone* (NOT *lonely*). In more formal English, a **lone** or **solitary** person or thing is simply the only one in a place, and therefore might seem a little lonely: *a lone figure in the middle of the field* (=it is the only one there). In spoken English, you are more likely to talk about: *a figure on its own in the middle of the field.* Sometimes **solitary** can suggest that you choose to be alone: *She is a very solitary person.*

a·long[1] /ə'lɔŋ/ *prep.* **1** by the side of something, and from one part to another part of it: *We took a walk along the river.* **2** in a line next to or on something: *They put up a fence along the sidewalk.* | *Wild strawberries grew along the trail.* **3** at a particular place on or by the side of something, usually something long: *The Martins' house is somewhere along this road.*

along[2] *adv.* **1** if someone or something moves along, they move forward: *I was driving along, listening to the radio.* | *He showed me the notes he had made as we went along.* **2 go/come/be along** to go to, come to, or be in the place where something is happening: *We're going to Ben's – do you want to **come along?*** **3 take/bring sb along** to take or bring someone with you somewhere: *Mandy had brought some of her friends along.* **4 along with sb/sth** in addition to someone or something, and at the same time: *Add milk to the flour mixture, along with the melted butter.* **5 come/go/get along** to improve, develop, or make progress in a particular way: *"How's she doing after her operation?" "Oh, she's **coming along fine.**"* | *The questions get harder as you go along.*

a·long·side /ə,lɔŋ'said/ *adv., prep.* **1** next to or along the side of something: *We parked alongside the road.* | *Serve the sandwiches with a fresh salad alongside.* **2** if you do something alongside someone else, you do it together with them: *The Italians have been working alongside French NATO troops.* **3** if different types of things, ideas etc. are used or exist alongside each other, they are used together or exist at the same time: *Norway is considered the favorite for the gold medal alongside the U.S.*

a·loof /ə'luf/ *adj.* **1** not friendly, especially because you think you are better than other people: *She was polite but aloof.* **2 remain/stay/keep etc. aloof** to not become involved with something: [+ **from**] *Ms. Morita has kept herself aloof from political activity.* —**aloofly** *adv.* —**aloofness** *n.* [U]

a·loud /ə'laud/ *adv.* **1** if you say something aloud, you say it in your normal voice: *The teacher read aloud to the class.* **2** LITERARY in a loud voice: *He cried aloud in pain.*

al·pac·a /æl'pækə/ *n.* **1** [C] an animal from South America that looks like a LLAMA **2** [U] the cloth made from the wool of an alpaca

al·pha /'ælfə/ *n.* [C usually singular] **1** the first letter of the Greek alphabet **2 the alpha and omega (of sth)** the beginning and the end, or the most important part of something

al·pha·bet /'ælfə,bɛt/ *n.* [C] a set of letters, arranged in a particular order, used in writing language: *the Cyrillic alphabet*

al·pha·bet·i·cal /,ælfə'bɛtɪkəl/ also **al·pha·bet·ic** /,ælfə'bɛtɪk/ *adj.* relating to the alphabet: *The dictionary is arranged in alphabetical order.* —**alphabetically** /-kli/ *adv.*

al·pha·bet·ize /'ælfəbə,taɪz/ *v.* [T usually passive] to arrange things in the order of the letters of the alphabet: *The books are alphabetized according to the author's last name.*

alpha male /,.. './ *n.* [C usually singular] **1** TECHNICAL the highest-ranking male in a group of animals such as CHIMPANZEES **2** HUMOROUS the man who has the most power and influence and the highest social position in a particular group

al·pha·nu·mer·ic /,ælfənu'mɛrɪk◂/ *adj.* using letters and numbers: *an alphanumeric code*

alpha ver·sion /'.. ,../ *n.* [C] TECHNICAL a new piece of SOFTWARE that is in its first stage of testing —compare BETA VERSION, DEMONSTRATION PROGRAM

al·pine /'ælpaɪn/ *adj.* **1** also **Alpine** relating to the Alps **2** alpine plants grow near the top of a mountain where trees cannot grow **3** alpine SKIing involves going down mountains, rather than across flat land

Alps, the /ælps/ a range of mountains in Europe that runs through France, Switzerland, Italy, Germany, and Austria

al·read·y /ɔl'rɛdi, ɔ'rɛdi/ *adv.* **1** by or before now, or before a particular time: *The design of the new house is similar to those that have already been built.* | *As I have already mentioned, we need to raise more political support.* | *"Do you want a cup of coffee?" "No thanks, I already have some."* | *"When are you going to do your homework?" "I already did it before dinner!"* **2** used to say that something has happened too soon or before the expected time: *Are you leaving already?* | *I can't believe I already forgot his phone number!* | *Is it already 5 o'clock?* **3** used to say that a situation, especially a bad one, now exists and it might get worse, greater etc.: *The building's already costing us way too much money as it is.* —see Usage Notes at JUST[1], STILL[1]

al·right /ɔl'raɪt, ɔ'raɪt/ *adj., adv.* NONSTANDARD a spelling of ALL RIGHT which is usually considered incorrect

al·so /'ɔlsoʊ, 'ɔsoʊ/ *adv.* **1** in addition to something else you have mentioned; as well as; too: *Six of Tom's friends were also arrested.* | *Nina runs a catering company. Also, she plans parties.* | *We talked to a counselor also.* | *The report has **not only** attracted much attention, **but also** some sharp criticism.* **2** used when saying that the same thing is true about another person or thing: *My girlfriend is also named Helen.*

USAGE NOTE: ALSO

WORD CHOICE: also, too, as well, either, neither
When you want to say that something exists or happens in addition to something else, **too** and **also** are more common than **as well** in informal and spoken English. In a formal article you might see: *The company manufactures beauty products and markets pharmaceuticals as well.* If the verb is negative, you use **either**: *"I don't like liver." "I don't like it either."* (NOT *I don't like it too* or *I don't also like it*, though *I also don't like it* is possible, but more formal). In informal English people usually say **not...either** rather than **neither**: *Lisa refused to help wash the dishes. She didn't do her homework either.* (If here you said: *Lisa neither helped wash the dishes nor did her homework*, it would sound very formal and unnatural.)

GRAMMAR
Also usually comes before the main verb: *The college also has a new swimming pool* (NOT usually *The college has also a new swimming pool*). | *Brad can also play the guitar* (NOT usually *...also can*). | *Many people were working full-time and also going to night school.* **Also** usually follows the verb *to be* where it is used alone as a main verb: *Seattle is also a very nice city.* **Too** and **as well** are not used at the beginning of a sentence, but **also** may be used at the beginning of a sentence, especially in speech and informal writing.

---

also-ran /'.. ,./ *n.* [C] someone who has failed to win a competition or election, or someone who you think is unlikely to be successful

A

al·tar /'ɔltɚ/ n. [C] **1** a table or raised surface that is the center of many religious ceremonies: *It was my job to light the candles on the altar.* **2** the part of a church, often at the front, where the priest or minister stands

altar boy /'.. ,./ n. [C] a boy who helps a Catholic priest during the church service

al·tar·piece /'ɔltɚ,pis/ n. [C] a painting or SCULPTURE behind an altar

s w **al·ter** /'ɔltɚ/ v. **1** [I,T] to change, or to make someone or something change: *Her face hadn't altered much over the years.* | *The plan will alter traffic patterns in the area.* **2** [T] to make a piece of clothing longer, wider etc. so that it fits better: *I got the dress altered for the wedding.*

al·ter·a·tion /,ɔltə'reɪʃən/ n. [C] **1** a small change that makes someone or something slightly different: *They're planning to make a few alterations to the house.* **2** a change in the shape or size of a piece of clothing to make it fit better

al·ter·ca·tion /,ɔltɚ'keɪʃən/ n. [C] FORMAL a short but noisy argument or fight, usually with someone you do not know

al·ter e·go /,.. '../ n. [C] **sb's alter ego 1** a character in a movie, television program etc. that is played by a particular actor, and may be better known to the public than the actor himself or herself **2** another part of your character that is very different from your usual character **3** FORMAL someone who you trust and who thinks about things in the same way as you do

s w **al·ter·nate**[1] /'ɔltɚnɪt/ adj. [only before noun] **1** able to be used or chosen instead of another person or thing of the same type: *an alternate juror* | *an alternate method of payment* **2** two alternate actions, situations, or states happen one after the other in a repeated pattern: *The walls were painted with alternate stripes of yellow and green.* **3** happening or doing something on one of every two days, weeks etc.: *He works alternate days.*

al·ter·nate[2] /'ɔltɚ,neɪt/ v. [I,T] if two things alternate or you alternate them, they change from one to the other in a repeated pattern: [+ **between**] *Her emotions alternated between outrage and sympathy.* | [**alternate sth with sth**] *Alternate alcoholic drinks with water to avoid drinking too much.* —**alternation** /,ɔltɚ'neɪʃən/ n. [C,U]

al·ter·nate[3] /'ɔltɚnɪt/ n. [C] someone who will do someone else's job if that person cannot do it; SUBSTITUTE[1] (2): *Madsen is listed as an alternate to tonight's starting pitcher.*

alternating cur·rent /,.... '../ n. [U] a flow of electricity that regularly changes direction at a very fast rate; AC —compare DIRECT CURRENT

al·ter·na·tive[1] /ɔl'tɚnətɪv/ adj. **1** [only before noun] an alternative idea, plan etc. is one that can be used instead of another one: *Jones' book details alternative ways of coping with stress.* **2** [only before noun] an alternative system or solution is considered less damaging or more effective than the old one: *alternative sources of energy* **3** not based on or believing in traditional social or moral standards: *an alternative lifestyle* | *alternative music* —**alternatively** adv.

s w **alternative**[2] n. [C] something that you can choose to do or use instead of something else: *Which alternatives are likely to reduce traffic?* | [+ **to**] *In this case, taking medication is a good alternative to surgery.* | *I had no alternative but (=I felt I had to) to report him to the police.* | *We don't want to lay off workers, but there seems to be no alternative.*

alternative med·i·cine /.,.... '.../ n. [U] one of the ways of treating illnesses that is not based on Western scientific methods

al·ter·na·tor /'ɔltɚ,neɪtɚ/ n. [C] an electric GENERATOR that produces an ALTERNATING CURRENT, used in motor vehicles —see picture at ENGINE

al·though /ɔl'ðoʊ, ɔ'ðoʊ/ conjunction **1** used to introduce a statement which is followed by another statement that may seem surprising: *Although she joined the company only a year ago, she's already been promoted twice.* | *Although the car's old, it still runs well.* **2** but; HOWEVER: *Patty may have left, although I'm not sure.* | *No, it's my responsibility, although I appreciate your offer.* —see Usage Note at DESPITE

al·tim·e·ter /æl'tɪmətɚ/ n. [C] an instrument used in aircraft that tells you how high you are

al·ti·tude /'æltə,tud/ n. [C] the height of an object or place above the surface of the ocean: *The plane normally flies at an altitude of 30,000 feet.* | **high/low altitude** *At high altitudes, it is difficult to get enough oxygen.* —compare ELEVATION

altitude sick·ness /'... ,../ n. [U] a feeling of sickness that people get when they travel to places that are very high in the mountains, because there is not enough OXYGEN in the air

al·to /'æltoʊ/ n. plural **altos** [C] a woman with a low singing voice —**alto** adj.

al·to·geth·er[1] /,ɔltə'gɛðɚ, 'ɔltə,gɛðɚ/ adv. **1** a word meaning "completely" or "thoroughly," that is used to emphasize what you are saying: *It seems to have vanished altogether.* | *Eventually they chose an altogether different design.* | *How this is to be achieved is altogether a different matter.* **2** used when you are stating a total amount: *There were five people altogether who attended the presentation.* | *How much do I owe you altogether?* **3** **not altogether** FORMAL used before an adjective, adverb, or verb to say that a situation is really closer to the opposite of that word: *The change is not altogether bad* (=it is fairly good). | *The boy was not altogether sure* (=he was fairly unsure) *the judge was talking to him.* **4** FORMAL used to make a final statement that gives the main idea of what you have been saying: *Latin America is a world where primitive ways of life exist near ultra-modern cities. Altogether, it is a continent full of vitality.*

altogether[2] n. **in the altogether** HUMOROUS wearing no clothes; NUDE: *The number of Americans sleeping in the altogether has risen to 16 percent.*

al·tru·ism /'æltru,ɪzəm/ n. [U] FORMAL the practice of thinking of the needs and desires of other people instead of your own —**altruist** n. [C] —**altruistic** /,æltru'ɪstɪk/ adj. —**altruistically** /-kli/ adv.

al·um /ə'lʌm/ n. [C] SPOKEN a former student of a school or college

a·lu·mi·num /ə'lumənəm/ symbol **Al** a silver-colored metal that is an ELEMENT and is light and easily made into different shapes

aluminum foil /.,... './ n. [U] a very thin sheet of shiny metal that you wrap around food to protect it

a·lum·na /ə'lʌmnə/ n. plural **alumnae** /-ni/ [C] FORMAL a woman who is a former student of a school or college

a·lum·ni /ə'lʌmnaɪ/ n. [plural] the former students of a school or college: *Berkeley alumni* | *alumni of Carleton College*

a·lum·nus /ə'lʌmnəs/ n. plural **alumni** [C] FORMAL a former student of a school or college

al·ve·o·lar /æl'viələ/ adj. TECHNICAL relating to a sound such as /t/ or /d/ that is made by putting the end of the tongue at the top of the mouth behind the upper front teeth —**alveolar** n. [C]

al·ways /'ɔlweɪz, -wiz, -wɪz, 'ɔwiz/ adv. **1** all the time, at all times, or each time: *Always lock your bicycle to something secure.* | *Grandma had always told us to be careful.* | *The wind is always blowing there.* **2** for as long as you can remember, or for a very long time: *I've always wanted to go to Paris.* | *He's always been very curious.* **3** if you say that you will always do something, you mean that you will do it forever: *I'll always remember that day.* **4** happening continuously or very often, especially in an annoying way: *My stupid car is always breaking down!* | *Jenna always talks too loud.* **5 you can/could always...** SPOKEN used to make a polite suggestion: *You could always take the test again next semester.*

USAGE NOTE: ALWAYS

GRAMMAR

Always usually comes after the first auxiliary or modal verb and before the main verb: *Sara always wanted a puppy* (NOT *Sara wanted always a puppy*). | *He had always lived there* (had is the auxiliary here). | *You should always be careful walking alone at night* (NOT *should be always careful*). **Always** usually follows the verb *to be* where it is used alone as a main verb: *Ed is always tired* (NOT *Ed always is tired*).

SPELLING

Remember it is **always** (NOT *allways* or *all ways*).

Alz·heim·er's Disease /'altshaimɚ dɪ,siz, 'altsaɪ-, 'æl-/ also **Alzheimer's** *n.* [U] an illness that attacks and gradually destroys parts of the brain, especially in older people, so that they forget things and lose their ability to take care of themselves

AM *n.* [U] a system for broadcasting radio programs that is not as clear as FM

am /əm; *strong* æm/ *v.* the first person singular of the present tense of the verb to BE

a.m., A.M. /,eɪ 'ɛm/ used when talking about times that are after MIDNIGHT but before NOON: *I start work at 9 a.m.* —compare P.M.

A.M.A., the the American Medical Association; an organization for doctors and people who do medical RESEARCH

a·mal·gam /ə'mælgəm/ *n.* **1** [C] FORMAL a mixture or combination of different things or substances: [+ of] *The band's songs are an interesting amalgam of different musical styles.* **2** [C,U] TECHNICAL a mixture of metals, used to fill holes in teeth

a·mal·gam·ate /ə'mælgə,meɪt/ *v.* [I + with, T] if two businesses or groups amalgamate, or if one business or group amalgamates with another, they join to form a bigger organization —**amalgamation** /ə,mælgə'meɪʃən/ *n.* [C,U]

am·a·ret·to /,æmə'rɛtoʊ, ,ɑ-/ *n.* [U] a type of strong alcohol made with the taste of ALMONDs (=a type of nut)

a·mass /ə'mæs/ *v.* [T] to gradually collect a large amount of money, knowledge, or power: *During the course of her lifetime, Mrs. Boone amassed over $5 million.*

am·a·teur¹ /'æmətʃɚ/ *adj.* **1** [only before noun] doing something only for pleasure or interest, not as a job: *an amateur golfer* | *an amateur orchestra* **2** amateurish: *The organization was woefully amateur in its methods and techniques.*

amateur² *n.* [C] **1** someone who plays a sport or does an activity for pleasure or interest, not as a job: *The cast was made up mostly of amateurs.* —compare PROFESSIONAL² **2** someone who is not skillful at a particular activity: *Compared to those guys, I'm an amateur.*

am·a·teur·ish /,æmə'tʃʊrɪʃ/ *adj.* not skillfully done or made: *It was a surprisingly amateurish movie.* —**amateurishly** *adv.* —**amateurishness** *n.* [U]

am·a·teur·ism /'æmətʃʊ,rɪzəm/ *n.* [U] **1** the belief that enjoying a sport or other activity is more important than earning money from it **2** lack of skill in doing an activity: *The failure of the discussion was caused by the amateurism of the President and his aides.*

am·a·to·ry /'æmə,tɔri/ *adj.* LITERARY expressing sexual or romantic love

a·maze /ə'meɪz/ *v.* [T] to make someone very surprised: *Some kids will amaze you with what they can do.* | *The beauty of the area **never ceases to amaze me** (=always surprises me).*

a·mazed /ə'meɪzd/ *adj.* [not before noun] extremely surprised: [+ (that)] *I was amazed that they'd show such a violent program on TV.* | [+ at] *We were amazed at his rapid recovery.* | [amazed to do sth] *Visitors are often amazed to discover how little the town has changed.*

a·maze·ment /ə'meɪzmənt/ *n.* [U] a feeling of great surprise: *We looked at each other **in amazement** when we heard the news.* | *To her amazement, Sheila discovered she was pregnant.*

a·maz·ing /ə'meɪzɪŋ/ *adj.* **1** extremely good, especially in a surprising and unexpected way: *It's an amazing ride. You really feel like you're flying.* | *an amazing bargain* **2** so surprising that it is hard to believe: *amazing stories of UFOs* —**amazingly** *adv.*: *an amazingly generous offer*

am·a·zon, Amazon /'æmə,zɑn/ *n.* [C] a tall strong woman with a forceful character, who may make men feel afraid —**amazonian, Amazonian** /,æmə-'zoʊniən/ *adj.*

Am·a·zon, the /'æmə,zɑn/ a river in South America which is the second longest river in the world, and which flows through the largest area of RAINFOREST in the world

am·bas·sa·dor /æm'bæsədɚ, əm-/ *n.* [C] an important official who represents his or her government in a foreign country —**ambassadorial** /æm,bæsə'dɔriəl/ *adj.* —**ambassadorship** /æm'bæsədɚ,ʃɪp/ *n.* [C,U]

am·ber /'æmbɚ/ *n.* [U] **1** a yellowish brown substance used to make jewelry **2** a yellowish brown color —**amber** *adj.*

ambi- /æmbɪ/ *prefix* **1** used to say that something has two parts or is done with two things: *ambidextrous* (=using either hand equally well) | *an ambiguous statement* (=one that could be understood in more than one way) **2** all around you: *ambient noise* (=noise that is all around you whenever you are in a place)

am·bi·ance /'æmbiəns, 'ɑmbiɑns/ *n.* [singular,U] another spelling of AMBIENCE

am·bi·dex·trous /,æmbɪ'dɛkstrəs/ *adj.* able to use either hand with equal skill for writing, playing sports etc.

am·bi·ence, ambiance /'æmbiəns, 'ɑmbiɑns/ *n.* [singular,U] FORMAL the qualities of a place that make you feel a particular way about it: *Prices aren't too high at the Osteria, and the ambience is bright and inviting.*

am·bi·ent /'æmbiənt/ *adj.* **1 ambient temperature/pressure/noise etc.** TECHNICAL the temperature, pressure etc. of the surrounding area or room **2** ambient music is played on electronic instruments, has no strong beat, and is meant to make you feel relaxed

am·big·u·ous /æm'bɪgyuəs/ *adj.* **1** having more than one meaning, so that it is not clear which meaning is intended: *an ambiguous question* **2** difficult to understand, or not certain: *McClane's position in the company is ambiguous.* —**ambiguously** *adv.* —**ambiguity** /,æmbɪ'gyuəti/ *n.* [C,U]

am·bit /'æmbɪt/ *n.* [singular] FORMAL the range or limit of something: *Unethical employment practices such as these are **within the ambit of** the law.*

am·bi·tion /æm'bɪʃən/ *n.* **1** [U] determination to be successful, rich, powerful etc.: *What can you do with a kid who has no ambition?* **2** [C] a strong desire to achieve something: *Kasich is thought to have grand political ambitions.* | [ambition to do sth] *It's been Bruce's lifelong ambition to climb Mt. Everest.*

am·bi·tious /æm'bɪʃəs/ *adj.* **1** determined to be successful, rich, powerful etc.: *Linda has always been an ambitious and hard-working manager.* **2** an ambitious plan, idea etc. shows a desire to do something good but difficult, involving a lot of work: *The Harbor Tunnel is one of the most ambitious engineering projects of modern times.* —**ambitiously** *adv.* —**ambitiousness** *n.* [U]

am·biv·a·lent /æm'bɪvələnt/ *adj.* not sure whether you want or like something or not: [+ about] *Many members of the parish were profoundly ambivalent about the protest.* —**ambivalence** *n.* [U] —**ambivalently** *adv.*

am·ble /'æmbəl/ *v.* [I always + adv./prep.] to walk in a slow relaxed way: [+ along/across etc.] *Joe ambled over to say hello.* —**amble** *n.* [singular]

A

am·bro·sia /æm'broʊʒə/ n. [U] **1** food or drink that tastes or smells extremely good **2** the food eaten by gods in ancient Greek stories

am·bu·lance /'æmbyələns/ n. [C] a special vehicle used for taking people who are very sick or badly injured to the hospital

ambulance chas·er /'... ,../ n. [C] DISAPPROVING a lawyer who uses a lot of pressure to persuade people who have been hurt in accidents to SUE other people or companies in court, so that the lawyer will get part of the money if they win

am·bu·la·to·ry /'æmbyələ,tɔri/ adj. TECHNICAL able to walk or move around: an ambulatory patient

am·bush¹ /'æmbʊʃ/ n. [C] a sudden attack by people who have been waiting and hiding, or the place where this happens: The three journalists were killed in an ambush.

ambush² v. [T] to attack someone from a place where you have been hiding

a·me·bic /ə'mibɪk/ adj. another spelling of AMOEBIC

a·me·lio·rate /ə'milyə,reɪt/ v. [T] FORMAL to make something better: Measures to ameliorate working conditions have had little effect. —**amelioration** /ə,milyə'reɪʃən/ n. [U]

a·men /,eɪ'mɛn, ,ɑ-/ interjection **1** Amen used at the end of a prayer: Blessed be the Lord. Amen. **2** used to show that you agree or approve: "I think we can end the meeting now." "Amen to that."

a·me·na·ble /ə'minəbəl, -'mɛ-/ adj. **1** willing to listen or to do something: [+ to] The administration is amenable to a compromise. **2** able to be changed or used in a particular way: [+ to] Not all jobs are amenable to flexible scheduling.

a·mend /ə'mɛnd/ v. [T] to make small changes or improvements to a law or document

SW **a·mend·ment** /ə'mɛndmənt/ n. [C,U] a written
2 change or improvement to a law or official document, or the process of doing this: [+ to] an amendment to the new banking bill

a·mends /ə'mɛndz/ n. **make amends** to say you are sorry for something bad you did that harmed someone, and try to make things better

a·men·i·ty /ə'mɛnəti, ə'mi-/ n. plural **amenities** [C usually plural] something such as a piece of equipment, store, or park that makes it easier to live somewhere: The small town has all the amenities of a large city. | Many live in simple huts with only the most basic amenities.

Am·er·a·sian /,æmə'reɪʒən/ n. [C] someone from Asia who has one American parent and one Asian parent —compare ASIAN-AMERICAN

A·mer·i·ca /ə'mɛrɪkə/ n. **1** the United States of America: the smallest state in America **2** the Americas [plural] North, Central, and South America considered together as a whole

A·mer·i·can¹ /ə'mɛrɪkən/ adj. **1** coming from or relating to the U.S.: American forces landed on the island at dawn. | The American writer William Burroughs **2** ESPECIALLY TECHNICAL coming from or relating to the CONTINENTs of North and South America: The frogs are a species found only in American rivers, especially in Brazil.

American² n. [C] someone from the U.S.

A·mer·i·ca·na /ə,mɛrə'kɑnə/ n. [U] objects, styles, people, stories etc. that are typical of the U.S.: Baseball cards and other pieces of Americana have become popular overseas.

American A·cad·e·my of Arts and Sci·enc·es, the /.,... .,... . ,. . '.../ an organization that helps scientists to work on particular problems and gives prizes for work in science and the arts

American As·so·ci·a·tion of Re·tired Per·sons, the /.,... .,... . '. ,../ abbreviation AARP an organization for people who are 50 or older, especially people who have stopped working

American Bar As·so·ci·a·tion, the /.,... '. ...,../ a large national organization for lawyers

American cheese /.,... './ n. [U] a type of yellowish-orange cheese that does not have a strong taste, is made in a factory, and is often bought in thin pieces wrapped in plastic

American Civ·il Lib·er·ties U·nion, the /.,... ,.. '... ,../ —see ACLU

American Civ·il War, the /.,... ,.. './ —see CIVIL WAR

American Coun·cil for the Arts, the /.,... ,... . './ an organization that helps artists, actors, and people who are teaching or learning about the arts

American dream /.,... './ n. **the American Dream** the belief that everyone in the U.S. has the opportunity to become successful and rich if they work hard

American In·di·an /.,... '.../ n. [C] another name for a NATIVE AMERICAN (=someone from one of the first groups of people who lived in America)

A·mer·i·can·ism /ə'mɛrɪkə,nɪzəm/ n. [C] a word, phrase, or sound that is part of the English language as it is used in the U.S.

A·mer·i·can·ize /ə'mɛrɪkə,naɪz/ v. [T] to make something American in character, for example a way of speaking or writing, or the way something is organized —**Americanization** /ə,mɛrɪkənə'zeɪʃən/ n. [U]

American League /.,... './ n. [singular] one of the two professional baseball teams in the U.S. and Canada

American Le·gion, the /.,... '../ a national organization for former members of the U.S. ARMED FORCES

American Sa·mo·a /ə,mɛrɪkən sə'moʊə/ a U.S. TERRITORY that consists of the eastern part of a group of islands in the South Pacific Ocean

American way /.,... './ n. **the American way** a way of doing things that is considered typically American and obeys the principles of the U.S.: I believe in the right to a trial by jury; it's the American way.

Am·er·ind /'æmə,rɪnd/ also **Am·er·in·di·an** /,æmə-'ɪndiən/ n. [C] TECHNICAL American Indian

am·e·thyst /'æməθɪst/ n. **1** [C,U] a valuable purple stone used in jewelry **2** [U] a light purple color —**amethyst** adj.

a·mi·a·ble /'eɪmiəbəl/ adj. friendly and easy to like: Kovitsky spoke in an amiable, conversational tone. —**amiably** adv. —**amiability** /,eɪmiə'bɪləti/ n. [U]

am·i·ca·ble /'æmɪkəbəl/ adj. FORMAL an amicable agreement, relationship etc. is one in which people feel friendly toward each other and do not want to argue: Both sides were able to reach an amicable settlement out of court. —**amicably** adv. —**amicability** /,æmɪkə'bɪləti/ n. [U]

a·mid /ə'mɪd/ prep. **1** happening while noisy, busy, or confused events are also happening: The dollar fell in value amid rumors of weakness in the U.S. economy. **2** among or surrounded by: Old farm houses could be seen amid the trees.

a·mid·ships /ə'mɪd,ʃɪps/ adv. TECHNICAL in the middle part of a ship

a·midst /ə'mɪdst/ prep. LITERARY amid

a·mi·go /ə'migoʊ/ n. plural **amigos** [C] SPOKEN a friend

a·mi·no ac·id /ə,minoʊ 'æsɪd/ n. [C] one of the substances that combine to form PROTEINs

A·mish /'ɑmɪʃ/ n. **the Amish** [plural] a Christian religious group that follows many strict rules, such as wearing plain traditional clothes and not using modern things such as telephones, cars, or televisions —**Amish** adj.

a·miss /ə'mɪs/ adj. **be amiss** also **see/notice/find etc. something amiss** if something is amiss or someone sees something amiss, there is a problem: Mr. McPherson insisted there was nothing amiss at his agency. | I felt something amiss, and looked down to find my pants unzipped.

am·i·ty /'æməti/ n. [U] FORMAL friendship, especially between countries: a spirit of perfect amity

Am·man /ɑ'mɑn/ the capital and largest city of Jordan

am·mo /'æmoʊ/ n. [U] INFORMAL: see AMMUNITION

am·mo·nia /ə'moʊnyə/ n. [U] **1** a clear liquid with a

strong bad smell that is used for cleaning or in cleaning products **2** a poisonous gas with a strong bad smell that is used in making many chemicals, FERTILIZERS etc.

am·mu·ni·tion /ˌæmyəˈnɪʃən/ n. [U] **1** bullets, SHELLS etc. that are fired from guns **2** information that you can use to criticize someone or win an argument against them: [+ against] *The oil spill gave environmentalists powerful new ammunition against the oil companies.*

am·ne·sia /æmˈniʒə/ n. [U] the medical condition of not being able to remember anything —**amnesiac** /æmˈniʒiˌæk, -ˈnizi-/ adj. —**amnesiac** n. [C]

am·nes·ty /ˈæmnəsti/ n. plural **amnesties** **1** **a)** [U] freedom from punishment that is officially given to prisoners or people who have done something illegal: *Congress granted amnesty to nearly 3 million illegal immigrants in 1986.* **b)** [C] an official order by a government that allows prisoners or people who have done something illegal to go free: *Mzukwa served just four years of his sentence before being released during a general amnesty in 1991.* **2** [C] a period of time when you can admit to doing something illegal without being punished: *Congressmen hope that an income-tax amnesty would encourage more people to pay.*

Amnesty In·ter·na·tion·al /ˌ... ...ˈ.../ an organization that defends people's HUMAN RIGHTS

am·ni·o·cen·te·sis /ˌæmnioʊsɛnˈtisɪs/ n. [C,U] a test to see if an unborn baby has any diseases or other problems, done by taking liquid from the mother's UTERUS

am·ni·ot·ic /ˌæmniˈɑtɪk◂/ adj. TECHNICAL relating to the SAC surrounding an unborn baby in its mother's UTERUS

a·moe·ba /əˈmibə/ n. plural **amoebas** or **amoebae** /-bi/ [C] a very small creature that has only one cell and a changeable shape —**amoebic** adj.

a·mok, amuck /əˈmʌk, əˈmɑk/ adv. **1** **run amok** to suddenly behave in an uncontrolled way in which things are destroyed: *Troops were allowed to run amok in the villages.* **2** **a sth run amok** something that is completely uncontrolled and is causing a lot of destruction: *Sheep ranches are being put in danger by a coyote population run amok.*

A·mon /ˈɑmən/ in Egyptian MYTHOLOGY, the god of life

a·mong /əˈmʌŋ/ also **a·mongst** /əˈmʌŋst/ prep. **1** affecting many people in a particular group, or shared by many people in a particular group: *There is widespread concern among scientists about the safety of storing nuclear waste underground.* | *Forbes dramatically increased his support among Republican voters statewide.* **2** through, between, or surrounded by: *We walked among the pines on the mountain slopes.* | *The letter is somewhere among these papers on her desk.* —see Usage Note at BETWEEN[1] **3** included in a group of people or things: *Yeltsin was among the first world leaders to arrive in Paris for the summit.* | *Innocent civilians were among the casualties.* | *My grandfather had among his possessions a portrait by Matisse.* | **among friends/strangers/ enemies etc.** *Jim relaxed, knowing he was among friends.* **4** **among other things** used to say that you are only mentioning one or two things from a much larger group of things: *At the meeting they discussed, among other things, recent events in Eastern Europe.* **5** if something is divided or shared among a group of people, each is given a part of it

a·mor·al /eɪˈmɔrəl, -ˈmɑr-/ adj. having no moral standards at all: *an amoral, greedy businessman* —**amorality** /ˌeɪməˈræləṭi/ n. [U] —compare IMMORAL

am·o·rous /ˈæmərəs/ adj. involving or expressing sexual love: *The park is a favorite spot for amorous couples.* —**amorously** adv. —**amorousness** n. [U]

a·mor·phous /əˈmɔrfəs/ adj. FORMAL having no definite shape or features, or without clear DEFINITION: *an amorphous mass of twisted metal*

am·or·tize /ˈæmərˌtaɪz/ v. [T] TECHNICAL to pay a debt by making regular payments —**amortizable** adj. —**amortization** /ˌæməṭəˈzeɪʃən/ n. [C,U]

a·mount[1] /əˈmaʊnt/ n. [C,U] **1** a quantity of something such as time, money, or a substance: *Please pay the full amount by the end of the month.* | [+ of] *a considerable amount of money* | *Cook the vegetables in a small amount of water.* | *There was **a fair amount of*** (=a fairly large amount of) *traffic on Highway 10.* | *No specific **dollar amounts** were mentioned in Shaw's report.* **2** the level or degree to which a feeling, quality etc. is present: [+ of] *Her case has attracted an enormous amount of public sympathy.* | *I felt **a certain amount of*** (=some) *embarrassment.* **3** **no amount of sth will/can etc. do sth** used to say that something has no effect: *No amount of persuasion could make her change her mind.*

USAGE NOTE: AMOUNT

GRAMMAR

Amount is usually used with uncountable nouns, and some people think this is the only correct use: *a large amount of money/food/electricity/hard work* (Note that you do not usually say a **high** or **big** amount). With plural countable nouns it is best to use **number**: *a large number of mistakes/people*. However, people often use **amount** with plural countable nouns when what they are talking about is thought of as a group: *We didn't expect such a large amount of people.* | *an enormous amount of problems*

amount[2] v.

amount to sth phr. v. [T not in progressive] **1** if numbers amount to a particular total, they equal that total when they are added together: *Time lost to sick leave amounted to 1,357 working days.* **2** if an attitude, remark, situation etc. amounts to something, it has the same effect: *The court's decision amounts to a not-guilty verdict.* **3** **not amount to much/anything** to not seem important, valuable, or successful: *Her academic achievements don't amount to much.* | *Jim's never going to amount to much.* **4** **amount to the same thing** to have the same result or effect: *She may not have killed him herself, but helping Dave to do it amounts to the same thing.*

a·mour /əˈmʊr, ɑ-, æ-/ n. [C] LITERARY OR HUMOROUS someone who you love and are having a sexual relationship with, often secretly

amp /æmp/ n. [C] **1** INFORMAL an AMPLIFIER **2** also **ampere** a unit for measuring electric current

am·per·age /ˈæmpərɪdʒ/ n. [singular,U] TECHNICAL the strength of an electrical current measured in amps

am·pere /ˈæmpɪr, -pɛr/ n. [C] TECHNICAL an amp

am·per·sand /ˈæmpərˌsænd/ n. [C] the sign "&" that means "and"

am·phet·a·mine /æmˈfɛṭəˌmin, -mɪn/ n. [C usually plural, U] a drug that gives you a feeling of excitement and a lot of energy

am·phib·i·an /æmˈfɪbiən/ n. [C] an animal, such as a FROG, that lives in water for the first part of its life and on land when it is an adult

am·phib·i·ous /æmˈfɪbiəs/ adj. **1** TECHNICAL able to live on both land and water **2** an amphibious vehicle is able to move on land and water **3** **an amphibious operation/force/assault etc.** a military action involving ships and land vehicles

am·phi·the·a·ter, amphitheatre /ˈæmfəˌθiəṭər/ n. [C] an outdoor theater with seats built in a half-circle shape on the side of a hill

am·ple /ˈæmpəl/ adj. [usually before noun] **1** more than enough: *You will have ample time to complete the test.* | *Every candidate will be given ample opportunity to be heard.* | *There is ample evidence that climate patterns are changing.* **2** **an ample bosom/ figure/torso etc.** part of a woman's body that is fairly fat —**amply** adv.: *Recent U.S. history has amply demonstrated the risks of foreign intervention.*

am·pli·fi·er /ˈæmpləˌfaɪər/ n. [C] a piece of electrical equipment that makes sound louder; AMP (1)

A

am·pli·fy /'æmpləˌfaɪ/ *v.* **amplifies, amplified, amplifying** [T] **1** to make a sound louder, especially musical sound: *an amplified guitar* **2** FORMAL to explain something by giving more information about it: *The Lockheed story amplifies how important top leadership is to an organization's success or failure.* **3** FORMAL to increase the effects or strength of something: *Critics say the Internet has amplified the problem of medical misinformation.* —**amplification** /ˌæmpləfə'keɪʃən/ *n.* [U]

am·pli·tude /'æmpləˌtud/ *n.* [U] **1** TECHNICAL the distance between the middle and the top or bottom of a WAVE² (8) such as a SOUND WAVE **2** the great size, strength, or loudness of something: *The current warming of the Pacific Ocean is unequaled in amplitude.*

am·pule /'æmpyul, -pul/ *n.* [C] a small container for medicine that will be put into someone with a special needle

am·pu·tate /'æmpyəˌteɪt/ *v.* [I,T] to cut off someone's arm, leg, finger etc. during a medical operation: *Two toes had to be amputated because of frostbite.* —**amputation** /ˌæmpyə'teɪʃən/ *n.* [C,U]

am·pu·tee /ˌæmpyə'ti/ *n.* [C] someone who has had an arm or a leg amputated

Am·ster·dam /'æmstɚˌdæm/ the capital city of the Netherlands

a·muck /ə'mʌk, ə'mʌk/ *adv.* another spelling of AMOK

am·u·let /'æmyəlɪt/ *n.* [C] a small piece of jewelry worn to protect against bad luck, disease etc.

A·mund·sen /'amənsən/, **Ro·ald** /'rouald/ (1872–1928) a Norwegian EXPLORER who was the first person to reach the SOUTH POLE in 1911

a·muse /ə'myuz/ *v.* [T] **1** to make someone laugh or smile: *Adams first began drawing cartoons to amuse his coworkers.* **2** to make someone spend time in an enjoyable way, without getting bored: *Most ski resorts offer activities to amuse children and even non-skiers.*

a·mused /ə'myuzd/ *adj.* **1** someone who is amused by something thinks it is funny, so that they smile or laugh: *Coach Montgomery seemed more amused than irritated at Shane's attempt to catch the ball.* | *James watched with an amused smile.* **2 keep sb amused** to entertain or interest someone for a long time so that they do not get bored: *Listening to the radio keeps me amused while I'm driving.* **3 sb is not amused** OFTEN HUMOROUS used to say that someone is angry about something: *I told Hardesty the damage was probably done by mice. He was not amused.*

a·muse·ment /ə'myuzmənt/ *n.* **1** [U] the feeling you have when you think something is funny: *Sheila was hardly able to conceal her amusement.* | *I tried my son's Rollerblades, **to the amusement** of the neighbors.* **2** [U] the process of getting or providing pleasure and enjoyment: *What do you do **for amusement** in this town?* **3** [C] something such as a movie or a game that entertains you and makes the time pass in an enjoyable way: *Video games and other manufactured amusements demand less imagination from kids.*

amusement park /.'.. ,./ *n.* [C] a large area with many special machines that you can ride on, such as ROLLER COASTERs and MERRY-GO-ROUNDs

a·mus·ing /ə'myuzɪŋ/ *adj.* funny and entertaining: *a charming and amusing book* —**amusingly** *adv.*

an /ən; *strong* æn/ *indefinite article, determiner* used instead of "a" when the following word begins with a vowel sound: *an orange* | *an X-ray* | *It's such an old house.* —see also A

an- /ən, æn/ *prefix* used instead of A-² in a word beginning with a vowel sound; NOT; WITHOUT: *anarchy* (=without government) | *anaerobic* (=without air or oxygen)

-an /ən/ *suffix* **1** [in adjectives and nouns] someone or something from a place, or relating to a place: *an American* | *Appalachian music* (=from Appalachia) | *suburban housing* **2** [in adjectives and nouns]

relating to the ideas of a particular person or group, or someone who follows these ideas: *Lutheran theology* (=relating to the teachings of Martin Luther) | *a Republican* (=someone who belongs to that political party) **3** [in adjectives] relating to or similar to a person, thing, or period of time: *the Roman Empire* —see also -EAN, -IAN

-ana /anə, ænə/ *suffix* [in U nouns] a collection of objects, papers, etc., relating to someone or something: *Americana* —see also -IANA

An·a·bap·tists /ˌænə'bæptɪsts/ a group within the Christian religion in the 16th century who thought that only people who really believed the religion should be baptized (BAPTIZE (1))

an·a·bol·ic ster·oid /ˌænbulɪk 'stɛrɔɪd, 'stɪr-/ *n.* [C] a drug that makes muscles grow quickly, sometimes used illegally in sports

a·nach·ro·nism /ə'nækrəˌnɪzəm/ *n.* [C] **1** someone or something that seems to belong to the past, not the present: *The law on mining is simply an anachronism in this day and age.* **2** something in a play, movie etc. that seems wrong because it is being shown in the wrong period of time —**anachronistic** /əˌnækrə'nɪstɪk/ *adj.* —**anachronistically** /-kli/ *adv.*

an·a·con·da /ˌænə'kandə/ *n.* [C] a large South American snake

an·aer·o·bic /ˌænɛ'roubɪk/ *adj.* TECHNICAL not needing oxygen in order to live

an·aes·the·sia /ˌænəs'θiʒə/ *n.* [U] another spelling of ANESTHESIA

an·aes·thet·ic /ˌænəs'θɛtɪk/ *n.* [C,U] another spelling of ANESTHETIC

a·naes·the·tist /ə'nɛsθəˌtɪst/ *n.* [C] another spelling of ANESTHETIST

a·naes·the·tize /ə'nɛsθəˌtaɪz/ *v.* [T] another spelling of ANESTHETIZE

an·a·gram /'ænəˌgræm/ *n.* [C] a word or phrase that is made by changing the order of the letters in another word or phrase: [+ **of**] *"Silent" is an anagram of "listen."*

a·nal /'eɪnl/ *adj.* **1** relating to the ANUS **2** also **anal retentive** INFORMAL showing too much concern with small details and keeping everything in order, especially in a way that annoys other people: *Stop being so anal!*

an·al·ge·sia /ˌænl'dʒiʒə, -ziə/ *n.* [U] TECHNICAL the condition of being unable to feel pain while conscious

an·al·ge·sic /ˌænl'dʒɪzɪk/ *n.* [C] TECHNICAL a drug that reduces pain —**analgesic** *adj.*

an·a·log¹, analogue /'ænlˌag, -ˌɔg/ *adj.* **an analog clock/watch/dial etc.** a clock, watch, or instrument that uses moving hands or a POINTER (3) to show information, instead of using changing numbers —compare DIGITAL

analog², analogue *n.* [C] FORMAL something that is similar to something else in some way: [+ **to/of**] *The Sierra Nevada mountains are the West Coast analogue of the Appalachians.*

analog com·pu·ter /ˌ... .'../ *n.* [C] a computer that calculates things by measuring changing quantities such as VOLTAGE rather than using a BINARY system of counting

a·nal·o·gous /ə'næləgəs/ *adj.* FORMAL similar to another situation or thing so that a comparison can be made: [+ **to/with**] *Scharf's findings are analogous with our own.*

a·nal·o·gy /ə'nælədʒi/ *n. plural* **analogies** [C,U] a comparison between two situations, processes etc. that seem similar, or the process of making this comparison: [+ **with/to/between**] *In class, we discussed analogies between human and animal behavior.* | **draw/make an analogy** *Norma drew an analogy between childbirth and the creative process.* | *Dr. Wood explained the movement of light **by analogy with** (=using an analogy of) the movement of water.*

an·a·lyse /'ænlˌaɪz/ *v.* [T] the British spelling of ANALYZE

a·nal·y·sis /ə'næləsɪs/ *n. plural* **analyses** /-siz/ **1** [C,U] a careful examination of something in order to understand it better: [+ of] *Collection and analysis of data on crime has become a priority.* **2** [C,U] a careful scientific examination of something to see what it consists of: [+ of] *Forensic experts are doing analyses of the samples.* **3** [C] a description or a report on something that is based on a careful examination of it: [+ of] *Our guests in the studio will provide a detailed analysis of the week's biggest news stories.* **4 in the final/last analysis** used when giving the most basic or important facts about a situation: *In the final analysis, the project was a failure.* **5** [U] a process in which a doctor makes someone talk about their past experiences, relationships etc. in order to help them with mental or emotional problems; PSYCHOANALYSIS

an·a·lyst /ˈænl-ɪst/ *n.* [C] **1** someone who makes a careful examination of events or materials in order to make judgments about them: *a stock market analyst* **2** someone such as a doctor who helps people who have mental or emotional problems by making them talk about their experiences and relationships —see also SYSTEMS ANALYST

an·a·lyt·ic /ˌænlˈɪtɪk/ / also **an·a·lyt·i·cal** /ˌænlˈɪtɪkəl/ *adj.* using methods that help you examine things carefully, especially by separating them into their different parts: *an analytic approach* | *analytical chemistry*

an·a·lyze /ˈænlˌaɪz/ *v.* [T] **1** to examine or think about something carefully, in order to understand it: *In a 1985 report, we analyzed the production costs of six different weapons systems.* **2** to carefully examine something using scientific methods and equipment to see what it consists of: *Experts are still analyzing the DNA evidence in the case.* **3** to examine someone's mental or emotional problems by using analysis; PSYCHOANALYZE

an·a·pest /ˈænəˌpɛst/ *n.* [C] TECHNICAL part of a line of poetry consisting of two short sounds then one long one

an·ar·chic /æˈnɑrkɪk/ *adj.* lacking any rules or order, or not following the moral rules of society: *a lawless, anarchic city*

an·ar·chism /ˈænərˌkɪzəm/ *n.* [U] the political belief that there should be no government and that ordinary people should work together to improve society

an·ar·chist /ˈænərˌkɪst/ *n.* [C] someone who believes that governments, laws etc. are not necessary —**anarchistic** /ˌænərˈkɪstɪk/ *adj.* —**anarchistically** /-kli/ *adv.*

an·ar·chy /ˈænərki/ *n.* [U] a situation in which there is no effective government in a country or no order in an organization or situation: *There was a state of near anarchy in the classroom.*

A·na·sa·zi /ˌɑnəˈsɑzi/ a Native American tribe who formerly lived in the southeastern area of the U.S.

a·nath·e·ma /əˈnæθəmə/ *n.* **sth is anathema (to sb)** used to say that someone strongly dislikes something or disapproves of it: *Cutting back on any government service is still anathema to liberals.*

an·a·tom·i·cal /ˌænəˈtɑmɪkəl/ *adj.* relating to the structure of human or animal bodies: *an anatomical model* —**anatomically** /-kli/ *adv.*: *an anatomically correct* (=showing all the body parts) *doll*

a·nat·o·mist /əˈnætəˌmɪst/ *n.* [C] someone who knows a lot about the anatomy of human or animal bodies

a·nat·o·my /əˈnætəmi/ *n. plural* **anatomies** **1** [U] the scientific study of the structure of human or animal bodies **2** [C usually singular] the structure of a body, or of a part of a body: [+ of] *the anatomy of the nervous system* **3 sb's anatomy** OFTEN HUMOROUS someone's body: *You could see a part of his anatomy that I'd rather not mention.* **4 the/an anatomy of sth a)** a study or examination of an organization, process etc. in order to understand and explain how it works: *Elkind's book is an anatomy of one man's discussion with his son about life.* **b)** the structure of an organization, process etc. or the way it works: *For the first time, we have a chance to examine the anatomy of a secret government operation.*

An·ax·ag·o·ras /ˌænækˈsægərəs/ (?500–428 B.C.) a Greek PHILOSOPHER

-ance /əns/ *suffix* [in nouns] **1** used to make nouns from verbs, to show a state, a quality, or a fact: *a sudden appearance* (=someone appeared suddenly) | *We need more assistance* (=more help). | *There's a resemblance between the two children* (=they look like each other). **2** used to make nouns from adjectives ending in -ANT: *Picasso's brilliance* (=great intelligence, from BRILLIANT) —see also -ENCE

an·ces·tor /ˈænˌsɛstə/ *n.* [C] **1** a member of your family who lived a long time ago: *Most of Luke's ancestors were Italian.* **2 the ancestor of sth** the form in which a modern machine, vehicle etc. first existed: *Babbage's invention was the ancestor of the modern computer.* —compare DESCENDANT —**ancestral** /ænˈsɛstrəl/ *adj.*

an·ces·try /ˈænˌsɛstri/ *n. plural* **ancestries** [C usually singular,U] the members of your family who lived a long time ago: *Quebec residents of French ancestry* (=who have French ancestors)

an·chor¹ /ˈæŋkə/ *n.* [C] **1** a piece of heavy metal that is lowered to the bottom of the ocean, a lake etc. to prevent a ship or boat from moving: *We dropped anchor a few yards offshore.* | *It was time to* **weigh anchor** (=lift the anchor) *on the cruise to Alaska.* **2** someone who reads the news on TV and introduces news reports **3** someone or something that provides a feeling of support and safety: *These ancient trees are a spiritual anchor that our culture needs to hold on to.* **4** someone on a sports team, usually the strongest member, who runs or competes last in a race or competition

anchor² *v.*
1 boat [I,T] to lower the anchor on a ship or boat to hold it in one place: *Three tankers were anchored in the harbor.* | *Captain Cook anchored in Opunohu Bay in the 1760s.*
2 tv news [T] to be the person who reads the news and introduces reports on TV: *The new hour-long program is anchored by Mark McEwen.*
3 fasten [T usually passive] to fasten something firmly so that it cannot move: *The panel was firmly anchored by two large bolts.*
4 support [T] to provide a feeling of support, safety, or help for someone or an organization: *The new company will be anchored by the Hobart food-equipment group.* | *Stevens anchors the team's defense.*
5 be anchored in sth to be strongly related to a particular system, way of life etc.: *Her personal ideals were anchored in her Irish heritage.*

An·chor·age /ˈæŋkərɪdʒ/ the largest city in the U.S. state of Alaska.

an·chor·age /ˈæŋkərɪdʒ/ *n.* **1** [C] a place where ships can anchor **2** [C,U] TECHNICAL a place where something can be firmly fastened: *91,000 cars had to be recalled because their seat belt anchorages were not strong enough.*

an·chor·man /ˈæŋkəˌmæn/ *n. plural* **anchormen** /-mɛn/ [C] a male ANCHOR¹ (2)

an·chor·per·son /ˈæŋkəˌpɔsən/ *n. plural* **anchorpersons** or **anchorpeople** /-ˌpipəl/ [C] an ANCHOR¹ (2)

an·chor·wom·an /ˈæŋkəˌwʊmən/ *n. plural* **anchorwomen** /-ˌwɪmɪn/ *n.* [C] a female ANCHOR¹ (2)

an·cho·vy /ˈænˌtʃoʊvi, -tʃə-, ænˈtʃoʊvi/ *n. plural* **anchovies** [C,U] a very small fish that tastes very salty

an·cient¹ /ˈeɪnʃənt/ *adj.* **1** belonging to a time long ago: *the ancient civilizations of Asia* **2 ancient history a)** the history of people and societies from long ago, especially in Greece and Rome **b)** SPOKEN HUMOROUS if you say that something is ancient history, you mean that it happened a long time ago and you do not want to talk about it anymore: *Will and I broke up a long time ago – that's ancient history now.* **3** having existed for a very long time: *an ancient walled city* **4** USUALLY HUMOROUS very old: *That picture makes me look ancient!*

ancient² *n.* **the ancients** LITERARY people who lived

A

long ago, especially the Greeks and Romans: *The ancients believed that the sun and moon were planets.*

an·cil·lar·y /ˈænsəˌlɛri/ *adj.* FORMAL relating to or supporting something else, but less important than it: *Film companies also make money in ancillary sales of T-shirts, toys, and so on.*

-ancy /ənsi/ *suffix* [in nouns] **1** the fact that something is being done: *a consultancy group* (=company that gives advice) | *the militancy of the union* (=its willingness to fight) **2** a state or a quality: *pregnancy* (=state of being PREGNANT) | *There was hesitancy in his voice* (=it showed he was not sure). —see also -ENCY

and /ən, n, ənd; *strong* ænd/ *conjunction* **1** used to join two words, parts of sentences etc.: *Do you want a pen and some paper?* | *The movie starred Sandra Bullock and Keanu Reeves.* | *We've dealt with items one, two, and eleven.* | *Try to eat less and get more exercise.* | *You need to know what rights you have and how to use them.* **2** then; afterward: *Tara picked up the book and put it on the shelf.* | *He opened the door and went in.* | *You'll have to* **wait and see** *what happens.* **3** used to say that something is caused by something else: *I missed supper and now I'm starving!* | *She took some medicine and threw up.* **4** used when adding numbers: *How much is fifteen and seven?* **5 come/go/try etc. and...** INFORMAL used instead of "to": *Let's go and have a cup of coffee.* | *I'll see if I can try and persuade her to come.* **6** SPOKEN used to introduce a statement, remark, question etc.: *And now I'd like to introduce our next speaker, Mrs. Thompson.* | *And where are you going on your vacation?* **7** used between repeated words to emphasize what you are saying: *More and more people are losing their jobs.* | *That was years and years ago.* | *We ran and ran.* **8** SPOKEN used to emphasize a particular quality, or that something is exactly the way you want it: *The Senator was good and mad.* | *Dennis, your steak is still nice and pink in the middle.* **9 three and three quarters, nineteen and a half etc.** used after the whole number and before the FRACTION or DECIMAL when saying numbers: *The baby is due in about two and a half months* (=2¹/₂ months). | *We had two and two tenths inches* (=2.2 inches) *of rain last week.* **10** used in descriptions of food and drink to mean served with: *Do you want some cake and ice cream?* | *I'll have a gin and tonic.* | *a slice of* **bread and butter** (=bread with butter spread on it) **11 and?** SPOKEN used when you want someone to add something to what they have just said: *"I'm sorry." "And?" "And I promise it won't happen again."*

an·dan·te /ɑnˈdɑnteɪ/ *n.* [C] a piece of music played or sung at a speed that is neither very fast or very slow —**andante** *adj., adv.*

An·der·sen /ˈændəˌsən/**, Hans Chris·tian** /hæns ˈkrɪstʃən/ (1805–1875) a Danish writer famous for his many FAIRY TALES

An·der·son, Max·well /ˈmækswɛl/ (1888–1941) a U.S. writer of historical plays

Anderson, Sher·wood /ˈʃɚwʊd/ (1876–1941) a U.S. writer famous for his short stories (SHORT STORY)

An·des, the /ˈændiz/ a range of high mountains along the west coast of South America

and·i·ron /ˈændˌaɪən/ *n.* [C] one of a pair of iron objects that holds wood in a FIREPLACE

An·dor·ra /ænˈdɔrə/ a very small country in the Pyrenees between France and Spain —**Andorran** *n., adj.*

Andorra la Vel·la /ænˌdɔrə lɑ ˈvɛlə/ the capital city of Andorra

andr- /ændr/ *prefix* TECHNICAL relating to males or men: *an android* (=machine that is like a man)

An·dret·ti /ænˈdrɛti/**, Ma·ri·o** /ˈmɑriou/ (1940–) a U.S. race car driver

An·drew, Saint /ˈændru/ (1st century A.D.) in the Bible, one of the 12 APOSTLES

An·drews /ˈændruz/**, Roy** /rɔɪ/ (1884–1960) a U.S. NATURALIST and PALEONTOLOGIST who made many

journeys in Central Asia and discovered the first DINOSAUR eggs

and·ro·gyn·ous /ænˈdrɑdʒənəs/ *adj.* **1** someone who is androgynous looks both female and male **2** TECHNICAL having both male and female parts —**androgyny** *n.* [U]

an·droid /ˈændrɔɪd/ *n.* [C] a ROBOT that looks like a real person

A·dro·pov /ænˈdroupɔv, -ˈdrɑpɔf/**, Yu·ri** /ˈyuri/ (1914–1984) the leader of the COMMUNIST PARTY of the former SOVIET UNION from 1982 to 1984

-andry /ændri/ *suffix* relating to males or men: *polyandry* (=having more than one husband at the same time)

an·ec·dot·al /ˌænɪkˈdoʊtl/ *adj.* consisting of short stories based on someone's personal experience: *The book is an anecdotal account of Kent's trip to Borneo.* | *Although statistics are hard to come by,* **anecdotal evidence** *suggests that there were fewer accidents ten years ago.*

an·ec·dote /ˈænɪkˌdoʊt/ *n.* [C] a short story based on your personal experience

a·ne·mi·a /əˈnimiə/ *n.* [U] a medical condition in which there are too few red cells in your blood

a·ne·mic /əˈnimɪk/ *adj.* **1** suffering from anemia **2** seeming weak and uninteresting: *It was an anemic performance from a usually intelligent actor.*

a·nem·o·ne /əˈnɛməni/ *n.* [C] **1** a SEA ANEMONE **2** a plant with red, white, or blue flowers

an·es·the·sia /ˌænəsˈθiʒə/ *n.* [U] **1** the use of anesthetics in medicine **2** the state of being unable to feel pain

an·es·the·si·ol·o·gist /ˌænəsˌθiziˈɑlədʒɪst/ *n.* [C] a doctor who gives anesthetics to a patient

a·nes·thet·ist /əˈnɛsθəˌtɪst/ *n.* [C] someone, such as a nurse, who is trained to give anesthetics

a·nes·the·tize /əˈnɛsθəˌtaɪz/ *v.* [T] to give someone an anesthetic so that they do not feel pain

an·es·thet·ic /ˌænəsˈθɛtɪk/ *n.* [C,U] a drug that stops you feeling pain: *Wisdom teeth are usually removed* **under anesthetic.** | *The surgery is done using* **a local anesthetic** (=one that only affects a particular area of your body). | *You will have to have* **a general anesthetic** (=one that affects your whole body and makes you unconscious) *for the surgery.*

an·eu·rysm, aneurism /ˈænyəˌrɪzəm/ *n.* [C] a small place on the surface of a BLOOD VESSEL that is swollen and full of blood, and that can kill you if it breaks open

a·new /əˈnu/ *adv.* LITERARY **1** if you do something anew, you start doing it again: *Fighting began anew on May 15.* **2 start/begin anew** to begin a different job, start to live in a different place etc., especially after a difficult period in your life: *Los Angeles was regarded as the place to begin life anew.*

an·gel /ˈeɪndʒəl/ *n.* [C] **1** a spirit who is believed to live with God in heaven, often shown as a person dressed in white with wings **2** someone who is very kind, very good, or very beautiful: *That little girl of theirs is an angel.* | *Clark admits he* **is no angel** (=sometimes behaves badly). **3** SPOKEN someone who helps or supports you when you need it, and who you can depend on: *Bernie, you're an angel. What would I do without you?* **4** SPOKEN a way of speaking to a child or woman you love: *Goodnight, angel.* **5 where angels fear to tread** if someone goes or does something where angels fear to tread, they do it in a dangerous place: *I didn't realize that cruising around at 3 a.m. could leave me with a bullet in my head – fools drive where angels fear to tread.* —see also **fallen angel** (FALLEN²), GUARDIAN ANGEL

angel dust /ˈ.. ˌ./ *n.* [U] SLANG an illegal drug

Angel Falls /ˌ.. ˈ./ a WATERFALL in southeast Venezuela that is the highest waterfall in the world

angel food cake /ˈ.. . ˌ./ *n.* [C,U] a type of light white cake that is made with the white part of eggs

an·gel·ic /ænˈdʒɛlɪk/ *adj.* **1** looking good, kind, and gentle, or behaving in this way: *Timmy has such an angelic face.* **2** relating to angels: *angelic beings* —**angelically** /-kli/ *adv.*

an·gel·i·ca /ænˈdʒɛlɪkə/ n. [U] a plant that smells sweet and is used in cooking

An·ge·lou /ˈændʒəlu/, **May·a** /ˈmaɪə/ (1928–) an African-American writer and poet

an·ger¹ /ˈæŋgə/ n. [U] a strong feeling of wanting to harm, hurt, or criticize someone because they have done something unfair, cruel, offensive etc.: *Our family has helped us deal with the grief and anger we felt over his death.* | *"It's a lie!" he shouted in anger.*

anger² v. [T] FORMAL to make someone angry: *The court's decision angered environmentalists.*

an·gi·na /ænˈdʒaɪnə/ n. [U] a medical condition in which you have bad pains in your chest because your heart is weak

an·gi·o·plas·ty /ˈændʒiəˌplæsti/ n. [C,U] a method of repairing or opening a closed or damaged BLOOD VESSEL, usually by putting a very small BALLOON filled with air into the BLOOD VESSEL to make it wider

An·gle /ˈæŋgəl/ one of the people from north Germany who settled in England in the fifth century A.D.

an·gle¹ /ˈæŋgəl/ n. [C] **1** the space between two straight lines or surfaces that touch or cross each other, measured in degrees: *a 45-degree angle* —see also RIGHT ANGLE **2** a way of considering a problem or situation: *Try approaching the problem from a different angle.* **3 at an angle** leaning to one side and not straight or upright: *The portrait was hanging at an slight angle.* **4** a position from which you look at something or photograph it: *The photograph was taken from an unusual angle.* **5** the shape formed when two lines or surfaces join: *I avoided the angle of the coffee table in the darkened room.*

angle² v. **1** [I,T] if you angle something in a particular direction or if it angles in that direction, it is not upright or facing straight ahead: *The mirror was angled to reflect light from a window.* | *Angle your forearms slightly downward.* **2 angle to do sth** to try to get something in an indirect and sometimes dishonest way: *Martin's been clumsily angling to get back into the tourist business in Phoenix.*

angle for sth phr. v. [T] to try to get something by making suggestions and remarks instead of asking directly: *I think she's angling for an invitation to the party.*

an·gler /ˈæŋglə/ n. [C] OLD-FASHIONED someone who catches fish as a sport —compare FISHERMAN

An·gli·can /ˈæŋglɪkən/ n. [C] a Christian who is a member of the official church of England or related churches, such as the Episcopal church —**Anglican** adj. —**Anglicanism** n. [U]

an·gli·cism /ˈæŋgləˌsɪzəm/ n. [C] an English word or expression that is used in another language

an·gli·cize /ˈæŋgləˌsaɪz/ v. [T] to make something or someone more English

an·gling /ˈæŋglɪŋ/ n. [U] the sport of catching fish

an·glo /ˈæŋgloʊ/ n. plural **anglos** [C] INFORMAL **1 Anglo** someone who belongs to the white race: *The school's teachers are almost all Anglos, while most of the students are black or Hispanic.* **2** CANADIAN an ANGLOPHONE —**Anglo** n. [C]

An·glo-, anglo- /ˈæŋgloʊ/ prefix **1** relating to England or Great Britain: *an anglophile* (=someone who likes England and its culture very much) **2** English or British and something else: *an Anglo-Scottish family* | *Anglo-American society*

Anglo-A·mer·i·can /ˌ.. .ˈ.../ adj. between or involving both England or the U.K. and the U.S.: *Anglo-American relations*

an·glo·phile /ˈæŋgləˌfaɪl/ n. [C] someone who is not English, but likes anything relating to England —**anglophilia** /ˌæŋgləˈfɪliə/ n. [U]

an·glo·phobe /ˈæŋgləˌfoʊb/ n. [C] someone who dislikes anything relating to England —**anglophobia** /ˌæŋgləˈfoʊbiə/ n. [U]

an·glo·phone /ˈæŋgləˌfoʊn/ n. [C] someone who speaks English as their first language —**anglophone** adj.

Anglo-Sax·on /ˌæŋgloʊ ˈsæksən/ n. **1** [C] a member of the race of people who lived in England from about 600 A.D. **2** [U] the language of the Anglo-

Saxons **3** [C] a white person, especially someone whose family originally came from England —**Anglo-Saxon** adj. —see also WASP

An·go·la /ænˈgoʊlə/ a country in southwest Africa next to the Atlantic Ocean —**Angolan** n., adj.

an·go·ra /æŋˈgɔrə/ n. **1** [C] a type of goat, rabbit, or cat with very long soft hair or fur **2** [U] wool or thread made from the fur of an angora goat or rabbit

an·gos·tur·a /ˌæŋgəˈstʊrə/ n. [U] a slightly bitter liquid used for adding taste to alcoholic drinks

an·gry /ˈæŋgri/ adj. **angrier, angriest 1** feeling strong emotions which make you want to shout at someone or hurt them because they have behaved in an unfair, cruel, offensive etc. way, or because you think that a situation is unfair, unacceptable etc.: *I was stunned and angry when I found out.* | *an angry letter* | [+ with/at] *She's still very angry with me for forgetting our anniversary.* | [+ about/over] *My folks were really angry about my grades.* | *The book is sure to make a lot of women very angry.* **2 angry with/at yourself** feeling strongly that you wish you had done something or had not done something: *David was angry with himself for trusting Michael.* **3** LITERARY an angry sky or cloud looks dark and stormy **4** LITERARY an angry wound etc. is painful and red and looks infected —**angrily** adv.: *"You're an idiot," he said angrily.*

angst /ɑŋst, æŋst/ n. [U] strong feelings of anxiety and unhappiness because you are worried about your life or your future: *angst-filled poems*

an·guish /ˈæŋgwɪʃ/ n. [U] mental or physical suffering caused by extreme pain or worry: *The anguish of not knowing the truth was almost unbearable.* —**anguished** adj.

an·gu·lar /ˈæŋgyələ/ adj. **1** thin and not having much flesh on your body, so that the shape of your bones can be seen: *a tall, angular young man* **2** having sharp and definite corners: *angular patterns* **3** [only before noun] TECHNICAL having or forming an angle: *Mercury's angular distance from the sun*

an·i·mal¹ /ˈænəməl/ n. [C] **1** a living creature that is not a plant or a person: *farm animals* | *wild animals in the jungle* | *Beth is an animal lover* (=someone who likes animals). **2** FORMAL OR TECHNICAL any living creature that is not a plant, including people: *Glycogen is found in a variety of animal tissues, particularly the liver.* **3** INFORMAL someone who behaves in a cruel, violent, or very rude way: *Get away from me, you animal!* **4 a very/completely different animal** something that is very different from the thing you have mentioned: *Communism in North Korea is a very different animal from the Eastern European model.* **5 a political/social animal etc.** INFORMAL someone who is interested in politics, in meeting other people etc. —see also **party animal** (PARTY¹)

animal² adj. [only before noun, no comparative] **1 animal urges/instincts etc.** human feelings, desires etc. that are related to sex, food, and other basic needs **2 animal products/fats/protein etc.** things that are made or come from animals

animal hus·band·ry /ˌ... ˈ.../ n. [U] farming that involves keeping animals and producing milk, meat etc.

animal rights /ˌ... ˈ./ n. [plural] the idea that people should treat animals well, and especially not use them in tests to develop medicines or other products | **animal-rights activists/protesters/groups** etc. (=people or groups who try to stop medical tests etc. involving animals)

an·i·mate¹ /ˈænəˌmeɪt/ v. [T] to give life or energy to something: *Laughter animated his face.*

an·i·mate² /ˈænəmɪt/ adj. FORMAL living: *animate beings* —opposite INANIMATE

an·i·mat·ed /ˈænəˌmeɪtɪd/ adj. **1 an animated cartoon/movie/show etc.** a movie or program made by photographing a series of pictures, clay models etc.

A

or by drawing a series of pictures with a computer **2** showing a lot of interest and energy: *We had a very animated discussion about women's rights.* —**animatedly** *adv.*

an·i·ma·tion /ˌænəˈmeɪʃən/ *n.* **1** [C,U] the process of making animated movies or television programs, or the movie or program itself **2** [U] excitement: *Marco spoke with real passion and animation.*

an·i·ma·tor /ˈænəˌmeɪtɚ/ *n.* [C] someone who makes animated movies or television programs

an·i·ma·tron·ics /ˌænəməˈtrɑnɪks/ *n.* [plural] real-looking moving models of animals or people, used in the entertainment industry —**animatronic** *adj.*

an·i·mism /ˈænəˌmɪzəm/ *n.* [U] a religion in which animals and plants are believed to have spirits —**animist** *adj.* —**animist** *n.* [C]

an·i·mos·i·ty /ˌænəˈmɑsəti/ *n. plural* **animosities** [C,U] strong dislike or hatred; HOSTILITY: [+ **between**] *There is a lot of animosity between Jerry and Frank.*

an·i·mus /ˈænəməs/ *n.* [singular,U] FORMAL strong dislike or hatred; HOSTILITY

an·ise /ˈænɪs/ also **an·i·seed** /ˈænɪsid/ *n.* [U] the strong-tasting seeds of a plant used in alcoholic drinks and in candy, especially LICORICE

An·ka·ra /ˈæŋkərə, ˈɑŋ-/ the capital city of Turkey

ankh /ɑŋk/ *n.* [C] a cross with a long tall circle at the top, used as a SYMBOL of life in ancient Egypt

s w **an·kle** /ˈæŋkəl/ *n.* [C] **1** the joint between your foot and your leg —see picture at BODY[1] **2 ankle socks/ boots** short socks or boots that only come up to your ankle

an·klet /ˈæŋklɪt/ *n.* [C] **1** a ring or BRACELET worn around your ankle **2** a short sock worn by girls or women that only comes up to your ankle

an·nals /ˈænlz/ *n.* [plural] **1 in the annals of sth** in the whole history of something: *No one can compete with Tiepolo in the annals of European painting for his mythological heroes.* **2** used in the titles of official records of events or activities: *the Annals of Internal Medicine*

An·nap·o·lis /əˈnæpəlɪs/ the capital of the U.S. state of Maryland

an·neal /əˈnil/ *v.* [T] TECHNICAL to make metal or glass hard by heating it and then slowly letting it get cold

an·nex[1] /əˈnɛks, ˈænɛks/ *v.* [T] to take control of a country or area next to your own, especially by using force: *Planning Director Jerry Flannery is attempting to annex 1260 acres of vacant land next to the city.* | *The Baltic republics were forcibly annexed by the Soviet Union in 1940.* —**annexation** /ˌænɛkˈseɪʃən/ *n.* [C,U]

an·nex[2] /ˈænɛks, -nɪks/ [C] **1** a separate building that has been added to a larger one **2** FORMAL a part that has been added to the end of a document, report etc.; APPENDIX

an·ni·hi·late /əˈnaɪəˌleɪt/ *v.* [T] **1** to destroy something or someone completely: *Just one of these bombs could annihilate a city the size of New York.* **2** to defeat someone easily and completely in a game, competition, or election: *Tyson annihilated his opponent in the second round.* —**annihilation** /əˌnaɪəˈleɪʃən/ *n.* [U]

an·ni·ver·sa·ry /ˌænəˈvɚsəri/ *n. plural* **anniversaries** [C] a date on which something special or important happened in a previous year: *our twentieth wedding anniversary* | [+ **of**] *A huge parade is held each year on the anniversary of the 1959 revolution.*

An·no Dom·i·ni /ˌænoʊ ˈdɑməni/ A.D.

an·no·tate /ˈænəˌteɪt/ *v.* [T usually passive] to add short notes to a book or piece of writing to explain parts of it: *Gardner wrote an annotated version of "Alice in Wonderland."* —**annotation** /ˌænəˈteɪʃən/ *n.* [C,U]

s w **an·nounce** /əˈnaʊns/ *v.* [T] **1** to officially tell people about a decision or something that will happen: *They announced plans to close 11 factories.* | [**announce**

(that)] *Weaver announced that he would retire in June.* **2 to be announced** used to say that a piece of information will be decided or given at a later time: *The meeting is in January, date and location to be announced.* **3** to give information to people, especially using a LOUDSPEAKER or MICROPHONE in a public place: *A man's voice announced the departure of the L.A. bus.* **4** to introduce a program, person, musical group etc. on television or radio

an·nounce·ment /əˈnaʊnsmənt/ *n.* **1** [C] an important or official statement: *The short written announcement gave no details.* | [+ **about/of/on**] *They've produced several public service announcements about the risks of smoking.* | [**announcement that**] *Beckwith's announcement that he would run for re-election came as a surprise.* | *Dillon made the announcement at a news conference.* **2** the act of telling people that something important is going to happen: *The announcement of the plan provoked demonstrations from the college's students.* **3** [C] a small advertisement or statement in a newspaper | a **wedding/birth/death announcement** *Their wedding announcement was in Sunday's paper.*

an·nounc·er /əˈnaʊnsɚ/ *n.* [C] someone who reads news or introduces people, musical groups etc., especially on television or radio

an·noy /əˈnɔɪ/ *v.* **annoys, annoyed, annoying** [T] to make someone feel slightly angry and unhappy about something: *The neighbor's kid walks across our lawn just to annoy us.* | *Brian talks to me like a child, which really annoys me.*

an·noy·ance /əˈnɔɪəns/ *n.* **1** [U] a feeling of slight anger: *He looked in annoyance at the hostess.* | *The meetings were held in secret, much to the annoyance of some members of Congress.* **2** [C] something that makes you slightly angry: *Smoking is a tremendous annoyance to non-smokers.*

an·noyed /əˈnɔɪd/ *adj.* slightly angry: [+ **at/with**] *I was really annoyed at him that time.* | [+ **about/by**] *Everyone is annoyed by the amount of traffic in the city.* | [**be annoyed (that)**] *I'm annoyed that he didn't show up when he said he would.* | *Rob gets so annoyed if you mix up his CDs.*

an·noy·ing /əˈnɔɪ-ɪŋ/ *adj.* making you feel slightly angry: *Corey is the most annoying little kid I've ever met.* | *Computerized telephone sales calls are really annoying.* —**annoyingly** *adv.*

an·nu·al[1] /ˈænyuəl/ *adj.* **1** happening once a year: *the annual school homecoming dance* **2** based on or calculated over a period of one year: *Her annual income is about $75,000.* —**annually** *adv.*

annual[2] *n.* [C] **1** a plant that lives for one year or season —compare BIENNIAL, PERENNIAL[2] **2** a book, especially for children, that is produced once a year with the same title but different stories, pictures etc. **3** a YEARBOOK

an·nu·al·ize /ˈænyuəˌlaɪz/ *v.* [T] to calculate a number or amount in a way that shows a rate that is based on a period of one year: *The values shown are annualized.* —**annualized** *adj.*

annual meet·ing /ˌ... ˈ../ *n.* [C] a meeting held once a year by a club, business, or organization

an·nu·i·ty /əˈnuəti/ *n. plural* **annuities** [C] a particular amount of money that is paid each year to someone, usually until they die

an·nul /əˈnʌl/ *v.* **annulled, annulling** [T often passive] TECHNICAL to officially end a marriage or legal agreement so that it is considered to have never existed —**annulment** *n.* [C,U]

an·ode /ˈænoʊd/ *n.* [C] TECHNICAL the part of a BATTERY (1) that collects ELECTRONS, often a wire or piece of metal with the sign (+) —compare CATHODE

an·o·dyne[1] /ˈænəˌdaɪn/ *adj.* expressed in a way that is unlikely to offend anyone: *anodyne topics of conversation*

anodyne[2] *n.* [C] **1** TECHNICAL a medicine that reduces pain **2** FORMAL an activity or thing that comforts people

a·noint /əˈnɔɪnt/ *v.* [T] to put oil or water on someone's head or body during a religious ceremony —**anointment** *n.* [C,U]

a·nom·a·lous /əˈnɑmələs/ *adj.* FORMAL a result, event, feature etc. that is anomalous is different from other similar results, events etc. —**anomalously** *adv.*

a·nom·a·ly /əˈnɑməli/ *n. plural* **anomalies** [C,U] something that is noticeable because it is different from what is usual: *Pohnpei is an anomaly – it's a Pacific island without a beach.*

a·non /əˈnɑn/ *adv.* LITERARY soon

anon. the written abbreviation of ANONYMOUS

a·non·ym·i·ty /ˌænəˈnɪmɪti/ *n.* [U] **1** the state of not letting your name be known: *Laws protect the anonymity of the rape victim.* | *One official, who* **spoke on condition of anonymity** (=he would only speak if his name was not published), *said the White House took the threat very seriously.* **2** the state of not showing who is involved in something: *The telephone used to give callers anonymity.* **3** the state of not having any unusual or interesting features: *the drab anonymity of the city*

W **a·non·y·mous** /əˈnɑnəməs/ *adj.* **1** not known by name: *The paper cited two anonymous sources.* | *A member of the office staff, who asked to* **remain anonymous**, *gave us the information.* **2** done, sent, or given by someone who does not want their name to be known: *The college received an anonymous $5 million gift.* | **an anonymous letter/phone call etc.** *Police were led to the scene by an anonymous phone tip.* **3** without any interesting features or qualities: *an anonymous hotel room* —**anonymously** *adv.* —see also ALCOHOLICS ANONYMOUS

a·noph·e·les /əˈnɑfəliz/ *n.* [C] a type of insect, known for spreading MALARIA to humans

an·o·rak /ˈænəˌræk/ *n.* [C] a PARKA

an·o·rex·i·a /ˌænəˈrɛksiə/ also **anorexia ner·vo·sa** /-nəˈvousə/ *n.* [U] a mental illness that makes people, especially young women, stop eating because they believe they are fat and want to be thin

an·o·rex·ic /ˌænəˈrɛksɪk/ *adj.* suffering from or relating to anorexia —**anorexic** *n.* [C]

W **an·oth·er** /əˈnʌðə/ *determiner, pron* **1** used to talk about one more person or thing of the same type: *Can I have another piece of cake?* | *I'll cancel that check and send you another.* | *The tape broke, so I'll have to make another one.* | **[+ of]** *Mary, another of Christine's close friends, was shocked by the news.* | *The failure of the bill was* **yet another** (=the last in a series of) *setback for the Democrats.* | *He's had* **one problem** *after* **another** (=without much time between them) *this year.* **2** a different person or thing, or some other type of person or thing: *They finally moved to another apartment.* | *Greg didn't like that dentist, so he went to another.* | *I'll see you another time.* | *Make sure you leave enough time to drive from one* **appointment** *to another.* | *Math will always be useful at some time* **or another**. | *There are a lot of people who,* **for one reason or another**, *can't have children.* | *They'll try to get the money* **one way or another**. | *You can try it, but whether it will work is* **another thing altogether** (=it is likely that it will not work). **3** in addition to a particular amount, distance, period of time etc.; FURTHER: *She'll be ready to retire in another three years.* | *Another 13 residents were taken to safety by firefighters.* **4** **one another** LITERARY used after a verb to show that two or more people or things do the same thing to each other: *We always call one another during the holidays.* **5** **another Chernobyl/another Babe Ruth etc.** used when talking about a situation or person that reminds you of another famous situation or person, especially because they have extremely good or extremely bad qualities

A·nou·ilh /ɑˈnuiː/**, Jean** /ʒɑn/ (1910–1987) a French writer of plays

W **an·swer**[1] /ˈænsə/ *v.*

1 **reply** **a)** [I,T] to say something to someone as a reply when they have asked you a question, made a suggestion etc.: *The waiters are happy to answer customers' questions.* | *She thought for a moment before answering.* | **[answer (that)]** *He answered that safety was the manager's responsibility.* | **[answer sb]** *I answered him as honestly as I could.* **b)** [T] to deal with someone's question in a satisfactory way:

No one in the city government satisfactorily answered that question.

2 **answer criticism/charges/accusations etc.** to explain why you did something when people are criticizing you: *Robinson appeared in court on Monday to answer the criminal charges against him.*

3 **test** [I,T] to write or say the answer to a question in a test, competition etc.: *Only one person answered all the questions correctly.*

4 **answer the phone/the door/a call** to pick up the telephone when it rings or open the door when someone knocks on it

5 **letter** [T] to send a reply to a letter, advertisement etc.: *Whitmore never answered any of my letters.*

6 **do sth as a reaction** [I,T] to do something as a reaction to criticism or attack: *The army answered by firing into the crowd.*

7 **deal with a problem** [T] to be a way of dealing with or solving a problem: *Officials have made every effort to answer trade concerns.* | *Our transportation system is designed to* **answer the needs** *of the city's commuters.*

8 **answer a description** if someone answers a description, they match that description: *A hiker spotted a man answering the description given by police.*

answer back *phr. v.* [I,T **answer sb ↔ back**] to reply to someone without delay

answer for sth *phr. v.* [T] **1** to explain to people in authority why you did something wrong or why something happened, and be punished if necessary: *The leaders will be made to answer for their actions.* **2** **have a lot to answer for** INFORMAL to be responsible for causing a lot of trouble: *That sister of yours has an awful lot to answer for.* **3** **I can answer for him/her etc.** SPOKEN used to say that you know what someone would say if they were with you: *Well, I can't answer for Pete.*

answer to sb/sth *phr. v.* [T] **1** to give an explanation to someone or be responsible to someone, especially about something that you have done wrong: *We need small schools that can answer to the community.* **2** **answer to the name of sth** to be called a particular name: *He's 6 foot 5, but he answers to the name of Shorty.*

USAGE NOTE: ANSWER

WORD CHOICE: answer, reply, respond, give an answer, get back to

Answer is the usual verb you use to talk about answering questions. **Reply** is used especially when you mention the actual words that were said: *I was so nervous I couldn't reply/answer.* | *"Absolutely not," Jake replied.* **Respond** is more formal and less common and often suggests that a criticism is being replied to: *The management has not yet responded to the negative reports in the press.* If you give someone a piece of information they have asked for, such as a decision you have made, you **give them an answer**: *If we offer you the job, when could you give us an answer?* If you think you can answer someone later but not right away, you say you will **get back to them**: *I'll have to get back to you later on that.*

GRAMMAR

You **answer** (*v.*) a question, advertisement etc. (NOT *to/ at it*). Normally you **answer** a person too. If you **answer to** someone, they are the person directly responsible for you in an organization, at work etc., and you have to explain to them if anything goes wrong or if you are not doing something correctly. You give the **answer** (*n.*) **to** a question or criticism (NOT *of it*). You get an **answer** (*n.*) **from** someone (NOT *of them*).

---

answer[2] *n.*

S W

1 **reply** [C,U] something you say when you reply to a question that someone has asked you: *What was her answer?* | *There was a question and answer period after the lecture.* | *No one seemed able to* **give an answer** *on how the law would affect employers.* | *I told you before,* **the answer is no**! | **In answer to**

A

the question, most employees said they were satisfied with their jobs.
2 [test/competition etc.] [C] something that you write or say in reply to a question in a test, competition etc.: *Score one point for each correct answer.*
3 [invitation/letter etc.] [C] a written reply to a letter, invitation, advertisement etc.: *Answers to the letters are as varied as the children who wrote them.*
4 [problem] [C] a way of dealing with a problem: *The obvious answer is to keep poisonous plants out of children's reach.* | [be the answer to sth] *This may not be the answer to the problems of our health-care system.*
5 [call/visit] [singular, usually in questions and negatives] a reply when you telephone someone, knock on their door etc.: *I called him but there was no answer and he hasn't phoned me back.*
6 sb's answer to sth someone or something that is considered to be just as good as a more famous person or thing: *The Space Needle is Seattle's answer to the Eiffel Tower.* —see Usage Note at ANSWER¹

an·swer·a·ble /ˈænsərəbəl/ *adj.* **1 be answerable** to have to explain your actions to someone in authority: [(to sb) for sth] *The agency is answerable to the governor.* **2** a question that is answerable can be answered

s w **an·swer·ing ma·chine** /ˈ... .ˌ./ *n.* [C] a machine
3 that records your telephone calls when you cannot answer them

answering serv·ice /ˈ... ˌ../ *n.* [C] a business that can receive your telephone calls when you are not able to do it yourself

ant /ænt/ *n.* [C] **1** a small insect that lives in large groups —see picture at INSECT **2 have ants in your pants** SPOKEN, HUMOROUS to be so excited or full of energy that you stay still

-ant /ənt/ *suffix* **1** [in nouns] someone or something that does something: *an assistant* (=someone who helps someone else) | *a disinfectant* (=substance that kills GERMS) **2** [in adjectives] having a particular quality: *pleasant* (=pleasing to someone) | *expectant* (=expecting someone) —see also -ENT

an·tac·id /ˌæntˈæsɪd/ *n.* [C] a substance that gets rid of the burning feeling in your stomach when you have eaten too much, drunk too much alcohol etc.

an·tag·o·nism /ænˈtægəˌnɪzəm/ *n.* [U] **1** hatred between people or groups of people: [+ between/to/toward] *The project aims to lessen the antagonism between racial groups.* **2** opposition to an idea, plan etc.: [+ to/toward] *There has been a lot of antagonism toward the new bridge building project.*

an·tag·o·nist /ænˈtægəˌnɪst/ *n.* [C] your opponent in a competition, battle, argument etc. —compare PROTAGONIST

an·tag·o·nis·tic /ænˌtægəˈnɪstɪk/ **1** showing opposition to or hatred for an idea or group: *During the Cold War, the two countries were fiercely antagonistic.* | [+ toward] *The public is often antagonistic toward politicians.* **2** wanting to argue or disagree; unfriendly: *Michaels was described by witnesses as being drunk and antagonistic.* —**antagonistically** /-kli/ *adv.*

an·tag·o·nize /ænˈtægəˌnaɪz/ *v.* [T] to make someone feel angry with you by doing something that they do not like: *The White House is reluctant to antagonize Beijing.*

An·ta·na·na·ri·vo /ˌæntəˌnænəˈrivoʊ/ the capital city of Madagascar

Ant·arc·tic /æntˈɑrktɪk, æntˈɑrtɪk/ *n.* **the Antarctic** the very cold most southern part of the world

Ant·arc·ti·ca /æntˈɑrktɪkə, ænˈɑrtɪkə/ **the** CONTINENT which is the most southern area of land on the Earth

Antarctic Cir·cle /.ˌ.. '../ *n.* **the Antarctic Circle** an imaginary line drawn around the world at a particular distance from its most southern point (the South Pole) —compare ARCTIC CIRCLE

an·te¹ /ˈænti/ *n.* **up/raise the ante** to increase your demands or try to get more things from a situation,

even though this involves more risks: *Sanctions upped the ante considerably in the Middle East crisis.* —see also PENNY ANTE

ante² *v.*
ante up *phr. v.* **anted** or **anteed, anteing** [I,T **ante up** sth] to pay an amount of money, especially in a game of chance: *Small businesses that want to expand must ante up large legal fees.*

ante- /ænti/ *prefix* coming or happening before something: *to antedate* (=exist before something else) | *the antebellum South* (=before the Civil War) —compare POST-, PRE-

ant·eat·er /ˈæntitɚ/ *n.* [C] an animal that has a very long nose and eats small insects

an·te·bel·lum /ˌæntɪˈbɛləm/ *adj.* existing before a war, especially the American Civil War: *antebellum Southern architecture*

an·te·ce·dent /ˌæntɪˈsidnt/ *n.* **1** [C] FORMAL an event, organization, or thing that is similar to the one you have mentioned, but that existed earlier: *The Byrds are seen as an antecedent of bands like R.E.M.* **2 antecedents** [plural] FORMAL the people in your family who lived a long time ago; ANCESTORS **3** [C] TECHNICAL a word, phrase, or sentence that is represented by another word, for example a PRONOUN —**antecedent** *adj.*

an·te·cham·ber /ˈæntɪˌtʃeɪmbɚ/ *n.* [C] a small room connected to a larger room

an·te·date /ˈæntɪˌdeɪt, ˌæntɪˈdeɪt/ *v.* [T] FORMAL to come from an earlier time in history than something else: *The economic troubles antedate the current administration.* —compare BACKDATE, POSTDATE, PREDATE

an·te·di·lu·vi·an /ˌæntɪdəˈluviən/ *adj.* FORMAL OR HUMOROUS very old-fashioned; OUTDATED: *antediluvian attitudes toward the disabled*

an·te·lope /ˈæntəlˌoʊp/ *n.* [C] an animal with long horns that can run very fast and is very graceful

an·te me·rid·i·em /ˌænti məˈrɪdiəm/ A.M.

an·ten·na /ænˈtɛnə/ *n.* [C] **1** *plural* **antennas** a piece of equipment on a television, car, roof etc. for receiving or sending television or radio signals —see pictures on pages 423 and 427 **2** *plural* **antennae** one of two long thin parts on an insect's head, that it uses to feel things —see picture at INSECT

an·te·ri·or /ænˈtɪriɚ/ *adj.* [no comparative] **1** TECHNICAL at or toward the front —opposite POSTERIOR² **2** FORMAL happening or existing before something else

an·te·room /ˈæntɪˌrum/ *n.* [C] a small room that is connected to a larger room, especially a small room where people wait to go into the larger room

an·them /ˈænθəm/ *n.* [C] **1** a formal or religious song: *the Olympic anthem* —see also NATIONAL ANTHEM **2** a song that a particular group of people considers to be very important: *"Surf City" was more or less the anthem of the surfer boys and girls of the '60s.*

an·ther /ˈænθɚ/ *n.* [C] TECHNICAL the part of a male flower that contains POLLEN

ant·hill /ˈæntˌhɪl/ *n.* [C] a place where ANTS live

an·thol·o·gy /ænˈθɑlədʒi/ *n. plural* **anthologies** [C] a set of stories, poems, songs etc. by different people, collected together in one book: *an anthology of American literature* —**anthologist** *n.* [C]

An·tho·ny /ˈænθəni/, **Su·san B.** /ˈsuzən bi/ (1820–1906) a U.S. woman who helped women get the right to vote

an·thra·cite /ˈænθrəˌsaɪt/ *n.* [U] a very hard type of coal that burns slowly and produces a lot of heat

an·thrax /ˈænθræks/ *n.* [U] a serious disease of cattle and sheep, that also can cause death in people

anthropo- /ænθrəpə, -poʊ/ *prefix* TECHNICAL like a human, or relating to humans: *anthropomorphic* (=having a human form or human qualities) | *anthropologist* (=someone who studies humans and their societies)

an·thro·poid /ˈænθrəˌpɔɪd/ *adj.* an anthropoid animal is very much like a human —**anthropoid** *n.* [C]

an·thro·pol·o·gy /ˌænθrəˈpɑlədʒi/ *n.* [U] the scientific

study of people, their societies, CULTURES etc.
—**anthropologist** n. [U] —**anthropological** /ˌænθrə-pəˈlɑdʒɪkəl/ adj. —compare ETHNOLOGY, SOCIOLOGY

an·thro·po·mor·phism /ˌænθrəpəˈmɔrfɪzəm/ n.
[U] **1** the belief that animals or objects have the same feelings and qualities as humans **2** TECHNICAL the belief that God can appear in a human or animal form —**anthropomorphic** adj.

anti- /ˈænti, ˈæntaɪ, ˈænti/ prefix **1** opposed to something; AGAINST: antinuclear (=opposing the use of atomic weapons and power) | anti-American feelings **2** the opposite of something: an anticlimax (=unexciting ending instead of the CLIMAX you expect) **3** acting to prevent something: antifreeze (=liquid that prevents an engine from freezing) | an antibiotic (=medicine that stops an infection) —compare ANTE-, PRO-

an·ti·air·craft /ˌæntiˈɛrkræft/ adj. [only before noun] antiaircraft weapons are used against enemy aircraft: antiaircraft missiles

an·ti·bac·ter·i·al /ˌæntibækˈtɪriəl, ˌæntaɪ-/ adj. stopping the growth of or killing BACTERIA: an antibacterial soap

an·ti·bal·lis·tic mis·sile /ˌæntibəlɪstɪk ˈmɪsəl, ˌæntaɪ-/ abbreviation **ABM** n. [C] a MISSILE that is used to destroy a BALLISTIC MISSILE while it is still in the air

an·ti·bi·ot·ic /ˌæntibaɪˈɑtɪk◂, ˌæntaɪ-/ n. [C usually plural] a drug that is used to kill BACTERIA and cure infections

an·ti·bod·y /ˈæntiˌbɑdi/ n. plural **antibodies** [C] a substance produced by your body to fight disease

an·ti·christ /ˈæntiˌkraɪst, ˈæntaɪ-/ n. **the Antichrist** also **the antichrist** the great enemy of Jesus Christ who represents the power of evil and is expected to appear just before the end of the world

W
3
an·tic·i·pate /ænˈtɪsəˌpeɪt/ v. [T] **1** to expect an event or situation to happen, and do something to prepare for it: Schools anticipate an increase in student test scores. | Sales are better than anticipated. | [anticipate that] I would anticipate that the poor harvest will increase the chance of famine. **2** to be ready for a question, request, need etc. before it happens: A skilled waiter can anticipate a customer's needs. **3** to think about something that is going to happen, especially something pleasant: The crowd sat quietly, anticipating the company's performance of "H.M.S. Pinafore." **4** to do something before someone else: In many ways, these comedies anticipated Romantic drama. **5** FORMAL to use or consider something before you should —**anticipatory** /ænˈtɪsəpəˌtɔri/ adj.

an·tic·i·pa·tion /ænˌtɪsəˈpeɪʃən/ n. [U] **1** a feeling of excitement because something good or fun is going to happen: The crowd's mood was one of anticipation. **2 do sth in anticipation of sth** to do something because you expect something to happen. Refineries are holding back supplies **in anticipation** of higher prices next year.

an·ti·cler·i·cal /ˌæntiˈklɛrɪkəl, ˌæntaɪ-/ adj. being opposed to priests having any political power or influence —**anticlericalism** n. [U]

an·ti·cli·max /ˌæntiˈklaɪmæks/ n. [C,U] a situation or event that is not as exciting as you had expected, often because it happens after something that was more exciting: After all the hype, the actual concert was something of an anticlimax.

an·tics /ˈæntɪks/ n. [plural] behavior that seems strange, funny, silly, or annoying: Three skydivers jumped off a skyscraper, but most skydivers disapprove of such antics.

an·ti·cy·clone /ˌæntiˈsaɪkloʊn/ n. [C] TECHNICAL an area of high air pressure that causes calm weather in the place it is moving over —see also CYCLONE

an·ti·de·pres·sant /ˌæntidɪˈprɛsənt, ˌæntaɪ-/ n. [C] a drug used to treat DEPRESSION (=a mental illness that makes people very unhappy)

an·ti·dote /ˈæntiˌdoʊt/ n. [C] **1** a substance that stops the effects of a poison: a nerve gas antidote | [+ to/for] an antidote for the venom of black widow spiders **2** something that makes a bad situation

better: [+ to] Shows such as "Sesame Street" are an antidote to the violence and commercialism of television.

An·tie·tam /ænˈtiṭəm/ a place in the U.S. state of Maryland where a battle was fought in the American Civil War

an·ti·freeze /ˈæntiˌfriz/ n. [U] a substance that is put in the water in car engines to stop it from freezing

an·ti·gen /ˈæntɪdʒən/ n. [C] TECHNICAL a substance that makes the body produce antibodies (ANTIBODY)

An·ti·gua and Bar·bu·da /ænˈtigə, -gwə ənd barˈbudə/ a country that consists of the islands of Antigua, Barbuda, and Redonda in the Caribbean Sea —**Antiguan** n., adj.

an·ti·her·o /ˈæntiˌhɪroʊ, ˈæntaɪ-/ n. [C] a main character in a book, play, or movie who is an ordinary or bad person and lacks the qualities that you expect a HERO to have

an·ti·his·ta·mine /ˌæntiˈhɪstəmin, -mɪn/ n. [C] a drug that is used to treat an ALLERGY (=a bad reaction to particular foods, substances etc.)

An·til·les, the /ænˈtɪliz/ the islands of the Caribbean Sea that form a curving line starting with Cuba near the east coast of Mexico and ending with Trinidad near the north coast of South America

anti-lock brakes /ˌ... ˈ./ n. [plural] an anti-lock braking system

anti-lock brak·ing sys·tem /ˌ... ˈ. ˌ../ n. [C] abbreviation **ABS** [U] a piece of equipment that makes a vehicle easier to control when you have to stop very suddenly

an·ti·ma·cas·sar /ˌæntiməˈkæsɚ/ n. [C] a piece of decorated cloth that is put on the back of a chair to protect it

an·ti·mat·ter /ˈæntiˌmætɚ, ˈæntaɪ-/ n. [U] a form of MATTER (=substance which the things in the universe are made of) consisting of antiparticles

an·ti·par·ti·cle /ˈæntiˌpɑrtɪkəl, ˈæntaɪ-/ n. [C] a very small part of an atom that has the opposite electrical charge to the one usually found in atoms

an·ti·pas·to /ˌæntiˈpɑstoʊ, ˌɑn-/ n. [U] an Italian dish consisting of cold food that you eat before the main part of a meal

an·ti·pa·thet·ic /ˌæntipəˈθɛtɪk/ adj. [+ to] FORMAL having a very strong feeling of disliking or opposing someone or something

an·tip·a·thy /ænˈtɪpəθi/ n. [U] a feeling of strong dislike or opposition toward someone or something: [+ to/toward] A survey showed a high level of antipathy toward lawyers.

an·ti·per·son·nel /ˌæntipɚsənˈɛl/ adj. [only before noun] an antipersonnel weapon is designed to hurt people rather than damage buildings, vehicles etc.

an·ti·per·spi·rant /ˌæntipɚˈspɚənt/ n. [U] a substance that prevents you from SWEATing, especially under your arms

An·tip·o·des /ænˈtɪpədiz/ n. **the Antipodes** Australia and New Zealand —**Antipodean** /ænˌtɪpəˈdiən/ adj.

an·ti·quar·i·an /ˌæntiˈkwɛriən/ adj. [only before noun] an antiquarian store sells old valuable things such as books

an·ti·quat·ed /ˈæntiˌkweɪṭɪd/ adj. old-fashioned and not suitable for modern needs or conditions; OUTDATED: antiquated laws

an·tique¹ /ænˈtik/ adj. **1** antique furniture, jewelry etc. is old and often valuable: an antique rosewood desk **2** LITERARY connected with ancient times, especially ancient Rome or Greece

antique² n. [C] a piece of furniture, jewelry etc. that was made a long time ago and is therefore valuable: The palace is full of priceless antiques. | an antiques dealer

an·tiq·ui·ty /ænˈtɪkwəṭi/ n. plural **antiquities 1** [U] ancient times: The common household fork was nearly unknown in antiquity. **2** [U] the fact or condition of being very old: the antiquity of Chinese culture **3** [C usually plural] a building or object

A

made in ancient times: *The museum contains Soane's personal collection of art and antiquities.*

an·ti-Sem·ite /ˌænti'sɛmaɪt, ˌæntaɪ-/ *n.* [C] someone who hates Jewish people —**anti-Semitic** /ˌæntisə'mɪtɪk, ˌæntaɪ-/ *adj.*

an·ti-Sem·i·tism /ˌænti'sɛməˌtɪzəm, ˌæntaɪ-/ *n.* [U] hatred of Jewish people

an·ti·sep·tic¹ /ˌæntə'sɛptɪk/ *n.* [C] a chemical substance that kills GERMS and helps stop wounds from becoming infected

antiseptic² *adj.* **1** helping to prevent infection: *antiseptic cream* **2** lacking emotion, interest, or excitement: *the antiseptic language of science*

an·ti·so·cial /ˌænti'soʊʃəl, ˌæntaɪ-/ *adj.* **1** violent and not behaving according to the normal moral rules of society: *Counselors confirmed that Steven had been showing signs of antisocial behavior.* **2** unwilling to meet people and talk to them, especially in a way that seems unfriendly or impolite: *Kip had always been shy, even antisocial.* **3** showing a lack of concern for other people: *Smoking cigarettes in public is increasingly considered antisocial.*

an·ti·tank /ˌænti'tæŋk, ˌæntaɪ-/ *adj.* [only before noun] an antitank weapon is designed to destroy enemy TANKS

an·tith·e·sis /æn'tɪθəsɪs/ *n.* **the antithesis of sth** FORMAL the exact opposite of something, or something that is completely different from something else: *Her style of writing is the antithesis of Dickens'.*

an·ti·thet·i·cal /ˌæntə'θɛtɪkəl/ *adj.* FORMAL completely different from something, and often showing or resulting from opposing ideas, beliefs etc.: [+ to] *The new law is clearly antithetical to the basic principles of free speech.*

an·ti·tox·in /ˌænti'tɑksɪn/ *n.* a substance produced by your body or put in a medicine to stop the effects of a poison

an·ti·trust /ˌænti'trʌst, ˌæntaɪ-/ *adj.* [only before noun] TECHNICAL intended to prevent companies from unfairly controlling prices: *antitrust laws*

ant·ler /'æntˈlɚ/ *n.* [C usually plural] one of the two horns of a male DEER, MOOSE etc. —see picture at MOOSE

Antoinette, Marie —see MARIE ANTOINETTE

an·to·nym /'æntəˌnɪm/ *n.* [C] a word that means the opposite of another word. For example, "good" is the antonym of "bad." —**antonymous** /æn'tɑnəməs/ *adj.* TECHNICAL —compare SYNONYM

ant·sy /'æntsi/ *adj.* INFORMAL nervous and unable to keep still, because you want something to happen

a·nus /'eɪnəs/ *n.* [C usually singular] the hole in your body through which solid waste leaves your BOWELS —see picture at DIGESTIVE SYSTEM

an·vil /'ænvɪl/ *n.* [C] a heavy iron block on which pieces of metal are shaped using a hammer

s w **anx·i·e·ty** /æŋ'zaɪəti/ *n. plural* **anxieties 1** [C,U] the
▢ feeling of being very worried about something that
3 may happen or may have happened, so that you think about it all the time: [+ about/over] *People's anxiety about the economy is increasing.* | *Tom often has anxiety attacks.* **2** [C] something that makes you worry: *the anxieties of parenthood* **3** [U] a feeling of wanting to do something very much, but being worried that you will not succeed: [**anxiety to do sth**] *In her anxiety to help, Laurie tripped and broke several wine glasses.*

anx·ious /'æŋkʃəs, 'æŋʃəs/ *adj.* **1** very worried about something that may happen or may have happened, so that you think about it all the time: *Gail was feeling anxious and depressed.* | *anxious employees* | [+ **about**] *Most children feel anxious about returning to school.* **2** an anxious time or situation is one in which you feel nervous or worried: *There were a few anxious moments for Morgan near the end of the match.* **3** feeling strongly that you want to do something or want something to

happen: [**anxious to do sth**] *Both countries are anxious to establish a closer relationship to the West.* —see Usage Note at NERVOUS —**anxiously** *adv.*: *I waited anxiously by the phone.*

an·y¹ /'ɛni/ *quantifier, pron.* **1** [with negatives and in s v
questions] some or even the smallest amount: *Few of* ▢
the students had any knowledge of classical music. | *I* 1
didn't pay any attention to what he said. | *She promised not to take any chances.* | *He had no friends and didn't deserve any.* | [+ **of**] *I don't understand what any of this stuff means.* | *I tried, but it wasn't any use* (=it was not successful). | *I don't think there will be more than a dozen left, if any* (=it is likely that there will be none left at all). | *Brad was not in any way upset by his wife's decision.* | *If I can help you in any way, let me know.* **2** used to say that it does not matter which person or thing you choose from a group: *Any student caught cheating will be suspended.* | *There are bad things about any job.* | *Before you sign any written agreement, read it over carefully.* | *These tiles are an ideal choice for any bathroom.* | [+ **of**] *Any of those will work okay.* | *Do any of you remember?* | *Are there any other comments?* **3** as much as possible; all: *We'll take any help we can get.* **4 in any case** also **at any rate** no matter what may happen; at least: *It wasn't a complete failure. At any rate, I learned something.* **5 just any** used to refer to something that is ordinary and not special: *You can't wear just any old clothes – you have to dress up.*

any² *adv.* [with negatives and in questions] **1** [with s
comparatives] used especially in negative statements ▢
to mean in the least; at all: *I don't see how things* 1
could get any worse. | *I can't walk any farther.* | *David could not stand it any longer.* | *Is Peggy feeling any better today?* **2** SPOKEN used to mean "at all" at the end of a sentence: *We tried talking to him, but that didn't help any.*

an·y·bod·y /'ɛniˌbɑdi, -ˌbʌdi, -bədi/ *pron.* INFORMAL s
ANYONE: *Is anybody home?* | *I don't think anybody's* ▢
going to come. 1

an·y·hoo /'ɛniˌhu/ *adv.* [sentence adverb] SPOKEN, NONSTANDARD used in order to continue a story, change the subject of a conversation, or finish saying something without all the details; ANYHOW

an·y·how /'ɛniˌhaʊ/ *adv.* [sentence adverb] INFORMAL: s
see ANYWAY: *Well, that's what Jeb told me anyhow.* | ▢
Anyhow, we have plenty of time to plan ahead. 3

an·y·more /ˌɛni'mɔr/ *adv.* **not...anymore** used to say s
that something does not happen or is not true now, ▢
although it used to happen or be true in the past; no 1
longer: *Nick doesn't live here anymore.* | *I don't want to talk to you anymore.*

an·y·one /'ɛniˌwʌn, -wən/ *pron.* **1** any person in a s
group or in the world, when it is not important to ▢
say exactly who: *Anyone can learn to swim in just a* 1
few lessons. | *Why would anyone want to do that?* | *Anyone foolish enough to believe in horoscopes needs a brain transplant.* | *Anyone else* (=any other person) *would have been embarrassed.* **2** [with negatives and in questions] a person or people: *Is anyone home?* | *If anyone sees Lisa, tell her to call me.* | *Is anyone new coming to tonight's meeting?* | *Do you know anyone else* (=a different person) *who wants a ticket?* —see also EVERYONE, SOMEONE¹

an·y·place /'ɛniˌpleɪs/ *adv.* INFORMAL anywhere: *Just set that down anyplace.* | *We didn't have anyplace else to go.*

an·y·thing /'ɛniˌθɪŋ/ *pron.* **1** any thing, event, situa- s
tion etc., when it does not matter exactly which: *If* ▢
you believe that, you'll believe anything! | *The cat will* 1
eat anything. | *Ron offered to hire investigators and do anything else* (=any different thing) *to help police find the killer.* **2** [with negatives and in questions or statements expressing possibility] nothing, or something: *You can't believe anything Kathy says.* | *Do you need anything from the store?* | *Have you heard anything about their new album?* | *Don't do anything stupid.* | [**anything to say/do etc.**] *It was a great resort, but there wasn't really anything to do in the evening.* | *Would you like anything else* (=any other thing) *to eat?* **3 anything but (clear/happy etc.)**

used to emphasize that someone or something is not clear, happy etc.: *The bridge is anything but safe.* | *Everyone said Troy was difficult to talk to, but when I met him he was anything but.* **4 ...or anything** SPOKEN or something that is similar: *Do you want a Coke or anything?* | *It wasn't like we were going steady or anything.* **5 anything like sb/sth** INFORMAL similar in any way to something or someone else: *Does Brenda look anything like her mother?* **6 not anything like/near sth** INFORMAL used to emphasize that someone or something is not in a particular condition or state: *We don't have anything like enough money to buy a new car.* **7 anything goes** used to say that anything is possible or acceptable: *Don't worry about what to wear – anything goes at Ben's parties.* **8 for anything** INFORMAL if you will not do something for anything, you will definitely not do it: *After what happened last time, I wouldn't work for them again for anything.* **9 like anything** SPOKEN if you do something like anything, you do it a lot or to a great degree: *Tom only left last week and I already miss him like anything.*

an·y·time /ˈɛniˌtaɪm/ *adv.* at any time: *Call me anytime – I'm always home.* | *The project won't be completed anytime soon.* | *They should arrive anytime between noon and 3 p.m.*

an·y·way /ˈɛniˌweɪ/ *adv.* [sentence adverb] **1** used to say that someone does something or that something happens in spite of something else: *He said he didn't know much about computers, but that he'd try and help us anyway.* | *It's just a cold, but you should see the doctor anyway.* **2** SPOKEN used in order to continue a story or change the subject of a conversation: *Anyway, what was I saying?* | *I think she's around my age, but anyway, she's pregnant.* | *Anyway, how about getting some lunch?* **3** SPOKEN used when you want to finish saying something or continue without all the details: *Anyway, I guess I'd better go now.* | *Anyway, after three months she made a full recovery.* **4** SPOKEN used when you are saying something that supports, limits, or adds information to what you have just said: *Sam didn't get the job, but he's not worried because it didn't pay well anyway.* | *Thanks for offering, anyway.* | *Hardly anyone's going to read it anyway.* **5** SPOKEN used in order to find out the real reason for something or what the real situation is: *So anyway, what were you doing in the park at two in the morning?* | *What is that thing for, anyway?*

an·y·ways /ˈɛniˌweɪz/ *adv.* [sentence adverb] SPOKEN, NONSTANDARD anyway

an·y·where /ˈɛniˌwɛr/ *adv.* **1** in or to any place, when it does not matter exactly where: *Sit anywhere – there are plenty of seats.* | *Tropical fruit used to be hard to find, but now you can buy it anywhere.* | [+ in] *It only costs $170 to fly anywhere in the U.S., if you buy your tickets this month.* | *Anywhere else* (=in or to a different place) *you'd have to pay airport tax, but not when you visit this Pacific island.* **2** [with negatives and in questions or statements expressing possibility] somewhere or nowhere: *I can't find my keys anywhere.* | *Do they need anywhere to stay for the night?* | *Did you go anywhere exciting on vacation this year?* | *These pictures are great – have you been anywhere else* (=any other place) *in Mexico?* **3 not anywhere near sth/sb** SPOKEN **a)** used to emphasize that someone or something is not near to another person or thing: *My car wasn't anywhere near yours. I couldn't have hit you.* **b)** used to emphasize that someone or something is not in a particular condition or state: *The money won't come anywhere near solving the school district's problems.* **4 not get anywhere** to not make any progress: *I'm trying to set up a meeting, but I don't seem to be getting anywhere.* **5 anywhere between/from one and ten etc.** used to mean any age, number, amount etc. between the numbers mentioned, when it is difficult to know exactly which age, number etc.: *She was one of those women who could be anywhere between forty-five and sixty years of age.* **6 it won't get you anywhere** SPOKEN used to tell someone that they will not be able to change a situation: *You can try writing to complain, but I don't think it will get you anywhere.*

A-OK /ˌeɪ ouˈkeɪ/ *adj.* INFORMAL in very good condition: *George had a physical six months ago, and he was A-OK.* —**A-OK** *adv.*

a·or·ta /eɪˈɔrtə/ *n.* [C] the largest ARTERY (=tube for carrying blood) in the body, taking blood from the heart

AP 1 TRADEMARK the abbreviation of ADVANCED PLACEMENT **2** the abbreviation of ASSOCIATED PRESS

a·pace /əˈpeɪs/ *adv.* FORMAL quickly | **grow/continue etc. apace** *Overall activity in the construction sector continues to grow apace.*

A·pach·e /əˈpætʃi/ a Native American tribe from the western region of the U.S. —**Apache** *adj.*

a·part /əˈpɑrt/ *adj., adv.*
1 *distance* if things are apart, they have an amount of space between them: *The two towns are fifteen miles apart.* | [+ from] *Families may be forced to sit apart from each other.*
2 *time* **two hours/six weeks etc. apart** if things are a particular time apart, they have that much time between them: *Our birthdays are only two days apart.* | *Carol's two daughters are three years apart* (=one was born three years after the other).
3 *separate* **a)** if you take or pull something apart, or something comes or falls apart, it is separated into many different parts or pieces: *The mechanics took the engine apart.* | *The upholstery had been ripped apart.* **b)** if you keep, pull, force etc. two things or people apart, you separate them: *Soldiers forced many families apart in the refugee camps.* | *We try to keep the cats apart as much as possible because they fight.*
4 *condition* if something is coming apart, falling apart etc., it is in a very bad condition: *My purse is starting to come apart.* | *The old house is falling apart.*
5 apart from sb/sth a) except for; not including: *Apart from a couple of spelling mistakes, this looks fine.* **b)** in addition to; besides: *Apart from being used as a school, the building is used for weddings, parties, and meetings*
6 *not with sb else* in a different place from someone else: *The twins were adopted and raised apart.* | *They got back together after two years apart.*
7 *country/group* if something such as a country or group comes apart, it stops being whole or stops having a single organization: *Civil war has ripped the country apart.*
8 grow/drift apart if people or groups grow apart, their relationship slowly ends: *I think Dan and Tina just grew apart.*
9 be worlds/poles apart if people, beliefs, or ideas are worlds or poles apart, they are completely different from each other
10 quite apart from sth FORMAL without even considering something; completely separately from something: *Quite apart from the stealth technology, the B-2 bomber's longer range makes it a more fearsome weapon.*
11 a sth apart FORMAL used to say that something is different in some way from other things of the same type: *We hope to find someone who will preserve the land as open space, a place apart.* —see also **fall apart** (FALL¹), **pull apart** (PULL¹), **set sb/sth apart** (SET¹), **take sb/sth apart** (TAKE¹), **tear sb/sth apart** (TEAR²)

a·part·heid /əˈpɑrtaɪt, -teɪt, -taɪd/ *n.* [U] **1** the former South African political and social system in which only white people had full political rights and people of other races, especially black people, were forced to go to separate schools, live in separate areas etc. **2** a situation in which people of different races and economic groups live in separate areas, do not have equal rights etc.: *The state could face social apartheid if minority students do not have access to higher education.*

a·part·ment /əˈpɑrtmənt/ *n.* [C] **1** a set of rooms within a larger building, usually on one level, where someone lives: *a one-bedroom apartment* **2** [usually plural] a large room with expensive furniture, decorations etc., used especially by an important person such as a president, prince etc.: *the presidential apartments*

a·part·ment build·ing /.'.. ,../ also **apartment house** /.'.. ,./ *n.* [C] a large building containing many apartments

a·part·ment com·plex /.'.. ,../ *n.* [C] a group of apartment buildings built at the same time in the same area —see picture on page 423

ap·a·thet·ic /ˌæpə'θɛtɪk◂/ *adj.* not excited and not caring about something, or not interested in anything and unwilling to make an effort to change and improve things: *Most people were just too apathetic to go out and vote.* —**apathetically** /-kli/ *adv.*

ap·a·thy /'æpəθi/ *n.* [U] the feeling of not being interested or not caring, either about a particular thing or about life: *Authoritarian management often leads to apathy among employees.*

ape[1] /eɪp/ *n.* [C] **1** a large monkey without a tail, or with a very short tail, such as a GORILLA or a CHIMPANZEE **2 go ape** SLANG to suddenly become very angry or excited: *Joe went ape when he found out.* **3** OLD-FASHIONED a man who behaves in a stupid or annoying way

ape[2] *v.* [T] to copy someone's behavior, especially in a silly way or because you cannot think of an original way to behave yourself

Ap·en·nines, the /'æpəˌnaɪnz/ a RANGE of mountains down the middle of Italy, from the northwest to the south

a·per·i·tif, apéritif /əˌpɛrə'tif, ɑ-/ *n.* [C] an alcoholic drink that is drunk before a meal

ap·er·ture /'æpətʃə/ *n.* [C] **1** the hole at the front of a camera or TELESCOPE, which can be changed to let more or less light in **2** TECHNICAL a small hole or space in something which is used for a particular purpose: *The box has 10 tiny apertures through which viewers can see 3-D images.*

ape·shit /'eɪpˌʃɪt/ *adj.* **go apeshit** VULGAR, SLANG to suddenly become very angry or excited

a·pex /'eɪpɛks/ *n.* [C] **1** TECHNICAL the top or highest part of something **2** FORMAL the most successful part: [+ of] *the apex of his career*

a·phid /'eɪfɪd/ *n.* [C] a type of very small insect that drinks the juices of plants

aph·o·rism /'æfəˌrɪzəm/ *n.* [C] a short wise phrase —**aphoristic** /ˌæfə'rɪstɪk◂/ *adj.*

aph·ro·dis·i·ac /ˌæfrə'dizi,æk, -'dɪ-/ *n.* [C] a food, drink, or drug that makes you want to have sex —**aphrodisiac** *adj.*: *The fruit is said to have aphrodisiac properties.*

Aph·ro·di·te /ˌæfrə'daɪti/ in Greek MYTHOLOGY, the goddess of love and beauty

A·pi·a /ə'piə/ the capital city of Western Samoa

a·pi·ar·y /'eɪpiˌɛri/ *n. plural* **apiaries** [C] TECHNICAL a place where BEES are kept

a·piece /ə'pis/ *adv.* [only after number or noun] costing or having a particular amount each: *Oranges are 20 cents apiece.* | *I bought a dozen cookies, so you can take three apiece.*

a·plen·ty /ə'plɛnti/ *adj.* [only after noun] OLD USE in large amounts or numbers, especially more than you need: *There was food aplenty.*

a·plomb /ə'plɑm, ə'plʌm/ *n.* [U] **with aplomb** in a confident and skillful way, especially when you have to deal with difficult problems or a difficult situation: *Morgan handled the media attention with aplomb.*

APO the abbreviation of "Army Post Office," used in writing addresses to people in the military

a·po·ca·lypse /ə'pɑkəˌlɪps/ *n.* [C] **1 the apocalypse** the destruction and end of the world **2** a dangerous, frightening, and very serious situation causing death, harm, or destruction: *Several leading scientists are predicting an environmental apocalypse.*

a·poc·a·lyp·tic /əˌpɑkə'lɪptɪk/ *adj.* **1** warning people about terrible events that will happen in the future: *an apocalyptic vision of the future* **2** relating to the final destruction and end of the world

a·poc·ry·phal /ə'pɑkrəfəl/ *adj.* an apocryphal story about a famous person or event is well known but probably not true

ap·o·gee /'æpədʒi/ *n.* [C] **1** FORMAL the most successful part of something: [+ of] *the apogee of his political career* **2** TECHNICAL the point where an object traveling through space is farthest from the Earth

a·po·lit·i·cal /ˌeɪpə'lɪtɪkəl/ *adj.* not having any interest in or involvement with politics

A·pol·lo /ə'pɑloʊ/ in Greek and Roman MYTHOLOGY, the god of the sun, medicine, poetry, music, and PROPHECY

a·pol·o·get·ic /əˌpɑlə'dʒɛtɪk/ *adj.* showing or saying that you are sorry that something has happened, especially because you feel guilty or embarrassed about it: *an apologetic letter* | [+ about] *Judi was very apologetic about forgetting my birthday.* —**apologetically** /-kli/ *adv.*: *"I know," she said apologetically.*

a·po·lo·gia /ˌæpə'loʊdʒə/ *n.* [C + for] LITERARY a statement in which you defend an idea that you believe in

a·pol·o·gist /ə'pɑlədʒɪst/ *n.* [C] LITERARY someone who tries to defend and explain an idea or system

a·pol·o·gize /ə'pɑləˌdʒaɪz/ *v.* [I] to tell someone that you are sorry that you have done something wrong: *The editors admitted the mistake and apologized.* | [+ for] *Torreo apologized for the delay in handling the order.* | *I apologized profusely for being late.* | [apologize to sb] *Marge should apologize to her daughter for reading her diary.*

a·pol·o·gy /ə'pɑlədʒi/ *n. plural* **apologies** [C] **1** something that you say or write to show that you are sorry for doing something wrong: [+ for] *The police chief issued an apology for the officer's behavior.* | *Black residents are demanding an apology from the mayor for his remarks.* | *It had nothing to do with Angela, and I owe her an apology.* | *Please accept my apologies.* | *The paper was forced to make an apology.* **2** LITERARY a statement in which you defend something you believe in after it has been criticized by other people

ap·o·plec·tic /ˌæpə'plɛktɪk◂/ *adj.* **1** so angry or excited that your face becomes red: *The colonel was apoplectic with rage.* **2** OLD-FASHIONED relating to apoplexy

ap·o·plex·y /'æpəˌplɛksi/ *n.* [U] OLD-FASHIONED an illness caused by a problem in your brain that can damage your ability to move, feel, or think; STROKE[1] (1)

a·pos·ta·sy /ə'pɑstəsi/ *n.* [U] FORMAL the act of changing your beliefs so that you stop supporting a religion, political party etc.

a·pos·tate /ə'pɑsteɪt, -tɪt/ *n.* [C] FORMAL someone who has stopped believing in and supporting a religion or political party

a pos·te·ri·o·ri /ˌɑ poʊstɪri'ɔri, ˌeɪ pɑ-/ *adj.* FORMAL using facts or results to form a judgment about what must have happened before. For example, "The streets are wet, so it must have been raining," is an a posteriori statement. —compare A PRIORI

a·pos·tle /ə'pɑsəl/ *n.* [C] **1** one of the 12 people chosen by Jesus Christ to teach and spread the Christian religion **2** FORMAL someone who believes strongly in a new idea and tries to persuade other people: [+ of] *an apostle of peace*

ap·os·tol·ic /ˌæpə'stɑlɪk◂/ *adj.* **1** relating to the POPE (=leader of the Catholic Church) **2** relating to one of Jesus Christ's 12 apostles

a·pos·tro·phe /ə'pɑstrəfi/ *n.* [C] **a)** the sign (') used in writing to show that numbers or letters have been left out, as in "don't" (=do not) and '96 (=1996) **b)** the same sign used before or after the letter "s" to show that something belongs to or is related to someone or something, as in "Joan's book," "Charles' mother," or "Clinton's last year as President" **c)** used before "s" to show the plural of letters and numbers, as in "Your r's look like v's."

a·poth·e·car·y /ə'pɑθə,kɛri/ *n. plural* **apothecaries** [C] someone who mixed and sold medicines in past times

a·poth·e·o·sis /ə,pɑθi'ousɪs, æ-/ *n.* **1** the apotheosis of sth FORMAL the best and most perfect example of something: *Bobby Darin is the apotheosis of '50s cool in "Too Late Blues."* **2** [U] LITERARY the state of getting to the highest level of something such as honor, importance etc.

Ap·pa·la·chi·ans, the /,æpə'leɪtʃənz, -'læ-/ also **the Appalachian Mountains** a long range of mountains in northeast America that go in a line southwest from Quebec in Canada to Alabama in the U.S.

ap·pall /ə'pɔl/ *v.* [T] to shock someone by being very bad or immoral: *The idea of killing animals for fur appalls me.* | *The social conditions appalled two physicians who fled their country shortly after the coup.*

ap·palled /ə'pɔld/ *adj.* very shocked by something very bad or immoral: *As one appalled witness later wrote, the fire spread out of control before the family could escape.* | [+ at] *I was appalled by John's rude behavior.*

ap·pall·ing /ə'pɔlɪŋ/ *adj.* **1** so bad or immoral that you are shocked: *the city's appalling pollution* **2** very bad: *The standard American diet is appalling in its lack of imagination.* —**appallingly** *adv.*: *appallingly cruel treatment*

ap·pa·loo·sa /,æpə'lusə/ *n.* [C] a type of horse that is a pale color with dark spots

ap·pa·ra·tchik /,ɑpə'rɑtʃɪk/ *n.* [C] an official working for a government or other organization who obeys orders without thinking

ap·pa·ra·tus /,æpə'rætəs, -'reɪtəs/ *n. plural* **apparatus** or **apparatuses** [C,U] **1** a tool, machine, or set of equipment used especially for scientific, medical, or technical purposes: *The astronauts have special breathing apparatus.* | *This wooden apparatus was used for weaving.* **2** a system or process for doing something: *The East German security apparatus used these kinds of devices to overhear conversations.*

ap·par·el /ə'pærəl/ *n.* [U] a word meaning "clothing," used especially by stores or the clothing industry: *an athletic shoe and apparel company* | *children's apparel*

ap·par·ent /ə'pærənt, ə'pɛr-/ *adj.* **1** seeming to be real or true, although it may not really be so: *There is no apparent connection between the murders.* | *the apparent failure of the device* **2** easily noticed or understood: [+ to] *Her embarrassment was apparent to everyone.* | [apparent (that)] *It was apparent that the company would shut down.* | **For no apparent reason**, *our daughter has started refusing to go to school.*

ap·par·ent·ly /ə'pærənt^li/ *adv.* **1** [sentence adverb] based on what you have heard is true, although you are not completely sure about it: *Nelson apparently committed suicide.* | *Apparently, it was a really good party.* **2** according to the way someone looks or a situation appears, although you cannot be sure: *Campaign funds have been used for apparently illegal activities.* —compare EVIDENTLY, OBVIOUSLY

ap·pa·ri·tion /,æpə'rɪʃən/ *n.* [C] something that you imagine you can see, especially the spirit of a dead person: *a ghostly apparition*

ap·peal¹ /ə'pil/ *n.* **1** [C] an urgent request for something important such as money or help, especially to help someone in a bad situation: [+ for] *an urgent appeal for medical supplies* | [appeal to sb to do sth] *An appeal to parents to supervise their children may help the situation.* | *Fowler went on the radio to make an appeal for law and order.* **2** [U] a quality that makes you like someone or something, be interested in them, or want them: [+ for] *The game has more appeal for older children.* | *Her music has wide appeal* (=liked by many people). | *He relies mainly on his sex appeal* (=the quality of being sexually attractive). **3** [C,U] a formal request to a court or to someone in authority asking for a decision to be changed: [+ to] *an appeal to the Supreme Court* —see also COURT OF APPEALS

appeal² *v.* **1** [I] to make a serious request for help, money, information etc.: [appeal (to sb) for sth] *The police are appealing to the public for information.* | *The Pope appealed for an end to the violence.* | [appeal to sb to do sth] *The water company appealed to everyone to reduce the amount of water used.* **2** [I,T] to make a formal request to a court or someone in authority asking for a decision to be changed: *The defendant is planning to appeal.* **3** appeal to sb's common sense/better nature/sense of honor etc. to try to persuade someone to do something by reminding them that it is a sensible, good, wise etc. thing to do

appeal to sb *phr. v.* [T] to seem attractive and interesting to someone: *The idea didn't appeal to me much.* | *The magazine is intended to appeal to working women in their 20s and 30s.*

ap·peal·ing /ə'pilɪŋ/ *adj.* **1** attractive or interesting: *Davies' books are an appealing blend of wit and wisdom.* | *Some men seem to find these qualities appealing in women.* **2** an appealing look/voice etc. FORMAL a look etc. that shows that someone wants help or sympathy: *She gave him an appealing look.* —**appealingly** *adv.*

appeals court /.'. ,./ *n.* [C usually singular] the COURT OF APPEALS

ap·pear /ə'pɪr/ *v.*
1 seem [linking verb, not in progressive] to seem: *Roger appeared very upset.* | *The city appeared calm after the previous night's fighting.* | [appear to be] *Karl appeared to be in his late twenties.* | [appear to do sth] *The gene appears to make people have a higher risk of developing cancer.* | *Police have found what appear to be* (=things that look like) *human remains.* | *The treatment would appear to be useful even in these cases* (=used when something is likely to be true, although you are not completely sure).
2 start to be seen [I] to start to be seen or to suddenly be seen: *An image appeared on the screen.* | *A face appeared at the window.* | *The dog appeared out of nowhere* (=suddenly appeared) *and began running alongside me.* | *Whole new industry sectors appear almost overnight* (=appear suddenly).
3 movie/play etc. [I] to take part in a movie, play, concert, television program etc.: [+ in/on] *Rogers appeared in 73 movies.* | [+ at] *Once in a while, a big band like the Rolling Stones appears at the club.*
4 be written/shown [I] to be written or shown on a list, in a book or newspaper, in a document etc.: *Lauren's name appears at the front of the book.* | *The story appeared in Thursday's paper.*
5 product/book [I] if a product or book appears, it becomes available to be bought for the first time: *When the book finally appeared on the shelves* (=became available in bookstores), *it was a huge success.*
6 sth new/different [I] if something new or surprising appears, it happens or exists for the first time: *Since Prozac appeared on the scene, research into similar drugs has increased dramatically.*
7 in court etc. [I] to be present in a court of law for a TRIAL that you are involved in, or to speak at a meeting of an official group: *Meeks is scheduled to appear in court February 5.* | [+ before/in front of] *Sen. Biden appeared before the Ways and Means Committee.*
8 arrive [I] to arrive, especially when people are not expecting you to: *Karen appeared at my house around 9 o'clock.*

ap·pear·ance /ə'pɪrəns/ *n.*
1 way sb/sth looks [C,U] the way someone or something looks or seems to other people: *O'Brien's article suggests ways to improve your appearance.* | *The Christmas lights gave the house a festive appearance.* | *Some of the Congressman's actions gave the appearance of* (=seemed) *being improper.*
2 arrival [C usually singular] the unexpected or sudden arrival of someone or something: [+ of] *The sudden appearance of several reporters at the hospital caused a lot of confusion.*

A

3 sth new [singular] the point or time at which something new begins to exist or starts being used: [+ of] *Viewing has increased since the appearance of cable TV.*

4 play/movie/sport etc. [C] the act of taking part in a movie, play, sports game etc.: *Thomas made his first appearance for Florida State in Friday's game.*

5 make an appearance also **put in an appearance** to go to an event for a short time, because you think you should: *Marc put in an appearance at the wedding, but didn't stay for the reception.*

6 court/meeting [C] the act of being present at a court of law or official meeting: *Ms. Lang made a brief appearance in court.*

7 to/by/from all appearances based on the way something seems to most people: *By all appearances, Craig has fully recovered from heart surgery.*

8 keep up appearances to continue to do things in the way you used to do them even though your situation has changed a lot: *For now, I can keep up appearances and still go to the same restaurants as my friends.*

ap·pease /ə'piz/ v. [T] to make someone less angry or stop them from attacking you by giving them what they want

ap·pease·ment /ə'pizmənt/ n. [C,U] FORMAL the act of trying to persuade someone not to attack you, or to make them less angry by giving them what they want, especially in politics

ap·pel·late court /ə,pɛlɪt 'kɔrt/ n. [C] a court in which people APPEAL[1] (3) against decisions made in other courts of law

ap·pel·la·tion /,æpə'leɪʃən/ n. [C] LITERARY a name or title

ap·pend /ə'pɛnd/ v. [T + to] FORMAL to add something to a piece of writing

ap·pend·age /ə'pɛndɪdʒ/ n. [C] FORMAL **1** something that is connected to a larger or more important thing **2** an arm, leg, or other body part

ap·pen·dec·to·my /,æpən'dɛktəmi/ n. plural **appendectomies** [C,U] a medical operation in which your APPENDIX (1) is removed

ap·pen·di·ci·tis /ə,pɛndə'saɪtɪs/ n. [U] an illness in which your APPENDIX (1) swells and causes pain

ap·pen·dix /ə'pɛndɪks/ n. plural **appendixes** or **appendices** /-dɪsiz/ [C] **1** a small part at the beginning of your large INTESTINE which has little or no use: *Joyce had her appendix out* (=had it removed) *when she was 18.* —see picture at DIGESTIVE SYSTEM **2** a part at the end of a book containing additional information

ap·per·tain /,æpɚ'teɪn/ v. FORMAL
appertain to sth phr. v. [T not in passive] to belong to or concern something

ap·pe·tite /'æpə,taɪt/ n. **1** [C,U] a desire for food: *Both of my kids have a healthy appetite* (=a desire to eat more than enough food). | *Watching open-heart surgery on TV made me lose my appetite* (=stop wanting to eat and feel slightly sick). | **spoil/ruin your appetite** (=stop being hungry for a meal because you have eaten something small) | *Walking all day, you can work up an appetite* (=get very hungry). **2** [C] a desire or liking for a particular activity: *Thompson claimed he had an insatiable sexual appetite.* | [+ for] *an appetite for new experiences* | *County officials have shown no appetite for further negotiations.* —see also **whet sb's appetite (for sth)** (WHET)

ap·pe·tiz·er /'æpə,taɪzɚ/ n. [C] a small dish eaten at the beginning of a meal, before the main part

ap·pe·tiz·ing /'æpə,taɪzɪŋ/ adj. food that is appetizing smells or looks very good: *an appetizing aroma* —**appetizingly** adv.

ap·plaud /ə'plɔd/ v. **1** [I,T] to hit your open hands together to show that you have enjoyed a play, concert, speaker etc.; CLAP[1] (1): *People laughed and applauded politely.* | *The President was applauded repeatedly during his 40-minute speech.* **2** to express strong approval of and praise for an idea, plan etc.: *We applaud the company's efforts to improve safety.* |

Caminiti's public remarks were applauded by his teammates.

ap·plause /ə'plɔz/ n. [U] **1** the sound of many people hitting their open hands together and shouting, to show that they have enjoyed something: *The audience burst into applause at Kramer's comments.* | *Let's give Ron a big round of applause* (=give someone a short period of applause)! **2** strong approval and praise for an idea, plan etc.: *Mowlam's statements and down-to-earth style have won applause among lawmakers in Washington.*

ap·ple /'æpəl/ n. [C,U] **1** a hard round fruit that has red, light green, or yellow skin and is white inside, or the tree this fruit grows on: *apple pie* —see picture at FRUIT[1] **2 be the apple of sb's eye** to be loved very much by someone: *Ben was always the apple of his father's eye.* **3 be as American as apple pie** to be typically or completely American: *The 9000 model cellular phone is made in Finland, but the technology inside is as American as apple pie.* **4 the apple doesn't fall far from the tree** used to say that children are usually similar to their parents, especially in a bad way —see also ADAM'S APPLE, **bob for apples** (BOB[1]), **a rotten apple** (ROTTEN[1]), **upset the apple cart** (UPSET[1])

apple-cheeked /'.. ,./ adj. having pink cheeks and looking healthy

ap·ple·jack /'æpəl,dʒæk/ n. [U] a very strong alcoholic drink made from apples

ap·ple pol·ish·er /'.. ,.../ n. [C] OLD-FASHIONED someone who tries to gain something, become popular etc. by praising or helping someone else without being sincere

ap·ple·sauce /'æpəl,sɔs/ n. [U] a food made from crushed cooked apples

Ap·ple·seed /'æpəl,sid/, **John·ny** /'dʒɑni/ (1774–1845) the popular name for John Chapman who walked around the eastern U.S. planting apple trees

ap·plet /'æplɪt/ n. TECHNICAL a small computer program that is used within another program

ap·pli·ance /ə'plaɪəns/ n. [C] a piece of electrical equipment such as a STOVE or WASHING MACHINE, used in people's homes —see Usage Note at MACHINE[1]

ap·pli·ca·ble /'æplɪkəbəl, ə'plɪkəbəl/ adj. affecting or relating to a particular person, group, or situation: [+ to] *These tax laws are not applicable to foreign companies.* —**applicability** /,æplɪkə'bɪləti, ə,plɪkə-/ n. [U]

ap·pli·cant /'æplɪkənt/ n. [C] someone who has formally asked, usually in writing, to be considered for a job, an opportunity to study at a college, permission to do something etc.: [+ for] *Applicants for immigrant visas must pay an additional $75 charge.*

ap·pli·ca·tion /,æplɪ'keɪʃən/ n.
1 written request [C,U] a formal, usually written, request to be considered for something such as a job, an opportunity to study at a college, or permission to do something: [+ for] *There were more than 30,000 applications for the 6,000 spaces in the freshman class.* | *Please fill out the application form and return it.* | *We received hundreds of job applications.*
2 computers [C] a piece of SOFTWARE: *New students will learn how to use word-processing and spreadsheet applications.*
3 practical use [C,U] the practical purpose for which a machine, idea etc. can be used, or the act of using it for this: *A computer has a wide range of applications for businesses.* | [+ to/in] *The article discusses the application of this theory to actual economic practice.*
4 put sth on sth **a)** [C,U] the act of putting something such as paint, liquid, medicine etc. onto a surface: [+ of] *The application of fertilizer increased the size of the plants.* **b)** [C] the amount of something that is put onto a surface at one time: *The larger bottle contains approximately 25 applications.*
5 effort [U] attention or effort over a long period of time: *Making your new business successful requires luck, patience, and application.*
6 relation to sth [U] the way in which something can affect or be used on something else: [+ to] *The*

Soviet model has important application to the American experience.

ap·pli·ca·tor /ˈæplɪˌkeɪtə/ n. [C] a special brush or tool used for putting paint, glue, medicine etc. on something

ap·plied /əˈplaɪd/ adj. [usually before noun] **applied science/physics/linguistics etc.** science, physics etc. that has a practical use —compare PURE —opposite THEORETICAL

ap·pli·qué /ˌæpləˈkeɪ/ n. [C,U] a piece of material that is sewn onto a piece of clothing etc. as a decoration, or the process of sewing pieces of material onto things —**appliqué** v. [T] —**appliquéd** adj.

_{s w} **ap·ply** /əˈplaɪ/ v. **applied, applies, applying**
_{1 1} **1** request for sth [I] to make a formal, usually written request to be considered for a job, an opportunity to study at a college, permission to do something etc.: [+ to] *I applied to four colleges and was accepted by all of them.* | [+ for] *Fletcher applied for the post of Eliot's secretary.*
2 use sth [T] to use something such as a method, idea, or law in a particular situation, activity, or process: *Some of the children seem unable to apply what they have learned.* | [apply sth to sth] *New technology is being applied to almost every industrial process.* | **apply force/pressure etc.** *The force applied to the walls is about 50 pounds per square foot.*
3 affect sb/sth [I,T not in progressive] to have an effect on or to concern a person, group, or situation: *Many of the restrictions no longer apply.* | [+ to] *The 20% discount only applies to club members.* | [apply when/where] *These tax laws apply when you borrow money to invest in a partnership.*
4 spread paint/liquid etc. [T] to put or spread something such as paint, liquid, or medicine onto a surface: *Apply the lotion evenly over the skin.*
5 make sth work [T] to do something in order to make something such as a piece of equipment operate: *On wet or icy roads, apply the brakes gently.* | *The crystal vibrates when a small electric current is applied to it.*
6 apply yourself to work hard with a lot of attention for a long time: *I wish Sam would apply himself a little more to his schoolwork.*
7 use a word [I,T] to use a particular word or name to describe something or someone in an appropriate way: [+ to/in] *The word "tragic" definitely applies in this situation.* | [apply sth to sth] *The term "mat" can be applied to any small rug.*

_w **ap·point** /əˈpɔɪnt/ v. [T] **1** to choose someone for a
₃ position or a job: *Pope John Paul II appointed several new bishops* | [appoint (sb) as sth] *Lisa Lore was appointed as an associate athletic director at USC.* | [appoint sb sth] *The company appointed Koontz chief financial officer.* | [appoint sb to sth] *He's been appointed to the State Supreme Court in California.* | [appoint sb to do sth] *DeGenoa appointed a police commission to investigate the scandal.* **2** FORMAL to arrange or decide a time or place for something to happen: *Judge Bailey appointed a new time for the trial.* —**appointed** adj.: *We met at the **appointed time** (=the arranged time).* —see also SELF-APPOINTED, WELL-APPOINTED

ap·point·ee /əˌpɔɪnˈtiː/ n. [C] FORMAL someone who is appointed to do a particular important job: *a presidential appointee*

_w **ap·point·ment** /əˈpɔɪntmənt/ n. **1** [C] an arrange-
₃ ment for a meeting at an agreed time and place, for some special purpose: *a doctor's appointment* | *a five o'clock appointment* | [+ with] *Judy's appointment with the doctor is at 10:30.* | [an appointment to do sth] *Do we need an appointment to see the manager?* | *I have an appointment at the clinic tomorrow morning.* | *Call Mrs. Reynolds' secretary and make an appointment.* **2** [C,U] the choosing of someone for an important position or job: [+ as/ to/of] *The President will make the appointment of a new Chief Justice this week.* **3** by appointment if you do something by appointment, you have to arrange it before you do it: *Dr. Sutton sees patients only by appointment.* **4** [C] a job or position, usually involving some responsibility: *Barron recently received an appointment as vice chairman.*

appointment book /ˈ.. ˌ./ also **appointment cal·en·dar** /ˈ.. ˌ.../ n. [C] a small book with a CALENDAR in it, in which you write the names of meetings, events, or other things you plan to do each day

Ap·po·mat·tox /ˌæpəˈmætəks/ a town in the U.S. state of Virginia, where General Robert E. Lee, the leader of the Confederate army surrendered (SURRENDER) to General Ulysses S. Grant, the leader of the Union army, and ended the American Civil War

ap·por·tion /əˈpɔrʃən/ v. [T] to decide how something should be shared among various people: [apportion sth among/between] *Apportioning funds fairly among the schools in the district has been difficult.* | *It's not easy to **apportion** blame* (=say who deserves the blame) *when a marriage breaks up.* —**apportionment** n. [C,U] —see also REAPPORTIONMENT

ap·po·site /ˈæpəzɪt/ adj. FORMAL appropriate to what is happening or being discussed: *Ms. Emerson made a few brief but apposite remarks about the incident.*

ap·po·si·tion /ˌæpəˈzɪʃən/ n. [U] TECHNICAL an arrangement in grammar in which one simple sentence contains two or more noun phrases that are used to give information about the same person or thing. For example, in the sentence "The defendant, a woman of thirty, denies kicking the policeman," the two phrases "the defendant" and "a woman of thirty" are in apposition.

ap·pos·i·tive /əˈpazətɪv/ n. [C] TECHNICAL a noun phrase that is used with another noun phrase that gives information about the same person or thing

ap·prais·al /əˈpreɪzəl/ n. [C,U] a statement or opinion judging the worth, value, or condition of something: [+ of] *an expert's appraisal of the antique clock* | *I took the necklace to a jewelry store for appraisal.*

ap·praise /əˈpreɪz/ v. [T] to officially judge how successful, effective, or valuable someone or something is; EVALUATE: [appraise sth at sth] *The house was appraised at $450,000.* —**appraiser** n. [C]

ap·pre·cia·ble /əˈpriʃəbəl/ adj. FORMAL large enough to be noticed or considered important: *Military leaders have seen no appreciable change in the situation.* —**appreciably** adv.: *Complaints of police abuse have increased appreciably.*

ap·pre·ci·ate /əˈpriʃiˌeɪt/ v. **1** [T not in progressive] _{s w} to be grateful for something someone has done: *Mom* ₁ *really appreciated the letter you sent.* | *I don't need* ₃ *any help, but I do appreciate your offer.* **2** [T not in progressive] to understand or enjoy the good qualities or value of someone or something: *Jan's abilities are not fully appreciated by her employer.* | *All the bad weather here makes me appreciate home.* **3 I would appreciate it if...** SPOKEN used to ask for something politely: *I'd really appreciate it if you could babysit the kids Friday night.* **4** [T not in progressive] to understand how serious a situation or problem is or what someone's feelings are: *I don't think you appreciate the difficulties this delay will cause.* | [appreciate how/why etc.] *At first he didn't appreciate how cold the winters are in Iowa.* **5** [I] to gradually become more valuable over a period of time: *Our house has appreciated over 20% in the last two years.* —opposite DEPRECIATE

ap·pre·ci·a·tion /əˌpriʃiˈeɪʃən, əˌpri-/ n. **1** a feeling of being grateful to someone for something: *Theo, we'd like to invite you to dinner in appreciation of your hard work this week.* | **show/express my appreciation** *I'd like to express my appreciation for all your help.* **2** [C,U] an understanding of the importance or meaning of something: *Murphy teaches classes in art appreciation to young children.* | [+ of] *Management does not have a realistic appreciation of the situation.* **3** [U] pleasure you feel when you realize something is good, useful, or well done: *As Lynn got older, her appreciation for her hometown grew.* **4** [singular,U] a rise in value, especially of land or possessions: *There has been an appreciation of 50% in property values.*

A

ap·pre·cia·tive /əˈpriʃətɪv/ adj. feeling or showing admiration or thanks: an appreciative audience | [+ of] I'm very pleased and appreciative of the support and kindness you have given me. —**appreciatively** adv.

ap·pre·hend /ˌæprɪˈhɛnd/ v. [T] **1** FORMAL if a criminal is apprehended, they are found and taken away by the police; ARREST[1] (1): Agents at the Interstate 8 station apprehended more than 3,100 undocumented workers. **2** OLD USE to understand something

ap·pre·hen·sion /ˌæprɪˈhɛnʃən/ n. **1** [C,U] anxiety about the future, especially the worry that you will have to deal with something bad: Dad has some apprehensions about having surgery. | Diplomats watched the events with growing apprehension. **2** [C,U] FORMAL the act of apprehending someone; ARREST[2]: A $100,000 reward is being offered for information leading to apprehension of the killer. **3** [U] OLD USE understanding: The discussion centered on our apprehension of the nature of God.

ap·pre·hen·sive /ˌæprɪˈhɛnsɪv/ adj. worried or nervous about something that you are going to do, or about the future: [+ about] Dave's always a little apprehensive about flying. —**apprehensively** adv.: I waited apprehensively for his reply.

ap·pren·tice[1] /əˈprɛntɪs/ n. [C] someone who agrees to work for an employer for a particular period of time in order to learn a particular skill or job: an apprentice chef —compare INTERN[2]

apprentice[2] v. [I,T] to make someone an apprentice, or to work as an apprentice: Jones apprenticed with the architect Frank Lloyd Wright. | [be apprenticed to sb] He's apprenticed to a plumber.

ap·pren·tice·ship /əˈprɛntɪˌʃɪp/ n. [C,U] the job of being an apprentice, or the period of time in which you are an apprentice

ap·prise /əˈpraɪz/ v. [T] FORMAL to inform or tell someone about something: [apprise sb of sth] The doctors will apprise you of your husband's progress.

s w **ap·proach**[1] /əˈprouʧ/ v.

1 move toward [I,T] to move toward or nearer to someone or something: Three people approached me, asking for money. | When I approached, the deer immediately ran away.

2 ask [T] to ask someone for something, or ask them to do something, especially when you are not sure they will be interested: Nash has already been approached by several pro football teams. | [approach sb/sth about (doing) sth] The company confirmed that it had been approached about a merger. —see also APPROACHABLE

3 future event [I,T] if an event or a particular time approaches, or you approach it, it is coming nearer and will happen soon: Everyone prepared celebrations as the year 2000 approached. | Warren was in his late fifties and approaching retirement.

4 almost reach sth [I,T] to almost reach a particular high level or amount, or an extreme condition or state: Temperatures could approach 100° today.

5 deal with [T] to begin to deal with a difficult situation in a particular way or with a particular attitude: Researchers are looking for new ways to approach the problem.

s w **approach**[2] n. **1** [C] a method of doing something or dealing with a problem: [+ to] a new approach to teaching languages | Higgins took a diplomatic approach. **2** [C] a request from someone, asking you to do something for them: Hanson made an approach regarding a company buyout. **3** [C] a road, path etc. that leads to a place, and is the main way of reaching it: The approach to the house was an old dirt road. **4** the approach of sth FORMAL the approach of a particular time or event is the fact that it is getting closer: The pillwort plant usually dies with the approach of winter. **5** [C,U] a movement toward or near something: The plane was on its final approach to the Birmingham airport when it crashed.

ap·proach·a·ble /əˈprouʧəbəl/ adj. friendly and easy to talk to: An excellent manager must be very approachable.

ap·pro·ba·tion /ˌæprəˈbeɪʃən/ n. [U] FORMAL official praise or approval

ap·pro·pri·ate[1] /əˈprouprit/ adj. correct or right for s w a particular time, situation, or purpose: We will take appropriate action once the investigation is over. | [+ for] The movie is appropriate for children age 12 and over. | [appropriate to do sth] It is not appropriate to ask such personal questions in an interview. | [+ to] They need to offer a salary appropriate to his experience and education. —**appropriately** adv.: The police responded appropriately. —**appropriateness** n. [U] —opposite INAPPROPRIATE

ap·pro·pri·ate[2] /əˈproupriˌeɪt/ v. [T] **1** to take something for yourself, when you have no right to do this: Carlin is suspected of appropriating company funds. **2** to take something, especially money, to use for a particular purpose: [appropriate sth for sth] Congress appropriated $11.7 billion for anti-drug campaigns. —see also MISAPPROPRIATE

ap·pro·pri·a·tion /əˌproupriˈeɪʃən/ n. [C,U] **1** the process of saving or using money for a particular purpose, especially by a business or government: [+ of] Congress discussed the appropriation of $2 million for improving school buildings. **2** the act of taking control of something, usually without asking permission, and using it for your own purposes: The exhibition focuses on Picasso's appropriation of photographs as the bases for his work.

ap·prov·al /əˈpruvəl/ n. **1** [C,U] the act of officially s w accepting a plan, decision, or person: Approval of the plans for the new science lab is expected by next month. | The FDA granted approvals for 105 new drugs last year. | The bill has been sent to the House for approval (=to be approved). | The project has won approval (=been approved) from the planning commission. | The budget proposals met with the Senate's approval. **2** [C,U] official permission to do something: We need parental approval before allowing students to go on field trips. | The county promised to speed up building approvals for people who lost their homes in the earthquake. **3** seal/stamp of approval a statement or sign that someone has accepted something or believes that it is good: In 1973, the Supreme Court gave its seal of approval to the principle that women should be entitled to the same benefits as men. **4** [U] the fact or belief that someone or something is good or is doing the right things: The crowd of young Democratic supporters roared with approval. —opposite DISAPPROVAL **5** on approval if you take something home from a store on approval, you get permission to take it home without paying for it, in order to decide whether you like it well enough to buy it

ap·prove /əˈpruv/ v. **1** [T] to officially accept a plan, s proposal etc.: The Senate approved a plan for federal funding of local housing programs. **2** [I] to think that someone or something is good or acceptable: Some women do not join unions because their husbands do not approve. | [+ of] Most people no longer approve of smoking in public places.

ap·prov·ing /əˈpruvɪŋ/ adj. showing support or agreement for something: an approving look —**approvingly** adv.: She smiled approvingly.

ap·prox. the written abbreviation of APPROXIMATELY

ap·prox·i·mant /əˈprɑksəmənt/ n. [C] TECHNICAL a CONSONANT sound such as /w/ or /l/ made by air passing between the tongue or lip and another part of the mouth without any closing of the air passage

ap·prox·i·mate[1] /əˈprɑksəmɪt/ adj. an approximate number, amount, or time is a little more or less than the exact number, amount etc.: The approximate cost of materials for the class should be around $25.

ap·prox·i·mate[2] /əˈprɑksəˌmeɪt/ v. [T] FORMAL to be similar to something, but not exactly the same: His snoring approximated the sound of a jet taking off.

ap·prox·i·mate·ly /əˈprɑksəmɪtli/ adv. a little more or less than an exact number, amount etc.; about: The plane will be landing in approximately 20 minutes. | Could you tell me approximately when you noticed the symptoms?

ap·prox·i·ma·tion /əˌprɑksəˈmeɪʃən/ *n.* [C,U] something that is similar to another thing, but not exactly the same: [+ of/to] *The restaurant serves a close approximation of French cuisine.*

ap·pur·te·nance /əˈpɜt⁀nəns/ *n.* [C usually plural] FORMAL things that you use or have with you when doing a particular activity

APR *n.* [C usually singular] Annual Percentage Rate; the rate of INTEREST that you must pay when you borrow money

ap·rès-ski /ˌæpreɪ ˈski, ˌɑ-/ *n.* [U] activities such as eating and drinking that you take part in after skiing —**après-ski** *adj.* [only before noun] *après-ski clothes*

ap·ri·cot /ˈeɪprɪˌkɑt, ˈæ-/ *n.* **1** [C] a small round fruit that is orange or yellow and has a single large seed **2** [U] the color of this fruit —**apricot** *adj.*

A·pril /ˈeɪprəl/ written abbreviation **Apr.** *n.* [C,U] the fourth month of the year, between March and May: *This office opened in April 1994.* | *My new job starts on April 3rd.* | *Jenni got her hair cut really short last April.* | *I'm going to Africa next April.* | *We got married April 8, 1982.* —see Usage Note at JANUARY

April fool /ˌ.. ˈ./ *n.* [C] someone who is tricked on April Fools' Day, or the trick that is played on them

April Fools' Day /ˌ.. ˈ. ˌ./ *n.* [C,U] [singular] April 1, a day when people play tricks on each other

a pri·o·ri /ˌeɪ priˈɔri, ˌɑ-, -praɪ-/ *adj., adv.* FORMAL using previous experiences or facts to decide what the likely result or effect of something will be. For example, "it is raining so the streets must be wet," is an a priori statement. —compare A POSTERIORI

a·pron /ˈeɪprən/ *n.* [C] **1** a piece of clothing that covers the front part of your clothes and is tied around your waist, worn to keep your clothes clean, especially while cooking **2 apron strings** INFORMAL the relationship between a child and its mother, especially in a relationship where the mother controls an adult son or daughter too much: *You're 25 years old, and you still haven't cut the apron strings.* | *It seems like Jeff is still tied to his mother's apron strings.* **3** the hard surface in an airport on which airplanes are turned around, loaded, unloaded etc. **4** the part of the stage in a theater that is in front of the curtain

ap·ro·pos[1] /ˌæprəˈpou, ˈæprəˌpou/ *adv.* FORMAL **apropos of sth** used to introduce a new subject that is related to something just mentioned: *She had nothing to say apropos of the latest developments.* | *Douglas paused and then, apropos of nothing* (=not relating to anything previously mentioned), *announced, "We could have been in New York by now."*

apropos[2] *adj.* [not before noun] appropriate for a particular situation: *I thought her remarks were very apropos.*

apse /æps/ *n.* [C] TECHNICAL the curved inside end of a building, especially the east end of a church

apt /æpt/ *adj.* **1 be apt to do sth** to have a natural tendency to do something: *Some of the employees are apt to arrive late on Mondays.* **2** exactly right for a particular situation or purpose: *Gibson refers to NARA as an organization, but "social club" might be a more apt description.* **3** FORMAL quick to learn and understand: *Fahey was obviously an apt pupil.* —**aptness** *n.* [U] —see also APTLY

apt. *n.* [C] the written abbreviation of "apartment"

ap·ti·tude /ˈæptəˌtud/ *n.* [C,U] **1** natural ability or skill, especially in learning: [+ for/in] *Becky has a real aptitude for mathematics.* **2 aptitude test** a test that measures your natural skills or abilities

apt·ly /ˈæptli/ *adv.* **aptly named/described/called etc.** named, described etc. in a way that seems very appropriate or right: *The hotel overlooking the ocean was aptly named The Lighthouse.*

aq·ua /ˈɑkwɑ, ˈæ-/ *n.* [U] a greenish-blue color —**aqua** *adj.*

aq·ua·cul·ture /ˈɑkwəˌkʌltʃə, ˈæ-/ *n.* the business of raising fish or SHELLFISH to sell as food

aq·ua·ma·rine /ˌɑkwəməˈrin, ˌæ-/ *n.* **1** [C,U] a greenish blue jewel, or the type of stone it comes from

2 [U] a greenish blue color —**aquamarine** *adj.*

a·quar·i·um /əˈkwɛriəm/ *n. plural* **aquariums** or **aquaria** /-riə/ [C] **1** a clear glass or plastic container for fish and other water animals **2** a building where people go to look at fish and other water animals

A·quar·i·us /əˈkwɛriəs/ *n.* **1** the eleventh sign of the ZODIAC, represented by a person pouring water and believed to affect the character and life of people born between January 20 and February 19 **2** [C] someone who was born between January 20 and February 19: *Dana's an Aquarius.*

a·quat·ic /əˈkwætɪk, əˈkwɑtɪk/ *adj.* **1** living or growing in water: *an aquatic plant* **2** involving or happening in water: *aquatic sports* —**aquatically** /-kli/ *adv.*

aq·ua·tint /ˈækwəˌtɪnt, ˈɑ-/ *n.* [C,U] a method of producing a picture using acid on a sheet of metal, or a picture printed using this method

aq·ue·duct /ˈækwəˌdʌkt/ *n.* [C] a structure, especially one like a bridge, that carries water over a river or valley

a·que·ous /ˈeɪkwiəs, ˈɑ-/ *adj.* TECHNICAL containing water or similar to water

aq·ui·fer /ˈækwəfə, ˈɑ-/ *n.* [C] a layer of stone or earth under the surface of the ground that contains water

aq·ui·line /ˈækwəˌlaɪn, -lən/ *adj.* **1 aquiline nose** an aquiline nose has a curved shape like the beak of an EAGLE **2** LITERARY like an EAGLE

A·qui·nas /əˈkwaɪnəs/, **St. Thomas** (1225–1274) an Italian THEOLOGIAN and PHILOSOPHER whose ideas had an important influence on the Catholic part of the Christian religion

AR the written abbreviation of Arkansas

-ar /ə, ɑr/ *suffix* **1** [in adjectives] relating to something: *stellar* (=relating to stars) | *polar* (=relating to the North or South Pole) —see also -ULAR **2** [in nouns] someone who does something: *a beggar* (=who asks people for money) | *a liar* (=who tells lies)

Ar·ab /ˈærəb, ˈɛr-/ *n.* [C] someone who language is Arabic and whose family is originally from Arabia, the Middle East, or North Africa

ar·a·besque /ˌærəˈbɛsk, ˌɛr-/ *n.* [C] **1** a position in BALLET, in which you stand on one foot with the other leg stretched out straight behind you **2** a decorative pattern of flowing lines

A·ra·bi·an[1] /əˈreɪbiən/ *adj.* coming from or relating to Arabia

Arabian[2] *n.* [C] a type of fast graceful horse

Ar·a·bic /ˈærəbɪk/ *n.* [U] the language or writing of the Arabs, which is the main language of North Africa, the Middle East, and Arabia —**Arabic** *adj.*

Arabic nu·mer·al /ˌ... ˈ.../ *n.* [C] the sign 1, 2, 3, 4, 5, 6, 7, 8, 9, or 0, or a combination of these signs, used as a number —compare ROMAN NUMERAL

ar·a·ble /ˈærəbəl, ˈɛr-/ *adj.* **arable land/soil** land or soil that is or can be used for growing crops

a·rach·nid /əˈræknɪd/ *n.* [C] TECHNICAL a small creature such as a SPIDER, that has eight legs and a body with two parts

a·rach·no·pho·bi·a /əˌræknəˈfoubiə/ *n.* [U] TECHNICAL a strong fear of SPIDERS

Ar·al Sea /ˈærəl, ˈɛr-/ a sea that is surrounded by land, between Kazakhstan and Uzbekistan

A·rap·a·ho /əˈræpəˌhou/ a Native American tribe from the Great Plains region of the U.S. —**Arapaho** *adj.*

Ar·a·wak /ˈærəˌwɑk, -ˌwæk/ a Native American tribe from the northwestern area of South America

ar·bi·ter /ˈɑrbətə/ *n.* [C] **1** someone who influences society's opinions about what is stylish, socially acceptable etc.: **arbiter of taste/fashion/culture etc.** *Totenberg and her colleagues are angry at losing their position as arbiters of American popular culture.* | *Havel was recognized as the moral arbiter for*

A

his country. **2** someone or something that settles an argument between two opposing sides: *The council is the final arbiter of the election process when there are disputes.*

ar·bi·trage /ˈɑrbəˌtrɑʒ/ *n.* [U] TECHNICAL the process of buying something such as a COMMODITY or CURRENCY in one place and selling it in another place at the same time —**arbitrager** also **arbitrageur** /ˌɑrbətrɑˈʒɚ/ *n.* [C]

ar·bi·trar·y /ˈɑrbəˌtrɛri/ *adj.* decided or arranged without any reason or plan, often unfairly: *The government has carried out numerous executions and arbitrary arrests.* —**arbitrariness** *n.* [U] —**arbitrarily** *adv.*

ar·bi·trate /ˈɑrbəˌtreɪt/ *v.* [I,T] to officially judge how an argument between two opposing sides should be settled: *Ms. Montoya was appointed to the commission that arbitrates disputes between businesses and employees.* | [+ **between**] *A committee will arbitrate between management and unions.* —**arbitrator** *n.* [C]

ar·bi·tra·tion /ˌɑrbəˈtreɪʃən/ *n.* [U] the process of judging officially how an argument should be settled: *The dispute is going to arbitration* (=someone is being asked to arbitrate). | *The school district and teachers agreed to binding arbitration* (=making judgments that they must accept and follow by law).

ar·bor /ˈɑrbɚ/ *n.* [C] a shelter in a park or yard made by making plants grow together on a frame shaped like an ARCH

ar·bo·re·al /ɑrˈbɔriəl/ *adj.* TECHNICAL OR LITERARY relating to trees, or living in trees

ar·bo·re·tum /ˌɑrbəˈritəm/ *n.* [C] a place where trees are grown for scientific study

ar·bor·ist /ˈɑrbərɪst/ *n.* [C] someone who studies and takes care of trees

Ar·bus /ˈɑrbəs/**, Di·ane** /daɪˈæn/ (1923–1971) a U.S. PHOTOGRAPHER

arc¹ /ɑrk/ *n.* [C] **1** a curved shape or line: *The islands lie in an arc in the eastern Caribbean.* **2** a flash of light formed by the flow of electricity between two points —see also ARC LIGHT, ARC WELDING

arc² *v.* [I] **1** [always + adv./prep.] to move in a smooth curved line: *The Space Shuttle arced high above the Atlantic after takeoff.* **2** if electricity or electrical wires arc, they produce a flash of light

ar·cade /ɑrˈkeɪd/ *n.* [C] **1** a special room or business where people go to play VIDEO GAMES **2** a passage or side of a building that has small stores next to it and is covered with an ARCHed roof **3** TECHNICAL a passage with an ARCHed roof supported by PILLARS

Ar·ca·di·a /ɑrˈkeɪdiə/ *n.* [singular,U] LITERARY a place or scene of simple pleasant country life

ar·cane /ɑrˈkeɪn/ *adj.* LITERARY secret and known or understood by only a few people: *the arcane language of lawyers*

arch¹ /ɑrtʃ/ *n.* [C] **1** a structure with a curved top and straight sides that supports the weight of a bridge or building **2** a curved structure above a door, window etc. **3** a curved structure of bones in the middle of your foot **4** a shape with a curved top and straight sides

arch² *v.* [I,T] to form or make something form a curved shape: *Two rows of trees arched over the driveway.* | *The dog arched its back and showed its teeth.*

arch³ *adj.* amused because you think you understand something better than other people: *an arch tone* —**archly** *adv.* —see also ARCH-

arch- /ɑrtʃ, ɑrk/ *prefix* belonging to the highest class or rank: *an archbishop* (=an important BISHOP) | *our archenemy* (=our worst enemy) | *the company's archrivals* (=main competitors)

ar·chae·ol·o·gy, archeology /ˌɑrkiˈɑlədʒi/ *n.* [U] the study of ancient societies by examining what remains of their buildings, graves, tools etc. —**archaeological** /ˌɑrkiəˈlɑdʒɪkəl/ *adj.*: *an archaeological dig* —**archaeologically** /-kli/ *adj.* —**archaeologist** /ˌɑrkiˈɑlədʒɪst/ *n.* [C]

ar·cha·ic /ɑrˈkeɪ-ɪk/ *adj.* **1** old and not used anymore: *The English used in Chaucer's plays is an archaic form of the language.* **2** old-fashioned and needing to be replaced: *an archaic sound system* **3** from or relating to ancient times: *archaic civilizations*

ar·cha·ism /ˈɑrkiˌɪzəm, -keɪ-/ *n.* [C] FORMAL an old word or phrase that is not used anymore

arch·an·gel /ˈɑrkˌeɪndʒəl/ *n.* [C] one of the chief ANGELS in the Jewish, Christian, and Muslim religions

arch·bish·op /ˌɑrtʃˈbɪʃəp/ *n.* [C] a priest with a very high rank, who is in charge of all the churches in a particular area

arch·di·o·cese /ˌɑrtʃˈdaɪəsɪs, -ˌsiz/ *n.* [C] the area that is governed by an archbishop

arch·duke /ˌɑrtʃˈduk/ *n.* [C] a prince who belonged to the royal family of Austria

arch·en·e·my /ˌɑrtʃˈɛnəmi/ *n. plural* **archenemies** [C] **1** someone's main enemy **2** the **Archenemy** LITERARY the DEVIL

ar·che·ol·o·gy /ˌɑrkiˈɑlədʒi/ *n.* [U] another spelling of ARCHAEOLOGY

arch·er /ˈɑrtʃɚ/ *n.* [C] someone who shoots ARROWS from a BOW

arch·er·y /ˈɑrtʃəri/ *n.* [U] the sport of shooting ARROWS from a BOW

ar·che·type /ˈɑrkɪˌtaɪp/ *n.* [C] **1** [usually singular] a perfect example of something, because it has all the most important qualities of things that belong to that type: [+ **of**] *For most of us, France is the archetype of the centralized nation-state.* **2** TECHNICAL a character in a story, movie etc. or a person who is very familiar to people and is considered a model for other characters etc.: *The biblical Mary is a powerful cultural archetype whose story has spoken to women across the centuries.* —**archetypal** /ˌɑrkɪˈtaɪpəl/ *adj.* —**archetypical** /ˌɑrkɪˈtɪpɪkəl/ *adj.*

Ar·chi·me·des /ˌɑrkəˈmidiz/ (287–212 B.C.) a MATHEMATICIAN and inventor in ancient Greece

ar·chi·pel·a·go /ˌɑrkəˈpɛləˌgoʊ/ *n. plural* **archipelagos** [C] a group of small islands

ar·chi·tect /ˈɑrkəˌtɛkt/ *n.* [C] **1** someone whose job is to design buildings and other large structures **2 the architect of sth** the person who originally thought of an important and successful idea: *Chubais was the chief architect of Russia's economic transition.*

ar·chi·tec·ture /ˈɑrkəˌtɛktʃɚ/ *n.* **1** [U] the style and design of a building or buildings: *medieval architecture* | *the architecture of Venice* **2** [U] the art and business of planning and designing buildings **3** [U] the structure of something: *Minerals are understood in terms of their molecular architecture.* **4** [C,U] TECHNICAL the structure of a computer system and the way it works —**architectural** /ˌɑrkəˈtɛktʃərəl/ *adj.*: *architectural features* —**architecturally** *adv.*: *The building plans were not architecturally appropriate for the neighborhood.*

ar·chive¹ /ˈɑrkaɪv/ *n.* [C] **1** a place where a large number of historical records are stored, or the records that are stored: *the Pacific Film Archive* | **archive photographs/recordings/tapes etc.** (=photographs etc. that are from an archive) **2** copies of a computer's FILEs that are stored on a DISK or in the computer's MEMORY in a way that uses less space than usual, so that the computer can keep them for a long time —**archival** /ɑrˈkaɪvəl/ *adj.*: *The program includes archival footage of the President's visit in 1969.*

archive² *v.* [T] **1** to keep documents, books information etc. in an archive: *NOAA will analyze and archive data from satellites.* **2** TECHNICAL to save a computer FILE in a way that uses less space than usual, because you are not likely to use that FILE often but may need it in the future

ar·chi·vist /ˈɑrkɪvɪst, -kaɪ-/ *n.* [C] someone who works in an archive

arch·ri·val /ˌɑrtʃˈraɪvəl/ *n.* [C] the person, team etc. who is your main competitor: *Hopkins High defeated their archrival Edison 3–2 in yesterday's game.*

arch·way /ˈɑrtʃweɪ/ *n. plural* **archways** [C] a passage or entrance under an ARCH¹ (1) or ARCHes

-archy /əki, ɑrki/ *suffix* [in nouns] used to talk about a particular type of government: *anarchy* (=no government) | *monarchy* (=having a king or queen)

arc light also **arc lamp** /ˈ. ./ *n.* [C] an electric light that produces a very bright light by passing electricity through a special gas

Arc·tic /ˈɑrktɪk, ˈɑrtɪk/ *n.* **the Arctic** the large area surrounding the North Pole

arc·tic /ˈɑrktɪk, ˈɑrtɪk/ *adj.* **1** also **Arctic** relating to or from the most northern part of the world **2** extremely cold: *arctic conditions*

Arctic Cir·cle /ˌ.. ˈ../ *n.* **the Arctic Circle** an imaginary line drawn around the world at a certain distance from the most northern point (the North Pole) —compare ANTARCTIC CIRCLE

Arctic O·cean, the /ˌ.. ˈ../ *n.* the ocean that surrounds the North Pole

arc weld·ing /ˈ. ˌ../ *n.* [U] a method or process of joining two pieces of metal together by heating them with a special tool

-ard /əd/ *suffix* [in nouns] someone who is usually or always in a particular state: *a drunkard*

ar·dent /ˈɑrdnt/ *adj.* [usually before noun] **1** showing strong positive feelings about an activity and determination to succeed at it: *an ardent advocate of gun control* **2** LITERARY showing strong feelings of love: *an ardent lover* —**ardently** *adv.*

ar·dor /ˈɑrdə/ *n.* [U] **1** very strong feelings of admiration or excitement: *He still has the fitness and ardor to climb the world's highest peaks.* **2** LITERARY strong feelings of love

ar·du·ous /ˈɑrdʒuəs/ *adj.* involving a lot of strength and effort: *an arduous trip through the mountains* —**arduously** *adv.* —**arduousness** *n.* [U]

are /ə; *strong* ɑr/ the present tense plural form of "be"

w **ar·e·a** /ˈɛriə/ *n.* [C] **1** a particular part of a country, city etc.: *Only cheeses made in this area may be labeled "Roquefort."* | *There were over 2 inches of rain in coastal areas.* | [+ of] *Many areas of Africa have suffered severe drought this year.* | *The police have searched the farm and the surrounding area* (=the area around a place). | *The fire in the downtown area* (=somewhere in or near downtown) *was quickly put out.* **2** a part of a house, office, yard etc. that is used for a particular purpose: *a no-smoking area* | *Their apartment has a large kitchen area.* **3** a particular subject, range of activities, or group of related subjects: *We're funding research in new areas like law enforcement technology.* | [+ of] *They have made some improvements in the area of human rights.* **4** the amount of space that a flat surface or shape covers: [+ of] *Use this formula to calculate the area of a circle.* —see **a gray area** (GRAY¹)

USAGE NOTE: AREA

WORD CHOICE: area, part of the world/the country/ town, region, district

Area is the most general word for a part of the Earth's surface. An **area** can be small or large, and is not usually thought of as a fixed land division: *one of the poorest areas of the city* | *a rural area of the country* | *the Houston area*. Informally you might talk instead about a **part of the world/the country/town**: *There's no post office in our part of town.* | *This part of the country is very mountainous.* A **region** is usually large, is usually part of a country, and may or may not be thought of as a fixed land division: *the arctic region of Canada*. A **district** is smaller than a **region**, and is usually an officially fixed area of a country or city: *Carla works in the financial district.* | *the central district of Hong Kong*

---

area code /ˈ... ˌ./ *n.* [C] a group of three numbers you use before a telephone number when you want to call someone in a different area of the U.S. or Canada

area rug /ˈ... ˌ./ *n.* [C] a RUG that covers part of the floor in a room

a·re·na /əˈrinə/ *n.* [C] **1** a building with a large flat

central area surrounded by seats, where sp[ ]entertainments take place: *The city is plann...ng to build a new sports arena.* **2** **the political/public/ international etc. arena** all the activities and people connected with politics, public life etc.: *Women are entering the political arena in larger numbers.*

A·rendt /ˈɛrənt, ˈɑr-/, **Han·nah** /ˈhænə/ (1906–1975) a U.S. political PHILOSOPHER

aren't /ˈɑrənt/ *v.* **a)** the short form of "are not": *They aren't here.* **b)** the short form of "am not," used in questions: *I'm in big trouble, aren't I?*

Ar·es /ˈɑriz, ˈɛriz/ in Greek MYTHOLOGY, the god of war

Ar·gen·ti·na /ˌɑrdʒənˈtinə/ a large country in the southern part of South America —**Argentinian** /ˌɑrdʒənˈtiniən/ *n., adj.*

ar·gon /ˈɑrgɑn/ *n.* [U] *symbol* **Ar** a chemically inactive gas that is an ELEMENT and is found in the air and is sometimes used in electric lights

ar·got /ˈɑrgət, -gou/ *n.* [C,U] expressions used by a particular group of people; JARGON: *A "Jim Wilson" is airline-industry argot for a dead body being shipped in cargo.*

ar·gu·a·ble /ˈɑrgyuəbəl/ *adj.* **1** not certain, or not definitely true or correct, and therefore easy to doubt: *Industry bosses oppose the new safety requirements because of the higher cost and arguable safety advantages.* | *Some items are frankly fakes; others are of arguable value.* **2** **it is arguable that...** used in order to give good reasons why something might be true: *There was nothing Iraq could do to stop us, and it is arguable that no force on Earth could.*

ar·gu·a·bly /ˈɑrgyuəbli/ *adv.* [sentence adverb] used to say that there are good reasons why something might be true, although some people may disagree: *arguably the best/biggest/worst etc. The air in El Paso is arguably the dirtiest in Texas.* | *Rowers are arguably the best-conditioned of all Olympic athletes.*

ar·gue /ˈɑrgyu/ *v.* **1** [I] to disagree with someone in s w words, often in an angry way: *We could hear the* ₂ ₁ *neighbors arguing.* | [+ with] *He was sent off the court for arguing with a referee.* | [+ about] *They were arguing about how to spend the money.* | [+ over] *The kids were arguing over which TV program to watch.* **2** [I,T] to state, giving clear reasons, that something is true, should be done etc.: *a well-argued case* | [**argue that**] *They argued that a dam might actually increase the risk of flooding.* | [**argue for/against doing sth**] *Baker argued against cutting the military budget.* | *Gore argued the case for keeping the affirmative action laws.*

ar·gu·ment /ˈɑrgyəmənt/ *n.* **1** [C] a situation in s w which two or more people disagree, often angrily: ₂ ₂ [+ with] *I broke the vase during an argument with my husband.* | *Henning told the police she and her husband had an argument before he left.* | *I got into an argument with the other driver.* | *Shelton and the woman had a heated argument* (=very angry argument). **2** [C] a set of reasons that show that something is true or untrue, right or wrong etc.: *Rose presented a good argument.* | [+ for/against] *a powerful argument against smoking* | [**argument that**] *She offered the familiar argument that a strong domestic steel industry is needed for national defense.* **3** [U] the act of disagreeing or questioning something: *Nathan accepted the decision without argument.* | *I'm not sure that's an accurate description, but for the sake of argument* (=in order to discuss all the possibilities) *I'll accept it.*

ar·gu·men·ta·tion /ˌɑrgyəmənˈteɪʃən/ *n.* [U] the way you organize your ideas and use language to support your views or to persuade people

ar·gu·men·ta·tive /ˌɑrgyəˈmɛntətɪv/ *adj.* someone who is argumentative often argues or likes arguing: *an argumentative lawyer*

ar·gyle /ˈɑrgaɪl/ *n.* [U] a pattern of DIAMOND shapes and crossed lines, used especially in clothing

a·ri·a /ˈɑriə/ *n.* [C] a song that is sung by only one person in an OPERA or ORATORIO

A

-arian /ɛriən/ *suffix* **1** [in nouns] someone who believes in or does a particular thing: *a vegetarian* (=someone who does not eat meat) | *a librarian* (=someone who works in a library) —see also -GENARIAN **2** [in adjectives] for people of this type, or relating to them: *a vegetarian restaurant* | *an egalitarian society*

ar·id /'ærɪd/ *adj.* **1** getting very little rain, and therefore very dry: *an arid climate* **2** an arid discussion, period of time etc. does not produce anything new —**aridity** /ə'rɪdəṭi/ *adj.*

Ar·ies /'ɛriz/ *n.* **1** [U] the first sign of the ZODIAC, represented by a RAM (=male sheep), and believed to affect the character and life of people born between March 21 and April 20 **2** [C] someone who was born between March 21 and April 20: *Laura's an Aries.*

a·right /ə'raɪt/ *adv.* OLD-FASHIONED **1** set sth aright to settle problems or difficulties: *Payne was helpful as the bank struggled to set itself aright.* **2** correctly

A·rik·a·ra /ə'rɪkərə/ a Native American tribe from the northern central area of the U.S.

a·rise /ə'raɪz/ *v.* past tense **arose** past participle **arisen** /ə'rɪzən/ [I] **1** if something arises from or out of a situation, event etc., it is caused or started by that situation etc.: *Several important legal questions arose in the contract negotiations.* | [+ from/out of] *The civil war arose from the social injustices present in the country.* **2** if a problem or difficult situation arises, it begins to happen: *More problems like those at the nuclear power plant are certain to arise.* **3** when/if the need arises also should the need arise when or if it is necessary: *They are ready to fight if the need arises.* **4** LITERARY to get out of bed, or stand up: *Daniel arose at dawn.* **5** LITERARY if a group of people arise, they fight for or demand something they want

ar·is·toc·ra·cy /ˌærə'stɑkrəsi/ *n. plural* **aristocracies 1** [C usually singular] the people in the highest social class, who traditionally have a lot of land, money, and power: *The nation's elite sends its children to boarding schools in the tradition of the British aristocracy.* **2** [U] TECHNICAL the system in which a country is governed by the people of the highest social class —compare DEMOCRACY

ar·is·to·crat /ə'rɪstə,kræt/ *n.* [C] someone who belongs to the highest social class

a·ris·to·crat·ic /ə,rɪstə'kræṭɪk/ *adj.* belonging to or typical of the aristocracy: *Pamela came from an aristocratic background.* | *He spoke with an aristocratic accent.*

Ar·is·toph·a·nes /ˌærɪ'stɑfəniz/ (?457–?385 B.C.) a writer from ancient Greece, famous for his humorous plays

a·rith·me·tic¹ /ə'rɪθmə,tɪk/ *n.* [U] the science of numbers involving adding, multiplying etc. —compare MATHEMATICS

ar·ith·met·ic² /ˌærɪθ'mɛṭɪk/ also **ar·ith·met·i·cal** /-'mɛṭɪkəl/ *adj.* TECHNICAL involving or related to arithmetic —**arithmetically** /-kli/ *adv.*

arithmetic pro·gres·sion /..,.. .'../ *n.* [C] a set of numbers in order of value in which a particular number is added to each to produce the next (as in 2, 4, 6, 8...) —compare GEOMETRIC PROGRESSION

Ar·i·zo·na /ˌærɪ'zoʊnə, ,ɛr-/ *written abbreviation* **AZ** a state in the southwestern U.S.

ark /ɑrk/ *n.* [C] **1** a large ship **2 the Ark** in the Bible, the large boat built by Noah to save his family and the animals from a flood that covered the earth

Ar·kan·sas /'ɑrkən,sɔ/ *written abbreviation* **AR** a state in the southern central part of the U.S.

Ark of the Cov·e·nant /ˌ. . . '.../ *n.* **the Ark of the Covenant** a box containing the laws of the Jewish religion that ancient Jews carried with them as they traveled through the desert

Ar·ling·ton Na·tion·al Cem·e·ter·y /ˌɑrlɪŋtən ,næʃənl 'sɛmə,tɛri/ a CEMETERY in Arlington, Virginia, where people who were in the U.S. army, navy, air force, or government are sometimes buried

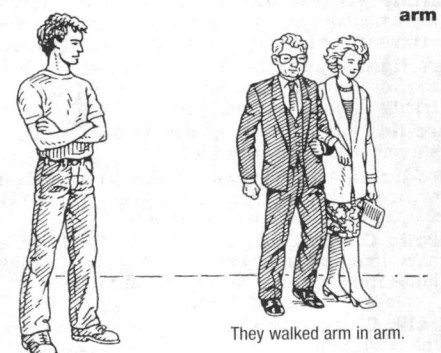

arm

They walked arm in arm.

He stood with his arms folded.

arm¹ /ɑrm/ *n.* [C]

S W
1

1 body one of the two long parts of your body between your shoulders and your hands: *Jens' mother put her arms around him.* | *Pat was carrying a large box under his arm.* | *Dana has a broken arm.* | *He had a pile of books in his arms.* | *An older couple were walking on the beach arm in arm* (=with their arms bent around each other's). | *She took him by the arm* (=led him by holding his arm) *and pushed him out of the door.* | *Jerry took Barbara in his arms* (=held her gently) *and kissed her.* | **cross/fold your arms** (=bend your arms so that they are resting on top of each other against your body) —see picture at BODY¹

2 weapons **arms** [plural] weapons used for fighting wars: *Sales of arms to the Middle East have dramatically increased.* | *nuclear arms* | *Boys as young as 13 are taking up arms* (=getting weapons and fighting) *to defend the city.* | *He appealed for the rebels to lay down their arms* (=stop fighting). —see also SMALL ARMS

3 furniture the part of a chair, SOFA etc. that you rest your arms on

4 clothing the part of a piece of clothing that covers your arm; SLEEVE

5 be up in arms to be very angry and ready to argue or fight: *Residents are up in arms about plans for a new road along the beach.*

6 with open arms if you do something with open arms, you show that you are happy to see someone or eager to accept an idea, plan etc.: *We welcomed Henry's offer with open arms.* | *My new in-laws accepted me with open arms.*

7 sb would give their right arm to do sth used to say that someone would be willing to do anything to get or do something: *These parents would give their right arms to get their kids into a prestigious school.*

8 at arm's length if you hold something at arm's length, you hold it away from your body

9 keep/hold sb at arm's length to avoid developing a relationship with someone: *Economic policies kept the Soviet Union and Japan at arm's length during the Cold War.*

10 as long as your arm INFORMAL a list or written document that is as long as your arm is very long

11 part of group a part of a large group that is responsible for a particular type of activity: *Epson America is the United States marketing arm of a Japanese company.*

12 object/machine a long part of an object or piece of equipment: *There is a 15-foot arm supporting the antenna.*

13 on your arm OLD-FASHIONED if a man has a woman on his arm, she is walking beside him holding his arm

14 design **arms** [plural] a set of pictures or patterns, usually painted on a SHIELD, that is used as the special sign of a family, town, university etc.; COAT OF ARMS —see also **arms akimbo** (AKIMBO), **brothers in arms** (BROTHER¹), **cost an arm and a leg** (COST²), **fold sb in your arms** (FOLD¹), **a shot in the arm** (SHOT¹), **twist sb's arm** (TWIST¹)

arm² *v.* [T] **1** to provide weapons for yourself, an army, a country etc. in order to prepare for a fight or a war: [arm sb with sth] *The local farmers have armed themselves with rifles and pistols.* —see also ARMED (1), UNARMED **2** to provide all the information, power etc. that are needed to deal with a difficult situation or argument: [arm sb with sth] *Arm yourself with all the facts you'll need to show you qualify for a loan.*

ar·ma·da /ɑrˈmɑdə/ *n.* [C] a large group of things, usually war ships

ar·ma·dil·lo /ˌɑrməˈdɪloʊ/ *n. plural* **armadillos** [C] a small animal that has a shell made of hard bone-like material, and lives in warm parts of North and South America

Ar·ma·ged·don /ˌɑrməˈgɛdn/ *n.* [singular,U] a terrible battle that will destroy the world: *a nuclear Armageddon*

ar·ma·ment /ˈɑrməmənt/ *n.* **1** [C usually plural] the weapons and military equipment used in an army: *nuclear armaments* **2** [U] the process of preparing an army or country for war by giving it weapons —compare DISARMAMENT

ar·ma·ture /ˈɑrmətʃɚ/ *n.* [C] TECHNICAL **1** a frame that you cover with clay or other soft material to make a model **2** the part of a GENERATOR, motor etc. that turns around to produce electricity, movement etc.

arm·band /ˈɑrmbænd/ *n.* [C] a band of material that you wear around your arm to show that you have an official position, or to show that someone you love has died

arm·chair¹ /ˈɑrmtʃɛr/ *n.* [C] a comfortable chair with sides that you can rest your arms on —see picture at CHAIR¹

armchair² *adj.* **an armchair traveler/critic etc.** someone who talks or reads about being a traveler, CRITIC etc., but does not have any real experience of doing it

▸w armed /ɑrmd/ *adj.* **1** carrying weapons, especially a gun: *The prisoners were kept under armed guard.* | [+ with] *The suspect is armed with a shotgun.* | *She got ten years in prison for armed robbery* (=stealing using a gun). | *The President fears that armed conflict* (=a war) *is possible.* | *There is very little support for an armed struggle* (=fighting with weapons) *against the government.* | *a heavily armed battleship* | *Many of the gangs are armed to the teeth* (=carrying a lot of weapons). **2** having something such as knowledge or skills that make it possible for you to do something or deal with something difficult: [+ with] *Valerie came to the meeting armed with all the facts and figures to prove us wrong.*

armed forc·es /ˌ. ˈ../ *n.* **the armed forces** PLURAL a country's military organizations that fight in wars, including the Army, Navy, and Air Force

armed ser·vic·es /ˌ. ˈ.../ *n.* **the armed services** PLURAL a country's military organizations, including the National Guard, Army, Navy etc.

Ar·me·ni·a /ɑrˈminiə/ a country in western Asia, north of Iran —**Armenian** *n., adj.*

arm·ful /ˈɑrmfʊl/ *n.* [C] the amount of something that you can hold in one or both arms: [+ of] *an armful of books*

arm·hole /ˈɑrmhoʊl/ *n.* [C] a hole in a shirt, dress, JACKET etc. that you put your arm through

ar·mi·stice /ˈɑrməstɪs/ *n.* [C] an agreement to stop fighting, usually for a short time —compare CEASE-FIRE, TRUCE

arm·load /ˈɑrmloʊd/ *n.* [C] the amount that you can carry in one or both arms: [+ of] *an armload of boxes*

ar·moire /ɑrmˈwɑr/ *n.* [C] a large piece of furniture with doors, and sometimes shelves, that you hang clothes in

ar·mor /ˈɑrmɚ/ *n.* [U] **1** metal or leather clothing that protects your body, worn by soldiers in battles in past times: *a suit of armor* **2** a strong metal layer that protects military vehicles: *armor-clad warships* **3** a strong layer or shell that protects some plants and animals —see also **a chink in sb's armor** (CHINK¹), **a knight in shining armor** (KNIGHT¹)

ar·mored /ˈɑrmɚd/ **1** armored vehicles have an outside layer made of metal to protect them from attack: *armored personnel carriers* **2** an armored car has special protection from bullets etc. and is used especially by important people **3** an armored army uses armored vehicles: *an armored division*

ar·mor·er /ˈɑrmərɚ/ *n.* [C] someone who makes or repairs weapons and ARMOR

armor-plat·ed /ˌ.. ˈ..◂/ *adj.* something, especially a vehicle, that is armor-plated has an outer metal layer to protect it —**armor plating** *n.* [U] —**armor plate** *n.* [U]

ar·mor·y /ˈɑrməri/ *n. plural* **armories** [C] **1** a place where weapons are stored **2** all the skills, information etc. someone has available to use in arguments, discussions etc.: *The computer industry didn't have anything special in its armory to tempt consumers last Christmas.*

arm·pit /ˈɑrmˌpɪt/ *n.* [C] **1** the hollow place under your arm where it joins your body —see picture at BODY¹ **2 the armpit of sth** SLANG the ugliest or worst place in a particular area: *Dale says the city of Butte is the armpit of Montana.*

arm·rest /ˈɑrmrɛst/ *n.* [C] a part of a chair that supports your arm

arms con·trol /ˈ. ˌ../ *n.* [U] the attempts by powerful countries to limit the number and type of war weapons that exist

arms race /ˈ. ˌ./ *n.* [C usually singular] the attempt by different countries to produce powerful weapons: *the nuclear arms race*

Arm·strong, /ˈɑrmstrɔŋ/, **Lou·is** /ˈlui/ (1900– 1971) a U.S. JAZZ musician and singer, who played the TRUMPET

Armstrong, Neil /nil/ (1930–) a U.S. ASTRONAUT who was the first man to step onto the moon, in 1969 —see picture on page 1330

ar·my /ˈɑrmi/ *n. plural* **armies 1 the army** the part of a country's military force that is trained to fight on land in a war: *The army is helping to clean up after the floods.* | *Neil joined the army when he was 17.* | *Both my sons are in the army.* **2** [C] a large organized group of people trained to fight on land in a war: *Rebel armies have taken control of the capital's radio station.* | *The Slovenians say they can raise an army* (=get enough people to fight) *of 20,000 men.* **3** [C] a large number of people or animals involved in the same activity: [+ of] *An army of ants overran our picnic.* —compare AIR FORCE, MARINES, NAVY¹

Ar·no, the /ˈɑrnoʊ/ a river in central Italy that flows westward from the Apennines and through the city of Florence

Ar·nold /ˈɑrnəld/, **Ben·e·dict** /ˈbɛnədɪkt/ (1741–1801) an American military leader in the American Revolutionary War, known for changing to support the British

a·ro·ma /əˈroʊmə/ *n.* [C] a strong nice smell: *the aroma of fresh coffee* —see usage note at SMELL¹

a·ro·ma·ther·a·py /əˌroʊməˈθɛrəpi/ *n.* [U] a treatment in which your body is rubbed with nice-smelling natural oils to reduce pain and make you feel well —**aromatherapist** *n.* [C]

ar·o·mat·ic /ˌærəˈmætɪk◂/ *adj.* **1** having a strong nice smell: *aromatic oils* **2** TECHNICAL aromatic chemical substances contain a ring of six CARBON atoms —**aromatically** /-kli/ *adv.*

a·rose /əˈroʊz/ the past tense of ARISE

A

a·round[1] /ə'raʊnd/ *prep.* **1** placed or arranged to surround something else: *We put a fence around the back yard.* | *The whole family was sitting around the dinner table talking.* | *She had a beautiful shawl wrapped around her shoulders.* **2** moving in a circular movement: *A few wolves were prowling around the cabin.* **3 around 200/5000 etc.** used when you do not know an exact number or amount to give a number or amount that is close to it; APPROXIMATELY: *Dodger Stadium seats around 50,000 people.* | *Greg must have drunk around 10 beers.* **4** in many places or parts of a particular area or place: *We took a walk around the park after breakfast.* | *Our company has branches around the world.* | *There were flowers all around the apartment.* **5** in or near a place: *I think Miguel lives somewhere around the high school.* | *Is there a bank around here?* **6** along or past the side of something, instead of through or over it: *We had to go around the lake.* **7** if something is organized around a particular person or thing, it is organized according to their needs, ideas, beliefs etc.: *Their whole society was built around the belief of reincarnation.* **8 get around sth** to avoid or solve a particular problem or difficult situation: *How do we get around the new tax laws?*

around[2] *adv.* **1** placed or arranged surrounding something else: *Reporters crowded around as Jensen left the courtroom.* | *The prison had high walls all around.* **2** [only after verb] used to say that someone or something is moving in a circular movement: *The children were dancing around in a circle.* | *Kevin spun his chair around to greet me as I walked into his office.* | *The helicopter continued flying **around and around**, searching for survivors.* **3 sit/stand/lie etc. around** to sit, stand etc. without doing anything in particular, especially so that people think you are wasting time: *A bunch of kids were hanging around outside.* **4** [only after verb] in many places or in many different parts of a particular area: *Don't leave all your clothes lying around.* | *When I finished college, I traveled around for a while before I got my first job.* | *Since it's your first day here, would you like me to show you around?* **5 a)** existing or available to use: *That joke's been around for years.* | *I think the B-52's were the best band around at the time.* **b)** if someone is around, they are in the same place as you: *It was 11:30 at night, and no one was around.* **6 fool/mess/play etc. around a)** used to mean that someone is wasting time by doing something stupid or dishonest: *Stop messing around! I know you hid my purse.* **b)** to have a secret sexual relationship with someone you should not have one with, for example someone's wife or husband: *I caught Jeff fooling around with my best friend.* **7 get around to (doing) sth** to finally do something that you have been intending to do for a long time: *I'll get around to painting the bedroom one of these days.* **8** toward or facing the opposite direction: *I'll turn the car around and pick you up at the door.* **9 2 feet/100 cm etc. around** measuring a particular distance on the outside of a round object: *Redwood trees can measure 30 or 40 feet around.* **10 have been around** INFORMAL **a)** to have had experience of many different situations, so that you can deal with new situations confidently **b)** HUMOROUS to have had many sexual experiences

around-the-clock /ˌ.ˌ. . '.ˌ/ *adj.* [only before noun] continuous through all hours of the day and night: *Ms. Jennings requires around-the-clock medical care.*

a·rou·sal /ə'raʊzəl/ *n.* [U] excitement, especially sexual excitement

a·rouse /ə'raʊz/ *v.* [T] **1 arouse interest/expectations etc.** to make you become interested, expect something etc.: *Why didn't Ames' behavior arouse suspicions at the CIA?* **2 arouse anger/fear/dislike etc.** to make someone feel very angry, afraid etc. **3** to make someone feel sexually excited **4** LITERARY to wake someone: [+ from] *Anne had to be aroused from a deep sleep.*

ar·peg·gi·o /ɑr'pɛdʒi,oʊ/ *n.* [C] the notes of a musical CHORD played separately rather than all at once

arr. 1 the written abbreviation of "arranged by" **2** the written abbreviation of "arrives" or "arrival"

ar·raign /ə'reɪn/ *v.* [T] TECHNICAL to make someone come to court to hear what the court says their crime is: [arraign sb on sth] *Thompson was arraigned on three charges of murder.* —**arraignment** *n.* [C,U]

ar·range /ə'reɪndʒ/ *v.* **1** [I,T] to organize or make plans for something such as a meeting, party, or trip: *Efforts to arrange a ceasefire have failed.* | [arrange to do sth] *Jessica arranged to pick us up.* | [arrange for sth] *I arranged for a private meeting between Donovan and the President.* | [arrange for sb to do sth] *Peter arranged for a friend to drive him there.* | [arrange sth with sb] *Dixon called to arrange an interview with Mrs. Tracy.* **2** [T] to put a group of things or people in a particular order or position: *We spent the morning arranging the jewelry in the display case.* **3** [T] to write or change a piece of music so that it is suitable for particular instruments: [+ for] *The symphony has been arranged for the piano.*

arranged mar·riage /.ˌ. '..ˌ/ *n.* [C,U] a marriage in which the parents choose a husband or wife for their child

ar·range·ment /ə'reɪndʒmənt/ *n.* **1** [C,U] something that has been organized or agreed on; agreement: *The clinics provide an opportunity for cooperative arrangements between health departments and academic centers.* | *Pets are permitted at the resort by prior arrangement.* **2** [C usually plural] the things that you must organize so that an event, meeting etc. can happen: *seating arrangements* | [+ for] *I've agreed to help with arrangements for our 10-year high school reunion.* | *The travel company made arrangements for our hotels and flights.* **3** [C,U] a group of things that have been arranged in an attractive or neat way, or the act of arranging a group of things in this way: *a beautiful flower arrangement* **4** [C,U] a piece of music that has been written or changed for a particular instrument: *a piano arrangement of an old folk song*

ar·rant /'ærənt/ *adj.* [only before noun] FORMAL used to emphasize how bad something is | **arrant nonsense/hypocrisy/fools etc.** *The article accused him of being "an arrant racist."*

ar·ray[1] /ə'reɪ/ *n. plural* **arrays 1** [C usually singular] a group or collection of things, usually arranged so that you can see them all: [+ of] *The museum has a vast array of Indian art.* **2** [C usually singular] a group of people, especially people who are important or special: [+ of] *a dazzling array of acting talent* **3** [C] TECHNICAL a set of numbers or signs, or of computer memory units, arranged in lines across or down

array[2] *v.* **arrays, arrayed, arraying** [T usually passive] **1** LITERARY to arrange something in an attractive way: *Nikulin's medals were arrayed on a cushion at the foot of his coffin.* **2** FORMAL to make something such as information, facts etc. ready and available for use, especially in an argument or disagreement: [be arrayed against sb/sth] *With such powerful interests arrayed against it, the reform plan had little chance of succeeding.* **3** FORMAL to put soldiers in position ready for battle

ar·rears /ə'rɪrz/ *n.* [plural] **1 be in arrears** if someone is in arrears or if their payments are in arrears, they are late in paying something that they should pay regularly, such as rent: *The rent money is two months in arrears.* | *The family fell into arrears* (=became late with payments) *when Ben lost his job.* **2** money that you owe someone because regular payments such as rent have not been paid at the right time: *When will America pay its arrears to the U.N.?*

ar·rest[1] /ə'rɛst/ *v.* [T] **1** if the police arrest someone, they take that person away because they think he/she did something illegal: *Police arrested 26 demonstrators.* | [arrest sb for sth] *Embry was arrested for assault.* **2** FORMAL to stop something that is happening, or to make it happen more slowly: *Powerful drugs are used to arrest the spread of the disease.* | *Smoking at an early age is thought to arrest growth in children.* **3 arrested development** HUMOROUS a situation in which someone behaves in a way that is not sensible and that seems more appropriate for someone much younger than they are: *As for your wimpy husband, he sounds like a pathetic case of arrested development.* **4 sb can't get arrested** HUMOROUS used to say that someone who used to be famous or popular is now not famous or popular at all

s w **ar·rest²** *n.* [C,U] the act of taking someone away and guarding them because they may have done something illegal: *The police expect to make an arrest soon.* | *Dillman is under arrest* (=kept by police) *for his role in the robbery.* | *Suu Kyi was placed under house arrest* (=forced by the police or government to stay in her house) *in 1989.*

s w **ar·riv·al** /əˈraɪvəl/ *n.* **1** [U] the act of arriving somewhere: *The arrival of Flight 227 was delayed by two hours.* | *Porter spoke to reporters shortly after his arrival.* | [+ at/in] *Today is the anniversary of my parents' arrival in New York from Puerto Rico.* | *Wyler was rushed to the hospital, but was dead on arrival* (=when he arrived). —opposite DEPARTURE **2 the arrival of sth** the time when an important new idea, method, or product is first used or discovered. *Demand for telephone numbers has skyrocketed since the arrival of fax machines in offices.* **3** [C] someone who has just arrived in a particular place to live, work etc.: *Las Vegas is America's fastest-growing city, with 6,000 new arrivals each month.* **4** HUMOROUS a baby: *Congratulations on your new arrival!*

s w **ar·rive** /əˈraɪv/ *v.* [I]

1 `get somewhere` to reach a particular place where you are going: [+ in/at/from] *What time does the plane arrive in New York?* | *We arrived at Carol's two hours late.*

2 `be delivered` if something arrives, it is brought or delivered to you: *The packages arrived the day before Christmas.*

3 `event` if an event or particular period of time arrives, it happens: *When the day of the wedding arrived, everything was ready.*

4 `sth new` if a new idea, method, product etc. arrives, it begins to exist or starts being used: *Toy sales have doubled since computer games arrived.*

5 `birth` to be born: *Sharon's baby arrived just after midnight.*

6 arrive at a conclusion/agreement/idea etc. to reach an agreement etc. after a lot of effort: *The jurors finally arrived at a verdict.*

7 `success` to achieve success: *When he saw his name printed on the door, he knew he'd arrived!* —see Usage Note at REACH¹

ar·ro·gance /ˈærəgəns/ *n.* [U] the quality of thinking that you are very important so that you behave in an impolite way

ar·ro·gant /ˈærəgənt/ *adj.* so proud of your own abilities or qualities that you behave as if you are much more important than anyone else: *an arrogant, selfish man* | *an arrogant smile* —**arrogantly** *adv.*

ar·ro·gate /ˈærəˌgeɪt/ *v.* **arrogate (to yourself) sth** FORMAL to claim that you have a particular right, position etc. without having the legal right to it

w **ar·row** /ˈæroʊ/ *n.* [C] **1** a weapon like a thin straight stick with a point at one end that you shoot with a BOW **2** a sign in the shape of an arrow, used to show people which direction to go or look in: *Follow the red arrows to the X-ray department.* —see also STRAIGHT ARROW

ar·row·head /ˈæroʊˌhɛd/ *n.* [C] a sharp pointed piece of metal or stone attached to one end of an arrow

ar·row·root /ˈæroʊˌrut/ *n.* [U] a type of flour made from the root of a tropical American plant

ar·se·nal /ˈɑrsənl/ *n.* [C] **1** a large number of weapons: [+ of] *NATO forces possess an arsenal of 700 surface-to-air missiles.* **2** a building where weapons are stored

ar·se·nic /ˈɑrsənɪk, ˈɑrsnɪk/ *n.* [U] *symbol* **As** a very poisonous substance that is an ELEMENT and is

sometimes used for killing rats and included in some chemicals used to kill insects or WEEDS

ar·son /ˈɑrsən/ *n.* [U] the crime of deliberately making something burn, especially a building —**arsonist** *n.* [C]

s w **art¹** /ɑrt/ *n.* **1** [U] the use of painting, drawing, SCULPTURE etc. to represent things or express ideas: *Picasso and other Cubists changed the course of modern art.* **2** [U,plural] objects that are produced by art, such as paintings, drawings etc.: *an art exhibit* | *The street fair will include dancing, arts and crafts, and food.* **3** [U] the skill of drawing or painting: *Ben was always good at art.* | *art class* **4 the arts** [plural] art, music, theater, movies, literature etc. all considered together: *Italians are proud of their country's contributions to the arts.* —see also **fine arts** (FINE ART), LIBERAL ARTS **5** [C,U] the ability or skill involved in doing or making something: *Phil has turned sandwich-making into an art.* | [the art of (doing) sth] *Television is ruining the art of conversation.* | *I have the early morning routine down to a fine art* (=can do it extremely skillfully).

art² *v.* **thou art** OLD USE used to mean "you are" when talking to one person

art dec·o /ˌɑrt ˈdɛkoʊ/ *n.* [U] a style of art and decoration that uses simple shapes and was popular in the U.S. and Europe in the 1920s and 1930s

art di·rec·tor /ˈ. .ˌ../ *n.* [C] someone whose job is to decide on the total appearance of a magazine, advertisement, movie, television program etc.

ar·te·fact /ˈɑrtɪˌfækt/ *n.* [C] another spelling of ARTIFACT

Ar·te·mis /ˈɑrtɪmɪs/ in Greek MYTHOLOGY, the goddess of hunting and the moon

ar·te·ri·al /ɑrˈtɪriəl/ *adj.* [only before noun] **1** involving the arteries: *arterial blood* **2 an arterial street/railroad etc.** a main road, railroad etc.

ar·te·ri·o·scle·ro·sis /ɑrˌtɪrioʊskləˈroʊsɪs/ *n.* [U] a disease in which your arteries become hard, which stops the blood from flowing through them smoothly

ar·ter·y /ˈɑrtəri/ *n. plural* **arteries** [C] **1** one of the tubes that carries blood from your heart to the rest of your body —compare VEIN **2** a main road, railroad, river etc.

ar·te·sian well /ɑrˌtiʒən ˈwɛl/ *n.* [C] a WELL from which the water is forced up out of the ground by natural pressure

art film /ˈ. ./ also **art mov·ie** /ˈ. ˌ../ *n.* [C] a movie that tries to express ideas rather than only entertain people

art·ful /ˈɑrtfəl/ *adj.* FORMAL **1** showing or resulting from a lot of skill and artistic ability: *The script is an artful adaptation of a novel by Rosa Guy.* **2** skillful at deceiving people: *artful misrepresentations* —**artfully** *adj.*: *artfully concealed pockets* —**artfulness** *n.* [U]

art gal·ler·y /ˈ. ˌ.../ *n.* [C] a building where important paintings are kept and shown to the public

art house /ˈ. ./ *n.* [C] a movie theater that shows mainly foreign movies, or movies made by small movie companies, or art films

ar·thri·tis /ɑrˈθraɪtɪs/ *n.* [U] a disease that causes a lot of pain in the joints of your body —**arthritic** /ɑrˈθrɪtɪk/ *adj.*: *arthritic fingers*

Ar·thur /ˈɑrθər/ in old European stories, a king of Britain —**Arthurian** /ɑrˈθʊriən/ *adj.*

Arthur, Ches·ter /ˈtʃɛstər/ (1829–1886) the 21st President of the U.S.

ar·ti·choke /ˈɑrtɪˌtʃoʊk/ *n.* [C] **1** also **globe artichoke** a plant with thick pointed leaves that are eaten as a vegetable **2** also **Jerusalem artichoke** a plant that has a root like a potato that you can eat

s w **ar·ti·cle** /ˈɑrtɪkəl/ *n.* **1** a piece of writing about a particular subject in a newspaper, magazine etc.: [+ about/on] *an article about the Hubble telescope* **2** a thing, especially one of a group of things: *Prisoners may receive some personal articles from their families.* | *She didn't take much with her, just a few*

A

articles of clothing. **3** a part of a law or legal agreement, especially a numbered part: *Article 1 of the U.S. Constitution guarantees freedom of religion.* **4** TECHNICAL a word used before a noun to show whether the noun refers to a particular example of something or to a general example of something. In English, "the" is the DEFINITE ARTICLE, and "a" or "an" are INDEFINITE ARTICLES. **5 an article of faith** FORMAL something that you feel very strongly about so that it affects how you think or behave

ar·tic·u·late¹ /ɑrˈtɪkyəlɪt/ *adj.* **1** able to talk easily, clearly, and effectively about things, especially difficult subjects: *bright, articulate 17-year-olds* —opposite INARTICULATE **2** writing or speech that is articulate is very clear and easy to understand even if the subject is difficult **3** TECHNICAL having joints: *articulate insects* —**articulately** *adv.* —**articulateness** *n.* [U]

ar·tic·u·late² /ɑrˈtɪkyəˌleɪt/ *v.* [I] **1** to express what you are thinking or feeling very clearly: *I was feeling emotions that I found difficult to articulate.* **2** to speak or pronounce your words clearly and carefully

ar·tic·u·lat·ed /ɑrˈtɪkyəˌleɪtɪd/ *adj.* TECHNICAL having two or more parts that are connected by a moving joint: *The X-ray device sits at the end of an articulated arm.*

ar·tic·u·la·tion /ɑrˌtɪkyəˈleɪʃən/ *n.* **1** [U] the production of speech sounds: *clear articulation* **2** [C,U] the expression of thoughts or feelings in words: *The report contains an articulation of the agency's mission statement.* **3** [C] TECHNICAL a joint, especially in a plant

ar·ti·fact /ˈɑrtɪˌfækt/ *n.* [C] an object that was made and used a long time ago, especially one that is studied by scientists: *Egyptian artifacts*

ar·ti·fice /ˈɑrtɪfɪs/ *n.* FORMAL **1** [U] the skillful use of tricks, especially used to deceive someone: *The documentary highlights the difference between Warren's real life and the artifice of her stage shows.* **2** [C] a trick that is used to deceive someone

ar·ti·fi·cial /ˌɑrtəˈfɪʃəl/ *adj.* [usually before noun] **1** not made of natural materials or substances, but made by people: *artificial sweeteners for coffee* | *Our ice cream contains no artificial colors or flavors.* **2** not real or natural, but deliberately made to look real or natural: *artificial Christmas trees* | *Glen wears an artificial leg.* **3** artificial behavior is not natural or sincere because someone is pretending to be something they are not: *an artificial smile* **4** happening because someone has made it happen and not as part of a natural process: *High import taxes give their goods an artificial advantage in the market.* —**artificially** *adv.*: *Food prices are being kept artificially low.* | *artificially flavored drinks* —**artificiality** /ˌɑrtəfɪʃiˈæləti/ *n.* [U]

artificial in·sem·i·na·tion /.....ˌ... ...ˈ../ *n.* [U] the process of making a woman or female animal PREGNANT using a piece of equipment, rather than naturally

artificial in·tel·li·gence /ˌ..... ˈ.../ *abbreviation* **AI** *n.* [U] the study of how to make computers do things that people can do, such as make decisions, see things etc.

artificial res·pi·ra·tion /ˌ..... ..ˈ..., ..,.. ..ˈ../ *n.* [U] a way of making someone breathe again when they have stopped, by blowing air into their mouth; MOUTH-TO-MOUTH RESUSCITATION

ar·til·ler·y /ɑrˈtɪləri/ *n.* [U] large guns, either on wheels or standing in a particular place

ar·ti·san /ˈɑrtəzən, -sən/ *n.* [C] someone who does skilled work with their hands; CRAFTSMAN —**artisanal** *adj.*

s w **art·ist** /ˈɑrtɪst/ *n.* [C] **1** someone who produces art,
2 2 especially paintings or drawings: *This exhibit of paintings and sculptures traces the artist's work during five decades.* **2** a professional performer, especially in music, dance, or the theater: *Many of the artists in the show donated their fee to charity.*

3 INFORMAL someone who is extremely good at something: *She's an artist in the kitchen.*

ar·tiste /ɑrˈtist/ *n.* [C] a professional singer, dancer, actor etc. who performs in a show

ar·tis·tic /ɑrˈtɪstɪk/ *adj.* **1** relating to art or CULTURE: *members of the artistic community* | *Creators of artistic works have a legal right to copyright.* **2** showing skill or imagination in any of the arts: *She's creative, artistic, and temperamental.* **3** an artistic arrangement, design etc. looks attractive and has been done with skill and imagination: *Chef Stroehl is known for the artistic presentation of his dishes.* —**artistically** /-kli/ *adv.*

art·ist·ry /ˈɑrtəstri/ *n.* [U] skill in a particular artistic activity: *The band's solos are displays of true artistry.*

art·less /ˈɑrtlɪs/ *adj.* LITERARY natural, honest, and sincere: *a naive, artless young woman* —**artlessly** *adv.* —**artlessness** *n.* [U]

art nou·veau /ˌɑrt nuˈvou/ *n.* [U] a style of art that used pictures of plants and flowers, popular in Europe and the U.S. at the end of the 19th century

art·sy /ˈɑrtsi/ *adj.* INFORMAL interested in art, seeming to know a lot about art, or showing qualities like those of art: *Celia's artsy friends* | *an artsy black-and-white movie*

artsy-craft·sy /ˌɑrtsi ˈkræftsi/ *adj.* someone who is artsy-craftsy makes things at home and does all kinds of art, especially in a way that is not very professional

artsy-fart·sy /ˌɑrtsi ˈfɑrtsi/ *adj.* INFORMAL someone who is artsy-fartsy tries too hard to show that they are interested in art

art·work /ˈɑrt¬wɔrk/ *n.* [C,U] **1** paintings, SCULPTURES etc. produced by artists **2** pictures that are made for a book or magazine, or for another product such as a computer program

art·y /ˈɑrti/ *adj.* ARTSY

a·ru·gu·la /əˈrugələ/ *n.* [U] a plant with leaves that are eaten in SALADS

-ary /ɛri, -əri/ *suffix* **1** [in adjectives] relating to something, or having a particular quality: *planetary bodies* (=that are PLANETS) | *customary* **2** someone who has a connection with something or who does something: *the beneficiaries of the will* (=people who get something from it) | *a functionary* (=someone with duties) **3** [in nouns] a thing or place relating to things of a particular kind, or containing these things: *a library* (=containing books) | *an ovary* (=containing eggs) —see also -ERY

Ar·y·an /ˈɛriən/ *n.* [C] someone from Northern Europe, especially someone with BLOND hair and blue eyes —**Aryan** *adj.*

as¹ /əz; *strong* æz/ *adv., prep.* **1** used when comparing things, or saying that they are like each other in some way: *These houses aren't as old as the ones downtown.* | *Jerry was as surprised as anyone when they offered him the job.* | *You can use cherries instead of plums – they work just as well.* | *Could you have Carol call me as soon as possible* (=as soon as you can)? **2** used when describing what someone's job, duty, or position is: *In the past, women were mainly employed as secretaries or teachers.* | *The kids dressed up as animals for Halloween.* **3** used when describing the way something is being used or considered: *John used an old blanket as a tent.* | *Settlers saw the wilderness as dangerous rather than beautiful.* **4 as a result of sth** because of something: *Several businesses went under as a result of the recession.* **5 be regarded as sth** to be considered to be something: *"Novecento" is regarded by many as Bertolucci's best film.* —see also **as a matter of fact** (MATTER¹), **as good as** (GOOD¹), **as/so long as** (LONG²), **as one** (ONE²), **as well as** (WELL¹), **such as** (SUCH¹)

as² *conjunction* **1** use when comparing things, or saying that they are like each other in some way: *I can't run nearly as fast as I used to.* | *Jim works in the same office as my sister does.* **2** in the way or manner mentioned: *Leave things as they are until the police arrive.* | *As I said earlier, this research has just started.* | *You'd better do as Mom says.* | *Roberta was late as usual.* **3** while or when something is

s 1

s 1

happening: *I saw Peter as I was getting off the bus.* | *Be patient with your puppy as he adjusts to his new home.* | *The phone rang just as I was leaving.* **4 as if.../as though... a)** in a way that suggests that something is true: *You look as if you're having a good time.* | *It sounds as though she's been really sick.* | *Mandy felt as if they were all against her.* | *Brian shook his head as if to say "don't trust her."* **b)** used to suggest a possible explanation for something, although you do not think that this is the actual explanation: *Joe always sounds as if he's drunk.* | *You make it seem as if you're being overworked.* **5 as to sth** concerning a particular subject or decision: *She offered no explanation as to why she'd left so suddenly.* | *I need some advice as to which college to choose.* | *The President asked for opinions as to the likelihood of war.* **6 as of today/December 15/next June etc.** starting from today, December 15 etc. and continuing: *The pay raise will come into effect as of January 1.* **7 as for sb/sth** concerning a person or subject that is related to what you were talking about before: *As for racism, much progress has been made, but there is still much to do.* | *As for you, young man, you're grounded.* **8 as it is a)** according to the situation that actually exists, especially when that situation is different from what you expected or need: *We were saving money to go to Hawaii, but as it is we can only afford to go on a camping trip.* **b)** already: *Just keep quiet – you're in enough trouble as it is.* **9** used to state why a particular situation exists or why someone does something; BECAUSE: *James decided not to go out as he was still really tired.* **10 as (of) yet** [used in negatives] until and including the present time: *Local election results have not as yet been announced.* | *As of yet, we don't believe it was a drive-by shooting.* **11** though: *Unlikely as it might seem, I'm tired too.* | *Try as she might, Sue couldn't get the door open.* | *As smart as Jake is, he doesn't know how to manage people well.* **12 so cold/heavy/quick etc. as to...** or **such an idiot/a disaster etc. as to...** FORMAL used to show the reason that makes something happen or not happen: *The water was so cold as to make swimming impossible.* | *How could he have been such an idiot as to trust them in the first place?* **13 so as to do sth** with the purpose of doing something: *The little boy ran off so as not to be caught* (=so that he would not be caught). **14 it's not as if...** SPOKEN used to say that something is definitely not true, about a situation or someone's behavior: *I don't know why Sally's grades are so low. It's not as if she can't do the work.* **15 as if you would/as if you care/as if it matters** SPOKEN used to say that someone would definitely not do something, does not care etc. or that something does not matter at all: *Margaret told me she'd never speak to me again – as if I cared* (=I do not care at all). | *"I think Ken's deliberately ignoring us." "As if he would* (=he would not ignore us)!*"* **16 as is/was/does sb/sth** FORMAL in the same way as someone or something else is, does etc.: *Dawn's very quiet, as was her mother.* | *I voted Republican, as did my wife.* **17 as it were** SPOKEN FORMAL used when describing someone or something in a way that is not completely exact: *He became famous, as it were, for never having a hit record.* **18 as against sth** in comparison with something: *Profits this year are $2.5 million as against $4 million last year.* —see also **as/so long as** (LONG²), **as soon as** (SOON), **not as such** (SUCH²), **as well** (WELL¹) —see Usage Note at THAN¹

ASAP, a.s.a.p. /ˌeɪ ɛs eɪ ˈpi/ *n.* the abbreviation of "as soon as possible": *Call him ASAP.*

as·bes·tos /æsˈbɛstəs, æz-, əs-, əz-/ *n.* [U] a gray mineral that does not burn easily, which was used as a building material or in protective clothing

as·cend /əˈsɛnd/ *v.* FORMAL **1** [I] to move up through the air: *The plane ascended rapidly.* **2** [T] to climb something or walk to a higher position, for example on a slope: *Ms. Goodman ascended a 10-foot aluminum ladder to the roof.* **3** [I,T] to move to a more important or responsible job, or to move higher in rank: [+ to] *Thomas ascended to the Supreme Court.* | *Jordan's King Hussein ascended the throne in 1952.* **4** [I,T] to lead or go up to a higher position: *Several ski lifts ascended the mountain.* **5 in ascending**

order if a group of things are arranged in ascending order, each thing is higher, or greater in amount, than the one before it —opposite DESCEND

as·cen·dan·cy, ascendency /əˈsɛndənsi/ *n.* [U] a position of power, influence, or control: *The U.S. gained ascendancy after World War II.* —**ascendance** *n.* [U]

as·cen·dant¹ /əˈsɛndənt/ *adj.* FORMAL becoming more powerful or popular: *an ascendant politician*

ascendant² *n.* **be in the ascendant** to be or become powerful or popular: *During this period, liberal ideas were in the ascendant.*

as·cen·sion /əˈsɛnʃən/ *n.* [U] the act of moving up

Ascension Day /.ˈ.. ˌ. / *n.* [U] a Christian holy day on the Thursday 40 days after Easter, when Christians remember when Jesus Christ went to heaven

as·cent /əˈsɛnt, ˈæsɛnt/ *n.* **1** [C usually singular] the act of climbing something or moving toward the top of something: *The final ascent of Kilimanjaro began at 5:00 a.m.* **2** [U] the process of becoming more important, powerful, or successful than before: *Yeltsin's ascent to the presidency of Russia* **3** [C usually singular] a path or way up to the top of something, for example a mountain: *a rugged and steep ascent* —opposite DESCENT

as·cer·tain /ˌæsərˈteɪn/ *v.* [I,T] FORMAL to find out something: *Read labels to ascertain the amount of fats in processed foods.* | [+ how/when/why etc.] *We're still trying to ascertain who was driving the car.* —**ascertainable** *adv.*

as·cet·ic /əˈsɛtɪk/ *adj.* living without any physical pleasures or comforts, especially for religious reasons: *They belonged to an ascetic Jewish sect called the Essenes* —**ascetic** [C] —**ascetically** /-kli/ *adv.* —**asceticism** /əˈsɛtəˌsɪzəm/ *n.* [U]

ASCII /ˈæski/ *n.* [U] TECHNICAL American Standard Code for Information Interchange; a system used in exchanging information between different computers by allowing them to recognize SYMBOLS, such as letters or numbers, in the same way

as·cot /ˈæskət, -kɑt/ *n.* [C] a wide piece of material worn by men loosely folded around their neck inside their collar

as·cribe /əˈskraɪb/ *v.*

ascribe sth to sb/sth *phr. v.* [T] FORMAL **1** to be fairly sure about what the cause of something is, and claim that this is true: *Doctors ascribed his death to a virus.* **2** to believe something or someone has a particular quality: *The natives ascribe healing properties to this fruit.* **3** to claim that someone is the artist, writer etc. who produced a particular piece of work: *These writings have been ascribed to Orpheus.* —**ascribable** *adj.* [+ to]

a·sep·tic /eɪˈsɛptɪk, ə-/ *adj.* a wound that is aseptic is completely clean without any harmful BACTERIA

a·sex·u·al /eɪˈsɛkʃuəl/ *adj.* **1** not having sexual organs, not able to have sex, or not involving sex: *asexual reproduction* **2 a)** not seeming to have any sexual qualities **b)** not interested in sexual relations —**asexually** *adv.*

ash /æʃ/ *n.* **1** [C,U] the soft gray powder that remains after something has been burned: *cigar ash* | *Investigators sifted through the ashes to find the cause of the fire.* **2 ashes** [plural] the ash that remains when a dead person's body is burned: *McCrea wanted his ashes scattered at sea.* **3** [C,U] a very hard wood, or the common type of forest tree that produces this wood —see also **rise from the ashes** (RISE¹)

a·shamed /əˈʃeɪmd/ *adj.* [not before noun] **1** feeling embarrassed and guilty about something you have done: [+ of/about] *Fritz is ashamed of the mess he's made.* | [**ashamed to do sth**] *Hassel was too ashamed to ask her family for help.* | [**be ashamed that**] *Later, I was ashamed that I hadn't helped.* | [**be ashamed of doing sth**] *He was ashamed of not being able to support his family.* | *The U.S. should be ashamed of itself for withholding economic aid.* **2** feeling uncomfortable or upset, especially because

A

someone does something that embarrasses you: [+ of] *I'm ashamed of the actions of my government.* | [**be ashamed to be/do sth**] *His behavior makes me ashamed to be seen with him in public.* —see Usage Note at GUILTY

ash·can /ˈæʃkæn/ *n.* [C] OLD-FASHIONED a GARBAGE CAN

Ashe /æʃ/, **Arthur** (1943– 1993) a U.S. tennis player famous for being the first African-American man to win the men's SINGLES competition at WIMBLEDON in 1975

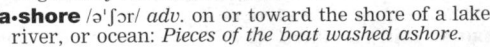
Arthur Ashe

ash·en /ˈæʃən/ *adj.* **1** very pale because of shock or fear: *Lisa's face had turned ashen.* **2** pale gray in color, like ash: *ashen hills*

Ash·er /ˈæʃɚ/ in the Bible, the head of one of the 12 tribes of Israel

Ash·ga·bat /ˈæʃkəˌbæt, -ˌbɑt/ the capital and largest city of Turkmenistan

a·shore /əˈʃɔr/ *adv.* on or toward the shore of a lake, river, or ocean: *Pieces of the boat washed ashore.*

ash·ram /ˈæʃrəm, -rɑm/ *n.* [C] a place where people who practice the Hindu religion live together, apart from other people

ash·tray /ˈæʃtreɪ/ *n. plural* **ashtrays** [C] a small dish where you put cigarette ASHes and used cigarettes

Ash Wednes·day /ˌ. ˈ../ *n.* [C,U] the first day of Lent

ash·y /ˈæʃi/ *adj.* **1** having a light gray color **2** covered with ASHes

A·sia /ˈeɪʒə/ the world's largest CONTINENT, which includes the countries of the Middle East and countries such as India, China, Japan, and part of Russia

Asia Mi·nor /ˌ.. ˈ../ the historical name for the main part of Turkey

A·sian¹ /ˈeɪʒən/ *n.* someone from Asia, especially Japan, China, Korea etc.

Asian² *adj.* from Asia or relating to Asia

Asian-A·mer·i·can /ˌ.. .ˈ.../ *n.* [C] an American citizen whose family was originally from Asia

A·si·at·ic /ˌeɪʒiˈætɪk, -zi-/ *adj.* TECHNICAL from Asia or relating to Asia

a·side¹ /əˈsaɪd/ *adv.* **1** put/set/leave etc. sth aside (for sth) **a)** to save an amount of money: *The company had set aside $140 million for bonus pay.* **b)** to keep something separate or not use it, especially because someone is going to buy or use it later: *Much of the forest was put aside for parkland.* **c)** to leave something to be considered or dealt with at another time: *During Thanksgiving, families try to put aside personal differences.* **d)** to stop using something and put it to one side: *Put grease in a baking pan and set it aside.* **2** step/stand/move etc. aside **a)** to stop doing something so that someone else can have a chance: *Ms. Lawrence said she was stepping aside as chairman.* **b)** to move, step etc. to the side: *Jim stepped aside to let me pass.* **3** aside from sb/sth **a)** except for: *Aside from coal, copper is the state's largest natural resource.* **b)** in addition to: *Aside from helpful tips, the book also contains a guide to the city's restaurants.* **4** used to show that something you have just said is not as important as what you are going to say next: *Sound problems aside, some of the acts stood out as winners.* **5** take/pull/call etc. aside to take someone a short distance to a more private place, so that you can talk to them: *A friend pulled him aside and told him to calm down.* **6** brush/ sweep sth aside to treat someone's idea or statement in a way that shows you do not think it is important: *The President brushed aside questions about this health.*

aside² *n.* [C] **1** a remark made in a low voice that you only intend particular people to hear **2** a remark or story that is not part of the main subject of a speech: *He noted as an aside that Mrs. Singer was also a member.* **3** words spoken by an actor to the people watching a play, that the other characters in the play do not hear

as·i·nine /ˈæsəˌnaɪn/ *adj.* extremely stupid or silly; RIDICULOUS: *asinine questions*

ask /æsk/ *v.*

SW
1 1

1 ▸**question**◂ [I,T] to say or write something in order to get an answer, a solution, or information: *"What's your name?" she asked.* | [**ask (sb) who/what/where etc.**] *She called and asked me what she should wear.* | [**ask sb sth**] *Don't ask me directions – I don't know where it is.* | [**ask sb**] *Why don't you just ask him?* | [**ask (sb) if/whether**] *Ask Jamie if she needs a ride home.* | *They asked a lot of questions about Medicare.* | [**ask (sb) about**] *Joe went and asked about getting a refund.* | *Everybody has a favorite restaurant, so ask around* (=ask a lot of people).

2 ▸**for help/advice etc.**◂ [I,T] to make a request for help, advice, information etc.: *Todd just went to the fridge and helped himself to a beer, without even asking.* | [**ask sb to do sth**] *She asked me to get her a cup of coffee.* | [**ask to do sth**] *Several employees asked to be given more time off.* | [+ for] *Mrs. Costello asked for a copy.* | [**ask sb for sth**] *I'm going to ask her for a raise.* | [**ask if you can do sth**] *Ask your mom if you can come with us.* —see Usage Note at REQUEST²

3 ▸**invite**◂ [T] to invite someone to your home, to go out with you etc.: *Did you ask her out?* (=ask someone, especially someone of the opposite sex, to go to a movie, a restaurant etc. with you) | *Why don't you ask them over for dinner?* (=invite someone to come to your home)

4 ▸**price**◂ [T] to want a particular amount of money for something you are selling: [**ask $30/$500 etc. for sth**] *How much is he asking for it?*

SPOKEN PHRASES

5 if you ask me used to emphasize your own opinion: *He's just plain crazy if you ask me.*
6 sb is asking for it used to say that someone deserves something bad that happens to them: *It's his own fault he got hit. I mean, he was asking for it.*
7 don't ask me used to say you do not know the answer to something: *"How does this thing work?" "Don't ask me!"*
8 don't ask used to say that something is too annoying or strange to explain: *"What did he want you to do?" "Oh, don't ask."*
9 I'm just asking used when you think someone was offended or annoyed by your question, to show that you did not mean to annoy or offend them: *"Yeah, but not now, Geri." "Okay, I was just asking."*
10 ask yourself to think carefully and honestly in order to find the answer to something: *And then I asked myself if what I was doing was really right.*
11 I ask you! OLD-FASHIONED used to express surprise at and disapproval of something stupid that someone has done

12 be asking for trouble to do something that is very likely to have a bad effect or result: *You'd better check the oil in your car. Otherwise you're just asking for trouble.*
13 for the asking if you can have something for the asking, you only have to ask for it and you can have it: *This kind of information is usually available for the asking.*

USAGE NOTE: ASK

WORD CHOICE: ask, want to know, inquire, question, interrogate

Ask is the usual verb for questions: *"How are you doing?" she asked.* | *That's a stupid question to ask.* Often people use **want to know** when they are talking about what someone else has asked: *He wanted to know what time it was.* **Inquire** has the same meaning but is more formal, and is not followed by a noun or pronoun object: *Be sure to inquire about local regulations well before your trip* (NOT *...inquire local regulations*). To **question** a person is to ask them a lot of questions, especially officially, and to **interrogate** suggests that someone is being held by force and asked questions that they are unwilling to answer, for example by the police or an enemy.

GRAMMAR

Remember that you do not follow **ask** with a direct question, unless you are repeating the exact words: *Ask Ben what kind of ice cream he wants* (NOT *Ask what kind of ice cream does he want*). | *I asked Ben, "What kind of ice cream do you want?"* You **ask** people certain things without using *for* or *about*: *I asked her the way/her name/the price/the time/a favor/permission/her advice* (NOT *asked to her the way*). You usually **ask for** or **about** most other things: *Should we stop and ask for directions?* | *Tom asked Sharon for a date* (NOT *Tom asked a date to Sharon*). | *Can I ask you about the grades on the test?* (NOT *of the grades*)

a·skance /əˈskæns/ *adv.* **look askance (at sb/sth)** to look at or consider something in a way that shows you do not believe it or approve of it

a·skew /əˈskyu/ *adv.* not exactly straight or in the right position: *There's Jerry, with his collar open and his tie askew.*

asking price /ˈ.. ˌ./ *n.* [C] the price that someone wants to sell something for: *The asking price for that car is $7500.*

ASL *n.* [U] American Sign Language; a language that uses hand movements instead of spoken words, used in the U.S. by people who cannot hear

a·slant /əˈslænt/ *adv.* [not before noun] FORMAL not straight up or down, but across at an angle —**aslant** *adj.*

³ᵂ **a·sleep** /əˈslip/ *adj.* [not before noun] **1** sleeping: *Kelly was asleep on the sofa.* | **fast/sound asleep** (=sleeping very deeply) **2 fall asleep** to begin to sleep: *Her three-year-old daughter fell asleep while we talked.* **3** an arm or leg that is asleep has been in one position for too long, so you cannot feel it **4 half asleep** INFORMAL not paying attention to something because you are tired: *Sorry, what did you say? I was half asleep.* —see also **go to sleep** (SLEEP²)

As·ma·ra /æzˈmɑrə, -ˈmærə/ the capital and largest city of Eritrea

a·so·cial /eɪˈsoʊʃəl/ *adj.* TECHNICAL **1** unwilling to meet people and talk to them, especially in a way that seems unfriendly **2** asocial behavior shows a lack of concern for other people —compare ANTI-SOCIAL

asp /æsp/ *n.* [C] a small poisonous snake from North Africa

as·par·a·gus /əˈspærəgəs/ *n.* [U] a green vegetable shaped like a small stick with a point at one end —see picture at VEGETABLE

ASPCA, the American Society for the Prevention of Cruelty to Animals; a CHARITY organization that takes care of animals

ᵂ **as·pect** /ˈæspɛkt/ *n.* **1** [C] one part of a situation, idea, plan etc. that has many parts: *How we are going to pay for it is one aspect we haven't discussed yet.* | [+ of] *She was active in many aspects of campus life.* **2** [C] the direction in which a window, room, front of a building etc. faces: *a south-facing aspect* **3** [C,U] LITERARY the appearance of someone or something: *When everything turns green, the countryside presents a truly beautiful aspect.* **4** [C,U] TECHNICAL the form of a verb in grammar that shows whether an action is continuing, or if it happens always, again and again, or once. For example, "he dances" is different from "he is dancing" in aspect.

as·pen /ˈæspən/ *n.* [C] a type of tree that grows in western North America, with leaves that make a pleasant noise in the wind

as·per·i·ty /æˈspɛrəti, ə-/ *n.* [C,U] FORMAL a way of speaking or behaving that is rough or severe

as·per·sion /əˈspɜrʒən, -ʃən/ *n.* **cast aspersions on sb/sth** to make an unkind remark or an unfair judgment: *They cast aspersions on his professional conduct.*

as·phalt /ˈæsfɔlt/ *n.* [U] a black sticky substance that becomes hard when it dries, used for making the surface of roads —**asphalt** *v.* [T]

as·phyx·i·a /əˈsfɪksiə, æ-/ *n.* [U] death caused by not being able to breathe

as·phyx·i·ate /əˈsfɪksiˌeɪt, æ-/ *v.* [I,T] TECHNICAL to be unable to breathe or to make someone unable to breathe, often resulting in death; SUFFOCATE (1) —**asphyxiation** /əˌsfɪksiˈeɪʃən/ *n.* [U]

as·pic /ˈæspɪk/ *n.* [U] a clear brownish JELLY made with juice from cooked meat, fish, or vegetables

as·pi·dis·tra /ˌæspəˈdɪstrə/ *n.* [C] a plant with broad green pointed leaves

as·pi·rant /ˈæspərənt/ *n.* [C + to/for] FORMAL someone who hopes to get a position of importance or honor

as·pi·rate¹ /ˈæspəˌreɪt/ *v.* TECHNICAL **1** [I,T] to breathe in, or to breathe something into your lungs by accident **2** [T] to make the sound of an "H" when speaking, or to blow out air when pronouncing some CONSONANTS

as·pi·rate² /ˈæspərɪt/ *n.* [C] TECHNICAL the sound of the letter "H," or the letter itself

as·pi·ra·tion /ˌæspəˈreɪʃən/ *n.* **1** [C usually plural,U] a strong desire to have or achieve something: *Did Cuomo have presidential aspirations?* | [+ to] *Cauther is a lawyer with aspirations to the bench* (=to become a judge). | [+ of] *the aspirations of average Americans* **2** [U] the sound of air blowing out that happens when some CONSONANTS are pronounced, such as the /p/ in pin

as·pire /əˈspaɪr/ *v.* [I] to desire and work toward achieving something important: [aspire to do sth] *Johnson aspires to become the city's first woman mayor.* | [+ to/after] *Kim aspires to a career as a travel agent.*

as·pi·rin /ˈæsprɪn/ *n.* [C,U] *plural* aspirin *or* aspirins a medicine that reduces pain, INFLAMMATION, and fever

ass /æs/ *n.* [C]

1 part of body VULGAR the part of your body that you sit on: *I fell down on my ass.*

2 stupid person VULGAR a stupid annoying person: *I heard him on TV. He's such an ass.* | *The dumb ass stuck his hand in the door while I was closing it.* | **make an ass of sb/yourself** (=do something stupid or embarrassing)

3 kick/whip sb's ass also **kick (some) ass** VULGAR to beat someone easily in a fight, game, or sport: *Marc, you break that chair and I'll kick your ass.* | *We played pool, and let me tell you, he kicked my ass.*

SPOKEN PHRASES

4 bad/big/cool etc. ass VULGAR an impolite phrase used to emphasize that something is very good, big etc.: *I have these big ass screws in my knee, now.*

5 get off your ass VULGAR used to tell someone to stop being lazy: *If you want to pass this test, you'd better get off your ass and study!*

6 get your ass in/out of/over here VULGAR used to tell someone to come in or go away from a place quickly: *Michael! Get your ass in here and help!*

7 sb's ass VULGAR used instead of words such as "me," "you," "him," etc. to emphasize what you are saying: *They could fire my ass, and I wouldn't care.*

8 be on sb's ass VULGAR **a)** used to say that someone is annoying you or telling you to do things you do not want to do: *I have deadlines and meetings and everyone's on my ass.* **b)** used to say that someone is driving very close to the back of another car

9 get your ass in gear also **move your ass** VULGAR used to tell someone to hurry: *You better get your ass in gear, you're late.*

10 sit on your ass VULGAR to do nothing, or to be lazy: *Are you just gonna sit on your ass all day?*

11 ass backwards VULGAR used to say that someone has done things in the wrong order

12 sb's ass is in a sling VULGAR said when someone is in trouble for something they have done: *My ass'll be in a sling if they find out I lost it.*

A

13 be ass out VULGAR, SLANG to be in trouble for something you have done

14 my ass! VULGAR said when you do not believe something: *"He says he ran twenty miles." "Twenty miles my ass!"*

15 sb doesn't know their ass from their elbow also **sb doesn't know their ass from a hole in the ground** VULGAR used to say that someone is stupid

16 sb goes around their ass to get to their elbow VULGAR used to say that someone does something in the most difficult way, when it should be very easy to do

17 animal OLD USE a DONKEY —see also HARD ASS, haul ass (HAUL[1]), sth/sb kicks ass (KICK[1]), kiss (sb's) ass (KISS[1]), be a pain in the ass/butt etc. (PAIN[1]), piece of ass (PIECE[1]), SMART ASS, work your butt/tail/ass off (WORK[1])

as·sail /ə'seɪl/ v. [T] **1** to criticize someone or something severely: [assail sb for sth] *Democrats have been assailing the Johnson camp for ignoring the needs of the middle class.* **2** [usually passive] LITERARY if a thought or feeling assails you, it worries or upsets you: *As soon as I'd finished the test, I was assailed by doubts.* **3** FORMAL to attack someone or something violently

as·sail·ant /ə'seɪlənt/ n. [C] FORMAL someone who attacks another person

as·sas·sin /ə'sæsən/ n. [C] someone who murders an important person: *Kennedy's assassin is assumed to have been Lee Harvey Oswald.*

as·sas·si·nate /ə'sæsə,neɪt/ v. [T] to murder an important person: *The CIA may have tried to assassinate Castro.* —see Usage Note at KILL[1]

as·sas·si·na·tion /ə,sæsə'neɪʃən/ n. [C,U] the act of assassinating someone: *the assassination of Lincoln | Reagan was wounded in an assassination attempt in 1981.* —see also **character assassination** (CHARACTER)

S W as·sault[1] /ə'sɔlt/ n. [C,U] **1** the crime of physically attacking someone: *She served three years in prison for assault. | an increase in sexual assaults* **2** a military attack to take control of a place controlled by the enemy: *The Combined Fleet made plans for an assault on Midway Island.* **3** assault on sth a strong spoken or written criticism of someone else's ideas, plans etc.: *The governor is continuing his assault on the welfare system.* **4** an attempt to achieve something difficult, especially using physical force: [+ on] *They made their assault on the south face of the glacier (=an attempt to climb or cross it).*

assault[2] v. [T] **1** to attack someone in a violent way: *A storekeeper was assaulted in an alley by eight youths.* **2** if a feeling assaults you, it affects you in a way that makes you uncomfortable or upset: *I stepped into the room and was assaulted by the heat and noise.* **3** to strongly criticize someone's ideas, plans etc.: *The Senator was assaulted with abuse from angry demonstrators.* **4** to try to do something very difficult, especially something that involves physical effort: *These routes are assaulted every winter by climbers.*

assault and bat·ter·y /ə,... . '.../ n. [U] LAW the official name for a violent attack and the threats that the attacker makes before it

as·say /æ'seɪ, 'æseɪ/ v. assays, assayed, assaying [T] to test a substance, especially a metal, in order to see how pure it is or what it is made of —assay /'æseɪ, æ'seɪ/ n. [C]

as·sem·blage /ə'sɛmblɪdʒ/ n. FORMAL **1** [C] a group of people or things that are together: *an assemblage of scholars* **2** [U] the act of putting parts together in order to make something

as·sem·ble /ə'sɛmbəl/ v. **1** [I] if a group of people assemble in one place, they all go there together: *Protesters started to assemble around 7 a.m.* **2** [T] to gather a large number of things or people together in one place or for one purpose: *Ohio State's basketball team was considered one of the best ever assembled.* **3** [T] to put all the parts of something together: *It was easy to assemble the bookcase myself.*

Assemblies of God /ə,... . './ a Pentecostal Christian church

as·sem·bly /ə'sɛmbli/ n. plural **assemblies 1** [C] a group of people who are elected to make laws for a particular country or area: *Jeffries is running for state Assembly in the 22nd District.* **2** [C] a group of people who have gathered together for a particular purpose: [+ of] *an assembly of leaders of Jewish community organizations* **3** [C,U] a meeting of all the teachers and students of a school **4** [U] the process of putting parts together in order to make something: *Some toy stores help with assembly.* **5 the right of assembly/freedom of assembly** LAW the right of any group to meet together in order to discuss things

assembly lan·guage /.'.. ,../ n. [C,U] TECHNICAL a computer language used in programs that are written to work with a specific kind of PROCESSOR

assembly line /.'.. ,./ n. [C] a system for making things in a factory, in which the products move past a line of workers who each make or check one part

as·sem·bly·man /ə'sɛmblimən/ n. [C] a male member of an ASSEMBLY (1)

as·sem·bly·wom·an /ə'sɛmbli,wumən/ n. [C] a female member of an ASSEMBLY (1)

as·sent[1] /ə'sɛnt/ n. [U] FORMAL approval or agreement from someone who has authority: *The court gave its assent.* —see also CONSENT[1], DISSENT[1]

assent[2] v. [I + to] FORMAL if someone who has authority assents, they agree to a suggestion, idea etc. after considering it carefully

as·sert /ə'sɔt/ v. [T] **1** to state firmly that something is true: *"It's a fairness issue," she asserted.* | [assert that] *All 12 leaders asserted that they had met their main goals.* **2 assert your rights/independence etc.** to state very strongly your right to do or have something **3 assert yourself** to behave in a determined way and say clearly what you think: *Don't be afraid to assert yourself in the interview.* **4 assert itself** if an idea, style, or belief asserts itself, it begins to influence something: *Islam began to assert itself in the seventh century.*

as·ser·tion /ə'sɔʃən/ n. [C] something that you say or write that you strongly believe: [assertion that] *Bennet denied assertions that she was mentally unstable.*

as·ser·tive /ə'sɔtɪv/ adj. behaving in a confident way so that people notice you: *an assertive, ambitious woman* —assertively adv. —assertiveness n. [U]

as·sess /ə'sɛs/ v. [T] **1** to make a judgment about a person or situation after thinking carefully about it: *Psychologists will assess the child's behavior.* | [assess what/how etc.] *It is difficult to assess how much has actually been done.* **2** to calculate the value or cost of something: [assess sth at] *The house was assessed at $170,000.*

as·sess·ment /ə'sɛsmənt/ n. **1** [C,U] a process in which you make a judgment about a person or situation: [+ of] *We start with an assessment of the student's abilities.* **2** [C,U] a calculation about the cost or value of something: *a tax assessment*

as·ses·sor /ə'sɛsɚ/ n. [C] **1** someone whose job is to calculate the value of something or the amount of tax someone should pay: *a property assessor* **2** someone who knows a lot about a subject or activity and who advises a judge or an official committee

as·set /'æsɛt/ n. [C] **1** [usually plural] the things that a company or person owns, that can be sold to pay debts: *Currently, they have $6,230,000 in assets.* **2** [usually singular] something or someone that is useful because they help you succeed or deal with problems: *The most powerful asset we have is our skilled, dedicated workforce.* | [+ to] *Ronnie has been a big asset to the team.* —compare LIABILITY, —see also LIQUID ASSETS

asset strip·ping /'.. ,../ n. [U] the practice of buying a company cheaply and then selling all the things it owns to make a quick profit

ass·hole /'æs,houl/ n. [C] VULGAR **1** someone who you think is very stupid and annoying **2** the ANUS

as·sid·u·ous /ə'sɪdʒuəs/ adj. FORMAL very careful to make sure that something is done correctly or completely: *an assiduous study of Austen's writings* —**assiduously** adv. —**assiduousness** n. [U]

as·sign /ə'saɪn/ v. [T] **1** to give someone a particular job or make them responsible for a particular person or thing: [assign sb to sb/sth] *Officer Crane was assigned to the vice squad.* | [assign sb to do sth] *Madison was assigned to investigate a balloon accident.* | assign a **task/job/duty** etc. *Troops have been assigned the task of securing all the roads in the region.* **2** to give money, equipment etc. to someone or decide it should be used for a particular purpose: [assign sb sth] *They assigned me a small room.* | [assign sth to sb] *Each of the children will be assigned to the appropriate classes.* **3** to decide that something should be done at or during a particular time

as·sig·na·tion /,æsɪg'neɪʃən/ n. [C] LITERARY a secret meeting, especially with someone you are having a romantic relationship with

as·sign·ment /ə'saɪnmənt/ n. **1** [C] a piece of work that is given to someone as part of their job, or that a student is asked to do: *a homework assignment* | *Half the workers were given different assignments.* **2** [U] the act of giving people particular jobs to do: *the assignment of chores* **3** [C] something such as a place to sit, piece of equipment etc. that you are given to use for a particular purpose: *an airplane seat assignment*

as·sim·i·late /ə'sɪmə,leɪt/ v. **1** [I,T] if people assimilate or are assimilated into a country or group, they become part of it and are accepted by other people in it: [+ into] *Many ethnic groups have been assimilated into American society.* **2** [T] to think about new ideas, information etc. so that you feel ready to use them: *Brubeck began to assimilate classical influences into his jazz performances.* **3** [T] TECHNICAL if you assimilate food, you take it into your mouth and DIGEST¹ (1) it

as·sim·i·la·tion /ə,sɪmə'leɪʃən/ n. [U] **1** the process of assimilating or being assimilated **2** TECHNICAL the process in which a sound in a word changes because of the effect of another sound next to it, for example the "p" in "cupboard"

As·sin·i·boin /ə'sɪnə,bɔɪn/ a Native American tribe from the northern U.S. and southern Canada

as·sist¹ /ə'sɪst/ v. FORMAL **1** [I,T] to help someone to do something that needs special skills, especially by doing all the less important things so that they can spend time doing difficult things: [assist (sb) with/in] *U.S. helicopters assisted in the rescue effort.* | *Ms. Allen assists immigrants with gaining citizenship.* **2** [T] to make it easier for someone to do something: *Citizens have a duty to assist the police.* —see Usage Note at HELP¹

assist² n. [C] an action that helps another player on your sports team to make a point

as·sist·ance /ə'sɪstəns/ n. [U] help or support: *financial assistance for students* | *Can I be of any assistance* (=can I help you)? | offer/provide/give **assistance** *The West can provide technical assistance to developing countries.* | *The research was conducted with the assistance of computer equipment.* | *I want to thank those who came to my assistance.* (=helped me) —see Usage Note at HELP²

as·sist·ant¹ /ə'sɪstənt/ adj. assistant **manager/director/cook** etc. someone whose job is just below the level of manager, DIRECTOR etc.

assistant² n. [C] someone who helps someone else in their work, especially by doing the less important jobs: *a sales assistant*

assistant pro·fes·sor, Assistant Professor /,... .'../ n. [C] the lowest rank of PROFESSOR —see Usage Note at PROFESSOR

assisted su·i·cide /,... '.../ n. [U] a situation when someone who is dying from an illness kills themselves with the help of someone else, usually a doctor: *Doctors are divided over the issue of assisted suicide.*

assn. n. a written abbreviation of "association"

assoc. n. a written abbreviation of "association"

as·so·ci·ate¹ /ə'souʃi,eɪt, -si,eɪt/ v. **1** associate **sb/sth with sth** to make a connection in your mind between one thing or person and another: *Ads try to associate drinking with fun.* **2** be associated (with **sb/sth**) to be related with a particular subject, activity, group etc.: *How did the colors red and green become associated with Christmas?* **3** associate with **sb** to spend time with someone, especially a group whom other people disapprove of: *Artie may have been associating with the criminals.*

as·so·ci·ate² /ə'souʃɪt/ n. [C] **1** someone with whom you work or do business with: *a sales associate* **2** someone who has an associate degree

associate³ adj. associate **member/director/head** etc. someone who does not have all of the same rights or responsibilities as a member, DIRECTOR etc.

associated com·pa·ny /.,.... '.../ n. [C] a company in which a different company owns 20 to 50 percent of the SHARES

Associated Press /.,.... './ abbreviation **AP** n. a company that employs REPORTERS in many different countries to send it news, so that it can sell these reports to many different newspapers

Associate of Arts /.,.... '.'./ also associate de·gree /.,.... '.'./ n. [C] a degree given after two years of study at a COMMUNITY COLLEGE

associate pro·fes·sor, Associate Professor /.,.... .'../ n. [C] a PROFESSOR at a college or university whose job is above the rank of ASSISTANT PROFESSOR and below the rank of FULL PROFESSOR —see Usage Note at PROFESSOR

as·so·ci·a·tion /ə,sousi'eɪʃən, -ʃi'eɪ-/ n. [C] **1** [C] an organization that consists of a group of people who have the same aims, do the same kind of work etc.: *the National Education Association* | *the college's alumni association* **2** [C,U] a relationship with a particular person, organization, group etc.: [+ with] *Franklin had a long association with Republican politics.* | *Lawyers said the charges were an attempt to prove guilt by association.* (=to prove someone is guilty because their friends are guilty) **3** [C] a connection or relationship between two events, ideas, situations etc.: *There is evidence of an association between headaches and computer use.* | *a word-association game* **4** in association with **sb/sth** made or done together with another person, organization etc.: *Sesame Street is produced by the Children's Television Workshop in association with PBS.* **5** [C] a feeling or memory that is related to a particular place, event, word etc.: *Foods served at holidays such as Thanksgiving have special associations.* —see also FREE ASSOCIATION

as·so·nance /'æsənəns/ n. [U] TECHNICAL similarity in the vowel sounds of words that are close together in a poem, for example between the words "born" and "warm"

as·sort·ed /ə'sɔrtɪd/ adj. of various different types: *a set of paintbrushes in assorted sizes* | *fruit and assorted cheeses*

as·sort·ment /ə'sɔrtʰmənt/ n. [C] a mixture of different things or of various types of the same thing: [+ of] *a wide assortment of merchandise*

asst. n. the written abbreviation of ASSISTANT

as·suage /ə'sweɪdʒ/ v. [T] LITERARY to make a bad feeling less painful or severe; RELIEVE (1): *Debra tried to assuage my fears*

as·sume /ə'sum/ v. [T] **1** to think that something is true, although you have no proof of it: [assume (that)] *I haven't heard from her, but I assume she's still going.* | *It is assumed that they will eventually join the EU.* | *I think we can safely assume* (=it is reasonably certain) *that this is legal unless we are told otherwise.* **2** to start to do a job, especially an important one | assume **control/power/responsibility** etc. *Stalin assumed control of the Soviet Union in 1941.* **3** assume a **manner/air/expression** etc.

A

FORMAL to behave in a way that does not show how you really feel, especially in order to seem more confident, cheerful etc. than you are: *When walking alone at night, assume an air of confidence.* **4 assume costs/responsibility/debts etc.** to agree to pay for something: *Her mother assumed responsibility for her debts.* | *The agency agreed to assume all the building costs.* **5** to start to have a particular quality or appearance: *Her family life assumed more importance after the accident.* **6** to be based on the idea that something else is correct; PRESUPPOSE: *Coen's economic forecast assumes a 3.5 percent growth rate.*

as·sumed /əˈsumd/ *adj.* **under an assumed name** using a false name: *Davis applied for a loan under an assumed name.*

as·sump·tion /əˈsʌmpʃən/ *n.* **1** [C] something that you think is true although you have no proof: *Don't make the assumption that stream water is safe to drink.* | *The pricing is based on the assumption that sales will increase.* | *The underlying assumption* (=belief that is used to support a statement or idea) *is that women are inferior athletes.* **2** [U] FORMAL the act of starting to have control or power: [+ of] *Castro's assumption of power in 1959*

as·sur·ance /əˈʃʊrəns/ *n.* **1** [U] a feeling of calm confidence in your own abilities, especially because you have a lot of experience; SELF-ASSURANCE: *She began to sing with assurance, an old, familiar song.* **2** [C] a promise that you will definitely do something or that something will definitely happen, especially to make someone less worried: *These jobs offer little assurance of long-term employment.* | [assurance that] *Despite assurances that the chemical leak did not threaten residents, officials said they were concerned.*

as·sure /əˈʃʊr/ *v.* **1 assure sb** to tell someone that something will definitely happen or is definitely true, so that they are less worried: [+ that] *Her doctors have assured us that she'll be fine.* | *It's very quiet there, and you'll be able to relax, I can assure you.* | [assure sb of sth] *Their guarantee assures customers of fast delivery.* —see also **rest assured (that)** (REST²) **2 be assured of sth** to be able to feel certain that something will happen: *The team is assured of a spot in the finals.* **3** [T] to make something certain to happen or to be achieved: *The new contract means that the future of the company is assured.* —see Usage Note at INSURE

as·sured /əˈʃʊrd/ *adj.* **1** certain to happen or to be achieved: *Her victory looks assured.* **2** confident about your own abilities; SELF-ASSURED: *a calm and assured manner*

as·sur·ed·ly /əˈʃʊrɪdli/ *adv.* FORMAL definitely or certainly: *Public reports on airline safety most assuredly influence their performance.*

As·syr·i·an /əˈsɪriən/ *n.* one of the people that lived in northern Mesopotamia from the 25th century to the seventh century B.C.

A·staire /əˈstɛr/, **Fred** /frɛd/ (1889–1987) a U.S. dancer, singer, and actor who appeared in many movies

as·ter·isk /ˈæstərɪsk/ *n.* [C] a mark like a star (*), used especially to show something interesting or important in a document —**asterisk** *v.* [T]

a·stern /əˈstɚn/ *adv.* in or at the back of a ship

as·ter·oid /ˈæstəˌrɔɪd/ *n.* [C] one of the many small PLANETS that move around the sun, especially between Mars and Jupiter

asth·ma /ˈæzmə/ *n.* [U] an illness that causes difficulties in breathing

asth·mat·ic /æzˈmætɪk/ *adj.* suffering from asthma —**asthmatic** *n.* [C] —**asthmatically** /-kli/ *adv.*

a·stig·ma·tism /əˈstɪgməˌtɪzəm/ *n.* [U] difficulty in seeing clearly, caused by the inner shape of the eye not being correct —**astigmatic** /ˌæstɪgˈmætɪk◂/ *adj.*

a·stir /əˈstɚ/ *adj.* [not before noun] LITERARY **1** excited about something **2** awake and out of bed

as·ton·ish /əˈstɑnɪʃ/ *v.* [T] to surprise someone very

much, especially because of being unusual or unexpected: *Einstein's work still astonishes physicists.* | **what astonished sb was that/the thing that astonished sb was that** *What astonished the doctors was that the wound healed without scarring.*

as·ton·ished /əˈstɑnɪʃt/ *adj.* very surprised about something, especially because it is unusual or unexpected: [+ at/by] *Miss Cotton was astonished at some of the responses.* | [be astonished to hear/learn/find etc.] *I was astonished to learn that he'd already written three books.*

as·ton·ish·ing /əˈstɑnɪʃɪŋ/ *adj.* so surprising that it is difficult to believe: *Their album has sold an astonishing 11 million copies.* —**astonishingly** *adv.*

as·ton·ish·ment /əˈstɑnɪʃmənt/ *n.* [U] complete surprise: *The crowd gasped in astonishment.* | *To everyone's astonishment, 27 people volunteered.*

As·tor /ˈæstɚ/, **John Jacob** (1763–1848) an American businessman who gave money for a public library in New York City

as·tound /əˈstaʊnd/ *v.* [T] to make someone very surprised, shocked, or feel admiration: *Turner's business sense continues to astound me.* —**astounded** *adj.*

a·stound·ed /əˈstaʊndɪd/ *adj.* very surprised or shocked, especially because something is impressive: *I was astounded at the depth of understanding the children showed.*

as·tound·ing /əˈstaʊndɪŋ/ *adj.* very surprising, especially because of being impressive: *Quincy has had astounding success as a painter.* —**astoundingly** *adv.*

as·tra·khan /ˈæstrəkən, -ˌkɑn/ *n.* [U] black or gray fur used for making coats and hats

as·tral /ˈæstrəl/ *adj.* FORMAL relating to stars: *astral bodies*

a·stray /əˈstreɪ/ *adv.* **1 go astray a)** to start doing something or behaving in a way that is different from how you should do it or behave: *The street is filled with teenagers who have gone astray.* **b)** to become lost: *The form you mailed must have gone astray.* **c)** OLD-FASHIONED, HUMOROUS to start behaving in an immoral way **2 lead sb astray a)** OFTEN HUMOROUS to encourage someone to do bad or immoral things that they would not normally do: *Pfeiffer plays a virtuous woman who is led astray.* **b)** to make someone believe something that is not true: *Gardeners shouldn't be led astray by these ideas.*

a·stride /əˈstraɪd/ *adv.* having one leg on each side of something: *An old portrait shows her sitting astride a horse.*

as·trin·gent¹ /əˈstrɪndʒənt/ *adj.* **1** criticizing someone very severely: *an astringent, humorous novel* **2** TECHNICAL able to make your skin less oily or stop a wound from bleeding **3** having an acid taste like a LEMON —**astringency** *n.* [U]

astringent² *n.* [C,U] TECHNICAL a substance used to make your skin less oily or to stop a wound from bleeding

astro- /æstroʊ, -trə/ *prefix* relating to the stars, the PLANETS, or space: *an astronaut* (=someone who travels in space) | *astronomy* (=science of the stars)

as·trol·o·ger /əˈstrɑlədʒɚ/ *n.* [C] someone who uses astrology to tell people about their character, life, or future

as·trol·o·gy /əˈstrɑlədʒi/ *n.* [U] the study of the relationship between the movements of the stars and PLANETS and their influence on people and events —**astrological** /ˌæstrəˈlɑdʒɪkəl/ *adj.* —**astrologically** /-kli/ *adv.* —see also HOROSCOPE, ZODIAC

as·tro·naut /ˈæstrəˌnɔt, -ˌnɑt/ *n.* [C] someone who travels and works in a SPACECRAFT

as·tron·o·mer /əˈstrɑnəmɚ/ *n.* [C] a scientist who studies the stars and PLANETS

as·tro·nom·i·cal /ˌæstrəˈnɑmɪkəl/ *adj.* **1** INFORMAL astronomical prices, costs etc. are extremely high **2** relating to the study of the stars —**astronomically** /-kli/ *adv.*

as·tron·o·my /əˈstrɑnəmi/ *n.* [U] the scientific study of the stars and PLANETS

as·tro·phys·ics /ˌæstroʊˈfɪzɪks/ *n.* [U] the scientific study of the chemical structure of the stars and the forces that influence them —**astrophysical** *adj.* —**astrophysicist** *n.* [C]

As·tro·Turf /'æstrou,tɜːf/ *n.* [U] TRADEMARK an artificial surface like grass that people play sports on

as·tute /ə'stuːt/ *adj.* able to understand situations or behavior very well and very quickly, especially so that you can be successful: *astute management* | *an astute judge of talent* —**astutely** *adv.* —**astuteness** *n.* [U]

A·sun·ción /ɑˌsunsi'oun/ the capital and largest city of Paraguay

a·sun·der /ə'sʌndə/ *adv.* **cast/tear/break** etc. **sth asunder** LITERARY to suddenly or violently separate something into pieces: *The family was torn asunder by war.*

As·wan High Dam /ˌæswɑn haɪ 'dæm/ a DAM built across the River Nile in southern Egypt

a·sy·lum /ə'saɪləm/ *n.* **1** [U] protection given to someone by a government because they have escaped from fighting or political trouble in their own country —see also POLITICAL ASYLUM **2** [C] OLD USE a hospital for people who are mentally ill **3** [C] OLD USE a home for children who have no parents

a·sym·met·ri·cal /ˌeɪsə'metrɪkəl/ also **a·sym·met·ric** /ˌeɪsə'metrɪk/ *adj.* **1** having two sides that are different in shape: *asymmetrical patterns* **2** FORMAL not equal —**asymmetrically** /-kli/ *adv.* —opposite SYMMETRICAL

a·symp·to·mat·ic /ˌeɪsɪmptə'mætɪk/ *adj.* if a person or the illness that they have is asymptomatic, there are no signs of the illness

at /ət; *strong* æt/ *prep.* **1** used to show a point in space where someone or something is, or where an event is happening: *Meet me at my house.* | *They sat down at a corner table.* | *I saw your mother at the supermarket.* | *Pete is at Jane's right now.* (=at Jane's house) **2 at a party/club/funeral** etc. at an event while it is taking place: *I met my wife at a dance.* | *They're all out at the movies.* **3 at school/work** etc. **a)** when you are in the place where you study, work etc.: *What did you do at school today?* **b)** in the place where you study, work etc.: *I'll be at work until 6:30.* **4 at lunch/dinner** etc. eating your LUNCH, dinner etc. in a place that is away from your office, CLASSROOM etc.: *She's at lunch; may I take a message?* **5** used to show a particular time: *The movie starts at 8 o'clock.* | *We're really busy at the moment* (=now). **6** used to show a particular period of time during which something happens: *Cliff works at night.* | *A lot of people get very lonely at Christmas.* **7** used to show the person or thing that an action is directed or aimed toward: *Those kids threw eggs at my car.* | *Look at that!* | *Stop shouting at me!* **8** used to show the person or thing that caused an action or feeling: *Nobody laughed at his jokes.* | *Andy, I'm surprised at you!* | *Dad got really mad at me for scratching the car.* **9** used to show the subject or activity that you are considering when making a judgment about someone's ability: *How's Kevin doing at his new job?* | **be good/bad** etc. **at sth** *Lisa's bad at saying what she really thinks.* | *She's really good at sports.* **10** used to show a continuous state or activity: *The two nations are at war.* | *Many children are still at risk from the disease.* **11** used to show a price, rate, level, age, speed etc.: *Gas is selling at about $1.35 a gallon.* | *You should have more sense at your age.* | *The car was going at about 50 mph.* | *Amanda rode off at a gallop.* **12 at least/worst/most** etc. the least, worst etc. thing possible: *John practices for at least half an hour every day.* | *At most, 50% of the population could be affected.* | **at the very most/worst** etc. *I think his car's worth about $1000 at the very most.* | **at sb's best/worst** etc. *This was Sampras at his best.* **13** used to show that you are trying to do something but are not succeeding or completing it: *I clutched at the rope but missed.* **14 at sb's invitation/command/request** because someone asks or orders you to do something: *Ms. Wintersteen attended the dinner at the chairman's request.* **15 at that a)** also or besides: *She's pregnant, and having twins at that!* **b)** after something happens or as a result of it; then: *Tess*

A

called him a liar and at that he stormed out of the room. —see also **leave it at that** (LEAVE[1]) **16 at a time** at the same time: *She ran up the steps two at a time.* **17 where sb is at** SPOKEN **a)** NONSTANDARD used when saying where someone or something is: *I don't know where we're at – give me the map.* **b)** INFORMAL someone's opinion or situation: *Dan's not very happy were he's at.* **18 where it's at** OLD-FASHIONED used to describe a place or activity that is very popular, exciting, and fashionable: *The Hacienda Club is where it's at.* —see also **(not) at all** (ALL[1] (3)), **while you're at it** (WHILE[1])

at·a·vis·tic /ˌætə'vɪstɪk/ *adj.* FORMAL atavistic feelings or behavior are like the feelings or ways of behaving that people have felt since humans have existed

ate /eɪt/ *v.* the past tense of EAT

-ate /ɪt, eɪt/ *suffix* **1** [in adjectives] full of a particular quality, or showing it: *very affectionate* (=showing love) **2** [in verbs] to make something have a particular quality: *to activate* (=make something start working) | *to regulate* (=control something or make it regular) **3** [in nouns] a group of people with particular duties: *the electorate* (=the voters) **4** TECHNICAL [in nouns] a chemical salt formed from a particular acid: *phosphate* **5** [in nouns] the job, rank, or degree of a particular type of person: *a doctorate* (=the degree of Doctor) —**-ately** /ɪtli/ *suffix* [in adverbs] *fortunately*

a·the·ist /'eɪθiɪst/ *n.* [C] someone who does not believe that God exists —**atheism** *n.* [U] —**atheistic** /ˌeɪθi'ɪstɪk/

A·the·na, Athene /ə'θinə/ in Greek MYTHOLOGY the goddess of WISDOM and the arts

Ath·ens /'æθənz/ the capital city of Greece

ath·lete /'æθlit/ *n.* [C] someone who is good at sports or who often does sports: *a good athlete*

athlete's foot /'.. ,./ *n.* [U] a medical condition in which the skin cracks and ITCHes on your foot and between your toes

ath·let·ic /æθ'letɪk/ *adj.* **1** relating to athletics: *the athletic department* **2** physically strong and good at sports: *her two athletic teenage daughters*

ath·let·ics /æθ'letɪks/ *n.* [U] physical activities such as sports and exercises

athletic sup·port·er /.'.. ,../ *n.* [C] FORMAL a JOCKSTRAP

-athon /əθɑn/ *suffix* INFORMAL [in nouns] an event in which a particular thing is done for a very long time, especially to collect money: *a swimathon* | *a walkathon*

a·thwart /ə'θwɔrt/ *prep.* LITERARY across

-ation /eɪʃən/ *suffix* [in nouns] the act, state, or result of doing something: *an examination of the contents* (=act of examining them) | *the combination of several factors*

-ative /ətɪv/ *suffix* [in adjectives] tending to do something or to have a particular quality: *talkative* (=liking to talk a lot) | *argumentative* (=tending to argue) | *imaginative* (=showing imagination)

At·lan·ta /ət'læntə, æt-/ the capital and largest city of the U.S. state of Georgia

Atlantic Ocean, the /ət'læntɪk/ the ocean between the east coast of North and South America and the west coast of Europe and Africa

at·las /'ætləs/ *n.* [C] a book of maps: *a world atlas*

At·las Moun·tains, the /'ætləs/ a system of mountain RANGES in northwest Africa, between the Mediterranean Sea and the Sahara Desert

ATM *n.* [C] Automated Teller Machine; a machine outside a bank that you use to get money from your account

at·mos·phere /'ætməs,fɪr/ *n.* [C,U] **1** the feeling that an event or place gives you: *Dim lighting creates a relaxing atmosphere.* | [+ **of**] *An atmosphere of mistrust has slowed the peace talks.* **2 the atmosphere** the mixture of gases that surrounds the Earth

A

3 the mixture of gases that surrounds something in space such as a PLANET **4** the air inside a room: *a smoky atmosphere*

at·mos·pher·ic /ˌætˈməsˈfɪrɪk◂/ *adj.* **1** [only before noun] relating to the Earth's atmosphere **2** if a place, event, sound etc. is atmospheric, it gives you a particular feeling, especially a pleasant or mysterious one: *a writer of atmospheric novels*

at·mos·pher·ics /ˌætˈməsˈfɪrɪks/ *n.* [plural] **1** features, events, or statements that make you have a particular feeling **2** continuous cracking noises that sometimes interrupt radio broadcasts, or the unusual conditions in the Earth's atmosphere that produce them

at·oll /ˈætɔl, -tal/ *n.* [C] a CORAL island in the shape of a ring

at·om /ˈætəm/ *n.* [C] **1** the smallest part of an ELEMENT that can exist alone or combine with other substances to form MOLECULES **2** a very small amount of something: *an atom of truth*

a·tom·ic /əˈtɑmɪk/ *adj.* **1** relating to the energy produced by splitting atoms or the weapons that use this energy: *atomic power* | *an atomic submarine* **2** relating to the atoms in a substance: *atomic weight*

a·tom·ic bomb /.ˌ.. ˈ./ also **atom bomb** /ˈ.. ./ *n.* [C] a NUCLEAR bomb that splits atoms to cause an extremely large explosion

a·tomic en·er·gy /.ˌ.. ˈ.../ *n.* [U] NUCLEAR ENERGY

at·om·iz·er /ˈætəˌmaɪzɚ/ *n.* [C] a thing inside a bottle used to make a liquid such as PERFUME come out in very small drops like mist

a·to·nal /eɪˈtoʊnl/ *adj.* a piece of music that is atonal is not based on a particular KEY —**atonally** *adv.* —**atonality** /ˌeɪtoʊˈnæləti/ *n.* [U]

a·tone /əˈtoʊn/ *v.* [I + **for**] FORMAL a word meaning to do something good after you have done something wrong, in order to make a situation better, used especially about religious actions

a·tone·ment /əˈtoʊnmənt/ *n.* [U] FORMAL something you do to make a bad situation better after you have done something wrong

a·top /əˈtɑp/ *prep.* LITERARY on top of something

-ator /eɪtɚ/ *suffix* [in nouns] someone or something that does something: *a narrator* (=someone who tells a story) | *a generator* (=machine that produces electricity)

at·risk /.ˌ. ˈ.◂/ *adj.* **at-risk children/patients etc.** people who need special care because they are likely to be in danger from violent parents, to become sick etc.

a·tri·um /ˈeɪtriəm/ *n.* [C] **1** a large high open space in a tall building **2** an AURICLE

a·tro·cious /əˈtroʊʃəs/ *adj.* extremely bad: *an atrocious crime* | *The traffic was atrocious.* —**atrociously** *adv.* —**atrociousness** *n.* [U]

a·troc·i·ty /əˈtrɑsəti/ *n. plural* **atrocities** [C usually plural,U] an extremely cruel and violent action, especially during a war

at·ro·phy /ˈætrəfi/ *v.* **atrophies, atrophied, atrophying** [I,T] to become weak or make something become weak because of lack of use or lack of blood: *His muscles had atrophied after the surgery.* —**atrophy** *n.* [U]

At·si·na /ætˈsɪnə/ a Native American tribe from the northern U.S. and southern Canada

at·ta /ˈætə/ **atta boy/girl!** SPOKEN used to tell a dog or a person that they have done something well: *You rolled double sixes again. Atta boy!*

at·tach /əˈtætʃ/ *v.* **1** [T] to connect one object to another: [**attach sth with sth**] *The note was attached with tape.* | [**attach sth to**] *Attach a bell to the cat's collar to warn birds.* | *a large house with an attached garage* **2** [T] to believe that someone or something has a particular quality or feeling related to it: [**attach sth to sth**] *We must help victims deal with the shame attached to rape.* | *Parry said he hadn't attached much importance to the decision.* | *No blame should be attached to my client for his actions.*

(=he should not be blamed) **3 be attached to sb/sth** to like someone or something very much, because you have known them or had them for a long time: *Regular babysitters can become deeply attached to the children they take care of.* **4** [T] to connect a document or FILE to an EMAIL (=electronic message) **5 be attached to sth a)** to work for part of a particular organization, especially for a short period of time: *We have 352 people attached to the embassy in Moscow.* **b)** to be part of a bigger organization: *The computer department is attached to the consumer products division.*

at·tach·é /ˌætæˈʃeɪ, ˌætə-/ *n.* [C] someone who works in an EMBASSY, and deals with a particular subject: *a military attaché*

attaché case /.ˈ.. ˌ./ *n.* [C] a thin hard container with a handle, used for carrying business documents

at·tach·ment /əˈtætʃmənt/ *n.* **1** [C,U] a feeling that you like or love someone or something and that you would be unhappy without them: *a romantic attachment* | [+ **to/for**] *Children form very strong attachments to their dolls.* **2** [C] a part that you can put onto a machine to make it do different things: *This vacuum cleaner comes with a range of attachments.* **3** [U] belief in and loyalty toward a particular idea: [+ **to/for**] *Many workers have little attachment to their companies.* **4** [C] a document or FILE that is sent by EMAIL that is separate from the message of the EMAIL

at·tack¹ /əˈtæk/ *n.*
1 in a war [C,U] the act of using weapons against an enemy in a war: *Their home was damaged in the attack.* | [+ **on**] *the attack on Pearl Harbor* | *The city is under attack* (=being attacked). | *Rebel forces launched an attack* (=started an attack) *late Sunday night.*
2 violence against sb [C] an act of deliberately using violence against someone: *She was left unconscious after an attack in her own home.* | [+ **on**] *Gibson was charged with an attack on his former girlfriend.*
3 criticism [C,U] a statement that criticizes someone strongly: [+ **on**] *recent attacks on the government's welfare policy* | *The company came under attack* (=was strongly criticized) *after plans to close three divisions were revealed.*
4 to stop sth [C,U] actions intended to get rid of or stop something such as a system, a set of laws etc.: [+ **on**] *the mayor's attack on organized crime*
5 illness [C] a sudden short period of suffering from an illness, especially an illness that you have often: *an asthma attack*
6 a panic/anxiety attack a short period of time when you feel extremely frightened, worried etc. and become unable to deal with the situation for a short period of time
7 sports [C,U] an attempt by a player or group of players to get points —see also HEART ATTACK

attack² *v.*
1 attack sb [I,T] to deliberately use physical violence against someone: *Brown Bears have been know to attack humans.* | *Snakes will only attack if you disturb them.* | [**attack sb with sth**] *He was arrested for attacking his brother with a knife.*
2 in a war [I,T] to start using guns, bombs etc. against an enemy in a war: *Guerrillas attacked an army patrol.*
3 criticize [T] to criticize someone or something very strongly: *The bill has been attacked because it will put loggers out of work.* | [**attack sb for sth**] *Newspapers attacked the President for failing to cut taxes.*
4 disease [T] to damage part of someone's body: *The virus attacks the body's immune system.*
5 begin doing sth [T] to begin doing a job or dealing with a problem with determination and eagerness: *There are several ways to attack the problem of rising rents.*
6 sports [I,T] to move forward and try to get points: *The Canadian team began to attack more in the second half of the game.* —**attacker** *n.* [C]

at·tain /əˈteɪn/ *v.* [T] FORMAL **1** to succeed in reaching a particular level or in getting something after trying for a long time: *Jean Arthur worked for a decade before attaining stardom.* | *India attained independence in 1947.* **2** to reach a high level: *The balloonists attained an altitude of 33,000 feet.* —**attainable** *adj.*: *an attainable goal*

at·tain·ment /əˈteɪnmənt/ *n.* FORMAL **1** [U] success in getting something or reaching a particular level: *a low level of educational attainment* **2** [C] something that you have succeeded in getting or learning, such as a skill

s w at·tempt¹ /əˈtɛmpt/ *v.* [T] **1** to try to do something that is difficult, dangerous, or has never been done before: ⌈**attempt to do sth**⌉ *He was charged with attempting to kill his wife.* | ⌈**attempt sth**⌉ *The plane crashed while attempting an emergency landing.* **2 attempted murder/assault/suicide etc.** an act of trying to kill someone, injure them etc.: *Hofmann was arrested for theft, arson, and attempted murder.*

s w attempt² *n.* [C] **1** an act of trying to do something, especially something difficult: *a field-goal attempt* ⌈**attempt to do sth**⌉ *All attempts to locate the missing climbers have failed.* | ⌈+ **at**⌉ *They've blocked every attempt at improving conditions for workers.* | *Authorities made no attempt to stop the march.* | *The truck crashed into a guard rail in an attempt to avoid a car going in the wrong direction.* **2 an attempt on sb's life** an act of trying to kill someone, especially someone famous or important

s w at·tend /əˈtɛnd/ *v.* **1** [I,T] to go to an event such as a meeting or a class: *More than 1000 people attended the conference.* | *Potential buyers were invited to attend.* **2** [I,T] to go regularly to a school, church etc.: *After attending church, the family would go home for dinner.* | *First-year students receive all the financial aid needed in order to attend.* **3** [T] if a doctor or nurse attends someone, they take care of them when they are sick: *the attending physician* **4** [T] FORMAL to happen or exist at the same time as something: *Uncertainty attends the future of the industry.*

attend to *phr. v.* [T] **1** [attend to sth] to deal with business or personal matters: *I have a few other things to attend to first.* **2** [attend to sth] to pay attention to something, especially when you are listening to it: *Sometimes, when I've read a book aloud often, I read it without really attending to it.* **3** [attend to sb] to take care of someone, especially because they are sick: *A nurse went to attend to the baby.* **4** [attend to sb] to help a customer in a store or a restaurant by serving them

at·tend·ance /əˈtɛndəns/ *n.* **1** [C,U] the number of people who attend a game, concert, meeting etc.: *an average attendance of 4000 fans per game* | ⌈+ **at**⌉ *Attendance at theme parks was down this year.* **2** [C,U] the act of going to a meeting, class etc. that is held regularly: ⌈+ **at**⌉ *Daily attendance at school has improved since the project began.* | *A student helped the teacher take attendance* (=count how many students are in class today). **3 be in attendance** FORMAL to be at a special or important event: *They had a private wedding with only a few close friends in attendance.* **4 be in attendance on sb** FORMAL to take care of someone or serve them

at·tend·ant¹ /əˈtɛndənt/ *n.* [C] **1** someone whose job is to help customers in a public place: *a gas station attendant* **2** someone who takes care of a very important person, such as a king or queen —see also FLIGHT ATTENDANT

attendant² *adj.* FORMAL **1** relating to something or caused by something: *aging and all its attendant medical problems* | ⌈+ **on**⌉ *Drugs are one of the usual difficulties attendant on running a school.* **2** with someone in order to help them: *a prince and his attendant servants*

at·tend·ee /əˌtɛnˈdi, ˌætɛn-/ *n.* [C] someone who is at an event such as a meeting or a class

w at·ten·tion /əˈtɛnʃən/ *n.*

1 ⌈**watch/listen/think carefully**⌉ [U] the state of carefully listening to, watching, or thinking about something that is happening or what someone is saying or doing: *Sorry, I guess I wasn't paying attention.* | ⌈+ **to**⌉ *These people were having a conversation rather than paying attention to the*

movie. | *I tried to give him some advice, but he paid no attention.* | **not pay any/much attention** *Jeff doesn't pay much attention to what anybody else thinks.* | *The NFL needs to give serious attention to the whole problem.* | **full/undivided attention** *You just got home from work and the kids want your undivided attention.* | ⌈+ **on**⌉ *My attention wasn't on the game.* | *The refinery explosion focused attention on safety issues.* | **hold/keep sb's attention** *These educational computer games kept our 5-year-old's attention for quite a while.*

2 ⌈**do sth carefully**⌉ **pay attention (to sth)** to be careful about what you are doing: *Stop talking and pay attention to your driving.* | *I wasn't paying attention and I stepped in a big puddle of oil.*

3 ⌈**interest**⌉ [U] the special interest that people show in someone or something: *The media has given Stone's new movie a lot of attention.* | *Jackie gets a lot of attention from the boys at school.* | *The Braves have been playing so well they have everyone's attention.* | *Rob always has to be the center of attention* (=the person everyone notices). | **public/press/media attention** *The new show is receiving a lot of attention from the press.*

4 ⌈**make sb notice**⌉ **a) attract/catch/get/draw sb's attention** to make someone notice you, especially because you want to speak to them or you need their help: *The ad was created to get the attention of people at risk for AIDS.* **b) attract attention** if someone or something attracts attention, people notice them, especially because they look very interesting or unusual: *He attracted attention in his late teens with his drawings and illustrations.* **c) get attention** to make someone notice you and be interested in what you are doing: *We thought he was whining just to get some attention.* **d) draw attention to sth** to make people notice and be concerned about something: *The march drew people's attention to women's concerns about breast cancer.* **e) draw/divert/turn attention away from sth** to make people stop being concerned about something such as a social problem: *It may have been an attempt to divert attention from the social unrest in the country.* **f) bring sth to sb's attention** to tell someone, especially someone in authority, about something such as a problem: *The case brought sexual harassment to the public's attention.* **g) come to sb's attention** FORMAL if something such as a problem comes to the attention of someone in authority, they find out about it **h) draw/call attention to yourself** to do something that makes people pay attention to you: *I tried to leave the meeting without calling attention to myself.*

5 ⌈**medical care**⌉ [U] treatment given to someone who is sick or injured: *Snake bites require immediate medical attention.*

6 ⌈**repair/clean**⌉ [U] something you do to repair or clean something, or make it work or be able to be used: *Grease the bike's chain and any other areas that need attention.*

7 ⌈**care**⌉ [C,U] things that you do to help or take care of someone or something: *Pets need a lot of care and attention.* | *Your plant looks like it needs some attention.* | *Attention to customers is increasingly important.*

8 stand at/to attention used to tell a soldier to stand up straight and stay still

9 Attention! used when ordering a group of soldiers to stand up straight

10 ⌈**speech/announcement**⌉ **a) may/can I have your attention?** SPOKEN, FORMAL used when you want people to listen to you **b) thank you for your attention** SPOKEN, FORMAL used at the end of a speech or statement to thank people for listening

11 ⌈**letter**⌉ **to the attention of sb** used on the front of an official letter when you want a particular person to read it or deal with it: *Enquiries should be sent to the attention of the Director.*

attention def·i·cit dis·or·der /.ˌ.. ˈ... .ˌ../ *abbreviation* **ADD** *n.* [U] a condition that affects especially children, causing them to be too active and not able to be quiet or pay attention for very long

A

attention span /.'.. ,./ *n.* [U] the amount of time that you are able to carefully listen or watch something that is happening: *Kids his age typically have a very short attention span.*

at·ten·tive /əˈtɛntɪv/ *adj.* **1** listening to or watching someone carefully because you are interested in them: *an attentive father* | [+ **to**] *Teachers are more attentive to good students.* **2** making sure someone has everything they need: *The waiters were attentive and friendly.* | [+ **to**] *They've built a business that is attentive to its customers.* —opposite INATTENTIVE —**attentively** *adv.* —**attentiveness** *n.* [U]

at·ten·u·at·ed /əˈtɛnuˌeɪtɪd/ *adj.* FORMAL made weaker or having less of an effect: *an attenuated form of the polio virus* —**attenuate** *v.* [T] —**attenuation** /əˌtɛnuˈeɪʃən/ *n.* [U]

at·test /əˈtɛst/ *v.* **1** [I,T] to show or prove that something is true: [+ **to**] *Young graduates attested to the value of the program.* | *She's an excellent cook, as her grandson can attest.* **2** [T] to officially state that you believe something is true, especially in a court of law

at·tes·ta·tion /ˌætɛˈsteɪʃən/ *n.* [C,U] FORMAL a legal statement made by someone in which they say that something is definitely true

at·tic /ˈætɪk/ *n.* [C] a space or room at the top of a house, often used for storing things —see picture on page 423

At·ti·la /əˈtɪlə, ˈætl-ə/ also **Attila the Hun** /.... ' ./ (?406–453) a king of the Huns (=an ancient tribe from Asia) who attacked and took control of large parts of the Roman Empire

at·tire /əˈtaɪɚ/ *n.* [U] FORMAL clothes: *business attire*

at·tired /əˈtaɪɚd/ *adj.* [not before noun] FORMAL dressed in a particular way: *Sean was properly attired in coat and tie.*

at·ti·tude /ˈætəˌtud/ *n.* **1** [C,U] the opinions and feelings that you usually have about something: *Some of the guys have a real macho attitude.* | [+ **toward/about**] *We can learn a great deal from the French attitude toward food.* **2** [C,U] the way that you behave toward someone or in a particular situation, especially when this shows how you feel: *The team just came out for the second half with a different attitude.* | [+ **toward**] *My boss has a patronizing attitude toward us.* | *Ben has a real attitude problem* (=he is not helpful or pleasant to be with). | **good/bad attitude** *Sarah's a good student with a good attitude.* | *Europeans have a different attitude about business.* **3** [U] INFORMAL a style, behavior etc. that shows you have the confidence to do unusual and exciting things without caring what other people think: *This is solid rock 'n' roll played with attitude.*

at·tor·ney /əˈtɚni/ *n. plural* **attorneys** [C] a word meaning a "lawyer," used in official letters and speech

attorney gen·er·al /.,.. '.../ *n.* [C] the chief lawyer in a state or of the government in the U.S.

at·tract /əˈtrækt/ *v.* **1** [T] to make someone interested in something, or make them want to take part in something: *The industry needs to focus on what attracts customers.* | [**attract sb to sth**] *What was it that attracted you to the sport?* | *Saturday's game attracted a lot of media attention.* **2 be attracted to sb** to feel that you like someone and want to have a sexual relationship with them: *She was obviously attracted to him from the start.* **3** [T] to make people or animals come to a place: *Disney World attracts millions of tourists each year.* | *The food mixture will attract a variety of wild songbirds.* | [**attract sb/sth to sth**] *These programs are designed to attract new business to the area.* **4** [T] to make someone like or admire something or have romantic feelings for someone: [**attract sb to sb**] *What attracted you to her in the first place?* **5** [T] if an object attracts another object, it makes that object move toward it: *Have the children see whether the magnet will attract paper clips, coins etc.*

at·trac·tion /əˈtrækʃən/ *n.* **1** [C,U] a feeling of liking someone, especially in a sexual way: *There was definitely a physical attraction between us.* | [+ **to**] *His attraction to other women has caused marital problems.* —opposite REPULSION **2** [C] something interesting or enjoyable to see or do: *"The Viper" is one of the theme park's most popular attractions.* | *the city's top tourist attraction* (=a place that many tourists visit) | *The beautiful beaches are the island's main attraction* (=most popular place, activity, etc.). **3** [C,U] a feature or quality that makes something seem interesting or enjoyable: *The hills of Provence have a magical attraction for many.* | [+ **of**] *Mexico's large labor force may have been the main attraction of the free trade agreement.* **4** [C,U] TECHNICAL a force which makes things move together or stay together: *magnetic attraction*

at·trac·tive /əˈtræktɪv/ *adj.* **1** someone who is attractive is good looking, especially in a way that makes you sexually interested in them: *an attractive young woman* | *Women seem to find him attractive.* **2** pleasant to look at: *an attractive outfit* **3** having qualities that make you want to accept something or be involved in it: *The interest rate makes these an attractive investment.* | [+ **to**] *Advertising campaigns make alcohol attractive to young people.* —see Usage Note at BEAUTIFUL —**attractively** *adv.* —**attractiveness** *n.* [U]

at·trib·ut·a·ble /əˈtrɪbyətəbəl/ *adj.* [not before noun] FORMAL likely to be caused by something: [+ **to**] *The price increase is attributable to a rise in the cost of paper.*

at·trib·ute[1] /əˈtrɪbyut/ *v.*
attribute sth to sb/sth *phr. v.* [T] **1** to say that a situation, state, or event is caused by something: *Doctors attributed his quick recovery to his physical fitness.* | *We tend to attribute a child's problems to the parent.* **2** to say that someone was responsible for saying or writing something, painting a famous picture etc., when you cannot be completely sure: *These paintings are attributed to Van Gogh.* **3** to say that someone or something has a particular quality: *The study shows that people attribute the most negative qualities to politicians.* —**attribution** /ˌætrəˈbyuʃən/ *n.* [U]

at·tri·bute[2] /ˈætrəˌbyut/ *n.* [C] a quality or feature, especially one that is considered to be good or useful: *Kindness is just one of her many attributes.*

at·trib·u·tive /əˈtrɪbyətɪv/ *adj.* describing and coming before a noun. For example, in the phrase "big city," "big" is an attributive adjective, and in the phrase "school bus," "school" is a noun in an attributive position —**attributively** *adv.*

at·tri·tion /əˈtrɪʃən/ *n.* [U] **1** a process in which the number of students or people who work for a company becomes smaller, because new people do not take the place of the people who leave: *Staff reductions could be achieved through attrition and early retirements.* **2** the process of gradually destroying your enemy or making them weak by attacking them continuously: *a war of attrition*

at·tuned /əˈtund/ *adj.* [not before noun] familiar with the way someone thinks or behaves so that you can react to them in an appropriate way: [+ **to**] *City government needs to be more attuned to the public.* —**attune** *v.* [T]

atty. *n.* a written abbreviation of ATTORNEY

ATV *n.* [C] all-terrain vehicle; a motor vehicle with three or four wheels that you can drive on rough ground

a·twit·ter /əˈtwɪtɚ/ *adj.* [not before noun] LITERARY very excited or nervous about something: *Washington is all atwitter with the latest scandal.*

a·typ·i·cal /eɪˈtɪpɪkəl/ *adj.* not typical or usual: *High school students who do volunteer work are not atypical.*

au·ber·gine /ˈoʊbəˌʒin/ *n.* [U] a very dark purple color —**aubergine** *adj.*

au·burn /ˈɔbɚn/ *adj.* auburn hair is a reddish brown color

au cou·rant /ˌoʊ kuˈrɑnt/ *adj.* knowing a lot about recent events or fashions

auc·tion[1] /'ɔkʃən/ n. [C] a public meeting where land, buildings, paintings etc. are sold to the person who offers the most money for them: *The painting sold at auction for $6,500.* | **put sth up for auction/go up for auction** *Items from Liberace's estate went up for auction.* | *It's the city's largest auction house.* (=company that arranges auctions)

auction[2] v. [T + off] to sell something at an auction

auc·tion·eer /,ɔkʃə'nɪr/ n. [C] someone who controls an auction, selling the goods to the people who offer the most money

au·da·cious /ɔ'deɪʃəs/ adj. brave and shocking: *a brilliant, audacious play* —**audaciously** adv.

au·dac·i·ty /ɔ'dæsəti/ n. [U] the quality of having enough courage to take risks or do things that are shocking or rude: *They had the audacity to use tax dollars to print this stuff.*

Au·den /'ɔdn/, **W. H.** /'dʌbəlyu eɪtʃ/ (1907–1973) a British poet

au·di·ble /'ɔdəbəl/ adj. a sound that is audible is loud enough for you to hear it: *There was an audible gasp from the audience.* | **barely/scarcely audible** *She replied in a voice that was barely audible.* —opposite INAUDIBLE —**audibly** adv. —**audibility** /,ɔdə'bɪləti/ n. [U]

au·di·ence /'ɔdiəns/ n. [C] **1** a group of people who watch and listen to a concert, speech, movie etc.: *The audience danced and clapped and swayed to the music.* **2** the number or type of people who regularly watch or listen to a particular program: *The ad was inappropriate for a family audience.* | *MTV's target audience* (=the kind of people that a program, advertisement etc. is supposed to attract) *is young people between 14 and 30.* **3** a formal meeting with a very important person: *We were granted an audience* (=given one) *with the Pope.*

au·di·o /'ɔdioʊ/ adj. [only before noun] relating to recording and broadcasting sound: *an audio signal*

au·di·ol·o·gy /,ɔdi'ɑlədʒi/ n. [U] the study of how people hear, especially the study of hearing problems —**audiologist** n. [C]

au·di·o·tape /'ɔdioʊ,teɪp/ n. [C,U] TECHNICAL a long thin band of MAGNETIC material used to record sound, put into a small plastic case so that it can be played easily

au·di·o·vis·u·al /,ɔdioʊ'vɪʒuəl/ adj. involving the use of pictures and recorded sound: *audiovisual equipment*

au·dit /'ɔdɪt/ v. [T] **1** to officially examine a company's financial records in order to check that they are correct: *The fund is audited annually by an accountant.* **2** to study a subject at college without getting a grade for it —**audit** n. [C]

au·di·tion[1] /ɔ'dɪʃən/ n. [C] a short performance by an actor, singer etc., which someone judges to decide if the person is good enough to act in a play, sing in a concert etc.: *an audition for the lead part*

audition[2] v. [I,T] to perform in an audition or judge someone in an audition: [+ for] *Judy said she auditioned for a yogurt commercial.* | [audition sb (for sth)] *We auditioned a lot of actors.*

au·di·tor /'ɔdɪtə/ n. [C] someone whose job is to officially examine a company's financial records

au·di·to·ri·um /,ɔdɪ'tɔriəm/ n. [C] **1** the part of a theater where people sit when watching a play, concert etc. **2** a large building used for concerts or public meetings: *the school auditorium*

au·di·to·ry /'ɔdɪ,tɔri/ adj. [only before noun] TECHNICAL relating to the ability to hear

Au·du·bon /'ɔdə,bɑn/, **John James** (1785–1851) a U.S. NATURALIST and painter of North American birds

Audubon So·ci·e·ty, the /'... ,.../ an organization that works to protect wild birds

Aug. n. the written abbreviation of August

au·ger /'ɔgə/ n. [C] a tool used for making a hole in wood or in the ground

aught /ɔt, ɑt/ pron. OLD USE anything

aug·ment /ɔg'mɛnt/ v. [T] FORMAL to increase the value, amount, effectiveness etc. of something: *State*

universities are looking for money from businesses to augment state funds.

au gra·tin /oʊ 'grɑt̚n/ adj. au gratin potatoes or vegetables are covered in cheese, butter, and bread CRUMBS and then baked

au·gur /'ɔgə/ v. **1** FORMAL to be a sign that something will be successful or unsuccessful: *Their attitudes do not augur well for the success of the peace talks.* **2** [I,T] LITERARY to use signs in order to say what will happen in the future

au·gu·ry /'ɔgyəri, -gə-/ n. [C] LITERARY a sign of what will happen in the future, or the act of saying what will happen

Au·gust /'ɔgəst/ written abbreviation **Aug.** n. [C,U] the eighth month of the year, between July and September —see Usage Note at JANUARY

au·gust /ɔ'gʌst/ adj. LITERARY old, famous, and respected

Au·gus·ta /ɔ'gʌstə, ə-/ the capital city of the U.S. state of Maine

Au·gus·tine, St. /'ɔgə,stin/ also **St. Augustine of Hippo** (354–430) a North African Christian leader, PHILOSOPHER, and writer whose books strongly influenced the development of Christianity

Au·gus·tus /ɔ'gʌstəs, ə-/ (63 B.C.–A.D. 14) the EMPEROR of Rome after Julius Caesar, and the first Roman emperor to be accepted by all the people and establish his power

au jus /oʊ 'ʒu, -'dʒus/ adj. served with a thin SAUCE made from the natural juices that come out of meat as it is cooking: *prime rib au jus*

auk /ɔk/ n. [C] a black and white bird with short wings that lives on or near the ocean

au lait /oʊ 'leɪ/ adj. with milk: *café au lait*

Auld Lang Syne /,oʊld læŋ 'zaɪn/ a Scottish song that people sing when they celebrate the beginning of the new year at 12 o'clock MIDNIGHT on December 31

aunt /ænt, ɑnt/ n. [C] **1** the sister of your father or mother, or the wife of your father's or mother's brother: *Aunt Mary* **2** INFORMAL a woman who is a friend of a small child's parents

aun·tie, aunty /'ænti/ n. [C] INFORMAL aunt

au pair /oʊ 'pɛr/ n. [C] a young woman who stays with a family in a foreign country to take care of their children

au·ra /'ɔrə/ n. [C] a quality or feeling that seems to surround a person or a place: [+ of] *The place has taken on an aura of success.*

au·ral /'ɔrəl/ adj. relating to the sense of hearing, or to someone's ability to understand a language —**aurally** adj.

au·re·ole /'ɔri,oʊl/ n. [C] LITERARY a bright circle of light; HALO

au re·voir /,oʊ rə'vwar, ɔr'vwar/ interjection goodbye

au·ri·cle /'ɔrɪkəl/ n. [C] one of the two spaces inside the top of your heart that push blood into the VENTRICLES

au·ro·ra bo·re·al·is /ə,rɔrə bɔri'ælɪs/ n. [singular] bands of moving light that you can see in the night sky in the far north; NORTHERN LIGHTS

aus·pic·es /'ɔspəsɪz, -,siz/ n. **under the auspices of sb/sth** FORMAL with the help and support of a particular organization: *A research project has been set up under the auspices of the University of Michigan.*

aus·pi·cious /ɔ'spɪʃəs/ adj. FORMAL showing that something is likely to be successful: *It was an auspicious beginning to her career as an author.*

Aus·sie /'ɔsi, 'ɑsi/ n. [C] INFORMAL someone from Australia —**Aussie** adj.

Aus·ten /'ɔstən/, **Jane** /dʒeɪn/ (1775–1817) a British writer of NOVELS

aus·tere /ɔ'stɪr/ adj. **1** someone who is austere is very strict and looks very serious: *a cold, austere woman* **2** plain and simple and without any decoration: *an austere style of painting* **3** an austere way of

A

life is very simple and has few things to make it comfortable or enjoyable —**austerely** *adv.*

aus·ter·i·ty /ɔ'stɛrəti/ *n.* [U] **1** bad economic conditions in which people do not have much money to spend: *Russians have faced years of austerity after communism's fall.* **2** the quality of being austere

Aus·tin /'ɔstɪn, 'ɑ-/ the capital city of the U.S. state of Texas

Aus·tral·a·sia /ˌɔstrə'leɪʒə, ˌɑ-/ *n.* [U] Australia and the islands that are close to it

Aus·tra·la·sian /ˌɔstrə'leɪʒən, ˌɑ-/ *adj.* relating to Australasia

Aus·tra·lia /ɔ'streɪlyə, ɑ-/ a country between the Indian Ocean and the southern Pacific Ocean, which is also a CONTINENT —**Australian** *n., adj.*

Aus·tri·a /'ɔstriə, 'ɑs-/ a country in central Europe, southeast of Germany —**Austrian** *n., adj.*

Austro- /ɔstroʊ, ɑ-, -strə/ *prefix* **1** Austrian and something else: *the Austro-Hungarian empire* **2** Australian and something: *Austro-Malayan*

au·tar·chy /'ɔtɑrki/ *n.* [U] FORMAL an AUTOCRACY

au·tar·ky /'ɔtɑrki/ *n.* TECHNICAL **1** [U] an economic system in which a country produces all the things it needs, as opposed to buying them from another country **2** [C] a country that has this economic system

au·then·tic /ɔ'θɛntɪk/ *adj.* **1** done or made in the traditional, correct, or original way: *an authentic Italian recipe for cannelloni | an authentic Texas Rangers uniform* **2** a painting, document, book etc. that is authentic has been proven to be the work of a particular person: *an authentic plaster statue by Michelangelo* **3** having a quality that makes something real or true: *DiMaggio was an authentic folk hero.* **4** based on facts: *an authentic account of the incident* —**authentically** /-kli/ *adv.*

au·then·ti·cate /ɔ'θɛntɪˌkeɪt/ *v.* [T] **1** to prove that something is real and not a copy: *Her company authenticates paintings and other works of art.* **2** to prove that something is true: *The Loch Ness Monster's existence has not been authenticated.* —**authentication** /ɔˌθɛntɪ'keɪʃən/ *n.* [U]

au·then·ti·ci·ty /ˌɔθən'tɪsəti/ *n.* [U] the quality of being real or true and not a copy: *Art experts have questioned the painting's authenticity.*

s w **au·thor¹** /'ɔθɚ/ *n.* [C] **1** someone who writes a book, play, story etc.: *The author has signed the book on the title page. | [+ of] Roald Dahl was a famous author of children's books.* **2** FORMAL the person who develops a plan or idea: [+ of] *Assemblyman Richard Floyd was the author of the helmet law.*

author² *v.* [T] to be the writer of a book, report etc.

au·thor·i·tar·i·an /əˌθɔrə'tɛriən, əˌθɑr-/ *adj.* strictly forcing people to obey a set of rules or laws, especially ones that are often wrong or unfair: *an authoritarian government | His management style has been criticized as authoritarian.* —**authoritarian** *n.* [C] —**authoritarianism** *n.* [U]

au·thor·i·ta·tive /ə'θɔrəˌteɪtɪv/ *adj.* **1** an authoritative book, account etc. is respected because the person who wrote it knows a lot about the subject: *an authoritative biography of Theodore Roosevelt* **2** behaving or speaking in a confident and determined way that makes people respect and obey you —**authoritatively** *adv.*

s w **au·thor·i·ty** /ə'θɔrəti/ *n. plural* **authorities**
1 power [U] the power you have because of your official position or because people respect your knowledge and experience: *Coach Harris has the authority to hire and fire players. | [+ over] The generals were given authority over particular regions of the country. | Do women and men who are in authority control situations differently?*
2 organization [C] an official organization or a local government department which controls public affairs, provides public services etc.: *the Regional Water Authority*
3 the authorities the people or organizations that

are in charge of a particular country or area: *Please report any suspicious activities to the authorities immediately.*
4 person with power [C] someone who has power because of their position or knowledge: *Al-Azhar is Egypt's highest religious authority.*
5 expert [C] someone who knows a lot about a subject and whose knowledge and opinions are greatly respected: [+ on] *Judith Martin is a widely read authority on etiquette.*
6 I have it on good authority used to say that you are sure that something is true because you trust the person who told you about it: *I have it on good authority that the school board wants to fire the principal.*
7 permission [C,U] official permission to do something: *The airline has been given authority to fly to several U.S. destinations.*

au·thor·i·za·tion /ˌɔθərə'zeɪʃən/ *n.* [C,U] official permission to do something, or the document giving this permission: *The company must get written authorization from the customer.*

au·thor·ize /'ɔθəˌraɪz/ *v.* [T] to give official or legal permission for something: [authorize sb to do sth] *The city council authorized staff to purchase a new computer system.*

authorized cap·i·tal /ˌ... '.../ *n.* [U] the largest amount of money a company is allowed to get by selling SHARES

au·thor·ship /'ɔθɚˌʃɪp/ *n.* [U] **1** the fact that you have written a particular book, document etc.: *Berg has denied authorship of the article and refused to comment further.* **2** the fact of being the person who thinks of and then makes a plan, piece of work, program etc. happen: *Both Democrats and Republicans have claimed authorship of the tax plan.* **3** FORMAL the profession of writing books

au·tism /'ɔˌtɪzəm/ *n.* [U] a severe mental illness that affects children and prevents them from communicating with other people —**autistic** /ɔ'tɪstɪk/ *adj.: an autistic child*

s w **au·to** /'ɔtoʊ/ *n.* [C] a car: *auto parts*

auto- /ɔtoʊ, -tə/ *prefix* **1** working by itself: *an automobile | an automatic camera* **2** relating to yourself, or done by yourself: *an autobiography (=a book about your life, written by yourself)*

au·to·bahn /'ɔtoʊˌbɑn, 'ɑtə-/ *n.* [C] a wide road in Germany for very fast traffic

au·to·bi·og·ra·phy /ˌɔtəbaɪ'ɑgrəfi/ *n. plural* **autobiographies 1** [C] the story of your life, written by yourself **2** [U] literature that is concerned with people writing about their own lives —**autobiographic** /ˌɔtəbaɪə'græfɪk/ *adj.* —**autobiographical** *adj.* —**autobiographically** /-kli/ *adv.* —compare BIOGRAPHY

au·toc·ra·cy /ɔ'tɑkrəsi/ *n. plural* **autocracies 1** [U] a system of government in which one person or group has unlimited power **2** [C] a country governed in this way

au·to·crat·ic /ˌɔtə'krætɪk◂/ *adj.* **1** making decisions and giving orders to people without asking them for their opinion: *an autocratic manager* **2** having unlimited power to govern a country: *an autocratic government* —**autocrat** /'ɔtəˌkræt/ *n.* [C] —**autocratically** /ˌɔtə'krætɪkli/ *adv.*

au·to·graph¹ /'ɔtəˌgræf/ *n.* [C] a famous person's name, written in their own writing: *Joe DiMaggio's autograph | She smiled and joked as she signed autographs.*

autograph² *v.* [T] if a famous person autographs a book, photograph etc., they write their name on it

au·to·im·mune dis·ease /ˌ... '. .ˌ./ *n.* [U] a condition in which substances that normally prevent illness in the body attack and harm parts of it instead

au·to·mak·er /'ɔtoʊˌmeɪkɚ/ *n.* [C] a word meaning a company that makes cars, used especially in newspapers or magazines

Au·to·mat /'ɔtəˌmæt/ *n.* [C] TRADEMARK a type of restaurant in which you put money in machines to get food, that existed from about 1900 until 1990

au·to·mate /'ɔtəˌmeɪt/ *v.* [T] to change to a system in which jobs are done or goods are produced by machines instead of people

au·to·mat·ed /'ɔtə,meɪtɪd/ *adj.* using machines to do a job or industrial process: *a highly automated factory*

s w **au·to·mat·ic¹** /,ɔtə'mætɪk◂/ *adj.* **1** an automatic machine, car etc. is designed to operate by itself after you start it, and can be operated using on a few controls: *an automatic weapon | a camera with automatic focus | Is the heating on automatic (=is it set to go on by itself)?* **2** something that is automatic is certain to happen, especially because of a rule or law: *The merit system replaced automatic yearly pay raises.* **3** done without thinking, especially because you have done the same thing many times before: *It takes a while before this kind of work feels automatic.*

automatic² *n.* [C] **1** a car with a system of GEARS that operate themselves without the driver needing to change them —compare STANDARD¹ **2** a weapon that can fire bullets continuously

s w **au·to·mat·i·cally** /,ɔtə'mætɪkli/ *adv.* **1** as the result of a situation: *Cancer is not automatically a death sentence.* **2** by the action of a machine, without a person making it work: *The gates rise automatically during high tide.* **3** without thinking about what you are doing: *After a while, driving just comes automatically.*

automatic pi·lot /,.... '../ *n.* [C] **1** a machine that flies an airplane by itself, without the need for a pilot to control it **2** be on automatic pilot INFORMAL to be doing something without thinking about it at all, especially because you have done it many times before or are very tired: *I wasn't really asleep – I was just kind of running on automatic pilot.*

automatic trans·mis·sion /...,.. .'../ *n.* [U] a system that operates the GEARS of a car without the driver needing to change them

au·to·ma·tion /,ɔtə'meɪʃən/ *n.* [U] the use of machines instead of people to do a job or industrial process

au·tom·a·ton /ɔ'tɑmə,tɑn/ *n.* [C] **1** someone who seems to be unable to feel emotions **2** a machine, especially one in the shape of a human, that moves without anyone controlling it

au·to·mo·bile /,ɔtəmə'bil, 'ɔtəmə,bil/ *n.* [C] a car: *the automobile industry*

au·to·mo·tive /,ɔtə'moʊtɪv◂/ *adj.* relating to cars: *automotive products*

au·ton·o·mous /ɔ'tɑnəməs/ *adj.* **1** having the power to govern an area, country etc. without being controlled by anyone else: *an autonomous region* **2** FORMAL having the ability to work and make decisions by yourself without any help from anyone else —**autonomously** *adv.*

au·ton·o·my /ɔ'tɑnəmi/ *n.* [U] **1** freedom to govern an area, country etc. without being controlled by anyone else: [+ from] *Rebel forces are fighting for autonomy from the central government.* **2** the ability to make your own decisions without being influenced by anyone else: *the autonomy of the individual*

au·to·pi·lot /'ɔtoʊ,paɪlət/ *n.* [C] AUTOMATIC PILOT

au·top·sy /'ɔ,tɑpsi/ *n. plural* **autopsies** [C] an examination of a dead body to discover the cause of death

au·to·route /'ɔtoʊ,rut/ *n.* [C] CANADIAN a HIGHWAY in Quebec

au·to·sug·ges·tion /,ɔtoʊsəg'dʒɛstʃən/ *n.* [U] TECHNICAL the process of making someone believe or feel something, without them realizing that you are doing this

au·to·work·er /'ɔtoʊ,wɜkɚ/ *n.* [C] someone who works in a factory making cars

au·tumn /'ɔtəm/ *n.* [C,U] the season between summer and winter, when leaves change color and the weather becomes slightly colder; FALL

au·tum·nal /ɔ'tʌmnəl/ *adj.* relating to or typical of autumn: *autumnal colors*

aux. the written abbreviation of AUXILIARY, especially of AUXILIARY VERB

aux·il·ia·ry¹ /ɔg'zɪləri, -'zɪlyəri/ *adj.* [only before noun] **1** providing additional help for someone: *auxiliary pilots* **2** an auxiliary motor, piece of

A

equipment etc. is kept ready to be used if the main one stops working or if another one is needed: *the auxiliary generator* —see also AUXILIARY VERB

auxiliary² *n. plural* **auxiliaries** [C] **1** a person or group that provides additional help for someone: *The auxiliary for the Symphony is holding a fund-raising party on Saturday.* **2** an auxiliary verb: *a modal auxiliary*

auxiliary verb /.'... , / *n.* [C] a verb that is used with another verb to show its tense, MOOD (8) etc. In English the auxiliary verbs are "be," "do," and "have" (as in "I am running," "I didn't go," "they have gone") and all the MODALS

AV, A.V. an abbreviation of AUDIOVISUAL

a·vail¹ /ə'veɪl/ *n.* FORMAL **be to/of no avail** if something you do is to no avail, you do not succeed in getting what you want: *We searched everywhere to no avail.*

avail² *v.* **avail yourself of sth** FORMAL to accept an offer or use an opportunity to do something: *Avail yourself of every opportunity to learn.*

a·vail·a·ble /ə'veɪləbəl/ *adj.* **1** something that is available is able to be used or can easily be bought s w or found: *More money may become available later in* 2 1 *the year. | We've used up all the available space. |* [+ for] *Spanish versions of the educational game are available for schools. |* [+ to] *The Inner Urban Areas Act helped to make more loans available to private firms. | Every available (=all the ones that can be used) ambulance rushed to the scene of the accident. | readily/freely available (=easy to get)* **2** [not before noun] someone who is available is not busy and has enough time to talk to you: *The mayor was not available for comment.* **3** someone who is available does not have a wife, BOYFRIEND etc., and therefore may want to start a new romantic relationship with someone else —**availability** /ə,veɪlə'bɪləti/ *n.* [U] *We want to increase the availability of health insurance to working families.*

av·a·lanche /'ævə,læntʃ, -,lɑntʃ/ *n.* [C] **1** a large amount of snow, ice, and rocks that falls down the side of a mountain —see picture on page 1333 **2** an avalanche of sth a very large number of things such as letters, messages etc. that arrive suddenly at the same time

avalanche

Av·a·lon /'ævə,lɑn/ in old stories about King ARTHUR, a holy island where Arthur was buried

a·vant-garde /,ævɑnt'gɑrd◂, ,ɑ-/ *adj.* **1** avant-garde music, literature etc. is extremely modern and often seems strange or slightly shocking **2** the avant-garde the group of artists, writers, musicians etc. who produce avant-garde books, paintings etc.

av·a·rice /'ævərɪs/ *n.* [U] FORMAL DISAPPROVING a strong desire to have a lot of money; GREED —**avaricious** /,ævə'rɪʃəs◂/ *adj.* —**avariciously** *adv.*

av·a·tar /'ævə,tɑr/ *n.* [C] **1** a person who represents an idea, principle etc. completely: [+ of] *Krisler is known as an avatar of traditional family values.* **2** a person, animal, or other character used by someone to represent himself or herself in a VIRTUAL computer world **3** the appearance of a Hindu god, especially Vishnu, in human or animal form

Ave. the written abbreviation of AVENUE (1): *6913 Broadway Ave.*

Av·e·don /'ævə,dɑn, -dən/, **Richard** (1923–) a U.S. fashion PHOTOGRAPHER

a·venge /ə'vɛndʒ/ *v.* [T] LITERARY to do something to hurt or punish someone because they have hurt or offended you: *He wanted to avenge his brother's death.* —**avenger** *n.* [C]

A

av·e·nue /'ævə,nu/ *n.* [C] **1** used in the names of streets in a town or city: *Fifth Avenue* | *Sherman Avenue* **2** a possible way of achieving something: [+ **for/of**] *Today, Yiddish still provides an avenue of communication.*

a·ver /ə'vɜ/ *v.* [T] FORMAL to say something firmly and strongly because you are sure that it is true

av·erage¹ /'ævrɪdʒ/ *adj.* **1** [only before noun] the average amount is the amount you get when you add together several quantities and divide this by the total number of quantities: *an average price of $9,000* | *What's the average rainfall in this area?* **2** an average amount or quantity is not unusually big or small: *I'd say he was of average height.* **3** having qualities that are typical of most people or things: *The laws were simplified so that the average person could understand.* | *In an average week, I drive about 250 miles.* **4** INFORMAL neither very good nor very bad: *The fishing is average around there – nothing special.*

average² *abbreviation* **avg.** *n.* **1** [C] the amount calculated by adding together several quantities, and then dividing this amount by the total number of quantities: *The average of 2, 4, and 9 is 5.* | *Prices have risen by an average of 1.5%.* | *the national/state/global etc. average* *The national average is a salary of about $20,000 per year.* **2 on average** based on a calculation about how many times something usually happens, how much money someone usually gets, how often people usually do something etc.: *On average, men are taller than women by several inches.* | *Japanese people, on average, live longer than Europeans.* **3** [C,U] the usual level or amount for most people or things in a group | **above/below average** (=better or worse than most other people's) *Paula's grades are well above average.* | **higher/lower than average** *higher than average levels of unemployment* —see also **law of averages** (LAW)

average³ *v.* [linking verb] **1** to usually do something, or usually happen a particular number of times, or usually be a particular size or amount: *Primary-care doctors said they averaged over 25 patients a day.* | *The fish averages about two inches in length.* **2** to calculate the average of quantities

average out *phr. v.* **1** if a set of numbers averages out to a particular number, or you average them out, their average is calculated to be that number: *650,000 teachers have been hired over five years; that averages out to 130,000 a year.* **2 sth averages out** used to say that sometimes there is more of one thing, amount, activity etc. than at other times, but that there is a balance over a longer period of time: *Sometimes I do the housework – sometimes she does. It all averages out.*

a·verse /ə'vɜs/ *adj.* **1 not be averse to (doing) sth** used to say that someone likes to do something sometimes, especially something that is slightly wrong or bad for them: *I don't drink much, but I'm not averse to the occasional glass of wine.* **2 be averse to (doing) sth** FORMAL to be unwilling to do something or to dislike something

a·ver·sion /ə'vɜʒən/ *n.* [singular,U] a strong dislike of something or someone: *These animals have an aversion to sunlight.*

a·vert /ə'vɜt/ *v.* [T] **1** to prevent something bad from happening: *Using an "automatic train stop" could have averted the disaster.* **2 avert your eyes/gaze etc.** to look away from something that you do not want to see

avg. the written abbreviation of "average"

a·vi·ar·y /'eɪvi,ɛri/ *n. plural* **aviaries** [C] a large CAGE or building where birds are kept

a·vi·a·tion /,eɪvi'eɪʃən/ *n.* [U] **1** the science or practice of flying in aircraft **2** the industry that makes aircraft

a·vi·a·tor /'eɪvi,eɪtə/ *n.* [C] OLD-FASHIONED a pilot

Av·i·cen·na /,ævə'sɛnə/ (980–1037) an Arab PHILOSO-PHER

av·id /'ævɪd/ *adj.* **1 avid reader/listener etc.** someone does something such as reading or listening to something as much as they can: *an avid sailor* | *an avid supporter of the arts* | **an avid fan** (=someone who likes a particular activity, type of music, etc. very much) **2 an avid interest/desire etc. (in sth)** a strong interest, desire etc.: *an avid interest in birds*

a·vi·on·ics /,eɪvi'ɑnɪks/ *n.* [U] TECHNICAL the science and development of the electronic systems used in aircraft

av·o·ca·do /,ævə'kɑdoʊ, ,ɑ-/ *n. plural* **avocados** [C] a fruit with a thick green or dark purple skin that is green inside and has a large seed in the middle

av·o·ca·tion /,ævə'keɪʃən/ *n.* [C] FORMAL an activity that someone does for pleasure; a HOBBY

a·void /ə'vɔɪd/ *v.* [T] **1** to do something to prevent something bad from happening: *Children quickly learn how to avoid punishment.* | [**avoid doing sth**] *We want to avoid disappointing our customers* **2** to deliberately stay away from someone or something: *Have you been avoiding me?* | *I managed to avoid the worst of the traffic.* | *She's at the age where she avoids boys like the plague.* **3** to not do something deliberately, especially because it is dangerous, bad etc.: *We must, above all, avoid involvement in the war.* | [**avoid doing sth**] *Bill had done everything he could to avoid talking to me.* —**avoidable** *adj.*

a·void·ance /ə'vɔɪdns/ *n.* [U] the act of avoiding someone or something: *Troops have received training in mine avoidance and detection.* | [+ **of**] *Her avoidance of issues such as tax reform could hurt her in the election.*

av·oir·du·pois /,ævədu'pwɑ, -'pɔɪ/ *n.* [U] the system of weighing things that uses the standard measures of the OUNCE, POUND, and TON —compare METRIC SYSTEM

a·vow /ə'vaʊ/ *v.* [T] FORMAL to say or admit publicly something you believe promise —**avowal** *n.* [C,U]

a·vowed /ə'vaʊd/ *adj.* **1 an avowed Communist/atheist/nonsmoker etc.** someone who publicly shows or admits their belief in a particular idea or way of living **2 avowed goal/purpose/intention etc.** a goal, purpose etc. that someone has stated publicly: *Hitler's avowed intention to defeat the Soviet Union*

a·vun·cu·lar /ə'vʌŋkyələ/ *adj.* LITERARY like an uncle in that you are kind to and concerned about someone who is younger: *Sam gave her an avuncular squeeze.*

a·wait /ə'weɪt/ *v.* [T] FORMAL **1** to wait for something: *The British army was trapped on the sands, awaiting destruction.* **2** if a situation, event etc. awaits you, it is going to happen in the future: *We knew that blizzard conditions awaited us in Boston.* —see Usage Note at WAIT¹

a·wake¹ /ə'weɪk/ *adj.* [not before noun] **1** not sleeping: *Are you awake?* | *I was* **wide awake** (=completely awake) *until 3 a.m.* | *The noise from the party* **kept us awake** (=stopped us from sleeping). | *I drank some coffee to try and* **stay awake**. | *My mother* **lay awake** *worrying all night.* **2 be awake to sth** to understand a situation and its possible effects: *Suddenly the world was awake to the dangers of nuclear weapons.*

awake² *v. past tense* **awoke** *past participle* **awoken** [I,T] **1** FORMAL to wake up, or to make someone wake up: *I awoke, feeling that someone was nearby.* **2** LITERARY if something awakes an emotion or if an emotion awakes, you suddenly begin to feel that emotion

awake sb ↔ to sth *phr. v.* [T] LITERARY to make someone understand a situation and its possible effects: *Artists finally awoke to the aesthetic possibilities of photography.*

a·wak·en /ə'weɪkən/ *v.* FORMAL **1** [T] to make someone feel an emotion or begin to understand something: *The exhibit is designed to awaken a deeper understanding of Mexican culture.* **2** [I,T] to wake up or to make someone wake up: *He was awakened by the phone.*

awaken sb ↔ to sth *phr. v.* [T] to make someone understand a situation and its possible effects:

People must be awakened to the danger to the environment.

a·wak·en·ing /ə'weɪkənɪŋ/ n. [C] **1** an occasion when you suddenly realize that you understand something or feel something: *a teenager's sexual awakening* | *a spiritual awakening* | *The sudden fall in stock prices was a **rude awakening** (=shocking moment when you realize the truth about something bad) for new investors.* **2** the act of waking from sleep

a·ward¹ /ə'wɔrd/ v. [T] **1** to officially give someone something such as a prize or money to reward them for something good they have done: [award sb sth] *Schultz was awarded a medal for bravery.* | [award sth to sb] *Prizes will be awarded to the top three runners.* **2** to officially decide that someone should receive a payment, a CONTRACT, or a particular legal decision: [award sb sth] *After seven years in court, he was awarded $750,000 compensation.* | [award sth to sb] *The contract was awarded to a small architectural firm.*

award² n. [C] **1** something such as a prize or money given to someone to reward them for something they have done: *Paltrow won the "Best Actress" award.* **2** something, especially money, that is officially given to someone as a payment or because of a decision made in a court: *She received a $700 legal award against her ex-landlord.*

a·ware /ə'wɛr/ adj. [not before noun] **1** if you are aware that something such as a problem or a dangerous situation exists, you realize that it exists: [aware that] *Were you aware that your son was taking drugs?* | [+ of] *Most people are aware of the dangers of drinking and driving.* | *Doctors want to **make** people **aware of** the risks.* | *"Does she have a boyfriend?" " **Not that I'm aware of.**"* | *well, ***acutely/fully aware** (=very aware)* **2** if you are aware of something, you notice it, especially because you can see, hear, or smell it: [aware that] *I slowly became aware that the room was getting colder.* | [+ of] *For the first time, Irene was aware of the people in the seats directly behind them.* **3** understanding a lot about what is happening around you and paying attention to it, especially because you realize possible dangers and problems | **politically/environmentally/socially etc. aware** *Many middle-class immigrant groups have become more politically aware.* **4 as/so far as I am aware** SPOKEN used to emphasize that there may be things that you do not know about a situation: *As far as I'm aware, only the managers are going to the meeting.*

a·ware·ness /ə'wɛrnɪs/ n. [U] **1** knowledge or understanding of a particular subject or situation: *political awareness* | *The 1500 mile walk was set up to **raise awareness about** (=improve people's knowledge about) domestic violence.* **2** the ability to notice something using your senses: [+ of] *an artist's awareness of light and color*

a·wash /ə'wɑʃ, ə'wɔʃ/ adj. [not before noun] **1** containing too many things or people of a particular kind: [+ with/in] *TV is awash with talk shows.* **2** covered with a liquid or light

a·way¹ /ə'weɪ/ adv. **1** to or at a distance from someone or something: *Go away!* | *The car quickly drove away.* | [+ from] *Please keep children away from the glass objects.* | *Move away from the fire!* | *Joe **looked away** (=turned his head in another direction), trying to control his anger.* **2 3 miles/5 kilometers etc. away** at a distance of 3 miles, 5 kilometers etc. from someone or something: *It's a town about 50 miles away from here.* **3 2 days/3 weeks etc. away** if an event is 2 days, 3 weeks etc. away, it will happen after 2 days etc. have passed: *Christmas is only a month away.* **4** into a safe or enclosed place: *Put all your toys away now, please.* **5** if someone is away from school, work, or home they are not there: *I'm sorry, Mrs. Parker is away this week.* | [+ from] *You need a note from your parents if you're going to be away from school.* **6** so as to be gone or used up: *All the water had boiled away.* | *Ruben gave all his money away to charity.* | *Support for the Democrats has dropped away.* | *The young lovers danced the night away (=danced all night).* **7** used to emphasize a continuous action:

He's been working away on the deck all afternoon. **8** if a team is away or is playing away, it is playing a game at its opponent's field, STADIUM etc.: *The Cubs are away in Los Angeles this week.* **9 away with sb/sth!** LITERARY used to tell someone to take someone or something away: *Away with the prisoner!* —see also **far and away** (FAR¹)

away² adj. [only before noun] an away game is played at your opponent's field, COURT etc. —opposite HOME¹

awe¹ /ɔ/ n. [U] **1** a feeling of great respect and admiration for someone or something: *I felt the wonder and awe of the first European explorers who looked at the mountain.* | *He spoke **with awe** of the nuns who started the hospital.* **2 be/stand in awe of sb** to have great respect and admiration for and sometimes a slight fear of someone: *Gelb was clearly in awe of his friend's strength and perseverance.*

awe² v. [T usually passive] if you are awed by someone or something, you feel great respect and admiration for them, and are often slightly afraid of them: *You can't help but be awed by the wonderful Alaskan scenery.* —**awed** adj. [only before noun] *an awed silence*

a·weigh /ə'weɪ/ adj. **anchors aweigh!** used to say that the ANCHOR of a ship has been lifted from the bottom of the ocean

awe·in·spir·ing /'. .,../ adj. extremely impressive in a way that makes you feel great respect and admiration: *an awe-inspiring ancient temple*

awe·some /'ɔsəm/ adj. **1** extremely impressive, serious, or difficult, so that you feel great admiration, worry, or fear: *The view was awesome.* **2** SLANG very good: *The food was totally awesome.* —**awesomely** adv.

awe·strick·en /'ɔ,strɪkən/ adj. awestruck

awe·struck /'ɔstrʌk/ adj. feeling extremely IMPRESSED by the importance, difficulty, or seriousness of someone or something: *Several of the ball players signed autographs for the awestruck kids.*

aw·ful¹ /'ɔfəl/ adj. **1** very bad, or not nice: *The weather was awful.* | *a really awful concert* | *I felt awful about not being able to help.* | *The soup tasted awful.* | *It sounds awful, but I just can't stand his parents.* **2** [only before noun] SPOKEN used to emphasize how much or how good, bad etc. something is: *She used the van an awful lot last month.* **3 look/feel awful** to look or feel sick: *You look awful – what's wrong?* **4** LITERARY making you feel great admiration or fear: *an awful power* —**awfulness** n. [U]

awful² adv. [+ adj./adv.] SPOKEN, NONSTANDARD very: *an awful cute kid*

aw·ful·ly /'ɔfli/ adv. SPOKEN very: *It's awfully noisy. Can we close the door?*

a·while /ə'waɪl/ adv. for a short time: *Gil stood at the window awhile, watching boats.* —compare **a while** (WHILE¹)

awk·ward /'ɔkwərd/ adj. **1** making you feel so embarrassed that you are not sure what to do or say: *It was really awkward, because she and Rachel don't get along.* | *an awkward silence* | *Saul's demands put Mr. McGuire in an awkward position* (=made it difficult for him to do or say something). **2** moving or behaving in a way that does not seem relaxed or comfortable; CLUMSY: *an awkward teenager* | *Seals are awkward on land, but graceful in the water.* **3** difficult to do, use, or handle: *Getting in and out of the water is awkward when you're wearing flippers.* | *The camera is awkward to use.* **4** not smoothly done or not skillful: *the awkward wording of the letter* **5** not convenient: *I'm sorry, have I called at an awkward time?* **6** an awkward person is deliberately unhelpful —**awkwardly** adv.: *"Excuse me, I mean, could you help me out?" she began awkwardly.* —**awkwardness** n. [U]

awl /ɔl/ n. [C] a pointed tool for making holes in leather

A

awn·ing /'ɔnɪŋ/ n. [C] a sheet of material hanging over a window, especially on a store, to keep off the sun or the rain

a·woke /ə'woʊk/ the past tense of AWAKE

a·wok·en /ə'woʊkən/ the past participle of AWAKE

AWOL /'eɪˌwɔl/ adj. absent without leave; absent from your military group without permission: *Two soldiers had gone AWOL the night before.*

a·wry /ə'raɪ/ adj. **1 go awry** if something goes awry, it does not happen in the way that was planned: *Your best financial plans can sometimes go awry.* **2** not in the correct position

aw-shucks[1] /'ɔʃʌks/ adj. [only before noun] an aw-shucks attitude, smile etc. is one that shows that someone is shy or embarrassed

aw shucks[2] /ɔ'ʃʌks/ interjection OLD-FASHIONED OR HUMOROUS used in a joking way to show that you feel shy or embarrassed

ax[1], **axe** /æks/ n. [C] **1** a tool with a heavy metal blade on the end of a long handle, used to cut down trees or split pieces of wood **2 get the ax** also **give sb the ax** INFORMAL **a)** to be dismissed from your job, or to dismiss someone from their job: *He had only been coaching for a year when he got the ax.* **b)** to get rid of something such as a system, service, program, position in a company etc., usually for financial reasons: *The management has not yet said which plants will get the ax.* **3 have an ax to grind** DISAPPROVING to have a personal reason for doing something: *I have no political ax to grind.*

ax[2], **axe** v. [T] INFORMAL **1** to suddenly dismiss someone from their job: *The nursing director says she was axed because the hospital couldn't afford her salary.* **2** to get rid of a system, service, program, position in a company etc., usually for financial reasons: *NBC axed the show after just three episodes.*

ax·i·om /'æksiəm/ n. [C] FORMAL a rule or principle that is generally considered to be true

ax·i·o·mat·ic /ˌæksiə'mæɾɪk/ adj. FORMAL not needing to be proved because you can easily see that it is true; SELF-EVIDENT —**axiomatically** /-kli/ adv.

ax·is /'æksɪs/ n. plural **axes** /'æksɪz/ [C] TECHNICAL **1** the imaginary line around which a large round object, such as the Earth, turns: *The Earth rotates on an axis between the North and South Poles.* **2** a line drawn across the middle of a regular shape that divides it into two equal parts **3** either of the two lines of a GRAPH, by which the positions of points are measured

Ax·is, the /'æksɪs/ the countries, including Germany, Italy, and Japan, who fought together during World War II against the Allies

ax·le /'æksəl/ n. [C] the bar connecting two wheels on a car or other vehicle —see picture at BICYCLE[1]

a·ya·tol·lah /ˌaɪjə'toʊlə, -'tɑ-/ n. [C] a religious leader of the Shiite Muslims, especially a very powerful one

aye /aɪ/ adv. SPOKEN, FORMAL used to say yes, especially when voting: *All those in favor say aye.* —opposite NAY[2] —**aye** n. [C] **The ayes have it** (=those who voted yes have won).

AZ a written abbreviation of Arizona

a·za·le·a /ə'zeɪlyə/ n. [C] a bush that produces bright-colored flowers

A·zer·bai·jan /ˌæzɚbaɪ'dʒɑn, ˌɑ-/ a country in western Asia, west of the Caspian Sea and north of Iran —**Azerbaijani** n., adj.

AZT TRADEMARK azidothymidine; a drug used to treat AIDS

Az·tec /'æztɛk/ [P] one of the tribes who lived in and controlled Mexico from the 14th century until the 16th century —**Aztec** adj.: *Aztec jewelry*

az·ure /'æʒɚ/ adj. having a bright blue color like the sky —**azure** n. [U]

B

B, b /bi:/ n. [C] plural **B's, b's** the second letter of the English alphabet

B /bi:/ n. **1 a)** the seventh note in the musical SCALE of C MAJOR **b)** the musical KEY based on this note **2** a grade given to a student's work, to show that it is good but not excellent *She earned mostly B's this semester.* **3** [U] a common type of blood —see also B-MOVIE, B-SIDE

b. the written abbreviation of "born": *Andrew Lanham, b. 1885*

B & B /,bi: ən 'bi:/ the abbreviation of BED AND BREAKFAST

B.A. n. [C] Bachelor of Arts; the title of a first college degree in a subject such as literature, history etc.: *a B.A. in English Literature* —compare B.S.

baa /bɑ, bæ/ v. [I] to make a sound like a sheep —**baa** n. [C]

Baal Shem Tov /,beɪl ʃɛm 'tɔv/ (1700?–1760) a Jewish religious leader who started Hasidism

Bab·bage /'bæbɪdʒ/, **Charles** (1792–1871) a British MATHEMATICIAN who designed a type of calculating machine which modern computers are based on

bab·ble¹ /'bæbəl/ v. **1** [I,T] to speak quickly in a way that is difficult to understand or sounds silly: *The woman was babbling incoherently and waving a gun.* **2** [I] to make a sound like water moving over stones —**babbler** n. [C]

babble² n. **1** the confused sound of many people talking at the same time: *the babble of a crowded party* **2** words and sentences that do not make sense: *an hour of babble about UFOs* **3** a sound like water moving over stones —see also PSYCHO-BABBLE

babe /beɪb/ n. **1** a way of speaking to someone you love, especially your wife or husband: *Hey, babe, how are you?* **2** APPROVING a word for an attractive young man or woman: *Brad's a total babe.* **3** a way of speaking to a young woman, often considered offensive **4** LITERARY a baby: *a woman with a babe in arms* (=a baby that has to be carried) **5 a babe in the woods** INFORMAL someone who can be easily deceived, because they do not know very much about life

ba·bel /'bæbəl, 'beɪ-/ n. [singular,U] LITERARY the confusing sound of many voices talking together: *a babel of conflicting opinions*

ba·boon /bæ'bu:n/ n. [C] a large monkey that lives in Africa and South Asia

ba·bush·ka /bə'buʃkə/ n. [C] **1** a SCARF worn by women that covers the hair and is tied under the chin **2** INFORMAL an old Russian woman

ba·by¹ /'beɪbi/ n. plural **babies** [C]

1 child a very young child who has not yet learned to talk: *A baby was crying upstairs.* | *They have a five-year-old boy and a baby girl.* | *My friend Joyce just had a baby!* | *Pam is expecting a baby in July* (=her baby will probably be born in July).

2 animal/plant a very young animal or plant: *baby birds*

3 baby carrots/corn/vegetables a special type of CARROT etc. that is smaller than normal

4 woman SPOKEN **a)** a way of speaking to someone that you love: *Bye, baby, I'll be back by six.* **b)** a way of speaking to a young woman, often considered offensive

5 thing SLANG a thing, especially a piece of equipment or a machine that you think is very good: *This baby will do 0–60 mph in 6 seconds.*

6 youngest a younger child in a family, especially the youngest: *I have three boys, but he's my baby.*

7 silly SPOKEN a word meaning someone who behaves in a stupid or silly way, used especially by children: *Don't be such a baby.*

---

8 have a baby on the way INFORMAL to be PREGNANT

9 responsibility INFORMAL something special that someone has developed or is responsible for: *The new chamber orchestra is Turner's baby.* —see Usage Note at CHILD

baby² v. **babies, babied, babying** [T] INFORMAL to treat someone or something with special care: *This 1956 Chevy has been babied, so that it's in near-perfect condition.*

baby blues /,.. '., '.. ,./ n. [plural] **1** INFORMAL a feeling of DEPRESSION that some women suffer from after they have had a baby **2** eyes that are a light blue color: *Tears began to fall from Carmen's beautiful baby blues.*

baby book /'.. ,./ n. [C] a book your parents make that has pictures of you and information about you when you were a baby

baby boom /'.. ,./ n. [C] a period when a lot of babies are born in a particular country, especially the period of 1946–1964 in the U.S.

baby boom·er /'.. ,../ n. [C] someone born during a period when a lot of babies were born, especially between 1946 and 1964 in the U.S.

baby car·riage also **baby bug·gy** /'.. ,../ n. [C] a thing like a small bed with four wheels, used for taking a baby from one place to another when you are walking —compare STROLLER

baby-faced /'.. ,./ adj. a baby-faced person has a round or fat face like a child

baby fat /'.. ,./ n. [U] fat around a child's or young person's face that makes their face look round

baby grand /,.. './ n. [C] INFORMAL a small GRAND PIANO —compare CONCERT GRAND

ba·by·hood /'beɪbihʊd/ n. [U] the period of time when someone is a baby

ba·by·ish /'beɪbiiʃ/ adj. like a baby or appropriate for a baby: *The games were a little babyish for nine-year-olds.*

Bab·y·lon /'bæbɪlən/ **1** an ancient city in Iraq **2** a place where people behave in an immoral way

ba·by's breath /'.. ,./ n. [C] small white flowers often used in arrangements of other flowers

ba·by·sit /'beɪbi,sɪt/ v. past tense and past participle **babysat** /-,sæt/ present participle **babysitting** [I,T] to take care of children while their parents are not at home

ba·by·sit·ter /'beɪbi,sɪtɚ/ n. [C] someone who takes care of children while their parents are not at home

ba·by·sit·ting /'beɪbi,sɪtɪŋ/ n. [U] the act of taking care of children while their parents are not at home: *She earns some extra cash by babysitting.* | *a babysitting service*

baby talk /'.. ./ n. [U] sounds or words that babies use when they are learning to talk

baby tooth /'.. ,./ n. [C] plural **baby teeth** a tooth from the first set of teeth that young children have

baby walk·er /'.. ,../ n. [C] a frame on wheels that is used to support a baby while it is learning to walk

bac·ca·lau·re·ate /,bækə'lɔːriɪt, -'lɑr-/ n. [C] FORMAL a BACHELOR'S DEGREE

bac·ca·rat /'bɑkərɑ, 'bæ-/ n. [U] a card game usually played for money

bac·cha·na·li·an /,bækə'neɪliən, ,bɑ-/ adj. LITERARY a bacchanalian party, celebration etc. involves alcohol, sex, and uncontrolled behavior

Bac·chus /'bækəs, 'bɑ-/ the Roman name for the god DIONYSUS

bach /bætʃ/ v. **bach it** OLD-FASHIONED if a man baches it, he lives on his own and does his own cooking, cleaning etc.

Bach /bɑk/, **Jo·hann Se·bas·tian** /'youhɑn sə'bæstʃən/ (1685–1750) a German musician, who wrote CLASSICAL music

bach·e·lor /'bætʃələ, 'bætʃlə/ n. [C] a man who has never been married: *Morgan was a confirmed bachelor* (=a man who has chosen to not ever marry). |

The Crown Prince was Japan's most **eligible bachelor** (=a rich young man who has not yet married).

bachelor par·ty /'... ,../ n. [C] a party for men only, on the night before a man's wedding —see also STAG PARTY

bach·e·lor's de·gree /'... .,./ n. [C] the first level of college degree; B.A.

ba·cil·lus /bə'sɪləs/ n. plural **bacilli** /-laɪ/ [C] TECHNICAL a long thin BACTERIA, of which some types cause diseases

B

s w **back¹** /bæk/ adv.
1 1
1 **return** in or into the place or position where someone or something was before: I should be back in time for dinner. | That's mine! Give it back! | We came back by bus.
2 **as before** in or into the condition that someone or something was in before: I woke up at 4 a.m. and couldn't get back to sleep. | Do you think Ron and his wife will get back together? | It's time I got back to work. | If a starfish loses a leg, it grows back.
3 **reply** as a reply or reaction to what someone has done: Can you call me back later? | I'll have to get back to you on that. | I'll pay you back on Friday. | I left a message, but I haven't heard anything back.
4 **not forward** in the direction that you have come from: Michelle looked back at him over her shoulder and smiled. | He stepped back and fell.
5 **home/town** in or to a place where you or your family lived before: She left home in 1995 and hasn't been back since. | Are you going **back home** for Christmas this year? | [+ in/at etc.] Once back in New York, Rockburne began working on the murals.
6 **again** once again: Play the tape back for me, okay? | I'll check back with you sometime next week.
7 **sit/lie/lean back** to sit or lie in a comfortable, relaxed way: Craig sighed and leaned back in his chair.
8 **the past** in or toward an earlier time: I was making $15 an hour back at the hospital. | [+ in/on] I had one of those VW Bugs back in high school. | This all happened about **three years back** (=three years ago). | Yeah, Jenny and I **go back** to sixth grade (=we have known each other since sixth grade). | **Looking back** (=thinking about the past), I see how hard it was for her.
9 **away from sb/sth** away from a surface, area, thing, or person: Hold the curtains back from the window. | Her hair was pulled back in a ponytail. | The rest of us stood back as the bride and groom took the floor.
10 **back and forth** if someone or something goes back and forth, they go in one direction then back to where they started from, and keep repeating this movement.: The chair squeaks when you rock back and forth. | Brach flies back and forth weekly, between New York and L.A.
11 **be back where you started** to have failed to do what you have been trying to do: If we lose tomorrow, we'll be back where we started.
12 **book** toward the beginning of a book: Turn back a page.
13 **pay/get sb back (for sth)** to do something bad to someone because they have done something bad to you or someone you care about: I'll get you back for this!
14 **go back on a promise/agreement etc.** to do the opposite of what you promised to do: Ken would never go back on his word.

s w **back²** n.
1 1
1 **body** [C] **a)** the side of a person's or animal's body that is opposite the chest and goes from the neck to the top of the legs: The cat wanted her back rubbed. | She had her hands tied behind her back. | Tom usually sleeps **on his back**. | Mrs. Ducin stood **with her back to** the camera. | Drexler fell **flat on his back** after bumping into Kosar. **b)** the bones that go from your neck to the top of your legs: Megan has some trouble with her back.
2 **part** [U] the part of something that is farthest from the direction in which it moves or faces: [+ of]

There was a small desk and chair in the back of the room. | the hairs on the back of your neck | Their house has a pool **in the back**. | Kids should always wear seatbelts, even **in back** (=in the seats behind the driver). | The pool is **in back of** the house. | Tom's working on the car out back (=behind a house or other building). —opposite FRONT¹ —see Usage Note at FRONT¹
3 **surface** [C usually singular] the less important side or surface of something such as a paper or card: What's written on the back? | [+ of] The back of the album had all the credits listed. —opposite FRONT¹
4 **chair** [C] the part of a seat that you lean against when you are sitting: [+ of] Jack leaned against the back of the chair.
5 **book/newspaper** [C usually singular] the last pages of a book or newspaper: [+ of] Answers to the exercises are at the back of the book.
6 **behind sb's back** if you do something behind someone's back, you do it without them knowing: Do you think people are talking about you behind your back?
7 **at/in the back of your mind** a thought or feeling that is at the back of your mind is influencing you even though you are not thinking about it: There was always a slight feeling of fear at the back of his mind.
8 **back to back a)** happening one after the other: We did three performances back to back that day. **b)** with the backs toward each other: Two rows of chairs were arranged back to back. —see also BACK-TO-BACK
9 **sports** [C] one of the defending players on a football, SOCCER, or HOCKEY team
10 **get off my back** SPOKEN said when you want someone to stop telling you to do something and you are annoyed about it: I'll do it in a minute. Just get off my back!
11 **be on sb's back** SPOKEN to keep telling someone to do something in a way that annoys them: The boss has been on my back about that report.
12 **know somewhere like the back of your hand** to know a place extremely well: McIlvie knows the island like the back of his hand.
13 **have your back to the wall** also **sb's back is against the wall** INFORMAL to be in a very difficult position with no choice about what to do: The general has his back to the wall – his army is too weak to defeat the rebels.
14 **turn your back on sb/sth** to refuse to help someone or be involved with something: Ron turned his back on a lucrative consulting job in Denver.
15 **at your back a)** behind you: Run into the wind so it's at your back as you return. **b)** LITERARY supporting you: Caesar marched into Rome with an army at his back.
16 **put your back into it** INFORMAL to work extremely hard at something: Come on, John. Stop messing around and put your back into it!
17 **be (flat) on your back** to be so sick that you cannot get out of bed: He's been flat on his back in the hospital for a week..

back³ v.
s
2
1 **move sb** [I always + adv./prep.,T always + adv./prep.] to move backward, or make someone else move backward: [back toward/across etc.] Hardaway backed slowly toward the door.
2 **move vehicle** [I,T] to make a car move backward: [back (sth) into/out of etc.] Marty backed into a parking space. | Teresa backed the car down the driveway.
3 **support** [T] to support someone or something, especially with money, power, or influence: The crime bill is backed by the Democrats. | government-backed loans
4 **back surface of sth** [T usually passive] to put something on the back surface of a flat piece of material: a plastic-backed shower curtain
5 **music** [T usually passive] if musicians back a singer or another musician, they play or sing the part of the music that is not the main part: The three tenors were backed by the Boston Philharmonic Orchestra.
6 **competition** [T] to risk money on whether a

horse, team etc. wins something: *Which team did you back for the Super Bowl?*

7 be behind [T usually passive] to be at the back of something or behind it: *The stage was backed by a light blue curtain.*

8 wind [I] TECHNICAL if the wind backs, it changes direction, moving around the COMPASS in the direction North-West–South-East

back away *phr. v.* [I] **1** to move backward, away from something, especially because you are afraid, shocked etc. [+ **from**] *We slowly backed away from the rattlesnake.* **2** to gradually stop taking part in something or supporting something: *The governor backed away from the controversial prison plan.*

back down *phr. v.* [I] to accept defeat in an argument, opinion, or claim: *Anderson forced the company to back down and rehire her*

back off *phr. v.* [I] **1** to stop trying to force someone to do or think something: *Back off! I don't want your advice.* **2** to move backward, away from something: *Back off, you're too close.* **3** to gradually stop taking part in something or supporting something: *The mayor backed off out of concern for public feelings.*

back onto sth *phr. v.* [T] if a building backs onto something such as a river or field, its back faces it: *The houses back onto a busy road.*

back out *phr. v.* [I] to decide not to do something that you had promised to do: *One potential buyer backed out when she learned what the taxes would be.* | [+ **of**] *The airline backed out of the deal.*

back up *phr. v.* **1** [I,T **back** sth ↔ **up**] to make a car go backward: *The truck stopped and then backed up.* **2** [I,T **back** sth ↔ **up**] if traffic, work etc. backs up, it stops moving, flowing, or being done quickly: *The accident backed up traffic for three hours.* | *Usually traffic is backed up all the way to Fair Oaks Avenue by 7:30.* **3** [I,T **back** sth ↔ **up**] to make a copy of the information on a computer PROGRAM or DISK **4** [T **back** sb/sth ↔ **up**] to say that what someone is saying is true or that what they are doing is correct: *Industry officials, backed up by the FDA, say the process is safe.* | *Brown's statement was backed up by witnesses.* **5** [T **back** sb ↔ **up**] to support someone by being ready to help them or to do what they usually do if necessary: *His shoulder may not last the game, but he's backed up by Tomczak.* **6** [I] to move backward: *Back up a bit so that everyone can see.*
—see also BACKUP

w **back**[4] *adj.* [only before noun] **1** at the back: *The kids should sit in the back seat.* | *They waited by the back entrance.* | *the back wall of the factory* —see also BACK DOOR —opposite FRONT[2] **2** behind something: *The car was later found parked on a back parking lot of the complex.* **3** from the back: *a back view* | *I took the back way out of town.* **4** a **back street/road etc.** a street, road etc. that is away from the main streets: *We explored the back streets of Florence.* **5** **back rent/taxes/pay** money that someone owes from an earlier date **6** a **back issue/copy/ number** an old copy of a magazine or newspaper: *a pile of back copies of National Geographic* **7** TECHNICAL a back vowel sound is made by raising your tongue at the back of your mouth —opposite FRONT[2]

back·ache /ˈbækeɪk/ *n.* [C,U] a pain in your back

back·al·ley /ˌ. ˈ...ˌ/ *adj.* [only before noun] a back-alley ABORTION is one that is done illegally

back·ba·con, **back bacon** /ˈbækˌbeɪkən/ *n.* [U] CANADIAN: see BACON

back·bit·ing /ˈbækˌbaɪtɪŋ/ *n.* [U] rude or cruel talk about someone who is not present —**backbiter** *n.* [C]

back·board /ˈbækbɔrd/ *n.* [C] the board behind the basket in the game of BASKETBALL

back·bone /ˈbækboʊn/ *n.* **1** **the backbone of sth** the most important part of an organization, set of ideas etc.: *The cocoa industry is the backbone of Ghana's economy.* **2** [C] the row of connected bones that go down the middle of your back; SPINE **3** [U] courage and determination: *Stuart doesn't have the backbone to be a good manager.*

back·break·ing /ˈbækˌbreɪkɪŋ/ *adj.* backbreaking work is physically very difficult and makes you very tired

back coun·try /ˈ. ˌ../ *n.* [U] an area, especially in the mountains, away from roads and towns

back·court /ˈbækˌkɔrt/ *n.* [C] the area farthest from the GOAL or net in a sport such as basketball or tennis, or the players who play in that area

back·date /ˌbækˈdeɪt/ *v.* [T] **1** to write an earlier date on a document or check than the date when it was actually written **2** to make something have its effect from an earlier date: [**backdate** sth **from/to** sth] *The pay increase will be backdated to January.* —compare ANTEDATE, POSTDATE, PREDATE

back door /ˌ. ˈ./ *n.* [C] **1** a door at the back or side of a building **2** a way of doing something that is not the usual way, and that is secret or slightly dishonest: *The job can be a back door into the bank's training program.*

back·door /ˈbækdɔr/ *adj.* [only before noun] secret, or not publicly stated as your intention: *a backdoor diplomatic solution*

back·drop /ˈbækdrɑp/ *n.* [C] **1** LITERARY the SCENERY behind something that you are looking at: *The snow-covered Rocky Mountains made a wonderful backdrop for the concert* **2** the conditions or situation in which something happens: *Their meeting will happen against a backdrop of increasing hardship for ordinary Russian citizens.* **3** a painted cloth hung across the back of a stage

-backed /bækt/ *suffix* **low-backed/straight-backed/ narrow-backed etc.** with a low, straight, narrow etc. back: *a high-backed chair*

back·er /ˈbækə/ *n.* [C] someone who supports a plan, especially by providing money: *backers of the local crime bill*

back·field /ˈbækfild/ *n.* **the backfield** the area behind the SCRIMMAGE line in football, or the group of players who play there

back·fire /ˈbækfaɪə/ *v.* [I] **1** if a plan or action backfires, it has the opposite effect to the one you intended **2** if a car backfires, it makes a sudden loud noise because the engine is not working correctly

back for·ma·tion /ˈ. ..ˌ../ *n.* [C] TECHNICAL a new word formed from an older word, for example "televise" formed from "television"

back·gam·mon /ˈbækˌgæmən/ *n.* [U] a game for two players, using flat round pieces and DICE on a special board

back·ground /ˈbækgraʊnd/ *n.* **1** [C] someone's S W family history, education, social class etc.: *All of the men have different religious backgrounds.* | *Steve has a background in computer engineering.* **2** [C,U] the events in the past that explain why something has happened in the way that it has: *The elections are taking place against a background of widespread unemployment.* | *It took five years for the author to research background information for her new book* **3** [C] the pattern or color on top of which something has been drawn, printed etc.: *The invitations had red lettering on a white background.* **4** **in the background a)** a sound that is in the background is present but is not the main thing that you are listening to: *A television was on in the background.* **b)** behind the main thing that you are looking at: *Palm trees swayed in the background.* **c)** someone who keeps or stays in the background tries not to be noticed: *Whitfield's mother stood in the background as he talked to reporters.* **5** [C,U] the sounds that you can hear, apart from the main thing that you are listening to: *All of the background noise made it difficult to have a phone conversation.*

back·hand /ˈbækhænd/ *n.* [C usually singular] a hit in tennis and some other games in which the back of your hand is turned in the direction of the hit —**backhand** *adj.*

back·hand·ed /ˈbækˌhændɪd/ *adj.* **1** a backhanded remark or COMPLIMENT seems to express praise or admiration but in fact is insulting **2** a backhanded shot etc. is made with a backhand

back·hand·er /ˈbækˌhændəʳ/ n. [C] a hit or shot made with the back of your hand

back·hoe /ˈbækhoʊ/ n. [C] a large digging machine used for making roads etc.

back·ing /ˈbækɪŋ/ n. **1** [U] support or help, especially with money **2** [C] material that is used to make the back of an object **3** [C] the music that is played with a singer's voice to make it sound better —**backing** adj.

back·lash /ˈbæklæʃ/ n. [C] a strong but usually delayed reaction against recent events, especially against political or social developments: [+ **against**] *The 1970s saw the first backlash against the emerging women's movement.*

back·less /ˈbæklɪs/ adj. a backless dress, SWIMSUIT etc. does not cover much or any of a woman's back

back·log /ˈbæklɔg, -lɑg/ n. [C usually singular] a large amount of work, especially work that should already have been completed: *a large backlog of orders*

back·lot /ˈbæklɑt/ n. [C] **1** land owned by a movie company, where movies or television programs are made **2** the area behind a company's main offices, where goods are stored

back of·fice /ˈ. ,../ n. [C] the department of a bank or other financial institution that managed or organizes the work of the institution, but that does not deal with customers

back or·der /ˈ. ,../ v. [I,T] to make a request for a product to be delivered when it becomes available —**back order** n. [C]

back·pack¹ /ˈbækpæk/ n. [C] a bag carried on your back, often supported by a light metal frame, used especially by climbers and HIKERS (=walkers) —SEE picture at BAG¹

backpack² v. [I] to go walking and camping carrying a backpack: *I've always wanted to go backpacking along the Appalachian trail.* —**backpacker** n. [C]

back·ped·al /ˈbækˌpɛdl/ v. [I] **1** to start to change your opinion or actions about something that you had promised: *The country's government is backpedaling on some of the reforms.* **2** to PEDAL backward on a bicycle **3** to start running back toward a position you were in before

back·rest /ˈbækrɛst/ n. [C] the part of a chair, SOFA etc. that supports your back

back·room /ˈbækrum/ adj. backroom deals, politics etc. happen in a private or secret way, when they should happen in public

back-scratch·ing, backscratching /ˈ. ,../ n. [U] the act of doing nice things for someone in order to get something in return, or to gain an advantage for yourself

back seat /ˌ. ˈ.·/ n. **1** [C] a seat at the back of a car, behind where the driver sits **2 a back seat driver** INFORMAL **a)** a passenger in the back of a car who gives unwanted advice to the driver about how to drive **b)** someone in business or politics who tries to control things that they are not really responsible for **3 take a back seat** to accept or be put in a less important position: *Women have often been forced to take a back seat in society.*

back·side /ˈbæksaɪd/ n. [C] INFORMAL the part of your body that you sit on

back·slap·ping /ˈbækˌslæpɪŋ/ n. [U] noisy cheerful behavior when people praise each other's achievements more than they deserve —**backslapper** n. [C]

back·slash /ˈbækslæʃ/ n. [C] a line (\) used in writing to separate words, numbers, or letters

back·slide /ˈbækslaɪd/ v. [I] to start doing the bad things that you used to do, especially after having improved your behavior: *Many of the patients backslide into drug and alcohol abuse.* —**backslider** n. [C]

back·space /ˈbækspeɪs/ n. [usually singular] the part of a TYPEWRITER or computer KEYBOARD that you press to move backward toward the beginning of the line

back·spin /ˈbækˌspɪn/ n. [U] a turning movement in a ball that has been hit so that the top of the ball turns backward as the ball travels forward

back·splash /ˈbæksplæʃ/ n. [C] TECHNICAL the area of a BATHROOM or kitchen wall that is behind the FAUCET and covered with TILE to protect the wall

back-stab·bing, backstabbing /ˈ. ,../ n. [U] the act of secretly doing bad things to someone else, especially saying bad things about them, in order to gain an advantage for yourself —**backstabber** n. [C]

back·stage /ˌbækˈsteɪdʒ/ adv. **1** behind the stage in a theater, especially in the actors' dressing rooms **2** in private, especially within the secret parts of an organization: *intensive backstage negotiations* —**backstage** adj.

back·stairs /ˈbækstɛrz/ adj. [only before noun] secret: *backstairs romantic encounters*

back·stop /ˈbækstɑp/ n. [C] **1** a type of fence or board that prevents balls or other objects from going outside of one part of a playing area **2** something that prevents a situation from getting worse: *The second medical test acts as a backstop to guard against false results.*

back·street /ˈbækstrit/ adj. backstreet activities are often illegal and done badly: *a backstreet abortion*

back·stretch, back stretch /ˈbækstrɛtʃ/ n. [singular] the straight part of a RACETRACK that is farthest away from the finish line: *Freeman is taking the lead down the backstretch.*

back·stroke /ˈbækstroʊk/ n. [U] a way of swimming on your back by moving first one arm then the other backward while kicking your feet

back·talk /ˈbæktɔk/ n. [U] INFORMAL a rude reply to someone who is telling you what to do

back-to-back /ˌ. . ˈ.·/ adj. [only before noun] happening one after another: *back-to-back victories*

back·track /ˈbæktræk/ v. [I] **1** to change your beliefs, statements etc. so that they are not as strong as they were earlier: *Don't worry about backtracking on a bad decision.* **2** to return by the same way that you came: *We had to backtrack about a mile.*

back·up /ˈbækʌp/ n. **1** [C] a copy of something that you can use if the original thing is lost or does not work: *Make a backup of any work you do on the computer.* **2** something or someone used to provide support and help when it is needed: *Several police cars provided backup for the officers.* **3 a backup plan/ system/generator** a plan or system that can be used if the main one does not work

back·ward¹ /ˈbækwəʳd/ also **backwards** adv. **1** in the direction that is behind you: *Hannah took a step backward.* | *Put the treat in front of the dog and walk backwards.* **2** toward the beginning or the past: *He can repeat the alphabet backwards.* **3** with the back part in front: *Your T-shirt is on backward.* —see picture at UPSIDE DOWN **4** toward a worse state: *The new law is seen by some as a major step backwards.* **5 backward and forward** also **backwards and forwards** first in one direction and then in the opposite direction, usually many times **6 bend over/lean over backward (to do sth)** to try as hard as possible to help or please someone: *Officials bent over backward to help downtown businesses.* —opposite FORWARD¹

backward² adj. [only before noun] made in a direction toward what is behind you: *a backward look* **2** developing slowly and less successfully than most others: *It's one of the more backward countries.* | *The people there are a little bit backward.* —compare FORWARD² —**backwardly** adv. —**backwardness** n. [U]

back·wash /ˈbækwɑʃ/ n. [U] **1** a backward flow of water, caused by an OAR, wave etc. **2** INFORMAL the SALIVA (=the liquid that is produced naturally in your mouth) and small pieces of food that sometimes goes into drink from your mouth when you are drinking something **3** the bad situation that remains after a something bad has happened: *I don't want to be left in the backwash when Gilson realizes the company's going bankrupt.*

back·wa·ter /'bæk,wɔtə/ n. **1** a very quiet place not influenced by outside events or new ideas: *a sleepy backwater town* **2** a part of a river away from the main stream, where the water does not move

back·woods /,bæk'wʊdz/ n. [plural] an area in the forest that is far away from any towns

back·woods·man /,bæk'wʊdzmən/ n. [C] someone who lives in the backwoods

back·yard, **back yard** /,bæk'yard/ n. **1** [C] an area of land behind a house, usually covered with grass **2 in sb's own back yard** INFORMAL very near where someone lives, works etc.: *Americans would probably react differently to the war if it was in their own back yard.* **3 not in my backyard** used to say that you do not want something to happen or be done near where you live —**backyard** adj. [only before noun] *a backyard barbecue*

ba·con /'beɪkən/ n. [U] **1** salted or smoked meat from the back or sides of a pig, often served in narrow thin pieces: *I want bacon and eggs for breakfast.* **2 bring home the bacon** INFORMAL to provide enough money to support your family —see also **save sb's skin/butt/bacon** (SAVE¹ (9))

Ba·con /'beɪkən/, **Fran·cis** /'frænsɪs/ (1909–1992) an Irish artist famous for painting people and animals in twisted shapes with dark strong colors

Bacon, Sir Francis (1561–1626) an English politician, PHILOSOPHER, and writer

bac·te·ri·a /bæk'tɪriə/ n. [plural] *singular* **bacterium** /-riəm/ very small living things, some of which cause illness or disease —compare VIRUS (1) —**bacterial** adj.: *a bacterial infection*

bac·te·ri·ol·o·gy /bæk,tɪri'alədʒi/ n. [U] the scientific study of bacteria —**bacteriologist** n. [C] —**bacteriological** /bæk,tɪriə'ladʒɪkəl/ adj.

Bac·tri·an cam·el /,bæktriən 'kæməl/ n. [C] a CAMEL from Asia with two HUMPS

bad¹ /bæd/ adj. *comparative* **worse** *superlative* **worst**
1 not good not good or not nice: *The bad weather caused huge traffic problems.* | *I thought things couldn't possibly get any worse.* | *a bad smell* | *Did you have a bad day at work?* —opposite GOOD¹
2 low quality low in quality or below an acceptable standard: *bad management* | *Your handwriting is so bad I can hardly read it.* | *Mrs. Carr was the worst teacher I ever had.* —opposite GOOD¹ (1)
3 harmful damaging or harmful: *Pollution in the lake is having a bad effect on fish stocks.* | *[+ for] Smoking is bad for your health.*
4 morally wrong morally wrong or evil: *He plays one of the bad guys in the movie.* —opposite GOOD¹ (15)
5 serious serious or severe: *Frank had a bad flu before Christmas.* | *The pain was really bad.* | *The traffic near the airport was even worse today than yesterday.*
6 a bad time/moment etc. a time at which it is very unlucky for something to have happened: *It's a bad time to borrow money because interest rates are so high.*
7 be bad for you to be harmful to you or to your health: *Too much salt can be bad for you.* | *It is bad for a young girl to be on her own so much.*
8 food food that is bad is not safe to eat because it has decayed: *This fish has gone bad.* | *bad apples*
9 bad at math/tennis/drawing etc. having no skill or ability in a particular activity: *I'm really bad at chess.* | *Strategic thinking is what so many companies are bad at.* —opposite GOOD¹ (3)
10 a bad heart/leg/back etc. a heart, leg etc. that is permanently injured or does not work correctly: *A childhood illness left him with a bad heart.* | *My eyes are getting worse.*
11 swearing bad language contains swearing or rude words: *a book full of bad language* | *Jacky said a bad word!*
12 in a bad temper/mood feeling annoyed or angry: *Watch out. Mom's in a really bad mood.*
13 feel bad to feel ashamed or sorry about something: *I felt bad about not being able to come last night.*
14 wrong behavior doing something you should not do, or behaving in a wrong way: *Katie was so bad*

B

today! She wouldn't listen to me at all. | *Bad cat! Get off the table!*

15 too bad a) used to say that you are sorry that something bad has happened to someone: *It's too bad she had to give up teaching when she got sick.* **b)** used to say that you do not care that something bad happens to someone: *"I've got plans this evening." "Too bad, I need you to stay till you've finished the report."*
16 not bad used to say that something is good or acceptable: *"How are you?" "Oh, not bad."* | *That's not a bad idea.*
17 bad girl/boy used when a child or pet behaves badly: *Bad girl! Don't touch the stove!*
18 *comparative* **badder** *superlative* **baddest** SLANG **a)** used when you think something is very good: *Now that's a bad car!* **b)** APPROVING someone who is bad is very determined and does not always obey rules
19 not that bad also **not as bad as sth** used to say that something is not as bad as someone says it is: *Oh, come one. Three miles isn't that bad.*
20 not too/so bad used to say that something is not as bad as expected: *The roads weren't too bad.*
21 it's bad enough... used to say that you already have one problem, so that you cannot worry about or deal with another one that makes the situation worse: *It was bad enough having to drive for eight hours straight, without it raining too.*

22 go from bad to worse to become even more difficult or lower in quality: *The schools have gone from bad to worse in this area.*
23 have/get a bad name also **give sth a bad name** to lose people's respect or trust: *Fighting gives hockey a bad name.*
24 bad blood angry or bitter feeling between people; HOSTILITY: *There'd been some bad blood between Jose and Arriola over a woman.*
25 bad news INFORMAL someone or something that always causes trouble: *Rich foods are bad news if you're on a diet.*
26 in bad faith if someone does something in bad faith they are behaving dishonestly and have no intention of keeping a promise: *In order to sue, you have to prove that the company was acting in bad faith.*
27 sth can't be bad used to tell someone that something is good or worth doing: *The kids get a multicultural education, and that can't be bad.*
28 be in a bad way OLD-FASHIONED to be very sick, injured, or upset
29 a bad penny OLD-FASHIONED, INFORMAL someone or something that causes trouble and is difficult to avoid —see also BAD-OFF —**badness** n. [U]

bad² n. **1 take the bad with the good** accept not only the good things in life but also the bad things **2 my bad!** SLANG used to say that you have made a mistake or that something is your fault **3 go to the bad** OLD-FASHIONED to begin living in a wrong or immoral way

bad³ adv. SPOKEN, NONSTANDARD badly: *He needed a drink pretty bad.*

bad-ass /'. ./ adj. SLANG **1** very good or impressive **2** APPROVING a bad-ass person is very determined and does not always obey rules —**bad ass** n. [C]

bad debt /,. './ n. [C] a debt that is unlikely to be paid

bade /bæd, beɪd/ v. the past tense and past participle of BID³

badge /bædʒ/ n. [C] **1** a small piece of metal, plastic etc. that you wear or carry to show people that you work for a particular organization, as for example a police officer: *Mulder showed his badge and asked a few questions.* | *You'll get a security badge that will allow you into the building.* **2** also **merit badge** a small piece of cloth with a picture on it, given to BOY SCOUTS or GIRL SCOUTS to show what skills they've learned: *a badge for photography* **3 a badge of honor/courage etc.** something that shows that you have a particular quality: *He now sees his war-time injuries as a badge of honor.*

badg·er¹ /'bædʒɚ/ *n.* [C] an animal which has black and white fur, lives in holes in the ground, and is active at night

badger² *v.* [T] to try to persuade someone by asking them something several times; PESTER: [**badger sb to do sth/badger sb into doing sth**] *Suppliers say they have to keep badgering the company to pay its bills.*

bad guy /'. ./ *n.* [C] INFORMAL someone who is bad, especially in a book or movie: *Jones has made a career of playing bad guys in movies.*

bad·i·nage /ˌbædn'ɑʒ/ *n.* [U] FORMAL OR HUMOROUS playful joking conversation

bad·lands /'bædlændz/ *n.* [plural] an area of land that is not useful for growing crops, with rocks and hills that have been worn into strange shapes by the weather

Badlands, the an area of land in the northern central U.S. in the states of South Dakota and Nebraska that is very dry with strangely shaped rocks and hills

SW bad·ly /'bædli/ *adv.* comparative **worse** superlative **worst 1** in an unsatisfactory or unsuccessful way: *a badly written story* | *It's often taught very badly.* | *badly made furniture* | *The Warriors didn't do too badly, even without their star player.* **2** to a great or serious degree: *She wanted to go so badly.* | *Did you sprain it badly?* | *The refugees badly need food and clean water.* | *It was badly damaged in the storm.*

bad·ly-off /ˌ.. '.◂ / *adj.* [not before noun] bad off

bad·min·ton /'bædˌmɪnt'n/ *n.* [U] a game like tennis but played with a BIRDIE (=small feathered object) instead of a ball

bad-mouth /'. ./ *v.* [T] INFORMAL to criticize someone or something: *Divorced parents shouldn't bad-mouth each other in front of the kids.*

bad off /ˌ. './ *adj.* comparative **worse off** superlative **worst off** [not before noun] INFORMAL **1** not having much money; poor: *We're not as bad off as some people, but we do get food stamps.* **2** in a bad situation: *If it doesn't rain much this year, the state's water supply will be bad off.*

bad-tem·pered /ˌ. '..◂ / *adj.* easily annoyed or made angry

baf·fle¹ /'bæfəl/ *v.* [T] if something baffles someone, they cannot understand or explain it at all: *The disease has baffled doctors, who are unable to treat it.* —**bafflement** *n.* [U] —**baffling** *adj.*: *a baffling mystery*

baffle² *n.* [C] TECHNICAL a board, sheet of metal etc. that controls the flow of air, water, or sound into or out of something

baf·fled /'bæfəld/ *adj.* unable to understand something at all: *Scientists are completely baffled by the results.*

SW bag¹ /bæg/ *n.* [C]
1 container **a)** a container made of paper, cloth etc., which usually opens at the top: *a paper bag* | *a garbage bag* —see picture at CONTAINER **b)** a large bag used to carry your clothes, things etc. when you are traveling: *Hand luggage and checked bags must go through Customs.* **c)** a PURSE: *an evening bag*
2 amount the amount that a bag will hold: [+ of] *Each family is given two bags of rice per month.*
3 sport one of the BASES in baseball
4 in the bag INFORMAL certain to be won or achieved: *They were ahead 6–2 in the eighth innings, and figured the game was in the bag.*
5 pack your bags INFORMAL to leave a place where you have been living, usually after an argument: *Tell him that if he doesn't shape up, he can pack his bags.*
6 eyes dark circles or loose skin around your eyes, usually because of old age or being tired
7 sb's bag INFORMAL, OLD-FASHIONED something that someone is very interested in or very good at: *Computers aren't really my bag.*
8 woman SPOKEN, OFFENSIVE an old woman who is

unattractive or not nice: *Some old bag was driving along at 15 miles an hour.*
9 a bag of bones INFORMAL a person or animal who is too thin —see also AIR BAG, SLEEPING BAG, **let the cat out of the bag** (CAT¹ (2)), **be left holding the bag** (HOLD¹ (28)), **a mixed bag** (MIXED (5))

bags

strap

purse

duffel bag

grocery bag

shaving bag

handle

tote bag

backpack

bag² *v.* **bagged, bagging 1** [T] to put materials or objects into bags: *He got a job bagging groceries.* **2** SPOKEN to decide not to do something: *I'm tired of waiting. Bag this – I'm leaving.* **3** [T] INFORMAL to manage to get something that a lot of people want, especially a prize or award: *Julie Gold bagged the top songwriter's award.* **4** [T] INFORMAL to kill or catch animals or birds: *We bagged a rabbit.* **5** [I] also **bag out** INFORMAL to hang loosely, like a bag

bag·a·telle /ˌbægə'tɛl/ *n.* **1** [U] a game played on a board with small balls that must be rolled into holes **2** [singular] something that is small and unimportant compared to everything else **3** [C] a short piece of CLASSICAL music

ba·gel /'beɪgəl/ *n.* [C] a small ring-shaped type of bread

bag·ful /'bægfʊl/ *n.* [C] *plural* **bagfuls** or **bagsful** the amount a bag can hold

bag·gage /'bægɪdʒ/ *n.* [U] **1** the SUITCASES, bags, boxes etc. carried by someone who is traveling; LUGGAGE: *carry-on baggage* **2** INFORMAL the beliefs, opinions, and experiences that someone has, which make them think in a particular way, especially in a way that makes it difficult to have good relationships: *Being abused as a child, she brings a lot of baggage into the marriage.*

baggage car /'.. ,./ *n.* [C] the part of a train where boxes, bags etc. are carried

baggage room /'.. ,./ *n.* [C] a place, usually in a train station, where you can leave your bags and collect them later

bag·gie /'bægi/ *n.* [C] TRADEMARK a small plastic bag used to keep food in

bag·gy /'bægi/ *adj.* baggy clothes hang in loose folds: *a baggy red sweater*

Bagh·dad /'bægdæd/ the capital and largest city of Iraq

bag la·dy /'. ,../ *n.* [C] INFORMAL an impolite word for a homeless woman who walks around carrying all her possessions with her

bag·pipes /'bægpaɪps/ *n.* [plural] a musical instrument played especially in Scotland, in which air

stored in a bag is forced out through pipes to produce the sound —**bagpipe** adj.

ba·guette /bæˈɡɛt/ n. [C] a long thin LOAF of bread

bah /bɑ/ interjection OLD-FASHIONED used to show disapproval of something: Bah! Christmas is too commercial.

Ba·ha'i /bəˈhaɪ/ a member of the Baha'i Faith

Ba·ha'i Faith, the /ˌ.. ˈ./ a religion started in 1863
and based on the belief that people should be peaceful and kind and respect all people, races, and re·li-
gions

Ba·ha·mas, the /bəˈhɑməz/ a country that consists
of a group of islands in the Atlantic Ocean, southeast
of Florida —**Bahamian** /bəˈheɪmiən/ n. adj.

Ba·haul·lah /bɑˌhaʊˈlɑ/ (1817–1892) a Persian religious leader, originally called Mirza Huseyn Ali,
who started the Baha'i Faith

Bah·rain, Bahrein /bɑˈreɪn/ a country consisting of
a group of islands in the Persian Gulf, near the coast
of Saudi Arabia —**Bahraini** n., adj

baht /bɑt/ n. [C] the standard unit of money used in
Thailand

Bai·kal, Lake /baɪˈkɑl/ a lake in southeast Russia
that is the largest FRESHWATER lake in the Eurasian
continent

bail¹ /beɪl/ n. [U] money left with a court of law to
prove that a prisoner will return when their TRIAL
starts: Harrell will be **released on bail** (=let out of
prison when bail was paid) until his trial. | Carpen-
ter is free **on bail** while he appeals his conviction. |
Veltman is being **held without bail** (=staying in
prison because bail is not allowed or cannot be paid)
after his arrest Thursday. | **post/stand bail** (=pay
the bail) | **jump/skip bail** (=to not return to trial as
you promised)

bail² v. **1** [I,T] to remove water from the bottom of a
boat **2** SPOKEN, SLANG to leave a place quickly: The
cops are coming! Let's bail!
bail out phr. v. **1** [T **bail** sb/sth ↔ **out**] to do something to help someone out of trouble, especially
financial problems: The state is helping bail out the
school districts by raising sales taxes. **2** [I] INFORMAL
to escape from a situation that you do not want to be
involved in anymore: After ten years in the business,
McArthur is bailing out. **3** [T **bail** sb ↔ **out**] to leave
a large sum of money with a court so that someone
can be let out of prison while waiting for their TRIAL:
He called me to bail him out. **4** [I] to escape from an
airplane, using a PARACHUTE **5** [I,T **bail** sth ↔ **out**] to
remove water from the bottom of a boat

bai·ley /ˈbeɪli/ n. [C] an open area inside the outer
wall of a castle

bail·iff /ˈbeɪlɪf/ n. [C] an official of the legal system who
watches prisoners and keeps order in a court of law

bail·i·wick /ˈbeɪliˌwɪk/ n. [C] FORMAL an area or subject that someone is interested in or responsible for

bail·out /ˈbeɪlaʊt/ n. [C] INFORMAL financial help given
to a person or a company that is in difficulty: A government bailout of the bank is being considered.

bait¹ /beɪt/ n. [singular,U] **1** food used to attract fish,
animals, or birds so that you can catch them: Worms
make excellent fish bait. | The trout just weren't
taking the bait (=eating it and being caught).
2 something used to make someone do something,
buy something etc., especially done in a way to
deceive people: Plenty of people **took the bait**
(=accepted what was offered) and ended up losing
their life savings. **3 rise to the bait** to become angry
when someone is deliberately trying to make you
angry: Sanders simply refused to **rise to the
bait**. **4 the (old) bait and switch** a situation in
which a customer is attracted by a low price on a
product, but pays much more for a different product

bait² v. [T] **1** to put bait on a hook to catch fish or in
a trap to catch animals **2** to deliberately try to make
someone angry by criticizing them, using rude
names etc.: Goodman refused to be baited into saying
anything bad about his co-star. **3 bear-baiting/bull-
baiting etc.** the activity of attacking a wild animal
with dogs

bait-and-switch /ˌ.. ˈ./ adj. if sellers used bait-and-

switch methods, they offer goods at extremely low
prices to attract customers, but then try to persuade
people to buy more expensive goods instead —**bait-
and-switch** n. [singular]

baize /beɪz/ n. [U] thick cloth, usually green, used
especially to cover tables on which games such as
POOL are played

Ba·ja Cal·i·for·nia /ˌbɑhɑ kælɪˈfɔrnyə/ also **Baja** a
PENINSULA in Mexico that is south of the U.S. state of
California

bake /beɪk/ v. **1** [I,T] to cook something using dry
heat, in an OVEN: Bake the mixture at 375 degrees for
20 minutes. | freshly baked cookies **2** [I,T] to make
something become hard by heating it: In former
times, bricks were baked in the sun. **3** [I] INFORMAL if
a person, place, or thing bakes, they become very
hot: Our apartment on the top floor bakes in the
summer —see also HALF-BAKED

baked beans /ˈ. ./ n. [plural] a food made with small
white beans that have been cooked for a long time in
a brown SAUCE, often sold in cans

Bake·lite /ˈbeɪklaɪt/ n. [U] TRADEMARK a hard plastic
used especially in the 1930s and 1940s

bak·er /ˈbeɪkə/ n. [C] someone who bakes bread,
cookies, cakes etc., especially in order to sell them in
a store

baker's doz·en /ˌ.. ˈ../ n. [singular] thirteen of something

bak·er·y /ˈbeɪkəri/ n. plural **bakeries** [C] a place
where bread and cakes are baked, or a store where
they are sold

bake sale /ˈ. ./ n. [C] an occasion when the members
of a school group, church organization etc. make
cookies, cakes etc. and sell them in order to make
money for the organization

bak·ing /ˈbeɪkɪŋ/ adj. INFORMAL very hot: a baking hot
day

baking pow·der /ˈ.. ˌ../ n. [U] a powder used in
baking cakes, cookies etc. to make them rise so that
they are light

baking sheet /ˈ.. ˌ./ n. [C] a flat piece of metal that
you bake food on

baking so·da /ˈ.. ˌ../ n. [U] a white powder used in
baking to make cakes, cookies lighter, and also used
in cleaning things; BICARBONATE OF SODA

baking tray /ˈ.. ˌ./ n. [C] a BAKING SHEET

ba·kla·va /ˌbɑkləˈvɑ/ n. [U] a sweet food from the
Middle East made from FILO DOUGH, nuts, and HONEY

bak·sheesh /bækˈʃiʃ, bɑk-/ n. [U] money that people
in the Middle East give to poor people, to someone
who has helped them, or as a BRIBE

Ba·ku /bɑˈku/ the capital and largest city of Azerbaijan

Ba·ku·nin, Mi·khail /bəˈkunɪn, -nyən/, /mɪˈkaɪl/
(1814–1876) a Russian REVOLUTIONARY who was an
ANARCHIST and opposed Karl Marx

bal·a·lai·ka /ˌbæləˈlaɪkə/ n. [C] a musical instrument
that has three strings, a long neck, and a TRIANGLE-
shaped body, played especially in Russia

bal·ance¹ /ˈbæləns/ n.
1 steady [U] a state in which all your weight is
evenly spread, so that you are steady and not likely
to fall. Riding a bike helps develop a child's sense of
balance. | I was leaning over and **I lost my balance**
(=could not stay steady). | One foot slipped on the ice,
but she managed to **keep her balance** (=stay steady
and not fall).
2 equality [singular,U] a state in which very different things have the right amount of importance or
influence in relation to each other: [+ **between**]
They need to find a balance between logging jobs and
the forest ecosystem. | [+ **of**] The sauce had a nice
balance of basil and oil. | The car's designers wanted
to **strike a balance** (=make sure two things have
equal importance) between safety and style. | His
recreational activities help keep his life **in balance**.
—opposite IMBALANCE

B

3 bank [C] the amount of money that you have in your bank account or that you still have to pay: [+ **of**] *a balance of $1,247*
4 off balance a) unable to stay steady or upright: *I was off balance when I threw the ball.* **b)** surprised or confused: *Kelly's remarks* **threw** *Avery* **off balance** *for a second or two.* | *The offense managed to* **keep** *the other team* **off balance.**
5 on balance if you think something on balance, you think it after considering all the facts: *On balance, it's a useful program, despite the problems.*
6 be/hang in the balance if the future or success of something hangs in the balance, you do not yet know whether the result will be bad or good: *The negotiations are continuing, with prospects for peace hanging in the balance.*
7 tip/swing the balance to influence the result of an event: *Your letter of recommendation swung the balance in his favor.*
8 sth that is left over the balance the amount of something that remains after some has been used or spent: [+ **of**] *Because of illness, Heinz will not serve the balance of his term in office.*
9 for weighing [C] an instrument for weighing things by seeing whether the amounts in two hanging pans are equal
10 opposite force/influence [singular] a force or influence on one side which equals an opposite force or influence: *Her practicality acts as a balance to this wild inventiveness.*
11 the balance of evidence/probability etc. the most likely answer or result produced by opposing information, reasons etc.

balance² *v.* **1** [I,T] to get into a steady position, without falling to one side or the other, or to put something into this position: [**balance sth on sth**] *She was balancing a plate of food on her knees.* [+ **on**] *I had to balance on top of the ladder to reach the last peach.* **2** [I,T] to be equal to something else in weight, amount, or importance, or to try to give something equal importance: *They asked state officials to balance giving jobs to men and women.* | [**balance sth with sth**] *It's not always easy to balance a career with a family.* **3** [T] to have an opposite effect to something else, so that a good result is achieved: *Its cranberry tartness is balanced with just a hint of sweetness.* **4** [T] to consider the importance of something in relation to the importance of something else: [**balance sth against sth**] *The public's right to know has to be balanced against national security.* **5** [I,T] to have equal amounts of money being paid and spent, or to make two amounts of money equal: *Congress may finally be forced to* **balance the budget.** **6 sth balances out** used to say that sometimes there is more of one thing, amount, activity etc. than at other times, but that the number, amount etc. becomes even over a longer period of time: *Sometimes I do the housework – sometimes she does. It all balances out.*

balance beam /ˈ.. ,./ *n.* [C] a long narrow wooden board on which a GYMNAST performs

bal·anced /ˈbælənst/ *adj.* **1** giving equal attention to all sides or opinions; fair: *a balanced account of the events* **2** arranged to include things or people of different kinds in the right amount: *a balanced approach to our transportation problems* | *It is very important for children to eat a* **balanced diet** (=containing a variety of good foods in the right amounts). **3 a balanced budget** a situation in which a government is not spending more than it has available **4** not giving too much importance to one thing: *He said he felt balanced and at peace with his choices.*

balance of pay·ments /ˌ... ˈ../ *n.* [singular] the difference between what a country spends in order to buy goods and services abroad, and the money it earns selling goods and services abroad

balance of pow·er /ˌ... ˈ../ *n.* **the balance of power** a situation in which political or military strength is shared evenly: *The election of so many Republicans to*

Congress has changed the balance of power in Washington.

balance of trade /ˌ... ˈ./ *n.* [singular] the difference in value between the goods a country buys from abroad and the goods it sells abroad

balance sheet /ˈ.. ,./ *n.* [C] a statement of how much money a business has earned and how much money it has paid for goods and services: *It's a healthy company with a strong balance sheet* (=it earns more than it pays out).

Bal·an·chine /ˌbælənˈʃin/, **George** (1904–1983) a Russian-born U.S. CHOREOGRAPHER who helped to start the New York City Ballet

Bal·bo·a /bælˈbouə/, **Vas·co de** /ˈvɑskou də/ (1475–1519) a Spanish EXPLORER who crossed the Isthmus of Darien in Panama, the narrow piece of land that joins North and South America, saw the Pacific Ocean, and officially claimed that it belonged to Spain

balcony

balcony

bal·co·ny /ˈbælkəni/ *n. plural* **balconies** [C] **1** a structure you can stand on that sticks out from the upstairs wall of a building **2** the seats upstairs at a theater

bald /bɔld/ *adj.* **1** having little or no hair on your head: *Dad started* **going bald** (=losing his hair) *when he was in his thirties.* **2** not having enough of what usually covers something: *The tires are bald and the car is in need of repair.* **3 bald statement/language/truth etc.** a statement etc. that is correct but gives no additional information to help you understand or accept what is said —**baldness** *n.* [U]

bald ea·gle /ˈ. ,../ *n.* [C] a large North American bird with a white head and neck, that is the national bird of the U.S. —see picture on page 429

bal·der·dash /ˈbɔldərˌdæʃ/ *n.* [U] OLD-FASHIONED talk or writing that is stupid nonsense

bald-faced /ˌ. ˈ.◂/ *adj.* making no attempt to hide that you know what you are doing or saying is wrong: *a bald-faced lie*

bald·ing /ˈbɔldɪŋ/ *adj.* a balding man is losing the hair on his head: *a balding, heavyset man*

bald·ly /ˈbɔldli/ *adv.* in a way that is true but makes no attempt to be polite: *Heather suggested baldly that Ms. Lane was mentally unstable.*

Bald·win /ˈbɔldwɪn/, **James** (1924–1987) an African-American writer of novels

bale¹ /beɪl/ *n.* [C] a large quantity of something such as paper or HAY that is tightly tied together, especially into a block: [+ **of**] *a bale of hay*

bale² *v.* [T] to tie something such as paper or HAY into a large block

bale·ful /ˈbeɪlfəl/ *adj.* LITERARY expressing anger, hatred, or a wish to harm someone: *a baleful look* —**balefully** *adv.*

Ba·li /ˈbɑli, ˈbɑli/ an island in Indonesia, to the east of Java

balk /bɔk/ *v.* **1** [I] to not want to or refuse to do something that is difficult, or frightening: [+ **at**] *Several of the managers balked at enforcing the decision.* **2** [I] in baseball, to stop in the middle of the action of throwing the ball to the player who is trying to hit it **3** [I + **at**] if a horse balks at a fence etc., it stops suddenly and refuses to jump or cross it **4** [T] to stop someone or something from getting what they want: *Their strategies to balk the enemy had failed.*

Bal·kan Mountains, the /'bɔlkən/ a RANGE of mountains in eastern Europe that runs from Serbia through Bulgaria, west of the Black Sea

Bal·kans, the /'bɔlkənz/ a large area in southeast Europe which includes Greece, Romania, Bulgaria, Albania, Slovenia, Croatia, Bosnia, and Serbia

balk·y /'bɔki/ *adj.* INFORMAL something or someone that is balky does not do what it is expected to do: *a balky air-conditioning system*

ball[1] /bɔl/ *n.* [C]
1 to play with a round object that is thrown, kicked, or hit in a game or sport *Mommy, where's my ball?* | *a big beach ball*
2 round shape something formed or rolled into a round shape: *a ball of string* | *Shape the dough into balls.*
3 on the ball INFORMAL thinking or acting quickly and intelligently: *A photographer who was on the ball got some great pictures of the incident.*
4 have a ball INFORMAL to have a very good time: *The kids had a ball building sandcastles.*
5 set/start the ball rolling to begin an activity or event or make sure it continues: *To start the ball rolling, you need to fill out a complaint form.*
6 baseball a ball thrown in baseball that the hitter does not try to hit because it is not within the correct area
7 a fast/good/curve etc. ball a ball that is thrown, hit, or kicked fast etc. in a game or sport: *He has a good curve ball.*
8 the ball of the foot/hand/thumb the rounded part of the foot at the base of the toe, rounded part of the hand at the base of the thumb or fingers, or the round part at the top of your thumb —see also EYE-BALL[1] (1)
9 the ball is in your court it is your turn to take action or to reply: *We'll see how they respond to the proposal. The ball's in their court.*
10 dance a large formal occasion at which people dance
11 balls [plural] VULGAR **a)** TESTICLES **b)** courage or determination: *That guy has balls.* **c)** said when you do not believe someone or something, or when you are annoyed about something
12 a ball-buster also **a ball-breaker** VULGAR **a)** a problem that is very difficult to deal with **b)** a woman who uses her authority over men in a way that other people do not think is appropriate for a woman to do
13 the whole ball of wax INFORMAL the whole thing; everything: *Benton is in charge of marketing, personnel, sales – the whole ball of wax.*
14 a ball of fire someone who has a lot of energy and is active and successful
15 bullet a round bullet fired from a type of gun that was used in past times —see also **play ball** (PLAY[1] (10))

ball[2] *v.* [T] **1** also **ball up** to form something into a small round shape so that it takes up less space **2** VULGAR to have sex with a woman

bal·lad /'bæləd/ *n.* [C] **1** a simple song, especially a popular love song **2** a short story in the form of a poem

bal·lad·eer /,bælə'dɪr/ *n.* [C] someone who sings love songs

bal·last[1] /'bæləst/ *n.* [U] **1** heavy material that is carried by a ship to make it more steady in the water **2** material such as sand that is carried in a BALLOON[1] (2) and can be thrown out to make it rise **3** broken stones that are used as a surface under a road, railroad lines etc.

ballast[2] *v.* [T] to fill or supply something with ballast

ball bear·ing /,. '../ *n.* [C] **1** an arrangement of small metal balls moving in a ring around a bar so that the bar can turn more easily **2** one of these metal balls

ball boy /'. ./ *n.* [C] a boy who picks up tennis balls for people playing in important tennis matches

ball·club /'bɔlklʌb/ *n.* [C] a baseball team

ball·cock /'bɔlkak/ *n.* [C] a hollow floating ball on a stick that opens and closes a hole, to allow water to flow into a container, for example in a TOILET

bal·le·ri·na /,bælə'rinə/ *n.* [C] a woman who dances in ballets

** bal·let** /bæ'leɪ, 'bæleɪ/ *n.* **1** [C] a performance in which a special style of dancing and music tell a story without any speaking: *"Swan Lake" is my favorite ballet.* **2** [U] this type of dancing **3** [C] a group of BALLET dancers who work together: *the Bolshoi ballet*

ballet danc·er /'.. ,.., '.. ,../ *n.* [C] someone who dances in ballets

ball game /'. ./ *n.* **1** a game of baseball, football, or BASKETBALL: *Dad was watching the ball game on TV.* **2 a whole new ball game** also **a different ball game** a situation that is very different from the one you are used to: *I used to be a teacher, so working in an office is a whole new ball game.*

ball girl /'. ./ *n.* [C] a girl who picks up tennis balls for people playing in important tennis matches

bal·lis·tic /bə'lɪstɪk/ *adj.* **go ballistic** SPOKEN to suddenly become very angry

ballistic mis·sile /,.. '../ *n.* [C] a MISSILE that is guided up into the air and then falls freely

bal·lis·tics /bə'lɪstɪks/ *n.* [U] the scientific study of the movement of objects that are thrown or fired through the air, such as bullets shot from a gun

bal·loon[1] /bə'lun/ *n.* [C] **1** a small brightly colored rubber bag that can be filled with air and used as a toy or decoration for parties **2** a large bag of strong light cloth filled with gas or heated air so that it can float in the air, and that has a basket hanging below it for people to stand in: *hot air balloon rides* **3** the circle drawn around the words spoken by the characters in a CARTOON **4 a balloon payment** money borrowed that must be paid back in one large sum after several smaller payments have been made: *Use the loan to pay off the balloon payment.* **5 go down like a lead balloon** INFORMAL if a joke, remark etc. goes down like a lead balloon, people do not laugh or react as you expected —see also TRIAL BALLOON

bal·loon[2] *v.* [I] **1** to become larger in amount: *The program's cost has ballooned from $270 million to more than $1 billion.* **2** to gain weight suddenly: *He ballooned to 300 pounds since college.*

bal·loon·ing /bə'lunɪŋ/ *n.* [U] the sport of flying in a balloon —**balloonist** *n.* [C]

bal·lot[1] /'bælət/ *n.* **1** [C,U] a system of secret voting or an occasion when you vote in this way: *November's general election ballot* | *There were 17 propositions on the ballot* (=17 things to be voted on). **2** [C] a piece of paper on which you make a secret vote **3** [C] the number of votes recorded

bal·lot[2] *v.* [I,T] to vote or to decide something by a vote *Baseball writers will be balloted on Hall of Fame candidates.*

ballot box /'.. ,./ *n.* **1** [C] a box that ballot papers are put in after voting **2 the ballot box** the system or process of voting in an election: *The issue will be decided at the ballot box.*

ball·park /'bɔl,park/ *n.* **1** a field for playing baseball, with seats for watching the game **2 in the (right) ball park** INFORMAL close to the amount, price etc. that you want or are thinking about: *The chief financial officer said that analysts' profit estimates are in the right ballpark.* **3 a ball park figure/estimate/ amount** a number or amount that is almost but not exactly correct: *Could you give me a ballpark figure for rebuilding the offices?*

ball·play·er /'bɔl,pleɪə/ *n.* [C] someone who plays baseball

ball·point /'bɔlpɔɪnt/ also **ballpoint pen** /,.. '../ *n.* [C] a pen with a ball at the end that rolls thick ink onto the paper

ball·room /'bɔlrum/ *n.* [C] a very large room used for dancing on formal occasions

ballroom danc·ing /,.. '../ *n.* [U] a type of dancing that is done with a partner and has different steps for particular types of music, such as the WALTZ¹ (2)

balls·y /'bɔlzi/ *adj.* SPOKEN, SLANG brave and determined

bal·ly·hoo /'bæli,hu/ *n.* [U] INFORMAL a situation in which people publicly express a lot of anger, excitement etc.: *A lot of the ballyhoo centered on the network's new hit show.* —**ballyhoo** *v.* [T]

balm /bɑm/ *n.* [C,U] **1** an oily liquid with a strong, pleasant smell that you rub into your skin, often to reduce pain: *lip balm* **2** LITERARY something that gives you comfort: *The performers were reassured by the balm of warm applause.*

balm·y /'bɑmi/ *adj.* **balmier, balmiest** balmy air, weather etc. is warm and pleasant: *a balmy summer night*

ba·lo·ney /bə'louni/ *n.* [U] **1** INFORMAL something that is silly or not true; nonsense **2** NONSTANDARD BOLOGNA

bal·sa /'bɔlsə/ *n.* [C,U] a tropical American tree or the wood from this tree, which is very light

bal·sam /'bɔlsəm/ *n.* [C,U] BALM, or the tree that produces it

bal·sam·ic vin·e·gar /bɔl,sæmɪk 'vɪnəgɚ/ *n.* [U] an expensive kind of dark-colored VINEGAR used especially in SALADs and Italian dishes

Bal·tic, the /'bɔltɪk/ also **the Baltic Sea** a sea that is part of the northern Atlantic Ocean and is surrounded by Denmark, Sweden, the Baltic States, and Poland

Baltic States, the /,.. '../ also **the Baltics** the countries of Estonia, Latvia, and Lithuania

Bal·ti·more /'bɔltɪ,mɔr/ the largest city in the U.S. state of Maryland

bal·us·trade /'bælə,streɪd/ *n.* [C] a row of upright pieces of stone or wood with a bar along the top, especially around a BALCONY

Bal·zac /'bɔlzæk, 'bæl-/, **Hon·o·ré de** /,ɑnə'reɪ də/ (1799–1850) a French writer of NOVELs

bam /bæm/ *interjection* **1** used in order to show that something happens quickly: *Just turn it on, and bam, you're ready to go.* **2** used to say that something has hit something else

Ba·ma·ko /,bɑmə'kou, ,bæ-/ the capital and largest city of Mali

bamboo

bamboo shelf

bamboo

bam·boo /,bæm'bu‹/ *n. plural* **bamboos** [C,U] a tall tropical plant with hollow stems, often used for making furniture

bam·boo·zle /bæm'buzəl/ *v.* [T] INFORMAL to deceive, trick, or confuse someone

ban¹ /bæn/ *n.* [C] an official order that forbids something from being used or done: [+ on] *a ban on logging in the forest* —see also TEST BAN

ban² *v.* **banned, banning** [T] to say that something must not be done, seen, used etc.: *Elephant ivory is banned in the U.S.* | [ban sb from doing sth] *The military government banned private citizens from carrying guns.* —see also BANNED

ba·nal /bə'næl, bə'nɑl, 'beɪnl/ *adj.* ordinary and not interesting, because of a lack of new or different ideas: *a banal argument* —**banality** /bə'næləti/ *n.* [C,U]

ba·nan·a /bə'nænə/ *n.* [C] a long curved tropical fruit with a yellow skin —see also SECOND BANANA —see picture at FRUIT¹

banana re·pub·lic /.,... '../ *n.* [C] DISAPPROVING a small poor country with a weak government that depends on financial help from other countries

ba·nan·as /bə'nænəz/ *adj.* INFORMAL **1 go bananas** to become very angry or excited: *Dad will go bananas when he sees this.* **2** crazy or silly: *You're bananas.*

banana split /.,... './ *n.* [C] a sweet dish with bananas and ICE CREAM

band¹ /bænd/ *n.* [C] **1** a group of musicians, especially a group that plays popular music: *a country-and-western band* | *There's a good band on Friday night at El Club.* **2** a group of people formed because of a common belief or purpose: *a small band of rebels* **3** a flat, narrow piece of material with one end joined to the other to form a circle: *an elastic band* | *a wide silk band* **4** a thick colored line: *There are orange bands around the snake's back.* **5** TECHNICAL a range of radio signals

band² *v.* [T] to put a band of color or material on or around something

band together *phr. v.* [I] to unite in order to achieve something: *Neighbors banded together to fight for a health clinic.*

ban·dage¹ /'bændɪdʒ/ *n.* [C] a narrow piece of cloth that you tie around a wound or around a part of the body that has been injured

bandage² *v.* [T] to tie or cover a part of the body with a bandage: *A paramedic bandaged his foot.*

Band-Aid /'bænd eɪd/ *n.* [C] TRADEMARK a piece of thin material that is stuck to the skin to cover cuts and other small wounds

ban·dan·na, bandana /bæn'dænə/ *n.* [C] a large brightly colored piece of cloth you wear around your head or neck: *The cowboy had a red bandana around his neck.*

Ban·dar Se·ri Be·ga·wan /,bʌndɚ ,seri bə'gɑwən/ the capital city of Brunei

B and B /,bi ən 'bi/ *n.* the abbreviation of BED AND BREAKFAST

band·box /'bændbɑks/ *n.* [C] a box for keeping hats in

ban·dit /'bændɪt/ *n.* [C] someone who robs people, especially one of a group of people who attack travelers: *The bandits took jewelry and cash.* —see also ONE-ARMED BANDIT —**banditry** *n.* [U]

band·mas·ter /'bænd,mæstɚ/ *n.* [C] someone who CONDUCTs a military band, MARCHING BAND etc.

ban·do·lier /,bændə'lɪr/ *n.* [C] a belt that goes over someone's shoulder and across their chest and is used to carry bullets

band·stand /'bændstænd/ *n.* [C] a small building in a park that has a roof but no walls and is used by a band playing music

band·wag·on /'bænd,wægən/ *n.* [C] **jump/climb/get on the bandwagon** to begin to do something that a lot of other people are doing: *A lot of cities are jumping on the bandwagon and putting cops back on foot, rather than in cars.*

band·width /'bænd,wɪdθ/ *n.* [U] TECHNICAL the amount of information that can be carried through a telephone wire, computer connection etc. at one time

ban·dy¹ /'bændi/ *adj.* bandy legs curve out at the knees —**bandy-legged** *adj.*

bandy² *v.* **bandies, bandied, bandying bandy words (with sb)** OLD-FASHIONED to argue with someone

bandy sth about *phr. v.* [T] to mention an idea, name, remark etc. several times, especially to appear impressive to someone: *A few names are being bandied about as possible stars of NBC's new sitcom.*

bane /beɪn/ *n.* [singular] something that causes trouble or makes people unhappy: [be the bane of sth] *Poison oak is the bane of campers.* | *This stupid* *computer has become **the bane of my existence** (=a cause of continual trouble).*

bane·ful /'beɪnfəl/ *adj.* LITERARY evil or bad —**banefully** *adv.*

bang[1] /bæŋ/ *v.*

1 **knock/hit sth** [I,T] to hit something hard against something else, making a loud noise: *I banged the phone down.* | *They were banging drums and chanting.* | [+ **on**] *Laramie was banging on the wall and yelling.*

2 **close sth** [I always + adv./prep.,T] to close something violently making a loud noise, or to make something close in this way: *He got out of the car and banged the door.* | *The screen door banged shut.*

3 **hit sth** [T] to hit a part of your body or something you are carrying against something, especially by accident; BUMP[1] (1): *I banged my toe on the door.* | *I slipped and banged the guitar against the door.*

4 **make noise** [I] to make a loud noise or noises: *The pipes bang when you turn the hot water on.* | [+ **around/away** etc.] *The shutters were banging in the wind.*

5 **bang your head against/on a (brick) wall** INFORMAL to be wasting your efforts by doing something that does not produce any results: *Trying to teach that class is like banging your head against a brick wall.*

6 **have sex** [T] VULGAR to have sex with someone

bang sth ↔ **out** *phr. v.* [T] INFORMAL **1** to play a tune or song loudly and badly on a piano **2** to write something in a hurry, especially on a TYPEWRITER: *As a journalist, you have to bang out a column for each day.*

bang sb/sth ↔ **up** *phr. v.* [T] INFORMAL to seriously damage something: *She banged up my car.*

bang[2] *n.* **1** [C] a sudden loud noise caused by something such as a gun or an object hitting a hard surface: *The front door slammed with a loud bang.* **2** **bangs** [plural] hair cut straight across your FOREHEAD **3** **get a bang out of sth** SPOKEN to enjoy something very much: *She got a real bang out of seeing the kids in the school play.* **4** **with a bang** very much in a way that is very exciting or noticeable: *Brewster finished the season with a bang.* **5** [C] a hard knock or hit against something: *He walked away from the accident with only a slight bang on the head.* **6** **more bang for the/your buck** something that gives you a good effect or a lot of value for the effort or money you spend on it: *You get more bang for your buck when you buy used textbooks.*

bang[3] *adv.* **1** INFORMAL directly or exactly: *It starts at eight, bang on the dot.* **2** SPOKEN in a sudden, violent way: *I lost my balance and fell, bang, on my back on the ice.*

bang[4] *interjection* used to make a sound like a gun or bomb: *"Bang, bang – you're dead," Tommy shouted.*

Bang·kok /'bæŋkɑk/ the capital and largest city of Thailand

Bang·la·desh /ˌbɑŋglə'dɛʃ, ˌbæŋ-/ a country in Asia that is east of India —**Bangladeshi** *n., adj.*

ban·gle /'bæŋgəl/ *n.* [C] a solid band of gold, silver etc. that you wear loosely around your wrist as jewelry

Ban·gui /bɑŋ'gi/ the capital and largest city of the Central African Republic

bang-up /'. ./ *adj.* INFORMAL very good: *They did a bang-up job on the display.*

ban·ish /'bænɪʃ/ *v.* [T] **1** to not allow someone or something to stay in a particular place: [**banish sth from/to**] *Smokers have been banished to an area outdoors.* **2** to send someone away permanently from their country or the area where they live, especially as an official punishment: [**banish sb from/to**] *Many Soviet dissidents were banished to Siberia.* **3** to prevent someone from doing something or something from happening: [**banish sb from sth**] *Pete Rose was banished from baseball.* **4** to try to stop thinking about something, especially something that worries you: *The study should banish any doubts about women's ability to handle the pressures of business.* —**banishment** *n.* [U]

ban·is·ter /'bænəstə/ *n.* [C] a row of upright sticks with a bar along the top, that stops you from falling over the edge of stairs —see picture on page 423

ban·jo /'bændʒoʊ/ *n. plural* **banjos** [C] a musical instrument with four or more strings, a long neck, and a round body used especially in COUNTRY AND WESTERN music

Ban·jul /'bɑndʒul/ the capital city of the Gambia

bank[1] /bæŋk/ *n.*

1 **place for money** [C] **a)** a business that keeps and lends money and provides other financial services: *The bill would force banks to lower credit card interest rates.* **b)** a local office of a bank: *I'll stop at the bank on the way home.*

2 **river/lake** [C] land along the side of a river or lake: *the grassy banks of the river* —see Usage Note at SHORE[1]

3 **a blood/sperm/organ etc. bank** a place where human blood etc. is stored until someone needs it

4 **pile** [C] a large pile of earth, sand, snow etc.: *He was drunk and drove into a snow bank.*

5 **a cloud/fog bank etc.** [C] a large amount of clouds, mist etc.

6 **a bank of televisions/elevators/computers etc.** a large number of machines, television screens etc. arranged close together in a row

7 **game** [singular] the money in a GAMBLING game that people can win —see also **break the bank** (BREAK[1] (48)), **it won't break the bank** (BREAK[1] (36))

8 **road** [C] a slope made at a curve in a road or RACETRACK to make it safer for cars to go around

9 **sb's money** [U] SLANG money: *Boy, you must have all kinds of bank after payday, huh?* —see also FOOD BANK, MEMORY BANK

bank[2] *v.*

1 **money** [T] to put or keep money in a bank: *She's managed to bank more than $300,000.*

2 **a particular bank** [I] to keep your money in a particular bank: [+ **with**] *Who do you bank with?* | [+ **at**] *They've always banked at Bank of America.*

3 **turn** [I] to make an airplane, MOTORCYCLE, or car slope to one side when turning: *The enemy fighter banked left, then right.*

4 **pile/rows** [T] to arrange something into a pile or into rows: *Dozens of candles were banked before the altar.*

5 **steep sides** to have steep sides like a hill: *The bobsled run has banked curves about a mile long.*

6 **cloud/mist** also **bank up** [T] to form a large amount of cloud, mist etc.: *Banked clouds promised rain.*

7 **fire** also **bank up** [T] to cover a fire with wood, coal etc. to keep it going for a long time: *Bank the hot coals on a grill.*

bank on sb/sth *phr. v.* [T] to depend on something happening or someone doing something: *Branson is banking on the media attention to attract advertisers* | [**bank on doing sth**] *I'd banked on being able to take that flight.*

bank·a·ble /'bæŋkəbəl/ *adj.* INFORMAL a bankable person or quality is likely to help you get money, success etc.: *Swayze has become a bankable star.*

bank ac·count /'. .,./ *n.* [C] an arrangement between a bank and a customer that allows the customer to pay in and take out money

bank bal·ance /'. ,../ *n.* [singular] the amount of money someone has in their bank account

bank book /'. ./ *n.* [C] a book in which a record is kept of the money you put into and take out of your bank account; PASSBOOK

bank card /'. ./ *n.* [C] a CREDIT CARD provided by your bank

bank draft /'. ./ also **banker's draft** /'.. ,./ *n.* [C] a check from one bank to another, especially a foreign bank, to pay a certain amount of money to a person or organization

bank·er /'bæŋkə/ *n.* [C] **1** someone who works in a bank in an important position **2** the player who is in charge of the money in some games

bank·ing /'bæŋkɪŋ/ *n.* [U] the business of a bank: *the international banking system*

B

bank note /'. ./ n. [C] a piece of paper money of a particular value that you use to buy things; BILL¹ (3)

bank rate /'. ./ n. [C] TECHNICAL the rate of INTEREST¹ (3) decided by a country's main bank

bank·roll¹ /'bæŋkroul/ n. [C] a supply of money

bankroll² v. [T] INFORMAL to provide the money that someone needs for a business, a plan etc.: *The company is bankrolled by a Swiss investor.*

bank·rupt¹ /'bæŋkrʌpt/ adj. **1** unable to pay your debts: *The state is virtually bankrupt.* | *a bankrupt steel manufacturer* **2 go bankrupt** to be unable to pay your debts and to have to sell your property and goods: *Several airlines have gone bankrupt since deregulation in 1978.* **3** completely lacking a particular good quality: *He claimed that American political leaders were morally bankrupt for not meeting welfare needs.*

bankrupt² v. [T] to make a person, business, or country bankrupt or very poor: *There are fears the new law could bankrupt some small businesses.*

bankrupt³ n. [C] someone who has officially said that they cannot pay their debts

bank·rupt·cy /'bæŋk,rʌptsi/ n. plural **bankruptcies 1** [C,U] the state of being unable to pay your debts: *Corporate bankruptcies increased last year.* | *School districts across the state are **declaring bankruptcy** (=officially saying they cannot pay their debts).* **2** [U] a total lack of a particular good quality: *the moral bankruptcy of this materialistic society*

Banks /bæŋks/, **Er·nie** /'ɚni/ (1931–) a U.S. baseball player who was the first African-American member of the Chicago Cubs team.

bank state·ment /'. ,../ n. [C] a document sent regularly by a bank to a customer that lists the amounts of money taken out of and paid into their BANK ACCOUNT

bank tell·er /'. ,../ n. [C] a TELLER

banned /bænd/ adj. not officially allowed to meet, exist, or be used: *Some fertilizers were found to contain the banned chemicals.*

ban·ner¹ /'bænɚ/ n. [C] **1** a long piece of cloth on which something is written, often carried between two poles: *The protesters were carrying anti-war banners.* **2** LITERARY a flag **3** a belief or principle: *Civil rights groups have achieved a lot **under the banner of** (=while supporting or believing in) fair and equal treatment.*

banner² adj. excellent: *a banner year for the team*

banner head·line /,.. '../ n. [C] words printed in very large letters across the top of the first page of a newspaper

Ban·nis·ter /'bænɪstɚ/, **Sir Rog·er** /'rɑdʒɚ/ (1929–) a British runner who was the first person to run a mile in less than four minutes

Ban·nock /'bænək/ a Native American tribe from the northwestern area of the U.S.

ban·quet /'bæŋkwɪt/ n. [C] a formal dinner for many people on an important occasion

banquet room /'.. ,./ n. [C] a large room in which banquets take place

ban·shee /'bænʃi/ n. [C] a spirit whose loud cry is believed to be heard when someone is going to die

ban·tam /'bæntəm/ n. [C] a type of small chicken

ban·tam·weight /'bæntəm,weɪt/ n. [C] a BOXER or WRESTLER who weighs between 112 and 118 pounds

ban·ter¹ /'bæntɚ/ n. [U] conversation that has a lot of jokes and teasing (TEASE) remarks in it: *lighthearted and amusing banter*

banter² v. [I] to joke with and TEASE someone —**bantering** adj. —**banteringly** adv.

ban·yan /'bænyən/ n. [C] an Indian tree with large branches that spread out and form new roots

bap·tism /'bæptɪzəm/ n. [C,U] **1** a Christian religious ceremony in which someone is touched with water or put completely in water to welcome them into a particular Christian faith, and sometimes to officially name them **2 a baptism by fire** a difficult or painful first experience of something: *We went straight into battle the next day. It was a baptism by fire I'll never forget.* —**baptismal** /bæp'tɪzməl/ adj.

Bap·tist /'bæptɪst/ n. [C] a member of a Christian group that believes that members should be baptized when they are old enough to understand its meaning

bap·tize /'bæptaɪz, bæp'taɪz/ v. [T] **1** to perform the ceremony of baptism on someone **2** to accept someone as a member of a particular Christian church by a ceremony of baptism: *Both boys were baptized Catholic.* **3** to give a child a name in a baptism ceremony: *Amy was baptized Amelia, but always called Amy.*

bar¹ /bɑr/ n. [C]

1 place to drink in a place where alcoholic drinks are served: *We went to a sports bar to watch the game and have a few beers.*

2 place to buy a drink the long table inside a bar where alcoholic drinks are served: *O'Keefe stood at the bar, drinking and watching the girls.*

3 block shape something, especially something solid, that is longer than it is wide: *a candy bar* | *the menu bar on your computer screen* | *[+ of] a bar of metal*

4 piece of metal/wood a length of metal or wood put across a door, window etc. to keep it shut or to prevent people going in or out: *A lot of houses had bars across the windows.*

5 a salad/coffee/sushi etc. bar a place where a particular kind of food or drink is served

6 lawyers the bar lawyers considered as a group, or the profession of being a lawyer: *I have to pass the bar exam before I can start practicing law.*

7 behind bars INFORMAL in prison

8 music a group of notes and RESTs, separated from other groups by VERTICAL lines, into which a line of written music is divided: *They played a few bars, then stopped.*

9 a bar to (doing) sth something that prevents you from achieving something that you want: *Homosexuality is a bar to becoming a priest in many churches.*

10 pile of sand/stones a long pile of sand or stones under the water at the entrance to a HARBOR: *One of the ships got stuck on a sand bar.*

11 color/light a narrow band of color or light

12 on uniforms a narrow band of metal or cloth worn on a military uniform to show rank —see also SALAD BAR, SNACK BAR

bar² v. **barred, barring** [T] **1** also **bar up** to shut a door or window using a bar or piece of wood so that people cannot get in or out **2** to officially prevent someone from entering a place or from doing something: [**bar sb from sth**] *Journalists are regularly barred from entering the country.* **3** to prevent people from going somewhere by placing something in their way: *She stood in the hall, barring my way.*

bar³ prep. **1 bar none** used to emphasize that someone is the best of a particular group: *They serve the best breakfast in town, bar none.* **2** FORMAL except: *No work's been done in the office today, bar a little typing.* —see also BARRING

Ba·ra·ka /bə'rɑkə/, **A·mir·i** /ə'mɪri/ (1934–) a U.S. writer of plays about the situation of African-American people

barb /bɑrb/ n. [C] **1** the sharp curved point of a hook, ARROW etc. that prevents it from being easily pulled out **2** a remark that is smart and amusing, but also cruel —see also BARBED (2)

Bar·ba·dos /bɑr'beɪdous/ an island in the Caribbean Sea, which is an independent country —**Barbadian** n., adj.

bar·bar·i·an /bɑr'bɛriən/ n. [C] **1** someone who does not behave correctly, or who does not show respect for education, art etc.: *His friends are a bunch of barbarians – they don't even wash their hands before they eat.* **2** someone from a different tribe or land, who people believe to be wild and violent and not CIVILIZED: *The barbarians conquered Rome.*

bar·bar·ic /bɑr'bærɪk, -'bɛrɪk/ adj. **1** very cruel and violent; BARBAROUS: *the barbaric treatment of women* prisoners **2** like or belonging to a wild or cruel group or society: *a barbaric custom*

bar·ba·rism /'bɑrbə,rɪzəm/ *n.* **1** [U] cruel and violent behavior **2** [U] a state or condition in which people are not educated, behave violently etc.

bar·bar·i·ty /bɑr'bærəti, -'bɛr-/ *n. plural* **barbarities** [C,U] a very cruel act, or cruel actions in general: *the barbarity of the Nazis*

bar·ba·rous /'bɑrbərəs/ *adj.* **1** extremely cruel in a way that is shocking; BARBARIC **2** wild and not CIVILIZED (1): *a savage, barbarous people* —**barbarously** *adv.*

bar·be·cue¹ /'bɑrbɪ,kyu/ *n.* [C] **1** a metal frame for cooking food on outdoors —see picture on page 423 **2** an outdoor party during which food is cooked and eaten outdoors: *The neighbors **had a barbecue** Saturday night.*

barbecue² *v.* [T] to cook food on a metal frame over a fire outdoors: *barbecued chicken*

barbed /bɑrbd/ *adj.* **1** a hook or ARROW that has one or more sharp curved points **2** a barbed remark is unkind

barbed-wire /ˌ. './ *n.* [U] wire with short sharp points on it: *a high barbed-wire fence*

bar·bell /'bɑrbɛl/ *n.* [C] a metal bar with weights at each end, that you lift to make you stronger

bar·be·que /'bɑrbɪ,kyu/ another spelling of BARBECUE

bar·ber /'bɑrbə/ *n.* [C] a man whose job is to cut men's hair and sometimes to SHAVE them

bar·ber·shop, **barber shop** /'bɑrbə ʃɑp/ *n.* **1** [C] a store where men's hair is cut **2** [U] a style of singing popular songs in four parts in close HARMONY: *a barbershop quartet*

barber's pole /ˈ.. ,./ *n.* [C] a pole with red and white bands, used as a sign outside a barbershop

bar·bi·can /'bɑrbɪkən/ *n.* [C] a tower for defense at the gate or bridge of a castle

bar·bi·tu·rate /bɑr'bɪtʃərɪt/ *n.* [C,U] a powerful drug that makes people calm and puts them to sleep

bar chart /'. ./ *n.* [C] a BAR GRAPH

bar code /'. ./ *n.* [C] a group of thin and thick lines from which a computer reads information about a product that is sold in a store

bard /bɑrd/ *n.* [C] **1** LITERARY a poet **2** **the Bard** INFORMAL William Shakespeare

Bar·deen /bɑr'din/**, John** (1908–1991) a U.S. scientist who worked on the development of an electronic TRANSISTOR and helped to develop the idea of SUPERCONDUCTIVITY

bare¹ /bɛr/ *adj.*
1 without clothes not covered by clothes: *Using her bare hands, she smears paint on the canvas.* | *bare-chested men*
2 land/trees not covered by trees or grass, or not having any leaves: *bare and treeless hills*
3 not covered/empty empty, not covered by anything, or not having any decorations: *Paint the bare wood with a primer.* | *a bare-looking room*
4 **the bare facts/truth** a statement that tells someone only what they need to know, with no additional details: *You only need to give the bare facts.*
5 smallest amount necessary [only before noun] the very least amount of something that you need to do something: *The measure passed by a bare majority of votes.* | *The refugees fled, taking only **the bare essentials**.* | *Try to keep administrative costs to a **bare minimum** (=the smallest amount possible).* | *There was only **the barest** (=smallest amount possible) flavor of coffee.* —see also BARE BONES
6 **lay sth bare a)** to uncover something that was previously hidden: *The excavation laid bare the streets of the ancient city.* **b)** to make known something that was secret: *The depth of the problem is laid bare in the fact that 40% of 18- to 25-year-olds are unemployed.*
7 **with your bare hands** without using a weapon: *They'll fight with their bare hands to protect their homeland.* —**bareness** *n.*

bare² *v.* [T] **1** to let something be seen, by removing something that is covering it: *The dog bared its teeth.* **2** **bare your soul** to tell your most secret feelings to someone

bare-assed /'. ./ *adj.* SLANG having no clothes on

bare·back /'bɛrbæk/ *adj. adv.* on the bare back of a horse, without a SADDLE: *Where did you learn to **ride bareback?***

bare bones /ˌ. './ *n.* **the bare bones** the least amount of something you need in order to do what you need to do: *I don't know how we can cut any more spending. We're down to the bare bones.*

bare-bones /'. ,./ *adj.* INFORMAL having only the most basic things, information, qualities etc. that are needed: *We only have a bare-bones staff.*

bare·faced /'bɛrfeɪst/ *adj.* a barefaced lie, remark etc. is clear and makes no attempt not to offend someone

bare·foot /'bɛrfʊt/ also **bare·foot·ed** /'bɛr,fʊtɪd/ *adj., adv.* without shoes on your feet: *As a kid, I loved **going barefoot**.*

bare-hand·ed /ˌbɛr'hændɪd◂/ *adj., adv.* having no GLOVES on, or having no tools or weapons: *They fought barehanded.*

bare-head·ed /ˌbɛr'hɛdɪd◂/ *adj., adv.* without a hat on your head: *These kids shouldn't be playing bareheaded in the snow.*

bare-leg·ged /'bɛr,lɛgd, -,lɛgɪd/ *adj., adv.* with no clothing on your legs

bare·ly /'bɛrli/ *adv.* **1** in a way that almost does not happen, exist etc.; just: *They lost, but just barely.* | *Dave barely noticed my new dress.* | *She was barely eighteen, and pregnant with her second child.* **2** in a way that is simple, with no decorations or details: *The room was furnished barely.* **3** used to emphasize that something happens immediately after a previous action: *I'd barely gotten home when the phone rang.*

Bar·ents Sea, the /'bærənts, 'bɑr-/ a part of the Arctic Ocean that is northeast of Scandinavia

barf /bɑrf/ *v.* [I] INFORMAL to VOMIT —**barf** *n.* [U] —**barfy** *adj.*

bar·fly /'bɑrflaɪ/ *n. plural* **barflies** [C] INFORMAL someone who spends a lot of time in bars —**barfly** *adj.*

bar·gain¹ /'bɑrgən/ *n.* [C] **1** something bought cheaply or for less than its usual price: *The 10-ounce can is a better bargain than the 4-ounce one.* | *Airlines aren't making money on bargain fares (=prices for plane travel that are very cheap).* | *The car was a bargain at $8500.* | *The clothes were a **real bargain**.* | *Hundreds of people go **bargain-hunting** in the sales after Christmas.* **2** an agreement, made between two people or groups, to do something in return for something else: *She had **made a bargain** and was now trying to back out of it.* | *The union representatives **drove a hard bargain** (=got an agreement favorable to them) in the talks.* | *They **struck a bargain** (=made an agreement) to marry and then divorce, in order to get him citizenship.* | *Negotiators are worried that the rebels will not **keep their side of the bargain** (=will not do whey they promised in the agreement).* —see also PLEA BARGAIN **3** **in the bargain** in addition to everything else: *It would be nice to get some exercise in the bargain.* **4** **make the best of a bad bargain** to do the best you can under difficult conditions —**bargainer** *n.* [C] *a wage bargainer*

bargain² *v.* [I] to discuss the conditions of a sale, agreement etc.: [bargain with sb] *The family refused to bargain with the kidnappers.* | [+ for] *Oliver's bargaining for a raise.*

bargain for sth *phr. v.* also **bargain on** sth [T usually in negatives] to expect that something will happen and make it part of your plans: [bargain on doing sth] *I hadn't bargained on it taking so long.* | *It turned out to be a **more** dangerous situation **than** he'd **bargained for** (=more than he'd expected).*

bargain base·ment /ˌ.. '../ *n.* [C] a part of a large store, usually in the floor below ground level, where goods are sold at reduced prices

bar·gain·ing /'bɑrgənɪŋ/ n. **1 bargaining chip** something that one person or group in a business deal or political agreement has, that can be used to gain an advantage in the deal **2 bargaining power** the power that a person or group has in a discussion or agreement: *When companies hire non-union workers, it weakens the bargaining power of the union.* **3 bargaining position a)** the fact of having bargaining power: **a good/strong bargaining position** *In paying for so much advertising, they were in a good bargaining position to dictate the movie's TV time slot.* **b)** the opinions and demands that one person or group has when starting a discussion or agreement: *The current Palestinian bargaining position is to negotiate limited self-rule in the occupied territories.*

bar·gain·ing chip /'... ./ n. [C] something that one person or group in a business deal or political agreement has, that can be used to gain an advantage in the deal: *We are against the use of hostages as bargaining chips.*

barge¹ /bɑrdʒ/ n. **1** [C] a large low boat with a flat bottom used mainly for carrying heavy goods on a CANAL or river **2** a large rowing boat used for an important ceremony

barge² v. [I always + adv./prep.] to move somewhere in an awkward way, often hitting against things: *A couple of kids barged past the guards at the door.* | *He barged his way through the room.*

barge in also **barge into** phr. v. [I] to enter or rush in rudely: *Chunovich barged into the office and demanded to see the boss.*

barge in on phr. v. [T] to interrupt someone rudely, especially by coming in while they are doing something: *She just barged in on Duncan and Jessica.*

barge·man /'bɑrdʒmən/ n. [C] someone who drives or works on a barge

barge pole /'. ./ n. [C] a long pole used to guide a barge

bar graph /'. ./ n. [C] a picture of boxes of different heights, in which each box represents a different amount, for example an amount of profit made in a particular month —see picture at CHART¹

bar·hop /'bɑrhɑp/ v. [I] INFORMAL to visit and drink at several bars, one after another

bar·i·tone /'bærə,toun/ n. [C] a male singing voice lower than a TENOR and higher than a BASS, or a male singer whose voice is in this range

bar·i·um /'bɛriəm, 'bær-/ n. [U] **1** *symbol* Ba a soft silvery-white metal that is an ELEMENT **2 a barium enema/swallow/meal** a substance containing barium that you swallow or that is put in your BOWELS before you have an X-RAY

bark¹ /bɑrk/ v. **1** [I] to make the short loud sound that dogs and some other animals make: [+ at] *Can you make the dog stop barking at the mailman?* **2** [T] also **bark out** to say something quickly in a loud voice: [+ at] *The sergeant barked orders at us.* **3 bark up the wrong tree** INFORMAL to have a wrong idea, especially about how to get a particular result: *You're barking up the wrong tree if you think Sam can help you.* **4 bark at the moon** INFORMAL to worry and complain about something that you cannot change, and that is not very important **5** [T] to rub the skin off your knee, elbow etc. by falling or knocking against something: *I barked my shin on the bed.*

bark² n. [C,U] **1** the sharp loud sound made by a dog **2** the outer covering of a tree **3** a loud sound or voice: *the bark of the guns* **4 sb's bark is worse than their bite** SPOKEN used to say that although someone talks in an angry way they would not behave violently **5** LITERARY BARQUE

bar·keep·er /'bɑr,kipə/ also **bar·keep** /'bɑrkip/ n. [C] someone who serves drinks in a bar; BARTENDER

bark·er /'bɑrkə/ n. [C] someone who stands outside a place at a CIRCUS, FAIR etc. shouting to people to come in

bar·ley /'bɑrli/ n. [U] a plant that produces a grain used for making food or alcohol

bar·maid /'bɑrmeɪd/ n. [C] a woman who serves drinks in a bar

bar·man /'bɑrmən/ n. [C] OLD-FASHIONED a BARTENDER

bar mitz·vah /,bɑr 'mɪtsvə/ n. [C] **1** the religious ceremony held when a Jewish boy reaches the age of 13 and is considered an adult in his religion **2** a boy for whom this ceremony is held —compare BAT MITZVAH

barn /bɑrn/ n. [C] **1** a large farm building for storing crops, or for keeping animals in **2** INFORMAL a large plain building: *a huge barn of a house* **3 close the barn door after the horse has left/escaped/fled etc.** to try to prevent something when it is too late and harm has already been done

bar·na·cle /'bɑrnəkəl/ n. [C] a small sea animal with a hard shell that sticks firmly to rocks and the bottom of boats

Bar·nard /'bɑrnɑrd/, **Chris·tiaan** /'krɪstʃən/ (1922–) a South African doctor who in 1967 performed the first-ever heart TRANSPLANT

barn·storm /'bɑrnstɔrm/ v. [I] **1** to travel from place to place making short stops to give political speeches or theater performances **2** to perform tricks and difficult movements in the air in a small airplane to entertain people —**barnstormer** n. [C] —**barnstorming** n. [U]

barn·yard /'bɑrnyɑrd/ n. [C] **1** a space surrounded by farm buildings **2 barnyard humor** humor about sex and body waste

ba·rom·e·ter /bə'rɑmətə/ n. [C] **1** an instrument for measuring changes in the air pressure and weather or calculating height above sea level **2** something that shows or gives an idea of changes that are happening: *Applications for building permits are a barometer of future construction activity.* —**barometric** /,bærə'mɛtrɪk◂/ adj. —**barometrically** /-kli/ adv.

bar·on /'bærən/ n. [C] **1** a businessman with a lot of power or influence: *media baron Rupert Murdoch* | *Colombian drug barons* **2** a man who is a member of the British NOBILITY, or of a rank of European NOBILITY —see also ROBBER BARON

bar·on·ess /'bærənɪs, -,nɛs/ n. [C] **1** a woman who is a member of the British NOBILITY **2** the wife of a baron

bar·on·et /'bærənɪt/ n. [C] a British KNIGHT who is lower in rank than a baron, whose title passes on to his son when he dies

ba·ro·ni·al /bə'rouniəl/ adj. **1** a baronial room is very large and richly decorated **2** belonging to or involving a BARON

ba·roque /bə'rouk/ adj. **1** belonging to the very decorated style of art, music, buildings etc. that was common in Europe in the 17th century: *a baroque composer* **2** very detailed and complicated —**baroque** n. [singular]

barque /bɑrk/ n. [C] a sailing ship with three, four, or five MASTS (=poles that the sails are attached to)

bar·racks /'bærɪks/ n. [plural] a group of buildings in which soldiers live

bar·ra·cu·da /,bærə'kudə/ n. [C] a large tropical fish that eats flesh

barracuda
dorsal fin
scales
gill

bar·rage¹ /bə'rɑʒ/ n. **1** [C usually singular] the continuous firing of guns, especially large heavy guns, to protect soldiers as they move toward an enemy: *a barrage of anti-aircraft fire* **2** [singular] a lot of actions, sounds, questions, etc. that happen at the same time or very quickly after each other: [+ of] *City officials faced a barrage of angry questions from local residents.*

bar·rage² /'bærɪdʒ/ n. [C] a wall of earth, stones etc. built across a river to provide water for farming or to prevent flooding

bar·rage bal·loon /.'. .,./ n. [C] a large bag that floats in the air to prevent enemy airplanes from flying near the ground

barred /bɑrd/ *adj.* **1** a barred window, gate etc. has bars across it **2** FORMAL having bands of different color: *red barred tail feathers* —see also BAR¹ (4)

bar·rel¹ /'bærəl/ *n.* [C] **1** a large curved container with a flat top and bottom, made of wood or metal: *The wine is aged in oak barrels.* —see picture at CONTAINER **2** also **barrelful** the amount of liquid that a barrel contains, used especially as a measure of oil: *The area may contain up to 2 billion barrels of oil.* **3** the part of a gun that the bullets are fired through **4 have sb over a barrel** to put someone in a situation in which they are forced to accept or do what you want: *The actor has the studio over a barrel – if they want to keep him, they have to pay him more money.* **5 be a barrel of laughs** [often in negatives] to be very enjoyable: *It wasn't a barrel of laughs, but I learned a lot.* —see also **lock, stock, and barrel** (LOCK² (2)), PORK BARREL, **scrape the bottom of the barrel** (SCRAPE¹ (4))

barrel² *v.* [I] INFORMAL to move very fast, especially in an uncontrolled way: *The train barreled down the tracks.* | *Smith barreled into him, knocking him over.*

barrel-chest·ed /'.. ,../ *adj.* a man who is barrel-chested has a round chest that sticks out

barrel or·gan /'.. ,../ *n.* [C] a musical instrument that you play by turning a handle, used especially in past times

bar·ren /'bærən/ *adj.* **1** land or soil that is barren has no plants growing on it: *the barren hillsides after the fire* **2** a room or area that is barren has nothing in it: *a barren apartment in a poor area* **3** OLD USE a woman or a female animal that is barren cannot produce children or baby animals; INFERTILE **4** a tree or plant that is barren does not produce fruit or seeds **5** LITERARY without any useful results: *a pointless and barren discussion*

bar·rette /bə'rɛt/ *n.* [C] a small metal or plastic object used for holding a woman or girl's hair in a particular position

bar·ri·cade¹ /'bærə,keɪd/ *n.* [C] a temporary wall or fence across a road, door etc. that prevents people from going through: *Soldiers fired over the barricades at the rioters.*

barricade² *v.* [T] to protect or close something by building a barricade: *Miners in Spain barricaded roads and clashed with police.* | *Faustino barricaded himself inside his home.*

Bar·rie /'bæri/, **J.M.** /dʒeɪ ɛm/ (1860–1937) a Scottish writer of plays and novels

bar·ri·er /'bæriə/ *n.* [C] **1** a rule, problem etc. that prevents people from doing something, or limits what they can do: *Their attempt to reduce trade barriers failed.* | [+ to] *A lack of education is a barrier to many good jobs.* | *Ballet is entertainment without a language barrier* (=problem caused by not speaking someone's language). **2** a type of fence or gate that prevents people from moving in a particular direction: *The police put up barriers to hold back the crowds.* | *a plexiglas barrier* **3** a physical object that keeps two areas, people etc. apart: [+ between] *The mountains form a natural barrier between the two countries.* **4 the 10 second/40% etc. barrier** a level or amount of 10 seconds, 40% etc. that is seen as a limit which it is difficult to get beyond: *It may be possible to push the inflation rate below the 3% barrier.* —see also SOUND BARRIER

barrier reef /,... './ *n.* [C] a line of CORAL (=pink stone-like substance) separated from the shore by water

bar·ring /'bɑrɪŋ/ *prep.* unless there are: *Barring power outages, the only use for candles is decorative.*

bar·ri·o /'bæri,oʊ/ *n. plural* **barrios** [C] a part of an American town or city where many poor Spanish-speaking people live

bar·ris·ter /'bærɪstə/ *n.* [C] a lawyer in the U.K. who can argue cases in the higher law courts —compare SOLICITOR

bar·room /'bɑr,rum/ *n.* [C] INFORMAL a BAR

bar·row /'bæroʊ/ *n.* [C] **1** a WHEELBARROW **2** a small vehicle like a box on wheels, from which fruits, vegetables etc. used to be sold **3** a large pile of earth like a small hill that was put over an important grave in ancient times

Bar·row /'bæroʊ/, **Clyde** /klaɪd/ (1909–1934) a young U.S. criminal who stole money from banks and businesses with Bonnie Parker

Bar·ry·more /'bæri,mɔr/ the family name of several U.S. actors who were famous in the late 19th and early 20th centuries. Ethel Barrymore (1879–1959) and John Barrymore (1882–1942) were famous for performing in plays and movies, and Lionel Barrymore (1878–1954) was famous for performing in movies.

bar·tend·er /'bɑr,tɛndə/ *n.* [C] someone who makes, pours, and serves drinks in a bar or restaurant

bar·ter¹ /'bɑrtə/ *v.* [I,T] to exchange goods, work, or services for other goods or services rather than for money: [barter (with sb) for sth] *We bartered with the local vendors for food in the bazaar.* | [barter sth for sth] *Pete barters plumbing or electrical work for groceries.*

barter² *n.* [U] **1** a system of exchanging goods and services for other goods and services rather than using money: *Many Soviet citizens were able to get what they needed by barter.* **2** goods or services that are exchanged in this kind of system: *Beads were used as barter in the early days of settlement.*

Barth /bɑrt, bɑrθ/, **Karl** /kɑrl/ (1886–1968) a Swiss Protestant religious teacher and writer

Barthes /bɑrt/, **Ro·land** /'roʊlɑn/ (1915–1980) a French writer famous for developing STRUCTURALISM

Bar·thol·o·mew /bɑr'θɑlə,myu/ in the Bible, one of the 12 APOSTLES

Bar·tók /'bɑrtɑk/, **Bé·la** /'beɪlə/ (1881–1945) a Hungarian musician who wrote CLASSICAL music

Bar·ton /'bɑrtn/, **Cla·ra** /'klærə/ (1821–1912) a U.S. nurse who started the American Red Cross in 1881

Ba·ruch /bə'ruk/ a book in the Apocrypha of the Protestant Bible and in the Old Testament of the Catholic Bible

Baruch, Ber·nard /bə'nɑrd/ (1870–1965) a U.S. FINANCIER and ECONOMIST who was a financial adviser to four U.S. presidents

Ba·rysh·ni·kov /bə'rɪʃnɪ,kɑf/, **Mik·hail** /mɪ'kaɪl/ (1948–) a Russian BALLET dancer and CHOREOGRAPHER who left the Soviet Union and came to live in the U.S.

ba·salt /bə'sɔlt, 'beɪsɔlt/ *n.* [U] a type of dark green-black rock

base¹ /beɪs/ *v.* [T] to establish or use somewhere as the main place for your business or work: [base sth in] *The toy company is based in Trenton, New Jersey.*

base sth on/upon sth *phr. v.* [T often passive] to use particular information or facts as a point from which to develop an idea, plan etc.: *The musical play is based on Hammett's "Thin Man" series.* | *Discrimination based on race or sex is forbidden by law.*

base² *n.*
1 lowest part [C usually singular] the lowest part of something, or the surface at the bottom of something: *a black vase with a round base* | [+ of] *Pour the concrete around the base of the post.* | *the base of a triangle* | *Spirit Lake is at the base of Mount St. Helens.*
2 knowledge/ideas [U] the most important part of something, from which new ideas develop: *India has a good scientific research base.* | *Both French and Spanish come from a Latin base.* | [+ for] *A good elementary school education provides a solid base for the rest of a child's school years.*
3 company/organization [C,U] the main place from which a group, company, or organization controls its activities: *Cuba was seen as a base for Communist activity throughout Latin America.* | *Microsoft's base is in Redmond, Washington.*
4 military [C] a place where people in a military organization live and work: *a naval base*
5 people/groups [C usually singular] the people,

money, groups etc. that form the main part of something: *Inviting new companies into the area is attempt to strengthen the city's economic base* (=things that produce jobs and money). | *The company's customer base* (=people who buy its goods) *is growing.* | *New jobs in the area will improve the city's tax base* (=the people who pay taxes). | *Volkswagen needed a manufacturing base* (=companies that make things) *in Asia to gain a share of the market.* —see also POWER BASE

6 body/plant [C usually singular] the point where part of your body or part of a plant joins with the rest: *Put a liquid fertilizer around the base of each plant.*

7 off base INFORMAL completely wrong: *If he thinks there was any discrimination involved, he's way off base.*

8 touch base (with sb) to talk with someone in order to find out what is happening about something: *It's important to touch base with our allies in this issue.*

9 sports [C] one of the four places that a player must touch in order to get a point in games such as baseball or SOFTBALL —see picture at BASEBALL

10 cover/touch all the bases to prepare for or deal with a situation thoroughly: *The police have called in experts to make sure they've covered all the bases.*

11 substance/mixture [singular,U] the main part of a substance to which something else is later added: *You should paint the outside walls with an oil base.* —see also BASE METAL

12 chemistry [C] TECHNICAL a chemical substance that combines with an acid to form a SALT[1] (5)

13 numbers [C usually singular] TECHNICAL the number in relation to which a number system or mathematical table is built up

base[3] *adj.* LITERARY not having good moral principles: *base passions*

base·ball /'beɪsbɔl/ *n.* **1** [U] an outdoor game between two teams of nine players, in which players try to get points by hitting a ball and running around four bases **2** [C] the ball used in this game

baseball cap /'.. ,./ *n.* [C] a hat that fits closely around your head, with a stiff round part that sticks out at the front —see picture at HAT

base·board /'beɪsbɔrd/ *n.* [C] a narrow board fastened to the bottom of indoor walls where they meet the floor

base·less /'beɪslɪs/ *adj.* FORMAL not based on facts or good reasons: *baseless rumors*

base·line /'beɪslaɪn/ *n.* **1** [C usually singular] TECHNICAL a standard measurement or fact to which other measurements or facts are compared, especially in medicine or science **2** the line at the back of the court in games such as tennis or VOLLEYBALL **3** the area that a player must run within, on a baseball field

base·man /'beɪsmən/ *n.* [C] *plural* **basemen** /-mən/ **first/second/third baseman** the person who plays one of three positions near the BASES in baseball

base·ment /'beɪsmənt/ *n.* [C] a room or area that is under the level of the ground —see picture on page 423

base metal /,. '.., '. ,../ *n.* [C,U] a metal that is not very valuable, such as iron or lead

bas·es /'beɪsiz/ *n.* the plural of BASIS

bash[1] /bæʃ/ *v.* [I,T] INFORMAL **1** to hit someone or something hard, in a way that causes pain or damage: [bash sth on/against sth] *I bashed my toe on the bedpost.* | [+ into/against] *He bashed into the car in front of him.* | **bash down/in/up etc.** (=destroy something by hitting it often) *They bashed in my locker and broke off the door.* **2** to criticize someone or something a lot: *The local newspaper has recently been bashing the city's court system.* —see also BASHING

bash[2] *n.* [C] INFORMAL a party or celebration: *a birthday bash*

bash·ful /'bæʃfəl/ *adj.* easily embarrassed in social situations; shy: *a bashful smile* | *Sheila was never bashful about asking a question.* —**bashfully** *adv.* —**bashfulness** *n.* [U]

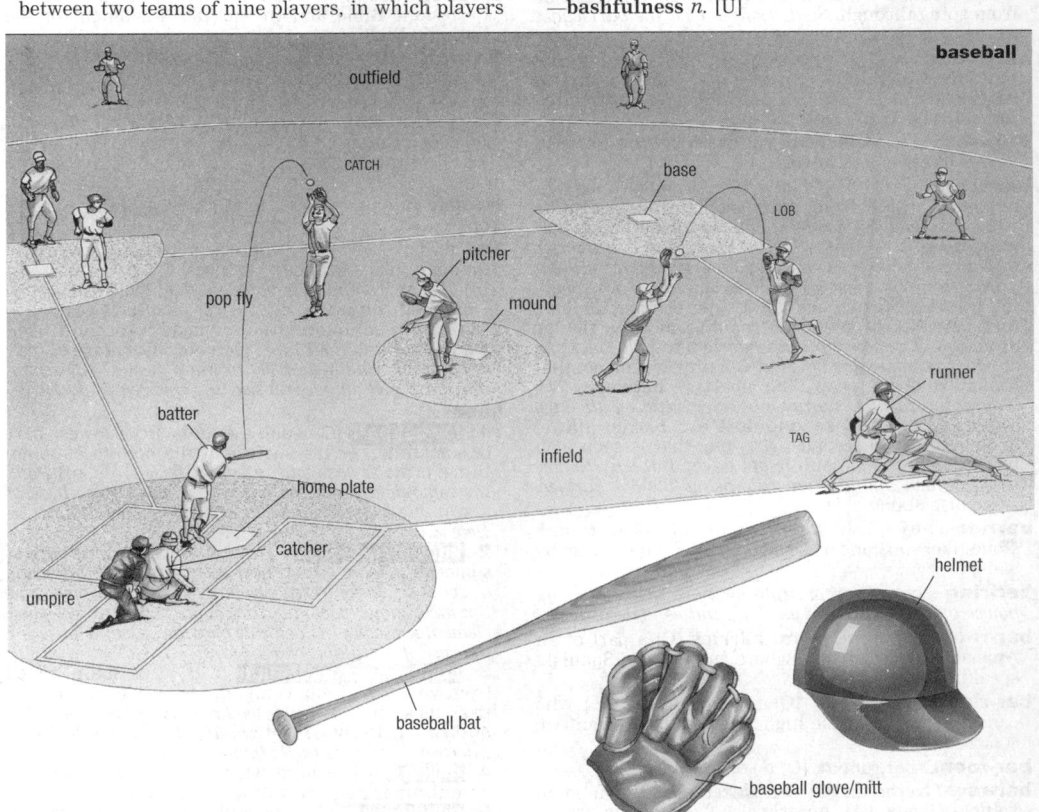

baseball

outfield

CATCH

base

LOB

pitcher

pop fly

mound

runner

batter

infield

TAG

home plate

catcher

umpire

helmet

baseball bat

baseball glove/mitt

bash·ing /'bæʃɪŋ/ n. **1 Congress-bashing/lawyer-bashing etc.** the act of criticizing a particular person or group: *There was a lot of Democrat-bashing in the last election.* **2 gay-bashing/Asian-bashing etc.** the act of physically attacking someone who belongs to a group of people the attacker dislikes: *Rivera was killed in a gay-bashing incident.*

Ba·sho /'bɑʃoʊ/, **Mat·su·o** /mæt'suoʊ/ (1644–1694) a Japanese poet famous as the first writer of HAIKU

Ba·sic /'beɪsɪk/ n. [U] a commonly used computer language

ba·sic /'beɪsɪk/ adj. **1** forming the main or most necessary part of something: *There are two basic problems here.* | *Tax money pays for basic services. People were standing in lines to buy basic goods such as bread, cheese, and milk.* | *the basic principles of mathematics* **2** at the simplest or least developed level: *a basic knowledge of scientific principles* | *The farm lacks even basic equipment.* | *basic healthcare for children* **3** [only before noun] basic desires, rights etc. are ones that everyone has: *Basic human rights are still denied in many countries.* **4 basic salary/pay etc.** the amount of money that you are paid before any special payments are added —see also BASICS

ba·si·cal·ly /'beɪsɪkli/ adv. **1** [sentence adverb] SPOKEN used when giving the most important reason or fact about something, or a simple explanation of something: *Basically, you just have to write what the teachers want.* | *Well, basically, she's just a lot of fun to work with.* **2** in the main or most important ways, without considering additional details or differences: *Norwegian and Danish are basically the same.* **3** in a very simple way, with only the things that are completely necessary: *The office was very basically equipped.*

ba·sics /'beɪsɪks/ n. [plural] **1** the most important and necessary facts about something, from which other possibilities and ideas may develop: *You can do fancier things later on, after you've learned the basics.* | *a class in **the basics of** first aid* **2 get/go back to basics** to return to teaching or doing the most important or the simplest part of something: *A lot of parents want the schools to get back to basics* (=to teach reading, writing, and mathematics thoroughly).

basic train·ing /ˌ.. '../ n. [U] the period when a new soldier learns military rules and does a lot of exercise

Ba·sie /'beɪsi/, **Count** /kaʊnt/ (1904–1984) a U.S. JAZZ musician who played the piano and led a famous band

ba·sil /'beɪzəl/ n. [U] a sweet-smelling HERB used in cooking

ba·sil·i·ca /bə'sɪlɪkə/ n. [C] a church in the shape of a long room with a round end: *the basilica of St. Peter's*

bas·i·lisk /'bæsəˌlɪsk, 'bæzə-/ n. [C] an imaginary animal in ancient stories, that is like a lizard and is supposed to be able to kill people by looking at them

ba·sin /'beɪsən/ n. [C] **1** an area of land that is lower at the center than at the edges, especially one from which water runs down into a river: *the Amazon Basin* **2** a large bowl, especially one for water **3** a bowl-shaped area containing water: *Water splashed in the basin of the fountain.*

ba·sis /'beɪsɪs/ n. plural bases /-siz/ [C] **1** the facts, ideas, or things from which something can be developed: *His claims have no **basis in fact**.* | [+ for] *Hamburger was used as the basis for many dinner recipes.* | [+ of] *Addams' characters, first drawn in the "New Yorker", **became the basis of** the television series.* | *The fear of Communism **formed the basis of** American foreign policy at that time.* **2 on the basis of sth** because of a particular fact or situation: *Employers are not allowed to discriminate on the basis of race or sex.* **3 on a daily/weekly etc. basis** every day, week etc.: *Meetings are held on a monthly basis.* **4 on a voluntary/part-time etc. basis** a system or agreement by which someone or something is VOLUNTARY etc.: *Donna was hired on a freelance basis.*

bask /bæsk/ v. [I] **1** to enjoy the approval or attention that you are getting from other people: [+ in] *Anderson basked in the glory of the victory.* **2 bask in sb's reflected glory** to share some of the importance and praise that belongs to someone close to you: *Perry happily basked in the reflected glory of his famous golf partner.* **3** to enjoy sitting or lying in the heat of the sun or a fire: [+ in] *A lizard was basking in the heat of the afternoon sun.*

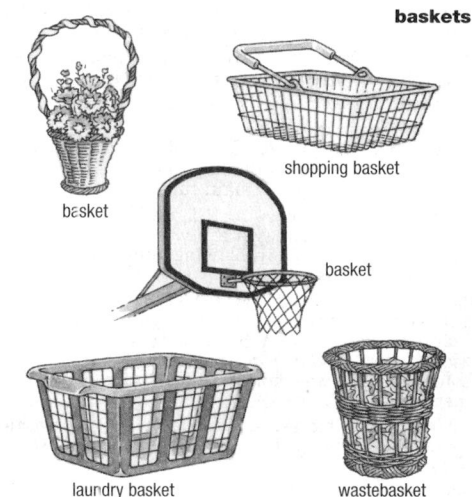

baskets

basket

shopping basket

basket

laundry basket

wastebasket

bas·ket /'bæskɪt/ n. [C] **1** a container made of thin pieces of plastic, wire, or wood woven together, used to carry things or put things in: *a shopping basket* | *a basket full of fruit* **2** a net with a hole at the bottom hung from a metal ring, through which the ball is thrown in basketball: *Johnson **made a basket** (=threw the ball into the basket) just as the buzzer sounded to end the game.* | *Vic and Tommy are out **shooting baskets** (=trying to throw the ball through the basket) in the park.* —see also **put/have all your eggs in one basket** (EGG[1] (4)), WASTEPAPER BASKET

bas·ket·ball /'bæskɪtˌbɔl/ n. [U] **1** a game played indoors between two teams of five players, in which each team tries to win points by throwing a ball through a net **2** the ball used in the game

basket case /'.. ˌ./ n. [C] INFORMAL someone who is so nervous or anxious that they cannot deal with simple situations: *Mom was a complete basket case at our wedding.*

bas·ket·ry /'bæskətri/ also **bas·ket·work** /'bæskətˌwək/ n. [U] **1** baskets or other objects made by weaving together thin dried branches **2** the skill of making baskets

bas·ma·ti rice /bɑzˌmɑti 'raɪs, bæs-/ n. [U] a type of high quality rice, often eaten with Indian food

basque /bæsk/ n. [C] a piece of underwear or part of a dress for a woman that covers her from under her arms to the top of her legs

bas-re·lief /ˌbɑ rɪ'lif/ n. [C,U] TECHNICAL a style of art in which stone or wood is cut so that shapes are raised above the surrounding surface —compare HIGH RELIEF

bass[1] /beɪs/ n. **1** [C] a man whose singing or speaking voice is very low **2** [singular] the part of a piece of music that this person sings **3** [U] the lower half of the whole range of musical notes —compare TREBLE[3] (1) **4** [C] a BASS GUITAR: *The band features Willie Dixon **on bass** (=playing the bass guitar).* **5** [C] a DOUBLE BASS —**bass** adj., adv.

bass[2] /bæs/ n. [C] plural bass or bases a fish that can be eaten and lives both in rivers and the ocean

bass clef /ˌbeɪs 'klɛf/ n. [C] a sign (𝄢) at the beginning of a line of written music that shows that the top line of the STAVE is the A below MIDDLE C

bass drum /ˌbeɪs ˈdrʌm/ n. [C] a type of large drum used for giving the main beat in a piece of music

bas·set /ˈbæsɪt/ also **basset hound** /ˈ.. ./ n. [C] a dog with short legs and long ears, used for hunting

Basse-terre /bɑsˈtɛr/ the capital city of St. Kitts and Nevis

bass gui·tar /ˌbeɪs gɪˈtɑr/ also **bass** n. [C] an electric musical instrument with four strings and a long neck, that plays low notes —**bassist** n. [C]

bas·si·net /ˌbæsɪˈnɛt/ n. [C] a small bed that looks like a basket, used for a very young baby

bass·ist /ˈbeɪsɪst/ n. [C] someone who plays a BASS GUITAR or a DOUBLE BASS

bass line /ˈbeɪs laɪn/ n. [C usually singular] a series of notes that make up the low sounds and RHYTHM of a piece of music, or its main tune

bas·soon /bəˈsun, bæ-/ n. [C] a very long wooden musical instrument with a low sound, that is held upright and played by blowing into a thin curved metal pipe —**bassoonist** n. [C]

bas·tard /ˈbæstɚd/ n. [C] 1 SPOKEN, OFFENSIVE a man who you do not like or are angry with: *You're such a lazy bastard!* | [**be a bastard to/with sb**] *He's a real bastard to his wife and kids.* 2 OLD-FASHIONED someone who was born to parents who were not married

bas·tard·ize /ˈbæstɚˌdaɪz/ v. [T] to spoil something by changing its good parts: *a bastardized version of the play*

bas·tard·y /ˈbæstɚdi/ n. [U] OLD USE the situation of having parents who were not married to each other when you were born

baste /beɪst/ v. [I,T] 1 to pour liquid or melted fat over meat that is cooking 2 to fasten cloth with long loose stitches, in order to hold it together so that you can sew it correctly later

bas·tion /ˈbæstʃən/ n. [C] 1 something that protects a way of life, principle etc. that seems likely to change or disappear: [+ **of**] *The region is a bastion of right-wing Republicanism.* 2 a place where a country or army has strong military defenses: *Pearl Harbor was the principal American bastion in the Pacific.* 3 TECHNICAL a part of a castle wall that sticks out from the rest

bat¹ /bæt/ n. [C] 1 a small animal like a mouse that flies around at night —see also FRUIT BAT 2 a long wooden stick with a special shape that is used in some sports and games: *a baseball bat* 3 **like a bat out of hell** INFORMAL very fast: *I drove like a bat out of hell to the hospital.* 4 **do sth right off the bat** INFORMAL to do something immediately: *I asked him to help, and he said yes right off the bat.* 5 **be at bat** to be the person who is trying to hit the ball in a game of baseball 6 **old bat** SPOKEN an old woman who is not nice and is often in a bad mood 7 **have bats in the belfry** OLD-FASHIONED to be slightly crazy —see also **as blind as a bat** (BLIND¹ (1))

bat² v. **batted, batting** 1 [I,T] to hit the ball with a bat in baseball 2 [I,T] to hit something lightly with your hand: [+ **at**] *Our kittens had fun batting at balls of paper.* 3 **not bat an eye/eyelid** INFORMAL to not seem to be shocked, surprised, or embarrassed: *He used to tell the worst lies without batting an eye.* 4 **bat your eyes/eyelashes** if a woman bats her eyes, she opens and closes them quickly, especially in order to look attractive to men 5 **go to bat for sb** INFORMAL to help and support someone: *Rene went to bat for me with the director and I ended up getting the part.* 6 **bat a thousand** also **bat a 1000** INFORMAL to be very successful: *She's been batting a thousand ever since she got that new job.*

bat sth ↔ around phr. v. [T] INFORMAL to discuss the good and bad parts of a plan, idea etc.

bat·boy /ˈbætˌbɔɪ/ n. [C] a boy whose job is to look after the equipment of a BASEBALL team

batch /bætʃ/ n. [C] 1 a quantity of food, medicine etc. that is produced or prepared at the same time: *a batch of cookies* 2 a group of people or things that arrive or are dealt with together: *the latest batch of reports*

batch pro·ces·sing /ˈ. ˌ.../ n. [U] a type of computer system in which the computer does several jobs one after the other, without needing instructions between each job

bat·ed /ˈbeɪtɪd/ adj. **with bated breath** feeling very anxious or excited: *The soldiers' families waited with bated breath for news.*

bath /bæθ/ n. [C] 1 an act of washing your body in a bathtub | **take/have a bath** (=wash yourself in a bathtub) | *Dan, will you give the kids a bath tonight* (=wash them)? 2 water that you sit or lie in to wash yourself: *I love to soak in a hot bath.* | *Lisa ran a bath* (=put water in a bathtub) *for herself.* 3 a word meaning a "bathroom," used by people who sell houses: *a three-bedroom, two-bath house* 4 **take a bath** INFORMAL to lose money, especially in a business deal: *We really took a bath on that deal.* 5 a container full of liquid in which something is placed for a particular purpose: *a bath of black dye* 6 **baths** a public building where people could go in past times to wash themselves: *the Roman baths* —see also BIRDBATH, BLOODBATH, BUBBLE BATH, **throw the baby out with the bath water** (THROW¹ (28)), TURKISH BATH

bathe /beɪð/ v. 1 [I,T] to wash yourself or someone else in a bathtub: *Brenda bathed and changed the baby.* 2 **be bathed in light/moonlight etc.** LITERARY an area or building that is bathed in light has light shining onto it in a way that makes it look pleasant or attractive: *The beach was bathed in bright sunlight.* 3 [T] to wash or cover part of your body with a liquid, especially as a medical treatment: *A nurse bathed her feet in medicine.* 4 **be bathed in tears/sweat etc.** LITERARY to be covered in tears, SWEAT etc.

bath·er /ˈbeɪðɚ/ n. [C] 1 someone who is taking a bath 2 OLD-FASHIONED someone who is swimming

bathing suit /ˈbeɪðɪŋ ˌsut/ n. [C] a piece of clothing that you wear for swimming —see also SWIMSUIT, SWIMMING TRUNKS

bath mat /ˈ. ./ n. [C] a piece of thick cloth that you put on the floor next to the bathtub

ba·thos /ˈbeɪθɑs/ n. [U] LITERARY a sudden change from discussing something that is beautiful, moral, or serious to something that is ordinary, silly, or not important: *a drama that is full of bathos*

bath·robe /ˈbæθroʊb/ n. [C] a long loose piece of clothing shaped like a coat, that you wear especially before or after you take a SHOWER or bath

bath·room /ˈbæθrum/ n. 1 [C] a room in a house where there is a toilet, a SINK, and a bathtub or SHOWER —see picture on page 423 2 [C] a room where there is a toilet, especially in a public place: *Excuse me, where's the bathroom?* 3 **go to the bathroom** to use a toilet: *Mommy, Mommy, I gotta go to the bathroom.*

bath salts /ˈ. ./ n. [plural] a substance that you put in bath water to make it smell nice

bath tow·el /ˈ. ˌ./ n. [C] a large TOWEL (=piece of material for drying yourself)

bath·tub /ˈbæθtʌb/ n. [C] a long large container that you fill with water and sit or lie in to wash yourself

bath·y·sphere /ˈbæθɪˌsfɪr/ n. [C] TECHNICAL a strong container used for going deep under the ocean, especially to look at plants, animals etc.

ba·tik /bəˈtik, bæ-/ n. 1 [U] a way of printing colored patterns on cloth that involves putting WAX over some parts of the cloth 2 [C,U] cloth that has been colored in this way

bat mitz·vah /ˌbæt ˈmɪtsvə/ n. [C] 1 the religious ceremony held when a Jewish girl reaches the age of 13 and is considered an adult in her religion 2 a girl for whom this ceremony is held —compare BAR MITZVAH

ba·ton /bəˈtɑn/ n. [C] 1 a short thin stick used by a CONDUCTOR (=the leader of a group of musicians) to direct the music 2 a light metal stick that is spun and thrown into the air by a MAJORETTE **3** a short thick stick used as a weapon by a police officer **4** a short light stick that is passed from one person to another during a race

Bat·on Rouge /ˌbætn 'ruːʒ/ the capital city of the U.S. state of Louisiana

bat·tal·ion /bə'tælyən/ n. [C] a large group of soldiers consisting of several companies (COMPANY (8))

bat·ten¹ /'bætn/ v. **batten down the hatches a)** INFORMAL to prepare yourself for a period of difficulty or trouble: *Businesses are focused on survival – everyone's battening down the hatches.* **b)** to firmly close the entrances to the lower part of a ship or SUBMARINE

batten² n. [C] a long narrow piece of wood that boards or SHINGLES are fastened to, or that is attached to other pieces of wood to keep them in place

bat·ter¹ /'bætɚ/ n. **1** [C,U] a mixture of flour, eggs, milk etc., used for making cakes, some types of bread etc.: *pancake batter* **2** [C] the person who is trying to hit the ball in baseball —see picture at BASEBALL

batter² v. [always + adv./prep.,T] **1** to hit someone or something again and again, in a way that hurts someone or causes damage: *Each year, perhaps 4 million women are battered by their husbands.* | [batter sth at/on/against etc.] *The storm battered the ship against the rocks.* **2** to make someone suffer from a loss, criticism etc.: *His campaign team was battered by a humiliating defeat in Iowa.* —**battering** n. [C,U]

bat·tered /'bætɚd/ adj. **1 battered woman/spouse etc.** a woman, wife, husband etc. who has been violently treated by their husband, BOYFRIEND, wife etc.: *The agency helps battered women.* **2** old and in bad condition: *a battered 1969 Ford*

bat·ter·ing ram /'... ,./ n. [C] a long heavy piece of wood or metal used to break through walls or doors

bat·ter·y /'bætəri/ n. plural **batteries 1** [C] an object that provides a supply of electricity for something such as a radio or a car: *This tape player operates on six C batteries.* | *I tried to start the car, but the battery was dead* (=stopped producing electricity). —see picture at ENGINE **2** [U] LAW the crime of hitting someone: *Ferguson was found guilty of battery.* —see also ASSAULT AND BATTERY **3 a battery of sth** a group of many things of the same type: *a battery of medical and psychological tests* **4** [C] several large guns used together: *He commands a battery of artillery.* **5 recharge your batteries** INFORMAL to rest or relax in order to get back your energy

bat·tle¹ /'bætl/ n. [C]

1 between armies [C,U] a fight between opposing armies, groups of ships etc., especially one that is part of a larger war: *the Battle of Bunker Hill* | *Sargent Merriman was killed in battle in 1943.* | *The vehicles are used to take troops into battle.*

2 between opponents [C] a situation in which opposing groups or people compete or argue with each other when trying to achieve success or control: *a long and costly legal battle* | [+ for] *a battle for the league title* | [+ between] *a four-month-long political battle between Congress and the White House* | [+ with] *a battle with Dawson for the mayor's job*

3 attempt an attempt to solve a difficult problem or change a bad situation: [+ against] *the battle against drug and alcohol abuse* | [+ with] *Williams died after a long battle with lung cancer.*

4 be half the battle to be a difficult or important part of what you have to do: *Just getting an interview is half the battle.*

5 fight/wage/be a losing battle to try to do something without being able to succeed: *Landon fought a losing battle with cancer.* | *They're trying to keep the Navajo language alive, but it may be a losing battle.*

6 do battle (with sb) to argue with someone or fight against someone: *The citizens group said they are prepared to do battle with City Hall over the passage of the bill.*

7 a battle of wits a disagreement that opposing sides try to win by using their intelligence

8 the battle of the sexes the relationship between

men and women when it is considered as a fight for power

9 the battle of the bulge INFORMAL, HUMOROUS to try to lose weight

battle² v. **1** [I,T] to try very hard to achieve something when this is very difficult: [battle sth] *Firefighters battled flames at a Detroit factory.* | [+ against/with] *Minorities must still battle against discrimination.* | [+ for] *Capra battled for freedom as a filmmaker.* | [battle to do sth] *Connors was battling to stay in the tournament.* | *They trailed 48–37, but **battled back** (=worked hard to win from a losing position) and won 57–51.* **2 battle it out** to keep fighting or opposing each other until one person or team wins: *The Yankees and the Red Soxs are battling it out for the championship.* **3** [I] LITERARY to take part in a fight or war: [+ with] *Rival gangs battled with knives and chains.*

battle ax, battle axe /'.. ,./ n. [C] **1** INFORMAL a woman who is unfriendly and not nice, and who tries to control other people **2** a large AX (=tool for cutting wood) used as a weapon in past times

battle cruis·er /'.. ,../ n. [C] a large fast ship used in war

battle cry /'.. ,./ n. [C usually singular] **1** a phrase used to encourage people, especially members of a political organization: *"Power to the people!" was their battle cry.* **2** a loud shout used in war to encourage your side and frighten the enemy

battle fa·tigue /'.. ,./ n. [U] a type of mental illness caused by the frightening experiences of war, in which someone feels very anxious and upset

bat·tle·field /'bætl,fild/ n. [C] **1** a place where a battle is being fought or has been fought **2** a BATTLEGROUND (1)

bat·tle·front /'bætl,frʌnt/ n. [singular] the place on a BATTLEFIELD where the opponents meet and start fighting

bat·tle·ground /'bætl,graʊnd/ also **bat·tle·field** /'bætl,fild/ n. [C] **1** a battlefield **2** a subject that people disagree or argue a lot about: *Prayer in schools has become a political battleground.*

bat·tle·ments /'bætlmənts/ n. [plural] a low wall around the top of a castle, that has spaces to shoot guns or ARROWS through

bat·tle·ship /'bætl,ʃɪp/ n. [C] a very large ship used in war, with very big guns

bat·ty /'bæti/ adj. INFORMAL crazy

bau·ble /'bɔbəl, 'ba-/ n. [C] a cheap piece of jewelry

Baude·laire /boʊd'lɛr/, **Charles** (1821–1867) a French poet

baud rate /'bɔd ,reɪt/ n. [C] TECHNICAL a measurement of how fast information is sent to or from a computer, for example through a telephone line

Baum /baʊm/, **L. Frank** (1856–1919) a U.S. writer who wrote the book "The Wonderful Wizard of Oz"

baux·ite /'bɔksaɪt, 'bak-/ n. [U] a soft substance that ALUMINUM (=a type of metal) is obtained from

Ba·var·i·a /bə'vɛriə/ a state in southeast Germany —**Bavarian** n., adj.

bawd·y /'bɔdi/ adj. bawdy songs, jokes, stories etc. are about sex and are funny, enjoyable, and often noisy: *a bawdy new comedy* —**bawdily** adv. —**bawdiness** n. [U]

bawdy house /'.. ,./ n. [C] OLD USE a BROTHEL

bawl /bɔl/ v. **1** [I] INFORMAL to cry loudly: *I couldn't help it, I just started bawling.* **2** [I,T] also **bawl out** to shout in a loud angry voice: *The captain stood at the front, bawling orders.*

bawl sb ↔ **out** phr. v. [T] INFORMAL to speak angrily to someone because they have done something wrong: *The coach bawled us out for being late to practice.*

bay¹ /beɪ/ n. plural **bays** [C]
1 ocean a part of the ocean that is enclosed by a curve in the land: *sailboats on the bay* | *the San Francisco Bay*

2 keep/hold sth at bay to prevent something dangerous or bad from happening or from coming too close: *Sandbags kept the floodwaters at bay.* | *The government hopes to keep inflation at bay.*
3 area an area within a larger area that is separated by shelves, walls etc.: *the space shuttle's cargo bay*
4 for vehicles a place where a vehicle can park for a short time: *a loading bay*
5 tree also **bay tree** a tree that has leaves which smell sweet and are often used in cooking
6 horse a horse that is a reddish brown color

bay² *v.* **bays, bayed, baying** [I] **1** if a dog bays, it makes a long high noise; HOWL: [+ **at**] *In the distance, wolves were baying at the moon.* **2** to speak or behave in a way that reminds people of a noisy dog: [+ **for**] *It was a room full of young, educated men baying for money on the bond market.*

bay³ *adj.* a bay horse is a reddish-brown color

Bay A·re·a, the /'. ,.../ the area of land around the San Francisco Bay in California, including cities such as San Francisco, Oakland, Berkeley, Palo Alto, and San José

bay leaf /'. ./ *n.* [C] a sweet-smelling leaf from the bay tree, often used in cooking

bay·o·net¹ /'beɪənɪt, -,nɛt, ,beɪə'nɛt/ *n.* [C] a long knife that is attached to the end of a RIFLE (=long gun)

bayonet² *v.* [T] to push the point of a bayonet into someone

bay·ou /'baɪu, 'baɪoʊ/ *n.* [C] a large area of water in the southeast U.S. that moves very slowly and has many water plants

bay win·dow /, '. ./ *n.* [C] a window that sticks out of the wall of a house, usually with glass on three sides

ba·zaar /bə'zɑr/ *n.* [C] **1** a place, usually outdoors, where a lot of different things are sold, especially in India or the Middle East **2** an occasion when a lot of people sell different things to collect money for a good purpose: *a church bazaar*

ba·zoo·ka /bə'zukə/ *n.* [C] a long light gun that rests on your shoulder and is used especially for firing at TANKS

B-ball /'. ./ *n.* [U] INFORMAL basketball

BB gun /'bibi ,gʌn/ *n.* [C] a gun that uses air pressure to shoot small round metal balls; AIR GUN

BBQ /'bɑrbɪ,kyu/ *n.* [C] an abbreviation of BARBECUE

B.C. *adv.* Before Christ; used after a date to show that it was before the birth of Jesus Christ: *The Great Pyramid dates from around 2600 B.C.* —compare A.D.

B.C.E. Before Common Era; used after a date to show that it is before the birth of Jesus Christ —compare C.E.

be¹ /bi/ *auxiliary verb* **1** used with a present participle to form the CONTINUOUS (2) tenses of verbs: [**be doing sth**] *I'm still living with my parents.* | *Angela was reading when the phone rang.* | *They've been asking a lot of questions.* | *Bruce is always telling us stories.* **2** used with past participles to form the PASSIVE²: *Smoking is not permitted on this flight.* | *I was shown a copy of the contract.* | *The house is being painted.* | *His arrival may have been delayed by snow.* **3** used to show what is or was planned: *Talks were to have begun two weeks ago.* | *I'll be leaving in about half an hour.* **4** FORMAL used to show what someone should do or what should happen: *What am I to tell her (=what should I tell her?) when she finds out?* | *He is more to be (=should be more) pitied than feared.* **5** used to show that cannot or could not happen: *Walker was nowhere to be found.* **6** used to give an order or to tell someone about a rule: *Fees are to be paid before classes begin.* | *The children are to go to bed by 8 o'clock.* **7** used to show what had to happen or what did happen: *It was to be one of the most important judgments the court made.* **8** used in CONDITIONAL² (2) sentences that describe a situation that does not or could not exist: *If Gore were to run, would you vote for him?* | *I know what I'd do if he*

were my son. **9** OLD USE used instead of "have" to form the PERFECT³ tenses of some verbs: *Christ is risen (=has risen) from the dead.*

be² *v.* **1** [linking verb] used to show that someone or something is the same as the subject: *Hi, it's me.* | *These are Len's dogs.* | *Christie is my girlfriend.* | *The truth is, I don't have enough money.* | *The problem is trying to get it done on time.* | *The goal is to raise about $200,000.* **2** [I always + adv./prep.] used to show position or time: *Where are the boys?* | *Jane's upstairs.* | *Mr. Smith's office is on the third floor.* | *How long has she been here?* | *The phone is in the hall.* | *When is the wedding?* **3** [linking verb] used to show that someone or something belongs to a group or has a particular quality: *Snow is white.* | *Horses are animals.* | *She wants to be a doctor when she grows up.* | *These shoes are mine.* | *We were lost.* | *I'm not ready.* | *Be careful!* | *It's hot today.* | *A saw is for cutting wood.* **4** used in short phrases and questions: *It's cold, isn't it?* | *You're not leaving, are you?* | *"That's not your coat" "Yes, it is!"* **5** [linking verb] used after "there" to show that something exists: *There's a hole in your sweater.* **6 be that as it may** FORMAL used to say that even though you accept that something is true it does not change a situation: *"Everyone knows it was your idea." "Be that as it may, we can present it together."* **7** [I] to exist: *That's just how it is.* **8 the be-all (and end-all)** the most important part of a situation or of someone's life: *Profit is important, but it is not the be-all and end-all.* —see also **let sb/sth be** (LET (8))

be- /bɪ/ *prefix* **1** [in verbs] used to mean that someone or something becomes a particular thing or is treated in a particular way: *Don't belittle him (=say he is unimportant).* | *He befriended me (=became my friend).* **2** [in adjectives] LITERARY used to mean that someone is wearing or is covered by a particular thing: *a bespectacled boy (=wearing glasses)* | *a bejeweled woman (=covered in jewels)*

beach¹ /bitʃ/ *n.* [C] *plural* **beaches** an area of sand or small stones at the edge of an ocean or a lake: *We sat there watching the waves breaking on the beach.* —see Usage Note at SHORE¹ —see picture on page 428

beach² *v.* [T] **1** if a WHALE or other sea animal beaches itself or is beached, it swims onto the shore and cannot get back in the water **2** to pull a boat onto the shore away from the water

beach ball /'. ,./ *n.* [C] a large colored plastic ball that you blow air into and use for playing games on the beach

beach bun·ny /'. ,../ *n.* [C] INFORMAL a very attractive young woman at a beach, usually considered offensive by women

beach chair /'. ./ *n.* [C] a folding chair with a seat and back made of cloth or plastic, which is used outdoors, especially at the beach

beach·comb·er /'bitʃ,koumə/ *n.* [C] someone who searches beaches for things that might be useful

beach·front /'bitʃfrʌnt/ *adj.* a beachfront building, piece of land etc. is on the edge of a beach: *beachfront hotels*

beach·head /'bitʃhɛd/ *n.* [C] an area of shore that has been taken from an enemy by force and where soldiers can go onto the land from ships

beach·wear /'bitʃwɛr/ *n.* [U] clothes that you wear for swimming, lying on the beach etc.

bea·con /'bikən/ *n.* [C] **1** a light that is put somewhere to warn or guide people, vehicles, or aircraft **2** a radio or RADAR signal used by aircraft or boats to help them find their position and direction: *Navigation was helped by a radio beacon set up by the Army on the island.* **3** a person, idea etc. that guides or encourages you: [+ **of**] *Havel has become his country's beacon of democracy and hope.* **4** a fire on top of a hill, used in past times as a signal

bead /bid/ *n.* [C] **1** one of a set of small, usually round, pieces of glass, wood, plastic etc., that you can put on a string and wear as jewelry **2** a small drop of liquid such as water or blood: *Beads of moisture have formed on the inside of the window.* **3 draw a bead on sb/sth** to aim carefully before shooting a weapon

bead·ed /'bidɪd/ adj. **1** decorated with beads: *a beaded evening gown* **2 beaded with sweat/perspiration** having drops of SWEAT (=liquid produced by your body when you are hot) on your skin

bead·ing /'bidɪŋ/ n. [U] **1** a lot of beads sewn close together on clothes, leather etc. as decoration **2** long thin pieces of wood or stone that are used as a decoration on the edges of walls, furniture etc.

bead·y /'bidi/ adj. **1** beady eyes are small, round, shiny, and unattractive, especially said about someone who you think looks dishonest or strange **2 have/keep your beady eye(s) on sb/sth** HUMOROUS to watch someone or something very carefully

bea·gle /'bigəl/ n. [C] a dog with short legs and smooth fur, sometimes used in hunting

beak /bik/ n. [C] **1** the hard pointed mouth of a bird —compare BILL¹ (7) —see picture on page 429 **2** HUMOROUS a large pointed nose

beak·er /'bikə/ n. [C] a glass cup with straight sides that is used in chemistry for measuring and heating liquids

beam¹ /bim/ n. [C] **1 a)** a line of light shining from the sun, a lamp etc.: [+ of] *the beam of the headlight* **b)** a line of light, energy etc. that you often cannot see: *a laser beam* | [+ of] *a beam of electrons* **2** a long heavy piece of wood or metal used in building houses, bridges etc.: *a 55-ton concrete beam* **3** a BALANCE BEAM **4** TECHNICAL the widest part of a ship from side to side **5** a wide happy smile: [+ of] *a beam of satisfaction*

beam² v. **1** [I] to smile very happily: *At the celebration, he beamed proudly.* **2** [T always + adv./prep.] to send a television or radio signal through the air, especially to somewhere very distant: *The images are beamed directly from a satellite.* **3** [I,T] to send out a line of light, heat, energy etc.: *The water sparkled and the sun beamed brightly.* **4** [T] also **beam sb ↔ up/out** OFTEN HUMOROUS an expression said when you want to leave a place because it is boring, strange etc., taken from the television program "Star Trek": *Beam me out of here!*

Beam·er, Beemer /'bimə/ n. [C] SPOKEN a BMW car

bean¹ /bin/ n. [C] **1 a)** a seed from one of many types of climbing plants, that is cooked as food: *Soak the beans overnight before cooking.* **b)** a POD (=seed case) from a bean plant that is used as food when the seeds are young: *chicken with rice and green beans* **2** a plant that produces beans **3** a seed used in making some types or food or drinks: *coffee beans* | *cocoa beans* **4 not know/care beans (about) sb/sth** INFORMAL to not know anything or care at all about someone or something: *Sorry, I don't know beans about fixing radios.* —see also **spill the beans** (SPILL¹ (3))

bean² v. [T] INFORMAL to hit someone on the head with an object: *Hughes got beaned by a wild pitch.*

bean bag /'. ./ n. [C] **1** also **bean bag chair** a very large cloth or plastic bag that is filled with small balls of plastic and that you can sit on **2** a small cloth bag filled with beans, used for throwing and catching in children's games

bean count·er, beancounter /'. ,../ n. [C] INFORMAL someone whose job is to study financial figures; ACCOUNTANT

bean curd /'. ./ n. [C] TOFU

bean·ie /'bini/ n. [C] a small round hat that fits close to your head

bean·pole /'binpoul/ n. [C] HUMOROUS a very tall thin person

bean sprout /'. ./ n. [usually plural] the small white stem from a bean seed that has just started growing, eaten as a vegetable

bear¹ /bɛr/ v. past tense **bore** past participle **borne** [T] **1** be responsible for FORMAL to be responsible for or accept something | **bear the cost/burden/expense etc.** *The company responsible for the oil spill should bear the expense of cleaning it up.* | **bear responsibility/the blame/the burden etc.** *U.N. agencies will bear the burden of resettling the refugees.* **2** deal with sth to bravely accept or deal with a painful, difficult, or upsetting situation: *He bore the pain stoically.* | *They had borne untold suffering and*

hardship. | *He wrote that he could hardly bear to be separated from her.* | *The rise in interest rates may be more than the economy can bear.* | *He constantly made rude comments, and I was expected to grin and bear it* (=accept something without complaining).
3 bear a resemblance/relation etc. to sb/sth to be similar to or related to someone or something else: *Ed bore little resemblance to the man she had described.* | *The final script bore absolutely no relation to the one I'd originally written.* | *The blaze bears several parallels to a previous fire last month.*
4 bear (sth) in mind to remember a fact or piece of information that is important or could be useful in the future: *Tourists must bear in mind that they are visitors in another country.* | *Thanks, I'll bear that in mind.*
5 sign/mark FORMAL to have or show a sign, mark, or particular appearance: *The list bore the names of people still missing after the disaster.* | *The melon rind bore traces of a rare type of the Salmonella bacteria.* | *The police are asking residents to keep an eye out for a person bearing this description.*
6 sb can't bear sb/sth a) to be so upset about something that you feel unable to accept it or let it happen: *I can't bear violence toward another human being.* | *I couldn't bear the thought of having to start all over.* | [can't bear to do sth] *She was the kind of person who just couldn't bear to throw anything away.* **b)** to dislike something or someone so much that they make you very annoyed or impatient: *I really can't bear him.* | [can't bear sb doing sth] *I can't bear swimming in cold water.*
7 support to be under something and support it: *The ice wasn't thick enough to bear his weight.* | *An oak table bore several photographs of the family.*
8 bear fruit a) if a plan, decision etc. bears fruit, it is successful, especially after a long period of time: *The project may not begin to bear fruit for at least two years.* **b)** if a tree bears fruit, it produces fruit
9 bear right/left to turn toward the right or left: *Bear left where the road divides.* | *The road bears to the right.*
10 baby FORMAL to give birth to a baby: *Jean will never be able to bear children.* | **bear sb a son/daughter/child** *She bore him five children.*
11 be affected by sth to show physical or emotional signs of something that has happened to you: *He would bear the scars of his experience for the rest of his life* (=it will always affect him).
12 carry LITERARY to carry someone or something, especially something important: *Several of the guests arrived bearing gifts.* | *They arrived in Israel on the same plane that bore Assad's coffin.*
13 wind/water/air LITERARY if wind, water, or air bears something, it carries it somewhere: *The seeds are borne long distances by the wind.*
14 bear the strain/pressure etc. to be strong enough or firm enough to continue despite problems: *His job requires long hours, and their marriage was unable to bear the strain.*
15 bear the brunt of sth to have to accept the most difficult or damaging part of something: *Our division is being forced to bear the brunt of the budget cuts.*
16 bear (sb) a grudge to continue to feel annoyed about something that someone did a long time ago: *The suspect appears to have borne a grudge against his former colleagues.*
17 bring influence/pressure etc. to bear (on) to use your influence or power to get what you want: *The agency has issued a series of warnings to bring pressure to bear on the companies it considers offenders.*
18 bear witness to sth FORMAL to show that something is true or exists: *Her latest book bears witness to her talent as a writer.*
19 sth doesn't bear thinking about used to say that something is so upsetting or shocking that you prefer not to think about it: *The reaction I'll get when my parents find out doesn't even bear thinking about.*
20 not bear examination/inspection etc. to not be appropriate or good enough to be tested or examined

thoroughly: *We suspect that their statistics will not bear close inspection.*
21 bear yourself FORMAL to walk, stand etc. in a particular way, especially when this shows your character: *Throughout the trial, she bore herself with great dignity.*
22 name/title FORMAL to have a particular name: *She bears the title of "Executive Director."*
23 bear sb no malice/ill will etc. FORMAL to not feel angry toward someone

bear down on sb/sth *phr. v.* [T] **1 a)** to move quickly toward a person or place in a threatening way: *Sweeney tried to leap over the car when it bore down on him.* | *A strong Pacific storm system is bearing down on the West Coast.* **b)** to behave in a threatening way toward a person or group: *Federal regulators have been bearing down on campaign contributors.* **2** to use all your strength and effort to push or press down on something

bear on/upon sth *phr. v.* [T] FORMAL to relate to and possibly influence something: *Her actions could influence voters and bear on whether Anderson is elected.*

bear sb/sth **out** *phr. v.* [T] if facts or information bear out a claim, story, opinion etc., they help to prove that it is true: *Silberman said more people are carrying pistols, and gun sales bear him out.*

bear up *phr. v.* [I] to show courage or determination during a difficult or upsetting time: *People who have hope bear up better in bad circumstances.*

bear with sb/sth *phr. v.* [T] **1 bear with me** SPOKEN used to ask someone politely to wait while you find out information, finish what you are doing etc.: *Bear with me for a minute while I check our records.* **2 bear with sth** to be patient or continue to do something that is difficult or not fun: *It's boring at first, but bear with it because it gets better.*

bear² *n.* [C] **1** a large strong animal with thick fur that eats flesh, fruit, and insects: *Visitors to the park are warned not to feed the bears.* —see also TEDDY BEAR, POLAR BEAR **2** INFORMAL something that is very difficult to do or to deal with: *The federal estate tax form is a real bear to fill out.* **3** INFORMAL a big man who behaves in a rough way or is in a bad mood **4** TECHNICAL someone who sells SHARES or goods when they expect the price to fall —compare BULL¹ (4)

bear·a·ble /'bɛrəbəl/ *adj.* something that is bearable is difficult or not nice, but you can deal with it: *The humidity was lower, making the high temperatures more bearable.* —**bearably** *adv.*

bear claw /'. ./ *n.* [C] a PASTRY filled with fruit that has a row of long cuts across the top

beard /bɪrd/ *n.* [C] **1** hair that grows on a man's chin and JAW —compare MUSTACHE —see picture at CLEAN-SHAVEN **2** something similar to a beard, such as hair growing on an animal's chin —**bearded** *adj.*

Beards·ley /'bɪrdzli/, **Au·brey** /'ɔbri/ (1872–1898) a British ILLUSTRATOR famous for his black and white pictures

bear·er /'bɛrɚ/ *n.* [C] **1** LAW the bearer of a legal document such as a PASSPORT is the person that it officially belongs to **2** someone who brings you information, a letter etc.: [+ of] *the bearer of bad news* **3** FORMAL someone whose job is to carry something such as a flag or a STRETCHER (=light bed for a sick person) —see also PALLBEARER

bear hug /'. ./ *n.* [C] an action in which you put your arms around someone and hold them very tightly because you like them or are pleased to see them —see also HUG²

bear·ing /'bɛrɪŋ/ *n.* **1 have a/some/no bearing on sth** to have an effect or influence on something, or not to have any effect or influence: *Really, Lieutenant, I can't see that this has any bearing on the case.* **2 lose your bearings a)** to become confused about where you are or what you should do next: *We lost our bearings in the fog and ended up 30 miles from home.* **b)** to become confused about what you

should do next in order to be successful: *When Kelly left, the company began to lose its bearings.* **3 get your bearings a)** to find out exactly where you are: *I had Mike climb up a tall tree to get our bearings.* **b)** to feel confident that you know what you should do next: *It will take a little time to get your bearings in new job.* **4** [C] TECHNICAL part of a machine that turns on another part, or in which a turning part is held **5** [C] TECHNICAL a direction or angle that is shown by a COMPASS (1) **6** [singular,U] FORMAL the way in which you move, stand, or behave, especially when this shows your character: *The lady is tall, strong, and dignified in her bearing.*

bear·ish /'bɛrɪʃ/ *adj.* **1 a)** someone who is bearish expects the prices of SHARES to decrease: [+ on] *Investors have turned bearish on Internet stocks.* **b)** a market that is bearish is one in which the prices of shares are decreasing **2** a man that is bearish is big and strong —**bearishly** *adv.* —**bearishness** *n.*

bear mar·ket /ˌ. '../ *n.* [C] a situation in which the value of STOCKS is decreasing

bear·skin /'bɛrˌskɪn/ *n.* [C,U] the skin of a bear: *a bearskin rug*

beast /bist/ *n.* [C] **1** an animal, especially a large or dangerous one: *I'm lucky that beast didn't bite my arm off.* **2** OLD-FASHIONED someone who is cruel or in a very bad mood: *Philip has a real beast of a father.* **3** INFORMAL something that is difficult to deal with: *The El Niño weather pattern is an unpredictable beast.* **4 the beast in sb** also **the beast within** the part of someone's character that makes them experience hatred, strong sexual feelings, violence etc. —see also **the nature of the beast** (NATURE (8))

beast·ly /'bistli/ *adj.* OLD-FASHIONED very bad or rude: *beastly weather* —**beastly** *adv.* —**beastliness** *n.* [U]

beast of bur·den /ˌ. . '../ *n.* [C] OLD USE an animal that does heavy work

beat¹ /bit/ *v. past tense* **beat** *past participle* **beaten**
1 defeat [T] **a)** to get the most points, votes etc. in a game, race, or competition: *The Pacers were beaten 71–68 by the Bulls.* | *Back then, girls were told that they could never beat a boy at tennis.* **b)** to successfully deal with a problem that you have been struggling with: *No one has figured out how to beat the problem of rodents eating the crops.* —see Usage Note at WIN¹
2 hit [I,T] to hit someone or something many times with your hand, a stick etc.: *He used to come home drunk and beat my mother.* | [+ on] *They were beating on the door.* | **beat sb to death/beat sb unconscious** (=hit someone until they die, become unconscious etc.) | *He was beaten black and blue* (=beaten until marks were made on his body) *by the crowd.* | *I'm going to beat the living daylights out of* (=hit him very hard) *Joe if I find out he's been lying to me.*
3 food [I,T] to mix food together quickly with a fork or special kitchen tool: *Beat the eggs and pour in the milk.* | *Gradually beat in the sugar.*
4 beat a record/score etc. if someone beats a record etc., they do something better, faster etc. than the person who did it best before: *Hank Aaron beat the record for home runs set by Babe Ruth.*
5 heart [I] when your heart beats, it moves in a regular RHYTHM as it pumps your blood: *On the ultrasound machine, I could see the baby's heart beating strongly.*

SPOKEN PHRASES

6 be better [T not in progressive] to be much better and more enjoyable than something else: *You should have the newspaper delivered to your house – it beats having to go out and buy one.* | *This car beats the hell out of my old one.* | *There's about 90 girls here, and only 12 guys. You can't beat that.*
7 beats me used to say that you do not know something or cannot understand or explain something: *"Who do you think is gonna win?" "Beats me." | How he caught that ball beats the hell out of me.*
8 beat the shit/crap/hell out of sb VULGAR to hit someone many times

9 beat it! used to tell someone to leave at once because they are annoying you or should not be there: *Go on, you kids! Beat it! Now!*

10 you can't beat sth (for sth) used to say that someone or something is better than anything else: *For romance, you can't beat the Rainbow Lodge.*

11 beat the pants off sb to defeat someone completely: *She beat the pants off me last time we played.*

12 beat your brains out to think about something very hard and for a long time: *Why should you beat your brains out fighting the environmentalists?*

13 if you can't beat 'em, join 'em used when you decide to take part in something although you disapprove of it, because everyone else is doing it and you cannot stop them

14 to beat the band in large amounts or with great force: *It's raining to beat the band.*

15 can you beat that/it? used to show that you are surprised or annoyed by something: *All I can remember of her as a baby is how much she loved butter. Can you beat that?*

16 beat your meat VULGAR, SLANG if a man beats his meat, he MASTURBATES

17 beat around the bush INFORMAL to avoid or delay talking about something embarrassing or upsetting: *Without beating around the bush, he stated, "If we don't expand, jobs will go elsewhere."*

18 beat sb to it INFORMAL to get or do something before someone else, especially if you are both trying to do it first: *I was going to have that last piece of pie but somebody beat me to it.*

19 beat the rush INFORMAL to do something earlier than normal in order to avoid problems when everyone does it: *I like to get to the theater early to beat the rush.*

20 beat the system to find ways of avoiding or breaking the rules of an organization, system etc., in order to achieve what you want: *There's a limit on how much luggage you can take on a plane, but there are ways to beat the system.*

21 drums [I,T] if you beat the drums or if drums beat, they make a regular continuous sound: *Children were beating on different kinds of drums.*

22 beat the drum for sb/sth to speak eagerly in support of someone or something: *Goodman rushed back to L.A. to beat the drum for his new movie.*

23 beat sb like a drum to defeat an opponent by a lot of points in a game or sport: *Seles beat her like a drum.*

24 hit against [I always + adv./prep.] to knock or hit against something continuously: [**beat on/against** etc.] *Waves beat against the cliffs.*

25 wings [I,T] if a bird beats its wings or its wings beat, they move up and down quickly and regularly

26 beat the rap INFORMAL to avoid being punished for something you have done: *He's been arrested on federal charges three times and has beaten the rap every time.*

27 beat a path (to sb's door) if people beat a path to your door, they are interested in something you are selling, a service you are providing etc.: *People are going to beat a path from all over to play these golf courses.*

28 beat time to make regular movements or sounds to show the speed at which music should be played: *a conductor beating time with his baton*

29 beat the heat INFORMAL to make yourself cooler: *Strawberries in wine is a festive way to beat the heat.*

30 take some beating a) if an achievement or SCORE will take some beating, it will be difficult for anyone to do better: *Schumacher has a twelve-second lead, which will take some beating.* **b)** to be better, more enjoyable etc. than almost anything else of the same type: *As a great place for a vacation, Florida takes some beating.*

31 metal [T] to hit metal with a hammer in order to shape it or make it thinner

32 hunting [I,T] to force wild birds and animals out of bushes, long grass etc. so that they can be shot for sport.

33 beat your breast LITERARY to show clearly that you are very upset or sorry about something —see also BEATEN, BEATING, **beat/flog a dead horse** (DEAD¹ (8))

beat down *phr. v.* **1** [I] if the sun beats down, it shines very brightly and the weather is hot **2** [I] if the rain beats down, it is raining very hard **3** [T **beat sb ↔ down**] SLANG to hit someone many times

beat off *phr. v.* **1** [T **beat sb/sth ↔ off**] to stop someone from trying to attack you, harm you, or compete against you: *McConnell beat off a challenge for his Senate seat.* **2** [I,T **beat sb ↔ off**] VULGAR, SLANG if a man beats off, he MASTURBATES

beat out *phr. v.* **1** [T **beat sb ↔ out**] to defeat someone in a competition [**beat sb out for sth**] *Michigan managed to beat out Penn State for the number one position in the country.* **2** [T **beat sth out**] if drums beat out a RHYTHM or you beat out a RHYTHM on the drums, they make a continuous regular sound **3** [T **beat sth out of sb**] to force someone to tell you something by beating them: *I had the truth beaten out of me by my father.* **4** [T **beat sth ↔ out**] to put out a fire by hitting it with something such as a wet cloth

beat up *phr. v.* **1** [T **beat sb ↔ up**] to hurt someone badly by hitting them: *Her boyfriend got drunk and beat her up.* **2 beat up on sb** to hit someone and hurt them, especially someone younger or weaker than yourself: *I used to beat up on my brothers when we were kids.* **3 beat up on yourself** also **beat yourself up** INFORMAL to blame yourself too much for something: *Stop beating yourself up – you couldn't have prevented it.*

beat² *n.* **1** [C] one of a series of regular movements or hitting actions: *a heart rate of 80 beats per minute* **2** [C usually singular] a regular repeated noise: [+ **of**] *the slow beat of the drum* **3** [singular] the main RHYTHM that a piece of music or a poem has: *a song with a beat you can dance to* **4** [singular] a subject or an area of a city that someone is responsible for as their job: *journalists covering the political beat | police officers **on the beat** (=working in their area)* **5** [C] one of the notes in a piece of music that sounds stronger than the other notes

beat³ *adj.* [not before noun] INFORMAL very tired: *I'm beat.*

beat·en /ˈbitˀn/ *adj.* [only before noun] **1** beaten metal has been shaped with a hammer to make it thinner **2 off the beaten path/track** not well known and far away from the places that people usually visit: *We stayed at a charming inn that's off the beaten path.* **3** a beaten path, track etc. has been made by many people walking the same way

beat·er /ˈbitˀ/ *n.* [C] **1** an object that is designed to beat something: *Using clean beaters, whip the cream. | a rug beater* **2 a wife/child beater** someone who hits his wife or child, especially someone who does this often **3** INFORMAL an old car in bad condition **4** someone who forces wild birds or animals out of bushes, long grass etc. so that they can be shot for sport —see also **fare beater** (FARE¹ (5)), WORLD-BEATER

be·a·tif·ic /ˌbiəˈtɪfɪk/ *adj.* LITERARY a beatific look, smile etc. shows great peace and happiness —**beatifically** /-kli/ *adv.*

be·at·i·fy /biˈætəˌfaɪ/ *v.* **beatifies, beatified, beatifying** [T] if the Catholic Church beatifies someone who has died, it says officially that they are a holy or special person —**beatification** /biˌætəfəˈkeɪʃən/ *n.* [U]

beat·ing /ˈbitɪŋ/ *n.* [C] **1** an act of hitting someone many times as a punishment or in a fight: *The patient died of head injuries inflicted during the beating.* **2 take a beating** to be defeated or criticized very badly: *The Mets took a real beating last Saturday.* —see also **take some beating** (BEAT¹ (30))

Beat·les /ˈbitlz/, **the** a British popular music group who made their first record in 1962 and became one of the most famous groups ever. They had a great influence on the development of popular music. The members of the Beatles were George Harrison, John Lennon, Paul McCartney, and Ringo Starr.

beat·nik /ˈbitˀnɪk/ *n.* [C] one of a group of young people in the late 1950s and early 1960s, who did not accept the values of society and showed this by their choice of clothes and the way they lived

Bea·ton /ˈbitˀn/**, Ce·cil** /ˈsɛsəl/ (1904–1980) a British photographer and designer

beat-up /ˌ. ˈ.◂/ *adj.* INFORMAL a beat-up car, bicycle etc. is old and in bad condition: *a beat-up old Chevy*

beau /boʊ/ *n.* [C] *plural* **beaux, beaus** OLD-FASHIONED **1** a woman's close friend or lover **2** a fashionable well-dressed man

beau·coup /ˈboʊku/ *quantifier* [only before noun] SPOKEN a lot or many: *He makes beaucoup bucks* (=earns a lot of money) *in that job.*

Beau·jo·lais /ˌboʊʒəˈleɪ/ *n.* [C,U] a type of French red wine

beaut /byut/ *n.* [singular] SPOKEN something that is very good, attractive, or impressive: *That necklace is a real beaut.*

beau·te·ous /ˈbyutiəs/ *adj.* POETIC beautiful —**beauteously** *adv.*

beau·ti·cian /byuˈtɪʃən/ *n.* [C] OLD-FASHIONED someone whose job is to cut your hair, put MAKEUP on you, color your FINGERNAILs etc.

beau·ti·ful /ˈbyutˀfəl/ *adj.* **1** someone or something that is beautiful is extremely attractive to look at and gives you a feeling of pleasure: *a beautiful woman!* | *The scenery was incredibly beautiful.* **2** very good or giving you great pleasure: *beautiful music* | *a beautiful catch* | *The weather was beautiful.* —**beautifully** *adv.*

USAGE NOTE: BEAUTIFUL

WORD CHOICE: beautiful, pretty, handsome, good-looking, attractive, sexy
Beautiful and **pretty** can be used about women, children, and things, but not usually about men, unless you want to suggest that they have female features: *a beautiful girl/house/view* | *a pretty child/picture/voice.* **Beautiful** is the strongest word to describe a very attractive appearance. It suggests that someone has almost perfect good looks. **Pretty** means good-looking in a more ordinary way, but not really beautiful. **Handsome** is not common in spoken English. It is usually used to describe men, especially if they have the strong features that men in romantic stories are supposed to have. **Good-looking** can be used about men and women, but not usually about things: *Gina and Barry are a good-looking couple.* **Attractive** can be used about men, women, and things: *an attractive color/idea/young man.* An **attractive** person may not be very **good-looking**, but makes other people sexually interested in them, though not as much as if they are **sexy**.

---

beau·ti·fy /ˈbyutəˌfaɪ/ *v.* **beautifies, beautified, beautifying** [T] to make someone or something beautiful: *Locals welcome any efforts to beautify the neighborhood.*

beau·ty /ˈbyuti/ *n. plural* **beauties**
1 attractive to look at **a)** [U] a quality that things, places, or people have that makes them very attractive to look at: *the beauty of America's national parks* | *Millions are spent every year on beauty products.* | *I was impressed by the beauty and warmth of the people.* **b)** [C] OLD-FASHIONED a woman who is very beautiful: *She was once considered quite a beauty.*
2 poem, song, emotion etc. [U] a quality that something such as a poem, song, emotion etc. has, which gives you pleasure or makes you feel happy: *Shaw was moved by the beauty of Handel's music.*
3 a good example of sth [C] SPOKEN a very good example of something or an object that is a particularly good, large, or impressive one of its type: *Eric's new car is a real beauty.*
4 the beauty of sth a particularly good quality that makes something especially appropriate or useful: *The beauty of this diet is that you never have to feel hungry.*
5 beauty is in the eye of the beholder used to say

that different people have different opinions about what is beautiful

beauty con·test /ˈ.. ˌ../ *n.* [C] a competition in which women are judged on how attractive they look; PAGEANT (1)

beauty mark /ˈ.. ˌ./ *n.* [C] a small dark mark on a woman's skin, especially one on her face

beauty pag·eant /ˈ.. ˌ../ *n.* [C] a beauty contest

beauty par·lor /ˈ.. ˌ../ *n.* [C] a beauty salon

beauty queen /ˈ.. ˌ./ *n.* [C] OLD-FASHIONED the winner of a beauty contest

beauty sa·lon /ˈ.. ˌ../ *n.* [C] a place in which you can receive treatments for your skin, or have your hair cut etc., so that you look more attractive

beauty shop /ˈ.. ˌ./ *n.* [C] a beauty salon

beauty sleep /ˈ.. ˌ./ *n.* [U] HUMOROUS enough sleep to keep you healthy and looking good: *I didn't get my beauty sleep last night.*

Beau·voir /boʊˈvwɑr/**, Si·mone de** /siˈmoʊn də/ (1908–1986) a French writer and FEMINIST famous for her book THE SECOND SEX

bea·ver /ˈbivər/ *n.* [C] **1** a North American animal that has thick fur, a wide flat tail, and cuts down trees with its teeth —see picture on page 429 **2** VULGAR the hairy area around a woman's sex organs —see also **eager beaver** (EAGER (3))

bea·ver·tail /ˈbivərteɪl/ *n.* [C] CANADIAN a wide flat FRIED PASTRY eaten in Canada

be·bop /ˈbibɑp/ *n.* [U] a type of JAZZ music

be·calmed /biˈkɑmd/ *adj.* LITERARY a ship or boat that is becalmed cannot move because there is no wind

be·came /bɪˈkeɪm/ the past tense of BECOME

be·cause /bɪˈkɔz, -ˈkʌz/ *conjunction* **1** for the reason that: *Mark couldn't come because he had to work.* | *She's studying because she has a test tomorrow.* | *"Why can't I go?" "Because you're not old enough."* **2 because of sb/sth** as a result of a particular thing or of someone's actions: *They're not playing baseball today because of the rain.* | *I got interested in wrestling because of Denny* (=Denny influenced me). **3 just because...** SPOKEN used to say that although one thing is true, it does not mean that something else is true: *Just because they're asking for $400 for it doesn't mean they won't sell it for less.* | *Pam seems to think that just because she's older than us she can tell us what to do.*

beck /bɛk/ *n.* **be at sb's beck and call** to always be ready to do what someone wants

Beck·et /ˈbɛkɪt/**, Saint Thomas** (1118–1170) an English priest who became the Archbishop of Canterbury. He had a serious argument with the king, Henry II, and was murdered by some of the king's soldiers

Beck·ett /ˈbɛkɪt/**, Samuel** (1906–1989) an Irish writer of plays, novels, and poetry, famous for his play WAITING FOR GODOT

beck·on /ˈbɛkən/ *v.* [I,T] **1** to make a signal to someone with your hand or arm, to show that you want them to come toward you: [+ **to**] *The woman beckoned to me to follow her.* | [**beckon sb forward/to/toward** etc.] *A guard beckoned the visitor onward.* **2** if something such as money or happiness beckons, it is so attractive that you want to get it: *The Sandcastle amusement park beckons visitors with water slides.* | *A brilliant future beckons.*

be·come /bɪˈkʌm/ *v. past tense* **became** *past participle* **become 1** [linking verb] to begin to be something, or to develop in a particular way: *Baker became head coach.* | *After the death of her father, she became the richest woman in the world.* | *The weather is becoming warmer.* | *These kinds of partnerships are becoming more common.* | *She started to become anxious about her son.* | *It is becoming harder to find decent housing in the city.* **2 what will/has become of...?** used to ask what will happen or what has happened to someone or something: *Workers who have been laid off are wondering what will become of their homes.* | *Whatever became of her, anyway?* **3** [T not in progressive] FORMAL to look good on someone or be appropriate for them: *I don't think that outfit really becomes you, Sheryl.*

B

WORD CHOICE: become, get, turn, go, come
Become and **get** can be used with most types of adjectives to describe changes in people and things. **Become** is more common in writing, and **get** in spoken English, especially where a quick change is involved: *Digital TVs are becoming more common.* | *It became clear that Daryl was lying.* | *It gets dark early in December.* | *I'm getting wet standing here.* | *Your dinner's getting cold.* When things change color or with some other changes in condition, **turn** can be used, or less formally **go**. Compare: *Jonathan turned/went pale when he heard the news.* | *The leaves turn a beautiful gold color in the fall.* | *Wait until the light turns green before you cross the street.* **Go** can also be used where someone's mind or body changes for the worse: *He went crazy/ blind/deaf/bald.* **Go** is used in a similar meaning with some things: *The milk will go bad if you leave it out.* | *Everything went wrong/haywire.* But in other situations **turn** is used: *If the weather turns bad, we can go to the mall.* | *The situation turned nasty.* **Come** is used only in a few expressions where something gets better: *All my dreams have come true* (NOT *become/get* true). Otherwise people use **become** or **get** again: *He eventually got better.*

GRAMMAR
Become is never followed by an infinitive with "to," though **come** can be followed by an infinitive with "to": *After a while, I came to like Chicago* (NOT *…became to like…*).

be·com·ing /bɪˈkʌmɪŋ/ *adj.* OLD-FASHIONED **1** making you look attractive: *Laura's hair is softer and more becoming.* **2** words or actions that are becoming are appropriate for you or for the situation you are in: *Bad language is not at all becoming.* —**becomingly** *adv.*

bed[1] /bɛd/ *n.*
1 sleep [C,U] a piece of furniture for sleeping on: *an old brass bed* | *a double bed* (=for two people) | *I was lying in bed reading.* | *Kim usually goes to bed at about eleven.* | *Have you made your bed* (=pulled the sheets, blankets etc. neatly into place)? | *I'll just put the kids to bed.* | *Come on Billy, it's time for bed* (=time to go to sleep). | *My wife got me out of bed to take the dog for a walk.*
2 go to bed with sb INFORMAL to have sex with someone
3 in bed with sb a) having sex with someone: *Mrs. Yates found her husband in bed with another woman.* **b)** people or organizations that are in bed with each other have a close involvement that gives them special advantages: *Everyone knows that the Mayor's in bed with the tobacco industry.*
4 river/lake/ocean [C] the flat ground at the bottom of a river, lake etc.: *the river bed*
5 get sb into bed INFORMAL to persuade someone to have sex with you
6 garden [C] an area of a garden, park etc. that has been prepared for plants to grow in: *rose beds*
7 base [C usually singular] a layer of something that forms a base that other things are put on top of: [+ of] *Our pasta salad is served on a bed of lettuce.*
8 put sth to bed INFORMAL if you put something such as a piece of work or problem to bed, you finish it or solve it
9 get up on the wrong side of the bed SPOKEN to feel slightly angry or annoyed for no particular reason: *Ooh, looks like somebody got up on the wrong side of the bed today.*
10 oyster/coral etc. bed an area of the bottom of the ocean where there are a lot of OYSTERS etc.
11 rock [C] a layer of rock —see also BEDROCK (2)
12 a bed of roses a phrase meaning a happy, comfortable, or easy situation, used especially in negative sentences: *Brian's life hasn't exactly been a bed of roses.*
13 you've made your bed and you have to lie in it SPOKEN used to say that you must accept the bad results of your actions

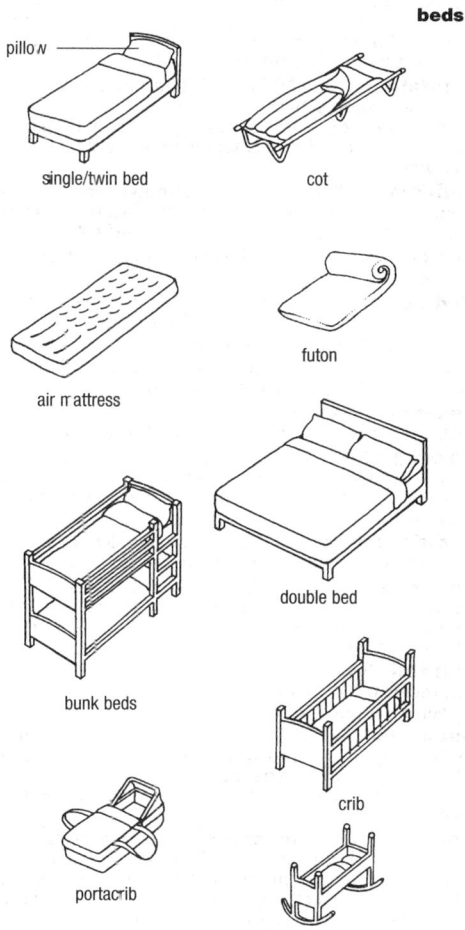

beds

pillow

single/twin bed

cot

air mattress

futon

bunk beds

double bed

crib

portacrib

cradle

bed[2] *v.* [T] **1** to put something firmly and deeply into something else: [+ in] *The foundations were bedded in cement.* **2 bed sb** OLD-FASHIONED to have sex with someone **3** also **bed out** to put plants into the ground so that they can grow
bed down *phr. v.* **1** [I] to make yourself comfortable for the night: *About 65 homeless people bedded down in a school gymnasium.* **2** [T bed sb/sth **down**] to make a person or animal comfortable for the night

bed and break·fast /ˌ. . ˈ../ *n.* abbreviation **B & B** [C,U] a private house or small hotel where you can sleep and have breakfast, or this type of place

be·daz·zle /bɪˈdæzəl/ *v.* [T] to make someone think that someone or something is extremely impressive: *The fireworks display bedazzled an estimated 50,000 spectators.*

bed·bug /ˈbɛdbʌg/ *n.* [C] an insect that sucks blood and lives in houses, especially in beds

bed·cham·ber /ˈbɛdˌtʃeɪmbɚ/ *n.* [C] OLD USE a BEDROOM

bed·clothes /ˈbɛdkloʊz, -kloʊðz/ *n.* [plural] OLD-FASHIONED the sheets, covers etc. that you put on a bed

bed·ding /ˈbɛdɪŋ/ *n.* [U] **1** sheets, covers etc. that you put on a bed: *All bedding is on sale at 30% off.* **2** something soft for animals to sleep on, such as dried grass or STRAW

be·deck /bɪˈdɛk/ *v.* [T usually passive] LITERARY to decorate something such as a building or street by hanging things all over it: *The ballroom was bedecked with flowers for the reception.*

be·dev·il /bɪˈdɛvəl/ v. [T usually passive] to cause a lot of problems and difficulties for someone or something: *The senator has been bedeviled by allegations of corruption.* —**bedevilment** n. [U]

bed·fel·low /ˈbɛdˌfɛloʊ/ n. [C] **strange/odd/uneasy etc. bedfellows** two or more people, ideas etc. that are related or working together in an unexpected way: *Politics and religion often make very uneasy bedfellows.*

bed·lam /ˈbɛdləm/ n. [U] a wild noisy place or situation: *The classroom erupted into bedlam whenever Miss Simpson left for longer than a minute.*

bed lin·en /ˈ. ˌ../ n. [U] the sheets and PILLOWCASEs for a bed

Bed·ou·in /ˈbɛduɪn/ one of the Arab tribes living in North Africa and West Asia who traditionally live in tents and travel from place to place

bed·pan /ˈbɛdpæn/ n. [C] a low wide container used as a toilet by someone who has to stay in bed

bed·post /ˈbɛdpoʊst/ n. [C] one of the four main supports at the corners of an old-fashioned bed

be·drag·gled /bɪˈdrægəld/ adj. looking messy and dirty, especially from being out in the weather: *Trucks carried hundreds of bedraggled refugees across the border.*

bed·rid·den /ˈbɛdˌrɪdn/ adj. unable to leave your bed, especially because you are old or very sick

bed·rock /ˈbɛdrɑk/ n. [U] **1** the basic ideas and principles of a belief, system, or set of ideas: *Facts are the bedrock of any trial.* **2** solid rock in the ground, below all the soil

bed·roll /ˈbɛdroʊl/ n. [C] a special thick BLANKET or a number of BLANKETs rolled together and used for sleeping outdoors

bed·room[1] /ˈbɛdrum/ n. [C] **1** a room for sleeping in: *a house with four bedrooms* —see picture on page 423 **2 have bedroom eyes** INFORMAL a look in your eyes that shows that you are sexually attracted to someone

bedroom[2] adj. **bedroom community/suburb** a place where people live but that does not have many businesses, so that people travel from there to work in a larger town every day: *Idaho Springs is a bedroom community forty miles west of Denver.*

bed·side /ˈbɛdsaɪd/ n. [C] the area around your bed: *The doctor sat by his bedside.* | *The clock on her bedside table said a quarter to four.* | *a bedside lamp*

bedside man·ner /ˈ.. ˈ../ n. [singular] a doctor's bedside manner is the way that he or she talks to the people that he or she is treating

bed·sore /ˈbɛdsɔr/ n. [C] a sore place on your skin caused by lying in bed in one position for a long time

bed·spread /ˈbɛdsprɛd/ n. [C] a cover for a bed that goes on top of all the other covers and is used for decoration

bed·stead /ˈbɛdstɛd/ n. [C] the wooden or metal frame of a bed

bed·time /ˈbɛdtaɪm/ n. [C,U] the time when you usually go to bed: *It's way past your bedtime!* | *a bedtime story*

bed wet·ting /ˈ. ˌ../ n. [U] the problem that some children have of passing URINE (=liquid waste from the body) while they are asleep —**bed-wetter** n. [C]

bee /bi/ n. [C] **1** a black and yellow flying insect with a round body that makes HONEY and can sting you: *a swarm of bees* —see also BUMBLEBEE, HONEYBEE **2 have a bee in your bonnet** INFORMAL to think something is so important, so necessary etc. that you keep mentioning it or thinking about it: *Dad has a bee in his bonnet about saving electricity.* **3 a sewing/quilting etc. bee** an occasion when people, usually women, meet in order to do a particular type of work **4 be the bee's knees** OLD-FASHIONED INFORMAL to be very good: *I think that show is just the bee's knees.* —see also **the birds and the bees** (BIRD (4)), **as busy as a bee** (BUSY[1] (9)), SPELLING BEE

beech /bitʃ/ n. [C,U] a large tree with smooth gray BARK (=outer covering), or the wood from this tree

beef[1] /bif/ n. **1** [U] the meat from a cow: *roast beef* **2** [C] INFORMAL a complaint: *Some guy who had a beef with the manager came in and yelled at him for half an hour.* **3 where's the beef?** SPOKEN used when you think someone's words and promises sound good, but you want to know what they actually plan to do: *"Where's the beef?" reporters asked Democratic leaders at a news conference.* —see also CORNED BEEF

beef[2] v. [I] INFORMAL to complain a lot: [+ about] *They're always beefing about how much work I give them.*

beef sth ↔ **up** phr. v. [T] INFORMAL to improve something, especially to make it stronger or more interesting: *Airport security has been beefed up.*

beef·cake /ˈbifkeɪk/ n. [C,U] INFORMAL a strong attractive man with large muscles, or men like this in general

beef·steak /ˈbifsteɪk/ n. [C,U] STEAK (1)

beef·y /ˈbifi/ adj. **beefier, beefiest** INFORMAL a man who is beefy is big, strong, and often fat: *beefy football players*

bee·hive /ˈbihaɪv/ n. [C] **1** a structure where BEES are kept for producing HONEY **2** a place with many people and a lot of activity: [+ of] *The convention was a beehive of workshops, seminars and speeches.* **3** a way of arranging a woman's hair in a high pile on the top of her head, which was popular in the 1960s

bee·keep·er /ˈbiˌkipɚ/ n. [C] someone who owns and takes care of BEES —**beekeeping** n. [U]

bee·line /ˈbilaɪn/ n. **make a beeline for sb/sth** INFORMAL to go quickly and directly toward someone or something: *I made a beeline for the food as soon as I arrived.*

Beem·er /ˈbimɚ/ n. [C] SPOKEN another spelling of BEAMER

been /bɪn/ **1** the past participle of BE **2 have/has been** used to say that someone has gone to a place and come back: [+ to] *I've never been to Japan.* | [have been to do sth] *Have you been to see Roger's new house?* **3 been there, done that** SPOKEN used to say that you are not interested in doing something, because you already have a lot of experience doing it

beep[1] /bip/ v. **1** [I] if a machine beeps, it makes a short high sound: *Dozens of arcade games were beeping and ringing along the wall.* **2** [I,T] if a car horn beeps or you make it beep, it makes a loud noise **3** [T] to telephone someone who has a beeper: *Beep Dr. Greene – he's needed in the E.R.*

beep[2] n. [C] **1** a short high sound made by an electronic machine: *Leave your message after the beep.* **2** the sound of a car horn **3** the action of telephoning someone who has a beeper

beep·er /ˈbipɚ/ n. [C] a small machine that you carry with you, that makes short high electronic sounds or moves slightly to tell you that you must telephone someone; PAGER

beer /bɪr/ n. **1** [U] an alcoholic drink made from MALT and HOPS: *a bottle of beer* **2** [C] a glass, bottle, or can of beer: *Want a beer, Pete?* —**beery** adj.

beer bel·ly /ˈ. ˌ../ also **beer gut** /ˈ. ./ n. [C] an unattractive fat stomach caused by drinking too much beer

bees·wax /ˈbizwæks/ n. [U] **1** a substance produced by BEES, used especially for making furniture polish and CANDLEs **2 none of your beeswax** SPOKEN used to tell someone rudely that what they have asked you is private or personal

beet /bit/ n. [C,U] **1** a plant with a round dark red root that you cook and eat as a vegetable **2** also **sugar beet** a vegetable that sugar is made from **3 red as a beet** INFORMAL having a red face, especially because you are embarrassed or sick

Beet·ho·ven /ˈbeɪˌtoʊvən/, **Lud·wig van** /ˈlʊdvɪg væn, vɑn/ (1770–1827) a German musician who wrote CLASSICAL music

bee·tle /ˈbitl/ n. [C] one of many types of insects with a round hard back, which is usually black —see picture at INSECT

be·fall /bɪˈfɔl/ v. past tense **befell** /bɪˈfɛl/ past participle **befallen** /bɪˈfɔlən/ [T] FORMAL if something bad or dangerous befalls you, it happens to you: *A similar crisis could befall the nation's banks.*

be·fit /bɪˈfɪt/ v. past tense and past participle **befitted** [T] FORMAL to be correct or appropriate for someone: *They gave him a funeral befitting a national hero.* —**befitting** adj. —**befittingly** adv.

be·fore¹ /bɪˈfɔr/ prep. **1** earlier than something: *I visited them just before Christmas.* | *No cookies before dinner, Andy.* | *Denise got there before me.* | [before doing sth] *We lived in Ogden before moving to Salt Lake City.* | *Larry got back from vacation **the day before yesterday** (=two days ago).* **2** ahead of someone or something else in a list or order: *This lady was before you, sir.* **3** FORMAL in front of: *The priest knelt before the altar.* | *The highway stretched out before them.* **4** if one quality or person comes before another, it is more important than it: *My son is most important – he comes before anyone.* | *Quality should come before quantity.* **5** if one place is before another place, it is a particular distance in front of that place as you travel toward it: *Turn left just before the traffic lights.* **6** in the same place, or in front of a person or crowd of people: *She gave a presentation before the board of directors.* **7** if something such as a report or EVIDENCE is put before a person or group of people, they must consider it and make a decision about it: *The proposal came before the city council a year ago.* **8** FORMAL if there is a job or situation before you, you have to do the job or face the situation soon: *There are great challenges that **lie before us**.* **9** FORMAL if a period of time is before you, it is about to start and you can do what you want during it: *We had the whole summer before us.* **10** FORMAL if you show a particular reaction before someone or something, you react in that way: *She trembled before the prospect of meeting him again.* —see Usage Note at FRONT¹

before² adv. **1** at an earlier time: *I know I've seen him somewhere before.* | *I've never been to this restaurant before.* | **the day/week/month etc. before** *Sales were up 14% from the year before.* | **as/like before** *I still get some fan letters, but not as many as before.* **2 before long** after not much time has passed: *Other stores will probably do the same thing before long.* | *Put it all in a compost pile, and before long you'll have a good fertilizer.* **3** OLD USE ahead of someone or something else: *The king's guards walked before.*

before³ conjunction **1** earlier than the time when something happens: *Anthony wants to see you before you go.* | *It will be a few days before we know the full results.* **2** so that something bad does not happen: *Lock up your bike before it gets stolen.* | *Take that dog indoors before it bites somebody.* **3** used to say that one thing will have to happen first or an amount of time will need to pass, in order for something else to happen: *There's a lot to do before we can submit the proposal.* | *We don't know how long it'll be before I get the cast off my arm.* **4 before you know it** SPOKEN used to say that something will happen very soon: *Spring break will be here before you know it.* **5** used to warn someone that you will do something mean or harmful to them if they do not do something: *Get out before I call the police.* **6** used to warn someone not to laugh at, criticize etc. someone or something because they have faults and WEAKNESSES themselves: *Before you get angry, try and remember what it was like to be fifteen.*

be·fore·hand /bɪˈfɔrˌhænd/ adv. before something else happens or is done: *You should have told me beforehand that you might be late.* | *Almost all the food was prepared beforehand.*

be·foul /bɪˈfaʊl/ v. [T] FORMAL to make something very dirty: *The oil spill befouled thousands of miles of the shoreline.*

be·friend /bɪˈfrɛnd/ v. [T] FORMAL to behave in a friendly way toward someone, especially someone who is younger or needs help: *A group of soldiers befriended my brothers and me during the war.*

be·fud·dled /bɪˈfʌdld/ adj. completely confused: *Dawn looked a little befuddled.*

B

beg /bɛg/ v. **begged, begging** [S W 3]

1 **ask** [I,T] to ask for something in an anxious or urgent way, because you want it very much: *Chad was begging and pleading.* | [beg (sb) to do sth] *The boy begged to be left alone.* | *I begged him to stay, but he wouldn't.* | [beg (sb) for sth] *My daughter is begging me for a kitten.* | *Money is so scarce in the school districts that principals are begging for donations.* | *One of the killers **begged** Mrs. Donaldson's **forgiveness** after the trial.*

2 **money/food** [I,T] to ask people to give you food, money etc. because you are very poor: *Children were begging in the streets.* | [beg for sth] *They were reduced to begging for food.* | [beg from sb] *An old man begged from people who walked by.*

3 **animal** [I] if an animal such as a dog begs, it asks for food: *Benji, stop begging.*

4 I beg your pardon SPOKEN **a)** used to politely ask someone to repeat what they have just said: *"And the year of your birth?" "I beg your pardon?" "When were you born?"* **b)** used to politely say you are sorry when you have made a mistake, or have said something wrong or embarrassing: *Oh, I beg your pardon. Are you all right?* **c)** said to show that you strongly disagree with something that someone has said, or think it is unacceptable, often used humorously: *"East Coast people are kind of uptight, aren't they?" "I beg your pardon!"*

5 beg, borrow, or steal an expression meaning to do whatever you must in order to get what you want or achieve something difficult, often used humorously: *The designers would beg, borrow, or steal in order to get the show ready.*

6 beg to differ FORMAL to firmly disagree with something that has been said: *Kreis begs to differ with the report or, him printed in the Star.*

7 beg the question a) if a statement begs the question, it avoids dealing with the question or subject being discussed, and makes you want to ask that question: [+ of] *All this activity to build and test nuclear missiles begs the question of who they will be aimed at.* **b)** to argue or discuss something as though the question you are arguing about is true or has been proved, when it may not be true: *The plan begs the question of whether the development is actually needed.* —**begging** n. [U]

be·get /bɪˈgɛt/ v. past tense and past participle **begot** or past tense **begat** /bɪˈgæt/ past participle **begotten** [T] **1** FORMAL to cause something or make it happen: *Poverty begets crime.* **2** OLD USE to become the father of a child

beg·gar¹ /ˈbɛgɚ/ n. [C] **1** someone who lives by asking people for food and money: *You can give beggars vouchers for food instead of cash.* **2 beggars can't be choosers** SPOKEN used to say that when you have no money, no power to choose etc., you have to accept whatever is available

beggar² v. [T] **1 beggar description/belief etc.** FORMAL to be impossible to describe, believe etc.: *For the terrorists to blame the police for their actions beggars belief.* **2** FORMAL to make someone very poor: *Floods combined with falling prices to beggar whole communities of farmers.*

beg·gar·ly /ˈbɛgɚli/ adj. LITERARY a beggarly amount of money or something is much too small

beg·gar·y /ˈbɛgəri/ n. [U] OLD USE the state of being very poor

be·gin /bɪˈgɪn/ past tense **began** /bɪˈgæn/, **begun** v. [S W 11]

1 **start doing/feeling** [I,T] to start doing something or start feeling a particular way: [begin to do sth] *After two weeks, I began to realize that she wasn't coming back.* | [begin doing sth] *Have you begun that new book yet?* | [begin doing sth] *I began working here in 1990.* | [+ with] *Shall we begin with a prayer?* | [begin by doing sth] *Ms. Black began by asking him about his background.*

2 **start happening** [I,T] if something begins, or you begin something, it starts to happen or exist: *Casting for the play will begin next week.* | *It was the coldest winter since records began.* | [+ at] *The*

B

funeral service will begin at 3 p.m. | **[begin (sth) as]** *The band began as a blues band before moving on to rock and roll.*
3 to begin with a) used to introduce the first or most important point that you want to make: *To begin with, much of this new housing is not affordable.* **b)** used to say that something was already in a particular condition before something else happened: *It might be on sale, but it was way overpriced to begin with.* **c)** during the first part of a process or activity: *To keep from going into debt to begin with, set a budget and stick to it.*
4 speech/book **[I]** if a speech, book, word etc. begins with something, it starts with a particular event, activity, letter etc.: **[+ with]** *The book begins with a letter from Barbara Bush.*
5 I can't begin to understand/imagine etc. SPOKEN used to emphasize how difficult something is to understand etc.: *I can't even begin to imagine what it must be like to live under those conditions.* —see Usage Note at COMMENCE
Be·gin /'beɪgɪn/, **Me·na·chem** /mə'nɑkəm/ (1913–1992) an Israeli politician who was PRIME MINISTER from 1977 to 1983, and signed a peace TREATY with President Sadat of Egypt which is called the Camp David Agreement
be·gin·ner /bɪ'gɪnɚ/ *n.* [C] **1** someone who has just started to do or learn something: *Beginners need to ski on easier slopes.* **2 beginner's luck** unusual success that you have when you start doing something new
be·gin·ning /bɪ'gɪnɪŋ/ *n.* **1** [C usually singular] the start or first part of an event, story, period of time etc.: **[+ of]** *The solstice marks the beginning of winter.* | **in/at/from the beginning** *He moved to a different school at the beginning of the school year.* | *There was something strange about the place* **right from the beginning**. | *The novel is exciting* **from beginning to end**. **2 beginnings** [plural] the early part or early signs of something that later develops and becomes bigger, more important etc.: *a report on the beginnings of the AIDS epidemic* | **from small/ humble etc. beginnings** *From humble beginnings in Dallas, the company has developed into one of the largest in America.* **3 the beginning of the end** the time when something starts to end or become less than it was before: *Mandela's release was the beginning of the end of apartheid.*

USAGE NOTE: BEGINNING

WORD CHOICE: at the beginning of, in the beginning
Something that happens at the very start of an event or period of time happens **at the beginning of** it: *At the beginning of the Civil War, Fort Sumter was attacked* (NOT *in the beginning of it*). | *There's a car chase at the beginning* (=at the start of the movie). If something happens **in the beginning** (not usually with *of*), it happens during a period of time near the start of an event or longer period of time: *In the beginning, the South had some success* (=during the early part of the Civil War). | *I was too shy to speak to her in the beginning* (=the first few times I saw her).
SPELLING
Remember that there are two "n"s in **beginning**.

---

be·gone /bɪ'gɔn/ *interjection* OLD USE used to tell someone to go away
be·go·nia /bɪ'goʊnyə/ *n.* [C] a plant with yellow, pink, red, or white flowers
be·got /bɪ'gɑt/ *v.* the past tense of BEGET
be·got·ten /bɪ'gɑtʰn/ *v.* the past participle of BEGET
be·grudge /bɪ'grʌdʒ/ *v.* [T] **1** to feel JEALOUS of someone because they have something which you think they do not deserve: **[begrudge sb sth]** *She is gracious and talented, and no one begrudged her good fortune.* **2** to feel annoyed or unhappy that you have to pay something, give someone something etc.: **[begrudge sb sth]** *I pay my taxes; I don't begrudge the government its share.* | **[begrudge doing sth]**

Most people don't begrudge tipping the waiter a little extra. —**begrudgingly** *adv.*
be·guile /bɪ'gaɪl/ *v.* [T] **1** to persuade or trick someone into doing something, especially by saying nice things to them: *a slick salesman who beguiles unwary investors* **2** LITERARY to do something that makes the time pass, especially in an enjoyable way: *They beguiled the hours away on a rowboat.*
be·guil·ing /bɪ'gaɪlɪŋ/ *adj.* attractive and interesting, but often in a way that deceives you: *beguiling green eyes* —**beguilingly** *adv.*
be·gun /bɪ'gʌn/ *v.* the past participle of BEGIN
be·half /bɪ'hæf/ *n.* **on behalf of sb/on sb's behalf** also **in behalf of sb/in sb's behalf a)** instead of someone, or as their representative: *Dante spoke on behalf of the Directors Guild of America.* | *She filed the lawsuit on her client's behalf.* **b)** because of someone: *Oh, don't go to any trouble on my behalf.*
be·have /bɪ'heɪv/ *v.* [I] **1** [always + adv./prep.] to do things in a particular way: *You behaved bravely in a very difficult situation.* **2** ALSO **behave yourself** to behave in a way that people think is good or correct, by being polite and obeying people, not causing trouble etc.: *Her kids just don't know how to behave.* | *If you behave yourself, I'll let you stay up to watch the movie.* | *a* **well-behaved** *young man* **3** [I] to do something according to natural laws: *Quantum mechanics is the study of the way atoms behave.*
be·hav·ior /bɪ'heɪvyɚ/ *n.* [U] **1** the way that a person or animal does or says things, or a particular example of this: *the behavior of lions in the wild* | *Make it very clear what is acceptable behavior and what is not.* | *criminal behavior* | **good/bad behavior** *Give the child a penalty for bad behavior.* **[+ toward]** *Men must examine their workplace behavior toward women.* **2 be on your best behavior** to behave as well and politely as you can, especially in order to please someone: *Both the lawyer and the client were on their best behavior.* **3** the things that an object, animal, substance etc. normally does: *a theory explaining the behavior of molecules in different substances* —**behavioral** *adj.*: *behavioral problems* —**behaviorally** *adv.*
be·hav·ior·ism /bɪ'heɪvyə,rɪzəm/ *n.* [U] TECHNICAL the belief that the scientific study of the mind should be based only on people's behavior, not on what they say about their thoughts and feelings —**behaviorist** *n.* [C]
be·hav·iour /bɪ'heɪvyɚ/ *n.* [U] the British and Canadian spelling of BEHAVIOR
be·head /bɪ'hɛd/ *v.* [T] to cut off someone's head as a punishment
be·he·moth /bɪ'himəθ/ *n.* [C] LITERARY something that is very large: *One of the new weapons is a $2.5 million behemoth: the M-1 tank.*
be·hest /bɪ'hɛst/ *n.* [singular] **at the behest of sb** FORMAL because someone has asked for something or ordered something to happen: *The committee was formed at the behest of Governor Sinclair.*
be·hind¹ /bɪ'haɪnd/ *prep.* **1** at or toward the back of something: *He sat behind me.* | *Is that your shoe behind the couch?* | *the mountains behind the city* | *I was driving behind a truck on the freeway.* | *I turned around and she was* **right behind** (=very close behind) *me.* **2** not as successful or advanced as someone or something else: *The Rams were 21 points behind the Falcons with only 10 minutes left to play.* | *American manufacturers are* **falling behind** (=becoming less and less successful than) *their global competitors.* | *Interstate 880 opened Tuesday, only three months* **behind schedule**. **3** supporting a person, idea etc.: *Surprisingly, Congress appears to be firmly behind the President on this issue.* **4** responsible for a plan, idea etc. or for organizing something: *The police believe a local gang is behind the killings.* | *The Chamber of Commerce is behind this year's annual fund-raising dinner.* **5** if an experience or situation is behind you, you are not taking part in it anymore, or it does not upset you or affect your life anymore: *Ronstadt's days as a rock star are behind her, for now.* | *The victim wants to* **put this behind** *her and get on with her life.* **6** if a reason,

experience, fact etc. is behind something, it is the reason why something exists or why it has happened: *It's interesting to learn the history behind the buildings.* | *What's behind Cooper's opposition to the changes?* | *The article examines the factors that lie behind his reluctance to compromise on the peace proposals.* **7** if you have experience behind you, you have learned valuable skills or gotten important qualities that can be used: *Gutierrez entered the race with six weeks of solid training behind her.* **8** if a quality or attitude is behind an appearance, you think that it exists although it is hidden: *Behind his gruff exterior, she finds a sweet soul.* —see also **behind sb's back** (BACK² (6)), **behind bars** (BAR¹ (7)) —see Usage Note at FRONT¹

behind² *adv.* **1** at or toward the back or something: *Anderson was in the lead, but several other runners followed close behind.* **2** **be/get/fall behind** to be late or slow in doing something: *He's always been a little bit behind developmentally.* | [**behind with sth**] *I don't know what to do – we're already three months behind with the rent.* **3** **stay/remain behind** to stay in a place when other people have left it or gone somewhere else: *You go ahead – I'll stay behind and wait for Harry.* **4** **leave sth behind** to leave something in a place where you were before or in a place after an event: *The beach was covered with litter left behind by the storm.* | *The movie is about a boy left behind by his family.* **5** **be/fall behind** to be less successful than other people: *The Bruins fell behind in the first quarter, but dominated the game after that.*

behind³ *n.* [C] INFORMAL a word used to mean your BUTTOCKS when you want to be polite

be·hind·hand /bɪˈhaɪndˌhænd/ *adv.* [+ **with, in**] FORMAL late or slow in doing something or paying a debt

be·hold /bɪˈhoʊld/ *v. past tense and past participle* **beheld** /-ˈhɛld/ [T] LITERARY OR OLD USE to see or to look at something —**beholder** *n.* [C] —see also **lo and behold** (LO)

be·hold·en /bɪˈhoʊldən/ *adj.* **feel/be beholden to sb** to feel that you have a duty to someone because they have done something for you: *Ludwig is beholden to the President, who gave him his job.*

be·hoove /bɪˈhuv/ *v.* **it behooves sb to do sth** FORMAL used to say that someone should do something because it is right or necessary or it will help them in some way: *As the war went on, America realized that it behooved them to do something more than sit by and watch.*

beige /beɪʒ/ *n.* [U] a pale dull yellow-brown color —**beige** *adj.*

Bei·jing /beɪˈdʒɪŋ/ the capital city of the People's Republic of China

be·ing¹ /ˈbiɪŋ/ *n.* **1** [C] a living thing, especially a person: *a human being* | *living beings* **2 come into being/be brought into being** to begin to exist: *New democracies have come into being since the end of the Cold War.* **3** [U] LITERARY the most important quality or nature of something, especially of a person | **the core/roots/whole of sb's being** *The fact that so many young people are killed each day shakes me to the core of my being.* | *I regret my actions with every fiber of my being* (=I regret them completely).

being² *v.* [linking verb] **1** the present participle of BE **2** used in explanations to give the most important facts about something: *Being young and single, I wasn't really worried about what might happen.* | *I wasn't surprised about the accident, kids being what they are.*

Bei·rut /beɪˈrut/ the capital and largest city of Lebanon

be·jew·eled /bɪˈdʒuəld/ *adj.* wearing jewels or decorated with jewels: *a bejeweled antique watch*

be·la·bor /bɪˈleɪbɚ/ *v.* [T] **1 belabor the point** to emphasize an idea or fact too strongly, especially by repeating it many times **2** OLD-FASHIONED to beat someone or something hard

Bel·a·rus /ˌbɛləˈrus/ a country in eastern Europe, east of Poland —**Belarussian** /ˌbɛləˈrʌʃən/ *n., adj.*

be·lat·ed /bɪˈleɪtɪd/ *adj.* happening or arriving late: *a belated birthday card* —**belatedly** *adv.*

be·lay /bɪˈleɪ/ *v.* [I,T] **1** TECHNICAL to attach a rope to a ship by winding it under and over in the shape of a figure 8 on a special hook **2** TECHNICAL to control a rope that a climber is attached to, in order to keep them safe while they climb, especially in the sports of ROCK CLIMBING or MOUNTAINEERING

belch /bɛltʃ/ *v.* **1** [I] to let air from your stomach come out loudly through your mouth —see also BURP (1) **2** [I] to give or send out large amounts of smoke, fire etc.: *smokestacks belching black smoke into the air* —**belch** *n.* [C]

be·lea·guered /bɪˈligɚd/ *adj.* FORMAL **1** having many difficulties, especially because everyone is criticizing you or causing trouble for you: *a beleaguered politician* **2** surrounded by an army and unable to escape: *A peace treaty has been accepted by the leaders of the beleaguered village.*

Bel·fast /ˈbɛlfæst/ the capital city of Northern Ireland

bel·fry /ˈbɛlfri/ *n. plural* **belfries** [C] a tower for a bell, especially on a church —see also **have bats in the belfry** (BAT¹ (7))

Belgian en·dive /ˌ.. ˈ../ *n.* [C] ENDIVE (1)

Bel·gium /ˈbɛldʒəm/ a country in northwest Europe between France, Germany, Luxembourg, and the Netherlands —**Belgian** *n., adj.*

Bel·grade /ˈbɛlgreɪd/ the capital city of The Federal Republic of Yugoslavia

be·lie /bɪˈlaɪ/ *v.* [T] FORMAL **1** to give someone a false idea about something: *With a quickness that belied her age, she ran across the road.* **2** to show that your words, hopes etc. are false or mistaken: *Two large tears belied Rosalie's brave words.*

be·lief /bəˈlif/ *n.* **1** [singular,U] the feeling that something is definitely or definitely exists: [+ **in**] *a belief in miracles* | [+ **that**] *Many of the letters to the editor expressed the belief that the two men were innocent.* | *It is my belief that we will find the cure to this disease within the next five years.* | *Most investors buy stocks in the belief that prices will rise in the long term.* | *Contrary to popular belief* (=unlike what most people believe) *pigs are actually very clean animals.* **2** [singular] the feeling that something is good and can be trusted: [+ **in**] *a belief in the value of hard work* | *The judge's decision shook my belief in the legal system.* (=made me doubt that it is good or can be trusted) **3** [C] an idea that you believe to be true, especially one that forms part of a system of ideas: *religious beliefs* | *Several members of the government still hold Marxist beliefs.* **4** **be beyond belief** to seem too strange or unreasonable to be true: *Their incompetence is beyond belief.* —see also **to the best of your knowledge/belief/ability** (BEST³ (10)) —compare DISBELIEF, UNBELIEF

be·liev·a·ble /bəˈlivəbəl/ *adj.* something that is believable can be believed because it seems possible, likely, or real: *Her story is told in a straightforward, believable fashion.* —**believably** *adv.*

be·lieve /bəˈliv/ *v.* [not in progressive]

1 be sure sth is true [T] to be sure that something is true or that someone is telling the truth: *You can't believe everything you read in the papers.* | *Students weren't sure who to believe.* | [**believe (that)**] *I can't believe that Rosen was offended.* | [**believe sb**] *His story wasn't very convincing, but I believed him.* | *She's charming and pretty, but you can't believe a word she says* (=you can't believe anything she says).

2 have an opinion [T] to think that something is true, although you are not completely sure: [**believe (that)**] *I believe that I should be receiving a refund.* | *"Is your mother coming to the picnic?" "Yes, I believe so."* (=think that it is true) | *At 115, Mrs. Jackson is believed to be one of the oldest people in the world.* | *The four men are widely believed* (=believed by a lot of people) *to have been killed by their captors.* | *We* **have reason to believe (that)** (=have information that makes you believe something) *she knew her killer.*

SPOKEN PHRASES

3 can't/don't believe sth said when you are very surprised or shocked by something: *When I saw the video, I was like, I don't believe it!* | *I can't believe you lied to me!*
4 believe (you) me used to emphasize that something is definitely true: *No, it's too far to walk, believe me.*
5 would you believe it! said when you are surprised or angry about something: *Would you believe it, she actually remembered my birthday!*
6 believe it or not used when you are going to say something that is true but surprising: *Well, believe it or not, we're getting married.*
7 you'd better believe it! used to emphasize that something is true: *"Do they make money on them?" "You'd better believe it!"*
8 can't believe your eyes/ears to be very surprised by something you see or hear: *I couldn't believe my ears when she told me the cheapest flight was $1,100.*
9 don't you believe it! used to emphasize that something is definitely not true
10 if you believe that, you'll believe anything used to say that something is definitely not true, and that anyone who believes it must be stupid
11 seeing is believing used to say that you will only believe that something happens or exists when you actually see it

12 religion [I] to have a strong religious faith: *Only those who believe will go to heaven.* —see also **make believe** (MAKE[1] (26))
believe in *phr. v.* [T] **1** [believe in sb] to be sure that someone exists: *Do you believe in God?* | *She still believes in Santa Claus.* **2** [believe in sth] to support or approve of something because you think it is good or right: *He believes in democracy.* [believe in doing sth] *They believe in maintaining small class sizes.* **3** [believe in sb/sth] to think that someone is good or that they can be trusted: *We're starting to believe in ourselves as a hockey team.* | *Many Americans no longer believe in their government.*

be·liev·er /bə'livɚ/ *n.* **1 be a (great) believer in sth** to believe strongly that something is good and brings good results: *I'm a great believer in regular exercise.* **2** [C] someone who believes in a particular religion, or system of beliefs

be·lit·tle /bɪ'lɪt̮l/ *v.* [T] FORMAL to make someone or something seem small or unimportant: *She has a way of speaking to employees that belittles them.*

Be·lize /bə'liz/ a country in Central America on the Caribbean Sea

S W
3 3
bell /bɛl/ *n.* [C] **1 a)** a hollow metal object shaped like an upside down cup, that makes a ringing sound when it is hit by a piece of metal that hangs down inside it: *church bells* **b)** a round ball of metal with another small ball inside it that makes a ringing sound: *Attach a bell to the cat's collar to warn birds.* —see picture at BICYCLE[1] **2** a piece of electrical equipment that makes a ringing sound, used as a signal or to get someone's attention: *The bell sounded to end the fight.* | *Please* **ring the bell** for assistance. **3** the sound of a bell ringing as a signal or a warning: *When you hear the bell, stop writing.* **4 with all the bells and whistles** with all the special features you can have: *The new Jeep comes with all the bells and whistles.* **5 have/get your bell rung** to be hit on the head, sometimes hard enough to make you unconscious: *a football player who had his bell rung too often* **6** something shaped like a bell: *the bell of a flower* **7 I'll be there with bells on** SPOKEN used to say that you will definitely be somewhere and ready to do what you have planned —see also **as clear as a bell** (CLEAR[1] (8)), DIVING BELL, **ring a bell** (RING[2] (4))

Bell /bɛl/**, Al·ex·an·der Gra·ham** /,ælɪg'zændɚ 'greɪəm/ (1847–1922) a Scottish scientist and inventor who lived in the U.S. and is famous for inventing the telephone in 1876 —see picture on page 1329

bel·la·don·na /,bɛlə'dɑnə/ *n.* [U] **1** a poisonous plant; DEADLY NIGHTSHADE **2** a substance from this plant, used as a drug

bell bot·toms /'. ,../ *n.* [plural] a pair of pants with legs that become wider at the bottom —**bell-bottomed** *adj.*

bell·boy /'bɛlbɔɪ/ *n. plural* **bellboys** [C] a bellhop

belle /bɛl/ *n.* [C] OLD-FASHIONED a beautiful girl or woman: *a Southern belle* | *Caroline was* **the belle of the ball** (=the most beautiful girl at a dance or party) *in her silver and white evening gown.*

belle é·poque /,bɛl eɪ'pɔk, -'pɑk/ *n.* [singular] a period of time in which art and CULTURE are very important, used especially about France in the early 20th century

belles let·tres /,bɛl 'lɛtrə/ *n.* [U] literature or writings about subjects relating to literature

bell·hop /'bɛlhɑp/ *n.* [C] a young man who carries bags, takes messages etc. in a hotel

bel·li·cose /,bɛləkoʊs/ *adj.* LITERARY always wanting to fight or argue; AGGRESSIVE —**bellicosity** /,bɛlə'kɑsət̮i/ *n.* [U]

-bellied /bɛlid/ [in adjectives] **black-bellied/fat-bellied/big-bellied** etc. having a black, fat etc. stomach: *a black-bellied duck*

bel·lig·er·ent /bə'lɪdʒərənt/ *adj.* **1** very unfriendly and mean, and wanting to argue or fight: *The police said that George was drunk and belligerent.* **2** [only before noun] FORMAL a belligerent country is at war with another country —**belligerence** —**belligerency** *n.* [U]

bel·low[1] /'bɛloʊ/ *v.* **1** [I,T] to shout loudly, especially in a deep voice: *"He's guilty and I'll prove it!" Sharpton bellowed.* **2** [I] to make the deep sound that a BULL makes

bellow[2] *n.* **1 bellows** [plural] **a)** an object that you use to blow air into a fire to make it burn better **b)** a part of a musical instrument that pushes air through pipes to produce sound, such as in an ORGAN **2** [C] the deep sound that a BULL makes

bell pep·per /,. '../ *n.* [C] a hollow red, green, or yellow vegetable; PEPPER[1] (3) —see picture at VEGETABLE

bell ring·er /'. ,../ *n.* [C] someone who rings a bell, especially in a church —**bell ringing** *n.* [U]

bell·weth·er /'bɛl,wɛðɚ/ *n.* [C] FORMAL something, especially a company or STOCK, that people consider to be a sign of how an economic situation is changing: *General Motors, a bellwether stock, rose several points.*

bel·ly[1] /'bɛli/ *n. plural* **bellies** [C] INFORMAL **1 a)** your stomach: *Everybody should go home with full bellies tonight.* **b)** the front part of your body between your chest and your legs: *She lay on her belly in the long grass.* —see also POTBELLY **2** the middle part of an animal's body, near its stomach **3 go belly up** to fail: *Tim's business went belly up in 1993.* **4** a curved or rounded middle part of an object: *the belly of an airplane* —see also -BELLIED

belly[2] *v.* **bellies, bellied, bellying**
belly up to sth *phr. v.* [T] INFORMAL to walk toward something and stand with your stomach next to it: *He bellied up to the bar and ordered a scotch.*

bel·ly·ache[1] /'bɛli,eɪk/ *n.* [C,U] a pain in your stomach

bellyache[2] *v.* [I] INFORMAL to complain a lot, especially about something that is not important: [+ about] *He just sat there, bellyaching about the price of the tickets.*

belly but·ton /'.. ,../ *n.* [C] INFORMAL the small hollow or raised place in the middle of your stomach; NAVEL

belly dance /'.. ,./ *n.* [C] a dance from the Middle East performed by a woman using movements of her stomach and HIPS —**belly dancer** *n.* [C]

belly flop /'.. ,./ *n.* [C] a way of jumping into water, in which the front of your body falls flat against the surface of the water —**belly flop** *v.* [I]

bel·ly·ful /'bɛli,fʊl/ *n.* **have had a bellyful of sth**

INFORMAL to be annoyed by something because you have heard or experienced too much of it: *Audiences have had a bellyful of gangster movies.*

belly-land·ing /'.. ,../ *n.* [C] the act of landing an airplane without using the wheels —**belly-land** *v.* [I]

belly laugh /'.. ,./ *n.* [C] INFORMAL a deep loud laugh

Bel·mo·pan /ˌbɛlmoʊ'pæn/ the capital city of Belize

be·long /bɪ'lɔŋ/ *v.* [I] **1** [always + adv./prep.] to be in the right place or situation: *Can you put that back where it belongs?* | [+ **in**] *The shopping center doesn't belong in the middle of a residential neighborhood.* **2** to be a member of a group or organization: [+ **to**] *They belong to the country club.* **3** to feel happy and comfortable in a place or situation, because you have the same interests and ideas as other people: *I felt I belonged there – I was important there.* | [+ **in**] *I taught in high schools, but I really belonged in the elementary schools.*

belong to [T] **1** [**belong to** sb/sth] to be the property of someone or of an organization: *Do the books belong to the school?* **2** [**belong to** sth] to be related to something or be a part of something: *cars that belong to a different era*

be·long·ings /bɪ'lɔŋɪŋz/ *n.* [plural] the things that you own, especially those that you can carry with you: *Soldiers searched through people's personal belongings.*

be·loved /bɪ'lʌvd, bɪ'lʌvɪd/ *adj.* LITERARY OR HUMOROUS **1** a beloved place, thing etc. is one that you love very much: *Tom's beloved 1965 Ford Mustang convertible* | [+ **by/of**] *The area has beautiful beaches, beloved by tourists and surfers alike.* **2** my/her etc. **beloved** LITERARY the person that you love most: *a visit from my beloved* —see also **dearly beloved** (DEARLY (4))

below

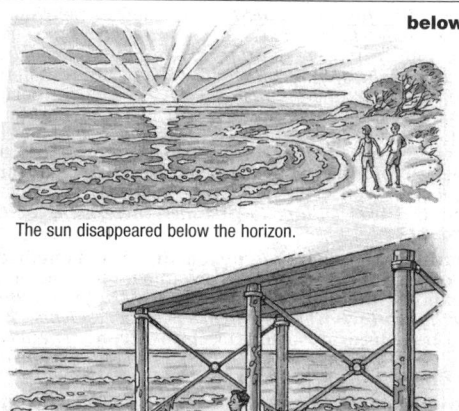

The sun disappeared below the horizon.

The boy was sitting under the pier.

be·low¹ /bɪ'loʊ/ *prep.* **1** in a lower place or position than something, or on a lower level than something: *The accident left him with no feeling below the waist.* | *Print your name below your signature.* —opposite ABOVE¹ **2** less than a particular number, amount, level etc.: *It was 20° below zero outside.* | *Many families in this area are living below the official poverty line.* | *Thompson scored only eight points, 14 below his season average.* | **way/well below** (=very much lower than a particular number etc.) | *a* **below average** (=not as good as the normal standard) *student* | *Temperatures are expected to remain* **below freezing** (=lower than the temperature at which water freezes) *for the rest of the week.* —opposite ABOVE¹ **3** in a lower less important job than someone else: *A captain is below a general.* —opposite ABOVE¹ —see Usage Note at UNDER¹

below² *adv.* **1** in a lower place or position, or on a lower level: *Water was dripping onto the ground below.* | *The wood is rotted below.* | *The colder water is* **down below***, with the warmer water on top.*

2 mentioned or shown lower on the same page or on a later page: *Answer each of the questions below.* | *For more information, see below.* —opposite ABOVE² **3** 10/15/20 **below etc.** if a temperature is 10, 15, 20 below etc., it is that number of degrees lower than zero **4** on the lower level of a ship or boat: *Captain Parker* **went below***, leaving Clooney in charge.* **5** less than a particular number, age, price etc.: *Designer clothing was offered at wholesale prices and below.* **6** in a lower less important rank or job: *officers of the rank of captain and below* **7** LITERARY on Earth rather than in Heaven

belt¹ /bɛlt/ *n.* [C] **1** a band of leather, cloth etc. that you wear around your waist, especially to hold up your pants **2** a circular band of a material such as rubber that connects or moves parts of a machine: *The pump belt was loose.* —see also CONVEYOR BELT, FAN BELT **3** a large area of land that has particular features: *America's farming belt* | *the sun belt states* (=states that have warm weather) **4 have/get sth under your belt** to have achieved something useful or important: *Once you've had a few lessons under your belt, you're ready to buy your own ski equipment.* **5 below the belt** INFORMAL unfair or cruel: *Some say the ads* **hit below the belt** (=are unfair). —see also CHASTITY BELT, GARTER BELT, SEAT BELT, **tighten your belt** (TIGHTEN (7))

belt² *v.* INFORMAL [T] to hit someone or something hard: *Maggie just turned around and belted him.*

belt sth ↔ out *phr. v.* [T] INFORMAL to sing a song very loudly: *My colleagues started belting out a chorus of "Happy Birthday."*

belt·ed /'bɛltɪd/ *adj.* fastened with a belt: *a belted jacket*

belt-tight·en·ing /'. ,.../ *n.* [U] the act or process of spending less money than before: *Raises won't be given during this period of belt-tightening.*

belt·way /'bɛltˌweɪ/ *n.* **1** [C] a road that goes around a city to keep traffic away from the center **2 the Beltway** the U.S. government in Washington, D.C., and the politicians, lawyers, LOBBYISTS etc. who are involved in it: *The idea isn't popular* **inside the Beltway***.*

be·lu·ga /bə'lugə/ *n.* **1** a type of WHALE **2** a type of expensive CAVIAR (=fish eggs) from a STURGEON

be·moan /bɪ'moʊn/ *v.* [T] to complain or say that you are disappointed about something: *For years, parents and teachers have bemoaned the fact that we do not have a national childcare policy.*

be·mused /bɪ'myuzd/ *adj.* someone who is bemused is slightly confused: *Edberg looked bemused by the questions.*

bench¹ /bɛntʃ/ *n.* **1** [C] a long seat for two or more people, used especially outdoors: *a long wooden bench* **2** [singular] **a)** a seat where members of a sports team sit when they are not playing: *We managed to win, even with Brian* **on the bench** (=not playing). | *Hayden came* **off the bench** (=he started playing) *to score 14 points.* **b)** the players who do not usually play at the start of a game, but who often play later in the game: *a team with a strong bench* **3 the bench a)** the job of being a judge in a court of law: *He was appointed to the bench in 1986.* | **serve/sit on the bench** (=to work as a judge) **b)** the seat where a judge sits in a court of law: *Smith approached the bench and asked for a delay.* **4** [C] a long heavy table used for working on with tools or equipment: *a carpenter's bench*

bench² *v.* [T] to not allow a sports player to play in a game, or to remove a player from a game: *Anderson has been benched for three weeks until his injury has healed.*

bench·mark /'bɛntʃmɑrk/ *n.* [C] **1** something that is used as a standard by which other things can be judged or measured: *The index rate is the benchmark used by lenders to set the mortgage rate.* **2** a mark made on a building, post etc. that shows its height above sea level, and is used to measure other heights and distances in a SURVEY

bench·warm·er /'bɛntʃ,wɔrmə/ *n.* [C] INFORMAL a sports player who does not play at the beginning of a game, but plays if someone else is injured or cannot play

bend[1] /bɛnd/ *v. past tense and past participle* **bent**

1 move your body [I always + adv./prep.,T] to move a part of your body so that it is not straight or so that you are not standing upright anymore: [+ **over**] *Levy bent over to pick up the coins.* | [+ **down**] *I bent down to tie my shoelaces.* | [+ **for-ward/toward/across** etc.] *Bending forward, he stroked the dog's head.* | *Relax your arms and bend your elbows slightly.*

2 curve **a)** [T] to push or press something into a curved shape or fold it at an angle: *You can't bend the steel without some kind of tool.* **b)** [I] to change to the shape of a curve, or to be in this shape: *If the Christmas tree is fresh, the needles will bend without breaking.* | *The metal bar bends in the middle.* —see picture on page 424

3 bend over backward (to do sth) also **bend over backward** to try very hard to be helpful: *The hotel employees bent over backward to please us.*

4 bend the rules to allow someone to do something that is not normally allowed, or to do something that is not usually allowed: *a tough street cop who bends the rules*

5 bend sb's ear SPOKEN to talk to someone, especially about something that is worrying you

6 on bended knee a) trying very hard to persuade someone to do something: *The TV network begged her on bended knee to return to the program.* **b)** in a kneeling position: *George asked her to marry him on bended knee.*

7 bend your mind/efforts/thoughts etc. to sth FORMAL to give all your energy or attention to one activity, plan etc.

bend[2] *n.* [C] **1** a curved part of something, especially a road or river: *The creek goes around a bend by the farm.* | [+ **in**] *a sharp bend in the road* **2** an action in which you bend a part of your body: *Start with a few knee bends.* **3 the bends** [plural] a very painful and serious condition that DIVERS get when they come up from under deep water too quickly

bend·a·ble /'bɛndəbəl/ *adj.* able to be bent: *bendable toys*

bend·er /'bɛndə/ *n.* [C] INFORMAL **go on a bender** to drink a lot of alcohol at one time

be·neath[1] /bɪ'niθ/ *prep.* FORMAL **1** in or to a lower position than something, or directly under something: *Plastic is used beneath the rocks to prevent weeds growing through.* | *the warm sand beneath her feet* **2** not appropriate for someone because of not being good enough: *She acted like even speaking to us was beneath her.* **3** a feeling or attitude that is beneath another feeling or attitude is covered or hidden by it: *racial tensions that lie beneath the surface of our society* **4** in a lower less important rank or job than someone else —see Usage Note at UNDER[1]

beneath[2] *adv.* in or to a lower position: *The whales are black or gray on top, with white beneath.* | *He stood on the bridge, looking at the river beneath.*

Ben·e·dict /'bɛnə,dɪkt/, **Saint** (?480–?547) an Italian religious leader who started the Benedictine group of Christian MONKS

Ben·e·dic·tine /,bɛnə'dɪktɪn, -tin/ *n.* [C] a member of a Christian religious order of MONKS —**Benedictine** *adj.*

ben·e·dic·tine /,bɛnə'dɪktɪn, -tin/ *n.* [C,U] a strong alcoholic drink that is a type of LIQUEUR

ben·e·dic·tion /,bɛnə'dɪkʃən/ *n.* [C,U] a type of prayer in the Christian religion that asks God to protect and help someone

Ben·e·dict XV /,bɛnədɪkt ðə fɪf'tinθ/, **Pope** (1854–1922) the POPE at the time of World War I

ben·e·fac·tion /,bɛnə'fækʃən/ *n.* FORMAL **1** [U] the act of doing something good, especially by giving money to someone who needs it **2** [C] money given in this way

ben·e·fac·tor /'bɛnə,fæktə/ *n.* [C] someone who gives money for a good purpose: *The museum received $5 million from an unnamed benefactor.*

ben·e·fac·tress /'bɛnə,fæktrɪs/ *n.* [C] OLD-FASHIONED a woman who gives money for a good purpose

ben·e·fice /'bɛnəfɪs/ *n.* [C] the pay and position of the priest of a Christian PARISH

be·nef·i·cent /bɪ'nɛfəsənt/ *adj.* FORMAL doing things to help people; generous —**beneficence** *n.* [U] —**beneficently** *adv.*

ben·e·fi·cial /,bɛnə'fɪʃəl/ *adj.* producing results that bring advantages: *beneficial changes* | [+ **to**] *an environmental program that is beneficial to all* —**beneficially** *adv.*

ben·e·fi·ci·ar·y /,bɛnə'fɪʃi,ɛri, -'fɪʃəri/ *n. plural* **beneficiaries** [C] **1** someone who gets advantages from an action or change: *Single mothers will be the chief beneficiaries of this new policy.* | [+ **of**] *the beneficiary of U.S. aid* **2** someone who receives money or property from someone else who has died: [+ **of**] *He was the main beneficiary of his father's will.*

ben·e·fit[1] /'bɛnəfɪt/ *n.* **1** [C usually plural] the money or other advantages that you get from something such as insurance or the government, or as part of your job: *The benefits include full medical cover when traveling abroad.* | *The company provides medical benefits.* | *social security benefits* **2** [C,U] something that gives you advantages or improves your life in some way: *the safety benefits of wearing bicycle helmets* | *Young mothers* **have the benefit of** *day care on campus.* | *Liu Han translated what he had said* **for my benefit** (=in order to help me). | *Even older heavy smokers can* **reap benefits** (=gain advantages) *from quitting smoking.* | *a new drug that may* **be of** *clinical benefit* (=be useful or helpful) *for a life-threatening disease* **3** [C] a concert, performance, dinner etc. arranged to make money for a CHARITY: *a benefit being held at a downtown hotel* | *a benefit concert for the Children's Hospital* **4 the benefit of the doubt** the act of accepting what someone tells you even though you think they may be lying: *I was willing to* **give her the benefit of the doubt**.

benefit[2] *v.* **benefited, benefiting** also **benefitted, benefitting 1** [T] to bring advantages to someone or improve their lives in some way: *New regulations will greatly benefit the region's poorest residents.* **2** [I] to be helped by something: [+ **by/from**] *The whole nation benefits by having skilled and educated workers.*

Be·ne·lux /'bɛnl,ʌks/ *n.* the countries of Belgium, the Netherlands, and Luxembourg, considered as a group

Be·nét /bə'neɪ/, **Ste·phen Vin·cent** /'stivən 'vɪnsənt/ (1898–1943) a U.S. writer of poems and short stories

be·nev·o·lent /bə'nɛvələnt/ *adj.* kind and generous: *a benevolent, kindly man* | *money for benevolent work* —**benevolence** *n.* [U] —**benevolently** *adv.*

Ben·ga·li /bɛn'gɔli/ *n.* **1** [U] the language of Bangladesh or West Bengal **2** [C] someone from Bengal —**Bengali** *adj.*

Ben-Gur·i·on /bɛn 'gurɪən/, **Da·vid** /'deɪvɪd/ (1886–1973) an Israeli politician, born in Poland, who is considered responsible for establishing the independent Jewish nation of Israel

be·night·ed /bɪ'naɪtɪd/ *adj.* having no knowledge or understanding —**benightedly** *adv.*

be·nign /bɪ'naɪn/ *adj.* **1** TECHNICAL not likely to hurt you or cause CANCER: *a benign tumor* **2** FORMAL kind and unlikely to harm anyone: *the animal's benign nature* —**benignly** *adv.* —**benignity** *n.* [U] —compare MALIGNANT

Be·nin /bə'nin, bə'nɪn, 'bɛnɪn/, **the People's Republic of** a country in West Africa, between Togo and Nigeria

Ben·ja·min /ˈbɛndʒəmɪn/ in the Bible, the youngest son of Jacob and the head of one of the 12 tribes of Israel

bent[1] /bɛnt/ v. the past tense and past participle of BEND[1]

bent[2] adj. **1 be bent on sth** to be completely determined to do something: *a society that seems bent on its own destruction* | **[be bent on doing sth]** *Rudi seems bent on finding a new job.* —see also HELL-BENT **2** curved and not flat or straight anymore: *The nail is bent.* **3 bent out of shape** SPOKEN very angry or annoyed: *Hey, don't get all bent out of shape!*

bent[3] n. [singular] a natural skill or ability: *Rebecca has an artistic bent.*

be·numbed /bɪˈnʌmd/ adj. FORMAL **1** made NUMB (=unable to feel anything) by cold **2** not doing anything or not working, especially because you are shocked or upset: *benumbed prison guards*

Benz /bɛnz/, **Karl** /karl/ (1844–1929) a German engineer who built the first gasoline-driven car in 1885

ben·zene /ˈbɛnzin, bɛnˈzin/ n. [U] a liquid obtained from coal and used for making plastics

ben·zine /ˈbɛnzin, bɛnˈzin/ n. [U] a liquid obtained from PETROLEUM and used to clean clothes

be·queath /bɪˈkwiθ, bɪˈkwið/ v. [T] FORMAL **1** to officially arrange for someone to have something that you own after your death: **[bequeath sth to sb]** *The letter was bequeathed to the museum by a collector.* **2** to pass knowledge, customs etc. to people who come after you or live after you

be·quest /bɪˈkwɛst/ n. [C] FORMAL money or property that you bequeath to someone: *a bequest of $50,000*

be·rate /bəˈreɪt/ v. [T] FORMAL to speak angrily to someone because they have done something wrong: **[berate sb for sth]** *An angry father berated the club's directors for not acting soon enough*

Ber·ber /ˈbɚbɚ/ one of the tribes from northwest Africa who live in the area between Morocco and Tunisia

be·reaved[1] /bəˈrivd/ adj. FORMAL having lost a close friend or relative because they have recently died: *a bereaved mother*

bereaved[2] n. **the bereaved** the person or people whose close friend or relative has just died: *Our sympathies go to the bereaved.*

be·reave·ment /bəˈrivmənt/ n. [C,U] FORMAL the fact or state of having lost a close friend or relative because they have died: *depression caused by bereavement or divorce*

be·reft /bəˈrɛft/ adj. FORMAL **1 bereft of hope/meaning/life etc.** completely without any hope etc.: *a city that is bereft of culture* **2** feeling very sad and lonely

be·ret /bəˈreɪ/ n. [C] a round hat with a tight band around the head and a soft loose top part —see picture at HAT

Berg·man /ˈbɚgmən/, **Ing·mar** /ˈɪŋmɑr/ (1918–) a Swedish movie DIRECTOR who is considered one of the most important directors ever

ber·i·ber·i /ˌbɛriˈbɛri/ n. [U] a disease of the nerves caused by lack of VITAMIN B

Be·ring Sea, the /ˈbɛrɪŋ, ˈbɪrɪŋ/ a part of the northern Pacific Ocean that is between Siberia and Alaska

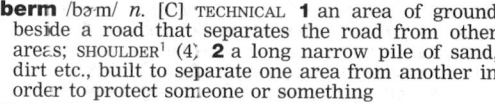
Irving Berlin

Bering Strait, the a narrow passage of water between Asia and North America that connects the Bering Sea to the Arctic Ocean

Ber·lin /bɚˈlɪn/ the capital city of Germany

Berlin, Ir·ving /ˈɚvɪŋ/ (1888–1989) a U.S. SONG-WRITER famous for his popular songs and MUSICALS

Ber·li·oz /ˈbɛrliouz/, **Hec·tor** /ˈhɛktɚ/ (1803–1869) a French musician who wrote CLASSICAL music

---

berm /bɚm/ n. [C] TECHNICAL **1** an area of ground beside a road that separates the road from other areas; SHOULDER[1] (4) **2** a long narrow pile of sand, dirt etc., built to separate one area from another in order to protect someone or something

Ber·mu·da /bɚˈmyudə/ a country that consists of a group of islands in the West Atlantic Ocean. Bermuda is a British COLONY, but has its own government.

Bermuda shorts /.ˌ.. ˈ./ also **Bermudas** n. [plural] short pants that end at the knee and are made from thin cloth, often in very bright colors

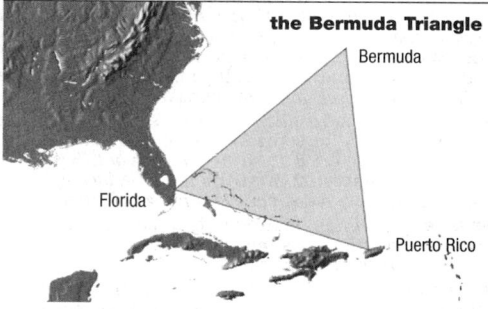
the Bermuda Triangle
Bermuda
Florida
Puerto Rico

Bermuda Tri·an·gle, the /.ˌ.. ˈ.../ an area in the Atlantic Ocean between Bermuda, Florida, and Puerto Rico where many ships and aircraft are believed to have strangely disappeared

Bern /bɚn, bɛrn/ the capital city of Switzerland

Ber·na·dette /ˌbɚnəˈdɛt/, **Saint** also **St. Berna·dette of Lourdes** (1844–1879) a French girl who claimed to have seen the Virgin Mary at Lourdes, which made Lourdes a place of PILGRIMAGE, especially for the sick

Bern·hardt /ˈbɚnhɑrt/, **Sa·rah** /ˈsærə/ (1844–1923) a French actress who is considered one of the best actresses ever

Ber·ni·ni /bɚˈnini/, **Gio·van·ni Lo·ren·zo** /dʒouˈvɑni ləˈrɛnzou/ (1598–1680) an Italian SCULPTOR, ARCHITECT, and PAINTER, famous for his work in the BAROQUE style

Bern·stein /ˈbɚnstaɪn, -stin/, **Leon·ard** /ˈlɛnɚd/ (1918–1990) a U.S. musician who wrote CLASSICAL music

ber·ry /ˈbɛri/ n. plural **berries** [C] a small soft fruit with small seeds

Ber·ry /ˈbɛri/, **Chuck** /tʃʌk/ (1926–) a U.S. musician and singer who was important in the development of ROCK 'N' ROLL

ber·serk /bɚˈsɚk, -ˈzɚk/ adj. **go berserk** to become very angry and violent: *The guy just went totally berserk and started hitting me.*

Leonard Bernstein

berth[1] /bɚθ/ n. [C] **1** a place for someone to sleep in a ship or on a train **2** a place where a ship can stop and be tied up —see also **give sb/sth a wide berth** (WIDE[1] (8))

berth[2] v. [I,T] to bring a ship into a berth or arrive at a berth

ber·yl /ˈbɛrəl/ n. [C] a valuable stone that is usually green or yellow

Ber·ze·li·us /bɚˈziliəs/, **Jäns** /yɑns/ (1779–1848) a Swedish scientist who established the system of ATOMIC weights

be·seech /bɪˈsitʃ/ v. past tense and past participle **beseeched** or **besought** [T] LITERARY to eagerly and anxiously ask someone for something

be·seem /bɪˈsim/ v. [T] OLD USE to be appropriate for something

be·set /bɪˈsɛt/ *v. past tense and past participle* **beset** *present participle* **besetting** [T] FORMAL **1** [usually passive] to make someone experience serious problems or dangers: [+ by/with] *Many families are beset by financial difficulties.* **2** besetting sin/weakness OFTEN HUMOROUS a particular bad feature or habit

be·side /bɪˈsaɪd/ *prep.* **1** next to or very close to someone or something: *Gary, come sit beside me.* | *a cabin beside the lake* **2** used to compare two people or things: *The loss of the port pales beside the gain of a peace treaty.* **3** be beside the point to not be directly related to the main subject or problem that you are talking about: *It's unrealistic, but that's beside the point – it's just good entertainment.* **4** be beside yourself (with sth) to feel so angry, excited etc. that you find it difficult to control yourself: *He was beside himself with joy when he won the lottery.*

be·sides[1] /bɪˈsaɪdz/ *adv.* **1** SPOKEN said when giving another reason for something after one that has just been mentioned: *I wanted to help her out. Besides, I needed the money.* **2** in addition to: *Besides going to aerobics twice a week, she rides horses on Saturdays.*

besides[2] *prep.* in addition to a point, statement, person etc. that has just been mentioned: *Who's going to be there besides me?*

be·siege /bɪˈsidʒ/ *v.* [T] **1** [usually passive] if people, thoughts etc. besiege you, you are surrounded by them: [+ by] *a movie star besieged by reporters and photographers* **2** be besieged with letters/demands/ requests etc. to receive a very large number of letters, requests etc.: *Her friends were besieged with calls.* **3** to surround a city, building etc. with a military force until the people inside let you take control: *opposition forces who besieged the parliament building*

be·smirch /bɪˈsmɚtʃ/ *v.* [T] LITERARY **besmirch sb's honor/reputation** to spoil the good opinion that people have of someone

be·sot·ted /bɪˈsɑtɪd/ *adj.* loving or wanting someone or something so much that you cannot think or behave sensibly: [be besotted with/by] *a father besotted with his new daughter*

be·sought /bɪˈsɔt/ *v.* the past tense and past participle of BESEECH

be·speak /bɪˈspik/ *v. past tense* **bespoke** /bɪˈspoʊk/ *past participle* **bespoken** /bɪˈspoʊkən/ [T] LITERARY to be a sign of something: *His speech bespoke the country's mood of hope and confidence.*

be·spec·ta·cled /bɪˈspɛktɪkəld/ *adj.* wearing glasses

best[1] /bɛst/ *adj.* [the superlative of "good"] **1** better than anything else or anyone else in quality, skill, effectiveness etc.: *Terry is the best player on our team.* | *What's the best way to get to El Paso?* | *Probably the best thing to do is to drop me off outside.* | *It's one of the best books I've ever read.* | *It's easily her best work in years.* | *Maui is by far the best base for whale watching.* | [be best to do sth] *It's best to have a bike shop check the bearings.* **2** best dress/ shoes/clothes etc. clothing that you only wear on special occasions: *Bobby was wearing his best shirt for the occasion.* **3** best friend the friend that you know and like better than anyone else **4** best wishes **a)** written in cards to say that you hope someone will be happy: [+ for/on] *Best wishes for your marriage!* **b)** used to say goodbye at the end of a letter **5** best of all used to introduce the one fact about a situation that is even better than the other good things: *You can lose five pounds a week on this diet. And best of all, you never have to feel hungry.* —see also **be on your best behavior** (BEHAVIOR (2)), **your best bet** (BET[2] (3)), **the next best thing** (NEXT[1] (5)), **the best/better part of sth** (PART[1] (6))

best[2] *adv.* [the superlative of "well"] **1** to the greatest degree; most: *I've met him a few times but Helen knows him best.* | *The judges liked the pumpkin pie from Gayle's Bakery best.* **2** in a way that is better than any other: *Try a few different skis and boots to see what works best for you.* | *Our new spring dresses have a look that can best be described as neat yet*

casual. | *the best-dressed man in the office* **3** as best you can SPOKEN as well as you can, even if this is not very good: *I'll deal with the problem as best I can.* **4** had best FORMAL ought to: *They had best be careful.* **5** for reasons best known to herself/himself used to say that you cannot understand why someone has done something: *For reasons best known to herself, she decided to quit her job and become a painter.*

best[3] *n.* **1** [singular] the person or thing that is better than any other: *She's the best of the new young writers.* | *The best is not always the most expensive.* **2** [singular] the most helpful, most successful etc. situation or result that you can achieve: *The acoustics in the auditorium weren't the best, but the audience didn't care.* | *All parents want the best for their children.* | *Playing once a week is about the best I can do* (=it is all I am able to do). **3** the best in sb the qualities that someone has that are good: *a teacher who can bring out the best in her students* **4** do the best you can also do your best to try as hard as you can to do something: *I'll play hard – I'll do the best I can.* | *Doctors did their best to stop the bleeding.* **5** at best used to emphasize that something is not very good, even when you try to think of all the good things about it: *At best, sales have been good but not great.* | *Public transportation is at best limited.* **6** at your/its best performing as well or effectively as you are able to: *The music, at its best, is almost unbearably beautiful.* | *Some vegetables are at their best nutritionally when eaten raw.* **7** make the best of sth to accept an unsatisfactory situation, and do whatever you can to make it better: *It's not going to be fun, but we might as well make the best of it.* **8** be for the best used to say that a particular event may not be as bad as it seems: *Even though I lost my job, I knew it was for the best. It gave me the chance to start again.* **9** hope for the best to hope that a bad or difficult situation will end in a way that is good: *We try to help the people who come in, and just hope for the best.* **10** to the best of your knowledge/belief/ability etc. used to say that something is as much as you know, believe, or are able to do: *To the best of my recollection, they never asked us for any money.* **11** the best of both worlds a situation in which you have the advantages of two different things without any of the disadvantages: *Job-sharing gives me the best of both worlds – I can be with my children and keep my professional status.* **12** at the best of times if something is not very good, enjoyable etc. at the best of times, it is usually even worse than this: *Even at the best of times the roads are dangerous.* **13** all the best used to express good wishes to someone for the future: *Tell him I said goodbye and wish him all the best.* —see also **sb's Sunday best** (SUNDAY)

best[4] *v.* [T] OLD USE to defeat someone

bes·tial /ˈbɛstʃəl, ˈbis-/ *adj.* FORMAL behaving like an animal, especially in a cruel way —**bestially** *adv.*

bes·ti·al·i·ty /ˌbɛstʃiˈælət̬i/ *n.* [U] **1** sexual relations between a person and an animal **2** FORMAL very cruel behavior

bes·ti·ar·y /ˈbɛstʃiɛri/ *n.* [C] an old book about strange animals, written in the Middle Ages

be·stir /bɪˈstɚ/ *v.* [T] **bestir yourself** FORMAL to start to do things, after relaxing or being lazy

best man /ˌ. ˈ./ *n.* [singular] the man who stands beside and helps the BRIDEGROOM (=the man getting married) at a wedding ceremony

be·stow /bɪˈstoʊ/ *v.* [T] FORMAL to give someone something of great value or importance: [bestow sth on/upon sb] *An award for poetry was bestowed on Philip Levine for his collection "What Work Is."*

be·stride /bɪˈstraɪd/ *v.* [T] LITERARY to sit or stand on or over something with one leg on each side of it

best·sell·er /ˌbɛstˈsɛlɚ/ *n.* [C] a very popular book which many people buy

best-sell·ing /ˌ. ˈ.·/ *adj.* [only before noun, no comparative] **1** a best-selling book, record etc. is very popular and has been bought by a large number of people **2** a best-selling AUTHOR has written a book that is very popular and has been bought by a large number of people

bet[1] /bɛt/ v. **bet, betting 1** [I,T] to risk money on the result of a race, game, competition, or other future event: [**bet sth on sb/sth**] *Todd bet fifty bucks on the Bears to win.* | [**+ on**] *In Oregon, ticket buyers can bet on sports games.* | [**bet that**] *A friend of mine bet that the Sharks would win 16 games this season.* | [**bet sb $10/$50 etc. that**] *I'll bet you ten bucks that it won't be ready on time.* **2** [T] to be fairly sure that something is true, that something will happen etc., although you cannot prove this: *I'll bet that made her mad!* | **You can bet (that)** *the lawyers will be looking for more wealthy clients like Martin.* | *I'd bet money that they weren't too happy about it.* **3 I/I'll bet** SPOKEN **a)** said to show that you understand or can imagine the situation that someone has just told you about: *"We went out on a fishing boat, it was great." "I'll bet."* | *"I'm tired." "I bet you are."* **b)** used when you are asking someone to guess something: *I bet you'll never guess who I saw this morning.* **c)** said to show that you do not believe what someone has just told you: *"I was really worried about you." "Yeah, I'll bet."* **4 you bet a)** SPOKEN said to emphasize that you agree with someone or to say that you are definitely going to do something: *"Are you taking the whole family?" "Sure, you bet."* | *Yeah, it helps to have a little more money – you bet it does.* **b)** SPOKEN used as a way of replying to someone when they thank you for something: *"All right, take care, thanks, Daphne." "You bet."* **5 don't bet on it** SPOKEN also **I wouldn't bet on it** used to say that you do not think something is true or will happen: *Maybe he's really a nice guy, but I wouldn't bet on it.* **6 (you) want to bet?** SPOKEN said when you disagree with someone and want to prove that you are right: *"You can't keep a secret." "Want to bet? I promise – I won't tell a soul."* **7 you can bet your life** INFORMAL also **you can bet your bottom dollar** used when you are sure that you know what someone will do or what will happen: *You can bet your life that when Mike takes the case there will be a battle.* **8 bet the ranch/farm** INFORMAL to risk everything that you own: *Do we really want to bet the ranch on this deal?* —see also BETCHA

bet[2] n. **1** [C] an agreement to risk money on the result of a race, game, competition etc.: *We had a bet, and he lost.* | *I had a bet on the Super Bowl and won $10.* | *People lined up at the windows to place a bet* (=choose a horse, team etc. and bet on it). **2** [C] money that you risk on a bet: *a $50 bet.* **3 your best bet** SPOKEN said when giving someone advice: *Well, your best bet would be to go back to Highway 218 and turn left.* **4 a good/safe bet** an action, situation, or thing that is likely to have the effect or produce the results you want: *The earrings seemed like a good bet for a birthday present.* **5 it's a safe/sure bet (that)** SPOKEN used to say that something seems almost certain: *It's a pretty safe bet that the Wilsons will be at that party.* **6 my/your/his etc. bet is (that)** SPOKEN used when saying what you expect to happen in the future: *My bet is that the store will continue to see rising profits.*

Be·ta /ˈbeɪtə/ n. [U] TRADEMARK a system for recording VIDEOTAPES, which used to be common in the U.S. —compare VHS

be·ta /ˈbeɪtə/ n. [singular] the second letter of the Greek alphabet, or β

beta-block·er /ˈ.. ,../ n. [C] a drug used to help prevent HEART ATTACKs

be·take /bɪˈteɪk/ v. **betake yourself to sth** LITERARY to go somewhere

beta ver·sion /ˈ.. , / n. [C] TECHNICAL a new piece of SOFTWARE that is not ready to be sold because it may still contain some problems or small mistakes —compare ALPHA VERSION, DEMONSTRATION PROGRAM

bet·cha /ˈbɛtʃə/ SPOKEN, NONSTANDARD **1** a short form of "bet you": *I betcha I can run faster than you.* **2 you betcha** used to tell someone that what they have just said is correct: *"So you're going to be there tonight." "You betcha."*

be·tel /ˈbiːtl/ n. [U] an Asian plant, the leaves of which are chewed as a STIMULANT

betel nut /ˈ.. ,./ n. [C] the seed of the betel plant that is wrapped in its leaves and chewed

bête noire /ˌbɛt ˈnwɑr/ n. [singular] LITERARY the person or thing that you dislike most

be·think /bɪˈθɪŋk/ v. OLD USE [T] to remember something or think about something

Beth·le·hem /ˈbɛθlɪˌhɛm, -həm/ a town on the West Bank of the River Jordan, near Jerusalem, thought to be where Jesus Christ was born

Be·thune /bəˈθuːn/, **Ma·ry Mc·Leod** /ˈmɛri məˈklaʊd/ (1875–1955) an African-American educator who started a college for African-American women and was an adviser to President Franklin D. Roosevelt

be·tide /bɪˈtaɪd/ v. **woe betide you** used, especially humorously, to say that someone will be in trouble if they do something: *Woe betide anyone who wakes the baby!*

be·times /bɪˈtaɪmz/ adv. OLD USE early or soon

be·to·ken /bɪˈtoʊkən/ v. [T] LITERARY to be a sign of something

be·tray /bɪˈtreɪ/ v. **betrays, betrayed, betraying** [T] **1** to be disloyal to someone who trusts you, so that they are hurt or upset: *Conservatives felt betrayed when Bush raised taxes.* | *My husband lied to me and betrayed me.* **2** to be disloyal to your country, for example by giving secret information to its enemies: *There are people who are prepared to betray their country for money.* **3 betray your beliefs/principles/ideals etc.** to stop supporting your old beliefs and principles, especially in order to get power or avoid trouble **4** [not in progressive or passive] to show feelings that you are trying to hide: *If he feels any bitterness, his voice doesn't betray it.* **5** to show the true condition, origin etc. of something, especially when this is not easily noticed: *The documents betray a deep anti-Semitism in the country.* **6** if your body betrays you, it will not move as you want it to move, especially because you are old or sick —**betrayer** n. [C]

be·tray·al /bɪˈtreɪəl/ n. [C,U] an act of betraying your country, a friend, or someone who trusts you: *Some politicians are calling the President's policy a betrayal of American principles.*

be·troth·al /bɪˈtroʊðəl/ n. [C] OLD USE an agreement that two people will be married; ENGAGEMENT (1)

be·trothed[1] /bɪˈtroʊðd/ adj. OLD USE **be betrothed to sb** to have promised to marry someone —**betroth** v. [T]

betrothed[2] n. [singular] **sb's betrothed** the person that someone has agreed to marry

bet·ter[1] /ˈbɛtɚ/ adj. [the comparative of "good"] **1** more useful, interesting, satisfactory, effective, appropriate etc. than someone or something else: *She bought a better car.* | *Here, this one is better – try it.* | *You'll get a better deal from a mail-order company.* | *A live performance is often better than a recording.* | **much better/far better/a lot better** *The restaurant across the street has much better food.* | *The more expensive running shoes weren't a lot better than the cheaper ones.* | *Gardening, walking, and other mild exercise are better than nothing.* —opposite WORSE[1] **2** [the comparative of "well"] **a)** more healthy or less sick or painful than before: *She's a little better than she was yesterday.* | *Do you feel any better than you did this morning?* | *You should exercise more – you'll feel better for* (=feel better as a result of) *it.* **b)** completely well again after being sick: *I don't think you should go swimming until you're better.* **3 get better a)** to improve: *Living conditions may get worse before they get better.* | *Braden's teams always get better as the season goes on.* **b)** to RECOVER from an illness or accident: *Get some rest and get better, okay?*

S W
1 1

---

4 that's better a) used to praise or encourage someone: *Try keeping your arm straight when you hit the ball. That's better!* **b)** used when you are trying to make someone feel less upset: *Come on, give me a hug. There, that's better, isn't it?* **5 be better (to do sth)** used to give advice: *It's better if she doesn't stand for too long.* | *It'd be better to eat a good breakfast.* **6 better luck next time** used to encourage someone who has done badly in a test, competition etc. **7 is that better?** used to ask someone if they are happier with something after you have changed it: *Sorry, I didn't mean to pull your hair. Here, is that better?* **8 it's better than doing sth** used to say that although something is not good, it is better than something else: *The water's been boiled, but it's better than drinking water you're not sure of.* **9 there's nothing better** used to say that something is perfect: *There's nothing better than curling up by the fireplace with a good book.* **10 have seen better days** INFORMAL to be in a bad condition or to not be as skillful at something as you were in past times: *Ms. Davis's car had certainly seen better days.* **11 better still** used to say that something is even better than the first thing you mentioned: *I quickly realized that she was someone who said what she meant and, better still, did what she said.* **12 against your better judgment** if you do something against your better judgment, you do it even though you think it may not be sensible: *She asked if she could go, and Max, against his better judgment, said yes.* **13 be no better than sth** to be almost as bad as something else: *The stock market is no better than a casino.* **14 better the devil you know (than the devil you don't)** used to say that something bad that you know about is better than something bad you know nothing about **15 sb's better nature** the part of someone's character that makes them want to be kind and generous, treat people well etc.

—see also **best/better part of sth** (PART¹ (6)), **your better/other half** (HALF² (9))

S W **better²** *adv.* [the comparative of "well"] **1** to a higher degree; more: *I liked his last movie better.* | *Vidal is better known as a novelist.* | *Mel knows the area a lot better than I do.* **2** at a higher standard or quality than before: *She looks better than she did in high school.* | *The car is running much better since I put in new spark plugs.* | *Hospitals are much better equipped now.* **3 do better** to perform better or reach a higher standard: *Some roses do better in different types of soil.* | *We did better than we expected.* **4 sb had better (do sth)** also SPOKEN, NONSTANDARD **(sb) better (do sth) a)** used to say what you or someone else should do: *"I'll call Randy right now." "Yeah, you'd better."* | *If a politician wants to be successful, he or she had better know how to use television.* | *Better wash your hands, Paige – it's dinnertime.* **b)** used to threaten someone: *You better shut up!* | *They'd better not be upstairs watching TV when I told them not to.* **5 better late than never** used to say that even if something happens late or someone arrives late, this is better than it not happening at all **6 better safe than sorry** used to say that it is more sensible to do something that will keep you safe or make you successful, than to not do it and be upset that something bad has happened: *Wear a bike helmet – better safe than sorry!* **7 go (sb) one better** INFORMAL to do something even more successfully than someone else who does it well: *If they can copy our popularity, or even go us one better, good for them.* —compare WORSE³ —see also BETTER OFF

S W **better³** *n.* **1 get the better of sb a)** if your feelings or wishes get the better of you, you do not control them when you should: *Kramer's temper sometimes gets the better of him.* **b)** to defeat someone or deal successfully with a problem: *Alison Leigh refuses to let circumstances get the better of her.* **2 for the better** in a way that improves the situation: *Anything they can do to improve children's health is for the better.* | *Smaller classes are definitely a change for the better.* | *The relationship between the two countries has recently taken a turn for the better.* (=improved) **3 the sooner/bigger/later etc. the better** used to emphasize that you would prefer

something to happen as soon as possible, be as big as possible etc.: *He needs counseling, and the sooner the better.* **4 the more... the better** used to say that something is improved if something else happens a lot: *The more liquid you can squeeze out, the better.* **5 the less... the better** used to say that something is improved if something else does not happen very much: *The less a wine is handled, the better.* **6 for better or (for) worse** used to say that something must be accepted, whether the results will be good or bad, because it cannot be changed: *The reality is that, for better or worse, the world of publishing has changed.* **7 so much the better** used to say that something would be even better or bring even more advantages: *If it makes illegal drug use even more difficult, so much the better.* **8 the better** used to mean the one that is better when you are comparing two similar people or things: [+ **of**] *I don't particularly like him, but he's the better of the two candidates.* **9 be all the better for sb/sth** SPOKEN to be improved by a particular action, change etc.: *If we put more drug dealers in jail, all the better for the people of this state.* **10** [C] another spelling of BETTOR **11 your betters** [plural] OLD-FASHIONED people who are more important than you or deserve more respect —compare WORSE²

better⁴ *v.* [T] **1** to be better than something in quality, amount etc.: *His total of five gold medals is unlikely to be bettered.* **2 better yourself** to improve your position in society by getting a better education or earning more money **3** FORMAL to improve something: *new laws aimed at bettering economic conditions*

Better Busi·ness Bu·reau, the /ˌ.. '.. ˌ../ an organization for businesses and their customers, which helps customers who believe they have been treated unfairly by a company or have bought a bad product

bet·ter·ment /ˈbɛtəmənt/ *n.* [singular] FORMAL improvement, especially in someone's social and economic position

better off /ˌ.. './ *adj.* [no comparative] **1** richer than you were before: *Are you better off than you were four years ago?* **2** happier, improved, more successful etc.: *The country would be better off if more women were serving in Congress.* | *I think you'd be better off if you just moved back to your mother's house for a while.* —compare WELL-OFF

bet·tor, better /ˈbɛtə/ *n.* [C] someone who bets on a game, sports event etc.

be·tween¹ /bɪˈtwin/ *prep.* **1** in or into the space or S time that separates two things or people: *the door-* 1 *way between my room and Laura's room* | *I had corn stuck between my teeth.* —see also IN-BETWEEN **2** in the time that separates two events: *Are you taking any time off between now and Thanksgiving?* | *You can barely get to your locker between classes.* —see also IN-BETWEEN **3** used to show a range of amounts, numbers, distances etc. especially when guessing a particular amount, number etc.: *She'll be here between seven and eight.* | *The project will cost between 10 and 12 million dollars.* **4** used to show the fact that something is divided or shared among two or more people, places, or things: *We had about two loads of laundry between us.* | *Linda and Dave split a milkshake between them.* | *Between the two of us, we used up all the stamps.* | [**between doing sth**] *Students alternated between scribbling notes and standing before the class giving reports.* **5** used to show the relationship between two situations, things, people etc.: *What's the difference between the two computers?* | *Trade relations between the countries have improved.* **6** used to show a connection between two places: *We have eight flights daily between New York and Boston.* | *the highway between Fresno and Visalia* **7 in between** at a point in space or time between two places, events, things etc.: *In between classes, she writes her memoirs on a battered typewriter.* | *Put a piece of waxed paper in between each layer.* | *It's somewhere in between Cedar Rapids and Des Moines.* **8** SPOKEN used when it is difficult to give an exact description of something, or a name to something, so that you have to compare it to two things that are similar to it: *It tastes like a cross* *between* an apple and a pear. **9 between you and me** SPOKEN said before telling someone something that you do not want them to tell anyone else: *Between you and me, I don't think she has a chance of getting that promotion.* **10 come between you/ them etc.** if something comes between two people, it causes an argument or problems between them: *I hope you don't let something as silly as that come between you.*

USAGE NOTE: BETWEEN

WORD CHOICE: between, among
Between is usually used to talk about two people, things, or groups, thought of separately or one after another: *a sense of cooperation between the two countries* | *We need to establish better communication between the sales and customer service departments* (NOT *among*). | *I had a piece of meat stuck between my teeth.* In spoken English you will often hear things like *There were a lot of arguments between the players*, though some people think only **among** is correct where more than two people, things, or groups are involved. **Among** is used to talk about of a group of three or more people or things together, especially using nouns that name groups: *Negotiations could reduce tensions among the nations involved.* | *Garcia's estate was divided equally among his four daughters.* | *I found this letter among Julia's papers* (*between the papers* would suggest that there were only two papers).

---

between[2] *adv.* in or into the space that separates two things or people, or in the time that separates two events: *two yards with a fence between* | *There are programs for the very young and the very old, but not much for those* **in between**. | **everyone/everything in between** (=used to emphasize that something includes everyone or everything) —see also IN-BETWEEN

be·twixt /bɪˈtwɪkst/ *prep.* **1** POETIC OR OLD USE between **2 betwixt and between** OLD-FASHIONED not completely belonging to one group or to another

bev·el /ˈbɛvəl/ *n.* [C] TECHNICAL **1** a sloping edge or surface, usually along the edge of a piece of wood or glass **2** a tool for making this kind of edge or surface

bev·eled /ˈbɛvəld/ *adj.* with a sloping edge: *a mirror with beveled edges*

bev·er·age /ˈbɛvrɪdʒ, ˈbɛvərɪdʒ/ *n.* [C] FORMAL a hot or cold drink: *alcoholic beverages*

bev·y /ˈbɛvi/ *n. plural* **bevies** [C] a large group of people of the same type, especially girls or young women: [+ of] *a limousine surrounded by a bevy of screaming teenagers*

be·wail /bɪˈweɪl/ *v.* [T] LITERARY to express deep sadness or disappointment about something

be·ware /bɪˈwɛr/ *v.* [I,T only in imperative and infinitive] used to warn someone to be careful because something is dangerous: [+ of] *Beware of the dog!* | *The department warned consumers to beware.*

be·wigged /bɪˈwɪgd/ *adj.* FORMAL wearing a WIG

be·wil·der /bɪˈwɪldɚ/ *v.* [T] to confuse someone

be·wil·dered /bɪˈwɪldɚd/ *adj.* totally confused: *The kids felt bewildered and betrayed by the divorce.*

be·wil·der·ing /bɪˈwɪldərɪŋ/ *adj.* confusing, especially because there are too many choices or things happening at the same time: *a bewildering number of options*

be·wil·der·ment /bɪˈwɪldɚmənt/ *n.* [U] a feeling of being very confused

be·witched /bɪˈwɪtʃt/ *adj.* **1** so interested in or attracted by someone or something that you cannot think clearly: *When he heard a recording of Brown playing the trumpet, Marsalis was bewitched.* **2** completely controlled by someone who has put a magic SPELL on you —**bewitching** *adj.*: *a bewitching smile* —**bewitch** *v.* [T]

be·yond[1] /bɪˈyɑnd/ *prep.* **1** on or to the farther side of something: *The park is a couple of streets beyond the school.* **2** not within someone's ability or skill: *The administration deserves no blame for events beyond its control.* | *an apple just beyond my reach* **3** outside the range or limits of something:

That topic is somewhat beyond the scope of this discussion. | *She's helped us* **above and beyond** the call of duty. **4 beyond belief/doubt/recognition etc.** used to say that you cannot believe something, doubt something etc.: *In just six years, the town had changed beyond all recognition.* | *The car has been damaged beyond repair.* **5** more or greater than a particular amount, level, or limit: *The rate of inflation has risen beyond 5%.* | *continuing to work beyond retirement age* **6** later than a particular time, date etc.: *The ban on hunting these animals has been extended beyond 2001.* **7 it is beyond me why/what etc.** SPOKEN used to say that something seems completely stupid and you cannot understand the reason for it: *It's beyond me why they ever got married at all.* **8 be beyond sb** ESPECIALLY SPOKEN to be too difficult for someone: *Calculus was always beyond me.* **9** used like "except" in negative sentences: *Santa Fe doesn't have much industry beyond tourism.* | *I can't really tell you anything beyond what you know already.*

beyond[2] *adv.* **1** on or to the farther side of something: *a view from the mountains with the plains beyond* **2** later than a particular time, date etc.: *planning for the year 2000 and beyond*

beyond[3] *n.* **the beyond** LITERARY whatever comes after this life

BFD *interjection* VULGAR a short way of saying "big fucking deal"; used to tell someone in an impolite way that you do not think that what they have just said is important

Bhu·tan /buˈtɑn, buˈtæn/ a country in the Himalayas, between India and China —**Bhutanese** /ˌbutnˈiz, -ˈis/ *n., adj.*

bi- /baɪ/ *prefix* two; twice: *bilingual* (=speaking two languages) | *a biannual meeting* (=happening twice a year) —compare SEMI- —see also DI-, TRI-

BIA —see BUREAU OF INDIAN AFFAIRS, THE

bi·an·nu·al /baɪˈænyuəl/ *adj.* happening twice each year: *a biannual report* —compare ANNUAL[1] (1), BIENNIAL (1)

bi·as[1] /ˈbaɪəs/ *n.* **1** [singular,U] an opinion about whether a person, group, idea is good or bad, that influences how you deal with it: *Conservatives say the press has a liberal bias.* | [+ against/toward/ in favor of] *Investigators found a pattern of bias against women and minorities among police officers.* **2** [singular] a natural skill or interest in one particular area: *Lydia has a strong artistic bias.* **3 on the bias** in a DIAGONAL direction: *cloth cut on the bias*

bias[2] *v.* [T] to unfairly influence attitudes, choices, or decisions

bi·ased /ˈbaɪəst/ *adj.* **1** unfairly influenced by someone's opinion: *If your advisor is also selling financial products, you may get biased advice.* | [+ against/ toward/in favor of] *Jurors may be biased against the defendant because he has been arrested.* **2** unfairly preferring one person or group over another: *racially biased reporting* | [+ against/toward/in favor of] *The news reports were heavily biased toward the government.*

bias tape /ˈ.. ˌ./ *n.* [U] cloth in the form of a narrow band, used when sewing edges

bi·ath·lon /baɪˈæθlɑn, -lən/ *n.* [C] a sports competition in which competitors SKI across country and then shoot a RIFLE —**biathlete** /baɪˈæθlit/ *n.* [C] —compare DECATHLON, PENTATHLON

bib /bɪb/ *n.* [C] **1** a piece of cloth or plastic tied under a baby's chin to keep food from falling on his or her clothes **2** the upper part of an APRON (1) or pair of OVERALLS that is above the waist

bi·ble, Bible /ˈbaɪbəl/ *n.* **1 the Bible** the holy book of the Christian religion, consisting of the OLD TESTAMENT and the NEW TESTAMENT **2** [C] a copy of the Bible **3** [singular] INFORMAL the most useful and important book on a particular subject: *This textbook is the computer programmer's bible.*

Bible Belt, the /ˈ.. ˌ./ an area in the south of the U.S. known for its very religious Christian people, who follow the teachings of the Bible very strictly

Bible thump·er /ˈ.. ˌ../ n. [C] an insulting expression for someone who tries to make other people believe their very strong Christian beliefs —**Bible-thumping** adj. [only before noun]

bib·li·cal, Biblical /ˈbɪblɪkəl/ adj. relating to the Bible

biblio- /ˈbɪbliou, -liə/ prefix relating to books: a bibliophile (=someone who likes books)

bib·li·og·ra·phy /ˌbɪbliˈɑgrəfi/ n. plural **bibliographies** [C] 1 a list of all the books and articles used in preparing a piece of writing 2 a list of everything that has been written about a particular subject —**bibliographer** n. [C]

bib·li·o·phile /ˈbɪbliəˌfaɪl/ n. [C] FORMAL someone who likes books

bib·u·lous /ˈbɪbyələs/ adj. HUMOROUS OR FORMAL liking to drink too much alcohol

bi·cam·er·al /baɪˈkæmrəl/ adj. [only before noun] a bicameral LEGISLATURE (=part of the government that makes laws) consists of two parts, such as the Senate and the House of Representatives in the U.S. Congress —compare UNICAMERAL

bi·car·bon·ate of so·da /baɪˌkɑrbənɪt əv ˈsoʊdə/ also **bicarbonate** or **bicarb** n. [U] TECHNICAL: see BAKING SODA

bi·cen·ten·ni·al /ˌbaɪsɛnˈtɛniəl/ n. [C] the day or year exactly 200 years after an important event: the bicentennial of the Declaration of Independence —**bicentennial** adj.: bicentennial celebrations

bi·cep /ˈbaɪsɛp/ n. [C usually plural] the large muscle on the front of your upper arm —see picture at BODY

bick·er /ˈbɪkɚ/ v. [I] to argue, especially about something very unimportant: I wish you two would stop bickering. | [+ about/over] The kids were bickering about who would sleep in the top bunk. —**bickering** n. [U]

bi·cy·cle¹ /ˈbaɪsɪkəl/ n. [C] a vehicle with two wheels that you sit on and make move by pushing its PEDALS with your feet; BIKE: Wear your helmet all the time you are **riding a bicycle**.

bicycle² v. [I always + adv./prep.] FORMAL to go somewhere on a bicycle —**bicyclist** n. [C]

bid¹ /bɪd/ n. [C] 1 an offer to do work or provide services for a specific price: [+ for] The city accepted the lowest bid for the bridge-building project. 2 an attempt to achieve or obtain something: [+ for] Wilson's successful bid for the senate | [**bid to do sth**] Workers dug beneath the ruins of the building in a desperate bid to reach any survivors trapped inside. 3 an offer to pay a particular price for something, especially at an AUCTION: [+ for] a bid of $300 for the painting 4 a statement of how many points you hope to win in a card game

bid² v. past tense and past participle **bid** present participle **bidding** 1 [I] to offer to do work or provide services for a specific price, in competition with other offers: [+ for] Four companies were invited to bid for the contract. 2 [I,T] to offer to pay a particular price for goods, especially in an AUCTION: [**bid (sb) sth for**] Jill bid $200,000 for an antique desk. 3 [I,T] to say how many points you think you will win in a game of cards —**bidder** n. [C]

bid³ v. past tense **bade** or **bid** past participle **bid** or **bidden** present participle **bidding** OLD USE OR LITERARY 1 bid sb good afternoon/good morning etc. to say good morning, good afternoon etc. to someone 2 [T] to order or tell someone what to do: [**bid sb (to) do sth**] The queen bade us to enter. 3 bid fair to do sth to seem likely to do something

bid·ding /ˈbɪdɪŋ/ n. [U] 1 the activity of offering to do work or providing services for someone at a particular price: The contract will be renewed with no bidding. 2 the activity of bidding for goods, especially in an AUCTION: The bidding was brisk and sales went well. 3 **do sb's bidding** LITERARY to obey someone's requests or orders 4 **at sb's bidding** FORMAL because someone has told you to

bide /baɪd/ v. past tense **bode** or **bided** 1 **bide your time** to wait until the right moment to do something: Investors are biding their time, trying to figure out

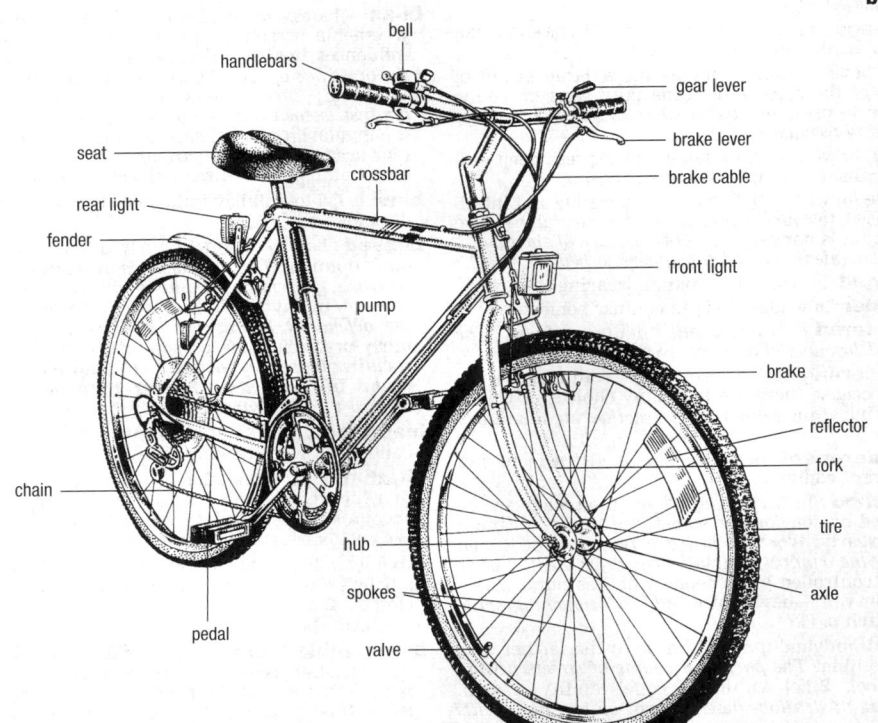

bicycle

bell
handlebars
gear lever
brake lever
seat
crossbar
brake cable
rear light
fender
front light
pump
brake
reflector
fork
chain
tire
hub
spokes
axle
pedal
valve

what the next successful stock will be. **2** [I] OLD USE to wait or stay somewhere, often for a long time

bi·det /biˈdeɪ/ *n.* [C] a small low bathtub that you sit on to wash the lower part of your body

bi·en·ni·al /baɪˈɛniəl/ *adj.* **1** a biennial event happens once every two years —compare ANNUAL[1] (1) BIANNUAL **2** a biennial plant stays alive for two years and produces seeds in the second year —compare ANNUAL[2] (1), PERENNIAL[2] —**biennally** *adv.*

bier /bɪr/ *n.* [C] a frame like a table on which a dead body or COFFIN is placed

Bierce /bɪrs/, **Am·brose** /ˈæmbroʊz/ (1842–?1914) a U.S. writer of short stories

biff /bɪf/ *v.* [T] INFORMAL to hit someone hard with your FIST —**biff** *n.* [C]

bi·fo·cals /ˈbaɪˌfoʊkəlz, baɪˈfoʊkəlz/ *n.* [plural] special glasses with an upper part made for seeing things that are far away, and a lower part made for reading —**bifocal** *adj.*

bi·fur·cate /ˈbaɪfərˌkeɪt/ *v.* [I] FORMAL if a road, river etc. bifurcates, it divides into two separate parts —**bifurcation** /ˌbaɪfərˈkeɪʃən/ *n.* [C,U]

big /bɪg/ *adj.* **bigger, biggest**
1 size **a)** of more than average size, amount, weight etc.: *a big tree* | *These jeans are too big.* | *The game works better if you have a bigger group.* | *a big difference in price* | *She's a cute baby with a big smile.* | *That boy gets bigger every time I see him.* | *Josie gave me a great big hug.* **b)** used to show the size of something: *How big a piece of cake do you want?* | *It's about as big as a dime.* —see Usage Note at WIDE[1]
2 important important or serious *The big game is on Friday.* | *Who's the big boss?* | *It's going to be a big adjustment for the kids whenever we move.* | *There will be some big changes in the way we work.* —see also BIG CHEESE, BIG NAME, BIG SHOT, BIG TIME[1]
3 popular/successful INFORMAL successful or popular, especially in business or entertainment: *Julia Roberts became a big star after "Pretty Woman".* | [+ in] *Microsoft is very big in the software business.* | *Cheerleading is big in Texas because football is big.* | *Can Shea make it big (=become very successful) in the NFL?* | *Small companies can still play with the big boys (=the most powerful people or companies) in the computer market.*
4 company a big company, organization, group etc. has a lot of people working for it: *one of the biggest companies in the insurance business*
5 older INFORMAL **a)** big sister/brother your older sister or brother **b)** used especially when speaking to children to mean older: *Sit up like a big girl and eat your dinner.*
6 a lot [only before noun] INFORMAL doing something to a very large degree: *I've never been a big jazz fan.* | **big eater/drinker/gambler etc.** *Sandra is used to serving a family of big eaters.*
7 bad [only before noun] used to emphasize how bad something is: *It's a simple repair that can prevent a big problem later.* | *You are such a big liar!*

SPOKEN PHRASES

8 in a big way SPOKEN very much, or to a large degree: *When they lose, they lose in a big way.*
9 be big on sth SPOKEN to like doing something very much or to be very interested in it: *I'm not big on foreign cars.*
10 what's the big idea? used when someone has done something annoying, especially when you want them to explain why they did it: *Hey, what's the big idea? Who said you could borrow my car?*
11 it is big of sb to do sth a) used to say that someone was very kind or generous to do something: *I think it was really big of Larry to admit that he made the wrong choice.* **b)** used when you really think that someone was not kind or generous at all: *A whole dollar! Gee, that was very big of her!*
12 big mouth used in some expressions to mean that someone cannot keep a secret: *That girl has a big mouth.* | *I'm sorry. I shouldn't have opened my big mouth.* | **me and my big mouth** (=said when you wish you had not told someone a secret)

---

13 have big ideas/plans to have impressive plans for the future: *Waller has big plans for her retirement.*
14 big money also **big bucks** INFORMAL a lot of money, or the chance to earn a lot of money: *In 1979, Shearer moved to California "to make big bucks in the electronics industry."*
15 letters INFORMAL a big letter is written in CAPITALS, for example G, R, A etc.
16 words INFORMAL big words are long or unusual and are difficult to read or understand
17 have/carry/wield a big stick INFORMAL to threaten to use your power to get what you want
18 be/get too big for your boots INFORMAL to be too proud of yourself
19 the big enchilada HUMOROUS the most important person or thing in an organization or the most important part of a particular subject: *The big enchilada is the U.S. Supreme Court, and we're going to go there and win.* —**bigness** *n.* [U] —see also BIG DEAL, **think big** (THINK (13))

USAGE NOTE: BIG

WORD CHOICE: big, large, great
Big and **large** are both often used to talk about the measurements of things or groups, though **large** is slightly more formal: *These shoes are too big for me.* | *a big/large room* | *a big crowd/company/gap* | *a large family/city/university.* None of these words are used with uncountable nouns for things you can touch: *There was a lot of traffic/land/space* (NOT *big traffic, large land* etc.). **Great** means famous or important for something good, or, when it is used about ordinary people, extremely nice: *Michelangelo was one of the greatest artists who ever lived.* | *You'll like Pat – he's a great guy.* **Great** used about the size of things or events is mainly found in literary writing or names and means "very large and impressive": *The great city of Samarkand.* | *A great crowd had gathered.* | *a great banquet* | *The Great Wall of China.* Otherwise **great** is used very informally of things just to mean extremely good: *You look great!* | *There's a great view from our hotel room.* | *We had a great time there* (=enjoyable, not necessarily long). You would usually use **great** rather than **big** to describe the size or extent of things you cannot touch: *She showed great courage/talent/ability.* | *We had great fun.* | *in great detail.* Where both can be used, **great** is stronger and suggests more importance: *It's a big/great pleasure to see you.* | *great/big problem/opportunity/danger.* But note that you usually say *a big difference/mistake/argument* | *It isn't a big deal* (informal=It's not serious or important). Note that **large** (less often **great** or **big**) is used with these quantity words: *a large amount/scale/number/quantity/extent/proportion/percentage/part/volume/area.* But note only **great** is used in: *a great deal* (=a lot) | *at great length* | *a great height/age*

---

big·a·my /ˈbɪgəmi/ *n.* [U] the crime of being married to two people at the same time —**bigamist** *n.* [C] —**bigamous** *adj.* —compare MONOGAMY, POLYGAMY

Big Ap·ple /ˌ. ˈ../ *n.* INFORMAL **the Big Apple** a name for New York City

big band /ˌ. ˈ./ *n.* [C] a large musical band, especially popular in the 1940s and 1950s, that plays JAZZ or dance music and has a leader who plays SOLOS[1] (1): *Tommy Dorsey's big band* —**big-band** *adj.*

Big Bang the·o·ry /ˌ. ˈ. ˌ.../ *n.* **the Big Bang theory** the idea that the universe began with a single large explosion (the "Big Bang"), and that the pieces are still flying apart —compare STEADY-STATE THEORY

Big Board /ˈ. ./ *n.* **the Big Board** the list of all the SHARE[2] (4) prices on the New York Stock Exchange: *Consolidated Aircraft's stock rose 50 cents to $12.625 on the Big Board.*

big-boned /ˈ. ./ *adj.* a big-boned person is large without being fat

big broth·er, **Big Brother** /ˌ. ˈ../ *n.* [singular, not with **the**] any person, organization, or system that

B

seems to want to control people's lives and restrict their freedom: *We don't permit smoking in the office, but we're not Big Brother. If people go outside to smoke, that's fine.*

Big Broth·ers /ˌ. ˈ../ an organization that helps boys, especially boys who have family problems, by giving each boy someone who meets him regularly to give advice, listen to his problems, etc.

big busi·ness /ˌ. ˈ../ *n.* [U] **1** very large companies, considered as a powerful group with a lot of influence **2** a product or type of activity that people spend a lot of money on: *Selling music to teenagers is big business.*

big cat /ˌ. ˈ./ *n.* [C] NOT TECHNICAL a large animal of the cat family, such as a lion or tiger

big cheese /ˌ. ˈ./ *n.* [C] INFORMAL, HUMOROUS an important and powerful person in an organization: *One of the big cheeses from NASA gave a speech.*

s w **big deal** /ˌ. ˈ./ *n.* [singular] SPOKEN **1** said when you
2 do not think something is as important as someone else thinks it is: *It's just a game. If you lose, big deal.* | *What's the big deal? It's only a birthday, not the end of the world.* **2 no big deal a)** said in order to show that you are not upset or angry about something that has happened: *It's no big deal. Everybody forgets things sometimes.* **b)** said in order to show that something is not important: *The kids won't get as many presents this year, but that's no big deal.* **3** an important or exciting event or situation: *This audition is a big deal for Joey.* **4 make a big deal about/over sth** also **make a big deal out of sth** to get too excited or upset about something, or make something seem more important than it is: *I know I'm probably making a big deal out of nothing, but I'm worried about you.* **5 big deal** used to say that you do not think something is as important or impressive as someone else thinks it is: *Anyway, he gave me a raise to $5.50. I mean, big deal.*

Big Dip·per /ˌ. ˈ../ *n.* the Big Dipper a group of seven bright stars in the shape of a bowl with a handle, seen only from northern parts of the world

Big·foot /ˈbɪgfʊt/ also **Sas·quatch** an animal like a large hairy human, which some people claim to have seen in the northwest U.S., but which has never been proved to exist

big game /ˌ. ˈ./ *n.* [U] large wild animals, such as lions and ELEPHANTs, hunted as a sport: *a big game hunter*

big·gie /ˈbɪgi/ *n.* [C] **1** INFORMAL something very large, important, or successful: *The latest Disney movie is a biggie.* **2 no biggie** SPOKEN said when something is not important, or when you are not upset or angry about something: *"Oh, I'm sorry." "That's okay, no biggie."*

big gov·ern·ment /ˌ. ˈ.../ *n.* [U] government, when people think it is controlling their lives too much: *Eisenhower worried that big government was threatening the old American values.* —**big-government** *adj.* [only before noun]

big gun /ˌ. ˈ./ *n.* [C] INFORMAL a person or company that has a lot of power or influence: *The software company has done well in areas ignored by big guns such as Microsoft and Lotus.*

big·head·ed /ˈbɪghɛdɪd/ *adj.* INFORMAL someone who is bigheaded thinks they are very important, smart etc.

big·heart·ed /ˌ. ˈ..◂/ *adj.* very kind and generous: *Larry's a big-hearted guy.*

Big·horn Moun·tains, the /ˈbɪghɔrn/ a RANGE of mountains in the northwestern U.S. that is part of the Rocky Mountains and is in the states of Wyoming and Montana

big·horn sheep /ˌbɪghɔrn ˈʃip/ *n.* [C] a wild sheep with long curved horns that lives in the mountains of western North America

bight /baɪt/ *n.* [C] **1** a slight bend or curve in a coast **2** a LOOP[1] (1) made in the middle of a rope when tying a knot

big-league /ˈ. ˌ./ *adj.* **1** also **big league** belonging or relating to the MAJOR LEAGUES **2** [no comparative] belonging or relating to an important company or group: *The Democrats are struggling to find a big-league presidential candidate.*

Big Man on Cam·pus /ˌ. . . ˈ../ *n.* [C] INFORMAL an important and popular male student at a college or university, especially someone who is good at sports

big mon·ey /ˌ. ˈ./ *n.* [U] INFORMAL a large amount of money: *Carter won big money in Vegas last year.* —**big-money** *adj.* [only before noun]

big·mouth /ˈbɪgmaʊθ/ *n.* [C] INFORMAL someone who cannot be trusted to keep secrets: *Who's the big mouth who told Carole about her surprise birthday party?* —see also **big mouth** (BIG (12))

big name /ˌ. ˈ.◂/ *n.* [C] a famous person or group, especially a musician, actor etc.: *None of the soloists are big names yet, but there's a lot of talent there.* —**big-name** *adj.* [only before noun] *big-name entertainers*

big·ot /ˈbɪgət/ *n.* [C] someone who has such strong opinions about race, religion, or politics that they are unwilling to listen to anyone else's opinions: *Toward the end of the campaign, he was reported to have called Jeff a "white, homophobic bigot".* —**bigoted** *adj.*

big·ot·ry /ˈbɪgətri/ *n.* [U] behavior or beliefs typical of bigots: *The newspaper condemned the former mayor's bigotry toward gays.*

big rig /ˈ. ./ *n.* [C] INFORMAL an extremely large truck, used for carrying goods; SEMI

big screen /ˌ. ˈ.◂/ *n.* the big screen the movies, rather than television or theater: *Filmmakers are hoping to bring several of Sandlin's works to the big screen.* —**big-screen** *adj.*

big-screen TV /ˌ.. . ˈ./ also **big-screen tel·e·vi·sion** /ˌ.. ˈ...../ *n.* [C] a large television with a very large screen

big shot /ˈ. ˌ./ *n.* [C] INFORMAL someone who has a lot of power or importance in a company or an area of business: *a media big-shot*

Big Sis·ters /ˌ. ˈ../ an organization that helps girls, especially girls with family problems, by giving each girl someone who meets her regularly to give advice, listen to her problems, etc.

big-tick·et /ˌ. ˈ.◂/ *adj.* [only before noun, no comparative] INFORMAL expensive: *Lower interest rates will encourage consumers to buy big-ticket items such as houses and cars.*

big time[1] /ˈ. ˌ./ *adv.* [no comparative] SPOKEN said in order to emphasize something, especially how bad or serious it is: *I lost, big time, on that investment.*

big time[2] *n.* INFORMAL the big time the position of being very famous or important, for example in the entertainment business or in politics: *He played in clubs for years before making it to the big time.*

big-time /ˈ. ./ *adj.* [only before noun, no comparative] INFORMAL **1** belonging or relating to someone or something that is important and successful: *Fuller's a player with a chance to make it into big-time football.* **2** SPOKEN used before nouns to emphasize them: *She's a big-time pain in the neck.*

big toe /ˌ. ˈ./ *n.* [C] the largest toe on your foot

big top /ˈ. ./ *n.* [C] the very large tent in which a CIRCUS (1) performance takes place

big·wig /ˈbɪgwɪg/ *n.* [C] INFORMAL an important person: *A few of the company bigwigs have their own jets.*

bike[1] /baɪk/ *n.* [C] INFORMAL **1** a bicycle: *The kids are out riding their bikes in the street.* | *Let's go for a bike ride before lunch.* **2** a MOTORCYCLE

bike[2] *v.* [I always + adv./prep.] to ride a bicycle: *She bikes to work every day.*

bike mes·sen·ger /ˈ. ˌ.../ *n.* [C] someone whose job is taking documents from one company in a big city to another, riding a bicycle in order to get there quickly

bik·er /ˈbaɪkɚ/ *n.* [C] **1** someone who rides a MOTORCYCLE, especially as part of a group: *Most of the bikers rode Harley-Davidsons.* **2** someone who rides a bicycle: *trails for bikers and hikers*

bi·ki·ni /bɪ'kini/ n. [C] a piece of clothing in two separate parts that women wear for swimming

Bi·ki·ni At·oll /bɪ,kini 'ætɔl/ one of the Marshall Islands in the Pacific Ocean

bikini line /.'.. ,./ n. [C] the place on a woman's legs where the hair around her sexual organs stops growing

bi·la·bi·al /baɪ'leɪbiəl/ n. [C] TECHNICAL a CONSONANT sound such as /p/ or /b/ that is made using both lips —see also LABIAL —**bilabial** adj.

bi·lat·er·al /baɪ'lætərəl/ adj. involving two groups or nations: *bilateral relations between the European Union and the U.S.* | **a bilateral agreement/arrangement/treaty etc.** (=between two countries or groups) —**bilaterally** adv. —compare MULTILATERAL, UNILATERAL

bile /baɪl/ n. [U] **1** a bitter green-brown liquid formed in the LIVER, which helps you to DIGEST[1] (1) fats —see picture at DIGESTIVE SYSTEM **2** LITERARY anger and hate

bilge /bɪldʒ/ n. **1** [C] the curved part of a ship that joins the bottom to the sides **2** [U] INFORMAL nonsense

bi·lin·gual /baɪ'lɪŋgwəl/ adj. **1** written or spoken in two languages: *a bilingual dictionary* **2** able to speak two languages equally well: *Their kids are completely bilingual.* —**bilingual** n. [C] —compare MONOLINGUAL, MULTILINGUAL

bil·ious /'bɪlyəs/ adj. **1** feeling sick to your stomach **2** very ugly or disgusting: *a bilious green color* **3** in a bad mood —**biliousness** n.

bilk /bɪlk/
bilk sb out of sth phr. v. [T] INFORMAL to cheat someone, especially by taking their money; SWINDLE

bill[1] /bɪl/ n. [C]
1 payment a written list showing how much you have to pay for services you have received, work that has been done etc.: **[+ for]** *The bill for the repairs came to $650.* | *Have you paid the phone bill?*
2 law a plan for a new law, that is written down for a government to decide on: *The House of Representatives passed a new gun-control bill.*
3 money a piece of paper money: *a five-dollar bill* —compare COIN[1] (1)
4 give sb/sth a clean bill of health to officially state that someone is in good health or that something is working correctly: *Maddox was given a clean bill of health by his doctor.*
5 fill the bill/fit the bill to be exactly what you need: *If you're looking for a good collection of stories for children, this book will fit the bill.*
6 concert/show etc. a program of entertainment at a theater, concert, the movies etc., with details of who is performing, what is being shown etc.: *Ray Charles and Etta James make a great **double-bill** (=program in two parts) at the Blues House tonight.*
7 bird a bird's beak
8 advertisement a printed notice advertising an event
9 part of a hat the front part that sticks out on a hat such as a BASEBALL CAP

bill[2] v. [T] **1** to send someone a bill: *Clients will be billed monthly.* **2 bill sth as sth** to advertise or describe something in a particular way: *The boxing match was billed as "the fight of the century."*

bill·a·ble /'bɪləbəl/ adj. [no comparative] relating to time, costs etc. that your customers will pay for

bill·board /'bɪlbɔrd/ n. [C] a large sign used for advertising

bil·let[1] /'bɪlɪt/ n. [C] a private house where soldiers live for a short time

billet[2] v. [T + on/with] to put soldiers in a private house to live there for a short time

bill·fold /'bɪlfould/ n. [C] a small flat leather case, used for carrying paper money, CREDIT CARDS etc. in your pocket; WALLET

bill·hook /'bɪlhʊk/ n. [C] a tool consisting of a curved blade with a handle, used for cutting off tree branches etc.

bil·liards /'bɪlyədz/ n. [U] a game played on a cloth-covered table in which balls are hit with a CUE (=a long stick) against each other and into pockets at the edge of the table —see also POOL[1] (2) —**billiard** adj. [only before noun] *a billiard table*

bill·ing /'bɪlɪŋ/ n. **give sb top/star billing** to name a particular performer, actor etc. as being the most important person in a show, play etc.

bil·lion /'bɪlyən/ plural **billion** or **billions** NUMBER 1,000,000,000: *$3 billion* | *Billions of dollars have been spent.* —see Usage Note at HUNDRED[1] —**billionth** adj., pron., n.

bil·lion·aire /,bɪlyə'nɛr, 'bɪlyə,nɛr/ n. [C] someone who has a billion or more than a billion dollars

bill of ex·change /,.. '.'./ n. [C] TECHNICAL a signed document ordering someone to pay someone else a particular amount of money

bill of fare /,. './ n. [C] OLD-FASHIONED a list of the food that is served in a restaurant; MENU (1)

bill of la·ding /,.. '../ n. [C] TECHNICAL a list of the goods being carried, especially on a ship

bill of rights /,.. '.'./ n. [C] a written statement of the most important rights of the citizens of a country or of a particular group

bill of sale /,.. '.'./ n. [C] a written document showing that someone has bought something

bil·low[1] /'bɪlou/ v. [I] **1** if something made of cloth billows, it moves in the wind: *Her long skirt billowed in the breeze.* **2** LITERARY if a cloud or smoke billows, it moves like a wave as it rises: *Smoke billowed out of the chimney.*

billow[2] n. [C usually plural] **1** LITERARY a wave, especially a very large one **2** a moving cloud or large amount of something such as smoke or cloth

bil·ly club /'bɪli klʌb/ n. [C] a short stick carried by a police officer

billy goat /'.. ./ n. [C] INFORMAL a word for a male goat, used especially by or to children —compare NANNY GOAT

bil·tong /'bɪltɔŋ, -tɑŋ/ n. [U] meat dried in the sun, eaten especially in some parts of Africa and Australia

bim·bo /'bɪmbou/ n. plural **bimbos** [C] OFFENSIVE an attractive but stupid young woman, especially one who you think has low moral standards

bi·month·ly /baɪ'mʌnθli/ adj. appearing or happening every two months or twice each month: *a bimonthly magazine* —**bimonthly** adv.

bin /bɪn/ n. [C] a large container for storing things, such as goods in a shop or substances in a factory

bi·na·ry /'baɪnɛri, 'baɪnəri/ adj. TECHNICAL **1 the binary system** a system of counting, used in computers, in which only the numbers 0 and 1 are used **2** consisting of two parts; double: *a binary star system*

bind[1] /baɪnd/ v. past tense and past participle **bound**
1 keep a promise [T] if an agreement, promise etc. binds someone, it forces them to do what they have agreed or promised: *The treaty binds the two countries to reduce the number of nuclear weapons.* | *The monks are bound by vows of silence.*
2 stick together [I,T] to stick together in a MASS, or to make small parts or pieces of something stick together: *The hydrogen molecule binds with the oxygen molecule.* | *Use 2 tablespoons of water to bind the flour and butter mixture.*
3 form a connection [T] to form a strong emotional or economic connection between two people, countries etc.: **[bind sb/sth together]** *A common history binds people together.*
4 tie/fasten [T] FORMAL OR LITERARY **a)** to tie someone so that they cannot move or escape: *He was found bound to a chair, barely alive.* | **bound and gagged** (=tied up, and with cloth tied around your mouth) **b)** also **bind up** to tie things firmly together with cloth or string: *The pile of newspapers were bound with string.*

B

5 book [T] to fasten the pages of a book together and put them in a cover

6 stitch [T] to strengthen or decorate something with a border of material: *The edges of the blanket were bound with ribbon.*

7 be bound over for trial TECHNICAL to be forced by law to appear in a court of law —see also BINDING[1], BOUND[2]

bind[2] *n.* an annoying or difficult situation: *The rise in fuel prices and the reduced number of customers has put the airlines in a bind.*

bind·er /'baɪndɚ/ *n.* **1** [C] a removable cover for holding loose sheets of paper, magazines etc. **2** [C] a person or machine that fastens the parts of a book together **3** [C,U] a substance that makes things stick together **4** [C] TECHNICAL an agreement in which you pay something to show that you intend to buy some property

bind·ing[1] /'baɪndɪŋ/ *adj.* **a binding contract/promise/agreement etc.** a promise, agreement etc. that legally forces someone to obey it

binding[2] *n.* **1** [C] a book cover **2** [U] material sewn or stuck along the edge of a piece of cloth for strength or decoration **3** [C usually plural] the metal part on a SKI that you step on so that your ski boot fastens to the ski

bind·weed /'baɪndwid/ *n.* [U] a wild plant that winds itself around other plants

binge[1] /bɪndʒ/ *n.* [C] a short period when you do too much of something, especially drinking alcohol: *an ice-cream binge* | *The fight sent Alexander off on a drinking binge.*

binge[2] *v.* [I] INFORMAL to eat a lot of food in a short time, especially because you have an EATING DISORDER: [+ **on**] *Whenever she's depressed, she binges on chocolate.*

bin·go[1] /'bɪŋgoʊ/ *n.* [U] a game played for money or prizes in which you win if a set of numbers chosen by chance are the same as one of the lines of numbers on your card

bingo[2] *interjection* said when you have just done something successfully or to tell someone that they have given the right answer: *Bingo! That's the one I've been looking for.*

bin·oc·u·lars /bɪ'nɑkyəlɚz, baɪ-/ *n.* [plural] a pair of special glasses that make distant objects look bigger or closer

bi·no·mi·al /baɪ'noʊmiəl/ *n.* [C] TECHNICAL a mathematical expression that has two parts connected by the sign + or the sign –, for example 3x + 4y or x – 7 —**binomial** *adj.*

bi·o /'baɪoʊ/ *n. plural* **bios** [C] INFORMAL a biography

bio- /baɪoʊ, baɪə/ *prefix* relating to living things: *biomedical*

bi·o·chem·is·try /ˌbaɪoʊ'kɛmɪstri/ *n.* [U] the scientific study of the chemistry of living things —**biochemist** *n.* [C] —**biochemical** *adj.*

bi·o·de·grad·a·ble /ˌbaɪoʊdɪ'greɪdəbəl/ *adj.* TECHNICAL materials, chemicals etc. that are biodegradable are changed naturally by the action of BACTERIA into substances that are not harmful to the environment —**biodegrade** *v.* [I]

bi·og·ra·pher /baɪ'ɑgrəfɚ/ *n.* [C] someone who writes a book about someone else's life

bi·og·ra·phy /baɪ'ɑgrəfi/ *n. plural* **biographies 1** [C] a book about a particular person's life, written by someone else: *Boswell's biography of Dr. Johnson* **2** [U] the part of literature that consists of biographies —**biographical** /ˌbaɪə'græfɪkəl/ *adj.* —**biographically** /-kli/ *adv.* —compare AUTOBIOGRAPHY

bi·o·log·i·cal /ˌbaɪə'lɑdʒɪkəl/ *adj.* **1** relating to biology: *biological studies* **2 sb's biological father/mother/parent** a child's natural parent, rather than someone who has become its parent through ADOPTION (1) —see also BIRTH FATHER, BIRTH MOTHER —**biologically** /-kli/ *adv.*

biological clock /...,... '../ *n.* [singular] **1** TECHNICAL the time system in plants and animals that controls behavior such as sleeping and eating; BODY CLOCK **2** the idea that when a woman reaches a certain age, she is too old to have a baby: *Jenny admits that her biological clock is ticking, but she doesn't want to get married.*

biological con·trol /...,... '../ *n.* [U] a method of controlling PESTS (=small insects that harm or destroy crops) by using other insects, birds, or animals to kill them

biological war·fare /...,... '../ *n.* [U] methods of fighting a war in which BACTERIA are used to poison people, damage crops etc. —compare CHEMICAL WARFARE

bi·ol·o·gy /baɪ'ɑlədʒi/ *n.* [U] **1** the scientific study of living things: *She has a degree in biology.* **2** the scientific laws that control the life of a particular type of animal, plant etc.: [+ **of**] *the biology of bacteria* —**biologist** *n.* [C]

bi·o·mass /'baɪoʊ,mæs/ *n.* [U] TECHNICAL plant and animal matter used to provide FUEL or energy

bi·on·ic /baɪ'ɑnɪk/ *adj.* INFORMAL much stronger or faster than a normal person usually because of having electronic arms or legs

bi·o·phys·ics /ˌbaɪoʊ'fɪzɪks/ *n.* [U] the scientific study of matter and natural forces in living things

bi·o·pic /'baɪoʊ,pɪk/ *n.* [C] INFORMAL a movie that tells the story of someone's life etc.: *"Kundun" is Martin Scorsese's biopic about the Dalai Lama.*

bi·op·sy /'baɪˌɑpsi/ *plural* **biopsies** *n.* [C] the removal of body TISSUE[3] from someone who is sick, in order to find out what is wrong with them

bi·o·rhythms /'baɪoʊ,rɪðəmz/ *n.* [plural] regular changes in the speed at which physical processes happen in your body, which some people believe can affect the way you feel and behave

bi·o·sphere /'baɪə,sfɪr/ *n.* [singular] TECHNICAL the part of the world in which animals, plants etc. can live

bi·o·tech·nol·o·gy /ˌbaɪoʊtɛk'nɑlədʒi/ *n.* [U] TECHNICAL the use of living things such as cells and BACTERIA in science and industry, for example to make drugs, destroy waste matter etc.

bi·par·ti·san /baɪ'pɑrtəzən/ *adj.* consisting of or representing two political parties: *a bipartisan agreement to balance the federal budget*

bi·par·tite /baɪ'pɑrtaɪt/ *adj.* **1** FORMAL shared by or agreed on by two different groups: *a bipartite treaty* **2** TECHNICAL having two parts: *a bipartite leaf* —compare TRIPARTITE

bi·ped /'baɪpɛd/ *n.* [C] TECHNICAL an animal with two legs, including humans —**bipedal** /baɪ'pɛdl/ *adj.* —compare QUADRUPED

bi·plane /'baɪpleɪn/ *n.* [C] an aircraft with two sets of wings, especially of a type built in the early 20th century —compare MONOPLANE

bi·po·lar /baɪ'poʊlɚ/ *adj.* **1** consisting of two opposite or clearly different ideas: *The bipolar world of the 1980s, where two opposing countries held all the power, disappeared very quickly.* **2** TECHNICAL someone who is bipolar has bipolar disorder

bipolar dis·or·der /.'.. .,../ *n.* [U] TECHNICAL: see MANIC DEPRESSION

bi·ra·cial /ˌbaɪ'reɪʃəl/ *adj.* representing or including people from two different races: *biracial families*

birch /bɚtʃ/ *n.* [C,U] a tree with smooth BARK (=outer covering) and thin branches, or the wood from this tree

bird /bɚd/ *n.* [C]
1 animal a creature with wings and feathers that lays eggs and can usually fly: *The tree was full of tiny, brightly colored birds.*
2 sth is for the birds SPOKEN said when you think something is useless, stupid, boring etc.: *Staying up late doing this kind of scheduling stuff is for the birds!*
3 give/flip sb the bird SLANG to make a very offensive sign by putting your middle finger up with the back of your hand toward someone
4 the birds and the bees HUMOROUS an expression meaning "sex," especially the things you tell children in order to explain sex to them

5 a bird in the hand (is worth two in the bush) used to say that something you already have is worth more than something which is better, but which you cannot be sure of getting

6 birds of a feather (flock together) used to say that two people or groups are very similar, do the same things etc.

7 person OLD-FASHIONED a person of a particular type, especially one who seems strange or unusual: *He's a strange old bird.* —see also **early bird** (EARLY¹ (11)), **sb eats like a bird** (EAT (13)), **kill two birds with one stone** (KILL¹ (12)), **a little bird told me** (LITTLE¹ (9))

bird·bath /ˈbɜdbæθ/ n. [C] a stone bowl filled with water for birds to wash in

bird·brain /ˈbɜdbreɪn/ adj. INFORMAL someone who is silly or stupid —**birdbrained** adj.

bird dog /ˈ. ./ n. [C] a dog that is trained to find and bring back birds that have been shot

bird·er /ˈbɜdə/ n. [C] INFORMAL a BIRD WATCHER

bird·house /ˈbɜdhaʊs/ n. [C] a small wooden box put in the yard for birds to live in

bird·ie¹ /ˈbɜdi/ n. [C] **1** SPOKEN a word meaning "bird," used especially by or to children **2** one STROKE¹ (3) less than PAR to get the ball in the hole in a game of GOLF **3** the small object that you hit across the net in a game of BADMINTON; SHUTTLECOCK

birdie² v. [T] to hit the ball into the hole in GOLF with one STROKE¹ (3) less than PAR

bird of par·a·dise /ˌ. . ˈ.../ n. [C] a brightly colored bird from New Guinea

bird of pas·sage /ˌ. . ˈ../ n. [C] **1** LITERARY someone who never stays in the same place for long **2** a bird that flies from one area or country to another, according to the seasons

bird of prey /ˌ. . ˈ./ n. [C] a bird that kills other birds or small animals for food

bird·seed /ˈbɜdsid/ n. [U] a mixture of seeds for feeding birds

bird's-eye view /ˌ. . ˈ./ n. [singular] a view of something from high above it: *From the road, you get a bird's-eye view across the Waipio Valley.*

bird·song /ˈbɜdsɔŋ/ n. [U] the musical noises made by birds: *The silence broken only by birdsong.*

bird watch·er /ˈ. ,../ n. [C] someone who watches wild birds and tries to recognize different types —**bird-watching** n. [U]

bi·ret·ta /bəˈrɛtə/ n. [C] a square cap worn by Catholic priests

Bir·ming·ham /ˈbɜmɪŋˌhæm/ a city in the U.S. state of Alabama

birth /bɜθ/ n. **1** [C,U] the time when a baby comes out of its mother's body: *Congratulations on the birth of your daughter!* | *What is your birth date* (=the date on which you were born)? | *He only weighed three pounds at birth.* | **the town/country etc. of your birth** (=the town, country etc. where you were born) **2 give birth (to sb)** if a woman gives birth, she produces a baby from her body: *At 9:40 Claudia gave birth to a nine-pound baby boy.* **3** the time when something new starts to exist: *the birth of photography* | *the birth of a nation* **4** [U] the character, language, social position etc. that you have because of the family or country you come from: *She is French by birth.* | *A large portion of the population is of foreign birth.*

birth cer·tif·i·cate /ˈ. .,.../ n. [C] an official document that shows when and where you were born

birth con·trol /ˈ. .,./ n. [U] the practice of controlling, by various methods, the number of children you have; CONTRACEPTION: *Have you discussed birth control with your daughter?*

birth·day /ˈbɜθdeɪ/ n. plural **birthdays** [C] **1** a day that is an exact number of years after the day when you were born: *It's my 18th birthday next week.* | **Happy Birthday!** (=what you say to someone on their birthday) | *a birthday present/card/party etc. I met Anna at your birthday party last year.* | **birthday boy/girl** (=the boy or girl whose birthday

it is) **2 in your birthday suit** HUMOROUS not wearing any clothes

birth de·fect /ˈ. .../ n. [C] a physical problem that a child is born with

birth fa·ther /ˈ. ,../ n. [C] a child's natural father, rather than someone who has become its father through ADOPTION (1)

birth·mark /ˈbɜθmɑrk/ n. [C] a permanent red or brown mark on your skin that you have had since you were born: *Paul has a birthmark on his left cheek.*

birth mo·ther /ˈ. ,../ n. [C] a child's natural mother, rather than someone who has become its mother through ADOPTION (1)

birth·place /ˈbɜθpleɪs/ n. [C usually singular] **1** the place where someone was born, especially someone famous: *We visited Elvis' birthplace in Tupelo, Mississippi.* **2** the place where something first started to happen or exist: *New Orleans is the birthplace of Jazz.*

birth·rate /ˈbɜθreɪt/ n. [C] the number of births for every 1000 people in a particular year in a particular place: *In California, the average birthrate was just slightly above the national pace.* —compare DEATH RATE

birth·right /ˈbɜθraɪt/ n. [C usually singular] **1** a basic right that you have because of the family or country you come from: *Freedom of speech is every American's birthright.* **2** property, money etc. that you have because it comes from your family

birth·stone /ˈbɜθstoʊn/ n. [C] a valuable stone that is used to represent the month of the year in which you were born: *Emerald is the birthstone of people born in May.*

Bis·cay, Bay of /ˈbɪskeɪ/ an area of the Atlantic Ocean between the west coast of France and the north coast of Spain

bis·cot·ti /bɪsˈkɑti/ n. [U] a type of Italian cookie eaten with coffee, often made with ALMONDS or HAZELNUTS

bis·cuit /ˈbɪskɪt/ n. **1** [C] a type of soft bread baked in small round pieces: *biscuits and gravy* **2** [U] a light yellowish-brown color **3** [C] BRITISH a cookie or a CRACKER

bi·sect /ˈbaɪsɛkt, baɪˈsɛkt/ v. [T] TECHNICAL to divide something, especially a line or angle, into two equal parts —**bisection** /baɪsɛkʃən, baɪˈsɛk-/ n. [U]

bi·sex·u·al /baɪˈsɛkʃuəl/ adj. **1** sexually attracted to both men and women —compare HETEROSEXUAL, HOMOSEXUAL **2** having qualities or features of both sexes: *a bisexual plant* —**bisexual** n. [C] —**bisexually** adv. —**bisexuality** /ˌbaɪsɛkʃuˌæləti/ n. [U]

Bish·kek /bɪʃˈkɛk/ the capital and largest city of Kyrgyzstan

bish·op /ˈbɪʃəp/ n. [C] **1** a priest with a high rank in some Christian churches, who is the head of all the churches and priests in a large area **2** a piece in the game of CHESS that can be moved any number of squares from one corner toward the opposite corner

bish·op·ric /ˈbɪʃəprɪk/ n. [C] **1** the area that a bishop is in charge of; DIOCESE **2** the position of being a bishop

Bis·marck /ˈbɪzmɑrk/ the capital city of the U.S. state of North Dakota

Bismarck, Ot·to von /ˈɑtoʊ vɑn/ (1815–1898) a German politician who was mainly responsible for joining all the separate German states together to form one country, and who them became CHANCELLOR of Germany

bis·muth /ˈbɪzməθ/ n. [U] symbol Bi a gray-white metal that is an ELEMENT and is often used in medicine

bi·son /ˈbaɪsən/ n. plural **bison** or **bisons** [C] TECHNICAL an animal like a large cow with long hair around the head and shoulders, which used to be common in western North America; BUFFALO (1) —see picture on page 429

bisque /bɪsk/ n. [U] a thick creamy soup, especially one made from SHELLFISH: *lobster bisque*

Bis·sau /bɪˈsaʊ/ the capital city of Guinea-Bissau

bis·tro /ˈbistroʊ/ n. *plural* **bistros** [C] a small restaurant or bar

bit¹ /bɪt/ n. [C]

1 **slightly/fairly** **a bit** INFORMAL slightly, but not very; a little: *I'm a little bit tired.* | *Let it warm up a little bit.* | *Prices have dropped a bit in the last few days.* | *Enrollment is down a bit from last year.* | *I'm feeling a bit better* | **a bit more/less** *This will make things a bit more difficult.*

2 **quite a bit** a fairly large amount, or to a fairly large degree: *She said she learned quite a bit.* | *He owes me quite a bit of money.*

3 **piece** a small piece of something: [+ **of**] *The floor was covered with tiny bits of broken glass.* | *making a mosaic out of bits and pieces of tiles* | *I tore the letter **to bits** (=into small pieces) and threw it away.*

4 **amount** INFORMAL a small amount, especially of something that is not a physical object: [+ **of**] *All that's needed is a bit of imagination.* | *There's been a bit of tension at the office lately.*

5 **computer** the smallest unit of information that can be used by a computer: *a 16-bit processor* —compare BYTE

6 **time** a short amount of time: *I'll come back to that point **in just a bit**.* | *I was a bit late.*

7 **not a bit** also **not the least bit** not at all: *"Did you regret not going to college?" "**Not a bit**."* | *He isn't the **least bit** afraid to look you in the eye and tell you you're wrong.*

8 **tool** the sharp part of a tool for cutting or making holes: *a drill bit*

9 **for a horse** a metal bar that is put in the mouth of a horse and used for controlling its movements

10 **every bit as...** just as much as: *I think she's every bit as pretty as her sister.*

11 **bit by bit** gradually: *Bit by bit, our apartment started to look like a home.*

12 **money** OLD USE 12½ cents: *I wouldn't give you two bits for that old book.* —see also **two bits** (TWO (5))

13 **do your bit** INFORMAL to do part of something that needs to be done, especially to help other people: *We wanted to do our bit for the boys fighting in the war.* —see also BIT PART, **be chomping at the bit** (CHOMP (2))

bit² the past tense of BITE¹

bitch¹ /bɪtʃ/ n. [C] **1** SPOKEN, OFFENSIVE a woman that you dislike or think is not nice: *It sounds like Carrie can be a real bitch sometimes.* **2 a bitch** SPOKEN, IMPOLITE something that causes problems or difficulties: *I drove his truck once – it was a bitch to drive.* **3 sb's bitch** IMPOLITE, SLANG **a)** a woman who is a boy's or man's GIRLFRIEND, or who is a PROSTITUTE working for a particular man **b)** a man in prison that another man controls and has sex with **4** a female dog —see also SON OF A BITCH

bitch² v. [I] SPOKEN, IMPOLITE **1** to say unkind things about someone or something: [+ **about**] *We were all bitching about the boss when she walked in.* **2** to complain continuously: *Stop bitching!* | [+ **at**] *Stop bitching at me and just tell me what your problem is!*

bitch·ing /ˈbɪtʃɪŋ/ also **bitch·in** /ˈbɪtʃɪn/ adj. SLANG very good; excellent: *That's a bitching car!*

bitch·y /ˈbɪtʃi/ adj. **bitchier, bitchiest** SPOKEN, IMPOLITE someone who is bitchy complains or is unkind about other people: *That's a bitchy thing to say.* | *She can be really bitchy sometimes.* —**bitchily** adv. —**bitchiness** n. [U]

bite¹ /baɪt/ v. *past tense* **bit** *past participle* **bitten**

1 **with your teeth** [I,T] to cut or crush something with your teeth: *Even a friendly dog will bite if it's scared.* | *Taryn, stop biting your fingernails!* | [+ **into**] *I felt something hard as I bit into the cake.* | [**bite sth off**] *His ear was bitten off in a fight.*

2 **insect/snake** [I,T] if an insect or snake bites you, it injures you by making a hole in your skin: *She was bitten by a rattlesnake.*

bite

peck

bite

nibble

chew

3 **bite the bullet** INFORMAL to bravely accept something bad: *A lot of companies had to bite the bullet and lay off a lot of their employees.*

4 **bite your tongue** to try hard to stop yourself from saying what you really think: *I'm just biting my tongue for now. If she wants to ask my advice, she can.*

5 **bite sb's head off** INFORMAL to answer someone or speak to them very angrily, when there is no good reason for doing this: *I never know if he's going to be in a good mood or if he's going to bite my head off.*

6 **bite the hand that feeds you** to harm someone who has treated you well or supported you: *If I put my prices up, it's like biting the hand that feeds me – it's economic suicide.*

7 **bite the dust** INFORMAL **a)** to die, fail, or be defeated: *Half of all new restaurants bite the dust in the first year.* **b)** to stop working completely: *My old car's finally bitten the dust.*

8 **bite off more than you can chew** to try to do more than you are able to do: *Many kids who leave home to live alone find they have bitten off more than they can chew.*

9 **sth bites (the big one)** SLANG an impolite expression meaning that something is very bad in quality or that a situation is very bad: *Your mom won't let you go? That bites.*

10 **bite me** VULGAR said when you are very angry with someone: *Hey, if she doesn't like it, she can bite me.*

11 **fish** [I] if a fish bites, it takes the fishing hook or the food on the hook in its mouth

12 **buy/believe** [I] to buy a product or believe what someone is telling you, especially when someone is trying very hard to make you do this: *The company withdraws its new products quickly if consumers fail to bite.*

13 **have an effect** [I] to have the effect that was intended, especially a negative or bad one: *The new tobacco taxes have begun to bite.*

14 **he/she won't bite** SPOKEN used to say that there is no need to be afraid of someone, especially someone in authority: *Well, go and ask him if he can help you – he won't bite!*

15 **be bitten by the bug/fever etc.** to develop a very strong interest in or desire for something: *Kinner had spent his time working on Model T Fords before being bitten by the flying bug.*

16 **not slip** [I] to hold firmly to a surface, or rest firmly against it: [+ **into**] *The ski's edge should bite into the snow.*

17 **cold/wind** [I] if cold weather or the wind bites, it makes you feel extremely cold

18 **once bitten twice shy** used to say that if you have failed or been hurt once, you will be very careful next time

bite back phr. v. **1** [T **bite** sth ↔ **back**] to stop yourself from saying something or telling someone what you really feel: *Tamara bit back the insult that sprang to mind and smiled instead.* **2** [I] to react strongly and angrily to something: *Shortly after the incident, Young bit back in court, filing a civil suit.*

    bite into sth *phr. v.* [T] to cut or press hard against a surface: *The knotted rope bit into my skin.*

**bite² ** *n.*
  1 `when you eat` [C] the act of cutting or crushing something with your teeth: *"The chicken's dry," said Kim, after* **taking a bite**. | *Can I* **have a bite** *of your steak?*
  2 `animal/insect` [C] a wound made when an animal or insect bites you: *You can get Lyme disease from a tick bite.*
  3 **a bite (to eat)** SPOKEN a small meal: *We had a bite to eat at Las Fuentes before the movie.* | *I'll just grab a bite on the way to work.*
  4 `cold` [singular] a sharp feeling of coldness: [+ **of**] *the bite of the November wind*
  5 `amount` [singular] an amount of money that is taken from something, especially by the government: *The state will be taking a bite out of money earned from local traffic tickets*
  6 `taste` [U] a pleasant, strong, slightly bitter, or sour taste: *The barbecue sauce lacked heat and bite.*
  7 `effectiveness` [U] a special quality in speech or writing that makes arguments or criticisms effective and likely to persuade people: *a protest song with bite and wit*
  8 `fish` [C] an occasion when a fish takes the food from a hook: *Sometimes I sit for hours and never get a bite.*
  9 `position of teeth` [C usually singular] the position of someone's upper teeth in relation to their lower teeth —see also SOUND BITE

bite-size also **bite-sized** /'. ,./ *adj.* [only before noun] **1** the right size to fit into your mouth easily: *bite-size pieces of chicken* **2** small enough to understand or deal with quickly and easily: *bite-size chunks of information*

bit·ing /'baɪtɪŋ/ *adj.* **1** a biting wind feels very cold **2** a biting criticism or remark is very unkind: *biting sarcasm* —**bitingly** *adv.*

bit·map /'bɪt˺mæp/ *n.* [C] TECHNICAL a computer image consisting of an arrangement of bits (BIT¹ (5)): *bitmap fonts*

bit part /'. ,./ *n.* [C] a very small acting performance in a play or movie: *She has a bit part in Mike Nichol's new movie.*

bit·sy /'bɪtsi/ *adj.* INFORMAL very small —see also ITTY-BITTY

bit·ten /'bɪt˺n/ *v.* the past participle of BITE¹

bit·ter /'bɪtɚ/ *adj.*
  1 `angry/upset` full of angry, JEALOUS, and unhappy feelings because bad things have happened to you or you have been treated unfairly: *I used to be very bitter and angry, but I've gotten over it.* | *She shot a bitter glance in his direction and left.* | [+ **about**] *Jensen sounded bitter about his team's fourth straight loss.*
  2 `full of hate` a bitter argument, attack, struggle etc. is one in which people oppose or criticize each other with strong feelings of hate and anger: *There has been bitter fighting in the hills to the north of the capital.* | *a bitter legal battle over custody of the children*
  3 `causing unhappiness` [only before noun] a bitter experience makes you feel very unhappy and upset: *The party suffered a bitter defeat in 1964.* | *The news was a* **bitter disappointment** *to NASA employees.* | *We know* **from bitter experience** (=because of your own very bad experiences) *that guns in the home end up killing children.*
  4 `taste` having a strong taste like black coffee without sugar, or very dark chocolate: *The medicine tasted bitter.* —compare SWEET¹ (1), SOUR¹ (1)
  5 `cold` extremely cold: *a bitter east wind* | *The children have to walk to school in the* **bitter cold**.
  6 **to/until the bitter end** continuing until the end, in spite of problems or difficulties: *We will* **fight until the bitter end** *to defend our land.*
  7 **a bitter pill (to swallow)** something very bad that you have to accept: *Losing the business was a bitter pill to swallow.*

  8 **bitter enemy** two people or groups who are bitter enemies hate each other and have been fighting or arguing for a long time: *The two countries are still bitter enemies after centuries of conflict.* —see also BITTERLY —**bitterness** *n.* [U]

bit·ter·ly /'bɪtɚli/ *adv.* **1** in a way that is full of anger or criticism: *The law was bitterly opposed by environmentalists.* **2** in a way that makes you very unhappy, or shows that you are very unhappy: *Ross complained bitterly that the state didn't care about the homeless.* | *It was a decision that she bitterly regretted later in her life.* **3** **bitterly cold** very cold

bit·tern /'bɪtɚn/ *n.* [C] a brown European bird with long legs that lives near water and makes a deep sound

bit·ters /'bɪtɚz/ *n.* [U] a bitter liquid made from a mixture of plant products and used to add taste to alcoholic drinks

bit·ter·sweet /ˌbɪtɚ'swit◂/ *adj.* **1** feelings, memories, or experiences that are bittersweet are happy and sad at the same time: *bittersweet memories of childhood* **2** a taste or smell that is bittersweet is both sweet and bitter at the same time **3** **bittersweet chocolate** chocolate that is not very sweet and that does not have a lot of milk in it

bit·ty /'bɪti/ *adj.* INFORMAL very small: *a small house with a little bitty yard* —see also ITTY-BITTY

bi·tu·men /bɪ'tyumən, -'tu-, baɪ-/ *n.* [U] BLACKTOP —**bituminous** *adj.*

bi·valve /'baɪvælv/ *n.* [C] TECHNICAL any sea animal that has two shells joined together, such as an OYSTER —**bivalved** *adj.*

biv·ou·ac¹ /'bɪvu,æk/ *n.* a temporary camp built outside without any tents

bivouac² ** *v.* **bivouacked, bivouacking [I] to spend the night outside without tents in a temporary camp: *The climbers bivouacked halfway up the mountain.*

bi·week·ly /baɪ'wikli/ *adj.* appearing or happening every two weeks or twice a week: *a bi-weekly magazine* —**biweekly** *adv.*

biz /bɪz/ *n.* [singular] INFORMAL a particular type of business, especially one connected with entertainment: *Ms. Francis reports on the music biz for the magazine.* —see also SHOWBIZ

bi·zarre /bɪ'zɑr/ *adj.* very unusual or strange: *The characters Arden creates are often odd and sometimes bizarre.* | *bizarre religious sects* —**bizarrely** *adv.*

blab /blæb/ *v.* [I,T] INFORMAL to talk too much about something, often something that should be secret: *Kerri told her agent, who then went and blabbed it to all the reporters.* | [+ **about**] *She's trying to lose weight, and she's always blabbing about her diet.*

blab·ber·mouth /'blæbɚ,maʊθ/ *n.* [C] INFORMAL someone who always talks too much and often says things that should be secret

black¹ /blæk/ *adj.*
  1 `color` having a color that is darker than every other color, like the sky at night: *a shiny black car* | *The letters were white on a black background.* | *She has* **jet-black** (=very dark black) *hair.* | *The room was* **pitch black** (=completely dark).
  2 `people` also **Black a)** someone who is black has dark-colored skin, and is from a family that is from Africa or was originally from Africa: *Most of the people in my neighborhood are black.* **b)** [only before noun] relating to or concerning black people: *politics from a black perspective* | *contemporary Black music*
  3 `coffee` black coffee does not have milk in it: *Do you take your coffee black?*
  4 `dirty` very dirty: *My hands were black from working on the car.*
  5 **a black mark (against sb)** if there is a black mark against you, someone thinks you have done something wrong or bad, and this makes them have a bad opinion of you: *It is almost impossible to borrow money if you have any black marks against you.*
  6 `without hope` sad and without much hope for the future; GLOOMY: *Tony was in a black mood.* | *It*

*was a **black day** (=when something very bad hap-pens) for the auto industry, with announcements of major job losses.*

7 angry full of feelings of anger or hate: *Denise gave me a black look.*

8 evil LITERARY very bad: *black deeds* | *a black-hearted villain* —see also BLACKLY —**blackness** n. [C]

black² n. **1** [U] the dark color of night or coal: *Black is his favorite color.* | *You look good **in black** (=wear-ing black clothes).* **2** [C] also **Black** someone who has very dark skin, and whose family is from Africa or was originally from Africa: *The laws were used to discriminate against blacks.* **3 be in the black** to have more money than you owe —opposite **be in the red** (RED² (3)) **4** [U] black paint, color, MAKEUP etc.: *Put some more black around your eyes.*

black³ v. [T]

black out phr. v. **1** [I] to become unconscious; FAINT: *The clerk was hit on the head and blacked out.* **2** [T **black** sth ↔ **out**] to put a dark mark over something so that it cannot be seen: *The censors had blacked out several words.* **3** [T **black** sth ↔ **out**] to hide or turn off all the lights in a town or city, espe-cially during war —see also BLACKOUT (1)

black·a·moor /'blækə,mʊr/ n. [C] OLD USE, OFFENSIVE a person with dark or black skin, especially a man

black and blue /,. . '. ./ adj. skin that is black and blue has BRUISES (=dark marks) on it as a result of being hit: *My leg was black and blue where the kid had kicked me.*

black and white /,. . '.◂/ adj. **1** showing pictures or images only in black, white, and gray: *old black and white movies* —opposite COLOR³ **2** considering things in a very simple way, as if there are clear differences between good and bad, right and wrong etc.: *The sit-uation is not black and white; we still don't know what to do.* | *A lot of people **see things in black and white**, and don't understand how complex the issue is.* **3 in black and white** in written form, and there-fore definite: *The rules are there in black and white for everyone to see.*

black art /,. './ n. [U] also **the black arts** [plural] BLACK MAGIC

black·ball /'blækbɔl/ v. [T] to make someone stop being part of a particular club, organization etc., especially by voting against them: *In 1962, Freed was fined $300 and blackballed from radio.*

black bear /'. . / n. [C] a North American bear with black or dark brown fur

black belt /'. . / n. [C] **1** a high rank in some types of Asian SELF-DEFENSE, especially JUDO and KARATE **2** someone who has this rank: *Sandy's a black belt in judo.*

black·ber·ry /'blæk,bɛri/ n. plural **blackberries** [C] a sweet black or dark purple BERRY

black·bird /'blækbɚd/ n. [C] a common European and American bird, the male of which is completely black

black·board /'blækbɔrd/ n. [C] a board with a dark smooth surface, used in schools for writing on with CHALK¹ (2) —compare WHITEBOARD

black box /,. './ n. [C] INFORMAL a piece of equipment on an airplane that records what happens and how the airplane operates during a flight; FLIGHT RECORDER

black com·e·dy /,. '.../ n. [C,U] a play, story etc. that is funny, but also shows a side of life that is not very nice

Black Death /,. './ n. **the Black Death** an illness that killed large numbers of people in Europe and Asia in the 14th century —see also BUBONIC PLAGUE, PLAGUE¹ (2)

black e·con·o·my /,. .'.../ n. **the black economy** business activity that takes place secretly, especially in order to avoid tax —compare BLACK MARKET

black·en /'blækən/ v. **1** [I,T] to become black, or make something black: *A few people, their faces blackened by the smoke, ran out of the building.*

2 blacken sb's name/character/reputation etc. to say things about someone that are not nice, in order to make other people have a bad opinion of them

black En·glish /,. '../ n. [U] the variety of English spoken by some African-American people in the U.S.; EBONICS

black eye /,. './ n. [C] darkness of the skin around your eye, because you have been hit: *How'd you get that black eye?*

black-eyed pea /,. . '. ./ n. [C] a small pale bean with a black spot on it

black-eyed Su·san /,blæk aɪd 'suzən/ n. [C] a yellow flower with a dark center that grows in North America

black·face /'blækfeɪs/ n. [U] someone who is in blackface has painted their face black, especially for a musical show popular in the early 1900s

Black·foot /'blækfʊt/ n. a Native American tribe from the northwest region of the U.S.

Black For·est, the /,. '../ an area of southwest Ger-many where there is a very large forest

black gold /,. './ n. [U] INFORMAL oil

black·guard /'blægɚd, 'blækgɑrd/ n. [C] OLD USE a man who treats other people very badly; SCOUNDREL

Black Hawk /'. ./ (1767–1838) a Sauk leader who fought against U.S. soldiers in 1832 in an attempt to get back his tribe's land

black·head /'blækhɛd/ n. [C] a small spot of dirt deep in someone's skin

black hole /,. './ n. [C] **1** TECHNICAL an area in outer space into which everything near it, including light, is pulled **2** INFORMAL something that uses up a lot of money: *The downtown area is an economic black hole.*

black hu·mor /,. '../ n. [U] jokes, funny stories etc. that deal with the parts of life that are not nice

black ice /,. './ n. [U] a thin layer of ice that is very difficult to see: *There may be black ice on the roads tonight, so drive carefully.*

black·ing /'blækɪŋ/ n. [U] OLD-FASHIONED a very thick liquid or polish that is put on objects to make them black

black·jack /'blækdʒæk/ n. **1** [U] a card game, usu-ally played for money, in which you try to get as close to 21 points as possible **2** [C] a weapon like a stick covered with leather, used to hit people

black knight /,. './ n. [C] SLANG a person or company that tries to buy most of the SHARES² (4) in a company whose owners do not want to sell them —compare WHITE KNIGHT

black·list¹ /'blæk,lɪst/ n. [C] a list of people, coun-tries, products etc. that are disapproved of, and should therefore be avoided or punished: *They are on the blacklist of companies that pollute the environ-ment.*

blacklist² v. [T] to put a person, country, product etc. on a blacklist: *More than 200 people in the movie industry were blacklisted during the McCarthy era.*

black lung /,. './ n. [U] a lung disease caused by breathing in coal dust over a long period of time, especially affecting MINERS

black·ly /'blækli/ adv. LITERARY in an angry, threaten-ing, or bad way: *Storm clouds blackly loomed over the valley.*

black mag·ic /,. '../ n. [U] magic that is believed to use the power of the Devil for evil purposes —see also WHITE MAGIC

black·mail¹ /'blækmeɪl/ n. [U] **1** the practice of get-ting money from someone or making them do what you want by threatening to tell secrets about them **2** an attempt to make someone do what you want by making threats or by making them feel guilty if they do not: *They said if I didn't do the over-time I'd lose my job – it was blackmail.* | *Using the picture of a sad little kid in their advertisement seems like **emotional blackmail** (=something that makes you feel guilty).*

blackmail² v. [T] to demand money or other things from someone by threatening to do something vio-lent or bad: *Ford had been blackmailing a gay naval* officer. | [**blackmail** sb **into doing** sth] *The President said he would not be blackmailed into making a hasty decision on balancing the budget.* —**blackmailer** *n.* [C]

black mar·ket /ˌ. ˈ.../ *n.* [C] the system by which people illegally buy and sell foreign money, goods that are difficult to obtain etc.: [+ **in**] *a black market in weapons* | *black market cigarettes* | *When you travel in these countries, never exchange money* **on the black market.** —compare BLACK ECONOMY

black mar·ket·eer /ˌblæk mɑrkɪˈtɪr/ *n.* [C] someone who sells things on the black market

Black Moun·tains /ˌ. ˈ../ a RANGE of mountains in the southeastern U.S. that is part of the Blue Ridge Mountains and is in the state of North Carolina

Black Mus·lim /ˌ. ˈ../ *n.* [C] a member of a group of African-American people who believe in the religion of Islam

black·out /ˈblækaʊt/ *n.* [C] **1** a period of darkness caused by a failure of the electricity supply: *Several neighborhoods in the San Francisco area experienced blackouts last night.* **2** an occasion when you suddenly lose consciousness: *Since the accident, Sharon has suffered from blackouts.* **3** also **news blackout** a situation in which particular pieces of news or information are not allowed to be reported: *The U.S. and Russia agreed to a news blackout for the remainder of the talks.* **4** a period during a war when all the lights in a town, city etc. must be turned off

black pep·per /ˌ. ˈ../ *n.* [U] pepper made from crushed seeds from which the dark outer covering has not been removed

Black Sea, the /ˌ. ˈ./ a large sea to the northeast of the Mediterranean that is surrounded by land, and is between Turkey, Bulgaria, Romania, Ukraine, Russia, and Georgia

black sheep /ˌ. ˈ./ *n.* [C usually singular] someone who is regarded by other members of their family or group as a failure or embarrassment: *My sister's* **the black sheep of the family.**

Black·shirt, Black Shirt /ˈblækʃɚt/ *n.* [C] a member of a FASCIST organization with a black shirt as part of its uniform

black·smith /ˈblæksmɪθ/ *n.* [C] someone who makes and repairs things made of iron, especially HORSESHOES

black·strap mo·las·ses /ˌblækstræp məˈlæsɪz/ *n.* [U] the darkest thickest MOLASSES (=thick sweet liquid) produced when sugar is taken from sugar plants

black-tie /ˈ. ˌ./ *adj.* a black-tie party or social occasion is one at which people wear special formal clothes, such as TUXEDOs for men: *a black-tie dinner* —compare WHITE-TIE

black·top /ˈblæktɑp/ *n.* **1** [U] a thick black sticky substance that becomes hard as it dries, used to cover roads **2 the blacktop** the surface of a road covered by this substance: *We left the blacktop and drove along a forest road.*

black·wa·ter fe·ver /ˌblækwɔtɚ ˈfivɚ/ *n.* [U] a very severe form of the disease MALARIA

Black·well /ˈblækwɛl/**, An·toi·nette** /ˈæntwɑˌnɛt/ (1825–1921) the first woman to be officially made a minister of a Protestant church in the U.S.

Blackwell, Elizabeth (1821–1910) a U.S. doctor who was the first woman to QUALIFY officially as a doctor in the U.S.

black wid·ow /ˌ. ˈ../ *n.* [C] a very poisonous type of SPIDER that is black with red marks

blad·der /ˈblædɚ/ *n.* [C] **1** an organ of the body that holds URINE (=waste liquid from the body) until it is passed out of the body **2** a bag of skin, leather, or rubber, for example inside a football, that can be filled with air or liquid —see also GALL BLADDER

blade /bleɪd/ *n.* [C] **1** the flat cutting part of a tool or weapon: *The blade should be kept sharp.* | *razor blades* —see picture at TOOL[1] **2** the flat wide part of an object that pushes against air or water: *a propeller blade* | *a ceiling fan with wooden blades* **3** a long flat leaf of grass or a similar plant: *a blade of grass* **4** the metal part on the bottom of an ICE SKATE —see also SHOULDER BLADE

blah[1] /blɑ/ *adj.* SPOKEN **1** not having an interesting taste, appearance, character etc.: *The chili was kind of blah.* **2** slightly sick or unhappy: *I feel really blah today.*

blah[2] *n.* [U] **blah, blah, blah** SPOKEN used when you do not need to complete what you are saying because it is boring or because the person you are talking to already knows it: *You know how Michelle talks: "Tommy did this, and Jesse did that, blah, blah, blah."*

blahs /blɑz/ *n.* INFORMAL **the blahs** a feeling of being sad and bored: *a case of the winter blahs*

blame[1] /bleɪm/ *v.* [T] **1** to say or think that someone or something is responsible for something bad: *Don't blame me – it's not my fault.* | [**blame** sb/sth **for** sth] *I used to blame my parents for messing up my life.* | *Dougan blamed the economy for weak Christmas sales.* | [**blame** sth **on** sb/sth] *The accident was blamed on pilot error.* **2 sb is to blame for sth** used to say that someone is responsible for something bad that happened: *Officials believe that more than one person may be to blame for the fire.* **3 don't blame me** SPOKEN used when you are advising someone not to do something: *Go ahead, but don't blame me if it doesn't work.* **4 I don't blame you/them etc.** SPOKEN used to say that you think it was right or reasonable for someone to do what they did: *I don't blame her for being mad – she didn't come all the way from Switzerland to be treated like that!* **5 only have yourself to blame** SPOKEN used to say that someone's problems are their own fault: *If they lose this game, they'll only have themselves to blame.*

blame[2] *n.* [U] responsibility for a mistake or for something bad: [+ **for**] *Much of the blame for homelessness should go on the state's welfare system.* | *Nathalie is older, and she usually* **gets the blame** *when the kids fight.* | **put/place/lay the blame on** sb (=say something is someone's fault)

blame·less /ˈbleɪmlɪs/ *adj.* FORMAL not guilty of anything bad; INNOCENT[1] (1): *In a divorce, no one is blameless.* | *a blameless life* —**blamelessly** *adv.*

blame·wor·thy /ˈbleɪmˌwɚði/ *adj.* FORMAL deserving blame or disapproval: *blameworthy conduct*

blanch /blæntʃ/ *v.* **1** [I] to become pale because you are frightened or shocked: [+ **at**] *Most customers blanch at the thought of paying $150 for kids' shoes.* **2** [T] to put vegetables, fruit, or nuts into boiling water for a short time: *Blanch the spinach for 30 seconds.* **3** [T] to make a plant become pale by keeping it away from light

bland /blænd/ *adj.* **1** without any excitement, strong opinions, or special character: *a bland suburban neighborhood* | *a few bland songs on the radio* **2** food that is bland has very little taste: *Tofu is a bland food made from soy beans.* —**blandly** *adv.* —**blandness** *n.* [U]

blan·dish·ments /ˈblændɪʃmənts/ *n.* [plural] FORMAL pleasant things you say that are intended to persuade or influence someone

blank[1] /blæŋk/ *adj.* **1** [no comparative] without any writing, print, or recorded sound: *a blank sheet of paper* | *I want to tape a show at 9:00. Are there any blank tapes?* **2** showing no expression, understanding, or interest: *I said hello, and she gave me a blank look.* | **a blank expression 3 go blank a)** to be suddenly unable to remember something: *I just went blank and couldn't remember his name for a minute.* **b)** to stop showing any images, writing etc.: *Suddenly the screen went blank.* —see also BLANKLY, BLANK VERSE —**blankness** *n.* [U]

blank[2] *n.* [C] **1** an empty space on a piece of paper, where you are supposed to write a word or letter: *Fill in the blanks with your name and address* **2** a form with empty spaces on it: *the competition entry blank* **3** a CARTRIDGE (=container for a bullet in a gun) that contains an explosive but no bullet: *We didn't know the guns were firing blanks.* —see also **draw a blank** (DRAW[1] (14)) —**blankness** *n.* [U]

blank³ v. **1** [T] INFORMAL to not allow your opponent or the opposing team to win points in a game or sport: *The Whalers blanked the Washington Capitals 2–0.* **2** also **blank out** [I] SPOKEN if your mind blanks, you are suddenly unable to remember something

blank sth ↔ **out** phr. v. [T] INFORMAL **1** to cover something so that it cannot be seen: *a picture with some of the names blanked out* **2** to completely forget something, especially deliberately: *My father's death forced me to face some things I'd blanked out for most of my life.*

blank car·tridge /ˌ. ˈ../ n. [C] a CARTRIDGE (2) in a gun that contains an explosive but no bullet

blank check /ˌ. ˈ./ n. [C] **1** a check that has been signed, but has not had the amount written on it **2** give sb a blank check to give someone permission to do whatever they think is necessary in a particular situation: *Congress gave President Johnson a blank check to wage war in Vietnam.*

s w **blan·ket¹** /ˈblæŋkɪt/ n. [C] **1** a cover for a bed, usually made of wool **2** a thick covering or area of something: [+ of] *The valley was covered with a blanket of mist.* —see also WET BLANKET, SECURITY BLANKET

blanket² v. [T usually passive] to cover something with a thick layer: [+ in/with] *The mountains were blanketed in snow.*

blanket³ adj. [only before noun] **a blanket statement/rule/ban etc. (on sth)** a statement, rule etc. that affects everyone or includes all possible cases: *a blanket ban on ivory trading*

blank·e·ty-blank /ˌblæŋkɪti ˈblæŋk‹/ adj. [only before noun] SPOKEN used to show annoyance when you want to avoid swearing: *That blankety-blank little idiot took my watch!*

blank·ly /ˈblæŋkli/ adv. in a way that shows no expression, understanding, or interest: *Joe stared blankly at the wall.*

blank verse /ˌ. ˈ./ n. [U] poetry that has a particular RHYTHM (1) but does not RHYME² (1): *Shakespeare's blank verse* —compare FREE VERSE

blare /blɛr/ v. [I,T] also **blare out** if a sound, radio etc. blares or if something blares music, voices etc., it makes a sound that is too loud: *Sirens blared as firefighters raced to the scene.* | *The radio was blaring out the news that an earthquake had hit just minutes before.* —**blare** n. [singular] *the blare of a horn*

blar·ney /ˈblɑrni/ n. [U] INFORMAL pleasant but untrue things that you say to someone in order to trick or persuade them

bla·sé /blɑˈzeɪ/ adj. not worried or excited about things that most people think are important, impressive etc.: *A trip to Disneyland excited even my blasé teenagers.*

blas·pheme /blæsˈfim, ˈblæsfim/ v. [I + against] to speak in a way that insults God or people's religious beliefs, or to use the names of God and holy things when swearing —**blasphemer** n. [C]

blas·phe·my /ˈblæsfəmi/ n. plural **blasphemies** [C,U] something you say or do that is insulting to God or people's religious beliefs —**blasphemous** adj.: *The book has been widely condemned as blasphemous.* —**blasphemously** adv.

blast¹ /blæst/ n.
1 air/wind [C] a sudden strong movement of wind or air: [+ of] *A blast of cold air swept through the hut.*
2 explosion [C] an explosion, or the very strong movement of air that it causes: *The blast was heard three miles away.* | *a shotgun blast*
3 fun a blast INFORMAL an enjoyable and exciting experience: *The concert was a blast.* | *We had a blast at the fair.*
4 full blast as strongly, loudly, or fast as possible: *The heating was on full blast.*
5 a blast from the past INFORMAL something from the past that you remember, see, or hear again, that reminds you of that time in your life: *The biggest blast from the past was '60s model, Peggy Moffat, whose famous haircut is back in style.*
6 noise [C] a sudden very loud noise: *The referee gave a blast on his whistle and we were off.*

blast² v.
1 criticize [T] to criticize something very strongly: *Environmental groups blasted the plan for more logging in the area.*
2 gun/bomb [T] to cause something to be damaged or destroyed, or someone to be injured or killed using a gun or a bomb: *Several Allied planes were blasted out of the sky.* | *The explosion blasted a hole in the county courthouse.*
3 music also **blast out** [I,T] to produce a lot of loud noise, especially music: *a radio blasting out music* | *Music blasted from the speakers in the living room.*
4 break sth into pieces **a)** [I,T] to break something into pieces using explosives, especially in order to build something such as a road: [+ through] *Four tunnels were made by blasting through the canyon rock.* | [blast sth through/in sth] *Slowly they blasted a path through the mountains.*
5 air/water [T] to direct air or water at something with great force: *A storm blasted the Florida coast with 75 m.p.h. winds.*
6 sports to beat another team very badly: *The Seahawks were blasted 35–14 by the Broncos at the start of the season.*
7 hit/kick sth [T] to hit or kick something very hard, especially a ball in a sport: *Newman blasted one into left field in the second inning.*
8 blast sb's hopes LITERARY to destroy someone's hope of doing something
9 blast! also **blast her/it etc.** SPOKEN, OLD-FASHIONED said when you are very annoyed about something: *Oh blast! I've forgotten my key.*

blast away phr. v. [I] to shoot at something or someone: *The police were blasting away at street lights, hoping that less light would mean less bloodshed.*

blast off phr. v. [I] if a SPACECRAFT blasts off, it leaves the ground —see also BLAST-OFF

blast·ed /ˈblæstɪd/ adj. [only before noun] SPOKEN OLD-FASHIONED used to express annoyance: *I wish that blasted dog would stop barking!*

blast fur·nace /ˈ. ˌ../ n. [C] a large industrial structure in which iron is separated from the rock that surrounds it

blast-off /ˈ. ./ n. [U] the moment when a SPACECRAFT leaves the ground: *10 seconds to blast-off*

bla·tant /ˈbleɪt‹nt/ adj. used to describe something bad that is happening, when it is so easy to notice that it shocks or surprises you: *blatant discrimination* | *At first I tried ignoring his blatant sexual hints and stares.* —**blatantly** adv. —**blatancy** n. [C]

blath·er /ˈblæðər/ v. [I] to talk for a long time about things that are not important —**blather** n. [U]

blaze¹ /bleɪz/ v. **1** [I] to burn very brightly and strongly: *A fire was blazing in the fireplace.* **2** [I] to shine with a very bright light: *Lights blazed in every room in the house.* **3** also **blaze away** [I] to fire bullets rapidly and continuously: *An enemy plane roared past with its guns blazing.* **4 blaze a trail** also **blaze the trail of sth** to discover or develop something new, or do something important that no one has done before: *Poland blazed the trail of democratic reform in eastern Europe.* **5** if someone's eyes blaze, they show a very strong emotion: [+ with] *"Get out!" he screamed, his eyes blazing with hate.* —see also ABLAZE, BLAZING

blaze² n.
1 fire **a)** [C] a word meaning a big dangerous fire, used especially in newspapers: *Six fire fighters were injured battling the blaze.* **b)** [singular] the strong bright flames of a fire: *a cheerful blaze in the fireplace*
2 light/color [singular] very bright light or color: [+ of] *a blaze of sunshine* | *In the fall, the trees are a blaze of color.*
3 guns [singular] the rapid continuous firing of a gun: [+ of] *Six passengers were killed in a blaze of automatic gunfire.*

4 in a blaze of glory/publicity etc. receiving a lot of praise or public attention: *The movie opened at theaters in a blaze of publicity.*

5 a blaze of anger/hatred/passion etc. a sudden show of very strong emotion: *He was surprised by the sudden blaze of anger in her eyes.*

6 what the blazes/who the blazes etc. SPOKEN, OLD-FASHIONED used to emphasize a question when you are annoyed: *What the blazes is he trying to do?*

7 like blazes OLD-FASHIONED as fast, as much, or as strongly as possible: *We're going to have to work like blazes to win this time!*

8 [mark] [C usually singular] a white mark, especially one down the front of a horse's face

blaz·er /'bleɪzɚ/ n. [C] a suit JACKET (=piece of clothing like a short coat), without matching pants: *a blue wool blazer*

blaz·ing /'bleɪzɪŋ/ adj. [only before noun, no comparative] **1** extremely hot: *We stood for hours in the blazing sun.* **2** brightly colored: *the blazing reds and oranges of the flowers* **3** full of strong emotions, especially anger

bla·zon¹ /'bleɪzən/ v. [T] **be blazoned across/on sth** to be written or shown on something in a very noticeable way: *The truck had "El Charro" blazoned across it in bright yellow letters.*

blazon² n. [C] a COAT OF ARMS

bldg. the written abbreviation of "building"

bleach¹ /blitʃ/ n. [U] a chemical used to make things white or to kill GERMS: *Soak the cloth in a mixture of bleach and water to get out the stains*

bleach² v. [T] to make something white, especially by using chemicals or SUNLIGHT: *I can't believe she bleached her hair.* | *The bones had been bleached in the desert sun*

bleach·ers /'blitʃɚz/ n. [plural] seats arranged in rows with no roof covering them, where you sit to watch a sport

bleak /blik/ adj. **1** without anything to make you feel cheerful or hopeful: *the bleakest year of the Depression* | *It looks pretty bleak for avocado growers here.* **2** cold and without any pleasant or comfortable features: *a bleak January afternoon* | *The snow-covered coast looked bleak and uninviting.* —**bleakly** adv. —**bleakness** n. [U]

blear·y /'blɪri/ also **bleary-eyed** /,.. '. / adj. unable to see very clearly, because you are tired or have been crying: *A messenger from the mill woke the bleary-eyed Thompson at 3:00 a.m.* —**blearily** adv. —**bleariness** n. [U]

bleat /blit/ v. to make the sound that a sheep or goat makes —**bleat** n. [C]

bleed /blid/ past tense and past participle **bled** /blɛd/ v.

1 [blood] a) [I] to lose blood, especially because of an injury: *A deep cut on her wrist was bleeding profusely.* | *He bled to death after being shot in the stomach.* b) [T] to take some blood from someone's body, done in the past in order to treat a disease

2 [money] [T] to make someone pay an unreasonable amount of money: *Marcia bled him for every penny he had.* | *The ten-year war had bled the country dry.*

3 [air/liquid] [T] to remove air or liquid from a system in order to make it work correctly, for example from a heating system: *The brake line had to be bled.*

4 [color] [I] to spread from one area of cloth or paper to another: *The dark blue bled into the white of the shirt.*

5 my heart bleeds (for sb) SPOKEN used to say that you feel a lot of sympathy for someone, but often said in a joking way when you do not think someone deserves any sympathy: *My heart bleeds for those poor children.* | *You can't afford a third car? My heart bleeds!*

bleed·er /'blidɚ/ n. [C] INFORMAL someone who tends to bleed a lot if they are injured

bleed·ing /'blidɪŋ/ n. [U] the condition of losing blood from your body: *Use pressure to control the bleeding.*

bleeding heart /,.. './ also **bleeding heart**

B

lib·e·ral /,.. . '.../ n. [C] INFORMAL someone who you think is too kind to people in society who are poor, have little education, etc.: *"These defense lawyers are all bleeding-heart liberals anyway," he growled.*

bleep¹ /blip/ n. [C] **1** a high electronic sound: *the bleeps of a video game* **2** SPOKEN a word used instead of a swear word, when you do not want to offend anyone: *What the bleep is going on here?*

bleep² v. **1** [T] also **bleep out** to prevent an offensive word being heard on television or the radio by covering it with a high electronic sound: *The TV network bleeped out the obscenities.* **2** [I] to make a high electronic sound; BEEP¹ (1)

blem·ish¹ /'blɛmɪʃ/ n. [C] a small mark, especially a mark on someone's skin or on the surface of an object, that spoils its appearance

blemish² v. [T often passive] to spoil the appearance, beauty, or PERFECTION of something —**blemished** adj. —see also UNBLEMISHED

blend¹ /blɛnd/ v. **1** [I,T] to mix together soft or liquid substances to form a single smooth substance: *Blend the sugar, eggs, and flour.* | [+ in] *Gradually blend in ¹/₂ cup of milk.* **2** [I,T] to combine different parts or features of something in a way that produces an effective or pleasant result, or to become combined in this way: *Children love the play because it blends the human and animal worlds.* | [+ with/together] *Rashad's sense of comedy blends well with Cosby's.* **3** [T usually passive] TECHNICAL to produce tea, tobacco, WHISKEY etc. by mixing several different types together

blend in phr. v. [I] also **blend into** sth [T] **1** if something blends in with the things around it, it looks similar to them in color or appearance, so that it is difficult to see that it is separate from the background: [+ with] *The bird blended in with the gray-brown reeds growing in the water.* | *Planners want to ensure that the structure blends into the landscape.* **2** if someone blends in with a group of people, they easily become part of the group because they are similar to the people in it: [+ with] *As much as I tried to blend in with my classmates, they knew my family was different.*

blend² n. [C] **1** a mixture of different qualities, foods, people etc. that combine together well: [+ of] *Santos' music is a fiery blend of Cuban and Puerto Rican rhythms* | *Curry is a blend of spices such as coriander, cloves, cinnamon, cardamom, turmeric, and more.* **2** a product such as tea, tobacco, or WHISKEY that is a mixture of several different types

blended fam·i·ly /,.. '.../ n. [C] a family in which both parents have children from earlier relationships

blend·er /'blɛndɚ/ n. [C] an electric machine that you use to mix liquids and soft foods together

bless /blɛs/ v. [T] **1 (God) bless you!** SPOKEN a) what you say when someone SNEEZES b) used to thank someone for doing something for you: *God bless you for all the help you have given people over the years.* **2** to ask God to protect someone or something: *May God bless you and keep you safe from harm.* **3 be blessed with sth** to have a special ability, good quality etc.: *He's blessed with the ability to laugh at himself.* | *The city is blessed with an excellent location.* **4** to make something holy: *Then the priest blesses the bread and wine.* **5 bless him/her** etc. SPOKEN used to show that you like someone, are amused by them, or are pleased by something they have done: *Bless him, he always helps when he can.* | *Joanie, bless her heart, brought me a card she'd made today.* **6 bless my soul!** also **I'll be blessed!** SPOKEN, OLD-FASHIONED used to express surprise

bless·ed /'blɛsɪd/ adj. **1** holy: *Blessed are the peacemakers.* | *the Blessed Virgin* **2** protected or helped by God: *We are truly blessed.* **3** [only before noun] very enjoyable or desirable: *a few minutes of blessed silence* **4** [only before noun] SPOKEN used to emphasize something: *I couldn't remember a blessed thing.* —**blessedly** adv. —**blessedness** n. [U]

bless·ing /'blɛsɪŋ/ *n.*
1 ❚approval❚ [U] someone's approval or encouragement for a plan, activity, idea etc.: *The book was adapted for the movie,* **with the author's blessing**. | *The city has* **given its blessing to** *$60 million worth of new housing construction.*
2 ❚sth good/helpful❚ [C] something that you have or something that happens which is good because it improves your life, helps you in some way, or makes you happy: *The store is a blessing for those on a budget.* | *It allows patients to live a more normal life, which is a blessing.* | *It's a blessing (that) no one was badly hurt.*
3 a mixed blessing a situation that has both good and bad parts: *The color printer is a mixed blessing – it looks good, but it takes a long time to print.*
4 ❚from god❚ [C,U] protection and help from God, or words spoken to ask for this: *The priest gave the blessing.*
5 a blessing in disguise something that seems to be bad or unlucky at first, but which you later realize is good or lucky: *The loss of fertilizer proved to be a blessing in disguise. It forced us to use compost, which is better for the soil and crops.*
6 count your blessings SPOKEN used to tell someone to remember how lucky they are, especially when they are complaining about something

blew /blu/ *v.* the past tense of BLOW¹

Bligh /blaɪ/, **Captain William** (1754–?1817) an officer in the British navy who was in command of the ship H.M.S. Bounty. Bligh was a very cruel leader, so the men on his ship attacked him and made him leave in a small boat

blight¹ /blaɪt/ *n.* **1** [U] a plant disease in which parts of the plants dry up and die **2** [singular] something that makes people unhappy or that spoils their lives or the environment they live in: [+ on] *Billboards are a blight on the community.* —see also **urban blight** (URBAN (2))

blight² *v.* [T] to spoil or damage something, especially by preventing people from doing what they want to do: *Rusty cans and plastic wrappers are blighting our wilderness areas.* | *The country is blighted by poverty.*

blight·ed /'blaɪtɪd/ *adj.* damaged or spoiled: *a blighted childhood*

blimp /blɪmp/ *n.* [C] **1** an aircraft without wings that looks like a very large BALLOON **2** SPOKEN an impolite word for a very fat person

blind¹ /blaɪnd/ *adj.*
1 ❚cannot see❚ **a)** unable to see: *My grandmother is almost totally blind.* | *In later stages of the disease, people often* **go blind** (=become blind). **b) the blind c)** [plural] people who are unable to see: *They're building a library for the blind.* **d) as blind as a bat e)** HUMOROUS not able to see well: *I'm as blind as a bat without my glasses.* —see also COLOR-BLIND
2 ❚ignore❚ **a) be blind to sth** to completely fail to notice or realize something: *The White House seems blind to the struggles of the middle class.* **b) turn a blind eye (to sth)** to deliberately ignore something that you know should not be happening: *Many landlords turn a blind eye to the fact that two families are sharing apartments.*
3 ❚feelings❚ **a) blind faith/loyalty/hate etc.** strong feelings that you have without thinking about why you have them: *a blind loyalty to the Communist Party* **b) a blind panic/rage etc.** strong feelings that are out of your control: *Tyrell went into a blind rage, punching and kicking at everyone.*
4 a blind study/test/experiment etc. a study or test of something in which the people being used to test a THEORY are not given any information about the things being tested because it might influence them: *a blind taste test* —see also DOUBLE-BLIND
5 a blind corner/curve/driveway etc. a corner, curve, etc. that you cannot see beyond when you are driving
6 the blind leading the blind OFTEN HUMOROUS used

to say that people who do not know much about what they are doing are helping or advising others who know nothing at all about it
7 blind flying/landing flying or landing an aircraft using only instruments because you cannot see through cloud, mist etc. —**blindness** *n.* [U] —see also BLINDLY

blind² *v.* [T] **1** to make it difficult for someone to see for a short time: *I was blinded by the truck's headlights.* **2** to make someone lose their good sense or judgment and be unable to see the truth about something: *Don't be blinded by emotion.* | [blind sb to sth] *Fear should not blind us to the necessity of fighting this disease.* **3** to permanently destroy someone's ability to see: *Richards had been blinded in the war.* **4 blind sb with science** to confuse or trick someone by using complicated language

blind³ *n.* [C] **1** a piece of cloth or other material that can be UNROLLed from the top of a window to cover it; WINDOW SHADE —see also VENETIAN BLIND —see picture on page 426 **2** a small shelter where you can watch birds or animals without being seen by them **3** a trick or excuse to stop someone from discovering the truth

blind⁴ *adv.* [no comparative] used in order to emphasize how complete or strong an action is: *They robbed us blind – everything was gone.*

blind al·ley /ˌ. '../ *n.* [C] **1** a small narrow street with no way out at one end **2** an attempt to achieve something, which does not produce useful results: *Al said the talks had temporarily gone down a blind alley, but he was sure the two companies could agree.*

blind date /ˌ. './ *n.* [C] an arranged meeting between a man and woman who have not met each other before

blind·ers /'blaɪndɚz/ *n.* [plural] **1** things fastened beside a horse's eyes to prevent it from seeing objects on either side **2** something that prevents you from noticing the truth about a situation: *People who dismiss the challenges of multi-cultural America are wearing blinders.*

blind·fold¹ /'blaɪndfoʊld/ *n.* [C] a piece of cloth used to cover someone's eyes to prevent them from seeing anything

blindfold² *v.* [T] to cover someone's eyes with a piece of cloth: *Blindfold the prisoner!*

blind·fold·ed /'blaɪndfoʊldɪd/ *adj.* **1** with your eyes covered by a piece of cloth —see picture at SEE¹ **2 sb can do sth blindfolded** INFORMAL used to say that it is very easy for someone to do something because they have done it so often: *Tomlinson could sail this boat blindfolded.*

blind·ing /'blaɪndɪŋ/ *adj.* **1 a blinding light/flash etc.** a very bright light that makes you unable to see for a short time **2 a blinding headache/pain etc.** a headache, pain etc. that is so strong that it makes you unable to think or behave normally

blind·ing·ly /'blaɪndɪŋli/ *adv.* very or extremely: *My brother's dislike for my wife became blindingly clear last month at a wedding reception.* | *blindingly beautiful scenery*

blind·ly /'blaɪndli/ *adv.* **1** not thinking about something or trying to understand it: *I'm not one of these people who blindly trust authority.* **2** not seeing or noticing what is around you: *He was found wandering blindly in the woods.*

blind man's bluff /ˌ. . './ *n.* [U] a children's game in which one player whose eyes are covered tries to catch the others

blind·side /'blaɪndsaɪd/ *v.* [T] INFORMAL **1** to hit the side of a car with your car in an accident: *Their car was blindsided by a bus at the intersection.* **2** to surprise someone so that they feel confused or upset: *I was blindsided by his suggestion.*

blind spot /'. ˌ./ *n.* [C] **1** something that you are unable or unwilling to understand: *Critics accuse him of having a blind spot on issues of ethics.* **2** the part of the road that you cannot see in front of you or in the mirrors when you are driving a car: *The other car was right in my blind spot.* **3** the point in your eye where the nerve enters, which is not sensitive to light

bli·ni /ˈblini/ n. [C] *plural* **blini** or **blinis** a small flat UNSWEETENED cake in the shape of a circle, often served with SALMON or CAVIAR on top

blink¹ /blɪŋk/ v. **1** [I,T] to close and open your eyes quickly: *He blinked as he walked out into the bright sunshine.* **2** [I] if lights blink, they go on and off continuously: *The neon lights on the theater blinked red and blue.* **3 not (even) blink** to not seem at all surprised or concerned: *Residents didn't even blink when the chemicals company set up business in town.*

blink² n. **1 in/with the blink of an eye** a very short period of time: *Now, even small TV stations can get a signal from anywhere in the world in the blink of an eye.* **2 on the blink** SPOKEN not working correctly: *The radio's on the blink again.* **3** [C] the action of quickly closing and opening your eyes

blink·er /ˈblɪŋkɚ/ n. [C] INFORMAL one of the small lights on a car that flash on and off to show which direction you are turning —see picture on page 427

blink·ered /ˈblɪŋkɚd/ adj. having a limited view of a subject or refusing to accept or consider ideas that are new or different: *a brilliant but blinkered scientist*

blintz /blɪnts/ n. [C] a type of thin PANCAKE usually filled with a cheese mixture

blip /blɪp/ n. [C] **1** a flashing light on a RADAR screen **2** a sudden and temporary change from the way something typically happens, especially when a situation gets worse for a while before it improves again: *Except for the blip this month, unemployment has continued to fall this year.*

bliss¹ /blɪs/ n. [U] perfect happiness or enjoyment: *If you like fish, this menu is bliss.* | **wedded/marital bliss** (=happiness in marriage)

bliss² v.

bliss out phr. v. [I] SPOKEN, INFORMAL to be completely happy and feel a lot of pleasure

bliss·ful /ˈblɪsfəl/ adj. **1** extremely happy or enjoyable: *blissful sunny days* **2 blissful ignorance** a situation in which you do not yet know about something bad or difficult to become upset or annoyed —**blissfully** adv.: *blissfully happy*

blis·ter¹ /ˈblɪstɚ/ n. [C] **1** a swelling on your skin containing clear liquid, caused for example by a burn or continuous rubbing: *New shoes always give me blisters.* **2** a swelling on the surface of metal, rubber, painted wood etc.

blister² v. **1** [I,T] to develop blisters or make blisters form: *The paint will blister in the heat.* **2** [T] to angrily criticize someone: *Brown blistered his players for their weak defensive game.* —**blistered** adj.: *blistered fingers*

blis·ter·ing /ˈblɪstərɪŋ/ adj. **1** extremely hot: *blistering summer days* | *the blistering heat of the sun* **2 blistering attack/criticism etc.** very angry and disapproving remarks: *blistering attacks in the press* —**blisteringly** adv.

blister pack /ˈ.. ˌ./ n. [C] a type of package for products, in which each object is enclosed in plastic that is shaped to fit around it, often attached to a piece of CARDBOARD: *Each blister pack contains 12 aspirins.*

blithe /blaɪð, blaɪθ/ adj. **1** seeming not to think or worry about the effects of what you do: *Mary spoke with blithe certainty about her future.* **2** LITERARY cheerful and having no worries

blithe·ly /ˈblaɪðli/ adv. **1** in a way that shows that you are not thinking about or do not care about the effects of what you do: *I remember my friend's mother blithely assuming that everyone celebrated Christmas.* **2** LITERARY happily and without worries

blith·er·ing /ˈblɪðərɪŋ/ adj. **blithering idiot** an insulting word for someone who behaves in a stupid way

blitz /blɪts/ n. [C usually singular] **1** a situation in football when several football players at one time run at the QUARTERBACK to try to stop him from throwing the ball **2** a situation when you use a lot of effort to achieve something, usually in a short time: *They've begun an advertising blitz to publicize the movie.* **3** a sudden military attack, especially from the air —**blitz** v. [T]

blitzed /blɪtst/ adj. SPOKEN very drunk

blitz·krieg /ˈblɪtskrig/ n. [U] a sudden surprise military attack that is intended to beat the enemy quickly

Blix·en /ˈblɪksən/, **Baroness Kar·en** /ˈkærən/ (1885–1962) a Danish writer of short stories who wrote in English using the man's name Isak Dinesen

bliz·zard /ˈblɪzɚd/ n. [C] **1** a severe storm with a lot of snow and wind —see picture on page 1333 **2** INFORMAL a sudden large amount of something that you must deal with: *a blizzard of memos*

bloat·ed /ˈbloʊtɪd/ adj. **1** much larger than usual because of being too full of water, gas, food etc.: *bloated fish, floating in the river* **2** feeling bad because you have eaten too much: *I felt so bloated after Thanksgiving dinner.* **3** INFORMAL an organization, company etc. that is bloated is too big and does not work well or effectively: *the bloated government bureaucracy*

bloa·ter /ˈbloʊtɚ/ n. [C] a large fish that is SMOKED and eaten

bloat·ing /ˈbloʊtɪŋ/ n. [U] swelling in part of the body, because it has too much gas or liquid in it: *Symptoms include severe cramps and bloating.*

blob /blɑb/ n. **1** a round MASS of liquid or sticky substance: [+ of] *a blob of oil* **2** something that is difficult to see clearly or see the shape of: *Astronomers say the comet will look like a fuzzy blob in the southwestern sky.*

bloc /blɑk/ n. [C usually singular] a large group of people or countries with the same political aims, working together: *the former Soviet bloc* —see also EN BLOC

block¹ /blɑk/ n. [C]
1 **street/streets** **a)** the distance along a city street from where one street crosses it to the next: *It's three blocks to the store from here.* **b)** a square area of houses or buildings formed by four streets: *We went for a walk around the block.* | *The Rosens were the first family on the block to get a satellite TV.* | **the 300/800/2000 block of sth** (=the area of houses on a particular road that have numbers between 300 and 399, 800 and 899, etc. in their addresses) *the 500 block of Stuart Street*
2 **solid mass** a solid MASS of hard material such as wood or stone with straight sides: [+ of] *a block of ice* | *a block of wood*
3 **related group** a group of things of the same kind, that are related in some way: [+ of] *We were given a block of shares in the company.* | *Jason says he can get a block of seats* (=seats next to each other) *for the concert.*
4 **a block of time** a length of time that is not interrupted by anything: *Set aside a block of time to do your homework.*
5 **a block of text** written sentences on a page or computer screen, considered as a group: *Highlight a block of text, then press delete.*
6 **toys** [usually plural] one of a group of pieces of wood, often shaped like a CUBE, that children use to build things with
7 **unable to think** [usually singular] the temporary loss of your normal ability to think, learn, write etc.: *I can't remember his name – I always have a mental block when I try to remember it.* | *After her first novel was published, she had writer's block for a year.*
8 **on the block** being sold, especially at an AUCTION
9 **sports** a movement in sports that stops an opponent going forward
10 **sb has been around the block (a few times)** INFORMAL used to say that someone has experienced many different situations, and can deal with new situations confidently
11 **large building** a large building divided into separate parts: *an apartment block*
12 **block voting** an arrangement that is made for a whole group to vote together

13 block computer a physical unit of stored information on a MAGNETIC TAPE or computer DISK

14 block printing a piece of wood or metal with words or line drawings cut into it, for printing

15 the block a solid block of wood on which someone's head was cut off as a punishment, in past times: *He was prepared to go to the block for his beliefs.* —see also BUILDING BLOCK, **be a chip off the old block** (CHIP¹ (7)), CHOPPING BLOCK, CINDER BLOCK, **knock sb's block off** (KNOCK¹ (8)), **the new kid on the block** (NEW (14)), ROADBLOCK, **stumbling block** (STUMBLE (5))

block² *v.* [T] **1** to prevent things from moving or flowing along something, such as a road or pipe, by putting something across it or in it: *The accident has blocked two lanes of traffic on the freeway.* | *The sink is blocked again.* **2** to prevent someone from moving to or toward a place: *I tried to get through, but there were too many people blocking my way.* **3** to stop something happening, developing, or succeeding: *The city council blocked the idea for a new shopping mall.* **4** to be in front of someone so that they cannot see a view, light, the sun etc.: *The view was blocked by two ugly high-rise apartment buildings.* **5** to prevent someone from making points, moving forward, or throwing or catching a ball in sports such as basketball, football, or HOCKEY **6** TECHNICAL to limit the use of a particular country's money: *a blocked currency*

block sth ↔ **off** *phr. v.* [T] to completely close a road or path: *Exit 31 is blocked off due to an accident.*

block sth ↔ **out 1** to stop yourself from thinking about something, or remembering it: *Carrie hears what she wants to hear and blocks out the rest.* **2** to prevent something from being seen or heard: *Heavy curtains blocked out the light.* | *Her face was blocked out of TV broadcasts by a large gray circle.* **3** to decide that you will use a particular time only for a particular purpose: *I try to block out two days a week for research* **4** to make a drawing of something that is not exact: *Block out the design on the rug using stencils.*

block·ade¹ /blɑˈkeɪd/ *n.* [C] a situation, during a war or time of political trouble, in which a place is surrounded by the military to stop people or supplies leaving or entering: *a naval blockade* | **lift/raise the blockade** (=to end a blockade) | *They've imposed an economic blockade on the country.*

blockade² *v.* [T] to put a blockade around a place: *Ships blockaded the port.*

block·age /ˈblɑkɪdʒ/ *n.* **1** [C] something that is stopping movement in a narrow place: *a blockage in the pipe* **2** [U] the state of being blocked or prevented

block and tack·le /ˌ. . ˈ../ *n.* [C usually singular] a piece of equipment made with wheels and ropes, used for lifting heavy things

block·bust·er /ˈblɑkˌbʌstɚ/ *n.* [C] INFORMAL a book or movie that is very good or successful: *a blockbuster from the summer of '99*

block·head /ˈblɑkhɛd/ *n.* [C] SPOKEN a very stupid person

block·house /ˈblɑkhaʊs/ *n.* [C] a small strong building used as a shelter from enemy guns

block let·ters /ˌ. ˈ../ *n.* [plural] CAPITAL letters

block par·ty /ˈ. ˌ../ *n.* [C] a party in the street for all the people living in the area near the street

bloke /bloʊk/ *n.* [C] BRITISH, INFORMAL a man

blond¹ /blɑnd/ *adj.* **1** another spelling of BLONDE **2** a man who is blond has pale or yellow hair

blond² *n.* [C] someone with pale or yellow-colored hair

blonde¹ /blɑnd/ *adj.* **1** blonde hair is pale or yellow in color **2** a woman who is blonde has pale or yellow hair **3 blonde bombshell** HUMOROUS an extremely attractive woman with light-colored hair

blonde² *n.* [C] INFORMAL a woman with pale or yellow-colored hair: *a beautiful blonde*

blood /blʌd/ *n.* [U]
1 in your body the red liquid that your heart

pumps around your body: *She lost a lot of blood in the accident.* | **give/donate blood** (=have blood taken from you and stored to be used when treating someone else)

2 draw blood a) to take blood from someone, especially during medical treatment **b)** to make someone BLEED: *The dog bit me, but it didn't draw blood.*

3 new/fresh blood new members in a group or organization who bring new ideas and energy: *The firm desperately needs some new blood.*

4 in cold blood in a cruel and deliberate way: *He murdered the old man in cold blood.*

5 sweat blood to work extremely hard to achieve something: *Donald sweated blood to build up his business.*

6 have sb's blood on your hands to have caused someone's death

7 your family/group the family or group to which you belong from the time that you are born: *There's French blood on his mother's side.* —see also BLOOD RELATIVE

8 be in sb's blood also **have sth in your blood** if an ability or tendency is in someone's blood, it is natural to them and others in their family

9 get sth in your blood to begin to like something so much that you want to do it all the time and it seems very natural to you: *The acting business gets in your blood, and you just don't want to do anything else.*

10 make your blood boil to make you extremely angry: *When I think about what she said to me, it still makes my blood boil.*

11 make your blood run cold to make you feel extremely frightened: *The sudden scream made my blood run cold.*

12 blood is thicker than water used to say that family relationships are more important than any other kind

13 can't get/take blood from a stone used to say that you have no money to give someone —see also **bad blood** (BAD¹ (24)), -BLOODED, **your own flesh and blood** (FLESH¹ (4)), RED BLOOD CELL, WHITE BLOOD CELL, **young blood** (YOUNG¹ (5))

blood-and-guts /ˌ. . ˈ./ *adj.* [no comparative] INFORMAL full of violence: *a blood-and-guts struggle between the two teams* | *a blood-and-guts horror movie*

blood bank /ˈ. ˌ./ *n.* [C] a place where human blood is kept to be used in hospital treatment

blood·bath /ˈblʌdbæθ/ *n.* [singular] the violent killing of many people at one time

blood broth·er /ˌ. ˈ../ *n.* [C] a man who shows loyalty to another, often in a ceremony in which the men's blood is mixed together

blood clot /ˈ. ./ *n.* [C] blood that has become thick in one place so that a BLOOD VESSEL becomes blocked

blood count /ˈ. ./ *n.* [C] a medical examination of someone's blood to see if it contains the right substances in the right amounts

blood·cur·dling /ˈblʌdˌkɚdl-ɪŋ/ *adj.* extremely frightening: *a bloodcurdling scream*

blood do·nor /ˈ. ˌ../ *n.* [C] someone who gives their blood to be used in the treatment of other people

blood drive /ˈ. ./ *n.* [C] an event at a local business, school etc. where many people can go to give blood for the treatment of others

-blooded /blʌdɪd/ *suffix* having a particular type of blood | **warm-blooded/cold-blooded** *Fish are cold-blooded.* —see also HOT-BLOODED

blood feud /ˈ. ./ *n.* [C] an argument that continues for many years between people or families and in which each side murders or injures members of the other side

blood·hound /ˈblʌdhaʊnd/ *n.* [C] a large dog with a very good sense of smell, often used for hunting

blood·less /ˈblʌdlɪs/ *adj.* **1** [no comparative] without killing or violence: *a bloodless invasion* —compare BLOODY¹ (2) **2** a bloodless part of your body is very pale: *His lips were thin and bloodless.* **3** lacking in human feeling —**bloodlessly** *adv.*

blood·let·ting /ˈblʌdˌlɛtɪŋ/ *n.* [U] **1** the act of killing people; BLOODSHED: *Troops are trying to stop the worst of the bloodletting in the capital.* **2** a situation in which a lot of people are forced to leave a company, political party etc.: *We've heard rumors that a major management bloodletting is about to happen.* **3** the medical practice in past times of treating people who were sick by removing some of their blood

blood·line /'blʌdlaɪn/ *n.* [C] the people in your family who lived in the GENERATIONS before you and from whom you get particular qualities: *Jim can trace his bloodlines to the Puritans.*

blood lust /'. ./ *n.* [U] a strong desire to be violent

blood·mo·bile /'blʌdmou,bil/ *n.* [C] a special vehicle with medical equipment where people can give their blood to be used for treating other people

blood mon·ey /'. ,../ *n.* [U] **1** money paid for murdering someone **2** money paid to the family of someone who has been murdered

blood or·ange /'. ,../ *n.* [C] an orange with red flesh and juice

blood poi·son·ing /'. ,.../ *n.* [U] a serious medical condition in which an infection spreads from a small area of your body through your blood

blood pres·sure /'. ,../ *n.* [U] the force with which blood travels through your body, that can be measured by a doctor: *high blood pressure*

blood-red /,. '.‹/ *adj.* dark red, like blood: *blood-red lips*

blood rel·a·tive /,. '.../ also **blood re·la·tion** /,. '.' ./ *n.* [C] someone related to you by birth rather than by marriage

blood·shed /'blʌdʃed/ *n.* [U] the killing of people, usually in fighting or war: *The two groups have a long history of bloodshed.*

blood·shot /'blʌdʃɑt/ *adj.* bloodshot eyes are slightly reddish in color

blood sport /'. ./ *n.* [C] a sport that involves the killing of animals or birds; HUNTING

blood·stain /'blʌdsteɪn/ *n.* [C] a mark or spot of blood: *There were bloodstains on the floor.* —**blood-stained** *adj.: a bloodstained shirt*

blood·stream /'blʌdstrim/ *n.* [singular] blood as it flows around your body: *The drug is injected directly into the bloodstream.*

blood·suck·er /'blʌd,sʌkəʳ/ *n.* [C] **1** a creature that sucks blood from the body of other animals **2** INFORMAL someone who tries to get a lot of money from someone else, especially by using BLACKMAIL

blood test /'. ./ *n.* [C] a medical examination in which a doctor takes blood from someone so that it can be checked to see if the person has a disease or medical problem

blood·thirst·y /'blʌd,θɜːsti/ *adj.* **bloodthirstier, bloodthirstiest 1** eager to kill or wound, or enjoying seeing killing or violence: *a bloodthirsty monster* | *a bloodthirsty crowd* **2** describing or showing violence: *bloodthirsty speeches* —**bloodthirstiness** *n.* [U]

blood trans·fu·sion /'. .,../ *n.* [C] the process of putting blood into someone's body as a medical treatment

blood type /'. ./ *n.* [C] one of the types into which human blood can be separated, including A, B, AB, and O

blood ves·sel /'. ,../ *n.* [C] any of the tubes through which blood flows in your body —see also **burst a blood vessel** (BURST¹ (7))

blood·y¹ /'blʌdi/ *adj.* **bloodier, bloodiest 1** covered in blood or BLEEDing: *a bloody nose* **2** with a lot of killing and injuries: *a bloody battle* **3 scream/yell bloody murder** INFORMAL to protest in a loud very angry way: *People were screaming bloody murder about the ridiculous prices.*

blood·y² *v.* **bloodies, bloodied, bloodying** [T] **1** FORMAL to injure someone so that blood comes, or to cover something with blood: *The boy punched Jack and bloodied his nose.* **2 bloodied but unbowed** affected badly by an argument or difficult situation, but not defeated by it

Bloody Mar·y /,.. '../ *n. plural* **Bloody Marys** [C] an alcoholic drink made by mixing VODKA, TOMATO juice, and SPICES

bloom¹ /blum/ *n.* **1** [C,U] a flower, or a group of flowers: *beautiful red blooms* | *a mass of bloom on the apple trees* **2 in bloom** a plant that is in bloom has flowers that are open: *The azaleas are in full bloom.* **3 the bloom of youth/love etc.** LITERARY the best or happiest time when you are young, in love etc.

bloom² *v.* [I] **1 a)** if a plant blooms, it produces flowers **b)** if a flower blooms, it opens **2** to become happy and healthy, or successful: *The experiment bloomed into a $50 million business.*

bloom·ers /'blumərz/ *n.* [plural] **a)** OLD-FASHIONED women's underwear like loose pants that end at your knees **b)** short loose pants that end in a tight band at your knees worn for sports by women in Europe and America in the late 19th century —see also **late bloomer/developer** (LATE¹ (8))

bloop /blup/ *v.* [T] to hit a ball in the air just past the INFIELD in a game of baseball

bloop·er /'blupəʳ/ *n.* [C] INFORMAL **1** an embarrassing mistake that you make in front of other people **2** a ball that is hit in the air just past the INFIELD in a game of baseball

blos·som¹ /'blɑsəm/ *n.* [C,U] **1** a flower, or all the flowers on a tree or bush: *The tree was covered in pink blossoms.* | *orange blossom* **2 in blossom** a bush or tree that is in blossom has flowers on it

blossom² *v.* [I] **1** if a tree blossoms, it produces flowers: *The apple trees are just beginning to blossom.* **2** also **blossom out** to become happier, more beautiful, more successful etc.: *Pete has really blossomed in his new school.*

blot¹ /blɑt/ *v.* **blots, blotted, blotting** [T] to dry a wet surface by pressing soft paper or cloth on it

blot sth ↔ **out** *phr. v.* [T] **1** to cover or hide something completely: *Gas and dust from the volcano blotted out the sun.* **2** to forget something, often deliberately: *She had blotted out all memory of the accident.*

blot sth ↔ **up** *phr. v.* [T] to remove liquid from a surface by pressing a soft cloth, paper etc. onto it

blot² *n.* [C] **1** a mark or spot that spoils something or makes it dirty: *ink blots* **2** a building, structure etc. that is ugly and spoils the appearance of a place: [+ on] *The oil rigs are a blot on the coastline.* **3** something that spoils the good opinion other people have of you: [+ on] *The massacre is one of the great blots on our nation's history.*

blotch /blɑtʃ/ *n.* [C] a small area of color on something, especially the skin, that makes it look unattractive: *The patient had purple blotches under his eyes.* | *That red blotch in the painting is supposed to be the sun.* —**blotchy** *adj.* —**blotched** *adj.*

blot·ter /'blɑtəʳ/ *n.* **1** [C] a large piece of blotting paper kept on the top of a desk **2** [C] a book in which an official daily record is kept: *the police blotter* **3** [U] SLANG the drug LSD

blotting pa·per /'.. ,../ *n.* [U] soft thick paper used for drying wet ink on a page after writing

blouse /blaʊs/ *n.* [C] a shirt for women: *a silk blouse*

blow¹ /blou/ *v. past tense* **blew** *past participle* **blown**   s w

1 wind a) [I] if the wind or a current of air blows, it moves: *A warm breeze was blowing from the south.* **b)** [I usually + adv./prep.,T] to move something or to be moved, by the force of the wind or a current of air: *Her hair was blowing in the breeze.* | *The wind must have blown the door shut.*

2 from your mouth [I,T] to send out a current of air from your mouth: *Blow on it, Ian – the oatmeal's very hot.* | *She blew the feather off her sleeve.*

3 explode/shoot [T] to damage or destroy something violently with an explosion or by shooting: [blow sth away/out/off] *His leg was blown off when he stepped on a landmine.* | **blow sth to pieces/bits/smithereens** *The railway station was blown to pieces and never repaired.*

B

4 ruin [T] INFORMAL to miss a good opportunity or ruin something, by making a mistake or by being careless: *Johnson had a chance to get the job, and he* **blew it**. | *She's worried that we've* **blown** *our* **chance** *to get any new contracts.* | *I can't act. I tried it once, and every time I stood up on stage I* **blew my lines** (=said the wrong thing).

5 **blow your nose** to clean your nose by forcing air through it into a cloth or a piece of soft paper

6 money [T] INFORMAL to spend all your money at one time in a careless way: *I blew it all on a trip to Hawaii.*

7 **sth blows your mind** SPOKEN to make you feel very surprised and excited by something: *Meeting her after so many years really blew my mind.* —see also MIND-BLOWING

8 **blow your top/stack/cool** also **blow a fuse** SPOKEN to become extremely angry quickly or suddenly: *My father blew his top when I told him I was quitting medical school.*

9 **blow the whistle on sb** INFORMAL to tell someone in authority about something wrong that is happening: *A few honest policemen were willing to blow the whistle on the captain.*

10 **blow sb/sth out of the water** to defeat or achieve much more than someone or something else you are competing with: *By then the Motown label had blown all the other record companies out of the water.*

11 **blow sth (up) out of (all) proportion** to make something seem much more serious or important than it is: *This case has been blown totally out of proportion because of the media attention.*

12 **blow your own horn** INFORMAL to praise yourself for your own achievements: *Borland has plenty of reason to blow his own horn – his company has just shown record profits.*

13 whistle/horn [I,T] if a horn or whistle blows or you blow it, it makes a sound when you pass air through it: *The whistle blew on the old steam engine.* | *The referee blew his whistle to start the game.*

14 make/shape sth [T] to make or shape something, such as a ring of smoke or a BUBBLE, by sending out a current of air from your mouth: *The kids were* **blowing bubbles** *in the backyard.* | *The ornaments are made of blown glass* (=glass shaped by blowing into it when it is very hot).

15 tire [I,T] if a tire blows, or if a car blows a tire, the tire bursts

16 electricity [I,T] if an electrical FUSE[1] (1) blows, or a piece of electrical equipment blows a FUSE, the electricity suddenly stops working

17 stop working [I,T] also **blow out** if a piece of equipment blows or if something blows it, it suddenly stops working completely: *You're lucky you didn't blow out the whole engine.*

18 secret [T] to tell someone about something that should be a secret: *Your coming here has blown the whole operation.* | **blow sb's cover** (=tell the names of people whose names must be kept secret because of the official work they do)

19 **blow sb a kiss** to kiss your hand and then pretend to blow the kiss toward someone: *Blow Grandma a kiss, Katie.*

20 **blow chunks** SLANG to VOMIT (=bring food or drink up from your stomach, because you are sick)

blow sb ↔ away *phr. v.* [T] SPOKEN **1** to make someone feel very surprised, often by something they like or admire: *It just blows me away, the way strangers say "Hi" to you in the street here.* **2** to kill someone by shooting them with a gun: *One move and I'll blow you away!* **3** to defeat someone completely, especially in a game: *Nancy blew away the rest of the skaters.*

blow down *phr. v.* [I,T **blow sth ↔ down**] if the wind blows something down, or if something blows down, the wind makes it fall: *Hundreds of trees were blown down in the storm.*

blow in *phr. v.* [I] also **blow into** sth [T] **1** if a storm or bad weather blows in, it arrives and begins to affect a particular area: *The first snowstorm blew in from the north.* **2** INFORMAL to arrive in a place, especially when you are only staying for a short time: *Jim blew in about an hour ago – did you see him?* | *Westheimer* **blew into town** *on Friday for a half-hour tour of the gallery's new exhibit.*

blow sb/sth off *phr. v.* [T] **1** SPOKEN to treat someone or something as unimportant, especially by not giving them any attention: *Tanya just blew me off – she said she didn't want to see me anymore.* | *I blew off my 8 a.m. class again.* **2** **blow the lid off sth** INFORMAL to tell something that was secret, especially something involving important or famous people: *Her book has blown the lid off the Reagan years.* **3** **blow sb's head off** INFORMAL to kill someone with a gun **4** **blow off steam** INFORMAL to get rid of anger or energy by doing something: *I went jogging to blow off some steam.*

blow out

Jan blew out all the candles on the cake.

blow out *phr. v.* **1** [I,T **blow sth ↔ out**] if you blow a flame or a fire out, or if it blows out, it stops burning: *Blow all the candles out.* | *The match blew out before I could light my cigarette.* **2** [I] if a tire blows out, it bursts **3** **sth blows itself out** if a storm blows itself out, it ends: *We sheltered in a barn waiting for the storm to blow itself out.* **4** [T **blow sb ↔ out**] SPOKEN to easily defeat someone: *We blew them out, 28 – zero.* **5** [I] if an oil or gas well blows out, oil or gas suddenly escapes

blow over *phr. v.* **1** [I,T **blow sth ↔ over**] if the wind blows something over, or it blows over, the wind makes it fall: *Our fence blew over in the storm.* | *The hurricane blew palm trees over.* **2** [I] if an argument or bad situation blows over, it does not seem important anymore or is forgotten: *Many people expected the scandal to blow over in a few days.* **3** [I] if a storm blows over, it comes to an end

blow up *phr. v.* **1** [I,T **blow sth ↔ up**] to destroy something, or to be destroyed, by an explosion: *Police cleared the waterfront before the ship blew up.* | *He was convicted of planning to blow up several New York City landmarks.* **2** [T **blow sth ↔ up**] to fill something with air or gas: *Ronnie was blowing up balloons for the party.* **3** [T **blow sth ↔ up**] if you blow up a photograph, you make it larger: *I had the picture of Mom and Dad blown up to an 8 x 10.* **4** [I] to become very angry with someone: [+ at] *Well, she blew up at me last Saturday for no reason.* **5** [I] if a situation, argument etc. blows up, it suddenly becomes important or dangerous: *A crisis had blown up over the peace talks.* **6** **blow up in sb's face** if something you plan blows up in your face, it does not work well, often so that it causes you serious problems: *Kristin knew that if anyone found out, the whole thing could blow up in her face.* **7** [I] if bad weather blows up, it suddenly arrives

blow[2] *n.*

1 hard hit [C] a hard hit with the hand, a weapon, or a tool: *a blow to the stomach* | *three heavy blows from the hammer*

2 bad effect [C] something that makes you feel unhappy, upset, or disappointed, or that damages your confidence: [+ to] *Losing the job was a blow to her pride.* | *The company* **suffered a** *major* **blow** *when its biggest customer canceled their order.* | *Farmers coping with the drought have been* **dealt** *another* **blow** *– wind storms.*

3 blowing air [C] an action of blowing air on something: *One blow and the candles were out.*

4 come to blows if two people come to blows, they get very angry and start hitting each other: *The police were called when their argument came to blows.*
5 a low blow SPOKEN something unkind you say to deliberately embarrass or upset someone
6 soften/cushion the blow to help someone accept something that is not nice or difficult to accept: *Some of the money will be used to soften the blow of budget cuts to education.*
7 `drug` [U] SLANG: see COCAINE
8 `wind` [singular] a strong wind or storm —see also BODY BLOW, **strike a blow to/at/against sth** (STRIKE¹ (19))

blow-by-blow /ˌ. . '.◂/ *adj.* [only before noun] a blow-by-blow story, account etc. gives every detail of an event in the order that they happened: *We were given a long, boring, blow-by-blow account of his last golf game.*

blow-dry /'. ./ *v.* **blow-dries, blow-dried, blow-drying** [T] to dry hair and give it shape by using a blow dryer —**blow-dry** *n.* [C] *a cut and blow-dry*

blow dry·er /'. ˌ../ *n.* [C] a small electric machine that you hold and use to blow hot air onto your hair in order to dry it

blow·er /'bloʊɚ/ *n.* [C] a machine that blows out air: *a snow blower* —see also GLASSBLOWER

blow·fly /'. ./ *n.* [C] a fly that lays its eggs on meat or wounds

blow·hard /'bloʊhɑrd/ *n.* [C] INFORMAL someone who talks too much and has very strong opinions

blow·hole /'bloʊhoʊl/ *n.* [C] **1** a hole in the top of the head of a WHALE, DOLPHIN etc. through which they breathe **2** a hole in the surface of ice to which water animals such as SEALs come to breathe

blow job /'. ./ *n.* [C] VULGAR the practice of touching a man's sexual organs with the lips and tongue to give him sexual pleasure

blown /bloʊn/ *v.* the past participle of BLOW¹

blow·out /'bloʊaʊt/ *n.* [C] **1** INFORMAL an easy victory over someone in a game: *a 30-point blowout* **2** also **blow-out** [usually singular] INFORMAL a big expensive meal or large social occasion: *We had a big blow-out at the club for our twenty-fifth anniversary.* **3** a sudden bursting of a TIRE: *A blow-out at this speed could be really dangerous.* **4** a sudden uncontrolled escape of oil or gas from a well

blow·pipe /'bloʊpaɪp/ *n.* [C] a tube through which you can blow small stones, poisoned ARROWS etc., used as a weapon

blow·sy, blowzy /'blaʊzi/ *adj.* **blowsier, blowsiest** **1** a blowsy woman is fat and has a messy appearance **2** blowsy hair is messy

blow·torch /'bloʊtɔrtʃ/ *n.* [C] a piece of equipment that produces a small very hot flame, used especially for removing paint

blow·up, blowup /'. ./ *n.* [C] **1** a photograph, or part of a photograph, that has been made larger **2** [C usually singular] a sudden noisy argument —see also **blow up** (BLOW¹)

blow·y /'bloʊi/ *adj.* blowy weather is windy

BLT *n.* [C] a SANDWICH made with BACON, LETTUCE, and TOMATO

blub·ber¹ /'blʌbɚ/ *v.* [I] to cry loudly, especially in a way that annoys people: *Quit blubbering!*

blubber² *n.* [U] **1** the fat of sea animals, especially WHALES **2** INFORMAL the fat on a person

blud·geon¹ /'blʌdʒən/ *v.* [T] **1** to hit someone several times with something heavy: *Ruddock had been bludgeoned to death in his beach-side home.* **2** [+ into/out of] to force someone to do something by making threats or arguing with them

bludgeon² *n.* [C] a heavy stick with a thick end, used as a weapon

blue¹ /blu/ *adj.* **1** having the color of the clear sky: *the blue waters of the lake | a dark blue sweater* **2** [not before noun] INFORMAL sad and without hope; DEPRESSED (1): *I've been feeling kind of blue lately.* **3 do sth till you're blue in the face** INFORMAL to do something a lot, without achieving anything: *You can argue with her till you're blue in the face, but*

she won't change her mind. **4** INFORMAL relating to sex in a way that might offend some people: *blue language* —see also BLUE MOVIE, **once in a blue moon** (ONCE¹ (13)), **talk a blue streak** (TALK¹ (27))

blue² *n.* **1** [C,U] the color of the sky on a clear day: *I especially like the rich blues and reds of the painting. | Carolyn's the one dressed in blue.* **2 blues** [plural] a slow sad style of music that came from the African-American CULTURE in the southern U.S.: *a blues singer* —see also RHYTHM AND BLUES **3 the blues** [plural] INFORMAL feelings of sadness: *A lot of women get the blues after the baby is born.* **4 out of the blue** INFORMAL suddenly and without warning: *Symptoms of the disease often appear out of the blue.* —see also **a bolt from the blue** (BOLT¹ (4)) **5 the blue** LITERARY the ocean or the sky —see also **the boys in blue** (BOY¹ (9))

blue ba·by /'. ˌ../ *n.* [C] a baby whose skin is slightly blue when it is born because it has problems with its heart or lungs

blue·bell /'blubɛl/ *n.* [C] a small plant with blue flowers that grows in woods

blue·ber·ry /'bluˌbɛri/ *n.* plural **blueberries** [C,U] the small blue fruit of a bushy plant, or the plant itself: *blueberry pie*

blue·bird /'blubɚd/ *n.* [C] a small blue bird that lives in North America —see picture on page 429

blue blood, blue-blood /ˌ. '.◂/ *n.* [C] someone who is born into a family that has a very high social position: *a spoiled blue blood* —**blue-blooded** also **blue-blood** *adj.*: *one of New York's blue-blooded families*

blue book /'. ./ *n.* [C] **1** a book with a list of prices that you can expect to pay for any used car **2** a book with a blue cover that is used in colleges for writing answers to test questions

blue cheese /ˌ. './ *n.* [C,U] a type of cheese with blue lines in it and a strong taste

blue chip /'. ˌ./ *adj.* [only before noun, no comparative] **1** a blue-chip company or INVESTMENT (1) earns profits and is safe: *blue chip stocks and shares* **2** a **blue-chip athlete** INFORMAL someone who is one of the best at playing a sport, especially someone who does not yet play for a PROFESSIONAL sports team —**blue chip** *n.* [C]

blue-col·lar /ˌ. '..◂/ *adj.* [only before noun] blue-collar workers are paid by the hour, rather than being paid a SALARY, and often do physically difficult work —compare PINK-COLLAR, WHITE-COLLAR

blue·fish /'blufɪʃ/ *n.* [C] plural **bluefish** a fish that lives in the Atlantic Ocean and is a bluish color

blue·grass /'blugræs/ *n.* [U] **1** a type of music from the southern and western U.S., played on instruments such as the GUITAR and VIOLIN **2** a type of grass found in North America, especially in Kentucky

blue gum /'. ./ *n.* [C] a tall Australian tree that is a type of EUCALYPTUS

blue hel·met /'. ˌ../ *n.* [C] someone who works for the United Nations as part of the organization's activities for keeping peace in countries that are at war

blue·jay /'bludʒeɪ/ *n.* plural **bluejays** [C] a common North American bird with blue feathers and feathers that form a point on its head —see picture on page 429

blue jeans /'. ./ *n.* [plural] dark blue pants made of a heavy material; JEANS

blue law /'. ./ *n.* [C] a law, used especially in the past in the U.S., that controls activities that are considered immoral, such as drinking alcohol, working on Sundays etc.

blue mov·ie /ˌ. '../ *n.* [C] a movie made in the past that showed more sexual activity than was considered appropriate at that time

blue·print /'bluˌprɪnt/ *n.* [C] **1** a plan for achieving something: *a blueprint for healthcare reform* **2** a plan for a building, machine etc. on special blue paper

B

blue rib·bon /ˌ. '.◂/ *n.* [C] a small piece of blue material that you give to the winner of a competition —**blue-ribbon** *adj.* [only before noun] *a blue-ribbon recipe*

Blue Ridge Moun·tains, the /ˌ. '. '../ also **the Blue Ridge** a range of mountains in the eastern U.S. that goes from southern Pennsylvania in the eastern U.S. to northern Georgia and is part of the Appalachians

blue-sky /ˌ. '.◂/ *adj.* [only before noun] blue-sky tests, RESEARCH etc. are done to test ideas and not for any practical purpose

blues·y /ˈbluzi/ *adj.* relating to blues (BLUE² (3)) music: *a bluesy rhythm*

bluff¹ /blʌf/ *v.* [I,T] **1** to pretend that you will do something, or that you know something, or that you are someone else, especially to get something you want when you are in a difficult or dangerous situation: *They're not bluffing when they say this could start a civil war.* | *Just remember a few tricks and you'll be able to* **bluff your way through** *the game.* | [bluff sb into doing sth] *Giuliani bluffed the guards into letting him in.* **2** to pretend you have better cards than you really do in a game of POKER

bluff² *n.* **1** [C,U] an attempt to deceive someone by making them think you will do something when you do not intend to do it: *Johnson said the threats were pure bluff.* | *Working as a trader makes me sensitive to the little bluffs people use.* **2 call sb's bluff** to tell someone to do what they threaten to do, because you believe they have no intention of doing it, and you want to prove it **3** [C] a very steep cliff or slope with a flat top

bluff³ *adj.* behaving in a loud cheerful way, without always considering the way other people feel: *a big, bluff man with a nice smile* —**bluffly** *adv.* —**bluffness** *n.* [U]

Blu·ford /ˈblufɚd/, **Gui·on** /ˈgaɪən/ (1942–) the first African-American ASTRONAUT

blu·ish /ˈbluɪʃ/ *adj.* slightly blue: *The patient's lips were bluish – I'd say she has a heart problem.*

blun·der¹ /ˈblʌndɚ/ *n.* [C] a careless or stupid mistake: *Major management blunders have led the company into bankruptcy.*

blun·der² *v.* **1** [I always + adv./prep.] to become involved in a situation or go somewhere by mistake: *They turned a corner and blundered into a group of soldiers.* **2** [I] to make a big mistake, especially because you have been careless or stupid: *Police admitted that they blundered when they let Wolie go.* **3** [I always + adv./prep.] to move in an unsteady way, as if you cannot see well: [blunder into/around/about] *I blundered into a table in the dark.* —**blunderer** *n.* [C]

blun·der·buss /ˈblʌndɚˌbʌs/ *n.* [C] a type of gun used in past times

blun·der·ing /ˈblʌndərɪŋ/ *adj.* [only before noun] careless or stupid

blunt¹ /blʌnt/ *adj.* **1** not sharp or pointed: *The victim was hit on the head with a blunt object.* —opposite SHARP¹ (1) **2** speaking in an honest way even if this upsets people: *blunt criticism* | *I'll be blunt. It's just not going to work.* —see also BLUNTLY —**bluntness** *n.* [U]

blunt² *v.* [T] **1** to make something less strong: *His senses were blunted by the whiskey.* | *The latest bombing has blunted residents' hopes for peace.* **2** to make the point of a pencil or the edge of a knife less sharp

blunt·ly /ˈblʌntli/ *adv.* speaking in a direct honest way that sometimes upsets people: *Several people bluntly questioned his ability to do the job.* | **To put it bluntly**, *the situation has gotten much worse.*

blur¹ /blɚ/ *n.* **a) a blur** a shape that you cannot see clearly: *Everything's a blur without my glasses.* | *A blur of horses ran past.* **b)** an unclear memory of something: *My wedding day is just a blur.*

blur² *v.* [I,T] **1** to make the difference between two ideas, subjects etc. less clear: *The show blurs the*

difference between information and entertainment. **2** to become difficult to see or make something difficult to see, because the edges are not clear: *Problems with the mirrors blurred the telescope's view.* —see also BLURRED —**blurry** *adj.*: *They have a few blurry pictures of their vacation.*

blurb /blɚb/ *n.* [C] a short description giving information about a book, new product etc.

blurred /blɚd/ *adj.* **1** unclear in shape, or making it difficult to see shapes: *a blurred image* **2** difficult to remember or understand clearly: *blurred memories*

blurt /blɚt/ *v.* [T] also **blurt sth ↔ out** to say something suddenly and without thinking, usually because you are nervous or excited: *Jackie blurted out that she was pregnant.*

blush¹ /blʌʃ/ *v.* [I] **1** to become red in the face, usually because you are embarrassed: *Carlos blushes every time he talks to her.* **2** sth that would **make sb blush** something you say or do that is so shocking that even someone who frequently says or does similar things is shocked by it: *She uses language that would make a construction worker blush.* | *Jones' political moves would even make a crooked politician blush.* **3 the blushing bride** HUMOROUS a young woman on her wedding day **4** to feel ashamed or embarrassed about something: [blush to do sth] *I blush to admit I've never read any of her books.* —**blushingly** *adv.*

blush² *n.* **1** [C] the red color on your face that appears when you are embarrassed, confused, or ashamed: *Susan confessed with a blush that she'd been watching him.* **2** [C,U] cream or powder used for making your cheeks slightly red **3 at first blush** FORMAL when first thought of or considered: *At first blush, this discovery seems to confirm his theory.* **4** [C,U] BLUSH WINE

blush·er /ˈblʌʃɚ/ *n.* [U] BLUSH² (2)

blush wine /ˈ. ./ *n.* [C,U] a wine with a slightly pink color

blus·ter¹ /ˈblʌstɚ/ *v.* [I] **1** to speak in a loud angry way and behave as if what you are doing is very important **2** if the wind blusters, it blows violently —**blustering** *adj.*: *blustering wintry weather*

bluster² *n.* [U] noisy proud talk

blus·ter·y /ˈblʌstəri/ *adj.* blustery weather is very windy: *a cold and blustery day*

blvd. the written abbreviation of BOULEVARD

Bly /blaɪ/, **Nel·lie** /ˈnɛli/ the PEN NAME of Elizabeth Cochrane Seaman (1867–1922), a U.S. JOURNALIST

B-mov·ie /ˌbi ˈmuvi/ *n.* [C] a cheaply made movie of low quality, especially one made in the 1950s

B'nai B'rith /bəˌneɪ ˈbrɪθ/ an international organization of Jewish people that works to oppose ANTI-SEMITISM and helps Jewish people all over the world

B.O. *n.* [U] body odor; a bad smell from someone's body caused by sweat

bo·a /ˈboʊə/ *n.* [C] **1** also **boa constrictor** a large snake that is not poisonous, but kills animals by crushing them **2** a FEATHER BOA

boar /bɔr/ *n.* [C] **1** a wild pig **2** a male pig —opposite SOW²

board¹ /bɔrd/ *n.*
1 information [C] a flat wide piece of wood, plastic etc. that has information shown or written on it: *Your homework assignment is written on the board.* | *I'll put an announcement up on the board.* —see also BLACKBOARD, BULLETIN BOARD, SCOREBOARD
2 group of people [C] a group of people in an organization who make the rules and important decisions: *a board meeting* | *the local school board* | *There's only one woman on the board of directors.* | *Several politicians sit on the company's board.*
3 for putting things on [C] a flat piece of wood, plastic etc. that you use for a particular purpose such as cutting things on, or for playing indoor games: *Where's the chess board?* | *a cutting board* —see also BREADBOARD
4 for building [C] a long thin flat piece of wood used for making floors, walls, fences etc.: *We got the cedar boards from an old fence.* —see also FLOORBOARD (1)

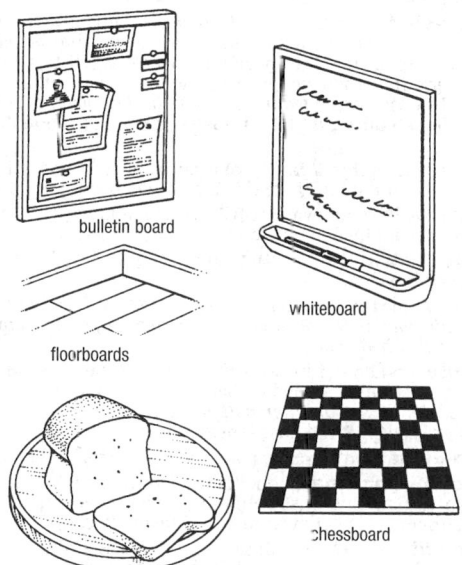

bulletin board

whiteboard

floorboards

chessboard

breadboard

5 on board a) on a ship or an airplane: *A light plane with four people on board crashed last night.* —compare ABOARD[1] **b)** involved in something or working for an organization: *The group has given more than 50 concerts to school groups since Morgan came on board.*
6 across the board if a plan or situation happens across the board, it affects everyone in a particular group, place etc.: *They're cutting 10% of their staff across the board.*
7 college/medical boards examinations that you take when you APPLY to a college or medical school
8 sports [C] INFORMAL a special board that you stand or lie on in sports such as SURFING, SKATEBOARDING etc. —see also BODY BOARD, SKATEBOARD, SNOWBOARD, SURFBOARD
9 the boards [plural] **a)** the low wooden wall around the area in which you play HOCKEY **b)** the plastic or wooden area to which a BASKETBALL HOOP (1) is attached **c)** the stage in a theater —see also **tread the boards** (TREAD[1] (4))
10 basketball [C usually plural] INFORMAL an act of REBOUND*ing* (REBOUND[1] (3)) the ball in a game of basketball
11 meals [U] the meals that are provided for you when you pay to stay somewhere: *Room and board is $3,000 per semester.*
12 go by the board/boards if a plan goes by the board, it is not possible anymore: *Plans for a skate park went by the board when the council decided it would be too expensive.*
13 take sth on board to listen to and accept a suggestion, idea etc.: *Our manager seemed to take our comments on board.*
14 electricity a CIRCUIT BOARD —see also ABOVEBOARD, DIVING BOARD, DRAWING BOARD, IRONING BOARD
board² *v.* **1** [I,T] FORMAL to get on a bus, airplane, train etc. in order to travel somewhere: *They boarded a flight for Israel.* | [+ at/to] *Please board to the rear of the aircraft.* **2** [I] if an airplane or a ship is boarding, passengers are getting onto it: *Flight 503 for Toronto is now boarding.* **3** [I always + adv./prep.] to pay to stay in a room in someone's house: *I board with the Nicholsons during the week.* **4** [I] to live at a school as well as studying there —see also BOARDING SCHOOL

board sth — up *phr. v.* [T] to cover a window or door with wooden boards: *The church has been boarded up because of the heavy damage.*

board·er /ˈbɔrdə/ *n.* [C] **1** someone who pays to live in another person's house with some or all of their

meals provided **2** a student who lives at a school as well as studying there
board game /ˈ. ./ *n.* [C] any indoor game in which pieces are moved around a specially designed board made of thick CARDBOARD or wood
board·ing /ˈbɔrdɪŋ/ *n.* [U] **1** the act of getting on a ship, an airplane etc. in order to travel somewhere: *Ladies and gentlemen, boarding will begin in just a few minutes.* **2** narrow pieces of wood that are fastened side by side, usually to cover a broken door or window
boarding card /ˈ.. ./ *n.* an official card that you have to show before you get onto an airplane
boarding house /ˈ.. ,./ *n.* [C] a private house where you pay to sleep and eat
boarding pass /ˈ.. ,./ *n.* [C] a boarding card
boarding school /ˈ.. ,./ *n.* [C] a school where students live as well as study
board·room /ˈbɔrdrum/ *n.* [C] a room where the members of the BOARD[1] (2) of a company or organization have meetings
board·walk /ˈbɔrdwɔk/ *n.* [C] a raised path made of wood, usually built next to the ocean —compare PIER (1)
boast¹ /boʊst/ *v.* **1** [I,T] to talk too proudly about your abilities, achievements, or possessions because you want to make other people admire you; BRAG: *I don't want to boast, but I was the first woman ever to win the competition.* | [+ about] *Scott was boasting about winning the game against Birmingham High.* | [+ of] *He boasted of having once sung with the Count Basie band.* | [boast that] *The company boasts that its packaging is recyclable.* **2** [T] if a place, object, or organization boasts a good feature or achievement, it has that good feature or achievement: *The new athletic center boasts an Olympic-size swimming pool.* —**boaster** *n.* [C]
boast² *n.* [C] something you talk too proudly about doing or having, so that it annoys other people: *Pat regretted her boast that she would be first to reach the top of the mountain.* | **sth is not an idle boast** (=something is true, not a boast)
boast·ful /ˈboʊstfəl/ *adj.* talking too proudly about yourself —**boastfully** *adv.* —**boastfulness** *n.* [U]
boat /boʊt/ *n.* [C] **1** a vehicle that travels across SW water: *a fishing boat* | *a motor boat* | *Many Cubans fled the island by boat.* **2** INFORMAL a ship, especially one that carries passengers **3 be in the same boat (as)** to be in the same bad situation as someone else: *Everyone was in the same boat during the Depression – we all went hungry sometimes.* —see also **burn your bridges** (BURN[1] (12)), GRAVY BOAT, **miss the boat** (MISS[1] (11)), **rock the boat** (ROCK² (3))
boat·er /ˈboʊtə/ *n.* [C] a hard STRAW (1) hat with a flat top
boat hook /ˈ. ./ *n.* [C] a long pole with an iron hook at the end, used to pull or push a small boat
boat·house /ˈboʊthaʊs/ *n.* [C] a building that small boats are kept in when they are not being used
boat·ing /ˈboʊtɪŋ/ *n.* [U] the activity of traveling in a small boat for pleasure: *The authorities decided not to allow boating on the lake.*
boat·load /ˈboʊtloʊd/ *n.* [C] the people or things that are or were on a boat: [+ of] *a boatload of refugees*
boat·man /ˈboʊtmən/ *n.* [C] a man whom you pay to take you out in a boat or for the use of a boat
boat peo·ple /ˈ. ,../ *n.* [plural] people who leave their country in small boats to escape from a bad situation
boat·swain /ˈboʊsən/ *n.* [C] an officer on a ship whose job is to organize the work and look after the equipment; BOSUN
boat·yard /ˈboʊtˈyɑrd/ *n.* [C] an area where boats are built, repaired, or kept when they are not in the water
bob¹ /bɑb/ *v.*
1 move in water [I] to move up and down when floating on the surface of water: *We could see swimmers bobbing up and down in the waves.*

2 [move somewhere] [I always + adv./prep.] to move quickly up or down in a particular direction: [+ **up/down/out** etc.] *Her blonde ponytail bobbed up and down as she talked.*
3 [hair] [T] to cut a woman's or girl's hair in a bob —see picture at HAIRSTYLE
4 bob and weave a) to move your body up and down and around an area, in order to avoid something or avoid being hit: *The two boxers were bobbing and weaving in the ring.* **b)** to avoid directly answering a question: *Davidovich bobs and weaves through the questions reporters shout to him.*
5 bob for apples to play a game in which you try to pick up apples floating in water, using only your mouth
6 bob your head to move your head down quickly as a way of showing respect, greeting someone or agreeing with them
7 bob (sb) a curtsy to make a quick small CURTSY to someone

bob² *n.* [C] **1** a way of cutting a woman's or girl's hair so that it hangs down to the level of her chin and is the same length all the way around: *a little girl with a short bob* **2** a quick up and down movement of your head or body, to show respect, agreement, greeting etc.: *The maid gave a little bob and left the room.* **3** a BOBSLED

bob·bin /'bɑbɪn/ *n.* [C] a small round object that you wind thread onto, especially for a SEWING MACHINE —compare SPOOL

bob·ble /'bɑbəl/ *v.* [T] to drop or hold a ball in an uncontrolled way; FUMBLE¹ (1): *The shortstop bobbled the ball and the runner ran home.*

bob·by /'bɑbi/ *n.* [C] OLD-FASHIONED, BRITISH a police officer

bobby pin /'.. ,./ *n.* [C] a thin piece of metal bent into a narrow U shape that a woman uses to hold her hair in place —see picture at PIN¹

bobby socks, bobby sox /'.. ,./ *n.* [plural] girls' short socks that have the tops turned over

bob·cat /'bɑbkæt/ *n.* [C] a large North American wild cat that has no tail; LYNX

bob·sled /'bɑbslɛd/ *n.* **1** [C] a small vehicle with two long thin metal blades instead of wheels, that is used for racing down a special ice track **2** [U] a sports event in which people race against each other in bobsleds: *Sixteen teams took part in the 400m bobsled.* —**bobsledding** *n.* [U] —**bobsledder** *n.* [C] —**bobsled** *v.* [I]

bob·tail /'bɑbteɪl/ *n.* [C] **a)** a horse or dog whose tail has been cut short **b)** a tail that has been cut short

bob·white /,bɑb'waɪt/ *n.* [C] a brown and white North American bird about the size of a chicken; QUAIL¹

bod /bɑd/ *n.* [C] INFORMAL someone's body: *He has a gorgeous bod!*

bo·da·cious /bou'deɪʃəs/ *adj.* SLANG **1** excellent: *a bodacious video* **2** brave and surprising or extreme: *Smith's bodacious promise*

bode /boud/ *v.* **1 bode well/ill (for sb/sth)** ESPECIALLY LITERARY to be a good or bad sign for the future: *The results of the opinion poll do not bode well for the Democrats.* **2** the past tense of BIDE

bo·de·ga /bou'deɪgə/ *n.* [C] a small store that sells food

Bo·dhi·dhar·ma /,boudi'dɑrmə/ (6th century A.D.) an Indian Buddhist religious leader who taught in China and is believed to have started Zen Buddhism

bo·dhi·satt·va /,boudi'sʌtvə/ *n.* [C] a Buddhist who has become holy enough to enter NIRVANA but chooses to stay on earth and help other people

bod·ice /'bɑdɪs/ *n.* [C] **1** the part of a woman's dress above her waist **2** a tight woman's VEST worn over a BLOUSE in past times **3** OLD USE a CORSET (1)

-bod·ied /bɑdid/ *suffix* **long-bodied/thick-bodied** etc. having a long thick etc. body: *They were thick-bodied men, used to hard labor.* —see also ABLE-BODIED, FULL-BODIED

bod·i·ly¹ /'bɑdl-i/ *adj.* [only before noun] relating to the human body: *bodily needs | bodily functions | the threat of death or serious bodily harm*

bodily² *adv.* by moving the whole of someone's body or by moving the whole of an object at once: *They lifted the child bodily aboard.*

body

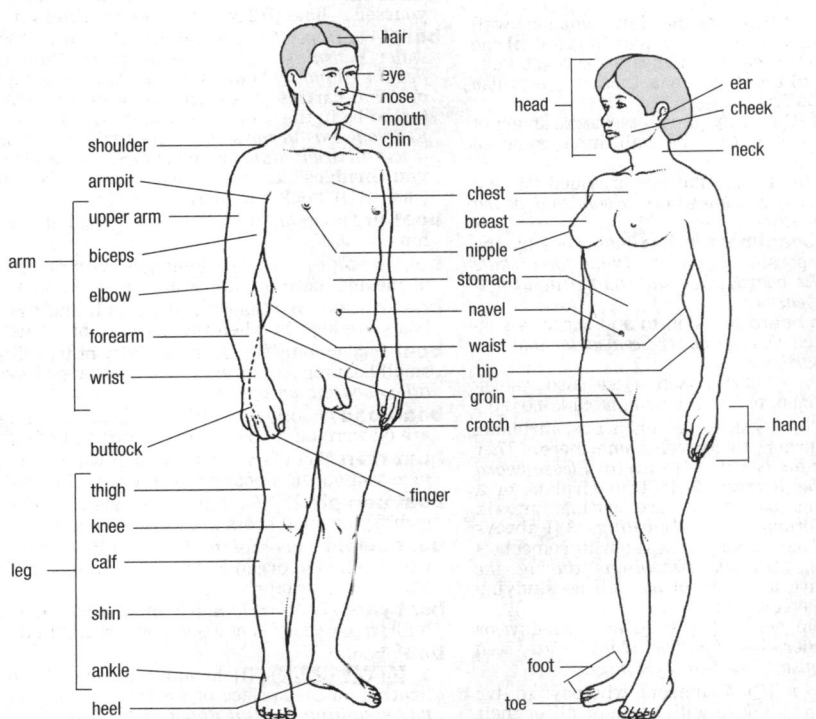

shoulder, armpit, upper arm, biceps, elbow, forearm, wrist, arm, buttock, thigh, knee, calf, shin, ankle, heel, leg, hair, eye, nose, mouth, chin, chest, breast, nipple, stomach, navel, waist, hip, groin, crotch, finger, head, ear, cheek, neck, hand, foot, toe

bod·kin /'bɑdkɪn/ n. [C] a long thick needle without a point

bod·y /'bɑdi/ n. plural **bodies**
1 sb's body [C] **a)** the physical structure of a person or animal: *a strong, healthy body* | *Many teenagers are self-conscious about their bodies.* | *body heat/temperature/weight etc. Babies undergo a rapid increase in body weight during the first weeks.* | *body image* (=the mental picture you have of your own body) **b)** the central part of a person or animal's body, not including the head, arms, legs, or wings: *a man with a short body and long legs*
2 dead body [C] the dead body of a person or animal: *His body was flown home to be buried.*
3 group of people [C] a group of people who work together to do a particular job or who are together for a particular purpose: [+ of] *the body of believers in the church* | *the governing body of the university* (=people in the government of the university) | *the President of the student body* (=all the students in a school or college)
4 a/the body of sth a) a large amount or collection of something: *the growing body of evidence* | *Davies' body of work consists of eleven novels and various collections of stories and essays.* **b)** the main, central, or most important part of something: *the body of the report*
5 vehicle [C] the main structure of a vehicle, not including the engine, wheels etc.: *The body of the plane broke in two.*
6 hair [U] if your hair has body, it is thick and healthy
7 a body of water a large area of water such as a lake
8 separate object [C] TECHNICAL an object that is separate from other objects: *There is some kind of foreign body* (=object that is not part of something) *irritating his eye.*
9 body and soul a) completely: *She devoted herself body and soul to the fight for women's rights.* **b)** all of someone: *It makes your body and soul feel better.*
10 keep body and soul together to continue to exist with just barely enough food, money etc.
11 in a body if people do something in a body, they do it together in large numbers: *The demonstrators marched in a body to the main square.* —see also -BODIED, **over my dead body** (DEAD[1] (17))

USAGE NOTE: BODY

WORD CHOICE: body, figure, build
A **body** consists of someone's arms, legs, head etc. and may be healthy, skinny, dead etc.: *I had a fever and my body ached all over.* If you say someone has a *lovely/good/beautiful body,* this may suggest you find them sexually attractive. Your **figure** is the shape of your **body. Figure** is usually used about women: *She has a really good figure.* | *It's better to avoid snacks if you're watching your figure* (=trying not to get fat). **Build** can be used for the size and shape of both men and women: *a man/woman with a small/heavy/slim build*

---

body ar·mor /'.. ,../ n. [U] clothing worn by the police that protects them against bullets
body bag /'.. ,./ n. [C] a large bag in which a dead body is put in order to remove it from a place
body blow /'.. ,./ n. [C] **1** a serious loss, disappointment, or defeat: *The corporation suffered a body blow when Williams resigned last week.* **2** a hard hit between your neck and waist during a fight
body board, bodyboard /'.. ,./ n. [C] a BOOGIE BOARD —**body boarding** n. [U] —**bodyboarder** n. [C]
body build·ing, bodybuilding /'.. ,../ n. [U] an activity in which you do hard physical exercise in order to develop big muscles —**body builder** n. [C]
body-check /'.. ,./ v. [T] to block an opponent in HOCKEY or LACROSSE by hitting them with your body —**body check** n. [C]
body clock /'.. ,./ n. [C] the system in your body that controls types of behavior which happen at regular times, such as sleeping or eating; BIOLOGICAL CLOCK
body count /'.. ,./ n. [C] **a)** the number of soldiers who are dead after a period of fighting, or the

number of people dead after a serious accident, shooting etc.: *We were horrified as the body count rose higher and higher.* **b)** the process of counting dead bodies
body dou·ble /'.. ,../ n. [C] someone whose body is used instead of an actor or actress's in a movie, especially in scenes in which they do not wear clothes
body En·glish /'.. ,../ n. [U] the way someone's body moves or twists after they have thrown or hit a ball, as if they can influence the direction of the ball while it is in the air
bod·y·guard /'bɑdi,gɑrd/ n. [C] **1** someone whose job is to protect an important person: *The agency provides bodyguards for movie and music stars.* **2** a group of people who work together to protect an important person
body lan·guage /'.. ,../ n. [U] changes in your body position and movements that show what you are feeling or thinking: *The man stared at Bonnie whose body language was screaming, "Leave me alone!"*
body o·dor /'.. ,../ n. [C] a bad smell from someone's body caused by SWEAT; B.O.
body pierc·ing /'.. ,../ n. [C,U] the process of putting holes in different parts of your body, so that you can wear jewelry there, or the holes produced in this way
body pol·i·tic /'.. ,../ n. [singular] FORMAL all the people in a nation forming a state that is under the control of a single government
body search /'.. ./ n. [C] a thorough search for drugs, weapons etc., that might be hidden on someone's body: *The reporter was subjected to a body search by presidential guards.* —**body-search** v. [T]
body shop /'.. ,./ n. [C] a place where the main structure of a car is repaired, not including the engine, wheels etc. —compare GARAGE[1] (2)
body snatch·er /'.. ,../ n. [C] someone in past times who dug up dead bodies and sold them to doctors for scientific study
body stock·ing /'.. ,./ n. [C] a close-fitting piece of clothing that covers the whole of your body
bod·y·suit /'bɑdisut/ n. [C] **1** a type of tight shirt worn by women that fastens between their legs **2** a piece of tight clothing that covers your whole body
bod·y·work /'bɑdi,wɔrk/ n. [U] **1** the metal frame of a vehicle, not including the engine, wheels etc.: *The bodywork is beginning to rust.* **2** work done to repair the frame of a vehicle, not including the engine, wheels etc.: *I know a garage that does good bodywork.*
Boer /bɔr, bʊr/ n. [C] someone from South Africa whose family came from the Netherlands —**Boer** adj.
bof·fo /'bɑfoʊ/ adj. [only before noun, no comparative] INFORMAL a word meaning "successful" or "impressive," used especially about movies or performances: *The movie did boffo business in theaters this summer.*
bog[1] /bɑg, bɔg/ n. [C,U] an area of low wet ground, sometimes containing bushes or grasses —compare MARSH, SWAMP[1]
bog[2] v.
bog sb/sth ↔ **down** phr. v. [T] **1** to become too involved in thinking about or dealing with one particular thing: [+ in/over] *The book gets bogged down in a lot of technical jargon.* **2** to become stuck in muddy ground and be unable to move: [+ in] *The tanks had bogged down in mud at the edge of the village.*
Bo·gart /'boʊgɑrt/, **Hum·phrey** /'hʌmfri/ (1899–1957) a U.S. movie actor
bo·gey /'boʊgi/ n. [C] **1** also **bogie, bogy** one STROKE[1] (3) more than PAR to get the ball into the hole in the game of GOLF **2** a problem or difficult situation that makes you feel anxious: [+ of] *the bogey of nuclear weapons in an unstable country* **3** a bogeyman
bo·gey·man /'boʊgi,mæn/ n. [C] an evil spirit, especially in children's imaginations or stories

bog·gle /'bɒgəl/ v. **the mind boggles (at sth)** INFORMAL also **sth boggles the mind** if your mind etc. boggles when you think of something, it is difficult for you to imagine or accept it: *The mind boggles at the huge amounts of money involved in the new space program.* —see also MIND-BOGGLING

bog·gy /'bɒgi/ adj. **boggier, boggiest** boggy ground is wet and muddy

bo·gie /'bougi/ v. [T] to use one more than PAR (=the usual number of strokes) to get the ball into the hole in GOLF —**bogie** n. [C]

Bo·go·tá /ˌbougə'tɑ, 'bougəˌtɑ/ the capital and largest city of Colombia

bo·gus /'bougəs/ adj. INFORMAL not true or real, although someone is trying to make you think it is; FAKE: *a bogus driver's license*

bo·gy /'bougi/ n. [C] a BOGEY

bo·he·mi·an /bou'hi:miən/ adj. living in a very informal or relaxed way and not accepting society's rules of behavior: *The tourist resort threatens to change Key West's bohemian culture.* —**bohemian** n. [C]

Bohr /bɔr/, **Niels Hen·rik Da·vid** /nils 'hɛnrɪk 'deɪvɪd/ (1885–1962) a Danish scientist who made important discoveries about the structure of atoms

boil[1] /bɔɪl/ v. **1** [I,T] when a liquid boils it is hot enough for BUBBLES to rise to the surface and for the liquid to change into gas: *Put the spaghetti into boiling, salted water.* | [+ at] *Water boils at 100 degrees centigrade.* | *Boil the water before drinking it.* **2** [I,T] to cook something in boiling water:

boil over

Boil the vegetables for 10 minutes. | *I've put the potatoes on to boil.* **3** [I] to be angry: [+ about/over] *Mike was still boiling over the letter to the editor in the local paper that morning.* **4** [T] to clean something using boiling water: *Clothes had to be boiled to prevent the disease from spreading.* —see also **make your blood boil** (BLOOD (10)), BOILING POINT

boil away phr. v. [I] if a liquid boils away, it disappears because it has been heated too much

boil down phr. v. **1 boil down to sth** INFORMAL if a long statement, argument etc. boils down to a single statement, that statement is the main point or cause: *In the end, the case will boil down to whether the jury believes Smith or not.* **2** [T **boil** sth ↔ **down**] to make a list or a piece of writing shorter by taking out anything that is not necessary or wanted: *The team boiled down a list of 75 candidates to six finalists.* **3** [I,T **boil** sth ↔ **down**] if a food or liquid boils down or you boil it down, the total amount of it becomes less after it is cooked: *Spinach tends to boil down a lot.*

boil over phr. v. [I] **1** if a liquid boils over, it rises and flows over the side of the container because it is boiling **2** if a situation or an emotion boils over, the people involved stop being calm: *In 1959 unrest among Africans boiled over into strikes, rioting, and looting.*

boil up phr. v. **1** [I] if a situation or emotion boils up, bad feelings grow until they reach a dangerous level: *That summer, ethnic tensions boiled up again in the city.* **2** [T **boil** sth ↔ **up**] to heat food or a liquid until it begins to boil: *Boil the fruit up with sugar.*

boil[2] n. **1** [singular] the act or state of boiling: *Bring the sauce to a boil and cook for 5 minutes.* | *Heat the mixture until it comes to a boil* (=begins to boil). **2** [C] a painful infected swelling under someone's skin

boil·er /'bɔɪlɚ/ n. [C] a container for storing or heating water, especially one in the heating system of a house or building

boiler room /'.. ,./ n. [C] **1** a room in a large building where the building's boiler is **2** SLANG a room or

office where people sell SHARES[2] (4) or services on the telephone, using unfair and sometimes dishonest methods

boiler-room /'.. ,./ adj. [only before noun] relating to very direct and often successful methods of persuading people to buy something, especially on the telephone: *Using boiler-room sales techniques, salespeople convinced clients to buy part ownership in hundreds of acres of desert.*

boil·ing /'bɔɪlɪŋ/ adj. **1** SPOKEN very hot: *It was a horrible weekend over here too. It was boiling.* | *His apartment is always boiling hot – I can't stand being in there.* **2** very angry: [+ with] *I was boiling with frustration.*

boiling point /'.. ,./ n. [C usually singular] **1** the temperature at which a liquid boils **2** a point when people cannot deal with a problem calmly anymore: *In 1988, popular frustration with the military government reached the boiling point.*

Boi·se /'bɔɪzi, -si/ the capital city of the U.S. state of Idaho

bois·ter·ous /'bɔɪstərəs/ adj. someone, especially a child, who is boisterous makes a lot of noise and has a lot of energy: *During his speech police in riot gear watched over a boisterous crowd.*

bok choy /ˌbɑk 'tʃɔɪ/ n. [U] a type of CABBAGE eaten especially in East Asia

bold /bould/ adj.

1 action/person behavior or actions that are bold show that you are extremely confident and not afraid to take risks: *The speech began with a bold statement about racism.* | *a bold leader* | *The Governor felt he had to make a bold move to provoke progress.* | *We must take bold steps to protect the environment.*

2 colors/shapes very clear and strong or bright, and therefore easy to notice: *wallpaper with bold stripes* | *bold illustrations*

3 in bold (type/print/letters) printed in letters that are darker and thicker than ordinary printed letters: *On Thursday they received a fax with "Warning" on it in bold letters.*

4 if I may be so bold SPOKEN used when asking someone a question, to show that you are slightly annoyed with them: *And what, if I may be so bold, is the meaning of this note?*

5 as bold as you please OLD-FASHIONED used to say that someone is being too confident or determined in a way that shocks people: *She just walked down the street in that skimpy outfit, as bold as you please.*

6 be/make so bold as to do sth OLD-FASHIONED to do something that other people feel is rude or not acceptable —**boldly** adv. —**boldness** n. [U]

bold·face /'bouldfeɪs/ n. [U] TECHNICAL a way of printing letters that makes them thicker and darker than normal —**boldface** adj. —**boldfaced** adj.

bold-faced /'bouldfeɪst/ adj. BALD-FACED

bole /boul/ n. [C] LITERARY the main part of a tree; TRUNK (1)

bo·le·ro /bə'lɛrou/ n. plural **boleros** [C] **1** a type of Spanish dance, or the music for this dance **2** a short JACKET for a woman

bol·i·var /bə'li:vɑr/ n. the standard unit of money used in Venezuela

Bol·i·var /bə'li:vɑr/, **Si·mon** /si'moun/ (1783–1830) **the Liberator** a South American soldier and political leader famous for fighting to win independence from Spain for Venezuela, Peru, Bolivia, Colombia, and Ecuador

Bo·liv·i·a /bə'lɪviə/ a country in the western part of South America, between Brazil and Peru —**Bolivian** n., adj.

boll /boul/ n. [C] the part of a cotton plant that contains the seeds

bol·lard /'bɑlɚd/ n. [C] a thick metal or stone post used for tying ships to

boll wee·vil /ˌ. '../ n. [C] an insect that eats and destroys cotton plants

bo·lo·gna /bə'louni/ n. a type of cooked meat often eaten in SANDWICHes[1]

bo·lo tie /'boʊloʊ ˌtaɪ/ n. [C] a thick string worn around your neck that you fasten with a decoration

Bol·she·vik /'boʊlʃəvɪk, 'bal-/ n. [C] **1** someone who supported the COMMUNIST[2] party at the time of the Russian Revolution in 1917 **2** OLD-FASHIONED an insulting word for someone who has LEFT-WING views —**bolshevik** adj.

bol·ster[1] /'boʊlstər/ v. [T] **1** also **bolster** sth ↔ **up** to improve something by making it stronger or bigger: *Additional soldiers were sent to bolster the defenses at two naval bases.* | *New camera and film technology will bolster the company's market share.* **2** also **bolster** sb/sth ↔ **up** to help someone to feel better and more positive: *Timman needs to win a game to bolster his confidence.*

bolster[2] n. [C] a long firm PILLOW[1] (1), usually shaped like a tube

bolt[1] /boʊlt/ n. [C]
1 lock a metal bar that you slide across a door or window to lock it
2 screw a screw with a flat top and no point, for fastening two pieces of metal together
3 a bolt of lightning LIGHTNING that appears as a white line in the sky —see also THUNDERBOLT
4 a bolt from the blue something that happens very suddenly and without warning: *The attack on the airbase was a bolt from the blue. We had no warning whatsoever.*
5 cloth a large long roll of cloth
6 gun a short metal bar that you slide into the BARREL[1] (3) of a gun to load bullets and hold them in place
7 weapon a short heavy ARROW (1) that is fired from a CROSSBOW —see also the **nuts and bolts of sth** (NUT (6))

bolt[2] v. **1** [I] to suddenly run somewhere very quickly, especially in order to escape or because you are frightened: *The dog bolted into the road, into the oncoming traffic.* **2** [T] to lock a door or window by sliding a bolt across: *Jason bolted the door and closed all the curtains.* **3** [T] also **bolt down** to fasten two things together using a bolt: [**bolt** sth **to** sth] *A wrought-iron bench was bolted to the patio.* **4** [T] also **bolt down** to eat very quickly: *I bolted down my breakfast and was out the door by 8:00.* **5 bolt the party** to leave a political party

bolt[3] adv. **sit/stand bolt upright** to sit or stand with your back very straight, often because something has frightened you: *We found her sitting bolt upright in bed with all the lights on.*

bolt-ac·tion /ˌ. '..◂/ adj. a bolt-action gun uses a bolt to load bullets and hold them in place

bomb[1] /bam/ n. [C]
1 weapon a weapon made of material that will explode: *A bomb exploded near the country's busiest airport before dawn today.* | *Warplanes began dropping the massive bombs last week.* | *No one claimed responsibility for planting the bomb* (=hiding it in order to destroy something). —see also ATOMIC BOMB, HYDROGEN BOMB, LETTER BOMB, NEUTRON BOMB, STINK BOMB, TIME BOMB
2 bad performance/event INFORMAL a play, movie, event etc. that is not successful: *This is just another one of Hollywood's bland and boring bombs.*
3 the bomb the ATOMIC BOMB or any NUCLEAR WEAPON: *What if the government decided to use the bomb?*
4 container a container in which insect poison, paint etc. is kept under pressure: *a flea bomb* (=used for killing FLEAS)
5 football a throw of a football that goes a very long way: *Billy Joe Tolliver threw a 44-yard bomb into the end zone.*
6 be the bomb SLANG to be very good or exciting —see also **drop a bombshell/bomb** (DROP[1] (25))

bomb[2] v. **1** [T] to attack a place by leaving a bomb there, or by dropping bombs on it from an airplane: *NATO warplanes bombed a dozen towns Thursday.* **2** [I] INFORMAL if a play, movie, event etc. bombs, it is not successful: *In 1986 they made "Shanghai Surprise," which bombed.* **3** [I,T] SPOKEN to fail a test very badly: *I just bombed the written section of the*

B

test. **4 bug-bomb/flea-bomb/paint-bomb etc.** to let insect poison, paint etc. out of a container where it has been kept under pressure, in order to fill or cover an area with that substance: *They had to bug-bomb the house yesterday, so we couldn't move in.* **5 be bombed out** if a building, bridge etc. is bombed out, it is completely destroyed by bombs: *He started the new school after his former school, the International College, was bombed out.* —see also BOMBED-OUT

bom·bard /bam'bard/ v. [T] **1** to attack a place for a long time using large weapons, bombs etc.: *Rockets bombarded residential areas of the Afghan capital Friday.* **2** to do something too often or too much, for example criticizing someone or giving too much information: [**bombard** sb **with** sth] *Already, the water department has been bombarded with complaints about the drinking water.*

bom·bar·dier /ˌbamba'dɪr/ n. [C] the person on a military aircraft responsible for dropping bombs

bom·bard·ment /bam'bardmənt/ n. [U] a long attack on a place using large weapons, bombs etc.: *Twenty-eight people have been killed in the past two days of* **heavy bombardment**. | **Aerial bombardment** (=attack by airplanes dropping bombs) *of rebel positions continued throughout the week.*

bom·bas·tic /bam'bæstɪk/ adj. using long words that sound important but have no real meaning: *His bombastic style made him unpopular with his colleagues.* —**bombast** /'bambæst/ n. [U]

bomb dis·pos·al /'. .ˌ../ n. [U] the job of dealing with bombs that have not exploded, and making them safe | **bomb disposal expert/squad/unit** (=person or group that makes bombs safe)

bombed /bamd/ adj. [not before noun] SLANG very drunk: *My dad used to get bombed every night.*

bombed-out /ˌ. '.◂/ adj. completely destroyed by bombs: *He showed us a bombed-out warehouse on the far side of the city.*

bomb·er /'bamər/ n. [C] **1** an airplane that carries and drops bombs **2** someone who hides a bomb somewhere in order to destroy something

bomber jack·et /'.. ˌ../ n. [C] a short JACKET which fits tightly around your waist

bomb·ing /'bamɪŋ/ n. [C,U] the use of bombs to attack a place: [+ of] *the bombing of Belgrade* | *Hundreds have been killed in the latest* **wave of bombings** (=series of attacks using bombs).

bomb·proof /'bampruf/ adj. strong enough not to be damaged by a bomb attack: *a bombproof shelter*

bomb scare /'. ./ n. [C] a situation in which people have to be moved out of a building or area because there may be a bomb there

bomb·shell /'bamʃɛl/ n. [C] INFORMAL an unexpected and very shocking piece of news: *Conley dropped another bombshell when she decided not to resign after all.* —see also **blonde bombshell** (BLONDE[1] (3))

bomb shel·ter /'. ˌ../ n. [C] a room or building that is built to protect people from bomb attacks

bomb site /'. ./ n. [C] a place where a bomb has destroyed one or more buildings in a town: *The library at the end of the road was built on a bomb site.*

bomb squad /'. ./ n. [C] a group of people, usually police officers, who deal with bombs that have not exploded and make them safe

bo·na fide /'boʊnə ˌfaɪd, 'banə-/ adj. real, true, and not intended to deceive anyone: *a bona fide job offer*

bo·nan·za /bə'nænzə, boʊ-/ n. [C] a lucky or successful situation in which people can make a lot of money: *The large jump in profits has resulted in a bonanza for Intel employees.*

Bo·na·parte /'boʊnə ˌpart/ —see NAPOLEON

bon ap·pe·tit /ˌboʊn æpeɪ'ti, apə-, ˌban-/ interjection said to someone before they start eating a meal, to tell them you hope they enjoy their food

bon·bon /'banban/ n. [C] a round piece of soft candy that is usually covered in chocolate

sw **bond¹** /band/ n.
1 relationship [C] something that unites two or more people or groups, such as love, or a shared interest or idea: [+ **with**] *Marilyn's bond with her mother was unusually strong.* | [+ **between**] *I felt that the troubles had strengthened the bond between us.* | **the bonds of friendship/marriage/family** etc. (=a special relationship that makes people loyal to each other)
2 money [C] an official document promising that a government or company will pay back money that it has borrowed, often with INTEREST¹ (3): *U.S. savings bonds* | *the bond market*
3 in a court [C,U] money given to a court of law so that someone can be let out of prison while they wait for their TRIAL; BAIL: *Maxwell's lawyers posted the $100,000 bond and he was released.*
4 with glue [C] the way in which two surfaces become attached to each other using glue
5 atoms [C] TECHNICAL the force that holds atoms together in a MOLECULE
6 bonds [plural] LITERARY something that limits your freedom and prevents you from doing what you want to do: [+ **of**] *the bonds of slavery*
7 bonds [plural] LITERARY chains, ropes etc. used for tying a prisoner
8 in bond or **out of bond** TECHNICAL in or out of a bonded warehouse
9 paper [U] BOND PAPER
10 promise [C] LITERARY a serious promise or agreement: *My word is my bond.* —see also BOND ISSUE

bond² v. **1** [I] to develop a special relationship with someone: [+ **with**] *Four months away from work gives new mothers a chance to bond with their babies.* **2** [I] if two things bond, they become firmly stuck together, especially after they have been joined with a substance such as glue: *It takes less than 10 minutes for the two surfaces to bond.* **3** [T] TECHNICAL to keep goods in a bonded warehouse

bond·age /'bandidʒ/ n. [U] **1** FORMAL the state of being a slave: *The men were accused of selling the 170 women and children into bondage.* **2** the practice of being tied up for sexual pleasure **3** FORMAL the state of having your freedom limited, or being prevented from doing what you want: [+ **of**] *Children should be guaranteed a life free from the bondage of drugs.*

bonded ware·house /,.. '../ n. [C] TECHNICAL an official place to keep goods that have been brought into a country before tax has been paid on them

bond·hold·er /'band,houldɚ/ n. [C] TECHNICAL someone who owns government or industrial BONDS¹ (2)

bond·ing /'bandɪŋ/ n. [U] **1** a process in which a special relationship develops between two or more people: *Difficult experiences, such as a death in the family, often result in bonding.* **2 male/female bonding** HUMOROUS the activity of doing things with other people of the same sex, so that you feel good about being a man or a woman: *Do a little female bonding – go shopping or out for a big lunch with a friend.* **3** TECHNICAL the connection of atoms or of two surfaces that are glued together

bond is·sue /'. ,../ n. [C] **1** an occasion when a government borrows public money to pay for something, which people must first approve of by voting for it: *They're hoping to get a bond issue passed so they can redo the aquarium.* **2** an occasion when a company sells BONDS¹ (2) to pay for something

bond pa·per /'. ,../ n. [U] a type of thick writing paper with a lot of cotton in it: *The first copy should be typed on good quality bond paper.*

sw **bone¹** /boʊn/ n.
1 body [C] one of the hard parts that form the frame of a human or animal body: *She broke two bones in her arm.* | *Did you give this bone to the dog?* | *Maxine has the right bone structure* (=shape of face) *to be a model.* | **thigh/arm/wrist** etc. **bone** *The boy's ankle bone had fractured.*

2 make no bones about (doing) sth to not feel nervous or ashamed about doing or saying something: *Mr. Stutzman makes no bones about his religious beliefs.*
3 be chilled/frozen to the bone to be extremely cold
4 a bone of contention something that causes arguments between people: *Her drinking became a bone of contention between them.*
5 I have a bone to pick with you SPOKEN used to tell someone that you are annoyed with them and want to talk about it: *I have a bone to pick with you! Why didn't you tell me Sheila was coming over tonight?*
6 feel/know sth in your bones to be sure that something is true, even though you have no proof and cannot explain why you are sure: *I know nothing's ever going to happen – I can feel it in my bones*
7 throw/toss sb a bone INFORMAL to help someone in a small way because you feel sorry for them —see also **bag of bones** (BAG¹ (9)), BARE-BONES, BIG-BONED, **cut sth to the bone** (CUT¹ (18)), **dry as a bone** (DRY¹ (1)), SMALL-BONED, **work your fingers to the bone** (WORK¹ (27))

bone² v. [T] **1** to remove the bones from fish or meat: *boned salmon* **2** SLANG to have sex with someone
bone up on sth *phr. v.* [T] INFORMAL to study a subject a lot, especially before a test: *I've spent the last two weeks boning up on medieval history.*

bone chi·na /,. '../ n. [U] delicate and expensive cups, plates etc. that are made partly with crushed bone

bone dry, bone-dry /,. '.◂/ adj. completely dry: *The Red River Valley soil is bone dry after three years of drought.*

bone·head /'boʊnhɛd/ n. [C] INFORMAL a stupid person

bone mar·row /'. ,../ n. [U] the soft substance in the hollow center of bones; MARROW (1): *a bone marrow transplant*

bone meal /'. ./ n. [U] a substance made of crushed bones that is used to feed plants

bon·er /'boʊnɚ/ n. [singular] **1** SLANG an ERECTION (1) **2** INFORMAL a stupid or embarrassing mistake

bone-tired /,. '.◂/ adj. [not before noun] extremely tired: *After supper, Paul sat in the rocker by the fire feeling bone-tired.*

bon·fire /'ban,faɪɚ/ n. [C] a large outdoor fire, either for burning waste, or for a celebration: *Dad had a bonfire going behind the garage.*

bong /baŋ/ n. **1** [C] an object used for smoking MARIJUANA in which the smoke goes through water to make it cool **2** [singular] a deep sound made by a large bell

bon·gos /'baŋgoʊz/ also **bongo drums** /'.. ,./ n. [plural] a pair of small drums that you play with your hands

Bon·hoef·fer /'banhoufɚ/, **Die·trich** /'ditrɪk/ (1906–1945) a German Protestant minister and religious teacher and writer, who opposed the Nazis

bon·ho·mie /,banə'mi, ,boʊ-/ n. [U] LITERARY a friendly feeling among a group of people: *The atmosphere of bonhomie was suddenly gone.*

bonk¹ /baŋk/ v. [T] INFORMAL to hit someone lightly on the head, or hit your head on something by mistake: *Casnoff was bonked by a piece of falling scenery during a performance.*

bonk² n. [C] INFORMAL **1** the action of hitting someone lightly on the head, or hitting your head against something **2** a sudden short deep sound, for example, when something hits the ground

bon·kers /'baŋkɚz/ adj. **1 go bonkers** to become crazy, or very excited: *He's going bonkers in his old age* | *The whole stadium went bonkers when we finally scored.* **2 drive sb bonkers** to make someone feel mad or annoyed: *The noise from the train tracks used to drive us bonkers.*

bon mot /boʊn 'moʊ, ban-/ n. [C] an intelligent remark

Bonn /ban/ a city in western Germany, which was the capital of West Germany

bon·net /'banɪt/ n. [C] **1** a type of hat that ties under the chin, worn by babies, and by women in past times **2** BRITISH a HOOD (1) —see also **have a bee in your bonnet** (BEE (2)) —see picture at HAT

Bon·nie and Clyde /ˌbani ən ˈklaɪd/ two young U.S. criminals, Bonnie Parker (a woman) and Clyde Barrow (a man), who stole money from banks and businesses in the U.S. in the 1930s

Bonnie & Clyde

bon·ny /ˈbani/ *adj.* OLD-FASHIONED pretty and healthy: *a bonny baby*

bon·sai /ˈbansaɪ, -zaɪ/ *n.* [C,U] a tree that is grown so that it always stays very small, or the art of growing trees in this way —**bonsai** *adj.*

bo·nus /ˈboʊnəs/ *n.* [C] **1** money added to someone's pay, especially as a reward for good work: *Did you get a Christmas bonus this year?* **2** something good that you did not expect in a situation: *The fact that the house is so close to the school is an added bonus.*

bon vi·vant /ˌboʊn viˈvɑnt, ˌbɑn-/ *n.* [C] LITERARY someone who enjoys good food and wine, and being with people

bon voy·age /ˌboʊn vɔɪˈɑʒ, ˌbɑn-/ *interjection* used to wish someone a good trip

bon·y /ˈboʊni/ *adj.* bonier, boniest **1** someone or part of their body that is bony is very thin: *bony fingers* **2** bony fish or meat contains a lot of small bones **3** a bony part of an animal consists mostly of bone

boo¹ /bu/ *v.* boos, booed, booing [I,T] to shout "boo" to show that you do not like a person, performance, idea etc.: *Some of the audience started booing.* | *Angry residents booed him off stage* (=shouted "boo" until he left the stage) *at a political rally last month.* —opposite CHEER¹

boo² *n. plural* boos [C] a noise made by someone who does not like a person, performance, idea etc.: *Mitchell ignored the boos and hit another home run.* —opposite CHEER²

boo³ *interjection* **1** a word you shout suddenly to someone as a joke, in order to frighten them **2** said loudly to show that you do not like a person, performance, idea etc. **3 not say boo** SPOKEN to not say anything at all

boob /bub/ *n.* **1** [C usually plural] SLANG a woman's breast **2** [C] INFORMAL a stupid or silly person

boob job /ˈ. ./ *n.* [C] SLANG an operation to make a woman's breasts larger or smaller

boo-boo /ˈ. ./ *n.* [C] SPOKEN **1** a word meaning a "silly mistake," often used when speaking to children: *Oh, I made a boo-boo.* **2** a word meaning a "small injury," used when speaking to children: *Do you have a boo-boo on your knee?*

boob tube /ˈ. ./ *n.* **the boob tube** SPOKEN television: *What's on the boob tube?*

boo·by /ˈbubi/ *n.* PLURAL boobies [C] **1** INFORMAL a stupid or silly person **2** a type of tropical SEABIRD **3** [usually plural] SLANG a woman's breast

booby hatch /ˈ.. ˌ./ *n.* [singular] OLD-FASHIONED a mental hospital

booby prize /ˈ.. ˌ./ *n.* [C] a prize given as a joke to the person who is last in a competition

booby trap /ˈ.. ˌ./ *n.* [C] **1** a hidden bomb that explodes when you touch something else that is connected to it **2** a trap that you arrange for someone as a joke —**booby-trapped** *adj.*: *a booby-trapped car*

boog·er /ˈbʊgɚ/ *n.* [C] SPOKEN **1** a thick piece of MUCUS from your nose **2** someone who annoys you or causes trouble for you: *Ben took my magazine home with him – the little booger!*

boog·ey·man /ˈbʊgiˌmæn/ *n.* [C] a BOGEYMAN

boog·ie¹ /ˈbʊgi/ *v.* [I] **1** INFORMAL to dance, especially to fast popular music: *Dance fans can boogie at Club Oasis and Paradise Beach.* **2** SLANG to go somewhere or do something quickly: *I've got to boogie – see you later.*

B

boogie² *n.* [U] BOOGIE WOOGIE

boogie board /ˈ.. ˌ./ *n.* [C] an object that you lie on to ride on ocean waves, that is half the length of a SURFBOARD —**boogie-boarder** *n.* [C] —**boogie-boarding** *n.* [U]

boog·ie·man /ˈbʊgiˌmæn/ *n.* [C] a BOGEYMAN

boogie woog·ie /ˌbʊgi ˈwʊgi/ *n.* [U] a type of music played on the piano with a strong fast RHYTHM (1)

boo hoo /ˈbu hu/ *interjection* used especially in children's stories or as a joke to show that someone is crying

book¹ /bʊk/ *n.* [C]   S W
1 1

1 printed pages a set of printed pages that are held together in a cover so that you can read them: *Have you read this book?* | [+ about/on] *a book about plants* | *Eric's reading a book by William Faulkner.* | *It's a pretty good book.*

2 to write in a set of sheets of paper held together in a cover so that you can write on them: *an address book*

3 books [plural] **a)** written records of the financial accounts of a business: *We saw their books, and they've lost $29 million this year.* | *For the past 6 months I've been working off the books* (=without the organization keeping written records, so you do not have to pay tax). **b)** the names of the people who use a company's services, or who are employed by a company: *We have over 100 VDU operators on our books* (=employed by our company) *at the moment.*

4 on the books a law that is on books of a particular city, area, or country, is part of the set of laws that are used to govern that place: *Canada has had gun control legislation on the books since 1978.*

5 set of things a set of things such as stamps, matches, or tickets, held together inside a paper cover: *a book of matches*

6 by the book exactly according to rules or instructions: *Rules are not to be broken – Barb does everything by the book.*

7 be in sb's good books SPOKEN used to say that someone likes or approves of someone else, especially when they often change their opinion about people: *I think I'm back in Corinne's good books again.*

8 in my book SPOKEN said when giving your opinion: *Well, in my book, if you steal, you deserve to get caught.*

9 part of a book one of the parts that a very large book such as the Bible is divided into: [+ of] *the Book of Genesis*

10 bring sb to book (for sth) to punish someone for breaking laws or rules, especially when you have been trying to punish them for a long time: *The brothers were finally brought to book for running illegal dog fights.* —see also **cook the books** (COOK¹ (5)), **one for the books** (ONE² (19)), **read sb like a book** (READ¹ (11)), STATUTE BOOK, **throw the book at sb** (THROW⁴ (25))

book² *v.* **1** [I,T] to arrange to stay in a place, eat in a   S W
3
restaurant etc. at a particular time in the future, or buy a ticket for a flight, performance etc. in the future: *I booked a table for two at 8:00.* | *You'll have to book by tomorrow if you want the lower price.* | *There are no tickets at the door – you have to book in advance* (=buy tickets before the event). | *I'm sorry sir, we're fully booked* (=there are no rooms, tables etc. available) *for the 14th.* | *a heavily booked flight* | *Classes are booked solid* (=completely full), *with many students unable to get the courses they need.* **2 be booked up a)** if a hotel, restaurant etc. is booked up, there are no more rooms or tables left **b)** if someone is booked up, they are extremely busy and do not have time to do anything new: *I'm all booked up this week, but I can see you on Monday.* **3** [T] to arrange for someone such as a speaker or singer to perform on a particular date: *Nelson was booked for a tour of Japan in August.* **4** [T] to put someone's name officially in police records, along with the charge made against them: *Dawkins was booked on suspicion of attempted murder.* **5** [I] SLANG

to go somewhere or do something fast: *Now, on Montana highways, you can really book.*

book sb into sth *phr. v.* [T] to arrange for someone to stay at a hotel: *We've booked you into the Sheraton. Is that all right?*

book sb on sth *phr. v.* [T] to arrange for someone to travel on a particular airplane, train etc.: *Could you book me on the next flight to Dallas?*

book·bind·ing /'buk,baɪndɪŋ/ *n.* [U] the art of fastening the pages of books inside a cover —**bookbinder** *n.* [C]

book·case /'buk-keɪs/ *n.* [C] a piece of furniture with shelves to hold books

book club /'. ./ *n.* [C] **1** a group of people who meet regularly to discuss books they have read **2** a club that offers books cheaply to its members

book·end¹ /'bukɛnd/ *n.* [C usually plural] one of a pair of objects that you put at each end of a row of books to prevent them from falling over

bookend² *v.* [T] if two similar things bookend something such as an event, performance, movie etc., they come at the beginning and the end of it: *The best parts are the two Reed songs that bookend the CD.*

book·ie /'buki/ *n.* [C] INFORMAL someone whose job is to collect money that people want to risk on the result of a race, competition etc., and who pays them if they guess correctly

book·ing /'bukɪŋ/ *n.* [C] **1** an arrangement in which a hotel, theater, AIRLINE etc. agrees to let you use a particular room, seat etc. at a particular time in the future: *Cheaper prices are available on early bookings.* | *We **canceled** our **booking** on the cruise and got a full refund.* **2** an arrangement made by a performer to perform at a particular place and time in the future

book·ish /'bukɪʃ/ *adj.* **1** someone who is bookish is more interested in reading and studying than in sports or other activities: *Bill was the studious, bookish type.* **2** seeming to come from books rather than from real experience: *bookish language*

book·keep·ing /'buk,kipɪŋ/ *n.* [U] the job or activity of recording the financial accounts of a company or organization —**bookkeeper** *n.* [C]

book·let /'buklɪt/ *n.* [C] a very short book that usually contains information: *a booklet on AIDS*

book·mak·er /'buk,meɪkɚ/ *n.* [C] a BOOKIE

book·mark /'bukmark/ *n.* [C] **1** a piece of paper, leather etc. that you put in a book to show you the last page you have read **2** TECHNICAL a way of marking a particular place on the Internet so that you can find it again quickly, by putting it on a list on your computer screen —**bookmark** *v.* [T]

book·mo·bile /'bukmoʊ,bil/ *n.* [C] a vehicle that contains a library and travels to different places so that people can use it

book·plate /'bukpleɪt/ *n.* [C] a decorated piece of paper with your name on it, that you stick in the front of your books

book re·port /'. ,./ *n.* [C] a report that children write at school, in which they describe a book they have read and give their opinion about it

book·rest /'buk-rɛst/ *n.* [C] a frame that holds a book upright so that you can read it without holding it in your hands

book·sell·er /'buksɛlɚ/ *n.* [C] a person or company that sells books

book·shelf /'bukʃɛlf/ *n. plural* **bookshelves** /-ʃɛlvz/ [C] a shelf on a wall, or a piece of furniture with shelves, used for holding books —see picture on page 426

book·sign·ing /'buk,saɪnɪŋ/ *n.* [C] an event where the AUTHOR of a book agrees to sign copies of the book for people who buy it, especially as a way to sell more books

book·stall /'bukstɔl/ *n.* [C] a small store on a street that has an open front and sells books

book·store /'bukstɔr/ *n.* [C] a store that sells books —compare LIBRARY —see picture at LIBRARY

book tour /'. ./ *n.* [C] a trip someone makes to advertise a book they have written

book val·ue /'. ,./ *n.* [C] **1** the value of a business after you sell all of its ASSETS (1) and pay all of its debts **2** how much something such as a car should be worth if it were sold —see also BLUE BOOK (1)

book·worm /'bukwɚm/ *n.* [C] **1** someone who likes reading very much **2** an insect that eats paper

boom¹ /bum/ *n.*
1 increase in business [singular] a rapid increase of business activity: [+ in] *a boom in new car sales* | *the post-war property boom* | **boom times/years** (=when profits are being made) —see also BOOM TOWN
2 when sth is popular [singular] a period when something suddenly becomes very popular or starts happening a lot: *The fitness boom started in the 1970s.*
3 sound [C] a deep loud sound that you can hear for several seconds after it begins, especially the sound of an explosion or a large gun: *Witnesses heard the first loud boom at 3:03 p.m.* —see also SONIC BOOM
4 long pole [C] **a)** a long pole on a boat that is attached to a sail at the bottom **b)** a long pole used as part of a piece of equipment that loads and unloads things **c)** a long pole that has a camera or MICROPHONE on the end
5 on a river [C] something that is stretched across a river or a BAY (1) to prevent things floating down or across it: *a log boom* —see also BABY BOOM

boom² *v.* **1** [I usually in progressive] if business, trade, or a particular area is booming, it is very successful: *We're happy to report that business is booming this year.* **2** [I] also **boom out** to make a loud deep sound: *Guns boomed in the distance.* **3** [T] also **boom out** to say something in a loud deep voice —**booming** *adj.*: *a booming economy*

boom box /'. ,./ *n.* [C] INFORMAL a large radio and TAPE DECK that you can carry around

boom·er /'bumɚ/ *n.* [C] INFORMAL a BABY BOOMER

boo·mer·ang¹ /'bumə,ræŋ/ *n.* [C] a curved stick that flies in a circle and comes back to you when you throw it

boomerang² *v.* [I] also **boomerang on sb** if a plan or action boomerangs on someone, it affects them badly instead of affecting the person who it was intended to affect: *Developing a close relationship with your students can boomerang – you may lose their respect.*

boom town /'. ,./ *n.* INFORMAL [C] a town or city that suddenly becomes very successful because there is a lot of new industry

boon /bun/ *n.* [C usually singular] something that is very useful and makes your life a lot easier or helps you make more money: [+ to/for] *"Mergers among the big banks have been a boon for our business," said Thompson.*

boon com·pan·ion /, .'. ./ *n.* [C] LITERARY a very close friend

boon·docks /'bundɑks/ *n.* INFORMAL **the boondocks** a place that is a long way from the nearest town: *Myra lives way out in the boondocks.*

boon·dog·gle /'bun,dɑgəl/ *n.* [singular] INFORMAL an official plan or activity that is very complicated and wastes a lot of time, money, and effort: *Republicans called the plan a boondoggle and a drain on federal highway funds.*

Boone /bun/, **Daniel** (1734–1820) one of the first white Americans to go to Kentucky

boon·ies /'buniz/ *n.* **the boonies** SPOKEN the BOONDOCKS

boor /bur/ *n.* [C] a man who behaves in a very rude way —**boorish** *adj.*: *boorish behavior* —**boorishly** *adv.*

boost¹ /bust/ *v.* **1** [T] to increase or improve something or make it more successful, especially because it is not as good or successful as it should be: *Perhaps year-round education would boost student performance.* | *The goal is to boost business for Zegna merchandise.* | **boost sb's confidence/morale/ego** *Free phone calls to home can help to boost the troops'* *morale*. **2** [T] also **boost sb up** to help someone reach a higher place by lifting or pushing them: *I boosted the kid up so he could reach the branch.* **3** [I,T] SLANG to steal something **4** [T] if a ROCKET or motor boosts a SPACECRAFT, it makes it go up into space or go in a particular direction

boost² *n.* [C usually singular] **1** something that gives someone more confidence, or that helps make an improvement or increase in something: *Some women may need an extra boost from vitamins.* | [+ for] *To win two games in a row is a big boost for this team.* | *These tax breaks have given the auto industry a tremendous boost.* | [+ in] *a boost in oil prices* **2** a lift or push that helps someone reach a higher place: *I can't reach the top shelf – can you give me a boost?*

boost·er /'bustə/ *n.* [C] **1** a small quantity of a drug that increases the effect of one that was given before, so that someone continues to be protected against a disease **2 confidence/ego/morale etc. booster** something that helps someone be more confident or less worried **3** someone who gives a lot of support to a person, organization, or an idea: *the Kennedy High School Booster Club* **4** a ROCKET¹ (1) that is used to provide additional power for a SPACECRAFT to leave the Earth

booster seat /'.. ./ *n.* [C] a special seat for a small child that lets them sit in a higher position in a car or at a table

boot¹ /but/ *n.* **1** [C] a type of shoe that covers your whole foot and the lower part of your leg: *a pair of hiking boots* **2 to boot** INFORMAL in addition to everything else you have mentioned: *The Corrado is a car that's small, quick, and stylish to boot.* **3 get the boot** INFORMAL to be forced to leave your job **4 give sb the boot** INFORMAL to dismiss someone from their job; FIRE² (1) **5** [C] a DENVER BOOT **6** [C] BRITISH a TRUNK (2) —see also **be/get too big for your boots** (BIG (18)), **lick sb's boots** (LICK¹ (6))

boot² *v.* **1** [I,T] also **boot up** TECHNICAL to start the PROGRAM that makes a computer ready to be used, before anything else can be done on the machine **2** [T] INFORMAL to force someone to leave a place, job, organization etc., especially because they have done something wrong: *If the usher caught you throwing popcorn, you were booted out of the theater.* **3** [T] INFORMAL to kick someone or something hard: *Jaeger booted a 37-yard field goal for the winning points.* **4** [T] to stop someone from moving their illegally parked vehicle by attaching a piece of equipment to one of its wheels

boot camp /'. ./ *n.* [C] a training camp for people who have just joined the Army, Navy, or Marine Corps

boot cut /'. ./ *adj.* boot cut pants are wide at the bottom so you can wear boots with them

booth /buθ/ *n.* [C] **1** a small partly enclosed place where one person can do something privately, such as use the telephone or vote: *a phone booth* | *a ticket booth* **2** a partly enclosed place in a restaurant with a table between two long seats **3** a small enclosed structure where you can buy things, play games, or find out information, usually at a FAIR² (1)

Booth /buθ/**, John Wilkes** /dʒɑn wɪlks/ (1838–1865) the man who shot and killed U.S. President Abraham Lincoln

boo·tie, bootee /'buti/ *n.* [C] a short thick sock that a baby wears instead of a shoe

boot·lace /'butleɪs/ *n.* [C usually plural] a long piece of string that you use to fasten a boot

boot·leg¹ /'butleg/ *adj.* [only before noun] bootleg products, such as alcohol or RECORDINGS, are made and sold illegally: *Police seized 30,000 bootleg tapes in a raid last night in Brooklyn.*

bootleg² *n.* [C] an illegal recording of a music performance, piece of computer SOFTWARE etc.

boot·leg·ging /'butlegɪŋ/ *n.* [U] illegally making or selling products such as alcohol or RECORDINGS —**bootlegger** *n.* [C] —**bootleg** *v.* [I,T]

boot·lick·ing /'butlɪkɪŋ/ *n.* [U] INFORMAL behavior that is too friendly to someone in a position of

authority, in order to get advantages for yourself —**bootlicker** *n.* [C] —**bootlicking** *adj.*

boot·straps /'butstræps/ *n.* [plural] **pull yourself up by your bootstraps** to improve your position and get out of a difficult situation by your own effort, without help from other people: *Davies believes that with support from family and friends, it is possible to pull yourself up by your bootstraps.*

boo·ty /'buti/ *n.* **1** [U] LITERARY valuable things that a group of people, especially an army that has just won a victory, take away or steal from somewhere **2** [C] SLANG the part of your body that you sit on; BOTTOM¹ (7) —see also **shake your booty** (SHAKE¹ (15))

booze¹ /buz/ *n.* [U] INFORMAL alcoholic drink: *a bottle of cheap booze*

booze² *v.* [I] INFORMAL to drink alcohol, especially a lot of it: *"The Champ" is a drama about a boozing fighter and his devoted son.*

booz·er /'buzə/ *n.* [C] INFORMAL someone who often drinks a lot of alcohol

booz·y /'buzi/ *adj.* showing signs that someone has drunk too much alcohol: *boozy laughter*

bop¹ /bɑp/ *v.* **bopped, bopping** INFORMAL **1** [T] to hit someone, especially gently: *I just bopped her on the head with the handbag.* **2** [I always + adv./prep.] INFORMAL to go somewhere: *We were bopping around town, doing some shopping.* **3** [I] to dance, especially to BEBOP music

bop² *n.* **1** [C] a gentle hit **2** [singular] another word for BEBOP

bo·rax /'bɔræks/ *n.* [U] a mineral used for cleaning things

Bor·deaux /bɔr'doʊ/ a city in southwest France

bor·del·lo /bɔr'dɛloʊ/ *n. plural* **bordellos** [C] LITERARY a BROTHEL

bor·der¹ /'bɔrdə/ *n.* [C] **1** the official line that separates two countries, states, or areas, or the area close to this line: [+ between] *the border between the U.S. and Canada* | [+ with] *Chile's border with Peru* | *It's a national park on the Utah border.* | *Refugees have been warned not to attempt to cross the border.* **2** a band along or around the edge of something, such as a picture or a piece of material: *a skirt with a red border* **3** an area of soil where you plant flowers or plants at the edge of an area of grass

border² *v.* [T] **1** if one area borders another area, it is next to it and shares a border with it: *Azerbaijan borders the Caspian Sea.* **2** to form a border along the edge of something: *Willow trees bordered the river.*

border on sth *phr. v.* [T] to be very close to reaching an extreme feeling or quality: *At first, Sandra thought her sister was bordering on insanity.*

bor·der·land /'bɔrdəˌlænd/ *n.* [singular] **1** the land near the border between two areas **2** a BORDERLINE² (1)

bor·der·line¹ /'bɔrdəˌlaɪn/ *adj.* **1** something that is borderline is very close to being unacceptable: *Caitlin's grades are borderline. She'll have to work harder.* **2** used to describe a person whose skills or qualities may or may not be acceptable: *a borderline student* | *Lower rates can help some borderline borrowers qualify for loans.* **3** [only before noun] borderline situations, statements, actions etc. have most of the qualities of another more extreme or worse situation, statement etc.: *Johnson's arguments range from ridiculous to borderline slander.* | **borderline anorexia/schizophrenia etc.** (=behavior with many or most of the signs of a particular psychological condition)

borderline² *n.* **1** [singular] the point at which one quality, condition, situation, emotion etc. ends and another begins: *the borderline between affection and love* | *We're on the borderline of having to ration water.* **2** [C] a BORDER² (1)

borderline³ *adv.* [only before adjectives] INFORMAL almost; PRACTICALLY: *The new sitcom is rude, insulting to viewers, and borderline immoral.*

bore¹ /bɔr/ v. **1** [T] to make someone feel bored: *Poetry bores me.* | [**bore sb with sth**] *Angela's always boring us with her stories about her family.* | **bore sb to death/tears** (=make someone extremely bored) **2** [I,T] to make a deep round hole in a hard surface: [**+ through/into**] *The drill is powerful enough to bore through solid rock.*

bore into sb *phr. v.* [T] if someone's eyes bore into you, they look at you in a way that makes you feel uncomfortable

bore² n. **1** [C] someone who makes other people feel bored, especially because they talk too much about something: *Winston is such a bore!* | **a theater/photography/science etc. bore** (=someone who talks too much about a particular subject) **2** [singular] a situation or a job you have to do that is not interesting to you: *Washing the dishes is a bore.* **3** [singular] the measurement of the size of the inside of a hole or hollow round object, especially a gun BARREL¹ (3): *a 12-bore shotgun* **4** [C] a borehole

bore³ v. the past tense of BEAR¹

bored /bɔrd/ adj. tired and impatient because you do not think something is interesting, or because you have nothing to do: *Mom, I'm bored!* | [**+ with**] *I don't know why he quit – I guess he was just bored with his job.* | *Anna looks **bored to tears** (=extremely bored).* | *Can't we do something else? I'm **bored stiff** (=extremely bored).* —see Usage Note at ADJECTIVE —see picture at BORING

bore·dom /'bɔrdəm/ n. [U] the feeling you have when you are bored: *I get more tired from boredom than from work.*

bore·hole /'bɔrhoul/ n. [C] a deep hole made using special equipment, especially in order to get water or oil out of the ground

Borg /bɔrg/, **Björn** /byɔrn/ (1956–) a Swedish tennis player who won the men's SINGLES competition every year from 1976 to 1980

Bor·ges /'bɔrhɛs/, **Jor·ge Lu·is** /'hɔrheɪ lu'is/ (1899–1986) an Argentinian poet and writer of short stories

Bor·gia /'bɔrdʒəz/, **the** a powerful wealthy Italian family in the 15th and early 16th centuries, known for their cruel determination to gain political power, including Lucrezia Borgia (1480–1519) and her brother Cesare Borgia (1476–1507), who was a successful soldier and ruler, and the Prince in Machiavelli's book "The Prince" is based on him

Bor·glum /'bɔrgləm/, **Gut·zon** /'gʌtsən/ (1867–1941) a U.S. SCULPTOR famous for his very large SCULPTURE of the heads of four U.S. Presidents on Mount Rushmore in South Dakota

boring

The teacher/lecture is boring. The students are bored.

bor·ing /'bɔrɪŋ/ adj. not interesting in any way: *The movie was boring.* | *He really is one of the most boring people I've ever met.* —opposite INTERESTING —see Usage Note at ADJECTIVE

born /bɔrn/ adj. **1 be born a)** when a person or animal is born, they come out of their mother's body or out of an egg: *Hey Mom, where were you born?* | [**+ in**] *Neil was born in Brooklyn, right?* | *Melissa was born in 1968.* | [**+ at**] *Were you born at home or in the hospital?* | [**+ on**] *Their daughter was born on June 7.* | [**+ with**] *Jenny was born with heart problems* (=she has had them since she was born). | [**+ to**] *More babies are being born to older parents* (=these are the people who are the parents). | *I was **born and raised** in Alabama* (=I grew up there). | **be born into wealth/poverty etc.** (=be born in a particular situation or type of family) | **be born blind/deaf etc.** (=be blind, deaf etc. when you were born) | **be born lucky/unlucky/free etc.** (=be lucky, unlucky etc. for your whole life) | **be born out of wedlock** (=be born to parents who are not married) **b)** when something is born, it starts to exist: *How a planet is born is a question that has only been partially answered.* **2 be born to do/be sth** to be very suitable for a particular job, activity etc.: *Jim was born to be a politician.* **3 a born leader/teacher/musician etc.** someone who has a strong natural ability to lead, teach etc.: *Lee is a born salesman with a New York accent.* **4 a born loser** someone who always seems to have bad things happen to them **5 sth is born (out) of sth** used to say that something exists as a result of a particular situation: *Labor unions were born out of a need for better working conditions.* **6 born and bred** born and having grown up in a particular place and having the typical qualities of someone from that place: *Meyer's a Texan, born and bred.* **7 be born with a silver spoon in your mouth** to be born into a rich family **8 be born under a lucky/unlucky star** to always have good or bad luck in your life

---

SPOKEN PHRASES

9 I wasn't born yesterday used to tell someone whom you think is lying to you that you are not stupid enough to believe them **10 there's one born every minute** used to say that someone has been very stupid or easily tricked **11 in all my born days** OLD-FASHIONED used to express surprise or annoyance at something that you have never heard about before: *Well, I've never heard of such a thing in all my born days!*

-born /bɔrn/ [in adjectives] **Australian-born/Moroccan-born/Canadian-born etc.** born in a particular country: *an Egyptian-born businessman*

born-a·gain /'. .,./ adj. **1 a born-again Christian** someone who has chosen to become an EVANGELICAL Christian **2 a born-again non-smoker/vegetarian etc.** INFORMAL someone who has recently stopped smoking, eating meat etc., and who keeps encouraging other people to do the same

borne¹ /bɔrn/ v. the past participle of BEAR¹

borne² adj. **be borne in on/upon sb** LITERARY if a fact is borne in on someone, they realize that it is true

-borne /bɔrn/ [in adjectives] **water-borne/air-borne/wind-borne etc.** carried by water, air etc.: *a blood-borne disease*

Bor·ne·o /'bɔrniou/ the largest island of the Malay Archipelago in southeast Asia. Part of it belongs to Malaysia and part of it to Indonesia, and it also includes the Sultanate of Brunei

bor·ough /'bɛrou, 'bʌrou/ n. [C] a town or part of a large city that is responsible for managing its own schools, hospitals, roads etc.: *the borough of Brooklyn in New York City*

bor·row /'bɛrou, 'bɔrou/ v. [I,T] **1** to use something that belongs to someone else and give it back to them later: *Can I borrow your car for the weekend?* | [**borrow sth from sb**] *Did you borrow those tools from your dad?* | *Many companies had **borrowed heavily** (=borrowed a lot of money) to cover their losses.* —compare LEND, LOAN² —see picture at LEND **2** to take or copy someone's ideas, words etc. and use them in your own work, language etc.: *Rogers discovered that his own humor worked better than jokes borrowed from other writers.* | [**+ from**] *English borrows words from many languages.* **3 borrow trouble** INFORMAL to worry about something when it is not necessary to do this —see also **be living on borrowed time** (LIVE[1] (19)) —see Usage Note at LEND

B

USAGE NOTE: BORROW

WORD CHOICE: borrow, lend, loan, rent, let someone use

You **borrow** something **from** another person who is willing to **lend** it to you: *Ben borrowed Ginger's bike for a couple of weeks.* | *I can lend the book to you if you want.* In less formal English, you can use **loan** instead of **lend**, especially when talking about money: *Actually, I loaned him ninety dollars.* If you **borrow** money you have to pay it back later, and you may have to pay for the use of it too, if you have borrowed it from a bank. If you **borrow** a car, a book etc., you give it back afterward, but you do not pay to use it. If you do pay to use it, you **rent** it: *Thanks for letting me borrow your car.* | *When do we have to return those videos we rented?* **Borrow**, **lend**, and **loan** are not used about large things that cannot be moved, such as rooms, houses etc., or about things that need to stay where they are, such as phones. If you pay for using this type of thing, you **rent** it. If you do not pay, someone **lets** you **use** it: *We've rented a summer place near Cape Cod.* | *The neighbors let us use their pool sometimes.*

---

bor·row·er /ˈbɑroʊɚ/ *n.* [C] someone who is borrowing money: *The bank is asking borrowers to repay their loans.*

bor·row·ing /ˈbɑroʊɪŋ/ *n.* **1** [plural,U] the activity of borrowing money, or the total amount of money that is borrowed: *Congress is likely to limit any more federal borrowing.* | *The Japanese company has invested its borrowings in government bonds.* **2** [C usually plural] something such as a word, phrase, or idea that has been copied from another language, book etc.: [+ from] *The work is original except for the borrowings from Archimedes.*

borrowing pow·ers /ˈ... ˌ.../ *n.* [plural] the amount of money that a company is allowed to borrow, according to its own rules

borscht /bɔrʃt/ *n.* [U] a soup made with BEETS, that you eat hot or cold

borscht belt /ˈ. ./ *n.* **the borscht belt** INFORMAL the vacation area in the Catskill Mountains with a lot of hotels that are used mainly by Jewish people

Bosch /bɑʃ/**, Hie·ron·y·mus** /ˌhaɪəˈrɑnɪməs/ (?1460–1516) a Flemish painter famous for his religious paintings showing strange and unnatural creatures and situations

bosh /bɑʃ/ *n.* [U] OLD-FASHIONED something that you do not believe or that does not make any sense —**bosh** *interjection*

Bos·ni·a /ˈbɑzniə/ also **Bosnia-Her·ze·go·vi·na** /-ˌhɛrtsəgoʊˈvinə/ a country in eastern Europe between Croatia and the Federal Republic of Yugoslavia. It was formerly a part of Yugoslavia —**Bosnian** *n., adj.*

bos·om /ˈbʊzəm/ *n.* **1** [C] OLD-FASHIONED a woman's breast or breasts **2 a bosom buddy/friend** a very close friend: *The late Malcolm Forbes was a bosom buddy of Elizabeth Taylor.* **3** [singular] LITERARY someone's chest, or the part of a piece of clothing that covers it **4 the bosom of the family/Church etc.** a situation in which you feel safe because you are with people who love and protect you **5** [singular] LITERARY a word meaning someone's feelings and emotions, used especially when these are bad: *Daniel harbored bitterness and anger in his bosom.*

bos·om·y /ˈbʊzəmi/ *adj.* INFORMAL having large breasts

Bos·po·rus /ˈbɑspərəs/ also **the Bos·pho·rus** /ˈbɑsfərəs/ the narrow sea between the European and Asian parts of Turkey, connecting the Black Sea with the Sea of Marmara

boss[1] /bɔs/ *n.* [C] **1** the person who employs you or who is in charge of you at work: *Can you ask your boss if she'll let you leave early today?* | *I've always wanted to **be my own boss** (=work for myself rather than be employed by someone else).* **2** INFORMAL someone with an important position in a company or other organization | **a party/political/union boss** *Since then, party bosses no longer choose the presidential candidates.* | **a crime/drug/mafia boss** *The alleged drug boss was shot through an open hospital window last night.* **3** the person who is the strongest in a relationship, who controls a situation etc.: *With these kids, you just have to **let them know who's boss** (=make sure you are in control).* **4** a round decoration on the surface of something such as the ceiling of an old building

boss[2] *v.* [T] also **boss sb around** to tell people to do things, give them orders etc., especially when you have no authority to do it: *Stop bossing me around!*

boss[3] *adj.* SLANG very attractive or fashionable: *That's a really boss surfboard.*

bos·sa no·va /ˌbɑsə ˈnoʊvə/ *n.* [C,U] a dance that comes from Brazil, or the music for this dance

boss·y /ˈbɔsi/ *adj.* **bossier, bossiest** always telling other people what to do in a way that is annoying: *Kevin's mother is really bossy.* —**bossily** *adv.* —**bossiness** *n.* [U]

Bos·ton /ˈbɔstən/ the capital city of the U.S. state of Massachusetts

bo·sun /ˈboʊsən/ *n.* [C] another spelling of BOATSWAIN

Bos·well /ˈbɑzwɛl/**, James** (1740–1795) a Scottish writer, famous for his book about the life of Samuel Johnson

bo·tan·i·cal /bəˈtænɪkəl/ *adj.* [only before noun] relating to plants or the scientific study of plants —**botanically** /-kli/ *adv.*

botanical gar·den /.ˌ... ˈ.../ *n.* [C] a large public garden where many different types of flowers and plants are grown for scientific study

bot·a·nist /ˈbɑtˈnɪst/ *n.* [C] someone whose job is to make scientific studies of wild plants

bot·a·ny /ˈbɑtˈn-i/ *n.* [U] the scientific study of plants

Bot·a·ny Bay /ˈbɑtˈn-i ˌ./ a BAY on the southeast coast of Australia, close to Sydney

botch[1] /bɑtʃ/ *v.* [T] INFORMAL also **botch up** to do something badly, because you have been careless or because you do not have the skill to do it well: *Defense lawyers are arguing that the police botched the investigation.* —**botcher** *n.* [C]

botch[2] *n.* [C] INFORMAL a piece of work, a job etc. that has been badly or carelessly done

both[1] /boʊθ/ *quantifier pron.* **1** used to talk about two people, things, situations etc. together: *They both went to Harvard.* | *Hold it in both hands.* | *Both the girls play the piano.* | *I'd like to try a little of both.* | [+ of] *Both of my grandfathers are farmers.* **2 you can't have it both ways** SPOKEN used to say that you cannot have the advantages from both of two possible situations: *It's either me or her. You can't have it both ways!* —see Usage Note at EACH[1]

both[2] *conjunction* **both...and...** used to emphasize that not just one person, thing, situation etc. is included in a statement, but also another: *Donny plays both football and baseball.* | *Both he and his wife enjoy tennis.* | *Jane's kids are both rude and spoiled.*

both·er[1] /ˈbɑðɚ/ *v.*
1 annoy [T] to annoy someone, especially by interrupting them when they are trying to do something: *"Why didn't you ask me for help?" "I didn't want to bother you."* | *Don't bother Ellen while she's reading.* | *Will it bother you if I play some music?*
2 worry [I,T] to make someone feel slightly worried or upset: *Something's bothering him but I'm not sure what.* | [bother sb with sth] *I don't want to bother you with my problems.* | [it bothers sb that] *It bothers me that he hasn't been telling me the truth.*
3 make an effort [I,T] to make the effort to do something: [not bother doing sth] *I'm not even going to bother studying.* | [not bother to do sth] *All my kids are gone and they don't even bother to write to me.* | [not bother with sth] *I don't think I'll bother with the coffee just yet.* | *"Do you want me to wait for you?" "No, please don't bother."* | *I tried to defend her but why bother? There's no point.* |

[**+ about**] *U.S. officials no longer bother about diplomatic politeness.*

4 sorry to bother you SPOKEN used as a very polite way of saying that you are sorry for interrupting someone when you want their attention: *Art, it's Lisa again – sorry to keep bothering you.*

5 `cause pain` [T] if a part of your body bothers you, it is painful or uncomfortable: *Actually, my back hasn't been bothering me.*

6 `frighten` [T only in progressive] to upset or frighten someone by continuously trying to hurt them, touch them sexually etc.: *Excuse me, Miss, is that man bothering you?*

7 sb can't be bothered (to do sth) used to say that someone thinks it is not worth the effort to do something: *See, they can't even plow snow right. They can't be bothered.*

bother² *n.* **1** [C] something or someone that slightly annoys or upsets you because of the trouble or problems they cause: *I hate to be a bother, but could I use your phone?* **2** [U] used in some expressions instead of the word "trouble" | **go to the bother of doing sth** (=make an effort to do something) | **sth is more bother than it's worth** (=something is too difficult to be worth doing) **3 (it's) no bother** SPOKEN used to say that you are not annoyed or that something does not cause you any problems: *"Sorry to bother you all." "That's okay, no bother."*

both·ered /ˈbɑðə·d/ *adj.* [not before noun] worried or upset: *Nobody seemed bothered that Grandpa wasn't there.* —see also **be hot and bothered** (HOT (34))

both·er·some /ˈbɑðə·səm/ *adj.* slightly annoying: *bothersome insects* | *a bothersome delay*

Bot·swa·na /bɑts'wɑnə/ a country in central southern Africa —**Botswanan** *adj.*

Bot·ti·cel·li /ˌbɑtɪˈtʃɛli/, **San·dro** /ˈsɑndroʊ/ (?1444–1510) an Italian PAINTER famous for his paintings based on Greek MYTHOLOGY

bottles

wine bottle

a bottle of pills

baby bottle

beer bottle

bot·tle¹ /ˈbɑtl/ *n.* [C] **1** a container with a narrow top for keeping liquids in, usually made of glass or plastic: *an empty wine bottle* | [**+ of**] *a bottle of shampoo* **2** also **bottleful** the amount of liquid that a bottle contains: *I only want one glass, not a whole bottle.* | *Egon managed to drink half a bottle of schnapps that night.* **3** a container for babies to drink from, with a rubber part on top that they suck on: *Do you want me to give Kayla her bottle?* **4 the bottle** a word meaning "alcoholic drink," usually used when talking about the problems that drinking can cause: *Peter let the bottle ruin his life.* | *After Sheila left him, Judd hit the bottle* (=started drinking a lot of alcohol regularly) *pretty hard.* —see also **bring your own bottle** (BRING (20))

bottle² *v.* [T] to put a liquid, especially wine or beer, into a bottle after you have made it: *wine bottled in Oregon* —see also BOTTLER

bottle sth ↔ up *phr. v.* [T] **1** to deliberately not allow yourself to show a strong feeling or emotion: *You bottle all your feelings up inside you – it's not good for you.* **2** to cause problems by delaying something: *The group hopes to bottle up the bill in Congress, so that it doesn't get to the President's desk to be signed.*

bottle cap /ˈ.. ˌ./ *n.* [C] a small metal lid on a bottle

bottled /ˈbɑtld/ *adj.* **bottled water/beer etc.** water, beer etc. that is sold in a bottle

bottle-feed /ˈ.. ˌ./ *v. past tense and past participle* **bottle-fed** [T] to feed a baby with milk from a bottle rather than from their mother's breast —**bottle-feeding** *n.* [U] —**bottle-fed** *adj.*

bottle green /ˌ.. ˈ. ◂/ *n.* [U] a very dark green color —**bottle green** *adj.*

bottleneck

bot·tle·neck /ˈbɑtlˌnɛk/ *n.* [C] **1** a place in a road where the traffic cannot pass easily, so that there are a lot of delays **2** a delay in one stage of a process that makes the whole process take longer: *Automatic packing machines should get rid of the bottlenecks in the process.*

bottle o·pen·er /ˈ.. ˌ.../ *n.* [C] a small tool used for removing the metal lids from bottles

bot·tler /ˈbɑtl-ə, ˈbɑtlə/ *n.* [C] a person or company that puts drinks into bottles or cans —**bottling** *n.* [U]

bottle rock·et /ˈ.. ˌ./ *n.* [C] a type of FIREWORK that you shoot from a bottle

bot·tom¹ /ˈbɑtəm/ *n.*
1 `lowest part` [C usually singular] the lowest part of something: [**+ of**] *Will you hold the bottom of this ladder for me?* | *At the bottom of the hill there was a dip in the road.* | *The answers are on the bottom of page 95.* | *They've got baggy pants with ripped bottoms.* | *Get me the books on that shelf second from the bottom* (=one shelf up from the bottom shelf). —opposite TOP¹

2 `lowest side` [C usually singular] the flat surface on the lowest side of an object: [**+ of**] *Something's hanging from the bottom of your car.* | *Oops, these plates are hot on the bottom.* | *What's that on the bottom of your shoe?*

3 `lowest inner part` [C usually singular] the lowest inner part of something such as a container: [**+ of**] *the bottom of a well* | *Spread the tomato sauce on the bottom of a large dish.* | *Heavy objects should be packed in the bottom of your suitcase.*

4 `lowest position` **the bottom** the lowest position in an organization or company, or on a list: *The Giants are at the bottom of the league.* | *Ben finally found his name at the very bottom of the list.* | *Watson is willing to start at the bottom* (=in a low position in a company) *and work his way up.* | **the bottom of the ladder/pile/barrel/heap** (=the lowest position in society, an organization etc.) —opposite **the top** (TOP¹)

5 `ocean/river` [C usually singular] the ground under an ocean, river etc., or the flat land in a valley: *the ocean bottom* | [**+ of**] *The bottom of the*

river is rocky. | *Frogs can stay all winter **at the bottom of** a pond.*
6 from the bottom up beginning by dealing with the most basic parts of something or with the people who have the least power: *Let's all prove that government will work from the bottom up.*
7 body [C] a word meaning BUTTOCKS (=the part of your body that you sit on), used especially when speaking to children: *Did you fall on your bottom?*
8 clothes [C usually plural] the part of a set of clothes that you wear on the lower part of your body: *pajama bottoms* —opposite TOP[1]
9 get to the bottom of sth INFORMAL to find out the cause of a problem or situation: *We're trying to get to the bottom of this, and see if she is lying.*
10 be at the bottom of the list to not be at all important to someone: *Surprisingly, safety was at the bottom of the list for airline passengers.*
11 the bottom of the first/fifth/ninth etc. (inning) the second half of an INNING in baseball: *The Blue Jays scored two runs in the bottom of the sixth inning.* —opposite TOP[1]
12 from the bottom of your heart used to show that you are very sincere about what you are saying: *Thank you, from the bottom of my heart.*
13 the bottom drops out (of the market) used to say that people suddenly stop buying a particular product: *The copper mines operated from 1911 until 1938, when the bottom dropped out of the market.*
14 bottoms up! SPOKEN used to tell someone to enjoy or finish their alcoholic drink
15 the bottom dropped out of sb's world/life used to say that something very bad suddenly happened to someone
16 ship [C] the part of a ship that is below water —compare TOP[1] —see also **you can bet your bottom dollar** (BET[1] (7)), -BOTTOMED, **knock the bottom out of sth** (KNOCK[1] (12)), ROCK BOTTOM, **(from) top to bottom** (TOP[1] (12))
bottom² *adj.* [only before noun] **1** in the lowest place or position: *The book is on the bottom shelf.* | *You have some peanut butter on your bottom lip.* | *the bottom right-hand corner of the page* —opposite TOP[2] **2** the least important or successful: *Tim is in the bottom 10% of his class.* —opposite TOP[2]
bottom³ *v.*
bottom out *phr. v.* [I] if a situation, price etc. bottoms out, it stops getting worse or lower, usually before improving again: *Interest rates are now at the lowest level since the rate bottomed out at 5.4 percent in 1977.*
-bottomed /bɑtəmd/ [in adjectives] **big-bottomed/ round-bottomed etc.** having a bottom or base that is big, round etc.
bot·tom·less /'bɑtəmlɪs/ *adj.* **1** a bottomless hole or area of water is extremely deep **2** seeming to have no end or limits: *the bottomless depths of the ocean* | *The U.S. is not a bottomless pit* (=a supply with no limits) *of aid money.* **3 a bottomless cup** a cup of coffee or a SOFT DRINK you buy in a restaurant, that you pay for once but that you can fill as many times as you want
bottom line /,.. './ *n.* **the bottom line 1** a situation or fact that is basic, true, or most important, and that must be accepted even if you do not like it: *Still, the bottom line is that Wisconsin won the game.* | *The bottom line is, men don't change very much after marriage.* **2** the profit or the amount of money that a business makes or loses: *Businesses are worried about the bottom line and a possible labor shortage.* **3** the lowest amount of money that you are willing to pay or take for something: *$2 million would pay for everything. That's the bottom line.* —**bottom-line** *adj.*
bot·tom·most /'bɑtəm,moʊst/ *adj.* [only before noun] in the lowest, farthest, or deepest position or place: *the bottommost rung of a ladder*
bot·u·lism /'bɑtʃə,lɪzəm/ *n.* [U] serious food poisoning caused by BACTERIA in preserved meat and vegetables
Bou·dic·ca /buˈdɪkə/, also **Bo·a·di·ce·a** /,boʊədɪˈsiə/ (died A.D. 60) the Queen of the Iceni tribe of eastern Britain, who led them in battle against the Romans

bou·doir /'budwar, bu'dwar/ *n.* [C] **1** the BEDROOM, especially considered as the place where people have sex: *secrets of the boudoir* **2** OLD USE a woman's BEDROOM or private sitting room
bouf·fant /buˈfɑnt/ *adj.* a bouffant hair style is brushed up and away from the head so that it stays high and full
bou·gain·vil·lea /,bugənˈvɪlyə/ *n.* [C,U] a South American plant that has red or purple flowers and grows up walls
bough /baʊ/ *n.* [C] LITERARY a main branch on a tree
bought /bɔt/ *v.* the past tense and past participle of BUY[1]
bouil·la·baisse /'buyə,beɪs, ,buyəˈbeɪs/ *n.* [C,U] a strong-tasting soup or STEW[1] made with fish
bouil·lon /'bulyɑn, 'bʊlyən/ *n.* [C,U] a clear soup made by boiling meat and vegetables in water
bouillon cube /'.. ,./ *n.* [C] a small square made of dried meats or vegetables, used to make soups and named SAUCES taste better
Boul·der /'boʊldə/ a city in the U.S. state of Colorado
boul·der /'boʊldə/ *n.* [C] a large stone or piece of rock: *Two huge boulders had to be moved out of the way before the trucks could get through.*
bou·le·vard /'bʊləvɑrd, 'bu-/ *n.* [C] **1** a wide road in a town or city, often with trees along the sides **2** a word used in the names of some roads: *Sunset Boulevard*
bounce¹ /baʊns/ *v.*
1 from a surface [I,T] if a ball or other object bounces, or if you bounce it, it immediately moves up or away from a surface after hitting it: *Two boys stood on the corner bouncing basketballs.* | [+ **off**] *Both of William's shots bounced off the rim of the basket.*
2 move up and down [I always + adv./prep.] to jump up and down continuously, for example on a soft surface: [+ **on**] *The kids were bouncing on the sofa.* | *Dooley was **bouncing up and down** with excitement.*
3 make sth move [I,T] if something bounces or something else bounces it, something makes it move up and down or from side to side: *I was in a sea plane with 10 others, bouncing in the air currents.* | *Her hair bounced when she walked.* | [+ **around**] *Put the disk drive in a place where it won't be bounced around.*
4 change situations [I,T] to move quickly from one situation, position, or place to another, or to make someone or something do this: *Doherty's case has bounced him from court to court.* | *Orders for products have **bounced up and down** (=become larger or smaller in number) throughout the year.*
5 change subjects [I] to change quickly from one subject, thought, idea etc. to another: *Grosso talks rapidly, bouncing from one thought to the next.*
6 check [I,T] if a check bounces or a bank bounces a check, the bank will not pay any money because there is not enough money in the account of the person who wrote it: *If the check bounces, the bank charges a fee of $18.*
7 computer [I,T] also **bounce back** if an EMAIL message that you send bounces or is bounced, it is AUTOMATICally returned to you because of a technical problem
8 walk [I always + adv./prep.] to walk quickly and with a lot of energy: [+ **across/along/in etc.**] *Laura came bouncing into the room with a smile on her face.*
9 light/sound [I,T] also **bounce off** if light or sound bounces or bounces off something, it hits a surface and REFLECTS (1) off it: *The radio signals are bounced off a satellite.*
10 make sb leave [T] INFORMAL to force someone to leave a place, job, or organization, especially because they have done something wrong: *That June, he bounced the other two leaders and named himself President.* | [**bounce sb from sth**] *Sean has already been bounced from three schools.*
11 be bouncing off the walls INFORMAL to be too

excited or too full of energy: *The sugar goes straight into your bloodstream and you start bouncing off the walls.*

12 bounce sb on your knee/lap to lift a child up and down while they are sitting on your knees

bounce around *phr. v.* [I] **1** if a person or their ideas bounce around, they move from one situation or idea to another without any planning or control: *He's got a Ph.D, but he's been bouncing around, working five jobs.* **2** if an object bounces around, something makes it keep moving in an uncontrolled way: *You don't want your stuff bouncing around in the back of the van, do you?*

bounce back *phr. v.* [I] to feel better quickly or become successful again, after having a lot of problems: *No matter what happens to Blanche, she always bounces back.* [+ **from**] *Farmers have bounced back from difficult times in the 1980s.*

bounce sth off sb *phr. v.* [T] to ask someone for their opinion about an idea, plan etc. before you make a decision: *Anytime I need to bounce ideas off someone, I give Debbie a call.*

bounce² *n.* **1** [U] a lot of energy: *Exercise is great. I feel like there's **a new bounce in my step**.* **2** [C] an action in which something immediately moves up or away from a surface after hitting it: *I caught the ball on the first bounce.* **3** [U] the ability to move up and down, or the ability of a surface to make something move up and down: *a basketball court with good bounce* **4** [U] hair that has bounce swings naturally and keeps its shape without looking stiff

bounc·er /'baʊnsɚ/ *n.* [C] someone whose job is to stand at the door of a club, bar etc. and stop unwanted people from coming in, or make people leave if they are behaving in a bad or offensive way

bounc·ing /'baʊnsɪŋ/ *adj.* **a bouncing baby boy/girl** a very healthy baby

bounc·y /'baʊnsi/ *adj.* **bouncier, bounciest 1** happy, confident, and full of energy: *bouncy country music* **2** moving up and down on hard surfaces very easily or too easily: *a bouncy ride over rough roads* **3** a bouncy surface moves up and down easily when someone is on it: *I love these bouncy chairs. They're really comfortable.* **4** hair that is bouncy swings naturally and keeps its shape without looking stiff —**bounciness** *n.* [U]

bound¹ /baʊnd/ *v.* the past tense and past participle of BIND¹

bound² *adj.* [no comparative]

1 **likely** **be bound to do sth** to be very likely to do something, to happen, to be true etc.: *The proposal is bound to fail without the committee's support.* | *Mom's bound to find out that you lied.* | *When two cultures are so different, there's bound to be conflict.*

2 **law/agreement** **be bound (by sth)** to have to do what a law, promise, agreement etc. says you must do: [**be bound (by sth) to do sth**] *The Foundation is bound by the treaty to help any nation that requests aid.* | *You are **legally bound** to report any change of address to the bank.*

3 **bound for college/Houston/Mexico** etc. also **college-bound/Houston-bound** etc. traveling toward a particular place, or intending to go there: *A plane bound for Peru crashed early Sunday morning.* | *After months of travel, we were at last **homeward bound**.* —see also EASTBOUND, NORTHBOUND, SOUTHBOUND, WESTBOUND

4 **bound and determined** very determined to do or achieve something, no matter how difficult it is: *Klein is bound and determined to win at least five races this year.*

5 **be bound up in sth a)** also **be bound up with sth** to be closely connected with a particular problem, situation etc.: *The history of music is, of course, bound up with the development of musical instruments.* **b)** to be so involved in a difficult situation etc. that you cannot think about anything else: *Jim's too bound up in his own worries to be able to help us.*

6 **be bound (together) by sth** to share a particular feature or quality: *The two groups were bound together by their hatred of the factory in which they worked.*

7 **book** a bound book or document is covered on the outside with paper, leather etc.: [+ **in**] *a notebook bound in red velvet* | *a **leather-bound** world atlas*

8 **I'll be bound** OLD-FASHIONED used when you are very sure that what you have just said is true

9 **a bound form** TECHNICAL a part of a word that is always found in combination with another form, such as "un-" and "-er" in the words "unknown" and "speaker"

bound³ *v.* **1** **be bounded by sth** if a country or area of land is bounded by something such as a wall, river etc., it has the wall etc. at its edge: *The U.S. is bounded in the north by Canada and in the south by Mexico.* **2** [I always + adv./prep.] to run with a lot of energy, because you are happy, excited, or frightened: [+ **up/toward/across** etc.] *George came bounding down the stairs.*

bound⁴ *n.*

1 **limits** **bounds** [plural] **a)** limits or rules that are given by law or exist because of social custom: *We're here to make sure that the police operate **within the bounds** of the law.* **b)** OLD-FASHIONED the edges of a town, city etc.

2 **go beyond the bounds of decency/reason** etc. to not follow the rules that people normally follow when doing something: *The humor in the movie goes beyond the bounds of good taste.*

3 **out of bounds a)** outside the legal playing area in a sport such as football or basketball **b)** if a place or subject is out of bounds, you are not allowed to go there or to talk about it: [+ **to/for**] *Those offices are out of bounds to non-management personnel.*

4 **in bounds** inside the legal playing area in a sport such as football or basketball

5 **jump** [C] LITERARY a long or high jump made with a lot of energy: *Superman can leap tall buildings in a single bound.* —see also **know no bounds** (KNOW¹ (23)), **by leaps and bounds** (LEAP² (2))

-bound /baʊnd/ [in adjectives] **1** **snow-bound/fog-bound/wheelchair-bound** etc. limited by something, so that you cannot do what you want or go where you want: *a fog-bound airport* | *Sarah has been wheelchair-bound since the accident* **2** **duty-bound/tradition-bound** etc. doing something because it is your duty, it is traditional etc. even though it is not the best thing to do, or not what you want to do: *I am duty-bound to express the management's position on this issue.*

bound·a·ry /'baʊndɚi, -dri/ *n. plural* **boundaries s 1** [C] a real or imaginary line that marks where one area of land is separate from other areas: [+ **between**] *The Mississippi River forms a natural boundary between Iowa and Illinois.* | *The property's **boundary line** is 25 feet from the back wall of the house.* | *In 1885, the state drew the southern boundary* (=decided where one area of land ends and another one starts) *for Linn County at the Lee River.* **2** [C usually plural] the highest or most extreme limit that something can reach or the limit of what is possible or acceptable: [+ **of**] *We are limited only by the boundaries of our imagination.* **3** **push the boundaries (of sth)** to change the way people think about an idea, belief etc., or to greatly increase their knowledge of something: *They pushed the boundaries of the way women were allowed to behave in society.* **4** [C] the point at which one feeling, quality etc. stops and another starts: [+ **of/between**] *the boundary between lust and love*

bound·en /'baʊndən/ *adj.* **your bounden duty** OLD-FASHIONED something that you should do because it is morally correct

bound·er /'baʊndɚ/ *n.* [C] OLD-FASHIONED, DISAPPROVING a man who has behaved in a way that you think is morally wrong

bound·less /'baʊndlɪs/ *adj.* having no limit or end: *boundless enthusiasm* —**boundlessly** *adv.* —**boundlessness** *n.* [U]

boun·te·ous /'baʊntiəs/ *adj.* LITERARY very generous

boun·ti·ful /ˈbaʊntɪfəl/ adj. LITERARY **1** if something is bountiful, there is more than enough of it: *a bountiful harvest* **2** generous: *God is bountiful.*

boun·ty /ˈbaʊnti/ n. plural **bounties 1** [C] an amount of money that is given to someone by the government as a reward for doing something, such as catching a criminal: *A bounty of $250,000 is being offered for the capture of the killer.* | [+ **on**] *There is a $50 bounty on each wolf that is captured.* **2** [U] LITERARY a large amount of something, especially food: *the bounty of the harvest* **3** [U] LITERARY the quality of being generous: *Mrs. Falzheim is known for her bounty to the poor.*

bounty hunt·er /ˈ.. ˌ../ n. [C] someone who catches criminals and brings them to the police in return for a reward

bou·quet /boʊˈkeɪ, bu-/ n. **1** [C] a bunch of flowers that you give to someone or carry on a formal occasion **2** [C,U] the smell of a wine: *It is a light wine with a clean bouquet and taste.*

Bour·bon /ˈbʊrbən/ the name of a family of French kings who ruled from 1589 to 1792

bour·bon /ˈbɜrbən/ n. [U] a type of WHISKEY

bour·geois[1] /bʊrˈʒwɑ, ˈbʊrʒwɑ/ adj. **1** belonging or relating to the MIDDLE CLASS: *bourgeois attitudes and values* **2** belonging to or typical of the MIDDLE CLASS people in society who are educated, own land etc., according to MARXISM: *a bourgeois capitalist* —see also PETTY BOURGEOIS —compare PROLETARIAN

bourgeois[2] n. plural **bourgeois** [C] **1** a member of the MIDDLE CLASS **2** someone who belongs to MIDDLE CLASS part of society and who is educated, owns land etc., according to MARXISM —compare PROLETARIAT

bour·geoi·sie /ˌbʊrʒwɑˈzi/ n. **the bourgeoisie a)** the MIDDLE CLASS people in a society who are educated, own land etc., according to MARXISM **b)** the MIDDLE CLASS

Bourke-White /ˌbɜrk ˈwaɪt/, **Mar·garet** /ˈmɑrgrɪt/ (1906–1971) a U.S. newspaper and magazine PHOTOGRAPHER

bout /baʊt/ n. [C] **1** a short period of time during which you suffer from a particular illness: [+ **of/with**] *Throughout his life, he often suffered bouts of depression.* | *Her bout with polio left her right leg paralyzed.* **2** a BOXING or WRESTLING competition **3** a short period of time during which you do something a lot, especially something that is bad for you: [+ **of**] *a bout of drinking*

'bout /baʊt/ adv. prep. SPOKEN, NONSTANDARD a short form of "about": *What are you talking 'bout?*

bou·tique /buˈtik/ n. [C] a small store that sells very fashionable clothes or other objects

bou·ton·niere /ˌbutⁿˈɪr, -ˈyɛr/ n. [C] a flower that a man wears in the LAPEL of his suit, especially at a wedding

bou·zou·ki /buˈzuki/ n. plural **bouzoukis** [C] a Greek musical instrument similar to a GUITAR

bo·vine /ˈboʊvaɪn/ adj. **1** TECHNICAL relating to cows: *bovine diseases* **2** slow and slightly stupid: *The woman smiled at us in a bovine sort of way.*

bow[1] /baʊ/ v. **1** [I] to bend the top part of your body forward, in order to show respect for someone important or as a way of thanking an AUDIENCE: *Archer bowed and left the stage.* | [+ **before/to** etc.] *We bowed before the king.* **2 bow your head** to bend your neck so that you are looking at the ground, especially because you want to show respect for God or because you are embarrassed or upset: *I bowed my head and prayed.* | *Jerry stood there with his head bowed in shame.* **3** [I,T] to bend your body over something, especially in order to see it more closely: [+ **over**] *Dr. Harris is usually in the lab, bowed over a microscope.* **4 bow and scrape** to show too much respect to someone in authority

bow down phr. v. [I] **1** to bend forward from your waist, especially when you are already kneeling, in order to show respect [+ **before/to** etc.] *Old women bowed down before the statue of Mary.* **2 bow down to sb** LITERARY to let someone give you orders or tell you what to do

bow out phr. v. [I] **1** to stop taking part in an activity, job etc., especially one that you have been doing for a long time: [**bow out of sth**] *Two more Republicans have bowed out of the presidential race.* **2** to not do something that you have promised or agreed to do: *Dreyfuss bowed out of the project at the last minute.*

bow to sb/sth phr. v. [T] to finally agree to do something that people want you to, even though you do not want to do it: *They eventually bowed to demands to withdraw military forces from the area.*

bow[2] /boʊ/ n. **1** [C] a knot of cloth or string with a curved part on each side, used especially for decoration: *She had a red bow in her hair.* **2** [C] a weapon used for shooting ARROWS, made of a long thin piece of wood held in a curve by a tight string **3** [C] a long thin piece of wood with a tight string fastened along it, used to play musical instruments that have strings, such as the VIOLIN **4 bow legs** legs that curve out at the knee —see also BOW-LEGGED

bow[3] /baʊ/ n. **1** [C] the act of bending the top part of your body forward to show respect for someone **2 take a bow** if someone takes a bow, they come on the stage at the end of a performance so that people can APPLAUD them **3** [C] the front part of a ship —compare STERN[2]

bow[4] /boʊ/ v. **1** [I] to bend or curve **2 be bowed** someone who is bowed is bent slightly, for example because they are old or tired or because they are carrying something heavy **3** [I,T] to play a piece of music on a musical instrument with a bow

bowd·ler·ize /ˈboʊdləˌraɪz/ v. [T] FORMAL to remove the parts of a book, play etc. that you think are offensive —**bowdlerized** adj.: *a bowdlerized edition of "Tom Sawyer"*

bow·el /ˈbaʊəl/ n. **1 bowels** [plural] the system of tubes inside your body in which food is made into solid waste material and through which it passes out of your body; INTESTINE | **move/empty your bowels** (=get rid of solid waste from your body) **2** [singular] one part of this system of tubes: *cancer of the bowel* **3 a bowel movement** FORMAL an act of getting rid of solid waste from your body **4 the bowels of sth** LITERARY the lowest or deepest part of something: *Most of the supplies were stored in the bowels of the ship.*

bow·er /ˈbaʊər/ n. [C] LITERARY **1** a pleasant place in the shade under a tree, especially in a garden: *a rose-scented bower* **2** a woman's BEDROOM in a castle

Bow·ie /ˈboʊi, ˈbui/, **James** (1799–1836) a U.S. soldier who was one of the leaders at the battle of the Alamo, when the Texans were fighting to be independent of Mexico

bow·ie knife /ˈboʊi ˌnaɪf/ n. [C] a large heavy knife with a long blade that is sharp on one side, used especially for HUNTING

bow·ing /ˈboʊɪŋ/ n. [U] the skill of using a BOW[2] (3) to play a musical instrument

bowl[1] /boʊl/ n. **1** [C] a wide round container that is open at the top, used to hold liquids, food etc.: *Mix the eggs and butter in a large bowl.* | **soup/salad/cereal etc. bowls** *a blue-striped salad bowl* **2** also **bowlful** [C] the amount that a bowl will hold: [+ **of**] *a bowl of chili* **3** [C] the part of an object such as a spoon, pipe, toilet etc. that is shaped like a bowl **4** [C usually singular] a special game played by the best football teams after the normal playing season: *the Rose Bowl* **5** [C usually singular] a STADIUM shaped like a bowl, where people go to watch special events such as sports games or music CONCERTS: *the Hollywood Bowl*

bowl[2] v. [I,T] to play the game of bowling

bowl sb ↔ **over** phr. v. [T] **1** to surprise, please, or excite someone very much: *I was bowled over by the hundreds of people who wrote to support me.* **2** to accidentally hit someone so that they fall down, because you are running too quickly: *Jackson bowls over linebackers like a runaway train.*

bow-leg·ged /ˈboʊ ˌlɛgɪd, -ˌlɛgd/ adj. having legs that curve out sideways at the knee

bowl·er /ˈboʊlə/ n. [C] **1** someone who plays the game of bowling **2** also **bowler hat** a DERBY (3)

bowl·ing /ˈboʊlɪŋ/ n. [U] an indoor game in which you roll a large heavy ball along a wooden track in order to knock down a group of PINS (=wooden objects shaped like bottles): *The kids and I went **bowling** (=went to a place to play this game) yesterday.* —see also LAWN BOWLING

bowl·ing al·ley /ˈ.. ˌ../ n. [C] a building where you play the game of bowling

bowling ball /ˈ.. ˌ./ n. [C] the heavy ball you use in the game of bowling

bowling green /ˈ.. ˌ./ n. [C] an area of grass where you play the game of LAWN BOWLING

bow·man /ˈboʊmən/ n. [C] a soldier in past times who shot ARROWS with a BOW

bow·sprit /ˈboʊsprɪt/ n. [C] a long pole on the front of a boat that the ropes from the sails are attached to

bow·string /ˈboʊstrɪŋ/ n. [C] the string on a BOW² (2)

bow tie /ˈboʊ taɪ/ n. [C] a short piece of cloth tied in the shape of a BOW² (1) that men wear around their neck

bow window /ˌboʊ ˈwɪndoʊ/ n. [C] a window that curves out from the wall

bow-wow¹, **bowwow** /ˈbaʊ waʊ/ interjection a word used to make the sound that a dog makes, used especially by small children

bow-wow², **bowwow** n. [C] a word meaning a "dog," especially used by small children

box¹ /bɑks/ n.
1 container [C] a container for putting things in, especially one with four stiff straight sides: *a cardboard box | five wooden boxes | toolbox/shoebox/lunchbox etc.* (=a box used for keeping tools, shoes etc. in) —see picture at CONTAINER
2 amount also **boxful** [C] the amount that a box can hold: [+ of] *a box of chocolates*
3 shape [C] **a)** a small square on a page that people mark to choose something such as an answer to a question: *Check this box if you would like information about our other products.* **b)** a square or RECTANGLE on a page where information is given or where an answer can be written: *The box on the left gives a short history of the Alamo.*
4 the box INFORMAL the television: *What's on the box tonight?*
5 in a court/theater etc. [C] a special area in a court, theater, STADIUM etc. that is separate from where other people are sitting: *the jury box* —see also SENTRY BOX
6 at a post office [C usually singular] a box with a number in it in a POST OFFICE where you can have mail sent to instead of your own address: *P.O. BOX*
7 area of a sports field [C] a special area of a sports field that is marked by lines and used for a particular purpose: *the penalty box | the batter's box* —see also BLACK BOX, **think outside the box** (THINK (18))

box² v. **1** [I,T] to fight someone as a sport by hitting them with your closed hands inside big leather GLOVES (2) **2** also **box up** [T] to put things in boxes —see also BOXED **3** [T] to draw a box around something on a page **4 box sb's ears** OLD-FASHIONED to hit someone on the side of their head
box sb/sth in phr. v. [T] **1** if a car is boxed in, other cars have parked around it so that it cannot move away: *Someone boxed me in.* **2** to surround someone so that they are unable to move freely: *My horse was winning the race until he got boxed in on the final curve.* **3 feel boxed in a)** to feel that you are limited in what you can do because of a particular situation or what someone else wants: *Married for only six months, Dawn already felt boxed in.* **b)** to feel that you cannot move freely, because you are in a small space
box sth off phr. v. [T] to separate a particular area from a larger one by putting walls around it: *We're*

going to box off that corner and make it a separate office.

box can·yon /ˈ. ˌ../ n. [C] a deep narrow valley with very straight sides and only one entrance

box·car /ˈbɑkskɑr/ n. [C] a railroad car with high sides and a roof, used for carrying goods

boxed /bɑkst/ adj. sold in a box or boxes: *a boxed set of CDs*

box end wrench /ˌ. . ˈ./ n. [C] a type of WRENCH with a hollow end that fits over a NUT (2) that is being screwed or unscrewed —see picture at TOOL¹

box·er /ˈbɑksər/ n. [C] **1** someone who BOXES² (1), especially as a job: *a heavyweight boxer* **2** a large dog with short light-brown hair and a flat nose

boxer shorts /ˈ.. ˌ./ also **boxers** n. [plural] loose underwear like SHORTS for men

box·ing /ˈbɑksɪŋ/ n. [U] the sport of fighting with closed hands while wearing big leather GLOVES (2)

boxing glove /ˈ.. ˌ./ n. [C] a big leather GLOVE used for boxing —see picture at GLOVE

boxing ring /ˈ.. ˌ./ n. [C] a raised square floor with ropes around it that is used for boxing

box lunch /ˌ. ˈ./ n. [C] a LUNCH that you take to school or work with you in a LUNCHBOX

box num·ber /ˈ. ˌ../ n. [C] an address of a box at a POST OFFICE that people can use instead of their own address

box of·fice /ˈ. ˌ../ n. **1** [C] the place in a theater, concert hall etc. where tickets are sold **2** [singular] used to describe how successful a movie, play, or actor is, by the number of people who pay to see them | **do well/badly/poorly etc. at the box office** (=be very successful or unsuccessful) | *Eddie Murphy went on to become one of the nation's biggest **box office draws** (=most successful actors who many people will pay to see).*

box spring /ˈ. ˌ./ n. [C usually plural] a set of metal springs inside a cloth cover that you put under a MATTRESS to make a bed

box·y /ˈbɑksi/ adj. **boxier, boxiest** something that is boxy is unattractive because it is too big and in the shape of a box: *a boxy car*

boy¹ /bɔɪ/ n. plural **boys**
1 child [C] a male child or young man: *There are only five boys in the class. | a polite little boy* (=young male child) | *Two small boys* (=young male child) *on bicycles led the way.*
2 son [C] a son: *My two boys are still in college. | How old is your little boy* (=young son)?
3 office/paper/delivery etc. boy a young man who does a particular job, usually one that is not paid well
4 city/local/country etc. boy INFORMAL a man of any age who is typical of people from a particular place or who feels a strong connection with the place he grew up in: *I'm just a country boy.*
5 rich/college/frat etc. boy INFORMAL a young man from a particular social group
6 the boys INFORMAL a group of men who are friends and often go out together: *Ted's out playing cards with the boys. | I've always just wanted to be one of the boys* (=popular with a group of men).
7 animal [C] a way of addressing a male animal, especially a dog, cat, or horse: *Good boy, Rover!*
8 job boys INFORMAL **a)** a group of men who do the same job: *The press boys are going to love this story.* **b)** men in the army, navy etc., especially those who are fighting in a war: *We need to support our boys stationed overseas.*
9 the boys in blue INFORMAL the police
10 boys will be boys used to say that you should not be surprised when boys behave badly, are noisy etc.
11 man OFFENSIVE an insulting word used to talk to a man when the person speaking considers him to be unimportant because of his race or position —see also MAMA'S BOY

boy² interjection **1** also **oh boy** used when you are excited or pleased about something: *Boy, that chicken was good!* **2 oh boy** used when you are slightly annoyed or disappointed about something: *Oh boy! My computer crashed again.*

boy·cott[1] /'bɔɪkɑt/ v. [T] to refuse to buy something, use something, or take part in something as a way of protesting about a situation, action etc.: *Six countries have threatened to boycott the Olympics.*

boycott[2] n. [C] an act of boycotting something, or the period of time when it is boycotted: [+ of/on/against] *The group is urging a nationwide boycott of toys manufactured with child labor.*

boy·friend /'bɔɪfrɛnd/ n. [C] a man that you are having a romantic relationship with: *Is he your new boyfriend?* —see also GIRLFRIEND

boy·hood /'bɔɪhʊd/ n. [U] the time of a man's life when he is a boy: *I spent my boyhood on a farm in Indiana.* —see also GIRLHOOD

boy·ish /'bɔɪ-ɪʃ/ adj. **1** a man who is boyish looks or behaves like a boy in a way that is attractive: *Chuck has blond hair and a smooth boyish face.* **2** a woman or girl who is boyish looks or behaves a little like a boy: *At 45, Nell still has a trim, boyish figure.* —**boyishly** adv. —**boyishness** n. [U]

Boyle /bɔɪl/, **Rob·ert** /'rɑbət/ (1627–1691) an Irish scientist famous for his new ideas that formed the beginning of modern chemistry

Boys and Girls Clubs of A·mer·i·ca /ˌ. . ˌ. . . ˈ. . ./ an organization for young people in the U.S., that arranges activities and gives help with problems

boy scout /'. ./ n. **1 Boy Scout** [C] a member of the Boy Scouts —compare GIRL SCOUT **2 the Boy Scouts** an organization for boys that teaches them practical skills and helps to develop their character **3** [C] a man or boy who you think is annoying because he always obeys rules and laws and always tries to do good things

Boy Scouts of A·mer·i·ca, the /ˌ. . . . ˈ. . ./ an organization of SCOUTS in the U.S., for boys from age seven to age 18

boy·sen·ber·ry /'bɔɪzənˌbɛri/ n. plural **boysenberries** [C] a small dark red or black berry, similar to a RASPBERRY

boy won·der /ˌ. ˈ. ./ n. [C] a young man who is very successful: *At age 27, Williams was the boy wonder of banking.*

bo·zo /'boʊzoʊ/ n. plural **bozos** [C] INFORMAL someone who you think is silly or stupid: *Who's that bozo in the purple shirt?*

BPOE —see ELKS

bps, BPS TECHNICAL the abbreviation of BITS per second; a measurement of how fast a computer or MODEM can send or receive information: *a 28,800 bps modem*

bra /brɑ/ n. [C] a piece of underwear that a woman wears to support her breasts

brace[1] /breɪs/ v. **1** [I,T] to prepare for something bad or difficult that is going to happen: [+ for] *Eastern Missouri braced for another six inches of snow.* | *Castro told Cubans to brace themselves for widespread shortages of fuel.* **2** [T] to push part of your body against something solid in order to make yourself more steady: [brace sth against sth] *Terry braced his back against the wall and pushed as hard as he could.* | *The pilot told passengers and crew to brace themselves for a crash landing.* **3** [T] to make something stronger by supporting it: *The building uses steel poles to brace the roof.* **4** [I,T] to make your body or part of your body stiff in order to prepare to do something difficult: *Alex braced his arms and pushed the car out of the road.*

brace[2] n. **1** [C] something that is used to strengthen, stiffen, or support something: *Diane had to wear a neck brace for eight weeks after the accident.* | *The steel beam serves as a brace for the ceiling.* **2 braces** [plural] a connected set of wires that people, especially children, sometimes wear on their teeth to make them straight **3** [C usually plural] a metal support that someone with weak legs wears to help them walk **4** [C usually plural] one of a pair of signs { } used to show that information written between them should be considered together —compare BRACKET[1] (2) **5 a brace of sth** OLD-FASHIONED two of something

brace·let /'breɪslɪt/ n. [C] a band or chain that you wear around your wrist or arm as a decoration

brac·er /'breɪsə/ n. [C] INFORMAL a drink, especially one that contains alcohol, that makes you feel more active or able to think quickly and clearly

bra·ce·ro /brɑ'sɛroʊ/ n. [C] someone from Mexico who has been allowed to come to the U.S. for a limited period of time to work on a farm

brac·ing /'breɪsɪŋ/ adj. **1** bracing air or weather is cold and makes you feel very awake and healthy: *a bracing ocean breeze* **2** exciting and interesting: *the bracing taste of ginger* | *a bracing musical experiment*

brack·en /'brækən/ n. [U] a plant that often grows in forests and becomes reddish brown in the fall

brack·et[1] /'brækɪt/ n. [C]
1 income/tax/age etc. bracket a particular range of incomes, taxes etc.: *The tax cut is good news for families in the lowest income bracket.*
2 printed sign [usually plural] one of a pair of signs [ ] used to show that information written between them should be considered together: *All grammar information is given in brackets.* —see also BRACE[2] (4)
3 support a piece of metal, wood, or plastic, often in the shape of the letter L, put in or on a wall to support something such as a shelf

bracket[2] v. [T] **1** to put brackets around a written word, piece of information etc., especially to show that the information given should be considered together: *Unpaid amounts have been bracketed.* **2** if two events bracket something, one happens before and the other after it: *The strong U.S. economy of the 1980s was bracketed by two recessions.* **3** if two things bracket something, one thing is on one side and the other thing is on the other side of it: *The airport's runway was bracketed on one end by power lines and on the other by a peach orchard.* **4** to decide which things, people, groups etc. belong together: [bracket sb with sb] *Arizona has been bracketed with Iowa in the tournament.*

brack·ish /'brækɪʃ/ adj. brackish water is not pure because it is slightly salty

brad /bræd/ n. [C] **1** a small metal object like a button that has two metal sticks on it that you put through several pieces of paper and fold down to hold the papers together **2** a small thin wire nail with either a small head or a part that sticks out to the side instead of a head

brad·awl /'brædɔl/ n. [C] a small tool with a sharp point for making holes in wood for brads or screws

Brad·bur·y /'brædbɛri/, **Ray** /reɪ/ (1920–) a U.S. writer of SCIENCE FICTION

Brad·ford /'brædfəd/, **William** (1590–1657) a leader of the Pilgrim Fathers who came from England in the Mayflower, who was elected GOVERNOR of the American COLONY of Plymouth 30 times

Brad·ley /'brædli/, **Bill** /bɪl/ (1943–) a U.S. basketball player and politician who was a CANDIDATE for U.S. President in 2000

Bradley, O·mar /'oʊmɑr/ (1893–1981) a general in the U.S. Army during World War II

Bra·dy /'breɪdi/, **James** also **Diamond Jim Brady** (1856–1917) a U.S. businessman who gave a lot of money to hospitals in Baltimore and New York City

Brady, Matthew B. (?1823–1896) a U.S. Civil War PHOTOGRAPHER

brag /bræg/ v. **bragged, bragging** [I,T] to talk too proudly about what you have done, what you own etc.; BOAST: [+ about] *Grandparents were happily bragging about their grandkids.* | [+ that] *A witness heard him bragging that he was responsible for all three murders.*

brag·ga·do·ci·o /ˌbrægə'doʊsioʊ, -tʃioʊ/ n. [U] ESPECIALLY LITERARY proud talk about something that you claim to own, to have done etc.

brag·gart /'brægət/ n. [C] DISAPPROVING someone who

B

is always talking too proudly about what they own or have done

Bra·he /'brɑə, 'brɑhi/, **Ty·cho** /'tikoʊ, 'taɪkoʊ/ (1546–1601) a Danish ASTRONOMER who made many exact and important OBSERVATIONS

Brah·man /'brɑmən/ n. [C] **1** also **Brahmin** someone belonging to the highest rank in the HINDU religion **2** also **Brahma** a cow developed in the southern U.S. that has a HUMP (=large raised part) on the front part of its back

Brah·man·i, Brahmanee /brɑ'mɑni/ n. [C] a woman belonging to the highest rank in the HINDU religion

Brah·man·ism /'brɑmə,nɪzəm/ the earliest stage in the development of Hinduism

Brah·min /'brɑmən/ n. [C] someone, especially someone from New England, who is from a wealthy upper-class family: *Walters was a Boston Brahmin, educated at Harvard.*

Brahms /'brɑmz/, **Jo·han·nes** /yoʊ'hɑnɪs/ (1833–1897) a German musician who wrote CLASSICAL music

braid¹ /breɪd/ n. **1** [C] a length of hair that has been separated into three parts and then woven together: *Sally likes wearing her hair in braids.* —see also PLAIT —see picture at HAIRSTYLE **2** [U] a narrow band of material formed by twisting threads together, used to decorate the edges of clothes: *a blue jacket with gold braid*

braid² v. [T] to weave or twist together three pieces of hair or cloth to form one length —**braided** adj.

braille /breɪl/ n. [U] a form of printing with raised round marks that blind people can read by touching

Braille /breɪl/, **Lou·is** /'lui/ (1809–1852) a French teacher who invented the BRAILLE form of printing that blind people can read by touch

S W
2 2
brain¹ /breɪn/ n.

1 organ [C] the organ inside your head that controls how you think, feel, and move: *The doctors have found a tumor in his brain.* | *The brain has trillions of cells.*

2 intelligence [singular] also **brains** [U] the ability to think clearly and learn quickly: *If you had any brains at all, you wouldn't ask such a stupid question.* | *Ted's got more money than brains* (=he doesn't spend his money wisely). | *Use your brain, John.*

3 person [C] INFORMAL someone who is intelligent, with good ideas and useful skills: *Some of the best brains in the country are here tonight.* | *Louis was the brain in our class.* —see also BRAIN DRAIN

4 brain dead also **brain-dead a)** in a state where your brain has stopped working correctly, even though your heart may still be beating **b)** INFORMAL in a state in which you behave stupidly, especially because you are tired: *What's the matter with you? Are you brain dead or something?*

5 be the brains behind/in sth to be the person who thought of and developed a particular plan, system, or organization, especially a successful one: *Silvetti is the brains behind the family business.*

6 have sth on the brain INFORMAL to be unable to stop thinking about something: *You always have food on the brain.* —see also **beat your brains out** (BEAT¹ (12)), BIRDBRAIN, FEATHER-BRAINED, HAREBRAINED, **pick sb's brain(s)** (PICK¹ (7)), **rack your brain(s)** (RACK² (1))

brain² v. [T] OLD-FASHIONED to hit someone very hard on the head: *I'll brain you if you don't shut up!*

brain·child /'breɪntʃaɪld/ n. [singular] INFORMAL an idea, plan, organization etc. that someone has thought of without any help from anyone else: [+ of] *The personal computer was the brainchild of a man named Steve Jobs.*

brain dam·age /'. ,../ n. [U] damage to someone's brain caused by an accident or illness: *Mrs. Wilson suffered severe brain damage in the accident.* —**brain-damaged** adj.

brain drain /'. ./ n. **the brain drain** the movement of highly skilled or professional people from their own country to a country where they earn more money

brain·less /'breɪnlɪs/ adj. INFORMAL stupid: *You brainless idiot!* —**brainlessly** adv.

brain stem, brainstem /'. ./ n. [C] the part of the brain that connects the SPINAL CORD to the front and main parts of the brain

brain·storm /'breɪnstɔrm/ n. [singular] a sudden intelligent idea: *I had a brainstorm about the project last night.*

brain·storm·ing /'breɪn,stɔrmɪŋ/ n. [U] the act of trying to develop ideas and think of ways to solve problems, done with a group of people: *The college is holding a brainstorming session to look at possible funding sources.* —**brainstorm** v. [I]

brain sur·ger·y /'. ,.../ n. [U] **1** the process of performing operations on people's brains **2 sth is not brain surgery** SPOKEN used to emphasize that something is easy or that it does not need intelligence to do it: *Playing baseball is not exactly brain surgery.* —**brain surgeon** n. [C]

brain·teas·er /'breɪn,tizɚ/ n. [C] a difficult problem that is fun to try to solve

brain trust /'. ./ n. [C] a group of very intelligent people who help a politician, company, team etc. make good decisions

brain·wash /'breɪnwɑʃ/ v. [T] to make someone believe something that is not true, by using force, confusing them, or continuously repeating it over a long period of time: *Kids are being brainwashed by the people who make these toy commercials.* | [brainwash sb into doing sth] *The Church is being sued by two former members who said they were brainwashed into joining it.* —**brainwashing** n. [U]

brain wave, brainwave /'. ./ n. [C] an electrical force that is produced by the brain and that can be measured

brain·y /'breɪni/ adj. **brainier, brainiest** INFORMAL able to learn quickly and think clearly: *It's my little sister who's the brainy one.*

braise /breɪz/ v. [T] to cook meat or vegetables slowly in a small amount of liquid in a closed container —**braised** adj.

brake¹ /breɪk/ n. [C] **1** a piece of equipment that makes a vehicle go more slowly or stop, usually operated by pressing on a bar with your foot or hand: *The back brake on my bike needs adjusting.* | **Apply the brakes** gently. | **put/slam on the brakes** *I managed to put on the brakes just in time.* —see also EMERGENCY BRAKE, HANDBRAKE, PARKING BRAKE —see pictures at BICYCLE¹ and on page 427 **2 put the brakes on sth** to stop something that is happening: *It's the government's latest effort to put the brakes on rising prices.* **3 act/serve as a brake on sth** to make something develop more slowly or be more difficult to do: *Rises in interest rates usually act as a brake on expenditure.*

brake² v. [I] to make a vehicle or bicycle go more slowly or stop by using its brake: *She had to brake suddenly to avoid a dog in the road.*

brake flu·id /'. ,../ n. [U] a liquid, used in certain kinds of brakes, that is put under pressure in order to make them work

brake light /'. ./ n. [C] a light on the back of a vehicle that comes on when you use the brake —see picture on page 427

brake pad /'. ./ n. [C] a block that presses against the DISC of a DISC BRAKE

brake shoe /'. ./ n. [C] one of the two curved parts that press against the wheel of a vehicle in order to make it go more slowly or stop

bram·ble /'bræmbəl/ n. [C] a wild plant with THORNS and berries

bran /bræn/ n. [U] the crushed outer skin of wheat or a similar grain, that is separated from the rest of the grain when making white flour

branch¹ /bræntʃ/ n. [C]

1 on a tree the part of a tree that grows away from the TRUNK (=main stem) and has leaves, fruit, or smaller branches growing from it: *A swing hung from the branch of a tree.* —see picture at OAK

2 store/office a store, office etc. in a particular

area that is part of a large company: *Her company has branches in Dallas and Chicago.* | *I was told to call the branch office in New Orleans.*
3 of an organization a part of a government or other organization that deals with one particular part of its work: *The President is in charge of the executive branch of our government.*
4 of a subject one part of a large subject of study or knowledge: [+ **of**] *The branch of international law that deals with war crimes has not always been enforced.*
5 of a family a group of members of a family who all have the same grandparents or ANCESTORS: *Jimmy's from the West Virginia branch of the family.*
6 smaller part a smaller less important part of something that leads away from the larger, more important part of it: *a branch of the Missouri River*

branch² v. [I] also **branch off** to separate from something and go in a different direction: *Turn off where the road branches to the right.* | [+ **from**] *We went into a passage that branched off from the main tunnel.*

branch off phr. v. [I] if a story, conversation etc. branches off, it changes from one subject to another, especially to a closely related subject: [+ **into**] *Then the conversation branched off into a discussion about movies.*

branch out phr. v. [I] to do something new in addition to what you usually do: *Some soybean farmers could branch out by growing crops as peanuts.* | [**branch out into doing sth**] *Foster has branched out into directing, as well as acting.*

brand¹ /brænd/ n. [C] **1** a type of product made by a particular company: [+ **of**] *Wal-Mart sells a brand of dog food named Ol' Roy.* | *It's been the **brand leader** (=the brand that sells the most) for the last two years.* | *I think there is less **brand loyalty** (=the tendency to always buy a particular brand) in computers than there was a few years ago.* | *The **store brand** (=product made and sold by a particular store) is usually cheaper than regular brands.* **2** a **brand of humor/politics/religion etc.** a particular type of humor, politics etc.: *Grade-school boys love Elliott's brand of nincompoop comedy.* **3** a mark made or burned on an animal's skin that shows who it belongs to **4** LITERARY a piece of burning wood **5** POETIC a sword

brand² v. [T] **1** to describe someone or something as a very bad type of person or thing, often unfairly: *Pete got **branded as** a troublemaker when he was just a kid.* **2** [usually passive] to make a mark on something such as an animal, especially by burning, in order to show who it belongs to: [**brand sth with sth**] *Henry Schmitt's cattle are branded with H lazy S.*

brand·ed /'brændɪd/ adj. [only before noun] a branded product is made by a well-known company and has the company's name on it

Bran·deis /'brændaɪs/, **Louis** (1856–1941) a judge on the U.S. Supreme Court

brand·ing i·ron /'.. ,../ n. [C] a piece of metal that is heated and used for burning marks on cattle or horses to show who they belong to

bran·dish /'brændɪʃ/ v. [T] to wave something around in a dangerous or threatening way, especially a weapon: *At one point, the suspect brandished a knife.*

brand name /'. ,./ n. [C] the name given to a product by the company that makes it: *Brand names such as Coca-Cola and Sony are recognized all over the world.* —compare NAME BRAND

brand-new /,bræn 'nu◄/ adj. new and never before used: *a brand-new motorcycle*

Bran·do /'brændoʊ/, **Mar·lon** /'mɑrlən/ (1924–) a U.S. actor who is considered one of the best movie actors ever

brand-spankin'-new, brand-spanking-new /,. .. './ adj. SPOKEN used to emphasize that something is new: *How can Ann afford a brand-spankin'-new sports car like that?* —see also SPANKING²

bran·dy /'brændi/ n. plural **brandies** [C,U] a strong alcoholic drink made from wine, or a glass of this drink

Braque /bræk, brɑk/, **Georges** /ʒɔrʒ/ (1882–1963) a French PAINTER famous for developing the style of CUBISM with Pablo Picasso

brash /bræʃ/ adj. **1** behaving in a way that is too confident and determined, and often speaking too loudly or behaving rudely: *a very brash young man* **2** a brash building, place, or object attracts attention by being very colorful, large, exciting etc., in a way that is very confident and does not seem to show respect: *The painting was bold, brash, and modern.* —**brashly** adv. —**brashness** n. [U]

Bra·si·lia /brə'zɪlyə/ the capital city of Brazil

brass /bræs/ n.
1 metal [U] a very hard bright yellow metal that is a mixture of COPPER and ZINC: *a brass bed*
2 the brass (section) the people in an ORCHESTRA or band who play musical instruments made of brass, such as the TRUMPET or horn
3 the (top) brass INFORMAL the people who hold the most important positions in a company, organization, the military etc.
4 get down to brass tacks INFORMAL to start talking about the most important details or facts
5 have the brass (to do sth) INFORMAL to have the self-confidence and lack of respect to do something that is rude: *I can't believe you had the brass to tell her what you really thought.*
6 decorations [C,U] an object made of brass, usually with a design cut into it, or several brass objects
7 in church [C] a picture and writing on brass, placed on the wall or floor of a church in memory of someone who died

brass band /,. './ n. [C] a band consisting mostly of brass musical instruments such as TRUMPETs or horns

bras·se·rie /,bræsə'ri/ n. [C] a cheap informal restaurant usually serving beer and other alcoholic drinks, and French food

bras·siere /brə'zɪr/ n. [C] FORMAL a BRA

brass knuck·les /,. '../ n. [plural] a set of connected metal rings worn over a person's fingers, used as a weapon

brass rub·bing /'. ,../ n. [C,U] the act of making a copy of a BRASS (7) in a church by putting a piece of paper over it and rubbing it with a soft pencil, or a picture made in this way

brass·y /'bræsi/ adj. **brassier, brassiest 1** like BRASS (1) in color **2** a woman who is brassy is too loud, confident, or brightly dressed **3** sounding hard and loud like the sound made by a musical instrument made of BRASS (1)

brat /bræt/ n. [C] INFORMAL a badly behaved child: *Stop acting like a spoiled brat.* —**bratty** adj.

Bra·ti·sla·va /,brɑtɪ'slɑvə/ the capital city of Slovakia

Brat·tain /'brætn/, **Wal·ter** /'wɔltə/ (1902–1987) a U.S. scientist who worked on the development of an electronic TRANSISTOR

bra·va·do /brə'vɑdoʊ/ n. [U] behavior that is deliberately intended to show how brave and confident you are, but that is often unnecessary: *The new recruits were full of youthful bravado.*

brave¹ /breɪv/ adj. **1** dealing with danger, pain, or difficult situations with courage and confidence: *Her brave fight against cancer is an inspiration to us all.* | *brave soldiers* **2** put on a brave face to pretend that you are happy when you are really very upset **3** very good: *It's a brave effort to compete with the big publishers.* **4** the brave brave people: *Today we remember the brave who died defending our country.* —**bravely** adv.

brave² v. [T] to deal with a difficult, dangerous, or bad situation: *Over 45,000 football fans braved the elements (=went out in bad weather) to watch Denver narrowly beat Miami.*

brave sth out phr. v. [T] to deal bravely with something that is frightening or difficult

brave³ n. [C] a young fighting man from a Native American tribe

brav·er·y /ˈbreɪvəri/ *n.* [U] actions, behavior, or an attitude that shows courage and confidence: *In 1944, he won the Military Cross for bravery.*

bra·vo /ˈbravoʊ, braˈvoʊ/ *interjection* said to show your approval when someone, especially a performer, has done something very well

bra·vu·ra /brəˈvyʊrə, -ˈvʊrə/ *n.* [U] **1** the act of showing a lot of skill in the way you perform, write, paint etc., especially when you do something very difficult **2** the act of showing great courage

brawl¹ /brɔl/ *n.* [C] a noisy fight among a group of people, especially in a public place: *a drunken brawl* —**brawler** *n.* [C]

brawl² *v.* [I] to fight in a noisy way, especially in a public place: *Fans brawled outside the stadium.*

brawn /brɔn/ *n.* [U] physical strength, especially when compared with intelligence: *Football players are known more for their brawn than their brains.*

brawn·y /ˈbrɔni/ *adj.* **brawnier, brawniest** very large and strong: *big brawny arms*

bray /breɪ/ *v.* **brays, brayed, braying** [I] **1** if a DONKEY brays, it makes a loud sound **2** if someone brays, they laugh or talk in a loud, slightly annoying way —**bray** *n.* [C] —**braying** *adj.*

bra·zen¹ /ˈbreɪzən/ *adj.* **1** not embarrassed or ashamed about doing something or behaving in a way that most people consider wrong or immoral: *She's just a brazen hussy* (=a woman who behaves this way, especially sexually). **2** a action that is brazen is shocking because the person responsible is not ashamed of it: *a brazen lie* | *Trade in illegal tapes and computer software is brazen in some parts of the world.* **3** LITERARY having a shiny yellow color

brazen² *v.*

brazen sth ↔ out *phr. v.* [T] to deal with a situation that is difficult or embarrassing for you by appearing to be confident rather than ashamed

bra·zen·ly /ˈbreɪzənli/ *adv.* without showing or feeling any shame: *She brazenly admitted she had spent the night with Greg.*

bra·zier /ˈbreɪʒɚ/ *n.* [C] a metal container that holds a fire and is used for cooking or keeping a place warm

Bra·zil /brəˈzɪl/ the largest country in South America —**Brazilian** *n., adj.*

Braz·za·ville /ˈbræzəˌvɪl, ˈbrɑ-/ the capital and largest city of the Republic of Congo

BRB, brb a written abbreviation of "be right back," used by people communicating in CHAT ROOMS on the Internet

breach¹ /britʃ/ *n.* **1** [C,U] an act of breaking a law, rule, or agreement between people, groups, or countries: *Selling the product to another distributor is a clear breach of the agreement.* | *The U.N. says there have been grave breaches of human rights.* | *You are in breach of the rules.* | *If you try to get out of the deal, I'll sue you for breach of contract.* **2** [C] an action that breaks the rules of what people consider good or moral behavior: *a breach of confidence/trust/etiquette etc. Showing this information to anyone outside the company would be regarded as a serious breach of trust.* **3** *a breach of security/duty etc.* the action and result of someone breaking a system, not doing their duty etc.: *We are investigating a major breach of security at the embassy.* **4** [C] a serious disagreement between people, groups, or countries, with the result that they do not have a good relationship anymore: *Britain could not risk a breach with the U.S. over the trade issue.* **5** **step into the breach** to help by doing someone else's job or work when they are suddenly unable to do it **6** [C] a hole or broken place in a wall or similar structure, especially one made during a military attack

breach² *v.* [T] **1** to break a law, rule, agreement etc.: *The court ruled that he had breached the terms of the agreement.* **2** to break a hole in a wall or similar structure so that something can pass through: *On Friday, flood waters breached the river's banks.*

bread¹ /brɛd/ *n.* [U] **1** a common food made from flour, water, and YEAST: *Please pass the bread.* | *Could you pick up a loaf of bread* (=large piece of bread that can be cut into pieces) *on your way home?* | *four slices of bread* (=thin pieces of bread that you cut from a loaf) *with butter and jam* | *white/wheat/rye etc. bread* (=bread made with white, wheat etc. flour) —see also FRENCH BREAD **2** OLD-FASHIONED, SLANG money **3** *sb's bread and butter* INFORMAL the thing that provides you with most of the money that you need in order to live or be successful: *Tourism is our bread and butter.* **4** *know which side your bread is buttered on* INFORMAL to know who to be nice to in order to get advantages for yourself **5** *sb's daily bread* OLD-FASHIONED INFORMAL the money that you need in order to live —see also *sth is the best/greatest thing since sliced bread* (SLICE² (4))

bread² *v.* [T] to put BREADCRUMBs on the outside of meat or a vegetable before it is cooked

bread-and-but·ter /ˌ. . '../ *adj.* [only before noun] a **bread-and-butter question/product/issue etc.** a question, product etc. that is concerned with the most important and basic things: *I think Americans care most about bread-and-butter issues like health care and education.* —see also *sb's bread and butter* (BREAD¹ (3))

bread·bas·ket /ˈbrɛdˌbæskɪt/ *n.* **1** [singular] INFORMAL the part of a country or other large area that provides most of its food: [+ of] *The midwest is the breadbasket of America.* **2** [C] a basket for holding or serving bread

bread·board /ˈbrɛdbɔrd/ *n.* [C] **1** a wooden board on which you cut bread —see picture at BOARD¹ **2** a model of a CIRCUIT BOARD that is used to test the design before it is produced

bread·box /ˈbrɛdbɑks/ *n.* [C] a container for keeping bread in so that it stays fresh —see picture at KITCHEN

bread·crumb, bread crumb /ˈbrɛdkrʌm/ *n.* [C usually plural] a very small piece of bread that is left after you have cut some bread, or very small pieces that are deliberately prepared this way to be used in cooking

bread·ed /ˈbrɛdɪd/ *adj.* covered in breadcrumbs: *breaded veal*

bread·fruit /ˈbrɛdfrut/ *n.* [C,U] a large tropical fruit that looks like bread

bread·line /ˈbrɛdlaɪn/ *n.* [C] a line of poor people waiting to receive food from an organization or government: *On most days, the breadline begins to form by seven o'clock in the morning.*

breadth /brɛdθ, brɛtθ/ *n.* **1** [C,U] the distance from one side of something to the other; width *This flower resembles a lily and may reach a breadth of four inches.* | *His research for the book took him across the full breadth of the country.* —compare LENGTH (1), WIDTH (1) **2** [U] the fact or quality of having a wide variety or range of something, especially used about someone's knowledge or experience: *One thing I noticed right away was the breadth of the training that the workers were given.* **3** **breadth of vision/mind/outlook etc.** an ability to consider and understand a range of ideas, attitudes, and customs that are very different from your own: *McFerrin's compositions displayed a breadth of vision and originality that was astonishing.* **4** [C,U] the quality of being very large from one side to the other: *the breadth of the ocean* —see also BROAD¹, HAIR'S BREADTH, **the length and breadth of sth** (LENGTH (10))

bread·win·ner /ˈbrɛdˌwɪnɚ/ *n.* [C] the member of a family who earns the money to support the others

break¹ /breɪk/ *v.* **past tense broke past participle broken** **1** **in pieces** [I,T] if something breaks or you break it, it separates into two or more pieces, for example because it has been hit, dropped, or bent: *Somebody broke the window and the car alarm went off.* | *Careful, those glasses break easily.* | [+ **off**] *Part of it broke off when I touched it.* | **break sth in two/in half/into pieces etc.** *The force of the explosion had broken the door into pieces.*

2 **part of your body** [T] if you break your leg, arm etc. or break a bone, the bone splits into two or more pieces: *Tanya went skiing and broke her leg.*

3 **not working** [I,T] to damage something such as a machine so that it does not work or cannot be used, or to become damaged in this way: *How did you manage to break the microwave? | I think the switch is broken. | We bought him a radio-controlled airplane and he broke it the first day! | It just broke. I didn't even touch it!*

4 **end a situation** [T] to stop a bad or boring situation from continuing: *We took turns driving, in order to try and break the monotony.* | **break the deadlock/stalemate** (=end a situation in which an agreement or a solution cannot be found)

5 **surface/skin** [I,T] if the surface of something breaks or if you break it, it splits or gets a hole in it: *Do not use this product if the seal has been broken*

6 **break a law/rule** to disobey a law or rule: *Smith was kicked off the team for breaking team rules.*

7 **break a promise/an agreement/your word/a contract etc.** to not do what you have promised to do or signed an agreement to do: *A good way to lose customers is to break promises.*

8 **break for lunch/coffee/dinner etc.** to stop working for a short time in order to eat or drink something: *What time do you want to break for lunch?*

9 **break a record** to do something faster or better than it has ever been done before: *Collins retired after she broke the world record.* | *Sales of their new CD have broken all records* (=been much better or much more successful than anything before).

10 **break the news to sb** to tell someone about something bad that has happened: *Penny didn't want to break the news to Mom.*

11 **news** [I] if news about an important event breaks, it becomes known by everyone, especially after having been a secret for a period of time: *The next morning the news broke that Senator Edmunds was dead.*

12 **break a/the habit** to stop doing something that you have regularly done for a long time, especially something that is bad for you: *I don't smoke anymore, but it was hard to break the habit.*

13 **break even** to neither make a profit nor lose money: *Thankfully, we broke even in our first year in business.*

14 **break sb's heart** to make someone very unhappy by ending a relationship with them or by doing something that they do not want you to do: *It really broke his heart when she told him it was over. | It'll break your father's heart if you tell him you're quitting the team.*

15 **day** [I] if the day or the DAWN breaks, light begins to show in the sky as the sun rises

16 **wave** [I] if a wave breaks, the top part starts to fall down, usually because it is hitting or getting near the shore: *Waves broke against the rocks.*

22 **break free/loose** to escape from someone or somewhere by using force: *The cattle had broken loose during the night.*

23 **break loose** if violent feelings or a violent situation breaks loose, they suddenly start to happen: *Debbie told him to shut up, he slapped her, and then all hell broke loose* (=people started behaving in a wild uncontrolled way).

24 **break sb's fall** to stop someone from falling straight onto the ground, so that they are not badly hurt: *Luckily some bushes at the bottom of the cliff broke his fall.*

25 **break sb's concentration** also **break sb's train of thought** to interrupt someone and stop them from being able to continue thinking or talking about something: *I never listen to music when I'm working – it breaks my concentration.*

26 **break the back of sb/sth** to defeat someone or something and destroy their chances of continued success: *If these men are convicted, it could break the back of organized crime in the entire state.*

27 **break a strike** to force workers to end a STRIKE: *The company has threatened to hire 700 new workers in order to break the 10-month-old strike.*

28 **break the silence/calm** to end a period of silence or calm by talking or making a noise: *Rhonda's laugh broke the silence.*

29 **break your silence** to start talking about something in public after refusing to do so for a long time: *Government officials have finally broken their silence about reports of nerve gas attacks.*

30 **voice** [I] **a)** if your voice breaks, it changes from one level to another suddenly, especially because of strong emotions: *Her voice breaks as she talks about her missing children.* **b)** if a boy's voice breaks, it gradually starts to sound lower, like a man's voice, sometimes doing this suddenly as he is speaking: *I think I was about 14 when my voice broke.*

31 **break sb** to completely destroy someone's chances of success or make them feel that they cannot continue: *The years of pressure and criticism finally broke him.*

32 **break the ice** to do something or say something to make someone who you have just met be less nervous and more willing to talk, for example at a party or meeting: *I tried to break the ice by offering her a drink, but she said no.* —see also ICEBREAKER (2)

33 **break a sweat** to begin SWEATING[1] (1), especially because you are working or exercising hard

34 **do sth without breaking a sweat** also **do sth and not break a sweat** to do something easily: *She can disarm the most complicated security systems without breaking a sweat.*

35 **break sb's spirit/resolve** to make someone stop trying to achieve something, or make them start doing what you want: *Being a political prisoner for 15 years had not broken her spirit.*

36 **it won't break the bank** used to say that you can afford to buy something: *Well, I don't think it'll break the bank if we only go away for a weekend.*

37 **break ranks** to behave differently from the other members of a group, who are expecting you to support them: *Surprisingly, nine of the 31 Republicans in the Assembly broke ranks to vote with the Democrats.*

38 **break fresh/new ground** to do something completely new that no one has ever done before, or find out new information about a subject: *With this agreement, the agency is breaking new ground in dealing with sex discrimination.*

39 **storm** [I] if a storm breaks, it suddenly begins: *The storm finally broke just as I was getting out of the car.*

40 **weather** [I] if the weather breaks, it suddenly changes: *Farmers are anxious for the cold weather to break.*

41 **code** [T] to succeed in understanding what the letters or numbers in a secret CODE mean: *We've finally managed to break their secret code.*

42 **break your ties/connection/links etc.** to end your connection or relationship with a person, group, organization etc.: *I broke all my ties with my father years ago.*

43 **break cover** to move out of a place where you have been hiding so that you can be seen: *Suddenly, one of the elephants broke cover and charged straight at them.*

44 **break camp** to pack tents and other equipment and leave the place where you have been camping

45 break wind FORMAL to allow gas to escape from your BOWELS, making a noise and a bad smell; FART
46 break (sb's) serve to win a game in tennis when your opponent is serving (SERVE[1] (10))
47 game [I] to begin a game of POOL, BILLIARDS etc. by being the first one to hit the ball: *I'll let you break next game.*
48 break the bank to win more money in a game of cards than a CASINO or a DEALER (3) is able to pay you
break away *phr. v.* [I] **1** to move away from someone or something, especially in order to escape: [+ from] *The woman broke away from police, but was later caught.* **2** to end your connection or relationship with a person, group, organization etc., usually because of a disagreement: [+ from] *During that time, Portugal's colonies broke away from colonial rule.*

break down

break down *phr. v.*
1 machine [I] if a large machine, especially a car, breaks down, it stops working: *My car broke down on the way to work.* | *The elevators in this building are always breaking down.*
2 fail [I] if a discussion, system etc. breaks down, it fails or stops existing: *The talks broke down completely in June 1982.*
3 door [T break sth ↔ down] to hit something, such as a door, so hard that it breaks and falls to the ground
4 break down (and do sth) to finally do something that you did not want to do, because someone has persuaded or forced you: *He finally broke down and admitted he'd stolen the money.*
5 change chemically [I,T break sth ↔ down] if a substance breaks down or is broken down, it is reduced or changed, usually as a result of a chemical process: *Glycogen is broken down to glucose in the liver.*
6 cry [I] to be unable to stop yourself from crying, especially in public: *Margaret broke down several times during the funeral.*
7 change ideas [T break sth ↔ down] to change the ideas or feelings that someone or a group of people have, so that they agree with yours: *No one has yet found a way to break down the hatred between the two ethnic groups.*
8 become sick [I] to become mentally or physically ill: *If Tim keeps working this hard, he'll break down sooner or later.*
9 make sth simple [T break sth ↔ down] to make something such as a job, report, plan etc. simpler or easier to understand by dividing it into parts: *You can break the exam question down into three parts to make it easier.*
10 sports [T break sb/sth ↔ down] to succeed in gaining points in a game in sports: *Seattle had no problem breaking down Dallas' defense.* —see also BREAKDOWN
break for sth *phr. v.* [T] to suddenly run or drive somewhere, especially in order to escape from someone: *Sullivan broke for the window, but was stopped by a security guard.*
break in *phr. v.* **1** [I] to enter a building by using force, in order to steal something: *It looks like they broke in through that window.* —see also BREAK-IN,

BREAKING AND ENTERING **2** [T break sb/sth ↔ in] to make a person or animal get used to a certain way of behaving or working: *They have a good training program for breaking in new employees.* **3** [I] to interrupt a conversation or activity by saying or doing something: *The operator broke in, saying, "You need another 75¢ to continue the call."* | *TV news anchors periodically broke in with updates on the incident.* | [+ on] *Sir, sorry to break in on your meeting, but your wife is outside.* **4** [I,T break sth ↔ in] if you break new shoes or boots in, or if they break in, they become less stiff and more comfortable because you have been wearing them
break into sth *phr. v.* [T]
1 steal to enter a building by using force, in order to steal something: *Someone broke into our house while we were on vacation.*
2 break into a run/gallop/trot etc. to suddenly start running etc.: *Brenda saw someone in the alley and broke into a run.*
3 new activity to become involved in a new activity, especially a business activity: *We think this product will help us to break into the Eastern European market.*
4 break into tears/laughter/cheers etc. to suddenly start crying, laughing etc. —see also **break into a sweat** (SWEAT[2] (5))
5 interrupt to interrupt an activity by saying or doing something: *Sorry to break into your lunch hour, but it's an emergency.*
6 money to start to spend money that you did not want to spend: *I was hoping we wouldn't have to break into our savings.*
break sb **of** sth *phr. v.* [T] to make someone stop having a bad habit: *You can break your dog of barking at the mailman by using the "stay" command.*
break off *phr. v.* **1** [T break sth ↔ off] to end a relationship, especially a political or romantic one: *The U.S. broke off diplomatic relations with Cuba over 30 years ago.* | *Did you hear? They've broken off their engagement.* **2** [T break sth ↔ off] to break a piece from the main part of something: *Can you break off a piece of that chocolate for me?* | *Large branches had been broken off by the wind.* **3** [I,T break sth ↔ off] to suddenly stop doing something, especially talking to someone: *Without explanation, management broke off contract negotiations.* | *She broke off, forgetting what she wanted to say.*
break out *phr. v.* [I] **1** if something bad such as a fire, war, or disease breaks out, it begins to happen: *War broke out six months later.* **2** to change the way you live or behave, especially because you feel bored | **break out of a rut/routine etc.** (=stop doing the same things all the time) **3** to begin to have red spots on your skin, especially on your face: *Chocolate makes me break out.* | *That soap made me break out in a rash.* **4** to escape from a prison or a similar place: [+ of] *They were caught trying to break out of jail.* —see also BREAKOUT[1]
break through *phr. v.* [I] **1** [I,T break through sth] to force a way through something *Our troops finally managed to break through enemy lines.* **2** [T break through sth] to deal successfully with something, especially unreasonable behavior or bad feelings: *Somehow we managed to break through the racial prejudices and get people talking.* **3** [I,T] if the sun or light breaks through, you can see it through something such as clouds or mist —see also BREAKTHROUGH
break up *phr. v.*
1 marriage/group [I] to end a marriage or romantic relationship, or to stop being together as a group: *Liz and I broke up last year.* | *What year did the Beatles break up?* —see also BREAKUP (1)
2 separate [T break sth ↔ up] to separate something into several smaller parts or groups: *The state-owned gas company was broken up into several smaller private companies.* | *I usually break the students up into pairs to practice using new vocabulary.*
3 break into pieces [I,T break sth ↔ up] to break into many small pieces, or to make something do this: *Increased traffic of heavy trucks will break up local roads.* | *The drug causes the clots that cause heart attacks to break up.*

4 *fight* [I,T] if a fight breaks up or someone breaks it up, the people stop fighting each other: *Rizzo stepped in to break up the fight.*

5 *crowd* [I,T **break** sth ↔ **up**] if a crowd or meeting breaks up or someone breaks it up, people start to leave: *Force was used to break up the rally.*

6 *make sb laugh* [T **break** sb **up**] INFORMAL to say or do something that is so funny that people cannot stop laughing: *His comment about football players broke everyone up.*

break with sb/sth *phr. v.* [T] **1** to leave a group of people or an organization, especially because you have had a disagreement with them: *Yugoslavia under Tito soon broke with Stalin's Russia.* **2 break with tradition** also **break with the past** to stop following old customs and do something in a completely different way

break² *n.*

1 *a rest* **a)** [C] a period of time when you stop what you are doing in order to rest, eat etc.: *I've been working since nine o'clock without a break.* | **coffee/lunch break** *When is your lunch break?* | *At 11, the band took a break.* **b)** [C] a short vacation: *We needed a break, so we went up to the mountains for a few days.* | **Thanksgiving/Spring/Christmas etc. break** (=the public or school holidays at Thanksgiving etc.) —see Usage Note at VACATION¹

2 *a pause in sth* [C] **a)** a period of time during which something stops, before continuing again: *There was a break of two years between his last book and this one.* | [+ **in**] *Elaine took a six-month break in her studies.* | [+ **from**] *I want you all to have a little break from your classroom work, so we're all going to the library.* **b)** a pause in a conversation or in what someone is saying: [+ **in**] *There was an awkward break in the conversation.* **c)** also **commercial break** a pause for advertisements during a television or radio program: *We'll be right back after the break.*

3 *give sb a break* SPOKEN said when you want someone to stop annoying, criticizing, or being mean to you or someone else: *Give me a break, you guys! I can't get the money until Friday.*

4 *give me a break* SPOKEN said when you do not believe something someone has just said or think that it was stupid: *"I thought this tie looked pretty good, actually." "Oh, give me a break!"*

5 *a chance* [C] INFORMAL a sudden or unexpected chance to do something, especially to be successful in your job | **a big/lucky break** *The band's big break came when they sang on a local TV show.*

6 *end/change* [C usually singular] an occasion when you end a relationship with a person, organization etc., or change the way that things have always been done in the past: [+ **from**] *Replacing human workers with machines would be a significant break from our company's manufacturing practices.* | [+ **with**] *This ruling represents a major break with the policies of the past 35 years.* | *In a break with tradition, the city council decided not to have a parade.* | *Why argue about the terms of the divorce when both of you just want a clean break* (=a very clear and definite end to a relationship)?

7 *a space* [C] a space between two things or between two parts of something: [+ **in**] *Occasionally you could see the moon through a break in the clouds.*

8 *make a break for sth* to suddenly start running toward something in order to escape from a place: *As soon as the guard's back was turned, they made a break for the door.* | *After the police fired tear gas, one hostage made a break for it* (=tried to escape).

9 *broken place* [C] the place where a bone in your body has broken: *The break has not healed correctly.*

10 *tennis* also **break of serve** [C] a situation in a game of tennis in which you win a game when your opponent is serving (SERVE¹ (10)): *Gonzales needs a break of serve to even the match up.* —see also BREAK POINT

11 the break of day LITERARY the time early in the morning when it starts getting light

12 *points* [C] the number of points won by a player when it is their turn to hit the ball in a game such as BILLIARDS

break·a·ble /'breɪkəbəl/ *adj.* made of a material such as glass or clay that breaks easily

break·age /'breɪkɪdʒ/ *n.* FORMAL **1** [U] the act of breaking **2 breakages** [plural] things that have been broken, especially things that belong to someone else that you must pay for: *You'll be required to pay for any breakages.*

break·a·way /'breɪkə,weɪ/ *adj.* **a breakaway group/party/movement etc.** a breakaway group, party etc. has been formed by people who left another group because of a disagreement: *This week saw continued fighting in two of the breakaway republics.* —**breakaway** *n.* [C]

break·dance /'breɪkdæns/ *v.* [I] to do a type of dance involving ACROBATIC movements —**breakdancing** *n.* [U] —**breakdancer** *n.* [C]

break·down /'breɪkdaʊn/ *n.* **1** [C,U] the failure of a system or relationship: *Many families experience marital breakdown.* | [+ **in**] *Is the problem due to a breakdown in our quality control system?* | [+ **of**] *The riots have been blamed on the breakdown of the peace process.* **2** [C] an occasion when a car or a piece of machinery breaks and stops working: *It seems like our copy machine has a breakdown every week.* **3** [C] a written statement explaining the details of something such as a bill or the cost of a plan: [+ **of**] *I'd like a breakdown of these figures, please.* **4** [C] a NERVOUS BREAKDOWN

break·er /'breɪkɚ/ *n.* [C] a large wave with a white top that rolls onto the shore —see also CIRCUIT BREAKER

break-e·ven /,. '../ *adj.* [only before noun] relating to the level of business activity at which a company is not making a profit or a loss | **the break-even point/level** *The company estimated this year's results at the break-even level or slightly above.* —**breakeven** *n.* [U] —see also **break even** (BREAK¹ (13))

break·fast /'brɛkfəst/ *n.* [C,U] the meal you have in the morning: *During breakfast, I usually read the paper.* | *I had bacon and eggs for breakfast.* | *Fewer than half of the children had eaten breakfast.* | *We met for a working breakfast* (=a breakfast at which you talk about business). —**breakfast** *v.* [I + **on**] —see also BED AND BREAKFAST, CONTINENTAL BREAKFAST

break-in /'. ./ *n.* [C] an act of entering a building illegally and by using force, especially in order to steal things: *The break-in occurred between midnight and six in the morning.*

breaking and en·ter·ing /,.. '.../ *n.* [U] LAW the crime of entering a building illegally and by using force

breaking point /'.. ,./ *n.* [singular] the point at which someone or something is not able to work well or deal with problems anymore: *Social services are stretched to the breaking point* (=the services are doing as much as they can possibly do).

break·neck /'breɪknɛk/ *adj.* **at breakneck pace/speed** extremely and often dangerously fast: *Everyone's working at breakneck pace to meet the deadline.* | *He was driving at breakneck speed.*

break·out¹ /'breɪkaʊt/ *n.* [C] an escape from a prison, especially one involving a lot of prisoners —compare OUTBREAK

breakout² *adj.* **a breakout game/performance/show etc.** a game, performance etc. in which you perform very well, especially after a time in which you were not very successful: *Atlanta pitcher John Smoltz hopes to have a breakout season.*

break point /'. ./ *n.* [C,U] a situation in tennis when you only have to win one more point to win a game when your opponent is serving (SERVE¹ (10))

break·through /'breɪkθru/ *n.* [C] an important new discovery in something you are studying, especially one made after trying for a long time: *Scientists have made an important breakthrough in the treatment of heart disease.*

break·up /'breɪkʌp/ n. [C] **1** the act of ending a marriage or other relationship: *I think Roger's still bitter about the breakup.* **2** the separation of a group, organization, or country into smaller parts, especially because it has become weaker or there are serious disagreements: [+ of] *the breakup of Yugoslavia*

break·wa·ter /'breɪk,wɔtɚ/ n. [C] a large strong wall built out into the ocean to protect the shore from the force of the waves

S W
2
3
breast¹ /brɛst/ n.
1 woman's body [C] one of the two round raised parts on a woman's chest that produce milk when she has a baby: *These bras are specially designed for women with large breasts.* | *breast cancer* —see picture at BODY
2 meat [U] meat that comes from the front part of the body of a bird such as a chicken: *turkey breast*
3 bird [C] the front part of a bird's body, between its neck and the stomach: *a robin with a red breast*
4 make a clean breast of it/things to admit that you have done something wrong: *He needs to go before the public and make a clean breast of it.*
5 chest [C] the part of your body between your neck and your stomach, especially the upper part of this area: *His arms were folded across his breast.*
6 emotions [C] LITERARY where your feelings of sadness, love, anger, fear etc. come from: *Anger swelled the young man's breast.* —see also **beat your breast** (BEAT¹ (33)), -BREASTED

breast² v. [T] FORMAL **1** to reach the top of a hill or slope **2** to push against something with your chest

breast·bone /'brɛstboʊn/ n. [C] the long flat bone in the front of your chest to which the top seven pairs of RIBs are connected —see picture at SKELETON

-breasted /brɛstɪd/ [in adjectives] **1 single-breasted/double-breasted** a coat, dress etc. that is single- or double-breasted has one or two rows of buttons down the front **2 small-breasted/bare-breasted etc.** having small breasts, no clothes over the breasts etc.

breast-feed /'. ,./ v. past tense and past participle **breast-fed** [I,T] if a woman breast-feeds, she feeds her baby with milk from her breast rather than from a bottle —**breast-fed** adj. [only before noun] *a breast-fed baby* —compare NURSE² (3), SUCKLE

breast im·plant /'. ,../ n. [C] a bag filled with a liquid or other substance that a doctor puts under the skin of a woman's chest, to make her breast bigger or to replace a breast that was removed

breast·plate /'brɛstpleɪt/ n. [C] a leather or metal protective covering worn over the chest by soldiers during battles in past times

breast pock·et /,. '../ n. [C] a pocket on the outside of a shirt or JACKET, above the breast

breast·stroke /'brɛststroʊk/ n. [U] a way of swimming in which you push your arms straight ahead and then bring them back in a circle toward your sides, while bending your knees toward your body and then kicking out

S W
2
3
breath /brɛθ/ n.
1 air you breathe **a)** [U] the air that you take in and send out of your lungs when you breathe: *I can smell alcohol on your breath.* | *If someone has bad breath* (=breath that smells bad), *should you tell them?* **b)** [singular,U] the act of breathing air into your lungs, or the amount of air that you breathe: *Let your breath out slowly.* | *Eric came running into the room, out of breath* (=having difficulty breathing because he had just been running, exercising etc.) *and red in the face.* | *Marge had to stop to get her breath back* (=breathe normally again after running or making a lot of effort) *after walking up the hill.* | *Do you ever find that you're short of breath* (=unable to breathe easily, especially because you are unhealthy) *after light exercise?* | *a big/deep breath* (=an occasion when you breathe in a lot of air once) **c)** [U] the process of breathing in and out: *Her breath was coming more easily now.*

2 hold your breath a) to breathe in and not breath out again, in order to keep the air in your lungs: *It stinks so bad you have to hold your breath until you come out.* **b)** to wait anxiously to see what is going to happen: *Patrice held her breath, waiting for Lettie's reply.*
3 don't hold your breath INFORMAL used to say that something is not going to happen soon: *If you're waiting for the Cubs to win the series, don't hold your breath.*
4 don't waste your breath also **save your breath** SPOKEN used in order to tell someone that what they want to say is not worth saying or will not change a situation: *Save your breath. He won't listen.*
5 a breath of fresh air a) something that is new and different in a way you think is exciting and enjoyable: *Moving to this big apartment was like a breath of fresh air.* **b)** the activity of going outside to breathe clean air in order to relax, especially because you are tired or hot: *I'm going outside for a breath of fresh air.*
6 take your breath away to be extremely beautiful or exciting: *The view from the overlook will take your breath away.*
7 under your breath in a very quiet voice: *"Son of a bitch," Bill muttered under his breath.*
8 in the same breath a) also **in the next breath** used to say that someone has said two things at once that are so different from each other they cannot both be true: *She said everything looked perfect, but in the same breath she suggested moving the couch more over to the window.* **b)** if you mention two people or things in the same breath, you show that you think they are alike: *He's a performer who is frequently mentioned in the same breath as Mick Jagger.*
9 with your last/dying breath at the moment when you are dying: *With his last breath, he told me he would always love me.*
10 a breath of air/wind LITERARY a slight movement of air: *Scarcely a breath of air disturbed the stillness of the day.* —see also **with bated breath** (BATED), **catch your breath** (CATCH¹ (24))

breath·a·ble /'briðəbəl/ adj. **1** clothing that is breathable allows air to pass through it easily: *a waterproof, breathable jacket* **2** able to be breathed: *breathable air*

breath·a·lyze /'brɛθə,laɪz/ v. [T] to make someone breathe into a special piece of equipment in order to see if they have drunk too much alcohol to be allowed to drive

Breath·a·lyz·er /'brɛθə,laɪzɚ/ n. [C] TRADEMARK a piece of equipment used by the police to see if drivers have drunk too much alcohol

S
2
breathe /brið/ v.
1 air [I,T] to take air into your lungs and send it out again: *My eyes began to sting and I couldn't breathe.* | *People are concerned about the quality of the air they breathe.* | *Relax and breathe deeply* (=take in a lot of air).
2 blow [I,T] to blow air, smoke, or smells out of your mouth: [+ on] *I breathed on my fingers to keep them warm.* | *It was cold, and everyone breathed clouds of vapor.*
3 breathe a sigh of relief to not be worried anymore about something that had been worrying or frightening you: *I breathed a sigh of relief that the boy had been found safe.*
4 be breathing down sb's neck INFORMAL to pay very close attention to what someone is doing, in a way that makes them feel nervous or annoyed: *I can't work with you breathing down my neck.*
5 not breathe a word to not tell anyone anything at all about something, because it is a secret: *You've got to promise not to breathe a word to anyone.*
6 breathe life/excitement/enthusiasm etc. into sth to change a situation so that people feel more excited or interested: *Some new teachers might breathe a little life into this school.*
7 breathe again/easy/easily to relax because something dangerous or frightening has finished: *With stocks going up, investors can breathe easily.*
8 wine [I] if you let wine breathe, you open the bottle to let the air get to it before you drink it

9 **say sth quietly** [T] to say something very quietly, almost in a whisper: *"Come closer," he breathed.*
10 breathe your last (breath) LITERARY to die
11 breathe fire to behave and talk very angrily
—see also **live and breathe sth** (LIVE[1] (18))

breathe in *phr. v.* **1** [I] to take air into your lungs: *Become aware of your breathing: breathe in, count, breathe out.* **2** [T **breathe** sth ↔ **in**] to breathe air, smoke, a particular kind of smell etc. into your lungs: *We stood on the sand, breathing in the fresh ocean air.*

breathe out *phr. v.* **1** [I] to send air out from your lungs: *OK, now breathe out slowly.* **2** [T **breathe** sth ↔ **out**] to send out air, oxygen, a particular kind of smell etc.: *Green plants breathe out oxygen in sunlight.*

breath·er /ˈbriðɚ/ *n.* **have/take a breather** INFORMAL to stop what you are doing for a short time in order to rest, especially when you are exercising

breath·ing /ˈbriðɪŋ/ *n.* [U] the process of breathing air in and out —see also **heavy breathing** (HEAVY[1] (13))

breathing space /ˈ.. ./ *n.* [U] also **breathing room 1** a short time when you stop doing something difficult, tiring etc., so that you have time to think more clearly about a situation or time to solve a problem: *This deal should give the company some extra breathing room before its loans are due.* **2** enough room to move or breathe easily and comfortably in: *He managed to create enough breathing space in the snow to survive until he could be rescued.*

breath·less /ˈbrɛθlɪs/ *adj.* **1** having difficulty breathing, especially because you are very tired, excited, or frightened: *Walking up ten flights of stairs left him breathless.* **2** LITERARY too hot, with no fresh air or wind: *a breathless August night* —**breathlessly** *adv.* —**breathlessness** *n.* [U]

breath·tak·ing /ˈbrɛθˌteɪkɪŋ/ *adj.* very impressive, exciting, or surprising: *the breathtaking scenery of the Rocky Mountains* | *The changes in the city since 1980 have been breathtaking.* —**breathtakingly** *adv.*

breath test /ˈ. ./ *n.* [C] a test in which the police make a car driver breathe into a special machine to see if he or she has drunk too much alcohol

breath·y /ˈbrɛθi/ *adj.* if someone's voice is breathy, you can hear their breath when they speak

Brecht /brɛkt/, **Ber·tolt** /ˈbɔtɔlt/ (1398–1956) a German writer of plays and poetry dealing with political ideas —**Brechtian** *adj.*

bred /brɛd/ *v.* **1** the past tense and past participle of BREED **2 -bred** combined with names of places or areas to show where someone was born or where something comes from: *I was a country-bred girl, trying to make it in the big city.* | *the young Georgia-bred singer* | *locally-bred small businesses* —see also PUREBRED, WELL-BRED

breech[1] /britʃ/ *adj.* if a baby is breech or is a breech delivery, the lower part of a baby's body comes out of its mother first when it is born

breech[2] *n.* [C] **1** the part of gun into which you put the bullets **2 breeches** *plural* **a)** short pants that fasten just below the knees: *riding breeches* **b)** OLD-FASHIONED long pants: BRITCHES

W **breed[1]** /brid/ *v. past tense and past participle* **bred 1** [T] to keep animals or plants in order to produce babies or new plants, or in order to develop animals or plants that have particular qualities: *Only some endangered animals can be bred in zoos.* | *These trees are bred to resist pollution.* **2** [I] if animals breed, they MATE[2] (1) in order to have babies: *This is a pond where ducks breed.* **3** [T] to cause a particular feeling or condition: *Poor living conditions breed violence and despair.* **4** [T] if a place, situation, or thing breeds someone, it influences the way they think and behave: *The music became a fixture on urban radio in the '80s and bred a generation of fans.* —see also **-bred** (BRED), **born and bred** (BORN (6)), WELL-BRED

W **breed[2]** *n.* [C] **1** a type of animal or plant, especially one that people have kept to breed, such as cats, dogs, and farm animals: *Spaniels are my favorite*

breed of dog. **2** a particular kind of person or type of thing: *Real cowboys are a dying breed* (=not many exist anymore). | *Roller blades are a new breed of roller skates.* | *He's one of the rare breed* (=there are not many of them) *of scientists who can explain his work to non-scientists.*

breed·er /ˈbridɚ/ *n.* [C] **1** someone who breeds animals or plants as a job: *a dog breeder* **2** DISAPPROVING, SLANG a word meaning HETEROSEXUAL, used by HOMOSEXUALS

breed·ing /ˈbridɪŋ/ *n.* [U] **1** the process of animals producing babies: *The disease often attacks during the birds' breeding season* (=time of the year when an animal has babies). **2** the activity of keeping animals or plants in order to produce new or better types: *the breeding of pedigree dogs* | *the sale of breeding stock* (=animals you keep to breed from) **3** polite social behavior that someone learns from their family: *a woman of wealth and good breeding*

breeding ground /ˈ.. ./ *n.* [C] **1** a place where animals go in order to breed: *The whales' breeding grounds are off the west coast of Mexico.* **2** a place or situation where something bad or harmful grows and develops: [+ **for**] *Overcrowded slums are breeding grounds for crime.*

breeze[1] /briz/ *n.* [C] **1** a gentle wind: *Flags waved in the breeze.* **2 be a breeze** SPOKEN to be something that is very easy to do: *Installing the program on your computer is a breeze.* —see also **shoot the breeze** (SHOOT[1] (13))

breeze[2] *v.* [I always + adv./prep.] to walk somewhere in a calm confident way: [+ **in/into/out** etc.] *Jenny breezed into the meeting thirty minutes late.*

breeze through sth *phr. v.* [T] to achieve something very easily: *The bill is expected to breeze through the Senate before Christmas.* | *Detroit breezed through the playoff games to win the championship.*

breez·y /ˈbrizi/ *adj.* **1** a breezy person is cheerful, confident, and relaxed: *She's a woman with a lot of breezy charm.* **2** breezy weather is when the wind blows strongly —**breezily** *adv.* —**breeziness** *n.* [U]

breth·ren /ˈbrɛðrən/ *n.* [plural] OLD-FASHIONED a way of addressing or talking about the members of an organization or association, especially a religious group

bre·vi·ar·y /ˈbriviˌɛri/ *n.* [C] a prayer book used in the Catholic Church

brev·i·ty /ˈbrɛvəti/ *n.* [U] FORMAL **1** the quality of expressing something in very few words: *Letters published in the newspaper are edited for brevity and clarity.* **2** shortness of time: *Fans were disappointed by the brevity of the concert.*

brew[1] /bru/ *v.* **1** [T] to make beer **2** [I,T] if tea or coffee brews or you brew it, you pour boiling water over it to make it ready to drink **3** [I] if a bad situation is brewing, it will happen soon: *An argument is brewing over the tax cuts.* **4** [I] if a storm is brewing, it will happen soon

brew[2] *n.* [C,U] **1** SPOKEN beer, or a can or glass of beer **2** a drink that is brewed, such as coffee or tea —see also HOME BREW

brew·er /ˈbruɚ/ *n.* [C] a person or company that makes beer

brew·er·y /ˈbruəri/ *n. plural* **breweries** [C] a building where beer is made, or a company that makes beer

brew·ski /ˈbruski/ *n.* [C] SPOKEN a can or glass of beer

Brezh·nev /ˈbrɛznɛf/, **Le·o·nid** /ˈliəˌnɪd/ (1906–1982) the leader of the Soviet Union from 1977 to 1982

bri·ar, **brier** /ˈbraɪɚ/ *n.* **1** [C,U] a wild bush with branches that have small sharp points **2** [C] a tobacco pipe made from a briar

bribe[1] /braɪb/ *n.* [C] money or gifts that you give someone to persuade them to do something, especially something dishonest: *A New York Supreme Court judge was charged with taking bribes.* —compare PAYOLA

bribe² *v.* [T] **1** to illegally pay money or offer gifts to an official, in order to persuade them to do something for you: [**bribe sb to do sth**] *Jones bribed officials to get government contracts.* **2** to offer someone, especially a child, something special in order to persuade them to do something they do not want to do: [**bribe sb with sth**] *I had to bribe the kids with the promise of lunch at McDonalds.*

brib·er·y /ˈbraɪbəri/ *n.* [U] the act of taking or offering bribes: *The drug bosses were using bribery to stay out of jail.* | *Several politicians are linked to the bribery and sex scandal.*

bric-a-brac /ˈbrɪk ə ˌbræk/ *n.* [U] small objects, especially things you have in your home, that are not worth very much money but are interesting or attractive: *The shelves in the living room were lined with bric-a-brac and religious figurines.*

SW **brick¹** /brɪk/ *n.* **1** [C,U] a hard block of baked clay used for building walls, houses etc.: *a brick wall* | [**+ of/with**] *Most of the houses were built of brick.* **2** [C] INFORMAL an attempt to throw the ball through the BASKET in basketball that fails, especially one that is so bad that it is embarrassing: *Jensen shot bricks all afternoon.* **3** [C] OLD-FASHIONED a good person who you can depend on when you are in trouble: *Janet's a real brick.* **4 you can't make bricks without straw** used to say you cannot do a job if you do not have the necessary materials —see also **bang your head against/on a (brick) wall** (BANG¹ (5)), **hit a brick wall** (HIT¹ (28)), **shit bricks** (SHIT² (3)), **sth is like talking to a brick wall** (TALK¹ (15)), **hit sb like a ton of bricks** (TON)

brick² *v.*

brick sth off *phr. v.* [T] to separate an area from a larger area by building a wall of bricks

brick sth up/in *phr. v.* [T] to fill or close a space using bricks

brick·bat /ˈbrɪkbæt/ *n.* [C] a criticism of something: *The plan has drawn both brickbats and praise.*

brick·lay·er /ˈbrɪkˌleɪə/ *n.* [C] someone whose job is to build walls, buildings etc. with bricks —**bricklaying** *n.* [U]

brick·work /ˈbrɪkwɜk/ *n.* [U] the way that bricks have been used to build something, or the skill or work of building something with bricks: *The brickwork was cracked and in need of repair.* | *We need someone to do the brickwork.*

brick·yard /ˈbrɪkyɑrd/ *n.* [C] a place where bricks are made

bri·dal /ˈbraɪdl/ *adj.* relating to a wedding or the woman who is getting married: *a bridal gown*

bridal par·ty /ˈ.. ˌ../ *n.* [C] a WEDDING PARTY

bridal reg·is·try /ˈ.. ˌ.../ *n.* **a)** [C] a list of things from a particular store that a couple who is getting married would like to receive as gifts **b)** [C,U] the service, provided by the store, of arranging this list

bridal show·er /ˈ.. ˌ../ also **shower** *n.* [C] a party for a woman who is going to be married, given by her friends and family

bride /braɪd/ *n.* [C] a woman at the time she gets married or just after she is married: *You may kiss the bride.*

bride·groom /ˈbraɪdgrum/ *n.* [C] a GROOM

brides·maid /ˈbraɪdzmeɪd/ *n.* [C] a girl or woman, usually unmarried, who helps the bride on her wedding day and stands with her at the wedding

bride-to-be /ˌ.. ˈ./ *n.* [C] a woman who is going to be married soon: *Suzanne is Jonathan's bride-to-be.*

SW **bridge¹** /brɪdʒ/ *n.*
1 **over a river/road etc.** [C] a structure built over a river, road etc., that allows people or vehicles to cross from one side to the other
2 **connection** [C] something that provides a connection or relationship between two things: [**+ between**] *His job is to serve as a kind of bridge between students and the college administration.* | *The mayor has been building bridges* (=making a

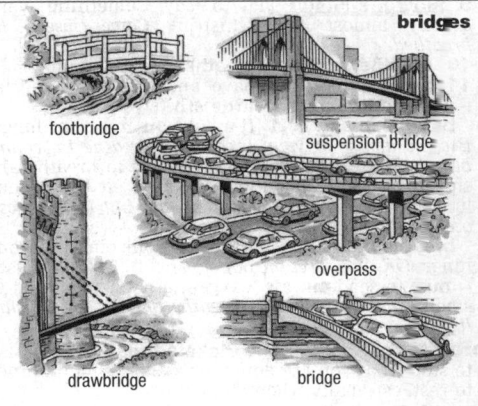

footbridge
suspension bridge
overpass
drawbridge
bridge

bridges

better relationship) *between ordinary citizens and public officials.*
3 **ship** [C] the raised part of a ship from which the officers control it
4 **card game** [U] a card game for four players who play in pairs
5 **part of nose** [C usually singular] the upper part of your nose between your eyes: *He had a small cut on the bridge of his nose.*
6 **pair of glasses** [C usually singular] the part of a pair of glasses that rests on the bridge of your nose
7 **musical instrument** [C usually singular] a small piece of wood under the strings of a VIOLIN or GUITAR, used to keep them in position
8 **for teeth** [C] a small piece of metal that keeps false teeth in place by attaching them to your real teeth —see also **burn your bridges** (BURN¹ (12)), **cross that bridge when you come to it** (CROSS¹ (9)), **be water under the bridge** (WATER¹ (6))

bridge² *v.* [T] **1** to reduce or get rid of the difference between two things: *The differences between our two cultures can be bridged if we continue to communicate.* | *We need a program to bridge the gap between the police and local youngsters.* **2** to build or form a bridge over something: *A log bridged the stream.*

bridge·head /ˈbrɪdʒhɛd/ *n.* [C] a good position far forward in enemy land from which an army can go forward or attack

bridge loan /ˈ. ./ also **bridg·ing loan** /ˈ.. ˌ./ *n.* [C] an amount of money that a bank lends you, to cover a short period of time before you receive a larger LOAN

Bridge·town /ˈbrɪdʒtaʊn/ the capital city of Barbados

bri·dle¹ /ˈbraɪdl/ *n.* [C] a set of leather bands put around a horse's head and used to control its movements

bridle² *v.* **1** [T] to put a bridle on a horse **2** [I,T] to become angry and offended about something: [**+ at**] *The coach bridled at suggestions that he'd made mistakes in the last game.*

bridle path /ˈ.. ˌ./ *n.* [C] a path that you ride a horse on

Brie, brie /bri/ *n.* [U] a soft French cheese

brief¹ /brif/ *adj.*
1 **time** continuing for a short time: *Police caught the man after a brief chase.* | *Let's keep the meeting as brief as possible.*
2 **speech/letter** using very few words or including few words: *The victim's parents read a brief statement to the press.*
3 **in brief a)** in as few words as possible: *In brief, the President plans to cut defense spending and lower taxes.* **b)** with very few details: *At 9:15, they give the foreign news in brief.*
4 **be brief** to say or write something using only a few words, especially because there is little time: *I'll be brief – a lot of changes are going to happen.*
5 **be brief with sb** to not say very much to someone in a way that seems impolite
6 **clothes** clothes which are brief are short and cover only a small area of your body: *a very brief bikini*

brief² v. [T] to give someone all the information about a situation that they will need [**brief sb on sth**] *Congress has been fully briefed on the current situation in Haiti.* —compare DEBRIEF

brief³ n. **1** [C] a short spoken or written statement giving facts about a law case: *The ACLU filed a brief* (=gave one to the court) *opposing the decision.* **2** [C] a short report about something, especially information about something that has happened recently: *I've prepared a brief on the economic situation in China.* **3 briefs** [plural] men's underwear that fits tightly to the body and covers only the BUTTOCKS and sexual organs —compare BOXER SHORTS **4** [C usually singular] official instructions that explain what someone's job is, what their duties are, how they should behave etc.

brief·case /'brifkeɪs/ n. [C] a flat suitcase with a handle, used especially by business people for carrying papers or documents —see picture at CASE¹

brief·ing /'brifɪŋ/ n. [C,U] information or instructions that you get before you do something, or the meeting at which this is done

W3 brief·ly /'brifli/ adv. **1** for a short time: *He worked briefly for Walt Disney Studios.* **2** using as few words as possible: *Sonia explained briefly how the machine works.* [sentence adverb] *Briefly, the problem was that I wanted a child and he didn't.*

bri·er /'braɪɚ/ n. [C] a BRIAR

brig /brɪg/ n. [C] **1** a military prison, especially on a ship **2** a ship with two MASTS (=poles) and large square sails

bri·gade /brɪ'geɪd/ n. [C] **1** a large group of soldiers forming part of an army **2** a group of people who are organized to do something: *In the Midwest, snowmobile brigades delivered food and medicine.* **3** INFORMAL, OFTEN HUMOROUS a group of people who have similar qualities and beliefs or wear similar clothes: *the back-to-nature brigade* —see also FIRE BRIGADE

brig·a·dier /ˌbrɪgə'dɪr/ n. [C] a high military rank, or someone holding this rank

brigadier-gen·e·ral /ˌ… '…/ n. [C] a high army rank, or someone holding this rank

brig·and /'brɪgənd/ n. [C] LITERARY a thief, especially one of a group that attacks people in mountains or forests

brig·an·tine /'brɪgən,tin/ n. [C] a ship like a BRIG but with fewer sails

W2 bright /braɪt/ adj. **1** [light] shining strongly or with plenty of light: *the bright afternoon sun* | *The light in here is not bright enough to read by.* | *a bright, airy room* **2** [colors] bright colors are strong and easy to see: *a bright red T-shirt* | *a book with bright, bold illustrations* | *Many of the houses were painted bright colors.* **3** [intelligent] intelligent and likely to be successful: *a bright eight-year-old girl* | *a bright idea* | *That wasn't a very bright thing to do.* **4** [future] likely to be successful: *a bright and promising career in the Navy* | *The outlook for the economy is not very bright.* | *Ruddock has a very bright future in the company.* **5** [cheerful] cheerful, happy, or full of life: *a bright smile* | *We try to make Christmas a little brighter for homeless people.* | [+ with] *Her eyes were bright with excitement.* **6 on the bright side** relating to the good points in a situation that is bad in other ways: *Look on the bright side – at least you learned something from the experience.* **7 bright and early** SPOKEN very early in the morning: *I'll be here bright and early to pick you up.* **8 the bright lights (of sth)** the interesting exciting life that people are supposed to have in big cities: *Bob left Iowa in search of the bright lights of New York.* **9 bright spot** an event or time that seems happy or good when everything else is upsetting or bad: *The show has a few bright spots, but is mainly uninspiring.* **10 as bright as a button** smart and full of life **11 bright-eyed and bushy-tailed** HUMOROUS completely awake and happy, even when it is very early

in the morning: *Christie was there, bright-eyed and bushy-tailed, at 6:30 a.m.* —**brightly** adv.: *The sun shone brightly.* —**brightness** n. [U]

bright·en /'braɪtn/ v. **1** [T] also **brighten** sth ↔ **up** to make something more attractive by adding something colorful to it: *Flowers are one way to brighten your surroundings.* | *New curtains would brighten up the room.* **2** [I,T] to become more successful or positive, or make something do this: *The political situation has brightened in recent months.* **3** [I,T] also **brighten** (sth ↔ **up**) to become happier or more excited, or make someone else feel like this: *I read an article in the paper that brightened my day.* | *Julie brightened up at the thought of visiting home.* **4** [I] to become brighter in color, or to shine with more light: *Fireworks brightened the sky.* **5** [I] also **brighten up** if the weather brightens or brightens up, the sun starts to shine a little and there are fewer clouds

brights /braɪts/ n. [plural] INFORMAL the HEADLIGHTS of a vehicle that shine more brightly than its regular HEADLIGHTS in order to help you see things far away —see also HIGH BEAM

bril·liance /'brɪlyəns/ n. [U] **1** a very high level of intelligence or skill: *Hendrix's brilliance as a rock guitarist has never been matched.* **2** brightness of color

bril·liant¹ /'brɪlyənt/ adj. **1** extremely intelligent or skillful: *a brilliant scientist* | *a brilliant idea* **2** brilliant light or color is very bright and strong: *the brilliant lights of the stadium* | *brilliant red and yellow flowers* **3** very successful: *a long and brilliant career* —**brilliantly** adv. —**brilliancy** n. [U]

brilliant² n. [C] TECHNICAL a valuable stone cut with a lot of surfaces that shine

Bril·lo pad /'brɪloʊ ˌpæd/ n. [C] TRADEMARK a ball of wire filled with soap, used for cleaning pans

brim¹ /brɪm/ n. [C] **1** the bottom part of a hat that sticks out to protect you from sun and rain —see picture at HAT **2** the top of a container such as a glass or bowl: *The cup was filled to the brim with coffee.*

brim² v. **brimmed, brimming** [I] to be very full of something: [+ with] *Andy's eyes brimmed with tears.* | *Her letter was brimming with happiness.*

brim over phr. v. [I] **1** if a container is brimming over, it is so full of a liquid or substance that the liquid etc. comes out over the top edge: [+ with] *The barrel was brimming over with water.* **2 brim over with confidence/excitement etc.** to be very confident, excited etc.: *In public, the American visitors were brimming over with optimism, but their reports to the President were less enthusiastic.*

brim·ful, brimfull /'brɪmfʊl/ adj. **be brimful (of/with sth)** to be very full: *The bucket was brimful of oil.*

brim·stone /'brɪmstoʊn/ n. [U] OLD USE SULFUR —see also **fire and brimstone** (FIRE¹ (11))

brin·dled /'brɪndld/ adj. a brindled cow, cat etc. is brown with marks or bands of another color

brine /braɪn/ n. [U] **1** water that contains a lot of salt, used for preserving food: *The sardines were soaked in brine.* **2** ocean water

bring /brɪŋ/ v. past tense and past participle **brought** [T] **1** [have sb/sth with you] to have something or someone with you when you go to a place: *Did you bring your coat?* | *I brought food for everyone.* | *Thanks for bringing me to work.* | [bring sb sth] *Could you bring me a glass of water?* **2** [make sth happen] to cause a particular type of result or reaction: *The tourist industry brings a lot of money into the area.* | *The article brought angry letters from readers.* **3** [legal case] if someone brings a legal action or charges against someone, they say officially that person has done something illegal: [bring sth against sb] *Ms. Burnett brought a libel suit against the National Enquirer.* | *The police did not have enough evidence to bring charges against the two men.*

4 time if a particular period of time brings something, it happens during that time: *Adolescence brings physical and emotional changes.* | *Who knows what the new year will bring?*

5 go somewhere if something such as an event or situation brings people to a place, it makes them go there: *The discovery of gold brought thousands of people to California in 1849.* | *"What brings you here?"* (=why have you come?) *"I need to talk to Mike."*

6 move sth to move something to a place or position: *Janine brought her hands slowly up to her face.* | *Always bring the car to a full stop at a stop sign.*

7 TV/radio sth is brought to you by sb if a television or radio program is brought to you by someone, they give money so that it can be broadcast, and advertisements for their product are shown during it: *This program is brought to you by Pepsi.*

8 bring sth to sb's attention/notice FORMAL to tell someone about something: *Thank you for bringing the problem to our attention.*

9 sth brings me (back) to sth SPOKEN if something brings you to a particular subject or brings you back to a particular subject when you are talking, you start talking about it or return to talking about it: *They haven't won a game all season, which brings me to the question of why.*

10 not bring yourself to do sth if you cannot bring yourself to do something, you cannot make yourself do it: *I couldn't bring myself to apologize to Stan.*

11 bring sth to an end/a close/a conclusion etc. to be the last thing that happens during an event or occasion: *The presentation of the trophy brought the tournament to an end.*

12 bring sth to bear FORMAL to use pressure, influence etc. to change a situation: *Pressure has been brought to bear on the governor by environmental groups.*

13 bring home the bacon INFORMAL to earn the money that your family needs to live

14 bring sth to the boil to heat liquid until it starts to boil

15 sell [T] to sell for a particular amount of money: *The painting brought $540,000 at the auction.*

16 bring a child into the world FORMAL **a)** if a woman brings a child into the world, she gives birth to it **b)** if a doctor brings a child into the world, he helps the mother give birth

17 bring tears to your eyes **a)** also bring a lump to your throat to make you start to feel strong emotions such as pity, sadness, or happiness: *The unexpected kindness brought tears to my eyes.* **b)** to make you feel enough pain that tears appear in your eyes: *The smoke brought tears to her eyes.*

18 bring sth into being FORMAL to make something start to exist: *The League of Nations was brought into being after World War I.*

19 sth brings with it sth used to say that a change, action etc. brings with it something such as a problem or advantage, the two things are connected and come together: *Every scientific advance brings with it its own risks.*

20 bring your own bottle *abbreviation* **BYOB** used when you invite someone to an informal party to tell them that they should bring their own bottle of alcoholic drink —see also bring sth home to sb (HOME² (4)), bring sth to a head (HEAD¹ (11)), bring sb to heel (HEEL¹ (8)), bring sb/sth to their knees (KNEE¹ (5)), bring sb to their senses (SENSE¹ (6))

bring sth **about** *phr. v.* [T] to make something happen: *Years of protest finally **brought about** change in the law.*

bring sb/sth **around** *phr. v.* [T] **1** to manage to persuade someone to do something or to agree with you: *He finally managed to bring his boss around to his point of view.* **2** to make someone become conscious again: *Paramedics eventually brought the man around.* **3** bring the conversation around to sth to deliberately and gradually introduce a new subject into a conversation: *I'll try to bring the conversation around to the subject of money.* **4** to bring someone or something to someone's house: *I'll bring Jody around tomorrow for you to meet.*

bring back *phr. v.* [T] **1** [bring sb/sth **back**] to take something or someone with you when you come back from somewhere: *I promised to bring them back for a visit.* | *I'll bring your books back on Wednesday.* | [bring sb **back** sth] *My dad brought me back a T-shirt from New York.* **2** [bring **back** sth] to make you remember something: *Watching the fire brought back memories of the day my own house burned down.* **3** [bring sth ↔ **back**] to start to use something such as a law, method, or process that was used in the past: *Many states have voted to bring back the death penalty.*

bring sb/sth ↔ **down** *phr. v.* [T] **1** bring down prices/costs/rates etc. to make prices, levels etc. be lower: *New taxes to help bring down the deficit.* | *Two pills, three times a day, should keep the fever down.* **2** bring down the government/President etc. to force the government, President etc. to stop ruling **3** to move your arm or a weapon, tool etc. quickly toward the ground: *He brought down the ax with a thud.* **4** to shoot at an airplane, bird, or animal so that it falls to the ground: *A bomber was brought down by anti-aircraft fire.* **5** bring down the house to perform so well that people APPLAUD (=hit their hands together to show they like something) a lot: *Fitzgerald brought down the house with her version of "Summertime."* **6** to fly an aircraft down to the ground and stop: *He brought the Cessna down in a hay-meadow by the river.*

bring sth **down on/upon** sb *phr. v.* [T] FORMAL to make something bad happen to someone, especially yourself: *What did I do to bring this down on myself?*

bring sth ↔ **forth** *phr. v.* [T] FORMAL to produce something or make it appear: *The smells from the kitchen brought forth happy memories of childhood.*

bring sth ↔ **forward** *phr. v.* [T] **1** to change the date or time of something so that something happens sooner than was originally planned: *The meeting's been brought forward to Thursday.* **2** bring forward legislation/plans/policies etc. to introduce or suggest a new plan or idea: *Gorbachev brought forward political reform in the former Soviet Union.* **3** TECHNICAL to move the total from one set of calculations onto the next page, so that more calculations can be done: *The balance brought forward is $21,765.*

bring in *phr. v.* [T] **1** [bring in sth] to earn a particular amount or produce a particular amount of profit: *The movie has brought in $30 million so far.* **2** [bring sb ↔ in] to involve someone in a job, situation, activity, etc.: *The police brought in the FBI to help.* | *D'Arezzo was brought in as the new marketing chief.* **3** bring in a verdict when a court or JURY brings in a verdict, it says whether someone is guilty or not

bring sth ↔ **off** *phr. v.* [T] to succeed in doing something very difficult: *It's a complicated play, and the actors don't quite bring it off.*

bring sth **on** *phr. v.* [T] to make something bad happen: *Abbot died of heatstroke brought on by the extremely high temperatures.* | *The destruction of the forest was brought on by pollution.*

bring sth **on/upon** sb *phr. v.* [T] to make something bad happen to someone: *They've brought this problem on themselves.*

bring out *phr. v.* [T] **1** [bring sb/sth ↔ out] to make something easier to see, taste, notice etc.: *Add a little salt to bring out the flavor.* | *The Christmas holidays have a way of bringing out the child in us.* **2** bring out the best/worst in sb to make someone behave in the best or worst way that they can: *Ingram always seems to bring out the best in his players.* **3** [bring sth ↔ out] to produce and begin to sell a new product, book, record etc.: *Companies are always bringing out improved versions of their products.*

bring sb **through** (sth) *phr. v.* [T] to help someone to successfully deal with a very difficult event or period of time: *My friends helped bring me through the divorce.*

bring sb ↔ **together** *phr. v.* [T] **1** to introduce two people to each other, or to be the thing that does this: *They've been friends ever since a school project* brought them together. **2** to make a group of people have fun together or work well together: *It's a good game that brings people together.*

bring up *phr. v.* [T] **1** [**bring** sb/sth ↔ **up**] to mention a subject or start to talk about it: *Some people laughed at the idea when I first brought it up.* | *Several safety questions were brought up in the last meeting.* **2** [**bring** sb **up**] [usually passive] to educate and care for a child until they are grown up: *He was born and brought up in Minneapolis.* | [**be brought up to do sth**] *All of our kids were brought up to respect other people.* | *I was brought up Lutheran* (=taught a particular religion as I grew up). —see Usage Note at RAISE¹ **3 bring sb up on charges** if the police, the courts etc. bring someone up on charges, they say officially that the person has done something illegal **4** [**bring** sth ↔ **up**] to VOMIT: *The ride was so scary I almost brought up my lunch.* **5 bring up the rear** to be behind everyone else when you are going somewhere as a group: *Dad was bringing up the rear to make sure no one got lost.*

USAGE NOTE: BRING

WORD CHOICE: bring, take, carry
Bring means to take someone or something with you to the place where you are now or to the place you have been talking about: *If you can come to the party, could you please bring a dessert?* | *Ellen brought her new boyfriend over to our place last night.* | *Did you bring your camera?* **Bring** is also used in the same way for taking something toward the person being spoken to or talked about: *Hold on, I'll bring you a towel.* | *They brought her everything she needed.* **Take** involves moving in the opposite direction of **bring**: *We went to Ann's party and took a dessert along.* | *Ellen took her boyfriend to her class reunion.* | *Take your camera when you go out* (NOT usually *carry* here). | *Can you take me home now?* **Carry** does not give any idea of the direction of movement, but suggests that you are holding something in your arms or with your hands: *Will you carry the baby/the groceries for me?*

---

brink /brɪŋk/ *n.* **1 the brink (of sth)** **a)** a time or situation just before something happens, especially something bad: *Hannah was **on the brink of** tears.* | *The people have been pushed to the brink of starvation by the drought.* | *The country is **at the brink of** revolution.* | *They hope to bring the birds **back from the brink** of extinction.* **b)** LITERARY the edge of a very high place such as a cliff **2 push/drive/shove etc. sb over the brink** to shock someone or to be so difficult to deal with that they cannot control their emotions and seem to go crazy: *Twerski's daughter's death pushed him over the brink.*

brink·man·ship /ˈbrɪŋkmənˌʃɪp/ also **brinks·man·ship** /ˈbrɪŋks-/ *n.* [U] a way of gaining advantage by getting involved in dangerous situations and taking unreasonable risks: *political brinkmanship*

brin·y /ˈbraɪni/ *adj.* containing a lot of salt, or having a strong salt taste

bri·oche /briˈoʊʃ, -ˈɑʃ/ *n.* [C] a type of sweet bread made with flour, eggs, and butter

bri·quette /brɪˈkɛt/ *n.* [C] a block of pressed coal dust that is burned in a fire or BARBECUE

brisk /brɪsk/ *adj.* **1** quick and full of energy: *a brisk walk* **2** trade or business that is brisk is very busy, with a lot of products being sold: *brisk sales* **3** weather that is brisk is cold and clear: *a brisk fall morning* **4** quick, practical, and showing that you want to get things done quickly —**briskly** *adv.* —**briskness** *n.* [U]

bris·ket /ˈbrɪskɪt/ *n.* [U] meat from an animal's chest, especially a cow

bris·tle¹ /ˈbrɪsəl/ *v.* [I] **1** to behave in a way that shows you are very angry or annoyed: [+ **with**] *Joan was bristling with rage.* | [+ **at**] *Teachers bristled at the criticism of their school.* **2** if an animal's hair bristles, it stands up stiffly because the animal is afraid or angry

bristle with sth *phr. v.* [T] to have a lot of something or be full of something: *The kids were bristling with energy.*

---

bristle² *n.* [C,U] **1** a sh... forms part of a brush —s...stiff hair, wire etc. that stiff hair that feels rough...ture at BRUSH¹ **2** short

bris·tly /ˈbrɪsəli, -sli/ *adj.* **1**... stiff **2** a bristly part of you... hair is short and hairs on it: *a bristly chin* ...has short stiff

Brit /brɪt/ *n.* [C] INFORMAL someon...

britch·es /ˈbrɪtʃɪz/ *n.* [plural] OLD... **2 be too big for your britches** INFO...ritain though you are more important or... really are **1** pants

Brit·ish /ˈbrɪtɪʃ/ *adj.* **1** from or connect...lave as Britain or the U.K.: *the British gover...you British people from Great Britain or the...*

British Co·lum·bi·a /ˌbrɪtɪʃ kəˈlʌmbiə/ *ab...* BC a PROVINCE in western Canada, next to th... Ocean

Brit·ish·er /ˈbrɪtɪʃə/ *n.* [C] OLD-FASHIONED son... from Great Britain or the U.K.

British Isles /ˌ.. ˈ./ *n.* the group of islands th... includes Great Britain, Ireland, and the smaller islands around them

Brit·on /ˈbrɪtn/ *n.* [C] FORMAL someone from Great Britain or the U.K.: *the ancient Britons*

Brit·ten /ˈbrɪtn/, **Benjamin** (1913–1976) a British musician who wrote modern CLASSICAL music

brit·tle¹ /ˈbrɪtl/ *adj.* **1** easily broken into many small pieces: *The paper was old and brittle.* **2** a system, relationship etc. that is brittle is easily damaged or destroyed: *Relations between the two countries are still very brittle.* **3** if someone's laugh, expression, PERSONALITY etc. is brittle, they seem to force themselves to show happiness or politeness that they do not feel

brittle² *n.* [U] PEANUT BRITTLE

bro /broʊ/ *n.* [C] SLANG **1** your brother **2** used by boys or men as a way of greeting a male friend

broach /broʊtʃ/ *v.* [T] **1 broach the subject/question/matter etc.** to mention a subject that may be embarrassing or upsetting, or that may cause an argument: *Parents often find it difficult to broach the subject of sex with their children.* **2** to open a bottle or BARREL containing wine, beer etc.

broad¹ /brɔd/ *adj.*
1 [including a lot] including many different kinds of things or people: *The program is now attracting broader audiences.* | *Michigan once provided the broadest welfare benefits in the U.S.* | *The committee will discuss **a broad range** of issues.*
2 [wide] a broad road, river, or part of someone's body etc. is wide: *Houston's broad streets* | *a tall, broad-shouldered man* —compare NARROW¹ (1) —see also BREADTH —see Usage Note at WIDE¹
3 [general] concerning the main ideas or parts of something rather than all the details: *Military officials gave a few broad statements about the bombing raid.* | *Successful business strategies fall into three broad categories.*
4 [large area] covering a large area of land or water: *the broad plains of lower Mesopotamia*
5 a broad grin/smile a big smile which clearly shows that you are happy
6 in broad daylight if something such as a crime happens in broad daylight, it happens in the daytime when you would expect someone to prevent it: *The attack happened in broad daylight, in one of the busiest parts of town.*
7 paint/tar (sb/sth) with a broad brush also **use a broad brush** to describe something or have an opinion about something without considering details: *Good people and bad may have been tarred with the same broad brush.*
8 [way of speaking] a broad ACCENT (1) clearly shows where you come from: *a broad Scottish accent*
9 broad humor/wit etc. humor that deals with sex —see also BREADTH

broad² *n.* [C] SPOKEN, OFFENSIVE a woman

broadband

broad·band /'brɔdbæ.../ n. [U] TECHNICAL a system of sending radio signals which allows several messages to be sent at the same time

broad·base /'.../ adj. [usually before noun] including many types of things, people, or subjects: *a broad-based student group* | *a broad-based* ...

broad-brush /'. ./ adj. [only before noun] dealing with the main parts of something, and not with details: *a broad-brush evaluation of the crisis (7))*

— **paint/tar (sb/sth) with a broad brush**

broad·cast¹ /'brɔdkæst/ n. [C] a program on television or the radio: *a news broadcast* | *CNN's live broadcast of the trial* (=one that you see or hear at the same time as the events are happening)

broadcast² v. past tense and past participle **broadcast** **1** [I,T] to send out television or radio programs: *The interview was broadcast Sunday on "Face the Nation."* | *CBS will broadcast the championship game live* (=as it happens). **2** [T] to tell something to a lot of people: *Don't go broadcasting what I've told you all over the office.*

broad·cast·er /'brɔd,kæstɚ/ n. [C] someone whose job is speaking on television or radio programs: *a well-known journalist and broadcaster*

broad·cast·ing /'brɔd,kæstɪŋ/ n. [U] the business of making television and radio programs: *a career in broadcasting*

broad·en /'brɔdn/ v. **1** [T] to increase something so that it includes more things or people, or affects more things or people: *The class is meant to broaden people's awareness of geography.* | *In 1995, the U.S. sought to broaden its ties with India and Pakistan.* | *I traveled to Japan to broaden my horizons* (=learn, understand, and do new things). **2** [I,T] to make something wider or to become wider: *The road broadens a little further on.* **3 broaden your mind** if an experience broadens your mind, it makes it easier for you to accept other people's beliefs, ways of doing things etc.: *Travel broadens the mind.*

broad jump /'. ./ n. [U] LONG JUMP

broad·ly /'brɔdli/ adv. **1** in a general way, covering the main facts rather than details: *She knows broadly what to expect.* | *The federal law applies broadly to all medical devices.* | *Broadly speaking, the cultures of the two countries are very similar.* | *Independent films, broadly defined, are movies that appeal to sophisticated audiences* **2 smile/grin broadly** to have a big smile on your face which clearly shows that you are happy or amused **3** including many different kinds of things, people, or subjects: *The company invests broadly, so that the risk is lessened.*

broad-mind·ed, broadminded /'. ,.../ adj. willing to respect opinions or behavior that are very different from your own: *Her parents are very broadminded.* —opposite NARROW-MINDED —compare SMALL-MINDED —**broad-mindedly** adv. —**broad-mindedness** n. [U]

broad·sheet /'brɔdʃit/ n. [C] a newspaper printed on large sheets of paper —compare TABLOID

broad·side¹ /'brɔdsaɪd/ n. [C] **1** a strong criticism of someone or something, especially a written one: *a broadside against abortion* **2** an attack in which all the guns on one side of a ship are fired at the same time

broad·side² /,brɔd'saɪd/ adv. with the longest side facing something: *His van was hit broadside by a speeding car.*

broad·side³ /'brɔdsaɪd/ v. [T] **1** to crash into the side of another vehicle: *Jerry's car was broadsided by a pickup truck.* **2** to strongly criticize someone

broad·sword /'brɔdsɔrd/ n. [C] a heavy sword with a broad flat blade

Broad·way /'brɔdweɪ/ n. a street in New York where there are many theaters, known as the center of the American professional theater industry: *a Broadway*

musical | *Miller's new play will soon open on Broadway.* —see also OFF-BROADWAY

Bro·ca /'broʊkə/, **Paul** (1824–1880) a French doctor who discovered the part of the brain that produces speech

bro·cade /broʊ'keɪd/ n. [U] thick heavy cloth which has a pattern of gold and silver threads and is used for decoration: *brocade curtains* —**brocaded** adj.

broc·co·li /'brɑkəli/ n. [U] a green vegetable with thick groups of small dark-green flower-like parts at the top —see picture at VEGETABLE

bro·chure /broʊ'ʃʊr/ n. [C] a thin book giving information or advertising something: *a travel brochure*

bro·gan /'broʊgən/ n. [C] a heavy work shoe that covers the ANKLE

brogue /broʊg/ n. [C] **1** a thick strong leather shoe with a pattern in the leather —see picture at SHOE **2** [usually singular] a strong ACCENT (=way of pronouncing words), especially the one used by the Irish or Scottish people

broil /brɔɪl/ v. [I,T] **1** if you broil something, or if it broils, you cook it under or over direct heat, or over a flame on a BARBECUE; GRILL: *broiled chicken* **2 be broiling** if it is broiling in a particular place, it is very hot there: *It was broiling in the classroom.*

broil·er /'brɔɪlɚ/ n. [C] a special part of an OVEN used for cooking food under direct heat

broil·ing /'brɔɪlɪŋ/ adj. broiling weather, sun etc. makes you feel extremely hot: *We worked all day in the broiling sun.*

broke¹ /broʊk/ v. the past tense of BREAK¹

broke² adj. [not before noun] **1** having no money: *I can't go – I'm broke.* | *Connie and her husband are flat broke* (=completely broke). **2 go broke** if a company or business goes broke, it cannot operate anymore because it has no money: *A lot of small businesses went broke during the recession.* **3 go for broke** INFORMAL to take big risks when you are trying to achieve something: *Jacobsen went for broke on the last nine holes and won the tournament.*

bro·ken¹ /'broʊkən/ the past participle of BREAK¹

broken² adj.

1 piece of equipment not working correctly: *The camera was broken, so none of my pictures turned out.* | *How did the lawn mower get broken?* (=become broken)

2 object in small pieces because it has been hit, dropped etc.: *broken beer bottles* | *Pack the cookies carefully so they won't get broken in the mail.*

3 bone cracked or split in more than one piece because you have had an accident: *The accident left her with three broken bones in her wrist.* | *a broken arm/leg/finger etc. My cat has a broken leg.*

4 interrupted interrupted and not continuous: *a broken white line* | *We had months of broken sleep* (=interrupted sleep) *before the baby finally slept through the night.*

5 person extremely mentally or physically weak because you have suffered a lot: *Gary returned from the war a broken man.*

6 a broken agreement/promise etc. an agreement, promise etc. in which someone did not do what they said they would do

7 broken English/French etc. English, French etc. that is spoken very slowly by someone who only knows a little of the language

8 family/marriage a broken relationship, family etc. is one that is destroyed by the separation of a husband and wife: *a broken marriage* | *Kids from broken homes* (=families that are separated) *sometimes have more trouble in school.*

9 a broken heart a feeling of extreme sadness, especially because someone you love has died or left you

bro·ken-down /,... '. ./ adj. broken, old, and needing a lot of repair: *a broken-down trailer*

broken-heart·ed /,.. '.. / adj. extremely sad, especially because someone you love has died or left you —**broken-heartedly** adv.

bro·ker¹ /'broʊkɚ/ n. [C] someone whose job is to buy and sell property, insurance etc. for someone else: *a real estate broker*

broker² v. [T] **broker a deal/settlement/treaty** etc. to help two groups agree on and arrange the details of a formal agreement: *a settlement brokered by the U.N.*

bro·ker·age /'broukərɪdʒ/ n. **1** [C] also **a brokerage house/firm** a company of brokers, or the place where they work **2** [U] the business of being a broker **3** [U] the amount of money a broker charges

bro·mide /'broumaɪd/ n. **1** [C,U] a chemical compound, sometimes used in medicine to make people feel calm **2** [C] FORMAL a statement which is intended to make someone less angry but which is not effective

bronc /brɑŋk/ n. [C] INFORMAL a BRONCO

bron·chi·al /'brɑŋkiəl/ adj. affecting the bronchial tubes: *a bronchial infection*

bronchial tube /'... ,./ n. [C usually plural] one of the small tubes that take air into your lungs

bron·chi·tis /brɑŋ'kaɪtɪs/ n. [C] an illness which affects your bronchial tubes and makes you cough —**bronchitic** /brɑŋ'kɪtɪk/ adj.

bron·co /'brɑŋkou/ n. plural **broncos** [C] a wild horse from the western U.S.

Bron·të /'brɑnti, -teɪ/ the family name of three English sisters who wrote some of the most famous English novels: Charlotte Brontë (1816–1855), Emily Brontë (1818–1848), and Anne Brontë (1820–1849)

bron·to·sau·rus /,brɑntə'sɔrəs/ n. [C] a large DINOSAUR with a small head and a long neck

Bronx, the /brɑŋks/ a COUNTY, and one of the five BOROUGHS of New York City

Bronx cheer /,. './ n. [C] INFORMAL a sound you make by putting your tongue between your lips and blowing, often considered rude; RASPBERRY (2)

bronze¹ /brɑnz/ n. **1** [U] a hard metal that is made of a mixture of COPPER and TIN **2** [U] the dark red-brown color of bronze **3** [C] a work of art such as a STATUE (=model of a person), made of bronze **4** [C] a BRONZE MEDAL

bronze² adj. **1** made of bronze: *a bronze statuette by Degas* **2** having the red-brown color of bronze: *bronze skin*

Bronze Age /'. ./ n. [singular] the time, between about 6000 and 4000 years ago, when bronze was used for making tools, weapons etc. —compare IRON AGE, STONE AGE

bronzed /brɑnzd/ adj. having skin that is attractively brown because you have been in the sun

bronze med·al /,. './ n. [C] a MEDAL made of bronze that is given to the person who comes third in a race or competition —see also GOLD MEDAL, SILVER MEDAL

bronze med·al·ist /,. '.../ n. [C] someone who has won a bronze medal

brooch /brout∫, brut∫/ n. [C] a piece of jewelry that a woman fastens to her clothes; PIN¹ (2)

brood¹ /brud/ v. [I] **1** to keep thinking for a long time about something that you are worried, angry, or upset about: *Ken had little to do except sit and brood.* | *[+ over/about/on] She's still brooding over what to do next.* **2** if a bird broods, it sits on its eggs to keep them warm until the young birds come out

brood² n. [C] **1** a family of young birds all born at the same time **2** HUMOROUS a family with a lot of children: *It takes at least an hour to get the whole brood ready to go to school.*

brood³ adj. **brood mare/sow** etc. a horse, pig etc. that is kept for the purpose of producing babies

brood·er /'brudə/ n. [C] **1** a heated structure for young birds to live in **2** someone who broods a lot

brood·ing /'brudɪŋ/ adj. **1** worrying and thinking about something: *a silent, brooding man* **2** mysterious and threatening: *a brooding, dark atmosphere* —**broodingly** adv.

brood·y /'brudi/ adj. silent because you are thinking or worrying about something —**broodily** adv. —**broodiness** n. [U]

brook¹ /brʊk/ n. [C] a small stream

brook² v. **brook no sth** FORMAL also **not brook sth** to

not allow something to happen or exist: *Mrs. Madison brooks no nonsense in her class.*

Brook·lyn /'brʊklən/ a BOROUGH and port area of New York City

broom /brum, brʊm/ n. **1** [C] a large brush with a long handle, used for sweeping floors —see picture a BRUSH¹ **2** [U] a large bush with small yellow flowers

broom·stick /'brum,stɪk/ n. [C] **1** the long handle of a broom **2** a broom that a WITCH is supposed to fly on in children's stories

Bros. the written abbreviation of Brothers, used in the names of companies: *Warner Bros.*

broth /brɔθ/ n. [U] soup made by cooking meat or vegetables in water and then removing them: *chicken broth*

broth·el /'brɑθəl, 'brɔ-, -ðəl/ n. [C] a house where men pay to have sex with PROSTITUTES

broth·er¹ /'brʌðə/ n. [C] **1** a male who has the same parents as you: *I have two brothers, James and Karl.* | *I have to walk my little brother* (=younger brother) *to school.* | *Michael's big brother* (=older brother) *is named Jonathan.* | *My kid brother* (=younger brother) *lives in Chicago.* **2** a member of a FRATERNITY (=a club of male university students) **3** SPOKEN a word for an African-American man, used especially by African-Americans **4** a male member of a group with the same interests, religion, profession etc. as you **5** plural **brothers** or **brethren** a male member of a religious group, especially a MONK **6 brothers in arms** soldiers who have fought together in a war —see also BIG BROTHER, BLOOD BROTHER

brother² interjection used to express annoyance or surprise: *Oh, brother – I really don't want to deal with this now.*

broth·er·hood /'brʌðə,hʊd/ n. **1** [U] a feeling of friendship between people: *All we want for our countries is peace and brotherhood.* **2** [C] an organization or society formed for a particular purpose, especially a religious one: *the Franciscan brotherhood* **3** [C] a union of workers in a particular trade **4** [U] the relationship between brothers

brother-in-law /'.. . ,./ n. [C] plural **brothers-in-law 1** the brother of your husband or wife **2** the husband of your sister **3** the husband of your husband's or wife's sister

broth·er·ly /'brʌðəli/ adj. showing the helpfulness, love, loyalty etc. that you would expect a brother to show: *brotherly love* | *He offered me some brotherly advice.* —**brotherliness** n. [U]

brougham /brum, 'brouəm/ n. [C] a light carriage used in the past which had four wheels and a roof and was pulled by a horse

brought /brɔt/ the past tense and past participle of BRING

brou·ha·ha /'bruhɑhɑ/ n. [C usually singular,U] INFORMAL a lot of noise or angry protest about something: *Budget cuts set off a whole new brouhaha at the university.*

brow /brau/ n. **1** [C] LITERARY the part of your face above your eyes and below your hair; FOREHEAD: **furrow/knit your brow** (=make lines appear on your brow because you are angry or worried) | **mop/wipe your brow** (=dry your forehead with your hand or a cloth because you are hot or nervous) **2** an EYEBROW **3 the brow of the hill** LITERARY the top part of a slope or hill

brow·beat /'braubit/ v. past tense **browbeat** past participle **browbeaten** /-,bit'n/ [T] to make someone do something by continuously asking them to, especially in a threatening way: *Clausen has been known to browbeat witnesses.*

brown¹ /braun/ adj. **1** having the color of earth, wood, or coffee: *dark brown hair* | *a brown shirt* **2** someone's skin that is brown has been turned brown by the sun: *Her skin gets really brown in the summer.* —see also TAN¹ (2)

brown[2] n. [C,U] the color of earth, wood, or coffee: *the browns and greens of the landscape*

brown[3] v. [I,T] **1** to heat food so that it turns brown or to become brown in this way by being heated: *Brown the meat in a frying pan.* **2** to become brown because of the sun's heat or to make something brown in this way: *The children's faces were browned by the sun.*

Brown /braʊn/, **John** (1800–1859) a U.S. CITIZEN who tried to use violence to end SLAVERY

Brown, Rob·ert /ˈrɑbət/ (1773–1858) a Scottish BOTANIST who made many important discoveries about the structure of plants

brown-and-serve also **brown-n-serve** /ˌ. . ˈ./ adj. [only before noun] brown-and-serve bread or SAUSAGES are partly cooked before you buy them, so that you only cook them for a short time before they are ready to eat

brown-bag /ˈ. ./ v. [I] **1** to bring your LUNCH to work, usually in a small brown paper bag: *I'm **brownbagging** it this week.* **2** to bring your own alcohol to a restaurant which does not serve alcohol —**brownbagging** n. [U]

brown bet·ty /ˌbraʊn ˈbeti/ n. [C] a baked DESSERT made of apples, RAISINS, BREADCRUMBS, sugar, butter, and SPICES

brown bread /ˈ. ./ n. [U] bread made with WHOLE WHEAT

brown·ie /ˈbraʊni/ n. **1** [C] a square piece of a type of heavy chocolate cake **2 the Brownies** [plural] the part of the Girl Scouts organization that is for younger girls **3 Brownie** [C] a member of this part of the Girl Scouts organization **4 get/earn brownie points** INFORMAL to do something so that people in authority have a good opinion of you: *Are you trying to get brownie points by getting here early?*

Brown·ing /ˈbraʊnɪŋ/, **E·liz·a·beth Bar·rett** /ɪˈlɪzəbəθ ˈbærət/ (1806–1861) an English poet who married the poet Robert Browning

Browning, Rob·ert /ˈrɑbət/ (1812–1889) an English poet

brown-nose /ˈ. ˌ./ v. [I,T] INFORMAL to try to make someone with authority like you by being very nice to them, in a way that is annoying to other people —**brown-noser** n. [C] —**brown-nosing** n. [U]

brown·out /ˈbraʊnaʊt/ n. [C] a reduction of electric power in an area that is caused by equipment failure or the use of too much electricity in the area

brown rec·luse /ˌ. ˈ..ˌ/ also **brown recluse spider** n. [C] a very poisonous brown SPIDER

brown rice /ˌ. ˈ./ n. [U] rice that still has its outer layer

brown·stone /ˈbraʊnstoʊn/ n. **1** [U] a type of reddish-brown stone, often used for building in the eastern U.S. **2** [C] a house with a front made of this stone, common especially in New York City —see picture on page 423

brown sug·ar /ˌ. ˈ../ n. [U] a type of sugar that contains MOLASSES

browse /braʊz/ v. **1** [I] to look through the pages of a book, magazine etc. without a particular purpose, just reading the most interesting parts: [+ **through**] *We browsed through a few travel books to get some ideas of where to go.* **2** [I] to look at the goods in a shop without wanting to buy any particular thing: *I enjoy browsing in bookstores.* **3** [I,T] to search for information on the Internet: *It's easy to spend hours just browsing the web without really finding anything.* **4** [I] if a goat, DEER etc. browses, it eats plants —**browsing** n. [U]

brows·er /ˈbraʊzə/ n. [C] a computer program that finds information on the Internet and shows it on your computer screen

brr /bə/ interjection said when you are cold

Brue·gel, Brueghel, Breughel /ˈbrʊgəl/, **Pie·ter** /ˈpitə/ **1 Bruegel the Elder** (?1525–1569) a Flemish PAINTER famous for his pictures of LANDSCAPES and ordinary people **2 Bruegel the Younger** (1564–1638) a Flemish PAINTER famous for his pictures of religious subjects

bru·in /ˈbruɪn/ n. [C] a bear

bruise[1] /bruz/ n. [C] **1** a purple or brown mark on your skin that you get because you have fallen, been hit etc. **2** a mark on a piece of fruit that spoils its appearance

bruise[2] v. [I,T] **1** if part of you body bruises or if you bruise it, a bruise appears because it has been hit: *Payton bruised his hip ten minutes into the game.* **2** if a piece of fruit bruises or is bruised, a bruise appears because it has been hit or dropped **3** if an experience bruises someone, they continue to feel upset and unhappy after it happens: *Not getting the promotion really bruised his ego.*

bruised /bruzd/ adj. **1** bruised ribs/knee/elbow etc. a part of your body with a bruise on it **2** upset or emotionally hurt by an experience

bruis·er /ˈbruzə/ n. [C] INFORMAL a big strong rough man: *I opened the door and saw this 250-pound bruiser standing there.*

bruis·ing /ˈbruzɪŋ/ n. **1** [U] purple or brown marks on your skin that you get because you have fallen, been hit etc.: *The woman suffered bruising to the face and head in the accident.* **2** [U] marks on a piece of fruit that spoil its appearance —see also **be cruising for a bruising** (CRUISE[1] (5))

bruit /brut/ v.
 bruit sth about phr. v. [T] FORMAL to tell a lot of people about something

brunch /brʌntʃ/ n. [C,U] a meal eaten in the late morning, as a combination of breakfast and LUNCH

Bru·nei /bruˈnaɪ/ also **Brunei Da·rus·sa·lam** /-dəˌrusəˈlɑm/ a small country on the island of Borneo —**Bruneian** n., adj.

bru·nette, brunet /bruˈnɛt/ n. [C] a woman with dark brown hair: *a slim brunette*

Brun·ner /ˈbrʊnə/, **E·mil** /ˈeɪmɪl/ (1889–1966) a Swiss Protestant religious writer and teacher

brunt /brʌnt/ n. **bear/take/suffer the brunt of sth** to receive the worst part of an attack, criticism etc.: *Schools will be bearing the brunt of the recent state staff cuts.*

brushes

hairbrush

toothbrush

nailbrush

paintbrushes

scrub brush

bristles

broom

brush[1] /brʌʃ/ n.
1 **for hair** [C] an object that you use to make your hair smooth and neat, consisting of thin pieces of plastic or BRISTLES attached to a handle; HAIRBRUSH

2 **for cleaning** [C] an object that you use for cleaning, painting etc., made with a lot of hairs, BRISTLES, or thin pieces of plastic or wire attached to a handle: *Use a wire brush to remove the rust.* —see also PAINT-BRUSH, TOOTHBRUSH

3 **bushes/trees** [U] **a)** small bushes and trees covering an open area of land: *a brush fire* **b)** branches which have broken off bushes and trees

4 a brush with death/a brush with the law etc. an occasion when something bad almost happens to you, but you manage to avoid it

5 **touch** [singular] a quick light touch, made by chance when two things or people pass each other: *I felt the brush of her sleeve as she walked past.*

6 **act of brushing** [singular] **a** movement which brushes something, to remove dirt, make something smooth etc.: *I'll just give my hair a quick brush.*

7 **tail** [C] the tail of a FOX

brush² *v.* **1** [T] to clean something or make something smooth and neat using a brush: *It's time for you kids to go brush your teeth.* **2** [I always + adv./prep.,T always + adv./prep.] to remove something with a brush or with your hand: [**brush sth → off/away etc.**] *Helen brushed away a tear.* | *I got up and brushed myself off* (=used my hands to clean myself after I fell). **3** [I always + adv./prep.,T] to put a liquid onto something using a brush: *Use small strokes to brush on the paint.* | *Brush the dough with melted butter.* **4** [I always + adv./prep.,T] to touch someone or something lightly by chance when passing them: *The car brushed the bush at the end of the driveway.* | [**brush (up) against sb/sth**] *I accidentally brushed up against the man in front of me.*

brush sb/sth aside *phr. v.* [T] to refuse to listen to or consider something: *The idea was quickly brushed aside by upper management.*

brush sb/sth off *phr. v.* [T] to refuse to listen to someone or their ideas, especially by ignoring them or saying something rude: *Robert usually just brushes off the neighbors' complaints.*

brush up (on) sth *phr. v.* [I] to quickly practice and improve your skills or knowledge: *I need to brush up on my Spanish.*

brushed /brʌʃt/ *adj.* [only before noun] a brushed cloth has been specially treated to make it feel much softer: *brushed cotton*

brush-off /'. ./ *n.* **give sb the brush-off** to ignore someone or make it clear that you do not want their friendship, invitations etc.

brush stroke /'. ./ *n.* [C] a line or mark that you make with a PAINTBRUSH, or the action of making this

brush-wood /'brʌʃwʊd/ *n.* [U] small dead branches broken from trees or bushes

brush-work /'brʌʃwɜːk/ *n.* [U] the particular way in which someone puts paint on a picture using a brush

brusque /brʌsk/ *adj.* using very few words in a way that seems rude but is not intended to be: *Her secretary was a little brusque on the phone.* —**brusquely** *adv.* —**brusqueness** *n.* [U]

Brus·sels /'brʌsəlz/ the capital city of Belgium and the city from which the business of the European Union and NATO is run

brus·sels sprout, Brussel sprout /ˌbrʌsəl 'spraʊt/ *n.* [C] a small round green vegetable that has a slightly bitter taste

bru·tal /'brʊtl/ *adj.* **1** very cruel and violent: *Three men were charged with the brutal murder.* **2** not nice, or not sensitive to people's feelings: *The brutal truth is that babies are starving to death there.* —**brutally** *adv.* —**brutality** /bruˈtæləti/ *n.* [C,U]

bru·tal·ize /'brʊtl̩aɪz/ *v.* [T usually passive] **1** to treat someone in a cruel or violent way: *Many of the prisoners were brutalized by soldiers.* **2** to affect someone so badly that they become cruel and violent: *Young men are often brutalized by their experiences in jail.* —**brutalization** /ˌbrʊtl̩əˈzeɪʃən/ *n.* [U]

brute¹ /bruːt/ *n.* [C] **1** a man who is rough, cruel, and not sensitive: *a drunken brute* **2** LITERARY an animal, especially a large or strong one

brute² *adj.* [no comparative] **brute force/strength etc.** physical strength rather than thought or intelligence: *Brute force is used far too often by police.*

brut·ish /'bruːtɪʃ/ *adj.* showing no human intelligence or feeling —**brutishly** *adv.* —**brutishness** *n.* [U]

Bry·an /'braɪən/**, Wil·liam Jen·nings** /'wɪljəm 'dʒɛnɪŋz/ (1860–1925) a U.S. lawyer and politician famous for his skill in public speaking

Bry·ant /'braɪənt/**, Paul "Bear"** /pɔl bɛr/ (1913–1983) a U.S. college football COACH who set a record for winning the most games

Bryant, Wil·liam Cul·len /'wɪljəm 'kʌlən/ (1794–1878) a U.S. poet and JOURNALIST

Bryl·creem /'brɪlkrim/ *n.* [U] TRADEMARK a substance used on men's hair to make it shiny and smooth

B.S. *n.* **1** [C usually singular] Bachelor of Science; a first college degree in a science subject: *a B.S. in Biology* —compare B.A. **2** [U] INFORMAL an abbreviation of BULLSHIT

BSE *n.* [U] a serious brain disease that affects cows

B-side /'bi saɪd/ *n.* [C] **1** the back side of a small record that has one song on each side. The front side has a popular song on it **2** the song on the back of this type of record

BTU *n.* [C] British Thermal Unit; a unit used to measure how much heat something produces

BTW, btw a written abbreviation of "by the way," often used in EMAIL, or by people communicating in CHAT ROOMs on the Internet —see **by the way** (BY¹ (11))

bub /bʌb/ *n.* [C] OLD-FASHIONED, BUDDY (3)

bub·ble¹ /'bʌbəl/ *n.* [C] **1** a ball of air in liquid: *soap bubbles* | *Grandma was blowing bubbles with us in the backyard.* **2** a small amount of air trapped in a solid substance: *Examine the glass carefully for bubbles.* **3** also **cartoon/ speech bubble** a circle around the words said by someone in a drawing or COMIC STRIP **4** a large clear plastic tent used to protect a seriously ill person from infection —see also **burst the/sb's bubble** (BURST¹ (6))

bubble

bubbles

bubble

bubble² *v.* **1** [I] to produce bubbles: *When the pancakes start to bubble, flip them over.* | [**+ up**] *Oil was bubbling up to the surface.* **2** [I] to make the sound that water makes when it boils: [**+ away**] *The water was bubbling away on the stove.* **3** [I] also **bubble over** to be full of a particular emotion, especially excitement: [**+ with**] *Boyer bubbled with enthusiasm.*

bubble bath /'.. ,./ *n.* **1** [U] a liquid soap that smells good and makes bubbles in your bath water **2** [C] a bath with bubbles in the water

bubble gum /'.. ,./ *n.* [U] a type of CHEWING GUM that you can blow into a BUBBLE¹ (2) —see picture at BUBBLE¹

bub·ble-gum /'.. ,./ *adj.* [only before noun] relating to music that is not serious and that only young people like: *The band resented the bubble-gum image the record companies had given them.*

bub·bler /'bʌblɚ/ *n.* [C] INFORMAL a piece of equipment in a public place that produces a stream of water for you to drink from; DRINKING FOUNTAIN

bubble wrap also **bubble pack** /'.. ,./ *n.* [U] a sheet of soft plastic covered with many small raised areas filled with air, used to protect things that are being moved, sent through the mail etc.

bub·bly¹ /'bʌbli/ *adj.* **1** full of BUBBLEs **2** someone who is bubbly always seems cheerful, friendly, and eager to do things: *I like Angie's bubbly personality.*

bubbly² *n.* [U] INFORMAL, CHAMPAGNE

Bu·ber /'bubɚ/**, Mar·tin** /'mɑrt̩n/ (1878–1965) an Austrian Jewish religious writer and teacher

bu·bon·ic plague /buˌbɑnɪk ˈpleɪg/ n. [U] a very serious disease spread by rats and FLEAs, that killed large numbers of people in the Middle Ages —see also BLACK DEATH, PLAGUE[1] (2)

buc·ca·neer /ˌbʌkəˈnɪr/ n. [C] **1** someone who attacks ships and steals from them; PIRATE **2** someone who succeeds, especially in business, by using any method, including cheating

Bu·chan·an /byuˈkænən/, **James** (1791–1868) the 15th president of the U.S. (1857–61)

Bu·cha·rest /ˈbukəˌrɛst/ the capital and largest city of Romania

sw **buck[1]** /bʌk/ n. [C]
1 money a dollar: *Could I borrow ten bucks?* | *He's paying his lawyer big bucks* (=a lot of money). | *Ellis will do anything to make a fast buck* (=make some money quickly, often dishonestly).
2 the buck stops here also the buck stops with sb used to say that a particular person is responsible for something: *It was my decision to close the hospital; the buck stops with me.*
3 animal plural **buck** or **bucks** a male animal, such as a DEER or rabbit —compare DOE
4 feel/look like a million bucks INFORMAL to feel or look very healthy, happy, and beautiful —see also more bang for the/your buck (BANG[2] (6)), pass the buck (PASS[1] (22))

buck[2] v.
1 horse [I] if a horse bucks, it kicks its back feet into the air, or jumps with all four feet off the ground
2 throw sb [T] to throw a rider off by bucking
3 car [I] if a car bucks, it moves forward in a way which is not smooth, but stops and starts suddenly
4 oppose INFORMAL [T] to oppose something in a direct way; RESIST: *The school bucked a national trend when its students showed improved SAT scores.* | *A lot of women just don't feel confident enough to buck the system* (=avoid the usual rules).
buck for sth phr. v. [T] to try very hard to get something, especially a good position at work: *Anne's bucking for a promotion.*
buck up phr. v. [I,T **buck** sb **up**] to become more cheerful, or make someone more cheerful: *Buck up! At least the insurance will pay to fix the car.*

buck[3] adv. **buck naked** wearing no clothes at all

Buck /bʌk/, **Pearl S.** /pɔrl ɛs/ (1892–1973) a U.S. writer who wrote novels about China

buck·a·roo /ˌbʌkəˈru, ˈbʌkəˌru/ n. [C] INFORMAL a COWBOY, used especially when speaking to children

buck·board /ˈbʌkbɔrd/ n. [C] a light vehicle which has four wheels and is pulled by a horse, used in the U.S. in the 19th century

sw **buck·et** /ˈbʌkɪt/ n. [C]
1 container an open container with a handle, used for carrying and holding things, especially liquids
2 also **bucketful** the quantity of liquid that a bucket can hold: [+ of] *I needed four buckets of water to wash the car.*
3 INFORMAL an occasion when the ball goes through the basket in basketball
4 part of a machine a part of a machine shaped like a large bucket and used for moving earth, water etc.
5 sweat/cry buckets INFORMAL to SWEAT or cry a lot
6 a large quantity INFORMAL a large quantity of a liquid: *He drinks beer by the bucket.* —see also sb can't carry a tune in a bucket (CARRY[1] (26)), a drop in the bucket/ocean (DROP[2] (7)), kick the bucket (KICK[1] (11))

bucket seat /ˌ.. ˈ./ n. [C] a car seat with a high back, with enough space for only one person

buck·le[1] /ˈbʌkəl/ v. **1** [I,T] to fasten a buckle or be joined together with a buckle: *The strap buckles on the side.* | *Frank buckled on his safety harness.* | *Buckle up, please* (=buckle your seatbelt in a car, airplane etc.). —see picture at FASTENER **2** [I,T] to become bent or curved because of heat or pressure,

or to make something bend or curve in this way: *The sidewalk was cracked and buckled from the earthquake.* **3** [I] if your knees or legs buckle, they become weak and bend **4** buckle under pressure/ strain etc. to do something you do not want to do, because a difficult situation forces you to: *Griffin buckled under pressure from investors to lay off workers.*
buckle down phr. v. [I] to start working seriously: *It's time to buckle down and do your homework.*
buckle under phr. v. [I] to do something you do not want to do, because someone forces you to: *I was determined to have my own room and determined not to buckle under.*

buckle[2] n. [C] a metal fastener used for joining the two ends of a belt or STRAP, for fastening a shoe, PURSE etc., or for decoration

buck·ler /ˈbʌklə/ n. [C] a small circular SHIELD with a raised center

buck·shot /ˈbʌkʃɑt/ n. [U] a lot of small metal balls that you fire together from a gun

buck·skin /ˈbʌkˌskɪn/ n. [U] strong soft leather made from the skin of a DEER or goat

buck teeth /ˌ. ˈ./ n. [plural] teeth that stick forward out of your mouth —**buck-toothed** /ˈ. ./ adj.

buck·wheat /ˈbʌkwit/ n. [U] a type of small grain used as food for chickens, and for making FLOUR

bu·col·ic /byuˈkɑlɪk/ adj. LITERARY relating to the land outside towns and cities: *a bucolic little town* —**bucolically** /-kli/ adv.

bud[1] /bʌd/ n. [C] **1** a young tightly rolled-up flower or leaf before it opens: *rose buds* **2** SPOKEN: see BUDDY —see also nip sth in the bud (NIP[1] (2)), TASTE BUD

bud[2] v. **budded, budding** [I] to produce buds

Bu·da·pest /ˈbudəˌpɛst/ the capital and largest city of Hungary

Bud·dha /ˈbudə, ˈbu-/ **1** the Buddha (?563–?483 B.C.) the title given to Gautama Siddhartha, a religious leader from India who taught the ideas on which the religion of Buddhism is based **2** [C] a STATUE or picture of the Buddha

Bud·dhis·m /ˈbudɪzəm, ˈbu-/ n. [U] a religion of east, south, and central Asia, based on the teachings of the Buddha that it is necessary to become free of human desires in order to escape from the suffering that is a part of life. Followers of Buddhism believe in REINCARNATION (=the idea that people are born again after they die, and that their next life depends on how they behaved in their previous life). —see also NIRVANA —**Buddhist** adj., n.: *a Buddhist monk* | *She became a Buddhist.*

bud·ding /ˈbʌdɪŋ/ adj. **1** a budding singer/actor/ writer etc. someone who is just starting to sing, act etc. and will probably be successful at it **2** [only before noun] beginning to develop: *a budding relationship*

bud·dy /ˈbʌdi/ n. plural **buddies** [C] **1** INFORMAL a s friend: *We're good buddies.* **2** SPOKEN, INFORMAL used to speak to a man or boy, especially one you do not know; BUD[1] (2): *Hey, buddy! Is this your car?* **3** also **buddy boy** SPOKEN used to speak to a man or boy that you are angry or annoyed with: *It doesn't matter to me what you think, buddy boy.*

buddy-buddy /ˌ.. ˈ../ adj. INFORMAL be buddy-buddy (with sb) very friendly with someone: *Lisa is being real buddy-buddy with James.*

buddy sys·tem /ˈ.. ˌ../ n. [C usually singular] a system in which people in a group are put in pairs to keep each other safe or to help each other

budge /bʌdʒ/ v. [usually in negatives] INFORMAL **1** [I,T] to move, or move someone or something from one place to another: *The car was stuck in the snow and we couldn't budge it.* | [+ from] *Will hasn't budged from his room all day.* | *I couldn't get the window to budge an inch.* **2** [I] to make someone change their opinion or accept something that is not exactly what they wanted: [+ on] *We offered more money for the house, but they wouldn't budge on the price.* | [+ from] *They refused to budge from their opposition to the plan.*

Budge /bʌdʒ/, **Don** /dɑn/ (1915–) a U.S. tennis player

budg·et¹ /'bʌdʒɪt/ n. [C] a plan of how a person or organization will spend the money that is available in a particular period of time, or the money itself: *the firm's annual budget* | *More cuts in the defense budget are expected.* | [+ of] *The organization has a budget of $35 million.* | *The state has a $14 billion budget deficit* (=a situation in which more money has been spent than is available). | *During his presidential campaign, he promised to balance the budget* (=make sure that only money available is spent). | **be over/under budget** (=to have spent more or less money than the amount allowed in the budget) | *They're on a tight budget* (=they do not have much money to spend).

budget² v. **1** [I,T] to carefully plan and control how much you spend: *No money was budgeted to widen the freeway.* | [+ for] *We'll be able to go if we budget for it.* **2** [I,T] to plan carefully how much of something will be needed: *Each question should take 20 minutes, so budget your time accordingly.*

budget³ adj. [only before noun, no comparative] very low in price; cheap: *a budget flight*

budg·et·ar·y /'bʌdʒə,tɛri/ adj. connected with the way money is spent in a budget: *budgetary restrictions*

Bue·nos Ai·res /,bwɛnəs 'æriz/ the capital and largest city of Argentina

buff¹ /bʌf/ n. **1** [C] **a movie/car/jazz etc. buff** someone who is very interested in movies, cars etc. and knows a lot about them **2** [U] a pale yellow-brown color **3 in the buff** INFORMAL having no clothes on; NAKED

buff² v. [T] to make a surface shine by polishing it with a dry cloth

buff³ adj. SPOKEN someone who is buff has a very attractive body, especially from doing exercise or physical work

Buf·fa·lo /'bʌfə,lou/ a city in the U.S. state of New York

buf·fa·lo /'bʌfə,lou/ n. plural **buffalos, buffaloes** or **buffalo** [C] **1** a large animal like a cow with a very large head and thick hair on its neck and shoulders; BISON **2** an African animal similar to a large black cow with long curved horns —see also WATER BUFFALO

Buffalo Bill /,... './ —see CODY, WILLIAM

buff·er¹ /'bʌfə/ n. [C]
1 **protection** something that protects something else: *Without the buffer of the trees, the noise from the highway would be unbearable.* | *Farmers want the government to set minimum prices as a buffer against market changes.*
2 **separation** something that keeps separate two things or people that might harm each other: *The U.N. forces will act as a buffer between the warring sides.*
3 **a buffer zone** an area between two armies, which is intended to separate them so that they do not fight: *After WWI, the Rhineland served as a buffer zone between France and Germany.*
4 **a buffer state** a smaller peaceful country between two larger countries, which makes war between them less likely
5 **computer** a place in a computer's memory for storing information for a short time
6 **for polishing** something used to polish a surface

buffer² v. [T] to reduce the bad effects of something: *Their savings helped to buffer the effects of the recession.*

buf·fet¹ /bə'feɪ, bu-/ n. [C] **1** a meal in which people serve themselves at a table and then move away to eat: *The restaurant offers a fabulous buffet lunch.* **2** the table that a buffet meal is served from **3** a piece of furniture in which you keep the things you use to serve and eat a meal

buf·fet² /'bʌfɪt/ v. [T usually passive] **1** if wind, rain, or the ocean buffets something, it hits it with a lot of force: *The coastline was buffeted by strong winds.* **2** to make someone have a lot of problems or bad experiences: *Local businesses have been buffeted by the troubled economy.* —**buffeting** n. [C]

buf·foon /bə'fun/ n. [C] OLD-FASHIONED someone who does silly things that make you laugh —**buffoonery** n. [U]

bug¹ /bʌg/ n. [C] **1** a small insect **2** INFORMAL a sickness that people catch very easily from each other, which is usually not very serious: *I missed school because of a stomach bug* (=sickness affecting her stomach). **3** a small fault in the system of instructions that operates a computer —see also DEBUG **4 the travel/ski/camera etc. bug** INFORMAL a sudden strong interest in doing something: *Donna's been bitten by the aerobics bug.* **5** a small piece of electronic equipment for listening secretly to other people's conversations

bug² v. **bugged, bugging** [T] **1** INFORMAL to annoy someone: *It really bugs me when the car behind me drives too close.* **2** to put a BUG¹ (5) somewhere secretly in order to listen to conversations: *The FBI had bugged his apartment.*
bug off phr. v. [I] INFORMAL used to tell someone to go away and stop annoying you

bug·a·boo /'bʌgə,bu/ n. [C] INFORMAL something that makes people feel upset or afraid: *Termite damage is one of the many bugaboos of owning a house.*

bug·bear /'bʌgbɛr/ n. [C] a bugaboo

bug-eyed /'bʌgaɪd/ adj. having eyes that stick out

bug·ger /'bʌgə/ n. [C] SPOKEN a person or thing: *You're a tough little bugger.*

bug·gy /'bʌgi/ n. plural **buggies** [C] **1** a light carriage pulled by a horse **2** a thing like a small bed on wheels, that a baby lies in to be pushed around outside

bu·gle /'byugəl/ n. [C] a musical instrument like a TRUMPET which is used in the army to call soldiers —**bugler** n. [C]

build¹ /bɪld/ v. past tense and past participle **built**
1 **make sth** [I,T] to make something, especially a building or something large: *They're going to build another runway at the airport.* | *We're planning to build near the lake.* | [build sb sth] *We'd like to build Katie a playhouse.*
2 **make sth develop** [T] to make something develop or form: *He built his political career on anti-Communism.* | *Ukraine wanted to build its own independent army.*
3 **feeling** [I,T] if a feeling builds or you build it, it increases gradually over a period of time: *Tension is building between the two countries.* | *The PTA is working to build support for the school in the community.*
4 **be built of sth** to be made using particular materials: *Many of the houses are built of brick.*
5 **be built on sth** to happen as a result of something: *The company's success is built on its line of popular home computers.*
6 **build bridges** to try to establish a better relationship between people who do not like each other: *The group has been trying to build bridges between Cuba and the U.S.* —see also -BUILT
build sth **around** sth phr. v. [T] to use an idea, process, or thing as the most basic or important part of something larger or more complicated: *The play is built around the shepherd's visit to the baby Jesus.* | *Grandmother often built meals around a kettle of beans or a hearty stew.*
build sth **in** phr. v. [T usually passive] to make something so that it is a permanent part of a wall, room etc.
build sth **into** sth phr. v. [T] **1** to make something so that it is a permanent part of a wall, room etc.: *A secret cupboard was built into the wall.* **2** to make something a permanent part of a system, agreement etc.: *A strict completion date was built into the contract.* —see also BUILT-IN
build on phr. v. [T] **1** [build on sth] to use your achievements as a base for further development: *We hope to build on current efforts to prevent teen pregnancy.* **2** [build sth on] to add another room etc. to a building in order to have more space —see also **be built of sth** (BUILD¹ (4))

B

build up *phr. v.*

1 increase gradually [I,T **build** sth **up**] if a substance, force, or activity builds up somewhere or you build it up, it gradually becomes bigger and stronger: *Both sides have built up huge stockpiles of arms.* | *Pressure built up as the water continued to flow into the clogged pipe.* —see also BUILD-UP (1)

2 feeling [I,T **build** sth **up**] if a feeling builds up or you build it up, it increases gradually over a period of time: *To make it in this business, you have to build up the customers' trust.*

3 build up sb's hopes to unfairly encourage someone to think that they will get what they hope for

4 make stronger [T **build** sb/sth ↔ **up**] to make someone or something well and strong: *These exercises help build up strength in your legs.*

5 praise [T **build** sb/sth ↔ **up**] to praise someone or something so that other people think they are really good, even if they are not: *My mom built him up so much, that when I met him I thought he was boring.*

build up to sth *phr. v.* [T] to prepare for a particular moment or event: *I could tell my sister was building up to telling me something.*

build² *n.* [singular,U] the shape and size of someone's body: *a powerful build* —see Usage Note at BODY

build·er /ˈbɪldɚ/ *n.* [C] a person or a company that builds or repairs buildings or other things

build·ing /ˈbɪldɪŋ/ *n.* **1** [C] a structure such as a house, church, or factory, that has a roof and walls: *The Sears Tower is one of the tallest buildings in the world.* | *an apartment building* **2** [U] the process or business of building things: *They made a documentary on the building of the State Capitol.* | *The new law will increase building costs.*

building block /ˈ.. ˌ./ *n.* **1 building blocks** [plural] the pieces or parts which together make it possible for something big or important to exist: *Amino acids are the fundamental building blocks of protein.* **2** [C] a BLOCK¹ (6)

building con·trac·tor /ˈ.. ˌ.../ *n.* [C] someone whose job is to organize the building of a house, office, factory etc.

building site /ˈ.. ˌ./ *n.* [C] a place where a house, building etc. is being built

build-up /ˈ. ./ *n.* **1** [singular,U] an increase over a period of time: *Scientists are warning of a dangerous build-up of chemicals in the water.* **2** [C] a description of someone or something in which you say they are very special or important, often when they are not: *Despite a big build-up in the press, the movie was disappointing.* —see also **build up** (BUILD¹)

built¹ /bɪlt/ the past tense and past participle of BUILD

built² *adj.* [not before noun] SPOKEN used by men to describe a woman with large breasts, considered offensive by many women

-built /bɪlt/ [in adjectives] **well-built/poorly-built etc.** used for describing how large someone is, what something is made of, how it was built, or who built it: *a heavily-built man* | *a well-built house* | *a Soviet-built tank*

built-in /ˌ. ˈ.◂/ *adj.* forming a part of something that cannot be separated from it: *The camera has a built-in flash.* —see also **build in** (BUILD¹)

built-up /ˌ. ˈ.◂/ *adj.* a built-up area has a lot of buildings and not many open spaces

Bu·jum·bu·ra /ˌbudʒəmˈbʊrə/ the capital and largest city of Burundi

bulb /bʌlb/ *n.* [C] **1** the glass-covered part of an electric light that the light shines from; LIGHT BULB: *a 100 watt bulb* **2** a root shaped like a ball that grows into a flower or plant: *tulip bulbs*

bul·bous /ˈbʌlbəs/ *adj.* fat, round, and unattractive: *a bulbous nose*

Bul·finch /ˈbʊlfɪntʃ/, **Thomas** (1796–1867) a U.S. writer famous for his retelling of European MYTHS

Bul·gar·i·a /bʌlˈgæriə, -ˈgɛr-/ a country in southeast Europe next to the Black Sea —**Bulgarian** *n., adj.*

bulge¹ /bʌldʒ/ *n.* [C] **1** a curved MASS on the surface of something, usually caused by something under or inside it: *The store detective had noticed an odd bulge under the suspect's clothes.* **2** a sudden temporary increase in the amount or level of something: *a bulge in the birthrate* —**bulgy** *adj.* —see also **battle of the bulge** (BATTLE¹ (9))

bulge² *v.* [I] **1** also **bulge out** to stick out in a rounded shape, especially because something is very full or too tight: [+ with] *His pockets were bulging with candy.* **2** [+ with] INFORMAL to be very full of people or things

bul·gur /ˈbʌlgɚ/ *n.* [U] a type of wheat which has been dried and broken into pieces

bu·li·mi·a /bəˈlimiə, bu-/ *n.* [U] an illness in which a person cannot stop themselves from eating too much, and then VOMITS¹ in order to control their weight —**bulimic** *adj.*

bulk¹ /bʌlk/ *n.* **1 the bulk (of sth)** the main or part of something: *The bulk of the book is about his experiences in Vietnam.* **2 in bulk** if you buy goods in bulk, you buy a large amount of something at one time **3** [U] the size of something or someone: *Let the dough rise until it is double in bulk.* **4** [C usually singular] a large quantity of something: *For its bulk, the whale is a graceful swimmer.*

bulk² *adj.* **1** [only before noun] bulk goods are sold or moved in large quantities: *We sell bulk coffee to restaurants.* **2 bulk mail/rate** if you send something bulk mail or bulk rate, you send large amounts of it for a smaller cost than usual **3 bulk buying/orders etc.** the buying, ordering etc. of goods in large quantities at one time

bulk³ *v.* [I] to swell or increase in size

bulk up *phr. v.* [I,T] INFORMAL **1** to deliberately gain weight or develop bigger muscles: *Quarterback Jeff George bulked up from 207 pounds to 230.* **2** to make something look bigger, better, or more important by adding something: *It's too bad the director has bulked up the movie with so many repetitions of the murder scene.*

bulk·head /ˈbʌlkhɛd/ *n.* [C] a wall which divides the structure of a ship or aircraft into separate parts

bulk·y /ˈbʌlki/ *adj.* **bulkier, bulkiest 1** something that is bulky is bigger than other things of its type and is difficult to carry: *a bulky package* | *The boxes were bulky and difficult to move.* **2** someone who is bulky is big and heavy —**bulkiness** *n.* [U]

bull¹ /bʊl/ *n.* [C]

1 animal **a)** an adult male animal of the cattle family **b)** the male of some other large animals such as the ELEPHANT or WHALE

2 sth you say [U] INFORMAL something someone says that is completely untrue; BULLSHIT: *People are saying that he stole the money, but that's a bunch of bull.*

3 take the bull by the horns to bravely or confidently deal with a difficult or dangerous problem: *We decided to take the bull by the horns and go to court, instead of paying the fine.*

4 business someone who buys SHARES² (4) because they expect prices to rise —compare BEAR² (4)

5 be like a bull in a china shop a) to behave in a way that is not sensitive to people's feelings or that shows you do not understand the rules or traditions in a situation: *The Senator may have a reputation on Capitol Hill as a bull in a china shop, but the voters love him.* **b)** to keep knocking things over, dropping things, breaking things etc. —see also PAPAL BULL, PIT BULL, **shoot the bull/breeze** (SHOOT¹ (13))

bull² *interjection* SLANG used to say that you do not believe or agree with what someone has said: *Bull! You could have come if you really wanted to.*

bull·dog /ˈbʊldɔg/ *n.* [C] a powerful dog with a large head, a short neck, and short thick legs

bull·doze /ˈbʊldoʊz/ *v.* [T] **1** to destroy buildings, structures etc. with a bulldozer **2** to push objects such as earth and rocks out of the way with a bulldozer **3** to force something to happen, or force someone to do something that they do not really want to do: *Congress is refusing to be bulldozed by the White House on the issue.*

bull·doz·er /'bʊl,doʊzɚ/ *n.* [C] a powerful vehicle with a broad metal blade, used for moving earth and rocks, destroying buildings etc.

bull dyke /'. ./ *n.* [C] OFFENSIVE a LESBIAN who behaves and dresses like a man —compare LIPSTICK LESBIAN

bul·let /'bʊlɪt/ *n.* [C] a small piece of metal that you fire from a gun: *He was killed by a single bullet.* | *One woman suffered a bullet wound to her leg.* —compare SHELL¹ (2), SHOT¹ (9) —see also **bite the bullet** (BITE¹ (3)), PLASTIC BULLET, RUBBER BULLET

bul·le·tin /'bʊlət̬n, 'bʊlət̬ɪn/ *n.* [C] **1** a letter or printed statement that a group or organization produces to tell people its news **2** a short news report on television or radio **3** an official statement that is made to inform people about something important: *The latest police bulletin described the suspect as a white male in his twenties.*

bulletin board /'... ,./ *n.* [C] **1** a board on the wall that you put information or pictures on —see picture at BOARD¹ **2** also **electronic bulletin board** a place in a computer information system where you can read or leave messages

bulletin board sys·tem /'... ,. ,../ abbreviation **BBS** *n.* [C] a place that people can connect to using a computer, to leave and receive messages about a particular subject

bul·let·proof /'bʊlɪt̚,pruf/ *adj.* designed to stop bullets from going through it: *a bulletproof vest*

bullet train /'.. ,./ *n.* [C] a word for a train that can go very fast, used especially about this type of train in Japan

bull·fight /'bʊlfaɪt/ *n.* [C] a type of entertainment popular in Spain, in which a man fights and kills a BULL¹ (1) —**bullfighter** *n.* [C] —**bullfighting** *n.* [U]

bull·frog /'bʊlfrɑg/ *n.* [C] a type of large FROG that makes a loud noise

bull·head·ed /'. '...◂/ *adj.* unwilling to change your opinion or a decision, even when people think you are being unreasonable or stupid —**bullheadedly** *adv.* —**bullheadedness** *n.* [U]

bull·horn /'bʊlhɔrn/ *n.* [C] a piece of equipment that you hold up to your mouth to make your voice louder; MEGAPHONE

bul·lion /'bʊlyən/ *n.* [U] bars of gold or silver: *gold bullion* —compare BOUILLON

bull·ish /'bʊlɪʃ/ *adj.* **1** [not before noun] feeling confident about the future: *We're very bullish about the company's prospects.* **2** TECHNICAL if a business market is bullish, the prices of STOCKs¹ (2) tend or seem likely to rise —**bullishly** *adv.* —**bullishness** *n.* [U]

bull mar·ket /'. '../ *n.* [C] if the STOCK MARKET is called a bull market, a lot of people are buying STOCKS

bull·necked /,bʊl'nɛkt◂/ *adj.* having a short and very thick neck

bul·lock /'bʊlək/ *n.* [C] a young male cow, especially one that has had its sex organs removed

bull·pen /'bʊlpɛn/ *n.* [C usually singular] **1** the area in a baseball field in which PITCHERs practice throwing **2** the PITCHERs on a BASEBALL team, especially those who only play at the end of the game, when the starting PITCHER becomes tired

bull·ring /'bʊlrɪŋ/ *n.* [C] the place where a BULLFIGHT is held

Bull Run /, '. ./ a place in the U.S. state of Virginia where there were two important battles in the American Civil War which the Union forces lost to Confederate forces

bull ses·sion /'. ,../ *n* [C] INFORMAL an occasion when a group of people meet to talk in a relaxed and friendly way: *an all-night bull session*

bull's-eye /'. ./ *n.* [C] the center of a TARGET that you try to hit when shooting or in games like DARTS

bull·shit¹ /'bʊl,ʃɪt/ *n.* [U] VULGAR something that is stupid and completely untrue: *That's total bullshit. You never said that.*

bullshit² *v.* [I,T] VULGAR to say something that is stupid or completely untrue, especially in order to deceive or to appear impressive to someone: *Don't bullshit me!* —**bullshitter** *n.* [C]

bull ter·ri·er /,. '.../ *n.* [C] a strong short-haired dog —see also PIT BULL

bull·whip /'bʊlwɪp/ *n.* [C] a large thick leather WHIP

bul·ly¹ /'bʊli/ *n. plural* **bullies** [C] someone who uses their strength or power to frighten or hurt someone who is weaker: *the school bully*

bully² *v.* **bullies, bullied, bullying** [T] to threaten to hurt someone or frighten them, especially someone smaller or weaker: *Ricky used to bully the younger kids in the neighborhood.* —**bullying** *n.* [U]

bul·rush /'bʊlrʌʃ/ *n.* [C] a tall plant that looks like grass and grows by water

bul·wark /'bʊlwɚk/ *n.* [C] **1** something that protects you from a bad situation: [+ **against**] *Politically, Japan became the main Asian bulwark against communism.* **2 bulwarks** [plural] the sides of a boat or ship above the DECK **3** a strong structure like a wall, built for defense

bum¹ /bʌm/ *n.* [C] INFORMAL **1** someone, especially a man, who you think is not doing a good job, or who is not doing what he should do: *She's always complaining about her husband, but she won't throw the bum out.* **2** someone, especially a man, who has no home or job, and who asks people for money **3 a beach/ski etc. bum** someone who spends all their time on the beach, SKIing² etc. **4 give sb the bum's rush** INFORMAL to make someone leave a place, especially a public place, quickly: *The protesters were given a polite bum's rush by the police.*

bum² *v.* **bummed, bumming** [T] SPOKEN to ask someone for something such as money, food, or cigarettes, without paying for them: *I bummed a ride from Sue.*

bum around sth *phr. v.* [T] INFORMAL to travel around without any real plan, living very cheaply: *I spent some time bumming around Europe.*

bum sb **out** *phr. v.* [T] SPOKEN to make someone feel sad or disappointed about something: *I don't want to bum you out, but we can't afford to go on vacation.* —see also BUMMED

bum³ *adj.* [only before noun, no comparative] **1** INFORMAL bad and useless: *He gave me a lot of bum advice.* **2 a bum ankle/leg/shoulder etc.** an ANKLE, leg etc. that is injured so that you cannot use it much **3 bum rap a)** an occasion when someone says that someone else has done something wrong or illegal even though it is not true: *Ted says he's gotten a bum rap. He claims he was at home on the night of the robbery.* **b)** an occasion when someone criticizes someone else or something unfairly: *The downtown area has been given a bum rap in the press.* **4 a bum steer** OLD-FASHIONED a piece of bad advice

bum·ble /'bʌmbəl/ *v.* [I always + adv./prep.] **1** to make a lot of mistakes when you do or say something: *Officials bumbled through their explanations of why the hospital had been bombed.* **2** to accidentally fall against things or knock things over when you walk —**bumbler** *n.* [C]

bum·ble·bee /'bʌmbəl,bi/ *n.* [C] a large hairy BEE —see picture at INSECT

bum·bling /'bʌmblɪŋ/ *adj.* [only before noun] behaving in a careless way and making a lot of mistakes: *a couple of bumbling burglars*

bummed /bʌmd/ also **bummed out** /,. './ *adj.* SPOKEN feeling sad or disappointed: *I was really bummed that I missed the game.*

bum·mer /'bʌmɚ/ *n.* [singular] SPOKEN a situation that is disappointing: *You can't go? What a bummer!*

bump¹ /bʌmp/ *v.* **1** [I always + adv./prep.,T] to hit or knock against something: [+ **against/into etc.**] *We bumped into each other in the hallway.* | [**bump sth on/against etc.**] *I bumped my head on the roof of the car as I got out.* **2** [T always + adv./prep.] INFORMAL to make someone change their place or position:

B

[bump sb up/out of/from etc.] *The airline bumped me up to first class! | The Super Bowl bumped "60 Minutes" from the number one spot in the TV ratings.* **3** [I always + adv./prep.] to move up and down as you move forward, especially in a vehicle: [+ along/across etc.] *We bumped along in an old white bus.* **4 bump and grind** INFORMAL to move your HIPS forward and back and around, usually while dancing, in a way that is intended to be sexually exciting **5 bump heads (with sb)** INFORMAL to argue with someone or compete with them: *The West Coast is a market where USAir bumps heads with United Airlines.*

bump into sb *phr. v.* [T] to meet someone that you know when you were not expecting to: *I bumped into Leo at the fair.*

bump sb **off** *phr. v.* [T] INFORMAL to murder someone

bump sth **up** *phr. v.* [T] INFORMAL to suddenly increase something by a large amount: *In the summer, they bump up the prices by ten percent.*

bump² *n.* [C] **1** an area of skin that is raised up because you have hit it on something: *Pam got a lot of bumps and bruises, but she's okay.* **2** a small raised area on a surface: *a bump in the road* **3** an occasion when something hits something else: *I was backing up when I felt a bump.* **4** the sound of something hitting a hard surface: *We heard a bump in the next room.* —see also GOOSEBUMPS, SPEED BUMP

bump·er¹ /ˈbʌmpɚ/ *n.* [C] a bar that is attached to the front and back of a car to protect it if it hits anything —see picture on page 427

bumper² *adj.* **a bumper crop (of sth) a)** an unusually large amount of a grain, vegetable, etc. produced in a particular year **b)** INFORMAL an unusually large number of something: *a bumper crop of congressional candidates*

bumper car /ˈ.. ˌ./ *n.* [C] a small electric car that you drive in a special area at a FAIR² (1) and deliberately try to hit other cars with

bumper stick·er /ˈ.. ˌ./ *n.* [C] a small sign on the bumper of a car, with a humorous, political, or religious message

bumper-to-bumper /ˌ... ˈ..ˑ/ *adj., adv.* with a lot of cars that are very close together and moving very slowly: *There's bumper-to-bumper traffic on the bridge. | I hate driving bumper-to-bumper.*

bump·kin /ˈbʌmpkɪn/ *n.* [C] INFORMAL someone from an area outside a city or town who is considered to be stupid: *These guys from Chicago come down and treat us like a bunch of country bumpkins.*

bump·tious /ˈbʌmpʃəs/ *adj.* too proud of your abilities in a way that annoys other people —**bumptiously** *adv.* —**bumptiousness** *n.* [U]

bump·y /ˈbʌmpi/ *adj.* **bumpier, bumpiest 1** a bumpy surface is flat but has a lot of raised parts so it is difficult to walk or drive on it: *bumpy dirt roads* —opposite SMOOTH¹ **2** a bumpy trip by car or airplane is uncomfortable because of bad road or weather conditions **3** having a lot of problems for a long time: *For many teenagers, getting to adulthood can be a bumpy road* (=a time when they have a lot of problems).

bun /bʌn/ *n.* [C] **1** a small round type of bread: *a hamburger bun* **2** a hairstyle in which a woman with long hair fastens it in a small round shape at the back of her head —see picture at HAIRSTYLE **3 buns** [plural] INFORMAL the part of your body that you sit on; BUTTOCKS **4 sb has a bun in the oven** SLANG used to say that a woman is PREGNANT

SW **bunch¹** /bʌntʃ/ *n.* [C] **1** [usually singular] a large number of similar things, or a large amount of something: *The doctor asked me a bunch of questions. | There are a whole bunch of good little restaurants on Ventura Boulevard. | This wine is the best of the bunch.* **2** [usually singular] a group of people: *There are always a bunch of kids hanging out at the beach. | Reporters are generally a cynical bunch.* **3** a group of similar things that are fastened or held

together: *a bunch of bananas | bunches of fresh grapes* —see also **thanks a bunch** (THANKS¹ (6))

bunch² *v.* [I,T] also **bunch together, bunch up 1** to stay close together in a group, or to move people or things together in a group: *The animals were bunched up along the river. | The soldiers bunched the prisoners together.* **2** to pull material together tightly in folds: *The shorts were bunched at the waist.*

Bunche /bʌntʃ/, **Ralph** /rælf/ (1904–1971) a U.S. DIPLOMAT who was involved in starting the UN and was the first African-American person to win the Nobel Peace Prize

bun·co, bunko /ˈbʌŋkoʊ/ *n.* [U] INFORMAL dishonest ways of tricking someone into giving you or paying you money

bun·dle¹ /ˈbʌndl/ *n.* [C] computer SOFTWARE and sometimes other services or equipment that is included with a new computer at no additional cost

bundle² *v.* [T] to include computer SOFTWARE or other services with a new computer at no extra cost

Bundt cake /ˈbʌnt keɪk/ *n.* [C] TRADEMARK a type of heavy cake baked in a special round pan with a hole in the middle

bung /bʌŋ/ *n.* [C] a round piece of rubber, wood etc. used to close the top of a container such as a BARREL

bun·ga·low /ˈbʌŋɡəˌloʊ/ *n.* [C] a small house, usually with only one STORY (=level)

bun·gee cord /ˈbʌndʒi ˌkɔrd/ also **bungee** *n.* [C] **1** a rope that stretches, used in bungee jumping **2** a short rope that stretches and has hooks on the ends, used to fasten things together

bungee jum·ping /ˈbʌn-dʒi ˌdʒʌmpɪŋ/ *n.* [U] a sport in which you jump off something very high with a rope that stretches tied to your legs, so that you go up again without touching the ground —**bungee jump** *n.* [C] —**bungee jump** *v.* [I] —**bungee jumper** *n.* [C] —see picture on page 1332

bungee jump

bun·gle /ˈbʌŋɡəl/ *v.* [T] to be unsuccessful, because you have made stupid mistakes: *Officers have bungled a number of recent criminal cases.* —**bungle** *n.* [C] —**bungler** *n.* [C] —**bungling** *n.* [U] —**bungled** *adj. a bungled rescue attempt*

bun·gling /ˈbʌŋɡlɪŋ/ *adj.* [only before noun] unsuccessful as a result of making stupid mistakes: *a movie about three bungling thieves*

bun·ion /ˈbʌnyən/ *n.* [C] a painful red sore area on the first joint of your big toe

bunk¹ /bʌŋk/ *n.* **1** [C] a narrow bed that is fastened to the wall, for example on a train or ship **2** [U] INFORMAL something someone says that is completely untrue; BUNKUM

bunk² *v.* [I] INFORMAL to sleep somewhere, especially in someone else's house: *I bunked with friends in Miami.*

bunk bed /ˈ. ./ *n.* [C usually plural] one of two beds that are attached together, one on top of the other —see picture at BED¹

bun·ker /ˈbʌŋkɚ/ *n.* [C] **1** a strongly built shelter for soldiers, usually located under the ground **2** a large hole on a GOLF COURSE that is filled with sand; SAND TRAP **3** a place where you store coal, especially on a ship or outside a house

bunk·house /ˈbʌŋkhaʊs/ *n.* [C] a building where workers sleep

bun·kum, buncombe /ˈbʌŋkəm/ *n.* [U] BUNK

bun·ny /ˈbʌni/ also **bunny rab·bit** /ˈ.. ˌ./ *n. plural* **bunnies** [C] a word for a rabbit, used especially by or to children —see also BEACH BUNNY, SNOW BUNNY

bunny slope /ˈ.. ˌ./ *n.* [C] the area of a mountain where people learn to SKI

bun·sen burn·er /ˈbʌnsən ˌbɜːnəʳ/ n. [C] a piece of equipment that produces a hot gas flame, for scientific EXPERIMENTS

bunt /bʌnt/ v. [I] to deliberately hit the ball toward the ground in BASEBALL by holding the BAT a special way —**bunt** n. [C]

bunt·ing /ˈbʌntɪŋ/ n. [U] small paper or cloth flags on strings, used to decorate buildings and streets on special occasions

Bun·yan /ˈbʌnyən/, **John** (1628–88) an English religious writer and PREACHER who wrote "The Pilgrim's Progress"

Bunyan, Paul in old American stories, a GIANT who changed the shape of the land as he traveled with his blue OX, Babe

buoy[1] /ˈbui, bɔɪ/ n. plural **buoys** [C] an object that floats on the ocean, a lake, etc. to mark a safe or dangerous area

buoy[2] also **buoy up** v. [T] **1** to make someone feel happier or more confident: Democrats were buoyed by election results. **2** to keep profits, prices etc. at a high level: Easier credit would help buoy economic growth. **3** to keep something floating

buoy·an·cy /ˈbɔɪənsi/ n. [U] **1** the ability of an object to float: the buoyancy of light wood **2** the power of a liquid to make an object float: Salt water has more buoyancy than fresh water. **3** a feeling of happiness and a belief that you can deal with problems easily **4** the ability of prices, a business etc. to quickly get back to a high level after a difficult period

buoy·ant /ˈbɔɪənt/ adj. **1** cheerful and confident: the buoyant 22-year-old dancer **2** buoyant prices, companies etc. tend to remain high or successful: a buoyant economy **3** able to float or keep things floating: Cork is a very buoyant material. —**buoyantly** adv.

bur /bɜːʳ/ n. [C] another spelling of BURR

bur·ble /ˈbɜːbəl/ v. **1** [I,T] to talk about something in a confused way that is difficult to understand **2** [I] to make a sound like a stream flowing over stones —**burble** n. [C]

burbs /bɜːbz/ n. **the burbs** INFORMAL the SUBURBS (=areas around a city where people live)

W 3 **bur·den**[1] /ˈbɜːdn/ n. **1** [C] something difficult or worrying that you are responsible for: I don't want to be a burden to my children when I'm old. | We need to reduce the tax burden of middle-income Americans. **2 the burden of proof** LAW the duty to prove that something is true **3** [C] something that is carried; LOAD[1] (1) **4** [singular] FORMAL the main meaning of what someone is saying —see also BEAST OF BURDEN

burden[2] v. **1 be burdened by/with sth** to have a lot of problems, be worried, or have a lot of work because of something: The company is burdened by debt. | Most social workers are burdened with large work loads. —see also UNBURDEN **2 be burdened with sth** to be carrying something heavy: The man, burdened with grocery bags, had trouble walking up the steps.

bur·den·some /ˈbɜːdnsəm/ adj. causing problems or additional work: burdensome responsibilities

W 2 **bu·reau** /ˈbyʊroʊ/ n. plural **bureaus** [C] **1** a government department or a part of a government department: the Federal Bureau of Investigation **2** an office or organization that collects or provides information: the visitor's information bureau **3** a piece of furniture with drawers, used for storing clothes

bu·reauc·ra·cy /byʊˈrɑːkrəsi/ n. plural **bureaucracies** [C,U] **1** a complicated official system which is annoying or confusing because it has too many rules, processes etc.: The company's huge bureaucracy limits creativity and independent thinking. **2** the officials who are employed rather than elected to do the work of a government, business etc.

bu·reau·crat /ˈbyʊrəˌkræt/ n. [C] someone who works in a bureaucracy and uses official rules very strictly

bu·reau·crat·ic /ˌbyʊrəˈkrætɪk/ adj. involving a lot of complicated official rules and processes —**bureaucratically** /-kli/ adv.

Bureau of Al·co·hol, To·bac·co and Fire·arms, the /ˌ.. .... ˈ../ a U.S. government organization that is concerned with the rules about the sale and use of alcohol, tobacco, guns, and explosives

Bureau of In·di·an Af·fairs, the /ˌ.. ...ˈ./ abbreviation **BIA** a U.S. government organization which is concerned with the WELFARE and education of Native Americans and with other legal matters concerning RESERVATIONS

burg /bɜːg/ n. [C] INFORMAL a small town

bur·geon /ˈbɜːdʒən/ v. [I] FORMAL to grow or develop quickly

bur·geon·ing /ˈbɜːdʒənɪŋ/ adj. [no comparative] increasing or developing very quickly: A larger water supply is needed for Denver's burgeoning population.

burg·er /ˈbɜːgəʳ/ n. [C] **1** GROUND BEEF in the shape of a circle, which is cooked and usually eaten with a BUN; HAMBURGER **2** another food that is cooked in a flat round shape, usually eaten with a BUN: a fish burger —see also **flip burgers** (FLIP[1] (3))

Bur·ger /ˈbɜːgəʳ/, **War·ren Earl** /ˈwɔːrən ɜːl/ (1907–1995) a CHIEF JUSTICE on the U.S. Supreme Court

burgh·er /ˈbɜːgəʳ/ n. [C] OLD USE someone who lives in a particular town, especially someone who is rich

bur·glar /ˈbɜːgləʳ/ n. [C] someone who goes into houses, stores etc. to steal things —see also CAT BURGLAR —see Usage Note at THIEF

burglar a·larm /ˈ.. .ˌ./ n. [C] a piece of equipment that makes a loud noise when someone tries to get into a building illegally

bur·glar·ize /ˈbɜːgləˌraɪz/ v. [T] to go into a building and steal things —see Usage Note at STEAL[1]

bur·gla·ry /ˈbɜːgləri/ n. plural **burglaries** [C,U] the crime of getting into a building to steal things: Burglaries in the area have risen by 5%.

bur·gun·dy /ˈbɜːgəndi/ n. plural **burgundies** **1** [U] a dark red color **2** [C,U] also **Burgundy** red or white wine from the Burgundy area of France

bur·i·al /ˈbɛriəl/ n. [C,U] the act or ceremony of putting a dead body into a grave

Bur·ki·na /bɜːˈkiːnə/ a country in west Africa, to the north of Ghana —**Burkinese** /ˌbɜːkɪˈniːz, -ˈnɪs/ n., adj.

bur·lap /ˈbɜːlæp/ n. [U] a type of thick rough cloth

bur·lesque[1] /bɜːˈlesk/ n. [C,U] **1** speech, acting, or writing in which a serious subject is made to seem silly or an unimportant subject is treated in a serious way **2** a performance involving a mixture of humor and STRIPTEASE, popular in America in the past

burlesque[2] v. [T] to make a serious subject seem silly to amuse people

bur·ly /ˈbɜːli/ adj. a burly man is big and strong —**burliness** n. [U]

Bur·ma /ˈbɜːmə/ the former name of Myanmar, a country in east Asia

Bur·mese[1] /bɜːˈmiːz/ n. **1** [C] someone who is from Myanmar **2** [U] one of the main languages spoken in Myanmar

Burmese[2] adj. coming from or relating to Myanmar

burn[1] /bɜːn/ v. past and past participle **burned** or **burnt**
1 produce heat [I] to produce heat and flames: The fire in the hills has been burning for a week.
2 destroy with fire [I,T] to be destroyed by fire or to destroy something with fire: Over 35 houses burned as wildfire swept through the town. | Most of the garbage is burned in a pit behind the building.
3 damage by fire/heat/sun [I,T] to damage something or hurt someone with fire, heat, or SUNLIGHT, or be hurt or damaged in this way: Marcus burned his hand on the stove. | Oh no, I burned the toast! | The best protection is to get out of the sun before you get burned.
4 burn (sth) to the ground if a building burns to the ground or if someone burns it to the ground, it is completely destroyed by fire

B

5 burn sth to a crisp to burn something until it is black, especially by cooking it for too long

6 `chemicals` [T] to damage or destroy something by a chemical action; CORRODE

7 be burned to death also **be burned alive** to be killed in a fire

8 `power/light/energy etc.` [I,T] if you burn a FUEL, or if it burns, it is used to produce power, heat, light etc.: *The engine only burns diesel fuel.*

9 `shine` [I] if a light or lamp burns, it shines or produces light: *Christmas lights burned brightly all around town.*

10 be/get burned INFORMAL **a)** to be emotionally hurt by someone or something: *Jo's afraid of getting burned if she gets involved with someone again.* **b)** to lose a lot of money, especially in a business deal: *A lot of people got burned buying junk bonds.*

11 `feel hot` [I,T] to feel too hot and uncomfortable or make part of your body feel like this; STING: *The ointment burns a little when you first apply it.* | *Cheap Scotch burns your throat.*

12 burn your bridges INFORMAL to do something so that you stop having a connection or relationship with someone or something: *Don't burn your bridges; you might want to work for them again.*

13 burn the candle at both ends INFORMAL to be very busy both at work and in your social life: *Back in the twenties, the Millay sisters were known in New York society for burning the candle at both ends.*

14 burn the midnight oil INFORMAL to work or study until late at night: *Lawmakers were burning the midnight oil last night, as the debate continued.*

15 burn a hole in your pocket INFORMAL if money is burning a hole in your pocket, you want to spend it as soon as you can: *Don't wait until the money's burning a hole in your pocket, plan ahead.*

16 burn your fingers also **get your fingers burned** INFORMAL to suffer the bad results of something that you have done: *Unless your business plan is very good, you can easily get your fingers burned.*

17 `be embarrassed` [I] if your face or cheeks are burning, they feel hot because you are embarrassed or upset

18 it burns me/her/him etc. that SPOKEN used to say that something makes someone feel angry or JEALOUS: *It really burns me the way he treats her.*

19 be burning to do sth to want to do something very much: *Hannah's burning to tell you her news.*

20 `go quickly` [I always + adv./prep.] *In Germany, sports cars burn along the highway at speeds over 100 mph.*

21 be burning with rage/desire etc. to feel an emotion very strongly

22 burn rubber INFORMAL to start a car moving so quickly that the tires make a loud high noise

23 burn sb at the stake to kill someone by tying them to a post on top of a fire —see also **crash and burn** (CRASH[1] (6)), **sb's ears are burning** (EAR (14))

burn away phr. v. [I,T] if something burns away or is burned away, it is destroyed or reduced to something much smaller by fire

burn down phr. v. **1** [I,T **burn** sth **down**] if a building burns down or is burned down, it is destroyed by fire: *The old school burned down thirty years ago.* **2** [I] if a fire burns down, the flames become weaker and it produces less heat —compare **burn out**, **burn up**

burn off phr. v. **1** [I] if FOG or MIST burns off, it disappears when the day becomes warmer and then sun gets higher in the sky **2** [T **burn** sth ↔ **off**] to remove something by burning it: *The nuts are roasted to burn off the poisonous oil.* **3 burn off energy/fat/calories etc.** to use energy etc. by doing physical exercise: *It takes one hour of running to burn off one chocolate bar.*

burn out phr. v.

1 `fire` [I,T **burn** sth **out**] if a fire burns out or burns itself out, it stops burning because there is no wood or FUEL left

2 `feel tired` [I] to feel very tired and not interested in things anymore, because you are working too hard: *A lot of teachers are burning out and quitting.* —see also BURNED OUT

3 be burned out a) if something is burned out, the inside of it is destroyed by fire: *Because of the war, entire cities were burned out.* **b)** if someone is burned out, they are very tired and no longer interested in things because they are working too hard

4 `engine` [I,T **burn** sth ↔ **out**] if an engine or electric wire burns out or is burned out, it stops working because it has been damaged by getting too hot

5 `aircraft` [I] if a ROCKET or JET burns out, it stops operating because all its FUEL has been used —see also BURNOUT (2)

burn up phr. v.

1 `destroy` [I,T **burn** sth ↔ **up**] if something burns up or is burned up, it is completely destroyed by fire or great heat

2 `burn brighter` [I] if a fire burns up, it gets stronger and brighter

3 `be hot` [I] SPOKEN if someone is burning up, they are very hot, especially because they have a fever

4 `make sb angry` [T **burn** sb **up**] INFORMAL to make someone angry: *It burns me up that they can charge so much for doing absolutely nothing!*

5 `go quickly` [T **burn up** sth] to run or dance very quickly, or travel very quickly in a car: *Matt and Jen were really burning up the dance floor.* | *cars burning up the race track*

6 burn up energy/fat/calories etc. to use energy etc. by doing physical exercise.

burn[2] n. [C] **1** an injury or mark caused by fire, heat, SUNLIGHT, or chemicals: *She was treated for minor burns on her hands.* **2 the burn** INFORMAL a painful hot feeling in your muscles when you exercise a lot

burned /bɔnd/ adj. damaged or hurt by burning: *burned trees*

burned out /ˌ. ˈ. ◂/ adj. so tired and bored because of working hard that you are not interested in anything: *By that time, I was totally burned out and ready to quit.*

burn·er /ˈbɔnɚ/ n. [C] **1** the part of a STOVE that produces heat or a flame **2 put sth on the back burner** INFORMAL to delay doing something until a later time: *I had to put sports on the back burner during college.*

burn·ing[1] /ˈbɔnɪŋ/ adj. [only before noun] **1** being damaged or destroyed by flames: *The two boys were rescued from the burning apartment building.* **2** feeling very hot: *burning cheeks* **3 a burning question/issue** a very important question or problem: *The burning issue of this election is the economy.* **4 a burning desire/ambition/need etc.** a very strong need etc.: *a burning desire to succeed*

burning[2] adv. **burning hot** very hot

bur·nish /ˈbɔnɪʃ/ v. [T] to polish metal until it shines —**burnished** adj.: *burnished copper*

bur·noose /bɔˈnus/ n. [C] a long loose dress or coat worn by Arab men and women

burn·out /ˈbɔnaʊt/ n. [C,U] **1** the feeling of always being very tired and uninterested in things, because you have been working too hard: *Nurses on these units have a high rate of burnout.* **2** the time when a ROCKET or JET has finished all of its FUEL and stops operating

Burns /bɔnz/, **Rob·ert** /ˈrɑbɚt/ (1759–96) a Scottish poet who wrote in the Scots dialect and is regarded as Scotland's national poet

burnt[1] /bɔnt/ a past tense and past participle of BURN[1]

burnt[2] adj. damaged or hurt by burning: *burnt toast*

burp /bɔp/ v. INFORMAL **1** [I] to pass gas loudly from your stomach out through your mouth; BELCH **2** [T] to help a baby to do this, especially by rubbing or gently hitting its back —**burp** n. [C]

burr /bɔ/ n. [C] **1** a fairly quiet regular sound like something turning quickly; WHIRR: *the burr of a sewing machine* **2** a rough spot on a piece of metal after it has been made, cut, or DRILLed[2] (1) **3** also **bur** a seed of some plants that is covered with PRICKLES that make it stick to things **4** a way of pronouncing English in which the tongue is used to make the /r/ sound very long, especially in Scottish ACCENTS —see also **roll your r's** (ROLL[1] (21))

Burr /bɜ/, **Aaron** (1756–1836) the Vice President of the U.S. under Thomas Jefferson

bur·ri·to /bəˈritoʊ/ n. plural **burritos** [C] a Mexican dish made with a TORTILLA (=flat thin bread) folded around meat or beans with cheese

bur·ro /ˈbɜoʊ, ˈbʊroʊ/ n. plural **burros** [C] a DONKEY, usually a small one

bur·row[1] /ˈbɜoʊ, ˈbʌroʊ/ v. **1** [I always + adv./prep., T] to make a hole or passage in the ground: [+ into/under etc.] Mother turtles burrow into the sand to lay their eggs. | The gophers were busy burrowing holes. **2** [I,T always + adv./prep.] to press your body close to someone or under something because you want to get warm, feel safe etc.: [+ into/under etc.] We burrowed under the blankets for warmth. **3** [I always + adv./prep.] to search for something that is in a container or under other things: [+ into/through etc.] Helen burrowed in her purse for some change.

burrow[2] n. [C] a passage in the ground made by a small animal such as a rabbit or FOX as a place to live

bur·sar /ˈbɜsɚ, -sɑr/ n. [C] someone at a college who is responsible for the money paid by students

bur·si·tis /bɜˈsaɪtɪs/ n. [U] the swelling of the area between a TENDON and a bone, especially around your knee or shoulder

burst[1] /bɜst/ v. past tense and past participle **burst 1** break open [I,T] if something bursts or you burst it, it breaks open or apart suddenly and violently so that the substance it contains comes out: The dam burst after heavy rains. | It's a game in which children try to burst balloons by sitting on them. **2 be bursting with sth** INFORMAL to be filled with something, or have a lot of something: The window boxes were bursting with flowers. | a story bursting with ideas | **be bursting with pride/confidence/ energy etc.** Her parents watched, bursting with pride, as she walked on stage. **3** move suddenly [I always + adv./prep.] to move somewhere suddenly or quickly, especially into or out of a place: [+ through/into/in etc.] Four men burst into the store and tied up the clerks. **4 bursting at the seams** so full that nothing or no one else can fit inside: All of our classrooms are bursting at the seams. **5 burst open** to suddenly be open: The door burst open and the kids piled into the house. **6 burst the/sb's bubble** to make someone suddenly realize that something is not as good as they believed or hoped: I hate to burst your bubble, but you look really dumb in that hat. **7 burst a blood vessel** SPOKEN to become extremely angry **8 be bursting to do sth** INFORMAL to want to do something very much

burst in on/upon sb/sth phr. v. [T] to interrupt something by entering a room, in a way that embarrasses you or other people: I burst in on them, thinking that the room was empty.

burst into sth phr. v. [T] **1** to suddenly begin to make a sound, especially to start singing, crying, or laughing: The crowd burst into cheers. | Believe it or not, Levy occasionally **bursts into song** at meetings. | Ken's sister suddenly **burst into tears** while we were eating. **2 burst into flames** to suddenly start to burn: The pickup hit the wall and burst into flames.

burst out phr. v. **1 burst out laughing/crying etc.** to suddenly start to laugh, cry etc.: Rubin burst out laughing as he read the letter. **2** [T] to suddenly say something in a forceful way: "I don't believe you!" she burst out angrily. —see also OUTBURST (1)

burst[2] n. [C] **1** the act of something bursting or the place where it has burst: I found a burst in the water pipe. **2** a short sudden increase in effort or activity: Finley's **burst of speed** on the last lap was what won the race for him. | They scored 14 points in a five-minute burst. | The drug gives you a **burst of energy**. **3 a burst of sth a)** a short sudden and usually loud sound: There were several sharp bursts of machine-gun fire behind the house. **b)** a sudden strong

feeling or emotion: She hit him in a burst of anger.

Bu·run·di /bʊˈrundi, -ˈrʊn-/ a country in east central Africa, west of Tanzania —**Burundian** n., adj.

bur·y /ˈbɛri/ v. **buries, buried, burying** [T] sw
1 put sb in a grave to put someone who has died in a grave: [bury sb in/at etc.] Uncle Bill was buried in the Milk River cemetery.
2 put sth under the ground to put something under the ground, often in order to hide it: Some of the phone lines are buried beneath the streets.
3 cover with sth [usually passive] to cover something with other things so that it cannot be found: [bury sth under/beneath/in etc.] Two cars were buried in the mudslide. | His glasses were buried under a pile of papers.
4 feeling/memory to ignore a feeling or memory and pretend that it does not exist: People may bury painful childhood memories to protect themselves.
5 hide facts to put a fact, report etc. in a place in a larger document where it is difficult to find, so that it is not likely to be read: The story was buried in the back of the business section of the paper.
6 end to make something end or stop: We hope to bury any speculation that there was a conspiracy.
7 defeat INFORMAL to defeat someone easily in a competition, business situation etc.: Tennessee buried Florida 45–3 in Saturday's game.
8 bury your face/head etc. (in sth) to press your face etc. into something soft, usually to get comfort, to avoid someone, or to be able to smell something: The girl buried her face in the fur of her dog's neck.
9 bury the hatchet to agree to stop arguing about something and become friends again: Surprisingly, Barbieri called Ryan two years later and suggested they bury the hatchet.
10 bury yourself in your work/studies etc. to give all your attention to something: After the divorce, she buried herself in her work.
11 bury your head in the sand to ignore a bad situation and hope it will stop if you do not think about it: If you bury your head in the sand now, you may lose your house.
12 push sth into a surface to push something, especially something sharp, into something else with a lot of force: The dog buried its teeth in my leg.
13 have sb die to have someone you love die: The hardest thing a mother can do is bury one of her children —see also **dead and buried** (DEAD[1] (18))

bus[1] /bʌs/ n. plural **buses** or **busses** [C] a large sw
vehicle that people pay to travel on: the bus to the airport | Traveling by bus is easy in the city. | Show your ticket to the driver as you **get on the bus**.

bus[2] v. **bused, busing** or **bussed, bussing** [T] **1** to take a group of people somewhere in a bus: [bus sb to/into etc.] Many children are being bused to schools in other areas. **2** to take away dirty dishes from the tables in a restaurant: I spent the summer busing tables.

bus·boy /ˈbʌsbɔɪ/ n. [C] a young man who works in a restaurant and whose job is to take away dirty dishes from the tables

bus·es /ˈbʌsɪz/ n. a plural of bus

bush /bʊʃ/ n. **1** [C] a low thick plant smaller than a sw
tree and with a lot of thin branches: a holly bush **2 the bush** wild country that has not been cleared, especially in Australia or Africa **3** [singular] VULGAR the area of hair on a woman's body above and around her sex organs —see also **beat around the bush** (BEAT[1] (17))

Bush /bʊʃ/, **George** (1924–) the 41st president of the U.S. and Vice President under Ronald Reagan

Bush, George W. (1946–) a U.S. POLITICIAN who was the GOVERNOR of Texas and was elected U.S. President in 2000

bush ba·by /ˈ. ˌ../ n. [C] a small African animal that lives in trees and has large eyes and ears, and a long tail

bushed /bʊʃt/ adj. [not before noun] INFORMAL very tired

bush·el /'bʊʃəl/ n. [C] a unit for measuring grain or vegetables equal to 8 gallons or 36.4 liters

bush league[1] /'. ./ adj. INFORMAL not skillful, or not skillfully made or done; AMATEURISH: *The bush-league agency that came up with that ad should be fired.*

bush league[2] n. [C] INFORMAL a MINOR LEAGUE baseball team

bush·man /'bʊʃmən/ n. [C] **1 Bushman** a member of a southern African tribe who live in the BUSH (2) **2** someone who lives in the Australian BUSH (2)

bush·whack /'bʊʃwæk/ v. **1** [T] to attack someone suddenly from a hidden place; AMBUSH **2** [I,T] to push or cut your way through thick trees or bushes —**bushwhacker** n. [C]

bush·y /'bʊʃi/ adj. **bushier, bushiest** bushy hair or fur is very thick: *a bushy tail* —**bushiness** n. [U]

bus·i·ly /'bɪzəli/ adv. in a busy way: *The children were painting busily at their easels.*

bus·i·ness /'bɪznɪs/ n.
1 buying or selling goods [U] the activity of buying or selling goods and services, done by companies: *As an M.B.A. student, you study all aspects of business.* | *This is a list of the major U.S. companies that do business in Russia.* | *The firm does a lot of business with oil companies.* | *The policy is backed by the international business community* (=people who work in business). | *the advertising/printing/shipping etc. business Paul's first job was in the movie business.* | *California's agricultural business.*
2 be in business or **go into business** to be operating as a company, or begin operating as a company: *She worked for Safeway before going into business for herself.* —opposite **go out of business**
3 work not pleasure [U] things you do as part of your job rather than for pleasure: *Jen went to Ohio on business* (=because of her job). | *business trip/lunch/meeting etc. a business trip to Dallas*
4 organization [C] an organization that produces or sells goods or services: *MacGrath owns a small business that only employs ten people.* | *Taylor runs an office equipment business.*
5 value/amount [U] the amount of work a company is doing or its value: *Lockheed expects defense work to account for 60% of its business.* | *Business has been slow for retailers this Christmas* (=they are not selling very much). | *Business is up this year* (=it is better than last year).
6 in a particular job/time [U] work that must be done in a particular job or during a period of time: *We discussed this week's business.* | *[+ of] the routine business of government*
7 your/sb's business SPOKEN used in phrases to tell someone that they do not have a right to know about something because it is private or personal: *Tell his mother to mind her own business.* | *My personal life is none of your business.* | *"Are you going out with Kate tonight?" "That's my business."*
8 sb was (just) minding their own business used to say that someone was not doing anything unusual or wrong at the time something unfair or bad happened to them: *I was just walking along, minding my own business, when this guy ran straight into me.*
9 make it your business to do sth to make a special effort to do something: *Ruth made it her business to get to know the customers.*
10 subject/activity [singular] used to talk about a subject, event, situation, or activity, especially one that you have a particular opinion of: *For kids, playing is serious business.* | *What's this business about you getting into a fight at school?*
11 sth general [U] SPOKEN used to talk about something in general without giving details: *He handles the mail and all that business.*
12 business as usual used to say that, although there have been problems, things are happening the way they normally happen, especially at a business: *Despite the fire damage, it's business as usual at the barber shop.*
13 get down to business to start dealing with an important subject: *Okay, let's get down to business.*
14 be in business INFORMAL to have all that you need to start doing something: *I have finger paints and paper for the kids, so we're in business.*
15 go about your business to do the things that you normally do: *The street was filled with ordinary people going about their business.*
16 have no business doing sth also **have no business to do sth** to behave wrongly in doing something: *He was drunk – he had no business driving.*
17 not in the business of doing sth not planning to do something, because it is thought to be wrong: *This newspaper is not in the business of sensationalism.*
18 business is business used to say that profit is the most important thing to consider: *For these guys, business is business and worker safety is not important.*
19 the business end (of sth) INFORMAL the end of a tool or weapon that does the work or causes the damage: *the business end of a gun*
20 be all business to be serious about the work you are doing, and not do or talk about other things: *We'd fool around in practice, but during the games we were all business.*
21 any other business subjects to be discussed in a meeting after the main subjects have been dealt with: *Before we end the meeting, is there any other business?*
22 give sb the business OLD-FASHIONED to make jokes and laugh at someone for fun or to criticize them —see also **BIG BUSINESS**, **sb means business** (MEAN[1] (22)), **monkey business** (MONKEY[1] (3)), **like nobody's business** (NOBODY[1] (2)), **SHOW BUSINESS**

business card /'.. ,./ n. [C] a card that shows a person's name, job, company, address, telephone number etc.

business class /'.. ,./ n. [U] traveling conditions on an airplane that are more expensive than COACH[1] (2) but not as expensive as FIRST CLASS (1) —compare ECONOMY CLASS

business hours /'.. ,./ n. [plural] the normal hours that stores and offices are open

busi·ness·like /'bɪznɪs,laɪk/ adj. effective and practical in the way that you do things: *a businesslike manner*

busi·ness·man /'bɪznɪs,mæn/ n. plural **businessmen** /-,men/ [C] a man who works in business

business park /'.. ,./ n. [C] an area where many companies and businesses have buildings and offices

busi·ness per·son /'.. ,../ n. plural **business people** [C] a person who works in business

business plan /'.. ,./ n. [C] a document which explains what a company wants to do in the future, and how it plans to do it

business suit /'.. ,./ n. [C] a suit that someone wears during the day at work, especially one that is CONSERVATIVE in style

busi·ness·wom·an /'bɪznɪs,wʊmən/ n. plural **businesswomen** /-,wɪmɪn/ [C] a woman who works in business

bus·ing /'bʌsɪŋ/ n. [U] a system in the U.S. in which students ride buses to schools that are far from where they live, so that a school has students of different races

bus lane /'. ./ n. [C] a part of a road that only buses are allowed to use

bus·load /'bʌsloʊd/ n. [C] the number of people on a bus that is full: *[+ of] a busload of people*

bus·man's hol·i·day /,bʌsmənz 'hɑlədeɪ/ n. [singular] a vacation spent doing the same work as you do in your job

bus pass /'. ./ n. [C] a ticket used for bus travel during a particular period of time such as a week or a month, which costs less than buying tickets for each trip

buss /bʌs/ v. [T] OLD-FASHIONED to kiss someone in a friendly rather than sexual way

bus·ses /'bʌsɪz/ n. a plural of bus

bus shel·ter /'. ,../ n. [C] a small structure with a roof that keeps people dry while they are waiting for a bus

bus sta·tion /'. ,../ n. [C] a place where buses start and finish their trips

bus stop /'. ./ *n.* [C] a place at the side of a road, marked with a sign, where buses stop for passengers

bust¹ /bʌst/ *v.* [T]
1 ***break*** [I,T] SPOKEN to break something: *Karl fell off his skateboard and busted his arm.* | *The window busted when the ball hit it.*
2 ***police*** [T] INFORMAL **a)** if the police bust someone, they charge them with a crime: **get/be busted (for sth)** *Her brother got busted for drunk driving* **b)** if the police bust a place, they go into it to catch people doing something illegal: *Federal agents busted several money-exchange businesses.*
3 ***money*** [T] INFORMAL to use too much money, so that a business etc. must stop operating: *The trip to Spain will probably bust our budget.*
4 -busting INFORMAL used with nouns to show that a situation is being ended or an activity is being stopped: *crime-busting laws* | *a drought-busting storm*
5 bust your butt/ass SPOKEN to work very hard to do something: *I busted my butt to get it done on time, and she didn't even say "Thank you."*
6 ***military*** [T] INFORMAL to give someone a lower military rank as a punishment; DEMOTE: *Jones was busted down to the rank of private.*
7 bust a gut SPOKEN **a)** to try extremely hard to do something: *We busted a gut trying to get home on time.* **b)** to laugh a lot: *The movie was hilarious. I just about busted a gut.*
8 bust your chops SLANG to work very hard in order to achieve something: *The players busted their chops this season.*
9 bust sb's chops to criticize or deliberately annoy someone as a joke: *Don't take it so seriously – I'm just busting your chops!*
10 bust a move SPOKEN, SLANG to make unusual and impressive movements while dancing to popular music
11 ...or bust! INFORMAL used to say that you will try very hard to go somewhere or do something: *San Francisco or bust!*
bust out *phr. v.* **1** [I] INFORMAL to escape from a place, especially prison **2** [T **bust** sb **out**] SLANG to strongly criticize someone: *I busted him out for forgetting to pay me back.*
bust up *phr. v.* **1** [T **bust** sb/sth ↔ **up**] INFORMAL to damage or break something, or to hit someone to injure them: *A bunch of bikers busted up the bar.* | *You could hear him on the tape, threatening to bust Michael up.* **2** [T **bust** sth ↔ **up**] SPOKEN to prevent an illegal activity or bad situation from continuing: *Last week the FBI busted up a big drug ring.* | *A couple of teachers stepped in to bust up the fight.* **3** [I,T **bust up** sth] to end a relationship or friendship: *The issue of money has busted up many friendships.* | *People were shocked when their marriage busted up.* **4** [I,T **bust** sth ↔ **up**] to force a large company to separate into smaller companies: *A federal judge busted up AT&T in a decision on monopolies.* —see also BUST-UP

bust² *n.* [C] **1** a woman's breasts, or the part of her clothes that covers her breasts **2** a measurement around a woman's breast and back: *a 36-inch bust* **3** INFORMAL a situation in which the police go into a place in order to catch people doing something illegal: *a drug bust* **4** a model of someone's head, shoulders and upper chest, made of stone or metal: [+ of] *a bust of Beethoven*

bust³ *adj.* INFORMAL **go bust** a business that goes bust cannot continue operating: *Most of the steel factories around here went bust in the 1980s.*

bust·ed¹ /'bʌstɪd/ *adj.* SPOKEN **1** broken: *The TV's busted again.* | *a busted arm* **2** SLANG caught doing something wrong and likely to be punished: *You guys are so busted!*

busted² *interjection* SLANG said when someone has been caught lying or doing something wrong

bust·er /'bʌstə/ *n.* **1** SPOKEN used when speaking to a man who is annoying you, or who you do not respect: *Keep your hands to yourself, buster!* **2** INFORMAL also **-buster** used with nouns to mean something that destroys or spoils something else: *The pilot of the plane, known as the tank buster, lost radio contact.* | *The Democrats' health-care bill has been*

---

called a *budget-buster* (=something that will force the government to spend too much money). | **price-buster/deal-buster** (=a price you pay for a product that is better than any other price)

bus·ti·er /'bʌstiə/ *n.* [C] a piece of woman's clothing that fits her chest tightly and has no SLEEVES. It can be worn alone or under a JACKET or BLOUSE

bus·tle¹ /'bʌsəl/ *v.* [I always + adv./prep.] to move around quickly, looking very busy: [+ **around/ through** etc.] *Grandma bustled around the kitchen.* —see also BUSTLING

bustle² *n.* **1** [U] busy and usually noisy activity: [+ **of**] *the bustle of a big city* —see also **hustle and bustle** (HUSTLE² (1)) **2** [C] a frame worn under women's skirts in the past to push out the back of the skirts

bus·tling /'bʌslɪŋ/ *adj.* a bustling place is very busy: *a small bustling Mexican restaurant*

bust-up /'. ./ *n.* [C] INFORMAL the end of a relationship: *the bust-up of their marriage* —see also **bust up** (BUST¹)

bust·y /'bʌsti/ *adj.* INFORMAL a woman who is busty has large breasts

bus·y¹ /'bɪzi/ *adj.* busier, busiest
1 ***short time*** someone who is busy at a particular time is working and is not available: *I'm kind of busy now, can I call you back?* | [+ **with**] *I'm sorry, Mrs. Daniels is busy with a customer.*
2 ***longer time*** using all or most of your time to do something: [**busy doing sth**] *Rachel's busy studying for her finals.* | [+ **with**] *My parents were always busy with work, but we still had time together.*
3 ***time*** a busy period of time is full of work or other activities: *December is the busiest time of year for the mall.*
4 ***place*** a busy place is very full of people or vehicles and movement: *a busy freeway* | *a busy airport*
5 ***works hard*** having very little free time because you always have so much to do: *She's a busy mother of four with a full time job.*
6 keep sb busy to find plenty of things to do: *Have plenty of projects planned to keep the kids busy during summer vacation.*
7 ***telephone*** if a telephone you are calling is busy, it makes a repeated sound to tell you the person you are calling is talking on their telephone: *It's busy. I'll call again later.*
8 ***pattern*** a pattern or design that is busy has too many small details
9 as busy as a bee INFORMAL very busy doing something, especially something active
10 ***sex*** **get busy** SLANG to have sex —**busily** *adv.*

busy² *v.* busies, busied, busying [T] **busy yourself with sth** to use your time by dealing with something: *I busied myself with answering letters.*

bus·y·bod·y /'bɪzi,bɑdi, -,bʌdi/ *n. plural* **busybodies** [C] someone who annoys people by being too interested in other people's private activities

busy sig·nal /'.. ,../ *n.* [C usually singular] the sound you hear on the telephone that tells you that the person you are trying to call is talking to someone else on their telephone

bus·y·work /'bɪzi,wɜrk/ *n.* [U] work that gives someone something to do, but that is not really necessary

but¹ /bət; *strong* bʌt/ *conjunction* **1** used to connect two statements or phrases when the second one is different from the first: *It's an old car, but it's very reliable.* | *Cara's going to the concert, but I'm not.* | *Mom hated the movie, but Dad thought it was good.* | *It's an expensive but very useful book.* **2** used like "however" to give a reason why something did not happen or why you did not do something etc.: *Carla was supposed to come tonight, but her husband needed the car.* | *I'd like to go, but I'm too busy.*

SPOKEN PHRASES

3 but then (again) a) used before a statement that makes what you have just said seem less true, useful, or valuable: *You feel really sorry for him, but*

B

then again it's hard to like him. **b)** used before a statement that may seem surprising, to say that it is not really surprising: *He doesn't have a strong French accent, but then he's lived here for twenty years.* **4** used to introduce a new subject in a conversation: *But now to the main issue.* | *That's why I've been so busy. But how are you, anyway?* **5** used after phrases such as "excuse me" and "I'm sorry:" *I'm sorry, but you can't smoke in here.* | *Excuse me, but aren't you Julie's sister?*

6 used after a negative to emphasize that it is the second part of the sentence that it is true: *They aren't doing this to make money, but to help the church.* | *We had no alternative but to fire him.* **7 you cannot but.../you could not but...** FORMAL used to say that you have to do something or cannot stop yourself from doing it: *I could not but admire her.* **8 but for sb/sth** FORMAL without or except for: *But for my family, I'd be having real difficulties.* **9** used to emphasize a word or statement: *It'll be a great party – everyone, but everyone, is coming.* **10** [usually in negatives] LITERARY used to emphasize that a statement includes every single person or thing: *Not a day goes by but that I think of Jeff* (=I think of Jeff every day).

USAGE NOTE: BUT

WORD CHOICE: but, however
But is very frequent in spoken English, where it is often used at the beginning of a sentence: *I didn't like the opening act at the concert. But the main band was great.* **But** is also used in writing, though not usually at the beginning of a sentence. **However** is used especially in more formal writing, often with commas before and after it in the middle of a sentence: *The first act was somewhat amateurish. The second, however, was excellent.*

GRAMMAR
But or **however** is never used in a main clause next to another clause with **although**: *Although they're very busy, I think they enjoy it* (NOT *...but/however I think they enjoy it*).

S W **but²** *prep.* except for: *There's no one here but me.* | *I could come any day but Thursday.* | *This car's been **nothing but** trouble* (=it has been a lot of trouble). | *The sales clerk was **anything but** helpful* (=the clerk was not helpful at all).

but³ *adv.* **1** ESPECIALLY LITERARY only: *You can but try.* **2** SPOKEN used to emphasize what you are saying: *They're rich, but I mean rich!*

but⁴ /bʌt/ *n.* **no buts (about it)** SPOKEN used to say that there is no doubt about something: *No buts, you are going to school today!*

bu·tane /ˈbyutein/ *n.* [U] a gas stored in liquid form, used for cooking and heating

butch¹ /bʊtʃ/ *adj.* INFORMAL **1** a woman who is butch looks, behaves, or dresses like a man **2** a man who is butch seems big and strong, and typically male

butch² *n.* [C] a LESBIAN woman who has the traditionally MALE part in a relationship with another woman —compare FEMME

butch·er¹ /ˈbʊtʃɚ/ *n.* [C] **1** someone who cuts and sells meat as a business **2** someone who has killed a lot of people cruelly and without reason

butcher² *v.* [T] **1** to kill animals and prepare them to be used as meat **2** to kill people cruelly or without reason, especially in large numbers **3** INFORMAL to spoil something by working carelessly: *The hairdresser really butchered my hair!*

butch·er·y /ˈbʊtʃɚi/ *n.* [U] **1** cruel and unnecessary killing: *the butchery of battle* **2** the preparation of meat for sale

but·ler /ˈbʌtlɚ/ *n.* [C] the main male servant of a house

S W **butt¹** /bʌt/ *n.* [C]
1 part of your body INFORMAL the part of your body that you sit on; BUTTOCKS

2 get your butt in/out/over used to tell someone rudely to go somewhere or do something: *Get your butt out of that bathroom now.*
3 work/play etc. your butt off to work, play etc. very hard: *I worked my butt off in college.*
4 get off your butt used to tell someone rudely to start doing something when they have been lazy: *Get off your butt, and go mow the lawn.*
5 sit on your butt to not do anything important or useful: *I've just been sitting on my butt, watching TV all day.*
6 butt ugly SLANG extremely ugly or unattractive: *Man, that dog Jake has is butt ugly!*

7 cigarette the end of a cigarette after most of it has been smoked
8 be the butt of sth to be the person or thing that other people often make jokes about: *Unfortunately for Ted, he's become the butt of jokes around the office.*
9 gun the thick end of the handle of a gun: *a rifle butt*
10 hitting with your head the act of hitting someone or something with your head —see also **bust your butt/ass** (BUST¹ (5)), HEADBUTT, **kick sb's) ass/butt** (KICK¹ (6)), **be a pain in the ass/butt** (PAIN¹ (3))

butt² *v.* [I,T] **1** to hit or push against someone or something with your head **2** if an animal butts someone or something, it hits them with its horns
butt in *phr. v.* [I] **1** to interrupt a conversation rudely: *Stop butting in!* **2** to become involved in a private situation that does not concern you: *I don't want you or anyone else butting in on my own business.*
butt out *phr. v.* [I] SPOKEN used to tell someone rudely that you do not want them to be involved in a conversation or situation: *Just butt out, OK? I don't want your advice.*

butte /byut/ *n.* [C] a very large rock with steep sides and a flat top, that sticks out of flat ground in the western U.S.

S W **but·ter¹** /ˈbʌtɚ/ *n.* [U] a solid yellow food made from milk or cream that you spread on bread or use in cooking: *Beat the butter and sugar together.* —**buttery** *adj.*

butter² *v.* [T] to spread butter on something: *buttered bread*
butter sb up *phr. v.* [T] INFORMAL to say nice things to someone so that they will do what you want: *Don't try to butter me up.*

but·ter·ball /ˈbʌtɚˌbɔl/ *n.* [C] INFORMAL someone who is fat, especially a child

butter bean /ˈ.. ˌ./ *n.* [C] a large pale yellow bean

but·ter·cup /ˈbʌtɚˌkʌp/ *n.* [C] a small shiny yellow wild flower

but·ter·fin·gers /ˈbʌtɚˌfɪŋgɚz/ *n.* [singular] INFORMAL someone who often drops things they are carrying or trying to catch

but·ter·fly /ˈbʌtɚˌflaɪ/ *n. plural* **butterflies** [C] **1** a type of insect that has large wings, often with beautiful colors —see picture at METAMORPHOSIS **2 butterflies** [plural] INFORMAL a very nervous feeling you have before doing something: *It was the first performance, and I **had butterflies in my stomach**.* **3** [U] a way of swimming by lying on your front and moving your arms together over your head **4** [C] someone who usually moves on quickly from one activity or person to the next: *Gwen's a real social butterfly.*

butterfly kiss /ˈ... ˌ./ *n.* [C] the action of opening and closing your eye very close to someone's cheek, so that your EYELASHes rub against it; used as a way of showing love, especially to your children

but·ter·milk /ˈbʌtɚˌmɪlk/ *n.* [U] the liquid that remains after butter has been made, used in BAKING

but·ter·scotch /ˈbʌtɚˌskatʃ/ *n.* [U] a type of candy made from butter and sugar boiled together

butt·hole /ˈbʌthoʊl/ *n.* [C] VULGAR **1** someone's ANUS **2** used to insult someone: *You butthole!*

butt·in·ski /bəˈdɪnski/ *n. plural* **buttinskis** [C] INFORMAL someone who is annoying because they are too interested in other people's private activities

but·tock /ˈbʌtək/ n. [C usually plural] one of the fleshy parts of your body that you sit on —see picture at BODY

but·ton¹ /ˈbʌt⌐n/ n. **1** [C] a small circular flat object on your shirt, coat etc. that you put through a hole to fasten it —see picture at FASTENER **2** [C] a small part or area of a machine that you press to make it do something: *Press the pause button.* | *To turn off the radio, push the button on the left.* **3** [C] TECHNICAL an area on a computer screen that you CLICK on to make the computer do a specific thing **4** a small metal or plastic pin with a message or picture on it **5 button nose/eyes** a nose or eyes that are small and round **6 on the button** INFORMAL exactly right, or at exactly the right time: *The weather forecast was right on the button.* | *She got to our house at two, on the button.* —see also **as bright as a button** (BRIGHT (10)), HOT BUTTON, **at/with the push of a button** (PUSH² (5)), **push sb's buttons** (PUSH¹ (10)), PUSH-BUTTON

button² v. [I,T] **1** also **button up** to fasten clothes with buttons, or to be fastened with buttons: *The pants button at the side.* | *Button up your coat, Nina – it's cold.* **2 button up** also **button your lip/mouth** SPOKEN used to tell someone in an impolite way to stop talking

But·ton /ˈbʌt⌐n/, **Dick** /dɪk/ (1929–) a U.S. FIGURE SKATER

button-down /ˈ.. ./ adj. a button-down shirt or collar has the ends of the collar fastened to the shirt with buttons

buttoned-up /ˌ.. ˈ.◂/ adj. INFORMAL someone who is buttoned-up is not able to express their feelings, especially sexual feelings

but·ton·hole /ˈbʌt⌐n,houl/ n. [C] a hole for a button to be put through to fasten a shirt, coat etc.

but·tress¹ /ˈbʌtrɪs/ n. [C] a brick or stone structure built to support a wall

buttress² v. [T] to support a system, idea, argument etc.: *Kotkin gave statistics to buttress his argument.*

bux·om /ˈbʌksəm/ adj. a woman who is buxom is attractively large and healthy and has big breasts

buy¹ /baɪ/ v. past tense and past participle **bought 1 a)** [I,T] to get something by paying money for it: *We bought a house in Atlanta.* | *We decided to buy instead of rent.* | [buy sb sth] *Can I buy you a drink?* | [buy sth for sb/sth] *I bought a T-shirt for Craig.* | *Teenagers can still buy cigarettes from vending machines.* | *Members can buy tickets for $5.* —opposite SELL¹ **b)** [T] if a sum of money buys something, that is what you can get with it: *A dollar doesn't buy much these days.* **2 buy time** to do something in order to get more time to finish something else: *The Russian President's action is a way of buying time to let the reforms work.* **3** [T] INFORMAL to believe an explanation or reason, especially one that is not very likely to be true: *She'll never buy that excuse.* **4** [T usually passive] INFORMAL to pay money to someone, especially someone in an official position, in order to persuade them to do something dishonest; BRIBE: *They say the judge was bought.* **5 (have) bought it** SPOKEN to have been killed, especially in an accident or war: *His brother almost bought it in Vietnam.* **6 (have) bought the farm** SPOKEN to have died or been killed: *Old Zeke just about bought the farm back then.*

buy into sth phr. v. [T] **1** to buy part of a business or organization, especially because you want to control it: *Television companies are buying into cable systems as quickly as they can.* **2** INFORMAL to believe an idea: *A lot of women have bought into the idea that they have to be thin to be attractive.*

buy sb **off** phr. v. [T] to pay someone money to stop them causing trouble or threatening you; BRIBE

buy out phr. v. [T **buy** sb/sth **out**] to buy someone's SHARES² (4) of a business that you previously owned together, so that you have complete control —see also BUYOUT

buy up sth phr. v. [T] to quickly buy as much as you can of something such as land, tickets, food etc.: *The park land is being bought up by two firms.*

---

buy² n. **be a good/bad** ... worth the price you pay ... $6.49. ... the wine is a good buy at

buy·er /ˈbaɪə/ n. [C] **1** someone ... expensive such as a house or ... who buys something should attract more buyers. —see Usage Note at CUSTOMER **2** someone ... house prices choose and buy the goods for a store; SELLER —see

buyer's mar·ket /ˈ.. ,../ n. [singular] ... the job is to which there is plenty of something avail... many buyers have a lot of choice and prices ten... in —opposite SELLER'S MARKET

buy·out /ˈbaɪaʊt/ n. [C] a situation in which sb... gains control of a company by buying all or mo... its SHARES² (4): *AT&T successfully negotiated a buy...of McCaw Cellular.*

buzz¹ /bʌz/ v.

1 make a sound [I] to make a continuous sound, like the sound of a BEE: *I hear something buzzing in the engine.*

2 move around **a)** [I always + adv./prep.] to move around in the air making a continuous sound like a BEE: [+ around/above etc.] *Dragonflies buzzed above the water.* **b)** to move quickly and in a busy way around a place: [+ around/over etc.] *We were buzzing around town like maniacs, trying to get the Christmas shopping done.*

3 excitement [I] if a group of people or a place buzzes, people are talking a lot and making noise because they are excited: *Local people were buzzing about the murder.* | [+ with] *The crowd buzzed with excitement.*

4 call [I,T] to call someone by pressing a BUZZER: *He buzzed at the security door, and I let him in.* | [buzz for sb] *I spilled my drink and had to buzz for the stewardess to bring some napkins.*

5 ears [I] if your ears or head are buzzing, you can hear a continuous annoying sound because you are not feeling well

6 sb's head/mind is buzzing (with sth) if your head or mind is buzzing with thoughts, ideas etc., your cannot stop thinking about them

7 aircraft [T] INFORMAL to fly an aircraft low and fast over buildings, people etc.

8 buzz off! SPOKEN used to tell someone rudely to go away

buzz² n. **1** [C] a continuous noise like the sound of a BEE: *From inside the house, we heard the buzz of helicopters overhead.* **2** [singular] the sound of people talking a lot in an excited way: [+ of] *the buzz of the crowd* **3** [singular] INFORMAL a strong feeling of excitement, pleasure, or success, or a similar feeling from drinking alcohol or taking drugs: *Playing well gives me a buzz.* | *Neil gets a buzz from drinking one beer.* **4 give sb a buzz** INFORMAL to call someone on the telephone **5 the buzz** INFORMAL unofficial news or information that is spread by people telling each other: *The buzz is that Jack is leaving.*

buz·zard /ˈbʌzəd/ n. [C] **1** a type of large bird that eats dead animals; VULTURE **2** a type of large HAWK in Europe and Asia

buzz·cut /ˈbʌzkʌt/ n. [C] a very short HAIRCUT

buzz·er /ˈbʌzə/ n. [C] a small thing like a button that makes a buzzing sound when you push it, for example on a door: *The buzzer sounded for the end of the quarter.*

buzz saw /ˈ. ./ n. [C] a SAW with a round blade that is spun around by a motor; CIRCULAR SAW

buzz·word /ˈbʌzwəd/ n. [C] a word or phrase from one special area of knowledge that people suddenly think is very important: *Multimedia has been a buzzword in the computer industry for years.*

BWL, bwl a written abbreviation of "bursting with laughter," used by people communicating in CHAT ROOMS on the Internet

by¹ /baɪ/ prep. **1** used especially with a PASSIVE verb to show who or what did something or what caused something: *Jim was bitten by a dog.* | *The building*

y. | *Everyone is worried* was designed by Frank G. 2 using or doing a particular thing: You | by the rise in violent crserve the tickets by phone. | ticular thing: You *ysitting.* | by car/train/plane/ Send it by air *from New York to Philadelphia by* extra money through or along a particular place: *go by the freeway.* | *Doris came in by* bus etc. 5 | *or.* 4 beside or near something: *She stood car. ndow looking out over the fields.* | *Jane went It by Patrick.* 5 come/go/stop by sth to visit o to a place for a short time when you intend to somewhere else after that: *Could you stop by the store and buy milk on your way home?* | *I need to drop by my house before we go to the club.* 6 if you move or travel by someone or something, you go past them without stopping: *He walked by me without saying hello.* | *I go by John's place on my way to work; I can pick him up.* 7 used to show the name of someone who wrote a book, produced a movie, wrote a piece of music etc.: *the "Unfinished Symphony" by Schubert* | *"Hamlet" was written by Shakespeare.* 8 not later than a particular time, date etc.: *The report must be ready by next Friday.* | *I'll be home by 9:30.* 9 according to a particular rule, method, or way of doing things: *By law, cars cannot pass a school bus while it is stopped.* | *Profits were $6 million, but by their standards this is low.* 10 used to show the amount or degree of something: *The price of oil fell by a further $2 a barrel.* | *I was overcharged by $3.* | *Reading was by far* (=by a large amount or degree) *my favorite activity as a child.* 11 by the way SPOKEN used to begin talking about a subject that is not related to the one you were talking about: *Oh, by the way, Vicky called while you were out.* 12 used when telling which part of a piece of equipment or of someone's body that someone takes or holds: *I picked the pot up by the handle.* | *She grabbed him by the arm.* 13 SPOKEN used when expressing strong feelings or making serious promises: *By God, we actually did it!* 14 used between two numbers that you are multiplying or dividing: *What's 48 divided by 4?* 15 used when giving the measurements of a room, container etc.: *The living room is 10 feet by 13 feet.* 16 used to show a rate or quantity: *Most restaurant workers are paid by the hour.* 17 day by day/little by little etc. used to show that something happens gradually or is done slowly and in small amounts: *Day by day he grew weaker.* | *Police searched the area house by house.* 18 used to show the situation or period of time during which you do something or something happens: *You'll ruin your eyes reading by flashlight.* | by day/night (=during the day or night) 19 used to show the relationship between one fact or thing and another: *Colette is French by birth.* | *It's fine by me if you want to go.* 20 as a result of an action or situation: *He brought over some of my mail that was delivered to his house by accident.* | *I deleted a whole afternoon's work on the computer by mistake.* 21 if a woman has children by a particular man, that man is the children's father: *Ann has two children by her ex-husband.* 22 (all) by yourself a) completely alone: *Dave spent Christmas all by himself.* b) without any help: *Katherine made the cookies all by herself.*

s w **by²** *adv.* 1 if someone or something moves or goes
1 1 by, they go past: *One or two cars went by, but nobody stopped.* | *Three hours went by before we heard any news.* | *James walked by without even looking in my direction.* 2 come/stop/go etc. by to visit or go to a place for a short time when you intend to go somewhere else after that: *I'll drop by and have a look at your car this afternoon.* | *Come by* (=come to my house, office etc.) *any time tomorrow.* 3 beside or near someone or something: *A crowd of people were standing by, waiting for an announcement.* 4 by and large used when talking generally about someone or something: *By and large, most of the people in the town work at the factory.* 5 by and by ESPECIALLY LITERARY soon 6 by the by SPOKEN, OLD-FASHIONED used

when mentioning something that may be interesting but is not particularly important: *By the by, John might come over tonight.*

by-, bye- /baɪ/ *prefix* less important than the main part of something or the main event: *a byproduct* (=something that is also produced when the main product is made)

s w **bye¹** /baɪ/ also **bye-bye** /. './ *interjection* SPOKEN good-
1 1 bye

bye² *n.* [C] a situation in a sports competition or SEASON¹ (2) in which a player or a team does not have an opponent to play against and continues to the next part of the competition

by·gone /ˈbaɪgɔn, -gɑn/ *adj.* bygone age/era/days etc. an expression meaning a "period of time in the past": *The buildings reflect the elegance of a bygone era.*

by·gones /ˈbaɪgɔnz/ *n.* let bygones be bygones to forget something bad that someone has done to you and forgive them

by·law /ˈbaɪlɔ/ *n.* a rule made by an organization to control the people who belong to it

by·line /. './ *n.* [C] a line at the beginning of some writing in a newspaper or magazine giving the writer's name

BYOB *adj.* Bring Your Own Bottle. Beer/Booze; used when inviting someone to an informal party to tell them that they must bring their own bottle of alcoholic drink: *By the way, the party at Hank's is BYOB.*

by·pass¹ /ˈbaɪpæs/ *n.* [C] 1 a heart bypass also bypass surgery an operation to direct blood through new VEINs (=blood tubes) outside the heart 2 a road that goes around a town or other busy area rather than through it 3 TECHNICAL a tube that allows gas or liquid to flow around something rather than through it

bypass² *v.* [T] 1 to avoid a place or situation by going around it: *This highway bypasses the downtown area.* | *The card allows you to bypass long lines at the bank.* 2 to avoid obeying a rule, system, or someone in an official position: *There should be no way of bypassing the security measures on the computer.*

by·play /ˈbaɪpleɪ/ *n.* [U] something that is less important than the main action, especially in a play

by·prod·uct /ˈbaɪˌprɑdəkt/ *n.* [C] 1 something additional that is produced during a natural or industrial process: *milk byproducts* 2 an unplanned additional result of something that you do or something that happens: [+ of] *Job losses are an unfortunate byproduct of the recession.* —compare END PRODUCT

Byrd /bɔrd/, **Richard** (1888–1957) a U.S. EXPLORER who led five EXPEDITIONs to Antarctica

By·ron, Lord /ˈbaɪrən/ (1788–1824) an English poet

by·stand·er /ˈbaɪˌstændər/ *n.* [C] someone who watches what is happening without taking part; ONLOOKER: *Two innocent bystanders were injured in the shooting.*

byte /baɪt/ *n.* [C] TECHNICAL a unit of computer information equal to eight BITS¹ (5) —see also GIGABYTE, KILOBYTE, MEGABYTE

by·way /ˈbaɪˌweɪ/ *n.* [C] a small road that is not used very much

by·word /ˈbaɪwɔrd/ *n.* 1 be a byword for sth someone or something that is so well known for a particular quality that it is used to represent that quality: *For Americans, Benedict Arnold is a byword for treason.* 2 [usually singular] a word, phrase, or saying that is very well known: *Caution should be a byword for investors.*

Byz·an·tine /ˈbɪzən,tin, -,taɪn/ 1 one of the people that lived in the Greek city of Byzantium in northern Turkey from the seventh century B.C. to the second century A.D. 2 one of the people that lived in the Byzantine Empire from the fourth century to the fifteenth century A.D.

byz·an·tine, Byzantine /ˈbɪzən,tin, -,taɪn/ *adj.* 1 complicated and difficult to understand: *byzantine tax laws* 2 relating to the Byzantines or the Byzantine Empire: *a 5th century Byzantine church*

C

C¹, c /si/ *n. plural* **C's, c's 1** [C] the third letter of the English alphabet **2** [C,U] **a)** the first note in the musical SCALE of C MAJOR **b)** the musical KEY based on this note **3** [C] a grade given to a student's work to show that it is of average quality: *Terry got a C in algebra.* **4** [C] the number 100 in the system of ROMAN NUMERALS

C² the written abbreviation of CELSIUS

c 1 the written abbreviation of "cent" **2** a written abbreviation of CIRCA (=about) **3** the written abbreviation of COPYRIGHT when printed inside a small circle **4** the written abbreviation of CUBIC

C&W *n.* [U] a written abbreviation of COUNTRY AND WESTERN music

CA a written abbreviation of California

ca. a written abbreviation of CIRCA (=about or approximately)

cab /kæb/ *n.* [C] **1** a car in which you pay the driver to take you somewhere; taxi: *Could you call me a cab please?* (=telephone to get a cab to come to you) | *You'll have better luck hailing a cab* (=attract the attention of a cab driver) *over on "M" Street.* **2** the part of a truck, bus, or train in which the driver sits **3** a carriage pulled by horses that was used like a taxi in past times

ca·bal /kə'bɑl, -'bæl/ *n.* [C] a small group of people who make secret plans, especially in order to have political or economic power

ca·ban·a /kə'bænə/ *n.* [C] a tent or small wooden structure used for changing clothes at a beach or pool

cab·a·ret /ˌkæbə'reɪ/ *n.* **1** [C,U] entertainment, usually with music, songs, and dancing, performed in a restaurant or club while the customers eat and drink **2** [C] a restaurant or club where this is performed

cab·bage /'kæbɪdʒ/ *n.* [C,U] a large round vegetable with thick green or purple leaves

cab·bie, cabby /'kæbi/ *n.* [C] INFORMAL a cab driver

cab driv·er, cabdriver /'. ,../ *n.* [C] someone who drives a CAB as their job

cab·in /'kæbɪn/ *n.* [C] **1** a small house, especially one made of wood, usually in a forest or the mountains: *a log cabin* **2** a small room on a ship in which you live or sleep **3** the area inside an airplane where the passengers or pilots sit

cabin boy /'.. ,./ *n.* [C] a young man who works as a servant on a ship

cabin class /'.. ,./ *n.* [U] the rooms on a ship that are better than TOURIST CLASS but not as good as FIRST CLASS

cabin crew /'.. ,./ *n.* [C] the group of people whose job is to take care of the passengers on a particular airplane

cabin cruis·er /'.. ,../ *n.* [C] a large MOTORBOAT with one or more cabins for people to sleep in

cab·i·net /'kæbənɪt/ *n.* [C] **1** a piece of furniture with doors and shelves or drawers, used for storing or showing things: *a display cabinet full of jewelry* | *the kitchen cabinets* —compare CUPBOARD —see also FILING CABINET **2** also **Cabinet** an important group of politicians who make decisions or advise the leader of a government: *a Cabinet meeting* | *She was appointed to the Cabinet as secretary of commerce.*

cab·i·net·mak·er /'kæbənɪt,meɪkɚ/ *n.* [C] someone whose job is to make wooden furniture

cabin fe·ver /'.. ,../ *n.* [U] INFORMAL a feeling of being upset and impatient, because you have not been outside for a long time

ca·ble¹ /'keɪbəl/ *n.* **1** [C,U] a plastic or rubber tube containing wires that carry telephone messages, electronic signals, television pictures etc.: *They're laying cable* (=putting a cable under the ground) *for the telephone company.* —see picture on page 426

2 [U] a system of broadcasting television by using cables that is paid for by the person watching it; CABLE TELEVISION: *I'll wait for the movie to come out on cable.* | *a cable channel* **3** [C,U] a thick strong metal rope used on ships, to support bridges etc. **4** [C] a TELEGRAM

cable² *v.* [I,T] to send someone a TELEGRAM

cable car /'.. ,./ *n.* [C] **1** a vehicle that is pulled along by a moving cable, used in cities to take people from one place to another **2** a vehicle that hangs from a cable and takes people up mountains

ca·ble·cast /'keɪbəl,kæst/ *n.* [C] a show, movie, sports event etc. that is broadcast on a cable television station: *The MTV Video Awards cablecast is almost as popular as the Grammy Awards.* —**cablecast** *v.* [T]

ca·ble·gram /'keɪbəl,græm/ *n.* [C] a TELEGRAM

cable rail·way /,.. '../ *n.* [C] a railroad on which vehicles are pulled up steep slopes by a moving CABLE¹ (3)

cable stitch /'.. ,./ *n.* [C,U] a knotted pattern of stitches used in KNITTING

cable tel·e·vi·sion /,.. '..../ also **cable TV** /,.. .'./ *n.* [U] CABLE¹ (2) —compare SATELLITE TELEVISION

ca·boo·dle /kə'budl/ *n.* **the whole (kit and) caboodle** INFORMAL everything: *He bought the whole kit and caboodle: computer, printer, and modem.*

ca·boose /kə'bus/ *n.* [C] a small railroad car at the back of a train, usually where the official in charge of it travels

Cab·ot /'kæbət/, **John** (?1450–?1498) an Italian EXPLORER who reached the coast of North America in 1497

Ca·bri·ni /kə'brini/, **St. Fran·ces Xa·vi·er** /'frænsɪs 'zeɪviɚ/ (1850–1917) also known as "Mother Cabrini"; a Catholic NUN who became the first U.S. citizen to be named a SAINT. Many churches and other institutions are named after her.

cab·ri·o·let /,kæbriə'leɪ/ *n.* [C] a word used in the names of cars to show that they are CONVERTIBLES

cab·stand /'kæbstænd/ *n.* [C] a TAXI STAND

ca·cao /kə'kaʊ/ *n.* [C] the seed from which chocolate and COCOA are made

cache¹ /kæʃ/ *n.* [C] **1** a number of things that have been hidden, or the place where they have been hidden: [+ of] *Police found a cache of weapons in a warehouse.* **2** TECHNICAL a special section of MEMORY in a computer that helps it work faster by storing DATA for a short time

cache² *v.* [T] **1** to hide something in a secret place **2** TECHNICAL to store DATA in a computer's MEMORY for a short time

ca·chet /kæ'ʃeɪ/ *n.* [singular,U] the respect and importance a person, organization, profession etc. has, because of their high position in society or the quality of their work: *It's a good university, but it lacks the cachet of Harvard or Princeton.*

cack·le¹ /'kækəl/ *v.* [I] **1** when a chicken cackles, it makes a loud high sound **2** to laugh in a loud way that does not sound nice, making short high sounds

cackle² *n.* [C,U] a short high laugh that does not sound nice: *loud cackles of amusement*

ca·coph·o·ny /kæ'kɑfəni/ *n.* [singular] a loud mixture of sounds that is not pleasant to listen to: [+ of] *A cacophony of voices in a dozen languages filled the train station.* —**cacophonous** *adj.*

cac·tus /'kæktəs/ *n. plural* **cacti** /-taɪ/ or **cactuses** [C] a desert plant with thick smooth stems and needles instead of leaves —see picture on page 428

cactus

C

CAD /ˌsi eɪ ˈdi, kæd/ n. [U] computer-aided design; the use of COMPUTER GRAPHICS to plan cars, aircraft, buildings etc.

cad /kæd/ n. [C] OLD-FASHIONED a man who cannot be trusted, especially one who treats women badly —**caddish** adj.

ca·dav·er /kəˈdævə/ n. [C] TECHNICAL a dead human body

ca·dav·er·ous /kəˈdævərəs/ adj. looking extremely pale, thin, and unhealthy: a cadaverous face

CAD/CAM /ˈkædkæm/ n. [U] computer-aided design and manufacture; the use of computers to plan and make industrial products

cad·dy¹ /ˈkædi/ n. plural **caddies** [C] **1** also **caddie** someone who carries the GOLF CLUBs for someone who is playing GOLF **2** a small box for storing tea

caddy², **caddie** v. [I + for] to carry GOLF CLUBs for someone who is playing GOLF

ca·dence /ˈkeɪdns/ n. [C] **1** the way someone's voice rises and falls, especially when reading out loud: She could imitate perfectly the cadence of my mother's voice. **2** a regular repeated pattern of sounds or movements: the cadence and rhythm of poetry **3** TECHNICAL a set of CHORDs at the end of a line or piece of music

ca·den·za /kəˈdɛnzə/ n. [C] TECHNICAL a difficult part of a CONCERTO in which the performer plays without the ORCHESTRA to show his or her skill

ca·det /kəˈdɛt/ n. [C] someone who is training to be an officer in the military or the police

cadge /kædʒ/ v. [I,T] INFORMAL to ask someone for something such as food or cigarettes, because you do not have any or do not want to pay; MOOCH

Cad·il·lac /ˈkædlˌæk/ n. [C] **1** TRADEMARK a very expensive and comfortable car made by an American company **2** INFORMAL something that is regarded as the highest quality example of a particular type of product: [+ of] the Cadillac of electric ovens

cad·mi·um /ˈkædmiəm/ n. [U] symbol **Cd** a type of metal that is an ELEMENT and is used in batteries (BATTERY (1))

ca·dre /ˈkædri, ˈkɑ-, -dreɪ/ n. FORMAL [C] a small group of specially trained people in a profession, political party, or military force: a cadre of highly trained scientists

ca·du·ce·us /kəˈduʃiəs/ n. [C] a sign consisting of two snakes around a stick that has wings at the top, used to represent a medical profession, especially that of doctors

Cae·sar /ˈsizə/, **Ju·li·us** /ˈdʒuliəs/ (100–44 B.C.) a Roman politician, military leader, and writer, who made himself the first Roman emperor

cae·sar·e·an /sɪˈzɛriən/ also **caesarean sec·tion** /ˌ.ˌ. ˈ../ n. [C] a CESAREAN

cae·su·ra /sɪˈzʊrə, sɪˈʒʊrə/ n. [C] TECHNICAL a pause in the middle of a line of poetry

ca·fé /kæˈfeɪ, kə-/ n. [C] **1** a small restaurant where you can buy drinks and simple meals **2** a place on a computer NETWORK, where people with similar interests discuss things by using computers

caf·e·te·ri·a /ˌkæfəˈtɪriə/ n. [C] a restaurant, often in a factory, school etc., where you choose from foods that have already been cooked and carry your own food to a table: Students complained about the cafeteria food.

caf·e·to·ri·um /ˌkæfəˈtɔriəm/ n. [C] a large room in a school that is used for activities such as preparing and eating food, exercising, and having meetings

caf·feine /kæˈfin, ˈkæfin/ n. [U] a chemical substance in tea, coffee, and some other drinks that makes you feel more active: Avoid caffeine (=drinks with caffeine) three to four hours before bedtime. | caffeine-free Coke (=Coke without caffeine) —**caffeinated** /ˈkæfəˌneɪtɪd/ adj.

caf·tan, kaftan /ˈkæftæn/ n. [C] a long loose piece of clothing like a dress, usually made of silk or cotton and worn in the Middle East

cage¹ /keɪdʒ/ n. [C] a structure made of wires or bars in which birds or animals can be kept —see also **rattle sb's cage** (RATTLE¹ (4))

cage² v. **1 feel caged in** to feel uncomfortable and annoyed because you cannot go outside or because a place is too small **2** [T] to put or keep an animal or bird in a cage

cag·ey /ˈkeɪdʒi/ adj. INFORMAL unwilling to tell people definitely what your plans, intentions, or opinions are: [+ about] The White House is being very cagey about the contents of the report. —**cagily** adv. —**caginess** n.

ca·hoots /kəˈhuts/ n. **be in cahoots (with sb)** INFORMAL to be working secretly with another person or group, especially in order to do something dishonest or illegal: Rogers is accused of being in cahoots with the mafia.

cai·man /ˈkeɪmən/ n. [C] a type of small CROCODILE that lives in tropical areas of North, Central, and South America

Cain /keɪn/ in the Bible, Adam and Eve's first son, who killed his younger brother, Abel, and became the first murderer

cairn /kɛrn/ n. [C] a pile of stones, especially at the top of a mountain, to mark a place

Cai·ro /ˈkaɪroʊ/ the capital and largest city of Egypt

cais·son /ˈkeɪsɑn, -sən/ n. [C] **1** a large box filled with air, that people go into to work under water **2** a large box with two wheels, used for carrying AMMUNITION

ca·jole /kəˈdʒoʊl/ v. [I,T] to gradually persuade someone to do something by being nice to them or making promises to them: **[cajole sb into doing sth]** Jacobs finally cajoled Beecher into taking the job.

Ca·jun /ˈkeɪdʒən/ n. a member of a group of people in southern Louisiana who had French-Canadian ANCESTORS —**Cajun** adj.

cake¹ /keɪk/ n. **1** [C,U] a soft sweet food made by baking a mixture of flour, butter, sugar, and eggs: a birthday cake | Do you want a piece of cake? **2** [C] a small piece of something, shaped into a block: [+ of] A thin cake of wax covered the jam to seal it. **3** a **fish/rice/potato etc. cake** fish, rice, potato etc. that has been formed into a flat round shape and then cooked **4 be a piece of cake** SPOKEN to be very easy: Getting tickets to the game will be a piece of cake. **5 have your cake and eat it too** INFORMAL to have all the advantages of something without any of the disadvantages **6 take the cake** INFORMAL to be worse than anything else you can imagine: You've done some pretty stupid things, but that really takes the cake! —see also **be selling/going like hotcakes** (HOTCAKE), PANCAKE

cake² v. **1 be caked with/in sth** to be covered with a layer of something thick and hard: Terry's elbow was caked with dried blood. **2** [I] if a substance cakes, it forms a thick hard layer when it dries

cake mix /'. ./ n. [C] a dry mixture that you buy and mix with eggs and milk to make a cake easily and quickly

cake pan /'. ./ n. [C] a metal container in which you bake a cake —see picture at PAN¹

cake·walk /ˈkeɪkwɔk/ n. [singular] INFORMAL a very easy thing to do, or a very easy victory: Don't expect the game against Florida to be a cakewalk.

cal. an abbreviation of CALORIE

cal·a·bash /ˈkæləˌbæʃ/ n. [C] a large tropical fruit with a shell that can be dried and used as a bowl

cal·a·mine lo·tion /ˈkæləmən ˌloʊʃən/ n. [U] a pink liquid used to treat sore, ITCHY, or SUNBURNed skin

ca·lam·i·ty /kəˈlæməti/ n. plural **calamities** [C] a terrible and unexpected event that causes a lot of damage or suffering: Hurricane George was just the latest calamity to hit the state. —**calamitous** adj. —**calamitously** adv.

cal·ci·fy /ˈkælsəˌfaɪ/ v. [I,T] TECHNICAL to become hard, or make something hard, by adding LIME

cal·ci·um /ˈkælsiəm/ *n.* [U] *symbol* **Ca** a silver-white metal that is an ELEMENT and that helps form teeth, bones, and CHALK

cal·cu·la·ble /ˈkælkyələbəl/ *adj.* [no comparative] something that is calculable can be measured by using numbers

S W **cal·cu·late** /ˈkælkyəˌleɪt/ *v.* [T] **1** to measure something or find out how much something will cost, how long something will take, etc. by using numbers: *These instruments calculate distances precisely.* | [**calculate (that)**] *Scientists have calculated that the sample is over 100,000 years old.* | [**calculate sth on sth**] *Rates are calculated on an hourly basis.* | **calculate how much/many etc.** *Use the formula to calculate how much water is wasted.* **2** to guess something using as many facts as you can find: *It's difficult to calculate what effect all these changes will have on the company.* **3 be calculated to do sth** to be intended to have a particular effect: *The commercials are calculated to attract young single consumers.*

calculate on sth *phr. v.* [T] if you calculate on something, you are depending on it for your plans to succeed: [**calculate on sb/sth doing sth**] *Ken hadn't calculated on Williams refusing his offer.*

cal·cu·lat·ed /ˈkælkyəˌleɪtɪd/ *adj.* [usually before noun] **1 a calculated risk/gamble** something risky that you do after thinking carefully about what might happen: *Investing in high-tech companies is a calculated risk.* **2** a calculated crime or dishonest action is deliberately and carefully planned: *It was a calculated attempt to make the governor look foolish.* —see also CALCULATE

cal·cu·lat·ing /ˈkælkyəˌleɪtɪŋ/ *adj.* [usually before noun] DISAPPROVING tending to make careful plans to get what you want, without caring about how it affects other people: *Yarbrough was a calculating troublemaker.*

cal·cu·la·tion /ˌkælkyəˈleɪʃən/ *n.* **1** [C usually plural,U] the act of adding, multiplying, dividing etc. numbers in order to find out an amount, price, or value: *By our calculations, it will cost about $12 million to build.* **2** [U] careful planning in order to get what you want

cal·cu·la·tor /ˈkælkyəˌleɪtɚ/ *n.* [C] a small electronic machine that can add, multiply, divide etc. numbers

cal·cu·lus /ˈkælkyələs/ *n.* [U] the part of mathematics that deals with changing quantities, such as the speed of a falling stone or the slope of a curved line

Cal·cut·ta /kælˈkʌtə/ the capital and largest city of the state of West Bengal in India

Cal·der /ˈkɔldɚ/, **Alexander** (1898–1976) a U.S. SCULPTOR best known for his large outdoor works of art and his large MOBILES

cal·dron /ˈkɔldrən/ *n.* [C] another spelling of CAULDRON

S W **cal·en·dar** /ˈkæləndɚ/ *n.* [C] **1** a set of pages that show the days, weeks, and months of a particular year, that you usually hang on the wall **2 a)** a book with separate spaces or pages for each day of the year, on which you write down the things you have to do; DATEBOOK **b)** all the things you plan to do in the next days, months etc.: *My calendar is full for the rest of the week.* **3** a system that divides and measures time in a particular way, usually starting from a particular event: *the Jewish calendar* **4** all the events in a year that are important for a particular organization or activity: *The Tour de France is the biggest race in the cycling calendar.*

calendar month /ˌ... ˈ./ *n.* [C] **1** one of the twelve months of the year: *Salaries will be paid at the end of the calendar month.* **2** a period of time from a specific date in one month to the same date in the next month

calendar year /ˌ... ˈ./ *n.* [C] the period of time from January 1st to December 31st

W **calf** /kæf/ *n. plural* **calves** /kævz/ **1** [C] the part of the back of your leg between your knee and your foot —see picture at BODY **2** [C] the baby of a cow, or of some other large animals such as the ELEPHANT **3** [U] calfskin **4 be in calf** if a cow is in calf, it is going to give birth

calf-length /ˈ. ./ *adj.* calf-length clothes cover your body to your calf: *a calf-length skirt* | *calf-length boots*

calf·skin /ˈkæfˌskɪn/ *n.* [U] the skin of a calf, which has been preserved and is used for making shoes, bags etc.

Cal·houn /kælˈhun/, **John C.** (1782–1850) a U.S. politician who supported the states' right not to accept laws passed by the national government

cal·i·ber /ˈkæləbɚ/ *n.* **1** [U] the level of quality or ability that someone or something has achieved: *He's a doctor of the highest caliber.* **2** [C] TECHNICAL **a)** the width of the inside of a gun or tube **b)** the width of a bullet

cal·i·brate /ˈkæləˌbreɪt/ *v.* [T] TECHNICAL to mark an instrument or tool so that you can use it for measuring

cal·i·bra·tion /ˌkæləˈbreɪʃən/ *n.* [C,U] TECHNICAL a set of marks on an instrument or tool used for measuring, or the act of making these tools correct

cal·i·co /ˈkælɪˌkoʊ/ *n.* **1** [U] light cotton cloth with a small printed pattern **2 calico cat** a cat that has black, white, and brown fur

Cal·i·for·nia /ˌkælɪˈfɔrnyə/ *written abbreviation* **CA** a state on the west coast of the U.S. —**Californian** *n. adj.*

California, the Gulf of a part of the Pacific Ocean that is between the PENINSULA of Baja California in western Mexico and the Mexican MAINLAND

Ca·lig·u·la /kəˈlɪgyələ/ (A.D. 12–41) a Roman emperor who was known for being extremely violent, cruel, and crazy

cal·i·pers /ˈkælɪpɚz/ *n.* [plural] a tool used for measuring thickness, the distance between two surfaces, or the DIAMETER (=inside width) of something

ca·liph /ˈkeɪlɪf, ˈkæ-/ *n.* [C] a MUSLIM ruler

ca·liph·ate /ˈkæləˌfeɪt, ˈkeɪ-/ *n.* [C] the country a caliph rules, or the period of time when they rule it

cal·is·then·ics /ˌkælɪsˈθɛnɪks/ *n.* [U] a set of physical exercises that are intended to make you strong, healthy, and graceful

CALL /kɔl/ *n.* [U] computer-assisted language learning; the use of computers to help people learn foreign languages

call[1] /kɔl/ *v.*   **S W** [1][1]

1 telephone [I,T] to talk to someone by telephone, or to attempt to do this: *Patty called when you were out.* | *I called Sue yesterday.* —see Usage Note at TELEPHONE[2]

2 describe [T] to use a particular word or phrase to describe someone or something that clearly shows what you think of them: [**call sb/sth sth**] *She drinks two cups of coffee and calls it breakfast!* | *Are you calling me a liar?* | *Artistic leaders called the bankruptcy of the symphony a "cultural catastrophe."*

3 ask/order by telephone [T] to ask someone to come to you by telephoning them: *Will somebody please call an ambulance?* | *Get out of here or I'll call the police!*

4 ask/order by speaking [T] to ask or order someone to come to you, either by speaking loudly or sending them a message: *Didn't you hear me calling you?* | [**call sb into/over**] *Later, the boss called Dan into her office.*

5 arrange [T] to arrange for something to happen at a particular time: *A meeting has been called for 3 p.m. Wednesday.*

6 say/shout [I,T] to say or shout something loudly because you want someone to hear you: *"Coming, Mom," I called.* | [+ **through/down/up**] *"Johnnie," Claire called through the door.*

7 name you use [T] to use a particular name or title when you speak to someone: *His name's actually Robert, but everyone just calls him Bob.* | *Do you want to be called Miss or Ms.?*

8 be called sth to have a particular name or title: *They live in this little town called Leroy, not far from Reed City.* | *What was that movie called again?*

C

9 give sb/sth a name [T] to give someone or something a name: [call sb/sth sth] *They're going to call her Amanda Margaret.*

10 call sb names to insult someone by using words that are not nice to describe them: *He went out and confronted him, calling him names.*

11 call yourself sth to claim that you are a particular type of person, although you do nothing to show this is true: *He calls himself a Christian, but he's not very nice to strangers.*

12 call the shots INFORMAL to be in a position of authority so that you can give orders and make decisions: *Here, democracy does not really exists. The generals call the shots.*

13 call it a day INFORMAL to decide to stop working, especially because you have done enough or you are tired: *Come on, guys, let's call it a day.*

14 call collect to make a telephone call that is paid for by the person who receives it

15 read names [T] also call out to read names or numbers in a loud voice in order to get someone's attention: *OK, when I call your name, raise your hand.*

16 court [T usually passive] to tell someone that they must come to a law court or official committee: [call sb to do sth] *I've been called to testify at Smith's trial.*

17 call into question to make people uncertain about whether something is right or true: *Bennett's ability as a leader has been called into question.*

18 be/feel called to do sth if you are called to do something, you feel strongly that it is your duty to do it or that you are the best person to do it: *Sandy felt called to do missionary work.*

19 call sb/sth to order FORMAL to tell people to obey the rules of a formal meeting: *I now call this meeting to order.*

20 call it $15/2 hours etc. SPOKEN used to ask someone to agree to a particular price, amount of time, limit etc., especially in order to make things simpler: *"How much do I owe you?" "Oh, just call it $15."*

21 call it/things even SPOKEN if you call a situation even, you are saying that someone who owes you something does not have to give you anything more than they have already given you: *Since you bought the movie tickets and I bought dinner, let's just call it even.*

22 call it a draw if two opponents in a game call it a draw, they agree that neither of them has won —see also **call it quits** (QUITS)

23 call attention to sth to ask people to pay attention to a particular subject or problem: *May I call your attention to item seven on the agenda.*

24 call sth to mind **a)** to remind you of something: *Fresno and Modesto are cities that call to mind the words "hot" and "dry."* **b)** to remember something: *Can you call to mind when you last saw her?*

25 call a huddle INFORMAL to arrange for people to come together to have a meeting

26 trains/ships [I] OLD-FASHIONED if a train or ship calls at a place, it stops there for a short time: [+ at] *This train will be calling at Yonkers, White Plains and Poughkeepsie.*

27 visit [I] OLD-FASHIONED to stop at a house or other place for a short time to see someone or do something: *Mr. Sweeney called while you were out.*

28 coin [I,T] to guess which side of a coin will land facing up after it is thrown in the air: *"OK, call it." "Heads."*

29 card game [I] to risk the same amount of money as the player who plays before you in a POKER game: *"I'll call your dollar – what have you got?" "Three nines".* —see also **call a spade a spade** (SPADE (3)), **call sb's bluff** (BLUFF² (2)), **draw/call attention to yourself** (ATTENTION (4)), SO-CALLED

call back *phr. v.* [I,T **call** sb **back**] to telephone someone again, especially because one of you was not in or was busy: *Okay, I'll call back around three.* | *I'm sorry, Mr. Dunbar is in a meeting, can he call you back later?*

call by *phr. v.* [I] OLD-FASHIONED to stop and visit someone when you are near the place where they live or work

call sb/sth ↔ **down** *phr. v.* [T] **1** to be asked to come to a particular place: *I was called down to the police station to answer a few questions.* **2** LITERARY to pray loudly that something bad will happen to someone or something: *The old man called down curses on us.*

call for sb/sth *phr. v.* [T] **1** to ask strongly and publicly for something to happen in order to change a situation: *Kerrey introduced a bill calling for nationwide health insurance.* **2** to demand or need a particular action, behavior, quality etc.: *I don't really think comments like that are called for, do you?* | *The beliefs of Orthodox Jews call for burial within 24 hours.* —see also UNCALLED FOR **3** to say that a particular kind of weather is likely to happen: *The weather forecast calls for more rain and high winds.* **4** OLD-FASHIONED to meet someone at their home in order to take them somewhere: *I'll call for you at seven o'clock.*

call sth ↔ **forth** *phr. v.* [T] FORMAL to make something such as a quality appear so that you can use it; SUMMON: *Calling forth all his strength, Arthur pulled the sword out of the stone.*

call in *phr. v.* **1** [T **call** sb/sth ↔ **in**] to ask or order a person or organization to help you with a difficult or dangerous situation: *The FBI has been called in to investigate.* **2** [I] to telephone somewhere, especially the place where you work, to tell them where you are, what you are doing etc.: *Why don't you just call in sick* (=telephone to say you are too sick to come to work)? **3** [I] to telephone a radio or television show to give your opinion or ask a question: *A number of people called in with good suggestions.* **4** call in a loan/favor to ask someone to pay back money or to help you with something, because you helped them earlier **5** [I] OLD-FASHIONED to visit a person or place while you are on your way somewhere else [+ at/on] *Could you call in on Grandma on your way home?*

call sb/sth ↔ **off** *phr. v.* [T] **1** to decide that a planned event will not take place; CANCEL: *The game was called off due to heavy rain.* **2** to order a dog or person to stop attacking someone: *Call off your dog!* **3** call off a strike/search etc. to decide officially that something should be stopped after it has already started: *Rescuers have been forced to call off the search until the weather improves.*

call on/upon sb/sth *phr. v.* [T] **1** to formally ask someone to do something: [call on sb to do sth] *Western countries have been called on to support the democratically elected government.* **2** to visit someone for a short time: *I spent most of the day calling on clients.*

call out *phr. v.* **1** [I,T **call** sth ↔ **out**] to say something loudly: *We'll call out your name when your order is ready.* | *I called out to you at the train station, but you didn't hear me.* **2** [T **call** sb/sth ↔ **out**] to ask or order a person or organization to help, especially with a difficult or dangerous situation: *Every fire engine in the city had been called out.*

call up *phr. v.* **1** [I,T **call** sb ↔ **up**] to telephone someone: *He called me up to tell me about it.* **2** [T **call** sth ↔ **up**] if you call up information on a computer, you make the computer show it to you **3** [T **call** sb/sth ↔ **up**] to make something appear again after it has gone or been forgotten: *The woman believes she can call up the spirits of the dead.* **4** [T **call** sb ↔ **up**] to move a baseball player from a MINOR LEAGUE team to a MAJOR LEAGUE team

call² n. [C]

1 telephone an attempt to speak to someone by telephone: *Have there been many calls?* | *We always get so many phone calls at suppertime.* | *I got a call from Pam yesterday.* | *Just give me a call from the airport when you arrive.* | *Excuse me, I have to make an important telephone call.* | *She never returns my calls.* (=telephones me back) | *I'll take the call* (=answer a telephone call) *in my office.* | a local/long-distance call (=a phone call made within the city or area where you are, or one made to somewhere far away) —see Usage Note at TELEPHONE¹

2 be on call if someone such as a doctor or engineer

is on call, they are ready to go and help whenever they are needed as part of their job: *She's on call at the hospital every other night.*
3 shout/cry **a)** the sound or cry that a bird or animal makes: [+ of] *the distinctive call of the hyena* **b)** a shout or cry that you make to get someone's attention: *a call for help*
4 request/order also **calling** a request or order for someone to do something or go somewhere: *Ambulances try to arrive within eight minutes of an emergency call.* | [call for sb (to do sth)] *Phillip felt a call from God to preach.* | *Democrats seemed not to be interested in the calls for reform.*
5 decision **a)** a decision made by a REFEREE (=judge) in a sports game: *When you play at your opponent's court, the calls tend to go against you.* | **make good/bad calls** *The referee made several bad calls.* **b)** INFORMAL a decision: *'Where should we eat tonight?' 'I don't know, it's your call.'* | **a hard/easy call** (=a difficult or easy decision) | *Guilty or innocent? You* **make the call** (=decide).
6 good/bad call! SLANG used to say that you agree or disagree with someone's decision about something
7 there is no call for sth also there is no call to do sth SPOKEN used to tell someone that their behavior is wrong and unnecessary: *There was no call for him to do that.*
8 visit a short visit, especially for a particular reason: *We should* **pay** *Jerry and his wife a call* (=visit them) *since we're driving through Ohio.*
9 airplane an official message at an airport that an airplane for a particular place will soon leave: *This is the last call for flight 372 to Atlanta.*
10 there isn't much call for sth used to say that something is not popular or is not needed: *There isn't much call for typewriters since computers got easier to use.*
11 the call of sth LITERARY the power that a place or way of life has to attract someone: *the call of the sea*
12 the call of nature INFORMAL a need to URINATE (=pass liquid from your body)
13 bank [U] TECHNICAL a demand by a bank or other financial institution for money that has been borrowed to be paid back immediately —see also **be at sb's beck and call** (BECK), PORT OF CALL, ROLL CALL

Cal·las /ˈkæləs/, **Ma·ri·a** /məˈriːə/ (1923–1977) a U.S. OPERA singer who is considered one of the greatest opera singers of the 20th century

call box /ˈ. ./ *n.* [C] a public telephone beside a street or FREEWAY, used to telephone for help

call·er /ˈkɔlə/ *n.* [C] **1** someone who is making a telephone call: *Didn't the caller say who she was?* **2** OLD-FASHIONED someone who visits your house

caller ID /ˌ. . ˈ./ *n.* [U] a special service on your telephone that lets you know who is calling before you answer the telephone

call for·ward·ing /ˈ. ˌ../ *n.* [U] a telephone service that allows you to send your calls to a different telephone number, so that people who call your usual number can reach you at the other number

call girl /ˈ. ./ *n.* [C] a PROSTITUTE who makes arrangements to meet men by telephone

cal·lig·ra·phy /kəˈlɪgrəfi/ *n.* [U] the art of producing beautiful writing using special pens or brushes, or the writing produced this way —**calligrapher** *n.* [C]

call-in /ˈ. ./ *n.* [C] a radio or television program in which people telephone to give their opinions

call·ing /ˈkɔlɪŋ/ *n.* [C] **1** a strong desire or feeling of duty to do a particular kind of work, especially work that helps other people; VOCATION: *Helping the poor was her calling in life.* **2** FORMAL someone's profession or trade

calling card /ˈ.. ˌ./ *n.* [C] a small card with a name and often an address printed on it, that people used to give to people they visited in past times

cal·li·o·pe /kəˈlaɪəpi/ *n.* [C] a large musical instrument like a piano, with large whistles that use steam to make sound, used especially in a CIRCUS

call let·ters /ˈ. ˌ../ *n.* [plural] a name made up of letters and numbers, used by people operating communication radios to prove who they are

call mon·ey /ˈ. ˌ../ *n.* [U] TECHNICAL the INTEREST rate that is charged on LOANS that a bank is asking to be paid back immediately

call num·ber /ˈ. ˌ../ *n.* [C] the numbers used on a library book to put it into a group with other books with the same subject, so that you can find it easily on the shelves

call op·tion /ˈ. ˌ../ *n.* [C] TECHNICAL the right to buy a particular number of SHARES at a particular price within a particular period of time

cal·lous /ˈkæləs/ *adj.* unkind and not caring that other people are suffering: *The company showed callous disregard for the safety of their employees.* | *the callous slaughter of thousands of civilians* —**callously** *adv.* —**callousness** *n.* [U]

cal·low /ˈkæloʊ/ *adj.* LITERARY young and without experience: *a callow young man*

call sign /ˈ. ./ *n.* [C] CALL LETTERS

cal·lus /ˈkæləs/ *n.* [C] an area of thick hard skin, caused by the skin rubbing against something such as shoes, a tool etc. over a long period of time: *calluses on her feet*

cal·lused /ˈkæləst/ *adj.* covered in calluses: *His hands were rough, callused. Workman's hands.*

call wait·ing /ˌ. ˈ../ *n.* [U] a telephone service that allows you to receive another call when you are already talking on the telephone, without ending the first call

calm¹ /kɑm/ *adj.* **1** relaxed and quiet, not angry, nervous, or upset: *His mother was a calm, slow-speaking woman.* | **keep/stay/remain calm** *The breathing exercises help you to stay calm.* **2** an ocean, lake etc. that is calm is smooth or has only gentle waves —see picture at CHOPPY **3** weather that is calm is not windy: *It was a calm, clear, beautiful day.* —**calmly** *adv.* —**calmness** *n.* [U]

calm² also **calm down** *v.* [I,T] **1** to become quiet and relaxed, after you have been angry, excited, nervous, or upset, or to make someone become quiet and relaxed: *Calm down, Morgan! Stop jumping around.* | *I waited until I'd calmed down a little, then went to talk to her.* | *Awareness of polio was high, and the government tried to* **calm people's fears**. **2** if a situation calms down, it becomes easier to deal with because there are fewer problems and it is not as busy as it was before: *It took about six months for things to calm down after we had the baby.*

calm³ *n.* **1** [singular,U] a time that is quiet and peaceful: *We sat on the patio, enjoying the calm of the evening.* **2** the calm before the storm a calm peaceful situation just before a big argument, problem etc.

ca·lor·ic /kəˈlɔrɪk/ *adj.* relating to calories: *The doctor told me to lower my caloric intake by 5%.*

cal·o·rie /ˈkæləri/ *n.* [C] **1** a unit for measuring the amount of ENERGY a particular food will produce: *An average potato has about 90 calories.* | *A long walk will help you* **burn off** *a few calories* (=control your weight by using the energy from the food you have eaten). | *My wife finally convinced me to start* **counting calories** (=trying to control my weight by calculating the number of calories I eat). **2** TECHNICAL the amount of heat that is needed to raise the temperature of one gram of water by one degree Celsius

cal·o·rif·ic /ˌkæləˈrɪfɪk◂/ *adj.* **1** food that is calorific tends to make you fat **2** TECHNICAL producing heat

ca·lum·ni·ate /kəˈlʌmniˌeɪt/ *v.* [T] FORMAL to say untrue and unfair things about someone; SLANDER²

cal·um·ny /ˈkæləmni/ *n.* FORMAL **1** [C] an untrue and unfair statement about someone that is intended to give people a bad opinion of them **2** [U] the act of saying things like this —see also SLANDER¹

cal·va·ry /ˈkælvəri/ *n.* [C] a model or STATUE that represents the death of Jesus Christ on the cross

calve /kæv/ *v.* [I] to give birth to a CALF (=baby cow)

calves /kævz/ *n.* the plural of CALF

Cal·vin /ˈkælvɪn/, **John** (1509–1564) a French-born Swiss religious leader, whose ideas had a strong

C

influence on the beginnings of the Protestant religion
—see also CALVINISM

Cal·vin·ism /'kælvə,nızəm/ *n.* [U] the Christian religious teachings of John Calvin, which are based on the idea that events on Earth are controlled by God, and which led to the establishment of the PRESBYTERIAN church

Cal·vin·ist /'kælvənɪst/ *adj.* **1** following the teachings of Calvinism **2** also **Calvinistic** having strict moral standards and tending to disapprove of pleasure; PURITANICAL —**Calvinist** *n.* [C]

ca·lyp·so /kə'lɪpsoʊ/ *n.* [C] a type of Caribbean song based on subjects of interest in the news

ca·lyx /'keɪlɪks/ *n. plural* **calyxes** or **calyces** /-lɪsiz/ [C] TECHNICAL the green outer part of a flower that protects it before it opens

cam /kæm/ *n.* [C] a wheel or part of a wheel that is shaped to change circular movement into backward and forward movement

ca·ma·rad·er·ie /kæm'rɑdəri, kɑm-/ *n.* [U] a feeling of friendship that a group of people have, especially when they work together: *I enjoy the camaraderie among the team.*

cam·ber /'kæmbə/ *n.* [C,U] TECHNICAL a slight curve from the center to the side of a road or other surface that makes water run off to the side

Cam·bo·di·a /kæm'boʊdiə/ a country in southeast Asia between Thailand and Vietnam —**Cambodian** *n., adj.*

cam·bric /'keɪmbrɪk/ *n.* [U] thin white cloth made of LINEN or cotton

cam·cord·er /'kæm,kɔrdə/ *n.* [C] a type of camera that you can hold in one hand to record pictures and sound onto VIDEOTAPE —see picture on page 426

came /keɪm/ *v.* the past tense of COME

cam·el /'kæməl/ *n.* [C] a large desert animal with a long neck and one or two HUMPS (=large raised parts) on its back —see also **the straw that breaks the camel's back** (STRAW (3))

cam·el·hair /'kæməl,hɛr/ *n.* [U] a thick yellowish brown cloth, usually used for making coats

ca·mel·lia /kə'milyə/ *n.* [C] a plant on which grow large sweet-smelling red, pink, or white flowers, or the flowers themselves

Cam·e·lot /'kæmə,lɑt/ according to old stories about King Arthur, the place where Arthur and his KNIGHTS lived

cam·em·bert /'kæməm,bɛr/ *n.* [C,U] a soft French cheese, that is white outside and yellow inside

cam·e·o /'kæmioʊ/ *n. plural* **cameos** [C] **1** a small part in a movie or play acted by a well-known actor: *Danny DeVito made a cameo appearance as a lawyer.* **2** a small piece of jewelry that has a raised shape, usually of a person's face, on a dark flat background: *a cameo brooch* **3** a short piece of writing that gives a clear idea of a person, place, or event

cam·er·a /'kæmrə, -ərə/ *n.* [C] **1** a piece of equipment used for taking photographs or making movies —see picture on page 426 **2** TECHNICAL the part of the equipment used for making television pictures that changes images into electrical signals **3 in camera** TECHNICAL a law case that is held in camera takes place secretly or privately

cam·er·a·man /'kæmrə,mæn, -mən/ *n.* [C] a man who operates a camera to film movies or television programs

camera-shy /'.. ,./ *adj.* not liking to have your photograph taken

cam·er·a·wo·man /'kæmrə,wʊmən/ *n.* [C] a woman who operates a camera to film movies or television programs

Cam·e·roon, Cameroun /,kæmə'run, 'kæmə,run/ a country in west Africa, east of Nigeria —**Cameroonian** /,kæmə'runiən/ *n., adj.*

ca·mi·sole /'kæmi,soʊl/ *n.* [C] a light piece of women's underwear that reaches to the waist and has narrow bands that go over the shoulders

cam·o·mile /'kæmə,mil/ *n.* [C,U] another spelling of CHAMOMILE

cam·ou·flage¹ /'kæmə,flɑʒ, -,flɑdʒ/ *n.* [U] **1** the way in which the color or shape of something makes it difficult to see in the place where it lives: *The stripes of the tiger provide important camouflage in its natural setting.* **2** a way of hiding something, especially a military object, using branches, paint etc.: *We used leaves and sticks as camouflage.* **3 camouflage clothing/ pants/ jacket etc.** camouflage clothes have green and brown patterns on them that make them hard to see in a forest **4** behavior that is designed to hide something: *Aggression is often a camouflage for insecurity.*

camouflage² *v.* [T] to hide something by making it look the same as the things around it, or by making it seem like something else: *Entrances to the tunnels were carefully camouflaged.*

camp¹ /kæmp/ *n.* **1** [C,U] a place where people stay in temporary shelters, such as tents, especially for a short time and in mountains or forests: *The camp is at the bottom of the Grand Canyon.* | *a mining camp in the Yukon* | *The soldiers broke camp* (=took down their tents, shelters etc.) *and left before dawn.* **2** [C,U] a place where children go to stay for a short time and take part in special activities, often as members of an organization: *scout camp* | *summer camp* | *The kids will be at camp all day.* —see also DAY CAMP **3 a prison/refugee/labor etc. camp** a place where people are kept for a particular reason, when they do not want to be there —see also CONCENTRATION CAMP **4** [C] a group of people or organizations who have the same ideas or principles,: *the extreme right-wing camp of the party* **5** [U] the act of behaving in a silly, unnatural way and expressing too much emotion when you are acting in a movie, television program, or play: *If you like camp, you'll probably enjoy the movie.* —see also BOOTCAMP, **camp sth ↔ up** (CAMP²), TRAINING CAMP

camp² *v.* [I] **1** to set up a tent or temporary shelter and stay there for a short time: *A family was camped on a sandy beach under the trees.* **2 go camping** to take a vacation in which you sleep in tents or other temporary shelters in the mountains, forest etc.: *Scouts frequently go hiking and camping.*

camp out *phr. v.* [I] **1** to sleep outdoors, usually in a tent: *People camp out overnight to get a good place to see the parade.* **2** to stay somewhere where you do not have all the usual things that you normally have at your house: *You can camp out in our living room until you find an apartment.*

camp sth ↔ **up** *phr. v.* [T] INFORMAL also **camp**

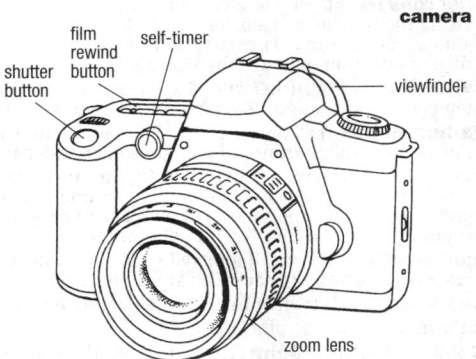
camera

film rewind button
self-timer
shutter button
viewfinder
zoom lens

it up to deliberately behave or act in a funny, unnatural way, with too much movement or expression

camp³ *adj.* INFORMAL **1** also **campy** clothes, decorations etc. that are camp are very strange, bright, or unusual: *That outfit is so camp.* **2** a man who is camp moves or speaks in the way that people used to think is typical of HOMOSEXUALS

cam·paign¹ /kæm'peɪn/ *n.* [C] **1** a series of actions intended to achieve a particular result, especially in politics or business: *the governor's election campaign* | *an advertising campaign* | [+ **for/against**] *a campaign against the death penalty* **2** a series of battles, attacks etc. intended to achieve a particular result in a war

campaign² *v.* [I] to lead or take part in a series of actions intended to achieve a particular result, especially in politics or business: [+ **for/against**] *Rosellini campaigned hard against the measure to cut welfare benefits.* —**campaigner** *n.* [C]

Cam·pa·nel·la /ˌkæmpə'nɛlə/, **Roy** /rɔɪ/ (1921–1993) a U.S. baseball player who was famous for his skill as a CATCHER, and was also one of the first African-American players in the Major Leagues

cam·pa·ni·le /ˌkæmpə'nili/ *n.* [C] a high bell tower that is usually separate from any other building

cam·pa·nol·o·gy /ˌkæmpə'nɑlədʒi/ *n.* [U] the skill of ringing bells —**campanologist** *n.* [C]

camp bed /'. ./ *n.* [C] a light bed that folds up

Camp·bell /'kæmbəl/, **Joseph** (1904–1987) a U.S. writer famous for his books on MYTHOLOGY

Camp Da·vid /ˌkæmp 'deɪvɪd/ the country home of the U.S. President, where the President goes to relax

camp·er /'kæmpɚ/ *n.* [C] **1** someone who is staying in a tent or temporary shelter **2** a vehicle or special type of tent on wheels that has beds and cooking equipment in it so that you can stay in it while you are on vacation **3** a child who is taking part in special activities at a camp **4 a happy camper** SPOKEN, HUMOROUS someone who seems to be happy with their situation

camp·fire /'kæmpfaɪɚ/ *n.* [C] a fire made outdoors by people who are camping

Camp Fire /'. ./ an organization for girls and boys, which teaches them practical skills and helps them develop their character

camp fol·low·er /'. ˌ.../ *n.* [C] **1** someone who supports an organization or a political party, but who is not actually a member of the main group **2** someone, especially a PROSTITUTE, who follows an army from place to place to provide services

camp·ground /'kæmpgraʊnd/ *n.* [C] an area where people can camp, that often has a water supply and toilets

cam·phor /'kæmfɚ/ *n.* [U] a white substance with a strong smell, that is used especially to keep insects away

camp meet·ing /'. ˌ../ *n.* [C] a religious meeting that often continues for more than one day, and that is usually held outside or in a very large tent

camp·out /'. ./ *n.* [C] an occasion when you sleep outdoors, especially in a tent: *a camp-out in the backyard*

camp·site /'kæmpsaɪt/ *n.* [C] a place, usually within a CAMPGROUND, where one person or group can camp

cam·pus /'kæmpəs/ *n.* [C] the land and buildings of a school, college, or university: *Work-study jobs are usually on campus, and the money earned pays for tuition.*

camp·y /'kæmpi/ *adj.* **campier, campiest** behaving or acting in a funny, unnatural way, with too much movement or expression: *a campy horror movie*

cam·shaft /'kæmʃæft/ *n.* [C] a metal bar that a CAM is attached to in an engine

Ca·mus /kæ'mu/, **Al·bert** /æl'bɛr/ (1913–1960) a French EXISTENTIALIST writer and PHILOSOPHER

can¹ /kən; *strong* kæn/ *modal verb past tense* **could 1** to be able to do something or know how to do

something: *Jean can speak French fluently.* | *There's hardly any traffic and you can really go fast.* | *I can't swim.* | *If you have a complaint, you can talk to the manager.* | *The police still haven't found her but they're doing all they can.* **2** to have permission to do something or to be allowed to do something: *You can't go in there.* | *I told her she can watch TV till bedtime.* | *In soccer, you can't touch the ball with your hands.* (=it is against the rules) **3** SPOKEN used when asking someone to do something or give you something: *Can I have the check, please?* | *Can we turn the air conditioner on?* **4** used to state a quality of something or a fact about how it is able to be used: *This knife can also be used as a can opener.* | *That kind of plastic can be molded into any shape.* **5** used to state what is possible or likely: *I'm sure we can finish in time.* | *The word "bill" can have several different meanings.* | *That can't be right.* | *There can be no doubt that he is guilty.* **6** used with the verbs "see," "hear," "feel," "smell," and "taste," and with verbs connected with thinking, to show that an action is happening: *Can you hear all right in the back row?* | *Oh, I can taste the lemon grass!* | *Nancy couldn't understand why I was so upset.* | *You can imagine how bad it smelled!* **7** [usually in questions and negatives] used especially when you think there is only one possible answer to a question or one possible thing to do in a particular situation: *Sure she's mad, can you blame her?* | *That's really nice of you, but I really can't accept it.* **8** to have to do something; must: *If you don't want to learn, you can leave right now.* **9** used especially in expressions of surprise: *You can't be serious!* | *Who can that be at the door?* | *They can't have left without me!* **10** used to show what sometimes happens or how someone sometimes behaves: *It can get pretty cold here at night.* | *He can be such a jerk sometimes.* —see also CANNOT, COULD

can² /kæn/ *n.* [C] **1** a metal container in which food or drinks are preserved without air, or the food contained in this: *soft drink cans* | [+ **of**] *a can of tuna fish* —see picture at CONTAINER **2** garbage/trash can a large metal or plastic container for holding GARBAGE (=waste food, paper etc.) **3** a special metal container that keeps the liquid inside it under pressure, letting it out as a SPRAY² (1) when you press the button on the lid: *a can of deodorant* **4** a metal container with a lid that can be removed, used for holding liquid: *You'll need three large cans of paint.* **5 a (whole) can of worms** a very complicated situation that causes a lot of problems when you start to deal with it **6 the can** SLANG **a)** a toilet **b)** OLD-FASHIONED a prison **7** SLANG your BUTTOCKS **8 in the can** INFORMAL a movie that is in the can is complete and ready to be shown

can³ *v.* **canned, canning** [T] **1** to preserve food by putting it into a closed container without air —see also CANNED (1) **2** SPOKEN to dismiss someone from their job: *Did you hear that they canned Linda?* **3 can it!** SPOKEN used to tell someone in an impolite way to stop talking or making noise

Can·a·da /'kænədə/ a country in North America, north of the U.S. —**Canadian** /kə'neɪdiən/ *n., adj.*

Canada Day /'... ˌ./ *n.* [C,U] the Canadian national holiday, celebrated on July 1st

Canada goose /ˌ... './ also **Canadian goose** /ˌ.... './ *n. plural* **Canada geese** [C] a common wild North American GOOSE, with gray feathers, a black head, and a white throat

Canadian ba·con /ˌ.... '../ *n.* [U] meat from the back or sides of a pig, cut in thin pieces, and that tastes similar to HAM —compare BACON (1)

ca·nal /kə'næl/ *n.* [C] **1** a long narrow stream of water for ships or boats to travel along, or to bring water from somewhere: *the Panama Canal* **2** a passage in the body of a person or animal —see also ALIMENTARY CANAL

canal boat /'. ˌ./ *n.* [C] a long narrow boat that is used on a canal

Ca·na·let·to /ˌkænl'ɛtoʊ/, **An·to·ni·o** /æn'toʊnioʊ/ (1697–1768) an Italian PAINTER famous for his paintings of Venice and of the Thames in London

can·a·lize /'kænl,aɪz/ v. [T] to make a river deeper, straighter etc., especially in order to make a canal or prevent flooding —**canalization** /ˌkænl-ə'zeɪʃən/ n. [U]

can·ap·é, canape /'kænəpi, -peɪ/ n. [C] a small piece of bread with cheese, meat, fish etc. on it, served with drinks at a party

ca·nard /kə'nɑrd/ n. [C] a statement or piece of news that is deliberately false: *A canard of anti-Semitism is that there is a secret group of powerful Jews running the country.*

ca·nar·y /kə'nɛri/ n. plural **canaries** [C] a small yellow bird that sings and is often kept as a pet

ca·nas·ta /kə'næstə/ n. [U] a card game in which two sets of cards are used

Can·ber·ra /'kænbərə, -ˌbɛrə/ the capital city of Australia

can·can /'kænkæn/ n. [C] a fast dance from France, in which women kick their legs high into the air during a show

can·cel /'kænsəl/ v. **canceled, canceling** also **cancelled, cancelling** [T] **1** to arrange that a planned activity or event will not now happen: *Classes were canceled for the day.* | *The comedy was canceled after just four episodes.* **2** to end an agreement or arrangement that exists in law: *I called and canceled the order.* **3** to stamp or mark a CHECK, stamp, or ticket so that it cannot be used again: *a canceled check*

   cancel sth **out** phr. v. [T] to have an equal but opposite effect on something, so that a situation does not change: *Increased advertising costs have canceled out our sales gains.*

can·cel·la·tion /ˌkænsə'leɪʃən/ n. [C,U] a decision or statement that a planned or regular activity will not happen: *Bad weather led to the cancellation of most flights out of O'Hare.*

Can·cer /'kænsɚ/ n. **1** [U] the fourth sign of the ZODIAC represented by a CRAB, and believed to affect the character and life of people born between June 21 and July 22 **2** [C] someone who was born between June 21 and July 22

cancer /'kænsɚ/ n. **1** [C,U] a very serious disease in which cells in a part of the body start to grow in a way that is not normal and that can cause death: *lung cancer* | *cancer of the liver* | *He died of cancer at the age of 63.* **2** [C] an activity that is increasing, and causes a lot of harm: *The mayor has called drug abuse "a cancer on our society."* —**cancerous** adj.: *a cancerous tumor*

can·de·la·bra /ˌkændə'lɑbrə/ also **can·del·a·brum** /-'lɑbrəm/ n. [C] a decorative holder for several CANDLES or lamps

can·did /'kændɪd/ adj. **1** directly truthful, even when the truth may be upsetting or embarrassing: *Myrdal's book is a candid biography of her famous parents.* **2** candid pictures or photographs are taken of someone who does not know that they are being photographed —**candidly** adv. —see also CANDOR

can·di·da /'kændədə/ n. [U] TECHNICAL a YEAST INFECTION

can·di·da·cy /'kændədəsi/ n. plural **candidacies** [C,U] the position of being one of the people who are competing to be elected to a position, especially a political position: *Cuomo's candidacy would have greatly changed the presidential race.*

can·di·date /'kændə,deɪt, -dɪt/ n. [C] **1** someone who is being considered for a job or is competing to be elected: *One candidate must receive a majority of the vote.* | [+ for] *Parcells seemed to be the leading candidate for the coaching job at Tampa Bay.* | *Zimmerman is the prime candidate* (=most likely candidate) *to take over the position of conductor.* **2** a person, group, or idea that is appropriate for something or likely to get something: [+ for] *His obvious*

intelligence makes him a strong candidate for a school for the gifted.

can·died /'kændid/ adj. cooked in or covered with sugar: *candied fruit*

can·dle /'kændl/ n. [C] **1** a round stick of WAX[1] (1) with a piece of string through the middle that you burn to produce light **2 can't hold a candle to sb/sth** INFORMAL to be not as good as someone or something else: *Basketball stars today can't hold a candle to Michael Jordan.* —see also **burn the candle at both ends** (BURN[1] (13))

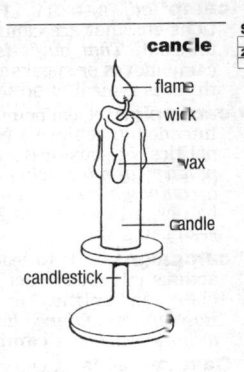

candle: flame, wick, wax, candle, candlestick

can·dle·light /'kændl,laɪt/ n. [U] the light produced when a candle burns: *We read by candlelight.* | *a candlelight dinner*

candle-lit /'.. ,./ adj. a candle-lit activity or place is one in which candles are used to produce light: *a candle-lit table*

can·dle·stick /'kændl,stɪk/ n. [C] a specially shaped metal or wooden object used to hold a candle —see picture at CANDLE

can-do /ˌ. './ adj. [only before noun] INFORMAL willing to try anything and expecting that it will work: *Denver is a world-class city with a can-do spirit.*

can·dor /'kændɚ/ n. [U] the quality of being honest and truthful: *Dietrich describes her Hollywood friends and rivals with her usual candor.* | *In all candor, I can say there isn't a quick and easy solution to these problems.* —see also CANDID

can·dy /'kændi/ n. plural **candies** [C,U] **1** a sweet food made of sugar or chocolate, or a piece of this: *a box of candy* **2 mind/brain/eye etc. candy** INFORMAL something that is entertaining or pleasant to look at, but that does not make you think: *Most video games are just brain candy.*

candy ap·ple /ˌ. '../ n. [C] an apple covered with a sticky brown or red candy

candy ass /'.. ,./ n. [C] SLANG someone who is weak and afraid to do things; WIMP —**candy-ass** adj. [only before noun]

candy bar /'.. ,./ n. [C] a long narrow bar of candy, usually covered with chocolate

candy cane /'.. ,./ n. [C] a stick of hard red and white sugar with a curved end

candy-striped /'.. ,./ adj. candy-striped cloth has narrow red or pink lines on a white background

candy strip·er /'kændi ,straɪpɚ/ n. [C] a young person, usually a girl, who does unpaid work as a nurse's helper in a hospital in order to learn about hospital work

cane[1] /keɪn/ n. **1** [C] a long thin stick with a curved handle, used to help someone walk: *He was walking slowly with a cane.* —see also STICK (5) **2** [U] thin pieces of the stems of plants, some types of which are used for making furniture, baskets etc.: *a cane and wicker rocker* | *raspberry canes* **3** [C] a long, hard, yellow stem of BAMBOO, used for supporting other plants in the garden **4** [C, singular] a long thin stick used especially in past times by teachers to hit children with as a punishment, or the punishment of being hit with a cane **5** [U] SUGAR CANE

cane[2] v. [T] to punish someone, especially a child, by hitting them with a long thin stick

cane sug·ar /ˌ. '../ n. [U] sugar that comes from SUGAR CANE

ca·nine /'keɪnaɪn/ adj. relating to dogs: *a police canine unit*

canine tooth /'.. ,./ n. [C] one of four sharp pointed teeth in the front of the human mouth; EYE TOOTH

can·is·ter /'kænəstɚ/ n. [C] a container with straight sides and a circular top, usually made of metal or plastic, in which you keep dry foods and some other types of objects: *a flour canister* | *canisters* of film **2** a round metal case that bursts when thrown or fired from a gun, scattering what is inside. *Police fired tear-gas canisters at the crowd of protesting students.* **3** a round metal container of gas

can·ker /'kæŋkə/ *n.* **1** [C] also **canker sore** a sore area on the flesh of people or animals, caused by illness or a disease **2** [C,U] an infected area on the wood of trees, or the disease that causes this —**cankerous** *adj.* —**cankered** *adj.*

can·na·bis /'kænəbɪs/ *n.* [U] TECHNICAL: see MARIJUANA

canned /kænd/ *adj.* [usually before noun] **1** canned food is preserved without air in a metal or glass container, and can be kept for a long time before it is opened: *canned peaches* **2 canned music/laughter/applause** music, laughter, applause that has been recorded and is used on television or in radio programs

can·nel·lo·ni /ˌkænə'louni/ *n.* [U] small tubes of PASTA filled with meat and sometimes cheese, and covered in SAUCE

can·ner·y /'kænəri/ *n.* [C] a factory where food is put into cans

can·ni·bal /'kænəbəl/ *n.* [C] **1** someone who eats human flesh **2** an animal that eats the flesh of other animals of the same kind —**cannibalism** *n.* [U] —**cannibalistic** /ˌkænəbə'lɪstɪk◂/ *adj.*

can·ni·bal·ize /'kænəbə,laɪz/ *v.* [T] to take something apart, especially a machine, so that you can use its parts to build something else

can·non /'kænən/ *n.* [C] a large, heavy, powerful gun, attached to the ground or on wheels, used in past times —see also **loose cannon** (LOOSE¹ (10))

can·non·ade /ˌkænə'neɪd/ *n.* [C] a continuous heavy attack by large guns

can·non·ball /'kænən,bɔl/ *n.* [C] a heavy iron ball fired from an old type of large gun

cannon fod·der /'.. ,../ *n.* [U] INFORMAL ordinary members of the army, navy etc., whose lives are not considered to be very important

can·not /'kænɑt, kə'nɑt, kæ-/ *modal verb* **1** a negative form of "can": *Many people cannot find affordable housing.* **2 cannot but** FORMAL used to say that you feel you have to do something: *If we are attacked with violence, we cannot but respond with violence.*

can·ny /'kæni/ *adj.* **cannier, canniest** smart, careful, not easily deceived, and understanding a situation very well, especially in business or politics: *Robinson has benefited from some canny marketing.* —**cannily** *adv.*

ca·noe¹ /kə'nu/ *n.* [C] a long light narrow boat that is pointed at both ends, which you move along using a PADDLE¹ (1) —compare KAYAK¹

canoe² *v.* [I] to travel by canoe —**canoeist** *n.* [C]

ca·no·la /kə'noulə/ *n.* [U] a plant with yellow flowers, grown as animal food and for its oil, which is used in cooking

can·on /'kænən/ *n.* [C] **1** FORMAL a generally accepted rule or standard on which an idea, subject, or way of behaving is based: *I knew that I was violating all the canons of journalistic ethics.* **2** an established law of the Christian church **3** a Christian priest who has special duties in a CATHEDRAL **4** a piece of music in which a tune is started by one singer or instrument and is copied by each of the others **5** FORMAL a list of books or pieces of music that are officially recognized as being the work of a certain writer: *He has now acted in all 37 plays of the Shakespeare canon.*

ca·non·i·cal /kə'nɑnɪkəl/ *adj.* according to canon law

can·on·ize /'kænə,naɪz/ *v.* [T] to officially state that a dead person is a SAINT (1) —**canonization** /ˌkænənə'zeɪʃən/ *n.* [C, U]

canon law /ˌ.. './ *n.* [U] the laws of the Christian church

ca·noo·dle /kə'nudl/ *v.* [I] OLD-FASHIONED if two people canoodle, they kiss and hold each other in a sexual way

can o·pen·er /'. ,../ *n.* [C] a tool for opening a can of food —see picture at KITCHEN

can·o·py /'kænəpi/ *n.* **plural canopies** [C] **1** a cover

attached above a bed, seat etc. as a decoration or as a shelter: *a canopy over the patio* **2** LITERARY something that spreads above you like a roof: *The tops of the trees in the rain forest are called the canopy.* —**canopied** *adj.*

canst /kənst; *strong* kænst/ *v.* **thou canst** OLD USE used to mean "you can" when talking to one person

can't /kænt/ *v.* **1** the short form of "cannot": *Sorry, I can't help you.* | *We can't afford a gardener.* **2** used as the opposite of "must," to say that something is impossible or unlikely: *You can't miss it – there's a huge Santa Claus in the front yard.*

cant¹ /kænt/ *n.* **1** [U] FORMAL insincere talk about moral or religious principles by someone who is pretending to be better than they really are: *His viewpoint is remarkably free of idealism or cant.* **2** [C,U] FORMAL special words used by a particular group of people, especially in order to keep things secret **3** [C] a sloping surface or angle

cant² *v.* [I,T] to lean, or make something lean: *The controls are canted toward the driver.*

can·ta·loupe /'kæntl,oup/ *n.* [C,U] a type of MELON with a hard green skin and sweet orange flesh —see picture at FRUIT¹

can·tan·ker·ous /kæn'tæŋkərəs/ *adj.* someone who is cantankerous is easily annoyed, difficult to be friends with, and complains a lot: *Brooks is the committee's cantankerous chairman.* —**cantankerously** *adv.* —**cantankerousness** *n.* [U]

can·ta·ta /kən'tɑtə/ *n.* [C] a piece of religious music sung by a CHOIR and single performers

can·teen /kæn'tin/ *n.* [C] **1** a small container for carrying water or other drinks, used especially by soldiers, HIKERS, or travelers **2** a store or place where people in the army, navy etc. can buy things or go to be entertained **3** a place in a factory, school etc. where meals are provided, usually cheap meals; CAFETERIA

can·ter¹ /'kæntə/ *v.* [I,T] to ride or make a horse run fairly fast, but not as fast as possible

canter² *n.* **1** [singular] the movement of a horse when it is running fairly fast, but not as fast as possible **2** [C] a ride on a horse at this speed

can·ti·cle /'kæntɪkəl/ *n.* [C] a short religious song, usually using words from the Bible

can·ti·le·ver /'kæntə,livə/ *n.* [C] a beam that sticks out from an upright post or wall and supports a shelf, the end of a bridge etc.

can·to /'kæntou/ *n.* **plural cantos** [C] one of the parts into which a very long poem is divided

can·ton /'kæntən/ *n.* [C] one of the areas with limited political powers that make up a country such as Switzerland

can·ton·ment /kæn'tɑnmənt/ *n.* [C] TECHNICAL a camp for soldiers

can·tor /'kæntə/ *n.* [C] **1** a man who leads the prayers and songs in a Jewish religious service **2** the leader of a CHOIR in some churches

Ca·nuck /kə'nʌk/ *n.* [C] INFORMAL a person from Canada

can·vas /'kænvəs/ *n.* **1** [U] a type of strong cloth used to make bags, tents, shoes etc. **2** [C] a painting done with oil paints, or the piece of cloth it is painted on

can·vass /'kænvəs/ *v.* **1** [I,T] to try to get information about something or support for something, especially a political party, by going from place to place within an area and talking to people: *Police canvassed the neighborhood but didn't find anyone who knew the man.* **2** [T] to talk about a problem, suggestion etc. in detail: *The suggestion is being widely canvassed as a possible solution to the dispute.* —**canvass** *n.* [C] —**canvasser** *n.* [C]

can·yon /'kænyən/ *n.* [C] a deep valley with very steep sides of rock that usually has a river running through it: *the Grand Canyon*

C

can·yon·ing /ˈkænyənɪŋ/ n. [U] the sport of swimming or floating along fast-flowing rivers in a CANYON

sw **cap**[1] /kæp/ n. [C]
1 hat **a)** a type of soft flat hat that has a curved part sticking out at the front: *a baseball cap* **b)** a covering that fits very closely to your head and is worn for a particular purpose: *a shower cap* **c)** a special type of hat that is worn with a particular uniform or by a particular group of people: *a nurse's cap* —see also STOCKING CAP
2 top/covering a protective covering that you put on the end or top of an object: *the lens cap for a camera* | *a bottle cap* —see also ICE CAP, TOECAP
3 limit an upper limit that is put on the amount of money that someone can earn, spend, or borrow: *Proposition 13 put a cap on property taxes.*
4 small explosive a small paper container with explosive inside it, used especially in toy guns
5 go cap in hand (to sb) to ask someone for something, especially money, in a very polite way that makes you seem unimportant: *Advertisers used to go to museums, cap in hand, to ask permission to use a painting for an advertisement.* —see also a **feather in your cap** (FEATHER[1] (2)), KNEECAP, **put on your thinking cap** (THINKING[1] (2))

cap[2] v. **capped, capping** [T] **1** to be the last and usually best thing that happens in a game, situation etc.: *Payton capped the game with three baskets in the final minute.* **2** to limit the amount of something, especially money, that can be used, allowed, or spent: *Some state colleges have capped enrollment for budgetary reasons.* **3** to cover the top of something: *The chain-link fence is capped with barbed wire.* | *snow-capped mountains* **4** to cover a tooth with a special hard white surface **5 to cap it all (off)** SPOKEN used before describing the worst, best, funniest etc. part at the end of a story or description: *I had a terrible day at work, and to cap it all off I got a flat tire.* **6** SLANG to shoot someone with a gun

cap. **1** also **caps.** the written abbreviation of "capital letter" **2** the written abbreviation of CAPACITY (1)

Cap·a /ˈkæpə/, **Rob·ert** /ˈrɑbət/ (1913–1954) a U.S. war PHOTOGRAPHER

ca·pa·bil·i·ty /ˌkeɪpəˈbɪləti/ n. plural **capabilities** [C] **1** the natural ability, skill, or power that makes a machine, person, or organization able to do something, especially something difficult: *The patrol plane has an infrared capability, so that searches can be made in the dark.* | [**the capability to do sth**] *The region had the capability to export two million barrels of oil per day.* | *I think the job was just beyond her capabilities.* (=too difficult) **2** the ability that a country has to take a particular kind of military action: *The country is nearing the capability to produce nuclear weapons.*

sw **ca·pa·ble** /ˈkeɪpəbəl/ adj. **1 be capable of (doing) sth** having the skills, power, intelligence etc. needed to do something: *These computerized weapons are capable of hitting almost any target.* | *We're definitely capable of playing much better than we are right now.* **2** skillful and effective, because you are very good at doing something: *a strong, capable woman* —**capably** adv.

ca·pa·cious /kəˈpeɪʃəs/ adj. FORMAL able to contain a lot: *a capacious theater* —**capaciousness** n. [U]

ca·pac·i·tor /kəˈpæsətə/ n. [C] a piece of equipment that collects and stores electricity for a short time

sw **ca·pac·i·ty** /kəˈpæsəti/ n. plural **capacities** **1** [singular, U] the amount of space a container, room etc. has to hold things or people: *The car's fold-down rear seat increases the trunk capacity.* | [+ of] *The theater had a seating capacity of 1,400 people.* | *Capacity crowds* (=people filling all the seats in a room, hall etc.) *are expected at the Christmas program.* | *Long-term parking spaces at the airport are expected to **fill to capacity** (=be completely full).* **2** [C,U] someone's ability to do something: [+ for] *The movie's characters show a capacity for change as the plot moves forward.* | [**capacity to do sth**] *The right person for the job must show a capacity to work independently.* **3** [singular] FORMAL someone's job, position, or duty; ROLE (3): *Rollins will be working in an advisory capacity on this project.* | [**do sth in your capacity as sth**] *Quan will continue to serve in his present capacity as treasurer.* **4** [singular,U] the amount of something that a factory, company, machine etc. can produce or deal with: *The company has the capacity to build 7 million cars a year.* | *The reactor had been operating at full capacity.*

ca·par·i·soned /kəˈpærəsənd/ adj. in MEDIEVAL times a caparisoned horse was one covered in a decorated cloth

cape /keɪp/ n. [C] **1** a long loose piece of clothing without SLEEVES, that fastens around your neck and hangs from your shoulders: *a black cape with a red stripe down the back* **2** a large piece of land surrounded on three sides by water: *Cape Cod*

Cape Ca·nav·er·al /ˌkeɪp kəˈnævrəl/ a CAPE (2) in the U.S. state of Florida which is famous for the Kennedy Space Center, where U.S. SPACECRAFT are sent into space. Cape Canaveral was formerly called Cape Kennedy. —see picture on page 1328

Cape Horn /ˌ. ˈ./ a PENINSULA at the southern end of South America, where the Atlantic Ocean meets the Pacific Ocean

Cape of Good Hope, the /ˌ. ... ˈ./ a PENINSULA at the southwestern end of South Africa, where the Atlantic Ocean meets the Indian Ocean

ca·per[1] /ˈkeɪpə/ n. [C] **1** a small dark green part of a flower used in cooking to give a sour taste to food **2** a planned activity, especially an illegal or dangerous one: *Stealing an inflatable King Kong may have been a student caper.* **3** a movie or story that is full of action, especially one about an activity that is illegal or dangerous: *This buddy/action caper will be released in December.* **4** a trick that is intended to make someone look silly **5** a short jumping or dancing movement

caper[2] v. [I always + adv./prep.] to jump around and play in a happy, excited way: *The dancers capered across the stage.*

Ca·pet /ˈkeɪpət, ˈkæ-, kæˈpeɪ/ the name of a family of French kings who ruled from 987 to 1328

Cape Verde /ˌkeɪp ˈvəd/ a country that consists of a group of islands in the Atlantic Ocean, West of Senegal —**Cape Verdean** n., adj.

cap·il·lar·y /ˈkæpəˌleri/ n. plural **capillaries** [C] **1** the smallest type of BLOOD VESSEL (=tube carrying blood) in the body —compare ARTERY (1), VEIN (1) **2** a very small tube as thin as a hair

capillary ac·tion /ˌ.... ˈ./ also **capillary at·trac·tion** /ˌ.... ˈ.../ n. [U] TECHNICAL the force that makes a liquid rise up a narrow tube

sw **cap·i·tal**[1] /ˈkæpətl/ n.
1 city [C] an important city where the main government of a country, state etc. is: *Albany is the capital of New York State.*
2 financial [U] money or property, especially when it is used to start a business or to produce more wealth: *Raley started a grocery business in the 1930s with $1000 in capital.* —see also VENTURE CAPITAL, WORKING CAPITAL
3 center of activity [C usually singular] a place that is a center for an industry, business, or other activity: [+ of] *Hollywood is the capital of the movie industry.*
4 letter [C] a letter of the alphabet written in its large form, for example at the beginning of a sentence or someone's name: *Please fill in your name and address in capitals.* —compare LOWER CASE
5 make capital out of/from sth to use a situation or event to help you get an advantage: *Johnson made political capital from his war career.*
6 building TECHNICAL the top part of a COLUMN (=a long stone post used in some buildings)

sw **capital**[2] adj. **1** relating to money or property that you use to start a business or to make more money: *The recycling industry is making huge capital investments* *in equipment.* **2** a capital letter is one that is written or printed in its large form, used for example at the beginning of a sentence or someone's name: *The company's logo is a large capital "B."* —compare LOWER CASE **3 a capital offense/crime etc.** an offense, crime etc. that may be punished by death **4** OLD-FASHIONED, SPOKEN excellent

capital as·sets /ˌ... '../ *n.* [plural] TECHNICAL machines, buildings, and other property belonging to a company

capital gains /ˌ... './ *n.* [plural] profits that you make by selling STOCKS, property, or possessions

capital gains tax /ˌ... '. ˌ./ *n.* [C] a tax that you pay on the profit you make when selling property etc.

capital goods /ˌ... './ *n.* [plural] goods such as machines or buildings that are made for the purpose of producing other goods —compare CONSUMER GOODS

capital·in·ten·sive /ˌ... .'..◂/ *adj.* a capital-intensive business, industry etc. needs a lot of money for it to operate well —compare LABOR-INTENSIVE

cap·i·tal·ism /ˈkæpəţlˌɪzəm/ *n.* [U] an economic and political system in which businesses belong mostly to private owners, not to the government —compare COMMUNISM, SOCIALISM

cap·i·tal·ist¹ /ˈkæpəţl-ɪst/ *n.* [C] **1** someone who owns or controls a lot of money and lends it to businesses, banks etc. to produce more wealth —see also VENTURE CAPITAL **2** someone who supports capitalism: *the capitalists of the West* —compare COMMUNIST¹ (1), SOCIALIST²

capitalist² also **cap·i·ta·lis·tic** /ˌkæpəţlˈɪstɪk/ *adj* using or supporting capitalism: *the seven richest capitalist countries*

cap·i·tal·ize /ˈkæpəţlˌaɪz/ *v.* [T] **1** to write or TYPE² (2) a letter of the alphabet using a CAPITAL letter: *Be sure to capitalize the first word of every sentence.* **2** [usually passive] TECHNICAL to supply a business with money so that it can operate: *There are a number of highly capitalized industries with imported technology in the north.* **3** [usually passive] TECHNICAL to calculate the value of a business based on the value of its STOCK or on the amount of money it makes: *The store's Japanese branches are capitalized at 2.8 million yen.* —**capitalization** /ˌkæpəţləˈzeɪʃən/ *n.* [U]

> **capitalize on** sth *phr. v.* [T] to get as much advantage out of a situation, event etc. as you can: *The Bulls managed to capitalize on the mistakes Houston made.*

capital mar·ket /ˈ... ˌ../ *n.* [C] TECHNICAL a place where businesses borrow money from other businesses such as banks and insurance companies

capital pun·ish·ment /ˌ... '...'/ *n.* [U] the punishment of legally killing someone for a crime after they have been found guilty in a court of law —compare DEATH PENALTY

cap·i·tol /ˈkæpəţl/ *n.* **1 the Capitol** the building in Washington, D.C., where the U.S. Congress meets **2** [C] the building in each U.S. state where the people who make laws for that state meet

Capitol Hill /ˌ... './ *n.* **1** the U.S. Congress **2** the hill in Washington, D.C. where the Capitol building stands

ca·pit·u·late /kəˈpɪtʃəˌleɪt/ *v.* [I] **1** to accept or agree to something that you have been opposing for a long time: [+ to] *Management finally capitulated to the union's demands.* **2** FORMAL to accept defeat by your enemies in a war; SURRENDER¹ (1) —**capitulation** /kəˌpɪtʃəˈleɪʃən/ *n.* [C,U]

cap·let /ˈkæplɪt/ *n.* [C] a small smooth PILL (=solid piece of medicine) with a shape that is slightly longer and narrower than a TABLET

ca·pon /ˈkeɪpɑn/ *n.* [C] a male chicken that has had its sex organs removed to make it grow big and fat

Ca·pone /kəˈpoʊn/, **Al** /æl/ (1899–1947) a U.S. GANG-STER (=criminal who works in a violent group), who was the leader of ORGANIZED CRIME in Chicago

Ca·po·te /kəˈpoʊti/, **Tru·man** /ˈtrumən/ (1924–1984) a U.S. writer or novels and short stories

Truman Capote

cap·puc·ci·no /ˌkæpəˈtʃinoʊ, ˌkɑ-/ *n. plural* **cappuccinos** [C,U] a drink made of ESPRESSO (=strong coffee) with hot milk on top, served in a small cup

Cap·ra /ˈkæprə/, **Frank** (1897–1991) a U.S. movie DIRECTOR

C

ca·price /kəˈpris/ *n.* LITERARY **1** [C] a sudden and unreasonable change in someone's opinion or behavior: *the caprices of a spoiled child* **2** [U] the tendency to change your mind suddenly or behave in an unexpected way

ca·pri·cious /kəˈprɪʃəs/ *adj.* **1** FORMAL done or used in a way that does not always seem to be reasonable: *Employees need legal protection against capricious and unfair actions by their employers.* **2** FORMAL likely to change your opinion suddenly or do things for no particular reason: *the capricious tastes of children* **3** LITERARY changing quickly and suddenly: *a capricious wind* —**capriciously** *adv.*

Cap·ri·corn /ˈkæprɪˌkɔrn/ *n.* **1** [U] the tenth sign of the ZODIAC, represented by a goat and believed to affect the character and life of people born between December 22 and January 19 **2** [C] someone who was born between December 22 and January 19: *Greg's a Capricorn.*

cap·si·cum /ˈkæpsɪkəm/ *n.* [C,U] TECHNICAL a type of PEPPER (=a hollow green, red, or yellow vegetable)

cap·size /ˈkæpsaɪz, kæpˈsaɪz/ *v.* [I,T] if a boat capsizes or if you capsize it, it turns over in the water

cap·stan /ˈkæpstən, -stæn/ *n.* [C] **1** a round machine shaped like a drum, used to wind up a rope that pulls or lifts heavy objects **2** a round part in a TAPE RECORDER that spins around to move the TAPE in a CASSETTE

cap·stone /ˈkæpstoʊn/ *n.* [C] **1** the last and usually best thing that someone achieves: *An appointment to the Supreme Court was the capstone of his career.* **2** a stone at the top of a building, wall etc.

cap·sule¹ /ˈkæpsəl/ *n.* [C] **1** a small closed tube with medicine inside that you swallow whole —see picture at MEDICATION **2** the part of a SPACECRAFT in which people live and work —see also TIME CAPSULE

capsule² *adj.* [only before noun] a capsule description, account etc. is short and includes only the most important details: *a capsule review of the latest movies*

Capt. the written abbreviation of "captain"

cap·tain¹ /ˈkæptən/ *n.* [C] **1** someone who commands a ship or aircraft **2** a military officer with a fairly high rank **3** someone who leads a team or other group of people: *Shauna's the captain of the volleyball team.* **4 a captain of industry** [usually plural] someone who owns an important company or has an important job at a large company

captain² *v.* [T] **1** to lead a group or team of people: *The Americans, captained by Arthur Ashe, won the Davis Cup.* **2** to be in charge of a ship, aircraft etc.

cap·tain·cy /ˈkæptənsi/ also **cap·tain·ship** /ˈkæptənˌʃɪp/ *n.* [U] the position of being captain of a team, or the period during which someone is captain

cap·tion¹ /ˈkæpʃən/ *n.* [C] words printed above or below a picture in a book or newspaper or on a television screen to explain what the picture is showing

caption² *v.* [T usually passive] to print words above or below a picture in a book or newspaper to explain what the picture is showing: *The photo was captioned, "Residents watch as firefighters struggle to put out the blaze."*

C

cap·tious /ˈkæpʃəs/ adj. LITERARY always criticizing unimportant things

cap·ti·vate /ˈkæptəˌveɪt/ v. [T often passive] to attract or interest someone very much: *I was captivated by her smile.*

cap·ti·vat·ing /ˈkæptəˌveɪtɪŋ/ adj. very attractive or interesting: *a captivating smile | a captivating account of his childhood*

cap·tive¹ /ˈkæptɪv/ adj. **1** [only before noun] unable to move around freely because of being kept in prison or in a small space: *captive soldiers | the breeding of captive animals* **2 take/hold sb captive** to take or keep someone as a prisoner: *The men were held captive in an abandoned garage for three days.* **3 a captive audience** people who listen or watch someone or something because they have to, not because they are interested **4 be captive to sth** to be unable to think or speak freely because of being influenced too much by another group or organization: *We want to cooperate with leading manufacturers without being captive to them.* **5 captive market** a situation in which people cannot choose between different types of a product or service, especially because there is only one person or company selling it

captive² n. [C] **1** someone who is kept as a prisoner, especially in a war **2 a captive of sth** someone who is not able to think or speak freely because they are influenced too much by another group or organization: *All of the top candidates for mayor are captives of the political establishment.*

cap·tiv·i·ty /kæpˈtɪvəti/ n. [U] the state of being kept as a prisoner, in a CAGE etc. and not allowed to go where you want: *Wilson was released from captivity just before the end of the war. | Many animals do not breed well **in captivity** (=when kept in a cage).*

cap·tor /ˈkæptər/ n. [C] someone who is keeping another person prisoner: *Mann was finally freed by his captors.*

cap·ture¹ /ˈkæptʃər/ v. [T]
1 **person** to catch someone in order to make them a prisoner: *Rebels wounded 1087 soldiers and captured 417.*
2 **place** to get control of a place that previously belonged to an enemy by fighting for it: *The town of Moulineuf was captured after a siege lasting ten days.*
3 **business/politics/sports** to get something or a share of something in a situation in which you are competing against other people, such as business, an election, or a sport: *Mayor Agnos captured 28.7% of the vote. | The Super Bowl always captures a large audience. | Cuba captured the first gold medal of the Olympic Games.*
4 **animal** to catch an animal after chasing or following it: *Many dolphins are accidentally captured in the nets of tuna fishermen.*
5 **book/painting/movie** to succeed in showing or describing a situation or feeling using words or pictures, so that other people can see, understand, or experience it: *Wilson's autobiography neatly captures the atmosphere of the late 19th century. | The TV camera captured Dad waving as he left the airplane.*
6 capture sb's imagination/attention etc. to make someone feel very interested and attracted: *Armstrong's landing on the moon captured the imagination of a generation.* —compare CAPTIVATE
7 capture sb's heart to seem attractive to someone so that they love you
8 **computers** TECHNICAL to put something in a form that a computer can use: *The data is captured by an optical scanner.*
9 **chess** to remove one of your opponent's PIECES from the board in CHESS

capture² n. **1** [U] the act of catching someone in order to make them a prisoner: *The government has offered $500,000 for information leading to Sanchez' capture. | avoid/evade/elude capture (=to avoid being captured)* **2 the capture of Rome/Jerusalem etc.** the act of getting control of a place that previously belonged to an enemy

car /kɑr/ n. [C] **1** a vehicle with four wheels and an engine, that you use to travel from one place to another: *Cars are parked on both sides of the road. | You can take my car to work today if you need to. | We decided to go across the U.S. **by car**.* **2** one of the connected parts of a train that people sit in or that goods are carried in: *I stayed in the dining car, drinking a glass of red wine.* **3** the part of an ELEVATOR in which people or goods are carried

Ca·ra·cas /kəˈrɑkəs/ the capital and largest city of Venezuela

ca·rafe /kəˈræf/ n. [C] **1** a glass container with a wide neck, used for serving wine or water at meals **2** a glass coffee pot that is part of an electric coffee maker

car alarm /ˈ. .ˌ./ n. [C] a special system for protecting cars against thieves, that makes a loud noise if anyone touches the car

car·a·mel /ˈkærəməl, -ˌmɛl, ˈkɑrməl/ n. **1** [C,U] a brown candy made of sticky boiled sugar and milk or cream **2** [U] burned sugar, used for giving food a special taste and color

car·a·mel·ize /ˈkærəməˌlaɪz, ˈkɑr-/ v. [I,T] if food caramelizes or is caramelized, the sugar in it burns slightly so that its color and taste change

car·a·pace /ˈkærəˌpeɪs/ n. [C] TECHNICAL a hard shell on the outside of some animals such as TURTLES or CRABS, that protects them

car·at /ˈkærət/ n. [C] a unit for measuring the weight of jewels, equal to 200 MILLIGRAMS —compare KARAT

Ca·ra·vag·gio, Mi·chel·an·ge·lo Me·ri·si da /ˌkɑrəˈvɑdʒou, -ˈvæ-, ˌmikəlˈændʒəlou məˈrisi də/ (1573–1610) an Italian PAINTER famous for his use of light and shadow in his paintings in the BAROQUE style

car·a·van /ˈkærəˌvæn/ n. [C] a group of people with animals or vehicles who are traveling together over a long distance, for example across a desert

car·a·van·se·rai /ˌkærəˈvænsəraɪ/ n. [C] LITERARY a hotel with a large open central area, used in the past in Middle Eastern countries by groups of people and animals traveling together

car·a·way /ˈkærəˌweɪ/ n. [U] a plant whose strong-tasting seeds are used to give a special taste to food

car·bine /ˈkɑrbaɪn/ n. [C] a short light RIFLE (=type of gun)

car·bo·hy·drate /ˌkɑrbouˈhaɪdreɪt, -drɪt, -bə-/ n. **1** TECHNICAL [C,U] one of several food substances such as sugar which consist of oxygen, HYDROGEN, and CARBON (1), and which provide your body with heat and energy **2 carbohydrates** [plural] foods such as rice, bread, and potatoes that contain carbohydrates

car·bol·ic a·cid /kɑrˌbɑlɪk ˈæsɪd/ n. [U] a liquid that kills BACTERIA, used for preventing the spread of disease or infection

car bomb /ˈ. ./ n. [C] a bomb hidden inside a car or stuck underneath it

car·bon /ˈkɑrbən/ n. **1** [U] symbol **C** a simple substance that is an ELEMENT and that exists in a pure form as DIAMONDS, GRAPHITE etc., or in an impure form as coal, gasoline etc. **2** [C,U] CARBON PAPER **3** [C] a CARBON COPY (1)

car·bon·at·ed /ˈkɑrbəˌneɪtɪd/ adj. carbonated drinks have a lot of small BUBBLES in them: *carbonated spring water* —**carbonation** /ˌkɑrbəˈneɪʃən/ n. [U]

carbon cop·y /ˌ.. ˈ../ n. plural **carbon copies** [C] **1** a copy, especially of something that has been TYPEd (TYPE² (1)), made using CARBON PAPER **2** someone or something that is very similar to another person or thing: [+ of] *Mozer is a carbon copy of Jane Pryce: same policies, same ideas.*

carbon dat·ing /ˈ.. ˌ../ n. [U] a method used by scientists to find out the age of very old objects

carbon di·ox·ide /ˌkɑrbən daɪˈɑksaɪd/ n. [U] abbreviation CO_2 the gas produced when animals and people breathe out, when carbon is burned in air, or when animal or vegetable substances decay

car·bon·if·er·ous /ˌkɑrbəˈnɪfərəs/ adj. TECHNICAL producing or containing carbon or coal: *carboniferous rocks*

car·bon·ize /ˈkɑrbəˌnaɪz/ v. [I,T] to change or make

something change into CARBON (1) by burning without air —**carbonized** *adj.*

carbon mon·ox·ide /ˌkɑrbən məˈnɑksaɪd/ *n.* [U] *abbreviation* **CO** a poisonous gas that is produced when CARBON (1), especially gasoline, burns in a small amount of air

carbon pap·er /ˈ.. ˌ../ *n.* [C] thin paper with a blue or black substance on one side, that you put between sheets of paper when writing with a TYPEWRITER, in order to make copies

Car·bo·run·dum /ˌkɑrbəˈrʌncəm/ *n.* [U] TRADEMARK an extremely hard substance made from CARBON and SILICON, used for polishing things

car·boy /ˈkɑrbɔɪ/ *n.* [C] TECHNICAL a large round bottle used for holding dangerous chemical liquids

carbs /kɑrbz/ *n.* [plural] SPOKEN INFORMAL foods such as rice, bread, and potatoes that contain CARBOHYDRATES: *Before a race, I make sure I eat plenty of carbs.*

car·bun·cle /ˈkɑrbʌŋkəl/ *n.* [C] **1** a large painful LUMP under someone's skin **2** LITERARY a red jewel, especially a GARNET

car·bu·re·tor /ˈkɑrbəˌreɪtə/ *n.* [C] a part of a car engine that mixes the gasoline that burns in the engine with air to provide power —see picture at ENGINE

car·cass /ˈkɑrkəs/ *n.* [C] **1** the body of a dead animal, especially one that is ready to be cut up as meat **2** the main structure of a building, ship etc.: *The ferry's carcass lies 220 feet underwater, on the floor of the Baltic Sea.* **3** sb's carcass SPOKEN someone's body, used especially when talking about someone who is tired or lazy: *Get your carcass out of my chair!*

car·cin·o·gen /kɑrˈsɪnədʒən/ *n.* [C] a substance that can cause CANCER

car·cin·o·gen·ic /ˌkɑrsɪnəˈdʒɛnɪk/ *adj.* likely to cause CANCER: *Blue asbestos is known to be highly carcinogenic.*

car·ci·no·ma /ˌkɑrsəˈnoumə/ *n.* [C] TECHNICAL an abnormal growth in the body caused by CANCER

card¹ /kɑrd/ *n.* [C]

1 **a library/membership/identity etc. card** a small piece of plastic or paper that shows who someone is, or shows that someone belongs to a particular organization, club etc.: *Employees must show their ID cards at the gate.* —see also GREEN CARD

2 birthday/christmas etc. a piece of thick stiff paper with a picture on the front, that you send to people on special occasions: *I need to send a card to Mom for Mother's Day.* | *a birthday card* —see also GREETING CARD

3 bank a small piece of plastic that you use to pay for goods or to get money from a special machine at a bank: *Lost or stolen cards must be reported immediately.* —see also CHARGE CARD, CREDIT CARD

4 vacation a card with a photograph or picture on one side, that you send to someone when you are on vacation; POSTCARD: *I got a card from Henry; he's in Colorado.*

5 games one of a set of 52 small piece of stiff paper with numbers or pictures on them, that are used for playing games: *We spent the entire evening playing cards* (=playing a game with cards) *and drinking.* | *a new deck of cards* (=set of cards)

6 information a small piece of stiff paper or plastic that shows information about someone or something, especially one that is part of a set used for storing information: *a recipe card* | *a card file*

7 **baseball/sports etc. card** a small piece of thick stiff paper with a picture of a baseball player etc. on one side and details about that player's CAREER on the other, that is part of a set which people collect

8 business a small piece of thick stiff paper that shows your name, job, and the company you work for; BUSINESS CARD: *Mr. Kim gave me his card and told me to call him.* —see also CALLING CARD

9 **be in the cards** to seem likely to happen: *The increase in price has been in the cards for some time.*

10 **put/lay your cards on the table** to tell people what your plans and intentions are in a clear, honest way after keeping them secret for some time: *They're willing to put all their cards on the table and negotiate.*

11 **your strong/strongest/best card** something that gives you a big advantage in a particular situation: *The promise of tax cuts proved to be the Republicans' best card.* —see also **your trump card** (TRUMP¹ (3))

12 computer [C] the thing inside a computer that the CHIPs are attached to, that allows the computer to perform specific operations

13 **play/keep/hold your cards close to your chest** also **play/keep/hold your cards close to your vest** to keep your plans, thoughts, or feelings secret: *The chairman is holding his cards close to his chest on the question of a merger.*

14 **hold all the cards** INFORMAL to have all the advantages in a particular situation so that you can control what happens: *In areas such as research, larger well-financed firms hold all the cards.*

15 **have a/another card up your sleeve** to have an advantage that you have been keeping secret, that you can use to be successful in a particular situation

16 person [usually singular] OLD-FASHIONED an amusing or unusual person: *Harold was always such a card!*

17 tool TECHNICAL a tool that is similar to a comb and is used for COMBing, cleaning and preparing wool or cotton for SPINning —see also **play your cards right** (PLAY¹ (15))

card² *v.* **1** [I,T] to ask someone to show a card proving that they are old enough to be in a particular place, especially a bar, or old enough to buy alcohol or cigarettes: *Clerks are supposed to card everyone buying alcohol who looks under 30.* **2** [T] to comb, clean, and prepare wool or cotton, before making cloth

car·da·mom /ˈkɑrdəməm/ *n.* [U] the seeds of an Asian fruit, used to give a special taste to Indian and Middle Eastern food

card·board¹ /ˈkɑrdbɔrd/ *n.* [U] a thick usually brown material like stiff paper, used especially for making boxes

cardboard² *adj.* **1** made from cardboard: *a cardboard box* **2** [only before noun] seeming silly and not real: *Most of these romantic novels are full of cardboard characters.*

cardboard cut·out /ˌ.. ˈ../ *n.* [C] **1** a picture drawn on cardboard and cut so that its shape follows the edges of the picture, with something attached to the back so that it can stand up on a surface **2** a person or character in a book, movie etc. who seems silly or unreal

card-car·ry·ing /ˈ. ˌ.../ *adj.* **a card-carrying member/Republican/liberal etc.** USUALLY DISAPPROVING someone who has paid money to an organization and is an involved member of it: *a card-carrying member of the ACLU*

card cat·a·log /ˌ. ˈ../ *n.* [C] a box of cards that contain information about something, especially about the books in a library, and are arranged in order

card·hold·er /ˈkɑrdˌhouldə/ *n.* [C] someone who has a CREDIT CARD

car·di·ac /ˈkɑrdiˌæk/ *adj.* [only before noun] TECHNICAL connected with the heart: *Patients with cardiac problems should avoid foods that are high in salt.*

cardiac ar·rest /ˌ... .ˈ./ *n.* [U] TECHNICAL a serious medical condition in which the heart stops beating; a HEART ATTACK

Car·diff /ˈkɑrdɪf/ the capital and largest city of Wales

car·di·gan /ˈkɑrdəgən/ also **cardigan sweat·er** /ˈ... ˌ../ *n.* [C] a SWEATER that is fastened at the front with buttons

car·di·nal¹ /ˈkɑrdn-əl, -nəl/ *n.* [C] **1** a priest of very high rank in the Catholic church **2** a North American bird, the male of which is a bright red color —see picture on page 429 **3** a CARDINAL NUMBER

cardinal² *adj.* [only before noun] very important or basic: *Having clean hands is one of the cardinal rules of food preparation.*

cardinal num·ber /,... '../ *n.* [C] a number such as 1, 2, or 3, that shows the quantity of something —compare ORDINAL NUMBER

cardinal sin /,... '../ *n.* [C] **1** something bad or stupid that you must avoid doing: *Senators who commit the cardinal sin of ignoring public opinion will soon be out of office.* **2** TECHNICAL a serious SIN in the Christian religion

cardinal vir·tue /,... '../ *n.* [C] FORMAL a moral quality that someone has which people greatly respect or value

cardio- /kɑrdioʊ, -diə/ *prefix* TECHNICAL concerning the heart: *a cardiograph* (=instrument that measures movements of the heart)

car·di·ol·o·gy /,kɑrdi'ɑlədʒi/ *n.* [U] the study or science of the heart —**cardiologist** *n.* [C]

car·di·o·pul·mo·nar·y /,kɑrdioʊ'pʊlmənɛri/ *adj.* [only before noun] TECHNICAL relating to the heart and the lungs

cardiopulmonary re·sus·ci·ta·tion /,...,.... .,..'../ *n.* [U] TECHNICAL: see CPR

car·di·o·vas·cu·lar /,kɑrdioʊ'væskyələ/ *adj.* TECHNICAL relating to the heart and the BLOOD VESSELS

card shark also **card sharp** /'. ./ *n.* [C] someone who cheats when playing cards in order to make money

card ta·ble /'. ,../ *n.* [C] a small light table with legs that you can fold, used for playing cards

care¹ /kɛr/ *v.* [I,T] **1** objects/events to feel that something is important, so that you are interested in it, worried about it etc.: [+ about] *Children care about the environment and want to help keep it clean.* | [care who/what/whether etc.] *I don't care whether we win or lose.* **2** people to be concerned about what happens to someone, because you like or love them: *She felt that nobody cared.* | *Some kids' parents don't care what they do.* | [+ about] *Just listening to somebody shows you care about them.* —see also CARING (1) **3 not care to do sth** to not like or want to do something: *It's not something I care to discuss.* | *Wyatt's old friends didn't care to visit, with a baby in the house.* **4 more...than sb cares to admit/remember etc.** used when something happens or is done more times than you think is acceptable: *Mistakes happen more often than doctors would care to admit.* | *That old bike's been in the basement for longer than I care to remember.*

SPOKEN PHRASES

5 who cares? used to say in an impolite or informal way that something does not worry or upset you, because you think it is not important: *So your house isn't perfectly clean. Who cares?*
6 I/he/they etc. couldn't care less also **I/he etc. could care less** NONSTANDARD used to say in an impolite way that you do not care at all about something: *I couldn't care less about the Super Bowl.*
7 what do I/you/they etc. care? used to say in an impolite way that someone does not care at all about something: *What does he care? He'll get his money whatever happens.*
8 for all sb cares used to emphasize that something does not matter at all to someone: *"Dave's moving to Boston." "He can move to Timbuktu, for all I care."*
9 would you care to do sth? FORMAL used to ask someone politely whether they want to do something: *Would you care to comment on that, Senator?*

care for sb/sth *phr. v.* [T] **1** to help someone who is old, sick, weak etc. and not able to do things for themselves: *Angie cared for her mother after her stroke.* | *The children are being well cared for in foster homes.* **2** to do things to keep something in good condition or working correctly: *Instructions on caring for your new sofa are in the brochure.* **3 not care for** sb to not like someone: *I don't really care for Jeff's parents.* **4 would you care for sth?** FORMAL used to politely ask someone if they want something: *Would you care for a drink?*

care² *n.* **1** helping sb [U] the process of doing things for someone or something, especially because they are weak, sick, old etc. and unable to do things for themselves: *Your father will need constant medical care.* | *All employees have been trained in the care of young children.* —see also CHILD CARE, DAYCARE, HEALTH CARE, INTENSIVE CARE, **tender loving care** (TENDER¹ (5)) **2** keeping sth in good condition [U] the process of doing things to something so that it stays in good condition and works correctly: *skin care lotions* | *With proper care, your washing machine should last for years.* **3** carefulness [U] carefulness to avoid damage, mistakes etc.: *The note on the box read, "Fragile – handle with care."* **4 take care of sb/sth a)** to watch and help someone and be responsible for them: *My mother said she'd take care of Luisa next weekend.* **b)** to keep something in good condition or working correctly: *The class teaches kids how to take care of their bikes.* **c)** to deal with all the work, arrangements etc. that are necessary for something to happen: *Her secretary will take care of the details.* **d)** an expression meaning "to pay for something," used when you want to avoid saying this directly: *Don't worry about the bill; it's taken care of.* **5 take care a)** SPOKEN used when saying goodbye to family and friends **b)** to be careful: *It's very icy, so take care driving home.* | [+ that] *Take care that the milk doesn't get too hot.* | [**take care to do sth**] *Hikers in the desert must take care to drink enough water.* **6 (in) care of sb** *abbreviation* **c/o** used when sending letters to someone at someone else's address: *Send me the package care of my cousins.* **7** problem/worry [C,U] LITERARY something that causes problems and makes you anxious or sad: *Movies set you free from your cares for a while.* | *Harry doesn't have a care in the world* (=does not have any problems or worries).

ca·reen /kə'rin/ *v.* [I always + adv./prep.] to move quickly forward without control, making sudden sideways movements: [+ down/over/around etc.] *Morillo's truck careened down the hillside and burst into flames.*

ca·reer¹ /kə'rɪr/ *n.* [C] **1** a job or profession that you have been trained for and intend to do for several years: *The win was the 250th in Anderson's coaching career.* | *Tina's interested in a career in banking.* | *After 15 years in teaching, I'm ready for a career change* (=I want to start a different job). **2** the period of time in your life that you spend doing a particular activity: *Will spent most of his career as a lawyer.* —see Usage Note at JOB

career² *adj.* **a career soldier/politician/diplomat etc.** someone who intends to be a soldier, politician etc. for most of their life, not just for a particular period of time

career³ *v.* [I always + adv./prep.] LITERARY to move forward very fast and often without control

career coun·sel·or /.'. ,.../ *n.* [C] someone whose job is to give people advice about what jobs and professional training might be appropriate for them —**career counseling** *n.* [U]

ca·reer·ist /kə'rɪrɪst/ *n.* [C] DISAPPROVING someone whose career is more important to them than anything else —**careerist** *adj.* —**careerism** *n.* [U]

career wom·an /.'. ,../ *n.* [C] a woman whose career is very important to her, so that she may not want to get married or have children

care·free /'kɛrfri/ *adj.* having no worries or problems: *a carefree summer vacation* | *carefree and fun-loving youngsters*

care·ful /'kɛrfəl/ *adj.* **1 (be) careful!** SPOKEN used in order to tell someone to think about what they are doing so that something bad does not happen: *Be careful – there's broken glass on the sidewalk.* **2** trying very hard to avoid doing anything wrong or damaging or losing something: *Jen's a very careful driver.* | **[be careful to do sth]** *Be careful to take all your litter with you when you leave a campsite.* | **[+ with]** *Consumers need to be careful with which insurance policies they buy.* | | **[+ about]** *The press ought to be very careful about how information is presented.* | **[be careful (that)]** *Parents must be careful that they don't frighten their children when teaching them to avoid strangers.* | **[careful who/what/how etc.]** *Grandma ought to be more careful who she lets into her apartment.* **3** paying a lot of attention to detail, so that something is done correctly and thoroughly: *Dr. Angelo made a careful examination.* | *Mona's careful planning made the festival a success.* **4 careful with money** not spending more money than you need to: *Napier hopes voters will remember that he's been careful with taxpayers' money.* **5 you can't be too careful** used in order to say that you should do everything possible to avoid problems or danger: *You can't be too careful where computer viruses are concerned.* —**carefulness** *n.* [U]

S W **care·ful·ly** /'kɛrfəli/ *adv.* in a careful way: *The book*
2 *must be handled carefully because of its age.* | **listen/ look/think etc. carefully** *City officials need to listen carefully to citizens' views.* | **examine/consider sth carefully** *It's confusing, but you should consider your options carefully.* | **carefully chosen/planned/controlled etc.** *The study was conducted on a small, carefully selected group.*

care·giv·er /'kɛr,gɪvɚ/ *n.* [C] someone who takes care of a child or sick person

care la·bel /'. ,../ *n.* [C] a small piece of cloth in a piece of clothing that tells you how to wash it

care·less /'kɛrlɪs/ *adj.* **1** not paying enough attention to what you are doing, so that you make mistakes, damage things etc.: *Officials suspect that the fire was started by careless campers.* | *Keaton got careless and left fingerprints at the scene of the crime.* **2** done without much effort or attention to detail: *a careless mistake* **3** natural and not done with any deliberate effort or attention: *He ran a hand through his hair with a careless gesture.* **4 careless of sth** LITERARY deliberately ignoring something: *Careless of the pain, she managed to climb up a 40-foot cliff to safety.* —**carelessly** *adv.* —**carelessness** *n.* [U]

care pack·age /'. ,../ *n.* [C] a package of food, candy etc. that is sent to someone living away from home, especially a student at college

ca·ress¹ /kə'rɛs/ *v.* [T] **1** to gently touch someone in a way that shows you love them: *Stan lovingly caressed my cheek.* **2** POETIC to touch something gently, in a way that seems pleasant or romantic: *Waves caressed the shore.*

caress² *n.* [C] a gentle loving touch

car·et /'kærət/ *n.* [C] TECHNICAL the mark (ʌ) or (ʌ) used in writing and printing to show where something is to be added

care·tak·er /'kɛr,teɪkɚ/ *n.* [C] **1** someone who takes care of a house or land while the person who owns it is not there **2** someone who takes care of other people, especially a teacher, parent, nurse etc. **3 a caretaker administration/government etc.** a government etc. that has power only for a short period of time between the end of one government and the start of another

care·worn /'kɛrwɔrn/ *adj.* looking sad, worried, or anxious: *a careworn face*

car·fare /'kɑrfɛr/ *n.* [U] OLD-FASHIONED the amount of money that it costs to travel on a bus or STREETCAR

car·go /'kɑrgoʊ/ *n. plural* **cargoes** or **cargos** [C,U] the goods being carried in a ship, airplane, truck etc.: *The ship was carrying a cargo of oil-drilling equipment.* | *a cargo plane*

car·hop /'kɑrhɑp/ *n.* [C] someone who carried food to people's cars at a DRIVE-IN restaurant, especially in past times

Car·ib /'kærɪb/ *a* Native American tribe from Central America and the northern area of South America

Car·ib·be·an /,kærɪ'biən, kə'rɪbiən/ *adj.* from or relating to the islands in the Caribbean Sea

Caribbean Sea, the also **the Caribbean** the part

of the western Atlantic Ocean between Central America, South America, and the Caribbean islands

ca·ri·bou /'kærəbu/ *n. plural* **caribou** or **caribous** [C] a North American REINDEER

caricature

car·i·ca·ture¹ /'kærəkətʃɚ, -,tʃʊr/ *n.* **1** [C] a funny drawing of someone that makes them look silly or stupid: *Klein began his career by drawing caricatures of local politicians in the paper.* **2** [C] a description of someone that shows only some parts of their character, especially parts that are silly or funny: *The young man looked like a caricature of a South American polo player.* **3** [U] the skill of making pictures, or writing about people in this way

caricature² *v.* [T] to draw or describe someone in a way that makes them seem silly or stupid: *Many celebrity customers have been caricatured and hung on the restaurant's walls.*

car·i·ca·tur·ist /'kærɪkə,tʃʊrɪst/ *n.* [C] someone who draws or writes caricatures

car·ies /'kɛriz/ *n.* [U] TECHNICAL decay in someone's teeth: *dental caries*

car·il·lon /'kærə,lɑn, -lən/ *n.* [C] a set of bells in a tower that are controlled from a piano KEYBOARD, or a tune played on these bells

car·ing /'kɛrɪŋ/ *adj.* **1** someone who is caring thinks about what other people need or would like, and tries to help them: *Roger's a warm and caring person.* | *a caring family* **2 a caring profession/career** a job that involves helping or taking care of other people, such as being a nurse or teacher

car·jack·ing /'kɑr,dʒækɪŋ/ *n.* [C,U] the crime of using a weapon to force the driver of a car to drive you somewhere or give you their car —**carjacker** *n.* [C] —**carjack** *v.* [T] —compare HIJACKING

car length /'. ./ *n.* [C] a distance that is equal to the length of a car: *Galles had a lead of about eight car lengths at one point in the race.*

car·load /'kɑrloʊd/ *n.* [C] the amount a car or a railroad car can hold: *a carload of kids* | *This year, the railroads carried 1.5 million carloads of chemicals.*

car·mak·er /'kɑr,meɪkɚ/ *n.* [C] a company that makes cars

Car·mel·ite /'kɑrmə,laɪt/ **1** a member of a Christian group of FRIARS **2** a member of a Christian group of MONKS or NUNS

car·mine /'kɑrmaɪn/ *n.* [U] a deep purplish red color —**carmine** *adj.*

car·nage /'kɑrnɪdʒ/ *n.* [U] the killing and wounding of many people, especially in a war: *TV cameras broadcast scenes of terrible carnage to U.S. audiences.*

car·nal /'kɑrnl/ *adj.* **1** relating to the body or sex, used especially in religious language: *carnal desires* **2 carnal knowledge/relations** BIBLICAL OR HUMOROUS sexual activity —**carnally** *adv.*

car·na·tion /kɑr'neɪʃən/ *n.* [C] a white, pink, or red flower that smells sweet and is often worn as a decoration at formal ceremonies

Car·ne·gie /'kɑrnəgi, kɑr'neɪgi/, **An·drew** /'ændru/ (1835–1919) a U.S. BUSINESSMAN who gave money to start many public libraries in the U.S. and for building Carnegie Hall

car·nel·ian /kɑr'niliən/ n. **1** [C,U] a dark red or red-dish-brown stone used in jewelry **2** [U] a dark red or reddish-brown color

car·ni·val /'kɑrnəvəl/ n. **1** [C] a noisy outdoor event at which you can ride on special machines and play games for prizes; FAIR **2** [C] an event held at a school in order to get money to pay for things at the school, in which students and other people play games for prizes; FAIR **3 Carnival** a celebration with dancing, drinking, and a PARADE through the streets, usually held just before the beginning of LENT (=a special period of time in the Christian calendar) —compare MARDI GRAS

car·ni·vore /'kɑrnəvɔr/ n. [C] **1** an animal that eats flesh —compare HERBIVORE, OMNIVORE **2** HUMOROUS someone who eats meat —**carnivorous** /kɑr'nɪvərəs/ adj. —compare VEGETARIAN

car·ny /'kɑrni/ n. plural **carnies** [C] INFORMAL someone who works in a CARNIVAL (1)

car·ob /'kærəb/ n. [U] the fruit of a Mediterranean tree, that tastes similar to chocolate and is sometimes eaten instead of chocolate

car·ol[1] /'kærəl/ also **Christmas carol** n. [C] a traditional Christmas song

carol[2] v. [I] to sing carols or other songs in a cheerful way, often going around in a group to people's houses —**caroler** n. [C]

Car·o·lin·gian /,kærə'lɪndʒən/ the name of a family of French kings who ruled from 751 to 987

car·om /'kærəm/ v. [I] if something caroms off something else, it hits that thing and then quickly moves away from it: [+ off] The puck caromed off Jovanovski's skate and into the net.

ca·rot·id ar·te·ry /kə,rɑtɪd 'ɑrtəri/ n. [C] TECHNICAL one of the two arteries (ARTERY) in your neck, that supply blood to your head

ca·rouse /kə'rauz/ v. [I] LITERARY to drink a lot, be noisy, and have fun —**carousal** n. [C,U]

car·ou·sel, carrousel /,kærə'sɛl/ n. [C] **1** a machine with painted wooden horses on it that turns around and around, which people can ride on for fun; MERRY-GO-ROUND **2** the circular moving belt that you get your bags and suitcases from at an airport **3** a circular piece of equipment that you put SLIDES into, in order to show them on a screen using a SLIDE PROJECTOR

carp[1] /kɑrp/ n. plural **carp** [C] a large fish that lives in lakes and rivers and can be eaten

carp[2] v. [I usually in progressive] to complain about something or criticize someone all the time: [+ about] Flight attendants are used to airplane passengers carping about the food.

car·pal tun·nel syn·drome /,kɑrpəl 'tʌnl ,sɪn-droum/ n. [U] TECHNICAL a medical condition in which someone gets a lot of pain and weakness in their wrist

car·pe di·em /,kɑrpeɪ 'diəm/ interjection a phrase meaning "seize the day," used to tell someone to do what they want to do, and not worry about the future: Carpe diem, Alan. I think you should take the job.

car·pen·ter /'kɑrpəntɚ/ n. [C] someone whose job is building wooden houses and making and repairing wooden objects

car·pen·try /'kɑrpəntri/ n. [U] the skill or work of a carpenter

s w **car·pet**[1] /'kɑrpɪt/ n. **1** [C,U] heavy woven material for covering all of a floor or stairs, or a piece of this material —compare RUG (1) **2 be/get called on the carpet** to be criticized by someone who has a higher rank than you, because you have done something wrong: Demmons was called on the carpet by the Board of Supervisors to explain his excessive spending. **3 a carpet of leaves/flowers etc.** LITERARY a thick layer of leaves etc. —see also MAGIC CARPET, **sweep sth under the rug/carpet** (SWEEP[1] (14))

carpet[2] v. [T] **1** [usually passive] to cover a floor with carpet: The hall was carpeted in a depressing shade of green. **2 be carpeted with grass/flowers** etc. LITERARY to be covered with a thick layer of grass etc.

car·pet·bag /'kɑrpɪt,bæg/ n. [C] OLD-FASHIONED a bag used by someone when they are traveling, usually made of carpet

car·pet·bag·ger /'kɑrpɪt,bægɚ/ n. [C] **1** someone from the Northern U.S. who went to the Southern U.S. after the Civil War of the 1860s in order to get rich, especially in a slightly dishonest or immoral way, without helping the people who lived there **2** someone who moves to a different place in order to help their political CAREER

carpet-bomb /'.. ,./ v. [T] to drop a lot of bombs over a small area to destroy everything in it. —**carpet bombing** n. [C]

car·pet·ing /'kɑrpətɪŋ/ n. [U] a carpet or carpets in general, or heavy woven material used for making CARPETS

carpet sweep·er /'.. ,../ n. [C] a simple machine that does not use electricity, used for sweeping CARPETS

car·pool[1], **car pool** /'kɑrpul/ n. [C] a group of people who travel together to work, school etc. in one car and share the costs

carpool[2], **car-pool** v. [I] if a group of people carpool, they travel together to work, school etc. in one car and share the costs

car·port /'kɑrpɔrt/ n. [C] a shelter for a car that has a roof but no door and sometimes no walls, and is often built against the side of a house —compare GARAGE[1] (1)

car·rel /'kærəl/ n. [C] a small enclosed desk for one person to use in a library

car·riage /'kærɪdʒ/ n. **1** [C] a vehicle with wheels that is pulled by a horse, used in past times —see also BABY CARRIAGE **2** [C] the movable part of a machine that supports another part: [+ of] the carriage of a typewriter **3** [C] something with wheels that is used to move a heavy object, especially a gun **4** [U] FORMAL the way someone walks and moves their head and body

s w **car·ri·er** /'kæriɚ/ n. [C] **1** a company that moves goods or passengers from one place to another, especially by airplane: a carrier with routes to the eastern U.S. **2** someone who carries something, especially as a job: a newspaper carrier | We give a gift to the letter carrier (=person who delivers mail) at Christmas. **3** a military vehicle or ship used to move soldiers, weapons etc. —see also AIRCRAFT CARRIER **4** TECHNICAL someone who passes a disease to other people without having it themselves **5** a company that provides a service such as insurance or telephones

carrier pi·geon /'... ,../ n. [C] a PIGEON (=type of bird) that has been trained to carry messages

car·ri·on /'kæriən/ n. [U] dead flesh that is decaying

Car·roll /'kærəl/, **Lew·is** /'luis/ (1832–1898) a British writer who wrote two very famous children's stories: "Alice's Adventures in Wonderland" and "Through The Looking Glass"

s **car·rot** /'kærət/ n. [C] **1** a plant with a long thick orange pointed root that you eat as a vegetable —see picture at VEGETABLE **2** something that is promised to someone in order to try and persuade them to work harder: One of the carrots that Dad always dangled in front of me (=promised me) was that he was going to send me to college. **3 a carrot-and-stick approach** a way of making someone do something that combines a promise of something good if they do it, and a threat of something bad if they do not do it: On Friday, a federal commission proposed a carrot-and-stick approach to punish and deter corporate crime.

car·rou·sel /,kærə'sɛl/ n. [C] another spelling of CAROUSEL

s **car·ry**[1] /'kæri/ v. **carried, carrying** **1** lift and take [T] to take something somewhere by holding it, supporting it etc.: Would you carry my suitcase for me? | 5000 people carrying banners and signs marched to the Capitol building. | [carry sth

around/out/to etc.] *I carried the bags out to the car.*
—see Usage Note at BRING

2 vehicle/ship/plane [T] to take people or things from one place to another: *We saw a lot of trucks carrying loads of grain.* | **[carry sth to/down/away etc.]** *The train from New York to Tampa normally carries 200 people.*

3 how sth is moved [T] if a pipe, road, wire etc. carries something such as liquid or electricity, the liquid etc. flows along it or on it: *Interstate 5 is carrying 50% more traffic than it did five years ago.* | **[carry sth down/through/across etc.]** *Pipes carry the water across the desert.*

4 store [T] if a store carries goods, it has a supply of them for sale: *Any good hardware store will carry bolts like that.* | *Bigger discount stores carry name-brand merchandise at low prices.*

5 have with you [T] to have something with you in your pocket, on your belt, in your bag etc.: *I don't usually carry that much cash on me.* | *How many teenagers carry guns or knives to school these days?*

6 newspaper/broadcast [T] if a newspaper or a television or radio broadcast carries news, a program, an advertisement etc., it prints it or broadcasts it: *The paper carried the story on the front page.* | *The local cable station carries a broad variety of shows.*

7 label/writing [T] if an object, container etc. carries information such as a warning, those words are written on it: *Ted keeps a card in his wallet that carries details of his blood type.*

8 have a quality [T] to have a particular quality such as authority or confidence that makes people believe or not believe you: *Laura carries an unmistakable air of authority.* | *Greenspan's views usually* **carry** great **weight** (=have influence) *with members of Congress.* | *Matthew's voice did not* **carry** much **conviction** (=he did not seem very sure).

9 disease [T] to have a disease and pass it to others, or to have a GENE that causes a disease: *Rats are known to carry diseases like the plague.* | *Doctors can perform tests to see if a woman carries the breast cancer gene.*

10 get/be carried away to be so excited, angry, interested etc. that you are not really in control of what you do or say anymore, or you forget everything else: *Norm tends to get carried away and talk too much.* | *I got a little carried away toward the end of the game.*

11 carry insurance/a guarantee etc. to have or include insurance etc.: *All our products carry a 12-month guarantee.*

12 crime/punishment [T] if a crime carries a particular punishment, that is the usual punishment for the crime: *Murder carries a life sentence in this state.*

13 election [T] if someone carries a state, COUNTY etc. they win an election in that area: *Reagan carried California in 1980.*

14 carry sth in your head/mind to remember information that you need, without writing it down: *The amount of knowledge Lee carries in her head is amazing.*

15 weight [T] to have a particular amount of weight on your body, especially when this is too much: *Mike carries 300 pounds on his 6-foot, 4-inch body.*

16 building [T] if a PILLAR, wall etc. carries something, it supports the weight of that thing: *These two columns carry the whole roof.*

17 persuade [T] to persuade people to accept your suggestions or support you: *Stephanie's arguments carried the meeting.* | *Jackson's common-sense attitude* **carried the day** (=persuaded people to support his ideas).

18 carry yourself to stand and move in a particular way: *It was obvious by the way they carried themselves that they were soldiers.*

19 carry sth too far/to extremes/to excess to do or say too much about something: *It was funny at first, but you've carried the joke too far.*

20 sound/smell [I] if a sound or smell carries to a particular place, it goes as far as that place: *The sounds of laughter carried as far as the lake.* | *Toni's high, thin voice did not carry well* (=it could not be heard very far away) *in such a large room.*

21 be carried if a suggestion, PROPOSAL etc. is carried, the people at a meeting approve it by voting: *The amendment to the bill was carried unanimously* (=everyone agreed to it). | *The motion was carried by 76 votes* (=76 more people voted for something than voted against it).

22 child [T] if a woman is carrying a child, she is PREGNANT (=going to have a baby)

23 carry a (heavy) load/burden to have a lot of work to do or a lot of responsibility for something: *Moore carries most of the load for the team.*

24 carry sb (to victory/to the top etc.) to be the reason that a person or group is successful: *Campaign workers are still looking for a message that will carry the Democrats to victory.* | *In the second half, Smith carried the team by scoring 35 points.*

25 carry a tune to sing the notes of songs correctly: *As long as you can carry a tune, you're welcome to join the choir.*

26 sb can't carry a tune in a bucket HUMOROUS used to say that someone is completely unable to sing the notes of any song

27 as fast as his/her legs could carry him/her LITERARY as fast as possible: *She ran to her mother as fast as her legs could carry her.*

28 mathematics [T] to put a number into the next row to the left when you are adding numbers together: *Nine and three make twelve, put down the two and carry the one.*

29 carry a torch for sb to secretly love and admire someone who does not love you: *Seth has been carrying a torch for Liz ever since high school.*

30 carry the torch of sth to continue to support a belief or tradition when no one else wants to: *Ancient Greeks carried the torch of scientific study for many centuries.*

31 ball [I] if a ball carries a particular distance, that is how far it travels when it is hit

32 carry everything before you LITERARY to be completely successful in a struggle against other people
—see also CARD-CARRYING, CARRIER

carry sth **forward** *phr. v.* [T] **1** to move a total to the next page in order to add it to other numbers on that page **2** to continue something that had been started earlier: *It would not be responsible to begin such a process and then leave, so that other people had to carry it forward.* **3** to make an amount of something such as money or vacation time available for use at a later time: *How many vacation days can be carried forward to next year?*

carry sth ↔ **off** *phr. v.* [T] **1** to do something difficult successfully: *Rubens carried off several important diplomatic missions.* **2** to win a prize: *Bancroft carried off the Oscar for Best Actress.*

carry on *phr. v.* **1** [I,T **carry on** sth] to continue doing something: *Wilde plans to carry on and finish writing the book.* | **[carry on with sth]** *I can't carry on with my life as though nothing had happened.* **2** [T **carry on** sth] to continue something that has been started by someone else: *Lundgaard's son will carry on the business.* | *June's daughters will carry on the family traditions.* **3 carry on a conversation** to talk to someone: *Don't you just hate people who carry on conversations in movie theaters?* **4** [I] SPOKEN to behave in a silly, excited, or anxious way: *We won't get anything done if you don't stop carrying on.* **5** [I] OLD-FASHIONED to have a sexual relationship with someone, when you should not: **[+ with]** *Deborah's husband had been carrying on with a young research assistant for over a year.*

carry sth **out** *phr. v.* [T] **1** to do something that needs to be organized and planned: *The attack was carried out by a group of 15 rebels.* | *Teenagers carried out a survey on attitudes to drugs.* **2 carry out an order/threat/instructions etc.** to do something that you have said you will do or that someone has told you to do: *The soldiers responded that they were only carrying out orders.*

carry sth **over** *phr. v.* [T] **1** if something is carried over into a new set of conditions, it continues to exist and influences the new conditions: *Being in* *good physical condition carries over mentally.* **2** to make an amount of something available to be used at a later time: *Only two days of vacation time can be carried over into next year.*

carry through *phr. v.* **1** [T **carry** sth **through**] to complete or finish something successfully, in spite of difficulties: *It's a good idea, and the team is determined to carry it through.* **2** [T **carry** sb **through** (sth)] to help someone to manage during an illness or a difficult period: *Troy's sense of humor carried him through his cancer treatments.* **3 carry through on sth** to completely finish doing something that you said you would do: *Fontana has been criticized for not carrying through on promised bank reforms.*

carry[2] *n.* [singular,U] TECHNICAL the distance a ball or bullet travels after it has been thrown, hit, or fired

car·ry·all /'kæri,ɔl/ *n.* [C] a large soft bag, usually made of cloth —see picture at BAG[1]

carrying charge /'... ,../ *n.* [C] a charge added to the price of something you have bought by INSTALLMENT PLAN (=paying over several months)

carry-on /'.. ,./ *adj.* [only before noun] carry-on bags are ones that passengers are allowed to take onto an airplane with them —**carry-on** *n.* [C]

car·ry·out, **carry-out** /'kæri,aʊt/ *n.* [C] food that you can take away from a restaurant to eat somewhere else, or a restaurant that sells food like this; TAKEOUT

car·ry·o·ver /'kæri,oʊvɚ/ *n.* [C] **1** something that affects an existing situation, but is the result of a past one: [+ **from**] *Some of the problems are a carryover from the bitter presidential campaign.* **2** an amount of money that has not been used and is available to use later: [+ **of**] *a carryover of funds to next year's budget* —see also **carry over** (CARRY[1])

car seat /'. ./ *n.* [C] a special seat for a baby or small child to hold them safely in a car

car·sick /'kɑrsɪk/ *adj.* feeling sick because you are traveling in a car —**carsickness** *n.* [U]

Car·son /'kɑrsən/, **Kit** /kɪt/ (1809–1868) a U.S. hunter and soldier who worked as a GUIDE for John C. Frémont on his trips through the western part of North America

Carson, Ra·chel /'reɪtʃəl/ (1907–1964) a U.S. scientist who was one of the first people to realize that PESTICIDES (=chemicals for protecting crops from insects) were damaging the environment

Carson Cit·y /,.. '../ the capital city of the U.S. state of Nevada

cart[1] /kɑrt/ *n.* [C] **1** a vehicle with two or four wheels that is pulled by a horse and used for carrying heavy things —see also HANDCART **2** also **shopping cart** a large wire basket on wheels that you use when shopping in a SUPERMARKET or some other large stores **3** a small table with wheels, used to move and serve food and drinks: *Then the waiter wheeled the dessert cart over to our table.* **4 put the cart before the horse** to do things in the wrong order —see also GOLF CART, **upset the apple cart** (UPSET[1] (6))

cart[2] *v.* [T always + adv./prep.] **1** INFORMAL to carry something somewhere, especially something that is awkward or heavy: *A burglar carted away all the family's Christmas presents.* | *After carting my equipment around the world, it's nice to be working closer to home.* **2** to carry something in a cart, truck etc.: [**cart** sth **away**] *Workers carted away several tons of trash.*

cart sb **away/off** *phr. v.* [T] INFORMAL to take someone away by force, especially to prison: *The sheriff carted him off to prison.*

carte blanche /,kɑrt 'blɑnʃ/ *n.* [U] complete freedom to do whatever you like in a particular situation, especially to spend money: *The director was given carte blanche to make his epic movie.*

car·tel /kɑr'tɛl/ *n.* [C] a group of companies or businesses that work together, especially to control prices and limit competition in an unfair way: *a drug cartel*

Car·ter /'kɑrtɚ/, **James (Jim·my)** /'dʒɪmi/ (1924–) the 39th President of the U.S.

cart·horse /'kɑrthɔrs/ *n.* [C] a large strong horse, often used for pulling heavy loads

Car·tier /kɑr'tyeɪ/, **Jacques** /ʒɑk/ (1491–1557) a French EXPLORER who traveled up the St. Lawrence River in Canada and claimed officially that the area belonged to France

Cartier-Bres·son /kɑr,tyeɪ brɛ'soʊn/, **Hen·ri** ɑn'ri/ (1908–) a French PHOTOGRAPHER

car·ti·lage /'kɑrtl-ɪdʒ/ *n.* [U] a strong substance that can bend and stretch, that is around the joints in a person's or animal's body and in places such as the outer ear and the end of the nose

cart·load /'kɑrtloʊd/ *n.* [C] the amount that a CART can hold: [+ **of**] *two cartloads of hay*

car·tog·ra·phy /kɑr'tɑgrəfi/ *n.* [U] the activity of making maps —**cartographer** *n.* [C]

car·ton /'kɑrt'n/ *n.* [C] **1** a box made of CARDBOARD (=stiff paper) that contains food or drinks: *a milk carton* | [+ **of**] *a carton of eggs* —see picture at CONTAINER **2** a large container with smaller containers of goods inside it: [+ **of**] *How many packs come in a carton of cigarettes?*

car·toon /kɑr'tun/ *n.* [C] **1** a short movie that is made by photographing a series of drawings: *We always watch cartoons on Saturday mornings.* **2** a funny drawing, often including a humorous remark, especially a drawing about events in the news or politicians: *an editorial cartoon* **3** a set of small boxes with drawings that tell a funny story or a joke, usually printed in newspapers; COMIC STRIP **4** TECHNICAL a drawing that is used as a model for a painting or other work of art

car·toon·ish /kɑr'tunɪʃ/ *adj.* like a cartoon in the way something is drawn or done: *Most action movies are full of cartoonish characters.*

car·toon·ist /kɑr'tunɪst/ *n.* [C] someone who draws CARTOONS —compare ANIMATOR

car·tridge /'kɑrtrɪdʒ/ *n.* [C] **1** a small piece of equipment or a container that you put inside something to make it work: *a computer game cartridge* | *Wind the film back into the cartridge before you open the camera.* **2** a tube containing explosive powder and a bullet that you use in a gun **3** the small part of a RECORD PLAYER containing the needle that takes sound signals from the record

cart·wheel /'kɑrt'wil/ *n.* [C] a movement in which you turn completely over by throwing your body sideways onto your hands while bringing your legs straight over your head | **do/turn cartwheels** *A few players turned cartwheels at the edge of the field to celebrate their victory.* —**cartwheel** *v.* [I]

carve /kɑrv/ *v.* **1** [T] to cut shapes out of solid wood or stone: [**carve** sth **from/out of** sth] *Michelangelo carved the statue from a single block of marble.* | [**carve** sth **into** sth] *Luke plans to carve the wood into candlesticks.* **2** [T] to cut a pattern or letter on the surface of something: [**carve** sth **on/in** etc.] *Someone's initials had been carved into the tree trunk.* —see also **not be carved/etched in stone** (STONE[1] (7)) **3** [T always + adv./prep.] to reduce the size of something by separating it into smaller parts or getting rid of part of it: [**carve** sth **into** sth/**out of** sth/**from** sth] *The land has been carved into 20-acre lots* | *The company needs to carve $1 million from its annual budget.* **4** [I,T] to cut a large piece of cooked meat into smaller pieces using a big knife: *What's the best way to carve a turkey?* | *Who's going to carve, Dad or Grandpa?* —see picture on page 425

carve sth **out** *phr. v.* [T] **carve out a career/niche/reputation etc.** to become successful and be respected: *Jenkins has carved out a very successful career for herself as a photographer*

carve sth ↔ **up** *phr. v.* [T] if two or more people, governments etc. carve up an area of land, they divide it into separate parts and share it between them: *After World War I, the British and French carved up the Ottoman Empire.*

carv·er /'kɑrvɚ/ *n.* [C] **1** someone who carves **2** a big knife used for cutting meat; CARVING KNIFE

Car·ver /'kɑrvɚ/, **George Washington** (1860–1943) a U.S. scientist who studied farming and crops and was one of the first African-American scientists —see picture on page 1329

carv·ing /'kɑrvɪŋ/ n. **1** [C] an object or pattern made by cutting a shape in wood or stone for decoration **2** [U] the activity or skill of carving

carving fork /'.. ,./ n. [C] a large fork used to hold cooked meat firmly while you are cutting it

carving knife /'.. ,./ n. [C] a large knife used for cutting cooked meat —see picture at KNIFE[1]

car wash /'. ./ n. [C] a place where there is special equipment for washing cars

car·y·at·id /ˌkæri'ætɪd/ n. [C] TECHNICAL a pillar (1) in the shape of a female figure

Cas·a·no·va /ˌkæsə'noʊvə/ n. [C] a man who has had, or says he has had, a lot of lovers: *Dave obviously thought he was a real Casanova.*

cas·bah /'kæzbɑ, 'kɑz-/ n. [C] an ancient Arab city, or the market in it

cas·cade[1] /kæ'skeɪd/ n. [C] **1** a small steep WATERFALL **2** something that hangs down in large quantities: [+ of] *Rebecca was tall and slim with a cascade of dark curly hair.* **3 a cascade of events** a series of events, each one affecting the next one: *The poison sets off a cascade of events including shock, organ failure, and often death.*

cascade[2] v. [I always + adv./prep.] to flow, fall, or hang down in large quantities: *Heavy rains caused a wall of mud to cascade down the hillside.*

Cas·cade Range, the /kæs'keɪd/ also **the Cascades** a range of mountains in the west of the U.S. and Canada, that runs from British Columbia in the north down to northern California, where they join with the Sierra Nevada

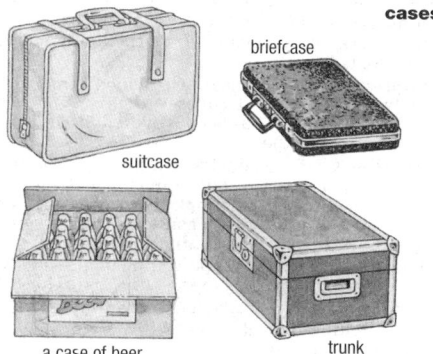

cases

briefcase

suitcase

a case of beer

trunk

w case[1] /keɪs/ n.

1 example/situation [C] a particular situation or problem that exists, or an example of a particular situation or problem: *In some cases, prices had gone up by 38 cents a gallon.* | [+ of] *Miller's actions were a clear case of sexual harassment.* | *In the case of these skeletons, 22 of 40 contained lead in dangerous amounts.* | *Many of these boys are from one-parent households, as in Mark's case.* | *Many southern cities are growing above the national average – Atlanta is a case in point* (=a clear example). | *This is a classic case of* (=a typical example of) *date rape.* | *85% of people mentioned in the newspapers are men. This is also the case for* (=the situation is also true for) *television news.*

2 law/crime [C] **a)** a question or problem that will be dealt with by a court of law: *a court case* | **win/lose a case** *Watson won the discrimination case against her employer.* | **a civil/criminal case** (=a case relating to private legal matters or crime) **b)** all the reasons that one side in a legal argument can give against the other side: *Ali's testimony strengthened the case for the prosecution.* | *The District Attorney's office says it has a clear case against Williams.* (=it has good enough arguments to go to court) **c)** an event or set of events that need to be dealt with by the police: [+ of] *Detroit police are*

investigating the case of a man found strangled on Tuesday. | *Luca is the investigator on the case.*

3 (just) in case a) as a way of being safe from something that might happen or might be true: *There are spare batteries in there, in case you need them.* **b)** used like "if": *In case you missed the last program, here's a summary of the story.*

4 reason/argument [C,U] the facts, arguments, or reasons for doing something, supporting something etc.: [+ for/against] *On Monday, they will present their case against allowing logging in national forests.* | *Smith made a good case for changing the way schools are run* (=he gave good reasons for it).

5 disease/illness [C] an example of a disease or illness, or the person suffering this disease or illness: *There were several food poisoning cases following the church picnic.* | [+ of] *Tara was treated for a slight case of frostbite.*

6 in any case used to say that a fact or part of a situation stays the same, even if other things change: *None of us here has ever been bitten, but in any case the spider's bite is not very poisonous.*

7 box/container [C] **a)** a large box or container in which things can be stored or moved: *a packing case* | [+ of] *a case of wine* **b)** a special box used as a container for holding or protecting something: *The exhibits were all in glass cases.* **c)** OLD-FASHIONED a SUITCASE —see also BOOKCASE, BRIEFCASE, PILLOWCASE

8 in case of sth used to describe what you should do in a particular situation, especially on official notices: *In case of fire, break the glass and push the alarm button.*

SPOKEN PHRASES

9 in that case used to describe what you will do, or what will happen, as a result of a particular situation or event: *"I'll be home late tonight." "Well, in that case, I won't cook dinner."*

10 be on sb's case to be criticizing someone continuously: *Dad's always on my case about getting a job.*

11 get off my case used to tell someone to stop criticizing you or complaining about you: *OK, OK, just get off my case, will you?*

12 make a (federal) case out of sth to complain or get very upset about something that has happened: *I just forgot! Don't make a federal case out of it.*

13 it is a case of sth used before describing a situation, especially when you use a familiar phrase to describe it: *Tim said that for him, it was a case of love at first sight.*

---

14 person [C] someone who is being dealt with by a doctor, a SOCIAL WORKER, the police etc. —see also BASKET-CASE

15 a case of the jitters/blahs/blues etc. INFORMAL an occasion when you feel a particular way: *McWilliams gave an excellent performance, despite admitting he had "a bad case of the jitters."* (=he was nervous)

16 grammar [C,U] TECHNICAL the way in which the form of a word changes, showing its relationship to other words in a sentence: *case endings* —see also LOWER CASE, UPPER CASE

case[2] v. [T] **1 be cased in sth** to be completely surrounded by a material or substance: *The reactor is cased in several feet of metal and concrete.* —see also CASING **2 case the joint** HUMOROUS to look around a place that you intend to steal from, in order to find out information

case·book /'keɪsbʊk/ n. [C] a detailed written record kept by a doctor, SOCIAL WORKER, or police officer of the cases they have dealt with

case his·to·ry /'. ,..., ,. '...' n. plural **case histories** [C] a detailed record of someone's past illnesses, problems etc. that a doctor or SOCIAL WORKER studies

case law /'. ./ n. [U] LAW a type of law that is based on decisions made by judges in the past

case·load /'keɪsloʊd/ n. [C usually singular] the number of people a doctor, SOCIAL WORKER etc. has to deal with

C

case·ment /'keɪsmənt/ also **casement win·dow** /'.. ˌ../ n. [C] a window that opens like a door with HINGES at one side

case stud·y /ˌ. '../ n. plural **case studies** [C] a detailed account of the development of a particular person, group, or situation that has been studied over a period of time

case·work /'keɪswɔrk/ n. [U] work that a SOCIAL WORKER does, which is concerned with the problems of a particular person or family that needs help —**caseworker** n. [C]

cash[1] /kæʃ/ n. [U] **1** money in the form of coins or bills rather than checks, CREDIT CARDs etc.: *By age 15, Sean was stealing cash from his mother to buy drugs.* | *He had about $150 in cash in his wallet.* | *Is there a discount if I pay cash?* | *You can't use checks there – they only take payment in hard cash* (=bills and coins). —see Usage Note at MONEY **2** INFORMAL money in the bank: *The firm is so short of cash* (=having very little money) *that it may not survive.* | *The country is strapped for cash* (=does not have enough money). **3 cash on delivery** C.O.D.; used when the customer must pay the person who delivers goods to them —see also PETTY CASH

cash[2] v. [T] **cash a check/money order etc.** to exchange a check etc. for the amount of money it is worth: *The company cashed my check but hasn't sent my order.*

cash in phr. v. **1** [I] to gain advantages from a situation: [+ on] *Miller can cash in on her basketball talent by advertising athletic shoes.* **2** [T **cash sth in**] to exchange something such as an insurance POLICY or a BOND[1] (2) for its value in money **3 cash in your chips** HUMOROUS to die: *Old Bill Fisher finally cashed in his chips last week.*

cash out phr. v. **1** [I] to add up the amount of money received in a store in a day so that it can be checked **2** [T **cash sth ↔ out**] to exchange something such as an insurance POLICY or a BOND[1] (2) for its value in money, especially before the date when you are supposed to do this

Cash /kæʃ/**, John·ny** /'dʒɑni/ (1932–) a singer and writer of COUNTRY AND WESTERN music

cash ad·vance /ˌ. .'./ n. [C] money that you can get from a bank, using a CREDIT CARD

cash bar /ˌ. './ n. [C usually singular] a place at an event such as a company party, wedding etc. where you can buy alcoholic drinks

cash box /'. ./ n. [C] a small metal box with a lock that you keep money in

cash cow /ˌ. './ n. [C usually singular] the part of a business you can always depend on to make enough profits: *The $8 billion video rental industry is the biggest cash cow ever developed in entertainment.*

cash crop /ˌ. './ n. [C] a crop grown in order to be sold, rather than to be used by the people growing it

cash dis·count /ˌ. '../ n. [C] an amount by which a seller reduces a price if the buyer pays immediately in cash or before a particular date

cash·ew /'kæʃu, kæ'ʃu/ n. [C] **1** a small curved nut **2** the tropical American tree that produces this nut

cash flow /'. ./ n. [singular,U] the movement of money into and out of a business or a person's accounts, which affects how much money they have available: *The translation business has been maintaining a healthy cash flow.* | *I've been having a few cash flow problems* (=have not had enough money) *lately.*

cash·ier[1] /kæ'ʃɪr/ n. [C] someone whose job is to receive or pay out money in a store, office etc.

cashier[2] v. [T usually passive] TECHNICAL to force an officer to leave the military because they have done something wrong

ca·shier's check /ˌ. '. ˌ./ n. [C] a special type of check that will definitely be paid because it uses money taken from a bank's own account

cash·less /'kæʃlɪs/ adj. done or working without using actual money: *a cashless transaction between two banks*

cash ma·chine /'. ˌ.ˌ./ n. [C] an machine in or outside a bank from which you can obtain money with a special plastic card; ATM

cash·mere /'kæʒmɪr, 'kæʃ-/ n. [U] a type of fine soft wool that comes from a particular type of goat: *a cashmere sweater*

cash price /'. ./ n. [C] the price that someone will sell something for if you pay for it immediately with money rather than with a CREDIT CARD

cash reg·is·ter /'. ˌ.../ n. [C] a machine used in stores to keep the money in and show how much customers have to pay

cash-strapped /'. ./ adj. not having enough money: *the cash-strapped school district*

cas·ing /'keɪsɪŋ/ n. [C] an outer layer that covers and protects something such as a wire, a bullet, or a SAUSAGE

ca·si·no /kə'sinoʊ/ n. plural **casinos** [C] a place where people try to win money by playing card games or ROULETTE

cask /kæsk/ n. [C] a round wooden container used for storing wine or other liquids, or the amount of liquid contained in this: [+ of] *a cask of rum*

cas·ket /'kæskɪt/ n. [C] **1** a long box in which a dead person is buried or burned; COFFIN **2** OLD-FASHIONED a small decorated box in which you keep jewelry and other valuable objects

Cas·pi·an Sea, the /'kæspiən/ the largest sea in the world that is surrounded by land, between southeast Europe and Asia. It is surrounded by Russia, Iran, Azerbaijan, Kazakhstan, and Turkmenistan.

Cas·satt /kə'sæt/**, Mary** (1845–1926) a U.S. painter who worked mainly in France with the IMPRESSIONISTS

cas·sa·va /kə'sɑvə/ n. [C,U] a tropical plant with thick roots that you can eat, or the flour made from these roots

cas·se·role /'kæsəˌroʊl/ n. [C] **1** food that is cooked slowly in liquid in a covered dish in the OVEN: *a chicken casserole* **2** a deep covered dish used for cooking food in the OVEN

cas·sette /kə'sɛt/ also **cassette tape** /'. ˌ./ n. [C] **1** a small flat plastic case containing MAGNETIC TAPE, that can be used for playing or recording sound or pictures; TAPE: **audio/video cassette** (=a cassette that records sound, or sound and pictures) **2** a closed container with photographic film in it, that can be put into a camera

cassette deck /'. ./ also **cassette play·er** /'. ˌ../ n. [C] a machine that plays cassettes

cassette re·cord·er /'. ˌ.ˌ./ n. [C] a machine used for recording sound or for playing cassettes; TAPE RECORDER

cas·sock /'kæsək/ n. [C] a long, usually black, piece of clothing worn by priests

cast[1] /kæst/ v. past tense and past participle **cast**
1 cast a vote also **cast a ballot** to vote in an election: *California residents will cast their votes today in the heated race for governor.*
2 cast doubt on sth to make people feel less certain about something: *Barry's lawyers tried to cast doubt on the FBI's evidence.*
3 cast a shadow a) if something casts a shadow over an event, period of time etc., it makes people feel less happy or hopeful because they are worried about it: [+ over] *At that time, the Cold War still cast a shadow over our children's future.* **b)** to make a shadow appear on a surface or area [+ on/over/ across etc.] *New York's skyscrapers cast shadows over the streets.*
4 cast a look/glance FORMAL to look at someone or something: [+ at/toward/around etc.] *Sandra waited, casting nervous glances over her shoulder.*
5 cast an eye over sth to check or look at something quickly: *While you are raking, cast an eye over your trees for broken branches.*
6 actors [T] to choose which people will act particular parts in a play, movie etc.: [**cast sb in sth**] *Before being cast in "Savannah", Luna attended culinary*

school. | [cast sb as sb] *Coppola cast Gary Oldman as Dracula.*

7 describe to describe or represent something in a particular way: *The meat industry complained that the nutrition chart cast its products in an unfavorable way.*

8 cast (a) light on/onto sth a) to provide new information which makes something easier to understand: *Tobin's research findings could cast new light on the origin of the universe.* **b)** LITERARY to send light onto a surface: *Candles cast a romantic light in the restaurant's dining room.*

9 cast a spell on/over sb/sth a) to use magic words or ceremonies to change someone or something: *The villagers accused her of being a witch who could cast evil spells.* **b)** to make someone feel very strongly attracted and keep their attention completely: *Within minutes, Sinatra's voice had cast its spell on the audience.*

10 metal [T usually passive] to pour liquid metal, plastic etc. into a MOLD (=specially shaped container), or to make an object in this way: *In the tomb they found a statue of a horse cast in bronze.*

11 cast blame/suspicion etc. on sb/sth to do or say something that blames someone or makes it seem that they have done something wrong: *People should take responsibility for their actions, and stop casting blame on society.*

12 fishing [I,T] to throw a fishing line or net into the water: *Cast your line across the current and upstream.*

13 throw [T always + adv./prep.] LITERARY to throw something somewhere: *Sparks leaped as more wood was cast onto the fire.*

14 cast aspersions on sb/sth FORMAL to make unfavorable remarks about someone or something: *The article called him a racist and cast aspersions on his professional conduct.*

15 cast sb as sb also **cast sb in the role of sb** to regard or describe someone as a particular type of person: *Barr refuses to be cast in the role of a victim of her childhood.*

16 cast your net wide to consider or try as many things as possible in order to find what you want: *NASA officials should cast their net wide for a cheaper way to return to the moon.*

17 cast your mind back to try to remember something that happened a long time ago: [+ to] *Cast your mind back to your first day at school.*

18 cast sb into prison/into a dungeon/into Hell etc. LITERARY to force someone to go somewhere bad: *Memet was cast into prison for life.*

19 be cast away LITERARY to be left alone on a shore or island, because the ship that you were on sank: *The story is about some sailors who were cast away on a desert island.*

20 cast sth from your mind LITERARY if you cast worries, fears, doubts etc. from your mind, you stop feeling worried, afraid etc.

21 cast a horoscope to calculate the details of someone's HOROSCOPE

22 cast pearls before swine LITERARY to offer something that is very valuable or beautiful to someone who does not understand how valuable it is —see also **cast your lot with sb** (LOT² (6)), **the die is cast** (DIE² (3))

cast around for sth *phr. v.* [T] to try to think of something to do or say: *In the 1950s, earth scientists were casting around for a project that would advance their field of study.*

cast sb/sth **aside** *phr. v.* [T] to get rid of someone or something because you do not like them or they are not useful anymore: *Hyde based his research on many of the scientific theories that are now being cast aside.*

cast off *phr. v.* **1** [T cast sb/sth ↔ off] LITERARY to get rid of something or someone that has been causing problems or difficulties: *One by one, Eastern European countries cast off Communism in the late 20th century.* **2** [I,T cast sth off] to untie the rope that fastens your boat to the shore so that you can sail away **3** [I,T cast sth off] to finish a piece of KNITTING by taking the last stitches off the needle in a way that stops them from coming apart

cast on *phr. v.* [I,T cast sth **on**] to start a piece of KNITTING by making the first stitches on the needle

cast sb/sth **out** *phr. v.* [T] LITERARY to force someone or something to go away: *Saint Guthlin is said to have cast out demons and performed miracles of healing.*

cast² *n.* [C]

1 actors [usually singular] all the people who act in a play, movie, or television program: *The cast includes Bruce Willis and Melanie Griffith.*

2 cast of characters all the characters in a play, movie, story etc., or all the people who are involved in an event: *The story's cast of characters includes Adele's grandfather and his boss, who owned peach orchards in Alabama.*

3 on your body a hard cover for a part of your body, that supports a broken bone while it gets better: *Mandy has to have her arm in a cast for six weeks.*

4 shape a) a MOLD (=specially shaped container) into which you pour liquid metal, plastic etc. in order to make an object of a particular shape **b)** an object made in this way: *McIntosh's work consists of plaster casts of the artist's own face.*

5 a cast of thousands HUMOROUS a very large number of people: *The President has a cast of thousands to remember facts for him.*

6 fishing an act of throwing a fishing line or net

7 color a small amount of a particular color: *The granite columns give a pinkish cast to the base of the building.*

8 sb's cast of mind LITERARY the way someone thinks or behaves: *Interpreting the stories depends on the reader's own cast of mind.*

cas·ta·net /ˌkæstəˈnɛt/ *n.* [C usually plural] a musical instrument made of two small round pieces of wood or plastic that you knock together in your hand

cast·a·way /ˈkæstəˌweɪ/ *n. plural* **castaways** [C] someone who is left alone on an island after their ship has sunk

caste /kæst/ *n.* **1** [C,U] one of the social classes into which Hindu people can be born, which cannot be changed, or the system of having these classes **2** [C] a group of people who have a particular position in society

cas·tel·lat·ed /ˈkæstəˌleɪtɪd/ *adj.* TECHNICAL built to look like a castle

cast·er, castor /ˈkæstɚ/ *n.* [C] a small wheel attached to the bottom of a piece of furniture so that it can move in any direction

cas·ti·gate /ˈkæstəˌgeɪt/ *v.* [T] FORMAL to criticize or punish someone severely: [castigate sb for doing sth] *In some countries, young couples would be castigated for kissing in public.* —**castigation** /ˌkæstəˈgeɪʃən/ *n.* [U]

cast·ing /ˈkæstɪŋ/ *n.* **1** [U] the process of choosing the actors for a movie or play: *a casting director* **2** [C] an object made by pouring liquid metal, plastic etc. into a MOLD (=specially shaped container) **3 the casting couch** HUMOROUS a situation in which an actor is persuaded to have sex in return for a part in a movie, play etc.

cast i·ron /ˌ. ˈ../ *n.* [U] a type of iron that is very hard but breaks easily, and that can be shaped in a MOLD

cast-i·ron /ˌ. ˈ../ *adj.* **1** made of cast iron: *a cast-iron skillet* **2 a cast-iron excuse/alibi/guarantee etc.** an excuse, alibi etc. that is very certain and cannot fail **3 a cast-iron stomach** someone with a cast-iron stomach can eat anything without feeling sick

cas·tle /ˈkæsəl/ *n.* [C] **1** a very large strong building, built in Europe in the past as a safe place that could be easily defended against attack **2** one of the pieces used in a game of CHESS; ROOK **3 build castles in the air** to make plans or imagine things that are unlikely ever to become real; DAYDREAM

cast-off /ˈkæstɔf/ *n.* [C usually plural] clothes or other things that someone does not want anymore, and gives or throws away: *We furnished the house with cast-offs from my parents' garage.*

cast-off /'. ./ *adj.* [only before noun] cast-off clothes or other goods that are not wanted or have been thrown away

cas·tor /'kæstə/ *n.* [C] another spelling of CASTER

castor oil /'.. ,./ *n.* [U] a thick oil made from the seeds of a plant, used in the past as a medicine to make the BOWELs empty

cas·trate /'kæstreɪt/ *v.* [T] to remove the sexual organs of a man or a male animal —**castration** /kæ'streɪʃən/ *n.* [U]

ca·stra·to /kæ'strɑtoʊ, kə-/ *n. plural* **castrati** /-ti/ or **castratos** [C] a male singer, especially one in past times, whose sexual organs were removed before he became an adult, so that he would not develop a deep voice

Cas·tries /'kæstriz, -tris/ the capital city of St. Lucia

Cas·tro /'kæstroʊ/, **Fi·del** /fi'dɛl/ (1927–) a Cuban COMMUNIST leader who led the opposition to the DICTATOR Batista, and became Prime Minister of Cuba, and later its President

casual

formal clothes

casual clothes

cas·u·al¹ /'kæʒuəl, -ʒəl/ *adj.*
1 clothes/style/event not formal, or not for a formal situation: *casual shoes | Are shorts appropriate at a casual party? | Plaid curtains give the room a casual look.*
2 relaxed/not caring relaxed and not worried about things, and sometimes seeming not to care: *Thompson's management style is casual but organized. | Society seems to have an increasingly casual attitude toward violence.*
3 without attention without any clear aim or serious interest: *Wayne just took a casual glance at the newspaper. | To the casual observer* (=to someone who is not looking very carefully), *everything seemed normal.*
4 not planned happening by chance, without being planned: *a casual encounter | Pete made a casual remark about Jo's hair style, and she got really mad* (=he said it for no particular reason and did not think about it carefully first).
5 casual sex sex that you have with someone, without intending to have a serious relationship with them
6 not regular/often using or doing something without doing it regularly or often: *Even casual visitors to the museum could save money with a membership card. | the casual use of marijuana*
7 casual worker/employment/labor etc. a worker, employment etc. that a company uses or offers only for a short period of time
8 a casual acquaintance someone you have met, but do not know well and do not see regularly —**casually** *adv.*: *a casually dressed young man* —**casualness** *n.* [U]

casual² *n.* **1** casuals [plural] informal clothes **2** [C usually plural] a worker who is not a regular EMPLOYEE at a company

cas·u·al·ty /'kæʒəlti, -ʒuəlti,/ *n. plural* **casualties 1** [C] someone who is hurt or killed in an accident or battle: *First reports of the air crash tell of more than 50 casualties. | There were heavy casualties* (=a lot of people hurt or killed) *in the first battle.*

2 be a casualty of sth to be someone or something that suffers as a result of a particular event or situation: *The Safer City Project became a major casualty of financial cutbacks.*

ca·su·ist /'kæʒuɪst/ *n.* [C] FORMAL someone who is skilled in casuistry

ca·su·ist·ry /'kæʒuəstri/ *n.* [U] FORMAL the use of intelligent but often false arguments to answer moral or legal questions

ca·sus bel·li /,kæsəs 'bɛli, ,keɪsəs 'bɛlaɪ/ *n.* [C] LAW an event or political action which directly causes a war

cat¹ /kæt/ *n.* [C]
1 animal **a)** a small animal with four legs that is often kept as a pet or used for catching mice **b)** also **big cat** a large animal that is related to this, such as a lion or tiger
2 let the cat out of the bag to tell a secret, especially without intending to
3 cat and mouse also a game of cat and mouse a situation in which someone who is trying to catch someone else pretends to let them escape, hoping that they will make a mistake that will make them easier to catch: *Since the first attack in 1993, police had been playing a dangerous game of cat and mouse with the brutal serial killer.*
4 look like something the cat dragged in to look very sick, tired, or messy
5 like a cat on a hot tin roof so nervous or anxious that you cannot keep still or keep your attention on one thing
6 when the cat's away (the mice will play) used to say that when someone with authority is not near, other people do not do what they should do
7 Cat got your tongue? SPOKEN used to ask someone, especially a child, why they are not talking
8 person OLD-FASHIONED SLANG a person: *That Jefferson is one cool cat.*
9 look like the cat that ate the canary to show too much satisfaction with your own intelligence or success —see also CATTY, **fat cat** (FAT¹ (5)), **it's raining cats and dogs** (RAIN² (4)), **there's not enough room to swing a cat** (ROOM¹ (6))

cat² *v.*
cat around *phr. v.* [I] OLD-FASHIONED be catting around to be looking for people to have sex with: *Al's probably out catting around again tonight.*

cat·a·clysm /'kætə,klɪzəm/ *n.* [C] LITERARY a violent and sudden event or change, such as a serious flood or EARTHQUAKE

cataclysmic /,kætə'klɪzmɪk/ *adj.* FORMAL a cataclysmic event or change is one that has a very extreme, usually negative, effect: *A cataclysmic event had shaken her parents' marriage.*

cat·a·comb /'kætə,koʊm/ *n.* [C] **1** [usually plural] an area of passages and rooms below the ground where dead people are buried **2** a place that has many passages and small rooms which make it easy to get lost: *The Isolation Plant is an immense underground catacomb of storage cells.*

cat·a·falque /'kætə,fælk, -,fɔlk/ *n.* [C] a decorated raised structure on which the dead body of an important person is placed before their funeral

Cat·a·lan /'kætə,læn, -,lɑn/ *n.* [U] a language spoken in the part of Spain around Barcelona

cat·a·log¹, **catalogue** /'kætl,ɔg, -,ɑg/ *n.* [C] **1** a book containing pictures and information about goods that you can buy: *a mail-order catalog | If they don't have your size in the store, see if you can order it from the catalog.* **2** a list of all the objects, paintings, books etc. in a place such as a MUSEUM or library —see also CARD CATALOG **3** a catalog of failures/disasters/errors etc. a series of failures DISASTERS etc. that happen one after the other and never seem to stop: *The commission's report is a catalog of horrors endured by innocent people.*

catalog², **catalogue** *v.* **catalogues, catalogued, cataloguing** [T] **1** to put a list of things into a particular order and write it in a catalog: *Fewer than 85,000 species native to Costa Rica have been scientifically described and catalogued.* **2** to give a list of all the events or qualities about someone or something:

Margaret catalogued her impressions of her class-mates in her diary.

ca·tal·y·sis /kəˈtæləsɪs/ *n.* [U] TECHNICAL the process of making a chemical reaction quicker by adding a catalyst

cat·a·lyst /ˈkætl-ɪst/ *n.* [C] **1** something or someone that causes an important change or event to happen: [+ for] *The women's movement acted as a catalyst for change in the workplace.* **2** a substance that makes a chemical reaction happen more quickly without being changed itself —**catalytic** /ˌkætlˈɪtɪk/ *adj.*

catalytic con·ver·ter /ˌ.... ˈ./ *n.* [C] a piece of equipment attached to the EXHAUST[2] (2) of a car that reduces the amount of poisonous gases sent out into the air when the engine is operating

cat·a·ma·ran /ˌkætəməˈræn, ˈkætəməˌræn/ *n.* [C] a sailing boat with two separate HULLS (=the part that goes in the water)

cat·a·pult[1] /ˈkætəˌpʌlt, -ˌpʊlt/ *n.* [C] **1** a large weapon used in former times to throw heavy stones, iron balls etc. **2** a piece of equipment used to send a military aircraft into the air from a ship

catapult[2] *v.* **1** [T always + adv./prep.] to push or throw something very hard so that it moves through the air very quickly: [catapult sb into/over/out etc.] *Two cars were catapulted into the air by the force of the blast.* **2** catapult sb to stardom/the top/fame etc. to suddenly make someone very famous or successful: *Erickson's pitching has helped catapult the Twins to the top of the league.*

cat·a·ract /ˈkætəˌrækt/ *n.* [C] **1** a medical condition of the eye in which the LENS (3) of your eye becomes white instead of clear, so that you cannot see well **2** LITERARY a large WATERFALL

ca·tas·tro·phe /kəˈtæstrəfi/ *n.* [C,U] **1** a terrible event in which there is a lot of destruction or many people are injured or die: *The oil spill will be an ecological catastrophe.* | *The governments of the world failed to act to prevent the catastrophe of World War II.* **2** an event or situation which is extremely bad for the people involved: *The economy seems to be moving toward catastrophe.* —**catastrophic** /ˌkætəˈstrɑfɪk/ *adj.*: *a catastrophic fall in the price of Internet stocks* —**catastrophically** /-kli/ *adv.*

cat·a·ton·i·a /ˌkætəˈtoʊniə/ *n.* [U] TECHNICAL a condition in which you cannot think, speak, or move any part of your body

cat·a·ton·ic /ˌkætəˈtɑnɪk/ *adj.* **1** TECHNICAL caused or affected by a condition in which you cannot think, speak, or move any part of your body: *Andrew was in a catatonic state for several months.* **2** NOT TECHNICAL not active, moving around, or reacting at all, or moving or reacting extremely slowly: *They were catatonic with disgust.*

Ca·taw·ba /kəˈtɔbə/ a Native American tribe from the southeastern area of the U.S.

cat·bird seat /ˈkætˈbɜd ˌsit/ *n.* INFORMAL be (sitting) in the catbird seat to be in a position where you have an advantage

cat bur·glar /ˈ. ˌ../ *n.* [C] a thief who gets into buildings by climbing up walls, pipes etc.

cat·call /ˈkætˌkɔl/ *n.* [C usually plural] a loud whistle or shout expressing dislike or disapproval of a speech or performance: *The mayor was greeted by jeers and catcalls from the audience.* —**catcall** *v.* [I]

w **catch**[1] /kætʃ/ *v. past tense and past participle* **caught**
 1 take and hold **a)** [I,T] to get hold of and stop an object such as a ball that is moving through the air: *Denise caught the bride's bouquet.* | *"Can I see that pen?" "Sure, catch."* | *Taylor caught 19 passes and ran for 180 yards.* **b)** [T] to suddenly take hold of someone or something: *Go on, jump. I'll catch you.* | *Rob caught hold of my sleeve and pulled me back.*
 2 stop/trap sb [T] **a)** to stop someone after you have been chasing them, and so prevent them from escaping: *"You can't catch me!" she yelled.* | *You choose sides, and one team hides and the other team tries to catch them.* **b)** if the police catch a criminal, they find the criminal and stop him or her from escaping: *State police have launched a massive operation to catch the murderer.* | *A lot of burglars never get caught.*

catch

catch

miss

C

 3 find sb doing sth [T] to find or see someone while they are doing something wrong or illegal: [catch sb doing sth] *The officer caught me going 70 miles an hour, so I got a ticket.* | *If you get caught stealing in some countries, they cut off your hand.* | *Milian was caught red-handed* (=caught while doing something wrong) *attempting to break into a house.* | *Several graffiti artists were caught in the act* (=caught while doing something wrong) *on the Brown River bridge.*
 4 illness [T] to get a disease or illness: *Kristen has the flu, so I guess we'll all catch it.* | *Dion caught a cold on vacation.* | [catch sth from sb] *The vet says you can't catch the disease from the cat.*
 5 catch sb by surprise/catch sb off guard also catch sb napping/unawares to do something or to happen when someone is not expecting it, so that they are not ready to deal with it: *My pregnancy caught us by surprise, but we're happy about it.* | *The public's reaction obviously caught the governor off guard.*
 6 animal/fish [T] to trap an animal or fish by using a trap, net, or hook, or by hunting it: *"We went fishing." "Did you catch anything?"* | *The cat caught a squirrel!* | *The kids were trying to catch tadpoles in the pond.*
 7 catch a train/plane/bus to get on a train etc. in order to travel, or to arrive early enough to get on it: *Kevin catches the bus home on Mondays and Wednesdays.* | *I should be able to catch the 12:05 train.* —see Usage Note at REACH[1]
 8 not miss sb/sth [T] to be early enough to see something, talk to someone, do something etc.: *If you call around 8:30, you might catch Shirley.* | *We send the letters out in November, to catch people who are thinking about giving Christmas donations.* | *I only caught about the last 20 minutes of the movie.* —opposite MISS[1]
 9 get stuck [I,T usually passive] if your hand, finger, clothing etc. catches or is caught in something, it becomes stuck or fastened there: *My pant leg caught on the fence and tore.* | *Steph's hair got caught in the machine, and they had to cut it.*
 10 catch sb's attention/interest/imagination etc. if something catches your attention etc., you notice it or feel interested in it: *Rainey first caught Coach O'Malley's attention at a football camp.* | *It's a story that will catch the imagination of every child.*

SPOKEN PHRASES

 11 hear/understand [T usually in questions or negatives] to hear or understand what someone says: *I didn't catch his first name.* | *Did you catch what the book's called?* | *It's a really funny play, but it went so fast I couldn't catch all the jokes.* | *Well, Jerry's not at Sue's apartment to play games, if you catch my drift.* (=used when you are saying something indirectly, and want to check that someone understands this)
 12 catch you later used to say goodbye: *Okay, Randy, catch you later.*
 13 do something [T] to go somewhere to do something: *I caught their act* (=saw them perform) *at the Blue Note Jazz Club.* | *Would you like to go to dinner, maybe catch a movie* (=go to a movie)?

14 catch a ride to go somewhere in someone's car: *Hey, Mike! Can I catch a ride with you?*

15 you won't catch me doing sth used to say that you would never do something: *You won't catch me ironing his shirts!*

16 catch it/hell to be punished very severely by someone who discovers that you have done something bad: *Dylan's going to catch hell when Mom gets home.*

17 notice [T not in progressive] to see, smell, or notice something: *It was a really stupid mistake; I'm surprised Rachel didn't catch it.* | *Oh, you caught the sarcasm in my voice, huh?* | *Hundreds of fans were eagerly trying to catch a glimpse of their idol.* | *We suddenly caught sight of the ocean.* | *Ugh, did you catch a whiff of* (=notice the smell of) *his aftershave?*

18 burn a) catch fire if something catches fire, it starts to burn accidentally: *Investigators said that a lit cigarette caused the curtains to catch fire.* **b)** [I] if a fire catches, it starts to burn: *For some reason the charcoal isn't catching.* —see picture at FIRE[1]

19 catch sb's eye a) to attract someone's attention and make them look at something: *All of a sudden, something red caught Barb's eye.* **b)** to look at someone at the same moment that they are looking at you: *I caught Ben's eye in the rear-view mirror and knew what he was thinking.*

20 catch yourself a) to suddenly realize that you are doing something: [catch yourself doing sth] *I caught myself watching everybody else instead of paying attention to the lecture.* **b)** to stop yourself from doing something quickly: *I was about to correct him, but I caught myself in time.*

21 problem [T] to discover a problem and stop it from developing any further: *More cases of breast cancer are being caught at the early stages.*

22 hit [T] to hit someone: *Tyson's punch caught him on the chin.*

23 in a bad situation be caught in/without etc. also **get caught in/without etc.** to be in a situation that is difficult, because you cannot easily get out of it or because you do not have what you need: *Jeff was driving through Montana and got caught in a snow storm.* | *Pack more than you think you need; you don't want to get caught without a diaper or a bottle of milk.*

24 catch your breath a) to pause for a moment after a lot of physical effort in order to breathe normally again: *Clark had to sit down to catch his breath.* **b)** to stop breathing for a moment because something has surprised, frightened or shocked you

25 container [T] if a container catches liquid, it is in a position where the liquid falls into it: *We had to put a bucket under the old sink to catch the dripping water.*

26 shine/light [T] if light catches something or if something catches the light or wind, the light shines on something and makes it look bright: *As Yvonne shook her head, her earrings caught the light from the candles.*

27 wind [T] if something catches the wind or the wind catches something, it blows on it: *Turn the boat so the sails catch the wind.*

catch at sth *phr. v.* [T] LITERARY to try to take hold of something: *The old man caught at Jason's wrist.*

catch on *phr. v.* [I] **1** to begin to understand or realize something: *Usually a couple of the children will catch on quickly and help the others.* | [+ to] *It's not that hard, once you catch on to it.* **2** to become popular and fashionable: *Mountain bikes caught on quickly and soon made up the bulk of bicycle sales.*

catch up *phr. v.* [I] **1** to reach the same standard as other people in your class, group etc.: *I missed a lot of school, and it was really hard to catch up.* | [+ with] *The U.S. spent a lot of money trying to catch up with the Soviet Union in space exploration.* **2** to come from behind and reach someone in front by going faster: *We had to run to catch up.* | [+ with/ to] *You go ahead. I'll catch up with you in a minute.* **3 be/get caught up in sth** to be or become involved in something, especially something bad: *We get caught up in the commercial aspects of Christmas.*

catch up on sth *phr. v.* [T] to do something that needs to be done, that you have not had time to do before: *I'll finally get a chance to catch up on some sleep.* | *It'll take a couple of days to get caught up on all this paperwork.*

catch up with sb *phr. v.* [T] **1** to find someone who has been doing something illegal and punish them, after trying to find them for a long time: *Alex hadn't paid taxes in five years, and the IRS finally caught up with him.* **2** if something bad catches up with you, you cannot avoid it anymore: *Amy eats a lot of junk food, and one day it'll catch up with her* (=it will start affecting her health).

catch² *n.* **1** [C] the act of catching something that has been thrown or hit: *That was a great catch!* **2** [U] a game in which two or more people throw a ball to each other: *The boys are out back playing catch.* **3** [C] INFORMAL a hidden problem or difficulty: *The deal comes with a catch – you have to buy one before June.* | *There is a catch. The software can only be used with the Windows program.* | *The airfare is great, but the catch is that you have a 4-hour stopover in St. Louis.* | *The whole thing almost sounds too simple. What's the catch?* **4** [C] a hook that fastens something and holds it closed: *The catch on my necklace is broken.* **5** [C] an amount of fish that has been caught: *Each morning, Troy goes down to the fish market to inspect the daily catch.* **6 a catch in your voice/throat** a short pause you make while speaking, because you feel very upset or are beginning to cry: *With a catch in his voice, Dan told her how proud he was.* **7 be a good catch** OLD-FASHIONED if a man is a good catch, he is regarded as a very desirable husband, because he is rich and good-looking

catch-22 /ˌkætʃ twɛnti'tu/ *n.* [singular] a situation in which you cannot do one thing until you do another thing, but you cannot do that until you have done the first thing, with the result that you can do neither thing: *It's a catch-22 – without experience you can't get a job, and without a job you can't get experience.*

catch-all¹, catch-all /'kætʃɔl/ *adj.* [only before noun] intended to include all situations or possibilities: *"Activity toys" is a catchall term that includes blocks and outdoor games.*

catchall², catch-all *n.* [C] a drawer, cupboard etc. where you put any small objects

catch·er /'kætʃɚ/ *n.* [C] the baseball player who SQUATS behind the BATTER in order to catch missed balls

catch·ing /'kætʃɪŋ/ *adj.* [not before noun] INFORMAL **1** a disease or illness that is catching is infectious: *I hope Shelly's cold isn't catching.* **2** an emotion or feeling that is catching spreads quickly among people

catch·ment /'kætʃmənt/ *n.* [C] a structure with an open top, used for collecting and storing water

catch phrase, catchphrase /'. ./ *n.* [C] a short phrase that is easy to remember and is used regularly by an entertainer or politician

catch·word /'kætʃwɚd/ *n.* [C] a word or phrase that is easy to remember and is repeated regularly by a political party, newspaper etc.; SLOGAN

catch·y /'kætʃi/ *adj.* **catchier, catchiest** a catchy phrase or song is easy to remember and nice to listen to: *We need a catchy advertising slogan.* | *a catchy tune* —**catchily** *adv.*

cat·e·chism /'kætəˌkɪzəm/ *n.* [C] a set of questions and answers about the Christian religion that people learn in order to become full members of the Catholic Church

cat·e·chize /'kætəˌkaɪz/ *v.* [T] to teach someone about the Christian religion by using a series of questions and answers

cat·e·gor·i·cal /ˌkætə'gɔrɪkəl, -'gɑr-/ *adj.* a categorical statement is a clear statement that something is definitely true or false: *Weber's agent issued a categorical denial that the incident had ever happened.*

cat·e·gor·i·cally /ˌkætəˈgɔrɪkˈi/ *adv.* in such a sure and certain way that there is no doubt: *I am categorically opposed to animal testing.* | **categorically deny/reject/refuse etc.** *Ms. Long categorically denied that she had had a relationship with Mr. Woods.* | **categorically false/untrue/wrong** *These allegations are categorically untrue.* | **say/state sth categorically** *Maris said categorically that he would not run for president.*

cat·e·go·rize /ˈkætəgəˌraɪz/ *v.* [T] **1** to put people or things into groups according to what type they are, or to say which group they are in; CLASSIFY: [**categorize sb/sth according to sth**] *The population is categorized according to age, gender, and occupation.* | [**categorize sb/sth by sth**] *In his book, Edwards categorizes businesses by start-up cost, income potential, and so forth.* **2** to describe someone or something in a particular way, for example by saying that they belong to a particular group because they have the same qualities: *How would you categorize your relationship with your parents?* | [**categorize sb/sth as sth**] *The Fire Department has categorized the fire as suspicious.* —**categorization** /ˌkætəgərəˈzeɪʃən/ *n.* [C,U]

cat·e·go·ry /ˈkætəˌgɔri/ *n. plural* **categories** [C] a group of people or things that all have the same particular qualities: *Housing authorities that enforce the policies will qualify for certain categories of bonus funding.* | *Voters* **fall into** (=belong to) *three main categories.*

category kil·ler /ˈ.... ˌ../ *n.* [C] a large store that sells only one type of product, usually at very low prices

ca·ter /ˈkeɪtə/ *v.* [I,T] to provide and serve food and drinks at a party, meeting etc., usually as a business: *a catered lunch* | [+ **for/at**] *The prize was a party catered for the winner and 50 guests.* | [**cater sth**] *Who's catering your daughter's wedding?*

    cater to/for sb/sth *phr. v.* [T] to provide a particular group of people with something that they need or want: *Big software stores cater mostly to the business market.* | *We need to focus on programs that cater to the needs of children.*

cat·er-cor·ner /ˈkætiˌkɔrnə, ˈkætə-, ˈkɪti-/ *adj.* another spelling of KITTY-CORNER

ca·ter·er /ˈkeɪtərə/ *n.* [C] a person or company that is paid to provide and serve food and drinks at a party, meeting etc.

ca·ter·ing /ˈkeɪtərɪŋ/ *n.* [U] the activity of providing and serving food and drinks at parties for money: *The restaurant also does take-out food and catering.*

cat·er·pil·lar /ˈkætəˌpɪlə, ˈkætə-/ *n.* [C] a small creature with a small rounded body and many legs, that eats leaves and is the YOUNG form of a BUTTERFLY or MOTH —see picture at METAMORPHOSIS

cat·er·waul /ˈkætəˌwɔl/ *v.* [I] to make a loud high annoying noise like the sound a cat makes —**caterwaul** *n.* [singular]

cat·fight /ˈkætˈfaɪt/ *n.* [C] INFORMAL a word for a fight between two women, considered insulting by many women

cat·fish /ˈkætˈfɪʃ/ *n.* [C,U] a common fish with long hair-like things around its mouth, that lives mainly in rivers and lakes

cat·gut /ˈkætˈgʌt/ *n.* [U] strong thread made from the INTESTINEs of animals and used for the strings of musical instruments, and for tennis RACKETS

ca·thar·sis /kəˈθɑrsɪs/ *n.* [singular,U] FORMAL a way of dealing with bad or strong feelings and emotions, by expressing or experiencing them through writing, talking, DRAMA etc.

ca·thar·tic /kəˈθɑrtɪk/ *adj.* helping you to deal with difficult emotions and get rid of them: *Talking to a counselor can be a cathartic experience.*

ca·the·dral /kəˈθidrəl/ *n.* [C] a large church, which is the main church of a particular area that a BISHOP is responsible for

Cath·er /ˈkæðə/, **Wil·la** /ˈwɪlə/ (1876–1947) a U.S. writer who wrote about Nebraska at the time when Europeans first went to live there

Cath·e·rine II /ˌkæθrɪn ðə ˈsɛkənd/ also **Catherine the Great** (1729–1796) the EMPRESS of Russia from 1762 to 1796 who greatly increased the size of the Russian EMPIRE

cath·e·ter /ˈkæθətə/ *n.* [C] a thin tube that is put into someone's body to take away liquids —**catheterize** *v.* [T]

cath·ode /ˈkæθoʊd/ *n.* [C] TECHNICAL the negative ELECTRODE from which electric current leaves a piece of equipment such as a BATTERY —compare ANODE

cathode ray tube /ˌ.. ˈ. ˌ./ *n.* [C] a piece of equipment used in televisions and computers, in which negative ELECTRONs from the cathode produce an image on a screen

Cath·o·lic /ˈkæθlɪk, -θəlɪk/ *adj.* belonging or relating to the part of the Christian religion whose leader is the Pope: *a Catholic school* —**Catholic** *n.* [C] —**Catholicism** /kəˈθɑləˌsɪzəm/ *n.* [U]

catholic *adj.* FORMAL not limited to only a few things: *an artist with catholic tastes* —**catholicity** /ˌkæθəˈlɪsəti/ *adj.*

cat·house /ˈkæthaʊs/ *n.* [C] INFORMAL a place where men can pay to have sex with PROSTITUTES; BROTHEL

cat·kin /ˈkætˈkɪn/ *n.* [C] a soft flower that grows in long thin groups and hangs from the branches of trees such as the WILLOW or BIRCH

Cat·lin /ˈkætlən/, **George** (1796–1872) a U.S. PAINTER famous for his pictures of Native Americans

cat lit·ter /ˈ. ˌ../ also **kitty litter** *n.* [U] a substance, like large grains of sand, that people put into boxes for cats that live indoors, which the cats use as a toilet

cat·nap /ˈkætˈnæp/ *n.* [C] INFORMAL a very short sleep: *New mothers learn to take catnaps while the baby is sleeping.* —**cat nap** *v.* [I]

cat·nip /ˈkætˈnɪp/ *n.* [U] a type of grass with a nice smell that cats are attracted to

cat-o'-nine-tails /ˌkæt ə ˈnaɪn ˌteɪlz/ *n.* [C] a whip made of nine strings with knots on the end, used in past times for punishing people

CAT scan /ˈkæt skæn/ also **CT scan** *n.* [C] **1** an image produced by a CAT scanner **2** the process of using a CAT scanner to produce an image of the inside of someone's body: *Todd underwent a CAT scan.*

CAT scan·ner /ˈkæt ˌskænə/ also **CT scanner** *n.* [C] an electronic machine used in a hospital to produce an image of the inside of someone's body

cat's cra·dle /ˌ. ˈ.../ *n.* [U] a game in which children wind string around their fingers and between their hands to make different patterns

Cats·kill Moun·tains, the /ˈkætskɪl/ also **The Catskills** a group of mountains in the southeast of New York state in the northeastern U.S. that is part of the Appalachians

cat·suit /ˈkætˈsut/ *n.* [C] a tight piece of women's clothing that covers all of the body and legs in one piece

cat·sup /ˈkɛtʃəp, ˈkæ-/ *n.* [U] another spelling of KETCHUP

Catt /kæt/, **Car·rie Chap·man** /ˈkæri ˈtʃæpmən/ (1859–1947) a U.S. woman who helped women get the right to vote

cat·tail /ˈkætˈteɪl/ *n.* [C] a plant that grows near water and has SAUSAGE-shaped groups of brown flowers and seeds

cat·tle /ˈkætl/ *n.* [plural] cows and BULLs kept on a farm for their meat or milk: *herds of cattle* | *The ranch has enough land to graze 7000 head of cattle* (=7000 cattle).

cattle call /ˈ.. ˌ./ *n.* [C] an event at which a large number of people who want to play a part in a play, movie etc. go and give a short performance for the people who are in charge of the play or movie

cattle guard /ˈ.. ˌ./ *n.* [C] a set of bars placed over a hole in the road, so that animals cannot go across but cars can

cat·tle·man /ˈkætlmən/ *n. plural* **cattlemen** /-mən/ [C] someone who owns cattle

cattle prod /ˈ.. ˌ./ *n.* [C] a type of stick that gives an electric shock to cattle, to make them move along

cat·ty /ˈkæti/ *adj.* deliberately not nice in what you say about someone: *Joyce made a catty comment about Sonia's clothes.* —**cattiness** *n.* [U]

cat·ty-cor·ner /ˈ.. ˌ../ *adv.* KITTY-CORNER

CATV *n.* [U] community antenna television; a type of television service for areas that normally do not receive television broadcasts clearly

cat·walk /ˈkætˌwɔk/ *n.* [C] **1** a long raised path that MODELS walk on in a fashion show; RUNWAY **2** a narrow structure for people to walk on that is built along something such as a bridge or above a stage in a theater

Cau·ca·sian /kɔˈkeɪʒən/ *adj.* FORMAL someone who is Caucasian belongs to the race that has pale skin —**Caucasian** *n.* [C]

Cau·ca·sus, the /ˈkɔkəsəs/ also **Cau·ca·sia** /kɔˈkeɪʒə/ an area between the Black Sea and the Caspian Sea that includes part of Russia, Georgia, Azerbaijan, and Armenia and contains the Caucasus Mountains

Caucasus Mountains, the a group of mountains in the Caucasus in southeast Europe

cau·cus /ˈkɔkəs/ *n. plural* **caucuses** [C] a local meeting of the members of a political party to choose people to represent them at a larger meeting, or to choose a CANDIDATE in an election

caught /kɔt/ *v.* the past tense and past participle of CATCH[1]

caul·dron, caldron /ˈkɔldrən/ *n.* [C] **1** a large round metal pot for boiling liquids over a fire **2** a situation that is dangerous and that may produce war, violence etc.: *If peace talks fail, the entire region could become a cauldron of destruction.*

cau·li·flow·er /ˈkɔliˌflaʊɚ, ˈka-/ *n.* [U] a vegetable with green leaves around a large firm white center made up of groups of flower-like parts —see picture at VEGETABLE

cauliflower ear /ˈ.... ˌ., ˌ.... ˈ./ *n.* [C] an ear permanently swollen into a strange shape, especially as a result of an injury

caulk[1] /kɔk/ also **caulk·ing** /ˈkɔkɪŋ/ *n.* [U] a substance used to fill in holes, cracks, or other empty spaces between two things or two parts of something so that air or water cannot get through

caulk[2] *v.* [I,T] to fill in holes, cracks, or other empty spaces between two things or two parts of something with caulk

caus·al /ˈkɔzəl/ *adj.* **1 a causal relationship/link/connection etc.** a relationship etc. that exists between two or more events or situations, where one causes the other to happen: *There is nothing to prove a causal relationship between violence on TV and violent crime.* **2** TECHNICAL a causal CONJUNCTION, for example "because," introduces a statement about the cause of something —**causally** *adv.*

cau·sal·i·ty /kɔˈzæləti/ *n.* [U] FORMAL the relationship between a cause and the effect that it has

cau·sa·tion /kɔˈzeɪʃən/ *n.* [U] FORMAL **1** the action of causing something to happen or exist **2** causality

caus·a·tive /ˈkɔzətɪv/ *adj.* **1** FORMAL acting as the cause of something: *Radon may be the major causative factor in many of these cancer cases.* **2** TECHNICAL a causative verb expresses an action that causes something to happen or be —**causatively** *adv.*

'cause /kəz/ *conjunction* SPOKEN an informal way of saying BECAUSE: *I have to go to the dentist, 'cause one of my back teeth hurts.*

cause[1] /kɔz/ *n.*
s w
1 1
1 what causes sth [C] a person, event, or thing that makes something happen, especially something bad: [+ of] *Airline officials refused to comment on the cause of the crash.* | **a major/primary/chief cause** *Pollution is a major cause of the global rise in* temperatures. | **the root/underlying cause** (=the basic or main cause) | *The man's death was from natural causes.* | *Heavy drinking may be both the cause and effect of sexual problems.* —see Usage Note at REASON[1]

2 good reason [U] something that makes it right or fair for you to feel or behave in a particular way: [+ for] *FAA officials see no cause for alarm in safety procedures.* | *Some experts believe there is cause for concern* (=a reason to be worried) *in the amount of time children spend on video games.* | *People are worried about the economy, and with good cause*

3 sth you support [C] an organization, principle, or aim that a group of people support or fight for: *Money from the charity dinner will go to causes chosen by the guests.* | [+ of] *Eleanor Roosevelt is remembered for her devotion to the cause of women's rights.*

4 be for a good cause if something you do is for a good cause, it is worth doing because it is intended to help other people, especially through a CHARITY: *I don't mind giving money if it's for a good cause.*

5 law TECHNICAL [C] a case that is brought to a court of law —see also **a lost cause** (LOST[1] (8)), **make common cause (with sb)** (COMMON[1] (12))

cause[2] *v.* [T] to make something happen, especially something bad: *Heavy traffic is causing long delays on the freeway.* | *The fire caused $500,000 in damage.* | [**cause sb/sth to do sth**] *Water flooded the ship in 10 minutes, causing it to sink.* | [**cause sth for sb**] *The industry's policies have caused problems for many retailers.* | [**cause sb sth**] *The classrooms are old and in disrepair, and this has caused parents some concern.*

cause cé·lè·bre /ˌkɔz sɛˈlɛbrə, ˌkooz-/ *n.* [C] FORMAL an event or legal case that a lot of people become interested in, because it is an exciting subject to discuss or argue about: *Gun control has become the cause célèbre since the recent high school shootings.*

cause·way /ˈkɔzweɪ/ *n.* [C] a raised road that goes across wet ground or an area of water

caus·tic /ˈkɔstɪk/ *adj.* **1** extremely unkind and full of criticism: *One of the lawyers made a caustic remark to the press.* **2** a caustic substance can burn through things by chemical action —**caustically** /-kli/ *adv.*

caustic soda /ˌ.. ˈ../ *n.* [U] a very strong chemical substance that you can use for some difficult cleaning jobs; LYE

cau·ter·ize /ˈkɔtəˌraɪz/ *v.* [T] TECHNICAL to burn a wound with hot metal or a chemical to stop the blood or to prevent it from becoming infected

cau·tion[1] /ˈkɔʃən/ *n.* **1** [U] the quality of being very careful, not taking any risks, and trying to avoid danger: *In rock climbing, no amount of skill will make up for a lack of caution.* | **treat/use etc. sth with caution** *The results of the survey must be treated with caution* (=thought about carefully, because they might not be correct). | **extreme/great caution** *Travelers in the area should use extreme caution.* | *The FBI said anyone receiving such a package should exercise* (=use) *caution when opening it.* **2 a word/note of caution** a warning to be careful: *A word of caution: learn from an experienced surfer.* **3 throw/fling/cast caution to the wind(s)** LITERARY to start to take more risks in what you do or say: *I decided to throw caution to the wind and say what I thought.*

caution[2] *v.* [T] to warn someone that something might be dangerous, difficult etc.: [**caution sb about/against sth**] *Shapiro cautioned doctors against using the new test until more research is done.* | [**caution (sb) that**] *A warning on the package cautioned customers that the toy contains small parts.* | [**caution sb to do sth**] *Garamendi cautioned consumers not to make a decision on price alone.*

cau·tion·ar·y /ˈkɔʃəˌnɛri/ *adj.* **1 a cautionary tale** a story about something bad that has happened, used to warn people about something that could happen to them: *The strike could be used in business schools as a cautionary tale for management.* **2** giving a warning or advice: *The group's latest album gives a cautionary account of chemical dependency.*

cau·tious /ˈkɔʃəs/ *adj.* careful to avoid danger or risks: *a cautious driver* | [+ **about**] *Doctors were cautious about releasing Sharon from the hospital too soon.* | *Both sides have expressed **cautious optimism** that an agreement will soon be reached* (=they are hoping for a good result, but are being careful not to expect too much). —**cautiously** *adv.*: *Sara opened the door cautiously and looked in.* —**cautiousness** *n.* [U]

cav·al·cade /ˌkævəlˈkeɪd, ˈkævəlˌkeɪd/ *n.* [C] **1** a line of people on horses or in cars moving along as part of a ceremony **2** a series of people or things: [+ **of**] *a cavalcade of dances and songs*

cav·a·lier /ˌkævəˈlɪr/ *adj.* not caring or thinking about other people: *Ron has **a very cavalier attitude** toward workers' safety.*

cav·al·ry /ˈkævəlri/ *n.* [U] **1** the part of a modern army that uses TANKS **2** the part of an army that fights on horses, especially in past times

cav·al·ry·man /ˈkævəlrimən/ *n.* [C] *plural* **cavalrymen** /-mən/ a soldier who fights on a horse

cave[1] /keɪv/ *n.* [C] a large natural hole in the side of a cliff or hill, or under the ground

cave[2] *v.*
cave in *phr. v.* [I] **1** to finally stop opposing something, especially because someone has persuaded or threatened you: [+ **to**] *The department **caved in to** pressure from environmental groups.* **2** if the top or sides of something cave in, they fall down or toward the inside: *Two miners were killed when a section of the mine caved in.* —**cave-in** *n.* [C]

ca·ve·at /ˈkævi,ɑt/ *n.* [C] FORMAL a warning that you must pay attention to something before you make a decision or take a particular action

caveat emp·tor /ˌkæviat ˈɛmptɔr, -tɔr/ *n.* [U] a phrase meaning, "let the buyer beware," used to express the principle that when goods are sold, the buyer is responsible for checking the quality of the goods

cave·man /ˈkeɪvmæn/ *n.* [C] *plural* **cavemen** /-mɛn/ **1** someone who lived in a CAVE many thousands of years ago **2** INFORMAL a man who behaves or thinks in a way that does not seem modern

cav·ern /ˈkævən/ *n.* [C] a large CAVE

cav·ern·ous /ˈkævənəs/ *adj.* a cavernous room, space, or hole is very large and deep —**cavernously** *adv.*

cav·i·ar, caviare /ˈkævi,ɑr/ *n.* [U] the salted eggs of various types of large fish, considered a special food that is usually very expensive

cav·il /ˈkævəl/ *v.* [I + **at**] FORMAL to make unnecessary complaints about someone or something —**cavil** *n.* [C]

cav·ing /ˈkeɪvɪŋ/ *n.* [U] the activity or sport of going deep under the ground in CAVES; SPELUNKING

cav·i·ty /ˈkævəti/ *n.* *plural* **cavities** [C] **1** a hole in a tooth made by decay **2** FORMAL a hole or space inside something: *The heart and lungs are located inside the chest cavity.*

ca·vort /kəˈvɔrt/ *v.* [I] to jump or dance around loudly in a playful or sexual way: *Annie's husband was pictured in newspapers cavorting with a fashion model.*

caw /kɔ/ *v.* [I] if a bird, especially a CROW, caws, it makes a loud sound —**caw** *n.* [C]

Cax·ton /ˈkækstən/, **William** (?1422-1491) an English printer, who was the first person in England to print books, after learning about printing in Germany

cay /ki, keɪ/ *n. plural* **cays** [C] a very small island formed from CORAL or sand

cay·enne pep·per /ˌkeɪɛn ˈpɛpə/ *n.* [U] red powder made from a PEPPER that has a very SPICY taste

cay·man /ˈkeɪmən/ *n. plural* **caymans** [C] a South American animal like an ALLIGATOR

Ca·yu·ga /keɪˈyugə, kaɪ-/ a Native American tribe from the northeastern area of the U.S.

Cay·use /kaɪˈyus/ a Native American tribe from the northwestern area of the U.S.

CB *n.* [U] Citizen's Band; a radio on which people can talk to each other over short distances, especially when they are driving

CBS *n.* Columbia Broadcasting System; one of the national companies that broadcasts television and radio programs in the U.S.

CBT *n.* [U] computer-based testing; a way of taking standard tests, such as the TOEFL or GRE, on a computer

cc 1 the abbreviation of "carbon copy;" used in a business letter or EMAIL to show that you are sending a copy to someone else: *To Neil Fry, cc: Andrea Baker, Matt Fox* **2** the abbreviation of CUBIC CENTIMETER: *an 800cc engine*

CD *n.* [C] **1** compact disc; a small circular piece of hard plastic on which high quality recorded sound or large quantities of information can be stored —compare CD-ROM **2** TECHNICAL the abbreviation of CERTIFICATE OF DEPOSIT

CD play·er /ˌ. ˈ.ˌ./ *n.* [C] a piece of equipment used to play music CDs

CD-ROM /ˌsi di ˈrɑm/ *n.* [C,U] compact disc read-only memory; a CD on which large quantities of information can be stored to be used by a computer —see picture on page 426

CDT the abbreviation of Central Daylight Time

C.E. Common Era; used after a date to show it was after the birth of Jesus Christ —compare B.C.E.

cease[1] /sis/ *v.* [I,T] **1** FORMAL to stop doing something or stop happening: *The newspaper has been forced to cease publication.* | *By noon the rain had ceased.* | [**cease doing sth**] *Hansen has ceased cooperating with the FBI investigation.* | [**cease to do sth**] *Without the Facilities Department, the university would soon cease to function.* | *East Germany ceased to exist in 1990, becoming a part of the Federal Republic of Germany.* | *The quality of Walters' music never ceases to amaze me* (=it always surprises me). **2 cease and desist** LAW to stop doing something —see also CEASE-FIRE, **wonders will never cease!** (WONDER[2] (5))

cease[2] *n.* **without cease** FORMAL without stopping

cease·fire /ˈsisfaɪr/ *n.* [C] an agreement to stop fighting for a period of time, especially so that a more permanent agreement can be made —compare ARMISTICE, TRUCE

cease·less /ˈsislɪs/ *adj.* FORMAL happening or existing for a long time without changing or stopping: *the ceaseless Arctic wind* —**ceaselessly** *adv.*

ce·dar /ˈsidə/ *n.* **1** [C] a large EVERGREEN tree with leaves shaped like needles **2** also **cedarwood** [U] the hard reddish wood of this tree, which smells good

cede /sid/ *v.* [T] FORMAL to give something such as an area of land or a right to a country or person, especially when you are forced to: *The military has refused to cede power to elected officials.* | *Much of the territory along the border was ceded to the United States.* —see also CESSION

ce·dil·la /sɪˈdɪlə/ *n.* [C] a mark put under the letter "c" in French and some other languages, to show that it is an "s" sound instead of a "k" sound. It is written "ç."

ceil·ing /ˈsilɪŋ/ *n.* [C] **1** the inner surface of the top part of a room —compare ROOF[1] (1) **2** the largest number or amount of something that is officially allowed: *Millions of federal employees may not receive paychecks unless Congress raises the debt ceiling.* | [+ **on**] *Gambling is allowed, but there is a $5 ceiling on bets.* **3** the height of the lowest layer of clouds over an area **4** TECHNICAL the greatest height at which an aircraft can fly or is allowed to fly —see also GLASS CEILING

cel·a·don /ˈsɛlə,dɑn/ *n.* [U] a pale or light green color —**celadon** *adj.*

ce·leb /səˈlɛb/ *n.* [C] INFORMAL a CELEBRITY

cel·e·brant /ˈsɛləbrənt/ *n.* [C] someone who performs or takes part in a religious ceremony

cel·e·brate /ˈsɛləˌbreɪt/ v. **1** [I,T] to do something special because of a particular event or special occasion: *We're celebrating Katie's birthday on Friday.* | *The graduation ceremony allows students to celebrate their achievements with family and friends.* | *When Peggy turned 40, she invited 40 friends to help her celebrate.* **2** [T] FORMAL to praise someone or something in speech, writing, or pictures: *His poems celebrate the joys of love.* **3** [T] to perform a religious ceremony, especially a Mass in the Catholic church

cel·e·brat·ed /ˈsɛləˌbreɪtɪd/ adj. famous or talked about a lot: *a celebrated professor* | [+ for] *Chicago is celebrated for its architecture.*

cel·e·bra·tion /ˌsɛləˈbreɪʃən/ n. **1** [C] an occasion or party when you celebrate something: *New Year's celebrations* | *Posadas is a nine-day celebration in Mexico before Christmas.* **2** [U] the act of celebrating: *There will be a party in celebration of Joan and Dave's 40th anniversary.* **3** [C,U] something that praises someone or something in speech, writing, or pictures: [+ of] *Her latest film is a celebration of motherhood.*

cel·e·bra·to·ry /ˈsɛləbrəˌtɔri/ adj. done in order to celebrate a particular event or occasion: *The celebratory event will mark the 75th anniversary of the university.*

ce·leb·ri·ty /səˈlɛbrəti/ n. plural **celebrities** **1** [C] a famous person, especially someone in the entertainment business **2** [U] FORMAL the state of being famous; FAME

ce·ler·i·ty /səˈlɛrəti/ n. [U] FORMAL great speed

cel·er·y /ˈsɛləri/ n. [U] a vegetable with long firm pale green stems, often eaten raw: *a stalk of celery*

ce·les·tial /səˈlɛstʃəl/ adj. LITERARY **1** relating to the sky or heaven: *Venus is the brightest celestial body* (=a star, moon, sun etc.) *after the moon.* **2** very beautiful: *celestial music*

cel·i·ba·cy /ˈsɛləbəsi/ n. [U] the state of not having sex, especially because of your religious beliefs: *Legend has it that the emperor had taken a vow of celibacy.* —compare ABSTINENCE

cel·i·bate /ˈsɛləbət/ adj. not having sex, especially because of your religious beliefs —**celibate** n. [C]

cell /sɛl/ n. [C] **1** the smallest part of a living thing that can exist independently: *cancer cells* | *red blood cells* **2** a small room in a police station or prison where prisoners are kept **3** a piece of equipment that produces electricity from chemicals, heat, or light: *alkaline battery cells* **4** a small group of people who are working secretly as part of a larger political organization: *Warren planned to find a communist cell and become a member.* **5** a small space that an insect or other small creature has made to live in or use: *the cells of a honeycomb* **6** a small room where someone sleeps in a MONASTERY or CONVENT

cel·lar /ˈsɛlə/ n. [C] **1** a room under a house or other building, often used for storing things —compare BASEMENT **2** also **wine cellar** a large number of bottles of wine that belong to a person, restaurant etc. **3 the cellar** INFORMAL the last position in a sports LEAGUE, held by the team that has lost the most games: *The Braves managed to climb from the cellar to first place.*

cell di·vi·sion /ˈ. .ˌ../ n. [U] the process by which plant and animal cells increase their numbers

Cel·li·ni /tʃəˈlini/, **Ben·ve·nu·to** /ˌbɛnvəˈnutoʊ/ (1500–1571) an Italian SCULPTOR famous for his work in gold and other metals

cel·list /ˈtʃɛlɪst/ n. [C] someone who plays the cello

cell·mate /ˈsɛlmeɪt/ n. [C] someone who shares a prison CELL with someone else

cel·lo /ˈtʃɛloʊ/ n. plural **cellos** [C] a large wooden musical instrument, shaped like a VIOLIN, that you hold between your knees and play by pulling a BOW (=SPECIAL STICK) across wire strings

cel·lo·phane /ˈsɛləˌfeɪn/ n. [U] thin transparent material used for wrapping things

cell phone /ˈ. ./ n. [C] a telephone that you can carry with you, that works by using a network of radio stations to pass on signals

cel·lu·lar /ˈsɛlyələ/ adj. **1** consisting of or relating to the cells of plants or animals: *cellular biology* **2** relating to cellular phones or the business of providing services for cellular phones: *a cellular network*

cellular phone /ˌ... ˈ./ n. [C] FORMAL a cell phone

cel·lu·lite /ˈsɛlyəˌlaɪt/ n. [U] fat that is just below someone's skin and that makes the surface of their skin look uneven and unattractive

cel·lu·loid[1] /ˈsɛlyəˌlɔɪd/ n. **1** the film used in past times to make movies: *Chaplin's comic genius is preserved on celluloid.* **2** [U] a substance like plastic, used in past times to make photographic film and other objects

celluloid[2] adj. relating to the movies, especially from the first half of the 20th century: *celluloid images of romance* | *America's celluloid heroes*

cel·lu·lose /ˈsɛlyəˌloʊs/ n. **1** the material that the cell walls of plants are made of, and that is used to make plastics, paper etc. **2** also **cellulose acetate** TECHNICAL a plastic that is used for many industrial purposes, especially making photographic film and explosives

Cel·si·us /ˈsɛlsiəs, -ʃəs/ abbreviation **C** n. [U] a temperature scale in which water freezes at 0° and boils at 100°; CENTIGRADE —**Celsius** adj.: *a Celsius thermometer* | *12° Celsius*

Celt /kɛlt, sɛlt/ **1** one of the people who lived in Britain and Ireland from about 400 B.C. before the arrival of the Romans in the first century B.C. **2** one of the people who lived in western Europe, especially in parts of France and Spain from about 1200 B.C. until the arrival of the Romans in the first century B.C.

Celt·ic /ˈkɛltɪk, ˈsɛltɪk/ adj. related to the Celts, an ancient European race, or to their languages

ce·ment[1] /sɪˈmɛnt/ n. [U] **1** a gray powder used in building things, that becomes hard when it is mixed with water and allowed to dry: *a cement wall* —compare CONCRETE[1] **2** a substance used for filling holes or as a glue **3** something that holds a relationship between people, countries etc. together or makes it strong: *Literary Arabic has always been the cement of Islam.*

cement[2] v. [T] **1** also **cement over** to cover something with cement: *Some of the graves are cemented over.* **2** to make a relationship between people or countries firm and strong: *Steven's marriage to Lucy Brett cemented important business ties with her family.*

cement mix·er /ˈ. ˌ../ n. [C] a machine with a round open container that turns around, into which you put cement, sand, and water to make CONCRETE; CONCRETE MIXER

cem·e·ter·y /ˈsɛməˌtɛri/ n. plural **cemeteries** [C] an area of land where dead people are buried —see also GRAVEYARD

cen·o·taph /ˈsɛnəˌtæf/ n. [C] a MONUMENT built to remind people of soldiers, SAILORS etc. who were killed in a war and are buried somewhere else

cen·sor[1] /ˈsɛnsə/ v. [T] to examine books, movies, letters etc. to remove anything that is offensive, morally harmful, or politically dangerous etc.: *Prisoners' letters were always heavily censored.*

censor[2] n. [C] someone whose job is to examine books, movies, letters etc. and remove anything that is offensive, morally harmful, or politically dangerous

cen·so·ri·ous /sɛnˈsɔriəs/ adj. FORMAL always disapproving of something and criticizing it: *Horowitz had been censorious of the peace movement in the 1960s.* —**censoriously** adv. —**censoriousness** n. [U]

cen·sor·ship /ˈsɛnsəˌʃɪp/ n. [U] the practice or system of censoring something: *Many community leaders have called for censorship of the Internet.*

cen·sure[1] /ˈsɛnʃə/ n. [U] FORMAL the act of officially expressing strong disapproval and criticism: *The governor could be pressured to resign by a vote of censure.*

censure² *v.* [T] FORMAL to officially criticize someone for something they have done wrong: *Several senators called for Hayes to be censured for his conduct.*

cen·sus /ˈsɛnsəs/ *n. plural* **censuses** [C] an official count of all the people in a country, including information about their ages, jobs etc.: *When was the first U.S. census taken?*

cent /sɛnt/ *n.* [C] **1** *written abbreviation* ¢ a unit of money that is worth 1/100th of a dollar. **2 put in your two cents' worth** INFORMAL to give your opinion about something, when other people do not want to hear it —see also **not one red cent** (RED¹ (7))

cen·taur /ˈsɛntɔr/ *n.* [C] a creature in ancient Greek stories that has the head, chest, and arms of a man and the body and legs of a horse

cen·te·nar·i·an /ˌsɛntəˈnɛriən/ *n.* [C] someone who is 100 years old or older

cen·ten·ni·al /sɛnˈtɛniəl/ also **cen·ten·a·ry** /sɛnˈtɛnəri, ˈsɛntˌnɛri/ *n.* [C] the day or year that is exactly 100 years after a particular event: *The orchestra will hold a concert to mark the centennial of Tchaikovsky's birth.*

cen·ter¹ /ˈsɛntər/ *n.* [C]
1 middle the middle of a space, area, or object, especially the exact middle: *a flower with yellow petals and a purple center* | [+ of] *There was an enormous oak table in the center of the room.* —see Usage Note at MIDDLE¹
2 place/building a place or building that is used for a particular purpose or activity: *the Fred Hutchinson Cancer Research Center* | *a huge shopping center* | *a new $3 million center for the elderly*
3 where things happen a place where most of the important things happen that relate to a particular business or activity: *His goal is to turn Stanford into a center for environmental policy.* | *a major banking center* | [+ of] *Nashville is still the center of the country music industry.*
4 attention/interest someone or something to which people give a lot of attention: *Some stars feel the need to be the center of attention on stage, but not Harris.* | *Linda soon found herself at the center of the scandal.*
5 center stage a position that attracts attention or importance. *The Republicans are hoping the issue of taxes takes center stage during the election.*
6 urban center also center of population an area where a large number of people live: *The wilderness area is only a few miles from a major urban center.*
7 politics the center a MODERATE (=middle) position in politics which does not support extreme ideas: *Seymour appeals to the party's broad political center.* | *right/left of center Environmental and left-of-center groups attended the protest in large numbers.*
8 basketball the player on a basketball team who is usually the tallest and who usually plays nearest to the basket
9 football the player on a football team who starts the ball moving in each PLAY² (3)

center² *v.* [T] **1** to move something to a position at the center of something else: *Use Shift-F4 to center the paragraph on the page.* **2 be centered** if an event or activity is centered at a particular place, the most important or largest part of it happens there: *Most of the fighting is centered in the southeast of the country.* | *The group of writers is centered at Vanderbilt University.*

center around sth *phr. v.* [T] if your thoughts, activities etc. center around something, it is the main thing that you think is important: *The investigation centered around drug use within the armed forces.*

center on/upon sth *phr. v.* [T] also **be centered on/upon** sth if an event or activity centers on something, that is the thing that people pay the most attention to: *The debate centered on the morality of abortion.* | *The dispute is centered on demands for higher pay.*

center di·vi·der /ˌ.. ..., ... ˈ../ *n.* [C] a fence or raised area in the middle of a wide road, that separates cars going in opposite directions

cen·tered /ˈsɛntərd/ *adj.* **1** having a particular

person or thing as the most important part of something: *a child-centered approach to education* **2** feeling calm and in control of yourself: *Meditation can make you feel centered and healthy.* —see also SELF-CENTERED

center field /ˌ.. ˈ./ *n.* [C] the area in baseball in the center of the OUTFIELD —**center fielder** *n.* [C]

cen·ter·fold /ˈsɛntərˌfoʊld/ *n.* [C] **1** a picture of a woman with no clothes on, that covers the two pages in the middles of a magazine: *Brandi was once a Playboy centerfold.* **2** the two pages that face each other in the middle of a magazine or newspaper, and that often have a picture on them: *The advertisement is a centerfold drawing of a vodka bottle.*

center of grav·i·ty /ˌ.. .. ˈ.../ *n.* [singular] **1** the point on an object where most of its weight seems to be, at which it will balance **2** the part of something that is most important or that people pay the most attention to: *Guichard wanted to halt the shift of Europe's center of gravity toward the east after the fall of Communism.*

cen·ter·piece /ˈsɛntərˌpis/ *n.* [C] **1** a decoration, especially an arrangement of flowers, in the middle of a table **2** the most important, noticeable, or attractive part of something: [+ of] *Health care reform was the centerpiece of the President's campaign.*

centi- /ˈsɛntə/ *prefix* also **cent-** **1** 100: *a centipede* (=a creature with 100 legs) **2** 100th part of a unit: *a centimeter* (=0.01 meters)

Cen·ti·grade /ˈsɛntəˌɡreɪd/ *n.* [U] CELSIUS —**Centigrade** *adj.*

cen·ti·gram /ˈsɛntəˌɡræm/ *n.* [C] a unit for measuring weight. There are 100 centigrams in one gram.

cent·i·li·ter /ˈsɛntəˌlitər/ *n.* [C] a unit for measuring liquid. There are 100 centiliters in one liter.

cen·time /ˈsɑntim/ *n.* [C] a unit of money that is worth 1/100 of a FRANC or of some other types of money, or a coin worth this amount

cen·ti·me·ter /ˈsɛntəˌmitər/ *written abbreviation* **cm** *n.* [C] a unit for measuring length. There are 100 centimeters in one meter

cen·ti·pede /ˈsɛntəˌpid/ *n.* [C] a very small creature with a long body and many legs

Cen·tral /ˈsɛntrəl/ *n.* a short form of Central Time: *The next episode is on Wednesday at 8:30 Eastern, 7:30 Central.*

cen·tral /ˈsɛntrəl/ *adj.* [no comparative] **1** [only before noun] in the middle of an object or an area: *the farming areas of central California* | *The central part of the building tends to be warmer in the winter.* **2** [only before noun] controlling or used by everyone or everything in a whole country, large organization, or system: *The computers are linked to a central database.* | *a house with central heating* **3** more important and having more influence than anything else: *Crime is going to be the central issue of the mayoral campaign.* | *Wingo is the troubled central character of Conroy's novel.* | [+ to] *Most of the foods central to Portuguese cooking are common in our kitchens.* | *Owen played a central role in the negotiations.* **4 party/comedy etc. central** INFORMAL a place where something is happening a lot: *Tim's house became party central for the band and their friends.* | *This bulletin board serves as communications central* (=a common place to leave a message for someone) *for the campus.* —**centrally** *adv.*: *Our office is centrally located.* —**centrality** /sɛnˈtræləti/ *n.* [U]

Central Af·ri·can Re·pub·lic, the /ˌ.. ˌ... ˈ../ a country in central Africa, that is north of Congo and west of Sudan

central bank /ˌ.. ˈ./ *n.* [C] a national bank that does business with the government, and that controls the amount of money available and the general system of banks of that particular country

Central Day·light Time /,.. '.. ,./ *written abbreviation* **CDT** *n.* [U] the time that is used in the east-central part of the U.S. for over half the year, including the summer, when clocks are one hour ahead of Central Standard Time

Central Eu·rope /,.. '../ *n.* countries in the middle of Europe, such as Poland, the Czech Republic, and Hungary —compare EASTERN EUROPE, WESTERN EUROPE

Central In·tel·li·gence A·gen·cy /,.. .'... ,../ *n.* the CIA

cen·tral·ism /'sɛntrə,lɪzəm/ *n.* [U] a way of governing a country or controlling an organization, in which one central group has power and tells people in other places what to do

cen·tral·ize /'sɛntrə,laɪz/ *v.* [T] to organize the control of a country or organization so that one central group has power and tells people in other places what to do: *Attempts to centralize the economy have failed.* —**centralized** *adj.*: *centralized planning* —**centralization** /,sɛntrələ'zeɪʃən/ *n.* [U] —compare DECENTRALIZE

central ner·vous sys·tem /,.. '.. ,../ *n.* [C] the main part of your NERVOUS SYSTEM, consisting of your brain and your SPINAL CORD

central pro·cess·ing u·nit /,.. '... ,../ *n.* [C] a CPU

Central Stan·dard Time /,... ,.. '., ,... '.. ,./ *written abbreviation* **CST** *n.* [U] the time that is used in the east-central part of the U.S. for almost half the year, including the winter —compare CENTRAL DAYLIGHT TIME

Central Time /'.. ,./ *written abbreviation* **CT** *n.* [U] the time that is used in the east-central part of the U.S.

cen·tre /'sɛntə/ the British and Canadian spelling of CENTER

cen·trif·u·gal force /sɛn,trɪfyəgəl 'fɔrs, -,trɪfə-/ *n.* [U] TECHNICAL a force which makes things move away from the center of something when they are moving quickly around that center

cen·tri·fuge /'sɛntrə,fyudʒ/ *n.* [C] a machine used especially by scientists that spins a container around very quickly so that the heavier liquids and any solids are forced to the outer edge or bottom

cen·trip·e·tal force /sɛn,trɪpətl 'fɔrs/ *n.* [U] TECHNICAL a force which makes things move toward the center of something when they are moving quickly around that center

cen·trist /'sɛntrɪst/ *adj.* having political beliefs that are not extreme; MODERATE[1] (2) —**centrist** *n.* [C] —**centrism** *n.* [U]

cen·tu·ri·on /sɛn'tʃʊriən/ *adj.* an army officer of ancient Rome, who was in charge of about 100 soldiers

s w
2 1
cen·tu·ry /'sɛntʃəri/ *n. plural* **centuries** [C] **1** one of the 100-year periods counted forward or backward from the year of Jesus Christ's birth: *It was the worst air disaster this century.* | *Cubism was one of the most significant art forms of the twentieth century* (=the years 1900–1999). | *The lake could be cleaned up by the turn of the century* (=the year that ends in "00"). **2** a period of time equal to 100 years: *Naismith invented basketball over a century ago.*

CEO *n.* [C] Chief Executive Officer; the person with the most authority in a large company

ce·phal·ic /sə'fælɪk/ *adj.* TECHNICAL relating to or affecting your head

ce·ram·ics /sə'ræmɪks/ *n.* **1** [U] the art of making pots, bowls, TILES etc. by shaping pieces of clay and baking them until they are hard **2** [plural] things that are made this way: *an exhibit of ceramics at the crafts museum* **3** [U] hard baked clay that pots, bowls, TILES etc. are made of: *Most of the things in the store are made of ceramic.* —**ceramic** *adj.*: *ceramic tiles*

s w
3
ce·re·al /'sɪriəl/ *n.* **1** [C,U] a breakfast food made from grain and usually eaten with milk: *a bowl of cereal* **2** [C] FORMAL a plant grown to produce grain for foods, such as wheat, rice etc.: *cereal crops*

cer·e·bel·lum /,sɛrə'bɛləm/ *n.* [C] TECHNICAL the bottom part of your brain that controls your muscles —compare CEREBRUM

ce·re·bral /sə'ribrəl, 'sɛrə-/ *adj.* **1** TECHNICAL relating to or affecting your brain: *a cerebral hemorrhage* (=bleeding in the brain) **2** thinking or explaining things in a very complicated way that takes a lot of effort to understand: *Winters' novel is cerebral, yet also scary and funny.*

cerebral pal·sy /,.. '.., ,... '../ *n.* [U] a disease caused by damage to the brain before or during birth that makes it very difficult to speak or control your movements

cer·e·bra·tion /,sɛrə'breɪʃən/ *n.* [U] FORMAL the process of thinking

cer·e·brum /sə'ribrəm/ *n.* [C] TECHNICAL the front, larger part of the brain, where thought and decision making processes happen —compare CEREBELLUM

cer·e·mo·ni·al[1] /,sɛrə'mooniəl/ *adj.* used in a ceremony or done as part of a ceremony: *The Vice Mayor is a largely ceremonial position.* | *Native American ceremonial robes*

ceremonial[2] *n.* [C,U] FORMAL a special ceremony, or the practice of having ceremonies: *an occasion for public ceremonial*

cer·e·mo·ni·ous /,sɛrə'mooniəs/ *adj.* paying great attention to formal, correct behavior, as if you were in a ceremony —**ceremoniously** *adv.*: *The flag should be lowered ceremoniously.*

s
3
cer·e·mo·ny /'sɛrə,mooni/ *n. plural* **ceremonies 1** [C] a formal or traditional set of actions used at an important social or religious event: *The wedding ceremony was held in the county park.* | *a graduation ceremony* **2** [U] the special actions and formal words traditionally used on particular occasions: *The Senator's problems overshadowed all the pomp and ceremony of the opening of the 105th Congress.* **3 without ceremony** in a very informal way: *The bodies were buried without ceremony in hastily dug graves.* —see also **not stand on ceremony** (STAND[1] (42))

Ce·res /'sɪriz/ the Roman name for the goddess Demeter

ce·rise /sə'ris, -'riz/ *n.* [U] a bright pinkish red color —**cerise** *adj.*

cert. the written abbreviation of CERTIFICATE

s
1
cer·tain[1] /'sət'n/ *determiner, pron.* **1** a certain thing, person, place etc. is a particular thing, person etc. that you are not naming or describing exactly, but that you could give details about if you needed to: *Some vegetables are only available at certain times of the year.* | *You have to be a certain height to go on some of the rides.* | *There are certain things I just can't talk to my mother about.* | *Mrs. Logan filed a lawsuit against the company and certain of its directors* (=several particular people that you are not naming). **2** some, but not a lot: *Tommy needs a certain amount of sleep or he gets really grumpy.* | *In certain ways Martha's good to work for, but she's really sarcastic.* **3 to a certain extent/degree** partly, but not completely: *To a certain extent, just about every business here is dependent on tourism.* | *Pollution can affect the acidity of water to a certain degree.* **4 a certain a)** enough of a particular quality to be noticed: *A baby was crying, and I felt a certain sympathy for it.* | *The restaurant has a certain charm.* **b)** FORMAL used to talk about someone you do not know, but whose name you have been told: *There's a certain Mrs. Myles on the telephone.*

s
3
certain[2] *adj.* **1** [not before noun] confident and sure, without any doubts: *Coaches should be certain before they challenge a referee's decision.* | **certain (that)** *I'm almost certain that Jackie was pregnant when they got married.* | **certain who/what/how etc.** *Doctors are not certain what causes the disease.* | **[+ of/about]** *Never eat a wild plant unless you are certain about what it is.* | *Smith said he was not certain of how the bomb was triggered.* —opposite UNCERTAIN **2 know/say/tell etc. for certain** to know, say, tell etc. something without any doubt: *We may not know for certain until next year.* | *No one can say for certain what will happen.* **3 make certain** to do something in order to be sure about a fact, about

what to do, or that something will happen: [**make certain (that)**] *I went back into the house to make certain the stove was turned off.* **4** if something is certain, it will definitely happen or is definitely true: *Her business faces certain bankruptcy.* | *The captain knew what the cargo was, but it is certain that the crew did not.* | [**certain to do sth**] *Beginning golfers are almost certain to get frustrated.* | [**it is not certain who/what/how sth**] *It is not certain whether the fires were set deliberately* (=no one knows for sure). **5 one thing is for certain** SPOKEN used when you are very sure about something, especially in a situation when you cannot be sure about other things: *One thing is for certain – we'll try our best.*

cer·tain·ly /ˈsɚtnli/ *adv.* [sentence adverb] **1** a word meaning "without any doubt," used to emphasize that something is really true or really happened: *We're certainly a lot better off than we were five years ago.* | *Certainly, a backpacking trip in the high Sierras is not for everyone.* | *Hollis was almost certainly a Soviet spy.* **2** SPOKEN FORMAL used to agree or give your permission: *"Would you turn up the sound?" "Certainly."* | *"Are you going to quit?" "Certainly not!"* (=I am not going to quit)

USAGE NOTE: CERTAINLY

WORD CHOICE: certainly, surely, sure, definitely, of course, naturally, obviously

Certainly shows that you strongly feel or believe something, in spite of what others think: *I'm certainly not going to let him stay overnight* (=I will not let him do this, ever if he expects it). **Certainly** often also suggests that there may be a condition about what you are saying, even if it is not actually followed by **but**: *Amy's certainly growing, but she's not gaining weight.* | *"Brian's a very good student, isn't he?" "Well, he certainly works very hard."* (=but I do not agree that he is very good). **Surely** is less common than **certainly** and is usually used to show that you believe something, and would be surprised if others did not agree: *Surely you don't expect me to call him* (=I hope you do not expect this, and I do not think you ought to). n informal spoken English, **sure** is often used, especially just before the verb to show that you strongly believe something and are surprised or annoyed by it: *Those kids sure eat a lot.* **Definitely** shows that you believe something so strongly that there is no doubt or question about it at all: *That movie is definitely not for small children.* **Of course**, **naturally**, and **obviously** show that you think something is true and that it is not surprising: *She hadn't seen me since I was four, so of course she didn't recognize me.*

---

cer·tain·ty /ˈsɚtnti/ *n. plural* **certainties 1** [C] something that is definitely true or that will definitely happen: *Further job cutbacks are a certainty.* **2** [U] the state of being completely certain: *No one can say with any certainty how much oil is there.* | *Scientists may never be able to predict earthquakes with absolute certainty.*

cer·ti·fi·a·ble /ˌsɚtəˈfaɪəbəl/ *adj.* **1** recognized as clearly true: *"The Silence of the Lambs" was a certifiable hit.* **2** OLD-FASHIONED crazy, especially in a way that is dangerous: *You'd have to be certifiable to do a bungee jump.* **3** good enough or correct enough to be officially approved: *grade A certifiable beef*

cer·tif·i·cate /sɚˈtɪfəkɪt/ *n.* [C] **1** an official document that states that a fact or facts are true | **a birth/marriage/death certificate** *Your application must be accompanied by a copy of your birth certificate.* **2** an official document stating that you have the required abilities to do a particular job: *Betsy earned a teaching certificate from San Jose State University.* **3** an official document stating that you have completed a short course of study —see also GIFT CERTIFICATE

cer·tif·i·cat·ed /sɚˈtɪfəˌkeɪtɪd/ *adj.* TECHNICAL having an official document that shows official facts, that something is of good quality etc.

certificate of de·pos·it /ˌ... ...ˈ.../ *abbreviation* **CD** *n.* [C] TECHNICAL a bank account that you must leave a particular amount of money in for a particular amount of time in order to get INTEREST

cer·ti·fi·ca·tion /ˌsɚtəfəˈkeɪʃən/ *n.* **1** [C,U] an official document that says that someone is allowed to do a certain job, that something is of good quality etc.: *To participate in the diving program, you must show proof of scuba certification.* **2** [U] the act of giving someone or something an official document that says that they are allowed to do a certain job, that something is of good quality etc.: *Additional funds are needed for training and certification of healthcare workers.*

cer·ti·fied /ˈsɚtəˌfaɪd/ *adj.* **1** having successfully completed a training course for a particular profession: *a certified medical assistant* **2** something that is certified has been signed by someone in an official position to show that it is correct or official: *a certified copy of your birth certificate*

certified check /ˌ... ˈ./ *n.* [C] TECHNICAL a check that you get from a bank for a particular amount of money, that the bank promises to pay

certified fi·nan·cial plan·ner /ˌ... ...ˈ.../ *n.* someone whose job is to help people plan how they will save and spend their money, and who have successfully completed a course of training to do this

certified mail /ˌ... ˈ./ *n.* [U] a method of sending mail in which the person who receives it must sign their name to prove they have received it

certified pub·lic ac·count·ant /ˌ... ... .ˈ.../ *n.* [C] a CPA

cer·ti·fy /ˈsɚtəˌfaɪ/ *v.* **certified, certifying** [T] **1** to officially state that something is correct or true, often after examining it or testing it: *Sellers should submit documents certifying the value of the artwork.* | *The aircraft must be certified to meet government safety standards.* | [**certify (that)**] *Two doctors certified that the patient had less than six months to live.* **2** to give an official paper to someone which states that they have completed a course of training for a profession: *Nancy was certified as a teacher in 1990.* **3** OLD-FASHIONED to officially state that someone is mentally ill

cer·ti·tude /ˈsɚtəˌtud/ *n.* [U] FORMAL the state of being or feeling certain about something

ce·ru·le·an /səˈruliən/ *n.* [U] TECHNICAL or LITERARY a deep blue color, like that of a clear sky —**cerulean** *adj.*

Cer·van·tes /sɚˈvɑntiz/**, Mi·guel de** /miˈgɛl deɪ/ (1547–1613) a Spanish writer, best known for his NOVEL "Don Quixote"

cer·vi·cal /ˈsɚvɪkəl/ *adj.* TECHNICAL **1** relating to the cervix: *cervical cancer* **2** relating to the neck: *cervical vertebrae* (=the bones in the back of your neck)

cer·vix /ˈsɚvɪks/ *n.* [C] the narrow passage into a woman's UTERUS

ce·sar·e·an /sɪˈzɛriən/ *also* **cesarean sec·tion** /.ˈ... ...ˈ.../ *n.* [C] an operation in which a woman's body is cut open to take a baby out

ces·sa·tion /sɛˈseɪʃən/ *n.* [C,U] FORMAL a pause or stop: [+ **of**] *a temporary cessation of nuclear tests*

ces·sion /ˈsɛʃən/ *n.* [C,U] FORMAL the act of giving up land, property, or rights, especially to another country after a war, or something that is given up in this way: [+ **of**] *Red Cloud refused to give his signature for the cession of Indian lands.* —see also CEDE

cess·pool /ˈsɛspul/ *n.* [C] **1** a place or situation that is very dirty, or in which people behave in an immoral way: *The downtown area has become a cesspool of poverty and crime.* **2** *also* **cesspit** a large hole or container under the ground in which waste from a building, especially from the toilets, is collected

c'est la vie /ˌseɪ lɑ ˈvi/ *interjection* used to say that a situation is typical of life and cannot be changed: *Fads come and go – c'est la vie.*

ce·ta·cean /sɪˈteɪʃən/ *n.* [C] TECHNICAL a MAMMAL (=an animal which feeds its babies on milk) that lives in the ocean, such as a WHALE —**cetacean** *adj.*

ce·vi·che /səˈvitʃeɪ/ *n.* [U] a dish originally from

Latin America, made from pieces of raw fish in LEMON or LIME juice, oil, and SPICES

Cey·lon /sɪˈlɑn, seɪ-/ the former name of Sri Lanka

Cé·zanne /seɪˈzæn/, **Paul** (1839–1906) a French PAINTER who influenced the development of CUBISM and ABSTRACT art

cf. used in writing to introduce something else that should be compared or considered

CFC *n.* also **chlorofluorocarbon** a gas used in REFRIGERATORS and AEROSOL cans and in making some plastics. The use of CFCs is believed to have damaged the OZONE LAYER.

CFO *n.* [C] Chief Financial Officer; the person with the most financial authority in a large company

ch. **1** the abbreviation of CHANNEL[1] (1) **2** the abbreviation of CHAPTER (1)

cha-cha /ˈtʃɑ tʃɑ/ also **cha-cha-cha** /ˈ. . ./ *n.* [C] a dance from South America with small, fast steps

Chad /tʃæd/ a country in north central Africa, west of Sudan —**Chadian** *n. adj.*

cha·dor /ˈtʃɑdɔr, -də/ *n.* [C] a long, loose, usually black piece of clothing that covers the whole body including the head, worn by Muslim women

chafe /tʃeɪf/ *v.* **1** [I] to be or become impatient or annoyed: [+ **at/under**] *Smokers are chafing under the new restrictions.* **2** [I,T] if a part of your body chafes or if something chafes it, it becomes sore because of something rubbing against it: *The boots have a soft lining to prevent your toes from chafing.* **3** [T] LITERARY to rub part of your body to make it warm

chaff /tʃæf/ *n.* [U] **1** the outer seed covers that are removed from grain before it is used as food **2** dried grasses and plant stems that are used as food for farm animals —see also **separate the wheat from the chaff** (SEPARATE[2] (8))

chafing dish /ˈ.. ./ *n.* [C] a container with a heat SOURCE such as a CANDLE under it, used for cooking food or for keeping food warm at the table

Cha·gall /ʃəˈgɑl, -ˈgæl/, **Marc** /mɑrk/ (1887–1985) a Russian artist who lived in France and painted in bright colors

cha·grin[1] /ʃəˈgrɪn/ *n.* [U] FORMAL annoyance and disappointment because something has not happened in the way you had hoped: *To the surfers' chagrin, the beach was closed during the storms that produced high waves.*

cha·grin[2] *v.* **be chagrined** FORMAL to feel annoyed and disappointed: *Lynch was chagrined at the delay.*

s w **chain**[1] /tʃeɪn/ *n.*
3/2 **1** line of rings [C,U] a series of rings, usually made of metal, connected together in a line, used as jewelry or for fastening things, supporting weights etc.: *A mugger tore Sylvia's gold chain from her neck.* | *The gates were held shut with a chain and a padlock.* —see picture at BICYCLE[1]
2 stores/hotels [C] a number of stores, hotels, restaurants etc. owned or managed by the same company or person: [+ **of**] *a chain of health clubs* | *a* **hotel/restaurant/retail** etc. **chain** *Leslie works for a major hotel chain.*
3 a chain of events/circumstances etc. a connected series of events, circumstances etc.: *No one could have predicted the chain of events that led to World War I.*
4 connected line [C] a group of mountains, lakes, or islands that are close together in a line: *It's the largest mountain chain in North America.*
5 the chains of sth LITERARY things such as rules or unfair treatment that limit your freedom: *Some residents want to see Puerto Rico freed from the chains of colonialism.*
6 in chains prisoners in chains have heavy chains fastened around their legs or arms, to prevent them from escaping
7 measure [C] a measurement of length, used in past times —see also CHAIN OF COMMAND, FOOD CHAIN, KEY CHAIN

chain[2] *v.* **1** to fasten someone or something to something else using a chain, especially in order to prevent them from escaping or being stolen: *The gates were chained shut.* | [**chain sb/sth to sth**] *I chained my bicycle to a tree.* | [**chain sb/sth up**] *The hostages were chained up and kept in a dark room.* | [**chain sb/sth together**] *Protesters chained themselves together across a road to prevent the logs from being trucked out.* **2 be chained to something** to have your freedom restricted because of a responsibility you cannot escape: *With a sick husband, Sandi's chained to the house all day.*

chain gang /ˈ. ./ *n.* [C] a group of prisoners who are chained together to work outside their prison

chain let·ter /ˌ. ˈ../ *n.* [C] a letter sent to several people asking them to send copies of the letter to more people

chain-link fence /ˌ. . ˈ./ *n.* [C] a type of fence made of metal wires twisted together to form DIAMOND shapes

chain mail /ˈ. ./ *n.* [U] protective clothing made by joining small metal rings together, worn by soldiers in past times

chain of com·mand /ˌ. . . ˈ./ *n.* [C usually singular] a system in an organization by which decisions are made and passed from people at the top of the organization to people lower down

chain re·ac·tion /ˌ. .ˈ.., ˈ. .ˌ./ *n.* [C] a series of related events or chemical reactions, each of which causes the next: *The atom splits, starting a nuclear chain reaction.* | *Interstate 35 was closed following a chain reaction crash that involved 93 vehicles.*

chain·saw, chain saw /ˈtʃeɪnsɔ/ *n.* [C] a tool used for cutting wood, consisting of a circular chain with teeth, driven by a motor around the edge of a metal bar —compare CIRCULAR SAW —see picture at TOOL[1]

chain-smoke /ˈ. .., ˈ. ./ *v.* [I,T] to smoke cigarettes continuously, one after another —**chain smoker** *n.* [C]

chain stitch /ˈ. ./ *n.* [C,U] a way of sewing in which each new stitch is pulled through the last one —**chain-stitch** *v.* [T]

chain store /ˈ. ./ *n.* [C] one of a group of stores, all of which are owned by one organization and which sell the same types of products —see also CHAIN[1] (2)

chairs

chair

armchair

stool

rocking chair

swivel chair

high chair

wheelchair

lounge chair

chair[1] /tʃer/ *n.* **1** [C] a piece of furniture for one person to sit on, which has a back, a seat, and legs: *Hey, you're sitting in my chair.* **2** [C] someone who is in charge of a meeting, a committee, or a college department: *Jones is the chair of the Committee on Science, Space, and Technology.* | *The U.S. is in the chair of the UN Security Council this month.* **3 the chair** the position of being in charge of a meeting or committee **4 the chair** INFORMAL the punishment of death by electric shock given in an ELECTRIC CHAIR: *If he is found guilty, Shogren could get the chair.*

chair² *v.* [T] to be the CHAIRPERSON of a meeting, committee, or college department: *Biden chaired the Senate hearings.*

chair·lift, chair lift /'tʃɛr,lɪft/ *n.* [C] a line of chairs hanging from a moving wire, used for carrying people up and down mountains, especially when they are SKIing²

chair·man /'tʃɛrmən/ *n. plural* **chairmen** /-mən/ [C] someone, especially a man, who is in charge of a meeting or directs the work of a committee, organization, or company: *the chairman of the board*

chair·man·ship /'tʃɛrmənˌʃɪp/ *n.* [U] the position of being a chairman, or the time when someone has this position: *Brown resigned the chairmanship of the committee in March.*

chair·per·son /'tʃɛrˌpɜrsən/ *n. plural* **chairpersons** [C] someone who is in charge of a meeting or directs the work of a committee, organization, or company

chair·wom·an /'tʃɛrˌwʊmən/ *n. plural* **chairwomen** /-ˌwɪmɪn/ a woman who is a chairperson

chaise /ʃeɪz/ *n.* [C] **1** a chaise longue **2** a light carriage pulled by one horse, used in past times

chaise longue, chaise lounge /ˌʃeɪz 'laʊndʒ/ *n.* [C] **1** a long chair with a back that can be upright for sitting, or can lie flat for lying down, usually used outside **2** a long chair with an arm only on one end, on which you can sit and stretch your legs out

cha·let /ʃæ'leɪ, 'ʃæleɪ/ *n.* [C] a house with a steeply sloping roof, common in places with high mountains and snow, such as Switzerland

chal·ice /'tʃælɪs/ *n.* [C] a gold or silver decorated cup, often used to hold wine in Christian religious services

chalk¹ /tʃɔk/ *n.* **1** [U] soft white or gray rock formed a long time ago from the shells of small animals that lived in the ocean: *chalk cliffs* **2** [C,U] small sticks of this substance that are white or colored, used for writing or drawing: *a piece of chalk*

chalk² *v.* [T] to write, mark, or draw something with chalk

chalk sth ← **up** *phr. v.* [T] INFORMAL **1** to succeed in getting or gaining something, especially points in a game: *Coach Montgomery has chalked up three winning seasons in a row.* **2** to record or report what someone has done, how much money they owe etc.: *Tire manufacturers chalked up a 5.1 percent rise in sales.* **3** to find out the reason or cause for something that has happened: [chalk sth up to sth] *Cain's success can be chalked up to a change in management style.* **4 chalk sth up to experience** to accept failure or disappointment calmly, and regard it as an experience that you can learn from **5 chalk one up for sb** INFORMAL used when someone has been successful at doing something: *Chalk one up for Sherry Richter – her campaign made the city change its mind about developing 5 acres of parkland.*

chalk·board /'tʃɔkbɔrd/ *n.* [C] a black or green smooth surface on the wall of a CLASSROOM that you write on with chalk —compare BLACKBOARD, WHITEBOARD

chalk talk /'. ./ *n.* [C] INFORMAL an occasion when a COACH (=person who trains a team in a sport) explains what he wants his team to do by drawing pictures on a chalkboard while talking to the team

chalk·y /'tʃɔki/ *adj.* similar to CHALK¹ (1), or containing chalk: *This medicine tastes chalky.* | *chalky desert sand* —chalkiness *n.* [U]

chal·lah /'hɑlə/ *n.* [U] a type of bread that is made with eggs and twisted into a BRAIDed shape

S W
chal·lenge¹ /'tʃæləndʒ/ *n.*
2
1 **sth difficult** [C,U] something that tests strength, skill, or ability, especially in a way that is interesting: *I like the challenge of learning new things.* | *Ms. Garvey now faces the challenge of* (=has to deal

with) *improving the city's public transportation system.* | **meet a challenge/rise to a challenge** (=be ready to deal successfully with something difficult)

2 **not right or legal** [C] the act of questioning whether something is right, fair, or legal: [+ to] *The court will hear a challenge to a ban on write-in votes.*

3 **invitation to compete** [C] an invitation to someone to try to defeat you in a fight, game etc.: *Holyfield accepted Lewis' challenge to fight for the title.*

4 **difficult person** [C usually singular] someone who is a challenge is difficult to talk to, work with, live with etc.: *In grade school, Clint was a real challenge to all of his teachers.*

5 **a demand to stop** [C] a demand from someone such as a guard to stop and give proof of who you are, and an explanation of what you are doing

6 **in law** [C] LAW a statement made before the beginning of a court case that a JUROR is not acceptable: *Each lawyer may issue up to six challenges.*

S W
challenge² *v.* [T]
2
1 **question sth** to question whether something is right, fair, or legal: *Billboard companies say they will challenge the new law in court.* | *Many doctors have challenged the accuracy of his findings.*

2 **demand that sb do sth** to demand that someone try to do something difficult: [challenge sb to do sth] *Civil rights activists have challenged the company to hire more minorities.*

3 **invite sb to compete** to invite someone to compete or fight against you: [challenge sb to sth] *She challenged him to a race and won.* —compare DARE¹ (1)

4 **test sb/sth** to test the skills or abilities of someone or something: *He's a good choir director – he really challenges us.* | [challenge sb to do sth] *Mrs. Eastman challenges her students to try new things.*

5 **make sb stop** to stop someone and demand proof of who they are, and an explanation of what they are doing: *Guards were ordered to challenge anyone entering the building.*

6 **make a statement in court** LAW to state that a JUROR is not acceptable before a TRIAL begins —challenger *n.* [C]

chal·lenged /'tʃæləndʒd/ *adj.* **visually/mentally/physically etc. challenged** a phrase meaning that someone has difficulty seeing, thinking, doing things etc., used in order to be polite

chal·leng·ing /'tʃæləndʒɪŋ/ *adj.* difficult in an interesting or enjoyable way: *a challenging game* | *Planning a wedding reception for over 1000 guests will be very challenging.* —challengingly *adv.*

S W
cham·ber /'tʃeɪmbə/ *n.*
3
1 **room** [C] a room used for a special purpose, especially a purpose that is not nice: **gas/torture chamber** (=a room used for killing people by gas or for hurting them)

2 chambers [plural] an office or offices used by a judge

3 **gun** [C] the place inside a gun where you put the bullet: *Always check to see if there is a bullet in the chamber.*

4 **people who make laws** [C] a group or part of a group of people who make laws for a country, state etc.: *In Poland, the Sejm is the lower chamber of parliament.*

5 **enclosed space** [C] an enclosed space, especially in your body or inside a machine: *The patient has an abnormal rhythm in the upper chamber of his heart.*

6 **meeting room** [C] a large room in a public building used for important meetings: *The council chamber is on the third floor.*

7 **private room** [C] OLD USE a BEDROOM or private room: *the Queen's private chambers*

cham·ber·lain /'tʃeɪmbəlɪn/ *n.* [C] an important official who organizes things such as cooking, cleaning, buying food etc. in a king's or NOBLEMAN's court

Cham·ber·lain /'tʃeɪmbəlɪn/, **Nev·ille** /'nɛvəl/ (1869–1940) the British Prime Minister at the beginning of World War II

Chamberlain, Wilt /wɪlt/ (1936–1999) a U.S. BASKETBALL player, known as "Wilt the Stilt" because of his height, who set several records for the number of points he won

cham·ber·maid /ˈtʃeɪmbəˌmeɪd/ n. [C] a female servant or worker whose job is to clean rooms, especially in a hotel, or, in past times, for a rich person

chamber mu·sic /ˈ.. ˌ../ n. [U] CLASSICAL MUSIC written for a small group of performers

chamber of com·merce, Chamber of Commerce /ˌ.. ˈ../ n. [C] a group of business people in a particular town or city whose aim is to encourage business: *The Nashville Chamber of Commerce sponsored the event.*

chamber or·ches·tra /ˈ.. ˌ../ n. [C] a small group of musicians who play CLASSICAL MUSIC together

chamber pot /ˈ.. ˌ/ n. [C] a round container used as a TOILET, kept in a BEDROOM under the bed in past times

cham·bray /ʃæmˈbreɪ, ˈʃæmbreɪ/ n. [U] a type of cloth used especially for shirts, that is plain and made of a white and a colored thread woven together

cha·me·leon /kəˈmilyən, kəˈmiliən/ n. [C] **1** a LIZARD (=type of animal) that can change its color to match the colors around it **2** someone who changes their ideas, behavior etc. to fit different situations: *The Congressman has a reputation as a political chameleon.*

cham·ois /ˈʃæmi/ n. **1** also **chamois leather** [C,U] soft leather prepared from the skin of chamois, sheep, or goats and used for cleaning or polishing, or a piece of this leather **2** [C] a wild animal like a small goat that lives in the mountains of Europe and southwest Asia

cham·o·mile /ˈkæməˌmil/ n. [C,U] a plant with small white and yellow flowers that are sometimes used to make tea

champ[1] /tʃæmp/ n. [C] INFORMAL a CHAMPION[1] (1): *They've been the league champs for the past five years.*

champ[2] v. [I,T] to bite food loudly; CHOMP

cham·pagne /ʃæmˈpeɪn/ n. [U] a French white wine with a lot of BUBBLES, often drunk on special occasions

cham·pi·on[1] /ˈtʃæmpiən/ n. **1** [C] a person, team etc. that has won a competition, especially in sports: *By 1978 Boitano was the national junior champion in ice skating.* | *the reigning national soccer champions* (=the champions right now) **2 a champion of sth** someone who publicly fights for and defends an aim or principle, such as the rights of a group of people: *Douglas has always been a champion of free speech.*

champion[2] v. [T] to publicly fight for and defend an aim or principle, such as the rights of a group of people: *Purcell championed social programs for the elderly.*

s w **cham·pi·on·ship** /ˈtʃæmpiənˌʃɪp/ n. **1** [C] also **championships** [plural] a competition or series of competitions to find which player, team etc. is the best in a particular sport: *Last year they won the national college basketball championship.* **2** [C] the position or period of being a champion: *Can she win the championship again this year?* **3** [U + of] the act of championing something or someone

Cham·plain, Lake /ʃæmˈpleɪn/ a large lake in the northeastern U.S., on the border between the states of New York and Vermont and with its most northern part in Canada

Champlain, Sam·u·el de /ˈsæmuəl də/ (1567–1635) a French EXPLORER who discovered many places in Canada and started the city of Quebec

Cham·pol·lion /ˌʃɑmpɔlˈyoʊn/, **Jean** /ʒɑn/ (1790–1832) a French ARCHEOLOGIST who discovered how to read ancient Egyptian writing

s w **chance**[1] /tʃæns/ n.

1 opportunity [C] a time or situation that you can use to do something that you want to do; opportunity: [**chance to do sth**] *I took the class because it was a chance to learn more about computers.* | *She never even gave me a chance to say goodbye.* | *I wanted to take this chance* (=use this opportunity) *to say how much I have appreciated your help over the years.* | **have/get a chance to do sth** *Tomorrow I might have a chance to look at your taxes.* | *Rachel jumped at the chance* (=eagerly and quickly used an opportunity) *to go to France for a year.* | *This is your last chance to prove you can be trusted.* | *Hey John, now's your chance to finally ask her for a date.* | *Given half a chance* (=if given even a small opportunity) *other firms would have done the same thing.* | *Getting that job was definitely the chance of a lifetime* (=an opportunity you are not likely to get more than once). | *a second/another chance* (=another chance, in which you hope to do better after failing the first time)

2 possibility [C,U] how possible or likely it is that something will happen or be true, especially something that you want: [+ of] *What do you think our chances of getting that contract are?* | *There's a chance that she left her keys in the office.* | *Chances are* (=it is likely), *someone you know has been burglarized.* | **a good/slight/fair chance** *There's a slight chance of showers this weekend.* | **some/no/little chance** *There seems to be little chance of a peaceful end to the conflict.* | *With the operation, he'll have a fifty-fifty chance* (=an equal chance of something happening or not happening) *of walking again.* | *a one in a million chance/a million to one chance* (=an extremely small chance)

3 stand/have a chance (of doing sth) if someone or something stands or has a chance of doing something, it is possible that they will succeed: *I think we stand a pretty good chance* (=are very likely to succeed) *of winning the World Series.* | *Polls show that Buchanan still has a fighting chance* (=has a small but real chance of success if a great effort can be made) *in the election.*

4 take a chance also **take (my/your/any etc.) chances** to do something that involves risk: *She knew she was taking a chance, but she decided to buy the house anyway.* | **take a chance on/with** *Thomas took a chance on Alvin Robertson by making him head coach.* | *Olympic officials were taking no chances of another terrorist attack.*

5 luck [U] the way some things happen without being planned or caused by people: *He supervises every detail of the business and leaves nothing to chance.* | *A tourist had filmed the robbery by chance* (=without being planned or intended). | *As chance would have it* (=happening in a way that was not expected or intended), *we both got jobs at the same hospital.* | **pure/sheer/blind chance** *Solving the crime was pure chance.*

6 sb's chances how likely it is that someone will succeed: *What are your chances of getting a college scholarship?*

7 by any chance SPOKEN used to ask politely whether something is true: *Would you, by any chance, know where a pay phone is?*

8 fat chance!/not a chance! SPOKEN used to emphasize that you are sure something could never happen: *"Everybody will chip in a couple of dollars." "Fat chance!"*

9 on the off chance if you do something on the off chance, you do it hoping for a particular result, although you know it is not likely: *I keep all of my old clothes on the off chance that they might come back into fashion.*

10 any chance of... SPOKEN used to ask whether you can have something or whether something is possible: *"Any chance of you two getting back together?" "I don't think so."* —see also **a game of chance** (GAME[1] (12)), **an outside chance** (OUTSIDE[3] (5))

chance[2] v. [T] **1** INFORMAL to do something that you know involves a risk: *We could save money by hitchhiking, but why chance it?* **2** LITERARY to happen in an unexpected and unplanned way: [**chance to do sth**] *She ended up marrying a man who chanced to come by looking for a room.*

chance on/upon sb/sth phr. v. [T] LITERARY to find something or meet someone when you are not expecting to: *Unknowingly, he had chanced upon the bathing place of the goddess Artemis.*

chance³ *adj.* [only before noun] not planned; accidental | **a chance meeting/encounter** (=an occasion when you meet someone by accident)

chan·cel /'tʃænsəl/ *n.* [C] the part of a church where the priests and the CHOIR (=singers) sit

chan·cel·ler·y /'tʃænsələri/ *n.* [C] **1** the building in which a chancellor has his office **2** the officials who work in a chancellor's office **3** the offices of an official representative of a foreign country; CHANCERY

chan·cel·lor, Chancellor /'tʃænsələr/ *n.* [C] **1** the head of some universities: *the Chancellor of Indiana University* **2** the head of the government in some countries: *Willy Brandt, the former West German Chancellor*

chan·cer·y /'tʃænsəri/ *n.* [singular] **1** the part of the legal system that deals with situations where the existing laws may not provide a fair judgment: *the Delaware Court of Chancery* **2** a government office that collects and stores official papers **3** the offices of an official representative of a foreign country; CHANCELLERY

chanc·y /'tʃænsi/ *adj.* **chancier, chanciest** INFORMAL uncertain or involving a lot of risk: *Making financial forecasts can be a very chancy business.* —**chanciness** *n.* [U]

chan·de·lier /ˌʃændə'lɪr/ *n.* [C] a large round structure that holds lights or CANDLEs, hangs from the ceiling, and is decorated with small pieces of glass

chan·dler /'tʃændlər/ *n.* [C] OLD USE someone who makes or sells CANDLES

Chan·dler /'tʃændlər/, **Ray·mond** /'reɪmənd/ (1888–1959) a U.S. writer of DETECTIVE stories whose best-known character is the PRIVATE DETECTIVE Philip Marlowe

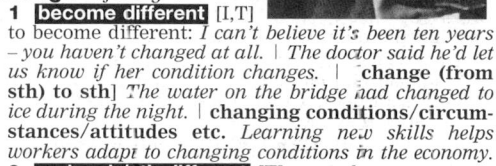
Raymond Chandler

Chang /tʃæŋ/, **the** also **the Chang Jiang** /ˌtʃæŋ 'dʒyɑŋ/ the longest river in China, that flows eastward from Tibet to the China Sea. It is also called the Yangtze

change¹ /tʃeɪndʒ/ *v.*

1 [become different] [I,T] to become different: *I can't believe it's been ten years – you haven't changed at all.* | *The doctor said he'd let us know if her condition changes.* | [**change (from sth) to sth**] *The water on the bridge had changed to ice during the night.* | **changing conditions/circumstances/attitudes etc.** *Learning new skills helps workers adapt to changing conditions in the economy.*

2 [make sb/sth different] [T] to make someone or something become different: *How does the President plan to change the tax system?* | *Going to college really changed my life.*

3 [from one thing to another] [I,T] to stop having or doing one thing and start having or doing something else instead: [**change (from sth) to sth**] *The company realized they could actually save money if we changed to a modern computerized system.* | *I think we'd better change the subject* (=talk about something else) *before we end up having an argument.* | **change your name/job/address etc.** *Many women choose not to change their name when they marry.* | **change jobs/cars/boyfriends etc.** *An unhappy worker can change jobs.* | **change course/direction** (=start to do something very different from what you were doing before)

4 change your mind to change your decision, plan, or opinion about something: [**+ about/on**] *The seller changed her mind about selling the house.*

5 [clothes] **a)** [I,T] to take off your clothes and put on different ones: *I'm just going upstairs to change.* | [**change into sth/change out of sth**] *We changed into our swimsuits and ran for the pool.* | *She has to get changed* (=put on different clothes) *before we go out.* **b)** [T] to put a clean DIAPER on a baby: *I'll be right back. I just have to change the baby.*

6 change the sheets to take SHEETs off a bed and put clean ones on it

7 [replace sth] [T] to put something new in place of something old, damaged, or broken: *I think the batteries need changing.* | *Sorry I'm late, I had to change a tire on the way here.*

8 [exchange money] [T] **a)** to exchange a larger unit of money for smaller units that add up to the same value: *Can you change a $10 bill?* **b)** to exchange money from one country for money from another: [**change sth into/for sth**] *I want to change my dollars into pesos, please.*

9 [airplanes/trains/buses] [I,T] to get out of one airplane, train, or bus and into another one in order to continue your trip: **change planes/trains/buses** *We had to change trains twice.* | [**+ at/in**] *All passengers bound for Boston should change at New Haven.*

10 change places (with sb) a) to give someone your place and take their place: *He immediately changed places so he could sit next to me.* **b)** to take someone else's social position or situation in life instead of yours: *Our lives are hard, but theirs are miserable. I would never change places.*

11 change hands to become someone else's property: *The theater recently changed hands.*

12 change your tune to start expressing a different attitude and reacting in a different way, after something has happened: *Newsome was originally against the plan, but later changed his tune.*

13 [wind] [I] if the wind changes, it starts to blow in a different direction

14 change gear/gears to put the engine of a vehicle into a higher or lower GEAR in order to go faster or slower: [**change into/out of gear**] *You'll have to change into third gear to get up this hill.*

change sth ↔ around *phr. v.* [T] to move things into different positions: *I didn't really rewrite it, I just changed a few paragraphs around.*

change into *phr. v.* [T] **1** [**change into** sth] to become something different: *Winter had finally changed into spring.* **2** [**change sb/sth into** sth] to make someone or something become something different: *In the ballet, the Nutcracker changes into a handsome prince.*

change over *phr. v.* [I] to stop doing or using one thing and start doing or using something different: [**+ to**] *We hope to change over to the new software by next month.*

change² *n.*

1 [things becoming different] [C,U] the process or result of something or someone becoming different: *Many people find it hard to accept change.* | [**+ in**] *A change in personality can mean your teenager has a drug problem.* | *Changes in diet can reduce the occurrence of some cancers.* | [**+ of**] *a change of temperature* | **change for the better/worse** *There has been a change for the worse in the environment as more trekkers reach Nepal.* | *Ms. Morris has had a change of heart* (=a change in attitude or decision), *and has agreed to speak at the conference.*

2 [from one thing to another] [C] a new or different thing or person used instead of something or someone else: *The car needs an oil change.* | [**change (from sth) to sth**] *The change from communism to democracy has been very difficult.* | [**+ of**] *There's been a change of plans – we can't leave until tomorrow.* | *Management has threatened to make sweeping changes if the situation does not improve.* | *I've sent out postcards telling everyone of our change of address.*

3 [pleasant new situation] [C usually singular] a situation or experience that is different from what happened before, and is usually interesting or enjoyable: [**+ from**] *Living in Iowa is certainly a big change from Florida.* | *The commute only took twenty minutes today, for a change.* | *Writing the biography was a change of pace for science fiction writer Henry Thibaud.* | *A change of scenery* (=a stay in a different place that is pleasant) *was just what I needed.*

4 [money] [U] **a)** the money that you get back when you pay for something with more money than it costs: *Here is your change, sir.* | *I was making change* (=calculating the right amount of money that a customer should get back) *for a customer when the phone rang.* **b)** money in the form of coins: *The clerk handed him $3 in change.* | *I put my spare change* (=coins that I do not need) *in a charity bucket.* | *We put our loose change* (=coins, usually the coins in your pocket when there are not very many of them) *aside each day and buy a small treat at the end of the week.* **c)** coins or small bills that you give in exchange for the same amount of money in a larger unit: *Excuse me, do you have change for $1?* | *Can you make change for a $20 bill?* —see Usage Note at MONEY

5 small change a) coins you have that do not have a high value: *Beggars were asking for small change.* **b)** used to emphasize that something is a small amount of money when it is compared to a larger amount: *The program costs $20 million a year, small change in Washington.* —see Usage Note at MONEY

6 a change of clothes/underwear etc. an additional set of clothes that you have with you, for example when you are traveling: *You'd better bring a change of clothes since we're staying overnight.*

7 [airplane/train/bus] [C] a situation in which you get off one airplane, train, or bus and get on another one in order to continue your trip

change·a·ble /ˈtʃeɪndʒəbəl/ *adj.* likely to change, or changing often: *We have very changeable weather here, especially in the winter.* —**changeableness** *n.* [U] —**changeably** *adv.* —**changeability** /ˌtʃeɪndʒə-ˈbɪləti/ *n.* [U]

changed /tʃeɪndʒd/ *adj.* **1 a changed man/woman** someone who has become very different from what they were before, as a result of a very important experience: *Marley said he was sorry for his crimes and insists he's a changed man.* **2 changed circumstances** a change in someone's financial situation: *Your changed circumstances may make you eligible for financial assistance.*

change·less /ˈtʃeɪndʒlɪs/ *adj.* LITERARY never seeming to change: *the changeless desert landscape* —**changelessly** *adv.*

change·ling /ˈtʃeɪndʒlɪŋ/ *n.* [C] LITERARY a baby that is said to have been secretly exchanged for another baby by fairies (FAIRY (2))

change of life /ˌ. . ˈ./ *n.* **the change of life** MENOPAUSE

change·o·ver /ˈtʃeɪnˌdʒoʊvɚ/ *n.* [C] a change from one activity, system, or way of working to another: *The country faces rising unemployment as it prepares for the painful changeover to a market economy.*

change purse /ˈ. ./ *n.* [C] a small bag in which some women keep coins

changing room /ˈ.. ./ *n.* [C] a room where people change their clothes when they play sports, go swimming, try on new clothes etc.

changing ta·ble /ˈ.. ˌ./ *n.* [C] a special piece of furniture that you put a baby on while you take off its DIAPER and put a clean one on

sw **chan·nel¹** /ˈtʃænl/ *n.*
2 2 **1** [television] [C] a particular television station and all the programs broadcast by it: *Brent works in the news department at Channel 9.* | *There's a good movie on Channel 5 tonight.*
2 [C usually plural] a system or method that is used to send or obtain information, goods, permission etc.: *New channels of communication have opened up between the two governments.* | *We need better distribution channels for our products.*
3 [ocean/river] [C] **a)** water that connects two larger areas of water: *the English Channel* **b)** the deepest part of a river, ocean etc., especially one that is deep enough to allow ships to sail in
4 [radio] [C] a particular range of SOUND WAVES which can be used to send and receive radio messages
5 [for water] [C] a long passage dug into the ground

that water or other liquids can flow along: *a channel for the water supply*
6 [in a surface] [C] a deep line cut into a surface or a deep space between two edges; GROOVE¹ (1 : *The sliding doors fit into these plastic channels.*

channel² *v.* [T] **1** to control and direct something such as money or energy toward a particular purpose: [channel sth into sth] *I channeled all my anger into running.* | [channel sth to sb] *The educational message is channeled primarily to school-children.* | [channel sth through sth] *The government routinely channels food and medicine through the Red Cross and other groups.* **2** to control or direct people or things to a particular place, work, situation etc.: [channel sb/sth into sth] *Women were more likely to be channeled into the lower-paying jobs.* | *Drugs from government pharmacies were being channeled into illegal drug markets.* **3** to send water through a passage: *These pipes will channel water to the settlement.* **4** to cut a deep line or space into something: *Water had channeled grooves in the rock.* **5** to allow a spirit to come into your body and speak through you, or to tell people a message that you have received in this way: *She claims to have channeled the spirit of a 2,000-year-old hunter.*

channel hop·ping /ˈ.. ˌ./ *n.* [U] CHANNEL SURFING

chan·nel·ing /ˈtʃænl-ɪŋ/ *n.* [U] a practice based on the belief that people can communicate with dead people by allowing a dead person's spirit to come into their body and speak through them —**channeler** *n.* [C]

channel surf·ing /ˈ.. ˌ./ *n.* [U] the activity of continuously changing from one television program to another, watching only a very small amount of each program —**channel surf** *v.* [I]

chant¹ /tʃænt/ *v.* [I,T] **1** to repeat a word or phrase again and again: *DiMaggio came to the window as the crowd chanted, "Joe, Joe!"* | *Protesters clapped and chanted.* **2** to sing or say a religious song or prayer in a way that involves using only one note or TONE: *We could hear monks chanting as we entered the monastery.*

chant² *n.* [C] **1** words or phrases that are repeated again and again: *Demonstrators blew whistles and screamed protest chants.* **2** a religious song or prayer with a regularly repeated tune, in which many words are sung or said using one note or TONE —**chanter** *n.* [C] —see also GREGORIAN CHANT

chan·tey /ˈʃænti, ˈtʃæn-/ *n.* [C] a song sung by SAILORS as they did their work in past times

chan·try /ˈtʃæntri/ also **chantry cha·pel** /ˈ.. ˌ./ *n.* [C] a small church or part of a church that is paid for by someone so that priests can pray for them there after they die

chant·y /ˈʃænti, ˈtʃæn-/ *n.* [C] another spelling of CHANTEY

Cha·nu·kah /ˈhɑnəkə/ *n.* [U] another spelling of HANUKKAH

cha·os /ˈkeɪɑs/ *n.* [U] **1** a situation in which everything is happening in a confused way and nothing is organized or arranged in order | **complete/utter/absolute etc. chaos** *It's been total chaos since Helen left on vacation.* | *At that time, East Germany's economy was in chaos* (=in a state of chaos). **2** the state of the universe before there was any order

cha·ot·ic /keɪˈɑtɪk/ *adj.* a situation that is chaotic is very disorganized and confusing: *The chaotic social and economic conditions could lead to civil war.*

chap /tʃæp/ *n.* [C] BRITISH **1 chaps** *plural* leather covers that fit over the sides of your pants, that protect your legs when you ride a horse through bushes, by fences etc. **2** a man, especially a man you know and like

chap., Chap. *n.* a written abbreviation of CHAPTER

chap·ar·ral /ˌʃæpəˈræl, -ˈræl/ *n.* [U] a word meaning a piece of land on which small trees or bushes grow close together, used especially of land in the southwest of North America

chap·book /ˈtʃæpbʊk/ *n.* [C] a small printed book, usually consisting of writings about literature, poetry, or religion

chap·el /'tʃæpəl/ n. [C] a small church or a room in a hospital, prison, church etc. in which Christians pray and have religious services: *a wedding chapel*

chap·er·on[1], **chaperone** /'ʃæpə,roʊn/ n. [C] **1** someone, usually a parent or teacher, who is responsible for young people on social occasions: *Three chaperons went with the Girl Scout group.* **2** LITERARY an older woman in past times who went out with a young unmarried woman on social occasions and was responsible for her behavior

chaperon[2], **chaperone** v. [T] to go somewhere with someone as their chaperon

chap·lain /'tʃæplɪn/ n. [C] a priest or minister who is responsible for the religious needs of a part of the army, a hospital etc.: *Reverend Edwards is the new prison chaplain.* —see Usage Note at PRIEST

chap·lain·cy /'tʃæplənsi/ n. [C] the position of a chaplain, or the place where a chaplain works

chap·let /'tʃæplɪt/ n. [C] LITERARY a band of flowers worn on the head

Chap·lin /'tʃæplɪn/, **Char·lie** /'tʃɑrli/ (1889–1977) a British movie actor and DIRECTOR who worked mainly in the U.S. in humorous SILENT FILMS (=films made with no sound) during the 1920s

chapped /tʃæpt/ adj. chapped lips or hands are sore, dry, and cracked, especially as a result of cold weather or wind —**chap** v. [T]

Chap Stick /'. ./ n. [U] TRADEMARK a stick of a WAX-like substance that you put on your lips to make them feel softer when they are chapped and to prevent them from becoming more chapped

chap·ter /'tʃæptɚ/ n. [C] **1** one of the parts into which a book is divided: *The Christmas story is told in Chapter 2, verses 1–20 of Luke.* | *For homework, read the first two chapters of the book.* **2** a particular period or event in someone's life or in history: [+ in] *Martin's death closed one of the more fascinating chapters of recent Bordeaux history.* **3** the local members of a large organization such as a club: *She was a volunteer with various chapters of the Junior League.* **4** all the priests belonging to a particular church or organization, or a meeting of these priests **5** give/quote sb chapter and verse to give someone exact details about where to find some information

chap·ter·house /'tʃæptɚ,haʊs/ n. [C] a building where the priests belonging to a particular church or organization meet

char /tʃɑr/ v. past tense and past participle **charred**, **charring** [I,T] to burn something so that its outside becomes black: *The fire had charred most of the inside of the house.* —see also CHARRED

char·ac·ter /'kærɪktɚ/ n.
1 all sb's qualities [C,U] the particular combination of qualities that makes someone a particular kind of person: *One of his strongest character traits is a very competitive spirit.* | *Poverty does not improve a man's character; rather, it makes him more selfish.* | **in character/out of character** (=typical of the way someone usually behaves, or very untypical) *Siefert described McCrea's strength of character* (=the qualities of being a good person) *in a difficult situation.* | **the American/Australian/French etc. character** (=the qualities that are typical of Americans, Australians etc.) —see CHARACTERISTIC[1]
2 qualities of sth [C,U] the particular combination of features and qualities that makes a thing or place different from all others: *Each neighborhood has its own unique character.* | [+ of] *Residents want to preserve the character of their neighborhoods.* | *The discussions were overwhelmingly political in character.*
3 interesting quality [U] a quality that makes someone or something special and interesting: *It's a red wine with an almost meaty character.* | *The town lacks character* (=is not interesting).
4 person [C] **a)** a person in a book, play, movie etc.: *She played the character of Alexis for seven years on television.* | *I found it hard to like the main character.* | *Children recognized "Old Joe," the Camel cigarette cartoon character* (=a drawing of a person, animal etc. that appears in a CARTOON) *as easily as Mickey Mouse.* **b)** a person of a particular kind: *He*

was a repulsive character. **c) a character** an interesting, and unusual person: *Max is quite a character!*
5 good qualities [U] a combination of qualities such as courage, loyalty, and honesty that are admired and regarded as valuable: *His actions during the war showed his character.* | *Ellis is a man of exceptional character.* | *The club promotes character building* (=activity aimed at developing these qualities) *activities for young boys.*
6 character assassination a cruel and unfair attack on someone's character
7 letter/sign [C] a letter, mark, or sign used in writing, printing, or on a computer: *That's the Chinese character for horse.* | *Only eight characters fit into the space for the document name.*

C

character ac·tor /'... ,../ n. [C] an actor who typically plays unusual characters

char·ac·ter·is·tic[1] /,kærɪktə'rɪstɪk/ n. [C usually plural] a special quality or feature of something or someone that is typical of them and easy to recognize: *Leadership and honesty are the characteristics of a good manager.* | *Can you describe the robber's physical characteristics?*

characteristic[2] adj. very typical of a particular thing or of someone's character: *Naomi is meeting the changes in her life with characteristic optimism.* | [+ of] *The vase is characteristic of 16th century Chinese art.* —**characteristically** /-kli/ adv.

char·ac·ter·i·za·tion /,kærɪktərə'zeɪʃən/ n. **1** [C,U] the way in which a writer makes a person in a book, movie, or play seem like a real person: *The characterization is believable, but it's still not a very good book.* **2** [U] the way in which the qualities of a real person or thing are described: [characterization of sb/sth as sth] *McComb objects to the letter's characterization of his supporters as "malcontents."*

char·ac·ter·ize /'kærɪktə,raɪz/ v. [T] **1** to describe the character of someone or something in a particular way: [characterize sb as sth] *Greenspan characterized the economy as "struggling."* **2** to be typical of a person, place, or thing: *He has the confidence that characterizes successful businessmen.*

char·ac·ter·less /'kærɪktɚlɪs/ adj. not having any special or interesting qualities: *a characterless hotel*

character ref·e·rence /'... ,../ n. [C] a REFERENCE (5)

character wit·ness /'... ,../ n. [C] someone who says at a TRIAL what someone's character (=qualities) and morals are like

cha·rade /ʃə'reɪd/ n. [C] a situation in which people pretend that something is true or serious and behave as if it were true or serious, when everyone knows it is not: *Without a firm commitment to peace, the talks will be a disappointing charade.*

cha·rades /ʃə'reɪdz/ n. [U] a game in which one person uses only actions to show the meaning of a word or phrase, and other people have to guess what it is

char·broil /'tʃɑrbrɔɪl/ v. [T] to cook food over a very hot charcoal fire —**charbroiled** adj.

char·coal /'tʃɑrkoʊl/ n. [U] a black substance made of burned wood, used as FUEL, or sticks of this substance used for drawing: *Add charcoal to the grill as needed.* | *charcoal drawings*

chard /tʃɑrd/ n. [U] a vegetable with large leaves

charge[1] /tʃɑrdʒ/ n.
1 price [C,U] the amount of money you have to pay for goods or services: *Interest charges on the loan totaled over $12,000.* | [+ for] *There is a $5 charge for each visit to the doctor.* | *We deliver free of charge* (=at no cost). | *Each meal comes with soup or salad and a dessert at no extra charge* (=without having to pay more money). —see Usage Note at COST[1]
2 control **a) in charge (of sth)** controlling or responsible for a group of people or an activity: *Ann Watterson is in charge of the business section of the paper.* | *The new position puts him in charge* (=gives him the responsibility) *of the computer systems throughout the company.* **b) take charge (of**

sth) to take control of a situation, organization, or group of people: *Anderson took charge of the firm in August, 1990.* —see Usage Note at CONTROL[2]

3 crime [C] an official statement made by the police saying that someone may be guilty of a crime: *Libel is a difficult charge to prove.* | [+ against] *Harris's office was informed of the charges against him.* | [+ of] *Jones will stand trial for three charges of sexual misconduct.* | **murder/drug/burglary etc. charges** *Police arrested him on three murder charges.* | *He'll be brought to the U.S. to* **face charges** (=go through the legal process that starts when the police say you may be guilty of a crime) *for the bombing.* | *Cathcart agreed to* **drop charges** (=say that someone will not have to go through the legal process) *against the restaurant.* | **press/bring charges** (=make official charges)

4 blame [C] a written or spoken statement blaming someone for doing something bad or illegal; ALLEGATION: [+ of] *There have been numerous charges of racism against the company.* | **deny/counter charges** *Wallace denied charges that he lied to investigators.*

5 get a charge out of sth SPOKEN to be excited by something and enjoy it very much: *I really get a charge out of watching the kids learn.*

6 be in/under sb's charge if someone or something is in your charge, you are responsible for taking care of them: *Soldiers under Bensen's charge say he was a harsh but fair commander.*

7 electricity [C] electricity that is put into a piece of electrical equipment such as a BATTERY: *There doesn't seem to be any charge coming from the outlet.*

8 effort [C usually singular] a strong effort to do something: *Seymour* **led the charge** *against rent control for the real-estate industry.*

9 basketball [C] an act of running into an opposing player while you have the ball, which results in a FOUL and the other team being given the ball: *Reed is not afraid to* **take a charge** (=allow another player to run into him, so that his team will get the ball) *when he has to.*

10 attack [C] an attack in which soldiers, wild animals etc. move forward quickly

11 explosive [C] an explosive put into a gun or weapon

12 someone you must take care of [C] FORMAL someone that you are responsible for taking care of: *Jill bought ice cream for her three young charges.*

13 strength of feelings [C] the power of strong feelings: *Cases of abuse have a strong emotional charge.*

14 an order to do sth [C] FORMAL an order to do something

s w **charge[2]** *v.*
1 1

1 money **a)** [I,T] to ask someone a certain amount of money for something you are selling: *The dry cleaners charges $1.25 a shirt.* | [+ for] *They charged me $2 for this candy bar.* **b)** [T] to pay for something with a CREDIT CARD: *I charged the flights on American Express.* | *I didn't have the money, I had to charge it.* **c) charge sth to sb's account/room** to record the cost of something on someone's account, so that they can pay for it later: *Charge the dinner to Room 455, please.*

2 with a crime [T] to state officially that someone may be guilty of a crime: [be charged with sth] *Her husband was charged with her murder.*

3 move to attack [I,T] to deliberately rush quickly toward someone or something in order to attack them: [+ at/toward/into] *Police charged into the house, guns ready.* | [charge sb] *The mother bear turned and charged us.*

4 rush [I always + adv./prep.] to deliberately run or walk somewhere quickly: [+ around/through/out etc.] *I could hear Willie and his friends charging down the stairs.*

5 blame sb [T] FORMAL to say publicly that you think someone has done something wrong: [charge that] *Hundreds have charged that police used excessive force during the demonstration.*

6 electricity also **charge up** [I,T] if a BATTERY charges or if you charge it, it takes in and stores electricity: *Did you charge the camcorder's batteries?* | *Leave it to charge overnight.*

7 order sb [T] FORMAL to order someone to do something or make them responsible for ... t: [be charged with doing sth] *His staff is charged with organizing all the training programs.*

8 gun [T] OLD USE to load a gun

charge·a·ble /'tʃɑrdʒəbəl/ *adj.* **1** chargeable costs must be paid: *chargeable expenses* **2** a chargeable offense is serious enough for the police to officially state that you may be guilty of it

charge ac·count /'. .ˌ./ *n.* [C] an account you have at a store that allows you to take goods away with you now and pay for them later

charge card /'. ./ *n.* [C] a plastic card that you can use to buy goods in a particular store and pay for them later

charged /tʃɑrdʒd/ *adj.* [usually before noun] a charged situation or subject makes people feel very angry, anxious, or excited, and is likely to cause arguments or violence: *The elections took place in the highly charged atmosphere of mass demonstrations.*

char·gé d'af·faires /ˌʃɑrʒeɪ dæ'fɛr/ *n.* [C] an official who represents a particular government during the absence of an AMBASSADOR or in a country where there is no ambassador

charg·er /'tʃɑrdʒɚ/ *n.* [C] **1** a piece of equipment used to put electricity into a BATTERY (1) **2** LITERARY a horse that a soldier or KNIGHT rides in battle

charge sheet /'. ./ *n.* [C] an official record kept in a police station of the crimes that the police say someone is guilty of

char·i·ot /'tʃæriət/ *n.* [C] a vehicle with two wheels, pulled by a horse, used in ancient times in battles and races

char·i·o·teer /ˌtʃæriə'tɪr/ *n.* [C] the driver of a chariot

cha·ris·ma /kə'rɪzmə/ *n.* [U] the natural ability to attract and interest other people and make them admire you: *Few Presidents have had the charisma of Kennedy.*

char·is·mat·ic[1] /ˌkæriz'mætɪk◂/ *adj.* **1** able to attract and influence other people because of a powerful personal quality you have: *Jackson was one of the most charismatic figures in sports.* **2** believing that God gives people special abilities such as healing people: *a charismatic church*

charismatic[2] *n.* [C] a Christian who believes that God gives people special abilities, such as curing people who have diseases

char·i·ta·ble /'tʃærətəbəl/ *adj.* **1** relating to money or gifts given to people who need help, or organizations that give this kind of help: *It's one of many excellent charitable organizations that work with the poor in the city.* **2** kind, generous, and sympathetic, especially in the way you judge people: *Johnson was not so charitable in calling the commission's decision "irresponsible."* —opposite UNCHARITABLE —**charitably** *adv.*

char·i·ty /'tʃærəti/ *n. plural* **charities 1** [C] an organization that gives money, goods, or help to people who are poor, sick etc.: *Several charities sent aid to the flood victims.* | **a charity event/dinner/concert etc.** (=an event organized to collect money for a charity) **2** [U] charity organizations in general: *He's donated over $200,000* **to charity.** **3** [U] money or gifts given to help people who are poor, sick etc.: *Pride makes it difficult for even the poorest peasant to* **accept charity** *from strangers.* **4** [U] FORMAL kindness or sympathy that you show toward other people: *Mother Teresa gained worldwide attention for her selfless acts of charity.* **5 charity begins at home** a phrase meaning you should help your own family, country etc. before you help other people

char·la·tan /'ʃɑrlətən/ *n.* [C] DISAPPROVING someone who pretends to have special skills or knowledge: *I think the voters will see him as the charlatan he really is.*

Char·le·magne /ˈʃɑrləˌmeɪn/ (742–814) the King of the Franks who gained control of most of western Europe in 800 by uniting its Christian countries, and had a great influence on European civilizations, by establishing a new legal system and encouraging art, literature, and education

Charles /tʃɑrlz/, **Prince** (1948–) the first son of the British Queen, Elizabeth II, who is expected to become the next British King. His official royal title is the Prince of Wales.

Charles·ton /ˈtʃɑrlstən/ n. **1** the capital city of the U.S. state of West Virginia **2** an old city in the U.S. state of South Carolina **3 the Charleston** a quick dance popular in the 1920s

char·ley horse /ˈtʃɑrli ˌhɔrs/ n. [C usually singular] INFORMAL a pain in a large muscle, for example in your leg, caused by the muscle becoming tight; CRAMP

Char·lotte /ˈʃɑrlət/ the largest city in the U.S. state of North Carolina

Charlotte Am·a·lie /ˌʃɑrlət ˈæməli/ the capital city of the U.S. TERRITORY of the Virgin Islands

Char·lotte·town /ˈʃɑrlətˌtaʊn/ the capital and largest town of the Canadian PROVINCE of Prince Edward Island

charm[1] /tʃɑrm/ n. **1** [C,U] the special quality someone or something has that makes people like them, feel attracted to them, or be easily influenced by them: *Vanessa has both charm and talent.* | *Beaufort has all the charm of the old South.* | *Wayne certainly knows how to* **turn on the charm** (=use charm) *when he wants something out of you.* **2** [C] a very small object worn on a chain or BRACELET: *a necklace with an angel charm* | *That diamond horseshoe is her* **lucky charm** (=a charm that will bring good luck). **3 work like a charm** to work exactly as you had hoped: *Our new accounting system works like a charm.* **4** [C] a phrase or action believed to have special magic powers; SPELL

charm[2] v. [T] **1** to attract someone and make them like you, especially so that you can easily influence them: *Goldie Hawn's high-pitched laugh has charmed fans for years.* **2** to please and interest someone: *It's a story that has charmed youngsters for generations.* **3** to gain power over someone or something by using magic

charmed /tʃɑrmd/ adj. always lucky, as if protected by magic: **lead/live/have a charmed life** *Cole admits he has led a charmed life.*

charm·er /ˈtʃɑrmər/ n. [C] someone who uses their charm to please or influence people: *Keen is a Texan charmer who delights in storytelling.* —see also SNAKE CHARMER

charm·ing /ˈtʃɑrmɪŋ/ adj. very pleasing or attractive; nice: *It's a very charming restaurant.* | *Gabby's parents thought Bill was charming.* —**charmingly** adv.

charm school /ˈ. ./ n. [C] a school where young women were sometimes sent in the past to learn how to behave politely and gracefully

char·nel house /ˈtʃɑrnl ˌhaʊs/ n. [C] LITERARY a place where the bodies and bones of dead people are stored

charred /tʃɑrd/ adj. something that is charred has been burned until it is black: *Police searched the charred remains of the building, looking for survivors.*

chart[1] /tʃɑrt/ n. **1** [C] information that is clearly arranged in the form of a simple picture, set of figures, GRAPH etc., or a piece of paper with this information on it: *This chart shows last year's sales figures.* | *medical charts* **2 the charts** [plural] a list, which comes out weekly, of the most popular records: *The song remains number one on the pop charts.* | *It was at the* **top of the charts** *for eleven weeks.* —see also CHART-TOPPING **3** [C] a detailed map, especially of an area of the ocean or of the stars —see also BAR CHART, FLOW CHART, PIE CHART

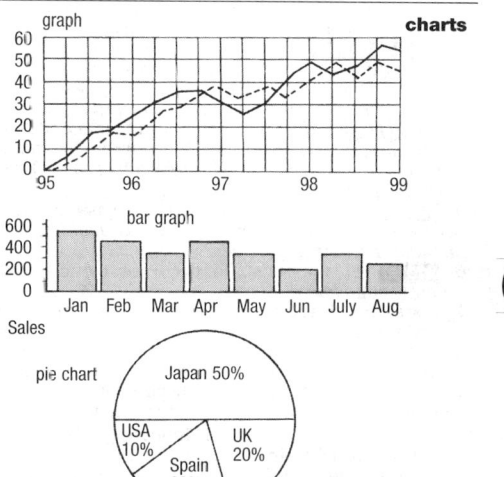

graph   charts

bar graph

Sales

pie chart — Japan 50% / UK 20% / Spain 20% / USA 10%

C

chart[2] v. [T] **1** to record information about a situation or set of events over a period of time, in order to see how it changes or develops: *Lydell has spent years charting the movement of these asteroids.* **2** to make a plan of what should be done to achieve a particular result: *Moore has the task of* **charting a course** *of expansion for the computer maker.* **3** to make a map of an area of land, ocean, or stars, or to draw lines on a map to show where you have traveled —see also UNCHARTED

char·ter[1] /ˈtʃɑrtər/ n. **1** [C] a statement of the principles, duties, and purposes of an organization: *Donating money to political groups goes against the union's charter.* **2** [C,U] the practice of paying money to a company to use their boats, airplanes etc., or the airplane, boat etc. that is used in this way: *The airline is now primarily a charter service.* **3** [C] a signed statement from a government or ruler that allows a town, organization, or university to officially exist and have special rights

charter[2] v. [T] **1** to pay a company for the use of their airplane, boat, train etc.: *I chartered a boat to take us to some of the smaller islands.* **2** to say officially that a town, organization, or university exists and has special rights

charter flight /ˈ.. ˌ./ n. [C] an airplane trip that is arranged for a particular group or for a particular purpose

charter mem·ber /ˌ.. ˈ../ n. [C] an original member of a club or organization

charter school /ˈ.. ˌ./ n. [C] a school to which the state government has given money and special permission to operate, but that is operated by parents, companies etc. rather than by the public school system

char·treuse /ʃɑrˈtruz, -ˈtrus/ n. [U] a bright yellow-green color

chart-top·ping /ˈ. ˌ../ adj. **a chart-topping record/group/hit etc.** a record, group etc. that has sold the most records in a particular week

char·wom·an /ˈtʃɑrˌwʊmən/ n. [C] OLD-FASHIONED a woman who cleans people's houses or offices

char·y /ˈtʃɛri, ˈtʃæri/ adj. **be chary about/of doing sth** to be unwilling to risk doing something: *The bank has become very chary about extending credit.*

chase[1] /tʃeɪs/ v. **1** [follow] [I,T] to quickly follow someone or something in order to catch them: *Stop chasing your sister!* | **[chase sb down/up/along etc.]** *Police chased the suspect along Stevens Creek Avenue.* | **[+ after]** *Our cat often chases after birds.* **2** [make sb/sth leave] [T] to make someone or some-

thing leave: [**chase sb away/off**] *A jeering, bottle-throwing crowd chased reporters away.*
3 man/woman [T] to try hard to make someone notice you and pay attention to you, because you want to have a romantic relationship with them: *He's been chasing some cute girl he met at the ice rink.*
4 try to get sth [I,T] to use a lot of time and effort trying to get something such as work or money: [+ **after**] *Do we really need three reporters chasing after the same story?*
5 hurry [I always + adv./prep.] to rush or hurry somewhere: *I chased around all day looking for a birthday present to give her.*
6 metal [T] TECHNICAL to decorate metal with a special tool: *chased silver*
7 chase the dragon SLANG to smoke the drug HEROIN
chase sth ↔ **down** *phr. v.* [T] **1** to run after someone or something and catch them: *Turner chased down the loose ball and ran it in for a touchdown.* **2** to find something you have been looking for: *Have you managed to chase down those contracts yet?*

chase² *n.* **1** [C] the act of following someone or something quickly in order to catch them: *Roswell's high-speed chase with police that ended in tragedy* **2 give chase** LITERARY to chase someone or something: *A patrol car spotted the vehicle and gave chase.* —see also **cut to the chase** (CUT¹ (19)), PAPER CHASE, WILD GOOSE CHASE

Chase /tʃeɪs/, **Sal·mon** /ˈsæmən/ (1808–1873) a CHIEF JUSTICE on the U.S. Supreme Court

chas·er /ˈtʃeɪsɚ/ *n.* [C] a weaker alcoholic drink that is drunk after a strong one, or a stronger alcoholic drink that is drunk after a weak one: *A shot of tequila and a beer chaser, please.*

chasm /ˈkæzəm/ *n.* [C] **1** [usually singular] a big difference between the opinions, experience, ways of life etc. of different groups of people, especially when this means they cannot understand each other: *Even today there is a chasm between white and black cultures in the Deep South.* **2** a very deep space between two high areas of rock or ice, especially one that is dangerous: *Winters died after her car plunged into the 40-foot chasm.*

chas·sis /ˈtʃæsi, ˈʃæ-/ *n. plural* **chassis** /-siz/ [C] **1** the frame on which the body, engine, wheels etc. of a vehicle are built **2** the landing equipment of an airplane **3** the frame in a radio, television, computer etc. that all of its electronic parts are attached to

chaste /tʃeɪst/ *adj.* **1** OLD-FASHIONED not having sex with anyone, or not with anyone except the person you are married to: *Girls were expected to remain chaste until marriage.* —compare CELIBATE —see also CHASTITY **2** simple and plain in style, and not showing much of someone's body; MODEST: *a chaste white dress* —**chastely** *adv.*

chas·ten /ˈtʃeɪsən/ *v.* [T usually passive] FORMAL to make someone realize that their behavior is wrong or mistaken: *Military leaders, chastened by Vietnam, have learned to be cautious.*

chas·tise /tʃæˈstaɪz, ˈtʃæstaɪz/ *v.* [T] **1** FORMAL to criticize someone severely: *Coleman chastised the board for not taking action sooner.* **2** OLD-FASHIONED to physically punish someone —**chastisement** *n.* [C,U]

chas·ti·ty /ˈtʃæstəti/ *n.* [U] the principle or state of not having sex with anyone, or not with anyone except the person you are married to: *Members of the group take vows of chastity (=a promise to not have sex), poverty, and obedience.*

chastity belt /ˈ... ˌ./ *n.* [C] a special belt with a lock, used in past times to prevent a woman from having sex

chas·u·ble /ˈtʃæzəbəl/ *n.* [C] a type of long loose coat without SLEEVEs worn by a priest at a religious service

chat¹ /tʃæt/ *v.* **chatted, chatting** [I] **1** to talk in a friendly informal way, especially about things that are not important: *The two women chatted all evening.* | [+ **about**] *Charlie and Kevin sat in the corner, chatting about life in the city.* | [+ **with/to**]

Dad really enjoys chatting with people from other countries. **2** to communicate with several people by computer, using a special Internet program that allows you to exchange written messages very quickly —see also CHAT ROOM

chat² *n.* [C,U] a friendly informal conversation: *Mr. Reynolds wants to have a chat with me about my report.* —see also CHIT-CHAT

châ·teau /ʃæˈtoʊ/ *n. plural* **châteaux** /-ˈtoʊz/ or **châteaus** [C] a castle or large house in the COUNTRYSIDE in France

chat·e·laine /ˈʃætlˌeɪn/ *n.* [C] FORMAL the female owner, or wife of the owner, of a castle or large house in the COUNTRYSIDE in France

chat line /ˈ. ./ *n.* [C] a telephone service that people call to talk to other people who have called the same service

chat room /ˈ. ./ *n.* [C] a place on the Internet where you can write messages to other people and receive messages back from them immediately, so that you can have a conversation

chat·tel /ˈtʃætl/ *n.* [C,U] LAW, OLD-FASHIONED something that belongs to you, that you can move from one place to another

chat·ter¹ /ˈtʃætɚ/ *v.* [I] **1** OLD-FASHIONED to talk quickly in a friendly way without stopping, especially about things that are not serious or important: [+ **about**] *What were you two chattering about?* **2** if birds or monkeys chatter, they make short high sounds **3** if your teeth are chattering, you are so cold or frightened that your teeth are knocking together

chatter² *n.* [U] **1** a friendly informal conversation, especially about something that is not serious or important **2** a series of short high sounds made by some birds or monkeys **3** a hard quick repeated sound made by your teeth knocking together or by machines: *I woke up to the chatter of helicopters flying overhead.*

chat·ter·box /ˈtʃætɚˌbɑks/ *n.* [C] OLD-FASHIONED someone, especially a child, who talks too much

chat·ty /ˈtʃæti/ *adj.* **chattier, chattiest** INFORMAL **1** liking to talk a lot in a friendly way: *Don Nobles is a chatty, energetic 75-year-old.* **2** a piece of writing that is chatty has a friendly informal style: *a chatty letter*

Chau·cer /ˈtʃɔsɚ/, **Geof·frey** /ˈdʒɛfri/ (?1340–1400) an English writer known for his long poem "The Canterbury Tales," one of the most important works in English literature

chauf·feur¹ /ˈʃoʊfɚ, ʃoʊˈfɚ/ *n.* [C] someone whose job is to drive a car for someone else

chauffeur² *v.* [T] **1** to drive a car for someone as your job **2** also **chauffeur around** to drive someone in your car, especially when you do not want to: *I've spent all day chauffeuring the kids around.*

chau·vin·ism /ˈʃoʊvəˌnɪzəm/ *n.* [U] **1** a belief that your own sex is better, more intelligent, or more important than the other sex, especially if you are a man: *The academy was labeled a stronghold of male chauvinism.* **2** a strong belief that your country or race is better or more important than any other: *national chauvinism*

chau·vin·ist /ˈʃoʊvənɪst/ *n.* [C] **1** someone, especially a man, who believes that their own sex is better, more intelligent, or more important than the other sex: *Call me a male chauvinist, but I want my wife to stay home with our kids.* **2** someone who strongly believes that their own country or race is better or more important than any other —**chauvinist** *adj.*

chau·vin·is·tic /ˌʃoʊvəˈnɪstɪk/ *adj.* **1** having the strong belief that your own country or race is better or more important than any other **2** having the belief that your own sex is better, more intelligent, or more important than the other sex, especially if you are a man: *He doesn't even try to hide his chauvinistic attitude toward women.* —**chauvinistically** /-kli/ *adv.*

Cha·vez /ˈtʃɑvɛz/, **Ce·sar** /ˈseɪzɑr/ (1927–1993) a Mexican-American who was the President of the United Farm Workers of America from 1966 to 1993

chaw /tʃɔ/ *n.* [C] a large piece of tobacco that you put in your mouth and chew

cheap¹ /tʃip/ *adj.*
1 price not expensive, or lower in price than you expected: *My flight to Reno was really cheap.* | *I bought the cheapest computer I could find.* | *Renting an apartment there is **dirt cheap** (=very low in price).*
2 charging less charging a low price: *The outlet mall is a lot cheaper than stores downtown.*
3 bad quality low in price and quality, or not worth much: *Who brought the nasty cheap beer?* | *a cheap leather jacket*
4 not generous not liking to spend money: *She's too cheap to take a cab.*
5 cheap to use not costing much to use or to employ: *Cheaper production facilities have helped boost profits.* | *The area's **cheap labor** has attracted many new businesses.*
6 unkind behaving in a way that is not kind, fair, or respectful to other people, especially people who cannot easily defend themselves: *I've had enough of his **cheap remarks** (=unkind criticism).* | *Burke's article was a **cheap shot** (=unkind criticism) at teenagers that did nothing to look past stereotypes.*
7 not deserving respect behaving in a way that shows you do not respect or care about yourself, so that other people do not respect you: *It's an ugly, mean little book that makes you **feel cheap** just for reading it.*
8 life is cheap used to say that it is not important if people die: *There is a feeling in the housing projects that life is cheap.*
9 on the cheap spending as little money as possible: *His new book tells how to visit New York on the cheap.*
10 a cheap thrill excitement that does not take much effort to get —**cheaply** *adv.*: *How do you feed a lot of people cheaply?* —**cheapness** *n* [U]

cheap² *adv.* **1** at a low price: *Old houses can sometimes be bought cheap and fixed up.* | *Comfort on this cruise ship **doesn't come cheap** (=is expensive).* | *Flights to Rio are **going cheap** (=selling for a lower price than usual).* **2** INFORMAL in a way that makes someone seem difficult to respect, because it makes them seem like they have low moral standards: *That dress makes her look real cheap.*

cheap·en /tʃipən/ *v.* [T] **1** to make something or someone seem to have lower moral standards than they had before: [**cheapen yourself by doing sth**] *Don't cheapen yourself by reacting to her insults.* **2** to make something seem to have less value or importance or to be less deserving of respect: *Using the national anthem as part of a comedy routine cheapens it.* **3** to become or make something lower in price or value: *The dollar's rise in value has cheapened imports.*

cheap·o /tʃipou/ also **el cheapo** *adj.* [no comparative] not of good quality and not costing very much: *I bought this cheapo camera during my vacation in Miami.*

cheap·skate /tʃipskeɪt/ *n.* [C] INFORMAL someone who does not like spending money and does not care if they behave in an unreasonable way to avoid spending it: *Don't be such a cheapskate – it's your turn to buy lunch.*

cheat¹ /tʃit/ *v.* **1** [I] to behave in a dishonest way in order to win or to get an advantage, especially in a competition, game, or test: *The movie's young heroine lies, cheats, and steals to get what she wants.* | [**+ on**] *Mrs. Mitchell caught me cheating on the history test.* | [**+ at**] *A guy named Bounce liked to cheat at dice.* | *You can't look at the cards, that's cheating.* **2** [T] to trick or deceive someone who trusts you: *He had cheated his clients by selling them worthless stocks.* | [**cheat sb (out) of sth**] *The airline's been accused of cheating its customers out of free bonus flights.* **3 feel cheated** to feel that you have been treated wrongly or unfairly and have not gotten what you deserve: *Many of the workers feel cheated by not getting their bonuses.* **4 cheat death/fate** to manage to avoid death or a very bad situation even though it seemed that you would not be able to

cheat on sb *phr. v.* [T] to be unfaithful to your husband, wife, or sexual partner by secretly having sex with someone else: *I would leave her if she ever cheated on me.*

cheat² *n.* [C] someone who is dishonest and cheats; CHEATER: *The law is aimed at catching tax cheats.*

Chech·nya /tʃetʃnyə, -ni,a/ a small area in Russia in the Caucasus Mountains, north of Georgia

check¹ /tʃɛk/ *v.*
1 find out [I,T] to do something or look at something to find out if it is done, correct, true, in good condition etc.: *"We have milk, don't we?" "Uh, I'll check."* | *I want to check my voice mail.* | [**+ whether/who etc.**] *The police will check whether the gun buyer has a criminal record.* | [**check (sth) for sth**] *It's a good idea to check for ticks after being out in the woods.* | [**+ that**] *We'll have to check that the forms have been filled out correctly.* | *Make sure you **double-check** (=check something twice) the spellings of these names.* | *My boss wants me to **check** the shipment **against** the order (=compare them to see if they are the same).*
2 ask sb [I] to ask someone for permission to do something or ask whether something is correct or true: *"Can I exchange this for a smaller size?" "You should be able to. Let me check."* | [**+ whether/ how/ who etc.**] *I need to check when the letter arrived.* | [**+ that**] *We'd better check that these are the right pills.* | [**check with sb**] *Check with Mrs. Jackson if you want to leave early.*
3 bags/coat etc. [T] to leave your bags, coat etc. at an official place, so they can be put on an airplane, train, bus etc. or so they can kept safe, or to take someone's bags in order to do this: *That bag's too large to take on the plane – I can check it for you.*
4 make a mark [T] to make a mark (✔) next to something to show that you have chosen it, that it is correct, or that you have dealt with it
5 not do sth [T] to suddenly stop yourself from saying or doing something because you realize it would be better not to: *I had to check the urge to laugh out loud.* | *I wanted to slap him, but managed to check myself.*
6 stop sth [T] to stop something bad from getting worse or continuing to happen: *Doctors are trying to check the spread of the disease with drugs.*
7 sports [T] to push another player very hard in HOCKEY

check in *phr. v.* **1** [I,T **check** sb **in**] to go to the desk at a hotel, airport, or hospital and report that you have arrived: *Has Mr. Walker checked in yet?* | *Airline employees were checking in passengers.* —see also CHECK-IN **2** [I] to call someone to tell them that you are safe or where you are: *Get the kids to check in with you by phone when they get home from school.*

check sth ↔ **off** *phr. v.* [T] to make a mark (✔) next to something to show that you have chosen it, that it is correct, or that you have dealt with it: *Good, now I can check that off the list.*

check on sb/sth *phr. v.* [T] to make sure that someone or something is safe, has everything they need, or is doing what they are supposed to be doing: *Dr. Stabler came by to check on Gilbert.* | *I need to check on the laundry.* —see Usage Note at CONTROL¹

check out *phr. v.*
1 make sure **a)** [T **check** sth ↔ **out**] INFORMAL to make sure that something is actually true, correct, or acceptable: *You should check that idea out with the boss first.* **b)** [I] if information checks out, it is proven to be true, correct, or acceptable: *We should see if his story checks out.*
2 look at sb/sth [T **check** sb/sth ↔ **out**] SPOKEN to look at someone or something because they are interesting or attractive: *Wow, check out that girl in the striped pants.* | *Check it out! They're selling hamburgers for 99 cents.*
3 hotel/hospital [I] to leave a hotel or hospital after paying the bill: *We have to check out by 1 p.m.*
4 examine/test sth [T **check** sth ↔ **out**] to test something to find out if it works, how it works,

whether it is appropriate for what you want etc.: *I'm going to check the car out today – Sue said it was making a clunking noise.*

5 get information [T **check** sb ↔ **out**] INFORMAL to get information about someone, especially to find out if they are appropriate for something: *We'd better check him out before we offer him the job.*

6 books [T **check** sth ↔ **out**] to borrow books from a library: *You can only check out three books at a time.* —see also CHECKOUT

check over *phr. v.* [T] **1** [**check** sth ↔ **over**] to look closely at something to make sure it is correct or acceptable: *I'll have my lawyer check over the contract.* **2** [**check** sb ↔ **over**] to examine someone to make sure they are healthy: *The doctor checked her over and couldn't find anything wrong.*

check up on sb/sth *phr. v.* [T] to try and make sure that someone is doing what they said they would do or what you want them to do, or that something is correct: *Mom's always checking up on me to see if I'm eating right.*

check² *n.*

1 from your bank [C] a printed piece of paper that you sign and write an amount of money on in order to pay for things: [+ **for**] *She gave the family a check for $2,450.* | *Can I pay by check?* | *I'll write you a check and put it in the mail today.* | *Have you cashed the check* (=asked a bank to give you the amount of money on a check) *yet?*

2 finding out [C] a process of finding out if something is safe, correct, true, or in the condition it should be: *a security check* | [+ **of**] *A check of phone records showed that the two men had been in contact with each other.* | [+ **on**] *I want you to run a check on* (=do the things needed to find out about sth) *his credit history.* | [+ **for**] *Ask the lab to do a check for any viruses.*

3 in a restaurant [C] a list that you are given in a restaurant that shows much you must pay for what you have eaten: *May I have the check, please?*

4 a control on sth [usually singular] something that controls something else and stops it from getting worse or continuing to happen: [+ **on**] *The commission serves as a check on telephone service monopolies.*

5 keep/hold sth in check to control something and prevent it from getting worse or continuing to happen: *The law is designed to keep rents in check.*

6 keep a check (on sb/sth) to watch or listen to someone or something regularly or continuously, in order to control something or gather information: *Keep a check on the engine temperature, so that it doesn't overheat.*

7 mark [C] a mark (✔) that you put next to something to show that you chose it, that it is correct, or that you have dealt with it

8 pattern [C,U] a pattern of squares, especially on cloth: *a tablecloth with red and white checks* | *a check shirt/tie/jacket etc.* (=a shirt, tie etc. made with this pattern on it) —see also CHECKED

9 checks and balances a system of rules in government or business that keeps any one person or group from having too much power or control

10 hat/coat check a) a place in a restaurant, theater etc. where you can leave your coat, bag etc. to be guarded until you go home **b)** a ticket that you are given so you can claim your things from this place

11 game [U] the position of the KING (=most important piece) in a game of CHESS when it can be directly attacked by the opponent's pieces —compare CHECKMATE

12 sports [C] an act of pushing another player very hard in HOCKEY

check·book /'tʃɛkbʊk/ *n.* [C] a small book of checks that your bank gives you

check card /'. ./ *n.* [C] a special plastic card that you can use to pay for things directly from your CHECKING ACCOUNT

checked /tʃɛkt/ *adj.* having a regular pattern of

colored squares, usually of white and one other color: *a checked skirt* —see also CHECK² (8)

check·er /'tʃɛkɚ/ *n.* [C] **1** someone who works at the CHECKOUT (1) in a SUPERMARKET **2 spell/grammar checker** a computer program that checks that the spelling of words or the grammar in a sentence is correct **3** someone who makes sure that something is written or done correctly: *a fact-checker for a magazine* **4** [C] one of a set of round wood or plastic objects used in the game of CHECKERS

check·er·board /'tʃɛkɚbɔrd/ *n.* [C] a board that you play checkers on, with 32 squares of one color and 32 squares of another color

check·ered /'tʃɛkɚd/ *adj.* **1** marked with squares of two different colors: *red and white checkered tiles* —see picture at PATTERN¹ **2 have a checkered history/past/career etc.** to have had periods of failure as well as successful times in your past: *Some banks won't give accounts to people with checkered credit histories.*

checkered flag /,.. './ *n.* [C] a flag covered with black and white squares that is waved at end of a car or MOTORCYCLE race

check·ers /'tʃɛkɚz/ *n.* [U] a game for two players, using 12 flat round pieces each and a special board with 64 squares, in which the purpose is to take the other player's pieces by jumping over them with your pieces —see also CHINESE CHECKERS

check-in /'. ./ *n.* **1** [U] the process of reporting your arrival at a hotel, airport, hospital etc.: *The hotel is hiring additional staff to make check-in easier.* **2** [C usually singular] a place where you report your arrival at a hotel, airport, hospital etc. | **check-in counter/desk** *When we got to the check-in counter, he couldn't find his ticket.* —see also **check in** (CHECK¹)

checking ac·count /'.. .,./ *n.* [C] a bank account that you can take money out of at any time, and for which you are given checks to use to pay for things —compare SAVINGS ACCOUNT

check-kit·ing /'. ,../ *n.* [U] the activity of obtaining money using illegal CHECKS

check·list /'tʃɛk,lɪst/ *n.* [C] a list that helps you by reminding you of the things you need to do or get for a particular job or activity: *She has a checklist she gives to the cleaning woman.*

check·mate /'tʃɛkmeɪt/ *n.* [U] the position of the KING (=most important piece) at the end of a game of CHESS when it is being directly attacked and cannot escape

check·out /'tʃɛk-aʊt/ *n.* **1** also **checkout counter/ stand** [C] the place in a SUPERMARKET or other store where you pay for the goods you want to buy: *Luckily, there was no line at the checkout.* **2** [C,U] the time by which you must leave a hotel room: *Check-out is at noon.* —see also **check out** (CHECK¹)

check·point /'tʃɛkpɔɪnt/ *n.* [C] a place, especially on a border, where an official person examines vehicles or people: *Tourist visas are issued at any border checkpoint.*

check·room /'tʃɛk-rum/ *n.* [C] a place in a restaurant, theater etc. where you can leave your coat, bags etc. to be guarded

check stub /'. ./ *n.* [C] **1** the part of a PAYCHECK that tells you the amount of taxes and other amounts taken out of it **2** the part of a check that is left when you tear it out of a CHECKBOOK, used for recording the amount you have spent

check·up, **check-up** /'tʃɛk-ʌp/ *n.* [C] an occasion when a doctor or DENTIST examines you to see if you are healthy: *It's been a couple of years since I had my last checkup.*

ched·dar, Cheddar /'tʃɛdɚ/ *n.* [U] a firm smooth yellow or orange cheese

cheek /tʃik/ *n.* **1** [C] the soft round part of your face below each of your eyes: *I kissed Mom on the cheek and said good night.* —see picture at BODY **2 cheek to cheek** if two people dance cheek to cheek, they dance very close to each other in a romantic way **3** [C] INFORMAL one of the two soft parts of your body that you sit on; BUTTOCK **4 turn the other cheek** to deliberately avoid reacting in an angry or violent way when someone has hurt or upset you: *It's hard to turn the other cheek when someone insults you.* **5 cheek by jowl** INFORMAL used to say that a group of people, things, or places are very close to each other: *Customers sat cheek by jowl along the counter of the bar.* **6** [singular,U] OLD-FASHIONED disrespectful or rude behavior, especially toward someone in a position of authority —see also -CHEEKED, TONGUE-IN-CHEEK

cheek·bone /'tʃikboʊn/ *n.* [C usually plural] one of the two bones above your cheeks, just below your eyes: *She has **high cheekbones** (=cheekbones that stick out and are considered attractive) and full lips.*

-cheeked /tʃikt/ [in adjectives] **red-cheeked/hollow-cheeked/rosy-cheeked etc.** having red, hollow etc. cheeks on your face

cheek·y /'tʃiki/ *adj.* **cheekier, cheekiest** OLD-FASHIONED badly behaved or not respectful, sometimes in a way that is amusing rather than rude —**cheekily** *adv.* —**cheekiness** *n.* [U]

cheep /tʃip/ *v.* [I] if a young bird cheeps, it makes a weak, high noise —**cheep** *n.* [C]

cheer[1] /tʃɪr/ *v.* **1** [I,T] to shout as a way of showing happiness, praise, approval, or support of someone or something: *Fans began to cheer as the teams entered the stadium.* | [cheer sb] *The crowd cheered the soldiers as they got into the plane.* —opposite BOO[1] **2** [T usually passive] to make someone feel more hopeful when they are worried: *Investors were cheered by news of the merger.* —**cheerer** *n.* [C]

cheer sb **on** *phr. v.* [T] to shout encouragement at a person or team to help them do well in a race or competition: *All of my friends were here to cheer me on.*

cheer up *phr. v.* **1** [I,T **cheer** sb ↔ **up**] to become happier, or to make someone feel happier: *Pizza also cheers me up.* | *I wish you would cheer up.* **2 cheer up!** SPOKEN used to tell someone not to be so sad: *Cheer up, it's not that bad!*

cheer[2] *n.* **1** [C] a shout of happiness, praise, approval, or encouragement: *The audience filled the theater with cheers.* | *Probably the biggest cheer of the evening was for General Powell.* —opposite BOO[2] **2** [C] a special CHANT (=phrase that is repeated) that the crowd at a sports game shouts in order to encourage their team to win: *The cheer, "Go Lions Go!" could be heard for over half a mile.* **3 three cheers for sb!** SPOKEN used to tell a group of people to shout three times as a way of showing support or praise for someone: *Three cheers for Coach Madison!* **4** [U] a feeling of happiness and confidence: *The rise in U.S. exports is certain to bring cheer to manufacturers.* —see also CHEERS

cheer·ful /'tʃɪrfəl/ *adj.* **1** behaving in a way that shows you are happy, for example by smiling or being very friendly: *The First Lady was cheerful and energetic during the press conference.* | *a cheerful voice* **2** something that is cheerful makes you feel happy because it is so bright or pleasant: *Salem is a cheerful, pleasant place.* | *a cheerful, spotlessly clean kitchen* **3** tending to be happy most of the time: *Mary Ellen is a cheerful and enthusiastic person.* **4** [only before noun] a cheerful attitude shows that you are willing to do whatever is necessary in a happy way: *a cheerful approach to the job* —**cheerfully** *adv.* —**cheerfulness** *n.* [U]

cheerleaders

pom pom

cheer·lead·er /'tʃɪr,lidə/ *n.* [C] **1** a member of a

team of people who encourage a crowd to cheer at sports games by shouting special words and dancing: *a high school cheerleader* **2** someone who encourages other people to do something: *Find a real estate agent who will be a cheerleader for your property.*

cheer·lead·ing /'tʃɪr,lidɪŋ/ *n.* [U] **1** the activity of being a cheerleader: *a cheerleading camp for girls* **2** the act of supporting an organization, idea etc. and not being willing to listen to criticism of it

cheer·less /'tʃɪrlɪs/ *adj.* cheerless weather, places, or times make you feel sad, bored, or uncomfortable: *Though brightly lit, the room was still somehow cheerless.* | *a cheerless winter sky* —**cheerlessly** *adv.* —**cheerlessness** *n.* [U]

cheers /tʃɪrz/ *interjection* used when you lift a glass of alcohol before drinking it, to say that you hope the people you are drinking with will be happy and have good health

cheer·y /'tʃɪri/ *adj.* **cheerier, cheeriest** cheerful, or making you feel happy: *A cheery fire burned in the fireplace.* —**cheerily** *adv.*

cheese /tʃiz/ *n.* [C,U] **1** a solid food made from milk, which is usually yellow or white and can be soft or hard: *half a pound of cheese* | *bagels and cream cheese* | *a tray of cheeses and cold meats* **2 say cheese** used to tell people to smile when you are going to take their photograph: *Come on everybody, say cheese!* —see also BIG CHEESE

cheese·board /'tʃizbɔrd/ *n.* [C] **1** a board used to cut cheese on **2** a board used for serving a variety of cheeses

cheese·burg·er /'tʃiz,bɔgə/ *n.* [C] a HAMBURGER served with a piece of cheese on top of the meat

cheese·cake /'tʃizkeɪk/ *n.* **1** [C,U] a cake made from a mixture containing soft cheese: *a slice of cheesecake* **2** [U] OLD-FASHIONED photographs of pretty young women with few clothes on

cheese·cloth /'tʃizklɔθ/ *n.* [U] thin light cotton cloth used for wrapping some types of cheeses, and in cooking

chees·y /'tʃizi/ *adj.* **cheesier, cheesiest** INFORMAL **1** cheap and not of good quality: *We went to some cheesy bar in Baltimore.* | *the cheesy music played in elevators* **2** tasting like cheese or containing cheese: *The enchiladas are extra cheesy but not greasy.* **3** not sincere: *a cheesy grin* —**cheesily** *adv.*

chee·tah /'tʃitə/ *n.* [C] a member of the cat family that has long legs and black spots on its fur, and can run extremely fast

Chee·ver /'tʃivə/**, John** (1912–1982) a U.S. writer of short stories and NOVELS

chef /ʃɛf/ *n.* [C] a skilled cook, especially the main cook in a restaurant or hotel: *a pastry chef*

chef d'oeu·vre /,ʃeɪ 'dʌvrə, -'dəv/ *n.* [C] FORMAL the best piece of work by a painter, writer, etc.; MASTERPIECE

Chek·hov /'tʃɛkɔf, -kav/**, An·ton** /'æntɑn/ (1860–1904) a Russian writer of plays and short stories —**Chekovian** /tʃəˈkoʊviən/ *adj.*

chem·i·cal[1] /'kɛmɪkəl/ *n.* [C] a substance that is used in or produced by a chemical process: *Farmers are moving away from the use of chemicals and pesticides.* | *a highly toxic chemical*

chemical[2] *adj.* relating to or used in chemistry, or involving the changes that happen when two substances combine: *a chemical analysis of the skeletons* | *chemical engineering* —**chemically** /-kli/ *adv.*: *chemically treated water*

chemical re·ac·tion /,... .'../ *n.* [C,U] a natural process in which the atoms of chemicals mix and arrange themselves differently to form new substances

chemical war·fare /,... '../ *n.* [U] methods of fighting a war using chemical weapons —compare BIOLOGICAL WARFARE

chemical weap·on /,... '../ *n.* [C] a poisonous substance, especially a gas, used as a weapon in war

C

che·mise /ʃə'miz/ n. [C] **1** a simple dress that hangs straight from a woman's shoulders **2** a piece of loose women's underwear worn on the top half of her body

chem·ist /'kɛmɪst/ n. [C] a scientist who has special knowledge and training in chemistry

chem·is·try /'kɛməstri/ n. [U] **1** the science that studies the structure of substances and the way that they change or combine with each other **2** if there is chemistry between two people or among a group, they like one other and work well together: *The chemistry between Hepburn and Tracy is obvious.* | *Teams with good chemistry win.* **3** the way substances combine in a particular process, thing, person etc.: *The drug may cause changes in a person's body chemistry.*

chemistry set /'... ,./ n. [C] a box containing equipment for children to do simple chemistry at home

chem·ist's /'kɛmɪsts/ n. [C] BRITISH a DRUGSTORE

che·mo /'kimoʊ/ n. [U] INFORMAL the short form of "chemotherapy"

che·mo·ther·a·py /ˌkimoʊ'θɛrəpi/ n. [U] the use of drugs to control and try to cure CANCER

che·nille /ʃə'nil/ n. [U] twisted thread with a surface like a soft brush, or cloth made from this and used for clothes, decorations etc.

cheque /tʃɛk/ n. the British and Canadian spelling of CHECK[2] (1)

cher·ish /'tʃɛrɪʃ/ v. [T usually passive] **1** to be very important to someone: *Sports has given me friendships that I cherish.* | *a cherished memory* | *The observance of Thanksgiving is a cherished tradition in the U.S.* **2** to love someone or something very much and take very good care of them: *They were forced to leave behind all their most cherished possessions.* | *Rosen's cherished wife, Eileen, died last year.*

Cher·o·kee /'tʃɛrəˌki/ a Native American tribe from the U.S. states of North Carolina and Tennessee

che·root /ʃə'rut/ n. [C] a CIGAR with both ends cut straight

cher·ry /'tʃɛri/ n. plural **cherries 1** [C] a small dark red round fruit with a long thin stem and a large seed: *cherry pie* | *a bunch of cherries* —see picture at FRUIT[1] **2 a)** [C] also **cherry tree** the tree on which this fruit grows **b)** [U] the wood of this tree, used for making furniture **3** [U] a bright red color **4 the cherry on (the) top** INFORMAL something additional that you did not expect, that is nice to have **5 lose your cherry** VULGAR SLANG to have sex for the first time

cherry bomb /'.. ,./ n. [C] a round red FIRECRACKER (=small loud explosive)

cherry bran·dy /ˌ.. '../ n. [U] a sweet alcoholic drink that tastes like cherries

cherry pick, cherry-pick /'.. ,./ v. [I,T] INFORMAL, DISAPPROVING to choose exactly the things or people you want from a group, especially in a way that is not fair to other people

cherry pick·er /'.. ,../ n. [C] a piece of equipment that has a long movable pole with a place for someone to stand at the end of it, used for doing work in high places

cherry to·ma·to /'.. ,../ n. plural **cherry tomatoes** [C] a very small TOMATO

cher·ub /'tʃɛrəb/ n. [C] **1** an ANGEL shown in paintings, SCULPTURE etc. as a fat pretty child with small wings: *marble cherubs over the entrance* **2** INFORMAL a young pretty child who behaves very well **3** plural **cherubim** BIBLICAL one of the ANGELS that guard the seat where God sits —**cherubic** /tʃə'rubɪk/ adj.: *a cherubic faced child*

cher·vil /'tʃɝvəl/ n. [U] a strong-smelling garden plant used as an HERB

Ches·a·peake Bay, the /'tʃɛsəˌpik/ a long narrow BAY of the Atlantic Ocean on the eastern coast of the U.S., in the states of Virginia and Maryland.

chess /tʃɛs/ n. [U] a game for two players, who move their playing pieces according to particular rules across a special board to try to trap their opponent's KING (=most important piece)

chess·board /'tʃɛsˌbɔrd/ n. [C] a square board with 64 black and white squares, on which you play chess —see picture at BOARD[1]

chess·man /'tʃɛsmæn, -mən/ also **chess·piece** /'tʃɛspis/ n. plural **chessmen** /-mɛn, -mən/ [C] one of the 16 black or 16 white playing pieces used in the game of chess

chest /tʃɛst/ n. [C] **1** the front part of your body, between your neck and your stomach: *Porter was shot in the chest.* | *When doing sit-ups, keep your hands crossed on your chest, rather than behind your neck.* —see also FLAT-CHESTED —see picture at BODY **2** a large, strong box with a lid, that you use to store things in or to move your personal possessions from one place to another: *a toy chest* | *We use a cedar chest to keep wool blankets in.* —see also HOPE CHEST, ICE CHEST, MEDICINE CHEST, WAR CHEST **3 chest pain** also **chest pains** pain in your chest that may mean you are having a HEART ATTACK (=condition in which your heart stops working correctly) **4 get something off your chest** to tell someone about something that has been worrying or annoying you for a long time, so that you feel better afterward: *People are able to get things off their chest in these meetings.* **5 chest-thumping/chest-pounding** the activity of telling other people how good you are or about the things you have done and are proud of: *Bryant's speech basically amounted to political chest-thumping.*

ches·ter·field /'tʃɛstɚˌfild/ n. [C] CANADIAN, BRITISH a large soft comfortable SOFA

chest·nut[1] /'tʃɛsnʌt/ n. **1** [C] a smooth red-brown nut that you can eat **2** also **chestnut tree** [C] the tree on which this nut grows **3** [U] a reddish-brown color **4** [C] a horse that is this color **5 an old chestnut** a joke or story that has been repeated many times —see also WATER CHESTNUT

chestnut[2] adj. red-brown in color: *Her face was framed by chestnut curls.*

chest of drawers /ˌ. . './ n. [C] a piece of furniture with drawers, used for storing clothes; DRESSER —see picture on page 426

chest·y /'tʃɛsti/ adj. **1** INFORMAL used to describe a woman with large breasts, when you want to avoid saying this directly **2** a chesty voice or cough comes from deep inside your chest

che·val glass /ʃə'væl ˌglæs/ n. [C] a long mirror in a frame which stands upright and can be moved backward and forward

chev·a·lier /ˌʃɛvə'lɪr, ʃə'væl,yeɪ/ n. [C] **1** a title for someone who has a high rank in a special association in France **2** a member of the lowest rank of the French NOBILITY in past times

chev·ron /'ʃɛvrən/ n. [C] **1** a pattern in a V shape **2** a piece of cloth in the shape of a V which soldiers have on their SLEEVES to show their rank

chew[1] /tʃu/ v. **1** [I,T] to bite food several times before swallowing it: *You can just swallow oysters or you can chew them a little bit first.* —see picture at BITE[1] **2** [I,T] to bite something repeatedly in order to taste it or because you are nervous: *My worst habit is chewing gum.* | *[+ on/at] I gave the baby my key ring to chew on.* **3 chew the fat** INFORMAL to have a long, friendly conversation **4 chew the cud a)** if a cow or sheep chews the cud, it repeatedly bites food it has brought up from its stomach **b)** INFORMAL to think very carefully before making a decision —see also **bite off more than you can chew** (BITE[1] (8))

chew on sth phr. v. [T] to think about something carefully for a period of time: *This program offers more than a little to chew on.*

chew sb ↔ **out** phr. v. [T] INFORMAL to talk angrily to someone in order to show them that you disapprove of what they have done: *I thought she was gonna chew me out for shrinking her sweater.*

chew sth **over** phr. v. [T] to think about something carefully for a period of time: *Let me chew it over for a few days, and then I'll let you have my answer.*

chew sb/sth ↔ **up** phr. v. [T] **1** to damage or

destroy someone or something by tearing it into small pieces: *The tape was chewed up by the VCR.* **2** INFORMAL to defeat or destroy someone, or use all of something: *The phone bill chewed up all but the last few dollars of my paycheck.* **3** to bite something repeatedly with your teeth so that you can make it smaller or softer and swallow it: *Take small bites of meat and chew them up well.*

chew² *n.* [C] **1** a piece of a special tobacco which you chew but do not swallow **2** something such as candy or cookies that you chew a lot to make it soft enough to swallow: *a recipe for chocolate walnut chews* **3** the act of biting something repeatedly with the teeth

chewing gum /'.. ,./ *n.* [U] GUM¹ (1)

chew·y /'tʃui/ *adj.* **chewier, chewiest** food that is chewy has to be chewed a lot to make it soft enough to swallow: *soft, chewy praline candy* | *Steak becomes tough and chewy when it is cooked too long.*

Chey·enne /ʃaɪˈyɛn, -ˈyɛn/ **1** a Native American tribe from the western region of the U.S. **2** the capital city of the U.S. state of Wyoming —**Cheyenne** *adj.*

Chiang Kai-shek /,tʃæŋ kaɪ 'ʃɛk/ (1887–1975) a Chinese soldier and politician, leader of the Chinese NATIONALIST Party, who was forced to move from mainland China to the island of Taiwan by the Communists in 1949, and ruled Taiwan as President until he died

chia·ro·scu·ro /,kyɑrəˈskyʊroʊ/ *n.* [U] the use of light and dark areas in a picture or painting

chic /ʃik/ *adj.* showing a good sense of what is attractive and good style: *a chic apartment* | *She is chic and witty.* —**chic** *n.* [U]

Chi·ca·go /ʃɪˈkɑgoʊ/ the largest city in the U.S. state of Illinois

Chi·ca·na /tʃɪˈkɑnə/ *n.* [C] a woman who is a U.S. citizen but who was born in Mexico or whose family came from Mexico —compare CHICANO

chi·can·er·y /ʃɪˈkeɪnəri/ *n.* [U] FORMAL the use of complicated plans or tricks to deceive people: *Many blacks were denied the right to vote through chicanery.*

Chi·ca·no /tʃɪˈkɑnoʊ/ *n.* [C] *plural* **Chicanos** a U.S. citizen who was born in Mexico or whose family came from Mexico —**Chicano** *adj.*: *the Chicano community*

chi-chi /'ʃi ʃi/ *adj.* INFORMAL, DISAPPROVING fashionable and expensive, and often very decorated: *a chi-chi Beverly Hills restaurant*

w **chick** /tʃik/ *n.* [C] **1** a baby bird: *a hen and her chicks* **2** SPOKEN, INFORMAL a word for a young woman, sometimes considered offensive: *"Who is he talking to?" "Some chick named Melanie."*

chick·a·dee /'tʃikədi/ *n.* [C] a North American bird with a black head

Chick·a·saw /'tʃikə,sɔ/ a Native American tribe from the southeastern area of the U.S.

w **chick·en¹** /'tʃikən/ *n.*

1 bird [C] a common farm bird that is kept for its meat and eggs: *We raise our own chickens.* —see also HEN, ROOSTER

2 meat [U] the meat from this bird, eaten as food: *fried chicken* | *Boy, that chicken smells good.*

3 lacking courage [C] INFORMAL someone who is not brave at all; COWARD: *I'm such a chicken when it comes to skiing.*

4 game [U] a game in which someone, especially a young person, must do something dangerous to show that they are brave

5 a chicken and egg situation/problem/thing etc. a situation in which it is impossible to decide which of two things happened first, or which action is the cause of the other: *That leaves the company in a chicken and egg dilemma.*

6 sb's chickens have come home to roost used to say that someone's bad or dishonest actions in the past have caused the problems that they have now

7 which came first, the chicken or the egg? used to say that it is difficult or impossible to decide which of two things happened first, or which action is the cause and which is the effect —see also **don't count your chickens (before they've hatched)** (COUNT¹ (8)), SPRING CHICKEN

chicken² *adj.* [not before noun] INFORMAL not brave enough to do something: *Dave's too chicken to ask her out.*

chicken³ *v.*

chicken out *phr. v.* [I] INFORMAL to decide at the last moment not to do something, because you are afraid: *Margaret chickened out of launching her own consulting firm.*

chicken feed /'.. ,./ *n.* [U] INFORMAL an amount of money that is too small to worry about: *The program will cost about $200 million to run, chicken feed compared to NASA's $16 billion budget.*

chicken-fried steak /,... '.../ *n.* [C,U] a thin piece of BEEF covered in small pieces of bread and cooked in hot oil

chicken-liv·ered /'.. ../ *adj.* not brave; COWARDLY

chick·en·pox /'tʃikən,paks/ *n.* [U] an infectious disease that causes ITCHY spots on the skin and a slight fever, and that usually affects children

chicken run /'.. ,./ *n.* [C] an area surrounded by a fence where you keep chickens

chick·en·shit /'tʃikən,ʃit/ *n.* [C] VULGAR **1** someone who is not brave at all; COWARD **2** a very small amount of money: *They worked hard, for chickenshit.* —**chickenshit** *adj.*

chicken wire /'.. ,./ *n.* [U] a type of thin wire net, used especially for making fences

chick·pea, chick pea, chick-pea /'tʃikpi/ *n.* [C] a large brown PEA that is cooked and eaten; GARBANZO

chick·weed /'tʃikwid/ *n.* [U] a plant that is a WEED with small white flowers

chic·le /'tʃikəl, 'tʃikli/ *n.* [U] the thick juice of a tropical American tree used for making CHEWING GUM

chic·o·ry /'tʃikəri/ *n.* [U] **1** a European plant with blue flowers whose bitter leaves are eaten in SALADs **2** the roots of this plant, used in coffee or instead of coffee

chide /tʃaɪd/ *v.* [I,T] LITERARY to speak angrily to someone who has done something wrong or done something you do not approve of; REBUKE: [**chide sb for (doing) sth**] *Harrell chides employees for not wearing their name tags.*

chief¹ /tʃif/ *adj.* [only before noun] **1** most important; main: *Advertising provides the radio station's chief form of revenue.* | *Troops have been stationed in the chief fortresses of the country.* —see also CHIEFLY **2** highest in rank: *the chief medical officer* | *Rehnquist is the Chief Justice of the Supreme Court.* **3 chief cook and bottle washer** HUMOROUS someone who does a lot of small jobs to make sure that something is successful

chief² *n.* [C] **1** the most important person in a company or organization: *the police chief* | *He was chief of SAS flight operations in Stockholm.* **2** the ruler of a tribe: *a Native American tribal chief* **3 the chief** INFORMAL the person in charge of the company or organization you work for: *The chief wants to see you right away.* **4 big/great white chief** OLD-FASHIONED HUMOROUS the person in charge of a group of people, company, organization etc. **5 too many chiefs and not enough Indians** used to say that there are too many people saying how something should be done and not enough people doing it

Chief Ex·ec·u·tive /,. .'.../ *n.* **the Chief Executive** the President of the U.S.

chief ex·ec·u·tive of·fi·cer /,. .,... '.../ also **chief executive** *n.* [C] a CEO

chief jus·tice /. '../ *n.* [C] the most important judge in a court of law, especially of the U.S. SUPREME COURT or of state SUPREME COURTS

chief·ly /'tʃifli/ *adv.* mostly but not completely; mainly: *Before 1849, travel was done chiefly on horseback.* | *Real estate prices have been falling, chiefly because of the lack of jobs in the area.*

chief of staff /,. . './ *n.* [C] *plural* **chiefs of staff** **1** an official of high rank who advises the man in charge of an organization or government: *the White*

House chief of staff **2** an officer of high rank in the army, navy etc. who advises the officer in charge of a particular military group or operation

Chief Rab·bi /ˌ. '../ *n.* **the Chief Rabbi** the main leader of the JEWISH religion in a country

chief·tain /'tʃiftən/ *n.* [C] the leader of a tribe, group, or a Scottish CLAN —**chieftainship** *n.* [C,U]

chif·fon /ʃɪ'fɑn/ *n.* [U] a soft thin silk or NYLON material that you can see through: *a red chiffon gown*

chif·fo·nier /ˌʃɪfə'nɪr/ *n.* [C] a tall CHEST OF DRAWERS

chig·ger /'tʃɪgɚ/ *n.* [C] a very small insect that lives in tall grass and bites animals and humans, causing severe ITCHING¹ (1)

chi·gnon /'ʃinyɑn/ *n.* [C] hair that is tied in a smooth knot at the back of a woman's head

chi·hua·hua /tʃɪ'wɑwɑ/ *n.* [C] a very small dog with smooth short hair, originally from Mexico

chil·blain /'tʃɪlbleɪn/ *n.* [C] a painful red area on your fingers or toes that is caused by cold weather

sw **child** /tʃaɪld/ *n. plural* **children** /'tʃɪldrən/ [C]
1 young person a young person who is not yet fully grown: *Admission is $5, children under 12 are free.* | *an attractive, happy child* | *He learned German as a child* (=when he was a child).
2 son/daughter a son or daughter of any age: *How many children does Jane have?* | *Vic was an only child* (=he had no brothers or sisters).
3 sb influenced by an idea someone who is very strongly influenced by the ideas and attitudes of a particular period of history: [+ of] *I am a child of the forties, of radio and World War II.*
4 sb who is like a child someone who behaves like a child or is not very experienced in doing something: *I don't want children – I'm married to a child and that's enough.*
5 children should be seen and not heard an expression meaning that children should be quiet and not talk, used when you disapprove of the way the children are behaving
6 be with child OLD USE to be PREGNANT
7 be heavy/great/big with child LITERARY to be almost ready to give birth —see also CHILD'S PLAY

USAGE NOTE: CHILD

WORD CHOICE: child, baby, infant, toddler, teenager, adolescent, youth, young people, kid

A **baby** (or more formally an **infant**) is a very young **child**, usually under one year old: *This seat is for infants up to 20 lbs.* | *Would you like to hold the baby?* A child who has just learned to walk is a **toddler**. Young people aged 13 to 19 are **teenagers** and a younger teenager may also be called an **adolescent**, but this word is fairly formal, and may show a negative attitude: *typical adolescent behavior.* The noun **youth** is often used for an older male teenager (15+) in official reports about crimes or bad behavior: *The police are seeking two youths in connection with the attack.* When it is used before a noun, **youth** includes both sexes: *a youth club/group/worker/center/hostel.* Often the phrase **young people** is used for this age group in everyday English: *There's nothing for young people to do in this town.* **Kid** is used both for a **child** (up to around 14): *The kids are playing in the yard,* and for **young people**: *We met a group of college kids.* **Child** may sound slightly formal in some contexts, and **kid** may be used instead in order to sound friendlier: *Can you pick up the kids after school today?*

GRAMMAR
Remember the plural of **child** is **children**, never *childs* or *childrens*. But in the possessive form you say: *this child's education* | *these children's education*

---

child·bear·ing /'tʃaɪldˌbɛrɪŋ/ *n.* [U] **1** the process of being PREGNANT and giving birth to a baby **2 child-bearing age/years** the period of time during a woman's life when she is able to have babies

child·birth /'tʃaɪldbɚθ/ *n.* [U] the act of giving birth: *a class on natural childbirth and parenting* | *He has*

three children by his first wife, who died in child-birth.

child care, childcare /'. ./ *n.* [U] an arrangement in which someone, especially someone with special training, takes care of children while their parents are at work: *She pays $700 a month for childcare.* | *a childcare center*

child·hood /'tʃaɪldhʊd/ *n.* [C,U] the period of time when you are a child: *They've been buddies since childhood.* | *Vince had a very unhappy childhood.* —see also SECOND CHILDHOOD

child·ish /'tʃaɪldɪʃ/ *adj.* **1** relating to or typical of a child: *the childish joys of cotton candy and carousels* **2** DISAPPROVING behaving in a silly way that makes you seem much younger than you really are: *I wish politicians would stop this childish name-calling.* —compare CHILDLIKE —**childishly** *adv.* —**childishness** *n.* [U]

child·less /'tʃaɪldlɪs/ *adj.* having no children: *a childless couple* —**childlessness** *n.* [U]

child·like /'tʃaɪldlaɪk/ *adj.* APPROVING having qualities that are typical of a child, especially qualities such as INNOCENCE and trust: *She has a childlike way of looking at things.* —compare CHILDISH

child prod·i·gy /ˌ. '.../ *n.* [C] a child who is unusually skillful at doing something such as playing a musical instrument

child·proof /'tʃaɪldpruf/ *adj.* something that is child-proof is designed to prevent a child from opening, damaging, or breaking it: *a childproof aspirin bottle*

chil·dren /'tʃɪldrən/ *n.* the plural of CHILD

child's play /'. ./ *n.* [U] INFORMAL something that it is very easy to do: *Working out the formula is child's play with a computer.*

child sup·port /'. .ˌ./ *n.* [U] money that someone pays regularly to their former wife or husband in order to support their children

Chil·e /'tʃɪli/ a country on the western coast of South America between the Pacific Ocean and the Andes mountains —**Chilean** *n., adj.*

chil·i /'tʃɪli/ *n. plural* **chilies** **1** [C] also **chile, chili pepper** a small type of PEPPER¹ (3) with a very strong, SPICY taste **2** [U] also **chili powder** a SPICY red powder made from this PEPPER¹ (3) and used in cooking **3** [U] also **chili con car·ne** /ˌtʃɪl kɑn 'kɑrni/ a SPICY dish made with chilies, meat, and beans

chil·i·dog /'tʃɪliˌdɔg/ *n.* [C] a HOT DOG (=meat in a tube-shape) with chili on it

chili pow·der /'.. ˌ../ *n.* [U] a powder that contains a mixture of SPICES, including chili and CUMIN, used in cooking

chill¹ /tʃɪl/ *v.* **1** [I,T] if you chill something such as food or drink, or if it chills, it becomes very cold but does not freeze: *Wrap the dough in plastic and chill for at least an hour.* | *I think the wine should be chilled enough by now.* **2** [I] also **chill out** SPOKEN, INFORMAL to relax instead of feeling angry or nervous: *Shelly, just chill out, okay.* **3** [T usually passive] to make someone very cold: *Chilled by the winds, people huddled under blankets.* **4** [T] LITERARY to frighten someone, especially by seeming very cruel or violent: *The look in her eye chilled me.*

chill² *n.* **1** [singular,U] a feeling of coldness: *There was frost on the windows and a chill in the air.* | *A small heater keeps off the night chill.* **2** [C] a feeling of fear or shock caused by something that is very upsetting, violent, or cruel: *Her description of the massacre sent a chill through the audience.* **3** [C] a feeling of being cold, caused by being sick: *Symptoms include fever, chills, and increased heart rate.* **4** [singular] a feeling that someone is not friendly, that you get from the way they behave or speak: *There was a definite chill in his voice when he answered.* **5** [singular] a situation in which something is not encouraged or is stopped: *The high price of oil put a chill on the auto industry.* —see also **send shivers/chills up (and down) your spine** (SEND (8))

chill³ *adj.* **1 take a chill pill** SPOKEN used to tell someone to stop being excited, nervous, or angry **2** [only before noun] LITERARY very cold *a chill wind*

chill·er /'tʃɪlɚ/ *n.* [C] INFORMAL a movie or book that is intended to frighten you: *the Stephen King chiller "The Shining"*

chil·ling /'tʃɪlɪŋ/ *adj.* **1** something that is chilling makes you feel frightened, especially because it is cruel, violent, or dangerous: *a chilling reminder of the war* **2** having a bad effect on what someone does: *Today's arrests should send a chilling message to anyone involved in insurance fraud.*

chil·lum /'tʃɪləm/ *n.* [C] a type of pipe used for smoking MARIJUANA

chill·y /'tʃɪli/ *adj.* **chillier, chilliest** **1** cold enough to make you feel uncomfortable: *A fire was needed against the chilly New England evenings.* **2** unfriendly: *His blue eyes had a chilly glint.* —**chilliness** *n.* [singular,U]

chime¹ /tʃaɪm/ *v.* **1** [I,T] if a bell or clock chimes, it makes a ringing sound, especially to tell you what time it is: *Church bells throughout France chimed to mark the occasion.* **2** [I] to be the same as something else or to have the same effect: [+ **with**] *Her views chime with my own.*
   chime in *phr. v.* [I] to say something in a conversation, especially to agree with what someone has just said: *"Chris and I like the same rides," Jimmy chimed in.*

chime² *n.* [C] **1 chimes** [plural] a set of bells or other objects that produce musical sounds: *Wind chimes hung from the tree branches.* **2** a ringing sound made by a bell or clock: *the chime of the doorbell*

chi·me·ra /kaɪ'mɪrə, -'mɛrə/ *n.* [C] **1** something, especially an idea or hope, that is not really possible and can never exist: *the chimera of a "universal language"* **2** an imaginary creature that breathes fire and has a lion's head, a goat's body, and a snake's tail

chi·mer·i·cal /kaɪ'mɛrɪkəl, -'mɪr-/ *adj.* LITERARY imaginary or not really possible

chim·ney /'tʃɪmni/ *n.* **plural chimneys** [C] **1** a pipe inside a building for smoke from a fire to go out through the roof: *Smoke drifted from a chimney.* —see picture on page 423 **2** a narrow opening in tall rocks or cliffs that you can climb up **3** the glass cover that is put over the flame in an oil lamp

chimney sweep /'.. ,./ *n.* [C] someone whose job is to clean CHIMNEYs using special long brushes

chimp /tʃɪmp/ *n.* [C] INFORMAL a CHIMPANZEE

chim·pan·zee /,tʃɪmpæn'zi/ *n.* [C] an intelligent African animal that is like a monkey without a tail

chin /tʃɪn/ *n.* [C] **1** the front part of your face below your mouth: *He smiled and rubbed his chin.* **2 (keep your) chin up!** SPOKEN used to tell someone to make an effort to stay cheerful when they are in a difficult situation: *Keep your chin up! We'll get through this together!* —see picture at BODY **3 take it on the chin** to be strongly criticized or put in a difficult situation and not complain about it: *I took it on the chin, but life goes on.*

Chi·na /'tʃaɪnə/ the largest country in eastern Asia —**Chinese** *n., adj.*

chi·na /'tʃaɪnə/ *n.* [U] **1** a hard white substance produced by baking a special type of clay at a high temperature: *a china tea cup* **2** also **chinaware** plates, cups etc. made of this substance: *We use our china only on special occasions.*

China Sea, the /,.. './ the western part of the Pacific Ocean that goes along the coast of China and Vietnam

Chi·na·town /'tʃaɪnətaʊn/ *n.* [C,U] an area in a city where there are Chinese restaurants, stores, and where a lot of Chinese people live

chin·chil·la /,tʃɪn'tʃɪlə/ *n.* **1** [C] a small South American animal bred for its fur **2** [U] the pale gray fur of the chinchilla: *a chinchilla coat*

Chi·nese¹ /,tʃaɪ'niz◂, -'nis◂/ *n.* **1** [U] the language of China **2 the Chinese** [plural] people from China

Chinese² *adj.* from or relating to China

Chinese cab·bage /,.. '../ *n.* [U] a type of CABBAGE with long leaves that have curly edges

Chinese check·ers /,.. '../ *n.* [U] a game in which you move small balls from hole to hole on a board that is shaped like a star

Chinese lan·tern /,.. '../ *n.* [C] a piece of folded colored paper that is put around a light for decoration

Chinese med·i·cine /,.. '.../ *n.* [U] a type of medicine that uses special dried plants and ACUPUNCTURE

Chink /tʃɪŋk/ *n.* [C] TABOO a Chinese person. Do not use this word.

chink¹ /tʃɪŋk/ *n.* **1 a chink in sb's armor** a weakness in someone's character, argument etc. that you can use to attack them: *Opponents are looking for chinks in his political armor.* **2** [C] a narrow crack or hole in something that lets light or air through: *Through a chink in the shutter we could see Ralph.* **3** [C] a short high ringing sound made by metal or glass objects hitting each other: *the chink of knives and forks*

chink² *v.* [I,T] if glass or metal objects chink or you chink them, they make a short high sound when they knock together: *A few pennies chinked in my pocket.*

chi·no /'tʃinoʊ/ *n.* **1** [U] a strong material made of woven cotton, often light brown in color **2 chinos** [plural] loose pants made from this material: *Bruce was wearing his baggy old chinos.*

Chi·nook /ʃə'nʊk, tʃə-/ a Native American tribe from the northwestern area of the U.S.

chin·strap /'tʃɪnstræp/ *n.* [C] a band of cloth that goes under your chin to keep a hat or HELMET in place

chintz /tʃɪnts/ *n.* [U] smooth cotton cloth that is printed with flowery patterns and used for making curtains, furniture covers etc.: *a chintz sofa*

chintz·y /'tʃɪntsi/ *adj.* **chintzier, chintziest** **1** INFORMAL cheap and badly made: *The car has chintzy uncomfortable seats.* **2** INFORMAL unwilling to give people things or spend money; STINGY: *Christina's Cafe tends to be a little chintzy with ingredients.*

chin up, chinup /'. ./ *n.* [C] an exercise in which you hang on a bar and pull yourself up until your chin is above the bar

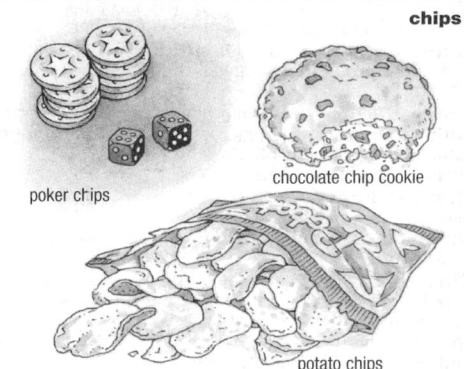

chips

poker chips

chocolate chip cookie

potato chips

chip¹ /tʃɪp/ *n.*
1 food [C usually plural] **a)** a thin dry flat piece of potato or TORTILLA cooked in very hot oil and eaten cold: *a bag of potato chips* | *chips and guacamole dip* **b)** BRITISH a FRENCH FRY: *fish and chips*
2 computer [C] **a)** a small piece of SILICON that has a set of complicated electrical connections on it and is used to store and PROCESS information in computers **b)** the main MICROPROCESSOR of a computer
3 piece [C] a small piece of wood, stone, metal etc., that has broken off something: *Chips of plaster littered the floor of the lobby.*
4 mark [C] a small crack or mark on a plate, cup etc. where a piece has broken off: [+ **in**] *Oh, the plate has a chip in it.*
5 have a chip on your shoulder to easily become offended or angry because you think you have been treated unfairly in the past: *The kid has had a chip on his shoulder ever since his parents divorced.*

6 **game** [C] a small flat colored piece of plastic used in games such as POKER and BLACKJACK to represent a particular amount of money

7 **be a chip off the old block** INFORMAL to be like one of your parents in the way you look or behave

8 **when the chips are down** SPOKEN in a serious or difficult situation, especially one in which you realize what is really true or important: *When the chips were down, you felt he could handle the situation.*

9 **let the chips fall (where they may)** to not worry about what the results of a particular action will be: *I decided to tell her my opinion and let the chips fall where they may.*

10 **sports** also **chip shot** [C] a hit or kick in GOLF or SOCCER that makes the ball go high into the air for a short distance —see also BLUE CHIP, **cash in your chips** at **cash in** (CASH²), CHOCOLATE CHIP, COW CHIP

chip² *v.* **chipped, chipping 1** [I,T] if something such as a plate chips or if you chip it, a small piece of it breaks off accidentally: *The ball hit him in the face and chipped a tooth.* | [+ off] *When he dropped the skillet on the counter, a small piece chipped off the tile.* **2** [I,T] to remove something by breaking it off in small pieces: *She tried to chip the ice off the windshield.* **3** [T] to make a GOLF or SOCCER ball go high into the air for a short distance

chip sth ↔ **away** *phr. v.* [T] to remove something, especially something hard that is covering a surface, by hitting it with a tool so that small pieces break off: *A drill was used to chip away the coal.* | [+ at] *Archeologists were carefully chipping away at the rock.*

chip away at sth *phr. v.* [T] to gradually make something less effective or destroy it: *Howe did little to chip away at his opponent's popularity.*

chip in *phr. v.* **1** [I,T] to give money, help, advice etc. to add to what other people are giving: *I was thinking we could all chip in $30 and buy Dad a new workbench.* | *Mercer chipped in with 16 points, giving the Eagles an easy win.* **2** [I] to interrupt a conversation by saying something that adds more detail: *Then I chipped in and said I'd like to go, too.*

chip·board /'tʃɪpbɔrd/ *n.* [U] a type of board made from small pieces of wood pressed together with glue

chip·munk /'tʃɪpmʌŋk/ *n.* [C] a small American animal similar to a SQUIRREL that has black lines on its fur

chipped /tʃɪpt/ *adj.* something that is chipped has a small piece broken off the edge of it: *chipped plates*

chipped

chipped

cracked

chipped beef /ˌ. './ *n.* [U] BEEF that has been dried and SMOKED and SLICED very thinly

Chip·pen·dale /'tʃɪpənˌdeɪl/, **Thomas** (1718–1779) an English furniture designer who had a great influence on the design of eighteenth-century furniture

chip·per /'tʃɪpɚ/ *adj.* INFORMAL cheerful and active: *You're looking very chipper this morning, Deborah.*

Chip·pe·wa, Ojibwa, Ojibway /'tʃɪpəˌwɔ-, -ˌwɑ/ *n.* a Native American tribe from the state of Michigan in the U.S.

Chi·ri·co /'kɪriˌkoʊ/, **Giorgio de** /'dʒɔrdʒoʊ deɪ/ (1888–1978) an Italian PAINTER whose paintings give the effect of dreams and influenced the development of SURREALISM in art

chi·ro·prac·tor /'kaɪrəˌpræktɚ/ *n.* [C] someone who treats sickness by pressing on and moving the bones in your back —**chiropractic** *n.* [U]

chirp /tʃɚp/ also **chir·rup** /'tʃɪrəp/ *v.* [I] **1** if a bird or insect chirps, it makes short high sounds **2** to speak in a cheerful, high voice: *"Good morning, Ricardo!" Judith chirped.* —**chirp** *n.* [C]

chis·el¹ /'tʃɪzəl/ *n.* [C] a metal tool with a sharp edge, used to cut wood or stone —see picture at TOOL¹

chisel² *v.* **chiseled, chiseling** also **chiselled, chiselling** [T] **1** to use a chisel to cut wood or stone, especially into a particular shape: [chisel sth into/from/in etc.] *Remove loose bricks, and then chisel out some of the old mortar underneath.* **2** OLD-FASHIONED to cheat or deceive someone —**chiseler** *n.* [C]

chis·eled /'tʃɪzəld/ *adj.* having a clear, sharp shape: *He was tall, with chiseled features and wide-set eyes.*

Chis·holm /'tʃɪzəm/, **Shir·ley** /'ʃɚli/ (1924–) a U.S. politician who was the first African-American woman to be elected as a member of Congress in 1969

Chisholm Trail, the /ˌ.. './ a path that was used for moving millions of cattle from Texas to Kansas during the 1800s

Chisinau, Kishinev /ˌkiʃi'naʊ/ the capital city of Moldova

chit /tʃɪt/ *n.* [C] a piece of paper that shows you owe money for something, which you sign and pay later: *He signed the bar chit.*

chit-chat /'tʃɪt-tʃæt/ *n.* [U] INFORMAL conversation about things that are not very important: *chit-chat about new cars* —**chit-chat** *v.* [I]

chit·ter·lings /'tʃɪtəˌlɪŋz/ also **chit·lins** /'tʃɪtlɪnz/ *n.* [plural] the INTESTINE of a pig eaten as food, especially in the southern U.S.

chiv·al·rous /'ʃɪvəlrəs/ *adj.* a man who is chivalrous behaves in a polite, kind, generous, and honorable way, especially toward women —**chivalrously** *adv.*

chiv·al·ry /'ʃɪvəlri/ *n.* [U] **1** behavior that is honorable, kind, generous, and brave, especially a man's behavior toward women **2** a system of religious beliefs and honorable behavior that KNIGHTS in the Middle Ages were expected to follow

chive /tʃaɪv/ *n.* [C usually plural] a long thin green plant that looks and tastes like an onion, and is used in cooking

chlo·ride /'klɔraɪd/ *n.* [C,U] TECHNICAL a chemical compound that is a mixture of chlorine and another substance: *sodium chloride*

chlo·ri·nate /'klɔrəˌneɪt/ *v.* [T] to add chlorine to water to kill BACTERIA —**chlorinated** *adj.*

chlo·rine /'klɔrin, klɔ'rin/ *n.* [U] *symbol* **Cl** a greenish-yellow gas with a strong smell that is a chemical ELEMENT, and is used to keep the water in swimming pools clean

chlo·ro·fluo·ro·car·bon /ˌklɔrəˌflʊroʊ'kɑrbən/ *n.* [C] TECHNICAL a CFC

chlo·ro·form /'klɔrəˌfɔrm/ *n.* [U] a liquid that makes you become unconscious if you breathe it —**chloroform** *v.* [T]

chlo·ro·phyll /'klɔrəˌfɪl/ *n.* [U] the green-colored substance in plants

choc·a·hol·ic /ˌtʃɑkə'hɔlɪk, -'hɑ-/ *n.* [C] another spelling of CHOCOHOLIC

chock /tʃɑk/ *n.* [C] a block of wood or metal put in front of a wheel, door etc. to prevent it from moving: *He pulled the chocks out from under the airplane's wheels.* —**chock** *v.* [T]

chock-a-block /'tʃɑk ə ˌblɑk/ *adj.* completely full of people or things: [+ with] *Best of all were the three libraries which were chock-a-block with rare and ancient books.*

chock-full /ˌ. './ *adj.* [not before noun] INFORMAL completely full: [+ of] *The bean soup, chock-full of smoked ham, was delicious.*

choc·o·hol·ic /ˌtʃɑkə'hɔlɪk, -'hɑ-/ *n.* [C] someone who likes chocolate very much and eats it all the time

choc·o·late /'tʃɑklɪt/ *n.* **1** [U] a sweet brown food made from COCOA that is eaten as candy, or used to give foods such as cakes a special sweet taste: *a chocolate bar* | *chocolate ice cream* **2** [C] a small candy that consists of something such as a nut or CARAMEL covered with chocolate: *a box of chocolates* —see also HOT CHOCOLATE

chocolate chip /ˌ.. './ *n.* [C] a small piece of chocolate put in foods such as cookies and cakes: *Stir in nuts and chocolate chips.*

chocolate chip cook·ie /ˌ.. . '../ *n.* [C] a type of COOKIE containing small pieces of chocolate —see picture at CHIP[1]

choco·lat·y, chocolatey /'tʃɑkləti/ *adj.* tasting or smelling like chocolate: *rich, chocolaty brownies*

Choc·taw /'tʃɑktɔ/ a Native American tribe from the southeastern region of the U.S. —**Choctaw** *adj.*

choice[1] /tʃɔɪs/ *n.*
1 |ability to choose| [singular] the right to choose or the chance to choose between two or more things: *I wouldn't ride without a helmet, but I think people should have the choice.* | *freedom of choice* (=the right to choose what you want to do) | [+ **between**] *a choice between right and wrong* | [+ **of**] *Dinner comes with bread and a choice of soup or salad.* | *Students have a choice of softball, football, or basketball.* | *With two seconds left, Stanford had no choice but to try for a 50-yard field goal* (=it was the only thing they could do). | *I'll give you a choice – we can rent a movie or go out for a pizza.* | *He was left with no choice but to resign.*
2 |range to choose from| [U] the range of people or things that you can choose from: *There's a small general store in town, but I don't think there will be much choice.* | *Parents should have a choice of where their children are educated.*
3 |thing chosen| [C usually singular] the person or thing that someone has chosen: *The choices you make now will affect you for many years.* | [+ **of**] *The choice of McLuhan seemed to please almost everyone.* | [**first/second etc. choice**] *My first choice would be to do track and field.*
4 |act of choosing| [C] the act of choosing something: *I think I made the right choice.* | [+ **of**] *That leaves politicians with the painful choice of raising taxes or cutting services.*
5 of your choice chosen by you without anything limiting what you can choose from: *The prize includes dinner for two at the restaurant of your choice.*
6 by choice if you do something by choice, you do it because you want to do it and not because you are forced to do it: *She is childless by choice.*
7 the drug/treatment/newspaper etc. of choice the thing that a certain group of people prefer to use: *Beer is the drink of choice among sports fans.* —see also CHOOSE

choice[2] *adj.* **choicer, choicest 1** FORMAL of a very high quality or standard, used especially of food: *choice apples* | *Chances are that most of the choice summer jobs have already been taken.* **2** choice meat, especially BEEF, is of a standard that is good but not the best: *choice steak* | *the choicest cuts of meat* **3 a few choice words/phrases** if you use a few choice words, you say what you mean in an angry way: *Meyer had a few choice words for federal bureaucrats after an error listed him as deceased.*

choir /kwaɪr/ *n.* **1** [C] a group of people who sing together, especially in a church or school: *the St. Joseph's Cathedral Choir* **2** [usually singular] in some churches, the part of the church where the choir sits

choir·boy /'kwaɪrbɔɪ/ *n.* [C] a young boy who sings in a church choir

choir loft /'. ./ *n.* [C] the part of a church, usually at the front, in which the choir sits

choir·mas·ter /'kwaɪrˌmæstɚ/ *n.* [C] someone who trains a choir; DIRECTOR (1)

choke[1] /tʃoʊk/ *v.*
1 |stop breathing| [I,T] to prevent someone from breathing, or to be prevented from breathing, because your throat is blocked or because there is not enough air: *Small parts on the toys could break off and choke young children.* | [+ **on**] *He choked on a wad of gum.*
2 |injure| [T] to prevent someone from breathing and hurt them by putting your hands around their throat and pressing on it: *The medical examiner concluded Perez had been choked to death.*
3 |voice| [I,T] if your voice is choked or you choke with laughter, sadness, or anger, your emotions make your voice sound strange and not very loud:

[+ **with**] *Deaton, red and almost choked with fury, thumped the table.*
4 |block| [I,T] to fill an area or passage so that it is difficult to move through it: *The roads were choked with traffic.*
5 |sports| [I] INFORMAL to fail at doing something, especially a sport, because there is a lot of pressure on you: *"I guess we choked," said Coach Landers after his team's last minute defeat.*
6 |plants| [I,T] also **choke out** to kill a plant by surrounding it with other plants that take away its light and room to grow: *Growth of the reed can choke out native water plants.*
7 choke a horse SPOKEN if you have enough of something to choke a horse, you have a lot of it: *I have enough kitchen gadgets to choke a horse.*
8 |say sth| [T] also **choke out** to say something one word or phrase at a time in a strange voice, because you are very upset or angry or because you have been laughing: *He began to sob, and choked out, "I have to go now."*

choke sth **back** *phr. v.* [T] to control your anger, sadness etc. so that you do not show it: *Kennedy paused and appeared to choke back tears.*

choke sth ↔ **down** *phr. v.* [T] **1** to eat something quickly or with difficulty, especially because it tastes bad or because you are sick or in a hurry: *I was barely able to choke down her tuna casserole.* **2** to control your anger, sadness etc. so that you do not show it: *Margaret put her napkin to her mouth to choke down a sob.*

choke off sth *phr. v.* [T] to prevent someone from doing something or stop something happening: *The Security Council imposed an embargo that will choke off their oil exports.*

choke up *phr. v.* [I] **be/get choked up** to feel like you are going to cry because you are upset about something: *I get choked up every time I hear that song.*

choke[2] *n.* **1** [C] a piece of equipment in a vehicle that controls the amount of air going into the engine, and that is used to help the engine start **2** [U] the controlling of the amount of air going into an engine by using this piece of equipment: *Give it a bit more choke.* **3** [C] the act or sound of choking

choke·cher·ry /'tʃoʊkˌtʃɛri/ *n.* [C] a North American tree that produces small sour fruit

choke col·lar /'. ˌ../ *n.* [C] a chain or band that is fastened around the neck of a dog in order to control it

chok·er /'tʃoʊkɚ/ *n.* [C] a piece of jewelry or narrow cloth that fits closely around your neck

chol·er /'kɑlɚ/ *n.* [U] LITERARY anger

chol·er·a /'kɑlərə/ *n.* [U] a serious disease of the stomach and BOWELS that is caused by infected water or food

chol·er·ic /'kɑlərɪk, kə'lɛrɪk/ *adj.* LITERARY angry or in a bad mood: *He was impatient and choleric.*

cho·les·ter·ol /kə'lɛstəˌrɔl, -ˌroʊl/ *n.* [U] a chemical substance found in fat, blood, and other cells in your body, which scientists think may cause heart disease

chomp /tʃɑmp/ *v.* **1** [I] to bite food loudly: *Nick noisily chomped on his gum.* **2 be chomping at the bit** to be impatient to do something or for something to happen: *Hollywood is chomping at the bit to remake this French hit movie.*

Chom·sky /'tʃɑmski/**, Noam** /noʊm/ (1928–) a U.S. LINGUIST famous for his important ideas about language, including the idea that everyone is born with knowledge about grammar, and for his political ideas

choo-choo /'tʃu tʃu/ *n.* [C] SPOKEN a word meaning a "train," used by children or when talking to children

choose /tʃuz/ *v. past tense* **chose** *past participle* **chosen** [I,T] **1** to decide which one of a number of things, possibilities, people etc. that you want, because it is the best or most appropriate: *The city chose a new mayor on Tuesday.* | *"Where do you want to go?" "You choose this time."* | [**choose to do sth**] *Six elementary schools have chosen to have year-round schedules.* | [**choose sb to do sth**] *There have*

you earn be reduced: *About 800 positions were on the chopping block.*

choppy

choppy

calm

been a lot of rumors about who will be chosen to take over Rubin's job. | [**choose sb/sth from sth**] *Jurors are chosen from lists of people who have driver's licenses or voter registration lists.* | [**+ between**] *Having to choose between shoes and school supplies for their kids is something no parent should have to face.* | [**choose which/when/what etc.**] *The hard part is choosing which software package to buy.* **2** to decide or prefer to do something or behave in a particular way: [**+ to**] *Both departments have chosen to ignore the situation.* —see also CHOICE[1]

choos·y /ˈtʃuːzi/ *adj.* **choosier, choosiest** someone who is choosy will only accept food, clothes, jobs etc. that they consider to be very good; PICKY: *These days, the Marine Corps is very choosy about who joins.*

chop

chopping down a tree   chopping up firewood

s w **chop**[1] /tʃɑp/ *v.* **chopped, chopping 1** [T] **chop up** to cut something such as food or wood into smaller pieces: *I think my mother chopped the nuts a little finer.* | [**chop sth into sth**] *Chop the carrots into bite-sized pieces.* | **finely/coarsely chopped** (=cut into small or large pieces) —see picture on page 425 **2** [I,T] to reduce the number or amount of something, especially a lot: *Over 200,000 jobs were chopped from the payrolls in November.* | [**+ off**] *The university chopped off $22 million from the budget.* **3** [I] to swing a heavy tool such as an AX in order to cut something: [**+ away/at**] *Volunteers chopped away the weeds and long grass that covered the field.* **4** [T] to hit a ball in a quick downward way, using a BAT, RACKET etc.

chop sth ↔ **down** *phr. v.* [T] to make a tree or large plant fall down by cutting it with a sharp tool such as an AX: *He chopped down the trees, planted crops, and built most of the farmhouse himself.*

chop sth **off** *phr. v.* [T] to remove something by cutting it with a sharp tool such as an AX so that it is not connected to something else anymore: *"Chop off his head!" ordered the king.*

chop[2] *n.* [C] **1** a small flat piece of meat on a bone, usually cut from a sheep or pig: *pork chops and applesauce* **2** a sudden downward movement with your hand: *a karate chop* **3 get the chop** INFORMAL **a)** to lose your job **b)** to officially stop something or reduce the amount you are spending on it **4 chops** [plural] INFORMAL the part of your face that includes your mouth and jaw: *The woman hit me right in the chops.* **5** the act of hitting something once with a sharp tool such as an AX —see also **lick your lips/chops** (LICK[1] (4))

chop-chop /ˌ. ˈ./ *interjection* an expression used when you want someone to hurry: *Come on! Chop-chop!*

Cho·pin /ˈʃoʊpæn/, **Fréd·é·ric** /ˈfrɛdərɪk/ (1810–1849) a Polish musician who wrote CLASSICAL music

Chopin, Kate /keɪt/ (1851–1904) a U.S. writer of short stories

chop·per /ˈtʃɑpɚ/ *n.* [C] **1** INFORMAL a HELICOPTER **2** a type of MOTORCYCLE on which the front wheel is in front of the HANDLEBARS instead of underneath them **3 choppers** [plural] SLANG teeth

chopping block /ˈ.. ˌ./ *n.* [C] **1** a large thick piece of wood that you cut food or wood on **2 be on the chopping block** to be in a situation in which you are going to lose your job, or have the amount of money

chop·py /ˈtʃɑpi/ *adj.* **choppier, choppiest 1** choppy water has many small waves and is very rough to sail on **2** stopping and starting a lot: *music with a choppy rhythm* —**choppiness** *n.* [U]

chop·stick /ˈtʃɑpˌstɪk/ *n.* [C usually plural] one of the two thin sticks used for eating food, especially by people in Asia

chop su·ey /ˌtʃɑp ˈsuːi/ *n.* [U] a Chinese dish made of BEAN SPROUTS and other vegetables and meat, served with rice

cho·ral /ˈkɔrəl/ *adj.* [only before noun] involving singing by a CHOIR (=group of people), or intended to be sung by a CHOIR: *Russian choral music of the 17th century* | *a choral symphony*

cho·rale /kəˈræl, -ˈrɑl/ *n.* [C] a piece of music praising God usually sung by a CHOIR (=group of people): *a Bach chorale*

chord /kɔrd/ *n.* [C] **1** a combination of two or more musical notes played at the same time —see Usage Note at CORD **2 strike/touch a chord** to do or say something that people feel is true or familiar to them: *The movie Thelma and Louise struck a chord with women.* **3** TECHNICAL a straight line joining two points on a curve

chore /tʃɔr/ *n.* [C] **1** a job that you have to do regularly, especially work that you do to keep a house clean: *household chores* | *Somehow he persuaded his sister to do his chores for him.* **2** something you have to do that is very boring or difficult: *Writing Christmas cards can be such a chore.*

cho·re·o·graph /ˈkɔriəˌgræf/ *v.* [T] to arrange how dancers should move during a performance

cho·re·og·ra·phy /ˌkɔriˈɑgrəfi/ *n.* [U] the art of arranging how dancers should move during a performance —**choreographer** *n.* [C]

cho·ris·ter /ˈkɔrɪstɚ, ˈkɑr-/ *n.* [C] a singer in a CHOIR, especially a boy in a church CHOIR

cho·ri·zo /tʃəˈrizoʊ/ *n.* [U] a type of SAUSAGE that is SPICY and is made from PORK (=the meat of a pig), used especially in Mexican and Spanish food

chor·tle /ˈtʃɔrtl/ *v.* [I] to laugh because you are very amused or pleased about something: *Sharon is still chortling over that stupid joke.* —**chortle** *n.* [C]

cho·rus[1] /ˈkɔrəs/ *n.* [C]
1 song the part of a song that is repeated after each VERSE
2 singers a large group of people who sing together —compare CHOIR (1) *a 100-voice chorus*
3 a chorus of thanks/disapproval/protest etc. something expressed by many people at the same time: *A loud chorus of boos greeted the governor's limousine.*
4 group in musical play a group of singers, dancers, or actors who act together in a show but do not have the main parts: *Oslin got her start in the chorus of musicals like "Hello, Dolly!" and "West Side Story."*
5 music a piece of music written to be sung by a large group of people: *the Hallelujah Chorus in Handel's Messiah*
6 in chorus if people say something in chorus, they say the same thing at the same time: *"Mom!" the kids cried, in chorus.*

7 [play] a) in ancient Greek plays, the chorus is the group of actors who give explanations or opinions about the play b) in English plays of the early 1600s, the chorus is usually one person who gives explanations or opinions about the play, especially at the beginning or the end

chorus[2] *v.* [T] if two or more people chorus something, they say it at the same time: *"What happened?" they chorused.*

chorus girl /'.. ,./ *n.* [C] a woman who sings and dances in a group in a play or movie

chorus line /'.. ,./ *n.* [C] a group of people who sing and dance together, especially while standing in a straight line, in a play or movie

chose /tʃouz/ *v.* the past tense of CHOOSE

cho·sen[1] /'tʃouzən/ *v.* the past participle of CHOOSE —see also WELL-CHOSEN

chosen[2] *adj.* **1 the chosen few** the small number of people to be invited or SELECTed: *Such information is made available only to the chosen few.* **2 the chosen people** also **God's chosen people a)** a phrase used in the Bible to describe Jewish people **b)** a name that a group of people who believe that God prefers them use for themselves: *The Puritans believed that they were God's new chosen people.*

chow[1] /tʃau/ *n.* **1** [U] SLANG food: *They don't serve anything fancy, just lots of good wholesome chow.* **2** also **chow chow** [C] a dog with long thick fur and a dark-colored tongue, originally from China

chow[2] *v.*

chow down *phr. v.* [I] INFORMAL to eat, especially in a noisy way or in a way that shows you are very hungry: *The kids were chowing down on a pepperoni pizza.*

chow·der /'tʃaudə/ *n.* [U] a thick soup usually made with CLAMS or fish, vegetables, and milk

chow·der·head /'tʃaudə,hɛd/ *n.* [C usually singular] SLANG a stupid person

chow mein /,tʃau 'mein/ *n.* [U] a Chinese dish made with meat, vegetables and NOODLES

Christ[1] /kraist/ *n.* **1** also **Jesus Christ, Jesus** the man on whose life, death, and teaching Christianity is based. who Christians believe to be the son of God **2 the Christ** the religious leader who Christians believe saves the world

Christ[2] *interjection* a word used to express annoyance, surprise etc., which may be offensive to some Christians: *Christ, they are all so stupid.* —see Usage Note at JESUS

chris·ten /'krisən/ *v.* [T] **1** to be officially given your name at a Christian religious ceremony soon after you are born: [be christened sth] *She was christened Mildred Mary Petre on Nov. 10, 1895.* **2** to officially give a name to something such as a ship, a business etc.: *Former first lady Barbara Bush officially christened the ship.* **3** to invent a name for someone or something because it describes them well: *Derek christened his new sports car "Lightning."* **4** INFORMAL to use something for the first time: *We christened the new mugs that same night.*

Chris·ten·dom /'krisəndəm/ *n.* [U] OLD-FASHIONED all the Christian people or countries in the world: *St. Peter's Basilica, the largest church in Christendom*

chris·ten·ing /'krisəniŋ/ *n.* [C,U] a Christian religious ceremony at which someone is officially given their name and becomes a member of a Christian church

Chris·tian[1] /'kristʃən, 'krıstʃən/ *n.* [C] **1** a person who believes in the ideas taught by Jesus Christ or belongs to a Christian church **2** INFORMAL a good person

Christian[2] *adj.* **1** believing the ideas taught by Jesus Christ, or belonging to a Christian church: *Christian ministers* **2** based on the ideas taught by Jesus Christ: *Christian doctrine* **3** also **christian** behaving in a good, kind way: *Laughing at his misfortune wasn't a very christian act.*

Christian e·ra /'.. ,.., ,.. '../ *n.* [singular] the period from the birth of Jesus Christ to the present

Chris·ti·an·i·ty /,kristʃi'ænəti/ *n.* [U] the religion based on the life and teachings of Jesus Christ

Christian name /'.. ,./ *n.* [C] someone's FIRST NAME, or the name someone is given when they are CHRISTENed: *His Christian name is Michael.*

Christian Sci·ence /,.. '../ *n.* [U] a religion which was started in the U.S. in 1866 whose members believe that they can cure their own illnesses using their minds rather than with medical help —**Christian Scientist** *n.* [C]

Chris·tie, Ag·a·tha /'kristi/, /'ægəθə/ (1890–1976) a British writer known for her many popular novels about murders and the DETECTIVEs who try to find out who committed them

Christ·mas /'krisməs/ *n.* **1** also **Christmas Day** December 25th, the day when Christians celebrate the birth of Jesus Christ: *What are you doing for Christmas?* **2** the period before and after this day: *Julie went snowboarding over Christmas.*

Christmas card /'.. ,./ *n.* [C] a card that you send to friends and relatives at Christmas with your good wishes

Christmas car·ol /'.. ,../ *n.* [C] a Christian song sung at Christmas; CAROL[1]

Christmas club /'.. ./ *n.* [C] a bank account that you put money into regularly during the year so that you have money to spend at Christmas

Christmas cook·ie /'.. ,../ *n.* [C] a special COOKIE made at Christmas, especially one shaped like a tree, star, SNOWMAN etc.

Christmas Day /,.. './ *n.* [C,U] December 25th, the day when Christians celebrate the birth of Jesus Christ

Christmas din·ner /,.. '../ *n.* [C] a special meal eaten on Christmas Day

Christmas Eve /,.. './ *n.* [C,U] December 24th, the day before Christmas Day: *an 11 p.m. church service on Christmas Eve*

Christmas stock·ing /'.. ,../ *n.* [C] a long sock that children leave out on Christmas Eve to be filled with small presents

Christ·mas·sy /'krisməsi/ *adj.* INFORMAL typical of or relating to Christmas: *a nice Christmassy atmosphere*

Christ·mas·time /'krisməs,taim/ *n.* [U] the period during Christmas when people celebrate

Christmas tree /'.. ,./ *n.* [C] a PINE or FIR tree that you put inside your house and decorate specially for Christmas

Chris·to·pher, Saint /'kristəfə/ (?A.D.–?250) a man who was supposed to have carried Jesus Christ across a river, and who, as a result, became the PATRON SAINT of travelers

chro·mat·ic /krou'mætik, krə-/ *adj.* **1** relating to or containing bright colors **2** relating to the musical scale that consists of HALF TONES: *the chromatic scale*

chrome /kroum/ *n.* [U] a hard ALLOY (=a combination of metals) of chromium and other metals, used for covering objects with a shiny protective surface: *a car with chrome bumpers*

chrome yel·low /,. '../ *n.* [U] a very bright yellow color

chro·mi·um /'kroumiəm/ *n.* [U] *symbol* **Cr** a blue or white metal that is an ELEMENT and is used for covering objects with a shiny protective surface

chro·mo·some /'kroumə,soum, -,zoum/ *n.* [C] TECHNICAL a part of every living cell that controls the character, shape etc. that a plant or animal has: *Humans have 46 chromosomes.*

chron- /kran/ *prefix* relating to time: *a chronic illness* (=that lasts a long time or keeps coming back)

chron·ic /'kranik/ *adj.* [usually before noun] **1** a chronic disease or illness is one that cannot be cured: *Steen suffers from chronic high blood pressure.* —compare ACUTE (2) **2** a problem or difficulty that you cannot get rid of or that keeps coming back: *California is trying to cope with chronic water shortages.* |

C

chronic unemployment **3 a chronic alcoholic/gambler etc.** someone who suffers from a particular problem or type of behavior for a long time and cannot stop —**chronically** /-kli/ *adj.*: *chronically ill*

chron·i·cle[1] /'krɑnɪkəl/ *n.* [C] a written record of a series of events, especially historical events, written in the order in which they happened: [+ **of**] *The book is a social and cultural chronicle of the years that Monet spent at Giverny.*

chronicle[2] *v.* [T] to give an account of a series of events in the order in which they happened: *Baer's film chronicles our government's sad history of dealing with the Indians.* —**chronicler** *n.* [C]

Chron·i·cles /'krɑnɪkəlz/ **1 Chronicles, 2 Chronicles** two books in the Old Testament of the Christian Bible

chrono- /krɑnoʊ, -nə/ *prefix* relating to time: *a chronometer* (=instrument for measuring time very exactly)

chron·o·graph /'krɑnə‚græf/ *n.* [C] a scientific instrument for measuring and recording periods of time

chron·o·log·i·cal /‚krɑnl'ɑdʒɪkəl/ *adj.* arranged according to when something happened: *We had to memorize all the presidents in chronological order.* —**chronologically** /-kli/ *adv.*

chro·nol·o·gy /krə'nɑlədʒi/ *n.* **1** [C] a list of events arranged according to when they happened: *a chronology of events in the Balkans* **2** [U] the science of giving times and dates to events

chro·nom·e·ter /krə'nɑmət̬ə/ *n.* [C] a very exact clock for measuring time, used for scientific purposes

chrys·a·lis /'krɪsəlɪs/ *n.* [C] a MOTH or BUTTERFLY at the stage of development when it has a hard outer shell, before becoming a LARVA and then an adult —see picture at METAMORPHOSIS

chry·san·the·mum /krɪ'sænθəməm/ *n.* [C] a garden plant with large round flowers that have many long thin PETALS

Chrys·ler /'kraɪslə/, **Wal·ter** /'wɔltə/ (1875–1940) a U.S. businessman who made cars and was the first President of the Chrysler Corporation

chub·by /'tʃʌbi/ *adj.* **chubbier, chubbiest** fat in a pleasant healthy-looking way: *He was this cute, chubby baby.* | *chubby cheeks* —see Usage Note at FAT —**chubbiness** *n.* [U]

chuck[1] /tʃʌk/ *v.* [T] INFORMAL **1** to throw something in a careless or relaxed way: *Somebody in the crowd chucked a bottle onto the field.* | [**chuck sth in/into/on** etc.] *I'll just chuck the shirt in the laundry basket.* **2** also **chuck out/away** to throw something away: *Just go ahead and chuck out the batteries.* **3** to stop doing something, especially something that is boring or annoying: *As much as I hate it, I'm not willing to chuck my job.* **4 chuck sb under the chin** to gently touch someone under their chin, especially a child

chuck sb/sth ↔ **out** *phr. v.* [T] to make someone leave a place or a job: *They ended up chucking thousands of employees out into the street.*

chuck[2] *n.* **1** [C] part of a machine that holds something so that it does not move: *a drill chuck* **2** CHUCK STEAK: *ground chuck*

chuck·le /'tʃʌkəl/ *v.* [I] to laugh quietly: *Coulter chuckled and shook his head.* | [+ **at**] *Kay chuckled at the idea.* —**chuckle** *n.* [C]

chuck·le·head /'tʃʌkəl‚hɛd/ *n.* [C] INFORMAL a stupid person

chuck steak /‚. './ *n.* [U] meat cut from the neck and shoulder area of a cow

chuck wag·on /'. ‚../ *n.* [C] OLD-FASHIONED a vehicle that carries food for a group of people

chug /tʃʌg/ *v.* **chugged, chugging** **1** [I] if a car, train etc. chugs, it moves slowly making a repeated low sound: [+ **along/around/up** etc.] *The Staten Island Ferry chugged across New York Harbor.* **2** [I] to make slow but steady progress: *Stocks chugged along*

most of the day Monday with no great gains or losses. **3** [T] also **chug-a-lug** INFORMAL to drink all of something in a glass or bottle without stopping: *Teddy sat back in his chair, chugging mineral water.* —**chug** *n.* [C usually singular]

chum /tʃʌm/ *n.* **1** [C] OLD-FASHIONED a friend: *I ran into an old high school chum.* **2** [U] small pieces of oily fish, used to catch other fish

Chu·mash /'tʃumæʃ/ a Native American tribe from the southwestern area of the U.S.

chum·my /'tʃʌmi/ *adj.* **chummier, chummiest** OLD-FASHIONED friendly: *I'd forgotten that Ellen and Gary had become chummy.* —**chummily** *adv.* —**chumminess** *n.* [U]

chump /tʃʌmp/ *n.* [C] INFORMAL someone who is silly or stupid, and who is easily tricked or deceived

chump change /'. ‚./ *n.* [U] an expression meaning a small amount of money, often used in negative sentences: *They're offering $10,000 in prize money, which is hardly chump change.*

chunk /tʃʌŋk/ *n.* [C] **1** a large piece of something that does not have an even shape: *pineapple chunks* | [+ **of**] *a 40 million-year-old chunk of amber* **2** a large part or amount of something: *The rent takes a large chunk out of my monthly salary.* | *You can move chunks of text directly from one document to another.* | *Lurie risked a pretty big chunk of change* (=a large amount of money) *on the race.*

chunk·y /'tʃʌŋki/ *adj.* **chunkier, chunkiest** **1** chunky food has large pieces in it: *chunky peanut butter* **2** thick, solid, and heavy: *chunky silver jewelry* **3** someone who is chunky has a broad, heavy body

church /tʃətʃ/ *n.* **1** [C] a building where Christians go to WORSHIP in religious services **2** [U] the religious ceremonies in a church: *Mrs. Dobson invited us to lunch after church.* | *Do you go to church every Sunday?* **3 the church** the profession of the CLERGY (=priests and other people employed by the church) **4** [singular,U] the Christian religion, considered as a whole: *Prayer in schools may be against the separation of church and state that the Constitution requires.* **5** [C] also **Church** one of the separate groups within the Christian religion: *the Catholic Church*

church·go·er /'tʃətʃ‚goʊə/ *n.* [C] someone who goes to church regularly

Chur·chill /'tʃətʃɪl/, **Win·ston** /'wɪnstən/ (1874–1965) a British politician who was Prime Minister during most of World War II and again from 1951 to 1955

church·key /'tʃətʃki/ *n.* [C] INFORMAL a BOTTLE OPENER

church·man /'tʃətʃmən/ *n.* [C] *plural* **churchmen** /-mən/ a priest; CLERGYMAN

Church of Je·sus Christ of Lat·ter-Day Saints, the /‚. . .. ‚. .‚... './ —see MORMONS, THE

church school /'. ./ *n.* [C] a private school that is supported by a particular religious group

church·yard /'tʃətʃyard/ *n.* [C] a piece of land around a church, in which people were buried in past times

churl·ish /'tʃəlɪʃ/ *adj.* not polite or friendly: *It seemed churlish to refuse his invitation.* —**churl** *n.* [C] —**churlishly** *adv.* —**churlishness** *n.* [U]

churn[1] /tʃən/ *n.* [C] a container in which milk or cream is shaken until it forms butter or ICE CREAM

churn[2] *v.* **1** [I] if your stomach churns you feel sick because you are nervous or frightened: *My stomach was churning on the day of the exam.* **2** [T] to make milk by using a churn **3** also **churn up** [I,T] if water churns or if it is churned it moves about violently

churn sth ↔ **out** *phr. v.* [T] to produce large quantities of something, especially without caring about quality: *The factory churns out thousands of these awful plastic toys every week.*

churn up *phr. v.* **1** [T **churn** sth ↔ **up**] to damage the surface of something, especially by walking on it or driving a vehicle over it: *The lawn had been churned up by the tractor.* **2** [I,T] to CHURN[2] (3)

chute /ʃut/ n. [C] **1** a long narrow structure that slopes down, so that things or people can slide down it from one place to another: *a laundry chute* **2** INFORMAL a PARACHUTE **3** a long narrow structure that guides cattle, people etc. toward a particular place as they walk along it: *Cows were led down a chute to be branded.*

chut·ney /'tʃʌtni/ n. [U] a SAUCE, originally from India, made with a mixture of fruits, SPICES and sugar, that is eaten with meat or cheese

chutz·pah /'hʊtspə/ n. [U] INFORMAL, APPROVING a lot of confidence and courage to do something, especially something that might involve being impolite to someone in authority: *It took a lot of chutzpah to quit your job like that.*

CIA n. **the CIA** the Central Intelligence Agency; the department of the U.S. government that collects information about other countries, especially secretly —compare FBI

ciao /tʃaʊ/ interjection INFORMAL used to say goodbye

ci·ca·da /sɪ'keɪdə/ n. [C] an insect that lives in hot areas, has large transparent wings, and makes a high singing noise

cic·a·trix /'sɪkə,trɪks/ also **cic·a·trice** /-,trɪs/ n. [C] TECHNICAL OR LITERARY a mark remaining from a wound; SCAR

Cic·e·ro /'sɪsəroʊ/, **Mar·cus Tul·li·us** /'markəs 'tʌliəs/ (106–43 B.C.) a Roman politician and ORATOR who is considered one of the greatest Latin writers

-cide /saɪd/ suffix [in nouns] another form of the SUFFIX -ICIDE: *genocide* (=killing a whole race of people) *suicide* (=act of killing yourself) —**cidal** suffix [in adjectives] —**cidally** suffix [in adverbs]

ci·der /'saɪdə/ n. [U] also **apple cider** a drink made from pressed apples

ci·gar /sɪ'gar/ n. [C] a thick, tube-shaped thing that people smoke, that is made from tobacco leaves that have been rolled up —see also **close, but no cigar** (CLOSE[2] (15))

cig·a·rette /,sɪgə'rɛt, 'sɪgə,rɛt/ n. [C] a thin tube-shaped thing that people smoke, that is made from finely cut tobacco leaves inside a tube of paper: *a pack of cigarettes* | *The ashtray was full of cigarette butts.*

cigarette hold·er /..'. ,..., '... ,../ n. [C] a long narrow tube that some people use to hold a cigarette while smoking it

cigarette light·er /..'. ,.., '... ,../ also **lighter** n. [C] a small object that produces a flame for lighting cigarettes, CIGARS etc.

cig·a·ril·lo /,sɪgə'rɪloʊ/ n. [C] plural **cigarillos** a small thin cigar

ci·lan·tro /sə'lantroʊ, -'læn-/ n. [U] the strong-tasting leaves of a small plant, used especially in Asian and Mexican cooking

Ci·ma·bu·e /,tʃimə'bueɪ/, **Gio·van·ni** /dʒoʊ'vani/ (?1240–?1302) an Italian PAINTER who is sometimes called the father of Italian painting because he began to develop a new and more LIFELIKE style

C-in-C /,si ɪn 'si/ n. an abbreviation of COMMANDER IN CHIEF

cinch[1] /sɪntʃ/ n. [singular] INFORMAL **1** something that will definitely happen, or someone who will definitely do something: [be a cinch to do sth] *The L.A. Dodgers are a cinch to win the division.* **2** something that is very easy: [be a cinch to do sth] *Good pie crust is a cinch to make.* **3** a cinch belt/strap etc. a thin belt etc. made of a material that stretches, that you pull so that it is very tight

cinch[2] v. [T] **1** to pull a belt, STRAP etc. tightly around something: *She had her dress cinched at the waist with a belt.* **2** to do something so that you can be sure something will happen: *Brown hopes to cinch the deal by Monday.*

Cin·cin·nat·i /,sɪnsɪ'næti/ a city in the southwest of the U.S. state of Ohio

cin·der /'sɪndə/ n. [C usually plural] a very small piece of burned wood, coal etc.: *Burning cinders fell onto the roof.* | *The cake was burned to a cinder* (=completely burned).

C

cinder block /'.. ,./ n. [C] a large gray brick used in building, made from CEMENT and cinders

Cin·der·el·la /,sɪndə'rɛlə/ n. [C] **Cinderella team/city etc.** a team, city etc. that becomes successful or popular after a long period of being unsuccessful or unpopular: *The Spurs were one of the NBA's Cinderella teams, helped by the arrival of David Robinson.*

cin·e·aste, cinéaste /'sɪneɪ,æst/ n. [C] FORMAL someone who is very interested in movies, especially ones with serious artistic value

cin·e·ma /'sɪnəmə/ n. **1** [U] the skill, industry, or art of making movies: *Dürrie is an important director in German cinema.* **2** [C] OLD-FASHIONED a building in which movies are shown; MOVIE THEATER: *Television and videos are replacing trips to the cinema.*

cin·e·mat·ic /,sɪnə'mætɪk/ adj. relating to movies: *Eisenstein invented cinematic techniques which are still in use today.*

cin·e·ma·tog·ra·phy /,sɪnəmə'tagrəfi/ n. [U] the skill or art of movie photography: *I loved the movie's beautiful cinematography of the African desert.* —**cinematographer** n. [C]

ci·né·ma vé·ri·té /,sineɪmə veɪri'teɪ/ also **cinema verite** /,sɪnəmə veri'teɪ/ n. [U] a style of filming a movie or television program in which people or events are filmed in a natural way or as they happen

cin·na·bar /'sɪnə,bar/ n. [U] **1** a type of red-colored rock from which MERCURY (=a poisonous liquid metal) is taken **2** a bright orange-red color

cin·na·mon[1] /'sɪnəmən/ n. [U] **1** a sweet-smelling brown SPICE that comes from the outer covering of a type of tree, used especially in the form of powder in baking cakes and cookies **2** a red-brown color

cinnamon[2] adj. having a red-brown color

CIO Congress of Industrial Organizations; an organization of UNIONS that is now part of the AFL-CIO

ci·pher /'saɪfə/ n. [C] **1** someone who is not important and has no power or influence: *The women are strong characters, but the men in this movie are mere ciphers.* **2** FORMAL a system of secret writing; CODE: *The embassy was ordered to destroy its cipher equipment and remaining codes.* **3** LITERARY the number 0; zero

cir·ca /'sə·kə/ prep., written abbreviation **ca.** FORMAL used before a date to show that it is not the exact date when something happened: *The manuscripts date from circa 1100 B.C.*

cir·ca·di·an /sə'keɪdiən/ adj. [only before noun] TECHNICAL relating to a period of 24 hours, used especially when talking about changes in people's bodies: *the body's circadian sleep-wake cycle*

circadian rhythm /.,... '../ n. [C] the regular series of changes that take place in your body at specific times during a twenty-four hour period, such as when you feel tired or hungry

cir·cle[1] /'sə·kəl/ n. [C]
1 shape **a)** a completely round line with no end, like the letter O: *This circle is 4 inches in diameter.* | *Draw a circle around the right answer.* **b)** a flat, completely round shape: *Cut the dough into several small circles.* —see picture at SHAPE[1]
2 group of people/things a group of people or things forming a round shape: *The women sat in a circle among the trees.* | *a circle of chairs*
3 social group a group of people who know each other: [+ of] *a large circle of friends* | *Today, people don't have the support of a wide family circle* (=the people in a family, including aunts, grandparents etc.). | *Johnson was part of the president's inner circle* (=the people who have the most influence).
4 political/literary/scientific etc. circles the people who are involved in politics, literature, science etc.: *Myers' new book has caused an uproar in literary circles.*

5 come/go full circle to end in the same situation in which you began, even though there have been changes in the time in between: *After the experiments of the 1960s, education has come full circle in its methods of teaching reading.*
6 go/run around in circles to think or argue about something a lot without deciding anything or making progress: *We've got to solve the problem instead of running around in circles, writing letters that never get answered.* —see also **square the circle** (SQUARE³ (6)), VICIOUS CIRCLE

circle² *v.* **1** [T] to draw a circle around something: *Glenn circled the date on his calendar.* **2** [I,T] to move in a circle around something: *Helicopters circled overhead.* | *Kelly hit the ball over the fence and circled the bases.*

cir·clet /ˈsɚklɪt/ *n.* [C] a narrow band of gold, silver, or jewels worn around someone's head or arm, especially in past times

cir·cuit /ˈsɚkɪt/ *n.* [C] **1 the tennis/lecture/college etc. circuit** all the places that are usually visited by someone who plays tennis etc.: *Vesey returned to the nightclub circuit as a singer.* **2** the complete circle that an electric current travels through **3** a trip around an area that forms a circle: *Gund did a circuit around the ice rink.* **4** an area in which a judge travels around regularly, so that a court of law can meet in several different places —see also CLOSED-CIRCUIT TELEVISION, PRINTED CIRCUIT, SHORT CIRCUIT

circuit board /ˈ.. ˌ./ *n.* [C] a set of connections between points on a piece of electrical equipment which uses a thin line of metal to CONDUCT (=carry) the electricity; PRINTED CIRCUIT

circuit break·er /ˈ.. ˌ../ *n.* [C] a piece of equipment that stops an electric current if it becomes dangerous

circuit court /ˌ.. ˈ./ *n.* [C] a court of law in a U.S. state that meets in different places within the area it is responsible for

cir·cu·i·tous /sɚˈkyuətəs/ *adj.* **1** going from one place to another in a way that is longer than the most direct way: *the river's circuitous course* **2** doing or achieving something in a way that is not very direct: *Lebeau took a circuitous route to academic life; he was a musician and a plumber first.* —**circuitously** *adv.*

cir·cuit·ry /ˈsɚkətri/ *n.* [U] a system of electric circuits

cir·cu·lar¹ /ˈsɚkyələ/ *adj.* **1** shaped like a circle: *a circular table* **2 a circular argument/discussion etc.** an argument etc. in which you always return to the same statements or ideas that were expressed at the beginning **3** moving around in a circle: *the moon's circular orbit* —**circularity** /ˌsɚkyəˈlærəti/ *n.* [U]

circular² *n.* [C] a printed advertisement, announcement etc. that is sent to a lot of people at the same time

circular saw /ˌ... ˈ./ *n.* [C] an electric tool with a round metal blade that has small sharp parts around the edge, used for cutting wood —compare CHAINSAW

cir·cu·late /ˈsɚkyəˌleɪt/ *v.* **1** [I,T] to move around within a system, or to make something do this: *Blood circulates around the body.* | *The vents circulate heat back into the room.* **2** [I,T] if information, facts, ideas etc. circulate or are circulated, people tell them to other people: *Rumors are circulating that the mayor's health is getting worse.* | *The propaganda Leary circulated soon attracted a great deal of publicity.* **3** [T] to send goods, facts, information etc. to a group of people: *Greenman circulated a petition for the city to install a traffic light last summer.* **4** [I] to talk to a lot of different people in a group, especially at a party

cir·cu·la·tion /ˌsɚkyəˈleɪʃən/ *n.* **1** [C,U] the movement of blood around your body: *The bandage is too tight – it's cutting off my circulation.* **2 in circulation** used by a group or society and passing from one person to another: *The government has reduced the*

number of $100 bills in circulation. —opposite **out of circulation 3** [C usually singular] the average number of copies of a newspaper, magazine, or book that are usually sold over a particular period of time: *The newspaper has a daily circulation of 55,000.* **4** [C,U] the movement of liquid, air etc. in a system: *Let's open the windows and get some circulation in here.* **5 out of circulation** INFORMAL not taking part in social activities for a period of time: *Joe's out of circulation until after his operation.*

cir·cu·la·tor·y /ˈsɚkyələˌtɔri/ *adj.* [usually before noun] relating to the movement of blood through the body: *Diabetes can cause circulatory problems.*

circum- /sɚkəm/ *prefix* all the way around something: *to circumnavigate the world* (=travel around it) | *to circumvent* (=avoid something by finding a way around it)

cir·cum·cise /ˈsɚkəmˌsaɪz/ *v.* [T] **1** to cut off the skin around the end of the PENIS (=male sex organ) **2** to cut off a woman's CLITORIS (=part of her sex organs)

cir·cum·ci·sion /ˌsɚkəmˈsɪʒən/ *n.* [C,U] the act of circumcising someone, or an occasion when a baby is circumcised as part of a religious ceremony

cir·cum·fer·ence /sɚˈkʌmfrəns/ *n.* [C,U] **1** the distance measured around the outside of a circle or any round shape: *the circumference of the Earth* | *The cable is 1 meter in circumference.* **2** the measurement around the outside of any shape: *The island is only nine miles in circumference.* —**circumferential** /sɚˌkʌmfəˈrɛnʃəl/ *adj.*

cir·cum·flex /ˈsɚkəmˌflɛks/ also **circumflex ac·cent** /ˈ... ˌ../ *n.* [C] a mark (ˆ) placed above a vowel in some languages to show that it is pronounced in a particular way, for example, â —compare GRAVE³, ACUTE (7)

cir·cum·lo·cu·tion /ˌsɚkəmlouˈkyuʃən/ *n.* [C,U] FORMAL the practice of using too many words to express an idea, instead of saying it directly —**circumlocutory** /ˌsɚkəmˈlʌkyəˌtɔri/ *adj.*

cir·cum·nav·i·gate /ˌsɚkəmˈnævəˌgeɪt/ *v.* [T] FORMAL to sail, fly, or travel completely around the Earth, an island etc. —**circumnavigation** /ˌsɚkəmnævəˈgeɪʃən/ *n.* [C,U]

cir·cum·scribe /ˈsɚkəmˌskraɪb/ *v.* [T] **1** [often passive] FORMAL to limit power, rights, or abilities; RESTRICT: *The church's role was tightly circumscribed by the new government.* **2** TECHNICAL to draw a shape around something: *In the middle of the drawing was a circle circumscribed by a square.*

cir·cum·spect /ˈsɚkəmˌspɛkt/ *adj.* FORMAL **1** thinking carefully about things before doing them; CAUTIOUS: *Walesa was circumspect in discussing his political actions.* **2** a circumspect action or answer is done or given only after careful thought —**circumspectly** *adv.* —**circumspection** /ˌsɚkəmˈspɛkʃən/ *n.* [U]

cir·cum·stance /ˈsɚkəmˌstæns/ *n.* **1** [C usually plural] the facts or conditions that affect a situation, action, event etc.: *The Soviet Union had been forced by circumstances to sign a pact with Nazi Germany.* | *Only in one particular circumstance could the court legally override the decision.* | *There are plenty of other people in similar circumstances.* | *The money will only be paid under certain circumstances* (=if particular conditions exist). | *Extensions on the loan can only be made in extenuating circumstances* (=in unusual situations). | *The woman was found dead in suspicious circumstances* (=in a way that makes you think something illegal happened). **2 under the circumstances** also **given the circumstances** used to say that a particular situation makes an action, decision, statement etc. necessary, acceptable, or true when it would not normally be: *Under the circumstances, she did the best job she could.* **3 under no circumstances** used to emphasize that something must definitely not happen: [+ verb/modal] *Under no circumstances should a baby be left alone in the house.* **4** [U] FORMAL the combination of facts, events etc. that influence your life, and that you cannot control: *Women of the same age and circumstance as you are less likely to live with* their parents. | *The workers who were laid off were purely victims of circumstance.* **5 in reduced circumstances** OLD-FASHIONED with much less money than you used to have —see also **pomp and circumstance** (POMP)

cir·cum·stan·tial /ˌsəkəm'stænʃəl◂/ *adj.* LAW making something seem like it is true, because of the events relating to it, but not definitely proving that it is true | **circumstantial evidence/case** *The case against McCarthy is based largely on circumstantial evidence.* —**circumstantially** *adv.*

cir·cum·vent /ˌsəkəm'vɛnt, 'səkəm,vɛnt/ *v.* [T] FORMAL **1** to avoid something, especially a rule or law that restricts you, especially in a dishonest way: *I had no intention of violating or circumventing Senate rules.* **2** to avoid something by changing the direction you are moving in —**circumvention** /ˌsəkəm'vɛnʃən/ *n.* [U]

cir·cus /'səkəs/ *n. plural* **circuses** [C] **1** a group of people and animals who travel to different places performing skillful tricks as entertainment, or a performance by these people and animals: *circus performers* | *Barnum and Bailey's three-ring circus* (=a circus that has three round areas where tricks are performed) **2** INFORMAL a meeting, group of people etc. that is very noisy and uncontrolled: *The media turned the trial into a circus.* **3** a place in ancient Rome where fights, races etc. took place, with seats built in a circle

cir·rho·sis /sɪ'roʊsɪs/ *n.* [U] a serious disease of the LIVER, often caused by drinking too much alcohol

cir·rus /'sɪrəs/ *n.* [U] a type of cloud that is light and shaped like feathers, high in the sky —compare CUMULUS, NIMBUS

CIS *n.* the Commonwealth of Independent States; the name given to a group of countries, the largest of which is Russia

cis·tern /'sɪstən/ *n.* [C] a large container that water is stored in

cit·a·del /'sɪtədəl, -,dɛl/ *n.* [C] **1** a strong FORT built in past times as a place where people could go for safety if their city was attacked **2 the citadel of sth** LITERARY a place or situation in which an idea, principle, system etc. that you think is important is kept safe: *The U.S. is often seen as the citadel of capitalism.*

ci·ta·tion /saɪ'teɪʃən/ *n.* [C] **1** an official order for someone to appear in court or pay a FINE for doing something illegal: [+ **for**] *Turner was issued a traffic citation for reckless driving.* **2** an formal statement or piece of writing publicly praising someone's actions or achievements: [+ **for**] *a citation for bravery* **3** a line taken from a book, speech etc. QUOTATION: *The Oxford English Dictionary's first citation for the word "garage" is from 1902.*

cite /saɪt/ *v.* [T] **1** to mention something as an example, especially one that supports, proves, or explains an idea or situation: *The judge cited a 1956 Supreme Court ruling in her decision.* | [**cite sth as sth**] *Wolfe cited Buick as a company that is working to attract older customers.* **2** to order someone to appear before a court of law or to pay a FINE, because they have done something wrong: [**cite sb for sth**] *Two protesters were cited for illegal camping.* **3** to give the exact words of something that has been written in order to support an opinion or prove an idea; QUOTE: *The passage cited above is from a Robert Frost poem.* **4** FORMAL to mention someone because they deserve praise: [**cite sb for sth**] *Twenty television programs were cited for excellence by Action for Children's Television.*

cit·i·fied /'sɪtɪ,faɪd/ *adj.* relating to the city or the way people in cities live, dress, and behave, especially used by people who consider this bad: *The novel is about three citified guys having a vacation on a ranch.*

cit·i·zen /'sɪtəzən/ *n.* [C] **1** someone who lives in a particular town, country, or state: *Parents have the responsibility of teaching our children to be good citizens.* | *The citizens of Ketchikan were excited to see the huge ship sail into their harbor.* **2** someone who legally belongs to a particular country and has rights and responsibilities there, whether they are

living there or not: *Laurent is a Swiss citizen.* —compare NATIONAL[2] —see also **second-class citizen** (SECOND-CLASS (2)), SENIOR CITIZEN

cit·i·zen·ry /'sɪtəzənri/ *n.* [U] FORMAL all the citizens in a particular place

citizen's ar·rest / ... .'./ *n.* [C] the act of preventing someone from leaving a place until the police arrive, because you think they have done something wrong: *Palmer made a citizen's arrest after tackling the robber as he tried to get away.*

citizens band, citizens' band, Citizens Band /ˈ... ,./ *n.* [U] —see CB

cit·i·zen·ship /'sɪtəzən,ʃɪp/ *n.* [U] **1** the legal right of belonging to a particular country: *Costas has dual citizenship* (=the legal right of being a citizen in two countries) *in the U.S. and the Philippines.* | **U.S./Canadian/French etc. citizenship** (=the state of being a citizen of the U.S., Canada etc.) **2** the quality of being a good citizen, for example being responsible and helping your COMMUNITY: *I believe Scout groups help teach good citizenship.*

cit·ric ac·id /ˌsɪtrɪk 'æsɪd/ *n.* [U] a weak acid found in some fruits, such as LEMONS

cit·ron /'sɪtrən/ *n.* [C] a fruit that comes from India that is like a LEMON, but bigger and with thick skin

cit·ro·nel·la /ˌsɪtrə'nɛlə/ *n.* [U] an oil used for keeping insects away

cit·rus /'sɪtrəs/ *n. plural* **citruses** [C] **1** also **citrus fruit** a fruit with thick skin, such as an orange or LEMON **2** also **citrus tree** a type of tree that produces citrus fruits —**citrus** *adj.*

cit·y /'sɪti/ *n. plural* **cities** [C] **1 a)** a large important town: *New York City* | *It's an old city with about 200,000 residents.* **b)** a town of any size that were officially given by the state government: *The city of Parlier is in Fresno county.* **2** [usually singular] the people who live in a city: *Panic swept the city after the earthquake.* **3 the city** the government of a city: *The city is working to improve public transportation.* **4 ...city** SPOKEN used in order to say that there is a lot or too much of a particular thing in a particular place or situation, or that a situation or place makes you feel something strongly: *It was sun city all weekend.* | *After we biked 60 miles, it was like tired city.* —see also INNER CITY, SISTER CITY

city coun·cil /ˌ.. '../ *n.* [C] the group of elected officials who are responsible for governing a city and making its laws

city desk /'.. ,./ *n.* [C usually singular] a department of a newspaper that deals with local news

city ed·i·tor /ˌ.. '.../ *n.* [C] a newspaper EDITOR who is responsible for local news

city fa·ther /ˌ.. '../ *n.* [C usually plural] **1** a member of the group of people who govern a city **2** a man who helped start or develop a city

city hall, City Hall /ˌ.. './ *n.* **1** [U] the government of a city: *The recycling program simply hasn't been a high priority at City Hall.* **2** [C usually singular] the building a city government uses as its offices: *The library is near City Hall.*

city plan·ning /ˌ.. '../ *n.* [U] the study of the way cities work best, so that streets, houses, services etc. can be provided effectively —**city planner** *n.* [C]

city slick·er /'.. ,../ *n.* [C] DISAPPROVING someone who lives and works in a city and has no experience of anything outside it

city-state /'.. ,./ *n.* [C] a city, especially in past times, that forms an independent country: *the city-state of Monaco*

cit·y·wide /ˌsɪti'waɪd◂/ *adj.* involving all the areas of a city: *They've started a citywide campaign to fight racism.*

civ·et /'sɪvɪt/ *n.* **1** [C] also **civet cat** a small wild animal like a cat, that lives in Asia and Africa **2** [U] TECHNICAL a strong-smelling liquid from a civet cat, used to make PERFUME

civ·ic /'sɪvɪk/ adj. [only before noun] **1** relating to a town or city: John Golden was an important civic and business leader. **2** relating to the people who live in a town or city: It is your civic duty to act as a juror. | The rebuilding program is designed to boost **civic pride** (=people's pride in their own city).

civic cen·ter /'.. ,../ n. [C] a large public building where events such as sports games and concerts are held

civ·ics /'sɪvɪks/ n. [U] a school subject dealing with the rights and duties of citizens and the way government works

civ·il /'sɪvəl/ adj. **1** [only before noun] relating to the people who live in a country: **civil unrest/war/conflict etc.** (=fighting between different groups of people in the same country) —see also CIVIL LIBERTY, CIVIL RIGHT **2** [only before noun] relating to the ordinary people or things in a country that are not part of military, government, or religious organizations: They were married in a civil ceremony in May. | civil aviation **3** [only before noun] relating to the laws concerning the private affairs of citizens, such as laws about business or property, rather than laws about crime: Many civil cases can be settled out of court. —see also CIVIL LAW —compare CRIMINAL[1] (2) **4** polite, but not really very friendly: I know you don't like Phil, but try to be civil. —**civilly** adv.

civil de·fense /,.. '.'./ n. [U] the organization of ordinary people to help defend their country from military attack

civil dis·o·be·di·ence /,.. ..'.../ n. [U] actions done, especially by a large group of people, in order to protest against the government, but without being violent

civil en·gi·neer·ing /,.. ..'../ n. [U] the planning, building, and repair of roads, bridges, large buildings etc. —**civil engineer** n. [C]

ci·vil·ian /sə'vɪlyən/ n. [C] anyone who is not a member of the military forces or the police: Many innocent civilians were killed during the war. —**civilian** adj.: Nigeria has returned to civilian government after years of military rule.

ci·vil·i·ty /sə'vɪləti/ n. plural **civilities 1** [U] polite behavior that most people consider normal: The annual meeting must be conducted with civility. **2** [C usually plural] FORMAL something that you say or do in order to be polite: Our conversations were little more than just exchanging civilities.

civ·i·li·za·tion /,sɪvələ'zeɪʃən/ n. **1** [C,U] a society that is well organized and developed: modern American civilization | [+ of] the ancient civilizations of Greece and Rome **2** [U] all the societies in the world considered as a whole: The book looks at the relationship between religion and civilization. **3** [U] HUMOROUS a place such as a city, where there is a lot to do or where you have things to make you feel clean and comfortable: After a week in the mountains, all I wanted to do was get back to civilization. **4** [U] the process in which societies become developed and organized: Our century has seen greater climate changes than any period since the dawn of civilization.

USAGE NOTE: CIVILIZATION

WORD CHOICE: civilization, culture
Civilization means societies that are advanced in their development and that have a particular type of culture and way of life: The Mayan civilization was at its height from 300 to 900 A.D. **Culture** is the art, music, literature etc. that a particular society has produced, and the way that society lives: Singapore is influenced by both Western and Asian cultures.

---

civ·i·lize /'sɪvə,laɪz/ v. [T] to improve a society so that it is more organized and developed: The Romans hoped to civilize all the tribes of Europe.

civ·i·lized /'sɪvə,laɪzd/ adj. **1** well organized and developed socially: Care for the disabled, old, and sick is essential in a civilized society. **2** HUMOROUS pleasant and comfortable: The Yosemite hotels are too civilized for Stacey's taste; she prefers sleeping in a tent. **3** behaving in a polite and sensible way: I tried talking to her in a civilized manner, but she refused to listen. **4 a civilized hour** HUMOROUS a time that is not too early in the morning: Can't we have the meeting at a more civilized hour?

civil law /,.. './ n. [U] the area of law that deals with the affairs of private citizens, such as laws about business or property, rather than laws about crime

civil lib·er·ty /,.. '.../ n. plural **civil liberties** [C,U] the right of all citizens to be free to do whatever they want while obeying the law and respecting the rights of other people

civil right /,.. './ n. [C usually plural] a right that every person should have, such as the right to vote or to be treated fairly by the law, whatever their sex, race, or religion: In the 1960s, King and others struggled for civil rights. | an important civil rights leader —see picture on page 1330

civil serv·ant /,.. '../ n. [C] someone who works in an office that is part of the civil service

civil serv·ice /,.. './ n. [singular] the government offices and departments that deal with all the work of the government, not including the military

civil war /,.. './ n. [C,U] **1** a war in which opposing groups of people from the same country fight each other in order to gain political control **2 the Civil War** the war that was fought from 1861 to 1865 in the U.S. between the northern and southern states over whether it was right to own slaves

civ·vies /'sɪviz/ n. [plural] INFORMAL a word meaning ordinary clothes, not military uniforms, used mainly by people in the military

ck. the written abbreviation of CHECK

cl the written abbreviation of CENTILITER

clack /klæk/ v. [I,T] if you clack something or if it clacks, it makes a continuous short hard sound: The keys clacked as she typed. —**clack** n. [C usually singular]

clad /klæd/ adj. LITERARY wearing a particular kind of clothing: [be clad in sth] The model was clad in silk and lace. | **warmly/poorly/scantily etc. clad** (=dressed in a particular way)

-clad /klæd/ [in adjectives] **snow-clad/ivy-clad etc.** LITERARY covered in a particular thing: an armor-clad ship

clad·ding /'klædɪŋ/ n. [U] a covering of hard material that protects the outside of a building, vehicle etc.

claim¹ /kleɪm/ v. [T] **1** to state that something is true, even though it has not been proven: [claim (that)] The report claims that 78% of male high school students have used illegal drugs. | [claim to have done sth] Doctors claim to have discovered a cure for the disease. | [claim to be sth] Tran claims to be the leader the gang. | [claim to do sth] George claims to remember exactly what the gunman looked like. | The Red Army Faction **claimed responsibility** (=said officially that they were responsible) for a number of bombings. **2** to officially demand or receive money from an organization that you have a right to receive: Congress intends to make welfare harder to claim. | Steiner filed a lawsuit **claiming damages** against her former employer. **3** to state that you have a right to something or to take something that belongs to you: Kashmir is claimed by both India and Pakistan. | Lost items can be claimed between 10 a.m. and 4 p.m. **4** if a war, accident etc. claims lives, people die because of it: The 12-year-old civil war had claimed 1.5 million lives. **5** if something claims someone's attention or time, they have to notice it or consider it

---

USAGE NOTE: CLAIM

WORD CHOICE: claim, demand
Use **claim** when you are asking for money and think that there is an official reason why someone should give it to you: Poor women with children may be able to claim food stamps. | You can claim certain deductions on your income tax return. Use **demand** when

you are asking for something strongly, but there is no official reason why someone should give it to you: *He demanded a pay raise.* | *People are demanding stricter gun control laws.*

s w **claim²** *n.* [C]

1 money **a)** a request for money, especially money that you believe you have a right to: [+ **for**] *There has been a rise in claims for unemployment benefits.* | *Ms. Byrd is **filing a claim** for unpaid child support.* | *You need to fill out a **claim form** (=an official form used in order to get money from an organization) in order to be reimbursed.* **b)** the sum of money you request when making such a claim: *They've paid out $30,000 in worker's compensation claims.*

2 statement a statement that something is true, even though it has not been proved: *Don't believe all of the health claims that are printed on food labels.* | [+ **that**] *There is no evidence to support claims that stolen dogs are being sold for research.* | *The cereal **makes claims** of helping to lower the risk of heart disease.* | *Wentworth **makes no claim to** literary greatness* (=he does not pretend he is a good writer). | *The lawsuit **disputes claims** (=says something is not true) that wearing motorcycle helmets saves lives.*

3 right to own or take sth a right to have or get something such as land, a title etc. that belongs to you: [+ **to**] *Alaska Natives have agreed to give up their claim to some of their lands.* | *have **claims on/to** The German leader said his country does not have territorial claims to any of its neighbors.* | *Both Serbs and Croats **lay claim to** (=say they have a right to own) the same land.*

4 *sb's/sth's claim to fame* an expression meaning a reason why someone or something is or should be famous: *Lane is a Broadway actor whose main claim to fame was his role as the voice of Timon in "The Lion King."*

5 land a piece of land that contains valuable minerals: *They have a mining claim on the Salmon River.*

6 *have a claim on sb* to have a right to demand someone's time, attention etc. —see also **jump a claim** (JUMP¹ (26)), **stake (out) a claim** (STAKE² (2))

claim·ant /ˈkleɪmənt/ *n.* [C] LAW **1** someone who claims something, especially money, from the government, a court etc., because they think they have a right to it: *Under the new system, claimants will receive their benefit checks three weeks earlier than before.* **2** someone who makes a claim, for example under a WILL² (2)

clair·voy·ant /klerˈvɔɪənt/ *n.* [C] someone who says they can see what will happen in the future —**clairvoyance** *n.* [U] —**clairvoyant** *adj.*

clam¹ /klæm/ *n.* [C] **1** a SHELLFISH that you can eat, which has a shell in two parts that open and close **2** *as happy as a clam* INFORMAL very happy **3** INFORMAL someone who does not say what they are thinking or feeling **4** [usually plural] OLD-FASHIONED, SLANG a dollar: *This shirt cost me fifty clams.*

clam² *v.* **clammed, clamming**
clam up *phr. v.* [I] INFORMAL to suddenly stop talking, especially when you are nervous, shy, or unhappy: *A lot of men just clam up when their marriages are in trouble.*

clam·bake /ˈklæmbeɪk/ *n.* [C] an informal party where clams are cooked and eaten outdoors, near the ocean

clam·ber /ˈklæmbɚ, ˈklæmɚ/ *v.* [I always + adv./prep.] to climb slowly, using your hands and feet: [+ **up/over/to** etc.] *They clambered over the slippery rocks.*

clam chow·der /ˌ. ˈ../ *n.* [U] a type of thick soup made with clams, potatoes, and milk

clam·my /ˈklæmi/ *adj.* **clammier, clammiest** feeling wet, cold, and sticky in a way that is not nice: *His hands were clammy.* —**clamminess** *n.* [U]

clam·or¹ /ˈklæmɚ/ *n.* **1** a very loud noise, often made by a large group of people or animals: *the clamor of factory machinery* **2** a complaint or a demand for something that is expressed by many people: [+ **for**] *There has been a national clamor for better schools.* —**clamorous** *adj.*

clamor² *v.* [I] **1** to demand or complain about something loudly, as part of a group of people: [+ **for**] *Youngsters clamored for Schwarzenegger's autograph.* **2** to talk or shout loudly, as part of a group of people: *We could hear children clamoring in the playground across the street.*

clamp¹ /klæmp/ *n.* [C] a piece of equipment that can fasten or hold things together

clamp² *v.* [T always + adv./prep.] **1** to fasten or hold two things together using a clamp: [**clamp sth together/onto/across** etc.] *Clamp the boards together until the glue dries.* **2** to put or hold something firmly in a position where it does not move: [**clamp sth over/between/around** etc.] *His cigar was clamped firmly between his teeth.*
clamp down *phr. v.* [I] to take firm action to stop a crime or other illegal activity from happening: [+ **on**] *The police are clamping down on drunk drivers.*

clamp·down /ˈklæmpdaʊn/ *n.* [C usually singular] a sudden action by the government, the police etc. to stop a particular activity: [+ **on**] *The governor has ordered a clampdown on illegal immigration.*

clan /klæn/ *n.* [C] **1** INFORMAL a large family, especially one that is all together at once: *Murphy, Jamie, and the rest of the O'Brien clan will be here for Thanksgiving.* **2** a large group of families who have the same ANCESTOR (=a member of your family who lived in past times), considered important in some societies —**clannish** *adj.*

clan·des·tine /klænˈdɛstɪn/ *adj.* clandestine activities or organizations are secret, and often illegal: *a clandestine meeting*

clang /klæŋ/ *v.* [I,T] if a metal object clangs or if you clang it, it makes a loud ringing sound —**clang** *n.* [C]

clan·gor /ˈklæŋɚ/ *n.* [U] a loud noise that continues for a long time

clank /klæŋk/ *v.* [I,T] if a metal object clanks or if you clank it, it makes a loud heavy sound —**clank** *n.* [C]

clans·man /ˈklænzmən/ *n.* [C] FORMAL a male member of a CLAN (2) —compare KLANSMAN

clans·wom·an /ˈklænzˌwʊmən/ *n.* [C] FORMAL a female member of a CLAN (2)

clap¹ /klæp/ *v.* **clapped, clapping 1** [I,T] **a)** if you clap or clap your hands, you hit your hands together loudly and continuously to show that you approve, agree, or have enjoyed something: *The audience clapped and cheered.* **b)** if you clap or clap your hands, you hit your hands together one or two times to attract someone's attention or to stop them from doing something: *Mrs. Phillips clapped her hands and yelled at the dog to come inside.* **2** *clap your hand on/over* etc. *sth* to put your hand somewhere quickly and suddenly: *She suddenly realized what she was saying, and clapped her hand over her mouth.* **3** *clap sb on the back/shoulder* to hit someone lightly on their back or shoulder with your open hand in a friendly way —**clapping** *n.* [U]

clap² *n.* **1** *a clap of thunder* a loud sound made by THUNDER **2** [C] a sudden loud sound that you make when you hit your hands together, especially to show that you enjoyed something or that you agree **3** *a clap on the back/shoulder* an act of hitting someone on the back or shoulder to show that you are friendly or amused **4** *the clap* SLANG: see GONORRHEA (=a disease that is passed from one person to another through sexual contact)

clap·board /ˈklæbɚd, ˈklæpbɔrd/ *n.* [C,U] a set of boards that cover the outside walls of a building, or one of these boards: *a clapboard house*

clap·per /ˈklæpɚ/ *n.* [C] the movable metal part inside a bell that hits the sides of the bell to make it ring

clap·trap /ˈklæptræp/ *n.* [U] INFORMAL stupid things that people say

clar·et /'klærət/ *n.* [U] **1** red wine from the Bordeaux area of France **2** a dark red color —**claret** *adj.*

clarified but·ter /... '../ *n.* [U] butter that has been made clear and pure by heating it: *Fry the mushrooms in two tablespoons of clarified butter.*

clar·i·fy /'klærə,faɪ/ *v.* **clarifies, clarified, clarifying** [T] to make something clearer and easier to understand by explaining it in more detail: *Illustrations are provided to help clarify the written instructions.* | **[clarify how/what etc.]** *City council members want to clarify how the smoking law would apply to restaurants and hotels.* | *Reporters asked the Congressman to clarify his position on welfare reform* (=tell people what he thinks about it and what he intends to do). —**clarification** /,klærəfə-'keɪʃən/ *n.* [C,U]

clar·i·net /,klærə'nɛt/ *n.* [C] a wooden musical instrument shaped like a long black tube, that you play by blowing into it and pressing KEYS[1] (3) to change the notes —**clarinetist** *n.* [C]

clar·i·on call /'klæriən ,kɔl/ *n.* [C usually singular] FORMAL a strong and direct request for people to do something: *Taken together, the studies are a clarion call to doctors to make drug therapy safer.*

clar·i·ty /'klærəti/ *n.* [singular,U] **1** the quality of expressing ideas or thoughts in a clear way: *The clarity of Irving's writing style makes his books a pleasure to read.* | *The war brought these countries together with a clarity of purpose* (=they had a clear reason for doing something). **2** the ability to be seen or heard clearly: *Compare the clarity of the pictures of these TVs.*

Clark /klɑrk/, **William** (1770–1838) a U.S. EXPLORER

clash¹ /klæʃ/ *v.* **1** [I] if two armies or groups of people clash, they suddenly start fighting each other: **[+ with]** *More than 3000 demonstrators clashed with police on Sunday.* **2** [I] if two people or groups of people clash, they argue because their opinions and beliefs are very different: **[+ with]** *Humphrey has often clashed with Republican leaders over tax cuts.* | **[+ over]** *The two lawyers clashed over the physical evidence.* **3** [I] if two colors or patterns clash, they look very bad together: **[+ with]** *No, the red tie will clash with your shirt.* **4** [I,T] if two pieces of metal clash or if you clash them, they make a loud ringing sound: *The cymbals clashed.*

clash² *n.* [C] **1** a short fight between two armies or groups of people: *In the last two months, there have been numerous border clashes.* | **[+ between]** *Johnson was killed in a clash between rival gangs.* | **[+ with]** *Ten soldiers were wounded in a clash with the rebels.* **2** an argument between two people or groups of people, because they have different opinions or beliefs: **[+ between]** *A clash between Democrats and Republicans in the Senate was expected.* | *The report reveals the clash of cultures between rural and urban areas.* | *Part of the problem seems to be a personality clash between Tyler and his teacher* (=they do not like each other because their characters are very different).* **3** a loud sound made by two metal objects being hit together: *the clash of swords* **4** a combination of two colors, designs etc. that look bad together

clasp¹ /klæsp/ *n.* **1** [C] a small metal object that fastens a bag, belt, piece of jewelry etc. **2** [singular] a tight hold; GRIP: *the firm clasp of her hand*

clasp² *v.* [T] to hold someone or something tightly, closing your fingers or arms around them: *The baby monkey clasped its mother's fur tightly.* | *Lie down with your hands clasped behind your head.* | *Jill clasped the doll to her chest* (=held it tightly against her chest) *and ran to her mother.*

s w **class¹** /klæs/ *n.*

1 group of students [C] **a)** a group of students who are taught together: *Today we only had a small class of ten people.* | *I was talking to a girl in my class about the math homework.* **b)** a group of students who finished college or HIGH SCHOOL in the same year: *My dad's going to his 40th class reunion this year.* |

Howard was a member of the class of '89 (=the group of students who finished in 1989).

2 teaching period [C,U] a period of time during which students are taught: *When's your next class?* | *I have class until ten tonight.* | *I'm sure we read that article in class* (=during the class).

3 subject [C] a set of lessons in which you study a particular subject: **[+ in]** *a class in computer design* | *She's taking a ballet class.* | *Spanish/maths/history etc. class* *I got a B+ in maths class.*

4 in a society **a)** [C] a group of people in a society that earn a similar amount of money, have similar types of jobs etc.: *The Republicans are promising tax cuts for the middle class.* —see also LOWER CLASS, MIDDLE CLASS, UPPER CLASS, WORKING CLASS **b)** [U] the system in which people are divided into such groups: *People were excluded from education based on class and race.*

5 quality [C] a group into which people or things are divided according to how good they are: *We can't afford to travel first class* (=the most expensive way) *on the plane.* | *As a tennis player, he's not in the same class* (=not as good) *as Sampras.* —see also BUSINESS CLASS, ECONOMY CLASS, FIRST CLASS, HIGH-CLASS, LOW-CLASS, SECOND CLASS, THIRD CLASS, TOURIST CLASS

6 be in a class of your/its own to be much better than all similar people or things: *Beene's designs are in a class of their own.*

7 style [U] INFORMAL style or skill in the way you do something, that makes people notice and admire you: *The players showed a lot of class under pressure.* | *Margaret's a person who really has class.* | *Harrison dealt with the problem with class and dignity.*

8 a class act INFORMAL someone or something that is very skillful, polite, attractive etc.: *Coach Williams is a real class act.*

9 group of people/things etc. [C] a group of people, animals, or other things that can be considered or studied together because they are similar in some way: *The treaty called for the elimination of an entire class of nuclear weapons.*

class² *v.* [T often passive] FORMAL to decide that **s** someone or something belongs in a particular group; CLASSIFY: **[class sb/sth as sth]** *Stewart's books are classed as romantic mysteries.*

class ac·tion /,. '../ *n.* [C,U] a type of LAWSUIT that a group of people bring to a court of law for themselves and other people with the same problem —**class-action** *adj.* [only before noun] *a class-action case*

class-con·scious /'. ,../ *adj.* always knowing what social class you and other people belong to, and often judging other people according to their social class —**class-consciousness** *n.* [U]

clas·sic¹ /'klæsɪk/ *adj.* **1** [usually before noun] considered important and of high quality, with a value that LASTS for a long time: *The Coca-Cola bottle is one of the classic designs of our century.* | *Orson Welles directed the classic film "Citizen Kane."* | *the classic rock music of the sixties* | *a classic car* **2 a classic example/case etc.** a typical or very good example of something: *This was a classic example of how to lose a football game.* | *The room is decorated in the classic country look.* | *It's the classic recipe for a club sandwich.* **3** [usually before noun] a classic style of art or clothing is attractive in a simple or traditional way, and is not influenced very much by changing fashions: *a classic blue suit* **4 That's classic!** SPOKEN said when you think something is very funny

clas·sic² *n.* [C] **1** something such as a book, movie, or music that is considered very good and important, and that has a value that has continued for a long time: *a collection of literary classics* | **[+ of]** *Barbecued ribs are one of the classics of Southern cuisine.* **2** something that is very good and one of the best examples of its kind: *Tuesday night's game against the Clippers was a classic.* **3 Classics** [U] the study of the languages, literature, and history of ancient Greece and Rome

clas·si·cal /'klæsɪkəl/ *adj.* **1** based on or belonging to a traditional style or set of ideas, especially in art or science: *The problem involves classical physics, as opposed to quantum physics.* | *The vase is a piece of modern art done in a classical Chinese style.* **2** relating to classical music: *a classical CD* | *Lima is one of Brazil's top classical pianists.* **3** relating to the language, literature etc. of ancient Greece and Rome: *classical architecture* | *Hargraves received a classical education* (=an education that includes studying Latin and Greek). **—classically** /-kli/ *adv.*

classical mu·sic /ˌ... '../ *n.* [U] a type of music, originally written in Europe, that includes OPERAS and SYMPHONIES, is played mainly on instruments such as the VIOLIN and piano, and is considered to have serious artistic value

clas·si·cism /'klæsəˌsɪzəm/ *n.* [U] a style of art that is simple, regular, and does not show too much emotion, based on the models of ancient Greece or Rome —compare REALISM, ROMANTICISM

clas·si·cist /'klæsəsɪst/ *n.* someone who studies Classics

clas·si·fi·ca·tion /ˌklæsəfə'keɪʃən/ *n.* **1** [C] a group or class into which something is put, along with things that are similar to it in some way: *job classifications* **2** [U] the process of putting something into the group or class it belongs to: *The classification of wines is often done according to their region.*

clas·si·fied¹ /'klæsəˌfaɪd/ *adj.* classified information or documents are ones that the government has ordered to be kept secret

classified² *n.* **the classifieds** [plural] INFORMAL the part of a newspaper where the classified ads are

classified ad /ˌ... './ *n.* [C] a small advertisement in a special part of a newspaper for jobs, houses, and things that people want to buy or sell, or for people who want to meet someone to begin a relationship with —see also WANT AD

clas·si·fy /'klæsəˌfaɪ/ *v.* **classifies, classified, classifying** [T] **1** to decide what group a plant, animal, book etc. belongs to according to a system: [**classify sth as sth**] *Whales are classified as mammals rather than fish.* **2** to make information or documents secret: *The military has classified the results of the weapons test.* **—classifiable** *adj.*

class·less /'klæslɪs/ *adj.* a classless society is one in which people are not divided into different social classes **—classlessness** *n.* [U]

class·mate /'klæsmeɪt/ *n.* [C] someone who is in the same class as you in a school or college

class ring /'. ˌ / *n.* [C] a ring that shows which high school or college you went to and the year you GRADUATED

class·room /'klæsrum/ *n.* [C] **1** a room in a school where students are taught: *Teachers often have to buy supplies to be used in classroom activities.* **2 in the classroom** in schools or classes in general: *Religion is rarely even discussed in the classroom.*

class strug·gle /ˌ. '..., '. ˌ../ *n.* [singular,U] the continuing struggle for political and economic power between CAPITALISTS (=the owners of land, factories etc.) and the PROLETARIAT (=the workers), according to Marxist THEORY

class·work /'klæswɚk/ *n.* [U] school work that you do during class, rather than at home —compare HOMEWORK

class·y /'klæsi/ *adj.* **classier, classiest** INFORMAL **1** stylish and fashionable, and usually expensive: *classy restaurants* **2** having style or skill in the way you do something, that makes people notice and admire you: *a classy woman*

clat·ter /'klætɚ/ *v.* **1** [I,T] to make a loud noise by hitting hard objects together: *All the pots clattered to the floor.* **2** [I always + adv./prep.] to move quickly and with a lot of noise: [**clatter over/down/along etc.**] *The cable cars clattered along the tracks.* **—clatter** *n.* [singular,U] *the clatter of dishes*

clause /klɔz/ *n.* [C] **1** a part of a written law or legal document covering a particular subject, condition etc.: *A clause in the contract states when payment must be made.* **2** in grammar, a group of words that contains a subject and a verb, but which is usually only part of a sentence. In the sentence "Jim is the

only one who knows the answer," "who knows the answer" is a clause —compare PHRASE¹ (2)

claus·tro·pho·bi·a /ˌklɔstrə'foubiə/ *n.* [U] a strong fear of being in a small enclosed space or among a crowd of people —compare AGORAPHOBIA

claus·tro·pho·bic /ˌklɔstrə'foubɪk◂/ *adj.* **1** feeling extremely anxious when you are in a small enclosed space: *I get claustrophobic in elevators.* **2** making you feel anxious and uncomfortable, because you are enclosed in a small space: *Cynthia's apartment is very claustrophobic.*

clav·i·chord /'klævəˌkɔrd/ *n.* [C] a musical instrument like a piano that was played especially in past times

clav·i·cle /'klævɪkəl/ *n.* [C] TECHNICAL a COLLARBONE —see picture at SKELETON

claw¹ /klɔ/ *n.* [C] **1** a sharp curved nail on the toe of an animal or bird —see picture on page 429 **2** [usually plural] the part of the body of some insects and sea animals such as CRABS that is used for attacking and holding things **3** a curved end of a tool or machine used for pulling nails out of wood and lifting things: *a claw hammer*

claw² *v.* [I,T] **1** to tear or pull at something using claws: *Their dog clawed all the paint off the doors.* | [**+ at**] *The cat's been clawing at the furniture again.* **2** to try very hard to get hold of something: *Marian's two-year-old toddler was clawing at her skirt.* **3** to move somewhere slowly by holding tightly onto things as you move: *Hundreds of searchers **clawed their way** up the stony hillsides.*

clay /kleɪ/ *n.* [U] **1** heavy soil that is soft and sticky when wet, but hard when dry or baked, and is used for making pots, bricks etc. **2** a soft sticky substance that can be pressed and formed into different shapes and made into figures etc., then dried or baked to make it hard —see also **feet of clay** (FOOT¹ (20)) **—clayey** *adj.*

Clay /kleɪ/, **Henry** (1777–1852) a U.S. politician who tried to establish an agreement between the states of the North and South before the American Civil War

Clay·ma·tion /kleɪ'meɪʃən/ *n.* [U] TRADEMARK a process in which clay figures are filmed so that they look as though they move and talk in movies or television programs

clean¹ /klin/ *adj.*   S W
                                                           2 2
1 ▮without dirt/mess▮ not dirty or messy: *Are your hands clean?* | *a clean towel* | *Gene always has the cleanest desk in the office.* | *I couldn't get the tiles any cleaner.* | *I want this room **nice and clean**.* | *The whole house was **as clean as a whistle** (=very clean).* | *The floor is **squeaky clean** (=very clean).*

2 ▮air/water/power etc.▮ not containing or producing anything that is dirty or harmful, such as poisons: *The river is a lot cleaner than it used to be.* | *Clean air and water is a necessity of life.* | *clean-burning natural gas*

3 ▮design▮ having a simple and attractive style or design: *the car's clean style* | *the clean lines of Morrison's drawings*

4 ▮no drugs/crime/weapons etc.▮ INFORMAL not involving taking drugs, doing anything illegal, carrying any weapons etc.: *Dave's been clean (=has not taken drugs) for over a year now.* | *The police searched Romero, but he was clean (=was not carrying a gun or drugs).* | *He's a **squeaky clean** kid – doesn't smoke, drink, or do drugs or anything.* | *Greene says vitamins and **clean living** (=not drinking alcohol, taking drugs, or behaving in an immoral way) are the keys to her long life.*

5 ▮fair/legal▮ **a)** honest, fair, and not breaking any rules: *a clean fight* | *Everyone wants a clean and honest election.* **b)** showing that you have followed the rules or the law: *Drivers with clean driving records pay less in insurance.*

6 come clean INFORMAL to finally tell the truth or admit that you have done something wrong: [**+ about**] *Roberts finally came clean about his involvement in the scheme.*

7 not offensive not offensive or not dealing with sex: *The resort offers good, clean fun for everyone.* | *The comedians were asked to keep it clean* (=asked not to use offensive language).

8 **a clean bill of health** a report that says you are healthy or that a machine or building is safe: *Three months after the operation, the doctors gave her a clean bill of health.*

9 **a clean slate** a situation that shows that someone has behaved well or not made any mistakes: *They've paid all their debts and can start off the year with a clean slate.*

10 **a clean sweep a)** a complete change in a company or organization, made by getting rid of people **b)** a victory in all parts of a game or competition, especially by winning the first three places: *Lewis, Burrell, and Mitchell made it a clean sweep for the U.S. in the 100 meters.*

11 **a clean break a)** an act of leaving a place, stopping a relationship, or stopping an activity, so that you do not have any more connections with that place, person, or activity: *The country is trying to make a clean break with its past.* **b)** a break in a bone or other object that is complete and has not left any small pieces

12 smooth having a smooth edge: *Fortunately, the glass made a clean cut on his leg.*

13 paper a clean piece of paper has not been used yet

14 clear pictures/writing looking clear and containing no mistakes: *The film produces clean, sharp images.* | *I need a clean copy; don't send a fax.*

15 movement a clean movement is skillful and exact: *The dancing was clean and brilliantly fast.*

16 **make a clean breast of it** SPOKEN to admit that you have done something wrong so that you do not feel guilty anymore

17 habits/appearance behaving in a way that keeps things clean or having a clean appearance: *Cats are very clean animals.* | *Monica is what I would call a clean freak* (=someone who thinks too much about making sure things are clean). —**cleanness** *n.* [U] —see also CLEAN-CUT, CLEANLINESS, CLEANLY, **keep your nose clean** (NOSE[1] (13))

s w **clean²** *v.* **1** [I,T] to remove dirt from something by rubbing or washing: *I need to clean the bathtub.* | *She's busy cleaning.* —see also DRY-CLEAN, SPRING-CLEANING **2** also **clean off/up** [T] to make something look neat by removing the things that make it look messy or by putting things in their correct places: *Manion cleaned his desk and answered a few emails before leaving for the day.* **3** [I,T] to clean a building or other people's houses as your job: *Anne comes in to clean twice a week.* | *We've hired a maid to clean our house.* **4** [T] to cut out the inside parts of an animal or bird that you are going to cook: *Simply place the whole cleaned fish in a greased pan.* **5 clean your plate** to eat all of the food that is on your plate **6 clean sb's clock** HUMOROUS to defeat or beat someone very severely: *In the 1992 presidential race, George Bush cleaned Buchanan's clock in every Southern state.*

clean sth ↔ **off** *phr. v.* [T] **1** to make the surface of something clean and neat, especially by removing things from it: *Logan Airport was closed so that snowplows could clean off the runways.* **2** to remove something from the surface of something else: *If your boots are muddy, use the hose to clean off the dirt.*

clean sb/sth **out** *phr. v.* [T] **1** [clean sth ↔ out] to make the inside of a room, house etc. clean and neat, especially by removing things from it: *I got rid of a lot of stuff when I was cleaning out my closets.* **2** [clean sb/sth ↔ out] INFORMAL to steal everything from a place or from someone: *One man held the gun, and the other cleaned out the cash register.* **3** [clean sb out] INFORMAL to be forced to spend all of your money on something, so that you have none left: *The car repair bill cleaned us out.*

clean up *phr. v.* **1** [I,T **clean** sth ↔ **up**] to make something clean and neat, especially by removing the things that make it look messy: *I have to clean up my room first.* | *They're working on a plan to clean up the bay.* **2** [I,T **clean** sb ↔ **up**] to wash yourself after you have gotten very dirty, or to wash someone else: *Go upstairs, get cleaned up, and then we can go.* | *It takes an hour to clean up the kids after soccer practice.* **3 clean up your act** INFORMAL to start behaving in a responsible way: *Gwen finally told her troubled son to clean up his act or get out of her house.* **4** [I] INFORMAL to win a lot of money or make a lot of money in a business deal: *Jack really cleaned up this time in Vegas.* **5** [T **clean** sth ↔ **up**] to improve moral standards in a place or organization: *We need someone to clean up City Hall.* —see also CLEANUP

clean³ *adv.* INFORMAL used to emphasize the fact that an action or movement takes place completely and thoroughly: [clean away/through/past etc.] *The gunmen got clean away.* | *The nail went clean through his finger.* | *Sorry, I clean forgot* (=completely forgot) *your birthday.*

clean-cut /ˌ. ˈ.◂/ *adj.* a clean-cut man or boy looks neat and clean, and appears to have a good moral character: *clean-cut college boys*

clean·er /ˈklinɚ/ *n.* [C] **1** a machine or substance used for cleaning: *a vacuum cleaner* | *Keep household cleaners away from children.* **2 the cleaners** a DRY CLEANERS: *I need to pick my suit up from the cleaners.* **3 take sb to the cleaners** INFORMAL **a)** to get all of someone's money, especially in business or in a court of law, in a way that is not honest: *Juanita threatened to take her former husband to the cleaners.* **b)** to defeat someone completely: *The Lakers took the Bulls to the cleaners, winning 96–72.* **4** someone whose job is to clean other people's houses, offices etc.: *Wayne had previously worked as a pool cleaner.*

clean·ing /ˈklinɪŋ/ *n.* [U] the process of making something clean and neat: *Women still do most of the cleaning in the home.*

cleaning la·dy also **cleaning woman** /ˈ.. ˌ../ *n.* [C] a woman who cleans offices, houses etc. as her job

clean·li·ness /ˈklɛnlinɪs/ *n.* [U] **1** the practice of keeping yourself or the things around you clean **2 cleanliness is next to godliness** OLD-FASHIONED, SPOKEN used to say that keeping yourself and other things clean is a sign of good moral character

clean·ly /ˈklinli/ *adv.* **1** quickly and smoothly in a neat way: *The branch snapped cleanly in two.* **2** if something burns cleanly, it does not produce any dirty or harmful substances as it burns

cleanse /klɛnz/ *v.* [T] **1** to make something completely clean: *Cleanse the wound with alcohol.* **2** LITERARY to remove everything that is immoral or bad from someone's character or from a place or organization: [cleanse sb/sth of sth] *The prisoners prayed that they would be cleansed of their sins.* —see also **ethnic cleansing** (ETHNIC (4))

cleans·er /ˈklɛnzɚ/ *n.* [C,U] **1** a chemical liquid or powder used for cleaning surfaces inside a house, office etc.: *household cleansers* **2** a liquid used for removing dirt or MAKEUP from your face

clean-shaven

Mike has a beard.

Paul is clean-shaven.

clean-shav·en /ˌ. ˈ..◂/ *adj.* a man who is clean-shaven does not have hair on his face

clean-up /ˈklinʌp/ *n.* [C usually singular] a process in which you get rid of dirt or waste from a place: *The cleanup of the oil spill took months.* | *The city must now pay millions of dollars in cleanup costs.*

clear¹ /klɪr/ *adj.*

1 easy to understand expressed in a simple and direct way so that people understand: *clear instructions* | *The test questions weren't very clear.* | *I'll give you until Monday to turn in your essay. Is that clear?* | [be clear about sth] *Smith was very clear about the school's policies on the issue.* | [be clear about what/when/how etc.] *Could you be more clear about how long it will take to do the job?* | [be clear on sth] *The manual is clear on how to operate the software.* | [be clear to sb] *It is clear to me that the company will have to make further job cuts.* | *Taylor's book* **makes** *the subject* **clear** *and even enjoyable.* | *The case* **made it clear that** *racial discrimination was still an important issue.* | *Klein said that Martin had not* **made himself clear** (=had not expressed something clear). | *Before asking for a raise, get* **a clear idea** (=a good understanding) *of what you plan to say.* | *We need to send kids a* **crystal-clear** (=very easy to understand) *message that drugs are dangerous.*

2 impossible to doubt impossible to doubt, question, or make a mistake about: *There was clear evidence of McCain's guilt.* | *Gun control laws are favored by a clear majority of Americans.* | [it is clear whether/why/how etc.] *It was not clear how many employees would be affected by the changes.* | *The tests* **make it clear that** *the drug is safe.* | **It is clear that** *the drug does benefit some patients.* | *Gwynn's lawyer said it was* **a clear case of** *sexual discrimination.*

3 be clear to feel certain that you know or understand something: [+ about/on] *There are a few points that I'm not really clear on.* | *Let me get this clear – you weren't even there at the time?*

4 see through easy to see through, rather than colored or dirty; TRANSPARENT: *clear glass bottles*

5 water/air clean and fresh: *a clear mountain lake*

6 weather without clouds, mist, smoke etc.: *a beautiful clear day*

7 easy to see having details, edges, lines etc. that are easy to see, or shapes that are easy to recognize: *Most of the photographs were sharp and clear.*

8 easy to hear easy to hear, and therefore easy to understand: *a clear speaking voice* | *The sound isn't very clear.* | *a good recording; the sound is as* **clear as a bell** (=very clear).

9 not blocked/covered not covered or blocked by anything that stops you from doing or seeing what you want: *The roads were fairly clear this morning.* | *We had a clear view of the ocean from our hotel room.* | [+ of] *Landowners are required to keep their property clear of trash.*

10 eyes very pure in color and without any redness: *clear blue eyes*

11 skin smooth and without any red spots

12 thinking able to think sensibly and quickly: *The organization suffers from a lack of new ideas and clear thinking.* | *Mario is able to keep a* **clear head** *even when things are going wrong.*

13 a clear conscience the knowledge that you have done the right thing: *Finley said that he had a clear conscience and that the charges were unfounded.*

14 as clear as mud SPOKEN, HUMOROUS used to say that something is very difficult to understand: *Joe's directions are as clear as mud.*

15 see your way clear (to doing sth) INFORMAL to have the necessary time or willingness to be able to do something: *If you can see your way clear, call this number to volunteer.*

16 not busy without any planned activities or events: *Next Monday is clear; how about 10 o'clock?*

17 be clear (of sth) to not be touching something, or to be past someone or something: *Put the rods at a height that will allow the curtains to be clear of the floor.* | *Drivers should not stop until they are clear of the construction area.*

18 after taxes a clear amount of profit, salary etc. is what is left after taxes have been paid on it; NET² (1): *Sullivan's company makes a clear $900,000 per year.* —**clearness** *n.* [U] —see also ALL-CLEAR, CLARITY, CLEARLY, **the coast is clear** (COAST¹ (2))

S W
2 2
clear² *v.*

1 surface/place [T] to make a place neat by removing things from it: [clear sth of sth] *Volunteers are working to clear the streets of sand, debris, and water.* | *Barbara, it's your turn to* **clear the table** (=take off the used plates, forks etc. after you have eaten).* | *We have to* **clear a space for** (=move things so there is room for something else) *some bookshelves.*

2 remove [T] to remove something that is blocking something else or causing a problem, or to make a place free from something that has been blocking it: *Snowplows have been out clearing the roads.* | [clear sb/sth from sth] *Trucks have just finished clearing the wreck from the road.* | [clear sth of sth] *The area was cleared of traffic as a safety precaution.*

3 crime/blame etc. [T usually passive] to prove that someone is not guilty of something: *Rawlings was cleared after new evidence was produced.* | [clear sb of (doing) sth] *The jury cleared Johnson of the murder.* | *Tucker's son is determined to* **clear** *his father's* **name** (=show that he is not guilty of something).

4 weather also **clear up** [I] if the weather, sky etc. clears, it becomes better or there is more sun: *The fog usually clears around noon.*

5 permission [T] **a)** to give or get official permission for something to be done: *The report was cleared by the State Department.* | [clear sth with sb] *I'll have to clear it with my boss first.* **b)** to give official permission for a person, ship, or aircraft to enter or leave a country: *Delta 7, you are cleared for takeoff.*

6 bank [I,T] if a check clears or if a bank clears it, the bank allows the money to be paid into the account of the person who received the check

7 earn [T] INFORMAL to earn a particular amount of money after taxes have been paid on it: *Wiley's business clears $300,000 a year.*

8 clear a debt/loan to get rid of a debt by paying what you owe

9 go over [T] to go over a fence, wall etc. without touching it: *The plane barely cleared the fence at the end of the runway.* | *Edwards cleared 18 feet in the pole vault.*

10 clear the way for sb/sth to make it possible for a process to happen: *This agreement will clear the way for further talks.*

11 clear your throat to cough in order to be able to speak with a clear voice

12 clear your head/mind to stop worrying or thinking about something, or get rid of the effects of drinking too much alcohol: *I go for a long walk at lunchtime to clear my head.*

13 clear the air to do something in order to end an argument or bad situation: *The White House hopes that the investigation will clear the air.*

14 clear sth through customs also **clear customs** to be allowed to take things through CUSTOMS

15 skin also **clear up** [I] to not have marks or PIMPLES on your skin anymore

16 liquid also **clear up** [I] if a liquid clears, it becomes more transparent

17 clear the decks to do a lot of work that needs to be done before you can do other things: *We're trying to clear the decks before Christmas.*

18 face/expression [I] if your face or expression clears, you stop looking worried or angry

clear sth ↔ **away** *phr. v.* [T] to make a place look neat by removing things or putting things where they belong: *Homeowners are clearing away brush near their houses to prevent fires.* | *The train station will be closed until the wreckage is cleared away.*

clear out *phr. v.* **1** [T clear sth ↔ out] to make a place neat by removing things from it: *I need to clear out that closet.* **2** [I] INFORMAL used in order to tell someone angrily to leave a place: *The campers were told to clear out by 9 a.m.*

clear up *phr. v.* **1** [T clear sth ↔ up] to explain something or make it easier to understand: *There are a lot of questions about the case that still haven't been cleared up.* **2** [T clear sth ↔ up] to make a place look neat by putting things where they belong: *Come on, it's time to clear up this mess.* **3** [I] if the weather clears up, it gets better: *I hope it clears up by the weekend.* **4** [I] if an illness or infection clears up, it disappears

s w **clear³** *adv.* **1** away from something, or out of the way: *Firefighters pulled the woman clear of the wreckage.* **2 steer/stay/keep clear (of sth)** to avoid someone or something because of possible danger or trouble: *The chicken is great, but steer clear of the coleslaw.* | *Drivers should stay clear of the I-40 bridge because of ice.* **3 clear to/through/across etc. sth** INFORMAL used to emphasize a long distance: *You can see clear to the mountains from here.* | *I had to walk clear across Oakland when my car broke down.* —see also **loud and clear** (LOUD¹ (4))

clear⁴ *n.* **in the clear a)** not guilty of something: *Martin's testimony showed that Buckley was in the clear.* **b)** not having difficulties because of something: *The debt is being paid off, but we're not in the clear yet.* **c)** not having a particular illness or infection anymore, so that your health or life is not in danger

clear·ance /'klɪrəns/ *n.* **1** [C,U] the process of getting official permission or approval for something: *Two months after his heart attack, Mason received medical clearance to go back to work.* | *Siegert helped the movie crew get clearance to film in the park.* | *Only personnel with a high-level **security clearance** are allowed in the building.* **2** [C,U] the amount of space around one object that is necessary for it to avoid touching another object: *We need twelve feet of overhead clearance for the truck.* **3** [C] a CLEARANCE SALE **4** [C,U] a SECURITY CLEARANCE **5** [C,U] a process by which a check goes from one bank to another **6** [C,U] the removal of unwanted things from a place: *The clearance of brush around houses helped prevent the fire from spreading.*

clearance sale /'.. ,./ *n.* [C] a sale in which goods are sold very cheaply in order to get rid of all of them

clear-cut¹ /ˌ. '.ˈ./ *adj.* **1** easy to understand or be certain about; DEFINITE: *There's no clear-cut distinction between severe depression and mental illness.* | *a clear-cut case of sexual harassment* **2** [only before noun] having a definite outer shape: *the clear-cut outline of the mountains*

clear-cut² *n.* [C] an area of forest in which all the trees have been cut down, or an act of cutting down all the trees in an area —**clear-cut** *v.* [T]

clear-head·ed /ˌ. '...ˈ./ *adj.* able to think in a clear and sensible way —**clear-headedly** *adv.* —**clear-headedness** *n.* [U]

clear·ing /'klɪrɪŋ/ *n.* [C] a small area in the middle of a forest where there are no trees

clear·ing·house, **clearing house** /'klɪrɪŋ haʊs/ *n.* [C] **1** an office that receives and gives out or sells information or goods for several other organizations: *The company serves as a clearinghouse for discount airline ticket sales.* **2** an office where banks exchange checks and other financial documents

s w **clear·ly** /'klɪrli/ *adv.* **1** [sentence adverb] without any doubt; OBVIOUSLY: *Clearly, the racial problems in America have no easy answers.* **2** in a way that is easy to see, hear, or understand: *Slow down and speak more clearly.* | *The map clearly shows all the trails where bikes are allowed.* **3** in a way that is sensible: *I'm sorry I forgot – I'm just not thinking clearly today.*

clear-sight·ed /ˌ. '..ˈ./ *adj.* able to understand a problem or situation well: *a clear-sighted analysis of the market* —**clear-sightedly** *adv.* —**clear-sightedness** *n.* [U]

cleat /klit/ *n.* [C] **1 cleats** [plural] a pair of sports shoes that have short pieces or rubber, plastic, or metal attached to the bottom of them, in order to prevent someone from slipping on the ground **2** [usually plural] a short piece of rubber, plastic, or metal that is attached to the bottom of a sports shoe **3** TECHNICAL a small bar with two short arms around which ropes can be tied, especially on a ship

cleav·age /'klivɪdʒ/ *n.* [C,U] **1** the space between a woman's breasts **2** FORMAL a difference between two people or things that often causes problems or arguments: *I am referring to the cleavage between the country's rulers and the population.*

cleave /kliv/ *v. past tense* **cleaved, clove, cleft** *past participle* **cleaved, cloven, cleft 1** [I always + adv./prep., T always + adv./prep.] LITERARY to cut something into separate parts using a heavy tool or to be able to be cut in this way: *The wooden door had been cleft in two.* **2** [T] FORMAL to divide something into two completely separate parts: *Our organization is trying to ease the racial problems that still cleave U.S. society.* **3 cleave the air/darkness etc.** LITERARY to move quickly through the air etc.: *His fist cleft the air.*

cleave to sb/sth *phr. v.* [T] **1** FORMAL to be faithful to an idea, belief, or person: *John still cleaves to his romantic ideals.* **2** LITERARY to stick to someone or something, or to seem to surround them

clea·ver /'klivɚ/ *n.* [C] a heavy knife with a wide blade that is used for cutting up large pieces of meat

Clea·ver /'klivɚ/, **El·dridge** /'ɛldrɪdʒ/ (1935–1998) a leader of the Black Panthers in the 1960s, who left the organization in 1975

clef /klɛf/ *n.* [C] a sign at the beginning of a line of written music to show the PITCH¹ (3) of the notes: *the treble clef*

cleft¹ /klɛft/ *n.* [C] **1** a natural crack in the surface of rocks or the Earth etc.: *a cleft in the granite cliff* **2** an area on the chin or lip that is goes slightly inward, so that the chin or lip is not smooth and rounded

cleft² *adj.* **1** a cleft chin is one that is not smooth and rounded, but that has a small area that goes inward **2 a cleft lip/palate** a split in someone's upper lip or the top of the inside of their mouth that makes it difficult for them to speak clearly

cleft³ a past tense and past participle of CLEAVE

clem·a·tis /'klɛmətɪs, klɪ'mætɪs/ *n.* [C,U] a plant with white or colored flowers that attaches itself to trees, buildings, fences etc. and covers them as it grows

Cle·men·ceau /ˌklɛmən'soʊ/, **Georges** /ʒɔrʒ/ (1841–1929) the Prime Minister of France at the end of World War I

clem·en·cy /'klɛmənsi/ *n.* [U] FORMAL forgiveness and less severe punishment for a crime, usually given by someone in power such as a governor or president: **grant/give sb clemency** *Ms. Aris was granted clemency after serving 10 years for killing her abusive husband.*

Clem·ens /'klɛmənz/, **Sam·u·el Lang·horne** /'sæmjuəl 'læŋhɔrn/ (1835–1910) the real name of Mark Twain

clem·ent /'klɛmənt/ *adj.* LITERARY clement weather is neither too hot nor too cold; MILD (3) —**clemently** *adv.* —opposite INCLEMENT

clem·en·tine /'klɛmən,tin, -,taɪn/ *n.* [C] a type of small sweet orange

clench /klɛntʃ/ *v.* [T] **1 clench your fist** to curl your fingers and thumb together very tightly, especially because you feel angry or determined: *Sonia clenched her fists in rage.* | *Morris faced the crowd and raised a clenched fist.* **2 a)** to hold two parts of your body together tightly, especially because you feel angry or determined | **clench your hands/teeth/jaws/buttocks** *I clenched my teeth and closed my eyes as the plane started to dive.* **b)** to hold something tightly in your hand or between your teeth: *Roosevelt smiled broadly, with his cigar clenched between his teeth.* —**clench** *n.* [C usually singular]

Cle·o·pat·ra /ˌkliə'pætrə/ (69–30 B.C.) a queen of Egypt who became the lover of Julius Caesar and later of Mark Antony

clere·sto·ry /'klɪr,stɔri/ *n. plura* **clerestories** [C] TECHNICAL the upper part of the wall of a large church, that has windows in it and rises above the lower roofs

cler·gy /'klɚdʒi/ *n.* **the clergy** [U] the official leaders of religious activities in organized religions, such as priests, RABBIS and MULLAHS: *Many members of the* *clergy were murdered during the civil war.* —see Usage Note at PRIEST

cler·gy·man /ˈklɚdʒimən/ *n. plural* **clergymen** /-mən/ [C] a male member of the clergy —see Usage Note at PRIEST

cler·gy·wom·en /ˈklɚdʒiˌwumən/ *n. plural* **clergy-women** /-ˌwɪmɪn/ [C] a female member of the clergy

cler·ic /ˈklɛrɪk/ *n.* [C] OLD-FASHIONED a member of the clergy

cler·i·cal /ˈklɛrɪkəl/ *adj.* **1** relating to office work: *a clerical error* | *The work you'll do is mainly clerical.* | *clerical staff* **2** relating to the clergy: *a clerical collar* (=a special black and white collar that priests wear)

clerk¹ /klɚk/ *n.* [C] **1** someone whose job is to help customers in a store: *a clerk at a convenience store* —see also SALESCLERK **2** someone whose job is to help people when they arrive at and leave a hotel: *Please return your keys to the clerk at the front desk.* **3** someone whose job is to keep records, accounts etc. in an office: *Right now I am working as a law clerk downtown.*

clerk² *v.* [I] to work as a clerk, especially either in a store or in a judge's or lawyer's office: [+ **for**] *Rehnquist clerked for Justice Robert Jackson early in his career.*

Cleve·land /ˈklivlənd/ a city in the U.S. state of Ohio

Cleveland, Gro·ver /ˈgrouvɚ/ (1837–1908) the 22nd and 24th President of the U.S., who was defeated in 1889 but elected again in 1893

clev·er /ˈklɛvɚ/ *adj.* **1** done or made in an unusual or interesting way: *It is a clever device that can chop onions in seconds.* | *a clever joke* **2** able to use your intelligence to do something, especially in a slightly dishonest way: *Tabloid reporters are very clever and persistent.* **3** showing ability or skill, especially at making things or finding new ways to do things: *Gibson met a clever classmate who had built his own radio transmitter.* **4** able to learn and understand things quickly; SMART: *In the story, the miller's daughter is a clever, beautiful girl.* —**cleverly** *adv.* —**cleverness** *n.* [U]

cli·ché, cliche /kliˈʃeɪ/ *n.* [C] DISAPPROVING an idea or phrase that has been used so much that it is not effective or does not have any meaning anymore: *The cliché that "truth is stranger than fiction" certainly applies here.* —**clichéd** *adj.*

---

click¹ /klɪk/ *v.*

1 ❚short hard sound❚ [I,T] to make a short hard sound, or make something produce this sound: *Both men smiled as the cameras clicked.* | *Mr. Samuelson clicked his tongue* (=made a short noise with his tongue) *in disapproval.* | *The door clicked shut.* | *The dancers jumped up, clicked their heels* (=knocked the heels of their shoes together), *and spun around.*

click

2 ❚happen in a good way❚ [I] INFORMAL to happen in a good or successful way: *Everything clicked for the team all season long.*

3 ❚computer❚ [I,T] to press a button on a computer MOUSE to choose something from the screen that you want the computer to do: [+ **on**] *Children can click on a sentence to hear it read aloud.* | [**click sth**] *Now click the "yes" button on the screen.* —see also RIGHT-CLICK

4 ❚suddenly understand sth❚ [I] INFORMAL to suddenly understand or realize something: *I had a lot of trouble with algebra, but the teacher was patient and one day it just clicked.*

5 ❚like and understand each other❚ [I] INFORMAL if two people click, they like, understand and agree with each other: *We just clicked from the moment we started working together.*

click² *n.* [C] **1** a short hard sound: *I heard a click, and the phone went dead.* **2** CANADIAN, SPOKEN a KILOMETER or one kilometer per hour: *They live about five clicks out of town.*

click·er /ˈklɪkɚ/ *n.* [C] SPOKEN a television REMOTE CONTROL

click·e·ty-clack /ˌklɪkəti ˈklæk/ also **clickety-click** *n.* [singular] a series of two different short hard sounds, especially the sound made by a moving train —**clickety-clack** *adv.*

cli·ent /ˈklaɪənt/ *n.* [C] **1** someone who pays for services or advice from a professional person, such as a lawyer or ARCHITECT, or from a company or organization: *Kilmer's attorney, Ralph Loeb, said that his client should not have to pay the government anything.* —compare CUSTOMER **2** someone who receives money, food, or help from a WELFARE organization or CHARITY (=organization that helps people): *Case workers deal with as many as a dozen clients a day.* **3** TECHNICAL a computer on a network that receives information from a SERVER (=main computer that contains information that the others use)

cli·en·tele /ˌklaɪənˈtɛl, ˌkliɑn-/ *n.* [C usually singular] all the people who regularly go to a store, restaurant etc.: *The Border Bar attracts a young clientele.*

client state /ˌ.. ˈ. ./ *n.* [C] a country that is dependent on the support and protection of a more powerful country

cliff /klɪf/ *n.* [C] a high, steep side of a large area of rock or mountain —see picture on page 428

cliff·hang·er /ˈklɪfˌhæŋɚ/ *n.* [C] INFORMAL **1** an ending of one part of a television or radio series that is very exciting because you do not know what will happen in the next part: *Actors have been told to keep the show's cliffhanger ending a secret.* **2** a competition or fight whose result is in doubt until the very end: *Malcome and Jones are in cliffhanger re-election races.* —**cliffhanging** *adj.*

cli·mac·tic /klaɪˈmæktɪk/ *adj.* forming a very exciting or important part of a story or event, especially near the end of it: *The identity of the killer is revealed in the movie's climactic ending.*

cli·mate /ˈklaɪmɪt/ *n.* [C] **1 a)** the typical weather conditions in a particular area: *Los Angeles has a warm, dry climate.* **b)** an area with particular weather conditions: *These flowers will not grow in cold climates.* **2** [usually singular] the general feeling or situation in a place at a particular time: *There is a climate of growing racial intolerance in the city.* | *economic/business/retailing climate Small businesses are finding it hard to survive in the present economic climate.*

cli·mat·ic /klaɪˈmætɪk/ *adj.* [only before noun] relating to the weather in a particular area: *harsh climatic conditions*

cli·max¹ /ˈklaɪmæks/ *n.* [C usually singular] **1** the most exciting or important part of a book, movie, situation etc., that usually happens at the end: [+ **of**] *King's famous "I have a dream" speech was the climax of a 1963 civil rights march.* | [+ **to**] *Mangione plays his trademark song as the climax to each show.* | *The crisis reached a climax last week, when two senators resigned.* **2** an ORGASM

climax² *v.* **1** [I,T] to reach the most important or exciting part of something such as a situation, story, or movie: [+ **with/in**] *The victim and another man got into an argument that climaxed with a stabbing.* **2** [I] to have an ORGASM

climb¹ /klaɪm/ *v.*

1 ❚move up/down❚ [I always + adv./prep.,T] to move up, down, or across something using your hands and feet, especially when this is difficult to do: *Burglars climbed a chain-link fence to gain access to the building.* | *The kids love climbing trees.* | [+ **up/down/along etc.**] *You have to climb down the cliff to get to the beach.* | *Some spectators climbed onto the roof to get a better view.* | *The wall is too high to climb over.*

2 ❚temperature/prices etc.❚ [I,T] to increase in number, amount, or level: *The temperature has climbed steadily since this morning.* | *Sales have*

climbed 11% this quarter. | [+ **to**] Stock prices climbed to record levels on Friday.
3 with difficulty [I always + adv./prep.] to move into, out of, or through something slowly and awkwardly: [+ **through/over/into** etc.] Ford climbed into a waiting limousine.
4 path/sun/airplane etc. [I,T] to move gradually to a higher position: The roller coaster climbs 91 feet and reaches speeds of 45 miles per hour. | [+ **to/into/up** etc.] Our plane climbed to 10,000 feet before we leveled off. | The trail climbs high into the mountain pass.
5 sport [I,T] to climb mountains or rocks as a sport: We saw a group of people climbing El Capitan in Yosemite. —see also CLIMBING
6 on a list [I,T] to move higher on a list of teams, records etc. as you become more popular or successful: [+ **to**] U2's new album has climbed to number two in the record charts.
7 plant [I] to grow up a wall or other structure: Ivy climbed up the front of the building.
8 in your job/life [I,T] to move to a better position in your professional or social life: Steve climbed rapidly through the sales division. | Women trying to **climb the** corporate **ladder** (=become more successful) still encounter discrimination.
9 be climbing the walls SPOKEN to become extremely anxious, annoyed, or impatient: If I drank another cup of coffee, I'd be climbing the walls.
climb² n. [C usually singular] **1** a process in which you move up toward a place, especially while using a lot of effort: It's a steep uphill climb all the way to the top. **2** an increase in value or amount: The dollar continued its climb against the Japanese yen. | [+ **in**] There has been a steady climb in house prices. **3** the process of improving your professional or social position: [+ **to**] Dreyer's climb to power in city government has been astonishing. **4** a process in which someone or something gets a higher position on a list or in a competition because of being popular or successful: Atlanta's climb from the bottom of the league to first place has increased ticket sales. | The song's **climb up the charts** has been steady. **5** a steep rock, cliff, or mountain that you climb up: Mount Rainier is a tough climb.
climb·er /'klaɪmɚ/ n. [C] **1** someone who climbs as a sport: a mountain climber **2** a person or animal that can climb easily: Monkeys are good climbers. **3** a plant that grows up a wall or other structure —see also **social climber**
climb·ing /'klaɪmɪŋ/ n. [U] the sport of climbing mountains or rocks: climbing equipment | Dan taught me the basic techniques of rock climbing. | She and her husband **go climbing** (=climb mountains or rocks as a sport) several times a week.
climbing wall /'.. ,./ n. [C] a special wall with small places to put your feet and hands as you climb up it, that rock climbers use for practice
clime /klaɪm/ n. [C usually plural] LITERARY the CLIMATE: They retired to sunnier climes.
clinch¹ /klɪntʃ/ v. **1** [T] to finally agree on something or get something after trying very hard: A last-minute touchdown clinched the game for the Saints. | Our company's CEO flew to Paris to clinch the deal. **2 clinch it** INFORMAL if an event, situation, process etc. clinches it, it makes someone finally decide to do something that they were already thinking of doing: The offer of a company car was what clinched it for me, and I accepted the job. **3** [I] if two people clinch, they hold each other's arms tightly, especially when they are fighting **4** [T] to fasten a nail firmly by bending the point over
clinch² n. [C] **1** a situation in which two people hold each other's arms tightly, especially when they are fighting **2** a situation in which two people who love each other hold each other tightly
clinch·er /'klɪntʃɚ/ n. [C] INFORMAL a fact, action, or argument that finally persuades someone to do something, or that ends an argument or competition:

Johnson's home run was the clincher for the Twins. | The clincher came when Munoz threatened to sue the city.
cline /klaɪn/ n. [C] TECHNICAL a range of very small differences in a group of things of the same kind; CONTINUUM
Cline /klaɪn/**, Pat·sy** /'pætsi/ (1932–1963) a U.S. singer of COUNTRY AND WESTERN music
cling¹ /klɪŋ/ v. past tense and past participle **clung** [I] **1** [always + adv./prep.] to hold someone or something tightly, especially because you do not feel safe: [+ **to/on/at** etc.] Passengers clung desperately to the lifeboats. **2** [always + adv./prep.] to stick to someone or something or seem to surround them: [+ **to/around** etc.] My wet shirt clung to my body. **3** to stay close to someone all the time because you are too dependent on them or do not feel safe: Some children tend to cling their first day at school.
cling to sth phr. v. [T] to continue to believe or do something, even though it may not be true or useful anymore: The village's inhabitants still cling to their traditions.
cling² n. —see STATIC CLING
cling·y /'klɪŋi/ adj. **clingier, clingiest 1** someone who is clingy is too dependent on another person: Samantha has become very clingy lately. **2** clingy clothing or material sticks tightly to your body and shows its shape
clin·ic /'klɪnɪk/ n. [C] **1** a place where medical treatment is given to people who do not need to stay in a hospital: a dental clinic **2** a place where medical treatment is given at a low cost: Glassman is one of several doctors who volunteer at the inner-city clinic. **3** a group of doctors who work together and share the same offices **4** a meeting at which a professional person gives help or advice to people: a marriage clinic | They're giving a free clinic on how to care for roses.
clin·i·cal /'klɪnɪkəl/ adj. **1** [only before noun] relating to treating or testing people who are sick: The drug has undergone a number of clinical trials. **2** relating to a hospital or clinic: Sound systems are now used in clinical settings, especially in psychiatrists' and dentists' offices. **3** considering only the facts and not influenced by emotions: a cold, clinical view of homelessness **4** a clinical building or room is very plain and clean, but not attractive or comfortable: The walls were painted a clinical white. **5** INFORMAL done in a very exact and skillful way, especially in sports: Klinsmann was absolutely clinical in scoring that goal. —**clinically** /-kli/ adv.: clinically-tested treatment methods
cli·ni·cian /klɪ'nɪʃən/ n. [C] FORMAL a doctor who treats and examines people, rather than one who does RESEARCH
clink¹ /klɪŋk/ v. [I,T] if two glass or metal objects clink or if you clink them, they make a short ringing sound because they have been hit together: The two men clinked their glasses in celebration.
clink² n. **1** [C usually singular] the short ringing sound made by metal or glass objects hitting each other **2 the clink** SLANG prison
clink·er /'klɪŋkɚ/ n. **1** [C] INFORMAL something or someone that is a total failure: Most of the album's songs are good, but there are a few clinkers. **2** [C] INFORMAL a wrong note in a musical performance: The singer hit a real clinker in the last verse. **3** [U] TECHNICAL the hard material like rocks which is left after coal is burned
Clin·ton /'klɪntʰn/**, Hil·la·ry Rod·ham** /'hɪləri 'rɑdəm/ (1946–) the wife of President Bill Clinton, considered to be a very successful lawyer
Clinton, William (Bill) (1946–) the 42nd President of the U.S.

Hillary Clinton

clip¹ /klɪp/ n.

1 [for fastening] [C] a small metal or plastic object that holds or fastens things together: *a paper clip* | *Fasten the microphone clip to your shirt.*
2 [movie] [C] a short part of a movie or television program that is shown by itself, especially as an advertisement: *They showed a few clips from Mel Gibson's new movie.*
3 [gun] [C] a container for bullets which passes them rapidly into the gun so that they can be fired
4 at a good/rapid/fast etc. clip quickly: *The car was going at a pretty good clip when it hit the tree.*
5 [newspaper] [C] an article that is cut from a newspaper or magazine for a particular reason; CLIPPING: *A friend sent me a clip from the Boston Globe.*
6 50 cents/$100 etc. a clip INFORMAL if things cost 50 cents, $100 etc. a clip, they cost that amount of money each

clip² v. clipped, clipping

1 [fasten] [I always + adv./prep.,T] to fasten something together or to be fastened together using a CLIP¹ (1): **[clip sth to/onto/together etc.]** *She'd clipped a business card to her letter.* | **[+ on/to etc.]** *The keys just clip onto your belt, like this.*
2 [cut] [T] to cut small amounts of something in order to make it neater: *Clip some of the bottom branches from the Christmas tree.*
3 [cut from newspaper] [T] to cut an article or picture from a newspaper, magazine etc.: **[clip sth out of/from sth]** *Kate regularly saves up to $7 with coupons she's clipped from the paper.*
4 [hit] [T] to hit something quickly at an angle, often by accident: *Jason swerved and clipped a truck in the next lane.*
5 [reduce] [T] to slightly reduce an amount, quantity etc.: **[clip sth off/from sth]** *Lewis clipped a second off the world record.*
6 clip sb's wings to restrict someone's freedom, activities, or power: *The economic troubles could clip the wings of entrepreneurs starting small businesses.* —see also CLIPPED

clip·board /'klɪpbɔrd/ n. [C] **1** a small flat board with a CLIP¹ (1) on top that holds paper so that you can write on it **2** TECHNICAL an area of computer MEMORY that holds information which is being moved or copied from one part of a computer DOCUMENT to another, or to a different computer document

clip-clop /'. ./ n. [C usually singular] the sound made by a horse as it walks on a hard surface —**clip-clop** v. [I]

clip joint /'. ./ n. [C] OLD-FASHIONED, SLANG a restaurant or NIGHTCLUB that charges too much for food, drinks etc.

clip-on /'. ./ adj. [only before noun] fastened to something with a CLIP¹ (1): *clip-on earrings* —**clip-on** n. [C]

clipped /klɪpt/ adj. **1** cut so that it is short and neat: *a clipped green lawn* **2** a clipped voice is quick and clear but not very friendly

clip·per /'klɪpə/ n. **1** [C] a fast sailing ship used in past times **2 clippers** [plural] a special tool with two blades for cutting small pieces from something: *hedge clippers*

clip·ping /'klɪpɪŋ/ n. [C] **1** an article or picture that has been cut out of a newspaper or magazine: *On the wall were a few press clippings of the trial.* **2** [usually plural] a small piece cut from something bigger: *Grass clippings can be recycled to make fertilizer.*

clique /klik, klɪk/ n. [C] DISAPPROVING a small group of people who think they are special and do not want other people to join their group, and are not friendly toward people who are not in their group

cliqu·ish /'klikɪʃ/ also **cliqu·ey** /'kliki/ adj. DISAPPROVING a cliquish organization, club etc. has a lot of cliques or is controlled by them

clit·o·ris /'klɪtərɪs/ n. [C] a small part of a woman's outer sexual organs, where she can feel sexual pleasure —**clitoral** adj.

cloak¹ /klouk/ n. **1** [C] a warm piece of clothing like a coat that hangs loosely from your shoulders and does not have SLEEVEs, worn mainly in past times **2** [singular] an organization, activity, or way

of behaving that deliberately protects someone or keeps something secret: **[+ of]** *A cloak of secrecy surrounds their decision-making process.* | **[+ for]** *The group uses a charity organization as a cloak for terrorist activities.* | *Some politicians, **under the cloak of** democratic changes, are trying to gain advantages for themselves.*

cloak² v. [T usually passive] **1** to deliberately hide facts, feelings etc. so that people do not see or understand them: *Production of the fighter plane was **cloaked in secrecy**.* **2 be cloaked in darkness/rust/snow etc.** LITERARY covered in darkness, snow etc.: *The dining area was cloaked in a blue haze of smoke.*

cloak-and-dag·ger /ˌ. . '../ adj. [only before noun] very secret and mysterious, and usually involving the work of spies (SPY¹): *a cloak-and-dagger operation*

cloak·room /'klouk-rum/ n. [C] a small room where you can leave your coat; COATROOM

clob·ber /'klɑbə/ v. [T] INFORMAL **1** to hit someone very hard: *He got clobbered by a kid on the playground.* **2** to defeat someone very easily in a way that is embarrassing for the person or group that loses: *The Lakers clobbered the Jazz, 83 to 66.* **3** to affect someone or something badly, especially by making them lose money: *We got clobbered last year by rising production costs.*

cloche /klouʃ/ n. [C] a hat shaped like a bell, worn by women in the 1920s

clock¹ /klɑk/ n. [C] **1** an instrument in a room or on a public building that shows what time it is: *One clock says it's a quarter after six, and the other says six.* | *Mary set her clock for 6:30 a.m.* (=made sure it would ring at 6:30). | *Just as we left, the clock struck two.* | **set the clock(s) back/ahead/forward** (=change the time shown on the clock to one hour earlier or later, when the time officially changes) | **the clock is slow/fast** (=the clock shows a time that is earlier or later than the actual time) —see also ALARM CLOCK, CUCKOO CLOCK, GRANDFATHER CLOCK, O'CLOCK —compare WATCH² (1) **2 put/turn/set the clock back** to go back to the way things were done before, rather than trying new ideas or methods: *Women's groups warned that the law would turn the clock back fifty years.* **3 around the clock** all day and all night without stopping: *The emergency telephone lines operate around the clock.* —see also ROUND-THE-CLOCK **4 race/work against the clock a)** to work quickly in order to finish something before a particular time: *Doctors are racing against the clock to find a cure for AIDS.* **b)** if you run, swim etc. against the clock, you run or swim a particular distance as fast as possible **5 the twenty-four hour clock** a system for measuring time in which the hours of the day and night have numbers from 0 to 23 **6 start/stop the clock** also **the clock starts/stops** to start or stop measuring how much time is left in a game or sport that has a time limit: *The clock is stopped when a player runs out of bounds with the ball.* **7 run out the clock** also **kill the clock** if a sports team runs out the clock at the end of a game, they play very slowly because they have a higher SCORE and they do not want to give their opponents a chance to earn any more points —see also BIOLOGICAL CLOCK, BODY CLOCK, **clean sb's clock** (CLEAN² (6)), TIME CLOCK, **watch the clock** (WATCH¹ (5))

clock² v. [T] **1** to travel at a particular speed, or to measure the speed at which someone or something is moving: **[clock sb/sth at sth]** *The police clocked her at 42 mph in a 35 mph zone.* | *Erickson's fastball was clocked at 84 mph.* **2** to record the time taken to travel a certain distance: *The runner from Lynbrook clocked the fastest time this season on the mile run.* **3** INFORMAL to hit someone in the head

clock in phr. v. [I] to record on a special card the time you arrive at or begin work; PUNCH in: *The employees clock in at 8:30.*

clock out phr. v. [I] to record on a special card the time you stop or leave work; PUNCH out: *Hansen clocked out early today.*

clock up sth phr. v. [T] to reach or achieve a

particular number or amount: *The Dodgers have clocked up six wins in a row so far this season.* | *I clocked up 90,000 miles in my old Ford.*

clock ra·di·o /ˌ. ˈ.../ *n.* [C] a clock that you can set to turn on a radio to wake you up

clock speed /ˈ. ./ *n.* [C] TECHNICAL a measurement of how quickly a computer's CPU (=main controlling part) can deal with instructions

clock·wise /ˈklɑk-waɪz/ *adv.* moving in the same direction in which the HANDS (=parts that point to the time) of a clock move: *Turn the dial clockwise.* —**clockwise** *adj.* —opposite COUNTERCLOCKWISE

clock·work /ˈklɑk-wɔ˞k/ *n.* [U] **1 like clockwork a)** if something happens like clockwork, it happens in exactly the way you planned and without any problems: *The charity event was well organized and ran like clockwork.* **b)** happening at the same time and in the same way every time: *At 6:30 every evening, like clockwork, Ari went out to milk the cows.* **2 with clockwork precision/accuracy** in an extremely exact way

clod /klɑd/ *n.* [C] **1** a lump of mud or earth **2** INFORMAL someone who is not graceful and behaves in a stupid way

clod·hop·per /ˈklɑdˌhɑpɚ/ *n.* **clodhoppers** [plural] HUMOROUS heavy strong shoes

clog[1] /klɑg/ also **clog up** *v.* [I,T] to block something or become blocked, especially with a large amount of one type of thing: *An increased number of arrests has clogged the court system.* | *Don't pour that grease down the drain, or the sink will clog up again.* | [**clog sth with sth**] *The freeways were clogged with traffic.* —**clogged** *adj.: a clogged drain*

clog[2] *n.* [C usually plural] a shoe made of wood or with a wooden bottom —see picture at SHOE[1]

cloi·son·né /ˌklɔɪzəˈneɪ, ˌklwɑ-/ *n.* [U] a method of decorating something in which different colors of ENAMEL are put on the object and separated by thin metal bars —**cloisonné** *adj.: cloisonné earrings*

clois·ter[1] /ˈklɔɪstɚ/ *n.* [C] **1** a building where MONKS or NUNS live, that is meant to be quiet and away from the public **2** [usually plural] a covered passage that surrounds one side of a square garden or area of grass near a church, MONASTERY etc.

cloister[2] *v.* **cloister yourself** FORMAL to spend a lot of time alone in a room or building, especially because you need to study or work

clois·tered /ˈklɔɪstɚd/ *adj.* **1** living in a cloister as a NUN or MONK, and having little or no communication with the world outside **2** protected from the difficulties and demands of ordinary life: *the cloistered world of the university* **3** a cloistered building contains cloisters

clone[1] /kloʊn/ *n.* [C] **1** TECHNICAL an exact copy of an animal or plant that has the same DNA as the original animal or plant, because it was produced from one cell of that animal or plant **2** TECHNICAL a computer that is built as an exact copy of a more famous computer: *an IBM clone* —compare COMPATIBLE[2] **3** INFORMAL someone or something that seems to be an exact copy of someone or something else: *Jackson's latest hit is a near-clone of one of his previous songs.*

clone[2] *v.* [T] **1** to make an exact copy of a plant or animal by taking a cell from it and developing it artificially **2** to copy the number of a CELLULAR PHONE and then use that number on a different telephone, so that the owner receives the telephone bill

clonk /klɑŋk/ *n.* [C] the sound made when a heavy object falls to the ground or hits another heavy object —**clonk** *v.* [I,T]

clop /klɑp/ *v.* **clopped, clopping** [I] if a horse clops, its hooves (HOOF[1]) make a loud sound as they touch the ground —**clop** *n.* [C,U]

SW
1 1 **close**[1] /kloʊz/ *v.*

1 **shut** [I,T] to move something that was open so that there is no space or hole anymore, or to become moved in this way: *Ann closed her book and stood up.* | *The door closed silently behind Mariko.* | *Close*

the curtains – it's getting dark.* | *Okay, close your eyes and make a wish.* —see Usage Note at OPEN[2]

2 **for a period of time** [I,T] to stop allowing the public to use a store, street, school etc. for a limited time, for example during the night: *What time does the mall close tonight?* | *The hotel is closed in the winter.* | [**close sth to sth**] *Larkin Street has been closed to traffic.*

3 **stop operating** also **close down** [I,T] if a company, store etc. closes or you close it, it stops operating permanently: *Hundreds of timber mills have been closed since World War II.* | *After 85 years, the local newspaper closed down last month.*

4 **book/speech etc.** [I,T always + adv./prep.] if a book, play, speech etc. closes or someone closes it, it ends in a particular way: *The novel closes when the family reunites in Prague.* | [**close sth with/by etc.**] *Professor Schmidt closed his speech with a quote from Tolstoy.* | *In his closing remarks (=the last part of an official speech), Merrill said that the plan "reflects the hard work of many people."*

5 **close an account** to stop having an account with a bank

6 **financial/economic** [I always + adv./prep.] if a CURRENCY or business STOCK closes at a particular price, it is worth that amount at the end of a day's trading on the STOCK MARKET: *WalMart shares closed only 4 cents down.*

7 **close a deal/sale/contract etc.** to successfully arrange a business deal, sale etc.: *We met at Olson's attorney's office to close the sale.*

8 **offer/process** [I] to finish on a particular date: *The special offer for tickets closes June 3.*

9 **distance/difference** [I,T] to make the distance or difference between two things smaller: *Society needs to close the gap between rich and poor.*

10 **not available anymore** [T] to make an activity or opportunity unavailable: *The legislation closes a lot of loopholes in the tax law.*

11 **hold sth** [I,T always + adv./prep.] if someone's hands, arms etc. close around something or they close them around something, they hold it firmly: [**+ around/over etc.**] *The baby's tiny hand closed over Ken's finger.*

12 **wound** also **close up** [I,T] if a wound closes or you close it, it grows back together and becomes healthy, or you sew it together for it to become healthy: *The cut should close up within a few days.*

13 **close ranks a)** if people close ranks, they join together to protect each other, especially because their group, organization etc. is being criticized: *The Republicans in Congress have closed ranks and refused to vote for the president's proposal.* **b)** if soldiers close ranks, they stand closer together

14 **close the book(s) on sth** to stop working on something, especially a police case, because you cannot continue: *Vallejo police closed the books on a bizarre kidnapping case when the victim refused to cooperate.* —see also CLOSED, CLOSING DATE, **close/shut your eyes to sth** (EYE[1] (13)), **shut/close the door on sth** (DOOR (9))

close down *phr. v.* [I,T **close sth ↔ down**] if a company, store etc. closes down or is closed down, it stops operating permanently: *Health department officials ordered the restaurant to be closed down.*

close in *phr. v.* [I] to move closer to someone or something, especially in order to attack them: *The lion closed in for the kill.* [**+ on/around/upon etc.**] *Warplanes and tanks closed in on the eastern cities.*

close sth off *phr. v.* [T] to separate a road, room etc. from the area around it so that people cannot go there or use it: *One of the lanes is closed off for repairs.*

close on sb/sth *phr. v.* [T] **1** to get nearer to someone or something that is moving in front of you, ahead of you in a competition etc.: *The other car was closing in on us fast.* | *New polls indicate that Marshall is closing on the leading Republican candidate.* **2** to successfully arrange a LOAN, especially in order to buy a house: *The day we closed on our place on Elm Lane, we celebrated with a bottle of champagne.*

close sth ↔ out *phr. v.* [T] **1** to finish something in a particular way or by doing something: *The 49ers closed out the NFL regular season with a win against* *the Bears.* **2** if a store closes out a type of goods, they sell all of them cheaply: *The women's depart-ment is closing out this line of swimwear.*

close up *phr. v.* **1** [I,T **close** sth ↔ **up**] to stop being open to the public for a period of time: *The public swimming pool closes up after August.* **2 close up shop** to stop doing something for a period of time or permanently: *Some of the big ad agencies close up shop early for the holidays.* **3** [I,T **close** sth ↔ **up**] if a group of people close up, they move nearer together **4** [I,T **close** sth ↔ **up**] if a wound closes up or if something closes it up, it grows together or is sewn together and becomes healthy again **5** [I] to deliberately not show your true emotions or thoughts: *Every time I ask Jenny about it, she just closes up.*

close with sb/sth *phr. v.* [T] LITERARY to get closer to someone or something in order to do something such as attack them, watch them carefully etc.: *In the final assault, the Marines planned to close with the enemy and destroy him.*

close² /klous/ *adj.*

1 near in space not far: *The grocery store on Vic-tory Boulevard is closer.* | [+ **to**] *Amy's house is close to the school.* | *The victim was shot at close range* (=from very near). | *Our office is in close proximity to* (=very near) *the airport.*
2 near in time near to something in time: *Our birthdays are close together.* | [+ **to**] *By the time we left, it was close to midnight.*
3 like/love if two people are close, they like or love each other very much: *Mom and I are a lot closer now than we were when I was a teenager.* | [+ **to**] *I'm very close to my brothers.* | *We were pretty close friends in high school.*
4 careful a close examination, INSPECTION, OBSERVA-TION etc. is one in which you give careful attention to details: *Take a closer look at the statistics, and you'll find that Sebert's conclusion is not valid.* | *Sci-entists are keeping a close watch on the volcano.* | *The school district keeps a close eye on students with poor attendance records.* | *The Justice Department has paid close attention to the merger.*
5 number/amount almost the same amount or almost at the same level: [+ **to**] *Inflation is now close to 6%.*
6 similar if two things are close, they are very sim-ilar: [+ **to**] *Do you have any shoes that are closer in color to the bridesmaid's dress?* | *The island was the closest thing to paradise I can imagine.*
7 likely to happen seeming likely to happen or to do something soon: *We haven't finished remodeling the kitchen yet, but we're close.* | [+ **to**] *Barnes was close to death.* | [**close to doing sth**] *The two coun-tries are close to signing a peace agreement.*
8 competition/elections etc. won or lost by a very small amount: *It's always frustrating to lose a close game.* | *Polls of voters showed Alioto running a close second to Agnos* (=he is behind Agnos by a very small amount). | *At this point, the game is too close to call* (=no one can say who the winner will be).
9 a close relative a member of your family such as your brothers, sisters, parents etc. —opposite DIS-TANT
10 almost bad INFORMAL used when you just manage to avoid something bad, such as an accident: *That was close! You almost got hit by that car!* | *It was a close call* (=situation in which something bad almost happens) *for the astronauts when Gemini 8 swung out of control.*
11 keep in close contact/touch also stay in close contact/touch if two people keep in close contact, they see, talk to, or write to each other regularly
12 work/talk together if a relationship, associa-tion etc. is close, the people in it work or talk together a lot: *The school encourages close partner-ships between teachers and parents.* | *Our job requires close contact with the sales manager.* | *What we need now is closer cooperation between the sales and marketing staffs.*
13 close/you're close/that's close SPOKEN used to tell someone that they have almost guessed or answered something correctly: *"How far is it, a*

hundred miles?" "Close – it's around 120 miles to Las Vegas."
14 too close for comfort INFORMAL if something that happens is too close for comfort, it frightens you or makes you nervous: *That car that came around the corner was just a little too close for comfort.*
15 close, but no cigar INFORMAL used when some-thing someone does or says is almost correct or successful
16 in/at close quarters in a place where people are close together and there is not very much room to move: *Tuberculosis spreads easily when people are sheltered in close quarters.*
17 a close shave **a)** a process in which someone's hair is cut very close to the skin **b)** INFORMAL a situ-ation in which you escape from something that is bad or dangerous
18 close work a process or activity which involves looking at or handling things in a very skillful and careful way: *Embroidery is very close work.*
19 be close with money FORMAL to not be generous; STINGY (1) —closeness *n.* [U] —see also CLOSELY

close³ /klous/ *adv.* **1** not far away; near: *She was holding her baby close.* | *The girls were sitting close together on the bench.* | *Her parents live close by.* | *Cuneo didn't know it, but the police had been follow-ing close behind in an unmarked car.* | *I couldn't get close enough to see what was happening.* **2 close up/up close** from only a short distance away: *When I saw her close up, I realized she wasn't Jane.* **3 come close to (doing) sth** to almost do something: *Carey came very close to victory.* | *I didn't hit her, but I was so angry I came close to doing it.* **4 hit/strike close to home a)** if a remark or criticism hits close to home, it makes someone feel embarrassed or uncom-fortable because it affects them, their feelings or someone close to them, even if it was not intended to: *Jokes aren't funny when they strike too close to home.* **b)** if something bad happens close to home, you are directly affected by it because you see it in your daily life: *The tragedy of the fire hit close to home.* **5 come close on the heels of sth** to happen very soon after something else: *Another bad snow-storm came close on the heels of the weekend bliz-zard.* **6** near to the surface of something: *An electric razor doesn't really shave as close as a blade.* —see also play/keep your cards close to your chest (CARD¹ (13)) —see Usage Note at NEAR¹

close⁴ /klouz/ *n.* [singular] FORMAL the end of an activity or of a period of time: [+ **of**] *At the close of trading, stock prices had risen 1.2%.* | *Mayor Menino is scheduled to speak at the close of the conference.* | *Millions of people were homeless as the war drew to a close* (=came to an end). | *A fireworks display will bring the festivities to a close on Saturday evening* (=they will end the celebration). | *As four days of talks came to a close* (=ended), *the opposing sides were still unable to agree.*

close-cropped /ˌklous ˈkrɑpt◂/ *adj.* close-cropped grass or hair is cut very short

closed /klouzd/ *adj.* **1** restricted to a particular group of people, vehicles, activities etc.: *Community leaders are having a closed meeting with the mayor.* **2 be closed to sb/sth** to be unavailable to be used by a particular group of people or for a par-ticular activity: *Jackson Creek is closed to salmon fishing* (=salmon fishing is not allowed there). | *This area is closed to mountain bikes.* **3** if a particular subject is closed, you are not willing to discuss it anymore: *I called March 6 to cancel my order and considered the matter closed after that.* **4** not will-ing to accept new ideas or influences: *During the period of the Cold War, many Communist countries were virtually closed societies.* | *We don't want mem-bers of the jury to have closed minds.* **5 behind closed doors** something that takes place behind closed doors happens secretly

closed cap·tioned /ˌ. ˈ...◂/ *adj.* if a television pro-gram is closed captioned, the words that are being said are also broadcast in written form, which can

C

be shown at the bottom of the screen if you have a special piece of equipment attached to your television —**closed captioning** n. [U] —**closed caption** n. [C usually plural]

closed-cir·cuit tel·e·vi·sion /ˌ... '..../ also **closed-circuit TV** /ˌ.. .. .'./ n. [U] a system in which television pictures of an event are shown on a television screen in another room or building while the event is happening, but are not broadcast

closed-door /ˌ. '.◂/ adj. [only before noun] closed-door meetings or talks take place secretly

close-down /'kloʊzdaʊn/ n. [C] a situation in which work in a company, factory etc. is stopped, either for a short time or permanently

closed shop /ˌ. '.◂/ n. [C] a company, factory etc. where all workers must belong to a particular UNION

close-fit·ting /ˌkloʊs 'fɪtɪŋ/ adj. close-fitting clothes are tight and show the shape of your body

close-knit /ˌkloʊs 'nɪt◂/ also **closely-knit** /ˌ.. '.◂/ adj. a close-knit group of people such as a family have good relationships with each other and care about each other: a close-knit team

s w **close·ly** /'kloʊsli/ adv. **1** if you look at or study something closely, you look at it in detail: Watch the area closely to make sure it does not become infected. | Voters should closely examine all the issues. **2** near to other things in space or time: The flash of lightning was closely followed by thunder. | We were so closely packed in the elevator that I could hardly move. **3** in a way that is similar to something or someone else: The unsuccessful holdup closely resembles two other bank robberies. **4** if you work closely with someone, you work with them often and help each other: Bush worked closely with Gorbachev to improve Soviet relations with the U.S. **5** in a way that shows two or more things are strongly related to each other: These two issues are closely linked, and it makes sense to consider them together.

close-mouthed /ˌkloʊs 'maʊθd◂,-'maʊθt◂/ also **closed-mouthed** adj. not willing to say much because you are trying to keep a secret

close-out /'kloʊzaʊt/ adj. a **closeout sale/price/goods** etc. a sale to get rid of goods cheaply, or something that is sold cheaply: They are having a closeout sale on swimwear at Macy's. —**closeout** n. [C]

close-set /ˌkloʊs 'sɛt◂/ adj. close-set eyes are very near to each other

s w **clos·et¹** /'klɑzɪt/ n. [C] **1** an area that you keep clothes and other things in, built behind the wall of a room with a door on the front: I have a closet full of clothes that don't fit. | The master bedroom has a **walk-in closet** (=a closet like a small room). —see picture on page 423 **2 come out of the closet** also **come out** INFORMAL **a)** to tell people that you are HOMOSEXUAL (=sexually attracted to people who are the same sex as you) after keeping that a secret **b)** to admit you believe something or to discuss something that was previously kept secret: The trial brought the issue of sexual harassment out of the closet. **3 be in the closet** INFORMAL to not tell people that you are HOMOSEXUAL —see also **a skeleton in the closet** (SKELETON (5)), WATER CLOSET

closet² adj. a **closet homosexual/liberal/alcoholic** etc. someone who is a HOMOSEXUAL, LIBERAL etc. but who does not say in public what they think or do in private

closet³ v. [T usually passive] to keep someone in a room away from other people in order to be alone or to discuss something private: Tom spent most of his time closeted in his study, surrounded by his books.

clos·et·ed /'klɑzɪtɪd/ adj. a closeted HOMOSEXUAL person is someone who has not told people publicly that they are sexually attracted to people of the same sex as themselves

close-up /'kloʊs ʌp/ n. [C,U] a photograph that someone takes from very near: I want to get a close-up of the children's faces. | Much of the movie is shot **in close-up** (=from very near).

clos·ing /'kloʊzɪŋ/ adj. [only before noun] happening or done at the end of a period of time or event: In his closing remarks, Pollard emphasized the need for more research. | The UN was set up during the closing stages of World War II.

closing date /'.. ,./ n. [C] the last official date on which it is possible to do something: The closing date on the deal is set for August 6.

clo·sure /'kloʊʒɚ/ n. **1** [C,U] the act of permanently closing a building, factory, school etc.: Several military bases are threatened with closure. **2 closure of a road/bridge** etc. a process in which a road, bridge etc. is blocked for a short time so that people cannot use it **3** [U] the act of bringing an event or a period of time to an end, or the feeling that something has been completely dealt with: Funerals help give people a sense of closure.

clot¹ /klɑt/ v. **clotted, clotting** [I,T] if a liquid such as blood or milk clots or something clots it, it becomes thicker and more solid

clot² n. [C] a thick, almost solid mass formed when blood, milk, or some other liquids dry

cloth /klɔθ/ n. **1** [U] material that is made from s w cotton, wool etc. and used for making things such as clothes: These pants are made with the finest wool cloth. | cloth napkins **2** [C] a piece of cloth used for a particular purpose: Put the bread dough in a bowl, and cover it with a damp cloth. | Dry the fruit thoroughly with a dish cloth. **3 a man of the cloth** FORMAL OR HUMOROUS a Christian priest or minister —compare CLOTHES —see Usage Note at CLOTHING

USAGE NOTE: CLOTH

WORD CHOICE: cloth, fabric, material
Use **cloth** as an uncountable noun to talk about the cotton, wool etc. that is used for making clothes: She bought some red cloth to make a dress. **Fabric** can be countable or uncountable, and can be used about clothes and things other than clothes: The sheets were made of a silky fabric. | fine Italian fabrics. When **material** is an uncountable noun, it means the same as **fabric**: There isn't enough material to make curtains.

---

clothe /kloʊð/ v. [T usually passive] FORMAL **1** to s w dress someone or be dressed in a particular way: The children were fast asleep on the bed, still **fully clothed** (=with all of their clothes on). **2** to provide clothes for someone: They could barely keep the family fed and clothed. **3 be clothed in sth** to be completely covered by something: We were served swordfish clothed in a pale, creamy sauce.

clothes

clothes

cloth/material

waterproof clothing

garments/ articles of clothing

clothes /klouz, klouðz/ n. [plural] the things that people wear to cover their bodies or to keep warm: *It's hard to find clothes that fit me.* | *Dana always wears such nice clothes.* | *Pete took his clothes off and went to bed.* | **work/school/play clothes** (=clothes that are appropriate for work, school etc.) —see also **a change of clothes/underwear** (CHANGE² (6)) —see Usage Note at CLOTHING

clothes·horse /'klouzhɔrs/ n. [C] INFORMAL someone who is too interested in clothes and who likes to have many different clothes

clothes·line /'klouzlaɪn/ n. [C] a rope on which you hang clothes outside to dry

clothes·pin /'klouzpɪn/ n. [C] a small wooden or plastic object that you use to fasten wet clothes to a clothesline —see picture at PIN

cloth·ier /'klouðyɚ/ n. [C] OLD-FASHIONED someone who makes or sells men's clothes or material for clothes

cloth·ing /'klouðɪŋ/ n. [U] clothes that people wear: *The church provides blankets and clothing for homeless children.* | *an expensive clothing store* | *Lab workers must wear protective clothing.* | **piece/item/article of clothing** | *Bring several warm pieces of clothing.*

USAGE NOTE: CLOTHING

WORD CHOICE: clothing, clothes, cloth, costume, garment, something to wear
Use **clothing** when you are thinking about clothes in general: *The refugees need food and clothing.* To talk about the particular things people wear, use **clothes**: *Here, take off those wet clothes and put this on.* **Cloth** is what clothes are made of: *a shirt made of cotton cloth.* **Costumes** are special clothes that people wear in a play or movie, or that people wear at Halloween to make themselves look like a particular type of person or an animal. An **item/piece of clothing** is one separate thing that you can wear. **Garment** is a formal word for a piece of clothing: *Only three garments may be taken into the fitting room.* When you are talking about clothes for a particular event, you often say **something to wear**: *I have to find something to wear to Nathan's wedding.*

---

clo·ture /'kloutʃɚ/ n. [C] TECHNICAL a way of ending an argument over a BILL¹ (2) in the U.S. government and forcing a vote on it

cloud¹ /klaud/ n.
1 in the sky [C,U] a white or gray mass in the sky that consists of very small drops of water: *Dark clouds gathered overhead.* | *The plane was unable to land due to strong winds and low cloud cover.*
2 in the air [C] a mass of something in the air, or a large number of things moving together in the air: *a cloud of flies* | **a cloud of dust/smoke/gas etc.** *The volcano shot clouds of smoke and ash into the air.*
3 problem [C] something that makes you feel afraid or worried: [+ of] *Businesses are worried by the clouds of a possible trade war.* | *With the budget problem not yet solved, there are some* **clouds on the horizon** (=things that may cause problems). | *Several players are injured, and this has* **cast a cloud over** (=caused problems for) *the rest of the season.*
4 under a cloud (of sth) INFORMAL if someone is under a cloud, people have a bad opinion of them because they did something wrong: *Rylan resigned under a cloud of suspicion.*
5 be on cloud nine INFORMAL to be very happy about something: *Adam was on cloud nine after the birth of his son.*
6 every cloud has a silver lining used to say that there is something good even in a situation that seems very sad or difficult —see also **have your head in the clouds** (HEAD¹ (36))

cloud² v.
1 glass/liquid also **cloud over/up** [T] if something clouds a transparent material such as glass or a liquid, it becomes less clear and more difficult to see through: *The display cases were clouded with dust.*
2 thoughts/memories [T] to make someone less able to think clearly or remember things: *The decision*

to put a parent in a nursing home can be clouded by guilt. | *Alcohol had clouded his judgment.*
3 spoil sth [T] to make something less nice than it should have been, because of problems or something bad that has happened: *The team's victory was clouded by the tragic events in their hometown.*
4 confuse [T] to make something difficult to understand, especially by introducing ideas or information that are not related to it: *The Supreme Court's latest decision has only* **clouded the issue** *of gun control.*
5 face also **cloud over** [I,T] LITERARY if someone's expression clouds or if something clouds it, they start to look angry or sad: *His face clouded when he saw her.*
6 cover with clouds [T] to cover something with clouds: *Thick mist clouded the mountaintops.*
cloud over phr. v. [I] **1** if the sky clouds over, it becomes dark and full of clouds **2** [I] if someone's expression clouds over, they start to look angry or sad: *Anne's face clouded over as she remembered.*
cloud up phr. v. **1** [I,T] if a transparent material such as glass or a liquid clouds up or if something clouds it up, it becomes less clear and more difficult to see through **2** [I] if the sky clouds up, it becomes dark and full of clouds

cloud·burst /'klaudbɚst/ n. [C] a sudden short rain storm

cloud·ed /'klaudɪd/ adj. **1** not clear, so that you cannot see through it easily: *clouded glass* **2** a clouded face or expression shows that someone is unhappy or angry

cloud·less /'klaudlɪs/ adj. a cloudless sky is clear and bright

cloud·y /'klaudi/ adj. cloudier, cloudiest **1** cloudy weather is dark because the sky is full of clouds: *a cloudy day* **2** cloudy liquids are not clear or transparent **3** cloudy thoughts, memories etc. are not very clear or exact

clout¹ /klaut/ n. [U] INFORMAL the power to influence other people's decisions | **political/economic clout** *Conservative Christian groups have been gaining political clout in Washington.*

clout² v. [T] INFORMAL to hit someone or something hard: *Mitchell has clouted 109 home runs in the last 3 years.*

clove¹ /klouv/ n. **1** [C] one of the separate pieces that a GARLIC (=a plant similar to an onion) plant consists of **2** [C,U] a dried flower BUD with a strong sweet smell that is used as a SPICE

clove² v. a past tense of CLEAVE

clo·ven /'klouvən/ v. a past participle of CLEAVE

cloven hoof /,.. './ n. [C] a HOOF that is divided into two parts, which animals such as goats or sheep have

clo·ver /'klouvɚ/ n. [U] **1** a small plant with three round leaves on each stem **2 a four-leaf clover** a clover plant that has four round leaves and is thought to bring good luck to the person who finds it **3 be in clover** INFORMAL to be living comfortably because you have plenty of money

clo·ver·leaf /'klouvɚlif/ n. [C] **1** a network of curved roads that connect two main roads where they cross, so that someone can drive from one road to the other without stopping **2** the leaf of a clover plant

clown¹ /klaun/ n. [C] **1** a performer who wears funny clothes and tries to make people laugh, especially at a CIRCUS **2** INFORMAL a stupid or annoying person: *Some clown cut in front of me on the freeway this morning and almost hit me.* **3** someone who often makes jokes or behaves in a funny or silly way: *Doug was the class clown* (=someone at school who behaves in a funny or silly way) *when we were in high school.*

clown² also **clown around** v. [I] to behave in a silly or funny way: *Stop clowning around and get back to work.*

clown·ish /'klaunɪʃ/ adj. silly or stupid —**clownishly** adv. —**clownishness** n. [U]

C

cloy·ing /ˈklɔɪ-ɪŋ/ *adj.* **1** a cloying attitude or quality annoys you because it is too nice and seems false: *The novel's plot is interesting, but the dialogue is just too cloying.* **2** cloying food or smells are too sweet and make you feel sick: *the cloying smell of cheap perfume*

cloze /kloʊz/ *adj.* **a cloze test/exercise/drill etc.** a test, exercise etc. in which students have to write the correct words into the spaces that have been left empty in a short piece of writing

club¹ /klʌb/ *n.* [C]
1 for an activity/sport an organization for people who share a particular interest or enjoy similar activities, or a group of people who meet together to do something they are interested in: *There is even a club for owners of Volkswagen buses.* | *I decided to join the ski club in college.* | *She belongs to a health club and works out three times a week.*
2 for dancing/music a place where people go to dance, listen to music, and meet socially, or where they go to listen to COMEDIANS: *a jazz club* | *a comedy club* | *They're going out for dinner and then to a club.*
3 building the building or place where people who belong to an organization meet in order to do activities or play sports: *The restaurant is located next to the fitness club.*
4 professional sport a professional organization including the players, managers, and owners of a sports team: *There are a number of clubs interested in getting a new quarterback.* | *The Red Sox are a hot ball club* (=baseball team) *this season.*
5 for hitting a ball a special stick used in GOLF to hit the ball; GOLF CLUB
6 a book/record club etc. an organization that people join in order to buy books, records etc. cheaply: *the Book-of-the-Month Club*
7 weapon a thick heavy stick used to hit people or things
8 in card games **a)** a black shape with three round leaves, printed on cards for games **b)** clubs [plural] the SUIT (=group of cards) that has this shape printed on them: *the ace of clubs*
9 for men **a)** an organization, usually for men only, that they pay to become members of so that they can relax and enjoy social activities with other members **b)** a room or building where members of this type of organization go to relax and enjoy social activities
10 join the club also **welcome to the club** SPOKEN used after someone has described a bad situation that they are in, to tell them that you are in the same situation: *"He never listens to my ideas." "Join the club."* —see also COUNTRY CLUB, FAN CLUB

club² *v.* **clubbed, clubbing** [T] to hit someone hard with a thick heavy object: *The teenage boy had been clubbed to death.*

club·bing /ˈklʌbɪŋ/ *n.* **1 go clubbing** INFORMAL to go to clubs where you can dance to popular music **2** [U] the action of hitting someone or something with a CLUB: *Two men were arrested for the clubbing and subsequent murder of Lester Monroe.* —clubber *n.* [C]

club foot /ˌ. ˈ./ *n.* [C,U] a foot that has been badly twisted since birth and that prevents someone from walking correctly, or the medical condition of having this

club·house /ˈklʌbhaʊs/ *n.* [C] **1** a DRESSING ROOM for a sports team at a STADIUM or sports field **2** a building used by a club **3** a building at a GOLF COURSE that usually has a small restaurant and a store where you can buy equipment

club sand·wich /ˌ. ˈ../ *n.* [C] a large SANDWICH consisting of three pieces of bread with meat and cheese between them

club so·da /ˌ. ˈ../ *n.* [C,U] water filled with BUBBLES that is often mixed with other drinks

cluck¹ /klʌk/ *v.* **1** [I] to make a noise like a HEN (=female chicken) **2** [I,T] to express sympathy, approval, or disapproval by saying something, or by

making a short low noise with your tongue: *Jessica clucked her tongue in sympathy when she saw his bruised arm.* | **[+ over/around/about]** *The older relatives were clucking over the new baby.* —clucking *adj.*

cluck² *n.* **1** [C] a low short noise made a HEN (=female chicken) **2** [C] a sound made with your tongue, used to show disapproval or sympathy: *Mrs. Newman shook her head with a disapproving cluck.* **3 dumb/stupid cluck** INFORMAL a stupid person: *You dumb cluck, why'd you tell him?*

clue¹ /klu/ *n.* [C] **1** an object, piece of information, reason etc. that helps you explain something or solve a crime: *The FBI sorted through the suspects' garbage in hopes of finding clues.* | **[+ to/about]** *Unexplained weight loss may be an early clue to a health problem.* | *Scientists examine fossils for clues about how dinosaurs lived and died.* | **[+ as to]** *Childhood experiences may provide a clue as to why some adults develop eating disorders.* | *Heyward police continued searching for clues in the death of a 43-year-old man.* **2 not have a clue** also **have no clue** INFORMAL **a)** to not have any idea about the answer to a question, how to do something, what a situation is etc.: *He doesn't seem to have a clue about the business.* | *Until I actually got there, I had no clue what I was going to say.* **3** a piece of information that helps you solve a PUZZLE, answer a question etc.: *I'll give you a clue – it's a kind of bird.* **4** a question that you must solve in order to find the answer to a CROSSWORD PUZZLE or other game

clue² *v.*
clue sb **in** *phr. v.* [T] INFORMAL to give someone information about something: **[+ on]** *Mark clued me in on how the computer system works.*

clued-in /ˌ. ˈ./ *adj.* INFORMAL knowing a lot about something

clue·less /ˈklulɪs/ *adj.* INFORMAL having no understanding or knowledge of something: *Joe's totally clueless.* | **[+ about]** *Many teachers are clueless about the needs of immigrant students.*

clump¹ /klʌmp/ *n.* **1** [C] a group of trees, bushes, or other plants growing very close together: **[+ of]** *a clump of daffodils* **2** [C + of] a small mass of something such as earth or mud **3** [U] the sound of someone walking with heavy steps —clumpy *adj.*

clump² *v.* **1** also **clump together** [I] to form a group or mass: *Humidity causes sugar to clump.* **2** [I always + adv./prep.] to walk with slow noisy steps: **[+ up/down/along etc.]** *The kids clumped up the stairs in their snowboots.* **3** [T always + adv./prep.] to put something heavy down with a loud noise

clum·sy /ˈklʌmzi/ *adj.* **clumsier, clumsiest 1** moving in an awkward way and tending to break things: *a clumsy, shy thirteen-year-old boy* | *Dana made a clumsy attempt to catch the ball.* **2** done carelessly or badly, without enough thought: *His writing is clumsy and unconvincing.* | *The show is a clumsy blend of news and entertainment.* **3** a clumsy object is not easy to use and is often large and heavy: *a clumsy camera* —clumsily *adv.* —clumsiness *n.* [U]

clung /klʌŋ/ *v.* the past tense and past participle of CLING

clunk /klʌŋk/ *n.* [singular] a loud sound made when two heavy objects hit each other —clunk *v.* [I,T]

clunk·er /ˈklʌŋkɚ/ *n.* [C] INFORMAL **1** an old car or other machine that does not work very well **2** something that is completely unsuccessful because people think it is stupid or wrong: *Studio executives should have put Jonathan Winters in a good show, not a clunker like this.*

clunk·y /ˈklʌŋki/ *adj.* **clunkier, clunkiest** heavy and awkward to wear or use: *a pair of clunky old boots*

clus·ter¹ /ˈklʌstɚ/ *n.* [C] **1** a group of things of the same kind that are very close together: **[+ of]** *a cluster of grapes* | *a cluster of office buildings* **2** a group of people all in the same place: **[+ of]** *A cluster of children stood around the ice cream van.* **3** a small piece of metal fastened to a soldier's uniform to show a high class of honor

cluster² *v.* [I always + adv./prep., T always + adv./prep.] to come together or be together in a group, or to be put together in a group: [+ **around/together** etc.] *Reporters had clustered together outside Fitzroy's office.*

cluster bomb /'.. ,./ *n.* [C] a bomb that sends out a lot of smaller bombs when it explodes —**cluster-bomb** *v.* [T]

clutch[1] /klʌtʃ/ *v.* [T] to hold something or someone tightly, especially because you are afraid, or you do not want to lose something: *Joanne clutched her mother's hand.* | [+ **at**] *Paxton fell, clutching at his knee.* —see also **be grasping/clutching at straws** (STRAW (4))

clutch[2] *n.*
1 vehicle [C] the PEDAL or LEVER in a vehicle that you press before you change GEARs, or the part that the pedal or lever controls | **push in/step on/put in the clutch** (=start to use the clutch) | **let out the clutch/release the clutch** *Put the car in first gear and slowly release the clutch.* —see picture at ENGINE and see picture on page 427
2 in the clutch INFORMAL in an important or difficult situation: *They need a player who can score consistently in the clutch.* | *Count on Tom to* **come through in the clutch** (=succeed in a difficult situation).
3 sb's clutches also **the clutches of sb** HUMOROUS the power, influence, or control that someone has over you: *Sam joined the Navy to escape from his mother's clutches.*
4 tight hold [singular] a tight hold that someone has on something: *I shook myself free of her clutch*
5 a clutch of sb/sth a small group of similar things or people: *A clutch of high school football players were suspended for drinking.*
6 eggs [C] the number of eggs a chicken produces at one time

clutch[3] *adj.* [only before noun] **1** done well during a difficult situation: *Clark made a clutch free throw to tie the game.* **2** able to perform well in a difficult situation: *Jordan's a good clutch player.*

clutch bag /'. ./ *n.* [C] a small PURSE that women carry in their hand, used especially on formal social occasions

clut·ter[1] /'klʌtər/ also **clutter up** *v.* [T] to make something messy by filling or covering it with things: *Piles of books and papers cluttered his desk.* | [**be cluttered (up) with sth**] *Their apartment was cluttered with photographs and books.* —**cluttered** *adj.*

clutter[2] *n.* [U] a lot of things that are scattered in a messy way: *I try to keep my desk free of clutter.*

cm the written abbreviation of CENTIMETER

Cmdr. the written abbreviation of Commander

CNN *n.* Cable News Network; an organization that broadcasts television news programs all over the world

C-note /'si noʊt/ *n.* [C] SLANG a 100 dollar bill

C.O. *n.* [C] Commanding Officer; an officer who commands a military unit

c/o the written abbreviation of "in care of," used when you are sending a letter for someone to another person who will keep it for them: *Send the letter to me c/o Anne Miller, 8 Brown St., Peoria, Illinois.*

CO *n.* the written abbreviation of Colorado

Co. 1 the written abbreviation of "company": *E.F. Hutton & Co.* **2** the written abbreviation of COUNTY

co- /koʊ/ *prefix* **1** together with someone or something else: *to coexist* (=exist together or at the same time) | *a coeducational school* (=with boys and girls together) **2** doing something with someone else, either with equal responsibility or with a little less: *my co-author* (=someone who wrote the book with me) | *the copilot* (=someone who helps a pilot)

s w **coach**[1] /koʊtʃ/ *n.* **1** [C] someone who trains a person or team in a sport: *a basketball coach* | *She's the coach of the volleyball team.* **2** [U] the cheapest type of seats on an airplane or a train: *Many business people have begun flying coach to save money.* **3** someone who gives private lessons in singing, acting etc.: *a drama coach* **4** [C] a large vehicle for people, pulled by horses and used in past times

5 [C] FORMAL a bus with space for suitcases under the seating area, used for trips between cities

coach[2] *v.* **1** [I,T] to train a person or team in a sport: *James used to coach high school football.* **2** [T] to give someone private lessons in singing, acting etc. **3** [T] to give someone instruction in what they should say or do in a particular situation, used especially when you disapprove of this: [**coach sb on sth**] *Kellogg coached the mayor on handling the questions from the press.* **4** [T] to give someone special help in preparing for a test

coach·ing /'koʊtʃɪŋ/ *n.* [U] **1** the process or job of training a person or team in a sport: *The difference between the two teams is the quality of the coaching.* **2** the process of helping someone prepare for an important test or prepare what they should say or do in a particular situation: *Coaching may raise some students' SAT scores.*

coach·man /'koʊtʃmən/ *n.* [C] someone who drove a COACH[1] (4) pulled by horses in past times

co·ag·u·late /koʊ'ægyə,leɪt/ *v.* [I,T] to change from a liquid into a thick substance or a solid: *The salt solution helps coagulate the soy milk into clumps.* —**coagulation** /koʊ,ægyə'leɪʃən/ *n.* [U]

coal /koʊl/ *n.* **1** [U] a black mineral that is dug from s w the earth and burned for heat: *coal miners* **2** [C usually plural] a small piece of something such as wood that is GLOWing because it is burning or has been burned: *Grill the steaks over medium-hot coals for 5–7 minutes on each side.* **3** [C usually plural] a piece of coal, especially one that is burning **4 bring/take coals to Newcastle** OLD-FASHIONED to take something to a place where there is already plenty of it available —see also **rake sb over the coals** (RAKE[2] (4))

co·a·lesce /,koʊə'lɛs/ *v.* [I] FORMAL to grow together or combine to form one single group: *A number of special interests are coalescing to protest against the bill.* —**coalescence** *n.* [U]

coal·field /'koʊlfild/ *n.* [C] an area where there is coal under the ground

coal gas /'. ./ *n.* [U] gas produced by burning coal, used especially for electricity and heating —compare NATURAL GAS

co·a·li·tion /,koʊə'lɪʃən/ *n.* **1** [C] a group of people s w who join together to achieve a particular purpose: *the California Coalition for Immigrant Rights* | *Community leaders hope to form a health-care reform coalition.* **2** [C] a union of separate political parties that allows them to form a government or fight an election together: *a three-party coalition* | *Italy's* **coalition government** (=a government that is run by different political parties working together) *collapsed in March.* **3** [U] a process in which two or more political parties or groups join together

coal mine, coalmine /'. ./ *n.* [C] a mine from which coal is dug —**coal miner** *n.* [C]

coal tar /'. ./ *n.* [U] a thick black sticky liquid made by heating coal without air, from which many medicines and chemical products are made

coarse /kɔrs/ *adj.* **1** feeling rough and thick, rather than smooth or fine: *A coarse cloth was made from the local wool.* | *coarse sand* **2** impolite and offensive, especially concerning sex: *Several comedians have been criticized for their coarse humor.* —**coarsely** *adv.* —**coarseness** *n.* [U]

coars·en /'kɔrsən/ *v.* [I,T] FORMAL **1** to become thicker or rougher, or to make something thicker or rougher: *Hard work had coarsened his hands.* **2** to become or to make someone less polite in the way they talk or behave: *The political process has become coarsened.*

coast[1] /koʊst/ *n.* **1** [C] the area where the land meets s w the ocean: *We drove along the Pacific coast to* Seattle. | *I enjoy bicycling along the Three Capes Route* **on the coast** (=on the land near the ocean) *of Oregon.* | *They live on a small island* **off the coast** (=in the ocean near the land) *of Scotland.* | *His business has grown to 29 stores from* **coast to coast**

(=across the whole country). **2 the coast is clear** INFORMAL used to say that it is safe for you to do something without risking being seen or caught: *We raced out the door as soon as the coast was clear.* —see Usage Note at SHORE[1]

coast[2] *v.* [I] **1** [always + adv./prep.] to keep moving in a car or on a bicycle without using more power: [+ **down/around/along** etc.] *Bev coasted downhill on her bicycle.* **2** to do something without using any effort: *She used to be an honor student, but now she's just coasting.* | [+ **to/through**] *Wilson coasted to victory in the election.* **3** TECHNICAL to sail in a boat along the coast while staying close to land

coast·al /'koʊstl/ *adj.* [only before noun] in the ocean or on the land near the coast: *the coastal waters of Florida*

coast·er /'koʊstɚ/ *n.* [C] **1** a small thin object you put under a glass or cup, to protect a table from heat or liquids **2** a ship that sails from port to port along a coast, but does not go further out into the ocean —see also ROLLER COASTER

coaster brake /'.. ,./ *n.* [C] a BRAKE on some types of bicycles that works when you move the PEDALS backward

Coast Guard /'. ./ *n.* **the Coast Guard** the part of the military that is in charge of watching for ships in danger and preventing illegal activities in the ocean —compare MARINES (1), NAVY[1] (1)

coast·line /'koʊstlaɪn/ *n.* [C] the land on the edge of the coast: *a rocky coastline*

s w **coat**[1] /koʊt/ *n.* [C] **1** a piece of clothing with long SLEEVES that you wear over your clothes to protect them or to keep warm: *her heavy winter coat* | *Billy! Put your coat on – it's cold outside!* | *The kids took off their coats and threw them on the floor.* **2** a JACKET that you wear as part of a suit **3** the fur, wool, or hair that covers an animal's body: *Huskies have a nice thick coat.* **4** a thin layer of something that covers a surface: [+ **of**] *a coat of paint* —see also -COATED, COATING

coat[2] *v.* [T] to cover a surface with a thin layer of something: *Dust coated all of the furniture.* | [**coat sth with/in sth**] *Next coat the fish with bread-crumbs.* —see also -COATED, SUGAR-COATED

coat check /'. ./ *n.* [C] a room in a public building where you can leave your coat, hat etc. while you are in the building; CLOAKROOM —**coat checker** *n.* [C]

-coated /koʊtɪd/ *suffix* **1** metal-coated/plastic-coated etc. covered with a thin layer of metal etc. —see also SUGAR-COATED **2** white-coated/fur-coated/winter-coated etc. wearing a white fur etc. coat

coat hang·er /'. ,../ *n.* [C] a HANGER

coat·ing /'koʊtɪŋ/ *n.* [C] a thin layer of something that covers a surface: *Rub a thin coating of oil onto the peppers, then put them on the grill.*

coat of arms /,. . './ *n. plural* **coats of arms** [C] a set of pictures or patterns painted on a SHIELD and used as the special sign of a family, town, university etc.

coat of mail /,. . './ *n. plural* **coats of mail** [C] a coat made of metal rings that was worn to protect the top part of a soldier's body in the Middle Ages

coat rack /'. ./ *n.* [C] a board or pole with hooks on it that you hang coats on

coat·room /'koʊtrum/ *n.* [C] a CLOAKROOM

coat stand /'. ./ *n.* [C] a tall pole with hooks at the top that you hang coats on

coat·tails /'koʊt-teɪlz/ *n.* [plural] **1** if someone or something uses someone's coattails to achieve something, they are helped by that person's success or power: *Alarcon rose to power on Bucaram's coattails.* **2** the cloth at the back of a TAILCOAT that is divided into two pieces

coax /koʊks/ *v.* **1** [I,T] to persuade someone to do something that they do not want to do by talking to them in a kind, gentle, and patient way: *"How about letting me borrow your car?" Santos coaxed.* | [**coax**

sb **into (doing) sth**] *Julie tried to coax her two children into smiling for a photo with Santa.* | [**coax sb to do sth**] *Scott coaxed him to give the new baby a kiss.* | [**coax sb out/down/back etc.**] *Members of the SWAT team coaxed Faustino out of his home.* **2** [T] to make something or someone do something by dealing with it in a slow, patient, and careful way: *Many bulbs can be coaxed into bloom early.* | [**coax sth out of sth**] *He hasn't lost his ability to coax outstanding performances out of his musicians.* | *They coax vegetables and rice from the poor soil.* —**coaxing** *n.* [U] —**coaxingly** *adv.*

cob /kɑb/ *n.* [C] **1** the long hard middle part of an EAR of corn: *We had hot dogs, hamburgers, and **corn on the cob**.* **2** a male SWAN **3** a type of horse that is strong and has short legs

co·balt /'koʊbɔlt/ *n.* [U] **1** *symbol* **Co** a shiny silver-white metal that is a chemical ELEMENT, and that is used to make some metals and to give a blue color to some substances **2** a deep blue color, or a bright blue-green color —**cobalt** *adj.*

Cobb /kɑb/**, Ty** /taɪ/ (1886–1961) a U.S. baseball player, known for being the first person to score 4000 BASE HITS

cob·ble[1] /'kɑbəl/ *v.* [T] **1** OLD-FASHIONED to repair or make shoes **2** to put COBBLESTONES on a street **cobble** sth **together** *phr. v.* [T] INFORMAL to quickly make something that is useful but not perfect: *Several officials worked late trying to cobble together an agreement.* | *They managed to cobble together a homemade radio.*

cobble[2] *n.* [C] a cobblestone

cob·bled /'kɑbəld/ *adj.* a cobbled street is covered with cobblestones

cob·bler /'kɑblɚ/ *n.* [C] **1** cooked fruit covered with a sweet, bread-like mixture: *warm peach cobbler* **2** OLD-FASHIONED someone who makes and repairs shoes

cob·ble·stone /'kɑbəl,stoʊn/ *n.* [C] a small round stone set in the ground, especially in past times, to make a hard surface for a road

co·bra /'koʊbrə/ *n.* [C] a poisonous African or Asian snake that can spread the skin of its neck to make itself look bigger

co·brand·ing /'koʊ,brændɪŋ/ *n.* [U] the activity of two companies helping each other to do business or sell products by using both company names, for example, having a particular bank inside a particular store

cob·web /'kɑbwɛb/ *n.* [C] **1** a very fine network of sticky threads made by a SPIDER to catch insects, that is covered in dust and makes a room look dirty —compare SPIDERWEB **2** blow/brush/clear etc. **the cobwebs** to do something, especially go outside, in order to help yourself to think more clearly and have more energy: [+ **off/away**] *I went for a walk to clear away the cobwebs.* —**cobwebbed** *adj.* —**cobwebby** *adj.*

co·ca /'koʊkə/ *n.* [U] a South American bush whose leaves are used to make cocaine

Co·ca-Co·la /,koʊkə 'koʊlə/ *n.* [C,U] TRADEMARK a sweet brown SOFT DRINK, or a glass of this drink; COKE

co·caine /koʊ'keɪn, 'koʊkeɪn/ *n.* [U] a drug, usually in the form of a white powder, that is taken illegally for pleasure or used in some medical situations to prevent pain —see also CRACK[2] (7)

coc·cyx /'kɑksɪks/ *n. plural* **coccyxes** or **coccyges** /'kɑksɪdʒiz, kɑk'saɪdʒiz/ [C] TECHNICAL the small bone at the bottom of your SPINE; TAILBONE —see picture at SKELETON

coch·i·neal /'kɑtʃə,nil, ,koʊ-/ *n.* [U] a red substance used to give food a red color

Co·chise /koʊ'tʃis, -'tʃiz/ (?1812–1874) a Native American chief of the Apaches who fought against U.S. soldiers from 1861 to 1872 in order to prevent them from taking land from his people

coch·le·a /'kɑkliə, 'koʊ-/ *n. plural* **cochleas** or **cochleae** /-li-i, -liaɪ/ [C] TECHNICAL a part of the inner ear

cock[1] /kɑk/ *n.*
1 sex organ [C] VULGAR a PENIS
2 chicken [C] a ROOSTER: *A cock crowed as morning approached.* —see also COCK-A-DOODLE-DOO

3 cock and bull story a story or excuse that is silly and unlikely but is told as if it were true: *He gave me a cock and bull story about the glass being smashed by hailstones.*
4 male bird [C] an adult male bird of any kind: *It's only legal to shoot the cocks, not the hens.*
5 control flow [C] something that controls the flow of liquid or gas out of a pipe —see also BALLCOCK, STOPCOCK
6 cock of the walk OLD-FASHIONED if you describe someone as behaving like the cock of the walk, they are behaving as if they were better or more important than other people —see also HALF-COCKED

cock[2] *v.* [T] **1** to lift a part of your body so that it is upright, or hold a part of your body at an angle: *She stood with her head* **cocked** *to one side and her hands on her hips.* | *Hardin cocked an eyebrow.* **2** to pull back the HAMMER of a gun so that it is ready to be fired: *The soldiers cocked their pistols, ready to fire.* **3** to put your hat on at an angle **4 keep an ear cocked** INFORMAL to pay close attention because you want to be sure you hear something you expect or think may happen

cock·ade /kɑˈkeɪd/ *n.* [C] a small piece of cloth used as a decoration on a hat to show rank, membership of a club etc.

cock·a·doo·dle·doo /ˌkɑk ə ˌdudl ˈduː/ *n.* [C] the loud sound made by a ROOSTER (=adult male chicken)

cock·a·ma·mie /ˈkɑkəˌmeɪmi/ *adj.* INFORMAL a cockamamie story, excuse, or idea is not believable or does not make sense: *Unemployment is not going to be solved by some cockamamie economic theory.*

cock·a·too /ˈkɑkəˌtu/ *n.* [C] an Australian PARROT with a lot of feathers on the top of its head

cock·crow /ˈkɑk-kroʊ/ *n.* [U] LITERARY the time in the early morning when the sun rises; DAWN[1] (1): *I was awakened before cockcrow by the sound of distant rifles.*

cocked hat /ˌ. ˈ./ *n.* [C] **1 knock/beat sb/sth into a cocked hat** to be a lot better than someone or something else: *Cavalli had no difficulty knocking the work of other composers into a cocked hat.* **2** a hat with the edges turned up on three sides, worn in past times

cock·er·el /ˈkɑkərəl/ *n.* [C] a young male chicken

cock·er span·iel /ˌkɑkə ˈspænyəl/ *n.* [C] a dog with long ears and long soft fur

cock·eyed /ˈkɑkaɪd/ *adj.* INFORMAL **1** an idea, situation, plan etc. that is cockeyed is strange and not practical: *a cockeyed comedy* | *Heller's theory is completely cockeyed.* **2** not straight or level: *a cockeyed grin*

cock·fight /ˈkɑkfaɪt/ *n.* [C] a sport, illegal in many countries, in which two male chickens are made to fight each other —**cockfighting** *n.* [U]

cock·le /ˈkɑkəl/ *n.* [C] **1** a common European SHELLFISH that is often used for food **2 warm the cockles of sb's heart** OLD-FASHIONED to make someone feel happy and full of good feelings toward other people

cock·le·shell /ˈkɑkəlˌʃɛl/ *n.* [C] **1** the shell of the cockle, that is shaped like a heart **2** LITERARY a small light boat

cock·ney, Cockney /ˈkɑkni/ *n.* **1** [C] someone, especially a WORKING CLASS person, who comes from the eastern area of London **2** [U] a way of speaking English that is typical of someone from this area —**cockney** *adj.*

cock·pit /ˈkɑkˌpɪt/ *n.* [C] **1** the part of an airplane, racing car, or small boat in which the pilot or driver sits **2** a small, usually enclosed area where COCKFIGHTS take place

cock·roach /ˈkɑk-roʊtʃ/ *n.* [C] a large black or brown insect that often lives where food is kept; ROACH (1) —see picture at INSECT

cocks·comb /ˈkɑks-koʊm/ *n.* [C] **1** the red flesh that grows from the top of a male chicken's head **2** the cap worn by a JESTER (=someone employed to amuse a king in past times)

cock·suck·er /ˈkɑkˌsʌkə/ *n.* [C] VULGAR a man whom you dislike very much, think is stupid etc.

cock·sure /ˌkɑkˈʃʊr/ *adj.* INFORMAL too confident of your abilities or knowledge, in a way that is annoying to other people: *She sounds confident, but not cocksure.*

cock·tail /ˈkɑkteɪl/ *n.* [C] **1** an alcoholic drink made from a mixture of LIQUOR and other drinks —see picture at GET **2 seafood/shrimp/lobster cocktail** a mixture of small pieces of fish, SHRIMP or LOBSTER, served cold with a special SAUCE and eaten at the beginning of a meal **3** a mixture of dangerous substances, especially one that you eat or drink: *He died after taking a lethal cocktail of alcohol and tranquilizers.* —see also FRUIT COCKTAIL, MOLOTOV COCKTAIL

cocktail bar /ˈ.. ˌ./ *n.* [C] a place where people can buy cocktails as well as beer and wine

cocktail dress /ˈ.. ˌ./ *n.* [C] a formal dress that reaches just above or below your knees, for wearing to parties or other evening social events

cocktail lounge /ˈ.. ˌ./ *n.* [C] a public room in a hotel, restaurant etc., where alcoholic drinks may be bought

cocktail par·ty /ˈ.. ˌ../ *n.* [C] a party at which alcoholic drinks are served and for which people usually dress formally

cocktail shak·er /ˈ.. ˌ./ *n.* [C] a container in which COCKTAILS are mixed

cocktail stick /ˈ.. ˌ./ *n.* [C] a short pointed stick on which small pieces of food are served

cocktail wait·ress /ˈ.. ˌ../ *n.* [C] a woman who serves drinks to people sitting at tables in a BAR

cock·y /ˈkɑki/ *adj.* **cockier, cockiest** INFORMAL too confident about yourself and your abilities, especially in a way that annoys other people: *a cocky 15-year-old boy* —**cockily** *adv.* —**cockiness** *n.* [U]

co·coa /ˈkoʊkoʊ/ *n.* [U] **1** a brown powder made from cocoa beans, used to make chocolate and in cooking to make cakes, cookies etc. **2** a sweet hot drink made with this powder, sugar, and milk or water: *a cup of cocoa*

cocoa bean /ˈ.. ˌ./ *n.* [C] the small seed of a tropical tree, that is used to make cocoa

cocoa but·ter /ˈ.. ˌ./ *n.* [U] a fat obtained from the seeds of a tropical tree, used in making some COSMETICS

co·coa·nut /ˈkoʊkəˌnʌt/ *n.* [C,U] another spelling of coconut

cocoa pow·der /ˈ.. ˌ./ *n.* [U] COCOA (1)

co·co·nut /ˈkoʊkəˌnʌt/ *n.* **1** [C] the large brown seed of a tropical tree, which has a hard shell containing liquid that you can drink and a white part that you can eat —see picture at FRUIT[1] **2** [U] the white part of this seed, often used in cooking: *shredded coconut*

coconut milk /ˈ... ˌ./ *n.* [U] the liquid inside a coconut

co·coon[1] /kəˈkun/ *n.* [C] **1** a bag of silky threads that young MOTHS and some other insects make to cover and protect themselves while they are growing **2** a place where you feel comfortable and safe: *These children live outside the cocoon of the middle class.* | *the cocoon of our hotel room* **3** something that wraps around you completely, especially to protect you: [+ of] *She is wrapped in a cocoon of blue silk.*

cocoon[2] *v.* [T] to protect or surround someone or something completely, especially so that they feel safe: *Pheiffer warns that we should not cocoon our daughters, even if it were possible.* —**cocooned** *adj.*

co·coon·ing /kəˈkunɪŋ/ *n.* [U] INFORMAL the activity of spending a lot of time in your own home because you feel comfortable and safe there: *They produce extra-wide armchairs for people with serious cocooning in mind.*

Coc·teau /kɑkˈtoʊ/, **Jean** /ʒɑn/ (1889–1963) a French writer and movie DIRECTOR, who was an important member of the SURREALIST movement

C.O.D. *adv.* the abbreviation of Cash On Delivery; a system in which you pay for something when it is delivered to you: *Send the equipment C.O.D.*

cod /kɑd/ *n.* **1** [C] a large ocean fish that lives in the North Atlantic **2** [U] the white meat from this fish: *baked cod with a mustard sauce*

co·da /'koʊdə/ *n.* [C] TECHNICAL **1** an additional part at the end of a piece of music that is separate from the main part **2** a separate piece of writing at the end of a work of literature or a speech

cod·dle /'kɑdl/ *v.* [T] to treat someone in a way that is too kind and gentle and that protects them from pain or difficulty: *Police Chief McBride says coddling young lawbreakers just creates more adult criminals.*

code¹ /koʊd/ *n.*

1 `behavior` [C] a set of rules that tell people how to behave in their life or in particular situations: *Churches help to teach children a strong moral code.* | **code of conduct/ethics** *Steinmetz said his own personal code of ethics prevented him from lying in court.*

2 `rules/laws` [C] a set of written rules or laws: *Building codes have been strengthened following the earthquake.* | *the income tax code* | *the school's **dress code** (=set of rules about what type of clothes people can wear)*

3 `secret message` [C,U] a system of words, letters, or signs that you use instead of ordinary writing when you want to send a secret message: *The code was used by the Japanese Navy during War II.* | *All government messages were to be sent **in code**.* | **break/crack a code** (=manage to understand a secret code)

4 `signs giving information` [C] a set of numbers, letters, or other marks that show what something is or that give information about it: *The code "ZZ35" on this cassette means it was imported from Europe.*

5 a code of silence an unwritten rule that that tells people not to say anything about someone they know who has done something wrong: *Axelrod denied that there was a code of silence over reporting cases of corruption in the police force.*

6 a code of practice a set of rules that people in a particular business or profession agree to obey: *Manufacturers agreed on a code of practice regarding the promotion of sweet alcoholic drinks.*

7 `computers` [C,U] a set of instructions that tell a computer what to do: *Some programmers write code for more than 12 hours straight.* —see also MACHINE CODE, SOURCE CODE

8 `sounds/signals` [C] a system of sounds or signals that represent words or letters when they are sent by machine: *a telegraphic code* —see also AREA CODE, BAR CODE, MORSE CODE, ZIP CODE

code² *v.* [T] **1** to put a set of numbers, letters, or signs on something to show what it is or give information about it: *Security badges are coded to show which buildings each person may enter.* **2** to put a message into a code so that it is secret **3 color code** to mark a group of things with different colors so that you can tell the difference between them: *color coded wires* —**coded** *adj.*: *a coded message*

co·deine /'koʊdin/ *n.* [U] a strong drug used to stop pain

code name /'. ./ *n.* [C] a name that is used instead of someone's or something's real name in order to keep it a secret, or to keep secret the aims, facts etc. of a plan —**code name** *v.* [T]

co-dependent, codependent /ˌ. .'..·/ *adj.* someone who is co-dependent thinks that they cannot be happy or successful without someone else, and so tries to keep that person happy without taking care of their own needs, in a way that seems unhealthy —**co-dependence, co-dependency** *n.* [U]

code word /'. ./ *n.* [C] **1** a word or phrase that has a different meaning than what it seems to mean, used to communicate something secretly **2** a word or expression that you use instead of a more direct one, used when you want to avoid shocking or upsetting someone: [+ for] *The fact is, "Japan bashing" is a phrase that's become a code word for racism.*

co·dex /'koʊdɛks/ *n.* plural **codices** /-dɪsiz/ [C] TECHNICAL an ancient book written by hand: *a sixth-century codex*

cod·fish /'kɑdˌfɪʃ/ *n.* [C] a COD

codg·er /'kɑdʒɚ/ *n.* [C] INFORMAL **old codger** a phrase meaning an "old man," used when you are not being respectful

cod·i·cil /'kɑdɪsɪl/ *n.* [C] LAW a document stating any changes or additions to a WILL (=legal document that says who you want your money and property to be given to after you die)

cod·i·fy /'kɑdəˌfaɪ, 'koʊ-/ *v.* **codifies, codified, codifying** [T] to arrange laws, principles, facts etc. in a system: *The agreement must still be codified by federal legislation.* —**codification** /ˌkɑdəfə'keɪʃən/ *n.* [C,U]

cod-liv·er oil /'. .. ˌ./ *n.* [U] a yellow oil from a codfish that contains many substances that are important for good health

cod·piece /'kɑdpis/ *n.* [C] a piece of colored cloth worn by men in the 15th and 16th centuries to cover the opening in the front of their pants

Co·dy /'koʊdi/**, William** (1846–1917) a U.S. soldier and hunter, known as **Buffalo Bill**, who organized a famous Wild West show, in which people showed their skill at shooting and riding horses and tried to show what life was like in the American West

co·ed¹, co-ed /ˌkoʊ'ɛd◂/ *adj.* using a system in which students of both sexes study or live together: *coed exercise classes* | *Wheaton College in Massachusetts went coed three years ago.* —opposite SINGLE-SEX

coed², co-ed *n.* [C] OLD-FASHIONED a woman student at a college or university

co·ed·u·ca·tion, co-education /ˌkoʊɛdʒə'keɪʃən/ *n.* [U] a system in which students of both sexes study or live together —**coeducational** *adj.* FORMAL

co·ef·fi·cient /ˌkoʊə'fɪʃənt/ *n.* [C] TECHNICAL in mathematics, the number by which an unknown quantity is multiplied: *In 8pq, the coefficient of pq is 8.*

co·e·qual /ˌkoʊ'ikwəl/ *adj.* FORMAL if people or groups are coequal, they have the same rank, ability, importance etc.: *The Supreme Court, the Congress, and the President are all coequal parts of the federal government.* —**coequally** *adv.*

co·erce /koʊ'ɚs/ *v.* [T] to force someone to do something they do not want to do by threatening them: [coerce sb into doing sth] *It's a bad idea to coerce a child into wearing something he or she doesn't like.*

co·er·cion /koʊ'ɚʃən, -ʒən/ *n.* [U] the use of threats or orders to make someone do something they do not want to do: *Coercion should not be used when questioning suspects.*

co·er·cive /koʊ'ɚsɪv/ *adj.* using threats or orders to make someone do something they do not want to do: *The police may have used coercive tactics to get confessions.* —**coercively** *adv.*

co·e·val /koʊ'ivəl/ *adj.* FORMAL happening or existing during the same period of time: [+ with] *The development of stone tools was coeval with the appearance of farming settlements.*

co·ex·ist /ˌkoʊɪg'zɪst/ *v.* [I] FORMAL to exist at the same time or in the same place, especially peacefully: *Can the two countries ever coexist peacefully?* | [+ with] *The article describes how Islam coexists with more traditional American religions.*

co·ex·is·tence /ˌkoʊɪg'zɪstəns/ *n.* [U] FORMAL **1** if two or more countries or people have a coexistence, they live close to each other without fighting: *North and South Korea signed an accord calling for **peaceful coexistence**.* **2** the state of existing together at the same time or in the same place —**coexistent** *adj.*

cof·fee /'kɔfi, 'kɑ-/ *n.* **1** [U] a hot, dark brown drink that has a slightly bitter taste: *Do you want **a cup of coffee** ?* | *What you need is some strong **black coffee** (=coffee with no milk added).* **2** [U] coffee beans, or the brown powder that is made by crushing coffee beans, used to make coffee: *a pound of coffee* | *Sorry, all I have is **instant coffee** (=a powder used to make coffee quickly).* **3** [C] a type of coffee that has a particular taste: *A variety of gourmet coffees are on sale.* **4** [C] a cup of this drink: *That's four coffees and two pieces of apple pie, right?* **5** [U] a light brown color —see also **wake up and smell the coffee** at **wake up** (WAKE¹)

coffee bar /'.. ,./ *n.* [C] **1** a place where people can buy coffee beans, cups of coffee, and sweet foods which they can eat and drink there or take away with them **2** a COFFEE HOUSE —compare COFFEE SHOP

coffee bean /'.. ,./ *n.* [C] the seed of a tropical tree that is used to make coffee

coffee break /'.. ,./ *n.* [C] a short time when you stop working to relax and drink something, and sometimes eat a little bit of food

coffee cake /'.. ,./ *n.* [C,U] a sweet heavy cake, usually eaten along with coffee

coffee grind·er /'.. ,../ *n.* [C] a small machine that crushes coffee beans

coffee house /'.. ,./ *n.* [C] a small restaurant where people go to talk and drink coffee, eat DOUGHNUTS (=a type of sweet cake) etc. —compare COFFEE BAR, COFFEE SHOP

coffee klatch /'kɔfi ,klætʃ/ *n.* [C] an informal social situation when people drink coffee and talk

coffee ma·chine /'.. ,../ *n.* [C] a machine that gives you a cup of coffee, tea etc. when you put money into it

coffee mak·er /'.. ,../ *n.* [C] an electric machine that makes a pot of coffee —see picture at KITCHEN

coffee mill /'.. ,./ *n.* [C] a COFFEE GRINDER

coffee pot /'.. ,./ *n.* [C] a container for making or serving coffee

coffee shop /'.. ,./ *n.* [C] a restaurant that serves cheap meals; DINER —compare COFFEE BAR, COFFEE HOUSE

coffee ta·ble /'.. ,../ *n.* [C] **1** a small low table in a LIVING ROOM for putting drinks and magazines on **2 coffee table book** a large expensive book that usually has a lot of pictures in it

cof·fer /'kɔfɚ, 'ka-/ *n.* [C] **1 coffers** [plural] the money that an organization, government etc. has available to spend: *The tax would add an estimated $500,000 to the city's coffers.* **2** a large strong box often decorated with jewels, silver, gold etc., and used to hold valuable or religious objects

cof·fer·dam /'kɔfɚ,dæm, 'ka-/ *n.* [C] a large box filled with air that allows people to work under water

cof·fin /'kɔfɪn/ *n.* [C] a long box in which a dead person is buried; CASKET —see also **a nail in sb's/sth's coffin** (NAIL[1] (3))

cog /kag/ *n.* [C] **1** a wheel with small parts shaped like teeth sticking out around the edge, which fit together with the teeth of another wheel as they turn around in a machine **2 a cog in the machine/wheel** someone who is not important or powerful, who only has a small job or part in a large business or organization **3** one of the small teeth that stick out on a cog

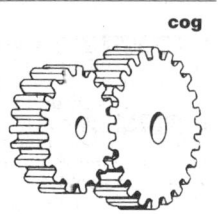
cog

co·gent /'koʊdʒənt/ *adj.* FORMAL something such as an argument that is cogent is reasonable, so that people are persuaded that it is correct: *The court will require clear, cogent evidence before its decision can be changed.* —**cogently** *adv.* —**cogency** *n.* [U]

cog·i·tate /'kadʒə,teɪt/ *v.* [I + about/on] FORMAL to think carefully and seriously about something —**cogitation** /,kadʒə'teɪʃən/ *n.* [U]

co·gnac /'kanyæk, 'kɔn-, 'koʊn-/ *n.* [C,U] a type of BRANDY (=alcoholic drink) made in France, or a glass of this drink

cog·nate[1] /'kagneɪt/ *adj.* cognate words or languages have the same origin

cognate[2] *n.* [C] a word in one language that has the same origin as a word in another language, or different words in the same language that have the same origin: *Classic, classical, and class are cognates.*

cog·ni·tion /kag'nɪʃən/ *n.* [U] **1** TECHNICAL the process by which you see or hear something, recognize it, and understand it: *Researchers still have little idea of how brain signals connect to cognition and*

C

feeling. **2** FORMAL understanding: *Political cognition rises with education.*

cog·ni·tive /'kagnətɪv/ *adj.* FORMAL OR TECHNICAL relating to the process of knowing, understanding, and learning something: *cognitive psychology* —**cognitively** *adv.*

cog·ni·zance /'kagnəzəns/ *n.* [U] FORMAL **1 take cognizance of sth** to understand something and consider it when you do something or make a decision **2** knowledge or understanding of something: *He has full cognizance of the risks involved.* **3** TECHNICAL responsibility for a particular area of knowledge, action etc.: *It was a military program developed under the cognizance of the Defense Department.*

cog·ni·zant /'kagnəzənt/ *adj.* [not before noun] having knowledge or information about something: *I'm cognizant of the fact that your client has tried to pay the debt.*

cog·no·men /kag'noʊmən, 'kagnə-/ *n.* [C] **1** FORMAL a name used instead of someone's real name, or a description added to someone's name, for example "the Great" in "Alexander the Great" **2** TECHNICAL a SURNAME (=last name or family name), especially in ancient Rome

co·gno·scen·ti /,kanyə'ʃɛnti, ,kagnə-/ *n.* **the cognoscenti** people who have special knowledge about a particular subject, especially art, literature, or food

cog·wheel /'kag-wil/ *n.* [C] a COG (1)

co·hab·it /,koʊ'hæbɪt/ *v.* [I] if two unmarried people cohabit, they live together as though they are married —**cohabitation** /,koʊhæbə'teɪʃən/ *n.* [U]

co·here /koʊ'hɪr/ *v.* [I] FORMAL **1** if the ideas or arguments in a piece of writing cohere, they are connected in a clear and reasonable way **2** if two objects cohere, they stick together

co·her·ence /koʊ'hɪrəns/ *n.* [U] **1** a reasonable connection or relation between ideas, arguments, statements etc.: *It is a challenge to tell these separate stories without losing overall coherence.* **2** if a group has coherence, its members are connected or united because they share common aims, qualities, or beliefs: *By 1924 the party had lost all discipline and coherence.*

co·her·ent /koʊ'hɪrənt/ *adj.* **1** if a piece of writing, set of ideas, plan etc. is coherent, it is easy to understand because it is clear and reasonable: *We would like to see a coherent federal housing program.* **2** if someone is coherent, they are talking in a way that is clear and easy to understand: *She was hysterical and screaming – not coherent at all.* —opposite INCOHERENT —**coherently** *adv.*

co·he·sion /koʊ'hiʒən/ *n.* [U] **1** if there is cohesion among a group of people, a set of ideas etc., all the parts or members of it are connected or related in a reasonable way to form a whole: *The article comments on the lack of cohesion and commitment within the administration.* **2** TECHNICAL a close relationship, based on grammar or meaning, between two parts of a sentence or the parts of a larger piece of writing —**cohesive** /koʊ'hisɪv, -zɪv/ *adj.* —**cohesively** *adv.* —**cohesiveness** *n.* [U]

co·hort /'koʊhɔrt/ *n.* [C] **1** a word meaning a person or group of people who work together or have the same aims, used especially when you disapprove of them: *Hawk and his cohorts cheated Jack out of a fortune.* **2** TECHNICAL a member of a particular age group, social class etc., or the group itself: *"Baby boomers" are the largest cohort of Americans living today.*

coif·fure /kwa'fyur/ *n.* [C] FORMAL a HAIRDO —**coiffured** *adj.*

coil[1] /kɔɪl/ *v.* [I,T] also **coil up** to wind or twist into a round shape, or to wind or twist something in this way: *A student discovered the 12-foot python coiled in a corner of the classroom.* | *Wrap the bar with heavy string, coiling it tightly for safety.* —**coiled** *adj.*

coil[2] *n.* [C] **1** a continuous series of circular rings into which something such as wire or rope has been wound or twisted: [+ **of**] *The embassy building is surrounded by high walls topped with coils of barbed wire.* **2** TECHNICAL a wire or a metal tube in a continuous circular shape that produces light or heat when electricity is passed through it: *There should be frost all over the freezer coil.* **3** TECHNICAL the part of a car engine that sends electricity to the SPARK PLUGS —see picture at ENGINE **4** a type of IUD

coin¹ /kɔɪn/ *n.* **1** [C] a piece of metal, usually flat and round, that is used as money: *I used to collect coins when I was a kid.* —compare BILL¹ (3) **2 toss/flip a coin** to choose or decide something by throwing a coin into the air and guessing which side of it will show when it falls: *We like to get out a map, and flip a coin to decide where to go.* **3** [U] money in the form of metal coins —see also COIN TOSS, **the other side of the coin** (SIDE¹ (27)), **two sides of the same coin** (SIDE¹ (28))

coin² *v.* **1** [T] to invent a new word or expression, especially one that many people start to use: *Freed was the disk jockey who coined the term "rock 'n' roll."* **2 to coin a phrase** said in a joking way when you use a very familiar expression that people often use too much, to show that you know it is used a lot: *Miller was trying to help his career and, to coin a phrase, snatch victory from the jaws of defeat.* **3** [T] to make coins from metal

coin·age /ˈkɔɪnɪdʒ/ *n.* **1** [C] a word or phrase that has been recently invented: *The book deals with cultural changes that prompted coinages such as "yuppie."* **2** [U] the system of money used in a country: *the coinage used in 16th century Italy* **3** [U] the use or making of new words or phrases **4** [U] the making of coins

co·in·cide /ˌkoʊɪnˈsaɪd/ *v.* [I] **1** to happen at the same time as something else: [+ **with**] *The demonstration is set for Sunday to coincide with World AIDS Day.* **2** [not in progressive] if two people's ideas, opinions etc. coincide, they are the same: *We work together when our needs coincide.*

co·in·ci·dence /koʊˈɪnsədəns/ *n.* **1** [C,U] a surprising and unexpected situation in which two things that are related happen at the same time, in the same place, or to the same people: *It was a coincidence that three earthquakes happened across the world in one week.* | **By coincidence**, *the designer had decorated the same house for the previous owner.* | *With those two athletes at the school,* **it's no coincidence** (=not something that happened by chance) *that they're leading the league.* | *"Ruby's dad gave her the exact same thing that she gave us for our wedding." "You're kidding!* **What a coincidence***."* | *It's a* **happy coincidence** *that Jackson and her mother gave birth on the same weekend.* | **be sheer/pure coincidence** (=happen completely by chance) **2** [singular] FORMAL an occasion when two ideas, opinions etc. are the same: [+ **of**] *There is a coincidence of opinion among the board members.*

co·in·ci·dent /koʊˈɪnsədənt/ *adj.* FORMAL existing or happening at the same place or time

co·in·ci·den·tal /koʊˌɪnsəˈdɛntl/ *adj.* happening completely by chance without being planned: *Any apparent similarities between the events of 1983 and the actual film were* **purely coincidental***.* —**coincidentally** *adv.* [sentence adverb]

co·in·sur·ance /ˌkoʊɪnˈʃʊrəns/ *n.* [U] **1** a type of insurance in which the payment is split between two people, especially between an employer and a worker: *health coinsurance* **2** insurance that will only pay for part of the value or cost of something

co·in·sure /ˌkoʊɪnˈʃʊr/ *v.* [T] to buy or provide insurance in which the payment is split between two people, or insurance that will only pay for part of the value or cost of something

coin toss /ˈ. ./ *n.* [C usually singular] an occasion when someone throws a coin into the air to see which side it falls on, in order to decide something: *The Mustangs won the coin toss and chose to defend first.*

coir /kɔɪr/ *n.* [U] the rough material that covers the shell of a COCONUT, used for making MATS, ropes etc.

coi·tus /ˈkɔɪtəs, ˈkoʊətəs/ *n.* [U] TECHNICAL the act of having sex; SEXUAL INTERCOURSE —**coital** *adj.*

Coke /koʊk/ *n.* [C,U] TRADEMARK the drink COCA-COLA, or a bottle, can, or glass of this drink: *Regular fries and a large Coke, please.*

coke /koʊk/ *n.* [U] **1** INFORMAL the drug COCAINE **2** a solid black substance produced from coal and burned to provide heat

col /kɑl/ *n.* [C] a low point between two high places in a mountain range

Col. *n.* the written abbreviation of COLONEL

col. the written abbreviation of COLUMN

col- /kəl, kɑl/ *prefix* used instead of CON- before the letter "l"; with: *to collaborate* (=work together)

COLA /ˈkoʊlə/ *n.* [singular] Cost of Living Adjustment; an increase in salary or SOCIAL SECURITY payments that is equal to the amount that prices, rents etc. have increased

co·la /ˈkoʊlə/ *n.* [C,U] a sweet brown SOFT DRINK, or a bottle, can, or glass of this drink

col·an·der /ˈkɑləndɚ, ˈkʌ-/ *n.* [C] a metal or plastic bowl with a lot of small holes in the bottom and sides, used to separate liquid from food

cold¹ /koʊld/ *adj.* **1** objects/surfaces/liquids/rooms etc. having a low temperature: *My car doesn't run very well when the engine's cold.* | *How about a nice cold beer?* | *The office always feels so* **cold** *first thing on Monday morning.* | *Come sit down – your coffee's* **getting cold***.* | **ice/stone/freezing cold** (=extremely cold) **2** weather when there is cold weather, the temperature of the air is very low: *a cold, clear night* | *They say it's the coldest winter for over 50 years.* | *I'd wear a hat – it's cold out.* | *It's supposed to* **get cold** (=become cold) *again during the weekend.* | *I can't believe it's* **turned so cold** (=become cold or colder, especially suddenly) *after the nice weather we had last week.* **3** **be/feel/look/get cold** if you are cold, your body is at a low temperature: *Aren't you cold?* | *Come inside before you get cold.* | *Oh, Jenny, your hands are* **as cold as ice** (=extremely cold). **4** food eaten cold cold food has been cooked, but is not eaten while it is warm: *I think we'll just have a cold buffet.* | *a selection of cold meats* —see also COLD CUTS **5** lacking feeling lacking normal human feelings such as sympathy, pity, humor etc.: *"He has abused his position," a cold and angry protester said.* | *a cold, pragmatic decision* **6** unfriendly unfriendly and behaving as though you do not care much about other people: *She gave us a polite but cold greeting.* **7** **leave sb cold** INFORMAL to not feel interested in or affected by something at all: *Ballet just leaves me cold.* **8** **get/have cold feet** INFORMAL to suddenly feel that you are not brave enough to do something you planned to do: *They later got cold feet and canceled the order.* **9** **give sb/sth the cold shoulder** INFORMAL to deliberately ignore someone or something, especially because you are upset or offended: *Haley is well-known for giving reporters the cold shoulder.* **10** **cold (hard) cash** INFORMAL money in the form of paper money and coins rather than checks or CREDIT CARDS **11** **take/need a cold shower** HUMOROUS used to say that you are sexually excited and the cold water will stop you feeling that way **12** **sb's trail/scent is cold** used to say that you cannot find someone because it has been too long since they passed or lived in a particular place: *The trail seemed cold until a woman in Mississippi recognized Pearson's face in a wanted poster.* **13** children's game SPOKEN used in a children's game to say that someone is far away from the hidden object they are trying to find: *No, you're getting colder.* —opposite WARM¹ (6) **14** **it's colder than a witch's tit** SPOKEN, HUMOROUS a phrase used to say the weather is very cold, which some people may think is offensive

15 color/light a cold color or light reminds you of things that are cold: *Pouring in from outside windows is cold, blue light.*

16 **in the cold light of day** in the morning, when you can think or understand things clearly

17 **cold steel** LITERARY a weapon such as a knife or sword —**coldness** *n.* [U] —see also **in cold blood** (BLOOD (4)), **cold/small comfort** (COMFORT¹ (7)), **a cold fish** (FISH¹ (6)), **pour cold water over/on sth** (POUR (6)), **a (cold) sweat** (SWEAT² (7))

s w **cold²** *n.* **1** [C] a common illness that makes it difficult to breathe through your nose and often makes your throat hurt: *He's had so many colds this winter.* | *I had a good time skiing, but I caught a cold* (=got one). —see also COMMON COLD **2 the cold** a low temperature or cold weather: *Nobody wanted to go out in the cold.* **3 leave sb out in the cold** INFORMAL to not include someone in an activity, group, process etc.: *These trade negotiations have left farmers out in the cold.* **4 come in from the cold** to become accepted or recognized, especially by a powerful group of people

s w **cold³** *adv.* **1** suddenly and completely: *Judy stopped cold, and waited for the laughter to finish.* **2 out cold** unconscious, especially because you have been hit on the head: *If he fights like he did last time, I'll knock him out cold* (=hit someone so that they become unconscious). **3** without preparation: *I can't just get up there and make a speech cold!*

cold-blood·ed /ˌ. '.ˌ/ *adj.* **1** not showing any emotions or any pity for other people's suffering: *a cold-blooded murderer* **2** a cold-blooded animal, such as a snake, has a body temperature that changes with the temperature of the air or ground around it —compare WARM-BLOODED —**cold-bloodedly** *adv.* —**cold-bloodedness** *n.* [U]

cold call /ˌ. './ *n.* [C] a visit or telephone call you make to someone you have never met to try to sell something to them

cold cream /'. ./ *n.* [U] a thick white oily cream used for cleaning your face and making it softer

cold cuts /'. ./ *n.* [plural] thinly cut pieces of cold cooked meat

cold front /'. ./ *n.* [C] TECHNICAL the front edge of a mass of cold air that is moving toward a place —compare WARM FRONT

cold-heart·ed /ˌ. '.ˌ/ *adj.* behaving in a way that shows no pity or sympathy: *a cold-hearted businessman* —**cold-heartedly** *adv.* —**cold-heartedness** *n.* [U]

cold·ly /'kouldli/ *adv.* without friendly feelings: *"No autographs," he said coldly.*

cold snap /'. ./ *n.* [C] a sudden short period of very cold weather

cold sore /'. ./ *n.* [C] a painful spot on your lip or inside your mouth that you may get when you are sick

cold spell /'. ./ *n.* [C] a period of several days or weeks of very cold weather

cold stor·age /ˌ. '../ *n.* [U] **1** if you keep something such as food in cold storage, you keep it in a cold place so that it will stay fresh and in good condition **2 put/go/be in cold storage** to not do something about a plan or idea until later in the future: *Patton's plan to defend Hawaii was put in cold storage in 1940.*

cold tur·key /ˌ. '../ *n.* [U] INFORMAL **quit/go/stop cold turkey** to suddenly stop smoking cigarettes or stop taking a drug: *Five years ago, Jay quit cold turkey, and hasn't touched a cigarette since.*

cold war /ˌ. './ *n.* **1** [singular,U] an unfriendly political relationship between two countries who do not actually fight with each other **2 the Cold War** this type of relationship between the U.S. and the Soviet Union, after World War II

Cole /koul/, **Thomas** (1801–1848) a U.S. PAINTER famous for his paintings of the American LANDSCAPE

Col·e·ridge /'kolərɪdʒ/, **Sam·u·el Tay·lor** /'sæmuəl 'teɪlə/ (1772–1834) a British poet

cole slaw, coleslaw /'koul slɔ/ *n.* [U] a SALAD made with thinly cut raw CABBAGE

Co·lette /kɔ'lɛt/ (1873–1954) a French writer of NOVELS

Col·gate /'kolgeɪt/, **William** (1783–1857) a U.S. businessman who made soap and started the Colgate Palmolive Peet company

col·ic /'kɑlɪk/ *n.* [U] severe pain in the stomach and BOWELS, especially in babies —**colicky** *adj.*

col·i·se·um /ˌkɑlə'siəm/ *n.* [C] a large structure with seats that has no roof, or a large building used for public events such as sports games, CONCERTS etc.

co·li·tis /kə'laɪtəs/ *n.* [U] TECHNICAL an illness in which part of your COLON swells, causing pain

col·lab·o·rate /kə'læbəˌreɪt/ *v.* [I] **1** to work together with another person or group in order to achieve something, especially in science or art: [+ on] *The author and illustrator wanted to collaborate on a book for children.* | [+ with] *Ella Fitzgerald regularly collaborated with some of the greatest musicians in jazz.* | [collaborate to do sth] *Six journalists have collaborated to produce a book on the history of Yugoslavia.* | [collaborate in doing sth] *He learned enough Chinese to collaborate in the writing of several books.* **2** to help a country that your country is at war with, or one that has taken control of your country: [+ with] *After the war, Mezeret was accused of collaborating with the Nazis.*

col·lab·o·ra·tion /kəˌlæbə'reɪʃən/ *n.* **1** [C,U] the act of working together with another person or group to achieve something, especially in science or art: [+ between] *A formal collaboration between our companies is good for everyone.* | [+ with] *Stromboli was Ingrid Bergman's first collaboration with director Roberto Rossellini.* | *The publication, produced in collaboration with Peterson's Guides, lists the 100 best schools in the state.* **2** [U] help given to a country that your country is at war with, or one that has taken control of your country: [+ with] *At least 216 Palestinians have been jailed, most on suspicion of collaboration with Israel.*

col·lab·o·ra·tive /kə'læbrətɪv/ *adj.* **collaborative project/effort/work etc.** a piece of work involving two or more people or groups working together to achieve something, especially in science or art

col·lab·o·ra·tor /kə'læbəˌreɪtə/ *n.* [C] **1** someone who helps their country's enemies, for example by giving them information, when the enemy has taken control of their country: *The three convicted collaborators have all been sentenced to death.* **2** someone who works with other people or groups in order to achieve something, especially in science or art: *Sansom's work will be continued by his son and long-time collaborator, Chip.*

col·lage /kə'lɑʒ, kou-/ *n.* **1** [C] a picture made by sticking other pictures, photographs, cloth etc. onto a surface **2** [U] the art of making pictures in this way

col·la·gen /'kɑlədʒən/ *n.* [U] a PROTEIN substance, sometimes put into women's face creams

col·lapse¹ /kə'læps/ *v.*
1 structure [I] if a building, wall, piece of furniture etc. collapses, it suddenly falls down or in because its structure is weak or because it has been hit with a sudden violent force: *Part of the floor collapsed as a result of water damage.*
2 illness/injury [I] to suddenly fall down or become unconscious because you are sick or injured: *Former Mayor Ed Koch collapsed this morning at a health club in midtown Manhattan.*
3 fail [I] if a system, idea, or organization collapses, it suddenly fails or becomes too weak to continue: *The U.S. auto industry nearly collapsed due to increased foreign competition.*
4 sit/lie [I] to suddenly sit or lie down, especially because you are very tired: *She finally took a break and collapsed in a chair.*
5 make sth smaller [I,T] if something collapses or you collapse it, you can fold it so that it becomes

C

smaller: *When folded in this way, the map collapses to pocket size.*
6 medical [I] if a lung or a BLOOD VESSEL collapses, it suddenly becomes flat because it does not have any air or blood in it anymore

collapse² *n.*
1 business/system/idea etc. [singular,U] a sudden failure in the way something works, so that it cannot continue: *He was sued for his role in the collapse of Southwest Savings and Loan.*
2 building/structure/furniture etc. [U] the act of suddenly falling down or in because of a weakness in something's structure or because something has hit it violently: *Buildings must be strengthened to prevent collapse from an earthquake.*
3 illness/injury [singular] an occasion when someone falls down or becomes unconscious because of a sudden illness or injury: *Roy is recovering from last week's collapse.*
4 money/prices etc. [singular] a sudden decrease in the value of something: *the collapse of the stock market in 1987*

col·laps·i·ble /kə'læpsəbəl/ *adj.* able to be folded up into a smaller size: *collapsible chairs*

col·lar¹ /'kɑlɚ/ *n.* [C]
1 clothing the part of a shirt, dress, coat etc. that fits around your neck
2 animal a narrow band of leather or plastic that is fastened around an animal's neck
3 hot under the collar INFORMAL angry or excited: *They got a little hot under the collar when they got the bill.*
4 colored fur/feathers a band of fur, feathers, or skin around an animal's neck that is a different color from the rest of the animal
5 work animal a thick leather ring put over the shoulders of a work animal to help it pull machinery or a vehicle
6 machine a part of a machine that is shaped like a ring
7 police SLANG if the police make a collar, they catch a criminal —see also BLUE-COLLAR, -COLLARED, DOG COLLAR, WHITE-COLLAR

collar² *v.* [T] INFORMAL **1** to catch someone and hold them so that they cannot escape: *The police collared two suspects less than twenty minutes after the robbery.* **2** to find someone so that you can talk to them: *Hugh was quickly collared by a salesperson.* **3** to put a special collar on an animal, especially so that you know where it is, for scientific reasons: *Seventeen Florida panthers have been collared.*

col·lar·bone /'kɑlɚ,boʊn/ *n.* [C] one of the pair of bones on your chest that go from the base of your neck to your shoulders —see picture at SKELETON

col·lard greens /'kɑlɚd ,grinz/ *n.* a vegetable with large green leaves, usually eaten cooked

-collared /kɑlɚd/ [in adjectives] **high-collared/blue-collared/open-collared etc.** having a particular type of collar: *a high-collared blouse*

collar stud /'.. ,./ *n.* [C] an object like a button, used to fasten old-fashioned collars to shirts

col·late /kə'leɪt, kɑ-, 'koʊleɪt, 'kɑ-/ *v.* [T] **1** to arrange sheets of paper in the correct order before they are put in a book, report etc.: *Please collate and staple ten copies of the report for the meeting.* **2** FORMAL to gather information together, examine it carefully, and compare it with other information to find any differences

col·lat·er·al¹ /kə'lætərəl/ *n.* [U] TECHNICAL property, money, or other goods that you promise to give to someone if you cannot pay back the money they lent you; SECURITY (6): *Trump was forced to put up his casinos as collateral* (=promise them in this way) *for a $65 million emergency loan.* —**collateralize** *v.* [T]

collateral² *adj.* FORMAL **1** relating to something or happening as a result of it, but not as important: *The ban on increased imports has the collateral effect of forcing up prices.* **2** **collateral damage** an expression meaning people who are hurt or property that

is damaged as a result of war, although they are not the main TARGET, used especially by the Army, Navy etc. **3** collateral relatives are members of your family who are not closely related to you

col·la·tion /kə'leɪʃən/ *n.* **1** [U] the examination and comparing of information **2** [U] the arranging of sheets of paper in the correct order **3** [C] FORMAL a small, usually cold, meal

col·league /'kɑlig/ *n.* [C] a word meaning someone you work with, used especially by professional people or managers: *my colleagues at the university* **s w** [2]

col·lect¹ /kə'lɛkt/ *v.* **s w** [2]
1 bring together [T] to get things of the same type from different places and bring them together: *After 25 years of collecting recipes, Barber has compiled them into a cookbook.* | *The planning process will involve collecting statistics on housing needs.* | *He's been collecting signatures of voters to get the measure on the ballot.*
2 keep objects [T] to get and keep objects because you think they are attractive or interesting: *Arlene collects teddy bears.*
3 money [T] to get money from people, the government etc.: *People who are collecting welfare checks usually really need them.* | *Rent is collected once a month.*
4 to help people [I,T] to ask people to give you money, goods etc. for a particular purpose: *Volunteers have collected and wrapped donated presents.* | [collect (sth) for sb/sth] *Some kids came by, collecting for UNICEF.*
5 increase in amount [I,T] if something collects in a place or you collect it there, it gradually increases in amount: *The building uses solar panels for collecting the sun's heat.* | *I didn't know what to do with it, so it just sat there, collecting dust.*
6 **collect yourself** also **collect your thoughts** to make an effort to remain calm and think clearly and carefully about something: *I got there early so I'd have a few minutes to collect my thoughts before the meeting began.*
7 obtain/win sth [T] to obtain or win something: *The team will soon collect its second NCAA title in three years.*
8 take sb/sth from a place [T] FORMAL to come to a particular place in order to take someone or something away: *I've come to collect Mr. Weinstein's order.*
9 crowd [I] FORMAL to come together gradually to form a group of people: *These games will help amuse all age groups of children that collect at family reunions.*

collect² *adv.* **call/phone sb collect** when you telephone someone collect, the person who received the call pays for it

collect³ *adj.* **a collect call** a telephone call that is paid for by the person who receives it

col·lect⁴ /'kɑlɪkt, -lɛkt/ *n.* [C] a short prayer in some Christian services

col·lect·ed /kə'lɛktɪd/ *adj.* **1** in control of yourself and your thoughts, feelings, etc.: *I thought I was prepared, I thought I'd be cool, calm and collected.* **2** put together in one book or as a collection: *A set of collected photographs of Ansel Adams are on display in the museum.*

col·lect·i·ble /kə'lɛktəbəl/ *adj.* something that is collectible is likely to be bought and kept as part of a group of similar things, especially because it might increase in value: *a selection of collectible cars* —**collectible** *n.* [C]

col·lec·tion /kə'lɛkʃən/ *n.* **s w** [2]
1 set/group [C] **a)** a set of similar things that are kept or brought together because they are attractive or interesting: *a coin collection* | *the Permanent Collection at the Whitney Museum* | [+ of] *a collection of antique vases* **b)** a group of things that are put together: *a collection of old newspapers*
2 bringing together [U] the act of bringing together things of the same type from different places to form a group: *The collection of data is not always something that a researcher can control.*
3 books/music [C] several stories, poems, pieces of music etc. that are in one book or on one record: *Perrault published his collection of fairy tales in 1697.*

4 **taking sth away** [C,U] the act of taking something from a place, especially when this is done regularly: *Christmas trees can be picked up with regular trash collection.*

5 **money** **a)** [C] the act of asking for money from people for a particular purpose: *Most Alcoholic Anonymous groups take up a collection at meetings to cover expenses.* **b)** [U] the act of obtaining money that is owed to you: *The new system should speed the collection of debts in the future.*

6 **clothes** [C] a number of different pieces of clothing designed by someone for a particular time of year: *Armani's summer collection*

7 **people** [C usually singular] a group of people, especially people you think are strange or unusual in some way: *They get together and behave like a real collection of idiots.*

col·lec·tion a·gen·cy /.'.. ,.../ n. [C] a company that finds people who owe money to other businesses and forces them to pay it: *I received a letter saying I owed interest, and the matter was being sent to a collection agency.*

collection box /.'.. ,./ n. [C] a container with a small opening in the top into which people put money for CHARITY

collection plate /.'.. ,./ n. [C] a large, almost flat dish in which you put money during some religious services

col·lec·tive¹ /kə'lɛktɪv/ adj. [only before noun] shared or made by all the members of a group together: *collective ownership* | *The decision to launch nuclear weapons must be collective.*

collective² n. [C] **1** a group of people who work together to run something such as a business or farm: *A women's collective runs the small cafe across the street.* **2** the business or farm that is run by this group

collective bar·gain·ing /.,.. '.../ n. [U] the discussions between employers and unions about pay, working conditions etc.

collective farm /.,.. './ n. [C] a large farm that is owned by the government and controlled by the farm workers

col·lec·tive·ly /kə'lɛktɪvli/ adv. as a group: *Commercial banks collectively earned $6.2 billion in the first three months of this year.*

collective noun /.,.. './ n. [C] TECHNICAL in grammar, a noun such as "committee" or "family" that is the name of a group of people or things considered as a unit

col·lec·tiv·ism /kə'lɛktɪ,vizəm/ n. [U] a political system in which all businesses, farms etc. are owned by the government —**collectivize** v. [T] —**collectivist** adj.

col·lec·tor /kə'lɛktə/ n. [C] **1** someone whose job is to collect things such as taxes, tickets, debts etc. from people **2** someone who collects things that are interesting or attractive: *a stamp collector* **3 a collectors' item** something that a collector would like to have: *Some of those bikes were collectors' items, probably worth a lot of money.*

col·lege /'kɑlɪdʒ/ n.
1 **advanced education** [C,U] **a)** a large school where you can study after HIGH SCHOOL and get a BACHELOR'S DEGREE: *He teaches at the college.* | *a college degree* | *It's a project for some college students.* | *Fran just finished her freshman year in college (=is a student at a college).* | *Older people are going back to college to get a diploma.* | *Recent college graduates have had trouble finding jobs.* —see also COMMUNITY COLLEGE, JUNIOR COLLEGE —compare UNIVERSITY **b)** a school for advanced education, especially in a particular subject or skill: *Tim's at business college to learn computer accounting.*
2 **part of university** [C] **a)** the part of a university that teaches a particular subject: *the College of Engineering* **b)** one of the groups of students that some universities are officially divided into, which usually has a particular character and particular classes the students must take: *Revell College at UC San Diego*
3 **students and teachers** [C] the students and teachers of a college: *Half of the college must've been at the demonstration.*

4 **organization** [C] a group of people who have special rights and duties within a profession or organization: *the American College of Surgeons* —see also ELECTORAL COLLEGE

5 give sth the (old) college try to try very hard to achieve a GOAL with your group or team, especially when it seems very difficult

College Boards /.' . ,./ n. [plural] TRADEMARK a set of tests taken by students in order to attend some universities

col·le·giate /kə'lidʒət/ adj. **1** relating to college or a college: *He won the Heisman Trophy as the nation's top collegiate football player.* **2** organized into COLLEGES (2): *a collegiate university*

col·lide /kə'laɪd/ v. [I] **1** to crash violently into something or someone: *The two players collided and Jordan fell to the floor.* | [+ with] *Her son was injured when his motorcycle collided with a car.* | *A pickup truck collided head-on with a car (=it hit a car moving directly toward it).* **2** to oppose a person or group, especially on a particular subject: [+ over/with] *The groups have collided over plans for a new cemetery.*

col·lie /'kɑli/ n. [C] a middle-sized dog with long hair, kept as a pet or trained to take care of sheep

col·lier /'kɑlyə/ n. [C] someone who works in a coal mine

col·lier·y /'kɑlyəri/ n. [C] a coal mine and the buildings and machinery relating to it

col·li·sion /kə'lɪʒən/ n. [C,U] **1** a violent crash in which two or more vehicles or people hit each other: [+ with] *Mike had a collision with another skier and broke his leg.* | *She was killed in a head-on collision (=between two vehicles moving directly toward each other) on Highway 218.* **2** a strong disagreement between two people or groups: [+ between] *a collision between police and demonstrators* **3 be on a collision course a)** to be likely to have serious trouble because your aims are very different from someone else's: *Newspaper reports say that the two nations are on a collision course that could lead to war.* **b)** to be moving in a direction in which you will hit another person or vehicle

col·lo·cate /'kɑlə,keɪt/ v. [I + with] TECHNICAL when words collocate with each other, they are often used together and sound natural together —**collocate** /'kɑləkɪt/ n. [C]

col·lo·ca·tion /,kɑlə'keɪʃən/ n. [C,U] TECHNICAL in grammar, the way in which some words are often used together, or a particular combination of words used in this way: *"Commit a crime" is a typical collocation in English.*

col·loid /'kɑlɔɪd/ n. [C] TECHNICAL a mixture of substances in which one substance is completely mixed with another but not DISSOLVEd (1) —compare SUSPENSION (4)

col·lo·qui·al /kə'loʊkwiəl/ adj. language or words that are colloquial are used mainly in informal conversations rather than in writing or formal speech: *colloquial expressions* —**colloquially** adv.

col·lo·qui·al·ism /kə'loʊkwiə,lizəm/ n. [C] an expression or word used mainly in informal conversation

col·lo·qui·um /kə'loʊkwiəm/ n. plural **colloquiums** or **colloquia** /-kwiə/ [C] an event at which someone such as a PROFESSOR gives a talk on a particular subject to a group of people

col·lo·quy /'kɑləkwi/ n. [C] FORMAL a conversation —compare SOLILOQUY

col·lude /kə'lud/ v. [I] FORMAL to work with someone secretly, especially in order to do something dishonest or illegal: [+ with] *Several customs officials have been accused of colluding with drug traffickers.*

col·lu·sion /kə'luʒən/ n. [U] FORMAL the act of agreeing secretly with someone else to do something dishonest or illegal

co·logne /kə'loʊn/ n. [U] a liquid that smells slightly like flowers or plants, which you put on your neck or wrists —compare PERFUME¹ (1)

Co·lom·bi·a /kəˈlʌmbiə/ a country in northern South America —**Colombian** *n.*, *adj.*

Co·lom·bo /kəˈlʌmboʊ/ the capital and largest city of Sri Lanka

co·lon /ˈkoʊlən/ *n.* [C] **1** the lower part of the INTESTINES, in which food is changed into waste matter —see picture at DIGESTIVE SYSTEM **2** the mark (:) used in writing and printing to introduce an explanation, example, list, QUOTATION (1) etc. —compare SEMICOLON

colo·nel, Colonel /ˈkɜnl/ *n.* [C] a high rank in the Army, Marines, or Air Force, or someone who has this rank

co·lo·ni·al¹ /kəˈloʊniəl/ *adj.* **1** relating to the control of countries by a more powerful distant country: *The goal of the uprising was to overthrow the colonial government.* **2** also **Colonial** made in a style that was common in the U.S. in the 18th century: *a Colonial-style brick house* **3** relating to the U.S. when it was under British rule: *The town was first established in colonial times.* —see also COLONY

colonial² *n.* [C] someone who lives in a COLONY (1) but who is a citizen of the country that rules the colony

co·lo·ni·al·ism /kəˈloʊniəˌlɪzəm/ *n.* [U] the principle or practice in which a powerful country rules a weaker one and establishes its own trade and society there —compare IMPERIALISM

co·lo·ni·al·ist /kəˈloʊniəlɪst/ *n.* [C] a supporter of colonialism —**colonialist** *adj.*

col·o·nist /ˈkɑlənɪst/ *n.* [C] someone who settles in a new COLONY (1): *In 1638, Swedish colonists settled in present-day Delaware.*

col·o·nize /ˈkɑləˌnaɪz/ *v.* [I,T] to establish political control over an area or over another country, and send your citizens there to settle —**colonization** /ˌkɑlənəˈzeɪʃən/ *n.* [U] —**colonizer** /ˈkɑlənaɪzə/ *n.* [C]

col·on·nade /ˌkɑləˈneɪd/ *n.* [C] a row of upright stone posts that usually support a roof or row of ARCHes —**colonnaded** *adj.*

col·o·ny /ˈkɑləni/ *n. plural* **colonies** [C] **1** a country or area that is ruled by a more powerful country, usually one that is far away: *Fighting is continuing in the former Belgian colony.* —see also DOMINION (3) PROTECTORATE **2** one of the 13 areas of land on the east coast of North America that later became the United States: *Many people who came to the colonies were escaping religious persecution.* **3** a particular group of people or the place where they live: *an artists' colony on the East Coast* | *a nudist colony* **4** a group of animals or plants of the same type that are living or growing together: *an ant colony* **5** a group of people who live in a colony

s w
col·or¹ /ˈkʌlə/ *n.*
1 red/blue etc. [C] red, blue, yellow, green, brown, purple etc.: *Red is her favorite color.* | *The paint complements the floor color.* | *How did the colors red and green become associated with Christmas?* | *I'd prefer a lighter color, please.* | *The atoms glow a yellowish color.* | *What color are his eyes?*
2 color in general [C,U] the appearance of something, especially something that has a lot of different colors: *In The Wizard of Oz, color was used for the imaginary world, while real life was in black-and-white.* | *Pale colors tend to be soft and feminine.* | *a color photograph* | *We pedaled through Vermont, which was ablaze with fall colors* (=the colors of the trees during the fall).
3 substance [U] a substance such as paint or DYE that makes something red, blue, yellow etc.: *Thiebaud applied color to black-and-white prints.*
4 sb's race [C,U] how dark or light someone's skin is, which shows which race they belong to: *The awards will be given without discrimination based on color, religion, or sex.* —see also COLORED²
5 a person/woman/man of color someone who is not white: *It's important that people of color become involved in government.*

6 sb's face/skin [U] the general appearance and color of someone's skin, especially when this shows the state of their health or emotions: *Kathy doesn't have much color in her cheeks, does she?* | *The baby was fine; he had good color and a strong heartbeat.*
7 in color a television program, movie, or photograph that is in color contains colors such as red, green, and blue, rather than just black and white: *She enjoys "I Love Lucy" even though the program isn't in color.* | *Of the 672 illustrations, 48 are in full color* (=they use all the colors). | *The difference was that we could see the Vietnam War in living color* (=in colors rather than black and white).
8 colors [plural] the colors that are used as a sign to represent a team, school, club etc.: *He always wears Raiders colors, silver and black.*
9 sth interesting [U] interesting and exciting details or qualities that a place or person has: *The play is performed with polish and color.* | *A few personal stories can help give color to your writing* (=make it more interesting). | *a color analyst/commentator* (=someone who gives interesting details about players, games in the past etc. while telling you about a sports game you are watching or listening to)
10 off-color jokes, stories etc. that are off-color are rude and often about sex
11 see the color of sb's money SPOKEN to have definite proof that someone has enough money to pay for something: *I wouldn't give him the books until I saw the color of his money.* —see also with flying colors (FLYING¹ (2)), show your true colors (SHOW¹ (16))

---

color in

color² *v.* **1** [T] to make something colored rather than just black, white, or plain: *She cut and colored Liz's hair.* | *Sweaters are colored with organic dyes.* | *Sunset came and colored the sky a brilliant orange.* **2** [I,T] to put color onto a drawing or picture, or to draw a picture using colored pencils, CRAYONS etc.: *Give Grandma the picture you colored, Jenny.* | *Cut out the square and color it red.* | *Jenny loves to color.* | [+ in] *The kids had sung, played games, and colored in pictures.* **3** [T] **color sb's judgment/opinions/attitudes etc.** to influence the way someone thinks about something, especially so that they become less fair or reasonable: *Critics say the plan is colored by party politics.* **4** [I] FORMAL when someone colors, their face becomes redder because they are embarrassed —see also **color code** (CODE² (3))

color³ *adj.* **a color television/photograph/movie etc.** a television, photograph etc. that produces or shows pictures in color rather than in black, white, and gray —opposite BLACK AND WHITE, MONOCHROME

Col·o·ra·do /ˌkɑləˈrædoʊ, -ˈræ-/ *written abbreviation* **CO** a state in the western central part of the U.S.

Colorado River /ˌ.... ˈ../ a long river in the western U.S., that flows southwest through the U.S. states of Colorado, Utah, and Arizona, and into Mexico

col·or·ant /ˈkʌlərənt/ *n.* [C] TECHNICAL a substance used to color something

col·or·a·tion /ˌkʌləˈreɪʃən/ *n.* [U] the way something is colored or the pattern these colors make; COLORING

col·or·a·tu·ra /ˌkʌlərəˈtʊrə, ˌkɑ-/ n. **1** [U] a difficult piece of music that is meant to be sung fast **2** [C] a woman, especially a SOPRANO, who sings this type of music

col·or·blind, color-blind /ˈkʌlərˌblaɪnd/ adj. **1** not able to see the difference between particular colors **2** treating people from different races equally and fairly: *In this court, justice is colorblind.* —**colorblindness** n. [U]

color-co·or·di·nat·ed /ˌ... .ˈ..../ adj. clothes or decorations that are color-coordinated have colors that look good together —**color-coordination** /ˌ... ...ˈ../ n. [U]

col·ored[1] /ˈkʌlərd/ adj. **1** having a color such as red, blue, yellow etc. rather than being black, white, or plain: *brightly colored bows and ribbons | cream-colored paper* **2** OLD-FASHIONED a word used to describe people who have dark or black skin, now considered offensive

colored[2] n. [C] OLD-FASHIONED a word for someone who has dark or black skin, now considered offensive

colored pen·cil /ˌ... ˈ../ n. [C] a pencil that writes in a particular color, rather than black

color·fast /ˈkʌlərˌfæst/ adj. cloth that is colorfast will not lose its color when it is washed —**colorfastness** n. [U]

col·or·ful /ˈkʌlərfəl/ adj. **1** having a lot of bright colors or a lot of different colors: *American Indian dancers in colorful costumes* **2** interesting, exciting, and full of variety: *a lecture full of colorful stories | Mr. Watson is one of the most colorful characters* (=interesting and unusual people) *I've ever met.* **3** colorful language, speech etc. uses a lot of swearing —**colorfully** adv.

col·or·ing /ˈkʌlərɪŋ/ n. **1** a substance used to give a particular color to food: *This is the same caramel coloring used in colas.* **2** [U] the activity of putting colors into drawings, or of drawing using CRAYONS, colored pencils etc.: *a coloring contest for children* **3** [U] the color of someone's skin, hair, and eyes: *People with light coloring tend to sunburn easily.* **4** [U] the colors of an animal, bird, or plant: *These birds resemble miniature penguins, with their black and white coloring.* —see also FOOD COLORING

coloring book /ˈ... ˌ./ n. [C] a book full of pictures that are drawn without color so that a child can color them in

col·or·ize /ˈkʌlərˌaɪz/ v. [T] to add color to an old movie that was made in BLACK AND WHITE —**colorization** /ˌkʌlərəˈzeɪʃən/ n. [U]

col·or·less /ˈkʌlərlɪs/ adj. **1** having no color: *a colorless gas* **2** not interesting or exciting; BORING: *Barker gave a completely colorless performance in his role as Hamlet.* —**colorlessly** adv. —**colorlessness** n. [U]

color line /ˈ.. ./ n. [singular] a set of laws in past times that did not let black people do the same things or go to the same places as white people: *Two black students crossed the color line at the previously all-white university.*

color scheme /ˈ.. ˌ./ n. [C] the combination of colors that someone chooses for a room, painting etc.: *an attractive color scheme*

co·los·sal /kəˈlɑsəl/ adj. extremely large: *Ramses ordered colossal statues carved in his honor. | It was a colossal disappointment.* —**colossally** adv.

Co·los·sians /kəˈlɑʃənz/ a book in the New Testament of the Christian Bible

co·los·sus /kəˈlɑsəs/ n. [C] someone or something that is very large or very important: *Entertainment colossus MCA Inc. was purchased for $6.6 billion.*

col·our /ˈkʌlər/ the British and Canadian spelling of COLOR, also used in the words, "colourant," "coloured," "colourfast," "colourful," "colouring," and "colourless"

Colt /koʊlt/ n. [C] TRADEMARK a type of PISTOL: *a Colt ·45 revolver*

colt /koʊlt/ n. [C] a young male horse —compare FILLY (1)

colt·ish /ˈkoʊltɪʃ/ adj. **1** a young person or animal that is coltish has a lot of energy but moves in an

awkward way **2** coltish arms or legs are long and thin

Col·trane /ˈkoʊltreɪn/, **John** (1926–1967) a U.S. JAZZ musician who played the SAXOPHONE and had a great influence on the development of modern jazz

Co·lum·bi·a[1] /kəˈlʌmbiə/ the capital city of the U.S. state of South Carolina

Columbia[2] —see DISTRICT OF COLUMBIA

Columbia River /ˌ.... ˈ../ a river that flows south from the Rocky Mountains in southeastern Canada and through the U.S. state of Washington to the Pacific Ocean

col·um·bine /ˈkɑləmˌbaɪn/ n. [C] a garden plant with delicate leaves and bright flowers that hang down

Co·lum·bus /kəˈlʌmbəs/ the capital city of the U.S. state of Ohio

Columbus, Christopher (1451–1506) an Italian sailor and EXPLORER who is traditionally thought of as the first European to discover America, in 1492. Most people now think that America was first discovered about 500 years earlier, by the Norwegian Leif Ericsson.

Columbus Day /ˈ.. ˌ./ n. [C] a holiday on the second Monday in October in the U.S. to celebrate the discovery of the New World in 1492 by Christopher Columbus

col·umn /ˈkɑləm/ n. [C] **1** a tall solid upright stone post used to support a building or as a decoration: *a row of Greek columns* **2** an article on a particular subject or by a particular writer that appears regularly in a newspaper or magazine: *an advice column | His column appears every other week in the local paper.* **3** something that has a long thin shape, like a column: *The car has an adjustable steering column. | [+ of] Firefighters battled columns of flames.* **4** one of two or more lines of print that go down the page of a newspaper or book and that are separated from each other by a narrow space: *The article I told you about is in the left column.* **5** a line of numbers or words written under each other that goes down a page: *The first column is for expenses.* **6** a long moving line of people or things: *Columns of factory workers waved banners.* —see also FIFTH COLUMN, SPINAL COLUMN

col·um·nist /ˈkɑləmnɪst, ˈkɑləmɪst/ n. [C] someone who writes articles, especially about a particular subject, that appear regularly in a newspaper or magazine

com /kɑm/ an abbreviation of "company," used in U.S. Internet addresses

com- /kəm, kɑm/ prefix used instead of CON- before the letters "b," "m," or "p"; WITH: *companion* (=someone you spend time with)

co·ma /ˈkoʊmə/ n. [C] a state in which someone is not conscious for a long time, usually after a serious accident or illness: *He's been in a coma since last week.*

Co·man·che n. /kəˈmæntʃi/ a Native American tribe from the southwestern region of the U.S. —**Comanche** adj.

Co·ma·neci /ˌkoʊməˈnitʃ/, **Na·di·a** /ˈnɑdiə/ (1961–) a Romanian GYMNAST famous for winning three GOLD MEDALS in the 1976 Olympic Games

co·ma·tose /ˈkoʊməˌtoʊs, ˈkɑ-/ adj. **1** TECHNICAL in a coma **2** INFORMAL so tired that you cannot think clearly: *We just sat comatose in front of the TV.*

comb[1] /koʊm/ n. **1** [C] a flat piece of plastic, metal etc. with a row of thin things like small sticks on one side, used to make your hair look neat **2** [C] a small flat piece of plastic, metal etc. with a row of thin things like small sticks on one side, used for keeping your hair back or for decoration **3** [C] the red piece of flesh that grows on top of a male chicken's head **4** [C] a HONEYCOMB —see also FINE-TOOTHED COMB

comb[2] v. [T] **1** to make your hair look neat with a comb: *His blond hair was neatly combed.* **2** to search

C

a place thoroughly: *Tugboats and helicopters combed the area before the body was finally found.* | [**comb sth for sb/sth**] *Police combed the forest for clues.*

comb sth ↔ **out** *phr. v.* [T] to make messy hair look neat and smooth using a comb: *The worst thing about having long hair is combing out the tangles.*

comb through *phr. v.* [T] to search through a lot of objects or information in order to find a specific thing or piece of information: *We spent weeks combing through huge piles of old documents.*

com·bat[1] /ˈkɑmbæt/ *n.* **1** [U] organized fighting, especially in a war: *The truce has not stopped combat in the civil war.* | *Vietnam lost about 1 million people* **in combat.** | **see combat** (=be involved in fighting in a war) | **combat vehicle/jacket/boots etc.** (=one that is used when fighting a war) **2** [C] a fight, argument, or battle: [**+ between/against**] *It seemed like my life was one long combat against my sister.* | *We observed a pair of lions,* **locked in mortal combat** (=fighting until one of the opponents dies). —**combat** *adj.*

com·bat[2] /kəmˈbæt, ˈkɑmbæt/ *v.* **combated, combating** [T] FORMAL **1** to try to stop something bad from happening or getting worse: *The Cabinet has recommended new measures to combat organized crime.* | *A conference will be held on how to combat pollution of the oceans.* **2** to fight against an enemy or opponent in order to try and defeat them, especially in a war

com·bat·ant /kəmˈbætˈnt/ *n.* [C] someone who fights in a war

combat fa·tigue /ˈ.. .,./ *n.* [U] TECHNICAL: see BATTLE FATIGUE

com·ba·tive /kəmˈbætɪv/ *adj.* showing eagerness to fight or argue: *Former Mayor Koch won a reputation for his combative style.* —**combatively** *adv.* —**combativeness** *n.* [U]

s w **com·bi·na·tion** /ˌkɑmbəˈneɪʃən/ *n.* **1** [C,U] two or
2 2 more different things, qualities, substances etc. that are used or put together: *I'll have the shrimp and chicken combination, please.* | [**+ of**] *Experts believe that a combination of bad weather and human error led to the accident.* | *Drinking and driving can be a* **lethal combination.** | *Use of the drug* **in combination with** *diet changes will help you lose weight.* **2** [C] a particular arrangement or way of putting two or more things together that have been chosen from a group: [**+ of**] *The design was a combination of Victorian and Tudor styles.* | *Language is flexible – we can all understand combinations of words we have never heard before.* **3** [C] the series of numbers or letters you need to open a combination lock: *What's the matter? Can't you remember the combination?* **4 a winning combination** a mixture of different people or things that work successfully together **5** [U] used before a noun in some phrases to mean that something does more than one job or uses more than one method: *The new device is a combination copier, fax, image scanner, and document printer.*

combination lock /ˌ.... ˈ./ *n.* [C] a lock that is opened by using a special series of numbers or letters

combination plate /ˌ.... ˈ./ *n.* [C] a plate with several different types of food on it, served to one person at a restaurant

s w **com·bine**[1] /kəmˈbaɪn/ *v.* **1** [I,T] if you combine two
2 or more different things, ideas, or qualities or if they combine, they begin to exist or work together: *Modern and traditional teaching methods are combined at the school.* | [**combine sth with sth**] *Diets are most effective when combined with exercise.* | [**combine to do sth**] *The beautiful weather and site combined to make the concert this year's most successful outdoor event.* | *Patients should be more aware of the* **combined effects** (=the result of several things used or mixed together) *of their medications.* **2** [I,T] two or more different substances combine or if you combine them, they mix together to produce a new substance: [**combine to do sth**]

Different amino acids combine to form proteins. | [**combine sth**] *Combine the rest of the ingredients in a small saucepan.* | [**combine sth with sth**] *Steel is produced by combining iron with carbon.* **3** [T] to do two different activities at the same time: [**combine sth with sth**] *It's hard to combine family life with a career.* | [**combine sth and sth**] *Most college students today combine school and work.* **4** [T] to add several numbers or amounts together to form a larger amount: *The highest possible score on each section is 800, for a combined score of 1600.* | *The banks plan to merge and combine their assets.* | *He makes more money than everyone else in the office combined.* **5** [I,T] if two or more groups, organizations etc. combine or if you combine them, they join or work together in order to do something: [**combine to do sth**] *The two car makers combined to form a new company.* | [**combine sth**] *The coach plans to combine best players from the two teams.*

com·bine[2] /ˈkɑmbaɪn/ *n.* [C] **1** a large machine used on a farm to cut a crop and separate the grain at the same time **2** a group of people, businesses etc. that work together: *The factory was sold to a European combine.*

com·bined /kəmˈbaɪnd/ *adj.* **1** [only before noun] done, made, or achieved by several people or groups working together: *It was a combined reunion, the class of 1965 with the class of 1970.* **2** having two very different feelings at the same time: *Ann felt a combined relief and sadness.*

com·bo /ˈkɑmboʊ/ *n. plural* **combos** [C] INFORMAL **1** a small group of musicians who play dance music **2** a combination of things, especially different foods at a restaurant: *I'll have the fish combo and a beer.*

com·bust /kəmˈbʌst/ *v.* [I] INFORMAL to start burning: *Scientists say that drying your clothes in the microwave might cause them to* **spontaneously combust.**

com·bus·ti·ble /kəmˈbʌstəbəl/ *adj.* able to begin burning easily: *Gasoline is* **highly combustible.**

com·bus·tion /kəmˈbʌstʃən/ *n.* [U] **1** the process of burning **2** TECHNICAL chemical activity that uses oxygen to produce light and heat **3 combustion chamber** an enclosed space in which combustion happens in an engine —see also INTERNAL-COMBUSTION ENGINE

come[1] /kʌm/ *v. past tense* **came** *past participle* **come** **s w**
[I]   **1 1**

1 move to to move to or toward a person who is speaking or to the place that they are talking about: *Come a little closer.* | *Sarah's coming later on.* | [**+ to/toward/back etc.**] *When are you coming back?* | *My boss didn't come to work today.* | [**+ for**] *What day are your parents coming for dinner?* | [**come and do sth**] *Can Anne come and play?* | [**come to do sth**] *A neighbor's boy comes to mow the grass on Saturdays.* | *Charlie,* **come here,** *quick.* | **come running/ flying/speeding etc.** *Jesse came flying around the corner and banged right into me.*

2 visit to visit somewhere, especially someone's house: *We come here every summer* | [**+ down/ over/up**] *Jerry and Julie will come down early on Saturday.* | *The Simpsons are coming over for dinner.* | *Why don't you come up to New York for the weekend?*

3 arrive to arrive: *The phone bill came at a bad time.* | *Christianity came to Russia in 989.* | *Her mother* **came home** *from vacation a day early.*

4 move with sb to move to a particular place with the person who is speaking: *Can Billy come too?* | [**+ with**] *Why don't you come to the concert with me?* | [**+ along**] *Brittany can come along too, if she wants.*

5 state/condition/position [always + adv./prep.] to begin to exist or be effective, used, understood, seen etc.: [**+ into**] *As we turned the corner, the town came into view.* | *The law will come into effect on June 1st.* | [**+ to**] *There is no reason they can't come to some sort of agreement.* | *The Communists came to power in China in 1949.* | *Have you come to a decision?* | *Buttons* **came into being** *first as ornaments rather than fasteners.* | *The science of pruning plants correctly* **comes into play** (=begins to be used) *when* *you learn how plants grow.* | *The extent of the financial crisis is just now* **coming into focus** (=beginning to be understood clearly).

6 `travel` to travel in a particular way or for a particular distance or time in order to get somewhere: *Some of the birds have come thousands of miles to winter here.* | *[+ by/on/with etc.]* *We came by train.*

7 `time/event` if a time or event comes, it arrives or happens: *Winter came early that year.* | *[+ before/after/later]* *The vote came after three hours of heated debate.* | *His comments came a day after the UN sent a peacekeeping force to the region.* | ***The time has come** for some radical changes.* | *Economists say* ***the worst is yet to come** (=worse things will happen in the future).* | ***Coming soon**, to a theater near you!* (=used especially in advertisements)

8 `be sold/available` to be sold, produced, or available: *The camera comes complete with batteries.* | *[+ in]* *These shoes don't come in size 11.* | *Houses like that **don't come cheap**.*

9 `list/order` *[always + adv./prep.]* to have a particular position in the order of something: *[+ before/after]* *No, the song comes before the Bible reading.* | **come first/second/next etc.** *Who comes third in the batting order?*

10 **come first** to be the most important thing to someone: *Alma's family will always come first with her.*

11 **come as a surprise/relief/shock etc. (to sb)** to make someone feel surprised, RELIEVED etc.: *It came as kind of a shock to me.* | *The food was excellent,* which should **come as no surprise** (=be expected) *to those who know the chef's reputation.*

12 `length/height` *[always + adv./prep.]* to reach a particular height or length: *[+ to]* *The grass came to my knees.* | *[+ up to/down to etc.]* *Carrie's hair comes down to her waist.*

13 **come open/undone/loose etc.** to become open, loose etc.: *Your shoelace just came untied.* | *The bottle came open in my backpack!*

14 **have come a long way** to have made a lot of progress: *Computer technology has come a long way since the 1570s.*

15 **years/weeks/days etc. to come** used to emphasize that something is still in the future or will continue into the future: *Nuclear waste will remain hazardous for years to come.* —see also COMING[1]

16 **have it coming** to deserve to be punished or to have something bad happen to you: *I don't feel sorry for Brad – he had it coming.*

17 **as big/heavy/good etc. as they come** also **as big/heavy etc. as it comes** having as much of a particular quality as is possible: *Roy Williams of Kansas is as smart as they come.* | *Burnett's "Moaning at Midnight" is blues as pure as it comes.*

18 `light` *[always + adv./prep.]* if light comes in or through something, you can see it in a particular place: *The morning sun came through the doorway.*

19 `sex` VULGAR to have an ORGASM

20 **come easily/naturally (to sb)** to be easy for someone to do, say etc.: *Acting has always come naturally to her.* | *Change doesn't always come easily.*

21 **come of age a)** to reach an age, usually 18 or 21, when you are considered by law to be an adult **b)** if an artist, style, or organization comes of age, they reach their best, most successful period of time: *Mozart's music came of age when the baroque style was at its height.*

22 **come what may** whatever happens: *I decided that, come what may, the three of us could handle it.*

23 **come sb's way** if something comes your way, you get or experience it, especially if you were not expecting it: *We're determined to take every opportunity that comes our way.*

24 **come calling a)** to attract someone's attention because you want to offer them something, get something from them, have them deal with something etc.: *After Troy's junior year in high school, colleges came calling with scholarship offers.* **b)** OLD-FASHIONED to visit someone: *Rudy did not come calling the next day.*

25 **not know whether you are coming or going**

INFORMAL to feel confused, especially because you have a lot of things to think about: *Andre's so in love he doesn't know whether he's coming or going.*

SPOKEN PHRASES

26 how come? used to ask someone why something has happened or why it is true: *How come Tyler's still here?* | *"She's moving to Alaska." "How come?"* | *How come the sky is blue?*

27 here comes sb said when someone is about to arrive at the place where you are: *Here comes Lori now.*

28 come to think of it said when you have just realized or remembered something: *Come to think of it, Cooper did mention it to me.*

29 take sth as it comes to accept something exactly as it happens or is given to you, without trying to change it or plan ahead: *I'm not going to worry about it. I'll just take each day as it comes.* | *I'll play in Monday's game and then take it as it comes.*

30 come July/next year/2010 etc. at a particular time in the future: *Come Monday, we'll be in our new house.*

31 come again? used to ask someone to repeat what they just said: *"She gave us tea from her samovar." "Come again?" "It's a kind of Russian teapot."*

32 come (now) OLD-FASHIONED said to comfort or gently encourage someone, or to tell them you do not like what they are doing: *Come, Sarah, don't cry.*

—see also **come clean** (CLEAN[1] (6)), **come to grips with sth** (GRIP[1] (3)), **come to life** (LIFE (13)) —see Usage Note at BECOME

come about *phr. v.* [I] to happen or develop: *High-tech solutions to the problem are not likely to come about soon.* | ***How did** this change **come about?***

come across *phr. v.* **1** [T not in passive **come across** sb/sth] to meet someone or find or discover something by chance: *I came across a picture of you when I was going through my stuff.* | *An airport employee came across the three kids alone in the terminal.* **2** [I] to make someone have a particular opinion of you: *Some candidates simply do not come across well on screen.* | **[come across as (being) sth]** *Sandi comes across as a really happy person.* | *Sometimes you come across as being kind of rude.* **3** [I] if an idea comes across to someone, they understand it clearly: *Your point really came across at the meeting.*

come after sb *phr. v.* [T not in passive] to look for someone so you can hurt them, punish them, or get something from them: *If I don't pay back the money soon, Vinnie's going to come after me.*

come along *phr. v.* [I] **1** to happen or arrive, especially at a time you do not know or expect: *Jobs like this don't come along very often!* | *We'd been married about a year when Joey came along* (=was born). **2** INFORMAL to develop or improve: *The corn crop is coming along fine this year.* | *Aaron has really come along – his reading is at third grade level now.*

come apart *phr. v.* [I] **1** to split or break into pieces, without anyone using force: *The book just came apart in my hands.* **2** if a situation comes apart, bad things start happening: *My marriage came apart that summer.* | *The lawsuit began **coming apart at the seams**.*

come around *phr. v.* **1** [I,T **come around** sth] to visit someone: *When's a good time to come around and drop off his present?* | *Stevens is a stockbroker now and still comes around the campus to advise students on their career prospects.* **2** [I] to decide to agree with someone, after disagreeing with them: *It took some persuading, but he finally came around.* **3** [I] if a regular event comes around, it happens as usual: *Christmas seems to come around so fast.* **4** [I] to become conscious again: *It was three weeks before she came around.*

come at sb/sth *phr. v.* [T not in passive] **1** to move toward someone in a threatening way: *The man came at me with a hammer.* **2** if information, work, people etc. come at you, they all have to be

C

dealt with at once, so that you feel confused or anxious: *At work, things keep coming at you all the time.* **3** INFORMAL to consider or deal with a problem: *We need to come at the problem from a different angle.*

come away *phr. v.* [I] **1** to become separated from something: [+ **from**] *Cook the tamales until they come away easily from the cornhusk.* **2** to be affected in a particular way after something has happened or after you have left a place: [+ **from**] *I came away from the interview feeling really good.* | [+ **with**] *Cannon came away with the impression that McFarlane would be a good man to work with.*

come back *phr. v.* [I] **1** to return from a place: *I won't be coming back tonight.* **2 come back to sb** SPOKEN to be remembered, especially suddenly: *Everything Williams had said suddenly came back to me.* **3** to become fashionable or popular again: *The styles of the seventies are coming back.* **4** to reply to something that someone said with a quick funny remark: [+ **with**] *I just wish I could have come back with a snappy remark when Todd said that about my hair.* —see also COMEBACK

come before sb *phr. v.* [T] FORMAL to be given or shown to someone in authority in order to be considered or judged: *Briggs' case may come before a jury within the next month.*

come between sb *phr. v.* [T not in passive] **1** to cause trouble between two or more people: *He never thought anything would come between us.* **2** to prevent someone from giving enough attention to something: *I don't let anything come between me and my work.*

come by sth *phr. v.* **1** [I,T not in passive] to visit someone or go to someone's house for a short time before going somewhere else: *I'll come by later to pick up Katrina.* | *Do you want to come by our place later?* **2** [T not in passive] to get something that is difficult to find: *How on earth did you come by these tickets?* | *Jobs are hard to come by* (=are hard to find) *these days.*

come down *phr. v.* [I]
1 become lower **a)** if a price, level etc. comes down, it becomes lower: *Wait until interest rates come down before you buy a house.* **b)** to offer or accept a lower price: [+ **on/to**] *They refused to come down on the price.* | *We need them to come down to $1.50 a square foot.*
2 building if a building comes down, it is destroyed by being pulled down: *The Berlin Wall came down in 1989.*
3 come (back) down to earth to begin dealing with ordinary practical problems in a practical way, after ignoring them for a time: *After first proposing huge raises, the union came down to earth.*
4 drugs [+ **off/from**] INFORMAL to stop being affected by a powerful illegal drug such as HEROIN or LSD that you have taken
5 come down in the world to become poorer or less successful than you used to be.
6 come down in sb's opinion/estimation to do something that makes someone respect you less: *John really came down in my opinion after that.* —see also COMEDOWN

come down on sb/sth *phr. v.* [T not in passive] **1** to punish someone or criticize them severely: *The first time the boss came down on Pete, he quit.* | [**come down on sb for doing sth**] *My parents really came down on me for being out so late.* | *I thought the movie was okay, but the critics came down hard on it.* **2 come down on the side of sth** to decide to support something: *The court came down on the side of the boy's father.*

come down to sb/sth *phr. v.* [T not in passive] **1** if a difficult or confusing situation comes down to one thing, that thing is the basic problem or the most important thing you have to do to solve it: *It came down to a choice between cutting wages or cutting staff.* **2 when it comes (right) down to it** used to say what the main or most important idea or thing is in a situation: *When it comes right down to it, I'd rather spend my money on hobbies like go-cart*

racing than on alcohol and cigarettes. **3** if a document, object, idea etc. comes down to someone, it has continued to exist from a long time ago until the present: *The text which has come down to us is only a fragment of the original.*

come down with sth *phr. v.* [T not in passive] INFORMAL to become infected with a particular illness.: *I think I'm coming down with a cold.*

come for sb/sth *phr. v.* [T] **1** to arrive to take someone or something away: *Did the guy come for the washing machine yet?* **2** to try to harm someone or take them away where they do not want to go: *An angry crowd came for the two men.*

come forward *phr. v.* [I] **1** to offer to help someone in an official position with a crime or problem, especially by giving them information: *Women are becoming more willing to come forward in cases of rape.* | [+ **with**] *Several students came forward with information on some of the vandals.* **2** to offer to do something: *There may be layoffs if not enough people come forward for early retirement.* | [**come forward to do sth**] *Community volunteers came forward to help build a new playground.* **3** to say publicly that something bad has happened to you or that you are responsible for something, especially when you would prefer to keep it a secret: *Johnson came forward to say that he had HIV.* | *One of the boys came forward and apologized.*

come from sb/sth *phr. v.* [T] **1** [not in progressive] to have been born in a particular place: "*Where do you come from?*" "*Texas.*" **2** [not in progressive] to have first existed, been made, or produced in a particular place, thing or time: *Milk comes from cows.* | *The lines she read come from a novel by Charles Dickens.* **3** if a sound comes from a particular place, it begins there: *Where's that music coming from?* **4 where sb's coming from** if you talk about where someone is coming from, you mean that what they are saying or doing is affected by their emotions, character, interests etc.: *Connie's really a right-wing religious person, and that's not where I'm coming from at all.*

come in *phr. v.*
1 enter [I] to enter a room or house: *Hi, Emma, come in.* | *I thought I recognized him when he came in.*
2 arrive [I] to arrive or be received: *Reports are coming in of a severe earthquake in Mexico.* | *What time does Kelli's plane come in?*
3 be involved [I] to be involved in a plan, deal etc.: *I need somebody to help, and that's where you come in.* | [+ **on**] *Jeanine might like to come in on the gift* (=buy it together) *with us.*
4 become fashionable [I] to become fashionable or popular to use: *Platform shoes came in again in the 1990s.* —opposite **go out of fashion/style** (GO[1])
5 come in first/second etc. to finish first, second etc. in a race or competition: *Jones came in fifth in the 100 meter dash.*
6 come in useful/handy to be useful: *My Swiss Army knife came in handy on our trip around Europe.*
7 [T **come in** sth] to exist or be available in a particular form: *Cats come in many shapes and sizes.*
8 ocean [I] when the TIDE (=level of the ocean) comes in, it rises —opposite **go out** GO[1] —see also **come in from the cold** (COLD[2] (4))

come in for sth *phr. v.* [T] **come in for criticism/blame/scrutiny** to be criticized, blamed etc. for something: *Thompson came in for sharp criticism from women's groups.*

come into sth *phr. v.* [T not in passive] **1 come into effect/force/operation** if a new law, system, rule etc. comes into effect, it begins to be used or to have an effect: *Government regulations came into effect this year that specify how much advertising can be shown during children's TV programs.* **2 come into being/existence** to begin to exist: *Before the specialized units came into being, polio patients were treated in general hospitals.* **3** to be involved in something or to influence it: *John came into the business as an equal partner.* | *I don't know if racism comes into it.* **4 come into money/a fortune** to receive money, land etc. after someone has died; INHERIT (1): *Last year they came into a large sum of* money when their Uncle Harry died. **5 come (back) into fashion** to become a popular thing to wear or do: *A-line skirts are coming into fashion again.* **6 come into your own** to become very good, useful, or important in a particular situation: *This season Brooks has really come into his own as a goal scorer.*

come of sth *phr. v.* [T] to result from something: *There was some discussion about buying some new equipment, but nothing ever came of it.*

come off *phr. v.*
1 not on/attached [I,T not in passive **come off** sth] to not be on something, connected to it, or fastened to it anymore: *A button came off my coat yesterday.* | *I can't get the lid to come off.* | [+ onto/on] *Some wet paint came off onto her hands.*
2 attitude/quality [I] to seem like you have a particular attitude or quality because of something you say or do: [+ as] *In the early scenes, Matt's supposed to be boyish and naive, but he comes off as stupid.* | [come off doing sth] *Some of these guys come off sounding like they think they're God's gift to women.* | *Marty came off looking like a fool.*
3 finish [T not in passive **come off** sth] if someone or something comes off something, they have just finished it before beginning something else: *Caan is coming off his most successful movie in 20 years.* | *The Warriors are coming off a 10-point loss to the Clippers.*
4 happen [I] to happen, especially in a particular way: *The wedding came off as planned.* | *If the deal does come off, it will involve a lot of money.*
5 succeed [I] to be successful or have the intended effect: *The joke just didn't come off very well.* | *Several songs came off better in concert than on their album.*
6 come off it! SPOKEN said when you think someone is being stupid or unreasonable, or when you do not believe something they have just said: *Oh, come off it, George. Sheila wouldn't do that.*
7 come off heroin/tranquilizers etc. to stop taking a drug that is ADDICTIVE (=makes you want to continue taking it)

come on *phr. v.*
1 come on! SPOKEN **a)** used to tell someone to hurry, or to come with you: *Come on! We're already late!* | *Here boy, come on Pecos, good dog.* **b) come on in/back/down etc.** used to tell someone to come to a particular place: *Joe! It's good to see you – come on in* (=come in to the room, office etc.). | *Roberto, come on back and help me lift this* | *come a room further inside in a building).* | *Come on down to Sky Ford, where the prices are unbeatable.* **c)** said in order to encourage someone to do something: *Come on, guys, you can do it!* | *Come on, Ben, I'll dance with you.* **d)** said when you do not believe what someone has just said: *Oh come on, don't lie to me!* **e)** used when you think what someone has said or done is stupid or unreasonable: *I mean, come on, is he really that naive?* | *Well, what was he supposed to do? Shoot him? Come on!* | *Come on, you know what I mean.*
2 light/machine [I] if a light or machine comes on, it starts working: *You clap your hands and the light comes on.*
3 TV/radio show [I] if a television or radio program comes on, it starts: *"Frasier" comes on at eight.*
4 illness [I usually in progressive] if an illness comes on, you start to have it: *Julie complained that she felt an asthma attack coming on.*
5 develop [I] to improve, develop, or progress: *Last year, Choe didn't play well, but this year she's coming on strong* (=improving a lot).
6 begin [I] if winter, spring, darkness etc. comes on, it begins: *The country is facing food shortages as winter comes on.*
7 come on strong/fast INFORMAL to make it very clear to someone that you think they are sexually attractive

come on to sb *phr. v.* [T] INFORMAL if someone comes on to another person, they make it very clear that they are sexually interested in them: *We were at a restaurant, and some girl was coming on to Jason.*

come out *phr. v.*
1 become known [I] to become publicly known, especially after being hidden: *It was several weeks*

before the truth came out. | *The news came out that the Mayor had had a heart attack.*
2 sell if a book, record etc. comes out, people are able to buy it: *When does Janowitz's new book come out?*
3 say publicly [always + adv./prep.] to say something publicly or directly: [+ for/against etc.] *Senator Peters came out strongly against abortion.* | *He'd like some grandchildren, but he won't just come right out and say it.*
4 dirt if dirt or a mark comes out of cloth, it can be washed out: *Ink stains will usually come out if you use a little stain remover first.* | [+ of] *I can't get these pen marks to come out of my shirt.*
5 be said if something you say comes out in a particular way, you say it that way or it is understood by someone in that way: *The words came out in little more than a whisper.* | *When I try to explain, it comes out all wrong* (=you do not say it in the way you intended), *and she gets mad.*
6 come out well/badly/ahead etc. to finish an action or process or to be finished in a particular way or with a particular result: *I figure I'll come out about $400 ahead every month with this new job.* | *I can never get cakes to come out right.* | *Some of the wedding photos didn't come out very well.*
7 homosexual if someone comes out, they say openly that they are HOMOSEXUAL
8 sun/moon if the sun, moon, or stars come out, they appear in the sky
9 flower if a flower comes out, it opens: *The crocuses are coming out.*
10 girl OLD-FASHIONED if a young woman comes out, she is formally introduced to upper-class members of society, usually at a dance

come out with sth *phr. v.* [T not in passive] **1** if a company comes out with a new product, they have made or developed it and are now making it available to be bought: *Chrysler has come out with a new line of minivans.* **2** SPOKEN to say something that is unexpected and funny or shocking: *I enjoyed playing the character of Stephanie because she was always coming out with funny quotes.*

come over *phr. v.* **1** [I] to travel or move from another country to the place where you are now: *Thousands of tourists come over every year.* | [+ to/from] *Her dad came over from Italy when he was in his twenties.* **2** [T not in passive **come over**] if a strong feeling comes over someone, they suddenly experience it: *A wave of sleepiness came over me.* | *I don't usually swear –* **I don't know what came over me!** (=I cannot explain why I behaved in a bad or strange way)

come through *phr. v.* **1** [T not in passive **come through** sth] to continue to live, exist, be strong, or succeed after a difficult or dangerous time: *Bill came through the operation all right.* | *Their house came through the storm without much damage.* **2** [I] if something such as a LOAN (=money you borrow from a bank) comes through, it arrives or is approved by someone: *I can't get a work-study job until my financial aid comes through.* | *It may take up to a month for your visa to come through.* **3** [I] to help or do something for someone, especially something you have promised to do: *Mike said he could get us tickets, so hopefully he'll come through.* | [+ with] *There is pressure on the West to come through with more aid.* **4** [I] if information, news etc. comes through, it becomes known or heard: *News of the coup came through late Tuesday night.*

come to *phr. v.* **1** [I] to become conscious again after having been unconscious: *He came to a few minutes later, unable to remember anything about the accident.* **2** [T **come to** sb] if an idea, thought, or memory comes to you, you suddenly realize or remember it: *The solution came to him late one night in a dream.* | *I've forgotten her name, but maybe it'll come to me later.* **3 come to $20/$3 etc.** to add up to a total of $20, $3 etc.: *That comes to $24.67, ma'am.* | *How much did the meal come to?* **4 when it comes to** sth INFORMAL **a)** relating to a particular subject: *I* can use a computer, but when it comes to repairing them I don't know a thing. **b)** when you are dealing with something: *When it comes to relationships, everyone makes mistakes.* **5 come to do sth** to begin to think or feel a particular way after knowing someone or doing something a long time: *That's the kind of behavior we've come to expect from Bryant.* | *We've come to cherish those memories.* **6 come to pass** LITERARY to happen after a period of time: *It came to pass that they had a son.*

come under sth *phr. v.* [T not in passive] **1 come under attack/fire/pressure etc.** to experience something bad such as an attack, criticism etc.: *The future of the orchestra has come under threat.* | *Courier came under investigation last April.* **2** to be governed, controlled, or influenced by something: *Moldova came under Soviet control in 1940.* **3** to say what type of thing something is, or put it or list it in a particular group: *Self-help books come under the psychology section of the store.* —see also **come/go under the hammer** (HAMMER[1] (2))

come up *phr. v.* [I]
1 move near to move near someone or something, especially by walking: *George came up and introduced himself to us.* | [+ **to/behind** etc.] *Come up to the front of the room so everyone can see you.*
2 mention to be mentioned or suggested: *A lot of new questions came up at the meeting.* | *Parson's name has come up for the position of head coach.*
3 happen if something, especially a problem, comes up, it suddenly happens: *Something's come up, so I won't be able to go with you on Thursday.* | *You should try to deal with each problem as it comes up.*
4 be coming up to be happening soon: *Alison's birthday is coming up.* | *Don't forget you have a test coming up on Thursday.*
5 appear to appear or be shown, especially by chance: *If my lotto numbers come up, I'll be a millionaire!* | *Click twice, and the encyclopedia program will come up on screen.*
6 sun/moon when the sun or moon comes up, it rises: *The sun came up around 5:30.*
7 job if a job comes up, it becomes available: *I've been out of work before, but something always comes up.*
8 plants when a plant comes up, you can see it start growing above the ground: *The tulips usually start coming up in late March.*
9 come up empty/empty-handed to not be able to find something or to not be successful in something you are trying to do: *Even the FBI has come up empty in its search for Weiss.*
10 coming (right) up! SPOKEN used to say that something, especially food or drink, will be ready very soon: *"Two martinis, please." "Coming right up!"*
11 come up in the world to become richer or more successful in society: *She had come up in the world since her days on the flower stall.*

come up against sth/sb *phr. v.* [T not in passive] to have to deal with difficult problems or people: *The novel's about a man who comes up against racism in a Midwest town.*

come up for sth *phr. v.* [T] **1 come up for review/renewal/discussion etc.** to have a time set for when something will be examined, changed etc.: *The contract comes up for renewal next year.* **2 come up for sale** to become available to be sold: *The house came up for sale last summer.* **3 come up for a vote** if something comes up for a vote, it is ready to be voted on at a meeting, in Congress etc. at a particular time: *The bill will come up for a vote in September.*

come up on sth *phr. v.* [T] **be coming up on sth** INFORMAL to be getting closer to a time, date, event etc.: *We're coming up on Labor Day, which means the summer is almost over.* | *It's coming up on two decades since a Tucson school won the high school football championship.*

come upon sth/sb *phr. v.* [T not in passive] LITERARY to find or discover something or someone by chance: *Suddenly we came upon two bears in a clearing in the forest.*

come up with sth *phr. v.* [T] **1** to think of an idea, plan, reply etc.: *Jordan has come up with some creative ideas for helping the homeless.* | *I do the music, and Trey comes up with the lyrics.* **2** to be able to get a particular amount of money: *We have to come up with $1500 to get the car fixed.*

come with *phr. v.* [I] SPOKEN, INFORMAL to go somewhere with someone else: *Danny and I are going to the Galleria. Do you want to come with?*

come[2] *n.* [U] SLANG another spelling of CUM

come-back /'kʌmbæk/ *n.* [C usually singular] **1** a return to being powerful, popular, or famous again after being unpopular or unknown for a long time: **make/stage a comeback** *The miniskirt made a comeback in the late 1980s.* **2** a situation in a sports competition in which a person or team begins playing better after playing badly: *The A's made a comeback in the eighth inning.* **3** a quick reply that is smart or funny; RETORT[2] (1): *I can never think of a comeback when I need one.* —see also **come back** (COME[1])

co·me·di·an /kə'midiən/ *n.* [C] **1** someone whose job is to tell jokes and make people laugh **2** INFORMAL someone who is amusing: *Dan was always trying to be the class comedian.*

co·me·dic /kə'midɪk/ *adj.* [usually before noun] FORMAL relating to comedy: *a comedic role*

co·me·di·enne /kə,midi'ɛn/ *n.* [C] OLD-FASHIONED a female comedian

come-down /'kʌmdaʊn/ *n.* [C usually singular] a situation that is not as good, important, interesting etc. as the one you had previously: *Teaching eighth-grade English must be a big comedown for a man with two PhDs.* —see also **come down** (COME[1])

com·e·dy /'kɑmədi/ *n. plural* **comedies 1** [C,U] a funny movie, television program, play etc. that makes people laugh, or this type of entertainment: *Capurro has been doing stand-up comedy (=telling jokes in front of people as a job) for about a year.* **2** [U] the quality in something such as a book or movie that makes you laugh; HUMOR[1] (1): *The movie swings from broad comedy to moving drama in a single scene.* **3 a comedy of errors** a situation in which a lot of things do not happen the way they should: *When the caterer canceled, the wedding turned into a comedy of errors.* **4 a comedy of manners** a comedy that shows how silly people's behavior is or can be —see also BLACK COMEDY, SITUATION COMEDY

come-hith·er /, . '../ *adj.* OLD-FASHIONED **come-hither look/eyes** a way of looking at someone that shows you think they are sexually attractive

come·ly /'kʌmli/ *adj.* LITERARY a comely woman has an attractive appearance —**comeliness** *n.* [U]

come-on /'. ./ *n.* [C] INFORMAL **1** something that someone does to try to make someone else sexually interested in them: *Rick's the kind of guy who thinks every smile is a come-on.* **2** an attempt to get people to buy something, by using an advertisement or giving something away free: *The free stationery is just a come-on; we want to get kids writing to penpals around the world.* —see also **come on** (COME[1])

com·er /'kʌmə/ *n.* **1 all comers** INFORMAL anyone who is interested, especially anyone who wants to take part in a competition: *The contest is open to all comers.* **2** [C usually plural] INFORMAL someone who is likely to be successful in a particular job: *These two young artists have been picked by critics as genuine comers.* —see also LATECOMER, NEWCOMER, UP-AND-COMER

co·mes·ti·bles /kə'mɛstəbəlz/ *n.* [plural] FORMAL food

com·et /'kɑmɪt/ *n.* [C] an object in space like a bright ball with a tail, that moves around the sun

come·up·pance /kʌm'ʌpəns/ *n.* [singular] INFORMAL a punishment or something bad that happens to you because you have done something bad: *The play is about a greedy man who gets his comeuppance.*

com·fort[1] /'kʌmfət/ *n.*
1 physical [U] a feeling of being physically relaxed and satisfied, so that you are not feeling any pain or

feeling too hot or cold: **be designed/made/crafted for comfort** *The chairs are designed for comfort and style.* | *Renting videos allows you to watch your favorite movies **in the comfort of** your own home.* | *After recovering from back surgery, I can finally sleep in comfort.*
2 |emotional| [U] a feeling of being calm or hopeful after you have been worried or sad: *Emilia goes to a women's group **for comfort and** emotional support.* | **take comfort from/in sth** *You can take some comfort in the fact that you did your best.* | **give/bring (sb) comfort** *Her faith gave her comfort during a very difficult time.* | **If it's any comfort**, *I got lost the first time I drove in Chicago too.*
3 |money/possessions| [U] a way of living in which you have everything you need to be happy: *Most American children have grown up **in comfort**, and cannot imagine the hardships of pioneer life.*
4 |sb/sth that helps| [C] someone or something that helps you feel happier or calmer when you have been worried or unhappy: [+ to/for] *The familiar surroundings were a comfort to the frightened children.* | *The program provides pets as a comfort for elderly people.* | **It's a comfort** *to know there's always someone to keep an eye on the kids.*
5 be too close for comfort something bad that is too close in distance or time: *The cars were whizzing past us much too close for comfort.*
6 comforts [plural] the things that make your life nicer and more comfortable, but that are not necessary: *The beach cabin has **all the comforts of home*** | *The cars are fast, but lack **creature comforts** (=things that make them comfortable for people to sit in).*
7 cold/small comfort a small piece of good news that does not make you feel better about a bad situation: *The business won't go bankrupt, but that's cold comfort for the 15 people who lost their jobs.* —**comfortless** *adj.* —see also COMFORT FOOD
comfort[2] *v.* [T] to make someone feel less worried or unhappy by being kind to them: *Lisa, in tears, was being comforted by her mother.* —**comforting** *adj.*: *It's comforting to know I can call my parents anytime.* —**comfortingly** *adv.*

W 2 com·fort·a·ble /'kʌmftəbəl, 'kʌmfətəbəl/ *adj.*
1 |feeling physically comfortable| feeling physically relaxed and satisfied, without feeling any pain or being too hot, cold etc.: *I was so comfortable and warm in bed I didn't want to get up.* | *Come in and **make yourself comfortable**.* | *My shoulder was hurting and I couldn't **get comfortable**.*
2 |clothes/furniture/places etc.| making you feel physically relaxed and satisfied: *Joyce has a comfortable apartment in Portland.* | *comfortable shoes* | *Our new sofa is really comfortable to sit on.*
3 |not worried| if you are comfortable with an idea, person, or activity, you do not feel worried about it: *Japanese is the language he's most comfortable with.*
4 |money| having enough money to live on without worrying about paying for things: *The Austins aren't rich, but they're comfortable.*
5 |sick/injured| if someone who is sick or injured is comfortable, they are not in too much pain
6 |race/competition| a number of points or a distance that will allow you to win easily: *The bill should pass in the House by a comfortable margin.* —opposite UNCOMFORTABLE
com·fort·a·bly /'kʌmftəbli, -fətəbli/ *adv.*
1 |physically comfortable| in a way that feels physically relaxed, without any pain or being too hot, cold etc.: *The Tough Traveler backpack will comfortably fit children up to 4'6" tall.* | *The mosquitoes aren't too bad here, so you should be able to sleep comfortably.*
2 |not worried| without feeling worried, unsure, or in danger: *Ellis won the race comfortably by 2.7 seconds over Conrad* | *Buick dealers were comfortably above average in the latest consumer survey.*
3 |money| with enough money to live well, without worrying about how to pay for things: *Analysts say that workers should save 18% of their income to live comfortably in retirement.* | *Mrs. Jenkins is still **comfortably off** (=fairly rich), with her own house.*

4 be resting comfortably to not be in too much pain after an accident or illness: *Taricini was resting comfortably at home last night after being released from the South Shore Medical Center.*
com·fort·er /'kʌmfətə/ *n.* [C] **1** a thick cover for a bed **2** someone who comforts you
comfort food /'.. ,./ *n.* [U] simple food that makes you feel relaxed and happy, especially because it is similar to the food your mother cooked when you were a child
comfort sta·tion /'.. ,../ *n.* [C] FORMAL a room where there are toilets for the public to use
com·fy /'kʌmfi/ *adj.* **comfier, comfiest** SPOKEN comfortable: *a comfy chair*
com·ic[1] /'kamık/ *adj.* **1** funny or amusing: *a comic novel* | *She is one of the most gifted comic actresses on television.* —opposite TRAGIC **2 comic relief** a funny part of a serious movie, book, situation etc.: *A beer-drinking dog provides the comic relief in this violent action movie.* **3 the comics** [plural] the part of a newspaper that has comic strips
comic[2] *n.* [C] **1** someone whose job is to tell jokes and make people laugh; COMEDIAN: *a stand-up comic* **2** a COMIC BOOK
com·i·cal /'kamıkəl/ *adj.* funny, especially in a strange or unexpected way: *Mrs. Hicks often wore large comical hats.* —**comically** /-kli/ *adv.*
comic book /'.. ,./ *n.* [C] a magazine that tells a story using pictures that are drawn like comic strips
comic ope·ra /,.. '../ *n.* [C,U] an OPERA in which the singers speak as well as sing, and that has an amusing story
comic strip /'.. ,./ *n.* [C] a series of pictures that are drawn inside boxes and that tell a story —compare CARTOON
com·ing[1] /'kʌmıŋ/ *n.* **1 the coming of sb/sth** the time when someone or something arrives or begins: *With the coming of the railroad, the population in the West grew quickly.* **2 sb's comings and goings** also **the comings and goings of sb** INFORMAL the movements of people as they arrive at and leave places: *Cameras record the comings and goings of the bank's customers.*
coming[2] *adj.* [only before noun] FORMAL happening soon: *The Pilgrims prepared for the coming winter.* —see also UP-AND-COMING
coming of age /,.. '. './ *n.* [singular] **1** the time in someone's life when society begins to consider them an adult: *It's a book about a young woman's coming of age in Berkeley during the 1960s.* **2** the time when something develops enough to be considered successful: *The popularity of these cars signals the coming of age of the Korean auto industry.*
Co·mis·key /kə'mıski/, **Charles** (1858–1931) a U.S. baseball player, manager and team owner who helped to organize the American League
com·i·ty /'kaməti/ *n.* [U] FORMAL behavior that is correct, respectful, and friendly
comm. 1 the written abbreviation of COMMISSION or COMMISSIONER **2** the written abbreviation of "committee" **3** the written abbreviation of "communication" or "communications"
com·ma /'kamə/ *n.* [C] the mark (,) used in writing to show a short pause or to separate single things in a list or parts of a sentence —see also COMMA SPLICE **S W 3 3**
com·mand[1] /kə'mænd/ *n.* **S W 3 3**
1 |control| [U] the control of a group of people or a situation: *The captain was drunk while **in command** of the ship.* | *McCormack took over in 1992, and the company has thrived **under his command**.* | *Janet **took command** (=began to control) of the situation and got everyone out of the building safely.* | *Each congressman has a large staff **at his command** (=available to be used).* | *Sergeant Lynch was **relieved of his command** (=his control over a group of people was taken away).*

C

2 |order| [C] an order that must be obeyed: *Fire when I give the command.*
3 command of sth knowledge of something, especially a language, or the ability to use something: *Employees should be able to demonstrate a basic command of reading, writing, and arithmetic.* | *Fujiko has a good command of English.*
4 |military| [C] **a)** a part of an army, navy etc. that is controlled separately and has a particular job: *These pilots belong to the Southern Air Command.* **b)** a group of officers or officials who give orders: *the Army High Command* **c)** the group of soldiers that an officer is in control of
5 |computer| [C] an instruction to a computer to do something
6 at your command if you have a particular skill at your command, you are able to use that skill well and easily: *Try to hire a carpenter with years of experience at his command.*
7 be in command of yourself to be able to control your emotions and thoughts: *Kathleen is a confident leader and in total command of herself.*

command² *v.*
1 |order| [I,T] to tell someone officially to do something, especially if you are a military leader, a king etc.: [**command sb to do sth**] *Captain Richardson commanded the crew to report to the main deck.*
2 |lead the military| [I,T] to be responsible for giving orders to a group of people in the Army, Navy etc.: *Lee commanded the 101st Airborne division in World War II.*
3 |deserve and get| [T] to get attention, respect etc. because you are important or popular: *Dr. Young commands a great deal of respect as a surgeon.* | *Traditionally, miners commanded higher wages than other workers.*
4 |control| [T] to control something: *Ford Motor Co. commands 16% of the market.*
5 |view| [T] if a place commands a view, you can see something clearly from it: *Giannuli's office commands a view of the Capitol Dome in Sacramento.*
—see Usage Note at ORDER²

com·man·dant /'kɑmən,dɑnt/ *n.* [C] the chief officer in charge of a military organization: *the commandant of a prison camp*

com·man·deer /,kɑmən'dɪr/ *v.* [T] to take someone else's property for your own use: *Two hijackers used fake explosives to commandeer the airliner.*

s w **com·mand·er** /kə'mændɚ/ *n.* [C] **1** an officer who is in charge of a group of soldiers, a particular military activity, a group of police officers etc.: *Mission Control told the shuttle commander that his first landing opportunity would be at 1 p.m.* | *Commander, here are the reports you asked for.* **2** an officer who has a middle rank in the Navy

commander in chief /.,... '. / *n.* [C usually singular] someone of high rank who is in control of all the military organizations in a country or of a specific military activity

com·mand·ing /kə'mændɪŋ/ *adj.* [usually before noun] **1** having the authority or position that allows you to give orders: *Wilmot is commanding officer of an Army Reserve unit.* **2** APPROVING having the confidence to make people respect and obey you: *Porter has a commanding voice and moves with authority.* **3** a commanding view or position is one from which you can see a long way: *The 2500-square-foot home has a commanding view of Whitby Island.* **4** being in a position from which you are likely to win a race or competition easily: *Polls have shown Isaacs to have a commanding lead.*

com·mand·ment /kə'mændmənt/ *n.* [C] **1** one of the ten rules given by God in the Bible that tell people how they should behave **2** LITERARY a command

command mod·ule /.'. ,../ *n.* [C] the part of a space vehicle from which its activities are controlled

com·man·do /kə'mændoʊ/ *n.* plural **commandos** or **commandoes** **1** [C] a group of soldiers who are specially trained to make quick attacks into enemy

areas: *a commando raid* **2** [C] a soldier who is a member of this group **3 go commando** SLANG to wear no underwear

command per·form·ance /.,. .'../ *n.* [C] a special performance at a theater that is given at the request of a president, king etc.

command post /.'. ,./ *n.* [C] the place from which military leaders and their officers control activities

comma splice /'.. ,./ *n.* [C] TECHNICAL a sentence with two or more main CLAUSEs joined using only a comma, such as "I'm tired, I want to go home." This is considered incorrect in English

com·mem·o·rate /kə'mɛmə,reɪt/ *v.* [T] to remember someone or something by a special action, ceremony, object etc.: *In the park, there is a plaque commemorating the town's 150th anniversary.* —**commemorative** /kə'mɛmrətɪv/ *adj.*

com·mem·o·ra·tion /kə,mɛmə'reɪʃən/ *n.* [C,U] a special action, ceremony, object etc. that makes you remember someone important or an important event in the past: *A 50th anniversary commemoration is planned for November.* | *The monument was built in commemoration of the people who died in the Vietnam war.*

com·mence /kə'mɛns/ *v.* [I,T] FORMAL to begin or to start something: *Work will commence on the new building immediately.* | *They will commence production in April.* | [+ **with**] *Volume 2 of the biography commences with Picasso at age 25.* | [**commence doing sth**] *The planes commenced bombing on Wednesday.*

USAGE NOTE: COMMENCE, BEGIN, START

FORMALITY
Commence is a very formal word that is used much more often in written language than in spoken. People use **start** in written language also, but it is the word most people use in spoken language. **Begin** is the most common word to choose in written language.

---

com·mence·ment /kə'mɛnsmənt/ *n.* FORMAL **1** [U] the beginning of something: [+ **of**] *the commencement of the trial* **2** [C,U] a ceremony at which college or high school students receive their DIPLOMAs; GRADUATION: *Colin Powell was asked to give the commencement address* (=a speech at the commencement).

com·mend /kə'mɛnd/ *v.* [T] FORMAL **1** to praise someone or something, especially in public: *The leadership Rodriguez displayed is to be commended.* | [**commend sb for sth**] *Judge Fein commended the two sides for reaching a fair settlement.* | *Bartholomew's work in the field of physics has been highly commended.* **2** FORMAL to tell someone that something is good or deserves attention; RECOMMEND: *The committee has commended achievement tests every four years.* **3** LITERARY to give someone to someone else to take care of: *The priest stepped forward to bless Tom's body and commend it to God.*

com·mend·a·ble /kə'mɛndəbəl/ *adj.* FORMAL deserving praise: *Baldwin answered with commendable honesty.* | *The team's recent record is highly commendable.* —**commendably** *adv.*

com·men·da·tion /,kɑmən'deɪʃən/ *n.* [C,U] FORMAL an honor or prize given to someone for being brave or successful

com·men·su·rate /kə'mɛnsərɪt, -ʃərɪt/ *adj.* FORMAL matching something in size, quality, or length of time: [+ **with**] *They should face legal sanctions commensurate with their actions.*

com·ment¹ /'kɑmɛnt/ *n.* **1** [C,U] an opinion that you express about someone or something: *Are there any questions or comments?* | [+ **about/on**] *Financial analysts have made positive comments about the company.* | *Barry often makes rude comments.* **2** [U] criticism or discussion of something that someone has said or done: *The jurors were not available for comment after the trial.* **3 No comment** SPOKEN said when you do not want to answer a question, especially in public or during an INTERVIEW **4 be a comment on sth** to be a sign of the bad quality of something: *The number of adults who cannot read is a sad comment on the quality of our schools.*

s w comment[2] *v.* [I,T] to give an opinion about someone or something: [+ **on**] *The police have refused to comment on the investigation until it is completed.* | [**comment that**] *Several critics have commented that the movie is unnecessarily violent.*

com·men·ta·ry /'kamən,teri/ *n.* *plural* **commentaries** [C,U] **1** a description of an event that is broadcast on the television or radio, or written in a newspaper: *Schuler will do the World Series commentary.* | [+ **on**] *Who's doing the commentary on the parade?* | *He's a former football coach who now does* **color commentary** *on television* (=he talks about players, game plans etc. rather than just saying what happens in the game). | *I sat behind a guy who gave a* **running commentary** (=continuous description) *during the whole movie.* **2** a book or article that explains or discusses something, or the explanation itself: *Garfield does political commentary on National Public Radio.* | [+ **on**] *The paper published a commentary on the abortion debate.* **3 be a sad/tragic etc. commentary on sth** to be a sign of how bad a particular situation is: *It's a sad commentary on our culture that we need constant entertainment.*

com·men·tate /'kamən,teit/ *v.* [I + **on**] to describe an event such as a sports game on television or radio

com·men·ta·tor /'kamən,teitə/ *n.* [C] **1** someone who knows a lot about a particular subject, and who writes about it or discusses it on the television or radio: *She was the former political commentator on the evening news.* **2** someone who describes an event as it is happening on television or radio: *a college basketball commentator*

s w com·merce /'kaməs/ *n.* [U] **1** the buying and selling of goods and services; TRADE[1] (1): *interstate commerce* (=among U.S. states) **2** OLD-FASHIONED relationships and communication between people —see also CHAMBER OF COMMERCE

s w com·mer·cial[1] /kə'məʃəl/ *adj.* **1** a commercial business or activity produces goods and services to be sold: *a large commercial fish farm* | *Theobald is a freelance commercial artist.* **2** relating to business and the buying and selling of goods and services: *Our top priorities must be profit and commercial growth.* | *Several commercial properties are vacant.* | *Guangzhou is the commercial capital of China's Pearl River area.* **3** relating to the ability of a product or business to make a profit: *The designer insists her clothing styles are commercial.* | *Spielberg's movie "The Lost World" was a huge* **commercial success.** **4 commercial TV/radio/broadcasting etc.** television or radio broadcasts that are produced by companies that earn money through advertising —compare PUBLIC TELEVISION **5** [only before noun] a commercial product is sold to the public rather than to businesses: *All commercial milk is pasteurized.* **6** DISAPPROVING more concerned with money than with quality: *I used to like their music, but they've become very commercial.*

w commercial[2] *n.* [C] an advertisement on television or the radio: *Networks show more toy commercials just before Christmas.* —compare AD

USAGE NOTE: COMMERCIAL
WORD CHOICE: commercial/advertisement
Commercial is used only about advertisements on the television and the radio. For advertisements in newspapers or magazines or on signs, use **advertisement**.

commercial bank /.,.. '.../ *n.* [C] TECHNICAL the kind of bank that most people use, that provides services for both customers and businesses

commercial break /.,.. '.../ *n.* [C] a time when advertisements are shown during a television or radio program

com·mer·cial·is·m /kə'məʃə,lizəm/ *n.* [U] DISAPPROVING the practice of being more concerned with making money than with the quality of what you sell or make: *At the last Olympics, sports seemed to be less important than the blatant commercialism of the merchandise suppliers.*

---

com·mer·cial·ize /kə'məʃə,laiz/ *v.* [T] **1** [usually passive] DISAPPROVING to be more concerned with making money from something than about its quality: *Christmas is getting so commercialized.* **2** to make a profit from something, especially by selling something that would not usually be sold: *Some space launches will be commercialized in order to help pay for more space research.* —**commercialization** /kə,məʃələ'zeiʃən/ *n.* [U]

com·mer·cial·ly /kə'məʃəli/ *adv.* **1** considering whether a business or product is making a profit: *Nintendo has been commercially successful.* | [sentence adverb] *Commercially, the movie was a flop.* **2** produced or used in large quantities as a business: *Much of the land around here is commercially farmed.* **3 commercially available** something that is commercially available can be bought in stores: *This type of weapon is commercially available in some states.*

com·mie /'kami/ *n.* [C] SPOKEN **1** an insulting word for a COMMUNIST **2** an insulting word for someone who expresses ideas that you think do not support traditional American beliefs

com·min·gle /kə'miŋgəl, ka-/ *v.* FORMAL **1** [I,T] to mix together, or to make different things do this: *Many towns allow recyclable items to be commingled for collection in a single container.* **2** [T] if a bank, insurance company, or other financial organization commingles, it mixes its own money with the money that belongs to one of its customers or that belongs to another part of the business, usually in an illegal way: *Southwest Securities consented to charges that it commingled firm and customer funds.*

com·mis·e·rate /kə'mizə,reit/ *v.* [I + **with**] FORMAL to express your sympathy for someone who is unhappy about something

com·mis·er·a·tion /kə,mizə'reiʃən/ *n.* FORMAL [U, plural] a feeling of sympathy for someone when something bad has happened to them: *Tom sent Julie's family a letter of commiseration.* | *We would like to express our commiserations to the losing team.* —compare CONDOLENCE

com·mis·sar /'kamə,sar/ *n.* [C] a Communist Party official whose job is to teach people about COMMUNISM and help them be loyal to it

com·mis·sar·y /'kamə,seri/ *n.* *plural* **commissaries** [C] **1** a store that supplies food and other goods in a military camp **2** a place where you can eat in a large organization such as a movie STUDIO, factory etc.

com·mis·sion[1] /kə'miʃən/ *n.* **s w**
1 people [C] a group of people who have been given the official job of finding out about something or controlling something: *The planning commission will allow 200 extra homes to be built on the site.*
2 money [C,U] an amount of money paid to someone for selling something: *Each dealer makes a 20% commission on his sales.* | *Jamil sells cars* **on commission** (=he is paid only according to what he sells).
3 job [C] **a)** a piece of work that someone, especially an artist or musician, is asked to do: *Ivanova has received a commission from the bank for a sculpture.* **b)** FORMAL a duty or job that you ask someone to do
4 out of commission a) not working or not able to be used: *The car's insured, but it's out of commission and I need to get to work.* **b)** INFORMAL sick or injured, and unable to go to work, play sports etc.: *My knee injury put me out of commission for two weeks.*
5 in commission if a military ship is in commission, it is still being used by the Navy
6 army/navy etc. [C] the position and authority given to an officer in the Army, Navy etc.: *Haley was asked to resign his commission.*
7 crime [U] FORMAL the commission of a crime is the act of doing it

commission[2] *v.* [T] **1** to formally ask someone to do something for you, such as write an official report, produce a work of art etc.: *The orchestra is commissioning new works from 14 composers.* | [**commission sb/sth to do sth**] *City Hall has commissioned a study to examine using fluoride in the drinking water.* **2 be commissioned** be given an officer's rank in the Army, Navy etc.

commissioned of·fic·er /.,.. '.../ *n.* [C] a military officer who has a commission

com·mis·sion·er /kə'mɪʃənɚ/ *n.* [C] **1** someone who is officially in charge of a police department, sports organization, government department etc. **2** a member of a COMMISSION¹ (1)

com·mit /kə'mɪt/ *v.* **committed, committing**
1 [crime] [T] to do something wrong or illegal: *Women **commit** fewer **crimes** than men.* | *Brady committed a series of brutal murders.* | *Isaacs denied trying to help his brother **commit suicide** (=kill himself deliberately).*
2 [say you will do sth] [I,T] to say that you will definitely do something or that you must do something: [**commit sb to doing sth**] *The scholarship commits students to teaching in public schools.* | [**commit sb to sth**] *The speech did not commit the rebels to a ceasefire.* | *It's common here for people to live together before **committing themselves** to marriage.*
3 [money/time] [T] to decide to use money, time, people etc. for a particular purpose: *The state of Florida will commit $58 million for a new research facility.* | [**commit sth to sth**] *They are unwilling to commit that many soldiers to the UN.*
4 [prison/hospital] [T] to order someone to be put in a hospital or prison: [**commit sb to sth**] *At age 26, she was committed to a mental institution.*
5 commit sth to memory to learn something so that you remember it
6 commit sth to paper FORMAL to write something down

com·mit·ment /kə'mɪt˺mənt/ *n.* **1** [C] a promise to do something or to behave in a particular way: *Marriage should be a lifelong commitment.* | [**+ to**] *Our company has a commitment to equal pay and opportunities.* | [**commitment to do sth**] *There is a growing commitment to fight poverty.* | *Volunteers must be able to **make a commitment** of four hours a week.* **2** [U] the hard work and loyalty that someone gives to an organization, activity etc.: *I was impressed by the energy and commitment shown by the players.* | [**+ to**] *Our employees' commitment to their work shows in their high-quality output.* **3** [C] something that you have promised you will do: *Many parents do not get involved in schools because they have too many other commitments.* **4** [U] the use of money, time, people etc. for a particular purpose: *The country is hoping for a commitment of $25 million in aid.* | *It's a part-time program, but it's still a big time commitment.*

com·mit·tal /kə'mɪtl/ *n.* [C,U] **1** the process in which a court sends someone to a mental hospital or prison **2** FORMAL the burying or burning of a dead person's body —see also NONCOMMITTAL

com·mit·ted /kə'mɪtɪd/ *adj.* willing to work very hard at something: *John is a very committed student.* | [**+ to**] *Residents are very committed to solving their neighborhood's problems.*

com·mit·tee /kə'mɪti/ *n.* [C] a group of people chosen to do a particular job, make decisions etc.: *the Senate Armed Forces Committee* | *A welcoming committee greets newcomers to the Parkside neighborhood.* | *Mary Ann is **on the finance committee**.*

com·mode /kə'moʊd/ *n.* [C] **1** a word meaning "toilet," used by people who do not like saying the word "toilet": *Bedford sat down on the commode.* **2** a chair with a bowl under the seat that can be used as a toilet by old or sick people **3** an old-fashioned piece of furniture with drawers or shelves

com·mo·di·ous /kə'moʊdiəs/ *adj.* FORMAL a house or room that is commodious is very big —**commodiously** *adv.*

com·mod·i·ty /kə'mɑdəti/ *n. plural* **commodities** [C]

1 TECHNICAL a product that is bought and sold: *agricultural commodities* **2** FORMAL a useful quality: *Time is a precious commodity.*

com·mo·dore /'kɑmə,dɔr/ *n.* [C] **1** a high rank in the Navy, or someone who has this rank **2** the CAPTAIN in charge of a group of ships that are carrying goods

com·mon¹ /'kɑmən/ *adj.*
1 [a lot] existing in large numbers: *Olson is a very common last name in Minnesota.* | *Foxes are very common around here.*
2 [happening often] happening often and to many people, or in many places: *A common reason for not hiring someone is their lack of writing skills.* | [**+ among**] *Osteoporosis, a bone disease, is common among older women.* | [**be common for sb to do sth**] *It's very common for new fathers to feel jealous of a baby.*
3 [same/similar] [usually before noun, no comparative] common aims, beliefs, ideas etc. are shared by several people or groups: *Students and faculty are working toward a common goal.* | [**+ to**] *The theme of the family is common to all Engle's novels.*
4 [ordinary] [only before noun, no comparative] ordinary and not special in any way: *common salt* | *The song is a tribute to **the common man** (=ordinary people).*
5 common ground facts, opinions, and beliefs that a group of people can agree on, in a situation in which they are arguing about something: *Democrats and Republicans did find some common ground in the debates about privacy.*
6 [shared by everyone] [usually before noun, no comparative] belonging to or shared by two or more people or things: *The Allies worked to defeat a common enemy.* | [**+ to**] *These problems are common to all big cities.* | *By **common consent** (=agreed by everyone), Joe was chosen as captain.*
7 the common good what is best for everyone in a society: *The government creates laws for the common good.*
8 common knowledge something that everyone knows: *Laura's drinking problem was common knowledge throughout the department.*
9 common practice a usual or accepted way of doing things: *Today it is common practice to let children choose their own topics for writing.*
10 common courtesy/decency a polite way of behaving that you expect from people: *Even at midnight, our neighbors don't have the common courtesy to turn the volume down.*
11 common touch the ability of someone in a position of power or authority to talk to and understand ordinary people: *Wilson's critics say his handling of the deal shows he has lost his common touch.*
12 make common cause (with sb) FORMAL to join with other people or groups for a particular purpose: *In the 1940s, the U.S. made common cause with the Soviet Union against Nazi Germany.* —see also COMMON DENOMINATOR

com·mon² *n.* **1 have sth in common (with sb)** to have the same interests, attitudes, qualities etc. as another person or group: *Terry and I have a lot in common.* | *I do not have much in common with the other kids in high school.* **2 have sth in common (with sth)** if objects or ideas have something in common, they share the same features: *The smaller boats actually have more in common with sailboards than with the huge yachts usually seen in marinas.* | *All these companies have one thing in common: they deal in small, inexpensive consumer items.* | *These paintings have little in common with traditional Chinese art.* **3** [C] a word meaning a "public park," used mostly in names: *Boston Common* —**commonality** /,kɑmə'næləti/ *n.* [C]

USAGE NOTE: COMMON

WORD CHOICE: common, general
When you have the same interests, attitudes, experiences etc. as someone else, you say that you have a lot **in common**. *As new parents, we have a lot in common.* When you mean that something happens or is true in most situations, use **in general**. *In general, new parents do not get enough sleep.*

common cold /ˌ.. './ n. [C usually singular] a slight sickness in which it is difficult to breathe normally, and your throat and head hurt

common de·nom·i·na·tor /ˌ.. .'....' n. [C usually singular] **1** an attitude or quality that all the different members of a group have: *The common denominator in these two election campaigns was money.* **2** TECHNICAL a number that can be divided exactly by all the DENOMINATORS (=bottom number) in a set of FRACTIONS **3 the lowest common denominator** the least attractive or least intelligent people or features of something or in a situation: *They produce trashy TV programs that appeal to the lowest common denominator.*

com·mon·er /'kɑmənə/ n. [C] someone who is not a member of the NOBILITY (1)

common frac·tion /ˌ.. '.., / n. [C] TECHNICAL a FRACTION (2) that is shown by a number above and a number below a line, such as ¹/₂, rather than as a DECIMAL²

common law /ˌ.. './ n. [U] the system of laws that are based on past decisions by courts of law: *Teachers may sue if they believe state common law has been violated.* —compare STATUTE LAW

common-law /'.. ,./ adj. [only before noun] **1 a common-law marriage/husband/wife** a relationship that is considered in law to be a marriage because the man and woman have lived together for a long time **2** LAW relating to or based on rules of law that developed over time through court decisions: *Dr. Williams' lecture notes were covered by common-law copyright.*

com·mon·ly /'kɑmənli/ adv. **1** usually or by most people: *Sodium chloride is more commonly known as salt.* | *Durum wheat is commonly used for making pasta.* **2** often, in many places or in large numbers: *Wilkins' column answers some of the most commonly asked questions about personal finance.* | *This bird is commonly found in Malaysia.*

common noun /'.. ,./ n. [C] any noun that is not the name of a particular person, place, or thing, for example "book" or "sugar" —compare PROPER NOUN —see also NOUN

com·mon·place¹ /'kɑmən,pleɪs/ adj. happening or existing in many places, and therefore not special or unusual: *Expensive foreign cars are commonplace in this Chicago suburb.*

commonplace² n. [C usually singular] something that happens or exists often or in many places, so that it is not considered unusual: *One-parent families are now a commonplace in our society.*

common sense /ˌ.. '.◂/ n. [U] the ability to behave in a sensible way and make practical decisions: *Use your common sense when deciding when children should go to bed.* —**common-sense** adj.: *a common-sense solution*

common stock /ˌ.. './ n. [C,U] the ordinary SHARES of a company, which give the people who own them a vote in how the company is run

com·mon·wealth /'kɑmən,wɛlθ/ n. [C] **1** the official legal title of some U.S. states, such as Massachusetts, Pennsylvania, Virginia, Maryland, and Kentucky: *the Commonwealth of Massachusetts* **2** FORMAL a group of countries that are related politically or economically, for example the group of countries that have a strong relationship with the U.K. **3** the official legal title of some places that are governed by the U.S. but are not states, such as Puerto Rico

com·mo·tion /kə'moʊʃən/ n. [singular,U] sudden noisy activity or arguing: *I heard a commotion outside.* | *The couple* **caused** *such a* **commotion** *that it woke the whole neighborhood up.*

com·mu·nal /kə'myunl/ adj. **1** shared by a group, especially a group of people who live together: *a communal bathroom* **2** relating or belonging to all the people in a particular community: *The pasture is located on communal land.* **3** relating to a commune: *Researchers did a study of children raised in communal situations.*

com·mune¹ /'kɑmyun/ n. [C] **1** a group of people who live together and who share the work and their possessions: *a religious commune* **2** a group of

people in a Communist country who work as a team, especially on a farm, and give what they produce to the government

com·mune² /kə'myun/ v.
   commune with sth/sb phr. v. [T] **1** if you commune with nature, animals etc., you seem as though you are trying to communicate with them without using words **2** FORMAL to try to communicate your thoughts and feelings to someone

com·mu·ni·ca·ble /kə'myunɪkəbəl/ adj. **1** a communicable sickness is infectious: *AIDS is not communicable by food or drink.* | *Measles is a dangerous* **communicable disease** *that can be prevented.* **2** FORMAL able to be communicated: *Her ideas were not easily communicable to others.*

com·mu·ni·cant /kə'myunɪkənt/ n. [C] **1** someone who receives COMMUNION (1) regularly in the Christian church **2** TECHNICAL someone who is communicating with someone else

com·mu·ni·cate /kə'myunə,keɪt/ v.   **s w**   **3 3**
   1 |exchange information| [I,T] to exchange information or conversation with other people, using words, signs, letters etc.: *Now that we live in different cities, we communicate by e-mail.* | [+ with] *They communicate with each other using sign language.* | [communicate sth to sb] *We established a policy and communicated it to everyone involved.*
   2 |express| [T] to express your thoughts and feelings clearly, so that other people understand them: *A baby communicates its needs by crying.* | [communicate sth to sb] *She unintentionally communicated her anxiety to her son.*
   3 |understand| [I] if two people communicate, they can easily understand each other's thoughts and feelings: *Jack and I just aren't communicating anymore.* | [+ with] *Parents sometimes find it difficult to communicate with their teenage children.*
   4 |disease| [T usually passive] to pass a disease from one person or animal to another: *Doctors are doing research into how the virus is communicated.*

com·mu·ni·ca·tion /kə,myunə'keɪʃən/ n. **1** [U] the   **s w**   **2 2** process of speaking, writing etc., by which people exchange information: *Good communication is vital in a large organization.* | *Radio was the pilot's only* **means of communication 2** [U] the way people express their thoughts and feelings or share information: *Family Services is offering a workshop called "Better Communication for Couples."* | *Some autistic children have limited* **communication skills** (=ways of expressing themselves clearly). **3 communications a)** [plural] ways of sending information, such as using radio, telephone, or computers: *Modern communications enable more and more people to work from home.* **b)** [U] the study of using radio, television, and movies to communicate: *a degree in communications* **4** [C] FORMAL a letter, message, or telephone call: *a communication from the IRS* **5 be in communication with sb** FORMAL to talk or write to someone regularly

communications sat·el·lite /...'.. ,.../ n. [C] a SATELLITE that is used to send radio, television, and telephone signals around the world

com·mu·ni·ca·tive /kə'myunɪkətɪv, -,keɪtɪv/ adj. **1** willing or able to talk or give information: *Customers complained that the sales clerks were not very communicative.* **2** relating to the ability to communicate, especially in a foreign language: *The test evaluates students' communication skills.*

com·mun·ion /kə'myunyən/ n. **1 Communion** also **Holy Communion** [U] the Christian ceremony in which people eat a small piece of bread and drink a small amount of wine as signs of Jesus Christ's body and blood **2** [U] FORMAL a special relationship with someone or something which makes you feel that you understand them very well: [+ between/with] *Prayer is a form of communion with God.* **3** [C] FORMAL a group of people or organizations that share the same religious beliefs; DENOMINATION: *He belongs to the Anglican communion.*

C

com·mu·ni·qué /kəˈmyunəˌkeɪ, -ˌmyunəˈkeɪ/ *n.* [C] an official report or announcement: *A military communiqué reported six soldiers killed.*

com·mu·nism, Communism /ˈkɑmyəˌnɪzəm/ *n.* [U] **1** a political system in which the government controls the production of all food and goods, and there is no privately owned property **2** the belief in this political system —compare CAPITALISM, SOCIALISM

S W **com·mu·nist¹** /ˈkɑmyənɪst/ *n.* [C] **1** someone who is a member of a political party that supports communism or who believes in communism —compare CAPITALIST¹, SOCIALIST² **2** SPOKEN an insulting word for someone who expresses ideas that you think do not support traditional American beliefs

communist², **Communist** *adj.* relating to communism: *Communist countries* | *a communist regime*

Communist bloc /ˌ... ˈ./ *n.* [singular] the group of countries, mostly in Eastern Europe, that had Communist governments and were controlled by the Soviet Union

S W **com·mu·ni·ty** /kəˈmyunəti/ *n. plural* **communities**
1 people [C] the people who live in the same area, town etc.: *An arts center will benefit the whole community.* | *Community leaders met with city officials to discuss the proposed golf course.*
2 town [C] a town, area etc. that a group of people live in: *Borrego Springs, a desert community, was the hottest place in the nation today.* —see also **bedroom community/suburb** (BEDROOM²)
3 particular group [C] a group of people who have the same interests, religion, race etc.: *Miami has a large Cuban exile community.* | *the gay community*
4 the community society and the people in it: *The police department wants to get officers out into the community.* | *The international community* (=all the countries of the world) *has rarely been so united in its purpose.*
5 sense of community the feeling that you belong to a particular community because people work together to help each other and improve the community
6 plants/animals [C] a group of plants or animals that live in the same environment: *These areas support diverse communities of birds and animals.*

community cen·ter /.ˈ... ˌ../ *n.* [C] a place where people from the same area can go for social events, classes etc.

community chest /.ˈ... ˌ./ *n.* [C] OLD-FASHIONED money that is collected by the people and businesses in an area to help poor people

community col·lege /.ˌ... ˈ../ *n.* [C] a college that people can go to, usually for two years, in order to learn a skill or to prepare to go to another college or university; JUNIOR COLLEGE

community prop·er·ty /.ˌ... ˈ.../ *n.* [U] LAW property that is considered to be owned equally by both a husband and wife

community serv·ice /.ˌ... ˈ./ *n.* [U] work that someone does to help other people without being paid, especially as punishment for a crime

com·mu·ta·tion /ˌkɑmyəˈteɪʃən/ *n.* **1** FORMAL [C,U] a reduction in how severe a punishment is: *Activists are campaigning for a commutation of Pollard's sentence.* **2** [U] FORMAL the act of commuting: *The bridge is a major commutation route.*

com·mu·ta·tive /kəˈmyutˌətɪv, ˈkɑmyəˌteɪtɪv/ *adj.* TECHNICAL a mathematical operation that is commutative can be done in any order

com·mute¹ /kəˈmyut/ *v.* **1** [I] to regularly travel a long distance to get to work: [+ to/from/between] *Jim commutes from Weehawken to Manhattan every day.* **2** [T] to change the punishment given to a criminal to one that is less severe: *Baldry's 20-year prison sentence was later commuted to three years.*

commute² *n.* [C usually singular] the trip made to work every day: *My morning commute takes 45 minutes.* | *Traffic congestion during peak commute hours is terrible.*

com·mut·er /kəˈmyutɚ/ *n.* [C] someone who travels a long distance to work every day

Com·o·ros /ˈkɑməˌroʊs/ a country consisting of several islands in the Indian Ocean, east of Mozambique —**Comoran** *n., adj.*

comp¹ /kɑmp/ *n.* [C] **1** INFORMAL a ticket for a play, sports game etc. that is given away free: *Gerry works for the theater, and gets two comps for every play.* **2** SPOKEN a short way of saying COMPENSATION (1) —see also COMP TIME, WORKERS' COMPENSATION

comp² *v.* [T] SPOKEN to give someone something such as a ticket free: *We comped tickets for some of the volunteers.*

com·pact¹ /ˈkɑmpækt, kəmˈpækt/ *adj.* **1** small, but arranged so that everything fits neatly into the available space: *The dormitory rooms are very compact, with a desk, bed, and closet built in.* | *a compact car* **2** packed or put together firmly and closely: *Look for plants with healthy leaves and a compact shape.* **3** small but solid and strong: *a short, compact-looking man* **4** expressing things clearly in only a few words —**compactly** *adv.* —**compactness** *n.* [U]

com·pact² /ˈkɑmpækt/ *n.* [C] **1** a small car: *a two-door compact* **2** a small flat container with a mirror, containing powder for a woman's face **3** FORMAL an agreement between two or more people, countries etc.

com·pact³ /kəmˈpækt/ *v.* [T] to press something together, so that it becomes smaller or more solid: *The dirt trail has been compacted from years of use.* —**compacted** *adj.*

compact disc /ˌkɑmpækt ˈdɪsk/ *n.* [C] a CD

com·pac·tor /kəmˈpæktɚ/ *n.* [C] a machine that presses something together, so that it becomes smaller or more solid: *a trash/garbage compactor The kitchen is also equipped with a dishwasher and trash compactor.*

com·pa·dre /kəmˈpɑdreɪ/ *n.* [C] INFORMAL a friend, or someone you spend a lot of time with

com·pan·ion /kəmˈpænyən/ *n.* [C] **1** someone you spend a lot of time with, especially someone who is a friend: *McCarthy and three companions were the first to arrive.* | *Sandy's doll, Pippi, is her constant companion* (=the doll is always with her). **2** one of a pair of things that go together or can be used together: [+ to] *Paul Simon has released a companion album to his Greatest Hits.* **3** used in the title of books that explain something about a particular subject: *the Fisherman's Companion* **4** someone, especially a woman, who is paid to live or travel with an older person

com·pan·ion·a·ble /kəmˈpænyənəbəl/ *adj.* nice and friendly: *They sat in companionable silence.* —**companionably** *adv.*

com·pan·ion·ship /kəmˈpænyənˌʃɪp/ *n.* [U] a friendly relationship with someone whom you see often: *Mrs. Greene keeps dogs for companionship and security.*

com·pa·ny /ˈkʌmpəni/ *n. plural* **companies**
1 business [C] an organization that makes or sells goods or services: *What company do you work for?* | *It's not company policy to exchange goods without a receipt.* | *the phone/electric/water etc. company I called the cable company about the bill.* | *Hutton runs his own contracting company.* —see also PUBLIC COMPANY
2 other people [U] the state of being with someone, so that they have someone to talk to or do not feel lonely: *I wasn't much company for Aunt Margaret tonight.* | *Come over for dinner – I could use the company.* | *Rita's husband is away, so I thought I'd go over and keep her company.* | *Owen is good company* (=he is fun to talk to). | *Bessie was glad to have the dog as company.* | *The paper published photos of Nina in the company of the head of the studio.* | *Some jokes are just not appropriate to tell in mixed company* (=in a group of both men and women).
3 guests [U] people who are visiting you in your home: *I have company right now, Dorothy. I'll call you back later.* | *The Hammils are expecting company* (=waiting for guests to arrive) *this weekend.*

4 friends [U] the group of people that you are friends with or spend time with: *People do tend to judge you by the company you keep* (=your friends). | *He's basically a nice guy who fell into some bad company* (=people who do things you disapprove of, especially illegal things).

5 performers [C] a group of actors, dancers, or singers who work together: *the Kirov Ballet company*

6 be in good company used to tell someone who has made a mistake that they should not be embarrassed because some important or famous people have made the same mistake: *If you can't program your VCR, you're in good company.*

7 sb and company INFORMAL used after a person's name to mean that person and their friends, often when you do not like or respect them: *Meanwhile, Balog and company raced to fix the ship's power supply.*

8 army [C] a group of about 120 soldiers, who are usually part of a larger group

9 two's company, three's a crowd INFORMAL used to suggest that two people would rather be alone together than have other people with them

10 in company with sth FORMAL if something happens in company with something else, both things happen at the same time: *Democracy progressed in company with the emancipation of women.* —see also part company (PART² (3)), present company excepted (PRESENT¹ (5))

company car /ˌ... ˈ./ *n.* [C] a car that your employer gives you to use while you work for them

company town /ˈ... ˌ./ *n.* [C] a town or city whose ECONOMY is dependent on one particular company or factory, because a large number of its people work there

com·pa·ra·ble /ˈkɑmpərəbəl/ *adj.* **1** similar to something else in size, number, quality etc., so that you can make a comparison: *Here are prices of three comparable homes that have sold in your neighborhood.* | [+ with/to] *Is the pay rate comparable to that of other companies?* | *The planet Pluto is comparable in size to the moon.* **2** being equally important, good, bad etc.: [+ with/to] *His poetry is hardly comparable with Shakespeare's.* —comparability /ˌkɑmpərəˈbɪləṭ/ *n.* [U]

com·pa·ra·bly /ˈkɑmpərəbli/ *adv.* in a similar way or to a similar degree: *Earnings have risen comparably in the computer industry.* | *The Senate's vote followed a comparably strong vote in the House of Representatives.*

com·par·a·tive¹ /kəmˈpærəṭɪv/ *adj.* **1 comparative comfort/freedom/wealth etc.** comfort, freedom etc. that is fairly good when measured or judged against something else, or against what the situation was before: *After a lifetime of poverty, his last few years were spent in comparative comfort.* **2 comparative study/analysis etc.** a study etc. that involves comparing something to something else that is similar: *The agent prepared a comparative market analysis.* **3 a comparative beginner/newcomer/ genius etc.** someone who is not really a beginner etc. but who seems to be one when compared to other people: *Even though we've lived here five years, we're still considered comparative newcomers.* **4** TECHNICAL the comparative form of an adjective or adverb shows an increase in size, quality, degree etc. For example, "bigger" is the comparative form of "big," and "more comfortable" is the comparative form of "comfortable." —compare SUPERLATIVE¹ (2)

comparative² *n.* **the comparative** TECHNICAL the form of an adjective or adverb that shows an increase in size, quality, degree etc. For example, "bigger" is the comparative of "big," and "more comfortable" is the comparative of "comfortable."

comparative lit·er·a·ture /ˌ...ˈ..../ *n.* [U] the study of literature from more than one country, which involves making comparisons between the writing from different countries

com·par·a·tive·ly /kəmˈpærəṭɪvli/ *adv.* as compared to something else or to a previous state: *The kids were comparatively well-behaved today.* | *Comparatively speaking, this part of the coast is still unspoiled.*

C

com·pare¹ /kəmˈpɛr/ *v.* **1** [T] to examine or judge two or more things in order to show how they are similar to or different from each other: *The report compares home computers currently available in stores.* | **[compare sth to/with sth]** *The police lab compared the suspect's fingerprints with those found at the crime scene.* | **Compare and contrast** (=describe the similarities and differences of) *the main characters of these two novels.* **2 compared to/with sth** used when considering the size, quality, or amount of something in relation to something similar: *Compared to Los Angeles, Santa Barbara almost seems rural.* | *Statistics show a 20% reduction in burglary compared with last year.* **3** [T] to say that something or someone is like someone or something else, or that it is equally good, large etc.: **[compare sth/sb to sth/sb]** *Davies' writing style has been compared to Dickens'.* | **[compare sth/sb with sth/sb]** *Edwards has been compared with former Giants coach Bill Parcells.* | **sth doesn't/can't compare with sth** *The rides at the fair just can't compare with the rides at Disneyland* (=they are not as good as the ones at Disneyland). | *The imported fabric is 30% cheaper and compares favorably* (=is as good) *in quality.* **4 compare notes (with sb)** INFORMAL to talk to someone in order to find out if their experience of something is the same as yours: *The New Moms group allows us to compare notes.*

compare² *n.* **beyond/without compare** LITERARY a quality that is beyond compare is the best of its kind: *The dancing in the show had a beauty that was beyond compare.*

com·par·i·son /kəmˈpærəsən/ *n.*

1 comparing [U] the process of comparing two people or things: [+ with] *Comparison with the director's earlier movies seems inevitable.* | **in comparison to/with** *In comparison to other recent video games, this one is dull.* | *Five ounces of coffee has about 150 mg of caffeine.* **By comparison**, *tea has about 40 mg.* | *The sales figures for 1996 were not available for comparison* (=for the purposes of comparing them). | *Her paintings invite comparison with those of the early Impressionists* (=they remind you of them).

2 judgment [C] a statement or examination of how similar or different two people, places, things etc. are: [+ of] *The EPA has issued a comparison of smog levels in various cities.* | [+ between] *The article makes a comparison between the two novels.*

3 be like sth [C] a statement that someone or something is like someone or something else: [+ to] *The comparison of the mall to a zoo seemed entirely appropriate.* | *You can't make a comparison between American and Japanese schools – they're too different.* | *Many writers have tried to draw comparisons between* (=show the similarities of) *the two presidents.*

4 there's no comparison SPOKEN used when you think that someone or something is much better than someone or something else: [+ between] *There's just no comparison between canned vegetables and fresh ones.*

5 grammar [U] a word used in grammar meaning the way an adverb or adjective changes its form to show whether it is COMPARATIVE¹ (4) or SUPERLATIVE¹ (2)

comparison-shop /.ˈ... ˌ./ *v.* [I] to go to different stores in order to compare the prices of things, so that you can buy things for the cheapest possible price —comparison shopping *n.* [U]

com·part·ment /kəmˈpɑrtmənt/ *n.* [C] **1** a smaller enclosed space inside something larger: *Put the ice cream back in the freezer compartment when you are finished.* **2** one of the separate areas into which a airplane, ship, or train is divided —see also GLOVE COMPARTMENT

com·part·men·tal·ize /kəmˌpɑrtˈmɛntl̩ˌaɪz/ *v.* [T] to divide things into separate groups, especially according to what type of things they are: *The brain does not neatly compartmentalize the areas used for* *language.* —**compartmentalized** *adj.* —**compartmentalization** /kəm,part'mɛntl-ə'zeɪʃən/ *n.* [U]

com·pass /'kʌmpəs/ *n.* **1** [C] an instrument that shows directions: *a map and compass* **2** [C] a V-shaped instrument with one sharp point and a pen or pencil at the other end, used for drawing circles or measuring distances on maps **3** [U] FORMAL the area or range of subjects that someone is responsible for or that is discussed in a book: [+ **of**] *Within the brief compass of a single page, the author covers most of the major points.*

com·pas·sion /kəm'pæʃən/ *n.* [U] a strong feeling of sympathy for people who are suffering, and a desire to help them: [+ **for**] *Many medical schools are trying to teach doctors to develop greater compassion for patients.* | **show/have/feel compassion** *The government needs to have more compassion for the poor.* | *Lieberman explores this sensitive topic* **with compassion** *and thoughtfulness.*

com·pas·sion·ate /kəm'pæʃənɪt/ *adj.* feeling sympathy for people who are suffering: *a caring, compassionate man* —**compassionately** *adv.*

compassionate leave /.,... './ *n.* [U] special permission to have time away from work because one of your relatives has died or is very sick

com·pat·i·bil·i·ty /kəm,pætə'bɪləti/ *n.* [U] **1** TECHNICAL the ability of one piece of computer equipment to be used with another one, especially when they are made by different companies **2** the ability to exist or be used together without causing problems **3** the ability to have a good relationship with someone, because you have similar interests, ideas etc.

com·pat·i·ble[1] /kəm'pætəbəl/ *adj.* **1** able to exist or be used together without causing problems: *The new software is IBM compatible* (=can be used with IBM computers). | [+ **with**] *The project is not compatible with the company's long-term aims.* **2** two people that are compatible are able to have a good relationship, because they have similar interests, ideas etc.

compatible[2] *n.* [C] a piece of computer equipment that can be used with another piece, especially one made by a different company: *Most software programs work with IBM compatibles.*

com·pa·tri·ot /kəm'peɪtriət/ *n.* [C] **sb's compatriot** someone who was born in or is a citizen of the same country as someone else: *Minh joined nearly 1 million of his compatriots in the West after being expelled from the Communist party in Vietnam.*

com·pel /kəm'pɛl/ *v.* **compelled, compelling** [T] **1** to force someone to do something: [**compel sb to do sth**] *The law will compel employers to provide health insurance.* | *Harris* **felt compelled to** *help after she saw the news story on television.* **2** FORMAL to make people have a particular feeling or attitude: *Chang's performance compels attention.* —compare IMPEL

com·pel·ling /kəm'pɛlɪŋ/ *adj.* **1** so interesting or exciting that you have to pay attention: *a compelling story* **2** a **compelling argument/reason/case etc.** an argument, reason etc. that makes you feel it is true or that you must do something about it: *Garcia presented a compelling case to the court.* —**compellingly** *adv.*

com·pen·di·um /kəm'pɛndiəm/ *n. plural* **compendiums** or **compendia** /-diə/ [C] FORMAL a book that contains a complete collection of facts, drawings etc. on a particular subject: *a baseball compendium*

com·pen·sate /'kampən,seɪt/ *v.* **1** [I] to reduce or balance the bad effect of something: [+ **for**] *More women will be promoted in order to compensate for discrimination in the past.* **2** [I,T] to pay someone money because they have suffered injury, loss, or damage: *The fund will compensate victims of smoking-related diseases.* | [**compensate sb for sth**] *The firm was ordered to compensate clients for their losses.*

com·pen·sa·tion /,kampən'seɪʃən/ *n.* **1** [U] money paid to someone because they have suffered injury or loss, or because something they own was dam-

aged: [+ **for**] *The fishermen have demanded compensation for the damage.* | *The jury awarded Tyler $1.7 million* **in compensation.** | *The parents are* **seeking compensation** *for the birth defects caused by the drug.* | *People who are wrongly arrested may be* **paid compensation.** | *The court* **awarded** *Jamieson $30,000* **compensation.** **2** [C,U] something that makes a bad situation better: *One of the few compensations of losing my job was seeing more of my family.* **3** [U] the money someone is paid to do their job: *Board members will receive compensation in the form of stock options, as well as salary.* **4** [C,U] actions, behavior etc. that replace or balance something that is lacking or bad: [+ **for**] *For some people, overeating can be a compensation for stress.*

com·pen·sa·to·ry /kəm'pɛnsə,tɔri/ *adj.* [usually before noun] **1** compensatory payments are paid to someone who has been harmed or hurt in some way: *The Court awarded Mitchel $650,000 in compensatory damages.* **2** intended to reduce the bad effects of something: *Officers can earn overtime pay or compensatory time off.*

com·pete /kəm'pit/ *v.* [I]

1 business to try to be more successful and sell more than another business: [+ **with/against**] *Fruit juice drinks do not compete directly with Coca-Cola.* | *The Toyota Paseo competes against such cars as the Honda CRX and the Saturn SL.* | [+ **for**] *The stores in the downtown area have to compete for customers in the Christmas season.* | [**compete to do sth**] *Several advertising agencies are competing to get the contract.* | *Small, independent bookstores simply* **can't compete** (=are unable to be more successful) *with the big national chains.*

2 person to try to gain something, or to be better or more successful than someone else: [+ **for**] *Sarah and Hannah are always competing for attention.* | [+ **against**] *I had to compete against 18 other people for the job.* | [+ **with**] *As a stepmother, don't even try to compete with the children's mother for their love.*

3 in a competition to take part in a competition or sports event: [+ **in/at**] *How many runners are competing in the Boston Marathon?* | *Professional athletes may now compete at the Olympics.* | [+ **against**] *Hodge will compete against some of the world's best swimmers at the Pan American games.* | [+ **for**] *Blair is competing for the starting quarterback position.*

4 **sb/sth can't compete with sb/sth** to not be as interesting, attractive etc. as someone or something else: *Melinda knew she couldn't compete with her sister when it came to boys.*

5 sound/smell if a sound or smell competes with another sound or smell, you can hear or smell both equally well: [+ **with**] *The songs of the birds competed with the sound of the church bells.*

6 ideas/arguments if two or more people or groups have competing ideas, arguments, claims etc., each one has a different solution to the same problem, and not everyone will be satisfied with the final result

com·pe·tence /'kampətəns/ *also* **com·pe·ten·cy** /-pətənsi/ *n.* **1** [U] the ability and skill to do what is needed: *Players are judged by their competence on the field.* **2** [U] LAW the legal power of a court of law to hear and judge something in court, or of a government to do something: *In the U.S., many legal issues are* **within the competence of** *the states rather than the federal government.* **3** [U] a special area of knowledge: *It is not* **within my competence** *to make such judgments.* **4** [C] FORMAL a skill needed to do a particular job

com·pe·tent /'kampətənt/ *adj.* **1** having enough skill or knowledge to do something to a satisfactory standard: *A competent mechanic should be able to fix the problem quickly.* | [**competent to do sth**] *He resigned amid questions of whether he was competent to manage the firm.* **2** satisfactory, but not especially good: *The roofers did a competent job.* **3** having normal mental abilities: *We believe the patient was not mentally competent.* | *A psychiatrist said McKibben was* **competent to stand trial.** **4** [not before noun] LAW having the legal power to deal with something in a court of law: [**be competent to do sth**]

This court is not competent to hear your case. —**competently** adv. —opposite INCOMPETENT

com·pet·ing /kəmˈpiːtɪŋ/ adj. **competing claims/interests/theories etc.** competing claims, interests etc. are two claims that cannot both be accepted: *Several people gave competing accounts of the accident.*

com·pe·ti·tion /ˌkɒmpəˈtɪʃən/ n. **1** [U] a situation in which people or organizations compete with each other: [+ **between/among**] *There was a lot of competition between me and my brother when we were kids.* | *The price reduction is due to competition among suppliers.* | [+ **for**] *Competition for the job was intense.* | **stiff/intense/fierce etc. competition** *They face strong competition from the three leading soap manufacturers.* | *Farmers say they are being hurt by foreign competition* (=competition from companies in foreign countries). | *Share prices have slipped in the face of stiff competition* (=in a situation in which they are competing) *from other automakers.* **2** [U] the people or groups that are competing against you, especially in business or in a sport: *The show's ratings are far behind the competition.* | *Lewis is bound to win the race; there's just no competition* (=no one who is likely to be better). **3** [C] an organized event in which people or teams compete against each other: *a photography competition* | [**a competition to do sth**] *The city is holding a competition to find a designer for the new airport.* | *She was the first woman ever to win the competition for National Small Business Leader of the Year.* | *Teams from all over the state have entered the competition.*

com·pet·i·tive /kəmˈpɛtətɪv/ adj. **1** determined or able to be more successful than other people or businesses: *Some U.S. industries are not as competitive as they have been in the past.* | *The merger will give the company a competitive edge* (=a better ability to compete) *in the market.* **2** relating to competition: *Competitive sports encourage children to work together as a team.* | **highly/very/intensely etc. competitive** *The market for airline companies is highly competitive.* **3** competitive prices, salary etc. are as good as or slightly better than prices or salary in other stores or companies: *Long distance phone companies offer very competitive rates.* | *The company offered a competitive bid for the contract.* **4** someone who is competitive is determined to win or to be more successful than other people: *Beth's so competitive, even with her friends.* —**competitively** adv.

com·pet·i·tive·ness /kəmˈpɛtətɪvnɪs/ n. [U] **1** the ability of a company or a product to compete with others: *New machinery has enhanced the company's productivity and competitiveness.* **2** the desire to be more successful than other people: *Keisha's enthusiasm and competitiveness rubbed off on the rest of the sales team.*

com·pet·i·tor /kəmˈpɛtətər/ n. [C] **1** a person, team, company etc. that is competing with another: *Last year they sold twice as many computers as their competitors.* **2** someone who takes part in a competition: *Two of the competitors failed to show up for the race.*

com·pi·la·tion /ˌkɒmpəˈleɪʃən/ n. **1** [C] a book, list, record etc. that puts together many different pieces of information, songs etc.: *a compilation of love songs* **2** [U] the process of compiling something: *the compilation of financial data*

com·pile /kəmˈpaɪl/ v. [T] **1** to make a book, list, record etc. using different pieces of information, music etc.: *A.C. Nielsen Co. compiles the television ratings.* | *The report was compiled from a survey of 5000 households.* **2** to put a set of instructions into a computer in a form that you can understand and use

com·pil·er /kəmˈpaɪlər/ n. [C] **1** someone who collects different pieces of information or facts to be used in a book, report, or list **2** TECHNICAL a set of instructions in a computer that changes a computer language known to the computer user into the form needed by the computer

com·pla·cen·cy /kəmˈpleɪsənsi/ also **com·pla·cence** /-ˈpleɪsəns/ n. [U] a feeling of satisfaction with a situation or with what you have achieved, so that you stop trying to improve or change things: *Doctors*

have warned against complacency in fighting common diseases.

com·pla·cent /kəmˈpleɪsənt/ adj. pleased with a situation, especially something you have achieved, so that you stop trying to improve or change things: *We've been winning, but we're not going to get complacent.* | [+ **about**] *The nation cannot become complacent about the quality of our schools.* —**complacently** adv.

com·plain /kəmˈpleɪn/ v. **1** [I,T not in passive] to say that you are annoyed, not satisfied, or unhappy about something or someone: *Residents are complaining because traffic in the area has increased.* | [+ **about**] *We called up to complain about the potholes in the road.* | [+ **of**] *Several women have complained of sexual harassment.* | [**complain (that)**] *Some scientists complained that manned space flight takes money away from other research.* | [**complain to sb**] *I complained to the landlord about the leak.* | *Some employees have complained bitterly about the layoffs.* **2 I can't complain** SPOKEN said when you think a situation is satisfactory, even though there may be a few problems: *I make a good living. I can't complain.*

complain of sth phr. v. [T] FORMAL to say that you feel sick or have a pain in a part of your body: *Van Buren went to the hospital complaining of chest pains.*

com·plain·ant /kəmˈpleɪnənt/ n. [C] LAW someone who makes a formal complaint in a court of law; PLAINTIFF

com·plaint /kəmˈpleɪnt/ n. **1** [C,U] a statement in which someone complains about something: *Complaints are dealt with by the customer services department.* | [+ **about**] *Keating was dismissed after complaints about the quality of his work.* | [**complaint that**] *The car's manufacturer received complaints that leaks were causing brake failures.* | *Amy and her friends made several complaints* (=complained formally) *to the school administrators.* | *The commission received over 10,000 letters of complaint.* | *If Ms. Weston's accusations of harassment are true, she has a legitimate cause for complaint* (=reason to complain). **2** LAW a formal statement saying that someone is guilty of a crime: [+ **against**] *All complaints against police officers are carefully investigated.* | *Prosecutors filed a complaint charging him with the murder of his wife.* **3** [C] something that you complain about: *The service was good, but my only complaint is the high prices.* **4** [C] FORMAL a sickness that affects a particular part of your body: *He is having treatment for a minor skin complaint.*

com·plai·sance /kəmˈpleɪsəns, -zəns/ n. [U] FORMAL willingness to do what pleases other people —**complaisant** adj. —**complaisantly** adv.

-complected /kəmˈplɛktɪd/ [in adjectives] **fair-complected/light-complected/dark-complected** having light or dark skin: *a dark-complected man*

com·ple·ment¹ /ˈkɒmpləmənt/ n. [C] **1** someone or something that emphasizes the good qualities of another person or thing: [+ **to**] *White wine makes an excellent complement to fish.* **2** the number or quantity needed to make a group complete: *The submarines are equipped with a full complement of 24 missiles.* **3** TECHNICAL in grammar, a word or phrase that follows a verb and describes the subject of the verb, or that follows the object of a verb and describes it. In the sentence "You look angry," "angry" is the complement, and in "They elected John chairman," "chairman" is the complement. **4** TECHNICAL an angle that together with another angle already mentioned makes 90 degrees —compare COMPLEMENT¹

com·ple·ment² /ˈkɒmpləˌmɛnt/ v. [T] to emphasize the good qualities of another person or thing, especially by adding something that was needed: *Buy a scarf that complements your shirt or dress.* | *For the show, the museum is borrowing twenty paintings that complement its own collection.* —compare COMPLIMENT²

The recent elections changed the complexion of the state assembly. —see also -COMPLECTED, -COMPLEXIONED

-complexioned /kəmplɛkʃənd/ [in adjectives] **light-complexioned/dark-complexioned** etc. having light or dark skin: *a chubby, dark-complexioned woman*

com·plex·i·ty /kəmˈplɛksəti/ n. plural **complexities 1** [U] the state or quality of being complicated and detailed: *Many people struggle with the complexity of the tax forms.* **2** [C usually plural] the details and problems that make something difficult to understand or deal with: *The article attempts to explain the affair's legal and political complexities.*

com·ple·men·ta·ry /ˌkɑmpləˈmɛntri, -ˈmɛntəri/ adj. **1** emphasizing the good qualities of someone or something, or adding qualities that the other person or thing lacks: *Bain and McCaskill have complementary skills – she is creative while he is highly organized.* **2** TECHNICAL two angles that are complementary add up to 90 degrees —compare SUPPLEMENTARY (2)

sw **com·plete**[1] /kəmˈplit/ adj. **1** including all parts,
²² details, facts etc. that are necessary or usual: *Older records of births, marriages, and deaths are not as complete as modern ones.* | *Scientists have unearthed a complete dinosaur skeleton in Montana.* | *We gave Vicki the complete works of Plato (=a book containing all of Plato's writings) as a present.* **2** [only before noun, no comparative] INFORMAL a word meaning "in every way," used in order to emphasize what you are saying; total: *The meeting was a complete waste of time.* | *I met Brad Pitt one time and made a complete fool of myself.* **3** [not before noun] finished: *Construction of the library is expected to be complete in February.* **4 complete with sth** having equipment or features: *The house comes complete with swimming pool and sauna.* —**completeness** n. [U]

com·pli·ance /kəmˈplaɪəns/ n. [U] FORMAL **1** the act or fact of obeying a rule, agreement, or law: [+ **with**] *Compliance with the law is expected of all citizens.* | *In compliance with Mrs. Kornfeld's wishes, she was buried next to her husband.* **2** the tendency to agree too willingly to someone else's wishes or demands —see also COMPLY

com·pli·ant /kəmˈplaɪənt/ adj. **1** willing to obey or agree to other people's wishes and demands: *Some patients are more compliant than others in the hospital.* **2** made, used, or done according to particular rules or standards: *All waste treatment facilities must be fully compliant with federal regulations.* —**compliantly** adv. —see also COMPLY

sw **complete**[2] v. [T] **1** to finish doing or making some-
²² thing, especially when it has taken a long time: *The book took five years to complete.* | *Scholarships will help more students to complete the program within two years.* **2** to make something whole or perfect by adding what is missing: *Once you've completed the questionnaire (=written all the information needed), put it in the blue box.* | *I need one more stamp to complete my collection.*

com·pli·cate /ˈkɑmpləˌkeɪt/ v. [T] **1** to make something more difficult to understand or deal with, especially by adding details to it: *The continued fighting has complicated the peace negotiations.* | *To complicate matters, sales taxes vary from state to state.* **2** [usually passive] to make a sickness worse: *Williams died on Monday from a heart condition complicated by pneumonia.*

com·plet·ed /kəmˈplitɪd/ adj. containing all the necessary parts or answers needed to finish something: *Be sure to mail your completed tax form by April 15.*

com·pli·cat·ed /ˈkɑmpləˌkeɪtɪd/ adj. **1** difficult to s
understand or deal with, because of the many details ²
or parts involved: *The new law is complicated and confusing.* | *a complicated set of instructions* | **extremely/very/highly** etc. **complicated** *The political situation in Northern Ireland is extremely complicated.* **2** consisting of many closely related or connected parts: *The human brain is an incredibly complicated organ.*

sw **com·plete·ly** /kəmˈplitli/ adv. in every way; totally: *I*
¹² *completely forgot that it was his birthday yesterday.* | *Muscle cells and fat cells are completely different kinds of tissue.* | *His knee is not completely healed.* | *Once the program is installed, it runs completely automatically.*

com·pli·ca·tion /ˌkɑmpləˈkeɪʃən/ n. **1** [C usually plural] an additional medical problem or sickness that happens while someone is already sick: *She died of complications following surgery.* **2** [C,U] a problem or situation that makes something more difficult to understand or deal with: *The drop in student numbers added further complications to the situation.*

com·ple·tion /kəmˈpliʃən/ n. [U] **1** the state of being finished: *Repair work is scheduled for completion in August.* **2** the act of finishing something. [+ **of**] *The vote will take place two days after the completion of the hearings.* | *Filming of the new series will begin on completion of Murphy's current project (=when the current project is completed).*

com·plic·i·ty /kəmˈplɪsəti/ n. [U] FORMAL the act of being involved in a crime with other people: [+ **in**] *He was charged with complicity in the murder of Sayers.* —**complicit** adj.

sw **com·plex**[1] /kɑmˈplɛks, kəm-, ˈkɑmplɛks/ adj. **1** con-
² sisting of many parts or details that are closely related and may make something or someone difficult to understand: *There is a complex network of roads connecting the two cities.* | *Few people understand the complex issues of environmental science.* | *a complex mathematical formula* | *a complex personality* **2** TECHNICAL a complex word or sentence contains a main part and one or more other parts. For example, the word "disadvantaged" is a complex word. The sentence "The picnic was canceled because of the rain" is a complex sentence.

com·pli·ment[1] /ˈkɑmpləmənt/ n. **1** [C] a remark that expresses admiration of someone or something: *"You look great!" "Thanks for the compliment."* | [+ **on**] *Paula got a lot of compliments on her dress.* | *Look, I was just paying you a compliment (=telling someone they look nice, did something well etc.).* | *Breslev returned the compliment (=said something nice to someone who has said something nice to him), saying that the students were "good boys and good athletes."* | *Mandy's always fishing for compliments (=trying to get people to say something nice about her).* **2 take sth as a compliment** if you take something as a compliment, you are pleased with what someone has said even though it really was not very nice: *I said he was a workaholic, and he seemed to take it as a compliment.* **3 pay sb the compliment of doing sth** to do something that shows you trust someone else and have a good opinion of them: *They paid me the compliment of electing me as their representative.* **4 compliments** [plural] praise, admiration, or good wishes: *Please give my compliments to the chef; the food was excellent.* **5 (with the) compliments of sb** also **with sb's compliments** used by a person or company when they send or give something to you: *Please accept these tickets with our compliments.* **6 a backhanded compliment** also a **left-handed compliment** something that someone says to you which is nice and not nice at the same

com·plex[2] /ˈkɑmplɛks/ n. [C] **1** a group of buildings or one large building with many parts used for a particular purpose: *Papp turned the old library into a huge six-screen movie complex.* | *Schneider manages an apartment complex in suburban Denver.* **2** an emotional problem in which someone is too anxious about something or thinks too much about something: *Jack has a complex about being short.* —see also ELECTRA COMPLEX, INFERIORITY COMPLEX, OEDIPUS COMPLEX

com·plex·ion /kəmˈplɛkʃən/ n. **1** [C,U] the natural color or appearance of the skin on your face: *Too much sun is bad for your complexion.* | *Alice is lighter in complexion than her mother.* | **a dark/ruddy/pale** etc. **complexion** *She had a long oval face with an olive complexion.* **2 the complexion of sth** the general character or nature of something:

time: *In one of those backhanded compliments that cops love, the drug dealers gave Captain Ragsdale an obscene nickname.* —compare COMPLEMENT[1]

com·pli·ment[2] /'kɑmplə,mɛnt/ *v.* [T] to say something nice to someone in order to praise them: [**compliment sb on sth**] *All of us complimented Joe on his cooking.* | [**compliment sb for sth**] *Health officials were complemented for their fast action.* —compare COMPLEMENT[2]

com·pli·men·ta·ry /,kɑmplə'mɛntri‹, -'mɛntəri‹/ *adj.* **1** given free to people: *Top students receive two complimentary tickets to a Dodgers game.* **2** expressing admiration, praise, or respect: *Bell had only complimentary things to say about the organization.*

com·ply /kəm'plaɪ/ *v.* **complies, complied, complying** [I] FORMAL to do what you must do or are asked to do: [+ **with**] *The gas stations that fail to comply with the law will be fined.* —see also COMPLIANCE

com·po·nent /kəm'pounənt/ *n.* [C] one of several parts that make up a whole machine or system: *Researchers have identified the substance's chemical components.* | *stereo components* —compare CONSTITUENT[1] (2)

com·port /kəm'pɔrt/ *v.* FORMAL **comport yourself** to behave yourself in a particular way: *Leo comported himself very professionally.*
  comport with sth *phr. v.* [T] FORMAL to follow or be in agreement with an idea, belief, rule etc.: *These practices do not comport with the principle of providing fair trials.*

com·port·ment /kəm'pɔrtmənt/ *n.* [U] FORMAL someone's behavior and the way they stand, walk etc.

com·pose /kəm'pouz/ *v.* **1 be composed of sth** to be formed from a group of substances or parts: *Water is composed of hydrogen and oxygen.* —compare COMPRISE (2) **2** [T not in progressive] to combine together with other things or people to form something: *The menu includes more than 60 small dishes from which you can compose a meal.* **3** [I,T] to write a piece of music: *Schumann was better at composing music than playing it.* **4 compose a letter/poem/ speech etc.** to write a letter, poem etc., thinking very carefully about it as you write it: *The class assignment was to compose a poem or short story.* **5** [T] to make yourself feel or look calm: *I needed a quiet place to compose my thoughts.* | *Weisberg took a few minutes to **compose herself** before she answered the question.* **6** [T] to put colors, shapes, or images together in a particular way to form a piece of art: *Olsen knows how to compose a visually interesting scene, but the script lets him down.* —see Usage Note at COMPRISE

com·posed /kəm'pouzd/ *adj.* **1** calm, rather than upset or angry: *The witness was composed and sure of her story.* **2** a composed SALAD is arranged carefully on a plate, rather than mixed together

com·pos·er /kəm'pouzɚ/ *n.* [C] someone who writes music

com·pos·ite[1] /kəm'pɑzɪt/ *adj.* [only before noun] made up of different parts or materials: *The police put together a composite sketch (=one drawn using different drawings of eyes, noses etc.).*

composite[2] *n.* [C] **1** something made up of different parts or materials: [+ **of**] *The plane's body is made of a composite of Kevlar and carbon fibers.* **2** a drawing of a possible criminal made by police from descriptions given by a WITNESS: *Several witnesses identified the man in the composite.*

com·po·si·tion /,kɑmpə'zɪʃən/ *n.*
1 making a whole [U] the way in which something is made up of different parts, things, members etc., or the different parts, things, members themselves: *The color of a star depends on its chemical composition and its mass.* | *Both factions disagree over the composition of a temporary government.*
2 music/art/writing **a)** [C] a piece of music or art, or a poem: *Blomstedt conducted a new composition by Charles Wuorinen.* **b)** [U] the art or process of writing pieces of music, poems, ESSAYS etc.: *Karina studied composition and music theory at the Juilliard School.*
3 photograph/picture [U] the way in which the different parts that make up a photograph or picture

are arranged, or the different parts themselves: *The paintings of each series differ in terms of color and composition.*
4 school subject [C,U] a short piece of writing about a particular subject that is done especially at school, or the art of writing about things: *We had to write a composition about our summer vacations.* | *Mrs. Blanchard teaches English and advanced composition.*
5 printing [U] TECHNICAL the process of arranging words, pictures etc. on a page before they are printed

com·pos·i·tor /kəm'pɑzətɚ/ *n.* [C] someone who arranges letters, pictures etc. on a page before they are printed

com·post[1] /'kɑmpoust/ *n.* [U] a mixture of decayed plants, leaves etc. used to improve the quality of soil: *The trees will be cut up and used to make compost.* | *Last year I started a **compost pile** (=a place where leaves etc. are left to decay) with raked leaves and grass cuttings.*

compost[2] *v.* [T] **1** to make plants, leaves etc. into compost **2** to put compost onto soil

com·po·sure /kəm'pouʒɚ/ *n.* [U] a calm feeling that you have when you feel confident about dealing with a situation: *The judge allowed the witness a few minutes to **regain her composure**.* | *This season, the team's basic problem is that the players **lose their composure** (=they become angry, anxious, or upset) under pressure.* | **keep/maintain your composure** (=stay calm)

com·pote /'kɑmpout/ *n.* [U] fruit that has been cooked in sugar and water and is eaten cold

com·pound[1] /'kɑmpaʊnd/ *n.* **1** [C] an area that contains a group of buildings and is surrounded by a fence or wall: *a prison compound* | *Marines protect the U.S. Embassy compound.* **2** [C] TECHNICAL a substance containing atoms from two or more ELEMENTS: *Sulfur dioxide is a compound of sulfur and oxygen.* | *an organic compound* **3** [C,U] something that consists of a combination of two or more parts, qualities etc.: *Seal all wall joints with joint compound and tape.* **4** [C] TECHNICAL in grammar, a noun or adjective made up of two or more words. For example, the noun "ice cream" is a compound.

com·pound[2] /kəm'paʊnd/ *v.* [T] **1** to make a difficult situation worse by adding more problems: *The country's economic woes were compounded by a seven-year civil war.* **2** to calculate INTEREST[1] (3) on both the sum of money and the interest that was paid or still owed before: *My bank compounds interest quarterly.* **3** to make something by mixing different parts or substances together: *Scientists are able to compound an increasing number of substances to produce new drugs.*

com·pound[3] /'kɑmpaʊnd, kɑm'paʊnd/ *adj.* **1 compound noun/adjective** TECHNICAL a noun or adjective that is made up of two or more words. For example, "ice cream" is a compound noun. **2 compound sentence** TECHNICAL a sentence made up of at least two INDEPENDENT CLAUSES joined by a CONJUNCTION. For example, "The door opened and Charlie walked in" is a compound sentence. **3 a compound eye/leaf etc.** TECHNICAL a single eye, leaf etc. that is made up of two or more parts or substances

compound frac·ture /,.. '../ *n.* [C] TECHNICAL a broken bone that cuts through someone's skin

compound in·ter·est /,.. '../ *n.* [U] INTEREST[1] (3) that is calculated on both the money that was lent or borrowed and on the interest already earned or charged —compare SIMPLE INTEREST

com·pre·hend /,kɑmprɪ'hɛnd/ *v.* [I,T not in progressive] FORMAL to understand something that is complicated or difficult: *Even scientists do not comprehend these phenomena.* | **comprehend how/ why/what** *It is difficult to comprehend how someone could harm a child.* | *Families are bound together in ways that cannot be **fully comprehended**.*

com·pre·hen·si·ble /,kɑmprɪ'hɛnsəbəl/ *adj.* easy to understand: *comprehensible instructions* | [+ **to**]

Most avant-garde music is not comprehensible to the average concertgoer. —**comprehensibly** *adv.* —**comprehensibility** /ˌkʌmprɪˌhɛnsəˈbɪləti/ *n.* [U] —opposite INCOMPREHENSIBLE

com·pre·hen·sion /ˌkʌmprɪˈhɛnʃən/ *n.* [U] the ability to understand something, or knowledge of something: *Some politicians seems to have no comprehension of what it's like to be poor.* | *The test includes a section on reading comprehension.* | *The Tongass National Forest is big, almost **beyond comprehension*** (=impossible to understand).

USAGE NOTE: COMPREHENSION

WORD CHOICE: comprehension, understanding
Comprehension means the ability to understand the meaning of something, especially something spoken or written: *He showed little comprehension of the judge's statements.* Don't use comprehension about someone's ability to understand other people's feelings, attitudes, or culture. Instead, use **understanding**: *Rhodes hoped the scholarships would contribute to world understanding and peace.*

---

com·pre·hen·sive /ˌkʌmprɪˈhɛnsɪv/ *adj.* including everything that is necessary: *The bill called for comprehensive health insurance for all Americans.* | *Jacobs is trying to make the university's policy clearer and more comprehensive.* —**comprehensively** *adv.* —**comprehensiveness** *n.* [U]

com·press¹ /kəmˈprɛs/ *v.* **1** [I,T] to press something or make it smaller so that it takes up less space, or to become smaller: *Scuba divers used cylinders of compressed air.* | *This program compresses computer files so they can be easily sent by email.* | *Some files compress more easily than others.* | [**compress sth into sth**] *The garlic is dried and then compressed into a pill.* **2** [T usually passive] to reduce the amount of time that it takes for something to happen or be done: [**compress sth into sth**] *Three years of training were compressed into eighteen months.* **3** [T] to write or express something using fewer words: *The play has been compressed from a huge book.* —**compressible** *adj.* —**compression** /kəmˈprɛʃən/ *n.* [U]

com·press² /ˈkʌmprɛs/ *n.* [C] a small thick piece of material that you put on part of someone's body to stop blood flowing out or to make it less painful: *Apply a **cold compress** to the injury.*

com·pres·sor /kəmˈprɛsɚ/ *n.* [C] a machine or part of a machine that compresses air or gas

com·prise /kəmˈpraɪz/ *v.* [not in progressive] FORMAL **1** [linking verb] to consist of particular parts, groups etc.: *The Sea Grant Program comprises over 300 colleges nationwide.* **2 be comprised of sth** to consist of particular parts, groups etc.: *The council is comprised of members of the nine tribes in the Hanford region.* —compare COMPOSE (1) **3** [T] to form part of a larger group: *Hindus comprise 82% of India's population.* —see also CONSTITUTE

USAGE NOTE: COMPRISE

WORD CHOICE: consist of, compose, comprise, make up, include
Use the phrases **comprise, consist of, be composed of** and **be made up of** to talk about the parts that things are made of, or the things that something contains. Each of the following sentences means the same thing, but the patterns are different: *The United States comprises 50 states.* | *The United States is composed of 50 states.* | *The United States consists of 50 states.* | *The United States is made up of 50 states.* You will sometimes hear people say "is comprised of," but some people think this is incorrect. It is also incorrect to say "is consisted of." **Comprise** is the most formal word, and **make up** is the most informal. If you only mention some of the parts that something is made of, you use **include**: *New York City includes Brooklyn and Queens.*
GRAMMAR
These words are not used in progressive (*-ing*) tenses in these meanings.

---

com·pro·mise¹ /ˈkʌmprəˌmaɪz/ *n.* [C,U] an agreement that is achieved after everyone involved accepts less than they wanted at first, or the act of making this agreement: *Decisions came only after a long process of compromise.* | [+ **between**] *The bill is the result of a compromise between Democrats and Republicans.* | *Talks are continuing in the hope that the two factions will **reach a compromise**.* | *I'm willing to **make compromises**, but you'll have to keep your side of the bargain.*

compromise² *v.* **1** [I] to end an argument by making an agreement in which everyone involved accepts less than what they wanted at first: *They compromised by alternating days on which each chose the activity.* | [+ **on**] *You need to be willing to compromise on the price.* | [+ **with**] *Nash High School students compromised with the principal on the song picked for their graduation ceremony.* **2** [T] to harm or damage something in some way, for example by behaving in a way that does not match a legal or moral standard: *We need to increase profits without compromising employees' safety.* | *The patient's immune system has been compromised by cancer treatments.* | *Watson has **compromised herself*** (=done something dishonest or embarrassing) *by accepting lobbyists' money for her election campaign.*

com·pro·mis·ing /ˈkʌmprəˌmaɪzɪŋ/ *adj.* proving that you have done something morally wrong, or making it seem as though you have done so | **compromising documents/materials/photos etc.** *Investigators found compromising documents in the files.* | *Brown claims to possess photographs showing Wilson in **compromising** (=embarrassing) **positions.***

comp time /ˈkʌmp ˌtaɪm/ *n.* [U] vacation time that you are given instead of money, because you have worked more hours than you were REQUIRED to work

comp·trol·ler /kənˈtroʊlɚ, kəmp-/ *n.* [C] FORMAL an official title for a CONTROLLER (1)

com·pul·sion /kəmˈpʌlʃən/ *n.* **1** [C] a strong and unreasonable desire to do something: *People may develop compulsions such as excessive cleaning or counting.* | [**a compulsion to do sth**] *George says he has an irresistible compulsion to gamble.* **2** [U] the act of forcing or influencing someone to do something they do not want to do, or the situation of being forced or influenced: *Compulsion is not the answer to get kids to perform better in school.* | *Remember, you are **under no compulsion** to sign the agreement.* —see also COMPEL

com·pul·sive /kəmˈpʌlsɪv/ *adj.* **1** compulsive behavior is very difficult to stop or control, and is often a result of or a sign of a mental problem: *Compulsive spending is often a symptom of deep unhappiness.* **2 a compulsive liar/gambler/drinker etc.** someone who has such a strong desire to lie etc. that they are unable to control it: *Not all compulsive eaters are overweight.* —**compulsively** *adv.* —**compulsiveness** *n.* [U]

com·pul·so·ry /kəmˈpʌlsəri/ *adj.* FORMAL something that is compulsory is REQUIRED to be done because of a rule or law; MANDATORY: *All young men are required to do two years of compulsory military service.* | *Attendance at the meeting is compulsory.* —**compulsorily** *adv.* —compare VOLUNTARY¹ (1)

com·punc·tion /kəmˈpʌŋkʃən/ *n.* [U] FORMAL **have/feel no compunction about sth** to not feel guilty or sorry about something, although other people may think that it is wrong: *He apparently felt no compunction about lying to us.*

com·pu·ta·tion /ˌkʌmpyəˈteɪʃən/ *n.* [C,U] FORMAL the process of calculating or the result of calculating: *Many workers lacked skills in language and computation.* —**computational** *adj.*

com·pute /kəmˈpyut/ *v.* [I,T] FORMAL **1** to calculate a total, answer, result etc.: *The machine can compute the time it takes a sound wave to bounce back.* **2** SPOKEN if facts, ideas etc. compute, they seem sensible or correct: *His ideas just don't compute.*

com·put·er /kəmˈpyutɚ/ *n.* [C] an electronic machine that stores information and uses programs to help you find, organize, or change the information: *Our office has switched to a different computer system.* |

computer software | *Many kids spend more time playing computer games than watching TV.* | *Complex computer graphics were used to create the film's special effects.* | *Dr. Fonseca's office now keeps all the patients' details on computer.* —see also LAPTOP, PERSONAL COMPUTER —see picture on page 426

computer-aid·ed de·sign /.,.. ... ..'./ *n.* [U] CAD

com·pu·ter·ate /kəm'pyutərɪt/ *adj.* INFORMAL knowing how to use computers with some skill: *Students need to be computerate as well as literate.*

com·put·er·ize /kəm'pyutə,raɪz/ *v.* [T] to use a computer to control the way something is done, to store information etc.: *They've computerized all the church records.* | *About 3,000 stocks were traded during two computerized auctions.* —**computerization** /kəm-,pyutərə'zeɪʃən/ *n.* [U]

computer jock·ey /.'.. ,../ also **computer jock** /.'.. ,./ *n.* [C] INFORMAL someone who is very good at writing computer PROGRAMS

computer-lit·er·ate /.,.. '.../ *adj.* able to use a computer —**computer literacy** *n.* [U]

computer mod·el·ing /.,.. '.../ *n.* [U] the representation of a problem, situation, or real object on a computer in a form which lets you see it from all angles

computer sci·ence /.,.. '../ *n.* [U] the study of computers and what they can do

computer vi·rus /.,.. '../ *n.* [C] a VIRUS (3)

com·put·ing /kəm'pyutɪŋ/ *n.* [U] the use of computers as a job, in a business etc.: *Personal computing is one of Jack's interests.*

com·rade /'kæmræd/ *n.* [C] **1** FORMAL a friend, especially someone who shares difficult work or danger: *Thirty-five of the Americans killed in the war were accidentally killed by their comrades* **2** someone who is a member of the Communist Party with you: *Comrade Yanayev has arrived.*

comrade in arms /,.. '.'./ *n.* [C] FORMAL someone who has worked or fought with you to achieve particular GOALS

com·rade·ship /'kæmræd,ʃɪp/ *n.* [U] FORMAL friendship and loyalty among people who work together, fight together etc.

Comte /kount/, **Au·guste** /ɔ'gust/ (1798–1857) a French PHILOSOPHER

con[1] /kɑn/ *v.* **conned, conning** [T] INFORMAL **1** to trick someone in order to get their money or get them to do something: [**con sb out of sth**] *He tried to con me out of $20.* | [**con sb into doing sth**] *Tyrell conned several millionaires into investing in his business.* **2 con yourself** to try to make yourself believe something that is not true: *If you think she'll take you back after this, you're just conning yourself.*

con[2] *n.* [C] **1** a trick to get someone's money or make them do something: *Newman and Redford play a couple of guys working an elaborate con.* **2** SLANG a prisoner; CONVICT[2] —see also EX-CON **3** something that is a disadvantage —see also **the pros and cons (of sth)** (PRO[1] (3))

con- /kən, kɑn/ *prefix* together or with: *to conspire* (=plan together) | *a confederation* (=a group of people or organizations working together) —see also COL-, COM-, COR-

Con·a·kry /'kɑnəkri/ the capital and largest city of Guinea

Con·an Doyle —see DOYLE

con art·ist /'. ,../ *n.* [C] INFORMAL someone who tricks or deceives people in order to get money from them —see also CON MAN

con·cat·e·na·tion /kɑn,kæt^n'eɪʃən, -,kætə'neɪ-/ *n.* [C,U + of] FORMAL a series of events or things joined together one after another

con·cave /,kɑn'keɪv/ *adj.* a concave surface is curved down or toward the inside in the middle: *a concave mirror* —**concavity** /kɑn'kævəti/ *n.* [C,U] —opposite CONVEX

con·ceal /kən'sil/ *v.* [T] FORMAL **1** to hide something carefully: *Customs officers found a kilogram of cocaine that Smith had concealed inside his suitcase.* **2** to hide your real feelings or the truth: [**conceal sth from sb**] *Dana concealed her pregnancy from her family and friends.* —**concealed** *adj.*: *a concealed weapon* —**concealment** *n.* [U]

con·cede /kən'sid/ *v.* **1** [T] to admit that something is true or correct, although you wish that it were not true: *"Well, she is a little bit rude," Ortega conceded.* | *Knowles refused to concede her error.* | [**concede (that)**] *Anderson is a large man who concedes that he is 40 pounds overweight.* **2** [I,T] to admit that you are not going to win a game, argument, battle etc.: *After three years of civil war, the rebels finally conceded.* | *Kavner conceded defeat after 75% of the vote had been counted.* **3** [T] to give something to someone unwillingly: [**concede sth to sb**] *He has stated repeatedly that he will not concede any territory to neighboring countries.* **4 concede a goal/point etc.** to not be able to stop your opponent from getting a GOAL, point etc. during a game: *The Lakers conceded 12 points in a row to the Suns.* **5** [T] to give something to someone as a right or PRIVILEGE (1): [**concede sth to sb**] *The richer nations will never concede equal status to the poorer countries.* —see also CONCESSION

con·ceit /kən'sit/ *n.* **1** [U] an attitude that shows you have too much pride in your own abilities, appearance etc. **2** [C] an unusual way of showing or describing something in a play, movie, work of art etc.: *The movie's design conceit uses color for the dream, and black and white for the real world.*

con·ceit·ed /kən'sitɪd/ *adj.* behaving in a way that shows too much pride in your abilities, appearance etc.: *I don't want to sound conceited, but we are the experts here.* —**conceitedly** *adv.* —**conceitedness** *n.* [U]

con·ceiv·a·ble /kən'sivəbəl/ *adj.* able to be believed or imagined: [**conceivable (that)**] *It is conceivable that the two jobs could be combined to save money.* | *The Olympic Games organizers are trying to prepare for every conceivable emergency.* —**conceivably** *adv.* —opposite INCONCEIVABLE

con·ceive /kən'siv/ *v.* [I,T] **1** FORMAL to imagine a situation or what something is like: *I don't believe an author could have conceived a more romantic first meeting.* | [**conceive what/why/how etc.**] *Most of us find it difficult to conceive what life is like on the space station.* | [**conceive of (doing) sth**] *Some people found it hard to conceive of voting for anyone but the party in power.* | *I can't conceive of anything we could have done better.* **2** to think of a new idea or plan: *Scientists first conceived the idea of the atomic bomb in the 1930's.* | [**conceive of sth**] *A large part of Brian's time is spent conceiving of new ways to increase production.* **3** to become PREGNANT: *Ben and Tracy are hoping to conceive a second child soon.*

con·cen·trate[1] /'kɑnsən,treɪt/ *v.* **1** [I] to think very carefully about something you are doing: *Okay, I'll stop talking so you can concentrate.* | [**+ on**] *Turn off the TV, so you can concentrate on your homework.* **2** [I,T] to be present in large numbers or amounts in a particular place, or to put a large number of things in one place: [**+ in/on/at etc.**] *Chipmunks concentrate their food in underground burrows.* | *Most of New Zealand's population is concentrated on the north island.* | *Never before had so many artists come so far to concentrate in one city.* **3** [T] to make a substance or liquid stronger by removing most of the water from it **4 concentrate your/the mind** FORMAL if something concentrates the mind, it makes you think very clearly

concentrate on sth *phr. v.* [T] to give most of your attention to one thing: *I concentrated on getting a better grade in biology.* | *The agency has concentrated its efforts on a new road safety education program.*

concentrate[2] *n.* [C,U] a substance or liquid that has been made stronger by removing most of the water from it: *orange juice concentrate*

con·cen·trat·ed /'kɑnsən,treɪtɪd/ *adj.* **1** a substance or liquid that is concentrated has had most of the water removed from it: *a concentrated detergent* **2** [only before noun] showing a lot of determination or effort: *Solutions to these problems will take time and concentrated effort.*

s w con·cen·tra·tion /ˌkɑnsənˈtreɪʃən/ *n.* **1** [U] the ability to think very carefully about something for a long time: *A good night's sleep will improve your concentration.* | *The noise outside is making me lose my concentration.* **2** [singular,U] a process in which you put a lot of attention, energy etc. into a particular activity: [+ **on**] *People want the government to shift toward a greater concentration on domestic issues.* **3** [C,U] a large amount of something in a particular place: [+ **of**] *California has the largest concentration of Vietnamese outside Vietnam.* **4** [C] TECHNICAL the amount of a substance contained in a liquid: [+ **of**] *Tests show high concentrations of chemicals in the water.*

concentration camp /..'.. ,./ *n.* [C] a prison where political prisoners and other people who are not soldiers are kept in very bad conditions without enough food, especially during a war

con·cen·tric /kənˈsɛntrɪk/ *adj.* TECHNICAL concentric circles have their centers at the same point —compare ECCENTRIC¹ (2)

con·cept /ˈkɑnsɛpt/ *n.* [C] an idea of how something **s w** is, or how something should be done: *The idea of a soul is a religious concept.* | [+ **of**] *It's difficult to grasp the concept of infinite space.* | *This Amazon tribe has no concept of privacy.*

con·cep·tion /kənˈsɛpʃən/ *n.* **1** [C,U] a idea about what something is like, or a basic understanding of something: [+ **of**] *You may not agree with your child's conception of how her room should look.* | **have little/no conception of sth** *The leaders still have little conception of how democracy works.* **2** [C,U] the process by which a woman or female animal becomes PREGNANT, or the time when this happens: *Rheinhold argues that life does not begin at conception.* **3** [U] a process in which someone forms a plan or idea: *Straczynski is responsible not only for the conception of the show, but for most of its scripts.*

con·cep·tu·al /kənˈsɛptʃuəl/ *adj.* FORMAL dealing with concepts, or based on them: *The mall's plans are still in the conceptual stage.* —**conceptually** *adv.*

conceptual art /..,... './ *n.* [U] TECHNICAL art in which the main aim of the artist is to show an idea, rather than to represent actual things or people

con·cep·tu·al·ize /kənˈsɛptʃuəˌlaɪz/ *v.* [I,T] to form an idea: *How do we as a nation conceptualize racial equality?* —**conceptualization** /kənˌsɛptʃuələˈzeɪʃən/ *n.* [C,U]

s w con·cern¹ /kənˈsən/ *n.*
1 worry **a)** [U] a feeling of worry about something important: *The recent rise in crime is a matter of considerable public concern.* | [+ **about/over**] *Youngsters expressed concern about being assaulted in their own neighborhoods.* | [**concern for sb/sth**] *Concern for human rights is basic to our foreign policy.* | [**concern (that)**] *There is concern that the gasoline additive will actually increase pollution.* | *Our principal expressed concern is that there would not be enough classrooms.* | *The depletion of the ozone layer is causing concern among scientists.* **b)** [C] something that worries you: *My main concern is that the project won't be finished on time.* | [+ **about/over**] *The new phone technology raises concerns about callers' privacy.* | [+ **for**] *Owens's biggest concerns were for his wife and family.* | [**concern that**] *The government responded to concerns that the election will not be free and fair.* | **express/voice concerns** *Several employees expressed concerns that jobs would be lost.*
2 sth important [C,U] something that is important to you or that involves you: *Mark's family is his first concern.* | [+ **for**] *Development of parkland is a major concern for the voters in this area.* | *The destruction*

of the rain forests is *of concern to* us all (=it is important to everyone).
3 feeling for sb [U] a feeling of wanting someone to be happy, safe, and healthy: *Lopez thanked them for their concern.* | [+ **for**] *Coach O'Brien was praised for his concern for students' well-being.*
4 business [C] a business or company: *Raytheon is a defense contractor and engineering concern.* | *There is doubt about the company's ability to continue as a going concern* (=a business that is making money).
5 not sb's concern also **none of sb's concern** FORMAL if something is not your concern, you do not need to worry about it or be involved with it: *How you spend your money is not my concern.*

concern² *v.* [T] **1** [not in passive] if an activity, situation, rule etc. concerns you, it affects you or involves you: *The tax changes will concern large corporations more than small businesses.* **2** to make someone feel worried or upset: *The potential for abuse of these products concerns me a great deal.* | *We are deeply concerned by America's neglect of its youth.* **3** [not in passive] if a story, book, report etc. concerns someone or something, it is about them: *Many of Woody Allen's movies concern life in New York.* **4 concern yourself with/about sth** to become involved in something that interests or worries you: *Our country's leaders must concern themselves with environmental protection.* **5 to whom it may concern** used at the beginning of a formal letter when you do not know the name of the person you are writing to —see also CONCERNED

con·cerned /kənˈsənd/ *adj.*
1 worried worried about something important: *Concerned parents approached the school about the problem.* | [+ **about**] *Zoo officials are concerned about the mother elephant.* | [+ **for**] *Rescuers are concerned for the safety of two men trapped in the cave.* | [**concerned that**] *The police are concerned that the protests may lead to violence.* —see Usage Note at NERVOUS
2 involved [not before noun] involved in something or affected by it: *Divorce is very painful, especially when children are concerned.* | [+ **in**] *Everyone concerned in the incident was questioned by the police.* | [+ **with**] *Businesses concerned with the oil industry do not support solar energy research.* | *The company's closure was a shock to all concerned.*
3 think sth is important [not before noun] believing that something is important [+ **with**] *They are more concerned with tourism than with preservation of the ruins.* | [+ **about**] *These days, people are concerned about good nutrition.*
4 as far as sb is concerned SPOKEN used to show what someone's opinion on a subject is or how it affects them: *It's a good deal, as far as I'm concerned.*
5 as far as sth is concerned also **where sth is concerned** SPOKEN used to show which subject or thing you are talking about: *Where taxes are concerned, savings bonds are better than certificates of deposit.*
6 love/care caring about someone and whether they are happy and healthy: [+ **for/about**] *One call came from a mother concerned for her thirteen-year-old daughter.*
7 be concerned with sb/sth if a book, story etc. is concerned with a person, subject etc. it is about that subject: *This story is concerned with a Russian family in the 19th century.*

con·cern·ing /kənˈsənɪŋ/ *prep.* FORMAL about or relating to: *The police are anxious for any information concerning the woman's whereabouts.* | *We have several questions concerning the report.*

con·cert /ˈkɑnsət/ *n.* **1** a performance given by musicians or singers: *a rock concert* | [+ **of**] *a concert of 20th century American music* | *I went to the Indigo Girls concert last weekend.* **2 in concert (with sb) a)** playing or singing at a concert: *The three tenors will be in concert at the Dorothy Chandler Pavilion.* **b)** FORMAL people who do something in concert do it together after having agreed on it: *Barr alleged the two had planted the bomb in concert with several others.*

con·cert·ed /kənˈsətɪd/ *adj.* [only before noun] **concerted effort/attempt/action** etc. something that is done by people working together in a carefully planned and very determined way: *Courtland County officials have made a concerted effort to raise the standards of education.* —**concertedly** *adv.*

con·cert·go·er /'kɑnsət͜,goʊɚ/ *n.* [C] someone who often goes to concerts, or someone who is at a particular concert

concert grand /,.. './ *n.* [C] a large GRAND PIANO that is used for concerts —compare BABY GRAND

concert hall /'.. ,./ *n.* [C] a large public building where concerts are performed

con·cer·ti·na /,kɑnsə'tinə/ *n.* [C] a small musical instrument like an ACCORDION that you hold in your hands and play by pressing in from each side

concertina wire /..'.. ,./ *n.* [U] RAZOR WIRE

con·cert·mas·ter /'kɑnsət͜,mæstɚ/ *n.* [C] the most important VIOLIN player in an ORCHESTRA

con·cer·to /kən'tʃɛrtoʊ/ *n. plural* **concertos** [C] a piece of CLASSICAL MUSIC, usually for one instrument and an ORCHESTRA

con·ces·sion /kən'sɛʃən/ *n.* **1** [C] something that you let someone have in order to end an argument: [+ to] *The government refused to give any concessions to the powerful drug barons.* | **make concessions on/about sth** *Neither side is willing to make concessions on the issue of pay.* —see also CONCEDE **2** [C] **a)** the right to have a business in a particular place, especially in a place owned by someone else: *The company owns valuable logging and mining concessions.* **b)** a small business that sells things in a place owned by someone else: *Joe runs a hamburger concession in the mall.* **3 concessions** [plural] the things sold at a concession stand **4** [C,U] FORMAL a special right given to someone by the government, an employer etc., or the act of giving someone this right: *tax concessions*

con·ces·sion·aire /kən͜,sɛʃə'nɛr/ *n.* [C] someone who has been given a CONCESSION (2), especially to run a business

con·ces·sion·ar·y /kən'sɛʃə͜,nɛri/ *adj.* given as a concession: *a concessionary agreement*

concession stand /.'.. ,./ *n.* [C] a small business that sells food, drinks, or other things at sports events, theaters etc.

conch /kɑŋk, kɑntʃ/ *n.* [C] the large twisted shell of a tropical sea animal that looks like a SNAIL

con·cierge /kɑn'syɛrʒ/ *n.* [C] someone in a hotel whose job is to help guests with problems, give them advice about local places to go etc.

con·cil·i·ate /kən'sɪliˌeɪt/ *v.* [I,T] FORMAL to do something to make people more likely to stop arguing, especially by giving them something they want: *Negotiators were called in to conciliate the warring factions.* —**conciliator** *n.* [C]

con·cil·i·a·tion /kən͜,sɪli'eɪʃən/ *n.* [U] the process of trying to get people to stop arguing and agree on something: *As a sign of conciliation, army troops were withdrawn from the area.*

con·cil·i·a·to·ry /kən'sɪliəˌtɔri/ *adj.* doing something that is intended to make someone stop arguing with you: *We need to take a more conciliatory approach in the negotiations.* | *The government has made a series of conciliatory gestures toward its neighbors.*

con·cise /kən'saɪs/ *adj.* short, with no unnecessary words: *The instruction manual is written in clear, concise English.* —**concisely** *adv.* —**conciseness** also **concision** /kən'sɪʒən/ *n.* [U] FORMAL

con·clave /'kɑŋkleɪv/ *n.* [C] **1** a private or secret meeting: *Puruggnan said the alliance was formed during a secret conclave.* **2** a meeting at which a group of CARDINALS chooses a new POPE

w
2
con·clude /kən'klud/ *v.* **1** [T] to decide that something is true after considering all the information you have: [conclude that] *The study concludes that California drivers would save money if insurance laws were changed.* | [conclude from sth that] *Taylor concluded from the smell that the substance was marijuana.* **2** [T] to complete something that you have been doing, especially after a long time: **conclude your work/investigation/research etc.** *The police hope to conclude their investigation of the*

murder within three months. **3** [I always + adv./prep.,T] if something such as a meeting or a speech concludes, or if you conclude it, you end it, often by doing or saying one final thing: *The sales convention will conclude as planned on Sunday.* | *The Giants conclude the three-game series tonight in Palm Springs.* | [+ with/by] *Our Wednesday night sessions usually conclude with an informal discussion.* | *Let me conclude by thanking you very much again for your participation.* **4 conclude an agreement/treaty/contract etc.** to finish arranging an agreement etc. successfully: *The United States and Japan concluded a new trade agreement on computer chips this month.*

C

con·clud·ing /kən'kludɪŋ/ *adj.* **concluding sentence/remark/stages etc.** the last sentence, stage etc. in an event or piece of writing: *Lester makes his position perfectly clear in the concluding paragraph.*

con·clu·sion /kən'kluʒən/ *n.* **1** [C] something you decide after considering all the information you have: *Becky came to the conclusion that Tim must have forgotten about their date.* | *The survey samples are too small for anyone to draw conclusions.* | *All the evidence pointed to the conclusion that he was guilty.* | *Don't jump to conclusions* (=make a decision too quickly) *– just because they're late doesn't mean they've had an accident!* **2** [C] the end or final part of something: [+ of] *Lucy was given a standing ovation at the conclusion of her speech.* **3 in conclusion** used in a piece of writing or a speech to show that you are about to finish what you are saying: *In conclusion, I want to thank all the people who have volunteered their time to our organization.* **4 be a foregone conclusion** to be certain to happen even though it has not yet officially happened: *It seemed like a foregone conclusion that Tiger Woods would win the tournament.*

sw
2

con·clu·sive /kən'klusɪv/ *adj.* showing without any doubt that something is true: *The investigation failed to turn up any conclusive evidence.* —**conclusively** *adv.* —opposite INCONCLUSIVE

con·coct /kən'kɑkt/ *v.* [T] **1** to invent a story, excuse, or plan, especially in order to deceive someone: *Lawyers claim that she's a nut who's concocted a story of date rape.* **2** to make something such as a food or drink by mixing different things, especially things that are not usually combined: *Debbie started the business by concocting recipes in her kitchen.*

con·coc·tion /kən'kɑkʃən/ *n.* [C] something such as a food or drink made by mixing different things, especially things that are not usually combined: *Jell-O shots are a bizarre concoction of sweet gelatin and vodka.*

con·com·i·tant[1] /kən'kɑmətənt/ *adj.* [only before noun] FORMAL existing or happening together, especially as a result of something: *Soldiers must be aware of the concomitant risks and responsibilities of military service.* —**concomitantly** *adv.*

concomitant[2] *n.* [C] FORMAL something that often or naturally happens with something else: [+ of] *The right to alter the facts is not a concomitant of a free press.*

Con·cord /'kɑŋkɚd/ the capital city of the U.S. state of New Hampshire

con·cord /'kɑŋkɔrd/ *n.* [U] **1** FORMAL the state of having a friendly relationship, so that you agree on things and live in peace: *international concord* **2** TECHNICAL in grammar, concord between words happens when they match correctly, for example when a plural noun has a plural verb following it

con·cor·dance /kən'kɔrdəns/ *n.* **1** [C] TECHNICAL an alphabetical list of all the words used in a book or set of books by one writer, with information about where they can be found and usually about how they are used **2** [U] FORMAL the state of being similar to something else or in agreement with it: *"There is apparent concordance among the unions,"* Buford said.

con·cor·dant /kən'kɔrdənt/ *adj.* FORMAL being in

agreement or having the same regular pattern: *concordant opinions*

con·course /'kɑŋkɔrs/ *n.* [C] a large hall or open place in a building such as an airport or train station: *Our sales office is on the lower concourse.*

con·crete[1] /'kɑŋkrit/ *n.* [U] a hard substance used for building things, made by mixing CEMENT, sand, small stones, and water

con·crete[2] /kɑn'krit, 'kɑŋkrit/ *adj.* **1** [only before noun] made of concrete: *a concrete floor* **2** clearly based on fact, rather than on beliefs or guesses: *Just tell him what you want in clear and concrete terms.* —compare ABSTRACT[1] (2) **3** definite and specific rather than general: *No mention is made of any concrete plans to address workers' complaints.* —**concretely** *adv.*

concrete jun·gle /,.. '../ *n.* [C usually singular] INFORMAL an ugly, possibly dangerous, area in a city that is full of tall buildings, with no open spaces

concrete mix·er /'.. ,../ *n.* [C] a CEMENT MIXER

con·cu·bine /'kɑŋkyə,baɪn/ *n.* [C] a woman who lives with and has sex with a man that she is not married to, especially when he already has a wife or wives —**concubinage** /kɑn'kyubənɪdʒ/ *n.* [U]

con·cur /kən'kɚ/ *v.* concurred, concurring [I] FORMAL **1** to agree with someone or have the same opinion as them: *"I think this was a sound decision,"* concurred Prof. Barbara Stevens. | [+ **with**] *The board members concurred with a recommendation by the district Superintendent.* | [+ **that**] *Umpire Bob Davidson concurred that the ball had hit the top of the fence.* **2** to happen at the same time; COINCIDE (1): *Everything concurred to produce the desired effect.*

con·cur·rence /kən'kɚəns, -'kʌr-/ *n.* FORMAL **1** [U] agreement: [+ **of**] *Any final decision must have the concurrence of the White House.* **2** [C] an occasion when several things happen at the same time: [+ **of**] *a strange concurrence of events*

con·cur·rent /kən'kɚənt, -'kʌrənt/ *adj.* **1** existing or happening at the same time: *A concurrent exhibition at the Museum of Modern Art offers a fuller look at Rothko's work.* **2** FORMAL in agreement: *concurrent opinions* —**concurrently** *adv.*: *Lee is serving two prison sentences concurrently.*

con·cus·sion /kən'kʌʃən/ *n.* [C] **1** an injury to the brain that makes you lose consciousness or feel sick for a short time, usually caused by something hitting your head: *The doctor said it could have been a mild concussion.* **2** FORMAL a violent shaking movement, caused by something such as an explosion: *The concussion blew him off his seat and shattered the window.* —**concuss** /kən'kʌs/ *v.* [T] —**concussed** *adj.*

con·demn /kən'dɛm/ *v.* [T]
1 [disapprove] to say very strongly that you do not approve of something or someone, especially because you think it is morally wrong: *Politicians were quick to condemn the bombing.* | *The French government condemned the killings and ordered an immediate investigation.* | [condemn sb for doing sth] *Ginny knew that society would condemn her for leaving her children.* | [condemn sth for sth] *The TV show was widely condemned for its violence.* | [condemn sb/sth as sth] *Other leaders have condemned Rev. Abernathy's story as false.*
2 [punish] to give someone a severe punishment after deciding they are guilty of a crime: *He was convicted of first degree murder and condemned to death.*
3 [force to do sth] if a particular situation condemns someone to do something, it forces them to live in a bad way or to do something bad: [condemn sb to (do) sth] *If you don't learn from the past, you're condemned to repeat its mistakes.* | *Having children could condemn a woman to a lifetime of economic dependence.*
4 [building] to state officially that a building is not safe enough to be used: *Inspectors condemned the three buildings after the fire.*

con·dem·na·tion /,kɑndəm'neɪʃən/ *n.* [C,U] an expression of very strong disapproval of someone or something: [+ **of**] *One of Grahame's frequent themes is the condemnation of intolerance.*

con·dem·na·to·ry /kən'dɛmnə,tɔri/ *adj.* FORMAL expressing strong disapproval: *a condemnatory attitude*

con·demned /kən'dɛmd/ *adj.* **1** a condemned person is going to be punished by being killed: *Chin spent the night locked in a jail cell with a condemned man.* **2** a condemned building is officially not safe to live in or use

con·den·sa·tion /,kɑndən'seɪʃən/ *n.* **1** [U] small drops of water that are formed when gas changes to liquid: *Condensation may develop on walls where moisture is a problem.* **2** [U] TECHNICAL the process of changing from gas to liquid: *the condensation of steam into water* **3** [C,U] FORMAL the act of making something shorter, or the thing that has been made shorter: *Next came a 15-minute condensation of Mozart's "Don Giovanni."*

con·dense /kən'dɛns/ *v.* **1** [I,T] if gas condenses or is condensed, it becomes a liquid as it becomes cooler: *Try insulating the water pipes to prevent moisture from condensing on them.* | [+ **into**] *The gaseous metal cools and condenses into liquid zinc.* **2** [T usually passive] to make a liquid thicker by removing some of the water: *condensed soup* **3** [T] to make something that is spoken or written shorter, by not giving as much detail or using fewer words to give the same information: *Medved's article was condensed in Reader's Digest.*

condensed milk /., ./ *n.* [U] milk which has been made thicker by removing some of the water, and has sugar added to it —compare EVAPORATED MILK

con·dens·er /kən'dɛnsɚ/ *n.* [C] **1** a piece of equipment that makes a gas change into liquid **2** a piece of equipment, for example in a car, that stores an electrical CHARGE for a short time; CAPACITOR

con·de·scend /,kɑndɪ'sɛnd/ *v.* [I] **1** to behave as if you think other people are not as good, intelligent, or important as you are: [+ **to**] *The best young people's magazines do not condescend to their readers.* **2** to do something in a way that shows you think it is below your social or professional position: [condescend to do sth] *Do you think the CEO would ever condescend to have lunch with us in the cafeteria?* —**condescension** /,kɑndɪ'sɛnʃən/ *n.* [U]

con·de·scend·ing /,kɑndɪ'sɛndɪŋ◂/ *adj.* behaving as though you think other people are not as good, intelligent, or important as you are: *English reviewers tended to take a condescending view of American writers.* —**condescendingly** *adv.*

con·di·ment /'kɑndəmənt/ *n.* [C] FORMAL something such as KETCHUP, MUSTARD, or another SAUCE, that you add to food when you eat it to make it taste better

con·di·tion[1] /kən'dɪʃən/ *n.*
1 [state] [singular,U] the particular state that someone or something is in, usually how good or bad it is: *Travel agents cannot guarantee the condition of the cruise ship or the food served aboard it.* | **in good/poor/satisfactory etc. condition** *The car has been well maintained and is in excellent condition.* | *What kind of condition is the house in?*
2 [conditions] [plural] the situation in which people live or work, especially the physical things such as pay or food that affect the quality of their lives: *Teachers voted to strike over pay and conditions.* | *The government promised improved **living conditions**.* | **in excellent/terrible etc. conditions** *Police discovered the children living in filthy conditions.*
3 [agreement/contract] [C usually plural,U] something that is stated in a contract or agreement that must be done or provided: [+ **of**] *Be sure you read and understand the conditions of participation in the program.* | [+ **for**] *The bank sets strict conditions for new loans.* | **Under the conditions of** the agreement, the work must be completed by the end of the month. | *Two employees agreed to speak to us **on condition that** they not be named.* | *Senator Dodd is leading a campaign to **impose** strict **conditions on** U.S.*

military aid. | **meet/satisfy a condition** (=obey what is demanded by a condition)
4 conditions [plural] the weather at a particular time, especially when you are considering how this will affect you: *Travelers are advised not to fly because of poor weather conditions.* | *Up to 10 inches of snow fell in blizzard conditions.*
5 necessary situation [C] something that must happen first before something else can happen: [+ for/of] *Finance ministers claim that all the conditions for an economic revival are in place.*
6 illness [C] an illness or health problem that affects you permanently or for a very long time: *Some people who have HIV show no outward signs of the condition.* | **a heart/lung/skin etc. condition** (=that affects a particular organ)
7 state of health [singular,U] a person or animal's state of health: *Her condition is good, but she's extremely tired.* | **in critical condition** (=dangerously sick or very badly injured)
8 be in no condition to do sth to be too sick, drunk, or upset to be able to do something: *I was in no condition to drive home after the party.*
con·di·tion² *v.* [T] **1** to make a person or an animal think or behave in a particular way by influencing or training them over a period of time: [condition sb to (do) sth] *The American public has been conditioned to think that this is just the way things are.* —see also CONDITIONING **2** to keep hair or skin healthy by putting a special liquid on it: *This shampoo conditions your hair and makes it smell great.* **3** FORMAL to make something depend on other facts being true or something else happening: *The administration has conditioned its support for the new laws.* —see also CONDITIONER
con·di·tion·al¹ /kən'dɪʃənəl/ *adj.* **1** if an offer, agreement etc. is conditional, it will only be done if something else happens: *a conditional contract* | [+ on/upon] *The deal is conditional on approval by the French authorities.* —opposite UNCONDITIONAL **2** in grammar, a conditional sentence is one that begins with "if" or "unless" and expresses something that must be true or that happens before something else can be true or happen —**conditionally** *adv.*
conditional² *n.* [C] a sentence or CLAUSE (2) that is expressed in a conditional form
con·di·tion·er /kən'dɪʃənɚ/ *n.* [C,U] a liquid that you put on your hair after washing it to make it softer
con·di·tion·ing /kən'dɪʃənɪŋ/ *n.* [U] **1** the process by which people or animals are trained to behave in a particular way when particular things happen: *Most adults are unaware of the social conditioning they have been subject to since childhood.* **2** the process of making your body used to a particular level or type of activity or exercise —see also AIR CONDITIONING
con·do /'kandou/ *n. plural* **condos** [C] INFORMAL a CONDOMINIUM
con·do·lence /kən'douləns/ *n.* [C usually plural,U] sympathy for someone that something bad has happened to, especially when someone has died: *a message of condolence* | **send/offer/extend your condolences** (=to formally express your sympathy when someone has died) —compare COMMISERATION
con·dom /'kandəm/ *n.* [C] a thin piece of rubber that a man wears over his PENIS (=sex organ) during sex, to prevent a woman from having a baby, or to protect against sexual diseases
con·do·min·i·um /ˌkandə'mɪniəm/ *n.* [C] **1** one apartment in a building with several apartments, each of which is owned by the people living in it **2** a building containing several of these apartments
con·done /kən'doun/ *v.* [T] to accept or forgive behavior that most people think is morally wrong: *Some parents feel that making birth control available to teenagers somehow condones sexual activity.*
con·dor /'kandor, -dɚ/ *n.* [C] a very large Californian or South American VULTURE (=bird that eats dead animals)
con·duce /kən'dus/ *v.*
   conduce to/toward sth *phr. v.* [T] FORMAL to help to produce a particular quality or state
con·du·cive /kən'dusɪv/ *adj.* **be conducive to sth**

FORMAL to provide conditions that make it easier to do something: *We want to create a disciplined environment that is conducive to learning.*
con·duct¹ /kən'dʌkt/ *v.*
1 do sth to get information [T] to do something, especially in order to get information or prove facts | **conduct a survey/test/poll etc.** *The experiments were conducted with three of the zoo's monkeys.* | *Advanced-level classes are conducted entirely in the foreign language.* | *A memorial service will be conducted Sunday for the missing woman.*
2 music [I,T] to stand in front of a group of musicians and direct their playing: *The Duke Ellington Orchestra is conducted by Mercer Ellington.*
3 conduct yourself FORMAL to behave in a particular way, especially in a situation where people judge your behavior: *Seidman has conducted himself with extraordinary grace and ability.*
4 electricity/heat [T] if something conducts electricity or heat, it allows the electricity or heat to travel along or through it: *Plastic and rubber won't conduct electricity, but copper will.*
5 show sb sth [T always + adv./prep.] to show someone a place or building by leading them around in it: *A guide will conduct us through the museum.*
con·duct² /'kandʌkt, -dəkt/ *n.* [U] FORMAL **1** the way someone behaves, especially in public, in their job etc.: *The Senator's conduct is being investigated by the Ethics Committee.* | *Prisoners' release dates depend on continued good conduct while in custody* **2** the way a business, activity etc. is organized: *Attending conferences and meetings is necessary to the conduct of our business.*
con·duc·tion /kən'dʌkʃən/ *n.* [U] the process by which electricity passes through wires, heat passes through metal, water passes through pipes etc.
con·duc·tive /kən'dʌktɪv/ *adj.* TECHNICAL able to conduct electricity, heat etc.: *Copper is a very conductive metal.* —**conductivity** /ˌkandʌk'tɪvəti/ *n.* [U]
con·duc·tor /kən'dʌktɚ/ *n.* [C] **1** someone who stands in front of a group of musicians or singers and directs their playing or singing **2** someone who is in charge of a train and collects payments from passengers or checks their tickets **3** something that allows electricity or heat to travel along or through it: *Wood is a poor conductor of heat.*
con·du·it /'kanduɪt/ *n.* [C] **1** a pipe or passage through which water, gas, electric wires etc. pass **2** a connection that allows people to pass ideas, news, money, weapons etc. from one place to another: [+ for] *Drug traffickers have used the country as a conduit for shipments to the U.S.*
cone /koun/ *n.* [C] **1** a solid or hollow shape with a round base, sloping sides, and a point at the top, or something with this shape: *Remember how they used to give you roasted chestnuts in a little cone of newspaper?* | *a volcanic cone* **2** a piece of thin cooked cake, shaped like a cone, that you put ICE CREAM in —see also ICE CREAM CONE, SNOW CONE **3** the fruit of a PINE¹ (1) or FIR¹ tree —see also CONIFER **4** an object shaped like a large cone, usually bright orange in color, that is put on a road to prevent cars from going somewhere or to warn drivers about something —see also NOSECONE **5** a CELL (1) in your eye that is shaped like a cone, that helps you see light and color —compare ROD (3)
Co·ney Is·land /ˌkouni 'aɪlənd/ an area of Brooklyn, New York, famous for its AMUSEMENT PARK and beach
con·fab /'kanfæb, kən'fæb/ *n.* [C] INFORMAL a friendly, usually private conversation or meeting: *We'll have a quick confab to talk about what he wants.*
con·fab·u·la·tion /kənˌfæbyə'leɪʃən/ *n.* FORMAL a private conversation or meeting —**confabulate** /kən'fæbyəˌleɪt/ *v.* [I]
con·fec·tion /kən'fɛkʃən/ *n.* [C] FORMAL **1** something sweet, such as candy, cake, or cookies: *a peanut butter confection* **2** a piece of clothing that is very delicate and complicated, or has a lot of decoration: [+ of] *a dreamy confection of pink beads and*

C

satin **3** something such as a movie or a song that is entertaining and not serious at all: *"Home Alone" is a simple little confection from John Hughes.*

con·fec·tion·er /kənˈfɛkʃənɚ/ *n.* [C] someone who makes or sells candy and other similar sweet things

confectioners' sug·ar /.ˈ... ˌ../ *n.* [U] POWDERED sugar

con·fec·tion·er·y /kənˈfɛkʃəˌnɛri/ *n. plural* **confectioneries** **1** [U] candy and other similar sweet things **2** [C] OLD-FASHIONED a store that sells candy and other similar sweet things

con·fed·er·a·cy /kənˈfɛdərəsi/ *n. plural* **confederacies** **1 the Confederacy** the southern states that fought against the northern states in the U.S. Civil War **2** [C] a CONFEDERATION

con·fed·er·ate¹ /kənˈfɛdərɪt/ *n.* [C] **1** someone who helps someone else do something, especially something secret or illegal: *A riot began when drug traffickers tried to free their jailed confederates.* **2 Confederate** a soldier from the southern states in the U.S. Civil War **3** a member of a confederacy —**confederate, Confederate** *adj.*

con·fed·er·ate² /kənˈfɛdəˌreɪt/ *v.* [I,T] FORMAL if groups, areas etc. confederate, or you confederate them, they join to become a confederation: [+ **with**] *In 1949, Newfoundland confederated with Canada.*

con·fed·e·ra·tion /kənˌfɛdəˈreɪʃən/ *n.* [C] a group of people, political parties, or organizations that have united for political purposes or trade

con·fer /kənˈfɚ/ *v.* **conferred, conferring** FORMAL **1** [I] to discuss something with other people, so that everyone can express their opinions and decide on something: [+ **with**] *Franklin leaned over and conferred with his attorneys.* **2** [T] to officially give someone an award, a degree, a right etc.: [**confer sth on/upon sb**] *I watched proudly as a Scout Court of Honor conferred a merit badge on our son.* —**conferment** *n.* [C,U]

s w **con·fer·ence** /ˈkɑnfrəns/ *n.* [C] **1** a private meeting
2 2 for a few people to discuss a particular subject: [+ **with**] *After a brief conference with his aides, Senator Bradley left for the airport.* | **have/hold a conference** *They're having parent-teacher conferences at my kids' school this week.* | *The meeting will be held in the second floor **conference room**.* —see also VIDEO CONFERENCING **2** a large formal meeting where a lot of people discuss important matters such as business, science, or politics, especially for several days: *Representatives from over 100 countries attended the International Peace Conference.* | [+ **on**] *The American Medical Association is sponsoring a conference on men's health.* —see also NEWS CONFERENCE, PRESS CONFERENCE **3** a group of sports teams that play against each other to see who is best: *Texas A&M won the Southwest Conference title last week with a 65–6 victory over SMU.*

conference call /ˈ.. ˌ./ *n.* [C] a telephone call in which several people in different places can all talk to each other at the same time

con·fer·enc·ing /ˈkɑnfrənsɪŋ/ *n.* [U] **video/telephone conferencing** the use of VIDEO or telephone equipment to make it possible for several people in different places to talk to each other at the same time

con·fess /kənˈfɛs/ *v.* [I,T] **1** to admit that you have done something wrong or illegal, especially to the police: *Woods was released from jail after the real murderers confessed.* | [**confess to (doing) sth**] *Edwards confessed to being a spy for the KGB.* | *Holmes confessed to the murders shortly before he died.* | [+ **that**] *An army captain confessed that he recruited soldiers to smuggle cocaine.* **2** to admit something that you feel embarrassed about: [+ **that**] *Marsha confessed that she didn't really know how to work the computer.* | [**confess to doing sth**] *Sid finally confessed to owning a pair of bell-bottom jeans.* | *I **must confess** I'm not very excited at the thought of dinner with the Martins.* **3** to tell a priest or God about the wrong things you have done so that

you can be forgiven: *Gary felt better after confessing his sins to one of the priests.*

con·fessed /kənˈfɛst/ *adj.* [only before noun] having admitted publicly that you have done something: *a confessed killer* —see also SELF-CONFESSED —**confessedly** /kənˈfɛsɪdli/ *adv.*

con·fes·sion /kənˈfɛʃən/ *n.* **1** [C] a formal statement that you have done something wrong or illegal: *Sanchez's confession was read out to the court.* | [+ **of**] *a confession of murder* | *At 3 a.m. Higgins broke down and **made a full confession**.* **2** [C] an act of saying that you have done something embarrassing or something that you are ashamed of: [+ **that**] *Carol overheard Mason's confession that he was drinking again.* **3** [C,U] a private statement to a priest or to God about the bad things that you have done: *Rita **goes to confession** at least once a month.* **4** [C] FORMAL a statement of what your religious beliefs are: [+ **of**] *a confession of faith*

con·fes·sion·al¹ /kənˈfɛʃənl/ *n.* [C] a place in a Catholic church, usually a small enclosed room, where a priest hears people make their confessions

confessional² *adj.* confessional speech or writing contains private thoughts or facts that you normally want to keep secret, especially private information about things you have done that were wrong

con·fes·sor /kənˈfɛsɚ/ *n.* [C] FORMAL the priest to whom someone regularly makes their confession

con·fet·ti /kənˈfɛti/ *n.* [U] small pieces of colored paper that you throw at events such as parties, PARADES etc.

con·fi·dant /ˈkɑnfəˌdɑnt/ *n.* [C] someone you tell your secrets to or who you talk to about personal things: *Steve's **closest confidant** is his brother Phil.*

con·fi·dante /ˈkɑnfəˌdɑnt/ *n.* [C] a woman you tell your secrets to or who you talk to about personal things: *Marcel viewed his mother as a confidante and best friend.*

con·fide /kənˈfaɪd/ *v.* [T] **1** to tell someone you trust about personal things that you do not want other people to know: [**confide (that)**] *Theodore confided that he was having a relationship with a woman he had met at one of his shows.* [**confide to sb (that)**] *Connie had confided to Michele that her marriage was in trouble.* **2** LITERARY to give something you value to someone you trust so they take care of it for you: [**confide sth to sb**] *Walter confided the money to his brother's safekeeping during the war.*

confide in sb *phr. v.* [T] to tell someone about something very private or secret, especially a personal problem, because you feel you can trust them: *Marian never really felt able to confide in her sister Amelia.*

con·fi·dence /ˈkɑnfədəns/ *n.*
1 ▌feeling sb/sth is good▐ [U] the feeling that you can trust someone or something to be good, work well, or produce good results: [+ **in**] *Our first priority is to maintain the customer's confidence in our product.* | **gain/lose confidence** *Opinion polls show that voters have lost confidence in the mayor.* | *At first, we didn't **have** any **confidence that** Tony's methods were going to work.* | *Gail can now drive a truck **with confidence**.*
2 ▌belief in yourself▐ [U] the belief that you have the ability to do things well or deal with situations successfully: *The key thing about being a quarterback is that you have to show confidence and lead the team.* | *Tom's a good student, but he **lacks confidence** in himself.* | *Living in a foreign country **gave** Jessica a lot of **confidence**.* | *Physical therapy gave Marianne **the confidence to** return to work.* | *She enrolled in karate to help **restore** her **confidence** after the mugging.*
3 ▌feeling sth is true▐ [U] the feeling that something is definite or true: *How can anyone say **with confidence** that the worst is over?* | *At that time he **had** little **confidence** that God existed.*
4 ▌feeling of trust▐ [U] a feeling of trust in someone, so that you can tell them something and be sure they will not tell other people: **earn/gain/win sb's confidence** *I only ask that you give me a chance to earn your confidence again.* | *I'm giving you this information **in the strictest confidence**.*

5 **a secret** [C] LITERARY a secret or a piece of information that is private or personal: *I later learned there were some confidences Richard hadn't shared with me.* —see also CONSUMER CONFIDENCE, VOTE OF CONFIDENCE, VOTE OF NO CONFIDENCE

con·fidence-build·ing /'... ,.../ *adj.* a confidence-building event, activity etc. increases your confidence: **confidence-building measures/gestures/steps etc.** *The outdoor training consists of several confidence-building activities for youngsters.*

confidence trick also **confidence game** /'... ,.../ *n.* [C] FORMAL a CON GAME

con·fi·dent /'kɑnfədənt/ *adj.* **1** sure that you can do something or deal with a situation successfully: *Sandi gave her a confident smile.* | [+ **about**] *I feel very confident about this game.* | [+ **of**] *The normally modest Baldwin is confident of victory in this year's Senate race.* **2** [not before noun] very sure that something is going to happen, or that you will be able to do something: [**confident (that)**] *William said he is confident the transplant will save his life.* —see also SELF-CONFIDENT —**confidently** *adv.*

con·fi·den·tial /,kɑnfə'denʃəl◂/ *adj.* **1** spoken or written in secret, and intended to be kept secret: *In 1965, a confidential report to President Johnson was leaked to the press.* | *Both sides agreed to **keep** their financial agreement **confidential**.* | *What I'm telling you is strictly confidential.* **2** a confidential way of speaking or behaving shows that you do not want other people to know what you are saying: *During the ride back home, Mom started to talk about her problems in a confidential way.* **3** a confidential secretary is one who is trusted with secret information —**confidentially** *adv.*

con·fi·den·ti·al·i·ty /,kɑnfə,denʃi'æləti/ *n.* [U] a situation in which you trust someone not to tell secret or private information to anyone else: *The relationship between attorneys and their clients is based on confidentiality.* | *It is a **breach of confidentiality** for a priest to reveal what someone has confessed.*

con·fid·ing /kən'faɪdɪŋ/ *adj.* behaving in a way that shows you want to tell someone about something that is private or secret: *All the people José interviewed were amazingly confiding and helpful.* —**confidingly** *adv.*: *Maggie put her hand confidingly in his.*

con·fig·u·ra·tion /kən,fɪgyə'reɪʃən/ *n.* [C,U] **1** FORMAL OR TECHNICAL the shape or arrangement of the parts of something; LAYOUT: [+ **of**] *The constellation appears as a cone-shaped configuration of bright stars.* **2** TECHNICAL the combination of equipment needed to run a computer system

con·fig·ure /kən'fɪgyə/ *v.* [T] TECHNICAL to arrange something, especially computer equipment, so that it works with other equipment

con·fine /kən'faɪn/ *v.* [T]
1 **keep sb in a place** to keep someone in a place that they cannot leave, such as a prison: [**confine sb to sth**] *The area was placed under curfew, confining all residents to their homes.* | [**be confined in sth**] *Stevenson was arrested for murder and confined in a hospital for psychiatric tests.*
2 **limit** to keep someone or something within the limits of a particular activity or subject; RESTRICT: [**be confined to sth**] *Thelma's cooking these days is confined to meals for herself.* | **confine yourself to sth** *The document confined itself to factual and accurate statements.*
3 **stop sth spreading** to stop something bad from spreading to another place: [**confine sth to sth**] *Although firefighters were able to confine the blaze to one room, the entire hotel was evacuated.*
4 **stay in one place** [usually passive] to have to stay in a place, especially because you are sick: *I had the flu and was **confined to bed**.* | *Scott's been **confined to a wheelchair** since the car crash.*
5 **be confined to sth** to affect or happen to only one group of people, or in only one place or time: *My theory is not confined to political events.*

con·fined /kən'faɪnd/ *adj.* a confined space or area is one that is very small: *It wasn't easy to sleep in such a confined space.*

con·fine·ment /kən'faɪnmənt/ *n.* **1** [U] the act of

putting someone in a room, prison etc., or the state of being there: *During his confinement, Wen taught himself how to read.* | *She was sentenced to 15 days' confinement in her cell for violating a direct order.* —see also SOLITARY CONFINEMENT **2** [C,U] LITERARY the period of time before and during which a woman gives birth to a baby

con·fines /'kɑnfaɪnz/ *n.* [plural] limits or borders: *The movie was filmed mostly **within the confines of** a studio.*

con·firm /kən'fəm/ *v.* [T] **1** to show that something is definitely true, especially by providing more proof: *New evidence has confirmed the first witness's story.* | [**confirm that**] *A study today confirms that fish oil appears to lower blood pressure.* | [**confirm what**] *This article confirms what many experts have been saying for years.* **2** to make an idea or feeling stronger or more definite: *The campaign has confirmed my worst instincts about politics.* **3** to say that something is definitely true: *U.S. officials said they could not confirm the report.* | [**confirm that**] *Tina called to confirm that you're working on Saturday.* | [**confirm what**] *My brother will confirm what I have told you.* | *Spokesmen for the agency would **neither confirm nor deny** reports that they were conducting an investigation.* **4** to tell someone that a possible arrangement, date, or time is now definite: *Could you confirm the dates we discussed?* | *I'll call the hotel and confirm our reservations.* **5** **be confirmed** to be made a full member of a Christian church in a special ceremony

con·fir·ma·tion /,kɑnfə'meɪʃən/ *n.* [C,U] **1** a statement or letter that says that something is definitely true, or the act of stating this: [+ **of**] *No independent confirmation of the report was available.* | [**confirmation that**] *McCarthy supplied the first confirmation that the hostages are still alive.* **2** a letter, message, etc. that tells you that a possible arrangement, date, or time is now definite: *I'm still waiting for confirmation from the travel agency about my tickets.* **3** a religious ceremony in which someone is made a full member of the Christian church

con·firmed /kən'fəmd/ *adj.* **a confirmed bachelor/alcoholic/vegetarian etc.** someone who seems unlikely to change the way of life they have chosen

con·fis·cate /'kɑnfəskeɪt/ *v.* [T] to officially take someone's property away from them, usually as a punishment: *An increasing number of guns have been confiscated in schools recently.* —**confiscation** /,kɑnfə'skeɪʃən/ *n.* [C,U] *the confiscation of private property* —**confiscatory** /kən'fɪskə,tɔri/ *adj.*

con·fla·gra·tion /,kɑnflə'greɪʃən/ *n.* [C] FORMAL **1** a very large fire over a large area that destroys a lot of buildings, forests etc.: *Bertha vividly remembers the conflagration that consumed her childhood home.* **2** a violent situation or war: *The conflict has the potential to become a major conflagration.*

con·flate /kən'fleɪt/ *v.* [T] FORMAL to combine two or more things to form a single new thing, whether it is correct or not: *Although we must not make the mistake of conflating Asians and Asian-Americans, we must recognize that international issues have domestic implications.* —**conflation** /kən'fleɪʃən/ *n.* [C,U]

con·flict¹ /'kɑn,flɪkt/ *n.* **1** [C,U] a state of disagreement or argument between people, groups, countries etc.: *serious political conflict* | *You've got nearly 2000 people here every day, so there are bound to be some conflicts.* | [+ **between**] *It's the age-old conflict between labor and management* | [+ **with**] *A school counselor helped Jason resolve a conflict with one of his teachers.* | *Nina seems to be permanently **in conflict with** her superiors.* | *Andy's management style has **brought** him **into conflict with** colleagues.* **2** [C,U] a situation in which you have to choose between two or more opposing things: [+ **between**] *It's the same conflict between doing what you want to and doing what you ought to.* | *The principles of democracy are sometimes **in conflict with** political reality.* **3** [C] something that you have to do at the same time that someone wants you to do something different: *Sorry, I have a conflict on Friday. Can we make it Monday?* **4** [C,U] fighting or a war: *a violent conflict* | *Armed conflict might be unavoidable.* **5** [C,U] a situation in which you have two opposite feelings about something: *Isn't it Freud who came up with the idea of inner conflict?*

con·flict² /kən'flɪkt/ *v.* [I] **1** if two ideas, beliefs, opinions etc. conflict, they cannot exist together or both be true: [+ **with**] *Large corporations' motives for making large profits often conflict with consumers' interests.* | **conflicting reports/opinions/statements etc.** *Javier and Jaime told conflicting stories of what happened.* **2** if two events or activities conflict, they happen at the same time so you cannot do both: [+ **with**] *Richard agreed to meet once a week; any more would conflict with his workouts.*

con·flict·ed /kən'flɪktɪd/ *adj.* FORMAL **be/feel conflicted** to be confused about what choice to make, especially when the decision involves strong beliefs or opinions: *Neither Jane nor Neil feels conflicted about pursuing their careers while raising children.*

conflict of in·ter·est /ˌ… '… '…/ *n. plural* **conflicts of interest** [C] a situation in which you cannot do your job fairly because your position or influence can affect another business that you have connections with: *Riegle returned the money because it could create the appearance of a conflict of interest.*

con·flu·ence /'kɑnfluəns/ *n.* [singular] **1** TECHNICAL the place where two or more rivers flow together: [+ **of**] *the confluence of the Missouri and Yellowstone rivers* **2** a situation in which two or more things happen or exist at the same time: [+ **of**] *a confluence of unhappy events* —**confluent** *adj.*

con·form /kən'fɔrm/ *v.* [I] **1** to behave in the way that most other people in your group or society behave: *Getting everyone on the team to conform has taken a long time.* **2** to obey or follow an established rule, pattern etc.: [+ **to**] *Most local buildings conform to an eight-story limit.* | [+ **with**] *Zach refuses to conform with school rules.* —see also CONFORMIST —**conformer** *n.* [C] —**conformance** *n.* [U]

con·for·ma·tion /ˌkɑnfɔr'meɪʃən, -fɚ-/ *n.* [C,U] TECHNICAL the shape of something or the way in which it is formed: [+ **of**] *the conformation of the earth*

con·form·ist /kən'fɔrmɪst/ *adj.* thinking and behaving like everyone else, because you do not want to be different: *Lagrange's outspoken views have left him well outside the conformist political mainstream.* —**conformist** *n.* [C] —opposite NONCONFORMIST

con·form·i·ty /kən'fɔrməti/ *n.* [U] **1** behavior that obeys the accepted rules of society or a group, and is the same as that of most other people: *Greg continued to resist conformity, later becoming a vegetarian.* **2 in conformity with sth** FORMAL in a way that obeys rules, customs etc.: *We took swift and decisive action in conformity with the First Lady's wishes.*

con·found /kən'faʊnd/ *v.* [T] **1** to confuse and surprise people by being unexpected: *Dan's speedy recovery confounded the medical experts.* **2** if a problem, question etc. confounds you, you cannot understand it or explain it: *Even travel agents are confounded by the logic of airline ticket pricing.* **3** LITERARY to defeat an enemy, plan etc. **4 confound it/him/them etc.** OLD-FASHIONED used to show that you are annoyed: *Confound it! What did I do with my glasses?*

con·found·ed /kən'faʊndɪd, 'kɑn,faʊn-/ *adj.* [only before noun] OLD-FASHIONED used to show that the thing you are talking about is annoying: *Where did that confounded dog get to?*

con·fra·ter·ni·ty /ˌkɑnfrə'tɚnəti/ *n.* [C] FORMAL a group of people, especially religious people who are not priests, who work together for some good purpose

con·frère, confrere /'kɑnfrɛr, kən'frɛr/ *n.* [C] FORMAL someone you work with or who belongs to the same organization as you: *Jerome preferred to spend his time surrounded by his confreres.*

con·front /kən'frʌnt/ *v.* [T] **1** [usually passive] to appear and need to be dealt with by someone: [**confront sb with sth**] *Laura is often confronted with questions about her father and brother.* **2** to behave in a threatening way toward someone, as though you are going to attack them: *They were confronted by about five men, one of whom had a gun.* **3** to ACCUSE someone of doing something by showing them the proof: *The play is about a woman who confronts the man who tortured her in prison.* | [**confront sb about/with sth**] *I'm afraid to confront Vivian about her drinking.* **4** to deal with something very difficult or bad in a brave and determined way: *We try to help people confront their problems.*

con·fron·ta·tion /ˌkɑnfrən'teɪʃən/ *n.* [C,U] **1** a situation in which there is a lot of angry disagreement between two people or groups with different opinions: *Julia had stayed in her room to avoid any more confrontation.* | [+ **with/between**] *There was a tense confrontation between Allen and the other commissioners.* **2** a fight or battle: *Two people were killed and several wounded in the confrontation.*

con·fron·ta·tion·al /ˌkɑnfrən'teɪʃənl/ *adj.* likely to cause arguments or make people angry: *Stern is a radio and TV talk show host known for his confrontational style.*

Con·fu·cian·ism /kən'fyuʃəˌnɪzəm/ *n.* [U] a Chinese way of thought which teaches that one should be loyal to one's family, friends, and rulers and treat others as one would like to be treated. Confucianism was developed from the ideas of Confucius. —**Confucian** *adj.*

Con·fu·cius /kən'fyuʃəs/ (551–479 B.C.) a Chinese PHILOSOPHER who taught social and moral principles that had a great influence on Chinese society and on the way the Chinese people think —see also CONFUCIANISM

con·fuse /kən'fyuz/ *v.* [T] **1** to make someone feel that they cannot think clearly or do not understand something: *I hope my explanation didn't confuse everybody.* | *The instructions just confused me more.* **2** to think wrongly that one person, thing, or idea is someone or something else: *The twins liked to confuse their teachers by switching seats.* | [**confuse sb/sth with sb/sth**] *In-line skating is not to be confused with roller skating.* **3 confuse the issue/situation** to make it even more difficult to think clearly about or deal with a situation or problem: *John kept asking unnecessary questions which only confused the issue.*

con·fused /kən'fyuzd/ *adj.* **1** unable to understand clearly what someone is saying or what is happening, or to think clearly about something: *Now I'm totally confused. Can you explain that again?* | [+ **about**] *If you're confused about anything, phone my office.* **2** not clear, or not easy to understand: *a lot of confused ideas* | *confused political thinking* —**confusedly** /kən'fyuzɪdli/ *adv.*

con·fus·ing /kən'fyuzɪŋ/ *adj.* difficult to understand because there is no clear order or pattern: *French wine labels can be very confusing.* | *Residents face confusing pricing and poor customer service from many local phone companies.* —**confusingly** *adv.*

con·fu·sion /kən'fyuʒən/ *n.* [U] **1** a state of not understanding what is happening or what something means because it is not clear: *I hope the meeting will clear up people's confusion.* | [+ **about/over/as to**] *There was some confusion over where the money had actually been hidden.* **2** a situation in which someone wrongly thinks that one person, thing, or idea is someone or something else: *To avoid confusion, the teams wore different colors.* | [+ **with/in**] *The seminar was going to begin at seven, but there was some confusion with the scheduling.* | [+ **between**] *Dan says there has been a lot of confusion between his name and his brother Don's.* **3** a feeling of not being able to think clearly about what you should say or do, especially in an embarrassing situation: *Jake's confusion at meeting Sherri at the party was obvious.* | *Terri stopped in confusion as everyone turned to look at her.* **4** a very confusing situation, usually with a lot of noise and action: *With all the confusion, nobody noticed the two boys leave.*

con·ga /ˈkɑŋgə/ n. [C,U] **1** a Latin American dance in which people hold onto each other and dance in a line, or the music for this **2** also **conga drum** a tall drum that is usually played by hitting it with your hands

con game /ˈ. ./ n. [C] a dishonest trick played on someone in order to get their money; CON² (1)

con·geal /kənˈdʒil/ v. [I] if a liquid such as blood congeals, it becomes thick or solid: *a puddle of congealed grease*

con·ge·nial /kənˈdʒinyəl/ adj. nice, in a way that makes you feel comfortable and relaxed: *a congenial atmosphere* | *Minnesotans are known for their congenial manner.* —**congenially** adv.

con·gen·i·tal /kənˈdʒɛnətl/ adj. **1** TECHNICAL a congenital medical condition or disease affects someone from the time they are born: *a congenital birth defect* | *a rare congenital disorder* **2** existing as a part of your character and unlikely to change: *The city seems to have a congenital inferiority complex.* | *Brian is a congenital liar.* —**congenitally** adv.

con·gest·ed /kənˈdʒɛstɪd/ adj. **1** a congested street, city etc. is very full of people or traffic: *Pedestrians picked their way across congested streets.* | *congested airports* **2** a congested nose, chest etc. is filled with thick liquid that does not flow easily, especially because you have a cold —**congestion** /kənˈdʒɛstʃən, -ˈdʒɛʃ-/ n. [U] *traffic congestion* | *nasal congestion*

con·glom·er·ate /kənˈglɑmərɪt/ n. **1** [C] a large business organization consisting of several different companies that have joined together: *a media and entertainment conglomerate* **2** [C,U] TECHNICAL a type of rock consisting of different sizes of stones held together by clay **3** [C] a group of different things or people gathered together: [+ of] *Russia expanded eastward to build a conglomerate of Slavs, Central Asians, and Siberian Eskimos.*

con·glom·er·a·tion /kənˌglɑməˈreɪʃən/ n. [C] a group of many different things gathered together: [+ of] *Scottsdale's Old Town is a conglomeration of loud bars, souvenir shops, and art galleries.*

Con·go, the /ˈkɑŋgoʊ/ a long river in central Africa that flows towards the Atlantic Ocean through both the Republic of Congo and the Democratic Republic of Congo

Congo, the Dem·o·crat·ic Re·pub·lic of a very large country in central Africa, which was called Zaïre between 1971 and 1997, and before that was called the Belgian Congo —**Congolese** /ˌkɑŋgəˈliz, -ˈlisʲ/ n., adj.

Congo, the Republic of a country on the Equator in the western part of central Africa, to the west of the Democratic Republic of Congo —**Congolese** /ˌkɑŋgəˈliz, -ˈlisʲ/ n., adj.

con·grats /kənˈgræts/ interjection INFORMAL a short form of CONGRATULATIONS

con·grat·u·late /kənˈgrætʃəˌleɪt/ v. [T] **1** to tell someone that you are happy because they have achieved something or because something good has happened to them: [congratulate sb on (doing) sth] *Let me congratulate you on getting the job done.* **2 congratulate yourself** to feel pleased and proud of yourself because you have achieved something or something good has happened to you: [+ for/on] *Squaw Valley ski resort is congratulating itself for installing new snow-making equipment in time for this season.* —**congratulatory** /kənˈgrætʃələˌtɔri/ adj.

con·grat·u·la·tion /kənˌgrætʃəˈleɪʃən/ n. **1 congratulations** [plural] words and expressions that you use to say that you are happy that someone has achieved something: *Donna was swamped with congratulations from friends and fellow reporters when she won the prize.* | *Sidney sent his congratulations.* | *I hear that congratulations are in order* (=something good has happened to you). **2 congratulations!** SPOKEN an expression used when you want to congratulate someone: *You got the job – congratulations!* | [+ on] *Congratulations on a superb performance!* **3** [U] the act of expressing your happiness that someone has achieved something: *Messages of approval and congratulation poured in from all over the world.*

con·gre·gant /ˈkɑŋgrɪgənt/ n. [C] FORMAL one of a group of people who come together, especially in a church, for religious WORSHIP

con·gre·gate /ˈkɑŋgrəˌgeɪt/ v. [I] to come together in a group: *Insects tend to congregate on the underside of leaves.*

con·gre·ga·tion /ˌkɑŋgrəˈgeɪʃən/ n. [C] **1** a group of people gathered together in a church: *When the prayer ended, the entire congregation sat down.* **2** the people who usually go to a particular church: *Several members of the congregation organized a bake sale to raise money for a new piano.* —**congregational** adj.

Con·gre·ga·tion·al /ˌkɑŋgrəˈgeɪʃənl/ adj. relating to a Protestant church in which each congregation is responsible for making its own decisions —**Congregationalism** n. [U] —**Congregationalist** n. [C]

con·gress /ˈkɑŋgrɪs/ n. **1 Congress** the group of people elected to make laws in the U.S., consisting of the Senate and the House of Representatives: *He predicted Congress will not accept the administration's proposal.* | *an act of Congress* **2** [C,U] a formal meeting of the members of a group, especially a political party, to discuss plans, exchange information etc.: *Jiang won a place on several committees at the Communist Party's August 1973 congress.* **3** [C] the group of people chosen or elected to make the laws in some countries —see also SEXUAL CONGRESS

con·gres·sion·al, Congressional /kənˈgrɛʃənl/ adj. [only before noun] relating to a congress, especially the U.S. House of Representatives: *a congressional subcommittee*

con·gress·man, Congressman /ˈkɑŋgrɪsmən/ n. [C] a man who is a member of a congress, especially the U.S. House of Representatives

con·gress·wom·an, Congresswoman /ˈkɑŋgrɪsˌwʊmən/ n. [C] a woman who is a member of a congress, especially the U.S. House of Representatives

con·gru·ent /kənˈgruənt, ˈkɑŋgruənt/ adj. **1** FORMAL fitting together well; appropriate: [+ with] *Many ancient societies had political systems that were congruent with their economic realities.* **2** TECHNICAL congruent TRIANGLES are the same size and shape —**congruence** n. [U] —**congruently** adv.

con·gru·ous /ˈkɑŋgruəs/ adj. FORMAL [+ with] fitting together well; appropriate —**congruity** /kənˈgruəti/ n. [C,U] —opposite INCONGRUOUS

con·ic /ˈkɑnɪk/ adj. TECHNICAL relating to or shaped like a CONE (1)

con·i·cal /ˈkɑnɪkəl/ adj. shaped like a CONE (1): *a conical roof*

conic sec·tion /ˌ.. ˈ../ n. [C] TECHNICAL a shape, such as an ELLIPSE or a PARABOLA, which is made in GEOMETRY when an imaginary flat surface is passed through a CONE (1)

con·i·fer /ˈkɑnəfɚ/ n. [C] TECHNICAL a tree, such as a PINE tree, that has needle-shaped leaves that stay on it during the winter, and produces brown CONES (3) that contain its seeds —**coniferous** /kəˈnɪfərəs, koʊ-/ adj.

conj. the written abbreviation of CONJUNCTION

con·jec·ture¹ /kənˈdʒɛktʃɚ/ n. FORMAL **1** [U] the act of guessing about things when you do not have enough information: *Jackson's political plans have been the subject of conjecture since he moved to Washington.* **2** [C] an idea or opinion formed by guessing: *My results show that this conjecture was, in fact, correct.* —**conjectural** adj.

conjecture² v. [I,T] FORMAL to form an idea or opinion without having much information to base it on; guess: *"Maybe Burt is jealous," Isabelle conjectured.* | [+ that] *Deckard conjectured that what happened to Dave might happen to him.*

con·join /kənˈdʒɔɪn/ v. [I,T] FORMAL **1** to join together, or to make things or people do this **2 conjoined twins** TECHNICAL: see SIAMESE TWINS

con·ju·gal /ˈkɑndʒəgəl/ adj. [only before noun]

FORMAL **1** relating to marriage or married people: *conjugal love* **2 a conjugal visit** a meeting between a married COUPLE, usually a prisoner and their husband or wife, during which they are allowed to have sex

con·ju·gate /ˈkɑndʒə‚geɪt/ *v.* TECHNICAL [T] to give the different grammatical forms of a verb in a particular order: *We have to conjugate these verbs in Latin.*

con·ju·ga·tion /‚kɑndʒəˈgeɪʃən/ *n.* [C] TECHNICAL **1** the way that a particular verb conjugates **2** a set of verbs in languages such as Latin that are conjugated in the same way

con·junct /ˈkɑndʒəŋkt/ *n.* [C] TECHNICAL a CONJUNCTIVE —**conjunct** *adj.*

con·junc·tion /kənˈdʒʌŋkʃən/ *n.* **1 in conjunction with sb/sth** FORMAL working, happening, or being used with someone or something else: *International driver's licenses are only valid in conjunction with a state license.* **2** [C usually singular] a combination of different things that have come together by chance: *Now we have the most attractive conjunction of home prices, incomes and interest rates since 1977.* **3** [C] TECHNICAL a word such as "but," "and," or "while" that connects parts of sentences, phrases, or CLAUSES (2)

con·junc·tive /kənˈdʒʌŋktɪv/ *n.* [C] TECHNICAL a word that joins phrases together —**conjunctive** *adj.*: *a conjunctive adverb*

con·junc·ti·vi·tis /kən‚dʒʌŋktɪˈvaɪtɪs/ *n.* [U] an infectious disease of the eyes that makes them red and makes the EYELIDS stick together

con·junc·ture /kənˈdʒʌŋktʃɚ/ *n.* [C] formal a combination of events or situations, especially one that causes problems: [+ of] *an accidental conjuncture of events*

con·jure /ˈkɑndʒɚ/ *v.* **1** [I,T] to perform tricks in which you seem to make things appear, disappear, or change as if by magic: *David conjured an endless succession of rabbits out of his hat.* **2 conjure an image/thought/memory etc.** to bring a particular image, thought etc. to someone's mind: *For me, Thanksgiving conjures images of Pilgrims and turkeys.* **3** [T] FORMAL to make something appear or happen suddenly, without any cause that people can see: *The threat of computer terrorists may be enough to conjure money for research from Congress.* —**conjuring** *n.* [U]

conjure sth ↔ **up** *phr. v.* [T] **1** to bring a thought, picture, idea, or memory to someone's mind: *The Beatles' music always conjures up happy memories of my teenage years.* **2** to make something appear when it is not expected, as if by magic: *Mrs. Keene graciously conjured up a smile and said: "I'm so glad you could make it."* **3** to make the spirit of a dead person appear by saying special magic words

con·jur·er, **conjuror** /ˈkɑndʒərɚ/ *n.* [C] someone who entertains people by performing tricks in which things appear, disappear, or change as if by magic

conk /kɑŋk/ *v.* [T] INFORMAL to hit someone hard, especially on the head

conk out *phr. v.* [I] INFORMAL **1** if a machine or car conks out, it suddenly stops working: *I was driving along on Highway 5 when my car conked out.* **2** if someone conks out, they fall asleep because they are very tired: *He just rolled over and conked out.*

con man /ˈ. ./ *n.* [C] someone who tries to get money or valuable things from people by tricking them —see also CON ARTIST

s w
2
con·nect /kəˈnɛkt/ *v.*
1 join [T] to join two or more things together: *The Kathmandu-Lhasa Highway connects Nepal and Tibet.* | [**connect sth to sth**] *After connecting the hose to the faucet, slide it into the drain and turn on the water.*
2 realize [T] to realize that two facts, events, or people are related to each other: *I'd probably know Phil by sight, but I just can't connect the face and the name.* | [**connect sb/sth with sth**] *They didn't connect Mrs. Jennings with the crime at first.*

3 electricity/gas etc. [T] also **connect up** to join something to the main supply of electricity, gas, or water, or to the telephone network: *Has the phone been connected yet?* —opposite DISCONNECT
4 airplane/train etc. [I] if one airplane, bus, etc. connects with another, it arrives just before the other one leaves so that you can continue your trip: *I missed the connecting flight.* | [+ **with**] *The #49 bus goes across the Dumbarton Bridge and connects with CalTrain in Palo Alto.*
5 telephone [T] to join two telephone lines so that two people can speak: *Please hold. I'll try to connect you.*
6 hit sth [I] to succeed in hitting someone or something: *In the first inning, Mitchell connected for his 19th home run of the season.*
7 understand people [I] if people connect, they feel that they like each other and understand each other: [+ **with**] *They valued Deanna's ability to empathize and connect with others.*
8 connect the dots an activity for children consisting of a piece of paper with small points on it that have numbers next to them, so that if you draw a line from one point to the next, it forms a picture

con·nect·ed /kəˈnɛktɪd/ *adj.* **1** if two facts, events, s
etc. are connected, they affect each other or are 3
related to each other: *Police are investigating whether the three shootings are connected.* | [+ **to**] *The incident did not appear to be connected to any political cause.* | [+ **with**] *Everything connected with Christmas is on sale this week.* | *The two ideas are closely connected, and should be dealt with together.* **2** if two things are connected, they are joined together: *The two continents were once connected.* | [+ **to**] *What's this cord connected to?* **3** having a social or professional relationship with someone: *a politically connected businessman* | [+ **with**] *Aren't they connected with his father's business in some way?* **4 well connected** having important or powerful friends or relatives

con·nect·ed·ness /kəˈnɛktɪdnɪs/ *n.* [U] the feeling of understanding and liking someone: *Education should expand the sense of connectedness a young child feels with the world.*

Con·nect·i·cut /kəˈnɛtɪkət/ *written abbreviation* **CT** a state in the northeastern U.S.

con·nec·tion /kəˈnɛkʃən/ *n.* s
2
1 sth that connects things [C,U] a relationship in which two or more facts, events, people etc. are related to each other, and one is affected or caused by the other: [+ **between**] *Today there is more awareness of the connection between food and health.* | [+ **with**] *The Atlanta Symphony has no connection with the new orchestra.* | *Police have yet to establish a connection between the two murders.* | *I never made the connection* (=realized there was a connection) *between Senator Bill Bradley and the New York Knicks.*
2 in connection with sth concerning or relating to something: *They're investigating safety matters in connection with the astronauts' experiences.*
3 people you know [plural] people whom you know who can help you by giving you money, finding you a job etc.: *Shirley used her connections in the country music industry to get a recording contract.*
4 electrical wire [C] a wire or piece of metal joining two parts of a machine or electrical system: *Your computer screen must have a loose connection somewhere.*
5 joining things together [U] the joining together of two or more things: [+ **to**] *The latest software makes connection to the Internet fast and easy.*
6 airplane/train etc. [C] an airplane, train, or bus that can be used by passengers from an earlier airplane, train, or bus who are continuing their trip: [+ **to**] *If this flight is delayed, we'll miss our connection to Paris.*
7 flight/road etc. [C] a road, path etc. that joins two places and allows people to travel between them
8 friendly feeling [C] a situation in which two people understand and like each other: *I felt an immediate connection with Luisa as soon as I met her.*

C

9 `telephone` [C] if you have a bad connection on the telephone, you are unable to hear well because there is a lot of noise in the telephone

10 `family` [plural] people who are related to you, but not very closely: *I believe Joe's family has Spanish connections.* —see Usage Note at RELATIONSHIP

con·nec·tive[1] /kəˈnɛktɪv/ *adj.* [only before noun] joining two or more things together: *Zwigoff, the director, brilliantly draws connective lines between the artist's life and work.*

connective[2] *n.* [C] TECHNICAL a word that joins phrases, parts of sentences etc.

connective tis·sue /.ˈ.. ˌ../ *n.* [U,plural] TECHNICAL parts of the body such as fat or bone that support or join organs and other body parts together

con·ning tower /ˈ.. ˌ../ *n.* [C] TECHNICAL the structure on top of a SUBMARINE (=ship that goes under water)

con·nip·tion /kəˈnɪpʃən/ also **conniption fit** /.ˈ.. ˌ./ *n.* [C] INFORMAL **have/throw a conniption** to become very upset because you disagree with something or do not want to do something: *Mom had a conniption fit the other day about Danni spending the night.*

con·nive /kəˈnaɪv/ *v.* **1 connive to do sth** to work together secretly to achieve something, especially something wrong; CONSPIRE: *The two connived to drive Diana and Mark apart.* **2** [I] to allow something wrong to happen without trying to stop it, even though you know it is wrong: [+ **with**] *Members of staff connived with outsiders to steal from the company.* —**connivance** *n.* [C] *We could not have escaped without the connivance of the guards.*

con·niv·ing /kəˈnaɪvɪŋ/ *adj.* behaving in a way that does not prevent something wrong from happening, or actively helps it to happen: *The main character, Fleur, is a conniving woman who will do almost anything to defeat her rivals.*

con·nois·seur /ˌkɑnəˈsɔ, -ˈsʊə/ *n.* [C] someone who knows a lot about something such as art, food, music etc.: *a wine connoisseur*

Con·nol·ly /ˈkɑnəli/, **Mau·reen** /mɔˈrin/ (1934–1969) a U.S. tennis player famous as the first woman to win the tennis GRAND SLAM

Con·nors /ˈkɑnəz/, **Jim·my** /ˈdʒɪmi/ (1952–) a U.S. tennis player who was considered one of the best players in the 1970s and 1980s

con·no·ta·tion /ˌkɑnəˈteɪʃən/ *n.* [C] a feeling or an idea that a word makes you think of: *Being a liberal has taken on negative connotations.* —compare DENOTATION —**connotative** /ˈkɑnəˌteɪtɪv/ *adj.*

con·note /kəˈnoʊt/ *v.* [T] FORMAL if a word connotes something, it makes you think of particular feelings and ideas: *The car's name is meant to connote luxury and quality.* —compare DENOTE

con·nu·bi·al /kəˈnubiəl/ *adj.* FORMAL relating to marriage: *Walt and Marge lived in connubial bliss* (=being happily married) *for over 50 years.*

con·quer /ˈkɑŋkə/ *v.* **1** [I,T] to take control of a land or country by attacking people or fighting a war: *Hernan Cortes led Spanish troops to conquer the Aztecs.* | *Alexander the Great conquered the world, but died at thirty-three.* | *a conquering hero* **2** [I,T] to defeat an enemy: *The Zulus conquered all the neighboring tribes.* —see also **divide and conquer/rule** (DIVIDE[1] (6)) **3** [T] to gain control over a feeling, or successfully deal with something that is difficult or dangerous: *Ari not only conquered his drinking problem, but he's found a new career.* | *The moral of the story is that love conquers all* (=love helps to solve any problem). **4** [T] to become very successful in a particular activity: *Disney's quest is to conquer the worlds of entertainment and leisure.* | **conquer sb's heart** (=make someone love you) **5** [T] to succeed in climbing to the top of a mountain when no one has ever climbed it before: *Sir Hillary and Sherpa Tenzing made history in 1953 by conquering Mount Everest.* —**conqueror** *n.* [C]

con·quest /ˈkɑŋkwɛst/ *n.* **1** [C,U] the act of defeating an army or taking land by fighting: *military conquests* | [+ **of**] *the Muslim conquest of Egypt* **2** [C] land that is won in a war: *French conquests in Asia*

3 [C] someone whom you have persuaded to love you or to have sex with you, although you do not love or respect them: *These men seek power through sexual conquests.* **4** [U] the act of gaining control of or dealing successfully with something that is difficult or dangerous: [+ **of**] *the conquest of space*

con·quis·ta·dor /kɑnˈkistəˌdɔr/ *n. plural* **conquistador** or **conquistadores** /kɑnˌkistəˈdɔreɪz/ [C] one of the Spanish conquerors of Mexico, Central, and South America in the 16th century

Con·rad /ˈkɑnræd/, **Joseph** (1857–1924) a British writer of novels, born in Poland, who is considered one of the greatest writers in English of the early 20th century

C

con·san·guin·i·ty /ˌkɑnsænˈgwɪnəti/ *n.* [U] LITERARY the state of being closely related

con·science /ˈkɑnʃəns/ *n.* **1** [C usually singular] the part of your mind that tells you whether the things you do are morally right or wrong: *I have to do what my conscience tells me.* | **a guilty/bad conscience** (=knowledge that you did something wrong) | *Smith says he has a clear conscience* (=knowledge that you have done nothing wrong) *about what happened.* | *A student's decision to attend or miss a class is a matter of conscience.* **2 have sth on your conscience** to feel guilty about something: *If anything happens to Emily, I'll always have it on my conscience.* **3** [U] a feeling of GUILT because you did something wrong: *Parker displayed a remarkable lack of conscience about what he had done.* | *She felt a pang of conscience at lying to him.* **4 in good conscience** FORMAL if you do something in good conscience, you do it because you think it is the right thing to do: *I could not, in good conscience, agree with his decision.* —see also PRISONER OF CONSCIENCE

conscience money /ˈ.. ˌ../ *n.* [U] money that someone gives to another person in order to make themselves feel less guilty about something bad that they have done

con·sci·en·tious /ˌkɑnʃiˈɛnʃəs/ *adj.* showing a lot of care and attention: *We have made a very conscientious effort to reduce spending.* | *a conscientious worker* —**conscientiously** *adv.* —**conscientiousness** *n.* [U]

conscientious ob·ject·or /ˌ.... .ˈ../ *n.* [C] someone who refuses to become a soldier because of their moral or religious beliefs —compare DRAFT DODGER

con·scious /ˈkɑnʃəs/ *adj.* **1** [not before noun] noticing or realizing something; AWARE: [+ **of**] *Frith was suddenly conscious of the fact that Laurie was frightened.* | [+ **that**] *Stanley was conscious that Mrs. Olenska was looking at him.* **2** awake and able to understand what is happening around you: *Francis was found in the car's trunk, covered in blood but conscious.* **3** thinking a lot about something that is important or that you are worried about: [+ **of**] *Lydia had always been very conscious of her foreign accent.* **4 a conscious effort/decision/attempt etc. (to do sth)** an effort, decision etc. that is deliberate and intended: *Vivien made a conscious effort to be friendly.* —**consciously** *adv.* —see also SELF-CONSCIOUS —opposite UNCONSCIOUS[1] [SW2]

-conscious /kɑnʃəs/ [in adjectives] **health-conscious/socially-conscious etc.** thinking a lot about something such as health, social position etc.: *Uniforms aren't very popular with fashion-conscious teenagers.*

con·scious·ness /ˈkɑnʃəsnɪs/ *n.* [U] **1** the condition of being awake and able to understand what is happening around you: *David lost consciousness* (=became unconscious) *and had to be taken to the hospital.* **regain consciousness** (=wake up after being sick and unconscious) **2** your mind and your thoughts: *The death of President Kennedy almost 40 years ago still lives in the national consciousness.* **3** someone's ideas, feelings, or opinions about politics, life etc.: *Yoga can have the effect of broadening your consciousness* (=helping you learn and [SW2] [SW3] accept new things). **4** the state of knowing that something exists or is true; AWARENESS: *The march is intended to raise people's consciousness about women's health issues.* —see also STREAM OF CONSCIOUSNESS

con·scious·ness rais·ing /'… ,../ *n.* [U] the process of making people understand and care more about a moral, social, or political problem —**consciousness-raising** *adj.* [only before noun]

cons·cript¹ /kən'skrɪpt/ *v.* [T] FORMAL **1** to make someone join the military; DRAFT² (2): [+ into] *Many young men were taken by soldiers and forcibly conscripted into the military.* **2** to make someone become a member of a group or take part in a particular activity: *Governor Davis wanted to conscript parents as homework helpers.* —compare RECRUIT¹

con·script² /'kɑnskrɪpt/ *n.* [C] FORMAL someone who has been made to join the military; DRAFTEE —compare RECRUIT² (1)

con·scrip·tion /kən'skrɪpʃən/ *n.* [U] FORMAL the practice of making people join the military; the DRAFT¹ (3)

con·se·crate /'kɑnsə,kreɪt/ *v.* [T] **1** to officially state in a special religious ceremony that something such as a place or building is holy and can be used for religious purposes: *The Pope will consecrate the new parish church during his visit to his homeland.* **2** to officially state in a special religious ceremony that someone is now a priest, BISHOP (1) etc. —**consecrated** *adj.*: *consecrated ground* —**consecration** /,kɑnsə'kreɪʃən/ *n.* [U]

con·sec·u·tive /kən'sɛkyətɪv/ *adj.* [only before noun] consecutive numbers, periods of time, or events follow one after the other without any interruptions: *It had rained for four consecutive days.* | *The Sharks have lost 10 consecutive games.* —**consecutively** *adv.*: *Number the pages consecutively.*

con·sen·su·al /kən'sɛnʃuəl/ *adj.* giving your permission for something or agreeing to do something: *The jury must decide whether it was consensual sex or rape.*

con·sen·sus /kən'sɛnsəs/ *n.* [singular,U] an opinion that everyone in a group will agree with or accept: *The group's task is to reach a consensus on the following questions.* | *We decided by consensus to head for shore on Shell Island to wait out the storm.*

consensus build·er /.'.. ,../ *n.* someone, especially a politician, who is good at helping people or groups reach agreements —**consensus building** *n.* [U]

s w **con·sent**¹ /kən'sɛnt/ *n.* [U] **1** permission to do something, especially from someone in authority or from someone who is responsible for something: *I want to read the form before I give my consent.* | *Schools cannot distribute condoms to students without parental consent.* | **written/verbal consent** *We have to get written consent from each participant.* —see also AGE OF CONSENT **2** agreement about something: *One woman left the training program early by mutual consent* (=by agreement between both people or groups involved). | *We have social rights and duties that are defined by common consent* (=by agreement from everyone involved). —see also ASSENT¹, DISSENT¹

consent² *v.* [I] to give your permission for something or agree to do something: [+ to] *Wendy's father reluctantly consented to the marriage.* | *Lee believes that sexual relations between consenting adults should not be the subject of laws.*

s w **con·se·quence** /'kɑnsə,kwɛns, -kwəns/ *n.* **1** [C usually plural] something that happens as a result of a particular action or situation: *We are very much aware of the consequences our actions will have.* | *Ignoring safety procedures can have potentially tragic consequences.* | [+ of] *The economic consequences of graffiti vandalism are enormous.* | **suffer/face the consequences** (=to accept and deal with bad results of something you did) **2 as a consequence (of sth)** as a result of something: *Tyler rarely paid for anything and, as a consequence, had no idea what things*

cost. **3 of little/no/any consequence** without much importance or value: *Your opinion is of little consequence to me.*

con·se·quent /'kɑnsəkwənt/ *adj.* [only before noun] FORMAL happening as a result of a particular event or situation: *The drought and consequent famine struck most of the country.* —compare SUBSEQUENT

con·se·quen·tial /,kɑnsə'kwɛnʃəl/ *adj.* FORMAL **1** important; SIGNIFICANT: *The NSC has taken an active and consequential role in providing guidance.* **2** happening as a direct result of a particular event or situation: *consequential effects of the policies* —**consequentially** *adv.* —opposite INCONSEQUENTIAL

con·se·quent·ly /'kɑnsə,kwɛntli, -kwənt-/ *adv.* [sentence adverb] as a result: *The book has no narrator or main character. Consequently, it lacks a traditional plot.* | *There was no fighting and consequently no casualties.* —see Usage Note at THUS

con·ser·van·cy /kən'sɜvənsi/ *n.* [C] a group of people who work to protect an area of land, a river etc.: *the Santa Monica Mountains Conservancy*

con·ser·va·tion /,kɑnsɚ'veɪʃən/ *n.* [U] **1** the protection of natural things such as animals, plants, forests etc., to prevent them being spoiled or destroyed: *wildlife conservation* **2** the act of preventing something from being lost or wasted: [+ of] *The organization promotes conservation of forest resources.*

conservation ar·e·a /..'.. ,../ *n.* [C] an area where animals and plants are protected from being destroyed

con·ser·va·tion·ist /,kɑnsɚ'veɪʃənɪst/ *n.* [C] someone who works to protect animals, plants etc. —**conservationism** *n.* [U]

con·serv·a·tism /kən'sɜvə,tɪzəm/ *n.* [U] **1** an attitude of not trusting change and new ideas: *They like the Pope's policy of conservatism on religious doctrine.* **2** conservative opinions and principles, especially on social and political subjects —compare LIBERALISM

s **con·serv·a·tive**¹ /kən'sɜvətɪv/ *adj.* **1** preferring to continue doing things the way they are being done or have been proven to work, rather than risking changes: *a conservative rural community* —compare LIBERAL¹ (1) **2** supporting political ideas that include less involvement by the government in business and people's lives, for example by encouraging everyone to work and earn their own money, and having strong ideas about moral behavior: *a conservative newspaper columnist* —compare LIBERAL¹ (2) **3** not very modern or fashionable in style, taste etc.: *Even conservative dressers should update their wardrobes from time to time.* | *Despite Dave's quiet, conservative appearance, he has a wicked sense of humor.* **4 a conservative estimate/guess** a guess which is deliberately lower than the real amount: *Conservative estimates indicate at least 150 people were killed in the military coup.* —**conservatively** *adv.*

s **conservative**² *n.* [C] someone with conservative opinions or principles: *According to a recent poll, the governor has lost support among conservatives.* —compare LIBERAL²

con·serv·a·tor /kən'sɜvətɚ/ *n.* [C] **1** LAW someone who is legally responsible for another person and their property because that person is not able to do it on their own **2** someone whose job is to preserve valuable things at a MUSEUM, library etc.

con·serv·a·to·ry /kən'sɜvə,tɔri/ *n. plural* **conservatories** [C] **1** a college where people are trained in music or acting: *the National Conservatory of Music* **2** a building made mostly of glass, where plants are kept for people to come and look at them

con·serve¹ /kən'sɜv/ *v.* [T] to prevent something from being wasted, damaged, or destroyed: *Try and rest frequently to conserve your energy.* | *Everyone needs to make efforts to conserve water.*

con·serve² /'kɑnsɜv/ *n.* [C,U] a sweet food made of pieces of fruit that are preserved by being cooked with sugar, usually eaten on bread —compare JAM¹ (1), PRESERVE² (3)

C

con·sid·er /kənˈsɪdəʳ/ v. [T]

1 **think about** to think about something, especially about whether to accept something or do something: *Bill paused to consider his options.* | *The boss says she's still considering my request for a raise.* | [**consider doing sth**] *Have you considered getting a new car?*

2 **have an opinion** to think of someone or something in a particular way: [**consider sb/sth (to be) sth**] *I consider New Mexico to be my home.* | *What do you consider your greatest achievement?* | *Okay, so what is considered a large dose of vitamin A?*

3 **remember to think about** to remember to think carefully about something before making a judgment or a decision: *Before you resign, you should consider the effect it will have on your family.* | [**consider that**] *Berenyi's victory is even more impressive when you consider that she's only sixteen years old.* | [+ **what/how/who etc.**] *We have to consider what's best for the students.*

4 **discuss formally** to discuss something such as a report or problem, so that you can make a decision about it: *Meanwhile, the Legislature is considering the committee's recommendations.*

5 **all things considered** SPOKEN used when giving your opinion or judgment after thinking about all the facts: *It wasn't the best game I've ever seen. But, all things considered, it wasn't too bad either.*

6 **people's feelings** to think about someone or their feelings etc. and try to avoid upsetting or hurting them: *The mayor needs to consider local residents when she decides where to put the new stadium.*

7 **consider yourself lucky** SPOKEN used to tell someone they should be glad that something is true or happened as it did: *Consider yourself lucky you weren't in the car at the time.*

8 **look at** FORMAL to look at someone or something carefully: *Henry considered the sculpture with an expert eye.*

con·sid·er·a·ble /kənˈsɪdərəbəl/ adj. large enough to be noticeable or to have noticeable effects: *A considerable amount of research was done here by our science department.* | *Attracting tourists to the area is going to take considerable effort* | *The difference between the two descriptions is considerable.* —compare INCONSIDERABLE

con·sid·er·a·bly /kənˈsɪdərəbli/ adv. in a noticeable or important way: *The sea turtle's natural habitat has been considerably reduced.* | **considerably more/larger/faster etc.** *A few of the paintings sold for considerably more than we had predicted.*

con·sid·er·ate /kənˈsɪdərɪt/ adj. always thinking of what other people need or want, and being careful not to upset them: *Natalie is considerate and responsible – a perfect daughter.* | [+ **of**] *It was very considerate of you to let us know you were going to be late.* —**considerately** adv. —**considerateness** n. [U] —opposite INCONSIDERATE

con·sid·er·a·tion /kənˌsɪdəˈreɪʃən/ n.

1 **thought** [U] FORMAL careful thought and attention: *Jackson is giving serious consideration to running for President again.* | *Several television movies about her life are currently under consideration* (=being thought about). | **full/due consideration** *The company promises to give due consideration to the results of the vote.*

2 **take sth into consideration** to remember to think about something important when you are making a decision or judgment: *Even when other factors were taken into consideration, shorter men had a higher risk of heart attacks.*

3 **sth that affects a decision** [C] something that you must think about when you are planning to do something, which affects what you decide to do: *Political rather than economic considerations influenced the location of the new factory.* | *Cost should not be your main consideration.*

4 **kindness** [U] the quality of thinking about other people's feelings or situation and taking care not to upset them: *The number of outdoor concerts has been reduced, out of consideration for the neighbors.* | *Jeff never shows any consideration for his mother's feelings.*

5 **discussion** [U] the act of thinking about or discussing something, especially in order to make a decision about it: *The Senate will return to its consideration of illegal immigration Monday.*

6 **in consideration of/for sth** FORMAL as a reward for something: *The payment was in consideration of Spira's help.*

7 **money** [singular] FORMAL a payment for a service: *I might be able to help you, **for a small consideration**.*

con·sid·ered /kənˈsɪdəʳd/ adj. **your considered opinion/judgment** FORMAL an opinion, decision etc. based on careful thought: *It is my considered opinion that you should now resign.*

con·sid·er·ing[1] /kənˈsɪdərɪŋ/ prep., conjunction used when describing a situation, before stating a fact that you know has had an effect on that situation: *Considering the weather and everything, the game wasn't that bad.* | [**considering (that)**] *Donald thinks he paid too much for the property, considering that the roof needed repair.* | [**considering who/how etc.**] *The service was pretty bad, considering how much we paid.*

considering[2] adv. SPOKEN used after you make a statement or give an opinion, to say that something is true in spite of another fact: *The office was busy, but it wasn't too bad, considering.*

con·sign /kənˈsaɪn/ v. [T] FORMAL **1** to make someone or something be in a particular situation, especially a bad one: [**consign sb/sth to sth**] *After being voted out of office, Rios Montt seemed consigned to political obscurity.* **2** to put someone or something somewhere, especially in order to get rid of them: [**consign sb/sth to sth**] *I've consigned all your oat bran and vitamins to the back of the pantry.* **3** to send or deliver something to someone who has bought it

con·sign·ee /ˌkɑːnsaɪˈniː, -sə-, kənˌsaɪˈniː/ n. [C] TECHNICAL the person that something is delivered to

con·sign·ment /kənˈsaɪnmənt/ n. **1** [C] a quantity of goods that is sent to someone at the same time, especially in order to be sold: [+ **of**] *a consignment of 5000 tons of rice* **2** **on consignment** goods that are on consignment are being sold by a store for someone else, for a share of the profit **3** [U] the act of delivering things

consignment shop /.ˈ.. ./ n. [C] a store where goods, especially used clothes and furniture, are sold by the store for someone else, for a share of the profit: *Consignment shops are a good place to look for cheap but good quality baby equipment.*

con·sig·nor /kənˌsaɪˈnɔːr, kənˈsaɪnəʳ/ n. [C] TECHNICAL the person who sends goods to someone else

con·sist /kənˈsɪst/ v.

consist in sth phr. v. [T not in progressive] FORMAL to be based on or depend UPON something: *The key element of the plan consists in sending in enough troops to completely surround the city.*

consist of sth phr. v. [T not in progressive] to be made of or contain a number of different parts or things: *Our condominium complex consists of 24 buildings.* | *The buffet consisted of several different Indian dishes.* —see Usage Note at COMPRISE

con·sist·en·cy /kənˈsɪstənsi/ n. plural **consistencies 1** [U] the quality of always being the same, always being good, or always behaving in an expected way: *Vardell's consistency helps the whole team.* | [+ **in**] *There has been a lack of consistency in carrying out democratic reforms.* —opposite INCONSISTENCY **2** [C,U] how firm or thick a substance is: [+ **of**] *Stir until the mixture thickens to the consistency of whipping cream.*

con·sist·ent /kənˈsɪstənt/ adj. **1** always having the same beliefs, behavior, attitudes etc.: *We need a quarterback who is consistent game after game.* | *Teaching by example has been a consistent theme in his work.* | [+ **in**] *When training animals, you must be consistent in commands and expectations.* **2** continuing to develop in the same way: *Until the second quarter of this year, the company had* been showing consistent growth. | We've seen a consistent improvement in the team's performance. **3 be consistent with sth** to say the same thing or follow the same principles as something else: *Her behavior was consistent with that of other rape victims.* **4** a consistent argument or idea is organized so that each part agrees with the others —**consistently** *adv.* —opposite INCONSISTENT

con·so·la·tion /ˌkɑnsəˈleɪʃən/ *n.* [C,U] **1** someone or something that makes you feel better when you are sad or disappointed: *Students sought consolation from school counselors.* | *You played better than you did last time, if that's any consolation.* | *Ryan White's family took consolation in the fact his short life made a difference for other AIDS sufferers.* **2** a **consolation game/semifinal etc.** a sports game played by two teams or players who lost a competition

consolation prize /...ˈ.. ˌ./ *n.* [C] a prize that is given to someone who has not won a competition, to make them feel better

con·so·la·to·ry /kənˈsoʊləˌtɔri, -ˈsɑ-/ *adj.* FORMAL intended to make someone feel better

con·sole¹ /kənˈsoʊl/ *v.* [T] to make someone feel better when they are feeling sad or disappointed: *I wanted to console my mother, but I did not know how.* | [**console sb with sth**] *Archer consoles himself with the thought that at least he tried hard.*

con·sole² /ˈkɑnsoʊl/ *n.* [C] **1** a flat board that contains the controls for a machine, piece of electrical equipment, computer etc.: *a Nintendo console* **2** a special cupboard in which a television, computer etc. is fitted

con·sol·i·date /kənˈsɑləˌdeɪt/ *v.* [I,T] **1** to join together a group of companies, organizations etc., or to become joined together: *We'll be consolidating departments and cutting the mayor's staff by 61%.* **2** to combine two or more things such as jobs, duties, or large amounts of money, especially to form a single thing that is more effective or easier to deal with: *They took out a loan to consolidate their credit card bills.* **3** to make your position of power stronger and more likely to continue: *Successful advertising helped them to consolidate their position as the largest computer company in Europe.* —**consolidated** *adj.* —**consolidation** /kənˌsɑləˈdeɪʃən/ *n.* [C,U]

con·som·mé /ˌkɑnsəˈmeɪ/ *n.* [U] a thin clear soup made from meat or vegetables

con·so·nance /ˈkɑnsənəns/ *n.* **1 in consonance with sth** FORMAL agreeing with something or existing together without any problems **2** [C,U] TECHNICAL a combination of musical notes that sounds pleasant; HARMONY (1) —compare DISSONANCE (2)

con·so·nant¹ /ˈkɑnsənənt/ *n.* [C] TECHNICAL **1** a speech sound made by partly or completely stopping the flow of air through the mouth **2** a letter of the English alphabet that represents one of these sounds. The letters "a," "e," "i," "o," and "u" represent vowels, and all the other letters are consonants.

consonant² *adj.* **1 be consonant with sth** FORMAL not seeming to show that a statement or belief is wrong: *The views of the black leadership are consonant with those of black Americans.* **2** TECHNICAL relating to a combination of musical notes that sounds pleasant

con·sort¹ /kənˈsɔrt/ *v.*
consort with sb *phr. v.* [T] FORMAL to spend time with someone, especially someone that other people do not approve of: *Williams was accused of consorting with drug dealers.*

con·sort² /ˈkɑnsɔrt/ *n.* [C] FORMAL **1 do sth in consort with sb** to do something together with someone else: *Our lawyers are acting in consort with the management of Central Hospital.* **2** the wife or husband of a ruler **3** a group of people who play music from past times or the group of old-fashioned instruments they use

con·sor·ti·um /kənˈsɔrʃiəm, -tiəm/ *n. plural* **consortiums** or **consortia** /-ʃiə, -tiə/ [C] a combination of several companies, organizations etc. working together to buy something, build something etc.: *The cost of making the programs was shared by a consortium of six public television stations.*

con·spic·u·ous /kənˈspɪkyuəs/ *adj.* **1** very easy to notice, especially because of being different from everything or everyone else: *Cuzco's few tourists are conspicuous as they explore the old cobbled streets.* **2 conspicuous consumption** the act of buying a lot of things, especially expensive things that are not necessary, in a way that people notice **3 conspicuous by sb/sth's absence** used to say that people noticed that someone or something was not in the place they expected them to be in **4** unusually good, bad, skillful etc.: *Johnson received a medal for conspicuous gallantry.* —**conspicuously** *adv.* —**conspicuousness** *n.* [U] —opposite INCONSPICUOUS

con·spir·a·cy /kənˈspɪrəsi/ *n. plural* **conspiracies** [C,U] a secret plan made by two or more people to do something that is harmful or illegal: [**conspiracy to do sth**] *Police have arrested six people for their involvement in a conspiracy to distribute heroin and cocaine.* | [**+ against**] *The conspiracy against Castro was led by several top military men.* | *There was then a conspiracy of silence* (=an agreement to keep quiet about something that should not be a secret) *about violations of regulations.* | *The book explores a new conspiracy theory* (=the idea that an event was caused by a conspiracy) *about President Kennedy's assassination.*

con·spir·a·tor /kənˈspɪrətər/ *n.* [C] someone who is involved in a secret plan to do something harmful or illegal

con·spir·a·to·ri·al /kənˌspɪrəˈtɔriəl/ *adj.* **1** relating to a secret plan to do something harmful or illegal **2** a **conspiratorial smile/giggle/wink etc.** a smile, giggle, wink etc. shared by two people who know a secret —**conspiratorially** *adv.*

con·spire /kənˈspaɪr/ *v.* [I] **1** to secretly plan with other people to do something harmful or illegal: [**conspire (with sb) to do sth**] *The company was accused of conspiring with local stores to fix prices.* | [**conspire against sb**] *He may have been connected to a group conspiring against the government.* **2** FORMAL if events conspire to make something happen, they happen at the same time and make something bad happen: [**conspire to do sth**] *Events conspired to ensure his defeat in the election.*

con·sta·ble /ˈkɑnstəbəl/ *n.* [C] **1** another name for a POLICE OFFICER, especially in Canada, the U.K., and Australia **2** a person who has some, but not all, of the powers of a police officer and who can officially give or send legal documents that order people to do something or not do something

Con·sta·ble /ˈkɑnstəbəl/**, John** (1776–1837) a British painter known for his paintings and drawings of the English countryside

con·stab·u·lar·y /kənˈstæbyəˌlɛri/ *n.* [C] the POLICE FORCE of a particular area or country, especially in Canada, Britain, and Australia

con·stan·cy /ˈkɑnstənsi/ *n.* [U] FORMAL **1** the quality of staying the same even though other things change: *It will be a long, slow and tedious process requiring patience and constancy of purpose.* **2** loyalty and faithfulness to a particular person

con·stant¹ /ˈkɑnstənt/ *adj.* **1** happening regularly or all the time: *The patient must be kept under constant supervision.* | *The winds are constant in winter.* **2** staying the same for a period of time: *You save more gas if you drive at a constant speed.* **3** LITERARY loyal and faithful: *a constant friend*

constant² *n.* [C] TECHNICAL **1** a number or quantity that never changes **2** FORMAL something that stays the same even though other things change —compare VARIABLE²

con·stant·ly /ˈkɑnstəntli/ *adv.* always, or very often: *That girl is on the phone constantly.* | *The English language is constantly changing.*

con·stel·la·tion /ˌkɑnstəˈleɪʃən/ *n.* [C] **1** a group of stars that forms a particular pattern and has a name **2** a **constellation of sth** LITERARY a group of people or things that are similar: *The term "sibling rivalry" refers to a constellation of feelings.*

con·ster·na·tion /ˌkɑnstəˈneɪʃən/ *n.* [U] a feeling of shock or worry that makes it difficult to decide what to do; DISMAY[1]: *President Cristiani expressed profound consternation at the deaths of the two journalists.*

con·sti·pa·tion /ˌkɑnstəˈpeɪʃən/ *n.* [U] the condition of having difficulty emptying your BOWELS —**constipated** /ˈkɑnstəˌpeɪtɪd/ *adj.* —**constipate** *v.* [T]

con·stit·u·en·cy /kənˈstɪtʃuənsi/ *n. plural* **constituencies** [C] **1** the people who live and vote in a constituency: *I'm voting the way my constituency wants me to, not the way the President wants me to.* **2** an area of a country that has one or more elected officials or representatives: *The governor will be visiting a rural constituency north of Charlotte.* **3** any group that supports or is likely to support a politician or a political party: *Students have never been the constituency of any single party.*

con·stit·u·ent[1] /kənˈstɪtʃuənt/ *n.* [C] **1** someone who votes and lives in a particular area represented by one or more elected official **2** FORMAL one of the parts that combine to form something: *Police found the constituents of a bomb inside an abandoned car.* —compare COMPONENT

constituent[2] *adj.* [only before noun] being one of the parts that makes a whole: *The treaty will give even greater powers to the country's 15 constituent republics.*

con·sti·tute /ˈkɑnstəˌtut/ *v.* FORMAL **1** [linking verb, not in progressive] to be considered to be something: *According to Marx, "money constitutes true power."* | *The company's action constituted fraud.* **2** [linking verb, not in progressive] if several parts constitute something, they form it together: *We may need to redefine what constitutes a family.* **3** [T] to make something from a number of different parts: *The thin layers that constitute the laser head are only 400 atoms thick.* —see also COMPRISE

con·sti·tu·tion /ˌkɑnstəˈtuʃən/ *n.* [C] **1** also **Constitution** a set of basic laws and principles that a DEMOCRATIC country is governed by, which cannot easily be changed by the political party in power: *The right to speak freely is written into the Constitution of the United States.* **2** [usually singular] the ability of your body to fight disease and illness: **a strong/ weak constitution** *She attributes her good health to a strong constitution, inherited from her mother.* **3** a set of rules and principles that an organization is governed by **4** FORMAL the way something is formed and how it is organized: [+ of] *the constitution of the committee*

con·sti·tu·tion·al[1] /ˌkɑnstəˈtuʃənəl/ *adj.* **1** officially allowed or restricted by the set of rules a government or organization has in a constitution: *We have a **constitutional right** to keep weapons for self-defense.* | *Great Britain is a **constitutional monarchy** (=a country ruled by a king or queen whose power is restricted by a constitution).* —opposite UNCONSTITUTIONAL **2** relating to the constitution of a country or organization: *The senate is voting on a proposed **constitutional amendment** (=change to the original set of laws in a constitution).* **3** relating to someone's health and their ability to fight illness —see also CONSTITUTIONALLY

constitutional[2] *n.* [C] OLD-FASHIONED a walk you take or physical activity you do because it is good for your health

con·sti·tu·tion·al·ism /ˌkɑnstəˈtuʃənəˌlɪzəm/ *n.* [U] the belief that a government should be based on a constitution —**constitutionalist** *n.* [C]

con·sti·tu·tion·al·i·ty /ˌkɑnstəˌtuʃəˈnæləti/ *n.* [U] the quality of being acceptable according to the constitution: *The Supreme Court agreed to review the constitutionality of the 1989 law.*

con·sti·tu·tion·al·ly /ˌkɑnstəˈtuʃənəli/ *adv.* **1** in a way that obeys the rules of a country that has a constitution: *Critics say the bill would interfere with constitutionally protected forms of protest.* **2** in a way that is related to someone's character or health and physical ability

con·strain /kənˈstreɪn/ *v.* [T] **1** to stop someone from doing what they want to do: *The bill actually*

constrains the legislature from doing what they are elected to do. **2** to prevent something from developing and improving: *Poor economies abroad may constrain demand for U.S. exports.*

con·strained /kənˈstreɪnd/ *adj.* **1** prevented from developing, improving, or doing what you really want: *Judge Leval was constrained by an earlier decision of the court.* **2** **be/feel constrained to do sth** to feel very strongly that you must do something: *I feel constrained to tell the truth.* **3** a constrained smile, manner etc. seems too controlled and is not natural —**constrainedly** /kənˈstreɪnɪdli/ *adv.*

con·straint /kənˈstreɪnt/ *n.* **1** [C] something that limits your freedom to do what you want; RESTRICTION: [+ on] *The bill could ease environmental constraints on the construction of a waterfront theme park.* | **financial/legal/cultural** etc. **constraints** *The program had to be postponed because of budget constraints.* **2** [U] control over the way people are allowed to behave, so that they cannot do what they want: *They have called on the military to show constraint.* **3** **under constraint** being controlled or being forced to do something

con·strict /kənˈstrɪkt/ *v.* [T] **1** to make something smaller, narrower, or tighter: *Avoid clothing that constricts the blood circulation in your legs.* **2** to limit someone's freedom to do what they want: *The law constricts people's choices about how to educate their children.* —**constricted** *adj.* —**constriction** /kənˈstrɪkʃən/ *n.* [C,U] —**constrictive** /-tɪv/ *adj.*

con·struct[1] /kənˈstrʌkt/ *v.* [T] **1** to build something large such as a building, bridge, or road: *The city has announced a plan to construct another runway at LaGuardia Airport.* | [construct sth of/from/in sth] *The mansion was constructed of wood with a brick facade.* **2** to form something such as a sentence, argument, or system by joining words, ideas etc. together: *Boyce has constructed a new theory of management.* **3** TECHNICAL to draw a mathematical shape: *Construct a square with 2-inch-long sides.* **s w** **3**

con·struct[2] /ˈkɑnstrʌkt/ *n.* [C] **1** an idea formed by combining pieces of knowledge: *It is these social constructs that determine our relations to each other.* **2** FORMAL something that is built or made

con·struc·tion /kənˈstrʌkʃən/ *n.* **s w** **2** **3**
1 buildings/roads etc. [U] the process or method of building something large such as a building, bridge, or road: *Construction of Highway 85 will begin soon.* | *The company is developing several new construction techniques.* | *Protective clothing must be worn by everyone visiting the **construction site** (=the place where something is being built).* | *A new water treatment plant is now **under construction** (=being built).*
2 making sth using many parts [U] the process or method of building or making something using many parts: *Most major toy companies have phone lines to help parents with the construction of toys.*
3 phrase [C] the order in which certain words are put together in a sentence, phrase etc.: *It's sometimes hard for students to understand complex grammatical constructions.*
4 ideas/knowledge [U] the method or process of forming something from knowledge or ideas: *the construction of sociological theory*
5 **of simple/strong** etc. **construction** FORMAL built in a simple way, built to be strong etc.: *The natives live in wooden huts of simple construction.*
6 sth built [C] FORMAL something that has been built: *"Time Passage" – a construction by Katherine Stutz-Taylor*
7 **put a construction on sth** FORMAL to think that a statement has a particular meaning or that something was done for a particular reason: *The law does not say that specifically, but people have chosen to put that construction on it.* —**constructional** *adj.*

construction pa·per /.ˈ.. ˌ../ *n.* [U] a thick colored paper that is used especially by children at school

con·struc·tive /kənˈstrʌktɪv/ *adj.* intended to be

helpful, or likely to produce good results: *Tribal leaders said they had "a very constructive conversation with the president" about the political situation in Rwanda.* | *Mrs. King says she welcomes* **constructive criticism** (=criticism that is intended to help her improve). —**constructively** *adv.* —**constructiveness** *n.* [U]

con·struc·tor /kən'strʌktɚ/ *n.* [C] a company or person that builds things

con·strue /kən'stru/ *v.* **1 construe sth as sth** to understand a remark or action in a particular way *Winston acknowledged that his comments could be construed as racist.* —opposite MISCONSTRUE **2** [I,T] FORMAL to translate each word in a piece of writing, especially one in Greek or Latin

con·sub·stan·ti·a·tion /ˌkɑnsəb,stænʃi'eɪʃən/ *n.* [U] TECHNICAL the belief that the real body and blood of Jesus Christ are present in the bread and wine offered by the priest at a Christian religious service —compare TRANSUBSTANTIATION

con·sul, Consul /'kɑnsəl/ *n.* [C] **1** a government official who lives in a foreign country and whose job is to help and protect citizens of their own country who also live or work there: *Molly Williamson, the U.S. Consul in East Jerusalem* **2** one of the two chief public officials of the ancient Roman REPUBLIC, each elected for one year —**consular** *adj.*: *consular services* —**consulship** *n.* [C,U]

con·sul·ate, Consulate /'kɑnsəlɪt/ *n.* [C] the official building where a consul lives and works

s w con·sult /kən'sʌlt/ *v.* [I,T] **1** to ask for information or advice from someone because it is their job to have the answers: *If your memory problems do not improve, consult your physician.* | [consult sb about sth] *An increasing number of people are consulting their accountants about the new tax laws.* | [+ with] *You should consider consulting with a lawyer.* **2** to ask for someone's permission or to discuss something with someone so that you can make a decision together: *Before making any changes, consult your family to find out which activities are most important to them.* | [+ with] *The administration is consulting with allies on the treatment of Libya.* **3** to look for information in a book, map, list etc.: *Consult the classified pages of any newspaper to find job offers.*

con·sul·tan·cy /kən'sʌltənsi/ *n.* [C] a company that gives advice and training in a particular area to people in other companies

s w con·sult·ant /kən'sʌltənt/ *n.* [C] someone with a lot of experience in a particular area whose job is to give advice about it: *Morris is a Democratic media consultant.*

con·sul·ta·tion /ˌkɑnsəl'teɪʃən/ *n.* **1** [C,U] a discussion in which people who are affected by a decision can say what they think should be done: *He urged "dialogue and consultation" to end the crisis.* | *The plan was worked out in consultation with* (=with the agreement and help of) *the World Bank.* **2** [C] a meeting with a professional person, especially a doctor, for advice or treatment: *Schweitzer took her daughter to the Mayo Clinic for a consultation.* **3** [U] advice given by a professional person: *Trained parenting experts are available for consultation by phone.* **4** [U] the act of looking for information or help in a book

con·sul·ta·tive /kən'sʌltətɪv, 'kɑnsəl,teɪtɪv/ *adj.* providing advice and suggesting solutions to problems: *The consultative committee will include representatives from all areas of the company.*

con·sult·ing[1] /kən'sʌltɪŋ/ *n.* [U] the service of providing financial advice to companies

consulting[2] *adj.* providing financial or other types of advice to companies: *Beth works at a consulting firm in Stamford, Connecticut.*

con·sume /kən'sum/ *v.* [T] **1** to completely use time, energy, goods etc.: *This year, health care costs will consume one-eighth of the average family's income.*

2 FORMAL to eat or drink something: *The college permits students who are 21 or older to consume alcoholic beverages in their dorm rooms.* **3 be consumed with guilt/passion/rage etc.** to have a very strong feeling that changes the way you behave and what you think about —see also CONSUMING **4** FORMAL if fire consumes something, it destroys it completely —see also TIME-CONSUMING

con·sum·er /kən'sumɚ/ *n.* **1** [C] someone who buys and uses products and services: *Consumers will soon be paying higher air fares.* **2** [singular] all the people who buy goods and services, considered as a group: *The travel agents' group want more protection for the consumer.* | *Consumer spending rose 0.7 percent in November.* —compare CUSTOMER (1), PRODUCER (1) —see Usage Note at CUSTOMER

consumer con·fi·dence /.,.. '.../ *n.* [U] a measure of how satisfied people are with the present economic situation, as shown by how much money they spend: *The report shows consumer confidence dipping to levels not seen since the severe 1981–82 recession.*

consumer goods /.'.. ,./ *n.* [plural] goods such as food, clothes, and equipment that people buy, especially to use in the home —compare CAPITAL GOODS

consumer group /.'.. ,./ *n.* [C] an organization that makes sure that consumers are treated fairly and that products are safe

con·sum·er·is·m /kən'sumə,rɪzəm/ *n.* [U] **1** the idea or belief that buying and selling products and services is the most important or useful activity a person or society can do **2** actions to protect people from unfair prices, advertising that is not true etc.

consumer price in·dex /.,.. '. ,../ *n.* [C] a list of the prices of certain products that is done to show how much prices have increased during a particular period of time

consumer so·ci·ety /.,.. '.../ *n.* [C] a society in which the buying of products and services is considered extremely important

con·sum·ing /kən'sumɪŋ/ *adj.* [only before noun] a consuming feeling is so strong that it controls you and often has a bad effect on your life: *She was possessed by a consuming rage.* | *Henry's consuming passion* (=something you are extremely interested in) *is birdwatching.*

con·sum·mate[1] /'kɑnsəmɪt/ *adj.* FORMAL **1** very skillful: *Johnson was a consummate team player.* **2** complete and perfect in every way: *Wagner's "Tristan und Isolde" is one of the consummate masterpieces of German opera.* **3** used to emphasize how bad someone or something is: *The newspaper accused Quigley of "consummate foolishness."* —**consummately** *adv.*

con·sum·mate[2] /'kɑnsə,meɪt/ *v.* [T] FORMAL **1** to make a marriage or a relationship complete by having sex **2** to make something such as an agreement complete: *A trustee was appointed to consummate the sale.*

con·sum·ma·tion /ˌkɑnsə'meɪʃən/ *n.* [U] FORMAL **1** the point at which something is complete or perfect: *They filed suit to prevent the deal's consummation.* **2** the act of making a marriage or relationship complete by having sex

con·sump·tion /kən'sʌmpʃən/ *n.* [U] **1** the amount of oil, electricity, gas etc. that is used: *Fuel consumption is predicted to rise.* **2** FORMAL the act of eating or drinking, or the amount of food or drink that is eaten or drunk: *The "Five-a-Day" promotion is meant to increase the consumption of fresh produce.* | *Dr. Boxhall said I should cut down on my alcohol consumption.* | **fit/unfit for human consumption** (=safe or not safe for people to eat) **3** the act of buying and using products: *an increase in the consumption of electrical products* | *Hong Kong was regarded as the world's capital of conspicuous consumption* (=buying expensive goods in order to show other people how rich you are). **4 for sb's consumption** if a piece of information or a remark is for a particular person or group's consumption, it is intended to be heard or read by them: *Senator McDonald's comments were not meant for public consumption.* **5** OLD-FASHIONED: see TUBERCULOSIS

con·sump·tive /kən'sʌmptɪv/ *adj.* a word used in the past to describe someone who had the lung disease TUBERCULOSIS —**consumptive** *n.* [C]

cont. the written abbreviation of CONTAINING, CONTENTS, CONTINUED, and CONTINENT

con·tact¹ /'kɑntækt/ *n.*

1 communication [C,U] communication or meetings with a person, organization, country etc., or the occasion on which the communication takes place: [+ with] *The Omaha tribe had more contacts with whites than most other tribes.* | *We don't have much contact with the Australian division of the company.* | [+ between] *The meeting was the highest level contact between the two countries since the 1979 war.* | **get/keep/stay in contact with sb** *Have you managed to stay in contact with any of the kids from the old neighborhood?* | *I've made contact with (=communicated with) most of the people on the list* | *We're afraid we'll lose contact with our granddaughters after our son's divorce.* | *Kathy's teacher should've put her in contact with (=given her the name or telephone number of someone) someone who could've helped.*

2 touch [U] the state of touching or being close to someone or something: *The disease cannot be spread through casual contact.* | [+ with] *Children need close physical contact and interaction with a caring adult.* | [+ between] *Termite problems are caused by contact between wood and the moist soil where termites nest.* | *Surgeons' gloves have to be strong because they are in contact with blood and other bodily fluids for long periods of time.* | *Health care workers who come in contact with flu victims should wash their hands frequently.* | *The weapon delivers an immobilizing electric shock on contact (=at the moment of touching something).* | **contact points/ areas/surfaces etc.** *Scrape the contact surfaces with a knife, then reattach the cables.*

3 come into contact with sb to meet someone: *Kevin annoys everyone he comes into contact with.*

4 person who can help [C] a person you know who may be able to help you or give you advice about something: *business contacts* | *I've made a few contacts in the industry.*

5 situation/problem [U] experience of dealing with a particular kind of situation or problem: *Dickens* worked in a factory, which **brought** him **into contact with** the poor conditions of the working classes.

6 eyes [C] a contact lens

7 electrical part [C] an electrical part that completes a CIRCUIT when it touches another part

8 point of contact a) a place that you go to or a person that you meet when dealing with an organization or trying to get something: *The new service center will serve as the single point of contact for general customer inquiries.* **b)** a way in which two very different things are related or connected: *It's difficult to find a point of contact between theory and practice.* —see also **eye contact** (EYE¹ (5))

contact² *v.* [T] to telephone or write to someone: *School officials immediately contacted the police.*

contact³ *adj.* [only before noun] **1** a contact number or address is a telephone number or address where someone can be found if necessary: *Did Mr. Warren leave a contact number?* **2** contact explosives or chemicals become active when they touch something: *Glue the tiles to the floor with contact cement.*

contact lens /'.. ,., ,.. './ *n.* [C] a small round piece of plastic you put on your eye to help you see clearly

con·ta·gion /kən'teɪdʒən/ *n.* **1** [U] TECHNICAL a situation in which a disease is spread by people touching each other or touching something that can infect them: *a serious risk of contagion* **2** [C] TECHNICAL a disease that can be passed from person to person by touch **3** [U] FORMAL a feeling or attitude that spreads quickly from person to person

con·ta·gious /kən'teɪdʒəs/ *adj.* **1** a disease that is contagious can be passed from person to person by touch: *Chicken pox is a highly contagious disease.* **2** a person who is contagious has a disease that can be passed to another person by touch: *People with measles are highly contagious.* **3** a feeling, attitude, or action that is contagious is quickly felt or done by other people: *Hardy has a booming voice and a contagious enthusiasm.* —**contagiousness** *n.* [U] —**contagiously** *adv.*

con·tain /kən'teɪn/ *v.* [T] **1** to have something inside, or have something as a part: *These alkaline batteries*

containers

a bag of potato chips

a tube of toothpaste

a pack of cigarettes

a packet of ketchup

a carton of milk

a box of matches

a package of cookies

a jar of pickles

a drum

a can of cola

a barrel

do not contain mercury. | *Buchanan's writing contains some of the same elements as Duke's.* **2** to keep a strong feeling or emotion under control: *I found it more and more difficult to contain my anger.* | *Shaw could hardly contain himself* (=control his emotions) *as the choirs sang "The Hallelujah Chorus" in his honor.* **3** to stop something from spreading or escaping: *Crews used booms to contain a large oil spill on the river.* —see also SELF-CONTAINED **4** FORMAL to surround an area or an angle: *How big is the angle contained by these two sides?*

con·tain·er /kənˈteɪnɚ/ n. [C] **1** something such as a box, bowl, or bottle that can be filled with something: *You'll need one small container of cottage cheese.* | *a container with a tight lid* **2** a very large metal box in which goods are packed to make it easy to lift or move them onto a ship or vehicle: *cargo containers*

con·tain·ment /kənˈteɪnmənt/ n. [U] **1** the act of keeping something under control: *cost containment* **2** the use of political actions to prevent an unfriendly country from becoming more powerful: *the Cold War policy of containment*

con·tam·i·nant /kənˈtæmənənt/ n. [C] TECHNICAL a dangerous or poisonous substance that makes something impure

con·tam·i·nate /kənˈtæməˌneɪt/ v. [T] **1** to spoil a place or substance by adding a dangerous or poisonous substance to it: *Lead in plumbing can contaminate drinking water.* **2** to influence someone or something in a way that has a bad effect: *Publicity before the trial can contaminate a jury.* —contamination /kənˌtæməˈneɪʃən/ n. [U]

con·tam·i·nated /kənˈtæməˌneɪtɪd/ adj. **1** water, food etc. that is contaminated has dangerous or harmful things in it, such as chemicals or poison: *Contaminated water leaked from the nuclear reactor.* **2** influenced in a way that produces a bad effect

contd the written abbreviation of "continued"

con·tem·plate /ˈkɑntəmˌpleɪt/ v. **1** [T] to think about something that you intend to do in the future: *A spokeswoman denied that job losses were being contemplated.* | [contemplate doing sth] *Have you ever contemplated committing suicide?* **2** [T] to accept the possibility that something is true: **too terrible/ horrible etc. to contemplate** *The thought that she might be dead was just too awful to contemplate.* **3** [I,T] to think seriously about something for a long time, especially in order to understand it better: *The rollercoaster stops briefly during each of the loops so that riders can contemplate their own mortality.*

con·tem·pla·tion /ˌkɑntəmˈpleɪʃən/ n. [U] quiet serious thinking about something, especially in order to understand it better: *Wente uses the hour for contemplation and study.*

con·tem·pla·tive¹ /kənˈtɛmplətɪv/ adj. spending a lot of time thinking seriously and quietly: *a contemplative life* —contemplatively adv.

contemplative² n. [C] FORMAL someone who spends their life thinking deeply about religious ideas

con·tem·po·ra·ne·ous /kənˌtɛmpəˈreɪniəs/ adj. FORMAL happening in the same period of time; CONTEMPORARY¹ (2): [+ with] *The bones are contemporaneous with some of the earliest human fossils.* —contemporaneously adv. —contemporaneity /kənˌtɛmpərəˈniəti, -ˈneɪəti/ n. [U]

con·tem·po·rar·y¹ /kənˈtɛmpəˌrɛri/ adj. **1** belonging to the present time; MODERN: *The cafe's decor is clean and contemporary.* | **contemporary art/ music/dance etc.** *a contemporary opera by John Adams* **2** happening or existing in the same period of time

contemporary² n. plural **contemporaries** [C] someone who lived in the same period of time or in the same place as a particular person or event: *Atkins is still working, long after many of his contemporaries have retired.*

con·tempt /kənˈtɛmpt/ n. [U] **1** a feeling that someone or something is not important and deserves no

respect: [+ for] *Jimmy has nothing but contempt for his boss.* | *Poor children are treated with contempt by the authorities.* | *A popular landscape artist, Chatham holds nearly all art gallery owners in contempt* (=feels contempt for them). | *Leaving litter in the wilderness is beneath contempt* (=so unacceptable that you have no respect for the person involved). **2** failure to obey or show respect toward a court of law: **find/hold sb in contempt (of court)** *She was found in contempt of court for not appearing on the day of the trial.* | *Morgan was jailed for contempt of court.* **3** complete lack of fear toward something difficult or dangerous: [+ for] *Her contempt for danger is something I do not understand.*

con·tempt·i·ble /kənˈtɛmptəbəl/ adj. so unacceptable that you have no respect for the person involved: *The union's tactics were contemptible.* —contemptibly adv.

con·temp·tu·ous /kənˈtɛmptʃuəs/ adj. **1** showing that you feel that someone or something is not important and deserves no respect: *a contemptuous attitude* | [+ of] *Franklin was contemptuous of the Iroquois and referred to them as savages.* **2** not feeling any fear in a dangerous situation: [+ of] *Contemptuous of the risks, she ran into the burning building.* —contemptuously adv.

con·tend /kənˈtɛnd/ v. **1** [I] to compete against someone in order to gain something: [+ for] *Ten teams are contending for the title.* **2** [T] to argue or state that something is true: *The government contended that most of the refugees were fleeing poverty, not persecution.*

contend with sth *phr. v.* [T] **have to contend with sth** also **have sth to contend with** to have to deal with something difficult or bad: *Those who choose to drive have to contend with traffic congestion.*

con·tend·er /kənˈtɛndɚ/ n. [C] someone who is involved in a competition or a situation in which they have to compete with other people: *Phillips is one of the top contenders for the middleweight championship of the world.*

con·tent¹ /ˈkɑntɛnt/ n. **1 contents** [plural] **a)** the things that are in a box, bag, room etc.: *The jewelry box and its contents are priceless.* | [+ of] *The contents of the safe had been removed.* **b)** the words or ideas that are written in a letter, book etc.: *He could not provide a copy of the report but outlined its contents.* | *Look in the table of contents* (=a list at the beginning of a book, which shows the different parts into which the book is divided) *to see how many chapters the book has.* **2** [singular] the amount of a substance that something contains: *Chestnuts have a high water content.* **3** [U] the ideas, facts, or opinions that are expressed in a speech, book etc.: *Many of the paintings are political in content.*

con·tent² /kənˈtɛnt/ adj. [not before noun] **1** happy and satisfied: [content to do sth] *We were content to just sit and listen.* | [+ with] *I am content with my job, my home, and my family.* **2 not content with sth** if someone is not content with doing something, they do not think that it is good enough, and so want to do more: *Not content with past creations, Leiber is always introducing new designs.* —see Usage Note at HAPPY

content³ v. [T] **1 content yourself with sth** to do or have something that is not what you really want, but is still satisfactory: *Firms in the industry realize they may have to content themselves with lower sales than before.* **2** to make someone feel happy and satisfied: *I was no longer satisfied with the life that had once contented me.*

content⁴ n. [U] **1 do sth to your heart's content** to do something as much as you want: *I was able to browse through the bookstore to my heart's content.* **2** LITERARY a feeling of quiet happiness and satisfaction

con·tent·ed /kənˈtɛntɪd/ adj. happy and satisfied because your life is good: *I'm pretty contented now.* | *a purring, contented cat* —contentedly adv. —opposite DISCONTENTED

con·ten·tion /kənˈtɛnʃən/ n. **1** [C] FORMAL a belief or opinion that someone expresses: [+ that] *It is my* contention *that bicycle helmets should be required at all times.* **2** [U] a situation in which people or groups are competing: *There are still six teams in* **contention** *for the playoffs.* **3** [U] FORMAL arguments and disagreement between people: *A key area of contention is the call for the wilderness to be opened to oil and gas drilling.* | *One of the issues in contention* (=being argued about) *is barriers to trade.* **4 a bone of contention** a subject that causes disagreement or argument: *The plans for the new library have been a real bone of contention for some time.*

con·ten·tious /kən'tɛnʃəs/ *adj.* **1** likely to cause a lot of argument and disagreement between people: *Logging on public lands is a contentious issue.* **2** someone who is contentious often argues with people —**contentiously** *adv.* —**contentiousness** *n.* [U]

con·tent·ment /kən'tɛntˉmənt/ *n.* [U] the state of being happy and satisfied: *The people of the village seem to live in peace and contentment.* —opposite DISCONTENT

con·test¹ /'kɑntɛst/ *n.* [C] **1** a competition, usually a small one: *They have a Halloween costume contest every year.* | *The essay contest is open to all teenagers.* **2** a struggle to win control or power: *a close contest for the mayor's job* **3 no contest** INFORMAL used to say that a choice or a victory is not difficult at all: *In the end, it was no contest with the Cardinals beating the Mets 9-2.* **4 plead no contest** LAW to say that you will not give any defense in a court of law for something you have done wrong: *He pleaded no contest to driving without a license.*

con·test² /kən'tɛst/ *v.* [T] **1** to say formally that you do not accept something or do not agree with it: *The pharmacy company contested the agency's findings.* **2** to compete for something or try to win it: *The ruling party will contest 156 seats in Algeria's elections.* —**contested** *adj.*: *a hotly contested mayoral election*

con·test·ant /kən'tɛstənt/ *n.* [C] someone who competes in a contest: *The next contestant is Diane Massa of Bay Ridge.*

con·text /'kɑntɛkst/ *n.* [C,U] **1** the situation, events, or information that are related to something, and that help you to understand it better: *The book sets economics in a historical context.* | **put/place/keep sth in context** (=consider something together with the related situation, events etc.) **2** the words and sentences that come before and after a particular word, and that help you to understand the meaning of the word: *English words can have several meanings depending on context.* **3 take/quote sth out of context** to repeat a sentence or statement without describing the situation in which it was said, so that its meaning is not clear: *Jennings accused the program of quoting him out of context.*

con·tex·tu·al /kən'tɛkstʃuəl/ *adj.* relating to a particular context: *contextual information* —**contextually** *adv.*

con·tex·tu·al·ize /kən'tɛkstʃuə,laɪz/ *v.* [T] to consider something together with the situation, events, or information that relate to it, rather than alone —**contextualization** /kən,tɛkstʃuələ'zeɪʃən/ *n.* [U]

con·tig·u·ous /kən'tɪgyuəs/ *adj.* FORMAL next to something, or near something in time or order: *the 48 contiguous states* (=the U.S. states that are next to each other) —**contiguously** *adv.* —**contiguity** /,kɑntə'gyuəti/ *n.* [U]

con·ti·nence /'kɑntənəns, 'kɑntˉn-əns/ *n.* [U] FORMAL the practice of controlling your desire for sex

con·ti·nent¹ /'kɑntənənt, 'kɑntˉn-ənt/ *n.* [C] one of the main masses of land on the earth: *the continent of Australasia*

continent² *adj.* **1** able to control your BLADDER (1) and BOWELS (1) **2** OLD USE controlling your desire to have sex —opposite INCONTINENT

con·ti·nen·tal /,kɑntən'ɛntl◂, ,kɑntˉn-/ *adj.* **1 the continental U.S./United States** all the states of the U.S. except for Alaska and Hawaii *Housing prices here are the highest in the continental United States.* **2** relating to a large mass of land: *The store is trying to expand into continental Europe.* **3** [only

before noun] belonging to the North American continent **4** typical of the warmer countries in Western Europe: *The cafe serves continental style cuisine.*

continental break·fast /,.... '../ *n.* [C] a breakfast consisting of coffee, juice, and a sweet ROLL (=type of bread)

continental drift /,.... './ *n.* [U] TECHNICAL the very slow movement of the CONTINENTs across the surface of the earth

continental shelf /,.... './ *n. plural* **continental shelves** [C] TECHNICAL the part of a CONTINENT¹ that slopes down under the ocean and ends in a steep slope down to the bottom of the ocean

con·tin·gen·cy /kən'tɪndʒənsi/ *n. plural* **contingencies 1** an event or situation that might happen in the future, especially one that might cause problems: *Businesses that store hazardous materials must have contingency plans for emergencies* (=a plan that you make in order to deal with a problem that might happen). | *A will should allow for contingencies.* **2 a contingency fee** an amount of money that a lawyer will be paid only if the person they are advising wins in court

con·tin·gent¹ /kən'tɪndʒənt/ *adj.* FORMAL dependent on something that may or may not happen in the future: [+ **on/upon**] *Erb's promotion was contingent upon finishing her a university degree.* —**contingently** *adv.*

contingent² *n.* [C] **1** a group of people who all have the same aim or are from the same area, and who are part of a larger group: [+ **of**] *A sizable contingent of my family attended the wedding.* **2** a group of soldiers sent to help a larger group: [+ **of**] *A large contingent of paratroopers was sent to the region.*

con·tin·u·al /kən'tɪnyuəl/ *adj.* **1** repeated often and over a long period of time, sometimes in an annoying way: *The continual news reports about the economy have scared many manufacturers.* | *We were kept awake by the continual buzz of small planes overhead.* **2** continuing for a long time without stopping: *The hostages lived in continual fear of violent death.* —**continually** *adv.*

USAGE NOTE: CONTINUAL

WORD CHOICE: continual, continuous
Continual describes separate, often annoying, actions which are repeated over a period of time: *These continual interruptions are making me angry.* | *Janet claims she was subjected to nine years of continual harassment by her supervisor.* **Continuous** describes things and events that go on without stopping or without being interrupted: *This product is the result of years of continuous development.* | *The plants must be kept in complete darkness for 14 continuous hours each night.* The uses just described are regarded by many as the correct ones, but many people use **continuous** like **continual** to describe repeated separate actions: *There were continuous interruptions.* Some people, however, consider this use of **continuous** to be incorrect.

---

con·tin·u·ance /kən'tɪnyuəns/ *n.* **1** [C usually singular] LAW the act of allowing the events in a court of law to stop for a period of time, usually so a lawyer can find more facts about the case **2** [singular,U] the state of continuing for a long period of time: *Last month's elections saw a continuance in power of the country's socialist party.*

con·tin·u·a·tion /kən,tɪnyu'eɪʃən/ *n.* **1** [C] something that follows after something else without stopping or changing: [+ **of**] *They favor continuation of Puerto Rico's status as a U.S. commonwealth.* **2** [U] The act or state of continuing for a long period without stopping: [+ **of**] *The continuation of family traditions is important to many immigrants.* **3** [C] something that is joined to something else as if it were part of it: [+ **of**] *The Gulf of Mexico is a continuation of the Caribbean Sea.*

continuation school /...'.. ,./ *n.* [C] a school for

children who are not able to study at a normal high school because of bad behavior or other problems

C

con·tin·ue /kənˈtɪnyu/ v. **1** [I,T] to keep happening, existing, or doing something without stopping: *Dry weather will continue through the weekend.* | *Soviet leaders said they would continue Gorbachev's democratic reforms.* | [+ **with**] *Despite his illness, he plans to continue with his normal work schedule.* | [**continue to do sth**] *The well should continue to produce oil for many years.* | [**continue doing sth**] *We continued drinking until after midnight.* **2** [I,T] to start doing something again after a pause: *The concert will continue after a brief intermission.* | *The state continues to raise taxes every year.* **3** [I] to go further in the same direction: [+ **on/down/in/after etc.**] *Route 66 continues on to Texas from here.* **4** [I,T] to say something else after you have been interrupted. *"That may be," he continued, "but the factory will still be closing at the end of the year."* **5 to be continued** used at the end of a television program to tell people that the story will not finish until a later program —see also CONTINUAL, DISCONTINUE

con·tin·ued /kənˈtɪnyud/ adj. [only before noun] continuing to happen for a long time, or happening many times: *The continued failure of the negotiations means that there will be no peace settlement before the winter.*

continuing ed·u·ca·tion /.,.... ..'../ n. [U] education for adults, usually in classes that are held in the evening and especially on subjects that are related to their jobs

con·ti·nu·i·ty /ˌkɑntəˈnuəti/ n. [U] **1** the state of continuing over a long period of time without being interrupted or changing: [+ **of**] *Long-term employees provide a continuity of service.* **2** TECHNICAL the organization of a movie or television program to give the appearance that the action happens without pauses or interruptions

con·tin·u·o /kənˈtɪnyuˌou/ n. [C] TECHNICAL a musical part consisting of a line of low notes with figures showing the higher notes that are to be played with them

con·tin·u·ous¹ /kənˈtɪnyuəs/ adj. **1** continuing to happen or exist without stopping or without being interrupted: *continuous news coverage* | *a continuous improvement in customer service* **2** something such as a line that is continuous does not have any spaces or holes in it: *a continuous trail along the ridge* —see Usage Note at CONTINUAL —**continuously** adv.

continuous² n. **the continuous** TECHNICAL in grammar, the form of a verb that shows that an action or activity is continuing to happen, and that is shown in English by the verb "be" followed by a PRESENT PARTICIPLE. In the sentence "She is watching TV," 'is watching" is in the continuous form.

con·tin·u·um /kənˈtɪnyuəm/ n. plural **continuums** or **continua** /-nyuə/ [C] FORMAL something that changes or develops very gradually, so that each part is very similar to previous and following parts; CLINE: *Mental development follows a set course along a continuum.*

con·tort /kənˈtɔrt/ v. [I,T] to twist something, especially your face or body, so that it does not have its normal shape and looks strange or unattractive, or to twist in this way: [+ **with**] *The boy's face was contorted with pain.*

con·tor·tion /kənˈtɔrʃən/ n. **1** [C] a twisted position or movement that looks strange: *Torrence dances with the lithe contortions of a cobra.* **2** [C] complicated activity in order to do something: *Some bills go through numerous legislative contortions before they are approved.* **3** [U] the act of twisting something, especially your face or body, so that it does not have its normal shape and looks strange or unattractive, or the fact of being twisted in this way: *the involuntary contortion of muscles*

con·tor·tion·ist /kənˈtɔrʃənɪst/ n. [C] someone who entertains people by twisting their body into strange and unnatural shapes and positions

con·tour /ˈkɑntʊr/ n. [C] **1** the shape of the outer edges of something, such as an area of land or someone's body: *An architect planned for a house that follows the contours of the hillside.* | [+ **of**] *the contours of the foot* **2** also **contour line** a line on a map that connects points of equal height above sea level, which together with others show hills, valleys etc.

con·toured /ˈkɑntʊrd/ adj. **1** shaped to fit closely next to something else, or in a shape like this: *The jacket is slightly contoured.* **2** having an attractive, curved shape: *a smoothly contoured golf course*

contra- /kɑntrə/ prefix **1** acting against something: *contraceptive devices* (=that prevent PREGNANCY) | *to contravene something* (=do something that is not allowed by a law or rule) **2** opposite: *plants in contradistinction to animals*

con·tra·band /ˈkɑntrəˌbænd/ n. [U] goods that are brought into or taken out of a country illegally, especially without tax being paid on them: *contraband cigarettes* —**contraband** adj.

con·tra·bass /ˈkɑntrəˌbeɪs/ n. [C] a DOUBLE BASS

con·tra·cep·tion /ˌkɑntrəˈsɛpʃən/ n. [U] the practice of making it possible for a woman to have sex without having a baby, or the methods for doing this; BIRTH CONTROL: *The pill is one of the most effective methods of contraception.*

con·tra·cep·tive /ˌkɑntrəˈsɛptɪv/ n. [C] a drug, object, or method used to make it possible for a woman to have sex without having a baby: *The clinic distributes contraceptives free of charge.* —**contraceptive** adj. [only before noun]

con·tract¹ /ˈkɑntrækt/ n. [C] **1** a legal written agreement between two or more people, companies etc. which says what each side must do for the other: *My contract guarantees me a 15% pay raise every year.* | [+ **with**] *McCaskill agreed to a three-year contract with the Chicago White Sox.* | *You should never sign a contract without getting legal advice first.* | *Nabb will enter into a lucrative contract with a soft drink company.* | *He said they fired him without cause, and sued them for breach of contract* (=something that is not allowed by the contract). **2** INFORMAL an agreement to kill someone for money: *The mob put a contract out on him.*

con·tract² /kənˈtrækt/ v. **1** [T] to get an illness: *He contracted the disease through an insect bite.* **2** [I] to become smaller, narrower, or tighter: *Metal contracts as it becomes cool.* | *In the 1980s, the economy contracted and many small businesses failed.* —opposite EXPAND **3** [I,T] to sign a contract in which you agree formally that you will do something: [**contract (with) sb for sth**] *The interior building work is not yet contracted for.* | [**contract to do sth**] *I'm contracted to work 35 hours a week.* **4 contract a marriage/alliance etc.** FORMAL to agree formally that you will marry someone or have a particular kind of relationship with someone

contract sth ↔ **out** phr. v. [T] to arrange to have a job done by a person or company outside your own organization: *The city has contracted its garbage collection out to an independent company.*

contract bridge /'.. ,./ n. [U] a form of the card game BRIDGE, in which one of the two pairs say how many TRICKS¹ (9) they will try to win

con·trac·tion /kənˈtrækʃən/ n. **1** [C] TECHNICAL a movement in which a muscle becomes tight, used especially when the muscles suddenly and painfully become tight when a woman is going to give birth **2** [U] the process of becoming smaller or narrower: *a contraction in economic activity* | *This type of plastic allows for expansion and contraction during temperature changes.* **3** [C] a short form of a word or words, such as "don't" for "do not"

con·trac·tor /ˈkɑnˌtræktɚ, kənˈtræk-/ n. [C] a person or company that makes an agreement to do work or provide goods in large amounts for another company: *a building contractor*

con·trac·tu·al /kənˈtræktʃuəl/ adj. agreed in a contract: *Carney has a contractual commitment to write two new books in the next four years.* —**contractually** adv.

con·tra·dict /ˌkɑntrəˈdɪkt/ v. **1** [T] if one statement, story etc. contradicts another one, it is very different or the opposite of the other one: *Smith gave an account that contradicted the woman's tearful testimony last week.* | *This information flatly contradicts North's statements.* **2** [I,T] to say that what someone else has said is wrong or not true, especially by saying that the opposite is true: [**contradict sb**] *Gillman contradicted her boss, saying that the name change occurred in 1972, not 1962.* **3 contradict yourself** to say something that is the opposite of what you said before: *During questioning, Robinson contradicted himself several times.* **4** [T] if one situation or event contradicts another, they cannot both happen at the same time or be true at the same time: *Heating the water to 150° F kills bacteria but contradicts efforts to save energy.*

con·tra·dic·tion /ˌkɑntrəˈdɪkʃən/ n. **1** [C] a difference between two statements, beliefs, or ideas about something that means they cannot both be true: *His speech was full of lies and contradictions.* | [**+ between**] *She pointed out the contradiction between Wilson's statements and his votes in the Senate.* **2** [C,U] if a person, situation, event etc. contains contradictions, it has many parts that are very different from or the opposite of each other: *Gage is a man of contradictions: a vegetarian who owns a cattle ranch.* | *America is a society rich in contradiction.* **3 a contradiction in terms** a combination of words in which one word describes the other word in a way that cannot be true, so that the phrase is confusing or not true: *In our business, the phrase "harmless error" is a contradiction in terms.* **4 in (direct) contradiction to sth** in a way that is opposite to a belief or statement: *Hatred is in contradiction to Christian values.* **5** [U] the act of saying that someone else's opinion, statement etc. is wrong or not true

con·tra·dic·to·ry /ˌkɑntrəˈdɪktəri/ adj. two statements, beliefs etc. that are contradictory are different and therefore cannot both be true: *Upon further questioning, the witnesses gave inconsistent and sometimes contradictory answers.* —see also SELF-CONTRA-DICTORY

con·tra·dis·tinc·tion /ˌkɑntrədɪˈstɪŋkʃən/ n. [C] **in contradistinction to sth** FORMAL as opposed to something

con·trail /ˈkɑntreɪl/ n. [C] FORMAL a line of white steam made in the sky by an airplane

con·tral·to /kənˈtræltoʊ/ n. [C] the lowest female singing voice, or a woman who has this voice

con·trap·tion /kənˈtræpʃən/ n. [C] INFORMAL a strange looking piece of equipment or machinery, especially one that you think is unlikely to work well: *It's a contraption for washing windows on tall buildings.*

con·trar·i·wise /ˈkɑntrəri,waɪz, kənˈtrɛr-/ adv. OLD-FASHIONED in the opposite way or direction; CONVERSELY

con·trar·y¹ /ˈkɑn,trɛri/ adj. **1** contrary ideas, opinions, or actions are completely different from each other and opposed to each other: *Some Congressmen are bound to express a contrary view.* | [**+ to**] *Thompson acted contrary to his client's best interests.* | *Contrary to his testimony, Pierce was personally involved in the fraud.* **2 contrary to popular belief/opinion** used to show that something is true even though people may believe or think the opposite: *Contrary to popular belief, gorillas are shy and gentle creatures.* **3** someone who is contrary deliberately does things differently from the way that other people do them, or from the way that people expect: *"Driving Miss Daisy" is the story of a contrary Southern lady and her wise chauffeur.* **4** FORMAL contrary weather conditions are ones that cause difficulties: *Contrary weather prevented the climb.* —**contrarily** adv. —**contrariness** n. [U]

contrary² n. FORMAL **1 on the contrary** used to show that the opposite of what has just been said is actually true: *"The war seems to be almost over." "On the contrary, more troops are being sent in to fight."* **2 to the contrary** showing that the opposite is true: *In*

spite of rumors to the contrary, I have no intention of leaving the country. **3 the contrary** the opposite of what has been said or suggested: *"Are the children too young to be taught about the Holocaust?" "Quite the contrary."*

con·trast¹ /ˈkɑntræst/ n. **1** [C,U] a difference between people, ideas, situations etc. that are being compared: [**+ between**] *The sharpest contrast between Vietnam and the Gulf War may be in the way the soldiers were treated when they came home.* | [**+ with**] *The Democrats said their budget offered a contrast with the President's when it came to children and working families.* **2 in/by contrast** used when you are comparing objects or situations and saying that they are completely different from each other: *About 1 in 4 Hispanic Americans are poor. By contrast, about 1 in 10 white Americans are below the poverty line.* | *The stock lost 60 cents a share, in contrast with last year, when it gained 21 cents.* | *In contrast to Brock's serious graduation speech, the rest of the ceremony was happy.* | **in sharp/ marked/stark etc. contrast to** *This year's record profits stand in sharp contrast to last year's $2 million loss.* **3** [C] something that is very different from something else: [**+ to**] *He wore a dark suit and tie, a contrast to the brightly colored shirts he usually wears.* **4** [U] the differences in color, or in light and darkness on photographs or paintings: *He's known for his use of contrast in his paintings.* **5** [U] the degree of difference between the light and dark parts of a television picture

con·trast² /kənˈtræst/ v. **1** [I] if two things contrast, the difference between them is very easy to see and is sometimes surprising: [**+ with**] *The sharpness of the vinegar contrasted with the sweetness of the nuts.* | *The German view contrasted sharply with the U.S. belief that food aid was not needed.* **2** [T] to compare two objects, ideas, people etc. to show how different they are from each other: *She has written a book contrasting the two prison systems.* | [**contrast sth with sth**] *The documentary contrasts the reality of war with its romanticized image.*

con·trast·ing /kənˈtræstɪŋ/ adj. two or more things that are contrasting are different from each other, especially in a way that is interesting or attractive: *Wear the jacket and skirt with contrasting pieces for a different look.*

con·tra·vene /ˌkɑntrəˈvin/ v. [T] FORMAL to do something that is not allowed according to a law or rule: *Critics said the ban on reporting contravened the public's democratic right to be informed.*

con·tra·ven·tion /ˌkɑntrəˈvɛnʃən/ n. FORMAL **1 in contravention of sth** in a way that is not allowed by a law or rule: *The company apparently shipped arms to the regime in contravention of the U.S. trade boycott.* **2** [C,U] the act of doing something that is not allowed by a law or rule

con·tre·temps /ˈkɑntrə,tɑn/ n. plural **contretemps** /-,tɑnz/ [C] LITERARY OR HUMOROUS **1** an argument **2** an unlucky and unexpected event, especially an embarrassing one

con·trib·ute /kənˈtrɪbyut, -yət/ v. **1** [I,T] to give money, help, ideas etc. to something that a lot of other people are also involved in: [**contribute sth to/toward sth**] *Volunteers contribute about 16,000 hours of work each year to the city.* | [**+ to**] *Japan contributed to the cost of the research.* **2 contribute to sth** to help make something happen: *Yellow fever contributed to Mudd's early death at age 19.* **3** [I,T] to write articles, stories, poems etc. for a newspaper or magazine: *Several hundred people contributed articles, photographs, and cartoons.*

con·tri·bu·tion /ˌkɑntrəˈbyuʃən/ n. **1** [C] something that you give or do in order to help something be successful: [**+ to/toward**] *The ships are Portugal's contribution to the multinational force.* | *The Chaos theory could make major contributions to accurate weather forecasting.* **2** [C] an amount of money that you give in order to help pay for something: *a* *campaign contribution* | [+ **to/toward**] *Contributions to charities are tax deductible.* | *In his memory,* **contributions** *can be* **made to** *the Muscular Dystrophy Association.* **3** [C] a regular payment that you make to your employer or to the government in addition to what they pay for BENEFITs that you will receive: *health-care insurance contributions* **4** [C] a story, poem, or piece of writing that you write and that is printed in a magazine or newspaper: *a journal with contributions from well-known writers* **5** [U] the act of giving money, time, help etc.

con·trib·u·tor /kən'trɪbyətə/ *n.* [C] **1** someone who gives money, help, ideas etc. to something that a lot of other people are also involved in: *The letter went to 800 of Durenberger's campaign contributors.* | [+ **to**] *Harris has been a major contributor to the Dodgers' success this season.* **2** FORMAL someone or something that helps to make something happen: [+ **to**] *Carbon dioxide is the primary contributor to the greenhouse effect.* **3** someone who writes a story, article etc. that is printed in a magazine or newspaper: [+ **to**] *Cannon had been a regular contributor to the monthly Ohio Magazine.*

con·trib·u·to·ry /kən'trɪbyə,tɔri/ *adj.* **1** [only before noun] being one of the causes of a particular result: *A poor diet may be a contributory factor in the disease.* **2** a contributory RETIREMENT or insurance plan is one that is paid for by the workers as well as by the company

contributory neg·li·gence /ˌ.ˌ... '.../ *n.* [U] LAW failure to take enough care to avoid or prevent an accident, so that you are partly responsible for any loss or damage caused

con trick /'. ./ *n.* [C] a CONFIDENCE TRICK

con·trite /kən'traɪt/ *adj.* feeling guilty and sorry for something bad that you have done, or showing that you feel this way: *A few days later, I received a contrite telephone call from the store, saying there had been a mistake.* —**contritely** *adv.* —**contrition** /kən'trɪʃən/ *n.* [U]

con·tri·vance /kən'traɪvəns/ *n.* FORMAL **1** a contrivance in a story or movie is something that seems artificial or not natural, but that makes something happen: *a plot contrivance* **2** [C] a machine or piece of equipment that has been made or invented for a special purpose: *This was a steam-driven contrivance used in 19th century clothing factories.* **3** [C,U] a plan to get something for yourself by deceiving someone, or the practice of doing this

con·trive /kən'traɪv/ *v.* [T] **1** FORMAL to succeed in doing something in spite of difficulties: [**contrive to do sth**] *The chef contrives to keep the fresh taste of the vegetables.* **2** to arrange an event or situation secretly or by deceiving people: *The lawsuit says oil companies contrived a gasoline shortage in the early 1970s.* **3** to make or invent something in a skillful way, especially because you need it suddenly: *Richter contrived a scale to measure the force of an earthquake.*

con·trived /kən'traɪvd/ *adj.* seeming false and not natural: *The script is contrived and unbelievable.*

s w **con·trol**[1] /kən'troʊl/ *n.*
¹¹

1 make sb/sth do what you want [U] the ability or power to make someone or something do what you want: [+ **over**] *He has editorial control over the publication.* | *Streiber has control of her classroom.* | *Strong winds sent the boat out of control* (=it could not be controlled). | *Have friends over to your place – that way you're in control of the menu.* | *Many people enter the welfare system because of changes that are mainly beyond their control* (=not possible for them to control). | *"Do you need any help?" "I've got it under control, thanks."* | *By age 5, Sidney's behavior problems were getting out of his parent's control* (=becoming impossible to control). | *The police think she was driving too fast, and just lost control of* (=was not able to control it any longer) *the car.* | *Captain Fisher parachuted to safety after being unable to regain control of the plane.*

2 your own life [U] the ability or power to behave in the way you want, deal with problems, and organize your own life: *Winfrey says she's letting go of the guilt and taking control of her own life.* | *The device allows handicapped people to have more control over their lives.* | *Weber's one of those guys who always seems to be in control.*

3 political/military power [U] the power to rule or govern a place, or the fact that you have more power than other political parties: *Croatian rebels battled for control of Vukovar.* | *Rebel forces were in control of the main communications building.* | *The Republicans have gained control of* (=they now control it, though they did not before) *both the Senate and the House.* | *Israel took control of the zone in 1985.* | *The plan is to keep most natural resources under state control* (=being controlled by the state). | *Most of the rebel fighters were under the control of the Khmer Rouge.* | **have control of/over sth** *Cities should have control over how their airports develop and operate.* | *It is feared that the troops may lose control of* (=not be able to control a place any longer) *several key defensive positions around the city.* | **under enemy/French/Communist etc. control** *The mountains to the south are now under Communist control.* | *Hussein started a campaign to regain control* (=gain control after it has been lost) *of the port.* | *The President has been executed and revolutionary forces have assumed control* (=got control of a country by defeating the government using military power).

4 way of limiting sth [C,U] a method or law for limiting the amount or growth of something: *price controls* | [+ **of**] *Our primary goal is the control of inflation.* | [+ **on**] *The Clean Air Act is designed to clean up the nation's air, largely through controls on pollutions from cars and industry.* | *Inflation appears to be out of control* (=it is not being limited). | *The company must keep costs under control* (=not allow costs to increase). | *an arms control* (=a limit on the number of weapons a country has) *treaty* | *We've hired an extra 200 security people to assist with crowd control.* | **tight/rigid/strict controls on sth** *Senator Landers favors tight controls on handguns.*

5 disease/fire etc. [U] the ability to stop something dangerous from getting worse or affecting more people: *Firefighters had the blaze under control by 7:30 a.m.* | *Exercise and diet have brought Young's weight under control* (=helped him lose weight). | *The situation quickly got out of control* (=it became much worse) *and the police were called in.* | *Ladybugs may help keep the whitefly pest problem under control.*

6 ability to control emotions [U] the ability to remain calm even when you feel very angry, upset, or excited: *Reynolds struggled for control as he told how much Dinah meant to him.* | *Moore managed to be in control throughout the birth of her child.* | *The argument ended violently when Winter's husband lost control* (=became unable to control his behavior). | *Most five-year-olds don't have a lot of self-control.* | *After panicking, Pierce regained control* (=succeeded in behaving calmly again after being upset or angry) *and worked at getting himself out of the situation.* | *Her rage was barely under control* (=being controlled).

7 company/organization [U] the power to make all the important decisions in an organization or part of an organization: *Simmons stepped into his battle for control of Lockheed.* | *Wilson is firmly in control of the board.* | **take/gain control** *Mr. Chang will take control of our Singapore offices in January of next year.* | *AT&T sought to gain control of NCR.* | *Wasserman has control of about 11.5 percent of MCA's stock.* | *Trump had to resolve the problems or risk losing control of the casino.* | *He plans to someday regain control of Lewis Oil.* | *The research department is now under the control of* (=being controlled by) *the Dallas office.*

8 computer also **control key** [usually singular] a particular button on a computer that allows you to do certain operations: *Press control and F2 to exit.*

9 your body [U] the ability to control the movements of your body by using your muscles when dancing or doing physical exercise: *The disease robs you of muscle control.* | *She hits the ball harder than Sabatini, but lacks her control.* | [+ of/over] *Babies are born with very little control over their movements.* | *Choose trails within your ability and ski* **under control** (=in a way in which your body does what you want).

10 `sports` [U] the ability to make points or win a game: *Hendricks* **took control** *of the ball and scored six straight points.* | *The Nuggets* **had control** *in the third quarter, extending their lead by 12 points.* | *St. Louis* **regained control** *of the game when Cavallini scored.* | *A basket by Basey put Logan High* **in control**.

11 `machine/vehicle` [C] the thing that you use to make a machine, vehicle, television etc. work: *a car with manual controls* | *the TV control* | *The train, with no one* **at the controls** (=controlling it) *derailed at 50 miles per hour.* —see also REMOTE CONTROL

12 `skill` [U] the ability to make very skillful movements with a ball, pencil, tool etc.: *Few people have better ball control than Jordan.*

13 `aircraft etc.` [U] the people who direct an activity, especially by giving instructions to an aircraft or SPACECRAFT: *air-traffic control*

14 `scientific test` TECHNICAL [C **a)** a person, group etc. against which you compare another person or group that is very similar, in order to see if a particular quality is caused by something or happens by chance: *The* **control group** *of 50 children averaged B's in reading.* **b)** a thing that you already know the result for that is used in a scientific test, in order to show that your method is working correctly —see also CONTROLLED EXPERIMENT

15 `checking sth` [U] the process of checking that something is correct, or the place where this is done: *Please stop at passport control.* —see also BIOLOGICAL CONTROL, BIRTH CONTROL, QUALITY CONTROL

control² *v.* **controlled, controlling** [T]

1 `company/organization` to own a company so that it does what you want, or to be the most important person or company in a particular industry: *Many U.S. corporations are controlled by foreign companies.*

2 `political/military power` to rule or govern a place, or to have more power than other political parties: *Republicans controlled more than two-thirds of the Senate.*

3 `machine/process/system` to make a machine, process, or system work in a particular way: *Insulin controls blood sugar levels in the body.* | *a radio-controlled car* | [control which/what/how etc.] *These switches control which track the trains are allowed to run on.*

4 `limit` to limit the amount or growth of something: *The export of these devices is strictly controlled.* | *She exercises to control her weight.* | *Health-care reform is intended to control costs and provide medical care for everyone.*

5 `disease/fire etc.` to stop something dangerous from getting worse or affecting more people: *We're trying to control the spread of AIDS by educating more young people.* | *The fire was controlled later Tuesday night.*

6 `emotion` to behave in a calm and sensible way, even if you feel angry, upset, or excited: *If you can't control your temper, you don't belong in this line of work.* | *Nathan tried to control his crying.* | *She fought to control herself* (=tried to stop crying, stop being angry etc.) *as she told me what they had gone through.* | **control your voice/face/expression** (=to make your voice, face etc. seem normal and not show your emotions)

7 `sports` to be winning in a game, or to have the ball so that you can make points: *Washington State controlled the ball for almost the whole game.*

8 `make sb/sth do what you want` to make someone or something do what you want or behave in the way you want them to behave: *If you can't control your dog, you should put it on a leash.* | *The Forestry Department is clearing 20 acres with a controlled burn* (=a fire that they make burn only a particular area).

9 `check sth` to make sure that something is done correctly: *The company strictly controls the quality of its products.*

C

USAGE NOTE: CONTROL

WORD CHOICE: control, manage, run, be in charge of, check on, inspect, monitor

Most meanings of **control** involve the idea of a person or other force having the power to change or stop something, without the people or things affected being able to do anything about it. People, organizations, machines etc. **control** other people or organizations, or their own or other people's actions, events etc., sometimes from far away. When you want to give the idea of people directing businesses etc., where the other people involved are nearby and perhaps allowed some influence over the activity, you may use **manage, run,** or **be in charge of:** *He's managing a hotel in Indianapolis.* | *Who's running the Boston office now that Harry's retired?* | *Peggy is in charge of the department while Mrs. Cohen is away.* When you want to talk about people, things, or activities, in order to see if they are correct, but without directly affecting them, you may use **check on** or **inspect:** *I have to go check on the roast.* | *The building is going to be inspected by the fire department next week.* **Monitor** is a word meaning to watch and check on someone or something over a period of time. This can be done by a person or by a machine, often in a technical or official way: *Doctors are monitoring the patient's condition.*

control freak /. '. ,./ *n.* [C] INFORMAL, DISAPPROVING someone who is too concerned about controlling all the details in every situation they are involved in

control key /. '. ,./ *n.* [C] a special button on a computer that allows you to do certain operations

con·trol·la·ble /kən'trouləbəl/ *adj.* able to be controlled: *Diabetes is a serious but controllable disease.*

con·trolled /kən'trould/ *adj.* **1** calm and not showing emotion, even if you feel angry, afraid etc.: *Hill, appearing calm and controlled, said Thomas made the remarks after she turned down his request for a date.* **2** a movement, action, situation etc. that is controlled is one that is carefully and deliberately done in a particular way, or made to have particular qualities: *Tharp displayed the smooth and controlled movements of an experienced dancer.* **3** limited by a law or rule: *Access to the site is controlled.*

controlled drug /.,. './ *n.* [C] LAW a CONTROLLED SUBSTANCE

controlled e·con·o·my /.,. .'.../ *n.* [C] an economic system in which the government controls all businesses

controlled ex·per·i·ment /.,. .'.../ *n.* [C] TECHNICAL a scientific test done in a way in which you can control all the things that might affect the test

controlled sub·stance /.,. '../ *n.* [C] LAW a drug that it is illegal to have or use: *They were charged with possession of a controlled substance.*

con·trol·ler /kən'troulə/ *n.* [C] **1** also **comptroller** FORMAL someone who is in charge of the money received or paid out by a company or government department: *the state controller* **2** someone who is in charge of a particular system or of part of an organization: *air traffic controllers*

controlling in·ter·est /.,.. '../ *n.* [C usually singular] TECHNICAL if you have a controlling interest in a company, you own enough SHARES to be able to make decisions about what happens to the company

control room /. '. ./ *n.* [C] the room from which a process, service, event etc. is controlled: *The satellite's launch brought cheers from the mission control room.*

control tow·er /. '. ,./ *n.* [C] a tall building at an airport from which people direct the movement of airplanes on the ground and in the air

con·tro·ver·sial /,kɑntrə'vəʃəl/ *adj.* causing a lot of disagreement, because many people have strong opinions about the subject being discussed: *Prozac is a controversial drug used to treat depression.* | **a controversial plan/decision/issue etc.** *In June, he made a controversial decision to increase the sales* tax. | *Maxwell soon became a **controversial** figure in the world of big business.* —**controversially** *adv.*

con·tro·ver·sy /'kɑntrə,vɜsi/ *n. plural* **controversies** [C,U] a serious argument or disagreement among many people over a plan, decision etc., over a long period of time: *Dahl's letter to "The Times" provoked controversy.* | *He resigned Tuesday after months of controversy.* | [+ **over/surrounding**] *Controversy over the drug's safety still continues.*

con·tu·ma·cious /,kɑntu'meɪʃəs/ *adj.* FORMAL disobedient in a very unreasonable way —**contumaciously** *adv.*

con·tu·me·ly /kən'tuməli/ *n.* [C,U] FORMAL behavior or language that is offensive or not respectful

con·tuse /kən'tuz/ *v.* [T] TECHNICAL to BRUISE² (1) someone or a part of the body

con·tu·sion /kən'tuʒən/ *n.* [C] TECHNICAL a BRUISE¹ (1)

co·nun·drum /kə'nʌndrəm/ *n.* [C] **1** a confusing and difficult problem: *The administration is facing a familiar conundrum.* **2** a person or situation that is strange or confusing: *King remains a conundrum, a man of both major strengths and serious character flaws.* **3** a trick question asked for fun; RIDDLE¹ (1)

con·ur·ba·tion /,kɑnɜ'beɪʃən/ *n.* [C] a group of towns that have grown and joined together to form an area with a high population, often with a large city as its center

con·va·lesce /,kɑnvə'lɛs/ *v.* [I] to spend time getting well after an illness or operation: *He will need about a week to convalesce after his hospital stay.*

con·va·les·cence /,kɑnvə'lɛsəns/ *n.* [singular,U] the length of time a person spends getting well after an illness or operation: *Mrs. Gwynn will continue her convalescence at home.*

con·va·les·cent¹ /,kɑnvə'lɛsənt/ *adj.* **a convalescent home/hospital etc.** a place where people stay when they need care from doctors and nurses but are not sick enough to be in a hospital —compare NURSING HOME

convalescent² *n.* [C] a person who is getting well after a serious illness or operation

con·vect /kən'vɛkt/ *v.* [I] TECHNICAL to move heat by convection

con·vec·tion /kən'vɛkʃən/ *n.* [U] the movement in a gas or liquid caused by warm gas or liquid rising, and cold gas or liquid sinking: *Convection takes place in liquids that are hotter at the bottom than at the top.*

convection ov·en /.'.. ,../ *n.* [C] a special OVEN that makes hot air move around inside it so that all the parts of the food get the same amount of heat

con·vene /kən'vin/ *v.* [I,T] if a group of people convene, or someone convenes them, they meet together, especially for a formal meeting: *A board was convened to judge the design competition.*

con·ven·ience /kən'vinyəns/ *n.* **1** [U] the quality of being appropriate or useful for a particular purpose, especially because it makes something easier or saves you time: *The new Accord station wagon offers safety and convenience.* | *People are willing to pay higher rent for the convenience of living near mass transit.* | *For convenience, the cheese is sold ready-sliced.* **2** [C] something that is useful because it saves you time or means that you have less work to do: *Being able to pay bills over the Internet is a real convenience.* **3** [U] what is easiest and best for someone: *I'll call in two weeks to arrange a meeting **at your convenience.*** **4 a marriage of convenience** a marriage that has been agreed for a particular purpose, not because the two people love each other: *Gerard Depardieu plays a French immigrant in a marriage of convenience with Andie McDowell.* **5 at your earliest convenience** FORMAL an expression meaning "as soon as possible," usually used in letters: *We should be grateful if you would reply at your earliest convenience.*

convenience food /.'.. ,./ *n.* [C,U] food that is frozen or that is in cans, packages etc., so that it can be prepared quickly and easily: *Convenience foods let you spend more quality time with your family.*

convenience store /.'.. ,./ *n.* [C] a store where you can buy food, alcohol, magazines etc., that is often open 24 hours each day

con·ven·ient /kən'vinyənt/ *adj.* **1** useful to you because it saves you time or does not spoil your plans or cause you problems: *The idea is to make it convenient to donate blood.* | *This is a safe and convenient way to dispose of chemicals.* | *Could we postpone the meeting until a more convenient t me?* | [+ **for**] *Is Friday convenient for you?* | *Drive-through restaurants are convenient for families with young children.* **2** close and easy to reach: *The bus stop around the corner is probably the most convenient.* | [+ **to**] *The airport is convenient to the city's downtown area.* —opposite INCONVENIENT

con·ven·ient·ly /kən'vinyəntli/ *adv.* **1** in a way that is useful to you because it saves you time or does not spoil your plans or cause you problems: *Each house for sale is conveniently listed by location and price.* **2** in a place that is near or easily reached: *The hotel is conveniently located near the airport.* **3** if someone has conveniently forgotten, ignored, or lost something, they do this because it helps them to avoid a problem or difficult situation: *People conveniently forget things that might be embarrassing to them.*

con·vent /'kɑnvɛnt, -vənt/ *n.* [C] a building or group of buildings where NUNS live —see also CONVENT SCHOOL

con·ven·tion /kən'vɛnʃən/ *n.* **1** [C] a large formal meeting of people who belong to the same profession, organization etc., or who have the same interests: *the Republican Convention* | *a convention for Star Trek fans* | *The issue will be voted on at the **annual convention**.* **2** [C,U] behavior and attitudes that most people in a society consider to be normal and right: *The handshake is a social convention.* | *Sand was a freethinker who refused to follow the conventions of her day.* | **By convention**, *the bride's father walks her down the aisle at her wedding.* —see HABIT —see Usage Note at HABIT **3** [C] a method or style often used in literature, art, the theater etc. to achieve a particular effect: *Italian neorealism breaks with film conventions of the past.* **4** [C] a formal agreement, especially between countries, about particular rules or behavior: *the European convention on human rights* —compare PACT TREATY

con·ven·tion·al /kən'vɛnʃənəl/ *adj.* **1** [only before noun] a conventional method, product, practice etc. is one that has been used for a long time and is considered the usual type: *Although expensive, it lasts longer and uses less energy than a conventional light bulb.* **2** always following the behavior and attitudes that most people in a society consider to be normal, right, and socially acceptable, so that you seem slightly boring: *She ended her letter with a conventional "Yours Sincerely."* | [+ **in**] *John is fairly conventional in his tastes.* —opposite UNCONVENTIONAL **3 (the) conventional wisdom** the opinion that most people consider to be normal and right: *Conventional wisdom says that gang members must be reached early to change.* **4** [only before noun] conventional weapons, wars, and FORCES (=armies) do not use NUCLEAR explosives or weapons —**conventionally** *adv.* —**conventionality** /kən,vɛnʃə'næləti/ *n.* [U]

conventional ov·en /.,... '.../ *n.* [C] an ordinary OVEN, not a MICROWAVE

convent school /'.. ,./ *n.* [C] a school for girls that is run by Catholic NUNS

con·verge /kən'vɜdʒ/ *v.* [I] **1** if groups of people converge in a particular place, they come there from many different places and meet together to form a large crowd: [+ **on**] *Hundreds of hippies converge on Stonehenge to celebrate the summer solstice.* **2** to come from different directions and meet at the same point to become one thing: *The delta is where the rivers converge and flow into the bay.* **3** if different ideas or aims converge, they become the same: *Here the two distinct theories converge.* —**convergence** *n.* [C,U] —opposite DIVERGE

con·ver·sant /kən'vɜsənt/ *adj.* [not before

noun] **1** FORMAL having knowledge or experience of something: [+ **with**] *Are you fully conversant with the facts of the case?* **2** able to have a conversation in a foreign language, but not to be able to speak it perfectly: [+ **in**] *Eban is conversant in 10 languages.*

con·ver·sa·tion /ˌkɑnvɚˈseɪʃən/ n. **1** [C,U] an informal talk in which people exchange news, feelings, and thoughts: *a telephone conversation* | *The buzz of conversation filled the hall.* | **have/hold a conversation** *He can't hold a conversation for more than five minutes without mentioning his new book.* | *A couple in their sixties were carrying on a conversation in Hebrew.* | *I struck up a conversation* (=started one) *with a fellow passenger.* | *Naturally, the conversation turned* (=people started to talk about something different) *to work and the problems at work.* | *I found Annie deep in conversation with her little sister.* **2 make conversation** to talk to someone to be polite, not because you really want to: *I'm not very good at making conversation.*

con·ver·sa·tion·al /ˌkɑnvɚˈseɪʃənl, -ʃnəl/ adj. **1** a conversational style, phrase etc. is informal and commonly used in conversation: *McGovern lectures in a conversational style.* **2** relating to conversation: *a class in conversational Spanish.* —**conversationally** adv

con·ver·sa·tion·al·ist /ˌkɑnvɚˈseɪʃənəˌlɪst/ n. [C] someone whose conversation is intelligent, amusing, and interesting: *Steve's a talented conversationalist with a gift for listening.*

conversation piece /.ˈ.. ˌ./ n. [C] something that provides a subject for conversation, often used in a joking way to describe objects that are very strange or unusual

con·verse¹ /kənˈvɚs/ v. [I] FORMAL to have a conversation with someone: [+ **with**] *She held a phone to each ear and conversed with two people at once.*

con·verse² /ˈkɑnvɚs/ n. FORMAL **the converse** the converse of a fact, word, statement etc. is the opposite of it: *If the project is successful, Dourif will get the credit, but the converse is also true; he will get the blame if it fails.*

con·verse³ /kənˈvɚs, ˈkɑnvɚs/ adj. FORMAL opposite: *a converse opinion*

con·verse·ly /kənˈvɚsli, ˈkɑnvɚsli/ adv. FORMAL used when one situation is the opposite of another: *Scandinavian cruises are very popular in the summer; conversely, the Caribbean is most popular in the winter.*

con·ver·sion /kənˈvɚʒən, -ʃən/ n. **1** [C,U] the act or process of changing something from one form, purpose, or system to a different one: [+ **to**] *Left-wing politicians are in favor of a slower conversion to capitalism.* | [+ **of**] *The conversion of an old warehouse into apartments will be finished in June.* **2** [C,U] an act of changing from one religion or belief to a different one: [+ **to**] *As a student, he experienced a fanatical conversion to Marxism.* **3** [C] the act of doing something in order to get more points after making a TOUCHDOWN in football: *The Aggies successfully completed a two-point conversion and led 24–21.*

con·vert¹ /kənˈvɚt/ v. **1** [I,T] to change from one form, system, or purpose to a different one, or to make something do this: [**convert sth into sth**] *Ms. McPartland is hoping to convert the building into a homeless shelter.* | [+ **to**] *Thousands of miles of old railroad lines have been converted to trails.* | *Beta carotene can be converted to vitamin A in the body.* **2** [I] to be able to be changed from one object into another: [+ **into**] *The train compartment's seats convert into beds.* **3** [I,T] to change your opinions or habits, or to make someone else do this: [+ **to**] *Young Japanese people are converting from tea to coffee.* | [**convert sb to sth**] *Jones was converted from an opponent to a supporter during the meeting.* **4** [I,T] to change from one religion or belief to another, or to make someone do this: [+ **to**] *Ron converted to Judaism so he could marry Beth.* **5** [I,T] to make a conversion in football

con·vert² /ˈkɑnvɚt/ n. [C] someone who has been persuaded to change their beliefs and accept a particular religion or opinion: *a convert to Buddhism*

con·vert·er, convertor /kənˈvɚtɚ/ n. [C] a piece of

equipment that changes the form of something, especially so that it can be more easily used: *Cable TV subscribers get a converter that unscrambles the pictures.* —see also CATALYTIC CONVERTER

con·vert·i·ble¹ /kənˈvɚtəbəl/ n. [C] a car with a roof that you can fold back or remove: *a 1965 Mustang convertible* —compare HARDTOP

convertible² adj. **1** an object that is convertible can be folded or arranged in a different way so that it can be used as something else: *a convertible sofa bed* **2** TECHNICAL money that is convertible can be exchanged for the money of another country **3** TECHNICAL a financial document such as an insurance arrangement or BOND that is convertible can be exchanged for money, STOCKS etc.: *My financial advisor suggested we invest in convertible preferred stock.* —**convertibility** /kənˌvɚtəˈbɪləti/ n. [U]

con·ver·tor /kənˈvɚtɚ/ n. [C] another spelling of CONVERTER

con·vex /ˌkɑnˈvɛks◂, kən-/ adj. curved toward the outside like the surface of the eye: *a convex lens* | *a convex mirror* —**convexly** adv. —**convexity** /kənˈvɛksəti/ n. [C,U] —opposite CONCAVE

con·vey /kənˈveɪ/ v. **conveys, conveyed, conveying** [T] **1** to communicate a message or information, with or without using words: *All this information can be conveyed in a simple diagram.* | *Her blond hair and blue eyes convey her Swedish origins.* | **convey a sense/an impression etc.** *Her clothes convey the impression that she's capable and confident.* **2** FORMAL to take or carry something from one place to another: *The guard was charged with conveying drugs to a prison inmate.* **3** LAW to legally change the possession of property from one person to another

con·vey·ance /kənˈveɪəns/ n. **1** [C] FORMAL a vehicle: *No wheeled conveyances of any kind were allowed in the park.* **2** [U] FORMAL the act of taking something from one place to another: *The company relies on trains for the conveyance of goods.* **3** [U] LAW the act of changing the ownership of land, property etc. from one person to another

con·vey·or, conveyer /kənˈveɪɚ/ n. [C] a conveyor belt or a machine that has one: *A conveyor carries lettuce from the fields into trucks.*

con·vey·or belt /.ˈ.. ˌ./ n. [C] a long continuous moving band of rubber, cloth, or metal, used in a place such as a factory or airport to move things from one place to another: *Baggage is placed on the conveyor belt to go through the X-ray machine.*

con·vict¹ /kənˈvɪkt/ v. [T] to prove or officially announce that someone is guilty of a crime after a TRIAL in a court of law: [**convict sb of sth**] *Smith was convicted of armed robbery.* | *a convicted murderer* —opposite ACQUIT

con·vict² /ˈkɑnvɪkt/ n. [C] someone who has been proven to be guilty of a crime and sent to prison: *Fifty-two convicts began a hunger strike on November 30th.* —compare EX-CON

con·vic·tion /kənˈvɪkʃən/ n. **1** [C] a very strong belief or opinion: *Americans held the conviction that anyone could become rich if they worked hard.* | **a deep/strong conviction** *The Dotens have a deep conviction that marriage is for life.* | **religious/political convictions** *Religious convictions have a strong influence on people's behavior.* **2** [C] a decision in a court of law that someone is guilty of a crime: *Mrs. Warren and her husband appealed the conviction.* | [+ **for**] *a conviction for driving while drunk* **3** [U] the feeling of being sure about something and having no doubts: *"No," she said, but without conviction.* | *He responded, "we will win," but his voice didn't carry conviction* (=it showed that he did not feel sure about what he was saying). **4** [U] the process of proving that someone is guilty in a court of law: *The trial and conviction of Jimmy Malone took over three months.* —opposite ACQUITTAL —see also **have the courage of your (own) convictions** (COURAGE (2))

con·vince /kən'vɪns/ v. [T] **1** to make someone feel certain that something is true: [convince sb (that)] Bell's evidence convinced us that the first reports were true. | It will be hard to convince voters it was a badly written law. | [convince sb of sth] He'll try to convince you of Mitchell's innocence. **2** to persuade someone to do something: [convince sb to do sth] Kevin convinced Lee Ann to go to the country club dance with him.

con·vinced /kən'vɪnst/ adj. [not before noun] feeling certain that something is true: [+ (that)] I am convinced that sooner or later we will succeed. | She was convinced he was dead when his car was found abandoned in Fort Bragg. | [be convinced of sth] We are convinced of the safety of these products. | I am **fully convinced** that this is necessary.

con·vinc·ing /kən'vɪnsɪŋ/ adj. **1** making you believe that something is true or right: No one seemed able to give a convincing answer to my question. | Investigators have not found a convincing motive for the crime. **2** a convincing victory/win an occasion when a person or team wins a game or competition by a lot of points: Kasparov scored a convincing win over Karpov. —**convincingly** adv.

con·viv·i·al /kən'vɪviəl/ adj. friendly and pleasantly cheerful: convivial conversation —**convivially** adv. —**conviviality** /kən,vɪvi'æləti/ n. [U]

con·vo·ca·tion /,kɑnvə'keɪʃən/ n. FORMAL **1** [C usually singular] a large formal meeting of a group of people, especially church officials: a convocation of Moslem clergy in Mecca **2** [C usually singular] the ceremony held when students have finished their studies and are leaving a college or university: Who's going to be the speaker at the convocation? **3** [U] FORMAL the process of arranging for a large meeting to be held

con·voke /kən'vouk/ v. [T] FORMAL to tell people that they must come together for a formal meeting: A conference was convoked to discuss the situation.

con·vo·lut·ed /'kɑnvə,lutɪd/ adj. **1** complicated and difficult to understand: The convoluted language in the UN resolution has caused confusion. | The loan approval process is very convoluted. **2** FORMAL having many twists and bends: a convoluted freeway interchange —**convolutedly** adv.

con·vo·lu·tion /,kɑnvə'luʃən/ n. [C usually plural] FORMAL **1** the complicated details of a story, explanation etc., which make it difficult to understand: The story's fascinating convolutions were inspired by real events. **2** a fold or twist in something which has many of them: the many convolutions of the brain

con·voy /'kɑnvɔɪ/ n. [C] a group of vehicles or ships traveling together, sometimes in order to protect one another: A 50-truck convoy was carrying food and medicine to the refugees. | Submarines sank all but one of the ships in the convoy.

con·vulse /kən'vʌls/ v. **1** [T] if something such as a war convulses a country, it causes a lot of problems and anxiety: In 1992, the city was convulsed by rioting and demonstrations. **2** be convulsed with laughter to be laughing so much that you shake and are not able to stop yourself: They were too convulsed with laughter to speak. **3** [I] if your body or a part of it convulses, it moves violently and you are not able to control it: She was suddenly convulsed by a hacking cough.

con·vul·sion /kən'vʌlʃən/ n. **1** [C usually plural] an occasion when someone cannot control the violent movements of their body, because they are sick: Pure wintergreen oil can cause convulsions if it is eaten. | His temperature was very high and he **went into convulsions**. **2** [C] an occasion when a country has a lot of problems or worries because of something such as a war: Half the country is starving, and that is a recipe for massive political convulsions. **3** be in convulsions (of laughter) INFORMAL to be laughing a lot: By the end of the first act, we were in convulsions.

con·vul·sive /kən'vʌlsɪv/ adj. sudden, violent and impossible to control: The coup led to convulsive changes in U.S.–Central American relations. —**convulsively** adv.

co·ny, coney /'kouni/ n. [C,U] OLD USE a rabbit or rabbit fur used in making coats

coo /ku/ v. [I] **1** to make the low soft cry of a DOVE or PIGEON **2** to make soft quiet sounds, or to speak in a soft quiet way: The baby cooed as I held her. —**coo** n. [C]

cook¹ /kʊk/ v. **1** [I,T] to prepare food for eating by using heat: Do you want me to cook some pasta or something? | Mom always says no when I offer to cook. | [cook sb sth] He decided to cook his parents a special meal for their wedding anniversary. | [cook for sb] She cooks for her family of seven. | cook dinner/supper/a meal etc. Dad cooks breakfast on weekends. **2** [I] to be prepared for eating by being heated: Cover and simmer until the chicken finishes cooking. **3** be cooking INFORMAL to be happening, especially in a secret way: Hey, guys! What's cooking? **4** be cooking with gas SPOKEN used to say someone is doing something very well: Put your hands together, like that – now you're cooking with gas! **5** cook the books to dishonestly change official records and figures in order to steal money: Officials at the bank were found to have cooked the books. —see also COOKING¹

cook sth ↔ **up** phr. v. [T] **1** INFORMAL to invent an excuse, reason, plan etc., especially one that is slightly dishonest or unlikely to work: Stevenson accused the Republicans of cooking up issues to embarrass the president. | He has a knack for cooking up new uses for old technology. **2** to prepare food, especially quickly: Dad's cooking up some T-bone steaks in the back yard.

USAGE NOTE: COOK

WORD CHOICE: cook, make, fix, prepare
Cook is used to talk about food that you prepare for eating by using heat: We cooked a ton of food for the party. | I cooked the beans for the chili yesterday. **Make** is used to talk about any food that you prepare for eating, whether you use heat or not: Can you make breakfast today, Liz? | Mom made pot roast for dinner. **Fix** is used the same way as **make** but is more informal: I can fix you a sandwich if you're hungry. | I have to be back by six to fix dinner. **Prepare** is a more formal word which is used especially when talking about food that is more difficult or complicated to make: A lot of work is involved in preparing shrimp. | Blanche prepared an excellent dinner for us.

---

cook² n. [C] **1** someone who prepares and cooks food, either as their job or because they enjoy it: She's a cook for one of the airlines. | a good/great/bad etc. cook My husband is a fabulous cook. —compare CHEF **2 too many cooks (spoil the broth)** used when you think there are too many people trying to do the same job at the same time, so that the job is not done well —see also **chief cook and bottle-washer** (CHEF¹ (3))

Cook /kʊk/, **Captain James** (1728–1779) a British sailor and EXPLORER who sailed to Australia and New Zealand, and was the first European to discover several islands in the Pacific Ocean, including Hawaii

cook·book /'kʊkbʊk/ n. [C] a book that tells you how to prepare and cook food: I got this recipe from the Green's cookbook.

cooked /kʊkt/ adj. cooked food is not raw and is ready for eating: Can I have a ¼ pound sliced cooked ham, please?

cook·er /'kʊkɚ/ n. [C] a piece of equipment that you cook food in: a rice cooker —see also PRESSURE COOKER (1)

cook·er·y /'kʊkəri/ n. [U] the art or skill of cooking: French provincial cookery

cook·house /'kʊkhaʊs/ n. [C] OLD-FASHIONED an outdoor kitchen where you cook food, especially in a military camp

cook·ie /'kʊki/ n. [C] **1** a small flat sweet cake: a

glass of milk and a cookie | molasses cookies **2 tough/smart cookie** INFORMAL someone who is smart and successful, and knows how to get what they want: *Barney's a tough cookie. He knows how to play politics.* **3 that's the way the cookie crumbles** SPOKEN, INFORMAL said when something bad has happened and you must accept things the way they are, even though you do not want to **4** TECHNICAL a set of information that a computer program on the Internet leaves in your computer so that it will recognize you when you use that program again **5** OLD-FASHIONED an attractive young woman

cook·ie cut·ter /'.. ,../ n. [C] a tool that cuts cookies into special shapes before you bake them

cookie-cut·ter /'.. ,../ adj. [only before noun] almost exactly the same as other things of the same type, and not very interesting: *Most movies have cookie-cutter plots.*

cookie sheet /'.. ,./ n. [C] a flat piece of metal that you bake cookies and some other foods on —see picture at KITCHEN

cook·ing¹ /'kʊkɪŋ/ n. [U] **1** the act of making food and cooking it: *Do you do a lot of cooking?* **2** food made in a particular way or by a particular person: *Gail's cooking is always good.* | *Southern cooking*

cooking² adj. **1** [only before noun] appropriate for cooking, or used in cooking: *Add the tomatoes and some of the cooking water.* **2 be cooking** SLANG to be doing something very well: *The band is really cooking tonight.*

cooking ap·ple /'.. ,../ n. [C] a type of apple used in cooking that is not very sweet —compare EATING APPLE

cooking oil /'.. ,./ n. [U] oil from plants, such as SUNFLOWERS or OLIVES

cook·out /'kʊk-aʊt/ n. [C] a party or occasion when a meal is cooked and eaten outdoors: *We're having a cookout on Memorial Day.* —compare BARBECUE¹ (2)

cook·ware /'kʊk wɛr/ n. [U] containers and equipment used for cooking: *ceramic cookware*

cool¹ /kul/ adj.

1 ⟨temperature⟩ low in temperature, but not cold, often in a way that feels nice: *Store the seeds in a cool, dry place.* | *It was a lot cooler and windier than earlier in the week.* | *When cool enough to handle, peel the eggs carefully.* —see COLD¹

2 ⟨approval⟩ INFORMAL said to show approval, especially of someone or something that is fashionable, interesting, attractive, or relaxed: *Madison is a really cool name for a girl.* | *Oh, look at you, you look so cool.* | *These are the coolest shoes.* | *This is really a cool book they've put together.* | *"Did you meet Nancy?" "Yeah, she's pretty cool."* | *I love these things. They are so cool.* | *Oh, look at all the kites, that's so cool.* | *"At the end they opened the cages and let all the doves fly out." "Cool."* | *I really liked her. I thought she was way cool* (=very cool).

3 ⟨agreement⟩ SPOKEN said to show that you agree with something, that you understand it, or that it does not annoy you: *"Okay, that'll do it, all done." "Cool."* | *Pizza, yeah, that would be cool* (=that is a good idea). | *Lisa wants to come, she seems pretty nice, so I said okay, that's cool.* | *"Sorry, I have to go." "It's okay, it's cool."* (=it does not upset me) | *Would Friday be cool with you guys?*

4 ⟨calm⟩ calm and not nervous, upset or excited: *She felt cool and in control until they called out her name.* | **stay/keep cool** *It can be hard to stay cool while listening to angry complaints.* | **Cooler heads prevailed**, *and the fight broke up before it started* (=calm people were able to persuade angry people not to fight). | *The witness seemed **cool, calm and collected**.* | *He's one **cool customer*** (=always behaves calmly).

5 ⟨not friendly⟩ behaving in a way that is not as friendly or interested as you expect: *Her gaze was decidedly cool.* | *[+ toward] Foley was cool toward the idea.* | *The proposal got a **cool reception** in Congress.*

6 ⟨color⟩ a cool color is one that is blue or has blue in it

7 a cool million/$200,000 etc. INFORMAL a surprisingly large amount of money that someone easily pays, earns etc.: *His new house cost a cool million.* —**coolness** n. [U] —**coolly** adv.

cool² v. **1** [I,T] also **cool down** to make something slightly colder or to become slightly colder: *Cool the cookies before storing them in an airtight container.* | *a drink that will cool you down on a hot summer day* **2** [I] if a feeling, emotion, or relationship cools, it becomes less strong: *Interest in the toys is finally cooling.* **3 cool it** SPOKEN **a)** to stop putting as much effort into something, or pressure on someone as you have been: *We already know who won, so cool it with the promos.* **b)** used to tell someone to stop being angry, violent etc.: *Cool it, guys. Just play the game.* **4 cool your heels** to be forced to wait: *I had to cool my heels in a long line at the checkout.*

cool down phr. v. [I] to become calm after being angry: *You need to give him some time to cool down.*

cool off phr. v. [I] **1** to return to a normal temperature after being hot: *The fans don't help at all – it doesn't cool off at night.* | *Your body sweats to cool off.* **2** to become calm after being angry: *I stayed in a motel for a few days until he'd cooled off.* **3** if sales, prices etc. cool off, they decrease

cool³ n. **1 keep your cool** to remain calm in a frightening or difficult situation: *The waitress was really busy, but she kept her cool.* **2 lose your cool** to stop being calm in a frightening or difficult situation: *Sam was a real gentleman who never lost his cool.* **3 the cool** a temperature that is pleasantly cold: *[+ of] Sweet peas grow best when planted in the cool of early spring.*

cool⁴ adv. **play it cool** to behave in a calm way because you do not want someone to know that you are really nervous, angry etc.: *Traci insists that she is going to play it cool with Brad.*

cool·ant /'kulənt/ n. [C,U] TECHNICAL a liquid or gas used to cool something, especially an engine —see picture at ENGINE

cool·er /'kulər/ n. [C] **1** a container in which you can keep food or drinks cold, especially so that you can keep them cold outdoors: *a cooler full of beer and soft drinks* **2** a WATER COOLER **3 the cooler** SLANG prison **4** an AIR CONDITIONER, especially one that only cools one room —see also WINE COOLER (1)

cool-head·ed /'. ,../ adj. not easily excited or upset: *Garnett is considered a cool-headed, professional manager.*

Coo·lidge /'kulɪdʒ/, **Calvin** (1872–1933) the 30th President of the U.S. and Vice President under Warren Harding

coo·lie /'kuli/ n. [C] OLD-FASHIONED an unskilled worker who is paid very little money, especially in parts of Asia

cooling-off pe·ri·od /,.. '. ,.../ n. [C] **1** a period of time when two people or groups who are arguing about something can go away and think about how to improve the situation: *The governor hoped a 60-day cooling-off period would avoid a strike.* **2** a period of time that you must wait after you have bought a gun, before you can receive the gun from the store: *A 28-day cooling-off period after buying a gun is required by law.*

cooling sys·tem /'.. ,../ n. [C] a system for keeping the temperature in a machine, engine etc. low: *the car's cooling system*

cooling tow·er /'.. ,../ n. [C] a large, round, tall building, used in industry for making water cool

coon /kun/ n. [C] **1** INFORMAL a RACCOON **2** TABOO an African-American. Do not use this word. **3 in a coon's age** INFORMAL in a long time

coon·skin /'kun,skɪn/ adj. made from the skin of a RACCOON: *a coonskin cap like Davy Crockett's*

co-op /'koʊap/ n. [C] a COOPERATIVE²

coop¹ /kup/ n. [C] a building for small animals, especially chickens —see also **fly the coop** (FLY¹ (22))

coop² v.

coop sb/sth **up** phr. v. [T usually passive] to make someone stay indoors, or in a small space: *[+ in] We spent half our vacation cooped up in a car.*

coo·per /'kupɚ/ *n.* [C] someone who makes BARRELS

Coo·per /'kupɚ/, **James Fen·i·more** /dʒeɪmz 'fɛnɪˌmɔr/ (1789–1851) a U.S. writer of novels about Native Americans and life on the American FRONTIER

co·op·er·ate /koʊ'ɑpəˌreɪt/ *v.* [I] **1** to work with someone else to achieve something that you both want: *The administration is willing to cooperate and work toward peace.* | [+ **with**] *Our company cooperates with environmental groups to encourage recycling.* | [+ **in**] *Unfortunately, Nixon and his family did not cooperate in the making of the film.* | [**cooperate to do sth**] *They're cooperating to achieve common goals.* | *The two countries will do their best to cooperate closely.* **2** to do what someone wants you to do: *We'll be all right if the weather cooperates* (=if the weather remains good). | [+ **with**] *Robbins will cooperate with an investigation into the fraud.*

co·op·er·a·tion /koʊˌɑpə'reɪʃən/ *n.* [U] **1** the act of working with someone else to achieve something that you both want: [+ **between**] *The Church has a duty to promote cooperation between Christians and Jews.* | *The documentary was produced in cooperation with KBC of Australia.* **2** willingness to work with other people, or to do what they ask you to do: *Thank you for your cooperation and your participation.* | **full/complete cooperation** *Paz promised full cooperation in anti-drug efforts.*

co·op·er·a·tive[1] /koʊ'ɑprətɪv/ *adj.* **1** willing to cooperate; HELPFUL: *a cooperative witness* | *A cooperative waiter helped us to order from the huge menu.* **2** made, done or owned by people working together: *Car companies have started several cooperative ventures.*

cooperative[2] also **co-op** *n.* [C] **1** an organization such as a company or factory in which all the people who work there own an equal share of it: *a potato farm cooperative in Pennsylvania* **2 a)** a building owned by a company that sells SHARES in it to people who can then live in one of the building's apartments: *a Park Avenue co-op* **b)** an apartment in this building —compare CONDOMINIUM

co-opt /koʊ'ɑpt/ *v.* [T] DISAPPROVING to use something that was not originally yours to help you do something, or to persuade someone to help you: *Mr. Bloom tried to co-opt her by offering her a better contract.* | *Most designers do nothing more than co-opt street fashion.*

co·or·di·nate[1] /koʊ'ɔrdnˌeɪt/ *v.* **1** [T] to organize people or things so that they work together well or succeed: *The Red Cross is coordinating relief aid to the refugees.* **2** [T] to make the parts of your body move and work together well: *Her movements on the balance beam were perfectly coordinated.* **3** [I] if clothes, decorations etc. coordinate, they look good together because they have similar colors and styles: *This wallpaper coordinates with the floral pattern on the bedspread.*

co·or·di·nate[2] /koʊ'ɔrdn-ɪt/ *n.* TECHNICAL **1** [C] one of a set of numbers which give the exact position of a point on a map, computer screen etc.: *The teacher gave the children coordinates to locate on the globe.* **2 coordinates** [plural] things such as women's clothes that can be worn or used together because their colors match or their styles are similar: *Have you seen our coordinates collection for spring?*

coordinate[3] *adj.* TECHNICAL **1** equal in importance or rank: *The coordinate clauses in this sentence are joined by "and."* —compare SUBORDINATE[2] **2** involving the use of coordinates

coordinating con·junc·tion /ˌ.ˌ......'.ˌ./ *n.* [C] a word such as "and" or "but," which joins two clauses of the same type

co·or·di·na·tion /koʊˌɔrdn'eɪʃən/ *n.* [U] **1** the way in which your muscles move together when you perform a movement: *Sam's coordination is still not a hundred percent after the accident.* | *It takes a lot of practice and good hand-eye coordination* (=the way your hands and eyes work together) *to play marbles.* **2** the organization of people or things so that they

work together well: *Sue will be responsible for the coordination of sales and marketing activities.*

co·or·di·na·tor /koʊ'ɔrdnˌeɪtɚ/ *n.* [C] someone who organizes the way people work together in a particular activity: *This is Ms. Darnell, the hospital's nursing coordinator.*

coot /kut/ *n.* [C] **1** a small black and white water bird with a short beak **2 old coot** INFORMAL an old man who you think is strange or mean: *He's a crazy old coot.*

coo·ties /'kutiz/ *n.* [plural] SPOKEN a word meaning lice (LOUSE[1] (1)), used by children as an insult when they do not want to play with or sit with another child: *I don't want to go with him – boys have cooties.*

cop[1] /kɑp/ *n.* [C] INFORMAL a police officer: *a motorcycle cop* | *There are more criminals out there than cops to chase them.*

cop[2] *v.* **copped, copping** [T] SPOKEN **1 cop a plea** to agree to say you are guilty of a crime in order to receive a less severe punishment: *Duckett copped a plea to avoid going to jail.* **2** to get or take something, often when it surprises people that you get it: *Linda Vernon copped the grand prize this year with her new novel.* **3 cop an attitude** to behave in a way that is not nice, especially by showing that you think you are better or more intelligent than other people **4 cop a buzz** to feel the effects of taking drugs or drinking alcohol **5 cop a feel** to touch someone in a sexual way when they do not want you to

cop out *phr. v.* [I] SLANG to not do something that you are supposed to do: *You're copping out by not apologizing to your husband.* —see also COP-OUT

co·pa·cet·ic /ˌkoʊpə'sɛtɪk/ *adj.* OLD-FASHIONED, SLANG excellent

cope[1] /koʊp/ *v.* [I] **1** to succeed in dealing with a difficult problem or job: [+ **with**] *Women must cope with working and taking care of the household and the family.* **2** to accept and deal with a particular situation: *The family is coping as best as possible following the mother's disappearance.* | *He's doing an experiment to see how frogs cope in a gravity-free environment.* **3** if a machine or system copes with a particular type or amount of work, it does it: *The automatic sorting machines cannot always cope with colored envelopes.*

cope[2] *n.* [C] a long loose piece of clothing worn by priests on special occasions

Co·pen·ha·gen /'koʊpənˌheɪgən, -ˌhɑ-/ the capital and largest city of Denmark

Co·per·ni·cus /kə'pɝnɪkəs, koʊ-/, **Nich·o·las** /'nɪkələs/ (1473–1543) a Polish ASTRONOMER who was the first person to suggest the idea that the Earth and the other PLANETS all travel in circles around the sun —**Copernican** *adj.*

cop·i·er /'kɑpiɚ/ *n.* [C] a machine that quickly copies documents onto paper by photographing them; PHOTOCOPIER

co·pi·lot /'koʊˌpaɪlət/ *n.* [C] a pilot who helps the main pilot fly an airplane

cop·ing /'koʊpɪŋ/ *n.* [C,U] a layer of rounded stones or bricks at the top of a wall or roof

co·pi·ous /'koʊpiəs/ *adj.* existing or being produced in large quantities: *Officer Gomez took copious notes.* —**copiously** *adv.*: *She wept copiously.*

Cop·land /'koʊplənd/, **Aaron** (1900–1990) a U.S. musician who wrote modern CLASSICAL music

cop-out /'. ./ *n.* [C] SLANG something you do or say in order to avoid doing or accepting something: *Putting the blame on your parents for your problems is a cop-out.*

cop·per /'kɑpɚ/ *n.* **1** [U] *symbol* **Cu** a reddish-brown metal that is an ELEMENT and is used for making wire, pipes etc. **2** [U] a reddish-brown color: *copper lipstick* **3** [C] OLD-FASHIONED a coin of low value made of copper or BRONZE

copper beech /ˌ.. './ *n.* [C] a large tree with purple-brown leaves

cop·per·head /'kɑpɚˌhɛd/ *n.* [C] a poisonous yellow and brown North American snake

copse /kɑps/ also **cop·pice** /ˈkɑpɪs/ n. [C] a group of trees or bushes growing close together: [+ of] *a copse of pine trees*

cop shop /ˈ. ./ n. [C] INFORMAL a POLICE STATION

cop·ter /ˈkɑptə/ n. [C] INFORMAL a HELICOPTER

cop·u·la /ˈkɑpyələ/ n. [C] TECHNICAL a type of verb that connects the subject of a sentence to its COMPLEMENT[1] (3); LINKING VERB. For example, in the sentence "The house seems big," "seems" is the copula.

cop·u·late /ˈkɑpyəˌleɪt/ v. [I] TECHNICAL to have sex —**copulation** /ˌkɑpyəˈleɪʃən/ n. [U]

cop·u·la·tive /ˈkɑpyələtɪv, -ˌleɪt̬ɪv/ n. [C] TECHNICAL a word or word group that connects other word groups —**copulative** adj.

copy out

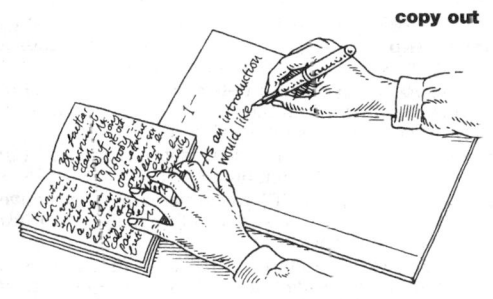

cop·y¹ /ˈkɑpi/ n. plural **copies 1** [C] something that is made to be exactly like another thing: *The application was sent in June, and this is a copy.* | [+ of] *The chair is a copy of a Mies van der Rohe design.* | *Make a copy of the check for your records.* **2** [C] one of many books, magazines, records etc. that are all exactly the same: *For a free copy, call 555-9121.* | [+ of] *an illegal copy of the software program* | *More than 85,000 copies of the magazine sold within three weeks.* **3** [U] TECHNICAL something written in order to be printed in a newspaper, magazine, advertisement etc.: *All copy must be on my desk by Monday morning.* **4 make good copy** INFORMAL to be an interesting piece of writing: *His flamboyant style always makes good copy.* **5** one of many GENES that are all exactly the same in each CHROMOSOME —see also HARD COPY

copy² v. **copies, copied, copying 1** [T] to make something exactly like another thing: *Copy the file onto a disk to save it.* | *Can you get the letter copied right away? I need 500 of them.* **2** [T] to do something that someone else has done, or to behave like someone else: *He began playing the guitar at age 7, copying his older brother Jimmie.* **3** [I,T] to cheat on a test, school work etc. by looking at someone else's work and writing the same thing that they have: *Several honors students were caught copying each other's answers.*

copy sb **in** phr. v. [T] to send someone a copy of an EMAIL message you are sending to someone else: [+ on] *Can you copy me in on the memo you're sending to Chris?*

cop·y·cat /ˈkɑpiˌkæt/ n. [C] **1** INFORMAL a word used by children to criticize someone who copies other people's clothes, behavior, work etc. **2 a copycat crime/killing etc.** a crime, murder etc. that is similar to a famous crime done by another person: *A highly publicized trial might encourage copycat killings.*

copy ed·i·tor /ˈ. ˌ. ./ n. [C] someone whose job is to be sure that the words in a book, newspaper etc. are correct and ready to be printed —**copy-edit** v. [I,T]

cop·y·ist /ˈkɑpiɪst/ n. [C] someone who made written copies of documents, books etc. in past times

copy ma·chine /ˈ. ˌ. ./ n. [C] a COPIER

cop·y·right /ˈkɑpiˌraɪt/ n. [C,U] the legal right to be the only maker or seller of a book, play, movie, or record for a specific length of time: *Mitchell's family owns the copyrights to her book.* | *a violation of copyright laws* —**copyright** adj. —**copyright** v. [T]

cop·y·writ·er /ˈkɑpiˌraɪt̬ə/ n. [C] someone who writes the words for advertisements

coq au vin /ˌkouk ou ˈvæn, ˌkɑk-/ n. [U] a dish of chicken cooked in red wine

co·quet·ry /ˈkoukətri, kouˈkɛtri/ n. [C,U] LITERARY behavior that is typical of a coquette: *Claudio was easily caught in her web of coquetry and lies.*

co·quette /kouˈkɛt/ n. [C] LITERARY a woman who tries to attract the attention of men without having sincere feelings for them; FLIRT[2] —**coquettish** adj. —**coquettishly** adv.

cor- /kə, kɔr, kɑr/ prefix used instead of CON- before the letter "r"; with: *to correlate* (=connect ideas together)

cor·a·cle /ˈkɔrəkəl, ˈkɑr-/ n. [C] a small round boat that you move with a PADDLE

cor·al¹ /ˈkɔrəl, ˈkɑrəl/ n. [U] a hard red, white, or pink substance formed from the bones of very small ocean creatures that live in warm water, that is often used to make jewelry: *a coral necklace*

coral² adj. pink or reddish orange in color: *The skirt was coral chiffon with a black velvet top.*

coral reef /ˌ.. ˈ./ n. [C] a line of hard rocks formed by coral, found in warm ocean water that is not very deep

Cor·bett /ˈkɔrbɪt/, **James (Gentleman Jim)** (1866–1933) a U.S. BOXER who was world CHAMPION from 1892 to 1897

cord /kɔrd/ n. **1** [C,U] an electrical wire or wires with a protective covering, usually for connecting electrical equipment to the supply of electricity: *The phone cord is all tangled.* | *I'll need an extension cord for the Christmas tree lights.* —see picture at PLUG² **2 cords** [plural] INFORMAL pants made from CORDUROY **3** [C,U] a piece of thick string or thin rope: *Her glasses hung around her neck on a silky cord.* **4** [C] a specific quantity of wood cut for burning in a fire: *Three cords of wood should last us all winter.* —see also CORDLESS, **cut the cord** (CUT¹ (35)), SPINAL CORD, UMBILICAL CORD, VOCAL CORDS

USAGE NOTE: CORD

SPELLING: cord, chord
These two words are pronounced the same way but they have different meanings. Use **cord** to talk about the electrical wire for connecting electrical equipment, such as televisions and telephones: *Have you seen the black cord for the TV?* **Cord** is also used to talk about a thick string or thin rope: *The cords for the blinds are all tangled.* **Chord** is used to talk about a combination of musical notes that are played at the same time: *How can you be in a band if you can only play one chord?*

cord·age /ˈkɔrdɪdʒ/ n. [U] rope or cord in general, especially on a ship

cor·dial¹ /ˈkɔrdʒəl/ n. [C, U] a strong sweet alcoholic drink; LIQUEUR: *We were offered an after-dinner cordial.*

cordial² adj. friendly, but formal and polite: *I received a cordial note from Mrs. Thomas thanking me for the present.* —**cordiality** /ˌkɔrdʒiˈæləti/ n. [U]

cor·dial·ly /ˈkɔrdʒəli/ adv. in a friendly but polite and formal way: *You are cordially invited to our wedding on May 9.*

cord·ite /ˈkɔrdaɪt/ n. [U] a smokeless explosive used in bullets and bombs

cord·less /ˈkɔrdlɪs/ adj. a piece of equipment that is cordless is not connected to its power supply by wires: *a cordless phone*

cor·don¹ /ˈkɔrdn/ n. [C] a line of police officers, soldiers or vehicles put around an area to stop people going there: *Rock-throwing protesters broke through the police cordon.*

cordon² v.

cordon sth ↔ **off** phr. v. [T] to surround and protect an area with police officers, soldiers, or vehicles: *Police cordoned off the area.*

cor·don bleu /ˌkɔrdoun ˈbluː, -dɑn-/ adj. [only before noun] relating to cooking of very high quality: *She* *attended the Cordon Bleu cooking school in Paris.* | *a cordon bleu chef*

cor·du·roy /ˈkɔrdəˌrɔɪ/ *n.* **1** [U] a thick strong cotton cloth with raised lines on it, used for making clothes: *a corduroy jacket* **2 corduroys** [plural] INFORMAL a pair of corduroy pants

S W
2
3

core¹ /kɔr/ *n.* [C]

1 fruit the hard central part of fruit such as an apple: *Remove the cores, fill with raisins and cinnamon, and bake the apples for 40 minutes.*

2 central part the most important or central part of something: [+ of] *This dish is the core of a traditional Portuguese Christmas dinner.* | *Math, science English, and history form the core of a high school education.*

3 people a number of people who form a strong group which is very important to an organization: *MTV's core audience is 18- to 24-year-olds.* | [+ of] *a core of dedicated volunteers*

4 core values/beliefs/concerns etc. the values, beliefs etc. that are most important to someone: *the core values of a large company*

5 to the core in a way that affects all of your feelings or your character, or all of something: *He's a military man to the core.* | *The financial system is rotten to the core* (=very bad).

6 planets the central part of the Earth or any other PLANET

7 nuclear reactor the central part of a NUCLEAR REACTOR: *Operator errors allowed the radioactive core to overheat.* —see also HARDCORE

core² *v.* [T] to take the center from a piece of fruit: *Core the apple and cut into ¼-inch slices.*

core cur·ric·u·lum /ˌ. .ˈ.../ *n.* [U] the basic subjects that someone must study in school

cor·er /ˈkɔrə/ *n.* [C] a specially shaped knife for taking the hard centers out of fruit

core time /ˈ. ./ *n.* [U] the period during the middle part of the day when a company or other place of work that has FLEXTIME expects all its people to be working

cor·gi /ˈkɔrgi/ *n. plural* **corgis** [C] a small dog with short legs and a pointed nose

co·ri·an·der /ˈkɔriˌændə/ *n.* [U] a plant used to give a special taste to food, especially in Asian and Mexican cooking; CILANTRO

Co·rin·thi·an /kəˈrɪnθiən/ *adj.* of a style of Greek ARCHITECTURE that uses decorations of leaves cut into stone: *a Corinthian column*

Co·rin·thi·ans /kəˈrɪnθiənz/ **1 Corinthians, 2 Corinthians** two books in the New Testament of the Christian Bible

cork¹ /kɔrk/ *n.* **1** [U] the BARK (=outer part) of a tree from southern Europe and North Africa, used to make things: *a cork bulletin board* **2** [C] a long round piece of cork that is put into the top of a bottle, especially a wine bottle, to keep liquid inside: *Announcement of the awards set champagne corks popping* (=people opened bottles to celebrate the awards).

cork² *v.* [T] to close a bottle by blocking the hole at the top tightly with a long, round piece of cork —opposite UNCORK

cork·age /ˈkɔrkɪdʒ/ *n.* [U] the charge made by a hotel or restaurant for allowing people to drink alcoholic drinks which they bought somewhere else: *The restaurant doesn't have a corkage fee.*

corked /kɔrkt/ *adj.* corked wine tastes bad because a decaying cork has allowed air into the bottle

cork·screw¹ /ˈkɔrkskru/ *n.* [C] a tool made of twisted metal that you use to pull a CORK out of a bottle

corkscrew² *adj.* [only before noun] twisted or curly; SPIRAL: *corkscrew curls* | *corkscrew pasta*

cor·mo·rant /ˈkɔrmərənt, -ˌrænt/ *n.* [C] a large black sea bird that has a long neck and eats fish

S W
2

corn /kɔrn/ *n.* **1** [U] a tall plant with large yellow or white seeds that grow together on a COB (=long hard

part), which are cooked and eaten as a vegetable or fed to animals: *The chickens are raised on a diet of corn and other grains.* | *an ear of corn* (=the top part of the plant where the yellow seeds grow) *Do you want corn on the cob* (=an ear of corn) *or green beans?* —see also INDIAN CORN —see picture at VEGETABLE **2** [C] a painful area of thick hard skin on your foot **3** [U] INFORMAL things such as songs, jokes, movies etc. which are old-fashioned, SENTIMENTAL, or silly

corn·ball /ˈkɔrnbɔl/ *adj.* [only before noun] INFORMAL cornball humor is too simple, old-fashioned, unoriginal, and silly: *Country and western songs always have such cornball titles.*

Corn belt /ˈ. ./ *n.* **the Corn Belt** the MIDWESTern part of the U.S., where there are a lot of farms

corn bread /ˈ. ./ *n.* [U] bread made from CORNMEAL

corn chip /ˈ. ./ *n.* [C] crushed corn formed into a small flat shape, cooked in oil and eaten cold

corn·cob /ˈkɔrnkɑb/ also **cob** *n.* [C] the hard part of a corn plant on which the yellow seeds grow: *a corncob pipe* (=made from a dried corncob)

corn dog /ˈ. ./ *n.* [C] a WIENER that is fried (FRY¹ (1)) in CORN BREAD and eaten on a stick

cor·ne·a /ˈkɔrniə/ *n.* [C] the transparent protective covering on the outer surface of your eye: *a cornea transplant* —**corneal** *adj.*

corned beef /ˌkɔrnˈbif/ *n.* [U] BEEF that has been covered in salt water and SPICES to preserve it: *a corned beef sandwich*

Cor·neille /kɔrˈneɪ/, **Pierre** /pyɛr/ (1606–1684) a French writer of plays

Cor·nell /kɔrˈnɛl/, **Ez·ra** /ˈɛzrə/ (1807–1874) a U.S. businessman who developed TELEGRAPH systems in the U.S. and started Cornell University

cor·ner¹ /ˈkɔrnə/ *n.*

S W
1
2

1 where two lines/edges meet [C] the point at which two lines, surfaces, or edges meet: *She picked the tablecloth up by the corners and folded it neatly.* | [+ of] *Gold tassels were sewn to the corners of the pillows.* | *The station's logo appears in the corner of the TV screen.* | *Jessie Olsen sat on the corner of her bed.*

2 streets the point where two streets, roads, or paths meet: [+ of] *The hotel is on the corner of Thornton and Sycamore.* | *Several women were standing at the corner, talking to two men.* | *The Greyhound depot consists of two worn chairs at the corner gas station* (=on the corner). | *Marnie's apartment is just around the corner from here.* | *The driver took the corner* (=went around it) *way too fast.*

3 corner of a room/box [C often singular] the place inside a room or box where two walls or sides meet: *A Christmas tree stood in the corner of the living room.*

4 mouth [C] the corners of your mouth are the sides of your mouth: *You have some mustard on the left corner of your mouth.*

5 distant place [C] a distant place in another part of the world: [+ of] *He sent a postcard from some remote corner of South Dakota.* | *the far/four corners of the world/earth/globe Spaniards traveled to the far corners of the globe in search of new lands.*

6 difficult situation [singular] a situation that is difficult to escape from: **back/force sb into a corner** *Interest payments and debts have backed the company into a corner.* | *With funding being cut, Pusani's program is in a tight corner.*

7 (just) around the corner likely to happen soon: *Economic recovery is just around the corner.*

8 see sth out of the corner of your eye to notice something by chance, without turning your head toward it or looking for it: *Out of the corner of her eye, she saw a man running out of the store.*

9 cut corners to do things too quickly, and not as carefully as you should, especially to save money or time: *The agency accused the airline of cutting corners on safety.*

10 sports [C] **a)** a kick in SOCCER that one team is allowed to take from one of the corners of their opponent's end of the field **b)** any of the four corners of the area in which the competitors fight in BOXING or WRESTLING

11 have a corner on sth to control, have more of, or be better at something than anyone else: *We like to brag about our system, but we no longer have a corner on knowledge or technology.* | *The company has a corner on the soybean market* (=controls the supply of the product).

12 cut a corner to go across the corner of something, especially a road, instead of keeping to the edges: *If we cut the corner too tight, the trailer will hit the fence.* —see also KITTY-CORNER

cor·ner² *v.* **1** [T] to force a person or animal into a position from which they cannot easily escape: *Hill cornered her at a party just before she left Washington.* **2 corner the market** to gain control of the whole supply of a particular kind of goods: *The company has cornered 98% of the fried chicken market.* **3** [I] if a car corners, it goes around a corner or curve in the road: *The new Audis corner very well.*

cor·ner·stone /'kɔrnəˌstoʊn/ *n.* [C] **1** something that is extremely important because everything else depends on it: [+ of] *The magazine became the cornerstone of MacFadden's publishing empire.* **2** a stone set at one of the bottom corners of a building, often put in place at a special ceremony: *The cornerstone was laid in 1848.* —compare FOUNDATION STONE

cor·net /kɔr'nɛt/ *n.* [C] a musical instrument like a small TRUMPET: *Dan played the cornet in the school band.*

corn-fed /'. ./ *adj.* used to talk about someone from the central part of the U.S. in order to say that they are big and strong with good moral values, but they do not know a lot about the world: *a corn-fed Kansas doctor*

corn·flakes /'kɔrnfleɪks/ *n.* [plural] small flat pieces of crushed corn, usually eaten for breakfast with milk

corn·flow·er /'kɔrnflaʊə/ *n.* [C] a wild plant with blue flowers

cor·nice /'kɔrnɪs/ *n.* [C] a decorative piece of wood or PLASTER along the top edge of a wall or door used for decoration: *A carved cornice ran around the high-ceilinged room.*

cor·niche /kɔr'niʃ/ *n.* [C] a road built along a coast: *The luxury hotel is located on a corniche by the Nile.*

corn liq·uor /'. ˌ../ *n.* [U] CORN WHISKEY

corn·meal /'kɔrnmil/ *n.* [U] a rough type of flour made from crushed dried corn: *In a large bowl, blend the cornmeal, flour, baking soda, and salt.*

corn on the cob /ˌ. . . './ *n.* [U] the top part of a corn plant, cooked and as a vegetable

corn pone /'kɔrnpoʊn/ *n.* [U] a type of bread made from cornmeal, made especially in the southern U.S.

corn-pone /'. ./ *adj.* silly and funny in a CORNY way: *Ford would sing and tell corn-pone jokes about growing up in Tennessee.*

corn·row /'kɔrnroʊ/ *n.* [C usually plural] a way of arranging hair in which it is put into small tight BRAIDS along the head

corn·starch /'kɔrnstɑrtʃ/ *n.* [U] a fine white flour made from corn, used in cooking to make soups, SAUCES etc. thicker

corn syr·up /'. ˌ../ *n.* [U] a very sweet thick liquid made from corn, used in cooking: *Combine the cream and corn syrup in a saucepan and bring to a boil.*

cor·nu·co·pi·a /ˌkɔrnə'koʊpiə/ *n.* **1** [C] a container in the shape of an animal's horn, full of fruit and flowers, used to represent ABUNDANCE (=a lot of food, good things etc.) **2** [singular] a lot of something: [+ of] *a cornucopia of talent*

corn whis·key also **corn liq·uor** /ˌ. '.., '. ˌ../ *n.* [U] a strong alcoholic drink made from corn

corn·y /'kɔrni/ *adj.* **cornier, corniest** INFORMAL old-fashioned, SENTIMENTAL, unoriginal, and silly: *a corny Hollywood romance* | *It may sound corny, but I enjoy helping people.* —**cornily** *adv.* —**corniness** *n.* [U]

cor·ol·lar·y /'kɔrəˌlɛri, 'kɑr-/ *n. plural* **corollaries** [C] FORMAL something that is the direct result of

something else: *Surprisingly, environmental improvement has been a corollary to economic growth.*

co·ro·na /kə'roʊnə/ *n.* [C] the shining circle of light seen around the sun when the moon passes in front of it in an ECLIPSE

Co·ro·na·do /ˌkɔrə'nɑdoʊ/, **Fran·cis·co de** /fran'siskoʊ deɪ/ (1510–1554) a Spanish EXPLORER who traveled in Arizona and New Mexico

cor·o·na·ry¹ /'kɔrəˌnɛri/ *adj.* relating to the heart: *coronary disease*

coronary² *n. plural* **coronaries** [C] a HEART ATTACK

cor·o·na·tion /ˌkɔrə'neɪʃən, ˌkɑr-/ *n.* [C] the ceremony at which someone is officially made king or queen

cor·o·ner /'kɔrənə/ *n.* [C] an official whose job is to discover the cause of someone's death, especially if they died in a sudden or unusual way: *The cause of death was listed by the coroner's office as a drowning.*

cor·o·net /ˌkɔrə'nɛt, ˌkɑr-/ *n.* [C] **1** a small CROWN worn by princes or other members of a royal family, especially on formal occasions **2** anything that you wear on your head that looks like a CROWN: *a coronet of flowers*

Corp. /kɔrp, kɔr/ **1** the abbreviation of CORPORATION: *Toyota Motors Corp.* **2** the abbreviation of CORPORAL¹

cor·po·ra /'kɔrpərə/ *n.* the plural of CORPUS

cor·po·ral¹ /'kɔrpərəl/ *n.* [C] a low rank in the Army or Marines: *a corporal in the 9th Virginia Regiment*

corporal² *adj.* FORMAL relating to the body: *corporal injury*

corporal pun·ish·ment /ˌ... '... ../ *n.* [U] a way of officially punishing someone by hitting them, especially in schools and prisons: *In 1987, California prohibited corporal punishment in schools.*

cor·po·rate /'kɔrpərɪt/ *adj.* [only before noun] **1** belonging or relating to a corporation: *The company's moving its corporate headquarters* (=main offices) *from St. Louis to Atlanta.* | *Vince is vice-president of corporate communications.* **2** shared by or involving all the members of a group: *corporate responsibility* | *a huge corporate farm* **3 corporate hospitality** the things companies do to entertain their customers, in order to gain business **4 corporate tax** another word for corporation tax (CORPORATION (2)) —**corporately** *adv.*

corporate raid·er /ˌ... '.. ../ *n.* [C] a person or an organization that tries to gain control of another company by buying most of that company's SHARES

cor·po·ra·tion /ˌkɔrpə'reɪʃən/ *n.* [C] **1** a big company, or a group of companies acting together as a single organization: *She's just been appointed chief financial officer of a major corporation.* | *a multinational corporation* **2 corporation tax** a tax paid by companies on their profits

cor·po·re·al /kɔr'pɔriəl/ *adj.* FORMAL **1** relating to the body as opposed to the mind, feelings, or spirit **2** able to be touched: *Ideas are presented as tangible and corporeal in the form of hands-on exhibits.*

corps /kɔr/ *n. plural* **corps** /kɔrz/ [C usually singular] **1** a group in an army with special duties: *the Navy medical corps* **2** TECHNICAL a trained army unit made of two or more DIVISIONS (=group of soldiers) **3** a group of people who work together to do a particular job: *the president's press corps* | *a ballet corps*

corpse /kɔrps/ *n.* [C] the dead body of a person

corps·man /'kɔrzmən/ *n. plural* **corpsmen** /-mən/ [C] someone in the Army who is trained to give medical treatment to soldiers who are hurt

cor·pu·lent /'kɔrpyələnt/ *adj.* FORMAL very fat and large —**corpulence** *n.* [U]

cor·pus /'kɔrpəs/ *n. plural* **corpora** /-pərə/ or **corpuses** [C] **1** FORMAL a collection of all the writing of a particular kind or by a particular person: *They aim to study the entire corpus of Shakespeare's works.* **2** TECHNICAL a collection of information or material to be studied: *a corpus of spoken English* —see also HABEAS CORPUS

cor·pus·cle /ˈkɔrˌpʌsəl/ n. [C] one of the red or white cells in the blood

cor·ral[1] /kəˈræl/ n. [C] a fairly small enclosed area where cattle, horses etc. are kept: *We stood around the corral watching a cowboy saddle the horse.*

corral[2] v. **corrals, corralled, corralling** [T] **1** to make animals move into a corral: *They corralled the cattle before loading them onto the truck.* **2** to make people move into a particular area, especially to control them or in order to talk to them: *Lewis couldn't be corralled for an interview.* | *Keep the kids corralled safely in the backyard.*

cor·rect[1] /kəˈrɛkt/ adj. **1** without any mistakes; RIGHT: *Score one point for each correct answer.* | *If predictions are correct, the sea level may increase more than four inches.* | *an architecturally correct model of the building* (=that is just like the original) **2** appropriate and right for a particular situation: *We are convinced our decision was correct.* | *When the heat is at the correct temperature, food cooks more evenly.* | [+ to] *I felt it was correct to keep the information private in order to protect everyone.* —see also POLITICALLY CORRECT **3** correct behavior is formal and polite: *What is the correct way to address a wedding invitation?* —**correctly** adv. —**correctness** n. [U] —opposite INCORRECT

correct[2] v. [T] **1** to make something better or make it work the way it should: *The problem was caused by faulty software and was corrected Sunday.* | *Speech therapy helped correct her lisp.* **2** to show someone that something is wrong, and make it right: *The figure was given as $500; it was later corrected to $1000.* | [correct sb] *Hilda corrected her very sharply.* **3** to make marks on a piece of work to show the mistakes in it: *She spent all night correcting her students' math tests.* **4 correct me if I'm wrong** SPOKEN used when you are not sure that what you are going to say is true or not: *Correct me if I'm wrong, but didn't you say you'd never met him before?* **5 I stand corrected** FORMAL, SPOKEN used to admit that something you have said is wrong after someone has told you it is wrong: *"It's a moose, not an elephant, Dad!" "Well, I stand corrected."*

cor·rec·tion /kəˈrɛkʃən/ n. **1** [C] a change made in something in order to make it right or better: *It just needs a few corrections before we can send it to the printer.* | *The mine will be shut until safety corrections are made.* **2** [U] the act of changing something in order to make it right or better: *Please hand in your papers for correction.* **3** [C] SPOKEN used to say that what you have just said is wrong and you want to change it: *That will basically cover fifty... correction eighty percent of all charges.*

correctional fa·cil·i·ty /.ˈ.. ..ˌ.../ n. [C] TECHNICAL OR HUMOROUS a prison

correction flu·id /.ˈ.. ..ˌ../ n. [U] FORMAL a special white liquid used for covering mistakes made when writing or typing (TYPE[2] (1)) something

cor·rec·ti·tude /kəˈrɛktɪˌtud/ n. [U] FORMAL correctness of behavior

cor·rec·tive[1] /kəˈrɛktɪv/ adj. FORMAL intended to make something right or better again: *Doctors performed corrective surgery to restore his sight.* | **corrective actions/measures** *The plan is a good start, but more corrective measures are needed.* —**correctively** adv.

corrective[2] n. [C] FORMAL something that is intended to make something right or better: [+ to] *The biography is a useful corrective to the myths that have grown about the man.*

cor·re·late[1] /ˈkɔrəˌleɪt, ˈkɑr-/ v. [I,T] if two or more facts, ideas etc. correlate, or you correlate them, they are closely related or one causes another: [+ with] *A lack of prenatal care correlates strongly with babies who are born too early.*

cor·re·late[2] /ˈkɔrəlɪt, ˈkɑr-/ n. [C] either of two things that correlate with each other

cor·re·la·tion /ˌkɔrəˈleɪʃən, ˌkɑr-/ n. **1** [C,U] a relationship between two ideas, facts etc., especially when one may be the cause of the other: [+ between] *Researchers have found a high correlation between athletic success and academic achievement* | **a strong/high/direct correlation** *There's a direct correlation between house prices and good schools.* **2** [U] the process of correlating two or more things

cor·rel·a·tive[1] /kəˈrɛlətɪv/ adj. **1** two or more facts, ideas etc. that are correlative are closely related or dependent on each other: *Profits are directly correlative to the popularity of the product.* **2** TECHNICAL two words that are correlative are frequently together but not usually used next to each other. For example, "either" and "or" are correlative conjunctions

correlative[2] n. [C] FORMAL one of two or more facts, ideas etc. that are closely related or that depend on each other

cor·re·spond /ˌkɔrəˈspɑnd, ˌkɑr-/ v. [I] **1** if two things or ideas correspond, the parts or information in one relate to the parts or information in the other: [+ to/with] *"Moderate" air pollution corresponds with a reading of 51–100 on the index.* | *Each colored line on the chart corresponds to the productivity level of each division of the company.* **2** to be very similar or the same as something else: [+ to] *What is happening in California corresponds to what happened in New England in June.* **3** if two people correspond, they write letters to each other: *Flaubert and Sand corresponded for many years.* | [+ with] *He hasn't seen or corresponded with his children in six years.*

cor·re·spond·ence /ˌkɔrəˈspɑndəns, ˌkɑr-/ n. [U] **1** letters exchanged between people, especially official or business letters: *I start my day by reading correspondence and scribbling replies.* **2** the process of sending and receiving letters: *And so began a long correspondence and a friendship with his distant cousin in Paris.* **3** a relationship or connection between two or more ideas or facts: [+ between] *There is a one-to-one correspondence between sound and alphabetical symbol in Spanish.*

correspondence course /.ˈ.. ..ˌ./ n. [C] a course of lessons that students receive by mail and do at home, and then send completed work to their teacher by mail: *a correspondence course in Chinese*

cor·re·spond·ent[1] /ˌkɔrəˈspɑndənt, ˌkɑr-/ n. [C] **1** someone whose job is to report news from a distant area or about a particular subject for a newspaper or for television: *a White House correspondent* | *I was stationed as a foreign correspondent for the New York Times in Warsaw.* **2** someone who writes letters

correspondent[2] adj. FORMAL appropriate for a particular situation: [+ with] *The result was correspondent with the government's intentions.*

cor·re·spond·ing /ˌkɔrəˈspɑndɪŋ, ˌkɑr-/ adj. [only before noun] **1** caused by or dependent on something you have already mentioned: *Rising real estate prices have had a corresponding effect on the area's rents.* **2** having similar qualities or a similar position to something you have already mentioned: *The corresponding chromosome in the other parent was found to be defective.* —**correspondingly** adv.

cor·ri·dor /ˈkɔrədər, -ˌdɔr, ˈkɑr-/ n. [C] **1** a long narrow passage between two rows of rooms: *A corridor led from the old schoolrooms to a modern building.* | *We were led down a long corridor in the airport terminal.* **2** an area of land between two large cities, where a lot of people live: *The Northeast corridor from Washington to Boston is Amtrak's busiest region.* **3** a narrow area of land, within a bigger area, that has particular qualities or features: *This industrial corridor connects Queretaro with Mexico City.* **4 corridors of power** the places where important government decisions are made: *Military strategists plotted war scenarios in their air-conditioned corridors of power.*

cor·rob·o·rate /kəˈrɑbəˌreɪt/ v. [T] FORMAL to provide information that supports or helps to prove someone else's statement, idea etc.: *Her statements were corroborated by the doctor's testimony.* —**corroboration** /kəˌrɑbəˈreɪʃən/ n. [U] —**corroborative** /kəˈrɑbəˌreɪtɪv, -rətɪv/ adj.

cor·rode /kəˈroʊd/ v. [I,T] to destroy something slowly, or to be destroyed slowly, especially by chemicals: *Acid rain has corroded the statue.*

cor·ro·sion /kəˈroʊʒən/ n. [U] **1** the process of something being destroyed slowly especially by chemicals: *If left unchecked, corrosion will eventually weaken the pipeline.* **2** a substance such as RUST (=weak red metal) that is produced by the process of corrosion: *To keep metal garbage cans free from corrosion, coat them lightly with used motor oil.*

cor·ro·sive /kəˈroʊsɪv/ adj. **1** a corrosive substance such as an acid can destroy metal, plastic etc.: *Hydrochloric acid is a colorless, corrosive acid.* **2** gradually making something weaker, and possibly destroying it: *We must fight the corrosive effect of discrimination.*

cor·ru·gat·ed /ˈkɔrəˌgeɪtɪd, ˈkɑr-/ adj. shaped in rows of folds that look like waves, or made like this in order to give something strength: *corrugated cardboard* | *a shack with a corrugated metal roof* —**corrugation** /ˌkɔrəˈgeɪʃən/ n. [C]

cor·rupt /kəˈrʌpt/ adj. **1** using your power in a dishonest or illegal way in order to get an advantage for yourself: *A grand jury accused the police department of being brutal and corrupt.* **2** very bad morally: *Politics has become a corrupt, big-money game.* **3** something that is corrupt is not pure or is not the way it was made or intended to be —**corruptly** adv. —**corruptness** n. [U] —see also INCORRUPTIBLE

corrupt[2] v. [T] **1** to encourage someone to start behaving in an immoral or dishonest way: *the corrupting influence of drugs* | *Power tends to corrupt, and absolute power corrupts absolutely.* **2** to change the traditional form of something, such as a language, so that it becomes worse than it was: *Excessive campaign spending is corrupting the American political system.* **3** TECHNICAL to change the information in a computer, so that the computer does not work correctly anymore: *Some of the files were corrupted and will have to be rewritten.* —**corruptible** adj. —**corruptibility** /kəˌrʌptəˈbɪləti/ n. [U]

cor·rup·tion /kəˈrʌpʃən/ n. **1** [U] dishonest, illegal, or immoral behavior, especially from someone with power: *The country's government has been accused of corruption and abuse of power.* **2** [U] the act or process of making someone dishonest or immoral: *The play is about the gradual corruption of a scientist.* **3** [C usually singular] a changed form of something, for example a word: *The word Thursday is a corruption of Thor's Day.*

cor·sage /kɔrˈsɑʒ/ n. [C] a group of small flowers that a woman fastens to her clothes or wrist on a special occasion, such as a wedding

cor·sair /ˈkɔrsɛr/ n. [C] OLD USE a North African PIRATE, or their ship

corse /kɔrs/ n. [C] OLD USE OR POETIC a CORPSE

cor·set /ˈkɔrsɪt/ n. [C] **1** a tightly fitting piece of underwear that women wore in past times to make them look thinner: *In those days, women wore corsets and up to five layers of petticoats.* **2** a strong, tightly fitting piece of clothing that supports your back when it is injured —**corseted** adj.

Cor·si·ca /ˈkɔrsɪkə/ a large island to the south of France in the Mediterranean Sea

cor·tege /kɔrˈtɛʒ/ n. [C] a line of people, cars etc. that move along slowly in a funeral

Cor·tés /kɔrˈtɛz/**, Her·nán** /hərˈnæn/ or **Her·nan·do** /hərˈnændoʊ/ (1485–1547) a Spanish soldier who defeated the Aztecs in 1521 and took control of Mexico for Spain

cor·tex /ˈkɔrtɛks/ n. plural **cortices** /-tɪsiz/ [C] TECHNICAL the outer layer of an organ such as your brain: *The eyes transmit electrical signals to the visual cortex in the brain.* —**cortical** /ˈkɔrtɪkəl/ adj.

cor·ti·sone /ˈkɔrtɪˌsoʊn, -ˌzoʊn/ n. [U] a HORMONE that is used especially in the treatment of diseases such as ARTHRITIS

cor·us·cat·ing /ˈkɔrəˌskeɪtɪŋ, ˈkɑr-/ adj. FORMAL **1** a speech, piece of writing etc. that is coruscating is intelligent, quick, and impressive **2** flashing with light: *coruscating jewels*

cos /kɑs, koʊs/ n. the abbreviation of COSINE

co·sign /ˈkoʊsaɪn/ v. [T] to sign a paper that has already been signed by someone else, especially a legal document: *I cosigned the loan for my brother-in-law.* —**cosigner** n. [C]

co·sig·na·to·ry /koʊˈsɪgnəˌtɔri/ n. [C] FORMAL one of a group of people who sign a legal document for their organization, country etc.: *We will need both cosignatories to sign the check.*

co·sine /ˈkoʊsaɪn/ n. [C] TECHNICAL a number relating to an ACUTE (6) angle in a RIGHT TRIANGLE that is calculated by dividing the length of the side next to the angle by the length of the HYPOTENUSE (=longest side) —compare SINE

cos·met·ic /kazˈmɛtɪk/ adj. [only before noun] **1** intended to make your skin or body look more attractive: *cosmetic products* | *80% of women who have surgery to enlarge their breasts do it for cosmetic reasons.* **2** dealing with the outside appearance rather than the important part of something; SUPERFICIAL: *The house needs no structural work, just a few cosmetic repairs.* **3** relating to cosmetics: *a cosmetic sponge* —see also COSMETICS, COSMETIC SURGERY

cos·me·ti·cian /ˌkazməˈtɪʃən/ n. [C] someone who is professionally trained to put cosmetics on other people

cos·met·ics /kazˈmɛtɪks/ n. [plural] **1** creams, powders etc. that you use on your face and body in order to look more attractive: *the cosmetics industry* | *People with acne problems should look for oil-free cosmetics.* **2** things that relate to the outside appearance rather than the important part of something: *The improvements to the subway system we plan are critical – they have nothing to do with cosmetics.*

cosmetic sur·ge·ry /.ˌ.. '.../ n. [U] medical operations that improve your appearance after you have been injured, or because you want to look more attractive

cos·me·tol·o·gy /ˌkazməˈtɑlədʒi/ n. [U] the art or skill of treating the face or body with cosmetics in order to make them more attractive —**cosmetologist** n. [C]

cos·mic /ˈkazmɪk/ adj. **1** relating to space or the universe: *The universe is believed to have been created about 15 billion years ago in a cosmic explosion.* **2** extremely large or important: *a scandal of cosmic proportions* —**cosmically** /-kli/ adv.

cosmic ray /ˌ.. '../ n. [C usually plural] a stream of RADIATION reaching the Earth from space

cos·mog·o·ny /kazˈmagəni/ n. [C,U] the origin of the universe, or a set of ideas about this: *His latest proposal flies in the face of conventional cosmogony.*

cos·mol·o·gy /kazˈmalədʒi/ n. [U] the science of the origin and structure of the universe, especially as studied in ASTRONOMY

cos·mo·naut /ˈkazməˌnɔt, -ˌnat/ n. [C] an ASTRONAUT from Russia or the former Soviet Union: *Cosmonaut Yuri Gagarin was the first man to orbit the Earth.*

cos·mo·pol·i·tan[1] /ˌkazməˈpalət n/ adj. **1** a cosmopolitan place consists of people from many different parts of the world: *Barcelona feels a lot more cosmopolitan than other Spanish cities.* **2** a cosmopolitan person, belief, opinion etc. shows a wide experience of different people and places: *Alexander, who speaks six languages, had a very cosmopolitan upbringing.*

cosmopolitan[2] n. [C] someone who has traveled a lot and feels at home in any part of the world: *Hassan is a French-speaking cosmopolitan.*

cos·mos /ˈkazmoʊs, -məs/ n. **the cosmos** the whole universe, especially when you think of it as a system: *Scientists continue looking for clues on how the cosmos was created.*

cos·set /ˈkasɪt/ v. **cossets, cosseted, cosseting** [T] to give someone as much care and attention as you can, especially when it is too much: *No one in the family gets as much cosseting as that cat!*

S W **cost**[1] /kɔst/ n. **1** [C,U] the amount of money that you have to pay in order to buy, do, or produce something: *Medical care costs keep rising.* | [+ **to**] *The cost of welfare to state taxpayers is over $5 billion.* | *Tenants pay a deposit to cover the cost of cleanup.* | *The 8-foot-tall granite sculpture was commissioned at a cost of $16,000.* | **high/low cost** *Both companies make low cost personal computers.* | *The stereo comes as standard equipment in the car, at no extra cost to you.* **2 costs** [plural] **a)** the money that you must regularly spend in a business, or on your home, car etc.: *The graph shows housing costs for Arizona, New York, Nevada, and Utah.* | *Pressure to cut costs* (=spend less money) *led to the firing of over 200 employees.* | *The change may dramatically increase transportation costs.* **b)** the money that you must pay to lawyers if you are involved in a legal case: *Bellisario won the case and was awarded costs.* **3** [C,U] something that you lose, give away, damage etc. in order to achieve something: *War is never worth its cost in human life.* | [+ **to**] *You should do what's right, despite the cost to yourself and your family.* | *He intends to hold onto power, whatever the cost.* **4 at cost** for the same price that you paid to buy or make something: *Most of the materials were bought at cost from local suppliers.* **5 at all costs/at any cost** whatever happens, or whatever effort is needed: *Margaret wants to have justice at all costs.* —see also COST OF LIVING

USAGE NOTE: COST

WORD CHOICE: cost, price, charge, fee, fare
Use **cost** to talk about how much you have to pay to buy, do, make, or use something: *What's the average cost of a CD in this store?* | *You have to add the cost of advertising to that.* Use **price** only to talk about the amount of money you have to pay to buy something in a store, restaurant, etc.: *The menu didn't have prices on it.* | *I got these shoes for half price.* Use **charge** to talk about how much you have to pay for a service or being allowed to use something: *It comes to $19.95, including the service charge.* Use **fee** to talk about the amount of money you have to pay to someone such as a lawyer or doctor for a professional service: Use **fare** to talk about how much money it costs to travel on a bus, plane etc.: *The price of the trip includes air fare and car rental.*

S W **cost**[2] v. past tense and past participle **cost** [T] **1** if something costs a particular amount of money, you have to spend that much in order to pay for it: *Cable TV service costs $19.95 a month.* | [**cost (sb) sth**] *The dental plan will cost you $7.50 each pay period.* | *It costs thirty-eight dollars per adult, round trip.* | *Michelle's college bills are costing me a fortune* (=it is expensive to pay them). **2** to lose something as a result of something that has happened or that you have done: *The field goal he missed cost the team the game.* **3 it'll cost you** SPOKEN used to say that something will be expensive: *Sure, tickets are still available, but they'll cost you.* **4 sth costs money** SPOKEN used to remind or warn someone that they should be careful because something is expensive: *Don't jump on the couch – this thing costs money!* **5 cost an arm and a leg** also **cost a pretty penny** INFORMAL to be extremely expensive: *Good childcare costs an arm and a leg.* **6 cost sb dearly** to do something that causes you a lot of trouble or makes you suffer: *Delays at the factory have cost us dearly.*

cost[3] v. past tense and past participle **costed** [T usually passive] to calculate the price to be charged for a job, the time someone spends working on something etc.: *The options are being costed and analyzed.*

co-star[1] /'koʊ stɑr/ n. [C] one of two or more main actors that work together in a movie, play, or television program: *Houston's co-star in "The Bodyguard" was Kevin Costner.*

co-star[2] v. [I] to be one of the main actors that work in a movie, play, or television program: [+ **with**] *Al Pacino co-stars with Jack Lemmon in "Glengarry Glen Ross."*

Cos·ta Ri·ca /ˌkɑstə 'rikə, ˌkoʊ-/ a country in Central America between Nicaragua and Panama —**Costa Rican** n. adj.

cost-ben·e·fit a·nal·y·sis /ˌ. '... .,.../ n. [C] TECHNICAL a way of calculating the business methods or plans that will bring you the most profits or advantages for the smallest cost

cost-ef·fec·tive, **cost effective** /'. .,./ adj. bringing the best possible profits or advantages for the lowest possible costs: *a cost-effective way to reduce pollution* —**cost-effectively** adv. —**cost-effectiveness** n. [U]

cost·ing /'kɔstɪŋ/ n. [C,U] the process of calculating the cost of a future business activity, product etc., or the act of calculating this: *Have we got the costings through yet?*

cost·ly /'kɔstli/ adj. **costlier, costliest 1** costing a lot of money, or too much money: *A lawsuit would be costly and we would probably lose.* **2** causing a lot of problems or trouble: *Taylor's pinched nerve has been the team's most costly injury this season.* —**costliness** n. [U]

cost of liv·ing /ˌ. . '../ n. [singular] the average amount that people spend to buy food, pay bills, own a home etc. in a particular area: *She's moving to Oregon to escape the high cost of living in Silicon Valley.*

cost-plus /ˌ. '.◂/ adj. TECHNICAL a cost-plus contract gives someone who is selling something or who is providing a service all of their costs, along with a specific PERCENTAGE as a profit

cos·tume /'kɑstum/ n. **1** [C] an unusual set of **S W** clothes that you wear to an event such as a party, that makes you look like an animal, a character **3** from a story, a GHOST etc.: *a Halloween costume* **2** [C,U] a set of clothes that is typical of a particular place or historical period of time: *All the guests attended the party in Victorian costume.* —see Usage Note at CLOTHING

costume dra·ma /'.. .,../ n. [C] a play, movie, television program etc. that is about a particular time in history, in which people wear costumes from that time

costume jew·el·ry /'.. ,..., .. '.../ n. [U] cheap jewelry that is designed to look expensive: *Many fashion boutiques carry costume jewelry priced under $20.*

co·sy /'koʊzi/ adj. **cosier, cosiest** another spelling of COZY

cot /kɑt/ n. [C] a light narrow bed that can be folded and stored: *Cots were set up in the local high school for flood victims.* —see picture at BED[1]

co·tan·gent /koʊ'tændʒənt, 'koʊtæn-/ n. [C] TECHNICAL a number relating to an angle in a RIGHT TRIANGLE that is calculated by dividing the length of the side next to the angle by the length of the side across from it —compare TANGENT (3)

Côte d'I·voire /ˌkoʊt di'vwɑr/ —see IVORY COAST

co·ter·ie /'koʊtəri/ n. [C] a small group of people who enjoy doing the same things together, and do not like including others in their group: *His loyal coterie of fans crowded the stage.*

co·til·lion /kə'tɪlyən, koʊ-/ n. [C] a formal occasion when people dance; BALL[1] (10)

cot·tage /'kɑtɪdʒ/ n. [C] a small house, especially in the country: *A few secluded cottages are located along the narrow winding road.*

cottage cheese /ˌ.. '.◂/ n. [U] a type of soft wet white cheese made from milk that has little fat in it

cottage in·dus·try /'.. ,../ n. [C] an industry that consists of people who do all the work in their homes: *Cake decorating is something of a cottage industry around here.*

cot·tag·ing /'kɑtɪdʒɪŋ/ n. [U] SLANG the practice of looking for male HOMOSEXUAL partners in public REST ROOMS —**cottager** n. [C]

cot·ton[1] /'kɑt⁻n/ n. [U] **1** cloth or thread made from the soft white FIBERS that surround the seeds of a cotton plant: *a white cotton shirt* | *The towels are 100% cotton.* **2** the plant that produces these FIBERS: *fields of cotton and corn*

cotton² *v.*

 cotton to *phr. v.* [T] INFORMAL **1** [cotton to sth] to like someone or something that is new to you: *Not everyone will cotton to the flavor of dry salt cod.* **2 cotton (on) to sth** to begin to understand something; REALIZE: *Other networks had not yet cottoned on to CNN's strategy.*

cotton ball /'.. ,./ *n.* [C] a small soft ball made from cotton, used for cleaning your skin, especially your face

cotton can·dy /,.. '../ *n.* [U] a type of sticky pink candy that looks like cotton, often sold at FAIRS² (1)

cotton gin /'.. ,./ *n.* [C] a machine that separates the seeds of a cotton plant from the cotton

cot·ton pick·ing /'.. ,../ *adj.* [only before noun] OLD-FASHIONED, SPOKEN used to emphasize that you are annoyed or surprised: *I paid $150 bucks for those cotton-picking shoes!*

cot·ton·tail /'katⁿ,teɪl/ *n.* [C] a small rabbit with a white tail

cot·ton·wood /'katⁿ,wʊd/ *n.* [C,U] a North American tree with seeds that look like white cotton

cot·y·le·don /,katə'lidn/ *n.* [C] TECHNICAL the first leaf that grows from a seed

s w **couch¹** /kaʊtʃ/ *n.* [C] **1** a comfortable piece of furniture, usually with a back and arms, on which more than one person can sit; SOFA: *Mandy curled up on the couch to watch television.* **2** a long low piece of furniture that you lie down on during PSYCHOANALYSIS: *After 20 years on the couch, Richard is finally giving up therapy.*

couch² *v.* [I] FORMAL to express something in a particular way in order to be polite or not offend someone: [couch sth in sth] *No matter what terms they couch it in, Danny is dying and there's no cure.*

couch po·ta·to /'. .,../ *n.* [C] INFORMAL someone who spends a lot of time sitting and watching television: *A lot of kids today are overweight couch potatoes.*

cou·gar /'kugɚ/ *n.* [C] a large brown wild cat from the mountains of Western North America and South America; MOUNTAIN LION —see picture on page 429

s w **cough¹** /kɔf/ *v.* **1** [I] to push air out of your throat with a sudden rough sound, especially because you are sick: *I've been coughing and sneezing all day.* **2** [I] to make a sound like a cough: *The old car coughed and sputtered before starting.*

 cough up *phr. v.* **1** [I,T cough sth ↔ up] INFORMAL to unwillingly give someone money, information etc.: *Business owners who do not put up "No smoking" signs will have to cough up a $100 fine.* **2** [T cough up sth] to get something out of your throat or lungs by coughing: *The woman was coughing up blood and was rushed to the hospital.*

cough² *n.* **1** [C] the sound made when you cough, or the act of coughing: *Disease can be spread by coughs.* **2** [singular,U] a medical condition that makes you cough a lot: *Ms. Meyers has this hacking smoker's cough.* | *I find honey is the best thing for a cough.*

cough drop /'. ./ *n.* [C] a type of medicine like a piece of candy that you suck to help you stop coughing

cough syr·up /'. ,../ *n.* [U] a thick liquid medicine that you take to help you stop coughing

w **could** /kəd; *strong* kʊd/ *modal verb* 3rd *person singular* **could** *negative short form* **couldn't 1** used to talk about what you were able to do: *Could you hear that all right?* | *Eleanor couldn't come last night.* | *Nobody could tell my hair was dirty.* **2** used to show that something might be possible or might happen: *I'm sure Francis could find out for you.* | *There's no way you could go by yourself, Kay.* | *I don't think I could live with someone like that.* **3** used instead of "can" when reporting what someone else said: *Dad said we could go swimming after lunch.* **4** used to politely ask someone to do something: *Could you have her call me back when she gets home, please?* | *Could you drop off the kids on your way to work?* **5** used to politely ask if someone is able or

allowed to do something: *What about Sam? Could he come along, too?*

SPOKEN PHRASES

6 used to suggest doing something: *We could use plastic cups, so we don't have to wash anything.* | *You guys could go to the Sirloin Saloon for a nice big steak.* **7 I couldn't care less** used to say that you are not interested at all in something: *I couldn't care less what happens to you and Peter.* **8** said when you are annoyed because you think someone should have done something: *You could have told me you were going to be late!* **9 I could have strangled/hit/killed etc. sb** used to emphasize that you were very angry with someone: *Brent forgot our anniversary again! I could have killed him!*

---

couldst /kʊdst/ *v.* OLD USE **thou couldst** an old form of "you could," used when talking to one person whom you know well

cou·lee /'kuli/ *n.* [C] a small valley with steep sides

coun·cil /'kaʊnsəl/ *n.* [C] **1** a group of people who are elected as part of a town or city government: *Feltz is running for city council in the fall elections.* | *a council meeting* **2** a group of people who make decisions for large organizations or groups, or who give advice: *the UN Security Council* | *Stuart is on the Regional Arts Council.* —see also STUDENT COUNCIL

coun·cil·man /'kaʊnsəlmən/ *n.* [C] a male councilor

coun·cil·or /'kaʊnsəlɚ/ *n.* [C] a member of a council: *Three city councilors resigned Monday to protest the mayor's decision.*

coun·cil·wom·an /'kaʊnsəl,wʊmən/ *n.* [C] a female councilor

coun·sel¹ /'kaʊnsəl/ *n.* TECHNICAL **1** [U] a lawyer or a group of lawyers who represent someone in a court of law, or who give legal advice: *The counsel for the defense gave her opening statement.* **2 keep your own counsel** to not talk about your private thoughts and opinions: *Even with those she loves most, Ginny tends to keep her own counsel.* **3** [U] FORMAL advice: *I'll miss her because I value her counsel.*

counsel² *v.* **counseled, counseling** *also* **counselled, counselling** [T] to listen to someone and give them support and advice about their personal problems: *Carvalho counsels cancer patients at a Rio hospital.*

coun·sel·ing /'kaʊnsəlɪŋ/ *n.* [U] advice given to people about their personal problems or difficult decisions: *The agency provides marriage and family counseling.*

coun·sel·or /'kaʊnsələ/ *n.* [C] **1** someone whose job is to help and support people with personal problems: *Erin works as a counselor at a drug and alcohol treatment center.* **2** someone, especially a young man or woman, who takes care of younger children at a summer CAMP¹ (2)

count¹ /kaʊnt/ *v.*

1 find the total [T] *also* **count up** to calculate the total number of things in a group: *Authorities counted 50 traffic deaths over the holiday weekend.* | *The computer can count how many words there are in a document you've written.*

2 say numbers [I] to say numbers in order, one by one or in groups: *The game teaches children to count and do simple addition and subtraction.* | [+ to] *Take a deep breath, count to ten and then breathe out.*

3 be allowed [I] to be allowed or accepted according to a standard, set of ideas, or set of rules: *If the ball is caught for the third out, the run doesn't count.* | [+ as] *Your sculpture class counts as a Humanities credit.*

4 include [T] to include someone or something in a total: *Counting playoff games, the Warriors have won 8 of the 9 games they've played against Utah.*

5 consider sth [T] to consider someone or something in a particular way: [count sb/sth as sth] *I think Mexico should be counted as part of Central America.* | *You should count yourself lucky that you weren't hurt.*

6 important [I] to be important or valuable: *First impressions do count, so look your best at the interview.* | [+ **for**] *I never vote – I feel my vote doesn't count for anything.*

7 I/you can count sth on one hand SPOKEN used to emphasize how small the number of something is: *Ten years ago, you could count on one hand the number of people who had computers in this neighborhood.*

8 don't count your chickens (before they're hatched) SPOKEN used to say that you should not make plans that depend on something good happening, because it might not: *You'll probably get the job, but don't count your chickens just yet.*

9 count sheep to imagine a line of sheep jumping over a fence, one at a time, and count them as a way of making yourself go to sleep

count sth ↔ **down** *phr. v.* [I,T] to count the number of days, minutes etc. left until a particular moment or event: *Robin is anxiously counting down the days until Jonathan arrives.* —see also COUNTDOWN

count sb in *phr. v.* [T] INFORMAL to include someone in an activity: *If you're going rock climbing this weekend, you can count me in.*

count on sb/sth *phr. v.* [T] **1** to depend on someone or something, especially in a difficult situation: *Maggie, I knew I could count on you.* | [**count on doing sth**] *She is counting on earning only about 45% of her previous salary in the first year.* **2** to expect someone to do something, or expect something to happen: *I didn't count on the fact that Morgan may not be able to take her car.* | [**count on sb/sth to do sth**] *You can count on him to get the work done on time.*

count out *phr. v.* [T] **1** [**count sb out**] INFORMAL to not include someone in an activity: *Well, you can count me out!* **2** [**count sb out**] to decide that someone or something is not important or worth considering: *They're the most improved team in the league – I wouldn't count them out.* **3** [**count** sth ↔ **out**] to put things down one by one as you count them: *Can you help me count out the ballots?*

S W count² *n.* [C]
2 3
1 total the process of counting, or the total that you get when you count things: *We've seen over 65 patients today, but we don't have an exact count.* | *Ms. Henderson said the final count may exceed 2,000.* | *At last count* (=the last and most recent time you counted), *76 readers had stopped their subscriptions.*

2 measurement a measurement that shows how much of a substance is present in a place, area etc. that is being examined: *My cholesterol count was a little high* (=there was a lot of it in my blood). | *High pollen counts and air conditioners may worsen allergies.*

3 lose count to forget a number you were calculating or a total you were trying to count: *Be quiet – you made me lose count!* | *I lost count after a hundred.*

4 keep count to keep a record of the changing total of something over a period of time: *Are you keeping count of how many people you've invited?*

5 on all/several/both etc. counts in every way or about every thing, in several ways or about several things etc.: *He proved many people in Washington wrong on several counts.*

6 law TECHNICAL one of the crimes that someone is charged with: *Davis was found not guilty on all counts.* | *Henderson pleaded guilty on one count of drunken driving.*

7 be out/down for the count a) to be defeated: *Many people felt he was down for the count and was considering bankruptcy.* **b)** to be in a deep sleep **c)** if a BOXER is out for the count, he has been knocked down for ten seconds or more

8 rank/title a European NOBLEMAN with a high rank: *the Count of Monte Cristo*

count·a·ble /'kaʊntəbəl/ *adj.* a countable noun is a noun such as "table," that has a singular and a plural form —opposite UNCOUNTABLE

count·down /'kaʊnt͡daʊn/ *n.* [C] the act of counting backward to zero before something happens, especially before a space vehicle is sent into the sky

coun·te·nance¹ /'kaʊntənəns/ *n.* FORMAL [C] your face or your expression: *Despite his troubles, his countenance was always friendly.*

countenance² *v.* [T] FORMAL to accept, support, or approve of something: *In no way will we countenance terrorism in order to advance our cause.*

coun·ter¹ /'kaʊntɚ/ *n.* [C] **1** a flat surface in the kitchen where you work, prepare food etc.: *Careful, you're going to spill it all over the counter.* | *a counter-top appliance* —see picture at KITCHEN **2** the place, usually a flat narrow surface, where you pay or are served in a store, bank, restaurant etc.: *The local supermarket has a good deli counter.* | *The cashier stood waiting behind the counter.* **3 over the counter** over the counter medicines and drugs can be bought without a PRESCRIPTION from a doctor **4 under the counter** if you buy something under the counter, you buy it secretly and usually illegally **5** a small object that you use in some games to mark a place on a board: *the blue counter* **6** a piece of electrical equipment that counts something: *Set the video counter to zero before you press play.* —see also GEIGER COUNTER

counter² *v.* **1** [I,T] to react to a statement, criticism, argument, action etc. by saying or doing something that will prove that the statement is not true or that will have an opposite effect: *Rodrigues countered the criticism by saying that the group does a lot of things for the area that go unnoticed.* **2** [T] to do something in order to reduce the bad effects of something, or to defend yourself against them: *Hospitals must offer better salaries to counter the shortage of nurses.*

counter³ *adv.* [not before noun] in a way that is opposite to something: *Sending troops abroad would run counter to Japan's anti-war constitution.*

counter- /kaʊntɚ/ *prefix* **1** the opposite of something: *Arguing is a counterproductive thing to do* (=producing results opposite to what you wanted). **2** done or given as a reaction to something, especially to oppose it: *proposals and counter-proposals* **3** matching something: *my counterpart in the Korean company* (=someone who has the same type of job that I have)

coun·ter·act /ˌkaʊntɚ'ækt/ *v.* [T] to reduce or prevent the bad effect of something, by doing something that has the opposite effect: *Taking vitamins can counteract some bad eating habits.* —**counteraction** /ˌkaʊntɚ'ækʃən/ *n.* [C,U]

coun·ter·at·tack /'kaʊntɚə͜tæk/ *n.* [C] an attack against someone who has attacked you, in a war, sport, or an argument: *Chavez unleashed a furious counterattack on his attacker.* —**counterattack** *v.* [I,T] —**counterattacker** *n.* [C]

coun·ter·bal·ance /ˌkaʊntɚ'bæləns, 'kaʊntɚˌbæləns/ *v.* [T] to have an effect that is the opposite of the effect of something else: *The company's success in Europe has counterbalanced its weak sales in the U.S.* —**counterbalance** /'kaʊntɚˌbæləns/ *n.* [C]

coun·ter·charge /ˌkaʊntɚ'tʃɑrdʒ/ *n.* [C] a statement that says someone else has done something wrong, made after they have said you have done something wrong: *The group denies the charge of election fraud, and makes a countercharge of violence against the opposition.*

coun·ter·clock·wise /ˌkaʊntɚ'klɑk-waɪz/ *adv.* moving in the opposite direction to the hands on a clock: *To remove the lid, turn it counterclockwise.* —opposite CLOCKWISE

coun·ter·cul·ture /'kaʊntɚˌkʌltʃɚ/ *n.* [U] the art, beliefs, behavior etc. of people, especially young people, who are against the usual or accepted behavior, arts etc. of society: *The environmental group had its roots in the counterculture of the 1960s.*

coun·ter·es·pi·o·nage /ˌkaʊntɚ'ɛspiənɑʒ/ *n.* [U] the process of trying to prevent someone from SPYing on your country: *He worked on counterespionage cases for the FBI.*

coun·ter·feit¹ /'kaʊntɚfɪt/ *adj.* made to look exactly like something else, in order to deceive people: *a counterfeit $20 bill* | *They were arrested for making counterfeit computer chips.*

counterfeit² *v.* [T] to copy something exactly in order to deceive people: *$100 dollar bills are the most likely to be counterfeited.*

coun·ter·foil /'kaʊntə,fɔɪl/ *n.* [C] FORMAL the part of something such as a check or ticket that you keep as a record

coun·ter·in·sur·gen·cy /,kaʊntərɪn'sɜdʒənsi/ *n.* [U] military action against people who are fighting against their own country's government

coun·ter·in·tel·li·gence /,kaʊntərɪn'telədʒəns/ *n.* [U] action that a country takes in order to stop other countries from discovering their secrets

coun·ter·mand /'kaʊntə,mænd/ *v.* [T] to officially tell people to ignore an order, especially by giving them a different one: *Goldstein was expelled for countermanding a direct order from the supervisor.*

coun·ter·mea·sure /'kaʊntə,mɛʒə/ *n.* [C usually plural] an action taken to prevent another action from having a harmful effect: *The rising incidence of drunken driving requires drastic countermeasures.*

coun·ter·of·fen·sive /'kaʊntərə,fɛnsɪv/ *n.* [C] a military attack on someone who has attacked you: *The city is the main target of the rebel counteroffensive.*

coun·ter·pane /'kaʊntə,peɪn/ *n.* [C] OLD-FASHIONED a BEDSPREAD

coun·ter·part /'kaʊntə,part/ *n.* [C] someone or something that has the same job or purpose as someone or something else in a different place: *Bars in Madrid offer more, and better, food than their American counterparts.*

coun·ter·point /'kaʊntə,pɔɪnt/ *n.* **1** [U] a way of writing music so that two or more tunes can be played together at the same time **2** [C] something that shows a clear difference when compared to something else: *Water chestnuts and snow peas provided a light counterpoint to the duck.*

coun·ter·pro·duc·tive /,kaʊntəprə'dʌktɪv/ *adj.* achieving the opposite result to the one that you want: *A confrontation is really going to be counterproductive for everyone.*

coun·ter·rev·o·lu·tion /,kaʊntərɛvə'luʃən/ *n.* [C,U] political or military actions taken to get rid of a government that is in power because of a previous REVOLUTION —**counter-revolutionary** *adj.*

coun·ter·rev·o·lu·tion·a·ry /,kaʊntərɛvə'luʃənɛri/ *n.* [C] someone who is involved in a counterrevolution

coun·ter·sign /'kaʊntə,saɪn/ *v.* [T] to sign a paper that has already been signed by someone else: *I'm supposed to countersign this check in their presence.*

coun·ter·ten·or /'kaʊntə,tɛnə/ *n.* [C] a man who is trained to sing with a very high voice

coun·ter·ter·ror·ist /,kaʊntə'tɛrərɪst/ *adj.* **a counterterrorist operation/squad etc.** a plan or group that tries to prevent the violent activities of political groups who use force: *a counterterrorist fighting squad* —**counterterrorist** *n.* [C]

coun·ter·vail·ing /,kaʊntə'veɪlɪŋ/ *adj.* FORMAL with an equally strong but opposite effect: *Some companies in the industry are in trouble, but there are countervailing forces that will help others survive.*

count·ess /'kaʊntɪs/ *n.* [C] a woman with the same rank as an EARL or a COUNT² (8)

counting house /'.. ,./ *n.* [C] an office where accounts and money were kept in past times

count·less /'kaʊntlɪs/ *adj.* too many to be counted: *We had to peel back countless layers of paint and wallpaper.* | *She spent **countless hours** knitting by the fire.*

count noun /'. ./ *n.* [C] TECHNICAL a COUNTABLE noun —compare UNCOUNT NOUN

coun·tri·fied /'kʌntri,faɪd/ *adj.* typical in appearance or behavior of the people or things that live outside towns and cities, or made to seem typical of this type of area: *You can add countrified curtains to enhance the rural charm of the kitchen.*

coun·try¹ /'kʌntri/ *n. plural* **countries** **1** [C] a nation or state with its land and people: *The ceremony was televised in over 30 countries.* —compare NATION (1) —see also MOTHER COUNTRY —see Usage Note at

NATION **2 the country a)** all the people who live in a particular country: *The President has the support of over 50 percent of the country.* **b)** land that is outside towns and cities, including land used for farming; the COUNTRYSIDE: *I've always wanted to live in the country.* **3 farm/Amish etc. country** land that is appropriate for a particular activity, or where a particular type of people live: *Doris grew up in Pennsylvania Dutch country.* **4** [U] country and western music: *I'm a big fan of country.* —see Usage Note at LAND

coun·try² *adj.* [only before noun] **1** the area outside cities or towns, or relating to this area: *twisting country roads* **2** relating to country and western music: *country music singer Dwight Yoakam*

country and west·ern /,.. '../ *n.* [U] a type of popular music from the southern and western U.S.: *She likes country and western.* | *a country and western song*

country bump·kin /,kʌntri 'bʌmpkɪn/ *n.* [C] someone who is considered to be stupid because they are from an area outside towns and cities

country club /'.. ,./ *n.* [C] a sports and social club, especially one for rich people

country cous·in /,.. '../ *n.* [C] **1** someone who does not have a lot of experience and who is confused by busy city life **2** an event, organization, place etc. that is not as big or exciting as another one of the same kind: *Fiddlefest was the country cousin to the New Orleans music festival staged earlier this year.*

country danc·ing /'.. ,../ *n.* [U] a traditional form of dance in which pairs of dancers move in rows and circles

coun·try·man /'kʌntrimən/ *n. plural* **countrymen** /-mən/ [C] someone from your own country: *President Pascal-Trouillot went on national television to urge her countrymen to vote.*

country mu·sic /'.. ,../ *n.* [U] COUNTRY AND WESTERN

coun·try·side /'kʌntri,saɪd/ *n.* [U] a word meaning the area outside cities and towns, used especially when you are talking about its beauty: *We marveled at the peacefulness of the Carolina countryside.*

coun·try·west·ern /'.. ,../ *adj.* COUNTRY AND WESTERN —**country-western** *adj.* [only before noun] *a country-western singer*

coun·try·wom·an /'kʌntri,wʊmən/ *n. plural* **countrywomen** /-,wɪmɪn/ [C] a woman who is from your own country

coun·ty /'kaʊnti/ *n. plural* **counties** [C] a large area of land within a state or country, that has its own government to deal with local matters: *Cedric County, Kansas* | *County elections are set for April 29.*

county court /,.. './ *n.* [C] in some states, a court that has authority in a county and deals with less important cases

county fair /,.. './ *n.* [C] an event that happens each year in a particular county, with games, competitions for the best farm animals, for the best cooking etc.: *Rosa's braided rug won first prize at the county fair.*

county seat /,.. './ *n.* [C] the town in a COUNTY where its government is: *The biggest town, Markleeville, is the county seat.*

coup /ku/ *n.* [C] **1** an action in which citizens or the army suddenly take control of the government by using violence or force; coup d'état: *Ben Bella was overthrown in a military coup in 1965.* **2** something you do that is successful and impressive, especially because you would not normally do it: *Getting to host the race was a coup for the Santa Cruz Yacht Club.*

coup de grâce /,ku də 'gras/ *n.* [singular] **1** an action or event that ends or destroys something that has gradually been getting weaker: *The coup de grace came when Smith dropped a ball, allowing the White Sox to score two runs.* **2** a hit or shot that kills someone or something

coup d'é·tat /,ku deɪ'ta/ *n. plural* **coups d'état** [C] (same pronunciation) a COUP (1)

coupe /kup/ *n.* [C] a type of car with two doors, which is shorter than a SEDAN: *a stylish little coupe*

Cou·pe·rin /ˌkupəˈræn/, **Fran·çois** /franˈswɑ/ (1668–1733) a French musician who wrote CLASSICAL music

SW
cou·ple¹ /ˈkʌpəl/ *n.* **1 a couple (of) sth a)** a small number of things: *Let's wait a couple more minutes. | I've run into Darryl a couple of times this summer.* **b)** two things or people of the same kind: *I'll have a couple of tacos, please. | The tape has a couple of Star Trek episodes on it.* **2** [C] two people who are married or having a sexual or romantic relationship: *It's increasingly common for unmarried couples to live together. | An elderly couple was sitting on the park bench.*

USAGE NOTE: COUPLE

WORD CHOICE: couple, pair
Use **couple** to talk about any two things of the same kind: *I haven't seen her for a couple of days.* Use **pair** to talk about something that has two main parts that are joined together: *a pair of shorts | a pair of glasses.* **Pair** can also be used to talk about two things that are used together as a set: *a new pair of shoes*
GRAMMAR
When you use **couple** to talk about two people, you can either use a singular noun, if you are considering them together: *A new couple is moving in next door*, or a plural noun, if you are considering them as two people: *A young couple were arguing at the next table.*

---

couple² *v.* **1** [T] to join or fasten two things together, especially two vehicles: *Efficiency is improved by coupling large numbers of boxcars together.* **2** [I] FORMAL to have sex
couple with *phr. v.* [T usually passive] to happen or exist together, and produce a particular result: *The system uses a radar unit coupled with a camera to photograph cars traveling over the speed limit.*

cou·plet /ˈkʌplɪt/ *n.* [C] two lines of poetry, one following the other, that are the same length: *a rhymed couplet*

cou·pling /ˈkʌplɪŋ/ *n.* [C] **1** something that connects two things together, especially two vehicles or pipes: *the coupling on the rear of the tractor* **2** FORMAL an act of having sex

SW
cou·pon /ˈkupɑn, ˈkyu-/ *n.* [C] **1** a small piece of printed paper that gives you the right to pay less for something or get something free: *This coupon is for 15 cents off paper towels.* **2** a printed form used when you order something, enter a competition etc. **3** TECHNICAL **a)** a piece of paper attached to some types of BONDs that you tear off and give to a bank or the seller of the bond in order to receive the INTEREST: *The notes will carry a coupon rate of 6⅛%.* **b)** the rate of INTEREST paid on BONDs: *a two-year bond with a 10% coupon*

cour·age /ˈkɝɪdʒ, ˈkʌr-/ *n.* [U] **1** the quality of being brave when you are in danger, in pain, in a difficult situation etc.: *Private Smith was recognized for her courage. | I just never had the courage to ask Lisa for a date. | It takes a lot of courage to go into combat, but that's my job.* **2 have the courage of your (own) convictions** to be brave enough to say or do what you think is right, even though other people may not approve or approve: *Larry displayed the courage of his convictions by saying no to his supervisor.*

cou·ra·geous /kəˈreɪdʒəs/ *adj.* brave: *King was a courageous leader who confronted the racist attitudes of his time. | Parker said the judge's decision was courageous.* —**courageously** *adv.* —**courageousness** *n.* [U]

Cour·bet /kʊrˈbeɪ/, **Gus·tave** /ˈgustɑv/ (1819–1877) a French PAINTER famous for painting ordinary scenes in a style that made them look real

cou·ri·er¹ /ˈkʊriɚ, ˈkɝ-/ *n.* [C] someone who is employed to take a package, documents etc. somewhere: *The invitations were sent out by courier.*

courier² *v.* [T] to send something somewhere by using a courier: *I'll courier the contracts out to you this afternoon.*

course¹ /kɔrs/ *n.*
1 of course a) used when what you or someone else has just said is not surprising, because it is what you expect: *We'll be spending more money, of course. | Shawn was ecstatic at winning the tournament, and of course, so was his father. | She was wearing her black dress, of course. | "Did his mother get it for him?" "Oh, of course."* **b)** used when mentioning something that you think other people already know or that they should know: *One reason literacy skills have decreased is, of course, television. | Of course, you have to go to the bank to do that.* **c)** also **course** SPOKEN used to agree with someone, or to give permission to someone: *"You're going to come, aren't you?" "Yes, of course, I'll be there."* **d)** also **course** SPOKEN used to emphasize that you are saying yes to something, or that what you are saying is true or correct: *"He'll do it, won't he?" "Of course he will!"* —see Usage Note at CERTAINLY
2 of course not/course not SPOKEN used to emphasize that you are saying no to something or that something is not true or correct: *"Do you mind if I come a little late?" "Of course not!"*
3 |class| [C] a class in a particular subject: *All hunters applying for licenses are required to take a hunting safety course. | [+ in/on] The university offers extensive courses in film. | Paul is taking a course on Marxist philosophy.* —see also CORRESPONDENCE COURSE, CRASH COURSE, REFRESHER COURSE
4 in the course of sth, during the course of sth FORMAL during a process or period of time: *If the card is used six times in the course of a year, there is no annual fee.*
5 |actions| [C] an action or series of actions that you could take in order to deal with a particular situation: *The council met last week to decide on a future course for peace. | We will now have to reconsider what the appropriate course of action will be.*
6 |way sth develops| [C] the usual or natural way that something happens, develops, or is done: *Scientists are monitoring the course of the measles epidemic throughout the state. | The coup against Gorbachev changed the course of the Soviet future. | Just relax and let nature take its course* (=allow something to happen in the usual way).
7 run its course to develop to the usual way and come to a natural end: *Greenspan suggested the recession might run its course by midyear.*
8 |direction| [C] the direction in which someone or something moves: *The plane had to change course to avoid the storm. | We had to paddle hard to keep the canoes on course* (=keep them going in the right direction). *| The boat had somehow gotten more than 150 miles off course* (=the wrong direction).
9 |part of a meal| [C] one of the separate parts of a meal: *The main course consists of pasta with chicken and peppers. | A three/five-course meal A three-course meal here costs only $15.*
10 on course likely to achieve something, especially because you have already had some success: *Western leaders put the trade talks back on course. | [on course to do sth] The party is on course to return to power.*
11 |sports| [C] an area of land or water on which some types of races are held or some sports are played: *The resort includes a yacht club, a golf course, and eight tennis courts. | a cross-country ski course* —see also OBSTACLE COURSE
12 |river| [C] the direction a river moves in: *The course of the water was marked by a line of willow trees.*
13 |bricks/stone| [C] a layer of bricks, stone etc. —see also **as a matter of course/routine** (MATTER¹ (20)), **in due time/course** (DUE¹ (5)), **be par for the course** (PAR (4)), **stay the course** (STAY¹ (7))

course² *v.* **1** [I always + adv./prep.] LITERARY if a liquid or electricity courses somewhere, it flows rapidly there: *[+ down/along/through etc.] Nicole turned her head away as tears coursed down her cheeks.* **2** [I always + adv./prep.] LITERARY if a feeling or thought courses through your body or mind, you feel it very strongly, or think it quickly: [+ **down/through**] *Fear coursed through Paul.* **3** [I] to move through something very quickly: *The storm system coursed through Georgia and Alabama.* **4** [I,T] to chase a rabbit with dogs as a sport

s w **court**[1] /kɔrt/ n.
2 **1**

1 law [C,U] a building or room where all the information concerning a crime is given so that it can be judged: *There was a large crowd of reporters gathered outside the court.* | *Within weeks of being released, the girl was back in court for trespassing.* | *My landlord is threatening to take me to court* (=have the case dealt with in a court). | *Our manager doesn't want this thing to go to court.* | *O'Toole's case was settled out of court* (=without going to a court).
2 the court a) the judges, lawyers, and JURY who officially decide whether someone is guilty of a crime and what the punishment should be: *On behalf of Mr. Sabich, we would ask the court to enter a plea of not guilty.* **b)** a particular court, especially the SUPREME COURT: *Thurgood Marshall was the court's first black justice.*
3 sport [C,U] an area that has been specially made for playing games such as tennis, basketball etc.: *a volleyball court* | *Agassi is back on the court, ready to resume play.*
4 king/queen etc. [C] **a)** the official place where a king or queen lives and works: [+ **of**] *the court of Versailles* **b)** the royal family and the people who work for them or advise them
5 hold court to speak in an interesting and amusing way so that people gather to listen to you: *The days when he held court at the hotel's supper club seem far away now.*
6 pay court to sb OLD-FASHIONED to give a lot of your attention to someone in order to seem attractive or impressive to them: *Elton had paid court to Miss Smith for a month, but had made no progress.*
7 castle/large house [C] a COURTYARD —see also **the ball is in your court** (BALL[1] (9)), FOOD COURT, **be laughed out of court** (LAUGH[1] (7))

court[2] v. **1** [T] to try to get support you want from other people, by doing something to please them: *Politicians are courting voters before the elections.* **2 court disaster/danger etc.** to behave in a way that makes danger etc. more likely: *People may be courting disaster by using over-the-counter pain relievers.* **3** [T] OLD-FASHIONED if a man courts a woman, he visits her, takes her out etc. because he hopes she will love him: *She finally married a gentleman who had been courting her for years.* **4** [I,T] OLD-FASHIONED if a man and a woman are courting, they are having a romantic relationship and may get married

cour·te·ous /ˈkɔrtiəs/ adj. having good manners (MANNER (3)) and respect for other people: *The officers were extremely courteous and well-trained.* | *They provide a fast and courteous service.* —opposite DISCOURTEOUS —**courteously** adv. —**courteousness** n. [U]

cour·te·san /ˈkɔrtəzən, -ˌzan/ n. [C] a woman in past times who had sex with rich or important men for money

cour·te·sy /ˈkɔrtəsi/ n. plural **courtesies** **1** [U] polite behavior that shows that you have respect for other people: *Even after midnight, they do not have the courtesy to turn the volume down.* —opposite DISCOURTESY **2** [C] something you do or say in order to be polite: *As a courtesy to other diners, we ask that all cell phones be left at the door.* **3 courtesy of sb/sth** by the permission or kindness of someone rather than by paying them: *Everyone on the flight was put up in a fancy hotel, all courtesy of the airline.*

courtesy bus /ˈ... ./ n. [C] a bus provided by a hotel near an airport that their guests can use to travel to and from the airport

courtesy call /ˈ... ./ n. [C] a visit to someone that you make to be polite or to show your respect for them

courtesy car /ˈ... ./ n. [C] a car that a garage, hotel etc. lends to its customers while they are having their own car fixed, are staying at the hotel etc.

courtesy phone /ˈ... ./ n. [C] a telephone in an airport, hotel etc. that you can use to talk to someone in the building without paying

court·house /ˈkɔrthaʊs/ n. [C] a building containing courts of law and government offices

court·i·er /ˈkɔrtiər/ n. [C] someone in past times who had an important position in a king or queen's COURT

court·ly /ˈkɔrtli/ adj. **courtlier, courtliest** graceful and polite: *a courtly, soft-spoken man* —**courtliness** n. [U]

court-mar·tial[1] /ˈ. ˌ../ n. plural **courts-martial** or **court-martials** [C] **1** a military court that deals with people who break military laws **2** an occasion on which someone is judged by one of these courts: *Corporal Spencer will be held in jail until his court-martial in 90 days.*

court-martial[2] v. past tense and past participle **court-martialed** [T] to hear and judge someone's case in a military court: *The Army decided against court-martialing him as a deserter.*

Court of Ap·peals /ˌ. . ˈ./ n. **the Court of Appeals** one of 12 law courts in the U.S. that deals with cases when people are not satisfied with the judgment given by a lower court —see also APPELLATE COURT

court of law /ˌ. . ˈ./ n. [C] FORMAL a place where law cases are judged; COURT

court or·der /ˈ. ˌ../ n. [C] an order given by a court of law that someone must do or must not do something: *She's under a court order to stay at least 500 yards away from her ex-husband.*

court re·por·ter /ˈ. .ˌ../ n. [C] someone who works in a court and records everything that is said during a case, on a special machine similar to a TYPEWRITER

court·room /ˈkɔrtrum/ n. [C] the room where a case is judged by a court of law

court·ship /ˈkɔrtʃɪp/ n. **1** [C,U] the period of time during which a man and a woman have a romantic relationship before getting married: *My parents got married after a two-week courtship.* **2** [U] special behavior used by animals to attract each other for sex

court·yard /ˈkɔrtyard/ n. [C] an open space that is completely or partly surrounded by walls or buildings: *Our hotel room faced out on to a lovely courtyard.*

cous·cous /ˈkuskus/ n. [U] a North African dish made of grains of crushed wheat, served with meat and vegetables

cous·in /ˈkʌzən/ n. [C] **1** the child of your UNCLE or AUNT —see also FIRST COUSIN, SECOND COUSIN, KISSING COUSIN **2** something that had a similar origin to something else: *The plantain is a large cousin of the banana.* **3** someone whose ANCESTOR (=member of your family who lived a long time ago) is the same as yours: *Apes may be distant cousins of humans.*

Cous·teau /kuˈstoʊ/, **Jacques** /ʒak/ (1910–1997) a French underwater EXPLORER, famous of making movies about plants and animals that live in the ocean

cou·ture /kuˈtʊr/ n. [U] very expensive and fashionable clothes

co·va·lent bond /koʊˌveɪlənt ˈband/ n. [C] TECHNICAL a chemical BOND between two atoms that forms when the atoms share one or more ELECTRONS

cove /koʊv/ n. [C] a small area on a coast that is partly surrounded by land, so that it is protected from the wind: *Lumahai is a perfect cove of white sand bordered by black lava rock.* —see picture on page 428

cov·en /ˈkʌvən/ n. [C] a group of 13 WITCHes

cov·e·nant /ˈkʌvənənt/ n. [C] a formal agreement between two or more people: [+ **of**] *the covenant of marriage* —**covenant** v. [T]

cov·er[1] /ˈkʌvər/ v. [T]
1 put sth over sth also **cover up** to put something over the top of something in order to hide or protect it: *Add salt and pepper, cover the pan, and let cook for 10–15 minutes.* | *Plaster can be used to cover the holes.* | [**cover sth with sth**] *We covered the sofa with a large blanket.*

2 [be over sth] to be on top of something or spread over something: *The roof was completely covered by snow.* | [be covered with/in sth] *We were covered in paint by the time we finished with the ceiling.* | *The floor of the basement was covered with ants.*

3 [deal with/include] to include or deal with something: *The story covers 12 years in the life of the troubled American actress.* | *A 32-page supplement covers European culture and lifestyle.* | *The awards ceremony covered a lot of ground* (=included a lot of things) – *rap, punk, rock, jazz, country and beyond.*

4 [insurance] if an insurance agreement covers someone or something, it states that money will be given to the person if they are injured, if something is damaged etc.: *Most health insurers don't cover any surgery that is done for cosmetic reasons.*

5 [news] to report the details of an event for a newspaper, television, or radio: *Michael Putzel now covers foreign affairs from Washington.*

6 [pay for sth] money that covers a cost is enough to pay for it: *Don't worry, I've got enough to cover your ticket.* | *Airlines are raising fares to cover the cost of fuel.*

7 [distance] to travel a particular distance: *A flight from Los Angeles to New York covers 2459 miles.* | *Donna drove 400 miles in one day – she really covered a lot of ground* (=traveled a long way).

8 [an area] to spread over an area: *The fire covered over 4000 acres.*

9 cover for sb a) to do the work that someone else usually does, because they are sick or not present: *Who's going to cover for you while you're on vacation?* **b)** to prevent someone from getting into trouble by lying about where they are or what they are doing: *Cindy refused to cover for him when his boss called.*

10 [guns] **a)** to protect someone by being ready to shoot anyone who attacks them: *We'll cover you while you run for the door.* **b)** to aim a gun at a person, or the door of a building with people in it, so that they cannot escape: *Mrs. Moss said the robber covered her with the machine gun and told her to open her door.*

11 [sports] to stay close to a member of the opposing team or a part of the field in a game, in order to prevent your opponents from gaining points: *Porter, who was covering Rice, was called for a foul.*

12 cover all (the) bases INFORMAL to make sure that you can deal with any situation or problem, so that nothing bad happens and no one can criticize you: *I want to make sure we cover all the bases in the new employee training class.*

13 [music] to perform or record a song that was originally recorded by another artist: *The Beatles' "Yesterday" has been covered more times than any other song.*

14 cover your back/butt etc. also **cover yourself** INFORMAL to do something now to avoid criticism or blame if something goes wrong in the future: *Take detailed notes of what you do for the client, in order to cover yourself.*

cover up *phr. v.* **1** [T cover sth ↔ up] to keep mistakes or unfavorable facts from being known about: *Criminals can cover up some of their illegal activities by dealing only in cash.* —see also COVER-UP **2 cover up for sb** to protect someone by hiding unfavorable facts about them: *High ranking military men were covering up for the murderers.* **3** [I,T cover yourself up] to put clothes on in order to keep warm or to prevent people from seeing your body: *I was completely covered up and I still wasn't warm enough.*

s w **cover²** *n.*
2̄2̄ **1** [sth that protects sth] [C] something that is put over or onto something to protect it, keep dirt out etc.: *a plastic cover* | *I need to buy a large casserole dish with a cover.*

2 [books] [C] the outer front or back page of a magazine, book etc.: *Clinton's on the cover of "Newsweek."* | *I read the magazine from cover to cover* (=read everything in it) *but I didn't see any coupons.*

3 the covers [plural] the sheets, BLANKETS etc. on a bed: *You're always stealing the covers!*

4 [shelter/protection] [U] shelter or protection from bad weather or attack: *The soldiers ran for cover when the shooting began.* | *The storm disrupted morning routines and sent people running for cover.* | *Come on, we can take cover in that barn over there!*

5 [U] something that hides something or keeps it secret, especially by seeming to be something else: [+ for] *He used a Miami aviation company as a cover for flights carrying drugs into the U.S.*

6 under cover pretending to be someone else in order to do something without being noticed: *Cobb worked on the case under cover for the FBI.* | *an undercover cop*

7 [music] also **cover version** [C] a performance or recording of a song that was originally recorded by someone else: *"The Bridge" was a tribute album of Neil Young covers.* | *I don't really like Clapton's cover of "I Shot the Sheriff."*

8 [cover charge] [C] a cover charge: *There's $5 cover because there's a band playing tonight.*

9 under cover of darkness/night hidden by darkness: *Most attacks take place under cover of darkness.*

10 under separate cover if a letter, check etc. is sent under separate cover it is in a separate envelope: *A $300 refund will be sent under separate cover.*

11 [insurance] [U] insurance against injury, damage etc.; COVERAGE

cov·er·age /'kʌvrɪdʒ/ *n.* [U] **1** the way in which a s w subject or event is reported on television or radio, or 3̄ in newspapers: *CNN intends to have continuous live coverage of the national party conventions.* **2** the amount of protection given to you by an insurance agreement: *Millions of people have no formal health care coverage.*

cov·er·alls /'kʌvɚˌɔlz/ *n.* [plural] a piece of clothing that you wear over all your clothes to protect them: *Brand stood before the judge wearing blue jail coveralls and leg irons.* —compare OVERALLS

cover charge /'.. ./ *n.* [C] money that you have to pay in a CLUB¹ (2) or bar in addition to the cost of the food and drinks, especially to go dancing or to hear a band: *On Wednesday and Thursday nights, the $5 cover charge is reduced to $3.*

covered wag·on /ˌ.. '../ *n.* [C] a large vehicle with a curved cloth top that is pulled by horses, used in past times in North America

cover girl /'.. ./ *n.* [C] a young attractive woman whose photograph is on the front cover of a magazine

cov·er·ing /'kʌvrɪŋ, -ərɪŋ/ *n.* [singular] something that covers or hides something: [+ of] *a light covering of snow*

cov·er·let /'kʌvɚlɪt/ *n.* [C] a cloth cover for a bed; BEDSPREAD

cover let·ter /'.. ,../ *n.* [C] a letter that you send with documents or a package explaining what it is or giving additional information: *Make sure to send a cover letter along with your resume.*

cover sto·ry /'.. ,../ *n.* [C] the story that goes with a picture on the cover of a magazine

co·vert¹ /'kouvɚt, 'kʌ-, kou'vɚt/ *adj.* secret or hidden: *A covert investigation was conducted to catch the drug-smuggling ring.* —opposite OVERT —**covertly** *adv.*

covert² *n.* [C] a group of small bushes growing close together in which animals can hide

cover-up /'.. ,./ *n.* [C] an attempt to prevent the public from discovering the truth about something: *People would suspect a cover-up if public hearings aren't held.* —see also **cover up** (COVER¹)

cov·et /'kʌvɪt/ *v.* [T] FORMAL to have a very strong desire to have something that someone else has: *Gatlin covets my job, which he has been in line for twice before.*

cov·et·ed /'kʌvətɪd/ *adj.* something that is coveted is something that many people want but that few people can get: *the highly coveted Pulitzer Prize*

cov·et·ous /'kʌvətəs/ *adj.* having a very strong desire to have something that someone else has, especially wealth: *They began to cast covetous eyes on their neighbors' fields.* —**covetously** *adv.* —**covetousness** *n.* [U]

cov·ey /'kʌvi/ *n.* [C] **1** a small group of birds **2** INFORMAL a small group of people or things: [+ **of**] *a covey of young girls*

SW
2
3**cow**[1] /kaʊ/ *n.* [C] **1 a)** a adult female animal that is large and is kept on farms for the milk it produces and for meat —compare BULL[1] (1) **b)** a male or female animal of this type: *a field full of cows* **2** the female of some large land and sea animals, such as the ELEPHANT or the WHALE **3 have a cow** SPOKEN to be very angry or surprised about something: *Pat had a cow because you didn't tell her about the party.* **4 till the cows come home** INFORMAL for a very long time, or forever: *They stay up and play cards till the cows come home.*

cow[2] *v.* [T] to make someone afraid, or to control them to by using violence or threats: *Dissidents were cowed into silence by the army.*

cow·ard /'kaʊərd/ *n.* [C] someone who is not brave at all: *They're cowards – they don't have the guts to confront me personally.*

Cow·ard /'kaʊərd/, **No·ël** /'noʊəl/ (1899–1973) a British actor, singer, and writer of songs and plays

cow·ard·ice /'kaʊərdɪs/ also **cow·ard·li·ness** /'kaʊərdlinɪs/ *n.* [U] lack of courage: *It would be an act of cowardice to avoid the debate.*

cow·ard·ly /'kaʊərdli/ *adj.* behaving in a way that shows that you are not brave: *Shooting at an animal that has just come out of a cage is cowardly.*

cow·bell /'kaʊbɛl/ *n.* [C] a bell that is put around a cow's neck so that it can be found easily

cow·boy /'kaʊbɔɪ/ *n.* **1** [C] a man whose job is to take care of cattle: *He'd been working as a cowboy on a Utah ranch.* **2 cowboys and Indians** a game played by children who pretend to be cowboys and Native Americans, fighting each other

cowboy hat /'.. ,./ *n.* [C] a hat with a wide circular edge and a tall, stiff top, worn by cowboys: *Today, the cowboy hat is an unmistakable symbol of America.* —see picture at HAT

cow·catch·er /'kaʊ ˌkætʃər/ *n.* [C] a piece of metal on the front of a train used to push things off the track

cow chip /'. ./ *n.* [C] a round flat mass of dry solid waste from a cow

cow·er /'kaʊər/ *v.* [I] to bend low and move back, especially because you are frightened: *They were cowering in the cellars, trapped by the shelling.*

cow·girl /'kaʊgərl/ *n.* [C] a woman whose job is to take care of cattle

cow·hand /'kaʊhænd/ *n.* [C] someone whose job is to take care of cattle

cow·hide /'kaʊhaɪd/ *n.* [C,U] the skin of a cow or the leather that is made from this

cowl /kaʊl/ *n.* [C] **1** a very large HOOD that covers your head and shoulders, especially worn by MONKS **2** a cover for a CHIMNEY that protects it from wind and rain

cow·lick /'kaʊˌlɪk/ *n.* [C] hair that sticks up on top of your head: *I can't brush this dumb cowlick down.*

cowl·ing /'kaʊlɪŋ/ *n.* [C] a metal cover for an aircraft engine

cowl neck /ˌ. './ *n.* [C] the neck on a piece of clothing that falls in folds at the front: *a cowl neck sweater*

co·work·er /'koʊ wɜrkər/ *n.* [C] someone who works with you and has a similar position

cow pie /'. ./ *n.* [C] a COW CHIP

cow·poke /'kaʊpoʊk/ *n.* [C] OLD-FASHIONED a COWBOY

cow·pox /'kaʊpɑks/ *n.* [U] a disease that cows suffer from, from which a VACCINE can be made and given to humans to protect them from SMALLPOX

cow·punch·er /'kaʊpʌntʃər/ *n.* [C] INFORMAL a COWBOY

cow·rie /'kaʊri/ *n.* [C] a shiny brightly-colored tropical shell, used in past times as money in parts of Africa and Asia

cow·shed /'kaʊʃɛd/ *n.* [C] a building where cows live in the winter, or where their milk is taken from them

323 · crack

cow·slip /'kaʊˌslɪp/ *n.* [U] a small European wild plant with sweet smelling yellow flowers

cox·comb /'kɑkskoʊm/ *n.* [C] another spelling of COCKSCOMB (2)

cox·swain /'kɑksən, -sweɪn/ also **cox** /kɑks/ *n.* [C] someone who controls the direction of a rowing boat, especially in races

coy /kɔɪ/ *adj.* **1** pretending to be shy in order to attract interest, or to avoid dealing with something difficult: *Ben thinks Leah is just being coy.* **2** unwilling to give information about something, especially because you want to keep an advantage: [+ **about**] *Gonzalez was coy about precisely where he's moving.* —**coyly** *adv.* —**coyness** *n.* [U]

coy·ote /kaɪ'oʊti, 'kaɪ-oʊt/ *n.* [C] a wild animal like a dog that lives in western North America and Mexico: *At night you can hear coyotes howling.* —see picture on page 429

coz /kʌz/ *n.* OLD USE used when speaking to your COUSIN

coz·en /'kʌzən/ *v.* [T] OLD USE to trick or deceive someone

co·zy /'koʊzi/ *adj.* **cozier, coziest 1** warm, soft and comfortable: *Who'd want to leave a warm cozy bed to go jogging in the middle of winter? | a cozy bathrobe* **2** a situation that is cozy is comfortable and friendly: *You and Mike looked pretty cozy at the party. | a cozy family gathering* —**cozily** *adv.* —**coziness** *n.* [U]

CPA *n.* [C] Certified Public Accountant; an ACCOUNTANT who has passed all their examinations

CPR *n.* [U] cardiopulmonary resuscitation; the act of breathing into someone's mouth and pressing on their chest to make them breathe again and to make their heart start beating again

Cpt. *n.* the written abbreviation of CAPTAIN

CPU *n.* [C] central processing unit; the part of a computer that controls and organizes what the computer does

crab[1] /kræb/ *n.* **1** [C,U] a sea animal with a round flat shell and two large CLAWS on its front legs, or the meat from this animal: *Alaskan king crabs | I'll have the crab cakes please.* —see picture at CRUSTACEAN **2** [usually singular] INFORMAL someone who easily becomes annoyed about unimportant things: *She's such a crab.* **3 crabs** [plural] a medical condition in which a type of LOUSE is in the hair around the sexual organs

SW
3

crab[2] *v.* **crabbed, crabbing** [I] to catch crabs

crab ap·ple /'. ,./ *n.* [C] a small apple that tastes sour, or the tree that it grows on

crab·bed /'kræbɪd/ *adj.* **1** crabbed writing is small and hard to understand: *His crabbed handwriting covered both sides of the page.* **2** OLD-FASHIONED easily annoyed; CRABBY: *Mr. Archer was a crabbed and unapproachable old man.*

crab·by /'kræbi/ *adj.* **crabbier, crabbiest** INFORMAL someone who is crabby easily becomes annoyed about unimportant things: *He's very crabby right now because he has a bad tooth.*

crab·grass /'kræbgræs/ *n.* [U] a type of rough grass

crack[1] /kræk/ *v.*

SW
2
3

1 break [I,T] to break something so that it gets one or more lines on its surface, or to break in this way: *Don't put delicate china in the dishwasher – it may crack. | Harding missed seven weeks of baseball practice after cracking a rib. | A strong earthquake cracked buildings in northwest China.*

2 loud sound [I,T] to make a sudden quick sound like the sound of something breaking, or to make something do this: *Her stiff joints cracked as she got out of her easy chair. | Cowboys cracked their whips as they herded cattle.*

3 hit sth [I always + adv./prep.,T always + adv./prep.] to accidentally hit something hard, especially part of your body: *Jim cracked his head on the bottom of the bunkbed. | [+ against/on] My elbow cracked against the edge of a shelf.*

4 voice [I] if your voice cracks, it changes from one level to another suddenly because of strong emotions: *Milken's voice cracked on the first word. "Guilty, your honor."*

5 egg/nut [T] to break the outside part of something, such as an egg or a nut, in order to get what is inside it: *Hold the egg in your hand and gently crack the shell with a knife.*

6 crack a joke INFORMAL to tell a joke: *He was relaxed and cracking jokes, despite his ordeal.*

7 lose control [I] also **crack up** to lose control of your emotions, become unable to think clearly or behave normally, or tell a secret, because you are very tired, worried, busy etc.: *If I don't get some time off soon, I'll be so stressed I'll crack up.* | **crack under the pressure/strain/burden etc.** *Some students crack under the strain.*

8 crack a window to open a window, especially one in a car, a small amount

9 stop working well [I] also **crack up** to be unable to continue doing something or working well because of a serious problem: *The whole political system is cracking up.*

10 be successful [T] to start being successful in a particular business or sport: *It's the first time the Spartans have cracked the top 20 in the rankings.*

11 solve [T] to solve a problem or find the way to use a CODE[1] (3): *Historians used the Rosetta stone to crack the code of Egyptian hieroglyphics.* | *Detectives finally cracked the murder case.*

12 crack a smile INFORMAL to smile when you have been serious, sad, or angry: *The security guard did not crack a smile.*

13 get cracking INFORMAL to start doing something or going somewhere as quickly as possible: *I'm going to the library – I've got to get cracking on this paper.*

14 not all it's cracked up to be INFORMAL not as good as people say it is: *Paper cups aren't quite the "green" product they were cracked up to be.*

15 crack open a bottle/the champagne etc. INFORMAL to open a bottle of alcohol for drinking: *Let's crack open a bottle to celebrate!*

16 steal [T] to open a SAFE illegally, in order to steal what is inside

17 crack the whip INFORMAL to make people you have control over work very hard: *As editor, Dorothy likes to crack the whip.*

crack down *phr. v.* [I] to become more strict in dealing with a problem and punishing the people involved: [+ on] *We have to crack down on software pirates.* —see also CRACKDOWN

crack up *phr. v.* INFORMAL [I,T] to laugh a lot at something, or to make someone laugh a lot: *Miranda sang us this cute song she learned in preschool and we were just cracking up.* | [**crack** sb **up**] *That joke still cracks me up.* —see also CRACKUP

sw **crack²** *n.* [C]

1 thin space a very narrow space between two things or two parts of something: [+ in] *Weeds grew from every crack in the sidewalk.* | [**open** sth **a crack**] *I crossed the room and opened the door a crack.*

2 break a thin line on the surface of something when it is broken but has not actually come apart: *Jagged cracks cut across the thick glass arch over the main entryway.* | [+ in] *The tremor caused cracks in the wall of older houses.*

3 problem a fault in an idea, system, or organization: *Cracks began to appear in the facade of their perfect family.* | [+ in] *Disagreements over such issues could cause cracks in the coalition.*

4 sound a sudden loud very sharp sound like the sound of a stick being broken: *There was a loud crack of thunder as the storm began.*

5 joke/remark INFORMAL a cruel joke or remark: *Roger made a crack about his girlfriend's weight.*

6 chance to do sth INFORMAL an opportunity or attempt to do something, especially for the first time: [+ at] *"This is Hearst's first crack at painting."* | *You should take another crack at that Camus book.*

7 drug [U] a very pure form of the illegal form of

COCAINE, that some people smoke for pleasure: *Shirley has been addicted to crack for four years.*

8 the crack of dawn very early in the morning: *They both had to get up at the crack of dawn the next morning.*

9 a crack in sb's voice a sudden change in the level of someone's voice, especially because they are very upset: *He noticed the crack in her voice as she tried to continue.*

10 sb's crack SLANG the space in the middle of someone's BUTTOCKS

crack³ *adj.* [only before noun] having a lot of skill: *She's an accomplished horse rider and a crack shot* (=good at shooting).

crack ba·by /'. ˌ../ *n.* [C] a baby that is born with medical and mental problems because its mother smoked CRACK² (7) before the baby was born

crack·down /'krækdaʊn/ *n.* [C usually singular] action that is taken in order to deal more strictly with a problem: [+ on] *Police have begun a major crackdown on drunk driving.* —see also **crack down** (CRACK¹)

cracked /krækt/ *adj.* **1** something that is cracked has thin lines on its surface because it has been damaged: *A cracked tile spoiled the look of the countertop.* —see picture at CHIPPED **2** someone's voice that is cracked sounds rough and uncontrolled because they are upset

crack·er /'krækɚ/ *n.* [C] **1** a type of hard dry bread that is thin and flat: *cheese and crackers* **2** a FIRE-CRACKER **3** TABOO a word used by African-Americans for a white person, especially a poor white person in the southeastern U.S. Do not use this word. sw 2

crack·er·jack /'krækɚˌdʒæk/ *adj.* having very good qualities or abilities: *a crackerjack police investigator*

crack·head /'krækhɛd/ *n.* [C] SLANG someone who uses the drug CRACK² (7)

crack house /'. ./ *n.* [C] a place where CRACK² (7) is sold, bought, and smoked

crack·le /'krækəl/ *v.* [I] to make a repeated short sharp sound like something burning in a fire: *There was a fire crackling in the big fireplace.* | *Welcome to St. Petersburg, a voice crackled over the intercom.* —**crackle** *n.* [singular]

crack·ling /'kræklɪŋ/ *n.* **1** [singular] the sound made by something when it crackles: *A loud crackling of papers and wrappers interrupted the movie.* **2** **cracklings** [plural] pieces of pig skin that have been cooked in oil and are eaten cold; PORK RINDS

crack·pot /'krækpɑt/ *adj.* slightly crazy or strange: *This theory is not just bad science – it's crackpot science.* —**crackpot** *n.* [C]

crack·up, crack-up /'kræk-ʌp/ *n.* INFORMAL **1** an accident on a vehicle such as a car or MOTORCYCLE: *Brian's had a couple of major crackups on his Harley.* **2** a NERVOUS BREAKDOWN —see also **crack up** (CRACK¹)

-cracy /krəsi/ *suffix* [in nouns] **1** government by a particular type of people or according to a particular principle: *democracy* (=government by the people) | *bureaucracy* (=government by officials who are not elected) **2** a society or country that is governed in this way, or in which a particular group of people have power: *a theocracy* (=government according to religious laws) **3** the group or type of people who have power in a particular society: *the aristocracy* (=people in the highest social rank) —see also -OCRACY

cra·dle¹ /'kreɪdl/ *n.* [C] **1** a small bed for a baby that you can ROCK (=move gently from side to side): *The baby rested peacefully in his cradle.* —see picture at BED¹ **2 the cradle of sth** the place where something important began: *Leipzig was the cradle of East Germany's pro-democracy movement.* **3 from the cradle to the grave** all through your life: *The colony provides for its people from cradle to grave.* **4** the part of a telephone where the part that you hold in your hand is put when it is not being used **5 from/in the cradle** from or in the earliest years of your life: *Joan's been a member of First Methodist since she was in the cradle.* —see also CAT'S CRADLE, **rob the cradle** (ROB (3))

cradle² *v.* [T] to gently hold someone or something in your hands or arms, as if to protect it: *Tamara was safely cradled in her mother's arms.* | *His arm was cradled in a sling.*

cradle-rob·ber /ˈ.. ˌ../ *n.* [C] someone who has a romantic relationship with someone much younger than they are: *Traci called Lee Ann a tramp and a cradle-robber.* —**cradle-rob** *v.* [I]

craft¹ /kræft/ *n.* **1** [C] *plural* **crafts** a job or activity that you need to have a lot of skill to do, especially one in which you make things: [+ **of**] *Karl learned the craft of knife-making in his hometown in Switzerland.* **2** [C] *plural* **craft** a boat, ship, or airplane: *Search and rescue craft were at the scene of the crash this morning.* **3** [U] skill in deceiving people: *Craft and cunning are necessary for the scheme to work.* —see also LANDING CRAFT

craft² *v.* [T usually passive] to make something using a special skill, especially with your hands: *a finely crafted Chinese serving platter* | *a hand-crafted Fabergé egg*

-craft /kræft/ *suffix* [in nouns] **1** a vehicle of a particular kind: *a spacecraft* | *a hovercraft* | *several aircraft* **2** skill of a particular kind: *witchcraft* (=ability to use magic) | *stagecraft* (=skill in acting or directing plays)

crafts·man /ˈkræftsmən/ *n. plural* **craftsmen** /-mən/ [C] someone who is very skilled at a particular craft: *The original designs were made by highly skilled craftsmen.*

crafts·man·ship /ˈkræftsmənˌʃɪp/ *n.* [U] **1** very detailed work that has been done using a lot of skill, so that the result is beautiful: *They make jewelry that is famous for its intricate craftsmanship.* **2** the special skill that someone uses to make something beautiful with their hands: *The design is inspired by Russian folk art and craftsmanship.*

crafts·wom·an /ˈkræftsˌwʊmən/ *n. plural* **craftswomen** /-ˌwɪmɪn/ [C] a woman who is very skilled at a particular craft

craft·y /ˈkræfti/ *adj.* **craftier, craftiest** good at getting what you want by planning what to do and secretly deceiving people; CUNNING¹ (1): *Willis plays a crafty policeman fighting international terrorists.* —**craftily** *adv.* —**craftiness** *n.* [U]

crag /kræg/ *n.* [C] a high and very steep rough rock or mass of rocks: *Massive slate crags rise above the river bank.*

crag·gy /ˈkrægi/ *adj.* **craggier, craggiest 1** a mountain that is craggy is very steep and covered in rough rocks: *the craggy peaks of the Sierra Madre* **2** having a face with many deep lines on it: *craggy good looks*

cram /kræm/ *v.* **crams, crammed, cramming 1** [T always + adv./prep.] to force something into a small space: [**cram sth into/onto etc.**] *I managed to cram all my stuff into the closet.* | [**cram sth with sth**] *Cars crammed with belongings left the disaster area.* **2** [T often passive] to fill an area with too many people: [**cram sth with sb**] *Store aisles were crammed with people looking for last minute gifts.* **3** [I] to prepare yourself for a test by learning a lot of information very quickly: *I've procrastinated all semester, so I have a lot of cramming to do.* | [**cram for sth**] *I have to cram for my chemistry test tomorrow.*

crammed /kræmd/ *adj.* completely full of things or people: *How can children learn in crammed classrooms?*

cramp¹ /kræmp/ *n.* **1** [C,U] a severe pain that you get in part of your body when a muscle becomes too tight, making it difficult for you to move that part of your body: *Muscle cramps often happen when you exercise in hot weather.* | **have/get a cramp** *Johnson got a cramp in his calf and had to be helped off the field.* —see also WRITER'S CRAMP **2 cramps** [plural] severe pains in the stomach, especially the ones that women get during MENSTRUATION

cramp² *v.* [T] **1** also **cramp up** to get a cramp in a muscle: *His muscles cramped so severely he had to stop playing.* **2** to prevent the development of

someone's ability to do something: *Federal guidelines are cramping the state's ability to adjust its own budget.* **3 cramp sb's style** to prevent someone from doing something they want to do, especially by going with them when they do not want you: *John said he broke up with her because she cramps his style.* —**cramping** *n.* [U]

cramped /kræmpt/ *adj.* **1** a cramped room, building etc. does not have enough space for the people in it: *I couldn't sleep on the plane – it was too cramped.* | *Five workers were packed into a cramped office.* **2** also **cramped up** unable to move much and uncomfortable because there is not enough space: *We all felt stiff from having been cramped up in the back of the car for so long.* **3** writing that is cramped is very small and difficult to read

cram·pon /ˈkræmpɑn/ *n.* [C usually plural] a piece of metal with sharp points on the bottom that you fasten onto your boots to help in mountain climbing in the snow

cran·ber·ry /ˈkrænˌbɛri/ *n. plural* **cranberries** [C] a small red sour fruit: *cranberry sauce*

crane¹ /kreɪn/ *n.* [C] **1** a large tall machine used by builders for lifting heavy things **2** a tall water bird with very long legs

crane² *v.* [I always + adv./prep.,T] to look around or over something by stretching or leaning: [**crane forward/over etc.**] *Curious passengers craned forward to see what the fuss was about.* | **crane your neck** *Parents and children craned their necks to see the parade.*

Crane /kreɪn/**, Hart** /hɑrt/ (1899–1932) a U.S. poet

Crane, Ste·phen /ˈstivən/ (1871–1900) a U.S. writer of NOVELS

cra·ni·um /ˈkreɪniəm/ *n.* [C] TECHNICAL the part of your head that is made of bone and covers your brain —**cranial** *adj.* —see picture at SKELETON

crank¹ /kræŋk/ *n.* **1** [C] a handle on a piece of equipment, that you turn in order to move something **2** [C] INFORMAL someone who easily gets angry or annoyed with people **3** [U] SLANG: see METHAMPHETAMINE (=an illegal drug)

crank² also **crank up** *v.* **1** SPOKEN to make something move by turning a crank: *You crank the engine while I try to connect these wires.* **2** SPOKEN to make the sound from a radio etc. louder: *They had it cranked up pretty loud.*

crank sth ↔ **out** *phr. v.* [T] INFORMAL to produce a lot of something very quickly: *He cranks out novels at the rate of two a year.*

crank call /ˈ. ./ *n.* [C] a telephone call intended as a joke or made in order to frighten, annoy, or upset someone: *We get quite a few crank calls at the office.*

crank·case /ˈkræŋkkeɪs/ *n.* [C] the container that encloses the crankshaft and other parts connected to the crankshaft

crank·shaft /ˈkræŋkʃæft/ *n.* [C] a long piece of metal in a vehicle that is connected to the engine and helps to turn the wheels

crank·y /ˈkræŋki/ *adj.* **crankier, crankiest** very easily annoyed or made angry, especially because you are tired: *Scott seems a little cranky this morning.* —**crankiness** *n.* [U]

Cran·mer /ˈkrænmər/**, Thomas** (1489–1556) an English priest who was the Archbishop of Canterbury and one of the leaders of the REFORMATION (=the start of the Protestant religion) in England

cran·ny /ˈkræni/ *n. plural* **crannies** [C] a small narrow hole in a wall or rock —**crannied** *adj.* —see also **nook and cranny** (NOOK (2))

crap¹ /kræp/ *n.*

1 something untrue [U] IMPOLITE something someone says that you think is completely wrong or untrue: *Jane doesn't really think we believe all that crap, does she?* | **a bunch/load of crap** *That's a bunch of crap! I never said that.* | *Greg's full of crap* (=says or said things that are untrue or

completely wrong). | *Len, just **cut the crap*** (=stop saying things that are untrue or completely wrong) *and tell me what happened.*
2 bad quality [U] IMPOLITE something that is very bad or is of bad quality: *They sell a lot of stuff cheap, but most of it is crap.* | **a bunch/load of crap** *The deal we worked out is a bunch of crap.*
3 things you do not want [U] IMPOLITE things that you do not need or want: *What is all this crap doing on my desk?*
4 bad treatment [U] IMPOLITE bad or unfair treatment: *I'm tired of you **giving me crap** (=saying bad things) about my long hair.* | *I'm not going to **take crap from you** (=allow you to treat me badly or say something bad about me) or anybody!* | *I **don't need this kind of crap** (=used when you are angry at the way someone is talking or behaving to you).*
5 solid waste [singular,U] VULGAR solid waste that is passed from your BOWELS: *I need to go **take a crap** (=pass solid waste from your bowels).*
6 sth is a crap shoot used to say that a situation contains a lot of risk and you do not know what will happen: *You can go to trial, but it's a crap shoot.*
7 craps [U] a game played for money in which you throw two DICE: *He's been out all night, **shooting craps** (=playing craps) with his friends.*

crap² *v.* **crapped, crapping** [I] VULGAR to pass solid waste matter from your BOWELS

crap·per /ˈkræpɚ/ *n.* VULGAR **the crapper** an impolite word meaning "the toilet"

crap·py /ˈkræpi/ *adj.* **crappier, crappiest** IMPOLITE not very good: *I've never seen such crappy acting.*

crash¹ /kræʃ/ *v.*
1 car/plane etc. [I,T] to have an accident in a car, airplane etc. by violently hitting another vehicle or something such as a wall or tree: *Witnesses say the jet crashed shortly after takeoff.* | *The tire blew, causing him to crash the car.* | [+ into/onto etc.] *Their car hit ice on a bridge and crashed into the side rail.*
2 hit sb/sth hard [I always + adv./prep.,T always + adv./prep.] to hit someone or something extremely hard while moving, in a way that causes a lot of damage or makes a lot of noise: [+ into/through etc.] *Suddenly, a baseball crashed through our living room window.* | *The plates **went crashing** to the floor.* | *A large branch **came crashing down**.*
3 computer [I,T] if a computer crashes or if someone or something crashes it, it suddenly stops working: *The system crashed and I lost three hours' worth of work.*
4 financial [I] if a STOCK MARKET crashes, the STOCKS suddenly lose a lot of value
5 sleep [I] SPOKEN **a)** to stay at someone's house for the night, especially when you have not planned to: *You can crash at our place if you can't get a ride home.* **b)** also **crash out** to go to bed, or to go to sleep very quickly, because you are very tired: *I crashed out on the sofa this afternoon.*
6 crash and burn INFORMAL to suddenly fail badly: *Minnelli's film career crashed and burned in the late '70s.*
7 party INFORMAL [T] to go to a party that you have not been invited to: *We crashed Stella's party last Friday.*
8 make a loud noise [I] to make a sudden, loud noise: *The cymbals crashed, and the symphony came to an end.*

crash² *n.* [C] **1** a very bad accident involving cars, airplanes etc. that have hit something: *Both drivers were injured in the crash.* | **a plane/car/bus etc. crash** (=a crash involving an airplane, car etc.) **2** an occasion when a computer or computer system suddenly stops working **3** an occasion on which the STOCKS in a STOCK MARKET suddenly lose a lot of value **4** a sudden loud noise made by something falling, breaking etc.: *The pile of books came down **with a crash**.*

crash course /ˌ. ˈ./ *n.* [C] a course in which you learn the most important things about a particular subject in a very short period of time: [+ in] *a crash course in computer programming*

crash di·et /ˌ. ˈ./ *n.* [C] an attempt to lose a lot of weight quickly by strictly limiting how much you eat

crash-dive /ˌ. ˈ./ *v.* [I] if a SUBMARINE crash-dives, it goes deeper into the water as fast as possible

crash hel·met /ˈ. ˌ../ *n.* [C] a hard hat that covers and protects your head, worn by race car drivers, people on MOTORCYCLEs etc.

crash land·ing /ˌ. ˈ./ *n.* **make a crash landing** to fly an airplane down so that it hits the ground hard but in as controlled a way as possible, in a situation in which a safe, normal LANDING is not possible

crass /kræs/ *adj.* offensive or rude, and not always knowing what is truly important or valuable: *We live in a time of crass materialism.* | *a crass remark* —**crassly** *adv.*

-crat /kræt/ *suffix* [in nouns] **1** a believer in a particular type or principle of government: *a democrat* (=who believes in government by the people) **2** a member of a powerful or governing social class or group: *an aristocrat* (=member of the highest social class) —see also -OCRAT

crate¹ /kreɪt/ *n.* [C] **1** a large wooden or plastic box used for moving things from one place to another or for storing them: *a big plastic crate for storing toys* | *a crate of beer* **2** OLD-FASHIONED a very old car or airplane that does not work very well

crate² also **crate up** *v.* [T] to pack things into a crate

cra·ter /ˈkreɪtɚ/ *n.* [C] **1** a round hole in the ground made by something that has fallen on it or exploded on it: *craters on the moon's surface* | *bomb craters* **2** the round open top of a VOLCANO

cra·vat /krəˈvæt/ *n.* [C] **1** FORMAL a TIE² (1) **2** a wide piece of loosely folded material that men wear around their necks; ASCOT

crave /kreɪv/ *v.* [T] to have an extremely strong desire for something: *Most little kids crave attention.*

cra·ven /ˈkreɪvən/ *adj.* FORMAL completely lacking courage; COWARDLY —**cravenly** *adv.* —**cravenness** *n.* [U]

crav·ing /ˈkreɪvɪŋ/ *n.* [C] an extremely strong desire for something: [+ for] *Parents should try to control their kid's cravings for fat-laden junk food.*

craw /krɔ/ *n.* [C] —see **stick in sb's craw** (STICK¹ (8))

craw·dad /ˈkrɔdæd/ also **craw·fish** /ˈkrɔˌfɪʃ/ *n.* [C] INFORMAL a CRAYFISH

crawl¹ /krɔl/ *v.* [I] **1** to move along on your hands and knees or with your body close to the ground: *When did Sam start crawling?* **2** if an insect crawls, it moves using its legs: [+ over/up etc.] *There's an ant crawling up your leg!* **3** if a vehicle crawls, it moves forward very slowly: *It took several hours to drive the 50 miles, crawling along through the snow.* **4 be crawling with sth** to be completely covered with insects, people etc.: *The apartments were crawling with rats and fleas.* **5 come crawling (back to sb)** INFORMAL to admit that you were wrong and ask for something that you refused to accept in the past: *In a few months, he'll come crawling back to us, wanting his old job.* —see also **make sb's skin crawl** (SKIN¹ (9))

crawl² *n.* **1** [singular] a very slow speed: *Traffic has slowed to a crawl.* **2 the crawl** a way of swimming in which you lie on your stomach and move one arm and then the other over your head

crash

cray·fish /ˈkreɪˌfɪʃ/ n. plural **crayfish** [C,U] a small animal like a LOBSTER that lives in rivers and streams, or the meat from this animal —see picture at CRUSTACEAN

cray·on /ˈkreɪɑn, -ən/ n. [C] a stick of colored WAX that children use to draw pictures

craze /kreɪz/ n. [C] a fashion, game, type of music etc. that becomes very popular for a short amount of time: The jogging craze began in the 1970s.

crazed /kreɪzd/ adj. [no comparative] wild, strange, or crazy: She was once attacked by a crazed fan.

-crazed /kreɪzd/ [in adjectives] **sex-crazed/sports-crazed/drug-crazed etc.** too interested in sex, sports etc.: fashion-crazed young women

cra·zy¹ /ˈkreɪzi/ adj. **crazier, craziest** INFORMAL
1 strange an action, idea, person, or type of behavior that is crazy is very strange or not sensible: Anybody who thinks they're a good team is crazy. | We're all grown up, but we still act like a couple of crazy kids. | Whose crazy idea was it to go camping in January? | **[be crazy to do sth]** It'd be crazy to try to drive home in this weather. | He often works 10 and 12 hours a day – it's crazy.
2 be crazy about sb/sth to like someone very much, or to be very interested in something: My sister's crazy about scuba diving.
3 angry angry or annoyed: Be quiet! You're driving me crazy! (=really annoying me) | Dad's going to go crazy (=be very angry) when he hears I quit my job.
4 like crazy very much or very quickly: These mosquito bites on my leg are itching like crazy. | We ran like crazy to the bus stop.
5 go crazy to do something too much, in a way that is not usual or not sensible, especially because you are excited: Don't go crazy and invest too much in stocks right now. | People went crazy with applause.
6 mentally ill mentally ill: I feel so alone, sometimes I wonder if I'm going crazy.
7 boy/girl crazy a phrase meaning too interested in having romantic relationships with boys or girls, usually used about young people: Stacy is sixteen and completely boy crazy.
8 crazy as a loon very strange and possibly mentally ill —**crazily** adv. —**craziness** n. [U]

crazy² n. [C] INFORMAL someone who is crazy

Cra·zy Horse /ˈ.. ./ (?1849–1877) a Native American chief of the Sioux tribe, famous for helping Sitting Bull to win a victory over General Custer's army at the Little Bighorn

crazy quilt /ˈ.. ./ n. [C] **1** a cover for a bed made from small pieces of cloth of different shapes and colors that have been sewn together **2 a crazy quilt of sth a)** several different kinds of things that form an unusual pattern together: The hayfields formed a crazy quilt of green. **b)** several different methods, styles, laws etc. that are used together or exist together, especially in a surprising or confusing way: What we have now is a crazy quilt of state insurance regulations.

creak /krik/ v. [I] if something such as a door, wooden floor, old bed, or stair creaks, it makes a long high noise when someone opens it, walks on it, sits on it etc.: The floorboards creaked as she walked. —**creak** n. [C]

creak·y /ˈkriki/ adj. **creakier, creakiest 1** something such as a door, floor, or bed that is creaky creaks when you open it, walk on it, sit on it etc., especially because it is old and not in good condition **2** an organization, company etc. that is creaky uses old-fashioned methods or ideas and does not work very well: a creaky national telephone system —**creakily** adv. —**creakiness** n. [U]

cream¹ /krim/ n. **1** [U] a thick yellow-white liquid that rises to the top of milk: Do you take cream or sugar in your coffee? —see also SOUR CREAM, WHIPPED CREAM **2** [U] a pale yellow-white color **3** [C,U] used in the names of foods containing cream or something similar to it: cream of chicken soup | banana cream pie **4** [C,U] a thick smooth substance that you put on your skin to make it feel soft, treat a medical condition etc.; LOTION: The doctor gave me some cream to put on my rash. **5 the cream of the crop** the best

people or things in a particular group: These students represent the cream of the academic crop.

cream² v. [T] **1** INFORMAL to hit someone very hard or easily defeat someone in a game, competition etc.: The Cougars creamed us last Saturday. | We got creamed 45–6. **2** to mix foods together until they become a thick smooth mixture: Next, cream the butter and sugar. **3** to take cream from the surface of milk

cream sb/sth ↔ off phr. v. [T] to choose the best people or things from a group, especially so that you can use them for your own advantage: Most of the best students are creamed off by the large companies.

cream cheese /ˌ. ˈ./ n. [U] a type of soft white smooth cheese

cream-col·ored /ˌ. ˈ..ˌ/ adj. yellow-white in color: a cream-colored purse

cream·er /ˈkrimə/ n. **1** [U] a white liquid or powder that you can use instead of milk or cream in coffee or tea **2** [C] a small container for holding cream

cream·er·y /ˈkriməri/ n. [C] OLD-FASHIONED a place where milk, butter, cream, and cheese are produced or sold; DAIRY (2)

cream of tar·tar /ˌ. . ˈ../ n. [U] a white powder used in baking and in medicine

cream puff /ˈ. ./ n. [C] **1** a light small sweet cake with WHIPped cream inside **2** someone who is weak or who cannot do difficult things: Professional wrestlers insist that wrestling is not for cream puffs.

cream·y /ˈkrimi/ adj. **creamier, creamiest 1** thick and smooth like cream: creamy peanut butter **2** containing cream: fresh creamy milk **3** yellow-white in color

crease¹ /kris/ n. [C] **1** a line on a piece of cloth, paper etc. where it has been folded, crushed, or pressed: I'll see if I can iron some of those creases out of your dress. **2** a fold in someone's skin

crease² v. [I,T] to become marked with a line or lines, or to make a line appear on cloth, paper etc. by folding or crushing it: These pants crease very easily. | Don't sit on my paper – you'll crease it! —see picture on page 424

cre·ate /kriˈeɪt/ v. [T] **1** to make something exist that did not exist before: Some believe the universe was created by a big explosion. | Several children created a disturbance. **2** to invent or design something: The software makes it easy to create colorful charts and graphs. | The pen pal program was created by teacher Cindy Lee.

cre·a·tion /kriˈeɪʃən/ n. **1** [U] the act of creating something: [+ of] The plan should result in the creation of 2000 new jobs. **2** [U] the whole universe and all living things: Are we the only thinking species in creation? **3** [C] something new that has been made or invented: Another of Marc's creations is a skirt with hand-painted flowers. **4 the Creation** the act by God of making the universe and everything in it, according to the Bible

cre·a·tion·ism /kriˈeɪʃənɪzəm/ n. [C] the belief that God created the universe in the way that is described in the Bible —**creationist** n. [C] —**creationist** adj.

creation sci·ence /.ˌ.. ˈ../ n. [U] a subject taught in some schools that is based on the idea that creationism can be proven scientifically

cre·a·tive¹ /kriˈeɪtɪv/ adj. **1** producing or using new and effective ideas, results etc.: I enjoy my job, but I'd like to do something more creative. | creative architectural designs **2** someone who is creative is very good at using their imagination and skills to make things: This year's prize goes to the creative young author Ben Williams. **3 creative accounting** the act of changing business accounts to achieve the result you want in a way that hides the truth, but is not illegal —**creatively** adv. —**creativeness** n. [U]

cre·a·tive² n. [C] SLANG someone such as a writer or artist who uses their imagination or skills to make things

C

cre·a·tiv·i·ty /ˌkrieɪˈtɪvəti/ n. [U] the ability to use your imagination to produce or use new ideas, make things etc.: *Companies need to encourage creativity and innovation.*

cre·a·tor /kriˈeɪtɚ/ n. **1** [C] someone who made or invented a particular thing: [+ of] *Walt Disney was the creator of Mickey Mouse.* **2 the Creator** God

s w **crea·ture** /ˈkritʃɚ/ n.
1 living thing [C] anything that is living, such as an animal, fish, or insect, but not a plant: *They found a fossil of a small, sparrow-like creature.* | *creatures of the deep* (=animals and fish that live in the ocean) | *Native Americans believe that all living creatures should be respected.*
2 imaginary or strange [C] an imaginary animal or person, or one that is very strange and sometimes frightening: *The movie's about creatures from outer space.*
3 a creature of sth someone who is a creature of something is influenced by it a lot, controlled by it, or has a quality produced by it: *Mimi is a creature of Hollywood, an aspiring actress.*
4 a creature of habit someone who always does things in the same way or at the same time
5 sth made or invented [C] something, especially something bad, that has been made or invented by a particular person or organization: *The Housing Board was a creature of Mayor Beller's design.*
6 stupid/adorable/horrid etc. creature OLD-FASHIONED someone who has a particular character or quality: *Get away from me, you horrid creature!*

creature com·forts /ˈ.. ˌ../ n. [plural] all the things that people need to feel comfortable, such as good food, a warm house, and comfortable furniture

crèche /krɛʃ/ n. [C] a model of the scene of Jesus Christ's birth, often placed in churches and homes at Christmas

cre·dence /ˈkridns/ n. [U] FORMAL the acceptance of something as true: *His ideas quickly gained credence* (=started to be believed) *among economists.* | *I don't give any credence* (=believe or accept something as true) *to these rumors.* | *The results of Dr. Young's study should lend credence* (=make something more believable) *to his theories on cell regeneration.*

cre·den·tial /krɪˈdɛnʃəl/ n. [C] **1** something, especially a document, that shows you have earned a particular position or are legally allowed to do a particular job: *He went back to college to get a teaching credential.* **2 credentials** plural **a)** someone's education, achievements, experience etc., that prove that they have the ability to do something: *His academic credentials include an M.A. and a Ph.D. from MIT.* **b)** a letter or other document that proves your good character or your right to have a particular position: *The commissioner presented his credentials to the State Department.*

cre·den·za /krəˈdɛnzə/ n. [C] a piece of furniture like a long low set of shelves with doors on the front, used for storing things, especially in offices

cred·i·bil·i·ty /ˌkrɛdəˈbɪləti/ n. [U] **1** the quality of deserving to be believed and trusted: *The scandal has ruined his credibility as a leader.* | [+ of] *There are serious questions about the credibility of these reports.* | **gain/lose credibility** *Harris has lost credibility among his colleagues.* **2 a/the credibility gap** the difference between what someone, especially a politician, says and what people can believe

cred·i·ble /ˈkrɛdəbəl/ adj. deserving or able to be believed or trusted: *Is she a credible witness?* —**credibly** adv.

s w **cred·it¹** /ˈkrɛdɪt/ n.
1 2
1 delayed payment [U] an arrangement with a store, bank etc. that allows you to buy something and pay for it later: *We bought a new stove on credit* (=using credit). | *One store offers six months of interest-free credit* (=credit with no INTEREST charges).
2 amount of money [C] an amount of money that is put into someone's bank account or added to another amount: *The company promised to provide refunds and credits to customers who had been charged too much.* —compare DEBIT¹
3 praise [U] approval or praise for doing something good: [+ for] *The credit for the team's winning season goes to the coach.* | *They never give Gene any credit for all the extra work he does.* | *If the economy improves, the White House will take credit for it.* | *To Navarro's credit, he was always accessible and cooperative.* | *The kids themselves deserve a lot of credit for the success of the program.*
4 in credit to have money in your bank account
5 the credits a list of all the people involved in making a television program or movie
6 be a credit to sb/sth also **do sb/sth credit** to be so successful or good that everyone who is connected with you can be proud of you: *Jo's a credit to her profession.*
7 university [C] a unit that shows you have successfully completed part of your studies at a school or college: *I don't have enough credits to graduate.*
8 responsibility for doing sth [U] the responsibility for achieving or doing something good: *She already has two best-selling novels to her credit.* | *Two companies have claimed credit for inventing the microprocessor.*
9 true/correct [U] the belief that something is true or correct: *The witness's story gained credit with the jury.*
10 a credit report/statement a document that gives details of whether someone has been responsible about paying for anything they have bought using credit

credit² v. [T not in progressive] **1** to add money to a bank account: [+ with] *For some reason, my account's been credited with an extra $76.* | [+ to] *The check has been credited to your account.* —compare DEBIT² (1) **2 credit sb with sth** to believe or admit that someone has a particular quality, or has done something good: *I wouldn't have credited him with that much intelligence.* **3 be credited to sb/sth** if something is credited to someone or something, they have achieved it or are the reason for it: *The revolutionary new drug is widely credited to Arthur Kessler.* **4** FORMAL to believe that something is true: *His statements are hard to credit.*

cred·it·a·ble /ˈkrɛdɪtəbəl/ adj. [only before noun] deserving praise or approval: *Bassett did a creditable job of impersonating the singer Tina Turner.* —**creditably** adv.

credit card /ˈ.. ˌ./ n. [C] a small plastic card that you s w use to buy goods or services and pay for them later: 2 *We accept all major credit cards.* —compare DEBIT CARD

credit his·to·ry /ˈ.. ˌ../ n. [C] someone's credit history says whether they have been responsible about paying for things they have bought using credit

credit lim·it /ˈ.. ˌ../ n. [C] the amount of money that you are allowed to borrow or spend using your credit card

cred·i·tor /ˈkrɛdətɚ/ n. [C] a person, bank, or company that you owe money to —compare DEBTOR

creditor na·tion /ˈ... ˌ../ n. [C] TECHNICAL a country that has INVESTed in or lent more money to other countries than other countries have INVESTed in or lent to it —compare DEBTOR NATION

credit rat·ing /ˈ.. ˌ../ n. [C] a judgment made by a bank or other company about how likely a person or business is to pay their debts

credit u·nion /ˈ.. ˌ../ n. [C] a business similar to a bank that is owned by the people who save money in it, and that also lends money to them for things such as cars or houses

cred·it·wor·thy /ˈkrɛdɪtˌwɚði/ adj. considered to be able to pay debts —**creditworthiness** n. [U]

cre·do /ˈkridoʊ/ n. plural **credos** [C] a short formal statement of the beliefs of a particular person, group, religion etc.: *American Express is emphasizing its "the customer is first" credo.*

cre·du·li·ty /krɪˈduləti/ n. [U] FORMAL **1** willingness or ability to believe that something is true **2 stretch/strain credulity** to make something hard to believe or accept as true: *Some sections of his testimony stretch credulity.*

cred·u·lous /ˈkrɛdʒələs/ *adj.* FORMAL always believing what you are told, and therefore easily deceived: *Quinn charmed hundreds of credulous investors out of millions of dollars.* —**credulously** *adv.* —**credulousness** *n.* [U]

Cree /kri/ *n.* a Native American tribe from the northern region of the U.S. and from Canada

creed /krid/ *n.* [C] **1** a set of beliefs or principles, especially religious: *The community center welcomes people of every creed* (=of all different religious beliefs), *color, and nationality.* **2 the Creed** a formal statement of belief spoken in some Christian churches

Creek /krik/ *n.* a Native American tribe from the southeastern region of the U.S.

creek /krik, krɪk/ *n.* [C] **1** a small narrow stream or river **2 be up the creek (without a paddle)** SPOKEN to be in a very difficult situation: *I'll really be up the creek if I don't get paid this week.*

creel /kril/ *n.* [C] a FISHERMAN's basket for carrying fish

creep¹ /krip/ *v.* past tense and past participle **crept** [I always + adv./prep.]
1 move quietly to move in a quiet, careful way, especially to avoid attracting attention: [+ into/over/around etc.] *A neighbor saw the guy creeping around our backyard.*
2 move slowly if something such as an insect, small animal, or car creeps, it moves slowly and quietly: [+ down/along/away etc.] *I got stuck behind a truck creeping along the highway at 25 mph.*
3 change slowly if prices, rates, levels etc. creep up or down, they slowly change from one price etc. to another: *The unemployment rate crept up to 5.7% in May.*
4 gradually occur to gradually begin to appear or happen in something and change it: [+ in/into/over etc.] *Bitterness crept into his voice.* | *Some English words have crept into Italian.*
5 plants if a plant creeps, it grows or climbs up or along a particular place: [+ up/over/around etc.] *All of the buildings have ivy creeping up their walls.*
6 mist/clouds etc. LITERARY if mist, clouds etc. creep, they gradually fill or cover a place: [+ into/over etc.] *Fog was creeping into the valley.*
7 make sb's flesh creep to make someone feel strong dislike or fear: *His touch made my flesh creep.*
creep up on sb/sth *phr. v.* [T] **1** to surprise someone by walking up behind them silently: *Don't creep up on me like that!* **2** if something creeps up on you, it gradually increases without you noticing it for a long time: *Lyme disease, caused by the bite of an infected tick, is an epidemic that has crept up on us.* **3** to seem to come sooner than you expect: *Somehow, the end of the semester had crept up on us.*

creep² *n.* **1** SPOKEN someone you dislike a lot: *Get lost, you little creep!* **2 give sb the creeps** if a person or place gives you the creeps, they make you feel nervous and a little frightened, especially because they are strange: *Tony gives me the creeps.*

creep·er /ˈkripɚ/ *n.* [U] a plant that grows up trees or walls, or along the ground

creep·y /ˈkripi/ *adj.* **creepier, creepiest** making you feel nervous and a little frightened: *There's something creepy about the building.*

creepy crawl·y /ˌ.. ˈ../ *n.* [C] SPOKEN a word meaning an "insect," especially one that you are frightened of, used especially by children

cre·mains /krɪˈmeɪnz/ *n.* [plural] what is left of a dead person's body after it has been CREMATED (=burned)

cre·mate /ˈkrimeɪt, krɪˈmeɪt/ *v.* [T] to burn the body of a dead person after a funeral —**cremation** /krɪˈmeɪʃən/ *n.* [C,U]

cre·ma·to·ri·um /ˌkriməˈtɔriəm/ **crem·a·to·ry** /ˈkriməˌtɔri, ˈkrɛm-/ *n.* plural **crematoriums, crematoria** /-riə/ *n.* a building in which the bodies of dead people are burned after a funeral

crème de la crème, creme de la creme /ˌkrɛm də

lɑ ˈkrɛm, -lə-/ *n.* [singular] the very best of a type of thing or group of people: *Tokyo University is the creme de la creme of Japanese universities.*

crème de menthe /ˌkrɛm də ˈmɛnθ/ *n.* [U] a strong sweet green alcoholic drink

cren·e·lat·ed /ˈkrɛnəˌleɪtɪd/ *adj.* TECHNICAL a wall or tower that is crenelated has BATTLEMENTS

cre·ole /ˈkrioʊl/ *n.* **1** [C,U] a language that is a combination of a European language and one or more other languages —compare PIDGIN **2 Creole a)** someone whose family was originally from both Europe and Africa **b)** someone whose family were originally French SETTLERS in the southern U.S. **3** [U] food prepared in the SPICY strong-tasting style of the southern U.S.: *Have you had the shrimp creole?* —**creole** *adj.*

cre·o·sote /ˈkriəˌsoʊt/ *n.* [U] a thick, brown, oily liquid used for preserving wood —**creosote** *v.* [T]

crepe, crêpe /kreɪp/ *n.* **1** [U] a type of light soft thin cloth with very small folded lines on its surface, made from cotton, silk, wool, etc. **2** [C] a very thin PANCAKE **3** [U] tightly pressed rubber used especially for making the bottoms of shoes

crepe pa·per /ˈ. ˌ../ *n.* [U] thin brightly colored paper with very small folded lines on its surface, used especially as a decoration at parties

crept /krɛpt/ *v.* [I always + adv./prep.] the past tense and past participle of CREEP¹

cre·scen·do /krəˈʃɛndoʊ/ *n.* [C] **1** a sound or a part of a piece of music that becomes gradually louder: *The violins had reached a crescendo* (=gradually become louder). | *Her voice rose to a crescendo* (=gradually became louder). —opposite DIMINUENDO **2** LITERARY a time when people are becoming more and more excited, anxious, or angry: *The mood on campus is building to a crescendo of excitement.* —**crescendo** *adj.*

cres·cent /ˈkrɛsənt/ *n.* [C] **1** a curved shape that is wider in the middle and pointed on the ends: *a crescent moon* —see picture at SHAPE¹ **2** this curved shape as a sign of the Muslim religion

cress /krɛs/ *n.* [U] a small plant with round green leaves that can be eaten and has a slightly SPICY taste

crest¹ /krɛst/ *n.* **1** [C usually singular] the top or highest point of something such as a hill or a wave: *the Pacific Crest Trail* | [+ of] *The planes flew in over the crest of the mountain.* **2 be riding the crest of sth** to be very successful, happy etc., especially for a limited period of time: *Minnesota is riding the crest of a six-game winning streak.* | *The President is currently riding the crest of a wave of popularity.* **3** [C] a pointed group of feathers on top of a bird's head **4** [C] a special picture used as a sign of a family, town, school etc.: *writing paper with the family crest* **5** [C] a decoration of bright feathers, worn, especially in past times, on top of soldiers' HELMETS

crest² *v.* **1** [I] if a wave, flood etc. crests, it reaches its highest point before it falls: *The Colorado River crested at 7 feet above flood stage.* **2** [T] FORMAL to reach the top of a hill, mountain etc.: *By afternoon, we had crested another ridge.*

crest·ed /ˈkrɛstɪd/ *adj.* [only before noun] **1** having a crest: *a red-crested cockatoo* **2** marked by a crest: *a crested navy blue jacket*

crest·fall·en /ˈkrɛstˌfɔlən/ *adj.* disappointed and sad, especially because you have failed to do something: *Stafford looked crestfallen when he was told about the layoffs.*

cre·ta·ceous /krɪˈteɪʃəs/ *adj.* TECHNICAL **1** similar to CHALK¹ (1) or containing CHALK **2 the Cretaceous period** the time when rocks containing CHALK were formed

Crete /krit/ the largest island belonging to Greece, in the southeast Mediterranean Sea

cre·tin /ˈkritˈn/ *n.* [C] someone who is extremely stupid: *Andy is one of the most incompetent cretins I've ever met!* —**cretinous** *adj.*

cre·vasse /krə'væs/ n. [C] a deep wide crack, especially in thick ice

crev·ice /'krɛvɪs/ n. [C] a narrow crack, especially in rock: *Yellow flowers grow in the crevices of the limestone cliffs.*

s w
2 2
crew[1] /kru/ n. **1** [C] all the people that work together on a ship, airplane etc.: *The crew of the space shuttle will hold a press conference Friday.* **2** [C] all the people working on a ship, airplane etc. except the most important officers: *I'd like to thank you on behalf of the officers and crew.* **3** [C] a group of people with special skills who work together on something: *Everyone in the movie's cast and crew has done a great job.* —see also GROUND CREW **4** [singular] a group of people: *We found a happy crew of foreign students in the hostel.* —see also **a motley crew/bunch/crowd etc.** (MOTLEY (1)) **5** [C] a team of people who compete in ROWING races: *Jason's on the Boston College crew.*

crew[2] v. [I,T] to be part of the crew on a boat: *The U.S.S. Mason was crewed entirely by black sailors.*

crew cut /'. ./ n. [C] a very short hair style for men —see picture at HAIRSTYLE[1]

crew·man /'krumən/ n. plural **crewmen** /-mən/ [C] a member, especially a male member, of a CREW[1] (2)

crew mem·ber /'. ,../ n. [C] a member of a CREW[1] (2)

crew neck /'. ./ n. [C] a plain round neck on a SWEATER —compare V-NECK

crew sock /'. ./ n. [C usually plural] a type of sock that is short, thick, and RIBBED (=having a pattern of raised lines)

crib[1] /krɪb/ n. [C] **1** a bed for a baby or young child, especially one with bars to keep the baby from falling out —see picture at BED[1] **2** SLANG the place where someone lives **3** an open box or wooden frame holding food for animals; MANGER

crib[2] v. **cribbed, cribbing** [I,T] to copy something dishonestly from someone else, especially school or college work: *He was accused of cribbing an article for his speech.* | **[crib sth off/from sb]** *Matt was caught cribbing the answers from his friend.*

crib·bage /'krɪbɪdʒ/ n. [U] a card game in which points are shown by putting small pieces of wood in holes in a small board

crib death /'. ./ n. [C] the sudden and unexpected death of a baby while it is asleep; SUDDEN INFANT DEATH SYNDROME

crib note also **crib sheet** /'. ./ n. [C] INFORMAL something on which answers to questions are written, usually used in order to cheat on a test

crick[1] /krɪk/ n. [C] a sudden painful stiffening of the muscles, especially in the back or the neck: **[+ in]** *I woke up with a crick in my neck.*

crick[2] v. [T] to do something that produces a crick in your back or neck

Crick /krɪk/, **Fran·cis** /'frænsɪs/ (1916–) a British scientist who worked with James Watson, and discovered the structure of DNA, the substance that carries GENETIC information in the cells of plants, animals, and humans

crick·et /'krɪkɪt/ n. **1** [C] a small brown jumping insect that makes a short loud noise by rubbing its wings together **2** [U] an outdoor game between two teams of 11 players, in which players try to get points by hitting a ball and running between two sets of special sticks

s w
1
crime /kraɪm/ n.
1 crime in general [U] illegal activity in general: *Compared to most cities, Cedar Rapids has very little crime.* | *This country has the fastest-growing crime rate* (=the amount of crime in a society) *in the world.* | *The last two years have seen a dramatic increase in violent crime.* | *Many blame the poor economy for the recent crime wave* (=a sudden increase in the amount of crime). | *At the age of twelve, he entered into a life of crime* (=a way of living and getting money by doing illegal activities). |

Kids in poor neighborhoods often turn to crime (=start doing illegal things). —see also **(a) petty crime** (PETTY (3))
2 a particular crime [C] a dishonest, violent, or immoral action that can be punished by law: **[+ against]** *Crimes against the elderly are becoming more common.* | *Paulson committed a number of crimes in the area.* | *Today, the jury was taken to the crime scene* (=place where a particular crime happened).
3 it's a crime SPOKEN said when you think something is completely wrong: *It's a crime to throw away all that food.*
4 crimes against humanity cruel crimes against a lot of ordinary people, that are considered unacceptable in any situation, even during a war: *Almost all the top party officials were freed despite their crimes against humanity.*
5 a crime of passion a crime, usually murder, that happens as a result of someone's sexual JEALOUSY
6 the perfect crime a crime in which the criminal is never discovered: *There is no such thing as the perfect crime.*
7 crime doesn't pay used to say that it is wrong to think that being involved in crime will bring you any advantage, because you will probably be caught and punished for it —see also HATE CRIME, ORGANIZED CRIME, **partner in crime** (PARTNER[1] (5)), WAR CRIME, **white-collar crime** (WHITE-COLLAR (2))

crim·i·nal[1] /'krɪmənəl/ adj. **1** relating to crime: *Gleason denied any involvement in criminal activity and was released.* | *Drinking and driving is a criminal offense* (=a crime that can be punished by law). | *None of his neighbors knew he had a criminal background* (=a history of doing illegal things). | *Ray got mixed up with the local criminal element* (=people within a particular group or area who do illegal things).* **2** [no comparative] relating to the part of the legal system that is concerned with crime: *Lawyers are not allowed to comment on current criminal cases.* | *the criminal justice system* | *The Justice Department is pursuing criminal charges* (=official statements saying that someone has done something illegal) *against the company as a result of the deaths.* —compare CIVIL (3) **3** INFORMAL wrong, dishonest, and unacceptable, but not illegal: *It's criminal to charge so much for popcorn at the movies!* —**criminally** adv.

s w
2

criminal[2] n. [C] someone who is involved in illegal activities or has been proven guilty of a crime: *We need to prevent young offenders from becoming hardened criminals* (=people who have been involved in crime for a long time).

crim·i·nal·ize /'krɪmənl,aɪz/ v. [T] to make something illegal: *In 1937, the U.S. government criminalized the use of marijuana.*

criminal law /,... './ n. [U] laws or the study of laws relating to crimes and their punishments —see also CANON LAW, CIVIL LAW, COMMON LAW

criminal rec·ord /,... '../ n. [C] an official record kept by the police of any crimes a person has done; RECORD[1] (4): *Judge Stevens noted that Osborn had no criminal record and no history of violence.*

crim·i·nol·o·gy /,krɪmə'nɑlədʒi/ n. [U] the scientific study of crime and criminals —**criminologist** n. [C]

crimp[1] /krɪmp/ n. **put a crimp in/on sth** to reduce or restrict something so that it is difficult to do something: *Falling wheat prices have put a crimp on farm incomes.*

crimp[2] v. [T] **1** to restrict the development, use, or growth of something: *The lack of effective advertising has crimped sales.* **2** to press something, especially cloth, paper etc. into small regular folds **3** to make your hair slightly curly by using a special heated tool

crim·son[1] /'krɪmzən/ n. [U] a dark slightly purple red color —**crimson** adj.

crimson[2] v. [I] FORMAL if your face crimsons, it becomes red because you are embarrassed

cringe /krɪndʒ/ v. [I] **1** to move back or away from someone or something, especially because you are afraid or in pain: *People cringed in terror as the* *shells hit the city around them.* **2** to feel embarrassed by something that seems stupid: *His blunt personality leaves even his supporters cringing.* | *Paul cringed at the thought of having to sing in public.* —**cringe** *n.* [C]

crin·kle[1] /'krɪŋkəl/ *v.* [I,T] also **crinkle up** to become covered with small folds, or to make something do this: *Mandy crinkled up her nose in disgust.* —**crinkled** *adj.* —compare WRINKLE[1]

crinkle[2] *n.* [C usually singular] a thin fold, especially in your skin or on cloth, paper etc. —compare WRINKLE[2]

crin·kly /'krɪŋkli/ *adj.* **1** having many thin folds: *The leaves turned brown and crinkly.* **2** hair that is crinkly is stiff and curly —**crinkliness** *n.* [U]

crin·o·line /'krɪnl-ɪn/ *n.* **1** [U] a stiff rough material used as a support on the inside of hats and other pieces of clothing **2** [C] a round frame worn under a woman's skirt in past times to support it and give it shape

cripes /kraɪps/ *interjection* OLD-FASHIONED said to express surprise or annoyance: *Oh, cripes! My mom'll kill me if she sees this!*

crip·ple[1] /'krɪpəl/ *v.* [T] **1** to hurt or wound someone so that they cannot use their arms or legs correctly or cannot walk: *The accident crippled her for life.* **2** to seriously damage or weaken something: *Asia's economy has been crippled by inflation.* —**crippled** *adj.* —**crippling** *adj.*

cripple[2] *n.* [C] **1** OFFENSIVE someone who cannot use their arms or legs correctly, especially someone who is physically unable to walk —compare DISABLED **2 emotional cripple** someone who is not able to deal with their own or other people's feelings: *Losing my family left me an emotional cripple.*

cri·sis /'kraɪsɪs/ *n. plural* **crises** /-siz/ [C,U] **1** a very bad or dangerous situation that might get worse, especially in politics or economics: *Cars lined up for gas during the energy crisis of 1972.* | *She's written a book about the Cuban missile crisis.* **2** a time when an emotional problem or illness is at its worst: *In times of crisis you find out who your real friends are.* **3 a crisis of/in confidence** a situation in which people do not believe that a government, ECONOMY, system etc. is working in the way that it should anymore, so that they will not support it, work with it etc. anymore: [+ in] *The disaster led to a crisis of confidence in NASA's leadership.* **4 crisis management** the skill or process of dealing with unusually dangerous or difficult situations —see also MIDLIFE CRISIS

crisp[1] /krɪsp/ *adj.* **1** pleasantly dry and hard enough to be easily broken: *His feet broke through the crisp outer layer of snow.* | *a crisp piece of bacon* **2** fruit and vegetables that are crisp are firm and fresh: *a crisp apple* | *a crisp salad* **3** paper or cloth that is crisp is fresh, clean, and new: *She handed me a crisp $20 bill.* **4** weather that is crisp is cold and dry: *It was a crisp winter morning.* **5** speech, behavior, or manner that is crisp is quick, confident, and shows no doubts or slowness: *The general's voice was crisp and clear as he addressed the meeting.* —**crisply** *adv.* —**crispness** *n.* [U]

crisp[2] *v.* [T] to make something become crisp, especially by cooking or heating it

crisp·y /'krɪspi/ *adj.* **crispier, crispiest** crisp and good to eat: *crispy fresh lettuce*

criss·cross[1] /'krɪskrɔs/ *v.* [I,T] **1** to travel many times from one side of an area to the other: *They spent a year crisscrossing the country by bus.* **2** to make a pattern of straight lines that cross over each other

crisscross[2] *n.* [C] a pattern made up of straight lines, usually a lot of them, that cross each other —**crisscross** *adj.*: *a crisscross pattern*

cri·te·ri·on /kraɪ'tɪriən/ *n. plural* **criteria** /-riə/ [C usually plural] a standard which is established so that a judgment or decision, especially a scientific one, can be made: [+ for] *What are the main criteria for awarding the prize?*

USAGE NOTE: CRITERION

GRAMMAR: criterion, criteria
Criterion is singular and **criteria** is plural. However, many people use the word **criteria** when they are speaking about a single reason for something.

crit·ic /'krɪtɪk/ *n.* [C] **1** someone whose job is to judge whether a movie, book etc. is good or bad: *She started as a food critic for a local paper.* **2** someone who expresses strong disapproval or dislike of a person, idea, organization etc.: [+ of] *Senator Wilson is an outspoken critic of the plan to close the old airport.* —see also **an armchair traveler/critic etc.** (ARMCHAIR[2])

crit·i·cal /'krɪtɪkəl/ *adj.*
1 ▊making severe judgments▊ someone who is critical makes severe and often unfair judgments of people or things: [+ of] *Dillard is very critical of the plan to reorganize the company.*
2 ▊important▊ very important, because what happens in the future depends on it: *We need an immediate decision on this critical issue.* | *This next phase is critical to the project's success.* | *Finding the cause of the power outage is of critical importance* (=very important).
3 ▊dangerous/uncertain▊ very serious, uncertain, or dangerous, because a situation could get worse: *Stan is at a critical stage in his recovery from the accident.*
4 ▊making fair judgments▊ making careful and fair judgments about whether someone or something is good or bad: *The article is a critical analysis of Faulkner's novels.*
5 ▊art/movies/books etc.▊ produced by or resulting from the work of critics: *The play was a critical success* (=liked by the critics).
6 in critical condition so sick that you could die: *The patient is in critical condition at Bellvue Hospital tonight.*
7 the critical list a list of people in the hospital who are so sick that they could die: *He was taken off the critical list last night, so we're very relieved.*
8 with a critical eye if you look at or examine something with a critical eye, you examine it carefully in order to judge its good and bad qualities

crit·i·cally /'krɪtɪkli/ *adv.* **1 critically ill/important/injured etc.** very seriously ill, very important etc.: *Ten people were critically injured in the accident.* | *Food supplies are critically low in the region.* **2** in a way that shows you have thought about the good and bad qualities of something: *College taught me to think critically about religion.* **3 critically acclaimed** praised by people who are paid to give their opinion on art, music etc.: *a critically acclaimed drama*

critical mass /ˌ... './ *n.* [C,U] TECHNICAL the amount of a substance necessary for an ATOMIC CHAIN REACTION to start

critical path a·nal·y·sis /ˌ... ˌ. '...ˌ ...'. ˌ.ˌ/ *n. plural* **critical path analyses** [C] TECHNICAL a method of planning a large piece of work so that there will be few delays and the cost will be as low as possible

crit·i·cism /'krɪtəˌsɪzəm/ *n.* **1** [C,U] the act of giving your opinion or judgment about whether someone or something is good or bad, or the written or spoken statements in which you do this: *Kathy doesn't take criticism* (=accept criticism) *very well.* | *I'm always willing to hear constructive criticism* (=advice that is intended to help someone or something improve). | *Graham's criticisms have no basis in fact.* | [+ of] *There is growing criticism of the President's decision.* **2 a)** [U] the activity of forming and expressing judgments about the good or bad qualities of books, movies, music etc.: *literary criticism* **b)** [C,U] the written work that results from this activity

crit·i·cize /'krɪtəˌsaɪz/ *v.* **1** [I,T] to express your disapproval of someone or something, or to talk about their faults: *Ron does nothing but criticize and* *complain all the time.* | [**criticize sb for (doing) sth**] Fowler has been criticized for misusing public funds. **2** [T] to judge whether something is good or bad: *I meet with several other artists and we criticize each other's work.*

cri·tique¹ /krɪˈtik/ *n.* [C,U] an article, book etc. that expresses judgments about the good and bad qualities of someone or something: [+ **of**] *The final article is a critique of John Updike's latest novel.*

critique² *v.* [I,T] to make remarks and judgments about the good and bad qualities of someone or something: *Doctors are taped and critiqued as they talk to patients.* | *Afterwards, the rest of the group will critique your presentation.*

crit·ter /ˈkrɪtɚ/ *n.* [C] INFORMAL an animal, fish, or insect; creature: *Frogs and toads are tough little critters.*

croak¹ /krouk/ *v.* **1** [I] to make a deep low sound like the sound a FROG makes **2** [I] INFORMAL to die **3** [I,T] to speak in a low rough voice, as if you have a sore throat: *"I don't feel very well," he croaked.*

croak² *n.* [C] **1** the sound a FROG makes **2** a low sound made in an animal's or person's throat, like one that a FROG makes

Cro·a·tia /krouˈeɪʃə/ a country in eastern Europe between Hungary and the Adriatic Sea —**Croatian** *n., adj.*

cro·chet /krouˈʃeɪ/ *v.* [I,T] to make clothes, hats etc. from YARN (1), using a special needle with a hook at one end —**crochet** *n.* [U] —**crocheting** *n.* [U] —compare KNIT¹ (1)

crock /krɑk/ *n.* [C] **1 a crock (of shit)** SPOKEN, IMPOLITE something that is not believable, not fair, not true etc.: *That's a crock. She'd never even met him before.* **2** OLD-FASHIONED a clay pot

crocked /krɑkt/ *adj.* [not before noun] SPOKEN drunk: *I was absolutely crocked last night.*

crock·er·y /ˈkrɑkəri/ *n.* [U] dishes made from clay

Crock·ett /ˈkrɑkɪt/, **Da·vy** /ˈdeɪvi/ (1786–1836) a famous American who lived on the FRONTIER and who became a member of the U.S. Congress and was later killed trying to defend the Alamo (=a church in Texas)

Crock-Pot /ˈ. ./ *n.* [C] TRADEMARK a large electric pot that cooks foods very slowly

croc·o·dile /ˈkrɑkəˌdaɪl/ *n.*
1 [C] a large REPTILE that has a long body and a long mouth with sharp teeth, and lives in hot wet areas **2** [U] the skin of this animal, used for making things such as shoes **3 crocodile tears** the expression of feeling

crocodile

sad, sorry, or upset when you do not really feel that way: **shed/cry crocodile tears** (=to pretend you feel sad, sorry, or upset)

cro·cus /ˈkroukəs/ *n.* [C] a small purple, yellow, or white flower that appears in early spring

crois·sant /krwɑˈsɑnt/ *n.* [C] a piece of bread, shaped in a curve and usually eaten for breakfast

Crom·well /ˈkrɑmwɛl/, **Ol·i·ver** /ˈɑlɪvɚ/ (1599–1658) an English military and political leader who led the army of Parliament against King Charles I in the English Civil War, defeated the King, and ruled until his death

crone /kroun/ *n.* [C] OLD-FASHIONED an ugly or mean old woman

Cro·nus, Kronos /ˈkrounəs/ in Greek MYTHOLOGY, a god, son of Uranus and one of the Titans, who became ruler of the universe until he was defeated by Zeus

cro·ny /ˈkrouni/ *n. plural* **cronies** [C usually plural] one of a group of people, who spend a lot of time with each other and will usually help each other, even if this involves doing things that are not honest or fair:

The senator gave positions of power to many of his political cronies.

cron·y·ism /ˈkrouniˌɪzəm/ *n.* [U] the practice of unfairly giving the best jobs to your friends when you are in a position of power —compare NEPOTISM

crook¹ /kruk/ *n.* [C] **1** INFORMAL someone who is not honest and who steals things, especially money: *Louisiana voters were faced with the choice of voting for a crook or a racist.* | *a petty crook* **2 the crook of your arm** the inside part of your arm where it bends, at the elbow: *He carried his jacket in the crook of his arm.* **3** a bend in something: *This type of cougar has a distinctive crook in its tail.* **4** a long stick with a curved end, used by people who take care of sheep —see also **by hook or by crook** (HOOK¹ (7))

crook² *v.* [T] if you crook your finger or your arm, you bend it: *Mrs. Garner crooked her finger at me, motioning for me to come over.*

crook·ed /ˈkrukɪd/ *adj.* **1** bent, twisted, or not in a straight line: *The picture's crooked – move it a little to the left.* | *crooked teeth* **2** dishonest: *a crooked cop* —**crookedly** *adv.* —**crookedness** *n.* [U]

croon /krun/ *v.* [I,T] to sing or speak in a soft gentle voice, especially about love: *On the store speakers, Bing Crosby was crooning "White Christmas."* —**crooner** *n.* [C]

crop¹ /krɑp/ *n.* [C] **1** a plant such as corn, wheat, rice etc. that is grown by a farmer and used as food: *Onions are one of the few crops that whitefly does not damage.* | *Most of the land is used for growing crops.* **2** the amount of corn, wheat, rice etc. that is produced in a single season: *Growers lost 80 percent of the apple crop in the storm.* | *We expect to have a bumper crop* (=a very large amount) *of barley.* **3 a crop of sb/sth** a group of people who begin doing a similar activity, job etc., or a group of new things or products that are similar: *a good crop of young authors* | *a new crop of luxury sport utility vehicles* **4** a short whip used in horse riding **5** the part under a bird's throat where food is stored **6** a very short HAIRSTYLE **7 a crop of hair/curls etc.** hair that is thick and attractive

crop² *v.* [T] **1** to cut someone's hair short **2** to cut a part off a photograph or picture so that it is a particular size or shape **3** if an animal crops grass or other plants, it makes them shorter by eating the top part

crop up *phr. v.* [I] **1** if something, especially a problem, crops up, it happens or appears suddenly and in an unexpected way: *Several problems cropped up soon after we bought the car.* **2** if something such as a name or a subject crops up, it appears in something you read or hear: *Your name kept cropping up in conversation.*

crop-dust·ing /ˈ. ,../ *n.* [U] the practice of using airplanes to spread chemicals that kill insects on crops

crop ro·ta·tion /ˈ. .,../ *n.* [U] the practice of changing the crops that you grow in a field each year to preserve the good qualities in the soil

cro·quet /krouˈkeɪ/ *n.* [U] an outdoor game in which you hit balls under curved wires using a wooden MALLET (=hammer with a long handle)

cro·quette /krouˈkɛt/ *n.* [C] a piece of crushed meat, fish, potato etc. that is made into a small round piece, covered in BREADCRUMBS, fried (FRY¹ (1)) and eaten

cross¹ /krɔs/ *v.*
1 go from one side to another [I,T] to go from one side of a road, river, room etc. to the other side: *Look both ways before crossing the street.* | *This is the point where Washington's army crossed the Delaware River.*
2 two roads/lines etc. [T] if two or more roads, lines etc. cross, they go across each other: *There's a post office where Oakland Road crosses 32nd Street.*
3 cross a line etc. [T] if you cross a line, track etc. you go over and beyond it: *Johnson crossed the finish line in first place.*
4 legs/arms/ankles [T] if you cross your legs, arms, or ANKLES, you put one on top of the other: *Doris sat down and crossed her legs.* —see picture at ARM¹
5 cross your mind if an idea, thought etc. crosses your mind, you begin to think about it: *It never*

crossed my mind that she might be sick. | "You could fly to Boston to visit him." **"The thought has crossed my mind."** (=used to tell someone you have thought of the thing they are suggesting)

6 `breed of plant/animal` [T] to mix two or more different breeds of animal or plant to form a new breed: *Some species of plants can be crossed very easily.* | [+ **with**] *If you cross a horse with a donkey, you get a mule.* —see also CROSS² (2), CROSSBREED¹

7 sb's paths cross also **cross sb's path** if two people's paths cross or if they cross paths, they meet without expecting it: *Our paths did not cross again until 1941.*

8 cross sb's face if an expression crosses someone's face, it appears on their face: *A look of horror crossed Ken's face.*

9 cross that bridge when you come to it SPOKEN used to say that you will not think or worry about something until it actually happens: *"What if they refuse?" "We'll cross that bridge when we come to it."*

10 cross my heart (and hope to die) SPOKEN used to say that you promise that you will do something or that what you are saying is true: *I didn't take it, cross my heart!*

11 cross your fingers a) used to say that you hope something will happen in the way you want: *People vote, cross their fingers, and hope for the best.* **b)** if someone crosses their fingers while they tell you something, what they are saying is not true: *A memo said that doctors were told "with crossed fingers" that the company was doing safety studies.*

12 cross swords (with sb) to argue with someone: *Japan and the U.S. have crossed swords on a number of trade issues.*

13 cross your eyes to look toward your nose with both of your eyes

14 `make sb angry` [T] to make someone angry by opposing their plans or orders: *I wouldn't cross her if I were you.*

15 cross yourself to move your hand in the shape of a cross across your chest and head, as Christians do in some churches, for example the Catholic Church —see also **cross the Rubicon** (RUBICON), **dot the i's and cross the t's** (DOT² (4)), **keep your fingers crossed** (FINGER¹ (2))

cross off *phr. v.* [I,T **cross** sth ↔ **off**] to draw a line through one or more things on a list because you have dealt with them or they are not needed anymore: *Cross off their names as they arrive.*

cross out

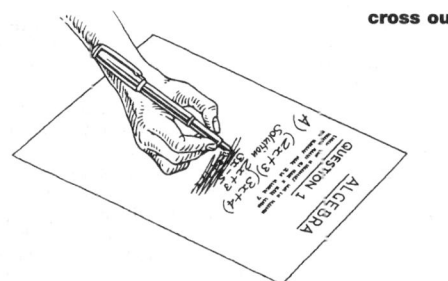

cross sth → **out** *phr. v.* [T] to draw a line or lines through something you have written or drawn, usually because it is wrong: *The salesman crossed out $222 and wrote $225.*

cross over *phr. v.* [I] **1** if a performer crosses over from one area of entertainment to another, they begin to produce work from the second one —see also CROSSOVER¹ **2** OLD USE to die

sw **cross²** *n.* [C]
3₃ **1** `christian sign` **a)** an upright wooden post with another post crossing it near the top, that people were nailed to and left to die on as a punishment in ancient times. Christians believe that Jesus died on a cross for our sins. **b)** an object or picture in the shape of a cross, used as a sign of the Christian faith: *Pauline wore a tiny gold cross around her neck.*
2 `mixture of things` a mixture of two or more things, breeds, qualities etc.: [+ **between**] *My dog is a cross between a whippet and a retriever.*

3 `a mark on paper` a mark (x or +) used on paper to represent where something is, or where something should be: *I've put a cross on the map to mark where our house is.*

4 `military award` a decoration in the shape of a cross that is worn as an honor, especially for performing military actions that show courage: *Jones was awarded the Distinguished Service Cross.*

5 `way of hitting` a way of hitting someone in the sport of BOXING in which your arm goes over theirs as they try to hit you: *Roberts was knocked out by a **right cross** (=a hit using his right hand) from Chavez.*

6 a (heavy) cross to bear a problem that makes you very unhappy or worried, often one that continues for a long time: *His mother's illness has been a very heavy cross to bear.* —see also **the sign of the cross** (SIGN¹ (7))

C

cross³ *adj.* OLD-FASHIONED angry or annoyed: *I'm sorry for **getting** so **cross with** you.*

cross- /krɔs/ *prefix* **1** going from one side of something to the other; ACROSS: *cross-country skiing* (=across fields) **2** going between two things and joining them: *cross-cultural influences*

cross·bar /'krɔsbɑr/ *n.* [C] **1** a bar that joins two upright posts, especially two GOALPOSTS **2** the metal bar between the seat and the HANDLEBARS on a man's bicycle —see picture at BICYCLE¹

cross·bones /'krɔsbounz/ *n.* [plural] —see SKULL AND CROSSBONES

cross·bor·der /'. ,../ *adj.* [only before noun] involving two countries that are next to each other: *cross-border trade*

cross·bow /'krɔsbou/ *n.* [C] a weapon like a small BOW² (2) attached to a longer piece of wood, used for shooting ARROWS (1) with a lot of force

cross·breed¹ /'krɔsbrid/ *v.* **a)** [T] to make one kind of a plant or animal breed with a different breed **b)** [I] if a plant or animal crossbreeds, it breeds with one of a different breed —**crossbred** /'krɔsbrɛd/ *adj.*

crossbreed² *n.* [C] an animal or plant that is a mixture of breeds —compare INTERBREED

cross·check /'krɔstʃɛk/ *v.* [T] to make sure that something is correct by using a different method to calculate it again —**cross-check** *n.* [C]

cross·coun·try¹ /,. '../ *adj.* **1** across fields and not along roads: *Denise enjoys cross-country running.* **2** from one side of a country to the other side: *He's on a cross-country flight from Los Angeles to Atlanta.* —**cross-country** *adv.: I went traveling cross-country with my uncle.*

cross-country² *n.* **1** [U] a sport in which you run across fields and not along roads or a track **2** [C] a race in which you run this way

cross-country ski·ing /,. .. '../ *n.* [U] the sport of moving across fields, through woods etc. on SKIS —compare DOWNHILL SKIING

cross-country skiing

cross-cul·tur·al /,. '../ *adj.* belonging to or involving two or more different societies, countries, or CULTURES (1): *cross-cultural communication*

cross·cur·rent /'krɔs-,kɜrənt/ *n.* [C] **1** an idea or attitude that is opposed to another one: *There is no easy solution to the area's complex crosscurrents of racial and religious conflict.* **2** a current in the ocean, a river etc. that moves across the general direction of the main current

crossed /krɔst/ *adj.* if a telephone line is crossed, it is connected by mistake to two or more telephones, so that you can hear other people's conversations —see also **get your wires crossed** (WIRE[1] (4))

cross·ex·am·ine /ˌ. .ˈ../ v. [T] to ask someone questions about something they have just said to see if they are telling the truth, especially in a court of law —**cross-examination** /ˌ. ...ˈ../ n. [C,U] —**cross-examiner** /ˌ. .ˈ.../ n. [C]

cross-eyed /ˈ. ./ adj. having eyes that look in toward the nose

cross·fer·til·ize /ˌ. ˈ.../ v. [T] **1** to combine the male sex cells from one type of plant with female sex cells from another **2** [often passive] to influence someone or something with ideas from other areas: *We hope to cross-fertilize the company with the expertise we've gained from other industries.* —**cross-fertilization** /ˌ. ...ˈ../ n. [U]

cross·fire /ˈkrɔsfaɪɚ/ n. **1** [U] bullets from two or more different directions that pass through the same area: *A bystander was killed when she was* **caught in the crossfire. 2** a situation in which people are arguing: *The crossfire exposed deep divisions within the party.* | *During a divorce, kids often get* **caught in the crossfire.**

cross-grained /ˈ. ./ adj. wood that is cross-grained has lines that go across it instead of along it

cross hairs /ˈ. ./ n. [plural] two very thin wires that cross in the middle, that help you to aim when you look through something such as a gun: *When the target reaches the center of the cross hairs, drop the bomb.*

cross·hatch·ing /ˈ. ,../ n. [U] lines drawn across part of a picture, DIAGRAM etc. to show that something is made of different material, or to produce the effect of shade

cross·ing /ˈkrɔsɪŋ/ n. [C] **1** a place where you can safely cross a road, railroad, river etc. **2** a place where two lines, roads, tracks etc. cross **3** a trip across the ocean: *The crossing took over two weeks.*

cross-legged

She sat with her legs crossed.   Paul was sitting cross-legged.

cross-leg·ged /ˈkrɔs ˌlɛgɪd, -ˌlɛgd/ adv. in a sitting position with your knees wide apart and your feet crossed: *All the children were sitting cross-legged on the floor.* —**cross-legged** adj.

cross·o·ver[1] /ˈkrɔsˌoʊvɚ/ n. **1** [C] the change a performer makes from working in one area of entertainment to another: [+ from] *Few actors have made a successful crossover from T.V. to movies.* **2** [C,U] the fact of liking, using, or supporting more than one type of thing or group, especially when these things or groups are considered to be very different from one another: *There is not much crossover among readers of romance and science fiction.* —see also **cross over** (CROSS[1])

crossover[2] adj. [only before noun] moving or changing from one type of group, music, style etc. to another: *The band's crossover album became an instant bestseller.*

cross·patch /ˈkrɔspætʃ/ n. [C] OLD-FASHIONED someone who is easily annoyed or is in a bad mood

cross·piece /ˈkrɔspis/ n. [C] something that lies across another thing, especially in a building, railroad track etc.

cross-pur·pos·es /ˌ. ˈ.../ n. **at cross-purposes** two people, plans, or ideas that are at cross-purposes disagree with each other and cause problems, usually without people realizing this at first: *Administration officials insist the two policies are not at cross-purposes.*

cross-re·fer /ˌ. .ˈ./ v. [I,T] to tell a reader of a book to look in another place in the book they are reading for more information

cross-ref·er·ence /ˈ. ,..., ˌ. ˈ.../ n. [C] a note that tells the reader of a book to look in another place in the book for more information

cross·roads /ˈkrɔsroʊdz/ n. *plural* **crossroads** [C] **1** a place where two roads meet and cross each other **2** a time in your life when you have to make a very important decision that will affect your future: *Warren's career was* **at a crossroads.**

cross sec·tion, cross-section /ˈ. ,../ n. [C] **1** something that has been cut in half so that you can look at the inside, or a drawing of this: *Page 112 shows a cross section of the human body.* **2** a group of people or things that is typical of a much larger group: *Managers from a cross-section of industries were interviewed.*

cross stitch, cross-stitch /ˈ. ./ n. [C,U] a stitch in the shape of the letter "x," used in sewing —**cross stitch** v. [I,T]

cross street /ˈ. ./ n. [C] a street that crosses another street: *The nearest cross street is Ellis Boulevard.*

cross·town /ˌkrɔsˈtaʊn◂/ adj. [only before noun] moving in a direction across a town or city: *Take the crosstown bus and get off at Jones Park.*

cross-train·er /ˌ. .ˈ./ n. [C usually plural] a type of shoe that can be worn for playing different types of sports

cross-train·ing /ˈ. ,../ n. [U] **1** the activity of training for more than one sport during the same period of time **2** the activity of learning different jobs during the same period of time —**cross-train** v. [I,T]

cross·walk /ˈkrɔswɔk/ n. [C] a specially marked place for people to walk across a street

cross·wind /ˈkrɔsˌwɪnd/ n. [C] a wind that blows across the direction that you are moving in

cross·wise /ˈkrɔsˌwaɪz/ adv. **1** cut/slice etc. sth crosswise to cut etc. something from one of its corners to the opposite corner **2** two things that are placed crosswise are arranged to form the shape of an "x" —compare LENGTHWISE

cross·word /ˈkrɔsˌwɚd/ also **crossword puz·zle** /ˈ.. ,../ n. [C] a game in which you write the words that are the answers to questions in a special pattern of numbered squares

crotch /krɑtʃ/ n. [C] the part of your body between the tops of your legs, or the part of a piece of clothing that covers this —see also BODY

crotch·et·y /ˈkrɑtʃəti/ adj. INFORMAL easily annoyed or made slightly angry: *a crotchety old man*

crouch /kraʊtʃ/ v. [I] also **crouch down 1** to lower your body close to the ground by bending your knees and back: *I crouched behind a bush as the soldiers marched by.* **2** if an animal crouches, it sits as low as possible, often because it is frightened or is going to attack something: *A black cat crouched in the corner.*

croup /krup/ n. [U] an illness in children which makes them cough and have difficulty breathing

crou·pi·er /ˈkrupiɚ/ n. [C] someone whose job is to collect and pay out money where people play cards, ROULETTE etc. for money

crou·ton /ˈkrutɑn/ n. [C] a small square piece of CRISP bread that is served with soup or on SALAD

Crow /kroʊ/ n. a Native American tribe from the northern region of the U.S. —**Crow** adj.

crow[1] /kroʊ/ n. **1** [C] a large shiny black bird that makes a loud sound **2** [singular] the loud sound a ROOSTER makes **3 as the crow flies** measured in a straight line: *My house is ten miles from here as the crow flies.* —see also **eat crow** (EAT (8))

crow[2] v. [I] **1** if a ROOSTER crows, it makes a loud high sound **2** to talk about what you have done in a very proud way: [+ **over/about**] *North and his supporters are still crowing about the court's decision.* **3** if a baby crows, it makes a noise that shows it is happy: *The baby crowed with delight at the toy.*

crow·bar /'kroubar/ *n.* [C] a heavy iron bar used to lift or open things

s w **crowd¹** /kraud/ *n.* **1** [C] a large group of people in a public place: *An enormous crowd gathered to watch the parade.* **2** [C] a large number of a particular kind of people or things: [+ **of**] *Kemp stepped out to face a crowd of cameras. | The streets were filled with crowds of angry people.* **3** [singular] INFORMAL a group of people who know each other, work together etc.: *I guess the usual crowd will be at the party.* **4 follow the crowd** also **go with the crowd** to always do what other people do, without thinking for yourself

s w **crowd²** *v.* **1** [I,T] if people crowd somewhere or around something, they gather together in large numbers, filling a particular place: *Angry protesters crowded the courthouse steps.* | [+ **around/into** etc.] *People crowded around the scene of the accident.* **2** [T] **a)** to make someone angry by moving too close to them: *Stop crowding me! There's plenty of room.* **b)** to make someone angry or upset by making too many unfair demands on them: *Stop crowding me! I need time to make this decision.* **3** [T] if thoughts or ideas crowd your brain, mind, head etc., they fill it: *A jumble of confused thoughts crowded my brain.*

crowd sb/sth ↔ out *phr. v.* [T] to force someone or something out of a place or situation: *For years, supermarket chains have been crowding out small grocery stores.*

crowd·ed /'kraudid/ *adj.* too full of people or things: *a crowded room* | [+ **with**] *The bus was crowded with schoolchildren.*

crowd-pleas·er /'. ,../ *n.* [C] someone or something that large groups of people enjoy watching very much: *Surya's backflips are real crowd-pleasers.* —**crowd-pleasing** *adj.*

crown¹ /kraun/ *n.*
1 hat for king/queen [C] **a)** a circle made of gold and decorated with jewels, worn by kings and queens on their heads **b)** a similar circle, sometimes made of other things such as leaves or flowers, worn by someone who has won a special honor
2 tooth [C] an artificial top for a damaged tooth
3 sports [C] INFORMAL the position you have if you have won an important sports competition: *A penalty kick gave McAteer High its first state soccer crown.*
4 king/queen **the crown a)** the position of being king or queen: *Prince Charles is next in line to the crown.* **b)** the government of a country such as Britain that is officially led by a king or queen: *The islands are possessions of the Crown.*
5 top part [C usually singular] the top part of a hat, head, or hill etc.: *His black hat had an unusually high crown.* —see picture at HAT
6 money [C] a unit of money in several European countries: *How much is $100 worth in Swedish crowns?*
7 picture [C] a mark, sign, BADGE etc. in the shape of a crown, used especially to show rank or quality

crown² *v.* [T] **1** to place a crown on someone's head, so that they officially become king or queen: *She was crowned at the age of eight.* **2** to do something or get something that is the best and usually last thing in a series of things you have done or gotten: [+ **by**] *His successful career was crowned by winning the best actor award.* **3** to put a protective top on a damaged tooth **4 be crowned with sth** LITERARY to have something on top: *All year round, the mountains are crowned with snow.* **5** OLD-FASHIONED to hit someone on the head

crowned head /,. './ *n.* [C usually plural] a king or queen: *All the crowned heads of Europe were present at the funeral.*

crown·ing /'kraunɪŋ/ *adj.* [only before noun] being the best and usually last of a series of things: *Winning a fourth championship was the crowning achievement of Ashton's basketball career.*

crown jew·el /,. './ *n.* **1** [C] the best, prettiest, or most valuable thing that a person or place has: *Innsbruck's crown jewel is the old town center.* **2 the crown jewels** the crown, sword, jewels etc. worn by a king or queen for special ceremonies

crown prince /,. './ *n.* [C] the son of a king or queen, who is expected to become the next king

crown prin·cess /,. './ *n.* [C] the daughter of a king or queen, who is expected to become the next queen

crow's feet /'. ./ *n.* [plural] very small lines in the skin near your eyes

crow's nest /'. ./ *n.* [C] a small box at the top of a ship's MAST from which someone can watch for danger, land etc.

CRT *n.* [C] **1** the abbreviation of CATHODE RAY TUBE **2** INFORMAL a computer screen that uses a CATHODE RAY TUBE

cru·cial /'kruʃəl/ *adj.* something that is crucial is extremely important, because everything else depends on it: *Learning to work together is a crucial part of the training program.* | [be crucial to/in (doing) sth] *The support of our fans was crucial to our winning the Super Bowl.* —**crucially** *adv.* s w

cru·ci·ble /'krusəbəl/ *n.* [C] **1** a situation that is very difficult, but that often produces something new or good: *New York and Los Angeles have arguably replaced Paris as the crucible of new artistic culture.* **2** a container in which substances are heated to very high temperatures

cru·ci·fix /'krusə,fɪks/ *n.* [C] a cross with a figure of Jesus Christ on it

cru·ci·fix·ion /,krusə'fɪkʃən/ *n.* **1** [C,U] in past times, the act of killing someone by fastening them to a cross and leaving them to die **2 the Crucifixion** the death of Jesus Christ in this way **3** [C] also **Crucifixion** a picture or other object representing Jesus Christ on the cross

cru·ci·form /'krusə,fɔrm/ *adj.* shaped like a cross

cru·ci·fy /'krusə,faɪ/ *v.* crucifies, crucified, crucifying [T] **1** to kill someone by fastening them to a cross **2** to criticize someone severely and cruelly for something they have done, especially in public: *If the newspapers find out, you'll be crucified.*

crud /krʌd/ *n.* [U] INFORMAL something that is very bad or disgusting to look at, taste, smell etc.: *What's this crud on my seat?*

crud·dy /'krʌdi/ *adj.* cruddier, cruddiest INFORMAL bad, dirty, or of poor quality: *Some of the workmanship is pretty cruddy.*

crude¹ /krud/ *adj.* **1** offensive or rude, especially in a sexual way; VULGAR (1): *crude pornographic pictures* | *Rudy was loud-mouthed and crude.* **2** not developed to a high standard, or made with little skill: *a crude homemade bomb* | *a crude map of the area* **3** done without attention to detail, but generally correct and useful: *The number of help-wanted advertisements can be used as a crude measure of the strength of the job market.* **4** in a natural or raw condition, before it is made more pure: *crude rubber* —**crudely** *adv.*: *crudely built shacks* —**crudity** also **crudeness** *n.* [C,U]

crude² also **crude oil** /'. ./ *n.* [U] oil that is in its natural condition, as it comes out of an OIL WELL, and before it is made more pure or separated to be used for different products: *About 700,000 gallons of crude oil spilled into Galveston Bay.*

cru·di·tés /,krudɪ'teɪ/ *n.* [plural] pieces of raw vegetable served before a meal

cru·el /'kruəl/ *adj.* **1** deliberately hurting people or animals: *Killing animals just for their skins seems cruel.* | [+ **to**] *Her mother could be cruel to her at times.* **2** making someone suffer or feel unhappy: *People say showbusiness can be very cruel.* | *a long cruel winter* | *Any cruel and unusual punishment is banned by the Eighth Amendment to the Constitution.* —**cruelly** *adv.*: *The child was cruelly neglected by his parents.*

cru·el·ty /'kruəlti/ *n. plural* **cruelties 1** [U] behavior that deliberately causes pain to people or animals: *There have been reports of cruelty and rape from the war zone.* | [+ **to**] *Cruelty to animals is punishable by law.* **2** [U] a willingness or desire to make people or animals suffer: *There was an edge of cruelty to their jokes.* **3** [C] a cruel action: *Khrushchev officially revealed the cruelties of Stalin's regime.*

cru·et /'kruət/ *n.* [C] a small bottle that holds oil, VINEGAR etc. on a table

cruise[1] /kruz/ *v.* **1** [I] to sail along slowly, especially for pleasure: *We spent the afternoon cruising on his yacht.* **2** [I] to move at a steady speed in a car, airplane etc.: *A car cruised by with a flag waving out the window.* **3** [I,T] to drive a car slowly through a place with no particular purpose: *It was Friday night and the kids were out cruising up and down Main Street.* **4** INFORMAL to do something well or successfully, without too much effort: *The Jayhawks cruised to a 7–0 victory over the Eagles.* **5 be cruising for a bruising** SPOKEN used to say that someone is being so annoying or stupid that they are very likely to get into trouble, a fight, an argument etc.: *The way you're talking, I'd say you're really cruising for a bruising.* **6** [I,T] SLANG to look for a sexual partner in a public place: *Let's go cruise some chicks* (=girls).

cruise[2] *n.* [C] **1** a vacation in which you travel on a large ship: *a Caribbean cruise* **2** a trip by boat for pleasure

cruise con·trol /'. .,./ *n.* [C] a piece of equipment in a car that makes it go at a steady speed, without you having to press with your foot on the ACCELERATOR

cruise lin·er /'. ,../ *n.* [C] a cruise ship

cruise mis·sile /'. ,../ *n.* [C] a large explosive weapon that flies close to the ground and can be aimed at an exact point hundreds of miles away

cruis·er /'kruzə/ *n.* [C] **1** a large fast ship used by a navy: *a battle cruiser* **2** a boat used for pleasure **3** a police car

cruise ship /'. ./ *n.* [C] a large ship with restaurants, bars etc. that people travel on for a vacation

cruis·ing /'kruzɪŋ/ *n.* [U] **1** the activity of driving a car slowly with no particular purpose: *The city council has banned cruising on 10th Street.* **2** the activity of going on a vacation on a large ship: *Special rates for children have made cruising one of the most affordable of family vacations.* **3** the activity of walking or driving around public places, looking for sexual partners

crul·ler /'krʌlə/ *n.* [C] a DONUT (=type of sweet bread) with a twisted shape

crumb /krʌm/ *n.* [C] **1** a very small piece of dry food, especially bread or cake: *Top the mixture with the remaining bread crumbs.* | *She stood up and brushed some crumbs off her uniform.* **2** a very small amount of something: [+ **of**] *The children gathered around their father, anxious for any crumb of affection.* **3** OLD-FASHIONED a person who is not nice, or not fun to be with

crum·ble[1] /'krʌmbəl/ *v.* **1** [I,T] to break apart into little pieces, or make something do this: *Crumble the bacon and set aside.* | *The rubber seal is crumbling and will need to be replaced.* **2** [I] if a building crumbles, it starts to fall down because it is old: *Rangoon's old buildings are crumbling from neglect.* **3** [I] to lose power, become weak, or fail: *His circle of advisers and associates is crumbling along with his empire.*

crumble[2] *n.* [U] a sweet dish of fruit covered with a dry mixture of flour, butter, and sugar and baked: *apple crumble*

crum·bly /'krʌmbli/ *adj.* something such as food or soil that is crumbly breaks easily into small pieces: *If you add too much flour, the cookies will be dry and crumbly.*

crum·my /'krʌmi/ *adj.* **crummier, crummiest 1** INFORMAL of bad quality: *The weather is still pretty crummy.* | *That's a crummy attempt at a French accent.* **2** INFORMAL bad or not pleasant: *Larry came home in a pretty crummy mood today.* | *Yeah, what a crummy job!* **3** SPOKEN used to show that you are angry or annoyed, or to emphasize what you are saying: *I didn't want your crummy toy anyway!*

crum·pet /'krʌmpɪt/ *n.* [C] a small round type of bread with holes in one side, that is eaten hot with butter

crum·ple /'krʌmpəl/ *v.* **1** [I,T] also **crumple up** to crush something so that it becomes smaller and bent, or to be crushed in this way: *He crumpled his shirt into a ball and threw it into the laundry basket.* | *The whole front of the car crumpled upon impact with the wall.* —see picture on page 424 **2** [I] if your body crumples, you fall in an uncontrolled way because you are unconscious, drunk etc.: *As the bullet tore through his leg, he crumpled to the ground.* **3** [I] if your face crumples, you suddenly look sad or disappointed, as if you might cry: [+ **with**] *Josh's face crumpled with disappointment.*

crum·pled /'krʌmpəld/ *adj.* **1** also **crumpled up** crushed into a smaller bent shape: *Jo pulled a crumpled piece of paper out of her pocket.* | *crumpled soda cans* **2** clothes that are crumpled have a lot of lines or folds in them: *Don't sit around in your suit. It'll get crumpled.* **3** someone who is crumpled is lying still in a strange position after they have fallen: *They found the boy crumpled on the pavement.*

crumple zone /'.. ,./ *n.* [C] part of a car that crumples easily in an accident to protect the people inside

crunch[1] /krʌntʃ/ *n.* **1** [singular] a noise like the sound of something being crushed: *I heard the crunch of footsteps on gravel road outside.* **2** [singular] a difficult situation caused by a lack of something, especially money or time: *Three new teachers were hired to help ease the crunch.* | **a budget/cash crunch** *Until the city's budget crunch is over, vacancies in the police department will go unfilled.* | *Arrests have increased so much that courts are **feeling the crunch**.* **3** also **crunch time** [singular] a period of time when you have to make the most effort to make sure you achieve something: *At crunch time the team really pulled together.* **4** [C] an exercise in which you lie on your back and lift your head and shoulders off the ground to make your stomach muscles strong

crunch[2] *v.* **1** [I] to make a sound like something being crushed: *Broken window glass crunched under foot.* **2** [I always + adv./prep.,T] to eat hard food in a way that makes a noise: [+ **on**] *The dog was crunching on a bone.* | *Kids were crunching graham crackers and drinking juice.* **3 crunch the numbers** INFORMAL to calculate a lot of numbers together: *We'll have to sit down and crunch the numbers before we commit to hiring any more people.* —see also NUMBER CRUNCHER, NUMBER CRUNCHING

crunch·y /'krʌntʃi/ *adj.* **crunchier, crunchiest** food that is crunchy is hard and makes a noise when you bite it: *crunchy carrot sticks* —**crunchiness** *n.* [U]

cru·sade[1] /kru'seɪd/ *n.* [C] **1** a determined attempt to change something, because you think you are morally right: [+ **to/for**] *a crusade for gun control* | [+ **against**] *Brown led a successful crusade against a major tobacco company.* **2** one of a series of wars fought in the 11th, 12th, and 13th centuries by Christian armies trying to take Palestine from the Muslims

crusade[2] *v.* [I] to take part in a crusade: [+ **against/for**] *The new mayor is actively crusading against drugs and gangs.* —**crusader** *n.* [C]

crush[1] /krʌʃ/ *v.* [T] **1** to press someone or something so hard that it breaks or is damaged: *Joe crushed his cigarette into an ashtray.* | *A zookeeper was **crushed to death** by a hippopotamus.* —see picture on page 424 **2** to press something in order to break it into very small pieces, or into a powder: *Add a handful of crushed dill to a bottle of white wine vinegar.* —see picture on page 425 **3** to completely defeat someone or something that is fighting against you or opposes you: *Seles crushed Sabatini in last night's match.* | **crush an uprising/revolt** *The military crushed the student-led uprising.* **4 crush sb's hopes/enthusiasm/confidence** etc. to make someone lose all hope, confidence etc.: *Not getting their bonus checks has crushed the staff's morale.* **5** to make someone feel extremely upset or shocked: *Pete was crushed by his wife's sudden death.*

crush² *n.* **1** [C] a word meaning a feeling of romantic love for someone, especially for someone you do not know very well, used especially about feelings that TEENAGERS (=young people from around age 12 to 18) have: *Actually, I had a big crush on Mel Gibson.* **2** [singular] a crowd of people pressed so close together that it is difficult for them to move: *Airports are expecting a record crush of passengers this holiday season.*

crush·ing /ˈkrʌʃɪŋ/ *adj.* **1** very hard to deal with, and making you lose hope and confidence: *Republicans in the state suffered a crushing defeat in last month's elections.* | *Latin American countries cannot afford the crushing burden of higher oil prices.* **2** a crushing remark, reply etc. expresses very strong criticism —**crushingly** *adv.*

s w **crust** /krʌst/ *n.* [C, U] **1** the hard brown outer surface of bread: *Jimmy only eats sandwiches with the crusts cut off.* **2** the baked outer part of foods such as PIES and PIZZAS: *a pizza with a thin, crispy crust* **3** a thin hard dry layer on the surface of something: *A hard gray crust had formed on the bottom of the tea kettle.* **4** the hard outer layer of the Earth: *the Earth's crust*

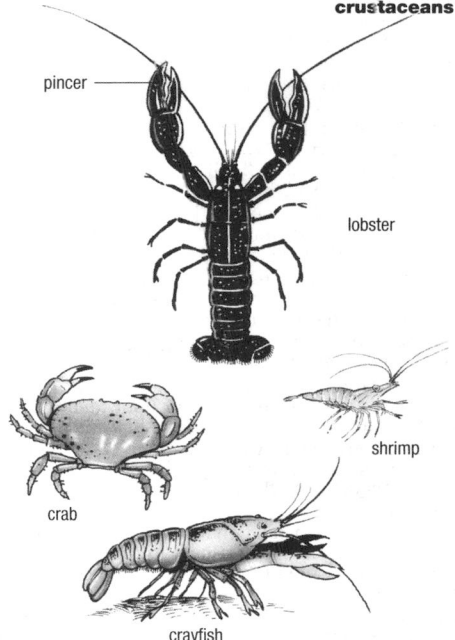

crustaceans

pincer

lobster

shrimp

crab

crayfish

crus·ta·cean /krʌˈsteɪʃən/ *n.* [C] TECHNICAL an animal such as a LOBSTER or a CRAB that has a hard outer shell and several pairs of legs, and usually lives in water —**crustacean** *adj.*

crust·ed /ˈkrʌstɪd/ *adj.* having a thin hard dry layer on the surface: [+ with] *Her boots were crusted with mud.*

crust·y /ˈkrʌsti/ *adj.* **1** bread that is crusty is pleasant to eat because it has a hard crust: *a crusty baguette* **2** INFORMAL easily annoyed and impatient: *a crusty old Kansas farmer* **3** having a thin dry hard layer of something on the surface: *There was a crusty ring around the rim of the ketchup bottle.* —**crustiness** *n.* [U]

crutch /krʌtʃ/ *n.* **1** [C usually plural] a special stick that you put under your arm to support you and help you walk when you have hurt your leg: *Dennis left the locker room on crutches, his knee heavily bandaged.* **2** something that gives you support or help: *Alcoholics use drinking as a crutch.*

cry

crux /krʌks/ *n.* the cru... problem, question, ar... ship between Trevor an... crux of this movie.

cry¹ /kraɪ/ *v.* third person s... past participle **cried** prese... **1** produce tears [I] to... eyes, usually because you... baby was crying, so I wen... [+ over/about] *I cried as...* [+ with/in] *Lin cried in a...* looked for her sons. | *Every...* would *cry himself to sleep.* |... out (=to cry a lot and be very s... **2** say loudly [T] to shout some... are we going to do?" she cried. **3** for crying out loud SPOKEN us... annoyed or impatient with some... front of you, for crying out loud. **4** animals/birds [I] if animals and... make a loud sound: *The seagulls on...* crying loudly. **5** cry foul to protest because you think... wrong or not fair: *Conservationists crie...* public land was put up for sale by the federa... ment. **6** cry over spilled milk to waste time feeling sorry about an earlier mistake or problem that cannot be changed: *It's no use crying over spilled milk.* **7** cry into your beer INFORMAL, DISAPPROVING to feel too much pity for yourself, especially because you think you have been treated unfairly **8** cry wolf to say that something bad is going to happen or has happened when it has not, so that people do not believe you when something bad really happens: *A weather forecaster who cried wolf led to the cancellation of the club's picnic* (=he said it was going to rain). —see also **a shoulder to cry on** (SHOULDER¹ (5))

cry out *phr. v.* **1** [I] to make a loud sound of fear, shock, pain etc. [+ in/with] *Even the smallest movement made him cry out in pain.* **2** [I,T] to shout something loudly: *"Another bourbon, waiter," the man cried out.* [+ for] *Chun cried out for his dead daughter.* **3** be crying out for sth INFORMAL to need something urgently: *The city's in trouble and is crying out for help.*

USAGE NOTE: CRY

WORD CHOICE: cry, weep, sob

If you **cry**, tears come from your eyes because you are upset or have hurt yourself: *The woman vanished, leaving the children crying on the sidewalk.* If you **weep**, you cry continuously and quietly because you are very sad: *Her lovely eyes were puffy from hours of weeping.* If you **sob**, you cry noisily and your body shakes because you are extremely upset: *He was led sobbing from the courtroom.* Both **weep** and **sob** are used especially in writing.

---

cry² *n.* plural **cries** **1** sound expressing feeling [C] a loud sound showing fear, pain, shock etc.: *a baby's cry* | **let out a cry/give a cry** *She let out a cry when he came up behind her suddenly.* | **a cry of delight/surprise/alarm/despair** etc. *She let out a cry of rage.* **2** shout [C] a loud shout: [+ of] *We heard a distant cry of warning.* | *From below came the hoarse cries of the injured workers.* **3** animal/bird [C] a sound made by a particular animal or bird: [+ of] *the cries of seagulls* **4** cry for help something someone says or does that shows that they are very unhappy and need help: *Janie's suicide attempt was obviously a cry for help.* **5** phrase [C] a phrase that is used to unite people in support of a particular action or idea: SLOGAN: *"Land and liberty" was the rallying cry of revolutionary Mexico.* —see also **be a far cry from sth** (FAR² (5)), **in full cry** (FULL¹ (23)), HUE AND CRY

crybaby ... *ural* **crybabies** [C] INFOR-
...ie, especially a child, who

cry·ba·by /ˈkraɪˌbeɪbi/ ... **it's a crying shame** used to
MAL, DISAPPROVIN... nd upset about something: *It
cries or com... shame if high ticket prices kept
...aseball games.* **2 a crying need**
cry·ing /ˈk... eed for something: *This is the kind
say ...*o... ylty has a crying need for.*
woul... /ˌkraɪə'dʒɛnɪks/ *n.* [U] the scientific
pe... low temperatures —**cryogenic** *adj.*
...n. [C] a room under a church, used in
...for burying people
...kriptik/ *adj.* deliberately mysterious, or
...secret meaning: *Indovina's lyrics are mostly
...and obscure.* —**cryptically** /-kli/ *adv.*
...- /kriptoʊ, -tə/ *prefix* FORMAL secret or hidden:
...pto-Communist

...p·to·gram /ˈkrɪptə,græm/ *n.* [C] a message writ-
...n in CODE[1] (3)

...ryp·tog·ra·phy /krɪpˈtɑgrəfi/ *n.* [U] the study of
secret writing and CODES[1] (3) —**cryptographer** *n.* [C]

crys·tal /ˈkrɪstəl/ *n.* **1** [C,U] rock that is clear like
ice, or a piece of this **2** [U] clear glass that is of very
high quality: *The table was set with the best china
and crystal.* **3** [C] a small regular-shaped piece of a
substance, formed naturally when this substance
becomes solid: *ice crystals* | *copper sulfate crys-
tals* **4** [C] the clear cover on a clock or watch **5** also
crystal meth [U] INFORMAL: see METHAMPHETAMINE

crystal ball /ˌ.. '. / *n.* [C] a glass ball that you can look
into to magically see what is going to happen in the
future

crystal clear /ˌ.. '. ◂ / *adj.* **1** very clearly stated and
easy to understand: *He has a gift for writing crystal
clear instructions.* **2** completely clean and clear:
Viewed from the air, the water looked crystal clear.

crys·tal·line /ˈkrɪstələn/ *adj.* **1** LITERARY very clear
or transparent, like crystal: *a crystalline blue
pool* **2** made of crystals: *a hormone in pure crystalline form*

crys·tal·lize /ˈkrɪstə,laɪz/ *v.* **1** [I,T] to make a substance form CRYSTALS: *Sea salt crystallizes from tidal
pools when the water evaporates.* **2** [I,T] if an idea,
plan etc. crystallizes or if you crystallize it, it
becomes very clear in your mind: *The recent events
really crystallized my opposition to war.* —**crystallization** /ˌkrɪstələ'zeɪʃən/ *n.* [U]

crys·tal·lized /ˈkrɪstə,laɪzd/ *adj.* crystallized fruit is
made by a special process which covers it with
sugar: *crystallized ginger*

crystal meth /ˌkrɪstəl 'mɛθ/ *n.* [U] INFORMAL: see
METHAMPHETAMINE

crystal set /ˈ.. ,. / *n.* [C] a very simple old-fashioned
radio

C-section /ˈsi ,sɛkʃən/ *n.* [C] INFORMAL a CESAREAN

CST the abbreviation of Central Standard Time

CT 1 a written abbreviation of Connecticut **2** the
written abbreviation of Central Time

ct. 1 the written abbreviation of CARAT: *a 24ct. gold
necklace* **2** a written abbreviation of "cent": *These
cost 75 cts.*

CT scan /si 'ti skæn, 'kæt skæn/ *n.* [C] another name
for a CAT SCAN

CU, cu a short way of writing "see you," used in
EMAIL, or by people communicating in CHAT ROOMS on
the Internet

cu. the written abbreviation of CUBIC: *40 cu. feet*

cub /kʌb/ *n.* [C] the baby of a wild animal such as a
lion, or a bear: *a seal cub* | *The older bears will teach
the cub how bears are supposed to behave in the wild.*

Cu·ba /ˈkyubə/ a country which is the largest island
in the Caribbean Sea —**Cuban** *n., adj.*

cub·by hole /ˈkʌbi ,hoʊl/ *n.* [C] a very small space or
a small room, used for storing or hiding things: *The
letters had been stuffed in a cubbyhole in the desk.*

cube[1] /kyub/ *n.* [C] **1** a solid object with six equal
square sides: *a sugar cube* | *Would you get me some
ice cubes out of the freezer?* | *cubes of Cheddar cheese*
—see picture at SHAPE **2** SPOKEN, INFORMAL a CUBICLE
3 the cube of sth the number you get when you
multiply a number by itself twice. For example, 4 ×
4 × 4 = 64, so the cube of 4 is 64

cube[2] *v.* [T] **1** to multiply a number by itself twice:
3 cubed is 27 **2** to cut food into cubes; DICE[2]: *The dish
is made with cubed pieces of steak.*

cube root /ˌ. './ *n.* [C] TECHNICAL the cube root of a
particular number is the number that when multiplied by itself twice will give that number: *5 is the
cube root of 125.*

cu·bic /ˈkyubɪk/ *adj.* **cubic feet/yards/inches etc.** a
measurement of space which is calculated by multiplying the length of something by its width and
height: *What's the cubic capacity of this engine?*

cu·bi·cle /ˈkyubɪkəl/ *n.* [C] a small partly enclosed
part of a room, especially in an office where several
people work: *I hate working in cubicles.*

cubic zir·co·ni·a /ˌkyubɪk zə'koʊniə/ *n.* [C,U] *plural* **cubic
zirconia** [C,U] an artificial DIAMOND

cub·ism /ˈkyu,bɪzəm/ *n.* [U] a 20th century style of
art, in which objects and people are represented by
GEOMETRIC shapes: *Picasso and Braques were the pioneers of cubism.* —**cubist** *adj.*: *cubist paintings*
—**cubist** *n.* [C]

cu·bit /ˈkyubɪt/ *n.* [C] OLD USE an ancient measure of
length equal to the length of your arm between your
wrist and your elbow

cub re·port·er /ˌ. .'../ *n.* [C] someone who has just
started to work as a REPORTER: *She got a job as cub
reporter at WTVJ in Miami.*

Cub Scout, cub scout /ˈ. ,./ *n.* **1 Cub Scouts**
[plural] the part of the BOY SCOUTS organization that
is for younger boys **2** a young boy who is a
member of the Cub Scouts

cuck·old /ˈkʌkəld, -koʊld/ *n.* [C] OLD USE a man whose
wife has deceived him by having sex with another
man —**cuckold** *v.* [T]

cuck·oo[1] /ˈkuku/ *n.* [C] a gray European bird that
puts its eggs in other birds' nests and that has a call
that sounds like its name

cuckoo[2] *adj.* [not before noun] INFORMAL crazy or
silly: *You're completely cuckoo.*

cuckoo clock /ˈ.. ,./ *n.* [C] a clock with a wooden
bird inside that comes out every hour and makes the
sound of a cuckoo to show what time it is

cu·cum·ber /ˈkyu,kʌmbər/ *n.* [C,U] a long thin
round vegetable with a dark green skin and a light
green inside, usually eaten raw —see picture at
VEGETABLE

cud /kʌd/ *n.* [U] **1** food that a cow has eaten, swallowed, and brought back into its mouth to CHEW a
second time **2 chew the cud** INFORMAL to think very
hard about something before making a decision

cud·dle[1] /ˈkʌdl/ *v.* [I,T] to hold someone or something
very close to you with your arms around them, especially to show that you love them: *Jenny sat on the
couch, cuddling a stuffed toy dog.* | *The couple cud-
dled and kissed all through dinner.*
   cuddle up *phr. v.* [I] to lie or sit very close to someone or something: *We cuddled up in bed to watch the
movie.*

cuddle[2] *n.* [C] an act of cuddling someone

cud·dly /ˈkʌdli/ *adj.* **cuddlier, cuddliest** someone or
something that is cuddly looks soft and makes you
want to cuddle them: *a cute and cuddly rabbit*

cudg·el[1] /ˈkʌdʒəl/ *n.* **1** [C] a short thick stick used as
a weapon **2 take up the cudgels** to start to fight for
an idea that you believe in: *In his latest collection,
Calvin Klein seems to have taken up the cudgels for
longer skirts.*

cudgel[2] *v.* [T] to hit someone with a cudgel

cue[1] /kyu/ *n.* [C] **1** an action or event that is a signal
for something else to happen: *Use the leash to give the
dog cues about what you want him to do.* | *Some
people can cope with hearing loss by using other cues
to meaning.* **2** a word or action that is a signal for

someone to speak or act in a play, movie etc.: *She stood nervously in the wings waiting for her cue.* | *Footage from Marilyn Monroe's last movie shows the star never **missed a cue*** | *The audience needs to laugh **on cue*** (=when they are given the signal). **3 on cue** happening or done at exactly the right moment: *I had been thinking of her, and as though on cue, Maria walked toward me.* **4 take your cue from sb** to use someone else's actions or behavior to show you what you should do or how you should behave: *The salesman controls the timing of a sale, but he should take his cues from the buyer.* **5** a long straight wooden stick used for hitting the ball in games such as POOL[1] (2) and BILLIARDS

cue² *v.* [T] to give someone a sign that it is the right moment for them to speak or do something, especially during a performance: *The studio manager will cue you when it's your turn to come on.*

cue ball /'. ./ *n.* [C] the ball which a player hits with the cue in a game such as POOL[1] (2)

cuff¹ /kʌf/ *n.* [C] **1** the end part of a SLEEVE (=the arm of a shirt, dress etc.) that often has a button on it to hold it closed around your wrist **2** a narrow band of cloth turned up at the bottom of your pants **3** an action in which you hit someone lightly on the head with your hand open **4 cuffs** [plural] INFORMAL HANDCUFFS —see also OFF-THE-CUFF

cuff² *v.* [T] **1** to put HANDCUFFS on someone: *His right hand was cuffed to the metal handgrip of the bus seat.* **2** to hit someone lightly, especially in a friendly way: *She cuffed him playfully on the side of the head.*

cuff link /'. ./ *n.* [C] a small piece of jewelry that a man uses instead of a button to hold the cuff on his shirt together

cui·rass /kwɪˈræs/ *n.* [C] a piece of metal or leather that covers a soldier's chest and back, worn for protection in battle in past times

Cui·sin·art /'kwizɪnˌɑrt/ *n.* [C] TRADEMARK a FOOD PROCESSOR

cui·sine /kwɪˈzin/ *n.* [U] **1** a particular style of cooking: *California cuisine* | [+ of] *the cuisine of Mediterranean countries* **2** the food cooked in a particular restaurant or hotel, especially when it is very good: *Enjoy the delicious cuisine created by our award-winning chef.*

CUL, cul a short way of writing "see you later," used in EMAIL, or by people communicating in CHAT ROOMS on the Internet

cul-de-sac /'kʌl də ˌsæk, 'kʊl-/ *n.* [C] **1** a street that is closed at one end so that there is only one way in and out **2** a situation in which you cannot make any more progress: *The administration finds itself in an ideological cul-de-sac that will be difficult to get out of.*

cul·i·nar·y /'kʌləˌnɛri, 'kyu-/ *adj.* [only before noun] FORMAL relating to cooking: *Deep-dish pizza is one of Chicago's culinary traditions.* | *Mary learned a lot of culinary skills from Gerard.*

cull¹ /kʌl/ *v.* **1** [T] FORMAL to find or choose information from many different places: *The anthology consists of 15 stories culled from literary reviews.* | *Names of potential jurors are culled from voter registration lists.* **2** [I,T] to kill the weakest animals in a group so that the size of the group does not increase too much: *Goats that are larger than average are culled from the herd.*

cull² *n.* [C] the act of killing the weakest animals in a group so that the size of the group does not increase too much

Cul·len /'kʌlən/, **Coun·tée** /kaʊnˈteɪ/ (1903–1946) a U.S. poet

cul·mi·nate /'kʌlməˌneɪt/ *v.* [I,T] FORMAL **1** to end after a long period of development: *Sunday's vote culminated a peaceful democratic revolution.* | [+ in/with] *Valerie's months of planning culminated in a beautiful wedding day.* **2** to reach the highest point of development: [+ in/with] *Cold War tensions culminated with the Cuban missile crisis.*

cul·mi·na·tion /ˌkʌlməˈneɪʃən/ *n.* [U] the final or highest point that is reached after a long period of

effort or development: culmination of months of ... carnival time in Rio is the culmination ... paration.

cu·lottes /kuˈlɑts, kuˈlɑts/ ... plural women's pants which stop at the knee and ... shaped to look like a skirt

cul·pa·ble /'kʌlpəbəl/ *adj.* ... responsible for something bad that has hap ... nd deserving blame; GUILTY: *Sloppy accounting ... able for the shortfall in revenue.* | **culpab** ... **de/negli·gence** *He pleaded guilty to culpab ... —cul·pably adv.* —**culpability** /ˌkʌlpəˈbɪ...

cul·prit /'kʌlprɪt/ *n.* [C] **1** someone w ... crime or of doing something wrong ... called in to help track down the culprit ... the reason for or cause of a particular prof ... ficulty: *Plaque is the culprit that causes too...*

cult /kʌlt/ *n.* **1** [C] an extreme religious gro ... not part of an established religion: *Two me ... a religious cult have been linked to the rece ... ders.* **2 a cult movie/figure/TV show etc.** a ... music group etc. that has become very popular ... only among a particular group of people: *Cu... favorite "South Park" will return in the fall TV schedule.* | *Bart Simpson fast became a cult hero.* **3** [C] a fashionable belief, idea, or attitude that influences people's lives: *Diet, therapy, exercise... It's all part of the cult of self-improvement.* **4** [C,U] FORMAL a system of religious beliefs and practices —see also PERSONALITY CULT

cul·ti·va·ble /'kʌltəvəbəl/ *adj.* land which is cultivable can be used to grow crops

cul·ti·var /'kʌltəˌvɑr/ *n.* [C] a type of plant that has been produced by breeding it over many years: *A tomato cultivar called "Yellow Pear" produces small, sweet tomatoes.*

cul·ti·vate /'kʌltəˌveɪt/ *v.* [T] **1** to prepare and use land for growing crops and plants: *The tribe cultivated the land and grew the food.* **2** to grow and take care of a particular crop. *Dozens of eucalyptus species are cultivated in the arboretum.* **3** to make an effort to help something grow or develop: *Baseball teams spend a lot on cultivating new talent.* | *Minnesota has long cultivated its cultural image.* **4** to develop a particular skill or quality in yourself: *He's spent years cultivating a knowledge of art.* **5** to make an effort to develop a friendly relationship with someone, especially someone who can help you.: *Her marriage allowed her to cultivate friendships with the Paris literary elite.*

cul·ti·vat·ed /'kʌltəˌveɪtɪd/ *adj.* **1** someone who is cultivated is intelligent and knows a lot about music, art, literature etc.: *Los Angeles are seen as less cultivated than San Francisco.* **2** crops or plants that are cultivated are grown in order to be sold: *You can use cultivated mushrooms, but a few wild ones add a better taste.* | *cultivated pearls* **3** land that is cultivated is used for growing crops or plants: *cultivated fields*

cul·ti·va·tion /ˌkʌltəˈveɪʃən/ *n.* [U] **1** the preparation and use of land for growing crops: *Almost every inch of the land is already **under cultivation**.* **2** the planting and growing of plants and crops: *Terraces for rice cultivation covered the hillsides.* | [+ of] *The ranch was used mainly for the cultivation of strawberries.* **3** the deliberate development of a particular quality or skill: [+ of] *Many parents think that the cultivation of manners in children requires constant nagging.*

cul·ti·va·tor /'kʌltəˌveɪtər/ *n.* [C] **1** FORMAL someone who grows crops or plants, especially a farmer **2** a tool or machine that is used to prepare land for growing crops

cul·tur·al /'kʌltʃərəl/ *adj.* **1** relating to a particular society and its way of life: *Puerto Rico has a distinct cultural identity.* | *Teachers must be equipped to deal with the linguistic and cultural diversity of the student body.* | *The New Orleans Spring Fiesta will spotlight the city's Spanish **cultural heritage**.* **2** relating to art, literature, music etc.: *Houston's cultural offerings are*

cul·tur·al·ly /ˈkʌlt...əli/ *adv.* **1** in a way that is related to the ideas, beliefs, or customs of a society: *someone's feelings are often culturally related to the* ... *in a way that is related to art, literature.* proc.: *The district is one of the most ... and culturally sophisticated in the ...* erature

... *for.* | *Vienna is a real cultural center for* ... *lovers.*

just what we were loo...

cul·ture ... /ˈkʌltʃə/ *n.* **1** [C,U] the ideas, beliefs, and customs shared and accepted by people in a society: *... out the book they give you examples of differ...tures and how they do things.* | **American/** ... **Mexican etc. culture** *I think it's part of* ... *erican culture to cater to kids.*

2 **in a group** [C,U] the attitudes and beliefs about something that are shared by a particular group of people or in a particular organization: *youth culture* | *The culture of the classroom should encourage children to be curious.* | *Superman and Batman have become a part of popular culture.* | *The two companies have very different corporate cultures.* —see also COUNTERCULTURE, SUBCULTURE

3 **art/music etc.** [U] activities relating to art, music, literature etc.: *Old San Juan is rich in history and culture.* —see Usage Note at CIVILIZATION

4 **society** [C] a society that existed at a particular time in history: *primitive cultures* | *the Ancient Greek and Roman cultures*

5 **science** [C,U] the process of growing BACTERIA for scientific use, or the BACTERIA produced by this: *The doctor ordered a throat culture.*

6 **crops** [U] TECHNICAL the practice of growing crops: *rice culture* —see also CULTURE SHOCK

cul·tured /ˈkʌltʃɚd/ *adj.* intelligent, polite, and interested in art, literature, music etc.: *I loved her combination of cultured sophistication and working-class humor.*

cultured pearl /ˌ.. ˈ./ *n.* [C] a PEARL that has been grown artificially

culture shock /ˈ.. ˌ./ *n.* [U] the feelings of surprise or anxiety that someone has when they visit a foreign country or a place for the first time: *I get culture shock every time I come back to this country.*

cul·vert /ˈkʌlvɚt/ *n.* [C] a pipe that takes a stream under a road, railroad etc.

cum¹ /kʊm, kʌm/ *prep.* FORMAL used between two nouns to show that something or someone has two purposes or does two things: *a bookstore-cum-coffeehouse* | *C.J. Stewart, a child psychologist-cum-karate teacher*

cum² /kʌm/ *n.* [U] VULGAR, SLANG a man's SEMEN (=liquid he produces during sex)

cum³ *v.* [I] VULGAR, SLANG to EJACULATE

Cum·ber·land Pla·teau, the /ˌkʌmbɚlənd plæˈtoʊ/ a part of the southwestern Appalachians, that runs from the state of West Virginia in the U.S. to the state of Alabama

cum·ber·some /ˈkʌmbɚsəm/ *adj.* **1** a process or system that is cumbersome is slow and difficult: *Leroy bitterly opposed the plan for being cumbersome and costly.* **2** heavy and difficult to move: *McMahon wore a cumbersome brace on his right leg.* **3** words or phrases that are cumbersome are long or complicated

cum·in /ˈkyumən/ *n.* [U] the seeds of a plant that have a sweet smell and are used especially in Mexican and Indian cooking, or the plant that they grow on

cum lau·de /kʊm ˈlaʊdə, kʌm-, -di/ *adv.* an expression meaning "with honors," used to show that you have finished high school or college at the third of the three highest levels of achievement that students can reach —compare MAGNA CUM LAUDE, SUMMA CUM LAUDE

cum·mer·bund /ˈkʌmɚˌbʌnd/ *n.* [C] a wide piece of cloth that a man wears around his waist as part of a

TUXEDO (=special pants and coat) worn on very formal occasions

cum·mings /ˈkʌmɪŋz/, **e.e.** /i i/ (1894–1962) a U.S. poet known for unusual ways of arranging the words in his poems, and for always using small letters

cu·mu·la·tive /ˈkyumyələt̬ɪv, -ˌleɪt̬-/ *adj.* increasing gradually as more of something is added or happens: *Learning is a cumulative process.* | *The cumulative effect of only two hours of unbroken sleep a night can make you very sick.*

cu·mu·lo·nim·bus /ˌkyumyələˈnɪmbəs/ *n.* [C] a type of thick large cloud that often produced rain storms or THUNDERSTORMS

cu·mu·lus /ˈkyumyələs/ *n.* [C,U] a thick white cloud with a flat bottom edge

cu·ne·i·form /ˈkyuniəˌfɔrm, kyuˈniəfɔrm/ *adj.* relating to the writing used by the people of ancient Mesopotamia —**cuneiform** *n.* [U]

cun·ni·lin·gus /ˌkʌnɪˈlɪŋgəs/ *n.* [U] TECHNICAL the act of touching the female sex organs with the lips and tongue in order to give sexual pleasure

cun·ning¹ /ˈkʌnɪŋ/ *adj.* **1** someone who is cunning is good at deceiving people in order to get what they want: *Diane was a cold and cunning woman who preyed upon lonely teenagers.* **2** behavior or actions that are cunning are dishonest and unfair, and are used to get what you want: *The coach quickly came up with a cunning counterattack.* **3** a cunning object or piece of equipment is unusual, very useful, well-designed etc.: *a cunning model of the world* **4** OLD-FASHIONED attractive: *There was a small black sofa with cunning red and blue cushions on it.* —**cunningly** *adv.*

cunning² *n.* [U] the ability to achieve what you want by deceiving people in a smart way: *The few people that escaped the crazed gunman did so by quick cunning, courage, and luck.*

Cun·ning·ham /ˈkʌnɪŋhæm/, **Im·o·gen** /ˈɪməˌdʒɪn/ (1883–1976) a U.S. PHOTOGRAPHER

Cunningham, Merce /mɚs/ (1919–) a U.S. dancer and CHOREOGRAPHER of modern dance

cunt /kʌnt/ *n.* [C] TABOO **1** a woman's vagina (=sex organ) **2** an extremely offensive word for someone you are angry with

cup¹ /kʌp/ *n.* [C]

1 **for drinking** a small round container with a handle, that you use to drink coffee, tea etc.: *a cup and saucer* | *a coffee/tea cup* *a set of china tea cups* —compare MUG¹ (1)

2 **drink** the liquid contained inside a cup: *Would you like another cup?* | *[+ of] Let me get you a cup of coffee.*

3 **amount of liquid** also **cupful** the amount of liquid or soft food a cup can hold: *The fish came with a little cup of tartar sauce.*

4 **measurement** an exact measure of quantity used in cooking: *Thoroughly mix the butter with 1 cup of powdered sugar until light and fluffy.*

5 **round thing** something round and hollow that is shaped like a cup: *acorn cups* | *[+ of] the cup of a flower* | *She held it in the cup of her hand.*

6 **sports** **a)** a specially shaped container that is given as a prize in a competition, especially a sports competition: *The winner stood on the platform, holding the cup above her head.* **b)** a sports competition: *When did Argentina win the World Cup?* **c)** a hole in the ground that you have to try to get the ball into in the game of GOLF

7 **women's clothing** the part of a BRA that covers a woman's breast

8 **men's clothing** a JOCKSTRAP

9 **not be your cup of tea** SPOKEN to not be the type of thing that you like: *Game shows just aren't my cup of tea.*

10 **a cup of joe** a cup of coffee

11 **my cup runneth over** used to say that you are very happy and have more than you need —see also LOVING CUP

cup² *v.* **cupped, cupping** [T] **1** to hold something in your hands, so that your hands form part of a circle around it: *He leaned an elbow on the desk and cupped* his chin in his hand. **2 cup your hand(s)** to make a shape like a cup with your hand or hands: *Sara cupped her hand around the match until it burned steadily.*

cup·board /'kʌbəd/ *n.* [C] a piece of furniture for storing clothes, plates, food etc. that is usually attached to a wall and has shelves and a door: *There's a lot of cupboard space in this kitchen.* —see picture at KITCHEN

cup·cake /'kʌpkeɪk/ *n.* [C] a small round cake

cup·ful /'kʌpfʊl/ *n.* [C] the amount that a cup can hold

Cu·pid /'kyupɪd/ *n.* **1** [singular] the Roman god of sexual love, usually represented as a beautiful boy with wings who carries a BOW and ARROW **2** [C] also **cupid** an image of this god, used to represent love: *The tablecloth had a pattern of hearts and cupids.* **3 play Cupid** to try to arrange for two people to fall in love with each other: *His attempt at playing Cupid for Selma and Mr. Skinner backfired.*

cu·pid·i·ty /kyu'pɪdəti/ *n.* [U] FORMAL very strong desire for something, especially money or property; GREED: *the cupidity of some businessmen*

cu·po·la /'kyupələ/ *n.* [C] a small round part on the roof of a building, that is shaped like an upside down bowl

cur /kɚ/ *n.* [C] OLD-FASHIONED **1** an unfriendly dog, especially one that is a mix of several breeds **2** a mean person

cur·a·ble /'kyʊrəbəl/ *adj.* an illness that is curable can be cured: *Cervical cancer is usually curable if it is detected early enough.* —opposite INCURABLE

cu·ra·çao /'kyʊrə,soʊ, 'kʊr-, ,kyʊrə'saʊ/ *n.* [U] a strong thick alcoholic drink that tastes like oranges

cu·ra·cy /'kyʊrəsi/ *n.* [C] the job or position of curate, or the period of time that someone has this position

cu·ra·re /kyu'rɑri/ *n.* [U] a poison made from a tropical plant, used as medicine and on ARROWS as a weapon

cu·rate[1] /'kyʊrət/ *n.* [C] a priest of the lowest rank, whose job is to help the priest who is in charge of an area

cu·rate[2] /'kyʊreɪt, kyʊ'reɪt/ *v.* [T] to decide what things will be shown in a MUSEUM, ZOO etc.: *The show at the Museum of Modern Art was curated by poet and critic Bill Berkson.*

cu·ra·tive /'kyʊrətɪv/ *adj.* able to or intended to cure illness: *The mud here has long been recognized for its curative properties.* —**curative** *n.* [C]

cu·ra·tor /'kyʊ,reɪtɚ, 'kyʊrətɚ, kyʊ'reɪtɚ/ *n.* [C] someone who is in charge of and decides what things are shown in a MUSEUM, ZOO etc.: *Michael is the mammal curator at the Los Angeles Zoo.*

curb[1] /kɚb/ *n.* [C] **1** the edge of a street, between where people can walk and cars can drive: *A car was parked at the curb.* —see picture on page 423 **2** something that helps to control or limit something: [+ **on**] *Right-wing politicians have called for a tight curb on immigration.*

curb[2] *v.* [T] to control or limit something in order to prevent it from having a harmful effect: *The city is trying new measures to curb pollution.*

curd /kɚd/ *n.* [C usually plural] the thick substance that forms in milk when it becomes sour, used to make cheese —see also BEAN CURD

cur·dle /'kɚdl/ *v.* [I,T] to become thicker or form curds, or to make a liquid do this: *Do not let the sauce boil or it will curdle.* —see also BLOODCURDLING

cure[1] /kyʊr/ *v.* [T] **1** to make an illness or an injury better, usually by medical treatment: *Penicillin or other antibiotics will cure most infections.* | *Prostate cancer can be cured if it is caught early.* **2** to solve a problem, or improve a bad situation: *The only thing that can cure grief is time.* | *Most economic ills cannot be cured by a simple infusion of cash.* | [**cure sb of sth**] *This simple solution cured me of biting my nails.* **3** to make someone who is sick well again: *Doctors won't consider her cured until she has been free of cancer for several years.* **4** to preserve food,

341

tobacco etc. by dry[...] covering it with salt [...] hanging it in smoke, or [...]

USAGE NOTE: CUR[...]

WORD CHOICE: cure, h[...]
Cure is used about treati[...] or an illness: *Although do[...] cannot yet cure it.* **Heal** is [...] about treating someone wh[o has a disease] *The doctor said the cut sho[...DS, they] won't even be a scar.* [...in talking about an injury:...]

cure[2] *n.* [C] **1** a medicine o[r ...] can cure an illness: *Preventi[...] cure.* | [+ **for**] *Scientists sti[ll ...] for the common cold.* **2** someth[ing ...] lem, or improves a bad situat[ion ...] *ment practices might be the c[...] problems.* **3** the act of making [...] after an illness: *Miraculous cure[s ...] in Lourdes.* **4 take the cure** OLD-[...] special hospital in order to impr[...] to make you stop drinking alcoho[l ...]

cure-all /'[...]./ *n.* [C] something that [...] cure any problem or illness: *The [...] used garlic as a cure-all for everythin[g...] bee stings.*

cur·few /'kɚfyu/ *n.* **1** [C] a law forcing eve[ryone to] stay indoors from a particular time in the ev[ening] until a particular time in the morning: *During [the] war, the government **imposed a curfew** in the capital.* | *The town and some surrounding villages were **under curfew**.* **2** [U] the time after which everyone must stay indoors, according to this law: *Residents blacked out their windows and stayed in **after curfew**.* **3** [C,U] the time by which a child must be indoors or asleep, as decided by their parents: *If your teenager keeps reasonable hours, there is no need to set a curfew.*

Cu·rie /kyʊ'ri/, **Ma·rie** /mə'ri/ (1867–1934) a Polish scientist, who with her husband Pierre Curie studied RADIOACTIVITY and discovered two new RADIOACTIVE substances, POLONIUM and RADIUM

Curie, Pierre /pyɛr/ (1859–1906) a French scientist who studied RADIOACTIVITY with his wife Marie Curie

cu·ri·o /'kyʊri,oʊ/ *n.* **plural curios** [C] a small object that is interesting or valuable because it is unusual, beautiful, or rare: *The street is lined with shops selling souvenirs and curios.*

cu·ri·os·i·ty /,kyʊri'asəti/ *n.* **plural curiosities** **1** [singular,U] the desire to learn about something or to know something: [+ **about**] *As human beings, we have great curiosity about how nature works.* | *Bebe went to the auction just **out of curiosity**.* | *Biographers try to **satisfy the curiosity** of readers by adding lots of little-known facts.* | **pique/stir/spark sb's curiosity** (=make someone curious about something) **2** [C] something that is interesting because it is unusual or strange: *The emperor's visit was treated as a curiosity rather than a political event.* **3 curiosity killed the cat** a phrase used to tell someone not to ask questions about something that does not concern them

cu·ri·ous /'kyʊriəs/ *adj.* **1** wanting to know or learn about something: *A few curious neighbors came out to see what was going on.* | [+ **about**] *All children are curious about the workings of things.* | **curious to hear/learn/know etc.** *I was curious to see if the plants would survive in lower temperatures.* **2** strange or unusual: *The principal's response to the problem was curious.* | [+ **that**] *It is curious that so many people are interested in something that happened over 20 years ago.* **3 the curious** people who are curious: *There are signs directing the curious to the museum.* —**curiously** *adv.*

s w
2
3

curl[1] /kɚl/ *n.* **1** [C] a small mass of hair that hangs in a curving shape: *a little girl with long blonde*

curl

curl

forms a curved shape: *A ... her cigarette.* | *Chocolate ...decoration for cakes and ...* **curls 2** [C] something ... **curl of smoke** r... ise in which you continu... **curls make** a... legs or stomach in order to ... **curls make 3** [C] ...ng: *Do two sets each of bicep ...* **desserts. 3** [... **curl of your lip/mouth** a move-... ously ben... in which you turn your lips ... make ...thing ... show that you disapprove of ... and ...rform a twisted or curved shape, or ... and ...ng do this: *I didn't have a chance to ... m...is morning.* | [+ **around**] *The phone ...* ...led around her hand.* **2** [I always ... ... always + adv./prep.] to move, form-... d or curved shape, or to make something ...nelope's fingers curled and uncurled ner-... her lap.* | [+ **across/along** etc.] *Morning ...led across the surface of the river.* **3** [I,T] if ... your lip, or if your lip curls, you move it up ...deways, to show that you disapprove of some-... something: *Her lip curled in contempt.* **4** [I] to ... a special stone toward a marked point on ice in ... sport of CURLING —see also **make sb's toes curl** ...E[1] (5)), **make your hair curl** (HAIR (12))

curl up *phr. v.* [I] **1** to lie or sit with your arms and legs bent close to your body: *The cat was curled up in the middle of our bed.* **2** if something flat curls up, its edges start to become curved and point up: *The leaves had turned yellow and curled up at the edges.*

curl·er /ˈkɚlɚ/ *n.* [C usually plural] **1** a small plastic or metal tube used for making hair curl: *Pink curlers were rolled into her hair.* **2** someone who plays the sport of curling

cur·lew /ˈkɚlu/ *n.* [C] a brown and gray bird with long legs and a curved beak, that lives near water or wet areas of land

curl·i·cue, curlycue /ˈkɚliˌkyu/ *n.* [C] a decorative twisted pattern

curl·ing /ˈkɚlɪŋ/ *n.* [U] a winter sport played on ice by sliding flat heavy stones toward a marked point

curl·ing i·ron /ˈ.. ˌ../ *n.* [plural] a piece of electrical equipment that you heat and use to curl your hair

curl·y /ˈkɚli/ *adj.* **curlier, curliest** having a lot of curls: *Mike is the guy with the curly blond hair.* —**curliness** *n.* [U]

curly en·dive /ˌ.. ˈ../ *n.* [U] ENDIVE (2)

cur·mudg·eon /kɚˈmʌdʒən/ *n.* [C] OLD-FASHIONED an old person who is often angry or annoyed —**curmudgeonly** *adj.*

cur·rant /ˈkɚənt, ˈkʌr-/ *n.* [C] a small round red or black BERRY used in cooking

s w **cur·ren·cy** /ˈkɚənsi/ *n. plural* **currencies 1** [C,U] the system or type of money that a particular country uses: *The Euro will eventually replace European national currencies.* | *The local currency is the cruzeiro.* —see also HARD CURRENCY —see Usage Note at MONEY **2** [U] the state of being generally accepted or used: *"Middle age" is a term which only gained currency after World War I.* | *The idea of time travel enjoys wide currency* (=is accepted by many people) *in 20th century fiction.*

s w **cur·rent¹** /ˈkɚənt/ *adj.* [only before noun] happening or existing now, but not likely to last for a long time: *What is your current occupation?* —see Usage Note at NEW

current² *n.* [C] **1** a continuous movement of water or air in a particular direction: *The current in the river was very strong.* **2** a flow of electricity through a wire: *Turn off the current before changing the fuse.*

current e·vents also **current af·fairs** /ˌ.. .ˈ./ *n.* [U] important political events or other events in society that are happening now: *I read the paper to keep up with current events.*

s w **cur·rent·ly** /ˈkɚəntli/ *adv.* at the present time: *The house is currently unoccupied.* | *Ken is currently*

working as a high school baseball coach. —see Usage Note at ACTUALLY

cur·ric·u·lum /kəˈrɪkyələm/ *n. plural* **curricula** /-lə/ or **curriculums** [C] the subjects that are taught at a school, college etc.: *The curriculum includes art and music classes.* —compare SYLLABUS **s w** 3

curriculum vi·tae /kəˌrɪkyələm ˈvitə, -ˈviti, -ˈvaɪti/ *n.* [C] a word for a RÉSUMÉ, used especially by people who are APPLYing for a teaching job at a college or university

Cur·ri·er and Ives /ˌkɚiɚ ən ˈaɪvz, ˌkʌr-/ a U.S. business firm, started by Nathaniel Currier (1813–1885) and James Merritt Ives (1824–1895), that produced very popular pictures showing scenes from daily life in 19th century America

cur·ry¹ /ˈkɚi, ˈkʌri/ *n. plural* **curries 1** [U] curry powder **2** [C,U] a type of food from India consisting of meat or vegetables covered in a thick SPICY liquid: *chicken curry and rice*

curry² *v.* **curries, curried, currying** [T] **1 curry favor with sb** to try to make someone like you or notice you in order to get something that you want: *Interest groups try to curry favor with lawmakers by donating to their campaigns.* **2** to comb a horse with a special metal comb

curry pow·der /ˈ.. ˌ../ also **curry** *n.* [U] a mixture of SPICEs that is used for giving food a SPICY taste

curse¹ /kɚs/ *v.* **1** [I] to swear: *A drunk started cursing and spitting.* | [+ **at**] *The cabbie cursed at her for giving him a lousy tip.* **2** [T] to say or think bad things about someone or something because they have made you angry: *I sat in my car, cursing the heavy traffic.* | [**curse sb for doing sth**] *Elsa cursed herself for being such a fool when it came to men.* **3** [T] to ask God or a magical power to harm someone: *People in many cultures believe witch doctors have the power to bless or curse their lives.*

curse sb **↔ out** *phr. v.* [T] INFORMAL to swear at someone who has made you angry: *This guy cursed me out because he thought I stole his parking place.*

curse² *n.* [C] **1** a swear word, or words, that you say because you are very angry: *Connors started shouting curses at the umpire who called the ball out.* **2** a word or sentence used to ask God or a magical power to do something bad to someone or something: *The witch put a curse on the baby princess.* **3** something that causes trouble, harm etc.: *Being a war hero has turned out to be both a blessing and a curse.* **4 the curse** OLD-FASHIONED a phrase meaning MENSTRUATION

cursed /kɚst/ *adj.* **1 be cursed with sth** to suffer because of a problem that you have and cannot get rid of: *The area is cursed with transportation problems.* **2** LITERARY suffering as a result of a punishment by God or a god: *Collins' novel is about a cursed jewel stolen from an idol's eye.* **3** [only before noun] OLD-FASHIONED bad, stupid, or annoying: *There was not a drink to be had after midnight in this cursed town.* —**cursedly** *adv.*

cur·sive /ˈkɚsɪv/ *adj.* written in a flowing rounded style of writing with the letters joined together: *cursive script* —**cursively** *adv.*

cur·sor /ˈkɚsɚ/ *n.* [C] a mark or a small light which can be moved around a computer screen to show where you are working

cur·so·ry /ˈkɚsəri/ *adj.* quick and done without much attention to details: *a cursory check/examination/inspection Even a cursory inspection would have shown how dangerous the bridge was.* —**cursorily** *adv.*

curt /kɚt/ *adj.* using very few words when you speak to someone, in a way that seems rude: *He responded with a curt, three-sentence letter.* —**curtly** *adv.* —**curtness** *n.* [U]

cur·tail /kɚˈteɪl/ *v.* [T] FORMAL to reduce or limit something: *Budget cuts forced schools to curtail after-school programs.* —**curtailment** *n.* [C,U]

cur·tain /ˈkɚtn/ *n.* [C] **1** a piece of hanging cloth that can be pulled across to cover a window, divide a room etc.: *a shower curtain* | **draw/pull the curtains** *Marie came in to draw the curtains and light* **s w** 3 the *fire*. **2** a sheet of heavy material that can be made to come down across the front of the stage in a theater: *Before the curtain went up, the dancers took their places on the stage.* **3 a** thick layer of something that stops anything behind it from being seen: *A dense curtain of fog caused traffic problems.* **4 draw/lower etc. the curtains on sth** to do something that stops or ends something else: *Officials are lowering the curtains on the fishing season because of low fish stocks.* **5 the curtain falls on sth** if the curtain falls on an event or period of history, it ends **6 be curtains for sb/sth** INFORMAL used to say that someone will die, or that something will end: *After 75 years, it's curtains for the town's movie theater.*

curtain call /'.. ,./ *n.* [C] the time at the end of a performance when the actors, dancers, musicians etc. come out to receive APPLAUSE: *Margot Fonteyn drew 48 curtain calls when she made her New York debut.*

curtain hook /'.. ,./ *n.* [C] a small hook that you put on the top of a curtain so that you can hang it up

curtain rail /'.. ,./ *n.* [C] a long bar of plastic or metal that you hang a curtain on

curtain rais·er, curtain-raiser /'.. ,../ *n.* [C] **1** a short play, movie, piece of music etc. that is performed or shown before the main one: *Dvorak's "Carnival" overture was a rousing curtain-raiser.* **2** a small thing that happens or is done just before something more important: *This leading part is likely to be the curtain raiser of her opera career.*

curt·sy, curtsey /'kɑtsi/ *v.* **curtsies, curtsied, curtsying** [I] if a woman curtsies to someone, she bends her knees while putting one foot behind the other as a sign of respect: *Sarah curtsied as the future queen entered the room.* —**curtsy** *n.* [C] —compare BOW[1] (1)

cur·va·ceous /kɑˈveɪʃəs/ *adj.* having an attractively curved body shape: *a curvaceous blonde woman* —**curvaceousness** *n.* [U]

cur·va·ture /'kɑvətʃɑ/ *n.* [C,U] TECHNICAL **1** the state of being curved, or the degree to which something is curved: [+ of] *the curvature of the Earth's surface* **2** a medical condition in which part of someone's body curves in a way that is not natural: [+ of] *a curvature of the spine*

curve[1] /kɑv/ *n.* [C] **1** a line or object which gradually bends like part of a circle: *Customers seem to like the car's curves and angles.* | [+ of] *the curve of the sword blade* **2** part of a road, river etc. that bends like part of a circle: *Will was killed when he lost control of his car in a curve.* **3** if sales, profits etc. are on a curve, they are increasing or decreasing compared to what they were doing before: *Sales are on an upward growth curve.* **4 throw sb a curve** to surprise someone with a question or problem that is difficult to deal with: *The governor threw them a curve when he announced that funding would be cut.* **5** also **curve ball** a throw in baseball toward the BATTER in which the ball spins so that it curves suddenly and is difficult to hit **6** a method of giving grades based on how a student's work compares with other students' work: *I'll be grading the test on a curve.* —see also LEARNING CURVE

curve[2] *v.* [I,T] to bend or move in the shape of a curve, or to make something do this: *Hurricane Gustav curved away from the Caribbean Islands and headed toward open ocean.*

curved /kɑvd/ *adj.* having a shape that is rounded and not straight: *An airplane wing is curved on top and flat on the bottom.*

curv·y /'kɑvi/ also **curv·ing** /'kɑvɪŋ/ *adj.* having a shape with several curves: *a curvy mountain road*

cush·ion[1] /'kʊʃən/ *n.* [C] **1** a cloth bag filled with soft material that you put on a chair, the floor etc. to make it more comfortable to sit or lie on: *She sat cross-legged on a cushion on the floor.* —compare PILLOW[1] (1) —see also WHOOPEE CUSHION **2** something that stops one thing from hitting another thing: *Good shoes should provide a cushion when running on concrete.* **3** something, especially money, that prevents you from being immediately affected by a bad situation: *The Red Wings had a three-point cushion in the second period.* | [+ against] *Banks should have money to act as a cushion against possible losses*

from loans. **4** the soft rubber edge of the table that is used for playing BILLIARDS or POOL[1] (2)

cushion[2] *v.* [T] **1** to make a fall or knock less painful, for example by having something soft in the way: *Mattresses on the ground cushioned his fall.* **2** to reduce the effects of something bad: **cushion the blow/impact (of sth)** *The law will cushion the blow for homeowners by gradually phasing in the tax increases.*

cush·y /'kʊʃi/ *adj.* **cushier, cushiest** INFORMAL **1** a cushy job is easy to do and pays well: *Peter just landed a cushy new job with a big firm.* **2** very comfortable: *I sank down on a cushy sofa.*

cusp /kʌsp/ *n.* [C] **1** TECHNICAL the point formed by two curves meeting **2** a time when something important is about to happen or begin: *The grizzly bear was chosen as the state animal when California was on the cusp of statehood.* **3** someone who was born on the cusp was born near the time when one STAR SIGN ends and another one begins: *I was born on the cusp of Cancer and Leo.*

cus·pi·dor /'kʌspəˌdɔr/ *n.* [C] FORMAL a SPITTOON

cuss[1] /kʌs/ *v.* [I,T] SPOKEN to swear because you are annoyed by something: *I didn't blow the horn, but I was cussing that driver for about a mile.*

cuss sb ↔ **out** *phr. v.* [T] to swear and shout at someone because you are angry: *She got mad and started cussing him out.*

cuss[2] *n.* [C] OLD-FASHIONED **a stubborn/stupid/ornery etc. cuss** someone who is annoying because they are STUBBORN, stupid etc.: *Gene is an arrogant little cuss.*

cuss word /'. ./ *n.* [C] a SWEAR WORD

cus·tard /'kʌstɑd/ *n.* [C,U] a soft mixture of milk, sugar, and eggs, that is usually baked

custard pie /,.. './ *n.* [C] a PIE filled with custard, which people throw at each other as a joke in movies, television shows etc.

Cus·ter /'kʌstɑ/, **George** (1839–1876) a general in the U.S. Civil War, who was killed by Native Americans from the Sioux tribe in the Battle of the Little Bighorn

cus·to·di·al /kʌˈstoʊdiəl/ *adj.* FORMAL **1** relating to the custody of someone, especially a child: *The mother is usually the custodial parent.* **2** relating to the work done by a CUSTODIAN (1): *the school's custodial staff*

cus·to·di·an /kəˈstoʊdiən/ *n.* [C] **1** someone who takes care of a public building: *a custodian at the stadium* **2** someone who is responsible for taking care of someone or something: *The state was named custodian of Kimberly and her two brothers.*

cus·to·dy /'kʌstədi/ *n.* [U] **1** a right to take care of a child, especially when the child's parents are legally separated from each other: [+ of] *Kephart got custody of his son after the divorce.* | *Mrs. Richburn has custody of her three children.* | *Harper and Moore have joint custody* (=they both have the right to take care of their child) *of their six-year-old son.* | **grant/award sb custody** (=if a court grants someone custody, it gives that person the right to take care of a child) | *The twins were placed in the custody of their grandparents.* **2 in custody** being kept in prison by the police until you go to court, because the police think you are guilty of a crime: *The youth was put in custody at juvenile hall.* | **hold/keep sb in custody** *The defendant will be kept in custody until the appeal.* | *As soon as the plane landed, they were taken into custody by waiting FBI men.* **3 in the custody of sb** FORMAL if something is in someone's custody, it is being kept and taken care of by them: *The records are in the custody of the government.*

cus·tom[1] /'kʌstəm/ *n.* **1** [C,U] something that is done by people in a particular society because it is traditional: *The Talmud is the Jewish book of law and custom.* | **a local/American/Mexican etc. custom** *The guide offers information on local*

C

customs. | It is Asia's **custom to** greet the New Year with firecrackers. | [**the custom of doing sth**] The custom of carving jack-o'-lanterns can be traced back to an old Irish folk tale. **2 customs** [plural] the place where your bag is checked for illegal goods when you go into a country: All bags must be inspected by customs officers. | We waited over two hours to **clear customs** (=be allowed through customs after being checked). **3** [C usually singular] ESPECIALLY LITERARY something that you usually do every day, or in a particular situation: It was his custom to attend Mass every Sunday. **4** [U] FORMAL the practice of regularly using a particular store or business: The service was not very good, so I've decided to take my custom elsewhere. —see Usage Note at HABIT

custom² adj. [only before noun] custom products and services are specially designed and made for a particular person or group: Temsco also offers custom tours to LeConte Glacier and Mount McKinley.

cus·tom·ar·y /ˈkʌstəˌmɛri/ adj. **1** something that is customary is normal because it is the way something is usually done: It is customary to wear new clothing for the Chinese new year. **2** someone's customary behavior is the way they usually do things: Whitworth performed with his customary brilliance. —**customarily** /ˌkʌstəˈmɛrəli/ adv.

custom-built /ˌ.. ˈ. ◄/ adj. something large that is custom-built has been specially designed and made for a particular person: a custom-built mountain bike —**custom-build** v. [T] —compare CUSTOM-MADE

cus·tom·er /ˈkʌstəmə/ n. [C] **1** someone who buys goods or services from a store, company etc.: Their typical customer earns more than $70,000. | British Airways was Boeing's largest customer for jet airplanes. | Hemingway was **a regular customer** (=someone who goes to a store, restaurant etc. often) of the cafe. **2 a cool customer** INFORMAL someone who is always calm and very confident, but sometimes in a way that is not nice

---

USAGE NOTE: CUSTOMER

WORD CHOICE: shopper, customer, buyer, consumer
If you are in a store, looking for things to buy, you are a **shopper**: Stores were crowded with shoppers looking for after-Christmas bargains. When you buy goods from a particular store, you are their **customer**: Customers will get $5 off all jeans purchased before May 25th. If you are buying something very expensive such as a car or a house, you are a **buyer**: first-time home buyers. **Consumers** are all the people who buy and use goods and services: Today's consumers face too many choices.

---

cus·tom·ize /ˈkʌstəˌmaɪz/ v. [T] to change something to make it more appropriate for you, or to make it look special or unusual: a customized pick-up truck

custom-made /ˌ.. ˈ. ◄/ adj. custom-made furniture, clothes etc. are specially made for a particular person: a custom-made guitar —compare CUSTOM-BUILT

cut¹ /kʌt/ v. past tense and past participle **cut** present participle **cutting**
1 divide into pieces [T] to use a knife, scissors etc. to divide something into two or more pieces, or to remove a piece from the main part of something: Would you cut some roses for the table? | [**cut sth in/into sth**] Cut the apples into four pieces. | [**cut sb sth**] Can you cut me a piece of bread too, please? | Use French bread, **cut in half**, for the sandwiches.
2 reduce [T] to reduce the amount of something, especially something such as prices, time, or money: This technology could cut our operating costs. | If you cut too many jobs, you overload the remaining employees. | People in the area might be forced to **cut** their water use **by half**.
3 wound [T] to injure yourself or someone else using a sharp object such as a knife, so that you start

bleeding: **cut your finger/hand/leg** etc. He cut his finger when a test tube broke in his hand. | I **cut myself** shaving this morning. | A man who tried to climb the fence **cut open** his leg.
4 make shorter [T] to make something shorter with a knife, scissors etc. especially in order to improve its appearance: The baby's fingernails need cutting again. | **have/get your hair cut** Have you had your hair cut? It looks good. | **cut the lawn/grass** I get two bucks a week for cutting the Gibson's lawn.
5 make a shape [T] to make something into a particular shape by using a sharp tool such as a knife: [**cut sth into/in sth**] Cut the chocolate into fairly small cubes.
6 make a hole [I,T] to make a hole in the surface of something, or to open it by using a sharp tool such as a knife: [+ into] Cut into the meat to see if it is done. | Somebody **cut a hole in** the tent and stole the bag. | Students will **cut open** a frog and dissect it.
7 cut sb free/loose to cut something such as a rope or metal in order to let someone escape: Firefighters cut her free from the wreckage of the car.
8 music/record [T] if a musician cuts a record, they record their music on a record, TAPE etc.: We cut this track in my studio at home.
9 movie/speech [T] **a)** to reduce the length of a movie, speech etc.: The original version was cut by more than 30 minutes. **b)** to remove part of a movie, speech, or piece of writing, because it is not right or it might offend people: Beresford cut the scenes of cannibalism. **c)** to put the parts of a movie together so that they make a continuous story, getting rid of the parts you do not want
10 cut corners to do something in a way that is not perfect, in order to save time, effort, or money: One airline was accused of cutting corners on safety.
11 cut your losses to stop trying to do something that is already failing in order to prevent the situation becoming even worse: At that point they just wanted to cut their losses and get out of the business.
12 cut in line/front to unfairly go in front of other people who are waiting to buy or do something: Tempers flared as cars tried to cut in line.
13 cut class/school to deliberately not go to a class that you ought to go to, or to not go to school when you ought to: She started cutting classes and fighting with her teachers and parents.
14 cut sth short to stop doing something earlier than was planned: The ten-day mission was cut short when one of the shuttle's navigation devices failed.
15 cut sb short to stop someone from finishing what they wanted to say: I tried to explain but she cut me short.
16 cut both ways INFORMAL used to say that something has advantages but also disadvantages: The new season cuts both ways for the team – they have a chance to prove themselves, but they are under pressure to do better than last year.
17 cut and paste TECHNICAL to take a part of a computer DOCUMENT or FILE and move it to another place in that or another document: You can edit your report by cutting and pasting.
18 cut sth to the bone to reduce costs, services etc. as much as possible: The company laid off employees and cut expenses to the bone.
19 cut to the chase INFORMAL to immediately start dealing with the most important part of something: In business meetings, Richardson likes to cut to the chase.

SPOKEN PHRASES

20 cut it/that out used to angrily tell someone to stop doing something because it is annoying you: Rusty, cut it out, I'm trying to study in here.
21 cut the crap an impolite way of telling someone to talk only about what is important, instead of wasting time on other things: Can we just cut the crap and start this meeting?
22 Cut! used by the director of a movie to tell everyone to stop acting, filming etc.: Cut, people! That's a wrap!

23 not cut it to not be good enough to do something or deal with something: *We could make a lot of excuses, but excuses won't cut it.* | *Players who can't cut it soon realize it and quit.*
24 cut it close to leave yourself just barely enough time or money to do something: *I don't know – leaving at six is cutting it kind of close.*
25 cut no ice also **not cut much ice** if something cuts no ice with someone, it will not persuade them to change their mind: *I don't think anything I say will cut much ice with him.*
26 cut the cheese also **cut one** HUMOROUS to make air come out of your BOWELS; FART

27 tooth if a baby cuts a tooth, the tooth starts to grow through the GUMS
28 divide an area [T] to divide an area into two or more parts: *The river cuts the valley in two.*
29 playing cards [I,T] to divide a DECK of cards into two before starting to play
30 cut and run INFORMAL to leave a situation suddenly when it becomes too difficult, especially when you should stay: *We sensed that Borden could cut and run at any moment.*
31 line [T] if a line cuts another line, they cross each other at a particular point
32 cut your teeth on sth to get your first experience of doing something by practicing on something simple: *After college, he cut his business teeth by working for his father's trucking firm.*
33 cut sb to the quick LITERARY to upset someone very much by saying something cruel: *His comments cut me to the quick.*
34 cut a fine/odd etc. figure LITERARY to have an impressive, strange etc. appearance: *With his flowing hair, Zhang cuts a striking figure on stage.*
35 cut the cord to stop depending on someone, especially your parents: *When I turned 18 I figured it was time to cut the cord and move away from home.*
36 illegal drug [T usually passive] to mix an illegal drug such as HEROIN with some other substance
37 not cut the mustard INFORMAL to be not good enough: *Athletes who can't cut the mustard don't make the team.* —see also **cut it fine** (FINE² (3)), **cut/give sb some slack** (SLACK² (6)), **to make/cut a long story short** (STORY (12)), **cut a swathe through sth** (SWATHE¹ (3))

cut across *phr. v.* [T] **1** if a problem or feeling cuts across different groups of people, they are all affected by it: *Johnson's popularity cuts across racial lines.* **2** to go across an area of land rather than around it: *Try not to cut across other people's campsites.*
cut away *phr. v.* **1** [T cut sth ↔ away] to remove the unwanted or unnecessary parts from something: *Cut away dead or diseased branches.* **2** [I] if a television program or movie cuts away from something, it moves away from or stops showing a particular thing: *Cut away from her face and focus on the puppies.*
cut back *phr. v.* **1** [I,T cut sth ↔ back] to reduce the amount, size, cost etc. of something: *She cut her class load back to spend more time with her family.* | [+ **on**] *Do you have any suggestions for cutting back on fats in cooking?* **2** [T cut sth ↔ back] to remove the top part of a plant in order to help it to grow: *In the early spring, cut the bushes back to five feet.* —see also CUTBACK
cut down *phr. v.* **1** [I,T cut sth ↔ down] to reduce the amount of something, especially something you do, eat, buy etc.: *You smoke too much – you should try to cut down.* | *The time it takes to bring a new product to the market has been cut down to six months.* | [+ **on**] *I'm trying to cut down on the amount of coffee I drink.* **2** [T cut sth ↔ down] to cut through the TRUNK of a tree so that it falls on the ground **3** [T cut sth ↔ down] to reduce the length of something such as a piece of writing: *Let's try to cut your speech down to six minutes.* **4** LITERARY [T cut sb ↔ down] to kill or injure someone with a gun, sword, knife etc.: *Dozens of terrified people were cut down as they tried to escape.* **5 cut sb down to size** to make someone realize that they are not as important, successful etc. as they think they are: *The team wants to cut UCLA down to size.*

cut in *phr. v.* **1** [I] to suddenly drive into the space between two moving cars in a dangerous way: *A small convertible suddenly cut in front of a truck.* **2** [I] to interrupt someone who is speaking or a conversation by saying something: *"Excuse me," I said, cutting in. "Just how much money are we talking about?"* **3** [I] to ask permission to dance with someone who is already dancing with someone else: *She was very popular, and everybody was cutting in and dancing with her.* **4** [I] if a part of a machine cuts in, it starts to operate when it is needed: *The safety device cuts in automatically when needed.* **5 cut sb in on sth** INFORMAL to allow someone to take part in a plan to make money, especially a secret or illegal plan: *Quinn said he'd cut him in on the profits.*

cut off *phr. v.* [T]
1 piece of sth [cut sth ↔ off] to separate something by cutting it from the main part: *Before cooking the mushrooms, cut off the tough stems.* | *I cut three inches off these pants and they're still too long.*
2 stop the supply [cut sth ↔ off] to stop the supply of something such as electricity, gas, water etc.: *They're going to cut the electricity off if you don't pay the bill.* | *Sniffing glue cuts off the oxygen to your brain.*
3 place/people [cut sth ↔ off] **a)** to surround a place so that the people there are completely separated from other places or people: *The resort town was cut off by a heavy snowfall.* **b) be cut off** if a place is cut off, it is difficult to get to and is a long way from any other place: *Accessible only by air, the town is cut off from the rest of the country.*
4 stop sb talking [cut sb off] to prevent someone from finishing what they are saying: *Don't cut him off before he had a chance to argue.*
5 driving [cut sb ↔ off] to suddenly drive in front of a moving car in a dangerous way: *A woman in a green station wagon cut me off at the on-ramp.*
6 get cut off to suddenly lose the telephone connection to someone that you were speaking to: *I don't know what happened – we just got cut off.*
7 stop being friendly [cut sb ↔ off] to stop having a friendly relationship with someone: *Don't let your son's divorce cut you off from your grandchildren.*
8 money/property [cut sb off] to take away someone's right to receive your money or property, especially when you die: *My parents threatened to cut me off without a penny if I married him.*
9 cut off your nose to spite your face to do something because you are angry, even though it will harm you

cut out *phr. v.*
1 remove or shape sth [T cut sth ↔ out] to remove something by cutting, or cut something in a particular shape: *Rescue workers cut the four men out of the car.* | *Children cut out and colored pictures of butterflies.*
2 stop doing sth [T cut sth ↔ out] to stop doing or eating something, especially because it is harmful to you: *Sheila's trying to cut sugar out of her diet.* | *I've cut out all expenses that aren't absolutely necessary.*
3 not involve sb/sth [T cut sb ↔ out] to stop someone or something from doing something or being part of something: *A new departmental structure will cut out a few layers of bureaucracy and red tape.*
4 piece of writing/news report etc. [T cut sth ↔ out] to take out part of a piece of writing, a news report etc., especially because it might offend people: *The movie was rebroadcast with the offending scenes cut out.*
5 motor [I] if a motor cuts out, it suddenly stops working: *The boat's engine cut out halfway across the lake.*
6 stop sth being seen [T] to prevent light from reaching somewhere, or prevent a particular view from being seen: *Tinted windows help cut out the sun's glare.*

7 cut sb out of your will to remove someone's name from the list of people who will receive your money or property when you die

8 be cut out for sth also **be cut out to be sth** to have the qualities that you need for a particular job or activity: *Sam is still a life guard – he's just not cut out for a nine-to-five job.* —see also **have your work cut out (for you)** (WORK² (12))

cut up *phr. v.* **1** [T **cut** sth ↔ **up**] to cut something into smaller pieces: *Just cut up the potatoes and throw them in with the meat.* **2** [I] if someone cuts up, they behave loudly, amusingly, and sometimes rudely: *kids who cut up in the classroom*

C

S W
2 2

cut² *n.* [C]

1 wound a wound that you get if a sharp object cuts your skin: *His hands were covered with cuts and scrapes.*

2 reduction [usually plural] a reduction in the size, number, or amount of something that someone has planned to make: *Teachers are expecting further cuts next year.* | **budget/job/tax/pay** etc. **cuts** *Democrats attacked the proposed spending cuts.* | [+ **in**] *They're proposing cuts in the number of troops in the area.*

3 hair [usually singular] INFORMAL **a)** the act of cutting someone's hair: *How much do they charge for a cut and blow-dry?* **b)** the style in which your hair has been cut: *That's a very flattering cut.* —see also CREW CUT

4 money [usually singular] INFORMAL someone's share of something, especially money: *Schools receive a 34% cut of the money the state lottery earns.*

5 clothes [usually singular] the style in which your clothes have been made: *The emphasis on comfort has changed the cut of men's suits.*

6 meat a piece of meat that is from a particular part of an animal, or the way a piece of meat has been cut: *It's a particularly tender cut of beef.*

7 hole/mark a hole in something, or a mark in the surface of something, made by something sharp: *Make the first cut fairly shallow, then push the saw deeper into the wood.*

8 remove part of writing etc. the action of removing part of a speech, piece of writing etc.: *The censors insisted on several cuts.*

9 movie the process of putting together the different parts of a movie and removing the parts that will not be shown: *Spielberg himself oversaw the final cut.*

10 be a cut above sth to be much better than someone or something else: *The lasagna at Bella Mia is a cut above other restaurants' versions.*

11 road a road that has been made through a hill

cut³ *adj.* **1 cut flowers** flowers whose stems have been cut so that they can be taken in the house, used as decoration etc. **2** SLANG having muscles whose edge and shape are clear and easy to see

cut and dried, **cut-and-dried** /ˌ. . '. ◂/ *adj.* a situation that is cut and dried is certain to happen because it has already been planned or decided, and nothing can be done to change it: *The outcome of the case seemed cut-and-dried until the prosecution found a new witness.*

cut·a·way /ˈkʌtəˌweɪ/ *adj.* a cutaway model, drawing etc. is open on one side so that you can see the details inside it

cut·back /ˈkʌtˈbæk/ *n.* [C usually plural] a reduction in something, such as the number of workers in an organization, the amount of money spent by the government etc.: [+ **in**] *Lansbury's new contract includes a cutback in her workload.* —see also **cut back** (CUT¹)

S W
1

cute /kyut/ *adj.* INFORMAL **1** cute people are attractive in the way they look and behave: *a cute, chubby baby* | *Julia Roberts is really cute in her new movie.* **2** cute things are attractive and pretty: *Pam always draws those cute little circles over her "i's."* | *Oh, aren't those shoes cute?* **3** smart in a way that can seem rude: *Their lawyer tried a cute trick.* —**cutely** *adv.* —**cuteness** *n.* [U]

cute·sy /ˈkyutsi/ *adj.* something that is cutesy is too pretty or smart in a way you think is annoying: *All the cottages had cutesy names like "Sea Shanty" painted above their doors.*

cut glass /ˌ. '. ◂/ *n.* [U] glass that has patterns cut into its surface

cut-glass /ˌ. '. ◂/ *adj.* made of cut glass: *a cut-glass chandelier*

cu·ti·cle /ˈkyuṭɪkəl/ *n.* [C] an outer layer of hard skin, especially around the base of your nails

cut·ie, cutey /ˈkyuṭi/ *n.* [C] SPOKEN someone who is attractive and nice: *Mike is such a cutie.*

cut·lass /ˈkʌtləs/ *n.* [C] a short sword with a curved blade, used by SAILORS or PIRATES in past times

cut·ler /ˈkʌtlər/ *n.* [C] OLD USE someone who makes or sells cutlery

cut·ler·y /ˈkʌtləri/ *n.* [U] knives, forks, spoons, and other tools used for eating with; SILVERWARE

cut·let /ˈkʌtlɪt/ *n.* [C] a small flat piece of meat: *turkey cutlets*

cut·off /ˈkʌtˌɔf/ *n.* [C] **1** a limit or level at which you must stop doing something: *By the mid-May cutoff date, we had received over 9000 entries.* **2** the act of stopping doing something, especially because it has reached a particular level or limit: [+ **of**] *a cutoff of foreign aid* **3** a SHORTCUT (1): *Take the San Pablo Ridge cutoff to the right.* **4** a part of a pipe that you open and shut to control the flow of gas or liquid **5 cutoffs** [plural] a pair of SHORTS that you make by cutting off the legs of an old pair of pants

cut·out /ˈkʌtaʊt/ *n.* [C] **1** the shape of a person, object etc. that has been cut out of wood or paper: *Cut-outs of pumpkins and witches decorated the room.* **2** a piece of equipment that stops a machine when something is not working correctly

cut-price /ˌ. '. ◂/ *adj.* CUT-RATE

cut-purse /ˈkʌtpɜrs/ *n.* [C] OLD USE a PICKPOCKET

cut-rate /ˌ. '. ◂/ *adj.* **1** sold at less than the usual price: *They sell cut-rate air fares.* **2** a cut-rate shop, supermarket etc. sells goods at reduced prices: *a cut-rate men's clothing store* **3** not of good quality: *The book is essentially a cut-rate Stephen King style novel.*

cut·ter /ˈkʌtər/ *n.* [C] **1** a small ship **2** [often plural] a tool that is used for cutting: *wire cutters*

cut·throat¹ /ˈkʌtˈθroʊt/ *adj.* willing to do anything to succeed, even if it is unfair: *a cutthroat divorce lawyer* | *The government protects some industries from cutthroat competition.*

cutthroat² *n.* [C] OLD USE a murderer

cut·ting¹ /ˈkʌtɪŋ/ *n.* a stem or leaf that is cut from a plant and put in soil or water to grow into a new plant

cutting² *adj.* **1** very unkind and intended to upset someone: *a cutting remark* **2** a cutting wind is very cold and you can feel it through your clothes

cutting board /ˈ.. ˌ./ *n.* [C] a large piece of wood or plastic used for cutting meat or vegetables on; CHOPPING BLOCK

cutting edge /ˌ.. './ *n.* **be at/on the cutting edge of sth** to be working at the most advanced stage or development of something: *State governments are at the cutting edge of changes that help employees juggle family needs and work.* —**cutting-edge** *adj.*: *cutting-edge technology*

cutting room /ˈ.. ˌ./ *n.* [C] a room where the final form of a movie is prepared by cutting the film and putting the different parts into the correct order

cut-up /ˈ. ./ *n.* [C] someone who makes other people laugh by doing amusing things, especially in a situation when they should not do this

Cu·vi·er /ˈkuvier, ˈkyu-/, **Georges** /ʒɔrʒ/ (1769–1832) a French scientist who developed a system for the CLASSIFICATION of animals

cuz /kəz/ *conjunction* SPOKEN, NONSTANDARD a short form of "because": *"Why do I have to go home?" "Cuz I said so!"*

cwt. the written abbreviation of HUNDREDWEIGHT

-cy /si/ *suffix* [in nouns] **1** the state or quality of being something: *privacy* (=state of being private) | *accuracy* | *bankruptcy* **2** a particular rank or position: *a presidency* (=the rank of a president)

cy·an /ˈsaɪ-æn, -ən/ *adj.* deep greenish blue —**cyan** *n.* [U]

cy·a·nide /ˈsaɪəˌnaɪd/ *n.* [U] a very strong poison

cyber- /saɪbə/ *prefix* relating to computers, especially to the messages and information on the Internet

cy·ber·ca·fé, **cyber café** /ˈsaɪbəˌkæˌfeɪ/ *n.* [C] a CAFÉ that has computers connected to the Internet for customers to use

cy·ber·crime, **cyber crime** /ˈsaɪbəˌkraɪm/ *n.* [C,U] criminal activity that involves the use of computers or the Internet

cy·be·ri·a /saɪˈbɪriə/ *n.* [U] CYBERSPACE

cy·ber·net·ics /ˌsaɪbəˈnɛtɪks/ *n.* [U] the scientific study of the way in which information is moved and controlled in machines, the brain, and the NERVOUS SYSTEM —**cybernetic** *adj.*

cy·ber·punk[1] /ˈsaɪbəˌpʌŋk/ *adj.* [only before noun] relating to computers and people who use computers and TECHNOLOGY but who dislike authority and society, especially in the future: *cyberpunk fiction*

cyberpunk[2] *n.* [U] **1** stories about imaginary events relating to computer science, usually set in the future **2** [C] someone who is able to use computers very well but who dislikes authority and society

cyber rage /ˈ.. ./ *n.* [U] HUMOROUS violence and angry behavior by people who are using the Internet

cyber·sex, **cyber sex** /ˈsaɪbəˌsɛks/ *n.* [U] sexual activity, pictures etc. discussed or shown on the Internet

cy·ber·space /ˈsaɪbəˌspeɪs/ *n.* [U] all the connections between computers in different places, considered as a real place where information, messages, pictures etc. exist: *ESPN's sports website is one of the most visited sites in cyberspace.*

cy·borg /ˈsaɪbɔrg/ *n.* [C] a creature that is partly human and partly machine

cy·cla·men /ˈsaɪkləmən, ˈsɪ-/ *n.* [C] a plant with pink, red, or white flowers

s w 3 **cy·cle**[1] /ˈsaɪkəl/ *n.* [C] **1** a number of related events that happen again and again in the same order: [+ of] *the life cycle of a fruit fly* | *The program is intended to help people who receive welfare break the cycle of poverty.* —see also LIFE CYCLE **2** the period of time needed for a machine to finish a process: *This washing machine has a 28-minute cycle.* **3** a group of songs, poems etc. that are all about a particular important event. *a song cycle about spring* **4** a bicycle or MOTORCYCLE

cycle[2] *v.* [I] **1** to travel by bicycle: *I run, cycle, or walk at least three times a week.* **2** [I,T] to go through or make something go through a series of related events again and again

cy·clic /ˈsaɪklɪk, ˈsɪ-/ also **cyc·li·cal** /ˈsaɪklɪkəl, ˈsɪ-/ *adj.* happening in cycles: *a cyclical downturn in the economy* —**cyclically** /-kli/ *adv.*

cy·clist /ˈsaɪklɪst/ *n.* [C] someone who rides a bicycle: *The old creek trail is used by hikers and cyclists.*

cy·clone /ˈsaɪkloʊn/ *n.* [C] a very strong wind that moves very fast in a circle —compare HURRICANE, TYPHOON

Cyclone fence /ˈ.. ./ *n.* [C] TRADEMARK a type of CHAIN-LINK FENCE

cy·clops /ˈsaɪklɑps/ *n.* [singular] a very big man in ancient Greek stories who only had one eye in the middle of his FOREHEAD

cyg·net /ˈsɪgnɪt/ *n.* [C] a young SWAN

cyl·in·der /ˈsɪləndə/ *n.* [C] **1** a shape, object, or container with circular ends and straight sides, such as a can: *a cylinder of oxygen* —see picture at SHAPE **2** the tube within which a PISTON moves forward and backward in an engine: *a four-cylinder engine* —see picture at ENGINE **3 run/hit/fire on all cylinders** to be operating or performing very well: *When we're hitting on all cylinders, we're hard to beat.*

cy·lin·dri·cal /səˈlɪndrɪkəl/ *adj.* in the shape of a cylinder: *a cylindrical oil tank*

cym·bal /ˈsɪmbəl/ *n.* [C] a musical instrument made of a thin round metal plate, played by hitting it with a stick or by hitting two of them together: *the clash of cymbals*

cyn·ic /ˈsɪnɪk/ *n.* [C] someone who is not willing to believe that people have good, honest, or sincere reasons for doing something: *Even hardened cynics believe the meeting is a step toward peace.* —**cynicism** /ˈsɪnəˌsɪzəm/ *n.* [U]

cyn·i·cal /ˈsɪnɪkəl/ *adj.* **1** unwilling to believe that people have good, honest, or sincere reasons for doing something: *a cynical journalist* **2** not following accepted standards of behavior: *They're using sex in a cynical attempt to sell more books.* | [+ about] *Voters have become cynical about the influence of interest groups on politicians.* —**cynically** /-kli/ *adv.*

cy·no·sure /ˈsaɪnəʃʊr, ˈsɪ-/ *n.* [C usually singular] FORMAL someone or something that everyone is interested in or attracted to

cy·pher /ˈsaɪfə/ *n.* [C] another spelling of CIPHER

cy·press /ˈsaɪprəs/ *n.* [C] a tree with dark green leaves and hard wood, that does not lose its leaves in winter

Cy·prus /ˈsaɪprəs/ a large island in the eastern Mediterranean Sea —**Cypriot** *n., adj.*

Cy·ril·lic /səˈrɪlɪk/ *adj.* Cyrillic writing is written in the alphabet used for Russian, Bulgarian, and other Slavonic languages

cyst /sɪst/ *n.* [C] a LUMP containing liquid that grows in your body or under your skin: *an ovarian cyst*

cys·tic fi·bro·sis /ˌsɪstɪk faɪˈbroʊsɪs/ *n.* [U] a serious medical condition, especially in children, in which breathing and DIGESTing[1] (1) food is very difficult

cys·ti·tis /sɪˈstaɪtɪs/ *n.* [U] an infection of the BLADDER, especially in women

cy·tol·o·gy /saɪˈtɑlədʒi/ *n.* [U] the scientific study of cells from living things —**cytologist** *n.* [C]

czar /zɑr/ *n.* [C] **1** a male ruler of Russia before 1917 **2 a banking/drug/health etc. czar** someone who is very powerful in a particular job or activity

cza·ri·na /zɑˈrinə/ *n.* [C] a female ruler of Russia before 1917, or the wife of a czar

czari·sm /ˈzɑrɪzəm/ *n.* [U] a system of government controlled by a czar, especially the system in Russia before 1917 —**czarist** *n.* [C] —**czarist** *adj.*

Czech·o·slo·va·ki·a /ˌtʃɛkəsləˈvɑkiə, -sloʊ-/ a former country in central Europe, which divided in 1993 into two separate countries, the Czech Republic and the Slovak Republic —**Czechoslovakian** *n., adj.*

Czech Republic, the /tʃɛk/ a country in central Europe, between Germany, Poland, the Slovak Republic, and Austria —**Czech** *n., adj.*

D

D, d /di/ *n. plural* **D's, d's** **1** [C] the fourth letter of the English alphabet **2** [C,U] **a)** the second note in the musical SCALE, of C MAJOR **b)** the musical KEY based on this note **3** [C] the number 500 in the system of ROMAN NUMERALS

D /di/ *n.* [C] **1** a grade that a teacher gives to a student's work, showing that it is not very good **2** a letter used to show that a television program contains conversations about sex —see also D AND C, D-DAY

d' /d/ *v.* SPOKEN the short form of "do": *D'you know how many people are going to be there?*

d. the written abbreviation of "died": *John Keats d. 1821*

'd /d/ *v.* **1** the short form of "would": *I asked if she'd be willing to help.* **2** the short form of "had": *Nobody knew where he'd gone.*

D.A. *n.* [C] the abbreviation of DISTRICT ATTORNEY

dab¹ /dæb/ *n.* [C] **1** a small amount of something that you put onto a surface with your hand, a cloth etc.: [+ **of**] *Add a dab of butter and some parsley.* **2** a light touch with your hand, a cloth etc.: *With big dabs of his brush, he began painting.*

dab² *v.* **dabbed, dabbing** **1** [I,T] to touch something lightly several times with something such as a cloth: *He dabbed his mouth with a napkin.* | [+ **at**] *Mrs. Copeland dabbed at her eyes with a tissue.* **2** [T] to put a small amount of a substance onto something with quick, light movements of your hand: [**dab sth on/onto/behind** etc.] *Diane dabbed perfume behind each ear.*

dab·ble /'dæbəl/ *v.* [I] to do something or be involved in something in a way that is not very serious: [+ **in/with**] *He was a vet who dabbled in writing.*

da·cha /'dɑtʃə, 'dɑʃə/ *n.* [C] a large country house in Russia

dachs·hund /'dɑkshʊnt, -hʊnd/ *n.* [C] a type of small dog with short legs and a long body

Da·cron /'deikrɑn/ *n.* [U] TRADEMARK a type of artificial material used especially for clothing

dac·tyl /'dæktl/ *n.* [C] TECHNICAL a repeated sound pattern in poetry, consisting of one long sound followed by two short sounds, for example as in the word "carefully" —**dactylic** /dæk'tɪlɪk/ *adj.*

dad, Dad /dæd/ *n.* [C] INFORMAL father: *She lives with her mom and dad.* | *Dad, can I help?*

Da·da·ism /'dɑdɑ,ɪzəm/ *n.* [U] a movement in European art and literature in the early 20th century in which artists and writers aimed to shock people by producing strange new ideas and images

dad·dy, Daddy /'dædi/ *n.* [C] a word meaning "father," used especially by or to young children: *My daddy is a pilot.* | *Look, Daddy's home!* —see also SUGAR DADDY

daddy long·legs /,dædi 'lɔŋlɛgz/ *n.* [C] an insect with long legs that is similar to a SPIDER

da·do /'deidou/ *n. plural* **dadoes** [C] the lower part of a wall that has a different surface or is decorated differently from the upper part of the wall

dae·mon /'dimən/ *n.* [C] a spirit in ancient Greek stories that is less important than the gods —compare DEMON

daf·fo·dil /'dæfə,dɪl/ *n.* [C] a tall yellow spring flower with a tube-shaped part in the middle

daf·fy /'dæfi/ *adj.* **daffier, daffiest** INFORMAL silly or crazy in an amusing way: *Sabina is beautiful but a little daffy.*

daft /dæft/ *adj.* INFORMAL silly or crazy

dag·ger /'dægə/ *n.* [C] **1** a short pointed knife used as a weapon **2** **look daggers at sb** to look at someone angrily: *The lady behind the counter looked daggers at me.* —see also CLOAK-AND-DAGGER

da·go /'deigou/ *n.* [C] TABOO someone from a Mediterranean country, especially Spain, Italy, or Portugal. Do not use this word

Da·guerre /də'gɛr/, **Lou·is** /'lui/ (1789–1851) a French artist and early PHOTOGRAPHER who invented the daguerrotype

da·guerr·o·type /də'gɛrou,taɪp, -rə-/ *n.* [C,U] an old type of photograph, or the process used to make it

dahl·ia /'dælyə/ *n.* [C] a large garden flower with a bright color

dai·kon /'daɪkɑn/ *n.* [C] a large white Asian RADISH (=type of root vegetable)

dai·ly¹ /'deɪli/ *adj.* [only before noun] **1** happening, done, or produced every day: *He has a daily radio show on KQFB.* | *a daily newspaper* **2** **daily life** the ordinary things that you usually do or experience: *VCRs have become a part of daily life in North America.* **3** relating to a single day: *The daily rate for parking downtown is $15.*

daily² *adv.* done or happening every day: *The zoo is open daily, from 9 a.m. to 5 p.m.*

daily³ *n.* **1** [C usually plural] a newspaper that is printed and sold every day, or every day except Sunday **2** **dailies** [plural] the prints of a movie as it is being made, which are looked at every day after filming ends and before changes are made to it; RUSHes² (8)

Daim·ler /'daimlə/, **Gott·lieb** /'gɑtlib/ (1834–1900) a German engineer who built one of the first cars

dain·ti·ly /'deɪntl-i/ *adv.* done in an extremely careful way, using small movements: *Mrs. Grant daintily sipped her tea.*

dain·ty¹ /'deɪnti/ *adj.* **daintier, daintiest** **1** small, pretty, and delicate: *a dainty white handkerchief* **2** extremely careful, and using small movements: *a dainty eater* —**daintiness** *n.* [U]

dainty² *n.* [C] OLD-FASHIONED something small that is good to eat, especially something sweet such as a small cake

dai·qui·ri /'dækəri/ *n.* [C] a sweet alcoholic drink made with RUM and fruit juice

dair·y /'dɛri/ *n. plural* **dairies** [C] **1** a company that sells milk and sometimes makes other things from milk, such as cheese **2** a place on a farm where milk is kept and butter and cheese are made

dairy cat·tle /'.. ,../ *n.* [plural] cows that are kept to produce milk rather than for their meat

dairy cow /'.. ,./ *n.* [C] a cow that is kept to produce milk rather than for its meat

dairy farm /'.. ,./ *n.* [C] a farm that has cows that produce milk

dair·y·maid /'dɛri,meɪd/ *n.* [C] a woman who worked in a dairy in past times

dair·y·man /'dɛrimən, -,mæn/ *n.* [C] a man who works in a DAIRY

dairy prod·uct /'.. ,../ *n.* [C] milk or a food made from milk, such as butter, cheese, or YOGURT

da·is /'deɪəs/ *n.* [C] a low stage or PLATFORM indoors that you stand or sit on so that people can see and hear you, for example when you are making a speech

dai·sy /'deɪzi/ *n. plural* **daisies** [C] a white flower with a yellow center —see also **be pushing up (the) daisies** (PUSH¹ (13))

daisy chain /'.. ,./ *n.* [C] daisies that are attached end to end to form a string that you can wear around your neck or wrist

dai·sy·wheel print·er /'deɪziwil ,prɪntə/ *n.* [C] a machine that prints from a computer using a round flat piece of plastic that has the letters around its edge

Da·kar /'dækɑr, də'kɑr/ the capital and largest city of Senegal

Dal·ai La·ma /,dɑli 'lɑmə, ,dɑleɪ/ *n.* **the Dalai Lama** the leader of the Tibetan Buddhist religion

dale /deɪl/ *n.* [C] OLD-FASHIONED a valley —see also **over hill and dale** (HILL (5))

Da·li /ˈdɑli/, **Sal·va·dor** /ˈsælvədɔr/ (1904–89) a Spanish painter famous for his work in the style of SURREALISM

Dal·las /ˈdæləs/ a city in the U.S. state of Texas

dal·li·ance /ˈdæliəns/ n. [C] a sexual relationship between two people that is not considered serious

dal·ly /ˈdæli/ v. **dallied, dallying** [I] OLD-FASHIONED to waste time, or do something very slowly: *Marshall complained that lawmakers dallied too long on major legislation.* —see also DILLY-DALLY
dally with sb phr. v. [T] OLD-FASHIONED to have a sexual relationship that is not serious with someone

Dal·ma·tian, **dalmatian** /dælˈmeɪʃən/ n. [C] a large dog with short white hair and black or brown spots

Dal·ton /ˈdɔltʰn/, **John** (1766–1844) a British scientist who made important discoveries about gases and developed the idea of the existence of atoms

dam¹ /dæm/ n. [C] **1** a special wall built across a river, stream etc. to stop the water from flowing, especially to make a lake or produce electricity: *the Hoover Dam in Nevada* **2** [usually singular] TECHNICAL the mother of a four-legged animal, especially a horse —compare SIRE¹ (2)

dam² v. **dammed, damming** [T] to stop the water in a river, stream etc. from flowing by building a special wall across it: *The East Branch River was dammed in 1952.*
dam sth ↔ **up** phr. v. [T] to make the water in a river, stream etc. stop flowing by blocking it: *The landslide dammed up the river.*

dam·age¹ /ˈdæmɪdʒ/ n. [U]
1 [physical harm] physical harm that is done to something or to a part of someone's body, so that it is broken or injured: [+ to] *There was a lot of damage to both cars.* | **cause/do damage** *Rabbits cause less damage to the land than goats.* | **serious/severe/major damage** *The earthquake caused major damage to the freeway system.* | **minor/minimal/superficial damage** (=damage that is not very serious) | **irreparable/irreversible/permanent damage** (=damage that cannot be repaired) | **flood/storm/water etc. damage** (=damage caused by a flood, storm, water etc.) | **brain/liver/lung etc. damage** *The treatment can cause permanent kidney damage.*
2 [emotional harm] harm that is done to someone's emotions or mind: *There is growing evidence of lasting psychological damage to children in broken families.*
3 [bad effect] a bad effect on something: [+ to] *Community leaders are not sure how to fix the damage to the city's reputation.*
4 damages LAW money that a court orders someone to pay to someone else as a punishment for harming them or their property: *The court awarded the families $33 million in damages.*
5 the damage is done SPOKEN used to say that something bad has happened that makes it impossible to go back to the way things were before it happened: *Ed apologized a week later, but the damage was already done.*
6 damage control an attempt to limit the bad effects of something: *Since the scandal broke, the Senator's staff have been busy doing damage control.*
7 What's the damage? SPOKEN HUMOROUS used to ask how much you have to pay for something

---

USAGE NOTE: DAMAGE

WORD CHOICE: damage, harm, hurt, injure, wound
Things or parts of your body (but NOT people) can be **damaged**: *The engine was too badly damaged to be repaired.* | *Clearly, smoking has damaged your lungs.* Both things and people can be **harmed**: *Experts disagree on whether unleaded gasoline will harm older cars.* | *I would never do anything to harm you!* People are **hurt** or **injured** in accidents: *Thank God no one was hurt!* | *A Carmel Valley plane crash left three people dead and a fourth injured Sunday.* Someone who is injured by a weapon, such as a gun or knife, is **wounded**: *The wounded soldiers were sent home for medical treatment.*

---

damage² v. [T] **1** to do physical harm to something or to part of someone's body, so that it is broken or injured: *The storm damaged hundreds of houses.* | *He slipped on some ice and damaged ligaments in his knee.* **2** if the good opinion that people have of a person or organization is damaged, something has happened to make them seem weaker or less important: *The crisis has badly damaged the President's authority.*

dam·ag·ing /ˈdæmɪdʒɪŋ/ adj. affecting someone or something in a bad way: *Wearing sunscreen can minimize the damaging effects of sunlight.* | [+ to] *Wigand's statements could be very damaging to the tobacco companies.*

Da·mas·cus /dəˈmæskəs/ the capital city of Syria

dam·ask /ˈdæməsk/ n. [U] a type of cloth with a pattern woven in it, often used to cover furniture: *a damask tablecloth*

Dame /deɪm/ n. [C] a title of honor given by the British king or queen to a woman as a reward for the good things she has done: *Dame Judi Dench*

dame /deɪm/ n. [C] OLD-FASHIONED a woman —see also GRANDE DAME

dam·mit /ˈdæmɪt/ interjection IMPOLITE a way of spelling "damn it" —see **damn it** (DAMN⁴ (1))

damn¹ /dæm/ interjection SPOKEN, IMPOLITE **1** used to show that you are very annoyed or disappointed: *Damn! I forgot the keys.* **2** used to show that something is impressive or surprising: *Damn, she's old.*

USAGE NOTE: DAMN

WORD CHOICE: damn, darn, dang
Although the spoken uses of **damn** are quite frequent in North America, they are still considered offensive by many people. **Darn** and **dang** are often used instead, and are not considered offensive: *That sweater is pretty darn expensive.* | *Dang it! We're going to be late.*

---

damn² adj. [only before noun] SPOKEN, IMPOLITE **1** used to show that you are angry or annoyed with someone or something: *Turn off that damn TV!* **2 not a damn thing** nothing at all: *He hasn't done a damn thing today.* **3** used to emphasize something negative: *It's your own damn fault.* | *It's a damn shame that you didn't get the job.* **4 a damn sight more/better etc.** a lot more, better etc.: *I don't know where we're going, but it's got to be a damn sight better than here.* —compare DAMNED¹

damn³ adv. [+ adj./adv.] SPOKEN, IMPOLITE **1** used to emphasize how good something is, how bad something is etc.; very: *Homes here are so damn expensive.* | *I just want to make damn sure we finish on time.* | *He was damn lucky he didn't have an accident.* **2 damn well** used to emphasize a statement: *You know damn well it's not true.* | *Marcus can do anything he damn well pleases* (=anything he wants). **3 damn near** almost: *He damn near killed himself trying to lose weight.* **4 damn straight/right** used to emphasize that something is completely true or right: *Damn straight I know what I'm talking about.* —compare DAMNED²

damn⁴ v.

SPOKEN PHRASES

1 damn it IMPOLITE used to show that you are extremely angry or annoyed: *Damn it, I'm late again!*
2 damn you/them etc. an offensive phrase used when you are extremely angry or annoyed with someone or something: *No, damn you! Just leave me alone.*
3 I'll be damned IMPOLITE used to show that you are surprised: *They came and got it already? I'll be damned.*
4 (I'll be/I am) damned if... IMPOLITE **a)** used to emphasize that you will not allow something to happen: *I'll be damned if I let her come into my house.* **b)** used to emphasize that you really do not know something: *"What kind of blood pressure medication are you on?" "Damned if I know."* (=I don't know)

D

5 damned if you do, damned if you don't IMPOLITE used to say that whatever you say or do will be considered wrong
6 be damned to be given the punishment of going to HELL (1) after you die: *Can the church really decide if I will be eternally damned or blessed?*
7 say sth is bad [T] IMPOLITE to state that something is very bad: *The play was damned by critics after opening night.*
8 damn sb with faint praise IMPOLITE to show that you think someone or something is not very good, by only praising them a little: *Johnson damned McNeil with faint praise, saying only, "He played a fine game."*

damn[5] *n.* [C usually singular] SPOKEN, IMPOLITE **1 not give a damn** used to show that you do not care about someone or something: *I don't give a damn about her.* **2 not be worth a damn** used to say that you think something has no value at all: *Her promise isn't worth a damn.*

dam·na·ble /'dæmnəbəl/ *adj.* OLD-FASHIONED very bad or annoying: *That's a damnable lie!* —**damnably** *adv.*

dam·na·tion[1] /dæm'neɪʃən/ *n.* [U] the act of deciding to punish someone by sending them to HELL (1) forever after they die, or the state of being in HELL forever

damnation[2] *interjection* OLD-FASHIONED used to show that you are very angry or annoyed

damned[1] /dæmd/ *adj.* [only before noun] IMPOLITE another form of DAMN[2], used especially in writing

damned[2] *adv.* [+ adj./adv.] IMPOLITE another form of DAMN[3], used especially in writing

damned[3] *n.* **the damned** [plural] the people whom God will send to HELL when they die because they have been so bad

damned·est /'dæmdɪst/ *adj.* SPOKEN, IMPOLITE **1** used to emphasize that something is strange or surprising: *"It's the damnedest case I've ever seen," said the sheriff.* **2 do/try your damnedest** to try very hard to do or achieve something: *We both tried our damnedest but it didn't work.*

damn-fool /'. ./ *adj.* [only before noun] SPOKEN, IMPOLITE very stupid: *That was the biggest damn-fool mistake I ever made.*

damn·ing /'dæmɪŋ/ *adj.* proving or showing that something is very bad or wrong: *The most damning evidence against the gang was four secretly recorded conversations.* | *a damning report on college athletics*

Dam·o·cles /'dæməˌkliz/ —see **a/the sword of Damocles** (SWORD (3))

damp[1] /dæmp/ *adj.* slightly wet, sometimes in a way that is not nice: *Just wipe off the surface with a damp paper towel.* | *My hair's still a little damp.* —**dampness** *n.* [U] —**damply** *adv.*

USAGE NOTE: DAMP

WORD CHOICE: damp, moist, humid
Damp is often used when something is slightly wet in a cold way that does not feel nice: *damp clothes* | *Our hotel room felt cold and damp.* **Moist** is used especially when something is a little wet, as it should be: *a moist chocolate cake* | *Keep houseplant soil moist.* **Humid** is a more technical word used mainly to describe the climate or weather: *Tokyo is very humid in the summer.*

---

damp[2] *v.* [T] **1** to make something less strong or lower in amount: *Political upheaval in the Soviet Union damped demand in that market.* | *The low price of soybeans has damped farmers' interest in the crop.* **2** TECHNICAL to make a sound less loud: *Damp the sound with the pedal after each beat.*

damp·en /'dæmpən/ *v.* [T] **1** to make something slightly wet: *a cloth dampened with alcohol* **2** to make a feeling such as interest or hope less strong: *My many mistakes didn't dampen my enthusiasm for gardening.* **3** to make something weaker or lower in amount: *Demand for gasoline has been dampened by the recession.*

damp·er /'dæmpə/ *n.* [C] **1 put a damper on sth** to stop something from being enjoyable or from having as good a result as expected: *The burglary put a damper on the family's Christmas.* **2** a small metal door in a FIREPLACE that is opened or closed to control how strongly a fire burns **3** a piece of equipment that stops a piano string from making a sound

dam·sel /'dæmzəl/ *n.* [C] **1** OLD-FASHIONED a young woman who is not married **2 damsel in distress** HUMOROUS a young woman who needs help

Dan /dæn/ in the Bible, the head of one of the 12 tribes of Israel

dance[1] /dæns/ *v.* **1** [I] to move your feet and body in a way that matches the style and speed of music: [+ **to**] *The audience clapped, swayed, and danced to the music.* | [+ **with**] *So there I was, dancing with all these girls.* **2** [T] to do a type of dance | **dance the waltz/tango/samba etc.** *They banged cymbals and danced jigs.* **3** [I,T] to dance in performances, especially in BALLET: *She danced with the San Francisco Ballet for six years.* | *Nakamura danced several solos in the "Nutcracker Suite."* **4** [I] to move up, down, and around quickly in a way that looks like dancing: *Red, white, and blue balloons danced in the wind.* **5 dance to sb's tune** to do what someone wants you to do in a way that shows you are obeying them completely: *They control all the funding so we have to dance to their tune.* —**dancing** *n.* [U] *I'd love to go dancing.*

dance[2] *n.* **1** [C] a social event where the main activity is dancing: *Alan took Amy to the dance last weekend.* | *school dances* **2** [C] a special set of movements that matches the style and speed of a particular type of music: *The waltz is an easy dance to learn.* | *The Blue Ridge Mountain Dancers did a clog dance.* **3** [C] an act of dancing to one piece of music: *May I have the next dance* (=will you dance with me?)? **4** [U] the activity or art of dancing, especially as a performance: *Twyla Tharpe's dance troupe* **5** [C] a piece of music that you can dance to: *The band was playing a slow dance.* —see also **a song and dance** (SONG (5))

dance band /'. ./ *n.* [C] a group of musicians who play music that you dance to

dance card /'. ./ *n.* [C] **1 sb's dance card is full** used to say that someone is very busy or has a lot of romantic partners **2** a card with a list of the men that a woman has promised to dance with at a formal party

dance floor /'. ./ *n.* [C] a special floor in a restaurant, club, hotel etc. for people to dance on

dance hall /'. ./ *n.* [C] a large public room where people paid to go and dance in past times

danc·er /'dænsə/ *n.* [C] **1** someone who dances as a profession: *Her childhood dream was to be a ballet dancer.* **2 be a good/bad dancer** to dance well or badly

D and C /ˌdi ən 'si/ *n.* [C] Dilation and Curettage; a medical operation to clean out the inside of a woman's UTERUS

dan·de·li·on /'dændəˌlaɪən/ *n.* [C] a wild plant with a small bright yellow flower, which later becomes a white ball of seeds that are blown away in the wind

dan·der /'dændə/ *n.* [U] **1 get sb's dander up** OLD-FASHIONED OR HUMOROUS to make someone angry: *Some recent columns have gotten readers' dander up.* **2** small pieces of dead skin that fall off an animal's body

dan·di·fied /'dændɪˌfaɪd/ *adj.* OLD-FASHIONED a man who is dandified wears very fashionable clothes in a way that shows he cares too much about his appearance

dan·dle /'dændl/ *v.* [T] OLD-FASHIONED to play with a baby or small child by moving them up and down in your arms or on your knee

dan·druff /'dændrəf/ *n.* [U] pieces of dead skin from someone's head that can be seen in their hair or on their shoulders

dan·dy[1] /'dændi/ *adj.* SPOKEN very good: *Everything is fine and dandy.*

dandy² *n.* [C] OLD-FASHIONED a man who spends a lot of time and money on his clothes and appearance

Dane /deɪn/ *n.* [C] someone from Denmark

dang /dæŋ/ *interjection* SPOKEN a word meaning DAMN that people consider less offensive: *Dang, another flat tire!* —see Usage Note at DAMN¹ —**dang** *adj., adv.*: *This software is too dang expensive.* —**dang** *v.* [T] *Dang it, anyway.*

s w **dan·ger** /'deɪndʒɚ/ *n.* **1** [U] the possibility that some-
2 one or something will be harmed or killed: *Danger! High Voltage.* | [+ **of**] *The danger of a fire in the home increases during the holidays.* | *Another 50-foot section of the bridge is **in danger** of falling* (=it might fall). | *None of the houses was **in immediate danger** from the volcano's lava flow.* | *The five injured sol-diers are **out of danger*** (=no longer likely to die). **2** [C usually plural] something or someone that may harm or kill you: *Few of the men used condoms even though they knew of **the dangers of** unprotected sex.* | [**be a danger to sb**] *Police said that Turner is a danger to herself and others.* **3** [C,U] the possibility that something bad will happen: [+ **(that)**] *I don't think there is any danger that there will be a misun-derstanding on this point.* | [+ **of**] *There is a danger of the conflict spreading into the bordering coun-tries.* | *Carlos is **in danger of** losing his job.*

s w **dan·ger·ous** /'deɪndʒərəs/ *adj.* **1** able or likely to
2 harm or kill you: *a dangerous dog* | *Neil thought the man looked dangerous.* | [+ **to**] *The paint they're using is dangerous to people and animals.* | [**be dan-gerous for sb to do sth**] *It's dangerous for a woman to walk alone at night.* | *a dangerous neighborhood* (=where you may be harmed or killed) —opposite SAFE¹ **2** involving a lot of risk, or likely to cause problems: *His followers warned him repeatedly that the agreement was **highly dangerous** politically.* **3 dangerous ground/territory** a situation or subject that could make someone very angry or upset: *You're on dangerous ground when you talk politics with Ed.* —**dangerously** *adv.*

danger pay /'.. ,./ *n.* [U] another word for HAZARD PAY

dan·gle /'dæŋgəl/ *v.* **1** [I,T] to hang or swing loosely, or make something do this: [+ **from**] *A cigarette dan-gled from her mouth.* | [**dangle sth over sth**] *I sat and dangled my legs over the side of the dock.* | [**dangle sth by sth**] *The phone had been left dangling by its cord.* **2** [T] to show or promise something that someone wants in order to make them do what you want: *Her parents actually **dangled** money and trips to Europe **in front of her** to try to get her to divorce Mikhail.* —compare TANTALIZE

Dan·iel /'dænyəl/ a book in the Old Testament of the Christian Bible

Dan·ish¹ /'deɪnɪʃ/ *n.* **1** [U] the language of Den-mark **2** [C] also **Danish pastry** a small sweet type of cake, often with fruit inside

Danish² *adj.* relating to the people or language of Denmark

dank /dæŋk/ *adj.* wet and cold, in a way that does not feel nice: *a dank prison cell* —**dankness** *n.* [U]

Dan·te /'dɑnteɪ/ also **Dante A·li·ghie·ri** /-,ɑli'gyɛri/ (1265–1321) an Italian poet

Dan·ton /dɑn'tɔn/, **Georges Jacques** /ʒɔrʒ ʒɑk/ (1759–1794) a French politician who became one of the leaders of the French Revolution

Dan·ube, the /'dænyub/ a long and important river in Eastern Europe, that starts in the Black Forest in Germany and runs through Austria, Hungary, and Romania into the Black Sea

dap·per /'dæpɚ/ *adj.* a man who is dapper is nicely dressed, has a neat appearance, and is usually small or thin: *Franklin looked dapper in his gray pin-striped suit.*

dap·ple /'dæpəl/ *v.* [T] LITERARY to mark something with spots of color, light, or shade: *The statue was dappled with light from a stained-glass window* —**dappled** *adj.*

dapple-gray /,.. '.◂/ *n.* [C] a horse that is gray with spots of darker gray

DAR —see DAUGHTERS OF THE AMERICAN REVOLUTION

Dar·da·nelles, the /,dɑrdn'ɛlz/ a long narrow area of ocean which connects the European and Asian parts of Turkey and was called the Hellespont in ancient times

dare¹ /dɛr/ *v.* **1** [T] to try to persuade someone to do something dangerous or embarrassing as a way of proving that they are brave: [**dare sb to do sth**] *One kid dared me to sneak into the back of the audito-rium.* | *Yeah, you tell him. **I dare you!*** **2** [I not in progressive] a word meaning to be brave enough to do something risky, used especially in questions and negative statements: *I don't dare tell my mom and dad.* | [+ **(to)**] *Who would dare to challenge the legal system, knowing they would be sued for every-thing they owned?* | *Even the sleaziest of the news-papers didn't dare publish the pictures.*

D

SPOKEN PHRASES

3 don't you dare! SPOKEN said to warn someone not to do something because it makes you angry: *Don't you dare hang up on me again!* **4 how dare you** SPOKEN said to show that you are very angry and shocked about what someone has done or said: *How dare you make fun of me like that!* **5 dare I say (it)** SPOKEN, FORMAL used when saying something that you think people may not accept or believe: *I found Shaw's play, dare I say it, boring.* **6 I dare say** also **I daresay** SPOKEN, OLD-FASHIONED used to say that you think or hope that something may be true: *I dare say things will improve.* **7 dare, double dare** said when you are trying to persuade someone to do something dangerous

---

dare² *n.* [C] something dangerous or difficult that you have dared someone to do: *Wilson said his idea for the invention started out as a dare.* | *Allen began his career as a comedian **on a dare** from a friend in 1979.*

dare·dev·il /'dɛr,dɛvəl/ *n.* [C] someone who likes doing dangerous things —**daredevil** *adj.*: *a daredevil sport*

dare·n't /'dɛrənt/ *v.* OLD USE the short form of "I dare not": *I daren't tell her.*

Dar-es-Sa·laam /,dɑr ɛs sə'lɑm/ the former capital and largest city of Tanzania

dar·ing¹ /'dɛrɪŋ/ *adj.* **1** involving danger, or willing to do something that is dangerous or that involves a lot of risk: *a daring rescue attempt* | *a daring pilot* **2** new or unusual in a way that is sometimes shocking: *Today she's wearing a daring two-piece suit in bold purple and orange.* | *Miller is exceptionally good in this daring film.* —**daringly** *adv.*

daring² *n.* [U] courage that makes you willing to take risks or do unusual things: *The young composer has shown considerable daring in his music.*

dark¹ /dɑrk/ *adj.*

1 place a dark place is one where there is little or no light: *The church was dark and quiet.* | *dark streets* | *Suddenly, the room **went dark*** (=became dark) *and somebody screamed.* —opposite LIGHT² —see also PITCH-BLACK

2 color closer to black than to white in color | *dark blue/green/brown etc. a dark blue shirt* —opposite LIGHT²

3 get/be dark to become night, or to be night: *Come on, let's go in. It's getting dark.* | *It's only 4:30 and it's already dark outside.*

4 hair/eyes/skin a dark person has brown or black hair, brown eyes, or brown skin: *a tall, dark man* —opposite FAIR¹

5 threatening/evil etc. mysterious or threatening in a way that makes you feel uncomfortable or afraid, especially when this involves something that you do not know enough about: *the dark side of his personality* | *a dark secret*

6 unhappy time a dark time is unhappy or with-out hope for the future: *The trials have been an unpleasant reminder of the **dark days** of terrorism.* | *It was your love that gave us strength in our **darkest hours**.*

7 showing little hope emphasizing the bad qualities of people or situations, often in a way that shows you do not think things will get better: *His songs are dark, intelligent, and have a message for our time.*
8 dark comedy/humor a way of writing or speaking that deals with very serious or sad subjects in a humorous way: *Patients joked among themselves with the dark humor common in difficult situations.*
9 feelings/thoughts LITERARY sad, and showing that you think something very bad may happen: *It was a tragedy she had never imagined in her darkest thoughts.*

dark² *n.* **1 the dark** a situation in which there is no light, usually because the sun has gone down: *Children are sometimes afraid of the dark.* | *Well, you certainly can't mow the lawn **in the dark**.* **2 after dark** after the sun goes down at night: *You shouldn't go into the park after dark.* **3 before dark** before the sun goes down at night: *You can go out to play, but make sure you come home before dark.* **4 in the dark** INFORMAL knowing nothing about something important because you have not been told about it: *Howard claims to be in the dark about when they will start filming the movie.* | *Board members were **kept in the dark** about the company's financial problems.* —see also **a shot in the dark** (SHOT¹ (12))

Dark Ag·es /ˈ. ˌ../ *n.* [plural] **the Dark Ages** the period in European history from A.D. 476 to about A.D. 1000

dark·en /ˈdɑrkən/ *v.* [I,T] **1** to become dark, or make something dark: *A cleaning solution shouldn't darken the wood.* | *The skies darkened and the wind grew stronger.* —opposite LIGHTEN (2) **2** to make a situation or someone's attitude less hopeful: *With the economy entering a slump, the computer industry's future could darken further.* | *The news darkened their view of the situation.* **3 never darken my door again** OLD-FASHIONED OR HUMOROUS used to tell someone that you do not want them in your house again

dark glass·es /ˌ. ˈ../ *n.* [plural] glasses with dark glass in them, that you wear to protect your eyes from the sun or to hide your eyes —compare SUNGLASSES

dark horse /ˌ. ˈ./ *n.* [C] someone who is not well known and who surprises everyone by winning a competition

dark·ie /ˈdɑrki/ *n.* [C] OLD-FASHIONED a word for a person with dark or black skin, now considered offensive

dark·ly /ˈdɑrkli/ *adv.* **1** in an sad, angry, or threatening way: *Her eyes turned darkly serious as she began to talk about her troubled past.* **2** having a dark color: *Sam was a darkly handsome young man.* **3 darkly funny/humorous/comic** dealing with something that is bad or upsetting in a funny way: *The show is a darkly comic look at medicine, money and morality.*

dark meat /ˈ. ./ *n.* [U] the darker-colored meat from the legs, THIGHS etc. of a chicken, TURKEY, or other bird —see also WHITE MEAT

dark·ness /ˈdɑrknɪs/ *n.* [U] **1** a place or time when there is no light: *Northern Alaska experiences eight weeks of 24-hour darkness.* | *He was one of the last players to finish as **darkness fell** (=it became night).* | *The clouds moved across the moon, leaving us **in complete darkness**.* **2 forces/powers of darkness** evil, or the DEVIL **3** the dark quality of a color: *The darkness of the lenses changes when you go into the sun.*

dark·room /ˈdɑrkrum/ *n.* [C] a special room with a red light or no light, where film from a camera is made into photographs

dar·ling¹ /ˈdɑrlɪŋ/ *n.* [C] **1** SPOKEN used when speaking to someone you love: *Hello darling. Did you have a good day?* **2** SPOKEN someone who seems very nice, generous, or friendly: *He's such a darling.* **3 the darling of sth** the most popular person or thing in a particular group: *Reno was the darling of the New York club scene.*

darling² *adj.* SPOKEN **1** used to say that you love someone: *This is my darling little sister.* **2** said when you think someone or something is attractive: *Those pants are darling.*

darn¹ /dɑrn/ *v.* [T]

> **SPOKEN PHRASES**
>
> **1 darn (it)** said when you are annoyed about something: *Darn, I forgot to put money in the parking meter.* **2 I'll be darned** SPOKEN said when you are surprised about something: *Did they really? Well, I'll be darned!* **3 (I'll be/I am) darned if... a)** used to emphasize that you will not allow something to happen: *I'll be darned if I let my kids talk that way.* **b)** used to emphasize that you really do not know something: *"Who's he?" "Darned if I know." (=I don't know)* **4 darn you/them etc.** used to show that you are extremely angry or annoyed with someone or something

5 to repair a hole in a piece of clothing by stitching it with thread —see Usage Note at DARN⁴

darn² also **darned** /dɑrnd/ *adj.* SPOKEN used to emphasize that something is bad or annoying: *Darned mosquito. It keeps flying around me.* —compare DAMN² (1)

darn³, darned *adv.* used to emphasize how bad or good someone or something is: **pretty darn nice/ stupid/exciting etc.** *You might think it's small, but it looks pretty darn good to me!* —compare DAMN³

darn⁴ *n.* [C] a place where a hole in a piece of clothing has been repaired neatly with thread

darn·ing /ˈdɑrnɪŋ/ *n.* [U] OLD-FASHIONED the repairing of holes in clothing by stitching them with thread, especially done to wool socks

Dar·row /ˈdæroʊ/, **Clar·ence** /ˈklærəns/ (1857–1938) a U.S. lawyer famous for the Scopes Trial, when he defended a teacher who was taken to court for teaching his students about EVOLUTION and the ideas of Charles Darwin

dart¹ /dɑrt/ *v.* **1** [I always + adv./prep.] to move suddenly and quickly in a particular direction: [+ across/out/out etc.] *A man darted out of the garage and down the street.* | *Brilliantly colored fish dart among the coral reefs.* **2** LITERARY to look at someone or something very quickly and suddenly: *His little black eyes darted around my office.*

dart² *n.* **1** [C] a small pointed object that is thrown or shot as a weapon or thrown in the game of darts: *Some South American Indians use poison darts for hunting.* **2 darts** [U] a game in which darts are thrown at a circular board with numbers on it **3** [singular] a sudden, quick movement in a particular direction: *The mouse **made a dart for** (=ran towards) its hole.* **4** [C] a small fold sewn into a piece of clothing to make it fit better

dart·board /ˈdɑrtbɔrd/ *n.* [C] a circular board used in the game of darts

Dar·win /ˈdɑrwɪn/, **Charles** (1809–1882) a British scientist who developed the THEORY OF EVOLUTION, the idea that plants and animals develop gradually from simpler to more complicated forms by NATURAL SELECTION

dash¹ /dæʃ/ *v.* **1** [I] to go or run somewhere very quickly: [+ into/across/behind etc.] *Duncan dashed across the lawn and climbed the fence.* **2 dash (sb's) hopes/dreams** to disappoint someone by showing or telling them that what they want will not happen: *Judge Turrone's decision dashed Montez's hopes of receiving a reduced prison sentence.* —opposite **raise sb's hopes** (RAISE¹ (6)) **3 dash (sth) against/ to/into etc.** LITERARY to hit violently against something, usually so that it breaks, or to make something do this: *Huge waves dashed the boats against the rocks.* | *The rushing wind and rain dashed against the thick stone walls.*

> **dash off** *phr. v.* **1** [T dash sth ↔ off] to write or draw something very quickly: *Ferraro quickly dashed off a letter of complaint to the judge.* **2** [I] to leave somewhere very quickly: *I called her before dashing off to the airport.*

dash² *n.*

1 `small amount` **a)** [C] a very small amount of a liquid or other substance, especially added to a drink or to food: [+ of] *Add a dash of salt to the beans.* **b)** [singular] a small amount of something such as a quality: [+ of] *It's fiction with a dash of history.*

2 `race` [singular] a race to find out who can run the fastest over a short distance: *the 40-yard dash*

3 make a dash for sth to run very quickly in order to get away from something or in order to reach something: *As the fire spread up the walls, Stan made a dash for safety.* | *We heard the whistle and made a mad dash* (=ran extremely quickly) *for the departing ship.*

4 `mark in a sentence` [C] a mark (–) used in informal writing or when representing spoken language to separate sentences or phrases, for example in the sentence "Don't talk to me now – I'm busy." —compare HYPHEN

5 `car` [C] INFORMAL a short form of DASHBOARD

6 `sound` [C] a long sound or flash of light used for sending messages in MORSE CODE —compare DOT¹ (5)

7 `style` [U] OLD-FASHIONED style, energy, and courage in someone such as a soldier

dash·board /'dæʃbɔrd/ also **dash** *n.* [C] the board that is in front of the driver of a car and has the controls on it —see picture on page 427

da·shi·ki /dəˈʃiki, dɑ-/ *n.* [C] a long loose brightly colored piece of clothing, worn especially in Africa

dash·ing /'dæʃɪŋ/ *adj.* OLD-FASHIONED a man or a thing that is dashing is very attractive and fashionable: *Custer first gained fame as a dashing Civil War military leader.* —**dashingly** *adv.*

das·tard·ly /'dæstɚdli/ *adj.* OLD-FASHIONED very cruel or evil

DAT *n.* digital audio tape; a system used to record music, sound, or information in DIGITAL form

da·ta /'deɪtə, 'dætə/ *n.* [plural] information or facts that have been gathered in order to be studied: *All the data shows that these animals are more adaptable than we thought.* | *The study collected data from 5,766 patients.*

data bank /'.. ,./ *n.* [C] **1** a place where information on a particular subject is stored, usually in a computer: *The national genetics data bank will be a storehouse of hundreds of blood samples.* **2** another word for DATABASE

da·ta·base /'deɪtəˌbeɪs/ *n.* [C] a large amount of data stored in a computer system and organized so that you can find and use it easily: *The library has a database of over 21 million book titles.*

data pro·cess·ing /'.. ,.../ *n.* [U] the use of computers to store and organize data, especially in business

date¹ /deɪt/ *n.* [C]

1 `day` a particular day of the month or year, shown by a number: *"What's the date today?" "September twenty-ninth."* | *The date on the newspaper is October 12, 1966.* | **date of birth/birth date** *Please write your name, address, and date of birth on the form.* | *Have you set a date* (=chosen a particular date) *for the wedding?*

2 `romantic` an occasion when you arrange to meet someone that you like in a romantic way: *Was that your first date?* | *I have a date tomorrow.* | *We're going on a date Friday night.* —see also BLIND DATE, DOUBLE DATE

3 at a later date FORMAL at some time in the future: *We'll deal with this problem at a later date.*

4 to date up to now: *This may be the winery's best Cabernet to date.*

5 `person` someone that you have a date with: *Can I bring my date to the party?*

6 `social` an arrangement to meet, especially socially, at a particular time or place: *We made a date to get together with Evan and Debbie for New Year's Eve.*

7 `fruit` a sweet sticky brown fruit with a long hard seed inside —see also CLOSING DATE, EXPIRATION DATE, OUT-OF-DATE, UP-TO-DATE

date² *v.* **1** [T] to write or print the date on something: *Oh, I forgot to date the check.* | *The internal memo, dated November 15, was from Watkins.* **2** [T]

to find out when something very old was made or formed, or when an ancient event happened: *Scientists have not yet dated the human remains found at these megalithic sites.* **3** [T] to have a romantic relationship with someone: *Is he still dating Sarah?* **4** [T] if something that you say, do, or wear dates you, it shows that you are fairly old: *Yes, I remember the moon landings – that dates me, doesn't it?* **5** [I] if clothing, art etc. dates, it looks old or old-fashioned: *His furniture designs have hardly dated at all.*

date from/date back to *phr. v.* [I] to have existed since a particular time in the past: *This church dates from the 13th century.*

date·book /'deɪtbʊk/ *n.* [C] a small book in which you write things you must do, addresses, telephone numbers etc.

dat·ed /'deɪtɪd/ *adj.* looking or seeming old or old-fashioned: *That dress looks dated now.* —compare OUT-OF-DATE

date·line /'deɪtlaɪn/ *n.* **1** [singular] the INTERNATIONAL DATE LINE **2** [C] the line at the top of a newspaper article that says the date and the city or place where the news is from —**dateline** *v.* [T usually passive]

date rape /'. ./ *n.* [C,U] a RAPE that happens during a date —**date rape** *v.* [T] —compare ACQUAINTANCE RAPE

date stamp /'. ./ *n.* [C] **1** a piece of equipment used for printing the date on letters, documents etc. **2** the mark that is made by this piece of equipment

dating ser·vice /'.. ,../ *n.* [C] a business that helps people to meet someone in order to have a romantic relationship with them

da·tive /'deɪtɪv/ *n.* [C] TECHNICAL a particular form of a noun in some languages such as Latin and German, which shows that the noun is the INDIRECT OBJECT of a verb —**dative** *adj.*

daub¹ /dɔb/ *v.* [T] to put paint or a soft substance onto a surface, without being very careful: *Anti-government slogans were daubed on the roads.*

daub² *n.* **1** [C] a small amount of a soft or sticky substance: [+ of] *a daub of glue* **2** [U] TECHNICAL mud or clay used for making walls

daugh·ter /'dɔtɚ/ *n.* [C] **1** someone's female child **2** TECHNICAL something new that forms or develops when something else divides or ends: *English is a daughter language of German and Latin.*

daughter-in-law /'... ,../ *n. plural* **daughters-in-law** [C] the wife of your son —compare SON-IN-LAW

daugh·ter·ly /'dɔtɚli/ *adj.* OLD-FASHIONED behaving in the way that a daughter is supposed to behave

Daughters of the A·mer·i·can Rev·o·lu·tion, also **DAR** /ˌ... . ˌ... .'../ an organization for women whose families have been in the U.S. since the American Revolutionary War

daunt /dɔnt, dɑnt/ *v.* [T usually passive] to make someone feel afraid or less confident: *The threat of lightning did little to daunt local golfers.*

daunt·ing /'dɔntɪŋ/ *adj.* frightening in a way that makes you feel less confident: *The interview process can be daunting.* | *Condensing the novel into a 90 minute script was a daunting task.*

daunt·less /'dɔntlɪs/ *adj.* LITERARY confident and not easily frightened: *dauntless courage* —**dauntlessly** *adv.*

dau·phin /'dɔfən, 'dou-/ *n.* [C] the oldest son of a King of France

dau·phine /dɔ'fin, dou-/ *n.* [C] the wife of the oldest son of a King of France

da·ven·port /'dævənˌpɔrt/ *n.* [C] a large SOFA, especially one that can be made into a bed

Da·vid /də'vid/, **Jacques-Lou·is** /ʒɑk lu'i/ (1748–1825) a French PAINTER famous for his paintings in the CLASSICAL style that supported the ideas of the French Revolution

Da·vid /'deɪvɪd/, **King** (died around 962 B.C.) in the Bible, one of the Kings of Israel, who is also believed to have written some of the Psalms. When David was a boy, he killed the GIANT (=a very tall strong man) Goliath.

Da·vis /'deɪvɪs/, **Jef·fer·son** /'dʒɛfɚsən/ (1808–1889) a U.S. politician who was the President of the Confederacy (=the Southern U.S. states) during the U.S. Civil War

Davis, Miles /maɪlz/ (1926–1991) a U.S. musician who played the TRUMPET and had an important influence on the development of JAZZ

da·vit /'deɪvɪt, 'dæ-/ n. [C] one of a pair of long curved poles that SAILORS swing out over the side of a ship in order to lower a boat into the water

Miles Davis

D

daw·dle /'dɔdl/ v. [I] to waste time by taking too long to do something or go somewhere: *Hurry up! Quit dawdling!* | [+ over] *I dawdled over a second cup of coffee.* —**dawdler** n. [C]

dawn¹ /dɔn/ n. [C, U] **1** the time at the beginning of the day when light first appears: *We talked almost until dawn.* | *An ice storm at dawn paralyzed St. Louis traffic.* | *When dawn broke* (=the first light of the day appeared) *Monday, the scope of the damage was clear.* | *On Thanksgiving, Mom always gets up at the crack of dawn* (=very early in the morning) *to put the turkey into the oven.* —compare DUSK **2 the dawn of civilization/time/man etc.** the time when civilization, time, man etc. first began or appeared: *People have been falling in love since the dawn of time.* | *Fear has ruled the world since the dawn of the atomic age.* **3 false dawn** something that seems positive or hopeful but really is not: *Our first quarter profits were a little bit of a false dawn.*

dawn² v. [I] **1** if day or morning dawns, it begins: *The morning dawned fresh and clear after the storm.* **2** LITERARY if a period of time or situation dawns, it begins: *As the Cold War dawned in 1949, Galvin was starting his military career.* **3** LITERARY if a fact dawns, you realize it or think of it for the first time

dawn on sb phr. v. [T not in passive] if a fact or idea dawns on you, you realize it or think of it for the first time: *Lucy thought for a minute before the solution dawned on her.* | *While I was teaching, it dawned on me that our class could help the refugees.*

day /deɪ/ n. plural **days**
1 24 hours [C] a period of time equal to 24 hours: *"What day is today?" "It's Friday."* | *Pressler spent four days in Cuba during a Caribbean tour.* | *One of my friends was in a car accident the day before yesterday.* | *I have a meeting with him the day after tomorrow.*
2 when it is light [C,U] the period of time between when it becomes light in the morning and the time it becomes dark: *It was cold and the days were getting shorter.* | *It rained all day.* | *Emily is an industrial engineer by day* (=during the day) *and a punk rock bass guitarist by night.*
3 when you're awake [C usually singular] the time during the day when you are awake: *His day begins at six.* | *It's been a very long day* (=a day when you were very busy or worked many hours). | *Frank eats all day long* (=continuously during the day). | *Gary smokes two packs of cigarettes a day* (=each day or per day).
4 when you're working [C] the time spent working during a 24-hour period: *I work an eight-hour day.* | *Did you have a good day at the office?* —see also WORKDAY
5 the other day a few days ago; recently: *I went to the library the other day to check out some children's books.*
6 one day on a particular day in the past: *One day, Barbara called him up to discuss her plans.*

7 one day, some day at an unknown time in the future: *One day the truth will be known about Kennedy's murder.*
8 these days used to talk about a situation now, especially if it used to be different: *These days, even permanent jobs don't pay well.*
9 day(s) off a day or days when you do not have to work: *He never took a day off.* | *Employees said they are negotiating to get three more days off.*
10 make sb's day to make someone very happy: *Your smile makes my day.*
11 the (good) old days the time in the past that you think was better that the present time: *Their songwriting isn't as good as in the old days.*
12 in those days during a period of time in the past: *In those days, a dime bought two double-dip ice cream cones.*
13 day by day slowly and gradually: *Day by day Jeffrey began to feel better.* | *We'll just take it day by day.*
14 one of these days INFORMAL at some time in the future: *One of these days, I am going to take a walk and I am not going to come back.*
15 to this day even now, after so much time has passed: *To this day, Harris continues to fire workers who support the union.*
16 from day one INFORMAL from the beginning of a process, activity etc.: *I've said from day one that I think the governor will sign the bill.*
17 from day to day used when you are comparing the differences that happen to something on different days: *Property values can vary from day to day.* —compare DAY-TO-DAY
18 day after day happening continuously for a long time so that you become annoyed or bored: *The same exercises can get boring if you do them day after day.*
19 up to/until/to the present day from a time in the past until now: *Indian pottery spans the prehistoric age to the present day.*
20 day and night, night and day all the time; continuously: *My neighbor's dog barks day and night.*
21 day in, day out every day for a long time: *Children really need consistent parents; the same people day in, day out.*
22 the day will/might come (when) used to emphasize that something will definitely happen or might happen at some time in the future: *Let's hope the day will come when we don't need such a big military force.*
23 in this day and age used when you are surprised or annoyed that something happens or still happens: *It seems incredible, in this day and age, that a ship can just disappear.*
24 have an off day to be less successful or happy than usual, for no particular reason: *His work isn't usually this bad – he must have had an off day.*

25 any day (now) very soon: *It's going to snow any day now.*
26 not have all day to not have much time to do something: *Hurry up, we don't have all day!*
27 it's not my/your/his day used when several bad things have happened to someone in one day: *This is just not my day. I was late to work, my computer crashed, and my boss yelled at me.*
28 it's (just) one of those days used when everything seems to be going wrong: *"Everything okay?" "Oh, it's just been one of those days."*
29 that'll be the day used to say that you think something is very unlikely to happen: *"Bill says he'll wash the dishes tonight." "That'll be the day!"*
30 those were the days used to say that a time in the past was better than the present time
31 it's your/his/my lucky day! used when something very good happens to someone: *It must be my lucky day. I just found a $10 bill on the floor.*
32 be on days, be working days to be working during the day during a job that you sometimes have to do at night, for example if you work in a hospital: *I'm on days this week.*
33 it's not every day (that) used to say that something does not happen often and is therefore very special: *It's not every day that a helicopter sits down in your backyard.*

34 (live to) see the day to experience something that you thought would never happen: *I never thought I'd see the day when our firm would have to lay people off.* | *I'd love to see the day that everyone is treated fairly.*

35 40/50/60 etc. if sb's a day used to emphasize that someone is at least as old as you are saying, especially because they look older *She's ninety if she's a day.*

36 in my day used to describe what things were like when you were young: *In my day, we didn't travel with children.*

37 make a day of it to decide to spend all day doing something, usually for pleasure: *We were going into New York for the concert anyway, so we decided to make a day of it.*

38 sb's day will come used to say that someone will have a chance to succeed in the future, even if they are not successful now: *The team is working hard, and our day will come.*

39 have had your day to not be successful, powerful, or famous anymore: *It seems as if Communism has had its day.*

40 by day's end by the time it becomes night on a particular day: *By day's end, 1000 firefighters had been called in to battle the fire.*

41 in his or her day during the most successful part of someone's life: *McClellan was the best organizer and trainer of troops in his day.*

42 sb's childhood/student/army etc. days the time when you were a child, student, soldier etc.: *Back in his student days in the late '70s, Hackmann lived with six others.*

43 the standards/fashion/wages etc. of the day the standards etc. that existed in a particular period of time in the past: *His first house was large by the standards of the day.*

44 five/three/nine etc. years to the day exactly five years, three years etc. ago: *It was 25 years to the day after they got married.*

45 sb's days someone's time or someone's whole life: *Mary spends her days writing love letters.* | *She ended her days in poverty.*

46 sb's days as/with sth a period of time in someone's life when they were doing a particular job or activity: *Michael knew Annette during her days as an off-Broadway actress.* | *She reminisced of her days with the Benny Goodman Orchestra.*

47 sb's/sth's days (as sth) are numbered someone or something will not continue to exist or be effective: *Most people think that Ms. Miller's days as CEO are numbered.*

48 from one day to the next if something changes from one day to the next, it does not stay the same for very long: *I never know where he'll be from one day to the next.*

49 soup/dish/fish of the day the special soup etc. that a restaurant serves on a particular day

50 the day of reckoning the time when you are punished or made to suffer for the things you have done wrong —see also **call it a day** (CALL¹ (13)), DAY JOB, **every dog has its/his day** (DOG¹ (5)), HALF-DAY, **have a field day** (FIELD DAY (1)), **it's (a little) late in the day** (LATE¹ (11)), **save the day** (SAVE¹ (13))

USAGE NOTE: DAY

WORD CHOICE: from day to day, day by day, day after day
Something that changes or goes on **day by day** or **from day to day** is a continuous action: *Day by day the weather is getting warmer.* | *Their love grew stronger day by day.* | *The polls can change from day to day.* Separate events that are repeated happen **day after day**: *I get tired of listening to their complaints day after day* (=the same thing happens every day).
GRAMMAR
Remember that *on* is used with the names of days and the word **day** itself: *on Thursday/on that day/on the same day/on the second day* (NOT **in** or **at**). However, **on** is never used with the phrase **the other day**, when you do not say the exact day when something happened: *I went to the beach the other day* (=a few days ago). Compare: *We spent two days in the mountains –*

---

on the first day we went hiking and on the second we went fishing. Note that you say **in those days** but **these days** (NOT "in these days"): *In those days, people rode trains, but these days everybody flies.* Remember the phrase **during the day:** *I couldn't get much work done during the day* (NOT "during day" or "in the day," though you can say *in the daytime*). You do not use **the** with **all day**. *Some people watch TV all day* (NOT "all the day").

Day /deɪ/, **Dor·o·thy** /ˈdɑrəθi/ (1897–1980) a U.S. writer and social REFORMER who started the Catholic Worker magazine and group of CHARITY workers

Da·yan /daɪˈɑn/, **Mosh·e** /ˈmoʃeɪ/ (1915–1981) an Israeli military leader and politician, who was responsible for Israel's victory in the Arab-Israeli War of 1967, and later became Israel's Foreign Minister

day·bed /ˈdeɪbɛd/ *n.* [C] a bed that can be used as a SOFA

day book /'. ./ *n.* [C] a book with all of a company's financial records in it, including the dates when things were bought, sold, delivered etc.

day·break /ˈdeɪbreɪk/ *n.* [U] the time of day when light first appears: *At daybreak, officers began a house-to-house search.*

day camp /'. ./ *n.* [C] a place where children go during the day to do activities, sports, art etc. on their summer vacation from school —compare CAMP¹ (2)

day·care, day care /ˈdeɪkɛr/ *n.* [U] **1** the care of babies and young children by people other than their parents, while their parents are at work: *Millions of parents have a hard time getting good daycare for their children.* | *I don't want to **put** the babies **in daycare**.* **2** the care of adults who are too sick or too old to take care of themselves, by someone who is paid to come to their house during the day

day care cen·ter /'. . ,../ *n.* [C] a place where babies and young children can be left and taken care of while their parents are at work

---

daydream

day·dream¹ /ˈdeɪdrim/ *v.* [I] to think about something nice, for example something you would like to happen, especially when this makes you forget what you should be doing: *Daniel was a quiet child who daydreamed in class.* | [+ about/of] *Many women daydream about having time to themselves.* —**daydreamer** *n.* [C] —**daydreaming** *n.* [U]

daydream² *n.* [C] pleasant thoughts you have while you are awake, that make you forget what you are doing

Day-Glo /ˈdeɪgloʊ/ *adj.* TRADEMARK having a very bright orange, green, yellow, or pink color: *a Day-Glo orange vest*

day job /'. ./ *n.* [C] **1** someone's main job that they do during the day from which they earn most of their money **2 don't quit your day job** also **don't give up your day job** SPOKEN, HUMOROUS used to tell someone that you do not think what they are doing is good or that their idea for making money will be successful

day la·bor /'. ,../ *n.* [U] physical work that someone is paid to do, one day at a time —**day laborer** *n.* [C]

day·light /'deɪlaɪt/ *n.* [U] **1** the time during the day when it is light: *The robberies usually occur during daylight hours.* | *The air search will continue* **at daylight** (=the time when it is first light in the morning) *on Friday.* **2** the light produced by the sun during the day: *Poinsettia plants need a lot of daylight to keep healthy.* **3 scare/frighten the (living) daylights out of sb** INFORMAL to frighten someone a lot **4 beat/ knock/pound the (living) daylights out of sb** INFORMAL **a)** to hit someone a lot and seriously hurt them **b)** to defeat someone in a game, race, election etc. by a large amount: *The home team got the daylights beaten out of it by Louisiana Tech.* —see also **in broad daylight** (BROAD¹ (6))

daylight sav·ing time /,.. '.. ,../ also **daylight savings** *n.* [U] the time from early April to late October when clocks are set one hour ahead of STANDARD TIME

day of judg·ment /,. . '../ *n.* [singular] JUDGMENT DAY

day room /'. ./ *n.* [C] a room in a hospital where PATIENTS can go to read, watch television etc.

day school /'. ./ *n.* [C,U] a school, especially a PRIVATE SCHOOL, where the students go home in the evening, rather than one where they live —compare BOARDING SCHOOL

day·time /'deɪtaɪm/ *n.* [U] the time during the day between the time when it gets light and the time when it gets dark; DAY (2): *Parking is difficult to find in the daytime when downtown is busiest.* | *Please include a daytime phone number* (=where you can be called during the day). —opposite NIGHTTIME

Day-Tim·er /'. ,../ *n.* [C] TRADEMARK a type of DATEBOOK

day-to-day /,. . '.< / *adj.* [only before noun] happening every day as a normal part of your life, your job etc.: *Resident managers are responsible for the day-to-day operations of the hotel.*

day trad·ing /'. ,../ *n.* [U] the activity of buying STOCK and selling it again very quickly in order to try to make a lot of money, which is considered very risky —**day trader** *n.* [C]

daze /deɪz/ *n.* **in a daze** unable to think clearly, especially because you have been shocked, surprised, or hurt: *Survivors wandered through the ruins in a daze.*

dazed /deɪzd/ *adj.* unable to think clearly, especially because you have been shocked, surprised, or hurt: *Anxious family members sat dazed in the waiting room.*

daz·zle /'dæzəl/ *v.* [T usually passive] **1** to make someone admire someone or something: *Staring out the train window, we were dazzled by the scenery.* | **[dazzle sb with sth]** *He routinely dazzles guests with his wit.* **2** if a very bright light dazzles you, it stops you from seeing well for a short time —**dazzle** *n.* [U]

daz·zling /'dæzlɪŋ/ *adj.* **1** very impressive, attractive, or interesting: *dazzling computer graphics* | *Johnston showed a dazzling display of football talent.* **2** a light that is dazzling makes you unable to see well for a short time: *the dazzling noonday sun*

dbl. *n., adj.* the written abbreviation of DOUBLE

D.C. District of Columbia; the area containing the city of Washington, the CAPITAL of the U.S.

D.C., dc the abbreviation of DIRECT CURRENT —compare AC (1)

D-Day /'di deɪ/ *n.* [C,U] **1** June 6, 1944; the day the American army, the British army, and other armies landed in France during World War II **2** INFORMAL a day on which an important action is planned to happen or begin: *Reports of a D-Day for layoffs at the factory turned out to be just rumors.*

DDT *n.* [U] a chemical used to kill insects that harm crops, which is now illegal

DE the written abbreviation of Delaware

de- /di, dɪ/ *prefix* **1** in some verbs, nouns, and adjectives, it shows an opposite: *a depopulated area* (=which all or most of the population has left) | *deindustrialization* (=becoming less industrial) **2** in some verbs, it means to remove something or remove things from something: *to debone the fish* (=remove its bones) | *The king was dethroned* (=removed from power). **3** in some verbs, it means to make something less; reduce: *to devalue the currency*

DEA *n.* [singular] Drug Enforcement Agency; an organization in the U.S. government that makes sure people obey the drug laws

dea·con /'dikən/ *n.* [C] a religious official in some Christian churches

de·ac·ti·vate /di'æktə,veɪt/ *v.* [T] **1** to do something to a system or a piece of equipment so that it cannot be used anymore: *In 1976, the old lighthouse was deactivated.* **2** a word meaning to remove a person or group from a larger group so that they are not a member of the group anymore, used especially in the army and by sports teams: *The San Francisco Giants deactivated wide receiver Chuck Robinson.*

dead¹ /dɛd/ *adj.*

1 ‖not alive‖ not alive anymore: *Her mother has been dead for ten years.* | *a dead tree* | **A dead body** (=a dead person) *was found in the park.* | *After I'm* **dead and gone** (=dead for a long time), *I would like to be remembered as a good person.* —compare ALIVE (1), LIVE² (1)

2 ‖not working‖ not working, especially because there is no electrical power: *Is the battery dead?* | *The phones went dead during the storm.*

3 ‖place/time‖ a place, period of time, or situation that is dead does not have anything interesting happening in it: *The bar is usually dead until around 10:00.*

4 a dead language a dead language is not used by ordinary people anymore —opposite **a living language** (LIVING¹ (4))

5 ‖tired‖ SPOKEN very tired: *I can't go out tonight. I'm dead.* | *Most of the soldiers were* **dead on their feet**.

6 ‖body part‖ a part of your body that is dead has no feeling in it for a short time: *I'd been sitting on my heels for so long my legs had* **gone dead**.

7 ‖in trouble‖ also **dead meat** SPOKEN if someone says you are dead or dead meat, you are in serious trouble and will probably be punished or hurt: *If anything happens to the car, you're dead!*

8 beat/flog a dead horse SPOKEN to waste time or effort by trying to do something that is impossible or talking about something that has already been decided

9 ‖land/water/planets‖ containing no life: *a dead moon of Jupiter* | *the Dead Sea*

10 be dead set on/against sth to be determined that something will or will not happen: *Key White House aides are dead set against the proposal.*

11 ‖in sports‖ when the ball is dead in some games, players must stop playing until the officials start the game again

12 a dead stop/silence/hush/loss etc. a complete stop, silence, hush, loss etc.: *It takes a lot of gas to get a car moving from a dead stop.*

13 ‖no emotion‖ showing no emotion or sympathy: *Jenny's eyes were cold and dead.*

14 dead center the exact center: *Hit the nail dead center so that it doesn't bend.*

15 dead on arrival a) someone who is dead on arrival is DECLAREd to be dead as soon as they are brought to a hospital **b)** a law, plan etc. that is dead on arrival is not worth considering even when it is first shown to the public: *Congress declared the President's budget dead on arrival.*

16 sb wouldn't be caught/seen dead said in order to emphasize that someone would never do something because it would be too embarrassing: **[sb wouldn't be caught/seen dead doing sth]** *Melanie wouldn't be seen dead wearing a dress like that!* | **[+ with/at/in]** *I wouldn't be caught dead at one of Val's parties.*

17 over my dead body SPOKEN used to say that you

are determined not to allow something to happen: *You'll marry him over my dead body!*
18 dead and buried an argument, problem, plan etc. that is dead and buried is not in use anymore, or is not worth considering anymore: *I thought the idea of us moving to New York was dead and buried.*
19 a dead duck INFORMAL **a)** someone who is in trouble or will be punished: *If he's not here on time, he's a dead duck.* **b)** something that is very likely to fail or become less successful: *The news program was once considered a dead duck.*
20 dead to the world very deeply asleep or unconscious: *Craig's upstairs, dead to the world.*
21 dead in the water something that is dead in the water is unable to work correctly and finish doing what it is supposed to do: *Right now the project is dead in the water.*
22 a dead ringer someone who looks exactly like someone else: *Dave's a dead ringer for Nicolas Cage.*
23 dead to rights in the act of doing something wrong: *They caught him dead to rights, smoking marijuana in his bedroom.*
24 dead as a doornail SPOKEN **a)** used to say that someone or something is clearly dead: *The rat was dead as a doornail.* **b)** used to say that a place is very quiet
25 in a dead faint completely unconscious: *The woman fell down in a dead faint.*
26 a dead eye someone who can shoot very well
27 the dead hand of sth a powerful bad influence that makes progress slower: *the dead hand of bureaucracy* —**deadness** *n.* [U] —see also **drop dead** (DROP[1] (12)) —see Usage Note at DIE[1]

—see Usage Note at DIE[1]

USAGE NOTE: DEAD

WORD CHOICE: dead, died
Use **dead** as an adjective to talk about things or people that are no longer alive: *I think this plant is dead.* **Died** is the past tense and past participle of "die": *He died on the way to the hospital.*

---

dead[2] *adv.* INFORMAL **1** extremely or completely: *Paula stopped dead when she saw us.* | *The baby was up all night and I'm dead tired.* | *The Kimballs are dead set against drinking.* **2** [+ adj./adv.] directly or exactly: *You can't miss it – it's dead ahead.*

dead[3] *n.* **1 the dead** [plural] people who have died, especially people who have been killed: *There wasn't even time to bury the dead.* **2 in the dead of night/winter** in the middle of the night or winter when everything is very quiet or cold: *We finally arrived at Aunt Claire's house in the dead of night.* **3 rise from the dead** also **come back from the dead** to become alive again after dying

dead·beat /'dɛdbit/ *n.* [C] INFORMAL **1** someone who is lazy and who has no plans in life **2** someone who does not pay their debts

deadbeat dad /ˌ. './ *n.* [C] INFORMAL a father who does not live with his children and avoids paying money to support them

dead·bolt /'dɛdboult/ also **deadbolt lock** /'.. ˌ./ *n.* [C] a type of lock that is built into a door and is very strong

dead cat bounce /ˌ. . './ *n.* [singular] SLANG an increase in the price of SHAREs after they have fallen, which may make you think that they will continue to increase even if they do not

dead·en /'dɛdn/ *v.* [T] to make a feeling or sound less strong: *He drank alcohol to deaden the pain.*

dead end[1] /ˌ. './ *n.* [C] **1** a street with no way out at one end **2** a situation from which no more progress is possible: *Working at the warehouse seemed like a dead end.* | *The negotiations have reached a dead end.* **3 a dead-end job** a job with low pay and no chance of progress

dead end[2] *v.* [I] if a road dead ends, there is no way out at one end of it: *Larkin Avenue dead ends into a large parking lot.*

Dead·head /'dɛdhɛd/ *n.* [C] INFORMAL someone who likes the band "The Grateful Dead"

dead heat /ˌ. './ *n.* [C usually singular] a race or competition in which two or more competitors are at exactly the same level, speed etc.

dead let·ter /ˌ. '../ *n.* [C] **1** a law, idea etc. that still exists but that people do not obey or are not interested in anymore: *An arts education is a dead letter for many students.* **2** a letter that cannot be delivered or returned

dead·line /'dɛdlaɪn/ *n.* [C] a date or time by which you have to do or complete something: *Can you meet the 5:00 deadline* (=Can you finish by 5:00?)*?* | *She missed the deadline* (=she was too late) *for entering the race.* | *Review the information and set a deadline* (=decide on a deadline) *for making your decision.* | *The department is working under a very tight deadline* (=a deadline that is difficult to meet).

dead·lock[1] /'dɛdlɑk/ *n.* [C] a situation in which a disagreement cannot be settled; STALEMATE: *The talks have reached a complete deadlock.*

deadlock[2] *v.* [I,T] if a group of people or something such as NEGOTIATIONs deadlocks, or if something deadlocks them, they are unable to settle a disagreement: [+ on] *The city planning commission deadlocked on the issue.*

dead·ly[1] /'dɛdli/ *adj.* **deadlier, deadliest**
1 very dangerous likely to cause death: *Hemlock is one of nature's oldest and most deadly poisons.*
2 a deadly enemy someone who will always be your enemy and who will try to harm you as much as possible: *Lawrence Caffey had been his deadly enemy since college.*
3 boring SPOKEN not interesting or exciting at all: *His lectures are deadly.*
4 very effective causing harm in a very effective way: *Hank can shoot with deadly precision.*
5 like death [only before noun] like death in appearance: *The woman's face had a deadly paleness.*
6 complete complete or total, often in a bad or frightening way: *We sat in deadly silence.* —**deadliness** *n.* [U]

deadly[2] *adv.* **deadly serious/quiet/dull etc.** very or extremely serious, quiet, dull etc.: *I'm deadly serious – this isn't a game!*

deadly night·shade /ˌ.. '../ *n.* [C,U] a poisonous European plant; BELLADONNA

dead-man's float /ˌ. . './ *n.* [singular] a way of floating in water with your body and face turned down in the water

dead·pan /'dɛdpæn/ *adj.* sounding and looking completely serious when you are really joking: *a deadpan expression* —**deadpan** *v.* [I] —**deadpan** *adv.*

dead reck·on·ing /ˌ. '.../ *n.* [U] the practice of calculating the position of a ship or airplane without using the sun, moon, or stars

Dead Sea /ˌ. './ a large lake between Israel and Jordan that is over 25% salt

dead weight /ˌ. '.*/ *n.* [C,U] **1** someone or something that you are responsible for that prevents you from being successful: *Many of its smaller stores are dead weight to the supermarket chain.* **2** something that is very heavy and difficult to carry: *He carried the dead weight of the unconscious man up the stairs.*

dead·wood /'dɛdwʊd/ *n.* [U] **1** the people or things within an organization that are useless or not needed anymore: *Mrs. Winston is quick to get rid of deadwood on her staff.* **2** dead branches or trees

deaf /dɛf/ *adj.* **1** physically unable to hear anything or unable to hear well: *Dad's partially deaf and needs a hearing aid.* —see also STONE DEAF, TONE-DEAF **2 the deaf** [plural] people who are deaf: *a school for the deaf* **3 deaf to sth** LITERARY unwilling to hear or listen to something: *She was deaf to his warnings.* **4 turn a deaf ear** to be unwilling to listen to what someone is saying or asking: *The factory owners turned a deaf ear to the demands of the workers.* **5 fall on deaf ears** if something you say falls on deaf ears, everyone ignores it: *Their requests fell on deaf ears.* —**deafness** *n.* [U]

deaf and dumb /ˌ. . ˈ.◂/ adj. OLD-FASHIONED a word meaning "unable to hear or speak," now usually considered offensive

deaf·en /ˈdɛfən/ v. [T usually passive] to make it difficult for you to hear anything: *We were deafened by the explosion.*

deaf·en·ing /ˈdɛfənɪŋ/ adj. noise or music that is deafening is very loud: *deafening bomb blasts*

deaf-mute /ˈ. ./ n. [C] OLD-FASHIONED a word for someone who is unable to hear or speak, now usually considered offensive

s w
1 1
deal¹ /dil/ n.
1 agreement [C] an agreement or arrangement, especially in business or politics: *The deal would create the nation's largest credit card company.* | *I got a really good deal on my car* (=I bought it at a very good price). | **strike/make/cut etc. a deal** (=produce an agreement)
2 a great/good deal a large quantity or amount of something: [+ of] *I've spent a good deal of time thinking about the project.* | *He knows a great deal more* (=a lot more) *about computers than I do.*
3 treatment [C usually singular] the way someone is treated in a particular situation: *Struthers felt she had gotten a raw deal* (=unfair treatment) *from her employer.*
4 game [singular] the process of giving out cards to players in a card game: *It's your deal, Alison.* —see also DEALER (3)

SPOKEN PHRASES

5 it's a deal used to say that you agree to do something: *"I'll give you $100 for it." "It's a deal."*
6 what's the deal? used when you want to know about a problem or something strange that is happening: *So what's the deal? Why is he so mad?*
7 good deal said when you are pleased by something someone else has just said: *"I've made all the arrangements for the trip." "Good deal."* —see also BIG DEAL

USAGE NOTE: DEAL

GRAMMAR: A great/good deal of...
is used only with uncountable nouns: *a great deal of time/money/difficulty/pressure etc.* Compare: *There's been a great deal of change* with: *There have been a large number of changes.* You cannot say, "There have been a great deal of changes."

s w
1 1
deal² v. past tense and past participle **dealt 1** [I,T] to give playing cards to each of the players in a game: *Whose turn is it to deal?* | *Deal three cards to each player.* **2** [I,T] INFORMAL to buy and sell illegal drugs: *He was arrested for dealing cocaine.* **3 deal sb/sth a blow** LITERARY **a)** to make someone or something less successful | **deal a crippling/decisive/fatal etc. blow** *The recession dealt the steel industry a crippling blow.* **b)** to hit someone or something
deal in sth phr. v. [T] **1** to buy and sell a particular type of product: *The store deals in high-quality jewelry.* —see also DEALER (1) **2** to let your work or behavior be guided by specific principles: *As a scientist, I do not deal in speculation.*
deal sb **in** phr. v. [T] INFORMAL to include someone in a plan or a deal: *If you ever want to start your own business, you can deal me in.*
deal sth ↔ **out** phr. v. [T] **1** to give playing cards to each of the players in a game: *You're supposed to deal the whole deck out.* **2** to give someone a punishment: *Chinese courts deal out harsh punishments to smugglers.*
deal with sb/sth phr. v. [T] **1** to take the correct action for a problem, piece of work etc.: *Who's dealing with the Sony account?* **2** to not lose confidence or to not become too upset in a difficult situation: *I can't deal with any more crying children today.* **3** to do business with someone or have a business connection with someone: *We've been dealing with their company for ten years.* **4** if a book, speech, work of art etc. deals with a particular subject, it is about that subject: *The book deals with art during the French Revolution.*

deal·er /ˈdilɚ/ n. [C] **1** someone who buys and sells a particular product, especially an expensive one: *a car dealer* **2** someone who sells illegal drugs **3** someone who gives out playing cards in a game —see also DOUBLE-DEALER

s w
3

deal·er·ship /ˈdilɚˌʃɪp/ n. [C] a business that sells a particular company's product, especially cars: *Ford dealerships*

deal·ing /ˈdilɪŋ/ n. **1 dealings** [plural] the business activities or relationships that someone has been involved in, especially those that seem dishonest or wrong: *The secret dealings of his department were made public.* | *We've had dealings with* (=had a business relationship with) *IBM for the past few years.* **2** [U] the buying and selling of things, especially things that are illegal: *The mayor wants to end all drug dealing in the city.*

dealt /dɛlt/ v. the past tense and past participle of DEAL²

dean /din/ n. [C] **1** someone in a college or university who is in charge of an area of study, or in charge of students and their behavior **2** a priest of high rank, especially in the Episcopal and Catholic Churches, who is in charge of several priests or churches **3** someone who has more experience than anyone else in a particular subject: *Donahue was the dean of TV talk show hosts.*

Dean /din/**, James** (1931–1955) a U.S. movie actor who became very famous, and became even more popular after dying in a car crash at the age of 24

James Dean

dean's list /ˈ. ./ n. [C usually singular] a list of students with high grades at a college or university

dear¹ /dɪr/ interjection **Oh dear** said when you are surprised, annoyed, or upset: *Oh dear, I can't find the meatloaf recipe anywhere.*

dear² n. [C] SPOKEN **1** used when speaking to someone you love: *How did the interview go, dear?* **2** a friendly way for an old person to speak to a young person: *What's your name, dear?* **3** someone who is very kind and helpful: *Be a dear and make me some coffee.*

dear³ adj. **1 Dear** used before someone's name or title when you begin a letter: *Dear Sally,...* | *Dear Dr. Ward:...* **2** FORMAL much loved and very important to you: *Mark had become a dear friend.* | *His sister was very dear to him.* **3 for dear life** if you run, hold on, fight etc. for dear life, you do so as fast or as well as you can because you are afraid: *Sherman held onto the bar for dear life.*

dear·est /ˈdɪrɪst/ n. [C] SPOKEN, OLD-FASHIONED used when speaking to someone you love: *Well, dearest, I was a little worried.*

dear·ie /ˈdɪri/ n. [C] OLD-FASHIONED OR HUMOROUS used as a way of speaking to someone you love or someone you want to be friendly to

dear John let·ter /ˌ. ˈ. ˌ../ n. [C] a letter to a man from his wife or GIRLFRIEND, saying that she does not love him anymore

dear·ly /ˈdɪrli/ adv. **1** if you love someone or something dearly or you miss them dearly etc., you do so with strong emotions: *She loves her children dearly.* **2 cost sb/sth dearly** to cost someone or something a lot of money or cause them a lot of trouble or suffering: *Vandalism costs schools dearly.* **3 pay dearly** to pay a lot of money or suffer a lot for something that you have done: *If we don't take action now, we'll pay dearly later.* **4 dearly beloved** SPOKEN used by a priest or minister when speaking to the people at a Christian religious service, especially a marriage or funeral

dearth /dɜθ/ n. [singular] FORMAL a lack of something: [+ of] *There is a dearth of qualified workers.*

death /dɛθ/ n.

1 the end of sb's life [U] the end of the life of a person or animal: *Maretti lived in Miami until his death.* | **bleed/burn/choke etc. to death** *Several people in the apartment burned to death.* | **shoot/beat etc. sb to death** *Ruby shot Oswald to death with a revolver.* | *The horse was so badly injured it had to be* **put to death** (=killed). | *Charlotte* **met her death** (=died) *in a train wreck.*

2 example of sb dying [C] a particular case of someone dying: *Authorities counted 50 traffic deaths over the holiday weekend.* | [+ from] *A new study says deaths from breast cancer are declining.*

3 **be scared/bored/worried etc. to death** INFORMAL extremely scared, bored, or worried etc.: *Ron's scared to death of dogs.*

4 way of dying [C] the way in which someone or something dies | **a horrible/terrible/agonizing etc. death** *The pilot and his crew must have died a horrible death.*

5 **the death of sth** the permanent end of an idea, custom etc.: *the death of American slavery* | *the death of the Soviet Union*

6 **death blow** an action or event that makes something fail or end: *The new law would be a death blow to casinos.*

7 **Death** [singular, not with **the**] a creature that looks like a SKELETON (1), used in paintings, stories etc. as a sign of death and destruction

8 **death's door** the point in time when someone is very sick and likely to die: *He looked like a man at* **death's door***.*

9 **you'll/he'll etc. be the death of me!** SPOKEN said about someone who makes you very worried and anxious, especially said in a humorous way: *That boy is going to be the death of me!*

10 **you'll catch your death (of cold)** SPOKEN OLD-FASHIONED said as a warning to someone when you think they are likely to become sick because it is wet or cold outside: *Don't go out without a coat! You'll catch your death of cold!*

11 **like death warmed over** INFORMAL if someone looks or feels like death warmed over, they look or feel very sick or tired: *What happened to you? You look like death warmed over.* —see also **be sick (and tired) of sth/be sick to death of sth** (SICK¹ (4)), BLACK DEATH, **fight to the death** (FIGHT¹ (14)), **sth is a matter of life and death** (MATTER¹ (27)), **the kiss of death** (KISS² (2))

death·bed /ˈdɛθbɛd/ n. [C] the point in time when someone is lying in bed and will die very soon: *Marquez flew home to be with his mother, who was on her deathbed* (=close to death).

death camp /ˈ. ./ n. [C] a place where large numbers of prisoners are killed or die, usually in a war

death cer·tif·i·cate /ˈ. .,../ n. [C] a legal document, signed by a doctor, that states the time and cause of someone's death

death knell /ˈdɛθ nɛl/ n. [singular] a sign that something will soon stop existing or stop being used: *Plans to build a bridge across the river* **sounded the death knell** *for ferry services.*

death·less /ˈdɛθlɪs/ adj. LITERARY something that is deathless does not die or go away: *Ben hated him with a bitter and deathless hatred.*

death·ly /ˈdɛθli/ adv. **1** if you are deathly afraid, or frightened, you are extremely afraid: *Mom's deathly afraid of flying.* **2** in a way that reminds you of death or of a dead body: *Rachel felt deathly cold.* | *He was in intensive care, lying deathly still.* —**deathly** adj. [only before noun]

death mask /ˈ. ./ n. [C] a model of a dead person's face, made by pressing a soft substance over their face and letting it become hard

death pen·al·ty /ˈ. .,../ n. **the death penalty** the legal punishment of being killed, used in some countries for serious crimes | **get/be given/receive the death penalty** *Jurors decided he should get the death penalty.*

death rate /ˈ. ./ n. [C] the number of deaths for every

100 or every 1000 people in a particular year and in a particular place —compare BIRTHRATE

death rat·tle /ˈ. ,../ n. [C] a strange noise sometimes heard from the throat or chest of someone who is dying

death row /ˌ. ˈ./ n. [usually singular] the part of a prison where prisoners are kept while waiting to be punished by being killed: *Jones is* **on death row** *for murdering five people.*

death sen·tence /ˈ. ,../ n. [C] **1** the punishment of death given by a judge: *Gilmore received a death sentence.* **2** something that causes the end of something or the death of someone: *Cancer is not automatically a death sentence.* | *A golf course will be a death sentence to the local ecosystem.*

death's head /ˈ. ./ n. [C] a human SKULL used as a sign of death

death squad /ˈ. ./ n. [C] a group of people who are ordered by a government to kill people, especially their political opponents

D

death throes /ˈ. ./ n. [plural] **1** the final stages before something fails or ends: *The regime seems to be in its death throes.* **2** sudden violent movements sometimes made by a person or an animal that is dying

death toll /ˈ. ./ n. [C] the total number of people who die in a particular accident, war etc.: *If the civil unrest continues, the death toll will rise.*

death trap /ˈ. ./ n. [C] INFORMAL a vehicle or building that is in such bad condition that it is dangerous and might kill someone: *The house looked like a real death trap.*

Death Val·ley /ˌ. ˈ../ an area of desert in the U.S. states of Nevada and California

death war·rant /ˈ. ,../ n. [C] **1** an official document stating that someone is to be killed as a punishment for their crimes **2** something that seems likely to cause you very serious trouble or even to cause your death: *Magnets are a death warrant to computer disks.* | *By not cutting back the brush around your home in fire season, you may be* **signing your own death warrant***.*

death wish /ˈ. ./ n. [singular] a desire to die: *You don't use your seatbelt? What do you have, a death wish?*

deb /dɛb/ n. [C] INFORMAL a DEBUTANTE

de·ba·cle /deɪˈbakəl, -ˈbæ-/ n. [C] an event or situation that is a complete failure

De Ba·key /də ˈbeɪki/**, Mi·chael** /ˈmaɪkəl/ (1908–) a U.S. doctor who was the first heart SURGEON to use an artificial heart in a person's body

de·bar /dɪˈbar/ v. **debarred, debarring** [T] to officially prevent someone from taking part in something: [**debar sb from sth**] *He was debarred from the golf club for misusing club funds.* —**debarment** n. [C,U] —compare DISBAR

de·bark /dɪˈbark, di-/ v. [I] to DISEMBARK —**debarkation** /ˌdibarˈkeɪʃən/ n. [U]

de·base /dɪˈbeɪs/ v. [T] **1** INFORMAL to reduce the quality or value of something: *Our society has been debased by war and corruption.* | *a debased currency* **2** if something debases you or if you debase yourself, you do something that makes people have less respect for you: *Women were forced to debase themselves by selling their bodies.* —**debasement** n. [C,U] —**debasing** adj.

de·bat·a·ble /dɪˈbeɪtəbəl/ adj. an idea or question that is debatable is one for which two or more different opinions or answers could be true or right: *It is debatable whether nuclear weapons actually prevent war.*

de·bate¹ /dɪˈbeɪt/ n. **1** [C,U] discussion or argument on a subject that people express different opinions about: [+ on/over/about] *There has been very little public debate on the Navy's new program.* | *The abortion debate is causing more women to run for office.* | **intense/heated/fierce debate** (=discussion involving very strong opinions) **2** [C] a formal discussion on a subject, in which each person has a chance to speak: [+ **on/about**] *The candidates will hold a debate on welfare reform next Tuesday.* **3 be open/subject to debate** also **be a matter for debate** if an idea is open to debate, no one has proved yet whether it is true or false: *Whether that would have made any difference is open to debate.* **4 under debate** being discussed: *The question of a third airport is still under debate.* **5 up for debate** able to be discussed or planned to be discussed: *Resolutions up for debate include raising the minimum wage.*

debate² *v.* [I,T] **1** to discuss a subject formally with someone. when you are trying to make a decision or find a solution: *The matter will be debated by the General Assembly.* | [**debate whether/what/how etc. (to do sth)**] *The council will debate whether to open the park to nonresidents.* | *Her conclusions are hotly debated* (=argued about strongly) *among academics.* **2** to seriously consider something: [**debate who/what/how etc. (to do sth)**] *Students debated whether holding the rally was necessary.* —**debater** *n.* [C] —**debating** *n.* [U]

de·bauch /dɪˈbɔtʃ, -ˈbɑtʃ/ *v.* [T] FORMAL to make someone behave in an immoral way, especially with alcohol, drugs, or sex

de·bauched /dɪˈbɔtʃt/ *adj.* someone who is debauched drinks too much alcohol, takes too many drugs, or has an immoral attitude about sex

de·bauch·er·y /dɪˈbɔtʃəri/ *n.* **1** [U] immoral behavior involving drugs, alcohol, sex etc. **2** [C] an occasion when someone behaves in this way

de·ben·ture /dɪˈbɛntʃə/ *n.* [C] TECHNICAL an official document given by a company, showing that it has borrowed money and that it will pay a particular rate of INTEREST, whether or not it makes a profit

de·bil·i·tat·ed /dɪˈbɪləˌteɪtɪd/ *adj.* **1** if someone is debilitated, their body or mind is weak from illness, heat etc.: *Millions of Americans are debilitated by alcohol.* **2** if an organization or structure is debilitated, its authority or effectiveness has become weak: *Civil war has left the country debilitated.* —**debilitate** *v.* [T]

de·bil·i·tat·ing /dɪˈbɪləˌteɪtɪŋ/ *adj.* **1** a debilitating disease or condition makes your body or mind weak: *He suffered a debilitating stroke last year.* **2** a debilitating action, result etc. makes an organization, structure etc. weak: *Negotiators are making every effort to end the debilitating trade war.*

de·bil·i·ty /dɪˈbɪləti/ *n. plural* **debilities** [C,U] FORMAL weakness, especially as the result of illness

deb·it¹ /ˈdɛbɪt/ *n.* [C] TECHNICAL a record of the money that you have taken out of your bank account —compare CREDIT¹ (2)

debit² *v.* [T] TECHNICAL **1** to take money out of a bank account: *How can they debit my account without me signing anything?* | [**debit sth from sth**] *The sum of $50 has been debited from your account.* **2** to record the amount of money taken from a bank account: [**debit sth against sth**] *Purchases are then debited against the customer's bank account.* —compare CREDIT² (1)

debit card /ˈ.. ˌ./ *n.* [C] a special plastic card that you can use to pay for things directly from your bank account —compare CHECK CARD, CREDIT CARD

deb·o·nair /ˌdɛbəˈnɛr/ *adj.* APPROVING a man who is debonair is fashionable and well dressed and behaves in an attractively confident way: *a stylish, debonair young man*

de·brief /diˈbrif/ *v.* [T] to ask someone such as a soldier for information about a job that they have just done or an important experience they have just had: *The returning bomber crews were debriefed.* —compare BRIEF² —**debriefing** *n.* [C,U]

de·bris /dəˈbri/ *n.* [U] all the pieces that are left after something has been destroyed in an accident, explosion etc.: *The beach was littered with debris.*

a U.S. LABOR leader who led an important railroad STRIKE and was the Socialist Party CANDIDATE for U.S. president in four elections

debt /dɛt/ *n.* **1** [C] money that you owe: [+ **of**] *The company has debts of around $1,000,000.* | *Brian ran up huge debts* (=borrowed a lot of money) *on his credit cards.* | **repay/clear etc. a debt** *Denise finally paid off her debts.* **2** [U] the state of owing money | **be ($10/$100/$1,000) in debt** *They are $40,000 in debt.* | **be heavily/deeply etc. in debt** *Bobby's up to his ears in debt.* | **go/get/fall etc. into debt** (=borrow more and more money) | **be/get out of debt** (=pay back all the money you owe) **3 owe a debt (of gratitude) to sb** also **be in sb's debt** to be grateful to someone for what they have done for you: *Our club owes a great debt of gratitude to Martha Graham.* **4 owe a debt to sb** to learn from or be influenced by someone else: *The singer owes a stylistic debt to Tina Turner.* —see also BAD DEBT, NATIONAL DEBT, **sb has paid their debt to society** (PAY¹ (13))

debt col·lec·tor /ˈ. .ˌ../ *n.* [C] someone whose job is to get back the money that people owe

debt·or /ˈdɛtə/ *n.* [C] a person, group, or organization that owes money —compare CREDITOR

debtor na·tion /ˈ.. ˌ../ *n.* [C] TECHNICAL a country that has borrowed a lot of money or in which other countries have INVESTed more money than that country has invested in other countries —compare CREDITOR NATION

debt re·tire·ment /ˈ. .ˌ../ *n.* [C,U] the act of paying back all of a sum of money you have borrowed, especially from a bank

de·bug /diˈbʌg/ *v.* **debugged, debugging** [T] **1** to take the mistakes out of a computer program **2** to find and remove secret listening equipment in a room or building

de·bunk /diˈbʌŋk/ *v.* [T] to show that an idea or belief is false: *The study debunks the myth that men are better at math than women.* —**debunker** *n.* [C]

De·bus·sy /ˌdɛbyuˈsi, ˌdeɪ-/, **Claude** /kloʊd/ (1862–1918) a French musician who wrote CLASSICAL music and developed musical IMPRESSIONISM

de·but¹ /deɪˈbyu, ˈdeɪbyu/ *n.* [C] the first public appearance of someone such as an entertainer or sports player or of something new and important: *Their debut album was recorded in 1991.* | *Foster made her debut in movies at age eighteen.*

debut² *v.* **1** [I] to appear in public for the first time or to become available to the public for the first time: *The show will debut Monday night at 8 p.m.* **2** [T] to introduce a product to the public for the first time: *Ralph Lauren debuted his new collection in Paris last week.*

deb·u·tante /ˈdɛbyuˌtɑnt/ *n.* [C] a young woman who goes to special parties as a way of being formally introduced to rich people's society

Dec. the written abbreviation of December

deca- /dɛkə/ *prefix* ten: *decaliter* (=ten liters) | *the decathlon* (=a sports competition with 10 different events)

dec·ade /ˈdɛkeɪd/ *n.* [C] a period of ten years

dec·a·dence /ˈdɛkədəns/ *n.* [U] the state of having low moral standards and being more concerned with pleasure than with serious matters

dec·a·dent /ˈdɛkədənt/ *adj.* having low moral standards and being more concerned with pleasure than with serious matters: *Pop music has been condemned as decadent and crude.* —**decadently** *adv.*

de·caf /ˈdikæf/ *n.* [U] SPOKEN decaffeinated coffee

de·caf·fein·at·ed /diˈkæfəˌneɪtɪd/ *adj.* coffee, tea, or COLA that is decaffeinated has had all or most of the CAFFEINE removed

de·cal /ˈdikæl/ *n.* [C] a piece of paper with a pattern or picture on it that you stick onto another surface

de·camp /dɪˈkæmp/ *v.* [I] to leave a place suddenly and usually secretly: *The secretary decamped with the organization's money.*

de·cant /dɪˈkænt/ *v.* [T] to pour liquid, especially wine, from one container into another

de·cant·er /dɪˈkæntɚ/ n. [C] a glass container for alcoholic drinks

de·cap·i·tate /dɪˈkæpəˌteɪt, diˈ-/ v. [T] to cut off someone's head —**decapitation** /dɪˌkæpəˈteɪʃən/ n. [C,U]

dec·ath·lon /dɪˈkæθlɑn, -lən/ n. [C] a competition involving ten running, jumping, and throwing sports —compare HEPTATHLON, PENTATHLON

de·cay¹ /dɪˈkeɪ/ v. **decays, decayed, decaying 1** [I,T] to be slowly destroyed by a natural chemical process, or to make something do this: *The decaying body of a man was found in a vacant warehouse.* **2** [I often in progressive] if things such as buildings or areas decay, their condition becomes worse, especially because they are not taken care of: *This decaying city was once the busiest port in the world.* **3** [I often in progressive] if traditional beliefs, principles, standards etc. decay, people do not believe in them or support them anymore: *the decaying moral values of American society*

decay² n. **1** [U] the natural chemical change that causes the slow destruction of something: *Fluoride is helpful in fighting* **tooth decay**. **2** [U] the part of something that has been destroyed by a gradual chemical change: *I have noticed decay in some of the floorboards.* **3** [singular,U] when traditional ideas, beliefs, standards etc. become weaker: [+ **in**] *a decay in educational standards* **4** [U] if there is decay in a system, government, economy etc., it is gradually getting weaker, less organized, or less strong: *the decay of the central government in Russia* **5** [U] the gradual destruction of buildings and structures caused by a lack of care: *The Civil War-era house was* **falling into decay** (=beginning to decay).

de·ceased /dɪˈsist/ adj. FORMAL **1** dead: *Mike's parents are both deceased.* **2 the deceased** someone who has died, especially recently: *The deceased left no will.*

de·ceit /dɪˈsit/ n. [U] behavior that is intended to make someone believe something that is not true, or the things people do or say that are not true: *The government has a sad history of deceit in its dealings with Indians.*

de·ceit·ful /dɪˈsitfəl/ adj. intending to make someone believe something that is not true: *a deceitful man* —**deceitfully** adv. —**deceitfulness** n. [U]

de·ceive /dɪˈsiv/ v. [I,T] **1** to make someone believe something that is not true in order to get what you want: *Kyl said voters had been deceived by supporters of the new bill.* | [**deceive sb into doing sth**] *Thousands of home buyers were deceived into buying homes at inflated prices.* **2 looks/appearances can be deceiving** used to say that the way someone or something looks may make you believe something about them that is not true: *The car looks just like any old station wagon. But looks can be deceiving: this is the only taxicab in Trinity County.* **3 deceive yourself** to pretend to yourself that something is not true, because you do not want to accept the truth: *Many parents deceive themselves about their children's behavior.* —**deceiver** n. [C] —see also DECEPTION

de·cel·er·ate /diˈsɛləˌreɪt/ v. [I] TECHNICAL **1** to go slower, especially in a vehicle **2** if the ECONOMY, sales, business etc. decelerates, it is not growing or improving anymore —**deceleration** /diˌsɛləˈreɪʃən/ n. [U] —opposite ACCELERATE

De·cem·ber /dɪˈsɛmbɚ/ written abbreviation **Dec.** n. [C,U] the twelfth and last month of the year, after November: *The semester ends* **in December**. | *Christmas is* **on December 25th**. | *Emily's baby is due* **December 10**. | **Last December** *I went to visit my parents.* | *I won't be spending the holidays at home* **next December**. —see Usage Note at JANUARY

de·cen·cy /ˈdisənsi/ n. [U] **1** the quality of being honest and polite, and respecting other people: *Everyone deserves to be treated with respect and decency.* **2** acceptable behavior, especially moral and sexual behavior: *News broadcasters who show pictures of dead bodies have no* **sense of decency**. | *It's* **common decency** (=basic standards of behavior that everyone should follow) *to let someone know if* you are going to arrive late. | *They have no sense of* **human decency** (=basic standards of how people should treat each other). **3 have the decency to do sth** to do something that you should do in order to be polite or to behave in a way that society approves of: *The media should have the decency to protect a rape victim's identity.*

de·cent /ˈdisənt/ adj. **1** acceptable or good enough: *Did you get decent seats for the game?* | *I need to get a decent night's sleep.* | *a decent salary* **2** treating people in a fair and kind way: *The coach was a pretty decent guy.* **3** following the standards of moral behavior accepted by most people: *Decent working people are frustrated at the level of crime in the cities.* **4** wearing enough clothes to not show too much of your body: *Don't come in – I'm not decent!* —opposite INDECENT —**decently** adv.

de·cen·tral·ize /diˈsɛntrəˌlaɪz/ v. [T] to move parts of a government, organization etc. from one central place to several different smaller ones —**decentralized** adj. —**decentralization** /diˌsɛntrələˈzeɪʃən/ n. [U]

de·cep·tion /dɪˈsɛpʃən/ n. [C,U] the act of deliberately making someone believe something that is not true: *The President has been accused of secrecy and deception.*

de·cep·tive /dɪˈsɛptɪv/ adj. **1** deliberately intended to make someone believe something that is not true: *States may soon be able to ban* **deceptive advertising**. **2** something that is deceptive seems to be one thing but is in fact very different: *There is a deceptive simplicity to Irving Berlin's songs* (=they are not as simple as they seem). —**deceptively** adj.: *Garbarek's melodies are deceptively simple.* —**deceptiveness** n. [U]

deci- /ˈdɛsɪ/ prefix ¹/₁₀ of a unit: *a deciliter* (=a tenth of a liter)

dec·i·bel /ˈdɛsəˌbɛl, -bəl/ n. [C] TECHNICAL a unit of measurement for the loudness of sound: *Noise levels in factories must not exceed 85 decibels.*

de·cide /dɪˈsaɪd/ v. **1** [I,T] to make a choice or judgment about something, especially after a period of not knowing what to do or in a way that ends disagreement: *Citizens must be allowed to decide their own futures.* | [**decide to do sth**] *Price decided to be a candidate for the city council.* | [**decide (that)**] *It was decided that women could compete in the biathlon.* | [**decide who/what/how etc.**] *Have you decided what to wear to the wedding?* | [**decide whether/if**] *Voters will decide if a new stadium should be built.* | [**+ between**] *I had to decide between paying the rent and paying for health insurance.* | [**decide for yourself**] *Restaurants should be able to decide for themselves* (=make their own choice) *whether to ban smoking.* —see also DECISION (1) **2** [T] if an event, action etc. decides something, it influences events so that one particular result will happen: *A 3-point basket in the final 5 seconds decided the game.* **3 deciding factor** the reason for making a particular decision: *Zimmer's testimony was the deciding factor in the case.* **4 deciding vote** the vote that makes the final decision, because all the other votes are equally divided: *Sen. McCorkle cast the deciding vote for the utilities tax.* **5 decide in favor of sth/decide against sth a)** to choose or not choose someone or something: *The former Longhorns basketball coach has decided in favor of appearing at the annual alumni game.* **b)** if a judge or JURY decides in favor of someone or against someone, they say in court that someone is guilty or not guilty: *The jury decided in favor of the plaintiff.*

decide on sth phr. v. [T] to choose one thing from many possible choices: *Have you decided on a date for your wedding?*

de·cid·ed /dɪˈsaɪdɪd/ adj. [only before noun] definite and easily noticed: *The new color is a decided improvement.*

de·cid·ed·ly /dɪˈsaɪdɪdli/ adv. **1** [+ adj./adv.] definitely or in a way that is easily noticed: *Some*

D

managers were decidedly uneasy about the changes.
2 in a way that shows that you are very sure and
determined about what you want to do: *"I'm not
going to do it," said Margaret decidedly.*

de·cid·u·ous /dɪˈsɪdʒuəs/ *adj.* deciduous trees lose
their leaves in winter —compare EVERGREEN[2]

dec·i·mal[1] /ˈdɛsəməl/ *adj.* a decimal system is based
on the number 10

decimal[2] *n.* [C] TECHNICAL a FRACTION (=a number less
than one) that is shown as a PERIOD followed by the
number of TENTHs, then the number of HUNDREDTHs
etc., for example in the numbers 0.5, 0.175, and 0.661

decimal place /'... ,./ *n.* [C] one of the positions after
a decimal point in a decimal number

decimal point /'... ,./ *n.* [C] the PERIOD in a decimal,
used to separate whole numbers from TENTHs,
HUNDREDTHs etc.

decimal sys·tem /'... ,.../ *n.* [C] a system of counting
that is based on the number 10 —see also DEWEY DEC-
IMAL SYSTEM

dec·i·mate /ˈdɛsəˌmeɪt/ *v.* [T usually passive] to
destroy a large part of something: *Whiteflies have
decimated the winter crop.* —**decimation** /ˌdɛsəˈmeɪ-
ʃən/ *n.* [U]

de·ci·pher /dɪˈsaɪfɚ/ *v.* [T] to find the meaning of
something that is difficult to read or understand:
*Illiterate people may be able to recognize and decipher
signs.* —see also INDECIPHERABLE

de·ci·sion /dɪˈsɪʒən/ *n.* **1** [C] a choice or judgment
that you make after a period of discussion or
thought: *The judges' decision is final.* | [**decision to
do sth**] *Navarro said it was his decision to resign.* |
[**+ about**] *Decisions about medical treatment should
not be based on cost.* | *The committee is due to **make
a decision** this week.* | *The department will make a
final decision this month.* | **tough/hard/difficult
decision** *Leaving my job was a tough decision.* | *The
jury debated for two days before **reaching a deci-
sion**.* | *Moving to New York was a **big decision** (=an
important decision).* **2** [U] the ability someone has
to make choices or judgments quickly and confidently: *This job requires the ability to act with speed
and decision.* —opposite INDECISION **3** [U] the act of
deciding something: *The burden of decision rests with
the Supreme Court.*

de·ci·sion-mak·ing /dɪˈsɪʒənˌmeɪkɪŋ/ *n.* [U] the
process of thinking about a problem, idea etc., and
then making a choice or judgment

de·ci·sive /dɪˈsaɪsɪv/ *adj.* **1** if an action, event, fact
etc. is decisive, it has a strong effect on the final
result of something: *the decisive battle of the war* |
*President Bush said the U.S. needed to **take decisive
action** (=do something to make something
happen).* | *Russia took a **decisive step** toward a
market economy in 1990.* | *The U.N. played a **deci-
sive role** in peace-making.* **2** good at making decisions quickly and with confidence: *a decisive
leader* **3** definite, having a clear result, and not able
to be doubted: *When asked about the possibility, his
answer was a decisive "no."* | *a decisive election vic-
tory* —**decisively** *adv.*

de·ci·sive·ness /dɪˈsaɪsɪvnɪs/ *n.* [U] the ability to
make decisions quickly with confidence and determination

deck[1] /dɛk/ *n.* [C] **1 a)** the outside top level of a ship,
that you can walk on: *I left my cabin and went out **on
deck**.* | *Most crewmen were sleeping **below
deck**.* **b)** one of the levels on a ship, airplane, bus, or
in a sports STADIUM: *a seat on the upper deck* **2** a
wooden floor built out from the back of a house,
where you can sit and relax —see picture on page
423 **3** a set of playing cards: *Let's open a new **deck of
cards**.* **4 cassette/tape/game etc. deck** a machine
into which you can put music TAPES, games etc.: *a
Nintendo game deck* **5 on deck** if a baseball player
is on deck, they have the next chance to hit the ball
—see also **clear the decks** (CLEAR[2] (17)), FLIGHT DECK,
hit the ground/deck/dirt (HIT[1] (24)), ON-DECK CIRCLE

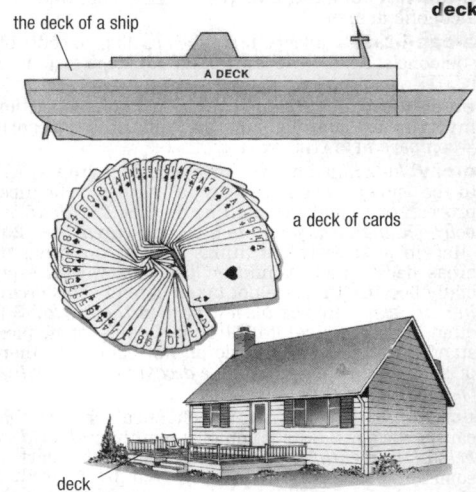

the deck of a ship

deck

A DECK

a deck of cards

deck

deck[2] *v.* [T] **1** also **deck sth ↔ out** [usually passive]
to decorate something with flowers, flags etc., especially for a special occasion: [**+ in**] *The altar was
decked in yellow flowers.* | [**+ with**] *The bridge is
decked out with lights during Christmas.* **2** SLANG to
hit someone so hard that they fall over: *Bill decked a
drunk guy who spilled his drink on Bobbie.*

deck sb out *phr. v.* [T usually passive] to dress in
fashionable clothes or to dress in a certain style of
clothes for a special occasion: [**+ in**] *Armstrong was
decked out in a leopard-skin toga.*

deck chair /'. ./ *n.* [C] a folding chair with a long seat
made of cloth, used especially on the beach

deck·hand /ˈdɛkhænd/ *n.* [C] someone who does
unskilled work on a ship

deck shoe /'. ./ *n.* [C] a flat shoe made of CANVAS
(=heavy cloth), with a rubber bottom

de·claim /dɪˈkleɪm/ *v.* [I,T] FORMAL to speak loudly,
sometimes with actions, so that people will notice
you —**declamation** /ˌdɛkləˈmeɪʃən/ *n.* [C,U]

de·clam·a·to·ry /dɪˈklæməˌtɔri/ *adj.* FORMAL a
declamatory speech or piece of writing expresses
your feelings and opinions very strongly

dec·la·ra·tion /ˌdɛkləˈreɪʃən/ *n.* [C,U] **1** an impor-
tant official statement: *a ceasefire declaration* | [**+ of**]
Congress issued a declaration of war. **2** an official
document giving information, especially about your
taxes or the things you are bringing into the country: *a customs declaration* **3** a statement strongly
expressing an idea or belief: [**+ of**] *Several audience
members responded by shouting declarations of love
for Martin.*

de·clar·a·tive /dɪˈklærətɪv, -ˈklɛr-/ *adj.* TECHNICAL a
declarative sentence has the form of a statement,
rather than a question

de·clare /dɪˈklɛr/ *v.*
1 **say officially** [T] to say officially and publicly
that a particular situation exists or that something
is true: *Severe flooding prompted the governor to
declare a state of emergency Tuesday.* | [**declare
that**] *Doctors declared that Maxwell died of natural
causes.* | [**declare sb/sth (to be) sth**] *Officials
declared Jackson the winner of the race.* | [**declare
yourself (to be) sth**] *Harris publicly declared herself
a candidate for governor.* | *Since the jury could not
make a decision, Judge Garcia was forced to **declare
a mistrial** (=state officially that a trial must be done
again).* | **declare sth illegal/unsafe/open etc.**
Police declared the protest illegal. | **declare sb dead/
unfit/insane etc.** *Burrus was declared dead at the
scene.*
2 declare independence to state officially that a
country or an area of a country is not ruled by any
other country: *The United States declared its independence from Britain in 1776.*

3 declare war (on sb) a) to decide and state officially that you will begin fighting another country **b)** to say that you will do everything you can to stop something that is bad or wrong: *The time has come to declare war on cancer.*
4 say what you think/feel [T] to say very clearly and publicly what you think or feel: *A majority of Republicans declared their support for the bill.* | [declare that] *Kerry declared that she knew the Sharks would win.*
5 money/property etc. [T] to make an official statement saying how much money you have earned, what property you own etc.: *All investment income must be declared on your 1040 tax form.*
6 declare bankruptcy to state officially that you are unable to pay your debts: *Richmond Unified School District was forced to declare bankruptcy.*
7 (Well) I declare! SPOKEN OLD-FASHIONED used as an expression of surprise —**declarable** *adj.*
　　declare for sth *phr. v.* [T] to state publicly that you are going to take part in an election etc.: *Toledo provided a list of the players who have declared for the draft so far.*

de·clared /dɪˈklɛrd/ *adj.* **declared policy/intention/wish etc.** a policy, intention, wish etc. that you have stated publicly: *Our declared policy is to help the refugees return to the south.*

de·clas·si·fied /diˈklæsəˌfaɪd/ *adj.* official information that is declassified was secret but is not secret anymore: *According to declassified government documents, officials were aware of the tests as early as 1967.* —**declassify** *v.* [T]

de·clen·sion /dɪˈklɛnʃən/ *n.* [C] TECHNICAL **1** the set of various forms that a noun, PRONOUN, or adjective can have according to whether it is the SUBJECT[1] (5), OBJECT[1] (5) etc. of a sentence in a language such as Latin or German **2** a particular set of nouns etc. that all have the same type of these forms

de·cline[1] /dɪˈklaɪn/ *v.*
1 become less [I,T] to decrease in quantity or importance: *Computer sales declined 2.1 percent this year.* | *Riker, a radio preacher, saw his popularity decline after World War II.*
2 say no [I,T] FORMAL to refuse when someone invites you somewhere, offers you something, or wants you to do something: *Ed asked me to run the new division for them, but I declined.* | *The pilot declined medical treatment after the accident.* | [decline to do sth] *FBI Agent Moran declined to comment.* —see Usage Note at REFUSE[1]
3 become worse [I] to become gradually worse in quality: *Water quality is declining due to too many dams and pumps.* | *Lambeth has been in declining health for several months.*
4 sb's declining years FORMAL the last years of someone's life
5 grammar TECHNICAL **a)** [I] if a noun, PRONOUN, or adjective declines, its form changes according to whether it is the SUBJECT[1] (5), OBJECT[1] (5) etc. of a sentence **b)** [T] if you decline a noun etc., you show these various forms that it can take

decline[2] *n.* [C usually singular, U] a gradual decrease in the quality, quantity, or importance of something: *Stock markets in Europe showed similar declines.* | [+ of] *Illegal hunting is leading to the decline of some birds.* | [+ in] *a decline in exports* | *During the last ten years, the construction industry has been in decline.*

de·code /diˈkoʊd/ *v.* **1** to translate a secret or complicated message, some DATA, or a signal into a form that can be easily understood: *The Allies were able to decode many enemy messages.* **2** TECHNICAL to understand the meaning of a word rather than use a word to express meaning —opposite ENCODE

de·cod·er /diˈkoʊdɚ/ *n.* [C] **1** a special machine that translates messages, DATA, or signals into a form that can be understood by people or used by another machine **2** a person who decodes secret messages

dé·col·le·tage /deɪˌkɑləˈtɑʒ/ *n.* [U] the top edge of a woman's dress that is cut very low to show part of her shoulders and breasts —**décolleté** /deɪˌkɑləˈteɪ/ *adj.*

de·col·o·nize /diˈkɑləˌnaɪz/ *v.* [T] to make a former COLONY politically independent —**decolonization** /diˌkɑlənəˈzeɪʃən/ *n.* [U]

de·com·mis·sion /ˌdikəˈmɪʃən/ *v.* [T] to officially stop using something such as a ship, airplane, or weapon and take it apart

de·com·pose /ˌdikəmˈpoʊz/ *v.* [I,T] **1** to decay, or to make something decay: *Diapers don't decompose in landfills.* | *A partly decomposed body was found late Saturday.* **2** TECHNICAL to divide into smaller parts, or to make something do this —**decomposition** /ˌdikɑmpəˈzɪʃən/ *n.* [U]

de·com·press /ˌdikəmˈprɛs/ *v.* **1** [I,T] to reduce the pressure of air on something: *The fire caused the plane's cabin to decompress.* **2** [T] TECHNICAL to do an operation on a computer that changes stored DATA into a normal form so that a computer can use it: *Most Macintosh computers can decompress files automatically.* —**decompression** /ˌdikəmˈprɛʃən/ *n.* [U]

decompression cham·ber /..ˈ.. ˌ../ *n.* [C] a special room where people go after they have been deep under water, in order to return slowly to normal air pressure

decompression sick·ness /..ˈ.. ˌ../ *n.* [U] a dangerous medical condition that people get when they come up from deep under water too quickly; the BENDS

de·con·gest·ant /ˌdikənˈdʒɛstənt/ *n.* [C,U] medicine that you can take if you are sick that will help you breathe more easily

de·con·struc·tion /ˌdikənˈstrʌkʃən/ *n.* [U] TECHNICAL a method used in PHILOSOPHY and the criticism of literature that says there can be no single explanation of the meaning of a piece of writing —**deconstructionism** *n.* [U] —**deconstructionist** *n.* [C] —**deconstructionist** *adj.* —**deconstruct** /ˌdikənˈstrʌkt/ *v.* [T]

de·con·tam·i·nate /ˌdikənˈtæməˌneɪt/ *v.* [T] to remove a dangerous substance from somewhere: *Workers are continuing to decontaminate the nuclear plant where the accident occurred.* —**decontamination** /ˌdikənˌtæməˈneɪʃən/ *n.* [U]

de·cor, décor /ˈdeɪkɔr, deɪˈkɔr/ *n.* [C,U] the way that the inside of a building is decorated: *The restaurant's decor is clean and contemporary.*

decorate

dec·o·rate /ˈdɛkəˌreɪt/ *v.* [T] **1** to make something look more attractive by putting something pretty on it: *Sliced kiwi fruit may be used to decorate the dessert.* | [+ with] *Christmas trees were decorated with ornaments and lights.* **2** to give someone a MEDAL as an official sign of honor: [+ for] *Charles Chappell, a wounded veteran, was decorated for heroism.*

dec·o·ra·tion /ˌdɛkəˈreɪʃən/ *n.* **1** [C usually plural] something pretty that you put on something else in order to make it more attractive: *Christmas tree decorations* **2** [U] the way in which something is decorated: *Liz studied design and interior decoration.* | *Thin slices of orange or lemon can be used for decoration.* **3** [C] something such as a MEDAL that is given to someone as an official sign of honor

dec·o·ra·tive /ˈdɛkərətɪv/ *adj.* pretty or attractive, but not always necessary or useful: *Cut out decorative shapes with a cookie cutter.* —**decoratively** *adv.*

dec·o·ra·tor /ˈdɛkəˌreɪtəʳ/ *n.* [C] someone whose profession is to chose furniture, WALLPAPER, CARPET etc. for houses, offices etc.

dec·o·rous /ˈdɛkərəs, dɪˈkɔrəs/ *adj.* FORMAL having the correct appearance or behavior for a particular occasion —**decorously** *adv.*

de·cor·um /dɪˈkɔrəm/ *n.* [U] FORMAL behavior that shows respect and is correct for a particular occasion: *Chauvin lacks a sense of decorum in professional matters.*

de·coy /ˈdikɔɪ/ *n. plural* **decoys** [C] **1** someone or something used to trick someone into going where you want them to go so that you can catch them, attack them etc.: *Officer Jane Langlois acted as a decoy to catch the rapist.* **2** a model of a bird used to attract wild birds so that you can watch them or shoot them —**decoy** /dɪˈkɔɪ/ *v.* [T]

de·crease¹ /dɪˈkris, ˈdikris/ *v.* [I,T] to become less in number, size, or amount, or to make something do this: *Sales in Japan decreased last quarter.* | *Birth control pills decrease the chances of getting pregnant.* —**decreasing** *adj.* —opposite INCREASE¹

de·crease² /ˈdikris/ *n.* [C] the process of reducing something, or the amount by which it reduces: [+ **in**] *Some illnesses cause a decrease in appetite.* | *a 19% decrease in prices*

de·cree¹ /dɪˈkri/ *n.* [C] **1** an official command or decision, especially one made by the ruler of a country: *The president issued a decree imposing a curfew on the capital city.* **2** a judgment in a court of law: *a court decree*

decree² *v.* [T] to make an official judgment or give an official command: [**decree that**] *The council decreed that leaf blowers could not exceed a certain noise level.*

de·crep·it /dɪˈkrɛpɪt/ *adj.* old and in bad condition: *decrepit wooden benches* —**decrepitude** *n.* [U]

de·crim·i·nal·ize /diˈkrɪmənəˌlaɪz/ *v.* [T] to reduce or remove the punishment for doing a particular illegal thing: *The chief of police believes marijuana use should be decriminalized.* —**decriminalization** /diˌkrɪmənələˈzeɪʃən/ *n.* [U] —compare LEGALIZE

de·cry /dɪˈkraɪ/ *v.* **decries, decried, decrying** [T] FORMAL to state publicly that you do not approve of something: *Loisel decried the election results.*

ded·i·cate /ˈdɛdəˌkeɪt/ *v.* [T] **1 a)** to say that something such as a book has been written, made, or sung to express love, respect etc. for someone: [**dedicate sth to sb**] *Greene dedicated the book to his mother.* **b)** to state in an official ceremony that something, especially a building, will be given someone's name in order to show respect for them: [**dedicate sth to sb**] *Murphy Hall is dedicated to one of the university's chancellors.* **2 dedicate yourself/ your life to sth** to decide to spend all your time on and put all your efforts into one particular thing: *Benavides dedicated himself to preserving Peru's environment.*

ded·i·cat·ed /ˈdɛdəˌkeɪtɪd/ *adj.* **1** someone who is dedicated works very hard at what they do because they care a lot about it: *Richard is a dedicated golfer.* | [+ **to**] *A group dedicated to saving nature celebrated by planting an oak tree.* **2** [only before noun] made or used for only one particular purpose: *One computer must be set aside as a dedicated network server.*

ded·i·ca·tion /ˌdɛdɪˈkeɪʃən/ *n.* **1** [U] the hard work or effort that someone puts into a particular activity because they care about it a lot: *I was impressed by LeMel's dedication in high school.* | [+ **to**] *Franklin was named "Man of the Year" for his dedication to community activities.* **2** [C] an act or ceremony of dedicating something to someone **3** [C] the words used in dedicating something to someone

de·duce /dɪˈdus/ *v.* [T] FORMAL to make a judgment about something, based on the information that you have: [**deduce that**] *Thompson deduced that the buyer was trying to increase the stock price.* | [**deduce sth from sth**] *The physical and chemical properties of the stars can be deduced from the data.* —**deducible** *adj.*

de·duct /dɪˈdʌkt/ *v.* [T] to take away an amount or part from a total; SUBTRACT: *Self-employed business owners could deduct all health insurance costs.* | [**deduct sth from sth**] *If you pay for repairs, you can deduct the cost from your rent.*

de·duct·i·ble¹ /dɪˈdʌktəbəl/ *adj.* an amount of money is deductible if you are allowed to subtract it from the amount of money you must pay taxes on: *Contributions to the American Cancer Society are tax-deductible.*

deductible² *n.* [C] the amount of money that you must pay a hospital, car repair shop etc. before your insurance company will pay the rest of the bill: *My health insurance policy has a $200 deductible.*

de·duc·tion /dɪˈdʌkʃən/ *n.* [C,U] **1** the process of making a judgment about something, based on the information that you have: *The game teaches children logic and deduction.* **2** the process of taking away an amount from a total, or the amount that is taken away: *The standard tax deduction* (=amount of money you do not have to pay taxes on) *for unmarried people is $3,600.*

de·duc·tive /dɪˈdʌktɪv/ *adj.* using the knowledge that you have in order to make a judgment about a fact or situation: *deductive reasoning*

deed /did/ *n.* [C] **1** LITERARY something that you do, especially something that is very good or very bad: *Parents can teach children their values by word and deed* (=by what they say and do). **2** LAW an official paper that is a record of an agreement, especially an agreement concerning who owns property: *My grandfather signed the deed for this land.* **3 your good deed for the day** HUMOROUS the one kind or helpful thing that you do during a day **4 in deed** according to what you do: *Schneider is known for his tireless political activism in deed and in word.*

deem /dim/ *v.* [T not in progressive] FORMAL to think of or consider something in a particular way | **deem sth appropriate/necessary/acceptable etc.** *Judges are free to give whatever punishment they deem appropriate.* [**deem that**] *The mission will be canceled if officials deem that the risks are too great.*

deep

shallow

deep

deep¹ /dip/ *adj.*

1 ▶**going far down**◀ going far down from the top or from the surface: *Snowboarders like deep snow.* | **5 inches/7 feet etc. deep** *The river is 40 feet deep in the middle.*

2 ▶**going far in**◀ going far in from the outside or from the front edge of something: *George got a deep cut on his arm in the accident.* | *a shelf 3 feet long and 8 inches deep*

3 ▶**feeling/belief**◀ a deep feeling or belief is very strong and usually sincere: *Tommy inherited his deep faith in God from his mother.* | *I grew up with this deep hatred for authority figures.*

4 ▶**sound**◀ a deep sound is very low: *Jones has a strong deep voice.*

5 ▶**color**◀ a deep color is dark and strong: *The women's uniforms are a deep blue-green.* —compare LIGHT² (1), PALE¹ (2)

6 breath a deep breath involves taking a lot of air into your lungs, especially before doing something difficult or after something upsetting has happened: *It's okay, just relax, take a deep breath.*

7 serious a) someone who is deep or has deep thoughts thinks very hard about things, often in a way that other people find difficult to understand: *Hal seems to be a very deep, sensitive type of person.* **b)** a deep book, conversation, thought etc. involves serious, complicated, or mysterious subjects that are often difficult to understand: *a deep conversation about religion*

8 deep sleep if someone is in a deep sleep it is difficult to wake them: *Finally, her mother fell into a deep sleep.*

9 be in deep trouble also **be in deep shit/doo-doo** SLANG to be in a bad or difficult situation, especially because you have done something wrong or stupid: *Everyone agrees this city is in deep financial trouble.*

10 in deep water in a difficult or serious situation, or in a situation where someone is angry with you

11 deep in thought/conversation etc. thinking so hard, talking so much, or paying so much attention to something that you do not notice anything else that is happening around you: *Moore was deep in prayer.*

12 go off the deep end INFORMAL to suddenly become crazy, angry, or violent: *Sara really went off the deep end and started taking drugs and stuff.* **—deepness** *n.* [U] —see also DEPTH

deep² *adv.* **1** [always + adv./prep.] a long way into or below the surface of something: [+ **down/below/inside** etc.] *She pushed her stick deep down into the mud.* | *With his flashlight, the fireman could see the boy deep inside the hole.* | *I work as a ranger* **deep in the woods** *of northern Maine.* **2 deep down a)** if you know or feel something deep down, that is what you really feel or know even though you do not admit it: *I always believed deep down that things would get better.* **b)** if someone is good, evil etc. deep down, that is what they are really like even though they usually hide it: *I regret my divorce, because deep down I'm a very old-fashioned woman.* **3 deep in debt** owing a lot of money: *After my surgery, we were deep in debt with doctor bills.* **4 run/go deep** if a feeling such as hatred or anger runs deep, you feel it very strongly, especially because of things that have happened in the past: *Bitterness runs deep among Kathy's family members.* —see also **still waters run deep** (STILL² (4)) **5 be in (too) deep** INFORMAL to be very involved in a situation, especially one that causes you problems: *I'm in too deep to get out of the business now.* **6 two/three/four etc. deep** if things or people are two, three, four etc. deep, there are two, three, four etc rows or layers of things or people: *People were packed ten deep along the parade route.* **7 deep into the night** until very late: *They talked deep into the night.*

deep³ *n.* **the deep** POETICAL the ocean

-deep /dip/ [in adjectives] **knee-deep/ankle-deep/ waist-deep etc.** deep enough to come up to your knees, ankles, waist etc.: *Kids waded barefoot through the knee-deep water.*

deep·en /'dipən/ *v.* [I,T] **1** if a serious situation deepens or something deepening it, it gets worse: *The recession may deepen still further.* | *Some principals worry that the decision will deepen divisions between rich and poor schools.* **2** if a feeling or relationship deepens or someone deepens it, it gradually becomes stronger: *The agreement will deepen the firm's ties to Japan's electronics companies.* **3** if you deepen your knowledge or understanding of something, you learn more about it and understand it better: *Traveling allows young people to deepen their understanding of other cultures.* **4** if a color deepens or you deepen it, it becomes or is made darker: *The natural fabric's color deepens over time.* **5** if a sound deepens or you deepen it, it becomes lower: *Johnny tried to deepen his voice to sound like a grown-up.* **6** if a body of water such as a river or stream deepens or someone deepens it, it is or is made deeper at a particular place: *The river deepens five feet from the shore.*

deep freeze /ˌ. './ *n.* [C] **1** a large metal box in which food can be stored at very low temperatures for a long time; FREEZER **2** very cold weather: *The surprise deep freeze brought temperatures of -20°.* **3 in a/the deep freeze a)** if something such as a piece of work is in the deep freeze, it is delayed or stopped for a period of time: *The movie was in the deep freeze for almost a year.* **b)** used to describe a difficult relationship between countries, especially when there is very little communication: *U.S.–Cuban relations have been in the deep freeze for years.*

deep-fry /ˈ. ./ *v.* [T] to cook food in a lot of hot oil **—deep-fried** *adj.*

deep·ly /ˈdipli/ *adv.* **1** used to emphasize that a belief, feeling, opinion etc. is very strong, serious, important, or sincere: *I am deeply honored.* | *Wood is a deeply religious man.* | *Congress is deeply concerned about unemployment.* **2** a long way into something, or a long way below the surface: *The daffodil bulbs were planted too deeply.* **3 breathe deeply** to completely fill your lungs with air **4 sleep deeply** to sleep very well

deep-pock·et·ed /ˌ. 'ˌ...◂/ *adj.* having a lot of money to spend: *the deep-pocketed tobacco industry*

deep-root·ed /ˌ. 'ˌ..◂/ also **deeply rooted** /ˌ... 'ˌ..◂/ *adj.* a deep-rooted habit, idea, belief etc. is so strong in a person or society that it is very difficult to change: *Collins has had to deal with deep-rooted prejudice against him.*

deep-seat·ed /ˌ. 'ˌ..◂/ *adj.* a deep-seated attitude, feeling, or idea is strong and is very difficult to change: *Many people in the community have a deep-seated distrust of the police.*

deep-set /ˌ. 'ˌ.◂/ *adj.* deep-set eyes seem to be farther back into the face than most people's

deep-six /ˌ. './ *v.* [T] INFORMAL to decide not to use something and to get rid of it: *Ritter finally deep-sixed his '70s comedy image with this fine dramatic performance.*

Deep South /ˌ. './ *n.* **the Deep South** the southeastern part of the U.S., including Alabama, Georgia, Mississippi, Louisiana, and South Carolina

deer /dɪr/ *n. plural* **deer** [C] a large wild animal that lives in forests, can run very fast, and has a short tail. The male has long horns that look like tree branches

Deere /dɪr/**, John** (1804–1886) the U.S. inventor of a new kind of PLOW

deer·stalk·er /ˈdɪrˌstɔkɚ/ *n.* [C] a type of soft hat with pieces of cloth that cover your ears

def /def/ *adj.* SLANG fashionable and attractive; COOL: *Hey, check out that def car.*

de·face /dɪˈfeɪs/ *v.* [T] to damage the surface or appearance of something, especially by writing or making marks on it: *Several office buildings were defaced by graffiti.* **—defacement** *n.* [U]

de fac·to /dɪ ˈfæktoʊ, di-/ *adj.* actually existing or happening without being approved of legally or formally: *Hyland is the department's de facto director.* **—de facto** *adv.* —compare DE JURE

def·a·ma·tion /ˌdɛfəˈmeɪʃən/ *n.* [U] FORMAL writing or saying something that makes people have a bad opinion about someone or something: *King is suing the show's producers for* **defamation of character**.

de·fame /dɪˈfeɪm/ *v.* [T] FORMAL to write or say something that makes people have an bad opinion of someone or something: *Religious leaders say the novel defames Islam.* **—defamatory** /dɪˈfæmətɔri/ *adj.*

de·fault¹ /dɪˈfɔlt/ *n.* **1 by default a)** if something happens by default, it happens because someone did not make a decision or take action: *The dollar is benefiting by default from the weakness of the yen.* **b)** if you win a game, competition etc. by default, you win because your opponent did not play or there were no other competitors **2** [C,U] FORMAL failure to do something that you are supposed to do according to the law or because it is your duty, especially not paying back money you borrowed: *The state government will pay off the mortgage in the event of a default.* | *The loan* is *in default.* **3** [C] TECHNICAL the way in which things will be arranged on a computer screen unless you decide to change them: *the default settings for my printer* **4 in default of sth** FORMAL because of the lack or absence of something: *A woman could inherit the throne in default of male heirs.*

default² *v.* [I] to not do something that you are legally supposed to, especially not to pay money you are supposed to pay: [+ **on**] *More than 35% of students defaulted on their loans.* —**defaulter** *n.* [C]

s w de·feat¹ /dɪˈfiːt/ *n.* **1** [C,U] failure to win or succeed: *an election defeat* | *Even in defeat, the Sandinistas are important politically in Nicaragua.* —see also **admit defeat** (ADMIT (6)) **2** [U] victory over someone or something: [+ **of**] *World leaders were pleased with the defeat of the military coup.* —opposite VICTORY

defeat² *v.* [T] **1** to win a victory over someone in a war, competition, game etc.; BEAT¹ (1): *In 1692, de Tourville's fleet was defeated near the coast of Cherbourg.* | [**defeat sb by 10 points/three runs etc.**] *Georgia defeated Fullerton State by 13 points.* —compare WIN¹ (1), BEAT¹ (1) **2** if something defeats you, you cannot understand it and therefore cannot deal with it: *Normally my hearing loss isn't a problem, but the telephone defeats me.* **3** to make something fail: *It was a lack of money, not effort, that defeated their plan.* —see Usage Note at WIN¹

de·feat·ist /dɪˈfiːtɪst/ *adj.* believing that you will not succeed: *a defeatist attitude* —**defeatist** *n.* [C] —**defeatism** *n.* [U]

def·e·cate /ˈdɛfəˌkeɪt/ *v.* [I] FORMAL to get rid of waste matter from your body out of your ANUS —**defecation** /ˌdɛfəˈkeɪʃən/ *n.* [U]

de·fect¹ /ˈdiːfɛkt/ *n.* [C] a fault or a lack of something that means that something is not perfect: *All the cars are tested for defects before they leave the factory.* | *a birth defect* —compare DEFECTIVE (1)

de·fect² /dɪˈfɛkt/ *v.* [I] to leave your own country or a group in order to go to or join an opposing one: [+ **from/to**] *Baryshnikov defected from the USSR in 1974.* —**defector** *n.* [C] —**defection** /dɪˈfɛkʃən/ *n.* [C,U]

de·fec·tive /dɪˈfɛktɪv/ *adj.* **1** not made correctly, or not working correctly: *Merchants will give refunds on any damaged or defective merchandise.* **2** TECHNICAL **defective verb** a verb such as "must" or "can" that cannot be used in all the forms that a verb can usually be used in —**defectively** *adv.* —**defectiveness** *n.* [U]

de·fence /dɪˈfɛns/ *n.* the British and Canadian spelling of DEFENSE¹

s w de·fend /dɪˈfɛnd/ *v.* **1** [I,T] to do something in order to protect someone or something from being attacked: [+ **against/from**] *The army's forces are the minimum needed to defend against an attack.* | *There is no longer a need to defend Europe against a Soviet invasion.* | [**defend yourself**] *Villagers have few weapons to defend themselves.* **2** [T] to use arguments to protect something or someone from criticism, or to prove that something is right: *Cox moved quickly to defend her record as state senator.* | [**defend sb/sth against sth**] *Hendricks defended himself against the charges.* **3** [I,T] to protect your GOAL in a sports game, to prevent your opponents from getting points **4** [T] to be a lawyer for someone who has been charged with a crime: *Freis defended a local radio station in a discrimination suit.* —compare PROSECUTE (2) **5** to do something in order to stop something from being taken away or in order to make it possible for something to continue: *The union said they would take action to defend their members' jobs.* **6 defend a title/championship** to take part in or win a competition that you won the last time it was held: *Tish Johnson will defend her title at next week's bowling championships.*

de·fend·ant /dɪˈfɛndənt/ *n.* [C] the person in a court of law who has been ACCUSEd of doing something illegal —compare PLAINTIFF

de·fend·er /dɪˈfɛndɚ/ *n.* [C] **1** one of the players in a sports game who have to defend their team's GOAL from the opposing team **2 a defender of the poor/of liberty/of privilege etc.** someone who defends a particular idea, belief, person etc. —see also PUBLIC DEFENDER

de·fense¹ /dɪˈfɛns/ *n.*

1 protecting **a)** [U] the act of protecting something or someone from attack or destruction: *Several people witnessed the attack, but no one came to her defense.* | *Sergeant Trapp said the officers fired at Clark in defense of their own lives.* —see also SELF-DEFENSE **b)** [C] something that can be used to protect someone or something against attack or destruction: [+ **against**] *Fire extinguishers are a good defense against small fires.*

2 military **a)** [U] all the systems, people, weapons etc. that a country uses to protect itself from attack: *the Department of Defense* | *There are plans to increase defense spending* (=money spent on weapons and armies) *by 6%.* **b) defenses** [plural] all the military forces and weapons that are available to defend a place: *The country plans to strengthen its defenses along the northern border.*

3 against criticism [C,U] something that you say or do in order to protect someone or something from criticism: *Senator Stevens spoke in defense of the bill to make handguns illegal.*

4 in a law court **a)** [C,U] the things that are said in a court of law to prove that someone is not guilty of a crime: *Martin decided to speak in his own defense.* | [+ **against**] *Medical necessity is not a defense against charges of marijuana-related crimes.* **b) the defense** all the people who are concerned with showing in a court of law that someone is not guilty of a crime: *The defense is relying largely on the testimony of Hernandez.* —compare PROSECUTION (1)

5 against illness [C] something that your body produces naturally as a way of preventing illness: [+ **against**] *Antibodies are the body's defense against disease.*

6 emotions [C] something you do or a way of behaving that prevents you from being upset or seeming weak: [+ **against**] *Mary Jo's religion gives her a defense against despair.*

de·fense² /ˈdiːfɛns/ *n.* [C,U] the players in a sports team whose main job is to try to prevent the other team from getting points: *Taylor plays defense for the New York Giants.* | [+ **against**] *The Eagles have the NFL's top-ranked defense against passing.* —compare OFFENSE²

de·fense·less /dɪˈfɛnslɪs/ *adj.* weak and unable to protect yourself from being hurt or criticized: *Troops fired on defenseless students, killing at least 50.*

defense mech·a·nism /.'. ˌ..../ *n.* [C] **1** a process in your brain that makes you forget things that are painful for you to think about **2** a reaction in your body that protects you from an illness or danger

de·fen·si·ble /dɪˈfɛnsəbəl/ *adj.* **1** a defensible opinion, idea, or action is one that seems reasonable, and you can easily support it: *Cooper believes the plan is fair and legally defensible.* —opposite INDEFENSIBLE **2** a defensible building or area is easy to protect against attack or damage —**defensibly** *adv.*

de·fen·sive¹ /dɪˈfɛnsɪv/ *adj.* **1** used or intended to protect people against attack: *defensive weapons* —compare OFFENSIVE¹ (4) **2** behaving in a way that shows you think someone is criticizing you even if they are not: *It has nothing to do with your work, so don't get defensive.* **3** relating to stopping the other team from getting points in a game: *a defensive player* —compare OFFENSIVE¹ (3) —**defensively** *adv.* —**defensiveness** *n.* [U]

defensive² *n.* **on the defensive** trying to protect yourself because someone is criticizing you: **be/go on the defensive** *The mayor has been on the defensive recently due to the continuing scandals.*

de·fer /dɪˈfɚ/ *v.* **deferred, deferring** [T] to delay something until a later date: *College loan payments are deferred until students finish their degrees.*

defer to sb/sth *phr. v.* [T] FORMAL to agree to accept someone's opinion or decision because you have respect for that person or because they have power over you: *The U.S. military is under civilian control; generals defer to elected leaders.*

def·er·ence /'defərəns/ *n.* [U] FORMAL polite behavior that shows that you respect someone and are willing to accept their opinions, judgment, or beliefs: *Visiting officials were treated with great deference.* | **in deference to sth/out of deference to sth** *In deference to Saudi custom, we cover our arms and wear longer skirts.* —**deferential** /,defə'renʃəl/ *adj.* —**deferentially** *adv.*

de·fi·ance /dɪ'faɪəns/ *n.* [U] behavior that shows you refuse to do what someone tells you to do, especially because you do not respect them: *a look of hatred and defiance* | *Many Americans have visited Cuba in defiance of U.S. law.*

de·fi·ant /dɪ'faɪənt/ *adj.* refusing to do what someone tells you to do, especially because you do not respect them: *"Nothing is going to change," said a defiant Miller after his trial.* —**defiantly** *adv.*

de·fi·cien·cy /dɪ'fɪʃənsi/ *n. plural* **deficiencies** [C,U] **1** a lack of something that is necessary: *Older women can suffer bone loss caused by estrogen deficiency.* **2** a weakness or fault in something: *Over 40% of rental housing contained structural deficiencies.*

de·fi·cient /dɪ'fɪʃənt/ *adj.* **1** not containing or having enough of something: [+ in] *a diet deficient in calcium* **2** not good enough: *As many as 2 million students leave school with deficient basic skills.*

def·i·cit /'defəsɪt/ *n.* [C] the difference between the amount of something that you have and the higher amount that you need: *a budget deficit of $20 million* | *The Chargers overcame a 13-point deficit to win 38–30.*

de·file /dɪ'faɪl/ *v.* [T] FORMAL to make something less pure, good, or holy, especially by showing no respect: *Tombstones in a Jewish cemetery had been defiled.*

de·fine /dɪ'faɪn/ *v.* [T] **1** to describe something correctly and thoroughly, and to say what standards, limits, qualities etc. it has that make it different from other things: *Jeffreys usually selects projects that meet a well-defined need.* | *The powers of the President are clearly defined in the Constitution.* **2** to explain the exact meaning of a particular word or idea: *Each of us might define the concept of freedom in a very different way.* | [**define sth as sth**] *A lie is defined as saying something in order to deceive someone.* | *Virtual reality is loosely defined* (=defined in a way that is less exact) *as putting real people into an environment made by a computer.* **3** to show the edge or shape of something clearly: *Leung draws his pictures with lines that are sharply defined, with clean angles and shadows.* —**definable** *adj.*

def·i·nite /'defənɪt/ *adj.* **1** clearly known, seen, or stated, and very certain: *Both Sally and John had definite ideas about how the new kitchen should look.* | *Jacinta's report card showed a definite improvement in math.* **2** a definite arrangement, promise etc. will happen in the way that someone has said: *The city has finally given a definite date to replace the street light.* | *Dorosin said she doesn't have any definite plans for the future.* **3** used to emphasize what you are saying: *Mark's studies take a definite back seat to football* (=they are not as important to him as football).

definite ar·ti·cle /,... '.../ *n.* [C] **1** the word "the" in English **2** a word in another language that is like "the" —compare INDEFINITE ARTICLE —see also ARTICLE (4)

def·i·nite·ly /'defənɪtli/ *adv.* [sentence adverb] certainly and without any doubt: *It's definitely cold and flu season.* | *According to the data, we can definitely say that pollution is increasing.* —see **of course** (COURSE[1] (1)), SURELY —see Usage Note at CERTAINLY

def·i·ni·tion /,defə'nɪʃən/ *n.* **1** [C] a phrase or sentence that says exactly what a word, phrase, or idea

means: [+ **of**] *What's the correct definition of the word "moot"?* | *It depends on your definition of success.* **2 by definition** if something has a particular quality by definition, it must have that quality because all things of that type have it: *Graffiti, no matter how well painted, is vandalism by definition.* **3** [U] the quality of being clear that something such as a picture or sound has: *This photograph lacks definition* (=is not clear).

de·fin·i·tive /dɪ'fɪnətɪv/ *adj.* **1** [usually before noun] a definitive book, description etc. is considered to be the best and cannot be improved: *She has written the definitive book on the poet Wordsworth.* **2** a definitive statement, VERDICT etc. is one that will not be changed and cannot be doubted —**definitively** *adv.*

de·flate /dɪ'fleɪt, di-/ *v.* **1** [I,T] if a tire, BALLOON, ball etc. deflates or if you deflate it, it gets smaller because the air or gas inside it comes out —opposite INFLATE **2** [T] to make someone feel less important or confident: *Learning new skills can boost egos that were deflated by losing a job.* **3** [T] to show that a statement, argument etc. is wrong: *The report will deflate arguments by city officials that they cannot reduce pollution.* **4** [T] TECHNICAL to change the economic rules or conditions in a country so that prices become lower or stop rising —**deflation** /dɪ'fleɪʃən/ *n.* [U] —compare INFLATE

de·flat·ed /dɪ'fleɪtɪd/ *adj.* feeling less cheerful or confident than before: *During the interview, Zak seemed deflated and shaken by his loss of power.*

de·fla·tion·ar·y /dɪ'fleɪʃə,neri/ *adj.* TECHNICAL causing a situation in which prices fall or stop rising

de·flect /dɪ'flekt/ *v.* **1** [I,T] to turn in a different direction, especially after hitting something else, or to make something do this: *The Stealth bomber is designed to deflect radar waves, making it "invisible."* | *Volek's shot deflected off the goalie's glove and into the goal.* **2 deflect attention/criticism/anger etc.** to stop people from thinking about something, criticizing something, getting angry about something etc.: *Harris deflected questions about the scandal.* **3** [T] to take someone's attention away from something: [**deflect sb from sth**] *Even the recession has not deflected the President's advisers from concentrating on the election.*

de·flec·tion /dɪ'flekʃən/ *n.* [C,U] **1** the action of changing direction after hitting something **2** TECHNICAL the degree to which the moving part on a measuring instrument moves away from zero

de·flow·er /di'flaʊə/ *v.* [T] LITERARY to have sex with a woman who has never had sex before

De·foe /də'foʊ/, **Daniel** (1660–1731) a British writer of NOVELS

de·fog /di'fag/ *v.* **defogged, defogging** [T] to remove the CONDENSATION from the windows inside a car, by using heat or warm air

de·fog·ger /di'fagə/ *n.* [C] a piece of electrical equipment in a car, that defogs the windows

de·fo·li·ant /di'foʊliənt/ *n.* [C,U] a chemical substance used on plants to make their leaves drop off —**defoliate** *v.* [T]

de·for·es·ta·tion /di,fɔrə'steɪʃən/ *n.* [U] the cutting or burning down of all the trees in an area: *Deforestation has been shown to cause floods and drought.* —**deforest** /di'fɔrɪst/ *v.* [T usually passive] —**deforested** *adj.*: *Parts of the Amazon Basin are totally deforested.* —opposite AFFORESTATION

de·form /dɪ'fɔrm/ *v.* [I,T] if you deform something, or if it deforms, its usual shape changes so that the thing's usefulness or appearance is spoiled: *The disease often causes joints to deform.*

de·for·ma·tion /,difɔr'meɪʃən, ,defə-/ *n.* [C,U] a change in the usual shape of something, especially one that makes it worse, or the process of changing something's shape: *deformation of the telescope's mirror*

de·formed /dɪ'fɔrmd/ *adj.* someone or something that is deformed has the wrong shape, especially because they have grown or developed in the wrong way: *a deformed foot*

de·form·i·ty /dɪˈfɔrməti/ *n. plural* **deformities** [C,U] part of someone's body that is not the normal shape, or the condition of having such a body part

de·fraud /dɪˈfrɔd/ *v.* [T] to trick a person or organization in order to get money from them: *Sanders was convicted of conspiracy to defraud the government.* | [**defraud sb/sth (out) of sth**] *He used his television show to defraud his followers of $4.8 million.*

de·fray /dɪˈfreɪ/ *v.* **defrays, defrayed, defraying** [T] **defray costs/expenses etc.** FORMAL to pay someone's costs, expenses etc.: *Donations will help defray costs of the school trip.*

de·frock /ˌdiˈfrɑk/ *v.* [T] to officially remove a priest, minister etc. from their job because they did something wrong —**defrocked** *adj.*

de·frost /dɪˈfrɔst/ *v.* **1** [I,T] if frozen food defrosts, or if you defrost it, it gets warmer until it is not frozen anymore **2** [I,T] if a FREEZER or REFRIGERATOR defrosts, or if you defrost it, it is turned off so that the ice inside it melts **3** [T] to remove ice from the windows of a car by blowing warm air onto them —compare DEFOG

deft /dɛft/ *adj.* **1** skillful at doing something, or showing skill: *The songs demonstrate Costello's deft wordplay.* **2** a deft movement is skillful, and often quick —**deftly** *adv.* —**deftness** *n.* [U]

de·funct /dɪˈfʌŋkt/ *adj.* not existing anymore, or not useful anymore: *Moyer played in the now-defunct Women's Basketball League.*

de·fuse /diˈfyuz/ *v.* [T] **1** to improve a difficult or dangerous situation, for example by making people less angry or by dealing with the causes of a problem: *Diplomats are trying to defuse the situation.* | *A joke can often defuse tension.* **2** to prevent a bomb from exploding

de·fy /dɪˈfaɪ/ *v.* **defies, defied, defying** [T] **1** to refuse to obey someone or something, or to refuse to do what is expected: *This celebration of Thanksgiving defies tradition.* | *Scopes was forbidden to teach Darwin's theory of evolution, but he defied the law.* **2** **defy reason/logic/the odds etc.** to not happen according to the principles you would expect: *The long period without a hurricane in the region defies all odds.* **3** **defy description/understanding/categorization etc.** to be almost impossible to describe, understand, categorize etc.: *The beauty of the scene defies description.* **4** **I defy sb (to do sth)** SPOKEN, FORMAL used when asking someone to do something that you think they cannot or will not do: *I defy anybody to prove otherwise.*

deg. the written abbreviation of DEGREE

De·gas /dɪˈgɑ/, **Ed·gar** /ˈɛdgɚ/ (1834–1917) a French Impressionist painter, known especially for his pictures of horse racing, theaters, CAFEs, and women dancing

de Gaulle /dɪˈgɔl, -ˈgoʊl/, **General Charles** (1890–1970) the President of France between 1959 and 1969

de·gen·er·ate¹ /dɪˈdʒɛnəˌreɪt/ *v.* [I] to become worse: [+ **into**] *These historic buildings have been allowed to degenerate into slums.* —**degeneration** /dɪˌdʒɛnəˈreɪʃən/ *n.* [U]

de·gen·er·ate² /dɪˈdʒɛnərɪt/ *adj.* **1** having very low standards or moral behavior: *a morally degenerate society* **2** FORMAL worse than before in quality: *Expressionism was at one time considered a degenerate form of art.* —**degeneracy** *n.* [U]

degenerate³ *n.* [C] someone whose behavior is considered to be morally unacceptable

de·gen·er·a·tive /dɪˈdʒɛnərətɪv/ *adj.* a degenerative illness gradually gets worse and cannot be stopped

deg·ra·da·tion /ˌdɛgrəˈdeɪʃən/ *n.* **1** [C,U] an experience, situation, or condition that makes you feel ashamed and angry: *a life of poverty and degradation* **2** [U] the process by which something changes to a worse condition **3** [U] TECHNICAL the process by which a substance, chemical etc. changes to a simpler form

de·grade /dɪˈgreɪd, di-/ *v.* **1** [T] to treat someone without respect and make them lose respect for themselves: *Winters says he never intended to degrade women in his movies.* **2** [T] to make a situation or the condition of something worse: *Erosion is degrading the land.* **3** [I,T] TECHNICAL if a substance, chemical etc. degrades, or if something degrades it, it changes to a simpler form: *Black plastic starts to degrade upon exposure to sunlight.* —**degradable** *adj.* —**degradability** /dɪˌgreɪdəˈbɪləti/ *n.* [U]

de·grad·ing /dɪˈgreɪdɪŋ/ *adj.* showing no respect for someone or making them feel very ashamed: *degrading racial comments* | [+ **to**] *Critics of welfare have long said that welfare is degrading to the recipient.*

de·gree /dɪˈgri/ *n.* **1** [C] a unit for measuring temperature or the size of an angle, often represented by the sign (°): *It got down to 27 degrees last night.* | *We had a 360-degree view of the city from the top of the building.* **2** [C,U] the level or amount of something: *To what degree is unemployment society's fault?* | [+ **of**] *All the students have different degrees of ability.* **3** [C] a QUALIFICATION given to someone who has successfully completed a course of study at a college or university: *a law degree* | [+ **in**] *a degree in history* | *Lori has a bachelor's degree from Harvard.* **4** **to a degree** also **to some degree, to a certain degree** partly, or to a particular level: *Kangaroos are trainable to a degree, but they're not as smart as dogs.* **5** **by degrees** very slowly; gradually: *Improvement will come by degrees.* **6** [U] OLD USE your position in society —see FIRST-DEGREE SECOND-DEGREE, THIRD-DEGREE BURN, **to the nth degree** (NTH (1)),

de·hu·man·ize /diˈhyuməˌnaɪz/ *v.* [T often passive] to treat people in a way that makes them not seem to have human qualities: *Terkel says today's society has been dehumanized by technology.* —**dehumanizing** *adj.* —**dehumanization** /diˌhyumənəˈzeɪʃən/ *n.* [U]

de·hu·mid·i·fi·er /ˌdihyuˈmɪdəˌfaɪɚ/ *n.* [C] a machine that removes water from the air in a building —**dehumidify** *v.* [T]

de·hy·drate /diˈhaɪdreɪt/ *v.* **1** [T] to remove all the water from something such as food or chemicals: *The milk is dehydrated and stored as powder.* **2** [I,T] to lose too much water from your body: *High temperatures make people dehydrate very quickly.* —**dehydrated** *adj.* —**dehydration** /ˌdihaɪˈdreɪʃən/ *n.* [U]

de·ice /ˌdiˈaɪs/ *v.* [T] to remove the ice from something, especially an airplane

de·i·fy /ˈdeɪəˌfaɪ, ˈdiə-/ *v.* **deifies, deified, deifying** [T] FORMAL to treat someone or something with a lot of respect and admiration, as if they were a god —**deification** /ˌdeɪəfəˈkeɪʃən/ *n.* [U]

deign /deɪn/ *v.* [T] **deign to do sth** HUMOROUS to agree to do something that you think you are too important to do: *Shelly finally deigned to join us for lunch.*

de·ism /ˈdiɪzəm, ˈdeɪ-/ *n.* [U] the belief in a God who made the world but has no influence on human lives —compare THEISM

de·i·ty /ˈdiəti, ˈdeɪ-/ *n. plural* **deities** [C] **1** a god or GODDESS **2 the Deity** FORMAL God

dé·jà vu /ˌdeɪʒɑ ˈvu/ *n.* [U] the feeling that what is happening now has happened before in exactly the same way: *Fans may have a feeling of déjà vu as they listen to Pauley's new album.*

de·ject·ed /dɪˈdʒɛktɪd/ *adj.* unhappy, disappointed, or sad: *My 12-year-old came home from school red-eyed and dejected.* —**dejectedly** *adv.* —**dejection** /dɪˈdʒɛkʃən/ *n.* [U]

de ju·re /ˌdi ˈdʒʊreɪ/ *adj.* FORMAL true or right because of a law —compare DE FACTO

De Klerk /dəˈklɛrk, -ˈklɛrk/, **F.W.** (1936–) the President of South Africa from 1989 to 1994 who ended the system of APARTHEID

de Koo·ning /dəˈkunɪŋ, -ˈkoʊ-/, **Wil·lem** /ˈwɪləm/ (1904–1997) a Dutch-American PAINTER famous for his ABSTRACT paintings

De·la·croix /ˌdɛləˈkrwɑ/, **Eu·gène** /yuˈdʒin/ (1798–

1863) a French PAINTER famous for his paintings in the style of ROMANTICISM

Del·a·ware /ˈdɛləˌwɛr/ **1** written abbreviation **DE** a small state in the northeastern U.S. **2** a Native American tribe from the northeastern area of the U.S.

Delaware Riv·er /ˌ... ˈ../ a river in the northeastern U.S. that flows southward from the state of New York to the state of Delaware

de·lay¹ /dɪˈleɪ/ v. **delays, delayed, delaying 1** [I,T] to wait until a later time to do something: *We cannot delay any longer.* | **[delay doing sth]** *The agency said it will delay mailing tax forms until after New Year's Day.* | *The manager wanted to **delay** the bad news **until** after Christmas.* **2** [T often passive] to make someone or something late: *Our flight was delayed by bad weather.* —**delayed** adj.

delay² n. plural **delays 1** [C] a situation in which someone or something is made to wait, or the length of the waiting time: *We went to the court and asked for a delay to continue preparing our defense.* | **[+ of]** *Delays of two hours or more are not uncommon.* | **[a delay in doing sth]** *There was some delay in asking for help.* | *There are **severe delays** on Highway 101 this morning because of an accident.* | **long/short delay** *The storm has caused long delays at some airports.* **2** [U] a situation in which something does not happen or start immediately or when it should: *You need to get those vegetables planted **without delay** (=immediately).* | *The reports will **be subject to delay** (=be likely to be delayed).*

delayed-ac·tion /ˌ.. ˈ..ˌ/ adj. [only before noun] designed to work or start only after a particular period of time has passed: *a delayed-action bomb*

delayed broad·cast /ˌ.. ˈ../ n. [C,U] a concert, sports event etc. that is broadcast on television or radio at a time after it originally happens —compare **live broadcast** (LIVE² (3))

delaying tac·tic /ˈ.. ˌ../ n. [C usually plural] something that you do deliberately to delay something, in order to gain an advantage for yourself

de·lec·ta·ble /dɪˈlɛktəbəl/ adj. FORMAL extremely good to taste, smell etc.: *a delectable chocolate souffle* —**delectably** adv.

de·lec·ta·tion /ˌdilɛkˈteɪʃən/ n. [U] FORMAL enjoyment, pleasure, or amusement

del·e·gate¹ /ˈdɛləgɪt/ n. [C] someone who has been elected or chosen to speak, vote, or make decisions for a group: *Delegates from 50 colleges met to discuss the issue of financial aid.*

del·e·gate² /ˈdɛləˌgeɪt/ v. **1** [I,T] to give part of your work or the things you are responsible for to someone in a lower position than you: *A good manager knows when to delegate.* | **[delegate sth to sb]** *McConnell delegated authority to the department heads.* **2** [T] to choose someone to do a particular job, or to be a representative of a group, organization etc.: **[delegate sb to do sth]** *We were delegated to represent our club at the state conference.*

dejected

del·e·ga·tion /ˌdɛləˈgeɪʃən/ n. **1** [C] a group of people who represent a company, organization etc.: *Kemp met with the California delegation on Monday afternoon.* **2** [U] the process of giving power or work

to someone else, so that they are responsible for part of what you normally do: *the delegation of authority*

de·lete /dɪˈlit/ v. [T] **1** to remove a letter, word etc. from a piece of writing: *Matt's name was deleted from the list.* **2** to remove a piece of information from a computer's memory: *I deleted that whole file by mistake.*

del·e·te·ri·ous /ˌdɛləˈtɪriəs/ adj. FORMAL damaging or harmful: *the deleterious effects of smoking*

de·le·tion /dɪˈliʃən/ n. **1** [U] the act or process of removing something from a piece of writing or a computer's memory **2** [C] a letter or word that has been removed from a piece of writing

del·i /ˈdɛli/ n. [C] a small store that sells cheese, cooked meat, SALADS, breads etc.

de·lib·er·ate¹ /dɪˈlɪbrɪt, -bərɪt/ adj. **1** intended or planned: *I believe this was a deliberate attempt to mislead the court.* **2** deliberate speech, thought, or movement is slow and careful: *Cirasola's style was very different from Perry's slow, deliberate manner of speaking.* —**deliberateness** n. [U]

de·lib·er·ate² /dɪˈlɪbəˌreɪt/ v. [I,T] to think about something very carefully: *The jury deliberated for three days before finding him guilty.* | **[+ about/on/over]** *Six committees deliberate on the defense budget each year.*

de·lib·er·ate·ly /dɪˈlɪbrɪtli/ adv. **1** done in a way that is intended or planned: *Somebody deliberately released the brakes and headed the truck downhill.* | *There were no signs that the fire had been set deliberately.* **2** done or said in a slow, careful way: *Tom paused deliberately before continuing.*

de·lib·er·a·tion /dɪˌlɪbəˈreɪʃən/ n. **1** [C usually plural, U] careful consideration or discussion of something: *The council concluded its deliberations on Monday.* | **After much deliberation**, *Diana decided to resign.* **2** [U] if you speak or move with deliberation, you speak or move slowly and carefully

de·lib·er·a·tive /dɪˈlɪbəˌreɪtɪv, -brətɪv/ adj. existing for the purpose of discussing or planning something

del·i·ca·cy /ˈdɛlɪkəsi/ n. plural **delicacies 1** [C] something good to eat that is expensive or rare: *Abalone are considered a delicacy in many fish restaurants.* **2** [U] a careful and sensitive way of speaking or behaving so that you do not upset anyone; TACT: *The issue is being handled with extreme delicacy.* **3** [U] the quality of being easy to harm, damage, or break: *a sculpture of great delicacy and subtlety*

del·i·cate /ˈdɛlɪkɪt/ adj. **1** easily damaged or broken; FRAGILE (1): *The delicate blossoms resemble lace.* **2** needing to be dealt with carefully or sensitively in order to avoid problems or failure: *The delicate operation took more than six hours.* **3** a part of the body that is delicate is small, attractive, and graceful: *Mrs. Archer extended her delicate hand.* **4** made skillfully and with attention to the smallest details: *The china has a delicate pattern of leaves.* **5** a taste, smell, or color that is delicate is pleasant and not strong: *delicate pinks and blues* **6** OLD-FASHIONED someone who is delicate is hurt easily or becomes sick easily: *Troy was a delicate child who spend most of his time indoors.* —**delicately** adv. —compare INDELICATE

del·i·cates /ˈdɛlɪkɪts/ n. [plural] clothes that are made from material that needs careful treatment

del·i·ca·tes·sen /ˌdɛlɪkəˈtɛsən/ n. [C] a DELI

de·li·cious /dɪˈlɪʃəs/ adj. **1** having a very enjoyable taste or smell: *The chocolate pie was delicious!* **2** LITERARY extremely pleasant or enjoyable: *He waited in delicious anticipation.* —**deliciously** adv.

de·light¹ /dɪˈlaɪt/ n. **1** [U] a feeling of great pleasure and satisfaction: *The kids rushed down to the beach, shrieking **with delight**.* | *The crowd roared **in delight** as the Bears scored.* | **To my delight**, *my first assignment was in Hawaii.* **2** [C] something that makes you feel very happy or satisfied: **[+ of]** *One of the delights of traveling east of Vienna is encountering the older,* *traditional Europe.* **3 take delight in (doing) sth** to enjoy something very much, often something that someone else thinks is not nice: *My dad took delight in calling me "The Big Ox" when I started growing taller than the other girls.*

delight² *v.* [T] to give someone a feeling of satisfaction and enjoyment: *This movie classic will delight the whole family.* | [**delight sb with sth**] *Jordan delighted the crowd with his spectacular talent.*

delight in sth *phr. v.* [T not in passive] to enjoy something very much, especially something that someone else thinks is not nice: *The twins delighted in confusing other people.*

de·light·ed /dɪˈlaɪtɪd/ *adj.* very pleased or happy: *Paul McCartney staged a concert for 50,000 delighted fans.* | [**be delighted to do sth**] *I'm delighted to have finally met you.* | [**delighted (that)**] *We're delighted that you'll be there.* | [+ **with/at**] *They were delighted with the results of the recent elections.* —**delightedly** *adv.*

de·light·ful /dɪˈlaɪtfəl/ *adj.* very nice and pleasant: *a delightful young man* | *This delightful Chianti has complex black cherry and herb flavors.* —**delightfully** *adv.*

deli meat /ˈ.. ˌ./ *n.* [C,U] cooked meat that is cut in the store and sold in SLICES

de·lim·it /dɪˈlɪmɪt/ *v.* [T] FORMAL to decide or say exactly what the limits of something are: *Once you have delimited the topic of your study, it is time to select your research strategy.* —**delimitation** /dɪˌlɪməˈteɪʃən/ *n.* [U]

de·lin·e·ate /dɪˈlɪniˌeɪt/ *v.* [T] FORMAL **1** to describe or draw something carefully so that it is easy to understand: *Kozol's book delineates the differences between urban and suburban schools.* **2** to make the border between two areas very clear: *The smoking section has been clearly delineated.* —**delineation** /dɪˌlɪniˈeɪʃən/ *n.* [U]

de·lin·quen·cy /dɪˈlɪŋkwənsi/ *n. plural* **delinquencies** **1** [U] illegal or socially unacceptable behavior, especially by young people: *Learning difficulties can often lead to juvenile delinquency and poor school performance.* **2** [C] FORMAL a debt that has not been paid on time

de·lin·quent¹ /dɪˈlɪŋkwənt/ *adj.* **1** a delinquent debt, account, LOAN etc. has not been paid when it should have been paid: *The federal government hopes to increase its collection of delinquent taxes.* **2** behaving in a way that is illegal or that society does not approve of: *Jail is not a good place to rehabilitate delinquent youths.*

delinquent² *n.* [C] someone, especially a young person, who breaks the law or behaves in ways their society does not approve of: *More than half of all juvenile delinquents have family members who have committed crimes.*

de·lir·i·ous /dɪˈlɪriəs/ *adj.* **1** confused, anxious, excited, and seeing things that are not there, especially because you are very sick: *One patient was delirious with a high fever.* **2** extremely excited or happy: *The freed citizens were delirious with joy.* —**deliriously** *adv.*

de·lir·i·um /dɪˈlɪriəm/ *n.* [singular, U] **1** a state in which someone is delirious, especially because they are very sick **2** extreme excitement: *The win brought on delirium among the fans.*

delirium trem·ens /dɪˌlɪriəm ˈtrɛmənz/ *n.* [U] TECHNICAL a medical condition, caused when someone who usually drinks too much alcohol stops drinking, in which their body shakes and they see things that are not there

ˢ ʷ de·liv·er /dɪˈlɪvɚ/ *v.*
1 [**take sth somewhere**] [I,T] to take a letter, package, message, goods etc. to a particular place or person: *Ask if the pizza place delivers.* | *As a boy, Ralph delivered newspapers on a bicycle.* | *He arranged to have the package delivered to her apartment.*

2 [**give a speech/performance**] [T] to give a speech or performance to a lot of people: *Rev. Whitman delivered a powerful sermon.*

3 [**do sth you are supposed to do**] [I,T] to do or provide the things that you are expected to or that you have promised to: *Budget cuts have affected the state's ability to deliver the services citizens expect.* | *Farrell said the team would win big, but he couldn't deliver the goods* (=do what he promised). | *Voters are angry that politicians haven't delivered on their promises.*

4 [**baby**] [T] to give birth to a baby, or to help a woman give birth to her baby: *Mrs. Arnold is due to deliver a baby girl in April.* | *Traditionally, local midwives would deliver all the babies in the area.*

5 [**judgment/ruling etc.**] [T] to officially give a formal decision, judgment, ruling etc.: *The packed courtroom was hushed as the jury delivered their verdict.*

6 [**votes**] [T] to get the votes or support of a particular group of people in an election: *Ford, a Democrat, is able to deliver the black vote in his hometown of Memphis.*

7 [**blow/shock etc.**] [T] to give something such as a blow, shock, or warning to someone or something: *If the animal ignores the command, the collar delivers a mild shock.*

8 [**person**] [T] LITERARY to put someone into someone else's control: [**deliver sb to sb**] *Judas delivered Christ to the Romans.*

9 [**make sb free of**] [T] LITERARY OR BIBLICAL to help someone escape from something bad or evil: [+ **from**] *Deliver us from evil.* —**deliverer** *n.* [C]

deliver sth **up** *phr. v.* [T] FORMAL to give something to someone else: *Voters now deliver up power not to a human being, but to an image on television.*

de·liv·er·ance /dɪˈlɪvərəns/ *n.* [U + **from**] FORMAL the state of being saved from harm or danger

de·liv·er·y /dɪˈlɪvri, -vəri/ *n. plural* **deliveries** **1** [C,U] the act or process of bringing goods, letters etc. to a particular place or person: *Pizza Mondo offers free delivery.* | *mail deliveries* **2** [C] something that is delivered: *Ask your neighbor to take any deliveries while you are on vacation.* **3** [C] the process of a baby being born: *She had a quick, easy delivery.* | *Mrs. Haims was rushed into the delivery room* (=hospital room where a baby is born) *at 7:42.* **4** [singular] the way in which someone speaks or performs in public: *The actor gives his usual gruff delivery, meant to convince us he's honest.* **5 take delivery of sth** to officially accept something large that you have bought

de·liv·er·y·man /dɪˈlɪvrimən, -ˌmæn/ *n.* [C] a man who delivers goods to people

delivery per·son /ˈ.. ˌ../ *n.* [C] someone who delivers goods to people

dell /dɛl/ *n.* [C] LITERARY a small valley with grass and trees

de·louse /diˈlaʊs/ *v.* [T] to remove lice (LOUSE¹ (1)) from someone's hair, clothes etc.

del·phin·i·um /dɛlˈfɪniəm/ *n.* [C] a tall garden plant with many blue flowers along its stem

del·ta /ˈdɛltə/ *n.* [C] **1** an area of low land where a river spreads into many smaller rivers near the ocean: *the Mississippi delta* **2** the fourth letter of the Greek alphabet

de·lude /dɪˈlud/ *v.* [T] to make someone believe something that is not true; DECEIVE: *Gamblers delude themselves that they can beat the odds and win.* —**deluded** *adj.* —**delusive** /dɪˈlusɪv/ *adj.*

del·uge¹ /ˈdɛlyudʒ/ *n.* [C usually singular] **1** a large flood, or a period of time when it rains continuously **2** a large amount of something such as letters or questions that someone gets at the same time: [+ **of**] *Are your savings being eroded by the deluge of bills that arrive every month?*

deluge² *v.* [T] **1** [usually passive] to send a lot of letters, questions etc. to someone at the same time: [+ **with**] *The radio station has been deluged with complaints.* **2** FORMAL to completely cover something with water

de·lu·sion /dɪˈluʒən/ *n.* **1** [C,U] a false belief about something: *Most of us are under the delusion that giving expensive gifts somehow makes us better people.* **2 delusions of grandeur** the belief that you are much more important or powerful than you really are —**delusional** *adj.*

de·luxe /dɪ'lʌks/ *adj.* [usually before noun] of better quality and more expensive than other similar things: *a deluxe hotel room*

delve /dɛlv/ *v.* [I always + adv./prep.] **1** to try to find more information about someone or something: [+ **into**] *Stewart's book delves into the history of traditional Christmas foods.* | *Hardy has studied kung fu, and wants to delve deeper into its spiritual side.* **2** to search for something by putting your hand deeply into a bag, container etc.: [+ **into**] *Laurie delved into her briefcase and pulled out a letter.* **3** [C usually singular] OLD USE to dig

Dem. the written abbreviation of Democrat or Democratic

de·mag·net·ize /di'mæɡnə,taɪz/ *v.* [T] to take away the MAGNETIC qualities of something —**demagnetization** /di,mæɡnətə'zeɪʃən/ *n.* [U]

dem·a·gogue /'dɛmə,ɡɑɡ/ *n.* [C] DISAPPROVING a political leader who tries to make people feel strong emotions in order to influence their opinions —**demagogy, demagoguery** *n.* [U] —**demagogic** /,dɛmə'ɡɑdʒɪk/ *adj.*

S W de·mand[1] /dɪ'mænd/ *n.*

1 desire for sth [U] the need or desire that people have for particular goods or services: [+ **for**] *There isn't much demand for leaded gasoline anymore.* | *As many as 300,000 new houses were needed to meet demand this year.* | *The candle-making class has been in great demand.* —see also SUPPLY AND DEMAND **2** firm request [C] a strong request for something that shows you believe you have the right to get what you ask for: [+ **for**] *Glover faced a demand for his resignation.* | [**demand that**] *Administrators finally bowed to demands that the university be renamed.* | *Managers thought that the union was making unreasonable demands.* —see Usage Note at CLAIM[1]

3 demands [C usually plural] something difficult, annoying, or tiring that you need to do or a skill you need to have; REQUIREMENT: *Some working moms worry about the conflicting demands of home and job.* | *Children can make heavy demands on parents' time and energy.*

4 by popular demand because a lot of people have asked for something to be done, performed etc.: *The run of the play was extended twice by popular demand.*

5 on demand done or given whenever someone asks: *Rahmer is opposed to abortion on demand.*

S W demand[2] *v.* [T] **1** to ask strongly for something, especially because you think you have a right to do this: *The President demanded the release of the hostages.* | [**demand (that)**] *Rainey demanded that his lawyer be called.* | *I demand to know what's going on here!* **2** to ask a question or order something to be done very firmly: *"Did you do this?" Kathryn demanded angrily.* | [**demand sth of sb**] *Some parents demand too much of their children* (=they ask them to do too much or do things they cannot yet do). **3** if something demands your time, skill, attention etc. it makes you use a lot of your time, skill etc.: *The baby demands most of Cindy's time.* —see Usage Note at REQUEST[2]

de·mand·ing /dɪ'mændɪŋ/ *adj.* **1** making you use a lot of your time, skill, attention etc.: *a very demanding job* **2** expecting a lot of attention or expecting to have things exactly the way you want them, especially in a way that is not fair: *a demanding boss*

de·mar·cate /dɪ'mɑrkeɪt, 'dimɑr,keɪt/ *v.* [T] FORMAL to decide or mark the limits of an area, system etc.

de·mar·ca·tion /,dimɑr'keɪʃən/ *n.* **1** the process of deciding on or marking the border between two areas of land: *Two conference buildings have been placed on the line of demarcation.* **2** the point at which one area of work, responsibility, activity etc. ends and another begins: [+ **between**] *There was no clear demarcation between work and play.*

de·mean /dɪ'min/ *v.* [T] to make someone or something less respectable: *Students should not demean the graduation ceremony with inappropriate behavior.*

de·mean·ing /dɪ'minɪŋ/ *adj.* showing less respect for someone than they deserve or making them feel embarrassed or ashamed: [+ **to**] *Protestors argued that the beauty pageant was demeaning to women.*

de·mean·or /dɪ'minɚ/ *n.* [singular,U] FORMAL the way someone behaves, dresses, speaks etc. that shows what their character is like: *a kind and gentle demeanor*

de·ment·ed /dɪ'mɛntɪd/ *adj.* **1** crazy or very strange: *Whoever committed these crimes was demented and sick.* | *a demented sense of humor* **2** OLD-FASHIONED suffering from dementia

de·men·tia /dɪ'mɛnʃə/ *n.* [U] TECHNICAL an illness that affects the brain and memory, and makes you gradually lose the ability to think and behave normally

de·mer·it /dɪ'mɛrɪt/ *n.* [C] **1** a warning or a mark showing that a warning that is given to a student or a soldier to tell them not to do something wrong again **2** [usually plural] a bad quality or feature of something

de·mesne /dɪ'meɪn/ *n.* [C] OLD USE a very big piece of land that one person owns, especially in past times

De·me·ter /dɪ'mitɚ/ in Greek MYTHOLOGY, the goddess of crops

demi- /dɛmi/ *prefix* half: *a demigod* (=half god and half human) | *a demitasse* (=a small cup for serving coffee)

dem·i·god /'dɛmi,ɡɑd/ *n.* [C] **1** someone who is so important and powerful that they are treated like a god **2** a man in ancient stories, who is partly god and partly human —**demigoddess** *n.* [C]

de·mil·i·ta·rize /di'mɪlətə,raɪz/ *v.* [T] to remove the weapons, soldiers etc. from a country or area so that there can be no fighting there: *The demilitarized zone between the two countries is heavily guarded.* —**demilitarization** /di,mɪlətərə'zeɪʃən/ *n.* [U]

De Mille /də 'mɪl/**, Ag·nes** /'æɡnɪs/ (1909–1993) a U.S. dancer and CHOREOGRAPHER of BALLET

DeMille, Ce·cil B. /'sisəl bi/ (1881–1959) a U.S. movie producer and director who is famous for making EPICS (=movies about people in the Bible and in history), using hundreds of actors

de·mise /dɪ'maɪz/ *n.* [U] **1** FORMAL the end of something that used to exist: [+ **of**] *the demise of the Cold War* **2** FORMAL OR LAW death: *My parents had mixed feelings about the President's demise.*

dem·i·tasse /'dɛmi,tɑs, -,tæs/ *n.* [C] a small cup for coffee

dem·o /'dɛmoʊ/ *n.* plural **demos** [C] INFORMAL **1** a recording containing an example of someone's music: *a demo tape* **2** a DISKETTE or CD-ROM that has a DEMONSTRATION PROGRAM on it **3** a DEMONSTRATION (2): *I'll give you a quick demo.* **4** an example of a product, especially a car, that is used to show how the product works and is later often sold at a lower price

demo- /dɛmə/ *prefix* relating to people or the population: *demographics* (=information about the population of a place)

de·mo·bil·ize /di'moʊbə,laɪz/ *v.* [I,T usually passive] to send home the members of an army, navy etc., especially at the end of a war: *Key points of the UN plan include disarming and demobilizing the rebel troops.* —**demobilization** /di,moʊbələ'zeɪʃən/ *n.* [U]

de·moc·ra·cy /dɪ'mɑkrəsi/ *n.* plural **democracies 1** [U] a system of government in which every citizen in the country can vote to elect its government officials **2** [C] a country that allows its people to elect its government officials **3** [C] a situation or society in which everyone is equal and has the right to vote, speak etc.: *The team's partnership is not a democracy – executives Larry Baer and Bob Quinn are the ones who make decisions.* **S W**

dem·o·crat /ˈdɛməˌkræt/ *n.* [C] **1 Democrat** a member or supporter of the Democratic Party of the U.S. —compare REPUBLICAN[2] (1) **2** someone who believes in or works to achieve democracy

dem·o·crat·ic /ˌdɛməˈkræṭɪk◂/ *adj.* **1 Democratic** belonging to or supporting the Democratic Party of the U.S.: *the Democratic nominee* **2** organized according to the principle that everyone has a right to vote, speak etc.: *Some people favor a more democratic style of parenting, saying they fear being too strict with their children.* **3** controlled by representatives who are elected by the people of a country: *a democratic government* —**democratically** /-klɪ/ *adv.*

Democratic Par·ty /ˌ.... ˈ../ *n.* **the Democratic Party** one of the two main political parties of the U.S. —compare REPUBLICAN PARTY

de·moc·ra·tize /dɪˈmɑkrəˌtaɪz/ *v.* [T] to change the way in which a government, company etc. is organized, so that it is more democratic —**democratization** /dɪˌmɑkrəṭəˈzeɪʃən/ *n.* [U]

De·moc·ri·tus /dɪˈmɑkrəṭəs/ (?460–?370 B.C.) a Greek PHILOSOPHER

dem·o·graph·ic /ˌdɛməˈɡræfɪk◂/ *n.* **1 demographics** [plural] information about the people who live in a particular area, such as how many people there are or what types of people there are: *the changing demographics of Southern California* **2** [singular] a part of the population that is considered as a group, especially for the purpose of advertising or trying to sell goods: *CBS has been trying to attract the 18-to-49 demographic with its hipper new shows.* —**demographic** *adj.* —**demographically** /-klɪ/ *adv.*

de·mog·ra·phy /dɪˈmɑɡrəfi/ *n.* [U] the study of how human populations change, for example the study of how many births, deaths, marriages etc. happen in a particular place at a particular time —**demographer** *n.* [C]

demolish

de·mol·ish /dɪˈmɑlɪʃ/ *v.* [T] **1** to completely destroy a building or other structure: *Several houses were demolished to make way for the new road.* **2** INFORMAL to end or ruin something completely: *The decision demolishes part of the city's civil rights legislation.* **3** INFORMAL if you demolish your opponent, you beat them completely: *Miami demolished Texas 46–3.*

dem·o·li·tion /ˌdɛməˈlɪʃən/ *n.* [C,U] the act or process of demolishing a building: *Several housing projects are scheduled for demolition.*

demolition der·by /ˌ..ˈ.. ˌ../ *n.* [C] a competition in which people crash old cars into each other until only one is left driving

de·mon /ˈdimən/ *n.* [C] **1** an evil spirit —compare DAEMON **2** an evil force that affects people's behavior or thoughts: *Spencer hoped that therapy would free her from her inner demons.* **3** HUMOROUS someone who is very good at something: *Paganini, the demon of the violin, transformed violin playing techniques.* —see also **speed demon** (SPEED[1] (6))

de·mo·ni·a·cal /ˌdiməˈnaɪəkəl/ also **de·mo·ni·ac** /dɪˈmoʊniæk/ *adj.* FORMAL wild and evil —**demoniacally** /-klɪ/ *adv.*

de·mon·ic /dɪˈmɑnɪk/ *adj.* **1** wild and cruel: *demonic laughter* **2** relating to a demon: *Some viewed the girl's shaking as a sign of demonic possession.* —**demonically** /-klɪ/ *adv.*

de·mon·ize /ˈdimənaɪz/ *v.* [T] to describe or represent someone as evil: *The U.S. government demonized the dictator as a new Hitler.* —**demonization** /ˌdimənəˈzeɪʃən/ *n.* [U]

de·mon·ol·o·gy /ˌdiməˈnɑlədʒi/ *n.* **1** [U] the study of or the belief in DEMONS **2** [C usually singular] a list of someone's enemies

de·mon·stra·ble /dɪˈmɑnstrəbəl/ *adj.* FORMAL able to be shown or proved: *There is a demonstrable link between smoking and lung cancer.* —**demonstrably** *adv.* —**demonstrability** /dɪˌmɑnstrəˈbɪləti/ *n.* [U]

dem·on·strate /ˈdɛmənˌstreɪt/ *v.* **1** [T] to show or prove something clearly: *The study demonstrates the link between poverty and malnutrition.* | [**demonstrate that**] *Scientific evidence demonstrates that smoking can cause birth defects.* | [**demonstrate how/what etc.**] *The power of the earthquake demonstrated how little control we actually have over our world.* **2** [T] to show or describe how to do something or how it works: *Aerobics instructors should always demonstrate each new movement first.* | [**demonstrate how/what etc.**] *This experiment demonstrates how electricity can be created.* **3** [I] to protest or support something in public with a lot of other people: *Supporters demonstrated outside the courtroom during the trial.* | [+ **against**] *Several thousand people came to demonstrate against abortion.* **4** [T] to show that a person or thing has a particular skill, quality, or ability: *Sloan demonstrated impressive leadership in building a company that took employees' needs into account.*

dem·on·stra·tion /ˌdɛmənˈstreɪʃən/ *n.* [C] **1** an event at which a lot of people meet to protest or support something in public: *The anti-affirmative action law sparked mass demonstrations.* | [+ **against**] *a demonstration against racism* | *In recent years farmers have held sometimes violent demonstrations against imported produce.* **2** an act of explaining and showing how to do something or how something works: *Laura gave a demonstration on how to use the electronic dictionary.* **3** an action, fact etc. that proves that someone or something has a particular quality, ability, emotion etc.: *Our polluted air is a clear demonstration of the need for tougher environmental laws.*

demonstration pro·gram /ˌ..ˈ.. ˌ../ *n.* [C] a computer PROGRAM that shows what a new piece of SOFTWARE will be able to do when it is ready to be sold —compare ALPHA VERSION, BETA VERSION

de·mon·stra·tive /dɪˈmɑnstrəṭɪv/ *adj.* **1** willing to show how much you care about someone: *Dave's not very demonstrative, but I know he loves me.* **2** showing or explaining something: *We use the dolls for demonstrative purposes in sessions with young children.* —**demonstratively** *adv.*

demonstrative pro·noun /ˌ.... ˈ../ *n.* [C] TECHNICAL a PRONOUN such as "that" or "this" that shows which person or thing is meant and separates it from others

dem·on·stra·tor /ˈdɛmənˌstreɪṭɚ/ *n.* [C] **1** someone who takes part in a DEMONSTRATION (1) **2** someone who shows people how something works or is done **3** an example of a product, that shows how it works

de·mor·al·ize /dɪˈmɔrəˌlaɪz, di-, -ˈmɑr-/ *v.* [T] to reduce or destroy someone's courage or confidence: *Gibson's home run demoralized the Astros.* —**demoralized** *adj.*: *exhausted and demoralized refugees* —**demoralizing** *adj.*: *a demoralizing defeat* —**demoralization** /dɪˌmɔrələˈzeɪʃən/ *n.* [U]

De·mos·the·nes /dɪˈmɑsθəˌniz/ (384–322 B.C.) a Greek ORATOR and writer of speeches

de·mote /dɪˈmoʊt, di-/ *v.* [T often passive] to make someone have a lower rank or a less important position than before —opposite PROMOTE —**demotion** /dɪˈmoʊʃən, di-/ *n.* [C,U]

de·mot·ic /dɪˈmɑṭɪk/ *adj.* FORMAL used by or popular with most ordinary people

Demp·sey /'dɛmpsi/, **Jack** /dʒæk/ (1895–1983) a U.S. BOXER who was world CHAMPION in 1919–1926

de·mur /dɪ'mɜ/ v. **demurred, demurring** [I] FORMAL to express doubt about or opposition to a plan or suggestion

de·mure /dɪ'myʊr/ adj. **1** someone, especially a girl or a woman, who is demure is shy and quiet and always behaves well **2** clothing that is demure is softly colored and does not allow very much of a person's body to be seen —**demurely** adv. —**demureness** n. [U]

de·mys·ti·fy /di'mɪstə,faɪ/ v. **demystifies, demystified, demystifying** [T] to make a subject that seems difficult or complicated easier to understand, especially by explaining it in simpler language: *The pamphlet demystifies the mortgage process.* —**demystification** /di,mɪstəfə'keɪʃən/ n. [U]

den /dɛn/ n. [C] **1** a room in a house where people relax, read, watch television etc. **2** the home of some types of animal, for example lions or FOXes **3** a place where secret or illegal activities take place: *an opium den* | *a den of thieves* **4** a group of CUB SCOUTS **5 den of iniquity** OFTEN HUMOROUS a place where activities that you think are immoral or evil happen

De·na·li /də'nɑli/ a mountain in central Alaska, which is the highest point in North America. It is also called Mount McKinley.

de·na·tion·al·ize /di'næʃənə,laɪz/ v. [T] to sell a business or industry that is owned by the government, so that it is then owned privately; PRIVATIZE —**denationalization** /di,næʃənələ'zeɪʃən/ n. [U]

Deng Xiao·ping /,dʌŋ ʃaʊ'pɪŋ/ (1904–1997) a Chinese politician who was the most powerful person in the Chinese Communist Party from 1977 until his death, and started important changes that helped China to develop its economy and industry

de·ni·al /dɪ'naɪəl/ n. **1** [C,U] a statement saying that something is not true: [+ of] *Diaz issued a firm denial of the rumor.* **2** [U] the act of refusing to allow someone to have or do something: [+ of] *the denial of basic human rights* **3** [U] a situation or condition in which you refuse to admit or believe that something bad exists or has happened: *My husband is still in denial about my rape.*

den·ier /'dɛnyɚ/ n. [U] a measure of how thin NYLON or silk threads are

den·i·grate /'dɛnɪ,greɪt/ v. [T] to do or say things to make someone or something seem less important or good: *remarks that denigrate women* —**denigration** /,dɛnɪ'greɪʃən/ n. [U]

den·im /'dɛnəm/ n. **1** [U] a type of strong cotton cloth, used especially to make JEANS **2 denims** [plural] OLD-FASHIONED a pair of pants made from denim; JEANS

den·i·zen /'dɛnəzən/ n. [C + of] LITERARY an animal, plant, or person that lives or is found in a particular place

Den·mark /'dɛnmɑrk/ a country in northern Europe, north of Germany and surrounded on three sides by seas —see also DANISH[1]

den moth·er /'. ,../ n. [C] a woman who leads a group of CUB SCOUTS

de·nom·i·nate /dɪ'nɑmə,neɪt/ v. [T] TECHNICAL to officially set the value of something according to one system or type of money: *Banks usually denominate loans to poorer countries in more stable currencies like the dollar.*

de·nom·i·na·tion /dɪ,nɑmə'neɪʃən/ n. [C] **1** a religious group that has slightly different beliefs from other groups who belong to the same religion: *Christians of all denominations attended the conference.* **2** the value of a coin, paper money, or a stamp: *U.S. bills in small denominations are useful for paying taxi fares in other countries.*

de·nom·i·na·tion·al /dɪ,nɑmə'neɪʃənəl/ adj. relating or belonging to a particular religious denomination: *Many campus Christian organizations cross denominational lines.* —see also NONDENOMINATIONAL

de·nom·i·na·tor /dɪ'nɑmə,neɪtɚ/ n. [C] TECHNICAL the number below the line in a FRACTION (2) —compare NUMERATOR —see also LOWEST COMMON DENOMINATOR

de·no·ta·tion /,dinoʊ'teɪʃən/ n. [C] TECHNICAL the thing that is actually described by a word, rather than the feelings or ideas it suggests —compare CONNOTATION

de·note /dɪ'noʊt/ v. [T] FORMAL to represent or mean something: *Each X on the map denotes 500 people.* —**denotative** adj. —compare CONNOTE

de·noue·ment /,deɪnu'mɑnt, deɪ'numɑnt/ n. [C] FORMAL the last part of a story or play that explains what happens after the CLIMAX[1] (1)

de·nounce /dɪ'naʊns/ v. [T] **1** to publicly express disapproval of someone or something: *Residents denounced the plan because of traffic and parking problems.* | [denounce sb/sth as sth] *Catholic bishops denounced the movie as immoral.* **2** to give information to the police or another authority about someone's illegal political activities: [denounce sb to sb] *Anja eventually denounced him to the secret police.* —see also DENUNCIATION

dense /dɛns/ adj. **1** made of or containing a lot of things or people that are very close together: *The jungle is so dense you cannot walk through it.* | *a dense population* **2** difficult to see through or breathe in: *dense smoke* **3** INFORMAL not able to understand things easily; STUPID: *Sometimes you just seem so dense!* **4** a dense piece of writing is difficult to understand because it contains a lot of information or uses complicated language **5** a substance that is dense has a lot of MASS[1] (6) in relation to its size: *Water is eight hundred times denser than air.* —**densely** adv.: *densely populated areas* —**denseness** n. [U]

den·si·ty /'dɛnsəti/ n. plural **densities** [C,U] **1** the degree to which an area is filled with things or people: *population density* **2** the relationship between something's MASS[1] (6) and its size

dent[1] /dɛnt/ n. [C] **1** a mark made when you hit or press something so that its surface is bent: [+ in] *There's a big dent in the side of my car.* **2** to reduce the amount of something: *This program won't even make a dent in the drug problem* | *The loss put a dent in the team's confidence.*

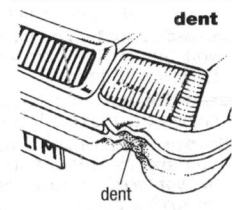

dent

dent[2] v. **1** [I,T] if you dent something, or if it dents, you hit or press it so that its surface is bent and marked: *Some idiot dented my car door last night.* **2** [T] to harm or reduce something: *Baseball's image was dented by the labor dispute.*

den·tal /'dɛntl/ adj. [only before noun] relating to your teeth: *dental treatment*

dental as·sist·ant /'.. ,../ n. [C] someone whose job is to help a DENTIST

dental floss /'.. ,./ n. [U] thin string that you use to clean between your teeth

dental hy·gien·ist /,.. '..., ,.. .'../ n. [C] someone who works with a dentist and cleans people's teeth or gives them advice about how to take care of their teeth

dental sur·geon /'.. ,../ n. [C] a dentist who performs operations in the mouth; ORAL SURGEON

den·ti·frice /'dɛntə,frɪs/ n. [U] FORMAL a PASTE[1] (3) or powder used to clean teeth

den·tist /'dɛntɪst/ n. [C] someone whose job is to treat people's teeth: *I'm going to the dentist this afternoon.*

den·tist·ry /'dɛntəstri/ n. [U] the medical study of the teeth and the mouth, or the work of a dentist

den·tures /'dɛntʃɚz/ n. [plural] a set of artificial teeth worn by someone who does not have their own teeth anymore; FALSE TEETH

de·nude /dɪ'nud/ v. [T usually passive] FORMAL to remove the plants and trees that cover an area of land: [denude sth of sth] *Meadows that were once denuded of plants by campers are now healing.*

de·nun·ci·a·tion /dɪˌnʌnsiˈeɪʃən/ n. [C] a public statement in which you criticize someone or something

Den·ver /ˈdɛnvɚ/ the capital city of the U.S. state of Colorado

Denver boot /ˌ.. ˈ./ n. [C] a metal object that the police attach to the wheel of an illegally parked car so that it cannot be moved

s w **de·ny** /dɪˈnaɪ/ v. **denies, denied, denying** [T]
2
3
1 not true/not believed to say that something is not true, or that you do not believe something: *I saw you do it, so don't try to deny it!* | [deny (that)] *Some groups deny that the Holocaust ever happened.* | [deny doing sth] *Fellowes denied trying to steal the jewelry.* | **flatly/categorically deny sth** (=deny very strongly)
2 not allow [often passive] to refuse to allow someone to have or do something: *Parry's appeal to the courts was denied.* | [deny sb sth] *Seven of the actors were denied visas.* | [deny sth to sb] *It's our policy to deny locker room access to all members of the opposite sex.*
3 **there's no denying (sth/that...)** SPOKEN used to say that it is very clear that something is true: *There's no denying that some U.S. workers will suffer from free trade.*
4 feelings to refuse to admit that you are feeling something: *I realized I'd been denying a lot of angry feelings toward my mother.*
5 **deny yourself sth** to decide not to have something that you would like, especially for moral or religious reasons or because you think it will be good for you in some way: *Mrs. Owens saved money by denying herself even the most basic comforts.*
6 principles LITERARY to do something that is the opposite of something you strongly believe in: *The act of stealing denied everything she had been taught.*

de·o·dor·ant /diˈoʊdərənt/ n. [C,U] a substance that you put on the skin under your arms to stop you from smelling bad

de·o·dor·ize /diˈoʊdəˌraɪz/ v. [T] to remove a bad smell or to make it less noticeable —**deodorizer** n. [C]

de·part /dɪˈpɑrt/ v. **1** [I,T] to leave, especially when you are starting a trip: *Travelers departing Ukraine do not need an exit visa.* | *Leopold stared after his departing nephew.* | [+ for] *All passengers departing for New York on flight UA179 should go to Gate 7.* | [+ from] *The train will depart from platform 5.*
2 **depart this life/earth** FORMAL to die —see also DEPARTURE
depart from sth *phr. v.* [T] to start to use new ideas or do something in an unusual or unexpected way: *The play departs from tradition in its form.*

de·part·ed /dɪˈpɑrtɪd/ adj. [only before noun] **1** a word meaning "dead," used to avoid saying this directly: *our dearly departed father* **2** LITERARY a period of time that is departed is gone forever

s w **de·part·ment** /dɪˈpɑrtˌmənt/ n. [C] **1** any of the groups of people working together that form part of a large organization such as a college, government, or business: *Vera works in the public relations department.* | *the Department of Motor Vehicles* **2** an area in a large store where a particular type of product is sold: *Ties are in the men's department* (=where clothes for men are sold). **3** **be sb's department** SPOKEN to be something that a particular person is responsible for or knows a lot about: *Don't ask me – cooking is John's department.* **4** a particular part of someone's character, or a particular part of a larger subject: *Fred has some problems in the humor department* (=he does not understand jokes). | *The movie tries to be both a comedy and a drama, without success in either department.* —**departmental** /dɪˌpɑrt-ˈmɛntl/ adj.: *a departmental meeting* —see also FIRE DEPARTMENT, POLICE DEPARTMENT

de·part·men·tal·ize /dɪpɑrt-ˈmɛntlˌaɪz, ˌdi-/ v. [T] to divide something into different departments —**departmentalization** /dɪpɑrtˌmɛntl-əˈzeɪʃən/ n. [U]

Department of Ag·ri·cul·ture, the /ˌ.ˌ.. ˈ.../ also **the Agriculture Department** the U.S. government department that is responsible for farming, food production, and the safety of food products

Department of Com·merce, the /ˌ.ˌ.. ˈ../ also **the Commerce Department** the U.S. government department that is concerned with trade and economic development

Department of De·fense, the /ˌ.ˌ.. .ˈ./ also **the Defense Department** the U.S. government department that is responsible for the military forces in the U.S., that is, the Army, Navy, Air Force, Marine Corps, and Coast Guard

Department of Ed·u·ca·tion, the /ˌ.ˌ.. ..ˈ../ also **the Education Department** the U.S. government department that is responsible for the education system, including education programs, laws for schools and colleges, standards for schools and teachers etc.

Department of En·er·gy, the /ˌ.ˌ.. .ˈ.../ also **the Energy Department** the U.S. government department that is concerned with supplies of FUEL, including coal, oil, gas and NUCLEAR energy

Department of Health and Hu·man Ser·vic·es, the /ˌ.ˌ.. ˌ.ˌ.. ˈ.../ the U.S. government department that is responsible for health programs and providing money and support for people who are poor, have no jobs, or are too old to work

Department of Hous·ing and Ur·ban De·vel·op·ment, the /ˌ.ˌ.. ˌ.ˌ.. .ˈ.../ —see HUD

Department of Jus·tice, the /ˌ.ˌ.. ˈ../ also **the Justice Department** the U.S. government department that deals with the law. Its work includes writing laws, representing the government in courts of law, and searching for information to solve crimes.

Department of La·bor, the /ˌ.ˌ.. ˈ../ also **the Labor Department** the U.S. government department concerned with how workers are treated by employers. It examines subjects such as fair wages, safety, and the number of hours worked each week.

Department of State, the /ˌ.ˌ.. ˈ./ also **the State Department** the part of the U.S. government that deals with the U.S.'s relations with other countries

Department of the In·ter·i·or, the /ˌ.ˌ.. ..ˈ.../ also **the Interior Department** the part of the U.S. government responsible for protecting the U.S.'s NATURAL RESOURCES such as minerals, water, natural energy etc.

Department of the Treas·ur·y, the /ˌ.ˌ.. .ˈ.../ also **the Treasury Department** the U.S. government department that is responsible for the money system of the country and the money that the government collects and spends

Department of Trans·por·ta·tion, the /ˌ.ˌ.. ..ˈ../ also **the Transportation Department** the U.S. government department that deals with TRANSPORTATION in the U.S., for example by making laws about road vehicles and airplanes, and by building and repairing roads

Department of Vet·er·ans' Af·fairs, the /ˌ.ˌ.. ˌ... .ˈ./ also **the Veterans' Department** the U.S. government department that gives help to soldiers, SAILORs etc. who have fought in a war and to their families

department store /.ˈ.. ˌ./ n. [C] a large store that sells many different products such as clothes, kitchen equipment etc.

de·par·ture /dɪˈpɑrtʃɚ/ n. **1** [C,U] an act of leaving a place, especially to travel in an airplane, car etc.: *You should be at the airport an hour before departure.* | [+ for] *Gregor's departure for the U.S. was delayed by visa problems.* **2** [C,U] an act of leaving an organization or position: [+ from] *Van Ness said his departure from the company was purely voluntary.* **3** [C] a change from what is usual or expected: *The plan is a radical departure from* (=a big change from) *the original.* **4** [C] a flight, train etc. that leaves at a particular time: *There are several departures for Minneapolis every day.* —opposite ARRIVAL

departure lounge /.ˈ.. ˌ./ n. [C] the place at an

airport where people wait until their airplane is ready to leave

S W **de·pend** /dɪˈpɛnd/ v. **(it/that) depends** SPOKEN used to say that you cannot give a definite answer to something because your answer will be affected by something else: "Are you going to Karla's party?" "It depends. I might have to work that weekend." | [it depends who/what/how/whether etc.] "Where's the best place to eat around here?" "It depends what kind of food you like."

depend on/upon sb/sth phr. v. [T] **1** if something depends on something else, it is directly affected or decided by that thing: Admission to the university depends solely on a student's performance. | [depend on who/what/how/whether etc.] Use 2 to 4 cups of stuffing, depending on how big the turkey is. **2** [not in progressive] to need the help or support of someone or something else in order to exist, be successful, be healthy etc.: The city depends heavily on tourism. | [+ for] Eastern Europe once depended on the Soviet Union for cheap oil. | [depend on sb/sth to do sth] Many people depend on food stamps to feed their families. **3** [not in progressive] to trust or have confidence in someone or something: I know I can depend on Bruce. | [depend on sb/sth to do sth] I can depend on my employees to take care of things.

de·pend·a·ble /dɪˈpɛndəbəl/ adj. able to be trusted to do what you need or expect: a dependable car —**dependably** adv. —**dependability** /dɪˌpɛndəˈbɪləti/ n. [U]

de·pend·ence /dɪˈpɛndəns/ n. [U] **1** the state of depending on the help and support of someone or something else in order to exist or be successful: [+ on/upon] We need to reduce our dependence on foreign oil. —opposite INDEPENDENCE **2** the state of being ADDICTED to drugs or alcohol

de·pend·en·cy /dɪˈpɛndənsi/ n. plural **dependencies 1** [U] a state of dependence **2** [C] a country that is controlled by another country

de·pend·ent[1] /dɪˈpɛndənt/ adj. **1** needing someone or something else in order to exist, be successful, be healthy etc.: Do you have any dependent children? | [+ on/upon] He is dependent on Karl, his Seeing Eye dog, to lead him. —compare CO-DEPENDENT **2 be dependent on/upon sth** to be directly affected or decided by something else: Your success is dependent on how hard you work. **3** ADDICTED (1) to drugs, alcohol etc.

dependent[2] n. [C] someone, especially a child, who depends on you for food, clothes, money etc.

dependent clause /.ˌ.. ˈ./ n. [C] TECHNICAL a CLAUSE (2) in a sentence that gives information related to the main clause, but cannot exist alone. For example, in the sentence, "I have hated cleaning since I was a child," the clause "since I was a child" is a dependent clause.

de·per·son·al·ize /diˈpɜsənlˌaɪz -snəˌlaɪz/ v. [T] to not consider someone as a person: Policemen dealing with murders sometimes depersonalize the victim. —**depersonalization** /diˌpɜsnələˈzeɪʃən/ n. [U]

de·pict /dɪˈpɪkt/ v. [T] to describe or show a person, situation, or event in a piece of writing or in art: The California state flag depicts a grizzly bear. | Critics said the article depicted Latinos negatively. | [depict sb/sth as sth] We know that New York is sometimes depicted as a cold and heartless city. —**depiction** /dɪˈpɪkʃən/ n. [C,U] Mayle's book offers an affectionate depiction of small-town life in Provence.

de·pil·a·to·ry /dɪˈpɪləˌtɔri/ n. plural **depilatories** [C] a substance that gets rid of unwanted hair from your body —**depilatory** adj. [only before noun]

de·plane /diˈpleɪn/ v. [I] to get out of an airplane

de·plete /dɪˈplit/ v. [T usually passive] to reduce the amount of something that is available: Salmon populations have been severely depleted recently. | Algae can block light and deplete oxygen from the water. —**depletion** /dɪˈpliʃən/ n. [U] the depletion of natural resources

de·plor·a·ble /dɪˈplɔrəbəl/ adj. FORMAL very bad, shocking, and deserving strong disapproval: American day care centers range from excellent to deplorable. | a deplorable mistake —**deplorably** adv.

de·plore /dɪˈplɔr/ v. [T] FORMAL to strongly criticize something that you disapprove of: "The Times" deplored the film's violence.

de·ploy /dɪˈplɔɪ/ v. **deploys, deployed, deploying** [I,T usually passive] **1 a)** to organize people or things, especially soldiers, military equipment etc., or to be organized so that they are in the right place and ready to be used: UN troops were deployed to keep the peace. **b)** to move soldiers, military equipment etc. or to be moved into action: Senior Marine Corps officers were preparing to deploy to the Gulf. **2** to move something or be moved into a particular position where it can be used: Air bags are only deployed when the car is struck from the front. —**deployment** n. [C,U]

de·po·lit·i·cize /ˌdipəˈlɪtəˌsaɪz/ v. [T] to remove political influence or control from a situation

de·pop·u·late /diˈpɑpyəˌleɪt/ v. [T usually passive] to greatly reduce the number of people living in a particular area —**depopulation** /diˌpɑpyəˈleɪʃən/ n. [U]

D

de·port /dɪˈpɔrt/ v. [T] **1** to make a person from a foreign country return to the country they came from: Many of the people who cross the border are quickly deported. **2 deport yourself** FORMAL to behave in a particular way, especially in the correct way

de·por·ta·tion /ˌdipɔrˈteɪʃən/ n. [C,U] the act of deporting someone: Pascual faces deportation shortly after Christmas.

de·por·tee /ˌdipɔrˈti/ n. [C] someone who has been deported or is going to be deported

de·port·ment /dɪˈpɔrtmənt/ n. [U] FORMAL the way that a person behaves in public

de·pose /dɪˈpouz/ v. **1** [T] to remove a ruler or political leader from their position of power: Clemens was deposed in a military coup. **2** [I,T] LAW to officially give information about something, after you have promised to tell the truth: He has not yet been deposed in this case, but he denies trying to sabotage Wilson's plans. —see also DEPOSITION (1)

de·pos·it[1] /dɪˈpɑzɪt/ n. [C] **1** the first part of the **S W** money that you pay for something, especially something large or expensive, so that it will not be sold to someone else: We put a $100 deposit down on (=paid a deposit for) a leather sofa. **2** money that you pay when you rent something such as an apartment or car, which will be given back if you do not damage it: We paid one month's rent in advance, plus a deposit of $500. | My landlord only returned half of my security deposit (=money you get back if you do not damage something). **3** an amount of money that is put into a bank account: I'd like to **make a deposit** into my savings account. **4** a layer of a mineral, metal etc. that is left in soil or rocks through a natural process: oil and mineral deposits **5** an amount or layer of a substance that gradually develops in a particular place: fatty deposits in the arteries leading to the heart

deposit[2] v. [T] **1** [always + adv./prep.] to put some- **S W** thing down or leave something in a particular place: [+ on/in/by etc.] Litter should be deposited in the green trash cans. **2** to leave a substance on top of something else: The Colorado River deposits large amounts of sediment in Lake Powell. **3** to put money or something valuable in a bank or other place where it will be safe: Deposit the check immediately. | I'd like to deposit this in my checking account.

deposit ac·count /.ˈ.. ..ˌ./ n. [C] TECHNICAL a bank account that earns INTEREST[1] (3) —see also CHECKING ACCOUNT, SAVINGS ACCOUNT

dep·o·si·tion /ˌdɛpəˈzɪʃən/ n. **1** [C] LAW a statement written or recorded for a court of law, by someone who has promised to tell the truth: Symington's deposition was taken as part of a lawsuit between the City of Tucson and the Metropolitan Water District. **2** [U] TECHNICAL the natural process of depositing a substance in rocks or soil **3** [C,U] the act of removing someone from a position of power

de·pos·i·tor /dɪ'pɑzɪtɚ/ *n.* [C] FORMAL someone who puts money in a bank or other financial organization

de·pos·i·to·ry /dɪ'pɑzə,tɔri/ *n. plural* **depositories** [C] a place where something can be safely kept —**depository** *adj.*

deposit slip /.'.. ,./ *n.* [C] a form that you use when you put money into your bank account

de·pot /'dipoʊ/ *n.* [C] **1** a place where large amounts of food and supplies are stored until they are needed: *a weapons depot* **2** a railroad station or bus station, especially a small one

de·praved /dɪ'preɪvd/ *adj.* completely evil or morally unacceptable: *a depraved and wicked man*

depravity /dɪ'prævəti/ *n.* [U] the state of being evil or morally unacceptable: *sexual depravity* —**deprava·tion** /,dɛprə'veɪʃən/ *n.* [U]

dep·re·cate /'dɛprə,keɪt/ *v.* [T] FORMAL to disapprove of or criticize something: *Javits deprecated the violence that had occurred during the demonstrations.* —**deprecation** /,dɛprə'keɪʃən/ *n.* [U]

dep·re·cat·ing /'dɛprə,keɪtɪŋ/ also **dep·re·ca·to·ry** /'dɛprəkə,tɔri/ *adj.* expressing criticism or disapproval: *His book includes a deprecating reference to Reagan's economic policy.* —**deprecatingly** *adv.* —see also SELF-DEPRECATING

de·pre·ci·ate /dɪ'priʃi,eɪt/ *v.* **1** [I] to decrease in value or price: *New cars depreciate quickly in the first two years.* —opposite APPRECIATE **2** [T] TECHNICAL to reduce the value of something over time, especially for tax purposes: *The entire cost of an asset is depreciated over a period of years.* **3** [T] LITERARY to make something seem unimportant: *Dana depreciates the value of his relationships with his friends in his poetry.*

de·pre·ci·a·tion /dɪ,priʃi'eɪʃən/ *n.* [U] a decrease in the value or price of something: *the depreciation of the dollar* —**depreciatory** /dɪ'priʃə,tɔri/ *adj.*

dep·re·da·tion /,dɛprə'deɪʃən/ *n.* [C usually plural] FORMAL an act of cruelty, violence, or destruction: *the depredations of war*

de·press /dɪ'prɛs/ *v.* [T] **1** to make someone feel very unhappy: *That movie depressed me for hours.* **2** to prevent something from working correctly or being as active as it usually is: *The governor thinks higher taxes will depress the state's economy.* **3** FORMAL to press something down, especially a part of a machine: *Depress the brake slowly.* **4** FORMAL to reduce the value of prices or pay: *Falling demand for wheat has depressed its market price.*

de·pres·sant /dɪ'prɛsənt/ *n.* [C] a substance or drug that makes your body's processes slower and makes you feel very relaxed or sleepy —**depressant** *adj.* —compare ANTIDEPRESSANT, STIMULANT

de·pressed /dɪ'prɛst/ *adj.* **1 a)** feeling very unhappy: *A lot of people eat too much when they're depressed.* | [+ about/over] *Morgan was depressed about the divorce.* **b)** suffering from a medical condition in which you are so unhappy that you cannot live a normal life: *Some patients were clinically depressed and suicidal.* **2** an area, industry etc. that is depressed does not have enough economic or business activity: *Most people enrolled in the food stamp program live in depressed urban areas.* **3** a depressed level or amount is lower than normal: *Symptoms of the illness include a depressed appetite.*

de·press·ing /dɪ'prɛsɪŋ/ *adj.* making you feel very sad: *It was a depressing book.* | *I find it really depressing that my old neighborhood has gotten so run-down.* —**depressingly** *adv.*

s w **de·pres·sion** /dɪ'prɛʃən/ *n.* **1** [C,U] **a)** a feeling of sadness in which you feel there is no hope for the future: *Keiffer's book is about her battle with depression.* | *He went into a deep depression when his wife died.* **b)** a medical condition that makes you feel extremely unhappy, so that you cannot live a normal life: *Up to 10% of Americans suffer from clinical depression* (=depression that a doctor says is a medical condition) *at some point in their lives.* **2** [C,U] a

long period when businesses do not buy, sell, or produce very much and a lot of people do not have jobs: *an economic depression* —compare RECESSION **3 the Depression** also **the Great Depression** the period in the 1930s when there was not much business activity and many people were very poor and had no jobs **4** [C] a part of a surface that is deeper or lower than the other parts: *a depression in the sand* **5** [C] TECHNICAL a mass of air that has a low pressure and usually causes rain

de·pres·sive[1] /dɪ'prɛsɪv/ *adj.* often feeling depressed, or having signs of depression

depressive[2] *n.* [C] someone who suffers from DEPRESSION —see also MANIC DEPRESSIVE

de·pres·sur·ize /di'prɛʃə,raɪz/ *v.* [I,T] to reduce the pressure of air or gas inside a container or especially in an airplane —**depressurization** /di,prɛʃərə-'zeɪʃən/ *n.* [U]

dep·ri·va·tion /,dɛprə'veɪʃən/ *n.* [C,U] a lack of something that you need or want: *Sleep deprivation causes memory loss, paranoia, and other problems.* | *A strong musical culture survived the deprivations of slavery.*

de·prive /dɪ'praɪv/ *v.*

deprive sb of sth *phr. v.* [T often passive] to take something from someone, especially something that they need or want: *The court ruled that the women had been deprived of their civil rights.*

de·prived /dɪ'praɪvd/ *adj.* not having the things that are considered to be necessary for a comfortable or happy life: *A deprived childhood can lead to emotional problems later.*

de·pro·gram /di'proʊgræm/ *v.* **deprogrammed, deprogramming** [T] to help someone who has been involved in a religious CULT to stop obeying its orders and to start thinking for themselves again

dept. the written abbreviation of DEPARTMENT

depth /dɛpθ/ *n.* s w

1 distance [C usually singular,U] **a)** the distance from the top surface of something, such as a river or hole, to the bottom of it: *The ship's navigational equipment can measure the depth of the water.* | *Buckeye Lake reaches depths of eight to ten feet.* | *Dig out the area to a depth of four inches.* | *All the quakes were centered at a depth of about three miles.* | *The pond is no more than 3 feet in depth.* **b)** the distance from the front of an object to the back of it: *The drawers have a depth of 16 inches.*

2 emotion/situation [U] how strong an emotion is or how serious a situation is: *The poll results indicate the depth of public concern about the economy.*

3 knowledge [U] APPROVING the quality of knowing or giving a lot of important details about a subject: *Network news coverage often lacks depth.*

4 the depths of the recession/war/crisis etc. a time when something is in its worst condition or state: *Unemployment is at its highest level since the depths of the 1982 recession.*

5 in depth considering all of the details of something: *Baker said he wanted to discuss the situation in depth with the Israeli leadership.* —see also IN-DEPTH

6 be out of your depth to be involved in a situation or activity that is too difficult for you to understand: *I was hopelessly out of my depth in college chemistry classes.*

7 team [U] the number of very skilled and experienced people on a team or in a group: *Their national team will have a little more depth this year.*

8 in the depths/depth of winter in the middle of winter, when it is very cold

9 the depths of the forest/universe etc. the place that is farthest away from any people: *the depths of the Amazon rain forest*

10 in/into the depths of despair feeling extremely unhappy

11 the depths LITERARY the deepest parts of the ocean

depth charge /. ./ *n.* [C] a bomb that explodes at a particular depth under water

dep·u·ta·tion /,dɛpyə'teɪʃən/ *n.* [C] FORMAL a group of people who are sent to talk to someone in authority, as representatives of a larger group

de·pute /dɪˈpyut/ v. [T] **depute sb to do sth** FORMAL to give someone the authority to do something instead of you

dep·u·tize /ˈdɛpyəˌtaɪz/ v. [T] to give someone below you in rank the authority to do your work for a short time, usually because you are unable to do it or need help: *Carter was deputized by Dodge to take command of the tanker.*

S W **dep·u·ty** /ˈdɛpyəti/ n. plural **deputies** [C] **1** someone who is directly below someone else in rank, and who is officially in charge when that person is not there: *the deputy district attorney* **2** someone whose job is to help a SHERIFF

de·rail /dɪˈreɪl, di-/ v. **1** [I,T usually passive] to make a train go off the railroad tracks, or to go off the tracks: *Forty-five people were injured when a passenger train derailed near Ottumwa, Iowa.* **2** [T] to spoil or interrupt a plan, agreement etc.: *Radicals are trying to derail the peace process.* —**derailment** n. [C,U]

de·rail·leur /dɪˈreɪlɚ/ n. [C] the piece of equipment on a bicycle that moves the chain from one GEAR to another

de·ranged /dɪˈreɪndʒd/ adj. behaving in a crazy or dangerous way: *a deranged gunman* —**derangement** n. [U]

der·by /ˈdɚbi/ n. plural **derbies** [C] **1** a type of horse race: *the Kentucky Derby* **2** a special race or competition: *a roller derby* (=a race on ROLLER SKATES) **3** a man's stiff round hat that is usually black

de·reg·u·late /diˈrɛgyəˌleɪt/ v. [T] to remove government rules and controls from some types of business activity: *The U.S. airline industry has been deregulated since 1978.* —**deregulation** /diˌrɛgyəˈleɪʃən/ n. [U]

der·e·lict[1] /ˈdɛrəˌlɪkt/ adj. **1** [usually before noun] a building or piece of land that is derelict is in very bad condition because it has not been used for a long time: *derelict homes and businesses* **2** not doing the things you should be doing or have the responsibility to do: *If Stewart was unaware of the problem, he was derelict in his duty* (=did not do what he should have done).

derelict[2] n. [C] DISAPPROVING someone who has no money or home and who has to live on the streets

der·e·lic·tion /ˌdɛrəˈlɪkʃən/ n. **1 dereliction of duty** FORMAL failure to do what you should do as part of your job: *The officer in charge was cleared of dereliction of duty.* **2** [U] the state of being derelict

de·ride /dɪˈraɪd/ v. [T] FORMAL to make statements or jokes that show you have no respect for someone or something: *Gavin has derided McLaughlin's crusade for gun control.* | [**deride sb/sth as sth**] *Jackson derided the plan as unworkable.*

de ri·gueur /də rɪˈgɚ/ adj. [not before noun] considered to be necessary and expected by other people: *Tuxedos are de rigueur at the event.*

de·ri·sion /dɪˈrɪʒən/ n. [U] statements or actions that show that you have no respect for someone or something: *Fans whistled in derision when Jones missed the catch.*

de·ri·sive /dɪˈraɪsɪv, -ˈrɪ-/ adj. showing that you have no respect for someone or something: *Fenton's remark drew derisive laughs.* —**derisively** adv.

de·ri·so·ry /dɪˈraɪsəri, -zə-/ adj. **1** an amount of money that is derisory is so small that it is not worth considering seriously: *Unions described the pay offer as derisory.* **2** derisive: *derisory comments* —**derisorily** adv.

der·i·va·tion /ˌdɛrəˈveɪʃən/ n. [C,U] the act or process of developing or coming from something else, such as the formation of a new word from another word: *What is the derivation of the word "redshirt"?*

de·riv·a·tive[1] /dɪˈrɪvəṭɪv/ n. [C] **1** something that has developed or been produced from something else: [+ **of**] *The drug is a derivative of Vitamin A.* **2** a type of financial INVESTMENT: *In the derivative market, insurance companies have scaled back their purchases of Remic securities.*

derivative[2] adj. DISAPPROVING not new or invented, but copied or taken from something else: *This season's TV shows are all pretty dull and derivative.*

de·rive /dɪˈraɪv/ v. **1** [T] to get something, especially a nice feeling or an advantage, from something or someone: [**derive sth from sth**] *Children derive comfort from familiar surroundings.* | *Many colleges derive most of their income from tuition fees.* **2** [I,T] to develop or come from something else: [**derive sth from sth**] *Hughes' music is derived from blues and jazz.* **3** [T] TECHNICAL to get a chemical substance from another substance: [**derive sth from sth**] *The enzyme is derived from human blood.*

der·ma·ti·tis /ˌdɚməˈtaɪṭɪs/ n. [U] a disease of the skin that causes redness, swelling, and pain

der·ma·tol·o·gy /ˌdɚməˈtɑlədʒi/ n. [U] the part of medical science that deals with the skin, its diseases, and their treatment —**dermatologist** n. [C]

der·mis /ˈdɚmɪs/ n. [U] TECHNICAL the layer of skin under the EPIDERMIS

der·o·gate /ˈdɛrəˌgeɪt/ v. [T] FORMAL to make something seem less important or less good

derogate from sth phr. v. [T] FORMAL to change from an expected or planned idea, action, or type of behavior

de·rog·a·to·ry /dɪˈrɑgəˌtɔri/ adj. insulting and disapproving | **derogatory remark/comment/term etc.** *"Cracker" is a derogatory term for a poor Southern white man.* —**derogatorily** adv.

der·rick /ˈdɛrɪk/ n. [C] **1** a tall tower built over an oil well that is used to raise and lower the DRILL[1] (1) **2** a tall machine used for lifting heavy weights, used especially on ships

Der·ri·da /ˌdɛriˈdɑ/, **Jacques** /ʒɑk/ (1930–) a French PHILOSOPHER

der·ri·ère /ˌdɛriˈɛr/ n. [C] HUMOROUS the part of the body that you sit on; BUTTOCKS

der·ring-do /ˌdɛrɪŋ ˈdu/ n. [U] HUMOROUS very brave actions like the ones that happen in adventure stories

der·rin·ger /ˈdɛrɪndʒɚ/ n. [C] a small gun with a short BARREL

der·vish /ˈdɚvɪʃ/ n. [C] a member of a Muslim religious group, some of whom dance fast and spin around as part of a religious ceremony

de·sal·i·nate /diˈsæləˌneɪt/ v. [T] TECHNICAL to remove the salt from ocean water so that it can be used in homes and factories —**desalination** /diˌsælənˈeɪʃən/ n. [U]

de·salt /diˈsɔlt/ v. [T] to desalinate

des·cant /ˈdɛskænt/ n. [C] a tune that is played or sung above the main tune in a piece of music

Des·cartes /deɪˈkɑrt/, **Re·né** /rəˈneɪ/ (1596–1650) a French mathematician and PHILOSOPHER

de·scend /dɪˈsɛnd/ v. **1** [I,T] FORMAL to move from a higher level to a lower one: *The plane started to descend.* | *Several climbers were descending the mountain.* | [+ **from/to/onto**] *The elevator descended to the 7th floor, and Anna got out.* —opposite ASCEND **2 in descending order** numbers, choices etc. that are in descending order are arranged from the highest or most important to the lowest or least important: *Food manufacturers must list ingredients in descending order by weight.* **3** [I] LITERARY if darkness, night etc. descends, it begins to get dark

descend from sb/sth phr. v. [T] **1 be descended from sb** to be related to someone who lived a long time ago: *Stu's mother is descended from Cherokee Indians.* **2** to have developed from something that existed in the past: *Some stretching exercises descend from yoga positions.*

descend into sth phr. v. [T] when a situation or place descends into something, it becomes worse than it was: *Yugoslavia descended into civil war.*

descend on/upon sb/sth phr. v. [T] **1** if a large group of people descends on a place, they go there together to do something or to meet or see someone: *Thousands of students will descend on Florida for spring break.* **2** LITERARY if a feeling descends on someone, they begin to feel it

descend to sth phr. v. [T] **1** to behave or speak in

an impolite way that is not what people expect from you: *The debate descended to name-calling.* **2 descend to sb's level** to behave or speak in the same impolite way as someone else

de·scend·ant /dɪ'sɛndənt/ *n.* [C] **1** someone who is related to a person who lived a long time ago: *Cristobal Colon is a direct descendant of* (=from one father or mother to the next) *Columbus.* —compare ANCESTOR **2** something that has been developed from something else: [+ of] *The owner of Ring's Super Burgers set out to create a direct descendant of a 1950s diner.*

de·scent /dɪ'sɛnt/ *n.* **1** [C,U] FORMAL the process of going down: *Passengers said the cabin shook violently during the plane's descent.* **2** [U] your family origins, especially in relation to the country where your family came from: *Today, about 65,000 people of Chinese descent live in Santa Clara County.* **3** [singular] a change to a bad condition or state: [+ into] *The diary chronicles a young girl's descent into drug abuse.* **4** [C] a path or road that goes steeply down: *a slippery descent* —opposite ASCENT

de·scram·bler /dɪ'skræmblə/ *n.* [C] a machine that can change a radio, television or telephone message that has been mixed up, into a form that can be understood

de·scribe /dɪ'skraɪb/ *v.* [T] **1** to say what something or someone is like by giving details about them: *This Navajo folk tale describes the creation of the Earth.* | *How would you describe yourself?* | [describe sb/sth as sth] *Nick's co-workers described him as fun and outgoing.* | [describe sb/sth to sb] *The woman described her attacker to police as tall and dark.* | [describe how/what/where etc.] *Children were asked to look at the painting and describe what they saw.* **2** FORMAL if something describes a shape, it follows the outside line of that shape: *Her hand described a circle in the air.*

de·scrip·tion /dɪ'skrɪpʃən/ *n.* **1** [C,U] a piece of writing or speech that gives details about what someone or something is like: [+ of] *The writer began with a description of the area.* | *One history textbook features a detailed description and illustration of a Seder.* | *"Outdated" would be an accurate description of the building.* | *The catalog gives a full description of each product.* | *There is a brief description of the book's plot.* | *Police stopped a van matching the general description of the vehicle.* | **fit/match a description** *Whitfield fit the description of the robbery suspect.* **2 be beyond description** also **defy description** to be too good, bad, big etc. to be described easily: *The death and destruction was beyond description.* **3 of every/some/any etc. description** also **of all descriptions** belonging to a group or type of things: *The police raid found drugs of every description.* | *Boats of all descriptions raced across Lake Michigan.*

de·scrip·tive /dɪ'skrɪptɪv/ *adj.* **1** giving a description of something in words or pictures: *A descriptive listing of 116 bed-and-breakfast inns is available.* **2** TECHNICAL describing how the words of a language are actually used, rather than saying how they ought to be used —compare PRESCRIPTIVE (2) —**descriptively** *adv.* —**descriptiveness** *n.* [U]

de·scry /dɪ'skraɪ/ *v.* [T] LITERARY to notice or see something, especially when it is a long way away

des·e·crate /'dɛsə,kreɪt/ *v.* [T] to spoil or damage something holy or respected: *Three skinheads admitted desecrating over 100 graves.* —**desecration** /,dɛsə'kreɪʃən/ *n.* [U]

de·seg·re·gate /di'sɛgrə,geɪt/ *v.* [T] to do something to end a system in which people of different races are kept separate: *School officials are still working to desegregate the district.* —opposite SEGREGATE —**desegregation** /di,sɛgrə'greɪʃən/ *n.* [U]

de·sen·si·tize /di'sɛnsə,taɪz/ *v.* **1** to make someone react less strongly to something by making them become used to it: [+ to] *Do war toys desensitize children to the reality of war?* **2** TECHNICAL to make PHO-

TOGRAPHIC material less sensitive to light —**desensitization** /di,sɛnsətə'zeɪʃən/ *n.* [U]

des·ert¹ /'dɛzət/ *n.* **1** [C,U] a large area of land where it is always very hot and dry and there is a lot of sand: *the Sahara Desert* —see also DESERT ISLAND **2** [C] a place where there is no activity or where nothing interesting happens: *Northern Iowa has long been seen as a cultural desert.* **3 get your just deserts** to be punished in a way that you deserve: *Seymour dreamed of a fairer world where the rich who exploited workers would get their just deserts.*

desert² /dɪ'zət/ *v.* **1** [T] to leave someone alone and refuse to help or support them anymore: *Paul feels that his father deserted him after the divorce.* **2** [I] to leave the military without permission: *U.S. officials say 1000 enemy soldiers have deserted.* **3** [T] to leave a place so that it is completely empty: *Goldilocks finds a house in the woods that seems to have been deserted by its owners.* **4** [T] if a feeling or quality deserts you, you do not have it anymore, especially at a time when you need it: *Mike's confidence seemed to have deserted him.*

de·sert·ed /dɪ'zətɪd/ *adj.* empty and quiet, especially because there are no people there: *Thirty years later, the steel mill town stands completely deserted.* | *a deserted street corner*

de·sert·er /dɪ'zətə/ *n.* [C] a soldier who leaves the military without permission

de·ser·tion /dɪ'zəʃən/ *n.* **1** [C,U] the act of leaving the military without permission: *Larsen was one of 42 Marines charged with desertion.* **2** [U] LAW the act of leaving your wife or husband because you do not want to live with them anymore

desert is·land /,.. '../ *n.* [C] a small tropical island that is far away from other places and that has no people living on it

de·serve /dɪ'zəv/ *v.* [T] **1** to have earned something by good or bad actions or behavior: *What had he done to deserve this punishment?* | [deserve to do sth] *It was the sort of game both teams deserved to win.* | *I worked hard for this award, and I deserve it.* | *Many people believe prisoners who suffer violence are getting what they deserve.* | *Homeless kids certainly deserve better* (=deserve nicer treatment). **2 deserve consideration/attention/mention etc.** if a suggestion, idea, or plan deserves consideration, attention, mention etc., it is good or sensible enough to be considered, paid attention to, mentioned etc.: *The recommendations in the report certainly deserve further consideration.* **3 sb deserves a medal** SPOKEN, HUMOROUS used to say that you admire the way someone has dealt with a situation or problem: *If you can sit through all 10 hours of lectures, you deserve a medal.*

de·served /dɪ'zəvd/ *adj.* earned because of good or bad behavior, skill, work etc.: *The company has a well-deserved reputation for providing very generous benefits.*

de·serv·ed·ly /dɪ'zəvɪdli/ *adv.* **1 deservedly famous/successful/celebrated etc.** famous, successful, celebrated etc. in a way that is right or deserved: *Bistro Roti is a deservedly popular restaurant.* **2 ...(and) deservedly so** used to say that you agree that something is right and deserved: *The play won the 1990 Pulitzer Prize for drama, and deservedly so.*

de·serv·ing /dɪ'zəvɪŋ/ *adj.* **1** [usually before noun] needing help and support, especially financial support: *The government has wrongly denied benefits to many deserving children.* **2 be deserving of sth** FORMAL to deserve something: *Howard is certainly deserving of the Heisman Trophy.*

de·sex·u·al·ize /di'sɛkʃuə,laɪz/ *v.* [T] to remove the sexual quality from something —**desexualization** /di,sɛkʃuələ'zeɪʃən/ *n.* [C,U]

dés·ha·billé /,deɪzæbi'eɪ/ also **dishabille** *n.* [U] LITERARY OR HUMOROUS the state of being only partly dressed, used especially of a woman

des·ic·cant /'dɛsɪkənt/ *n.* [C,U] TECHNICAL a substance that takes water from the air so that other things stay dry

des·ic·cate /ˈdesɪˌkeɪt/ v. [T] FORMAL to remove all the water from something —**desiccated** adj. —**desiccation** /ˌdesɪˈkeɪʃən/ n. [U]

de·sid·er·a·tum /dɪˌsɪdəˈrɑtəm, -ˈreɪ-/ n. plural **desiderata** [C] LITERARY something that is wanted or needed

de·sign¹ /dɪˈzaɪn/ n.

1 pattern [C] a style or pattern used for decorating something: *The arched ceiling is bordered with a hand-painted, floral design.* | *Tom has several tattoos, and they're all Native American designs.*

2 arrangement of parts [C,U] the way that something has been planned and made, including its appearance, how it works etc.: *The car's design has been greatly improved.* | *the design of consumer products*

3 process of planning [U] the art or process of making a drawing of something to show how you will make it or what it will look like: *Dorn has done a great deal of design work on the new city hall.* | *graphic design*

4 drawing [C] a drawing showing how something will be made or what it will look like: [+ **for**] *The President will unveil the design for a new World War II memorial on the National Mall.*

5 intention [C,U] a plan that someone has in their mind: *The law firm is all-female, though not **by design*** (=intentionally).

6 have designs on sth to be interested in something because you want it for yourself, especially if it will bring you money: *Several developers have designs on the two-acre beachfront property.*

7 have designs on sb to want a sexual relationship with someone

de·sign² v. **1** [I,T] to make a drawing or plan of something that will be made or built: *The office complex was designed by Mitchell Benjamin.* **2 well-designed/badly-designed/specially-designed** etc. made well, made badly, made especially etc.: *Hong Kong has a clean, cheap, and well-designed urban subway system.* **3** [T usually passive] to plan or develop something for a specific purpose: [**design sth to do sth**] *These exercises are designed to develop and strengthen muscles.* | [**be designed for sth**] *The kitchen is designed for two cooks, with double work areas.* | [**be designed as sth**] *The new Saturn models were designed as fun-to-drive, affordable cars.* —see also DESIGNER¹

des·ig·nate¹ /ˈdezɪɡˌneɪt/ v. [T usually passive] **1** to choose someone or something for a particular job or purpose: [**designate sth as/for sth**] *Funds were designated for projects in low-income areas.* | [**designate sb to do sth**] *Sullivan is the second crew member designated to walk in space during the mission.* **2** to show or mean something, especially by using a special name or sign: *Buildings are designated by red squares on the map.*

des·ig·nate² /ˈdezɪɡnət, -neɪt/ adj. [only after noun] FORMAL a word used after the name of an official job showing that someone has been chosen for that job but has not yet officially started work: *the ambassador designate*

designated driv·er /ˌ.... '../ n. [C] someone who agrees to not drink alcohol when they go out to a party, bar etc., so that they can drive their friends home

designated hit·ter /ˌ.... '../ n. [C] **1** a baseball player who replaces the PITCHER when it is the PITCHER's turn to hit the ball **2** INFORMAL someone who does a job for someone else, especially in politics or business

des·ig·na·tion /ˌdezɪɡˈneɪʃən/ n. **1** [U] the act of choosing someone or something for a particular purpose, or of giving them a particular description: *Lott opposed the designation of Martin Luther King Jr.'s birthday as a national holiday.* **2** [C] FORMAL a description or title that someone or something is given: *Erik's official designation is Senior Developmental Director.*

de·sign·er¹ /dɪˈzaɪnɚ/ n. [C] someone whose job is to make plans or patterns for clothes, furniture, equipment etc.: *I recommend hiring a professional designer.* | *a software designer*

designer² adj. [only before noun] made by a well-known and fashionable designer: *designer jeans*

designer drug /ˈ.. ˌ./ n. [C] a drug that is made to have a pleasant, exciting, or relaxing effect but that is not used for medical reasons, especially a drug similar to COCAINE or HEROIN but having a slightly different chemical structure

de·sign·ing /dɪˈzaɪnɪŋ/ adj. [only before noun] someone who is designing tries to deceive people in order to get what they want

de·sir·a·ble /dɪˈzaɪrəbəl/ adj. FORMAL **1** something that is desirable is worth having or doing because it is useful, popular, or good: *Oak Hills is one of the area's most desirable neighborhoods.* | *Ellman's goal is **highly desirable*** (=very desirable), *but unfortunately not realistic.* —compare UNDESIRABLE **2** someone who is desirable is sexually attractive —**desirably** adv. —**desirability** /dɪˌzaɪrəˈbɪləti/ n. [U]

de·sire¹ /dɪˈzaɪɚ/ n. **1** [C,U] a strong hope or wish: [+ **for**] *Teenagers' desire for independence can cause problems for their parents.* | [**desire to do sth**] *One woman had expressed a strong desire to learn to read.* | [**desire that**] *It was Mr. Hertzog's desire that there be no funeral service.* | *I **have no desire to*** (=used to emphasize that you do not want to do something) *work in a restaurant.* | *All my life I've had a **burning desire** (=a very strong desire) to travel.* | *If either country **expresses a desire** for peace, this represents progress.* **2** [U + **for**] FORMAL a strong wish to have sex with someone

desire² v. [T not in progressive] **1** FORMAL to want or hope for something very much: *I think the Israelis as a people desire peace.* | [**desire to do sth**] *Power is used by those desiring to fulfill their objective.* | *Add lemon juice **if desired*** (=if you want to). **2** FORMAL to want to have sex with someone —**desired** adj. —see also **leave something/a lot/ much to be desired** (LEAVE¹ (24))

de·sir·ous /dɪˈzaɪrəs/ adj. [+ **of**] FORMAL wanting something very much

de·sist /dɪˈzɪst, dɪˈsɪst/ v. [I] FORMAL to stop doing something: [+ **from**] *The government urged the rebels to desist from their terrorist actions.* —see also **cease and desist** (CEASE¹ (2))

desk /desk/ n. [C] **1** a piece of furniture like a table, usually with drawers in it, that you sit at to write and work **2** the place in a hotel where you pay for and get the key for your room, or the area of a business or hospital where you can get information: *A nurse was seated at the reception desk.* | *Check in at the front desk.* **3** an office that deals with a particular subject, especially in newspapers or television: *Lloyd is running the sports desk.* —see picture on page 426

desk clerk /ˈ. ./ n. [C] someone who works at the main desk in a hotel

de·skill /ˌdiˈskɪl/ v. [T] to remove or reduce the need for skill in a job, usually by changing to machinery

desk job /ˈ. ./ n. [C] a job that involves working mostly at a desk in an office

desk jock·ey /ˈ. ˌ../ n. [C] INFORMAL, HUMOROUS someone who works at a desk instead of doing something that involves physical activity

desk·top /ˈdesktɑp/ n. [C] **1** the main area on a computer where you can find the ICONs that represent PROGRAMs, and where you can do things to manage the information on the computer **2** the top surface of a desk

desktop com·put·er /ˌ.. .'../ n. [C] a computer that is small enough to be used on a desk —compare LAPTOP

desktop pub·lish·ing /ˌ.. '.../ n. [C] the work of producing magazines, books, signs etc. with a desktop computer

Des Moines /dəˈmɔɪn/ the capital city of the U.S. state of Iowa

des·o·late[1] /'dɛsəlɪt/ adj. **1** a place that is desolate is empty and looks sad because there are no people there and not much activity: *Radin's body was found in a desolate canyon about 65 miles north of Los Angeles.* **2** someone who is desolate feels very sad and lonely —**desolately** adv. —**desolation** /ˌdɛsə'leɪʃən/ n. [U]

des·o·late[2] /'dɛsə,leɪt/ v. [T usually passive] LITERARY **1** to make someone feel very sad and lonely: *Andropulos was desolated by the deaths of his friends.* **2** to cause so much damage to a place that it is almost completely destroyed: *Drought had desolated the farming town.*

de So·to /dɪ'soʊtoʊ/, **Her·nan·do** /hɚ'nændoʊ/ (?1500–1542) a Spanish EXPLORER who discovered the Mississippi River

de·spair[1] /dɪ'spɛr/ n. [U] **1** a feeling that you have no hope at all: *I could understand her despair at her homelessness.* | *Snyder hanged himself in despair over problems in his marriage.* | *To the despair of 15,000 workers, the company announced the closure of eight factories.* **2** **be the despair of sb** OLD-FASHIONED to make someone feel very worried, upset, or unhappy, especially by your bad behavior

despair[2] v. [I] FORMAL to feel that there is no hope at all: *Despite his illness, Ron never despaired.* | [**despair of (doing) sth**] *By the end of the day, I despaired of ever learning to ski.*

de·spair·ing /dɪ'spɛrɪŋ/ adj. showing a feeling of despair: *We are disappointed with the rate of progress, but we are not despairing.* —**despairingly** adv.

des·per·a·do /ˌdɛspə'radoʊ/ n. plural **desperadoes** or **desperados** [C] OLD-FASHIONED a violent criminal who is not afraid of danger

des·per·ate /'dɛsprɪt, -pərɪt/ adj. **1** willing to do anything to change a very bad situation, and not caring about danger: *I had no money left and was desperate.* | *TV stations broadcast an appeal from the teenager's desperate parents.* | [**be desperate to do sth**] *Many East Germans were desperate to leave their homeland.* **2** needing or wanting something very much: [+ **for**] *Desperate for ideas, Hollywood often recycles movie plots.* | *The American Red Cross said it was in desperate need of blood.* **3** a desperate situation is very bad or serious: *There was a desperate shortage of doctors.* **4** a desperate action is something that you only do because you are in a very bad situation: *Several POWs made a desperate attempt to escape.* | *The country is taking desperate measures to improve the economy.*

des·per·ate·ly /'dɛsprɪtli/ adv. **1** in a desperate way: *We're desperately trying to avoid laying off people.* **2** very much: *Lori wanted desperately to have a child.* | *Steady winter rains are desperately needed to bring the city water supply back to normal.*

des·per·a·tion /ˌdɛspə'reɪʃən/ n. [U] a strong feeling that you will do anything to change a very bad situation: *a look of desperation* | *Larson resorted to high-risk investments out of desperation.* | *In desperation, the boy grabbed at his rescuer's hands.*

de·spic·a·ble /dɪ'spɪkəbəl/ adj. extremely bad, immoral, or cruel: *Abusing a child is a despicable act.* —**despicably** adv.

de·spise /dɪ'spaɪz/ v. [T not in progressive] to dislike someone or something very much: *If you fly a lot on business, then you probably despise most airports.*

de·spite /dɪ'spaɪt/ prep. **1** without being prevented by something; even though something else exists or is true: *Despite international pressure, progress has slowed in the peace talks.* | *Lorin said he and his sister make a good team, despite the fact that they sometimes argue.* **2** **despite yourself** if you do something despite yourself, you do it although you did not intend to: *Jessie realized that, despite herself, she cared about Edward.*

WORD CHOICE: despite, in spite of, although
Despite and **in spite of** (prepositions) can only be followed by a noun or gerund: *Marla's a good worker, despite her problems at home.* | *Despite being one of the largest cities in the world, Mexico City was relatively safe.* Unlike **although** (a conjunction), **despite** and **in spite of** cannot introduce a clause that has a finite verb such as "was." Compare: *Despite owning two cars, he can't drive.* | *In spite of owning two cars, he can't drive.* | *Although he owns two cars, he can't drive.*

de·spoil /dɪ'spɔɪl/ v. [T] LITERARY **1** to make a place much less attractive by removing or damaging things: *The sandy beaches are being despoiled by an oil spill.* **2** to steal from a place or people using force, especially in a war

de·spond·ent /dɪ'spandənt/ adj. unhappy and without hope: [+ **about/over**] *She said her husband had been despondent about his cancer.* —**despondency** n. [U] —**despondently** adv.

des·pot /'dɛspət, -pat/ n. [C] someone such as a ruler who uses power in a cruel and unfair way —**despotic** /dɛ'spatɪk, dɪ-/ adj. —**despotically** /-kli/ adv.

des·pot·ism /'dɛspə,tɪzəm/ n. [U] rule by a despot

des·sert /dɪ'zɚt/ n. [C,U] sweet food served after the main part of a meal: *What's for dessert, Mom?*

dessert wine /.'. ,./ n. [C,U] a sweet wine served with dessert

de·sta·bi·lize /di'steɪbə,laɪz/ v. [T] **1** to make something such as a government or ECONOMY become less successful or powerful, or less able to control events: *Apparently the CIA acted to destabilize Communist governments.* **2** to make something unsteady or weak: *The train wreck destabilized a gas pipeline that later exploded.* **3** TECHNICAL to make a chemical separate into simpler ELEMENTs —**destabilization** /diˌsteɪbələ'zeɪʃən/ n. [U]

des·ti·na·tion /ˌdɛstə'neɪʃən/ n. [C] the place that someone or something is going to: *Allow plenty of time to get to your destination.* | *Maui is a popular tourist destination.*

des·tined /'dɛstənd/ adj. **1** [not before noun] seeming certain to happen at some time in the future: [+ **for**] *Beautiful and young, Carmen seemed destined for stardom on Broadway.* | [**be destined to do sth**] *Miyazawa was destined to succeed Toshiki Kaifu as Prime Minister.* **2** **(be) destined for sth** to be traveling or taken to a particular place: *The new trade rules do not apply to exports destined for Europe.*

des·ti·ny /'dɛstəni/ n. plural **destinies 1** [C usually singular] the things that will happen to someone in the future, especially those that cannot be changed or controlled; FATE (1): *Nancy wondered whether it was her destiny to live in England and marry Melvyn.* **2** [U] the power that some people believe decides what will happen to them in the future; FATE (2)

des·ti·tute /'dɛstə,tut/ adj. **1** having no money, no food, no place to live etc.: *The floods left many people destitute.* **2** **be destitute of sth** LITERARY to be completely without something: *a man destitute of compassion* —**destitution** /ˌdɛstə'tuʃən/ n. [U]

de·stroy /dɪ'strɔɪ/ v. **destroys, destroyed, destroying** [T] **1** to damage something so badly that it does not exist anymore or cannot be used or repaired: *Pollution may destroy the 17th century shrine.* | *An accident destroyed her ballet career.* **2** **destroy sb** to ruin someone's life completely, so that they have no hope for the future: *The information would destroy Walken and his reputation.* **3** INFORMAL to defeat an opponent easily or by a large number of points: *The Bears destroyed the Detroit Lions, 35–3.* **4** to kill an animal, especially because it is sick or dangerous —see also DESTRUCTION, **search-and-destroy mission/operation** (SEARCH[2] (7))

USAGE NOTE: DESTROY

WORD CHOICE: destroy, ruin, spoil
Destroy means to damage something so badly that it does not exist or cannot be used or repaired anymore: *About 28,000 buildings were destroyed by the earthquake.* | *The radiation treatments are designed to destroy cancer cells.* | *The tribe's traditional way of life has been destroyed.* If you **ruin** or (less strong) **spoil** something good or useful, it usually still exists, but does not have its good qualities or features anymore: *Too much sugar can ruin your teeth.* | *I hope this conversation hasn't spoiled your meal.*

de·stroy·er /dɪ'strɔɪɚ/ *n.* [C] **1** a small fast military ship with guns **2** someone or something that destroys things or people: *Dams have been destroyers of fish habitats.*

de·struc·tion /dɪ'strʌkʃən/ *n.* [U] **1** the act or process of destroying something or of being destroyed: [+ of] *Belarus agreed to the destruction of its nuclear weapons.* **2** the damage caused by something: *The president flew in to look at the destruction caused by the earthquake.* —see also DESTROY

de·struc·tive /dɪ'strʌktɪv/ *adj.* causing damage to people or things: *Jealousy is a very destructive emotion.* | *Residents were awed by the earthquake's destructive force.* —**destructively** *adv.* —**destructiveness** *n.* [U]

des·ul·to·ry /'dɛsəl,tɔri/ *adj.* FORMAL done without any particular plan or purpose: *a desultory conversation*

Det. the written abbreviation of DETECTIVE

de·tach /dɪ'tætʃ/ *v.* [I,T] **1** if you detach something or if it detaches, it becomes separated from something that it was attached to: *Please detach and fill out the application form.* | *The tires on the toy cars may detach and become a hazard to small children.* | [detach sth from sth] *Workers detached the power lines from the old, rotting poles.* **2** detach yourself from sb/sth to try to be less involved with or less concerned about someone or something: *In order to do her job during the war, she detached herself from her feelings.*

de·tach·a·ble /dɪ'tætʃəbəl/ *adj.* able to be removed and put back: *The coat has a detachable lining.*

de·tached /dɪ'tætʃt/ *adj.* **1** not reacting to or becoming involved in something in an emotional way: *Wheeler sings in a detached, passionless way.* | [+ from] *Perhaps people feel detached from the war because of the technology involved.* **2** a detached house or garage is not connected to another building on any side

de·tach·ment /dɪ'tætʃmənt/ *n.* **1** [U] the state of not expressing or feeling strong emotions about something: *Doctors need to have some degree of emotional detachment.* **2** [C] a group of soldiers who are sent away from the main group to do a special job **3** [U] the state of being separate from something or not involved in it: [+ from] *Several people reported a sense of detachment from their bodies after taking the drug.*

detail

s w **de·tail**[1] /'diteɪl, dɪ'teɪl/ *n.* **1** [C,U] a single feature, **2 2** fact, or piece of information about something: [+ of] *Barr would not discuss details of the research.* | *Demand that the house plans show everything, down*

to the last detail (=completely). **2** [U] all the separate features and pieces of information about something: *Dr. Blount described the process in detail* (=using a lot of details). | *McDougal was reluctant to go into detail* (=give a lot of details) *about the company's earnings.* | *Her hard work and attention to detail helped make the store a success.* **3 details** [plural] information that helps to complete what you know about something: *It wasn't until 1945 that the full details were revealed.* | *For further details, please consult your tax adviser.* **4** [singular,U] TECHNICAL a specific duty that is given to a soldier, or the person or group who have that duty: *The Secretary of State was accompanied by a small security detail.*

de·tail[2] /dɪ'teɪl/ *v.* [T] **1** to list things or give all the facts or information about something: *The story detailed Tyson's charitable donations.* **2** to clean a car very thoroughly, inside and out **3 detail sb to (do) sth** to officially order someone, especially soldiers, to do a particular job: *Vance, you're detailed to the night watch.*

de·tailed /dɪ'teɪld, 'diteɪld/ *adj.* **1** containing or using a lot of information or details: *detailed lesson plans* **2** having decorations or a lot of small features that are difficult to produce: *Furniture makers produced beautifully detailed chairs.*

de·tail·ing /'diteɪlɪŋ/ *n.* [U] **1** decorations that are added to something such as a car or piece of clothing **2** the process of cleaning a car very thoroughly, inside and out

de·tain /dɪ'teɪn/ *v.* [T] **1** to officially prevent someone from leaving a place: *Police detained two suspects for questioning.* **2** to stop someone from leaving a place as soon as they expected: *Mrs. Flanagan was detained in Washington on urgent business.* —**detainment** *n.* [U]

de·tain·ee /di,teɪ'ni/ *n.* [C] FORMAL someone who is officially kept in a prison, usually because of their political views

de·tan·gle /,di'tæŋgəl/ *v.* [T] to remove the knots in hair

de·tect /dɪ'tɛkt/ *v.* [T] to notice or discover something, especially something that is not easy to see, hear etc.: *Many forms of cancer can be cured if detected early* | *Though the yellow tomatoes are pretty, I couldn't detect much difference in flavor.* —**detectable** *adj.*

de·tec·tion /dɪ'tɛkʃən/ *n.* [U] the process of detecting, or the fact of being detected: *By flying low, the plane was able to avoid detection by enemy radar.*

de·tec·tive /dɪ'tɛktɪv/ *n.* [C] **1** a police officer whose job is to discover information about crimes and catch criminals: *Anyone with information is being asked to call Detective Mike Place.* —see also STORE DETECTIVE **2** someone who is paid to discover information about someone or something: *a private detective* **3 detective work** efforts to discover information, find out how something works, answer a difficult question etc.: *It takes some detective work to trace the symptom back to its cause.* **4 detective story/novel etc.** a story, novel etc. about a crime, often a murder, and a detective who tries to find out who did it

de·tec·tor /dɪ'tɛktɚ/ *n.* [C] a machine or piece of equipment that finds or measures something: *Fred's belt buckle set off the metal detector at the airport.* —see also LIE DETECTOR, SMOKE DETECTOR

de·tente, détente /deɪ'tɑnt/ *n.* [U] FORMAL a time or situation in which two countries that are not friendly toward each other agree to behave in a more friendly way

de·ten·tion /dɪ'tɛnʃən/ *n.* **1** [C,U] the state of being kept in prison, or the time someone is kept in prison: *Sanchez has been released without charge after five days' detention.* **2** [U] a punishment in which children who have behaved badly are forced to stay at school for a short time after the others have gone home: *I got detention for talking in class.*

detention camp /.ˈ.. ˌ../ *n.* [C] a camp where a lot of military prisoners, political prisoners, REFUGEES etc. are kept by a government

detention cen·ter /.ˈ.. ˌ../ *n.* [C] a prison, often for a particular type of person such as children or women

de·ter /dɪˈtɚ/ *v.* deterred, deterring [T] to stop something happening, or to stop someone from doing something, by making it seem difficult or threatening people with punishment: *It is not clear whether the death penalty deters crime.* | [**deter sb from doing sth**] *The study's results may have deterred women from getting regular checkups.* —see also DETERRENT

de·ter·gent /dɪˈtɚdʒənt/ *n.* [C,U] a liquid or powder similar to soap, used for washing clothes, dishes etc.

de·te·ri·o·rate /dɪˈtɪriəˌreɪt/ *v.* [I] **1** to become worse: *Ethel's health deteriorated to the point that she could no longer walk.* | *Relations between the two countries have deteriorated since the agreement was signed.* **2** to develop into a bad situation: [+ **into**] *They got into an argument that deteriorated into a fistfight.* —**deterioration** /dɪˌtɪriəˈreɪʃən/ *n.* [U]

de·ter·mi·nant /dɪˈtɚmɪnənt/ *n.* [C + of] FORMAL something that strongly influences what you do or how you behave

de·ter·mi·nate /dɪˈtɚmənɪt/ *adj.* FORMAL strictly controlled or limited

de·ter·mi·na·tion /dɪˌtɚməˈneɪʃən/ *n.* [C,U] **1** the quality of trying to do something even when it is difficult: *Determination and hard work led Sanders from poverty to success.* | [**determination to do sth**] *Yuji shows great determination to learn English.* | *Hansen has vision and dogged (=strong) determination.* **2** FORMAL the act of deciding something officially: *He had not yet made a determination on whether to keep the U.S. embassy open.* **3** TECHNICAL the act of finding the exact level, amount, or causes of something: *The inquiry is trying to make a final determination of what caused the accident.* —see also SELF-DETERMINATION

S W **de·ter·mine** /dɪˈtɚmɪn/ *v.* [T] **1** to find out the facts
1
2 about something: [**determine how/what/who etc.**] *Using sonar, they determined exactly where the ship had sunk.* | [**determine that**] *Investigators have determined that the signature was forged.* **2** to officially decide something: *The date of the court case is yet to be determined.* | [**determine how/what/who etc.**] *The tests will help the doctors determine what treatment to use.* **3** if something determines something else, it directly influences or decides it: *The amount of available water determines the number of houses that can be built.* | [**determine how/whether/what etc.**] *How hard the swimmers work now will determine how they perform in the Olympics.* **4** **determine to do sth** FORMAL to decide to do something, even if it is difficult or not nice: *Turner makes no excuses, just determines to work harder.*

S W **de·ter·mined** /dɪˈtɚmɪnd/ *adj.* having or showing a strong desire to do something even if it is difficult:
3 *Gwen is a very determined woman.* | [**determined to do sth**] *Harold was determined to marry Esther.* | [**determined (that)**] *I was determined that it would never happen again.* | *Many Asian governments have made a determined effort to reduce population growth.*

de·ter·min·er /dɪˈtɚmənɚ/ *n.* [C] TECHNICAL in grammar, a word that is used before a noun in order to show which thing you mean. In the phrases "the car" and "some cars," "the" and "some" are determiners

de·ter·min·ism /dɪˈtɚməˌnɪzəm/ *n.* [U] the belief that what you do and what happens to you are caused by things that you cannot control —**deterministic** /dɪˌtɚməˈnɪstɪk/ *adj.*

de·ter·rent /dɪˈtɚənt/ *n.* [C] **1** something that stops someone from doing something or stops something bad from happening, by making people realize it will be difficult or have bad results: *The small fines for copying software were not much of a deterrent.* | [+ **to**] *Car alarms can be an effective deterrent to burglars.* **2 nuclear deterrent** NUCLEAR weapons that a country has, that are supposed to prevent other countries from attacking —**deterrence** *n.* [U]

de·test /dɪˈtɛst/ *v.* [T not in progressive] FORMAL to hate someone or something very much: *The other girls detested her.* | *Stalin detested the monument and had it demolished.* —**detestation** /ˌditɛsˈteɪʃən/ *n.* [U]

de·test·a·ble /dɪˈtɛstəbəl/ *adj.* FORMAL very bad and deserving to be criticized or hated —**detestably** *adv.*

de·throne /dɪˈθroʊn/ *v.* [T] **1** to remove someone from a position of authority or importance: *Democrats picked an unlikely candidate to try to dethrone the Republican senator.* **2** to defeat an opponent in sports and take their position as the best or highest-ranking person or team: *Douglas dethroned Tyson in a fight that rocked the boxing world.* **3** to remove a king or queen from power —**dethronement** *n.* [U]

det·o·nate /ˈdɛtnˌeɪt, -təˌneɪt/ *v.* [I,T] to explode, or to make something explode: *Nuclear bombs were detonated in tests in the desert.*

det·o·na·tion /ˌdɛtnˈeɪʃən, -təˈneɪ-/ *n.* [C,U] an explosion, or the action of making a bomb explode

det·o·na·tor /ˈdɛtnˌeɪtɚ, -təˌneɪtɚ/ *n.* [C] a small object that is used to make a bomb explode

de·tour¹ /ˈditʊr/ *n.* [C] a way of going from one place to another that is longer than the usual way because you want to avoid traffic problems, go somewhere special etc. | **make/take a detour** *We took a detour to avoid the street repairs.*

detour² *v.* [I] to make a detour

de·tox /ˈditɑks/ *n.* [U] INFORMAL a special treatment to help people stop drinking alcohol or taking drugs: *She spent a month in detox.* —**detox** /diˈtɑks/ *v.* [I,T]

de·tox·i·fi·ca·tion /diˌtɑksəfəˈkeɪʃən/ *n.* [U] **1** the process of removing harmful chemicals or poison from something **2** detox: *a detoxification program* —**detoxify** /diˈtɑksəfaɪ/ *v.* [T]

de·tract /dɪˈtrækt/ *v.* [I] to make something seem less good than it really is: [+ **from**] *The billboards lining the streets detract from the city's beauty.* —**detraction** /dɪˈtrækʃən/ *n.* [C,U]

de·trac·tor /dɪˈtræktɚ/ *n.* [C] someone who says bad things about someone or something, in order to make them seem less good than they really are: *Even the President's detractors admit the decision was good.*

det·ri·ment /ˈdɛtrəmənt/ *n.* [U] FORMAL harm or damage that is done to something: *Americans spend too much time at work, to the detriment of their families.*

det·ri·men·tal /ˌdɛtrəˈmɛntl/ *adj.* FORMAL causing harm or damage: [+ **to**] *Smoking is detrimental to your health.* —**detrimentally** *adv.*

de·tri·tus /dɪˈtraɪtəs/ *n.* [U] FORMAL small pieces of waste that remain after something has been broken up or used

De·troit /dɪˈtrɔɪt/ a city in the U.S. state of Michigan

deuce /dus/ *n.* **1** [C] a playing card with the number two on it **2** [U] the situation in tennis when both players have 40 points, after which one of the players must win two more points to win the game **3 a deuce of a time/job etc.** OLD-FASHIONED a very difficult or bad time, job etc.

deu·te·ri·um /duˈtɪriəm/ *n.* [U] TECHNICAL a type of HYDROGEN that is twice as heavy as normal hydrogen

Deu·ter·on·o·my /ˌdutəˈrɑnəmi/ a book in the Old Testament of the Christian Bible

Deutsch·mark /ˈdɔɪtʃmɑrk/ *n.* [C] the standard unit of money in Germany; MARK² (16)

de·val·ue /diˈvælyu/ *v.* **1** [I,T] TECHNICAL to reduce the value of a country's money, especially in relation to the value of another country's money: *The rouble has been devalued.* **2** [T] to make someone or something seem less important or valuable: *History has tended to devalue the contributions of women.* —**devaluation** /diˌvælyuˈeɪʃən/ *n.* [C,U]

dev·as·tate /ˈdɛvəˌsteɪt/ *v.* [T] **1** to make someone feel extremely shocked and sad: *Her mother's early death from cancer devastated Lianne.* **2** to damage something very badly, or to destroy something completely: *Bombing raids devastated the city of Dresden.* —**devastated** *adj.*

dev·as·tat·ing /'dɛvə,steɪtɪŋ/ *adj.* **1** badly damaging or destroying something: *The drought has had a devastating effect on crops.* **2** making someone feel extremely sad or shocked: *The news of her sister's death was devastating.* **3** said or done in a very amusing, intelligent, and effective way: *The movie is a devastating parody of the star's life.* **4** extremely attractive. *a devastating smile* —**devastatingly** *adv.*

dev·as·ta·tion /,dɛvə'steɪʃən/ *n.* [U] **1** very bad damage or complete destruction: *Japan took years to recover from the wartime devastation.* **2** very bad emotional damage: *Many of the children have suffered the devastation of divorce.*

S W
1 1
de·vel·op /dɪ'vɛləp/ *v.*
1 grow [I,T] to grow or change into something bigger, stronger, more advanced, or more severe, or to make someone or something do this: *Knowledge in the field of genetics has been developing very quickly.* | [+ from] *New growth will develop from the bud on the branch.* | [+ into] *Scouting helps teenagers develop into responsible adults.* | [develop sth] *These exercises will develop muscle strength.*
2 plan/product [T] to work on a new idea or product to make it successful: *The organization has developed a successful program to increase parents' involvement in schools.*
3 start to have [T] to gradually begin to have a quality, feature, or illness: *The oil tank had developed a small crack.* | *One in nine women will develop breast cancer.*
4 start to happen [I] to gradually begin to happen, exist, or be noticed: *Clouds are developing over the mountains.*
5 land [T] to use land for the things that people need, for example by taking minerals out of it or by building on it: *We would like to see the land developed for low-cost housing.*
6 photography [T] to make pictures out of film from a camera
7 idea/argument [T] to make an argument or idea clearer, by studying it more or by speaking or writing about it in more detail: *Bradley develops these ideas further in his book.*

de·vel·oped /dɪ'vɛləpt/ *adj.* **1** bigger, stronger, more advanced, or more severe than before: *Plants with well developed root systems will survive the drought better.* | *A child's social skills aren't fully developed.* **2** a developed country is one of the rich countries of the world and has many industries, comfortable living for most people, and usually an elected government: *energy consumption in the developed world* | **developed country/nation** *Most developed countries have a sizable middle class.* —compare DEVELOPING, UNDERDEVELOPED

de·vel·op·er /dɪ'vɛləpɚ/ *n.* **1** [C] someone who makes money by buying land and then building houses, factories etc. on it **2** [C] a person or an organization that works on a new idea, product etc. to make it successful: *The company was an early developer of computer-controlled robots.* **3** [C] someone who is in the process of learning new skills: *Reggie was a late developer* (=he learned more slowly than others), *but he's turned out to be one of our best players.* **4** [C,U] TECHNICAL a chemical substance used for developing photographs

de·vel·op·ing /dɪ'vɛləpɪŋ/ *adj.* **1** growing or changing: *the developing crisis in the Middle East* | *a developing fetus* (=unborn baby) **2** a developing country is a poor country that is trying to increase its industry and trade and improve life for its people: *Millions of people in the developing world get around by bicycle or scooter.* | **developing country/nation** *Many residents of developing countries are moving to the cities.* —compare DEVELOPED, UNDERDEVELOPED

S W
2 1
de·vel·op·ment /dɪ'vɛləpmənt/ *n.*
1 changing [U] the process of becoming bigger, stronger, more advanced, or more severe: *The class teaches new mothers the stages of child development.* |

[+ of] *The development of modern religious practices has taken thousands of years.*
2 event [C] a new event that changes a situation: *NATO allies will be discussing developments in the Balkans.*
3 planning [U] the process of working on a new product, plan, idea etc. to make it successful | **under/in development** *Spielberg has several interesting projects under development.*
4 improvement [C] a change that makes a product, plan, idea etc. better: *Developments in radar and engine designs have changed the shape of the plane.*
5 building process [U] the process of planning and building new houses, streets etc. on land: *Several hundred acres of wetland have been sold for development.*
6 houses/offices etc. [C] a group of new buildings that have all been planned and built together on the same piece of land: *a new housing development*
7 economic activity [U] the process of increasing business, trade, and industrial activity: *The program promotes economic development in the inner city.* —**developmental** /dɪ,vɛləp'mɛntl/ *adj.* —**developmentally** *adv.*

de·vi·ant /'diviənt/ *adj.* FORMAL different, in a bad way, from what is normal or acceptable: *deviant sexual behavior* —**deviant** *n.* [C] —**deviance, deviancy** *n.* [U]

de·vi·ate¹ /'divi,eɪt/ *v.* [I] FORMAL to be or become different from what is normal or expected: [+ from] *The screenplay does not deviate very much from the book.*

de·vi·ate² /'diviət/ *adj.* FORMAL deviant —**deviate** *n.* [C]

de·vi·a·tion /,divi'eɪʃən/ *n.* FORMAL **1** [C,U] a noticeable difference from what is expected or normal: [+ from] *Midwives consult with a doctor if there is any deviation from normality during the birth.* **2** [C] TECHNICAL a difference between a number or measurement in a set and the average of all the numbers or measurements in that set —see also STANDARD DEVIATION

de·vice /dɪ'vaɪs/ *n.* [C] **1** a machine or other small object that does a special job: *a birth control device* | **[device to do sth]** *The company makes devices to detect carbon monoxide.* | **[+ for]** *a device for separating metal from garbage* —see Usage Note at MACHINE¹ **2** a way of achieving a particular purpose: *Testing yourself with information on cards is a useful device for studying.* **3** a trick that gets someone to do what you want: *The phone call was just a device to keep him from leaving.* **4** a bomb or other weapon that explodes: *an explosive device* **5** TECHNICAL the special use of words in literature, or of words, lights etc. in a play, to achieve an effect: *Rahman uses dreams as a device to fill in the characters' backgrounds.* —see also **leave sb to their own devices** (LEAVE¹ (35))

S W
3 2

dev·il /'dɛvəl/ *n.*
1 a) the devil also **the Devil** the most powerful evil spirit in some religions, especially in Christianity; Satan **b)** [C] any evil spirit: *The villagers believed a devil had taken control of the old woman.*
2 little devil INFORMAL, HUMOROUS someone who behaves very badly, especially a child

SPOKEN PHRASES

3 lucky/poor etc. devil someone who is lucky, unlucky etc.: *Some lucky devil in Cedar Falls won the lottery.*
4 what/who/why etc. the devil? used to emphasize that you are surprised or annoyed when you are asking a question: *How the devil should I know what she's thinking?*
5 do sth like the devil to do something very fast or using a lot of force: *They rang the doorbell and ran like the devil.*
6 a devil of a time/job etc. OLD-FASHIONED a very difficult or bad time, job etc.: *We had a devil of a time trying to get rid of her.*

7 the devil made me do it HUMOROUS used to make an excuse for something bad you have done

8 better the devil you know (than the devil you don't) used to say that it is better to deal with someone or something you know, even if you do not like them, than to deal with someone or something new that might be worse

9 play/be (the) devil's advocate to pretend that you disagree with something so that there will be a discussion about it: *Letting people play devil's advocate too much can really slow a meeting down.*

10 bad person OLD-FASHIONED someone who is very bad or evil

11 have the devil to pay to have a lot of trouble because of something you have done: *If we don't get this in on time, we'll have the devil to pay.*

12 give the devil his due to praise someone that you do not like for something good they have done: *Give the devil his due – he did a lot for foreign policy.*

—see also **speak of the devil** (SPEAK (12))

dev·iled /ˈdɛvəld/ adj. deviled food is cooked in or mixed with very hot pepper: *deviled eggs*

dev·il·ish /ˈdɛvəlɪʃ/ adj. **1** very bad, difficult, or evil: *devilish torture techniques* **2** like the devil in appearance or behavior, but often in a way that is amusing or attractive: *Dalton looked at her with a devilish grin.* —**devilishly** adv.

devil-may-care /ˌ.. . ˈ.ˌ/ adj. [only before noun] cheerful, careless, and willing to take risks: *a reckless, devil-may-care attitude*

dev·il·ment /ˈdɛvəlmənt/ n. [U] LITERARY: see DEVILTRY

devil's food cake /ˈ.. .ˌ./ n. [C,U] a type of chocolate cake

dev·il·try /ˈdɛvəltri/ also **dev·il·ry** /ˈdɛvəlri/ n. LITERARY **1** [U] wild or bad behavior that causes trouble: *Backstage, the children are mischievous and full of deviltry.* **2** [C,U] evil or an evil act

de·vi·ous /ˈdiviəs/ adj. **1** using tricks or lies to get what you want: *Their method of collecting money was devious, but not illegal.* **2** FORMAL not going in the most direct way to get to a place: *a devious route* —**deviously** adv. —**deviousness** n. [U]

de·vise /dɪˈvaɪz/ v. [T] to plan or invent a way of doing something: *A teacher devised the game as a way of making math fun.*

de·void /dɪˈvɔɪd/ adj. **be devoid of sth** to not have a particular quality at all: *The food was completely devoid of taste.*

dev·o·lu·tion /ˌdɛvəˈluʃən/ n. [U] **1** the act of giving power from a national government to a group or organization at a lower or more local level **2** the process of becoming worse: *Cronkite expressed surprise at the devolution of TV news into little more than soundbites.* —**devolutionist** adj.

de·volve /dɪˈvɑlv/ v. FORMAL **1** [I,T] if you devolve work, responsibility, power etc. on a person or group at a lower level, or if it devolves on them, it is given to them: [+ **on/upon**] *Half of the cost of the study will devolve upon the firm.* | [**devolve sth to sb/sth**] *The federal government has devolved responsibility for welfare to the states.* **2** [I] if land, goods etc. devolve to a person or group they become the property of that person or group

de·vote /dɪˈvoʊt/ v. [T] **1 devote time/money/attention etc. to sth** to give your time, money, attention etc. to do something or help something be successful: *Graham wants to devote more time to his family, and less to the business.* **2 devote yourself to sth** to do everything you can to achieve something or help someone: *Roper retired and devoted himself to charity work.* **3** to use a particular area, period of time, or amount of space for a specific purpose: [+ **to**] *In his autobiography, Laughlin devotes a chapter to his personal philosophy.*

de·vot·ed /dɪˈvoʊtɪd/ adj. giving someone or something a lot of love, concern, and attention: *Mark is a devoted father.* | [+ **to**] *a museum devoted to photography* —**devotedly** adv.

dev·o·tee /ˌdɛvəˈti, -ˈteɪ, -voʊ-/ n. [C] **1** someone who enjoys or admires someone or something very much: *Opera devotees were disappointed with the performance.* **2** a very religious person: [+ **of**] *a devotee of Buddhism*

de·vo·tion /dɪˈvoʊʃən/ n. **1** [U] a strong feeling of love that you show by paying a lot of attention to someone or something: [+ **to**] *As a child I was always aware of my parents' devotion to each other.* **2** [U] the act of spending a lot of time and energy on something, especially in order to make it successful: [+ **to**] *Escalante should be admired for his devotion to improving education.* | [+ **of**] *the devotion of the team's fans* **3 devotions** [plural] prayers and other religious acts **4** [U] strong religious feeling

de·vo·tion·al¹ /dɪˈvoʊʃənəl/ adj. relating to or used in religious services: *devotional music*

devotional² n. [C] **1** a short religious reading, or a book containing a group of these **2** a short religious meeting

de·vour /dɪˈvaʊɚ/ v. [T] **1** to eat something quickly because you are very hungry: *An eagle, perching on a cactus, was devouring a snake.* **2** to read something, especially something that is long, quickly and eagerly: *Kandel devours novels and magazines.* **3** to quickly use or destroy a limited amount of something such as money: *The new fighter plane is devouring public funds.* **4 be devoured by sth** to be filled with a strong feeling that seems to control you: *Howard was devoured by hatred for his co-workers.* **5 devour sb/sth with your eyes** LITERARY to look eagerly and not very nicely at someone or something and notice everything about them

de·vout /dɪˈvaʊt/ adj. **1** having very strong and sincere beliefs, especially religious or political ones: *a devout Muslim* **2** LITERARY a devout hope, wish etc. is one that you feel very strongly and sincerely: *It is my devout hope that we can work together and solve this crisis.* —**devoutly** adv. —**devoutness** n. [U]

De Vries /də ˈvris/, **Hu·go** /ˈhyugoʊ/ (1848–1935) a Dutch BOTANIST who studied plant GENETICS and developed ideas about EVOLUTION

dew /du/ n. [U] the small drops of water that form on outdoor surfaces during the night

dew·drop /ˈdudrɑp/ n. [C] a small drop of dew: *Dewdrops sparkled in the morning sunlight.*

Dew·ey /ˈdui/, **John** (1859–1952) a U.S. PHILOSOPHER and EDUCATIONALIST

Dewey Dec·i·mal Sys·tem /ˌ.. ˈ...ˌ./ n. **the Dewey Decimal System** a system for organizing books in a library in which different subjects are given different numbers

dew·fall /ˈdufɔl/ n. [U] LITERARY the forming of DEW or the time when DEW begins to appear

dew·lap /ˈdulæp/ n. [C] a fold of loose skin hanging under the throat of an animal such as a cow or dog

dew point /ˈ. ./ n. **the dew point** TECHNICAL the temperature at which the air cannot hold any more water, so that DEW forms on surfaces outdoors

dew·y /ˈdui/ adj. wet with drops of DEW: *dewy grass*

dewy-eyed /ˈ.. ˌ./ adj. having eyes that are slightly wet with tears

dex·ter·i·ty /dɛkˈstɛrəti/ n. [U] skill and speed in doing something, especially with your hands, or in speaking: **manual/verbal/physical dexterity** *Computer games can improve children's manual dexterity.*

dex·ter·ous /ˈdɛkstrəs/ adj. skillful and quick in using your hands or body, or in speaking —**dexterously** adv.

dex·trose /ˈdɛkstroʊs/ n. [U] a type of sugar that is found naturally in many sweet fruits

dex·trous /ˈdɛkstrəs/ adj. another spelling of dexterous

Dha·ka /ˈdækə, ˈdɑ-/ the capital and largest city of Bangladesh

dho·ti /ˈdoʊti/ n. [C] a piece of clothing worn by some Hindu men, consisting of a piece of cloth that is wrapped around the waist and between the legs

dhow /daʊ/ n. [C] an Arab ship with one large sail

di- /daɪ, dɪ/ *prefix* two; double; twice: *a diphthong* (=a vowel made by two sounds) —see also BI-, TRI-

di·a·be·tes /ˌdaɪə'biːtiz, -'biːtɪs/ *n.* [U] a disease in which there is too much sugar in the blood

di·a·bet·ic¹ /ˌdaɪə'bɛtɪk/ *adj.* **1** having diabetes: *Anne is diabetic.* **2** caused by diabetes: *a diabetic coma* **3** produced for people who have diabetes: *diabetic chocolate*

diabetic² *n.* [C] someone who has diabetes

di·a·bol·i·cal /ˌdaɪə'bɑlɪkəl/ also **di·a·bol·ic** /ˌdaɪə'bɑlɪk/ *adj.* very bad, evil, or cruel: *a diabolical serial killer* —**diabolically** /-kli/ *adv.*

di·a·chron·ic /ˌdaɪə'krɑnɪk/ *adj.* TECHNICAL dealing with something, especially a language, as it changes over time —**diachronically** /-kli/ *adv.*

di·a·crit·ic /ˌdaɪə'krɪtɪk/ also **diacritical mark** /..'... ,./ *n.* [C] TECHNICAL a mark placed over, under, or through a letter in some languages, to show that the letter should be pronounced differently from a letter that does not have the mark —**diacritical** *adj.*

di·a·dem /'daɪəˌdɛm/ *n.* [C] LITERARY a circle of jewels that you wear on your head, usually to show that you are a queen, PRINCESS etc.

di·ag·nose /ˌdaɪəg'nous, 'daɪəgˌnous/ *v.* [T usually passive] to find out what illness a person has or what is wrong with something: *A technician diagnosed a bad pump in the engine.* | **[diagnose sb with sth]** *Her mother was diagnosed with cancer.* | **[diagnose sb as having sth]** *Roger was diagnosed as having hepatitis.*

di·ag·no·sis /ˌdaɪəg'nousɪs/ *n. plural* **diagnoses** /-siz/ [C,U] the process or result of diagnosing someone or something: **[+ of]** *a diagnosis of heart disease* | *Dr. Pool was unable to **make a diagnosis** (=decide what was wrong).* —compare PROGNOSIS

di·ag·nos·tic /ˌdaɪəg'nɑstɪk/ *adj.* relating to or used for diagnosis: *diagnostic tests* —**diagnostics** *n.* [U]

di·ag·o·nal /daɪ'ægənəl/ *adj.* **1** following a sloping angle: *diagonal parking spaces* **2** a diagonal line is straight and joins two opposite corners of a flat shape, usually a square: *He drew a diagonal line across the page* —compare HORIZONTAL¹, VERTICAL¹ —see picture at VERTICAL¹ —**diagonal** *n.* [C] —**diagonally** *adv.*

di·a·gram¹ /'daɪəˌgræm/ *n.* [C] a drawing that shows how something works, where something is, what something looks like etc.: **[+ of]** *a diagram of the building's heating system* —**diagrammatic** /ˌdaɪəgrə'mætɪk/ *adj.*

diagram² *v.* [T] **1** to show or represent something in a diagram: *Ms. Johnson spent four hours measuring and diagramming every room in the 80-year-old house.* **2 diagram a sentence** to examine and describe the GRAMMATICAL purpose of all the words in a sentence, especially as an exercise in school

di·al¹ /'daɪəl/ *v.* [I,T] to turn the wheel with numbers on a telephone, or to press the buttons on a telephone: *Dial 911 – there's been an accident.*

dial² *n.* [C] **1** the round part of a clock, watch, machine etc. that has numbers that show you the time or a measurement **2** the part of a piece of equipment, such as a radio or THERMOSTAT, that you turn in order to do something, such as find a different station or set the temperature: *Don't touch that dial. Stay tuned to WXRB.* **3** the wheel with holes for fingers on some telephones

di·a·lect /'daɪəˌlɛkt/ *n.* [C,U] a form of a language that is spoken in one area which is different from the way it is spoken in other areas: *a dialect of Arabic* | *The children speak only in the local dialect.* —compare ACCENT¹ (1)

di·a·lec·tic /ˌdaɪə'lɛktɪk/ *n.* [C,U] also **dialectics** [plural] a method of finding the truth, in which two opposing ideas are compared in order to find a solution that includes them both —**dialectical** *adj.*

di·a·logue, dialog /'daɪəˌlɔg, -ˌlɑg/ *n.* [C,U] **1** a conversation in a book, play, or movie: *The movie has almost no dialogue.* —compare MONOLOGUE (1) **2** a formal discussion between countries or groups in order to solve problems: **[+ with/between]** *The U.S. pressured Israel to start a dialogue with the Palestinians.*

dialogue box, dialog box /'... ,./ *n.* [C] a box that appears on your computer screen when the program you are using needs to ask you a question before it can continue to do something, and on which you can CLICK on one of two or more choices to give your answer

dial tone /'.. ,./ *n.* [C] the sound you hear when you pick up a telephone, that lets you know that you can make a call

di·al·y·sis /daɪ'æləsɪs/ *n.* [U] the process of taking harmful substances out of someone's blood using a special machine, because their KIDNEYs do not work correctly: *Bill will probably have to spend the rest of his life **on dialysis** (=receiving dialysis treatments).*

di·am·e·ter /daɪ'æmətɚ/ *n.* [C,U] a line or measurement from one side of a circle to the other that passes through the center: *Shape the dough into balls about 1 inch **in diameter**.*

di·a·met·ri·cal·ly /ˌdaɪə'mɛtrɪkli/ *adv.* **diametrically opposed/opposite** completely different or opposite: *The women hold diametrically opposed views on abortion.*

dia·mond /'daɪmənd, 'daɪə-/ *n.* **1** [C,U] a clear, very hard valuable stone, used in jewelry and in industry: *a diamond necklace* **2** [C] a shape with four straight sides of equal length that stands on one of its points: *Cut the cookie dough into diamonds.* —see picture at SHAPE¹ **3** [C] **a)** the area in a baseball field that is within the diamond shape formed by the four BASES **b)** the whole playing field used in baseball **4** [C] a playing card with red diamond shapes on it: *the king of diamonds* **5 a diamond in the rough** someone or something that has the possibility of being good, valuable or attractive, but needs improvement

diamond an·ni·ver·sa·ry /ˌ.. ....'.../ *n.* [C] the date that is exactly 60 or 75 years after the beginning of something, especially a marriage —compare GOLDEN ANNIVERSARY, SILVER ANNIVERSARY

diamond lane /'.. ,./ *n.* [C] a special LANE on a road or street that is marked with a diamond shape and can be used only by buses, taxis etc. and sometimes private cars with more than one passenger

Di·an·a /daɪ'ænə/ the Roman name for the goddess Artemis

dia·per /'daɪpɚ, 'daɪə-/ *n.* [C] a piece of cloth or other soft material that is put between a baby's legs and fastened around its waist to hold its body wastes: *I think we need to **change the baby's diaper** (=put on a new one).* —**diaper** *v.* [T]

diaper rash /'.. ,./ *n.* [U] sore red skin between a baby's legs and on its BUTTOCKS, caused by a wet diaper

di·aph·a·nous /daɪ'æfənəs/ *adj.* LITERARY diaphanous cloth is so fine and thin that you can almost see through it: *a diaphanous silk gown*

di·a·phragm /'daɪəˌfræm/ *n.* [C] **1** the muscle between your lungs and your stomach that controls your breathing **2** a round rubber object that a woman can put inside her VAGINA to stop her from getting PREGNANT **3** TECHNICAL a thin round object, especially in a telephone or LOUDSPEAKER, that is moved by sound or that moves when it produces sound **4** TECHNICAL a round flat part inside a camera that controls the amount of light that enters the camera

di·ar·rhe·a /ˌdaɪə'riə/ *n.* [U] an illness in which waste from the BOWELs is watery and comes out often

di·a·ry /'daɪəri/ *n. plural* **diaries** [C] a book in which you write down important or interesting things that happen to you each day; JOURNAL (1): *I kept a diary (=wrote in it regularly) during high school.* —**diarist** *n.* [C]

Di·as /'diəs, 'diɑʃ/, **Bar·tol·o·me·u** /bɑrˌtɑlə'meɪu/ also **Diaz** /'diəz/ (?1450–1500) a Portuguese EXPLORER whose ship was the first to sail around the Cape of Good Hope at the southern end of Africa

D

di·as·po·ra /daɪˈæspərə/ n. **1 the Diaspora a)** the movement of the Jewish people away from ancient Palestine, to settle in other countries **b)** all the Jewish people who have moved away from ancient Palestine and live in other countries around the world **2** [U] FORMAL the spreading of people from a national group to other areas

di·a·ton·ic /ˌdaɪəˈtɑnɪk◂/ adj. TECHNICAL relating to music that uses a set of eight notes with a particular pattern of spaces between them: *the diatonic scale* —compare CHROMATIC

di·a·tribe /ˈdaɪəˌtraɪb/ n. [C] FORMAL an angry speech or piece of writing that criticizes someone or something very severely: [+ against/on] *He delivered a diatribe against church policy on women's rights.*

dibs /dɪbz/ n. [plural] INFORMAL the right to have, use, or do something: *Freshmen have first dibs on dormitory rooms* (=they get to have them).

dice¹ /daɪs/ n. **1** [plural] *singular* **die** two or more small blocks of wood, plastic etc. with a different number of spots on each side, used in games: *It's your turn to roll the dice.* **2 no dice** SPOKEN said when you refuse to do something: *I asked if I could borrow the car, but she said no dice.* **3** [U] a game of chance that is played with dice **4** [plural] small square pieces of food: *Cut the potatoes into ½" dice.*

USAGE NOTE: DICE

GRAMMAR: die, dice
Die is singular and **dice** is plural. However, many people use the word **dice** when they are speaking about a single **die**.

---

dice² v. also **dice up** [T] to cut food into small square pieces —see picture on page 425

dic·ey /ˈdaɪsi/ adj. INFORMAL risky and possibly dangerous: *The future looks pretty dicey for small businesses.*

di·chot·o·my /daɪˈkɑtəmi/ n. plural **dichotomies** [C] FORMAL the difference between two things or ideas that are not like each other at all, and that usually cannot both be true: [+ between] *The artist is concerned with the dichotomy between the way something appears and reality.*

dick¹ /dɪk/ n. [C] **1** VULGAR a PENIS **2** VULGAR a stupid annoying person, especially a man: *Chuck's acting like a complete dick.* | [be a dick to sb] *The other day I saw this guy being a real dick to the waiter.* **3** OLD-FASHIONED **a private dick** a PRIVATE DETECTIVE

dick² v.
   dick sb **around** phr. v. VULGAR to cause a lot of problems for someone, especially by changing your mind often or preventing them from getting what they want: *The phone company's been dicking me around for three months.*

dick·ens /ˈdɪkənz/ n. SPOKEN, OLD-FASHIONED **1 what/who/where the dickens?** used when asking a question to show that you are very surprised or angry: *What the dickens is the matter with her?* **2 as pretty/smart etc. as the dickens** INFORMAL used to emphasize that someone is very pretty, smart etc. **3 have a dickens of a time (doing sth)** SPOKEN to have a difficult time doing something: *I had a dickens of a time trying to get the VCR to work.*

Dick·ens /ˈdɪkənz/, **Charles** (1812–1870) a British writer famous for his NOVELs which made him the most popular British writer of the 19th century, and which are still very popular today

Dic·ken·si·an /dɪˈkɛnziən/ adj. Dickensian buildings, living conditions etc. are poor, dirty, and not nice: *He describes his childhood as Dickensian in its poverty and hardship.*

dick·er /ˈdɪkɚ/ v. [I] INFORMAL to argue about or discuss the conditions of a sale, agreement etc.: *"The prices on the vehicles are the real prices. We don't dicker," Olsen said.*

dick·ey /ˈdɪki/ n. another spelling of DICKY

dick·head /ˈdɪkhɛd/ n. [C] VULGAR, OFFENSIVE a stupid annoying person, especially a man: *Don't be such a dickhead!*

Dick·in·son /ˈdɪkənsən/, **Em·i·ly** /ˈɛməli/ (1830–1886) a U.S. poet whose clever and original work is still very popular

Emily Dickinson

dick·less /ˈdɪklɪs/ adj. VULGAR, OFFENSIVE not having the courage to do something: *Barry couldn't even tell me the truth – he's so dickless.*

dick·y /ˈdɪki/ n. [C] **1** a false shirt front or collar sometimes worn under a suit or dress **2** OLD-FASHIONED a small bird

dict. n. the abbreviation of DICTIONARY

Dic·ta·phone /ˈdɪktəˌfoʊn/ n. [C] TRADEMARK an office machine on which you can record speech so that someone can listen to it and TYPE it later

dic·tate¹ /ˈdɪkteɪt, dɪkˈteɪt/ v. **1** [I,T] to say words for someone else to write down: [dictate a letter/memo etc. to sb] *Dr. Frakes dictated a resignation letter to his secretary.* **2** [I,T] to tell someone exactly what they must do or how they must behave: *Fashion designers no longer dictate skirt lengths.* | [dictate sth to sb] *The board does not want to dictate teaching methods to schools.* | [dictate to sb (sth)] *Fazio said, "We're not trying to dictate to the governor."* | [dictate who/what/how etc.] *I will not let them dictate how I should run my personal life.* | [dictate that] *The Postal Service dictates that all mail leaving the San Peninsula go to San Francisco for sorting.* | *Federal funds have to be used as dictated by Washington.* **3** [T] if something dictates another thing, it controls or influences it; DETERMINE (3): *The amount of funds we receive dictates what we can do.* | [dictate that] *Islamic custom dictates that women should be fully covered.*

dic·tate² /ˈdɪkteɪt/ n. [C] FORMAL an order, rule, or principle that you have to obey: *The city's policy clearly violates the dictates of the Fair Labor Standards Act.*

dic·ta·tion /dɪkˈteɪʃən/ n. **1** [U] the act of saying words for someone to write down, usually so that they can write a letter, message etc. for you: *As a secretary, I often have to take dictation* (=to write down the words someone says). **2** [C] a piece of writing that a teacher reads out to test your ability to hear and write the words correctly: *I hate doing French dictations.*

dic·ta·tor /ˈdɪkteɪtɚ/ n. [C] **1** a ruler who has complete power over a country, especially when their power has been gained by force: *Pinochet was a military dictator who took power in a 1973 coup.* **2** someone who tells other people what they should do, in a way that seems unreasonable: *dictators of fashion*

dic·ta·to·ri·al /ˌdɪktəˈtɔriəl/ adj. **1** a dictatorial government or ruler has complete power over a country: *a corrupt, dictatorial regime* **2** a dictatorial person tells other people what to do in an unreasonable way: *dictatorial parents* | *A Senate chairman cannot be dictatorial.* —**dictatorially** adv.

dic·ta·tor·ship /dɪkˈteɪtɚˌʃɪp, ˈdɪkteɪtɚ-/ n. **1** [C,U] government by a ruler who has complete power: *The country has been moving toward dictatorship.* | *Residence permits are a remnant of Stalin's dictatorship.* **2** [C] a country that is ruled by one person who has complete power

dic·tion /ˈdɪkʃən/ n. [U] **1** the way in which someone pronounces words: *His diction is generally poor and his words often inaudible.* **2** the choice and use of words and phrases to express meaning, especially in literature or poetry: *In matters of diction, the author has a taste for folksy slang.*

dic·tion·ar·y /ˈdɪkʃəˌnɛri/ n. plural **dictionaries** [C] **1** a book that gives a list of words in alphabetical order and explains their meanings in the same or another language: *a Korean–English dictionary* **2** a book like this that deals with the words and phrases used in a particular subject: *a dictionary of business terms*

dic·tum /'dɪktəm/ *n. plural* **dicta** /-tə/ or **dictums** [C] **1** a formal statement of opinion by someone who is respected or has authority: *the Catholic Church's dictum against birth control* **2** a short phrase that expresses a general rule or truth: *Gertrude Stein's most famous dictum was "a rose is a rose is a rose."*

did /dɪd; *strong* dɪd/ *v.* the past tense of DO¹ and DO²

di·dac·tic /daɪ'dæktɪk/ *adj.* **1** something such as a speech or movie that is didactic is intended to teach people a moral lesson: *Kubrick made the movie with both didactic and creative intentions.* **2** someone who is didactic is too eager to teach people things or give instructions: *a didactic priest* —**didactically** /-kli/ *adv.*

did·dle /'dɪdl/ *v.* [I always + adv./prep.] INFORMAL to do something in a way that is not very serious: *In high school, he often diddled around on the piano.*

did·dly /'dɪdl-i, 'dɪdli/ *also* **did·dly·squat** /'dɪdli-,skwɑt/ *n.* **not know/mean diddly** INFORMAL to know or mean nothing at all: *Bradley doesn't know diddly about running his own business.* —compare SQUAT³ (2)

Di·de·rot /,dido'rou, 'didorou/, **De·nis** /dɪ'ni/ (1713–1784) a French PHILOSOPHER and writer

did·ge·ri·doo /,dɪdʒəri'du/ *n.* [C] a long wooden musical instrument, played especially in Australia

did·n't /'dɪdnt/ *v.* the short form of "did not": *I didn't want to go.*

Did·rik·son (Za·har·i·as) /'dɪdrɪksən zə'hæriəs/, **Mil·dred** /'mɪldrɪd/ *also* **Babe Didrikson** (1914–1956) a U.S. ATHLETE who is considered one of the best female athletes of this century

didst /dɪdst/ *v.* **thou didst** OLD USE you did

die¹ /daɪ/ *v. past tense and past participle* **died** *present participle* **dying** [I]

1 *become dead* to stop living and become dead: *He was very sick and we knew he might die.* | *Her husband had died two years earlier.* | *[+ of/from] My mother died of cancer when I was 10 years old.* | *The youths died from burns and smoke inhalation.* | *[+ for] Crowds of young men shouted their willingness to die for their faith.* | **die young/happy/poor** etc. *Franklin died young, at only 32.* | **die a hero/martyr/pauper** etc. *Marine William G. Windrich died a hero at the Chosin Reservoir.* | **die a natural/horrible/quick** etc. **death** *The elder Chamoun died a natural death in August 1987.*

2 do sth to your dying day to do something or feel something until the day you die: *I'll regret it to my dying day.*

3 *disappear* to disappear or stop existing: *Broadway classics like "A Chorus Line" will never die.* | *Being the only son, the family name will **die with him** (=disappear or be finished when he dies).*

4 *machines* INFORMAL to stop working: *The engine coughed and died.* | *There I was in the middle of the intersection and my car just **died on me** (=stopped working while I was using it).*

5 dying breath/wish someone's very last breath or wish before they die: *Marcos insists that her husband's dying wish was to be buried in Manila.*

6 die by your own hand LITERARY to kill yourself: *Doctors confirmed that Foster died by his own hand.*

7 die on the vine LITERARY if an idea, process, or business dies on the vine, it fails, especially at an early stage, because of a lack of support: *Several new businesses in the downtown area are dying on the vine, and the city is not helping much.*

8 die without issue OLD USE or LAW to die before you have any children

SPOKEN PHRASES

9 be dying for sth to want something very much: *I'm dying for a cup of coffee.*

10 be dying to do sth to want to do something very much, so that it is difficult to wait: *They made a movie out of the book, and I'm dying to see it.*

11 be dying of hunger/thirst to be very hungry or thirsty: *I'm dying of thirst. Do you have anything to drink?*

12 I nearly died, I could have died said when you felt very surprised, shocked, or embarrassed: *I checked prices on new models and nearly died!*

13 I'd rather die used to say very strongly that you do not want to do something: *I'd rather die than work for my uncle.*

14 be dying used to say that you are becoming very tired while you doing something: *"I was dying on the last three laps of the race," Feingold said.*

15 be to die for if something is to die for, it is very good: *Their French dip sandwich is to die for.*

16 die laughing to laugh a lot: *Rebecca told me this joke on the phone today, and I almost died laughing.*

die away *phr. v.* [I] if a sound or feeling dies away, it becomes gradually weaker and finally stops: *Her footsteps died away.*

die back *phr. v.* [I] if a plant dies back, it dies above the ground but remains alive at its roots: *Prune the plant after it dies back in the fall.*

die down *phr. v.* [I] **1** if something such as the wind or a noise dies down, it becomes less strong or violent: *I hope the wind has died down.* **2** if something such as an activity dies down, fewer people are taking part in it: *The crowds at the mall have died down now that the Christmas season is over.* | *Rumors about a new round of layoffs still haven't died down.*

die off *phr. v.* [I] if a group of people, animals etc. die off, they die one by one until there are no more of them: *Many insects die off in the winter when there are no crops to feed them.*

die out *phr. v.* [I] to disappear or stop existing completely: *If the ocean becomes too salty, certain types of marine life die out.* | *Ten years ago, Turner predicted that newspapers would die out.* —see Usage Note at DEAD¹

USAGE NOTE: DIE

WORD CHOICE: die, be dead
When you are talking about an event, use **die** (**dying, died, died**). When you are talking about a condition or state, use **be dead**. Compare: *He died in the ambulance on the way to the hospital.* | *By the time the ambulance reached the hospital, he was dead.*

die² *n.* [C] **1** a metal block used to press or cut something into a particular shape **2** the singular of DICE¹ (1) **3 the die is cast** used to say that a decision has been made and cannot now be changed

die cast·ing /'. ,../ *n.* [U] the process of making metal objects by putting liquid metal into a hollow container that has a particular shape, and then allowing it to become hard

die·hard, die·hard /'daɪhɑrd/ *adj.* **1** opposing change and refusing to accept new ideas: *Brock has been a diehard opponent of new taxes.* **2 die-hard fan/communist/supporter** etc. someone who is very loyal to a team, political party, person etc.: *I've been a die-hard Dodgers fan since I was a boy.* —see also **old habits die hard** (HABIT (8))

di·e·re·sis /daɪ'ɛrəsɪs/ *n. plural* **diereses** /-siz/ [C] TECHNICAL a sign (¨) that is put over the second of two VOWELS to show that it is pronounced separately from the first, for example in the word "naïve"

die·sel /'dizəl, -səl/ *n.* **1** [U] a type of heavy oil used instead of gas in a special type of engine **2** [C] INFORMAL a vehicle that uses DIESEL, especially a large truck: *a diesel truck*

die·sel en·gine /,.. '../ *n.* [C] an engine that burns DIESEL, used especially for buses, trains, and goods vehicles

diesel fu·el /,.. '.., '.. ,../ *also* **diesel oil** /,.. '., '.. ,./ *n.* [U] DIESEL

di·et¹ /'daɪət/ *n.* **1** [C,U] the type of food that someone eats each day: *The Italians have a good healthy diet and lifestyle.* | *a vegetarian diet* | *[+ of] Prisoners were given a diet of hard bread and breadcrumbs.* | *It is important to have a **balanced diet** (=a diet that includes all of the foods you need to stay healthy).*

2 [C] a plan to eat only particular types or amounts of food, especially because you want to get thinner or because you have a health problem | **go/be on a diet** *Ted has gone on a diet three times in the last two years.* | *Since his heart attack, Brice has been on a salt-free diet.* **3 a diet of sth** something such as an activity, entertainment etc. that is used or done regularly: *The local theater has provided a steady diet of entertainment for young and old.* **4** [C] OLD USE an official meeting to discuss political or church matters

diet² *v.* [I] to limit the amount and type of food that you eat in order to become thinner: *Janet dieted for months before her wedding.*

di·e·tar·y /ˈdaɪəˌteri/ *adj.* relating to someone's diet: *The dietary guidelines can be achieved by eating more fruits and vegetables.*

di·e·tet·ics /ˌdaɪəˈtɛtɪks/ *n.* [U] the science that is concerned with what people eat and drink and how this affects their health

di·e·ti·cian, dietitian /ˌdaɪəˈtɪʃən/ *n.* [C] someone who is specially trained in dietetics

dif·fer /ˈdɪfɚ/ *v.* **1** [I] to be different from something in some way: [+ from] *Harris adds that many of his views differ from those of his partner's.* | *Interest rates **differ from** bank **to** bank.* | **differ greatly/widely** *The amount of preparation students do differs widely.* **2** [I] to have different opinions: [+ on/over/about] *Experts differ on how profitable the recycling business will be.* —see also **I beg to differ** (BEG (6))

dif·fer·ence /ˈdɪfrəns/ *n.* **1** [C] a way in which two or more things or people are not like each other: [+ between] *There are many differences between public and private schools.* | *The argument highlighted the difference between the two parties.* | *How can you **tell the difference** (=see or notice the difference) between the twins?* **2** [singular,U] the fact of not being the same as something else, or an amount by which one thing is not the same as another: *The trade deficit is the difference between imports and exports.* | [+ in] *Holmgren said he hasn't noticed any difference in the way Rice plays since the injury.* | *There's a big **difference in** maturity level **between** a 13- and 15-year-old.* | [+ of] *There is a temperature difference of up to 15 degrees between the valley and the coast.* —see also **a world of difference** (WORLD¹ (14)) **3 make a (big) difference, make all the difference** to have an important effect on a thing or a situation: *Working together, we can make a difference.* | **[make a difference in sth]** *New drugs have made an enormous difference in the way the disease is treated.* | **[make a difference to sb/sth]** *A salesperson's attitude can make all the difference to a customer.* **4 their/our/your etc. differences** the disagreements that people have: *Although Charlie and I **have** our **differences**, I respect his intelligence a lot.* | *Penny and Thea have managed to **overcome** their **differences**.* **5 difference of opinion** a slight disagreement: *My husband and I **have a difference of opinion** regarding the disciplining of our 13-month-old child.* **6 make no difference a)** to have no effect at all on a situation: *Unfortunately, the drugs made no difference to the spread of the cancer.* **b)** to be unimportant to someone: **[make no difference to sb]** *Mamet says it makes no difference to him what a movie costs, as long as it's a good movie.* **7 with a difference** used to express approval about something that is different and better: *These are children's book reviews with a difference – the children are writing the reviews.* —see also **split the difference** (SPLIT¹ (7))

USAGE NOTE: DIFFERENCE

WORD CHOICE: difference of, difference in
Difference of is only used to compare numbers. *There is a difference of $500 between the sale price and the regular price.* **Difference in** is used to compare particular features, practices, or qualities: *In the U.S., I noticed a big difference in social behavior.*

dif·fer·ent /ˈdɪfrənt/ *adj.* **1** not like something or someone else, or not the same as before: *He looked so different that his own daughter didn't recognize him.* | [+ from] *The heat in Arizona is different from the heat here. It's very dry.* | [+ than] *"College campuses look a lot different than they did years ago," Nidiffer said.* **2** [only before noun] a word meaning "separate," used when you are speaking about or comparing things of the same kind: *He took the photo from three different angles.* | *The bookstore has many different books on Kennedy.* | *Alice transferred to a different school last year.* | **[a different sth from sth]** *North Pacific humpback whales sing a different song from humpbacks in the North Atlantic.* **3** SPOKEN unusual, often in a way that you do not like: *"Do you like my new shoes?" "Well, they sure are different."* **4 different strokes (for different folks)** INFORMAL used to say that different people like different types of things —**differently** *adv.*: *The twin wear their hair differently so that they look less alike.*

USAGE NOTE: DIFFERENT

GRAMMAR
We use both **different from** and **different than** to talk about two things that are not the same: *My new school is different from/than my old one.* However, most teachers prefer **different from**. Note that we never say **different of.**
SPELLING
The noun is **difference**: *the difference between your country and mine*

dif·fer·en·tial¹ /ˌdɪfəˈrɛnʃəl/ *n.* [C] **1** an amount or degree of difference between two quantities, especially relating to money: *The wage differential between managers and workers is huge.* **2** a differential gear

differential² *adj.* [only before noun] **1** based on or depending on a difference: *Differential pay will be given to teachers who oversee student club meetings.* **2** TECHNICAL relating to differential calculus

differential cal·cu·lus /ˌ.... ˈ.../ *n.* [U] TECHNICAL a type of mathematics that deals with how a mathematical quantity changes according to how other quantities change

differential gear /ˌ..ˈ.. ˌ./ *n.* [C] an arrangement of GEARs that allows one back wheel of a car to turn faster than the other when the car goes around a corner

dif·fer·en·ti·ate /ˌdɪfəˈrɛnʃiˌeɪt/ *v.* **1** [I,T] to recognize or express the difference between things or people: [+ between] *Most people couldn't differentiate between the two types of soft drink.* | **[differentiate sb/sth from sb/sth]** *It's easy to differentiate the male birds from the female ones.* **2** [T] to make someone or something different from someone or something else: **[differentiate sb/sth from sb/sth]** *Quality is what differentiates our product from our competitors'.* **3** [I] to behave differently toward someone or something, sometimes in an unfair way; DISCRIMINATE (1): [+ between] *Their religion does not differentiate between the rich and poor.* —**differentiation** /ˌdɪfəˌrɛnʃiˈeɪʃən/ *n.* [U]

dif·fi·cult /ˈdɪfəˌkʌlt/ *adj.* **1** not easy to do or understand: *a difficult job* | *A lot of students find calculus difficult.* | **[be difficult (for sb) to do sth]** *Tickets for the Super Bowl are always difficult to get.* **2** involving a lot of problems and causing a lot of trouble or worry: *My wife and I have gone through some difficult times.* | *The bus strike is **making life difficult for** commuters.* **3** someone who is difficult is never satisfied, friendly, or helpful: *Stop being difficult!*

dif·fi·cul·ty /ˈdɪfɪˌkʌlti/ *n. plural* **difficulties 1** [C usually plural,U] trouble, or a problem that causes trouble: **[have difficulty (in) doing sth]** *Stephen's having difficulty finding an apartment.* | **mechanical/technical difficulties** *Mechanical difficulties caused the flight to be delayed.* | *She will be 76 next month and walks **with difficulty** (=it is not easy for her to walk).* | *We **ran into difficulties** (=had trouble) when we tried to exchange the tickets.* | *Their* business is **in financial difficulty**. **2** [U] the quality of being hard to do or understand: *The books vary in level of difficulty.*

dif·fi·dent /'dɪfədənt/ *adj.* FORMAL lacking confidence in your abilities, and therefore unwilling to make decisions, say your opinion, or make people notice you: *Her former classmates say she was shy and diffident in school.* —**diffidence** *n.* [U] —**diffidently** *adv.*

dif·frac·tion /dɪ'frækʃən/ *n.* [U] TECHNICAL the process or result of dividing sound or light waves into smaller waves, by sending them around something or through a small hole —**diffract** /dɪ'frækt/ *v.* [I,T]

dif·fuse[1] /dɪ'fyuz/ *v.* **1** [T] FORMAL to make a bad feeling less strong or the effects of a situation, especially a bad one, less severe: *Many presidential candidates have used humor to diffuse criticism.* **2** [T] to spread something over a larger area or to more people, often so that it becomes less strong: *Critics believe that such action will diffuse the power of Congress.* **3** [T] TECHNICAL if something diffuses light, it spreads it over a larger area and makes it softer and less bright **4** [I,T] FORMAL if you diffuse information, ideas etc., or if they diffuse, they become available to many people: *The history of the house has been diffused through family legend.* **5** [I,T] TECHNICAL if you diffuse a liquid or a gas, or if it diffuses, it spreads over a larger area and mixes with the surrounding gases or liquids, becoming less strong: *The wind quickly diffused any toxic vapors that may have leaked out.* —**diffused** *adj.*: *diffused lighting* —**diffusion** /dɪ'fyuʒən/ *n.* [U]

dif·fuse[2] /dɪ'fyus/ *adj.* **1** spread over a large area or in many places: *The new opposition party continues to be a diffuse organization.* **2** using a lot of words and not explaining things clearly or directly —**diffusely** *adv.* —**diffuseness** *n.* [U]

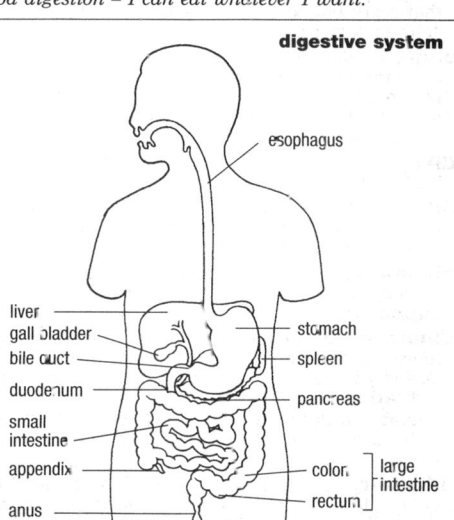

dig[1] /dɪg/ *v. past tense and past participle* **dug** *present participle* **digging**
1 move sth [I,T] to break and move earth, stone, snow etc. with a tool, your hands, or a machine: *Jessica dug in the sand with a small shovel.* | [+ **for**] *They're digging for dinosaur bones.* | [**dig sth**] *Our dog had dug a big hole behind the roses.*

dig

2 look for sth [I] to move many things such as papers, boxes, rocks, or clothing in order to find something: [+ **for**] *She reached into her daypack to dig for her keys.* | [+ **through**] *I dug through my drawers until I found the note.* | [+ **into**] *Julie dug into her purse for some spare change.*

3 find information [I] find more information about someone or something: [+ **into**] *I wasn't sure if I really wanted to dig deeper into my family's past.* | [+ **for**] *Boyden is digging for details about Thompson's activities.*

4 **dig a hole for yourself** also **dig yourself into a hole** to do or say something that makes a problem or situation so bad that it is difficult to make it better: *The mayor dug himself into a hole when he promised 3000 new jobs.*

5 remove sth from the ground [T] to remove something from the ground: *The whole family was out in the fields digging potatoes.*

6 **dig your own grave** to do something that will make you have serious problems later: *By continuing to make racist comments before the committee, he really dug his own grave.*

SPOKEN PHRASES

7 understand sth [I,T] OLD-FASHIONED, SLANG to understand something: *"She says she doesn't want to get pregnant." "Yeah, I can dig that."*

8 like sb/sth [T] OLD-FASHIONED, SLANG to like someone or something: *I really dig that dress.*

9 **Dig that...!** [T] OLD-FASHIONED, SLANG used to tell someone to notice or look at something: *Dig that funky hat she has on!*

dig in *phr. v.* **1** [I] SPOKEN, INFORMAL to start eating food that is in front of you: *Come on everyone – dig in!* **2 dig in your heels** also **dig your heels in** to refuse to do or accept something in spite of other people's efforts to persuade you: *Let's not dig our heels in over issues that really aren't important.* **3** [I,T **dig yourself in**] if soldiers dig in or dig themselves in, they make a protected place for themselves by digging

dig into *phr. v.* **1** [T **dig sth into** sth] to push hard into something, or to make something do this: *She dug her fingernails into my arm.* **2** [T **dig into sth**] to start using a supply of something, especially money: *I'm going to have to dig into my savings again.*

dig out *phr. v.* **1** [I,T **dig sth ↔ out**] to get someone or something out from under something or inside something by using a tool, your hands, or a machine: *Rescue workers spent the day digging survivors out from under the rubble.* **2** [T **dig sth ↔ out**] to find something you have not seen for a long time, or that is not easy to find: *Mom dug her wedding dress out of the closet.*

dig sth ↔ **up** *phr. v.* [T] **1** to remove something from under the ground with a tool, your hands, or a machine: *Beth is out back digging up weeds.* **2** INFORMAL to find hidden or forgotten information by careful searching: *See what you can dig up on the guy.*

dig[2] *n.* **1** [C] an unkind thing you say to annoy someone: *Sally keeps making digs about my work.* **2** [C] a small quick push that you give someone with your finger or elbow: *He gave me a dig in the ribs.* **3** [C] the process of digging in a place to find ancient objects to study: *an archeological dig* **4 digs** [plural] a room or apartment that you pay rent to live in **5** [C] an act of hitting the ball back up into the air when it is near the ground or floor in VOLLEYBALL

di·gest[1] /daɪ'dʒɛst, dɪ-/ *v.* [I,T] **1** if food digests or if you digest it, it changes in the stomach into a form your body can use: *Some babies can't digest cow's milk.* | *You shouldn't go swimming until your food has had a chance to digest.* —compare INGEST **2** to understand new information after thinking about it carefully: *It took a while to digest the theory.* —**digestible** *adj.*

di·gest[2] /'daɪdʒɛst/ *n.* [C] a short piece of writing that gives the most important facts from a book, report etc.

di·ges·tion /daɪ'dʒɛstʃən/ *n.* [U] the process of digesting food, or your ability to digest it: *I've always had good digestion – I can eat whatever I want.*

digestive system

- esophagus
- liver
- gall bladder
- bile duct
- duodenum
- small intestine
- appendix
- anus
- stomach
- spleen
- pancreas
- colon ⎱ large
- rectum ⎰ intestine

di·ges·tive /daɪ'dʒɛstɪv/ *adj.* [only before noun] relating to the process of digestion

digestive sys·tem /.'.. ,../ *n.* [C] the system of organs in your body that DIGESTs food

dig·ger /'dɪgɚ/ *n.* [C] **1** a person who digs: *a clam digger* **2** a machine or tool that is used to dig —see also GOLD DIGGER

dig·gings /'dɪgɪŋz/ *n.* [plural] a place where people are digging for metal, especially gold

dig·it /'dɪdʒɪt/ *n.* [C] **1** a written sign that represents any of the numbers from 0 to 9: *a seven-digit phone number* **2** FORMAL a finger or toe

dig·i·tal /'dɪdʒɪtl/ *adj.* **1** using a system in which information is represented in the form of numbers, usually numbers in the BINARY system: *This camera can take digital pictures.* **2** giving information in the form of numbers: *a digital clock* **3** FORMAL relating to the fingers and toes

digital au·di·o·tape /,... '..../ *n.* [C] a DAT

dig·i·tal·is /,dɪdʒə'tælɪs/ *n.* [U] a medicine made from FOXGLOVE that makes your heart beat faster

dig·i·tize /'dɪdʒə,taɪz/ *v.* [T] to put information into a digital form: *To create special effects, engineers digitize the film and then work with it on computer.*

dig·ni·fied /'dɪgnə,faɪd/ *adj.* calm, serious, and making people feel respect: *We were charmed by the dignified and unassuming Tibetan people.*

dig·ni·fy /'dɪgnəfaɪ/ *v.* dignified, dignifying [T] to make something or someone seem better, more impressive, or more important than they really are, especially by reacting to them in a particular way or calling them a good name: *A huge portrait of the couple dignified the living room wall.* | [dignify sb/sth with sth] *I'm not even going to dignify that last comment with a response.*

dig·ni·tar·y /'dɪgnə,tɛri/ *n. plural* dignitaries [C] someone who has an important official position: *Foreign dignitaries from 20 countries were invited to attend.*

dig·ni·ty /'dɪgnəti/ *n.* [U] **1** calm serious behavior, even in difficult situations, that makes people respect you: *Juana Alvarez was a woman of compassion and dignity.* | *In the prison camp, it was hard to retain some human dignity.* **2** the quality of being serious, formal, and respectable: *Lawyers must respect the dignity of the court.* **3** be beneath sb's dignity if something is beneath your dignity, you think you are too good or important to do it: *It seemed that even doing his own laundry was beneath his dignity.*

di·graph /'daɪgræf/ *n.* [C] TECHNICAL a pair of letters that represent one sound, such as "ea" in "head" and "ph" in "phrase"

di·gress /daɪ'grɛs, dɪ-/ *v.* [I] FORMAL to move away from the main subject that you are talking or writing about: *During the lecture, Miller often digressed to give the history behind each theory.* —digression /daɪ'grɛʃən/ *n.* [C,U] —digressive /daɪ'grɛsɪv/ *adj.*

dike, dyke /daɪk/ *n.* [C] a wall or bank built to keep back water and prevent flooding

dik·tat /dɪk'tat/ *n.* [C,U] an order that is forced on people by a ruler or government: *Lithuania refused to give in to the diktat from Moscow.*

di·lap·i·dat·ed /də'læpə,deɪtɪd/ *adj.* old, broken, and in very bad condition: *a dilapidated house* —dilapidation /də,læpə'deɪʃən/ *n.* [U]

di·late /daɪ'leɪt, 'daɪleɪt/ *v.* [I,T] to become wider or more open, or to cause something to do this: *The doctor put drops in my eyes to dilate my pupils.* —dilation /dɪ'leɪʃən, daɪ-/ *n.* [U]

dilate on/upon sth *phr. v.* [T] FORMAL to speak or write a lot about something: *He dilated upon their piety.*

dil·a·to·ry /'dɪlə,tɔri/ *adj.* FORMAL slow and tending to delay decisions or actions: *Their unreasonable demands had a dilatory effect on the peace process.*

dil·do /'dɪldoʊ/ *n.* [C] INFORMAL an object shaped like a PENIS, which is used for sexual pleasure

di·lem·ma /də'lɛmə/ *n.* [C] a situation in which you have to make a difficult choice between two, or sometimes more than two, actions: *Many single parents struggle with the dilemma of dividing time between work and children.* | *We're in a dilemma about whether to move or not.* —see also be on the horns of a dilemma (HORN[1] (8))

dil·et·tante /'dɪlə,tant/ *n.* [C] FORMAL, DISAPPROVING someone who is interested in a subject or activity but does not really know very much about it and is not serious about learning: *Morrison is no dilettante – the music is clean and professional.* —dilettante *adj.* —dilettantism *n.* [U]

dil·i·gent /'dɪlədʒənt/ *adj.* **1** someone who is diligent works hard and carefully: *Tony is a very diligent student.* **2** carefully and thoroughly done: *The book required ten years of diligent research.* —diligence *n.* [U] —diligently *adv.*

dill /dɪl/ *n.* [U] a plant whose seeds and leaves are used in cooking

Dil·lin·ger /'dɪlɪndʒɚ/, **John** (1903–1934) a famous U.S. bank ROBBER and murderer

dill pick·le /, '../ *n.* [C] a CUCUMBER that has been preserved in VINEGAR (=a sour-tasting liquid)

dil·ly /'dɪli/ *n.* [C] OLD-FASHIONED someone or something that is exciting or special: *Hey, listen to this joke – it's a dilly.*

dilly-dal·ly /'.. ,../ *v.* dilly-dallied, dilly-dallying [I] INFORMAL to waste time or do something very slowly, especially because you cannot decide about something: *Stop dilly-dallying and get dressed!*

di·lute[1] /dɪ'lut, daɪ-/ *v.* [T] **1** to make a liquid weaker by adding water or another liquid: *Add some red wine to dilute the tomato sauce.* | [dilute sth with sth] *Dilute the paint with a little oil.* **2** to make a quality, belief etc. weaker or less effective, especially by adding something: *Opening NATO to new members may dilute its strength.* —diluted *adj.*: *diluted fruit juice* —dilution /dɪ'luʃən/ *n.* [U]

dilute[2] *adj.* [only before noun] a dilute liquid has been made weaker by the addition of water or another substance: *dilute hydrochloric acid*

dim[1] /dɪm/ *adj.* dimmer, dimmest

1 **dark** not bright: *I was led through a dim hallway to his office.* | *The lights were dim.*

2 **shape** a dim shape is not easy to see well because it is far away or there is not enough light: *We could only see a dim outline of a ship in the distance.*

3 **a dim recollection/awareness etc.** something that is difficult for someone to remember, understand etc.: *Laura had only a dim memory of the conversation.*

4 **take a dim view of sth** to disapprove of something, or to expect someone or something to fail: *Management took a dim view of union organizing efforts.*

5 **future chances** if your chances of success in the future are dim, they are not good: *Prospects for an early settlement of the dispute are dim.*

6 **unintelligent** INFORMAL not intelligent: *The boy's just a little dim.* —see also DIMWIT

7 **long ago** long ago and not related to the present time: *For many students the 1970s are dim history.*

8 **eyes** LITERARY dim eyes are weak and cannot see well —dimly *adv.*: *a dimly lit room* | *She was only dimly aware of the risk.* —dimness *n.* [U]

dim[2] *v.* dimmed, dimming **1** [I,T] if a light dims, or if you dim it, it becomes less bright: *Can you dim the lights? I have a headache.* **2** [I,T] if a feeling or quality dims, or if something dims it, it grows weaker: *The painful memory began to dim.* | *Her words dimmed our hopes of a peaceful settlement.* **3** dim your headlights/lights to lower the angle of the front lights of your car, especially when someone is driving toward you

Joe Di Maggio

Di Mag·gio /dɪ 'mædʒioʊ/, **Joe** /dʒoʊ/ (1914–1999) a U.S. baseball player who is considered one of the greatest players ever

sw **dime** /daɪm/ n. [C] **1** a coin worth 10 cents (=1/10 of a dollar), used in the U.S. and Canada **2 a dime a dozen** very common and not valuable: *Jobs like his are a dime a dozen.* **3 on a dime** within a very small space, or within a very short period of time: *Her new car can stop on a dime.*

dime bag /'. ./ n. [C] SLANG a small package of an illegal drug that costs ten dollars —compare NICKEL BAG

dime nov·el /'. ,./ n. [C] a cheap book with a story that contains a lot of exciting events

di·men·sion /dɪˈmɛnʃən, daɪ-/ n. **1** [C] a part of a situation that affects the way you think about it; ASPECT (1): *The baby brought a new dimension to the Porter family.* | *Stacy is also Tom's twin, which adds another dimension to the story.* | **the political/ human/spiritual etc. dimension** *Ron always paid attention to the personal dimension of issues at work.* **2** [C] used in PHYSICS to describe the measurement of physical objects in length, time etc.: *The use of perspective allows us to represent three dimensions on a flat page.* —see also FOURTH DIMENSION **3 dimensions** [plural] the size of something, especially when this is given as its length, height, and width: *When decorating your house, you should consider the dimensions of each room.* **4** [C,U] how great or serious a problem is: *The plant closure could have an impact of unknown dimension on the local economy.*

dime store /'. ./ n. [C] a store that sells many different types of inexpensive goods, especially for the house; FIVE-AND-DIME

di·min·ish /dɪˈmɪnɪʃ/ v. **1** [I,T] to become smaller or less important, or to make something do this: *The time Foreman spent with his children gradually diminished.* | *Tate said the fences threaten to diminish property values in the neighborhood.* **2** [T] to deliberately make someone or something appear less important or valuable than they really are: *"I'm not going to diminish the fact that I was upset with Harbaugh," McMahon said.* **3 diminishing returns** the idea that a point can be reached at which the profits or advantages you are getting stop increasing in relation to the effort you are making: *Technologies that helped rescue developing countries from famine in the 1970s have reached the point of diminishing returns.*

diminished ca·pac·i·ty /.,.. .'.../ also **diminished re·spon·si·bil·i·ty** /.,.. ...'.../ n. [U] LAW a condition in which someone is not considered to be responsible for their actions because they lack the mental ability to be able to COMMIT a certain crime

di·min·u·en·do /dɪˌmɪnyuˈɛndoʊ/ n. [C] TECHNICAL a part in a piece of music where it becomes gradually quieter —opposite CRESCENDO

dim·i·nu·tion /ˌdɪməˈnuʃən/ n. [C,U] FORMAL a reduction in the size, number, or amount of something: [+ of/in] *The design can be changed with no diminution in the value of the product.*

di·min·u·tive[1] /dɪˈmɪnyətɪv/ adj. FORMAL very small or short: *Brennan is a diminutive man with a quick smile.*

diminutive[2] n. [C] TECHNICAL a word formed by adding a diminutive suffix

diminutive suf·fix /.,... '../ n. [C] TECHNICAL an ending that is added to a word to express smallness, for example "-ling" added to "duck" to make "duckling"

dim·mer /'dɪmə/ also **dimmer switch** /'.. ,./ n. [C] an electric SWITCH that can change the brightness of a light

dim·ple /'dɪmpəl/ n. [C] a small hollow place on your cheek or chin, especially one that forms when you smile —**dimpled** adj.: *dimpled cheeks*

dimple

dimple

dim sum /dɪm ˈsʌm/ n. [U] a Chinese meal in which small amounts of many different types of food are served, usually a few at a time

dim·wit /'dɪmˌwɪt/ n. [C] SPOKEN a stupid person: *Don't let that dimwit Larry near my computer.* —**dimwitted** adj.

din[1] /dɪn/ n. [singular,U] FORMAL a loud continuous noise that sounds bad: *We couldn't hear ourselves talk above the din of the crowd.*

din[2] v. **dinned, dinning**
din sth into sb phr. v. [T] FORMAL to make someone learn and remember something by repeating it to them again and again: *Respect for our elders was dinned into us in school.*

di·nar /'dinɑr, dɪˈnɑr/ n. [C] the standard unit of money used in the former Yugoslavia and in some Middle Eastern countries

dine /daɪn/ v. [I] FORMAL to eat dinner, especially at a formal occasion: *We dined at the Ritz.* —see also **wine and dine sb** (WINE²)
dine on sth phr. v. [T] FORMAL to eat a particular kind of food for dinner, especially expensive food: *We dined on lobster and strawberries.*
dine out phr. v. [I] FORMAL to eat dinner in a restaurant; EAT OUT: *They would dine out together once a month.*

din·er /'daɪnə/ n. [C] **1** a small restaurant that serves inexpensive meals **2** someone who is eating in a restaurant

Di·ne·sen /'dinəsən, 'dɪ-/, **I·sak** /'isɑk/ —see Karen BLIXEN

di·nette /daɪˈnɛt/ n. [C] a small area, usually in or near the kitchen in a house, where people eat meals

dinette set /.'. , / n. [C] a table and matching chairs

ding[1] /dɪŋ/ n. [C] **1** a small hollow area in the surface of something, usually caused by something hitting it: *There are a few dings in the car door, but nothing serious.* **2** a sharp ringing sound, usually from a bell or piece of metal

ding[2] v. INFORMAL **1** [T] to damage something slightly by hitting it: *Pete just dinged the rear bumper a little.* **2** [I,T] to make a sound like a bell, or to make a bell do this

ding-a-ling /'dɪŋ ə ˌlɪŋ/ n. [C] SPOKEN a stupid person: *Some ding-a-ling parked too close to us.*

ding·bat /'dɪŋbæt/ n. [C] SPOKEN a stupid person: *I had to talk to that dingbat Myrtle at the church picnic.*

ding-dong /'dɪŋ dɔŋ, -dɑŋ/ n. **1** [U] the sound made by a bell **2** [C] SPOKEN a stupid person

ding·hy /'dɪŋi/ n. plural **dinghies** [C] a small open boat used for pleasure, or for taking people between a ship and the shore

din·go /'dɪŋgoʊ/ n. plural **dingoes** [C] an Australian wild dog

din·gy /'dɪndʒi/ adj. **dingier, dingiest** a dingy room, street, or place is dirty and in bad condition: *a dark, dingy basement* —**dinginess** n. [U]

din·ing car /'.. ,./ n. [C] a special car on a train where meals are served

S W 3 **dining room** /ˈ.. ˌ./ *n.* [C] a room where you eat meals in a house, hotel etc. —see picture on page 423

dining ta·ble /ˈ.. ˌ../ *n.* [C] a table at which you eat meals —compare DINNER TABLE

dink[1] /dɪŋk/ *v.*

dink around *phr. v.* [I] SPOKEN to waste time doing something unimportant: *What are you doing dinking around, getting drunk all the time?*

dink[2] *n.* [C] SPOKEN a stupid person —see also RINKY-DINK

din·ky /ˈdɪŋki/ *adj.* **dinkier, dinkiest** SPOKEN too small, and often of poor quality: *I can't believe they charge $8.95 for this dinky salad!*

S W 1 2 **din·ner** /ˈdɪnə/ *n.* **1** [C,U] the main meal of the day, eaten in the evening or in the middle of the day: *We're having fish for dinner tonight.* | **have/eat dinner** *Josh's family was still eating dinner when I called.* **2 Sunday/Christmas/Thanksgiving etc. dinner** a special meal eaten on Sunday, at Christmas, at Thanksgiving etc.: *This year Lee plans to eat Christmas dinner with his grandchildren in Kansas.* **3** [C] a formal occasion when an evening meal is eaten, often to celebrate something: *Allen and Wanda celebrated their anniversary at a dinner hosted by their children.* —see also TV DINNER

dinner dance /ˈ.. ˌ./ *n.* [C] a social event in the evening, that includes a formal meal and music for dancing

dinner jack·et /ˈ.. ˌ../ *n.* [C] a black or white JACKET (2) worn by men on very formal occasions, usually with a BOW TIE as part of a TUXEDO

dinner par·ty /ˈ.. ˌ../ *n.* [C] a social event when people are invited to someone's house for an evening meal

dinner serv·ice /ˈ.. ˌ../ also **dinner set** /ˈ.. ./ *n.* [C] a complete set of plates, dishes etc., used for serving meals

dinner ta·ble /ˈ.. ˌ../ *n.* **the dinner table a)** an occasion when people are eating dinner together: *Many of the photographs are not suitable for the dinner table.* **b)** the table at which people eat dinner —compare DINING TABLE

dinner the·a·ter /ˈ.. ˌ../ *n.* [C,U] a restaurant in which you see a play after your meal, or this type of entertainment

din·ner·time /ˈdɪnəˌtaɪm/ *n.* [U] the time when you usually have dinner, usually between 5 p.m. and 7 p.m. or between noon and 1 p.m.: *He always seems to call me at dinnertime.*

dinosaur

S W 3 **di·no·saur** /ˈdaɪnəˌsɔr/ *n.* [C] **1** one of many types of REPTILE that lived millions of years ago **2** something very large and old-fashioned that does not work well or effectively anymore: *The Maine dam is a dinosaur which should be removed.* **3** INFORMAL an insulting way of describing someone who is old and does not have modern ideas: *Some of the dinosaurs of heavy metal music will be on tour this summer.*

dint /dɪnt/ *n.* **by dint of sth** by using a particular method: *By dint of hard work, Marshall excelled in the field of law.*

di·o·cese /ˈdaɪəsɪs, -ˌsiz/ *n.* [C] the area under the control of a BISHOP in some Christian churches —**diocesan** /daɪˈɑsəsən, ˌdaɪəˈsisən/ *adj.*

di·ode /ˈdaɪoʊd/ *n.* [C] TECHNICAL a piece of electrical equipment that makes an electrical current flow in one direction

Di·og·e·nes /daɪˈɑdʒəniz/ (?412–?323 B.C.) an ancient Greek PHILOSOPHER

Di·o·ny·sus /ˌdaɪəˈnaɪsəs/ in Greek MYTHOLOGY, the god of wine and FERTILITY, usually connected with uncontrolled behavior involving drinking, parties, and sex

di·o·ram·a /ˌdaɪəˈræmə, -ˈrɑmə/ *n.* [C] a box or glass case that contains a model of a scene from history or from a story, often made by children in school

di·ox·ide /daɪˈɑksaɪd/ *n.* [C,U] TECHNICAL a chemical compound containing two atoms of oxygen to every atom of another ELEMENT —see also CARBON DIOXIDE

di·ox·in /daɪˈɑksən/ *n.* [C,U] a very poisonous chemical used for killing plants

dip[1] /dɪp/ *v.* **dipped, dipping 1** [T] to put something into a liquid and quickly lift it out again: **[dip sth in/into sth]** *Dip vegetables into the batter, then fry for 3–4 minutes.* —see picture on page 425 **2** [I] to go down: *The temperature may dip to –10 at some places near Tahoe tonight.* | **[+ in/into/down etc.]** *The trail dipped into the dark rain forest.* **3** [T] to put pets or other animals in a bath containing a chemical that kills insects on their skin —see also SKINNY-DIPPING **S W 3**

dip into sth *phr. v.* [T] **1** to use some of an amount of money that you have: *City officials were forced to dip into other funds to pay for snow removal.* | *Due to lack of funds, public school teachers often **dip into their pockets** (=pay for something with their own money) for new school supplies.* **2** to take something from inside something such as a box or container: *When drugs weren't available, he'd dip into the liquor at home.* **3** to read short parts of a book, magazine etc., but not the whole thing: *It's the kind of book you can dip into now and again.*

dip[2] *n.*
1 food [C,U] a thick mixture that you can dip food into before you eat it: *The sauce also works well as a dip for raw vegetables.*
2 swim [C] INFORMAL a quick swim: *Let's **take a quick dip** in the pool.*
3 decrease [C] a slight decrease in the amount of something: *There's been a dip in revenue because of the recession.*
4 in a surface [C] a place where the surface of something goes down suddenly, and then goes up again: *There's a dip in the road at the bottom of the hill.*
5 person [C] SPOKEN a stupid person
6 for animals [C,U] a liquid that contains a chemical which kills insects on pets and other animals

diph·the·ri·a /dɪfˈθɪriə, dɪp-/ *n.* [U] a serious infectious throat disease that makes breathing difficult

diph·thong /ˈdɪfθɔŋ, ˈdɪp-/ *n.* [C] TECHNICAL **1** a compound vowel sound made by pronouncing two vowels quickly one after the other; for example, the vowel sound in "my" is a diphthong **2** a DIGRAPH

di·plo·ma /dɪˈploʊmə/ *n.* [C] an official paper showing that a student has successfully completed their HIGH SCHOOL or college education: *a high school diploma*

di·plo·ma·cy /dɪˈploʊməsi/ *n.* [U] **1** the management of relationships between countries: *We hope to end the conflict through diplomacy rather than force.* **2** skill in dealing with people and persuading them to agree to something without upsetting them: *Bill handles personnel problems with tact and diplomacy.* —see also **gunboat diplomacy** (GUNBOAT (2))

dip·lo·mat /ˈdɪpləˌmæt/ *n.* [C] **1** someone who officially represents their government in a foreign country **2** someone who is good at dealing with people without upsetting them: *As a natural diplomat, Baxter found it easy to get the two sides to agree.*

dip·lo·mat·ic /ˌdɪpləˈmætɪk◂/ *adj.* **1** relating to the work of diplomats: *Robert's next diplomatic assignment was at the Paris embassy.* **2** good at dealing with people politely and skillfully without upsetting them: *Jen tried to be diplomatic as she explained the problem.* **3 diplomatic relations** also **diplomatic ties** the arrangement between two countries that each should keep representatives at an EMBASSY in the other's country: *Sweden established diplomatic relations* (=began diplomatic relations) *with Ukraine several years ago.* | *The U.S. broke off diplomatic relations* (=ended diplomatic relations) *with Cuba in the early 1960s.* —**diplomatically** /-kli/ *adv.*

diplomatic corps /..'.. ,./ *n.* [U] all the diplomats working in a particular country

diplomatic im·mu·ni·ty /..,.. ..../ *n.* [U] LAW a diplomat's special rights in the country where they are working, which protect them from local taxes and PROSECUTION (2)

di·plo·ma·tist /dɪˈploʊmətɪst/ *n.* [C] FORMAL a DIPLOMAT

dip·per /ˈdɪpə/ *n.* [C] **1** a large spoon with a long handle, used for taking liquid out of a container **2** a small bird that feeds in quick-moving streams —see also BIG DIPPER, LITTLE DIPPER

dip·py /ˈdɪpi/ *adj.* **dippier, dippiest** INFORMAL acting silly or crazy

dip·shit /ˈdɪpʃɪt/ *n.* [C] VULGAR, OFFENSIVE a stupid person

dip·so·ma·ni·ac /ˌdɪpsəˈmeɪniæk/ *n.* [C] TECHNICAL someone who has a very strong desire for alcoholic drinks, which they cannot control —**dipsomania** *n.* [U] —compare ALCOHOLIC[1]

dip·stick /ˈdɪpstɪk/ *n.* [C] **1** a stick used for measuring the amount of liquid in a container, especially the amount of oil in a car's engine —see picture at ENGINE **2** SPOKEN a stupid person

dip·tych /ˈdɪptɪk/ *n.* [C] a picture made in two parts which can be closed like a book —compare TRIPTYCH

dire /daɪə/ *adj.* **1** extremely serious or terrible: *The situation doesn't seem as dire as you described it.* | *At the time, rebels were in dire need of arms.* | *Increasing housing prices will have dire consequences for the poor.* **2 be in dire straits** to be in an extremely difficult or serious situation: *Peggy realized what dire financial straits she was in when her husband died.* **3 a dire warning/prediction/outlook** something that warns people about something terrible that will happen in the future: *Analysts' dire predictions about the economy have failed to come true.*

ˢ ʷ **di·rect**[1] /dəˈrɛkt, daɪ-/ *adj.*
⅔ **1** without others involved done without involving other people, actions, processes etc.: *I have direct access to the company's database.* | *Sue has direct control over the business.* | *I'm not in direct contact with them.*
2 from one place to another going straight from one place to another, without stopping or changing direction: *We can get a direct flight to New York.* | *Shade Road would be a more direct route to the freeway.*
3 effect likely to change something immediately: *Cutbacks in defense spending will have a direct impact on 80,000 jobs.*
4 a direct result/consequence something that happens only because of one particular thing: [+ of] *Authorities report that 32 people died as a direct result of the explosion.*
5 behavior/attitude saying exactly what you mean in an honest clear way: *It's best to be direct when talking with the management.* | *a direct question/answer Gaylord avoided giving direct answers to most of the reporters' questions.*
6 exact [only before noun] exact, complete, or total: *Tyler's fierce public image was a direct contrast to his tender love for his family.* | *Weight increases in direct proportion to mass.* | *The study includes direct quotes* (=their exact words) *from several people suffering from drug addiction.*
7 a direct hit an occasion when something such as a bomb or a very bad storm exactly hits a place, causing a lot of damage: *Monday night's air raids resulted in direct hits on the presidential palace.*
8 a direct descendant someone who is related to someone else through their parents and grandparents, not through their AUNTS, UNCLES, brothers, sisters etc.: *Kevin says he's a direct descendant of Benjamin Franklin.*

9 direct sunlight/heat strong heat or sunlight that someone or something is not protected from: *Never leave a videocassette in direct sunlight.* —opposite INDIRECT

direct[2] *v.*
ˢ ʷ
⅔
1 [T always + adv./prep.] to aim something in a particular direction or at a particular person, group etc.: [+ at/toward/away from etc.] *Her angry comments were not directed at us.* | *How could scientists direct deadly meteorites away from the earth?*
2 [T] to be in charge of something or control it: *Steinberg directed Argonne's chemistry division from 1982 to 1988.*
3 [I,T] to give the actors in a play, film, or television program instructions about what they should do
4 [T] FORMAL to tell someone the way to a place: [direct sb to sth] *A nurse directed us down the hallway to the birthing room.* —see Usage Note at LEAD[1]
5 tell sb to do sth [T] FORMAL to tell someone what they should do: [direct sb to do sth] *The border guard directed me to hand over my passport.* | [direct that] *Burns' will directed that the money be used for college scholarships.*

D

direct[3] *adv.* **1** without stopping or changing direction: *I'm flying direct to Dallas from Los Angeles.* **2** without dealing with anyone else first: *It's usually cheaper to buy the goods direct from the wholesaler.*

direct ac·tion /.,. '..◄/ *n.* [U] an action such as a STRIKE or a protest which is intended to make a company or government make changes such as increasing workers' pay or stopping development of the country

direct cur·rent /.,. '../ *n.* [U] a flow of electricity that moves in one direction; DC —compare ALTERNATING CURRENT

direct de·pos·it /.,. .'../ *n.* [U] a method of paying someone's salary directly into their bank account —**direct deposit** *v.* [T] *My paycheck is direct deposited into my checking account.*

direct dis·course /.,. '../ *n.* [U] DIRECT SPEECH

di·rec·tion /dəˈrɛkʃən, daɪ-/ *n.*
1 toward [C] the way something or someone moves, faces, or is aimed: *Did you see which direction they went?* | *The trucks headed in the direction of* (=toward) *town.* | *A car coming in the opposite direction struck Sandi's car.* | *Hurricanes can change direction in a matter of hours.* | *I saw smoke coming from the direction of the parking lot.* | *People started running in all directions.* | *in a northerly/easterly etc. direction Continue in a southerly direction until you reach the road.*
ˢ ʷ
⅔
2 way sth develops [C] the general way in which someone or something changes or develops: *This decision could determine the direction in which our lives will move.* | *take a different/new/exciting etc. direction "We decided that the campaign should take a different direction," said Faso.*
3 directions [plural] instructions about how to get from one place to another, or about how to do something: *Could you give me directions to Times Square?* | *You'd better read the directions before you put the bicycle together.*
4 control [U] control, management, or advice: *The company has been successful under Meyer's direction.*
5 purpose [U] a general purpose or aim: *Officials have complained that there is a lack of direction in the mayor's office.*
6 movie [U] the instructions and advice given to actors and other people in a movie, play etc. —see also **sense of direction** (SENSE[1] (11))

di·rec·tion·al /dəˈrɛkʃənəl, daɪ-/ *adj.* [only before noun] TECHNICAL **1** pointing in a particular direction: *directional signs* **2** a directional piece of equipment receives or gives out radio signals from some directions more strongly than others: *a directional antenna*

di·rec·tive[1] /dəˈrɛktɪv/ *n.* [C] an official order or instruction to do something: *All government agencies received a directive to reduce their staffs.*

directive² *adj.* giving instructions: *It is important in these cases that doctors take a less directive approach.*

s w **di·rect·ly** /dəˈrɛktli, daɪ-/ *adv.* **1** with no other
2 2 person, action, process etc. involved: *New evidence directly linked Nathanson to the killing.* | *The new law won't affect us directly.* **2** exactly: *Have you noticed how he never looks directly at us,* | *Mike and his wife sat directly behind us.* **3 speak/ask/answer etc. directly** to say exactly what you mean without trying to hide anything: *Strauss refused to comment directly on the board meeting.*

direct mail /.,. ˈ./ *n.* [U] advertisements that are sent by mail to many people

direct meth·od /.,. ˈ../ *n.* [singular] a method of teaching a foreign language without using the student's own language

direct ob·ject /.,. ˈ../ *n.* [C] TECHNICAL in grammar, the person or thing that receives the direct action of a TRANSITIVE verb. In the sentence "He eats bread," "bread" is the direct object. —compare INDIRECT OBJECT

s w **di·rec·tor** /dəˈrɛktɚ, daɪ-/ *n.* [C] **1** the person who
2 1 gives instructions to the actors, CAMERAMEN etc. in a movie, play etc. —compare PRODUCER (2) **2** someone who controls or manages a company, organization, or activity: *Miller has been appointed to the position of sales director.*

di·rec·tor·ate /dəˈrɛktərɪt/ *n.* [C] the BOARD (=committee) of directors of a company, or the people who are in change of a large government AGENCY: *the CIA's Operations Directorate*

di·rec·tor·ship /dəˈrɛktɚʃɪp/ *n.* [C,U] the position of being in charge of a company, organization, or activity: *Sales increased by 25% under Danoff's directorship.*

di·rec·to·ry /dəˈrɛktəri, daɪ-/ *n.* plural **directories** [C] **1** a book or list of names, facts etc., usually arranged in alphabetical order: *Sam's number should be listed in the telephone directory.* | *a directory of city tours* **2** a list of computer FILES kept on a DISK or in the part of the computer where information is stored

directory as·sist·ance /.,.... ˈ.../ *n.* [U] a service on the telephone network that you can use to find out someone's telephone number

direct speech /.,.. ˈ./ *n.* [U] TECHNICAL the style used to report what someone says by giving their actual words, for example "'I don't want to go,' said Julie" —compare INDIRECT SPEECH, REPORTED SPEECH

direct tax /.,. ˈ./ *n.* [C,U] TECHNICAL a tax, such as income tax, which is collected from the person who pays it, rather than a tax on goods or services which companies pay —**direct taxation** /.,. .ˈ../ *n.* [U] —opposite INDIRECT TAXATION

dirge /dɚdʒ/ *n.* [C] **1** a slow sad song that is sung or played at a funeral **2** a song or piece of music that is too slow and boring

dir·i·gi·ble /ˈdɪrədʒəbəl, dəˈrɪ-/ *n.* [C] an AIRSHIP —see also BLIMP (1)

s w **dirt** /dɚt/ *n.* [U] **1** earth or soil: *Put the seeds in the*
2 3 *pot and cover them with dirt.* | *They live at the end of a dirt road* (=with a surface made of dirt). **2** any substance that makes things dirty, such as mud or dust: *The floor was covered with dirt.* **3** INFORMAL information about someone's private life or activities which could give people a bad opinion of them if it became known: *Reporters contacted Cox's former girlfriend, trying to **dig up dirt on** (=find embarrassing things about) him.* **4** talk, writing, movies etc. that are considered bad or immoral because they are about sex —see also **dish the dirt** (DISH²), **hit paydirt** (PAYDIRT), **hit the ground/deck/dirt** (HIT¹ (24))

dirt bag, dirtbag /ˈ. ./ *n.* [C] a person who is disgusting and immoral, who does bad things to other people, and who you do not respect

dirt bike /ˈ. ./ *n.* [C] a small MOTORCYCLE for young people, usually ridden on rough paths or fields

dirt-cheap /,. ˈ.‹/ *adj., adv.* INFORMAL extremely inexpensive: *Air fares to Chicago are dirt-cheap right now.*

dirt farm·er /ˈ. ,../ *n.* [C] a poor farmer who works to feed himself and his family, without paying anyone else to help

dirt-poor /,. ˈ.‹/ *adj.* INFORMAL extremely poor

dirt·y¹ /ˈdɚti/ *adj.* **dirtier,**
dirtiest

s w
2
3

1 not clean covered in dirt, or marked with dirt: *How did the floor get so dirty?* | *Take off those dirty jeans.*

2 sex relating to sex, in a way that is considered bad or immoral: *Do you know any **dirty jokes** in Spanish?* | *My parents found a bunch of **dirty magazines** (=magazines with pictures of naked people) in my room.*

3 bad/immoral used to emphasize that you think something is bad, dishonest, or immoral: *Having to lay employees off is a dirty job.* | *The government led a dirty war against its own citizens.* | *Journalists have discovered the mayor's **dirty little secret**: his criminal record for drug possession.*

4 a dirty word a word that people find offensive or disapprove of, especially because it is about sex: *A lot of the dirty words were removed from the script before filming began.* | *Has "individualism" become a dirty word in America?*

5 dirty tricks dishonest or illegal activities, especially done by a government, political group, or company, such as spreading false information about their competitors or opponents: *Denser accused Hubert of running **a dirty tricks campaign** (=a series of planned dirty tricks).*

6 give sb a dirty look to look at someone in a very disapproving way: *Amy kept crying, and everybody was giving us dirty looks.*

7 do sb's dirty work to do a bad or dishonest job for someone so that they do not have to do it themselves: *Tell Fran I'm not going to do her dirty work for her.*

8 wash your dirty laundry/linen in public also **air your dirty laundry/linen in public** to discuss something embarrassing or bad about yourself where everyone can know, see, or hear

9 dirty pool unfair or dishonest behavior: *They shouldn't charge you for that. It's just dirty pool.*

10 drugs SLANG containing or possessing illegal drugs

dirty² *adv.* **1 dirty rotten** SPOKEN extremely dishonest or unkind: *What a dirty rotten trick!* **2 play dirty** INFORMAL **a)** to behave in a very unfair and dishonest way: *Warren was willing to play dirty in order to get the job.* **b)** to cheat in a game: *I hate playing basketball with Bill – he always plays dirty.* **3 talk dirty** INFORMAL to talk about sex using words that are offensive or OBSCENE: *She said Smith paid her to pose naked and talk dirty to him.*

dirty³ *v.* **dirties, dirtied, dirtying** [T] **1** to make something dirty: *There were cigarette butts and dirtied napkins everywhere.* **2 dirty your hands (with sth)** to involve yourself in something that you disapprove of: *I don't want to dirty my hands with illegal drugs.*

dirty blond /,.. ˈ.‹/ *adj.* dirty blond hair is a dull light brown color —**dirty blond** *n.* [C]

dirty old man /,.. . ˈ./ *n.* [C] INFORMAL, DISAPPROVING an older man who is too sexually interested in younger women

dis /dɪs/ v. **dissed, dissing** [T] SLANG to make unfair and unkind remarks about someone

dis- /dɪs/ prefix **1** shows an opposite or negative: I disapprove (=do not approve). | his dishonesty (=lack of honesty) | a discontented look **2** [in verbs] shows the stopping or removing of a condition: Disconnect the machine from the electrical supply (=so that it is no longer connected). | Disinfect the wound first.

dis·a·bil·i·ty /,dɪsə'bɪləti/ n. plural **disabilities 1** [C] a physical or mental condition that makes it difficult for someone to do the things most people are able to do: She manages to lead a normal life in spite of her physical disabilities. **2** [U] money that is given by the government to people who are disabled: Eschbach has been living on disability for ten years. **3** [U] the state of having a disability, especially not being able to use parts of your body: The group is for people who are learning to live with disability.

dis·a·ble /dɪs'eɪbəl/ v. [T] **1** [often passive] to make someone unable to use a part of their body in a way that most people can: Don had been permanently disabled in a car accident. **2** to deliberately stop a machine or piece of equipment from working: Somehow, the robbers were able to disable the gallery's alarm system. —**disablement** n. [C,U]

dis·a·bled /dɪs'eɪbəld/ adj. **1** someone who is disabled cannot use a part of their body in a way that most people can: One of their daughters is severely disabled. | disabled parking/restroom/entrance etc. (=a service, room, entrance etc. for disabled people) **2 the disabled** [plural] people who are disabled: Doors should be wide enough to provide access for the disabled. —compare HANDICAPPED —see Usage Note at HANDICAPPED

disabled list /.'.. ,./ n. **the disabled list** the players on a professional sports team who are unable to play because of injuries: Sheffield has already been **on the disabled list** twice this season.

dis·a·buse /,dɪsə'byuz/ v. [T] FORMAL to persuade someone that what they believe is untrue: [**disabuse sb of sth**] I hope to disabuse you of the notion that all employees are lazy.

dis·ad·van·tage /,dɪsəd'væntɪdʒ/ n. [C,U] **1** something that may make someone less successful than other people: Your main disadvantage is your lack of job experience. | Jen's small size **puts** her **at a disadvantage** in the game. **2** something that is not favorable, or that causes problems: [+ of] The biggest disadvantage of her work is the long hours. | [+ to] One disadvantage to this plan is that you can't choose your own doctor.

dis·ad·van·taged /,dɪsəd'væntɪdʒd/ adj. **1** having social problems, such as a lack of money or education, which make it more difficult for you to succeed than other people: Improved nutrition will help disadvantaged children perform better in school. **2 the disadvantaged** [plural] people who are disadvantaged: In a letter to his clients, Romer told them he had given their money to the disadvantaged.

dis·ad·van·ta·geous /,dɪsædvæn'teɪdʒəs, -vən-/ adj. [+ to/for] unfavorable and likely to cause problems for you —**disadvantageously** adv.

dis·af·fect·ed /,dɪsə'fɛktɪd/ adj. FORMAL not loyal anymore because you are not satisfied with your leader, ruler etc.: Candidates are trying to attract disaffected voters. —**disaffection** /,dɪsə'fɛkʃən/ n. [U]

dis·af·fil·i·ate /,dɪsə'fɪli,eɪt/ v. [I,T + from] if an organization disaffiliates from another organization or is disaffiliated from it, it breaks the official connection between them —**disaffiliation** /,dɪsəfɪli-'eɪʃən/ n. [U]

dis·a·gree /,dɪsə'gri/ v. [I] **1** to have or express a different opinion from someone else: I totally disagree, Mike. It's not a problem at all. | [+ **with**] Every time I disagree with somebody, they go running to the boss. | [+ **on/about**] We often disagree on politics. | Jane and Rob disagreed about how to use the money they won. **2** if two or more sets of statements, reports, or numbers which are about the same thing, disagree, they are different from each other

disagree with sb phr. v. [T] if something such as food or weather disagrees with you, it has a bad effect on you or makes you sick: Spicy food really disagrees with me.

dis·a·gree·a·ble /,dɪsə'griəbəl/ adj. FORMAL **1** unfriendly and in a bad mood: He's the most disagreeable man I've ever met. **2** not enjoyable or pleasant: a very disagreeable task —**disagreeably** adv.

dis·a·gree·ment /,dɪsə'grimənt/ n. **1** [C,U] a situation in which people express different opinions about something and sometimes argue: We've had a few disagreements, but we're still good friends. | [+ **about/over**] There was some disagreement about the age of the mummies. | [+ **with**] Gavin was afraid to express his disagreement with company policies. | [+ **among/between**] The brawl apparently started with a disagreement between two students over a female. | Diana shook her head **in disagreement**. **2** [U] differences between two statements, reports, numbers etc. that ought to be similar: [+ **between**] There is considerable disagreement between these two estimates.

dis·al·low /,dɪsə'laʊ/ v. [T] to officially refuse to allow something such as a tax BENEFIT, an action in a court of law, or a GOAL in sports, because a rule has been broken: Judge Nisen disallowed certain evidence containing confidential information.

D

dis·ap·pear /,dɪsə'pɪr/ v. [I] **1** to become impossible to see anymore: The scars will disappear in a year or two. | [+ **into/behind/from** etc.] The railway tracks disappear into a hole in the side of the mountain. | **disappear from sight/view** She watches her grandchildren until they disappear from sight. **2** to become impossible to find or to be lost: The two girls disappeared while walking home from school. | "The Little Mermaid" video quickly disappeared from the stores (=it sold so quickly that it was impossible to find it in the stores). —see Usage Note at LOSE **3** to stop existing: Small companies will disappear by being merged into big ones.

dis·ap·pear·ance /,dɪsə'pɪrəns/ n. [C,U] **1** the act or state of becoming impossible to see or find: He notified police of the girl's disappearance. **2** the state of not existing anymore: the disappearance of ancient forests

dis·ap·point /,dɪsə'pɔɪnt/ v. [I,T] **1** to make someone feel unhappy because something they hoped for does not happen or is not as good as they expected: Of course our kids disappoint us sometimes, but we don't stop loving them. | Bolton promised a great performance, and he didn't disappoint. **2 disappoint sb's hopes/plans/expectations** FORMAL to fail to make something happen, or to prevent something from happening, that someone hoped for or expected: If we disappoint the hopes of these people, much of what we have accomplished with them will be lost.

dis·ap·point·ed /,dɪsə'pɔɪntɪd/ adj. **1** unhappy because something you hoped for did not happen, or because someone or something was not as good as you expected: Disappointed tourists were turned away from the Washington Monument today, which was closed for repairs. | [**disappointed (that)**] Steve is very disappointed that he couldn't go. | [+ **with/at/about**] Stockholders were disappointed with the company's third-quarter profits. | We are saddened and disappointed about this decision. | [+ **in**] I was disappointed in the quality of the food. | [**disappointed to hear/see/learn** etc.] We are very disappointed to see her go. | **deeply/terribly/bitterly disappointed** Arnold said he was deeply disappointed by the verdict. **2** a disappointed **hope/plan/expectation** something you hope for, plan, or expect that does not happen or is not as good as you expected: Disappointed expectations arise sometimes from unrealistic hopes.

dis·ap·point·ing /,dɪsə'pɔɪntɪŋ/ adj. not as good as you expected or hoped something would be: The delay of the flight was disappointing news for the travelers. | It rained most of the time we were in England, which was pretty disappointing. —**disappointingly** adv.

D

dis·ap·point·ment /ˌdɪsəˈpɔɪntˀmənt/ *n.* **1** [U] a feeling of sadness because something is not as good as you expected or has not happened in the way you hoped: *Julie tried to smile, but her disappointment showed through.* | [+ **with**] *The Pope described his disappointment with the recent course of Western history.* | [+ **over**] *Waters expressed disappointment over the company's decision to lay off more workers.* | [**disappointment (that)**] *It was a **great disappointment** that my marriage didn't work.* | [+ **at/in**] *The company accepted the ruling, but stressed its disappointment in the outcome of the trial.* | *McGee **expressed disappointment** at not being chosen for the job.* | *To her great disappointment* (=she was very disappointed), *she was turned down for the transfer.* **2** [C] someone or something that is not as good as you hoped or expected: *The Giants have been a disappointment all season.* | [**be a disappointment to sb**] *Kate feels like she's a disappointment to her family.* | [**be a disappointment for sb**] *Low sales of the album have been a disappointment for the band.*

dis·ap·pro·ba·tion /ˌdɪsæprəˈbeɪʃən/ *n.* [U] FORMAL disapproval of someone or something because you think they are morally wrong

dis·ap·prov·al /ˌdɪsəˈpruvəl/ *n.* [U] a feeling or opinion that someone is behaving badly or that something is bad: [+ **of**] *Public disapproval of smoking has increased.* | *Marion shook her head **in disapproval**.*

dis·ap·prove /ˌdɪsəˈpruv/ *v.* **1** [I] to think that someone or something is bad, wrong etc.: [+ **of**] *His journal shows he disapproved of slavery.* | *My grandmother strongly disapproves of couples living together before marriage.* **2** [T] FORMAL to not agree to something that has been suggested: *The board of directors disapproved the sale.*

dis·ap·prov·ing /ˌdɪsəˈpruvɪŋ/ *adj.* showing that you think someone or something is bad, wrong etc.: *Her disapproving parents refused to attend her wedding.* —**disapprovingly** *adv.*

dis·arm /dɪsˈɑrm/ *v.* **1** [I] to reduce the size of your army, navy etc. and the number of your weapons: *Both sides must disarm before the peace talks.* **2** [T] to take away someone's weapons: *U.N. peacekeepers will disarm both forces.* **3** [T] to make someone less angry and more friendly: *She uses humor to disarm people.* —see also DISARMING **4** [T] to take the explosives out of a bomb, MISSILE etc.

dis·ar·ma·ment /dɪsˈɑrməmənt/ *n.* [U] the reduction in numbers or size of a country's weapons, army, navy etc.: *The world appears to be moving toward **nuclear disarmament*** (=a reduction in the number of atomic weapons). —compare ARMAMENT (2)

dis·arm·ing /dɪsˈɑrmɪŋ/ *adj.* making you feel less angry and more friendly or trusting: *a disarming smile* —**disarmingly** *adv.*

dis·ar·range /ˌdɪsəˈreɪndʒ/ *v.* [T] FORMAL to spoil the organization of something, or to make something messy —**disarrangement** *n.* [U]

dis·ar·ray /ˌdɪsəˈreɪ/ *n.* [U] FORMAL the state of being messy or not organized: *The company's files were in disarray.* | *fall into disarray/throw sth into disarray The Soviet economy has fallen into disarray.*

dis·as·sem·ble /ˌdɪsəˈsɛmbəl/ *v.* [T] to take apart something that is made of many connected pieces: *You'll have to disassemble the bed frame in order to move it.* —**disassembly** *n.* [U]

dis·as·so·ci·ate /ˌdɪsəˈsoʊʃiˌeɪt, -siˌeɪt/ *v.* [T] another form of DISSOCIATE

dis·as·ter /dɪˈzæstɚ/ *n.* [C,U] **1** a sudden event such as a flood, storm, or accident that causes great harm or damage: *The 1986 nuclear disaster in Chernobyl spread radiation worldwide.* | *If disaster strikes during a school day, Newark elementary students know what to do.* **2** a complete failure: *The party was a total disaster.* **3** INFORMAL something that is very messy or dirty, or that looks very bad: *I'd invite you in, but my place is a disaster.* —see also NATURAL DISASTER

disaster ar·e·a /.ˈ.. ˌ..../ *n.* [C] **1** a place where a flood, storm, fire etc. has happened and caused a lot of damage, used especially when the government agrees to give disaster relief: *The town was **declared a disaster area** after the floods.* **2** INFORMAL a place that is very messy or dirty: *Her bedroom is a disaster area.*

disaster re·lief /.ˈ.. .ˌ./ *n.* [U] money and supplies that are given to people after their property has been damaged by a very bad flood, storm, fire etc.: *Congress pledged $3 million in disaster relief to the hurricane victims.*

dis·as·trous /dɪˈzæstrəs/ *adj.* very bad, or ending in failure: *A disastrous pesticide spill killed all water life along 40 miles of the river.* | *a disastrous early marriage* —**disastrously** *adv.*

dis·a·vow /ˌdɪsəˈvaʊ/ *v.* [T] FORMAL to say that you are not responsible for something, that you do not know about it, or that you are not involved with it: *The bus drivers' union has disavowed any involvement in the violence.* —**disavowal** *n.* [C,U]

dis·band /dɪsˈbænd/ *v.* [I,T] to stop existing as an organization, or to make something do this: *Yeltsin disbanded the Soviet Interior Ministry.*

dis·bar /dɪsˈbɑr/ *v.* **disbarred, disbarring** [T] to make a lawyer leave the legal profession: *Estrada was fired from his job as an assistant U.S. attorney and disbarred.* —**disbarment** *n.* [U] —compare DEBAR

dis·be·lief /ˌdɪsbəˈlif/ *n.* [U] a feeling that something is not true or does not exist: *Her first reaction to winning the award was disbelief.* | *Bill stared at him **in disbelief**.* —compare BELIEF, UNBELIEF

dis·be·lieve /ˌdɪsbəˈliv/ *v.* [I,T] FORMAL to not believe something or someone: *The jury had no reason to disbelieve the witnesses.* —**disbelieving** *adj.* —**disbelievingly** *adv.*

dis·burse /dɪsˈbɚs/ *v.* [T] FORMAL to pay out money, especially from a large sum that is available for a special purpose: *The bank disbursed a record $2.5 billion in loans last year.* —**disbursement** *n.* [C,U] —**disbursal** *n.* [C,U]

disc /dɪsk/ *n.* [C] another spelling of DISK —see also COMPACT DISC, LASER DISC

dis·card¹ /dɪˈskɑrd/ *v.* **1** [T] to get rid of something: *Cut the olives into small slices and discard the pits.* **2** [I,T] to put down unwanted cards in a card game: *Wait! You forgot to discard.* —**discarded** *adj.*

dis·card² /ˈdɪskɑrd/ *n.* [C] **1** something that you get rid of because you do not want it anymore: *People pay him to haul away their discards.* **2** an unwanted card that is put down in a card game

disc brakes /ˈ. ./ *n.* [plural] BRAKES that work by means of a pair of hard surfaces pressing against a DISK (3) in the center of a car wheel

dis·cern /dɪˈsɚn, dɪˈzɚn/ *v.* [T not in progressive] FORMAL to see, notice, or understand something by looking at it or thinking about it carefully; PERCEIVE (2): *Politicians are good at discerning public opinion.* | *The telescope can discern objects incredibly distant in space.* | [**discern what/whether/how** etc.] *Because of the camera angle, it was impossible to discern whether Harper had scored.* —**discernible** *adj.* —**discernibly** *adv.*

dis·cern·ing /dɪˈsɚnɪŋ/ *adj.* APPROVING able to make good judgments about people, styles, and things: *The book will charm discerning readers.* | *the discerning ear/eye/nose* etc. (=someone who is able to make good judgments about what they hear, see, smell etc.)

dis·cern·ment /dɪˈsɚnmənt/ *n.* [U] FORMAL the ability to make good judgments about people, styles, and things

dis·charge¹ /dɪsˈtʃɑrdʒ/ *v.*
1 send sb away [T] to officially allow someone to go or to send them away from a place, especially after they have been in a hospital or working in the Army, Navy etc.: [**discharge sb from sth**] *Hazlett was medically discharged from the Army in 1989.*
2 let sth out [I always + adv./prep.,T usually passive] to send, pour, or let out something from

something else, especially a liquid or a gas: [**discharge sth into sth**] *Raw sewage was discharged into the ocean.* | [+ **into**] *The pond discharges into Matadero Creek.*
3 shoot [I,T] FORMAL if you discharge a gun, or if it discharges, it shoots a bullet: *Jefferson's gun accidentally discharged, killing him.*
4 duty/responsibility [T] FORMAL to perform a duty or keep a promise, etc.: *The president called upon the soldiers to discharge their duty with honor.*
5 electricity [I,T] if a piece of electrical equipment discharges or is discharged, it sends out electricity
6 a wound [T] if a wound or body part discharges a substance such as PUS (=infected liquid), the substance slowly comes out of it
7 debt [T] FORMAL to pay a debt
8 goods/passengers [T] FORMAL to unload goods or passengers from a ship, airplane etc.: *The captain gave the order to discharge the cargo.*
dis·charge² /'dɪstʃɑrdʒ/ *n.* **1** [U] the action of officially sending someone or something away, especially from the hospital or the Army, Navy etc.: [+ **from**] *After his discharge from the army, Jim got married.* —see also DISHONORABLE DISCHARGE, HONORABLE DISCHARGE **2** [C,U] the act of sending a substance out of something else, or the substance that comes out: [+ **of**] *The discharge of harmful chemicals into drinking water is banned.* **3** [U] a substance that comes out of a wound or out of a part of your body such as your nose: *Pain and a nasal discharge may mean the patient has a sinus infection.* **4** [U] the act of shooting a gun: *the discharge of a firearm* **5** [C,U] electricity that is sent out by a piece of equipment, a storm etc. **6** [U] the act of doing a duty or paying a debt
dis·ci·ple /dɪˈsaɪpəl/ *n.* [C] **1** a follower of a great teacher or leader, especially a religious one: *Mirabai gave up family and fortune to become a wandering disciple of Krishna.* **2** one of the 12 original followers of Jesus Christ
dis·ci·ple·ship /dɪˈsaɪpəlʃɪp/ *n.* [U] the period of time when someone is a disciple, or the state of being one
dis·ci·pli·nar·i·an /ˌdɪsəpləˈnɛriən/ *n.* [C] someone who believes that people should obey orders and rules, and who makes them do this: **strict/stern disciplinarian** *He was kind, but a strict disciplinarian.*
dis·ci·pli·nar·y /ˈdɪsəpləˌnɛri/ *adj.* relating to trying to make someone obey rules, or to the punishment of someone who has not obeyed rules | **disciplinary action/measures** *The department is considering disciplinary action against the officers.*
SW dis·ci·pline¹ /ˈdɪsəplɪn/ *n.* **1** [C,U] a way of training someone so that they learn to control their behavior and obey rules: *Windell's book gives parents advice on discipline.* | *Disciplines such as yoga improve mental and physical fitness.* **2** [U] controlled behavior in which people obey rules and orders: *Many schools are lacking in discipline.* **3** [U] the ability to control your own behavior and way of working: *Working from home requires a good deal of discipline.* | *Martial arts teach respect, discipline, and cooperation.* —see also SELF-DISCIPLINE **4** [U] punishment for not obeying rules: *Employees who joined the strike face discipline.* **5** [C] an area of knowledge or teaching, especially one such as history, chemistry, mathematics etc. that is studied at a college or university: *History and economics only became separate academic disciplines in the 20th century.*
discipline² *v.* [T] **1** to punish someone for not obeying rules: *Six workers were disciplined last year for not doing their jobs.* **2** to train someone to obey rules and control their own behavior: *Disciplining children takes patience and consistency.* **3** **discipline yourself (to do sth)** to control the way you work or how regularly you do something, because you know it is good for you
dis·ci·plined /ˈdɪsəplɪnd/ *adj.* obeying rules and controlling your behavior: *a loyal and disciplined army* | *We're very disciplined when it comes to money.* —opposite UNDISCIPLINED

disc jock·ey /'. ˌ../ *n.* [C] someone whose job is to play the music on a radio show or in a club where you can dance
dis·claim /dɪsˈkleɪm/ *v.* [T] FORMAL to state, especially officially, that you are not responsible for something, that you do not know about it, or that you are not involved with it: *The group has disclaimed all responsibility for the attack.*
dis·claim·er /dɪsˈkleɪmɚ/ *n.* [C] a statement that you are not responsible for something, that you do not know about it etc., often used in advertising: *The diet pills include the disclaimer: "For many dieters, weight loss is temporary."*
dis·close /dɪsˈkloʊz/ *v.* [T] **1** to make something known publicly, especially after it has been kept secret: *GM did not disclose details of the agreement.* | [**disclose that**] *Councilman Horton disclosed last night that he is gay.* **2** FORMAL to show something by removing the thing that covers it
dis·clo·sure /dɪsˈkloʊʒɚ/ *n.* [C,U] a secret that someone tells people, or the act of telling this secret: *Following sensational disclosures concerning his personal life, he has offered to resign.* | *the disclosure of classified information*
dis·co /ˈdɪskoʊ/ *n. plural* **discos** [C] **1** a type of dance music with a strong repeating beat that was first popular in the 1970s **2** a place where people can dance to recorded popular music
dis·cog·ra·phy /dɪˈskɑgrəfi/ *n.* [C] a list of the music and songs recorded by a musician or musical group
dis·col·or /dɪsˈkʌlɚ/ *v.* [I,T] to change color, or to make something change color, so that it looks unattractive: *His teeth were discolored from smoking.*
dis·col·or·a·tion /dɪsˌkʌləˈreɪʃən/ *n.* **1** [C] a place on the surface of something where it has become discolored: *The victims suffered a purplish discoloration of the skin.* **2** [U] the process of becoming discolored
dis·com·bob·u·lat·ed /ˌdɪskəmˈbɑbyəˌleɪtɪd/ *adj.* HUMOROUS completely confused or upset —**discombobulate** *v.* [T]
dis·com·fit /dɪsˈkʌmfɪt/ *v.* [T] FORMAL to make someone feel uncomfortable, annoyed, or embarrassed: *Foley's announcement discomfited some Democrats.* —**discomfited** *adj.* —**discomfiting** *adj.* **discomfiture** /dɪsˈkʌmfətʃɚ/ *n.* [U]
dis·com·fort /dɪsˈkʌmfɚt/ *n.* **1** [U] slight pain or a bad feeling: *A cushion will help ease the discomfort of sitting on the floor.* **2** [U] a feeling of embarrassment, shame, or worry: [+ **at**] *Kage admits discomfort at seeing the peace symbol used as a fashion statement.* **3** [C] something that makes you uncomfortable: [+ **of**] *The new book stand eliminates the discomforts of reading in bed.*—**discomfort** *v.* [T] —**discomforting** *adj.*
dis·com·mode /ˌdɪskəˈmoʊd/ *v.* [T] FORMAL to cause trouble or difficulties for someone
dis·com·po·sure /ˌdɪskəmˈpoʊʒɚ/ *n.* [U] FORMAL the state of feeling worried and not calm anymore —**discompose** *v.* [T]
dis·con·cert /ˌdɪskənˈsɚt/ *v.* [T] to make someone feel slightly confused, worried, or embarrassed
dis·con·cert·ed /ˌdɪskənˈsɚtɪd/ *adj.* feeling slightly confused, worried, or embarrassed: *Sabach is slightly disconcerted by his success.*
dis·con·cert·ing /ˌdɪskənˈsɚtɪŋ/ *adj.* making you feel slightly confused, worried, or embarrassed: *Waters asked a few disconcerting questions.* —**disconcertingly** *adv.*
dis·con·nect /ˌdɪskəˈnɛkt/ *v.* **1** [I,T] to separate something from the thing it is connected to, or to become separated: *Salazar's family agreed to disconnect the life support system.* | [+ **from**] *Two freight cars disconnected from the train engine and fell into a river near Dhaka.* **2** [T] to remove the supply of power from a machine or piece of equipment: *Disconnect the battery and recharge it.* **3** [T] to stop supplying a service, such as water, telephone,

D

electricity, or gas, to a house or other building: *I tried to call the company, but the phone number had been disconnected.* **4** [T] to break the telephone connection between two people: *I'll have to call him back – we got disconnected.* —**disconnection** /ˌdɪskə-ˈnɛkʃən/ *n.* [C,U]

dis·con·nect·ed /ˌdɪskəˈnɛktɪd/ *adj.* not related to anything else, and often difficult to understand: *The plot is disconnected and unbelievable.*

dis·con·so·late /dɪsˈkɑnsəlɪt/ *adj.* extremely sad and hopeless: *A few disconsolate men sat with their hats in their hands.* —**disconsolately** *adv.*

dis·con·tent /ˌdɪskənˈtɛnt/ also **dis·con·tent·ment** /ˌdɪskənˈtɛntˈmənt/ *n.* [U] a feeling of not being happy or satisfied: [+ **with**] *The election results were attributed to discontent with economic reform among voters.* | [+ **over**] *The Oklahoma teacher says there is widespread discontent over math education.* —opposite CONTENTMENT —**discontent** *v.* [T]

dis·con·tent·ed /ˌdɪskənˈtɛntɪd/ *adj.* unhappy or not satisfied: *Discontented workers joined the protests.*

dis·con·tin·ue /ˌdɪskənˈtɪnyu/ *v.* [T] to stop doing, producing, or providing something: *The airline plans to discontinue daily flights from L.A. to Osaka.* —**discontinued** *adj.*: *a discontinued china pattern* —**discontinuance** *n.* [U] —**discontinuation** /ˌdɪskəntɪnyuˈeɪʃən/ *n.* [U]

dis·con·ti·nu·i·ty /ˌdɪskɑntˈnˈuəti -təˈnuəti/ *n.* FORMAL **1** [U] the fact of a process not being continuous **2** [C] a sudden change or pause in a process

dis·con·tin·u·ous /ˌdɪskənˈtɪnyuəs/ *adj.* FORMAL not continuous

dis·cord /ˈdɪskɔrd/ *n.* **1** [U] FORMAL disagreement between people: *The verdict has increased racial discord in the country.* **2** [C,U] an annoying sound produced by a group of musical notes that do not go together well —compare HARMONY

dis·cor·dant /dɪsˈkɔrdnt/ *adj.* **1 a discordant note** LITERARY something that shows disagreement, or that seems strange and wrong in relation to everything around it: *The modern decor* ***strikes a discordant note*** *in this 17th century building.* **2** a discordant sound is annoying because it is made up of musical notes that do not go together well: *Strange discordant music emanated from the woods.* **3** not in agreement: *The two experiments gave us discordant results.*

dis·co·theque /ˈdɪskəˌtɛk, ˌdɪskəˈtɛk/ *n.* [C] a DISCO (2)

dis·count¹ /ˈdɪskaʊnt/ *n.* [C] a reduction in the usual price of something: *Tickets are $9, with a $2 discount for kids.* | [+ **on**] *Disney gives shareholders a discount on visits to Disneyland.* | *Vendors were selling the posters* ***at a discount****.* | *Rochelle gets a 15%* ***employee discount*** *(=a discount for workers at a particular place).* | **discount fare/price** *discount airfares to Europe* | *Wal-Mart has quickly become one of the largest* ***discount stores*** *(=stores where you can buy goods cheaply) in the nation.*

dis·count² /ˈdɪskaʊnt, dɪsˈkaʊnt/ *v.* [T] to reduce the price of something: *Some games were discounted to sell for as little as $5.*

dis·count³ /dɪsˈkaʊnt/ *v.* [T] to regard something as unlikely to be true or important: *Scientists discounted his method of predicting earthquakes.* | *It would be foolish to* ***discount the possibility*** *of violence in such a tense situation.*

dis·coun·te·nance /dɪsˈkaʊntˈn-əns/ *v.* [T] FORMAL to show your disapproval of something or of someone's behavior: *The Russians were anxious to discountenance the war.*

dis·count·er /ˈdɪskaʊntɚ/ *n.* [C] a store or a person that sells goods cheaply

discount rate /ˈ.. ˌ./ *n.* **the discount rate** the interest rate that the Federal Reserve Bank charges other banks

dis·cour·age /dɪˈskɚɪdʒ, -ˈskʌr-/ *v.* [T] **1** to persuade someone not to do something, especially by making it seem difficult or bad: *The cameras should discourage*

shoplifters. | [**discourage sb from doing sth**] *Schools discourage youngsters from being involved in gangs.* **2** to make someone less confident or less willing to do something: *Trying to lose weight fast will only discourage you.* **3** to make something become less likely to happen: *Put the plant in a cold room to discourage growth.* —opposite ENCOURAGE

dis·cour·aged /dɪˈskɚɪdʒd/ *adj.* no longer having the confidence you need to continue doing something: *The game is simple enough that beginners won't* ***get discouraged****.*

dis·cour·age·ment /dɪˈskɚɪdʒmənt/ *n.* **1** [U] a feeling of being discouraged: *Our reaction to the court's decision is one of discouragement and disappointment.* **2** [U] the act of trying to discourage someone from doing something: *the country's discouragement of religion* **3** [C] something that discourages you: *Despite early discouragements, she eventually became a successful songwriter.*

dis·cour·ag·ing /dɪˈskɚɪdʒɪŋ/ *adj.* making you lose the confidence you need to continue doing something: *a discouraging report on the economy*

dis·course¹ /ˈdɪskɔrs/ *n.* **1** [U] serious discussions between people, especially about a particular subject: *Rational discourse on public policy is vital to a democracy.* | *Racist language is not acceptable in* ***public discourse*** *(=discussions of subjects by politicians, business leaders etc.).* **2** [C] a serious speech or piece of writing on a particular subject: [+ **on/upon**] *The book opens with a discourse on the environment.* **3** [U] the language used in particular kinds of speech or writing: *the restraints of diplomatic discourse*

dis·course² /dɪsˈkɔrs, ˈdɪskɔrs/ *v.*
   discourse on/upon sth *phr. v.* [T] to make a long formal speech about something, or to discuss something seriously: *Hitchins discoursed on his view of the political situation.*

dis·cour·te·ous /dɪsˈkɚtiəs/ *adj.* FORMAL not polite, and not showing respect for other people: *The sales staff were discourteous and slow.* —**discourteousness** *n.* [U] —**discourteously** *adv.*

dis·cour·te·sy /dɪsˈkɚtəsi/ *n.* [C,U] FORMAL an action or behavior that is not polite, or does not show respect

dis·cov·er /dɪˈskʌvɚ/ *v.* [T] **1** to find something that was hidden or that people did not know about before: *Police discovered 500 pounds of dynamite in the house.* | *The Vikings may have discovered America long before Columbus.* —compare INVENT **2** to find out something that is a fact, or the answer to a question: [**discover that**] *Simmons discovered that one employee was using the computer system to bet on horses.* | [**discover who/what/how etc.**] *Did you ever discover who sent you the flowers?* **3** to notice or try something for the first time and start to enjoy it: *The two girls were inseparable until Veronica discovered boys.* **4** to notice someone who is very good at something and help them to become successful and well-known: *She used to go to Hollywood parties, hoping to be discovered.* —see Usage Note at INVENT —**discoverer** *n.* [C]

dis·cov·er·y /dɪˈskʌvri, -vəri/ *n. plural* **discoveries** **1** [C] a fact, thing, or answer to a question that someone discovers: *Einstein* ***made an*** *important* ***discovery*** *about the nature of energy.* | [**discovery that**] *The discovery that the budget was short by $9 million caused immense problems.* **2** [U] the act of discovering something that was hidden or not known before: [+ **of**] *The discovery of oil in Alaska was a boon to the economy.*

dis·cred·it¹ /dɪsˈkrɛdɪt/ *v.* [T] **1** to make someone or something less respected or trusted: *Lawyers for the defense tried to discredit her testimony.* **2** to cause an idea not to be believed anymore: *Some of Freud's theories have now been discredited.*

dis·cred·it² *n.* the loss of other people's respect or trust: *Wilson's actions* ***brought discredit on*** *the entire Senate.*

dis·cred·it·a·ble /dɪsˈkrɛdɪtəbəl/ *adj.* bad or wrong, and making people lose respect for you or trust in you

dis·creet /dɪˈskrit/ *adj.* **1** careful about what you say or do so that you do not upset or embarrass people, especially by keeping a secret: *Chambers was discreet about the affair.* **2** done, said, or shown in a careful or polite way so that you do not upset or embarrass people: *He followed at a discreet distance.* | *Skirt lengths are a discreet inch above the knee.* **3** APPROVING not easily noticed, especially because small in size, and showing good judgment about style, politeness etc.: *discreet jewelry* | *A discreet nod indicated that he was ready to leave.* —**discreetly** *adv.* —opposite INDISCREET —compare DISCRETE, DISCRETION

dis·crep·an·cy /dɪˈskrɛpənsi/ *n. plural* **discrepancies** [C,U] a difference between two amounts, details etc. that should be the same: [+ **in**] *There were discrepancies in the expense accounts.* [+ **between**] *An employee noticed a discrepancy between the two signatures.*

dis·crete /dɪˈskrit/ *adj.* FORMAL clearly separate: *The developing insect passes through several discrete stages.* —compare DISCREET

dis·cre·tion /dɪˈskrɛʃən/ *n.* [U] **1** the ability to deal with situations in a way that does not offend or embarrass people, especially by keeping other people's secrets: *The hotel has built a reputation on its discretion for the past 25 years.* —see also **be the soul of discretion** (SOUL (7)) **2** the ability and right to decide what should be done in a particular situation: *Hiring is at the discretion of fire department administrators.* | *Decisions about attendance policies are left to the discretion of individual schools* (=each school can decide). **3 parental/viewer discretion is advised** SPOKEN said on television before programs that might offend some people because they contain violence, swearing, sex etc. **4 discretion is the better part of valor** used to say that it is better to be careful than to take unnecessary risks

dis·cre·tion·a·ry /dɪˈskrɛʃəˌnɛri/ *adj.* **1** not controlled by strict rules, but left for someone to make a decision about in each particular situation: *Judges have discretionary powers over sentencing of criminals.* **2 discretionary income/money** money that you can spend in any way you want, as opposed to money that must be used to pay bills, rent etc.

dis·crim·i·nate /dɪˈskrɪməˌneɪt/ *v.* **1** [I] to treat a person or a group differently from another in an unfair way: [+ **against**] *Hartman claims the new welfare laws discriminate against the poor.* | [+ **in**] *The court ruled that the company does not discriminate in its hiring practices.* | *The report called for lawmakers to discriminate in favor of* (=give better treatment to) *the inner cities when providing funds.* **2** [I,T] to recognize a difference between things: [+ **between**] *Young babies can discriminate between pleasant and unpleasant odors.* | [**discriminate sth from sth**] *The parties have become so similar it is difficult to discriminate Republicans from Democrats.*

dis·crim·i·nat·ing /dɪˈskrɪməˌneɪtɪŋ/ *adj.* able to judge what is of good quality and what is not: *Discriminating travelers return to Italy year after year.*

dis·crim·i·na·tion /dɪˌskrɪməˈneɪʃən/ *n.* [U] **1** the practice of treating a person or a group differently from another in an unfair way: *Many women still face sex discrimination in the military.* | *racial discrimination* | [+ **against**] *The 1990 Act prohibits discrimination against people with disabilities.* | *The university does not allow discrimination in favor of* (=better treatment of) *or against anyone on the basis of race.* —see also REVERSE DISCRIMINATION **2** the ability to judge what is of good quality and what is not

dis·crim·i·na·to·ry /dɪˈskrɪmənəˌtɔri/ *adj.* tending to treat a person or a group of people differently from other people in an unfair way: *a discriminatory hiring policy*

dis·cur·sive /dɪˈskɜsɪv/ *adj.* discussing many different ideas, facts etc., without always having a clear purpose: *Rich's novels are circling and discursive.* —**discursively** *adv.* —**discursiveness** *n.* [U]

dis·cus /ˈdɪskəs/ *n.* [C] **1** a heavy plate-shaped object which is thrown as far as possible for sport **2** the sport in which this is thrown

dis·cuss /dɪˈskʌs/ *v.* [T] **1** to talk about something with someone or a group in order to exchange ideas or decide something: *White House officials met to discuss the budget.* | [**discuss sth with sb**] *Doctors should discuss possible treatments with the patient.* | [**discuss what/who/where etc.**] *I discussed what had happened with Pat.* **2** to talk or write about something in detail and consider different ideas or opinions about it: *The book discusses Columbus's voyages, including his landings in America.*

dis·cus·sant /dɪˈskʌsənt/ *n.* [C] FORMAL someone who is part of a formal discussion

dis·cus·sion /dɪˈskʌʃən/ *n.* [C,U] **1** the act of discussing something, or a conversation in which people discuss something: [**have a discussion (about sth)**] *We had a heated discussion about politics.* | *Changes in the airline's mileage program are now under discussion* (=being discussed). | *Salaries will be up for discussion* (=able to be discussed and possibly changed) *in November.* **2** a piece of writing about a subject that considers different ideas or opinions about it: *The report includes a discussion of global warming.*

dis·dain[1] /dɪsˈdeɪn/ *n.* [U] FORMAL a complete lack of respect that you show for someone or something because you think they are not important or good enough. [+ **for**] *They expressed disdain for Western pop culture.* | *Mr. Rodriguez spoke of his tenants with disdain,* blaming them for the poor condition of the apartment.

disdain[2] *v.* **1** [T] to not like or to have no respect for someone or something, because you think they are not important or good enough: *He disdains New York and the art that is produced there.* **2 disdain to do sth** to refuse to do something because you are too proud to do it: *Tom Butler disdained to reply to such a trivial question.*

dis·dain·ful /dɪsˈdeɪnfəl/ *adj.* showing that you do not respect someone or something because you think they are not important or good enough: *a long disdainful look* | [+ **of**] *Porter is disdainful of professors he believes are incompetent or lazy.* —**disdainfully** *adv.*

dis·ease /dɪˈziz/ *n.* **1** [C,U] an illness or unhealthy condition of the body or mind, which can be named: **heart/lung/liver etc. disease** *Heart disease is a leading cause of death in the U.S.* | *Tina suffers from a rare brain disease.* | *Scientists are working to block the viruses that cause disease.* | *She contracted the fatal disease* (=she became infected with the disease) *through a blood transfusion.* | *Unclean drinking water can spread disease* (=cause other people to become infected). | **infectious/contagious/communicable disease** (=disease that is passed from one person to another) **2** [C] a bad or harmful condition or behavior of a group, such as society: *Nationalism can be a serious disease.* —**diseased** *adj.* —compare ILLNESS —see also HEART DISEASE, SOCIAL DISEASE, VENEREAL DISEASE

USAGE NOTE: DISEASE

WORD CHOICE: illness, disease, sickness
Illness can be used about the general state of being sick: *Janey missed a lot of school because of illness.*
Diseases have medical names and must usually be cured before you are well again: *a sexually transmitted disease* | *Alzheimer's disease.* However, you would usually talk about *mental illness* or a *terminal/critical illness.* A **Sickness** is often a less serious type of illness and may go away by itself: *motion sickness*

---

dis·em·bark /ˌdɪsɪmˈbɑrk/ *v.* [I,T] FORMAL to get off or to be taken off a vehicle, such as a ship or airplane: [+ **from**] *Seventeen women and five children disembarked from the plane at Orly airport.* —**disembarkation** /ˌdɪsɪmbɑrˈkeɪʃən/ *n.* [U]

dis·em·bod·ied /ˌdɪsɪmˈbɑdid/ *adj.* **1** a disembodied sound or voice comes from someone who cannot

be seen **2** without a body or separated from a body:
*Some believe the dead return to earth as disembodied
spirits.*

dis·em·bow·el /ˌdɪsɪmˈbaʊəl/ v. [T] to remove someone's BOWELs —**disembowelment** n. [U]

dis·en·chant·ed /ˌdɪsɪnˈtʃæntɪd/ adj. disappointed
with someone or something, and not believing in
their value anymore: [+ **with**] *Voters seem disenchanted with government in general.* —**disenchant-
ment** n. [U]

dis·en·fran·chised /ˌdɪsɪnˈfræntʃaɪzd/ adj. not
having any rights, especially the right to vote, and
not feeling part of society: *South Africa finally
extended rights to the disenfranchised black majority.*
—**disenfranchise** v. [T] —**disenfranchisement** n.
[U]

dis·en·gage /ˌdɪsɪnˈgeɪdʒ/ v. **1** [I,T] if you disengage
a machine or DEVICE, or if it disengages, it stops operating because two parts are separated from each
other: *Disengage the gears before you start the car.* |
The cruise control does not disengage when it should.
2 [I,T] to separate yourself from another person or
group, so that you are not involved with them:
[+ **from**] *The council pressured Pike to disengage
from the project.* | *Yoko disengaged herself from
John's side.* **3** [I,T] if an army disengages, or if
someone disengages it, it stops fighting and removes
its soldiers from the area: *After the Gulf War, the
U.S. disengaged quickly from the Middle East.* |
*Troops moved in Thursday to disengage the two war-
ring factions.* **4** [T] to separate something from
something else that was holding it or connected to it:
He removed the screws and disengaged the back panel.
—**disengagement** n. [U]

dis·en·gaged /ˌdɪsɪnˈgeɪdʒd/ adj. not involved with
something or someone, and feeling separate from
them: [+ **from**] *The singer seemed completely disengaged from the audience.*

dis·en·tan·gle /ˌdɪsɪnˈtæŋgəl/ v. [T] **1** to separate
different things, especially ideas or pieces of information, that have become confused together: *Investigators had to disentangle Maxwell's complicated
financial affairs.* **2 disentangle yourself (from sb/
sth)** to remove yourself from a complicated situation
that you are involved in: *The President was eager to
disentangle himself from the scandal.* **3** to remove
knots from ropes, strings etc. that have become
twisted or tied together —**disentanglement** n. [U]

dis·e·qui·lib·ri·um /ˌdɪsikwəˈlɪbriəm/ n. [U] FORMAL a
lack of balance in something: *Interest rates reflect the
disequilibrium between supply and demand.*

dis·es·tab·lish /ˌdɪsəˈstæblɪʃ/ v. [T] FORMAL to officially decide that a particular system, organization,
or church is not the official system, organization, or
church etc. of your state or country anymore

dis·fa·vor /dɪsˈfeɪvɚ/ n. [U] FORMAL a feeling of dislike
and disapproval: *Statues of Lenin are difficult to find
since Communism fell into disfavor* (=became
unpopular).

dis·fig·ure /dɪsˈfɪgyɚ/ v. [T] to ruin the appearance of
someone or something —**disfiguring** adj.: *a disfiguring disease* —**disfigurement** n. [C,U]

dis·fig·ured /dɪsˈfɪgyɚd/ adj. ruined in appearance: *a
boy severely disfigured by burns*

dis·fran·chise /dɪsˈfræntʃaɪz/ v. [T] another form of
DISENFRANCHISE —**disfranchisement** n. [U]

dis·gorge /dɪsˈgɔrdʒ/ v. **1** [T] LITERARY if a vehicle or
building disgorges people, they come out of it in a
large group: *Black limousines disgorged movie stars.*
2 [T] if something disgorges what was inside it, it
lets it pour out: *Chimneys in the valley were disgorg-
ing smoke into the air.* **3** [T] to give back something
that you have taken illegally: *The trustee was forced
to disgorge the funds.* **4** [T] to bring food back up
from your stomach through your mouth **5** [I,T] if a
river disgorges, it flows into the ocean —**disgorge-
ment** n. [U]

dis·grace¹ /dɪsˈgreɪs, dɪˈskreɪs/ n. **1 sth is a disgrace**

used to say that something is extremely wrong or
bad, or is in very bad condition, and should not be
allowed to continue the way it is: [**it is a disgrace
that**] *It is a disgrace that we've been cutting these
ancient trees.* | *The schools in Fremont are an
absolute disgrace.* **2** [U] the complete loss of other
people's respect because you have done something
they strongly disapprove of: *It was the first time an
American president resigned in disgrace.* **3 be a
disgrace (to sb/sth)** to have a very bad effect on the
opinion that people have of your family or the group
that you belong to: *Players who only think of their
paychecks are a disgrace to the game of baseball.*
4 sth is no disgrace used to say that you should not
feel ashamed about a particular situation or action:
It's no disgrace to be out of work.

disgrace² v. [T] to do something so bad that people
lose respect for your family or for the group you
belong to: *Many say Lonetree has disgraced his people
and his country.* | *a disgraced Senator* | [**disgrace
yourself**] *I was hoping I wouldn't disgrace myself by
spilling a drink down my front.*

dis·grace·ful /dɪsˈgreɪsfəl/ adj. a situation or behavior that is disgraceful is morally wrong or
extremely embarrassing to other people: *The most
disgraceful thing is that the airline has refused to pay
money to the families of the crash victims.* —**dis-
gracefully** adv.

dis·grun·tled /dɪsˈgrʌntld/ adj. annoyed and not satisfied because things have not happened in the way
that you wanted: *Disgruntled employees are leaving
to work for other firms.*

dis·guise¹ /dɪsˈgaɪz, dɪˈskaɪz/ v. [T] **1** to change your
appearance so that people cannot recognize you: *The
robber was wearing a paper bag over his head to dis-
guise his face.* | [**disguise yourself as sb/sth**] *To get
into the building, I disguised myself as a reporter.*
2 to change the usual appearance, sound, taste etc.
of something so that people do not recognize it: *The
park's waterfalls disguise the traffic noise from the
freeway.* | [**disguise sth as sth**] *Well, it may be hard
to disguise junk as health food.* **3** to hide a fact or
feeling so that people will not notice it: *Larry could-
n't disguise his satisfaction at seeing his competitor go
out of business.* | *His thinly disguised* (=not well
hidden at all) *hatred of rock-n-roll had made him an
unpopular journalist.* | *Daranna Gidel's exotic name
disguises the fact that she was born in California
and lives in New York.*

disguise² n. **1** [C,U] something that you wear to
change your appearance and hide who you are, or
the act of wearing this: *The army does not officially
admit that it uses disguises.* | *Friends gave us long
robes and veils for disguise.* **2 in disguise a)** made
to seem like something else: *"Tax reform" is just a
tax increase in disguise.* | *I've always told my kids to
treat every obstacle as an opportunity in disguise.*
b) wearing a disguise: *Perhaps the officer thought the
cameraman was a student protester in disguise.* —see
also **a blessing in disguise** (BLESSING (5))

dis·gust¹ /dɪsˈgʌst, dɪˈskʌst/ n. [U] **1** the feeling you
have when you are annoyed or upset because a situation or someone's behavior is completely unacceptable: [+ **with**] *The voters have expressed their disgust
with the way Congress handles public money.* | [+ **at**]
*Meg tried to hide her disgust at what she had just
heard.* | *Barber walked out of the meeting in dis-
gust.* | *To my disgust, I found that there were no
nonsmoking tables available.* **2** a very strong feeling
of dislike that almost makes you sick because something is so bad: *Lula's face was twisted with disgust
as she remembered the rape.*

disgust² v. [T] **1** to make someone feel very annoyed
or upset about something that they think is completely unacceptable: *Many parents said they were
disgusted by the amount of violence contained in "children's shows."* **2** to be so bad to see, feel, think
about etc. that it makes someone feel almost sick:
The thought of dissecting a frog disgusts me.

dis·gust·ed /dɪsˈgʌstɪd/ adj. annoyed or upset
because of something that you think is completely
unacceptable: *More than 200 disgusted parents
jammed the auditorium to discuss the new policies.* |

a disgusted look | [+ **with**] *I had over $3000 worth of dental work done and I'm disgusted with it.*

dis·gust·ing /dɪsˈgʌstɪŋ/ *adj.* **1** extremely unpleasant, and making you feel sick: *I think chewing tobacco is a disgusting habit.* | *It was kind of disgusting – she had something hanging out of her nose.* **2** shocking, or completely unacceptable: *It's disgusting, men looking at pictures of 12-year-old naked girls.* | *Fifteen dollars for a salad? That's disgusting.* —**disgustingly** *adv.*: *They're disgustingly rich.* —compare NAUSEATING

dish[1] /dɪʃ/ *n.* [C] **1** a round container with low sides, used for holding food: *a serving dish* | *a casserole dish* —compare BOWL[1] (1), PLATE[1] (1) **2 the dishes** all the plates, cups, bowls etc. that have been used during a meal: *Could you put away the dishes for me?* | **do/wash the dishes** *No, we never wash the dishes until morning.* **3** food cooked or prepared in a particular way as a meal: *a classic Creole dish* | *This salad is substantial enough to be served as a* **main dish.** —see also SIDE DISH **4** OLD-FASHIONED a sexually attractive person, especially a woman —see also SATELLITE DISH

dish[2] *v.* [I] INFORMAL also **dish the dirt** to spend time talking about other people's private lives and saying unkind or shocking things about them: *He goes on to dish the dirt about which Hollywood actors wear toupees.*

dish sth ↔ **out** *phr. v.* [T] **1** INFORMAL to give something to a number of people in a careless way: *My uncle's always dishing out unwanted advice.* **2** to serve food to people: *Volunteers dished out ham, potatoes, and apple pie to the homeless in the area.* **3** to pass the ball or PUCK to another player in basketball or HOCKEY so that they can SCORE points easily: *Fields scored 17 points, made nine steals, and dished out six assists.* **4 sb can dish it out, but they can't take it** used to say that someone often treats other people in a particular way, for example by criticizing them, but does not like to be treated that way by others

dish sth ↔ **up** *phr. v.* [T] to put food for a meal onto dishes, or to serve food to people: *Hand me your plate and I'll dish up some rice for you.*

dis·ha·bille /ˌdɪsəˈbil/ *n.* [U] another form of the word DÉSHABILLÉ

dis·har·mo·ny /dɪsˈharməni/ *n.* [U] FORMAL disagreement about important things, which makes people be unfriendly to each other: *Racial disharmony is what makes the news; when people get along, we don't hear about it.* —**disharmonious** /ˌdɪsharˈmouniəs/ *adj.*

dish·cloth /ˈdɪʃklɔθ/ *n.* [C] a cloth used for washing dishes

dish drain /ˈ. ./ *n.* [C] a DRAINER (1)

dis·heart·ened /dɪsˈhartnd/ *adj.* FORMAL disappointed, so that you lose hope and do not feel determined to continue doing something anymore: *Each day, Lou came back from the mailbox disheartened.* —**dishearten** *v.* [T]

dis·heart·en·ing /dɪsˈhartn-ɪŋ/ *adj.* making you lose hope and determination: *For many college graduates, job hunting can be a disheartening struggle.* | [**disheartening to hear/see/know etc.**] *It's disheartening to see what little progress has been made.*

di·shev·eled /dɪˈʃɛvəld/ *adj.* if someone or what they are wearing is disheveled, they look very messy: *Clarke appeared tired and disheveled.*

dis·hon·est /dɪsˈanɪst/ *adj.* not honest: *I don't think he was being dishonest – he just didn't know the truth.* | *a dishonest lawyer* —**dishonestly** *adv.*

dis·hon·est·y /dɪsˈanɪsti/ *n.* [U] behavior in which someone lies or tries to hide the truth from others: *Dishonesty and corruption will not be tolerated in this agency.*

dis·hon·or[1] /dɪsˈanɚ/ *n.* [U] FORMAL loss of respect from other people because you have behaved in an unacceptable way or have done something immoral: *He thought about shooting himself, but he knew that suicide would* **bring dishonor on** *his family.*

dishonor[2] *v.* [T] **1** FORMAL to make your family,

country, profession etc. lose the respect of other people: *Failure to build a memorial would dishonor the American soldiers who lost their lives in the war.* **2** TECHNICAL if a bank dishonors a check, it refuses to pay out money for it

dis·hon·or·a·ble /dɪsˈanərəbəl/ *adj.* not morally correct or acceptable: *There's nothing dishonorable in making people pay for your advice.*

dishonorable dis·charge /ˌ.,.... ˈ../ *n.* [C,U] an order to someone to leave the military because they have behaved in a morally unacceptable way: *Sergeant Baum was sentenced to a year in prison and given a dishonorable discharge.*

dish·pan /ˈdɪʃpæn/ *n.* [C] **1** a large bowl that you wash dishes in **2 dishpan hands** INFORMAL hands that look dry and old because you wash dishes a lot

dish rack /ˈ. ./ *n.* [C] an object that holds dishes while they dry, that is usually kept next to the kitchen SINK

dish-rag /ˈdɪʃræg/ *n.* [C] an old cloth that is used for washing dishes

dish tow·el /ˈ. ˌ../ *n.* [C] a cloth used for drying dishes —see picture at KITCHEN

dish·ware /ˈdɪʃwɛr/ *n.* [U] a set of dishes, cups, bowls etc.

dish·wash·er /ˈdɪʃˌwaʃɚ/ *n.* [C] **1** a machine that washes dishes —see picture at KITCHEN **2** someone whose job is to wash dirty dishes in a restaurant

dishwashing de·ter·gent /ˈ... ˌ../ *n.* [U] soap used to wash dishes, especially in a dishwasher

dishwashing liq·uid /ˈ... ˌ../ *n.* [U] liquid soap used to wash dishes —see picture at KITCHEN

dish·wa·ter /ˈdɪʃˌwɔtɚ/ *n.* [U] dirty water that dishes have been washed in —see also **(as) dull as dishwater** (DULL[1] 8))

dishwater blond /ˌ... ˈ./ *adj.* OLD-FASHIONED dishwater blond hair is a dull pale brown color —see also DIRTY BLOND

dish·y /ˈdɪʃi/ *adj.* OLD-FASHIONED sexually attractive

dis·il·lu·sion /ˌdɪsəˈluʒən/ *v.* [T] to make someone realize that something which they thought was true or good is not really true or good: *I hate to disillusion you, but you'll probably never get your money back from them.* —**disillusionment** *n.* [U]

dis·il·lu·sioned /ˌdɪsəˈluʒənd/ *adj.* disappointed because you have lost your belief that someone or something is good or right: [+ **by/with**] *After working on several campaigns, Laura grew increasingly disillusioned with politics.*

dis·in·cen·tive /ˌdɪsɪnˈsɛntɪv/ *n.* [C] something that makes people not want to continue doing something anymore: [+ **to**] *Higher taxes may act as a disincentive to savings and investment.*

dis·in·clined /ˌdɪsɪnˈklaɪnd/ *adj.* **be/feel disinclined to do sth** FORMAL to be unwilling to do something: *The President said that he was disinclined to send in American troops.* —**disinclination** /ˌdɪsɪŋkləˈneɪʃən/ *n.* [C,U]

dis·in·fect /ˌdɪsɪnˈfɛkt/ *v.* [T] to clean something with a chemical that destroys BACTERIA: *First, use some iodine to disinfect the wound.*

dis·in·fect·ant /ˌdɪsɪnˈfɛktənt/ *n.* [C,U] a chemical or a cleaning product that destroys BACTERIA

dis·in·for·ma·tion /ˌdɪsɪnfɚˈmeɪʃən/ *n.* [U] false information which is given deliberately in order to hide the truth or confuse people, especially in political situations: *Wallace says his job was to spread government disinformation to extremist groups.* —compare MISINFORMATION

dis·in·gen·u·ous /ˌdɪsɪnˈdʒɛnyuəs/ *adj.* FORMAL not sincere and slightly dishonest, perhaps trying to trick people: *It's disingenuous of politicians to blame journalists for leaks that appear in the press.* —**disingenuously** *adv.*

dis·in·her·it /ˌdɪsɪnˈhɛrɪt/ *v.* [T] to prevent someone, especially your children, from receiving any of your money or property after your death —**disinheritance** *n.* [U]

dis·in·te·grate /dɪsˈɪntəˌgreɪt/ v. **1** [I,T] to break into very small pieces and be destroyed, or to make something do this: *A large section of the roadway apparently disintegrated after the first few cars passed over it.* **2** [I] to become weaker or not whole anymore, and then be destroyed: *It seemed to him that his home life was disintegrating all at once.* | *As the news spread of the general's death, the army disintegrated.* —**disintegration** /dɪsˌɪntəˈgreɪʃən/ n.

dis·in·ter /ˌdɪsɪnˈtɚ/ v. **disinterred, disinterring** [T] FORMAL to remove a dead body from a grave —opposite INTER —**disinterment** n. [U]

dis·in·terest /dɪsˈɪntrɪst/ n. [U] a lack of interest: [+ **in**] *He's already showing a widespread disinterest in politics.*

dis·in·terest·ed /dɪsˈɪntrɪstɪd, -ˈɪntəˌrɛstɪd/ adj. **1** not personally involved in a situation, and therefore able to judge the situation fairly; OBJECTIVE[2] (1): *The transaction is subject to approval by a panel of disinterested directors.* **2** NONSTANDARD sometimes used to mean "UNINTERESTED," although many people think this is incorrect: [+ **in**] *Police appeared disinterested in halting the fighting.*

dis·in·vest·ment /ˌdɪsɪnˈvɛstmənt/ n. [U] TECHNICAL another form of the word DIVESTMENT

dis·joint·ed /dɪsˈdʒɔɪntɪd/ adj. disjointed speaking or writing is not easy to understand, because the words or ideas are not connected in an understandable way: *Rambling, disjointed notes found in Brady's apartment gave no clues as to his disappearance.* —**disjointedly** adv. —**disjointedness** n. [U]

disk /dɪsk/ n. [C] **1** a small flat round piece of plastic or metal used for storing electronic or computer information **2** a FLOPPY DISK —see also HARD DISK —see picture on page 426 **3** something that is flat and round, or that looks this way: *When over half the moon's disk is visible, we have a "gibbous" moon.* **4** a flat piece of CARTILAGE between the bones in your back —see also **slip a disk** (SLIP[1] (11)), SLIPPED DISK

disk brakes /'. ./ n. [plural] another spelling of DISC BRAKES

disk drive /'. ./ n. [C] a piece of equipment in a computer that is used to get information from a disk or to store information on it

disk·ette /dɪˈskɛt/ n. [C] a FLOPPY DISK

dis·like[1] /dɪsˈlaɪk/ v. [T, not in progressive] to not like someone or something: *Why do you dislike her so much?* | [**dislike doing sth**] *Many men dislike shopping.*

dislike[2] n. **1** [C,U] a feeling of not liking someone or something: [+ **of**] *She shared her mother's dislike of housework.* | [+ **for**] *Everyone knew of their dislike for each other.* | *I wondered why I had **taken an instant dislike to** the man* (=immediately did not like him). **2** [C usually plural] something that you do not like: *Describe your **likes and dislikes**, and the type of person you'd like to meet.*

dis·lo·cate /dɪsˈloʊkeɪt, ˈdɪsloʊˌkeɪt/ v. [T] **1** to injure a joint so that the bone at the joint is moved out of its normal position: *Hawkins dislocated a shoulder in the third game of the season.* **2** to cause so many changes to a system or to someone's life that things cannot work normally: *Thousands of workers have been dislocated by recent military base closures.* —**dislocation** /ˌdɪsloʊˈkeɪʃən/ n. [C,U]

dis·lodge /dɪsˈlɑdʒ/ v. [T] **1** to force or knock something out of a place where it was held or stuck: *Heavy rains had dislodged a boulder at the mouth of Thompson Canyon.* | *It was 30 minutes before rescuers could dislodge the food from his throat.* **2** to make someone leave a place or lose a position of power: *Army commanders were preparing to dislodge the militia from the capital.* —compare LODGE[2] (1) —**dislodgement** n. [U]

dis·loy·al /dɪsˈlɔɪəl/ adj. doing or saying things that do not support your friends, your country, or the group you belong to: [+ **to**] *My opinion is that she was disloyal to her family and a traitor to her race.* —**disloyalty** n. [C,U]

dis·mal /ˈdɪzməl/ adj. if a situation or place is dismal, it is so bad that it makes you feel very unhappy and hopeless: *The couple lived in a dismal apartment in the poorest section of town.* | *a dismal, gray afternoon* | *dismal economic news* | *Mitchell called the policy a **dismal failure**.* —**dismally** adv.

dis·man·tle /dɪsˈmæntl/ v. [T] **1** to take a machine or piece of equipment apart so that it is in separate pieces: *Chris had dismantled the entire bike in five minutes.* **2** to get rid of a system or organization, especially in a gradual way: *No one is suggesting that we dismantle the Social Security system.* **3** to defeat an opponent in a game by a large number of points: *The Detroit Tigers dismantled the Chicago White Sox 16-0.*

dis·may[1] /dɪsˈmeɪ/ n. [U] the worry, disappointment, or unhappiness you feel when something bad happens: *Many women discover **with dismay** that their salaries will not pay for child care.* | *Neighbors stared **in dismay** at the damage the tornado had caused.* | *To the dismay of his parents, he's moving back in with them.* | *Members of Congress **expressed dismay** at the cost of the new bombers.*

dismay[2] v. [T] to make someone feel worried, disappointed, and upset: *The President's policies have dismayed some conservative groups.*

dis·mayed /dɪsˈmeɪd/ adj. worried, disappointed, and upset: [+ **at**] *Students were dismayed at the number of classes which were already full.* | [**dismayed that**] *I am dismayed that the park service is allowing commercial development of the land.* | [**dismayed to see/ hear/read etc.**] *Health experts were dismayed to discover an increase in the number of young smokers.*

dis·mem·ber /dɪsˈmɛmbɚ/ v. [T] FORMAL **1** to cut or tear a body into pieces: *His dismembered body was dumped near Hoover Dam.* **2** to divide a country, area, or organization into smaller parts: *Mr. Corry might have to dismember the company more than he wants to.* —**dismemberment** n. [U]

dis·miss /dɪsˈmɪs/ v. [T] **1** to refuse to consider someone or something seriously because you think they are silly or not important: *Richards dismissed criticism that the Red Cross has not educated the public about AIDS.* | [**dismiss sth as sth**] *Some doctors still dismiss the disease as being just another type of flu.* **2** if a court CASE is dismissed, a judge decides that it should not continue, often because there is not enough information available to make a decision about the case: *The murder charge against Beckwith has been dismissed.* **3** to remove someone from their job or position: [+ **from**] *He became defense secretary in 1950, but was dismissed from the post in 1956.* | [+ **for**] *Employees may still be dismissed for using illegal drugs at work.* **4** if someone in authority dismisses a person or a group, they send them away or allow them to leave: *You all know your homework assignment? All right, **class dismissed**.*

dis·miss·al /dɪsˈmɪsəl/ n. **1** [C,U] the act of removing someone from their job or position: *Rader's dismissal had been rumored for weeks.* **2** [C,U] the act of stopping a court CASE from continuing: *the dismissal of a lawsuit* **3** [U] the act of refusing to consider someone or something seriously **4** [C,U] the act of allowing someone to leave, or of sending them away

dis·mis·sive /dɪsˈmɪsɪv/ adj. refusing to consider someone or something seriously: *Collins has been criticized for her dismissive attitude toward the investigations.* —**dismissively** adv.

dis·mount[1] /dɪsˈmaʊnt/ v. **1** [I] to get off a horse, bicycle, or MOTORCYCLE: *Seidman's horse reared up when he tried to dismount.* **2** [T] to take something, especially a gun, out of its base or support

dis·mount[2] /ˈdɪsmaʊnt/ n. [C] the final movements that a GYMNAST performs in a particular event, especially to get off a piece of equipment

Dis·ney /ˈdɪzni/, **Walt** /wɔlt/ (1901–1966) a U.S. PRODUCER who is famous for making CARTOON movies for children, and for inventing cartoon characters including Mickey Mouse and Donald Duck

dis·o·be·di·ent /ˌdɪsəˈbidiənt/ *adj.* deliberately not doing what you are told to do by your parents, teacher, employer etc.: *a disobedient child* —**disobedience** *n.* [U] —see also CIVIL DISOBEDIENCE

dis·o·bey /ˌdɪsəˈbeɪ/ *v.* **disobeys, disobeyed, disobeying** [I,T] to refuse to do what someone in authority tells you to do, or refuse to obey a rule or law: *Pilots who disobey orders to land can face up to five years in prison.* —see picture at OBEY

dis·or·der /dɪsˈɔrdɚ/ *n.* **1** [C] a mental or physical problem that can affect your health for a long time: *a serious heart disorder* | *After two years of therapy, Duane was able to conquer his eating disorder.* **2** [U] a situation in which many people disobey the law, especially in a violent way, and are difficult to control: *Most urban areas were generally free of civil disorder.* **3** [U] a situation in which things are not organized at all: *The smallest problem can throw all their services into disorder.*

dis·or·dered /dɪsˈɔrdɚd/ *adj.* **1** not arranged, planned, or done neatly or in a clear order: *Conflicts between departments result in disordered priorities.* **2** if someone is mentally disordered, their mind is not working in a normal and healthy way

dis·or·der·ly /dɪsˈɔrdɚli/ *adj.* **1** behaving in a noisy way and causing trouble in a public place: *Cole was arrested for disorderly conduct.* **2** messy or lacking order: *We formed a sort of disorderly semicircle with our chairs.* —**disorderliness** *n.* [U]

dis·or·ga·nized /dɪsˈɔrgənaɪzd/ *adj.* not arranging or planning things in a clear order, or not planned at all: *I'm sorry I'm so disorganized – I just haven't had time to get everything ready.* | *The meeting was completely disorganized.* —compare UNORGANIZED

dis·o·ri·ent /dɪsˈɔriˌɛnt/ *v.* [T] **1** to make someone uncertain about what is happening around them and unable to think clearly: *Grandpa's doctor told me the medicine might disorient him.* **2** to make someone not know which direction they have come from or are going in: *The maze of hallways can disorient visitors who are unfamiliar with the building* —**disorienting** *adj.* —**disorientation** /dɪsˌɔriənˈteɪʃən/ *n.* [U]

dis·o·ri·ent·ed /dɪsˈɔriˌɛntɪd/ *adj.* **1** confused and not understanding what is happening around you: *At first, the fire had left them shocked and disoriented.* **2** confused about which direction you are facing or which direction you should go: *The pilot became disoriented in bad weather over the ocean.*

dis·own /dɪsˈoʊn/ *v.* [T not in progressive] to say that you do not want to have any connection with someone or something anymore, especially a member or members of your family: *Jen's parents threatened to disown her if she married Omar.*

dis·par·age /dɪˈspærɪdʒ/ *v.* [T] FORMAL to criticize someone or something in a way that shows you do not think they are very good or important: *"The comments were not meant to disparage any company's products,"* stated the publisher. —**disparagement** *n.* [C,U]

dis·par·ag·ing /dɪˈspærədʒɪŋ/ *adj.* criticizing someone or something, and showing that you do not think they are very good or important: *Tyler also made disparaging remarks about her ex-husband on a national talk show.* —**disparagingly** *adv.*

dis·par·ate /ˈdɪspərɪt/ *adj.* FORMAL very different and not related to each other: *Many disparate forms of information can be linked together in the database.* —**disparately** *adv.*

dis·par·i·ty /dɪˈspærəti/ *n.* plural **disparities** [C,U] FORMAL a difference between things, especially an unfair difference: [+ in/between] *We are still seeing a disparity between men's and women's salaries.* —see also PARITY

dis·pas·sion·ate /dɪsˈpæʃənɪt/ *adj.* not easily influenced by personal feelings: *Weber's report provides a dispassionate analysis of the conflict.* —**dispassionately** *adv.*

dis·patch[1] /dɪˈspætʃ/ *v.* [T] **1** to officially send someone or something somewhere for a particular purpose: *The agency dispatched an 11-member team to*

Texas to investigate the crash. | *Mike Pappas dispatches taxis from his office on 39th Street.* **2** to completely defeat an opponent: *Sampras quickly dispatched his opponent in straight sets.* **3** LITERARY to deliberately kill a person or animal **4** OLD-FASHIONED to finish all of something

dis·patch[2] *n.* **1** [C] a message sent between military or government officials: *Our unit received a dispatch from headquarters ordering us to tighten security.* **2** [C] a report sent to a newspaper from one of its writers who is in another town or country: *In one dispatch from Washington, negotiators were said to be close to an agreement.* **3** the act of sending people or things to a particular place: [+ of] *The dispatch of U.S. military forces did not seem likely at that time.* **4** with dispatch FORMAL if you do something with dispatch, you do it well and quickly: *Most cases are investigated with dispatch.*

dis·patch·er /dɪˈspætʃɚ/ *n.* [C] someone whose job is to send out vehicles such as police cars, taxis, or AMBULANCEs to places where they are needed

dis·pel /dɪˈspɛl/ *v.* **dispelled, dispelling** [T] FORMAL to stop someone from believing or feeling something, especially because it is harmful or not correct: *We hope to dispel the belief that scientists work in isolation in windowless rooms.*

dis·pen·sa·ble /dɪˈspɛnsəbəl/ *adj.* not really needed, and therefore easy to get rid of: *Part-time workers are considered dispensable in times of recession.* —opposite INDISPENSABLE

dis·pen·sa·ry /dɪˈspɛnsəri/ *n.* plural **dispensaries** [C] a place where medicines are prepared and given out, especially in a hospital —compare PHARMACY

dis·pen·sa·tion /ˌdɪspənˈseɪʃən, -pɛn-/ *n.* **1** [C,U] special permission from someone in authority or from a religious leader to do something that is not usually allowed: *You may be able to get special dispensation from a rabbi to eat non-kosher food.* **2** [U] FORMAL the act of providing people with something as part of an official process: *The dispensation of the land around Fort Ord should be a regional decision.* **3** [C] FORMAL a religious or political system that has control over people's lives at a particular time in history

dis·pense /dɪˈspɛns/ *v.* [T] **1** FORMAL to give or provide something to people, especially in a particular amounts as part of an official activity: *More than 100 writers came to hear Wentworth dispense advice.* | [**dispense sth to sb**] *Volunteers helped dispense food and blankets to people involved in the accident.* **2** to officially provide medicine to people: *The Reed County Clinic dispenses medication and makes referrals.* **3** if a machine dispenses a product or substance, it gives you a particular amount of the product when you press a button or put money in the machine

dispense with sb/sth *phr. v.* [T] FORMAL to not use or do something that you usually use or do, because it is not necessary anymore: *Some national leaders hope that one day Europe will dispense with borders.*

dis·pens·er /dɪˈspɛnsɚ/ *n.* [C] a machine that provides a particular amount of a product or substance when you press a button or put money into it: *a soap dispenser* | *a candy dispenser*

dis·per·sal /dɪˈspɚsəl/ *n.* [U] the act of spreading something over a wide area or to a large number of people: *Our goal is a wider geographic dispersal of economic aid.*

dis·perse /dɪˈspɚs/ *v.* [I,T] **1** if a group of people disperses or is dispersed, they separate and go away in different directions: *One resident said the student protesters dispersed peacefully.* **2** if something disperses or is dispersed, it spreads thinly and evenly over a wide area: *The oil had been dispersed by chemicals sprayed on the water.* —**dispersion** /dɪˈspɚʒən/ *n.* [U] FORMAL

dis·pir·it·ed /dɪˈspɪrɪtɪd/ *adj.* FORMAL without hope or confidence: *Pernkopf returned to Vienna a broken and dispirited man.*

dis·place /dɪsˈpleɪs/ v. [T] **1** if a bad event or situation displaces people or animals, they cannot stay where they normally live anymore: *An estimated 500,000 refugees have been displaced by the civil war.* | *Flooding caused by the dam may displace up to a million people.* **2** to force someone or something out of a place or position, and take that place or position instead: *Compact discs displaced records in the late 1980s.* | *The displaced workers* (=people whose jobs do not exist anymore) *have access to a job assistance center.*

displaced per·son /ˌ.. ˈ../ n. *plural* **displaced persons** [C] FORMAL someone who has been forced to leave their country because of war or cruel treatment; REFUGEE

dis·place·ment /dɪsˈpleɪsmənt/ n. **1** [U] the act of forcing a group of people or animals to leave the place where they usually live **2** [singular,U] TECHNICAL the weight or VOLUME (4) of liquid that something such as a ship takes the place of when it floats on that liquid, used especially as a way of describing how large or heavy that object is

dis·play¹ /dɪˈspleɪ/ n. *plural* **displays**

1 arrangement [C] an arrangement of things for people to look at: *The store's window display is the idea of designer David Wolfgang.* | *[+ of] In the lobby there's a display of photos of the theater from its early days.*

display

2 performance [C] a public performance of something that is intended to entertain people: *a fireworks display* | *[+ of] a display of traditional dance*

3 on display a) something that is on display is in a place where people can look at it: **[put sth on display]** *Owen said the fossil would be put on display in about a month.* | **be/go on display** *Benner's works will be on display through Feb. 15 at the Berman Gallery.* **b)** a quality, feeling etc. that is on display is shown very clearly and is easy to notice: *There's a tremendous amount of creativity on display in this school.*

4 a display of anger/affection/loyalty etc. an occasion when someone clearly shows a particular feeling, attitude, or quality: *I was shocked by their display of unbelievably bad manners.*

5 on equipment [C] a part of a piece of equipment that shows changing information, for example the screen of a computer

display² v. **displays, displayed, displaying** [T] **1** to show an object or a specially arranged group of objects to people, or to put them where people can easily see them: *The Van Gogh Museum will display 135 of his paintings.* | *One of the robbers displayed what the victims thought was a handgun.* **2** to clearly show a feeling, attitude, or quality by what you do or say: *Laura's friend displayed little emotion in court.* | *Early in life, Frederick displayed an interest in poetry.* **3** if a computer or notice displays information, it shows information in a way that can be clearly seen: *Local train and bus times are displayed in the station.*

dis·pleased /dɪsˈplizd/ adj. FORMAL very unhappy and fairly angry about something: *[+ with] City officials said they are displeased with the lack of progress.* —**displease** v. [T]

dis·pleas·ure /dɪsˈplɛʒɚ/ n. [U] FORMAL the feeling of being unhappy and fairly angry with someone or something: *[+ with/over] The letter expressed his displeasure with the management.*

dis·port /dɪˈspɔrt/ v. **disport yourself** OLD-FASHIONED to amuse yourself by doing active, enjoyable things

dis·pos·a·ble /dɪˈspoʊzəbəl/ adj. **1** intended to be used once or for a short time and then thrown away: *disposable diapers* **2 disposable income** the amount of money you have left to spend after you have paid your taxes, bills etc. **3** DISAPPROVING not interesting, of poor quality, and not likely to be remembered for very long: *disposable pop songs*

dis·pos·al /dɪˈspoʊzəl/ n. **1** [U] the act of getting rid of something: *[+ of] There is no site in the county for the disposal of hazardous waste.* **2 at sb's disposal** available for someone to use: *Hadden has some of the best medical advice in the country at his disposal.* **3** [C] a GARBAGE DISPOSAL **4** [U] FORMAL the act of putting people or things in a particular place or in a particular order

dis·pose /dɪˈspoʊz/ v.
dispose of sth *phr. v.* [T] **1** to get rid of something, especially something that is difficult to get rid of: *Companies must be held responsible for the cost of disposing of industrial wastes.* **2** to get rid of something by selling it: *Garage sales give people an opportunity to dispose of unwanted furniture.* **3** to defeat an opponent: *Hingis disposed of Williams in three straight sets.*

dis·posed /dɪˈspoʊzd/ adj. **1 be/feel disposed to do sth** FORMAL to feel willing to do something or behave in a particular way: *Johnson disagreed, but did not feel disposed to argue.* **2 be favorably/well/pleasantly etc. disposed toward sth** to like or approve of something such as an idea or plan: *Most board members were favorably disposed toward Anne's proposal.* **3 be disposed to sth** FORMAL to tend to do, have, or use something | **be naturally/genetically disposed to sth** *The new drug could help men who are genetically disposed to baldness.*

dis·po·si·tion /ˌdɪspəˈzɪʃən/ n. FORMAL **1** [C] the way someone tends to behave: **have a nervous/cheerful/sunny etc. disposition** *Thena has such a sweet disposition.* **2** [U] FORMAL the way that something is sold, given away, or gotten rid of, or the act of dealing with it: *[+ of] The disposition of an individual's estate need not be a difficult thing.* **3** [U] FORMAL the way that a situation is dealt with or that things are arranged: *[+ of] There are questions about the disposition of thousands of American troops in Germany.* **4** [singular] someone's willingness to do something: *Neither side shows a disposition to compromise in the dispute.*

dis·pos·sess /ˌdɪspəˈzɛs/ v. [T usually passive] FORMAL to take land or other property away from someone: *[be dispossessed of sth] Many black South Africans had been dispossessed of their homes.* —**dispossession** /ˌdɪspəˈzɛʃən/ n. [U]

dis·pos·sessed /ˌdɪspəˈzɛst◂/ n. **the dispossessed** [plural] FORMAL people who have had their land or other property taken away from them

dis·pro·por·tion /ˌdɪsprəˈpɔrʃən/ n. [C,U] FORMAL a situation in which two or more things do not have an equal or appropriate relationship

dis·pro·por·tion·ate /ˌdɪsprəˈpɔrʃənɪt/ adj. too much or too little in relation to something else: *Do you find yourself spending a disproportionate amount of time reading junk mail?* —**disproportionately** adv.

dis·prove /dɪsˈpruv/ v. [T] to prove that something is false or wrong: *Only the government has information which can disprove these claims.*

di·sput·a·ble /dɪˈspyutəbəl/ adj. something that is disputable is not definitely true or correct, and therefore is something that you can argue about; DEBATABLE —opposite INDISPUTABLE —**disputably** adv.

dis·pu·ta·tion /ˌdɪspyəˈteɪʃən/ n. [C,U] FORMAL a formal discussion about a subject which people cannot agree on

dis·pu·ta·tious /ˌdɪspyəˈteɪʃəs/ adj. FORMAL tending to argue a lot; ARGUMENTATIVE

dis·pute¹ /dɪˈspyut/ n. **1** [C,U] a serious argument or disagreement: *[+ between] Several disputes have*

broken out between businesses competing for the best locations. | [+ **over**] Kahane killed the man in a dispute over money. | The key issue **in dispute** (=being argued about) is the church's plan to expand its bookstore. | Several unions are **in dispute with** the company over retirement benefits. | Employees are involved in a **labor dispute** (=argument between a union and a company) with GenCo and may go on strike. **2 be beyond dispute** FORMAL if something is beyond dispute, everyone agrees that it is true or that it really happened: Ellen's honesty is beyond dispute.

dispute² v. **1** [T] to say that you think something such as a statement or idea is not correct or true: Local residents disputed the police's version of the incident. | [**dispute sth with sb**] Then I disputed the charges with my credit card company. **2** [I,T] to argue or disagree with someone: What happened next is **hotly disputed** (=argued about with strong feelings). **3** [T usually passive] to argue with another country, group, or person about who owns or controls something: **disputed territory/region/area** Shienken Street is still disputed territory in the divided city.

dis·qual·i·fy /dɪsˈkwɑləˌfaɪ/ v. disqualifies, disqualified, disqualifying [T] to stop someone from taking part in an activity or competition, or from doing a job, usually because they have broken a rule: [**disqualify sb from sth**] Certain crimes could disqualify you from entering the United States. | [+ **for**] Tillery was disqualified for kicking Bowe after the first round. —disqualification /dɪsˌkwɑləfəˈkeɪʃən/ n. [C,U]

dis·qui·et /dɪsˈkwaɪət/ n. [U] FORMAL feelings of being anxious or not satisfied about something: People felt a growing sense of disquiet over levels of crime in the neighborhood.

dis·qui·si·tion /ˌdɪskwəˈzɪʃən/ n. [C] FORMAL a long speech or written report

Dis·rae·li /dɪzˈreɪli/, **Benjamin** (1804–1881) a British politician who was Prime Minister in 1868 and from 1874 to 1880

dis·re·gard¹ /ˌdɪsrɪˈgɑrd/ v. [T] to ignore something or treat it as unimportant: Please disregard any notes written in the margins.

disregard² n. [singular,U] the act of ignoring something, in a way that annoys other people because they think it is important: [+ **for/of**] Native Americans complain that the deals have shown disregard for their rights. | **blatant/reckless/flagrant disregard** Byrd acted in blatant disregard of party rules.

dis·re·pair /ˌdɪsrɪˈpɛr/ n. [U] buildings, roads etc. that are in disrepair are in bad condition because they have not been repaired or cared for: The landmark Sainte Claire Hotel **fell into disrepair** and closed in 1988.

dis·rep·u·ta·ble /dɪsˈrɛpyətəbəl/ adj. FORMAL not respected, and often thought to be involved in dishonest or illegal activities: Jack usually got his information from fairly disreputable sources. —disreputably adv.

dis·re·pute /ˌdɪsrəˈpyut/ n. [U] a situation in which people do not trust or respect a person or an idea: Today, such ideas have **fallen into disrepute**. | Gordon knew his illegal payments would **bring disrepute** to him and the game of baseball.

dis·re·spect¹ /ˌdɪsrɪˈspɛkt/ n. [U] **1** lack of respect for someone or for something such as the law: Teenagers who show disrespect for authority are more likely to get involved in drugs. **2 no disrespect (to sb)** SPOKEN used when you are criticizing someone or something to show that you do not want to seem impolite: No disrespect to your son, but I think it's better for an adult to do this. —disrespectful adj. —disrespectfully adv.

disrespect² v. [T] INFORMAL to show a lack of respect to someone, especially by saying impolite things to them: Hicks accused Williams of disrespecting him at a record company party.

dis·robe /dɪsˈroʊb/ v. [I] FORMAL to take off your clothes

dis·rupt /dɪsˈrʌpt/ v. [T] to prevent a situation, event, system etc. from continuing in its usual way by causing problems: We hope the move to Kansas won't disrupt the kids' schooling too much.

dis·rup·tion /dɪsˈrʌpʃən/ n. [C,U] a situation in which something is prevented from continuing in its usual way because of problems and difficulties: The strike caused widespread disruption to flight schedules.

dis·rup·tive /dɪsˈrʌptɪv/ adj. disruptive behavior prevents something from continuing in its usual way and causes trouble: Stephen's teacher said he was often disruptive in class. —disruptively adv.

dis·sat·is·fac·tion /dɪˌsætɪsˈfækʃən, dɪsˌsæ-/ n. [U] a feeling of not being satisfied, especially because something is not as good as you had expected: [+ **with**] Sue's expression showed her dissatisfaction with the food and the service.

dis·sat·is·fied /dɪˈsætɪsˌfaɪd/ adj. not satisfied, especially because something is not as good as you had expected: [+ **with**] We hope to attract customers who are dissatisfied with their present health insurance. —dissatisfying adj.

dis·sect /dɪˈsɛkt, daɪ-/ v. [T] **1** to cut up the body of a dead animal or person to study it **2** to examine something in great detail so that you discover its faults or understand it better: The book dissects historical data to show how Napoleon ran his army.

dis·sec·tion /dɪˈsɛkʃən/ n. [C,U] the act of cutting up the body of a dead animal or person to study it

dis·sem·ble /dɪˈsɛmbəl/ v. [I,T] FORMAL to hide your true feelings, ideas, desires etc. especially in order to deceive someone

dis·sem·i·nate /dɪˈsɛməˌneɪt/ v. [T] FORMAL to spread information, ideas etc. to as many people as possible, especially in order to influence them: Racist messages are being widely disseminated via the Internet. —dissemination /dɪˌsɛməˈneɪʃən/ n. [U]

dis·sen·sion /dɪˈsɛnʃən/ n. [C,U] FORMAL disagreement and argument among a group of people: Recent defeats had caused dissension in the army ranks.

dis·sent¹ /dɪˈsɛnt/ n. **1** [C,U] disagreement with an official rule or law, or with an opinion that most people accept: The arrests are part of a government effort to suppress **political dissent**. **2** [C] a judge's written statement, giving reasons for disagreeing with the other judges in a law CASE **3** [U] OLD USE a disagreement with accepted religious beliefs, especially one that makes someone leave an established church —see also CONSENT¹, ASSENT¹

dissent² v. [I] to say that you strongly disagree with an official opinion or decision, or one that is accepted by most people: [+ **from**] Four of the panel's members dissented from the majority's opinion. —dissenter n. [C]

dis·ser·ta·tion /ˌdɪsɚˈteɪʃən/ n. [C] a long piece of writing about a particular subject, especially one that you write as part your work for a Ph.D. degree from a university

dis·serv·ice /dɪˈsɚvɪs, dɪsˈsɚ-/ n. **do sb/sth a disservice** to do something that harms someone or something, especially by giving other people a bad opinion about them: The fans' rude behavior has done the game a great disservice.

dis·si·dent /ˈdɪsədənt/ n. [C] someone who publicly criticizes a government or political party in a country where this is not allowed —dissident adj.: a group of dissident writers —dissidence n. [U]

dis·sim·i·lar /dɪˈsɪmələ, dɪsˈsɪ-/ adj. FORMAL very different: Several countries have legal systems which are **not dissimilar to** our own. —dissimilarity /dɪˌsɪməˈlærəti/ n. [C,U]

dis·sim·u·late /dɪˈsɪmyəˌleɪt/ v. [I,T] FORMAL to hide your true feelings or intentions, especially by lying to people

dis·si·pate /ˈdɪsəˌpeɪt/ v. FORMAL **1** [I,T] to scatter or disappear, or to make something do this: The gas

D

cloud had dissipated by late morning. | An evaporation system is used to dissipate heat from the sun and protect the shuttle's electronics. **2** [T] to gradually waste something such as money or energy by trying to do a lot of different or unnecessary things: They dissipated their inheritance money in a very short period of time.

dis·si·pat·ed /'dɪsəˌpeɪtɪd/ adj. LITERARY spending too much time on physical pleasures such as drinking, smoking etc., in a way that is harmful to your health

dis·si·pa·tion /ˌdɪsəˈpeɪʃən/ n. [U] FORMAL **1** the process of making something disappear or scatter: A heavy coat makes heat dissipation difficult. **2** the enjoyment of physical pleasures that are harmful to your health: Conrad lived a life of luxury and dissipation. **3** the act of wasting money, time, energy etc.

dis·so·ci·ate /dɪˈsouʃiˌeɪt, -siˌeɪt/ also **disassociate** v. [T] FORMAL **1 dissociate yourself from sb/sth** to do or say something to show that you do not agree with a person, organization, or action, especially so that you avoid being criticized or blamed: The Student League dissociated itself from the violence of June 13. **2 dissociate sb/sth from sb/sth** to consider two things or people as separate and not related to each other: Citizens demanded that the President dissociate the U.S. from the actions of its allies. —**dissociation** /dɪˌsouʃiˈeɪʃən/ n. [U]

dis·so·lute /'dɪsəˌlut/ adj. FORMAL having an immoral way of life, for example by drinking too much alcohol, having sex with many people etc. —**dissolutely** adv.

dis·so·lu·tion /ˌdɪsəˈluʃən/ n. [U] **1** the act of formally ending a marriage, a business arrangement, an organization etc.: A third woman had filed for divorce but never completed the dissolution. | the dissolution of the Soviet Union **2** the process by which something gradually becomes weaker and disappears: the dissolution of America's farmland

dissolve

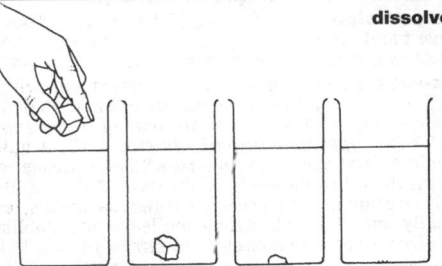

The sugar cube slowly dissolved in water.

dis·solve /dɪˈzɑlv/ v.
1 sth solid **a)** [I] if something solid dissolves, it mixes with a liquid and becomes part of it: [+ in] Sugar dissolves in water. **b)** [T] to make something solid become part of a liquid by putting it in a liquid and mixing it: [dissolve sth in sth] Dissolve the yeast in lukewarm water.
2 marriage/business/organization [T usually passive] to formally end a marriage, business arrangement, or organization: The law suit began ten months after the Rossi marriage had been legally dissolved.
3 become weaker [I] to become weaker and disappear: Maria's objections to the plan began to dissolve.
4 dissolve into laughter/tears LITERARY to start to laugh or cry: When Harriet learned about Edward's affair, she dissolved into tears.
5 government [T] to formally end a LEGISLATURE or PARLIAMENT before an election

dis·so·nance /'dɪsənəns/ n. **1** [C usually singular,U] FORMAL a lack of agreement between ideas, opinions, or facts: [+ between] As a young girl, Claudia felt tremendous dissonance between her Catholic school and her home in the ghetto. **2** [C,U] an annoying sound made by a group of musical notes that do not

go together well; DISCORD (2): a choral piece full of dissonance and odd rhythms —compare CONSONANCE (2) —opposite HARMONY —**dissonant** adj.

dis·suade /dɪˈsweɪd/ v. [T] to make someone decide not to do something: He wanted to come with me, and nothing I said could dissuade him. | [dissuade sb from doing sth] Hopefully the movie will dissuade teenagers from drinking and driving. —**dissuasion** /dɪˈsweɪʒən/ n. [U] —compare PERSUADE

dis·tance¹ /'dɪstəns/ n.   S W / 2 2
1 how far [C,U] the amount of space between two places or things: [+ from] Measure the distance from the top of the closet to the shelf below it | [+ between] The distance between St. Petersburg and Moscow is 593 miles. | **a short/long distance** Police found the body a short distance from the scene of the crime. | The church is still **some distance** (=a fairly long distance) away. | Bird feeders should be placed **at a distance of** at least six feet from a bush or tree.
2 a place that is far [singular] a point or place that is far away, but close enough to be seen or heard: The ruins look very impressive **from a distance**. | That's Mt. St. Helens **in the distance** over there. | Even **at a distance** he could see she was in a bad mood.
3 within walking/driving/striking etc. **distance** near enough to walk to, drive to, hit etc.: [+ of] The subway is within walking distance of my house.
4 keep your distance a) to stay far enough away from someone or something to be safe: Shots were fired into the air to force the police to keep their distance. **b)** also **keep sb at a distance** to avoid becoming too friendly with someone or too closely involved in something: Men tend to keep their children at more of a distance than women.
5 difference [C usually singular] a difference or separation between two things: [+ between] The economic distance between rich and poor will only cause more trouble for society. | Simmons was quick to **put some distance between** the ambassador's remark and the administration's official position (=he emphasized what the differences were).
6 time [U] the amount of time between two events: Now that there's some distance between us and the accident, it's easier to talk about.
7 unfriendly feeling [C usually singular] a situation in which two people do not tell each other what they really think or feel, in a way that seems unfriendly: [+ between] There was still a certain distance between me and my father.
8 go the distance INFORMAL if you go the distance in a sport or competition, you continue playing or competing until the end —see also LONG-DISTANCE, MIDDLE DISTANCE

distance² v. **1 distance yourself** to say that you are not involved with someone or something, or to try to become less involved with someone or something: [+ from] Rosen tried to distance himself from the controversy over fund-raising. **2** [T] to make someone have a less friendly relationship with someone else or a less positive attitude toward something: [distance sb from sb] Woods claims that his work has distanced him from his teenage daughter.

distance learn·ing /'. .ˌ../ n. [U] a method of studying that involves watching television programs, using the Internet etc. and sending work to teachers instead of going to school

dis·tant /'dɪstənt/ adj. **1** far away from where you are now: There was no sound other than the distant roar of the ocean. | Travelers came from distant lands to visit the shrine. **2** at a time that was very long ago, or that will be very far in the future: The book tells about societies **in the distant past** (=from a long time ago). | Wilde thinks there will be a black president **in the not too distant future** (=sometime fairly soon). **3** seeming unfriendly and showing no emotion: Jeff's been kind of distant lately. **4** [only before noun] not very closely related to you: Howard is a distant cousin of my mother's. —opposite CLOSE²
5 be/finish a distant second, come in a distant second [only before noun] to be the person, company etc. who finishes next after the winner of a competition, race etc., but to be much worse, slower etc.

than the winner: *Rolley finished the tournament a distant second.* —**distantly** *adv.*

dis·taste /dɪsˈteɪst/ *n.* [U] a feeling of dislike for someone or something that you think is annoying or offensive: [+ **for**] *The two men became friends, and spoke often of their distaste for war.*

dis·taste·ful /dɪsˈteɪstfəl/ *adj.* very disgusting or offensive: *We may **find** the songs **distasteful** today, but they are historically important.* —**distastefully** *adv.* —**distastefulness** *n.* [U]

dis·tem·per /dɪsˈtɛmpɚ/ *n.* [U] an infectious disease that affects dogs and cats

distended /dɪˈstɛnd/ *adj.* stretched larger than the normal size because of pressure from inside: *One child had a distended belly, like the stomachs of famine victims.* —**distend** *v.* [I,T] —**distention, distension** /dɪˈstɛnʃən/ *n.* [U]

dis·till /dɪˈstɪl/ *v.* [T] **1** to make a liquid purer by heating it so that it becomes a gas, and then letting it cool, or to make a strong alcoholic drink by this method: [**distill sth from sth**] *"Brandy" usually refers to spirits distilled from wine.* **2** to get ideas, information etc. from a large amount of knowledge or experience: [**distill sth from sth**] *Our organization attempts to distill information from a variety of sources.* —**distilled** *adj.*: *distilled water* —**distillation** /ˌdɪstəˈleɪʃən/ *n.* [C,U]

dis·til·late /ˈdɪstəlɪt, -ˌleɪt, dɪˈstɪlɪt/ *n.* [C] TECHNICAL a liquid that has been distilled from another liquid, for example GASOLINE that has been made from oil

dis·till·er /dɪˈstɪlɚ/ *n.* [C] a person or company that makes strong alcoholic drinks such as WHISKEY

dis·till·er·y /dɪˈstɪləri/ *n.* *plural* **distilleries** [C] a factory where strong alcoholic drinks are produced by distilling

dis·tinct /dɪˈstɪŋkt/ *adj.* **1** clearly different or separate: *African and Asian elephants are distinct species.* | [+ **from**] *The hill people are ethnically distinct from lowland Laotians.* | *Heraclitus repeatedly speaks of "God" **as distinct from** "the gods"* (=as if the two are clearly different ideas). **2** clearly seen, heard, understood etc.: *I have a distinct memory of my grandma sitting in the rocking chair, knitting.* **3** [only before noun] a distinct possibility, feeling, quality etc. definitely exists or is definitely important and cannot be ignored: *I get the distinct impression that you don't like her very much.* | *a distinct advantage*

s w **dis·tinc·tion** /dɪˈstɪŋkʃən/ *n.* **1** [C] a clear difference between things: [+ **between**] *"It is important to remember the distinction between rights and laws," he wrote.* | **make/draw a distinction between** (=to be careful to say what the difference between two or more things is) **2** [C] something that makes a person or thing special: *Neil Armstrong **had the distinction of** being the first man on the moon.* **3** [U] the quality of being unusually good: *He graduated **with distinction** in all subjects.* | *a poet of distinction*

dis·tinc·tive /dɪˈstɪŋktɪv/ *adj.* having a special quality, character, or appearance that is easy to recognize and is different from others of the same type: *A black widow spider has a distinctive red hourglass marking on its stomach.* —**distinctively** *adv.* —**distinctiveness** *n.* [U]

dis·tinct·ly /dɪˈstɪŋktli/ *adv.* **1** clearly, and without any doubt: *I distinctly told you to be home before 11:00.* | *Several witnesses **distinctly remember** Sanders starting the fight.* **2** used with adjectives to emphasize that something is clear, easy to recognize, or important: *New Orleans has a distinctly European feel to it.*

s w **dis·tin·guish** /dɪˈstɪŋgwɪʃ/ *v.* **1** [I,T] to recognize or understand the difference between two similar things, people etc.: [+ **between**] *Young children often can't distinguish between TV programs and commercials.* | [**distinguish sb/sth from sb/sth**] *The twins are so alike it's difficult to distinguish one from the other.* **2** [T not in progressive] to be able to see, hear, or taste something, even if this is difficult: *I couldn't distinguish the words, but his tone was clear.* **3 distinguish yourself** to do something so

well that people notice you, praise you, or remember you: *Eastwood distinguished himself as an actor before becoming a director.* **4** [T not in progressive] to be the thing that makes someone or something different from other people or things: [**distinguish sb/sth from sb/sth**] *The bright feathers distinguish the male peacock from the female.* —**distinguishing** *adj.* [only before noun] *a distinguishing feature*

dis·tin·guish·a·ble /dɪˈstɪŋgwɪʃəbəl/ *adj.* easy to notice or to recognize as being different from other things or people: *By December the quasar should be distinguishable in the night sky.*

dis·tin·guished /dɪˈstɪŋgwɪʃt/ *adj.* **1** very successful and therefore respected and admired: *He quit his job at Cornell, ending a distinguished academic career.* | *Ms. Dixon comes from a distinguished Washington family.* —see Usage Note at FAMOUS[1] **2** looking important and serious in a way that makes people respect you: *a tall, distinguished-looking man*

distort

D

dis·tort /dɪˈstɔrt/ *v.* **1** [T] to explain a fact, statement, idea etc. in a way that makes it seem to mean something different from what it really means: *Some say that the President has distorted facts in order to win the election.* **2** [I,T] if a sound, shape, or character distorts, or someone distorts it, it changes so that it is strange or unclear: *Funhouse mirrors, which are not flat, cause images to be distorted.* —**distorted** *adj.*: *a badly distorted TV picture* —**distortion** /dɪˈstɔrʃən/ *n.* [U]

dis·tract /dɪˈstrækt/ *v.* [I,T] to do something that takes someone's attention away from what they should be paying attention to: *Don't distract me while I'm driving!* | [**distract sb from sth**] *To distract myself from the pain, sweat, and effort of exercising, I check out the men's bodies.* | [+ **from**] *The instruments distract from his voice instead of supporting it.* | *Events in Europe must not **distract attention from** problems in the third world.* —**distracting** *adj.*

dis·tract·ed /dɪˈstræktɪd/ *adj.* unable pay attention to what you are doing, because you are worried or thinking about something else: *Amanda is very easily distracted – she takes forever to do anything.* —**distractedly** *adv.*

dis·trac·tion /dɪˈstrækʃən/ *n.* **1** [C,U] something that takes your attention away from what you are doing: *There are too many distractions in this office – it's hard for me to get anything done.* **2** [C] a pleasant and not very serious activity that you do for amusement: *Tennis has become a welcome distraction for Rudy and his whole family.* **3 drive sb to distraction** to annoy someone so much that they become angry, upset, and not able to think clearly anymore: *Mrs. Swanson was being driven to distraction by her mischievous son.*

dis·traught /dɪˈstrɔt/ *adj.* so anxious or upset that you cannot think clearly: *A policewoman was trying to calm the boy's distraught mother.*

dis·tress¹ /dɪˈstrɛs/ *n.* [U] **1** a feeling of being extremely worried and upset: *Children suffer emotional distress when their parents divorce.* | *The girl was crying and clearly **in distress**.* **2** a situation in which someone or something needs help, for example because they are in a dangerous situation or they do not have food or money: *The Family Shelter meets the needs of families* **in distress**. | **a distress signal/ call** *The Ship sank west of Auckland after sending out a distress signal at 3:20 a.m.* **3** FORMAL severe physical pain, or injury to the muscles: *Symptoms of panic attacks can include chest pain and abdominal distress.*

distress² *v.* [T] to make someone feel extremely upset and worried: *The prospect of a painful death distresses most people.* | [**it distresses sb to hear/see/learn etc.**] *It distresses me to think how many people in this area don't earn enough money to live on.* | [**it distresses sb that**] *It distressed her that women could not fully take part in the church.*

dis·tressed /dɪˈstrɛst/ *adj.* **1** extremely worried or upset: [**+ about/at/over**] *Homeowners are already distressed about their high property taxes.* | *When he came to see me, he was* **deeply distressed**. | [**distressed to hear/see/learn etc.**] *His manager said they were distressed to learn of his accidental death.* | [**distressed that**] *I am distressed that more progress has not been made.* **2** FORMAL needing help, money etc.: *The chief problem in distressed urban communities is unemployment.* **3** distressed furniture or cloth has been deliberately treated in a way that makes it look old and used **4** experiencing a lot of pain: *The animal was clearly distressed.* **5** distressed property is offered for sale at a lower than usual price because the owner cannot afford to keep it: *distressed real estate*

dis·tress·ing /dɪˈstrɛsɪŋ/ also **dis·tress·ful** /dɪˈstrɛsfəl/ *adj.* making you feel extremely worried or upset: *The front page news was shocking and distressing.* —**distressingly** *adv.*

dis·trib·ute /dɪˈstrɪbyət/ *v.* [T] **1** to give something such as food, medicine, or information to each person in a group: *Copies of the report were distributed shortly after the meeting* | [**distribute sth to/ among sb**] *The Red Cross is distributing food and clothing to the refugees.* **2** to supply goods to stores, companies etc. in a particular area so that they can be sold: *The tape costs $19.95 and is distributed by American Video.* **3** to divide something such as power or an amount of money fairly among different people or organizations so that they can share it: *The National Science Foundation is responsible for distributing the grant money.* **4** to spread something over an area or through a substance: *Each panel distributes sound evenly in all directions.*

dis·tri·bu·tion /ˌdɪstrəˈbyuʃən/ *n.* **1** [U] the act of giving things to each person in a group or of supplying goods to stores, companies etc.: *The cost of packaging and distribution ranges from $3 to $4 per videotape.* | [**+ of**] *a law prohibiting the free distribution of cigarettes* **2** [C,U] the way in which people or things are spread out over an area or through a substance: *This map shows the population distribution of Canada.* **3** [U] the way in which money, property etc. is shared among different groups: *The conference called for a more equitable distribution of wealth and power among nations.* —**distributional** *adj.* —**distributive** /dɪˈstrɪbyətɪv/ *adj.*

dis·trib·u·tor /dɪˈstrɪbyətɚ/ *n.* [C] **1** a company or person that supplies goods to stores or other companies **2** the part of a car's engine that sends electricity to the SPARK PLUGS —see picture at ENGINE

dis·trib·u·tor·ship /dɪˈstrɪbyətɚˌʃɪp/ *n.* [C] a company that supplies goods to stores or other companies

dis·trict /ˈdɪstrɪkt/ *n.* [C] a particular area of a city, country etc., especially an area that is officially divided from others: *Blaine works in the financial district.* —see Usage Note at AREA

district at·tor·ney /ˌ.. .ˈ../ *n.* [C] a lawyer who works for the government in a particular district and brings people who may be criminals to court

district court /ˌ.. ˈ./ *n.* [C] a U.S. court of law where people are judged in situations that involve national rather than state law

District of Co·lum·bi·a, the /ˌ.. . .ˈ.../ *written abbreviation* **D.C.** the special area of the eastern U.S. next to Maryland and Virginia, which includes Washington, the capital of the U.S.

dis·trust¹ /dɪsˈtrʌst/ *n.* [U] a feeling that you cannot trust someone: *Many people regard politicians with distrust.* | [**+ of**] *a deep distrust of authority* —**distrustful** *adj.* —compare MISTRUST¹

distrust² *v.* [T] to not trust someone or something: *He distrusts banks.*

dis·turb /dɪˈstɚb/ *v.* [T] **1** to annoy someone or interrupt what they are doing by making noise, asking a question etc.: *Please avoid disturbing me during the day unless it's an emergency.* | *a* **Do Not Disturb** *sign* (=that you put on your hotel door to tell people not to wake you up) **2** to make someone feel worried or upset: *The high rate of teenage pregnancy disturbs me a great deal.* **3** to do something that changes the position or condition of things, usually in a bad way: *When drying the flowers, be careful not to disturb the petals.* | *Cutting down rainforests disturbs the Earth's balance.* **4 disturb the peace** LAW to behave in a noisy and annoying way in public

dis·turb·ance /dɪˈstɚbəns/ *n.* **1** [C,U] something that annoys you or interrupts you so that you cannot continue what you are doing, or the act of annoying or interrupting someone: *Residents complained about the disturbance caused by the work on the roads.* **2** [C] a situation in which people fight or behave violently in public: *A sheriff's deputy went to investigate a family disturbance.* | **create/cause a disturbance** *Several people tried to create a disturbance in the courtroom.* **3** [C,U] a change in the normal condition or order of something, or in someone's mental or physical health: *There is a fast-moving weather disturbance passing through Utah.* | *Henderson claims he was suffering from extreme emotional disturbance when he attacked the woman.*

dis·turbed /dɪˈstɚbd/ *adj.* **1** worried or upset: [**+ about**] *Baker was disturbed about the restrictions put on the freedom to travel.* | [**disturbed to hear/ read/learn etc.**] *I was very disturbed to learn that many teenagers have no trouble buying alcohol.* | [**disturbed that**] *His parents are disturbed that he's dating a much older woman.* **2** not behaving in a normal way because of mental or emotional problems: *The defendant is mentally and emotionally disturbed.*

dis·turb·ing /dɪˈstɚbɪŋ/ *adj.* making you feel worried or upset: *It's very disturbing, the way they're getting rid of older employees.*

dis·u·nited /ˌdɪsyuˈnaɪtɪd/ *adj.* FORMAL not working together the way the members of a group should: *a disunited political party* —**disunite** *v.* [I,T]

dis·u·ni·ty /dɪsˈyunəti/ *n.* [U] FORMAL a state in which a group of people cannot agree with each other or work together: *The Vatican conference ended in disunity.*

dis·use /dɪsˈyus/ *n.* [U] a situation in which something is not used anymore: *A lot of farmland fell* **into disuse** (=stopped being used) *during the war.* —**disused** /ˌdɪsˈyuzd‹/ *adj.*

di·syl·lab·ic /ˌdaɪsəˈlæbɪk‹/ *adj.* TECHNICAL having two SYLLABLES

ditch¹ /dɪtʃ/ *n.* [C] a long narrow open hole that is dug in the ground for water to flow through, usually at the side of a road or in a field: *I fell asleep on the way home and drove my car into a ditch.* | **an irrigation/drainage ditch** *a drainage ditch blocked with leaves and mud* —see also LAST-DITCH

ditch² *v.* **1** [T] INFORMAL to get rid of something because it is not useful to you anymore: *Investors ditched stocks that were performing badly.* **2** [T] SPOKEN, INFORMAL to not go to school, class etc. when you should; SKIP¹ (1): *Let's ditch school and go to the park.* **3** [T] SPOKEN, INFORMAL to leave someone somewhere without telling them that you are leaving: *I'm mad at Charlene – she ditched me at the party last night.* **4** [T] SPOKEN, INFORMAL to end a romantic relationship with someone: *If I were you, I'd ditch her.* **5** [I,T] to land an airplane on water in a controlled crash: *The pilot had no choice but to ditch the plane in the Atlantic Ocean.*

dith·er[1] /'dɪðəʳ/ *v.* [I] to keep changing your opinion or decision about something, especially to avoid making a final decision: [+ **on/over**] *The ethics committee has been dithering over what to do about Cranston.* —**ditherer** *n.* [C]

dither[2] *n.* **be/get (all) in a dither** to be nervous and confused because you cannot decide what to do: *The British press gets in a dither whenever Americans touch visiting royalty.*

dit·sy /'dɪtsi/ *adj.* another spelling of DITZY

dit·to[1] /'dɪtoʊ/ *interjection* used to say that you have exactly the same opinion as someone else about something, or that something is also true for you: *"I read that book in about three days." "Ditto."*

ditto[2] *adv.* used to say that what is true about one thing or situation is also true about another: *The Monterey Jack cheese was tasteless; ditto for the mild cheddar.*

ditto[3] *n. plural* **dittos** [C] **1** also **ditto mark** a mark ('') that you write beneath a word in a list so that you do not have to write the same word again **2** a copy of a letter, form etc. made on an old-fashioned machine that was used before PHOTOCOPIERS

dit·ty /'dɪti/ *n.* [C] HUMOROUS a short simple poem or song

ditz /dɪts/ *n.* [C] SPOKEN someone who is silly, forgetful, or stupid: *My art teacher is a total ditz.*

dit·zy /'dɪtsi/ *adj.* INFORMAL silly, forgetful, or stupid: *Someone once told her she looked like Betty Boop, the ditzy cartoon character.*

di·u·ret·ic /ˌdaɪjəˈrɛtɪk/ *n.* [C] a substance that increases the flow of URINE —**diuretic** *adj.*

di·ur·nal /daɪˈɜrnl/ *adj.* TECHNICAL **1** happening or being active in the daytime: *diurnal animals such as cows* **2** happening every day: *The plains have a wide range of diurnal and annual temperatures.*

Div. *n.* the written abbreviation of DIVISION (2)

di·va /'divə/ *n.* [C] a woman who is a very good singer, especially of OPERA music —compare PRIMA DONNA (2)

di·van /dɪˈvæn, ˈdaɪvæn/ *n.* [C] OLD-FASHIONED a long low soft seat that has no arms, which is often used as a bed

dive[1] /daɪv/ *v. past tense* **dived** or **dove** *past participle* **dived** [I]

1 **jump into water** to jump into the water with your head and arms going in first: [+ **into/off etc.**] *Then Gabby dived into the swimming pool.* | *Diving off the cliffs is very dangerous.*

2 **jump/move quickly** [always + adv./prep.] to jump or move quickly in a particular direction or into a particular place: [+ **after/under/aside etc.**] *Ripken dived to his left and caught the ball.* | *Calabia said he dove under a table when the earthquake struck.*

3 **swim under water** to swim under water using special equipment to help you breathe: *The men use scuba gear to dive for abalone.*

4 **go deeper** to go deeper under water: *Slowly, the submarine began to dive.*

5 **aircraft/bird** if an airplane or a bird dives, it suddenly flies toward the ground very steeply: *Flight 776 from Orlando suddenly lost cabin pressure and dived nearly four miles.*

6 **numbers** if numbers, prices etc. dive, they fall very quickly and suddenly: *The dollar dived against the Japanese yen in Tokyo today.* —see also NOSEDIVE[2], SCUBA DIVING, SKYDIVING

dive in *phr. v.* [I] **1** to immediately start doing something eagerly and with a lot of energy: *Children fantasize about superheroes who can dive in and solve their problems.* **2** **dive in!** SPOKEN, INFORMAL used to invite people to start eating a meal

dive into sth *phr. v.* [T] to quickly become completely involved in an activity, a subject etc.: *Plummer was eager to dive into the kind of opportunity the college offers.*

dive[2] *n.* [C]

1 **sudden movement** a jump or sudden movement in a particular direction or into a particular place: *Vincenze made a dive for the ball.*

2 **amount/value** a sudden drop in the amount or value of something: *Their sales have taken a dive.*

3 **bar/hotel/restaurant** INFORMAL a place such as a bar or a hotel that is cheap and dirty: *It was a dive, but it was the only place to go that was near the airport.*

4 **jump** a jump into deep water with your head and arms going in first

5 **airplane/bird** an occasion when an airplane or a bird suddenly flies toward the ground very steeply

6 **take a dive** to deliberately do something in order to lose a game, competition etc.: *The game show producers forced Stempel to take a dive after weeks of success.*

7 **swim** an occasion when someone swims under water using special equipment to breathe

8 **submarine** an occasion when a SUBMARINE goes deeper under the water

dive-bomb /'. ./ *v.* [I,T] **1** to attack someone or something by flying down toward them and dropping a bomb: *The plane grew louder as it dive-bombed a bunker.* **2** INFORMAL if a bird dive-bombs someone or something, it quickly flies down and attacks them

dive bomb·er /'. ˌ../ *n.* [C] a type of military airplane that flies low over a place and drops bombs on it

div·er /'daɪvəʳ/ *n.* [C] **1** someone who swims or works underwater using special equipment to breathe: *a deep sea diver* **2** someone who jumps into deep water with their head and arms first

di·verge /dəˈvɜrdʒ, daɪ-/ *v.* [I] **1** if two things such as opinions, interests, or plans diverge, they are similar at the beginning but then begin to develop in different ways: [+ **from**] *Russia does not intend to diverge from the United Nations position on this issue.* **2** if two lines or paths that are next to each other diverge, they begin to go in different directions —opposite CONVERGE

di·ver·gence /dəˈvɜrdʒəns/ *n.* [C,U] a difference between two or more things such as opinions or interests: [+ **between/of**] *There is a divergence of views between Washington and Berlin on how to deal with the issue.*

di·ver·gent /dəˈvɜrdʒənt/ *adj.* divergent opinions, ideas, interests etc. are very different from each other: *Americans have divergent attitudes toward alcohol and cigarettes.*

di·vers /'daɪvərz/ *adj.* [only before noun] OLD-FASHIONED of many different kinds; VARIOUS

di·verse /dəˈvɜrs, daɪ-/ *adj.* a place or group that is diverse has many different types of people or things in it: *New York is one of the most culturally diverse cities in the world.* | *I never realized that the terrain in Africa is so diverse.*

di·ver·si·fy /dəˈvɜrsəˌfaɪ/ *v.* **diversifies, diversified, diversifying** [I,T] **1** if a company or a country's ECONOMY diversifies, or if someone diversifies it, it begins to make a larger range of products or to become involved in new types of business: [+ **into**] *In recent years Western Union has diversified into other communications businesses.* **2** to put your money into several different types of INVESTMENT instead of only one or two: *Most financial planners recommend that investors diversify their assets.* **3** to increase the variety of things that you do: *As a singer, she began to diversify, performing songs in many languages.* —**diversification** /dəˌvɜrsəfəˈkeɪʃən/ *n.* [U]

di·ver·sion /dəˈvɜrʒən, daɪ-/ *n.* **1** [C,U] a change in the direction or purpose of something, or the act of changing it: *Water diversions such as dams and canals are threatening the fish population.* | [+ **of**] *Easton was certainly aware of the diversion of funds into the military budget.* **2** [C,U] an enjoyable activity that you do so that you are not bored: *Everybody needs a diversion and college basketball is mine.* | *People who used to rent videos regularly are now looking for diversion elsewhere.* **3** [C] something that takes your attention away from something that you should be giving your attention to: *Four prisoners* *created a diversion* to allow the others time to escape.

di·ver·sion·a·ry /dəˈvɚʒəˌnɛri/ *adj.* intended to take someone's attention away from something: *The bombing was apparently a diversionary tactic, while the Navy landed its troops ashore.*

di·ver·si·ty /dəˈvɚsɪti, daɪ-/ *n.* **1** [U] the quality of being made up of a range of different people, ideas, or things: *Mayor Hannah wants to bring more ethnic diversity to the city council* (=she wants people from various races to be members). | [+ of] *The diversity of their merchandise is better than anywhere else.* **2** [C usually singular] a range of different people, ideas, or things; VARIETY (3): [+ of] *It's natural that there is a diversity of opinions within the organization.*

di·vert /dəˈvɚt, daɪ-/ *v.* [T] **1** to change what something such as money or time is used for: [**divert sth to/into sth**] *Oregon voters do not want public tax dollars diverted to private education.* | [**divert sth from sth**] *Police resources are being diverted from investigating real crimes.* **2** to change the direction in which something flows or travels: *Farmers were illegally diverting water to save their crops.* **3** to stop someone from paying attention to something, by giving them something else to notice: *They say that Republicans want to divert people's attention from the recession.* **4** FORMAL to amuse or entertain someone: *Bring games in the car to divert the children during a long trip.*

di·vert·ing /dəˈvɚtɪŋ/ *adj.* FORMAL entertaining and amusing: *a diverting play*

di·vest /dəˈvɛst, daɪ-/ *v.* [I,T] TECHNICAL if you divest something such as a company or an INVESTMENT, or if it is divested, it is sold or gotten rid of: *The operations that will be divested include factories in New Hampshire.*

divest sb of sth *phr. v.* [T] **1** TECHNICAL to sell a company or an INVESTMENT: [**divest yourself of sth**] *Pinkerton's is divesting itself of $120 million in unprofitable business.* **2** FORMAL to take off something you are wearing or carrying **3** FORMAL to take something away from someone —**divestment** *n.* [U]

di·ves·ti·ture /dəˈvɛstɪtʃɚ/ *n.* [C,U] TECHNICAL the act of selling a company or an INVESTMENT

s w
2 2 **di·vide¹** /dəˈvaɪd/ *v.*

1 separate [I,T] to separate something into two or more parts, groups etc., or to become separated in this way: *Cancer cells divide rapidly.* | [**divide sth into sth**] *Divide the dough into four parts and make each into a ball.* | [+ into] *The class divided into groups of four and five.*
2 keep separate [T] to keep two areas separate from each other: *The Berlin Wall used to divide East and West Berlin.* | [**divide sth from sth**] *The living room is divided from the kitchen area by a white brick wall.*
3 share [T] also **divide up** to separate something into two or more parts and share it among two or more people, groups, places etc.: [+ between] *She divides her time between New York and Paris.* | [+ among] *The money will be divided up equally among his children.*
4 mathematics **a)** [T] to calculate how many times one number contains a smaller number: [**divide sth by sth**] *Divide 21 by 3.* | [**divided by sth**] *12 divided by 4 is 3.* **b)** [I] to be contained in another number one or more times: [+ into] *8 divides into 64 eight times.* —compare MULTIPLY (2)
5 disagree [T] to make people disagree with each other and form groups with different opinions: *The choice of a new rabbi has divided the entire congregation.* | [**be divided over/about**] *Congress is divided over the issue of impeachment.*
6 divide and conquer/rule to defeat or control people by making them argue or fight with each other instead of opposing you: *The authorities continued to practice divide and rule policies.* —**divided** *adj.*

divide² *n.* [C usually singular] **1** a strong difference between two groups of people, especially in their beliefs or way of life, that separates them and can result in fighting: *The racial divide between the city and its suburbs is deepening.* **2** a line of very high ground from which water flows to two different river systems; WATERSHED (2): *The Continental Divide runs along the length of the Rocky Mountains.*

divided high·way /.,.. '../ *n.* [C] a main road on which the traffic traveling in opposite directions is kept apart by a piece of land or a low wall

div·i·dend /ˈdɪvəˌdɛnd, -dənd/ *n.* [C] **1** a part of a s w company's profit that is paid to people who have 3 SHARES in the company **2** TECHNICAL a number that is to be divided by another number —compare DIVISOR

di·vid·er /dəˈvaɪdɚ/ *n.* [C] **1** something such as a wall or SCREEN that separates one area from another: *the center divider of the Lawrence Expressway* | *a room divider* **2** a piece of stiff paper used to keep pages separate: *a set of notebook dividers* **3 dividers** [plural] an instrument used for measuring or marking lines or angles, that consists of two pointed pieces of metal joined together at the top

dividing line /.'.. ,./ *n.* [C] **1** the difference between two types or groups of similar things: [+ between] *It's hard to draw a dividing line between scientific issues and moral and religious ones.* **2** a line or border that separates two areas or things: *The car swerved across the dividing line of a two-lane highway.*

div·i·na·tion /ˌdɪvəˈneɪʃən/ *n.* [U] FORMAL the act of finding out what will happen in the future by using special powers, or the practice of doing this

di·vine¹ /dəˈvaɪn/ *adj.* **1** coming from God or a god: *Perhaps it was divine intervention* (=help from God) *that brought the survivors through.* **2** relating to God or a god, or like a god: *The emperor was considered the nation's divine spiritual leader.* **3** OLD-FASHIONED unusually good; WONDERFUL: *Singer Sarah Vaughan was often called "the Divine Sarah."*

divine² *v.* **1** [T] LITERARY to discover or guess something: *He had apparently divined from my expression that I was not prepared.* **2** [I] to search for water or minerals that are under the ground using a special Y-shaped stick —**diviner** *n.* [C]

divine³ *n.* **1 the Divine** God, or someone who has qualities like a god's: *St. John the Divine* **2** [C] FORMAL a priest or minister

divine right /.,. './ *n.* [singular] **1** INFORMAL the right to do what you want without having to ask permission: *Some bicyclists apparently think they have a divine right to ride wherever they want.* **2** the right given to a king or queen by God to rule a country, that in past times could not be questioned or opposed

div·ing /ˈdaɪvɪŋ/ *n.* [U] **1** the sport of swimming under water using special equipment to breathe: *They went diving in the Florida Keys on their vacation.* **2** the activity of jumping into water with your head and arms first: *a diving competition*

diving bell /'.. ,./ *n.* [C] a metal container shaped like a bell, in which people can work under water

diving board /'.. ,./ *n.* [C] a board above a SWIMMING POOL from which you can jump into the water

diving suit /'.. ,./ *n.* [C] a special protective suit that is worn when someone is swimming deep under water

divining rod /.'.. ,./ *n.* [C] a special stick shaped like the letter Y that some people use to find water and minerals that are under the ground

di·vin·i·ty /dəˈvɪnəti/ *n. plural* **divinities 1** [U] the study of God and religious beliefs; THEOLOGY: *a Master of Divinity degree* **2** [U] the state of being a god, or the quality of being like a god: *After 1946, the Emperor no longer claimed divinity.* **3** [C] God or a god **4** [U] a soft white candy, often containing nuts

divinity school /.'... ,./ *n.* [C] a college where students study to become priests or ministers

di·vis·i·ble /dəˈvɪzəbəl/ *adj.* able to be divided, especially by another number: [+ by] *15 is divisible by 3.* —**divisibility** /dəˌvɪzəˈbɪləti/ *n.* [U]

di·vi·sion /dəˈvɪʒən/ n.

1 separation [C,U] the act of separating something into two or more parts or groups, or the way that these parts are separated or shared: [+ **of**] *The Constitution clearly calls for the division of church and state.* | [**division of sth between/among sb**] *The documents explain the division of the estate among his children.* | [**division of sth into sth**] *The division of Korea into North and South took place in 1948.*

2 part of an organization [C] a group that does a particular job within a large company, organization etc.: *The company's Credit Data Division is based in Orange County.*

3 disagreement [C,U] a disagreement among the members of a group: *Both elections revealed a deep division within the Republican party.* | [+ **between**] *"There are divisions between the band and myself," she says.*

4 mathematics [U] the process of finding out how many times one number contains a smaller number —compare MULTIPLICATION (1) —see also LONG DIVISION

5 sports [C] a group of teams that a sports LEAGUE or competition is divided into: *The Warriors are currently first in the Pacific division.*

6 military [C] a large military group: *The entire division of 18,000 troops will be home in about a month.*

di·vi·sion·al /dəˈvɪʒənl/ adj. relating to a sports or military division: *the divisional championship game*

division of la·bor /ˌ... .. ˈ../ n. [C,U] a way of organizing work in which each member of a group has a particular job to do

di·vi·sive /dəˈvaɪsɪv, -ˈvɪs-/ adj. causing a lot of disagreement among people: *Abortion is one of the most divisive issues in America.*

di·vi·sor /dəˈvaɪzɚ/ n. [C] TECHNICAL the number by which another number is to be divided —compare DIVIDEND (2)

di·vorce[1] /dəˈvɔrs/ n. **1** [C,U] the legal ending of a marriage: *Half the marriages in this country end in divorce.* | *Tony said he and Karen are **getting a divorce**.* | *Packer has **filed for divorce** (=begun the divorce process) from his wife of 25 years.* | *a **messy/bitter divorce** a prolonged and bitter divorce* | *He had to pay her $10 million as part of the **divorce settlement** (=the legal decision about how much money, property etc. each person gets after a divorce).* —compare SEPARATION (3) **2** [C] a separation of ideas, subjects, values etc.: [+ **between**] *We hope to avoid a complete divorce between research and practice.*

divorce[2] v. **1** [I,T] to legally end a marriage: *We divorced after six years of marriage.* | *She's afraid of what her husband might do if she tries to divorce him.* | [+ **from**] *Tran was divorced from his wife Inge in 1974.* **2** [T] to separate two ideas, values, organizations etc.: [**divorce sth from sth**] *Carlin says he divorces philosophy from his religion.* | *Some of his ideas **are** completely **divorced from reality** (=not based on real experience or sensible thinking).* **3 divorce yourself from sth** to stop being involved with an activity, an organization etc.

di·vorced /dəˈvɔrst/ adj. not married to your former wife or husband anymore: *divorced women* | [+ **from**] *He's been divorced from Delores for years.* | *My parents **got divorced** (=legally ended their marriage) when I was ten.*

di·vor·cee, **divorcée** /dəˌvɔrˈseɪ, -ˈseɪ/ n. [C] a woman who has legally ended her marriage

div·ot /ˈdɪvət/ n. [C] a small piece of earth and grass that you dig out accidentally while playing GOLF

di·vulge /dəˈvʌldʒ, daɪ-/ v. [T] to give someone information, especially about something that was secret: *A spokeswoman for the company would not divulge the salaries paid to top managers.* | [**divulge sth to sb**] *I have not divulged any information to the police.* | [**divulge what/where/whether etc.**] *The Navy refuses to divulge whether any of the ships are carrying nuclear weapons.*

div·vy /ˈdɪvi/ v. **divvies, divvied, divvying**
divvy sth ↔ **up** phr. v. [T] INFORMAL to divide

something among two or more people: *Divvy up the cookies between you.*

Dix /dɪks/, **Do·ro·the·a** /ˌdɔrəˈθiə, ˌdɑr-/ (1802–1887) a U.S. social REFORMER who worked to improve conditions for people who were in prison or mentally ill

Dix·ie /ˈdɪksi/ n. [U] INFORMAL the southeastern states of the U.S. that fought against the North in the U.S. Civil War

dix·ie·land /ˈdɪksiˌlænd/ also **dixieland jazz** /ˈ... ˌ./ n. [U] a type of JAZZ with a strong RHYTHM

diz·zy /ˈdɪzi/ adj. **dizzier, dizziest 1** having a feeling of not being able to balance, especially after spinning around or because you feel sick: *The thin mountain air made Trautmann feel dizzy.* | *She suffers from high blood pressure and **dizzy spells** (=short periods when you feel dizzy).* **2** confused or excited: [+ **from/with**] *Rapid economic development has left the people of Eastern Europe dizzy with change.* **3** INFORMAL silly or stupid: *a dizzy blonde* **4** another form of DIZZYING —**dizzily** adv. —**dizziness** n. [U]

diz·zy·ing /ˈdɪziɪŋ/ adj. **1** making someone feel confused or excited: *Voters will choose from a dizzying number of parties.* **2** making someone feel unable to balance: *The view from Cyril's restaurant is dizzying.* —**dizzy** v. [T]

DJ n. [C] a DISC JOCKEY

Dji·bou·ti /dʒɪˈbuti/ a small country on the coast of northeast Africa —**Djiboutian** n., adj.

djinn /dʒɪn/ n. [C] a magical spirit in Islamic stories that can appear as a human or an animal and influence people in good or bad ways —compare GENIE

DMV n. **the DMV** the Department of Motor Vehicles; the organization in many U.S. states where you can get a DRIVER'S LICENSE, REGISTER your car etc.

DMZ n. [C] Demilitarized Zone; a phrase meaning an area from which all weapons, soldiers etc. have been removed so that there can be no fighting there, used especially about the area between North and South Korea

DNA n. [U] TECHNICAL deoxyribonucleic acid; an acid that carries GENETIC information in a cell

DNA pro·fil·ing /ˌ... ˈ.../ n. [U] the act of examining DNA to find out who did a particular crime

do[1] /də; strong du/ auxiliary verb, past tense **did** past participle **done** 3rd person singular present tense **does 1** used with another verb to form questions or negatives: *Do you know Nancy?* | *What time does he take his morning nap?* | *She didn't think she would have time.* | *Where do you live?* | *Doesn't Rosie look fat?* | *Don't just stand there – help me!* | *Why don't you let me carry that (=please let me carry that for you)?* **2** SPOKEN used at the end of a sentence to make a question or to show that you expect someone to agree with it: *It looks just like new, doesn't it?* | *You didn't go there alone, did you?* **3** used to emphasize the main verb in a sentence: *He hasn't been here in a while, but he does come to visit us most weekends.* | *"Why didn't you tell me?" "I did tell you – you just forgot."* **4** used to avoid repeating another verb: *"Have you called him yet?" "I did yesterday."* | *Emilio speaks much better English than he did a year ago.* | *"That's where I always get confused." "I do too."* | *"I definitely need to get more exercise." "Yeah, so do I."* | *"She didn't have any lunch." "Neither did I."* **5** used to change the order of the subject and the verb when a negative adverb or adverbial phrase starts a sentence: *Not only did she change her address, she also changed her name.*

do[2] /du/ v. past tense **did** past participle **done** 3rd person singular present tense **does**
1 do an action [T] to perform an action or an activity: *Do your homework before you watch TV.* | *It's Jim's turn to **do the dishes/laundry**.* | *"What are you doing?" "Making cookies."* | *It's a pleasure **doing business** with you.* —see Usage Note at MAKE[1]
2 succeed/fail [I only in progressive] used to ask or say whether someone is being successful: *How are you doing? Are you nearly finished?* | [+ **with/in**

etc.] *Is Erica doing okay with the new baby?* | *Neil is **doing** very **well** this year at school.*

3 **have an effect** [T] to have a particular effect on someone or something: *The new car factory has **done a lot for** (=had a good effect on) the local economy.* | *If she doesn't like Kevin, you can't **do anything about** that* (=you cannot change that). | *Come on, let's go to the beach. It'll **do you good** (=make you feel better or happier).* | *Red **doesn't do a thing for her** (=doesn't make her look good).* | *Moving to the city has **done wonders for** (=has really improved) my social life.*

4 **what sb does (for a living)** what someone's job is: *"And what about Ann, what does she do?" "She's an attorney."* | *Both men are darn good at what they do for a living.*

5 **do sb's hair/nails/makeup etc.** to spend time arranging someone's hair, painting their nails etc.: *It takes her a half an hour to do her hair in the morning.* | *Who did your nails? They look great!*

6 **travel fast/far** to travel at a particular speed, or to travel a particular distance: *Wiegert said the car did 0 to 60 miles per hour in 3.5 seconds.* | *We did 300 miles on the first day.*

7 **be acceptable/enough** [I,T not in progressive] to be acceptable or be enough: *The recipe calls for butter, but margarine will do.* | *I wanted to get a new dress for the wedding, but my blue one **will have to do**.* | *"Do you want a small glass like this size?" "Yeah, **that'll do**."* | *Two mediums and one extra large. Okay, I think **that'll do me**.* —see Usage Note at ADEQUATE

8 **spend time** [T] INFORMAL to spend a period of time doing something difficult or something that you have to do: *He did two years at the University of Tennessee after he left here.* —see also **do time** (TIME[1] (41))

9 **make food** [T] INFORMAL to make a particular type of food: *I was thinking of doing a casserole tonight.*

10 **copy** [T] INFORMAL to copy someone's behavior, in order to entertain people: *He does Clinton very well.*

11 **provide a service** [T] to provide a particular service: *They do music for weddings and school dances mostly.* | *We do both interior and exterior design.*

12 **visit** [T] to visit a particular place, especially when you are going to see a lot of other places: *Let's do the Empire State Building today and the Statue of Liberty tomorrow.*

13 **take a drug** [T] to use an illegal drug, especially regularly: *When I do speed, I can't think straight.*

14 **perform a play** [T] to perform a particular play: *We did "Our Town" and "Guys and Dolls" when I was in high school.*

SPOKEN PHRASES

15 **what is sb/sth doing...?** used to ask why someone or something is doing something or why they are in a particular place, especially when you do not approve: *What's this cake doing on the floor?* | *What are you doing eating that cookie when I'm about to fix dinner?*

16 **do lunch/a meeting/a movie etc.** INFORMAL to have lunch, have a meeting, see a movie etc. with someone else: *Let's do lunch next week.*

17 **do it** a phrase meaning "have sex," used humorously or when you do not want to say this directly: *I had to tell the officer about these people I saw doing it in the park.*

18 **that'll do** used to tell a child that you want them to stop being noisy, angry, excited etc.: *Sit down, sit down, that'll do.*

19 **what will you do for sth?** used to ask someone what arrangements they have made to deal with something: *What will you do for money if you quit your job?*

20 **what can I do you for?** HUMOROUS used to ask someone what you can do to help them, for example in a store: *Good morning, Mitch! What can I do you for today?*

21 **do sb** VULGAR to have sex with someone: *Are you gonna do her?*

22 **happen** [I] SLANG to happen: *What's doing at your place tonight?*

23 **sb would do well to do sth** used to advise someone that they should do something: *Nelson would do well to keep his political views out of her work.*

24 **decorate** [T] to paint or decorate something such as a room or a house: *We're going to do my office in blue.*

25 **behave** [I] to behave in a particular way: *Do as I say, not as I do.*

26 **do sth to death** to talk about or do something so often that it becomes boring: *That joke has been done to death.*

27 **allow/accept** [T] to allow a particular behavior, or to consider it acceptable: *In China, putting your fingers in your mouth **just isn't done**.*

28 **do well by sb** to treat someone well: *He's left home, but he still does well by his kids.* —see also **be done for** (DONE[2] (4)), DO-OR-DIE, **how do you do** (HOW[1] (15))

do away with *phr. v.* [T] **1** [**do away with** sth] to get rid of something: *Maybe the Scouts should do away with uniforms.* **2** [**do away with** sb] INFORMAL to kill someone: *In the movie, she hires two thugs to do away with her husband.*

do sb **in** *phr. v.* [T] **1** to make someone feel extremely tired: *That bike ride really did me in.* **2** INFORMAL to kill someone or kill yourself: *I don't think Stan is going to do himself in.*

do sb **out** of sth *phr. v.* [T often passive] INFORMAL to cheat someone by not giving them something that they deserve, or something that they are owed: *The reporters were afraid that the out-of-court settlement would do them out of a story.*

do sth **over** *phr. v.* [T] **1** to do something again, especially because you did it wrong the first time: *If you make too many mistakes, the teacher'll make you do it over.* | *If I had it to do over, I'd have given myself more time to relax.* **2** to decorate a room, wall etc. in a different way than before: *They're going to do the whole apartment over in an art deco style.*

do up *phr. v.* **1** [I,T **do** sth ↔ **up**] if something does up or you do it up in a particular way, it is fastened or tied in that way: *I don't like blouses that do up in the back.* | *For the birthday party, she did her hair up with a ribbon.* **2** [T **do** sth ↔ **up**] to decorate something so that it looks attractive: *The bar was done up like a plush salon from 100 years ago.* **3** [T **do** sb ↔ **up**] to make yourself or another person look neat and attractive, or to dress them in a particular way: *Sue took forever doing herself up for her date.* | [+ **in/with**] *The girls were all done up in white robes and tinsel for the Christmas procession.*

do with sth *phr. v.* [T] **1** (**have**) to do with sth to be about something, related to something, or involved in something: *What does this have to do with learning?* | *The overdose had nothing to do with the patient's death* (=it was not related to the death). | *Scientists think the El Niño current had something to do with the drought* (=it is related to the dry weather, but they are not sure exactly how).

SPOKEN PHRASES

2 **what have you/has he etc. done with sth?** used to ask where someone has put something: *What have you done with the scissors?* **3** **what you do with yourself/what sb does with himself etc.** what someone spends their time doing: *My dad doesn't know what to do with himself since he retired.* **4** **what are you/is she etc. doing with sth?** used to ask why someone has something: *What are you doing with my wallet?* **5** **what should I do with sth?** used to ask what you should use something for, or where you should put it: *Mom, what should I do with this frying pan?* **6** **I/he/she etc. could do with sth** used to say that someone needs or wants something: *I could do with a cold beer right now.*

do without *phr. v.* **1** [I,T **do without** sth] to manage to continue living or doing something without having a particular thing: *City residents need to think about what services they can do without.*

2 I can/could do without sth SPOKEN used to say that something is annoying you or making things difficult for you: *I could do without that constant racket in the next room.*

do³ *n.* [C] INFORMAL **1 dos and don'ts** things that you should or should not do in a particular situation: *the dos and don'ts of office dating* **2** a party or other social event: *a family do* **3** a HAIRDO

do⁴, doh /dou/ *n.* [singular,U] the first note in a musical SCALE according to the SOL-FA system

DOA *adj.* the abbreviation of "dead on arrival" —see **dead on arrival** (DEAD¹ (15))

do·a·ble /'duəbəl/ *adj.* INFORMAL able to be completed or done: *doable recipes for home cooks*

d.o.b. *n.* the written abbreviation of "date of birth"

Do·ber·man pin·scher /,doubəmən 'pintʃɚ/ also **Doberman** *n.* [C] a large black and brown dog with very short hair, often used for guarding houses or buildings

doc /dak/ *n.* [C] SPOKEN a short form of DOCTOR¹ (1)

do·cent /'dousənt/ *n.* [C] someone who guides visitors through a MUSEUM, church, garden etc.

doc·ile /'dasəl/ *adj.* quiet, calm, and easy to control: *Kangaroos are not as docile as they look.* —**docilely** /'dasəl-li/ *adv.* —**docility** /da'sıləti/ *n.* [U]

dock¹ /dak/ *n.* [C] **1** the structure in a port from which boats or ships are loaded or unloaded, or the area around it: *The boat crossed the bay and let them off at the dock, directly below the hotel.* | *The ship is now in dock for repairs.* —see also DRY DOCK **2** a wooden structure built out into a lake or river, that you can use to get on and off boats: *Cyril sat on the dock and stared out over the water.* **3** a LOADING DOCK **4** an enclosed area in some law courts where the DEFENDANT (=person charged with a crime) sits or stands

dock² *v.* **1** [I,T] if a ship docks or you dock it, it sails into a dock: *The ship docked in Honolulu on November 1.* **2 dock sb's wages/pay** to reduce the amount of money you pay someone, especially because they have done something wrong: *Roman was docked two hours' pay for the incident.* **3** [I] if two spaceships dock, they join together in space: *The repair ship docked with the space station Mir last night.* **4** [T] to cut an animal's tail short

dock·et /'dakıt/ *n.* [C] **1** LAW a list of legal cases that will take place in a particular court: *The court's docket of civil rights cases is light compared to last year's.* **2** a list of things to be done or discussed; AGENDA: *So what's on the docket for today's meeting?* **3** TECHNICAL a short document that shows what is in a package or describes goods that are being delivered

dock·side /'daksaɪd/ *n.* [singular] the area around the place in a port where ships are loaded and UNLOADed

dock·work·er /'dak,wɚkɚ/ *n.* [C] someone who works on a DOCK, especially loading and UNLOADing ships

dock·yard /'dakyard/ *n.* [C] a place where ships are repaired or built

doc·tor¹, Doctor /'daktɚ/ *n.* [C] **1** someone whose job is to treat people who are sick: *I made an appointment with Doctor Sangha for next Monday.* | **go to the doctor/see a doctor** *See a doctor if the fever lasts more than three days.* **2** someone who has the highest level of degree given by a university: *a Doctor of Law*

doctor² *v.* [T] **1** to change something, especially in a way that is not honest: *Photographs can easily be doctored.* **2** to add a substance, especially a drug or poison, to food or drink: *Nancy likes to doctor her coffee with a shot of whisky.* **3** to give medical treatment to someone or something: *Gina gently doctored Clint's injured hand.*

doc·tor·al /'daktərəl/ *adj.* [only before noun] relating to or done as part of work for the university degree of DOCTOR¹ (2): *Hasse wrote his doctoral dissertation on ragtime music.*

doc·tor·ate /'daktərıt/ *n.* [C] a university degree of the highest level

Doctor of Phi·los·o·phy /,.. . .'...'.../ *n.* [C] a PH.D.

doctor's de·gree /'.. .,./ *n.* [C] INFORMAL a doctorate

doc·tri·naire /,daktrə'nɛr/ *adj.* FORMAL certain that your beliefs or opinions are completely correct, and not willing to change them: *Scalia is perhaps the most doctrinaire of the court's conservative judges.*

doc·trine /'daktrın/ *n.* [C] a strong belief or set of beliefs that form an important part of a religion or system of ideas: *the Hindu doctrine of the immortality of the soul* —**doctrinal** *adj.*

doc·u·dra·ma /'dakyə,dramə/ *n.* [C] a movie, usually for television, that is based on a true story

doc·u·ment¹ /'dakyəmənt/ *n.* [C] **1** a piece of paper that has official information written on it, or a collection of these papers: *legal documents* | *The company was given a 55-page document detailing the criminal charges.* **2** a piece of work that you write on a computer

doc·u·ment² /'dakyə,mɛnt/ *v.* [T] **1** to write about something, film it, photograph it etc. in order to record information about it: *The photographs documented the anguish of the Great Depression.* **2** to support something with facts: *It is well documented that people using car phones are more likely to have accidents.* **3** to provide someone with official documents, especially so they can work legally —**documented** *adj.*

doc·u·men·ta·ry¹ /,dakyə'mɛntri, -'mɛntəri/ *n. plural* **documentaries** [C] a movie or television program that gives facts and information about something [+ **on/about**] *a documentary on humpback whales*

documentary² *adj.* **1 documentary film/program** a movie or television program that gives facts and information about something **2** [only before noun] documentary proof or EVIDENCE is proof in the form of documents: *Lehder provided no documentary evidence to support his claims.*

doc·u·men·ta·tion /,dakyəmən'teıʃən/ *n.* [U] **1** official documents, reports etc. that are used to prove that something is true or correct: *Parents are required to take documentation of the child's health screening to the school.* **2** the process of writing about something, filming it, photographing it etc. in order to record information about it, or the papers, photographs etc. that are produced: *The local library wants documentation of the fire for its history exhibit.*

DOD the written abbreviation of the U.S. Department of Defense

dod·der /ˈdɑdɚ/ *v.* [I] to walk in an unsteady way while shaking slightly, especially because you are very old

dod·der·ing /ˈdɑdərɪŋ/ *adj.* shaking slightly, walking with difficulty, and often confused because you are old or sick: *a doddering old man*

dodge

duck

dodge

dodge

dodge[1] /dɑdʒ/ *v.* **1** [I,T] to move quickly and avoid someone or something: *Cyclists should take care to dodge the potholes and bumps in the road.* | [+ into/out/behind etc.] *George dodged around the truck.* **2** [T] to avoid talking about something or doing something that you do not want to do: *Senator O'Brian skillfully dodged the reporter's question.* | *When asked about his enormous salary, he dodged the issue, saying, "I don't like discussing cash."* **3 dodge a bullet** to avoid something that could hurt you or make you fail: *The space shuttle crew dodged a bullet by making a successful flight with a badly damaged temperature sensor.*

dodge[2] *n.* [C] **1** INFORMAL something dishonest that you do to avoid a responsibility or a law: *Flanders insisted he was not using his medical condition as a dodge to avoid testifying.* | *IRS attorneys have called the church a **tax dodge** (=a way to avoid paying taxes).* **2** a sudden forward or sideways movement to avoid someone or something

dodge ball /ˈ. ./ *n.* [U] a game played by children in which you try to avoid being hit by a large rubber ball thrown by the other players

Dodge Cit·y /ˌdɑdʒ ˈsɪti/ a city in the U.S. state of Kansas

dodg·er /ˈdɑdʒɚ/ *n.* [C] **a tax/draft dodger** someone who uses dishonest methods to avoid paying taxes or serving in the army

do·do /ˈdoʊdoʊ/ *n.* [C] **1** a large bird that was unable to fly and does not exist anymore **2** INFORMAL a stupid person

doe /doʊ/ *n.* [C] a female DEER, rabbit, and some other animals —compare BUCK[1] (3)

do·er /ˈduɚ/ *n.* [C] someone who does things instead of just thinking or talking about them: *The people of our grandparents' generation were doers, not talkers.* —see also EVILDOER, WRONGDOER

does /dəz; *strong* dʌz/ *v.* the third person singular of the present tense of DO[1] and DO[2]

does·n't /ˈdʌzənt/ *v.* the short form of "does not": *She doesn't want to go.*

doff /dɑf, dɔf/ *v.* [T] OLD-FASHIONED to take off a piece of clothing, especially your hat: *Lasorda doffed his cap and bowed.* —opposite DON[1]

dog[1] /dɔg/ *n.* [C]
1 animal a very common animal with four legs that is often kept as a pet or used for guarding buildings: *the family dog*
2 woman INFORMAL, OFFENSIVE an ugly woman: *Most of the women he goes out with are dogs.*
3 dog eat dog used when describing a situation in which people compete against each other and will do anything to get what they want: *The media lead young people to believe that we live in a dog-eat-dog world.*
4 go to the dogs INFORMAL if an organization, company etc. is going to the dogs, it is getting much worse and will be difficult to improve: *This country's really going to the dogs.*
5 every dog has its/his day an expression used to mean that even the most unimportant person has a time in their life when they are successful and noticed
6 food INFORMAL a HOT DOG[1] (1)
7 it's a dog's life SPOKEN used to say that life is difficult and full of hard work and worry, with very little pleasure
8 poor quality INFORMAL something that is not of good quality: *It was a dog of a movie.*
9 he is/you are a (dirty) dog INFORMAL used to say that a man is not nice or respectable: *He's such a dog. I can't believe he would cheat on you like that.*
10 feet dogs [plural] INFORMAL feet: *Boy, my dogs really hurt.*
11 put on the dog OLD-FASHIONED to behave or dress in a way that makes people notice how wealthy, intelligent etc. you are, especially when this annoys people
12 a dog in the manger someone who will not let other people use or have something, even though they do not need it themselves
13 dog and pony show INFORMAL a talk on a particular subject, especially one that uses a lot of pictures, CHARTS[1] (1), and GRAPHs and that is used to try to get people's approval
14 male animal a male dog, FOX, and some other animals —compare BITCH[1] (4) —see also **be in the doghouse** (DOGHOUSE (2)), **a/the hair of the dog (that bit you)** (HAIR (13)), **(you) lucky dog!** (LUCKY (8)), SHAGGY-DOG STORY, **let sleeping dogs lie** (SLEEP[1] (7)), **it's (a case of) the tail wagging the dog** (TAIL[1] (12)), **top dog** (TOP[2] (6))

dog[2] *v.* **dogged, dogging** [T] **1** if a problem, bad luck etc. dogs you, it does not go away and causes trouble for a long time: *Plans for the new campus have been dogged by controversy from the start.* **2** to follow closely behind someone: *The press dogged him relentlessly.* **3 dog sb** SLANG **a)** to make jokes about someone and laugh at them in order to embarrass them, in either a friendly or an unkind way: *Those guys kept dogging me about my beard, so I finally shaved it off.* **b)** to defeat someone badly, especially in a sport or a game **4 dog it** INFORMAL to not try as hard as you should or need to in order to do something: *Quit dogging it and do your work.*

dog bis·cuit /ˈ. ,../ *n.* [C] a small dry hard cookie for dogs

dog·catch·er /ˈdɔgˌkætʃɚ/ *n.* [C] someone whose job is to catch dogs that are loose or that do not have owners

dog col·lar /ˈ. ,../ *n.* [C] **1** a collar worn by dogs, onto which a LEASH (=a piece of rope used to control a dog) can be attached **2** INFORMAL a stiff round white collar worn by priests

dog days /ˈ. ./ *n.* [plural] LITERARY **1** the hot uncomfortable days in July and August: *the dog days of summer* **2** a period of time when not very much is done or when someone is not successful: *Another loss proves that these are truly dog days for the Broncos.*

dog door /ˈ. ./ *n.* [C] a small door cut in a door of the house that a dog or cat can go in and out of

doge /doʊdʒ/ *n.* [C] the highest government official in Venice and in Genoa in the past

dog-eared /ˈ. ./ *adj.* dog-eared books or papers have been used so much that the corners are turned down or torn: *Ruth clutched a dog-eared Bible in one hand.* —**dog-ear** *v.* [T]

dog·fight /ˈdɔgfaɪt/ *n.* [C] **1** an organized fight between dogs **2** a fight between armed airplanes

dog·fish /ˈdɔgˌfɪʃ/ *n. plural* **dogfish** [C] a type of small SHARK

dog·ged /ˈdɔgɪd/ *adj.* dogged actions or behavior show that you are very determined to continue doing something: *He was admired for his dogged determination to learn the language.* —**doggedly** *adv.* —**doggedness** *n.* [U]

dog·ge·rel /'dɔgərəl, 'da-/ *n.* [U] poetry that is silly or funny and not intended to be serious: *The Fool in "King Lear" speaks mostly doggerel.*

dog·gie /'dɔgi/ *n.* [C] another spelling of DOGGY

dog·gone /ˌdɔ'gɔn◂/ *v.* [T] SPOKEN **doggone it** used when you are annoyed: *Doggone it! I can't find my purse.* —**doggone, doggoned** SPOKEN *adj.*: *Why is she trying to look so doggone young?*

dog·gy, doggie /'dɔgi/ *n.* [C] a word meaning "dog," used especially by or when speaking to young children

doggy bag /'.. ˌ./ *n.* [C] a small bag for taking home food that is left over from a meal, especially from a restaurant

doggy pad·dle /'.. ˌ../ *n.* [C] DOG PADDLE

doggy style /'.. ˌ./ *n.* [adv.] SLANG if two people have sex doggy style, the man is above and behind his partner

dog han·dler /'. ˌ../ *n.* [C] a police officer who works with a trained dog

dog·house /'dɔghaʊs/ *n.* **1** [C] a small house made for a dog to sleep in **2 be in the doghouse** INFORMAL to be in a situation in which someone is annoyed with you because you have done something wrong: *I'm in the doghouse for forgetting Valentine's Day.*

do·gie /'dougi/ *n.* [C] a CALF (=baby cow) without a mother

dog·leg /'dɔgleg/ *n.* [C] a place in a road, path etc. where it changes direction suddenly: *Poppy Hills Golf Course is filled with doglegs.* —**dogleg** *v.* [I]

dog·ma /'dɔgmə, 'dagmə/ *n.* [C,U] a particular belief or set of beliefs that people are expected to accept without questioning them: *The dogma of the free market should be re-examined.*

dog·mat·ic /dɔg'mætɪk/ *adj.* having ideas or beliefs that you will not change and that you expect other people to accept: *Her employees find her bossy and dogmatic.* —**dogmatically** /-kli/ *adv.*

dog·ma·tis·m /'dɔgmə,tɪzəm/ *n.* [U] attitudes or behavior that are dogmatic —**dogmatist** *n.* [C]

dog·ma·tize /'dɔgmə,taɪz/ *v.* [I + **about**] to speak, write, or act in a dogmatic way

do-good·er /'du ˌgʊdɚ/ *n.* [C] someone who does things to help people who are poor or need help, but who sometimes is annoying because they get involved when they are not wanted

dog pad·dle /'. ˌ../ also **doggy paddle** INFORMAL *n.* [singular] a simple way of swimming by moving your legs and arms like a swimming dog

dog show /'. ./ *n.* [C] a competition in which dogs are judged according to their appearance and sometimes according to the things they can do

dog·sled /'dɔgsled/ *n.* [C] a SLED (=low flat vehicle on metal blades) pulled by dogs over snow

dog tag /'. ./ *n.* [C] a small piece of metal that soldiers wear on a chain around their necks that has their name, blood type, and number written on it

dog-tired /ˌ. '.◂/ *adj.* INFORMAL extremely tired

dog·wood /'dɔgwʊd/ *n.* [C,U] an eastern North American tree or bush with flat white or pink flowers

d'oh /dou/ *interjection* HUMOROUS said when you have just realized that you did something stupid

Do·ha /'douha/ the capital city of Qatar

doi·ly /'dɔɪli/ *n.* [C] a circle of paper or cloth with a pattern cut into it, used for decoration, especially on a plate before you put cakes etc. on it

do·ing /'duɪŋ/ *n.* **1 be sb's (own) doing** if something bad is someone's doing, they did it or did things that caused it: *Nixon may blame others, but the scandal was his own doing.* **2 take some doing** to be hard work: *Getting this old car to run is going to take some doing.* **3 doings** [plural] INFORMAL events or activities: *Fan magazines will bring you up-to-date on the doings of your favorite stars.*

do-it-your·self /ˌ. . .'.◂/ *adj.* **1** a do-it-yourself job, repair etc. is one that you do yourself instead of

paying someone else to do it: *The Yokums' home is a do-it-yourself remodeling job.* **2** a do-it-yourself book, store etc. tells you how to make or repair things yourself, sells you things you need to do this etc.: *His shelves are filled with do-it-yourself manuals.*

Dol·by /'doulbi/ *n.* [U] TRADEMARK a system for reducing unwanted noise when you record music or sounds

dol·drums /'douldrəmz, 'dal-/ *n.* [plural] INFORMAL **1** a state in which something is not improving or developing. *The stock market is much improved from the doldrums of 1990.* | *The manufacturing sector is still in the doldrums, analysts say.* **2** a state in which you feel sad and bored; DEPRESSION: *Beat the summer doldrums by spending a day at the zoo.* | *Fourteen-year-old Trevor is in the doldrums.* **3 the doldrums** an area in the ocean just north of the EQUATOR where the weather can be so calm that sailing ships cannot move

dole¹ /doul/ *v.*
dole sth out *phr. v.* [T] INFORMAL to give something such as money, food, advice etc. in small amounts to a lot of people: [**dole sth out to sb**] *The bill would dole out $850 million to school districts around the country.*

dole² *n.* **the dole** money given by the government to people who need financial help; WELFARE (1)

dole·ful /'doulfəl/ *adj.* very sad: *a doleful look* —**dolefully** *adv.* —**dolefulness** *n.* [U]

doll¹ /dal/ *n.* [C] **1** a child's toy that looks like a small person or baby **2** a very nice person: *Thanks, you're a doll.* **3** OLD-FASHIONED a word used to talk to an attractive young woman, now considered offensive: *Hey, doll, why don't you get me a cup of coffee?*

doll² *v.*
doll sb up *phr. v.* [T] INFORMAL if a woman dolls herself up, she puts on attractive clothes and MAKEUP: *The wives were all dolled up in fancy cocktail dresses.*

dol·lar /'dalɚ/ *n.* [C] **1** written abbreviation **$** the standard unit of money in the U.S., Canada, Australia, New Zealand, and other countries: *These pants cost $26.* **2** a piece of paper money or a coin of this value **3 the dollar** the value of U.S. money in relation to the money of other countries: *The pound rose once again against the dollar.* —see also **feel/look like a million bucks/dollars** (MILLION (5)), **you can bet your bottom dollar** (BET¹ (7))

USAGE NOTE: DOLLAR

SPOKEN-WRITTEN
We say "a two billion dollar debt" or "a fifty dollar loan," but we write "a $2 billion debt" or "a $50 loan."

---

dollar di·plo·ma·cy /ˌ.. .'...◂/ *n.* [U] a way of getting support from other countries for American ideas and aims, by giving them money or by INVESTing in them: *The U.S. has always relied to some degree on dollar diplomacy to fulfill its objectives.*

dol·lar·i·za·tion /ˌdalərə'zeɪʃən/ *n.* [U] the process by which a country's ECONOMY becomes dependent on the U.S. dollar instead of its own money: *The government has taken steps to halt further dollarization of the Russian economy.*

dollars-and-cents /ˌ.. . '.◂/ *adj.* considered in a financial way: *It's an interesting idea, but from a dollars-and-cents point of view it just won't work.*

dollar sign /'.. ˌ./ *n.* [C] **1** a sign ($) that means dollar or dollars: *$1* (=one dollar) | *$3* (=three dollars) **2 see dollar signs** to think that a situation is likely to give you an opportunity to make a lot of money: *Some are unsure about the product, but others see nothing but dollar signs.*

doll·house /'dalhaʊs/ *n.* [C] a small toy house for DOLLS (DOLL¹ (1))

dol·lop /'daləp/ *n.* [C] a small amount of soft food, usually dropped from a spoon in a rounded shape: [**+ of**] *a large dollop of whipped cream* —**dollop** *v.* [T]

dol·ly /'dɑli/ *n. plural* **dollies** [C] **1** another word for a DOLL[1] (1), used by children and when talking to children **2** TECHNICAL a flat frame on wheels used for moving heavy objects

dol·men /'doʊlmən, 'dɑl-/ *n.* [C] TECHNICAL two or more large upright stones supporting a large flat piece of stone, built in ancient times

dol·phin /'dɑlfɪn, 'dɔl-/ *n.* [C] an intelligent ocean animal like a large gray fish with a long pointed nose

dolphin-safe /'.. ,./ *adj.* dolphin-safe fish are caught in a way that does not harm DOLPHINS: *I only buy dolphin-safe tuna.*

dolt /doʊlt/ *n.* [C] OLD-FASHIONED a silly or stupid person —**doltish** *adj.* —**doltishly** *adv.*

-dom /dəm/ *suffix* **1** [in U nouns] the state of being in a particular condition or having a particular quality: *freedom* (=state of being free) | *boredom* (=state of being bored) | *wisdom* (=state of being wise) **2** [in C nouns] **a)** an area ruled in a particular way: *a kingdom* (=place ruled by a king) **b)** a particular rank: *He was rewarded with a dukedom* (=was made a DUKE). **3** [in U nouns] INFORMAL all the people who share the same set of interests, have the same job etc.: *officialdom* (=all government officials)

do·main /doʊ'meɪn, də-/ *n.* [C] FORMAL **1** a particular activity that is controlled by one person, group, organization etc.: *Work in skilled trades and union jobs remains a male domain.* **2** the range of things that are included in a particular subject, type of art, or activity: *The discovery of X-rays added to the domain of natural science.* **3** an area of land owned or controlled by one person, group, or government: *The building was once the domain of the Soviet KGB.* **4** TECHNICAL the set of possible quantities by which something can vary in mathematics —see also EMINENT DOMAIN, PUBLIC DOMAIN

dome /doʊm/ *n.* [C] **1** a round roof on a building or room **2** a shape like a ball cut in half: *the dome of his bald head*

domed /doʊmd/ *adj.* covered with a dome, or shaped like a dome: *Toronto, with its big domed stadium, is a likely site for the Olympic games.*

do·mes·tic[1] /də'mɛstɪk/ *adj.* **1** happening or produced within one country and not involving any other countries: *Most Americans listed domestic issues as their top priority.* | *The airline serves mainly domestic routes.* | *domestic wine* **2** [only before noun] relating to family relationships and life at home: *Manley was arrested for assault and domestic violence* (=violence between husband and wife). **3** someone who is domestic enjoys spending time at home and is good at cooking, cleaning etc. **4** [only before noun] a domestic animal lives on a farm or in someone's home **5** [only before noun] used in the house or home: *Whirlpool is the number one maker of large domestic appliances.* —**domestically** /-kli/ *adv.*

domestic[2] *n.* [C] OLD-FASHIONED a servant who works in a house

do·mes·ti·cate /də'mɛstɪ,keɪt/ *v.* [T] to make an animal able to live with people as a pet or to work for them, especially on a farm —compare TAME[2] (1) —**domestication** /də,mɛstɪ'keɪʃən/ *n.* [U]

do·mes·ti·cat·ed /də'mɛstɪ,keɪtɪd/ *adj.* animals or plants that are domesticated are raised by people and are able to be used for work or food: *The area is populated by domesticated birds such as geese and turkeys.* —opposite WILD[1]

do·mes·tic·i·ty /,doʊmɛ'stɪsəti/ *n.* [U] life at home with your family, or the state of enjoying this life: *a scene of happy domesticity*

domestic part·ner /.,.. '../ *n.* [C] a phrase meaning someone that you live with and have a romantic relationship with, but whom you are not married to —**domestic partnership** *n.* [C,U]

dom·i·cile /'dɑmə,saɪl, 'doʊ-/ *n.* [C] LAW a place where someone lives

dom·i·ciled /'dɑmə,saɪld/ *adj.* LAW **be domiciled in** to live in a particular place

dom·i·cil·i·a·ry /,dɑmə'sɪli,ɛri/ *adj.* FORMAL **domiciliary services/care/visits** etc. care or services at someone's home

dom·i·nance /'dɑmənəns/ *n.* [U] the fact of being more powerful, more important, or more noticeable than other people or things: *military dominance* | [+ in] *Microsoft has grown to dominance in the software market.* | [+ over] *The Buffalo Sabres continued their dominance over the Boston Bruins with a 5–0 win.* | [+ of] *the dominance of Hollywood's film industry*

dom·i·nant[1] /'dɑmənənt/ *adj.* **1** stronger, more important, more common, or more noticeable than other people or things: *TV is the dominant source of information in our society.* **2** controlling other people or things, or showing this quality: *dominant and aggressive behavior* **3** TECHNICAL a physical feature that is dominant can appear in a child even if it has been passed on from only one parent: *Brown eyes are dominant.* —compare RECESSIVE

dominant[2] *n.* [singular] the fifth note of a musical SCALE of eight notes

dom·i·nate /'dɑmə,neɪt/ *v.* **1** [I,T] to control someone or something, or to have more power or importance than them: *Movie directing is a profession dominated by men.* | *New Orleans dominated throughout the game.* **2** [I,T] to be the most important feature of something: *The murder trial has dominated the news this week.* **3** [T] to be larger or more noticeable than anything else in a place or situation: *A pair of red-and-gold boots dominated the display.* —**dominating** /'dɑmə,neɪtɪŋ/ *adj.* —**domination** /,dɑmə'neɪʃən/ *n.* [U]

dom·i·na·trix /,dɑmɪ'neɪtrɪks/ *n.* [C] a woman who is the stronger partner in a sado-masochistic (SADO-MASOCHISM) sexual relationship

dom·i·neer·ing /,dɑmə'nɪrɪŋ/ *adj.* someone who is domineering tries to control other people without considering how they feel or what they want: *a domineering mother* —**domineer** *v.* [I]

Dom·i·nic /'dɑmɪnɪk/, **Saint** (?1170–1221) a Spanish religious leader who started the Dominican group of Christian FRIARS

Dom·i·ni·ca /,dɑmə'nikə, də'mɪnɪkə/ a country which is an island in the Caribbean Sea —**Dominican** *n.*, *adj.*

Do·min·i·can /də'mɪnɪkən/ *n.* [C] a member of a Christian religious group who leads a holy life —**Dominican** *adj.*

Do·min·i·can Re·pub·lic, the /də,mɪnɪkən rɪ'pʌblɪk/ a country in the Caribbean Sea on the island of Hispaniola, which it shares with Haiti —**Dominican** *n.*, *adj.*

Do·min·i·cans, the /də'mɪnɪkənz/ a Christian religious ORDER of MONKS —**Dominican** *adj.*

do·min·ion /də'mɪnyən/ *n.* **1** [U] LITERARY the power or right to rule people or control something | **have/hold dominion over sb/sth** *Alexander the Great held dominion over a vast area.* **2** also **Dominion** [C] one of the countries that was a member of the British Commonwealth in past times: *Canada became a self-governing dominion of Great Britain in 1867.* **3** [C] FORMAL the land owned or controlled by one person or a government —see also COLONY (1), PROTECTORATE

dom·i·no /'dɑmə,noʊ/ *n. plural* **dominoes 1** [C] a small piece of wood, plastic etc. with a different number of spots on each half of its top side, used in playing a game **2 the domino effect** a situation in which one event or action causes several other things to happen, one after the other: *The workers' strike delayed production and had a domino effect on several other deadlines.*

dom·i·noes /'dɑmə,noʊz/ *n.* [U] the game played using dominoes

don[1] /dɑn/ *v.* **donned, donning** [T] FORMAL to put on a hat, coat etc. —opposite DOFF

don[2] *n.* [C] the leader of a Mafia organization

do·nate /'dooneɪt, doo'neɪt/ v. [I,T] **1** to give something useful to a person or an organization that needs help: [donate sth to sb/sth] *One school donated $500 to the Red Cross.* **2 donate blood/organs etc.** to give some of your blood or part of your body to be used for medical purposes: *There is no risk of getting AIDS when donating blood.*

do·na·tion /doo'neɪʃən/ n. **1** [C] something, especially money, that you give to a person or an organization that needs help: *Please make a donation to UNICEF.* **2** [U] the act of giving something to help a person or an organization: *The booklet provides information about organ donation and transplants.*

done¹ /dʌn/ v. the past participle of DO¹ and DO²

done² adj. [not before noun, no comparative] **1** finished or completed, or at the point of completion: *The job's almost done.* | *Well, I'm done. I'm going home.* | [+ **with**] *Do you want to read this magazine? I'm done with it.* **2** cooked enough to be eaten: *I think the hamburgers are done.* —compare OVERDONE, UNDERDONE **3 it's a done deal** INFORMAL used to mean that an agreement has been made and it cannot be changed **4 be done for** INFORMAL to be in serious trouble and likely to fail or die: *If we get caught we're done for.* **5 be done in** INFORMAL to be extremely tired: *I've got to sit down – I'm done in.* **6 be done** to be considered acceptable behavior in social situations: *Showing affection in public just isn't done in Japan.* **7 be/have done with sth** to stop talking about or doing something: *Oh, buy it and have done with it!* —see also DO²

done³ interjection said in order to accept a deal that someone offers you: *"How about I give you $25 for it?" "Done!"*

dong /dɑŋ, dɔŋ/ n. [C] **1** the unit of money in Vietnam **2** VULGAR the male sex organ

don·gle /'dɑŋgəl, 'dɔŋ-/ n. [C] a small piece of equipment that you attach to a computer in order to use particular SOFTWARE

Don Juan /ˌdɑn 'wɑn/ n. [C] a man who is good at persuading women to have sex with him

don·key /'dɑŋki, 'dʌŋ-, 'dɔŋ-/ n. plural **donkeys** [C] a gray or brown animal similar to a horse, but smaller and with long ears

Donne /dʌn/, **John** (?1572–1631) an English poet known for his love poetry and religious poems

do·nor /'doonɚ/ n. [C] **1** a person, group etc. that gives something, especially money, to help an organization: *The museum received $10,000 from an anonymous donor.* **2** someone who gives some of their blood or part of their body to be used for medical purposes: *Finding a liver donor may be difficult.*

donor card /'.. ˌ./ n. [C] a card that you carry to show that when you die, a doctor can take parts of your body to use for medical purposes

do·no·thing /'. ˌ../ adj. [only before noun] INFORMAL lazy or unwilling to make any changes, especially in politics: *The voters are fed up with this do-nothing Congress.* —**do-nothing** n. [C]

Don Qui·xo·te /ˌdɑn ki'ooti, -'hooti/ n. [singular] someone who is determined to change what is wrong, but who does it in a way that is silly or not practical —see also QUIXOTIC

don't /doont/ v. **1** the short form of "do not": *Don't worry!* | *You know him, don't you?* —see also **dos and don'ts** (DO³ (1)) **2** SPOKEN, NONSTANDARD an incorrect short form of "does not": *She don't like it.*

do·nut /'doonʌt/ n. [C] another spelling of DOUGHNUT

doo·bie /'dubi/ n. [C] OLD-FASHIONED, SLANG a MARIJUANA cigarette

doo·dad /'dudæd/ n. [C] INFORMAL a small and unnecessary object, especially one whose name you have forgotten or do not know: *The hotel gift shop sells souvenirs and other doodads.*

doo·dle /'dudl/ v. [I,T] to draw shapes, lines, or patterns without really thinking about what you are doing: *Margo was doodling on a legal pad.* —**doodle** n. [C]

doo·doo /'dudu/ n. [U] INFORMAL a word for solid

waste from your body, used especially by or when speaking to children —**doo-doo** v. [I]

doo·fus /'dufəs/ n. [C] INFORMAL a silly or stupid person

doo·hick·ey /'duˌhɪki/ n. [C] a small object whose name you have forgotten or do not know, especially a part of a machine

doom¹ /dum/ v. [T usually passive] to make someone or something certain to fail, be destroyed, or die: *The threat of a costly legal battle doomed the proposal.* | [doom sb/sth to do sth] *Are we doomed to lose our memory as we get older?* | [doom sb/sth to sth] *Over 50,000 species a year are being doomed to eventual extinction.* | *The marriage seems doomed to failure.* —**doomed** adj.

doom² n. [U] **1** destruction, death, or failure that you are unable to avoid: *I sat there, overwhelmed by a sense of imminent doom* (=death, failure etc. that will come very soon). | *The poor performances do not necessarily spell doom for the movie* (=mean that it will fail). | *Thousands of soldiers met their doom* (=died, on this very field). **2 doom and gloom** HUMOROUS a state or attitude in which there is no hope for the future: *The article is full of doom and gloom about the environment.*

doom·say·er /'dumˌseɪɚ/ n. [C] someone who says that bad things are going to happen: *Doomsayers predict that one day California will tumble into the sea.*

Dooms·day /'dumzdeɪ/ n. [C,U] **1** till/until Doomsday INFORMAL forever: *You could wait till Doomsday and he'd never show up.* **2** the last day of the Earth's existence

doom·ster /'dumstɚ/ n. [C] INFORMAL someone who always thinks something bad is going to happen: *Doomsters are predicting a rough Christmas season for merchants.*

door /dɔr/ n. [C] **1** the large flat piece of wood, glass etc. that you push or pull in order to go into a building, room, car etc. | **open/close/shut the door** *She closed the garage door and headed to the house.* | **front/back/side door** *A Christmas wreath hung on the front door.* | **kitchen/bathroom/office etc. door** *Leave the bathroom door open when you're done in the shower.* | **knock on/at the door** *I knocked on the door, but there was no answer.* | *He slammed the door* (=shut it very hard) *and stormed off.* | [+ **to**] *This is the door to the fitness center.* —compare GATE (1) **2** the space made by an open door; DOORWAY | **out/through a door** *Go out the double doors and turn left.* **3 get the door** to open or close a door: *Bob, would you get the door? My hands are full.* **4 at the door** if someone is at the door, they are waiting for you to open it and have usually knocked: *I think there's somebody at the door.* **5 two/three etc. doors down** a place that is a particular number of rooms, houses etc. away from where you are: *Her office is two doors down.* **6 (from) door to door a)** between one place and another: *If you drive, it should take you 20 minutes door to door.* **b)** going to each house in a street or area to sell something, collect money etc.: *We went door to door asking people to sponsor us in the race.* —see also DOOR-TO-DOOR **7 show/see sb to the door** to walk with someone to the main door of a building: *My secretary will show you to the door.* **8 out of doors** outside; OUTDOORS **9 shut/ close the door on sth** to make something impossible: *A loss in this election will not necessarily close the door on the campaign.* —see also **answer the phone/the door/a call** (ANSWER¹ (4)), **at death's door** (DEATH (8)), BACK DOOR, **behind closed doors** (CLOSED (5)), FRONT DOOR, **lay sth at sb's door** (LAY¹ (18)), NEXT DOOR, OPEN DOOR POLICY, **show sb the door** (SHOW¹ (14)), **work the door** (WORK¹ (28))

door·bell /'dɔrbɛl/ n. [C] a button outside a house or apartment that you push so that people inside know you are there, or the bell that this button rings: *I rang the doorbell and waited.*

do-or-die, **do or die** /ˌ. . '. './ adj. something do-or-die has to be done or you will fail completely: *The airline* *spent $120 million in a do-or-die effort to save the company.*

door·jamb /'dɔrdʒæm/ *n.* [C] one of two upright posts on either side of a doorway; DOORPOST

door·keep·er /'dɔr,kipɚ/ *n.* [C] someone who guards the main door of a large building and lets people in and out

door·knob /'dɔrnɑb/ *n.* [C] a round handle that you turn to open a door

door·knock·er /'dɔr,nɑkɚ/ *n.* [C] a heavy metal ring or bar on a door, that visitors use to knock with

door·man /'dɔrmæn, -mən/ *n. plural* **doormen** /-men, -mən/ [C] a man who works in a hotel or apartment building watching the door, helping people find taxis etc. —compare PORTER (3)

door·mat /'dɔrmæt/ *n.* [C] **1** a thick piece of material just outside or inside a door for you to clean your shoes on **2** INFORMAL someone who lets other people treat them badly and who never complains about it

D

door·nail /'dɔrneɪl/ *n.* [singular] —see **dead as a doornail** (DEAD[1] (24))

door·plate /'dɔrpleɪt/ *n.* [C] a flat piece of metal attached to the door of a house or building, that shows the name of the person or company that lives or works inside

door·post /'dɔrpoust/ *n.* [C] a DOORJAMB

door prize /'. ./ *n.* [C] a prize given to someone who has the winning number on their ticket for a show, dance etc.

door·sill /'dɔr,sɪl/ *n.* [C] the part of a door frame that you step across when you go through a DOORWAY

door·step /'dɔrstɛp/ *n.* [C] **1** a step just outside a door to a house or building: *A cat sat patiently on the doorstep.* **2 on/at sb's doorstep a)** at your home, or very near to it: *Janet turned up on her sister's doorstep, needing a place to stay.* **b)** affecting a particular person or group, rather than happening somewhere far away: *Today, there's a new racial conflict on our doorstep.*

door·stop /'dɔrstɑp/ *n.* [C] **1** something you put under or against a door to keep it open: *They'd been using the encyclopedia as a doorstop.* **2** a rubber object attached to a wall to stop a door from hitting it when it is opened

door-to-door, door to door /,. . '. ./ *adj., adv.* visiting each house in a street or area, usually to sell something, collect money, or ask for votes: *a door-to-door salesman* | *In 1964, I campaigned door to door for Lyndon Johnson.*

door·way /'dɔrweɪ/ *n.* [C] **1** the space where a door opens into a room or building: *a wide doorway into the kitchen* **2** a way for you to get what you want in order to succeed: *Large corporations are seeking a doorway to the markets of the Far East.*

door·yard /'dɔryɑrd/ *n.* [C] OLD-FASHIONED the area in front of the door of a house

doo·zy, doozie /'duzi/ *n.* [C] INFORMAL something that is extremely good, bad, strange, big etc.: *Then I went on a drinking binge that was a real doozy.*

do·pa·mine /'doupə,min/ *n.* [U] a chemical in the brain that is necessary for the normal control of muscle movements

dope[1] /doup/ *n.* INFORMAL **1** [U] a drug that is not legal, especially MARIJUANA: *I used to smoke dope all the time.* **2** [C] SPOKEN someone who is stupid or has done something stupid: *Pam, you dope!* **3** [U] new information about someone or something, especially information that not many people know: [+ on] *Reporters were anxious for the latest dope on Bo Jackson.* **4** [U] medicine, especially medicine that makes you sleep easily

dope[2] also **dope sb up** *v.* [T] INFORMAL to take a drug or to give a person or animal a drug, in order to sleep, feel better, or work better: *They dope the elephants in order to tag them.* —see also DOPING

dope[3] *adj.* SLANG good or satisfactory: *If we got to be friends, that'd be dope.*

dope·head /'douphɛd/ *n.* [C] SLANG someone who takes a lot of illegal drugs

dop·ey /'doupi/ *adj.* INFORMAL **1** slow to react mentally or physically, as if you have taken a drug: *I feel really dopey, and I've had a headache all day.* **2** slightly stupid: *What is it that makes politicians do such dopey things?*

dop·ing /'doupɪŋ/ *n.* [U] the practice of taking drugs to improve your performance in a sport: *Several athletes at the Pan American Games failed a doping test.*

dop·pel·gang·er /'dɑpəl,gæŋɚ, -,gɛŋɚ/ *n.* [C] **1** an imaginary spirit that looks exactly like a living person, but behaves very differently **2** someone who looks exactly like someone else

Dop·pler ef·fect /'dɑplɚ ɪ,fɛkt/ *n.* [singular] a change in how someone hears a sound or sees a light that is moving toward or away from them, so that a sound seems higher as it is moving closer to them, and a light seems more blue

Do·ri·an /'dɔriən/ *n.* [C] one of the people that lived in the southern part of ancient Greece from the 11th century B.C.

Dor·ic /'dɔrɪk, 'dɑr-/ *adj.* in the oldest and simplest of the Greek building styles: *a Doric column* —compare CORINTHIAN, IONIC

dork /dɔrk/ *n.* [C] INFORMAL someone who you think is stupid, because they behave strangely or wear strange clothes: *The people who go there are dorks.* —**dorky** *adj.*

dorm /dɔrm/ *n.* [C] INFORMAL a DORMITORY: *Yeah, I know him, he lived in my dorm.* | *Each dorm room is shared by two students.*

dor·mant /'dɔrmənt/ *adj.* **1** not active or not growing right now, but able to be active later: *Wait to prune your roses until they are fully dormant in January.* | *a dormant volcano* | *The virus can lie dormant in the blood for up to 12 years.* **2** not used or not active for a period of time: *Accounts that remain dormant for three years must be reported to the state.* —**dormancy** *n.* [U]

dor·mer /'dɔrmɚ/ also **dormer win·dow** /'.. ,../ *n.* [C] a window built upright in the slope of a roof, so that it sticks out from the roof

dor·mi·to·ry /'dɔrmə,tɔri/ *n. plural* **dormitories** [C] **1** a large building at a college or university where students live **2** a large room for several people to sleep in, for example in a prison or a HOSTEL: *The second riot began just after 6 p.m. at a medium security dormitory.*

dor·mouse /'dɔrmaus/ *n.* [C] a small European forest animal similar to a mouse, with a long furry tail

dor·sal /'dɔrsəl/ *adj.* [only before noun] TECHNICAL relating to the back of an animal or fish: *a shark's dorsal fin* —compare VENTRAL —see picture at BARRACUDA

do·ry /'dɔri/ *n. plural* **dories** [C] a boat that has a flat bottom and is used for fishing —see also HUNKY-DORY

DOS /dɑs, dɔs/ *n.* [U] TRADEMARK Disk Operating System; SOFTWARE that is loaded onto a computer system to make all the different parts work together

dos·age /'dousɪdʒ/ *n.* [C usually singular] the amount of medicine that you should take at one time: *Lowering the dosage can stop some side effects.*

dose[1] /dous/ *n.* [C] **1** a measured amount of a medicine: [+ of] *a dose of heart medicine* | *Doctors say that a low dose is just as effective as a high dose, and causes fewer side effects.* **2** an amount of something such as a chemical or poison that affects you: [+ of] *People living near the Hanford site were exposed to doses of radiation.* | *Niacin can be harmful if used in large doses* (=if you take a lot each time you take it). **3** an amount of something that you do or experience at one time: *The banks need a healthy dose of competition.* | *It's a very amusing book if read in small doses* (=a little at a time).

dose[2] *v.* [T] also **dose up** to take medicine or another type of drug, or to give this to someone: [+ with] *The mental patients were all dosed with psychotropic drugs.*

do-si-do /,dou si 'dou/ *n.* [singular] an action in

SQUARE DANCING in which partners walk around each other with their backs toward each other —do·si·do v. [I]

Dos Pas·sos /dɑs ˈpæsəs/**, John** (1896–1970) a U.S. writer of NOVELS

dos·si·er /ˈdɑsi‚eɪ, ˈdɔ-/ n. [C] a set of papers containing detailed information about a person or subject; FILE¹ (1): *The U.S. government kept a secret dossier on him for 27 years.*

dost /dʌst/ v. **thou dost** OLD USE or BIBLICAL you do

Dos·to·yev·sky /‚dɑstəˈyɛfski, ‚dɑstɔɪ-/**, Fy·o·dor** /ˈfiədər/ also **Dostoevsky** (1821–1881) a Russian writer, famous for his NOVELS

dot¹ /dɑt/ n. **1** [C] a round mark or spot: *His fabric prints include lots of roses, hearts, and dots.* —see also **connect the dots** (CONNECT (8)) **2** [C] SPOKEN what you say when you read the sign (.) in an Internet address or a computer CODE: *You can visit our website at www.awl.com* (=said as, "W-W-W dot A-W-L dot com"). **3 on the dot** INFORMAL exactly at a particular time: *I'm leaving work at twelve-thirty on the dot.* **4** [C] something that looks like a small spot because it is so far away: *The plane was just a dot in the sky.* **5** [C] a short sound or flash of light used when sending messages by MORSE CODE —compare DASH² (6) —see also POLKA DOT

dot² v. **dotted, dotting** [T] **1** to mark something by putting a dot on it or above it: *She never dots her i's.* **2** [usually passive] to spread things far apart from each other over a wide area: *Chalet-style homes dot the forested hillside.* | [be dotted with sth] *The hills of Tejon are dotted with California live oaks.* | [be dotted around sth] *There were little piles of toys dotted around the room.* **3** to put a very small amount of something on a surface, or in several places on a surface: *Dot the apples with butter cut into small pieces.* **4 dot the i's and cross the t's** INFORMAL to deal with all the details when you are finishing something: *Well, we haven't dotted the i's and crossed the t's, but the contract's nearly ready.* —dotted adj. —see also DOTTED LINE

dot·age /ˈdoʊtɪdʒ/ n. **in your dotage** when you are old: *Thurmond is as mean in his dotage as he was in his younger days.*

dot-com, dot.com, dot com /‚dɑt ˈkɑm/ adj. [only before noun] INFORMAL relating to a company whose business involves the Internet —dot-com n. [C] —dot-com v. [T] *We'll have to decide whether to dot-com our business.*

dote /doʊt/ v.
dote on/upon sb phr. v. [T] to love someone very much and to show this by your actions: *He doted on Dorothy, his 6-year-old niece.* —doting adj. [only before noun] *a doting parent* —dotingly adv.

doth /dʌθ/ v. OLD USE OR BIBLICAL an old form of "does"

dot-ma·trix print·er /‚.. .. ‚../ n. [C] a machine connected to a computer, that prints letters, numbers etc. using many small DOTS

dotted line /‚.. ˈ./ n. [C] a series of printed or drawn DOTS that form a line: *Cut along the dotted lines.*

dot·ty /ˈdɑti/ adj. OLD-FASHIONED slightly crazy or likely to behave strangely: *a dotty old lady*

dou·ble¹ /ˈdʌbəl/ adj.
1 of two parts consisting of two parts that are similar or exactly the same: *She drove over the double yellow line and crashed head-on into a truck.* | *a double cheeseburger* (=one with two layers of meat) **2 twice as big** twice as big, twice as much, or twice as many as usual, or twice as big, much, or many as something else: *Leave the dough in a warm place to rise until it is double in bulk.* | *These classes are taught over a double class period by one teacher.* **3 for two people** made to be used by two people: *a double room* —compare SINGLE¹ (5) **4 with two different uses** combining two different uses, reasons, qualities etc.; DUAL: *She's doing a double major in political science and economics.* | *Mortensen had a double motive for going to San Francisco: to see his kids and to apply for a job.* **5 a double meaning/nature/life etc.** two very different or opposite meanings, qualities, lives etc. that one thing or person has at the same time: *The title*

has a double meaning. | *It was a shock to find out that Dad was leading a double life* (=he had two very different lives, each one of which is a secret from the other) *all those years.* **6** flower a double flower has more than the usual number of PETALS —see also DOUBLY

double² n.
1 twice the size [C,U] something that is twice the size, quantity, value, or strength of something else: *Scotch and water, please – make it a double.* **2** similar person [C] someone who looks very much like someone else: *Caroline is virtually her mother's double.* **3** in movies [C] an actor who takes the place of another actor in a movie, especially because the acting involves doing something dangerous: *a stunt double* | *Goodrich worked as a double for John Wayne.* **4** baseball [C] a hit in baseball that allows the BATTER to reach second BASE: *Hrbek led the inning with a double.* **5** tennis doubles [U] a game played between two pairs of players: *the men's doubles* —compare **singles** (SINGLE² (3)) —see also MIXED DOUBLES **6** room a room in a hotel for two people: *Rooms cost $95 for a double.* **7 on the double** very quickly and without any delay: *I headed for the Commander's office on the double.* **8 double or nothing** a decision in a game when you must decide to do something that will either win you twice as much money or make you lose it all

double³ v. **1** [I,T] to become twice as large or twice as much, or to make something twice as large or twice as much: *Building costs have doubled since then.* | *The federal government has doubled its tax on liquor.* | [+ in] *Our house has doubled in value since we bought it.* **2** also **double sth over/up** [T] to fold something in half: *Ralph doubled up his blankets and put them at the foot of the bed.* **3** [I] if a BATTER in a game of baseball doubles, he hits the ball far enough to run to second BASE safely **4 double your fists** to curl your fingers tightly to make FISTS, usually in order to be ready to fight
double as sb/sth phr. v. [T] to have a second use, job, or purpose as something else: *Sidewalks double as parking lots.*
double back phr. v. [I] to turn around and go back the way you have come: *I doubled back and headed south.*
double up phr. v. **1** also **double over** [I,T **double** sb **up**] to suddenly bend at the waist because you are laughing too much or are in pain and cannot stand up: *We doubled over, laughing so hard it hurt.* | *be doubled up/over with* *He was doubled up with cramps from the greasy stew.* **2** [I] to share something, especially a house or a BEDROOM: [+ with] *Many can't afford their own homes and double up with family.*

double⁴ adv. **1 see double** to have something wrong with your eyes so that you see two things instead of one: *Selma complained of seeing double.* **2 be bent double** to be bent over a long way: *The old man was bent double under his load.* **3 fold sth double** to fold something in half to make it twice as thick

double⁵ quantifier twice as much or twice as many: *The new library will be double the size of the present one.*

double-act /ˈ.. ‚./ n. [C] two actors, especially COMEDIANS, who perform together

double a·gent /‚.. ˈ../ n. [C] someone who finds out an enemy country's secrets for their own country, but who also gives secrets to the enemy —compare SPY¹

double-bar·reled /‚.. ˈ..‚/ **1** a double-barreled gun has two places where the BULLETS come out **2** with two purposes: *a double-barreled question* **3** very strong or using a lot of force: *a double-barreled threat*

double bass /ˌdʌbəl 'beɪs/ also **bass** n. [C] a very large musical instrument shaped like a VIOLIN that the musician plays standing up

double bed /ˌ.. './ n. [C] a bed made for two people to sleep in —see picture at BED

double bill /ˌ.. './ n. [C] an occasion when two plays, performances, movies etc. are shown or performed one after the other at a theater: *The jazz festival features the double bill of singers Mel Torme and Cleo Laine.* —compare DOUBLE FEATURE

double bind /ˌ.. './ n. [C usually singular] a situation in which any choice you make will have bad results

double-blind /ˌ.. '.◂/ adj. TECHNICAL a double-blind EXPERIMENT or study compares two or more groups in which neither the scientists nor the people being studied know which group is being tested and which group is not

double bluff /ˌ.. './ n. [C] an attempt to deceive someone by telling them the truth, hoping that they will think you are lying

double boil·er /ˌ.. '../ n. [C] a pot for cooking food, consisting of one pan resting on top of another pan with hot water in it

double-book /ˌ.. './ v. [I,T] to promise the same seat in a theater, on an airplane etc. to more than one person —**double-booking** n. [U]

double-breast·ed /ˌ.. '..◂/ adj. a double-breasted JACKET, coat etc. has two sets of buttons —compare SINGLE-BREASTED

double-check /ˌ.. './ v. [I,T] to check something again so that you are completely sure that it is safe, ready, correct etc.: *Double-check that all the information was copied correctly.*

double chin /ˌ.. './ n. [C] a fold of loose skin under someone's chin that looks like a second chin

double-cross /ˌ.. './ v. [T] to cheat someone, especially after you have already agreed to do something dishonest with them: *He was killed for double-crossing his Mob bosses.* —**double cross** n. [C] —**double-crosser** n. [C]

double date /ˌ.. './ n. [C] an occasion when two COUPLES meet to go to a movie, restaurant etc. together —**double-date** v. [I,T]

Dou·ble·day /'dʌbəlˌdeɪ/, **Ab·ner** /'æbnɚ/ (1819–1893) a U.S. army officer who is known as the inventor of baseball

double-deal·er /ˌ.. '../ n. [C] INFORMAL someone who deceives other people —**double-dealing** n. [U]

double-deck·er /ˌ.. '..◂/ n. [C] **1** a bus with two levels **2** a SANDWICH made with meat, cheese etc. between three pieces of bread

double-di·git /ˌ.. '..◂/ adj. relating to the numbers 10 to 99, especially as a PERCENTAGE: *double-digit inflation* —see also DOUBLE FIGURES

double-dip¹ /ˌ.. './ n. [C] an ICE CREAM CONE with two balls of ice cream

double-dip² v. [I] to get money from two places at once, usually in a way that is not legal or not approved of: *Some farmers double-dip into federal irrigation and crop subsidies.*

double-dip re·ces·sion /ˌ.. . .'../ n. [C usually singular] INFORMAL a situation in which a country's ECONOMY is weak, starts to get strong again, then becomes weak again

double-dutch /ˌ.. './ n. [U] a game in which one child jumps over two long ropes that are being swung around in a circle by other children

double du·ty /ˌ.. '../ n. do double duty to do more than one job or be used for more than one thing at the same time: *Choose a sofa that will do double duty as a guest bed.*

double-edged /ˌ.. '.◂/ adj. **1 a double-edged sword** something good that also has a bad effect: *For Lansbury, the series has been a double-edged sword: the more popular it becomes, the harder she has to work.* **2** having two very different meanings: *a double-edged joke* **3** having two cutting edges: *a double-edged knife*

dou·ble en·ten·dre /ˌdubəl ɑn'tɑndrə, ˌdʌbɑ-/ n. [C] a word or phrase that may be understood in two different ways, one of which is often sexual

double fault /ˌ.. './ n. [C] two mistakes, one after another, when you are serving (SERVE¹ (10)) in tennis, that make you lose a point

double fea·ture /ˌ.. '..◂/ n. [C] **1** an occasion when two movies are shown one after the other at a theater **2** a VIDEO or a LASER DISC with two movies on it: *a double feature of two early John Wayne westerns*

double fig·ures /ˌ.. '..◂/ n. [plural] a number such as 10, 25, 43 etc., that is made up of two figures: *All five Washington State starters scored in double figures.* —see also DOUBLE-DIGIT

double-head·er /ˌ.. '../ n. [C] two baseball games played one after the other

double he·lix /ˌ.. '..◂/ n. [C] TECHNICAL a shape consisting of two parallel SPIRALs that twist around the same center, found especially in the structure of DNA

double in·dem·ni·ty /ˌ.. .'.../ n. [U] LAW a feature of a life insurance POLICY that allows twice the value of the contract to be paid in the case of death by accident

double jeo·par·dy /ˌ.. '.../ n. [U] LAW the act of taking someone to court a second time for the same offense, in some rare situations

double-joint·ed /ˌ.. '..◂/ adj. able to move the joints in your fingers, arms etc. backward as well as forward

double neg·a·tive /ˌ.. '.../ n. [C] a sentence in which two NEGATIVE words are used when only one is needed in correct English grammar, for example in the sentence "I don't want nobody to help me!"

double-park /ˌ.. './ v. [I,T] to leave a vehicle on a road beside another vehicle that is already parked there

double play /ˌ.. './ n. [C] the action of making two runners in a game of baseball have to leave the field by throwing the ball quickly from one BASE to another before the runners reach either one

double-spaced /ˌ.. './ adj. double-spaced lines of words on a printed page have one empty line between them, rather than being close together —**double-space** v. [T] —**double spacing** n. [U] —compare SINGLE-SPACED

double stand·ard /ˌ.. ' ./ n. [C] a rule, principle etc. that is unfair because it treats one group or type of people more severely than another in the same situation: *Society has a double standard when it comes to teen sex: it is seen as natural for boys but forbidden for girls.*

dou·blet /'dʌblɪt/ n. [C] a man's shirt, worn in Europe from about 1400 to the middle 1600s

double take /'.. ˌ./ n. [C] **do a double take** to look at someone or something again because you are surprised by what you originally saw or heard

double-talk /'.. ˌ./ n. [U] INFORMAL speech that seems to be serious and sincere, but has another meaning or is a mixture of sense and nonsense: *legal double-talk* —**double-talk** v. [I,T] —**double-talker** n. [C]

dou·ble·think /'dʌbəlˌθɪŋk/ n. [U] a dishonest belief in two opposing ideas at the same time

double time /'.. ˌ./ n. [U] **1** twice the amount of regular pay given when someone works on a day or at a time when people do not normally work —compare TIME AND A HALF **2** a fast military march

dou·ble-time, **double time** /'.. ˌ./ adj., adv. twice as fast as usual, or as quickly as possible: *She works at what seems a double-time pace.*

double vi·sion /ˌ.. '../ n. [U] a medical condition in which you see two of everything, for example after hitting your head or drinking too much alcohol

double wham·my /ˌdʌbəl 'wæmi/ n. [C] INFORMAL two bad things that happen together, or one after the other: *Farmers have faced the double whammy of a freeze and a drought this year.*

double whole note /ˌ.. '. ./ n. [C] a musical note that continues for twice the length of a WHOLE NOTE

double-wide /ˈ.. ˌ./ also **double-wide trail·er** /ˌ.. '../ n. [C] a type of inexpensive house that is made in two halves in a factory and then put together at the place where it is meant to stand

dou·bloon /dʌˈblun/ n. [C] a gold coin used in the past in Spain and Spanish America

dou·bly /ˈdʌbli/ adv. **1** by twice the amount, or to twice the degree: *Be doubly careful when driving in fog.* **2** in two ways or for two reasons: *You are doubly mistaken.*

doubt¹ /daʊt/ n. **1** [C,U] the feeling of being unable to trust or believe in someone or something: [+ about/as to] *We have strong doubts about his effectiveness as a leader.* | [doubt whether/who/what etc.] *There was doubt whether he would be well enough to play.* | [doubt (that)] *Our team has little doubt that this deal will be made.* | *Several scientists expressed serious doubts about the study.* | *I have doubts about his qualifications for the job.* | *The recent bombing errors have raised doubts about the military's competence.* | *The case has been proved beyond a shadow of a doubt* (=there is no doubt at all). | *There is an element of doubt* (=a slight doubt) *as to whether the deaths were accidental.* | *Neighbors quickly cast doubt on Hill's version of the story.* (=said that it might not be true) **2 no doubt** used when emphasizing that you think something is probably true: *No doubt you'll have your own ideas.* | *The budget cuts will hurt, no doubt about it* (=it is certainly true). **3 have your doubts (about sb/sth)** used to say that you have reasons for not feeling certain about something or someone: *Bradley says he'll be ready to play, but the coach has his doubts.* **4 if/when (you're) in doubt...** used when advising someone what to do: *If you're in doubt about what to wear to the interview, dress conservatively.* **5 be in doubt a)** to not be certain what will happen or what to do: *The outcome of the case never seemed in doubt.* **b)** to not be sure that something will be able to succeed or continue: *Prospects for progress in the peace talks are very much in doubt.* **6 be beyond doubt** if something is beyond doubt, it is completely certain: *The test showed beyond doubt that Montand was the girl's father.* **7 reasonable doubt** LAW something that makes you think that a law case has not been completely proved: *After a week of listening to testimony, the jurors felt there was reasonable doubt.* | *They proved beyond a reasonable doubt that alcohol played a part in the accident* (=they showed that it was certain). **8 without/beyond doubt** FORMAL used to emphasize an opinion: *It is, without doubt, wrong to kill dolphins for no reason.* —see also **the benefit of the doubt** (BENEFIT¹ (4)), **be open to question/doubt** (OPEN¹ (16)), SELF-DOUBT

USAGE NOTE: DOUBT

GRAMMAR
When you use the verb **doubt** in a statement, it can be followed by the words "that," "if," or "whether":
I doubt that they would be willing to pay $20 each. | *Sara doubted if/whether Al would show up.* However, if **doubt** is used with a negative, it can only be followed by "that" or a clause: *I never doubted (that) Jake would be able to help us* (= I always believed that he would be able to help). When you use the noun **doubt** after "no" or "not," it is always followed by "that" or a clause: *There is no doubt that Jenkins is guilty.*

---

doubt² v. [T not in progressive] **1** to think that something may not be true or that it is unlikely: *The Navy never seriously doubted the inquiry's findings.* | [doubt (that)] *Doctors doubted that surgery would be necessary.* | [doubt if/whether] *Researchers doubted if any of the three remaining eggs would hatch.* | *He might show up later, but I doubt it* (=I don't think he will). **2** to not trust or have confidence in someone: *I never doubted myself.* | *I knew I could play at that level.* | *I have no reason to doubt his word* (=think that he is lying). —**doubter** n. [C]

doubt·ful /ˈdaʊtfəl/ adj. **1** probably not true or not likely to happen: *Prospects for a lasting peace remain*

---

doubtful. | [it is doubtful if/whether] *It is doubtful whether the budget will be passed before the elections in July.* | [it is doubtful that] *It is doubtful that voters will approve the bill.* **2** not sure or not certain about something: *I could see that Holmes still looked doubtful.* | [doubtful if/whether] *Bruno was doubtful whether you'd even notice the difference.* **3** probably false or of no value; DUBIOUS: *Doblado accepted the doubtful honor of organizing the fund-raiser.* **4** if a sports player is doubtful for a game, it is not likely that they will play, especially because they are injured **5** unable to be trusted or believed: *The general expressed his concern about the number of citizens with doubtful loyalties.* —**doubtfully** adv.

doubting Thom·as /ˌ.. '../ n. [C] someone who tends to doubt things if they have not seen proof of them

doubt·less /ˈdaʊtlɪs/ adv. FORMAL very likely: *Your payments will doubtless rise in the second year.*

douche /duʃ/ n. [C usually singular] a mixture of water and something such as VINEGAR, that a woman can use to wash her VAGINA, or the instrument that is used to do this —**douche** v. [I,T]

douche bag /ˈ. ./ n. [C] VULGAR, OFFENSIVE a stupid or weak person

dough /doʊ/ n. **1** [singular,U] a mixture of flour and water ready to be baked into bread, PASTRY etc. **2** [U] INFORMAL money

dough·nut /ˈdoʊnʌt/ n. [C] **1** a small round cake, often in the form of a ring **2 do doughnuts** INFORMAL to make a car spin around in circles

dough·ty /ˈdaʊti/ adj. [only before noun] LITERARY brave and determined: *a doughty fighter*

dough·y /ˈdoʊi/ adj. **1** looking and feeling like DOUGH (1) **2** doughy skin is pale and soft and looks unhealthy

Doug·lass /ˈdʌgləs/, **Fred·erick** /ˈfrɛdrɪk/ (1817–1895) an African-American who was born a SLAVE, famous for working to get rid of SLAVERY (=the practice of having slaves) and writing a book about his life

dour /ˈdaʊɚ, dʊɚ/ adj. **1** severe and never smiling **2** making you feel anxious or afraid; GRIM: *a dour reminder* —**dourly** adv.

douse, **dowse** /daʊs/ v. [T] **1** to put out a fire by pouring water on it **2** [+ with/in] to cover something in water or other liquid

dove¹ /dʌv/ n. [C] **1** a type of small white PIGEON (=bird), often used as a sign of peace **2** someone in politics who prefers peace and discussion to war —opposite HAWK¹

dove² /doʊv/ v. a past tense of DIVE¹

dove·cote /ˈdʌvkoʊt, -kɑt/ n. [C] a small house built for doves to live in

Do·ver /ˈdoʊvɚ/ the capital city of the U.S. state of Delaware

dove·tail¹ /ˈdʌvteɪl/ v. **1** [I, T] to fit perfectly together, or to make two plans, ideas etc. fit together perfectly: [+ with] *New mail-handling systems dovetail with the Post Office's push for efficiency.* **2** [T + together] to join two pieces of wood by means of dovetail joints

dovetail² also **dovetail joint** /ˈ. ˌ./ n. [C] a type of JOINT fastening two pieces of wood together

a dovetail joint

dov·ish /ˈdʌvɪʃ/ adj. preferring peace and discussion to war

dow·a·ger /ˈdaʊədʒɚ/ n. [C] **1** a woman from a high social class who has land or a title from her dead husband: *the dowager empress* **2** INFORMAL a respected and impressive old lady

dow·dy /ˈdaʊdi/ *adj.* **1** unattractive or unfashionable: *a dowdy uniform* **2** a dowdy woman wears clothes that are old-fashioned or that are not attractive —**dowdily** *adv.* —**dowdiness** *n.* [U]

dow·el /ˈdaʊəl/ *n.* [C] a wooden pin for holding two pieces of wood, metal, or stone together

Dow Jones Ave·rage /ˌdaʊ dʒoʊnz ˈævrɪdʒ/ *n.* TRADEMARK **the Dow Jones average** a daily INDEX¹ (4) of the prices of SHARES on the New York Stock Exchange, based on the share prices of a small group of companies

down¹ /daʊn/ *adv.*

1 `from higher to lower` from a higher place or position toward a lower place or position: *David bent down to tie his shoelace.* | *The next day, the sky was clear and the sun beat down.* | *Do you want me to take that poster down* (=take it off the wall) *for you?* | *Ken fell asleep face down* (=with his face toward the ground) *on the couch.*

2 `from standing to lying/sitting` from a position in which someone or something is standing into a position in which they are lying flat or sitting: *Angie, why don't you sit down and relax?* | *I think I'll go and lie down for a while.* | *Lots of trees were blown down onto houses when a tornado hit Cleveland County.*

3 `to the south` toward or in the south: [+ to] *Why don't you come down to Albuquerque?* | *The only thing I don't like about living down here is the traffic.*

4 `from more to less` at or toward a lower level or amount: *Keep your speed down.* | *Can I turn the TV down a little?* | *House prices have come down in recent months.*

5 `from bigger to smaller` to a smaller size: *Grit and sand can wear down every moving part in your bike.* | [+ to] *Sharif cut his report down to only three pages.*

6 `in a low place` in a lower place or position: *There's a parking lot down there, below the cliff.* | *We've got most of the old Tarzan books down in the basement.*

7 `recorded` written on paper, or recorded on something such as a TAPE: *I have his number down somewhere.* | *Okay, write "return library books" down on your list.* | *Put me down to bring the dessert.* | *Let me take down your details and I'll have her call you back.*

8 `firmly` firmly and tightly into a place or position: *Well, we could tape the mat down with duct tape.*

SPOKEN PHRASES

9 `away from sb` **a)** in a direction that is away from the person who is speaking: *We're going down to the mall and look at those cars they have there.* | [+ from] *You know their neighbor, the one that lives two doors down from them?* **b)** used to emphasize where something is when it is in a different place from the person who is speaking: *Were there many people down at the beach today?*

10 Down! used to tell a dog not to jump on you or someone else

11 Down with...! used to say that you strongly oppose a government, leader etc. and do not want them to have any power anymore: *Hundreds of students were shouting, "Down with dictatorship!"*

---

12 be down to sth to have only a small amount left from a larger amount: *Now we're down to our last eight dollars.*

13 `from one person to another` from an older person to a younger one, from someone with a high rank to someone with a lower rank etc.: *Chu prefers traditional recipes, handed down through generations.* | *Information in the form of orders is passed down through the chain of command.*

14 go/come/be down to the wire to have very little time left to finish or achieve something: *We were in a couple of games that went right down to the wire.*

15 `in payment` paid to someone immediately in CASH as part of the payment for something: *Lease a new Ford today for no money down and low monthly payments.* —see also DOWN PAYMENT

16 down to sb including something or someone at a low level or rank: *Everyone uses the cafeteria, from the CEO down to the mailroom staff.*

17 get/keep sth down to be able to swallow something or keep it in your stomach after you have eaten it: *I had food poisoning, and for a week I couldn't keep anything down.* —see also **come down to sth** (COME¹), **come down with sth** (COME¹)

USAGE NOTE: DOWN

GRAMMAR

The word **down** is often used to make phrasal verbs. Some of these verbs show that you have moved from a higher level to a lower one. For example, **quiet down** means "to become quieter after being noisy," **calm down** means "to become more calm after being excited," and **dumb down** is an informal phrasal verb that means "to make something much easier to understand than it was." Another common use of **down** as a phrasal verb is to show that something is done very thoroughly. For example, **wash down** means to wash something completely using a lot of water.

---

down² *adj.*

1 `sad` [not before noun] INFORMAL sad and without confidence: *She feels very down, and doesn't like herself or anything.*

2 `in a game` [not before noun] behind an opponent by a particular number of points: *We were down by 17 points at half-time.*

3 `computer` [not before noun] if a computer is down, it is not working because there is something wrong with the NETWORK it is connected to: *Our computers are down right now so I can't give you an account balance.* —opposite UP² (8)

4 `less/lower` [not before noun] less in amount than before, or at a lower level or place than before: *At lunchtime, the stock market was down 77 points.* | *The lake level is down but fishing is still good.*

SPOKEN PHRASES

5 be down on sb/sth to have a bad opinion of someone or something: *I thought, "I can't do anything right." And I was really down on myself.*

6 `completed` [not before noun] used to say that a particular number of things have been finished, when there are more things left to do: *"One down, five to go," Howell thought, wishing he didn't have to paint all those chairs.*

7 be down with sth SLANG to agree with or accept something

---

8 be down on your luck to have very little money because you have had a lot of bad luck recently: *Here, parents who are down on their luck can pick out toys for their children.*

9 be down in the dumps/mouth INFORMAL feeling sad and not very interested in life; DEPRESSED: *Sometimes I get down in the dumps and still wonder why it happened to me*

10 a down escalator/staircase/elevator an ESCALATOR (=set of moving stairs) that takes you down to a lower floor, stairs that lead to a lower floor etc.

down³ *prep.* **1** along something, or toward the far end of something: *Look who's coming down the hall.* | *There's a great Vietnamese restaurant down the street.* | *We were driving down the freeway, and it was so slick we just slid off.* **2** toward the ground or a lower place, or in a lower position: *Just walk down the stairs.* | *Do you want to go down the slide?* | *The hospital is just down the hill, in Berkeley.* **3 down the road/line/pike** INFORMAL at some time in the future: *Down the road, it's going to be worth less than you paid for it.* **4 down the river** in the direction of a river's current; DOWNRIVER: *At sunset, the boats were loaded and the whole party floated down the river.*

down⁴ *v.* [T] **1** to drink or eat something very quickly: *Jack downed three beers with his steak and fries.* **2** to defeat an opponent in sports: *Malone added 20 points as Utah downed Orlando in Salt Lake City.* **3** to make something that is usually upright or in the air fall to the ground: *More than 60 electrical*

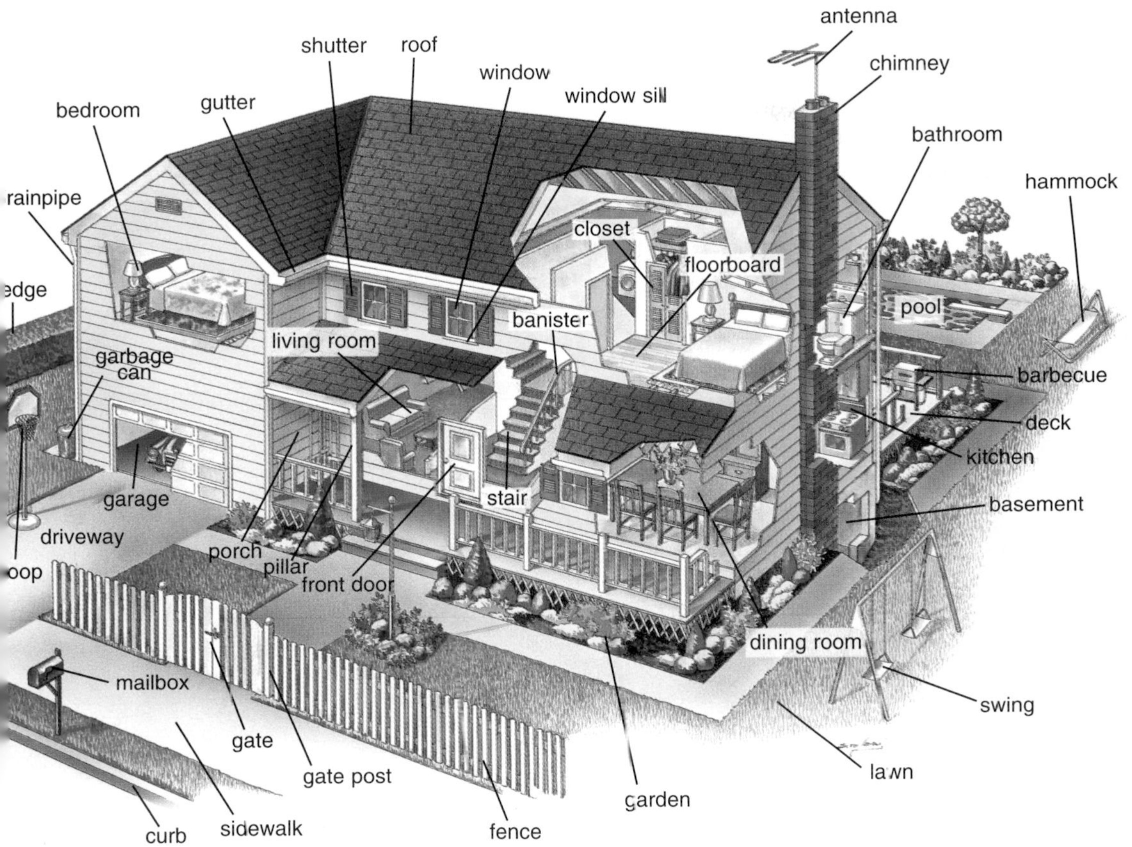

antenna

chimney

shutter roof

window

bedroom

gutter

window sill

bathroom

rainpipe

hammock

closet

floorboard

edge

pool

garbage can

living room

banister

barbecue

deck

kitchen

garage

stair

basement

driveway

porch

pillar

front door

oop

dining room

mailbox

swing

gate

gate post

lawn

curb

sidewalk

fence

garden

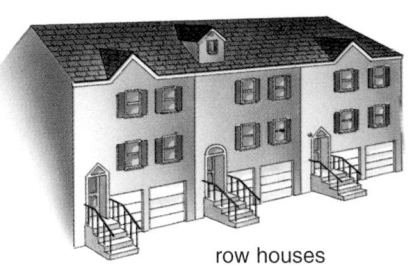

row houses

brownstone

apartment complex

mobile home

shatter

squash

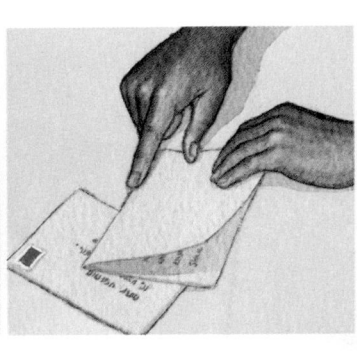

fold

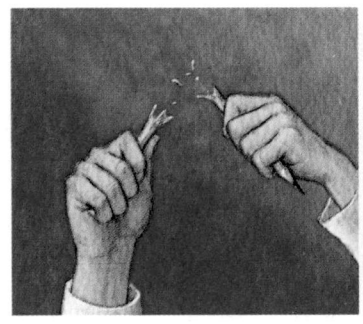

snap

melt

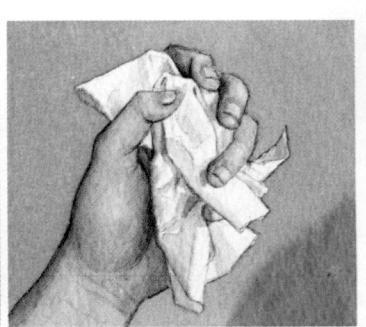

crumple

flatten

burst

bend

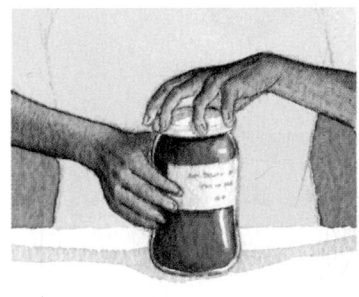

twist

warp

crease

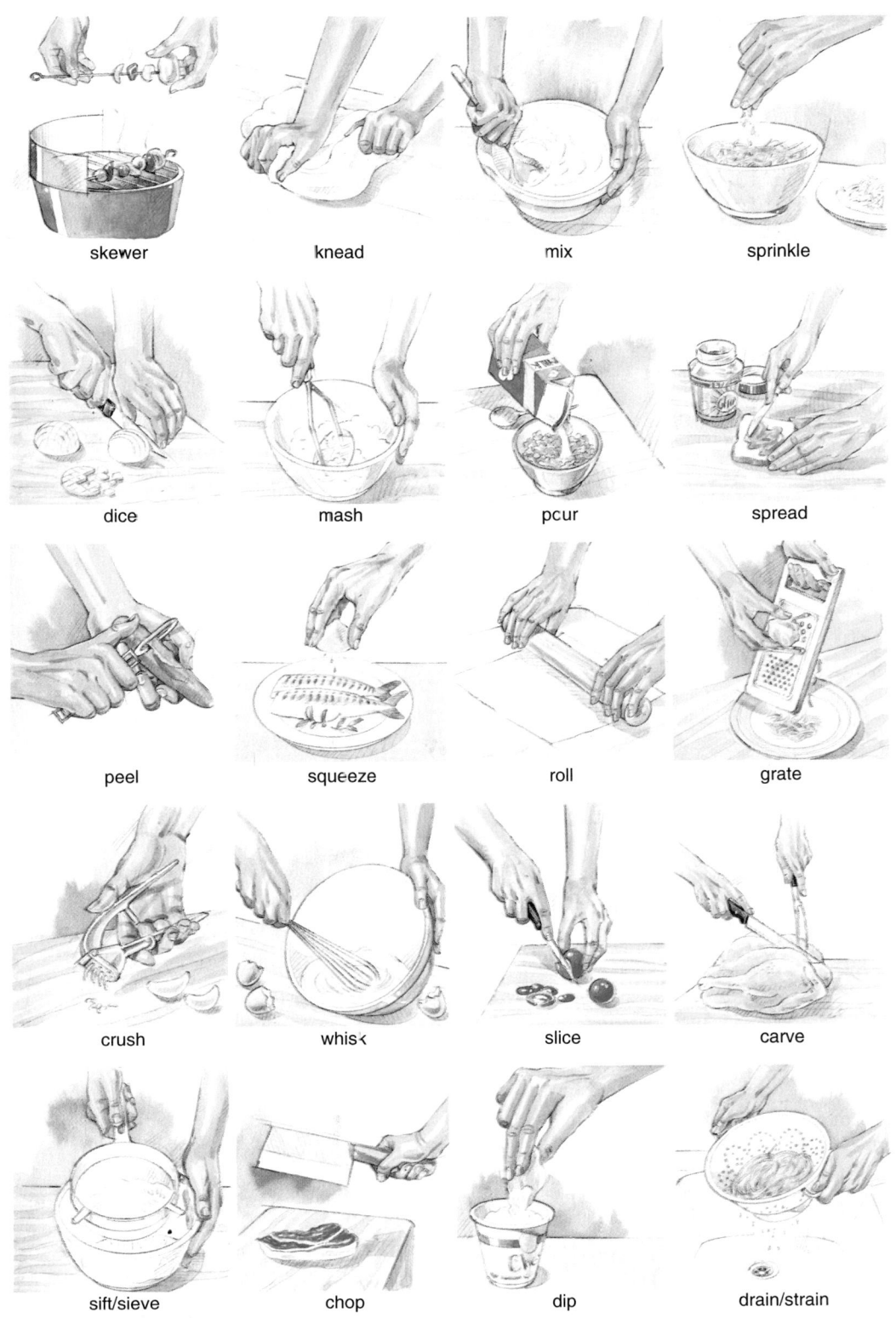

skewer	knead	mix	sprinkle
dice	mash	pcur	spread
peel	squeeze	roll	grate
crush	whisk	slice	carve
sift/sieve	chop	dip	drain/strain

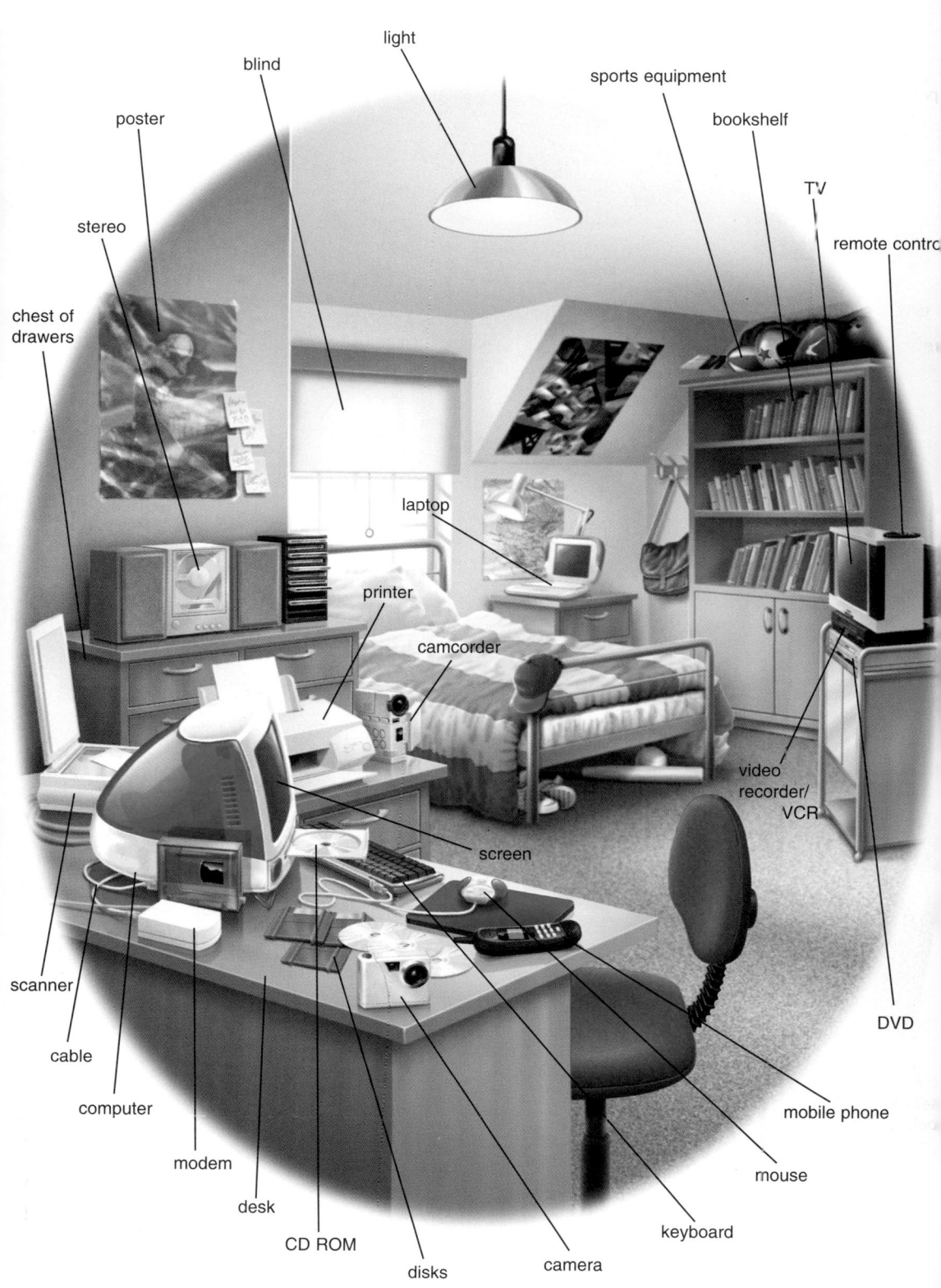

light

blind

sports equipment

poster

bookshelf

TV

stereo

remote control

chest of drawers

laptop

printer

camcorder

video recorder/ VCR

screen

scanner

cable

DVD

computer

mobile phone

modem

mouse

desk

keyboard

CD ROM

camera

disks

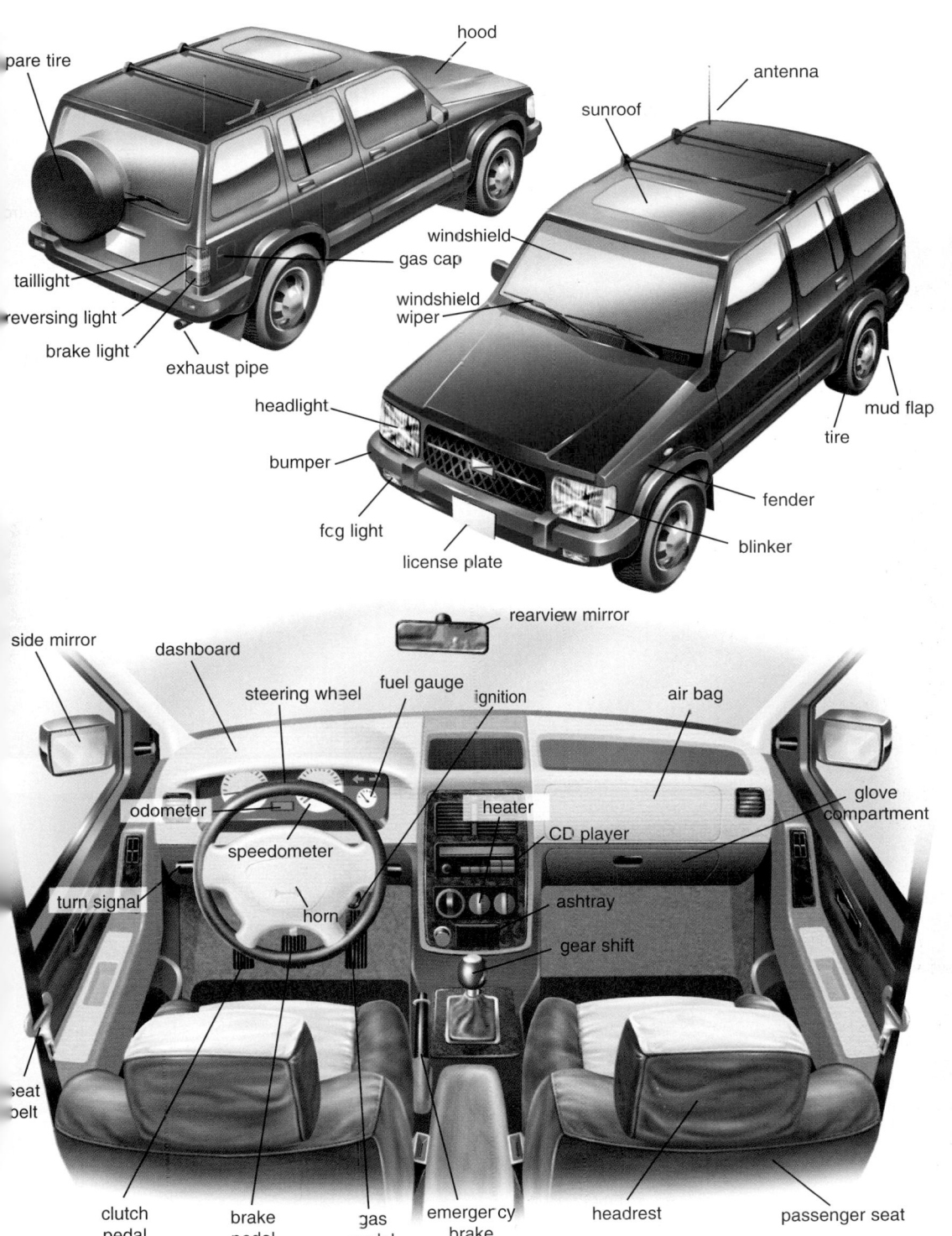

hood

antenna

spare tire

sunroof

windshield

gas cap

taillight

windshield wiper

reversing light

brake light

exhaust pipe

headlight

bumper

fcg light

license plate

mud flap

tire

fender

blinker

rearview mirror

side mirror

dashboard

fuel gauge

steering wheel

ignition

air bag

odometer

heater

glove compartment

CD player

speedometer

turn signal

horn

ashtray

gear shift

seat belt

clutch pedal

brake pedal

gas pedal

emergency brake

headrest

passenger seat

mountains

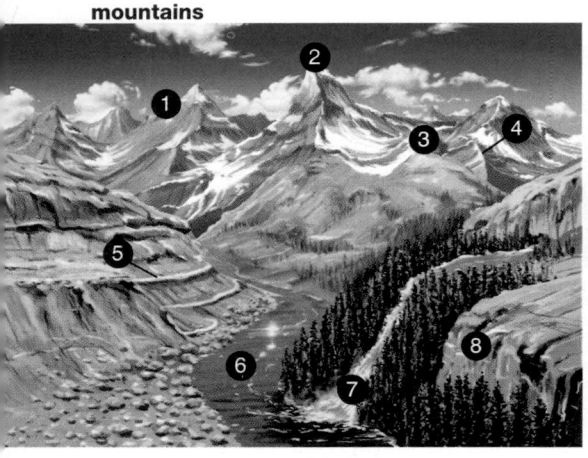

swamp

desert

coast

lake

redwood forest

1. peak
2. summit
3. pass
4. ridge
5. trail
6. river
7. waterfall

8. cliff
9. swamp
10. reeds
11. egrets
12. alligator
13. sand dune
14. cactus

15. beach
16. forest
17. cave
18. lighthouse
19. wave
20. ocean
21. cove

22. headland
23. hill
24. lake
25. shore
26. sequoia

bison

horn

beaver

cougar

haunch

whiskers

tail

bluebird

mockingbird

beak

bald eagle

wing

blue jay

talon

muzzle

grizzly bear

coyote

claws

cardinal

going to the amusement park

using the internet

eating out

playing in a band

hanging out at the mall

having fun at the beach

going in-line skating

going to the movies

wires were downed by the wet, heavy snow. **4** to force an airplane to crash by shooting it or exploding it: *He claimed the rebels downed 35 government aircraft.*

down⁵ *n.* **1** [U] the soft fine feathers of a bird, often used between layers of material to make warm clothes and bed covers: *Bring a down jacket and a pair of gloves, and you'll be fine.* | *a down comforter* —see also EIDERDOWN, GOOSEDOWN **2** [C] one of the four chances that a football team has to move forward at least ten YARDS in order to keep the ball: *In the second quarter, he sprinted up the field 13 yards for a first down.* **3** [U] soft hair like a baby's **4 downs** [plural] low round hills covered with grass —see also **ups and downs** (UP⁴ (1))

down- /daʊn/ *prefix* **1** toward a lower position, or toward the bottom of something: *downstairs* | *downriver* (=nearer to where it flows into an ocean or lake) **2** used to show that something is being made smaller or less important: *to downsize a company* (=reduce the number of jobs in it) | *to downgrade a job* (=make it less important) **3** used to show that something is bad or negative: *the downside of a situation* (=the negative part of it) —compare UP-

down-and-out /ˌ. '. ./ *adj.* INFORMAL having no luck or money: *a down-and-out actor* —**down-and-outer** *n.* [C]

down-beat¹ /ˈdaʊnbit/ *adj.* not hopeful that the future will be good: *Mubarak gave a downbeat assessment of the situation in the Middle East.* —opposite UPBEAT

downbeat² *n.* [C] **1** the first note in a MEASURE of music **2** the movement a CONDUCTOR makes to show when this note is to be played or sung

down-cast /ˈdaʊnkæst/ *adj.* **1** sad or upset because something bad has happened: *Hardaway seemed downcast after the Warriors' fourth loss in a row.* **2** downcast eyes are looking down: *He said nothing and kept his eyes downcast.*

down-draft /ˈdaʊndræft/ *n.* [C] **1** a DOWNWARD movement of air: *The plane experienced a sudden downdraft.* **2** a situation in which prices, STOCKS etc. go down, or when business becomes worse —compare UPDRAFT

Down East /ˌ. '. / *adv.* INFORMAL in or to New England, especially the state of Maine —**Down Easter** *n.* [C]

down-er /ˈdaʊnə/ *n.* [C] INFORMAL **1** [usually singular] a person or situation that stops you from feeling cheerful or happy: *The book is a real downer.* **2** a drug that makes you feel very relaxed or sleepy —compare UPPER² (2)

down-fall /ˈdaʊnfɔl/ *n.* [singular] **1** the complete loss of your money, moral standards, social position etc., or the sudden failure of an organization: *Bad investment eventually led to Roberts' downfall.* **2** something that causes a complete failure or loss of someone's money, moral standards, social position etc.: *Greed would later prove to be Barnett's downfall.*

down-grade¹ /ˈdaʊngreɪd/ *v.* [T] **1** to make a job less important, or to move someone to a less important job: *After the merger, many reporters were reassigned or downgraded.* | [**downgrade sb/sth to sth**] *Harris was downgraded to assistant manager.* **2** to make something seem less important or valuable than it is, or to state that something is not as serious as it was: [**downgrade sth to sth**] *Hurricane Bob was downgraded to a tropical storm late Monday.* —compare UPGRADE

downgrade² *n.* [C] TECHNICAL the angle at which something such as a hill or a road goes down

down-heart-ed /ˌdaʊnˈhɑrtɪd/ *adj.* sad or hopeless: *When no job offers came, I began to feel downhearted.*

down-hill¹ /ˌdaʊnˈhɪl/ *adv.* **1** toward the bottom of a hill or lower land: *The truck rolled downhill into a parked car.* —opposite UPHILL² **2 go downhill** to become worse: *After he lost his job, things went downhill.*

down-hill² /ˈdaʊnhɪl/ *adj.* **1** on a slope that goes down to a lower point: *a downhill slide* —opposite UPHILL¹ **2 be (all) downhill a)** to become easier to

do, especially after you have been doing something difficult: *After my Chemistry final is over, it's all downhill from here.* **b)** to become worse: *The best growth rates were in '93 and '94, and it's been downhill ever since.*

downhill ski-ing /ˌ.. '../ *n.* [U] the sport of moving fast down a mountain on SKIS —compare CROSS-COUNTRY SKIING

down-home /ˈ. ./ *adj.* [only before noun] relating to the simple values and customs of people who live in the COUNTRYSIDE, especially in the southern U.S.: *Bubba's Grill serves authentic, down-home cooking.*

down-load /ˈdaʊnloʊd/ *v.* [I,T] if information, a program etc. downloads, or if you download it, you move it from a large computer system to a computer which is connected to the system: [+ **from/off**] *It's easy to download sound files from the Internet.* —**download** *n.* [C] —compare UPLOAD

down-mar-ket /ˈdaʊnˌmɑrkɪt/ *adj.* DOWNSCALE¹ —opposite UPMARKET

down pay-ment /ˌ. '../ *n.* [C] the first payment that you make on something expensive, which you will continue to pay for over a longer period of time: *We almost have enough to* **make a down payment on** *a house.*

down-play /ˈdaʊnpleɪ/ *v.* **downplays, downplayed, downplaying** [T] to make something seem less important than it really is; PLAY DOWN: *Grandma downplays the seriousness of her health problems.*

down-pour /ˈdaʊnpɔr/ *n.* [C usually singular] a lot of rain that falls in a short time

down-range /ˌdaʊnˈreɪndʒ/ *adv.* in the direction away from where something such as a MISSILE or gun is fired: *The rockets dropped into the Atlantic about 130 miles downrange.*

down-right /ˈdaʊnraɪt/ *adv.* [+ adj./adv.] INFORMAL used to emphasize that someone or something is completely good, bad etc.: *Tom can be downright nasty sometimes.* —**downright** *adj.* [only before noun] *a downright idiot*

down-riv-er /ˌdaʊnˈrɪvə/ *adv.* in the direction that the water in a river is flowing: *The bridge was a mile downriver.* —opposite UPRIVER —compare DOWNSTREAM

down-scale¹ /ˈdaʊnskeɪl/ *adj.* not expensive, and usually not of good quality: *a downscale motel* —opposite UPSCALE

downscale² *v.* [T] to reduce something in size, or to make something less expensive: *The military forces have been downscaled since the end of the Cold War.*

down-shift /ˈdaʊnʃɪft/ *v.* [I,T] to move the GEAR SHIFT in a car or truck to a lower GEAR

down-side /ˈdaʊnsaɪd/ *n.* [singular] the negative part or disadvantage of something: *Digital cell phones offer more security, but the downside is that they have less power.* —opposite UPSIDE

down-size /ˈdaʊnsaɪz/ *v.* [I,T] if a company or organization downsizes, or downsizes its operations, it reduces the number of people it employs in order to reduce costs —**downsizing** *n.* [U] —compare RIGHTSIZE

down-spout /ˈdaʊnspaʊt/ *n.* [C] a pipe that carries water away from the roof of a building; DRAINPIPE

Down's syn-drome /ˈdaʊnz ˌsɪndroʊm/ *n.* [U] a condition that someone is born with, that stops them from developing in a normal way, both mentally and physically

down-stage /ˌdaʊnˈsteɪdʒ/ *adv.* toward or near the front of the stage in a theater —**downstage** /ˈdaʊnsteɪdʒ/ *adj.* —compare UPSTAGE²

down-stairs /ˌdaʊnˈsterz/ *adv.* to or on a lower floor of a building, especially a house: *Rosie ran downstairs to answer the door.* | *The washing machine is downstairs.* —**downstairs** /ˈdaʊnsterz/ *adj.* [only before noun] *a downstairs bedroom* —compare UPSTAIRS¹

down-state /ˌdaʊnˈsteɪt/ *adv.* in or to the southern part of a state —**downstate** /ˈdaʊnsteɪt/ *adj.* [only before noun] *downstate Illinois* —compare UPSTATE

down·stream /ˌdaʊn'strim/ *adv.* in the direction the water in a river or stream is flowing: *The body had drifted at least three miles downstream.* —opposite UPSTREAM

down·swing /'daʊnswɪŋ/ *n.* [C usually singular] a time during which business activity is reduced and conditions become worse: *There has been a downswing in lumber prices in recent years.* —opposite UPSWING

down·time /'daʊntaɪm/ *n.* [U] **1** the time when a machine or equipment is not working **2** INFORMAL time spent relaxing

down-to-earth /ˌ. . '.◂/ *adj.* practical and direct in a sensible honest way: *Fran's a very friendly, down-to-earth person.*

down·town /ˌdaʊn'taʊn/ *adv.* to or in the main business area of a town or city: *Stacy works downtown.* | *I have to go downtown later.* —**downtown** /'daʊn taʊn/ *adj.* [only before noun] *downtown restaurants* —compare UPTOWN

down·trend /'daʊntrɛnd/ *n.* [C] a time in which business activities, prices etc. decrease: *After an eight-month downtrend in the car market, sales jumped sharply in February.* —opposite UPTREND

down·trod·den /'daʊnˌtrɑdn/ *adj.* LITERARY downtrodden people, workers etc. are treated badly and without respect by people who have power over them

down·turn /'daʊntən/ *n.* [C usually singular] a time during which business activity, production etc. is reduced and conditions become worse: [+ in] *an economic downturn in the auto industry* —opposite UPTURN

Down Un·der /ˌ. '../ *adv.* in or to Australia or New Zealand: *After a few days Down Under, you'll get used to the heat.*

down·ward[1] /'daʊnwəd/ also **downwards** *adv.* **1** toward a lower level or position: *Tim pointed downward to his shoes.* **2** down to and including the lowest person or position in a group or set: *Everyone from the chairman downward is taking a pay cut.* —opposite UPWARD[1]

downward[2] *adj.* [only before noun] going or moving to a lower level or place: *a gentle downward slope* | *Stock prices continued their downward trend.* —opposite UPWARD[2]

down·wind /ˌdaʊn'wɪnd/ *adv.* in the direction that the wind is moving: *Residents who lived downwind from the explosion were evacuated.*

down·y /'daʊni/ *adj.* covered in, filled with, or made of soft fine hair or feathers: *a baby's downy hair*

dow·ry /'daʊri/ *n. plural* **dowries** [C,U] property and money that a woman gives to her husband when they marry in some societies

dowse[1] /daʊz/ *v.* [I + for] to look for water or minerals under the ground using a special stick that points to where they are; DIVINE[2] (2) —**dowser** *n.* [C]

dowse[2] /daʊs/ *v.* [T] another spelling of DOUSE

dows·ing rod /'.. ./ *n.* [C] a special stick in the shape of a Y, used for dowsing for water or minerals

dox·ol·o·gy /dɑk'sɑlədʒi/ *n.* [C] a special HYMN or prayer used to praise God

doy·en /'dɔɪən, 'dwɑyɛn/ *n.* [C] the oldest, most respected, or most experienced member of a group: *the doyen of sports commentators*

doy·enne /dɔɪ'ɛn, dwɑ'yɛn/ *n.* [C] the oldest, most respected, or most experienced woman in a group: *the doyenne of gossip columnists*

Doyle /dɔɪl/, **Sir Ar·thur Con·an** /'ɑrθə ˌkɑnən/ (1859–1930) a British doctor and writer of stories about the DETECTIVE Sherlock Holmes

doz. the written abbreviation of DOZEN

doze /doʊz/ *v.* [I] to sleep lightly for a short time: *Kevin often dozes in his chair instead of going to lunch.*

  doze off *phr. v.* [I] to go to sleep, especially when you did not intend to: *I was just dozing off when the phone rang.*

doz·en /'dʌzən/ *written abbreviation* **doz.** *n.* **1** **a/two/three dozen etc. (sth)** one, two, three etc. groups of twelve: *two dozen eggs* | *half a dozen* (=six of something) **2** **dozens (of sth)** INFORMAL a lot of something: *Three men were killed in the fighting and dozens were injured.* | *They collected dozens and dozens of shells on the beach.* —see also BAKER'S DOZEN, **a dime a dozen** (DIME (2)), **it's six of one and half a dozen of the other** (SIX (3))

USAGE NOTE: DOZEN

PLURAL FORMS: dozen, dozens (of)
Dozen, without an "s," is used after numbers. **Dozens (of)** is used in an informal way when the exact number of what you are talking about is not important.
Compare: *I bought two dozen apples* (=24 apples) and *I bought dozens of apples* (=a lot of apples).

---

do·zy /'doʊzi/ *adj.* INFORMAL not feeling very awake

DP the abbreviation of DATA PROCESSING

D.Phil. /di 'fɪl/ an abbreviation of Doctor of Philosophy

DPT also **DTP** *n.* [U] a VACCINE against the diseases DIPHTHERIA, TETANUS, and PERTUSSIS

Dr. **1** the written abbreviation of DOCTOR **2** the written abbreviation of DRIVE[2] (10): *88 Park Dr.*

drab /dræb/ *adj.* **1** not bright in color: *The walls were painted a drab green.* **2** boring: *Paul grew tired of his drab, depressing life.* —see also DRIBS AND DRABS

drach·ma /'drækmə, 'drɑk-/ *n. plural* **drachmas** or **drachmae** /-mi/ [C] **1** the unit of money in modern Greece **2** an ancient Greek silver coin and weight

dra·co·ni·an /dræ'koʊniən/ *adj.* FORMAL very strict and cruel: **draconian laws/measures/methods** etc. *County hospitals have been forced into making draconian budget cuts.*

draft[1] /dræft/ *n.*
1 **unfinished form** [C] a piece of writing, a drawing, or a plan that is not yet in its finished form: *I read a draft of the first chapter and thought it was very good.* | **a first/rough draft** (=the first plan for something)
2 **a/the final draft** the finished form of a piece of writing, a drawing, or a plan
3 **military the draft a)** a system in which people must join the military, especially when there is a war **b)** [C usually singular] the group of people who are ordered to do this
4 **air** [C] a current of air, especially cold air: *Could you close the window? There's a draft in here.*
5 **sports** [C usually singular] a system in some sports in which professional teams choose players from colleges to join their teams
6 **money** [C] a written order for money to be paid by a bank, especially from one bank to another: *We were asked for a bank draft payable in French francs.*
7 **on draft** beer that is on draft is served from a large container, rather than from a bottle or can

draft[2] *v.* [T] **1** to write a plan, letter, report etc. that will need to be changed before it is in its finished form: *Ballou drafted a proposal which was later presented to the school board.* **2** [usually passive] to order someone to serve in their country's military, especially during a war: [be/get drafted into sth] *My dad was eighteen when he got drafted into the army.* **3** to choose an ATHLETE to play for a professional sports team: *Craigwell was the first player drafted by the Chicago Blackhawks.* **4** to choose someone to do something such as a PROJECT: *Somehow my boss drafted me into filing these reports.*

draft[3] *adj.* **1** **a draft proposal/copy/version etc.** a piece of writing that is not yet in its finished form: *The draft proposal was given to managers for their comments.* **2** **draft beer** beer that is served from a large container, rather than a bottle or can **3** **a draft horse/animal** an animal such as a horse which is used for pulling heavy loads

draft board /'. ./ *n.* [C] the committee that decides who will be ordered to join the military

draft card /'. ./ *n.* [C] a card that is sent to someone, telling them they have been ordered to join the military

draft dodg·er /'. ,../ *n.* [C] someone who illegally avoids joining the military, even though they have been ordered to join —compare CONSCIENTIOUS OBJECTOR

draft·ee /dræf'ti/ *n.* [C] someone who has been ordered to join the military

draft pick /'. ./ *n.* [C] a person who has been chosen to play for a professional sports team during a DRAFT[1] (5)

drafts·man /'dræftsmən/ *n. plural* **draftsmen** /-mən/ [C] **1** someone whose job is to make detailed drawings of a building, machine etc. that is being planned **2** FORMAL someone who puts a suggested law or a new law into the correct words

draft·y /'dræfti/ *adj.* **draftier, draftiest** with currents of air flowing through: *a drafty old house*

drag[1] /dræg/ *v.* **dragged, dragging**
1 pull along the ground [T] to pull someone or something along the ground, often because they are too heavy to carry: [drag sb/sth away/along/through etc.] *Ben dragged his sled through the snow.* | *Several protesters were dragged away by police.*
2 not gently [T always + adv./prep.] to pull someone or something somewhere in a way that hurts or damages them: *Mumphrey dragged her up a flight of stairs and beat her repeatedly.* | *Secret Service agents* **dragged** *the man* **to the ground** (=pulled the man down to the ground).
3 **drag yourself up/down/into etc.** to move somewhere with difficulty: *Jacob was so tired he could hardly drag himself up the stairs.*
4 persuade sb to go [T always + adv./prep.] INFORMAL to persuade or force someone to come somewhere when they do not want to: *Mom dragged us to a Barry Manilow concert last night.* | *Can you* **drag yourself away from** *that video game for a few minutes?*
5 computer [T always + adv./prep.] to move something on a computer screen by pulling it along with the MOUSE (1)
6 touch the ground [I] if something is dragging along the ground, part of it is touching the ground as you move: [+ along/in/on] *Kayle's scarf dragged along the sidewalk as she walked.*
7 boring [I] if time or an event drags, it seems to go very slowly because nothing interesting is happening: *The last two hours of the play really dragged.*
8 **drag your feet** INFORMAL to take too much time to do something because you do not want to do it: *The police have been accused of dragging their feet on the investigation.*
9 **drag a lake/river/pond etc.** to look for something in a lake, river, pond etc. by pulling a heavy net along the bottom: *They dragged the lake for the missing girl's body.*
10 **drag sb's name through the mud** to tell about the bad things that someone has done, so that others will have a bad opinion of them
11 **drag sb kicking and screaming into sth** HUMOROUS to force someone to do something or become involved in something that they do not want to: *Mim will have to be dragged kicking and screaming into the 21st century.*
12 boat [T] if a boat drags its ANCHOR[1] (1), it pulls the anchor away from its place on the bottom of a lake, river etc.
drag sb/sth ↔ **down** *phr. v.* [T] **1** to make something such as the ECONOMY or prices become weaker or smaller: *The widespread decline in stocks dragged down computer share prices.* **2** to make someone feel unhappy: *Fuhr said that losing his job dragged him and his whole family down.*
drag sb/sth **in** *phr. v.* [T] to start to talk about someone or something that is not connected with what you are talking or arguing about: *They're trying to drag in all kinds of other issues to distract us.* —see also **look like something the cat dragged in** (CAT[1] (4)), **look what the cat dragged in!** (LOOK[1] (21))
drag sb/sth **into** sth *phr. v.* [T] to make someone or an organization get involved in a particular situation, discussion etc., even though they do not want to: *I'm sorry I dragged you into this mess.*

drag on *phr. v.* [I] if an event drags on, it seems to continue for longer than is necessary, often because you are bored: [+ for/into] *The board's discussions dragged on for several hours.* | *The meeting dragged on into the evening.*
drag sth ↔ **out** *phr. v.* [T] to make a meeting, an argument etc. last longer than is necessary: *How long are you going to drag this discussion out?*
drag sth **out of** sb *phr. v.* [T] to make someone tell you something when they had not intended to or were not supposed to do so: *It took me all day to drag it out of her.*
drag sth **up** *phr. v.* [T] to mention a subject or event that is not nice to think about, even though it is not necessary and it upsets the people who were involved in it: *Why does he have to drag that up again?*

drag[2] *n.*
1 a drag INFORMAL **a)** something or someone that is boring: *Don't be such a drag! Come to the party.* **b)** something that is annoying and continues for a long time: *It's a major drag having to share a bathroom with four people.*
2 be a drag on sb/sth a person or thing that is a drag on someone makes it hard for them to make progress toward what they want: *Maggie thinks marriage would be a drag on her career.*
3 cigarette [C] the act of breathing in smoke from your cigarette: *Frank took a deep drag on his cigarette.*
4 the main drag INFORMAL the biggest or longest street that goes through a town, especially the middle of a town: *Our hotel is right on the main drag.*
5 in drag INFORMAL wearing clothes that are intended for people of the opposite sex, especially for fun or entertainment
6 force [singular,U] the force of air that pushes against an airplane or a vehicle that is moving forward: *The car's low profile and rounded edges reduce its drag.*

drag·gled /'drægəld/ *adj.* LITERARY: see BEDRAGGLED

drag·gy /'drægi/ *adj.* INFORMAL if something is draggy, it is boring or seems to happen too slowly: *Shepherd's delightful performance makes up for the play's draggy parts.*

drag·net /'drægnet/ *n.* [C] **1** a net that is pulled along the bottom of a river or lake, to bring up things that may be there **2** a system in which the police look for criminals, using very thorough methods: *a police dragnet*

drag·on /'drægən/ *n.* [C] a large imaginary animal that is like a LIZARD with wings and a long tail and can breathe out fire —see also **chase the dragon** (CHASE[1] (7))

dragon breath /'.. ,./ *n.* [U] HUMOROUS breath that smells very bad

drag·on·fly /'drægən,flaɪ/ *n. plural* **dragonflies** [C] a brightly colored insect with a long thin body and transparent wings

dragon la·dy /'.. ,../ *n.* [C] HUMOROUS a woman with power who is cruel toward other people

dra·goon[1] /drə'gun, dræ-/ *n.* [C] a European soldier in past times who rode a horse and carried a gun and sword

dragoon[2] *v.*
dragoon sb **into** sth *phr. v.* [T usually passive] to force someone to do something they do not want to do: *Monica was dragooned into helping Kira and Dave move.*

drag queen /'. ./ *n.* [C] SLANG a HOMOSEXUAL man who dresses as a woman, especially as an entertainer

drag race /'. ./ *n.* [C] a car race over a very short distance —**drag racing** *n.* [U]

drag·ster /'drægstɚ/ *n.* [C] a long narrow low car used in drag races

drain[1] /dreɪn/ *v.*
1 liquid **a)** [T] to make the water or liquid in something flow away: *A week later, the pond was*

drained and the fish were inspected. | [**drain sth from sth**] *Brad drained all the oil from the engine.* | **well/poorly etc. drained** *Carrots grow best in well-drained soil.* **b)** [I] if liquid drains, it flows away: [+ **away/off**] *After the floodwaters drained away, Shahar returned to her village.* **c)** [I] if something drains, the liquid that is in it or on it flows away and it becomes dry: *Open ditches drain very efficiently.* —see picture on page 425
2 **make tired** [T] to make someone feel very tired: *Listening to customers' complaints all day really drains me.*
3 **use too much** [T usually passive] to use too much of something so that there is not enough left: *The federal insurance fund has been drained by recent bank failures.* | [**be drained of sth**] *Parents can become so drained of energy that they just give up.*
4 **color** [I always + adv./prep.] if the color or blood drains from your face, your skin becomes very pale usually because you are frightened or shocked: [+ **from/away** etc.] *All the blood drained from Collins' face as the verdict was read.*
5 **drain a glass/cup etc.** to drink all the liquid in a glass, cup etc.: *Lori quickly drained her cup.*
  drain sth **off** *phr. v.* [T] to make water or a liquid flow off something, leaving it dry: *Drain off the fat from the meat after frying.*

drain² *n.* [C] **1** a pipe or hole that dirty water or waste liquids flow into: *The drain in the bathtub is clogged.* **2 a drain on sth** something that continuously uses time, money, strength etc.: *Owning this boat is a big drain on my finances.* **3 down the drain** INFORMAL wasted or having no result: *Well, there's another fifty dollars down the drain.* —see also BRAIN DRAIN

drain·age /'dreɪnɪdʒ/ *n.* [U] **1** a system of pipes or passages in the ground for carrying away water or waste liquids: *drainage ditches* **2** the process by which water or waste liquid flows away: *A handful of pebbles in the flowerpot can help improve drainage.*

drain board /'. ./ also **draining board** /'.. ‚./ *n.* [C] a slightly sloping flat area next to a SINK where you put dishes to dry

drained /dreɪnd/ *adj.* very tired, and without any energy: *Steve felt so drained he could hardly make it to the car.*

drain·er /'dreɪnɚ/ *n.* [C] **1** a flat object made of RUBBER that you put under a DISH RACK to catch the water from wet dishes **2** INFORMAL someone who often asks for a lot of attention and support from you, so that you feel tired after dealing with them: *I love Tammy, but she's a real drainer.*

drain·pipe /'dreɪnpaɪp/ *n.* [C] **1** a pipe that carries waste water away from buildings **2** a pipe that carries rain water away from the roof of a building —see picture on page 423

drake /dreɪk/ *n.* [C] a male duck

Drake /dreɪk/**, Sir Fran·cis** /'frænsɪs/ (?1540–1596) an English sailor and EXPLORER, who was the first English man to sail around the world, and was one of the leaders of the English navy when it defeated the Spanish Armada in 1588

dram /dræm/ *n.* [C] a small unit of weight or of liquid

s w **dra·ma** /'drɑmə, 'dræmə/ *n.* **1** [C] a movie, television program, play etc. that is serious rather than humorous —compare COMEDY (1) **2** [U] the study of acting and plays: *Jeb graduated from drama school in 1997.* **3** [C,U] an exciting and unusual situation or set of events: *The drama of this year's World Series helped boost the network's ratings.*

drama queen /'.. ‚./ *n.* [C] DISAPPROVING **a)** a woman, especially an actress, who demands too much attention by trying to make situations seem worse than they are **b)** a HOMOSEXUAL man who behaves this way

s w **dra·mat·ic** /drə'mætɪk/ *adj.* **1** sudden, surprising, and often impressive | **dramatic change/improvement/results** etc. *There has been a dramatic increase in temperature since yesterday.* **2** exciting

and impressive: *Firemen carried out a dramatic rescue of the boy trapped in the burning house.* **3** connected with drama or the theater: *a collection of Shakespeare's dramatic works* **4** showing a lot of emotion in a way that makes other people notice: *Stop being so dramatic. It's embarrassing.* —**dramatically** /-kli/ *adv.*: *Output has increased dramatically.*

dramatic i·ro·ny /‚... '.../ *n.* [U] a way of giving information in a play in which the people watching know something that the characters in the play do not, and can understand the real importance or meaning of what is happening

dra·mat·ics /drə'mætɪks/ *n.* **1** [plural] behavior that shows too much feeling, and that is often insincere; HISTRIONICS: *I've had enough of Betty's dramatics.* **2** [U] the study or practice of skills used in drama, such as acting

dram·a·tis per·so·nae /‚dræmətɪs pɚ'souni, -naɪ/ *n.* [plural] FORMAL the characters in a play

dram·a·tist /'dræmətɪst, 'drɑ-/ *n.* [C] someone who writes plays, especially serious ones; PLAYWRIGHT

dram·a·tize /'dræmə‚taɪz/ *v.* [T] **1** to make a book or event into a play, movie, television program etc.: *Twigg's search for her daughter was dramatized in a TV movie.* **2** to make a situation seem more exciting, terrible etc. than it really is: *Some newspapers tend to dramatize reports of property crimes.* —**dramatization** /‚dræmətə'zeɪʃən/ *n.* [C,U]

dra·me·dy /'drɑmədi, 'dræ-/ *n.* [C] INFORMAL a television program that is both serious and humorous

drank /dræŋk/ the past tense of DRINK¹

drape /dreɪp/ *v.* [T usually passive] **1** to let something hang or lie somewhere loosely: [**drape sth over/around/across etc. sth**] *Twinkling lights were draped across the balconies.* **2** to cover or decorate something with a cloth: [**drape sth over/around/with etc. sth**] *The soldiers' coffins were draped with American flags.*

drap·er·y /'dreɪpəri/ *n.* **1 draperies** [plural] long heavy curtains **2** [U] cloth that is arranged in folds

drapes /dreɪps/ *n.* [plural] long heavy curtains

dras·tic /'dræstɪk/ *adj.* strong, sudden, and often severe: *NATO threatened more drastic action if its terms were not met.* —**drastically** /-kli/ *adv.*: *The size of the army was drastically cut.*

drat /dræt/ *interjection* OLD-FASHIONED used to show you are annoyed: *Drat! The car won't start!*

draught /dræft/ *n.* [C] the British spelling of DRAFT¹ (4)

draw¹ /drɔ/ *v. past tense* **drew** *past participle* **drawn**
1 **picture** [I,T] to make a picture of something with a pencil or pen: *Amy loves to draw cartoons.* | [**draw sb sth**] *Could you draw me a diagram?* | [**draw sth for sb**] *I'll draw a map for you if you don't know where my house is.*
2 draw (sb's) attention to sth to make someone notice something: *We want to draw attention to the unpaid work that housewives do.* | *I'd like to draw your attention to the wonderful paintings on the ceiling.*
3 draw a conclusion/moral etc. to decide that a particular fact or principle is true after thinking carefully about it: [+ **from**] *I certainly hope it's true, but it's too early to draw that conclusion from the data.*
4 draw a distinction/comparison etc. to show why two things are different from or similar to each other: [+ **between**] *It's important to draw a distinction between business and non-business expenses.*
5 draw praise/criticism/laughter etc. to get a particular kind of reaction from someone because of something you have said or done: *Phillips has drawn criticism recently for canceling a national concert tour.* | *The development plans have drawn fire from* (=been criticized by) *local residents.*
6 draw the line (at sth) to set a limit on what you are willing to do, or refuse to do something, especially because you disapprove of something: *I don't mind a little mess, but I draw the line at wearing work boots in the house.*
7 draw a line in the sand to warn someone that if they do something you have told them not to do, they

will have to fight you or be punished by you: *It's time to draw a line in the sand against the threats to education funding.*

8 **attract** [T] to attract someone: [+ **to**] *Zayyad said he was drawn to engineering because it seemed to be a respectable profession.* | *The new Children's Museum is drawing huge crowds.*

9 **draw blood a)** to take blood from someone, especially at a hospital: [+ **from**] *The nurse drew some blood from Toni's arm.* **b)** to make someone BLEED: *Sand flies are tiny insects that swarm and bite, sometimes drawing blood.* **c)** to have a very negative effect on something, especially in business or politics: *The next social program cuts will draw blood.*

10 **draw a gun/knife/sword etc.** to take a weapon from its container or from your pocket: *The next thing I knew was that he had drawn a knife and was pointing it at me.*

11 **take out** [T always + adv./prep.] to remove something from its place or from a container: *She reached in her purse and drew out a silver cigarette case.*

12 **move in one direction** [I always + adv./prep.] to move steadily in a particular direction, especially toward someone or something: *Maria grew nervous as the men drew closer.* | [**draw alongside/beside/ toward etc.**] *The crowd shouted as the boat drew away from the dock.*

13 **pull** [T] to make someone or something move by pulling them: *The carriage was drawn by six white horses.* | [**draw sb/sth aside/around/up etc.**] *Jackie drew me aside to ask what was wrong.* | *Ben drew his chair up to the fireplace.*

14 **draw a blank** SPOKEN to not be able to think of or find an answer to a question: *I just drew a blank on the last test question.*

15 **draw the curtains** to close the curtains

16 **be paid** [T] to receive an amount of money regularly from your employer or from the government: *I've been drawing unemployment benefits for six months.*

17 **draw a check (on sth)** to write a check for taking money out of a bank: *Records show that the check was drawn on a Swiss bank.*

18 **get sth important** [T] to get something that you need or that is important from someone or something: [**draw sth from sth**] *I drew a lot of comfort from her kind words.*

19 **liquid** [T] to take water, beer etc. from a well or container

20 **into your lungs** [T] to take air or smoke into your lungs: *Brooks can speak for several minutes without drawing a breath.*

21 **draw (sb) a picture** to describe something in detail, in speech or in writing: *It was impossible to draw a complete picture of the damage.*

22 **draw sb's eyes (to sth)** if something draws your eyes, it is so interesting that you notice it: *My eyes were drawn to the tall woman beside Ken.*

23 **playing card/ticket** [I,T] to choose a card, ticket etc. by chance: *The winning lottery numbers will be drawn on Saturday evening.*

24 **draw to a stop/end/close** FORMAL to gradually stop or finish

25 **draw near** to move closer in time or space: *Summer vacation is drawing near.*

26 **draw straws** to decide who will do something, especially something bad, by having each person pick one STRAW, stick, pencil etc. from a group of different-sized ones, with the loser being the person who picks the shortest one: *Crawford, Schepler, and Ravi had to draw straws to determine their playing order.*

27 **draw the short straw** used to say that someone has been unlucky because they were chosen by chance to do a job that no one wants to do: *I'm only here because I drew the short straw.*

28 **draw lots** to decide who will do something by taking pieces of paper etc. out of a container: *We drew lots to see who would go first.*

29 **draw a bath** LITERARY to fill a BATHTUB with water

30 **draw a bow** to bend a BOW² (2) by pulling back the string in order to shoot an ARROW (1)

draw back *phr. v.* [I] **1** to move backward and away from something: *The crowd drew back to let the police through.* **2** to decide not to do something: [+ **from**] *The company drew back from its initial agreement of a 3% pay raise.*

draw sb **in** also **draw sb into sth** *phr. v.* [T] to attract someone or involve them in something, often when they do not really want to take part: *Keith refused to get drawn into the argument.* | *We hope our lower prices will draw in more first-time Internet users.*

draw sth **off** *phr. v.* [T] to remove some liquid from a larger supply: *Some of the river water will be drawn off into a network of canals.*

draw on sth *phr. v.* [T] **1** also **draw upon sth** to use supplies, experiences etc. for a particular purpose: *As an actor, you have to draw upon your experience to create believable characters.* **2 draw on a cigarette/cigar etc.** FORMAL to breathe in smoke from a cigarette etc.

draw sb/sth ↔ **out** *phr. v.* [T] **1** to make someone feel less nervous and more willing to talk: *Mr. Monroe has helped draw Billy out of his shyness.* **2** to make an event last longer than usual: *The final questions drew the meeting out for another hour.* **3** to remove money from a bank account; WITHDRAW: *She went to the bank and drew out all the money they had saved.*

draw up *phr. v.*
1 **list/contract etc.** [T **draw** sth **up**] to prepare a written document: *The committee has drawn up a list of finalists.*
2 **vehicle** [I] to arrive somewhere and stop: *A huge black limousine drew up outside the gates.*
3 **draw yourself up** to stand up very straight because you are angry or determined about something: *Drawing himself up to his full height, he ordered me out of the room.*
4 **soldiers** [T usually passive **draw** sb **up**] to arrange people in a special order: *The troops were drawn up in ranks for inspection by the general.*

draw² *n.* [C] **1** the final result of a game or competition in which both teams or competitors have the same number of points, or when it becomes impossible for anyone to win; TIE: *The third game in the chess tournament ended in a draw.* **2** a person, thing, or place that a lot of people are interested in seeing or going to: *New York is always a big draw for tourists.* **3** the act of choosing someone or something by chance, especially in a game or LOTTERY (1): *The jackpot for Saturday's draw is over $5 million.* —see also **the luck of the draw** (LUCK¹ (17)), **be quick on the draw** (QUICK¹ (10)), **a quick draw** (QUICK¹ (11))

draw·back /'drɔbæk/ *n.* [C] a disadvantage of a situation, product etc.: [+ **to/of (doing) sth**] *One drawback is that it will take a long time.*

draw·bridge /'drɔbrɪdʒ/ *n.* [C] a bridge that can be pulled up to let ships go under it, or to stop people from entering or attacking a castle —see picture at BRIDGE¹

draw·down /'drɔdaʊn/ *n.* [C] the act, process, or result of reducing the level or amount of something: *a large drawdown in world grain supplies*

drawer /drɔr/ *n.* **1** [C] part of a piece of furniture, such as a desk, that is like a box that slides in and out and that you can keep things in | **the bottom/ top drawer** *There are some pens in the top drawer.* —see also TOP-DRAWER —see picture at KITCHEN **2 drawers** OLD-FASHIONED underwear worn between the waist and the top of the legs

draw·ing /'drɔ-ɪŋ/ *n.* **1** [C] a picture that you make with a pencil, pen etc.: [+ **of**] *a drawing of the building* **2** [U] the art or skill of making pictures with a pen, pencil etc.: *Katherine enjoys drawing.* **3** [C] a contest in which a winning number, ticket etc. is chosen by chance: *The church social will include a buffet dinner and prize drawing.*

drawing board /'.. ,./ *n.* **1** (go) back to the drawing

board also **send sb/sth back to the drawing board** to start working on a plan or idea again after an idea that you have tried has failed, or to make someone do this: *Voters rejected the bridge expansion plan, so it's back to the drawing board for city engineers.* **2** in the process of being planned or prepared: *A remake of the movie is on the drawing board.* **3** [C] a large flat board that artists and DESIGNERS[1] work on

drawing card /'.. ,./ n. [C] a feature that attracts people to an area, a concert, a competition etc.: *This week's drawing card is cellist Yo-Yo Ma.*

drawing room /'.. ,./ n. [C] OLD-FASHIONED a room, especially in a large house, where you can entertain guests or relax

drawl /drɔl/ n. [singular] a way of speaking in which vowels are longer than normal: *a Texas drawl* —**drawl** v. [I,T]

drawn[1] /drɔn/ v. the past participle of DRAW[1]

drawn[2] adj. someone who looks drawn has a thin pale face, usually because they are sick or worried

drawn-out /, . '.‹/ adj. taking more time than usual or more time than you would like: *Getting parents involved in schools is **a long drawn-out process**.*

draw·string /'drɔstrɪŋ/ n. [C] a string through the top of a bag, piece of clothing etc. that you can pull tight or make loose

dray /dreɪ/ n. [C] a flat CART with four wheels that was used in past times for carrying heavy loads, especially BARRELS of beer

dread[1] /drɛd/ v. [T] to feel anxious about or afraid of something, especially something in the future: *The icy weather had citrus growers dreading the effects of frost.* | [**dread doing sth**] *I dread spending time with Sue because she's such an angry person.* | **I dread to think** (=I do not want to think about it because I think it will be bad) *what might happen if he gets elected.*

dread[2] n. **1** [U] strong fear of something, especially something in the future: *I felt a sense of dread as I walked into the interview.* **2 dreads** [plural] INFORMAL: see DREADLOCKS

dread·ed /'drɛdɪd/ also **dread** LITERARY OR HUMOROUS adj. [only before noun] making you feel anxious or afraid: *cancer and other dreaded diseases*

dread·ful /'drɛdfəl/ adj. FORMAL very bad: *Young made two dreadful mistakes.*

dread·ful·ly /'drɛdfəli/ adv. FORMAL **1** [+ adj./adv.] extremely: *I am dreadfully sorry for any damage I may have caused.* **2** very badly: *The team played dreadfully.*

dread·locks /'drɛdlɑks/ n. [plural] hair that hangs in a lot of thick pieces that look like rope —see picture at HAIRSTYLE

s w **dream[1]** /drim/ n.
1 2
1 `images while sleeping` [C] a series of thoughts, pictures, and feelings that you have when you are asleep: *You and Bobby were in my dream last night.* | *I had a really weird dream last night.* | *Horror movies give me **bad dreams** (=frightening dreams).*

2 `wish` [C] something you hope for and want to happen very much: *Alfonso's dream was to be a professional ball player.* | [+ **of**] *She was able to realize her lifelong dream of opening a little boutique.* | *The store has succeeded **beyond our wildest dreams** (=better than anything we hoped or imagined).* | *In law school Stuart met the woman **of his dreams**.*

3 a/sb's dream (come true) something that is perfect for someone, or something that they have wanted to happen for a long time: *The food festival is a pasta lover's dream come true.* | *Our evening together was so perfect – it was like a dream.*

4 `other thoughts` [C usually singular] a set of thoughts that make you forget about the things happening around you; DAYDREAM[2]: *Ben seemed lost in a dream.*

5 a dream car/job/vacation etc. the best car, job etc. that you can imagine

---

6 be/live in a dream world to have ideas or hopes that are not practical or likely to happen: *If you think he'll change, you're living in a dream world.*

7 never in my wildest dreams used to say that you could not possibly have imagined or expected something: *Never in my wildest dreams did I expect him to apologize.*

8 in your dreams used to say in a rude way that something is not likely to happen: *"I can beat you, no problem." "Yeah, in your dreams."*

9 like a dream extremely well or effectively: *The new car drives like a dream.*

10 a dream OLD-FASHIONED, INFORMAL a very attractive person or thing: *Her latest boyfriend is an absolute dream.*

—see also AMERICAN DREAM, **pipe dream** (PIPE[1] (4)), WET DREAM

dream[2] v. past tense and past participle **dreamed** or s w
dreamt 1 [I,T] to think about something that you would like to happen: [+ **of/about**] *It was the kind of vacation I'd always dreamed about.* | [**dream (that)**] *King dreamt that white and black people would join together as equals.* **2** [I,T] to have a dream while you are asleep: [+ **about**] *I dreamt about her last night.* | [**dream (that)**] *I often dream that I'm falling.* **3** to think about something else and not give your attention to what is happening around you; DAYDREAM[1]: *Most of the students were dreaming during the lecture.* **4** [I,T] to imagine that you do, see, or hear something that you really do not: *I was sure I mailed the letter yesterday, but I must have dreamed it.* **5 sb wouldn't dream of (doing) sth** SPOKEN used to say that you would never do something, because you do not approve of it or think it is bad: *We wouldn't dream of making you stay in a hotel – you'll stay with us.*

dream sth ↔ **away** phr. v. [T] to waste time by thinking about what may happen: *We used to lie on the beach and dream away the hours.*

dream on phr. v. [I] SPOKEN used to tell someone that they are hoping for something that will not happen: *You think I'm going to help you move? Dream on!*

dream sth ↔ **up** [T] to think of a plan or idea, especially an unusual one: *Who dreams up these silly TV commercials?*

dream·boat /'drimboʊt/ n. [C] INFORMAL someone who is very good-looking and attractive

dream·er /'drimɚ/ n. [C] **1** someone who has ideas or plans that are not practical: *Their second daughter is a dreamer and a tomboy.* **2** someone who dreams

dream·i·ly /'driməli/ adv. thinking about pleasant things and not about what is actually happening: *She looked dreamily at the sky.*

dream·land /'drimlænd/ n. [U] **1** a happy place or situation that exists only in your imagination **2** INFORMAL sleep: *Most of the kids were on their way to dreamland.*

dream·less /'drimlɪs/ adj. dreamless sleep is very deep and peaceful

dream·like /'drimlaɪk/ adj. as if happening or appearing in a dream: *The film had a dreamlike quality.*

dreamt /drɛmt/ v. a past tense and past participle of DREAM[2]

dream·y /'drimi/ adj. **dreamier, dreamiest 1** pleasant, peaceful, and relaxing: *dreamy melodies* **2** having a quality like a dream: *The photos have a dreamy look.* **3** someone who is dreamy likes to imagine things: *a dreamy 14-year old girl* **4** OLD-FASHIONED, INFORMAL very attractive and desirable: *a dreamy new sports car* —**dreaminess** n. [U]

drear·y /'drɪri/ also **drear** /drɪr/ LITERARY adj. **drearier, dreariest** dull, uninteresting, and not cheerful: *dreary weather*

dreck /drɛk/ n. [U] INFORMAL something that is of very bad quality: *There's just so much dreck on TV this season.*

dredge /drɛdʒ/ v. **1** [I,T] to remove mud or sand from the bottom of a river, HARBOR[1] etc., or to search for something by doing this: *Fearing more floods, the state had the river dredged.* **2** [T + **in**] to cover food lightly with flour, sugar etc.

dredge sth ↔ **up** *phr. v.* [T] **1** INFORMAL to start talking again about something that happened a long time ago: *Why do the papers have to dredge up that old story?* **2** to pull something up from the bottom of a river: *Weapons crews dredged up the unexploded bombs.*

dredg·er /'drɛdʒə/ also **dredge** *n.* [C] a machine or ship used for digging or removing mud and sand from the bottom of a river, HARBOR etc.

dregs /drɛgz/ *n.* **1** [plural] small solid pieces in a liquid such as wine or coffee that sink to the bottom of the cup, bottle etc. **2 the dregs of society/humanity etc.** OFFENSIVE people that are considered by the person speaking to be the least important or useful in society

drei·del /'dreɪdl/ *n.* [C] a TOP (=toy that you spin) with a Hebrew letter on each of its four sides and a point at the bottom, used in a game played during Hanukkah

Drei·ser /'draɪsə, -zə/, **The·o·dore** /'θiə,dɔr/ (1871–1945) a U.S. writer of NOVELS

drench /drɛntʃ/ *v.* [T] to make something or someone completely wet: *I forgot my umbrella and got drenched.* —**drenching** *adj.*

drenched /drɛntʃt/ *adj.* **1** completely wet: [+ **with/in**] *I was drenched in sweat from mowing the lawn.* **2** completely covered in something: [+ **in**] *She was drenched in cheap perfume.* | **sun-drenched/syrup-drenched etc.** *Phoenix is a sun-drenched city of one million inhabitants.*

dress

He got dressed.

He put on a jacket.

He wore a dark suit.

s w **dress¹** /drɛs/ *v.*

1 put on clothes [I,T] to put clothes on someone or yourself: *Can you dress the kids while I make breakfast?* | *It's a costume party, so she's dressing as a clown.* | *Patty's just learning to dress herself.* | [+ **for**] *The players came in and started dressing for the game.* —see also DRESSED

2 wear clothes [I] to wear a particular kind of clothes: *Dress warmly – it's cold out.* | *How do most of the people dress at your office?* | *He once taught a course in how to dress for success* (=dress in a way that will help you to be successful in business). | *The entire family dressed for dinner* (=put on formal clothes for dinner).

3 wound/cut etc. [T] to put medicine and BANDAGES

on a wound: *Clean the area thoroughly before dressing the wound.*

4 make clothes for sb [T] to make or choose clothes for someone: *Versace dressed some of the most famous people in Hollywood.*

5 meat/chicken/fish [T] to clean and prepare a dead animal so that it is ready to cook or eat: *Ask Mom if she needs help dressing the turkey.*

6 vegetables [T] to put a DRESSING¹, salt etc. onto a SALAD: *Dress the salad with lemon, olive oil, and a little black pepper.*

7 window [T] to put an attractive arrangement in a store window

8 soldiers [I,T] TECHNICAL to stand in a line, or to make soldiers do this

9 horse [T] to brush a horse in order to make it clean

10 hair [T] FORMAL to arrange someone's hair into a special style

dress down *phr. v.* **1** [I] to wear clothes that are more informal than you would usually wear: *Many offices dress down on Fridays.* **2** [T **dress** sb ↔ **down**] to speak angrily or severely to someone about something they have done wrong: *Carter had no problem dressing down his staff.* —see also DRESSING DOWN

dress up *phr. v.* **1** [I,T **dress** sb ↔ **up**] to wear special clothes, shoes, etc. for fun, or to put such clothes on someone: *We dressed the kids up as tigers.* | [**dress up as sb/sth**] *Jane dressed up as a witch for Halloween.* | [+ **in**] *I keep a box of old clothes for the kids to dress up in.* **2** [I] to wear clothes that are more formal than you would usually wear: *Do we have to dress up?* **3** [T **dress** sth **up**] to make something more interesting or attractive: [**dress sth up with sth**] *Buy simple cards and dress them up at home with glue and glitter.*

D

USAGE NOTE: DRESS

WORD CHOICE: dress, get dressed, put on, dress up, dress yourself, have on, wear, dress in, be (dressed) in
Use **dress** (a slightly formal word) or **get dressed** to mean "put on all your clothes." But use **put on** if you mention the particular piece or pieces of clothing or things like glasses and jewelry that you are putting on your body: *David dressed quickly.* | *Go and get dressed – it's almost time for school.* | *Wait while I put my shoes on.* Use **dress up** when you talk about putting on special clothes, often for a special occasion. These may be formal clothes: *We always used to dress up to go to church.* Or they may be unusual clothes that make you look like someone else, for example if you are acting in a play: *He had to dress up as a clown for the parade.* You only talk about someone **dressing themselves** if a special effort is involved: *Can Tara dress herself yet?* (=Tara is a small child) | *He hasn't been able to dress himself since the accident.* After you have **put on** your clothes, shoes etc., you **have** them **on**: *They all had black athletic shoes on.* **Wear** means to **have** clothes, jewelry etc. **on** your body and is often used to describe someone's usual style of dressing: *He always wears a tie and jacket to work.* | *All visitors to the site must wear a protective helmet.* You can also use **dress (in)** to describe someone's usual style of dressing and **be (dressed) in** to talk about what clothes someone is wearing: *She always dresses casually.* | *Sal tends to dress in dark colors.* | *Some of the Girl Scouts wore costumes, but others were dressed in uniforms.*

dress² *n.* **1** [C] a piece of clothing worn by a woman or girl, that covers the top of her body and some or all of her legs: *Do you like my new dress?* —compare SKIRT¹ (1) **2 casual/informal/formal dress etc.** clothes that are casual, informal, formal etc. in style: *It's casual dress for dinner tonight.* **3 evening/national etc. dress** special clothes that you wear for a particular occasion: *All of the dancers wore traditional Austrian dress.* **4 dress shirt** a formal shirt with buttons **5 dress shoe** a type of shoe that you wear with formal clothes such as a SUIT

dres·sage /drə'saʒ, drɛ-/ *n.* [U] a competition in which a horse performs a complicated series of actions in answer to signals from its rider

dress code /'. ./ *n.* [C] a set of rules for what you should wear for a particular situation: *More schools are starting strict dress codes.*

dressed /drɛst/ *adj.* **1 get dressed** to put your clothes on: *Rob got dressed in a hurry.* **2** having your clothes on, or wearing a particular type of clothes: *Aren't you dressed yet?* | [+ **in/as**] *Ten thousand people dressed in white marched down the street.* | *Mrs. Russell is always neatly dressed.* | **half/fully dressed** (=with half or all of your clothes on) **3 dressed up** wearing more attractive or formal clothes than you would usually wear: *What are you doing all dressed up?* **4 dressed to kill** INFORMAL wearing very attractive clothes so that everyone notices you: *In her black velvet cocktail dress, Elaine Russell was dressed to kill.* **5 dressed to the nines** INFORMAL wearing your best or most formal clothes: *Johnson was dressed to the nines in a handsome tailored suit.* —see also WELL-DRESSED

dress·er /'drɛsɚ/ *n.* [C] **1** a piece of furniture with drawers for storing clothes, sometimes with a mirror on top; CHEST OF DRAWERS **2 a fashionable/stylish/sloppy etc. dresser** someone who dresses in a fashionable, stylish, sloppy etc. way: *Kendall is known as a sharp dresser.* **3** someone who takes care of someone's clothes and helps them dress, especially someone who helps an actor in the theater —see also HAIRDRESSER

dress·ing /'drɛsɪŋ/ *n.* **1** [U] a mixture of liquids, often made from oil and VINEGAR, that you put on raw vegetables or SALAD —see also FRENCH DRESSING, SALAD DRESSING **2** [C,U] STUFFING (1) **3** [C,U] a special piece of material used to cover and protect a wound: *Change the dressing twice a day.* —see also WINDOW DRESSING

dressing down /,.. './ *n.* [singular] an act of talking angrily to someone and criticizing them because they have done something wrong: *Bennet gave Koch a dressing down for not getting the contract.*

dressing gown /'.. ,./ *n.* [C] FORMAL a ROBE[1] (2)

dressing room /'.. ,./ *n.* [C] **1** an area in a store where you can put on clothes to see how they look; FITTING ROOM **2** a room where an actor, performer, sports team etc. can get ready, before going on stage, appearing on television, playing a game etc. **3** a small room in some houses where you get dressed, put on MAKEUP etc.

dressing ta·ble /'.. ,../ *n.* [C] a piece of furniture that you use when you are brushing your hair, putting on MAKEUP etc., that is like a table with a mirror on top and sometimes has drawers

dress·mak·er /'drɛs,meɪkɚ/ *n.* [C] someone who makes clothes for other people as a job —compare SEAMSTRESS —**dressmaking** *n.* [U]

dress re·hear·sal /'. .,../ *n.* [C] the last time actors practice a play, OPERA etc., using all the clothes, objects etc. that will be used in the real performance

dress u·ni·form /'. ,.../ *n.* [C,U] a uniform that officers in the army, navy etc. wear for formal occasions or ceremonies

dress-up /'. ./ *n.* [U] a children's game in which they put on special clothes and pretend that they are someone else —see Usage Note at DRESS[1]

dress·y /'drɛsi/ *adj.* **dressier, dressiest 1** formal and fashionable: *a dressy silk suit* **2** someone who is dressy likes to wear very attractive or formal clothes: *Older customers are dressier than most 18- to 25-year-olds.*

drew /dru/ *v.* the past tense of DRAW[1]

drib·ble[1] /'drɪbl/ *v.* **1** [I,T] to have liquid or soft food come out of your mouth onto your face: *My son's enchilada dribbled sauce all over his shirt.* **2** [I always + adv./prep.] if a liquid dribbles, it flows in a thin irregular stream: [+ **down/from/out etc.**] *Sweat was dribbling down my face.* **3** [I,T] to move a ball or PUCK forward by bouncing (BOUNCE[1] (1)), kicking, or hitting it: *Mullin dribbled the ball down the floor.* **4** [I always + adv./prep.] if something such as money or news dribbles somewhere, it comes or goes in small irregular amounts: *Money is finally dribbling back into the country now.* **5** [T] to pour something out slowly in an irregular way: *She dribbled cream in her coffee.*

dribble[2] *n.* **1** [U] a small amount of liquid or soft food that has come out of your mouth **2** [C] a small amount of liquid: *The oil spill sent dribbles of tar onto beaches in New Jersey.* **3** [C] an act of bouncing (BOUNCE[2] (2)) or kicking a ball, or of hitting a PUCK to move it forward

dribs and drabs /,drɪbz ən 'dræbs/ *n.* [plural] **in dribs and drabs** in small irregular amounts or numbers over a period of time: *News of the accident is coming through in dribs and drabs.*

dried /draɪd/ *adj.* dried substances, such as food or flowers, have had the water removed

dried milk /,. './ *n.* [U] milk that is made into a powder and can be used by adding water

dri·er /'draɪɚ/ *n.* [C] another spelling of DRYER

drift[1] /drɪft/ *v.* **1** [I] to be moved slowly and quietly through the air or on the surface of water, or to move in this way: [+ **out/toward etc.**] *The boat had drifted out to sea.* | *Black clouds of smoke drifted over the city.* **2** [I always + adv./prep.] to move or go somewhere without any plan or purpose: [+ **around/along etc.**] *Many of these kids will drift though life without any goals.* | [**drift from sth to sth**] *For five years he drifted from one job to another.* **3** [I] to gradually change from being in one condition, situation etc. into another: *All night Julie drifted in and out of consciousness.* | *Vargas Llosa's politics gradually drifted to the right.* **4** [I] if values, prices, STOCKS etc. drift, they gradually change: *The dollar drifted lower against the yen today.* **5** [I,T] if snow, sand etc. drifts, or if the wind drifts it, the wind blows it into large piles

drift apart *phr. v.* [I] if people drift apart, their relationship gradually ends: *After college, we both got busy and just drifted apart.*

drift off *phr. v.* [I] **a)** to gradually fall asleep, or to stop giving attention to something: *I kissed her goodnight as she drifted off to sleep.* **b)** to move away slowly: *One by one the people at the table got up and drifted off.*

drift[2] *n.* **1** [C] a large pile of snow, sand etc. that has been blown by the wind: *All the roads to Denver were blocked by snow drifts.* **2 catch/get the drift (of sth)** INFORMAL to understand the general meaning of what someone is saying: *I heard enough of the speech to get the drift of it.* | *She was very friendly to me – if you catch my drift* (=I hope you understand what I am trying to say). **3** [singular] a gradual change or development in a situation, people's opinion etc.: *The party has experienced a drift toward the right in the last two years.* **4** [U] very slow movement, especially movement caused by wind or water —see also CONTINENTAL DRIFT

drift·er /'drɪftɚ/ *n.* [C] **1** someone who is always moving from one job or place to another **2** a fishing boat that uses a floating net

drift ice /'. ./ *n.* [U] pieces of broken ice floating in an ocean, river etc.

drift·wood /'drɪftwʊd/ *n.* [U] wood floating in the ocean or left on the shore

drill[1] /drɪl/ *n.* **1** [C] a tool or machine used for making holes in something: *an electric drill* | *a dentist's drill* **2** [C] a method of teaching students, soldiers, sports players etc. something by making them repeat the same lesson, exercise etc. many times: *multiplication drills* | *a marching drill* **3 fire/emergency etc. drill** an occasion when you practice what you should do during a dangerous situation such as a fire **4 the drill** the usual expected way that something is done: *You know the drill – Christmas at my parents' and New Year's at Aunt Jill's.* **5** [U] a type of strong cotton cloth **6** [C] a machine for planting seeds in rows **7** [C] a row of seeds planted by machine

drill[2] v. **1** [I,T] to make a hole in something using a drill: *We'll have to drill some holes here to put up the shelves.* | *Oil companies still **drill for oil** (=make a hole in the earth to find oil) off Santa Barbara.* **2** [T] to teach students, soldiers, sports players etc. something by making them repeat the same exercise, lesson etc. many times: [**drill sb in sth**] *The game is designed to drill children in the letters of the alphabet.* | *Our flight crew is **well-drilled** in handling emergencies.* **3** [T] to plant seeds in rows using a machine

drill sth into sb phr. v. [T] to keep telling someone something until they know it very well: *Mom drilled it into my head that I should never talk to strangers.*

drilling plat·form /'.. ,../ n. [C] a large structure in the ocean used for drilling for oil, gas etc.

drill team /'. ./ n. [C] a team in a school, the army, navy etc. whose members perform together a series of complicated movements with their bodies or with pieces of equipment

dri·ly /'draili/ adv. another spelling of DRYLY

drink[1] /drɪŋk/ v. past tense **drank** past participle **drunk 1** [I,T] to pour a liquid into your mouth and swallow it: *What do you want to drink?* | *Charlie drinks way too much coffee.* | *Do you want something to drink?* **2** [I] to drink alcohol, especially too much or too often: *"Whiskey?" "No thanks, I don't drink."* | *You really shouldn't **drink and drive** (=drive after you have drunk too much alcohol).* | *Luke **drinks like a fish** (=regularly drinks a lot of alcohol).* | *Robin can **drink** any man **under the table** (=drink more alcohol than them without becoming as drunk as them).* **3 drink yourself unconscious/silly etc.** to drink so much alcohol that you become unconscious, silly etc.: *I'm going out tonight and drink myself silly.*

drink sth ↔ **in** phr. v. [T] LITERARY to listen to, look at, feel, or smell something in order to enjoy it: *From the balcony, I drank in the beauty of the valley below.*

drink to sth phr. v. [T] **1** to have an alcoholic drink after wishing someone success, good luck, good health etc.: *Let's drink to their happiness as a married couple.* **2 I'll drink to that!** SPOKEN used to agree with what someone has said

drink sth ↔ **up** phr. v. [I,T] to finish drinking something, or to drink all of something: *Drink up, they're closing.* | *Drink up your milk, Kelsey.*

drink[2] n. **1** [C,U] liquid that you can drink, or an amount of liquid that you drink: *a drink of water* | *Do you want a drink?* | *There will be plenty of food and drink available at the fair.* **2** [C,U] alcohol, or an alcoholic drink: *There's a nice bar nearby where we can **have a drink**.* —compare SOFT DRINK **a stiff drink/whiskey etc.** (STIFF[1] (7)), SOFT DRINK **3 the drink** INFORMAL the ocean, a lake, or another large area of water: *The car rolled down the hill and ended up in the drink.*

drink·a·ble /'drɪŋkəbəl/ adj. **1** water that is drinkable is safe to drink **2** wine, beer etc. that is drinkable is of good quality and tastes good

drink·er /'drɪŋkɚ/ n. [C] someone who regularly drinks alcohol or another type of drink: *Greg's always been a **heavy drinker** (=has always drunk a lot).* | *a coffee/wine/beer etc. drinker* (=someone who regularly drinks coffee, wine, beer etc.)

drinking foun·tain /'.. ,../ n. [C] a piece of equipment in a public place that produces a stream of water for you to drink from; WATER FOUNTAIN

drinking wa·ter /'.. ,../ n. [U] water that is pure enough for you to drink

drip[1] /drɪp/ v. **dripped, dripping 1** [I,T] to let liquid fall in the shape of small drops: *The faucet's dripping again – you'd better call the plumber.* | [**drip sth**] *A cut on her head dripped blood.* **2** [I] to fall in the shape of a small drop: [+ **down/from etc.**] *Sweat was dripping off his arms.* **3 be dripping with sth a)** if someone or something is dripping with water, it is so wet that small drops are falling off it: *My coat was dripping with snow.* **b)** to have, wear etc. a lot or too much of something: *As usual Ms. Vanderwegh arrived dripping with jewels.* **c)** to be filled with a strong emotion, or to show this emotion clearly: *Mulroy's voice was dripping with sarcasm.*

drip[2] n. **1** [C] one of the small drops of liquid that falls from something: *Before painting, lay a cloth on the floor to catch any drips.* **2** [singular,U] the sound or action of a liquid falling in very small drops: *Everything was quiet except for the drip of rain from the roof.* **3** [C] an IV **4** [C] INFORMAL someone who is boring and annoying

drip-dry /,. '.◂/ adj. drip-dry clothing can be hung up wet and dried without needing to be IRONED —**drip-dry** v. [I,T]

drip·ping /'drɪpɪŋ/ adj. extremely wet: *Take off that jacket, you're **dripping wet**.*

drip·pings /'drɪpɪŋz/ n. [plural] the oil and liquid that comes out of meat when you cook it

drip·py /'drɪpi/ adj. **drippier, drippiest** very emotional in a silly way: *The movie is nothing but a drippy melodrama.*

drive[1] /draɪv/ v. past tense **drove** past participle **driven**

1 | operate a vehicle | [I,T] to make a car, truck, bus etc. move and control where it goes: *I learned how to drive when I was fifteen.* | *Jeff drives a green Volvo.*
2 | travel somewhere | [I,T] to travel somewhere in a car, truck etc.: *On our trip to Florida, I drove 300 miles in one day.* | **drive up/down (to somewhere)** *We're driving down to Chicago this weekend.*
3 | take sb somewhere | [T] to take someone somewhere in a car, truck etc.: *Can you drive me to the airport next Friday?* | *Let me drive you home.*
4 | make sb/sth move | [T] to make people, animals, or an activity move somewhere: *Gang activity has driven business away from downtown.*
5 | make sb/sth do sth | [T] to strongly influence someone to do something or feel a particular way: *My love of competition is what drives me.* | [**drive sb/sth to do sth**] *Years of emotional abuse drove her to kill.* | *This job's enough to **drive you to drink** (=make you feel so bad that you begin to drink alcohol).* | [+ **by**] *Driven by financial pressures, doctors may be sending newborn babies home too soon.*
6 drive sb crazy/nuts/insane etc. to make someone feel very annoyed and angry: *I can't remember his name and it's driving me crazy.*
7 drive sb crazy/wild to make someone feel very sexually excited: *Her tight dresses drive all the guys wild.*
8 sb/sth drives sb up the wall also **sb/sth drives sb out of their mind** to make someone feel very annoyed and angry: *All that barking is driving me up the wall!*
9 | hit sth into sth | [T] to hit something, such as a nail, into something else: *Drive the nail into the wall at a downward angle.*
10 | make sb/sth work | [T] to make someone or something work hard: *Don't **drive yourself too hard** (=work too hard).*
11 | sports | [I,T] **a)** to move a ball or PUCK in a game of baseball, GOLF, HOCKEY etc. by hitting or kicking it hard and fast: *McGwire drove the ball into right field.* **b)** to run with the ball toward the GOAL in sports such as basketball or football
12 | provide power | [T] to provide the power for something: *The ship is driven by nuclear energy.*
13 | rain/wind etc. | [I always + adv./prep.] if rain, snow, wind etc. drives somewhere, it moves very quickly in that direction: *Snow drove against the windows.*
14 drive a hard bargain to demand a lot or refuse to give too much when making an agreement: *Well, you drive a hard bargain, but you've got yourself a deal.*
15 drive a wedge between sb/sth to do something that makes people or groups disagree or start to dislike each other: *My husband says I'm trying to drive a wedge between him and his mother.*

drive at sth phr. v. **what sb is driving at** the thing someone is really trying to say: *She didn't mention "sexual harassment," but I knew what she was driving at.*

drive sb/sth **away** phr. v. [T] to make someone or

something leave or stay away from someone or something: *If you keep on drinking, I guarantee you'll drive her away.* | [+ **from**] *Such strict laws drive drug addicts away from getting treatment.*

drive sth ↔ **home** *phr. v.* [T] to make something completely clear and meaningful: *Cox wanted to drive home the point that the team can't afford to lose another game.*

drive sb/sth ↔ **in** *phr. v.* [T] to hit the ball so that another player can SCORE a RUN² (2) in baseball: *Gant drove in 105 runs this season.*

drive off *phr. v.* **1** [I] if a driver or a car drives off, they leave: *After the accident, the other car just drove off.* **2** [T **drive** sb/sth ↔ **off**] to force someone or something to go away from you: *The army used tear gas to drive off the rioting crowds.*

drive sb/sth ↔ **out** *phr. v.* [T] to force someone or something to leave an area: *Cattle tend to drive out wild animals that eat the same grass.*

drive sth ↔ **up** *phr. v.* [T] to make prices, costs etc. increase: *The price of gasoline was driven up by at least 5% during the war.*

drive² *n.*

1 in a car [C] a trip in a car: *The beach is just a 20-minute drive from the city.* | *Let's go for a drive this afternoon.*

2 natural need [C] a strong natural need, such as the need for food, that people or animals must satisfy: *The male sex drive is not necessarily stronger than the female.*

3 effort [C singular] an effort to achieve something, especially an effort by an organization for a particular purpose: *Union High School is holding a blood drive (=an effort to collect blood) on December 19.* | [+ **for**] *The drive for civil rights is an on-going process.*

4 computers [C] a piece of equipment in a computer that is used to get information from a DISK or to store information on it: *Put your disk in the "A" drive and click on "save."*

5 determination [U] determination and energy to succeed: *Greg certainly has the drive to become a good lawyer.*

6 power [U] the power from an engine that makes the wheels of a car, bus etc. turn: *The pickup has four-wheel drive.*

7 baseball/tennis etc. [C] an act of hitting a ball hard, especially in baseball, tennis, or GOLF: *Griffey hit a long, high drive to right field.*

8 military attack [C] a series of military attacks: *The infantry made a drive deep into enemy territory.*

9 animals [C] an act of bringing animals such as cows or sheep together and making them move in a particular direction: *Brown was hired to lead a cattle drive north to the Canadian border.*

10 a road [C] a road for cars and other vehicles, especially a beautiful one or a small one that leads to a house: *You can park in the drive.* | *a scenic drive* —see also DISK DRIVE

drive-by shoot·ing /ˌ.. '../ also **drive-by** /'. ./ *n.* [C] a situation in which someone shoots someone else from a moving car

drive-in /'. ./ *n.* [C] **1** a place where you can watch movies outdoors while sitting in your car **2** a restaurant where you are served and eat in your car

driv·el /'drɪvəl/ *n.* [U] something that is said or written that is stupid, silly, or does not mean anything: *Most of these essays are just full of drivel.* —**drivel** *v.* [I]

driv·en¹ /'drɪvən/ *v.* the past participle of DRIVE¹

driven² *adj.* **1** trying extremely hard to achieve what you want: *John is a very driven young man.* **2** driven snow is snow that has been blown by the wind and is in piles —see also **as pure as the driven snow** (PURE (10))

driv·er /'draɪvɚ/ *n.* [C] **1** someone who drives a car, bus etc. **2** TECHNICAL a piece of computer SOFTWARE that makes a computer work with another piece of equipment such as a PRINTER or a MOUSE **3** **in the driver's seat** in control of a situation: *Foreign*

investors think that Latin America's need for them puts them in the driver's seat. **4** a GOLF CLUB with a wooden head —see also **back seat driver** (BACK SEAT (2)), SLAVE DRIVER

driver's ed·u·ca·tion /ˌ... ..'../ also **driver's ed** /ˌ.. './ *n.* [U] a course that teaches you how to drive, which you usually take in high school

driver's li·cense /'.. ,../ *n.* [C] an official document or card that says you are legally allowed to drive, which has your name and address on it, and usually a picture of you

drive shaft /'. ./ *n.* [C] TECHNICAL a part of a car, truck etc. that takes power from the GEARBOX to the wheels

drive-through, drive-thru /'. ./ NONSTANDARD *adj.* [only before noun] a drive-through restaurant, bank etc. can be used without getting out of your car: *We'll just get a couple of burgers at the drive-through window.* —**drive-through** *n.* [C]

drive·way /'draɪvweɪ/ *n.* plural **driveways** [C] the area or road for cars between a house and the street —see picture on page 423

driv·ing /'draɪvɪŋ/ *adj.* **1 driving rain/snow** rain or snow that falls very hard and fast **2 driving force/ambition** someone or something that strongly influences people or situations and makes them do something or change: *Hawksworth was the driving force behind the project.*

driving range /'.. ,./ *n.* [C] an open outdoor area where people practice hitting GOLF balls

driving school /'.. ,./ *n.* [C] a business that teaches you to how to drive a car

driving test /'.. ,./ *n.* [C] the official test that you must pass in order to be legally allowed to drive

driz·zle¹ /'drɪzəl/ *v.* **1** it drizzles if it drizzles, light rain and mist come out of the sky: *It's been drizzling all day.* **2** [T] to let a liquid fall on something else in a small stream or small drops, or to cover something with a liquid in this way: *Drizzle chocolate sauce over the sliced bananas.*

drizzle² *n.* [singular, U] weather that is a combination of mist and light rain: *A light drizzle had started by the time we left.* —**drizzly** *adj.*

droll /droʊl/ *adj.* amusing in an unusual way —**drolly** *adv.* —**drollness** *n.* [U]

drom·e·dar·y /'drɑmə,dɛri/ *n.* [C] a CAMEL with one raised HUMP¹ (2) on its back

drone¹ /droʊn/ *v.* **1** to make a continuous low noise: *A plane droned overhead.* **2** also **drone on** to speak in a boring way, usually for a long time: [+ **about**] *Lawyers were droning on about documentation.*

drone² *n.* **1** [U] a continuous low noise: [+ **of**] *The drone of the traffic was keeping him awake.* **2** [C] a male BEE that does no work **3** [C] someone who does a lot of dull work without many rewards: *Shelby was one of the drones on the factory floor.* **4** [C] an airplane or piece of equipment that does not have a person inside it, but is operated by radio: *The police use high-tech radar drones to catch speeders.* **5** [C] someone who has a good life but does not work to earn it: *She was labeled a welfare drone.*

drool¹ /drul/ *v.* [I] **1** to have SALIVA (=the liquid in your mouth) come out of your mouth: *This stupid dog drools all over the place.* —compare DRIBBLE¹ (1), SLOBBER **2** to show in a silly way that you like someone or something a lot: [+ **over**] *Sarah was drooling over the lead singer through the whole concert.*

drool² *n.* [U] a flow of SALIVA (=the liquid in your mouth) that comes out of your mouth

droop /drup/ *v.* **1** [I,T] to hang or bend down, or to make something do this: *Can you water the plants? They're starting to droop.* **2** [I] to become sad or weak: *Consumer spending could revive the drooping economy.* —**droop** *n.* [singular] —**droopy** *adj.*

drop¹ /drɑp/ *v.*

1 let sth fall [T] to suddenly or accidentally stop holding or carrying something, so that it falls: *One of the waiters tripped and dropped a tray full of food.* | *Allied planes began dropping bombs at midnight Tuesday.*

2 **fall** [I] to fall, especially from a high place: *The bottle rolled off the table and dropped to the floor*

3 **lower your body** [I always + adv./prep.,T] to lower yourself or part of your body suddenly: [+ **to/into/down** etc.] *The blow was so hard that he dropped to his knees.* | [**drop sth**] *Hearst dropped his head and shoulders and ran for the end zone.*

4 **take sb somewhere** [T always + adv./prep.] also **drop off** to take someone to a place in a car when you are going on to somewhere else: *I'll drop you at the corner, okay?* | *She drops the kids off at school on her way to work.*

5 **drop in/by/over** to visit someone when you have not arranged to come at a particular time: *Doris and Ed dropped by on Saturday.* | [**drop in on sb**] *Every now and then I drop in on my brother Art.*

6 **decrease** [I,T] to decrease to a lower level, amount, temperature etc., or to make something do this: *Stock prices dropped sharply Wednesday.* | [+ **to/from**] *The temperature dropped to 50 below zero.* | [**drop sth**] *The major phone companies have all dropped their prices recently.*

7 **stop doing sth** [T] to stop doing something or stop planning to do something: *Schultz threatened to resign and Reagan dropped the idea.* | *When the alarm sounded, we dropped everything (=stopped everything we were doing) and ran for safety.*

8 **move to a lower position** [I] to move to a lower position in relation to someone or something else, especially in a competition: [+ **to/from**] *Georgia dropped from 18th to 21st after losing to Virginia.*

9 **leave sth somewhere** [T always + adv./prep.] also **drop off** to take something to a place and leave it there for a short time: *You can drop your stuff at my place and pick it up after the concert.* | *I need to drop off these papers at Bob's.*

10 **stop including/using** [T] to decide not to include or use someone or something: [+ **from**] *Morris has been dropped from the team.*

11 **stop discussing** [I,T] to stop talking about something, especially because it is upsetting someone: *She didn't understand, so I let it drop.* | *Just drop it, man. It's late and I'm tired.*

12 **drop dead a)** to die suddenly: *One day he just dropped dead in the street.* **b)** SPOKEN said when you are angry with someone to tell them rudely to stop annoying you, go away etc.

13 **stop studying sth** [T] to stop taking a course at a high school or college, or to stop studying a particular subject: *If you take four classes you can drop one later if you need to.*

14 **lose weight** [I,T] to lose weight: *I have to drop 25 pounds to fit in the costume.*

15 **end a relationship** [T] to stop having a relationship with someone, especially suddenly: *Marian has dropped all her old friends since she started college.* | *After a few dates, he dropped her like a hot potato (=ended his relationship with her very suddenly).*

16 **work/run/shop etc. till you drop** INFORMAL to do something until you are extremely tired

17 **drop sb a line/note** to write and send a short letter to someone: *Drop us a line sometime.*

18 **drop a hint** to say something in a way that is not direct: *I've dropped a few hints about what I want for my birthday.*

19 **drop the ball** to not do a job that you are expected to do, especially because you make mistakes: *Investigators dropped the ball in the murder investigation.*

20 **airplane** [T] to drop someone from an airplane with a PARACHUTE[1]: *Soldiers were dropped behind enemy lines.*

21 **drop your pants/trousers** to pull down your pants, usually as a joke or to be rude

22 **be dropping like flies** INFORMAL used to say that a lot of people are dying or getting sick at the same time: *Players from both teams are dropping like flies.*

23 **slope** [I always + adv./prep.] if a path, land etc. drops, it goes down suddenly, forming a steep slope: *The road crosses the highway and then drops down to Chesbro Lake.*

24 **not pronounce a letter** [T] to not pronounce a particular sound: *Not all Southerners drop their r's.*

25 **drop a bombshell/bomb** INFORMAL to suddenly tell someone a shocking piece of news: *Last week Carson dropped the bombshell that she would resign.*

26 **lower your voice** [I,T] if your voice drops, or if you drop it, you speak more quietly or lower: *Barbara dropped her voice so Nelson wouldn't hear.*

27 **drop acid** INFORMAL to swallow ACID[1] (2) (=an illegal drug)

28 **lose games** [T] to lose a point, game etc. in a sports competition: *The Knicks dropped all three games on their West Coast trip.*

29 **drop your eyes/gaze** to stop looking at someone and look down, usually because you feel embarrassed or uncomfortable: *They dropped their eyes and pretended not to notice him.*

30 **lose/spend money** [T] INFORMAL to lose money in business, a game etc., or to spend a lot of money on something: *Pearl dropped $600 at the blackjack table in Vegas last weekend.*

31 **drop anchor** to lower a boat's ANCHOR to the bottom of the ocean, lake etc. so that the boat stays in the same place

32 **hit sb** [T] to hit someone so hard that they fall down: *Getz dropped McCallum with a right blow to the jaw.*

33 **drop names** to use the names of famous or important people in conversations to make yourself seem important

34 **drop a load** SLANG to pass solid waste out of your body through your BOWELS

35 **drop a stitch** to let the YARN (1) fall off the needle when you are KNITting

drop away *phr. v.* [I] to become lower in level or amount: *Sales have dropped away in recent months.* | *The roadside dropped away into the canyon.*

drop back *phr. v.* [I] to move backward, especially in football before throwing the ball: *Bono dropped back and threw a game-winning touchdown.*

drop behind *phr. v.* [I] to move or make progress more slowly than other people or things, so that they move ahead of you: *An hour into the hike, two of the boys had already dropped behind.*

drop off *phr. v.* **1** [I] to begin to sleep: *The baby dropped off to sleep in the car.* **2** [I] to become lower in level or amount: *The demand for leaded fuel dropped off in the late 1970s.*

drop out *phr. v.* [I] **1** to stop going to school or stop an activity before you have finished it: [+ **of**] *Kelly dropped out of college after one semester.* **2** to move away from or refuse to take part in society, because you do not agree with its principles: *In the 60s, many young people just wanted to drop out.* **3** if a word or expression drops out of a language, it is not used anymore —see also DROPOUT

drop[2] *n.*

1 **liquid** [C] a very small amount of liquid that falls in a round shape: [+ **of**] *Big drops of rain splashed on the sidewalk.* | *a tear drop*

2 **a small amount** [C] INFORMAL a small amount of liquid [+ **of**] *The glass in the kitchen still had a drop of milk in it.*

3 **eye/ear/nose etc. drops** medicine that you put in your eye, ear, nose etc. in drops

4 **distance** [singular] a distance from the top of something that is high to the bottom of it: *It's a twenty-five-foot drop from this cliff.*

5 **decrease in amount** [singular] a decrease in the amount, level, or number of something: [+ **in**] *Declining orders could mean a drop in production and a loss of jobs.*

6 **a fall** [C] a fall from a higher position to a lower position: *There was a sudden drop in the plane's altitude.*

7 **a drop in the bucket/ocean** an amount of something that is too small to have any effect: *Five thousand is a drop in the bucket compared to the $14 million we need.*

8 **at the drop of a hat** at any time without preparation or warning: *He's willing to organize anything guests want at the drop of a hat.*

9 **deliver** [C] an act of dropping or leaving something, such as food or medical supplies, especially from an airplane: *Despite the air drops of food and tents, the refugees continue to suffer.* —see also MAIL DROP

10 a lemon/chocolate/fruit etc. drop a small piece of candy that tastes like or is made of LEMON, chocolate, fruit etc. —see also COUGH DROP

11 drops [plural] special liquid medicine that you put in your eyes, ears, or nose in small drops —see also EYE DROPS, EAR DROPS

12 not touch a drop to not drink any alcohol at all: *I haven't touched a drop in years.*

drop cloth /'. ./ n. [C] a large cloth for covering furniture, floors etc. in order to protect them from dust or paint

drop-dead /'. ./ adv. SPOKEN extremely: *drop-dead gorgeous*

drop-in /,. '.‹ / adj. [only before noun] a drop-in place or time is a place where you can go or a time that you can go there without having to make arrangements first: *The drop-in center provides food and clothing for the homeless.*

drop kick /'. ./ n. [C] a kick made by dropping a ball and kicking it immediately —**drop-kick** v. [T]

drop·let /'draplɪt/ n. [C] a very small drop of liquid

drop-off¹ /'. ./ n. [C] **1** a decrease in something: *The remarkable drop-off in customers was partly due to the recession.* **2** a place where the level of the land goes down sharply: *There's a drop-off of about 50 feet.* **3** a place where you leave something for someone else

drop-off² adj. [only before noun] a drop-off place or container is a place where something can be left for someone else: *Local malls will set up drop-off bins for toys for needy kids.*

drop·out /'drap-aut/ n. **1** [C] someone who leaves school or college before they have finished: *About half of the prisoners are high-school dropouts.* **2** [C] someone who refuses to be involved in ordinary society, because they do not agree with its social practices, moral standards etc. **3** [C,U] TECHNICAL a short loss of signal when an electronic machine is working

drop·per /'drapə/ n. [C] a short glass tube with a hollow rubber part at one end, used for measuring liquid in drops

drop·pings /'drapɪŋz/ n. [plural] solid waste from birds or other animals

drop shot /'. ./ n. [C] an action of hitting the ball very lightly in sports such as tennis so that it barely goes over the net

drop·sy /'drapsi/ n. [U] OLD-FASHIONED, NOT TECHNICAL a medical condition in which liquid forms in parts of your body; EDEMA

dross /dras, drɔs/ n. [U] waste or useless substances, especially the waste separated from gold when gold is REFINEd

drought /draut/ n. [C,U] a long period of dry weather when there is not enough water

drove¹ /droov/ v. the past tense of DRIVE¹

drove² n. **1** [C] a group of animals that are being moved together **2 droves** [plural] a large crowd of people or animals: *The sunny weather has brought out boaters in droves.*

drov·er /'droovə/ n. [C] someone who moves cattle or sheep from one place to another in groups

drown /draun/ v. **1** [I,T] to die from being under water for too long, or to kill someone in this way: *He nearly drowned before friends rescued him.* | *The floods drowned scores of livestock.* **2** [T] to cover something completely with liquid: [**drown sth in/ with sth**] *The beef was drowned in red-wine gravy.* **3** [I,T] to have so much of something bad that it is almost impossible to deal with, or to put someone in this situation: *The country is drowning in debt.* **4 drown your sorrows** to drink a lot of alcohol in order to forget your problems

drown sb/sth ↔ **out** phr. v. [T] to prevent a sound from being heard by making a loud noise or sound: *Godchaux's fiddle drowned out the other instruments.* —**drowning** n. [C,U]

drowse /drauz/ v. [I] to be in a light sleep: *We were content to drowse in the warm sunlight on the beach.*

drows·y /'drauzi/ adj. **drowsier, drowsiest 1** tired and almost asleep, sometimes because you have eaten, taken drugs, or because you are in a warm place: *Cold medicines can make you feel drowsy.* **2** so peaceful that you feel relaxed and sleepy: *a drowsy rice-farming village* —**drowsily** adv. —**drowsiness** n. [U]

drub·bing /'drʌbɪŋ/ n. [C] INFORMAL **1** an occasion when something or someone is criticized a lot: *Taylor's latest movie has **taken a drubbing** from the critics.* **2** an occasion when one team easily beats another team in a game: *The Dodgers held first place after a 10–4 drubbing of the Cincinnati Reds.* —**drub** v. [T]

drudge /drʌdʒ/ n. [C] someone who does hard boring work: *Some drudge in the post office wouldn't give me any tape for my package.* —**drudge** v. [I]

drudg·er·y /'drʌdʒəri/ n. [U] hard boring work: *the endless drudgery of housework*

drug¹ /drʌg/ n. [C] **1** an illegal substance that people take, smoke, INJECT etc. for pleasure: *Four teenagers were arrested for selling drugs.* | *take/use/do drugs* *My cousin's been using drugs for years.* | *Look for signs that your child may be **on drugs** (=using drugs).* | *The program was designed to reduce the flow of **illegal drugs** into the United States.* **2** a medicine or a substance for making medicines: *Many researchers think that the drug may help prevent prostate cancer.* —see also DESIGNER DRUG, DRUG ABUSE

drug² v. **drugged, drugging** [T] **1** to give a person or animal a drug, especially in order to make feel them tired or go to sleep: *Collins says she was drugged and then raped on their first date.* **2** to add drugs to someone's food or drink to make them feel tired or go to sleep: *The wine had been drugged.* —**drugged** adj.

drug a·buse /'. .,./ n. [U] the use of illegal drugs, or the use of other drugs in way that is not good for you: *Drug abuse is becoming more common in higher-income neighborhoods.*

drug ad·dict /'. .,./ n. [C] someone who cannot stop taking drugs, especially illegal drugs —**drug addiction** /'. .,./ n. [U]

drug czar /'. ./ n. [C] an official employed by the U.S. government to try to stop people from using illegal drugs

drug deal·er /'. ,../ n. [C] someone who sells illegal drugs

Drug En·force·ment Ad·min·i·stra·tion, the /,. .'. ..,../ a U.S. government organization which makes sure that people and companies obey the laws about dangerous drugs

drugged-out /,. '.‹/ adj. INFORMAL using drugs a lot or being influenced by drugs: *a drugged-out hippie*

drug·get /'drʌgɪt/ n. [C,U] rough heavy cloth used especially as a floor covering, or a piece of this material

drug·gie /'drʌgi/ n. [C] INFORMAL someone who often takes illegal drugs

drug·gist /'drʌgɪst/ n. [C] OLD-FASHIONED a PHARMACIST

drug lord /'. ./ n. [C] someone who leads an organization that sells large quantities of illegal drugs

drug re·hab·il·i·ta·tion /'. .....,../ also **drug re·hab** /'drʌg ,rihæb/ n. [U] the process of helping someone to live without drugs after they have been ADDICTED to them

drug run·ner /'. ,../ n. [C] someone who brings illegal drugs from one country to another

drug·store /'drʌgstɔr/ n. [C] a store where you can buy medicine, beauty products etc.; PHARMACY

dru·id, Druid /'druɪd/ n. [C] a member of an ancient Celtic group of priests, in Great Britain, Ireland, and France, before the Christian religion —**Druidism** n. [U]

drum¹ /drʌm/ *n.* [C] **1** a musical instrument with a skin stretched over a circular frame, that you play by hitting it with your hand or a stick: *a snare drum* | *The band feature Frank Vilardi on drums* (=playing the drums). | **play (the) drums** *Jones quit school to play drums with a band.* **2** a large round container for storing liquids such as oil, chemicals etc.: *a 50-gallon drum of paint thinner* —see picture at CONTAINER **3** something that looks like a drum, especially part of a machine: *The rear brake drums on the car need replacing.* —see also **beat sb like a drum** (BEAT¹ (23)), **beat the drum for sb/sth** (BEAT¹ (22)), DRUM ROLL

drum² *v.* **drummed, drumming 1** [I] to play a drum **2** [I,T] to hit something again and again in a way that sounds like a drum: *Rain drummed on the windows.* | *He drummed his fingers* (=hit lightly with his fingers) *on the wood box a few times.*

drum sth into sb *phr. v.* [T] to keep telling someone something until they cannot forget it: *Patriotism was drummed into us at school.*

drum sb out *of sth phr. v.* [T] to force someone to leave an organization: *He was drummed out of football for writing a very revealing book.*

drum sth up *phr. v.* [T] to obtain something by asking a lot of people for help, information etc.: *We've been working hard to drum up business on the East Coast.*

drum·beat /'drʌmbit/ *n.* [C] the sound made by hitting a drum

drum brake /'. ./ *n.* [C usually plural] a system used for stopping a vehicle which uses two BRAKE SHOES that press against a metal CYLINDER that looks like a drum

drum ma·jor /'. ,../ *n.* [C] the leader of a MARCHING BAND

drum ma·jor·ette /,. ..'./ *n.* [C] a MAJORETTE

drum·mer /'drʌmə/ *n.* [C] someone who plays drums

drum·ming /'drʌmɪŋ/ *n.* [U] the act of playing a drum or the sound a drum makes

drum roll /'. ./ *n.* [C] a quick continuous beating of a drum, usually used to introduce an important event

drum·stick /'drʌm,stɪk/ *n.* [C] **1** the leg of a chicken or other bird, cooked as food **2** a stick that you use to hit a drum

drunk¹ /drʌŋk/ *v.* the past participle of DRINK¹

drunk² *adj.* **1** [not before noun] unable to control your behavior, speech etc. because you have drunk too much alcohol: *He gets in fights when he's drunk.* | *One of the salesman got drunk while entertaining clients.* | [+ **on**] *University police confronted about 500 youths who were apparently drunk on beer.* | *Michael's drunk as a skunk* (=very drunk). | *The old man was drunk off his ass* (=very drunk). **2 drunk and disorderly** LAW the crime of behaving in a violent noisy way in a public place when you are drunk: *Miller was fined $700 for being drunk and disorderly aboard a plane in October.* **3 drunk on/with sth** so excited by a feeling that you behave in a strange way: *We were drunk with freedom.* —compare DRUNKEN, SOBER¹ (1) —see also PUNCH-DRUNK, **roaring drunk** (ROARING (3))

drunk³ also **drunk·ard** /'drʌŋkəd/ *n.* [C] someone who is drunk or often gets drunk —compare ALCOHOLIC¹

drunk driv·er /,. '../ also **drunken driver** /,.. '../ *n.* [C] someone who illegally drives while drunk on alcohol

drunk-driv·ing /,. '../ also **drunken driving** /,.. '../ *n.* [U] driving a car after having drunk too much alcohol —**drunk-driving** *adj.*: *a drunk-driving accident*

drunk·en /'drʌŋkən/ *adj.* [only before noun] **1** drunk, or showing that you are drunk: *A drunken teenager was arrested for vandalism.* | *He hit her in a drunken rage.* **2 a drunken party/brawl/orgy etc.** a party, brawl, orgy etc. at or in which people are drunk: *Two men were killed in drunken brawl inside a cafe.* —**drunkenly** *adv.* —**drunkenness** *n.* [U]

drunk tank /'. ./ *n.* [C] INFORMAL a room in a prison for people who have drunk too much alcohol

druth·ers /'drʌðəz/ *n.* **if I had my druthers...** also **given my druthers...** SPOKEN used to say what you would wish if you could have whatever you wanted: *If I had my druthers, I wouldn't even take the trip.*

Druze, Druse /druz/ *n. plural* **Druze** [C] a member of a group of people in Syria, Lebanon, and Israel whose religion includes features from Islam, Christianity, and Judaism —**Druze** *adj.*

dry¹ /draɪ/ *adj.* **drier, driest**
1 not wet having no water or liquid inside or on the surface: *Can you check to see if the laundry's dry?* | *When the paint is completely dry, carefully peel off the masking tape.* | *The vehicle was found upside down in a dry creek bed.* | *My steak is dry as a bone* (=very dry). | **wipe/shake/rub etc. sth dry** *Pat the lettuce dry with a paper towel.*
2 weather having very little rain or MOISTURE: *In Arizona, the air is often extremely dry.* | *The weather tomorrow will be sunny and dry.* | *a dry winter*
3 dry mouth/skin/lips etc. a mouth, skin, lips etc. that is dry does not have enough of the normal liquid or MOISTURE that is usually there: *His mouth was dry, and he swallowed nervously.*
4 dry wine/sherry etc. wine, sherry etc. that is not sweet: *I prefer a dry white wine with fish dishes.*
5 dry wit/humor also **a dry sense of humor** someone with a dry sense of humor pretends to be serious when they are really joking: *Harman's dry humor enlivens the lectures.* —see also DRYLY
6 boring someone or something such as a movie or book that is dry is boring and too serious: *Scientists can be so dry and unexciting.*
7 voice very serious and showing no emotion: *His voice was dry as he told of his time as a prisoner of war.*
8 a dry cough a cough that does not produce any PHLEGM: *A dry cough is one of the features of altitude sickness.*
9 run/go dry if a lake, river etc. runs dry, all the water gradually disappears, especially because there has been no rain: *The reservoir ran dry during the drought.*
10 dry toast TOASTed bread that does not have butter or JAM on it
11 not a dry eye in the house used to say that everyone was crying because something was very sad: *There wasn't by a dry eye in the house after Marvin finished his graduation speech.*
12 dry land land rather than water: *After three weeks at sea we were glad to be back on dry land again.*
13 the dry heaves the action of continuing to VOMIT even though nothing comes out through your mouth anymore
14 town/county not allowing any alcohol to be sold there: *Conway is in a dry county.* —**dryness** *n.* [U] —see also DRIP-DRY

dry² *v.* **dries, dried, drying** [I,T] to become dry or to make something dry: *After you press the two parts together, let the glue dry for at least an hour.* | *It'll only take a few minutes to dry my hair.* —see also CUT AND DRIED, DRIED

dry off *phr. v.* [I,T **dry sb/sth off**] to become dry or make something dry, especially on the surface: *The best time to moisturize the skin is after you shower and dry off.* | *He dried his bicycle seat off with a towel.*

dry out *phr. v.* **1** [I,T **dry sth ↔ out**] to become completely dry or make something completely dry after it has been very wet: *Farmers will have to wait for fields to dry out before they can harvest their soybeans.* | *Hang your towel over the chair to dry it out.* **2** [I,T **dry sb out**] to stop drinking alcohol after you have become an ALCOHOLIC: *Miller spent a month drying out at the Betty Ford Center.*

dry up *phr. v.* **1** [I,T **dry sth ↔ up**] a river, lake, or area of land that dries up has no more water in it: *Lake Elizabeth will not dry up, but its water level could drop.* **2** [I] if supplies or money dry up, they come to an end and there is no more available: *If the*

D

network money begins to dry up, team owners may increase the price of tickets. **3** [I,T **dry sth ↔ up**] if a sore or wound dries up, it stops having liquid inside or on it: *Calamine lotion helps to dry up poison ivy sores very effectively.*

dry·ad /ˈdraɪæd, -əd/ *n.* [C] a female spirit who lives in a tree, in ancient Greek stories

dry bat·te·ry /ˌ. ˈ..../ also **dry cell** /ˌ. ˈ./ *n.* [C] an electric BATTERY containing chemicals that are not in a liquid form

dry-clean, **dry clean** /ˈ. ./ *v.* [T] to clean clothes, BLANKETS etc. with chemicals instead of water

dry clean·ers /ˈ. ˌ../ *n.* [C] a store where you can take clothes to be dry-cleaned

Dry·den /ˈdraɪdn/, **John** (1631–1700) an English writer of poetry and plays

dry dock /ˈ. ./ *n.* [C] a place where a ship can be taken out of the water for repairs

dry·er /ˈdraɪɚ/ *n.* [C] a machine that dries things, especially clothes

dry-eyed /ˈ. ./ *adj.* not crying

dry goods /ˈ. ./ *n.* [plural] **1** foods that are dry and will stay fresh without being in a REFRIGERATOR, such as coffee **2** things that are made from cloth, such as clothes, sheets, and curtains: *a dry goods store*

dry-hump /ˌ. ˈ./ *v.* [I,T] VULGAR if someone dry-humps something, they rub their sexual organs against it while they are wearing clothing —**dry humping** *n.* [U]

dry ice /ˌ. ˈ./ *n.* [U] CARBON DIOXIDE in a solid form, often used to keep food and other things cold or used to make mist in a theater or NIGHTCLUB

dry·ly, **drily** /ˈdraɪli/ *adv.* speaking seriously, although you are really joking: *"If you're lucky," said Harrison dryly, "they'll only hang you."*

dry mea·sure /ˌ. ˈ.., ˌ. ˌ../ *n.* [U] a system of measuring the VOLUME, instead of the weight, of things such as grain, fruit, and vegetables —see also BUSHEL, PECK[2] (3)

dry rot /ˈ. ./ *n.* [U] a disease in wood that turns it into powder

dry run /ˌ. ˈ./ *n.* [C] an event that you use as a way of practicing for a more important event: *Both the parties are treating the local elections as a dry run.*

dry-shod /ˈ. ./ *adv.* LITERARY without getting your feet wet

dry·wall /ˈdraɪwɔl/ *n.* [U] a type of board made of two large sheets of CARDBOARD with PLASTER between them, used to cover walls and ceilings —**dry-wall** *v.* [I,T]

DST *n.* [U] Daylight Saving Time

DTP *n.* [U] **1** DPT **2** the abbreviation of DESKTOP PUBLISHING

DT's /ˌdi ˈtiz/ *n.* **the DT's** HUMOROUS: see DELIRIUM TREMENS

du·al /ˈduəl/ *adj.* [only before noun] **dual nationality/ controls/purpose etc.** having two nationalities, sets of controls, purposes etc. —**duality** /duˈæləti/ *n.* [U]

dual cit·i·zen·ship /ˌ.. ˈ..../ *n.* [U] the state of being a citizen of two countries at the same time

dub /dʌb/ *v.* **dubbed, dubbing** [T] **1** [usually passive] to give something or someone a humorous name that describes their character: *Johnson was dubbed "Magic" while playing high school basketball.* **2** to replace the original sound recording of a movie, television show etc. with another sound recording, especially in another language: [**dub sth into sth**] *Most martial arts movies are poorly dubbed into English.* **3** to copy a recording from an AUDIOTAPE or CD to another tape **4** LITERARY if a king or queen dubs someone, they give the title of KNIGHT to that person in a special ceremony

du·bi·e·ty /duˈbaɪəti/ *n.* [U] FORMAL a feeling of doubt

du·bi·ous /ˈdubiəs/ *adj.* **1** making you doubt whether someone or something is honest or correct: *Newsome failed to explain his dubious personal finances.* **2** making you doubt whether something is useful, safe, or dependable: *The new strategy of stopping drug smugglers is untested and dubious.* **3 a dubious honor/distinction/pleasure etc.** something that is actually bad or the opposite of an honor etc.: *The Stephens had the dubious honor of being the 100th homeowners to lose their home to the fire.* **4 be dubious (about sth)** to have doubts about whether something is good or true: *I am dubious about the safety of my car's airbags.* —**dubiously** *adv.* —**dubiousness** *n.* [U]

Dub·lin /ˈdʌblɪn/ the capital and largest city of the Republic of Ireland

Du Bois /duˈbɔɪs/, **W.E.B.** (1868–1963) an African-American writer and educator who helped to start the NAACP

du·cal /ˈdukəl/ *adj.* relating or belonging to a DUKE

duc·at /ˈdʌkət/ *n.* [C] a gold coin that was used in several European countries in the past

Du·champ /duˈʃɑmp/, **Mar·cel** /mɑrˈsɛl/ (1887–1968) a French PAINTER famous for his work in the style of Cubism and Dadaism

duch·ess /ˈdʌtʃɪs/ *n.* [C] a woman with the highest social rank below a PRINCESS, or the wife of a DUKE: *the Duchess of York*

duch·y /ˈdʌtʃi/ *n. plural* **duchies** [C] the land and property of a DUKE or DUCHESS; DUKEDOM

duck[1] /dʌk/ *n.* **1** [C] a common water bird with short legs and a wide beak, that is used for its meat, eggs, and soft feathers **2** [C] a female duck —compare DRAKE **3** [U] the meat of this bird used as food: *roast duck* —see also **a dead duck** (DEAD[1] (19)), LAME DUCK, **take to something like a duck to water** at **take to sth** (TAKE[1]), **like water off a duck's back** (WATER[1] (8))

duck[2] *v.* **1** [I,T] to lower your head or body very quickly, especially to avoid being seen or hit: *It was a good thing that I ducked when the wind blew the sail around.* | [+ **under**] *The bank teller ducked under the counter and pushed the alarm button.* | *Lewis ducked his head to avoid the ball.* **2** [I] to go into a place quickly, especially to avoid being seen or to get away from someone: [+ **into**] *The three men ducked into a subway entrance and disappeared.* —see picture at DODGE[1] **3** [I] to visit a place, especially for only a short time: [+ **into**] *When I'm in the area, I'll occasionally duck into the place to have a beer.* **4** [T] to try to avoid something, especially a difficult duty or something that you do not want to do: *Glazer ducked a question about his involvement in the bank scandal.* **5** [T] OLD-FASHIONED to push someone or something under the water; DUNK

duck out *phr. v.* [I] INFORMAL **1** to avoid doing something that you have to do or have promised to do: [+ **of/on**] *I can't believe he would duck out of his promise to help me.* **2** to leave quickly, especially without anyone noticing: [+ **of**] *As he ducked out of the meeting, Shirakawa was immediately surrounded by reporters.*

duck-billed plat·y·pus /ˌdʌkbɪld ˈplætəpʊs, -pəs/ *n.* [C] a PLATYPUS

duck·boards /ˈdʌkbɔrdz/ *n.* [plural] long narrow boards that you use to make a path over muddy ground

duck·ing stool /ˈ.. ˌ./ *n.* [C] a seat on the end of a long pole, used to DUCK[2] (5) a person in water as a punishment in the past

duck·ling /ˈdʌklɪŋ/ *n.* [C] a small young duck

duck·weed /ˈdʌkwid/ *n.* [U] a plant that grows on the surface of fresh water

duck·y[1] /ˈdʌki/ *n. plural* **duckies** [C] INFORMAL a word meaning a DUCK, used especially when speaking to children: *a rubber ducky for the bathtub*

ducky[2] *adj.* OLD-FASHIONED perfect or satisfactory: *Well, that's just ducky.*

duct /dʌkt/ *n.* [C] **1** a pipe or tube for carrying liquids, air, CABLES etc.: *an air-conditioning duct* **2** a thin narrow tube that carries air, liquid etc. inside your body, in a plant etc.: *tear ducts*

duc·tile /ˈdʌktl, -taɪl/ *adj.* ductile substances can be pressed or pulled into shape without breaking —**ductility** /dʌkˈtɪləti/ *n.* [U]

duct·less gland /ˌdʌktlɪs ˈglænd/ n. [C] an ENDOCRINE GLAND

duct tape /ˈ. ./ n. [U] a silver-gray cloth TAPE that is used for repairs in a house such as PLUMBING

dud /dʌd/ n. [C] INFORMAL **1** something that is useless, especially because it does not work correctly: *Critics have labeled the new telescope a dud.* **2** a person, movie, book etc. that is not interesting, entertaining, or successful: *Pauley's last performance was a major dud.* **3** duds [plural] OLD-FASHIONED clothes —dud adj.

dude /dud/ n. [C] **1** SLANG a man: *Come on dude, play your card.* | *Dude, check out that car.* **2** OLD-FASHIONED a man from a city, who is living in or visiting the COUNTRYSIDE, especially a RANCH

dude ranch /ˈ. ./ n. [C] a vacation place where you can ride horses and live like a COWBOY

dudg·eon /ˈdʌdʒən/ n. **in high dudgeon** FORMAL angry because someone has treated you badly: *Simons ended the interview and left in high dudgeon.*

due¹ /du/ adj. [no comparative]
1 be due a) to be expected to happen or arrive at a certain time or date: *When is your baby due (=expected to be born)?* | *The bus is due any minute now.* | [+ at/on etc.] *The flight from Chicago is due at 6:30 p.m.* | [+ in] *Dr. Rankin is due in surgery in about an hour.* | [+ for] *After working eight days in a row, I'm due for (=expect to get) a day off.* | [be due to do sth] *Our book's not due to be published until December.* | [be due back/out/in etc.] *Mike is due back today.* **b)** to need to be paid or given on a particular date: [+ at/on/by etc.] *Larry's mortgage payments are always due at the end of the month.* | *My library books aren't due until next week.*
2 due to sth because of: *Her success is due to her hard work.* | *Our flight was delayed due to fog.* | *Frank will not be here this afternoon due to an illness in the family.*
3 owed [not before noun] owed to someone either as a debt or because they have a right to it: *I was assured that any money due me would be sent immediately.* | *She should be given the respect due a great educator.* | [+ to] *After he was fired, the company failed to pay him the commissions due to him.*
4 with (all) due respect (to sb) SPOKEN used when you disagree with someone or criticize them in a polite way: *With due respect, this is not the time for council members to argue about their salaries.* | *With all due respect to Ramsay, I don't agree with him.*
5 in due time/course at some time in the future when it is the right time, especially after a process has been completed: *In due time, Medicare should fully insure about 34 million elderly Americans.*
6 appropriate [only before noun] FORMAL appropriate or correct: *The community association must use due care to make responsible decisions.* —see also DULY

due² adv. **due north/south/east/west** directly or exactly north, south, east, or west etc.: *At noon, the storm was 150 miles due east of New York City.*

due³ n. **1 sb's due** things such as respect, money, justice etc. that someone deserves: *Women composers rarely get their due.* | *Cheatham wasn't given his due until he was well into his seventies.* **2 dues** [plural] regular payments you make to an organization of which you are a member: *Lawyers were formerly required to pay yearly dues to the Bar Association.* —see also **pay your dues** (PAY¹ (17)) **3 give sb his/her due** to admit that someone has good qualities even though you often criticize them: *Let's give the man his due – he's very good at turning a profit.* —see also **give the devil his due** (DEVIL (12))

due date /ˈ. ./ n. [usually singular] **1** the date on which a baby is expected to be born, which is calculated by a doctor: *Fewer than 5 percent of women deliver on their due date.* **2** a DEADLINE

du·el¹ /ˈduəl/ n. [C] **1** a situation in which two ATHLETES or teams compete very hard against each other: *Bob Welch won a pitching duel with Jack Morris by the score of 3–1.* **2** a situation in which two people or groups are involved in an angry disagreement: *A verbal duel at the conference showed the depth of disagreement between the two countries.* **3** a

fight with weapons between two people, used in past times to settle an argument: *In 1779, Decatur was killed in a duel.*

duel² v. dueled, dueling also duelled, duelling [I + with] to fight a duel

due proc·ess /ˌ. ˈ. ./ n. [U] LAW the correct process that should be followed in law and is designed to protect someone's legal rights

du·et /duˈɛt/ n. [C] a piece of music for two performers —compare QUARTET (1), SOLO¹ (1), TRIO (3)

duff /dʌf/ n. [C usually singular] INFORMAL **1 get off your duff** used to say that someone should stop being lazy and start doing something: *Tell him to get off his duff and get a job!* **2** your BUTTOCKS

duf·fel bag, duffle bag /ˈdʌfəl ˌbæg/ n. [C] a cloth bag with a round bottom and a string at the top to tie it closed —see picture at BAG¹

duffel coat, duffle coat /ˈdʌfəl ˌkoʊt/ n. [C] a coat made of rough heavy cloth, usually with a HOOD and TOGGLES (=a type of long button)

duff·er /ˈdʌfɚ/ n. [C] **1** INFORMAL someone who plays GOLF fairly badly **2 old duffer** INFORMAL an old man who cannot think clearly anymore **3** OLD-FASHIONED someone who is stupid or not very good at something

dug /dʌg/ v. the past tense and past participle of "dig"

dug·out /ˈdʌgaʊt/ n. [C] **1** a low shelter at the side of a sports field, especially a baseball field, where players and COACHES (COACH¹ (1)) sit **2** a small boat made by cutting out a hollow space in a tree TRUNK: *a dugout canoe*

duh /dʌ/ also **no duh** interjection INFORMAL used to say that what someone else has just said or asked is stupid or unnecessary because it is very easy to understand: *"You mean I can't park there?" "Duh, that's what I said."*

DUI n. [C,U] driving under the influence; the crime of driving when you have drunk too much alcohol: *McKay was charged with DUI.*

du jour /du ˈʒʊr, də ˈʒɚ/ adj. [only after noun] used in restaurants to show that a dish is not part of the usual MENU but has been specially made for that day: *soup du jour*

duke¹ /duk/ n. [C] **1** a man with the highest social rank below a PRINCE: *the Duke of Norfolk* —compare DUCHESS **2 put up your dukes** INFORMAL to hold up your FISTS to get ready to fight

duke² v. INFORMAL **duke it out (with sb)** to fight or compete: *Manwaring and Decker will duke it out for the starting catcher job next season.*

duke·dom /ˈdukdəm/ n. [C] **1** the rank of a DUKE **2** the land and property belonging to a DUKE

Duke of Wellington, the /ˌduk əv ˈwɛlɪŋtən/ (1769–1852) a British soldier and politician, famous for defeating Napoleon at the Battle of Waterloo in 1815

dul·cet /ˈdʌlsɪt/ adj. **1 sb's dulcet tones** HUMOROUS someone's voice **2** LITERARY dulcet sounds are soft and pleasant to hear

dul·ci·mer /ˈdʌlsəmɚ/ n. [C] **1** a musical instrument with up to 100 strings, played with light hammers **2** a small instrument with strings that is popular in American FOLK MUSIC, and is played with it sitting across your knees

dull¹ /dʌl/ adj.
1 boring not interesting or exciting: *This place gets really dull at times.* | *Margaret has such a dull personality.*
2 never a dull moment USUALLY HUMOROUS used to say that a lot of interesting things are happening or that you are very busy: *"We talk about everything, whatever's going on," Faso said. "There's never a dull moment."*
3 color/light not bright or shiny: *When a plant changes color from bright green to dull gray-green, it needs water.*
4 sound not clear or loud: *His head hit the floor with a dull thud.*

D

D

5 [pain] a dull pain is not severe but does not stop: *a dull headache*
6 [knife/blade] not sharp; BLUNT: *Here, use this knife – that one's dull.* —see picture at SHARP[1]
7 [not intelligent] OLD-FASHIONED not able to think quickly or understand things easily: *a dull student*
8 (as) dull as dishwater INFORMAL very boring: *It's supposed to be political satire, but it's dull as dishwater.*
9 [trade] if business on the Stock Exchange is dull, few people are buying and selling: *A dull opening Wednesday on Wall Street kept stock prices at low levels.* —**dullness** n. [U] —**dully** adv.

dull² v. [T] to make something such as pain or a feeling become less sharp, less clear etc.: *Three times a day, he takes medication to dull the pain from back problems.*

dull·ard /'dʌlɚd/ n. [C] OLD-FASHIONED someone who is stupid and has no imagination

du·ly /'duli/ adv. in the appropriate or expected way: *The gift was duly noted by the Secretary of State in his annual financial disclosure form.*

Du·mas /du'mɑ/, **Al·ex·an·dre** /,ælɪg'zɑndrə/ (1802–1870) a French writer of NOVELS and plays

dumb¹ /dʌm/ adj. **1** INFORMAL stupid: *That's a dumb idea.* | *I can't get my dumb car to start.* | *She's just a dumb blonde.* (=a woman with BLONDE hair who is pretty, but seems stupid) **2** OLD-FASHIONED a word used to describe someone who is permanently unable to speak, now considered offensive by most people —see also DEAF AND DUMB **3** unable to speak, because you are angry, surprised, shocked etc.: *He stared in dumb misery at the wreckage of the car.* | *The crowd was **struck dumb** by the sight of the hanging.* **4 dumb luck** the way in which something good happens in a completely unexpected way, especially if it is not deserved: *The cleanup of the oil spill was helped by good weather and a lot of dumb luck.* **5 dumb animals** used to emphasize that animals cannot speak and that people often treat them badly —**dumbly** adv. —**dumbness** n. [U]

dumb² v.
dumb sth ↔ down phr. v. [T] INFORMAL, DISAPPROVING to make something very simple, so that anyone can understand it: *They've dumbed down the TV news so much it's not really worth watching anymore.*

dumb ass /'. ./ n. [C] SLANG, OFFENSIVE a stupid person: *Stop acting like a dumb ass.* —**dumb-ass** adj. [only before noun]

dumb·bell /'dʌmbɛl/ n. [C] **1** two weights connected by a short bar, that you can lift in each hand to strengthen your arms and shoulders **2** INFORMAL someone who is stupid

dumb·found /dʌm'faʊnd, 'dʌmfaʊnd/ v. [T] to shock or surprise someone so much that they are very confused

dumb·found·ed /'dʌm,faʊndɪd/ adj. so surprised that you are confused and cannot speak: *He was dumbfounded when Ryskamp didn't apologize.*

dum·bo /'dʌmboʊ/ n. [C] INFORMAL someone who is stupid

dumb·struck /'dʌmstrʌk/ adj. so shocked or surprised that you cannot speak: *Millions of Americans were dumbstruck by the news of the bombing.*

dumb ter·mi·nal /'. ,.../ n. [C] a type of computer that is not able to store information or do things without being connected to another computer —compare INTELLIGENT TERMINAL

dumb·wait·er /dʌm'weɪtɚ/ n. [C] a small ELEVATOR used to move food, plates etc. from one floor of a restaurant, hotel etc. to another

dum-dum /'dʌm dʌm/ n. [C] **1** also **dum-dum bullet** a soft bullet that causes serious wounds because it breaks into pieces when it hits you **2** SPOKEN a stupid person

dum·my¹ /'dʌmi/ n. plural **dummies** [C] **1** INFORMAL a stupid person: *That's what I just said, dummy.* | *She's no dummy.* **2** a large DOLL in the shape of a

person, which has a mouth that can be moved so that it looks as though it is talking **3** a large model in the shape of a person, especially used when you are making clothes or to show them in a store: *a dressmaker's dummy* **4** an object that is made to look like a tool, weapon, vehicle etc. but which you cannot use **5** cards that are placed on the table by one player for all the other players to see in a game of BRIDGE

dummy² adj. [only before noun] a dummy tool, weapon, vehicle etc. is made to look like a real one, but you cannot use it: *a dummy rifle*

dummy³ v. **dummies, dummied, dummying**
dummy up phr. v. [I] SLANG to stay silent and not speak: *When I asked her name she just dummied up.*

dummy run /,.. '. / n. [C] an occasion when you practice doing something in complete detail to see if it works: *In a recent dummy run, the 4th Marine Brigade stormed a beach on Catalina Island.*

dump¹ /dʌmp/ v.
1 [put sth somewhere] [T always + adv./prep.] to pour something out or put something somewhere in a careless, messy, or quick way: [dump sth in/on/under etc.] *Just dump your bags over there in the corner.*
2 [end relationship] [T] to end a romantic relationship, especially in a sudden way that shows you do not care about that person: *I mean he just used her emotionally and then dumped her.*
3 [throw away] [T] to get rid of something you do not want, especially by pouring it out: *Should I dump this coffee? It's cold.* | *Hill had to drive six miles just to dump her garden waste.*
4 a dumping ground a place where you send people or things that you want to get rid of: *The lawyers say the agency is using the shelter as a dumping ground for unwanted teen-agers.*
5 [copy information] [T] TECHNICAL to copy information stored in a computer's memory onto a DISK or MAGNETIC TAPE
6 [sell goods] [T] to sell goods at a very low price, when they should cost much more, in order to beat the competition: *They were accused of dumping computer chips on the U.S. market.*
dump on phr. v. [T] INFORMAL **1** [dump on sb] to criticize someone very strongly and often unfairly: *Students will always dump on the teachers.* **2** [dump on sb] to tell someone all your problems: *Sorry to dump on you like that – I just needed someone to listen.* **3** [dump sb/sth on sb] to give someone an unwanted job or responsibility: *Don't dump your kids on me. I've got work to do.*

dump² n. [C] **1** a place where unwanted waste is taken and left: *a garbage dump* **2** INFORMAL a place that is not nice to live in because it is dirty, ugly, messy etc.: *How can you live here? This place is a dump.* **3** a place where military supplies are stored, or the supplies themselves: *an ammunition dump* **4 take a dump** SLANG to pass solid waste from your BOWELS **5** TECHNICAL the act of copying the information stored in a computer's memory onto something else, such as a DISK —see also **be down in the dumps** (DOWN² (9))

dump·ling /'dʌmplɪŋ/ n. [C] **1** a small round mass of flour and fat mixed with water, cooked in boiling liquid and served with meat: *chicken and dumplings* **2** a sweet dish made of PASTRY filled with fruit: *apple dumplings*

Dump·ster /'dʌmpstɚ/ n. [C] TRADEMARK a large metal container used for waste

Dumpster div·ing /'.. ,../ n. [U] INFORMAL the activity of looking through Dumpsters for used clothes, food, furniture etc. that other people have thrown away

dump truck /'. ./ n. [C] a vehicle with a large open container at the back that can move up at one end to pour sand, soil etc. onto the ground

dump·y /'dʌmpi/ adj. INFORMAL someone who is dumpy is fat, short, and unattractive: *a dumpy little man*

dun /dʌn/ n. [C,U] a dull brownish-gray color —**dun** adj.

Dun·bar /'dʌnbɑr/, **Paul** (1872–1906) a U.S. poet famous as one of the first African-American writers to become well known

Dun·can /'dʌŋkən/, **Is·a·do·ra** /ˌɪzəˈdɔrə/ (1878–1927) a U.S. dancer who had a great influence on MODERN DANCE

Isadora Duncan

dunce /dʌns/ n. [C] OLD-FASHIONED someone who is slow at learning things: *the dunce of the class*

dunce cap /'. ./ n. [C] a tall pointed hat that a stupid student had to wear in school in the past

dun·der·head /'dʌndə-ˌhɛd/ n. [C] OLD-FASHIONED someone who is stupid

dune /dun/ n. [C] a hill made of sand near the ocean or in the desert; SAND DUNE

dune bug·gy /'. ˌ../ n. plural dune buggies [C] a car with big wheels and no roof, that you can drive across sand

dung /dʌŋ/ n. [U] solid waste from animals, especially cows

dun·ga·rees /ˌdʌŋgəˈriz, 'dʌŋgəˌriz/ n. [plural] OLD-FASHIONED heavy cotton pants used for working in; JEANS

dun·geon /'dʌndʒən/ n. [C] a dark prison that is below the surface of the earth, especially under a castle, used in past times

dunk /dʌŋk/ v. 1 [T] to quickly put something into a liquid and take it out again, especially something you are eating: *The old men sit around the table talking and dunking donuts into their coffee.* 2 [I,T] to jump up toward the basket and throw the ball down into it in the game of basketball: *Keefe dunked to bring Stanford's lead to 10 points.* 3 [T] to push someone under water for a short time, especially as a joke —**dunk** n. [C] SLAM DUNK

dun·no /dəˈnoʊ/ SPOKEN, NONSTANDARD a way of saying "I don't know": *"What are you doing tonight?" "I dunno."*

du·o /'duoʊ/ n. plural duos [C] two people who do something together, especially sing or play music

du·o·dec·i·mal /ˌduəˈdɛsəməl/ adj. TECHNICAL a duodecimal system of numbers is based on the number 12, instead of the usual system based on ten

du·o·de·num /ˌduəˈdinəm, ˌduˈadn-əm/ n. [C] TECHNICAL the beginning part of your SMALL INTESTINE, below your stomach —**duodenal** /ˌduəˈdinl, ˌduˈadn-əl/ adj.

du·op·o·ly /duˈapəli/ n. plural duopolies [C usually singular] TECHNICAL the control of all or most of a business activity by only two companies, so that other organizations cannot easily compete with them

dupe¹ /dup/ n. [C] 1 someone who is tricked, especially into becoming involved in something illegal 2 the act of duping someone

dupe² v. [T usually passive] to trick or deceive someone: [dupe sb into doing sth] *Many elderly people have been duped into buying worthless insurance.*

du·plex /'duplɛks/ n. [C] a type of house that is divided so that it has two separate homes in it

du·pli·cate¹ /'dupləkɪt/ n. [C] 1 an exact copy of something that you can use in the same way: *a duplicate of the key* 2 **in duplicate** if something is written in duplicate, there are two copies of it —**duplicate** adj.: *a duplicate copy*

du·pli·cate² /'dupləˌkeɪt/ v. [T] 1 to copy something exactly: *The video had been duplicated illegally.* | *Give the plant a lot of bright light, to duplicate outdoor conditions.* 2 FORMAL to succeed in repeating something: *Scientists raced to duplicate Fleishmann's experiments.* —**duplication** /ˌdupləˈkeɪʃən/ n. [U]

du·plic·i·ty /duˈplɪsəti/ n. [U] FORMAL dishonest behavior that is intended to deceive someone —**duplicitous** adj.

Du Pont /du 'pant/, **Pierre Sam·u·el** /pyɛr ˈsæmuəl/

(1870–1954) a U.S. businessman who greatly developed the Du Pont company, especially by adding the making of chemicals to its activities

Du Pont de Ne·mours /du 'pant də nəˈmʊr/, **El·eu·thère** /ˌɛluˈθɛr/ (1771–1834) a U.S. businessman, born in France, who made explosives and started the Du Pont company

dur·a·ble /'dʊrəbəl/ adj. 1 staying in good condition for a long time, even if used a lot: *Plastic window frames are more durable than wood.* 2 continuing for a long time: *We hope to have created a durable peace between the two countries.* —**durably** adv. —**durability** /ˌdʊrəˈbɪləti/ n. [U]

durable goods /ˌ... './ n. [plural] large things such as cars, televisions, and furniture that last a long time, and that you do not buy often

Du·rant /dʊˈrænt/, **William** (1861–1947) a U.S. businessman who organized the car companies Buick, Chevrolet, and General Motors

du·ra·tion /dʊˈreɪʃən/ n. [U] FORMAL the length of time that something continues: *To avoid injuries, increase the duration of your exercise gradually.* | *The site manager will be in Japan **for the duration of the project** (=until the end of the project).*

Dü·rer /'dʊrə/, **Al·brecht** /'ælbrɛkt/ (1471–1528) a German artist famous for his drawings and ENGRAVINGS

du·ress /dʊˈrɛs/ n. [U] FORMAL illegal or unfair threats: *Williams said he agreed to the new settlement **under duress** (=as a result of illegal or unfair threats used against him).*

dur·ing /'dʊrɪŋ/ prep. 1 all through a period of time: *During the summer, she worked as a lifeguard.* | *There are always significant traffic problems during commuting hours.* 2 at some point in a period of time: *There will be six meetings during the college's winter quarter.* | *During the second week in December, the jobless rate fell by two percent.* **s w 1 1**

USAGE NOTE: DURING

WORD CHOICE: during, for
During can be used to answer the question "when?": *"When did you learn Italian?" "I learned it during my year abroad in Venice."* **For** can be used to answer the question "how long?": *"How long have you been in the U.S.?" "I've been here for three months."* When you want to talk about the time within which something happens, you use **during**: *Call me sometime during your trip.* | *Thieves broke in during the night.* When you are talking about how long something lasts, you use **for**: *I was only out of the room for a few minutes.* | *They were married for 20 years.* **During** is common with words for something that continues for a length of time: *during the program/the semester/the war/a conversation.* You also use it to talk about specific periods of time: *during office hours/the day/that year/the 80s.* **For** is more usual with phrases used to measure length of time: *for two hours/a week/many years.*
GRAMMAR
During is never used in a clause like **while**: *While I was at home, I saw Jerri.* You can say: *During my time at home,...* but NOT "during I was at home,..." Also, you can say: *I did the dishes while you were asleep* (NOT "during you were asleep").

Durk·heim /'dʊrkhaɪm/, **É·mile** /eɪ'mil/ (1858–1917) a French university teacher who helped to establish the principles of SOCIOLOGY

durst /dəst/ v. OLD USE the past tense of DARE

Du·shan·be /duˈʃambə, -ˈʃæm-/ the capital city of Tajikistan

dusk /dʌsk/ n. [U] the time just before it gets dark, when the sky is becoming darker: *The street lights go on **at dusk**.* —compare DAWN¹ (1)

dusk·y /'dʌski/ adj. dark or not very bright in color: *a dusky museum* | **dusky pink/orange/blue etc.** *a dusky pink room* s w **dust¹** /dʌst/ n. **1** [U] extremely small pieces of dirt, sand etc. that are like a dry powder: *a thick layer of dust on the furniture* | *The eruption of Mount Pinatubo produced a massive **cloud of dust**.* **2** gold/coal/pollen etc. dust [U] powder consisting of extremely small pieces of gold, COAL, POLLEN etc. **3** the dust settles used to say that the details of a situation become clearer and less confused: *When the dust finally settled after the layoffs, only two senior managers were left in the department.* | *We'll just have to **wait for the dust to settle**.* —see also bite the dust (BITE¹ (7)), DUSTY, **leave sb in the dust** (LEAVE¹ (36))

dust² v. **1** [I,T] to clean the dust from a surface by moving something such as a soft cloth across it: *A maid dusted the furniture.* **2** [T] to cover something with a fine powder: *Dust the top of the cake with cinnamon.* | *[be dusted with sth] The landscape below was barely dusted with snow.*

dust sth **off** phr. v. [T] **1** to clean something by brushing it or rubbing it with a cloth or with your hands: *She dusted the snow off Billy's coat.* **2** to get something ready in order to use it again after not using it for a long time: *Investors are dusting off their check books as the economy recovers.*

dust bowl /'. ./ n. [C] an area of land that has DUST STORMs and very long periods without rain

dust bun·ny /'. ,../ also **dust mouse** n. plural **dust bunnies** [C] INFORMAL a small ball of dust that forms in a place that is not cleaned regularly, such as under a piece of furniture

dust cov·er /'. ,../ n. [C] a DUST JACKET

dust·er /'dʌstə/ n. [C] **1** a cloth or piece of equipment used for removing dust from furniture **2** a light coat that you wear to protect your clothes from dust **3** INFORMAL a DUST STORM

dust jack·et /'. ,../ n. [C] **1** a folded paper cover that fits over the cover of a book, used to protect it; DUST COVER **2** a CARDBOARD cover that a record is sold in

dust mouse /'. ./ n. plural **dust mice** [C] a DUST BUNNY

dust·pan /'dʌstpæn/ n. [C] a flat container with a handle, that you use with a brush to remove dust and waste from the floor

dust storm /'. ./ n. [C] a storm with strong winds that carries large amounts of dust

dust-up /'. ./ n. [C] SLANG, OLD-FASHIONED a fight or argument

dust·y /'dʌsti/ adj. **dustier, dustiest 1** covered with dust: *The shelves are really dusty.* | *a dusty road* **2** dusty blue/pink etc. blue etc. that is not bright but is slightly gray: *The curtains had faded to a dusty pink.*

Dutch¹ /dʌtʃ/ n. **1** [U] the language of the Netherlands **2** the Dutch [plural] people from the Netherlands —see also DOUBLE-DUTCH

Dutch² adj. **1** from or relating to the Netherlands **2** go Dutch (with sb) INFORMAL to share the cost of a meal in a restaurant **3** Dutch treat an occasion when you share the cost of something such as a meal in a restaurant

Dutch barn /ˌ. './ n. [C] a farm building with a curved roof on a frame that has no walls, used for storing HAY

Dutch elm dis·ease /ˌ. '. .,./ n. [U] a disease that kills ELM trees

Dutch·man /'dʌtʃmən/ n. [C] someone from the Netherlands

Dutch ov·en /ˌ. '../ n. [C] a large heavy pot with a lid, used for cooking

du·ti·a·ble /'dutiəbəl/ adj. dutiable goods are those that you must pay DUTY on

du·ti·ful /'dutifəl/ adj. always obeying other people, doing what you are supposed to do, and behaving in a loyal way: *All my life I have been an obedient, dutiful daughter.*

du·ti·ful·ly /'dutifəli/ adv. if you do something dutifully, you do it because you think it is the correct way to behave: *Palmer always dutifully signs autographs without complaint.*

du·ty /'duti/ n. plural **duties** s w 2 2

1 sth you must do [C,U] something that you have to do because you think it is right, or because it is legally right: [+ to/toward] *Dennis feels a sense of duty toward his parents.* | *Parents have a duty to make sure their kids behave in school.* | *It is the duty of the state to make laws for the common good.* | *You must do your duty and report him to the police.* —see also JURY DUTY

2 part of your job [C usually plural, U] something you have to do as part of your job: *Your duties will also include answering the phone and typing letters.* | *Report for duty at General Peckham's office* (=go to the office to work or to be told what to do). | *Eldrige devoted too much of his time to official duties and not enough to his family.* —see also DOUBLE DUTY, **in the line of duty** (LINE¹ (25)), TOUR OF DUTY

3 be on/off duty to be working or not working at a particular time, especially in a job which people take turns to do so that someone is always doing it: *The night shift goes off duty at six a.m.* | *Boncoeur was on duty at the switchboard.* —see also **active duty/service** (ACTIVE¹ (5))

4 tax [C,U] a tax you pay on something you buy, especially goods you bought in another country: *Last month the customs duty was raised on luxury cars.* —compare TAX¹ (1)

5 kitchen/laundry/garbage etc. duty a job, especially in the house, that you must do: *My wife has me on kitchen duty tonight* (=I have to cook dinner, wash the dishes etc.).

6 do duty as/for sth to be used as something: *The home office may also do duty as a sitting or dining room.*

duty-bound /'.. ,./ adj. having to do something because of a feeling of duty: *Agency employees are duty-bound to enforce the rules.*

duty-free /ˌ.. '.◂/ adj. duty-free goods can be brought into a country without paying tax on them: *the duty-free shop* | *duty-free cigarettes* —**duty-free** adv.

du·vet /du'veɪ/ n. [C] a COMFORTER (1)

DVD n. [C] Digital Video Disc or Digital Versatile Disc; a special type of CD that can store large amounts of DATA such as movies, music, or computer information —see picture on page 426

Dvo·řák /'dvɔrʒɑk/, **An·to·nín** /'æntənin/ (1841–1904) a Czech musician who wrote CLASSICAL music

dwarf¹ /dwɔrf/ n. plural **dwarves** /dwɔrvz/ or **dwarfs** [C] **1** an imaginary creature that looks like a small man: *Snow White and the Seven Dwarfs* **2** a word meaning someone who does not grow to a normal height because of a medical condition, considered offensive by some people

dwarf² adj. [only before noun] a dwarf plant or animal is much smaller than the usual size: *a dwarf cherry tree*

dwarf³ v. [T usually passive] to be so big that other things are made to seem very small: *The cathedral is dwarfed by the surrounding skyscrapers.*

dweeb /dwib/ n. [C] SLANG a weak slightly strange person who is not popular or fashionable

dwell /dwel/ v. past tense and past participle **dwelled** or **dwelt** [I] LITERARY to live in a particular place: *A woodsman and his family dwelt in the middle of the forest.*

dwell on/upon sth phr. v. [T] to think or talk for too long about something, especially something that is not nice to think about: *Depressed people tend to dwell on the bad things that have happened to them.*

dwell·er /'dwelə/ n. [C] a city/town/cave/forest dweller a person or animal that lives in a city, town etc.: *City dwellers suffer from higher pollution levels.*

dwell·ing /'dwelɪŋ/ n. [C] FORMAL a house, apartment etc. where people live

dwelt /dwelt/ v. a past tense and past participle of DWELL

DWI n. [C,U] driving while intoxicated; DUI

dwin·dle /'dwɪndl/ v. [I] also **dwindle away** to gradually become less and less or smaller and smaller:

The money available to build new parks has dwindled. | **dwindle (away) to nothing/one/two etc.** *The inquiries for our product have dwindled to about three a day.* —**dwindling** *adj.: a dwindling population*

Dyck /daɪk/, **An·tho·ny Van** /ˈænθəni væn/ —see VAN DYCK

dye[1] /daɪ/ *n.* [C,U] **1** a substance you use to change the color of your clothes, hair etc.: *hair dye* **2 a dye job** INFORMAL someone who has had a dye job has used a substance to change the color of their hair

dye[2] *v.* **dyes, dyed, dyeing** [T] to give something a different color using a dye | **dye sth black/blue/blond etc.** *Priscilla's hair was dyed jet black.* —**dyed** *adj.*

dyed-in-the-wool /ˌ. . . ˈ.◂/ *adj.* having strong beliefs, likes, or opinions that will never change: *Allen is a dyed-in-the-wool New Yorker.*

dy·ing /ˈdaɪ-ɪŋ/ the present participle of "die"

dyke /daɪk/ *n.* [C] OFFENSIVE **1** a LESBIAN (=woman who is sexually attracted to women) **2** another spelling of DIKE (1)

Dy·lan /ˈdɪlən/, **Bob** /bɑb/ (1941–) a U.S. singer and SONGWRITER famous for his songs from the 1960s on the subjects of war and the CIVIL RIGHTS movement

Bob Dylan

dy·nam·ic[1] /daɪˈnæmɪk/ *adj.* **1** full of energy and new ideas, and determined to succeed: *a dynamic young businesswoman* **2** continuously moving or changing: *Markets are dynamic and a company must learn to adapt.* **3** TECHNICAL relating to a force or power that causes movement —**dynamically** /-kli/ *adv.*

dynamic[2] *n.* **1 dynamics a)** [plural] the way in which things or people behave, react, and affect each other: *The racial and ethnic dynamics of the situation are very important.* | *the dynamics of capitalist economies* —see also GROUP DYNAMICS **b)** [U] the science concerned with the movement of objects and with the forces related to movement **c)** [plural] changes in how loudly music is played or sung **2** [singular] FORMAL something that causes action or change: *Feminism is seen as a dynamic of social change.*

dy·na·mism /ˈdaɪnəˌmɪzəm/ *n.* [U] the quality of being dynamic

dy·na·mite[1] /ˈdaɪnəˌmaɪt/ *n.* [U] **1** a powerful explosive used especially for breaking rock **2** OLD-FASHIONED something or someone that is very exciting or is likely to cause a lot of trouble: *They've only been playing together for six months but they're dynamite.*

dynamite[2] *v.* [T] to damage or destroy something with dynamite

dy·na·mo /ˈdaɪnəˌmoʊ/ *n.* *plural* **dynamos** [C] **1** INFORMAL someone who has a lot of energy and is excited about what they do: *Jasso is the 5 foot 2 inch dynamo who is in charge of the teaching program.* **2** something that has a very strong effect on something else, and that makes things happen: *Oil production is the dynamo that drives Iraq's economy.* **3** a machine that changes some other form of power directly into electricity: *Bicycle lights are usually powered by a dynamo.*

dy·nas·ty /ˈdaɪnəsti/ *n.* *plural* **dynasties** [C] **1** a family of kings or other rulers whose parents, grandparents etc. have ruled the country for many years: *The Habsburg dynasty ruled in Austria from 1278 to 1918.* **2** a period of time when a particular family ruled a country or area: *the Ming dynasty* **3** INFORMAL a group or family that controls a particular business or organization for a long period of time —**dynastic** /daɪˈnæstɪk/ *adj.*

dys·en·ter·y /ˈdɪsənˌtɛri/ *n.* [U] a serious disease of your BOWELS that makes them bleed and pass much more waste than usual

dys·func·tion·al /dɪsˈfʌŋkʃənl/ *adj.* TECHNICAL **1** not following the normal patterns of social behavior, especially with the result that someone cannot behave in a normal way or have a satisfactory life: *a dysfunctional family* **2** not working correctly or normally

dys·lex·i·a /dɪsˈlɛksiə/ *n.* [U] TECHNICAL a condition that makes it difficult for someone to read —**dyslexic** *adj.: a dyslexic child*

dys·pep·si·a /dɪsˈpɛpsiə, -ˈpɛpʃə/ *n.* [U] TECHNICAL a problem that your body has in dealing with the food you eat; INDIGESTION

dys·pep·tic /dɪsˈpɛptɪk/ *adj.* **1** suffering from dyspepsia **2** OLD-FASHIONED in a bad mood

dys·to·pi·a /dɪsˈtoʊpiə/ *n.* [C] an imaginary place where life is extremely difficult and a lot of unfair or immoral things happen —**dystopian, dystopic** *adj.* —compare UTOPIA

dys·tro·phy /ˈdɪstrəfi/ —see MUSCULAR DYSTROPHY

D

about two people or things, and **one another** when talking about more than two: *The two leaders shook hands with each other.* | *All the leaders shook hands with one another.* **One another** is more formal than **each other.**

E

E, e /i/ *plural* **E's, e's** *n.* **1** [C] the fifth letter of the English alphabet **2** [C,U] **a)** the third note in the musical SCALE of C MAJOR **b)** the musical KEY based on this note

E /i/ **1** the written abbreviation of "east" or "eastern" **2** SLANG the abbreviation of ECSTASY (2), an illegal drug

e-, E- /i/ *prefix* a PREFIX meaning "electronic," relating to the Internet: *e-commerce* (=business on the Internet) | *e-money* (=money that can be used to buy things on the Internet) —see also CYBER-, EMAIL

each[1] /itʃ/ *quantifier, pron.* **1** every one of two or more things or people, considered separately: *Lift each leg eight times.* | *There are four bedrooms, each with its own shower.* | *John and I have each been to Greece twice.* | *"There are chocolate chip cookies and brownies." "Can I have one of each* (=one of both kinds)*?"* | [+ of] *Each of the children got a piece of candy.* **2 each and every one/member/person etc.** used to emphasize that you are talking about every single person or thing in a group: *I'm proud of each and every member of the team.* **3 to each his own** used to mean that we all have different ideas about how to do things, what we like etc.: *I don't like dating older men, but like you said, to each his own.*

USAGE NOTE: EACH

WORD CHOICE: each, every, both, all
Use **each** and **every** with a singular countable noun to mean "every person or thing in a group": *Each/Every child got a balloon to take home.* Use **both** with a plural countable noun to mean "the two things or people in a pair, considered together": *I have blisters on both feet.* Use **all** with a plural countable noun to mean "every member of a group of three or more things or people": *All the leaves have fallen off the trees.* Compare: *Both our children are in college* (=we have two children). | *All our children are married* (=we have more than two children).

GRAMMAR: each, every
You can use **each** or **every** before a singular countable noun, and the verb that follows is always singular: *Each/every part of the country has* (NOT *have*) *had unusual weather this year.* You can use **each of** or **every one of** before plural nouns or pronouns. Most teachers think that the verb that follows should be singular: *Each of the girls was wearing a red and white uniform.* | *Every one of them has promised to help.* In informal English, however, people sometimes use a plural verb in these sentences, especially when there are a lot of words between **each of** and the verb: *Each of the kids arriving for the first time are shown around the school.* If **each** comes after a plural noun or pronoun, the verb is also always plural: *They each have their own phone line.* | *The kids each drink about two glasses of milk a day.*

---

each[2] *adv.* to, for, or by every one in a group: *The tickets cost $10 each.* | *You get two cookies each.*

each oth·er /ˌ. '../ *pron.* [not used as the subject of a sentence] used to show that each of two or more people does something to the other or others: *José and his uncle hate each other.* | *The two kids played happily with each other all morning.* | *It's normal for people to ignore each other in an elevator.* —see also **be at each other's throats** (THROAT (5))

USAGE NOTE: EACH OTHER

WORD CHOICE: each other, one another
Some teachers prefer to use **each other** when talking

---

ea·ger /'igɚ/ *adj.* **1** having a strong desire to do, have, or experience something: *a group of eager volunteers* | [eager to do sth] *The students here are eager to learn.* | [eager for sth] *Rural towns are eager for any business they can attract.* **2 eager to please** willing to do anything to be helpful to people: *Mika is a very hard worker and very eager to please.* **3 an eager beaver** INFORMAL someone who works harder and is more excited about the work than others who are doing the same thing: *You came in to work on the weekend? Well, aren't you an eager beaver!* —**eagerly** *adv.*: *Her new novel has been eagerly awaited for over a year.* —**eagerness** *n.* [U]

ea·gle /'igəl/ *n.* [C] a very large strong bird with a beak like a hook that eats small animals

eagle-eyed /ˈ.. ˌ./ *adj.* very good at seeing or noticing things: *The error was caught by an eagle-eyed bank employee.*

ea·glet /'iglɪt/ *n.* [C] a young EAGLE

Ea·kins /'eɪkənz/, **Thomas** (1844–1916) a U.S. PAINTER famous for his REALISTIC style

-ean /iən/ *suffix* [in adjectives and nouns] another form of the SUFFIX -AN: *Mozartean* (=of or like Mozart)

ear /ɪr/ *n.*
1 part of your body [C] one of the two organs on either side of your head that you hear with, or just the part of these organs that you can see from the outside: *Stop shouting in my ear!* —see picture at BODY
2 hearing [C,U] the ability to hear sounds: *The new recording technique fools the ear into thinking sounds are coming from different parts of the room.* | *Wow, you really have good ears. I didn't hear anything at all.*
3 corn [C] the part of a corn plant where the grain grows: *Pick up a few ears of corn for dinner tonight.*
4 have an ear for music/languages etc. to be very good at hearing, recognizing, and copying sounds from music, languages etc.: *The author has an ear for the way present-day New Yorkers talk.*
5 smile/grin etc. from ear to ear to smile a lot because you are very happy: *Brandon held the baby at arm's length and grinned from ear to ear.*
6 go in one ear and out the other INFORMAL to be heard and then forgotten immediately: *You can tell me all you like about computers, but it just goes in one ear and out the other.*
7 by ear by listening, and without looking at something written down: *He learned to play the piano by ear.* —see also **play it by ear** (PLAY[1] (8))
8 be up to your ears in sth to be very busy with something, or to have too much of something: *I'm up to my ears in work right now. Can I call you back?*
9 be all ears INFORMAL to be very interested in listening to someone: *Go ahead, I'm all ears.*
10 be out on your ear INFORMAL to be forced to leave a place, especially because of something you have done wrong: *If you keep taking two-hour lunches, you'll be out on your ear.*
11 have sb's ear to be able to get someone important to listen to what you have to say, especially because they trust you: *He used to boast to his friends that he often had the president's ear.*
12 keep your/an ear to the ground to make sure that you always know what is happening or is going to happen in a situation: *I haven't heard any more news, but I'll keep my ear to the ground.*
13 shut/close your ears to sth to refuse to listen to something, especially to bad news: *The administration seems to have shut their ears to the economic crisis.*
14 sb's ears are burning used to say that someone thinks that people are talking about them: *I bet your ears were burning – Tom and I were just talking about you.* —see also **bend sb's ear** (BEND[1] (5)), **turn a deaf ear** (DEAF (4)), **lend an ear** (LEND (6)), **wet behind the ears** (WET[1] (4))

ear·ache /'ıreık/ *n.* [C usually singular] a pain inside your ear

ear drops /'. ./ *n.* [plural] medicine to put in your ear

ear·drum /'ırdrʌm/ *n.* [C] a tight thin MEMBRANE (1) (=layer like skin) over the inside of your ear that allows you to hear sound

-eared /ırd/ *suffix* **long-eared/short-eared** etc. having long, short etc. ears: *a long-eared rabbit*

ear·ful /'ırfʊl/ *n.* **give sb an earful** or **get an earful** INFORMAL to tell someone about something you are upset or angry about, or to be told by someone else about something they are upset or angry about: *The chancellor got an earful when he asked the students for feedback.*

Amelia Earhart

Ear·hart /'ɛrhɑrt/, **A·me·li·a** /ə'miliə/ (1898–1937) a U.S. pilot known for being the first woman to fly across the Atlantic Ocean alone, and for mysteriously disappearing while flying across the Pacific Ocean

earl /ɔl/ *n.* [C] a man with a high social rank in Europe, especially in the United Kingdom: *the Earl of Warwick*

ear·li·est /'ɔliıst/ *n.* **the earliest** the soonest time that is possible: *The earliest I can meet you is 4:00.* | *He'll arrive on Monday at the earliest.*

ear·lobe /'ırloʊb/ *n.* [C] the soft piece of flesh at the bottom of your ear

ear·ly /'ɔli/ *adj.* **earlier, earliest**
1 near the beginning [only before noun] near the beginning of a period of time, event, story, or process: *By early 1995, the business was close to bankruptcy.* | *Early detection of cancer improves the chances of survival.* | *a man in his early twenties*
2 before the usual time arriving, happening, ready etc. before the usual or expected time: *The train was ten minutes early.* | *Hey, you're early! It's only five o'clock.*
3 before others [only before noun] existing or happening before other people, machines, events etc. of the same kind: *early automobiles* | *Many of the earliest settlers here were from Sweden.*
4 at/from an early age at or since a time when you were very young: *She started reading at an early age.*
5 the early days the time when something has just started to be done or exist: *In the early days of the company, our office was in my garage.*
6 the early hours the time between MIDNIGHT and morning: *Order was restored in the prison in the early hours of June 25th.*
7 get (off to) an early start **a)** to start doing something earlier than you had expected: [+ on] *Jonathon got an early start on getting to know his baby sister – he helped deliver her.* **b)** also **make an early start** to start an activity, trip etc. very early in the day: *If we want to get to Las Vegas by noon, we'll have to make an early start.*
8 early riser someone who always gets up early in the morning: *My father has always been an early riser.*
9 an early night a night when you go to bed earlier than usual: *I think I'm going to make it an early night tonight.*
10 an early warning system/aircraft/radar etc. a system, airplane etc. that gives a warning when something bad, especially an enemy attack, is going to happen
11 early bird someone who gets up early or arrives early, or something that is made for or given to

someone like this: *Early bird discount tickets will be available to the first 100 customers.*
12 the early bird gets/catches the worm SPOKEN used to say that someone is successful because they were the first to be somewhere or to do something
13 an early grave a death that comes before it should: *Heroin was responsible for sending Morrison to an early grave.*

early² *adv.* **earlier, earliest 1** before the usual, arranged, or expected time: *You should get there early if you want a good seat.* | *I left work early to go to the dentist.* **2** near the beginning of a particular period of time: *early in the century* | *The flowers were planted earlier in the spring.* **3** near the beginning of an event, story, process etc.: *I realized early on that the relationship wasn't going to work.*

ear·mark¹ /'ırmɑrk/ *v.* [T usually passive] to decide that something, especially money, will be used for a particular purpose in the future: [earmark sth for] *$40,000 will be earmarked for providing drug treatment for prisoners.*

earmark² *n.* [C] a feature that makes something easy to recognize: *The case has all the earmarks of a political cover-up.*

ear·muffs /'ırmʌfs/ *n.* [plural] two pieces of material attached to the ends of a band that you wear over your head to keep your ears warm

earmuffs

earn /ɔn/ *v.*
1 get money [T] to get money by working: *Alan earns $30,000 a year.*
2 make a profit [T] to make a profit from business or from putting money in a bank, lending it etc.: *The company earned $187 million in 1998.* | [earn sth from sth] *I earned $5000 from my investments last year.*
3 get sth you deserve [T] to get something that you deserve, because of your qualities or actions: *Enjoy your vacation – you've earned it!* | *Gail earned her place on the team by practicing hard.* | [earn (sb) sth] *Chavez earned himself a reputation for being unfair.*
4 earn a living to make money in order to pay for the things you need: *It's hard to earn a living as a writer.*
5 earn your keep to do jobs as a way of paying the owner of the place where you live: *Philip lived in the attic and earned his keep by tutoring the officer's son.*
6 earn your stripes INFORMAL to do something to deserve a particular rank or position —see Usage Note at GAIN¹

earned in·come /,. '../ *n.* [U] money that you receive for work you have done, used on official documents such as tax forms —compare UNEARNED

earn·er /'ɔnɚ/ *n.* [C] **1** the main/top/worst etc. earner something that earns you the most, least etc. money: *The portable radio is the company's second highest earner.* **2** someone who earns money for the job that they do: **high-income/low-income/high-wage etc. earners** *Taxes rose for low-income earners last year.* —see also WAGE EARNER

ear·nest¹ /'ɔnıst/ *adj.* very serious and sincere: *Friends described Jackson as an earnest, hard-working young man.* **—earnestly** *adv.* **—earnestness** *n.* [U]

earnest² *n.* **1** in earnest happening more seriously or with greater effort than before: *After the war, Kempton began his acting career in earnest.* **2** be in earnest FORMAL to be serious about what you are saying: *I believe he was in earnest when he said he was leaving.*

Earn·hardt /'ɔnhɑrt/, **Dale** /deıl/ (1952–) a U.S. race car driver who has been STOCK CAR racing champion seven times

earn·ings /'ɔnıŋz/ *n.* [plural] **1** the money that you get by working: *The average worker's earnings have not kept up with inflation.* **2** the profit that a company makes: *Company earnings are up 18% over last year's.*

Earp /ɔp/, **Wy·att** /ˈwaɪət/ (1848–1929) a famous U.S. MARSHAL (=law official) and GAMBLER who lived in the western U.S.

ear·phone /ˈɪrfoʊn/ n. [C usually plural] a piece of electrical equipment that you put over or in your ear to listen to a radio, CD PLAYER etc.

ear·piece /ˈɪrpis/ n. [C] **1** a piece of electrical equipment that you put into your ear to hear a recording, message etc. **2** the part of a telephone that you listen through **3** one of the two pieces at the side of a pair of glasses that go over your ears

ear·plug /ˈɪrplʌg/ n. [C usually plural] a small piece of rubber, FOAM¹ (2) etc. put inside your ear to keep out noise or water

ear·ring /ˈɪrɪŋ/ n. [C] a piece of jewelry that you fasten to your ear

ear·shot /ˈɪrʃɑt/ n. **within earshot** near enough to hear what someone is saying: *The police would not question the victims while the press was within earshot.* —opposite **out of earshot** (OUT¹)

ear-split·ting /ˈ. ˌ../ adj. very loud: *ear-splitting music*

earth /ɔθ/ n.

1 [word] [singular] also **(the) Earth** the world that we live in, especially considered as a PLANET (1), or its surface: *The temperature of the Earth's core may be as high as 9,000 degrees Fahrenheit.* | *planet earth* | *The space shuttle will return to earth next week.* —compare WORLD¹ (1) —see Usage Note at LAND¹

2 the biggest/tallest/most expensive etc. on earth the biggest, tallest etc. example of something that exists: *She's the most beautiful woman on earth.*

3 what/why/how etc. on earth...? SPOKEN said when you are asking a question about something that you are very surprised or annoyed about: *What on earth did you do to your hair?*

4 nothing/nowhere etc. on earth used to emphasize that you mean nothing, nowhere etc. at all: *Nothing on earth could make her change her decision.*

5 [soil] [U] the substance that plants, trees etc. grow in: *The message was freshly scratched in the earth.*

6 down/back to earth to a sensible or practical way of thinking, behaving, or living: *He believes that fashion designers need to come down to earth and make clothes for real people.*

7 earth to sb! SPOKEN used to tell someone that you think they are being unreasonable or are not paying attention to what is happening: *Earth to Cathy! You're not the only one with problems.* —see also DOWN-TO-EARTH, **move heaven and earth** (HEAVEN (11)), **the salt of the earth** (SALT¹ (2))

USAGE NOTE: EARTH

WORD CHOICE: earth, world
The **earth** (or the **Earth**) is the planet we live on, as compared to the moon, the sun, other planets etc.: *The Earth is the third planet from the sun.* The **world** is the planet we live on considered with all the people and places on it: *In some parts of the world, clean drinking water is very hard to find.* | *China is one of the largest countries in the world.* **On earth** (NOT "in earth") can also be used in the same way as **in the world** (NOT "on the world"): *Mt. Everest is the highest mountain on earth.*

---

earth·bound /ˈɔθbaʊnd/ adj. unable to move away from the surface of the Earth: *The Hubble space telescope takes clearer pictures of stars than earthbound telescopes.*

earth·en /ˈɔθən, -ðən/ adj. [only before noun] made of dirt or baked clay: *an earthen floor* | *an earthen pot*

earth·en·ware /ˈɔθənwɛr, -ðən-/ adj. an earthenware cup, plate etc. is made of very hard baked clay —**earthenware** n. [U]

earth·ling /ˈɔθlɪŋ/ n. [C] a word used by creatures from other worlds in SCIENCE FICTION stories, to talk about a human

earth·ly /ˈɔθli/ adj. **1 no earthly reason/use/solution** etc. no reason, use etc. at all: *I had no earthly idea she was a drug addict.* **2** [only before noun] LITERARY relating to life on earth rather than in heaven: *Buddha taught that earthly existence is full of suffering.*

earth moth·er /ˌ. ˈ../ n. [C] a woman who has a natural appearance and does not wear much MAKEUP, who cares about other people, especially children, and who is interested in SPIRITUAL things and nature —see also MOTHER EARTH

earth·quake /ˈɔkweɪk/ n. [C] a sudden shaking of the earth's surface that often causes a lot of damage: *Kobe was devastated by the 1995 earthquake.* —see picture on page 1330

earth·shak·ing /ˈɔθˌʃeɪkɪŋ/ adj. **1** surprising or shocking and very important: *Results of the research were interesting, but nothing earthshaking.* **2** making the earth shake: *an earthshaking explosion*

earth-shat·ter·ing /ˈ. ˌ.../ adj. surprising, upsetting, or shocking and very important: *Being diagnosed with cancer was an earth-shattering experience.*

earth tone /ˈ. ./ n. [C usually plural] one of the colors within the range of brownish colors

earth·ward /ˈɔθwɔd/ also **earthwards** adv. in a direction toward the earth's surface: *The missile fell earthward.* —**earthward** adj.

earth·work /ˈɔθwɔk/ n. [C usually plural] a large long pile of dirt used to stop attacks

earth·worm /ˈɔθwɔm/ n. [C] a common type of long thin light brown WORM that lives in soil

earth·y /ˈɔθi/ adj. **earthier, earthiest 1** tasting, smelling, or looking like earth or soil **2** natural, relaxed, and enjoying life: *The part is played by the sassy and earthy Juliet Stevenson.* **3** talking in a direct and impolite way, usually about sex and the human body: *an earthy sense of humor* —**earthiness** n. [U]

ear trum·pet /ˈ. ˌ../ n. [C] a type of tube that is wide at one end, used by old people in the past to help them hear

ear·wig /ˈɪrˌwɪg/ n. [C] a long brown insect with two curved pointed parts at the back of its body

ease¹ /iz/ n. [U] **1 at ease a)** feeling relaxed in a situation in which most people might feel a little nervous: *Mr. Pratt uses games to make the new students feel at ease.* | *Dave always looks ill at ease* (=not relaxed) *in a suit.* | *News of their safe return put everyone at ease.* | *His explanation put my mind at ease* (=made me feel less worried and nervous). **b)** SPOKEN used by officers in the military to tell soldiers to stand in a relaxed way with their feet apart **2** the quality of doing something easily or of being done easily: *Randy learns new languages with ease.* | *I was surprised by the ease with which I had gotten reservations.* **3 a life of ease** a comfortable life, without problems or worries: *Rachel has always lived a life of ease.* **4** the ability to feel or behave in a natural or relaxed way: *I'm amazed at the sense of ease he has with children.* **5 ease of use/application** etc. how easy it is to use, APPLY etc. something: *Ease of use and price are two main factors in buying a computer.*

ease² v.

1 [become less severe] [I,T] if something bad eases, or if you ease it, it gradually becomes less severe: *Tensions in the region have eased slightly.* | [ease sth] *He was given drugs to ease the pain.* | *Increased police patrols have helped ease the fears of residents.*

2 [make easier] [T] to make something, especially a process, happen more easily: *Congress may ease import restrictions on grain.* | *The central bank eased credit* (=made it easier to borrow money) *twice last year.*

3 [move sth] [I,T always + adv./prep.] to move slowly and carefully into another place, or to move something this way: [ease (sth) into/onto etc.] *Large crates of food were eased onto the ship.* | *She eased herself onto the couch.*

4 ease your grip (on sth) a) to allow your control of something to become weaker: *The military has no plans to ease its grip on the region.* **b)** to hold something less tightly

5 ease sb's mind to make someone feel calmer and

less nervous or worried about something: *Knowing that he's getting good medical care does ease my mind.*

ease sb ↔ **out** *phr. v.* [T] to deliberately try to make someone leave a job, a position of authority etc. without officially saying anything: *They're trying to ease out some of the older staff to save money.*

ease up *phr. v.* [I] **1** also **ease off** if something, especially something bad or annoying, eases up or eases off, it becomes less or gets better: *The rain is starting to ease up.* | *Why don't you wait until the traffic eases off a little?* —see also **let up** (LET) **2** to stop demanding so much from someone: [**ease up on sb**] *Ease up on Sean – he's trying really hard.* **3** to do something more slowly or with less effort than before, especially because you have been going too fast, working too hard etc.: *Doctors have told him to ease up in practice to avoid further injury.* **4** to stop pressing so hard on something: [+ **on**] *If your tires start to skid, ease up on the brakes.*

ea·sel /'izəl/ *n.* [C] a frame that you put a painting on while you paint it

ease·ment /'izmənt/ *n.* [C] LAW **1** an agreement that allows a person, organization, or government to use land that belongs to someone else **2** the area of land that is being used

eas·i·ly /'izəli/ *adv.* **1** without problems or difficulties: *The bike can easily be assembled in thirty minutes.* | *I'll easily finish the report by Friday.* **2** without doubt; DEFINITELY: *He is easily the highest paid player in baseball.* **3 could/can easily** used to say that something is possible or is very likely to happen: *They could easily wait till next year to hire a replacement for her.* **4** in a relaxed way: *She smiled easily when I asked about her hometown.* —see also **breathe again/easy/easily** (BREATHE (7))

east¹, **East** /ist/ *n.* **1** [U] written abbreviation **E.** the direction from which the sun rises, that is on the right of a person facing north: *Which way is east?* | *The wind was blowing from the east.* | *Five miles to the east of the cabin lay the blue waters of Lake Michigan.* **2 the east** the eastern part of a country: [+ **of**] *The rebel strongholds are located in the east of the republic.* **3 the East a)** the part of the U.S. east of the Allegheny Mountains, especially the states north of Washington, D.C.: *She was born in the East, somewhere in New Jersey, but now lives in California.* **b)** the countries in Asia, especially China, Japan, and Korea: *The martial arts originated in the East.* **c)** the countries in the eastern part of Europe especially the ones that had Communist governments: *American relations with the East were at their worst in the late 1950s.* **4 back East** back to the northeast part of the U.S. after being further west: *Glen went to college back East.* —compare **out West** (WEST¹ (4)) **5 East-West relations/trade etc.** political relations, trade etc. between countries in eastern Europe or Asia and those in Europe or North America —compare FAR EAST, MIDDLE EAST, NEAR EAST —see Usage Note at NORTH¹

east² *adj.* **1** written abbreviation **E.** in, to, or facing the east: *We sailed down the east coast of the island.* | [+ **of**] *The town is 12 miles east of Portland.* **2** an east wind comes from the east

east³ *adv.* toward the east: *Go east on I-80 to Omaha.* | *The apartment faces east.*

East bloc, **East Bloc** /ˌ. '.ˌ/ *n.* [singular] the former name for the group of countries including the former Soviet Union and other eastern European countries with Communist governments, that had a close military and trade relationship

east·bound /'istbaʊnd/ *adj. adv.* traveling or leading toward the east: *eastbound traffic* | *The truck was traveling eastbound on Blossom Hill Road.*

East Coast /ˌ. '.ˌ/ *n.* **the East Coast** the part of the U.S. that is next to the Atlantic Ocean, especially the states north of Washington, D.C.

Eas·ter /'istɚ/ *n.* [C,U] **1** a Christian holiday on a Sunday in March or April to celebrate Jesus Christ's return to life after his death **2** the period of time just before and after this day: *We went skiing in Vermont at Easter.*

Easter Bun·ny /'..ˌ../ *n.* **the Easter Bunny** an imaginary rabbit that children believe brings colored eggs and chocolate at Easter

Easter egg /'..ˌ/ *n.* [C] **1** an egg that has been colored and decorated, to celebrate Easter **2** chocolate in the shape of an egg, eaten around the time of Easter

Easter Is·land /ˌ.. '.ˌ/ a small island in the Pacific Ocean, which belongs to Chile

east·er·ly /'istɚli/ *adj.* **1** in or toward the east **2** an easterly wind comes from the east

East·ern /'istɚn/ *n.* **1** SPOKEN a short form of Eastern Time **2** the TIME ZONE in the eastern part of the U.S.

east·ern /'istɚn/ *adj.* **1** in or from the east of a country or area: *There was heavy snow in eastern Minnesota yesterday.* **2** in or from the countries in Asia, especially China, Japan, or Korea: *Eastern philosophies* **3** in or from the countries in the east part of Europe, especially the countries that used to have Communist governments

Eastern Day·light Time /ˌ.. '.ˌ ˌ./ *abbreviation* **EDT** *n.* [U] the time that is used in the eastern part of the U.S. for over half the year, including the summer, when clocks are one hour ahead of Eastern Standard Time

East·ern·er /'istɚnɚ/ *n.* [C] someone who lives in or comes from the eastern U.S., north of Washington, D.C.

Eastern Eu·rope /ˌ.. '.ˌ/ *n.* the eastern part of Europe, especially the countries that used to have Communist governments, such as Poland and Bulgaria —compare CENTRAL EUROPE, WESTERN EUROPE

east·ern·most /'istɚnˌmoʊst/ *adj.* farthest east: *Punta Maisi is the easternmost point in Cuba.*

Eastern Or·tho·dox Church, the /ˌ.. ˌ... '.ˌ/ the group of Christian churches that include the Greek Orthodox Church and the Russian Orthodox Church

Eastern Stan·dard Time /ˌ.. ˌ. '.ˌ, ˌ.. '.. ˌ./ *abbreviation* **EST** *n.* [U] the time that is used in the Eastern U.S. for almost half the year, including the winter —compare EASTERN DAYLIGHT TIME

Eastern Star, Order of the /ˌ.. '.ˌ/ an organization of Masons and women related to them, that does CHARITY work

Eastern Time /'..ˌ ˌ./ *abbreviation* **ET** *n.* [U] the time that is used in the eastern part of the U.S.

East In·dies, the /ist 'ɪndiz/ **1** Indonesia **2** a name that was formerly given to the countries of Southeast Asia and, before that, to the Indian SUBCONTINENT

East·man /'istmən/, **George** (1854–1932) a U.S. inventor and businessman who started the Kodak company, and made the first camera that was cheap and easy to use —see picture on page 1329

East Riv·er, the /ˌ. '.ˌ/ a river in the northeastern U.S. that flows into New York Harbor, separating Manhattan from Long Island

east·ward /'istwɚd/ also **eastwards** *adj.* toward the east: *To get to the island, we had to first fly eastward toward Hawaii.* —**eastward** *adv.*

eas·y¹ /'izi/ *adj.* **easier, easiest**
1 not difficult not difficult, and not needing much physical or mental effort: *Word processing is easier than it looks.* | *There's no easy way to solve this problem.* | [**sth is easy (for sb) to do**] *I want a book that's easy to read.* | [**it is easy (for sb) to do sth**] *Around Christmas time, it's easy for a parent to feel exhausted.* | *Having a personal assistant will definitely make things a lot easier at work.* | *The shopping center is within easy walking distance* (=near enough to walk to) *of the stadium.* —opposite HARD¹ (2)
2 not causing problems not causing many problems, or not making many demands: *This is not an easy time to be traveling.* | *I think Paul's had a pretty easy life.* | *Mr. Taylor is an easy teacher.* | [**be easy on sb/sth**] *The judge has been criticized for being too easy on marijuana growers.*

E

3 relaxed relaxed, comfortable, and not nervous: *Ms. Morrell is a small woman with a soft voice and an easy smile.*

4 I'm easy SPOKEN used to say that you do not mind what choice is made: *"Do you want to stop at the mall now or on the way home?" "I'm easy."*

5 take the easy way out to end a difficult situation in a way that seems easy, but is not the best or smartest way: *Too many people take the easy way out of financial trouble by declaring bankruptcy.*

6 that's easy for you to say SPOKEN said when someone has given you some advice that would be difficult for you to follow: *"Just ignore her when you don't want to talk to her." "That's easy for you to say."*

7 easy money money that you do not have to work hard to get: *The thought of easy money draws many people to drug dealing.*

8 easy prey/an easy mark someone who can be easily attacked, tricked, treated badly etc.: *The elderly are often easy prey for conmen.*

9 have an easy time (of it) to have no problems or difficulties: *She hasn't had an easy time of it since Jack left.*

10 easy on the eye/ear pleasant to look at or listen to: *I like jazz because it's usually easy on the ear.*

11 easy as pie SPOKEN very easy

12 it's as easy as falling off a log SPOKEN used to say that something is very easy to do

13 sex OLD-FASHIONED, DISAPPROVING a woman who is easy has a lot of sexual partners

14 be on easy street OLD-FASHIONED to be in a situation in which you have plenty of money —**easiness** *n.* [U] —see also EASE[1], EASILY, OVER-EASY

s w **eas·y**[2] *adv.* **easier, easiest** INFORMAL **1 take it easy**
a) also **take things easy** to relax and not do very much: *I'm going to take it easy this weekend.* **b)** SPOKEN used to tell someone to slow down or become less upset or angry: *Take it easy – everything's going to be just fine.* **c)** SPOKEN used to say goodbye to someone: *"See you next week." "Yeah, take it easy."* **2 go easy on/with sth** to not use too much of something: *Go easy on the cheese – it has a lot of fat.* **3 go easy on sb** to be more gentle and less strict or angry with someone: *Go easy on Peter – he's having a hard time at school.* **4 get off easy** to escape severe punishment for something that you have done wrong: *You got off pretty easy if you only had to pay a $33 fine.* **5 easier said than done** used to say that it would be difficult to actually do what someone has suggested: *I should just tell him to go away, but that's easier said than done.* **6 easy does it** SPOKEN used to tell someone to be careful, especially when they are moving something **7 easy come, easy go** said when something, especially money, was easily obtained and is quickly used, spent, or taken away **8 rest/sleep/breathe easy** to stop worrying: *I won't rest easy until I know she's safe.*

easy chair /'.. ,./ *n.* [C] a large comfortable chair with arms, which is covered with soft material

eas·y·go·ing /ˌizi'gouɪŋ◂/ *adj.* not easily upset, annoyed, or worried: *Ted's an easygoing, nice guy.*

easy lis·ten·ing /ˌ.. '../ *n.* [U] music that is relaxing to listen to

s w **eat** /it/ *v. past tense* **ate** *past participle* **eaten**
1 food [I,T] to put food in your mouth and swallow it: *Eat your dinner.* | *Would you like something to eat* (=some food)? | *I try to exercise and eat right* (=eat food that keeps you healthy).
2 meal [I,T] to have a meal: *What time do we eat?* | *eat breakfast/lunch/dinner Let's eat dinner in the dining room tonight.*
3 eat your words to admit that what you said was wrong: *They think we can't compete with them – I'll make them eat their words.*
4 eat your heart out to be upset or ENVIOUS because someone is better than you or has something that you want: *I just bought a new convertible. Eat your heart out, Jay.*

5 eat sb alive also **eat sb for breakfast** to show that you are very angry with someone, or to defeat them completely: *If I miss a mortgage payment, the bank's going to eat me alive.*
6 use also **eat up** [I always + adv./prep.,T] to use a lot of something: *That big old car of mine just eats money.*
7 eat sb out of house and home to eat a lot of someone's supply of food, especially when you are living with them: *Our sixteen-year-old is eating us out of house and home.*
8 eat crow also **eat humble pie** to admit that you were wrong, especially in an embarrassing situation: *Critics who said CNN would never survive are now eating crow.*
9 eating out of sb's hand very willing to believe someone or to do what they want: *Young and beautiful, Lamour had the world eating out of her hand.*

SPOKEN PHRASES

10 what's eating you? used to ask why someone seems annoyed or upset
11 I could eat a horse used to say you are very hungry
12 sb eats like a horse if someone eats like a horse, they eat a lot
13 sb eats like a bird if someone eats like a bird, they eat very little
14 I'll eat my hat OLD-FASHIONED used to say that you think something is not true or will not happen: *If the Democrats win, I'll eat my hat!*
15 I couldn't eat another bite/thing used to say that you are full
16 eat me! VULGAR used to show that you are extremely angry with someone

---

—see also EATS

eat sth ↔ **away** *phr. v.* [T] to gradually remove or reduce the amount of something until it is gone: *The liquid is a strong acid that can eat away clothes and burn your skin.*

eat away at *phr. v.* [T] **1** [eat away at sth] to gradually remove or reduce the amount of something: *Rising production costs are eating away at profits.* **2** [eat away at sb] to make someone feel very worried or upset over a long period of time: *Economic anxiety is eating away at working people in this country.*

eat in *phr. v.* [I] to eat at home instead of going to a restaurant: *I don't have any money, so it looks like we're eating in tonight.*

eat into sth *phr. v.* [T] **1** to gradually reduce the amount of time, money etc. that is available: *Costs of cleaning up the military bases will eat into the savings of closing them.* **2** to damage or destroy something: *The acid eats into the surface of the metal.*

eat out *phr. v.* [I] to eat a meal in a restaurant: *I don't feel like cooking. Let's eat out tonight.*

eat up *phr. v.* **1** [T] [eat sth ↔ up] INFORMAL to use a lot of something or all of something until it is gone: *The program eats up too much of the memory on my computer.* **2** [I,T] SPOKEN to eat all of something: *Come on, Katie, eat up!* | [eat sth ↔ up] *Who ate up all the cookies I baked for the party?* **3 eat it up** to enjoy something very much: *We use games to teach children math, and the kids eat it up.* **4** [eat sb up] to make someone feel very upset and full of sadness: *It eats me up to see those starving kids on TV.* **5 be eaten up with anger/jealousy/curiosity etc.** to be very angry, JEALOUS etc., so that you cannot think about anything else

eat·a·ble /'itəbəl/ *adj.* in a good enough condition to be eaten —see also EDIBLE

eat·en /'itⁿn/ the past participle of EAT

eat·er /'itɚ/ *n.* [C] **a big/light/fussy etc. eater** someone who eats a lot, not much, only particular things etc.: *Stacy's not much of a meat eater.*

eat·e·ry /'itəri/ *n. plural* **eateries** [C] INFORMAL a restaurant or other place to eat

eating ap·ple /'.. ,../ *n.* [C] an apple that you eat raw rather than cooked —compare COOKING APPLE

eating dis·or·der /'.. ,../ *n.* [C] a medical condition in which you do not eat normal amounts of food or do not eat regularly —see also ANOREXIA, BULIMIA

eats /its/ n. [plural] INFORMAL food, especially for a party: *The bar is cozy, and the eats aren't bad either.*

eau de co·logne /ˌou də kəˈloʊn/ n. [U] COLOGNE

eaves /ivz/ n. [plural] the edges of a roof that stick out beyond the walls: *Birds had nested under the eaves.*

eaves·drop /ˈivzdrɑp/ v. **eavesdropped, eavesdropping** [I] to listen secretly to other people's conversations: [+ **on**] *For months the FBI had been eavesdropping on Martin's phone conversations.* —**eavesdropper** n. [C] —compare OVERHEAR

eavesdrop

eaves·trough /ˈivzˌtrɔf/ n. [C] ESPECIALLY CANADIAN a GUTTER[1] (2) on the edge of a roof

ebb[1] /ɛb/ n. **1 ebb and flow** a situation or state in which something increases and decreases in a type of pattern: *Manufacturers need to anticipate the ebb and flow of consumer demand.* **2 be at a low ebb** to be in a bad state or condition: *I was at my lowest ebb after the kidney surgery.* **3** a decrease in the amount of something: *The latest setback is another sign of the ebb in the governor's influence.* **4** [singular] also **ebb tide** the flow of the ocean away from the shore, when the TIDE[1] (1) goes out —opposite FLOOD TIDE

ebb[2] v. [I] **1** also **ebb away** to gradually decrease: *I could feel my courage ebbing away.* **2** if the TIDE ebbs, it flows away from the shore

E·bon·ics, ebonics /iˈbɑnɪks/ n. [U] BLACK ENGLISH

eb·o·ny[1] /ˈɛbəni/ n. [U] a type of hard black wood

ebony[2] adj. LITERARY black: *She had long ebony hair.*

Eb·ro, the /ˈibroʊ/ a river that flows through Spain from mountains near its northern coast to the Mediterranean Sea

e·bul·lient /ɪˈbʌlyənt, ɪˈbʊl-/ adj. very happy and excited: *Supporters of the amendment were ebullient at the outcome of the vote.* —**ebullience** n. [U]

EC n. **the EC** the European Community; the former name of the EUROPEAN UNION

ec·cen·tric[1] /ɪkˈsɛntrɪk/ adj. **1** behaving or appearing in a way that is unusual and different from most people: *an eccentric millionaire* **2** TECHNICAL eccentric circles do not have the same center point —compare CONCENTRIC —**eccentrically** /-kli/ adv.

eccentric[2] n. [C] someone who behaves in a way that is different from what is usual or socially accepted: *Many of Dr. Brook's colleagues consider him an eccentric.*

ec·cen·tric·i·ty /ˌɛksənˈtrɪsəti/ n. plural **eccentricities 1** [U] strange or unusual behavior: *Kate's mother had a reputation for eccentricity.* **2** [C] a feature, action, or opinion that is strange or unusual: *In his films, Levinson chronicles Baltimore's eccentricities and charms.*

Ec·cle·si·as·tes /ɪˌkliziˈæstiz/ a book in the Old Testament of the Christian Bible

ec·cle·si·as·tic /ɪˌkliziˈæstɪk/ n. [C] FORMAL a priest or minister, usually in a Christian church

ec·cle·si·as·ti·cal /ɪˌkliziˈæstɪkəl/ also **ec·cle·si·as·tic** /ɪˌkliziˈæstɪk/ adj. relating to the Christian church or its priests or ministers: *ecclesiastical history*

Ec·cle·si·as·ti·cus /ɪˌkliziˈæstɪkəs/ a book in the Apocrypha of the Protestant Bible and in the Old Testament of the Catholic Bible

ECG n. [C] an EKG

ech·e·lon /ˈɛʃəlɑn/ n. [C] **1** also **echelons** [plural] a rank or level of responsibility in an organization, business etc., or the people at that level: *Even the highest echelons of management could not explain the decision.* **2** TECHNICAL a line of ships, soldiers, airplanes etc. arranged in a pattern that looks like a series of steps

ech·o[1] /ˈɛkoʊ/ v. present tense **echoes** past tense and past participle **echoed 1** [I] if a sound echoes, it is

heard again, sometimes repeatedly, because it was made near something such as a wall or hill: *Thunder echoed over the mountains.* | *Their voices echoed through the cave.* **2** [T] to repeat or copy an idea, a style, or what someone has said or done: *Results of the study echo the findings of recent newspaper polls.* **3 echo with sth** if a place echoes with a sound, it is filled with it: *The theater echoed with laughter and applause.* **4 it echoes** SPOKEN if it echoes in a place, sounds that are made there are heard again, sometimes repeatedly: *Hey, listen – it echoes in here.*

echo[2] n. plural **echoes** [C] **1** a sound that you hear again, sometimes repeatedly, because it was made near something such as a wall or a hill: *The echo of the bells rang through the town.* **2** something that is very similar to something that has happened or been said before: [+ **of**] *The uprising was an echo of the student protests in the '60s.*

é·clair /eɪˈklɛr, ɪ-/ n. [C] a small cake with a long narrow shape, covered with chocolate and filled with whipped cream

é·clat /eɪˈklɑ/ n. [U] LITERARY **1** praise and admiration: *Miller's new play has been greeted with great éclat.* **2** a way of doing something with a lot of style, especially in order to attract attention: *Pinckney has served in Congress with ability and éclat.*

e·clec·tic[1] /ɪˈlɛktrɪk/ adj. including a mixture of many different things or people, especially so that you can use the best of all of them: *The album features an eclectic collection of old blues, jazz, and romantic pop standards.* —**eclectically** /-kli/ adv. —**eclecticism** /ɪˈlɛktəˌsɪzəm/ n. [U]

eclectic[2] n. [C] FORMAL someone who chooses the best or most useful parts from many different ideas, methods etc.

e·clipse[1] /ɪˈklɪps/ n. **1** [C] an occasion when the sun or the moon cannot be seen because one of them is passing between the other one and the Earth: *I've never seen a total eclipse of the sun* (=an occasion when the sun is completely blocked by the moon so that the sun cannot be seen). —see also LUNAR ECLIPSE, SOLAR ECLIPSE **2** [U] FORMAL a situation in which someone or something loses their power or fame, because someone or something else has become more powerful or famous: *the eclipse of Europe's prestige after World War I* **3 be in eclipse/ go into eclipse** FORMAL to be or become less famous or powerful than before: *Left-wing political ideas seem to be in eclipse among young people.*

eclipse[2] v. [T] **1** if the moon eclipses the sun or the earth eclipses the moon, the sun or the moon cannot be seen for a short time because the moon or earth passes in front of it **2** to become more important, powerful, famous etc. than someone or something else, so that they are not noticed anymore: *Zubero's time of 1:56.57 eclipsed the world record.*

e·clip·tic /ɪˈklɪptɪk/ n. [singular] TECHNICAL the path along which the sun seems to move

eco- /ikoʊ/ prefix concerned with the environment, or not harmful to the environment: *eco-education* | *eco-toys*

e·co·friend·ly /ˌikoʊˈfrɛndli/ adj. not harmful to the environment: *eco-friendly detergents*

E. co·li /ˌi ˈkoʊlaɪ/ n. [U] a type of BACTERIA that can make you very sick if you eat food that contains it

e·co·log·i·cal /ˌikəˈlɑdʒɪkəl, ˌɛ-/ adj. [only before noun] **1** relating to how plants, animals, and people are related to each other and to their environment: *an ecological disaster* **2** interested in protecting the environment: *ecological groups* —**ecologically** /-kli/ adv.

e·col·o·gist /ɪˈkɑlədʒɪst/ n. [C] a scientist who studies ecology

e·col·o·gy /ɪˈkɑlədʒi/ n. [singular,U] the way in which plants, animals, and people are related to each other and to their environment, or the scientific study of this: *the ecology of the Red Sea*

e-com·merce /ˈ, ˌ-/ n. [U] the activity of doing business using the Internet

e·con /'ikɑn/ n. [U] SPOKEN, ECONOMICS (1), especially as a subject of study at a college or university

sw **ec·o·nom·ic** /ˌɛkə'nɑmɪk‹, ˌi-/ adj. **1** [only before noun] relating to trade, industry, and the management of money: *The President's number one priority is economic growth.* | *The country may be headed for an economic crisis.* | *a difficult economic climate* **2** relating to money or to making a profit: *The spies' motives were not political but economic* (=they wanted to make money from what they were doing).

USAGE NOTE: ECONOMIC

WORD CHOICE: economy, economic, economical
The adjective of the word **economy** [C], referring to the economy of a country or region, is **economic** (NOT **economical**). *We are faced with a deepening economic crisis.* | The adverb of both **economic** and **economical** is **economically**: *The country is not economically stable.* | *You can live here very economically.*

---

ec·o·nom·i·cal /ˌɛkə'nɑmɪkəl/ adj. using money, time, goods etc. carefully and without wasting any: *It might be more economical to buy the video, rather than renting it so many times.* —see Usage Note at ECONOMIC

ec·o·nom·i·cal·ly /ˌɛkə'nɑmɪkli/ adv. **1** in a way that is related to systems of money, trade, or business: *economically depressed areas* | [sentence adverb] *Economically, our city has never been stronger.* **2** in a way that uses money, goods, time etc. without wasting any: *We did the printing as economically as we could possibly make it.*

sw **ec·o·nom·ics** /ˌɛkə'nɑmɪks/ n. **1** [U] the study of the way in which money and goods are produced and used **2** [plural] the way in which money influences whether a plan, business etc. will work effectively: *The economics of building new subway lines are being studied.* —see also HOME ECONOMICS

USAGE NOTE: ECONOMICS

WORD CHOICE: economics, economy
The study of economies and their money systems is called **economics** (uncountable): *Tammy majored in history and economics* (NOT **economic** or **economy**). | *Economics is my favorite subject* (NOT *are my favorite subject*).

---

sw **e·con·o·mist** /ɪ'kɑnəmɪst/ n. [C] someone who studies the way in which money and goods are produced and used, and the systems of business and trade

e·con·o·mize /ɪ'kɑnəˌmaɪz/ v. [I] to reduce the amount of money, time, goods etc. that you use: [+ **on**] *We're looking for ways to help farmers economize on chemicals and fertilizer.*

sw **e·con·o·my**[1] /ɪ'kɑnəmi/ n. plural **economies** **1** [C] the system by which a country's money and goods are produced and used, or a country considered in this way: *Low interest rates will help the economy.* | *a capitalist economy* **2** [U] the careful use of money, time, goods etc. so that nothing is wasted: *For reasons of economy, the armed forces keep equipment in service for 15 to 20 years.* **3 a false economy** something that seems cheaper than something else at first, but which will cause you to spend more money later: *Getting rid of our in-house technical support staff just looks like a false economy to me.* **4 economies of scale** the financial advantages of producing something in very large quantities, because the cost per piece is lower **5 a mixed economy** an economic system in which some industries are owned by the government and some are owned by private companies —see also MARKET ECONOMY —see Usage Notes at ECONOMIC and ECONOMICS

economy[2] adj. [only before noun] **economy size/pack/package etc.** a large product that costs less per pound, piece etc. compared to smaller-sized packages

economy class /.'... ˌ./ n. [U] the cheapest type of seats in an airplane —compare BUSINESS CLASS, FIRST CLASS —**economy class** adj.: *There were only two economy class seats left.*

e·co·pol·i·tics /ˌikoʊ'pɑlətɪks/ n. [U] a type of political activity that is concerned with preserving the world's environment

e·co·sys·tem /'ikoʊˌsɪstəm/ n. [C] all the animals and plants in a particular area, and the way in which they are related to each other and to their environment

e·co·tour·ism /ˌikoʊ'tʊrɪzəm, 'ikoʊˌtʊrɪzəm/ n. [U] the business and activity of traveling to places on vacation, being careful not to damage the natural environment

ec·ru /'ɛkru, 'eɪkru/ n. [U] a very light brown color —**ecru** adj.

ec·sta·sy /'ɛkstəsi/ n. plural **ecstasies** **1** [C,U] a feeling of extreme happiness: *Fans sang along in ecstasy as McCartney performed.* **2 Ecstasy** [U] an illegal drug, usually in the form of a PILL, which is taken to give a feeling of happiness, love, and energy

ec·stat·ic /ɪk'stætɪk, ɛk-/ adj. feeling extremely happy and excited: *Jacqueline was ecstatic to see her old friends again.* —**ecstatically** /-kli/ adv. —see Usage Note at HAPPY

ECT n. [U] electroconvulsive therapy; another word for ELECTROSHOCK

-ectomy /ɛktəmi/ suffix [in nouns] the removing of a particular part of someone's body by an operation: *an appendectomy* (=removing the appendix)

Ec·ua·dor /'ɛkwəˌdɔr/ a country in northern South America, between Peru and Colombia, and next to the Pacific Ocean —**Ecuadorian** /ˌɛkwə'dɔriən/ n., adj.

ec·u·men·i·cal /ˌɛkyə'mɛnɪkəl/ adj. supporting the idea of uniting the different branches of the Christian religion —**ecumenically** /-kli/ adv.

ec·ze·ma /'ɛksəmə, 'ɛgzəmə, ɪg'zimə/ n. [U] a condition in which your skin becomes dry, red, swollen, and ITCHY

ed /ɛd/ n. [U] INFORMAL, SPOKEN education as a subject of study: *We learned how to check the oil in drivers' ed class.*

ed. 1 the written abbreviation of "education" **2** the written abbreviation of EDITION **3** the written abbreviation of EDITOR

-ed /d, ɪd, t/ suffix [in adjectives] having a particular thing: *a bearded man* (=a man with a beard) | *a red-haired girl*

E·dam /'idəm, -dæm/ n. [U] a type of yellow cheese from the Netherlands, usually covered in red WAX

ed·dy[1] /'ɛdi/ n. plural **eddies** [C] a circular movement of water, wind, dust etc.

eddy[2] v. **eddies, eddied, eddying** [I + **around**] if water, wind, dust etc. eddies, it moves around with a circular movement

Ed·dy /'ɛdi/, **Ma·ry Ba·ker** /'mɛri 'beɪkə·/ (1821–1910) a U.S. religious leader, who started a new form of Christianity called Christian Science in 1866

e·de·ma /ɪ'dimə/ n. [U] a medical condition in which a part of the body, such as the legs, lungs, or brain, becomes swollen and filled with liquid

E·den /'idn/ n. [U] **1** also the **Garden of Eden** in the Bible story, the garden where Adam and Eve, the first humans, lived **2** [singular] a place of happiness, INNOCENCE, or beauty: *In those days, California seemed like an agricultural Eden.*

edge[1] /ɛdʒ/ n. [C]
1 side the part of an object or an area that is farthest from its center: *Don't put your glass so close to the edge of the table.* | *My uncle's house is on the edge of town near the freeway.*
2 knife the thin sharp part of a blade or tool that is used for cutting: *You'll need a knife with a very sharp edge.*
3 advantage a quality that you have, that gives you an advantage over other people: *Some athletes lose their edge by their mid-20s.* | *American companies have an edge over their competition in this technology.*

on the edge of a cliff

at the water's edge

4 be on edge to be nervous, especially because you are expecting something bad to happen: *What's wrong, Sue? You've been on edge all morning.*
5 an edge (of sth) a small amount of a particular quality, such as an emotion: *Jenny's voice took on an edge of impatience.*
6 be on the edge to be behaving in a way that makes it seem as if you are going crazy
7 be on the edge of your seat to be very excited and interested in something that is happening: *Star Trek fans will be waiting on the edge of their seats for the next movie.*
8 the edge of sth the limit of something, or the point at which it may start to happen: *She and her family live on the edge of poverty.*
9 take the edge off (sth) to make something less bad, strong etc.: *Try this. It should take the edge off the pain.*
10 go over the edge to go crazy or have a NERVOUS BREAKDOWN: *Nick needs to get some help before he goes completely over the edge.* —see also CUTTING EDGE, **have rough edges** (ROUGH¹ (7))

edge² *v.* **1** [I,T always + adv./prep.] to move slowly and gradually, or to make something do this: *As he edged closer, Jan became more nervous.* | [edge sth in/across/toward etc.] *Dan edged his chair closer to the fireplace.* **2** [I,T always + adv./prep.] to develop gradually, or to make something do this: [edge (sth) up/down/toward etc.] *The dollar edged lower against the Japanese yen.* **3** [T usually passive] to have or put something on the edge or border of something: [edge sth with/in sth] *The sleeves were edged with lace.* **4** [T] to defeat someone by a small number of points or by a short distance: *Fontes edged Gibbs in the voting for NFL Coach of the Year.* **5** [T] to cut the edges of an area of grass so that they are neat and straight

edge sb/sth ↔ **out** *phr. v* to win by a small number of points or by a short distance: *Carr edged out Durelle in a battle for second place.*

edge·wise /ˈɛdʒwaɪz/ *adv.* with the edge or thinnest part forward; sideways —see also **not get a word in edgewise** (WORD¹ (16))

edg·ing /ˈɛdʒɪŋ/ *n.* [C,U] something that forms an edge or border: *a white handkerchief with blue edging*

edg·y /ˈɛdʒi/ *adj.* **edgier, edgiest** nervous and worried: *Residents are still edgy over a series of student killings last summer.*

ed·i·ble /ˈɛdəbəl/ *adj.* something that is edible can be eaten: *The meal was barely edible.* | *edible plants* —opposite INEDIBLE

e·dict /ˈidɪkt/ *n.* [C] FORMAL an official public order made by someone in a position of power, sometimes unfairly: *Perpich learned how much state employees resented edicts sent down from the senior management.*

ed·i·fice /ˈɛdəfɪs/ *n.* [C] FORMAL **1** a building or structure, especially a large one: *The Times is housed in an imposing edifice on 1st Street.* **2** a complicated system of beliefs or ideas: *The whole edifice of the family's thinking rested on the notion of hard work.*

ed·i·fy /ˈɛdəˌfaɪ/ *v.* **edifies, edified, edifying** [T] FORMAL to be good for your mind or moral character by teaching you something: *The movie neither edifies nor entertains its viewers.* —**edification** /ˌɛdəfəˈkeɪʃən/ *n.* [U] FORMAL OR HUMOROUS *For your edification, I'm enclosing an article on our local fishing festival.* —**edifying** /ˈɛdəˌfaɪ-ɪŋ/ *adj.*

Ed·in·burgh /ˈɛdnbərə/ the capital city of Scotland

Ed·i·son /ˈɛdɪsən/**, Thomas Al·va** /ˈtɑməs ˈælvə/ (1847–1931) a U.S. inventor who made over 1300 electrical inventions and is most famous for inventing the LIGHT BULB —see picture on page 1329

Thomas Edison

ed·it /ˈɛdɪt/ *v.* [T] **1** to remove mistakes or inappropriate parts from a book, article, television program etc.: *Viewing and editing documents on screen can be much quicker than working on paper.* **2** to prepare a book, article etc. for printing by deciding what to include and how to arrange and put together the parts **3** to be in charge of a newspaper, magazine etc. and make decisions about what types of information to include: *Gupta founded and edited a newspaper in colonial East Africa.* **4** to arrange and put together the parts of a movie, television program, or sound recording —**edit** *n.* [C]

edit sth ↔ **out** *phr. v.* [T] to remove something when you are preparing a book, piece of film etc. for printing or broadcasting: *If you make a mistake, don't worry – we can edit it out before the interview is shown.*

e·di·tion /ɪˈdɪʃən/ *n.* [C] **1** the form in which a book, newspaper, product etc. is printed or made at a particular time: *Vogel's textbook is now in its fourth edition.* | *Publishers expect to bring out a paperback edition later in the year.* **2** the number of copies of a particular book, newspaper, product etc. that are printed or made at one time: *This beautiful hand-painted plate is available in an edition of 5,000.* **3** one copy of a book, newspaper etc.: *Wilson owns a rare 1853 edition of the poetry collection.* **4** one television or radio program that is part of a series: *I saw a report on cancer treatments on Thursday's edition of the local news.* —see also LIMITED EDITION

ed·i·tor /ˈɛdət̬ə/ *n.* [C] **1** the person who is in charge of a newspaper, magazine etc. and decides what should be included in it **2** someone who prepares a book, article etc. for printing by deciding what to include and by checking for any mistakes **3** someone who arranges and puts together the parts of a movie, television program, or sound recording **4** someone who decides what should be included in a television or radio program, especially a news program **5** TECHNICAL a computer program that is used to make changes in FILES

ed·i·to·ri·al¹ /ˌɛdəˈtɔriəl/ *adj.* **1** relating to the work of an editor: *Sharon is an editorial assistant in the sports department.* **2** [only before noun] expressing an opinion, rather than just giving facts: *the editorial pages in the newspaper* | *editorial comments*

editorial² *n.* [C] a piece of writing in a newspaper that gives the editor's opinion about something, rather than just reporting facts

ed·i·to·ri·al·ize /ˌɛdəˈtɔriəˌlaɪz/ *v.* [I] to give your opinion and not just the facts about something, especially publicly: [+ on/about/against etc.] *The Clarion-Ledger has editorialized in favor of increased funding for AIDS drugs.*

ed·i·tor·ship /'ɛdətə‚ʃɪp/ n. [U] the position of being the editor of a newspaper or magazine, or the time during which someone is an editor

Ed·mon·ton /'ɛdməntən/ the capital city of the Canadian PROVINCE of Alberta

EDT the abbreviation of Eastern Daylight Time

edu /‚i di 'yu/ the abbreviation for "educational institution," used in U.S. Internet addresses

ed·u·ca·ble /'ɛdʒəkəbəl/ adj. able to learn or be educated: *educable mentally handicapped students*

s w **ed·u·cate** /'ɛdʒə‚keɪt/ v. [T] **1** to teach or train someone, especially at a school or college: *Many of the women had been educated at the best universities abroad.* **2** to give someone information about a particular subject, or to show them a better way to do something: [educate sb about sth] *Young people need to be educated about the dangers of alcohol abuse.* —see Usage Note at TEACH

ed·u·cat·ed /'ɛdʒə‚keɪtɪd/ adj. **1** having knowledge as a result of studying or being taught: *The First Lady was also a highly educated woman.* | **college-educated/Harvard-educated/high-school-educated** etc. *Young is the Berkeley-educated son of an immigrant.* **2 an educated guess** a guess that is likely to be correct because you have enough information: *Dearborn was making an educated guess when he said that 170 positions would be cut over six months.*

s w **ed·u·ca·tion** /‚ɛdʒə'keɪʃən/ n. **1** [singular,U] the process by which your mind develops through learning at a school or college: *It can cost a lot to give your kids a college education.* | *Jody's grandmother only had five years of formal education* (=education in a school). **2** [U] the general area of work or study connected with teaching: *He earned his bachelor's degree in elementary education.* —see also HIGHER EDUCATION, SPECIAL EDUCATION

s w **ed·u·ca·tion·al** /‚ɛdʒə'keɪʃənəl/ adj. **1** relating to education: *After retiring, he remained active in educational programs at the laboratory.* **2** teaching you something you did not know before: *educational TV programs*

ed·u·ca·tion·ist /‚ɛdʒə'keɪʃənɪst/ also **ed·u·ca·tion·al·ist** /‚ɛdʒə'keɪʃənl‚ɪst/ n. [C] FORMAL an EDUCATOR

ed·u·ca·tor /'ɛdʒə‚keɪtə/ n. [C] FORMAL **1** a teacher **2** someone who knows a lot about methods of education

ed·u·tain·ment /‚ɛdʒu'teɪnmənt/ n. [U] movies, television programs, or computer SOFTWARE that educate and entertain at the same time

Ed·ward·i·an /ɛd'wɑrdiən, -'wɔr-/ adj. relating to the time of King Edward VII of Great Britain (1901–1910): *Edwardian furniture*

Ed·wards /'ɛdwədz/, **Jon·a·than** /'dʒɑnəθən/ (1703–1758) a U.S. THEOLOGIAN and religious leader, who succeeded in persuading large numbers of people to become Christians

-ee /i/ suffix [in nouns] **1** someone who is being treated in a particular way: *a payee* (=someone who is paid) | *a trainee* | *an employee* **2** someone who is in a particular state or who is doing something: *an absentee* (=someone who is absent) | *an escapee*

EEC n. **the EEC** the European Economic Community; the former name for the EC and a former name of the EU

EEG n. [C] **1** electroencephalograph; a piece of equipment that records the electrical activity of your brain **2** electroencephalogram; a drawing made by an ELECTROENCEPHALOGRAPH

eek /ik/ interjection an expression of sudden fear and surprise: *Eek! A mouse!*

eel /il/ n. [C] a long thin fish that looks like a snake and can be eaten

e'en /in/ adv. POETIC the short form of EVEN[1]

ee·ny /'ini/ **eeny meeny miny mo** SPOKEN the first line of a short poem that children say to help them choose between different possibilities

EEO n. [U] equal employment opportunity; the principle that some businesses follow, stating that a person's race, sex, religion etc. cannot be a reason for not getting the job

EEOC —see EQUAL EMPLOYMENT OPPORTUNITY COMMISSION

e'er /ɛr/ adv. POETIC the short form of "ever"

-eer /ɪr/ suffix [in nouns] someone who does or makes a particular thing, often something bad: *an auctioneer* (=someone who runs auction sales) | *a profiteer* (=someone who makes unfair profits)

ee·rie /'ɪri/ adj. strange and frightening: *The wind made an eerie sound outside.*

ef·face /ɪ'feɪs/ v. [T] **1** FORMAL to destroy or remove something so that it cannot be seen or noticed: *Carbon dioxide and moisture threaten to efface the Lascaux cave drawings.* | *Communist historians tried to efface whole segments of their nation's past.* **2 efface yourself** LITERARY to behave in a way that makes other people not notice you —see also SELF-EFFACING

ef·fect[1] /ɪ'fɛkt/ n.
1 change/result [C,U] the way in which an event, action, or person changes someone or something: [+ of] *Most people are aware of the harmful effects of smoking.* | *Seeing my father in such pain really had an effect on my mom.* | *In order to produce the desired effect* (=achieve the result you want) *of losing weight permanently, you must alter your eating habits.* | **to good/great/little etc. effect** *Arai mixes and sculpts the metallic fibers to breathtaking effect.* —see also SIDE EFFECT
2 put/bring sth into effect to make a plan or idea happen: *The council will need more money to put the regulations into effect.*
3 go/come into effect if a new law, rule, or system goes into effect, it officially starts: *The treaty went into effect in May 1997.*
4 take effect a) to start to produce results: *It will be a few minutes before the drugs start to take effect.* **b)** if a law, rule, or system takes effect, it officially begins: *The controversial bike-helmet law will take effect January 1.*
5 be in effect if a law, rule, or system is in effect, it must be obeyed now or it is being obeyed now: *The benefits listed are those in effect as of December 16.*
6 in effect used when you are describing what the real situation is, especially when it is different from the way that it seems to be: *In effect we're earning less than last year because of inflation.*
7 to this/that/the effect used when you are giving the general meaning of what someone says, rather than the exact words: *Barkley's response was, "Go away," or words to that effect.* | *The letter said something to the effect that her job was no longer safe.*
8 idea/feeling [C usually singular] an idea or feeling that an artist, speaker, book etc. tries to make you think of or feel: *Storni's use of rhythm creates an effect of tension in her poems.*
9 for effect if someone does something for effect, they do it in order to make people notice: *Dangerfield rolled his eyes for effect as he told the joke.*
10 movie [C usually plural] an unusual or impressive sound or image that is artificially produced for a movie, play, or television or radio program
11 effects [plural] the things that someone owns; BELONGINGS: *Don's few personal effects were in a suitcase under the bed.*
12 with immediate effect FORMAL beginning immediately: *Both armies were ordered to cease all attacks with immediate effect.* —see also SOUND EFFECTS, SPECIAL EFFECT —see Usage Note at AFFECT[2]

effect[2] v. [T] FORMAL to make something happen: *Conley saw religion as a way to effect real change in her family life.*

ef·fec·tive /ɪ'fɛktɪv/ adj. **1** producing the result that was wanted or intended: *The less expensive drugs were just as effective in treating arthritis.* —opposite INEFFECTIVE **2** [no comparative] if a law, agreement, or system becomes effective, it officially starts: *His resignation is effective April 8.* **3** done with skill, or having a skillful way of doing things: *The effective* use of color can make a small room look much bigger. **4** [no comparative; only before noun] real, rather than what is officially intended or generally believed: *Rapid advancements in technology have reduced the effective lifespans of computers.* —**effectiveness** n. [U]

ef·fec·tive·ly /ɪˈfɛktɪvli/ adv. **1** in a way that produces the result that was intended: *Unlike many academics, Rice can communicate her knowledge effectively.* **2** used to describe what the real situation is as a result of something that has happened: *Most of the urban poor are effectively excluded from politics.*

ef·fec·tu·al /ɪˈfɛktʃuəl/ adj. FORMAL producing the result that was wanted or intended; effective —opposite INEFFECTUAL —**effectually** adv.

ef·fec·tu·ate /ɪˈfɛktʃuˌeɪt/ v. [T] FORMAL to make something happen

ef·fem·i·nate /ɪˈfɛmənɪt/ adj. a man who is effeminate looks or behaves like a woman —**effeminacy** n. [U] —**effeminately** adv.

ef·fer·vesce /ˌɛfəˈvɛs/ v. [I] TECHNICAL a liquid that effervesces produces small BUBBLES of gas

ef·fer·ves·cent /ˌɛfəˈvɛsənt/ adj. **1** a liquid that is effervescent produces small BUBBLES of gas **2** someone who is effervescent is very cheerful and active: *an effervescent personality* —**effervescence** n. [U]

ef·fete /ɛˈfit, ɪ-/ adj. FORMAL **1** an effete man looks or behaves like a woman **2** weak and powerless in a way that you dislike: *the effete intellectuals in New York society* —**effetely** adv.

ef·fi·ca·cious /ˌɛfəˈkeɪʃəs/ adj. FORMAL producing the result that was intended, especially when dealing with an illness or a problem: *More efficacious treatments may soon be available.* —**efficaciously** adv. —**efficacy** /ˈɛfɪkəsi/ n. [U]

ef·fi·cien·cy /ɪˈfɪʃənsi/ n. **1** [U] the quality of doing something well and effectively, without wasting time, money, or energy: *A new furnace could give you increased efficiency and more heat output.* | **fuel/energy efficiency** *Auto makers are working to meet fuel efficiency requirements for new cars.* **2** **efficiencies** [plural] the amounts of money, supplies etc. that are saved by finding a better or cheaper way of doing something: *Using new technology has helped us achieve dramatic efficiencies in production.* **3** [C] an efficiency apartment

efficiency a·part·ment /.ˈ... .../ n. [C] a small apartment, usually with only one room, that is meant to be easy to take care of

ef·fi·cient /ɪˈfɪʃənt/ adj. a person, machine, or organization that is efficient works well and effectively without wasting time, money, or energy: *Service at the restaurant is efficient and friendly.* | **fuel-/energy-efficient** *an energy-efficient heating system* —**efficiently** adv.

ef·fi·gy /ˈɛfədʒi/ n. plural **effigies** [C] **1** a figure made of wood, paper, stone etc., that looks like a person, especially one that makes the person look ugly or funny: [+ of] *Protesters unveiled an effigy of the mayor.* **2** **burn/hang sb in effigy** to burn or hang a figure of someone at a political DEMONSTRATION because you hate them

ef·flo·res·cence /ˌɛfləˈrɛsəns/ n. [U] FORMAL OR TECHNICAL the action of flowers, art etc. forming and developing, or the period of time when this happens

ef·flu·ent /ˈɛfluənt/ n. [plural,U] liquid waste, especially chemicals or SEWAGE

ef·fort /ˈɛfət/ n.

1 physical/mental energy [U] the physical or mental energy that is needed to do something: *Starting an exercise program takes a lot of effort.* | *City management needs to put more effort into promoting our airport.* | *Driving an automatic takes all the effort out of driving* (=makes it much easier).

2 attempt [C,U] an attempt to do something, especially when this involves a lot of hard work or determination: [+ at] *Further efforts at negotiation have broken down.* | **effort(s) to do sth** *Tom's efforts to lose weight haven't been very successful.* | *Team officials continue to negotiate in an effort to reach an* agreement with Parcells. | *We should make an effort* (=try very hard) *to include everyone in the process.* | *Board members made no effort* (=did not try at all) *to hide their disgust.*

3 **be an effort** to be difficult or painful to do: *I was so weak that even standing up was an effort.*

4 **a good/bad/poor etc. effort** something that has been done well, badly etc.: *That's a good effort for a beginner!*

5 **an effort of will/imagination/concentration etc.** FORMAL the determination needed to do something: *Birdwatching requires a real effort of patience sometimes.*

ef·fort·less /ˈɛfətlɪs/ adj. done in a skillful way that makes it seem easy: *Garner's effortless performance makes the show a pleasure to watch.* —**effortlessly** adv.: *It was amazing how she could run effortlessly mile after mile.*

ef·fron·ter·y /ɪˈfrʌntəri/ n. [U] OLD-FASHIONED behavior that you think someone should be ashamed of, although they do not seem to be: *I can't believe that they have the effrontery to ask us to help.*

ef·ful·gent /ɪˈfʊldʒənt/ adj. LITERARY beautiful and bright

ef·fu·sion /ɪˈfyuʒən/ n. [C,U] **1** LITERARY an uncontrolled expression of strong feelings: *His letters were filled with effusions of love.* **2** FORMAL the action of something such as gas flowing out

ef·fu·sive /ɪˈfyusɪv/ adj. showing strong excited feelings: *Simpson began his speech with effusive praise for his wife.* —**effusively** adv. —**effusiveness** n. [U]

EFL n. [U] English as a foreign language; the methods used for teaching English to people whose first language is not English, and who do not live in an English-speaking country —compare ESL

EFT n. [C,U] an ELECTRONIC FUNDS TRANSFER

e.g. the written abbreviation of "for example": *midwestern states, e.g., Iowa and Illinois*

e·gal·i·tar·i·an /ɪˌɡæləˈtɛriən/ adj. believing that everyone is equal and should have equal rights: *an egalitarian society* —**egalitarianism** n. [U]

egg¹ /ɛɡ/ n. [C]

1 bird a round object with a hard SHELL, that contains a baby bird, snake, insect etc. and which comes out of a female bird, snake, or insect: *Blackbirds usually lay their eggs in March.* | *an ostrich egg*

2 food an egg, especially one from a chicken, that is used for food: *We had fried eggs for breakfast.*

3 animals/people also **egg cell** a cell produced by a woman or female animal that combines with SPERM (=male cell) to make a baby

4 **put/have all your eggs in one basket** to depend completely on one thing or one course of action in order to get success: *When planning your investments, it's unwise to put all your eggs in one basket.*

5 **have egg on your face** if someone, especially someone in authority, has egg on their face, they look silly because something embarrassing has happened: *Economists who had predicted a recession emerged with egg on their faces after news of the stock market boom.*

6 **a good egg** OLD-FASHIONED someone who you can depend on to be honest, nice etc. —see also **lay an egg** (LAY¹ (19))

egg² v.

egg sb ↔ on phr. v. [T] to encourage someone to do something, especially something that they should not do or do not want to do: *Susan didn't want to ask Bob on a date, but her friends kept egging her on.*

egg cream /ˈ. ./ n. [C] a drink made with chocolate SYRUP, milk, and CARBONATED water (=water that has a lot of BUBBLES in it)

egg·head /ˈɛɡhɛd/ n. [C] HUMOROUS someone who is very intelligent, and only interested in ideas and books

egg·nog /ˈɛɡnɑɡ/ n. [U] a drink made with milk, eggs, SPICES, and often alcohol such as BRANDY, drunk mainly in the winter

egg·plant /ˈɛgplænt/ n. **1** [C,U] a large vegetable with smooth purple skin **2** [U] a dark purple color —see picture at VEGETABLE

egg roll /ˈ. ./ n. [C] a type of Chinese food consisting of vegetables and sometimes meat rolled inside a piece of thin DOUGH that is then cooked in oil

eggs Ben·e·dict /ˌɛgz ˈbɛnəˌdɪkt/ n. [U] a dish made with a POACHed egg on an ENGLISH MUFFIN with a piece of HAM, with a white SAUCE poured over it

egg·shell /ˈɛgʃɛl/ n. **1** [C,U] the hard outside part of a bird's egg **2** [U] a very pale yellowish-white color **3** eggshell paint a type of paint that is slightly shiny when it is dry —see also **be walking on eggshells/ eggs** (WALK¹ (8))

egg tim·er /ˈ. ˌ../ n. [C] a small glass container with sand in it that runs from one part to the other in about 3 to 5 minutes, used for measuring the time it takes to boil an egg

egg white /ˈ. ./ n. [C,U] the transparent part inside an egg that turns white when it is cooked —compare YOLK

e·go /ˈigoʊ/ n. plural egos [C] **1** the opinion that you have about yourself: *Skinner has a big ego* (=thinks he is very smart and important). | *Losing 50 pounds was the ego boost* (=something that makes you feel good about yourself) *he needed.* | *Jan's co-workers became increasingly annoyed with her inflated ego* (=the thought that you are smarter or more important than you are). —see also ALTER EGO **2 an ego trip** INFORMAL something that you do because it makes you feel important: *Phillips has been on an ego trip ever since he got promoted to vice president.* **3** [usually singular] TECHNICAL the part of your mind with which you think and take action, according to Freudian PSYCHOLOGY —compare ID, SUPEREGO

e·go·cen·tric /ˌigoʊˈsɛntrɪk/ adj. thinking only about yourself and not thinking about what other people might need or want —**egocentricity** /ˌigoʊsɛnˈtrɪsəti/ n. [U] —**egocentric** n. [C]

e·go·ism /ˈigoʊˌɪzəm/ n. [U] EGOTISM —**egoist** n. [C] —**egoistic** /ˌigoʊˈɪstɪk/ adj.

e·go·ma·ni·ac /ˌigoʊˈmeɪniˌæk/ n. [C] someone who thinks that they are very important, and tries to get advantages for themselves without caring about how this affects other people

e·go·tism /ˈigəˌtɪzəm/ n. [U] the belief that you are much better or more important than other people, or behavior that shows this

e·go·tis·ti·cal /ˌigəˈtɪstɪkəl/ adj. believing that you are much better or more important than other people: *Rigby often seems egotistical and arrogant.*

e·gre·gious /ɪˈgridʒəs/ adj. FORMAL an egregious mistake, failure, problem etc. is extremely bad and noticeable: *The situation at Zefco was one of the most egregious examples of discrimination we have seen.* —**egregiously** adv.

e·gress /ˈigrɛs/ n. [U] FORMAL OR LAW the act of leaving a building or place, or the right to do this

e·gret /ˈigrət, -ɛt/ n. [C] a bird that lives near water and has long legs and long white tail feathers —see picture on page 428

E·gypt /ˈidʒɪpt/ a country in northeast Africa, next to the Mediterranean Sea and the Red Sea —**Egyptian** /ɪˈdʒɪpʃən/ n., adj.

E·gyp·tol·o·gy /ˌidʒɪpˈtɑlədʒi/ n. [U] the study of the history, society, buildings, and language of ancient Egypt —**Egyptologist** n. [C]

eh /eɪ, ɛ/ interjection SPOKEN used when you want someone to reply to you or agree with something you have said: *Pretty cold out, eh?*

ei·der·down /ˈaɪdəˌdaʊn/ n. **1** [U] the soft fine feathers of a particular type of DUCK **2** [C] OLD-FASHIONED a thick warm cover for a bed, filled with feathers

Eif·fel /ˈaɪfəl/, **Gus·tave** /ˈgustav/ (1832–1923) a French engineer who built many bridges and the Eiffel Tower

Eiffel Tow·er, the /ˈ.. ˌ../ a 300 meter-high metal tower in Paris, completed in 1889

eight /eɪt/ number **1** 8 **2** 8 o'clock: *Let's have break-fast at eight.* **3 be behind the eight ball** SPOKEN to be in a difficult or risky situation: *We can't afford to lose any more money – we're behind the eight ball already.*

eight·een /ˌeɪˈtin/ number 18

eight·eenth¹ /ˌeɪˈtinθ/ adj. 18th; next after the seventeenth: *the eighteenth century*

eighteenth² pron. **the eighteenth** the 18th thing in a series: *Let's have dinner on the eighteenth* (=the 18th day of the month).

eighteen-wheel·er /ˌ.. ˈ../ n. [C] a large truck consisting of two connected parts, used for carrying goods over long distances

eighth¹ /eɪtθ/ adj. 8th; next after the seventh: *This is the eighth day in a row that he has been late.*

eighth² pron. **the eighth** the 8th thing in a series: *Classes start on the eighth* (=the 8th day of the month).

eighth³ n. [C] ⅛; one of eight equal parts: *Divide the pie into eighths.* | *An eighth of the students said they had no opinion on the subject.* | **one-eighth/three-eighths/seven-eighths etc.** *Shares fell five-eighths of a point yesterday.*

eighth note /ˈ. ./ n. [C] a musical note that continues for an eighth of the length of a WHOLE NOTE —see picture at MUSIC

eight·i·eth¹ /ˈeɪtiɪθ/ adj. 80th; next after the seventy-ninth: *It's my grandmother's eightieth birthday tomorrow.*

eightieth² pron. **the eightieth** the 80th thing in a series

eight·y /ˈeɪti/ number **1** 80 **2 the eighties** also **the '80s** the years from 1980 through 1989 **3 sb's eighties** the time when someone is 80 to 89 years old | **in your early/mid/late eighties** *My grandfather's in his early eighties.* **4 in the eighties** if the temperature is in the eighties, it is between 80° and 89° FAHRENHEIT: **in the high/low eighties** *The temperature was in the low eighties and sunny.*

eighty-six /ˌ.. ˈ./ v. [T] INFORMAL to refuse to serve a customer, or to make them leave a bar or restaurant: *Rob got eighty-sixed from the club for not wearing a jacket.*

Ein·stein /ˈaɪnstaɪn/ n. [C usually singular] INFORMAL a name you call someone who is very smart, or that you use humorously when someone has just done or said something stupid: *You don't have to be an Einstein to know it's not going to work.*

Einstein /ˈaɪnstaɪn/, **Al·bert** /ˈælbət/ (1879–1955) a U.S. PHYSICIST and MATHEMATICIAN born in Germany, who developed the THEORY OF RELATIVITY, which completely changed the way that scientists understand space and time. —see picture on page 1329

Ei·sen·how·er /ˈaɪzənˌhaʊə/, **Dwight Da·vid** /dwaɪt ˈdeɪvɪd/ (1890–1969) the 34th President of the U.S., who had been a general in the U.S. Army during World War II

Ei·sen·stein /ˈaɪzənˌstaɪn/, **Ser·gei Mi·khai·lo·vich** /ˈsɛrgeɪ mɪˈkeɪləvɪtʃ/ (1898–1948) a Russian movie DIRECTOR who is considered one of the greatest directors ever

ei·ther¹ /ˈiðə, ˈaɪ-/ conjunction used to begin a list of two or more possibilities, separated by "or": *You can choose either french fries, baked potato, or mashed potatoes.* | *Either eat some more, or take some of those meatballs home with you.* —compare OR (1) —see Usage Note at ALSO

USAGE NOTE: EITHER

GRAMMAR: either…or and neither…nor
When you use these phrases in formal speech or writing, use a singular verb if the second noun is singular: *If either my parents or Will calls, tell them I'm not here.* | *Neither Brad nor Mike was at the party.* If the second noun is plural, use a plural verb: *If either my sister or my parents come, can you let them in?* In informal speech, the verb is usually plural.

s w **either**[2] *determiner* **1** one or the other of two things or people: *Do you have insurance on either one of these cars?* —compare ANY[1], NEITHER[1] **2** one and the other of two things or people; each: *Sandy's brothers were standing on either side of her.* | *There are gas stations at either end of the block.* **3 either way** SPOKEN used to say that something will be the same, whichever of two possible choices you make: *Either way, it's going to be expensive.* **4 within two feet/ten years/one hour etc. either way** two feet, ten years etc. more or less than the correct amount or measurement: *Chris says he can guess anyone's age within two years either way.* **5 sth could go either way** if a situation could go either way, both results are equally possible: *The race for governor could still go either way.* **6 an either-or situation** a situation in which you cannot avoid having to make a decision or choice

---

USAGE NOTE: EITHER

GRAMMAR: either, neither, none, any
In formal speech and writing, use these pronouns with a singular verb: *None/Neither of us has seen the show.* In informal speech and writing, you can use a plural verb: *Have either of you ever been to New York?*

---

s w **either**[3] *pron.* one or the other of two things or people: *I brought chocolate and vanilla ice cream – you can have either.* | *Do either of you have 50 cents I could borrow?*

s w **either**[4] *adv.* **1** [only in negatives] also: *"I didn't know you could go skiing in Hawaii." "I didn't either."* | *"Didn't she tell you her name?" "No, and I didn't introduce myself, either."* **2 me either** SPOKEN, NONSTANDARD used to say that something is also true about you: *"I've never had a broken bone." "Me either."* —compare NEITHER[2], TOO (2)

e·jac·u·late /ɪ'dʒækyə,leɪt/ *v.* **[I,T] 1** when a man ejaculates, SEMEN comes out of his PENIS **2** OLD-FASHIONED to suddenly shout or say something, especially because you are surprised —**ejaculation** /ɪ,dʒækyə-'leɪʃən/ *n.* [C,U]

e·ject /ɪ'dʒɛkt/ *v.* **1** [T] to push or throw out with force: *The driver was ejected when the car hit an embankment and rolled over.* **2** [I] to jump out of an airplane when it is going to crash **3** [T] to make something come out of a machine by pressing a button: *Press the stop button again to eject the tape.* **4** [T] to make someone leave a place or building by using force: [+ **from**] *Protesters where ejected from the courtroom for shouting obscenities.* —**ejection** /ɪ'dʒɛkʃən/ *n.* [C,U]

ejection seat /.'.. ,./ *n.* [C] a special seat that throws the pilot out of an airplane when it is going to crash

eke /ik/ *v.*

eke sth ↔ **out** *phr. v.* [T] LITERARY **1 eke out a living/existence** to succeed in getting the things you need to live, even though you have very little money or food: *Cliff's family worked in the cotton fields to eke out a meager living.* **2 eke out a profit/victory** etc. to just barely succeed in making a profit, winning a competition etc.: *If they're lucky, they might eke out a tiny profit for the year.* **3** to make a small supply of something such as food or money last longer by carefully using small amounts of it: *The library has worked hard to eke out extra space for books.*

EKG *n.* [C] **1** a piece of equipment that records electrical changes in your heart; ELECTROCARDIOGRAPH **2** a drawing produced by an ELECTROCARDIOGRAPH; ELECTROCARDIOGRAM

e·lab·o·rate[1] /ɪ'læbrɪt/ *adj.* **1** having a lot of small details or parts that are connected to each other in a complicated way: *an elaborate tattoo of an eagle* **2** carefully planned and produced with many details: *Cho and Lee celebrated their new partnership at an elaborate banquet.* —**elaborately** *adv.*: *an elaborately carved statue* —**elaborateness** *n.* [U]

e·lab·o·rate[2] /ɪ'læbə,reɪt/ *v.* [I] to give more details or new information about something: [+ **on**] *Lally refused to elaborate on her earlier statement.* —**elaboration** /ɪ,læbə'reɪʃən/ *n.* [U]

é·lan /eɪ'lɑn/ *n.* [U] LITERARY a style that is full of energy and determination: *Collins' story was filmed with real intelligence and élan.*

e·lapse /ɪ'læps/ *v.* [I not in progressive] FORMAL if a particular period of time elapses, it passes: *More than five years have elapsed since the kidnapping.*

e·las·tic[1] /ɪ'læstɪk/ *n.* **1** [U] a type of rubber material that can stretch and then return to its usual length or size: *The gloves have elastic at the wrist for a snug fit.* **2** ESPECIALLY CANADIAN [C] a RUBBER BAND

elastic[2] *adj.* **1** made of elastic: *an elastic waistband* **2** a material that is elastic can stretch or bend and then go back to its usual length, size, or shape: *Children's bones are far more elastic than adults'.* **3** a system or plan that is elastic can change or be changed easily: *The demand for air travel is less elastic in the Caribbean.* —**elasticity** /ɪlæ'stɪsəti, ,ɪlæ-/ *n.* [U]

e·lat·ed /ɪ'leɪtɪd/ *adj.* extremely happy and excited, especially because you have been successful: *We were elated to find out Sue was pregnant again.*

e·la·tion /ɪ'leɪʃən/ *n.* [U] a feeling of extreme happiness and excitement

el·bow[1] /'ɛlboʊ/ *n.* [C] **1** the joint where your arm bends —see picture at BODY **2** the part of a shirt, coat etc. that covers your elbow **3 give sb the elbow** INFORMAL to tell someone that you do not like them or want them to work for you anymore, and that they should leave **4 elbow grease** INFORMAL hard work and effort, especially when cleaning or polishing something: *You'll need to use some elbow grease to get that floor clean.* **5 elbow room** enough space in which to move easily: *Let's sit in a booth. There's more elbow room there.* **6** a curved part of a pipe

s w

elbow[2] *v.* [T] to push someone with your elbows, especially in order to move past them: *Greene had to leave the game after being elbowed in the face.*

El·brus, Mount /'ɛlbrus/ the highest mountain in the Caucasus Mountains

El Cid /ɛl 'sɪd/ (?1043–1099) a Spanish soldier who appears in many stories and poems as a perfect example of CHIVALRY, Christian values, and love of his country

el·der[1] /'ɛldə/ *adj.* **1** OLD-FASHIONED OR FORMAL **an elder brother/daughter/sister etc.** an older brother, daughter etc.: *John's elder brother died in the war.* **2 the elder a)** OLD-FASHIONED OR FORMAL the older one of two people: *The elder of his two daughters sat next to him.* **b) the Elder** used after the name of a famous person who lived in the past, to show that they are the older of two people with the same name, usually a father and son: *Pliny the Elder* —compare YOUNGER —see Usage Note at OLD

elder[2] *n.* [C] **1** a member of a tribe or other social group who is important and respected because they are old: *the tribal elders* **2 your elders** people who are older than you are: *Young people should have respect for their elders.* **3** someone who has an official position of responsibility in some Christian churches **4 elder abuse** the crime of harming an old person **5** a small wild tree with white flowers and black berries

---

USAGE NOTE: ELDER

USAGE: elder, eldest
Elder and **eldest** are fairly formal words and were used more in the past. **Older** and **oldest** are used more often now. Note that you CANNOT say "elder than": *My sister is two years older* (NOT "elder") *than I am.*

---

el·der·ber·ry /'ɛldə,bɛri/ *n.* [C] the fruit of the elder tree

el·der·care /'ɛldə,kɛr/ *n.* [U] medical care for old people

el·der·ly /'ɛldəli/ *adj.* **1** old, especially used in order to be polite: *Some elderly residents cited concerns over crime levels.* **2 the elderly** [plural] people who are **s w**

E

old: *What services are available for the elderly in this neighborhood?* —see Usage Note at OLD

elder states·man /,.. '../ *n.* [C] someone old and respected, especially a politician, who people ask for advice because of his knowledge and experience

el·dest /'ɛldɪst/ *adj.* OLD-FASHIONED OR FORMAL **1 the eldest son/sister/child etc.** the oldest son, sister etc. among a group of people, especially brothers and sisters: *Her eldest child is at college now.* **2 the eldest** the oldest one in a group of people, especially brothers and sisters: *I have two brothers, but I'm the eldest.*

s w **e·lect¹** /ɪ'lɛkt/ *v.* **1** [T usually passive] to choose **2** someone for an official position by voting: [**elect sb to sth**] *Brock was elected to the state legislature.* | **elect sb president/governor etc.** *Brown was elected mayor two years ago.* **2 elect to do sth** FORMAL to choose to do something: *The committee elected not to fire Johnson.*

elect² *adj.* **president-elect/governor-elect/mayor-elect etc.** the person who has been elected as president etc., but who has not yet officially started their job

s w **e·lec·tion** /ɪ'lɛkʃən/ *n.* **1** [C] an occasion when **1** people vote to choose someone for an official position: *This year's presidential election will take place on November 4.* **2** [U] the fact of being elected to an official position: *This is Sanders' fourth trip to Washington since his election as governor.* —see also GENERAL ELECTION

e·lec·tion·eer·ing /ɪ,lɛkʃə'nɪrɪŋ/ *n.* [U] speeches and other activities intended to persuade people to vote for a particular person or political party —**electioneer** *n.* [C]

e·lec·tive¹ /ɪ'lɛktɪv/ *n.* [C] a course students can choose to take, but they do not have to take in order to GRADUATE

elective² *adj.* FORMAL **1** an elective position or organization is one for which there is an election **2** elective medical treatment is treatment that you choose to have, although you do not have to

e·lec·tor /ɪ'lɛktɚ, -tɔr/ *n.* [C] **1** someone who has the right to vote in an election **2** a member of the Electoral College

e·lec·tor·al /ɪ'lɛktərəl/ *adj.* [only before noun] **1** relating to elections and voting: *the electoral system* **2** relating to the people who are allowed to vote in an election: *an electoral list*

electoral col·lege /.,... '../ *n.* **1 the Electoral College** an official group of people who come together to elect the U.S. President and Vice President, based on the votes of people in each state **2** [C] a similar group in other countries

e·lec·tor·ate /ɪ'lɛktərɪt/ *n.* [singular] all the people who are allowed to vote in an election

E·lec·tra com·plex /ɪ'lɛktrə ,kɑmplɛks/ *n.* [C usually singular] TECHNICAL the unconscious sexual feelings that a girl has toward her father, according to the ideas of Sigmund Freud —compare OEDIPUS COMPLEX

s w **e·lec·tric** /ɪ'lɛktrɪk/ *adj.* **1** needing electricity to **3 3** work, produced by electricity, or used for carrying electricity: *The cabin has an electric heater.* | *Is the stove electric or gas?* | *an electric shock* | *an electric cable* **2** making people feel very excited: *There was an almost electric atmosphere in the stadium.*

USAGE NOTE: ELECTRIC

WORD CHOICE: electric, electronic, electrical

Use **electric** as an adjective with the names of things that need electricity to work or that carry electricity: *an electric guitar* | *electric lights.* Use **electronic** for equipment that uses electricity, but in a special way by passing the electricity through smaller, more complicated pieces of equipment: *an electronic game* | *an electronic calculator.* Use **electrical** as a more general word to talk about people and their work, or about general types of things that use or produce electricity: *an electrical engineer* | *My dad's company imports electrical goods.*

---

e·lec·tri·cal /ɪ'lɛktrɪkəl/ *adj.* **1** relating to electri- **s w** city: *an electrical technician* **2** using electricity: **3** *electrical equipment* | *The changing magnetic fields create an electrical current.* —see Usage Note at ELECTRIC —**electrically** /-kli/ *adv.*

electrical storm /.'... ,./ *n.* [C] a violent storm with a lot of LIGHTNING

electric blan·ket /.,.. '../ *n.* [C] a special BLANKET (=large cloth on a bed) with electric wires in it, used for making a bed warm

electric blue /.,.. '. ◂/ *adj.* very bright blue —**electric blue** *n.* [C,U]

electric chair /.'.. ,./ *n.* **the electric chair** a chair in which criminals are killed using electricity, in order to punish them for crimes such as murder

electric eel /.,.. './ *n.* [C] a large South American fish that looks like a snake, and can give an electric shock

electric eye /.,.. './ *n.* [C] NOT TECHNICAL a PHOTO-ELECTRIC CELL (1)

e·lec·tri·cian /ɪ,lɛk'trɪʃən, i-/ *n.* [C] someone whose job is to connect or repair electrical wires or equipment

e·lec·tric·i·ty /ɪ,lɛk'trɪsəti/ *n.* [U] **1** the power that is **s w** carried by wires, CABLES¹ (1) etc. and is used to pro- **3** vide light or heat, to make machines work etc.: *The electricity went out* (=it stopped working) *during the storm.* **2** a feeling of excitement: *You could feel the electricity in the air.*

e·lec·tri·fy /ɪ'lɛktrə,faɪ/ *v.* electrified, electrifying [T] **1** to make people feel very excited or interested: *Standing on stage, Los Lobos electrified the audience.* **2** to make a particular area or a system such as a railroad able to use electricity: *Mackenzie had electrified the Toronto streetcar system.* **3** to supply something with electricity: *the electrified third rail in the subway* —**electrifying** *adj.*: *It's standing room only for the group's electrifying concerts.* —**electrification** /ɪ,lɛktrəfə'keɪʃən/ *n.* [U] *a rural electrification program*

electro- /ɪlɛktroʊ, -trə/ *prefix* TECHNICAL **1** relating to electricity, or made to work by electricity: *an electromagnet* | *to electrocute someone* (=kill them with electricity) **2** electric and something else: *electromechanical*

e·lec·tro·car·di·o·gram /ɪ,lɛktroʊ'kɑrdiə,græm/ *n.* [C] TECHNICAL an EKG (2)

e·lec·tro·car·di·o·graph /ɪ,lɛktroʊ'kɑrdiə,græf/ *n.* [C] TECHNICAL an EKG (1)

e·lec·tro·con·vul·sive therapy /ɪ,lɛktroʊkən,vʌlsɪv 'θɛrəpi/ *n.* [U] TECHNICAL: see ELECTROSHOCK

e·lec·tro·cute /ɪ'lɛktrə,kyut/ *v.* [T usually passive] to kill someone by passing electricity through their body —**electrocution** /ɪ,lɛktrə'kyuʃən/ *n.* [U]

e·lec·trode /ɪ'lɛktroʊd/ *n.* [C] a small piece of metal or a wire that is used to send electricity through a system or through someone's body

e·lec·tro·en·ceph·a·lo·gram /ɪ,lɛktroʊɪn'sɛfələ,græm/ *n.* [C] TECHNICAL an EEG (2)

e·lec·tro·en·ceph·a·lo·graph /ɪ,lɛktroʊɪn'sɛfələ,græf/ *n.* [C] TECHNICAL an EEG (1)

e·lec·trol·y·sis /ɪ,lɛk'trɑlɪsɪs/ *n.* [U] **1** the process of using electricity to destroy hair roots and remove hair from your face, legs etc. **2** TECHNICAL the process of separating or changing the chemical parts of a substance by passing an electric current through it

e·lec·tro·lyte /ɪ'lɛktrə,laɪt/ *n.* [C] a substance, especially a liquid, that carries electricity by using IONS

e·lec·tro·mag·net /ɪ,lɛktroʊ'mægnɪt, ɪ'lɛktroʊ,mægnɪt/ *n.* [C] a piece of metal that becomes MAGNETIC (=able to attract metal objects) when an electric current is turned on —**electromagnetic** /ɪ,lɛktroʊmæg'nɛtɪk/ *adj.*

e·lec·tro·mag·net·ism /ɪ,lɛktroʊ'mægnə,tɪzəm/ *n.* [U] TECHNICAL a force relating to electric and MAGNETIC FIELDS, or the study of this force

e·lec·tron /ɪ'lɛktrɑn/ *n.* [C] a very small piece of matter with a negative electrical CHARGE¹ (7) that moves around the NUCLEUS (=central part) of an atom —compare NEUTRON, PROTON

e·lec·tron·ic /ɪˌlɛkˈtrɑnɪk/ *adj.* **1** electronic equipment, such as computers or televisions, uses electricity that has passed through CHIPS[1] (2), TRANSISTORS (1) etc.: *an electronic keyboard* —see Usage Note at ELECTRIC **2** using or produced by electronic equipment: *electronic banking | electronic music* —**electronically** /-kli/ *adv.*

electronic funds trans·fer /ˌ...ˌ. ˈ. ˌ../ *n.* [C,U] the process by which money is moved from one bank account, business etc. to another using the telephone or a computer

electronic mail /..ˌ.. ˈ./ *n.* [U] EMAIL

electronic mon·ey /..ˌ.. ˈ../ *n.* [U] E-MONEY

electronic or·gan·iz·er /..ˌ.. ˈ..../ *n.* [C] a small piece of electronic equipment that you can use to record addresses, telephone numbers, meetings etc.

electronic pub·lish·ing /..ˌ.. ˈ..../ *n.* [U] a system of producing books, magazines and newspapers in which the documents are on DISKETTES, CD-ROMS, or WEB SITES, and can be read on a computer

e·lec·tron·ics /ɪˌlɛkˈtrɑnɪks/ *n.* **1** [U] the study or industry of making equipment, such as computers or televisions, that uses electricity that has passed through CHIPS[1] (2), TRANSISTORS (1) etc. **2** [plural] electronic equipment: *American homes are filled with VCRs and other electronics.*

electron mi·cro·scope /.ˌ.. ˈ../ *n.* [C] a very powerful MICROSCOPE (1) (=scientific instrument used for looking at small objects) that uses ELECTRONS instead of light to make things look larger

e·lec·tro·plate /ɪˈlɛktrəˌpleɪt/ *v.* [T usually passive] to put a very thin layer of metal onto the surface of an object, using ELECTROLYSIS (2)

e·lec·tro·shock ther·a·py /ɪˈlɛktroʊˌʃɑk/ also **electroshock** /.ˌ.. ˈ../ *n.* [U] a method of treatment for mental illness that involves sending electricity through someone's brain

el·e·gant /ˈɛləgənt/ *adj.* **1** very beautiful and graceful: *The plain black dress set off her elegant neck. | elegant handwriting* **2** an idea or a plan that is elegant is very intelligent yet simple: *an elegant solution* —**elegantly** *adv.* —**elegance** *n.* [U]

el·e·gi·ac /ˌɛləˈdʒaɪək‹/ *adj.* LITERARY **1** showing that you feel sad or upset about someone or something that happened in the past or that does not exist anymore: *He spoke of his childhood in elegiac tones.* **2** relating to elegies: *elegiac verse*

el·e·gy /ˈɛlədʒi/ *n.* [C] *plural* **elegies** a poem or song written to show sadness for someone or something that does not exist anymore: *a funeral elegy*

el·e·ment /ˈɛləmənt/ *n.* [C]
1 part one part or feature of a whole system, plan, piece of work etc., especially one that is basic or important: *Vegetables are a vital element of the human diet. | The movie has all the elements of a great love story. | If I told you the plan, that would spoil the element of surprise.*
2 an element of danger/truth/risk etc. a definite amount, usually small, of danger, truth etc.: *There's an element of truth in what he says.*
3 people USUALLY DISAPPROVING a group of people who can be recognized by particular behavior or beliefs: *The clubs also tend to attract a criminal element* (=people who do illegal things).
4 chemistry a simple chemical substance such as CARBON, oxygen, or gold that is made of only one type of atom —compare COMPOUND[1] (2)
5 the elements weather, especially bad weather: *The tent was their only protection from the elements.*
6 the elements of sth the most basic and important features of something, or the things that you have to learn first about a subject: *His imaginative stories use the elements of poetry – rhythm, rhyme, alliteration.*
7 be in your element to be in a situation that you enjoy because you are good at it: *On the soccer field is where Christina really feels like she is in her element.*
8 be out of your element to be in a situation that makes you uncomfortable because you are not good at it: *Miller is completely out of her element in this sci-fi role.*
9 heat the part of a STOVE or other piece of electrical equipment that produces heat

10 earth/air/fire/water one of the four substances from which people used to believe that everything was made

el·e·men·tal /ˌɛləˈmɛntəl/ *adj.* **1** simple, basic, and important: *Love and fear are two of the most elemental human emotions.* **2** TECHNICAL existing as a simple chemical element that has not been combined with anything else: *elemental carbon*

el·e·men·ta·ry /ˌɛləˈmɛntri, -ˈmɛntəri/ *adj.* **1** [only before noun] relating to elementary school: *elementary education* **2** [only before noun] relating to the first and easiest part of a subject: *Billy is taking elementary algebra this year.* **3** simple or basic: *The right to defend itself is an elementary right of every state.*

elementary par·ti·cle /ˌ.... ˈ.../ *n.* [C] TECHNICAL one of the types of pieces of matter, including ELECTRONS, that make up atoms and are not made up of anything smaller

elementary school /..ˈ.. ˌ./ also **grade school** *n.* [C] a school in the U.S. that is typically for the first six years of a child's education

el·e·phant /ˈɛləfənt/ *n.* [C] a very large gray animal with four legs, big ears, and a TRUNK (3) (=very long nose) that it can use to pick things up —see also WHITE ELEPHANT

el·e·phan·tine /ˌɛləˈfæntin, -taɪn/ *adj.* FORMAL very large, or slow and awkward, like an elephant: *elephantine bureaucracy*

el·e·vate /ˈɛləˌveɪt/ *v.* [T] **1** FORMAL to move someone or something to a higher or more important level or rank, or make them better than before: *Store owners hope to elevate the mall's image to help improve business.* | [**elevate sb/sth to sth**] *Sloane was elevated to the rank of captain.* **2** to increase the amount, temperature, pressure etc. of something: *This drug tends to elevate body temperature.* **3** to lift someone or something to a higher position: *Lie down and elevate your feet.* **4** FORMAL to make someone feel happier, more moral, or more intelligent: *We need candidates who can elevate and inspire the American people.*

el·e·vat·ed /ˈɛləˌveɪtɪd/ *adj.* **1** raised off the ground: *A section of the elevated highway collapsed. | an elevated pipeline* **2** FORMAL elevated levels, temperatures etc. are higher than normal: *Elevated cholesterol levels may lead to a heart attack.* **3** elevated thoughts, words etc. seem to be intelligent or of a high moral standard: *Jack had more elevated interests than his colleagues' drinking parties.* **4** [only before noun] an elevated position or rank is very important and respected: *Vans and RVs have reached elevated status among young professionals.*

el·e·va·tion /ˌɛləˈveɪʃən/ *n.* **1** [C] a height above the level of the ocean: [**+ of**] *We camped at an elevation of 10,000 feet.* **2** [U] FORMAL an act of moving someone to a more important rank or position: *Many tried to block the judge's elevation to the Supreme Court.* **3** [C,U] FORMAL an increase in the amount or level of something: *Elevation of blood pressure can cause headaches.* **4** [C] TECHNICAL an upright side of a building, as shown in a drawing done by an ARCHITECT (=person who plans buildings): *the front elevation of a house* **5** [C] TECHNICAL the angle made with the HORIZON by pointing a gun: *The cannon was fired at an elevation of 60 degrees.*

el·e·va·tor /ˈɛləˌveɪtɚ/ *n.* [C] **1** a machine in a building that takes people and goods from one level to another **2** a tall building used for storing and lifting grain

elevator mu·sic /ˈ.... ˌ../ *n.* [U] INFORMAL the type of music that is played in stores and public places, and is usually thought to be boring

e·lev·en /ɪˈlɛvən/ *number* **1** 11 **2** 11 o'clock: *I have an appointment at eleven.*

e·lev·enth[1] /ɪˈlɛvənθ/ *adj.* **1** 11th; next after the tenth: *Tomorrow is her eleventh birthday.* **2** at the eleventh hour at the latest possible time: *The arrival of additional troops at the eleventh hour turned a potential catastrophe into a victory.*

E

eleventh[2] *pron.* **the eleventh** the 11th thing in a series: *The meeting is on the eleventh* (=the 11th day of the month).

ELF *n.* [U] TECHNICAL extremely low frequency; a type of RADIATION (1) (=energy wave) that comes from electrical equipment such as computer screens and televisions

elf /ɛlf/ *n. plural* **elves** /ɛlvz/ [C] a small imaginary person with pointed ears and magical powers

el·fin /'ɛlfən/ *adj.* **1** someone who looks elfin is small and delicate: *Winona's face is small, almost elfin, with pale skin and big eyes.* **2** liking to have fun, especially by playing tricks on other people: *an elfin charm*

El·gar /'ɛlgɑr/**, Ed·ward** /'ɛdwɚd/ (1857–1934) a British musician who wrote CLASSICAL music

El Grec·o /ɛl 'grɛkoʊ/ (1541–1614) a Spanish PAINTER famous for his paintings of religious subjects

e·lic·it /ɪ'lɪsɪt/ *v.* [T] FORMAL to get information, a reaction etc. from someone, especially when this is difficult: *Short questions are more likely to elicit a response.* | [**elicit sth from sb**] *The circus act elicited "oohs" and "ahs" from the crowd.* —**elicitation** /ɪ,lɪsɪ'teɪʃən/ *n.* [U]

e·lide /ɪ'laɪd/ *v.* [T] to leave out the sound of a letter or of a part of a word: *Most English speakers elide the first "d" in Wednesday.* —**elision** /ɪ'lɪʒən/ *n.* [C,U]

el·i·gi·ble /'ɛlədʒəbəl/ *adj.* **1** able or allowed to do something: [+ **for**] *If you're over 65, you're eligible for a discount.* | [**eligible to do sth**] *You're eligible to vote when you turn 18.* **2** [only before noun] an eligible man or woman would be good to marry because they are rich, attractive etc. and not married: *He's America's most eligible bachelor.* —**eligibility** /,ɛlədʒə'bɪləti/ *n.* [U]

e·lim·i·nate /ɪ'lɪmə,neɪt/ *v.* [T] **1** to get rid of something completely: *The car maker said it will eliminate 74,000 jobs over the next four years.* | [**eliminate sth from sth**] *Try to eliminate high-calorie foods from your diet.* **2** [usually passive] to defeat a team or person in a competition, so that they do not take part in it anymore: *The Colts were eliminated in the first round of the playoffs.* **3** to kill someone in order to prevent them from causing trouble: *The dictator eliminated anyone who might be a threat to him.*

e·lim·i·na·tion /ɪ,lɪmə'neɪʃən/ *n.*
1 removal of sth [U] the removal or destruction of something: [+ **of**] *The elimination of unemployment is still our goal.*
2 defeat [C,U] the defeat of a team or player in a competition, so that they may not take part anymore: *We were all disappointed by Iowa's elimination in the semi-finals.*
3 killing [U] the act of killing someone, especially to prevent them from causing trouble: [+ **of**] *The elimination of Gustavo has weakened the drug cartel.*
4 body process [U] TECHNICAL the process of getting rid of substances that your body does not need anymore: *Fiber will speed the elimination of digested food from the body.* —see also **process of elimination** (PROCESS[1] (4))

El·i·ot /'ɛliət/**, George** (1819–1880) a British woman writer, famous for her NOVELs, whose real name was Mary Ann (or Marian) Evans

Eliot, T.S. (1888–1965) a U.S. poet who lived in England, and is considered one of the most important writers of the 20th century

e·lite[1]**, élite** /eɪ'lit, ɪ-/ *adj.* [only before noun] limited to a small number of the best, most skilled, most experienced etc. people: *The competition is only open to an elite group of athletes.*

elite[2]**, élite** *n.* [C also + plural verb] a small group of people who are powerful or important because they have money, knowledge, special skills etc.: *The ruling elite have resisted all attempts at reform.*

e·lit·ist /eɪ'litɪst/ *adj.* DISAPPROVING an elitist system, government etc. is one in which a small group of people have much more power or advantages than other people —**elitism** *n.* [U] —**elitist** *n.* [C]

e·lix·ir /ɪ'lɪksɚ/ *n.* **1** [C] something that is supposed to solve problems as if by magic: *Nutritionists warn that artificial fat is no magic elixir for weight loss.* **2** [C,U] LITERARY OR HUMOROUS a magical liquid that is supposed to cure people of illness, make them younger etc. **3** [C,U] TECHNICAL a type of sweet liquid medicine

E·liz·a·beth I, Queen /ɪ,lɪzəbəθ ðə 'fɚst/ (1533–1603) the Queen of England from 1558 until her death

Elizabeth II, Queen /ɪ,lɪzəbəθ ðə 'sɛkənd/ (1926–) the British Queen since 1952, and also head of the British Commonwealth. She is married to Prince Philip, and they have four children.

E·liz·a·be·than /ɪ,lɪzə'biθən/ *adj.* relating to the period 1558-1603 when Elizabeth I was the Queen of England: *Elizabethan drama* —**Elizabethan** *n.* [C]

elk /ɛlk/ *n.* [C] **1** *plural* **elk** or **elks** a large DEER with a lot of hair around its neck —compare MOOSE **2 Elk** a member of the Elks

Elks /ɛlks/ **the Elks** an organization for men which does charity work, with groups in many small towns and cities in the U.S.

El·ling·ton /'ɛlɪŋtən/**, Duke** /duk/ (1899–1974) a U.S. JAZZ musician who played the piano, wrote music, and was a band leader

el·lipse /ɪ'lɪps/ *n.* [C] a curved shape like a circle, but with two slightly longer and flatter sides; OVAL

el·lip·sis /ɪ'lɪpsɪs/ *n. plural* **ellipses** /-siz/ **1** [C] the sign (...) in writing, used to show that some words have deliberately been left out of a sentence **2** [C,U] an occasion when words are deliberately left out of a sentence, though the meaning can still be understood, often shown by the sign (...) in writing

el·lip·ti·cal /ɪ'lɪptɪkəl/ also **el·lip·tic** /ɪ'lɪptɪk/ *adj.* **1** having the shape of an ellipse: *Kepler first discovered the elliptical orbits of the planets.* **2** elliptical speech or writing is difficult to understand because more is meant than is actually said: *The theme is often hard to find in his elliptical storytelling*

El·li·son /'ɛlɪsən/**, Ralph** /rælf/ (1914–1994) a U.S. writer famous for his NOVEL "The Invisible Man"

Ells·worth /'ɛlzwɚθ/**, Oli·ver** /'alɪvɚ/ (1745–1807) a CHIEF JUSTICE on the U.S. Supreme Court

elm /ɛlm/ *n.* [C,U] a type of large tree with broad leaves, or the wood from this tree

El Ni·ño /ɛl 'ninjoʊ/ *n.* [singular without **the**] the condition when the surface of the Pacific Ocean becomes warmer near the west coast of South America, affecting the weather around the ocean

el·o·cu·tion /,ɛlə'kyuʃən/ *n.* [U] good clear speaking in public, involving voice control, pronunciation etc.: *elocution lessons* —**elocutionary** *adj.* —**elocutionist** *n.* [C]

e·lon·gate /ɪ'lɔŋgeɪt, i-/ *v.* [I,T] to become longer, or make something longer than normal: *Wearing high-heeled shoes elongates the leg.* —**elongation** /ɪ,lɔŋ'geɪʃən/ *n.* [C,U]

e·lon·gat·ed /ɪ'lɔŋgeɪtɪd/ *adj.* longer and thinner than normal: *The picture shows two elongated figures dancing.*

e·lope /ɪ'loʊp/ *v.* [I] to go away secretly with someone in order to get married: *My parents didn't approve, so we eloped.* —**elopement** *n.* [C,U]

el·o·quent /'ɛləkwənt/ *adj.* **1** able to express your ideas or opinions well, especially in a way that influences people: *He gave an eloquent speech after dinner.* **2** showing a feeling or meaning clearly without using words: *The photographs are an eloquent reminder of the horrors of war.* —**eloquently** *adv.* —**eloquence** *n.* [U]

El Sal·va·dor /ɛl 'sælvə,dɔr/ a country in Central America, on the coast of the Pacific Ocean —**Salvadorean** /,sælvə'dɔriən/ *n., adj.*

else /ɛls/ *adv.* **1** a word meaning "in addition" or "besides," used after words beginning with "any-," "no-," or "some-," and after question words: *Clayton needs someone else to help him.* | *There's nothing else to do.* | *What else can I get you?* **2** a word meaning "different" or "instead," used after words beginning with "any-," "every-," "no-," or "some-," and after question words: *Is there anything else to eat?* | *She's wearing someone else's coat* (=not her coat). | *Everyone else gets to go – why can't I?* **3 or else... a)** used when saying what the result of not doing something will be: *They said she'd have to pay, or else she'd go to jail.* **b)** used when saying what another possibility might be: *She'll be here any minute, or else she's gotten lost again.*

SPOKEN PHRASES

4 anything else? used to ask someone if they want to buy another thing, say another thing etc.: *"I'll have a cheeseburger and a large Coke." "Anything else?" "No, thanks."* **5 if nothing else** used to say that a situation gives you one opportunity, or has one good result, even though there are no others: *It's boring, but if nothing else, I can get my homework done.* **6 what else?/who else?/where else? etc.** used to say that it is easy to notice that the thing, person, place etc. that has been mentioned is the only one possible: *"Was he with Andrea?" "Of course, who else?"* **7 what else can sb do/say?** used to say that it is impossible to do or say anything apart from what you have mentioned: *I told her it looked good. What else could I say?* **8 ...or else!** used to threaten someone: *You'd better not tell Mom, or else!*

else·where /'ɛlswɛr/ *adv.* FORMAL in, at, or to another place: *Prices continue to rise in Moscow and elsewhere in the country.*

e·lu·ci·date /ɪ'lusə,deɪt/ *v.* [I,T] FORMAL to explain very clearly something that is difficult to understand: *The studies elucidate the history of alcohol problems in men.* —**elucidation** /ɪ,lusə'deɪʃən/ *n.* [C,U]

e·lude /ɪ'lud/ *v.* [T] **1** to avoid being found or caught by someone, especially by tricking them: *Jones eluded the police for six weeks.* | **elude arrest/capture/discovery etc.** *She hid in the bushes to elude detection.* **2** if something that you want eludes you, you fail to find, catch, or achieve it: *Till now a college degree has eluded her.* **3** if a fact, idea etc. eludes you, you cannot completely understand it: *The distinction between the two philosophies largely eludes me.*

e·lu·sive /ɪ'lusɪv/ *adj.* **1** difficult to find, or not often seen: *The fox is a sly elusive animal.* **2** an elusive result is difficult to achieve: *The team came within one game of the elusive state championship.* **3** an elusive idea or quality is difficult to describe or understand: *the elusive key to corporate success* —**elusively** *adv.* —**elusiveness** *n.* [U]

elves /ɛlvz/ the plural of ELF

em /əm/ *pron.* SPOKEN, INFORMAL a short form of "them": *Tell the kids I'll pick 'em up after school.*

em- /ɪm, ɛm/ *prefix* used instead of EN- before the letters "b," "m," and "p": *an embittered man* (=made to feel extremely disappointed) | *empowerment* (=when someone is given control of something)

e·ma·ci·at·ed /ɪ'meɪʃi,eɪtɪd/ *adj.* extremely thin from lack of food or illness: *His emaciated body shivered uncontrollably.* —see Usage Note at THIN —**emaciate** *v.* [I,T] —**emaciation** /ɪ,meɪʃ'eɪʃən/ *n.* [U]

e·mail, e-mail, E-mail /'imeɪl/ *n.* **1** [U] a system that allows you to send and receive messages by computer; ELECTRONIC MAIL **2** [C] a message that is sent from one person to another using this system: *I'll send you an email when I know more about it.* —**email** *v.* [I,T] *Ryan emailed me as soon as he arrived in Japan.*

em·a·nate /'ɛmə,neɪt/ *v.* **1** [I] to come from or out of something: [+ from] *Wonderful smells were emanating from the kitchen.* **2** [T] to produce a smell, light, heat etc., or to show a particular quality: *Bould is a wonderful young actor; he emanates a brooding loneliness without speaking a word.* —**emanation** /,ɛmə'neɪʃən/ *n.* [C,U]

e·man·ci·pate /ɪ'mænsə,peɪt/ *v.* [T] FORMAL to make someone free from social, political, or legal restrictions that limit what they can do —**emancipation** /ɪ,mænsə'peɪʃən/ *n.* [U] *the emancipation of slaves*

e·man·ci·pat·ed /ɪ'mænsə,peɪtɪd/ *adj.* **1** socially, politically, or legally free **2** an emancipated woman is not influenced by old-fashioned ideas about how women should behave

e·mas·cu·late /ɪ'mæskyə,leɪt/ *v.* [T often passive] **1** to make a man feel weaker and less male: *Barry worried that working for a woman would emasculate him in his girlfriend's eyes.* **2** to make someone or something weaker or less effective: *The Clean Air Act has been emasculated by tobacco industry pressure.* **3** TECHNICAL to remove all or part of a male's sex organs; CASTRATE —**emasculation** /ɪ,mæskyə'leɪʃən/ *n.* [U]

em·balm /ɪm'bɑm/ *v.* [T] to treat a dead body with chemicals, oils etc. to prevent it from decaying —**embalmer** *n.* [C]

em·bank·ment /ɪm'bæŋkmənt/ *n.* [C] a wide wall of earth or stones built to stop water from flooding an area, or to support a road or railroad

em·bar·go[1] /ɪm'bɑrgoʊ/ *n. plural* **embargoes** [C] an official order to stop trade with another country: [+ on] *an embargo on wheat* | [+ against] *The UN imposed an arms embargo against the country.* | *Many allies are pushing to lift the oil embargo* (=end it).

embargo[2] *v.* [T] to officially stop particular goods from being traded with another country: *Several countries embargoed arms shipments to Yugoslavia.*

em·bark /ɪm'bɑrk/ *v.* **1** [I,T] to go onto a ship or an airplane, or to put or take something onto a ship or an airplane: *Passengers will have to pay a fee at the airport where they embark.* —opposite DISEMBARK **2** to begin a trip: [+ for] *The ship embarks for Honolulu at 10:00.* —**embarkation** /,ɛmbɑr'keɪʃən/ *n.* [C,U]

embark on/upon sth *phr. v.* [T] to start something, especially something new, difficult, or exciting: *Hal is embarking on a new career.*

em·bar·rass /ɪm'bærəs/ *v.* [T] **1** to make someone feel ashamed, nervous, or uncomfortable, especially in front of other people: *I hope my little dance didn't embarrass you.* **2** to do something that causes problems for a government, political organization, or politician, and makes it look bad: *The release of these secret documents has embarrassed the administration.*

em·bar·rassed /ɪm'bærəst/ *adj.* ashamed, nervous, or uncomfortable, especially in front of others: *The chair broke when Tim sat on it – he was pretty embarrassed.* | *an embarrassed grin* | *Lori's a good singer, but she gets embarrassed if we ask her to sing.* | [be embarrassed to do sth] *He was embarrassed to buy a condom.* | [+ about] *I felt embarrassed about how dirty my house was.* —see Usage Note at GUILTY

em·bar·rass·ing /ɪm'bærəsɪŋ/ *adj.* making you feel ashamed, nervous, or uncomfortable: *She asked a lot of embarrassing questions.* —**embarrassingly** *adv.*: *Student numbers are embarrassingly low in our department.*

em·bar·rass·ment /ɪm'bærəsmənt/ *n.* **1** [U] the feeling you have when you are embarrassed: *Will looked down and tried to hide his embarrassment.* | [+ at] *She suffered extreme embarrassment at not knowing how to read.* **2** [C] an event or action that causes a government, political organization etc. problems, and makes it look bad: *Stich's arrest was an embarrassment to the agency because they had often criticized foreign governments of corruption.* **3** [C] someone who behaves in a way that makes you feel ashamed, nervous, or uncomfortable, or their behavior: [+ to] *Tim's drinking has made him an embarrassment to the whole family.* **4 financial embarrassment** debts or a lack of money that causes problems for you, or makes you feel ashamed **5 an embarrassment of riches** so many good things that it is difficult to decide which one you want —see Usage Note at SHAME[1]

em·bas·sy /'ɛmbəsi/ *n.* [C] *plural* **embassies** a group of officials who represent their government in a foreign country, or the building they work in: *the American Embassy in Paris*

em·bat·tled /ɪmˈbætld/ *adj.* FORMAL **1** [only before noun] an embattled person, organization, etc. has many problems or difficulties: *The embattled mayor explained his position in an interview after the rally.* **2** surrounded by enemies, especially in war or fighting: *Helicopters carried 300 women and children from two embattled villages*

em·bed /ɪmˈbɛd/ *v.* **embedded, embedding 1** [I,T usually passive] to put something firmly and deeply into something else, or to be put into something else in this way: [+ **in**] *A piece of glass was embedded in her hand.* | *Part of the club broke off and embedded in his skull.* **2** [T usually passive] to make something an important or basic part of something else, or to make it difficult to remove: *Her feelings of guilt are deeply embedded in her personality.*

em·bel·lish /ɪmˈbɛlɪʃ/ *v.* [T] **1** to make something more beautiful by adding decorations to it: [+ **with**] *The dress is embellished with gold threads.* **2** to make a story or statement more interesting by adding details that are not true: *Lynn couldn't help embellishing the story.* —**embellishment** *n.* [C,U]

em·ber /ˈɛmbər/ *n.* [C usually plural] a piece of wood or coal that stays red and very hot after a fire has stopped burning

em·bez·zle /ɪmˈbɛzəl/ *v.* [I,T] to steal money from a place where you work: *Two managers were charged with embezzling $400,000 over a ten-year period.* —**embezzlement** *n.* [U] —**embezzler** *n.* [C]

em·bit·tered /ɪmˈbɪtərd/ *adj.* angry, sad, or full of hate because of bad or unfair things that have happened to you: *Steven is an embittered man who lost a leg while fighting in the war.* —**embitter** *v.* [T]

em·bla·zon /ɪmˈbleɪzən/ *v.* [T] to put a name, design etc. on something so that it can easily be seen: *She arrived wearing a T-shirt emblazoned with a political slogan.*

em·blem /ˈɛmbləm/ *n.* [C] **1** a picture, shape, or object that is used to represent a country, organization etc.: [+ **of**] *The hammer and sickle is the emblem of the Communist Party.* **2** something that represents an idea, principle, or situation: [+ **of**] *Many Californians view the mountain lion as an emblem of the state's vanishing wilderness.* —compare SYMBOL

em·blem·at·ic /ˌɛmbləˈmætɪk/ *adj.* FORMAL seeming to represent or be a sign of something: [+ **of**] *The cowboy is emblematic of not only an era, but a nation.*

em·bod·i·ment /ɪmˈbɑdɪmənt/ *n.* **the embodiment of sth** someone or something that represents or is very typical of an idea or quality: *Many people think Wall Street is the embodiment of greed.*

em·bod·y /ɪmˈbɑdi/ *v.* **embodied, embodying** [T] **1** to be a very good example of an idea or quality: *Mrs. Miller embodies everything I admire in a teacher.* **2** FORMAL to include something: *The limits on nuclear weapons are embodied in two treaties from the 1970s.*

em·bold·en /ɪmˈboʊldən/ *v.* [T] FORMAL to give someone more courage: *Emboldened by her smile, he asked her to dance.*

em·bo·lism /ˈɛmbəˌlɪzəm/ *n.* [C] TECHNICAL something such as a hard mass of blood or a small amount of air that blocks a VESSEL carrying blood through the body: *a coronary embolism*

em·boss /ɪmˈbɔs, ɪmˈbɑs/ *v.* [T usually passive] to decorate the surface of metal, paper, leather etc. with a raised pattern: [**emboss sth with sth**] *She was given a Bible embossed with her name.* —**embossed** *adj.*: *embossed stationery*

s w **em·brace¹** /ɪmˈbreɪs/ *v.* **1** [I,T] to put your arms around someone and hold them in a caring way: *He jumped up and embraced his lawyer with both arms.* **2** [T] FORMAL to eagerly accept new ideas, opinions, religions etc.: *We hope these regions will embrace democratic reforms.* **3** [T] FORMAL to include something as part of a subject, discussion etc.: *This course embraces several different aspects of psychology.* —see also ALL-EMBRACING

embrace² *n.* [C] an act of holding someone close to you, especially as a sign of love: *They held each other in a tender embrace.*

em·broi·der /ɪmˈbrɔɪdər/ *v.* **1** [I,T] to decorate cloth by sewing a picture, a pattern, or words on it with colored threads **2** [T] to make a story or report of events more interesting or exciting by adding details that are not true; EMBELLISH (2): *He embroidered his stories and kept us entertained for hours.* —**embroidered** *adj.*: *a richly embroidered jacket*

em·broi·der·y /ɪmˈbrɔɪdəri/ *n.* [U] **1** a decoration, pattern, or words sewn onto cloth, or the act of making this **2** imaginary details that are added to make a story seem more interesting or exciting: *Lasher refused to comment on the embroidery and speculation in the article.*

embroidery floss /.ˈ... ˌ./ *n.* [U] silk or cotton thread used in embroidery

embroidery hoop /.ˈ... ˌ./ *n.* [C] a circular wooden frame used to hold cloth firmly in place while patterns are being sewn into it

em·broil /ɪmˈbrɔɪl/ *v.* [T usually passive] to involve someone or something in a difficult situation: [**embroil sb/sth (in sth)**] *Morgan is embroiled in a child custody battle with her ex-husband.*

em·bry·o /ˈɛmbriˌoʊ/ *n. plural* **embryos** [C] an animal or human that has not yet been born, and has just begun to develop —compare FETUS

em·bry·ol·o·gy /ˌɛmbriˈɑlədʒi/ *n.* [U] the scientific study of embryos —**embryologist** *n.* [C]

em·bry·on·ic /ˌɛmbriˈɑnɪk/ *adj.* in a very early stage of development: *Her plan is still in the embryonic stage.*

em·cee /ˌɛmˈsi/ *n.* [C] MASTER OF CEREMONIES; someone who introduces the performers on a television or radio program or at a social event: *a beauty pageant emcee* —**emcee** *v.* [I,T]

e·mend /iˈmɛnd/ *v.* [T] FORMAL to take the mistakes out of something that has been written —compare AMEND —**emendation** /ˌiˌmɛnˈdeɪʃən, ˌimɛn-/ *n.* [C,U]

em·er·ald /ˈɛmərəld/ *n.* **1** [C] a valuable bright green stone that is often used in jewelry **2** [U] a bright green color —**emerald** *adj.*

e·merge /ɪˈmɚdʒ/ *v.* [I] **1** to appear or come out from s w somewhere: *Insects emerge in the spring and start multiplying rapidly.* | [+ **from**] *The sun emerged from behind the clouds.* **2** if facts emerge, they become known after having been hidden or secret: *New evidence has emerged to contradict earlier claims.* | [**it emerges that**] *After the crash, it emerged that bomb warnings had been issued to airlines.* **3** to come out of a difficult experience, often with a new quality or position: [+ **from**] *She emerged from the divorce a stronger person.* **4** to begin to be known or noticed: *Marlena Fischer is emerging as a top fundraiser for the charity.* —see also EMERGENT, EMERGING

e·mer·gen·cy /ɪˈmɚdʒənsi/ *n. plural* **emergencies** s w [C] an unexpected and dangerous situation that you must deal with immediately: *Don't call me unless it's an emergency.* | **emergency exit/supplies/surgery etc.** (=done or used in an emergency) —see also STATE OF EMERGENCY

emergency brake /.ˈ... ˌ./ *n.* [C] a piece of equipment in a car that stops the car from moving or rolling down a slope if the regular BRAKES fail —see picture on page 427

emergency med·i·cal tech·ni·cian /.ˌ... ˈ... ˌ./ *n.* [C] an EMT

emergency room /.ˈ... ˌ./ *n.* [C] *abbreviation* **ER** the part of a hospital that immediately treats people who have been hurt in accidents or who are extremely sick

emergency ser·vic·es /.ˈ... ˌ.../ *n.* [plural] the official organizations, such as the police or the fire department, that deal with crime, fires, and injuries

e·mer·gent /ɪˈmɚdʒənt/ *adj.* [only before noun] beginning to develop and be noticeable: *She is widely perceived as the emergent leader of the movement.*

e·merg·ing /ɪˈmɚdʒɪŋ/ *adj.* [only before noun] in an early state of development: *Opinions vary on emerging markets such as China and Indonesia.*

e·mer·i·ta /ɪ'mɛrətə/ *adj.* **professor/director etc.** emerita used about a woman who is RETIRED, but has kept her previous job title as an honor

e·mer·i·tus /ɪ'mɛrətəs/ *adj.* **professor/director etc.** emeritus used about a man who is RETIRED, but has kept his previous job title as an honor

Em·er·son /'ɛmərsən/, **Ralph Wal·do** /rælf 'wɔldou/ (1803–1882) a U.S. poet and writer who had great influence on the religious and PHILOSOPHICAL thought of his time

em·er·y /'ɛmri, 'ɛməri/ *n.* [U] a very hard mineral that is used for polishing things and making them smooth

emery board /'... ,./ *n.* [C] a NAIL FILE made from a piece of stiff paper with emery powder on it

e·met·ic /ɪ'mɛtɪk/ *n.* [C] TECHNICAL something that you eat or drink in order to make yourself VOMIT (=bring up food from your stomach) —**emetic** *adj.*

em·i·grant /'ɛməgrənt/ *n.* [C] someone who leaves their own country to live in another country —compare IMMIGRANT

em·i·grate /'ɛmə,greɪt/ *v.* [I] to leave your own country in order to live in another country: [+ from/to] *Maria emigrated from Mexico three years ago.* —**emigration** /,ɛmə'greɪʃən/ *n.* [C,U] —compare IMMIGRATE

USAGE NOTE: EMIGRATE

WORD CHOICE: emigrate, immigrate, migrate
Use **emigrate** about people who have left their country in order to live in another one: *My grandparents emigrated from Italy.* Use **immigrate** about people who are entering a country in order to live there: *Jae-won immigrated to the U.S. last year.* Use **migrate** about birds or animals that go to another part of the world in the fall and the spring. You can also use **migrate** about people who move from one place to another, especially to find work: *After World War II, many African-Americans migrated to cities in the North to get jobs.*

é·mi·gré /'ɛmɪ,greɪ/ *n.* [C] someone who leaves their own country to live in another, usually for political reasons: *Many Cuban émigrés have made Miami their home.*

em·i·nence /'ɛmɪnəns/ *n.* **1** [U] the quality of being famous and important: *De Mille has a perspective that comes only with age and eminence.* **2 your/his Eminence** a title used when talking to or about a CARDINAL (=priest of high rank in the Catholic Church) **3** [C] LITERARY a hill or area of high ground

em·i·nence grise /,ɛmɪnəns 'griz/ *n.* [C] someone who has a lot of power in an organization, but who often works secretly or in an unofficial way

em·i·nent /'ɛmənənt/ *adj.* famous and admired by many people: *an eminent anthropologist* —compare IMMANENT, IMMINENT —see Usage Note at FAMOUS

eminent do·main /,... .'./ *n.* [U] LAW the right of the U.S. government to take private land for public use, usually by paying for it

em·i·nent·ly /'ɛmənəntli/ *adv.* FORMAL, APPROVING completely and without a doubt: *Woods is eminently qualified for the job.*

e·mir /ɛ'mɪr, i-/ *n.* [C] a Muslim ruler, especially in Asia and parts of Africa: *the emir of Bahrain*

em·ir·ate /'ɛmərɪt, ɪ'mɪrət/ *n.* [C] the country ruled by an emir, or his position

em·is·sar·y /'ɛmə,sɛri/ *n. plural* **emissaries** [C] someone who is sent with an official message, or who must do other official work: *Japan is sending two emissaries to Washington to discuss trade issues.*

e·mis·sion /ɪ'mɪʃən/ *n.* **1** [C usually plural] a gas or other substance that is sent out into the air: *U.S. emissions of carbon dioxide are still increasing.* | *Your car has to pass an emissions test* (=a test to make sure the gases your car sends out are at the right level). **2** [U] the act of sending out light, heat, gas, sound etc.

e·mit /ɪ'mɪt/ *v.* **emitted, emitting** [T] to send out gas, heat, light, sound etc.: *The kettle emitted a shrill whistle.*

Em·my /'ɛmi/ *n. plural* **Emmys** [C] a prize given

---

every year to the best programs, actors etc. on U.S. television

e·mol·lient /ɪ'malyənt/ *adj.* FORMAL **1** making something, especially your skin, softer and smoother **2** making you feel calmer when you have been angry: *emollient words* —**emollient** *n.* [C]

e·mol·u·ment /ɪ'malyəmənt/ *n.* [C] FORMAL money or another form of payment for work you have done

e-money /'i ,mʌni/ *n.* [U] money from your CREDIT CARD that you use to pay for something on the Internet; ELECTRONIC MONEY

e·mote /ɪ'mout/ *v.* [I] to clearly show emotion, especially when you are acting: *Siskind encourages the children to emote to the music as they dance.*

e·mot·i·con /ɪ'mouti,kɑn/ also **smiley** *n.* [C] a set of special signs that are used to show emotions in EMAIL and on the Internet, often by making a picture that you look at sideways. For example, the emoticon :-) looks like a smiling face and means that you have made a joke

e·mo·tion /ɪ'mouʃən/ *n.* [C,U] a strong human feeling such as love, hate, or anger: *David usually tries to hide his emotions.* | *Her voice was full of emotion as she spoke.*

e·mo·tion·al /ɪ'mouʃənəl/ *adj.* **1** making people have strong feelings: *It was an emotional game for all of us.* **2** having strong feelings and showing them to other people, especially by crying: *He's an emotional guy.* | *Please don't get emotional* (=start crying). **3** [only before noun] relating to your feelings or how they are controlled: *Ann suffered from a number of emotional disturbances.* **4** influenced by what you feel, rather than what you know: *The busing plan got an emotional response from the community.* **5 an emotional cripple** DISAPPROVING someone who is not able to deal with their own or other people's feelings —**emotionally** *adv.*

e·mo·tion·al·ism /ɪ'mouʃənə,lɪzəm/ *n.* [U] a tendency to show or feel too much emotion

e·mo·tion·less /ɪ'mouʃənlɪs/ *adj.* not feeling or showing your emotions: *He delivered a precise, emotionless speech.*

e·mo·tive /ɪ'moutɪv/ *adj.* making people have strong feelings: *an emotive drama*

em·pa·na·da /,ɛmpə'nɑdə/ *n.* [C] a food made with DOUGH which has been filled with SPICY meat or something sweet, then folded over and baked or cooked in hot oil

em·pan·el /ɪm'pænl/ *v.* [T] another spelling of IMPANEL

em·pa·thize /'ɛmpə,θaɪz/ *v.* [I] to be able to understand someone else's feelings, problems etc., especially because you have had similar experiences: [+ with] *My mother died last year, so I can really empathize with what he's going through.* —compare SYMPATHIZE (1)

em·pa·thy /'ɛmpəθi/ *n.* [U] the ability to understand other people's feelings and problems: [+ for/with] *We have a lot of empathy for those who are having hard times.* —**empathetic** /,ɛmpə'θɛtɪk/ also **empathic** /ɛm'pæθɪk/ *adj.* —compare SYMPATHY

em·per·or /'ɛmpərə/ *n.* [C] a man who is the ruler of an EMPIRE —compare EMPRESS

em·pha·sis /'ɛmfəsɪs/ *n. plural* **emphases** /-siz/ [C,U] **1** special attention or importance: [+ on] *Menu items have a Southern flair, with an emphasis on fresh fish.* | *Jamieson's report places emphasis on the need for better working conditions.* **2** special importance that is given to a word or phrase by saying it louder or higher, or by printing it in a special way: *The emphasis should be on the first syllable.*

em·pha·size /'ɛmfə,saɪz/ *v.* [T] **1** to show that an opinion, idea, quality etc. is especially important: *My teacher always emphasized the importance of studying hard.* | [**emphasize that**] *Both leaders emphasized that there are no plans to raise taxes.* **2** to say a word or phrase louder or higher than others to give it more importance: *She emphasized the "Ms." when she introduced herself.*

em·phat·ic /ɪmˈfætɪk/ *adj.* done or said in a way that clearly shows something is important or should be believed and not doubted: *Dale's answer was an emphatic "No!"* | *an emphatic victory* —**emphatically** /-kli/ *adv.*

em·phy·se·ma /ˌɛmfəˈzimə, -ˈsi-/ *n.* [U] a serious disease that affects the lungs, making it difficult to breathe

s w **em·pire** /ˈɛmpaɪɚ/ *n.* [C] **1** a group of countries that are all controlled by one ruler or government: *the Roman empire* **2** a group of organizations that are all controlled by one person or company: *a media empire*

Empire State Build·ing, the /ˌ.. ˈ. ˌ./ also the **Empire State** a famous very tall office building in New York City, which has 102 floors. It was built in 1931, and for many years it was the tallest building in the world

Empire State Building

em·pir·i·cal /ɪmˈpɪrɪkəl, ɛm-/ *adj.* [only before noun] based on scientific testing or practical experience, not on ideas: *His theory is inconsistent with the empirical evidence.* —**empirically** /-kli/ *adv.*

em·pir·i·cism /ɪmˈpɪrəˌsɪzəm, ɛm-/ *n.* [U] the belief in basing your ideas on practical experience —**empiricist** *n.* [C]

em·place·ment /ɪmˈpleɪsmənt/ *n.* [C] a special position prepared for a gun or other large piece of military equipment: *a cannon emplacement*

s w **em·ploy¹** /ɪmˈplɔɪ/ *v.* **employs, employed, employing** [T] **1** to pay someone to work for you: *The factory employs over 2000 people.* | [**employ sb as sth**] *Kelly is currently employed as a motorcycle mechanic.* | [**employ sb to do sth**] *He is a computer analyst, employed to investigate new technologies.* —see also SELF-EMPLOYED, UNEMPLOYED¹ **2** to use a particular object, method, skill etc. in order to achieve something: *The equipment employs laser beams to make the computer chips.* **3** FORMAL to spend your time doing a particular thing: *We have lively discussions which pleasantly employ our time and our thoughts.*

employ² *n.* [U] **in sb's employ** FORMAL working for someone: *Mr. Morton had a number of servants in his employ.*

em·ploy·a·ble /ɪmˈplɔɪəbəl/ *adj.* having skills or qualities that are necessary to get a job: *She's highly employable, so she shouldn't have any trouble finding work.*

s w **em·ploy·ee** /ɪmˈplɔɪ-i, ˌɪmplɔɪˈi, ˌɛm-/ *n.* [C] someone who is paid to work for someone else: *a government employee* | *The restrooms are for employees only.* | *Sara gets an employee discount at Carson's.*

s w **em·ploy·er** /ɪmˈplɔɪɚ/ *n.* [C] a person, company, or organization that employs people: *The shoe factory is the largest employer in this area.*

s w **em·ploy·ment** /ɪmˈplɔɪmənt/ *n.* [U] **1** the act of paying someone to work for you: [+ of] *Mexican law prohibits the employment of children under 14.* **2** the condition of doing work to earn money: *Steve's still looking for full-time employment.* | *How many times were you promoted during your employment at the company?* **3** the number of people who have jobs: *Nationwide employment now stands at 95%.* | *Many economists consider full employment (=a situation in which everyone in society has a job) an unrealistic goal.* —opposite UNEMPLOYMENT **4** FORMAL the use of a particular object, method, skill etc. to achieve something: [+ of] *The pact calls for the continued employment of economic sanctions.*

employment a·gen·cy /.ˈ.. ˌ.../ *n.* [C] *plural* **employment agencies** a business that makes money by finding jobs for people

em·po·ri·um /ɪmˈpɔriəm/ *n. plural* **emporiums** or **emporia** /-riə/ [C] a large store

em·pow·er /ɪmˈpaʊɚ/ *v.* [T] **1** to give someone more control over their own life or situation: *The Voting Rights Act was needed to empower minority groups.* **2** FORMAL to give an organization the power or legal right to do something: [**be empowered to do sth**] *The President is empowered to appoint judges to the Supreme Court.* —**empowerment** *n.* [U]

em·press /ˈɛmprɪs/ *n.* [C] a female ruler of an EMPIRE, or the wife of an EMPEROR

emp·ties /ˈɛmptiz/ *n.* [plural] bottles or glasses that are empty: *Put the empties in that bag.*

emp·ti·ness /ˈɛmptɪnɪs/ *n.* [U] **1** a feeling of great sadness and loneliness: *A lot of people have a sort of emptiness in their lives.* **2** the state of being empty or containing nothing in a place: [+ of] *Most tourists are awed by the barren emptiness of the Mojave Desert.*

emp·ty¹ /ˈɛmpti/ *adj.* **emptier, emptiest**

s w **1** container having nothing inside: *Could you pick up the empty beer cans over there?* | *The gas tank's almost empty.*

2 room/building an empty room, building etc. does not have any people in it: *I hate coming home to an empty house late at night.* | *Half the classroom was empty.*

3 not used not being used by anyone: *Is this seat empty?*

4 person/life unhappy because nothing seems interesting or important, or because you feel your life has no purpose: *After the divorce, he felt alone and empty.*

5 empty words/promises/gestures etc. words, promises etc. that are not sincere, or have no effect: *His repeated promises to pay them back were just empty words.*

6 do sth on an empty stomach to do something without having eaten any food first: *I overslept and had to go to class on an empty stomach.*

7 empty nest also **empty nest syndrome** a situation in which parents become sad because their children have grown up and moved out of their house

8 be empty of sth to not contain a particular type of thing, or not have a particular quality: *Mrs. Payne was tired and empty of emotion.* —**emptily** *adv.* —see also EMPTIES

empty² *v.* **empties, emptied, emptying 1** [T] also **empty out** to remove everything that is inside of something: *Did you empty the dishwasher?* | *You can empty those glasses out in the sink.* **2** [T] to pour the things that are in a container into or onto something else: [**empty sth into/onto etc.**] *Empty the muffin mix into a medium bowl.* **3** [I,T] to leave a place, or to make everyone leave a place: *The judge emptied the courtroom when fighting almost broke out between members of the defendant's family.*

empty into sth *phr. v.* [T] if a river empties into a larger area of water, it flows into it: *The Mississippi River empties into the Gulf of Mexico.*

empty-hand·ed /ˌ.. ˈ../ *adj.* without getting what you hoped or expected to get: *Hearing police sirens in the distance, the robber was forced to leave the bank empty-handed.*

empty-head·ed /ˌ.. ˈ.. ◂/ *adj.* INFORMAL stupid, silly, and unable to think or behave seriously

EMS *n.* **1** [singular] European Monetary System; a system for limiting how much the different currencies (CURRENCY (1)) of countries within the European Union can go up and down in value in relation to each other **2** [U] emergency medical services; a type of medical service that gives medical treatment to people before taking them to a hospital

EMT *n.* [C] emergency medical technician; a person who is trained to give medical treatment to people before they are taken to a hospital

e·mu /'imyu, ' imu/ *n.* [C] a large Australian bird that can run very fast, but cannot fly

em·u·late /'ɛmyə,leɪt/ *v.* [T] **1** to try to do something or behave in the same way as someone else, especially because you admire them; IMITATE: *Davis was encouraged to emulate the style of trumpet player Bobby Hackett.* **2** TECHNICAL if one computer or piece of electronic equipment emulates another, it works in a similar way: *Procomm can connect with and emulate virtually any computer terminal.* —**emulation** /,ɛmyə'leɪʃən/ *n.* [U]

e·mul·si·fi·er /ɪ'mʌlsə,faɪɚ/ *n.* [C] a substance that is added, especially to food, to prevent liquids and solids from separating

e·mul·si·fy /ɪ'mʌlsə,faɪ/ *v.* **emulsifies, emulsified, emulsifying** [I,T] to combine to become a smooth mixture, or to make two liquids do this: *Gradually stir in the oil until the mixture emulsifies.*

e·mul·sion /ɪ'mʌlʃən/ *n.* [C,U] **1** a mixture of liquids that do not completely combine, such as oil and water **2** TECHNICAL the substance on the surface of photographic film or paper that makes it react to light

en- /ɪn, ɛn/ *prefix* [in verbs] **1** to make someone or something be in a particular state, or have a particular quality: *to enlarge* (=make something bigger) | *to endanger* (=put someone in danger) | *to enrich* (=make better) **2** to go completely around something, or include all of it: *to encircle* (=surround everything)

-en /ən/ *suffix* **1** [in adjectives] made of a particular material or substance: *a golden crown* | *wooden seats* **2** [in verbs] to make something have a particular quality: *to darken* (=make or become dark) | *ripening fruit* | *This strengthened his resolve* (=made it stronger).

en·a·ble /ɪ'neɪbəl/ *v.* [T] **1** to give someone what they need to be able to do something: [**enable sb to do sth**] *The goal of the training is to enable employees to work as a team.* **2** FORMAL to make something possible: *Our main goal is to enable healthy change and growth.*

en·a·bler /ɪ'neɪblɚ/ *n.* [C] **1** DISAPPROVING someone who makes it possible for someone else to continue behaving badly, for example by dealing with their problems for them: *Fleiss became his daughter's enabler by continuing to lend her money.* **2** someone or something that makes it possible for someone to do something or for something to happen

en·a·bling /ɪ'neɪblɪŋ/ *adj.* [only before noun] TECHNICAL an enabling law is one that makes something possible or gives someone special legal powers

en·act /ɪ'nækt/ *v.* [T] **1** to make a new rule or law: *Under a new law, universities must enact smoke-free policies on their campuses.* **2** FORMAL to perform a play or story by acting: *The characters wear colorful outfits and enact their scenes center stage.* —see also RE-ENACT —**enactment** *n.* [C,U]

en·am·el[1] /ɪ'næməl/ *n.* [U] **1** a glass-like substance that is put on metal, clay etc. for decoration or protection **2** the hard, smooth outer surface of your teeth **3** a type of paint that produces a shiny surface when it is dry —**enamel** *adj.*

enamel[2] *v.* [T usually passive] to cover or decorate something with enamel

en·am·ored /ɪ'næmɚd/ *adj.* [not before noun] **1** liking something very much: [+ of/with] *Charley was never really enamored of Paris.* **2** in love with someone, or caring about them very much: [+ of/with] *They tend to become enamored of pretty young women.*

en bloc /ɑn 'blɑk/ *adv.* all together as a single unit, rather than separately: *You cannot dismiss these stories en bloc.*

en·camp /ɪn'kæmp/ *v.* **be encamped** to be staying in a camp, especially a military one, somewhere: *Troops remained encamped two miles east of the border.*

en·camp·ment /ɪn'kæmp'mənt/ *n.* [C] a large temporary camp, especially of soldiers: *a military encampment*

en·cap·su·late /ɪn'kæpsə,leɪt/ *v.* [T] **1** to put the main facts or ideas of something in a short form or a small space: *Two lines of the song neatly encapsulate Gregg's romantic philosophy.* | [**encapsulate sth in sth**] *The teachings of Zen were encapsulated in short statements.* **2** to completely cover something with something else, especially in order to protect it: [**encapsulate sth in sth**] *It will cost at least $4 million to encapsulate the leaking fuel rods in lead.* —**encapsulation** /ɪn,kæpsə'leɪʃən/ *n.* [C,U]

en·case /ɪn'keɪs/ *v.* [T often passive] to cover or surround something completely: [**encase sth in sth**] *Andre's right arm was encased in a cast.*

-ence /əns/ *suffix* [in nouns] **1** used to make nouns from verbs, to show a state, a quality, or a fact: *existence* (=the fact of existing) | *an occurrence* (=something that has happened) | *dependence* (=the state of depending on someone or something) **2** used to make nouns from adjectives ending in -ENT: *permanence* (=from "permanent") —compare -ANCE

en·ceph·a·li·tis /ɪn,sɛfə'laɪtɪs/ *n.* [U] a serious medical condition carried by insects which involves swelling of the brain

en·chant /ɪn'tʃænt/ *v.* [T usually passive] **1** to attract and hold someone's attention and make them feel very interested, happy, or excited: *Sue was a college student, enchanted by Baum's storytelling abilities.* **2** LITERARY to use magic on something or someone

en·chant·ed /ɪn'tʃæntɪd/ *adj.* **1** someone who is enchanted with someone or something is attracted to them and feels happy and excited: [+ with] *From the moment we met, I was completely enchanted with her eyes.* —compare DISENCHANTED **2** an enchanted object or place has been changed by magic, so that it has special powers: *an enchanted castle*

en·chant·er /ɪn'tʃæntɚ/ *n.* [C] LITERARY someone who uses magic on people and things

en·chant·ing /ɪn'tʃæntɪŋ/ *adj.* very pleasant or attractive in a way that makes you feel very interested, happy, or excited: *an enchanting tale a boy and his magic toy horse* —**enchantingly** *adv.*

en·chant·ment /ɪn'tʃænt'mənt/ *n.* **1** [C,U] a feeling of pleasure or excitement that strongly interests or attracts you: *Cleveland's production of the "Nutcracker" is full of enchantment.* **2** [C,U] LITERARY a change caused by magic, or the state of being changed by magic

en·chant·ress /ɪn'tʃæntrɪs/ *n.* [C] **1** OLD-FASHIONED a woman whom men find very attractive and interesting **2** LITERARY a woman who uses magic on people and things

en·chi·la·da /,ɛntʃə'lɑdə/ *n.* [C] **1** a Mexican food consisting of a TORTILLA (=flat piece of bread) that is rolled up and filled with meat or cheese, and covered with a SPICY SAUCE **2 the big enchilada** INFORMAL something that is the most important or biggest of its type: *We're aiming our products at the big enchilada – the home computer market.* **3 the whole enchilada** INFORMAL all of something: *Wells should sell the whole enchilada to get the best price.*

en·cir·cle /ɪn'sɚkəl/ *v.* [T] to surround someone or something completely: *The city is nearly encircled by rebel troops.* —**encirclement** *n.* [U]

encl. the written abbreviation of ENCLOSURE, used in formal letters to show that something else has been included in the envelope

en·clave /'ɛnkleɪv, 'ɑŋ-/ *n.* [C] a place or a group of people that is surrounded by people or areas that are different from it: *Nagorno-Karabakh is a mainly Armenian enclave within Azerbaijan.*

en·close /ɪn'kloʊz/ *v.* [T] **1** to put something inside an envelope with a letter: *I am enclosing my résumé and three letters of reference.* **2** [usually passive] to surround something, especially with a fence or wall, in order to make it separate: *The pool area is enclosed by a six-foot wall.* —**enclosed** *adj.*: *Smoking is banned in most enclosed public places.*

en·clo·sure /ɪnˈkloʊʒɚ/ *n.* **1** [C] an area surrounded by a wall or fence, and used for a particular purpose: *The animals were placed in a large enclosure behind the barn.* **2** [U] the act of making an area separate by putting a wall or fence around it: *Holden's lawsuit led to the enclosure of freeway overpasses with fencing.* **3** [C] something that is put inside an envelope with a letter

en·code /ɪnˈkoʊd/ *v.* [T] to put a message or other information into CODE —opposite DECODE

en·com·pass /ɪnˈkʌmpəs/ *v.* [T] **1** to include a wide range of ideas, subjects, etc.: *Birnbaum's career encompassed television, radio, newspapers, and guidebooks.* **2** to completely cover or surround something: *The Presidio encompasses 1,400 acres and 848 buildings.*

en·core[1] /ˈɑŋkɔr/ *n.* [C] an additional or repeated part of a performance, especially a musical one: *The band came back on stage for an encore.*

encore[2] *interjection* said when you have enjoyed a musical performance very much and want the performer to sing or play more

en·coun·ter[1] /ɪnˈkaʊntɚ/ *v.* [T] **1** to experience problems, difficulties, or opposition when you are trying to do something: *Matheu's efforts to establish the clinic encountered a number of setbacks.* **2** FORMAL to meet someone or experience something without planning to: *If your dog encounters poison oak, do not pet it until you clean its fur.*

encounter[2] *n.* [C] **1** an occasion when you meet someone, especially when it is not planned or expected: *A bus ride from New York to Miami brings encounters with all kinds of people.* | *Bernstein began training the young conductor after **a chance encounter** (=a meeting that happened by luck or chance).* **2** a short dangerous or frightening meeting between people, groups, or things: [+ **with**] *The U.S. had won its first encounter with the North Vietnamese army.* | *If you've ever had **a close encounter** (=a frightening situation in which you get too close to something) with a moose, you know just how big they are.*

encounter group /.'.. ,./ *n.* [C] a group of people, usually led by someone with special training, that meets to discuss emotions, personal problems, experiences etc.

en·cour·age /ɪnˈkɚɪdʒ, -ˈkʌr-/ *v.* [T] **1** to say or do something that helps someone have the courage or confidence to do something: *Her letters really encouraged me throughout my illness.* | [**encourage sb to do sth**] *Barber's parents encouraged her to stay in school.* **2** to make something more likely to happen, or make people more likely to do something: *This insurance plan will be too hard to administer and will encourage fraud.* | [**encourage sb to do sth**] *We want to encourage businesses to invest and create jobs.* —**encouragement** *n.* [C,U] —opposite DISCOURAGE

en·cour·ag·ing /ɪnˈkɚɪdʒɪŋ/ *adj.* giving you hope and confidence: *His condition after the surgery looks very encouraging.* —**encouragingly** *adv.*

en·croach /ɪnˈkroʊtʃ/ *v.* [I always + prep.] **1** to gradually cover more and more of an area, so that something is affected or threatened: [+ **on/upon/into**] *Booming urban development is encroaching on rural land.* **2** to gradually take more and more control of someone's time, possessions, rights etc.: [+ **on/upon**] *Gordimer doesn't allow her political activities to encroach on her writing.* —**encroaching** *adj.*: *The road curved through the encroaching jungle.* —**encroachment** *n.* [C,U]

en·crust·ed /ɪnˈkrʌstɪd/ *adj.* covered with a hard layer of something, or covered all over with small hard things: [+ **with/in**] *The hull of the ship had become encrusted with ice.* | **jewel-encrusted/ ice-encrusted/mud-encrusted** etc. *a diamond-encrusted bracelet* —**encrustation** /ɪnˌkrʌsˈteɪʃən/ *n.* [C,U]

en·crypt /ɪnˈkrɪpt/ *v.* [I,T] to change the form of computer information so that it cannot be read by people who are not supposed to see it —**encryption** /ɪnˈkrɪpʃən/ *n.* [U]

en·cum·ber /ɪnˈkʌmbɚ/ *v.* [T usually passive] FORMAL to make it difficult for someone to move easily or for something to happen in the usual way or make progress: [+ **with**] *Belarus' economy is still encumbered with inefficient state-owned factories.* —**encumbrance** *n.* [C]

-ency /ənsi/ *suffix* [in nouns] the state or action of doing something, or the quality of being a particular way: *the Presidency* (=the state of being President) | *fluency in French* (=the ability to speak it very well) —compare -ANCY

en·cyc·li·cal /ɪnˈsɪklɪkəl/ *n.* [C] TECHNICAL a letter sent by the Pope to all Catholic BISHOPS or to members of the Catholic Church

en·cy·clo·pe·di·a /ɪnˌsaɪkləˈpidiə/ *n.* [C] a book, set of books, or computer program which contains facts about many different subjects, or about one particular subject

en·cy·clo·pe·dic /ɪnˌsaɪkləˈpidɪk/ *adj.* encyclopedic knowledge, memory etc. has a very large amount of information in it: *Haspiel has an encyclopedic knowledge of baseball.*

end[1] /ɛnd/ *n.* [C]

1 `last part` the last part of something such as a period of time, activity, book, or movie: *I liked the story, except when the hero dies at the end.* | *Rob's moving to Maine at the end of September.*

2 `farthest point` the farthest point of a place or thing: *We were told to go to the end of the line.* | *Their house is located on the north end of the lake.* | *I don't like to swim in the deep end of the pool.* | *Put the two tables **end to end** (=in a line with the ends touching).*

3 `finish` a situation in which something is finished or does not exist anymore: *Community activists are calling for an end to selling cigarettes to children.* | *This could mean the party's 75 years of power **are at an end**.* | *Lieber's baseball career **came to an end** Friday after nineteen seasons.* | *The fall of the Berlin Wall **brought** the Cold War **to an end**.*

4 put an end to sth to stop or finish something: *We're hoping to put an end to the use of dangerous chemicals in foods.*

5 `goal` a result that you hope to achieve: *Officials want to encourage small business expansion. **To that end**, they have proposed tax cuts.* | *Ryan didn't realize Thompson would use the information **for his own ends**.* | *Learning to play the piano was **an end in itself** (=something you do because you want to, not in order to get any other advantage) for me.* | *We've had decades of school reform, **to what end** (=what are the goals or results)?*

6 in the end after a period of time; FINALLY: *In the end, we decided to go to Florida.* —see Usage Note at LASTLY

7 make ends meet to have just enough money to buy what you need: *With the car repairs, I just don't see how we're going to make ends meet this month.*

8 for days/hours/weeks etc. on end for many days, hours etc. without stopping: *When Wright was a child, he would play with blocks for hours on end.*

9 to no end SPOKEN very much: *It would make me happy to no end to see her get her Ph.D.*

10 no end of sth a lot of something: *There seems to be no end of traffic laws in this country.*

11 the end of the road/line the end of a process or activity: *Monday's loss was the end of the line for Martin, who finished third in the tournament.*

12 put/stand sth on end to put something in a position so that its longest edge is upright —see also **make sb's hair stand on end** (HAIR (11))

13 `part of an activity` INFORMAL the particular part of a job, activity, place etc. that you are involved in, or that affects you: *She works in the sales end of the company.* | *Let's hope they keep their end of the bargain.* | *What's the weather like **at your end** (=where you are)?*

14 no end in sight (to sth) no way of stopping or limiting something that you know of: *There seems to be no end in sight to the amount of power a personal computer can have.*

15 be at the end of your rope to have no more PATIENCE or strength to deal with something: *I'm at the end of my rope here. What should I do?*

16 it's not the end of the world SPOKEN used to say that a possible problem is not really as bad or serious as someone thinks: *If you don't get the job, it's not the end of the world.*

17 at the end of the day SPOKEN used to say what the final result of something is: *At the end of the day, it's just too much money to spend.*

18 the end justifies the means used to say that the result you want makes it acceptable to do bad things in order to get it

19 death [C usually singular] INFORMAL a word meaning "death," used because you want to avoid saying this directly: *James was with his father at the end.*

20 until/till the end of time LITERARY forever: *He promised that his love for her would last till the end of time.*

21 go to the ends of the earth to do everything you can, even if it is very difficult, in order to have or achieve something: *Brad would go to the ends of the earth to make his wife happy.*

22 go to such/those ends to do sth to use a lot of effort in order to achieve something: *Most women would not go to those ends to make their house look nice.*

23 sb/sth is the living end SPOKEN used as an expression of strong approval or disapproval: *What will she do next? She's the living end!* —see also **the be-all (and end-all)** (BE² (8)), **go off/until the bitter end** (BITTER (6)), **DEAD END¹, go off the deep end** (DEEP¹ (12)), **be at loose ends** (LOOSE¹ (14)), **loose ends** (LOOSE¹ (11)), ODDS AND ENDS, **get the short end of the stick** (SHORT¹ (20)), **the tail end of sth** (TAIL¹ (7)), **be at your wits' end** (WIT² (5))

SW 11 **end²** *v.* **1** [I,T] to finish or stop, or to make something finish or stop: *The conference ends on Saturday.* | *Janet's party didn't end until 4 o'clock in the morning.* | *A knee injury ended Brotherton's basketball season.* **2 end your life** to kill yourself: *Mabel tried to end her life after her husband died.* **3 end your days** if you end your days in a particular place or doing a particular thing, you spend the last part of your life there or doing that: *I would like nothing more than to end my days fly fishing in Montana.* **4 end it all** to kill yourself

end in sth *phr. v.* [T not in passive] to have a particular result, or finish in a particular way: *Papp's first three marriages ended in divorce.* | *Last year 23 high-speed car chases ended in accidents.*

end up *phr. v.* [linking verb] INFORMAL **1** to come to be in a particular situation or state, especially when you did not plan it: *You could end up dead if you're not careful.* [+ **with/in/on** etc.] *Cochrane ended up with 12 percent of the vote.* | [**end up doing** sth] *Whenever we go out to dinner with them, I always end up paying the bill.* **2** to arrive in a place you did not plan to go to: *Landau decided to see the world and ended up in New Orleans.*

en·dan·ger /ɪnˈdeɪndʒɚ/ *v.* [T] to put someone or something in a dangerous situation: *Smoking during pregnancy can endanger your baby's health.*

en·dan·gered /ɪnˈdeɪndʒɚd/ *adj.* in danger of being killed or destroyed, or of not existing anymore: *The organization has planted trees and bought endangered forests.*

endangered spe·cies /.,.. '../ *n.* [C] a type of animal or plant that may soon not exist anymore: *The bald eagle has been taken off the endangered species list* (=the official list of these animals and plants).

en·dear /ɪnˈdɪr/ *v.*

endear sb **to** sb *phr. v.* [T] to make someone popular and liked: *Comments like that won't endear Hill to the fans.*

en·dear·ing /ɪnˈdɪrɪŋ/ *adj.* making someone love or like you: *Will's sense of humor is one of his most endearing qualities.* —**endearingly** *adv.*

en·dear·ment /ɪnˈdɪrmənt/ *n.* [C,U] an action or word that expresses your love for someone: *It's better not to use such terms of endearment* (=names for someone you love) *as "sweetie" on the first date.*

en·deav·or¹ /ɪnˈdɛvɚ/ *n.* **1** [C] FORMAL an attempt or effort to do something new or different: *His latest endeavor is a Chinese restaurant in the Beacon Hill neighborhood.* **2** [U] efforts or activities that have a useful purpose: *Soon, nearly every area of **human endeavor*** (=all the activities that people do) *will be dominated by the computer chip.*

endeavor² *v.* [I] FORMAL to try very hard: [**endeavor to do** sth] *Judge Harris said he will endeavor to be fair to both sides.*

en·dem·ic /ɛnˈdɛmɪk, ɪn-/ *adj.* an endemic disease or problem is always present in a particular place, or among a particular group of people: *Cholera was endemic in Mexico in the 19th century.* —compare EPIDEMIC

end·game /ˈɛndɡeɪm/ *n.* [C usually singular] **1** the last part of a long process or series of events: *The war is now in its most difficult phase of all – the complex and delicate endgame.* **2** TECHNICAL the last part of a game of CHESS, when most of the pieces have been removed from the board

end·ing /ˈɛndɪŋ/ *n.* [C] **1** the way in which a story, movie, etc. finishes: *The story has a happy ending.* **2** a part that can be added to the end of a word: *Gerunds have the ending "-ing."*

en·dive /ˈɛndaɪv/ *n.* [C,U] **1** also **Belgian endive** a vegetable with long pointed bitter-tasting pale green leaves that is eaten raw or cooked **2** also **curly endive, frisee** a vegetable with curly bitter-tasting leaves that is eaten raw in SALADS

end·less /ˈɛndlɪs/ *adj.* **1** continuing for a very long time, especially in a way that is annoying: *We had to sit through endless meetings.* **2** with no limit to the number, size, or amount of something: *The possibilities for the use of plastics seems endless.* **3** [only before noun] TECHNICAL an endless belt, chain etc. is circular with its ends fastened together —**endlessly** *adv.*: *Mrs. Allen talked endlessly about her grandchildren.*

en·do·crine /ˈɛndəkrɪn/ *adj.* [only before noun] TECHNICAL relating to HORMONES in your blood: *an endocrine gland*

en·do·cri·nol·o·gy /ˌɛndəkrəˈnɑlədʒi/ *n.* [U] the scientific and medical study of the GLANDS (=a type of organ) in the body and the HORMONES that they produce —**endocrinologist** *n.* [C]

en·dor·phin /ɛnˈdɔrfɪn/ *n.* [U,plural] a chemical produced by the brain, that reduces the feeling of pain and can affect emotions

en·dorse /ɪnˈdɔrs/ *v.* [T] **1** to officially say that you support or approve of someone or something: *NATO leaders have endorsed a new strategy that creates smaller military forces.* **2** to say in an advertisement that other people should buy a particular product: *These days, Jenner endorses products including health foods and sunglasses.* **3 endorse a check** to sign your name on the back of a check —**endorsement** *n.* [C,U] **SW 3**

en·dow /ɪnˈdaʊ/ *v.* [T] to give a college, hospital etc. a large sum of money that will provide it with an income over a long period of time, especially for a specific purpose or department: *Donna's parents plan to endow a scholarship fund in memory of their daughter.*

endow sb **with** sth *phr. v.* [T] **1 be endowed with sth** to naturally have a good feature or quality: *She was endowed with both good looks and brains.* **2** FORMAL to give someone or something a good quality or ability: *This law does not endow judges with the power to raise taxes.* —see also WELL-ENDOWED

en·dow·ment /ɪnˈdaʊmənt/ *n.* **1** [C,U] a sum of money that is given to a place such as a college or hospital to give it an income over a long period of time, or the giving of this money **2** [C] a quality or ability that someone or something has naturally: *the island's natural endowments of white sandy beaches and clean water*

end·point /ˈɛndpɔɪnt/ n. [C] the place or stage at which something ends: *No one thinks the trend toward smaller computers has reached its endpoint.*

end prod·uct /ˌ. ˈ../ n. [C] something that is produced as the result of a long process: *The F-15 jets were the end product of a research program that began in 1965.* —compare BYPRODUCT

end re·sult /ˌ. .ˈ./ n. [C usually singular] the final result of a process or activity: *Despite all our efforts, the end result was a product that no one could use.*

end ta·ble /ˈ. ˌ../ n. [C] a small low table, usually used in a LIVING ROOM next to a SOFA or chair

en·due /ɪnˈdu/ v.
  endue sb **with** sth phr. v. [T] LITERARY to give someone a good quality; ENDOW

en·dur·ance /ɪnˈdʊrəns/ n. [U] the ability to suffer difficulties or pain with strength and patience for a long period of time: *Swimming helps to increase your strength and endurance.*

en·dure /ɪnˈdʊr/ v. **1** [T] to suffer pain or deal with a very bad situation for a long time, especially with strength and patience: *Many cancer patients have to endure a great deal of pain.* **2** [I] to remain alive, or continue to exist: *Scott's popularity endured well beyond his death in 1832.* —**endurable** adj.

en·dur·ing /ɪnˈdʊrɪŋ/ adj. continuing to exist for a long time, especially in spite of difficulties: *Negotiators are working toward establishing an enduring peace in the region.*

end us·er /ˌ. ˈ.. ◂/ n. [C] the person who actually uses a particular product: *Engineers have to be able to write things the end user can understand.*

end·ways /ˈɛndweɪz/ adv. SPOKEN with the end forward

end zone /ˈ. ./ n. [C] the place at each end of a football field where players take the ball in order to gain points

en·e·ma /ˈɛnəmə/ n. [C] the process of putting a liquid into someone's RECTUM in order to make them empty their BOWELs, or the liquid that is used in this process

sw en·e·my /ˈɛnəmi/ n. plural **enemies** [C] **1** someone who hates you and wants to harm you, or someone who opposes you and wants to prevent you from doing something: *She's a dangerous enemy to have.* | *For years, Ball and Dutra were bitter enemies* (=enemies who hate each other very much). | *He made enemies of everyone – the media and other teams.* | *Taylor has been Johnson's sworn enemy* (=an enemy that is determined never to end their disagreement) *since that dispute.* | *Harris said his political enemies are behind the rumor.* **2** [often singular] the person or group of people you are fighting against in a war: *The enemy is likely to attack after dark.* | *There are reports that enemy forces* (=the army, navy etc. of the country or group that you are fighting against) *have entered the capital.* | *enemy soldiers/missiles etc. Enemy aircraft were spotted 20 miles east of the border.* **3 the enemy of sth** LITERARY something that changes something else or makes it weaker: *Jealousy is the enemy of love.* —see also **With friends like that, who needs enemies?** (FRIEND (7)), NATURAL ENEMY, **sb is his/her own worst enemy** (WORST¹ (3))

en·er·get·ic /ˌɛnɚˈdʒɛtɪk/ adj. very active because you have a lot of energy: *Captain Nagumo was a capable, intelligent, and energetic officer.* —**energetically** /-kli/ adv.: *They are working energetically on local problems that affect our daily lives.*

en·er·gize /ˈɛnɚˌdʒaɪz/ v. [T] **1** to make someone feel more determined and energetic: *Woods said the women's movement has not been so energized since the mid-1970s.* **2** [usually passive] to make a machine work: *The cars' electric motors are energized by solar cells.* —**energizing** adj.

sw en·er·gy /ˈɛnɚdʒi/ n. **1** [U] the physical and mental strength that makes you able to be active: *Watkins will need more than energy and experience to turn the department around.* | *She came back full of energy*

after her vacation. | *Joking around is often a sign of nervous energy* (=energy that you have because you feel nervous). **2** [U] power that is used to produce heat and make machines work: *the world's energy resources* | *nuclear energy* **3 energies** [plural] the effort that you use to do things: *Paskowitz says he quit his medical practice to devote all of his energies to his children.*

en·er·vat·ed /ˈɛnɚˌveɪtɪd/ adj. FORMAL having lost energy and feeling weak: *Feeling both enervated and threatened, they refused to continue.*

en·er·vat·ing /ˈɛnɚˌveɪtɪŋ/ adj. FORMAL making you feel weak

en·fant ter·ri·ble /ˌɑnfɑn tɛˈriblə/ n. [C] LITERARY a young person who behaves in a way that shocks and amuses other people: *Venturi is the former enfant terrible of architecture.*

en·fee·ble /ɪnˈfibəl/ v. [T] LITERARY to make someone weak —**enfeebled** adj.

en·fold /ɪnˈfoʊld/ v. [T] LITERARY to enclose or surround someone or something: **[enfold sb/sth in sth]** *He enfolded her in his arms.*

en·force /ɪnˈfɔrs/ v. [T] **1** to make people obey a rule or law, especially by punishing those who do not obey it: *The police are strict here about enforcing the speed limit.* **2** to make something such as a feeling or a particular type of behavior happen, especially by threats or force: *It's difficult to enforce discipline in these surroundings.* | *a period of enforced silence* —**enforceable** adj. —**enforcement** n. [U] —see also LAW ENFORCEMENT

en·forc·er /ɪnˈfɔrsɚ/ n. [C] **1** someone such as a police officer who makes sure that people obey rules and laws **2** a player in sports such as basketball and hockey who plays roughly in order to make his opponents afraid to get close to the GOAL: *Edmonton enforcer Kelly Buchberger scored twice in last night's game.*

en·fran·chise /ɪnˈfræntʃaɪz/ v. [T] **1** FORMAL to give a group of people rights, especially the right to vote: *South Africa's new constitution enfranchised 28 million blacks.* —compare DISENFRANCHISED **2** OLD USE to free a slave —**enfranchisement** n. [U]

en·gage /ɪnˈgeɪdʒ/ v. FORMAL **1** [T] to attract someone and keep their interest: *She is a storyteller who can engage the children's imagination.* **2** [T] FORMAL to arrange to employ someone: **[engage sb to do sth]** *The board engaged Thompson to conduct a series of seminars.* **3** [I,T] to make one part fit into another part of a machine: *She engaged the clutch and put the car into first gear.* | **[+ with]** *The wheel engages with the cog and turns it.* —opposite DISENGAGE **4** [I,T] to begin to fight with an enemy: *The two armies engaged at dawn.*
  engage in sth FORMAL phr. v. [T] **1** to take part or become involved in an activity: *The two companies are engaged in a price war.* **2 engage sb in conversation** to start talking to someone and involve them in a conversation.

en·gaged /ɪnˈgeɪdʒd/ adj. **1** two people who are engaged have agreed to get married: *They've been engaged for six months.* | **[+ to]** *Shari's engaged to Joe.* | *Vicki and Tyler got engaged last week.* **2 be otherwise engaged** FORMAL to be unable to do something because you have arranged to do something else: *Duffy, who was otherwise engaged, has been replaced by another actor.*

en·gage·ment /ɪnˈgeɪdʒmənt/ n. **1** [C,U] an agreement to marry someone: *They've officially announced their engagement.* | *Carla and I have broken off our engagement* (=said we do not want to get married anymore). **2** [C] an arrangement to do something or meet someone: *Mrs. Dole had to leave for a speaking engagement* (=an occasion when you give a speech) *in Ohio.* | *I won't be able to make it – I have a previous engagement* (=an arrangement you have already made). **3** [C] TECHNICAL a battle between armies, navies etc. **4** [U] the state of being joined together with other working parts of a machine

engagement ring /.ˈ.. ˌ./ n. [C] a ring, often with a diamond on it, that a man gives to a woman when they decide to get married

en·gag·ing /ɪnˈgeɪdʒɪŋ/ *adj.* attracting people's attention and interest: *Her engaging personality has helped make her television's favorite talk-show hostess* —**engagingly** *adv.*

En·gels /ˈɛŋgəlz/**, Frie·drich** /ˈfriːdrɪk/ (1820–1895) a German political thinker and REVOLUTIONARY who, together with Karl Marx, wrote "The Communist Manifesto" and developed the political system of Communism

en·gen·der /ɪnˈdʒɛndɚ/ *v.* [T] FORMAL to be the cause of something such as a situation, action, or emotion: *Their financial success has engendered jealousy among their neighbors.*

s w **en·gine** /ˈɛndʒɪn/ *n.* [C] **1** a piece of machinery with moving parts that changes power from steam, electricity, oil etc. into movement: *The car's engine tends to be noisy as it builds to highway speeds.* | *a jet engine* —compare MOTOR[1] **2** a vehicle that pulls a train: *a diesel engine* —compare LOCOMOTIVE[1] **3 an engine of change/destruction etc.** FORMAL something that causes change etc.: *Investments will be the engine of growth for the future.* —see also FIRE ENGINE, SEARCH ENGINE

s w **en·gi·neer**[1] /ˌɛndʒəˈnɪr/ *n.* [C] **1** someone who designs the way roads, bridges, machines etc. are built: *a civil engineer* | *a software engineer* **2** someone who drives a train **3** someone who controls the engines on a ship or airplane: *a flight engineer* **4** a soldier in the army who designs and builds roads, bridges etc. **5 the engineer of sth** someone who plans something and uses skill to make it happen: *Tiller has been the engineer of many Republican victories in the state.*

engineer[2] *v.* [T] **1** to arrange something by skillful secret planning: *Sakakida engineered the escape of nearly 500 prisoners of war.* **2** [usually passive] to design and plan the building of roads, bridges, machines, etc.: *This computer has been specially engineered to run the latest operating systems.*

s w **en·gi·neer·ing** /ˌɛndʒəˈnɪrɪŋ/ *n.* [U] the profession and activity of designing the way roads, bridges, machines etc. are built —see also CIVIL ENGINEERING, GENETIC ENGINEERING

Eng·land /ˈɪŋglənd/ the largest country in the U.K.

Eng·lish[1] /ˈɪŋglɪʃ/ *n.* [U] **1** the language used in countries such as the U.S., the U.K., Canada, and Australia **2** the study of the English language and its literature, or a course in this: *an English teacher* | *What grade did you get in English?* **3 the English** [plural] people from England, or sometimes from all of Great Britain

English[2] *adj.* **1** from or relating to England or Great Britain **2** relating to the English language

English horn /ˌ.. ˈ./ a musical instrument similar to an OBOE, but larger

Eng·lish·man /ˈɪŋglɪʃmən/ *n. plural* **Englishmen** /-mən/ [C] a man from England

English muf·fin /ˌ.. ˈ../ *n.* [C] a round thick flat piece of bread that you cut in half and TOAST[2] (2) before eating

Eng·lish·wom·an /ˈɪŋglɪʃˌwʊmən/ *n. plural* **Englishwomen** /-ˌwɪmɪn/ [C] a woman from England

en·gorged /ɪnˈgɔrdʒd/ *adj.* having become larger or filled with something: [+ with] *The river was engorged with water from the recent rains.* —**engorgement** *n.* [U] —**engorge** *v.* [T]

en·grave /ɪnˈgreɪv/ *v.* [T] **1** to cut words or pictures into the surface of metal, wood, glass etc.: [engrave sth on sth] *The names of soldiers who were killed are engraved on two marble walls.* | [engrave sth with sth] *She wore a thin gold band engraved with the initials O.M.O.* **2 be engraved in your memory/mind/heart** FORMAL to be impossible to forget: *Their last conversation is deeply engraved in his memory.* **3** to prepare a special metal plate for printing **4** to print something using a specially prepared metal plate —**engraver** *n.* [C]

en·grav·ing /ɪnˈgreɪvɪŋ/ *n.* **1** [C] a picture printed from an engraved metal plate **2** [U] the art or work of cutting words or pictures into the surfaces of things

en·gross /ɪnˈgroʊs/ *v.* [T] **1 be engrossed in sth** to be so interested in something that you do not notice anything else: *Motorists who are engrossed in conversation on their cell phones are more likely to get into*

E

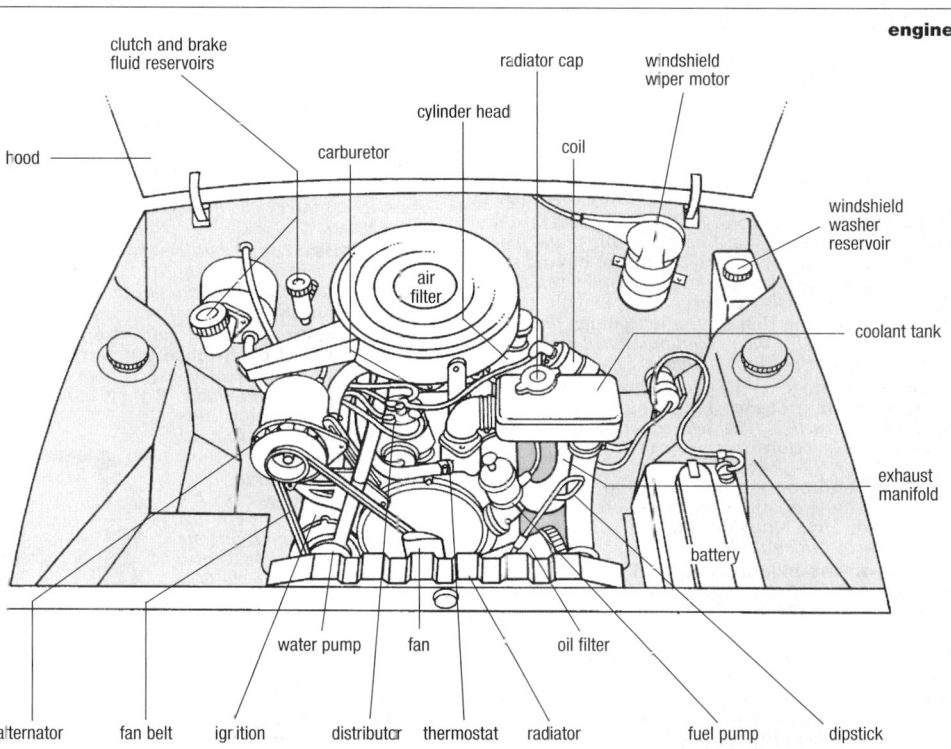

engine

clutch and brake fluid reservoirs

radiator cap

windshield wiper motor

cylinder head

hood

carburetor

coil

air filter

windshield washer reservoir

coolant tank

exhaust manifold

battery

water pump   fan   oil filter

alternator   fan belt   ignition   distributor   thermostat   radiator   fuel pump   dipstick

accidents. **2** to be or become very interesting to someone, so that they do not notice anything else: *The murder trial had engrossed the small northern Ohio city for months.* —**engrossing** *adj.*: *an engrossing story*

en·gulf /ɪnˈgʌlf/ *v.* [T] **1** to suddenly affect someone so strongly that they feel nothing else: *Fear engulfed him as he approached the microphone.* **2** if a war, social change etc. engulfs a place, it affects it so much that the place changes completely: *Civil war has completely engulfed the country.* **3** [usually passive] to completely surround or cover something: *Coast Guard boats arrived to find the boat engulfed in flames.*

en·hance /ɪnˈhæns/ *v.* [T] to make something such as a taste, feeling, or ability better: *We're using technology to enhance our levels of service.* —**enhancement** *n.* [C,U]

e·nig·ma /ɪˈnɪgmə/ *n.* [C] a person, thing, or event that is strange or mysterious and difficult to understand or explain: *Lorraine remains an enigma who is easy to admire but impossible to get to know.*

en·ig·mat·ic /ˌɛnɪgˈmætɪk◂/ *adj.* mysterious, and difficult to understand or explain: *an enigmatic smile* —**enigmatically** /-kli/ *adv.*: *"You'll find out soon," she said enigmatically.*

en·join /ɪnˈdʒɔɪn/ *v.* [T] **1** LAW to legally forbid an activity **2** FORMAL to order someone to do something

en·joy /ɪnˈdʒɔɪ/ *v.* enjoys, enjoyed, enjoying [T] **1** to get pleasure from something: *Greg says he enjoys his new job.* | [**enjoy doing sth**] *Thena enjoys working with children.* **2** to have something good such as success or a particular ability or advantage: *The team has enjoyed some success this season.* **3 enjoy yourself** to be happy and experience pleasure in a particular situation: *David seemed to be enjoying himself at the concert.* **4 enjoy!** SPOKEN used when you give someone something and you want them to get pleasure from it: *Here's your dinner. Enjoy!*

USAGE NOTE: ENJOY

GRAMMAR

Enjoy is almost always followed by a noun phrase, a pronoun, or by a verb with *-ing*: *"Did you enjoy your vacation?" "Yes, I enjoyed it a lot."* (NOT *I enjoyed with/of it.*) | *I really enjoyed myself last night at the party.* (NOT *I enjoyed at the party*). | *He enjoys playing golf very much* (NOT *He enjoys very much playing golf* and NOT *He enjoys to play golf*).

---

en·joy·a·ble /ɪnˈdʒɔɪəbəl/ *adj.* giving you pleasure: *It was a very enjoyable afternoon.* —**enjoyably** *adv.*

en·joy·ment /ɪnˈdʒɔɪmənt/ *n.* **1** [U] the pleasure that you get from something: *I now play the piano mostly for enjoyment.* **2** [U] FORMAL the fact of having something: *Some state laws regulated the enjoyment of civil rights on the basis of race.* **3** [C usually plural] FORMAL something that you enjoy doing: *The others were absorbed in their economic problems, social enjoyments, and political activities.*

en·large /ɪnˈlɑrdʒ/ *v.* [I,T] to become bigger, or to make something bigger: *I'm going to get these two pictures enlarged.* | *The left chamber of the heart often enlarges before there are other signs of heart failure.*

enlarge on/upon sth *phr. v.* [T] to provide more facts or details about something you have already mentioned: *Mrs. Maughan did not enlarge on what she meant by "unsuitable."*

en·large·ment /ɪnˈlɑrdʒmənt/ *n.* **1** [C] a photograph that has been printed again in a larger size —opposite REDUCTION (2) **2** [C,U] an increase in size or amount

en·larg·er /ɪnˈlɑrdʒɚ/ *n.* [C] a piece of equipment used for making photographs larger

en·light·en /ɪnˈlaɪtˈn/ *v.* [T] FORMAL to explain something to someone so that they understand: *I see teaching as an opportunity to enlighten students, not just*

inform them. —**enlightening** *adj.*: *an enlightening experience*

en·light·ened /ɪnˈlaɪtˈnd/ *adj.* **1** treating people in a kind and fair way and understanding their needs and problems: *Apple promotes itself as an enlightened, progressive company.* **2** showing a good understanding of something, and not believing things about it that are false: *enlightened readers*

en·light·en·ment /ɪnˈlaɪtˈnmənt/ *n.* [U] **1 the Enlightenment** a period in the eighteenth century when many writers and scientists believed that science and knowledge, not religion, could improve people's lives **2** FORMAL the state of understanding something clearly, or the act of making someone understand something clearly **3** the state in the Buddhist and Hindu religions, of not having any more human desires, so that your spirit is united with the universe

en·list /ɪnˈlɪst/ *v.* **1 enlist sb's help** to persuade someone to help you: *I enlisted the help of four friends to help move the piano.* **2** [I] to join the army, navy etc.: [**+ in**] *In the first year of the war, a million men enlisted in the armed forces.* **3** [T **+ in/into**] to persuade people to join your organization —**enlistment** *n.* [C,U]

en·list·ed /ɪnˈlɪstɪd/ *adj.* **an enlisted man/woman** someone in the army, navy etc. whose rank is below that of an officer

en·liv·en /ɪnˈlaɪvən/ *v.* [T] to make something more interesting or amusing: *Paintings by West Marin artists enliven their living room.*

en masse /ɑn ˈmæs, -ˈmɑs, ɛn-/ *adv.* if a group of people do something en masse, they all do it together: *The senior management resigned en masse.*

en·meshed /ɪnˈmɛʃt/ *adj.* [not before noun] very involved in a bad or complicated situation: [**+ in**] *Congress is worried about becoming enmeshed in a foreign war.*

en·mi·ty /ˈɛnməti/ *n. plural* **enmities** [C,U] FORMAL the feeling of hatred or anger toward someone: *For many years, there has been deep enmity between the two ethnic groups.*

en·no·ble /ɪˈnoʊbəl, ɛ-/ *v.* [T] FORMAL **1** if something ennobles you, it improves your character **2** [usually passive] to give someone an official title and make them part of the NOBILITY —**ennoblement** *n.* [U] —**ennobling** *adj.*

en·nui /ɑnˈwi/ *n.* [U] LITERARY a feeling of being tired and bored, especially as a result of having nothing to do

e·nor·mi·ty /ɪˈnɔrməti/ *n.* [U] **1** the enormity of a situation, event etc. is how serious it is or how big an effect it will have: *The enormity of our country's economic problems is overwhelming.* **2** the enormity of a problem, subject, job etc. is how large or difficult it is: *In his interview, he discussed the enormity of the agency's task.*

e·nor·mous /ɪˈnɔrməs/ *adj.* extremely large in size or amount: *Their house is enormous.* | *He has an enormous amount of work to finish before Friday.* —**enormousness** *n.* [U]

e·nor·mous·ly /ɪˈnɔrməsli/ *adv.* **1 enormously popular/successful/destructive etc.** very popular, successful etc.: *"I'm enormously proud of the music we've created," said Judd.* **2** very much: *America's Hispanic population has grown enormously in recent years.*

e·nough¹ /ɪˈnʌf/ *adv.* **1** as much as is necessary: *It's getting late, and you two have talked enough for one day.* | **tall/nice/fast etc. enough** *I couldn't see well enough to read the sign.* | [**+ for**] *Our car wasn't big enough for all of the suitcases.* | *The song "Silent Night" is easy enough for a child to play.* | *You'll have to rewrite this paper – it's just **not good enough*** (=not

enough

He wasn't tall enough to reach the shelf.

Her coat wasn't big enough.

satisfactory or acceptable). **2 strangely/oddly/ funnily enough** used to say that although something seems unlikely, it is true: *Oddly enough, both authors begin their stories with the same incident.* **3** not very, but in an acceptable way: *She's nice enough when I see her, but I don't think she really likes me.* —see also **it's bad enough...** (BAD¹ (21)), **fair enough** (FAIR¹ (12)), **sure enough** (SURE² (1)) —see Usage Note at ADEQUATE

s w **enough**² *determiner, pron.* **1** as much or as many as
1 1 may be necessary: *Could you please move over? I don't have enough room.* | **[+ for]** *Don't grab. There's enough for everyone.* **[enough sth to do sth]** *We simply didn't win enough games to go to the play-offs.* | *We have **nowhere near enough** space in our car for everyone's suitcase.* | *Two years of college were **more than enough** (=too much) for Rainis, who dropped out in 1978.* | *Ten years was **time enough** for the forest to recover from the volcano's eruption.* | **enough to do/eat** etc. *It's sad that there are so many children who don't have enough to eat.*

SPOKEN PHRASES

2 have had enough (of sth) to be very annoyed with someone or something: *I'd had enough of the neighbors' noise, so I called the police.* **3 enough is enough** used to say that you are annoyed because something has been continuing for too long, or there is too much of it: *Finally my grandmother said, "Enough is enough," and left him after 35 years of suffering.* **4 enough about sb/sth** used to say that you want to stop talking about someone or something and talk about someone or something else: *Enough about politics. Let's talk about sports.* **5 that's enough** used to say that you want someone to stop behaving like they are because they are annoying you: *That's enough, you two. Now sit down and do your homework.* **6 enough said** used to say that there is no need to say any more because you understand everything: *"I saw her coming out of his room at 6 o'clock this morning." "Enough said."*

en·pas·sant /ˌɑn pɑˈsɑn/ *adv.* LITERARY if you say something en passant, you say a few words about it while you are talking about something else

en·quire /ɪnˈkwaɪɚ/ *v.* [I,T] another spelling of INQUIRE

en·quir·y /ɪnˈkwaɪɚri, ˈɪŋkwəri/ *n. plural* **enquiries** [C,U] another spelling of INQUIRY

en·rage /ɪnˈreɪdʒ/ *v.* [T] to make someone extremely angry: *The governor's racist comments enraged civil rights activists.* —**enraged** *adj.*: *an enraged bull*

en·rap·ture /ɪnˈræptʃɚ/ *v.* [T usually passive] FORMAL to make someone feel such pleasure and happiness that they cannot think of anything else: *Darwin was so enraptured by orchids that he wrote an entire book about them.* —**enraptured** *adj.*: *The orchestra played before an enraptured audience.*

en·rich /ɪnˈrɪtʃ/ *v.* [T] **1** to improve the quality of something, especially by adding things to it: *The goal of the course is to enrich our understanding of other cultures.* | *Fruit juices are added to cheap port wine to enrich its color and flavor.* **2** to make someone richer —**enrichment** *n.* [U]

en·roll /ɪnˈroʊl/ *v.* [I,T] to officially arrange to join a school, college, class, organization etc., or arrange for someone else to do this: **[+ in]** *He plans to enroll in a vocational school.*

en·roll·ment /ɪnˈroʊlmənt/ *n.* **1** [U] the process of arranging to join a school, college, organization etc. **2** [C] the number of people who have

arranged to join a school, college, class, organization etc.: *College enrollments are up again this fall.*

en route /ɑn ˈrut, ɛn-/ *adv.* on the way: *The refugees drove north toward the border, bribing the guards en route.* | **[+ to/from]** *The bus was en route to Denver when it ran off the road.*

en·sconce /ɪnˈskɑns/ *v.* **be ensconced** to be in a comfortable or safe place, usually with no intention of moving or being moved: **[+ in]** *Gavigan was firmly ensconced in the top job in sales.*

en·sem·ble /ɑnˈsɑmbəl/ *n.* **1** [C] a small group of musicians who play together regularly **2** [C usually singular] a set of clothes that are worn together **3** [C usually singular] a set of things that go together to form a whole

en·shrine /ɪnˈʃraɪn/ *v.* [T usually passive] **1** FORMAL if something such as an idea is enshrined in something, it is preserved and protected as a law or in a CONSTITUTION: **[+ in]** *The right of free speech is enshrined in the U.S. Constitution.* **2** if someone is enshrined in a place, their picture or possessions are placed in a public place so that people will remember them: **[+ in]** *Hunter will be enshrined in the Baseball Hall of Fame at a ceremony this week.*

en·shroud /ɪnˈʃraʊd/ *v.* [T] LITERARY to cover or hide something: *A dense fog enshrouded the mountain tops.*

en·sign /ˈɛnsən/ *n.* [C] **1** a low rank in the U.S. Navy, or an officer who has this rank **2** a flag on a ship that shows what country the ship belongs to **3** a small piece of metal on your uniform that shows your rank

en·slave /ɪnˈsleɪv/ *v.* [T usually passive] **1** FORMAL to trap someone in a situation that they cannot easily escape from: *Many Americans are enslaved in credit-card debt.* **2** to make someone into a slave: *The Tahltans often enslaved the women of other tribes.* —**enslavement** *n.* [U]

en·snare /ɪnˈsnɛr/ *v.* [T] **1** FORMAL to catch someone doing something that is illegal or wrong, or to involve someone in something like this, especially by tricking them: *Benson, who was ensnared in the investment scandal, received a short prison term.* **2** to be caught in something so that you cannot get away, especially in a TRAP¹ (1) or net: *Park rangers found three deer that had become ensnared in traps.*

en·sue /ɪnˈsu/ *v.* [I] to happen after something, especially as a result of it: *When police told them to leave, an argument ensued.* | **the ensuing year/months/ weeks etc.** *In the ensuing weeks, she began to get disturbing phone calls at night.* | **the ensuing battle/ argument/panic etc.** *Fred was knocked to the ground in the ensuing fight.*

en·sure /ɪnˈʃʊr/ *v.* [T] to make certain that something **s w** will happen: *All the necessary steps had been taken to* **3** *ensure their safety.* | **[+ that]** *The new law will ensure that criminals serve their full prison terms.* —compare INSURE —see Usage Note at INSURE

-ent /ənt/ *suffix* [in adjectives and nouns] someone or something that does something, or that has a particular quality: *local residents* (=people who live here) | *different* —see also -ANT

en·tail /ɪnˈteɪl/ *v.* [T] **1** to make it necessary to do something: *Repairs would entail the closure of the bridge for six months.* | **[entail doing sth]** *The surgery entailed placing a screw into a bone in her wrist.* **2** OLD USE to arrange for your property to become the property of a particular person, especially your son, after your death

en·tan·gle /ɪnˈtæŋgəl/ *v.* [T usually passive, always + adv./prep.] **1** to become involved in an argument, a situation that is difficult to escape from, or a relationship that causes problems etc.: **[entangle sb in sth]** *They lost all their money after getting entangled in a bad real estate deal.* | **[entangle sb with sb]** *Sue became romantically entangled with her boss.* **2** to become twisted and caught in a rope, net etc.: **[+ in/with]** *Penguins have been found entangled in lengths of fishing net.* —**entangled** *adj.*

en·tan·gle·ment /ɪn'tæŋgəlmənt/ n. [C,U] a difficult situation or relationship that is hard to escape from: *political entanglements*

en·ten·dre /ɑn'tɑndrə/ [C] n. —see DOUBLE ENTENDRE

en·tente /ɑn'tɑnt/ n. [C,U] a situation in which two countries agree to work together in some areas, even though they may not be friendly with each other

s w
2 1
en·ter /'ɛntɚ/ v.

1 go into **a)** [I,T] to go or come into a place: *When the bride entered the church, everyone stood up.* | *Army tanks entered the main square of the city.* **b)** [T] if an object or disease enters part of something, it goes inside it: *The infection hasn't entered the bloodstream.*

2 start working [T] to start working in a particular profession or organization, or to start studying at a college or university: *Jason plans to enter the Navy.* | *This fall she will enter the University of North Carolina.*

3 start an activity [T] to start to take part in an activity, such as a sports game: *Reese entered the game with five minutes left in the first half.*

4 computer [T] **a)** to put information into a computer by pressing the keys: *Enter your user name and hit the return key.* **b)** if you enter a computer system, you are given permission to use it by the computer

5 write information [T] to write information on a particular part of a form, document etc.: *Enter your address and telephone number in the spaces provided.*

6 competition/exam [I,T] to arrange to take part in something such as a competition, or to arrange for someone else to take part: *She entered the drawing competition and won.* | *A friend of mine entered me in the 10K race.*

7 period of time [T] **a)** to begin a period of time when something happens: *Our economy is entering a period of growth.* **b)** enter its third week/sixth day/second year etc. if something enters its third week, its sixth day etc., it continues for a third week, a sixth day etc.: *The hostage crisis has now entered its third day.*

8 a) enter a plea (of guilty/of not guilty) to officially say that you are guilty or not guilty of a particular crime in a court of law: *Sarkin is scheduled to enter a plea Tuesday.* **b)** to officially give something to a court of law, such as EVIDENCE for a TRIAL: *Judge Laney allow them to enter the knife as evidence.* —see also SUBMIT (1)

9 sth never entered my mind/head SPOKEN used to say that you have not considered a possibility, especially if you are surprised that something has happened: *It never entered my mind that I might break the world record.*

10 change [T] if a particular quality enters something, it starts to exist in it and change it, especially suddenly: *A note of panic entered her voice.*

11 enter sb's life if someone or something enters your life, you start to know them or be affected by them: *Brandy's friends noticed a big difference in her after Jerry entered her life.*

12 start discussing [T] to start to discuss or study a particular subject: *Last week, the governor entered the public debate on health-care reform.*

13 enter an offer/complaint/objection etc. FORMAL to officially make an offer, complaint etc.

enter into sth *phr. v.* [T] **1** enter into an agreement/contract etc. to officially make an agreement to do something: *Turner Inc. said it had entered into a partnership agreement with Scientific-Atlanta Inc.* **2** to start doing something, especially discussing or studying something: *Lawyers often avoid entering into discussions about personal and legal ethics.* **3** [usually with a negative] to affect a situation and be something that you must consider when you make a choice: *Money didn't enter into my decision to leave the company.* **4** enter into the spirit of it/ things to take part in a game, party etc. in an eager way

enter upon/on sth *phr. v.* [T] FORMAL to start doing something or being involved in it: *Our nation is entering upon a new era of racial harmony.*

en·ter·i·tis /ˌɛntə'raɪtɪs/ n. [U] a painful condition that affects your INTESTINES

en·ter·prise /'ɛntɚˌpraɪz/ n. **1** [C] a company, organization, or business, especially a new one: *He is the CEO of a multimillion-dollar enterprise.* **2** [U] the activity of starting and running businesses: *Private enterprise is the backbone of this country.* **3** [C] a large and complicated plan or process that is done with other people or groups: *The U.S. and Russia are working together on a new scientific enterprise.* **4** [U] the ability to think of new activities or ideas and make them work: *She's a woman of great enterprise and creativity.* —see also FREE ENTERPRISE, PRIVATE ENTERPRISE

en·ter·pris·ing /'ɛntɚˌpraɪzɪŋ/ adj. able and willing to think of new activities or ideas, and make them work: *An enterprising student was selling copies of the answers to the test.* —**enterprisingly** adv.

en·ter·tain /ˌɛntɚ'teɪn/ v. **1** [I,T] to do something that amuses or interests people: *It's Scott's personality that really inspires and entertains.* | [entertain sb with sth] *He still occasionally entertains his family with his accordion playing.* **2** [I,T] to invite people to your home for a meal or party, or take your company's customers to have a meal, drinks etc.: *Donna entertains at home on a regular basis.* | *Mike often gets home late when he's entertaining business clients.* **3** entertain an idea/thought/doubt etc. to consider or think about something: *Since last year, he's been entertaining the idea of retiring.*

en·ter·tain·er /ˌɛntɚ'teɪnɚ/ n. [C] someone who tells jokes, sings etc. to amuse people: *a nightclub entertainer*

en·ter·tain·ing[1] /ˌɛntɚ'teɪnɪŋ/ adj. amusing and interesting: *an entertaining movie*

entertaining[2] n. [U] the practice of inviting people for meals or to parties, especially for business reasons

en·ter·tain·ment /ˌɛntɚ'teɪnmənt/ n. [U] things such as movies, television shows, performances etc. that amuse or interest people: *So what do you do for entertainment in this town?* | *the entertainment industry*

en·thrall /ɪn'θrɔl/ v. [T usually passive] to make someone so interested and excited that they listen to or watch something very carefully: *The new video game has enthralled millions of children.* | be enthralled by/with sth *We were attracted by her beauty and enthralled by her talk.* —**enthralling** adj.: *an enthralling story*

en·throne /ɪn'θroʊn/ v. [T usually passive] to officially give a new king, queen, or other person in a very high position the power to rule in a special ceremony in which they sit on a THRONE (=special chair) —**enthronement** n. [C,U]

en·thuse /ɪn'θuz/ v. **1** [I,T] to talk about something in a way that shows you are very excited: *"It's an opportunity learn from the best," enthused Rossi.* **2** [T] to make someone interested in something or excited by it: *Does your spouse still stimulate and enthuse you?*

en·thused /ɪn'θuzd/ adj. [not before noun] excited about or interested in something: [+ about] *Overall, they're enthused about students' response to the new textbooks.*

en·thu·si·asm /ɪn'θuziˌæzəm/ n. [U] a strong feeling of interest and enjoyment about something, and an eagerness to be involved in it: *She sang the national anthem with great enthusiasm.* | [+ for] *Even the President's supporters showed little enthusiasm for his decision.*

en·thu·si·ast /ɪn'θuziˌæst/ n. [C] someone who is very interested in a particular activity or subject: *a sports enthusiast*

en·thu·si·as·tic /ɪnˌθuzi'æstɪk/ adj. showing a lot of interest and excitement about something: *There is enthusiastic support for a new high school.* | [+ about] *Rachel is enthusiastic about going to kindergarten.* —**enthusiastically** /-kli/ adv.

en·tice /ɪn'taɪs/ v. [T] to persuade someone to do

something by offering them something nice: [**entice sb to do sth**] *Beulah tried to entice him to eat the ham she had prepared.* —**enticement** *n.* [C,U]

en·tic·ing /ɪn'taɪsɪŋ/ *adj.* very pleasant or interesting, so that you feel strongly attracted: *the enticing smell of fresh bread* —**enticingly** *adv.*

en·tire /ɪn'taɪɚ/ *adj.* [only before noun] whole or complete, used to emphasize what you are saying: *Dad spent the entire day in the kitchen.* | *Gary was so hungry that he ate an entire chicken for dinner.*

en·tire·ly /ɪn'taɪɚli/ *adv.* completely and in every possible way: *Jeff and Mike come from entirely different backgrounds.* | *The sculpture is made entirely of old car tires.* | *Aikman's arm is not entirely healed.*

en·tire·ty /ɪn'taɪɚti, -'taɪrəti/ *n.* **in its/their entirety** FORMAL as a whole, and including every part: *The speech will published in its entirety in tomorrow's paper.*

en·ti·tle /ɪn'taɪtl/ *v.* [T] **1** to have the right to have or do something, or to give someone this right: [be **entitled to (do) sth**] *Only full-time employees are entitled to receive health insurance.* | [**entitle sb to (do) sth**] *Membership entitles you to the full use of our fitness facilities.* **2 be entitled sth** if a book, play etc. is entitled something, that is its name: *The last song is entitled "Into the Woods."*

en·ti·tle·ment /ɪn'taɪtlmənt/ *n.* **1** [C] an entitlement program **2** [C,U] the official right to have or receive something, or the amount that you receive: [+ **to**] *People's entitlement to compensation may be affected by state and local laws.*

entitlement pro·gram /.'... ,../ also **entitlement** *n.* [C] a government program or system that gives money or help to anyone who meets a particular standard: *The President refuses to make cuts in Social Security, the biggest entitlement program for the elderly.*

en·ti·ty /'ɛntəti/ *n. plural* **entities** [C] something that exists as a single and complete unit: *The two school districts are separate legal entities.*

en·tomb /ɪn'tum/ *v.* [T often in passive] LITERARY to bury or trap someone under the ground: *Burns' body was entombed at Forest Lawn Cemetery.*

en·to·mol·o·gy /,ɛntə'malədʒi/ *n.* [U] the scientific study of insects —**entomologist** *n.* [C] —**entomological** /,ɛntəmə'ladʒɪkəl/ *adj.*

en·tou·rage /,antu'raʒ/ *n.* [C usually singular] a group of people who travel with an important person: *Mr. Stallone and his entourage arrived half an hour late.*

en·trails /'ɛntreɪlz/ *n.* [plural] the inside parts of an animal or person's body, especially their INTESTINES

en·trance[1] /'ɛntrəns/ *n.* **1** [C] a door, gate etc. that you go through to enter a place: [+ **to/of**] *Meet us at the main entrance to the school.* —opposite EXIT[1] **2** [U] permission to become a member of or become involved in a profession, university, organization etc.: *college entrance examinations* | *In 1987, Walls gained entrance to Yale.* **3** [C usually singular] the act of entering a place or room: *Their conversation was interrupted by the entrance of four visitors.* —opposite EXIT[1] **4** [U] the right or ability to go into a place: *The price includes most meals and entrance fees to museums.* | *No one is sure how the men gained entrance to (=got into) the factory.* **5 make your/an entrance a)** to enter a room, especially in a way that makes everyone notice you: *With her long fur coat, she always made a dramatic entrance.* **b)** to come onto the stage in a play: *The hero doesn't make his entrance until Act II, Scene 2.*

en·trance[2] /ɪn'træns/ *v.* [T usually passive] to seem very interesting and attractive, so that people will be sure to pay attention: *I was entranced by her sheer beauty.* —**entrancing** *adj.*

en·trant /'ɛntrənt/ *n.* [C] someone who enters a competition, race etc.

en·trap /ɪn'træp/ *v.* **entrapped, entrapping** [T] FORMAL to trap someone, especially by tricking or deceiving them: *Clark said that he was entrapped into committing illegal acts.*

en·trap·ment /ɪn'træpmənt/ *n.* [U] the act of

trapping someone by tricking them, especially to make them do something illegal that they would not have done on their own

en·treat /ɪn'trit/ *v.* [T] FORMAL to ask someone, in a very emotional way, to do something for you: *Rayburn entreated them to hand over their guns.*

en·treat·y /ɪn'triti/ *n.* [C,U] *plural* **entreaties** FORMAL a serious request in which you ask someone to do something for you

en·trée, **entree** /'antreɪ/ *n.* **1** [C] the main dish of a meal **2** [C,U] FORMAL the right or freedom to enter a place or to join a group of people: [+ **to/into**] *They began making use of their connections to gain entree to the White House.*

en·trenched /ɪn'trɛntʃt/ *adj.* strongly established, and not likely to change: *Some people are so deeply entrenched in their views that it's impossible to discuss things with them.*

en·trench·ment /ɪn'trɛntʃmənt/ *n.* [U] the process in which an attitude, belief etc. becomes firmly established

en·tre·pot /'antrə,poʊ/ *n.* [C] TECHNICAL a place, especially a large building at an airport or a port, where large quantities of goods are stored before they are sent somewhere else

en·tre·pre·neur /,antrəprə'nɚ, -'nʊr/ *n.* [C] someone who starts a company, arranges business deals, and takes risks in order to make a profit —**entrepreneurial** *adj.*: *entrepreneurial skills*

en·tro·py /'ɛntrəpi/ *n.* [U] TECHNICAL a measure of the lack of order in a system, that includes the idea that the lack of order increases over a period of time

en·trust /ɪn'trʌst/ *v.* [T] to make someone responsible for doing something important, or for taking care of something or someone: [**entrust sb with (doing) sth**] *Bergen was entrusted with depositing the money at the bank.* | [**entrust sth to sb**] *Carter entrusted the negotiations to Richard Holbrooke.*

en·try /'ɛntri/ *n. plural* **entries**
1 act of entering [C,U] the act of coming or going into something: [+ **into**] *An alarm will signal any unauthorized entry into the lab.* | *The thieves gained entry* (=got into a place) *through an open kitchen window.*
2 becoming involved [C,U] a situation in which someone starts to take part in a system, a particular kind of work etc., or joins a group of people: *The entry of women into the work force was one of the most significant changes in our society.* | *Several Eastern European countries hope to soon gain entry* (=become involved) *to the European Union.*
3 dictionary [C] a short piece of writing in a dictionary, list etc.: *Look up the entry for George Washington in the encyclopedia.*
4 a) competition [C] something such as a performance, set of answers, a picture etc. that is intended to win a competition: *The winning entry was a short film from France.* **b)** [C usually singular] a group of people or things who take part in a competition
5 computer [U] the act of writing of information onto a computer: *data entry*
6 door [C] a door, gate, or passage that you go through to enter a place —see also ENTRANCE[1] (1)

entry-lev·el /'.. ,../ *adj.* [only before noun] an entry-level job, activity, course etc. is for people with little or no experience: *I'm looking for an entry-level position in a bank.*

en·try·way /'ɛntri,weɪ/ *n.* [C] a passage or small room that you go through to enter a place

en·twine /ɪn'twaɪn/ *v.* [I,T often passive] **1** to twist two things together, or to wind one thing around another: *Fresh flowers were entwined in her hair.* **2 be entwined (with sth)** to be closely connected with something in a complicated way: *Carnegie Hall is entwined completely with the artistic growth of this country.*

e·nuff /ɪ'nʌf/ NONSTANDARD, SLANG a way of spelling ENOUGH

e·nu·mer·ate /ɪ'numə,reɪt/ v. [T] FORMAL to name a list of things one by one: *Hunt said things looked bad, and went on to enumerate the reasons why.*

e·nun·ci·ate /ɪ'nʌnsi,eɪt/ v. **1** [I,T] to pronounce words clearly and carefully: *Be sure to enunciate when you speak into the microphone.* —see also ARTICULATE² (2) **2** [T] FORMAL to express an idea clearly and exactly: *Here, Paul utilizes the principle he enunciated in Chapter 3.* —**enunciation** /ɪ,nʌnsi'eɪʃən/ n. [U]

en·ure /ɪ'nʊr/ v. [T] another spelling of INURE

en·vel·op /ɪn'vɛləp/ v. [T] to cover something, or wrap it up completely: [envelop sth in/with sth] *They entered an area enveloped in thick mist.* —**envelopment** n. [U]

en·ve·lope /'ɛnvə,loʊp, 'ɑn-/ n. [C] **1** a thin paper cover in which you put a letter **2** a layer of something that surrounds something else: [+ of] *A bluish envelope of flame surrounds the particle as it burns.* **3** push the envelope to try to do more than what people think is possible, sensible, or right: *Each time Walters asked his employees to push the envelope, he said, "If you can dream it, you can do it."*

en·vi·a·ble /'ɛnviəbəl/ adj. [only before noun] an enviable quality, position, or possession is good and other people would like to have it: *Burns is now in the enviable position of being able to make any film he wants.* —**enviably** adv.

en·vi·ous /'ɛnviəs/ adj. wishing you had something that someone else has: [+ of] *She had always been envious of her cousin's long blond hair.* —see also JEALOUS —see Usage Note at JEALOUS —**enviously** adv.

en·vi·ron·ment /ɪn'vaɪrənmənt/ n. **1** the environment the air, water, and land in which people, animals, and plants live: *Recycling paper and cans is one easy way to preserve the environment.* **2** [C,U] all the situations, events, people etc. that influence the way in which people live or work: *Our company tries to maintain a pleasant work environment.* | *It's not a very safe environment for children there.*

en·vi·ron·men·tal /ɪn,vaɪrən'mɛntl/ adj. concerning or affecting the air, land, or water on Earth: *An oil spill of that size will cause a lot of environmental damage.* —**environmentally** adv. —see also ENVIRONMENTALLY FRIENDLY

environmental im·pact state·ment /.,.... '.. ,../ n. [C] a report by a group that wants to build on or change an area of land that explains what effect the change will have on the environment, and that is given to an official government department for approval

en·vi·ron·men·tal·ist /ɪn,vaɪrən'mɛntl-ɪst/ n. [C] someone who is concerned about protecting the environment —**environmentalism** n. [U]

environmentally friend·ly /......,... '../ also **environment-friendly** /.,... '../ adj. things such as soaps, containers etc. that are environmentally friendly do not harm the environment

en·vi·rons /ɪn'vaɪrənz, ɛn-/ n. [plural] FORMAL the area surrounding a place: *We became very familiar with Boston and its environs.*

en·vis·age /ɪn'vɪzɪdʒ/ v. [T] FORMAL to imagine something that will happen in the future: *The changes have been greater than we ever envisaged.*

en·vi·sion /ɪn'vɪʒən/ v. [T] to imagine something, especially as a future possibility: *He envisions a day when every household will have access to the Internet.*

en·voy /'ɛnvɔɪ, 'ɑn-/ n. plural **envoys** [C] someone who is sent to another country as an official representative of their government

en·vy¹ /'ɛnvi/ v. **envied, envying** [T] **1** to wish that you had someone else's possessions, abilities, qualities etc.: *Everyone in the neighborhood envied Bob Green's expensive new luxury car.* **2** not envy sb sth used to say that you are glad you do not have to have or deal with something that someone else does: *We don't envy them their task.*

envy² n. [U] **1** the feeling of wanting something that someone else has: *He stared with envy at Robert's new car.* **2** be the envy of sb/sth to be something that other people admire and want to have very much: *We enjoy living standards which are the envy of the world.* —compare JEALOUSY —see also **be green with envy** (GREEN¹ (5))

en·zyme /'ɛnzaɪm/ n. [C] a chemical substance produced by living cells in plants and animals, that causes changes in other chemical substances

e·on /'iən, 'iɑn/ n. [C usually plural] an extremely long period of time

-eous /iəs/ suffix [in adjectives] used to make adjectives; -OUS: *gaseous* (=in the form of a gas) *beauteous* (=having great beauty) —see also -IOUS

ep·au·let, epaulette /,ɛpə'lɛt, 'ɛpə,lɛt/ n. [C] a shoulder decoration on a shirt or military uniform

é·pée, epee /'ɛpeɪ, eɪ'peɪ/ n. [C] a narrow sword with a sharp point, used in the sport of FENCING (1)

e·phem·er·a /ɪ'fɛmərə/ n. [plural] things such as newspapers, letters etc. that are only popular or important for a short time

e·phem·er·al /ɪ'fɛmərəl/ adj. FORMAL existing for only a short time —**ephemerally** adv.

E·phe·sians /ɪ'fiʒənz/ a book in the New Testament of the Christian Bible

ep·ic¹ /'ɛpɪk/ n. [C] **1** a book, movie etc. that tells a long story that is full of action and events **2** a long poem that tells the story of what gods or important people did in ancient times: *"The Iliad" is perhaps the most studied epic of all time.*

epic² adj. [only before noun] **1** epic stories, poems, movies etc. are long and full of action and events **2** of epic proportions very big or impressive: *The country is facing a famine of epic proportions.*

ep·i·cen·ter /'ɛpə,sɛntə/ n. [C usually singular] a place on the Earth's surface that is above the point where an EARTHQUAKE begins

ep·i·cure /'ɛpɪ,kyʊr/ n. [C] LITERARY someone who enjoys good food and drinks; GOURMET

ep·i·cu·re·an /,ɛpɪkyʊ'riən, -'kyʊriən/ adj. LITERARY gaining or giving pleasure through the senses, especially through good food and drinks —**epicurean** n. [C]

ep·i·dem·ic /,ɛpə'dɛmɪk/ n. [C] **1** a large number of cases of a particular infectious disease happening at the same time: *a cholera epidemic* **2** a sudden increase in the amount of times that something bad happens: [+ of] *There has been a recent epidemic of car thefts.* —**epidemic** adj.: *Violence is reaching epidemic proportions in the inner cities.*

ep·i·de·mi·ol·o·gy /,ɛpə,dimi'ɑlədʒi/ n. [U] the study of the causes and control of diseases among people —**epidemiologist** n. [C] —**epidemiological** /,ɛpə,dimiə'lɑdʒɪkəl/ adj.

ep·i·der·mis /,ɛpə'dəmɪs/ n. [C,U] TECHNICAL the outside layer of your skin —**epidermal** adj.

ep·i·dur·al /,ɛpɪ'dʊrəl/ n. [C usually singular] a medical process in which a drug is put into your lower back to prevent you from feeling pain, especially when you are having a baby

ep·i·glot·tis /,ɛpə'glɑtɪs/ n. [C] a thin piece of flesh at the back of your throat, that covers part of your throat when you swallow

ep·i·gram /'ɛpə,græm/ n. [C] a short poem or phrase that expresses an idea in an amusing way —**epigrammatic** /,ɛpəgrə'mætɪk/ adj. —**epigrammatically** /-kli/ adv.

ep·i·lep·sy /'ɛpə,lɛpsi/ n. [U] a medical condition in the brain that can suddenly make you become unconscious, and often make you move your body in an uncontrolled way

ep·i·lep·tic¹ /,ɛpə'lɛptɪk/ adj. caused by epilepsy: *an epileptic seizure*

epileptic² n. [C] someone who has epilepsy

ep·i·logue, epilog /'ɛpə,lɑg, -,lɔg/ n. [C] a speech or piece of writing added to the end of a book, movie, or play to give more information about what happened later —compare PROLOGUE

e·piph·a·ny /ɪˈpɪfəni/ n. **1** [C] plural **epiphanies** a moment of sudden very strong emotions, when someone suddenly understands something **2 Epiphany** a Christian holy day on January 6 that celebrates the Three Wise Men's visit to the baby Jesus Christ

e·pis·co·pa·cy /ɪˈpɪskəpəsi/ also **e·pis·co·pate** /ɪˈpɪskəpət/ n. [U] TECHNICAL **1** the rank of a BISHOP (=a priest of high rank in charge of a large area), or the time during which someone is bishop **2** all the bishops, or the system of the church government by bishops

e·pis·co·pal /ɪˈpɪskəpəl/ adj. **1 Episcopal** relating to the Episcopal Church **2** TECHNICAL relating to a BISHOP

Episcopal Church /ˌ... ˈ.../ n. the Episcopal Church a PROTESTANT church in America that developed from the official Church of England

E·pis·co·pa·li·an /ɪˌpɪskəˈpeɪliən/ n. [C] a member of an Episcopal church —**Episcopalian** adj.

s w 3

ep·i·sode /ˈɛpəˌsoʊd/ n. [C] **1** a television or radio program that is one of a series of programs telling one story: The final episode will be broadcast next week. **2** an event or a short period of time during which something specific happened: Susan has had several episodes of depression lately.

ep·i·sod·ic /ˌɛpəˈsɑdɪk/ adj. FORMAL **1** happening at times that are not regular: This illness is characterized by episodic neck pain. **2** consisting of separate parts which together form a series: an episodic TV program —**episodically** /-kli/ adv.

e·pis·tle /ɪˈpɪsəl/ n. [C] **1** FORMAL a long or important letter **2 Epistle** one of the letters written by the first Christians which are in the New Testament of the Bible

e·pis·to·lar·y /ɪˈpɪstəˌlɛri/ adj. TECHNICAL an epistolary book is written in the form of a series of letters

ep·i·taph /ˈɛpəˌtæf/ n. [C] a short piece of writing on the stone over someone's grave

ep·i·thet /ˈɛpəˌθɛt/ n. [C] a word or short phrase used to describe someone, especially when saying something bad about them: Perez was the target of a **racial epithet** (=something negative said about someone's race) by an angry co-worker.

e·pit·o·me /ɪˈpɪtəmi/ n. **the epitome of sth** the best possible example of something: Haneberg is the epitome of the successful executive.

e·pit·o·mize /ɪˈpɪtəˌmaɪz/ v. [T not in progressive] to be a very typical example of something: Cass Avenue epitomizes the city's economic and social depression.

e pluribus unum /i ˌplʊrəbəs ˈyunəm/ a Latin phrase meaning "out of the many, one," printed on U.S. money. It expresses the idea that many different people can work together under a single government

ep·och /ˈɛpək/ n. [C] a period of history, especially one in which important events take place: The Russian Revolution marked the beginning of a new epoch in history. —see also ERA

epoch-mak·ing /ˈ.. ˌ../ adj. [only before noun] very important in changing or developing people's lives: an epoch-making event

e·pon·y·mous /ɪˈpɑnəməs/ adj. [only before noun] an eponymous television show, CD, book etc. takes its name from a person, group, character etc. involved in it: The Indigo Girls' eponymous debut album (=it was called) "The Indigo Girls" won a Grammy award in 1988. —**eponymously** adv.

ep·ox·y /ɪˈpɑksi/ n. [U] a type of very strong glue

Ep·som salts /ˈɛpsəm ˌsɔlts/ n. [plural] a white powder that can be mixed with water and used as a type of medicine

eq·ua·ble /ˈɛkwəbəl/ adj. **1** TECHNICAL having weather or conditions that are neither too hot nor too cold: an equable climate **2** FORMAL calm and not easily annoyed —**equably** adv. —**equability** /ˌɛkwəˈbɪləti/ n. [U]

s w 2 3

e·qual¹ /ˈikwəl/ adj.
1 size/value/number the same in size, value, amount, number etc. as someone or something else: Divide the dough into three equal parts. | [+ to] The

$2.42 million is equal to 3% of the department's budget. | **of equal height/weight/strength etc.** They want three people of equal height for the show.
2 same rights/chances having the same rights, opportunities etc. as everyone else, or allowing everyone to have the same rights: The Declaration of Independence says that all men are created equal. | We are equal partners in the business. | This company is **an equal opportunity employer** (=it allows any person to have the same chances of employment, pay etc. as anyone else). | The fight for a constitutional amendment guaranteeing **equal rights** for women is over.
3 on equal footing/terms with neither side having any advantage over the other: Teachers say that wearing uniforms helps to **put** rich and poor students **on equal footing** with each other.
4 be equal to sth a) to be able to deal with a problem, piece of work etc. successfully: I'm not sure he's equal to the job. **b)** to have as high a standard or quality as something else: The museum's collection is equal to any in Europe.
5 all (other) things being equal SPOKEN used when saying what is most likely or what you prefer, if there are no special facts to consider: All other things being equal, schools where parents are highly involved are more likely to run effectively.

equal² v. **equaled, equaling 1** [linking verb] to be the same in size, number, or amount as something else: Three plus three equals six. | The average retired worker gets $720 a month in benefits, which equals about 42% of earnings before retirement. **2** [T] to be as good as someone or something else: Butcher will attempt to equal Swenson's win record. **3** [T] to directly produce a particular result or effect: Americans are finding out the hard way that drug possession equals jail in foreign countries.

s w 3

equal³ n. [C] **1** someone who is as important, intelligent etc. as you are, or who has the same rights and opportunities as you do: My boss treats her employees as equals. **2 be without equal** also **have no equal** FORMAL to be better than everyone or everything else of the same type: His paintings are without equal in the Western world.

Equal Em·ploy·ment Op·por·tu·ni·ties Com·mis·sion, the /ˌ.. .ˌ.. .ˈ.. .ˌ../ a U.S. government organization whose aim is to make sure that people are not prevented from getting jobs because of their race, religion, age, sex etc., and to make sure that all workers are treated fairly and equally

e·qual·i·ty /ɪˈkwɑləti/ n. [U] the state of having the same rights, opportunities, etc. as everyone else: America continues to strive for **racial** and **sexual equality** (=equality between all races and between men and women).

e·qual·ize /ˈikwəˌlaɪz/ v. [T] to make two or more things the same in size, value, amount etc.: The Legislature has failed again to equalize spending between rich and poor school districts. —**equalization** /ˌikwələˈzeɪʃən/ n. [U]

e·qual·iz·er /ˈikwəˌlaɪzɚ/ n. [C] **1** something that affects all people or groups the same way, even if their position in society is very different: Farmers markets are **great** social **equalizers** where famous chefs shop alongside housewives. **2** the part of a piece of electronic equipment such as a radio, that you use to change the quality of high and low sounds: a graphic equalizer

e·qual·ly /ˈikwəli/ adv. **1** [+ adj./adv.] to the same degree or amount: The candidates are equally qualified for the job. **2** in the same way: He treats all the customers equally. **3** in parts or amounts that are the same size: We'll divide the work equally. **4** [sentence adverb] also **equally important** used when introducing a second idea or statement that is as important as your first one: Many business people do not know what sexual harassment is. Equally important, they do not know how to prevent it.

s w 3

equal sign /ˈ.. ˌ./ n. [C] a sign (=) used in mathematics to show that two things are the same size, number, or amount

e·qua·nim·i·ty /ˌikwəˈnɪməti, ˌɛk-/ *n.* [U] FORMAL calmness in a difficult situation: *He received the news with surprising equanimity.*

e·quate /ɪˈkweɪt/ *v.* [T] to consider that one thing is the same as something else: [**equate sth with sth**] *Don't equate criticism with blame.*

e·qua·tion /ɪˈkweɪʒən/ *n.* **1** [C] a statement in mathematics, science etc., showing that two quantities are equal, for example $2x + 4 = 10$ **2** [U] a problem or situation with many different parts that must all be considered together: *If you're trying to get healthy by losing weight, exercise should be part of the equation.* | *An applicant's sex does not* **enter into the equation** (=affect the situation) *when we make hiring decisions.* **3** [U] the act of equating two things

e·qua·tor, Equator /ɪˈkweɪt̬ə/ *n.* **the equator** an imaginary line around the Earth, that divides it equally into its northern and southern halves

e·qua·to·ri·al /ˌɛkwəˈtɔriəl/ *adj.* relating to the equator, or near the equator: *an equatorial rainforest*

E·qua·to·ri·al Guin·ea /ˌɛkwətɔriəl ˈgɪni/ a small country in west central Africa north of Gabon —**Equatorial Guinean** *n., adj.*

eq·uer·ry /ˈɛkwəri, ɪˈkwɛri/ *n.* [C] a personal servant to a powerful person, especially a member of the British royal family

e·ques·tri·an /ɪˈkwɛstriən/ *adj.* relating to horse riding: *equestrian events* —**equestrian** *n.* [C]

equi- /ikwə, ɛkwə/ *prefix* equal or equally

e·qui·dis·tant /ˌikwəˈdɪstənt, ˌɛkwə-/ *adj.* FORMAL at an equal distance from or between two places: [**+ from/between**] *The asteroids are located at a point equidistant from Jupiter and the Sun.*

e·qui·lat·er·al /ˌikwəˈlæt̬ərəl/ *adj.* TECHNICAL having all sides the same length: *an equilateral triangle* —**equilateral** *n.* [C]

e·qui·lib·ri·um /ˌikwəˈlɪbriəm/ *n.* [singular,U] **1** a balance between opposing forces, influences etc.: *The supply and the demand for money must be kept* **in equilibrium**. **2** a calm balance of emotions, attitudes, feelings etc.: *The shock of Freddie's death had upset her equilibrium.*

e·quine /ˈikwaɪn, ˈɛ-/ *adj.* FORMAL relating to horses, or looking like a horse

e·qui·nox /ˈikwəˌnɑks, ˈɛ-/ *n.* [C] one of the two times in a year when day and night are equal in length everywhere —**equinoctial** /ˌikwəˈnɑkʃəl/ *adj.* —compare SOLSTICE

e·quip /ɪˈkwɪp/ *v.* **equipped, equipping** [T usually passive] **1** to provide a person, group, building etc. with the things that are needed for a particular activity or type of work: *It will cost over $2000 to equip the entire team.* | [**equip sb with sth**] *The school will be equipped with 70 brand new computers.* | [**equip sb/sth to do sth**] *The hospital is not equipped to provide the care the veterans need.* | [**equip sb/sth for sth**] *Guides are equipped with radios for emergencies.* | **fully/well/poorly equipped** *There are four cabins, each with a fully equipped kitchen.* | *The report says city police are poorly equipped and underpaid.* **2** to provide someone with the skills, training, or education that they need for a particular purpose: [**equip sb for sth**] *She is not equipped for the public role she has been forced to play.* —see also ILL-EQUIPPED

s w
2 2
e·quip·ment /ɪˈkwɪpˈmənt/ *n.* [U] **1** the special tools, machines, etc. that you need for a particular activity or type of work: *camera equipment* | *We bought several new* **pieces of equipment** *for the chemistry lab.* **2** the process of equipping someone or something

eq·ui·ta·ble /ˈɛkwət̬əbəl/ *adj.* FORMAL fair and equal to everyone involved: *We need a more equitable tax system.* —**equitably** *adv.*

Eq·ui·ty /ˈɛkwəti/ a UNION for actors and other theater workers in the U.S.

eq·ui·ty /ˈɛkwəti/ *n.* **1** [U] TECHNICAL the value of something you own, such as a house or SHARES² (4) after you have taken away the amount of money you still owe on it **2** [U] FORMAL a situation in which everyone is treated fairly: *All human beings want to be treated with equity and respect.* **3 equities** [plural] TECHNICAL trading in companies' SHARES² (4) on a STOCK MARKET, rather than on other types of markets

s w
3

e·quiv·a·len·cy /ɪˈkwɪvələnsi/ *n. plural* **equivalencies** [C,U] **1 equivalency degree/diploma/certificate etc.** a test that you try to pass to show that you have the same knowledge or skills as other people who have passed a course or GRADUATED from a particular school or college —see also GED **2** the state of being equal in value, meaning, or effect to something else

e·quiv·a·lent¹ /ɪˈkwɪvələnt/ *n.* [C] something that has the same value, size etc. as something else: *Some Thai words have no English equivalents.* | [**+ of**] *A typhoon is the Eastern Hemisphere's equivalent of a hurricane.*

equivalent² *adj.* equal in value, purpose, rank etc. to someone or something else: *no more than 12 bottles of beer or an equivalent amount of alcohol* | [**+ to**] *Each barrel of oil is equivalent to about 40 gallons of gasoline.* —**equivalence** *n.* [U] —**equivalently** *adv.*

e·quiv·o·cal /ɪˈkwɪvəkəl/ *adj.* **1** deliberately not clear or definite in meaning: *His answer was evasive and equivocal.* **2** not certain, or difficult to understand or explain: *The results of the test were equivocal.* —**equivocally** /-kli/ *adv.* —compare AMBIGUOUS

e·quiv·o·cate /ɪˈkwɪvəˌkeɪt/ *v.* [I] FORMAL to say something that has more than one possible meaning, in order to avoid giving a clear or direct answer: *Wilson continues to equivocate about what action he will take.* —**equivocation** /ɪˌkwɪvəˈkeɪʃən/ *n.* [C,U]

ER *n.* [C] TECHNICAL the abbreviation of EMERGENCY ROOM

er /ə/ *interjection* a sound you make when you want to correct something you have just said, or when you do not know exactly what to say next: *We'll never forgive – er, forget – her accomplishments.*

-er /ə/ *suffix* **1** [in adjectives] used to form the COMPARATIVE of many short adjectives and adverbs: *hot, hotter* | *My car is fast, but hers is faster.* —see also -IER **2** [in nouns] someone who does something or who is doing something: *a dancer* (=someone who dances or is dancing) | *the diners* (=people having dinner) **3** [in nouns] something that does something: *a dishwasher* (=machine that washes dishes) **4** [in nouns] someone who makes a particular type of thing: *a potter* (=someone who makes things from clay) **5** [in nouns] someone who lives in or comes from a particular place: *a New Yorker* (=someone from New York) | *the villagers* (=people who live in the village) **6** [in nouns] someone skilled in a particular subject: *a geographer* (=someone who studies GEOGRAPHY) **7** [in nouns] something that has something: *a three-wheeler* (=a vehicle with three wheels) —see also -AR, -IER, -OR

e·ra /ˈɪrə, ˈɛrə/ *n.* [C] a period of time in history that is different in some way from other periods, or that begins with a particular date or event: *a new era of global cooperation* —see also EPOCH

s w
2

e·rad·i·cate /ɪˈrædɪˌkeɪt/ *v.* [T] to completely get rid of or destroy something: *He spoke about what is necessary to eradicate AIDS.* —**eradication** /ɪˌrædəˈkeɪʃən/ *n.* [U]

e·rase /ɪˈreɪs/ *v.* [T] **1** to completely remove information from a computer memory or recorded sounds from a TAPE: *Ben erased one of my favorite tapes.* **2** to remove marks or writing so that they cannot be seen anymore: *Be sure to completely erase any incorrect answer.* **3** FORMAL to get rid of or destroy something so that it does not exist anymore: *Today's rise in prices erases yesterday's losses.* | *The fall of the Berlin Wall erased the border between the two Germanys.* **4 erase sth from your mind/memory** to make yourself forget something bad that has happened: *After the rape, I just wanted to erase it from my mind.*

s w
3

e·ras·er /ɪˈreɪsə/ *n.* [C] **1** a piece of rubber used to remove pencil or pen marks from paper **2** an object used for cleaning marks from a BLACKBOARD

E·ras·mus /ɪˈræzməs/, **Des·i·der·i·us** /ˌdɛzɪˈdɛriəs/ (?1466–1536) a Dutch writer and teacher who criticized the Catholic Church but opposed the Protestant Reformation

e·ra·sure /ɪˈreɪʃɚ/ *n.* FORMAL **1** [C] a mark that is left when words or letters are removed with an eraser **2** [U] the act of completely removing or destroying something: *the erasure of the debt*

ere /ɛr/ *prep., conjunction* OLD USE OR POETIC before

Er·e·bus, Mount /ˈɛrəbəs/ a mountain on Ross Island in Antarctica that is an active VOLCANO

e·rect[1] /ɪˈrɛkt/ *v.* [T] FORMAL **1** to build a building, wall, STATUE etc.: *Officials plan to erect a monument in Lindbergh's honor.* **2** to put something together in an upright position: *The tents for the fair were erected overnight.* **3** erect barriers/obstacles etc. to make a law, rule, or system that stops someone from doing something: *The Secretary of Commerce said that the agreement would not erect any serious trade barriers.*

erect[2] *adj.* **1** in a straight upright position: *The 8-year-olds sat erect at their desks.* **2** an erect PENIS or NIPPLE is stiff and bigger than it usually is —**erectly** *adv.* —**erectness** *n.* [U]

e·rec·tile /ɪˈrɛktl, -taɪl/ *adj.* TECHNICAL relating to a man's erection

e·rec·tion /ɪˈrɛkʃən/ *n.* **1 have an erection** if a man has an erection, his PENIS becomes stiff because he is sexually excited **2** [U] the act of building something or putting it in an upright position: *the erection of a new temple*

erg /ɚg/ *n.* [C] TECHNICAL a unit used to measure work or energy

er·go /ˈɛrgoʊ, ˈɚgoʊ/ *adv.* FORMAL [sentence adverb] therefore

er·go·nom·ics /ˌɚgəˈnɑmɪks/ *n.* [U] the study of how the design of equipment affects how well people can use it and do their work —**ergonomic** *adj.* —**ergonomically** /-kli/ *adv.*

Er·ics·son, Leif /ˈɛrɪksən, lif/ also **Eriksson** (10th century A.D.) an EXPLORER from Norway, who was probably the first European to discover America. He landed in Newfoundland in the late 10th century.

Er·ic the Red /ˌɛrɪk ðə ˈrɛd/ (10th century) a Norwegian EXPLORER who sailed along the coast of Greenland and brought people to settle there

E·rie, Lake /ˈɪri/ one of the Great Lakes of North America, between the U.S. and Canada

Erie Ca·nal, the /ˌ… .ˈ./ a CANAL in the U.S. state of New York that connects Lake Erie and the Hudson River

Er·i·tre·a /ˌɛrɪˈtriə/ a country in northeast Africa, south of Sudan and north of Ethiopia —**Eritrean** *n., adj.*

er·mine /ˈɚmən/ *n.* **1** [U] an expensive white fur, used especially for the clothes of judges, kings, and queens **2** [C] a small thin animal of the WEASEL (1) family whose fur is white in winter

Ernst, Max /ɛrnst, mæks/ (1891–1976) a German PAINTER famous for his work in Dadaism and Surrealism

e·rode /ɪˈroʊd/ *v.* **1** [I,T] if wind, water, or acid erodes a substance, or it erodes, the substance or it is gradually broken up until it is destroyed: *The hard rains have eroded topsoil in the Midwest.* **2** [I,T] to gradually reduce someone's power, authority, confidence etc., or to become weaker: *A strong president would further erode the power of the Congress.* —see also EROSION

e·rog·e·nous /ɪˈrɑdʒənəs/ *adj.* sensitive to touching and giving you sexual pleasure: *the body's erogenous zones*

Er·os /ˈɛrɑs, ˈɛroʊs, ˈɪr-/ **1** in Greek MYTHOLOGY, the god of sexual and romantic love **2** [U] sexual love

e·ro·sion /ɪˈroʊʒən/ *n.* [U] **1** the process of being gradually destroyed by rain, wind, the ocean etc.: *soil erosion* | *the erosion of our beaches* **2** the process of gradually making something weaker: *the erosion of civil liberties* —**erosive** /ɪˈroʊsɪv/ *adj.*

e·rot·ic /ɪˈrɑtɪk/ *adj.* relating to sex, or making you feel sexually excited: *erotic pictures* —**erotically** /-kli/ *adv.*

e·rot·i·ca /ɪˈrɑtɪkə/ *n.* [U] erotic writing, drawings etc. —compare PORNOGRAPHY

e·rot·i·cism /ɪˈrɑtəˌsɪzəm/ *n.* [U] a style or quality that expresses strong feelings of sexual love and desire, especially in works of art: *the lush eroticism of the Kama Sutra*

err /ɛr, ɚ/ *v.* [I] **1 err on the side of caution/mercy etc.** to be too careful, kind etc. rather than risk making a mistake: *Doctors would prefer to err on the side of caution by keeping newborns in the hospital longer.* **2** FORMAL to make a mistake: *Cannon errs in labeling his critics as mindless pessimists.* **3 to err is human, (to forgive divine)** used to say that it is very easy to make mistakes, so we should all try to forgive them

er·rand /ˈɛrənd/ *n.* [C] a short trip that you take to deliver a message, buy something etc.: *Could you run/do an errand for Grandma?* | *His mother sent him on an errand.*

er·rant /ˈɛrənt/ *adj.* [only before noun] FORMAL OR HUMOROUS **1** moving in the wrong direction: *Rainer caught the errant pass.* **2** behaving in a bad or irresponsible way: *an errant husband*

er·rat·ic /ɪˈrætɪk/ *adj.* changing often, moving, or behaving in an irregular way, without any reason or pattern: *The erratic winds made fighting the fire more difficult.* —**erratically** /-kli/ *adv.*: *Police observed him driving erratically and stopped him.*

er·ra·tum /ɛˈrɑtəm/ *n. plural* **errata** /-tə/ [C] TECHNICAL a mistake in a book, shown in a list that is added after the book is printed

er·ro·ne·ous /ɪˈroʊniəs/ *adj.* FORMAL incorrect or wrong: *At least 15 million Americans still hold the erroneous view that cancer is contagious.* —**erroneously** *adv.*

er·ror /ˈɛrɚ/ *n.* **1** [C,U] a mistake, especially one that causes problems: *We know now that the plane crash was the result of human error* (=by a person rather than a machine). | *Kovitz apologized yesterday for his error in judgment* (=a decision that was a mistake). | **computer/technical/administrative etc. error** *The company says a computer error was responsible for the enormous bill.* **2** a mistake in written or spoken language: *a spelling error* | *She made several errors on the typing test.* **3 see the error of your ways** LITERARY OR HUMOROUS to realize that you have been behaving badly and decide to stop **4** a throw or catch in baseball that you do not make successfully when you should have: **make/commit an error** *They committed two errors, and only scored two runs.* **5 be in error** FORMAL **a)** to be wrong or have made a mistake: *The company has admitted to the court that it was in error.* **6 do sth in error** FORMAL to do something that is wrong without intending to do it: *It was discovered that the funds had been withdrawn in error.* —see also **by/through trial and error** (TRIAL (4))

USAGE NOTE: ERROR

WORD CHOICE: error, mistake

Mistake is a word for something that you do by accident or that is the result of not knowing or understanding something: *I'm sorry – I took your pen by mistake.* | *Maybe we made a mistake in buying the car.* **Error** is a more formal word than **mistake.** It is used more frequently in writing than in speech, especially in phrases like the ones shown in the entry above.

---

er·satz /ˈɛrsɑts, ˈɛrzɑts/ *adj.* [usually before noun] artificial, and not as good as the real thing: *ersatz coffee*

erst·while /ˈɚstwaɪl/ *adj.* [only before noun] FORMAL former or in the past: *He has won over many of his erstwhile critics.*

er·u·dite /'ɛryə,daɪt, 'ɛrə-/ *adj.* showing a lot of knowledge: *"The Cunning Man" is an intricate and erudite work.* —**erudition** /,ɛryə'dɪʃən/ *n.* [U]

e·rupt /ɪ'rʌpt/ *v.* [I] **1** if fighting, violence etc. erupts, it starts suddenly: *A controversy has erupted over the price of the new weapons system.* **2** if a VOLCANO erupts, it explodes and sends smoke, fire, and rock into the sky **3** if a place or situation erupts, there is a sudden increase in activity or strong emotion: [+ into] *The memorial service for the slain leader erupted into a riot Saturday.* | *In 1999 the housing market suddenly erupted into a buying frenzy.* **4 erupt into laughter/coughs etc.** to start laughing, coughing etc. suddenly and loudly **5** if spots erupt on your body, they suddenly appear on your skin —**eruption** /ɪ'rʌpʃən/ *n.* [C,U]

Er·ving /'ɚvɪŋ/, **Ju·li·us** /'dʒuliəs/ (1950–) a basketball player often called "Dr. J"

-ery /əri/ *suffix* [in nouns] **1** a quality or condition: *bravery* (=quality of being brave) | *slavery* (=condition of being a slave) **2** things of a particular kind: *modern machinery* (=different types of machines) | *her finery* (=beautiful clothes) **3** a place where a particular activity happens: *a bakery* (=where bread is baked) | *an oil refinery* | *a fish hatchery* —see also -ARY

es·ca·late /'ɛskə,leɪt/ *v.* [I,T] **1** if fighting, violence, or an bad situation escalates, or if someone escalates it, it becomes much worse: *A dispute on the dance floor quickly escalated into violence.* **2** to become higher or increase, or to make something do this: *Land costs are escalating, causing concern among local builders.* —**escalation** /,ɛskə'leɪʃən/ *n.* [C, U]

es·ca·la·tor /'ɛskə,leɪtɚ/ *n.* [C] a set of stairs that move and carry people from one level within a building to another

escalator

es·ca·pade /'ɛskə,peɪd/ *n.* [C] **1** a sexual relationship that is exciting or risky, but that is not considered serious: *Do you think I should tell her about her husband's little escapades?* **2** an adventure, trick, or series of events that is exciting or risky: *In her most outlandish escapade, she faked her own death.*

s w **es·cape¹** /ɪ'skeɪp/ *v.*

1 get away [I,T] **a)** to get away from a place or dangerous situation, especially when someone is trying to catch you or stop you: *The prisoner was shot as he attempted to escape.* | *The two men escaped with $6,000.* | [+ from/through/over etc.] *Many people were killed trying to escape from the war zone.* **b)** to get away from a bad situation: *I could see no way of escaping the boredom of the small-town social scene.*
2 avoid [I,T] to avoid something bad happening to you: *Until now he has managed to escape criticism and even attract glowing media coverage.* | *Hare escaped death by testifying against his partner, who was later hanged.*
3 forget [I,T] to do something else in order to forget a bad situation for a short time: *People are willing to pay $10 for a movie ticket to escape their problems.*
4 gas/liquid etc. [I] if gas, liquid, light, heat etc. escapes from somewhere, it comes out, especially when you do not want it to: *A cloud of poisonous gas escaped from the chemical plant.*
5 escape (sb's) attention/notice to not be noticed by someone: *Nothing escapes Bill's attention.*
6 sound [I,T] if a sound escapes from someone's mouth, they accidentally make that sound
7 the name/date/title escapes me SPOKEN said

when you cannot remember something: *I know I've met him before, but his name escapes me.*
8 there's no escaping sb/sth used to emphasize that something cannot be avoided or must be thought about: *There's no escaping the fact that he was with another woman.* —**escaped** *adj.* [only before noun] *escaped prisoners*

escape² *n.* **1** [C,U] **a)** the act of getting away from a place or dangerous situation, especially when someone is trying to catch you: *The three men made a daring escape from jail.* **b)** the act of getting away from a bad situation: *There is no escape from the difficulties of growing up.* **2** [singular,U] a way to forget about a bad situation for a short time: *Books are a good form of escape.* **3** [singular,U] an amount of gas, liquid etc. that comes out of a place, especially when you do not want it to: *Methane blocks the escape of heat from the atmosphere.* —see also FIRE ESCAPE

escape clause /.'. ,./ *n.* [C] a part of a contract that explains the conditions under which the person who signs it would not have to obey the contract

es·cap·ee /ɪ,skeɪ'pi, ,ɛskeɪ'pi/ *n.* [C] someone who has escaped from somewhere

escape ve·loc·i·ty /.'. .,.../ *n.* [C,U] the speed that a ROCKET¹ (1) must travel at in order to get into space

es·cap·ism /ɪ'skeɪp,ɪzəm/ *n.* [U] activities or entertainment that help you forget about bad or boring things for a short time: *The world looks to Hollywood for escapism.* —**escapist** *adj.*

es·cap·ol·o·gy /ɪ,skeɪ'pɑlədʒi, ,ɛskə-/ *n.* [U] the skill of escaping from ropes, chains etc. as part of a performance —**escapologist** *n.* [C]

es·car·got /,ɛskɑr'goʊ/ *n.* [C] a SNAIL (1) that has been prepared for you to eat

es·ca·role /'ɛskə,roʊl/ *n.* [U] a vegetable like LETTUCE with curly leaves

es·carp·ment /ɪ'skɑrpmənt/ *n.* [C] a high steep slope or cliff that joins two levels on a hill or mountain

es·cheat /ɪs'tʃit/ *n.* [C] LAW a legal process in which someone's money and property is given to the state after they die if they do not have a WILL² (2), or if there is not someone else with the legal right to receive their money or property

es·chew /ɛs'tʃu/ *v.* [T] FORMAL to deliberately avoid doing, using, or having something: *Quintera was a man who eschewed violence.*

es·cort¹ /ɪ'skɔrt, 'ɛskɔrt/ *v.* [T] **1** to go somewhere with someone to protect or guard them: *Armed guards escorted the prisoners into the courthouse.* **2** to go somewhere with someone to show them the way, show them the place etc.: *Kedge escorted Streisand on a tour of the house.* **3** to go with someone to a social event: *She sat with Jackson in the front row and later escorted him to a party.*

es·cort² /'ɛskɔrt/ *n.* [C] **1** a person or a group of people or vehicles that go with someone in order to protect or guard them: *The governor travels with a police escort.* | *The three were sent back to Baghdad under escort* (=with an escort). **2** someone who goes with someone to a formal social event: *His first wife, Tammy, was his escort at the White House party.* **3** someone who is paid to go out with someone socially **4** also **escort girl, male escort** a PROSTITUTE, especially one who also goes to social events or on trips with the person who pays them

escort serv·ice /.'.. ,../ also **escort a·gen·cy** /.'.. ,.../ *n.* [C] a business that arranges occasions for people to meet escorts or PROSTITUTEs

es·cri·toire /'ɛskrə,twɑr/ *n.* [C] a small writing desk

es·crow /'ɛskroʊ/ *n.* [U] LAW something such as a written contract, money etc. that is held by someone who is not directly involved in an agreement while the agreement is being achieved

es·cu·do /ɪ'skudoʊ/ *n.* [C] the unit of money used in Portugal

es·cutch·eon /ɪ'skʌtʃən/ *n.* [C] FORMAL a SHIELD¹ (1) on which someone's COAT OF ARMS (=family sign) is painted

-ese /iz/ *suffix* **1** [in nouns] a person from a particular country or place, or their language: *the Taiwanese*

(=people from Taiwan) | *learning Japanese* (=language of Japan) **2** [in adjectives] belonging to a particular country or place: *Chinese music* **3** [in nouns] language or words used by a particular group, especially when it is difficult to understand: *journalese* (=language used in newspapers) | *officialese* (=language used in official or legal writing)

Es·ki·mo /ˈɛskə,moʊ/ *n. plural* **Eskimo** or **Eskimos** [C] a word for a member of one of the Native American tribes in Alaska, northern Canada, etc., that may be considered offensive —compare INUK

ESL *n.* [U] English as a second language; the teaching of English to people whose first language is not English, who are living in an English-speaking country —compare EFL

ESOL /ˌi ɛs oʊ ˈɛl, ˈisɒl/ *n.* [U] English for speakers of other languages —see also TESOL

e·soph·a·gus /ɪˈsɑfəgəs/ *n.* [C] the tube from your mouth to your stomach —see picture at DIGESTIVE SYSTEM

es·o·ter·ic /ˌɛsəˈtɛrɪk / *adj.* known and understood by only a few people who have special knowledge about something: *esoteric religious teachings* —**esoterically** /-kli/ *adv.*

ESP *n.* [U] **1** extrasensory perception; the ability to know what another person is thinking, or to know what will happen in the future, not by seeing or hearing things, but in a way that cannot be explained **2** English for special purposes; the teaching of technical English to business people, scientists etc.

esp. the written abbreviation of "especially"

es·pa·drille /ˈɛspə,drɪl/ *n.* [C] a light shoe that is made of cloth and rope

es·pe·cial /ɪˈspɛʃəl/ *adj.* FORMAL: see SPECIAL

S W 1 1
es·pe·cial·ly /ɪˈspɛʃəli/ *adv.* **1** [sentence adverb] used to emphasize that something is more important than usual, or that something happens to a higher degree with one particular person, group, or thing than with others: *Drive carefully, especially with all this fog.* | *Everyone's excited about the trip, especially Wendy.* | *Families, especially those with young children, benefit from the program.* **2** to a particularly high degree, or much more than usual: *I'm especially interested in hearing about your trip to China.* | *"Do you want to help me paint?" "Not especially."* **3** for a particular person, purpose etc.: [+ **for**] *I bought the flowers especially for her, and she didn't even thank me.* —compare SPECIALLY

USAGE NOTE: ESPECIALLY

GRAMMAR
Don't use **especially** at the beginning of a sentence or clause. You would usually say: *Young people especially need plenty of sleep* (NOT *Especially young people need plenty of sleep*). You can, however, use **especially** before a clause that begins with "if," "when," "because" etc.: *I think he'll do it, especially if you pay him.*

Es·pe·ran·to /ˌɛspəˈræntoʊ, -ˈrɑntoʊ/ *n.* [U] a language invented in 1887 to help people from different countries in the world speak to each other

es·pi·o·nage /ˈɛspiə,nɑʒ/ *n.* [U] the activity of finding out secret information and giving it to a country's enemies or a company's competitors

es·pla·nade /ˈɛsplə,neɪd, ˌɛsplə'neɪd/ *n.* [C] a flat open space or wide street, especially next to the ocean in a town

ESPN *n.* [singular, not with **the**] a CABLE TELEVISION station that broadcasts sports programs

es·pouse /ɛˈspaʊz, ɪ-/ *v.* [T] **1** FORMAL to believe in and support a political, religious etc. idea or PHILOSOPHY: *Followers of the sect espouse pure love and nonviolence.* **2** OLD USE to marry —**espousal** *n.* [singular,U]

es·pres·so /ɛˈsprɛsoʊ/ *n. plural* **espressos** [C,U] very strong coffee that you drink in small cups

es·prit de corps /ɛˌspri də ˈkɔr/ *n.* [U] feelings of loyalty toward people who are all involved in the same activity as you

---

es·py /ɪˈspaɪ/ *v.* [T] LITERARY to see someone or something that is far away or difficult to see

Esq. Esquire; a title of respect that is put after the names of lawyers: *Peter Niemeyer, Esq.*

-esque /ɛsk/ *suffix* [in adjectives] **1** in the manner or style of a particular person, group, or place: *Kafkaesque* (=in the style of the writer Franz Kafka) **2** having a particular quality: *picturesque* (=pleasant to look at)

Es·quire /ˈɛskwaɪr, ɪˈskwaɪr/ *n.* ESQ.

-ess /ɛs, ɪs/ *suffix* [in nouns] a woman who does something, or a female: *an actress* (=female actor) | *a waitress* | *two lionesses*

S W 3
es·say¹ /ˈɛseɪ/ *n. plural* **essays** [C] **1** a short piece of writing about a particular subject, especially as part of a class at school or college: [+ **on/about**] *an essay on democracy and education* **2** FORMAL an attempt to do something: [+ **into**] *an essay into politics*

es·say² /ɛˈseɪ, ˈɛseɪ/ *v.* [T] FORMAL to attempt to do something: *He swayed to the music and essayed a little dance step.*

es·say·ist /ˈɛseɪ-ɪst/ *n.* [C] someone who writes essays, especially as a form of literature

es·sence /ˈɛsəns/ *n.* **1** [U] the most basic and important quality of something: [+ **of**] *The essence of war is violence.* **2 in essence** FORMAL used to emphasize the most basic and important part of a statement, idea, or situation: *In essence, leadership involves accomplishing goals with and through people.* **3** [C,U] a liquid obtained from a plant, flower etc. that has a strong smell or taste and is used especially in cooking: *essence of garlic* **4 time/speed is of the essence** used to say that it is important to do something as quickly as possible

S W 3
es·sen·tial¹ /ɪˈsɛnʃəl/ *adj.* **1** important and necessary: *If you're going walking in the mountains, strong boots are essential.* | [+ **for/to**] *Good food is essential for your health.* | [**it is essential (that)**] *In a crisis situation, it is essential that the pilot remain calm.* | [**it is essential to do sth**] *It is essential to keep tropical plants warm.* **2** an essential part, quality, or feature of something is the most basic one; FUNDAMENTAL: *What is the essential difference between these two books?* —opposite NONESSENTIAL —see also ESSENTIAL OIL

essential² *n.* [C usually plural] something that is important and necessary: *The budget provides money for food, transportation, and other essentials.* | *We provide the homeless with the bare essentials* (=the most basic and necessary things) *such as food and clothing.* **2 the essentials** [plural] the basic and most important information or facts about a particular subject: *the essentials of English grammar*

S W 2 3
es·sen·tial·ly /ɪˈsɛnʃəli/ *adv.* in the most important or basic form or state: *Polk clearly states her belief that the world is essentially a good place.* | [sentence adverb] *Essentially, "domicile" is just a legal term for the place where you live.*

essential oil /.ˌ.. ˈ./ *n.* [C] an oil from a plant that has a strong smell and is used for making PERFUME¹ (1) or in AROMATHERAPY etc.

EST the abbreviation of Eastern Standard Time

est. **1** the written abbreviation of "established": *H. Perkins and Company, est. 1869* **2** the written abbreviation of ESTIMATED

-est /ɪst/ *suffix* used to form the SUPERLATIVE of many short adjectives and adverbs: *cold, colder, coldest* | *the survival of the fittest* —see also -ER, -IEST

S W 1 3
es·tab·lish /ɪˈstæblɪʃ/ *v.* [T] **1** to start a company, organization, system etc. that is intended to exist or continue for a long time: *The university was established in 1922.* | *A committee hopes to establish a new drug policy by the end of the month.* **2** to begin a relationship with someone or a situation that will continue: *Matt hoped to establish a caring relationship with Sandy.* **3** to find out facts that will prove that something is true: *Investigators have not established a reason for the attack.* | *His lawyer established that*

Shepherd did not know the victim. | *Doctors have* **established a link between** *smoking and cancer.* **4 establish yourself** to make people accept that you can do something, or that you have a particular quality: *Stevens has* **established himself as** *an expert in the field of psychology.*

es·tab·lished /ɪˈstæblɪʃt/ *adj.* [only before noun] **1** already in use or existing for a long period of time: *a well-established teaching method* **2** known to do a particular job well, because you have done it for a long time: *an established scientist*

es·tab·lish·ment /ɪˈstæblɪʃmənt/ *n.* **1** [C] FORMAL a business, store, institution etc.: *The smaller retail establishments in town serve mainly tourists.* **2 the establishment** the organizations and people in a society who have a lot of power and influence, and are often opposed to change and new ideas: **the medical/legal/military etc. establishment** (=the people who control the medical, legal etc. system) **3** [U] the act of establishing an organization, relationship, system etc.: [+ of] *Experts have called for the establishment of new health guidelines.*

es·tate /ɪˈsteɪt/ *n.* **1** [C usually singular] all of someone's property and money, especially everything that is left after they die: *Mrs. Graham left her entire estate to her three children.* **2** [C] a large area of land in the country, usually with one large house on it and one owner —see also FOURTH ESTATE, REAL ESTATE

estate sale /.ˈ. ˌ./ *n.* [C] a sale of used furniture, clothes etc. from someone's house, usually after the owner has died —compare GARAGE SALE

estate tax /.ˈ. ˌ./ *n.* [C,U] a tax on the money and possessions of a dead person that other people, especially family members, have to pay before they can get these things —see also INHERITANCE TAX

es·teem[1] /ɪˈstim/ *n.* [U] a feeling of respect and admiration for someone: *In order to be elected, you've got to attract the support and esteem of the population.* | **[hold sb in high/great etc. esteem]** *In the 1960s, lawyers were still held in very high esteem.* | *Please accept this gift* **as a token of our esteem** (=as a sign of our respect for you). —see also SELF-ESTEEM

esteem[2] *v.* [T usually passive] to respect and admire someone: *No writer is more* **highly esteemed** *by the Japanese than Soseki.* | *The Church teaches people to esteem others more than themselves.*

Es·ther /ˈɛstər/ a book in the Old Testament of the Christian Bible

es·thete /ˈɛsθit/ *n.* [C] another spelling of AESTHETE

es·thet·ic /ɛsˈθɛtɪk/ *adj.* another spelling of AESTHETIC —**esthetically** /-kli/ *adv.*

es·thet·ics /ɛsˈθɛtɪks/ *n.* [U] another spelling of AESTHETICS

es·ti·ma·ble /ˈɛstəməbəl/ *adj.* [only before noun] FORMAL deserving respect and admiration: *Before long, the estimable Dick Cheney took over the top job.*

es·ti·mate[1] /ˈɛstəˌmeɪt/ *v.* [T] to try to judge the value, size, speed, cost etc. of something, partly by calculating and partly by guessing: *The committee did not estimate how much such a program would cost.* | *We* **estimate that** *over 75% of our customers are women.* —**estimated** *adj.*: *The World Cup is watched on TV by* **an estimated** *one billion people.* —**estimator** *n.* [C]

es·ti·mate[2] /ˈɛstəmɪt/ *n.* [C] **1** a calculation or judgment of the value, size, amount etc. of something: *According to a government estimate, the number of refugees is at least 18 million.* | **A rough estimate** (=not an exact number; a guess) *is that vehicles cause about half the smog here.* —see also GUESSTIMATE **2** a statement of how much it will probably cost to build or repair something: *We got two or three estimates on the car.*

es·ti·ma·tion /ˌɛstəˈmeɪʃən/ *n.* **1** [U] your opinion or judgment of the value, nature etc. of someone or something: *In my estimation, he has been a great mayor.* **2** [C,U] a calculation or judgment about a number, amount, price etc. that is not exact: *To aid*

the estimation of moving costs, we will assume that each room is of average size. **3** [U] FORMAL respect or admiration for someone; ESTEEM[1]

Es·to·ni·a /ɛˈstouniə/ a small country in northeastern Europe on the Baltic Sea, west of Russia and north of Latvia —**Estonian** *n., adj.*

es·trange /ɪˈstreɪndʒ/ *v.* [T] to behave in a way that makes other people unfriendly toward you: *Joey seems to estrange everyone he meets.*

es·tranged /ɪˈstreɪndʒd/ *adj.* **1** not living with your husband or wife anymore, used especially in news reports: *Anderson's* **estranged wife** *declined to comment.* **2** not having any connection anymore with a relative or friend, especially because of an argument: [+ from] *Nagle said she had been estranged from her father for 14 years.* **3** not feeling any connection anymore with something that used to be important in your life: [+ from] *Simmons gradually became estranged from the religious group.* —**estrangement** *n.* [C,U]

es·tro·gen /ˈɛstrədʒən/ *n.* [U] a sex HORMONE (=chemical substance) that is produced in a woman's body

es·tu·ar·y /ˈɛstʃuˌɛri/ *n.* [C] *plural* **estuaries** the wide part of a river where it goes into the ocean

ET the written abbreviation of Eastern Time

ETA *n.* the abbreviation of "estimated time of arrival"; the time when a person or an airplane, ship etc. is expected to arrive: *What's our ETA?*

et al. /ˌɛt ˈæl, ˌɛt ˈɑl/ *adv.* FORMAL written after a list of names to mean that other people are also involved in something: *The exhibition will include works from Picasso, Pollock, Warhol, et al.*

etc. *adv.* the written abbreviation of "et cetera," used after a list to show that there are many other similar things or people that could be added: *Combine the champagne with fruit juices such as orange, pineapple, etc.* | *Simpson has traveled all over the country: Boston, Memphis, Dallas, etc., etc.* (=used to emphasize that a list is very long, or that you are annoyed or bored by the list you are giving)

et cet·er·a /ɛt ˈsɛtrə, -tərə/ *adv.* FORMAL the full form of "etc."

etch /ɛtʃ/ *v.* **1** [I,T] to cut lines on the surface of a metal plate, piece of glass, stone etc. in order to write something or make a picture or design: *The design is etched onto the glasses using a laser.* **2 be etched in your memory/mind** LITERARY if an experience, name etc. is etched in your memory or mind, you cannot forget it and you think of it often: *The war seems to be etched forever in my memory.* **3 be etched with sth** LITERARY if someone's face is etched with pain, sadness etc. you can see these feelings from their expression: *We could see that the man's face was etched with fatigue.* —**etched** *adj.*: *etched glass* —**etcher** *n.* [C,U] —see also **not be carved/etched in stone** (STONE[1] (7))

etch·ing /ˈɛtʃɪŋ/ *n.* [C] a picture made by printing from an etched metal plate

e·ter·nal /ɪˈtɜnl/ *adj.* **1** continuing forever, and having no end: *Church members express a belief in eternal life after death.* | *people searching for eternal youth* **2** seeming to continue forever, especially because of being boring or annoying: *Night after night, Manson was aware of his eternal hunger.* **3 eternal truths/verities** FORMAL principles that are always true —see also **hope springs eternal** (HOPE[2] (6))

e·ter·nal·ly /ɪˈtɜnl-i/ *adv.* **1** always, or for a very long time: *Roger seems eternally optimistic, but even he realized that the Giants couldn't win the championship.* **2** without end; forever: *We are eternally loved by God.* **3 eternally grateful** FORMAL very grateful: *I am eternally grateful for your encouragement.*

e·ter·ni·ty /ɪˈtɜnəti/ *n.* [U] **1 an eternity** a very long time, or a period of time that seems very long because you are annoyed, anxious etc.: *We only waited five minutes, but it seemed like an eternity.* **2** the whole of time, without any end: *The cause of the crash will continue to be a mystery* **for all eternity.** **3** the state of existence after death that some people believe continues forever

-eth /ɪθ/ *suffix* also **-th** OLD USE OR BIBLICAL used to form the third person singular of verbs: *he goeth* (=he goes)

eth·a·nol /ˈɛθəˌnɔl, -ˌnoʊl/ *n.* [U] TECHNICAL: see ETHYL ALCOHOL

e·ther /ˈiθɚ/ *n.* **1** [U] a clear liquid that was used in past times to make people go to sleep before a medical operation **2 the ether** LITERARY the air or the sky

e·the·re·al /ɪˈθɪriəl/ *adj.* LITERARY very delicate and light, in a way that does not seem real: *ethereal beauty* —**ethereally** *adv.*

e·ther·net /ˈiθɚˌnɛt/ *n.* [U] TRADEMARK a special system of wires used for connecting computers into a network in an office, building etc.

s w **eth·ic** /ˈɛθɪk/ *n.* **1** [singular] a general idea or set of moral beliefs that influences people's attitudes: *the Judeo-Christian ethic* —see also WORK ETHIC **2 ethics** [plural] moral rules or principles of behavior for deciding what is right and wrong: *Mallett is highly respected for his professional ethics* (=the moral rules relating to a particular profession). **3 ethics** [U] the study of the moral rules and principles of behavior in society, and how they influence the choices people make

eth·i·cal /ˈɛθɪkəl/ *adj.* **1** relating to principles of what is right and wrong: *Emmanuel Hospital is devoted to quality care and high ethical standards.* **2** morally good or correct: *This type of advertisement may be legal, but is it ethical?* —**ethically** /-kli/ *adv.* —opposite UNETHICAL

E·thi·o·pi·a /ˌiθiˈoʊpiə/ a country in northeast Africa on the Red Sea —**Ethiopian** *n., adj.*

s w **eth·nic** /ˈɛθnɪk/ *adj.* **1** relating to a particular race, nation, or tribe and their customs and traditions, especially when it is different from the main one in a particular country or area: *Employers cannot discriminate on the basis of racial or ethnic background.* | **ethnic group/minority** *Asian-Americans are the largest ethnic group at the university.* **2 ethnic cooking/food/clothes etc.** cooking, food etc. from different countries or races that are considered very different and unusual **3 an ethnic joke/remark/slur etc.** a joke, remark etc. that may be intended to be funny, but that insults people of a particular race or nationality **4 ethnic cleansing** the act of forcing people to leave their homes or killing them because they belong to a particular RACIAL (2), religious, or national group —**ethnically** /-kli/ *adv.*

eth·nic·i·ty /ɛθˈnɪsəti/ *n.* [C,U] *plural* **ethnicities** the race or national group that someone belongs to

eth·no·cen·tric /ˌɛθnoʊˈsɛntrɪk/ *adj.* based on the idea that one race, nation, group etc. is better or more important than any other —**ethnocentrism** *n.* [U] —**ethnocentricity** /ˌɛθnoʊsɛnˈtrɪsəti/ *n.* [U]

eth·nog·ra·pher /ɛθˈnɑgrəfɚ/ *n.* [C] someone who studies ethnography

eth·nog·ra·phy /ɛθˈnɑgrəfi/ *n.* [U] the scientific study of different races of people —**ethnographic** /ˌɛθnəˈgræfɪk/ *adj.* —**ethnographically** /-kli/ *adv.*

eth·nol·o·gy /ɛθˈnɑlədʒi/ *n.* [U] the scientific study and comparison of the origins and organization of different races of people —compare ANTHROPOLOGY, SOCIOLOGY —**ethnologist** *n.* [C] —**ethnological** /ˌɛθnəˈlɑdʒɪkəl/ *adj.* —**ethnologically** /-kli/ *adv.*

e·thos /ˈiθɑs/ *n.* [singular] the set of ideas and moral attitudes belonging to a person or group: *In the late '60s, thousands of people lived according to an ethos of sharing and caring.*

eth·yl al·co·hol /ˌɛθəl ˈælkəhɔl/ *n.* [U] TECHNICAL the type of alcohol in alcoholic drinks

E-tick·et /ˈi ˌtɪkɪt/ *n.* [C] electronic ticket; a ticket, especially a ticket for an airplane, that is stored in a computer and is not given to the customer in the form of paper

e·ti·o·lat·ed /ˈitiəˌleɪtɪd/ *adj.* **1** LITERARY pale and weak **2** TECHNICAL a plant that is etiolated is white because it has not received enough light —**etiolation** /ˌitiəˈleɪʃən/ *n.* [U]

e·ti·ol·o·gy /ˌitiˈɑlədʒi/ *n.* [C,U] *plural* **etiologies** TECHNICAL the cause of a disease, or the scientific study of the causes of diseases —**etiological** /ˌitiəˈlɑdʒɪkəl/ *adj.* —**etiologically** /-kli/ *adv.*

et·i·quette /ˈɛtɪkɪt/ *n.* [U] the formal rules for polite behavior in society or in a particular group

Et·na /ˈɛtnə/ also **Mount Etna** a mountain in Sicily, southern Italy, which is an active VOLCANO

é·touf·fée, etouffee /ˌeɪtuˈfeɪ/ *n.* [U] a SPICY dish popular in traditional Cajun cooking from Louisiana, made with SEAFOOD and vegetables cooked in liquid

E·trus·can /ɪˈtrʌskən/ one of the people that lived in northern Italy from the eighth century to the fourth century B.C.

-ette /ɛt/ *suffix* [in nouns] **1** a small thing of a particular type: *a kitchenette* (=small kitchen) | *a statuette* (=small statue) **2** OLD-FASHIONED a woman who does a particular job: *an usherette* (=a female USHER)

et tu /ɛt ˈtu/ *interjection* HUMOROUS said to someone when you are disappointed to learn that they think the same way as other people, because you expected them to be better: *"If a man doesn't have money, I'm not interested." "Et tu, Diane?"*

e·tude /ˈeɪtud/ *n.* [C] a piece of music that is intended to improve your skill at playing an instrument

et·y·mol·o·gy /ˌɛtəˈmɑlədʒi/ *n.* **1** [U] the study of the origins, history, and changing meanings of words **2** [C] *plural* **etymologies** a description of the history of a particular word —**etymologist** *n.* [C] —**etymological** /ˌɛtəməˈlɑdʒɪkəl/ *adj.* —**etymologically** /-kli/ *adv.*

EU the abbreviation of the European Union

eu·ca·lyp·tus /ˌyukəˈlɪptəs/ *n.* [C,U] a tall tree, originally from Australia, that produces an oil with a strong smell which is used in medicines

Eu·cha·rist /ˈyukərɪst/ *n.* **the Eucharist** the holy bread and wine, representing Jesus Christ's body and blood, used during a Christian ceremony, or the ceremony itself —**Eucharistic** /ˌyukəˈrɪstɪk/ *adj.*

Eu·clid /ˈyuklɪd/ (about 300 B.C.) a Greek MATHEMATICIAN who developed a system of GEOMETRY (=the study of angles, shapes, lines etc.) called Euclidean geometry

Eu·clid·e·an /yuˈklɪdiən/ *adj.* relating to the GEOMETRY described by Euclid, who made statements about what was possible by connecting facts and reasons in a clear and sensible way

eu·gen·ics /yuˈdʒɛnɪks/ *n.* [U] the scientific idea that it is possible to improve the mental and physical abilities of people by choosing who should become parents, often using threats or force from the government

eu·lo·gize /ˈyuləˌdʒaɪz/ *v.* [I,T] to praise someone or something very much, especially at a funeral: *Wilkes was eulogized as a caring, helpful man and a good father.* —**eulogist** *n.* [C] —**eulogistic** /ˌyuləˈdʒɪstɪk/ *adj.* —**eulogistically** /-kli/ *adv.*

eu·lo·gy /ˈyulədʒi/ *n. plural* **eulogies** [C,U] a speech or piece of writing in which you praise someone or something very much, especially at a funeral

eu·nuch /ˈyunək/ *n.* [C] a man whose TESTICLES have been removed, especially someone who guarded a king's wives in some Eastern countries in past times

eu·phe·mism /ˈyufəˌmɪzəm/ *n.* [C] a polite word or expression that you use instead of a more direct one, to avoid shocking or upsetting someone: *"Pass away" is a euphemism for "die."*

eu·phe·mis·tic /ˌyufəˈmɪstɪk/ *adj.* using polite words and expressions to avoid shocking or upsetting people: *Simon's euphemistic descriptions of wartime crimes have been heavily criticized.* —**euphemistically** /-kli/ *adv.*

eu·pho·ni·ous /yuˈfoʊniəs/ *adj.* LITERARY words or sounds that are euphonious are pleasant to listen to

eu·pho·ri·a /yuˈfɔriə/ *n.* [U] a feeling of extreme happiness and excitement

E

eu·phor·ic /yuˈfɔrɪk/ *adj.* feeling very happy and excited —**euphorically** *adv.*

Eu·phra·tes, the /yuˈfreɪtiz/ a long river that flows from Turkey through Syria and Iraq into the Persian Gulf

Eur·a·sia /yʊˈreɪʒə/ the large area of land that consists of the CONTINENTs of Europe and Asia

Eur·a·sian[1] /yʊˈreɪʒən/ *adj.* relating to both Europe and Asia

Eurasian[2] *n.* [C] OLD-FASHIONED someone who has one white parent and one Asian parent

eu·re·ka /yʊˈrikə/ *interjection* OFTEN HUMOROUS used to show how happy you are that you have discovered the answer to a problem, found something etc.

Eu·rip·i·des /yʊˈrɪpə،diz/ (?480–406 B.C.) an ancient Greek writer of plays

Euro- /yʊroʊ/ *prefix* **a)** relating to Europe, especially western Europe: *Europop* (=European popular music) | *Euromoney* **b)** European and something else: *Euro-American relations*

euro /ˈyʊroʊ/ *n. plural* **euros** [C] the unit of money used in the European Union

Eu·rope /ˈyʊrəp/ *n.* one of the seven CONTINENTs, that includes land north of the Mediterranean Sea and west of the Ural Mountains

Eu·ro·pe·an[1] /،yʊrəˈpiən،/ *adj.* from or connected with Europe: *European law*

European[2] *n.* [C] someone from Europe

European U·nion /،.... ˈ../ *n.* **the European Union** a European political and economic organization that encourages trade between the countries that are members, and makes laws for all these countries

Euro·trash /ˈyʊroʊ،træʃ/ *n.* [U] SLANG an insulting word for people from Europe who have a lot of money, wear fashionable clothes, go to fashionable clubs and events, but who are considered lazy and too interested in their social lives

Eu·sta·chian tube /yuˈsteɪʃiən ،tub, -ʃən/ *n.* [C] one of the pair of tubes inside your head and neck that connect your ears to your throat

eu·tha·na·sia /،yuθəˈneɪʒə/ *n.* [U] the painless killing of people who are very sick or very old in order to stop them from suffering; MERCY KILLING

eu·than·ize /ˈyuθə،naɪz/ *v.* [T] to kill animals or people in a painless way, especially because they are very sick or old

e·vac·u·ate /ɪˈvækyu،eɪt/ *v.* **1** [T] to move people from a dangerous place to a safe place: [**evacuate sb from/to**] *Some 2,500 campers were evacuated from Yosemite Valley due to a wildfire.* **2** [I,T] to empty a place by making all the people leave: *The stock exchange was quickly evacuated after receiving a bomb threat.* **3** [T] TECHNICAL to empty your BOWELs —**evacuation** /ɪ،vækyuˈeɪʃən/ *n.* [C,U]

e·vac·u·ee /ɪ،vækyuˈi/ *n.* [C] someone who is moved away from a place that it is dangerous, for example because there is a war

e·vade /ɪˈveɪd/ *v.* [T] **1** **evade the subject/question/issue etc.** to avoid talking about something, especially because you are trying to hide some information: *We tried to get a straight answer from the mayor, but he kept evading the question.* **2** to avoid doing something that you should do according to the law, such as paying taxes: *Fisher pleaded guilty to evading taxes on $51,000 of income.* **3** to avoid being caught or hurt by someone or something: *For six years, Harris has evaded capture* (=avoided being caught) *by federal agents.* **4** to find a way of not doing something you should do, by using skill or tricks: *Jones is now doing everything he can to evade responsibility for his mistake.* **5** FORMAL if success, the truth etc. evades you, you cannot achieve it or understand it

e·val·u·ate /ɪˈvælyu،eɪt/ *v.* [T] to carefully consider someone or something in order to make a judgment about them, especially about how good or useful they

are: *Your work will be evaluated by members of the management team.*

e·val·u·a·tion /ɪ،vælyuˈeɪʃən/ *n.* [C,U] the act of considering and judging someone or something, especially to decide how skillful or useful they are, or a document in which this is done: *Inspectors will have to do a thorough evaluation of the project before we can continue.*

ev·a·nes·cent /،ɛvəˈnɛsənt/ *adj.* LITERARY something that is evanescent disappears quickly

e·van·gel·i·cal[1] /،ivænˈdʒɛlɪkəl, ،ɛvən-/ *adj.* **1** evangelical Christians and beliefs emphasize a personal relationship with God and the importance of the Bible, as well as telling others about this **2** very eager to talk about your ideas and beliefs in order to persuade people to accept them: *Kemp is very evangelical about eating healthy food.*

evangelical[2] *n.* [C] a person who is a member of an evangelical Christian church

e·van·ge·list /ɪˈvændʒəlɪst/ *n.* [C] **1** someone who travels from place to place, trying to persuade people that they should become Christians **2** **Evangelist** Matthew, Mark, Luke, or John, one of the four writers of the books in the Bible called the Gospels —**evangelism** *n.* [U] —**evangelistic** /ɪ،vændʒəˈlɪstɪk/ *adj.*

e·van·gel·ize /ɪˈvændʒə،laɪz/ *v.* [I,T] to try to persuade people that they should become Christians

E·vans /ˈɛvənz/**, Mar·y Ann** /ˈmɛri æn/ the real name of the writer George Eliot

e·vap·o·rate /ɪˈvæpə،reɪt/ *v.* **1** [I,T] if a liquid evaporates or if something evaporates it, it changes into a gas **2** [I] if a feeling evaporates, it slowly disappears: *Support for the idea had evaporated by that time.* —**evaporation** /ɪ،væpəˈreɪʃən/ *n.* [U]

evaporated milk /ɪ،.... ˈ./ *n.* [U] a type of milk, often used in cooking, which has been made thicker by removing some of the water from it —compare CONDENSED MILK

e·va·sion /ɪˈveɪʒən/ *n.* [C,U] **1** the act of avoiding doing something that you should do: *Henning went to prison on charges of tax evasion.* **2** an act of deliberately avoiding talking about something or dealing with something: *Uncle Harry's style of evasion was to pretend he didn't hear the question.*

e·va·sive /ɪˈveɪsɪv/ *adj.* **1** not willing to answer questions directly: *an evasive answer* **2** **evasive action** action to avoid being injured or harmed: *The pilots took evasive action to avoid hitting the other plane.* —**evasively** *adv.* —**evasiveness** *n.* [U]

Eve /iv/ in the Bible, the first woman, who lived in the Garden of Eden with Adam, the first man

eve /iv/ *n.* **1** [C usually singular] the night or day before an important religious day or holiday: *Christmas Eve* (=December 24) | *New Year's Eve* (=December 31) **2** **the eve of sth** the time just before an important event: *On the eve of the election, some candidates were showing signs of strain.* **3** [C usually singular] POETIC evening: *one summer's eve*

e·ven[1] /ˈivən/ *adv.* **1** used to emphasize something that is unexpected or surprising: *Even Al was bored with the game, and he loves baseball.* | *I can't believe that Carrie doesn't even like cookies.* **2** **even bigger/better/worse etc.** used to emphasize a comparison: *Jeff knows even less than I do about cars.* **3** **even though** used to emphasize that although something happens or is true, something else also happens or is true: *I still look fat, even though I've been exercising fairly regularly.* **4** **even if** used to say that something will not have any effect on a situation: *Even if he gets accepted to Harvard, he won't be able to afford the tuition.* **5** **even so** used to mean that something is different from or opposite of what you would expect, based on a statement that was just made: *"It was the cheapest hotel we could find." "Even so, it still costs $200 a night."* **6** **even with sth** despite something: *Even with his disability, Ryan's one of the best students in the class.* **7** **even as** used to emphasize that something happens at the same time as something else: *Families somehow survived, even as they were being torn apart by the war.* | *Marge is preparing dinner even as we speak* (=while we are having this conversation). **8 even now/then** in spite of what has happened, what you have done, or what is true: *Even now I find it hard to believe Brenda's story.* | *Her only hope is an operation, but even then she may not get well.* **9** used to add a stronger, more exact word to what you are saying: *Molly looked depressed, even suicidal.* | *The bride looked beautiful – radiant, even.*

even² *adj.*
1 surface completely flat, level, or smooth: *Make sure the floor is even before you lay the carpet.* | *an even stretch of road*
2 not changing an even rate, temperature etc. is steady and does not change much: *These chemicals must be stored at an even temperature.* | *an even rhythm*
3 divided equally divided equally, so that there is the same amount of something in each place, for each person etc.: *Shape the dough into eight even balls.* | *an even distribution of wealth*
4 amount/measurement an even amount, measurement, price etc. can be expressed as an exact number of units: *Our grocery bill came to an even $30.00.*
5 even number a number that can be divided exactly by two, such as 2, 4, 6, 8 etc. —opposite ODD
6 line of things regularly spaced and neat-looking: *an even row of telephone poles*
7 get even (with sb) to harm someone just as much as they have harmed you: *I'll get even with you – just wait!*
8 be even INFORMAL to not owe someone something anymore, especially money: *If you pay for my ticket, we'll be even.*
9 be even (with sth) to be at the same height or level as something: *Line up the boards so their ends are even.* | *The top of the picture should be even with the window frame.* —**evenness** *n.* [U] —compare UNEVEN —see also **break even** (BREAK¹ (13)), EVEN-TEMPERED, **stay/remain on an even keel** (KEEL¹ (2))

even³ *v.*
even out *phr. v.* [I,T] to become equal or level, or to make something do this: *This year, the supply and demand for cherries are expected to even out.* | [even sth ↔ out] *The $1.3 billion plan is an attempt to even out spending in rich and poor school districts.*
even sth ↔ up *phr. v.* [T] to make a situation or competition equal: *O'Malley hit a home run to even up the score.*

even-hand·ed /ˌ.. '..◂/ *adj.* giving fair and equal treatment to everyone; IMPARTIAL: *Doug Pray's first film is an impressively even-handed documentary on the Seattle music scene.* —**even-handedly** *adv.*

eve·ning /ˈivnɪŋ/ *n.* **1** [C,U] the late part of the day between about 6:00 and the time when most people go to bed: *I have a class Thursday evening.* | *We like to go for walks in the evening.* | *I'm going out for the evening.* | *early/late evening Their flight didn't arrive until late evening.* —compare AFTERNOON
2 Good evening SPOKEN, FORMAL also **Evening** said as a greeting in the evening: *Good evening, ladies and gentlemen, and welcome to the show.*

evening dress /ˈ.. ˌ./ *n.* **1** [C] an evening gown **2** [U] EVENING WEAR

evening gown /ˈ.. ˌ./ *n.* [C] a long dress worn by women to formal meals, parties etc. in the evening

eve·nings /ˈivnɪŋz/ *adv.* during the evening: *After the end of this month, she'll be working evenings.*

evening star /ˌ.. './ *n.* **the evening star** the PLANET Venus, seen as a bright star in the western sky in the evening before the other stars can be seen —compare MORNING STAR

evening wear /ˈ.. ˌ./ *n.* [U] special clothes that you wear for formal occasions in the evening

e·ven·ly /ˈivənli/ *adv.* **1** with equal amounts or numbers of something in every part of a particular area, or divided equally among a group of people: *Spread the coating evenly over the entire surface.* | *The money was divided evenly among all four brothers.* **2** in a steady or regular way: *The patient was breathing evenly.* | *In the front yard, they had an evenly spaced row of rose bushes.* **3** dealing with or affecting all

parts of something in the same way: *Turn the chicken pieces so that they cook evenly.* **4 evenly matched** if two competitors are evenly matched, they have an equal chance of winning: *The teams seem pretty evenly matched, so it's hard to say who will win.* **5** if you say something evenly, you say it in a calm way, trying not to show any emotion: *"You can do whatever you like," she said evenly.*

even-ste·ven /ˌivən ˈstivən/ *adj.* SPOKEN if you are even-steven with someone, you do not owe them anything: *Here's your five dollars back. Now we're even-steven.*

e·vent /ɪˈvɛnt/ *n.* [C]
1 interesting/exciting something that happens, especially something important, interesting, or unusual: *Our special December issue lists the most important events of the past year.* | *Investigators are working to find out the sequence of events (=the order in which events happened) that led to the plane crash.* | *We couldn't have done anything to change the course of events (=the way that each event caused the next one, without being planned).* —see also CURRENT EVENTS
2 competition/performance/party an important performance, sports competition, party etc. which has been arranged for a particular date and time: *The presidential victory party was the social event of the year.*
3 in a sports competition any of the races, competitions etc. arranged as part of a day's sports: *The next event will be the men's 100-meter dash.*
4 in any event used just before or after a statement to emphasize that it is true or will happen, even if something else is not clear: *Some people claim that the show was a fake. In any event, it was good television.*
5 in the event of rain/fire/an accident etc. also **in the event that** used to tell people what they should do or what will happen if something else happens: *In the event of fire, the boat is equipped with fire extinguishers.*

even-tem·pered /ˌ.. '..◂/ *adj.* not becoming angry easily; calm

e·vent·ful /ɪˈvɛntfəl/ *adj.* full of interesting or important events: *She's led a very eventful life.* | *an eventful meeting* —**eventfully** *adv.*

e·ven·tide /ˈivənˌtaɪd/ *n.* [U] POETIC evening

e·ven·tu·al /ɪˈvɛntʃuəl/ *adj.* [only before noun] happening or achieving something at the end of a process: *Sweden was the eventual winner of the tournament.* | *No one was sure what the eventual outcome of the war would be.*

e·ven·tu·al·i·ty /ɪˌvɛntʃuˈæləti/ *n. plural* **eventualities** [C] FORMAL a possible event or result, especially a bad one: *We have to be prepared for every eventuality.*

e·ven·tu·al·ly /ɪˈvɛntʃəli, -tʃuəli/ *adv.* after a long time, especially after a long delay or a lot of problems: *Seventy-two percent of people eventually found work, but mainly in low-paid service jobs.* | *Eventually, the sky cleared up and we went to the beach.*

e·ven·tu·ate /ɪˈvɛntʃuˌeɪt/ *v.*
eventuate in sth *phr. v.* [T] FORMAL to have something as a final result: *Some officials feared the violence might eventuate in social revolution.*

ev·er /ˈɛvɚ/ *adv.*
1 anytime a word meaning "at any time," used mostly in questions, negatives, comparisons, or sentences with "if": *I don't remember ever seeing him before.* | *If you're ever in Wilmington, give us a call.* | *Nothing ever makes Ted mad.* | *That's the biggest fish I've ever seen.* | *"Have you ever eaten snails?" "Yes, I have."* | *It's hotter than ever (=than it has ever been) outside.* | *Mrs. Russell is as talkative as ever (=as she has always been).* | *Brent hardly ever (=almost never) calls me anymore.*
2 ever since continuously since a time or event in the past: *Ever since the accident, Martha's been too afraid to drive.* | *We moved to Springfield in 1985 and have lived here ever since.*

3 always always: *Ever optimistic, Jen gave him another chance.* | *Stan, ever the leader, made all the decisions.* | **ever-growing/-increasing/-worsening etc.** *We need to keep up with ever-changing trends in the market.*

4 ever so slightly very little; by a very small amount: *Meg looked at us and smiled ever so slightly.*

5 if ever there was (one) used to say that someone or something is a typical example of something: *Clapton is a living legend if ever there was one.* | *If ever there was an avoidable war, this is it.*

6 was sb ever...! SPOKEN used to add force to a statement: *Boy, was he ever mad (=he was extremely angry)!*

7 did you ever OLD-FASHIONED used to show your surprise, disbelief etc.: *Did you ever hear of such a thing?*

Ev·er·est /'ɛvrɪst/ also **Mount Everest** a mountain in the Himalayas, on the border between Tibet and Nepal, that is the highest mountain in the world

ev·er·glade /'ɛvəˌgleɪd/ *n.* [C] an area of low flat land that is covered with water and tall grass

Ev·er·glades, the /'ɛvəˌgleɪdz/ an area of low, wet, warm land in the southeastern U.S., in the state of Florida, covering about 5000 square miles and famous for its special plants and animals

ev·er·green[1] /'ɛvəˌgrin/ *n.* [C] a tree or bush that does not lose its leaves in the winter

evergreen[2] *adj.* **1** an evergreen tree or bush does not lose its leaves in winter —compare DECIDUOUS **2** always popular and never becoming unfashionable: *The group's name matches the evergreen quality of Farrar's songs.*

ev·er·last·ing /ˌɛvəˈlæstɪŋ◂/ *adj.* a word used especially in religious writing, meaning continuing to exist forever; ETERNAL (1): *Traditionally, weddings signify everlasting fidelity and love.*

Ev·ers /'ɛvəz/, **Med·gar** /'mɛdgə/ (1925–1963) a U.S. CIVIL RIGHTS worker in Mississippi who was shot dead by a member of the Ku Klux Klan

Ev·ert /'ɛvət/, **Chris** /krɪs/ (1954–) a U.S. tennis player famous for winning many women's tennis CHAMPIONSHIPS

ev·ery /'ɛvri/ *quantifier* **1** each one of a group of people or things: *Every athlete in the tournament must take a drug test.* | *Every one of the bags has a hole in it.* | *These two dresses are identical in every way, except for the price tag.* **2 every single** used to emphasize that you are talking about all the things, people etc. in a group: *Every single person in the office has a cold.* | *There aren't any cookies left – Dan ate every single one.* **3 every day/every 3 weeks/ every 10 miles etc.** used to say that something happens at regular periods of time, after a certain distance etc.: *Every year on her birthday, Jackie holds a party at the Vineyard House.* | *You should change your car's oil every 5,000 miles.* **4 every time** used to emphasize that each time one thing happens, something else also happens; whenever: *It seems like every time I play basketball, I get hurt.* **5 one in every hundred/two out of every thousand/five for every thousand etc.** used to say how often something affects a particular group of people or things: *There are more than 50 phone lines for every 100 residents in the U.S.* **6 every other day/week/one etc.** the first, third, fifth etc. or the second, fourth, sixth etc. of things that can be counted: *We go jogging every other day (=Monday, Wednesday, Friday etc.).* | *Concerts are held every other Saturday in Winsett Park.* **7 every now and then** also **every so often** sometimes, but not often: *Grandma still bakes us cookies every now and then.* **8 every which way** INFORMAL in every direction: *People were running every which way when the fire started.* **9 every bit as good/ important/much etc.** used to emphasize that something is just as good, important as something else: *The cake was every bit as good as I remembered.* **10 every Tom, Dick, and Harry** SPOKEN everyone or anyone: *I didn't want every Tom, Dick, and Harry*

knowing about my private life. **11 every chance/ reason/opportunity etc.** as much chance, reason etc. as possible: *We have every reason to believe that Melinda is still alive.* **12 every last drop/bit/scrap etc.** INFORMAL every single drop, piece etc.: *Billy always eats every last spoonful of his ice cream.* —see Usage Note at EACH[1]

ev·ery·bod·y /'ɛvriˌbɑdi, -ˌbʌdi/ *pron.* everyone —see Usage Note at EVERYONE

ev·ery·day /'ɛvriˌdeɪ/ *adj.* [only before noun] ordinary, usual, or happening every day: *The book is written in simple everyday language.* | *Stress is just part of everyday life.*

USAGE NOTE: EVERYDAY

SPELLING

Every day is spelled as two words as an adverb, but only one word as an adjective: *She swims every day.* | *the everyday life of a business executive.* Note that you never say **every days**.

Eve·ry·man /'ɛvriˌmæn/ *n.* [singular without **the**] LITERARY a typical ordinary person

ev·ery·one /'ɛvriˌwʌn/ *pron.* **1** every person involved in a particular activity or in a particular place; everybody: *Is everyone ready to go?* | *Everyone who ran in the race got a T-shirt.* | *I was still awake, but everyone else (=all the other people) had gone to bed.* | *Everyone but (=all the people except) Lisa got there on time.* —compare ANYONE, SOMEONE[1] **2** all people in general: *Everyone has bad days now and then.*

USAGE NOTE: EVERYONE

SPELLING

Everyone, written as one word, means "all the people in one group": *Everyone is waiting for you.* **Every one**, written as two words, means "each single thing or person in a group." It is always used with an *of* phrase, either stated or suggested: *Every one of the books has a torn page.* | *There are torn pages in every one (of them).* **Everybody** is written as one word. **Every body** written as two words means "every dead body."

GRAMMAR

Note that words like **everyone, everybody,** and **everything** must be used with a singular verb: *Everybody was* (NOT *were*) *glad to be home.*

---

ev·ery·place /'ɛvriˌpleɪs/ *adv.* SPOKEN everywhere

ev·ery·thing /'ɛvriˌθɪŋ/ *pron.* **1** each thing, or all things: *Maria has succeeded at almost everything she has tried to do.* | *Do you have everything you need?* | *Her photo album was saved, but she lost everything else (=all her other things) in the fire.* **2** used when talking in general about your life or about a situation: *"How's everything at work?" "Very busy."* **3 be/ mean everything (to sb)** to be the thing that is most important to you and that you care about the most: *Walt's family means everything to him.* **4 ...and everything** SPOKEN and so on: *Ben's all worried about getting married and everything.* **5 have everything going for you** to have all the qualities that are likely to give you an advantage over other people and make you succeed: *Dan seemed to have everything going for him in college.* —see also **everything but the kitchen sink** (KITCHEN (2))

ev·ery·where /'ɛvriˌwɛr/ *adv.* **1** in, at, or to every place: *They searched everywhere for Jen's keys.* | *Everywhere I go, I hear people worrying about the future.* | *People here are the same as everywhere else (=in every other place).* **2 be everywhere** to be very common: *Microchips seem to be everywhere – even in washing machines.* —compare NOWHERE

e·vict /ɪ'vɪkt/ *v.* [T] to legally force someone to leave the house they are living in: *Frank was evicted from his apartment four months ago.* —**eviction** /ɪ'vɪkʃən/ *n.* [C,U]

ev·i·dence[1] /'ɛvədəns/ *n.* **1** [U] facts, objects, or signs that make you believe that something exists or is true: [+ of/for] *Alex's father says he never saw any evidence of his son's mental illness.* | *There was no*

evidence that *either driver had been drinking.* | *Medical evidence shows that men are more likely to have heart attacks than women.* **2** [U] information, statements, and objects that are given in a court of law in order to prove that someone is guilty or not guilty: *The defense presented some new evidence from the victim's next-door neighbor.* **3 be in evidence** FORMAL to be present and easily seen or noticed: *The police were very much in evidence at the protest.* —see also STATE'S EVIDENCE

ev·i·dence² *v.* [T usually passive] FORMAL to show that something exists or is true: *The volcano is still active, as evidenced by the recent eruption.*

ev·i·dent /ˈevədənt/ *adj.* easily noticed or understood; OBVIOUS: *Carlos' frustration was evident in his comments.* | *It became evident that his football career would soon be over.* —see also SELF-EVIDENT

ev·i·dent·ly /ˈevəˌdəntli, ˌevəˈdentli/ *adv.* **1** seeming likely, based on the information that you have: *The man outside was evidently a visitor.* | [sentence adverb] *Evidently, the two of them have gotten back together.* **2** in a way that is very easy to see and understand: *Amelio evidently liked what he saw during Carey's concert.*

s w
2
3
e·vil¹ /ˈivəl/ *adj.* **1** someone who is evil deliberately does very cruel things to harm other people: *In the movie, the hero has to rescue the world from an evil scientist.* **2** having a very harmful influence on people: *Sue says that TV talk shows are evil.* **3** connected with the Devil or having special powers to harm people: *evil spirits* **4 the evil eye a)** the power which some people believe makes particular people able to harm others by looking at them **b)** HUMOROUS a way of looking at someone which shows that you are very angry at them: *Brad's been giving me the evil eye all night.* **5** very bad or disgusting: *There's an evil smell coming from the fridge.* —**evilly** *adv.*

evil² *n.* **1** [U] actions and behavior that are morally wrong and cruel, or the power that makes people do bad things: *It's a classic tale about the struggle between good and evil.* **2** [C] something that has a very bad or harmful influence or effect: *Dad gave us a lecture on the evils of smoking* —see also **the lesser of two evils** (LESSER (2)), **necessary evil** (NECESSARY (2))

e·vil·do·er /ˌiːvəlˈduɚ/ *n.* [C] OLD-FASHIONED someone who does evil things

evil-mind·ed /ˌ..ˈ..ˌ/ *adj.* an evil-minded person is always thinking of evil things to do

e·vince /ɪˈvɪns/ *v.* [T] FORMAL to show a feeling or quality very clearly in what you do or say: *Gumbel has evinced little interest in the new network so far.*

e·vis·cer·ate /ɪˈvɪsəˌreɪt/ *v.* [T] FORMAL OR TECHNICAL to cut the organs out of a body

e·voc·a·tive /ɪˈvɑkətɪv/ *adj.* FORMAL making people remember something by producing a feeling or memory in them: [+ of] *Twyman's drawings are strangely evocative of the paintings of Egon Schiele.*

e·voke /ɪˈvoʊk/ *v.* [T] to produce a strong feeling or memory in someone: *Jackson's speech evoked strong responses from the audience.* —**evocation** /ˌivəˈkeɪʃən, ˌevə-/ *n.* [C,U]

ev·o·lu·tion /ˌevəˈluʃən/ *n.* [U] **1** the scientific idea that plants and animals develop gradually from simpler to more complicated forms **2** the gradual change and development of an idea, situation, or object: *The table below shows the evolution of the English alphabet.*

ev·o·lu·tion·ar·y /ˌevəˈluʃəˌneri/ *adj.* **1** connected with scientific evolution: *evolutionary biology* **2** connected with gradual change and development: *an evolutionary process*

s w
3
e·volve /ɪˈvɑlv/ *v.* [I,T] to develop by gradually changing, or to make something do this: [+ from/into] *SuperMart was a small family store that evolved into a national supermarket chain.*

ewe /yu/ *n.* [C] a female sheep

ex /ɛks/ *n.* [C usually singular] INFORMAL someone's former wife, husband, GIRLFRIEND, or BOYFRIEND: *I didn't know my ex was going to be at the party.*

ex- /ɛks/ *prefix* **1** no longer in a particular relationship

---

or position, but still alive: *my ex-wife* | *an ex-President* —compare FORMER¹ (1), LATE¹ (7) **2** out of something, or away from something: *to exhale* (=let the air out of your lungs) | *to be excommunicated* (=not be allowed to remain a member of a church)

ex·ac·er·bate /ɪgˈzæsɚˌbeɪt/ *v.* [T] FORMAL to make a bad situation worse: *Howe's unkind remarks have exacerbated racial tensions in the community.* —**exacerbation** /ɪgˌzæsɚˈbeɪʃən/ *n.* [U]

ex·act¹ /ɪgˈzækt/ *adj.*

s w
2

1 correct correct and including all the necessary details: *It is difficult to determine the exact number of homeless people.* | *Doctors do not know the exact cause of the disease.* | *The exact time is 2:37 p.m.*
2 the exact color/moment/type etc. used to emphasize how similar or close two things are: *He came into the room at the exact moment I mentioned his name.* | *The red car over there is the exact one I've been looking for.*
3 the exact same thing/one etc. SPOKEN, INFORMAL used to emphasize that something is exactly the same as something else: *Carla was saying the exact same thing yesterday.*
4 to be exact SPOKEN, FORMAL used to emphasize that what you are saying is exact: *It was more than 20 years ago, to be exact.*
5 the exact opposite someone or something that is as different as possible from another person or thing: [+ of] *Nelson is friendly and outgoing, but his brother is the exact opposite of him.*
6 sth is not an exact science used to say that an activity involves opinions, guessing etc. rather than just calculating and measuring things: *Therapy is not an exact science because everyone responds differently.*
7 careful person someone who is exact is very careful and thorough in what they do

exact² *v.* [T] FORMAL to demand and get something from someone by using threats, force etc.: [+ from] *Gomez would exact a monthly fee from each vendor at the market.*

ex·act·ing /ɪgˈzæktɪŋ/ *adj.* demanding a lot of effort and attention: *Only a few applicants meet our very exacting standards.* —**exactingly** *adv.*

ex·ac·ti·tude /ɪgˈzæktəˌtud/ *n.* [U] FORMAL the state of being exact

ex·act·ly /ɪgˈzæktli/ *adv.* **1** used to emphasize that a particular number, amount, or piece of information is completely correct: *The baby was born almost exactly a year after they were married.* | *That's exactly right.* **2** used to emphasize a statement or question, and usually to show disapproval or annoyance: *I'm sure he knew exactly what he was doing.*

s w
1
2

SPOKEN PHRASES

3 exactly used to say that you agree with what someone has said: *"So you're saying there's no money left?" "Exactly."* **4 not exactly a)** used to say that you think that what someone has said is not completely correct or true: *"Dan's spent about a million dollars fixing up his house." "Not exactly. It was just a few thousand."* **b)** used when you say the opposite of what you mean, either as a humorous remark, or to show that you are annoyed: *I wouldn't bother asking Dave – he's not exactly Einstein* (=he is stupid). | *Well, they didn't exactly rush over to help us* (=they came very slowly, or not at all). **5 why/ what/where etc. exactly...?** used when asking someone to tell you the exact place, reason, thing etc.: *What exactly do you do at your company?* **6 that's exactly what....** used to say that what someone has said, done etc. is exactly the same as what you or another person said, did etc.: *"I think they should just get married." "That's exactly what Frank said too."*

---

ex·ag·ger·ate /ɪgˈzædʒəˌreɪt/ *v.* [I,T] to make something seem better, larger, worse etc. than it really is: *Rob said he caught a 20-pound fish, but I think he was exaggerating.* | *Hanley didn't exaggerate when he said Geary was the best basketball player the team ever had.*

ex·ag·ger·at·ed /ɪgˈzædʒəˌreɪtɪd/ *adj.* **1** described as better, more important etc. than is really true: *greatly exaggerated reports* **2** an exaggerated sound or movement is emphasized to make people notice it: *exaggerated hand gestures* —**exaggeratedly** *adv.*

ex·ag·ger·a·tion /ɪgˌzædʒəˈreɪʃən/ *n.* [C,U] a statement or way of saying something that makes something seem better, more important etc. than it really is: *It would be an exaggeration to say that we were close friends.*

ex·alt /ɪgˈzɔlt/ *v.* [T] FORMAL to praise someone or something very much: *The poem was written to exalt the Roman empire.*

ex·al·ta·tion /ˌɛgzɔlˈteɪʃən, ˌɛksɔl-/ *n.* [C,U] FORMAL **1** very high praise, or something that expresses this **2** a very strong feeling of happiness, power etc.

ex·alt·ed /ɪgˈzɔltɪd/ *adj.* FORMAL **1** having a very high rank and highly respected **2** filled with a feeling of great happiness

S W **ex·am** /ɪgˈzæm/ *n.* [C] **1** a spoken or written test of knowledge, especially an important one at the end of a school year or course of study: *a chemistry exam* | *Do you have to take an exam in French?* | *When are your final exams?* —compare TEST¹ (1) **2** a set of medical tests: *an eye exam*

ex·am·i·na·tion /ɪgˌzæməˈneɪʃən/ *n.* **1** [C,U] the process of looking at something carefully in order to see what it is like: *The judge ordered a detailed examination of Cowley's financial records.* | *The proposals are still under examination.* | *Upon closer examination, technicians found several more defective parts.* **2** [C] FORMAL a spoken or written test of knowledge; exam: *The examination scores will be announced next week.* **3** [C] a set of medical tests **4** [C,U] TECHNICAL the process of asking questions to get specific information, especially in a court of law: *Darden's examination of the witness produced no startling evidence.*

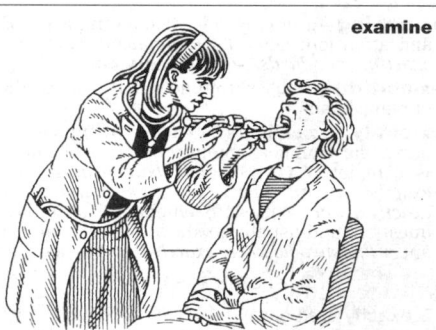

examine

examining a patient

S W **ex·am·ine** /ɪgˈzæmɪn/ *v.* [T] **1** to look at something carefully, in order to make a decision, find something, check something etc.: *Several hotels have examined ways to provide better access to wheelchair users.* | [examine sth for sth] *Investigators examined the gun for fingerprints.* **2** if a doctor examines you, he or she looks at your body to check that you are healthy **3** TECHNICAL to officially ask someone questions in a court of law **4** FORMAL to ask someone questions to test their knowledge of a subject —see also CROSS-EXAMINE

ex·am·in·er /ɪgˈzæmɪnɚ/ *n.* [C] someone whose job is to look at something carefully, find something, check something etc.: *a bank examiner* —see also MEDICAL EXAMINER

S W **ex·am·ple** /ɪgˈzæmpəl/ *n.* [C] **1** a specific fact, idea, person, or thing that is used to explain or support a general idea, or to show what is typical of a larger group: [+ of] *Can anyone give me an example of a transitive verb?* | *She cited a number of recent examples to support her theory.* | a good/typical/prime example of sth *This church is a good example of Roman architecture.* **2 for example** used before mentioning something that shows what you mean or shows that your idea is true: *It's extremely expensive to live in New York. For example, I pay $1250 for a one-bedroom apartment.* | *Japanese pop music sounds different from what we're used to.* **Take** the group Pizzicato Five, **for example**... **3** someone whose behavior is very good and should be copied by others, or this type of behavior: [+ to] *His determination is an example to us all.* | *Parents should* set an example for *their children.* | *I suggest you* follow *Rosie's* example (=copy her behavior) *and get more exercise.* **4 make an example of sb** to punish someone so that other people will be afraid to do the same thing

ex·as·per·ate /ɪgˈzæspəˌreɪt/ *v.* [T] to make someone very annoyed by continuing to do something that upsets them: *His refusal to cooperate has exasperated his lawyers.* —**exasperation** /ɪgˌzæspəˈreɪʃən/ *n.* [U]

ex·as·per·at·ed /ɪgˈzæspəˌreɪtɪd/ *adj.* very annoyed and upset: *an exasperated look* | [+ with] *Cindy was completely exasperated with her son.* —**exasperatedly** *adv.*

ex·as·per·at·ing /ɪgˈzæspəˌreɪtɪŋ/ *adj.* extremely annoying: *Marsha has this exasperating way of talking to me like a child.* —**exasperatingly** *adv.*

Ex·cal·i·bur /ɛksˈkælɪbɚ/ the name of the sword belonging to King Arthur

ex·ca·vate /ˈɛkskəˌveɪt/ *v.* [I,T] **1** if a scientist or ARCHAEOLOGIST excavates an area of land, they dig carefully to find ancient objects, bones etc.: *Work is under way to excavate the ancient city.* **2** to dig a big hole in the ground —**excavation** /ˌɛkskəˈveɪʃən/ *n.* [C,U]

ex·ca·va·tor /ˈɛkskəˌveɪtɚ/ *n.* [C] **1** a large machine that digs and moves earth and soil **2** someone who digs to find things that have been buried under the ground for a long time

ex·ceed /ɪkˈsid/ *v.* [T] **1** to be more than a particular number, amount, etc.: *Construction costs for the bridge could exceed $230 million.* **2** to go beyond the limits of something: *Nearly 100 cities have air pollution that exceeds federal standards.* | *The youngest player in the league has far* **exceeded** *his coaches' expectations* (=done better than he was expected to). **S W**

ex·ceed·ing·ly /ɪkˈsidɪŋli/ *adv.* extremely: *I've become exceedingly worried about the future of our nation.*

ex·cel /ɪkˈsɛl/ *v.* **excelled, excelling** [I not in progressive] to do something very well, or much better than most people: [+ at/in] *Rick has always excelled at foreign languages.*

ex·cel·lence /ˈɛksələns/ *n.* [U] the quality of being excellent

Ex·cel·len·cy /ˈɛksələnsi/ *n.* **your/his/her Excellency** FORMAL a way of talking to or about someone who has a high position in the government or the church: *his Excellency the Egyptian Secretary of State*

ex·cel·lent /ˈɛksələnt/ *adj.* **1** extremely good or of very high quality: *Nancy's in excellent health.* | *That was an excellent meal.* **2** SPOKEN said when you approve of something: *"I'll bring the books over tonight." "Excellent."* —**excellently** *adv.* **S W**

ex·cept¹ /ɪkˈsɛpt/ *prep.* also **except for** used before the people or things that are not included in a statement: *Everyone went to the show, except for Scott and Dan.* | *We're open every day except Monday.* | [+ in/by/up etc.] *There is wall-to-wall carpeting in every room, except in the kitchen and bathrooms.* **S W**

except² *conjunction* used for giving a reason why something is not true or not completely true: [except (that)] *I have earrings just like those, except they're blue.* | *A date book would make a great gift, except that a lot of people already have one.* | [except to do sth] *Since the accident he has been unable to speak, except to say "mama."* | [except when/what/where etc.] *I don't smoke except when I'm drinking.* **S W**

except³ *v.* [T] FORMAL to not include something:

[+ from] *High-technology equipment would be excepted from the trade agreement.*

ex·cept·ed /ɪk'sɛptɪd/ *adj.* **sb/sth excepted** used to mean that someone or something is not included in a statement: *Fred's not interested in anything, politics excepted.* —see also **present company excepted** (PRESENT¹ (5))

ex·cept·ing /ɪk'sɛptɪŋ/ *prep.* FORMAL except: *It is a desert with no animals of any kind, excepting a few lizards.*

s w ex·cep·tion /ɪk'sɛpʃən/ *n.* [C,U] **1** someone or something that is not included in a rule, does not follow the expected pattern etc.: *It's been very cold, but today's an exception.* | *We don't usually accept checks, but for you we'll **make an exception** (=not include you in this rule).* | *Most actresses never retire and Tandy **was no exception**.* | *John took all the books to college, **with the exception of** his cookbooks.* | *While most of the city's high schools are overcrowded, East High School **is the exception to the rule**.* | *Successful two-career couples with children are still **the exception not the rule** (=used to emphasize that something is unusual).* **2 take exception to sth** to be offended and angry about what someone says and complain about it: *Jones took exception to a comment I made about his weight.* **3 without exception** used to say that something is true of all the people or things in a group: *Without exception people were unbelievably friendly during our trip through the South.* **4 sb/sth is the exception that proves the rule** SPOKEN used to say that the fact that something is not true or does not exist in one situation emphasizes the fact that it is true or exists in general: *Most people our age have finished school, and Mike is the exception that proves the rule.*

ex·cep·tion·a·ble /ɪk'sɛpʃənəbəl/ *adj.* FORMAL an exceptionable remark, criticism etc. is a statement that other people will probably disagree with

ex·cep·tion·al /ɪk'sɛpʃənəl/ *adj.* **1** unusually good or impressive: *an exceptional athlete* **2** unusual or not likely to happen often: *The flood victims are doing their best under exceptional circumstances.* **3** having mental or physical problems that make it necessary to go to a special school: *a class for exceptional children*

ex·cep·tion·al·ly /ɪk'sɛpʃənəli/ *adv.* [+ adj./adv.] unusually or extremely: *Gloria is an exceptionally gifted singer.*

ex·cerpt /'ɛksɚpt/ *n.* [C] a short part taken from a book, poem, piece of music etc.: [+ of/from] *An excerpt of the speech appeared in the Sunday paper.* —**excerpt** /ɪk'sɚpt/ *v.* [T]

ex·cess¹ /'ɛksɛs, ɪk'sɛs/ *adj.* [only before noun] additional and more than is needed or allowed: *The airline charged me $75 for excess baggage.* | *Cut any excess fat from the meat before cooking.*

excess² *n.* **1 in excess of sth** more than a particular amount: *The director earns an annual salary in excess of $100,000.* **2** [singular,U] a larger amount of something than usual, needed, or allowed: [+ of] *There is an excess of writer-actors in Los Angeles.* **3 do sth to excess** to do something too much or too often, so that it may harm you: *Irwin admitted he often used alcohol and drugs to excess.* **4 excesses** [plural] actions that are socially or morally unacceptable because they are too harmful or too extreme: *The people have not forgotten the excesses of the military regime.* **5** [U] behavior that is not acceptable because it is too harmful or extreme: *The '80s were a period of excess for many American businesses.*

ex·ces·sive /ɪk'sɛsɪv/ *adj.* much more than is reasonable or necessary: *Don's wife left him because of his excessive gambling.*

s w ex·change¹ /ɪks'tʃeɪndʒ/ *n.*

1 giving/receiving [C,U] the act of giving someone one thing and receiving something else from them at the same time: [+ of] *Negotiators are considering the exchange of land for peace.* | *I gave Larry my bike **in exchange for** some video games.*

2 sth you buy [C,U] the act of giving something you have bought back to the store where you bought

---

it, for example because it does not work, fit etc., and taking something else instead: *The store's policy is not to allow returns or exchanges.*

3 argument/discussion [C] a short conversation, usually between two people who are angry with each other: [+ of] *Collins had a brief exchange of words with some reporters.* | *There were several **heated exchanges** (=angry arguments) but no injuries during the demonstration.*

4 an exchange of ideas/information etc. an act of discussing or sharing ideas, information, etc., or the situation in which this happens: *The organization is dedicated to the free exchange of information.*

5 place [C] a place where things are bought, sold, or traded: *a commodities exchange* —see also STOCK EXCHANGE

6 students/teachers [C,U] an arrangement in which a student, teacher etc. visits another school or country to work or study: *Elke first came to the U.S. in 1994 **on an exchange with** her university in Germany.* —see also EXCHANGE PROGRAM, EXCHANGE STUDENT

7 jobs/homes etc. [C] an arrangement in which you stay in someone's home, do someone's job etc. for a short time while that person stays in your home, does your job, etc.: *Kate's in New York on an employee exchange so she can get some more training.*

8 guns [C] an event during when two people, armies etc. use weapons against each other: *an exchange of gunfire*

9 money **a)** [U] the process in which you change money from one CURRENCY to another: *Most capital cities have extensive exchange facilities.* **b)** [C] the EXCHANGE RATE

10 telephone a TELEPHONE EXCHANGE

exchange² *v.* [T]

1 give/get sth better to give someone something so that they will give you something that is better, more appropriate, or more useful for you: *This shirt is too big. Can I exchange it?* | [exchange sth for sth] *In 1960 a trade agreement was made to exchange Cuban sugar for Soviet oil.*

2 give/receive to give someone something and receive the same kind of thing from them: *My family still exchanges gifts at Christmas.* | *We exchanged phone numbers, but I don't think I'll call him.*

3 do the same thing if two or more people exchange something, they do the same thing to each other: *City council members **exchanged greetings with** the group of business leaders.* | *The two men **exchanged a few words** (=talked to each other) and then left the park in opposite directions.* | *exchange glances/looks The two women exchanged glances and laughed.*

4 change money to change money from one type of CURRENCY (1) to another: *Did you exchange any money before your trip?* | [exchange sth for sth] *I need to exchange these dollars for pesos.*

5 exchange words (with sb) to argue with someone: *The pitcher exchanged words with the umpire and was thrown out of the game.*

6 exchange information/ideas etc. to discuss something or share information, ideas etc.: *It's a place where people can chat and exchange ideas.* —**exchangeable** *adj.*

exchange pro·gram /.'. ,../ *n.* [C] a program in which people, especially students, travel to another country to work or study for a particular length of time —compare FOREIGN EXCHANGE

exchange rate /.'. ,./ *n.* [C] the value of the money of one country compared to the money of another country

exchange stu·dent /.'. ,../ *n.* [C] a student who goes to a foreign country to study, usually as part of a program

ex·cise¹ /'ɛksaɪz, -saɪs/ also **excise tax** /'.. ,./ *n.* [C,U] a government tax that is put on particular goods produced and used inside a country

ex·cise² /'ɛksaɪz, ɪk'saɪz/ *v.* [T] FORMAL to remove or get rid of something, especially by cutting it out:

Offensive scenes were excised from the film. —**exci·sion** /ɪkˈsɪʒən/ *n.* [C,U]

ex·cit·a·ble /ɪkˈsaɪtəbəl/ *adj.* easily excited: *Louis is an excitable, quick-tempered person.* —**excitability** /ɪkˌsaɪtəˈbɪləti/ *n.* [U]

ex·cite /ɪkˈsaɪt/ *v.* [T] **1** [not in progressive] to make someone feel very happy, interested, or eager because of something good: *The movie was okay, but it didn't excite me that much.* **2** to cause a particular feeling or reaction: *The murder trial has excited a lot of public interest.* **3** [not in progressive] to make someone feel nervous or upset: *Don't excite him – he needs his rest.* **4** TECHNICAL to make an organ, nerve etc. in your body react or increase its activity: *The signal excites the neurons in the brain.* **5** to make someone feel sexual desire

s w
2
ex·cit·ed /ɪkˈsaɪtɪd/ *adj.* **1** feeling very happy, interested, or eager because of something good: *Police tried to hold back the excited crowd.* | *Before the first day of school, I get so excited that can't sleep.* | [+ about] *The kids are really excited about our trip to Mexico.* | *His latest novel is nothing to get excited about* (=not very good or interesting). | [+ by] *Everyone was excited by Alton's discovery.* | [excited to do sth] *We're excited to be here tonight.* | [excited (that)] *I'm very excited that our song was chosen.* **2** very nervous and upset about something: [+ about] *People don't get as excited about noise pollution as they probably should.* **3** feeling sexual desire —**excitedly** *adv.*: *They ran excitedly to the lake and jumped in.* —compare EXCITING

ex·cite·ment /ɪkˈsaɪtˈmənt/ *n.* **1** [U] the feeling of being excited: [+ of] *I love the excitement of opening night at the opera.* | [+ at] *Anna couldn't hide her excitement at the possibility of meeting the band.* | *In his excitement, he knocked over a lamp.* **2** [C] an exciting event or situation: *We were both new to the excitements of life in the big city.*

s w
2
3
ex·cit·ing /ɪkˈsaɪtɪŋ/ *adj.* making you feel very happy, interested, or eager: *an exciting story* | *It must have been so exciting to watch the first men land on the moon.* —**excitingly** *adv.* —compare EXCITED

ex·claim /ɪkˈskleɪm/ *v.* [I,T] to say something suddenly because you are surprised, excited, or angry: *"Wow!" exclaimed Bobby, "Great car!"*

ex·cla·ma·tion /ˌɛkskləˈmeɪʃən/ *n.* [C] a sound, word, or short sentence that you say suddenly because you are surprised, excited, or angry: [+ of] *The air was filled with exclamations of praise for Kendrick.*

exclamation point also **exclamation mark** /..ˈ.. ˌ./ *n.* [C] **1** the mark (!) used in writing after a sentence or word that expresses surprise, excitement, or anger **2** INFORMAL something that you do or say that has a big effect on a situation: *Johnson put an exclamation point on the Olympics by setting records in both races.*

ex·clude /ɪkˈsklud/ *v.* [T] **1** to not allow someone to enter a place or to do something: [exclude sb from (doing) sth] *Potter was excluded from military service due to his poor eyesight.* **2** to deliberately not include something: [exclude sth from sth] *Several of the incidents were excluded from the report.* **3** to decide that something is not a possibility: *France has refused to exclude the possibility of a military attack.* —opposite INCLUDE

ex·clud·ing /ɪkˈskludɪŋ/ *prep.* not including something: *The trip costs $1300, excluding airfare.* —opposite INCLUDING

ex·clu·sion /ɪkˈskluʒən/ *n.* **1** [C,U] the act of not allowing someone to do something or of not including something, or a situation in which this happens: *The resolution ended the exclusion of professional athletes from the Olympics.* **2 do sth to the exclusion of sth** to do something so much that you do not do, include, consider, or have time for something else: *The countries agreed to trade as much as possible among themselves, to the exclusion of outsiders.* **3 exclusion zone** an area that the government does not allow people to enter, because it is dangerous or because secret

things happen there: *a military exclusion zone* —**exclusionary** *adj.*: *exclusionary business practices*

ex·clu·sive¹ /ɪkˈsklusɪv, -zɪv/ *adj.* **1** available to only one person or group, and not shared: *Our figure skating club has exclusive use of the rink on Mondays.* | *Stay tuned for our exclusive interview with Boris Yeltsin.* **2** an exclusive group, organization etc. is difficult to be part of: *These students are part of an exclusive group of high achievers.* **3** exclusive restaurants, hotels etc. are for people who have a lot of money, or who belong to a high social class: *an exclusive Manhattan hotel* **4** concerned with only one thing: *The committee's exclusive focus will be to improve public transportation.* **5** deliberately not allowing someone to do something or be part of a group: *a racially exclusive hiring policy* —opposite INCLUSIVE **6 exclusive of sth** not including: *The college offers 25 full sports scholarships, exclusive of football.* —**exclusivity** /ˌɛksklusˈɪvəti, ˌɪks/ *n.* [U] —**exclusiveness** /ɪkˈsklusɪvnɪs/ *n.* [U] —see also **mutually exclusive/contradictory** (MUTUALLY (2))

exclusive² *n.* [C] an important news story that is in only one newspaper, magazine, television news program etc.

ex·clu·sive·ly /ɪkˈsklusɪvli/ *adv.* only: *This offer is available exclusively to those who call now.*

ex·com·mu·ni·cate /ˌɛkskəˈmyunəˌkeɪt/ *v.* [T] to punish someone by not allowing them to be a member of the Catholic Church anymore —**excommunication** /ˌɛkskəˌmyunəˈkeɪʃən/ *n.* [C,U]

ex·con /ˌɛks ˈkɑn/ *n.* [C] INFORMAL a criminal who has been in prison but who is now free —compare CONVICT²

ex·co·ri·ate /ɪkˈskɔriˌeɪt/ *v.* [T] FORMAL to express a very bad opinion of a book, play, person etc.: *The Boston Globe excoriated the first American exhibition, calling it a hotbed of Bolshevism.* —**excoriation** /ɪkˌskɔriˈeɪʃən/ *n.* [C,U]

ex·cre·ment /ˈɛkskrəmənt/ *n.* [U] FORMAL the solid waste material from a person's or animal's BOWELS

ex·cres·cence /ɪkˈskrɛsəns/ *n.* [C] FORMAL **1** an addition that is not wanted or not needed **2** an ugly growth on an animal or plant

ex·cre·ta /ɪkˈskriṭə/ *n.* [plural] FORMAL the solid or liquid waste material that people and animals produce and get rid of from their bodies

ex·crete /ɪkˈskrit/ *v.* [I,T] FORMAL to get rid of waste material from your body through your BOWELS, your skin etc. —**excretory** /ˈɛkskrɪˌtɔri/ *adj.* —compare SECRETE (1)

ex·cre·tion /ɪkˈskriʃən/ *n.* **1** [U] the process of getting rid of waste material from your body **2** [C,U] the waste material that people or animals get rid of from their bodies

ex·cru·ci·at·ing /ɪkˈskruʃiˌeɪtɪŋ/ *adj.* **1** extremely painful: *The pain in my knee was excruciating.* **2** extreme in a negative or upsetting way: *Witnesses described the brutal attack in excruciating detail.* —**excruciatingly** *adv.*

ex·cul·pate /ˈɛkskəlˌpeɪt/ *v.* [T] FORMAL to prove or decide that someone is not guilty of something: *The grand jury exculpated local authorities for their handling of the riots.* —**exculpatory** /ɪkˈskʌlpəˌtɔri/ *adj.*: *exculpatory evidence* —**exculpation** /ˌɛkskəlˈpeɪʃən/ *n.* [U]

ex·cur·sion /ɪkˈskɚʒən/ *n.* [C] **1** a short trip, usually made by a group of people: *The tour includes an three-day excursion to Disneyland.* **2 excursion into sth** FORMAL an attempt to experience, learn, or talk about something, especially something that is new to you: *During the meeting, the two leaders made brief excursions into the issue of Asian security.*

ex·cus·a·ble /ɪkˈskyuzəbəl/ *adj.* excusable behavior or reasons are easy to forgive —opposite INEXCUSABLE

ex·cuse¹ /ɪkˈskyuz/ *v.* [T]
1 excuse me SPOKEN **a)** said when you want to politely get someone's attention or interrupt them, especially to ask a question: *Excuse me. Is this the right bus to the airport?* **b)** used to say that you are sorry when you have done something embarrassing or impolite: *Oh, excuse me. I didn't know you were*

s v
1

standing in line. **c)** used to politely tell someone that you are leaving a place: *Excuse me for a minute. I'll be right back.* **d)** used to ask someone to repeat something that they have just said: *"What time is it?" "Excuse me?" "I asked what time it is."* **e)** used to politely ask someone to move so that you can walk past: *Excuse me. I need to get through.* **f)** used to show that you disagree with someone or are very surprised or upset by what they have just said: *"You're going to pay, right?" "Excuse me? Of course I am."* **g)** used to say you are sorry when you hit someone accidentally, make a small mistake etc.: *Oh, excuse me. Did I mispronounce your name?*
2 **forgive** to forgive someone, usually for something that is not very serious: *Please excuse my bad handwriting.* | [**excuse sb for (doing) sth**] *You'll have to excuse me for being late – my car broke down.* | *After the way the team played last Friday, he can be excused for being upset.*
3 **explain** to make someone's bad or unusual behavior seem more acceptable by giving reasons for it: *I'm sorry, but that explanation doesn't excuse what he did.*
4 **from a place** to give someone permission to leave a place: *May I please be excused from the table?*
5 **excuse yourself** to say politely that you need to leave a place: *Richard excused himself and went to his room.*
6 **from a duty** to allow someone not to do a duty or not to do something they are supposed to do: [**excuse sb from (doing) sth**] *Please excuse Sherry from gym class today. She has had the flu.*
7 **excuse me (for living)!** SPOKEN said when someone has offended you or told you that you have done something wrong

USAGE NOTE: EXCUSE (v.)

WORD CHOICE: (I'm) sorry, excuse me, pardon (me), (I) beg your pardon

Say **I'm sorry** or **excuse me** to someone if you accidentally get in their way, touch them, or push against them, or if you make a small mistake. *Sorry. I didn't mean to bump you.* | *"You're blocking the doorway." "Oh, excuse me."* Use **I'm sorry** when you have done something more seriously wrong or have upset someone: *I'm sorry I didn't call you – I forgot.* If you are ate, it is polite to say **I'm sorry** and give a reason: *I'm sorry I'm late. The traffic was bad.* Say **excuse me** to get someone's attention or before speaking to someone you don't know: *Excuse me. Can you tell me where the post office is?* Say **sorry, excuse me, pardon (me)** or **(I) beg your pardon** (old-fashioned) as a question if you want someone to repeat something, especially because you did not understand it or hear it correctly: *"Hi, my name's Maria Dallaglio." "Sorry?" "Maria Dallaglio."*

ex·cuse[2] /ɪkˈskyus/ *n.* [C] **1** a reason that you give to explain why you did something wrong: [+ for] *His excuse for being late wasn't very good.* | *There's no excuse for yelling in a restaurant like that.* | *I'm sure Mike has a good excuse for not coming to practice.* **2** a false reason that you give to explain why you are or not doing something: [**an excuse to do sth**] *I need an excuse to call her.* | [+ for] *I think this vacation is just an excuse for her to buy new clothes.* | *I'll make an excuse and get away from the party early.* | *The conference gives me an excuse to visit Atlanta.* **3 a poor/bad etc. excuse for sth** used when you think someone is very bad at something they are doing or at their job: *Her paintings are a pretty poor excuse for artwork.* **4** a note written by one of your parents or a doctor explaining why you were not at school on a particular day

USAGE NOTE: EXCUSE (n.)

WORD CHOICE: reason, explanation, excuse, pretext

If you call someone's explanation for what they have done a **reason**, you either believe it, or you are just repeating what they have said: *His reason for being late was that his alarm clock was broken* (=either you know his alarm clock was broken, which made him late, or that was simply the reason he gave you). If you call someone's reasons an **explanation**, you are just repeating what they said: *His explanation for being late was that his alarm clock was broken* (= that was the reason he gave – it may or may not be true). An **explanation** often sounds more like a personal opinion, a **reason** more like a fact. If you call someone's explanation an **excuse**, it suggests that you may not believe it is true or, if it is true, you do not believe that it really explains what happened: *His excuse for being late was that his alarm clock was broken* (=maybe his alarm clock was broken, or maybe it was not, OR you think it was broken, but that is not really a good enough reason for being late). If you say *My excuse is....* you are giving a reason that you know is not really good enough to explain what you did. If you call someone's explanation a **pretext**, you definitely think that it is not true or not the real reason: *His pretext for being late was that his alarm clock was broken* (=you do not believe it was broken, OR it was broken, but you know there was another reason that he was really late).

ex·ec /ɪgˈzɛk/ *n.* [C] INFORMAL an EXECUTIVE[1] (1)

ex·e·cra·ble /ˈɛksəkrəbəl/ *adj.* FORMAL extremely bad: *execrable wine*

ex·e·crate /ˈɛksəˌkreɪt/ *v.* [T] LITERARY to express strong disapproval or hatred for someone or something

ex·e·cute /ˈɛksɪˌkyut/ *v.* [T] **1** to kill someone, especially legally as a punishment for a serious crime: *The general was executed for war crimes.* —see Usage Note at KILL[1] **2** FORMAL to do something that has been planned or agreed to: *Franklin is in charge of executing the company's reorganization plan.* **3** FORMAL to perform something, especially a difficult action or movement: *The show's dance routines were well executed.* **4** TECHNICAL if a computer executes a program or a COMMAND (=instruction), it makes the program or command work or happen: *This program automatically executes the commands once a day.* **5** LAW to make sure that the instructions in a legal document are followed: *Brock's attorney has yet to execute the will.* **6** FORMAL to produce a painting, movie, book etc.: *a boldly executed story*

ex·e·cu·tion /ˌɛksɪˈkyuʃən/ *n.* **1** [C,U] the act of killing someone, especially as a legal punishment for a serious crime: *The execution has been delayed one month.* **2** [U] FORMAL a process in which you do something that has been planned or agreed to: [+ of] *Our office is responsible for the execution of the new marketing plan.* **3** [U] FORMAL the performance of something, especially a difficult action or movement: *Davis' execution on his last jump was perfect.* **4** [U] LAW the process of making sure that the instructions in a legal document are followed: *the execution of a search warrant* **5** [U] FORMAL the act of producing a painting, movie, book etc., or the way it is produced: *Many of Dali's paintings are witty in design and execution.* **6** TECHNICAL [C,U] the act or result of making a computer program work, or a COMMAND (=instruction) happen

ex·e·cu·tion·er /ˌɛksɪˈkyuʃənɚ/ *n.* [C] someone whose job is to legally kill someone else as a punishment for a serious crime

ex·ec·u·tive[1] /ɪgˈzɛkyətɪv/ *n.* **1** [C] someone who manages others in an organization, especially a business or company, or helps decide what the organization will do: *a senior company executive* **2 the executive** the executive branch of government —see also CHIEF EXECUTIVE

executive[2] *adj.* [only before noun] **1** relating to making decisions and organizing, especially in a company or a business: *an executive committee* **2** for the use of people who are important managers in a company or organization: *the executive washroom* —see also CHIEF EXECUTIVE OFFICER **3 the executive branch** the part of a government that approves decisions and laws and is responsible for making them work —compare **the judicial branch** (JUDICIAL (2)), **the legislative branch** (LEGISLATIVE (3))

ex·ec·u·tive priv·i·lege /.,... '.../ n. [C] the right of a president or other government leaders to keep official records and papers secret

ex·ec·u·tor /ɪɡ'zɛkyətə/ n. [C] someone who deals with the instructions in someone's WILL[2] (2)

ex·e·ge·sis /,ɛksə'dʒisɪs/ n. [C,U] FORMAL a detailed explanation of a piece of writing, especially one about the Bible

ex·em·plar /ɪɡ'zɛmplɑr, -plə/ n. [C] FORMAL a good or typical example

ex·em·pla·ry /ɪɡ'zɛmpləri/ adj. **1** excellent and used as an example to follow: *exemplary leadership skills* **2** [only before noun] severe and used as a warning: *an exemplary punishment*

ex·em·pli·fy /ɪɡ'zɛmplə,faɪ/ v. **exemplifies, exemplified, exemplifying** [T] to be a very typical example of something, or to give an example like this: *Moore's case exemplifies the difficulty in diagnosing unusual illnesses.* —**exemplification** /ɪɡ,zɛmpləfə'keɪʃən/ n. [C,U]

ex·empt[1] /ɪɡ'zɛmpt/ adj. having special permission not to do a duty, pay for something etc.: [+ **from**] *Their income is exempt from state taxes.*

exempt[2] v. [T] to give someone special permission not to do a duty, pay for something etc.: [**exempt sb from sth**] *Disabled students are exempted from paying the fee.*

ex·emp·tion /ɪɡ'zɛmpʃən/ n. [C] **1** an amount of money that you do not have to pay tax on in a particular year: *a tax exemption for a dependent child* **2** [C,U] special permission not to do a duty, pay for something etc.

sw **ex·er·cise[1]** /'ɛksə,saɪz/ n.

22 **1** for health [U] physical activity that you do in order to stay healthy and become stronger: *Let's walk. It'll be good exercise.* | *I don't get a lot of exercise during the week.*
2 for a body part [C] a movement or set of movements that you do regularly in order to keep your body strong and healthy: *a stretching exercise for my back* | *Have you done your stomach exercises today?*
3 for school [C] a set of written questions that test your skill or knowledge: *For homework, do exercises 1 and 2.*
4 army/navy etc. [C] a set of military actions that are not part of a war, but that allow soldiers to practice their skills: *a naval exercise*
5 a quality/result [C usually singular] an activity or situation that has a particular quality or result: [+ **in**] *Fighting the rising waters was an exercise in futility.*
6 use [C,U] FORMAL the use of power, a right etc.: [+ **of**] *The law protects the exercise of our freedom of speech.*
7 for a skill [C] an activity or process that helps you practice a particular skill, such as playing a musical instrument or singing: *fingering exercises for the piano*

sw **exercise[2]** v. **1** [I] to do physical activities so that you stay strong and healthy: *Karl exercises by playing racquetball twice a week.* **2** [T] to make a particular part of your body move in order to make it stronger: *Swimming exercises all the major muscle groups.* **3** FORMAL to use power, a right etc.: *Our manager exercised her influence to get Rigby the position.* **4** [T] to make an animal walk or run in order to keep it healthy and strong

exercise bike /'... ,./ also **exercise bi·cy·cle** /'... ,.../ n. [C] a bicycle that does not move and is used indoors for exercise

ex·ert /ɪɡ'zət/ v. [T] **1 exert authority/influence etc.** to use your authority, influence etc. to make something happen: *The UN is exerting pressure on the countries' leaders to stop the war.* **2 exert yourself** to make a strong physical or mental effort: *It's important not to exert yourself – it'll take a few weeks to recover.*

ex·er·tion /ɪɡ'zəʃən/ n. [C,U] **1** strong physical or

mental effort: *A little physical exertion helps me think more clearly at work.* **2** the use of authority, influence etc. to make something happen: *the exertion of legislative power*

ex·e·unt /'ɛksi,ʌnt/ v. a word written in the instructions of a play to tell two or more actors to leave the stage

ex·hale /ɛks'heɪl, ɛk'seɪl/ v. [I,T] to breathe air, smoke etc. out of your mouth or nose: *Take a deep breath; then exhale slowly.* —**exhalation** /,ɛksə'leɪʃən, ,ɛkshə-/ n. [U] —opposite INHALE

ex·haust[1] /ɪɡ'zɔst/ v. [T] **1** to make someone very tired: *The trip totally exhausted us.* | [it **exhausts sb to do sth**] *It exhausts me to think of all the things I have to do before the move.* **2** to use all of something: *We are in danger of exhausting the world's oil supply.* **3 exhaust a subject/topic** to talk about something so much that you have nothing more to say about it: *Well, it looks like we've exhausted that topic. Let's move on to the next question.*

exhaust[2] n. **1** [U] the gas or steam that is produced when a machine is working **2 the exhaust** also **the exhaust system** the parts of a car that exhaust passes through as it leaves the engine —see picture at ENGINE

ex·haust·ed /ɪɡ'zɔstɪd/ adj. **1** extremely tired and having no energy: [+ **from/by**] *Ron was exhausted from studying all night.* **2** having or containing no more of a particular thing or substance: *an exhausted coal mine*

ex·haust·ing /ɪɡ'zɔstɪŋ/ adj. making you feel extremely tired: *an exhausting trip*

ex·haus·tion /ɪɡ'zɔstʃən/ n. [U] **1** a state of being extremely tired | **mental/physical exhaustion** *Neil is suffering from mental exhaustion.* **2** the act of using all of a substance, material etc., or all the substances in something else, so that there are none left: [+ **of**] *Poor farming techniques have led to the exhaustion of the soil.*

ex·haus·tive /ɪɡ'zɔstɪv/ adj. extremely thorough: *The rescue team made an exhaustive search of the area.* —**exhaustively** adv.

exhaust pipe /.'. ,./ n. [C] a pipe on a car or a machine that gas or steam comes out of —see picture on page 427

ex·hib·it[1] /ɪɡ'zɪbɪt/ v. **1** [I,T] to put something in a public place so that people can see it, learn about it etc.: *The gallery will exhibit some of Monet's paintings.* **2** [T] FORMAL to show a particular quality, sign, emotion, etc. so that it is easy to notice: *Some of the patients exhibit aggressive and violent behavior.*

exhibit[2] n. [C] **1** an exhibition: *a new sculpture* sw *exhibit at the museum* **2** something or a collection of 3 things that is put in a public place so that people can see it, learn about it etc.: *The children's museum has several hands-on exhibits.* **3** LAW an object, piece of clothing etc. that is used in a court of law to prove that someone is guilty or not guilty: *Exhibit A is the bloody glove.*

ex·hi·bi·tion /,ɛksə'bɪʃən/ n. **1** [C] a public show where you put something so that people can go to see it: [+ **of**] *an exhibition of Impressionist painters* **2** [U] the act of showing something such as a painting in a public place: [+ **of**] *She never agreed to the public exhibition of her sculptures while she was still alive.* | *A collection of rare books is on exhibition at the city library.* **3** an exhibition of rudeness/jealousy/temper etc. behavior that shows rudeness, jealousy etc.: *Stilwell's actions were a startling exhibition of his disregard for others.* **4 make an exhibition of yourself** behave in a silly or embarrassing way: *Sam got drunk and made an exhibition of himself as usual.*

ex·hi·bi·tion·ism /,ɛksə'bɪʃə,nɪzəm/ n. [U] **1** behavior that makes people notice you, but that most people think is not acceptable: *Getting up and singing like that is pure exhibitionism.* **2** a mental problem which makes someone like to show their sexual organs to other people in public places —**exhibitionist** n. [C] —**exhibitionistic** /,ɛksə,bɪʃə'nɪstɪk/ adj.

E

ex·hib·i·tor /ɪgˈzɪbɪtə/ n. [C] someone who is showing something in a public place so that people can see it, learn about it etc.: *an exhibitor at a trade show*

ex·hil·a·rat·ed /ɪgˈzɪləˌreɪtɪd/ adj. feeling extremely happy and excited: *Our walk to the waterfall left us tired but exhilarated.* —**exhilarate** v. [T] —**exhilaration** /ɪgˌzɪləˈreɪʃən/ n. [U]

ex·hil·a·ra·ting /ɪgˈzɪləˌreɪtɪŋ/ adj. making you feel extremely happy and excited: *Sky-diving is an exhilarating experience.* —**exhilaratingly** adv.

ex·hort /ɪgˈzɔrt/ v. [T] FORMAL to try very hard to persuade someone to do something, especially through a speech: [**exhort sb to do sth**] *He exhorted the workers to end the strike.* —**exhortation** /ˌɛksɔrˈteɪʃən, ˌɛgzɔ-/ n. [C,U]

ex·hume /ɪgˈzum, ɛksˈhyum/ v. [T usually passive] FORMAL to remove a dead body from the ground after it has been buried —**exhumation** /ˌɛkshyuˈmeɪʃən, ˌɛgzu-/ n. [C,U]

ex·i·gen·cies /ˈɛksədʒənsiz, ɪgˈzɪdʒənsiz/ n. [plural] FORMAL what you need to do to deal with a particular situation: *the exigencies of war*

ex·i·gent /ˈɛksədʒənt/ adj. FORMAL an exigent situation is urgent, so that you must deal with it very quickly —**exigency** also **exigence** n. [U] FORMAL

ex·ig·u·ous /ɪgˈzɪguəs/ adj. FORMAL very small in amount: *exiguous earnings*

ex·ile[1] /ˈɛgzaɪl, ˈɛksaɪl/ n. **1** [singular,U] a situation in which someone is forced to leave their country to live in another country, especially for political reasons: *Some of her best works were written while she was in exile.* | *The King went into exile after the revolution.* **2** [C] someone who has been forced to live in exile

exile[2] v. [T usually passive] to force someone to leave their country, especially for political reasons: [**exile sb to**] *Several of the student leaders have been exiled to France.* —**exiled** adj. [only before noun]

W2 **ex·ist** /ɪgˈzɪst/ v. [I not in progressive] **1** to be real, or to be alive: *Do ghosts really exist?* | *Only about 50 Florida panthers are believed to exist.* **2** to happen or be present in a particular situation or place: *The custom of arranged marriages still exists in many countries.* **3** to stay alive, especially in difficult conditions: *Poor families in our city are barely able to exist during the winter.* | [**+ on**] *Brian exists on pizza and soft drinks.*

W2 **ex·ist·ence** /ɪgˈzɪstəns/ n. **1** [U] the state of existing: [**+ of**] *Do you believe in the existence of God?* | *Similar laws are already in existence.* | *The museum's very existence depends on contributions like yours.* | *Scientists have many theories about how the universe first came into existence* (=started to exist). **2** [C usually singular] the type of life that someone has, especially when it is bad or unhappy: *Pablo led a lonely existence when he first moved to San Juan.* —see also **eke out a living/existence** (EKE (1))

ex·is·tent /ɪgˈzɪstənt/ adj. FORMAL existing now —compare NONEXISTENT

ex·is·ten·tial /ˌɛgzɪˈstɛnʃəl/ adj. [only before noun] relating to the existence of humans or to existentialism: *an existential novel*

ex·is·ten·tial·ism /ˌɛgzɪˈstɛnʃəˌlɪzəm/ n. [U] the belief that people are alone in a meaningless world, that they are completely free to choose what to do, and that their actions shape their character and nature —**existentialist** adj. —**existentialist** n. [C]

W3 **ex·ist·ing** /ɪgˈzɪstɪŋ/ adj. [only before noun] present or being used now: *Forbes suggests getting rid of the existing tax system.*

W3 **ex·it**[1] /ˈɛgzɪt, ˈɛksɪt/ n. [C] **1** a door or space through which you can leave a room, building etc.: *There are two exits at the back of the plane.* | *an emergency exit* **2** [usually singular] the act of leaving a place such as a room or theater stage: *Kennedy made a quick exit after his speech.* —opposite ENTRANCE **3** a small road that you drive on to leave a larger road: *Take the 14th Street exit and then turn right.* **4** [usually singular] an occasion when someone stops being involved in a situation, event etc., often because they have not been successful or have done something

wrong: *Surprisingly, Pratt made an early exit from the tournament.*

exit[2] v. **1** [I] to leave a place: [**+ from/through**] *The band exited through a door behind the stage.* **2** [I,T] to stop using a computer program: *Push F3 to exit.* **3** [I,T] a word used in the instructions of a play to tell an actor to leave the stage: *Exit Hamlet, carrying the body of Polonius.*

exit poll /ˈ.. ˌ./ n. [C] a process of asking people how they have voted as they leave a voting place in order to discover the likely result of the election

Ex·o·dus /ˈɛksədəs/ the second book in the Old Testament of the Christian Bible

ex·o·dus /ˈɛksədəs/ n. [singular] a situation in which a lot of people leave a particular place at the same time: [**+ from/to**] *a mass exodus of Cubans to Miami*

ex of·fi·ci·o /ˌɛks əˈfɪʃiou/ adj. FORMAL an ex-officio member of an organization is only a member because of their rank or position —**ex officio** adv.

ex·on·er·ate /ɪgˈzɑnəˌreɪt/ v. [T] FORMAL to officially say that someone who has been blamed for something is not guilty: [**exonerate sb from/of sth**] *Ross was exonerated of all charges of child abuse.* —**exoneration** /ɪgˌzɑnəˈreɪʃən/ n. [U]

ex·or·bi·tant /ɪgˈzɔrbətənt/ adj. an exorbitant price, demand etc. is much higher or greater than is reasonable or usual: *It's a nice hotel, but the prices are exorbitant.* —**exorbitance** n. [U] —**exorbitantly** adv.

ex·or·cise /ˈɛksɔrˌsaɪz, -sə-/ v. [T] **1** to forget or be able to deal with bad memories or bad experiences, or to make someone do this: **exorcise demons/ghosts** etc. *Starting my own family has helped exorcise the demons of my past.* **2** to try to force evil spirits to leave a place or someone's body by using special words and ceremonies

ex·or·cism /ˈɛksɔrˌsɪzəm/ n. [C,U] a process by which someone tries to force evil spirits to leave a place or someone's body by using special words and ceremonies

ex·or·cist /ˈɛksɔrsɪst/ n. [C] someone who tries to force evil spirits to leave a place or someone's body

ex·ot·ic /ɪgˈzɑtɪk/ adj. APPROVING unusual and exciting because of a connection with a foreign country: *exotic birds from New Guinea* —**exotically** /-kli/ adv.

ex·ot·i·ca /ɪgˈzɑtɪkə/ n. [plural] unusual and exciting things, especially ones that come from foreign countries

exotic danc·er /.ˌ.. ˈ../ n. [C] a dancer who takes off their clothes while dancing —see also STRIPTEASE

SW2,3 **ex·pand** /ɪkˈspænd/ v. **1** [I,T] to become larger in size, number, or amount, or to make something become larger: *Heat makes the gas in the container expand.* | *The population of Texas expanded rapidly in the '60s.* | [**expand sth**] *This exercise is a good way to expand the chest.* | *The study will be expanded to include inner-city youth.* —opposite CONTRACT[2] **2** [I,T] if a company, business etc. expands or if someone expands it, they open new stores, factories etc.: *Pepsi has aggressive plans to expand overseas.* —**expandable** adj.: *an expandable garment bag*

expand on/upon sth phr. v. [T] to add more details or information to something that has already been said: *Wilson refused to expand upon what action would be taken.*

ex·panse /ɪkˈspæns/ n. [C] a very large area of water, sky, land etc.: [**+ of**] *the vast expanse of the Pacific Ocean*

SW3 **ex·pan·sion** /ɪkˈspænʃən/ n. **1** [C,U] the act or process of increasing in size, number, amount, or range: *the expansion of the local stadium* **2** [C,U] a period of increased business activity: *Most regions are enjoying rapid economic expansion.* **3** [U] the act or process of making a company or business larger by opening new shops, factories etc.: *The airline has plans for expansion into Asia.* **4** [C] a detailed idea, story etc. that is based on one that is simpler or

E

more general: *The novel is an expansion of a short story he wrote about forty years ago.*

expansion card also **expansion board** /.'.. ,./ *n.* [C] TECHNICAL a piece of electronic equipment that allows a computer to do more things, such as make sounds, receive FAXes, and play CD-ROMs

ex·pan·sion·ism /ɪk'spænʃə,nɪzəm/ *n.* [U] the practice of increasing the amount of land or power that a country has, used especially when you disapprove of this —**expansionary** *adj.* —**expansionist** *adj.* —**expansionist** *n.* [C]

expansion team /.'.. ,./ *n.* [C] a new professional sports team in the U.S. whose members usually come from other teams

ex·pan·sive /ɪk'spænsɪv/ *adj.* **1** very large in area, or including a large variety of things: *an expansive view of the beach* | *an expansive selection of food* **2** very friendly and willing to talk a lot: *Our visitors became more expansive after a few beers.* **3** relating to the ability of a business to grow: *The new office building represents the company's expansive ambitions.* —**expansively** *adv.* —**expansiveness** *n.* [U]

ex·pat /'ɛks,pæt/ *n.* [C] INFORMAL an expatriate

ex·pa·ti·ate /ɛk'speɪʃi,eɪt/ *v.*
  expatiate on/upon sth *phr. v.* [T] FORMAL to speak or write in detail about a particular subject: *Bill likes to expatiate on the benefits of a free market economy.*

ex·pa·tri·ate /ɛks'peɪtriɪt/ *n.* [C] someone who lives in a foreign country —**expatriate** *adj.* [only before noun] *Hong Kong's expatriate community*

ex·pa·tri·a·tion /ɛks,peɪtri'eɪʃən/ *n.* [T] a situation in which someone is forced to leave their country and go to live in another country, especially because they have broken the law —**expatriate** /ɛks'peɪtri-,eɪt/ *v.* [T] —compare EXILE[1]

ex·pect /ɪk'spɛkt/ *v.* [T]
  1 think sth will happen to think that something will happen or will be true, because it seems likely or has been planned: *Light rain is expected today in the Bay Area.* | [expect sb/sth to do sth] *I didn't expect him to stay.* | [expect to do sth] *She expects to graduate next spring with a degree in psychology.* | [expect (that)] *Analysts expect that stock prices will improve this year.* | *She fully expected to be criticized for her decision.* | *As expected*, Maggie Smith *won the best actress prize* (=everyone knew this would happen). | *This type of weather damage is to be expected* (=is not surprising) *with older houses.*
  2 demand to demand that someone do something, especially because it is their duty: *At these prices, I expect better service.* | [expect sb to do sth] *You are expected to return all books by Monday.* | *Wanda's parents expect too much of her* (=think she should do more than she really can).
  3 be expecting (a baby) to be going to have a baby soon: *They're expecting their first child September 5.*
  4 think to think that someone or something has a particular quality or does a particular thing: *She's shorter than I expected.*
  5 be waiting for sb/sth to believe that someone or something is going to arrive: *How many people are you expecting?* | *I'm expecting a call from him soon.* | *Forecasters expect snow in the mountains.*
  6 what do/can you expect? SPOKEN used to say that something should not surprise you: *"This printer doesn't do color printing." "Well, what do you expect for that price?"*
  7 how do/can you expect...? used to say that it is unreasonable to think that something will happen or be true: *How can you expect to do well in college if you study a subject that doesn't interest you?*
  8 half expect to think that something might happen, although you know it really will not: *I half expected the kids to burn down the house while we were gone.*
  9 I expect SPOKEN used to say that you think something is probably true: *I expect you're right.* —see Usage Note at WAIT[1]

ex·pect·an·cy /ɪk'spɛktənsi/ *n.* [U] the feeling that something pleasant or exciting is going to happen: *We celebrate Passover with joy and expectancy.* —see also LIFE EXPECTANCY

ex·pect·ant /ɪk'spɛktənt/ *adj.* **1 expectant mother/father/couple** a mother, father etc. whose baby will be born soon **2** hopeful that something good or exciting will happen, or showing this: *The children were looking at the gifts with expectant expressions.* —**expectantly** *adv.*

ex·pec·ta·tion /,ɛkspɛk'teɪʃən/ *n.* **1** [C usually plural,U] what you think or hope will happen: [expectation that] *These figures are based on the expectation that the economy will continue to improve.* | *The size of the audience was far below expectations* (=worse than expected). | *Meetings between the two leaders have raised expectations* (=made people more hopeful) *that an agreement is likely.* | *Sales results have exceeded expectations* (=been much better than expected). | *Sandbags were placed in expectation of the river rising another foot.* | on expectations of/that *Boeing's stock price rose on expectations of an order from Korean Airlines.* **2** [C usually plural] a feeling or belief about the way something should be or how someone should behave: *Viking fans have high expectations for this season* (=they expect the team to be successful). | *Parents and teachers must raise their expectations of students.* | meet sb's expectations/live up to sb's expectations (=be as good as someone thinks it should be)

ex·pect·ed /ɪk'spɛktɪd/ *adj.* [only before noun] **1** an expected event or result is one you think will happen: *When he didn't get his expected bonus, he quit his job.* **2** an expected person or group is one you think will arrive: *an expected crowd of 80,000*

ex·pec·to·rant /ɪk'spɛktərənt/ *n.* [U] FORMAL a type of medicine that you take to help you cough up PHLEGM (=a sticky substance) from your lungs

ex·pec·to·rate /ɪk'spɛktə,reɪt/ *v.* [I] FORMAL to force liquid out of your mouth; SPIT[1] (1)

ex·pe·di·en·cy /ɪk'spidiənsi/ also **ex·pe·di·ence** /ɪk'spidiəns/ *n. plural* **expediencies** [C,U] what is quickest or most effective to do in a particular situation, rather than what is morally right: *The governor vetoed this bill out of political expediency rather than principle.*

ex·pe·di·ent[1] /ɪk'spidiənt/ *adj.* **1** quick and effective, but sometimes not morally right: *a politically expedient compromise* **2** useful or appropriate for a particular situation: [expedient to do sth] *It is expedient to reduce unnecessary expenditure.* —opposite INEXPEDIENT —**expediently** *adv.*

expedient[2] *n.* [C] a quick and effective way of dealing with a problem

ex·pe·dite /'ɛkspə,daɪt/ *v.* [T] to make a process, action etc. happen more quickly: *More money would, of course, expedite the construction.*

ex·pe·di·tion /,ɛkspə'dɪʃən/ *n.* **1** [C] a long and carefully organized trip, especially to a dangerous or unfamiliar place, or the people that make this trip: *an expedition to the North Pole* **2** [C] a short trip, usually made for a particular purpose: *a shopping expedition* **3** [U] the act of doing something more quickly than you would usually

ex·pe·di·tion·ar·y /,ɛkspə'dɪʃə,nɛri/ *adj.* **1 expeditionary army/force** etc. an army, group of soldiers etc. that is sent to a battle in another country **2** relating to an expedition

ex·pe·di·tious·ly /,ɛkspə'dɪʃəsli/ *adv.* FORMAL in a quick and effective way: *The board understands that it must resolve this issue expeditiously.* —**expeditious** *adj.*

ex·pel /ɪk'spɛl/ *v.* **expelled, expelling** [T] **1** to officially make someone leave a school, organization, country etc., especially because they have broken rules: *The government is trying to expel all foreign journalists.* | [expel sb from sth] *Jakes had been expelled from the Communist Party.* | [expel sb for doing sth] *Leon got expelled for bringing a knife to school.* **2** to force air, water, gas etc. out of something —see also EXPULSION

ex·pend /ɪkˈspɛnd/ v. [T] FORMAL to use money, time, energy etc. to do something: *Carrying small weights increases the calories you expend when walking for fitness.* | [**expend sth on sth**] *Billions of dollars have been expended on research.*

ex·pend·a·ble /ɪkˈspɛndəbəl/ adj. **1** not needed enough to be kept or saved: *Everyone is expendable. No one's job is safe.* **2** able to be spent: *expendable income*

ex·pend·i·ture /ɪkˈspɛndətʃə/ n. [C,U] FORMAL **1** the total amount of money that a government, organization, or person spends: [+ **on**] *The state's expenditure on welfare programs went down by 5% last year.* —compare INCOME —see also PUBLIC FUNDING **2** the action of spending or using time, money, energy etc.: *The new regulations will require unnecessary expenditure of time and money.*

ex·pense /ɪkˈspɛns/ n. **1** [C,U] the amount of money that you spend on something: *Most of my paycheck just goes to living expenses* (=what it costs to pay for food, a house etc.). | *Melissa's parents spared no expense on her wedding* (=they spent all the money necessary to buy the best things). | **go to considerable/great expense** (=spend a lot of money) **2 expenses** [plural] money that you spend on travel, hotels, meals etc. as part of your job, and that your employer gives back to you later **3 at the expense of sb/sth** if something is done at the expense of someone or something else, it is only achieved by doing something that could harm the other person or thing: *The cars were produced quickly, at the expense of safety.* | *He did not want to devote more time to his business at the expense of his family* **4 at sb's expense a)** if you do something at someone's expense, they pay for you to do it: *Several state senators traveled to Asia at taxpayers' expense.* **b)** if you make jokes at someone's expense, you laugh about them and make them seem stupid or silly: *Louis kept making jokes at his wife's expense.* **5 all expenses paid** having all of your costs for hotels, travel, meals etc. paid for by someone else *The prize is an all-expenses-paid trip to Hawaii.*

expense ac·count /.ˈ. .ˌ./ n. [C] money that is available to someone who works for a company so that they can pay for meals, hotels etc. when traveling or entertaining people for work

ex·pen·sive /ɪkˈspɛnsɪv/ adj. costing a lot of money: *Smoking can be an expensive habit.* | *an expensive restaurant* | [**sth is expensive to do**] *Children's hospitals are expensive to run.* —**expensively** adv.

ex·pe·ri·ence¹ /ɪkˈspɪriəns/ n.

1 knowledge/skill [U] knowledge or skill that you gain from doing a job or activity, or the process of gaining this: *The job requires two years of teaching experience.* | [+ **in/with**] *Do you have any previous experience in sales?* | *He didn't get the job because of his lack of experience with computers.* | *Chuck gained valuable work experience while he was still in college.*

2 knowledge of life [U] knowledge that you gain about life and the world by being in different situations and meeting different people, or the process of gaining this: *In my experience, training programs are almost always worth it.* | **know/learn/speak from experience** *The computer actually learns from experience and can change its game strategy.* | **personal/past experience** *Robbins wrote a story about climbing based on personal experience.* | *Experience shows that older adults can quit smoking as successfully as young ones.*

3 sth that happens [C] something that happens to you or something that you do, especially when this has an effect on what you feel or think: *A lot of the other kids had had the same experience.* | [+ **of/with**] *Nothing had fully prepared me for the experience of childbirth.* | [+ **for**] *Losing the tournament was a difficult experience for her.* | **a memorable/unforgettable experience** *A trip down the Colorado River is an unforgettable experience.*

4 the American/immigrant/black etc. experience events or knowledge shared by the members of a particular society or group of people: *No writer has ever expressed the black experience with such passion*

as Toni Morrison. —see also **first-hand experience/ knowledge/account** (FIRST-HAND)

experience² v. [T] **1** if you experience a problem, event, situation etc., you are involved with it and it influences or affects you: *Many regions are experiencing a shortage of food.* | *As it grew, the city experienced an increase in crime.* | *I have experienced first hand* (=seen or heard directly) *the problems caused by lack of cooperation.* **2** to feel a particular emotion, pain etc.: *You may experience some dizziness after taking the medicine.*

ex·pe·ri·enced /ɪkˈspɪriənst/ adj. having particular skills or knowledge because you have done something often or for a long time: *an experienced skier* | [+ **in**] *He's not very experienced in politics.*

ex·pe·ri·en·tial /ɪkˌspɪriˈɛnʃəl/ adj. based on experience, or relating to experience: *experiential approaches to learning*

ex·per·i·ment¹ /ɪkˈspɛrəmənt/ n. [C,U] **1** a scientific test done to find out how something will react in a particular situation, or to find out if a particular idea is true: [**an experiment to see/test etc.**] *The lab has designed experiments to test the ability of dogs to see color.* | [+ **on/with**] *Early humans' first experiments with agriculture were failures.* | **perform/conduct/do an experiment** *Finnish scientists plan to conduct an experiment on gravity during the eclipse.* **2** a process in which you try a new idea, method etc. to find out if it is useful or effective: [+ **in**] *The Gallo Winery is trying an experiment in farming without using chemicals.*

ex·per·i·ment² /ɪkˈspɛrəˌmɛnt/ v. [I] **1** to try using various ideas, methods, materials etc. to find out how good or effective they are: [+ **with**] *Schools have experimented with desktop publishing in English classes.* **2** to do a scientific test to find out if a particular idea is true or to obtain more information: [+ **on**] *The research involves experiments on mice and guinea pigs.* **3** to use an illegal drug to find out what it feels like: [+ **with**] *Several politicians admitted experimenting with marijuana.* —**experimenter** n. [C]

ex·per·i·men·tal /ɪkˌspɛrəˈmɛntəl/ adj. **1** used for, relating to, or resulting from experiments: *an experimental drug* | *experimental research* **2** using new ideas or methods: *an experimental theater group* —**experimentally** adv.

ex·per·i·men·ta·tion /ɪkˌspɛrəmɛnˈteɪʃən/ n. [U] **1** the process of testing various ideas, methods, materials etc. to find out how good or effective they are: [+ **with/in**] *Experimentation in health-care reform should be left to each state.* **2** the process of performing scientific tests to find out if a particular idea is true or to obtain more information: [+ **on**] *medical experimentation on cats* **3** [+ **with**] the use of an illegal drug to find out what it feels like

ex·pert¹ /ˈɛkspɚt/ n. [C] someone who has a special skill or special knowledge of a subject, gained as a result of training or experience: [+ **on/in**] *He's an expert on ancient Egyptian art.* | [+ **at**] *Mrs. Taus became an expert at making desserts.*

expert² adj. **1** having a special skill or special knowledge of a subject: *an expert watchmaker* **2** relating to or coming from an expert: *expert advice* —**expertly** adv. —**expertness** n. [U]

ex·per·tise /ˌɛkspɚˈtiz/ n. [U] special skills or knowledge in a particular subject, that you learn by experience or training: *the expertise of trained teachers* | [+ **in**] *He has expertise in the biotechnology industry.*

expert sys·tem /ˌ.. ˈ../ n. [C] a computer system containing a lot of information about one particular subject, so that it can help someone find an answer to a problem

expert wit·ness /ˌ.. ˈ../ n. [C] someone with special knowledge about a subject who is asked to give their opinion about something relating to that subject in a court of law

ex·pi·ate /'ɛkspi,eɪt/ v. [I,T] FORMAL to do something to show that you are sorry and to improve the situation after you have done something wrong: *He spent the rest of his life trying to expiate for his sins.* —**expiation** /,ɛkspi'eɪʃən/ n. [U]

ex·pi·ra·tion /,ɛkspə'reɪʃən/ n. [U] the end of a period of time during which an official document or agreement is allowed to be used: *the expiration of the treaty*

expiration date /..'.. ,./ n. [C] the date after which something is not safe to eat or cannot be used or sold anymore: *Write in the credit card number and the expiration date.*

ex·pire /ɪk'spaɪr/ v. [I] **1** if a document, agreement, contract etc. expires, it cannot be legally used anymore: [+ on/at/in] | *My driver's license expires on October 12.* **2** if a period of time when someone has a particular authority expires, it ends: *The chairman's term of office expires at the end of March.* **3** LITERARY to die **4** FORMAL to breathe out air

s w **ex·plain** /ɪk'spleɪn/ v. **1** [T] to describe something in a way that makes it clear or easier to understand: [explain sth to sb] *Could you explain the rules to me again?* | [explain why/how/what etc.] *The guide explains how to identify edible mushrooms.* | [explain to sb why/how/what etc.] *The book explains to buyers how to get the best home loan.* | [explain that] *The doctor explained that my ear problem was related to my sinuses.* **2** [I,T] to give a reason for something, or to be a reason for it: *Wait! I can explain.* | [explain sth (to sb)] *There wasn't even an announcement to explain the delay.* | [explain why/how/what etc.] *He was obviously drunk, which explains why he was acting strangely.* | [explain that] *Marta explained that the bus had broken down, which was why she was late.* **3 explain yourself a)** to tell someone who is angry or upset with you the reasons why you did something: *John doesn't make excuses or explain himself to anybody.* **b)** to say clearly what you mean: *No, that's not what I meant. I guess I didn't explain myself very well.*

explain sth ↔ **away** phr. v. [T] to make something seem less important, or not your fault, by giving reasons for it: *Children will often try to explain away bruises caused by abuse.*

s w **ex·pla·na·tion** /,ɛksplə'neɪʃən/ n. **1** [C,U] the reasons you give for why something happened or why you did something: *Coach Green wasn't willing to accept his explanation.* | [+ for] *a scientific explanation for the change* | [+ of] *The report gave a technical explanation of the accident.* | **give/provide an explanation** *The terrorists gave no explanation for the killing.* —see Usage Note at EXCUSE[2] **2** [C] what you say or write to make something easier to understand: [+ of] *Ms. White gave the kids an explanation of how butter was made.*

ex·plan·a·to·ry /ɪk'splænə,tɔri/ adj. giving information about something or describing how something works, in order to make it easier to understand: *The information desk has maps and explanatory pamphlets.* —see also SELF-EXPLANATORY

ex·ple·tive /'ɛksplətɪv/ n. [C] FORMAL a strong impolite word that you use when you are angry or in pain, for example "DAMN"

ex·pli·ca·ble /ɪk'splɪkəbəl, 'ɛksplɪ-/ adj. [often in negatives] able to be easily understood or explained —opposite INEXPLICABLE

ex·pli·cate /'ɛksplə,keɪt/ v. [T] FORMAL to explain a work of literature, an idea etc. in detail: *explicating a poem* —**explication** /,ɛksplə'keɪʃən/ n. [C,U]

ex·plic·it /ɪk'splɪsɪt/ adj. **1** language or pictures that are explicit describe or show sex or violence very clearly: *There are several very explicit love scenes in the movie.* **2** expressed in a way that is very clear: *A health inspector gave explicit instructions on how to correct the problem.* **3 be explicit** to say something very clearly and directly: *Be explicit when you talk about money with your family.* | [+ about] *Angela was very explicit about her reasons for wanting a*

divorce. —compare IMPLICIT —**explicitly** adv. —**explicitness** n. [U]

s w **ex·plode** /ɪk'sploud/ v. **1** **burst** [I,T] to burst into small pieces, usually making a loud noise and causing damage, or to make something do this: *In 1949 the USSR exploded its first atomic bomb.* | *Firefighters were called when a gas tank exploded in the back yard of a home on Clayton Road.* —compare IMPLODE

2 **increase suddenly** [I] to suddenly increase greatly in number, amount, or degree: *Florida's population exploded after World War II.* | *"Country music's popularity has exploded," says Billy Dean.*

3 **get angry** [I] to suddenly become angry: *"Damn it!" Bill exploded. "Don't push me, Harry."*

4 **become dangerous** [I] if a situation explodes, it is suddenly not controlled anymore, and is often violent: *A fight exploded at the roller-skating rink last Friday.* | [+ in/with/into] *The student protests exploded into a violent revolution that toppled the government.*

5 explode the myth to prove that something which is believed by many people is actually wrong or not true: *The report explodes the myth that pollution is only a problem for rich countries.*

6 **make a loud noise** [I] to make a very loud noise: *A clap of thunder exploded overhead.* | [+ into] *The entire room exploded into applause.*

7 **do sth suddenly** [I] to suddenly begin moving or doing something very quickly: [+ into] *The audience exploded into laughter.*

exploded view /.,.. './ n. [C] TECHNICAL a drawing, model etc. that shows the parts of something separately, but in a way that shows how they are related or put together

ex·ploit[1] /ɪk'sploɪt/ v. [T] **1** to treat someone unfairly in order to earn money or gain an advantage: *The factory's largely Hispanic workforce is underpaid and exploited.* **2** to use something such as materials or skills effectively or completely in order to gain an advantage or profit: *We need to do a better job of exploiting our natural resources.* | *Christmas has been exploited for commercial reasons.* —**exploitable** adj. —**exploiter** n. [C]

ex·ploit[2] /'ɛksploɪt/ n. [C usually plural] a brave, exciting, and interesting action: *Kids will love these stories about Annie Oakley's exploits.*

ex·ploi·ta·tion /,ɛksploɪ'teɪʃən/ n. [U] **1** a situation in which someone treats someone else unfairly in order to earn money or gain an advantage: *The company was fined for the exploitation of its immigrant workers.* **2** a process in which something such as materials or skills are used effectively or completely in order to gain an advantage or profit: *They are working to control the exploitation of the rain forests.*

ex·ploit·a·tive /ɪk'sploɪtətɪv/ adj. treating people unfairly to earn money or gain an advantage: *a sexually exploitative movie*

ex·plo·ra·tion /,ɛksplə'reɪʃən/ n. **1 a)** [U] the process of trying to find out what something is like or to find something you are looking for: *oil exploration* | [+ of] *the exploration of Mars by robot* **b)** [C] a trip that is made in order to do this: *In explorations of the Japan Sea, scientists examined the sea bottom.* **2** [C,U] the act of trying to find out more about something by discussing it, thinking about it etc.: [+ of/into] *an exploration of spiritual issues*

ex·plo·ra·to·ry /ɪk'splɔrə,tɔri/ adj. done in order to find out more about something: *Watkins will have exploratory surgery on his knee.*

ex·plore /ɪk'splɔr/ v. **1** [I,T] to travel around an unfamiliar area to find out what it is like: *We spent a week exploring the Oregon coastline.* **2** [T] to discuss, examine, or think about something carefully: *James plans to explore offers from other companies before making a decision.*

ex·plor·er /ɪk'splɔrə/ n. [C] someone who travels through an area about which little is known or which has not been visited before

ex·plo·sion /ɪk'splouʒən/ n. **1** [C,U] the action of something exploding, or the act of making something explode: *a nuclear explosion* | [+ of] *The* explosion of the space shuttle *Challenger* shocked the nation. **2** [C] a sudden or quick increase in the number or amount of something: [+ **of**] *During the past three years there has been an explosion of interest in Latin music and dance.* | *Rabbits and ducks have been contributing to a population explosion in the park.* **3** [C] a sudden increase in anger, violence, disagreement etc.: *An explosion of conflict last month left at least six people dead in the town.* **4** [C] a sudden very loud noise: *an explosion of laughter*

ex·plo·sive[1] /ɪkˈsploʊsɪv/ *adj.* **1** able or likely to explode: *Dynamite is **highly explosive**.* | *an explosive device* (=that can explode or make a bomb explode) **2** likely to suddenly become violent: *Overcrowding and lack of jobs in the area have created an explosive situation.* | *a man with an explosive temper* **3** able to make people argue and become angry: *the explosive issue of abortion* | *The paper's editors knew they had an explosive story.* **4** increasing suddenly or quickly in amount, number, or degree: *the explosive growth of the computer industry* **5** relating to or like an explosion: *an explosive force of 15,000 tons of TNT* | *an explosive sound* —**explosively** *adv.* —**explosiveness** *n.* [U]

explosive[2] *n.* [C] a substance that can cause an explosion —see also HIGH EXPLOSIVE, PLASTIC EXPLOSIVE

ex·po /ˈɛkspoʊ/ *n.* [C] INFORMAL an EXPOSITION (1)

ex·po·nent /ɪkˈspoʊnənt, ˈɛkspoʊ-/ *n.* [C] **1** someone who supports or explains an idea, belief etc.: [+ **of**] *the world's leading exponent of yoga* —compare PROPONENT **2** TECHNICAL a sign written above and to the right of a number or letter to show how many times that quantity is to be multiplied by itself, for example 2^2 **3** someone whose work or methods provide a good example of a particular skill, idea, or activity: [+ **of**] *The poet Goethe is a supreme exponent of the Romantic response to nature.*

ex·po·nen·tial /ˌɛkspəˈnɛnʃəl/ *adj.* TECHNICAL **1 exponential growth/increase** a rate of growth that becomes faster as the amount of the thing that is growing increases **2** using a sign that shows how many times a number is to be multiplied by itself, such as y^3 —**exponentially** *adv.*

w **ex·port**[1] /ˈɛkspɔrt/ *n.* **1** [U] the business of selling and sending goods to other countries: *An international agreement restricts the export of missiles.* | *Mexico is California's third largest **export market**.* **2** [C] a product that is sold and sent to another country: *Wheat is one of our country's chief exports.* —opposite IMPORT[1]

ex·port[2] /ɛkˈspɔrt, ˈɛkspɔrt/ *v.* **1** [I,T] to sell and send goods to another country: [**export sth to sb**] *The U.S. hopes to export more cars to Asia next year.* **2** [T] to introduce an activity, idea etc. to another place or country: *The influence of African music has been exported to many parts of the western world.* **3** [T] TECHNICAL to move computer information from a computer you are working on to another one, or from a computer document you are working on to another one —opposite IMPORT[2] —**exportation** /ˌɛkspɔrˈteɪʃən/ *n.* [U]

ex·port·er /ɪkˈspɔrtɚ, ˈɛkspɔrtɚ/ *n.* [C] a person, company, or country that sells and sends goods to another country —compare IMPORTER

w **ex·pose** /ɪkˈspoʊz/ *v.* [T]
1 **put in danger** to put someone or something in a situation or position that could be harmful or dangerous, without any protection against what may happen: [**expose sb to sth**] *The test will tell you if you've been exposed to the virus.* | [**expose sth to sth**] *Horses' shoes break up the trails and leave them exposed to erosion.*
2 **show** to uncover or show something that is usually covered or not able to be seen: *The boy lifted his T-shirt to expose a jagged scar across his belly.* | [**expose sth to sth**] *Flowers will develop only if the plants are exposed to sunlight daily.*
3 **let sb experience sth** to make it possible for someone to experience ideas, events, methods etc. that are new to them: [**expose sb to sth**] *Children often aren't exposed to classical music.*
4 **tell the truth** to tell people the truth about an event or situation that is not acceptable, especially because it involves something dishonest or illegal:

Two reporters exposed corruption in Philadelphia's court system. | [**expose sb as sth**] *Guillaume was exposed as an East German spy.*
5 **expose yourself** if a man exposes himself, he deliberately shows his sexual organs to someone in a public place, usually because he is mentally ill
6 **make a photograph** to allow light onto a piece of film in a camera in order to take a photograph
7 **show feelings** to show other people feelings that you usually hide, especially when this is not planned: *I'm afraid to expose my innermost thoughts and emotions to anyone.* —see also EXPOSURE

ex·po·sé /ˌɛkspoʊˈzeɪ/ *n.* [C] a television program, newspaper story, or movie that tells people the truth about an event or situation in which someone did something dishonest or illegal: [+ **of**] *"Through the Wire" is an exposé of human rights abuses in the U.S. prison system.*

ex·posed /ɪkˈspoʊzd/ *adj.* not covered or protected from harm or danger: *Exposed areas, such as the nose, ears, and fingers, are more likely to get frostbite.*

ex·po·si·tion /ˌɛkspəˈzɪʃən/ *n.* **1** [C] a large public event at which you show or sell products, art etc.: *the Southwestern Exposition and Rodeo* **2** [C,U] the act of giving a clear and detailed explanation, or the explanation itself: *a professor of Bible exposition*

ex post fac·to law /ˌɛks poʊst ˌfæktoʊ ˈlɔ/ *n.* [C] LAW a law that makes a particular action into a crime, and then punishes people who took that action before it had legally become a crime

ex·pos·tu·late /ɪkˈspɑstʃəleɪt/ *v.* [I] FORMAL to say something angrily because you do not agree with something, disapprove of it, or are not satisfied with it

ex·po·sure /ɪkˈspoʊʒɚ/ *n.*
1 **danger** [C,U] the state of being put into a harmful or bad situation or position without having any protection against what may happen: *radiation exposure* | [+ **to**] *Skin cancer is often caused by too much exposure to the sun.*
2 **experience** [C,U] the opportunity to experience ideas, events, methods etc. that are new to you: [+ **to**] *Exposure to a second language should take place in elementary school.*
3 **truth** [C,U] the action of telling people about a dishonest person, event, or situation: [+ **of**] *The paper won an award for its exposure of the scandal in the Oakland school district.*
4 **public attention** [U] things that are said and written on television and in newspapers that make a person or event known to a lot of people: *The convention brought money and media exposure to this small city.* | *Doing an exercise video is one way of getting exposure.*
5 **photography** **a)** [C] a length of film in a camera that is used for producing one photograph: *a roll of 36-exposure film* (=that has enough space for 36 photographs to be taken) **b)** [C] the amount of time a piece of film is EXPOSEd to the light when making a photograph: *a timed exposure*
6 **effect of cold weather** [U] the harmful effects on your body that happen when you stay outside for a long time when the weather is extremely cold: *Three climbers died of exposure in the Himalayas this weekend.*
7 **direction** [C usually singular] the direction in which a building, hill etc. faces: *a window with a southern exposure*
8 **show** [C + **of**] the act of exposing or showing something that is usually covered or unable to be seen
9 **business risk** [C,U] the amount of financial risk that a company has: [+ **to**] *California and Idaho limit an owner's or manufacturer's exposure to damages.* —see also INDECENT EXPOSURE

ex·pound /ɪkˈspaʊnd/ *v.* [I,T] FORMAL to explain or talk about something in detail: [+ **on/upon**] *texts that expound on Jewish beliefs*

s w **ex·press¹** /ɪkˈsprɛs/ v. [T] **1** to tell or show what you are thinking or feeling by using words, actions, looks etc.: *She doesn't express her emotions as much as he does.* | [express sth in/by/through sth] *Your father may be expressing his wish to die by refusing to eat.* | *It's hard sometimes for children to* **express themselves** (=say what they think or feel). | **express your views/opinions** *Even people who knew little about the subject were ready to express their opinions.* | *She expressed an interest in seeing the old map.* | **express gratitude/thanks for sth** *Hector expressed his thanks for the help the community had given his family.* | **Words cannot express** (=it is impossible to describe) *how much we miss her.* **2 sth expresses itself** if a feeling expresses itself, it becomes noticeable: *Sometimes public outrage expresses itself in extreme ways.* **3** to show or describe a particular feeling: *Many of Munch's paintings express a deep feeling of despair.* **4** TECHNICAL to show a mathematical idea in a particular form: *Express three-quarters as a decimal.* **5** if a woman expresses milk, she presses milk out of her breast in order to feed it to her baby later

express² adj. [only before noun] **1** designed to help you move through a place more quickly: *express lanes on the freeway* | *an express line at the supermarket* (=where people with few things to buy can buy them more quickly) **2** sent more quickly than usual: *an express package* **3 express train/bus** a train or bus that does not stop in many places and therefore can travel more quickly —compare **local train/bus** (LOCAL¹ (2)) **4** an express command, desire, aim etc. is very clear and very specific, so that everyone understands exactly what it means: *It was her express wish that you inherit her house.*

express³ n. **1** [C usually singular] a train or bus that does not stop in many places, and can therefore travel more quickly —compare LOCAL² (3) **2** [U] a service that delivers letters and packages very quickly: *We'll send it by express.* —see also EXPRESS MAIL

express⁴ adv. **send/deliver sth express** to send or deliver a letter, package etc. quickly using a special mail service

s w **ex·pres·sion** /ɪkˈsprɛʃən/ n.
1 a look [C] a look on someone's face that shows what they are thinking or feeling: *Each of the statues has a different facial expression.* | [+ of] *an expression of contentment*
2 words/actions etc. [C,U] something you say, write, do, or make that shows what you think or feel: [+ of] *Crying is an acceptable and healthy expression of grief.* | *Student leaders also have demanded greater* **freedom of expression** (=the right to say what you think without being punished). | **political/artistic/religious expression** *All forms of religious expression are protected by the First Amendment.* | *The film* **gave expression to** *the way many people in her community felt.*
3 a word/phrase [C] a word or phrase that is used to express a particular idea or feeling: *You use the expression "break a leg" to wish an actor good luck.* | *Knight was a quiet man whose favorite expression was "shucks."*
4 music [U] the quality of singing or playing a musical instrument with feeling: *Try to put a little more expression into the slow passage.*
5 mathematics [C] TECHNICAL a sign or group of signs that show a mathematical idea in a particular form: $x^2 + 4$ *is an algebraic expression.*
6 pardon/forgive/excuse the expression SPOKEN said when you have used a word that you think may offend someone: *She's kind of a bitch, if you'll pardon the expression.*

ex·pres·sion·ism /ɪkˈsprɛʃəˌnɪzəm/ n. [U] a style of art and literature that uses unusual images, colors, and forms to emphasize feelings, rather than showing images or telling stories in a traditional way —**expressionist** n. [C] —**expressionist** adj.

ex·pres·sion·less /ɪkˈsprɛʃənlɪs/ adj. an expressionless face, feature, or voice does not show what someone thinks or feels: *dark expressionless eyes* —**expressionlessly** adv.

ex·pres·sive /ɪkˈsprɛsɪv/ adj. **1** showing what someone thinks or feels: *Achuff's dancing is versatile and expressive.* | *She has large, expressive eyes.* **2 be expressive of sth** showing a particular feeling or influence: *Art deco designs are expressive of the modern technology of the 1920s.* —**expressiveness** n. [U] —**expressively** adv.

ex·press·ly /ɪkˈsprɛsli/ adv. FORMAL **1** in a detailed or exact way: *Congress had* **expressly forbidden** *sending arms to Iran.* **2** for a specific purpose: *Three songs were written expressly for the movie version of "Show Boat".*

express mail /ˈ. ./ n. [U] a mail service that delivers letters and packages very quickly

ex·press·way /ɪkˈsprɛsˌweɪ/ n. [C] a wide road in a city on which cars can travel very quickly without stopping —see also FREEWAY

ex·pro·pri·ate /ɛksˈproʊpriˌeɪt/ v. [T] FORMAL to take away someone's private property, especially for public use: *The police station is in a private home that the Communists expropriated in 1948.* —**expropriation** /ɛksˌproʊpriˈeɪʃən/ n. [C, U]

ex·pul·sion /ɪkˈspʌlʃən/ n. [C,U] FORMAL **1** the official act of making someone leave a country, school, organization etc.: [+ from] *All the students responsible for the prank face expulsion from school.* **2** the process of sending a person or group of people away from a place, often by using force: [+ from] *the expulsion of rebel forces from the area* **3** the act of forcing air, water, or gas out of something: [+ from] *the expulsion of air from the lungs* —see also EXPEL

ex·punge /ɪkˈspʌndʒ/ v. [T] FORMAL **1** to remove something such as a name or piece of information from a list, book etc.: *Their criminal records were expunged in return for their testimony.* **2** to forget something bad: [expunge sth from sth] *Howard tried to expunge the whole episode from his memory.*

ex·pur·gat·ed /ˈɛkspəˌɡeɪtɪd/ adj. FORMAL an expurgated book, play etc. has had some parts removed because they are considered harmful or offensive: *an expurgated version of "A Streetcar Named Desire"* —**expurgate** v. [T] —compare ABRIDGED —opposite UNEXPURGATED

ex·quis·ite /ɪkˈskwɪzɪt, ˈɛkskwɪ-/ adj. **1** extremely beautiful or delicate, and seeming to be perfect: *an exquisite piece of jewelry* | *Dessert at Bellino's was exquisite.* **2** very sensitive and nearly perfect in the way you do things, or showing this: *She has exquisite taste.* | *Miller is an exquisite dancer.* **3** LITERARY exquisite pain or pleasure is felt extremely strongly —**exquisitely** adv. —**exquisiteness** n. [U]

ext. n. the written abbreviation of EXTENSION (2)

ex·tant /ˈɛkstənt, ɛkˈstænt/ adj. FORMAL still existing in spite of being very old: *This is one of the few extant manuscripts.*

ex·tem·po·ra·ne·ous /ɪkˌstɛmpəˈreɪniəs, ɛk-/ adj. spoken or done without any preparation or practice: *an extemporaneous speech* —**extemporaneously** adv.

ex·tem·po·re /ɪkˈstɛmpəri/ adj. FORMAL spoken or done without any preparation or practice: *His remarks were extempore and may need to be qualified.* —**extempore** adv.

ex·tem·po·rize /ɪkˈstɛmpəˌraɪz/ v. [I] FORMAL to speak without preparation, especially during a performance; AD-LIB —**extemporization** /ɪkˌstɛmpərəˈzeɪʃən/ n. [C,U]

ex·tend /ɪkˈstɛnd/ v. **s w**
1 affect more than before [T] to make something affect more people, situations, areas etc. than before: *Derkin vows to fight any effort to extend sales taxes on food.* | [extend sth to sb/sth] *The group was unable to agree on a way to extend insurance coverage to all Americans.*
2 continue longer [I always + adv./prep.,T] to continue to happen or exist for a longer period of time than planned or expected, or to make something do this: *The stock market headed lower today, extending*

its month-long decline. | **[extend sth for/ by/until etc.]** *The deadline has been extended till next Monday.* | **[+ for/into/over etc.]** *The hot weather extended into late September.*

3 reach/spread [I always + adv./prep.] to reach a particular distance, or spread over a particular area: **[+ across/over/through etc.]** *The plantation extends across 7,500 acres along the Georgia-Florida border.* | **extend 5 inches/six feet/40 miles etc. from sth** *The shelf extends six inches from the wall.* | *The business area extends about nine miles from the center of town.*

4 affect/include [I always + adv./prep.] to affect or include people, things, or places **[+ to/beyond/over etc.]** *His influence extends far beyond the company where he works.*

5 offer/give [T] FORMAL to offer or give help, sympathy, thanks etc. to someone: *We'd like to extend a warm welcome to our Mongolian visitors.* | *A German bank has extended credit to the city for most of the cost of the project* (=has allowed it to borrow money).

6 continue winning [T] to increase the number of points, games etc. by which one person or team is ahead of other competitors: **[extend sth to/by sth]** *The Titans will attempt to extend their winning streak to 23 games.*

7 arms/legs etc. [T] to stretch out a part of your body: *"Hello, Tom," he said, extending his hand.*

8 make sth bigger [T] to make a room, building, road etc. bigger or longer: *The developer plans to extend Thomas Road to meet Tenth Street.* —see also OVEREXTEND

ex·tend·ed /ɪkˈstɛndɪd/ *adj.* **extended period (of time)** a period of time that is fairly long, or longer than expected: *Some pills are designed to release medication over an extended period of time.*

extended fam·i·ly /.ˌ.. '../ *n.* [C] a family group that includes not only parents and children but also grandparents, AUNTS, UNCLES etc —compare NUCLEAR FAMILY

s w **ex·ten·sion** /ɪkˈstɛnʃən/ *n.*
3
1 more time [C] an act of making something continue longer than expected or planned, or an additional period of time that is given to do something: *Professor Lohman gave me a one-week extension on my paper.*

2 telephone **a)** [C] the set of additional numbers for a particular telephone line in a large building: *Hello, I'd like extension 2807, please.* **b)** [C] one of the telephones in a house that all have the same number

3 making sth bigger/longer [C,U] the process of making something bigger or longer, or the part that is added in this process: *The city is building an extension to the subway line.*

4 by extension used to say that something is true about one thing, because it is also true about another thing that is related to it: *Women lawyers, and by extension all professional women, looked for ways to balance family and work.*

5 affecting more [singular,U] the process of making something affect more people, situations, areas etc. than before, or a development that does this: **[+ of]** *What is needed is an extension of copyright laws to cover on-line materials.*

6 university/college [U] part of a university or college that offers courses to people who cannot come to classes at the usual time or place: *an extension course*

7 computer [C] TECHNICAL a set of letters that follow the name of a computer FILE to show what type of file it is. For example, the extension ".doc" shows that a file is a written document.

8 offering/giving [U] FORMAL the act of offering or giving something to someone: *the extension of credit to newer customers*

9 stretching an arm/leg etc. [U] the position of a part of the body when it is stretched, or the process of stretching it: *"I've been having some problems getting extension,"* Clark said about his elbow.

extension cord /.'.. ,./ *n.* [C] an additional electric CORD that you attach to another cord to make it longer

ex·ten·sive /ɪkˈstɛnsɪv/ *adj.* **1** containing a lot of

information, details, work etc.: *Adelman has done* s w *extensive research into the effects of stress.* **2** very large in size, amount, or degree: *Forests were* 3 *destroyed due to extensive logging.* —**extensively** *adv.*: *He read extensively on the subject.* —**extensiveness** *n.* [U]

ex·tent /ɪkˈstɛnt/ *n.* **1** [singular] the degree, size, or s w limit of something: **[+ of]** *There is disagreement* 3 3 *about the extent of American influence in Europe.* | *We were shocked by* **the full extent** *of the damage.* **2** **to such an extent that, to the extent that, to the extent of** used when saying that something is affected or influenced so much that something else happens: *The schools have deteriorated to such an extent that parents don't want to send their children to school.* | *We hope the connections have not been damaged to the extent that we cannot repair them.* **3** **to what extent, to that extent, to the extent that** used when talking about to what degree something is true: *To the extent that exercise can help people lose weight, it is a useful addition to medical treatment.* | *To what extent is your life more exciting since you fell in love* (=how much more exciting is it?)? **4** **to some extent, to a certain extent, to a large extent a)** used to say that something is partly but not completely true: *The divorce means that I am losing my wife and, to some extent, my children.* **b)** used to say that something will have an effect or influence on something, but will not change it completely: *Salinas' plan could weaken his party to some extent.* **5** [U] the size of a large area: *the extent of the palace grounds*

ex·ten·u·at·ing /ɪkˈstɛnuˌeɪtɪŋ/ *adj.* **extenuating circumstances** FORMAL facts about a situation which make a wrong or illegal action easier to understand or excuse: *I admit to running the red light, but there were* **extenuating circumstances**. —**extenuate** *v.* [T]

ex·te·ri·or¹ /ɪkˈstɪriɚ/ *n.* [C] **1** [usually singular] the appearance or outside surface of something: *the exterior of a house* **2** behavior that others see, but which often hides a different feeling or attitude: *Belle finds a sweet soul behind his gruff exterior.* **3** an outdoor scene in a picture, part of a movie etc. —opposite INTERIOR¹

exterior² *adj.* **1** on the outside or outside surface of something: *the car's sleek exterior design* **2** appropriate for use outside: *exterior paint* —opposite INTERIOR²

ex·ter·mi·nate /ɪkˈstɚməˌneɪt/ *v.* [T] to kill most or almost all members of a particular group of people, animals, or insects: *Ranchers systematically exterminated prairie dogs on their land.* —**extermination** /ɪkˌstɚməˈneɪʃən/ *n.* [C,U]

ex·ter·mi·na·tor /ɪkˈstɚməˌneɪtɚ/ *n.* [C] someone whose job is to kill insects or small animals that have been causing problems in people's houses or other buildings

ex·ter·nal /ɪkˈstɚnl/ *adj.* **1** coming from outside something such as an organization, group, or business: *Dickins has been resisting external pressure to resign as the head of the organization.* | *information from external sources* **2** relating to the outside of something: *This medicine is* **for external use only** (=to be used on the outside of the body and not swallowed). **3** relating to foreign countries: *external affairs* **4** **external ear/gill/genitals etc.** TECHNICAL a part of a person's or animal's body that is on the outer surface of the body rather than inside it —**externally** *adv.* —opposite INTERNAL

ex·ter·nal·ize /ɪkˈstɚnlˌaɪz/ *v.* [T] FORMAL to express your feelings in words or actions —**externalization** /ɪkˌstɚnl·əˈzeɪʃən/ *n.* [C,U]

ex·ter·nals /ɪkˈstɚnlz/ *n.* [plural] the way that a situation or thing appears to be, although this may not be true: *The religions are similar in essence, though they differ widely in externals.*

ex·tinct /ɪkˈstɪŋkt/ *adj.* **1** an extinct animal, plant, language etc. does not exist anymore: *Dinosaurs*

E

have been extinct for millions of years. **2** an extinct VOLCANO does not ERUPT anymore

ex·tinc·tion /ɪkˈstɪŋkʃən/ *n.* [U] the state of being extinct: *Greenpeace believes that whales are in danger of extinction.* | *Their traditional way of life seems doomed to extinction.*

ex·tin·guish /ɪkˈstɪŋgwɪʃ/ *v.* [T] FORMAL **1** to make a fire or light stop burning or shining: *Please extinguish all cigarettes.* **2** LITERARY to destroy an idea or feeling, or make it stop existing: *The news extinguished all hope of his return.* —see Usage Note at FIRE

ex·tin·guish·er /ɪkˈstɪŋgwɪʃə/ *n.* [C] INFORMAL a FIRE EXTINGUISHER

ex·tir·pate /ˈɛkstəˌpeɪt/ *v.* [T] FORMAL to completely destroy something that is bad or not wanted

ex·tol /ɪkˈstoʊl/ *v.* **extolled, extolling** [T] FORMAL to praise something very much: *Scott was **extolling the virtues of** being a vegetarian.*

ex·tort /ɪkˈstɔrt/ *v.* [T] to illegally force someone to give you money by threatening them: [**extort sth from sth**] *The police officers were actually extorting money from drug dealers.* —**extortion** /ɪkˈstɔrʃən/ *n.* [U] —**extortionist** *n.* [C]

ex·tor·tion·ate /ɪkˈstɔrʃənɪt/ also **ex·tor·tion·a·ry** /ɪkˈstɔrʃəˌnɛri/ *adj.* an extortionate price, demand etc. is extremely high or unfair: *an extortionate price for car insurance* —**extortionately** *adv.*

ex·tra¹ /ˈɛkstrə/ *adj.* more than the usual or standard amount of something, or more than you need: *a large mushroom pizza with extra cheese* | *I need some extra time to finish.* | *Will you bring me an extra napkin, please?*

extra² *adv.* **1 extra nice/special/hard etc.** SPOKEN, INFORMAL used with adjectives to mean "extremely": *If you're extra good, I'll buy you an ice cream cone.* **2 extra large/small** used in sizes to show that something is extremely large or small

extra³ *n.* [C] **1** something that is added to a basic product or service and that usually costs more: *a car with extras such as a sun roof and CD player* **2** an actor who is not a main character in a movie but who pretends to be part of a crowd in some scenes **3** something additional or helpful that you do, but that you are not paid for: *Shirley worked really hard and did a lot of little extras for the clients.* **4** a special EDITION of a newspaper containing important news: *Extra! Extra! Read all about it!*

extra⁴ *pron.* **1 cost/pay/charge etc. extra** to cost, pay etc. more money than the usual amount: *You have to pay extra if you want to fly first class.* | *It'll cost you a little extra.* | *Whipped cream is 50 cents extra.* **2** something additional of the same type: *So whose hamburger is this, or did I make extra?* *"Would you like some cough drops?" "Yeah, do you have extra?"*

extra- /ɛkstrə/ *prefix* outside of; BEYOND: *extracurricular activities* (=activities a student does in addition to their usual classes) | *extramarital sex* (=between people who are not married to each other)

ex·tract¹ /ɪkˈstrækt/ *v.* [T] **1** to remove an object from somewhere, especially by pulling it: *I'm having my wisdom teeth extracted.* | [**extract sth from sth**] *He uses pliers to extract the hook from the fish's mouth.* **2** to remove a substance from another substance which contains it, using a machine, chemical process etc.: [**extract sth from sth**] *The laboratories are able to extract DNA from bones and teeth.* **3** to make someone give you information, money etc. that they do not want to give: [**extract sth from sb**] *The police were unable to extract a confession from him.* **4 extract yourself from sth** to leave a place or situation that is difficult to leave: *The singer finally extracted himself from the crowd of admirers.* **5** to take a small part from a report, book, poem etc. to use as an example —**extractor** *n.* [C]

ex·tract² /ˈɛkstrækt/ *n.* **1** [C,U] a substance that is removed from a root, flower etc. by a special process:

vanilla extract **2** [C] a small part taken from a story, poem, song etc.: [**+ from**] *an extract from 'A Midsummer Night's Dream"*

ex·trac·tion /ɪkˈstrækʃən/ *n.* **1** [C,U] the process of removing an object or substance from something else: [**+ of**] *the extraction of coal and other natural resources* **2 be of German/Chinese/Indian etc. extraction** to be part of a family that comes from a particular country, although you were born in another country

ex·tra·cur·ric·u·lar /ˌɛkstrəkəˈrɪkyələ/ *adj.* extracurricular activities are sports or other activities that you do in addition to your usual classes

ex·tra·dit·a·ble /ˈɛkstrəˌdaɪtəbəl/ *adj.* FORMAL an extraditable crime is one for which someone can be sent back to the country or state where the crime happened, in order to be judged in a court of law

ex·tra·dite /ˈɛkstrəˌdaɪt/ *v.* [T] to use a legal process to send someone who may be guilty of a crime back to the country or state where the crime happened so that they can be judged in a court of law: [**extradite sb to/from**] *Drexel was arrested and extradited to Germany.* —**extradition** /ˌɛkstrəˈdɪʃən/ *n.* [C,U]

ex·tra·ju·di·cial /ˌɛkstrədʒuˈdɪʃəl/ *adj.* FORMAL beyond or outside the ordinary powers of the law

ex·tra·mar·i·tal /ˌɛkstrəˈmærətl◂/ *adj.* an extramarital sexual relationship is one that someone has with a person who is not their husband or wife

ex·tra·mu·ral /ˌɛkstrəˈmyʊrəl◂/ *adj.* **1** involving students from different schools: *extramural sports* —compare INTRAMURAL **2** happening or done outside of a particular place or organization, but relating or belonging to it: *the director of extramural research* (=research for a company that is done outside the company)

ex·tra·ne·ous /ɪkˈstreɪniəs/ *adj.* FORMAL **1** not important, or not directly related to a particular subject or problem; IRRELEVANT: *Her report contains too many extraneous details.* **2** coming from outside: *extraneous military forces*

ex·traor·di·naire /ɪkˌstrɔrdnˈɛr/ *adj.* [only after noun] able to do something very well: *a violin player extraordinaire*

ex·traor·di·nar·i·ly /ɪkˌstrɔrdnˈɛrəli/ *adv.* [+ adj./ adv.] in an unusual or surprising way; EXTREMELY: *She looks extraordinarily beautiful tonight.*

ex·traor·di·nar·y /ɪkˈstrɔrdnˌɛri/ *adj.* **1** extremely good, special, or impressive: *He's the most extraordinary man I've ever met.* | *The show's ratings were extraordinary – it was a huge success.* **2** very unusual or surprising: *According to Shafer, many people in high positions hold some extraordinary beliefs.* **3 extraordinary meeting/session etc.** FORMAL a meeting that takes place in addition to the usual ones **4 envoy/ambassador/minister extraordinary** an official who is employed for a special purpose, in addition to the usual officials

ex·trap·o·late /ɪkˈstræpəˌleɪt/ *v.* [I,T] **1** to use facts that you already know about a situation or group in order to make a guess about how true those facts are generally, or about what will happen in the future: [**extrapolate from sth to sth**] *The survey interviews members of 49,000 households and extrapolates from that to the entire nation.* **2** TECHNICAL to guess a value that you do not know by continuing a curve which is based on values that you already know —**extrapolation** /ɪkˌstræpəˈleɪʃən/ *n.* [C, U]

ex·tra·sen·so·ry per·cep·tion /ˌɛkstrəsɛnsəri pəˈsɛpʃən/ *n.* [U] ESP (1)

ex·tra·ter·res·tri·al¹ /ˌɛkstrətəˈrɛstriəl/ *n.* [C] a living creature that people think may live on another PLANET

extraterrestrial² *adj.* relating to things that do not come from Earth or do not exist or happen on Earth: *extraterrestrial exploration*

ex·tra·ter·ri·to·ri·al /ˌɛkstrəˌtɛrəˈtɔriəl/ *adj.* LAW extraterritorial rights, powers etc. are governed from outside a particular country or area: *an extraterritorial jurisdiction treaty* —**extraterritoriality** /ˌɛkstrəˌtɛrəˈtɔriˈæləti/ *n.* [U]

ex·trav·a·gant /ɪkˈstrævəgənt/ *adj.* **1** spending a lot of money on things that are not necessary: *Van Jong's personal life was notably extravagant.* **2** very impressive because something is very expensive, beautiful etc.: *The gifts, though not extravagant, were nice.* **3** ideas or behavior that are extravagant are too extreme and are not reasonable: *extravagant marketing claims* **4 extravagant with sth** using too much of something or wasting it —**extravagantly** *adv.* —**extravagance** *n.* [C,U]

ex·trav·a·gan·za /ɪkˌstrævəˈgænzə/ *n.* [C] an event or performance that is very large and impressive: *a fireworks extravaganza*

ex·tra·vert /ˈɛkstrəˌvət/ *n.* [C] another spelling of EXTROVERT

extra vir·gin ol·ive oil /ˌ.. .. ˈ.. ˌ./ *n.* [U] oil that is taken from OLIVES the first time they are pressed, without using any heat

ex·treme¹ /ɪkˈstrim/ *adj.* **1** [only before noun] very great in degree: *The refugees face a winter of extreme hardship.* | *extreme temperatures* **2** extreme opinions, beliefs, or organizations, especially political ones, are considered by most people to be very unusual and unreasonable: *The organization says they consider Kahane's views to be extreme.* | *extreme nationalists* **3 an extreme example/case** the strangest, most severe, or most unlikely possibility: *In extreme cases, insurance premiums may double.* | *an extreme example of child abuse* **4 extreme south/end/limits etc.** the extreme south etc. is the place furthest toward the south etc.

extreme² *n.* [C] **1** something that goes beyond normal limits, so that it seems very unusual or bad: *Seals are quite comfortable in* **the extremes** *of the Arctic climate.* | *Fans of car racing have* **taken** *their love of the sport* **to an extreme**. | *People were willing* **to go to extremes** (=do things that go beyond normal limits of behavior) *to prevent the prison from being built near their homes.* **2 in the extreme** to a very great degree: *Historians note that some Indian tribes were brutal in the extreme.*

s w 2 2 **ex·treme·ly** /ɪkˈstrimli/ *adv.* to a very great degree: *Quitting my old job was an extremely difficult decision.* —see Usage Note at ALMOST

extremely low fre·quen·cy /ˌ... . ˈ.../ *n.* [U] TECHNICAL: see ELF

extreme sport /.ˈ. ˌ./ *n.* [C usually plural] a sport such as ROCK CLIMBING or SNOWBOARDING that is new and dangerous

extreme unc·tion /ɪkˌstrim ˈʌŋkʃən/ *n.* [U] LAST RITES

ex·tre·mis /ɪkˈstrimɪs/ *n.* —see IN EXTREMIS

ex·trem·ism /ɪkˈstriˌmɪzəm/ *n.* [U] opinions, ideas, and actions, especially political or religious ones, that most people think are unusual and unreasonable

ex·trem·ist /ɪkˈstrimɪst/ *n.* [C] someone who has extreme political opinions and aims, and who is willing to do unusual or illegal things in order to achieve them: *right-wing political extremists* —**extremist** *adj.*

ex·trem·i·ty /ɪkˈstrɛməti/ *n. plural* **extremities 1** [C usually plural] one of the parts of your body that is furthest away from the center, for example your hands and feet **2** [U] the degree to which a belief, opinion, situation, or action goes beyond what is usually thought to be acceptable or usual: *The committee was uncomfortable about the extremity of the proposal.* **3** [C] the part that is furthest away from the center of something: *Alviso is a mostly Hispanic area in the city's northern extremity.*

ex·tri·cate /ˈɛkstrəˌkeɪt/ *v.* [T] **1** to remove someone or something from a place in which they are trapped: *It took firemen almost an hour to extricate the driver from the wrecked car.* **2** to escape from a difficult, embarrassing, bad etc. situation: [+ **from**] *Hasenfus spent more than $57,000 extricating her husband from jail.* | [**extricate yourself from sth**] *Fewer black women than white women manage to extricate themselves from low-paying jobs.* —**extrication** /ˌɛkstrəˈkeɪʃən/ *n.* [U]

ex·trin·sic /ɛkˈstrɪnzɪk/ *adj.* **1** on the outside of something, or coming from the outside: *Some teachers*

believe students need extrinsic rewards to motivate them to learn (=they need rewards such as money or gifts, instead of the reward of learning something). **2** not directly related to a particular subject or problem

ex·tro·vert /ˈɛkstrəˌvət/ *n.* [C] someone who is active and confident, and who enjoys being with other people: *Willie is a total extrovert who will talk to any stranger.* —**extrovert** *adj.* —opposite INTROVERT

ex·tro·vert·ed /ˈɛkstrəˌvətɪd/ *adj.* confident and enjoying being with other people: *Smokers are measurably more extroverted than non-smokers.* —**extroversion** /ˌɛkstrəˈvəʒən/ *n.* [U] —opposite INTROVERTED

ex·trude /ɪkˈstrud/ *v.* [T] FORMAL **1** to push or force something out through a hole **2** TECHNICAL to force plastic or metal through a hole so that it has a particular shape —**extrusion** /ɪkˈstruʒən/ *n.* [C,U]

ex·u·ber·ant /ɪgˈzubərənt/ *adj.* **1** happy and cheerful, and full of energy and excitement: *He is energetic and exuberant.* | *an exuberant celebration* **2** plants that are exuberant are healthy and growing very quickly —**exuberance** *n.* [U] —**exuberantly** *adv.*

ex·ude /ɪgˈzud, ɪkˈsud/ *v.* **1 exude confidence/enthusiasm etc.** if you exude a particular quality or feeling, it is easy to see that you have a lot of it or feel it strongly: *He exudes enough confidence for us both.* **2** [I,T] to flow out slowly and steadily, or to push a liquid out in this way: *Like all bamboo buds, the flowers exude no fragrance.*

ex·ult /ɪgˈzʌlt/ *v.* [I] FORMAL to show that you are very happy and proud, especially because you have succeeded in doing something: *"It was a great day,"* *Martin exulted.* | [+ **in/over/at**] *Republicans exulted in the election results.* —**exultation** /ˌɛksəlˈteɪʃən, ˌɛgzəl-/ *n.* [U]

ex·ul·tant /ɪgˈzʌltənt/ *adj.* FORMAL very happy or proud, especially because you have succeeded in doing something: *Crowds of exultant people waved flags and sang.* —**exultantly** *adv.*

-ey /i/ *suffix* [in adjectives] used to show that something has a particular quality: *gooey candy*

Eyck /aɪk/**, Jan van** /yɑn væn/ (?1390–1441) a Flemish PAINTER famous as the first important northern European painter of the early Renaissance, who painted pictures of people with bright colors and a lot of detail

eye¹ /aɪ/ *n.* [C]
1 body part one of the two parts of the body that you see with: *Elika has green eyes.* | *Close your eyes and go to sleep.* | *Her eyes were bright with happiness.* —see picture at BODY
2 keep an eye on sb/sth INFORMAL **a)** to carefully watch someone or something, especially because you do not trust them or you need to see what happens: *Clerks are keeping an eye on the groups of teenagers who come into their stores.* | *Firefighters kept a wary eye on the dry hills.* **b)** to take care of someone or something and make sure that they are safe: *Could you keep an eye on my luggage while I go the bathroom?* | *His parents should have kept a closer eye on the boy.* **c)** to carefully watch something, especially in order to do something with it: *Keep your eye on the ball and swing the bat evenly.*
3 in the eyes of the law/the world/the police etc. in the opinion or judgment of the law, the world, the police etc.: *Almost overnight he became a hero in the eyes of millions.*
4 lay/set eyes on sb/sth an expression meaning "to see someone or something," used especially when you are surprised or shocked: *The McCrackens loved the house from the moment they set eyes on it.*
5 eye contact if you have eye contact with someone, you look directly at them and they look directly at you: *I don't trust people who don't* **make eye contact** *with me.*
6 all eyes are on sb/sth, all eyes focus on sb/sth everyone is looking at or paying attention to something or someone: *The score was 3–3, and all eyes were on the batter.* | *All eyes were on the President during the recent crisis.*

that shows you find them sexually attractive: *Janet spent the whole evening making eyes at other men.*

29 an eye for an eye the idea that people should be punished by hurting them in the same way as they hurt someone else: *The government's eye-for-an-eye justice could lead to further human rights abuses.*

30 one eye on sth (and the other on sth) paying attention to one thing while you are also doing or watching something else: *Responsible companies should **keep one eye on** profits and the other on the environment.*

31 needle the hole in a needle that you put thread through

32 be all eyes to watch carefully what is happening or what someone is doing: *Five-year-old Ryan was all eyes during his first trip to the ballpark.*

33 eyes glued to sth if your eyes are glued to something, you watch it so carefully that you do not notice anything else: *Their eyes were glued to the news report on TV.*

34 take your eye off sth to stop watching something carefully: *Don't take your eye off the ball.*

35 potato a dark spot on a potato from which a new plant can grow

36 only have eyes for sb if someone only has eyes for someone else, they only love and are interested in that one person: *Mark only had eyes for his wife.*

37 (for your) eyes only said or written when something is secret and must only be seen by one particular person

38 storm the calm center of a storm, especially a HURRICANE or CYCLONE

39 clothing a small circle or U-shaped piece of metal used together with a hook for fastening clothes
—see also **be the apple of sb's eye** (APPLE (2)), **not bat an eye/eyelid** (BAT² (3)), BIRD'S-EYE VIEW, BLACK EYE, **turn a blind eye (to sth)** (BLIND¹ (2)), **catch sb's eye** (CATCH¹ (19)), **see sth out of the corner of your eye** (CORNER¹ (8)), **the evil eye** (EVIL¹ (4)), -EYED, **look sb in the eye/face** (LOOK¹ (14)), **there's more to sb/sth than meets the eye** (MEET¹ (12)), **in your mind's eye** (MIND¹ (43)), **here's mud in your eye** (MUD (4)), **open sb's eyes (to sth)** (OPEN² (8)), PRIVATE EYE, RED-EYE, **a sight for sore eyes** (SIGHT¹ (13)), SNAKE EYES, **in the twinkling of an eye** (TWINKLING (1)), **keep a weather eye on sth** (WEATHER¹ (5)), **pull the wool over sb's eyes** (WOOL (4))

eye² *v.* present participle **eyeing** or **eying** [T] to look at someone or something with interest, especially because you do not trust them or because you want something: *The dog sat there eyeing my sandwich as I ate.*

eye·ball¹ /ˈaɪbɔl/ *n.* [C] **1** the round ball that forms the whole of your eye, including the part inside your head **2 eyeball-to-eyeball** if two people are eyeball-to-eyeball, they are directly facing each other, especially in an angry or threatening way: *All of a sudden, I was eyeball-to-eyeball with a crocodile.*

eyeball² *v.* [T] **1** INFORMAL to look directly and closely at something, especially when you are thinking carefully about it: *They eyeballed us suspiciously before speaking.* **2** to guess the size, length etc. of something by just looking at it, without using any measuring tools

eye·brow /ˈaɪbraʊ/ *n.* [C] **1** the line of short hairs above your eye **2 raise your eyebrows** to move your eyebrows up in order to show surprise or disapproval **3 be up to your eyebrows in sth** SPOKEN to have a lot of things to do or to deal with: *Stein is up to his eyebrows in debt.*

eyebrow pen·cil /ˈ.. ˌ../ *n.* [C,U] a special pencil you can use to make your eyebrows darker

eye can·dy /ˈ. ˌ../ *n.* [U] INFORMAL people or things that are very attractive and nice to look at, but do not make you think very hard: *It's one of those movies that is full of eye candy.*

eye-catch·ing /ˈ. ˌ../ *adj.* something eye-catching is unusual or attractive in a way that makes you notice it: *an eye-catching dress* —**eye-catchingly** *adv.*

-eyed /aɪd/ [in adjectives] **blue-eyed/one-eyed/bright-eyed etc.** having blue eyes, one eye, bright eyes etc.

---

7 keep an eye out for sth to watch something or look for something in order to notice or find it: *Art dealers are being asked to keep an eye out for the stolen paintings.*

8 with your eyes open knowing fully what the problems, difficulties, results etc. of a situation might be: *They went into the deal with their eyes open.*

9 have a (good) eye for sth to be good at noticing and recognizing what is attractive, valuable, of good quality etc.: *Greene has an eye for detail.*

10 cannot take your eyes off sb/sth to be unable to stop looking at someone or something, especially because they are very attractive or interesting: *She was so beautiful I simply couldn't take my eyes off her.*

11 the naked eye if you can see something with the naked eye, you can see it without using any artificial help such as a TELESCOPE or MICROSCOPE: *The comet will be visible to the naked eye.*

12 see eye to eye if two people or groups see eye to eye, they have the same opinions about something: *Lifland and his wife don't always see eye to eye.*

13 close/shut your eyes to sth to ignore something or pretend that you do not know it is happening: *We can't close our eyes to the fact that our town has a gang problem.*

14 with your eyes closed/shut easily and without any difficulty: *You could run that place with your eyes shut.*

15 have your eye on sth to have noticed something that you want to buy or have: *Rodrigues has his eye on the major leagues (=he wants to play professional baseball).* | *We have our eyes on a nice little house near the beach.*

16 have your eye on sb to notice someone, especially because you think they are attractive: *I've had my eye on my sister's roommate for a while.*

17 with an eye to/toward sth if you do something with an eye to something else, you do it in order that a second thing will happen: *Chavez become involved in city government with an eye to someday becoming a city manager.*

18 eye to eye if you are eye to eye with someone or something, they are not far away from you: *A lot of business people prefer doing business eye to eye.*

SPOKEN PHRASES

19 in front of/before your (very) eyes an expression meaning "happening in a way that is clear to see," used especially when what you see is surprising or shocking: *The Soviet Union fell apart before our eyes.*

20 sb has eyes bigger than their stomach, sb's eyes are bigger than their stomach said when you take more food than you are able to eat: *I can't finish this cake – my eyes are bigger than my stomach!*

21 keep your eyes open/peeled to watch or look carefully for something: *Keep your eyes peeled for bargains at the farmers' market.*

22 not be able to believe your eyes said when you see something very surprising: *I couldn't believe my eyes – there she was, stark naked!*

23 have eyes in the back of your head to know what is happening all around you, even when this might seem impossible: *You need to have eyes in the back of your head to be a teacher.*

24 have eyes like a hawk to notice every small detail or everything that is happening, and therefore to be difficult to deceive: *My mother had eyes like a hawk.*

25 my eye! OLD-FASHIONED said when you are surprised or when you think something is not true: *A diamond necklace my eye! That was glass!*

26 drop/lower your eyes to look down, especially because you are shy, embarrassed, or ashamed: *Suzanne dropped her eyes and blushed.*

27 eyes pop out (of your head) INFORMAL used when you are very surprised, excited, or shocked by something you see: *A few years ago, Grillo spotted a 16-year-old hockey player who made his eyes pop out.*

28 make eyes at sb to look at someone in a way

eye drops /'. ./ *n.* [plural] a special liquid that you put in your eyes when they feel dry or sore

eye·ful /'aɪfʊl/ *n.* [C] **1 get an eyeful** SPOKEN to see something shocking or surprising: *Two boys got an eyeful when a video labeled "Cinderella" turned out to be pornography.* **2** an amount of liquid, dust, or sand that has gone into someone's eye **3** OLD-FASHIONED something or someone, especially a woman, who is very attractive to look at: *Alyson is an eyeful, standing there in her miniskirt.*

eye·glass /'aɪglæs/ *n.* [C] **1** a MONOCLE **2** an EYEPIECE

eye·glass·es /'aɪ,glæsɪz/ *n.* [plural] a pair of glasses (GLASS (4))

eye·lash /'aɪlæʃ/ *n.* [C usually plural] **1** one of the small hairs that grow along the edge of your EYELIDS **2 flutter/bat your eyelashes** if a woman flutters her eyelashes, she moves them up and down very quickly, especially in order to look sexually attractive

eye·less /'aɪlɪs/ *adj.* having no eyes

eye·let /'aɪlɪt/ *n.* **1** [C] a hole surrounded by a metal ring, which is put in leather or cloth so that a string can be passed through it, especially in a shoe —see picture at SHOE[1] **2** [U] a type of cloth with small holes in it

eye lev·el /'. ,../ *n.* [singular] a height equal to the level of your eyes: *Pictures should be hung at eye level.*

eye·lid /'aɪ,lɪd/ *n.* [C] the two pieces of skin that cover your eye when it is closed —see also **not bat an eye/eyelid** (BAT[2] (3))

eye·lin·er /'aɪ,laɪnɚ/ *n.* [C,U] a colored substance that you put along the edges of your eyelids to make your eyes look bigger or more noticeable —see picture at MAKEUP

eyeliner pen·cil /'... ,../ *n.* [C,U] a type of pencil used for putting on eyeliner

eye-o·pen·er /'. ,.../ *n.* [C] a situation, event etc. from which you learn something surprising, or something that you did not know before: *A visit to a farm is an eye-opener to a city child.* —see also **open sb's eyes (to sth)** (OPEN[2] (8))

eye patch /'. ./ *n.* [C] a piece of material worn over one eye, usually because that eye has been damaged

eye·piece /'aɪpis/ *n.* [C] the glass piece that you look through in a MICROSCOPE or TELESCOPE

eye shad·ow /'. ,../ *n.* [C,U] a colored substance that you put on your eyes to make your eyes look more attractive —see picture at MAKEUP

eye·sight /'aɪsaɪt/ *n.* [U] your ability to see

eye·sore /'aɪsɔr/ *n.* [C] something that is very ugly, especially a building surrounded by other things that are not ugly: *Many residents consider the old house an eyesore.*

eye strain /'. ./ *n.* [U] a pain you feel in your eyes, for example because you are tired or have been reading a lot

eye tooth /'. ./ *n.* [C] **1** one of the long pointed teeth at the corner of your mouth; CANINE TOOTH **2 give your eye teeth for sth** SPOKEN used when you want something very much: *I'd give my eye teeth to be able to play the piano like her.*

eye·wit·ness /,aɪ'wɪtˈnɪs, 'aɪ,wɪtˈnɪs/ *n.* [C] someone who has seen something such as a crime happen, and is able to describe it later: *Sheriff's detectives had no eyewitnesses to the shootings.*

ey·ing /'aɪ-ɪŋ/ *v.* the present participle of EYE[2]

E·ze·ki·el /ɪ'zikiəl/ a book in the Old Testament of the Christian Bible

Ez·ra /'ɛzrə/ a book in the Old Testament of the Christian Bible

E

F

F, f /ɛf/ *n. plural* **F's, f's** **1** [C] the sixth letter of the English alphabet **2** [C,U] the fourth note in the SCALE¹ (9), or the musical KEY¹ (4) based on this note

f the written abbreviation of FORTE²

F¹ /ɛf/ *n.* a grade that a teacher gives to a student's work, showing that the student has failed: *Tony got an F in chemistry and has to take the class again over the summer.*

F² **1** the written abbreviation of FAHRENHEIT: *Water boils at 212°F.* **2** the written abbreviation of FEMALE **3** the written abbreviation of FALSE

fa /fɑ/ *n.* [singular] the fourth note in a musical SCALE according to the SOL-FA system

FAA —see FEDERAL AVIATION ADMINISTRATION, THE

fab /fæb/ *adj.* [no comparative] OLD-FASHIONED extremely good

Fa·ber·gé /ˌfæbəˈʒeɪ/, **Peter** (1846–1920) a Russian GOLDSMITH and JEWELER famous for making beautiful Easter eggs decorated with jewels for the Russian royal family

fa·ble /ˈfeɪbəl/ *n.* **1** [C] a traditional short story, often about animals, that teaches a moral lesson: *My favorite is the fable of the race between the tortoise and the hare.* **2** [U] such stories considered as a group: *monsters of fable and legend*

fa·bled /ˈfeɪbəld/ *adj.* [only before noun] famous and often mentioned in traditional stories: *Statues of fabled warriors stood in the city square.*

fab·ric /ˈfæbrɪk/ *n.* **1** [C,U] cloth used for making clothes, curtains etc.; MATERIAL¹ (1): *The company creates fabrics for jackets and coats.* | *special fabric for Christmas decorations* —see Usage Note at CLOTH **2** the fabric (of sth) the basic structure of a society, its way of life, and its relationships and traditions: *Freeman feared that welfare policies threatened the economic and social fabric of the nation.*

fab·ri·cate /ˈfæbrəˌkeɪt/ *v.* [T] **1** to invent a story, piece of information etc. in order to deceive someone: *Branson later admitted that he had fabricated the whole story.* **2** TECHNICAL to make or produce goods or equipment; MANUFACTURE¹ (1): *At their small workshop, they fabricate parts for jet engines.*

fab·ri·ca·tion /ˌfæbrɪˈkeɪʃən/ *n.* **1** [C,U] a piece of information or a story that someone has invented in order to deceive people; LIE: *A report about abuse at the school was found to be a fabrication.* **2** [U] TECHNICAL the process of making or producing something

fabric soft·en·er /ˈ.. ˌ.../ *n.* [C,U] a liquid that you put in water when washing clothes in order to make them feel softer

fab·u·lous /ˈfæbyələs/ *adj.* **1** extremely good or impressive: *You look fabulous!* | *That was really a fabulous meal.* **2** [only before noun] FORMAL unusually large: *The painting was sold for a fabulous sum.* **3** LITERARY [only before noun] fabulous creatures, places etc. are mentioned in traditional stories, but do not really exist

fab·u·lous·ly /ˈfæbyələsli/ *adv.* **fabulously expensive/rich/successful etc.** extremely expensive, rich, successful etc.

fa·cade, façade /fəˈsɑd/ *n.* **1** [C usually singular] a way of behaving that hides your real feelings or character: *Behind her cheerful facade, she's really a lonely person.* **2** [C] the front of a building, especially a large and important one: *Work is underway to repair the Taj Mahal's marble facade.*

face¹ /feɪs/ *n.* [C]
1 front of your head the front part of your head, where your eyes, nose, and mouth are: *Jodi has such a pretty face.* | *One of the victims had scratches all over his face.* | *Uncle Gene had a surprised look on his face.* —see Usage Note at FRONT¹

2 expression an expression on someone's face: *I could see the children's happy faces.* | *Matt, stop making faces at your sister* (=making expressions with his face to annoy her or make her laugh). | *You should have seen his face* (=used to say how angry, surprised etc. someone looked) *when I told him I was leaving the company.* | *Joan's face brightened* (=she started to smile and look happy) *when I told her how much I liked her painting.* | *The kids' faces lit up* (=they started to smile and look happy) *when they saw Santa Claus.* | *Darren's face fell* (=he started to look disappointed or upset) *when I told him about the test results.* | *Hey, Eddie, why the long face* (=unhappy or worried expression)?

3 person a) a new/different face someone who you have not seen before or not met yet: *There seem to be quite a few new faces in the department since I left.* b) a famous/well-known face someone who is famous from television, magazines, movies etc.

4 face to face a)** if two people are face to face, they are very close and in front of each other: *Actually, I've never met her face to face.* b) in a situation where you have to accept or deal with something bad: *It was the first time he'd ever come face to face with death.* —see also FACE-TO-FACE

5 in the face of sth** in a situation where there are many problems, difficulties, or dangers: *It is amazing how Daniels has survived in the face of such strong political opposition.*

6 lose face** to make other people lose their respect for you: *They want to negotiate a ceasefire without either side losing face.*

7 save face** if you do something to save face, you do it so that people will not lose their respect for you: *Rather than admit defeat, Franklin compromised in order to save face.*

8 mountain/cliff a steep, high side of a mountain, cliff etc.: *We climbed the north face of Mount Rainier.*

9 clock the front of a clock, where the numbers are

10 face down/downward with the face or front toward the ground: *The body was lying face down on the carpet.*

11 face up/upward with the face or front toward the sky: *She laid the cards out face upward.*

12 on the face of it** used to say that something seems true but that you think there may be other facts about it which are not yet clear: *It looks, on the face of it, like a pretty minor change in the regulations.*

13 say sth to sb's face** to say something to someone directly: *I'd never say it to her face, but her hair looks terrible.*

14 the face of sth a)** the way in which an organization, system etc. appears to people: *Roosevelt's bold policies changed the face of the nation.* b) the general appearance of a particular place: *It's a new book about the changing face of the suburbs.*

15 outside surface one of the outside surfaces of an object or building: *A cube has six faces.*

16 the face of the Earth a)** the outside part of the Earth: *It's one of the last unexplored places on the face of the Earth.* b) used to emphasize that something affects everyone on Earth, or that it is the best, worst etc. that anyone knows about or has done: *It's the greatest adventure on the face of the Earth.* | *The polio vaccine lifted a terrible curse from the face of this Earth.*

17 in your face** SLANG behavior, remarks etc. that are in your face are very direct and often make people feel shocked or surprised: *Bingham has a real "in your face" writing style.*

18 get in sb's face** SPOKEN to annoy someone and try to tell them what to do

19 sports the part of a RACKET, GOLF CLUB etc. that you use to hit the ball

20 get out of my face** SPOKEN used to tell someone in an impolite way to go away because they are annoying you

21 blow up in sb's face** if a situation blows up in your face, it goes badly, especially in an embarrassing way: *It was kind of funny watching the presentation blow up in Harry's face.*

22 disappear/vanish from the face of the Earth INFORMAL used to say that you do not know where someone is because you have not seen them in a long time: *It was like the woman vanished from the face of the Earth for 19 years.*

23 put a brave face (on) to make an effort to behave in a happy cheerful way when you are upset or disappointed: *Although he was disappointed, Frank still managed to put on a brave face.*

24 put your face on INFORMAL to put MAKEUP on: *Jill's still busy putting on her face.*

25 mine the part of a mine from which coal, stone etc. is cut —see also **do sth till you're blue in the face** (BLUE[1] (3)), **have egg on your face** (EGG[1] (5)), -FACED, **fly in the face of sth** (FLY[1] (19)), **laugh in sb's face** (LAUGH[1] (6)), **not just another/a pretty face** (PRETTY[2] (5)), **show your face** (SHOW[1] (18)), **shut your mouth/trap/face!** (SHUT (2)), **a slap in the face** (SLAP[2] (2)), **be staring sb in the face** (STARE[1] (2)), **a straight face** (STRAIGHT[2] (5)), WHAT'S-HER-FACE, WHAT'S-HIS-FACE, **wipe the smile/grin off sb's face** (WIPE[1] (4)), **have sth written all over your face** (WRITE (5))

face[2] *v.* [T]
1 difficult situation if you face a difficult situation or if it faces you, you must deal with it: *Weber is facing the biggest challenge of his career.* | *If found guilty, Jones could face up to 20 years in jail.* | *The city council is faced with* (=is in a situation where they have to deal with) *the task of making budget cuts.*

2 admit a problem exists to accept that a difficult situation or problem exists, even though you would prefer to ignore it: *We have to face the fact that we'll be playing teams that are better than we are.* | *Let's face it, people change.* | *Arts groups don't like the funding cuts, but they have to face facts.* | *He had to face the awful truth that there was no cure for the disease.*

3 can't face sth if you cannot face something, you feel unable to do it because it seems too bad or difficult: *I don't want to go back to school again – I just can't face it.* | [can't face doing sth] *Mr. MacArthur can't face selling the store.*

4 point in a particular direction to be turned or pointed in a particular direction or toward someone or something: *Dean turned to face me.* | *My house faces the bay.* | **face east/north/up/down etc.** *The bedroom window faces west.*

5 opponent/team to be in a position in which you are going to play against an opponent or team in a game or competition: *The Jets face the Dolphins in two weeks.*

6 difficult person to deal with someone who is difficult to deal with, or talk to someone who you do not want to talk to: *You're going to have to face her sooner or later.*

7 face the music INFORMAL to accept criticism or punishment for something you have done

8 be faced with stone/concrete etc. a building that is faced with stone, CONCRETE etc. is built with it on its outside surface

face sb ↔ **down** *phr. v.* [T] to deal in a strong and confident way with someone who opposes you: *Harrison successfully faced down the mob of angry workers.*

face off *phr. v.* [I] to get in a position in which you are ready to fight, argue, or compete with someone: *The two candidates will face off in a televised debate on Friday.* —see also FACE-OFF (1)

face up to sth *phr. v.* [T] to accept and deal with a difficult fact or problem: *Kids need to face up to the consequences of their actions.*

face card /'. ./ *n.* [C] the king, queen, or JACK in a set of playing cards

-faced /feɪst/ [in adjectives] **1 pale-faced/round-faced/hawk-faced etc.** having a face that has a particular shape or color: *Police are looking for a wide-faced youth, about six feet tall.* —see also RED-FACED **2 grim-faced/sad-faced/solemn-faced etc.** showing a particular expression on your face: *happy-faced children* —see also BAREFACED, POKER-FACED, STONE-FACED, TWO-FACED

face·less /'feɪslɪs/ *adj.* a faceless person, organization etc. is boring, not easily noticed, or not known: *These victims should not remain faceless.* | *a faceless committee*

face·lift, face-lift /'feɪslɪft/ *n.* [C] **1** work or repairs that make something look newer or better: *The 57th Street auditorium is scheduled to be given a $10 million facelift.* **2** a medical operation in which doctors make loose skin tighter on someone's face in order to make them look younger: *Roberts denied that she has had a face-lift.*

face-off /'. ./ *n.* [C] **1** INFORMAL a fight or argument: *The face-off between soldiers and demonstrators ended with hundreds being arrested.* —see also **face off** (FACE[2]) **2** the start of play in a game of HOCKEY

face sav·er /'. ,../ *n.* [C] something that helps you not to lose other people's respect: *These tax cuts were the face saver the President needed after the latest economic figures were released.* —**face-saving** *adj.* [only before noun] —see also **save face** (FACE[1] (7))

fac·et /'fæsɪt/ *n.* [C] **1** one of several parts of someone's character, a situation etc.; ASPECT: [+ of] *You've only seen one facet of her personality.* **2** one of the flat sides of a cut jewel

-faceted /'fæsətɪd/ [in adjectives] **multi-faceted/many-faceted** consisting of many different parts: *Feeding the hungry is a multi-faceted issue, and there are no easy answers.*

face time /'. ./ *n.* [U] time that you spend at your job because you want other people, especially your manager, to see you there and to think that you are working, even if you are not

fa·ce·tious /fə'tiʃəs/ *adj.* saying things that are intended to be funny but which annoy people, especially because they are said in a serious situation: *At the risk of sounding facetious, I have to ask who really cares about all this?* —**facetiously** *adv.* —**facetiousness** *n.* [U]

face-to-face /,. . '. ./ *adj.* [only before noun] a face-to-face meeting, conversation etc. is one where you are actually with another person and talking to them: *This was the first face-to-face meeting the two leaders have had.*

face val·ue /'. ,../ *n.* **1** [C,U] the value that is written on something such as a coin, STOCK[1] (2) etc., but that may not actually be what the coin etc. is worth: *Super Bowl tickets with a face value of $300 are being sold for $2,000.* **2 take sth at face value** to accept a situation or accept what someone says, without thinking there may be a hidden meaning: *The newspapers have taken this propaganda at face value, without questioning it.*

fa·cial[1] /'feɪʃəl/ *adj.* on the face, or relating to the face: *facial hair* | *The patient has a few small cuts and facial abrasions.*

facial[2] *n.* [C] a beauty treatment in which creams are rubbed into your face in order to clean and improve your skin: *Saturday morning I went downtown to have a facial.*

fac·ile /'fæsəl/ *adj.* FORMAL **1** a facile remark, argument etc. is too simple and shows a lack of careful thought or understanding: *The senator is known for making facile judgments on current issues.* **2** [only before noun] a facile achievement or success has been obtained too easily to be respected or to be satisfying: *a facile victory* —**facilely** *adv.* —**facileness** *n.* [U]

fa·cil·i·tate /fə'sɪlə,teɪt/ *v.* [T] to make it easier for a process or activity to happen: *Dividing students into small groups usually helps facilitate discussion.* —**facilitation** /fə,sɪlə'teɪʃən/ *n.* [U]

fa·cil·i·ta·tor /fə'sɪlə,teɪtə/ *n.* [C] **1** someone who helps a group of people discuss things with each other or do something effectively **2** TECHNICAL something that helps a process to take place

fa·cil·i·ty /fə'sɪləti/ *n. plural* **facilities 1** [C] a place or building used for a particular activity or industry, or for providing a particular type of service: *Money is being raised to build a new sports facility.* | *The* *college has excellent research facilities.* **2** [singular] a natural ability to do or learn something easily and well: [+ **for**] *Dr. Lao has a facility for remembering names and faces.* **3** [C usually singular] FORMAL a useful additional system or piece of equipment that makes it possible to do something: *The phone is equipped with a call-back facility.* **4 with great facility** FORMAL very easily: *McKelvey writes with great facility in a style similar to Samuel Barber.* **5 the facilities** SPOKEN a word meaning the "toilet," used to be polite: *Excuse me, I have to use the facilities.*

fac·ing /ˈfeɪsɪŋ/ *n.* [C,U] **1** an outer surface of a wall or building that is made of a different material from the rest, in order to make it look attractive **2** material fastened to the inside of a piece of clothing to strengthen it

fac·sim·i·le /fækˈsɪməli/ *n.* [C] **1** an exact copy of a picture, piece of writing etc. **2** FORMAL a FAX[1] (1) —**facsimile** *adj.*

fact /fækt/ *n.*

1 ❚true information❚ [C] a piece of information that is known to be true: *Newspapers have a duty to provide readers with the facts.* | [+ **of/in**] *What are the facts of this case?* | [+ **about**] *The book is full of interesting facts about plants.* | **get your facts right/straight** (=make sure you are right about something) | **stick/keep to the facts** (=only say what you know is true) | *It's a well-known fact that most deaths from lung cancer are caused by smoking.* | *I know for a fact that* (=used to say that you definitely know that something is true) *the company won't be giving out any Christmas bonuses this year.* —see also **the bare facts/truth** (BARE[1] (4)), **hard facts/information/evidence etc.** (HARD[1] (9))

2 the fact (that) used when talking about a situation and saying that it is true: *He refused to help me despite the fact that I've done many things for him.* | *The company's poor financial situation is largely due to the fact that* (=because) *the price of raw materials has increased dramatically.*

3 ❚real events/not a story❚ [U] situations, events etc. that really happened and have not been invented: *Much of the novel is based on fact.*

4 in fact also **in actual fact a)** used when you are adding something, especially something surprising, to emphasize what you have just said: *I know the mayor really well – in fact, I had dinner with her last week.* **b)** used to say what the real truth of a situation is, especially when this is different from what people think or say it is: *In fact, it's cheaper to fly than it is to drive.* | *Her teachers said she was a slow learner, but in actual fact she was partially deaf.*

5 ...and that's a fact SPOKEN used to emphasize that something is definitely true or that something definitely happened: *This car will get over 60 miles to a gallon of gas and that's a fact.*

6 the fact is also **the fact of the matter is** SPOKEN used when you are telling someone what is actually true in a particular situation, especially when this is different from what people believe: *The fact of the matter is that without government help this industry couldn't survive.*

7 facts and figures the basic details, numbers etc. relating to a particular situation or subject: *The report contained some interesting facts and figures about the Saturn Corporation.*

8 sth is a fact of life used to say that a situation exists and must be accepted: *Violent crime just seems to have become a fact of life.*

9 the facts speak for themselves used to say that the things that have happened or the things someone has done show clearly that something is true: *She obviously knows what she's doing – the facts speak for themselves.*

10 the facts of life a) the details about sex and how babies are born: *Most parents have difficulty talking to their children about the facts of life.* **b)** the way life really is, with all its problems and difficulties

11 the fact remains used to emphasize that a situation is true and people must realize this: *The fact*

remains that without raising taxes we won't be able to pay for any of these programs.

12 in view of the fact that... used when saying that a particular fact influences your judgment about something or someone: *In view of the fact that this is Mr. Farrar's first offense, the court has decided to dismiss the case.*

13 after the fact after something has happened or been done, especially after a mistake has been made: *Few people even heard about the concert until after the fact.* —see also **as a matter of fact** (MATTER[1] (11)), **in point of fact** (POINT[1] (26))

fact-find·ing /ˈ. ˌ../ *adj.* **a fact-finding trip/tour/mission etc.** a trip during which you try to find out facts and information about something for your organization, government etc.

fac·tion /ˈfækʃən/ *n.* **1** [C] a small group of people within a larger group, who have different ideas from the other members: *The warring factions are attempting to negotiate an end to the conflict.* **2** [U] FORMAL disagreement or fighting within a group or a political party —**factional** *adj.*

fac·ti·tious /fækˈtɪʃəs/ *adj.* FORMAL **1** not based on facts or truth **2** made artificially rather than naturally

fac·toid /ˈfæktɔɪd/ *n.* [C] INFORMAL a small interesting piece of information, that is often not important

fac·tor[1] /ˈfæktɚ/ *n.* [C] **1** one of several things that influence or cause a situation: *The rise in crime is mainly due to social and economic factors.* | [+ **in**] *The weather could be a factor in tomorrow's game.* | **a key/crucial factor** *Donovan's support was a key factor in Ventura's election win.* | **the deciding/decisive/determining factor** *We liked both cars, but in the end the deciding factor was the price.* **2** a particular level on a scale that measures the force or effectiveness of something: *Doctors recommend putting factor 30 sun lotion on children.* | *With **the wind chill factor*** (=the degree to which the air feels colder because of the wind), *it feels like 20 below zero.* **3 by a factor of five/ten etc.** if something increases or decreases by a factor of five, ten etc., it increases or decreases by five times, ten times etc.: *The number of cars with airbags has increased by a factor of ten since 1993.* **4** TECHNICAL a number that divides into another number exactly: *3 is a factor of 15.* **5** a financial company that pays a business for all the money it is owed by other companies, in return for a small PERCENTAGE, and that then collects the money owed for itself

factor[2] *v.* [T] TECHNICAL to divide a number into factors

factor sth ↔ in also **factor sth into sth** *phr. v.* [T] to include a particular thing in your calculations about how long something will take, how much it will cost etc.: *Interest payments will have to be factored in.*

factor sth ↔ out *phr. v.* [T] to not include something in your calculations about how long something will take, how much it will cost etc.: *Real wages, after factoring out inflation, rose eleven percent.*

fac·to·ri·al /fækˈtɔriəl/ *n.* [C] TECHNICAL the result when you multiply a whole number by all the numbers below it: *factorial 3 = 3 x 2 x 1*

fac·tor·ing /ˈfæktərɪŋ/ *n.* [C] the business of being a FACTOR[1] (5)

fac·to·ry /ˈfæktəri/ *n. plural* **factories** [C] **1** a building or group of buildings in which goods are produced in large quantities, using machines: *a shoe factory* | *factory workers* **2 on the factory floor** among the ordinary workers in a company: *There's been a lot of talk on the factory floor about more layoffs in the spring.*

factory farm /ˈ... ˌ./ *n.* [C] a farm where animals such as chickens or pigs are kept inside, in small spaces or small CAGEs, and made to produce eggs or grow very quickly —**factory farming** *n.* [U]

fac·to·tum /fækˈtoʊtəm/ *n.* [C] FORMAL a servant or worker who has to do many different kinds of jobs for someone

fact sheet /ˈ. ./ *n.* [C] a piece of paper giving all the most important information about something

fac·tu·al /ˈfæktʃuəl/ adj. [no comparative] based on facts or relating to facts: *Try to keep your account of events as factual as possible.* | *The report contained a number of factual errors* (=pieces of information that are wrong). —**factually** adv.

fac·ul·ty /ˈfækəlti/ n. plural **faculties** **1** [C,U] all the teachers in a particular school or college, or in a particular department of a school or college: *A drop in enrollment will affect students, faculty, and administrators.* | *representatives from the history faculty* **2** [C] FORMAL a particular skill that someone has: [+ for] *Margret had a great faculty for absorbing information.* **3** [C] FORMAL a natural ability, such as the ability to see, hear, or think clearly: [+ of] *The patient's faculty of hearing has been greatly damaged.* | *Mrs. Darwin is no longer in full possession of all her faculties* (=able to see, hear, think etc. well).

fad /fæd/ n. [C] something that someone likes or does for a short time, or that is fashionable for a short time: *The popularity of organic food is more than just a passing fad.* —**faddish** adj. —**faddishness** n. [U]

fade /feɪd/ v. **1** [I] also **fade away** to gradually disappear: *Hopes of an early end to the strike are beginning to fade.* | *Over the years her beauty had faded a little.* **2** [I,T] to lose color or brightness, or to make something do this: *He's wearing a red shirt and faded jeans.* | *The sun had faded the curtains.* **3** [I] if someone fades, they stop doing something as well as they did before: *The Broncos faded in the second half.* **4** also **fade away** [I] to become weaker physically, especially so that you become very sick or die
fade in phr. v. [I,T **fade sth ↔ in**] to appear slowly or become louder, or to make a picture or sound do this —**fade-in** n. [C]
fade out phr. v. [I,T **fade sth ↔ out**] to disappear slowly or become quieter, or to make a picture or sound do this: *The radio signal faded out.* —**fade-out** n. [C]

faer·ie /ˈfɛri/ n. [C] OLD USE a FAIRY (2)

fag /fæg/ n. [C] **1** OFFENSIVE a HOMOSEXUAL man **2** BRITISH, INFORMAL a cigarette

fag·got /ˈfæɡət/ n. [C] OFFENSIVE: see FAG (1)

fag-hag, **fag hag** /ˈ. ./ n. [C] OFFENSIVE a woman who spends a lot of time with HOMOSEXUAL men

Fahr·en·heit /ˈfærənˌhaɪt/ n. [U] a scale of temperature in which water freezes at 32° and boils at 212°

fail¹ /feɪl/ v.
1 try but fail [I] to be unsuccessful in something that you want to do: *Peace talks between the two countries have failed.* | [**fail to do sth**] *Doctors failed to save the girl's life.* | *Millions of people have tried to quit smoking and failed miserably* (=been completely unsuccessful in a way that it is embarrassing).
2 not do what is expected [I] to not do what is expected, needed, or wanted: [**fail to do sth**] *Unfortunately, Larry failed to submit his proposal on time.* | **fail in sb's duty/responsibility** *She said she felt as if she had failed in her duty as a parent.*
3 exam/test **a)** [I,T] to not pass a test or examination: *I failed my math test.* | [+ **on**] *Sam passed the written test but failed on the driving test.* **b)** [T] to decide that someone has not passed a test or examination: *Her work was so bad that I had no choice but to fail her.*
4 I fail to see/understand used to show that you are annoyed by something that you do not accept or understand: *I fail to see the humor in this situation.*
5 bank/company [I] if a bank, company etc. fails, it has to stop operating because of a lack of money: *A very high percentage of small businesses fail within their first year.*
6 machine/body part [I] if a part of a machine or an organ in your body fails, it stops working: *The engine failed just after the plane took off.* | *His heart failed and there was nothing we could do to save him.*
7 failing sight/health sight or health that is becoming worse
8 never fail (to do sth) to do something or happen so regularly that people expect it: *The show never fails to entertain me.* | *His use of the term never failed to annoy her.* | *Never fails*, (=used to say that something always happens, especially something annoying) *the*

light always turns red just as you get there.
9 fail sb to not do what someone has trusted you to do: *I feel I've failed my children by not spending more time with them.* —see also **words fail me** (WORD¹ (30))
10 crops [I] if crops fail, they do not grow or produce food: *Across the state, corn crops failed due to the drought.*
11 your courage/nerve fails (you) if your courage, nerve etc. fails or fails you, you suddenly do not have it when you need it: *Jim's nerve failed and he left without asking for her phone number.*
12 rains [I] if the RAINS (=a lot of rain that happens at a particular time each year) fail, they do not come at the usual time of the year

fail² n. **without fail a)** if you do something without fail, you always do it: *Danny comes over every Sunday without fail.* **b)** used when telling someone that they must do something: *I want that work finished by tomorrow, without fail!*

failed /feɪld/ adj. [only before noun] **a failed actor/writer etc.** someone who wanted to be an actor, writer etc. but was not successful

fail·ing¹ /ˈfeɪlɪŋ/ n. [C] a fault or weakness: *He loved her in spite of her failings.*

failing² prep. used to say that if one thing is not possible or available, there is another one you could try: *We will probably have the conference at the Hyatt, or failing that, at the Fairmont.*

fail-safe /ˈ. ˌ./ adj. **1** a fail-safe machine, piece of equipment etc. contains a system that makes the machine stop working if one part of it fails **2** a fail-safe plan is certain to succeed

fail·ure /ˈfeɪljɚ/ n.
1 lack of success [C,U] a lack of success in achieving or doing something: *Winston is not someone who accepts failure easily.* | **end/result in failure** *His last attempt at directing a movie ended in failure.*
2 unsuccessful person/thing [C] someone or something that is not successful: *I feel like such a failure.* | **a total/complete failure** *The plan to expand the company overseas was a complete failure.* | *A series of crop failures have driven many farmers out of business.*
3 machine/body part [C,U] an occasion when a machine or part of your body stops working in the correct way: **heart/liver/kidney etc. failure** *If your condition is left untreated, you could die of heart failure.* | [+ **in**] *The power outage was the result of a failure in the computer system.*
4 failure to do sth an act of not doing something that should be done or that people expect you to do: *Failure to show proof of car insurance to an officer will result in a fine.*
5 bank/company [C,U] a situation in which a bank, company etc. has to stop operating because of a lack of money: *It has become the most expensive bank failure in U.S. history.*

fain /feɪn/ adv. OLD USE **sb would fain do sth** if someone would fain do something, they would like to do it

faint¹ /feɪnt/ adj. **1** difficult to see, hear, smell etc.: *We heard a faint noise coming from the room.* | *I could just make out the faint outline of the cliffs.* **2 a faint possibility/chance etc.** a very small or slight possibility etc.: *There's still a faint hope that they might be alive.* **3 not have the faintest idea** to not know anything at all about something: *I don't have the faintest idea what you're talking about.* **4 sth is not for the faint of heart** HUMOROUS used to say that a particular activity or job is not good for people who are nervous or easily frightened: *Being an inner-city cop is not for the faint of heart.* —see also FAINT-HEARTED **5** feeling weak and as if you are about to become unconscious because you are very sick, tired, or hungry: [+ **with**] *He was faint with hunger.* —**faintly** adv.: *a wine with a faintly sweet taste* —**faintness** n. [U] —see also **damn sb with faint praise** (DAMN⁴ (8))

F

faint² *v.* [I] **1** to suddenly become unconscious for a short time: *It was hot and crowded, and several people fainted.* **2 I almost fainted** SPOKEN used to say that you were very surprised by something: *I almost fainted when they told me the price.*

faint³ *n.* [C usually singular] an act of becoming unconscious: *She fell down in a faint.*

faint-heart·ed, fainthearted /ˌ. ˈ..‹/ *adj.* **1** not trying very hard, because you do not want to do something, or because you are not confident that you can succeed: *She made a rather faint-hearted attempt to stop him from leaving.* **2 sth is not for the faint-hearted** HUMOROUS used to say that a particular activity or job is not good for people who are nervous or easily frightened —see also **sth is not for the faint of heart** (FAINT¹ (4))

s w
2 2
fair¹ /fɛr/ *adj.*
1 reasonable and acceptable a situation, system, or way of treating people that is fair, seems reasonable and acceptable and right: *My grandfather used to say that life isn't always fair.* | *What do you think is the fairest solution?* | *All we're asking for is a fair wage.* | [be fair to do sth] *It seems fair to give them a second chance.*
2 treating everyone equally a fair situation, judgment, description etc. is one in which everyone is treated equally: *Why does Eric get to go and I don't? It's not fair!* | *Any new changes in the law must be fair to everyone, regardless of their age.* | *It's only fair that everyone has access to the same information.*
3 according to the rules a fair fight, game, or election is one that is played or done according to the rules: *The new government has promised to hold free and fair elections.*
4 fair person someone who treats everyone in a reasonable, equal way: *Mrs. Anderson is strict but she's fair.*
5 level of ability neither particularly good nor particularly bad; AVERAGE: *Jenny excels in science, but her grades in English are just fair.*
6 have had more than your fair share of sth to have had more of something, especially something bad, than seems reasonable or fair: *Tim's had more than his fair share of bad luck this year.*
7 skin/hair someone who is fair, or has fair skin or hair, has skin or hair that is light in color: *Julia has blue eyes and fair hair.* | *Both her children are very fair.* —opposite DARK¹
8 weather weather that is fair is pleasant and not windy, rainy etc.: *It should be generally fair and warm for at least the next three days.*
9 it's fair to say (that) used when you think what you are saying is correct or reasonable: *It's fair to say that most of our customers are well-educated.*
10 give/get a fair shake INFORMAL to treat someone, or to be treated, fairly, so that everyone has the same chances as everyone else: *It's true that women don't always get a fair shake in business.*
11 a fair size/number/amount/distance etc. INFORMAL a fairly large size, number, amount, distance etc.: *There's a fair amount of unemployment around here.* | *We had traveled a fair way by lunch time.*

SPOKEN PHRASES
12 fair enough used to say that you agree with someone's suggestion or that something seems reasonable: *"I'll trade you my tennis racket for your skates." "Okay, fair enough."*
13 to be fair said when adding something after someone has been criticized, which helps to explain or excuse what they did: *He's not playing very well but, to be fair, he did have a pretty serious injury.*
14 be fair! used to tell someone not to be unreasonable or criticize someone too much: *Come on, be fair, the poor girl's trying her hardest!*
15 fair's fair said when you think it is fair that someone should do something, especially because of something that has happened earlier: *Come on, fair's fair – I paid last time, so it's your turn.*

16 beauty LITERARY beautiful: *Welcome to our fair city.* | *a fair maiden*
17 have a fair idea of sth to know a lot about something: *I think I have a pretty fair idea of what she's like.*
18 all's fair in love and war used to say that in some situations any method of getting what you want is acceptable
19 by fair means or foul using any method to get what you want, including dishonest or illegal methods
20 fair comment used to say that a remark or criticism seems fair: *I think that the article criticizing Governor Bateman went beyond fair comment* (=was not fair).

fair² *n.* [C] **1** an outdoor event, at which there are s w large machines to ride on, games to play, and sometimes farm animals being judged and sold: **a state/county fair** (=a fair for the whole state or county) **2 craft/stamp/book/science etc. fair** an event at which people can look at a lot of things of the same type that are made or sold by many different people, often in order to buy them or judge them for a competition: *Kelly made that, it's her science fair project for school.* | *There's a craft fair in Balboa Park this Sunday.* **3 a trade/job etc. fair** a regular event where companies show their newest products in order to advertise them, where people go to find out information about jobs etc.

fair³ *adv.* **1 fair and square** in a fair and honest way: *They won fair and square.* **2 play fair** to do something in a fair and honest way: *In international trade, very few countries play fair.*

Fair·banks /ˈfɛrbæŋks/, **Doug·las** /ˈdʌɡləs/ (1883–1939) a U.S. actor famous for performing in movies

fairer sex /ˌ.. ˈ./ *n.* [U] OLD-FASHIONED **the fairer sex** also **the fair sex** women

fair game /ˌ. ˈ./ *n.* [U] if someone or something is fair game, it is appropriate to criticize or attack them: *The paper seems to think that just because I'm a politician, my entire family is fair game.*

fair·ground /ˈfɛrɡraʊnd/ *n.* [C] an open space on which a fair takes place

fair-haired boy /ˌ. ˈ. ˈ./ *n.* [C] INFORMAL someone who is likely to succeed because someone in authority likes them: *Jones is the boss's fair-haired boy.*

fair·ly /ˈfɛrli/ *adv.* **1** more than a little, but much less s w than very: *The house had a fairly large garage.* | *She* 2 3 *speaks English fairly well.* —see Usage Note at RATHER **2** in a way that is fair, honest, and reasonable: *I felt I hadn't been treated fairly.*

fair-mind·ed /ˈ. ˌ../ *adj.* able to understand and judge situations fairly and always considering other people's opinions: *I think he's been fair-minded in all his dealings with us.*

fair·ness /ˈfɛrnɪs/ *n.* [U] **1** the quality of being fair **2 in fairness (to sb)** used after you have just criticized someone, in order to add something that explains their behavior or performance: *In fairness to Principal Montara, the school hasn't received funding to hire better teachers.*

fair play /ˌ. ˈ./ *n.* [U] **1** playing according to the rules of a game, without cheating **2** fair treatment of people, without cheating or being dishonest: *Claiming credit for other people's work violates our society's sense of fair play.* —see also **turnabout is fair play** (TURNABOUT (2))

fair sex /ˌ. ˈ./ *n.* **the fair sex** OLD-FASHIONED: see FAIRER SEX

fair-to-mid·dling /ˌ. . ˈ../ *adj.* INFORMAL neither particularly good nor particularly bad; SO-SO: *"How're you doing?" "Oh, fair-to-middling."* | *Jonathan considers himself a fair-to-middling saxophone player.*

fair·way /ˈfɛrweɪ/ *n.* [C] the part of a GOLF COURSE that you hit the ball along toward the hole

fair-weath·er friend /ˌ. .. ˈ./ *n.* [C] someone who only wants to be your friend when you are successful

fair·y /ˈfɛri/ *n. plural* **fairies** [C] **1** a very small imaginary creature with magic powers, that looks like a small person with wings **2** OFFENSIVE a HOMOSEXUAL man

fairy god·moth·er /ˌ.. '.../ n. [C] a woman with magic powers who saves people from trouble, especially in children's stories

fair·y·land /'fɛriˌlænd/ n. **1** [U] an imaginary place where fairies live **2** [singular] a place that looks very beautiful and special: *Mitford's downtown at Christmas is a fairyland.*

fairy tale /'.. ˌ./ n. [C] **1** a story for children in which magical things happen: *In traditional fairy tales, the hero is rewarded and the enemy punished.* **2** a story that someone has invented and that is difficult to believe

fai·ry·tale /'fɛriˌteɪl/ adj. [only before noun] extremely happy, lucky etc. in a way that usually only happens in children's stories: *Their fairytale marriage turned into a nightmare.*

fait ac·com·pli /ˌfeɪt əkɑm'pli, ˌfɛt ækɔm'pli/ n. [singular] FORMAL something that has already happened or been done and cannot be changed

faith /feɪθ/ n.

SW 2 3

1 ‖trust/belief in sb/sth‖ [U] a strong belief that someone or something can be trusted to be right or to do the right thing: *I have a lot of faith in her.* | *destroy/restore faith in Seeing how people worked together after the hurricane has restored my faith in human nature.* | *The public has quite simply lost faith in the political process.*
2 ‖belief in god/religion‖ **a)** [U] belief and trust in God: *He's a man of deep religious faith.* | [+ in] *Her faith in God is unshakable.* **b)** [C] one of the main religions in the world: *The center welcomes people from all faiths.* | *the Jewish faith*
3 good faith honest and sincere intentions: *As a sign of his good faith, the company has agreed to replace the defective parts for free.* | *The guy who sold me the car claimed he had acted in good faith* (=without intending to deceive someone).
4 bad faith intentions that are not honest or sincere: *If the board acted in bad faith* (=if they were deliberately not fair or broke an agreement), *the teacher who was dismissed should get her job back.*
5 break faith with sb/sth to stop supporting or believing in a person, organization, or idea: *Officials have denied reports that the U.S. had broken faith with the island's government.*
6 keep faith with sb/sth to continue to support or believe in a person, organization, or idea: *The military regime has not kept faith with its promises of democratic reform.*
7 keep the faith used to encourage someone to continue to believe in a principle, religion etc.
8 an act of faith something you do that shows you trust someone or believe that something will happen: *Allowing Ken to be in charge of the project was a total act of faith.*

faith·ful¹ /'feɪθfəl/ adj. **1** remaining loyal to a person, belief, political party etc. and continuing to support them: *Mary's always been a trustworthy and faithful friend.* | [+ to] *Reynolds has remained faithful to his principles.* **2** representing an event or an image in a way that is exactly true or that looks exactly the same: *I did my best to give a faithful account of what happened* | *It's a faithful reproduction of the original picture.* **3** loyal to your wife, husband, BOYFRIEND etc. by not having a sexual relationship with anyone else: [+ to] *I know she hasn't always been faithful to me, but I love her anyway.* —**faithfulness** n. [U]

faithful² n. **1 the faithful a)** the people who are very loyal to a leader, political party etc. and continue to support them: *Eighty percent of the party faithful will vote for whatever candidate we choose.* **b)** the people who believe in a religion: *The progressive wing of the Church has encouraged the faithful to press for social reform.* **2** [C] a loyal follower, supporter, or member: *There were only a handful of old faithfuls at the meeting.*

faith·ful·ly /'feɪθfəli/ adv. in a faithful way: *Every year we faithfully make a trip to see my parents.*

faith heal·ing /'. ˌ../ n. [U] a method of treating illnesses by praying —**faith healer** n. [C]

faith·less /'feɪθlɪs/ adj. FORMAL someone who is faith-

less cannot be trusted: *a faithless husband* —**faithlessly** adv. —**faithlessness** n. [U]

fa·ji·ta /fə'hitə, fɑ-/ n. [C usually plural] a TEX-MEX food made with GRILLED onions, peppers, and chicken or meat that are put in a TORTILLA

fake¹ /feɪk/ n. [C] **1** a copy of a valuable object, painting etc. that is intended to deceive people: *Beware of fakes when buying antiques.* **2** someone who is not what they claim to be or does not have the skills they say they have: *It turned out her doctor was a fake.* **3** an action in which you pretend to move in one direction when you are really moving in another, or that makes you think one thing is happening when something else is really happening

fake² adj. [usually before noun] **1** made to look like a real material or object in order to deceive people: *a fake fur coat* **2** pretending to be something you are not in order to deceive people: *a fake police officer*

fake³ v. **1** [I,T] to pretend to be sick, or to be interested, pleased etc. when you are not: *I thought he was really hurt, but he was just faking it.* **2** [I,T] to pretend to move in one direction, but then move in another, especially when playing a sport: *Elway faked a pass and ran with the ball.* **3** [T] to make an exact copy of something in order to deceive people: *He faked his grandfather's signature on the check.*

fake sb out phr. v. [T] to deceive someone by making them think you are planning to do one thing when you are really planning to do something else

fa·kir /fə'kɪr, 'feɪkə/ n. [C] a traveling Hindu or Muslim holy man

fal·con /'fælkən, 'fɔl-/ n. [C] a large bird that kills and eats other animals and can be trained to hunt

fal·con·er /'fælkənə, 'fɔl-/ n. [C] someone who trains falcons to hunt

fal·con·ry /'fælkənri, 'fɔl-/ n. [U] the skill or sport of using falcons to hunt

Falk·land Is·lands, the /ˌfɔklənd 'aɪləndz/ also **the Falklands** a group of islands, under British control, in the southwest Atlantic Ocean off the coast of Argentina. The Argentineans believe that the islands belong to Argentina, and call them the Malvinas.

F

fall

fall   drop

fall¹ /fɔl/ v. past tense **fell** past participle **fallen**
1 ‖move downward‖ [I] to move or drop down from a higher position to a lower position: *I sat in bed, listening to the rain fall.* | [+ out of/from/on] *We picked up the apples that had fallen from the trees.* | [+ down] *A large tree in our backyard fell down during the storm.* | *The little boat rose and fell with the movement of the waves.*
2 ‖person falling‖ [I] to suddenly go down onto the ground, especially without intending to, after you have been standing, walking, or running: *Katie fell and scraped her knee.* | *Don't worry – I'll catch you if you fall.* | [+ down] *I slipped and fell down the stairs.* | [+ on/into etc.] *Dennis lost his balance and fell into the water.* | *She fell flat on her face* (=fell so that she was lying facing the ground) *in the mud.* | *Father Reilly fell to his knees* (=moved down

SW 1 1

from a standing position so that his body was resting on his knees) *and began to pray.*

3 `lower amount/level etc.` [I] to become lower in price, amount, level etc.: *Temperatures should fall below zero tonight.* | *The number of traffic fatalities fell by 15% last year.* | *Interest rates **fell sharply** (=quickly became lower).*

4 fall asleep/ill/silent etc. to start to be asleep, sick etc.: *I fell asleep.* | *Everyone fell silent as Beth entered.*

5 fall in love to begin to love someone or something very much: *Your father and I fell in love during the war.* | [+ **with**] *I fell in love with her the moment I met her.* | *Rick fell in love with New York after his first visit there.*

6 `group/pattern` [I] to be part of a particular group, pattern, or range of things or people: [+ **into**] *These substances fall into two categories.* | [+ **under**] *Her earlier books would fall under the heading of historical fiction.*

7 fall into place a) if parts of a situation that you have been trying to understand fall into place, you start to understand how they are related to each other: *Gradually the clues started falling into place, and it became clear who the murderer was.* **b)** if the parts of something that you want to happen fall into place, they start to happen in the way that you want: *Things are finally falling into place for the team.*

8 `happen` [I] to happen on a particular day or date: [+ **on**] *Christmas falls on a Thursday this year.*

9 night/darkness/dusk falls LITERARY used to say that the night begins and that it starts to become dark: *The lights came on as darkness fell on the city.*

10 `light/shadow` [I always + adv./prep.] to shine on a surface or go onto a surface: *The last rays of sunlight were falling on the fields.* | *A shadow fell across his face, hiding his expression.*

11 `hang down` [I always + adv./prep.] to hang down loosely: *Maria's hair fell over her shoulders.*

12 fall short (of sth) to fail to achieve the result, amount, or standard that is needed or that you want: *Her newest book fell short of many critics' expectations.*

13 fall flat if a joke, remark, or performance falls flat, it fails to interest or amuse people: *Your joke about the nuns really fell flat, didn't it?*

14 fall into decay/disrepair/disrepute etc. to become decayed, in bad condition, not respected anymore etc.: *Over the years the old family home had been allowed to fall into disrepair.*

15 fall to pieces to become damaged or not be able to work well: *If reforms are not carried out soon, the economy will simply fall to pieces.*

16 fall into sb's lap if an opportunity or something good falls into your lap, you get it by chance and good luck, without trying to get it: *I've always wanted to open my own restaurant and this opportunity sort of fell into my lap.*

17 `be killed` [I] LITERARY to be killed in a war: *He reportedly fell in battle on June 17th.*

18 `lose power` [I] if a leader or a government falls, they lose their position of power: *The previous administration fell after only 6 months in office.*

19 `take control of a place` [I] if a place falls in a war or an election, a group of soldiers or a political party takes control of it: [+ **to**] *After three weeks of heavy fighting, the city finally fell to the rebel army.*

20 fall into sth INFORMAL to get into a place very quickly because you are in a hurry or very tired: *She fell into bed the moment she got home.* | *I'm just going to go home and fall into a hot bath.*

21 be falling to pieces/bits to be in very bad condition, especially because of being very old: *The walls were dirty and the furniture was falling to pieces.*

22 fall to pieces a) to break into many pieces: *The vase fell to pieces as soon as it hit the floor.* **b)** if something such as a plan or a relationship falls to pieces, it stops happening in the way that it should **c)** to become so sad and upset that you cannot do anything: *Stacy would fall to pieces if she knew Gary was cheating on her.*

23 fall out of fashion/favor to stop being popular or fashionable

24 fall into the hands/clutches of sb if something or someone falls into the hands of an enemy or dangerous person, the enemy, dangerous person etc. gets control or possession of them: *Somehow, the plans fell into the hands of an enemy spy.*

25 fall victim/prey to sth to get a very serious illness: *She fell victim to a rare blood disorder.*

26 fall victim/prey to sb to be attacked or deceived by someone: *The elderly are most likely to fall prey to con men.*

27 fall into the habit of sth to start doing something, especially something that you should not do: *He soon fell into the habit of stopping at the bar every night before going home.*

28 fall into a trap also **fall into the trap of sth** to make a mistake that many people make: *Don't fall into the trap of thinking you're smarter than others.*

29 fall back into your old ways to start doing things or behaving in the way that you used to, especially in a way that other people disapprove of: *Brian soon fell back into his old ways and started drinking again.*

30 fall by the wayside a) to become unsuccessful after being successful at first: *A lot of marriages fall by the wayside because couples cannot talk to each other.* **b)** to not deal with something and forget about it: *Congress has let many important issues fall by the wayside this session.*

31 fall into line to obey someone or do what other people want you to do, especially when you do not want to do it at first: *If you can persuade her, the others will soon fall into line.*

32 fall on hard times to have problems because you do not have enough money: *Within a few years, the factory fell on hard times and he was forced to declare bankruptcy.*

33 fall into step with sb/sth a) to start doing something in the same way as the other members of a group: *The other countries on the Security Council are expected to fall into step with France.* **b)** to start to walk next to someone else, at the same speed as them

34 fall down on the job INFORMAL to not do your work or duties as well as you should: *I'd be falling down on my job if I didn't take an interest in the welfare of my staff.*

35 fall from grace/favor to stop being liked by people in authority: *I don't think she'll get the promotion – she's kind of fallen from grace recently.*

36 fall foul of sb/sth to do something that makes someone angry or that breaks a rule, with the result that you are punished: *Edwards fell foul of the authorities and was ordered to leave the country.*

37 fall on deaf ears if someone's words fall on deaf ears, no one pays any attention to them: *His pleas for mercy fell on deaf ears.*

38 `voice/sound` [I] if someone's voice or a sound falls, it becomes quieter or lower

39 sb's eyes/gaze/glance falls on sth used to say that someone sees something when they are looking at or for something else: *As I looked over in the corner, my eyes instantly fell on the young woman.*

40 silence/sadness/calm etc. falls LITERARY used to say that a group of people or a place becomes quiet, sad, calm etc.: [+ **on/upon**] *As she entered the ballroom, a great silence fell on the crowd.*

41 `hit` [I always + adv./prep.] to hit a particular place or a particular part of someone's body: *The first punch fell right on his nose.*

42 the stress/accent/beat falls on sth used to say that a particular part of a word, phrase, or piece of music is emphasized or is played more loudly than the rest: *In the word "spoken," the stress falls on the first syllable.*

43 I almost fell off my chair SPOKEN used to say that you were very surprised when something happened

44 fall at sb's feet to kneel in front of someone, especially to ask them to do something or to show your respect

45 fall from sb's lips LITERARY if words fall from someone's lips, they say them —see also **it's as easy as falling off a log** (EASY¹ (12)), **stand or fall by/on** (STAND¹ (41))

fall apart *phr. v.* [I] **1** to separate into small pieces: *The old book fell apart in my hands.* **2** if an organization, system etc. falls apart, it stops working effectively and has a lot of problems: *Our department is **falling apart at the seams**.* **3 be falling apart** to be in very bad condition: *That car of yours is falling apart.* **4** if your life, your world etc. falls apart, you suddenly have a lot of personal problems: *When she left me, my world just fell apart.*

fall away *phr. v.* [I] **1** if something such as a feeling, a quality, or a noise falls away, it gradually becomes weaker or quieter and disappears: *Upon closing the door behind me, the music outside fell away.* **2** to become separated from something after being attached to it: *There were places where the plaster had fallen away from the walls.* **3** to become fewer in number and stop being able to be seen as you move through an area: *As we drove out of the city, the rows of houses started to fall away and we could see open farmland.* **4** FORMAL to slope down: *After the next bend, the road falls away to the valley.*

fall back *phr. v.* [I] **1** if soldiers fall back, they move back because they are being attacked: *He ordered the men to fall back.* **2** LITERARY to move backward because you are very surprised, frightened etc.: *They fell back in horror.*

fall back on sth *phr. v.* [T] **1** to use something that already exists or depend on someone's help when dealing with a difficult situation, especially after you have tried using other methods or tried to deal with it yourself: *Theaters are falling back on old favorites rather than risking money on new plays.* | *Well, at least she **has** her father's money **to fall back on**.* **2** to use a particular method, argument etc. because it seems simple and easy, not because it is the best one to use: *They tend to fall back on the same tired old arguments.*

fall behind *phr. v.* [I,T] **1** to fail to finish a piece of work or fail to pay someone money that you owe them at the right time: *The manufacturers have fallen behind schedule.* | [+ with/on] *We fell behind with the payments on the car.* **2** to become less successful than someone else: *If we don't release the new software soon, we risk falling behind our competitors.* **3** to go more slowly than other people, so that they gradually move further ahead of you: *The older walkers soon fell behind.*

fall down *phr. v.* [I] **1 be falling down** if a building is falling down, it is in very bad condition **2** if an argument, plan, system etc. falls down, it fails to work because of a particular fault: *That's where the whole argument falls down.*

fall for *phr. v.* [T] INFORMAL **1** [**fall for** sth] to be tricked into believing something that is not true: *I can't believe he fell for it when we told him we were French!* | *He told me I'd double my money in six months and I **fell for it hook, line, and sinker** (=was completely deceived).* **2** [**fall for** sb] to suddenly feel romantic love for someone: *Jackie's fallen for a man half her age.*

fall in *phr. v.* [I] **1** if the roof, ceiling etc. falls in, it falls onto the ground **2** if a group of soldiers fall in, they form neat lines behind each other so that an officer can check them

fall in behind sb *phr. v.* [T] to form a line behind someone

fall into sth *phr. v.* **1** to start to have a particular mood, especially suddenly: *She's unstable and liable to fall into sudden fits of rage.* **2** to contain two or more different parts: *The agreement falls into two distinct parts.* **3 fall into a conversation/discussion/argument** etc. FORMAL to start talking or arguing with someone: *Half an hour after we met, Kirk and I fell into a heated discussion about the space program.*

fall in with sb *phr. v.* [T] to begin to spend time with someone, especially someone who is bad or does illegal things: *I don't like the crowd he's fallen in with.*

fall off *phr. v.* **1** [I,T] if part of something falls off, it becomes separated from the main part: *This button keeps falling off.* **2** [I] if the amount, rate, or quality of something falls off, it becomes less: *Demand for records has fallen off dramatically.*

fall on/upon *phr. v.* [I] **1** [**fall on/upon** sb] FORMAL if a duty or responsibility falls on you, you are given that duty or responsibility: *The duty has fallen on me to announce that we will be going out of business at*

the end of the year. **2** [**fall on/upon** sb] LITERARY to suddenly attack or get hold of someone: *Rebel forces fell upon the small outpost during the night.* **3** [**fall on/upon** sth] LITERARY to eagerly start eating or using something: *The kids fell upon the pizza as if they hadn't eaten in weeks.*

fall out *phr. v.* [I] **1** if something such as a tooth or your hair falls out, it comes out: *My dad's hair fell out when he was only 30.* **2** to have an argument with someone, so that you do not agree with them anymore or are not friendly with them anymore: [+ with] *Walker has recently fallen out with his publisher.* **3** if a group of soldiers who are standing together fall out, they leave and go to different places

fall over *phr. v.* [I] **1** [I,T] if someone falls over or if they fall over something, they fall onto the ground: *I got dizzy and fell over.* | *Tommy fell over one of the electric cables.* **2** if something falls over, it falls from an upright position onto its side: *The fence fell over in the wind.* **3 be falling over yourself to do sth** to be very eager to do something, especially something you do not usually do: *Sylvia was falling over herself to be nice to me.*

fall through *phr. v.* [I] if an agreement, plan etc. falls through, it is not completed successfully: *The deal fell through at the last minute.*

fall to *phr. v.* [T] **1** [**fall to** sb] FORMAL if a duty, especially a difficult one, falls to someone, it is their responsibility to do it: *The job fell to me to give her the bad news about her father.* **2** [**fall to** sth] FORMAL to start doing something with a lot of effort: *We immediately fell to work on the project.* **3 fall to doing something** LITERARY to start doing something: *When things really started to go wrong, they fell to arguing among themselves.*

fall² *n.*

1 season [singular,U] the season between summer and winter, when the weather becomes cooler; AUTUMN: *Fall is my favorite season.* | *Brad's going to Georgia Tech **in the fall**.* | *They were married in the fall of 1957.* | *I met her **last fall** (=the last time it was fall).* | *The new building opens **next fall** (=the next time it will be fall).*

2 decrease [C] a decrease in the amount, level, price etc. of something: [+ in] *The government is worried about the recent fall in house prices.* | *There was a dramatic fall in temperature overnight.* —opposite RISE²

3 movement downward [C] movement down toward the ground or toward a lower position: *I sat listening to the fall of the rain on the roof.* | *A few years ago Don **had a bad fall** (=he fell onto the ground and hurt himself) from a ladder.* | *Luckily there were some bushes next to the house which **broke my fall** (=prevented me from falling too quickly and hurting myself too much).*

4 water falls [plural] a place where a river suddenly goes straight down over a cliff: *Niagara Falls*

5 lose power/become unsuccessful [singular] a situation in which someone or something loses their position of power or becomes unsuccessful: [+ from] *Until his party's fall from power last year, Andrews was one of the most important men in Washington.* | *It's a book about **the rise and fall** (=the period of success and then failure) of communism in eastern Europe.*

6 defeat [singular] a situation in which a country, city etc. is defeated by an enemy: *It's a movie about the fall of France in 1940.*

7 fall from grace a situation in which someone stops being respected by other people or loses their position of authority, especially because they have done something wrong: *Jackson's fall from grace came in the fourth game, when he struck out three times in a row.*

8 sports [C] an act of forcing your opponent onto the ground in WRESTLING or JUDO

9 amount of snow etc. [C] an amount of snow, rocks etc. that has fallen to the ground: *It's one of the heaviest falls of snow on record.*

10 the fall the occasion in the Bible when Adam

F

S W
2 **1**

and Eve did not obey God, and as punishment they had to leave the Garden of Eden

fal·la·cious /fəˈleɪʃəs/ *adj.* FORMAL containing or based on false ideas: *a fallacious argument* —**fallaciously** *adv.*

fal·la·cy /ˈfæləsi/ *n. plural* **fallacies 1** [C] a false idea or belief, especially one that a lot of people believe is true: *Don't believe the fallacy that money brings happiness.* **2** [C,U] FORMAL a weakness in someone's argument or idea that is caused by a mistake in the way they have thought about that argument or idea

fall·back /ˈfɔlbæk/ *n.* [C] something that can be used if the usual supply, method etc. fails: *Do you have an alternative plan to use as a fallback?*

fall·en[1] /ˈfɔlən/ *v.* the past participle of FALL[1]

fallen[2] *adj.* **1** on the ground after falling down: *The road was blocked by a fallen tree.* **2 fallen angel** someone who is now having difficulties in their life because they behaved in an immoral way or did something wrong, but who had been an honest, good person before **3 a fallen woman** OLD-FASHIONED a woman who has had a sexual relationship with someone she is not married to **4 the fallen** FORMAL soldiers who have been killed in a war

fall guy /ˈ. ./ *n.* [C] INFORMAL **1** someone who is punished for someone else's crime or mistake; SCAPEGOAT: *Biondi's defenders say he was the fall guy for troubles at the company.* **2** someone who is easily tricked or made to seem stupid

fal·li·ble /ˈfæləbəl/ *adj.* [no comparative] able to make mistakes or be wrong: *Steyer's murder trial showed that the justice system is fallible.* —**fallibility** /ˌfæləˈbɪləti/ *n.* [U] —opposite INFALLIBLE

falling-out /ˌ.. ˈ./ *n.* **have a falling-out (with sb)** INFORMAL to have a bad argument with someone: [+ **over**] *Richard and Jeff had a falling-out over what to do with the inheritance.*

falling star /ˌ.. ˈ./ *n.* [C] a SHOOTING STAR

fall line /ˈ. ./ *n.* [C] the natural slope of a hill straight down from top to bottom

fall·off, fall-off /ˈfɔlɔf/ *n.* [C] a quick decrease in the level, amount, or number of something: *The recent falloff in technology stock prices has investors worried.*

fal·lo·pi·an tube /fəˌloupiən ˈtub/ *n.* [C] one of the two tubes in a female's body through which her eggs move to her UTERUS

fall·out /ˈfɔlaʊt/ *n.* [U] **1** the dangerous RADIOACTIVE dust that is left in the air after a NUCLEAR explosion and that slowly falls to earth **2** the bad results or effects of a particular event, especially when they are unexpected: *The fallout from the scandal cost him his job.*

fallout shel·ter /ˈ.. ˌ../ *n.* [C] a building under the ground where people can go to protect themselves from a NUCLEAR attack

fal·low /ˈfæloʊ/ *adj.* **1** fallow land is dug or PLOWed but is not used for growing crops, in order to let the soil become better **2** not doing anything or not working; INACTIVE: *They've started producing films again after a two-year fallow period.*

false /fɔls/ *adj.*
1 not true a statement, story etc. that is false is not true at all: *Please decide whether the following statements are true or false.* | *We were given false information about his background.* | *Rosenberg had supplied a false name and address.* —opposite TRUE[1] (1)
2 wrong based on incorrect information or ideas: *Many false assumptions were made about the planet Jupiter.* | *Large profits over the last two years have given stock investors a false sense of security* (=a feeling of being safe when you are really not). | *The marketing of the drug raised false hopes that a cure was available.*
3 false eyelashes/fingernails etc. made from artificial material

4 not sincere not sincere or honest, and pretending to have feelings that you do not really have: *Her smile and welcome seemed false.* | *It would be false modesty* (=pretending to be unwilling to talk about your abilities or achievements) *to say that we win games on luck alone.*
5 one false move used when warning someone that if they disobey you, make a mistake, or move suddenly, something very bad will happen to them: *One false move, and I'll shoot!*
6 under false pretenses if you get or do something under false pretenses, you get it or do it by deceiving people: *In violation of the Privacy Act, a reporter gained information under false pretenses.*
7 false imprisonment/arrest the illegal act of putting someone in prison or ARRESTing them for a crime they have not done
8 a false positive/negative a result of a scientific or medical test that shows signs of what is being looked for even though it is not really there, or shows that it is not there even though it really is: *A number of drugs can cause false positives on the screening tests.*
9 false friend a word in a foreign language that seems similar to one in your own, so that you wrongly think they both mean the same thing
10 sail/fly under false colors to pretend to be something that you are not

false a·larm /ˌ. .ˈ./ *n.* [C] a situation in which people think that something bad is going to happen, when this is a mistake: *Firefighters responded to a false alarm at one of the college's dormitories.*

false bot·tom /ˌ. ˈ../ *n.* [C] a part of a container that looks like the bottom of it, but is used to cover a small space for hiding things: *The drugs were found in a suitcase with a false bottom.*

false dawn /ˌ. ˈ./ *n.* [C] a situation in which something good seems likely to happen, but it does not: *The first quarter's sales figures were sort of a false dawn.*

false e·con·o·my /ˌ. .ˈ.../ *n.* [C] something that you think will save money but that will really cost you more: *To cut the city's budget for waste disposal is a false economy.*

false·hood /ˈfɔlshʊd/ *n.* FORMAL **1** [C] a statement that is not true; lie **2** [U] the practice of telling lies

false start /ˌ. ˈ./ *n.* [C] **1** an unsuccessful attempt to begin a process or event: *After several false starts, the concert finally began.* **2** a situation at the beginning of a race when one competitor starts too soon and the race has to start again

false step /ˌ. ˈ./ *n.* [C] a step in the wrong direction, especially one that makes you fall off something

false teeth /ˌ. ˈ./ *n.* [plural] a set of artificial teeth worn by someone who has lost their natural teeth; DENTURES

fal·set·to /fɔlˈsɛtoʊ/ *n. plural* **falsettos** [C] a very high male voice, that is much higher than the man's normal voice and is done when he is singing or speaking —**falsetto** *adj., adv.*

fals·ies /ˈfɔlsiz/ *n.* [plural] INFORMAL pieces of material inside a BRA, used to make a woman's breasts look larger

fal·si·fy /ˈfɔlsəˌfaɪ/ *v.* **falsified, falsifying** [T] to change figures, records etc. so that they contain false information: *Mitchell joined the Navy at 16 by falsifying his birth certificate.* —**falsification** /ˌfɔlsəfəˈkeɪʃən/ *n.* [C,U]

fal·si·ty /ˈfɔlsəti/ *n.* [U] FORMAL the quality of being false or not true

fal·ter /ˈfɔltɚ/ *v.* [I] **1** to become weaker and unable to continue in an effective way: *The peace talks seem to be faltering.* **2** to speak in a voice that sounds weak and uncertain, and keeps stopping: *Laurie's voice faltered as she tried to thank him.* **3** to become less certain and less determined that you want to do something: *We must not falter in our resolve to end the conflict.* **4** FORMAL to move in an unsteady way because you suddenly feel weak or afraid: *Langetta faltered as he made his way up the steps.*

fal·ter·ing /ˈfɔltərɪŋ/ *adj.* nervous and uncertain or unsteady: *With faltering steps, the old lady left the office.* —**falteringly** *adv.*

Fal·well /ˈfɔlwɛl/, **Jer·ry** /ˈdʒɛri/ (1933–) a U.S. Christian leader who started a RIGHT-WING political group called the Moral Majority in 1979

fame /feɪm/ *n.* [U] the state of being known about by a lot of people because of your achievements: *The novel's main character has a choice between fame and love.* | **win fame/rise to fame/gain fame** *Elizabeth Taylor first rose to fame in the movie "National Velvet."* | *In 1967, the Beatles were* **at the height of** *their fame.* | *Lee set off for California to find* **fame and fortune.** | *Macaulay Culkin, of "Home Alone"* *fame* (=used to show what someone is famous for) —see also **sb's/sth's claim to fame** (CLAIM² (4))

famed /feɪmd/ *adj.* known about by a lot of people: **[+ for]** *The Blue Ridge Mountains are famed for their beauty.*

fa·mil·ial /fəˈmɪliəl/ *adj.* [only before noun] FORMAL relating to a family or typical of a family: *familial relationships*

s w **fa·mil·iar¹** /fəˈmɪlyɚ/ *adj.*
2 2
1 easy to recognize someone or something that is familiar is easy to recognize because you have seen or heard them many times before: *That's a familiar tune – what is it?* | *Your face looks familiar to me.* | *She seems* **vaguely familiar** (=a little familiar), *but I can't quite remember where I know her from.*
2 be familiar with sth to know something well because you have seen it, read it, or used it many times before: *Are you familiar with his books?*
3 place/situation a familiar place, situation etc. is one that you know well: *It was a relief to be back in the familiar surroundings of my hometown.*
4 common a familiar sight, problem, story etc. is one that you see or hear about often, because it is part of a common social problem: *Homeless beggars are becoming an* **all-too-familiar** *sight* (=seen or heard so much that it becomes almost normal).
5 informal style informal and friendly in speech, writing etc.: *Sanders has an easy, familiar style of writing.*
6 be on familiar terms with sb to know someone well and be able to talk to them in an informal way: *He's on familiar terms with all the teachers.* —see also FAMILIARLY

familiar² *n.* **1** [C] a cat or other animal that is controlled by an evil spirit, and is used by a WITCH to do magic **2 familiars** OLD USE close friends

fa·mil·iar·i·ty /fəˌmɪliˈærəti, -ˌmɪliˈær-/ *n.* [U] **1** a good knowledge of a particular subject or place: **[+ with]** *If readers don't have a familiarity with the Bible, many literary references are missed.* **2** a feeling of being relaxed and comfortable because you are in a place you know well or with people you know well: *Sometimes I really miss the familiarity of home.* **3 familiarity breeds contempt** an expression meaning that if you know someone too well, you find out their faults and respect them less

fa·mil·iar·ize /fəˈmɪlyəˌraɪz/ *v.* **familiarize sb/yourself etc. with sth** to learn about something so that you understand it, or to teach someone else about something so that they understand it: *Booklets will help familiarize restaurant owners with the new regulations.* | *I spent the first week* **familiarizing** *myself with the neighborhood.* —**familiarization** /fəˌmɪlyərəˈzeɪʃən/ *n.* [U]

fa·mil·iar·ly /fəˈmɪlyəli/ *adv.* in an informal or friendly way: *The FBI is looking for Tom Charles, familiarly known as Charlie the Kid.*

s w **fam·ily** /ˈfæmli, -məli/ *n. plural* **families**
1 1
1 people who are closely related [U] a group of people who are related to each other, especially a mother, father, and their children: *Do you know the family next door?* | *The house is big enough for* **a family of five.** | *Terry wants to work in the* **family business** (=a small business owned by one family). | *His essay deals with the effect of divorce on the* **nuclear family** (=a family consisting of a mother, father, and their children). | **one-parent families/single-parent families** (=families in which there is only one parent) | *The report deals with the suspect's* **family background** (=information about the sort of family someone comes from). | *The Wongs have a*

---

very large **extended family** (=all the people in a family, including grandparents, COUSINS etc.). | *I usually charge a fee for giving legal advice, but it's free since you're family* (=used to say that the relationship is special because someone is related to you).
2 all the people related to you [C,U] all the people you are related to, including those who are now dead: *I'm moving to Detroit because I have some family there.* | **[be in sb's family]** *The house has been in my family for over 200 years.* | *Heart disease* **runs in our family** (=is common in our family).
3 children [C] children: *The resort isn't really the place for people with young families.* | *Steve and Linda want to* **start a family** (=have children) *next year.* | *We didn't know anything about the problems of* **raising a family** (=educating and caring for your children) *when we first got married.* | **family movies/shows/restaurants etc.** (=movies, shows, restaurants etc. that are appropriate for children as well as adults)
4 family size/pack etc. a product sold in a large container or package that holds enough for a whole family: *When I buy detergent, I usually get the family size.*
5 group of animals/things [C] TECHNICAL a group of related animals, plants, languages etc.: *tigers and other members of the cat family* | *Spanish and Italian are part of the Romance language family.*
6 be in the family way OLD-FASHIONED to be PREGNANT

family cir·cle /ˌ.. ˈ../ *n.* [C usually singular] a group of people who are related to each other, especially a mother, father, and their children

family doc·tor /ˌ.. ˈ../ *n.* [C] a doctor trained to treat the general health problems of families and people of all ages

family jew·els /ˌ.. ˈ../ *n.* [plural] HUMOROUS, SLANG a man's TESTICLES

family man /ˈ.. ˌ./ *n.* [C] **1** a man who enjoys being with his wife and children **2** a man with a wife and children

family name /ˈ.. ˌ./ *n.* [C] the name someone shares with all the members of their family; SURNAME, LAST NAME

family plan·ning /ˌ.. ˈ../ *n.* [U] the practice of controlling the number of children that are born by using CONTRACEPTIVES

family prac·tice /ˌ.. ˈ../ *n.* [U] a part of medical practice in the U.S. in which doctors learn to treat general health problems of families and people of all ages

family prac·ti·tion·er /ˌ.. ..ˈ.../ *n.* [C] a FAMILY DOCTOR

family room /ˈ.. ˌ./ *n.* [C] a room in a house where the family can play games, watch television and relax

family tree /ˌ.. ˈ./ *n.* [C] a drawing that gives the names of all the members of a family over a long period of time, and shows how they are related to each other

family val·ues /ˌ.. ˈ../ *n.* [plural] an expression that means traditional principles or ideas about what is right or wrong and what families should be like, used especially in politics

fam·ine /ˈfæmɪn/ *n.* [C,U] a situation in which a large number of people have little or no food for a long time and many people die

fam·ished /ˈfæmɪʃt/ *adj.* [not before noun] INFORMAL extremely hungry: *What's for dinner? I'm absolutely famished.*

s w **famous¹** /ˈfeɪməs/ *adj.* **1** known about or recognized
2 2 by a lot of people: *a famous actress* | **[+ for]** *Yosemite is famous for its giant sequoia trees.* | **[+ as]** *Lake Winnebago is famous as a fishing destination.* | *The San Diego Zoo is* **world-famous** (=recognized by everyone all over the world) *for its world breeding endangered animals.* **2 famous last words** SPOKEN used when someone has said too confidently that they can do something or that something will happen: *So he said, with those famous last words, "Don't worry, everything will be fine."* **3** OLD-FASHIONED very good; excellent

F

famous² *n.* **the famous** people who are famous: *The old hotel is all that is left of the 1850s resort for **the rich and famous**.*

fa·mous·ly /ˈfeɪməsli/ *adv.* **1 get along famously** OLD-FASHIONED to have a friendly relationship with someone **2** FORMAL in a way that is famous

fans

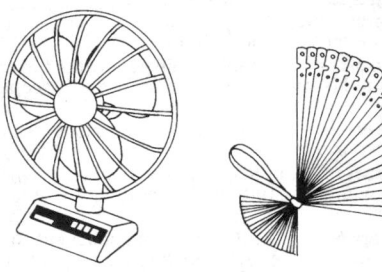

sw **fan¹** /fæn/ *n.* [C] **1** someone who likes a particular
22 sport, kind of music etc. very much, or who admires a famous person: *I'm not much of a basketball fan, but I love baseball.* | *He's **a big fan of** Elvis Presley.* **2** a machine, or a thing that you wave with your hand, that makes the air move so you become cooler: *a beautiful, delicate Japanese fan* —see also FAN CLUB, FAN MAIL

fan² *v.* **fanned, fanning** [T] **1** to make air move around by waving a fan, piece of paper etc. so that you feel cooler: *Gina fanned herself with a newspaper.* **2** also **fan out** to spread something out, especially a group of things, so that they make the shape of a half-circle: *If the bird fans its tail and has a shiny black breast color, it's a male.* **3** to make someone feel an emotion more strongly: *Some politicians are deliberately fanning nationalist emotions.* | *Comments like that will only **fan the flames** of distrust and fear.* **4 fan a fire/blaze** to make a fire burn more strongly, for example by blowing on it: *Fanned by a steady wind, the fire destroyed more than 100 acres.*

fan out *phr. v.* [I] if a group of people fan out, they walk forward while spreading over a wide area

fa·nat·ic /fəˈnætɪk/ *n.* [C] **1** someone who has extreme political or religious ideas and is often dangerous: *Gandhi was killed by a religious fanatic.* **2** someone who likes a particular thing or activity very much: *Ron's an exercise fanatic.* —**fanatical** *adj.* —**fanatically** /-kli/ *adv.*

fa·nat·i·cism /fəˈnætəˌsɪzəm/ *n.* [U] extreme political or religious beliefs that are often dangerous

fan belt /ˈ. ./ *n.* [C] the belt that operates a FAN which keeps a car engine cool —see picture at ENGINE

fan·ci·er /ˈfænsiɚ/ *n.* **cat/wine/opera** etc. **fancier** someone who is very interested in a particular kind of animal, food, music etc.

fan·ci·ful /ˈfænsɪfəl/ *adj.* **1** full of unusual and very detailed shapes or complicated designs: *the fanciful horses on an old-fashioned merry-go-round* **2** imagined rather than based on facts: *I dismissed the rumors as fanciful.* | *a fanciful idea* —**fancifully** *adv.*

fan club /ˈ. ./ *n.* an organization for FANS¹ (1) of a particular team, famous person etc.

fan·cy¹ /ˈfænsi/ *adj.* **fancier, fanciest 1** fancy hotels, restaurants, cars etc. are expensive and fashionable: *We stayed in this really fancy hotel in the mountains.* **2** having a lot of decoration or bright colors, or made in a complicated way: *fancy soaps in seashell shapes* | *The restaurant's food is **nothing fancy**, but it's good family fare.* **3** complicated and needing a lot of skill: *fancy skiing* | *Negotiating a good deal can take some **fancy footwork** (=skill at discussing things).* **4** [only before noun] fancy food is very high quality: *fancy butter*

fan·cy² *n.* OLD-FASHIONED **1** [singular] a feeling that you would like something or someone: *Cora **took a fancy to** a neighbor boy, and eventually married him.* | *Concerns about the environment are not just some **passing fancy** (=an idea that does not last long).* **2** [C,U] imagination or something that you imagine: *The poet Emily Dickinson is known for her brilliant fancies.* | *Her **flights of fancy** (=occasions when she imagines many things) were a refuge from her strict homelife.* **3 tickle sb's fancy** to seem attractive or amusing to someone **4 take your fancy** if something takes your fancy, you like it or want to have it **5** [C] an idea or opinion that is not based on fact: *Oh, that was just a fancy of his.*

fan·cy³ *v.* **fancies, fancied, fancying** [T] **1** to consider that something is true, even if it is not really: *Archer fancied that she had been told of his coming.* | *She **fancies herself** an intellectual.* **2** OLD-FASHIONED to like or want something, or want to do something: *Do you fancy a walk in the park, Estelle?*

fan·cy-free /ˌ. ˈ. ./ *adj.* [not before noun] able to do anything you like because you do not have a family or other responsibilities: *No, I'm not married – still **footloose and fancy-free**.*

fan·cy·work /ˈfænsiwɚk/ *n.* [U] pretty sewing; EMBROIDERY

fan·dan·go /fænˈdæŋgoʊ/ *n.* [C] a fast Spanish or South American dance, or the music for this dance

fan·fare /ˈfænfɛr/ *n.* [C] **1** a lot of attention from people, or actions that are meant to attract attention: *Goldin resigned last week with little fanfare.* **2** a short, loud piece of music played on a TRUMPET to introduce an important person or event

fang /fæŋ/ *n.* [C] a long sharp tooth of an animal such as a snake or dog

fan·light /ˈfænlaɪt/ *n.* [C] **1** a small window above a door or a larger window; TRANSOM **2** a window shaped like a half circle

fan mail /ˈ. ./ *n.* [U] letters sent to famous people by their FANS¹ (1)

fan·ny /ˈfæni/ *n.* *plural* **fannies** [C] INFORMAL the part of your body that you sit on; BOTTOM

fanny pack /ˈ. . ˌ./ *n.* [C] a small bag that someone wears around their waist to carry money, keys etc.

fan·ta·sia /fænˈteɪʒə/ *n.* [C] **1** a piece of music that does not have a regular form or style **2** a piece of music consisting of a collection of well-known tunes

fan·ta·size /ˈfæntəˌsaɪz/ *v.* [I,T] to imagine something strange or very pleasant happening to you: [+ about] *Boys idolize athletes, and fantasize about playing in the pros.* | [fantasize (that)] *Judith fantasizes that her sons will grow up to be doctors.*

fan·tas·tic /fænˈtæstɪk/ *adj.* **1** extremely good, sw attractive, enjoyable etc.: *My mom's sixty this year, but she still looks fantastic.* | *He's done a fantastic* 3 *job.* **2** SPOKEN used when someone has just told you something good: *"He got a scholarship." "Fantastic!"* **3** a fantastic amount is extremely large: *Teenagers spend fantastic amounts of money on clothes.* **4** [only before noun] a fantastic story, creature, or place is very strange or unreal: *fantastic stories of invisible men* **5** a plan, suggestion etc. that is fantastic is not likely to be possible —**fantastically** /-kli/ *adv.*

fan·tas·ti·cal /fæn'tæstɪkəl/ *adj* strange and unreal: *He described a fantastical world populated by mermaids.*

fan·ta·sy /'fæntəsi, -zi/ *n. plural* **fantasies 1** [C,U] an exciting and unusual experience or situation you imagine happening to you but which will probably never happen: *Sometimes I hate this fantasy about opening a campground there.* | *Young children sometimes can't distinguish between fantasy and reality.* | *a young woman's romantic fantasies* | *Carlos retreats into a fantasy world in which everyone adores him.* **2** [singular,U] an idea or belief that is based only on imagination, not on real facts: *Psychologists say that memories can sometimes be pure fantasy, rather than actual recollections.*

fan·zine /'fænzin/ *n.* [C] a magazine written by and for people who admire and support a popular musician, a sports team etc.

FAQ *n.* [C usually plural] a frequently asked question

far[1] /far/ *adv. comparative* **farther** or **further** *superlative* **farthest** or **furthest**
1 long distance over a long distance: *I don't want to drive very far.* | *As a parent, I think two miles is too far for a small child to walk to school.* | *Let's see who can swim the farthest.* | *How far away does Sue live?* | *I've started parking farther away from the office in order to get a cheaper rate.* | **far above/below/across** etc. *Laughter could be heard far above us, on the canyon's rim.*
2 as far as sth up to a particular point or distance: *Boatmen traded goods up the Missouri River as far as Yellowstone.*
3 far stronger/faster/sooner/more etc. much stronger, faster etc.: *Jake has a far bigger appetite than I do.* | *Holly had decided that women were far more interesting than men.*
4 much to a great degree: *I'm afraid this gift is far too expensive.* | *Life on the farm is far removed from* (=very different from) *the hustle and bustle of life in the city.* | **far above/below** *Half of the students scored far below grade level on the test.*
5 effect used to describe how much effect something will have on a situation: *The implications of the plan go far beyond the classroom.* | *Republicans complained that the bill did not go far enough to limit immigration.*
6 so far up to a particular time, point, degree etc.: *I think he's done a great job so far.*
7 sb will/should go far used to say that you think someone will be successful in the future: *The Sharks can expect their new player, Pat Falloon, to go far in the league.*
8 by far also **far and away** used to say that something is much better, worse etc. than anything else: *In most places, the car is still far and away the preferred form of travel.*
9 as far as sb is concerned used to show what someone's opinion about something is: *As far as I'm concerned, this is the council's decision, not mine.*
10 as far as sth is concerned also **as far as sth (goes)** used to show which particular subject or thing you are talking about: *As far as bilingual education is concerned, the schools are not doing a good enough job.*
11 go so far as to do sth to behave in a way that seems surprising or extreme: *Many ranchers go so far as to block public access roads with gates.*
12 go too far also **take/carry sth too far** to do something too much or in an extreme way, especially so that people get angry: *The court ruled that the police went too far when they handcuffed Rooney to a chair.*
13 not go far a) if money does not go far you cannot buy very much with it: *A dollar doesn't go very far these days.* b) if a supply of something does not go far, it is not enough: *This pizza won't go far if everyone wants some.*
14 as far as possible as much as possible: *We try, as far as possible, to use local produce.*

SPOKEN PHRASES

15 as far as I know also **as far as I can tell/remember** said when you think that something is

true, although you do not know or cannot remember all the facts: *He's planning to be there for Christmas, as far as I know.* | *As far as I could tell, she wasn't angry about it.*
16 so far so good used to say that things have been happening successfully until now: *"How's your new job?" "So far so good."*
17 how far have you gotten (with sth)? said when asking or talking about how much of something someone has done or how much they have achieved: *How far have you gotten with painting the kitchen?*
18 go so/as far as to say sth used when you give a particular idea or opinion, in order to show that the opinion is extreme or unlikely to be true: *Some people go as far as to say that a kiss is more intimate than sex.* | *I wouldn't go so far as to say that this is as important an invention as the computer mouse.*
19 far from it used to say that the opposite of what someone says is true; certainly not: *"Did you enjoy yourself?" "Far from it!"*
20 far be it from me to do sth used when you are going to criticize someone or give them advice, and you want to pretend that you do not want to do this: *Far be it from me to tell you what to wear.*

21 far from used to say that the opposite of something is true, or the opposite of what you expect happens: [**far from doing sth**] *Far from allowing more trade, the new regulations actually make it harder to do business in Eastern Europe.* | *The company's troubles are far from over.* | *What happened shows that the U.S., far from being in decline, is still the most powerful nation in the world.* | **far from pleased/happy** etc. *Critics are far from satisfied.*
22 as far as it goes used to say that an idea, suggestion, plan etc. is satisfactory, but only to a limited degree: *What Kroll said was accurate, as far as it goes.*
23 as far as the eye can see up to the longest distance away that you can see: *There was nothing but snow covered peaks as far as the eye could see.*
24 long time a long time in the past or the future, or a long time into a particular period: *As far back as 400 B.C. Hippocrates was using herbs to treat his patients.* | *Spring was not far off* (=going to happen soon). —see also FAR-OFF (2)
25 far and wide over or from a large area: **travel/wander** etc. **far and wide** *I have traveled far and wide, and have never eaten at a worse diner.* | **hunt/search far and wide** *We've been searching far and wide for new talent.*
26 not be far off/wrong INFORMAL to be almost correct: *His estimates weren't too far off.* —see also INSOFAR AS

far[2] *adj. comparative* **farther** or **further** *superlative* **farthest** or **furthest 1** a long way away: *We can walk if it's not far.* | *In the far distance she could see the outlines of several tall buildings.* | *Denver's farther away than I thought.* | *Aim at the target that's farthest from you.* | *Excuse me, how far is it to Times Square?* **2 the far end/side** etc. the end or side that is farthest from you: *The parking lot is on the far side of the building.* **3 the far north/south** etc. the part of a country or area that is farthest in the direction of north, south etc.: *The plains are in the far west of the country.* **4 the far left/right** people who have extreme LEFT-WING or RIGHT-WING political opinions **5 be a far cry from sth** to be very different from something else: *Europe was a far cry from what we'd been led to expect.*

far·a·way /'fɑrə,weɪ/ *adj.* **1** [only before noun] LITERARY distant: *She was lost and alone in a faraway place.* | *We sat around the fire listening to faraway noises.* **2 a faraway look** an expression on your face which shows that you are around you but thinking about something very different

farce /fɑrs/ *n.* **1** [singular] an event or a situation that is badly organized and does not happen in the way that it should: *The speed limits on that stretch of road are a farce.* **2** [C] a humorous play in which people are involved in silly situations: *a farce by Feydeau* **3** [U] the style of writing or acting that is concerned with this kind of play

far·ci·cal /'fɑrsɪkəl/ *adj.* **1** extremely silly and badly organized: *a farcical trial* **2** having the qualities of a farce: *farcical characters* —**farcically** /-kli/ *adv.*

fare¹ /fɛr/ *n.* **1** [C] the price you pay to travel by bus, train, airplane etc.: *The fare is cheaper on Saturdays and Sundays.* | **air/bus/train/cab fare** *His brother is a pilot, so he got a discount on the air fare.* —see Usage Note at COST¹ **2** [U] food, especially food that you can buy in a restaurant or that you eat on a special occasion: *Goose, duck, and turkey are typical holiday fare in the Netherlands.* **3** [U] entertainment that someone else provides for you: *The movie is suitable family fare.* **4** [C] a passenger in a taxi **5** **a fare beater** INFORMAL someone who avoids paying for a ticket on a train, SUBWAY, or bus

fare² *v.* **fare well/badly/better etc.** FORMAL to be successful, unsuccessful etc.: *The show is faring well in the ratings.*

Far East /ˌ. './ *n.* **the Far East** the countries in the eastern part of Asia, such as China, Japan, Korea etc. —**Far Eastern** *adj.* —compare MIDDLE EAST, NEAR EAST

fare·well¹ /ˌfɛr'wɛl/ *n.* **1** [C,U] the action of saying goodbye: *a farewell speech* | *Grantson met with employees to* **bid** *them* **farewell** (=say goodbye to them). **2** **a farewell party/drink** a party or drink that you have because someone is leaving a job, city etc.

farewell² *interjection* OLD-FASHIONED goodbye

far-fetched /ˌ. '.ˑ/ *adj.* extremely unlikely to be true or to happen: *At the time, his ideas were considered far-fetched.*

far-flung /ˌ. '.ˑ/ *adj.* **1** very distant: *He's gone off hiking in some far-flung corner of Alaska.* **2** spread out over a very large area: *The company operates a number of far-flung offices.*

Far·go /'fɑrgoʊ/ the largest city in the U.S. state of North Dakota

far gone /ˌ. './ *adj.* [not before noun] INFORMAL very sick, drunk, crazy etc.: *She's too far gone to understand what's happening.*

farm¹ /fɑrm/ *n.* [C] an area of land, used for growing crops or keeping animals: *a farm in southern Alberta* | *farm animals* | **live/work etc. on a farm** *He grew up on a farm in Iowa.* | **a chicken/pig/wheat etc. farm** *a rice farm in Thailand* —see also **bet the ranch/farm** (BET¹ (8)), FACTORY FARM, FARM TEAM, FISH FARM, FUNNY FARM

farm² *v.* [I,T] **1** to use land for growing crops, keeping animals etc.: *My family has farmed here since 1901.* **2** farmed fish/salmon/trout etc. fish that have been raised in a special place in order to be sold as food, rather than fish that live in the wild

farm sth ↔ out *phr. v.* [T] to send work to other people instead of doing it yourself: *Most of the editing is farmed out to freelancers.*

farm belt /'. ./ *n.* [C] an area where there are many farms

farm·er /'fɑrmɚ/ *n.* [C] **1** someone who owns or manages a farm **2** **a farmer's tan** SPOKEN someone with a farmer's tan has dark skin from the sun on their arms, face, and neck, but a pale chest, because they were wearing a shirt while they were outside

farmers' mar·ket /ˌ.. ˌ../ *n.* [C] a place where farmers bring their fruit and vegetables to sell directly to people

farm·hand /'fɑrmhænd/ *n.* [C] someone who is employed to work on a farm

farm·house /'fɑrmhaʊs/ *n.* [C] the main house on a farm, where the farmer lives

farm·ing /'fɑrmɪŋ/ *n.* [U] the practice or business of growing crops or keeping animals on a farm

farm·land /'fɑrmlænd/ *n.* [U] land used for farming

farm·stead /'fɑrmstɛd/ *n.* [C] a farmhouse and the buildings around it

farm team /'. ./ *n.* [C] a MINOR LEAGUE baseball team that trains players for a particular MAJOR LEAGUE team

farm·yard /'fɑrmyɑrd/ *n.* [C] the area next to or around farm buildings

far-off /ˌ. '.ˑ/ *adj.* LITERARY **1** a long way from where you are: *They knew that invaders would come from a far-off land.* **2** a long time ago: *Life was simpler in those far-off days when we were young.*

far-out /ˌ. '.ˑ/ *adj.* **1** very strange or unusual: *Dave has some pretty far-out beliefs about UFOs.* **2** OLD-FASHIONED SLANG extremely good: *The concert was really far out.*

Far·ra·khan, Lou·is /'færəˌkɑn, 'luɪs/ (1933–) the leader of the Nation of Islam

far-reach·ing /ˌ. '.ˑ/ *adj.* having a big influence or effect: *a far-reaching law on environmental protection*

far·ri·er /'færiɚ/ *n.* [C] someone who makes special metal shoes for horses' feet

Far·si /'fɑrsi/ *n.* [U] the language of Iran; PERSIAN

far·sight·ed /'fɑrˌsaɪtɪd/ *adj.* **1** able to see or read things clearly only when they are far away from you —opposite NEARSIGHTED **2** APPROVING considering what will happen in the future: *Even farsighted advisers were surprised by the speed of political change.* —**farsightedly** *adv.* —**farsightedness** *n.* [U]

fart¹ /fɑrt/ *v.* [I] IMPOLITE to make air come out of your BOWELS

fart around *phr. v.* [I] IMPOLITE to waste time, especially by seeming to be busy when you are not: *Stop farting around and get to work!*

fart² *n.* **1** INFORMAL an act of making air come out of your BOWELS (1) **2** SLANG a stupid and uninteresting person

far·ther /'fɑrðɚ/ *adj., adv.* the COMPARATIVE of "far"

USAGE NOTE: FARTHER

WORD CHOICE: farther and further
Use **farther** to talk about distance: *I can't run any farther.* | *There's a gas station a few miles farther down the road.* Use **further** to talk about time, quantities, or amounts: *Prices will probably increase further next year.* | *Patty refused to discuss the matter any further.* People often use **further** to talk about distance, but many teachers consider this use incorrect.

---

far·thest /'fɑrðɪst/ *adj., adv.* the SUPERLATIVE of "far"

far·thing /'fɑrðɪŋ/ *n.* [C] a British coin, used in past times, that was worth one quarter of a PENNY

fas·ci·a /'feɪʃə/ *n. plural* **fascias** or **fasciae** /-ʃi-i/ [C] **1** the flat outside surface of a building, which is meant to be pretty rather than being part of the structure of the building **2** a band of material in your body that separates, attaches, or surrounds muscles, organs etc.

fas·ci·nate /'fæsəˌneɪt/ *v.* [I,T not in progressive] to attract or interest someone very much: *Baseball still fascinates Americans.* | *Parsons, playing Miss Margarida, entertains, seduces, and fascinates.*

fas·ci·nat·ed /'fæsəˌneɪtɪd/ *adj.* [not before noun] extremely interested by something or someone: [+ by] *As a schoolboy, Martin was fascinated by aviation.* | **be fascinated to discover/hear/learn etc.** *We were fascinated to learn she had grown up in Kenya.*

fas·ci·nat·ing /'fæsəˌneɪtɪŋ/ *adj.* extremely interesting: *a fascinating woman* | *I* **found** *Rutherfurd's book on Russia* **fascinating.** —**fascinatingly** *adv.*

fas·ci·na·tion /ˌfæsəˈneɪʃən/ *n.* **1** [singular,U] the state of being very interested in something, so that you want to look at it, learn about it etc.: [+ with/for] *Most children share a fascination with dinosaurs.* | *Kucher has* **had a fascination with** *bugs since childhood.* | *The audience watched* **in fascination.** **2** [C,U] something that interests you very much, or the quality of being very interesting: **have/hold fascination for sb** *The idea of space travel will always hold great fascination for me.*

fas·cism /'fæʃɪzəm/ *n.* [U] an extreme political system in which people's lives are completely controlled by the state and no political opposition is allowed

fas·cist /'fæʃɪst/ *n.* [C] **1** someone who supports fascism **2** INFORMAL someone who is cruel and unfair and does not like people to argue with them: *My children have occasionally accused me of being a fascist.* —**fascist** *adj.*

fash·ion[1] /'fæʃən/ *n.* **1** [singular,U] the popular style of clothes, hair, behavior etc. at a particular time, that is likely to change: *The color black is always in fashion.* | *Harper carries classic styles that never go out of fashion* (=stop being popular). | *His ideas are coming back into fashion.* | *Our typical customer is very fashion conscious* (=always wanting to wear the newest fashions). | *Bottled mineral water was the fashion in the late 1980s.* **2** [C] a style of clothes, hair etc. that is popular at a particular time: *This year's men's fashions are brighter and more casual than ever before.* | *Platform sandals are this summer's fashion.* | *She always buys the latest fashions.* | *Nightclubbers and teenagers prompted the fashion of body piercing.* **3** [U] the business or study of making and selling clothes, shoes etc. in new and changing styles: *Diane is the assistant fashion editor at "Vogue."* | *She is studying fashion and hopes to work in the fashion industry.* **4 in a... fashion** FORMAL in a particular way: *He failed to correct the error in a timely fashion* (=he did not do it quickly). **5 like it's going out of fashion** INFORMAL if you eat, drink, or use something like it's going out of fashion, you eat, drink, or use a lot of it: *She's been spending money like it's going out of fashion.* **6 after the fashion of sb** in a style that is typical of a particular person: *His early work is very much after the fashion of Faulkner and O'Connor.* **7 after a fashion** FORMAL if you do something after a fashion, you can do it, but not very well: *The group learns to ride and lasso after a fashion.* —see also FASHION PLATE, FASHION SENSE, FASHION SHOW, FASHION VICTIM

fashion[2] *v.* [T] **1** FORMAL to shape or make something, using your hands or only a few tools: [**fashion sth from sth**] *Several prisoners were armed with weapons fashioned from razor blades.* | [**fashion sth into sth**] *As a boy, he had fashioned pieces of wood into homemade baseball bats.* **2** [usually passive] to influence and form someone's ideas and opinions or a particular situation: *Our attitudes to politics are fashioned by the media.*

-fashion /fæʃən/ *suffix* [in adverbs] like something, or in the way that a particular group of people does something: *They ate Indian-fashion, using their fingers.*

fash·ion·a·ble /'fæʃənəbəl/ *adj.* **1** popular, especially for a short period of time: *The fleece tops for children come in fashionable colors.* **2** popular with, or used by, rich people: *He runs a very fashionable restaurant in Sag Harbor.* **3** someone who is fashionable wears good clothes, goes to expensive restaurants etc. —opposite UNFASHIONABLE

fash·ion·a·bly /'fæʃənəbli/ *adv.* **1 fashionably late** a little late, especially because you want people who are waiting for you to pay special attention to your arrival: *Lucy and Rose arrived fashionably late.* **2** according to the current style: *You don't have to dress fashionably, just warmly.*

fashion house /'.. ,./ *n.* [C] a company that produces new and expensive styles of clothes

fashion plate /'.. ,./ *n.* [C] INFORMAL someone who likes to wear very fashionable clothes

fashion sense /'.. ,./ *n.* [U] the ability to choose clothes that make you look attractive

fashion show /'.. ,./ *n.* [C] an event at which new styles of clothes are shown to the public

fashion state·ment /'.. ,../ *n.* [C] an unusual way of wearing clothes that makes people notice you and shows them what your feelings, attitudes, or opinions are: *She wears old army uniforms as a fashion statement.*

fashion vic·tim /'.. ,../ *n.* [C] INFORMAL someone who always tries to wear what is fashionable, even though it makes them look bad

fast[1] /fæst/ *adj.* S W
1 moving quickly **a)** moving or traveling quickly: *He's one of the fastest sprinters in the world.* | *The first pitch was fast and hard.* **b)** able to travel or move very quickly: *The new convertible is fast and fun to drive.*
2 in a short time **a)** doing something or happening in a short time: *The subway is the fastest way to get downtown.* | *We hope Arlene will make a fast recovery.* **b)** able to do something in a short time: *I'm a pretty fast reader.* **c)** happening without delay: *One man's fast response saved a heart-attack victim's life.*
3 clock [not before noun] a clock that is fast shows a later time than the real time: *Is it really 6:45, or is my watch fast?* | *I keep the clock five minutes fast, so I won't be late.*
4 fast track a way of achieving something more quickly than it is normally done: *The agency is looking at a fast track for approving drugs for life-threatening illnesses.* | *Women have sought business degrees to get on the fast track at big corporations.*
5 the fast lane a) an exciting way of living that involves dangerous or expensive activities: *McCravey lived his life in the fast lane for 27 years.* **b)** the part of a large road, especially a HIGHWAY, that is used by fast vehicles
6 fast film/lens a film or LENS that can be used when there is not much light, or when photographing something that is moving very quickly
7 color a color that is fast will not change when clothes are washed —see also COLORFAST
8 sports a fast surface is one on which a ball moves very quickly, or one on which a person, horse, or dog can run very quickly
9 fast talker someone who talks quickly and easily but is often not honest or sincere: *Lenny Clarke is a fast talker, which might explain why he was torn between politics and comedy.*
10 fast friends LITERARY two people who are very friendly for a long time
11 sb's a fast worker INFORMAL used to say that someone can get what they want very quickly, especially in starting a sexual relationship with another person
12 woman OLD-FASHIONED becoming involved quickly in sexual relationships with men
13 make sth fast to tie something such as a boat or tent firmly to something else —see also **make a fast buck** (BUCK[1] (1)), **pull a fast one** (PULL[1] (11)), FAST FOOD, FAST FORWARD

fast[2] *adv.* S W
1 quickly moving quickly: *The car was going pretty fast when it went off the road.* | *Burglars work fast.* | *Just keep skiing as fast as you can.* | *Johnny ran off as fast as his legs could carry him* (=running as quickly as he could).
2 in a short time **a)** in a short time: *Prices aren't rising as fast as they were a year ago.* | *Kids grow up so fast these days.* | *a fast-growing community* | **be fast becoming/developing/disappearing** *Many Asian countries are fast becoming real economic powers.* **b)** soon and without delay: *Two of these will get rid of your headache fast.* | *How fast can you get it ready?*
3 fast asleep sleeping very deeply: *Most of the household was still fast asleep.*
4 tightly firmly or tightly, and unable to move: *The front of the boat was stuck fast in the mud.* | *The opening is held fast with a slide.*
5 hold fast (to sth) to continue to believe in or support an idea, principle etc.: *Bush urged the party to hold fast to its traditions.*
6 not so fast SPOKEN **a)** used to tell someone to do something more slowly or carefully: *Not so fast! You'll scrape the paint!* **b)** used to say that something has not yet happened or is not yet true: *Not so fast, guys. One win doesn't make a championship season.*
7 fast and furious done very quickly with a lot of

effort and energy, or happening very quickly with a lot of sudden changes: *With elections about a year away, proposals for tax cuts are coming fast and furious.*
8 fast by sth LITERARY very close to something: *We stood on a rock, fast by the river.* —see also **play fast and loose with sb/sth** (PLAY¹ (24)), **stand fast/firm** (STAND¹ (20)), **thick and fast** (THICK² (2))

fast³ *v.* [I] to eat little or no food for a period of time, especially for religious reasons: *Muslims fast during Ramadan.*

fast⁴ *n.* [C] a period during which someone eats little or no food, especially for religious reasons: *a one-day fast for charity* | *The group will **break** its **fast*** (=end the fast by eating or drinking something) *at a Friday evening religious service.*

fast·ball /'fæstbɔl/ *n.* [C] a ball that is thrown very hard and quickly toward the BATTER in a game of baseball

fast day /'. ,./ *n.* [C] a day when you do not eat any food, especially for religious reasons

fas·ten /'fæsən/ *v.*
1 clothes/bag etc. also **fasten up a)** [T] to join together the two sides of a coat, shirt, bag etc. so that it is closed: *Please fasten your seat belts.* | *With the strap fastened, you should not be able to get the bike helmet off.* —opposite UNFASTEN **b)** [I] to become joined together with buttons, hooks etc.: *Many children's shoes now fasten with Velcro.*
2 attach sth to sth [T] to attach something firmly to another object or surface: *The chains were fastened with steel locks.* | [**fasten sth to/onto sth**] *A pulley is fastened to the ceiling of the warehouse.*
3 fasten your eyes on sb/sth to look at someone or something for a long time: *Her dark eyes fastened on Arthur's face.*
4 fasten your attention on sth to think a lot about one particular thing
5 window/gate etc. [I,T] to firmly close a window, gate etc. so that it will not open, or to become firmly closed: *Make sure all the windows are securely fastened before you leave.* —opposite UNFASTEN
6 fasten blame on sb/sth to blame someone or something, often in a way that is not fair
7 fasten your arms/legs around sth to hold something firmly with your arms or legs
fasten on/upon sth *phr. v.* [T] to decide quickly and eagerly that an idea is the best one: *Brennan's campaign has fastened on budget problems as a way to get voters' attention.*

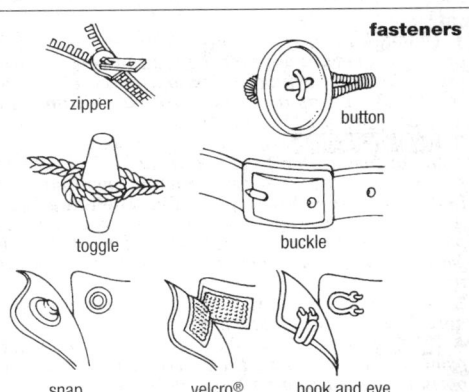

fasteners

zipper

button

toggle

buckle

snap

velcro®

hook and eye

fas·ten·er /'fæsənɚ/ also **fas·ten·ing** /'fæsənɪŋ/ *n.* [C] something that you use to join something together, for example a button on a piece of clothing: *a Velcro fastener*

fast food /, '. '. / *n.* [U] inexpensive food, for example HAMBURGERS, that is prepared and served quickly in a restaurant: *a fast-food restaurant*

fast for·ward, fast-forward /, '. '. ./ *v.* **1** [I,T] to wind a TAPE forward quickly in a machine by pressing a button: *Listeners can fast forward and rewind the taped audio.* **2** [I] to move quickly to a later point in a story or stage of development: *Now fast forward to 1976 when Bolin met his future wife.* —**fast forward** *n.* [U] *He watched the whole movie on fast forward.*

fas·tid·i·ous /fæ'stɪdiəs, fə-/ *adj.* very careful about small details in your appearance, work etc.: *A cat is a fastidious animal that washes itself frequently.* —**fastidiously** *adv.* —**fastidiousness** *n.* [U] —compare FUSSY (1)

fast·ness /'fæstnɪs/ *n.* [C] LITERARY a safe place that is difficult to reach: *mountain fastnesses*

fat¹ /fæt/ *adj.* **fatter, fattest**
1 flesh weighing too much because you have too much flesh on your body: *He's short and fat.* | *I always look so fat in pictures.* | *a **big fat** kid* | *The cat's starting to **get fat**.*
2 thick or wide thick or wide: *There was a nice fat letter waiting for him the next morning.* | *fat red plastic earrings*
3 money [only before noun] INFORMAL containing or worth a large amount of money: *He left the waitress a nice fat tip.*
4 a fat lip a lip that is swollen because it has been injured
5 fat cat INFORMAL, DISAPPROVING someone who has too much money and uses it to influence political decisions
6 grow fat on sth to become rich because of something: *These stock brokers grow fat on other people's money.*

<table>
<tr><td colspan="1">SPOKEN PHRASES</td></tr>
</table>

7 fat chance used to say that something is very unlikely to happen: *You want tickets for the big game? Fat chance.*
8 be in fat city OLD-FASHIONED to have plenty of money
9 a fat lot of good/use something that is not useful or helpful at all: *He practiced, but a fat lot of good it did him* (=the practice did not help him). —**fatness** *n.* [U]

—compare PHAT

USAGE NOTE: FAT

WORD CHOICE: fat, overweight, large, heavy, plump, chubby, stout, tubby, obese
If you want to be polite about someone, do not say that they are **fat**. Saying that they are **overweight, large** or **heavy** is a more polite way of saying the same thing. **Plump** is most often used about women and children, and it means slightly fat, usually in a way that looks nice. **Chubby** is most often used about babies and children and also means pleasantly fat and healthy-looking. When you are describing adults, **stout** means slightly fat and heavy and **tubby** means short and fat, especially around the stomach. If someone is extremely fat and unhealthy, they are **obese**. Obese is also the word used by doctors.

fat² *n.*
1 person or animal [U] a substance that is under the skin of people and animals, that helps to keep them warm: *A roll of fat bulged over his belt.* | *Take two chicken breasts, and cut off all the fat.*
2 in food [C,U] an oily substance in some foods: *A portion of tuna packed in water contains 1.2 grams of fat.* | **high/low in fat** *Crisp, crunchy cookies are usually high in fat.* | **high-/low-fat** *low-fat cottage cheese*
3 for cooking [C,U] an oily substance taken from animals or plants and used in cooking: *Fry the potatoes in oil or bacon fat.*
4 money [U] money used to buy things that you do not really need: *Most people are trying to **trim the fat** out of their budgets this Christmas.*
5 the fat is in the fire used to say that there will be trouble because of something that has happened
6 live off the fat of the land to get enough money to live comfortably without doing much work
7 run/go to fat to start to become fat, especially

because you are getting older or do not do much exercise —see also BABY FAT, **chew the fat** (CHEW[1] (3)), **not have an ounce of fat on you** (OUNCE (4))

fa·tal /ˈfeɪtl/ *adj.* **1** resulting in someone's death: *The gas can be fatal if inhaled in large amounts.* | **a fatal accident/illness/injury** etc. *Ultimately, AIDS is still a fatal disease.* | *German measles can prove fatal* (=make someone die) *to an unborn baby.* **2** having a very bad effect, especially making someone fail or stop what they are doing: [**be fatal to sth**] *This approach will be fatal to real reform.* | *The loss could prove fatal to their championship hopes.* | *Her fatal mistake was to marry too young.* | *The developments dealt a fatal blow to the government's peace plan.* | *There are fatal flaws* (=serious weaknesses) *in this computer program.*

fa·tal·ism /ˈfeɪtl,ɪzəm/ *n.* [U] the belief that there is nothing you can do to prevent events from happening —**fatalist** *n.* [C]

fa·tal·is·tic /ˌfeɪtlˈɪstɪk/ *adj.* believing that there is nothing you can do to prevent things from happening: *Emma was fatalistic about her future.* —**fatalistically** /-kli/ *adv.*

fa·tal·i·ty /feɪˈtæləti, fə-/ *n. plural* **fatalities 1** [C,U] a death in an accident or violent attack: *This year there have been 15% fewer traffic fatalities.* | *Airplane fatality rates are low.* **2** [U] FORMAL the fact that a disease is certain to cause death: *New drugs have reduced the fatality of the disease.* **3** [U] FORMAL the feeling that you cannot control what happens to you

fa·tal·ly /ˈfeɪtl-i/ *adv.* **1** in a way that causes death: **fatally wounded/injured/burned** etc. *Eight children were fatally injured in the explosion.* **2** in a way that will make something fail or be unable to continue: *The strategy is fatally flawed.*

fate /feɪt/ *n.* **1** [C] the things that will happen to someone or something, especially bad events: [+ **of**] *These rulings will affect the fate of more than 6,000 refugees.* | *So far, Nintendo has not suffered the same fate as other toy fads.* | **decide/settle/seal sb's fate** *A three-man, three-woman jury will decide Chambers's fate.* | **leave/abandon sb to their fate** (=leave someone when something bad is likely to happen to them) **2** [U] also **Fate** a power that is believed to control what happens in people's lives: *He felt that fate had been very unfair to him.* | *By a lucky twist of fate* (=completely unexpected event), *we were on the same plane.* —compare PROVIDENCE **3 a fate worse than death** HUMOROUS an experience that seems like the worst thing that could happen to you: *I knew that Grandma's visit would be a fate worse than death.* **4 the Fates** the three GODDESSES who, according to the ancient Greeks, controlled what happened to people —see also **tempt fate** (TEMPT (3))

fat·ed /ˈfeɪtɪd/ *adj.* LITERARY certain to happen or to do something because a mysterious force is controlling events: [**be fated to do sth**] *Achilles was fated to die after Hector.* —see also ILL-FATED

fate·ful /ˈfeɪtfəl/ *adj.* having an important, usually bad, effect on future events: *People were glued to their televisions on that fateful day when Kennedy was killed.* —**fatefully** *adv.*

fat farm /ˈ. ./ *n.* [C] INFORMAL a place where people who are fat can go to lose weight and improve their health

fat-free /ˌ. ˈ.◂/ *adj.* food that is fat-free does not have any fat in it: *fat-free yogurt*

fat·head /ˈfæthɛd/ *n.* [C] SLANG a stupid person —**fatheaded** *adj.*

fa·ther¹ /ˈfɑðə/ *n.* **1** [C] a male parent: *Pianto has been working with his father for 21 years.* | **a father of two/three** etc. *Hernandez, the father of five, has not been able to work since July.* **2 Father a)** a priest, especially in the Catholic church: *Have you met Father Simmons?* **b)** a way of speaking to or about God, used in the Christian religion: *Heavenly Father, please forgive us our sins.* **3 the father of sth** the man who was responsible for starting something: *George Washington is the father of our country.* **4 father figure** an older man who you trust and respect **5 like father, like son** used to say that a boy

behaves like his father, especially when this behavior is bad **6 fathers** [plural] FORMAL people related to you who lived a long time ago; ANCESTORS: *Our fathers came to a new country with new hope.* —see also CITY FATHER, FOREFATHER

father² *v.* [T] **1** to make a woman have a baby: *Taylor denies fathering her 4-month-old son.* **2** to start an important new idea or system: *Roosevelt fathered the concept of Social Security.*

fa·ther·hood /ˈfɑðə,hʊd/ *n.* [U] the state of being a father

father-in-law /ˈ.. . ,./ *n. plural* **fathers-in-law** [C] the father of your husband or wife

fa·ther·land /ˈfɑðə,lænd/ *n.* [singular] a word meaning the place where someone or their family was born —see also MOTHER COUNTRY, MOTHERLAND

fa·ther·ly /ˈfɑðəli/ *adj.* kind and gentle in a way that is considered typical of a good father: *He spoke in a warm, fatherly tone.*

Father's Day /ˈ.. ,./ *n.* [C] a holiday in the U.S. and Canada on the third Sunday of June, on which people give cards and presents to their father

fath·om¹ /ˈfæðəm/ *v.* [T] to understand what something means, especially something very difficult to understand, after thinking about it carefully: *The jury had difficulty fathoming the technical details.*

fathom² *n.* [C] a unit for measuring how deep water is, equal to 6 feet or 1.83 meters

fath·om·less /ˈfæðəmlɪs/ *adj.* LITERARY **1** too deep to be measured **2** too complicated to be understood

fa·tigue /fəˈtig/ *n.* [U] **1** extreme tiredness: *Stoklos was showing signs of fatigue after a difficult game.* **2** TECHNICAL weakness in a substance such as metal, caused when it is bent or stretched many times, which is likely to make it break **3 fatigues** [plural] loose-fitting army clothes —**fatigue** *v.* [T] FORMAL —see also COMBAT FATIGUE

fa·tigued /fəˈtigd/ *v.* [T] FORMAL extremely tired

fat·so /ˈfætsoʊ/ *n.* [C] SPOKEN an insulting word for someone who is fat

fat·ten /ˈfætⁿn/ *v.* [I,T] **1** to make an animal become fatter so that it is ready to eat, or to become fat and ready to eat **2** to make an amount larger: *Increased profits will fatten the bonuses of the managers.*

fatten sb/sth ↔ **up** *phr. v.* [T] to make a thin person or animal fatter: *Cattle are sent to the feedlot to be fattened up.*

fat·ten·ing /ˈfætⁿn-ɪŋ/ *adj.* likely to make you fat: *a fattening dessert*

fat·ty¹ /ˈfæti/ *adj.* **fattier, fattiest** containing a lot of fat: *fatty foods*

fatty² *n.* [C] SPOKEN an insulting word for someone who is fat

fatty ac·id /ˌ.. ˈ../ *n.* [C] TECHNICAL an acid that a cell needs to use food effectively

fat·u·ous /ˈfætʃuəs/ *adj.* FORMAL stupid or FOOLISH: *fatuous speeches* —**fatuously** *adv.* —**fatuousness** *n.* [U]

fat·wa /ˈfɑtⁿwɑ/ *n.* [C] an official order made by an important Islamic religious leader

fau·cet /ˈfɔsɪt/ *n.* [C] the piece of equipment that you turn on and off to control the flow of water from a pipe; TAP —see picture at KITCHEN

Faulk·ner /ˈfɔknə/**, William** (1897–1962) a U.S. writer of NOVELs about the Deep South of the U.S.

fault¹ /fɔlt/ *n.*
1 be sb's fault if something bad that has happened is someone's fault, they should be blamed for it, because they made a mistake or failed to do something: [**be sb's fault (that)**] *It's your fault we're late.* | [**be sb's fault for doing sth**] *Somehow, people seem to think it's my fault for letting him in.* | *It's partly their own fault if they don't get promoted.*
2 at fault a person, organization, or system that is at fault is responsible for something bad that has happened: *The accident report found both drivers at fault.*

3 `sth wrong with sth` [C] **a)** something that is wrong with a machine, system, design etc., which prevents it from working correctly: *Check the ignition system for faults.* | [+ **in**] *a fault in the airplane's fuel system* **b)** something that is wrong with something, which could be improved: *Despite its faults, the novel is suspenseful.* | *The treaty was a great achievement, for all its faults* (=in spite of its faults). **c)** a mistake in the way that something was made: [+ **in**] *a fault in the new microchips*
4 `sb's character` [C] a bad or weak part of someone's character: *Denney is aware of his faults.* | *For all her faults* (=in spite of her faults), *I still love her.*
5 through no fault of sb's own used to say that something bad that happened to someone was not caused by them: *The program is designed to help people who lose their jobs through no fault of their own.*
6 `crack` [C] a large crack in the rocks that form the Earth's surface: *The San Andreas fault runs right through the middle of this valley.*
7 generous/kind etc. to a fault extremely generous, kind etc., especially to a degree that is unnecessary: *Our cat is friendly to a fault.*
8 `tennis` [C] a mistake made when a player is serving the ball in a game of tennis —see also **find fault with sb/sth** (FIND[1] (16))

fault[2] v. [T] to criticize someone or something for a mistake: *The Mars project has been faulted by some scientists who say it has little research value.* | *The meal was a little bland, but you **couldn't fault** the service* (=the service was good).

fault·less /ˈfɔltlɪs/ adj. having no mistakes; PERFECT: *a faultless memory* —**faultlessly** adv. —**faultlessness** n. [U]

fault·y /ˈfɔlti/ adj. **1** something such as a machine that is faulty has something wrong with it that stops it from working correctly, or it was not made correctly: *The report said the fire was started by faulty electrical wiring.* **2** a faulty way of thinking about something contains a mistake that results in a wrong decision: *Weston's article contained some interesting but faulty reasoning.* —**faultily** adv.

faun /fɔn, fɑn/ n. [C] an ancient Roman god with the body of a man and the legs and horns of a goat

fau·na /ˈfɔnə, ˈfɑ-/ n. [C,U] TECHNICAL all the animals living in a particular place or at a particular time in history —compare FLORA

Faust /faʊst/, **Jo·hann** /ˈyoʊhɑn/ also **Dr. Faustus** a German doctor and SCHOLAR of the early 16th century, who appears in many stories, plays, etc. as a man who sold his soul to the Devil in exchange for knowledge and power

fauv·ism /ˈfoʊˌvɪzəm/ n. [U] a style of painting that uses pure bright colors, which was developed in the early 20th century —**fauvist** n. [C]

faux /foʊ/ adj. [only before noun] artificial, but made to look real: *faux pearls*

faux pas /ˌfoʊ ˈpɑ/ n. [C] an embarrassing mistake in a social situation: *Talking business at dinner is a faux pas in France.*

fa·va bean /ˈfɑvə ˌbin/ n. [C] a large flat pale green bean

fave /feɪv/ n. [C] INFORMAL a favorite person or thing: *The band Helen Keller Plaid, a local fave, kicks off the show.* —**fave** adj.

s w fa·vor[1] /ˈfeɪvɚ/ n.
1 `help` [C] something that you do for someone in order to help them or be kind to them: *Could you **do me a favor** and watch the baby for half an hour?* | *I need to **ask you** both **a huge favor**.* | *I **have a favor to ask** – could you call Eric for me?* | *Landis offered to direct the video **as a favor to** Jackson.* | *I flew to Vermont to conduct a seminar for a friend to whom I **owed a favor** (=I felt that I should help my friend because he helped me in the past).* | *Thanks for all your help – I'll **return the favor** (=help you because you have helped me) sometime!*

2 `support/approval` [U] support or approval for something such as a plan, idea, or system: *A number of politicians **are in favor of** term limits.* | *I'm **all in favor of** (=completely approve of) people doing whatever they want as long as they don't bother anyone else.* | *Will **all in favor say aye** (=used when taking a vote)?* | *Plans to increase spending have **lost favor** (=stopped being supported) among the President's inner circle.* | *We're hoping the board will **look with favor** (=use its power to help something succeed) our plan.* | **find/gain/win favor** *It's hoped that the proposal will gain favor with local residents.* | **find/rule in favor of sb/sth** (=make a legal decision that supports someone or something)
3 do sth in favor of sth/sb if you decide not to use one plan, idea, system, or person in favor of another, you choose the other one because you think it is better: *Taylor was dropped from the starting position in favor of Louis Stewart.* | *Martinelli abandoned his restaurant in favor of a catering business.*
4 in sb's favor if something is in someone's favor, it gives them an advantage over someone else: *The vote was 60–54 in Warren's favor.* | *In an interview, a good first impression **works in your favor** (=gives you an advantage).* | *Everyone knows that you can't win in gambling because **the odds are stacked in** the dealer's favor (=he has a big advantage).*
5 `popular` [U] if someone or something is in favor or out of favor, people like and approve of them at the present time, or do not like and approve of them anymore: *Lefebvre isn't **in favor with** the team's management.* | *I never thought old-time movie stars like her would be **back in favor** (=popular again).* | *Although he's **out of favor**, some people still read his books.* | *Once a presidential candidate **falls out of favor** (=stops being liked), it is very difficult for him to regain popularity.* | *That kind of teaching method **went out of favor** (=stopped being used) in the 1970s.*
6 be thankful/grateful for small favors to be pleased that a bad situation is not as bad as it could be
7 `gift` [C] a small gift given to guests at a party: *inexpensive party favors in plastic bags*
8 `sex` favors [plural] a sexual relationship that a woman agrees to have with a man: *Several women said they had been pressured for **sexual favors**.*
9 `unfair support` [U] support that is given to one person or group and not to others in a way that does not seem fair; FAVORITISM —see also **curry favor with sb** (CURRY[2] (1)), **without fear or favor** (FEAR[1] (4))

favor[2] v. [T]
1 to support or approve of one plan, idea etc., especially when there are several to choose from: *The president is believed to favor further tax cuts.*
2 to prefer something and choose it instead of something else: *This year's styles are based on loose clothing of the type favored in some Middle Eastern countries.*
3 `give an advantage` to treat someone much better than someone else, in an unfair way: *It's yet another tax cut that favors the rich.*
4 `help` to provide the right conditions for something to happen: *These are exactly the wind conditions that favor sailing.*
5 `look like` OLD-FASHIONED to look like one of your parents or grandparents: *I think he favors his Uncle Dean.*
favor sb with sth phr. v. [T] FORMAL to give someone something that gives them an advantage or that pleases them: *The factories in Mexico were favored with tax and tariff breaks.*

fa·vor·able /ˈfeɪvərəbəl/ adj. **1** a favorable report, opinion, or reaction shows that you think that someone or something is good or that you agree with them: *They expect a favorable ruling from the court.* | *Responses from audiences have been overwhelmingly favorable.* **2** appropriate and likely to make something happen or succeed: [+ **for/to**] *Unfortunately, the wind conditions were favorable for fires to spread.* **3** favorable conditions are reasonable and not too expensive or difficult: *Banks are now offering favorable financing terms.* **4** making people like or approve of someone or something: *Dress appropriately in order to* **make a favorable impression**. —**favorably** adv.

fa·vored /ˈfeɪvəd/ adj. [only before noun] **1** receiving special attention, help, or treatment, especially in an unfair way: *Congress approved "most favored nation" trade status for the country.* **2** chosen or preferred by many people: *"Time out," rather than spanking, is now the favored form of discipline for many parents.* **3** a favored team, player etc. is one that is expected to win: *Kansas City is favored by 4 points.* —see also ILL-FAVORED

fa·vor·ite¹ /ˈfeɪvrɪt, -vərɪt/ adj. **1** [only before noun] someone or something that you like more than any other one of its kind: *Everyone has a favorite recipe.* **2 a favorite son** a politician, sports player etc. who is popular with people in the area that they come from

favorite² n. [C] **1** something that you like more than other things of the same kind: *Apple fritters are my favorite.* | *Sunol Regional Park is a favorite with dog owners.* | *This song is* **an old favorite** *of mine.* **2** someone who receives more attention and approval than is fair: *Parents shouldn't have favorites.* | *The recession hasn't* **played favorites**; *everyone has suffered.* —see also FAVORITISM **3** the team, person etc. that is expected to win a race or competition: *Feinstein is considered a favorite to win a seat in Congress.*

fa·vor·it·ism /ˈfeɪvrəˌtɪzəm/ n. [U] a way of treating one person or group better than others in an unfair way: *School district employees believed that promotions were based on favoritism.*

fa·vour /ˈfeɪvə/ n., v. the British and Canadian spelling of FAVOR, also used in the words "favourable," "favoured," "favourite," and "favouritism"

fawn¹ /fɔn, fɑn/ v. [I] to praise someone and be friendly to them in an insincere way, because you want them to like you or give you something: [+ on/over] *People were fawning over him, hoping for tickets.*

fawn² n. **1** [C] a young DEER **2** [U] a pale yellow-brown color

fawn³ adj. having a pale yellow-brown color

fax¹ /fæks/ n. **1** [C] a document that is sent in electronic form through a telephone line and then printed using a special machine: *Did you get my fax?* **2** [C] also **fax machine** a machine used for sending and receiving faxes: *What's your fax number?* **3** [U] the system of sending documents using a fax machine: *Send this letter* **by fax**, *Judy.*

fax² v. [T] to send someone a document using a fax machine: [fax sb sth] *She said they'll fax us the contract by 4:30.* | [fax sth to sb] *Can you fax the order to Reynolds as soon as possible?*

fay /feɪ/ n. [C] POETIC a FAIRY (2)

faze /feɪz/ v. [T] INFORMAL if a new or difficult situation fazes you, it makes you feel confused or shocked: *The intense heat of the Cuban summer doesn't faze Vasquez.*

FBI, the n. the Federal Bureau of Investigation; the police department of the U.S. government that collects information about crime and is concerned with FEDERAL law rather than state law —compare CIA

FCC, the —see FEDERAL COMMUNICATIONS COMMISSION, THE

FDA, the Food and Drug Administration; a U.S. government organization which makes sure that foods and drugs are safe enough to be sold

fe·al·ty /ˈfiəlti/ n. [U] OLD-FASHIONED loyalty to a King, Queen, President, political party etc.

fear¹ /fɪr/ n. **1** [C,U] the feeling you get when you are afraid or worried that something bad is going to happen: *Curiosity overcame her fear.* | *McCarthy exploited deep-seated fears about communism among the American people.* | [+ of] *the fear of nuclear war* | *a fear of flying* | [fear that] *There is real fear that the situation in Yugoslavia will deteriorate.* | [+ for] *Two men refused to testify in court out of fear for their lives.* | *He was never caught, and I* **live in fear of** (=am always afraid of) *being raped again.* | *A small boy was crouched* **in fear** (=feeling afraid) *behind a tree.* **2 for fear of sth** also **for fear (that)** because you are worried that you will make something happen: *She would not give her name, for fear that her abusive husband would find her.* **3 put the fear of God into sb** INFORMAL to make someone feel that they must do something, by making sure they know what will happen if they do not do it: *The IRS tries to put the fear of God into people who don't pay enough tax.* **4 without fear or favor** FORMAL in a fair way: *We will investigate without fear or favor.*

fear² v. [T] **1** to feel afraid or worried that something bad may happen: *Fearing a blizzard, many people stayed home.* | [fear (that)] *Analysts fear that war could spread to that area as well.* | [fear to do sth] *Many old people fear to leave their own homes.* **2 fear for sb/sth** to feel worried about someone or something because you think something bad might happen to them: *I'm not afraid for myself, but I fear for my daughter, if something should happen to me.* | *Sometimes I* **fear for the future** *of this country.* | **fear for sb's safety/life** *Residents fear for their children's safety on the busy road.* **3 fear the worst** to think that the worst possible thing has happened or might happen: *Rescuers feared the worst for the men trapped in the mine.* **4** to be afraid of someone or something and what they might do: *He was a ruthless dictator, feared by the entire country.* **5 I fear** FORMAL used when telling someone that you think that something bad has happened or is true: *I fear that we must accept the limitations of medicine.* **6 fear not** also **never fear** FORMAL used to tell someone not to worry: *Never fear, we'll fix it somehow.* —see also GOD-FEARING

fear·ful /ˈfɪrfəl/ adj. **1** FORMAL frightened that something might happen: [+ of] *Even doctors are fearful of getting the disease.* | [fearful (that)] *Many economists are fearful that consumers will cut back even further on spending.* **2** OLD-FASHIONED [only before noun] frightening: *a fearful noise* —**fearfulness** n. [U]

fear·ful·ly /ˈfɪrfəli/ adv. **1** in a way that shows you are afraid: *Rosario fearfully clutched her 3-month-old infant as the bombs continued to fall.* **2** [+ adj./adv.] OLD-FASHIONED extremely

fear·less /ˈfɪrlɪs/ adj. not afraid of anything: *These animals are fearless and very aggressive.* —**fearlessly** adv. —**fearlessness** n. [U]

fear·some /ˈfɪrsəm/ adj. very frightening: *Stalin's fearsome secret police*

fea·si·ble /ˈfizəbəl/ adj. a plan, idea, or method that is feasible is possible and is likely to work: *Solar heating is technically and economically feasible.* —**feasibly** adv. —**feasibility** /ˌfizəˈbɪləti/ n. [U]

feast¹ /fist/ n. [C] **1** a large meal for a lot of people, to celebrate a special occasion: *The last day of Kwanzaa is marked by a lavish feast.* | *a Thanksgiving Day feast* **2** a very good, large meal: *On Tuesdays the restaurant offers a prime rib feast.* **3** an occasion when there are a lot of enjoyable things to see or do: [+ for] *The wonderful, detailed illustrations are a feast for the eyes.* **4** a day or period when there is a special religious celebration

feast² v. **1** [I] to eat and drink a lot to celebrate something: *On the first Thanksgiving, the Pilgrims feasted for three days.* **2 feast your eyes on sb/sth** to look at someone or something with great pleasure: *Just feast your eyes on the car's leather seats and walnut dashboard.* **3 feast on/upon sth** to eat a lot of a particular food with great enjoyment: *Hundreds of people, young and old, feasted on free hot dogs, hamburgers, and ice cream..* **4** [T usually passive] FORMAL to treat someone with a lot of respect by giving them a special meal

feat /fit/ n. [C] something that someone does that is impressive because it needs a lot of skill, strength etc.: *acrobatic circus feats* | [+ of] *The tunnel is a remarkable feat of engineering.* | **perform/accomplish/**

F

achieve a feat *Steger crossed Antarctica, and performed a similar feat at the North Pole.* | **no mean/ small/easy feat** (=something that is very difficult to do)

feath·er[1] /ˈfɛðɚ/ *n.* [C] **1** one of the light soft things that cover a bird's body: *an eagle feather* | **a feather bed/pillow/comforter etc.** (=a bed etc. that is filled with feathers) **2 a feather in your cap** something you have done that you should be proud of —see also **birds of a feather** (BIRD (6)), **light as air/as light as a feather** (LIGHT[2] (2))

feather[2] *v.* [T] **1 feather your nest/bed** to get money by dishonest methods **2** OLD-FASHIONED to put feathers on an ARROW —see also **tar and feather sb** (TAR[2] (4))

feath·er bed·ding /ˈ.. ˌ../ *n.* [U] INFORMAL the practice of letting workers keep their jobs even if they are not needed or do not work well

feather bo·a /ˌ.. ˈ./ *n.* [C] a long SCARF made of feathers and worn around someone's neck

feather-brained /ˈ.. ˌ./ *adj.* extremely silly: *a feather-brained scheme*

feather dust·er /ˈ.. ˌ../ *n.* [C] a stick with feathers on the end, used for removing dust

feath·ered /ˈfɛðɚd/ *adj.* **1** having feathers, or made from feathers **2 a feathered friend** a bird

feath·er·weight /ˈfɛðɚˌweɪt/ *n.* [C] a BOXER who is heavier than a BANTAMWEIGHT but lighter than a LIGHTWEIGHT

feath·er·y /ˈfɛðəri/ *adj.* **1** made of a lot of soft thin pieces: *dark brown, feathery hair* **2** soft and light: *feathery snow*

fea·ture[1] /ˈfitʃɚ/ *n.* [C] **1** a part of something that you notice because it seems important, interesting, or typical: *Air bags are a standard feature in most new cars.* | [+ **of**] *These protein deposits are a feature of Alzheimer's disease.* | *The crescent moon is a **common feature** of the flags of Islamic countries.* **2** a piece of writing about a subject in a newspaper or a magazine, or a special treatment of a subject on television or the radio: [+ **on**] *Ferriss won an award for her feature on the children of migrant farmworkers.* **3** a movie being shown at a theater: *The Plaza Theater is showing a classic science fiction **double feature** (=two movies the same evening).* **4** a part of the land, especially part that you can see: *The maps show mountains, rivers, vegetation and other **geographical features**.* **5** [usually plural] a part of someone's face such as their eyes, nose etc.: *Her eyes are her best feature.* | *She had a small face with delicate features.*

feature[2] *v.* **1** [T] to show a particular person or thing in a movie, magazine, show etc.: *Wilson's first solo album features her version of "Love Child."* | [**feature sb as sth**] *The movie features Frank Sinatra as Nathan Detroit.* | [**be featured in sth**] *Their house was featured in "Ebony" magazine last month.* **2** [I] to be included in something and be an important part of it: [+ **in**] *Violence features too strongly in many TV shows.* **3** [T] to show or advertise a particular kind of product: *Sales have gone up for items featured on money-off coupons.* **4** [T] a word meaning "to include something new or unusual," used especially in advertisements: *The cordless telephone featured 900-megahertz circuitry.* **5** to show a movie, play etc.: *Opera San Jose will feature operas by Puccini and Verdi this spring.*

feature film /ˈ.. ˌ./ *n.* [C] a movie that has a story and is acted by professional actors, which people would usually go to see in a theater

fea·ture·less /ˈfitʃɚləs/ *adj.* a featureless place has no interesting features: *a large featureless expanse of desert*

feb·rile /ˈfibraɪl, ˈfɛ-/ *adj.* **1** LITERARY full of nervous excitement or activity: *a febrile atmosphere* **2** TECHNICAL relating to or caused by a fever

Feb·ru·ar·y /ˈfɛbyuˌɛri, ˈfɛbruˌɛri/ written abbreviation **Feb.** *n.* [C,U] the second month of the year,

between January and March: *Eric's new job starts on February 4.* | *The new bridge opened in February 1997.* | *I came back last February.* | *I'm going to France next February.* | *Our game is February 25th.* —see Usage Note at JANUARY

fe·ces /ˈfisiz/ *n.* [plural] FORMAL solid waste material from the BOWELS —**fecal** /ˈfikəl/ *adj.*

feck·less /ˈfɛklɪs/ *adj.* FORMAL lacking determination, and not achieving anything in your life: *a feckless young man* —**fecklessly** *adv.* —**fecklessness** *n.* [U]

fe·cund /ˈfikənd, ˈfɛkənd/ *adj.* FORMAL able to produce many children, young animals, or crops; FERTILE: *fecund agricultural land* —**fecundity** *n.* [U]

Fed /fɛd/ *n.* **the Fed** INFORMAL **a)** the FEDERAL RESERVE SYSTEM **b)** the FEDERAL RESERVE BOARD

fed[1] /fɛd/ *v.* the past tense and past participle of FEED[1] —see also FED UP

fed[2] *n.* [C] INFORMAL a police officer in the FBI

fed·er·al /ˈfɛdərəl/ *adj.* **1** relating to the central government of a country such as the U.S., rather than to the government of one of its states: *It is against federal law to discriminate against someone because of religion.* | *federal income tax* **2** a federal country or system of government consists of a group of states that control their own affairs but are controlled by a central government: *The Federal Republic of Germany was the official name of West Germany.*

Federal A·vi·a·tion Ad·min·i·stra·tion, the /ˌ... ...ˈ.. ...ˌ../ *n.* a U.S. government organization which is responsible for making sure that aircraft and airports are safe for people to use

Federal Bu·reau of In·ves·ti·ga·tion, the /ˌ... ˌ.. . ...ˈ./ *n.* the FBI

Federal Com·mu·ni·ca·tions Com·mis·sion, the /ˌ... ...ˈ. .ˌ../ *n.* a U.S. government organization which makes rules that control broadcasting on radio, television, CABLE and SATELLITE television in the U.S.

Federal De·pos·it In·sur·ance Com·mis·sion, the /ˌ... ˌ.. .ˈ. .ˌ../ *n.* a U.S. government department that provides insurance against the failure of banks and controls their activities

fed·er·al·ism /ˈfɛdərəˌlɪzəm/ *n.* [U] belief in or support for a federal system of government —**federalist** *n.* [C]

Federal Re·serve Bank /ˌ... .ˈ. ˌ./ *n.* [C] one of the 12 banks that are part of the Federal Reserve System

Federal Reserve Board /ˌ... .ˈ. ˌ./ *n.* [singular] the official organization that controls the Federal Reserve System

Federal Reserve Sys·tem /ˌ... .ˈ. ˌ../ *n.* [singular] the main system of banks in the U.S., in which a group of seven officials and 12 banks control the way the country's banks work

fed·er·ate /ˈfɛdəˌreɪt/ *v.* [I + **with**] if a group of states federate, they join together to form a federation

fed·er·a·tion /ˌfɛdəˈreɪʃən/ *n.* **1** [C] a group of organizations, clubs, or people that have joined together to form a single group: *the U.S. Gymnastics Federation in Indianapolis* **2** [C] a group of states that have joined together to form a single group: *the Russian Federation* **3** [U] the act of joining together to form a group

fed up /ˌ. ˈ./ *adj.* [not before noun] INFORMAL annoyed or bored, and wanting something to change: [+ **with**] *City golfers are fed up with conditions on the course.* | *In the end, she just got fed up and left.*

fee /fi/ *n.* [C] **1** an amount of money that you pay to do something: *The fee is $50 for a six-week art class.* | *No shipping fee is charged.* | *The 10K run has an entry fee* (=a fee to take part) *of $15.* | *State parks charge a small entrance fee* (=a fee to enter a place). **2** an amount of money that you pay to a professional person for their work: *Insurance covered most of the doctor's fees.* | *legal/medical etc. fees Losers of the suit will have to pay the winner's legal fees.* —see Usage Notes at COST[1] and PAY[2]

fee·ble /ˈfibəl/ *adj.* **1** extremely weak: *a feeble voice* | *a feeble elderly woman in a wheelchair* **2** not very good or effective: *Such a feeble case should not have gone to court.* | *Sales have gone up only by a feeble 0.1 percent.*

feeble-mind·ed /'.. ,../ *adj.* **1** unable to think clearly and decide what to do **2** OLD-FASHIONED having much less than average intelligence —**feeble-mindedly** *adv.* —**feeble-mindedness** *n.* [U]

SW 1 2 **feed¹** /fid/ *v. past tense and past participle* **fed**

feed

1 give food [T] **a)** to give food to a person or animal: *Did you feed the dog?* | *Hospital officials said she is no longer able to feed herself.* | [**feed sth to sb**] *We fed the scraps to the pig.* **b)** to provide enough food for a group of people: *Ismail's wages are hardly enough to feed his family.* | *This recipe feeds six.*

2 plant [T] to give a special substance to a plant, which makes it grow: *Feed chrysanthemums with a house plant fertilizer.*

3 supply sth [T] to supply something, especially a liquid or gas, in a continuous flow: *The public baths are fed by natural springs.*

4 increase sth [T] to do something that increases an activity or makes something bigger or stronger: *There has been a boom in tourism, fed by publicity about the movie filmed there.* | [**feed sth with sth**] *Blanca fed the fire with sticks she had brought in.*

5 **well-fed/under-fed/poorly-fed etc.** having plenty of food or not enough food: *Well-fed chickens produce healthier offspring.*

6 animal/baby [I] if a baby or an animal feeds, they eat: *Humpback whales come to the California coast to feed each summer.*

7 put sth into sth [T] to put something such as a tube or a wire slowly into something else: *The tube was fed into the patient's stomach.*

8 computer [T] to put information into a computer over a period of time: [**feed sth into sth**] *The locations of the icebergs are fed into computer models.*

9 information [T] to give someone information or ideas over a period of time, especially false information: [**feed sth to sb**] *She fed celebrity gossip to "People" magazine.*

10 **feed your face** INFORMAL to eat a lot of food

11 **feed sb's guilt/vanity/paranoia etc.** to do something that makes someone feel more guilty etc.: *He's doing this just to feed his ego* (=make himself feel important).

12 **feed lines/jokes to sb** to say things to another performer so that they can make jokes

13 **feed sb a line** INFORMAL to tell someone something which is not true so that they will do what you want: *She fed him a line about being busy on Saturday.*

14 sports [T] to throw or hit a ball or a PUCK to someone else on your team, especially so that they can make a point

15 **feed a meter** to keep putting money into a machine so that you can park your car

16 tv/radio [T] to send a television or radio program somewhere so that it can be broadcast —see also BREAST-FEED, FEEDING, FORCE-FEED, **mouth to feed** (MOUTH¹ (10)), SPOON-FEED

feed into sth *phr. v.* [T] to flow or move into something that is larger, or to provide it with something: *Six elementary schools feed into Jefferson High.*

feed off sth *phr. v.* [T] **1** if an animal feeds off something, it gets food from it: *The bears are feeding off the town's garbage.* **2** to use something to increase, become stronger, or succeed: *In new parents, exhilaration and exhaustion feed off one another.* | *The Rockets feed off the energy that Elie has on court.* **3** DISAPPROVING to use something bad or negative to help you succeed, or use something in a bad or negative way to help you succeed: *The careers of those who feed off scandal have blossomed.*

feed on sth *phr. v.* [T] **1** if an animal feeds on a particular food, it usually eats that food: *The young fish feed on brine shrimp.* **2** to use something to

increase, become stronger, or succeed: *The uprising has fed on widespread unhappiness with the government.*

feed sb **up** *phr. v.* [T] to give someone a lot of food to make them more healthy

feed² *n.* **1** [U] food for animals: *cattle feed* **2** [C] an action of sending a television or radio program somewhere so that it can be broadcast, or the connection that is used to do this: *a live satellite feed* **3** [C] a tube which supplies a machine with FUEL **4** [C] OLD-FASHIONED a big meal —see also CHICKEN FEED

feed·back /'fidbæk/ *n.* [U] **1** advice, criticism etc. about how successful or useful something is: [+ **on**] *It is important to provide employees with feedback on their job performance.* **2** a high noise that is not nice to listen to, heard when a MICROPHONE is too close to an AMPLIFIER **SW 3**

feed·bag /'fidbæg/ *n.* [C] a bag put around a horse's head, containing food

feed·er /'fidɚ/ *n.* [C] **1** a container with food for animals or birds **2** a small road or railroad line that takes traffic onto a main road or railroad line

feeder school /'.. ,./ *n.* [C] a school from which many students go to a high school in the same area

feed·ing /'fidɪŋ/ *n.* [C] one of the times when you give milk to a small baby: *a midnight feeding*

feeding fren·zy /'.. ,../ *n.* [C] **1** INFORMAL a situation in which many people all try to get something, especially information, at the same time in an uncontrolled way: *It became a media feeding frenzy with each TV show reporting more sensational details.* **2** a situation in which a group of SHARKS or other fish attack and eat something

F

feeding ground /'.. ,./ *n.* [C] a place where a group of animals or birds find food to eat

feel¹ /fil/ *v. past tense and past participle* **felt** **SW 1 1**

1 feeling/emotion [linking verb, T] to experience a particular feeling or emotion: *I feel sorry for her.* | *She felt okay last night, but she had a fever this morning.* | *I don't really feel hungry yet.* | *He's feeling guilty for not writing her back.* | [+ **like**] *The Lees made me feel like their own son.* | [+ **as if/though**] *I felt as if I had won a tremendous victory.* | [**feel sth**] *Stop running if you feel any pain.*

2 physical [linking verb] to give someone a particular physical feeling, especially when touched or held: *The room felt cool and comfortable.* | *The clothes still feel slightly damp.* | [+ **like**] *Her hands felt like ice.* | [+ **as if/though**] *My arm feels as though it might be broken.*

3 experience/event [linking verb] if a situation, event etc. feels good, strange etc., that is the emotion or feeling that it gives you: *It felt great to be up in the mountains.* | *How does it feel to be home?* | *It felt kind of weird being back in school.* | [+ **like**] *It felt like I'd known them all my life.*

4 have an opinion [linking verb, T not usually in progressive] to have a particular opinion, especially one that is based on your feelings, not on facts: [+ **about**] *The survey asked what people felt about abortion.* | [**feel (that)**] *I felt I should've helped more.* | [+ **like**] *I feel like I'm being treated unfairly.* | *"I think it's a good idea." "I hope you still feel that way tomorrow."* | **feel sure/certain (that)** *I felt certain that the other jurors agreed with me.*

5 touch [T] to touch something with your fingers to find out about it: *Doctor Wright felt the baby's stomach, checking that it was not hard.* | **feel how hard/soft/rough etc. sth is** *Can you feel how smooth it is now that it's been sanded?*

6 notice sth [T not in progressive] to notice something that is happening to you, especially something that is touching you: *The earthquake was felt as far south as Carpenteria.* | [**feel sth do sth**] *Ann felt him brush against me and turned to face him.* | [**feel sb/sth doing sth**] *I felt myself blushing.*

care. | [+ on] *Please send us your thoughts and feelings on the subject.* | [+ about] *Polls ask consumers for their feelings about current economic conditions.* | *Mothers sometimes* **have mixed feelings** (=are not sure what they feel or think) *about going to work.*

3 have/get the feeling to think that something is probably true, or will probably happen: *Mike* **got the feeling that** *she didn't believe him.* | *I* **had a bad feeling about** *this from the beginning* (=I thought something bad would happen).

4 general attitude [singular,U] a general attitude among a group of people about a subject: [+ against] *Johnson underestimated the strength of public feeling against the war in Vietnam.*

5 heat/cold/pain etc. [C] something that you feel in your body such as heat, cold, pain etc.: *It's not very painful, just a feeling of discomfort.*

6 ability to feel [U] the ability to feel heat, cold, pain etc. in part of your body: *She has no feeling in her legs.*

7 put your feelings into words to express clearly what you want to say: *I'm not very good at putting my feelings into words, but I'll try to explain.*

8 the feeling is mutual SPOKEN said when you have the same feeling about someone as they have toward you: *Well, if Dave doesn't want to play with me, then the feeling is mutual.*

9 with feeling in a way that shows you feel very angry, happy etc.: *Baktiar spoke of Iran with deep feeling.*

10 bad/ill feeling anger, lack of trust etc. between people, especially after an argument or unfair decision: *There have been bad feelings between area residents and police.* | **harbor/bear ill feelings (toward sb)** (=to be angry or unhappy with someone)

11 I know the feeling SPOKEN said when you understand how someone feels because you have had the same feeling: *"She makes me so mad I could scream!" "I know the feeling."*

12 effect of a place/book etc. [singular] the effect that a place, book, movie etc. has on people and the way it makes them feel: *Her descriptions evoke a feeling of America as it is for new immigrants.*

13 a feeling (for sth) a) an ability to do something or understand a subject, which you get from experience: *The experiments give kids a better feeling for what magnetism is.* **b)** a natural ability to do something: *All the people in this course have a feeling for the theater.*

14 emotions not thought [U] a way of reacting to things using your emotions, instead of thinking about them carefully: *The Romantic writers valued feeling above all else.* —see also **hard feelings** (HARD[1] (15))

feeling[2] *adj.* showing strong feelings: *A feeling look came across her face.* —**feelingly** *adv.*

feet /fit/ *n.* the plural of FOOT —see also **get/have cold feet** (COLD[1] (8)), **have feet of clay** (FOOT[1] (20)), **have itchy feet** (ITCHY (3))

feign /feɪn/ *v.* [T] FORMAL to pretend to have a particular feeling or to be sick, asleep etc.: *Bernstein returned to his desk, feigning unconcern.*

feint[1] /feɪnt/ *n.* [C] a movement or an attack that is intended to deceive an opponent, especially in BOXING

feint[2] *v.* [I,T] to pretend to hit someone in BOXING

feist·y /ˈfaɪsti/ *adj.* **feistier, feistiest** APPROVING having a strong, determined character and being willing to argue with people: *She's a pretty feisty kid, isn't she?*

feld·spar /ˈfɛldspɑr/ *n.* [U] a type of gray or white mineral

fe·lic·i·ta·tions /fɪˌlɪsəˈteɪʃənz/ *interjection* FORMAL said to wish someone happiness

fe·lic·i·tous /fɪˈlɪsətəs/ *adj.* FORMAL well-chosen and appropriate: *Lincoln's felicitous words about government* —**felicitously** *adv.*

fe·lic·i·ty /fɪˈlɪsəti/ *n.* FORMAL **1** [U] happiness: *He demonstrated a concern for the felicity of his children.* **2** [singular,U] the quality of being well-chosen or appropriate: *a felicity of language*

SPOKEN PHRASES

7 feel like (doing) sth to want to have something or do something: *I just don't feel like doing anything tonight.* | *Joe says he feels like Mexican food.*

8 feel free used to tell someone that they can do something if they want to: *"Could I use your phone for a minute?" "Feel free."* | [**feel free to do sth**] *Feel free to add your own ingredients.*

9 I know how you feel said to express sympathy with a remark someone has just made: *"It's so embarrassing." "I know how you feel."*

10 not feel yourself to not feel as healthy or happy as usual: *I just haven't been feeling myself lately.*

11 feel the force/effects/benefits etc. of sth to experience the good or bad results of something: *Patients will feel the effects of the operation for weeks.*

12 feel your way to move carefully with your hands out in front of you because you cannot see well: *He felt his way across the room, and found the door handle.*

13 feel around/on/in etc. sth (for sth) to search for something with your fingers: *Ben felt in his pocket for a handkerchief.*

14 feel the need to do sth to have the feeling that you need to do something: *Some magazines feel the need to be controversial.*

15 feel your age to realize that you are not as young or active as you used to be: *You really start to feel your age when you spend time around these kids.*

16 feel your oats INFORMAL to feel full of energy

17 feel the cold to suffer because of cold weather: *Old people tend to feel the cold more.*

18 feel a death/loss etc. to react very strongly to a bad event, especially someone's death

feel for sb *phr. v.* [T] to feel sympathy for someone: *All I could do was let him know that I felt for him and that I cared.*

feel sb ↔ **out** *phr. v.* [T] INFORMAL to find out what someone's opinions or feelings are without asking them directly: *Party leaders began to feel out residents of poor areas, to see how to get their votes.*

feel sb ↔ **up** *phr. v.* [T] SPOKEN to touch someone sexually

feel up to sth *phr. v.* [T] INFORMAL to have the strength, energy etc. to do something: *I don't really feel up to going out tonight.*

feel[2] *n.* [singular] **1** a quality that something has that makes you feel or think a particular way about it: *The movie has the feel of a big summer hit.* | *The car has a sporty feel to it.* | *The house had a nice* **feel about it.** **2** the way that something feels when you touch it: *I love the feel of leather.* | *The seats look good and have a sturdy feel.* **3 have/get a feel for sth** INFORMAL to have or develop an understanding of something and skill in doing it: *Kingston is starting to get a good feel for the position, and is playing well.* **4 get the feel of sth** to become comfortable with something: *You'll soon get the feel of the car.*

feel·er /ˈfilɚ/ *n.* **1 put/send out feelers** to start to try to discover what people think about something that you want to do: *Possible presidential candidates are already putting out feelers.* **2** [C usually plural] one of the two long things on an insect's head that it uses to feel or touch things —see picture at INSECT

feel-good /ˈ. ./ *adj.* **feel-good movie/program/music etc.** a movie etc. whose main purpose is to make you feel happy and cheerful

SW feel·ing[1] /ˈfilɪŋ/ *n.*
1 anger/sadness/happiness etc. [C] something that you feel such as anger, sadness, or happiness: *It's always a great feeling to win a game at home.* | [+ of] *The group of women talk about their feelings of shame and anger.* | *Exercise gives a feeling of accomplishment.* | *It was the last game of the season, and* **feelings were running high** (=people were very angry or excited).

2 opinion [C] a belief or opinion about something, especially one that is influenced by your emotions: *My personal feeling is that most voters just don't*

fe·line¹ /'filaɪn/ adj. **1** relating to cats or other members of the cat family, such as lions or tigers **2** looking like or moving like a cat: *A feline grin spread over his face.*

feline² n. [C] TECHNICAL a cat or a member of the cat family, such as a lion or a tiger

fell¹ /fɛl/ v. the past tense of FALL¹

fell² v. [T] **1** to cut down a tree **2** to knock someone down with a lot of force

fell³ adj. **in one fell swoop** doing a lot of things at the same time, using only one action: *A single company can eliminate 74,000 jobs in one fell swoop.*

fel·la /'fɛlə/ n. [C] SPOKEN, OLD-FASHIONED **1** a man **2** a boy or man with whom you have a romantic relationship; BOYFRIEND

fel·la·ti·o /fə'leɪʃiou/ n. [U] TECHNICAL the practice of touching a man's PENIS with the lips and tongue to give sexual pleasure —compare CUNNILINGUS

fel·ler /'fɛlə/ n. [C] SPOKEN, OLD-FASHIONED a man

Fel·li·ni /fə'lini/, **Fed·e·ri·co** /ˌfɛdə'rikou/ (1920–1993) an Italian movie DIRECTOR who had an important influence on the cinema

sw **fel·low¹** /'fɛlou/ n. [C] **1** OLD-FASHIONED a man: *He said a fellow named LeRoy was the best pilot.* **2** a GRADUATE student who has a fellowship in a university **3** a member of an ACADEMIC society

fellow² adj. **1 fellow workers/students/countrymen etc.** people who work, study etc. with you: *Try to maintain good relationships with your fellow workers.* **2 our fellow man** other people in general: *We must all help our fellow man.* **3 fellow feeling** LITERARY a feeling of sympathy and friendship toward someone because they are like you: *As an only child myself, I had a certain fellow feeling for Laura.*

fel·low·ship /'fɛlouʃɪp, -lə-/ n. **1** [C] **a)** money given to a student to allow them to continue their studies at an advanced level: *She has been awarded a Nieman Fellowship at Harvard University.* **b)** a group of officials who decide which students will receive this money: *He received a gold medal from the Artists' Fellowship in New York.* **2** [C] a group of people who share an interest or belief, especially Christians who have religious ceremonies together **3** [U] a feeling of friendship resulting from shared interests or experiences: *Who can resist the message of warmth and good fellowship?*

fellow trav·el·er /ˌ.. '.../ n. [C] someone you disapprove of because they agree with the aims of the Communist Party

fel·on /'fɛlən/ n. [C] LAW someone who is guilty of a serious crime: *Williams, a **convicted felon** (=criminal who is sent to prison), decided to represent himself at his appeal.*

fel·o·ny /'fɛləni/ n. plural **felonies** [C,U] LAW a serious crime such as murder —compare MISDEMEANOR

felt¹ /fɛlt/ v. the past tense and past participle of FEEL¹

felt² n. [U] a thick soft material made of wool, hair, or fur that has been pressed flat

felt tip pen /ˌ. '. ./ n. [C] a pen that has a hard piece of felt at the end that the ink comes through

fem. adj. the written abbreviation of FEMALE or FEMININE

sw **fe·male¹** /'fimeɪl/ n. [C] **1** a person or animal that belongs to the sex that can have babies or produce eggs **2** OLD-FASHIONED a word for a woman or girl, now usually considered offensive —opposite MALE² —see Usage Note at MASCULINE

sw **female²** adj. **1** belonging to the sex that can have babies or produce eggs: *Notice the distinguishing marks of the female spider.* **2** a female plant or flower produces fruit **3** TECHNICAL a female part of a piece of equipment has a hole into which another part fits —**femaleness** n. [U] —opposite MALE¹

female con·dom /ˌ.. '../ n. [C] a loose rubber tube with one end closed, that fits inside a woman's VAGINA when she is having sex, so that she will not have a baby

fem·i·nine /'fɛmənɪn/ adj. **1** having qualities that are considered to be typical of women, especially by being gentle, delicate and pretty: *How can I persuade my tomboy daughter to wear feminine clothes?* | *Lane stressed the importance of feminine values like non-competition.* **2** relating to being female: *Amelia's report describes the experience from a feminine point of view.* **3** TECHNICAL a feminine noun or PRONOUN has a special form that means it REFERS to a female, such as "actress" or "her" —compare MASCULINE —see Usage Note at MASCULINE

feminine hy·giene /ˌ... '../ n. [U] feminine hygiene products are things that women use when they are having their monthly PERIOD, or that they use to clean their sexual organs

fem·i·nin·i·ty /ˌfɛmə'nɪnəṭi/ n. [U] qualities that are considered to be typical of women, especially qualities that are gentle, delicate, and pretty: *The color pink is associated with femininity.* —compare MASCULINITY

fem·i·nism /'fɛməˌnɪzəm/ n. [U] the belief that women should have the same rights and opportunities as men —**feminist** adj.: *feminist principles*

fem·i·nist /'fɛmənɪst/ n. [C] someone who supports the idea that women should have the same rights and opportunities as men: *She's been well-known as an outspoken feminist for over 20 years.*

femme /fɛm/ n. [C] a LESBIAN who has a traditionally FEMININE part in a relationship with another woman —**femme** adj. —compare BUTCH²

femme fa·tale /ˌfɛm fə'tɑl, -'tæl/ n. [C] a beautiful woman who men find very attractive, even though she may make them unhappy

fe·mur /'fimə/ n. [C] TECHNICAL the bone in your THIGH —**femoral** /'fɛmərəl/ adj. —see picture at SKELETON

fence¹ /fɛns/ n. **1** [C] a structure made of wood, metal etc. that surrounds a piece of land —see picture on page 423 **2** [C] SLANG someone who buys and **sw** sells stolen goods **3** [C] a wall or other structure that horses jump over in a race or competition —see also **mend (your) fences** (MEND¹ (4)), **sit on the fence** (SIT (9))

fence² v. **1** [T] to put a fence around something **2** [I] to fight with a long thin sword as a sport **3** [I + with] to answer someone's questions in a skilled way in order to get an advantage in an argument

fence sb/sth **in** phr. v. [T] **1** to surround a place with a fence **2** to make someone feel that they cannot leave a place or do what they want: *I felt fenced in at home – I was happier at work.* —**fenced-in** adj.

fence sb/sth ↔ **off** phr. v. [T] to separate one area from another area with a fence: *The main building was fenced off as a possible hazard.*

fenc·er /'fɛnsə/ n. [C] someone who fights with a long thin sword as a sport

fence-sit·ter /'. ˌ../ n. [C] someone who avoids saying which side of an argument they support or what their opinion is about a particular subject: *Wilson will have a hard job winning over Democratic fence-sitters.* —**fence-sitting** n. [U] —see also **sit on the fence** (SIT (9))

fenc·ing /'fɛnsɪŋ/ n. [U] **1** the sport of fighting with a long thin sword **2** fences, or the pieces of wood, metal etc. used to make them

fend /fɛnd/ v. **fend for yourself** to take care of yourself without help from other people: *Young birds are left to fend for themselves soon after they hatch.*

fend sb/sth **off** phr. v. [T] **1** to defend yourself against someone who is attacking you: *Mrs. Spencer tried to fend off the mugger with her umbrella.* **2** to defend yourself from something such as competition, difficult questions, or a situation you do not want to deal with: *ITT managed to fend off the hostile takeover bid.*

fend·er /'fɛndə/ n. [C] **1** the part of a car's body that covers the wheels —see picture on page 427 **2** a curved piece of metal over the wheel of a bicycle —see picture at BICYCLE¹ **3** a low metal wall around a FIREPLACE that prevents burning wood or coal from falling out **4** an object such as an old tire used to protect the side of a boat

fend·er-bend·er /'.. ,../ *n.* [C] INFORMAL a car accident in which little damage is done

feng shui /ˌfɛŋ 'ʃuɪ/ *n.* [U] a Chinese system of organizing the furniture and other things in a house or building in a way that people believe will bring good luck and happiness

fen·nel /'fɛnl/ *n.* [U] a pale green plant whose seeds are used to give a special taste to food and which can also be eaten as a vegetable

fe·ral /'fɛrəl, 'fɪrəl/ *adj.* feral animals used to live with humans but have become wild: *a pack of feral dogs*

Fer·di·nand and Is·a·bel·la /ˌfɔdn-ænd ənd ˌɪzə'bɛlə/ King Ferdinand of Spain (1452–1516) and his wife, Queen Isabella of Spain (1451–1504), who are famous for giving Christopher Columbus the money and ships to make the trip on which he discovered America

fer·ment[1] /fɔ'mɛnt/ *v.* [I,T] if fruit, beer, wine etc. ferments or if it is fermented, the sugar in it changes to alcohol —**fermented** *adj.* —**fermentation** /ˌfɔmən-'teɪʃən/ *n.* [U]

fer·ment[2] /'fɔmɛnt/ *n.* [U] a situation of great excitement or trouble in a country, especially caused by political change: *In the 1960s, American society was in ferment.* | **political/intellectual/social etc. ferment** *Michelangelo lived in a time of perhaps the greatest artistic ferment the world has known.*

Fer·mi /'fɛrmi/, **En·ri·co** /ɛn'rikoʊ/ (1901–1954) a U.S. scientist, born in Italy, who did important work on RADIOACTIVITY and produced the first controlled NUCLEAR REACTION

fern /fɔn/ *n.* [C] a type of plant with green leaves shaped like large feathers, but no flowers —**ferny** *adj.*

fe·ro·cious /fə'roʊʃəs/ *adj.* **1** violent, dangerous, and frightening: *Gang members have committed ferocious acts of violence.* | *a ferocious hammerhead shark* **2** very strong, severe, and bad: *Ferocious competition has pushed computer prices down.* —**ferociously** *adv.* —**ferociousness** *n.* [U]

fe·roc·i·ty /fə'rɑsəti/ *n.* [U] the state of being extremely violent, cruel, and severe: *the ferocity of the fighting in the former Yugoslavia*

fer·ret[1] /'fɛrɪt/ *v.*
ferret sb/sth ↔ out *phr. v.* [T] **1** to succeed in finding a piece of information that is difficult to find: *Political corruption is difficult to ferret out.* **2** to find and usually get rid of someone who is causing a problem: *The new program is meant to ferret out problem cops.* **3** INFORMAL to search for something, especially inside a drawer, box etc.: *Ferret out some Chinese paper lanterns to decorate the yard.*

ferret[2] *n.* [C] a small animal with a pointed nose and soft fur, used for hunting rats and rabbits

fer·ris wheel /'fɛrɪs ˌwil/ *n.* [C] a very large upright wheel with seats on it for people to ride on in an AMUSEMENT PARK

fer·rous /'fɛrəs/ *adj.* TECHNICAL containing iron, or relating to iron: *ferrous metals*

fer·rule /'fɛrəl/ *n.* [C] a piece of metal or rubber put around a stick or pipe to make it stronger

fer·ry[1] /'fɛri/ *n. plural* **ferries** [C] a boat that carries people or goods across a river or a narrow area of water

ferry[2] *v.* **ferries, ferried, ferrying** [T always + adv./prep.] to carry people or goods a short distance from one place to another in a boat or other vehicle: **[ferry sth (from sth) to sb/sth]** *Four helicopters ferried food, medicine, and blankets to the survivors.*

fer·ry·boat /'fɛriˌboʊt/ *n.* [C] a ferry

fer·ry·man /'fɛrimən/ *n.* [C] someone who guides a ferry across a river

fer·tile /'fɔtl/ *adj.* **1** fertile land or soil is able to produce good crops: *fertile farmland* **2** able to produce babies, young animals, or new plants —opposite INFERTILE **3 a fertile imagination/mind** an imagination that is able to produce a lot of interesting and unusual ideas **4 fertile ground/field/territory etc.** a situation where new ideas, political groups etc. can easily develop and succeed: *Central Asia is considered fertile soil for a growth in Islamic fundamentalism.*

fer·til·i·ty /fɔ'tɪləti/ *n.* [U] **1** the ability of the land or soil to produce good crops **2** the ability of a person, animal, or plant to produce babies, young animals, or seeds

fertility drug /.'... ,./ *n.* [C] a drug given to a woman to help her have a baby

fer·til·ize /'fɔtlˌaɪz/ *v.* [T] **1** to put fertilizer on the soil to help plants grow **2** to make new animal or plant life develop: *After the egg has been fertilized, it will hatch in about 6 weeks.* —**fertilization** /ˌfɔtlə'zeɪʃən/ *n.* [U]

fer·til·iz·er /'fɔtlˌaɪzɔ/ *n.* [C,U] a substance that is put on the soil to help plants grow

fer·vent /'fɔvənt/ *adj.* believing or feeling something very strongly and sincerely: *There were fervent arguments both for and against gun control.* | **a fervent believer/admirer/supporter etc.** *My children are fervent believers in Santa.* —**fervency** *n.* [U] —**fervently** *adv.*

fer·vid /'fɔvɪd/ *adj.* FORMAL believing or feeling something too strongly —**fervidly** *adv.*

fer·vor /'fɔvɔ/ *n.* [U] very strong belief or feeling: *The country has not seen such patriotic fervor since the war.*

'fess /fɛs/ *v.*
'fess up *phr. v.* [I] SPOKEN to admit that you have done something wrong, although it is not very serious: *Nobody 'fessed up to owning it.*

fest /fɛst/ *n.* **a beer/song/food etc. fest** an informal occasion when a lot of people do a fun activity together, such as drinking beer, singing songs, or eating food —see also LOVEFEST, SLUGFEST

fes·ter /'fɛstɔ/ *v.* [I] **1** if a bad feeling or problem festers, it gets worse because it has not been dealt with: *Disputes between environmentalists and loggers have been festering for decades.* **2** if a wound festers, it becomes infected **3** if waste material or dirty objects fester, they decay and smell bad: *The animal parts were allowed to fester in the hot sun.*

fes·ti·val /'fɛstəvəl/ *n.* [C] **1** an occasion when there are performances of many movies, plays, pieces of music etc., which happens in the same place every year: *the music festival in Salzburg* —see picture on page 1330 **2** a special occasion when people celebrate something such as a religious event: *Hannukah is an eight-day Jewish festival.*

fes·tive /'fɛstɪv/ *adj.* **1** looking or feeling bright and cheerful in a way that seems appropriate for celebrating something: *Fondue is an easy and festive dish for a party.* | *The mood was happy and festive.* **2 a festive occasion** a day when you celebrate something special, such as a holiday **3 the festive season** the period around Christmas

fes·tiv·i·ty /fɛ'stɪvəti/ *n.* [U] **1** a happy and cheerful feeling that exists when people celebrate something: *Carnivals are about excitement and festivity.* **2 festivities** [plural] things such as drinking, dancing, or eating that are done to celebrate a special occasion: *Fourth of July festivities at Huntington Beach*

fes·toon[1] /fɛ'stun/ *v.* [T usually passive] to cover something with flowers, long pieces of material etc., especially as a decoration: **[be festooned with sth]** *The steps of the courthouse were festooned with banners and flags.*

festoon[2] *n.* [C] FORMAL a long thin piece of material, used especially as a decoration

fet·a /'fɛtə/ *n.* [U] a white cheese from Greece made from sheep's milk or goat's milk

fe·tal /'fitl/ *adj.* TECHNICAL relating to a FETUS

fetal po·si·tion /'.. .,../ *n.* [C] a body position in which your body is curled up, and your arms and legs are pulled up against your chest

fetch¹ /fɛtʃ/ v. [T] **1** to be sold for a particular amount of money, especially at a public sale: *Some properties have fetched prices in the $4 million range.* **2** OLD-FASHIONED to go and get something, and bring it back: *Rushworth went to fetch the key to the gate.* | [fetch sth from sth] *She fetched water from the well.* **3** **fetch and carry** OLD-FASHIONED to do simple and boring jobs for someone as if you were their servant

fetch² n. **play fetch** if you play fetch with a dog, you throw something for the dog to bring back to you

fetch·ing /'fɛtʃɪŋ/ adj. OLD-FASHIONED a word meaning "attractive," used especially about a woman: *a fetching young woman* —**fetchingly** adv.

fete¹ /feɪt/ v. [T usually passive] to honor someone by having a public celebration for them: *Mandela will be feted at a government banquet.*

fete² n. [C] a special occasion to celebrate something: *a farewell fete in honor of the mayor*

fet·id /'fɛtɪd/ adj. FORMAL having a strong, bad smell: *the fetid streets of the slum*

fet·ish /'fɛtɪʃ/ n. [C] **1** a desire for sex that comes from seeing a particular type of object or doing a particular activity, especially when the object or activity are considered unusual: *a foot fetish* **2** something you are always thinking about, or spending too much time doing: *The suspect has had a gun fetish for a long time.* **3** an object that is treated like a god and is thought to have magical powers

fet·ish·ist /'fɛtɪʃɪst/ n. [C] someone who gets sexual pleasure from unusual objects or activities —**fetishism** n. [U] —**fetishistic** /ˌfɛtɪ'ʃɪstɪk/ adj.

fet·lock /'fɛtlɑk/ n. [C] the back part of a horse's leg, just above the HOOF

fet·ter /'fɛtə/ v. [T usually passive] FORMAL **1** to restrict someone's freedom and prevent them from doing what they want to do *The industry is fettered by debt.* **2** to put chains on a prisoner's hands or feet

fet·ters /'fɛtəz/ n. [plural] **1** FORMAL the things that prevent someone from doing what they want to do: *Ordinary citizens are in political fetters, unable to control their own lives.* **2** chains that were put around a prisoner's feet in past times

fet·tle /'fɛtl/ n. **in fine fettle** OLD-FASHIONED healthy or working correctly

fet·tuc·ci·ne /ˌfɛtə'tʃini/ n. [U] thin flat pieces of PASTA

fe·tus /'fitəs/ n. [C] TECHNICAL a young human or animal before birth —compare EMBRYO

feud¹ /fyud/ n. [C] an angry and often violent argument between two people or groups that continues for a long time: [+ with/between] *Several companies became involved in feuds with Microsoft.* | [+ over] *the bitter national feud over abortion*

feud² v. [I] to continue arguing for a long time, often in a violent way: [feud (with sb) over sth] *Turkey and Greece have long been feuding over the island of Cyprus.*

feud·al /'fyudl/ adj. [only before noun] relating to feudalism: *the feudal system*

feu·dal·is·m /'fyudlˌɪzəm/ n. [U] a system that existed in the Middle Ages, in which people received land and protection from someone of a higher rank when they worked and fought for him

feu·dal·is·tic /ˌfyudl'ɪstɪk/ adj. based on a system in which only a few people have all the power

fe·ver /'fivə/ n. **1** [C,U] an illness or a medical condition in which you have a very high temperature: *She's running a fever* (=has a fever). | *a high/low/slight fever* *The illness begins with a high fever, followed by a rash.* —see also HAY FEVER, SCARLET FEVER, YELLOW FEVER **2** [U] a state in which a lot of people are excited about something in a crazy way: *Academy Award fever is taking over Hollywood.* | *The incident raised racial tensions to a fever pitch* (=an extreme level of excitement) *in the city.* —see also CABIN FEVER

fever blis·ter /'.. ˌ../ n. [C] a COLD SORE

fe·vered /'fivəd/ adj. [only before noun] LITERARY **1** extremely excited or worried: *Security kept the band's fevered fans away from the stage.* **2** suffering from a fever; FEVERISH: *She smoothed the child's fevered brow* (=a hot forehead caused by a fever). **3** **a fevered imagination/mind** someone who has a fevered imagination imagines strange things and cannot control their thoughts

fe·ver·ish /'fivərɪʃ/ adj. **1** suffering from a fever: *Parents comforted their feverish, aching children.* **2** very excited or worried about something: *The pace slowed after two days of feverish activity.* —**feverishly** adv.

few /fyu/ quantifier, pron. **1** **a few/the few** [no comparative] a small number of something: *Let's wait a few minutes and see if Amy shows up.* | *I just need to stop at the store for a few things.* | [+ of] *I've seen a few of those new cars around.* | *Don has seemed really happy these last few weeks* (=the weeks just before this). | *You'll have to work hard over the next few months* (=the months just after this time). | *There are a few more things I'd like to talk about before we go.* | *Grant's one of the few people I know who can tell stories well.* | *I've seen only a very few* (=not many) *of his movies.* **2** **quite a few** also **not a few** a fairly large number of things or people: *Quite a few people came to the meeting.* | *Ed's been this drunk on not a few occasions.* **3** not many or not enough people or things: *There are few events that are as exciting as having a baby.* | *There may be few options open to you.* | *Many people expressed concern, but few were willing to help.* | *Give me the one with the fewest calories.* | [+ of] *Very few of the teachers actually live here.* **4** **be few and far between** to be rare, or to be not happening or available often: *Good jobs are few and far between these days.* **5** **as few as** used to emphasize how small a number is: *As few as 10% of the patients treated at Highland pay anything for their care, even though many are employed.* **6** **no fewer than** used to emphasize how large a number is; at least: *I tried to contact him no fewer than ten times.* —see Usage Note at LESS¹ **7** **precious few (of sth)** a very small number: *Only a small percentage of the seeds germinated and precious few of those survived.* **8** **have a few (too many)** INFORMAL to have too much alcohol to drink: *I think I may have had a few too many at the office party.* —opposite MANY —see also **the chosen few** (CHOSEN² (1)), **to name (but) a few** (NAME² (5))

USAGE NOTE: FEW

WORD CHOICE: few, a few, little, a little
Use **few** with plural countable nouns to mean "not many": *Few people actually bother to get involved.* **Few** used alone is fairly formal, and you would most often use it with **very**: *Very few people come here now.* Use **a few** with plural countable nouns to mean "some": *A few people arrived late, but most of them got there on time.* With words for time, use **a few**: *After a few minutes I decided to leave.* | *I didn't see her again until a few years later.* Use **little** with uncountable nouns to mean "not much": *Unfortunately he now has little money left.* Again, **little** used alone is fairly formal, and you would most often use it with **very**: *There's usually very little traffic this early in the morning.* Use **a little** with uncountable nouns to mean "some, but not a lot": *There's only a little ice cream left.*

---

fey /feɪ/ adj. someone who is fey is attractive or interesting but in a slightly strange or childish way

Feyn·man /'faɪnmən/, **Richard** (1918–1988) a U.S. scientist who did important work on RADIOACTIVITY and won a Nobel Prize

fez /fɛz/ n. [C] a round red hat with a flat top and no BRIM

ff the written abbreviation of "and following," used in a book to mean the pages after the one you have mentioned: *Please see pages 54ff.*

fi·an·cé /ˌfianˈseɪ, fiˈɑnseɪ/ *n.* [C] the man whom a woman is going to marry

fi·an·cée /ˌfianˈseɪ, fiˈɑnseɪ/ *n.* [C] the woman whom a man is going to marry

fi·as·co /fiˈæskoʊ/ *n. plural* **fiascoes** or **fiascos** [C,U] something that is completely unsuccessful, in a way that is very embarrassing or disappointing: *The new mall has been an economic fiasco.*

fi·at /ˈfiæt, -ɑt, -ət/ *n.* [C] FORMAL an official command given by someone in a position of authority, without considering what other people want: *Public policy issues cannot be settled by fiat.*

fib¹ /fɪb/ *n.* [C] INFORMAL a small unimportant lie: *His mother says that he sometimes tells fibs.*

fib² *v.* **fibbed, fibbing** [I] INFORMAL to tell a small unimportant lie: *He fibbed about his age.* —**fibber** *n.* [C]

fi·ber /ˈfaɪbɚ/ *n.* **1** [U] parts of plants that you eat but cannot DIGEST, which help food to move quickly through your body: *high-fiber foods such as oatmeal* **2** [C,U] the part of some plants that is used for making materials such as rope or cloth: *Sisal carpeting is made from the fiber of the agave plant.* **3** [C] a natural or artificial thread that is used to make cloth or rope: *The coffee filter has thin fibers to trap the particles that cause bitterness.* **4 nerve/muscle fibers** [plural] the thin pieces of flesh that form the nerves or muscles in your body **5 with every fiber of your being** LITERARY if you feel something with every fiber of your being, you feel it very strongly: *I regret my decision with every fiber of my being.*

fi·ber·board /ˈfaɪbɚˌbɔrd/ *n.* [U] a special type of board made from wood fibers pressed together

fi·ber·fill /ˈfaɪbɚˌfɪl/ *n.* [U] an artificial substance used to fill PILLOWS, SLEEPING BAGS etc.

fi·ber·glass /ˈfaɪbɚˌglæs/ *n.* [U] a light material made from small glass threads pressed together, used for making racing cars, small boats etc.

fiber op·tics /ˌ.. '../ *n.* [U] the use of long thin threads of glass or plastic to carry information in the form of light, especially on telephone lines —**fiber-optic** *adj.: fiber-optic cables*

fi·brous /ˈfaɪbrəs/ *adj.* consisting of many fibers or looking like fibers: *The coconut has a fibrous outer shell.*

fib·u·la /ˈfɪbyələ/ *n.* [C] TECHNICAL the outer bone of the two bones in your leg below your knee

fiche /fiʃ/ *n.* [C,U] a MICROFICHE

fick·le /ˈfɪkəl/ *adj.* **1** someone who is fickle is always changing their opinions or feelings about what they like or want, so that you cannot depend on them: *Teenagers are fickle and switch brands frequently.* **2** something that is fickle, such as weather, often changes suddenly: *fickle winds* —**fickleness** *n.* [U]

fic·tion /ˈfɪkʃən/ *n.* **1** [U] books and stories about imaginary people and events: *The best fiction conveys the richness of life.* | *science-fiction novels* —opposite NONFICTION **2** [C] something that someone wants you to believe is true, but which is not true: *It is a fiction that unemployment can be solved by some economic theory.*

fic·tion·al /ˈfɪkʃənəl/ *adj.* fictional people, events etc. are imaginary and from a book or story: *Holmes is a popular fictional character.* | *The novel is set in the fictional German town of Kreiswald.*

fic·tion·al·ize /ˈfɪkʃənəˌlaɪz/ *v.* [T] to make a movie or story about a real event, changing some details and adding some imaginary characters: *"Zoot Suit" is Valdez's fictionalized version of a famous murder case.* —**fictionalization** /ˌfɪkʃənələˈzeɪʃən/ *n.* [C,U]

fic·ti·tious /fɪkˈtɪʃəs/ *adj.* not true, or not real: *The setting is a fictitious island in the Chesapeake River.*

fic·tive /ˈfɪktɪv/ *adj.* fictive events, people etc. are imaginary and not real

fid·dle¹ /ˈfɪdl/ *v.* [I] **1** to keep moving and touching things, especially because you are bored or nervous: *I sat and fiddled at the computer for a while.* **2** to play a VIOLIN

fiddle around *phr. v.* [I] to waste time by doing things that are not important: *If you keep fiddling around we're going to be late!*

fiddle around with sth also **fiddle with** sth *phr. v.* [T] to keep making changes to something, especially in a way that is stupid, annoying, or dangerous: *The bus company is always fiddling with the schedules.*

fiddle with sth *phr. v.* [T] to keep moving something or touching something with your fingers because you are bored, nervous, or want to change something: *Rosie fiddled with the lock, trying different combinations.*

fiddle² *n.* [C] INFORMAL a VIOLIN —see also **fit as a fiddle** (FIT³ (3)), **play second fiddle (to sb)** (PLAY¹ (16))

fid·dle-fad·dle /ˈfɪdl ˌfædl/ *n.* [U] OLD-FASHIONED nonsense

fid·dler /ˈfɪdlɚ/ *n.* [C] someone who plays the VIOLIN, especially someone who plays FOLK MUSIC

fid·dle·sticks /ˈfɪdlˌstɪks/ *interjection* OLD-FASHIONED said when you are slightly angry or annoyed about something

fid·dling¹ /ˈfɪdlɪŋ/ *n.* [U] the activity of playing the fiddle

fiddling² *adj.* [only before noun] unimportant and annoying: *a fiddling little job*

fi·del·i·ty /fəˈdɛləti, faɪ-/ *n.* [U] **1** loyalty to your husband, wife etc., shown by having sex only with them: *Kip was beginning to doubt Jessica's fidelity.* **2** FORMAL the quality of not changing something when you are producing it again in a different form, by recording, translating, making a movie etc.: *The sound fidelity of CDs is much better than that of records.* | [+ to] *Wilson and Nabokov argued over the translation's fidelity to the original text.* **3** the quality of being faithful and loyal, or of not doing anything that is against your beliefs: *fidelity to religious beliefs* —see also FAITHFUL¹, HIGH FIDELITY

fidg·et¹ /ˈfɪdʒɪt/ *v.* [I] to keep moving your hands or feet, especially because you are bored or nervous: *A few students fidgeted nervously in their chairs.* | [fidget with sth] *He fidgeted with paper and pen.*

fidget² *n.* [C] INFORMAL **1** someone who keeps moving and is not able to sit or stand still **2 get/have the fidgets** to be unable to stop moving

fidg·et·y /ˈfɪdʒəti/ *adj.* INFORMAL tending to fidget a lot: *Two fidgety toddlers stood with their mothers.*

fi·du·ci·ar·y¹ /fɪˈduʃiˌɛri/ *n.* [C] TECHNICAL someone who has legal control of the money or property belonging to other people, a company, or an organization

fiduciary² *adj.* TECHNICAL relating to the legal control of someone else's money or property

fie /faɪ/ *interjection* OLD USE **fie on sb** used to express anger or disapproval toward someone

fief /fif/ *n.* [C] an area of land that belonged to a LORD in past times

field¹ /fild/ *n.*
1 farm [C] an area of land where crops are grown or animals feed on grass: *fields full of cotton* | **a corn/wheat/rice etc. field** (=an area of land where corn, wheat, rice etc. is grown)
2 sports **a)** [C] an area of ground where outdoor games such as baseball or football are played: *The fans cheered as he walked off the field.* | *The Trojans will take the field* (=go onto the field in order to begin a game) *against Arizona State this afternoon.* | **a baseball/football/soccer field** *Students gathered at the side of the football field before the game.* **b) the field** the team that is throwing and catching the ball in a game such as baseball, rather than the team that is hitting
3 subject [C] a subject that people study or are involved in as part of their work: [+ of] *There is much that is new in the field of health care.* | *He has an engineering degree, but couldn't find a job in his field.*
4 practical work [singular] work or study that is done in the field is done in the real world or in the area where something is happening, rather than in a CLASSROOM or LABORATORY: *Firefighters in the field*

F

called for more help. | **field testing/trial etc.** *Seven months of field testing have shown the device to be reliable.* —see also FIELD TEST

5 competitors [singular] **a)** all the people, companies, or products who are competing against each other: *Bartlett defeated a crowded field of candidates for the job of mayor.* | *Motorola led the field* (=was the most successful company) *in wireless communication devices.* **b)** all the horses or runners in a race: *Dusty Nell is leading the field as they come around the final bend.*

6 coal/oil/gas field a large area where coal, oil, or gas is found

7 field of view/vision the whole area that you are able to see without turning your head: *The goggles limit your field of vision.*

8 magnetic/gravitational/force field an area where a natural force is felt or has an effect

9 the field (of battle) the time or place where there is fighting in a war: *Civilians walked miles to villages away from the field of battle.* | *The new tank has yet to be used in the field.*

10 snow/ice etc. field a large area covered with snow etc.

11 field of fire the area that you can hit by shooting from a particular position

12 computers [C] an amount of space made available for a particular type of information: *The field for the user's name is 25 characters long.* —see also **play the field** (PLAY¹ (22))

field² *v.* **1 field a question** to answer a difficult question: *Blair fielded questions on everything from pensions to landmines.* **2 field a (phone) call** to answer a telephone call, especially when there are a lot of calls from people asking questions: *The college spokeswoman has fielded numerous calls from the media.* **3** [T] if you field a team, or an army, they represent you or fight for you in a competition or war: *He fielded a soccer team with Argentinean and Brazilian talent.* **4** [T] if you field the ball in a game of baseball, you stop it after it has been hit: *Carlton fielded all five grounders his way.* **5 be fielding** the team that is fielding in a game of baseball is the one that is throwing and catching the ball, rather than the one hitting it

field corn /ˈ. ./ *n.* [U] corn that is grown to use as grain or to feed to animals, rather than to be eaten by people

field day /ˈ. ./ *n.* [C] **1 have a field day** INFORMAL to have a chance to do a lot of something you enjoy, especially a chance to criticize someone or something: *Politicians and the media have had a field day with the incident.* **2** a day when students at a school have sports competitions

field·er /ˈfildɚ/ *n.* [C] one of the players who tries to catch the ball in a game of baseball

field e·vent /ˈ. .,./ *n.* [C] a sports activity such as jumping over bars or throwing heavy things that is part of an outdoor competition —compare TRACK EVENT

field glass·es /ˈ. ,../ *n.* [plural] BINOCULARS

field goal /ˈ. ./ *n.* [C] **1** the act of kicking the ball over the bar of the GOAL for three points in football **2** the act of putting the ball through the BASKET to get points in basketball

field hock·ey /ˈ. ,../ *n.* [U] an outdoor game in which two teams of 11 players using special sticks try to hit a ball into their opponents' GOAL

field house /ˈ. ./ *n.* [C] a large building used for indoor sports events such as basketball

field test /ˈ. ./ *n.* [C] a test of a new product or system that is done outside the LABORATORY in real conditions —**field-test** *v.* [T]

field trip /ˈ. ./ *n.* [C] an occasion when students go somewhere to learn about a particular subject: *Teachers have organized a field trip to a recycling factory.*

field·work /ˈfildwɚk/ *n.* [U] **1** the study of scientific or social subjects that is done outside the CLASSROOM or LABORATORY **2** work that is done in farmers' fields to help crops grow —**fieldworker** *n.* [C]

fiend /find/ *n.* [C] **1** a dope/drug/cocaine etc. fiend

someone who takes drugs regularly **2 a sex fiend** DISAPPROVING someone who wants to have sex a lot **3** someone who likes something much more than other people do: *a sports fiend* **4** a very cruel or evil person **5** LITERARY an evil spirit

fiend·ish /ˈfindɪʃ/ *adj.* **1** LITERARY very bad in a way that seems evil: *Napalm is among the most fiendish of chemical weapons.* **2** FORMAL extremely difficult or bad: *a plot of fiendish complexity* —**fiendishly** *adv.*

fierce /fɪrs/ *adj.* **1** done with a lot of energy and strong feelings, and sometimes violent: *The fiercest fighting took place in the West Woods.* | *Rogers is a young player with a fierce love for the game.* | *Despite fierce competition within the industry, prices are unlikely to drop any further.* **2** a fierce person or animal is angry or ready to attack, and looks very frightening: *The peregrine falcon is one of nature's fiercest predators.* **3** fierce cold, heat, or weather is much colder, hotter etc. than usual: *It was one of the region's fiercest storms in years.* **4 something fierce** SPOKEN more loudly, strongly etc. than usual: *It rained something fierce.* —**fiercely** *adv.* —**fierceness** *n.* [U]

fi·er·y /ˈfaɪəri/ *adj.* **1** containing or looking like fire: *a fiery sunset* **2** making people feel strong emotions such as anger or excitement, or showing these types of emotion: *a fiery labor leader* | *music with a fiery rhythm* **3** becoming angry very quickly: *Nansen is fiery and emotional.* **4** fiery foods taste very strong and hot **5** bright red: *He has fiery red hair.*

fi·es·ta /fiˈɛstə/ *n.* [C] **1** a religious holiday with dancing, music etc., especially in Spain and Latin America **2** a party

fife /faɪf/ *n.* [C] a small musical instrument like a FLUTE, often played in military bands

fif·teen¹ /ˌfɪfˈtin◂/ *number* 15

fif·teenth¹ /ˌfɪfˈtinθ◂/ *adj.* 15th; next after the fourteenth: *the fifteenth century*

fifteenth² *pron.* **the fifteenth** the 15th thing in a series: *Let's have dinner on the fifteenth* (=the 15th day of the month).

fifth¹ /fɪfθ/ *adj.* 5th; next after the fourth: *We came in fifth place in the race.*

fifth² *pron.* **1 the fifth** the 5th thing in a series: *Her party is on the fifth* (=the 5th day of the month). **2 take/plead the fifth (amendment)** to refuse to answer a question about a crime in a court of law, because you are afraid by answering you might give the court information that would show you are guilty

fifth³ *n.* [C] **1** 1/5; one of five equal parts: *Only a fifth of the students are boys.* | **one-fifth/two-fifths/three-fifths etc.** *Four-fifths of doctors are unhappy with the amount of government funding.* **2** an amount of alcohol equal to 1/5 of a gallon, sold in bottles: *a fifth of bourbon*

fifth col·umn /ˌ. ˈ../ *n.* [C] a group of people who work secretly during a war to help the enemies of the country they live in —**fifth columnist** *n.* [C]

fifth wheel /ˌ. ˈ./ *n.* [C] **1 feel like a fifth wheel** INFORMAL to feel that the people you are with do not want you to be there **2** a piece of equipment, shaped like a wheel on its side, used to attach a TRAILER to a large vehicle such as a truck

fif·ti·eth¹ /ˈfɪftiɪθ/ *adj.* 50th; next after the forty-ninth: *It's my parents' fiftieth anniversary next week.*

fiftieth² *pron.* **the fiftieth** the 50th thing in a series

fif·ty /ˈfɪfti/ *number* **1** 50 **2 the fifties** also **the '50s a)** the years from 1950 through 1959: *Were you born in the fifties?* **3 sb's fifties** the time when someone is 50 to 59 years old | **in your early/mid/late fifties** *I'll be in my early fifties when the kids leave home.* **4 in the fifties** if the temperature is in the fifties, it is between 50° and 59° FAHRENHEIT | **in the high/low fifties** *The temperatures are only going to be in the low fifties.*

fifty² *n. plural* **fifties** [C] a piece of paper money worth $50: *He pulled out this huge pile of fifties and handed me one.*

F

fifty-fifty /ˌ.. '..ˌ/ *adj., adv.* SPOKEN **1** divided or shared equally between two people: *We split the money fifty-fifty.* **2** having an equal chance of happening in one of two ways: *I think we **have a fifty-fifty chance of** winning.*

fig /fɪg/ *n.* [C] **1** a soft sweet fruit with a lot of small seeds, often eaten dried, or the tree on which this fruit grows —see picture at FRUIT[1] **2** **not care/give a fig (about sb/sth)** SPOKEN, OLD-FASHIONED to not care at all about someone or something

fig. 1 the written abbreviation of "figure" **2** the written abbreviation of FIGURATIVE

fight[1] /faɪt/ *past tense and past participle* **fought** *v.*
1 war [I,T] to take part in a war or battle: *Pancho Villa fought a battle near here.* | [+ **in**] *My father fought in the Pacific during World War II.* | [+ **against/with**] *He fought against the Nazis during World War II.* | [+ **about/over/for**] *The two countries started fighting over control of the northern plains.* | [**fight sb**] *Vietnam fought France and then the U.S. over 30 years.* | *North and South Korea **fought a** three-year **war** in the early 1950s.*
2 hit people [I,T] if someone fights another person, or if two people fight, they hit and kick each other in order to hurt each other: *The children fought and pushed in line.* | [+ **with**] *Stop fighting with each other, you two!* | [+ **about/over/for**] *Apparently they were fighting over a woman.* | [**fight sb**] *Did you fight him?*
3 argue [I] to argue about something: *My mother and my grandmother fight all the time.* | [+ **with**] *The kids seem to fight with each other constantly.* | [+ **about/over**] *Most married couples fight occasionally about money.*
4 try to do sth [I,T] to try hard to get, change, or prevent something: *Civil rights groups have vowed to fight the changes.* | [+ **for/against**] *The union fought for a better health care package.* | [**fight to do sth**] *I had to really fight to stay awake, I was so tired.* | [**fight sb (on sth)**] *Citizens' groups intend to fight the mayor on the freeway plan.* | *The closing of the school was **fought tooth and nail** (=opposed with a lot of energy) by neighborhood groups.*
5 compete [I,T] to compete strongly for something, especially a job or political position or in a sport: [+ **for**] *Party members are fighting for power.* | [**fight sb for sth**] *He had to fight several other applicants for the job.*
6 sport [I,T] to fight someone as a sport; BOX: *The two former champions fought again in Las Vegas.*
7 fight a fire/blaze etc. to try to stop a fire from burning
8 emotion [T] also **fight back** to try very hard not to show your feelings or not to do something you want to do: *"I'm devastated," Weston said, **fighting back tears**.*
9 fight your way to move through a group of people by pushing past them, or through a difficult or dangerous area: *Firefighters fought their way into a bedroom and rescued a 3-year-old boy.*
10 have a fighting chance to have a chance to do something or achieve something if you work very hard at it: *All children must have a fighting chance at a good education.*
11 fight fire with fire to use the same methods as your opponents in an argument, competition etc.
12 fighting spirit the desire to fight or compete
13 fighting words something you say that makes someone want to fight or argue with you: *To Chapman, those are fighting words.*
14 fight to the death a) to fight until one person is killed **b)** to fight very hard to achieve something even if it means that you suffer —see also **fight/wage/be a losing battle** (BATTLE[1] (5))

fight back *phr. v.* **1** [I] to use violence or arguments against someone who has attacked you or argued with you: *If you're mugged, don't fight back. Give them your wallet.* **2** [I] to work hard to prevent something bad happening: *Victims of discrimination often don't have the power to fight back.*

fight sb/sth ↔ **off** *phr. v.* [T] **1** to try to keep someone or something away or stop someone from doing something, especially by using violence: *The company managed to fight off a hostile takeover attempt.* **2** to try hard to get rid of something, especially a feeling or an illness: *White blood cells help to fight off infections.*

fight sth **out** *phr. v.* [T] to argue or use violence until a disagreement is settled: *The two groups will **fight it out** in the courts.*

fight[2] *n.*
1 hit [C] an act of fighting in which two people or groups hit, push etc. each other: [+ **between**] *A fight between them on New Year's Day left Paula with a black eye.* | *What was the fight about?* | *You **got in a fight** ? Are you all right?* | **pick/start a fight** *A drunk tried to pick a fight with him.*
2 battle [C] a battle between two armies, especially the fighting that happens at one particular place and time: [+ **for**] *the fight for independence from France*
3 argument [C] an argument: *A good fight once in a while can clear the air.* | *We used to **have fights about** who got to sit in the front seat.*
4 achieve/prevent sth [singular] the process of trying to achieve something, change something, or prevent something: [+ **against**] *Conservative voters led a fight against forced school busing.* | [+ **for**] *We have made progress in the fight for equality and justice.* | *He'll **have a fight on his hands** (=have to oppose someone to achieve something) to get Malone acquitted.*
5 sports [C] an act of fighting as a sport: *Tyson's fight against Evander Holyfield*
6 energy [U] the energy and desire to keep working hard for something you want to achieve: *They're not going to give up – they **have a lot of fight left** in them.*
7 put up a good fight to work very hard to fight or compete in a difficult situation
8 a fight to the finish/death a fight that continues until one side is completely defeated

fight·er /ˈfaɪtɚ/ *n.* [C] **1** someone who keeps trying to achieve something in difficult situations: *Dad was a fighter, but he couldn't beat cancer.* | *a crime fighter* **2** someone who fights as a sport; BOXER **3** also a **fighter plane/jet** a small, fast military airplane that can destroy other planes —see also FIREFIGHTER, FREEDOM FIGHTER

fig leaf /ˈ. ./ *n.* [C] **1** the large leaf of the FIG tree, sometimes shown in paintings as covering people's sex organs **2** INFORMAL something that is intended to hide embarrassing facts

fig·ment /ˈfɪgmənt/ *n.* [C] **a figment of sb's imagination** something that you imagine to be real, but does not exist: *These two men actually lived; they weren't figments of some writer's imagination.*

fig·u·ra·tive /ˈfɪgyərətɪv/ *adj.* **1** a figurative word or expression is used in a different way from the usual one, to give you a picture in your mind —compare LITERAL (1) **2** TECHNICAL figurative art shows objects, people, or nature in the way they really look —compare ABSTRACT[1] (3) —**figuratively** *adv.*

fig·ure[1] /ˈfɪgyɚ/ *n.* [C]
1 number **a)** a number representing an amount, especially an officially printed number: *sales figures* | *Ohio's employment figures for December are not available.* **b)** a number from 0 to 9, written as a sign rather than spelled with letters: *Five players scored in **double figures** (=numbers between 10 and 99).*
2 amount of money a particular amount of money: *He offered to buy the team for the figure of $140 million.* | *Until he lost his job, Carl was earning a **six-figure** (=over $100,000) salary as a top sales executive.*
3 woman's body the shape of a woman's body, used when describing how attractive it is: *Caroline really has a terrific figure.* | **keep/lose your figure** (=keep your body in an attractive shape as you get older, or to not do this) —see Usage Note at BODY
4 father/mother/authority figure someone who is considered to be like a father or mother, or to represent

authority, because of their character or behavior: *A young girl needs a strong mother figure.*
5 `important person` someone who is important in a particular way: *Ali was one of the great sports figures of this century.* | *The central figure of the movie is a 13-year-old girl.*
6 **give an exact figure** also **put an exact figure on it** to say exactly how much something is worth, or how much or how many of something you are talking about: *I know it's worth a lot of money but I really couldn't give you an exact figure.*
7 `person's shape` the shape of a person, especially one that is far away or is difficult to see: *a figure in a red robe* | *Freddy's bent figure limped in front of him.*
8 `drawing` a numbered drawing or a DIAGRAM in a book
9 `mathematical shape` a GEOMETRIC shape: *A hexagon is a six-sided figure.*
10 **a fine figure of a man/woman** OLD-FASHIONED someone who is tall and has a good body
11 `painting/model` a person in a painting, a model, or a small STATUE: *a rare 16th century Japanese figure* | *Star Wars action figures* (=a toy shaped like a person) —compare FIGURINE
12 `on ice` a pattern formed in FIGURE SKATING
13 **a figure of fun** someone who people laugh at

S W
1 2
figure² *v.* **1** [I] to be important or included in something, and to be noticed because of this: [+ **in**] *Lott figured prominently in the Chiefs' win last night.* **2** [T] to calculate an amount: *I'm just figuring my expenses.*

SPOKEN PHRASES

3 [T] to form a particular opinion after thinking about a situation: [**figure (that)**] *I buy the pie shell because I figure that's easier than making it.* **4** **that figures** also **(it) figures a)** said when something happens or someone behaves in a way that you expect, but do not like: *"They're out of hot chocolate." "Figures."* **b)** used to say that something is reasonable or makes sense: *Well, it sort of figures that she'd be mad at you after what you did.* **5** **go figure** said to show that you think something is strange or difficult to explain: *"He didn't even leave a message." "Go figure."*

---

figure on sth *phr. v.* [T] SPOKEN to include something, especially a number or a time, in your plans: *Figure on 40 minutes from Gilroy to Tamian Station.*
figure sb/sth ↔ **out** *phr. v.* [T] **1** to think about a problem or situation until you find the answer or understand what has happened: *If I have a map, I can figure it out.* | *Don't worry, we'll figure something out* (=find a way to solve the problem). | [**figure out how/what/why**] *I could hear them talking but I couldn't figure out what they were saying.* **2** to understand why someone behaves in the way they do: *Women. I just can't figure them out.*

fig·ured /ˈfɪɡəd/ *adj.* [only before noun] FORMAL decorated with a small pattern
figure eight /ˌ.. ˈ./ *n.* [C] the pattern or shape of a number eight, as seen in a knot, dance, SEATING etc.
fig·ure·head /ˈfɪɡəˌhɛd/ *n.* [C] **1** someone who seems to be the leader of a country or organization, but who has no real power: *Norway's King Harald V is a figurehead.* **2** a wooden model of a woman that used to be placed on the front of ships
figure of speech /ˌ... ˈ./ *n.* [C] a word or expression that is used in a different way from the usual meanings of the words, in order to give you a picture in your mind: *He said he used the phrase as a figure of speech, and did not mean to imply she was a coward.*
figure skat·ing /ˈ.. ˌ../ *n.* [C] a kind of skating (SKATE² (1)) in which you move in patterns on the ice —**figure skater** *n.* [C]
fig·u·rine /ˌfɪɡjəˈrin/ *n.* [C] a small model of a person or animal made of CHINA (=baked clay), used as a decoration —compare FIGURE¹ (11)
Fi·ji /ˈfidʒi/ a country in the southwestern Pacific Ocean made up of two main islands and hundreds of smaller islands —**Fijian** *n., adj.*
fil·a·ment /ˈfɪləmənt/ *n.* [C] a very thin thread, especially the thin wire in a LIGHT BULB

---

fil·bert /ˈfɪlbət/ *n.* [C] a HAZELNUT
filch /fɪltʃ/ *v.* [T] INFORMAL to steal something, especially something small or not very expensive: *Peters filched thousands of coins from the city's parking meters.*
file¹ /faɪl/ *n.* [C] **1** a collection of information about a particular person or subject, usually kept by an official organization: *I put Callahan's file back in the drawer.* | [+ **on**] *Mendoza read over the file on the murders again.* | *The CIA does not **keep files on** (=collect and keep information on) American citizens.* **2** a box or folded piece of heavy paper that is used to keep papers organized or separate from other papers: *a stack of blue and yellow files* **3** a collection of information on a computer that is stored under a particular name: *The statistics are in the file called "stats.doc."* **4** **on file a)** kept in a file so that it can be used later: *Some of the information on file is confidential.* **b)** officially recorded: *More than four million patents are on file in the U.S.* **5** a metal tool with a rough surface, used to make other surfaces smooth or to cut through wood, metal etc. —see also NAIL FILE —see picture at TOOL¹; —see RANK AND FILE, SINGLE FILE

S W
1 2

file² *v.* **1** [I always + adv./prep., T] to officially record something such as a complaint, law case, official document etc.: [+ **for**] *I heard she decided to file for divorce.* | *The district attorney **filed charges** against him.* | **file a claim/suit** *O'Brien will file a $1 million civil damage suit against the Committee.* **2** also **file away** [T] to keep papers with information on them in a particular place, so that you can find them easily: *Slawa filed a copy of the contract he'd signed.* | *I filed away my notes and manuscripts.* **3** [I always + adv./prep.] to walk in a line of people, one behind the other: [+ **past/into/through etc.**] *He shook hands with each member as they filed out.* **4** [I always + adv./prep.,T] to rub something with a metal tool or a NAIL FILE to make it smooth or cut it: *Alice sat at her desk, filing her nails.* | [+ **through/away/down etc.**] *File down the sharp edges.*

S W
2 2

file cab·i·net /ˈ. ˌ.../ *n.* [C] a FILING CABINET
file ex·ten·sion /ˈ. .ˌ../ *n.* [C] TECHNICAL an EXTENSION (7)
file·name /ˈfaɪlneɪm/ *n.* [C] the name of a particular computer FILE
fil·et /fɪˈleɪ/ *n.* [C] a piece of meat or fish without bones: *salmon filets*
file trans·fer /ˈ. ˌ../ *n.* [C] TECHNICAL the process by which computer information is sent from one computer to another, especially over the Internet
fil·i·al /ˈfɪliəl/ *adj.* FORMAL relating to the way in which a son or daughter should behave toward their parents: *filial duty*
fil·i·bus·ter /ˈfɪləˌbʌstə/ *v.* [I] to try to delay action in the Senate by making very long speeches —**filibuster** *n.* [C]
fil·i·gree /ˈfɪləˌgri/ *n.* [U] delicate decoration made of gold or silver wire
fil·ing /ˈfaɪlɪŋ/ *n.* [U] **1** the activity of putting papers or documents into the correct FILES¹ (1): *I should go do some filing.* **2** **filings** [plural] very small sharp pieces that come off a piece of metal when it is FILED² (4)
filing cab·i·net /ˈ. ˌ.../ *n.* [C] a piece of office furniture with drawers for keeping letters, reports etc.
Fil·i·pi·no /ˌfɪləˈpinoʊ/ *n.* [C] someone from the Philippines —**Filipino** *adj.*
fill¹ /fɪl/ *v.*
1 `make sth full` **a)** also **fill up** [T] to put enough of a liquid, substance, or material into a container to make it full: *Just turn on the faucet and fill it up.* | *I found a clean mug and filled it.* | [**fill sth with sth**] *George filled a couple of sacks with newspapers.* **b)** **be filled with sth** if a container is filled with something, it has had as much of something as possible put inside it: *His black bag was filled with medicines.*

S W
1 1

F

fill in

form

2 **become full** also **fill up** [I] if a place, building, or container fills, it gradually becomes full of people, things, or a particular substance: *After heavy rains in March, the reservoirs began to fill up.* | [+ **with**] *Quickly the streets began to fill with angry protesters.*
3 **not leave any space** also **fill up** [T] if a lot of people or things fill a place, there are so many of them that there seems to be no room for anyone or anything else: *Boxes and piles of magazines filled every room in the house.* | *Computers used to fill up entire rooms.* | [**be filled with sth**] *Crowded stores were filled with shoppers.*
4 **hole/crack** also **fill in** [T] to put a substance in a hole or crack in order to make a surface smooth again: *Fill the hole with a mixture of compost and sand.*
5 **sound/smell/light** [T] if a sound, smell, or light fills a place or space, you notice it because it is very loud or strong: *The smell of smoke filled the house.* | *The days were hot, filled with sunshine and clear skies.*
6 **fill a need/demand etc.** to give people something they want but which they have not been able to have until now: *The project will fill a need for affordable housing.*
7 **fill a job/position etc. a)** to find someone to do a particular job: *Many corporations hire older workers to fill temporary positions.* **b)** to do a particular job: *Women do not fill combat positions in the military.*
8 **emotions a)** [T] if an emotion fills you, you feel it very strongly: *A feeling of joy filled his heart.* | [**be filled with sth**] *He gave me a smile that was filled with pride.* **b)** [I] if someone's eyes fill with tears, they begin to cry
9 **time** [T] if you fill a period of time with a particular activity you use most of your time doing it: [**fill sth with sth**] *I filled every minute with activity, trying to forget.* | [**fill sth doing sth**] *I fill most of my spare time reading and listening to music.*
10 **fill sb's shoes** to be able to do a job as well as the person who did it before you: *New mayor Susan Hammer had to prove she could fill McEnery's shoes.*
11 **fill yourself** also **fill yourself up** INFORMAL to eat so much food that you cannot eat any more: [**fill yourself with sth**] *Don't fill yourself up with candy, it's almost dinner time.*
12 **fill (in) the gaps** to do something that makes something more complete: *A number of projects try to fill in the gaps in social service programs.*
13 **fill a role** to do something or be an important part of something: *Roberts is expected to fill a significant role in Michigan's offense.*
14 **fill an order** to supply the goods a customer has asked for
15 **teeth** [T] to put a FILLING¹ (1) in a tooth
16 **sail** [I,T] if a sail fills or the wind fills a sail, the sail has a rounded shape rather than hanging down loosely —see also **fill the bill/fit the bill** (BILL¹ (5))

fill in *phr. v.* **1** [T **fill** sth ↔ **in**] to write all the necessary information in special places on a document:

He updated the records, filling in expenses and income. | *Check the second box, and **fill in the blanks** in that section.* **2** [T **fill** sth ↔ **in**] to make something more complete, especially by giving more information: *This picture of events will be corrected or filled in by new evidence.* **3** [T **fill** sb ↔ **in**] to tell someone about things that have happened recently, especially because you have not seen them for a long time: [**fill sb in on sth**] *She never fills me in on the details.* **4** [T **fill** sth ↔ **in**] to paint or draw over the space inside a shape: *He doodled as he talked, filling in the letters.* **5** [I] to do someone's job or work because they are unable to do it [**fill in for sb**] *Beth, I need you to fill in for Tina while she's on vacation.*

fill out *phr. v.* **1** [T **fill** sth ↔ **out**] to write all the necessary information in special spaces on a document: *She filled out the order form in purple ink.* **2** [T **fill** sth ↔ **out**] to make a description, story, idea etc. more complete: *Different scholars fill out Irigaray's ideas quite differently.* **3** [I] if your body fills out it becomes rounded or large in a way that is considered attractive: *At puberty, a girl's body begins to fill out.*

fill up *phr. v.* **1** [T **fill** sb **up**] INFORMAL food that fills you up makes you feel you have eaten a lot when you have only eaten a small amount: *I used to have just a sandwich for lunch, but that doesn't fill me up anymore.* **2** [T **fill** sth ↔ **up**] to put enough of a liquid or substance in a container to make it full: *I filled up my plate with food.* **3** [I] to gradually become full of people, things, or a substance: [+ **with**] *After school, the pool starts filling up with kids.*

fill² *n.* **1 have your fill of sth** to not be able to accept a bad situation anymore: *I've had my fill of noisy, smoky parties.* **2 eat/drink your fill** to eat or drink as much as you want or need

filled gold /ˌ. ˈ.◂/ *n.* [U] filled gold jewelry is made of an inexpensive metal such as COPPER covered with a thin layer of gold

fill·er /ˈfɪlə/ *n.* [U] **1** stories, information, drawings, songs etc. that are not important but are used to fill space in a newspaper or magazine, on a CD etc.: *His latest album consists of two great singles and ten tracks of filler.* **2** something that is added to food in order to increase its weight or size, so that the food can be sold cheaply: *The crab cakes were 80% crab, with very little filler.* **3** a substance used to fill cracks in wood, walls etc., especially before you paint them **4** also **fill** a soft substance such as cotton or feathers used to fill PILLOWS, COMFORTERS etc.

fil·let¹ /fɪˈleɪ/ *n.* [C] a piece of meat or fish without bones: *salmon fillets*

fillet² *v.* [T] to remove the bones from a piece of meat or fish: *Salmon is a relatively easy fish to fillet.*

fill-in /ˈ. ./ *n.* [C] someone who does someone else's job while they are away, sick etc.: *Hahn is scheduled to announce tonight's game as a fill-in for Joe Starkey.*

fill·ing¹ /ˈfɪlɪŋ/ *n.* **1** [C] a small amount of metal that is put into your tooth to replace a decayed part that has been removed **2** [C,U] the food that is put inside something such as a PIE, cake etc.: *Roll the tortilla around the filling.*

filling² *adj.* food that is filling makes your stomach feel full: *A casserole makes a basic but filling meal.*

filling sta·tion /ˈ.. ˌ../ *n.* [C] a GAS STATION

fil·lip /ˈfɪlɪp/ *n.* [singular] something that adds excitement or interest to something: *Cardin still knows how to give a fillip to classic styles.*

Fill·more /ˈfɪlmər/, **Mil·lard** /ˈmɪləd/ (1800–1874) the 13th President of the U.S.

fil·ly /ˈfɪli/ *n. plural* **fillies** [C] **1** a young female horse —compare COLT **2** OLD-FASHIONED a young girl who has a lot of energy

film¹ /fɪlm/ *n.* **1** [U] the material used in a camera for taking photographs or recording movies: *I've got a roll of film that I have to take in and get developed.* | *An onlooker captured the Kennedy assassination on film.* **2** [C] a MOVIE: *They're showing some classic French films at the Rialto.* **3** [U] the making of movies, considered as an art or a business: *Raymond was well-known in film and television.* | *the Hollywood*

film industry 4 [singular,U] a very thin layer of something on the surface of something else: [+ **of**] *A thin film of perspiration appeared on his forehead.*

S W
3
film² *v.* [I,T] to use a camera to record a story or real events so that it can be shown in movie theaters or on television: *They filmed the movie off the west coast of Ireland.* | *We need permission to film in some of those old churches.*

film fes·ti·val /'. ,.../ *n.* [C] an event at which a lot of movies are shown, and sometimes prizes are given for the best ones: *the Cannes film festival*

film·mak·er /'fɪlm,meɪkɚ/ *n.* [C] someone who makes movies, especially a DIRECTOR or PRODUCER —**film-making** *n.* [U]

film star /'. ./ *n.* [C] OLD-FASHIONED a MOVIE STAR

film·strip /'fɪlm,strɪp/ *n.* [C] a photographic film that shows photographs, drawings etc. one at a time, not as moving pictures, especially used in a class

fil·o dough /'filou ,dou/ *n.* [U] another spelling of PHYLLO DOUGH

S W
3
fil·ter¹ /'fɪltɚ/ *n.* [C] 1 something that you put gas or liquid through, in order to remove unwanted substances: *a water filter* 2 a piece of glass or plastic that changes the amount or color of light allowed into a camera or TELESCOPE 3 a piece of equipment that only allows certain sounds to pass through it

filter² *v.* 1 [T] to clean a liquid or gas by passing it through a special substance or piece of equipment: *In remote areas, you will need to filter or boil your drinking water.* 2 [I always + adv./prep.] if news or information filters somewhere, people gradually hear about it: [+ **back/through** etc.] *Unofficial reports of the violence began to filter out of the capital within days.* 3 [I always + adv./prep.] if people filter somewhere, they move gradually in that direction through a door, passage etc.: [+ **in/out** etc.] *Chattering noisily, the crowd began to filter into the auditorium.* 4 [I always + adv./prep.] if light or sound filters into a place, it can be seen or heard only slightly: [+ **through/into**] *Sunshine filtered through a stained glass window.*

filter sth ↔ **out** *phr. v.* [T] 1 to remove something by using a filter: *The metals, if not filtered out, can clog pipes and diminish water pressure.* 2 to remove inappropriate people or things from a group: *New pre-employment screening programs have filtered out 125,000 applicants who could not meet standards.*

filter tip /'.. ,./ *n.* [C] 1 the special end of a cigarette that removes some of the harmful substances from the smoke 2 a cigarette that has a special end on it to remove some of the harmful substances from the smoke —**filter-tipped** *adj.*

filth /fɪlθ/ *n.* [U] 1 an extremely dirty substance: *Look at all that filth on the windshield!* 2 very impolite or offensive language, stories, or pictures about sex: *I am deeply offended by some of the filth they show on television.*

filth·y¹ /'fɪlθi/ *adj.* **filthier, filthiest** 1 extremely dirty: *Get your filthy feet off the couch!* | *The bathroom was absolutely filthy.* 2 showing or describing sexual acts in a very offensive way: *I was horrified by the filthy language the kids were using.* —**filthily** *adv.* —**filthiness** *n.* [U]

filthy² *adv.* **1 filthy rich** INFORMAL an expression meaning "extremely rich," used when you think someone has too much money: *Everyone assumed the members at the golf club were filthy rich.* **2 filthy dirty** SPOKEN extremely dirty: *Pete came in filthy dirty from playing in the backyard.*

fil·trate /'fɪltreɪt/ *n.* [C] TECHNICAL a substance that has been removed from something else by using a FILTER¹ (1)

fil·tra·tion /fɪl'treɪʃən/ *n.* [U] the process of being cleaned by passing through a FILTER¹ (1): *a water filtration system*

fin /fɪn/ *n.* **1** [C] one of the thin body parts that a fish uses to swim —see picture at BARRACUDA **2** [C] part of an airplane that sticks up at the back and helps it to fly smoothly **3** [C] also **tailfin** a thin piece of metal that sticks out from something such as a car, as a decoration **4** [C usually plural] a FLIPPER

fi·na·gle /fə'neɪgəl/ *v.* [T] INFORMAL to obtain something that is difficult to get by using unusual methods: *How he finagled four front row seats to the game, I'll never know.* —**finagling** *n.* [U]

S W
3
fi·nal¹ /'faɪnl/ *adj.* **1** [only before noun] last in a series of actions, events, parts of a story etc.: *Mulligan will coach his final game on Saturday.* | *Paul just started writing the final draft of his novel.* **2** if a decision, offer, agreement etc. is final, it cannot be changed: *The final decision rests with the client.* | *When it comes to discipline, parents have the final say.* | *You can't go, and that's final!* **3** [only before noun] being the result at the end of a process: *The drug is now in its final stage of testing.* | *What was the final score?*

S W
3
final² *n.* [C] **1** an important test taken in a particular class at the end of each year in high school or college: *I really shouldn't go out – my biology final is tomorrow.* **2** [usually plural] the last and most important game, race, or set of games in a competition: *Sue qualified for the finals in the 100-meter backstroke but finished sixth.* | *the NBA finals*

fi·nal·e /fɪ'næli, -'nɑ-/ *n.* [C] the last part of a piece of music, a performance etc.: *The grand finale was accompanied by fireworks.*

fi·nal·ist /'faɪnl-ɪst/ *n.* [C] one of the people or teams that reaches the final part in a competition or set of sports games

fi·nal·i·ty /faɪ'næləti, fə-/ *n.* [U] FORMAL the quality or feeling that something has when you know it is finished or done and cannot be changed: *She announced her impending departure with finality and sadness in her voice.*

fi·nal·ize /'faɪnl,aɪz/ *v.* [T] to finish the last part of a plan, business deal etc.: *The first draft of the script has been completed, but no casting has been finalized yet.* —**finalization** /,faɪnl-ə'zeɪʃən/ *n.* [U]

S W
1 1
fi·nal·ly /'faɪnl-i/ *adv.* **1** after a long time: *I was put on hold for about ten minutes before I finally got to speak to my dad.* | *We finally found a decent apartment close to campus.* **2** [sentence adverb] as the last of a series of things: *And finally, I'd like to thank the cast and crew for all their hard work.* —see Usage Note at LASTLY **3** FORMAL in a way that does not allow further change: *The Senate ethics committee has not yet acted finally in the Cranston case.*

S W
2
fi·nance¹ /fə'næns, 'faɪnæns/ *n.* **1** [U] the management of money, especially money controlled by a government, company, or large organization: *Wahl has an impressive knowledge of corporate finance and budgeting.* | *The Mayor was accused of breaking campaign finance laws.* | *There are several articles on* **personal finance** *(=managing your own bank accounts etc.) in the paper each week.* **2 finances** [plural] the money that a person, company, organization etc. has available, or the way they manage this money: *The school's finances are unlikely to improve in the coming year.* | *Mason is going to help me straighten out my finances.*

S W
2
finance² *v.* [T] **1** to provide money, especially a large amount of money, to pay for something: *More than $100,000 was donated to help finance Ryan's heart transplant.* **2** [T] to make an arrangement to pay for something over a long period of time: *We financed the new house through the credit union.*

finance charge /'.. ,./ *n.* [C] the money that a bank or finance company charges someone who has borrowed money from them to start a business, buy something etc. —compare INTEREST¹ (3)

finance com·pa·ny /'.. ,.../ *n.* [C] a company that lends money, especially to businesses

S W
1
fi·nan·cial /fə'nænʃəl, faɪ-/ *adj.* relating to money, or the management of money: *I'll have to speak to my financial advisors before I can give you an answer.* | *A baby would be a heavy financial burden.* | *Buyers need a financial incentive to choose more efficient cars.* | *Some establishments offer estate planning and other* **financial services.** | *Bank Boston's headquarters are*

F

located in the **financial district** (=the part of a city where many banks, financial institutions etc. are located). —**financially** adv.: People who are retired or financially independent have more time to travel.

financial aid /.,.. './ n. [U] money that is given or lent to college or university students to pay for their education

financial in·sti·tu·tion /.,.. ..'../ n. [C] a business or organization that lends and borrows money, for example a bank

financial mar·ket /.,.. '../ n. [C usually plural] TECHNICAL a bank or other financial institution that makes business contracts with other similar organizations

financial year /.,.. './ n. [C] BRITISH a FISCAL YEAR

fin·an·cier /ˌfaɪnænˈsɪr, fəˌnæn-, ˌfɪnən-/ n. [C] someone who controls or lends large sums of money

fi·nanc·ing /ˈfaɪnænsɪŋ/ n. [U] money that you borrow from a bank or FINANCE COMPANY to start a business, buy something etc., and which you pay back over an agreed period of time: Ron still has to arrange financing for his fitness center project.

finch /fɪntʃ/ n. [C] a small wild bird with a short beak

S W
1 1
find[1] /faɪnd/ past tense and past participle **found** v. [T]
1 by searching to discover or see something, either by searching for it or by chance: I found a wallet full of cash and credit cards in the parking lot. | Have you found your plane ticket yet? | I have a better chance of winning the lottery than of finding a man to marry. | [**find sb sth**] I found Trudy a nice blouse for her birthday.
2 by study to discover or learn something by study, tests, or thinking about a problem: Scientists still haven't found a cure for AIDS. | [+ **that**] Researchers have found that 67% of all American mothers now work outside the home.
3 by experience to learn or know something by experience: [+ (**that**)] She's found that people aren't always eager for change. | One thing I find about living in the big city is that people are more friendly than I expected.
4 arrive to discover that someone or something is in a particular condition or doing a particular thing when you arrive or first see them: He wasn't surprised to find the marsh blanketed in a thick fog. | [**find sb doing sth**] They were shocked to find their father working as a bartender downtown.
5 think/feel to have a particular feeling or idea about something | **find sth easy/difficult etc.** Are you finding it easy to adjust to the culture? | I found Stan's comments very offensive. | **find sb appealing/annoying etc.** Lots of women I know find him attractive.
6 money/time/energy to have enough money, time, energy etc. to be able to do something you want to do: I'd love to learn a foreign language, but I can't find the time right now. | Where will she find the money to send her son to college?
7 realize to notice or realize something, especially something you did not expect: [+ (**that**)] If Marie waits too long, she may find that even Arnold is no longer interested in her. | I found I was really looking forward to going back to work.
8 be found [always + adv./prep.] if something is found somewhere, it lives or exists there: This species of butterfly is only found in West Africa.
9 find your way to reach a place by discovering the right way to get there: I can probably find my way to your house if I use a map.
10 find its way [always + adv./prep.] if something finds its way somewhere, it arrives or gets there after some time or in a way that is not clear: Some water had found its way between the boards and warped the wood. | Virtually every major U.S. newspaper has found its way onto the Internet.
11 find yourself doing sth to gradually realize that you are doing something, although you had not intended or planned to do it: Marc found himself smiling at the thought of seeing Rosa again.

12 find yourself in/at etc. **a)** to realize that you are in a particular situation, especially a bad one, that you did not expect: If you have limited work experience, you might find yourself in a no-win situation. | Despite what Sheila knew about him, she found herself attracted to this strange man. **b)** to realize that you have arrived somewhere without intending to go there: After wandering around, we found ourselves back at the hotel.
13 find yourself OFTEN HUMOROUS to discover what you are really like and what you want to do: She went to India to find herself.
14 find sb guilty/not guilty/innocent to officially decide that someone is guilty or not guilty of something: Galbraith was found not guilty and set free. | [+ **of**] Morgan was found guilty of kidnapping.
15 have a feeling to experience a good feeling because of something: He found great satisfaction in kneading the dough and baking the bread.
16 find fault with sb/sth to criticize someone or something, often unfairly and frequently: The sergeant seemed to find fault with everything Maddox did.
17 find favor with sb be liked or approved of by someone: The film received mixed reviews from critics, but has found favor with audiences.
18 find in sb's favor to judge that someone is right or not guilty: A jury found in the employees' favor, although it did not award them monetary damages.
19 be found wanting FORMAL to not be considered good enough: The policy has been severely tested over the last 16 months and has been found wanting.
20 find its mark/target if an ARROW (1), bullet etc. finds its target, it hits what it is supposed to hit
21 find your voice **a)** also **find your tongue** to become able to speak again after being too nervous, surprised etc. to say anything **b)** if a writer, speaker, politician etc. finds their voice, they decide what they want to say and how to say it effectively
22 find your feet to get used to a new situation, especially one that is difficult at first: Susie said I could stay at her place for a while, just until I found my feet. —see Usage Note at KNOW[1]

find out phr. v. **1** [I,T **find** sth ↔ **out**] to learn information, either by chance or after trying to discover it: From the minute Joyce found out she had cancer, she lost all hope. | [+ **who/what/how** etc.] Can't you call those guys and find out where our pizza is? | [+ **that**] When I got to the airport, I found out that the flight had been canceled. | [+ **about**] You find out a lot about people on these trips. | [+ **if/whether**] I had some tests done to find out if I have any food allergies. **2** [T **find** sb **out**] to discover that someone has been doing something dishonest or illegal: After years of stealing from the company, Andrews was finally found out.

find against sb phr. v. [T not in passive] LAW to judge that someone is wrong or guilty: The defendants realized that the jury might find against them.

find for sb phr. v. [T not in passive] LAW to judge that someone is right or not guilty: The jury found for the plaintiffs on both counts.

find[2] n. [C usually singular] something very good or valuable that you discover by chance: That little Greek restaurant was a real find.

find·er /ˈfaɪndər/ n. [C] **1** someone who finds something **2** finders keepers (losers weepers) SPOKEN used to say that if someone finds something, they have the right to keep it, even if the person who lost it is unhappy about this **3** finder's fee money that is paid to someone who finds something for someone else, or who introduces people to each other so that they can make a business deal: Bowell used an agency to find a nanny, and said the finder's fee was worth it.

fin de siè·cle, fin-de-siècle /ˌfæn də siˈɛklə/ adj. [only before noun] typical of the end of the 19th century, especially typical of the art, literature, and attitudes of the time: fin-de-siècle architecture

find·ing /ˈfaɪndɪŋ/ n. [C] **1** [usually plural] the information that someone has learned as a result of their studies, work etc.: The findings show a high level of
S W
3

alcohol abuse among teenagers. **2** LAW a decision made by a judge or JURY

fine¹ /faɪn/ adj.

1 very good of a very high quality or standard, or very expensive: *Many people regard Beethoven's fifth symphony as his finest work.* | *Trinity Church is a fine example of Gothic architecture.* | *fine jewelry* | *It handles like a fine sports car.*

2 thin very thin, or in small pieces or drops: *Cut the onion into fine slices.* | *A fine coating of dust covered most of the furniture.* —see also FINE PRINT —see picture at THIN¹

3 small details involving differences, changes, or details that are difficult to understand or notice: *the fine tuning on the radio* | *Scientists are now able to measure fine distinctions between levels of sleep depth.*

SPOKEN PHRASES

4 good enough; ALL RIGHT: *"I could cook something for dinner." "That's okay – a sandwich is fine with me."* | *"Did you want some more coffee?" "No, I'm fine, thank you."*

5 healthy and well: *"How are you?" "Fine, thanks."* | *So far, mother and baby are both just fine.*

6 that's/it's fine used when you agree to something: *If you want to do that, it's fine with me.*

7 used when you are angry because you really think that something is not good or satisfactory at all: *Fine, then, I'll do it myself.*

8 SLANG used when you think someone is attractive: *I met this fine Italian girl at school.*

9 a fine line if you say that there is a fine line between two different things, you mean that there is a point at which one can easily become the other: *Roth's novels have always walked a fine line between fiction and fact.*

10 fine features someone with fine features has a small and attractively-shaped nose, mouth etc.

11 a fine man/woman/person a good person that you have a lot of respect for: *Your father is a fine man, a real gentleman.*

12 a fine figure of a man/woman OLD-FASHIONED someone who looks big, strong and physically attractive: *Vellios was a fine figure of a man.*

13 not to put too fine a point on it FORMAL used to show that you are going to criticize something in a plain and direct way: *The dishes we tried tasted, not to put too fine a point on it, like gasoline.*

14 sb's/sth's finest hour an occasion when someone or something does something very well or successfully: *The festival's finest hour was the production of "Henry V."*

fine² adv. **1** SPOKEN in a way that is satisfactory: *"How's it going?" "Fine, thanks."* | *I called the repairman, but of course the TV worked fine when he tried it.* **2 do fine** SPOKEN to be good enough, or to do something well enough: *Standard hooks and nails should do just fine for hanging the painting.* | *Once Hutton relaxes, he should do fine in the role.* **3 cut it fine** INFORMAL to leave yourself just barely enough time to do something: *If we don't leave now, we'll be cutting it fine for the bus.*

fine³ v. [T] to make someone pay money as a punishment: *Hill was fined $115 for driving alone in the carpool lane.*

fine⁴ n. [C] money that you have to pay as a punishment: *She faces up to 90 days in jail and a $1,000 fine.*

fine art /ˌ. ˈ./ n. **1** [U] paintings, drawings, music, SCULPTURE etc. that are of very good quality and have serious artistic value: *Dixon collected fine art and antique cars.* **2 fine arts** [plural] activities such as painting, music, and SCULPTURE that are concerned with producing beautiful rather than useful things: *Virginia is head of the fine arts department.* **3** [singular] something you are very good at, because you have practiced it a lot: *While some reports are excellent, most require the fine art of reading between the lines.* | *Tropical resorts have honed honeymoon planning to a fine art, often including the wedding itself in the package.*

fine·ly /ˈfaɪnli/ adv. **1** into very thin or very small pieces: *In a food processor, finely chop the peppers and onions.* **2** to a very exact degree: *a finely*

polished mirror | *He's a finely tuned athlete – he notices everything.* **3** beautifully and delicately: *finely detailed furniture*

fine print /ˈ. ./ n. [U] the part of a contract or other document that has important information which you may not notice, often written in smaller letters than the rest of the document: *Before you buy insurance, you should ask questions and read the fine print.*

fi·ne·ry /ˈfaɪnəri/ n. [U] FORMAL clothes and jewelry that are beautiful or very expensive, and are worn for a special occasion: *They all turned out in their best Sunday finery.*

fi·nesse¹ /fɪˈnɛs/ n. [U] delicate and impressive skill: *It's not easy to decorate a small room, but our designer did it with considerable finesse.*

finesse² v. [T] **1** to handle a situation well, but in a way that is slightly deceitful: *Kemp uses his creativity to find excuses which are meant to finesse problematic moments.* **2** to do something with style and delicate skill: *Roberts finessed his arrival, speaking to Fernandez privately about their shared responsibilities.*

fine-toothed comb, fine-tooth comb /ˌ. ˈ./ n. [C] **go through/over sth with a fine-toothed comb** to examine something very carefully and thoroughly: *A lender will go over your credit report and application with a fine-toothed comb.*

fine-tune /ˌ. ˈ./ v. [T] to make very small changes to something, especially a machine or system, so that it works as well as possible: *The natural gas industry continues to fine-tune its structure and business strategies.* —**fine tuning** n. [U]

fin·ger¹ /ˈfɪŋgər/ n. [C]

1 part of your hand one of the four long thin parts on your hand, not including your thumb: *She ran a finger along the spine of the book.* | *Ted anxiously tapped his fingers on the table.* —see also INDEX FINGER, LITTLE FINGER, MIDDLE FINGER, RING FINGER —see picture at BODY

2 keep your fingers crossed also **cross your fingers** to hope that something will happen the way you want: *Keep your fingers crossed that I get this job.*

3 not lift/raise a finger to not make any effort to help someone with their work: *I do all the work around the house – Frank never lifts a finger.*

4 put your finger on sth to realize exactly what is wrong, different, or unusual about a situation: *I can't put my finger on it, but there's something different about you.*

5 give sb the finger to show someone you are angry with them in a very offensive way by holding up your middle finger with the back of your hand facing them

6 long thin shape anything that is long and thin, like the shape of a finger, especially a piece of land, an area of water, or a piece of food: *Fingers of flame spread in all directions.*

7 drink an amount of an alcoholic drink that is as high in the glass as the width of someone's finger: *In the glass was a finger of pale gold wine.*

8 have/keep your finger on the pulse to always know about the most recent changes or developments in a situation or organization: *Brokers have to keep their fingers on the pulse of the international markets.*

9 twist/wrap sb around your little finger to be able to persuade someone to do anything that you want: *Before long, Jennifer had Carlos wrapped around her little finger.*

10 have a finger in every pie to be involved in many activities and have influence over them, used especially when you think someone has too much influence —see also **burn your fingers** (BURN¹ (16)), **-FINGERED, have a green thumb** (GREEN¹ (7)), **lay a finger/hand on sb** (LAY¹ (5)), **point the finger at sb** (POINT² (5)), **slip through your fingers** (SLIP¹ (8)), **snap your fingers** (SNAP¹ (4)), **have sticky fingers** (STICKY (4)), **work your fingers to the bone** (WORK¹ (27))

finger² v. [T] **1** to touch or handle something with your fingers: *She fingered the beautiful cloth with* *envy.* **2** SLANG if someone, especially a criminal, fingers another criminal, they tell the police what the other person has done: *Casey was only fingered as the mastermind of the operation after he was dead.*

finger bowl /'.. ,./ *n.* [C] a small bowl in which you wash your fingers at the table during a formal meal

-fingered /fɪŋgəd/ [in adjectives] **1 long-fingered/delicate-fingered etc.** having long fingers, delicate fingers etc.: *Collins began his rise to success as the lightning-fingered* (=able to move his fingers very fast) *guitarist for Lynyrd Skynyrd.* —see also LIGHT-FINGERED **2 two-fingered/three-fingered etc.** using two, three etc. fingers to do something: *I've gotten pretty fast, even with my two-fingered typing.*

fin·ger·ing /'fɪŋgərɪŋ/ *n.* [U] the positions in which a musician puts their fingers to play a piece of music, or the order in which they use their fingers

fin·ger·nail /'fɪŋgəˌneɪl/ *n.* [C] the hard flat part that covers the top end of your finger: *Stop biting your fingernails.*

finger paint /'.. ,./ *n.* [U] special paint that children paint pictures with, using their fingers —**finger-paint** *v.* [I] —**finger painting** *n.* [U]

fin·ger·print[1] /'fɪŋgəˌprɪnt/ *n.* **1** [C usually plural] the mark made by the pattern of lines at the end of a person's finger: *His fingerprints were all over the gun.* | *Detective Blake* **took** *the suspects'* **fingerprints** (=pressed their fingers on ink and then onto paper to make a picture of them). **2** [C] a mark or special feature that can be used to correctly name something or someone: *DNA testing provides a genetic fingerprint that can be extremely accurate.* | *Now this is a policy that's got Kevin McBride's fingerprints all over it* (=it is obvious that he was involved in it).

fingerprint[2] *v.* [T] to press someone's finger on ink and then press it onto paper in order to make a picture of the pattern of the lines at the end of the finger

fin·ger·tip /'fɪŋgəˌtɪp/ *n.* [C] **1** the end of a finger: *Darla touched Tom's ear with her fingertip.* **2 at your/their fingertips** if you have something at your fingertips, it is ready and available to use very easily: *Keep travel information at your fingertips with the Interstate Travelmate.*

fin·ick·y /'fɪnɪki/ *adj.* someone who is finicky only likes particular types of food, clothes, music etc. and is difficult to please: *Tonya was a finicky eater when she was little.*

fin·ish[1] /'fɪnɪʃ/ *v.*

1 stop doing sth [I,T] to come to the end of doing or making something, so that it is complete: *Marv moved to New York when he finished college.* | [**finish doing sth**] *Let's go play after you finish eating.* | *Just leave it on the table when you finish.*

2 complete [I,T] to complete an event, performance, piece of work etc. by doing one final thing: *In 1953, the Army Corps of Engineers finished the job by building a flood control channel.* | [**+ with**] *We finished dinner with a salad of fresh fruit.* | *The concert finished with a sing-along version of "You're a Grand Old Flag."*

3 eat/drink [T] to eat or drink all of something, so there is none left: *Angrily, she finished her beer and threw the can away.*

4 race [I,T] to be in a particular position at the end of a race, competition etc.: *In March, he finished second in the Las Vegas Amateur Bowlers Tour.*

5 surface [T] to give the surface of something a particular appearance by painting, polishing, or covering it: *The furniture had been attractively finished in a walnut veneer.*

6 the finishing touch the final detail or details that make something complete: *The hat added the finishing touch to her outfit.*

finish off *phr. v.* **1** [T **finish** sth ↔ **off**] to use or eat all of something, so there is none left: *Who finished off the cake?* **2** [T **finish** sb/sth ↔ **off**] to kill or defeat a person or animal when they are weak or wounded: *Several of the victims were finished off with shots to the head as they lay on the ground.* **3** [T

finish sth ↔ **off**] to end a performance, event etc. by doing one final thing: *We finished off the trip with a visit to the spectacular harbor.* **4** [T **finish** sb **off**] to take away all of someone's strength, energy etc.: *Coming home to a house full of screaming children just finished me off.*

finish sth ↔ **up** *phr. v.* **1** to eat or drink all the rest of something: *Why don't you finish up the pie?* **2** to end an event, situation etc. by doing one final thing: *He finished up his summer with a week on the Cape.*

finish with sth *phr. v.* [T] to not need something that you have been using anymore: *Can you hand me the scissors when you finish with them?*

finish[2] *n.* **1** [C] the end or last part of something: *It was a* **close finish** (=when competitors in a race are very close at the end), *but Jarrett won.* | *Their new album is a good listen* **from start to finish**. **2** [C,U] the appearance of the surface of something after it has been painted, polished etc.: *The paint should dry to a smooth, glossy finish.* **3 fight to the finish** to fight until one side is completely defeated

fin·ished /'fɪnɪʃt/ *adj.* **1** [not before noun] at the end of an activity: *I'm almost finished.* | [**+ with**] *Are you finished with my tools yet?* | [**be finished doing sth**] *We can go as soon as Troy is finished drying his hair.* **2** [only before noun] fully made or completed: *It took a long time to do, but the* **finished product** *was worth it.* —opposite UNFINISHED **3** [not before noun] not able to do something successfully anymore: *If the bank refuses to give us the loan, we're finished!*

finishing school /'... ,./ *n.* [C] a private school where girls from rich families go to learn social skills

finish line /'.. ,./ *n.* **the finish line** the line at which a race ends —compare STARTING LINE

fi·nite /'faɪnaɪt/ *adj.* **1** having an end or a limit: *Oil is a finite resource.* —compare INFINITE **2** TECHNICAL a finite verb form shows a particular tense or subject. "Am," "was," and "are" are examples of finite verb forms, but "being" and "been" are non-finite.

fink[1] /fɪŋk/ *n.* [C] OLD-FASHIONED, INFORMAL **1** someone who tells the police, a teacher, or a parent when someone else breaks a rule or a law **2** a person who you do not like or respect

fink[2] *v.* [I] OLD-FASHIONED, INFORMAL to tell the police, a teacher, or a parent that someone has broken a rule or a law: [**+ on**] *I would never fink on a friend.*

Fin·land /'fɪnlənd/ a country in northeast Europe that is west of Russia and east of Sweden —**Finnish** *n.*, *adj.*

fiord /fyɔrd/ *n.* [C] another spelling of FJORD

fir /fɚ/ *n.* [C] a tree with leaves shaped like needles, that do not fall off in the winter

fire[1] /faɪɚ/ *n.*

1 burning [U] the flames, light, and heat produced when something burns: *The house is* **on fire** (=burning). | *Fireworks stored in a shed* **caught fire** (=started to burn) *and caused a massive explosion.* | *Protesters seized the police van and* **set it on fire** (=made it start to burn).

2 uncontrolled flames [C] uncontrolled flames, light, and heat that destroys or damages things: *Winds quickly spread the fire across the valley.* | *Police believe the fire in the store was started deliberately.* | *It took firemen several hours to* **put out the fire** (=stop it burning). | *Lightning will increase the possibility of* **forest fires**.

3 controlled flames [C] burning material used to heat a room, cook food etc.: **build/light a fire** (=make a fire, or start burning one) *Matt built a fire to dry his wet clothes.* | *We roasted marshmallows over the* **open fire**.

4 shooting [U] an act of shooting, especially of many guns at the same time: *They just heard a car coming and* **opened fire** (=started shooting). | *The truck she was in* **came under fire** (=was shot at) *as it tried to deliver supplies to the front lines.*

5 be/come under fire to be criticized very strongly: *Campbell came under fire for his handling of the negotiations.*

Lisa lit the candles.

He set fire to the car.

The curtain caught fire.

6 `emotion` [U] a very strong emotion that makes you want to think about nothing else: [+ of] *Nothing could dampen the fire of his enthusiasm for music.*
7 have a fire in your belly INFORMAL to have a strong desire to achieve something
8 `injury` a part of your body that is on fire feels very painful: *My feet were on fire after the trek up the mountain.*
9 set the world on fire to do something that is very good, or will make you very famous and popular: *Pitt's new movie isn't exactly setting the world on fire.*
10 light a fire under sb SPOKEN to do something that makes someone who is being lazy start doing their work
11 fire and brimstone a phrase describing Hell, used by some religious people —see also CEASE-FIRE, **fight fire with fire** (FIGHT[1] (11)), **do sth like a house on fire** (HOUSE[1] (12)), **play with fire** (PLAY[1] (17)), **there's no smoke without fire** (SMOKE[1] (6))

USAGE NOTE: FIRE

WORD CHOICE: light, set fire to, catch fire, put out, go out, extinguish
If you want something to burn, you usually **light** it: *She casually lit a cigarette.* You can also **set fire to** things, especially things that are not supposed to be burned: *Several prisoners set fire to their bedding.* When something begins to burn, especially by accident it **catches fire**: *The blaze started when some oily rags caught fire.* To stop a fire you **put** it **out**, or else it may **go out** on its own (NOT *go off*). On official signs and instructions you may see **extinguish**: *Please extinguish all cigarettes before takeoff.*

S W
2 2 **fire²** *v.*

1 `job` [T] to force someone to leave their job: *The company fired a top executive for his role in improper financial dealings.* | *Brad got fired from the pizzeria last week.*
2 `shoot` [I,T] to shoot bullets from a gun, or to shoot small bombs: *Several shots were fired, but no one was injured.* | [+ at/on/into] *It was reported that several missiles were fired at the army base* | [**fire a gun/rifle etc.**] *Van Gogh ended his life by firing a rifle into his chest.* | [**fire sth at sb**] *The police officer fired two shots at the suspects before they surrendered.*
3 `questions` [T] to ask someone a lot of questions quickly, often in order to criticize them: [**fire sth at**

sb] *Dozens of reporters fired non-stop questions at him.*
4 `excite` [T] also **fire up** to make someone feel very excited or interested in something; INSPIRE: [**be fired with sth**] *After reading Steinbeck, Joel was fired with the ambition to become a writer.*
5 fire away SPOKEN used when you are ready to answer someone's questions: *"I have a few questions." "Fire away."*
6 `engine` [I] if a vehicle's engine fires, the gas is lit to make the engine work
7 `clay` [T] to bake clay pots etc. in very high heat in a KILN: *fired earthenware*
8 not firing on all cylinders HUMOROUS acting strangely, or not thinking sensibly
fire back sth *phr. v.* [I,T] to quickly and angrily give an answer or a reply to something that someone has said: *Lawrence fired back with a statement denying his co-star's claims.*
fire sth ↔ **off** *phr. v.* [T] **1** to shoot a weapon, often so that there are no bullets etc. left: *A number of accidents were caused by people firing off pistols in New Year's Eve celebrations.* **2** to quickly send an angry letter to someone: *When Jen's car kept breaking down, she fired off an irate letter to the manufacturer.*
fire sth/sb ↔ **up** *phr. v.* [T] INFORMAL **1** to start a machine or piece of equipment, especially one that burns gas: *If you don't feel like firing up the grill, the meat can also be sautéed.* **2** [usually passive] to make someone very excited and eager: *Kelly always comes home **all fired up** after those environmental meetings.*

fire a·larm /'. ., / *n.* [C] a piece of equipment that makes a loud noise to warn people of a fire in a building: *He was already in bed when he heard the hotel fire alarm go off.*
fire ant /'. ./ *n.* [C] a type of insect that lives in groups in large piles of earth that they build, and that can give a very painful bite
fire·arm /'faɪərɑrm/ *n.* [C usually plural] FORMAL a gun: *Rudolph was charged with illegal possession of firearms.*
fire·ball /'faɪərbɔl/ *n.* [C] a large, hot fire, such as the very hot cloud of burning gases formed by an atomic explosion
fire·bomb¹ /'faɪərbɑm/ *n.* [C] a bomb that makes a fire start burning when it explodes
firebomb² *v.* [T] to attack a place with a firebomb —**firebombing** *n.* [C]
fire·brand /'faɪərbrænd/ *n.* [C] FORMAL **1** someone who tries to make people angry about a law, government etc. so that they will try to change it: *Devlin, the former Irish nationalist firebrand, has been shot and jailed.* **2** LITERARY a large burning piece of wood
fire·break /'faɪərbreɪk/ *n.* [C] a narrow piece of land without any plants and trees on it, made to prevent fires from spreading
fire·brick /'faɪərbrɪk/ *n.* [C] a brick that is not damaged by heat, used in CHIMNEYs
fire bri·gade /'. ., / *n.* [C] a group of people who work together to stop fires, but are not paid to do this
fire·bug /'faɪərbʌg/ *n.* [C] INFORMAL someone who deliberately starts fires to destroy property
fire chief /'. , / *n.* [C] someone who is in charge of all the fire departments in a city or area
fire·crack·er /'faɪərˌkrækər/ *n.* [C] a small FIREWORK that explodes loudly, usually used when celebrating a special day
fire de·part·ment /'. ., ,.. / *n.* [C] an organization that works to prevent fires and stop them from burning
fire door /'. ./ *n.* [C] a heavy door in a building that is kept closed to help to prevent a fire from spreading
fire drill /'. ./ *n.* [C] an occasion when people practice how to leave a burning building safely: *We had a fire drill today in school.*
fire eat·er /'. ,.. / *n.* [C] an entertainer who puts burning sticks into their mouth —**fire eating** *n.* [U]

F

fire en·gine /ˈ. ˌ../ *n.* [C] a special large truck that carries people and equipment to stop fires from burning

fire engine red /ˌ. … ˈ./ *n.* [U] a very bright red color —**fire-engine-red** *adj.*

fire es·cape /ˈ. .ˌ./ *n.* [C] metal stairs on the outside of a building, that people can use to escape from the building if there is a fire

fire ex·tin·guish·er /ˈ. .ˌ.../ *n.* [C] a metal container with water or chemicals in it, used for stopping small fires

fire·fight /ˈfaɪəfaɪt/ *n.* [C] a short gun battle, usually involving soldiers or the police

fire·fight·er /ˈfaɪəˌfaɪtə/ *n.* [C] someone who stops fires from burning, either as their job or as a special helper during forest fires or wars —**firefighting** *n.* [U]

fire·fly /ˈfaɪəflaɪ/ *n. plural* **fireflies** [C] an insect with a tail that shines in the dark; LIGHTNING BUG

fire·house /ˈfaɪəhaʊs/ *n.* [C] a small FIRE STATION, especially in a small town

fire hy·drant /ˈ. ˌ../ *n.* [C] a piece of equipment near a street and connected to a large water pipe under the ground, used to get water for stopping fires from burning

fire i·ron /ˈ. ˌ../ *n.* [C] a metal tool used for arranging a fire in a FIREPLACE

fire·light /ˈfaɪəlaɪt/ *n.* [U] the light produced by a small fire: *The room glowed cozy and warm in the firelight.*

fire·man /ˈfaɪəmən/ *n.* [C] **1** a man whose job is to stop fires from burning; FIREFIGHTER **2** someone who takes care of the fire in a steam train engine or a FURNACE

fire·place /ˈfaɪəpleɪs/ *n.* [C] an opening in the wall of a room, connected to a CHIMNEY, where you can burn wood: *The family sat in front of the fireplace until late in the evening.*

fire·plug /ˈfaɪəplʌg/ *n.* [C] INFORMAL a FIRE HYDRANT

fire·pow·er /ˈfaɪəˌpaʊə/ *n.* [U] TECHNICAL the number of weapons that an army, military vehicle etc. has available: *The battle was won by classic military tactics and superior firepower.*

fire·proof /ˈfaɪəpruf/ *adj.* a building, piece of cloth etc. that is fireproof cannot be badly damaged by fire —**fireproof** *v.* [T]

fire sale /ˈ. ./ *n.* [C] a sale of things that have been slightly damaged by a fire, or of goods that cannot be stored because of a fire

fire screen /ˈfaɪəskrin/ *n.* [C] a large frame with woven wire in the middle that is put in front of a FIREPLACE to protect people

fire·side /ˈfaɪəsaɪd/ *n.* [C usually singular] the area close to or around a small fire, especially in a home: *A cat dozed in the chair by the fireside.*

fire sta·tion /ˈ. ˌ../ *n.* [C] a building where the equipment used to stop fires from burning is kept, and where FIREFIGHTERS stay until they are needed

fire·storm /ˈfaɪəstɔrm/ *n.* [C] **1** a very large fire that is kept burning by the high winds that it causes **2** an occasion when something such as a plan or decision causes a serious argument or disagreement: [+ of] *The court's ruling created a firestorm of criticism.*

fire·trap /ˈfaɪətræp/ *n.* [C] a building that would be very dangerous if a fire started there

fire truck /ˈ. ./ *n.* [C] a FIRE ENGINE

fire·wall /ˈfaɪəwɔl/ *n.* [C] **1** a wall that will not burn, used to keep a fire from spreading **2** TECHNICAL a system that protects a computer network from being used or looked at by people who do not have permission to do so, especially over the Internet

fire·wat·er /ˈfaɪəˌwɔtə/ *n.* [U] INFORMAL strong alcohol, such as WHISKEY

fire·wood /ˈfaɪəwʊd/ *n.* [U] wood that has been cut in order to be burned: *A pile of freshly chopped firewood stood next to the cabin door.*

fire·works /ˈfaɪəwəks/ *n.* [plural] **1** colorful explosives that people burn when celebrating a special day: *a Fourth of July fireworks display* **2 there'll be fireworks** SPOKEN used to say that someone will be angry if something happens: *There'll be fireworks if your dad finds out about this.*

fir·ing line /ˈ.. ˌ./ *n.* **be on the firing line** to be in a position or situation in which you can be attacked or criticized: *As Communications Director, Hall is constantly on the firing line.*

fir·ing squad /ˈ.. ˌ./ *n.* [C] a group of soldiers whose duty is to punish prisoners by shooting and killing them: *In December, Beria was found guilty and sent before a firing squad.*

firm¹ /fəm/ *n.* [C] a small company, especially one involved in law, ENGINEERING etc.: **a law/engineering/design etc. firm** *Stan works for one of the best architectural firms in Michigan.* S W 1

firm² *adj.*
1 hard not completely hard, but not soft and not easy to bend: *What you need is a firmer mattress.* | *Cook macaroni until tender but still firm.* | *a firm red tomato*
2 in control showing that you are in control of a situation and not likely to change your mind about something: *Cal replied with a polite but firm "no."* | *We're going to have to be very firm with her, but still treat her with respect.*
3 definite definite and not likely to change: *Argentina has the firm intention of recovering control of the Falkland Islands.* | *Both sides held firm about their demands.*
4 not likely to move strongly fastened or placed in position, and not likely to move or break: *Make sure the ladder is firm before you climb up.* | *A dam about a mile upriver from the city held firm during the earthquake.*
5 not likely to end/change not likely to end, or be easily changed or destroyed: *Janos gave us a firm offer of $2.5 million for the ranch.*
6 a firm grip/hold/grasp etc. if you have something in a firm grip, hold, grasp etc. you are holding it tightly and strongly: *He took a firm grip of my arm and marched me toward the door.* | *Her firm handshake and bright smile inspired confidence in everyone who met her.*
7 money not falling in value: *The dollar began Friday on a firm note.* —**firmly** *adv.*: *"We still can't afford it," Brenda said firmly.* | *Richards' reputation as a chef had become firmly established by 1997.* —**firmness** *n.* [U]

firm³ *v.* [T] to make something harder or more solid, especially by pressing down on it
firm sth ↔ up *phr. v.* [T] **1** to make arrangements, ideas etc. more definite and exact: *Jane will call later to firm up the details.* **2** to make a part of your body have more muscle and less fat by exercising **3** if a company or organization firms up the price or value of something, it does something to keep it at a particular level: *Some European economies may need to firm up interest rates in order to stabilize their currencies.*

fir·ma·ment /ˈfəməmənt/ *n.* LITERARY the firmament the sky or heaven

firm·ware /ˈfəmwɛr/ *n.* [U] TECHNICAL instructions to computers that are stored on CHIPs so that they can be done much faster, and cannot be changed or lost —compare HARDWARE, SOFTWARE

first¹ /fəst/ *adj.* **1** happening or done before other events or actions of the same kind: *She made her first appearance on the stage in the 1950s.* | *Was that the first time that you met Ted?* **2** at the beginning of a row, line, series, period of time etc.: *I read the first chapter and got so scared I couldn't finish the book.* | *Put the first five ingredients into a large pot and simmer gently for an hour.* | *Jenkins left his first wife after only two years of marriage.* | *the first Monday of every month* **3** most important; MAIN: *Our first priority is to maintain the quality of the product.* **4 at first sight/glance a)** the first time you see someone: *Do you believe in love at first sight?* **b)** when you first start considering something, without noticing much detail: *At first sight, it may seem strange to treat three such diverse nations as a group.* S W 1 1

5 first thing as soon as you get up in the morning, or as soon as you start work: *Sharon wants that report on her desk first thing tomorrow.* | *I'll call her first thing in the morning.* **6 in the first place** used to give a fact or reason that proves what you are saying in an argument: *Well, in the first place, Quinn would never say such a thing.* **7 not know the first thing about sth** to not know anything about a subject, or not know how to do something: *My dad doesn't know the first thing about sports.* **8 first things first** used to tell someone to deal with things in order of importance: *Okay people, first things first: does everybody have their safety helmets?*

9 first choice the thing or person you like best: *Brittany was our first choice as a name for the baby.* **10 (at) first hand** if you hear or experience something first hand, you hear or experience it directly, not through other people: *Students in the program are exposed first hand to college life.* —see also FIRST-HAND **11 first prize** the prize that is given to the best person or thing in a competition: *My jam won first prize at the county fair.* **12 first come, first served** used to say that the first people who arrive somewhere, ask for something etc. will be dealt with before others: *Seating is available on a first come, first served basis.* **13 make the first move** to be the person who does something when everyone is nervous or uncomfortable about starting to do something: *Everybody's waiting for the other person to make the first move.* **14 first light** the time when the sun is just beginning to appear, very early in the morning: *They left camp at first light and were in the mountains by nightfall.*

---

first² adv. **1** before anything or anyone else: *It's mine – I saw it first.* | *Who's going first?* | *Shall we fill in the forms first, and get that out of the way?* | *Johnson finished first in the 100-meter dash.* **2** at the beginning of a situation or activity: *When we were first married, we lived in Toronto.* | *We first became friends when we were teenagers.* **3** done for the first time: *Simmons' book was first published in Australia last year.* | *When I first heard about what happened, I thought it was a joke.* **4** before doing anything else, or before anything else happens: *You can borrow the book, but first I've got to find it.* | *First of all, we'd better make sure we have everything we need.* **5** [sentence adverb] used to give an important fact or reason that will be followed by others: *First, Jack would not allow it, and second, I don't think Mom would like it much either.* **6 come first** to be the most important thing to someone: *For me, over the years, work came first, family came second.* **7 put sth first** to make something the most important thing: *It's refreshing to see a school district that puts quality education first.* **8 first and foremost** as the main reason or purpose of something: *Mayor Agnos is a conservative Christian, but he considers himself first and foremost an American.* **9 first off** SPOKEN used to introduce a fact, reason, or statement that will be followed by others, especially when you are annoyed about something: *Well, first off, I want to know what you've done with the money I gave you.*

USAGE NOTE: FIRST

WORD CHOICE: first, first of all, at first
First and **first of all** are used at the beginning of a sentence to talk about the first or most important thing in a series of things: *First, we have to notify the police.* | *First of all, you have to figure out how much money you have available.* Use **at first** to talk about what happened at the beginning of an event or s tuation, before a change or something different that happened: *At first I didn't recognize the voice on the phone, but then I realized it was my old buddy Tyler from college.*

---

first³ n. **1 at first** in the beginning: *At first, exercising seemed like an obligation, but now I really enjoy it.* —compare **at last** (LAST³ (2)) **2** [C usually singular] something that has never been done or happened before: *This project is a first for the city.* | *"Dad actually washed the dishes after dinner*

tonight." "That's a first." **3 from the (very) first** FORMAL from the beginning: *The relationship was doomed to failure from the first.*

first⁴ pron. **1 the first** the 1st thing or person in a series: *Can we meet on the first* (=the 1st day of the month)? | [be the first to do sth] *She's the first in her family to go to college.* **2 the First** abbreviation **I** used after the name of a King, Queen, POPE etc. who has the same name as someone who held that position at a later time: *Queen Elizabeth the First* (=written as "Queen Elizabeth I") **3 the first I (have) heard of sth** SPOKEN used when you have just found out about something that other people already know, and are slightly annoyed about it: *The first I heard of it was on the night of August 23.*

first aid /ˌ. ˈ./ n. [U] basic medical treatment that is given as soon as possible to someone who is injured or who suddenly becomes sick: *The victims were all given first aid at the scene of the accident.*

first-aid kit /ˌ. ˈ. ˌ./ n. [C] a special box containing BANDAGES and medicines to treat people who are injured or suddenly become sick

first base /ˌ. ˈ./ n. [C] **1 a)** the first of the four places in a game of baseball that a player must touch before gaining a point **b)** the position of a defending player near this place: *He plays first base for the Red Sox.* **2 get to first base a)** to reach the first stage of success in an attempt to achieve something: *If you don't have a decent-looking résumé, you won't even get to first base in your job search.* **b)** OLD-FASHIONED, INFORMAL an expression meaning "to kiss or hold someone in a sexual way," used especially by young men

first·born /ˈfəstbɔrn/ n. [singular] your first child —**firstborn** adj.

first class /ˌ. ˈ.◄/ n. **1** [U] the best and most expensive seats or rooms on an airplane, boat etc.: *Ron was already sitting in first class when we boarded the plane.* —compare BUSINESS CLASS, CABIN CLASS, ECONOMY CLASS **2** [U] the class of mail used in the U.S. for ordinary business and personal letters —compare SECOND CLASS, THIRD CLASS

first-class /ˌ. ˈ.◄/ adj. **1** of very good quality, and much better than other things of the same type: *Their recent production of "Our Town" was first class.* | *She's doing a first-class job of running this company.* **2** using the first class of mail: *a first-class package* **3** using the first class of seats and rooms in an airplane, boat etc.: *a first-class passenger*

first cous·in /ˌ. ˈ../ n. [C] a child of your AUNT or UNCLE; COUSIN (1)

first-de·gree /ˌ. .ˈ.◄/ adj. [always before noun] **1 first-degree murder** murder of the most serious type, in which someone deliberately kills someone else —compare MANSLAUGHTER **2 first-degree burn** a burn that is not very serious

first e·di·tion /ˌ. .ˈ../ n. [C] one of the first copies of a book that was produced, which is often valuable: *Peter had an impressive collection of 19th-century first editions on his shelves.* —**first-edition** adj.: *a first-edition copy of "Brideshead Revisited"*

first-ev·er /ˌ. ˈ.◄/ adj. [only before noun] happening for the first time: *It was the first-ever visit to China by an American president.*

first fam·ily, First Family /ˌ. ˈ../ n. [C usually singular] the family of the President of the U.S.

first gen·er·a·tion /ˌ. ..ˈ..◄/ n. [singular] **1 a)** the children of people who have moved to live in a new country **b)** people who have moved to live in a new country **2** the first type of a machine to be developed: [+ of] *The first generation of digital TV sets cost over $2000 each.* **3** the first people to do something: [+ of] *Levebre and her friends were among the first generation of radical feminists.* —**first-generation** adj.: *first-generation Americans*

first-hand /ˌ. ˈ.◄/ adj. [only before noun] **first-hand experience/knowledge/account etc.** experience, knowledge, an account etc. that has been learned or gained by doing something yourself: *Wilson knew from first-hand observation how cruel students could be to each other.* —compare SECONDHAND —see also **(at) first hand** (FIRST[1] (10))

S W **first la·dy,** First Lady /ˌ. ˈ../ *n.* [C usually singular] the wife of the President of the U.S., or of the GOVERNOR of a U.S. state

first lieu·ten·ant /ˌ. .ˈ..◂/ *n.* [C] a middle rank in the U.S. Army, Marines, or Air Force, or someone who has this rank

first·ly /ˈfəstli/ *adv.* [sentence adverb] used to say that the fact or reason that you are going to mention is the first one and will be followed by others: *Firstly, I would like to thank everyone who has contributed to this project.*

first mate /ˌ. ˈ./ *n.* [C] the officer on a non-military ship who has the rank just below CAPTAIN

S W **first name** /ˈ. ./ *n.* [C] **1** the name that is your own name, and that comes before your other names in English: *What's your mom's first name?* **2 be on a first-name basis** to know someone well enough to call them by their first name: *Flores is on a first-name basis with most of the employees at the hospital.* —compare LAST NAME, MIDDLE NAME

first of·fend·er /ˌ. .ˈ../ *n.* [C] someone who is guilty of breaking the law for the first time

first of·fi·cer /ˌ. ˈ...◂/ *n.* [C] a FIRST MATE

first per·son /ˌ. ˈ..◂/ *n.* TECHNICAL **1 the first person** a form of a verb or a pronoun that is used to show that you are the speaker. For example, "I," "me," "we," and "us" are pronouns in the first person, and "I am" is the first person singular of the verb "to be." **2 in the first person** a story in the first person is told as if the writer or speaker were involved in the story: *Ulrich's novel is written in the first person.* —**first-person** *adj.* [only before noun] *a first-person narrative* —compare SECOND PERSON, THIRD PERSON

first-rate /ˌ. ˈ.◂/ *adj.* of the very best quality: *She's a first-rate surgeon.*

first-string /ˌ. ˈ.◂/ *adj.* [only before noun] a first-string player on a team plays when the game begins because they are one of the best players —compare SECOND-STRING

first-time buy·er /ˌ. . ˈ../ *n.* [C] someone who is buying a house or a car for the first time

First World /ˌ. ˈ.◂/ *n.* **the First World** the rich industrial countries of the world, which do not have COMMUNIST governments —**first-world** *adj.* [always before noun] —compare THIRD WORLD

First World War /ˌ. . ˈ./ *n.* **the First World War** WORLD WAR I

S W **fis·cal** /ˈfɪskəl/ *adj.* FORMAL connected with money, taxes, debts etc., especially those relating to the government: *The administration needs to come up with a sound fiscal policy.* —**fiscally** *adv.*

fiscal year /ˌ.. ˈ./ *n.* [C] a 12-month-long period of time over which a company calculates its profits and losses, or a government calculates its income and spending

S W **fish**[1] /fɪʃ/ *n. plural* **fish** or **fishes** [C] **1** an animal that lives in water, and uses its FINS (1) and tail to swim: *Ronny caught three huge fish this afternoon.* **2** [U] the flesh of a fish used as food: *We're having fish for supper.* **3 feel like a fish out of water** to feel uncomfortable because you are in an unfamiliar place or situation: *I'd feel like a fish out of water if I had to live in the big city.* **4 there are more/other fish in the sea** used to tell someone whose relationship is finished that there are other people they can have a relationship with, in order to make them feel less sad **5 have other/bigger fish to fry** INFORMAL to have other things to do, especially more important things: *I can't deal with this now – I've got other fish to fry.* **6 a cold fish** an unfriendly person who seems to have no strong feelings **7 a big fish in a small/ little pond** someone who is important or who has influence over a very small area **8 neither fish nor

fowl** neither one thing nor another: *We were caught between two generations, neither fish nor fowl.*

fish[2] *v.* **1** [I] to try to catch fish: [+ **for**] *We're fishing for trout.* **2** [I,T always + adv./prep.] to search through a bag, pocket, container etc. trying to find something: [**fish sth out**] *Eric fished a piece of candy out of the bag.* | [+ **around**] *She fished around in her purse and pulled out a picture.* | [+ **for**] *Chris fished in his pocket for a coin.* **3 be fishing for compliments** to try to make someone say something nice about you, usually by asking a question **4 fish or cut bait** SPOKEN used to tell someone to do something they say they will, when they have been talking about doing it for too long **5** [T] FORMAL to try to catch fish in a particular area of water: *Other nations are forbidden to fish the waters within 200 miles of the coast.* **6 be fishing for information/ news/gossip etc.** to try to find out secret information: *When Wilkinson's door was closed, it usually meant he was fishing for information on the phone with somebody.* **S W** [3]

fish sb/sth **out** *phr. v.* [T] to pull someone or something out of water: *Police divers fished the body out of the East River a week later.*

fish and chips /ˌ. . ˈ./ *n.* [U] a meal consisting of fish covered with a mixture of flour and milk and cooked in oil, served with thick FRENCH FRIES

fish·bowl /ˈfɪʃboul/ *n.* [C] **1** a glass bowl that you can keep fish in **2** a place or situation in which you cannot do anything in private: *In a small town like this, you're in a fishbowl.*

fish·cake /ˈfɪʃkeɪk/ *n.* [C] a small round flat food consisting of cooked fish mixed with cooked potato

fish·er·man /ˈfɪʃ˭mən/ *n. plural* **fishermen** /-mən/ [C] someone who catches fish as a sport or as a job

fish·er·y /ˈfɪʃəri/ *n. plural* **fisheries** [C] a part of the ocean where fish are caught as a business

fish-eye lens /ˌfɪʃaɪ ˈlɛnz/ *n.* [C] a type of curved LENS (=piece of glass on the front of a camera) that allows you to take photographs of a wide area

fish farm /ˈ. ./ *n.* [C] a place where fish are bred as a business

fish fry /ˈ. ./ *n.* [C] an event, usually held outdoors to raise money for an organization, at which fish is fried and eaten with other foods

fish·hook /ˈfɪʃhʊk/ *n.* [C] a small hook with a sharp point at one end, that is fastened to the end of a long string in order to catch fish

fish·ing /ˈfɪʃɪŋ/ *n.* [U] **1** the sport or business of catching fish: *Fishing is one of Mike's hobbies.* | *Terry's going fishing at Lake Arrowhead next weekend.* **2 be on a fishing expedition** INFORMAL to try to find out secret information

fishing line /ˈ.. ˌ./ *n.* [U] very long string made of strong material and used for catching fish

fishing rod also **fishing pole** /ˈ.. ˌ./ *n.* [C] a long thin pole with a long string and a hook attached to it, used for catching fish

fishing tack·le /ˈ.. ˌ../ *n.* [U] equipment used for fishing, such as hooks and BAIT

fish meal /ˈ. ./ *n.* [U] dried fish that have been crushed into a powder, in order to be put on the land to help plants grow or used as food for farm animals

fish·mon·ger /ˈfɪʃˌmɑŋgɚ, -ˌmʌŋ-/ *n.* [C] OLD-FASHIONED someone who sells fish

fish·net /ˈfɪʃnɛt/ *n.* [U] a type of material with a pattern of small holes that look like a net: *fishnet stockings*

fish stick /ˈ. ./ *n.* [C] a long piece of fish that has been covered with small pieces of dried bread, usually sold frozen to be cooked at home

fish·tail /ˈfɪʃteɪl/ *v.* [I] if a vehicle or airplane fishtails, it slides from side to side, usually because the tires are sliding on water or ice

fish·y /ˈfɪʃi/ *adj.* **1** INFORMAL seeming bad or dishonest: *There's something very fishy about his business deals.* **2** tasting or smelling like fish

fis·sile /ˈfɪsəl/ *adj.* TECHNICAL **1** able to be split by atomic fission **2** tending to split along natural lines of weakness

fis·sion /ˈfɪʃən/ *n.* [U] TECHNICAL **1** the process of splitting an atom to produce large amounts of energy or an explosion **2** the process of dividing a cell into two or more parts —compare FUSION

fis·sure /ˈfɪʃə/ *n.* [C] a deep crack, especially in rock or earth

fist /fɪst/ *n.* [C] a hand with the fingers curled in toward the PALM, especially in order to express anger or to hit someone: *She held the money tightly in her fist.* | *Mark **clenched** his **fists** (=held his fists very tightly closed) in rage.* —see also HAM-FISTED, **make/spend/lose money hand over fist** (HAND¹ (27)), TIGHT-FISTED

fist·fight /ˈfɪstfaɪt/ *n.* [C] a fight in which you use your BARE hands to hit someone

fist·ful /ˈfɪstfʊl/ *n.* [C] an amount that is as much as you can hold in your hand: [+ of] *a fistful of cash*

fist·i·cuffs /ˈfɪstɪˌkʌfs/ *n.* [plural] OLD-FASHIONED a fistfight

fit

Susan's old dress didn't fit her anymore.

These socks don't match.

fit¹ /fɪt/ *v.* past tense and past participle **fit** or **fitted** present participle **fitting**

1 `right size` [I,T not in progressive] to be the right size and shape for someone or something: *The pants fit fine, but the jacket's too small.* | [fit sb] *I wonder if your wedding dress still fits you?* | *I tried it on and it **fits like a glove** (=fits perfectly).*

2 `fit a space` [I always + adv./prep., not in progressive] to be the right size and shape for a particular space, and not be too big or too small: *I'm looking for the puzzle piece that fits here.* | [+ **in/into/under/through** etc.] *A queen-sized bed will never fit in this room.*

3 `put in place` [I always + adv./prep.,T always + adv./prep.] to put or join something in a particular place where it is meant to go: [fit sth **in/over/together**] *You have to fit the plastic cover over the frame.* | *I tried to fit them together like the directions said, but I couldn't.*

4 `find space for` [I always + adv./prep.,T always + adv./prep.] to find enough space for something in a room, vehicle, container etc.: [fit sth **in/into/through** etc.] *We couldn't fit the couch through the door unless we turned it on its side.* | *Can you **fit in** another person in the back seat?*

5 `appropriate` [T not in progressive] to have the qualities, experience etc. that are appropriate for a particular situation, job etc.: *We wanted an experienced journalist, and Watts **fit the bill** (=had the right qualities or experience).*

6 `belong` [I,T] to belong to a particular group or set of ideas: [+ **into**] *Being young and single made it hard to fit into my sister's circle of married friends.* | *It's obvious that having a girlfriend just doesn't **fit in with** your plans.*

7 `description` [T not in progressive] if someone or something fits a description, it describes them exactly: *A man fitting that description was seen running from the park.*

8 `match/be part of` [I,T not in progressive] if something fits a system, idea etc., it matches it or is able to be a part of it: [+ **in/into**] *Our books on tape are designed to fit into your busy lifestyle.* | [fit sth] *Your clothes should fit the way you live.* | *The takeover bid **fit in with** Merrill's strategy of expansion.*

9 `equipment/part` [T] to put a small piece of

equipment into a place, or a new part onto a machine, so that it is ready to be used: *I'm going to have a new exhaust system fitted next week.* | [fit sth **on/to** etc.] *A driver's airbag is fitted in all our new cars.* —see also FITTED, FITTING², **if the shoe fits, (wear it)** (SHOE¹ (4))

fit in *phr. v.* **1** [I] to be accepted by other people in a group because you have the same attitudes and interests: *A lot of our new students have a hard time fitting in.* | [+ **with**] *Lonnie doesn't seem to fit in with the other children.* **2** [T fit sb/sth ↔ **in**] to manage to do something or see someone, even though you have a lot of other things to do: *Dr. Lincoln can fit you in on Monday at 4:00.*

USAGE NOTE: FIT

WORD CHOICE: fit, fit in, match, go together, go with
If something is not too big and not too small for a person or other thing, it **fits**: *This blouse doesn't fit – it's too small.* | *Do those screws fit?* If people **fit in**, they have a good social relationship with the other people in a group, and share the same attitudes, interests etc.: *When I first moved to Middleville I felt awkward, but I soon began to fit in with the other kids.* If things are almost the same in some way and look good together, they **match**: *Your shirt doesn't match your tie* (= they are not the same pattern or color). If things look right together in style, color etc., they **go together** or they **go with** each other: *Do my shoes and hat go together?* | *The curtains don't go with the carpet.* Things can **go together** in other ways too: *Fish and white wine go particularly well together.*

GRAMMAR
Although both **fit** and **fitted** can be used in the past tense, most people generally use **fit**: *Two years ago, these pants fit me perfectly.*

---

fit² *n.*
1 **have/throw a fit** SPOKEN to become very angry or shocked and shout a lot: *Mom's going to have a fit when she sees what you've done.*

2 `stop being conscious` [C] a short period of time when someone stops being conscious and cannot control their body because their brain is not working correctly: *He sometimes **has** epileptic **fits**.*

3 `emotion` [C] a very strong emotion that you cannot control: [+ **of**] *In a fit of rage he slammed the door in her face.* | *a fit of depression*

4 **be a good/tight/close etc. fit** to fit a person or a particular space well, tightly, closely etc.: *I thought they'd be too big, but these shelves are a perfect fit.*

5 `laugh/cough` [C] a period during which you laugh or cough a lot: *I had a coughing fit that lasted nearly an hour.* | *He had the entire audience **in fits of laughter** (=laughing a lot).*

6 **in/by fits and starts** repeatedly starting and stopping: *Electoral reform is moving ahead in fits and starts.*

7 `appropriate` [singular] FORMAL a relationship between two things, systems, organizations etc. in which they match each other or are appropriate for each other: [+ **between**] *There must be a fit between the children's needs and the education they receive.*

fit³ *adj.* **fitter, fittest**
1 `appropriate` having the qualities that are appropriate for a particular job, occasion, purpose etc.: [+ **for**] *They're making people live in buildings that aren't fit for animals to live in.* | [fit **to do sth**] *That woman's not fit to be a mother!* | **be fit to eat/drink** *The cafeteria food isn't fit to eat.* | *That dinner was **fit for a king** (=of the highest quality).* —opposite UNFIT

2 **see/think fit (to do sth)** an expression meaning to decide that it is right or appropriate to do a particular thing, used especially when you do not agree with this decision: *The government has seen fit to start testing more nuclear weapons.*

3 `strong` healthy and strong, especially because you exercise regularly: *Sandy's very fit – he runs almost 30 miles a week.* | *Rowers have to be extremely*

F

physically fit. | *She's 86, but fit as a fiddle* (=completely healthy).

4 fit to be tied SPOKEN very angry, anxious, or upset: *I was absolutely fit to be tied when I found out who got the promotion.*

5 fit to wake the dead OLD-FASHIONED a noise that is fit to wake the dead is extremely loud

6 fit to drop OLD-FASHIONED extremely tired after using a lot of effort or energy

7 be in a fit state/condition (to do sth) to be healthy enough, after being sick or drunk, to be able to do something —see also **survival of the fittest** (SURVIVAL (2))

fit·ful /'fɪtfəl/ *adj.* happening for short and irregular periods of time: *He finally fell into a fitful sleep.* —**fitfully** *adv.*

fit·ness /'fɪtʰnɪs/ *n.* [U] **1** the condition of being healthy and strong enough to do hard work or sports: *Join a health club to improve your fitness.* | *Running marathons requires a high level of physical fitness.* **2** the quality of being appropriate or good enough for a particular situation or purpose: [+ **for**] *They were still unsure of his fitness for the priesthood.* | [**fitness to do sth**] *Wyatt questioned Lindsey's fitness to serve as judge.*

fit·ted /'fɪtɪd/ *adj.* **1** fitted clothes are designed so that they fit closely to someone's body: *a fitted black jacket* **2 be fitted (out) with sth** to have or include something as a permanent part: *The law requires that all new buildings be fitted with water meters.*

fitted sheet /ˌ.. './ *n.* [C] a sheet that has ELASTIC at the corners to hold it on a MATTRESS on a bed

fit·ting¹ /'fɪtɪŋ/ *adj.* FORMAL right or appropriate for a particular situation or occasion: *The victory was a fitting end to a near-perfect season.* | *It seemed fitting that it rained the day of his funeral.* | *It's only fitting that the convention center be named after the mayor.*

fitting² *n.* [C] **1** an occasion when you put on a piece of clothing that is being made for you to find out if it fits **2** [usually plural] a part of a piece of equipment that makes it possible for you to use it: *They're putting in a new sink with chrome fittings* (=handles).

fitting room /'.. ˌ./ *n.* [C] a DRESSING ROOM (1)

Fitz·ger·ald /fɪts'dʒɛrəld/, **El·la** /'ɛlə/ (1918–1996) a U.S. JAZZ singer famous for her beautiful voice and her skill in SCAT singing

Fitzgerald, F. Scott /ɛf skɑt/ (1896–1940) a U.S. writer of NOVELs

five¹ /faɪv/ *number* **1** 5 **2** 5 o'clock: *Meet me at five.* —see also HIGH-FIVE, NINE-TO-FIVE

five² *n.* [C] **1** a piece of paper money worth $5: *Do you have two fives for a ten?* **2 give sb five** INFORMAL to hit the inside of someone's hand with the inside of your hand to show that you are very pleased about something **3 take five** SPOKEN used to tell people to stop working and rest for a few minutes

F. Scott Fitzgerald

five-and-dime /ˌ. . './ also **five-and-ten (cent store)** *n.* [C] OLD-FASHIONED a DIME STORE

five o'clock shad·ow /ˌ.. . '../ *n.* [singular] the dark color on a man's face where the hair has grown during the day

five-spot /'. ./ *n.* [C] OLD-FASHIONED a piece of paper money worth $5

five-star /'. ./ *adj.* [only before noun] a five-star hotel or restaurant is very good

five star gen·e·ral /ˌ. . '../ *n.* [C] the highest rank in the Army

fix¹ /fɪks/ *v.* [T]

1 repair to repair something that is broken or not working correctly: *Gale waited while Seldon fixed the projector.*

2 prepare to prepare a meal or drinks: *I have to fix supper now.* | [**fix sb sth**] *Sit down. I'll fix you a martini.* —see Usage Note at COOK¹

3 fix a time/day/place etc. to decide on a particular time etc. when something will happen: *Have you fixed a date for the wedding yet?*

4 limit to decide on a limit for something, especially prices, costs etc., so that they do not change: [+ **at**] *The interest rate has been fixed at 6.5%.*

5 arrange also **fix up** to make arrangements for something: *If you want a chance to meet the Senator, I can fix it.*

6 hair/face to make your hair or MAKEUP look neat and attractive: *Let me fix my hair first and then we can go.* | *Terry was in the bathroom, fixing her face* (=putting makeup on it to make it look attractive).

7 attach to attach something firmly to something else, so that it stays there permanently: [**fix sth to/on sth**] *We fixed the shelves to the wall with steel bolts.*

8 cat/dog INFORMAL to do a medical operation on a cat or dog so that it cannot have babies

9 result to make dishonest arrangements so that an election, game etc. has the result that you want: *If you ask me, the whole thing was fixed.*

10 injury INFORMAL to treat an injury on your body so that it is completely better: *The doctors don't know if they can fix my kneecap.*

11 punish SPOKEN to harm or punish someone for something they have done: *I'll fix her! Just you wait!*

12 fix your attention/eyes/mind etc. on sb/sth to think about or look at someone or something carefully: *All eyes were fixed on Mayor Wilkins as he walked into the crowded room.*

13 fix sb with a stare/glare/look etc. to look directly into someone's eyes for a long time: *Rachel fixed him with an icy stare.*

14 be fixing to do sth SPOKEN, INFORMAL to prepare to do something: *I'm fixing to go to the store. Do you need anything?*

15 paintings/photographs to use a chemical process on paintings, photographs etc. that makes the colors or images permanent

fix on sth/sb *phr. v.* [T] to choose an appropriate thing or person, especially after thinking about it carefully: *We've finally fixed on a date for the family reunion.*

fix up *phr. v.* [T] **1** [**fix sth ↔ up**] to make a place look attractive by doing small repairs, decorating it again, etc.: *The landlord refused to fix up the property, even after repeated warnings.* **2** [**fix sb ↔ up**] INFORMAL to find a romantic partner for someone: *Dean fixed him up with a girl from his class.* **3** [**fix sb ↔ up**] to provide someone with something they want: [+ **with**] *Can you fix me up with a bed for the night?*

fix² *n.* **1** [C, usually singular] an amount of something, such as an illegal drug, that you often use and badly want: *I need to have my coffee fix in the morning before I speak to anyone.* | *The streets are filled with drug addicts looking for a fix.* **2 be in a fix** to have a problem that is difficult to solve: *We're going to be in a real fix if we miss the last bus.* **3 get a fix on sb/sth a)** to find out exactly where someone or something is: *Have you managed to get a fix on the plane's position?* **b)** to understand what someone or something is really like: *I sat there, trying to get a fix on the situation.* **4** [singular] something that has been dishonestly arranged: *The election was a fix!* —see also **a quick fix** (QUICK¹ (3))

fix·ate /'fɪkseɪt/ *v.*

fixate on sb/sth *phr. v.* [T] to always think or talk about one particular person or thing

fix·at·ed /'fɪkseɪtɪd/ *adj.* **1** always thinking or talking about one particular thing: [+ **on**] *She becomes fixated on pursuing justice at all costs.* **2** TECHNICAL having stopped developing emotionally or mentally

fix·a·tion /fɪk'seɪʃən/ *n.* [C] **1** an extreme, unhealthy interest in or love for someone or something: [+ **on/**

about/with] *Their attitudes reflected the fixation on money common in the 1980s.* **2** TECHNICAL a type of mental illness in which someone's mind or emotions stop developing, so that they are like a child

fix·a·tive /'fɪksətɪv/ *n.* [C,U] **1** a substance used to glue things together or to hold things such as hair or false teeth in place **2** a chemical used on a painting or photograph so that the colors do not change

fixed /fɪkst/ *adj.* **1** not changing or not able to be changed: *A fixed number of tickets will be on sale the day of the show.* | *The symbols must be used in a fixed order.* **2** firmly fastened to something and in a particular position: [be fixed to/in/on sth] *The ship's tables are fixed to the floor.* **3 fixed ideas/opinions etc.** ideas or opinions which you will not change and that are often unreasonable: *Lloyd has very fixed ideas about religion.* **4 a fixed expression/smile/frown etc.** a fixed expression, smile, frown etc. does not change and does not seem to express real emotions **5 have no fixed address** to not have a permanent place to live **6 how are you fixed for sth?** SPOKEN used to ask someone how much of something they have: *Hey Mark, how are you fixed for cash?*

fixed as·sets /ˌ. '../ *n.* [plural] TECHNICAL land, buildings, or equipment that a business owns and uses

fixed cap·i·tal /ˌ. '.../ *n.* [U] TECHNICAL buildings or machines that a business owns and that can be used for a long time to produce goods

fixed charge /ˌ. './ *n.* [C] a cost that does not change for a long time

fixed cost /ˌ. './ *n.* [C usually plural] a cost, such as rent, that a business has to pay even when it is not producing anything

fix·ed·ly /'fɪksɪdli/ *adv.* without looking at or thinking about anything else: *She stared fixedly at the highway.*

fix·er /'fɪksə/ *n.* [C] someone who is good at arranging events, situations etc. for other people so that they have the results they want, especially by using dishonest or illegal methods

fix·ings /'fɪksɪŋz/ *n.* **the fixings** the vegetables, bread etc. that are eaten with meat at a large meal: *We had turkey with all the fixings.*

fix·i·ty /'fɪksəti/ *n.* [U] FORMAL the state of not changing or not becoming weaker

fix·ture /'fɪkstʃə/ *n.* **1** [C usually plural] a piece of equipment that is attached inside a house or building, such as an electric light or a toilet, and is sold as part of the house **2 be a (permanent) fixture** to be always present and not likely to move or go away: *Jerry's Hamburger Haven has been a fixture on Third Avenue for over 20 years.*

fizz¹ /fɪz/ *n.* [singular,U] the BUBBLES of gas in some kinds of drink, or the sound that they make —**fizzy** *adj.*

fizz² *v.* [I] if a liquid fizzes, it produces a lot of BUBBLES and makes a continuous sound: *The champagne fizzed in the glasses.*

fiz·zle /'fɪzəl/ *v.* [I] INFORMAL also **fizzle out** to gradually stop being interesting, and therefore stop happening: *The project fizzled and Turner left the company.*

fjord /fyɔrd/ *n.* [C] a narrow area of ocean between high cliffs

FL a written abbreviation of Florida

flab /flæb/ *n.* [U] INFORMAL soft, loose fat on a person's body: *My workout video will help you get rid of that flab.*

flab·ber·gast·ed /'flæbəˌgæstɪd/ *adj.* INFORMAL extremely surprised or shocked: *Studio executives were flabbergasted at the film's extraordinary success.*

flab·by /'flæbi/ *adj.* **flabbier, flabbiest** INFORMAL **1** having too much soft loose fat instead of strong muscles: *She's gotten flabby since she stopped swimming.* **2** a flabby argument, excuse etc. is weak and not effective —**flabbiness** *n.* [U]

flac·cid /'flæsɪd/ *adj.* TECHNICAL soft and weak instead of firm: *flaccid muscles* —**flaccidity** /flæ'sɪdəti/ *n.* [U]

flack /flæk/ *n.* [U] another spelling of FLAK

flag¹ /flæg/ *n.* [C] **1** a piece of cloth with a colored pattern or picture on it, that represents a particular country or organization: *The children waved flags as the President's car drove by.* | *the state flag of Montana* | **Flags were flying** (=they were shown on poles) *at half-mast after the bombing of the embassy.* **2** a colored piece of cloth used as a signal: *The flag went down, and the race began.* **3 under the flag of sth** if a group of people do something under the flag of a particular country or organization, they do it as representatives of that country or organization **4 keep the flag flying** to achieve success for your country in a competition **5 the flag** an expression meaning a country or organization and its beliefs, values, and people: *Captain Schrader has shown undying loyalty to the flag.* **6** a FLAGSTONE —see also RED FLAG, WHITE FLAG

flag² *v.* **flagged, flagging 1** [I] to become tired, weak, or less interested in something: *Japan's economic growth was beginning to flag.* **2** [T] make a mark against something to show that it is important: *I've flagged the sections I have questions about.*

flag sb/sth ↔ **down** *phr. v.* [T] to make the driver of a vehicle stop by waving at them: *She tried to flag down a passing car.*

flag·el·lant /'flædʒələnt, flə'dʒɛlənt/ *n.* [C] FORMAL someone who whips themselves as a religious punishment

flag·el·late /'flædʒəˌleɪt/ *v.* [T] FORMAL to whip yourself or someone else, especially as a religious punishment

flag foot·ball /'. ˌ../ *n.* [U] a game like football in which players tear off flags from around other players' waists instead of knocking them down —compare TOUCH FOOTBALL

flagged /flægd/ *adj.* covered with FLAGSTONES

flag·ging /'flægɪŋ/ *adj.* becoming tired, weaker, or less interested: *the nation's flagging economy*

flag·on /'flægən/ *n.* [C] a large container for liquids, used in the past

flag·pole /'flægpoʊl/ *n.* [C] a tall pole used for hanging flags

fla·grant /'fleɪgrənt/ *adj.* a flagrant action is shocking because it is done in a way that is easily noticed and shows no respect for laws, truth, someone's feelings etc.: *The arrests are a flagrant violation of human rights.* —**flagrantly** *adv.*

flag·ship /'flægˌʃɪp/ *n.* [C] **1** the most important ship in a group of Navy ships, on which the ADMIRAL sails **2** the best and most important product, building etc. that a company owns or produces: *The new Mustang is the flagship of the new Ford range.*

flag·staff /'flægstæf/ *n.* [C] FORMAL a flagpole

flag·stone /'flægstoʊn/ *n.* [C] a smooth flat piece of stone used for floors, paths etc.

flag-wav·ing /'. ˌ../ *n.* [U] the expression of strong feelings of support for your country, especially when these feelings seem too extreme

flail¹ /fleɪl/ *v.* **1** [I,T] to wave your arms or legs in a fast and uncontrolled way: *Flailing his arms, Sam nearly knocked the vase to the floor.* | [+ away/around] *McGuire flailed away at the drums.* **2** [I] to do something in an uncontrolled way, especially because you do not know exactly how to do it or do not have a plan: [+ around] *Lasch flailed around, trying to answer the question.* **3** [T] to beat someone or something violently, usually with a stick **4** [I,T] to beat grain with a flail

flail² *n.* [C] a tool consisting of a stick that swings from a long handle, used in the past to separate grain from wheat by beating it

flair /flɛr/ *n.* **1** [singular] a natural ability to do something very well: *She credits her father for her business flair.* | *He's a normal 11-year-old kid, but he has a flair for math.* **2** [U] a way of doing things that is interesting and shows imagination: *Bates is bringing her comedic flair to the show.*

flak /flæk/ *n.* [U] **1** INFORMAL strong criticism: **get/take/catch flak** *Belzer has taken some flak for his* *adult-oriented comedy.* **2** bullets or SHELLs that are shot from guns on the ground at enemy airplanes —see also FLAK JACKET

flake¹ /fleɪk/ *v.* **1** [I] also **flake off** to break off or come off in small thin pieces: *Paint was flaking off the doors and window frames.* **2** [I,T] to break fish or another food into small thin pieces, or to break in this way: *Poach the fish until it flakes easily.*

flake off

   flake out *phr. v.* [I] SPOKEN **1** to do something strange or forgetful, or to not do what you said you would do: [**flake out on sb**] *Kathy kind of flaked out on us today – said she couldn't take the stress.* **2** to fall asleep because you are extremely tired: *When I got home, Karl was already flaked out on the sofa.*

flake² *n.* [C] **1** SPOKEN someone who easily forgets things, does strange things, or does not do what they say they will do: *He's such a flake, but he's fun to work with.* **2** a very small flat thin piece that breaks off easily from something else: *flakes of chocolate on a cake* —see also SNOWFLAKE

flak jack·et /'. ,../ *n.* [C] a special coat made of heavy material with metal inside it to protect soldiers and police officers from bullets

flak·y /'fleɪki/ *adj.* **flakier, flakiest 1** tending to break into small pieces: *rich, flaky croissants* **2** SPOKEN someone who is flaky easily forgets things or does strange things: *Brown, though flaky, shows a restless intelligence.* —**flakiness** *n.* [U]

flam·bé /flɑm'beɪ/ also **flam·béed** /flɑm'beɪd/ *adj.* food that is flambéed has an alcoholic drink such as BRANDY poured over it and then is lit to produce flames

flam·boy·ant /flæm'bɔɪənt/ *adj.* **1** behaving or dressing in a confident or surprising way that makes people notice you: *Gotti was a flamboyant New York mobster.* **2** brightly colored, expensive, big etc., and therefore easily noticed: *a flamboyant red sequined dress* —**flamboyantly** *adv.* —**flamboyance** *n.* [U]

flame¹ /fleɪm/ *n.* [C,U] **1** hot bright burning gas that you see when something is on fire: *Flames poured out of the windows.* | *The room was dimly lit by the flame of a single candle.* | *The plane crashed and* ***burst into flames*** *(=began burning suddenly and strongly) upon impact.* | *By the time the firemen arrived the whole house was* ***in flames*** *(=burning strongly).* —see picture at CANDLE **2 a flame of passion/desire/vengeance etc.** LITERARY a strong feeling —see also **naked flame** (NAKED (4)), **old flame** (OLD (6))

flame² *v.* **1** [I] LITERARY to become suddenly bright with light or color, especially red or orange: *Seeing the mockery in Johnny's eyes, Claire's cheeks flamed.* **2** [I] also **flame up** to suddenly burn more strongly or brightly **3** [T] to send someone an angry or insulting message by EMAIL or through a BULLETIN BOARD SYSTEM, especially one that is written only in CAPITALS

fla·men·co /flə'mɛŋkoʊ/ *n.* [C,U] a fast and exciting Spanish dance, or the music that is played for this dance

flame·proof /'fleɪmpruf/ also **flame re·sist·ant** /'. .,../ *adj.* something that is flameproof is specially made or treated with chemicals so that it does not burn easily

flame·throw·er /'. ,../ *n.* [C] a machine like a gun that shoots flames or burning liquid, used as a weapon or for burning away plants

flam·ing /'fleɪmɪŋ/ *adj.* [only before noun] **1** very

bright: *She had flaming red hair.* **2** burning strongly and brightly: *the flaming wreckage of the helicopter*

fla·min·go /flə'mɪŋgoʊ/ *n.* plural **flamingos** or **flamingoes** [C] a tall tropical bird with very long thin legs, pink feathers, and a long neck

flam·ma·ble /'flæməbəl/ *adj.* something that is flammable burns very easily: *Caution! Highly flammable chemicals.* —opposite NONFLAMMABLE —compare INFLAMMABLE

USAGE NOTE: FLAMMABLE

WORD CHOICE: flammable, inflammable
Both of these words mean the same thing, but we usually use **flammable** to avoid confusion. The opposite of both of these words is **nonflammable**.

---

flan /flæn, flɑn/ *n.* [C] a sweet soft baked food made with eggs, milk, and sugar

Flan·ders /'flændəz/ a flat area consisting of part of Belgium, the Netherlands, and northern France. It is known for the many battles that were fought there in World War I.

flange /flændʒ/ *n.* [C] the flat edge that stands out from the main surface of an object such as the wheel on a railroad car, to keep it in the right position

flank¹ /flæŋk/ *n.* [C] **1** the side of an animal's or person's body, between the RIBS and the HIP **2** the side of an army in a battle or war: *We were attacked on our left flank.* **3** FORMAL the side of a hill, mountain, or very large building

flank² *v.* [T usually passive] to be on both sides of someone or something: [**be flanked by sb/sth**] *Rushdie arrived, flanked by police bodyguards.*

flan·nel /'flænl/ *n.* [U] soft light cotton or wool cloth that is used for making warm clothes: *a flannel shirt*

flan·nel·ette /,flænl'ɛt/ *n.* [U] soft cotton cloth used especially for baby clothes and sheets

flap¹ /flæp/ *v.* **flapped, flapping 1** [T] if a bird flaps its wings, it moves its wings up and down in order to fly **2** [I] if a piece of cloth, paper etc. flaps, it moves around quickly and makes noise: *The ship's sails flapped in the wind.* **3 flap your lips/gums** SPOKEN to talk a lot without saying anything important

flap² *n.* **1** [C] a thin flat piece of cloth, paper, skin etc. that is attached by one edge to a surface, which you can lift up easily: *The return address was on the flap of the envelope.* **2** [C] INFORMAL a situation in which people are excited, confused, and upset: *Kelly resigned over a flap about videotaping interviews with job seekers.* **3** [singular] the noisy movement of something such as cloth in the air: *All we could hear was the flap of the sails.* **4** [C] a part of the wing of an airplane that can be raised or lowered to help the airplane go up or down

flap·jack /'flæpdʒæk/ *n.* [C] a PANCAKE

flap·per /'flæpə/ *n.* [C] a fashionable young woman in the late 1920s who wore short dresses, had short hair, and had ideas that were considered very modern

flare¹ /flɛr/ *v.* **1** [I] also **flare up** to suddenly begin to burn, or to burn more brightly for a short time: *A match flared in the darkness.* **2** [I] also **flare up** if strong feelings flare, people suddenly become angry, violent etc.: *Violence has flared up again in the Middle East.* **3** [I,T] to become wider toward the bottom end or edge, or to make something do this: [**+ out**] *The plant has dainty, white, tubular flowers that flare out at the lip.* | *The bull* ***flared*** *its* ***nostrils*** *and charged.* **4** [I] also **flare up** if a disease or illness flares, it suddenly becomes worse: *My allergies tend to flare up in humid weather.*

flare² *n.* **1** [C] a piece of equipment that produces a bright flame, or the flame itself, used outdoors as a signal: *Flares marked the landing site.* **2** [C usually singular] a sudden bright flame **3 flares** [plural] pants that become wide near the bottom of the leg

flare path /'. ./ *n.* [C] a path for an airplane to land on that is lit with special lights

flare-up /'. ./ *n.* [C] **1** a situation in which a person or group suddenly becomes angry or violent, especially when they have not been violent for a period of time: *a flare-up in the dispute between Armenians and Azerbaijanis* **2** a situation in which a disease or illness suddenly becomes bad again, after not causing any problems for a long time: *She's following a low-fat diet, and hasn't had a flare-up in months.*

flash¹ /flæʃ/ v.
1 shine [I,T] to shine suddenly and brightly for a very short time, or to make something shine in this way: *Lightning flashed and thunder rolled.* | [**flash sth into/at/toward sb**] *Why did that guy flash his headlights at me?* | *A big red warning light flashed on and off* (=shone for a short time and then stopped shining).
2 pictures [I always + adv./prep.] to be shown quickly on television or in a movie etc.: [+ **across/onto/past etc.**] *New pictures from the surface of Mars flashed across the screen.* | *The message flashed across Gibbs' computer screen.*
3 memories/images [I always + adv./prep.] if thoughts, images, memories etc. flash through your mind, you suddenly think of them or remember them: [+ **across/through/into**] *Stories about what happened to captured pilots flashed through his mind.*
4 flash a smile/glance/look/sign etc. at sb to smile or look at someone quickly, or to make a quick movement with a particular meaning: *Counter flashed a broad grin and waved to reporters.* | *Reed flashed a "V" for victory sign.*
5 show sth quickly [T] to show something to someone for only a short time: *Detective Mallory flashed his badge as he walked through the door.*
6 news/information [T always + adv./prep.] to send news or information somewhere quickly by radio, computer, or SATELLITE: [**flash sth across/over etc.**] *Brady's comments flashed across the newswires.*
7 move quickly [I always + adv./prep.] to move very quickly: [+ **by/past**] *An ambulance flashed past.*
8 eyes [I] if your eyes flash, they seem to be very bright for a moment, especially because of a sudden emotion: [+ **with**] *Anne's eyes flashed with excitement.*
9 sex organs [I,T] INFORMAL if a man flashes or flashes someone, he shows his sexual organs in public
10 sb's life flashes before their eyes if someone's life flashes before their eyes, they suddenly remember many events from their life, especially because they are in great danger and might die
11 time [I always + adv./prep.] if a period of time flashes by, past etc., it seems to end very quickly: [+ **by/past**] *Our vacation seemed to just flash by.*
flash sth **around** phr. v. [T] to use something in a way that will make people notice you and think you have a lot of money: *He's always flashing his money around.*
flash back phr. v. [I] to think about or show something that happened in the past, especially in a movie, book etc.: [+ **to**] *From here the movie flashes back to Billy's first meeting with Schultz.*
flash forward phr. v. [I] if a movie, book etc. flashes forward, it shows what is happening in the future: *The movie then flashes forward to their daughter's fifth birthday.*

flash² n.
1 light [C] a bright light that shines for a short time and then stops shining: *a flash of lightning*
2 camera [C,U] a special bright light used with a camera when taking photographs indoors or when there is not enough light: *Did the flash go off?*
3 in/like a flash also **quick as a flash** very quickly: *The computer can sort and edit a mailing list in a flash.*
4 a flash of brilliance/inspiration/anger etc. if someone has a flash of brilliance, anger etc., they suddenly have a very good idea or suddenly have a particular feeling: *His work shows occasional flashes of brilliance.*
5 a flash in the pan a sudden success that ends quickly and is unlikely to happen again: *Beene's new novel proves that he isn't just a flash in the pan.*

6 bright color/sth shiny [C] if there is a flash of something brightly colored or shiny, it appears suddenly for a short time: [+ **of**] *The bird stood watching for the underwater flash of a turning fish.*
7 signal [C] the act of shining a light as a signal: *Two flashes mean danger.* —see also HOT FLASH

flash³ adj. [only before noun] happening very quickly or suddenly, and continuing for only a short time: *Flash fires swept through the Los Angeles foothills last night.* —see also FLASH FLOOD

flash·back /'flæʃbæk/ n. **1** [C,U] a scene in a movie, play, book etc. that shows something that happened before that point in the story: *The events of the hero's childhood are shown as a series of flashbacks.* **2** [C] a sudden very clear memory of something that happened to you in the past: *Amado **has flashbacks** to his experiences in Vietnam.* **3** [C] an occasion when someone has the same bad feeling that they had when they took an illegal drug in the past: *Many users of this drug experience chronic depression and flashbacks.* **4** [C] TECHNICAL a burning gas or liquid that moves back into a tube or container

flash bulb /'. ./ n. [C] a small BULB (=a bright light) used when you take photographs indoors or when there is not enough light

flash burn /'. ./ n. [C] a burn that you get from being near a sudden, very hot flame, for example an explosion

flash·card /'flæʃkɑrd/ n. [C] a card with a word or picture on it, used in teaching

flash·er /'flæʃɚ/ n. [C] INFORMAL a man who shows his sex organs to women in public

flash flood /ˌ. './ n. [C] a sudden flood that is caused by a lot of rain falling in a short period of time

flash freeze /ˌ. './ v. [T] to freeze food quickly so that its quality is not damaged

flash·gun /'flæʃgʌn/ n. [C] a piece of equipment that lights a special bright light when you press the button on a camera to take a photograph

flash·light /'flæʃlaɪt/ n. [C] a small electric light that you can carry in your hand

flash·point /'flæʃpɔɪnt/ n. [C] **1** a place where trouble or violence might easily develop suddenly and be hard to control: *Vukovar was one of the early flashpoints in the former Yugoslavia.* **2** [usually singular] TECHNICAL the lowest temperature at which a liquid such as oil will produce enough gas to burn if a flame is put near it

flash·y /'flæʃi/ adj. **flashier, flashiest** INFORMAL too big, bright, or expensive in a way that other people disapprove of: *a flashy new sports car*

flask /flæsk/ n. [C] **1** a small flat bottle used to carry alcohol in your pocket **2** a glass bottle with a narrow top, used in a LABORATORY

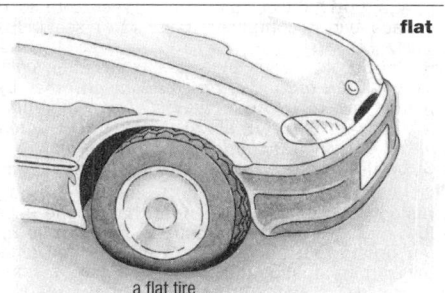

flat

a flat tire

flat¹ /flæt/ adj. **flatter, flattest** $^{SW}_{2\ 2}$
1 surface smooth and level, without raised or hollow areas, and not sloping or curving: *Stack the crepes on a flat plate.* | *We swam out to a flat rock to sunbathe.* | *That part of the state is **as flat as a pancake*** (=very flat).
2 tire/ball a tire or ball that is flat has no air or not enough air inside it

3 [drink] a drink that is flat does not taste fresh because it has no more BUBBLES of gas in it: *This Coke is completely flat.*

4 [business/trade] if prices, economic conditions, trade etc. are flat, they have not increased or gotten better over a period of time: *Home prices have stayed flat for the past year.* | *Worries over the economy have kept attendance flat at California's theme parks.*

5 [musical sound] a musical note that is flat is played or sung slightly lower than it should be: *The horn was a little flat.* —see picture at MUSIC

6 E flat/B flat/A flat etc. a musical note that is one half STEP[1] (13) lower than the note E, B, A etc.

7 a flat rate/price/fee etc. a flat rate, price, amount of money etc. that you pay that does not change or have anything added to it: *We charge a flat fee of $3 a day for each video.*

8 [not interesting] [not before noun] a performance, book etc. that is flat seems fairly boring: *The game just seemed kind of flat, like they didn't care.*

9 [voice] not showing much emotion, or not changing much in sound as you speak: *"He's dead," she said in a flat voice.*

10 a flat refusal/denial etc. something you say that is definite and that you will definitely not change: *Our requests were met with a flat refusal.*

11 be flat on your back a) to be lying down so that all of your back is touching the floor or the ground: *Arthur was flat on his back under the car.* **b)** to be very sick so that you have to stay in bed for a period of time: *I've been flat on my back with the flu all week.*

12 [shoes] flat shoes have very low heels

13 [not deep] not very deep, thick, or high, especially in comparison to its width or length: *The cake came out of the oven flat, not fluffy.*

14 [light] having little variety of light and dark: *Flat lighting is typical of Avedon's portraits.* —**flatness** *n.* [U]

flat² *adv.*

1 [flat position] in a straight position or stretched against a flat surface: *The box can be folded flat for storage.* | *I have to **lie flat on my back** when I sleep.* | *My first time out on the ice I **fell flat on my face** (=fell so I was lying on my chest).*

2 10 seconds/two minutes etc. flat INFORMAL in exactly ten seconds, two minutes etc.: *I was out of the house in ten minutes flat.*

3 fall flat INFORMAL **a)** if a joke or story falls flat, people are not amused by it: *Koppel's clumsy joke fell flat.* **b)** if something you have planned falls flat, it is unsuccessful or does not have the result you wanted: *At first, Gorbachev's political ideas fell flat.* | *A lot of people expected the team to **fall flat on its face** (=be unsuccessful in an embarrassing way).*

4 [music] if you sing or play music flat, you sing or play slightly lower than the correct note so that it sounds bad —compare SHARP² (2) —see picture at MUSIC

5 flat out INFORMAL **a)** as fast as possible: *They were working flat out to get the job done on time.* **b)** completely, or in a direct way: *O'Leary flat out loves teaching.* | **ask/tell sb sth flat out** *Clinton was asked flat out if he had ever had an affair.*

6 be flat broke INFORMAL to have no money at all

flat³ *n.* [C] **1** a tire that does not have enough air inside it **2 a)** a musical note that is one HALF STEP lower than a particular note **b)** the sign (♭) in written music that shows that a note is one HALF STEP lower than a particular note —compare NATURAL² (2), SHARP³ (1) **3 flats** [plural] **a)** a pair of women's shoes with very low heels **b)** an area of land that is at a low level, especially near water: *the mud flats near the beach* **4 the flat of sth** the flat part or flat side of something: *She hit me with the flat of her hand.* **5** BRITISH an APARTMENT

flat·car /'flæt‑kɑr/ *n.* [C] a railroad car without a roof or sides, used for carrying goods

flat-chest·ed /ˌ. '...‹/ *adj.* a woman who is flat-chested has small breasts

flat feet /ˌ. './ *n.* [plural] a medical condition in which someone's feet rest flat on the ground because the middle of each foot is not as curved as it should be

flat·fish /'flæt‑fɪʃ/ *n.* [C] a type of ocean fish with a thin flat body, such as COD or SOLE

flat-foot·ed /ˌ. ‚.../ *adj.* **1 catch sb flat-footed** to surprise someone so that they cannot do something in the way they ought to: *The recent recession caught managers flat-footed and unprepared.* **2** having flat feet **3** INFORMAL moving in an awkward way; CLUMSY: *Leonard was flat-footed and slow during the match.* **4** if art, writing, music etc. is flat-footed, it is slightly awkward and does not express emotion or thoughts well **5** INFORMAL dealing with situations in a way that is not sensitive to other people's thoughts or feelings

Flat·head /'flæthɛd/ a Native American tribe from the northwestern area of the U.S.

flat·i·ron /'flæt‚aɪrən/ *n.* [C] a type of IRON (=object that you use to make your clothes smooth) used in the past that was not heated by electricity

flat·ly /'flætli/ *adv.* **1 flatly refuse/deny/oppose etc.** to say something in a direct and definite way that is not likely to change: *He flatly rejected calls for his resignation.* **2** without showing any emotion: *He said flatly that there was no chance of a reconciliation.*

flat·ten /'flætn/ *v.* **1** [I,T] also **flatten out** to make something flat or flatter, or to become flat or flatter: *Flatten the cardboard boxes and stack them in the corner.* | *The hills flatten out near the coast.* —see picture on page 424 **2** [T] to destroy a building or town by knocking it down, bombing it etc.: *More than 10,000 houses were flattened by the quake.* **3** [T] INFORMAL to defeat someone completely and easily in a game, argument etc.: *The Packers flattened the Saints 42–6.* **4 flatten yourself against sth** to press your body against something: *I flattened myself against the wall.* **5** [T] INFORMAL to hit someone very hard: *Shut up or I'll flatten you!*

flat·tened /'flætnd/ *adj.* [not before noun] unhappy and embarrassed because of what someone has said about you

flat·ter /'flætɚ/ *v.* **1 be flattered** to be pleased because someone has shown you that they like or admire you: *If a woman called me for a date I'd be flattered.* **2** [T] to praise someone in order to please them or get something from them, even though you do not really mean it: *Don't try to flatter me!* **3** [T] to make someone look as attractive as they can: *That dress really flatters your figure.* **4** [T] to make something look or seem more important or better than it really is: *Lewis' novel doesn't flatter Midwestern attitudes and morals.* **5 flatter yourself** if you flatter yourself that something is true about your abilities or achievements, you make yourself believe it is true, although it is not: *"I think you like me more than you'll admit." "Don't flatter yourself."*

flat·ter·er /'flætərɚ/ *n.* [C] someone who FLATTERS (2) people

flat·ter·ing /'flætərɪŋ/ *adj.* clothes, pictures etc. that are flattering make someone look as attractive as they can or make something as good as possible, even if is not really very good: *It's not a very flattering photograph, is it?*

flat·ter·y /'flætəri/ *n.* [U] praise that you do not really mean

flat·top /'flæt‚tɑp/ *n.* [C] a type of hair style that is very short and looks flat on top —see picture at hairstyle

flat·u·lence /'flætʃələns/ *n.* [U] FORMAL the condition of having too much gas in your stomach —**flatulent** *adj.*

flat·ware /'flæt‚wɛr/ *n.* [U] a word meaning knives, forks, and spoons; CUTLERY

Flau·bert /floʊˈbɛr/, **Gus·tave** /ɡʊstɑv/ (1821–1880) a French writer of NOVELS

flaunt /flɔnt, flɑnt/ *v.* [T] **1** to show your money, success, beauty etc. so that other people notice it: *Limousines aren't necessarily a way of flaunting your wealth.* **2 if you've got it, flaunt it** SPOKEN, HUMOROUS used to tell someone not to hide their beauty, wealth, or abilities

flau·tist /ˈflaʊtɪst/ n. [C] a FLUTIST

s w
2/3
fla·vor[1] /ˈfleɪvə/ n. **1** [C] the particular taste of a food or drink: *It has a tangy citrus flavor.* **2** [U] the quality of tasting good: *The meat was cooked exactly right and was full of flavor.* **3** [U] an idea of what the typical qualities of something are: *The language is simple, but gives readers the flavor of the sailing ship period.* **4** [singular] a quality or feature that makes something have a particular style or character: *The stories have a strong regional flavor.* **5 flavor of the month** the idea, person, style etc. that is the most popular one for a short time: *Environmentalism seems to have become Hollywood's flavor of the month.*

flavor[2] v. [T] to give something a particular taste or more taste: *Before roasting, flavor the beef with salt, pepper, and fresh garlic.*

fla·vored /ˈfleɪvəd/ adj. having had a flavor added: *flavored coffees*

-flavored /ˈfleɪvəd/ [in adjectives] **chocolate-flavored/strawberry-flavored etc.** tasting like chocolate, strawberries etc.: *cheese-flavored crackers*

fla·vor·ful /ˈfleɪvəfəl/ adj. having a strong pleasant taste: *a flavorful Mexican dish*

fla·vor·ing /ˈfleɪvərɪŋ/ n. [C,U] a substance used to give something a particular flavor: *This yogurt contains no artificial flavorings.*

fla·vour /ˈfleɪvə/ the British and Canadian spelling of FLAVOR, also used in the words "flavoured," "flavourful," and "flavouring"

flaw /flɔ/ n. [C] **1** a mistake, mark, or weakness that makes something not perfect; DEFECT: *It was half price because of a slight flaw.* | [+ **in**] *The property inspector missed several major flaws in the home.* **2** a mistake in an argument, plan, or set of ideas: *There are **fatal flaws** (=very important mistakes that make something certain to fail) in this program that make it unworkable.* | *The report illustrates a **fundamental flaw** in the way we deal with new product development.* **3** a fault in someone's character: *Jealousy is Othello's major flaw.* | *a character flaw*

flawed /flɔd/ adj. spoiled by having mistakes, weaknesses, or damage: *a flawed but entertaining movie*

flaw·less /ˈflɔlɪs/ adj. perfect, with no mistakes, marks, or weaknesses: *He spoke in flawless Armenian.* | *the flawless skin of a baby* —**flawlessly** adv.

flax /flæks/ n. [U] **1** a plant with blue flowers, used for making cloth and oil **2** the thread made from this plant, used for making LINEN

flax·en /ˈflæksən/ adj. LITERARY flaxen hair is very light in color

flay /fleɪ/ v. **flays, flayed, flaying** [T] **1** FORMAL to criticize someone very severely: *Congressmen have flayed the President for neglecting domestic issues.* **2** LITERARY to whip or beat someone very severely

flea /fli/ n. [C] a very small insect without wings that jumps and bites animals and people to eat their blood

flea·bag /ˈflibæg/ n. [C] INFORMAL a cheap dirty hotel

flea·bite /ˈflibaɪt/ n. [C] the bite of a flea

flea col·lar /ˈ. ,../ n. [C] a special collar, worn by a dog or cat, that contains chemicals to keep fleas away from them

flea mar·ket /ˈ. ,../ n. [C] a market, usually in the street, where old or used goods are sold

flea·pit /ˈfli,pɪt/ n. [C] OLD-FASHIONED, HUMOROUS a cheap dirty place, especially a movie theater

fleck /flɛk/ n. [C] a small mark or spot: [+ **of**] *Kathy's eyes have flecks of gray in them.*

flecked /flɛkt/ adj. having small marks or spots: *red cloth flecked with white*

fledged /flɛdʒd/ adj. —see also FULL-FLEDGED

fledg·ling[1] /ˈflɛdʒlɪŋ/ adj. [only before noun] a fledgling state, organization etc. has only recently been formed and is still developing: *Democratic reforms are beginning to take hold in this fledgling republic.*

fledglings

fledgling[2] n. [C] a young bird that is learning to fly

flee /fli/ v. past tense and past participle **fled** /flɛd/ [I,T] to leave somewhere very quickly, in order to escape from danger: *When they saw the police car, his attackers turned and fled.* | [+ **from/to/into**] *Thousands of people have fled from the area.* | *The President was forced to **flee the country** after the revolution.*

s w
3

fleece[1] /flis/ n. [C] **1** the woolly coat of a sheep, especially the wool and skin of a sheep when it has been made into a piece of clothing: *fleece-lined slippers* **2** an artificial soft material used to make warm coats

fleece[2] v. [T] INFORMAL to charge someone too much money for something, usually by tricking them: *American taxpayers are used to **getting fleeced**.*

fleec·y /ˈflisi/ adj. soft and woolly, or looking soft and woolly: *a fleecy bathrobe*

fleet[1] /flit/ n. [C] **1** a group of ships, or all the ships in a navy: *There are unconfirmed reports that the seventh fleet is moving into the area.* **2** a group of vehicles that are controlled or owned by one company: *We have the largest fleet of trucks in the state.*

fleet[2] adj. LITERARY very fast or quick: *Atalanta was good with a bow and **fleet of foot** (=able to run quickly).*

fleet admiral, Fleet Admiral /ˈ. ,.../ n. [C] the highest rank in the Navy, or someone who has this rank

fleet·ing /ˈflitɪŋ/ adj. [usually before noun] continuing for only a short time: *I caught a fleeting glimpse of them as they drove past.* —**fleetingly** adv.

Flem·ing /ˈflɛmɪŋ/, **Alexander** (1881–1955) a British scientist who discovered PENICILLIN, a substance that is used as a medicine to destroy BACTERIA

Fleming, Peg·gy /ˈpɛgi/ (1948–) a U.S. woman who was world FIGURE SKATING CHAMPION in 1966–1968

Flem·ish /ˈflɛmɪʃ/ n. [U] a language like Dutch that is spoken in northern Belgium —**Flemish** adj.

flesh[1] /flɛʃ/ n. [U] **1** the soft part of the body of a person or animal that is between the skin and the bones: *a freshwater fish with firm, white flesh* | *She was treated for a **flesh wound** (=a slight injury from a knife or bullet) and released.* **2** the soft part of a fruit or vegetable that can be eaten: *Cut the melon in half and scoop out the flesh.* —see picture at FRUIT[1] **3 see/meet sb in the flesh** if you see or meet someone in the flesh, you see or meet someone who you previously had only seen in pictures, in movies etc.: *I never thought I'd actually meet him in the flesh.* **4 your own flesh and blood** someone who is part of your family: *He raised those kids like they were his own flesh and blood.* **5 make sb's flesh crawl/creep** to make someone feel very frightened, nervous, or uncomfortable: *His touch makes my flesh crawl.* **6 the flesh** LITERARY the physical human body, as opposed to the mind or spirit | *the **temptations/pleasures of the flesh** (=things such as drinking, eating a lot, or having sex)* **7 put flesh on sth** to give more details about something to make it clear, more interesting etc.: *Medical experts put flesh on the statistical data for the audience.* **8 more than flesh and blood can stand/bear** used to describe something that you find too bad, difficult etc. to think about **9 go the way of all flesh** LITERARY to die —see also **get/take etc. a pound of flesh** (POUND¹ (5)), **press the flesh** (PRESS¹ (13)), **the spirit is willing but the flesh is weak** (SPIRIT¹ (15))

flesh² *v.*

flesh sth ↔ out *phr. v.* [T] to add more details to something in order to improve it: *Fleshing out the details of the plan may be difficult.*

flesh·col·ored /'. ,../ *adj.* having a slightly pink color like that of white people's skin: *flesh-colored pantyhose*

flesh·ly /'flɛʃli/ *adj.* [only before noun] LITERARY physical, especially sexual

flesh·pots /'flɛʃpɑts/ *n.* [plural] INFORMAL areas in a city or town where there are many places that people go to for pleasure, especially sexual pleasure: *the fleshpots of the south side of the city*

flesh·y /'flɛʃi/ *adj.* **1** having a lot of flesh: *a round, fleshy face* **2** having a soft, thick inner part: *The plant has dark green fleshy leaves.*

flew /flu/ *v.* the past tense of FLY¹

flex /flɛks/ *v.* [T] **1** to bend or move part of your body so that your muscles become tight **2 flex your muscles** to show your ability to do something, especially your skill or power: *This new position should give you the chance to really flex your muscles.*

flex·i·bil·i·ty /ˌflɛksəˈbɪləti/ *n.* [U] **1** the ability to change or be changed easily to suit a different situation: *Cities now have flexibility in deciding how to spend federal transportation money.* **2** the ability to bend or be bent easily: *Stretching exercises will help your flexibility.*

flex·i·ble /'flɛksəbəl/ *adj.*
1 a person, plan etc. that is flexible can change or be changed easily to suit any new situation: *My work schedule is fairly flexible.* —opposite INFLEXIBLE
2 something that is flexible can bend or be bent easily: *It's made out of a tough but extremely flexible plastic.* —**flexibly** *adv.*

flexible

flex·time /'flɛks-taɪm/ *n.* [U] a system in which people work a particular number of hours each week or month, but can change the times at which they start and finish working each day

flick¹ /flɪk/ *v.* **1** [T] to make something move by hitting or pushing it suddenly or quickly, especially with your thumb and finger: [**flick sth from/off/into etc. sth**] *Barry flicked the ash from his cigarette into the ashtray.* **2** [I always + adv./prep., T always + adv./prep.] to move with a sudden, quick movement, or to make something move in this way: [+ **from/ up/down**] *The cow's tail flicked from side to side.* | [**flick sth up/into/down etc.**] *Jackie flicked her long hair back.* **3** [T] to make a light, machine etc. stop or start working by pressing or moving a button: [**flick sth on/off**] *As I drove away, I flicked on the radio.* **4** [T] if you flick something such as a whip or rope, you move it so that the end moves quickly away from you: *Ricky, stop flicking that towel at me!*

flick

flick through sth *phr. v.* [T] to look at a book, magazine, set of photographs etc. quickly

flick² *n.* **1** [C] INFORMAL a movie: *an action flick* **2** [C] a short, light, sudden movement or hit with your hand, a whip etc.: *With a flick of the wrist, Ferguson*

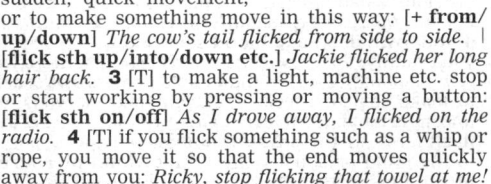

sent the ball into the opposite court. **3 a flick of a switch** used to emphasize how easy it is to start a machine and use it: *Brokers can move huge amounts of stock with the flick of a switch.*

flick·er¹ /'flɪkɚ/ *v.* [I] **1** to burn or shine with an unsteady light that goes on and off quickly: *The overhead lights suddenly flickered and went out.* **2** [always + adv./prep.] if an emotion or expression flickers on someone's face or through their mind, it exists or is shown for only a short time: [+ **across/ through/on etc.**] *A look of remembrance flickered across Mrs. Esterman's face.* **3** to quickly make a sudden small movement or series of movements: *Penny's eyelids flickered for a moment, then she slept.*

flick·er² *n.* [C] **1** an unsteady light that goes on and off quickly: [+ **of**] *the flicker of firelight* **2 a flicker of interest/remorse/guilt etc.** a feeling or expression that continues for a very short time: *As the verdict was read, Farley showed not even a flicker of emotion.* **3** a quick sudden movement or series of movements

fli·er /'flaɪɚ/ *n.* [C] **1** a piece of paper advertising something, which is given to people in the street, sent in the mail etc. **2** INFORMAL a pilot or someone who travels on an airplane —see also FREQUENT FLIER

flies /flaɪz/ *n.* the plural of FLY² (1)

flight /flaɪt/ *n.* S W
1 travel [C] a trip in an airplane or space vehicle: *It's only an hour's flight to Detroit from here.*
2 plane [C] an airplane making a particular trip: *United Flight 202 from Denver is now arriving.* | *I have to go – my flight's been called* (=it has been announced that the airplane is ready to leave). —see also CHARTER FLIGHT
3 flying [U] the act of flying through the air: *a photograph of eagles in flight* | *Thousands of birds took flight* (=began flying) *at our approach.*
4 stairs [C] a set of stairs between one floor and the next: *Each room contains a sink, but the bathroom is one flight up.* | *He can't climb a flight of stairs without becoming breathless.*
5 escape [U] the act of avoiding a dangerous or difficult situation by leaving or escaping: [+ **from**] *The monks protected Jews in flight from Nazi persecution.* | *Residents took flight* (=ran away in order to escape) *from Dohuk to escape the fighting.*
6 flight of imagination/fancy/fantasy thoughts, ideas etc. that are full of imagination but that are not practical or sensible
7 birds [C] LITERARY a group of birds all flying together
8 put sb to flight OLD-FASHIONED to make someone run away in order to try and escape —see also IN-FLIGHT, TOP-FLIGHT

flight at·tend·ant /'. ,.../ *n.* [C] someone who is responsible for the comfort and safety of the passengers on an airplane

flight deck /'. ,./ *n.* [C] **1** the room in an airplane where the pilot sits to control the airplane **2** the flat surface of a ship from which military airplanes can fly into the air

flight·less /'flaɪtlɪs/ *adj.* a flightless bird is unable to fly

flight path /'. ./ *n.* [C] the course that an airplane or space vehicle travels along

flight re·cord·er /'. ,.../ *n.* [C] a piece of equipment on an airplane that records what happens and how the airplane operates during a flight; BLACK BOX

flight sim·u·la·tor /'. ,..../ *n.* [C] a machine that copies the movements of an airplane, used to train pilots

flight·y /'flaɪti/ *adj.* someone who is flighty changes their ideas or activities a lot without finishing them or being serious about them —**flightiness** *n.* [U]

flim·flam /'flɪmflæm/ *n.* OLD-FASHIONED, INFORMAL **1** [U] stories, information etc. that do not seem serious or true **2** [C usually singular] a trick intended to cheat someone —**flimflam** *v.* [T]

flim·sy /'flɪmzi/ *adj.* **flimsier, flimsiest** DISAPPROVING **1** flimsy cloth or clothing is light and thin, and can tear easily: *a flimsy summer dress* **2** flimsy equipment, buildings etc. are not made very well and are easily broken: *a shantytown of flimsy wood and tin* structures **3** a flimsy argument, excuse etc. is hard to believe: *The evidence against him is very flimsy.* —**flimsily** *adv.* —**flimsiness** *n.* [U]

flinch /flɪntʃ/ *v.* [I] **1** to make a sudden small backward movement when you are hurt or afraid of something: *Everyone flinched as shells exploded all around us.* **2** to avoid doing something because you dislike it or are afraid of it: *While the price will make you flinch, in the end the lightbulbs save you money.* | [**flinch from doing sth**] *Writer LaPlante does not flinch from showing the ugly side of Tennison's character.* **3 sb didn't (even) flinch** used to say that someone did not seem surprised about something: *McCracken didn't flinch when told the price was $150,000.*

fling[1] /flɪŋ/ *v.* past tense and past participle **flung** [T] **1** throw [always + adv./prep.] to throw something quickly with a lot of force: *Shoes and socks lay where they had been flung.* | [**+ down**] *Jimmy flung down his coat and ran upstairs.* | [**+ off**] *The catcher flung off his mask.* | [**fling sth at/into/on etc.**] *Carmen was flinging a tennis ball high into the air.* **2** body [always + adv./prep.] to move yourself or part of your body suddenly and with a lot of force: [**fling sth around/toward/back etc.**] *When I came in, Katie flung her arms around me and kissed me.* | *Polly flung herself down on the bed beside him.* **3 fling yourself into sth** to begin to do something using a lot of effort: *Mas flung himself into the economic and political life of America.* **4 fling a door/window etc. open** to quickly and suddenly open a door, window etc.: *She flung open her cabin door and waved.* **5 fling sb in prison/jail** to put someone in prison, often without having a good reason: *After the revolution, opposition leaders were flung into jail.*

fling[2] *n.* [C usually singular] **1** a short and not very serious sexual relationship: *We had a brief fling twenty years ago.* **2** a short period of time during which you enjoy yourself or are interested in something: *Long after your child has had his or her fling with cowboys, this book will be worth keeping.*

flint /flɪnt/ *n.* **1** [C,U] a type of smooth hard black or gray stone, or a piece of this stone **2** [C] a piece of this stone or a small piece of metal that makes a small flame when you strike it with steel

flint·lock /ˈflɪntlɑk/ *n.* [C] a gun used in past times

flint·y /ˈflɪnti/ *adj.* a flinty expression or person does not show emotions

Flip /flɪp/ *n.* [C] TABOO someone from the Philippines. Do not use this word.

s w
2

flip[1] /flɪp/ *v.* **flipped, flipping 1** [I,T] to turn something over or put into a different position with a quick, sudden movement, or to turn over in this way: [**+ over**] *The whole helicopter flipped over and landed in a field upside down.* | [**flip sth back/across/over etc.**] *She flipped her hair across one shoulder.* | *Flip the tortilla over and cook for 1 to 2 minutes.* **2** [T] to throw something flat such as a coin up so that it turns over in the air; TOSS: *In the end we flipped a coin* (=tossed a coin in the air to help decide something, according to which side lands upward). **3 flip burgers** INFORMAL to work in a FAST FOOD restaurant, cooking food such as HAMBURGERS: *In his teens, Armstrong was already winning major races while his friends were flipping burgers.* **4** [I] also **flip out** or **flip your lid** INFORMAL to suddenly become very angry or upset, or start behaving in a crazy way: *The guy just flipped out and started shooting.* | *When Jerry found out about the money we took, he completely flipped his lid.* **5** [T] to quickly start or stop electrical equipment by pressing or moving a button: [**flip sth on/off**] *I flipped the answering machine off and stared at it.* **6** [I + over] OLD-FASHIONED, INFORMAL to feel very excited and like something very much

flip for sb *phr. v.* [T] INFORMAL to suddenly begin to like someone very much: *Ben has really flipped for Laura, hasn't he?*

flip sb ↔ **off** *phr. v.* [T] SLANG also **flip sb the bird** to make an offensive sign at someone by raising your middle finger and keeping your other fingers down

flip through sth *phr. v.* [T] to look at a book, magazine etc. quickly

flip[2] *n.* [C] **1** a movement in which you jump up and turn over in the air, so that your feet go over your head: *a backward flip* **2** a quick, light hit with your thumb or finger, especially one that makes a flat object turn over in the air: *It'll be decided by a flip of a coin.*

flip[3] *adj.* INFORMAL: see FLIPPANT

flip chart /ˈ. ./ *n.* [C] large pieces of paper that are connected at the top so that the pages can be turned over to present information to groups of people

flip-flop[1] /ˈ. ./ *n.* **1** [C] INFORMAL an occasion when someone changes their opinion or decision about something: *There's been yet another administration flip-flop on domestic policy.* **2** [C usually plural] a summer shoe, usually made of rubber, with only a V-shaped band across the front to hold your feet **3** a movement in GYMNASTICS in which you flip over backward with your hands touching the floor

flip-flop[2] *v.* [I] INFORMAL to change your opinion or decision about something

flip·pant /ˈflɪpənt/ *adj.* not serious about something that other people think you should be serious about, so that they think you do not care: *Kalb gave a flippant answer to the question.* —**flippantly** *adv.* —**flippancy** *n.* [U]

flip·per /ˈflɪpɚ/ *n.* [C] **1** a flat part on the body of some large sea animals, used for pushing themselves through water **2** a large flat rubber shoe that you use to help you swim faster

flip side /ˈ. ./ *n.* [singular] **1** used when you describe the bad effects of something, after you have just described the good effects: *On the flip side, the medicine may cause nausea.* **2** the side of a record that has a song on it that is less popular than the song on the other side

flirt[1] /flɚt/ *v.* [I] to behave toward and talk to someone as though you are sexually attracted to them, but not in a very serious way: *We flirted a little but that was as far as it went.* | [**+ with**] *The waitress was flirting with some of the customers at the bar.*

flirt with sth *phr. v.* **1** [T not in passive] to consider doing something, but not be very serious about it: *Who hasn't flirted with the idea of giving up work and escaping to paradise?* **2 flirt with danger/disaster etc.** to take an unnecessary risk and not be worried about it: *Even some high school athletes have flirted with these drugs.*

flirt[2] *n.* [C] someone who often behaves toward and talks to people as though she or he is sexually attracted to them, but not in a very serious way

flir·ta·tion /flɚˈteɪʃən/ *n.* **1** [U] behavior that shows a sexual attraction to someone, though not in a serious way **2** [C] a short period of time during which you are interested in something or in which you try something: [**+ with**] *the magazine's flirtation with taboo topics* **3** [C] a short sexual relationship which is not serious

flir·ta·tious /flɚˈteɪʃəs/ *adj.* behaving in a way that deliberately tries to attract sexual attention, but not in a serious way: *Graham plays Benedict's flirtatious daughter.* —**flirtatiously** *adv.* —**flirtatiousness** *n.* [U]

flit /flɪt/ *v.* **flitted, flitting** [I always + adv./prep.] to move lightly or quickly from one place to another: *In the greenhouse birds flit among the plants.*

float[1] /floʊt/ *v.*

s w
3 3

1 on water [I] **a)** to stay or move on the surface of a liquid without sinking: *If the egg floats in a glass of water, it's not fresh.* | *Tim was floating on his back in the pool.* | [**+ along/down/past etc.**] *Gerard held up his oars in greeting as he floated past the dock.* **b)** [T] to put something on the surface of a liquid so that it does not sink: *Children were floating small boats made of banana leaves.*

F

float

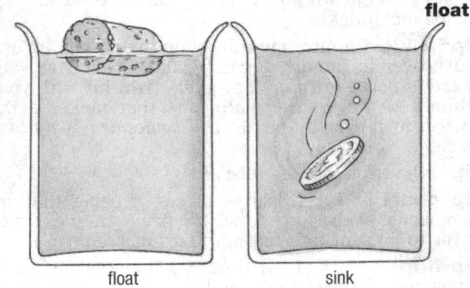

float   sink

2 in the air [I always + adv./prep.] if something floats, especially something very light or filled with air, it moves slowly in the air or stays up in the air: [+ **up/down/through** etc.] *The satellite floated gracefully away from the space shuttle's cargo bay.*
3 suggest [T] to suggest an idea or plan, especially in order to find out what people think about it: *Butler floated proposals for a number of films.*
4 company [T] to sell STOCK in a company or business to the public for the first time
5 money [I,T] TECHNICAL if a country floats its money or its money floats, the value of the money is allowed to change freely in relation to money from other countries: *Russia floated the rouble on the foreign exchange market.*
6 music/sounds/smells etc. [I always + adv./prep.] if sounds, smells etc. float somewhere, people in another place can hear or smell them: [+ **down/ toward/into** etc.] *The notes seemed to float up from somewhere far in the distance.*
7 move gracefully [I] to move gracefully and lightly: *She turned, her hair floating around her face.*
8 no definite purpose [I always + adv./prep.] to keep changing what you are doing without having any particular ideas or plans: *Speck was a drifter who had floated in and out of trouble for most of his life.*
9 **float sb a loan** INFORMAL to allow someone to borrow money from you
10 check [T] to write a check that you do not have enough money in the bank to pay —**floater** *n.* [C] —see also **whatever floats your boat** (WHATEVER[1] (8))

float[2] *n.* [C] **1** a large vehicle that is decorated to be part of a PARADE: *You can see the Rose Parade floats being made.* **2** a SOFT DRINK that has ICE CREAM floating in it: *a root-beer float* **3** a small amount of money that a bank, store etc. keeps so that they have enough money to pay for things, give change to people etc.

float·ing /ˈfloʊtɪŋ/ *adj.* **1** changing according to what the situation is at a particular time: *Employees are asking for three floating holidays each year.* **2** TECHNICAL an organ or part of your body that is floating is not connected correctly or is not in the usual place

flock[1] /flɑk/ *n.* **1** [C] a group of sheep, goats, or birds: *a flock of geese* —compare HERD[1] (1) **2** [C usually singular] a large group of the same kind of people: [+ **of**] *A flock of celebrities was expected at the movie's premiere.* **3** [C usually singular] a priest's or minister's flock is the group of people who regularly attend his church **4** [U] FORMAL small pieces of wool, cotton etc. used for filling the CUSHIONs of chairs and other furniture **5** [U] also **flock·ing** a soft woolly substance used to make patterns on the surface of WALLPAPER, curtains etc.

flock[2] *v.* [I always + adv./prep.] to go to a place in large numbers because something interesting or exciting is happening there: [+ **to/into/around** etc.] *Disney expects millions of kids to flock to its new movie.*

flocked /flɑkt/ *adj.* decorated with patterns made of a soft woolly material: *flocked wallpaper*

floe /floʊ/ *n.* [C] an ICE FLOE

flog /flɑg, flɔg/ *v.* **flogged, flogging** [T] **1** to beat a person or animal with a whip or stick as a punishment: *People caught breaking the liquor laws may be flogged.* **2** INFORMAL to sell something: *He's been on a lot of TV shows, flogging his new book.* —see also **beat/flog a dead horse** (DEAD[1] (8))

flog·ging /ˈflɑgɪŋ/ *n.* [C] a punishment in which someone is severely beaten with a whip or stick

flood[1] /flʌd/ *v.*
1 cover with water [I,T] to make a place become covered with water, or to become covered with water: *The fire department showed up and flooded the hall with their hoses.* | *The whole town flooded last summer.*
2 arrive/go in large numbers [I,T] to arrive or go somewhere in large numbers or amounts: *Donations flooded the newspaper and the school.* | [+ **in/into/ out/across** etc.] *Refugees flooded across the border.*
3 send in large amounts [T] to send a large number of things such as letters or complaints to an organization so that it is difficult for people there to deal with them: [**flood sb/sth with sth**] *Campaigners flooded Congress with letters of protest.* | *I was flooded with* (=received a lot of) *calls from just that one advertisement.*
4 flood the market to sell something or be sold in very large numbers or amounts, especially so that the price goes down: *Special sports drinks are now flooding the market.* | [+ **with**] *The country has recently flooded the market with crude oil.*
5 engine [I,T] if an engine floods or you flood it, it has too much gas in it, so that it will not start
6 light [I,T] if light floods a place or floods into it, it makes it very light and bright: *The small room was flooded with light.*
7 be flooded out to be forced to leave your home because of a flood
8 feeling [I,T] LITERARY if a feeling or memory floods someone, they feel or remember it very strongly: *Loneliness flooded her as she watched J.D. walk away.* | [+ **over/back/through**] *New energy flooded through me.*
9 flood with tears if someone's eyes or face flood with tears, they cry a lot

flood[2] *n.* **1** [C,U] a very large amount of water that covers an area that is usually dry: *The town was completely destroyed by floods.* **2 flood of sb/sth** a very large number of people or things that arrive at the same time: *The station has received a flood of complaints about last night's show.* **3 the Flood** the great flood described in the Bible story, that covered the world —see also FLASH FLOOD

flood·gate /ˈflʌdgeɪt/ *n.* **1 open the floodgates** to suddenly make it possible for a lot of people to do something, by removing laws and rules which had previously prevented or controlled it: *Any change in the law could open the floodgates to increased immigration.* **2** [C usually plural] a gate used to control the flow of water from a large lake, river etc.

flood·ing /ˈflʌdɪŋ/ *n.* [U] a situation in which an area of land becomes covered with water, for example because of heavy rain —see picture on page 1333

flood·light /ˈflʌdlaɪt/ *n.* [C usually plural] a very bright light, used at night to light the outside of buildings, sports fields etc.

flood·lit /ˈflʌdˌlɪt/ *adj.* lit at night by floodlights: *a floodlit football field*

flood plain /ˈ. ./ *n.* [C] the large area of flat land on either side of a river that is sometimes covered with water

flood tide /ˈ. ./ *n.* [C] **1** the flow of the TIDE[1] (1) in toward the land —opposite **ebb tide** (EBB[1]) **2 the flood tide of sth** a very large number or amount of something that arrives at the same time: *Fans can create their own collection of favorites from the flood tide of new Mozart releases on compact disc.*

flood·wa·ter /ˈflʌdˌwɔtɚ/ *n.* [U, plural] water that covers an area during a flood: *2500 residents were forced out of their homes by floodwaters.*

floor[1] /flɔr/ *n.*
1 flat surface [C] the flat surface on which you

F

stand indoors: *Cody spilled his milk on the kitchen floor.* —see Usage Note at LAND[1]

2 [level in building] [C] one of the levels in a building: *My office is **on the** third **floor**.*

3 ocean/forest floor the ground at the bottom of the ocean, the forest etc.: *These sea creatures live on the ocean floor.*

4 the floor a) the part of a government or public building where people discuss things: *The delegates crowded the floor of the House.* **b)** the people attending a public meeting: *Are there any questions from the floor?*

5 take the floor a) to begin speaking at an important public meeting **b)** to begin dancing: *The bride and groom took the floor for the first dance.*

6 have the floor to be speaking or have the right to speak at an important public meeting: *The Senator from Wyoming has the floor.*

7 [area for particular purpose] [C] a large area on one level in a building, used for a particular purpose: *The stock market floor was wildly busy.* | *Ray and Lisa were the first ones on the dance floor.* | *The manager's office is above the **shop floor** (=the area in a factory where people work using machines).*

8 go through the floor if a price, amount etc. goes through the floor, it becomes very low: *In the past few years, stock prices have gone through the floor.*

9 [limit] [singular] an officially agreed limit so that something cannot go below a certain value: *The French government tried to **put a floor under** the value of the franc.* —see also **be/get in on the ground floor** (GROUND FLOOR (2)), **wipe the floor with sb** (WIPE[1] (5))

floor[2] *v.* [T] **1** to surprise or shock someone so much that they do not know what to say or do: *We were floored that so many people came.* **2** to hit someone so hard that they fall down: *The champion floored Watson with a single punch.* **3** INFORMAL to make a car go as fast as possible by pressing the ACCELERATOR all the way down: *She floored the Audi and took off.* | *The other cars crowded in and Williams floored it.*

floor·board /'flɔrbɔrd/ *n.* [C] **1** [usually plural] a board in a wooden floor —see picture at BOARD[1] —see picture on page 423 **2** the floor in a car

floor·ing /'flɔrɪŋ/ *n.* [U] material used to make or cover floors: *vinyl flooring*

floor lamp /'. ./ *n.* [C] a tall lamp that stands on the floor

floor-length /'. ./ *adj.* [only before noun] long enough to reach the floor: *a floor-length evening gown*

floor mod·el /'. ,../ *n.* [C] a piece of furniture or equipment for the home, such as a washing machine, that has been in a store for people to look at and is often sold at a cheaper price because it may have been slightly damaged

floor plan /'. ./ *n.* [C] a drawing that shows the shape of a room or rooms in a building and the positions of things in it, as seen from above

floor show /'. ./ *n.* [C] a performance by singers, dancers etc. at a NIGHTCLUB

floo·zy, floozie /'fluzi/ *n. plural* **floozies** [C] INFORMAL DISAPPROVING a woman whose sexual behavior is considered immoral

flop[1] /flɑp/ *v.* **flopped, flopping 1** [I always + adv./prep.] also **flop down** to sit or lie down in a relaxed way, by letting all your weight fall heavily onto a chair etc.: [+ in/onto/across etc.] *Karl came in and flopped onto the sofa.* **2** [I always + adv./prep.,T always + adv./prep.] to move or fall, or put something down, in an awkward or uncontrolled way: [+ around/along/onto etc.] *A bird with an injured wing flopped helplessly along the ground.* | *Dave flopped his arm over the edge of the bathtub.* **3** INFORMAL if something such as a product, play, or plan flops, it is completely unsuccessful: *The musical flopped after its first week on Broadway.*

flop[2] *n.* **1** [C] INFORMAL a movie, play, product etc. that is completely unsuccessful: *"Heaven's Gate" was a box-office flop.* | *Gino's party was a total flop.* **2** [singular] a heavy falling movement or the noise that something makes when it falls heavily: *He*

landed with a flop in the water. —see also BELLY FLOP, FLIP-FLOP[1]

flop·house /'flɑphaʊs/ *n.* [C] a cheap dirty hotel, that often has many beds in one room

flop·py /'flɑpi/ *adj.* **floppier, floppiest** soft and hanging down loosely: *a dog with long, floppy ears* | *a floppy hat* —**floppiness** *n.* [U]

floppy disk /,.. './ also **floppy** *n.* [C] a small square plastic object with a DISK in it, that can be put into a computer and used for storing or moving information —compare HARD DISK

flo·ra /'flɔrə/ *n.* [U] TECHNICAL OR LITERARY all the plants of a particular place, or of a particular period of time: *the flora of the Alps* —compare FAUNA

flo·ral /'flɔrəl/ *adj.* decorated with or made of flowers: *floral designs on the curtains* | *a floral display*

Flor·en·tine /'flɔrəntin, -taɪn/ *adj.* **1** relating to or coming from Florence, Italy **2** [only after noun] made with SPINACH: *eggs Florentine*

flor·et /'flɔrət/ *n.* [C usually plural] **1** one of the small flower-like parts of vegetables such as BROCCOLI or CAULIFLOWER **2** a small flower-like part of a plant

flor·id /'flɔrɪd, 'flɑrɪd/ *adj.* LITERARY **1** having too much decoration or detail: *a florid romance novel* **2** skin that is florid is red: *florid cheeks* —**floridly** *adv.*

Flor·i·da /'flɔrɪdə, 'flɑr-/ *written abbreviation* **FL** a state in the southeastern U.S.

flo·rist /'flɔrɪst, 'flɑr-/ *n.* [C] **1** someone who owns or works in a store that sells flowers **2** a store that sells flowers: *Dean stopped at the florist on the way home.*

floss[1] /flɔs, flɑs/ *n.* [U] **1** DENTAL FLOSS **2** EMBROIDERY FLOSS

floss[2] *v.* [I,T] to clean between your teeth with DENTAL FLOSS

flo·ta·tion /floʊ'teɪʃən/ *n.* [C,U] **1** **flotation ring/ compartment/device etc.** something that helps something or someone float in water: *Every boat carries one flotation device per passenger.* **2** the act of offering STOCK in a company to the public for the first time: *The money from the share flotation will be used to strengthen the company's financial position.*

flo·til·la /floʊ'tɪlə/ *n.* [C] a group of small ships

flot·sam /'flɑtsəm/ *n.* [U] **1** broken pieces of wood, plastic etc. that are floating in the ocean or scattered on the shore —compare JETSAM **2** also **flotsam and jetsam** things or people that are not useful or needed anymore: *the plastic foam flotsam of fast-food restaurants*

flounce[1] /flaʊns/ *v.* [I always + adv./prep.] to walk quickly while making a big movement with your head or shoulders, especially to show that you are angry: [+ out/off/past etc.] *Sandra frowned and flounced out of the room.*

flounce[2] *n.* [C] a band of cloth that is stitched into folds as a decoration on a piece of clothing, furniture etc.

flounced /flaʊnst/ *adj.* decorated with flounces

floun·der[1] /'flaʊndə/ *v.* [I] **1** to have great difficulty saying or doing something, especially because you are not sure what to do: *The team was floundering in the first half of the season (=they had difficulty playing well).* **2** to have so many problems that it is difficult to continue: *Brando's career was floundering when he was offered the role.* **3** [always + adv./prep.] to move awkwardly or with difficulty, especially in water, mud etc.: *The lifeguard saw some little kids floundering in the shallow water.*

floun·der[2] *n. plural* **flounder** or **flounders** [C,U] a flat ocean fish, or the meat of this fish

flour[1] /flaʊɚ/ *n.* [U] a powder made from grain, usually wheat, and used for making bread, cake etc.: *Mix the flour and sugar.* | *Add 1 cup of **all-purpose flour** (=flour that can be used for making bread or cake) to the mixture.*

flour[2] *v.* [T] to cover a surface with flour: *a lightly floured board*

flour·ish[1] /ˈflɚɪʃ, ˈflʌrɪʃ/ v. **1** [I] to develop well and be successful: *a flourishing black market* | *Foley's career has flourished.* **2** [I] to grow well and be very healthy; THRIVE: *The plants flourished in the warm sun.* **3** [T] to wave something in your hand in order to make people notice it: *Ellie ran in, flourishing her acceptance letter.*

flour·ish[2] n. **1** [C] something such as a decoration or detail that is not necessary: *Lucas' speech was full of rhetorical flourishes.* **2 with a flourish** with a large confident movement that makes people notice you: *Mr. Darcy swept back his hat with a flourish.* **3** [C] a curved line in writing, done for decoration **4** [C] a loud part of a piece of music, played especially when an important person enters: *a flourish of trumpets*

flour·y /ˈflaʊri/ adj. covered with flour, or tasting or feeling like flour

flout /flaʊt/ v. [T] FORMAL to deliberately disobey a law, rule etc.: *Too many people regularly flout traffic laws.*

flow[1] /floʊ/ v. [I]

1 `liquid` if a liquid flows, it moves in a steady continuous stream: [+ **over/down/through** etc.] *Even if water flows over the top of the dam, the dam won't collapse.* | *Tears still **flow freely** when Sara thinks of her mother.*

2 `goods/information/cars etc.` to move or be supplied easily, smoothly, and continuously from one place to another: *The widened freeway should help keep traffic flowing.* | [+ **in/out/through/from** etc.] *Money has been flowing into the country from Western aid agencies.*

3 `alcohol` if alcohol flows at a party, people drink a lot and there is a lot available: *The whiskey usually **flows freely** at Sean's parties.*

4 `words/ideas` **a)** if conversation or ideas flow, people talk or have ideas without being interrupted: *The conversation flowed from one topic to another.* **b)** if the ideas or words of a speech or piece of writing flow, they seem to go well together and make sense: *If I change this paragraph, do you think it will flow better?*

5 `clothes/hair` if clothing, hair etc. flows, it hangs loosely and gracefully

6 `feelings` if an emotion flows, someone feels it strongly: [+ **through/into/from** etc.] *Compassion for Mary flowed through her.*

7 `ocean` if the TIDE[1] (1) flows, it moves toward the land —compare EBB[2] (2)

flow[2] n.

1 `movement of liquid` [C usually singular] a smooth steady movement of liquid: *a lava flow* | [+ **of**] *Smoking affects the flow of blood to the brain.*

2 `supply/movement` [C usually singular] a continuous supply or movement of something from one place to another: *The road repairs should not affect traffic flow.* | [+ **of**] *The agency is coordinating the flow of food and medicine into the country.*

3 `words/ideas` [U] actions, words, or ideas that are produced continuously: [+ **of**] *Putting in a quote there breaks the flow of your speech.*

4 `ocean` [singular] the movement of the TIDE[1] (1) toward the land: *the ebb and flow of the tide*

5 go with the flow INFORMAL **a)** to do what is easiest in your situation, and not try to do something difficult or different: *If you want to stay sane, just go with the flow.* **b)** to do what other people are doing

6 go against the flow INFORMAL to do something very different from what other people are doing —see also CASH FLOW, **ebb and flow** (EBB[1] (1))

flow chart /ˈ. ./ also **flow di·a·gram** /ˈ. ,../ n. [C] a drawing that uses shapes and ARROWS to show how a series of actions or parts of a system are connected with or related to each other

flow·er[1] /ˈflaʊɚ/ n. **1** [C] the colored part of a plant or tree that produces seeds or fruit: *Amelia was holding a huge bouquet of flowers.* **2** [C] a plant that is grown for the beauty of this part: *Mrs. Coulter planted a few flowers in her front yard.* **3 in flower** a plant or tree that is in flower has flowers on it: *Buy plants with buds rather than ones that are in flower.* **4 the flower of sth** LITERARY the best or most perfect part of something: *The flower of the nation's youth was lost in the war.*

flower[2] v. [I] **1** to produce flowers: *Hardly any of the gladioli I planted actually flowered.* **2** FORMAL to develop and reach a high level of achievement: *Communal living flowered briefly in the 1960s.*

flower ar·rang·ing /ˈ.. ,../ n. [U] the art of arranging flowers in an attractive way

flow·er·bed, flower bed /ˈflaʊɚˌbɛd/ n. [C] an area of ground in which flowers are grown

flower child /ˈ.. ,./ n. plural **flower children** [C] a young person in the 1960s and 1970s who wanted peace and love in society

flow·ered /ˈflaʊɚd/ adj. decorated with pictures of flowers: *a flowered dress* —see picture at PATTERN[1]

flow·er·et /ˈflaʊɚət, flaʊəˈrɛt/ n. [C] a FLORET (1)

flower girl /ˈ.. ,./ n. [C] a young girl who carries flowers in a wedding ceremony —compare BRIDESMAID

flow·er·ing /ˈflaʊərɪŋ/ n. **the flowering of sth** a successful period in the development of something: *Reforms paved the way for a flowering of democracy in Eastern Europe.*

flow·er·pot /ˈflaʊɚˌpɑt/ n. [C] a pot in which you grow plants

flower pow·er /ˈ.. ,../ n. [U] the idea that peace and love are the most important things in life and can change the way people live. This idea was common among young people in the 1960s and 1970s.

flow·er·y /ˈflaʊəri/ adj. **1** decorated with pictures of flowers: *flowery fabrics* **2** flowery speech or writing uses complicated and rare words instead of simple clear language: *a flowery description*

flow·ing /ˈfloʊɪŋ/ adj. [usually before noun] moving, curving, or hanging gracefully: *long, flowing white hair* | *the flowing lines of the car's design*

flown /floʊn/ v. the past participle of FLY[1]

fl. oz. n. the written abbreviation of FLUID OUNCE

flu /flu/ n. [U] a common infectious disease that makes your throat sore, makes it difficult for you to breathe, gives you a fever, and makes you feel very tired; INFLUENZA: *Flu shots are recommended for people 55 and older.* | *Arlene has the flu.* | *Glen is home sick with the flu.*

flub /flʌb/ v. flubbed, flubbing [T] INFORMAL to make a mistake or do something badly: *Several cast members flubbed their lines.*

flub up phr. v. [I] INFORMAL to make a mistake or do something badly: *You can totally flub up by missing just one step.*

fluc·tu·ate /ˈflʌktʃueɪt/ v. [I] to change very often, especially from a high level to a low one and back again: *The state's income from sales taxes fluctuates with the economy.* | [+ **between**] *Pearce's writing style fluctuates between the conversational and the strictly formal.* | [**fluctuate from sth to sth**] *McWhirter's weight fluctuates from 265 to 285 pounds.* | **fluctuate widely/greatly/wildly** *Stock prices fluctuated wildly in the following weeks.*

fluc·tu·a·tion /ˌflʌktʃuˈeɪʃən/ n. [C,U] a sudden change in the amount, value, or price of something: *price fluctuations* | [+ **in**] *These plants are affected by fluctuations in temperature.*

flue /flu/ n. [C] a pipe through which smoke or heat from a fire can pass out of a building: *a chimney flue*

flue·gel·horn /ˈflugəlˌhɔrn/ n. [C] another spelling of FLUGELHORN

flu·ent /ˈfluənt/ adj. **1** able to speak a language very well: [+ **in**] *Sutherland is fluent in French.* **2 fluent French/Japanese etc.** someone who speaks fluent French etc. speaks it like a person from that country: *They were surprised when I gave my speech in fluent Chinese.* **3** speaking, writing, or playing a musical instrument confidently and without long pauses: *Johansson is a fluent and expressive fiddler.* —**fluently** adv. —**fluency** n. [U]

fluff[1] /flʌf/ n. [U] **1** something that is pretty or interesting, but not really serious or important: *The magazine is a mix of fashion, fluff, and some serious journalism.* **2** small soft light pieces of thread or dust that have come from clothing or other materials: *fluff under the bed* **3** soft light hair or feathers, especially from a young bird or animal —compare DOWN[5] (1)

fluff[2] v. [T] also **fluff up, fluff out 1** to make something soft appear larger by shaking or brushing it: *Fluff the couscous with a fork.* | *We made the bed and fluffed up the pillows.* **2** if a bird fluffs its feathers, it raises them and makes itself look bigger

fluff·y /'flʌfi/ adj. **fluffier, fluffiest 1** made of or covered with something soft and light, such as wool, hair, or feathers: *a fluffy little kitten* | *He had fluffy white hair.* **2** food that is fluffy is made soft and light by shaking, or beating so that air is mixed into it: *Mix the butter and sugar until fluffy.* | *a light, fluffy cheesecake* —**fluffiness** n. [U]

flu·gel·horn /'flugəl,hɔrn/ n. [C] a musical instrument similar to a TRUMPET

flu·id[1] /'fluɪd/ n. [C,U] a liquid: *Be sure and drink plenty of fluids.* | *brake fluid* **body/bodily fluids** (=liquids that come from your body, such as blood or URINE)

fluid[2] adj. **1** fluid movements are relaxed and graceful: *Clark throws with a fluid motion.* **2** having a moving, flowing quality: *The sculptures are admired for their round shapes and fluid lines.* | *a fluid guitar solo* **3** [not before noun] likely to change often, or able to change: *Our plans for the project are still somewhat fluid.* —**fluidity** /flu'ɪdəti/ n. [U]

fluid ounce /,.. '. / n. [C] *written abbreviation* **fl. oz.** a unit for measuring liquids, equal to $\frac{1}{16}$ of a PINT or 0.0296 liters

fluke /fluk/ n. [C] **1** INFORMAL something that only happens because of chance or luck: *We wanted to show that beating Arizona State was not just a fluke.* **2** TECHNICAL one of the two flat parts of a WHALE's tail —**fluky** adj.

flume /flum/ n. [C] a long narrow structure built for water to slide down, used to move water or LOGS from one place to another or for people to slide down for fun

flum·mox /'flʌməks/ v. [T usually passive] to completely confuse someone: *I was totally flummoxed by his last question.*

flung /flʌŋ/ v. the past tense and past participle of FLING[1]

flunk /flʌŋk/ v. INFORMAL **1** [I,T] to fail a test or class: *Tony flunked chemistry last semester.* | *Yesterday I took my driving test and flunked – for the sixth time.* **2** [T] to give someone low grades on a test or for a class so that they fail it: *She didn't do any of the work, so I flunked her.*

flunk out phr. v. [I] INFORMAL to be forced to leave a school or college because your work is not good enough: [+ of] *Leo flunked out of Yale in his junior year.*

flun·ky /'flʌŋki/ n. plural **flunkies** [C] INFORMAL **1** someone who does the boring or physical work that someone else tells them to do: *the office flunky* **2** DISAPPROVING someone who is always with an important person and treats them with too much respect

flu·o·res·cent /flu'rɛsənt, flɔ-/ adj. **1** fluorescent colors are very bright: *a fluorescent pink T-shirt* **2 fluorescent light/lamp** a light that contains a gas-filled tube that produces a very bright light when electricity is passed through it **3** TECHNICAL a fluorescent substance or something containing a fluorescent substance produces light when electricity passes through it —**fluorescence** n. [U]

fluor·i·date /'flɔrə,deɪt, 'flu-/ v. [T usually passive] to add fluoride to water in order to protect people's teeth —**fluoridation** /,flɔrə'deɪʃən/ n. [U]

fluor·ide /'flɔraɪd/ n. [U] a chemical that helps to protect teeth against decay

fluor·ine /'flɔrin, 'flu-/ n. [U] *symbol* **F** a chemical substance that is an ELEMENT and is usually in the form of a poisonous gas

fluor·o·car·bon /,flɔrou'karbən, 'flɔrou,karbən/ n. [C] any chemical that contains the substances fluorine and CARBON (1) —see also CFC

flur·ry /'flɜi, 'flʌri/ n. plural **flurries 1** [C usually singular] an occasion when there is suddenly a lot of activity for a short period of time: [+ of] *After his statement, Orr's office received a flurry of phone calls.* **2** [usually plural] a small amount of snow that falls: *Colder temperatures and snow flurries are expected tonight.*

flush[1] /flʌʃ/ v. **1** [I,T] if you flush a toilet or if it flushes, you make water go through it to clean it: *People who neglect to flush public toilets may be fined.* | *I can't get the toilet to flush.* | *Joe flushed the dead goldfish down the toilet.* **2** [I] to become red in the face: *Flushing slightly, Lesley looked away.* **3** [T] also **flush out** to clean something by forcing water or another liquid through it: *Drinking water after exercise flushes out the wastes released from the muscles.* | *Deep watering flushes salts from the soil around the plant's roots.*

flush sb ↔ out phr. v. [T] to make someone leave the place where they are hiding: *Police used tear gas to flush out the gunman.*

flush[2] n. **1 a flush of pride/embarrassment etc.** a sudden feeling of pride, excitement etc.: *The hoax caused a flush of embarrassment to a leading newspaper.* **2 the (first) flush of youth/success etc.** LITERARY the beginning of a period of time when something is still new and exciting: *The family bought a new house and car in the first flush of affluence.* **3** [C] the act of flushing a toilet: *The average toilet uses 5 gallons of water per flush.* **4** [singular] a red color that appears on your face or body, especially because you are embarrassed, sick, or excited **5** [C] if someone playing a game of cards has a flush, they have a set of cards that are all of the same SUIT[1] (4)

flush[3] adj. **1** if two surfaces are flush, they are at exactly the same level, so that the place where they meet is flat: [+ with] *Make sure that the cupboard is flush with the wall.* **2** INFORMAL if someone or an organization is flush, they have plenty of money: *Jamie has $600 saved; Adam isn't quite so flush.*

flush[4] adv. **1** fitting together so that the place where two surfaces meet is flat: *The door should fit flush into its frame.* **2** directly onto something: *Williams was hit flush on the helmet by a fastball.*

flushed /flʌʃt/ adj. **1** red in the face: *Nona was feverish and flushed.* | [+ with] *Her face was flushed with pride.* **2 flushed with success/excitement** excited and eager because you have achieved something: *Charles was flushed with pride.*

flus·tered /'flʌstəd/ adj. feeling confused and nervous: *Jay got all flustered and forgot what he was going to say.* —**fluster** v. [T]

flute /flut/ n. [C] **1** a musical instrument shaped like a pipe, that you play by holding it across your lips, blowing into it, and pressing KEYS to change the notes **2** also **champagne flute** a tall narrow glass used for some alcoholic drinks, especially CHAMPAGNE

flut·ed /'flutɪd/ adj. decorated with long narrow upright curves or folds: *a fluted cake pan*

flut·ist /'flutɪst/ n. [C] someone who plays the flute

flut·ter[1] /'flʌtə/ v. **1** [I,T] if a bird or insect flutters its wings or if its wings flutter, its wings move quickly and lightly up and down: *Butterflies fluttered from flower to flower.* **2** [I] to wave or move gently in the air: *Flags from a hundred nations fluttered in the breeze.* **3** [I,T] if your heart or your stomach flutters, you feel very excited or nervous **4** if your heart flutters, it beats in a rapid or irregular way **5 flutter your eyelashes (at sb)** if a woman flutters her eyelashes at a man, she uses her sexual attractiveness to influence him

flut·ter[2] n. **1** [C usually singular] a fluttering movement: *a flutter of wings* **2** [singular] the state of being nervous, confused, or excited: *Laurie was in a flutter of excitement at the idea of a party.* **3** [C] TECHNICAL an irregular heart beat **4** [U] TECHNICAL a shaking movement that stops a machine from working correctly

flu·vi·al /ˈfluːviəl/ *adj.* TECHNICAL relating to or produced by rivers

flux /flʌks/ *n.* [U] **be in (a state of) flux** to be changing a lot so that you cannot be sure what will happen: *Fashion is always in flux.* | *The country's economy is in a state of flux.*

fly¹ /flaɪ/ *v. past tense* **flew** *past participle* **flown**
1 through air [I,T] to move through the air, or to make something do this: *Fighter jets fly at incredibly high speeds.* | *Flocks of seagulls flew overhead.* | *Some kids were flying kites in the park.* | *Papers were flying around in the wind.*
2 travel [I] to travel by airplane: *Are you going to fly or drive?* | *We're flying nonstop from Milwaukee to Orlando.*
3 airline [I,T] to use a particular AIRLINE or use a particular type of ticket when flying: *I flew Aeroflot out of Moscow.* | *We usually fly coach.*
4 pilot [I,T] to be the pilot of an airplane: *Brenda's learning to fly.* | *Stan flew helicopters in Vietnam.*
5 send goods/people [T] to carry or send goods or people by airplane: [**fly sth into/out of**] *Food and medicine are being flown into the area.*
6 over/across an area [T] to fly an airplane over a large area: *Lindbergh was the first man to fly the Atlantic.*
7 move [I always + adv./prep.] to suddenly move somewhere quickly: [+ **down/across/out of etc.**] *Timmy flew down the stairs and out the door.* | [+ **open/shut/back etc.**] *The door suddenly flew open.*
8 time if time flies, it passes very quickly: *Is it 5:30 already? Boy, time sure flies!* | *Last week just seemed to fly past.*
9 **be flying high** to be very successful, and often to feel very happy about it: *The Rams are flying high after winning the Super Bowl.*
10 **send sb/sth flying** to make someone or something move through the air, especially after being hit by something: *A glass beaker shattered and sent glass flying around the classroom.*
11 **go flying** to suddenly move through the air, especially after being hit by something or someone: *He tripped over a crack in the sidewalk and went flying.*
12 hair/coat [I] if your hair, coat etc. is flying, it moves freely and loosely in the air: *Her long hair was flying in the wind.*
13 flag [I,T] if a flag flies, or if you fly it, it is fastened to a pole or a building, ship etc.: *The ship is flying the Dutch flag.* | *Banners were flying in the breeze.*
14 **fly off the handle** INFORMAL to suddenly become angry, especially about something that does not seem very important: *Linda called me back and apologized for flying off the handle.*
15 **fly into a temper/rage** to suddenly become extremely angry: *He flew into a rage and demanded his money back.*
16 **rumors/accusations etc. are flying** if RUMORS, ACCUSATIONS etc. are flying about something, a lot of people are saying things about it: *Rumors are flying around the capital about a possible military takeover.*
17 plan [I] INFORMAL a plan that will fly is good or useful: *Not everyone is convinced the home banking idea is going to fly.*
18 **let fly** INFORMAL **a)** to suddenly say something angrily to someone: [+ **with**] *Hayes let fly with some unprintable swear words.* **b)** to suddenly attack someone: [+ **with**] *The boys let fly with a torrent of rocks.*
19 **fly in the face of sth** to be the opposite of what most people think is reasonable, sensible, or normal: *Eysenck's claim flies in the face of all the evidence.*
20 **go fly a kite** SPOKEN said when you want someone to go away because they are being annoying

21 **fly a kite** to make a suggestion to see what people will think of it
22 **fly the coop** INFORMAL to leave or escape from a place where you were not free: *All my children have flown the coop now.*
23 escape [T] OLD-FASHIONED to leave somewhere in order to escape: *They were forced to fly the country in 1939.* —see also **as the crow flies** (CROW¹ (3)), **sparks fly** (SPARK¹ (7))
fly at sb also **fly into** sb *phr. v.* [T] to suddenly rush toward someone because you are very angry with them: *The old man flew at her in rage.*

fly² *n. plural* **flies** [C]
1 insect a small flying insect with two wings: *The flies were swarming around the garbage cans.* —see picture at INSECT
2 pants the part at the front of a pair of pants that you can open: *Your fly is unzipped.*
3 baseball a fly ball
4 fishing a hook that is made to look like an insect, used for catching fish
5 **on the fly** while you are doing something else: *Sometimes you have to make decisions on the fly.*
6 **sb wouldn't hurt a fly** SPOKEN used to say that someone is very gentle and is not likely to hurt anyone: *Duane wouldn't hurt a fly. I can't imagine him fighting in a war.*
7 **drop/die like flies** INFORMAL used to say that a lot of people are becoming sick, or that a lot of people are dying: *Napoleon's under-dressed soldiers died like flies in the winter of 1812.*
8 **a fly in the ointment** INFORMAL the thing that spoils something and prevents it from being successful
9 **be a fly on the wall** to be able to watch what happens without other people knowing that you are there: *I wish I'd been a fly on the wall during that conversation.*

fly³ *v. past tense and past participle* **flied** [I] to hit a baseball high into the air, especially so that the ball is caught by the other team: *Harper flied out to left field* (=the ball was caught so that Harper was out).

fly⁴ *adj.* SLANG very fashionable, attractive, relaxed etc.; COOL: *Mmm, that Sharlene is one fly girl.*

fly ball /ˌ. ˈ./ *n.* [C] a ball that has been hit high into the air in a baseball game

fly·boy /ˈflaɪbɔɪ/ *n. plural* **flyboys** [C] OLD-FASHIONED a pilot

fly·by /ˈflaɪbaɪ/ *n. plural* **flybys** [C] **1** an occasion when a space vehicle or SATELLITE passes a PLANET: *During the flyby, the spacecraft will measure gases in the atmosphere.* **2** an occasion when a plane flies over a particular position

fly-by-night /ˈ. . ˌ./ *adj.* [only before noun] INFORMAL a fly-by-night organization cannot be trusted and is not likely to exist very long

fly·er /ˈflaɪɚ/ *n.* [C] a FLIER

fly fish·ing /ˈ. ˌ../ *n.* [U] the sport of fishing in a river or lake, using special hooks that are made to look like insects, that you move through the water

fly·ing¹ /ˈflaɪ-ɪŋ/ *adj.* [only before noun] **1** able to fly: *a flying insect* **2 with flying colors** if you do something with flying colors, you are very successful at it: *The President passed his health exam with flying colors.* **3 get off to a flying start** to begin something such as a job or race very well **4 a flying jump/leap** a long high jump made while you are running **5 not give a flying fuck (about sb/sth)** SPOKEN, TABOO to not care at all about someone or something

fly·ing² *n.* [U] the activity of traveling by plane or of being a pilot: *She's afraid of flying.*

flying but·tress /ˌ.. ˈ../ *n.* [C] part of an ARCH¹ (1) that sticks out from and supports the top of an outside wall of a large building such as a church

flying fish /ˌ.. ˈ./ *n.* [C] a tropical fish that can jump out of the water

flying fox /ˌ.. ˈ./ *n.* [C] a FRUIT BAT

flying sau·cer /ˌ.. ˈ../ *n.* [C] a space vehicle shaped like a plate, that some people believe carries creatures from another world; UFO

fly leaf /ˈ. ./ *n.* [C] a page at the beginning or end of a book, on which there is usually no printing

fly·o·ver /ˈflaɪˌoʊvə/ n. [C] a group of planes that fly close together for people to watch on a special occasion

fly·pa·per /ˈflaɪˌpeɪpə/ n. [U] paper that is covered with a sticky substance and is used to catch and kill flies

fly·speck /ˈflaɪspɛk/ n. [C] **1** something that is very small: *The islands are just flyspecks in the ocean.* **2** a small spot of waste matter from a fly

fly·swat·ter /ˈflaɪˌswɑtə/ n. [C] a plastic square fastened to a long handle, used for killing flies

fly·weight /ˈflaɪweɪt/ n. [C] a BOXER who belongs to the lightest class of BOXERs and weighs under 112 pounds

fly·wheel /ˈflaɪwil/ n. [C] a heavy wheel that keeps a machine working at a steady speed because of its weight

FM n. [U] a system of broadcasting radio programs which produces a clear sound —compare AM

foal[1] /foʊl/ n. [C] a very young horse

foal[2] v. [I] to give birth to a foal

foam[1] /foʊm/ n. [U] **1** a lot of very small BUBBLES on the surface of something: *White foam from the top of the waves left lines on the beach.* **2** a light solid substance filled with many very small BUBBLES of air: *foam packing material* | *a dirty foam mattress* **3** a soft liquid substance made of very small BUBBLES: *The fire extinguisher uses a chemical foam rather than water.* —**foamy** adj. —see also STYROFOAM

foam[2] v. [I] **1** to produce foam: *Beat the cream until it foams.* **2** foam at the mouth **a)** to have a lot of very small BUBBLES come out of your mouth because you are sick **b)** to be very angry: *Some senators are foaming at the mouth over what they say is obscene art.*

foam rub·ber /ˌ. ˈ../ n. [U] soft rubber full of air BUBBLES that is used in PILLOWs, chair seats, beds etc.

fob[1] /fɑb/ v. **fobbed, fobbing**
fob sth off phr. v. [T] to get rid of something that is broken or of poor quality by tricking someone: [**fob sth off on sb**] *Don't let them fob off a cheap brand on you.*

fob[2] n. [C] a short chain or piece of cloth to which a fob watch is fastened

fob watch /ˈ. ./ n. [C] a watch that fits into a pocket, or is pinned to a woman's dress

fo·cac·cia /foʊˈkɑtʃə/ n. [U] a type of Italian bread

fo·cal length /ˈfoʊkəl ˌlɛŋθ/ n. [C] TECHNICAL the distance between the center of a LENS and the focal point

fo·cal point /ˈfoʊkəl ˌpɔɪnt/ n. **1** the thing, activity, or person in a situation that is the most interesting or most important: *The kitchen is usually the focal point of the home.* **2** TECHNICAL the point on a LENS or a mirror where light RAYs meet

focus

in focus   out of focus

s w **fo·cus**[1] /ˈfoʊkəs/ v. [I,T] **1** to pay special attention to a particular person or thing instead of others: *He stared out the window for a moment, trying to focus his thoughts.* | [**+ on**] *The gallery's show focuses on works painted after 1945.* | *The recent civil war has focused attention on the southern region.* **2** to change the position of the LENS on a camera, TELESCOPE etc., so that you can see something clearly: [**focus (sth) on sth**] *He focused his binoculars on the*

building opposite. **3** if your eyes focus, or if you focus your eyes, you become able to see something clearly **4** if you focus beams of light or if they focus, they pass through a LENS and meet at a point

focus[2] n. **1** [C usually singular] a subject or situation that people pay special attention to: *The organization has a simple focus – keeping kids in school.* | [**+ of**] *The war in the former Yugoslavia became the focus of worldwide attention.* | *The company's focus is on growth.* **2** [U] special attention that is given to one particular subject or situation: [**+ on**] *Despite the merger, the company plans to keep its central focus on the music industry.* | *The case has brought the problem of child abuse sharply into focus* (=made people pay attention to it). **3** in focus/out of focus if a photograph, camera, TELESCOPE etc. is in focus, the edges of the things you see are clear; if it is out of focus, the edges are not clear **4** [C] TECHNICAL plural **foci** /ˈfoʊsaɪ/ the point where beams of light or waves of sound meet after their direction has been changed

fo·cused /ˈfoʊkəst/ adj. paying careful attention to what you are doing, in a way that shows you are determined to succeed: *As a player, she's a lot more focused this year.*

focus group /ˈ.. ˌ./ n. [C] a group of people who are asked their opinions about a particular product or subject

fod·der /ˈfɑdə/ n. [U] **1** something for people to talk or write about: [**+ for**] *Gangsters have been fodder for movies virtually since movies began.* **2** food for farm animals —see also CANNON FODDER

foe /foʊ/ n. [C] LITERARY an enemy

fog[1] /fɑg, fɔg/ n. **1** [C,U] thick cloudy air near the ground that is difficult to see through: *Thick fog is making driving conditions hazardous.* —compare MIST[1] (1) —see picture on page 1333 **2** in a fog INFORMAL confused and unable to think clearly: *Stillman seems to be in a fog.*

fog[2] v. **fogged, fogging 1** also **fog up** [I,T] if glass fogs or becomes fogged, it becomes covered in very small drops of water so you cannot see through it: *My glasses fogged up as soon as I stepped outside.* **2** be fogged in to be completely surrounded by fog: *Kennedy Airport was fogged in, so we landed in Newark.*

fog·bound /ˈfɑgbaʊnd/ adj. prevented from traveling or working normally because of fog: *Interstate 5 was fogbound early Monday morning.*

fo·gey, fogy /ˈfoʊgi/ n. plural **fogeys** or **fogies** [C] DISAPPROVING someone who is old-fashioned and does not like change: *Don't listen to that old fogey.*

fog·gy /ˈfɑgi/ adj. **foggier, foggiest 1** not clear because of fog: *a damp and foggy morning* **2 not have the foggiest (idea)** SPOKEN said in order to emphasize that you do not know something: *I don't have the foggiest idea what his address is.* —**foggily** adv. —**fogginess** n. [U]

Fog·gy Bot·tom /ˌfɑgi ˈbɑtəm/ n. [U] the part of Washington, D.C. where the offices of the U.S. State Department are

fog·horn /ˈfɑghɔrn/ n. [C] **1** a loud horn used by ships in fog to warn other ships of their position **2 like a foghorn** HUMOROUS very loud: *He has a voice like a foghorn.*

fog light also **fog lamp** /ˈ. ./ n. [C usually plural] a strong light on the front of a car that helps drivers to see in fog —see picture on page 427

foi·ble /ˈfɔɪbəl/ n. [C usually plural] FORMAL a habit that someone has that is slightly strange or silly: *Her act is full of funny observations on human foibles.*

foie gras /ˌfwɑ ˈgrɑ/ n. [U] the LIVER of a duck or GOOSE, usually eaten as a PÂTÉ

foil[1] /fɔɪl/ n. **1** [U] metal sheets that are thin like paper, used for wrapping food: *Cover the turkey with foil and bake in a hot oven.* **2 be a foil to sb/sth** to make the good qualities of someone or something more noticeable, especially by being very different

F

from them: *Roasted red peppers are a sweet foil to the slightly bitter spinach.* **3** [C] a light narrow sword used in FENCING (1)

foil² *v.* [T often passive] to prevent someone from doing something they had planned to do, especially to prevent someone from doing something illegal: *The escape attempt was foiled by police guards.*

foist /fɔɪst/ *v.*

foist sth **on/upon** sb *phr. v.* [T] to make someone accept something they do not want: *Don't try to foist a major change on your employees without preparing them first.*

-fold /fould/ *suffix* **1** [in adjectives] relating to a particular number of kinds: *The purpose of a window is twofold: to let light in, and to let people see out.* **2** [in adverbs] a particular number of times: *The value of the house has increased fourfold* (=it is now worth four times as much as before).

fold

fold

roll up

F

SW
3 3

fold¹ /fould/ *v.*

1 **bend** [T] to bend a piece of paper, cloth etc. so that one part covers another part: *Doug folded the check and put it in his wallet.* | *Roll the dough out on a floured board and fold it in half.* | **[fold sth under/over/down etc.]** *Fold the hem under and press it with an iron.* —see picture on page 424

2 **make sth smaller/neater** [T] also **fold up** to fold something several times so that it makes a small neat shape: *Fold up your clothes, don't just throw them on the floor!* | *The blankets were folded at the bottom of the bed.*

3 **furniture etc.** [I,T] if something such as a piece of furniture folds or you fold it, you make it smaller or move it to a different position by bending it or closing it: *The chairs fold flat for easy storage.* | **[fold sth forward/up/down etc.]** *Fold the seat forward so Becky can get in.* | **[+ away/up/down etc.]** *The computer screen folds down over the keyboard.*

4 **fold your arms** to bend your arms so they are resting across your chest: *George stood silently with his arms folded.* —see picture at ARM¹

5 **business** [I] if a business folds, it fails and is not able to continue: *One of the most important newspapers in the region has folded.*

6 **cover** [T] to cover something, especially by wrapping it in material: **[fold sth in sth]** *Some old pennies were folded in the handkerchief.*

7 **fold sb in your arms** LITERARY to hold someone closely by putting your arms around them

fold sth **in/into** *phr. v.* [T] to gently mix another substance into a mixture when you are preparing food: *Fold in the sugar and whisk until stiff.* | *Whip the cream and fold it into the cooled custard.*

fold² *n.* [C]

1 **loose skin/material** [usually plural] the folds in material, skin etc. are the loose parts that hang over other parts of it: *He hid the knife in the folds of his robe.* | *Camels have an extra fold of skin on their eyelids to keep out the sand.*

2 **line** a line made in paper, cloth etc. when you fold one part of it over another: *Bend back the cardboard and cut along the fold.*

3 **the fold** the group of people that you belong to or have the same beliefs as: *Democrats have to find some*

way to make voters **return to the fold** (=vote for them again). | *With Jordan in the fold, it is likely that coach Phil Jackson will return to the team.*

4 **sheep** LITERARY a small area of a field where sheep are kept for safety

5 **rock** TECHNICAL a bend in layers of rock, caused by movements under the earth

fold·a·way /ˈfouldəˌweɪ/ *adj.* [only before noun] a foldaway bed, table etc. can be folded so that it uses less space

fold·er /ˈfouldə/ *n.* [C] **1** a large folded piece of hard paper or plastic, in which you keep loose paper **2** a picture on a computer screen that shows you where a FILE is kept: *The program allows you to group related documents in folders.*

SW
2

fold·ing /ˈfouldɪŋ/ *adj.* [only before noun] **1** a folding bicycle, bed, chair etc. can be folded so that it is smaller and easier to carry or store **2** **folding money** HUMOROUS paper money: *You'll need folding money to play any of the games of chance.*

fo·li·age /ˈfouliɪdʒ/ *n.* [U] the leaves of a plant

fo·li·o /ˈfouliou/ *n. plural* **folios** [C] TECHNICAL **1** a book made with very large sheets of paper **2** a single numbered sheet of paper from a book

folk¹ /fouk/ *n.* **1** also **folks** [plural] INFORMAL people: *Most folk around here are pretty friendly.* | *Some old folks just shouldn't be driving anymore.* | *Congressmen are very aware that they need to please the folks back home.* **2** **folks** SPOKEN said when you are talking to a group of people in a friendly way: *Hi folks, it's good to see you all here tonight!* **3** **sb's folks a)** your parents: *I need to call my folks sometime this weekend.* **b)** all of your family, including AUNTS, UNCLES, grandparents etc.: *Betty's folks are having a family reunion next summer.* **4** **country/city/farming etc. folk(s)** [plural] INFORMAL people who live in a particular area or do a particular kind of work: *The ranch serves city folks who want to try cowboy life.* **5** [U] FOLK MUSIC

SW
1 1
3

folk² *adj.* [only before noun] **1** folk art, dance, knowledge etc. is traditional and typical of the ordinary people who live in a particular area: *folk tales* | *Spanish folk songs* **2** **folk medicine/remedy** a traditional type of medical treatment that uses plants etc. rather than modern scientific methods

folk dance /ˈ. ˌ./ *n.* [C] a traditional dance from a particular area, or a piece of music for this dance —**folk dancer** *n.* [C] —**folk dancing** *n.* [U]

folk he·ro /ˈ. ˌ../ *n.* [C] someone who people in a particular place admire very much because of something they have done

folk·ie /ˈfouki/ *n.* [C] INFORMAL someone who sings or who likes folk music

folk·lore /ˈfouk-lɔr/ *n.* [U] the traditional stories, customs etc. of the ordinary people of a particular area: *Hawaiian folklore tells of the movements of the volcano goddess Pele.* —**folkloric** *adj.*

folk mu·sic /ˈ. ˌ../ *n.* [U] **1** a style of popular music in which people sing and play GUITARS, without any electronic equipment **2** traditional music that has been played by the ordinary people in a particular area

folk·sy /ˈfouksi/ *adj.* INFORMAL **1** friendly and informal: *The town of Colville has a folksy charm.* **2** in a style that is typical of traditional country speech or customs: *a funny folksy radio show*

folk·way /ˈfoukweɪ/ *n.* [C usually plural] the way a group of people who live in a particular area behave: *The book looks with affection at Southern folkways.*

fol·li·cle /ˈfɑlɪkəl/ *n.* [C] one of the small holes in the skin that hairs grow from

fol·low /ˈfɑlou/ *v.*

SW
1 1

1 **come behind** [I,T] to walk, drive, run etc. behind or after someone else: *I'll drive, and you can follow us.* | *The president came in, followed by a crowd of photographers.* | *You go ahead, I'll follow later.*

2 **happen after** [I,T] to happen immediately after something else: *There was a major increase in immigration in the years following World War I.* | *The huge fire that followed the 1906 San Francisco* *earthquake virtually destroyed the city.* | *Thunderstorms today are likely to be **followed by** more rain tonight and tomorrow.* | *The wedding is at 2:30, with a reception **to follow**.* | *In the days/weeks that **followed**, the police received hundreds of calls.* —see also FOLLOWING[1]

3 [in order to watch sb] [T] to go closely behind someone in order to watch them and find out where they go: *Marlowe looked over his shoulder to make sure no one was following him.*

4 [come after] [I,T] to come immediately after something else, for example in a book or a series of things: *A full report follows this chapter.* | *In English the letter "Q" is always **followed by** a "U."*

5 follow instructions/rules/advice etc. to do something according to the instructions, rules or instructions that say how it should be done: *If you're going to live in my house, you have to follow my rules.* | *Investors who followed Murphy's advice made a large profit.* | *If you don't **follow** the recipe **to the letter** (=exactly), the cake won't rise.*

6 follow the signs/directions to go in the direction that the signs say you should go or that someone has told you to go: *Go in the double doors and follow the signs down the hallway.*

7 [go in a particular direction] [T] **a)** to continue along a particular road, river etc.: *Follow the Iceberg Lake trail until you reach the shore.* **b)** to go in the same direction as something else, especially something that is very close: *The road follows the river for the next six miles.*

8 [do same thing] [I,T] to do the same thing or the same type of thing as someone else: [**follow sb into sth**] *Cox's son Robert followed him into the family business.* | *He praised Suu Kyi, and encouraged others to **follow her example** (=do the same things as her) of non-violence.* | *When Allied Stores reduced their prices, other companies were forced to **follow suit** (=do the same thing).*

9 a hard/tough act to follow SPOKEN someone or something that is so good that it will be difficult for the next person or thing to be as good or as successful: *Muriel knew her glamorous older sister would always be a hard act to follow.*

10 follow (in) sb's footsteps to do the same job as someone else, especially a member of your family: *My father never pressured me to follow in his footsteps, but I know he was disappointed when I dropped out of college.*

11 [understand] [I,T] to understand something such as an explanation or story: *Sorry, **I don't follow you**.* | *The plot was pretty **hard to follow**.*

12 [be interested] [T] to be interested in something, especially a sport, and pay attention to it: *Do you follow baseball at all?*

13 [believe/obey] [T] to believe in and obey a particular set of religious or political ideas, or a leader who teaches these ideas: *They still follow the teachings of Gandhi.*

14 it follows (that) FORMAL used in order to show that something must be true as a result of something else that is true: *Interest rates are going down, so it follows that house sales will improve.*

15 follow a trend/pattern/course etc. to continue to happen or develop in a particular way: *In Australia, the weather follows a fairly predictable pattern.*

16 [be about] [T] to show or describe someone's life or a series of events, for example in a movie or book: *The novel follows a group of students during the sixties.*

17 [think about/study] [T] to study or think about a particular idea or subject and try to find out more about it: *Several biotech companies are following the same line of research.*

18 [watch carefully] [T] to carefully watch someone move: *It was one of those paintings where the eyes follow you.* | *The dogs in the pens perked up and followed her with their eyes as she passed.*

19 as follows FORMAL used to introduce a list of names, instructions etc.: *The winners in the color photography category are as follows: J. Robinson, D. Smith, R. Lewis.*

20 follow your instincts to do something in the way

that you feel is best: *If you feel uncomfortable with a guy, follow your instincts and leave.*

21 follow your nose INFORMAL **a)** to do something in the way that you feel is right: *I don't really have a career plan – I just follow my nose.* **b)** to go straight forward: *Turn left on 6th Avenue, then just follow your nose.*

22 follow your heart to do what you most want to do and what will make you happy: *Her father encouraged her to follow her heart, and run competitively.*

23 follow the herd/crowd to do the same thing as other people, without really thinking about what you want to do

follow along *phr. v.* [I] to read a book or written document while someone says or sings the words in it out loud: [+ **with**] *Jurors were given a typed transcript to follow along with the tape.*

follow sb **around** *phr. v.* [T] to keep following someone everywhere they go: *Jamie follows Andrew around everywhere.*

follow through *phr. v.* **1** [I,T **follow** sth ↔ **through**] to do what needs to be done to complete something or make it successful: *The college will make every effort to follow the proposal through.* | [+ **on**] *The airline apparently didn't follow through on its promise.* | [+ **with**] *If thousands of viewers complain and follow through with a boycott, you can be sure the networks will change.* **2** [I] to continue moving your arm after you hit the ball in tennis, GOLF etc. —see also FOLLOW-THROUGH

follow up *phr. v.* [I,T **follow** sth ↔ **up**] to find out more about something, or to do more about something: [+ **on**] *Did Jay ever follow up on that job possibility in Tucson?* | [**follow sth up with sth**] *Follow up the letters with a phone call.* —see also FOLLOW-UP[1]

fol·low·er /ˈfɑloʊɚ/ *n.* [C] someone who believes or supports a particular leader, team, or set of ideas: *Duke lost the governor's race, but his followers want him to run for president.* | [+ **of**] *The early followers of Jesus were mostly Jews.*

fol·low·ing[1] /ˈfɑloʊɪŋ/ *adj.* **1 the following day/year/chapter etc.** the day, year, chapter etc. after the one just mentioned: *Once you have given your notice, you only have to pay rent for the following 30 days.* **2 the following example/way etc.** the example, way etc. that will be mentioned next: *Payment may be made in any of the following ways: check, cash, or credit card.* **3 a following wind** TECHNICAL a wind that is blowing in the same direction as a ship, and helps it to move faster —opposite PRECEDING

following[2] *n.* **1** [C usually singular] a group of people who support or admire someone such as a performer: *I was playing in clubs and I'd gotten a following there.* **2 the following** [plural] the people or things that you are going to mention next: *Typical examples of opposites include the following: small and large, cold and hot...*

following[3] *prep.* immediately after an event or as a result of it: *There will be time for questions following the lecture.* | *Thousands of refugees left the country following the outbreak of civil war.*

follow-on /ˈ.. ./ *adj.* [only before noun] done or existing in addition to something or in order to continue something that was done before: *The Land System Survey is a 15-year follow-on program begun in 1985.*

follow-the-lead·er /ˌ.. . ˈ../ *n.* [U] **1** a children's game in which one of the players does actions which all the other players must copy **2** if companies or groups of people play follow-the-leader, they all do something that one of the companies has done: *If one car manufacturer cuts prices, the others usually **play follow-the-leader**.*

follow-through /ˈ.. ˌ./ *n.* [singular] **1** the continued movement of your arm after you have thrown a ball or hit the ball in tennis, GOLF and other sports **2** the things that someone does in order to complete a plan: *The budget covers not only the main project but the follow-through.*

follow-up[1] /ˈ.. ˌ./ *adj.* [only before noun] done in

F

order to find out more or do more about something: *Weiss is doing a follow-up study to his research on children raised in single-parent families.* —see also **follow up** (FOLLOW)

follow-up[2] *n.* **1** [C,U] something that is done to make sure that earlier actions have been successful or effective: *We're fairly sure the data is accurate, but we will be doing a follow-up.* **2** [C] a book, movie, article etc. that comes after another one that has the same subject or characters: *Spielberg says he's planning to do a follow-up next year.*

fol·ly /ˈfɑli/ *n. plural* **follies 1** [C,U] FORMAL a very stupid thing to do: [+ of] *the follies of youth* | *In 1914, President Wilson said it would be folly to enter the war.* **2** [C] LITERARY an unusual building that was built in past times as a decoration, not to be used or lived in **3 Follies** used in the name of a theater show that has dancing, singing, and other types of entertainment: *Agnes was a dancer in the Greenwich Village Follies in the 1920s.*

fo·ment /ˈfoʊmɛnt, foʊˈmɛnt/ *v.* FORMAL **foment war/revolution/unrest etc.** to do something that encourages people to cause a lot of trouble in a society: *The students were accused of fomenting rebellion.* —**fomentation** /ˌfoʊmənˈteɪʃən/ *n.* [U]

fond /fɑnd/ *adj.* **1 be fond of sb** to like someone very much, especially when you have known them for a long time and almost feel love for them: *I haven't seen Ed for a while, but I'm very fond of him.* | *Over the years we've grown very fond of each other.* **2 be fond of sth** to like something, especially something you have liked for a long time: *Aubrey's not very fond of strawberries or grapes.* | *I'd grown fond of Burlington and it was difficult to leave.* **3 fond memories** a memory that makes you happy when you think of it: *I have fond memories of my first trip to Europe.* | *The park brings back fond memories of family gatherings.* **4 be fond of doing sth** to enjoy doing something, and to do it often: *Sue's very fond of hiking and backpacking.* | *"The only reason I make money is so I can give it away," Quigley is fond of saying.* **5** [only before noun] a fond look, smile, action etc. shows you like someone very much: *We wish you a fond farewell.* **6 a fond belief/hope** FORMAL a belief or hope that something will happen, especially something that does not seem likely to happen: *David holds the fond hope that he will be able to put the incident behind him.* —**fondness** *n.* [U] —see also FONDLY

fon·dle /ˈfɑndl/ *v.* [T] **1** DISAPPROVING to touch someone's body in a sexual way: *He reached under her blouse and fondled her breasts.* **2** FORMAL to touch someone or something in a gentle way that shows love: *Jack fondled the silver beads and recited a prayer.*

fond·ly /ˈfɑndli/ *adv.* **1** in a way that shows you like someone or something very much: *Greta smiled fondly at him from across the room.* | *Both sisters spoke fondly of their daredevil brother.* **2 fondly remember/recall** to feel happy when you remember what you like about a person or place: *The Frank brothers fondly recalled the games they played as children.* **3 fondly imagine/believe/hope etc.** FORMAL to believe something that is untrue, hope for something that will probably not happen etc.: *Some people fondly believe that these herbs will cure them.*

fon·due /fɑnˈdu/ *n.* [U] a hot food made of melted cheese or chocolate, into which you DIP small pieces of meat, fruit etc. on the end of a stick or fork

Fon·ga·fa·le /ˈfɔŋɡəˌfɑleɪ/ the capital city of Tuvalu

font /fɑnt/ *n.* [C] **1** a set of letters that are printed or on a computer screen, of a particular size and shape **2** a container for the water used in the ceremony of BAPTISM in a Christian church

food /fud/ *n.* **1** [U] things that people and animals eat, such as vegetables or meat: *The food's great and it's not that expensive.* | *North Korea faces severe food shortages.* **2** [C,U] a particular type of food: *I'd never tried Indian food before.* | *To lose weight, cut down on*

sweet and fatty foods. | *It's a fast food* (=food in a restaurant that is ready immediately) *pasta restaurant.* | *Tim eats way too much junk food* (=food that is not healthy for you). | *There's a health food* (=food that is healthy for you) *store on Lassen Street.* | **cat/dog/fish etc. food** (=food for cats, dogs, fish etc.) **3 food for thought** something that makes you think carefully: *The study on poverty certainly offers food for thought to America's leaders.*

Food and Drug Ad·min·i·stra·tion, the /ˌ. . ˈ. ..ˌ../ —see FDA, THE

food bank /ˈ. ./ *n.* [C] a place that gives food to poor people

food chain /ˈ. ./ *n.* **the food chain 1** animals, insects, and plants considered as a group in which a plant is eaten by an insect or animal, which is then eaten by another animal and so on: *Pollution is having a long-term impact on the food chain in the bay.* **2** the system in society or an organization in which people at each rank have authority and control over the people in the rank below them: *Those higher on the political food chain, such as manufacturers and oil companies, will benefit most.*

food col·or·ing /ˈ. ˌ.../ *n.* [U] a special colored liquid used to give cookies, FROSTING, and other foods a color

food cou·pon /ˈ. ˌ../ *n.* [C] **1** a small piece of paper given to poor people by an organization, that they can use to buy food **2** a FOOD STAMP

food court /ˈ. ./ *n.* [C] the area in a shopping MALL where there are many small restaurants

food drive /ˈ. ./ *n.* [C] an event at a business, school, church etc. at which people can give food in cans to help poor people

food group /ˈ. ./ *n.* [C] one of the groups that types of food are divided into, such as meat, vegetables or milk products: *A balanced diet includes foods from all the food groups.*

food·ie /ˈfudi/ *n.* [C] INFORMAL someone who is very interested in cooking and eating good-quality food

food poi·son·ing /ˈ. ˌ.../ *n.* [U] an illness caused by eating food that contains harmful BACTERIA, in which you usually VOMIT often

food pro·ces·sor /ˈ. ˌ.../ *n.* [C] a piece of electrical equipment for preparing food, that cuts or mixes food very quickly —see picture at KITCHEN

food serv·ice /ˈ. ˌ../ *n.* [U] the department of a school, hospital etc. whose job is to provide food: *Food service officials say that pizza is kids' favorite food.*

food stamp /ˈ. ./ *n.* [C] an official piece of paper that the US government gives to poor people so they can buy food

food·stuff /ˈfudstʌf/ *n.* [C usually plural, U] a word meaning "food," used especially when talking about supplying, producing, or selling food: *Prices of most foodstuffs and consumer goods have gone down.*

fool[1] /ful/ *n.* [C]

1 stupid person a stupid person: *What does that fool think he's doing?* | *Anyone who thinks TV news gives you enough information is a fool.* | *I felt like such a fool when I locked my keys in the car.*

2 make a fool of yourself to do something stupid that you feel embarrassed about later and that makes you seem silly: *I met Sylvester Stallone one time and made a complete fool of myself.*

3 make a fool of sb to deliberately try to make someone seem stupid: *Why did you try to make a fool of me in public?*

4 be no fool/be nobody's fool to be difficult to trick or deceive, because you have a lot of experience and knowledge about something: *Claire is no fool – she knows how to take care of herself.*

5 any fool can do sth SPOKEN used to say that it is very easy to do something or to see that something is true: *Any fool can make a baby, but it takes a real man to raise his children.*

6 entertainer a man whose job was to entertain a king or other powerful person in past times, by doing tricks, singing funny songs etc.

7 play/act the fool to behave in a silly or stupid

F

way: *Don't play the fool with me. You know why I moved away.*

8 be living in a fool's paradise FORMAL to feel happy and satisfied, and believe there are no problems, when in fact this is not true

9 send sb on a fool's errand FORMAL to make someone go somewhere or do something for no good reason —see also APRIL FOOL

fool² *v.* **1** [T] to trick or deceive someone: *Even the art experts were fooled.* | *The recording fooled the enemy about troop movements.* | [**fool sb into doing sth**] *Don't be fooled into buying more insurance than you need.*

SPOKEN PHRASES

2 be fooling yourself to try to make yourself believe something you know is not really true: *You're fooling yourself if you think exercise alone will make you lose weight.* **3 you could have fooled me** said when you do not believe what someone has told you: *"Look, we're doing our best to fix it." "Well, you could have fooled me."* **4 no fooling** used to say that what you have just said is really true, even though it seems unlikely: *They're celebrating Thanksgiving in April. No fooling!* **5 sb is just fooling** used to say that someone is not serious and is only pretending that something is true: *Don't pay any attention to Henry. He's just fooling.*

---

fool around *phr. v.* [I] **1** to spend time doing something that you enjoy: *We spent the day fooling around at the beach.* **2** to waste time by doing things that are not important: *Stop fooling around and start studying!* | *It was an intensive training session – we didn't fool around.* **3** to behave in a silly or careless way: [+ **with**] *Stop fooling around with those scissors before you hurt yourself!* **4** to have a sexual relationship with someone else, especially when you should not: [+ **with**] *Matt thinks his wife is fooling around with someone.*

fool with sth *phr. v.* [T] INFORMAL **1** to do something that could be dangerous or could ruin something: *A hacker had been fooling with the hospital computers.* **2** to touch something or move it, especially when you should not: *Who's been fooling with the volume knob?*

fool³ *adj.* [only before noun] SPOKEN silly or stupid: *What did you say a fool thing like that for?*

fool·er·y /ˈfuləri/ *n.* [U] OLD-FASHIONED silly or stupid behavior

fool·har·dy /ˈful͵hɑrdi/ *adj.* taking stupid and unnecessary risks: *Holding onto a moving car while wearing skates is illegal and foolhardy.* —**foolhardiness** *n.* [U]

fool·ish /ˈfuliʃ/ *adj.* **1** not sensible or wise: *a foolish decision* | *It is foolish to ride a motorcycle without a helmet.* | *The place is guarded by dogs who will attack anyone foolish enough to try to get in.* **2** a foolish person behaves in a silly way or looks silly: *a foolish grin* —**foolishly** *adv.*: *She foolishly agreed to go with them.* —**foolishness** *n.* [U]

fool·proof /ˈfulpruf/ *adj.* a foolproof method, plan, system etc. is certain to be successful: *Condoms aren't a foolproof method of preventing pregnancy.*

fools·cap /ˈfulskæp/ *n.* [U] a large size of paper, especially paper used for writing

fool's gold /͵. ʹ./ *n.* [U] **1** a kind of yellow metal that exists in some rocks and looks like gold, but is not valuable; iron PYRITES **2** something that you think will be very exciting, very attractive etc. but in fact is not

Foos·ball /ˈfusbɔl/ *n.* [U] TRADEMARK a game played on a special table, in which two players move rods with small figures of people on them, in order to hit a ball toward a hole at the end of the table

foot¹ /fʊt/ *n.* [C]

1 body part *plural* **feet** the part of your body that you stand on and walk on: *My foot hurts.* | *Is Daddy tickling your feet, Lisa?* —see picture at BODY

2 measurement *written abbreviation* **ft.** *plural* **feet** or **foot** a unit for measuring length, equal to 12 inches or 0.3048 meters: *He's six feet tall, with blonde hair and a mustache.* | *a two-foot-long board*

3 on foot if you go somewhere on foot, you walk there: *The best way to see Yosemite is on foot.*

4 bottom part **the foot of sth** the lowest part of something such as a mountain, tree, or set of stairs, or the end of a bed: *Our Great Dane sleeps at the foot of the bed.* | *a stunningly beautiful lake at the foot of the mountain*

5 on your feet a) standing or walking for a long time without having time to sit down: *Waitresses are on their feet all day.* **b)** having enough money again, or successful again after having problems: *Dan got a job, so we should be back on our feet soon.* **c)** feeling better again after being sick and in bed: *It's good to see you on your feet again!* **d)** standing up: *Ellis was hurt but managed to stay on his feet* (=remain standing).

6 off your feet sitting or lying down, rather than standing or walking: *The doctor told me to stay off my feet for a few days.* | *It was a relief to get off my feet for a while.*

7 set foot in sth to go into a place: *The last time Molly set foot in that house was 26 years ago.*

8 get/jump/rise etc. to your feet to stand up after you have been sitting or after you have fallen: *The fans cheered and bounded to their feet.*

9 put your feet up INFORMAL to relax and rest, especially by sitting with your feet supported on something

10 put your foot down to say very firmly what someone must do or must not do: *I wanted to take a year off before college, but my mother put her foot down.*

11 get your foot in the door to get your first opportunity to work in a particular organization or industry: *I auditioned for a commercial and got it, and that's how I got my foot in the door.*

12 put your foot in your mouth to say something that is embarrassing or that upsets someone, because you have not thought carefully about what you are saying

13 have one foot in the grave HUMOROUS to be old: *She sounded like she had one foot in the grave.*

14 be/get under your feet to annoy you by always being in the same place as you and preventing you from doing what you want: *The kids have been under my feet all day long.*

15 get/start off on the wrong foot to start a relationship or activity badly: *The interview got off on the wrong foot and never got any better.*

16 get/start off on the right foot to start a relationship or activity well: *I was pleased to participate and help get things off on the right foot.*

17 put your best foot forward to try to be polite, helpful etc. so that other people will have a good opinion of you from the beginning

18 have/keep both feet on the ground to be sensible and practical in the way you do things: *She's really creative, but she also has her feet firmly on the ground.*

19 have two left feet INFORMAL to be very CLUMSY and unable to dance well

20 have feet of clay someone that you admire who has feet of clay has faults that you did not realize they had

21 foot soldier/patrol a soldier or a group of soldiers that walks and does not use horses or vehicles

22 foot pedal/brake/pump etc. a machine or part of a machine that you operate using your feet

23 sock the part of a sock that covers your foot: *There's a run in the foot of my nylons.*

24 poetry TECHNICAL a part of a line of poetry in which there is one strong BEAT and one or two weaker ones —see also **get/have cold feet** (COLD¹ (8)), **drag your feet** (DRAG¹ (8)), **find your feet** (FIND¹ (22)), **-FOOTED, (from) head to foot/toe** (HEAD¹ (7)), **land on your feet** (LAND² (7)), **pull the rug (out) from under sb** (RUG (2)), **stand on your own two feet** (STAND¹ (36)), **sweep sb off their feet** (SWEEP¹ (11)), UNDERFOOT

foot² *v.* **foot the bill** INFORMAL to pay for something, especially something expensive: [+ **for**] *Our insurance company should foot the bill for the damage.*

F

foot·age /ˈfʊtɪdʒ/ n. [U] film that shows a particular event: [+ **of**] black-and-white footage of the 1936 Olympics

foot-and-mouth dis·ease /ˌ. . ˈ. .ˌ./ n. [U] a serious disease that kills cows and sheep

s w
2 2
foot·ball /ˈfʊtˌbɔl/ n. **1** [U] a game in which two teams of 11 players carry, kick or throw an OVAL ball into an area at the end of a field to win points: college football games —compare SOCCER **2** [C] the OVAL ball used in this game **3** [U] BRITISH —see SOCCER —see also FLAG FOOTBALL, **political football** (POLITICAL (5))

foot·bridge /ˈfʊtˌbrɪdʒ/ n. [C] a narrow bridge that people can walk over —see picture at BRIDGE[1]

foot·drag·ging /ˈfʊtˌdrægɪŋ/ n. [U] the act of deliberately being slow to do something: The police were accused of foot-dragging on the investigation.

-footed /fʊtɪd/ suffix [in adjectives] **flat-footed/four-footed etc.** having a particular type or number of feet: a four-footed animal | a flat-footed man

foot·er /ˈfʊtɚ/ n. **1** **six-footer/eighteen-footer etc.** someone or something that measures six feet tall, eighteen feet long etc.: Hardaway made a 20-footer for a two point lead with 10 seconds left (=he made points by throwing the ball 20 feet into the basket). **2** [C] information at the bottom of a page, especially things such as page numbers that appear on each page in a document

foot·fall /ˈfʊtfɔl/ n. [C,U] LITERARY the sound of each step when someone is walking; FOOTSTEP

foot fault /ˈ. ./ n. [C] a mistake in tennis when the person who is serving (SERVE[1] (10)) is not standing behind the line

foot·hill /ˈfʊtˌhɪl/ n. [C usually plural] one of the low hills at the bottom of a group of high mountains: the foothills of the Rockies

foot·hold /ˈfʊthoʊld/ n. [C] **1** [usually singular] a position from which you can start to make progress and achieve your aims: The sport is **gaining a foothold** in Northern California. **2** a place where you can safely put your foot when climbing a rock or mountain

foot·ing /ˈfʊtɪŋ/ n. **1** [singular] the conditions or arrangements under which something exists or operates: The city hopes to start the new year **on a** stronger **financial footing**. | Microsoft has a **firm/ solid footing** in the market for software. | The device allows younger players to play the video games **on a** more **equal footing** with more skillful competitors. **2** [singular] a firm hold with your feet on a SLIPPERY or dangerous surface: A local boy **lost his footing** and fell 200 feet down a steep bank. | We were struggling to **keep** our **footing** on the icy trail. **3** [C] a base that supports a bridge or structure and fastens it firmly to the ground: The swing should be anchored in concrete footings at least 12 inches deep.

foot·lights /ˈfʊtlaɪts/ n. [plural] a row of lights along the front of the stage in a theater

foot lock·er /ˈ. ˌ../ n. [C] a large strong plain box that you can keep your things in, used especially by soldiers

foot·loose /ˈfʊtlus/ adj. OLD-FASHIONED able to do what you want and enjoy yourself because you have no responsibilities: Europe is filled with footloose students every summer. | No, I'm not married – still **footloose and fancy free!**

foot·man /ˈfʊtˌmən/ n. plural **footmen** /-mən/ [C] a male servant in past times who opened the front door, announced the names of visitors etc.

foot·note /ˈfʊtˌnoʊt/ n. [C] **1** a note at the bottom of the page in a book, that gives more information about something on that page **2** something that is not very important but that is mentioned because it is interesting or helps you understand something: I don't see this affair as anything more than an interesting historical footnote.

foot·path /ˈfʊtpæθ/ n. [C] a TRAIL[2] (1)

foot·print /ˈfʊtˌprɪnt/ n. [C] **1** a mark made by a foot or shoe: a deer's footprints in the snow **2** a word used to describe the amount of space that a particular piece of computer equipment covers on the surface of a desk or on the floor

foot·rest /ˈfʊtˌrɛst/ n. [C] a part of a chair that you can raise or lower in order to support your feet when you are sitting down

foot·sie /ˈfʊtsi/ n. **play footsie** INFORMAL **a)** to secretly touch someone's feet with your feet under a table, to show that you think they are sexually attractive **b)** to work together and help each other in a dishonest way: [+ **with**] Morris continued to play footsie with prominent Republicans.

foot·step /ˈfʊtstɛp/ n. [C] the sound of each step when someone is walking: He heard someone's footsteps in the hall. —see also **follow (in) sb's footsteps** (FOLLOW (10))

foot·stool /ˈfʊtstul/ n. [C] a low piece of furniture used to support your feet when you are sitting down

foot·wear /ˈfʊtˌwɛr/ n. [U] things that people wear on their feet, such as shoes or boots: athletic footwear

foot·work /ˈfʊtˌwɚk/ n. [U] **1** skillful use of your feet when dancing or playing a sport **2** skillful methods that you use to achieve something: Government attorneys' **fancy** legal **footwork** has raised doubts about their motives.

fop /fɑp/ n. [C] OLD-FASHIONED, DISAPPROVING a man who is too interested in his clothes and appearance —**foppish** adj. —**foppishness** n. [U]

s v
1 1
for[1] /fɚ; strong fɔr/ prep. **1** intended to be given to or used by a particular person or group: I have a present for you. | Save a piece of cake for Noah. **2** intended to be used in a particular situation: Leave the chairs out – they're for the concert. | We made cookies for the party. **3** used to show the purpose of an object, action etc.: a knife for cutting bread | The dining room is just large enough for the table and four chairs. | What did you **do** that **for** (=why did you do it?)? | What's this gadget **for** (=what is its purpose?)? **4** in order to have, do, or get something: Alison is looking for a job. | Several people were standing there, waiting for the bus. | Are the Gardiners coming for dinner tonight? | You should see a lawyer for some advice. | For more information, write to the address below. | Let's **go for** a walk. | We just play poker **for fun**, not for money. **5 for sale/rent** used to show that something is available to be sold or rented: They've just put their house up for sale. **6** in order to help someone: I'm babysitting for Jo on Friday night. | Let me lift that box for you. | The doctor said that there was nothing he could do for her (=he could not make her well). | What can I **do for you** (=used by someone in a store, in order to ask if they can help you)? **7** used to show the time when something is planned to happen: I made an appointment for October 18th. | It's **time for** supper (=we are going to have supper now). **8** used to express a length of time: Bake the cake for 40 minutes. | I've known Kim for a long time. | Can I borrow your drill **for a while**? —see Usage Notes at DURING and SINCE[1] **9** because of or as a result of something: The award for the highest sales goes to Pete McGregor. | It won't print pictures for some reason. | [for doing sth] Mia got a ticket for driving through a red light. **10** used to state where a person, vehicle etc. is going: I usually leave for work at 7:30. | The plane for Las Vegas took off an hour late. **11** used to express a distance: We walked for miles. | The mountains went on for as far as the eye could see. **12** used to show a price or amount: a check for a hundred dollars | He placed an order for 200 copies. | **for free/nothing** I got this stereo for nothing from my cousin. **13 for breakfast/lunch/ dinner etc.** used in order to say what you ate or will eat at breakfast, LUNCH, dinner etc.: We had steaks **for dinner** last night. | "What's for lunch?" "Chicken noodle soup." **14 for Christmas/ sb's birthday etc.** in order to celebrate Christmas, someone's birthday etc.: What did you get for your birthday? | We went to my grandmother's for Thanks-

F

giving last year. **15 for now** used to say that a situation is temporary and can be changed later: *We'll have to keep the cat in the house for now.* | *Just put the pictures in a box for now.* **16** if you work for a company, play for a team etc., the one mentioned is the one in which you work, play etc.: *Amelia worked for Exxon until last year.* | *He writes for the "Washington Post".* **17 for sb/sth to do sth a)** used when discussing what is happening, what may happen, or what can happen: *The plan is for us to leave on Friday to pick up Joe.* | *It's unusual for it to be so cold in June.* | *There's nothing worse than for a parent to hit a child.* | *The cat is too high in the tree for me to reach her.* **b)** used when you are saying what someone or something is able to do: *It's easy for a computer to keep a record of this information.* | *The dolphin was near enough for me to reach out and touch it.* | *It's too difficult for me to explain.* **c)** used when you are explaining a reason for something: *He must have had some bad news for him to be so quiet.* | *I left my coat for it to be cleaned.* **18** supporting, or agreeing with someone or something: *How many people voted for Mulhoney?* | *Please discuss the case for and against nuclear energy.* | *Three cheers for Mr. Sheridan!* | **I'm all for** (=I approve of) *making to-do lists, but you have to stay flexible, too.* **19** when you consider a particular fact: *It's cold for this time of year.* | *Libby is very tall for her age.* | *For someone who is supposed to have very good taste, Jo wears some strange clothes.* **20** relating to or concerning someone or something: *I'm sure she's the ideal person for the job.* | *Fortunately for Tim, he can swim.* | *Congratulations! I'm really happy for you.* | *Nate has a lot of respect for his teachers.* | *The success rates for each task are given in Table 4.* | *You're too quick for me* (=used to say that someone does something much more quickly than you do)! | *City life is **not** for me.* **21** meaning or representing something: *What's the Spanish word for "oil"?* | *Red is for stop, green is for go.* **22 for all I know/care** SPOKEN used to say that you really do not know or care: *For all I know, the story just could be true.* | *Their religion doesn't matter; they can howl at the moon for all I care.* **23 for all a)** considering how little: *For all the good I did, I shouldn't have even tried to help.* **b)** considering how much or how many: *For all the plays Ruby's seen, she still hasn't seen "Hamlet".* | *For all his expensive education, Leo doesn't know very much.* **24 for each/every sth** used to say something happens or is true each or every time another thing happens or is true: *For each mistake, you'll lose half a point.* | *For every three people who agree, you'll find five who don't.* **25 I wouldn't do sth for anything** SPOKEN used to emphasize that you definitely would not do something: *I would not go through that again for anything.* **26 I, for one...** SPOKEN used to say what your opinion is or what you will do: *I, for one, believe that many sports stars are not good role models.* | *As a resident, I, for one, will refuse to participate.* **27 for one thing... (and for another)** used when you are giving reasons for a statement you have made: *No, I'm not going to buy it. For one thing I don't like the color, and for another it's way too expensive.* **28 now for sb/sth** SPOKEN used to introduce a new subject: *Okay, now for the news.* | *Now for the first graders, each one needs a bag lunch.* **29 if it weren't for/if it hadn't been for sb/sth** if something had not happened, or if a situation were different: *If it hadn't been for you, I would not be alive now.* | *If it weren't for Michelle's help, we'd never get this job done.* **30 (well,) that's/there's...for you!** SPOKEN **a)** used to say that something is typical of a particular type of thing, especially when you expect that thing to be of low quality: *I apologize for the behavior of the students. That's the younger generation for you, I guess.* **b)** used to say that something is the complete opposite of what you were saying: *She didn't even thank me; there's gratitude for you!* **31 be in for it** to be likely to be blamed or punished, or to have something bad happen to you: *The hills are very dry; if we get any more hot winds we could be in for it* (=there could be fires). —see also **once and for all** (ONCE[1] (8)), **for sure** (SURE[1] (6))

USAGE NOTE: FOR

Use verbs such as "buy" or "make" without **for** only when you are talking about buying or making something for a person or animal: *He bought a new dish for his dog* or *He bought his dog a new dish.* | *She made a new dress for her daughter* or *She made her daughter a new dress.* If you are talking about buying or making something for an object, you must use **for**: *I bought a new tablecloth for the kitchen table.* Don't say "I bought the table a new tablecloth."

for[2] *conjunction* LITERARY used to introduce the reason for something; because: *He found it increasingly difficult to read, for his eyes were failing.*

for·age[1] /'fɔrɪdʒ, 'far-/ *v.* [I] **1** to go around searching for food or other supplies: [+ **for**] *Horses are able to forage for grass even under deep snow.* **2** to search for something, especially with your hands: *Writers who need a good title have often foraged in Shakespeare or the Bible.* —**forager** *n.* [C]

forage[2] *n.* [U] food supplies for horses and cattle

for·ay[1] /'fɔreɪ, 'fɑreɪ/ *n. plural* **forays** [C] **1** a short attempt at doing a particular job or activity, especially one that is very different from what you usually do: [+ **into**] *After an unsuccessful foray into politics, Ramsey went back to his law practice.* **2** a short sudden attack by a group of soldiers, especially in order to get food or supplies: [+ **into**] *The soldiers made nightly forays into enemy territory.* **3** a short trip somewhere in order to get something or do something: [+ **into**] *It was Louise's first foray into the mountains since she'd moved to the area.*

foray[2] *v.* [I + **into**] FORMAL **1** to go out and make a sudden attack against the enemy, especially in order to get food or supplies **2** to make a trip somewhere, especially somewhere you do not normally go

for·bade /fɚ'bæd/ *v.* the past tense of FORBID

for·bear[1] /fɔr'bɛr, fɚ-/ *v. past tense* **forbore** *past participle* **forborne** [I] LITERARY to not do something that you could do because you think it is wiser not to: [**forbear to do sth**] *They were all silly games, which Thornton forbore to join.* | [+ **from**] *He forbore from commenting on my appearance.*

for·bear[2] /'fɔrbɛr/ *n.* [C] another spelling of FOREBEAR

for·bear·ance /fɔr'bɛrəns/ *n.* [U] LITERARY the quality of being patient, having control over your emotions, and being willing to forgive someone

for·bear·ing /fɔr'bɛrɪŋ/ *adj.* FORMAL patient and willing to forgive: *Carlos was tactful and forbearing even when I was impatient and angry.*

for·bid /fɚ'bɪd/ *v. past tense* **forbade** or **forbid** *past participle* **forbidden** [T] **1** to order someone not to do something: *At that time, the state law forbade the teaching of evolution.* | [**forbid sb from doing sth**] *Women are forbidden from going out without a veil.* | [**forbid sb to do sth**] *Post Office rules forbid employees to accept tips.* | *The law **strictly forbids** racial or sexual discrimination in hiring.* **2 God/Heaven forbid** SPOKEN said in order to emphasize that you hope that something will not happen: *God forbid you should have an accident.* **3** FORMAL to make it impossible for someone to do something: *Lack of space forbids the listing of all those who contributed.*

USAGE NOTE: FORBID

WORD CHOICE: forbid, prohibit, not let/allow
Forbid and **prohibit** are formal words that are usually used when a government, law, or person in authority orders someone not to do something: *The law forbids smoking in public buildings.* | *Some countries prohibit the export of local currency.* They are much more common in written English than in spoken English. In less formal writing and in speech, it is more common to use phrases such as **say that someone can't do something, not let someone do something**, and **not allow someone to do something**: *My mother says I can't sleep over at your house on Friday.* | *Dad won't let me use*

the car this weekend. | The school does not allow students to wear gang colors.

for·bid·den /fɚˈbɪdn/ *adj.* **1** not allowed, especially because of an official rule: *Alcohol is forbidden in the dormitories.* | *You can't smoke inside the hospital – it's strictly forbidden.* | [**be forbidden to do sth**] *As a child, I was simply forbidden to watch more than an hour of TV daily.* | [**be forbidden from sth**] *The union is forbidden from striking.* | **It is forbidden to** *marry someone who is not a member of the same faith.* **2** a forbidden place is one that you are not allowed to go to: *The Great Mosque is forbidden to Christians.* **3** a forbidden activity, object etc. is one that seems exciting because you are not allowed to do it or have it: *I was curious about the forbidden pleasures of the city.* | *The ads tempt children to smoke – it's a forbidden fruit* (=something you should not have, that you think will make you happy).

for·bid·ding /fɚˈbɪdɪŋ/ *adj.* having a frightening or unfriendly appearance: *The mountains looked more forbidding as we got closer.* —**forbiddingly** *adv.*

for·bore /fɔrˈbɔr, fɚ-/ *v.* the past tense of FORBEAR

for·borne /fɔrˈbɔrn, fɚ-/ *v.* the past participle of FORBEAR

force¹ /fɔrs/ *n.*
1 [military] [C] a group of people who have been trained to do military or police work: *the Air Force* | *Barnes is a member of the St. Paul Police Force.* | *Rebel forces are seeking to overthrow the government.*
2 [military action] [U] military action used as a way of achieving your aims: *The UN tries to limit the use of force in conflicts.* | *Change must come by negotiation, not by force.* | *This has been a war fought more with technology than brute force* (=physical violence).
3 [violence] [U] violent physical action used to get what you want: *The police used force to break up the demonstration.* | *A ten-year-old girl was taken away by force outside a local supermarket.*
4 [natural power] **a)** [U] the natural power that is used or produced when one thing moves or hits another thing: *The force of the explosion shook buildings several blocks away.* | *Waves were hitting the rocks with tremendous force.* | *Sometimes you have to use sheer brute force to get these things open.* **b)** [C,U] TECHNICAL a natural power that produces movement in another object: *Centrifugal force can be greater than the force of gravity.*
5 [sb/sth that influences] [C] something or someone that has a strong influence or a lot of power: *Mandela was the driving force behind the changes* (=the one who made them happen). | *He has emerged as a strong force for political and economic reform.* | *Kessler has made the agency a force to be reckoned with* (=an organization with a lot of power and influence). | *Americans have been frightened by job losses and other forces beyond their control.*
6 [strong effect] [U] the powerful effect of what someone says or does: *Even after 30 years, the play has lost none of its force.* | *The force of public opinion stopped the highway project.*
7 [organized group] [C] a group of people who have been trained and organized to do a particular job: *The college must cut 10% of its teaching force for the fall semester.* | *the company's sales force*
8 **join/combine forces** to join together so that you can deal with a problem, defend yourselves etc.: *Local churches have joined forces to help the homeless.* | [+ **with**] *Workers are joining forces with the students to protest the new bill.*
9 **in force** **a)** if a law or a rule is in force, it must be obeyed: *Similar rules on appearance are in force at all Disney amusement parks.* | *A curfew went into force* (=started to operate) *on May 31.* **b)** in a large group: *Residents showed up in force at Tuesday's planning meeting.* | *The mosquitoes were out in force tonight.*
10 **the forces of evil/darkness** also **dark forces** LITERARY someone or something, especially the Devil,

that has a strong bad influence on a person or situation: *"A Wrinkle in Time" is about two children who travel through time and space to save their father from the forces of evil.*
11 **by/from force of habit** because you have always done a particular thing: *Ken puts salt on everything from force of habit.*
12 **the forces of nature** natural forces such as wind, rain, or EARTHQUAKES
13 **gale/hurricane force wind** an extremely strong wind that does a lot of damage —see also LABOR FORCE, TASK FORCE, TOUR DE FORCE

USAGE NOTE: FORCE

WORD CHOICE: force, power, strength
Force is the natural power that something has: *The force of the wind knocked the fence down.* **Power** is the ability and authority that you have to do something, or the energy that is used in order to make something work: *Congress has the power to make laws.* | *Their home is heated by solar power.* **Strength** is the physical quality that makes you strong: *I don't have the strength to lift this.*

---

force² *v.* [T]
1 [make sb do sth] **a)** to make someone do something they do not want to do: [**force sb to do sth**] *Nobody's forcing you to get married.* | [**force sb/sth into doing sth**] *It's pretty hard to force a kid into eating something he doesn't want to.* | *I had to force myself to get up this morning.* **b)** if a situation forces you to do something, it makes you do it, even though you do not want to: *The economy has forced a lot of companies out of business.* | [**force sb to do sth**] *The storms forced 84,000 people to flee their homes in the Philippines.* | [**force sb into (doing) sth**] *Illness forced her into canceling the concert tour.*
2 [make sb/sth move] to make someone or something move in a particular direction or into a different position or place, especially using physical force: *Some idiot forced Laura off the road yesterday.* | [**force sb into/out of sth**] *Prisoners were forced into concentration camps.* | *Ciccino was forced out of his car and taken hostage.*
3 **force your way in/out/through etc.** to push and use physical force to get into, out of, through etc. something: *Four men, wearing masks, forced their way into the house.* | *Demonstrators forced their way past police barricades.*
4 [open sth] to use physical force to open something: *Firefighters had to force the lock.* | *Thieves forced open a kitchen window and escaped with $5000 worth of goods.*
5 **force the issue** to do something that makes it necessary for someone to make decisions or take action: *What you are asking your tenants to do is reasonable, but you may decide not to force the issue.*
6 **force sb's hand** to make someone do something that they do not want to do, or to do it earlier than they had intended: *The governor is trying to force the legislature's hand on this issue.*
7 **force a smile/laugh etc.** to make yourself smile, laugh etc. even though you feel upset or annoyed
force sth **back** *phr. v.* [T] to try hard and stop yourself from showing your emotions: *Janet forced back her tears.*
force sth **down** *phr. v.* [T] **1** to make yourself swallow something that you do not want to eat or drink: *I managed to force down a piece of toast.* **2** to make a plane have to land by threatening to attack it
force sth **on/upon** sb *phr. v.* [T] to make someone accept something even though they do not want it: *Many children have piano lessons forced upon them.* | *No man has the right to force himself upon a woman* (=make her have sex with him).
force sth **out of** sb *phr. v.* [T] to make someone tell you something by asking them many times, threatening them etc.: *I wasn't going to tell Matt, but he forced it out of me.*

forced /fɔrst/ *adj.* **1** done because you must do something, not because of any sincere feeling: *The applause seemed forced rather than appreciative.*

2 done suddenly and quickly, because a situation makes it necessary: *The plane had to make a forced landing in a field.*

force-feed /'. ./ *v. past tense and past participle* **force-fed** [T] to force someone to eat by putting food or liquid down their throat —**force-feeding** *n.* [U]

force·ful /'fɔrsfəl/ *adj.* **1** a forceful person expresses their opinions very strongly and clearly and people are easily persuaded by them: *Gage is outspoken and forceful.* **2** forceful arguments, reasons etc. are strongly and clearly expressed, and help persuade you that something is true: *When accused of embezzlement, Sharon made a forceful denial.* —**forcefully** *adv.* —**forcefulness** *n.* [U]

force ma·jeure /ˌfɔrs mɑ'ʒɚ/ *n.* [U] LAW unexpected events that prevent you from doing what you intended or promised: *The company declared force majeure on its shipping commitments.*

for·ceps /'fɔrsəps, -sɛps/ *n.* [plural] a medical tool used for picking up, pulling, or holding things

forc·i·bly /'fɔrsɪbli/ *adv.* using physical force: *The police threatened to forcibly remove the protesters.* —**forcible** *adj.*

ford[1] /fɔrd/ *n.* [C] a place in a river that is not deep, so that you can walk or drive across it

ford[2] *v.* [T] to walk or drive across a river at a place where the water is not deep

Ford /fɔrd/, **Ger·ald** /'dʒɛrəld/ (1913–) the 38th President of the U.S.

Ford, Henry (1863–1947) a U.S. businessman and engineer, who established the Ford Motor Company, and developed the idea of the ASSEMBLY LINE for producing cars in large numbers —see picture on page 1329

Ford, John (1895–1973) a U.S. movie DIRECTOR known especially for his WESTERNS (=films about the American west in the 19th century)

Ford Foun·da·tion /'. .ˌ. ./ *n.* an organization that gives money and supports programs to improve social conditions and opportunities for education and employment, in the U.S. and other countries

fore- /fɔr/ *prefix* **1** before: *to forewarn someone | forethought* (=careful thinking before you do something) **2** at the front, or in the most important position: *a horse's forelegs | the factory foreman* (=the person in charge of a group of people) **3** the front part of something: *his strong forearms* (=the lower part of his arms) *| in the foreground* (=in the nearest part of a picture)

fore[1] /fɔr/ *n.* **to the fore** in a position of importance or influence: *Environmental issues came to the fore* (=became important) *in the 1980s. | This case has brought to the fore a lot of racial tensions.*

fore[2] *adj.* [only before noun] TECHNICAL the fore parts of a ship, plane, or animal are the parts at the front —opposite AFT

fore[3] *interjection* used in the game of GOLF to warn people that you have hit the ball toward them

fore·arm /'fɔrɑrm/ *n.* [C] the lower part of the arm, between the hand and the elbow —see picture at BODY —see also **forewarned is forearmed** (FOREWARN (2))

fore·bear /'fɔrbɛr/ *n.* [C usually plural] FORMAL someone who was a member of your family a long time in the past; ANCESTOR

fore·bod·ing /fɔr'boudɪŋ/ *n.* [U] a feeling that something bad is going to happen soon: *We waited for news of the men with a sense of foreboding.*

fore·cast[1] /'fɔrkæst/ *n.* [C] a description of what is likely to happen in the future, based on information you have now: *the weather forecast | Apex Corp. has issued its annual sales forecast.*

forecast[2] *v. past tense and past participle* **forecast** or **forecasted** [T] to make a statement saying what is likely to happen in the future, based on information that you have now: *Wind and rain has been forecast for this weekend. | [forecast (that)] The Federal Reserve Bank forecast that the economy will grow by 2% this year.*

fore·cast·er /'fɔrkæstɚ/ *n.* [C] someone who says what is likely to happen in the future, especially the person on television who explains the weather

fore·cas·tle /'fouksəl, 'fɔrˌkæsəl/ *n.* [C] TECHNICAL the front part of a ship, where the SAILORs live

fore·close /fɔr'klouz/ *v.* [I] to take away someone's property because they cannot pay back the money that they borrowed to buy it: [+ on] *Ms. Harvey's mortgage company has threatened to foreclose on her Houston home.* —**foreclosure** /fɔr'klouʒɚ/ *n.* [C,U]

fore·fa·ther /'fɔrˌfɑðɚ/ *n.* [C usually plural] **1** the people, especially men, who were part of your family a long time in the past: *None of David's forefathers died in World War I.* **2** someone in the past who did something important that influences your life today: *We seem to have less of a work ethic than did our forefathers. | Two hundred years ago our forefathers established a new nation.*

fore·fin·ger /'fɔrˌfɪŋgɚ/ *n.* [C] the finger next to your thumb; INDEX FINGER

fore·front /'fɔrfrʌnt/ *n.* **in/at/to the forefront (of sth)** in an important and leading position among a group of people or organizations, especially a group that is trying to achieve something: *The Pasteur Institute has been at the forefront of research into the AIDS virus.*

fore·go /fɔr'gou/ *v.* [T] another spelling of FORGO

fore·go·ing /'fɔrˌgouɪŋ/ *adj.* **the foregoing sth** FORMAL that have just been mentioned: *None of the foregoing concerns were addressed at the meeting.*

fore·gone con·clu·sion, forgone conclusion /ˌfɔrgɔn kən'kluʒən/ *n.* **be a foregone conclusion** if something is a foregone conclusion, it is certain to have a particular result, even though it has not yet happened: *The last three elections were all foregone conclusions* (=people knew what the results would be).

fore·ground /'fɔrgraund/ *n.* **1 the foreground** the nearest part of a scene in a picture or a photograph: *A young girl in the foreground plays in the water of the fountain.* **2 in/to the foreground** regarded as important and receiving a lot of attention: *Trade issues are currently in the foreground of the talks.*

fore·hand /'fɔrhænd/ *n.* [singular] a way of hitting the ball in tennis, with the flat part of your hand facing the direction of the ball —**forehand** *adj.*

fore·head /'fɔrhɛd, 'fɔrɪd, 'fɑrɪd/ *n.* [C] the part of your face above your eyes and below your hair

for·eign /'fɑrɪn, 'fɔrɪn/ *adj.* **1** not from your own country or the country you are talking about: *The tour went through seven foreign countries in two weeks. | "Journey of Hope" won the Oscar in 1991 for best foreign-language film. | Toyota is the leading foreign car company.* **2** [only before noun] involving or dealing with other countries: *America's foreign policy | The budget calls for cuts in foreign aid.* **3 be foreign to sb** FORMAL **a)** to seem strange and not familiar to someone: *I knew the tune, but the words were foreign to me.* **b)** to not be typical of someone's usual character: *This type of thinking is completely foreign to the Republicans.* **4 foreign body/matter/object** FORMAL something that is inside something else, but should not be there: *Make sure you remove all foreign matter from the wound.* —**foreignness** *n.* [U]

foreign af·fairs /ˌ... ˈ./ *n.* [plural] politics, business matters etc. that affect or concern the relationship between your country and other countries

for·eign·er /'fɑrənɚ/ *n.* [C] someone who comes from a different country: *About 40 million foreigners visited the US last year.*

USAGE NOTE: FOREIGNER

POLITENESS

It is not polite to call someone from another country a **foreigner** because this can sometimes mean that they are strange or different in some way that you do not like. You should say that someone is "from Canada/ Japan/Russia" or use a noun referring to their nationality instead: *More Americans and Europeans have visited Nagano since the Olympics.*

foreign ex·change /ˌ.. .ˈ./ *n.* **1** [U] the system of buying and selling foreign money: *The foreign exchange markets reacted quickly to the cut in German interest rates.* **2** [U] foreign money, especially money obtained by selling goods to a foreign country: *Coffee is a valuable source of foreign exchange for Uganda.* **3** [C] a program in which people, especially students, travel to another country to work or study for a particular length of time: *Rotary club members discussed plans to host a foreign exchange student.*

fore·knowl·edge /ˈfɔrˌnɑlɪdʒ/ *n.* [U] FORMAL knowledge that something is going to happen before it actually does

fore·leg /ˈfɔrlɛɡ/ *n.* [C] TECHNICAL one of the two front legs of a four-legged animal

fore·lock /ˈfɔrlɑk/ *n.* [C] LITERARY a piece of hair that falls over someone's FOREHEAD

fore·man /ˈfɔrmən/ *n. plural* **foremen** /-mən/ [C] **1** someone who is in charge of a group of workers, for example in a factory: *Her father is a retired mining foreman.* **2** the leader of a JURY, who announces the jury's decision in court

Fore·man /ˈfɔrmən/, **George** (1949–) a U.S. BOXER who was world CHAMPION in 1973–1974 and again in 1994–1995

fore·most /ˈfɔrmoʊst/ *adj.* **1** the foremost scientist/ expert/writer etc. the most famous, important, and respected scientist, expert, writer etc.: *Rostropovich was long considered the world's foremost cellist.* **2** the most important idea or thing: *Economic concerns are foremost on many voters' minds.* —see also **first and foremost** (FIRST² (8))

fo·ren·sic /fəˈrɛnsɪk, -zɪk/ *adj.* [only before noun] **1** relating to the methods for finding out about a crime: *DNA tests have revolutionized forensic science.* | *Forensic evidence showed that the woman had been raped before being murdered.* | *a forensic expert* **2** relating to arguments and DEBATE: *a politician's forensic skill* —**forensics** *n.* [U]

fore·or·dain /ˌfɔrɔrˈdeɪn/ *v.* [T usually passive] FORMAL to decide or arrange how something will happen before it actually happens —**foreordained** *adj.*

fore·per·son /ˈfɔrˌpɚsən/ *n.* [C] the leader of a JURY, who announces the jury's decision in court

fore·play /ˈfɔrpleɪ/ *n.* [U] sexual activity such as kissing and touching the sexual organs, before having sex

fore·run·ner /ˈfɔrˌrʌnɚ/ *n.* [C] **1** someone or something that is an early example or a sign of something that comes later: [+ of] *The Warriors started in 1926 as part of the American Basketball League, a forerunner of the NBA.* **2** a sign or warning that something is going to happen: [+ of] *Cirrus clouds are usually forerunners of a cold front.*

fore·see /fɔrˈsi/ *v. past tense* **foresaw** /-ˈsɔ/ *past participle* **foreseen** /-ˈsin/ [T] FORMAL to know that something will happen before it happens: *Scientists foresee humans living on Mars within the next 200 years.* | [foresee that] *Few analysts foresaw that oil prices would rise so steeply.*

fore·see·a·ble /fɔrˈsiəbəl/ *adj.* **1 for the foreseeable future** for as long as anyone can know about: *He expects that people will want their news on paper, rather than computer screen, for the foreseeable future.* **2 in the foreseeable future** fairly soon: *There is a possibility of water shortages in the foreseeable future.* **3** foreseeable difficulties, events etc. are ones that you know will happen in the future: *Employers must be told in advance when a leave of absence is foreseeable – such as for the birth of a baby.*

fore·shad·ow /fɔrˈʃædoʊ/ *v.* [T] to be a sign of something that will happen in the future: *The events in Spain in the 1930s foreshadowed the rise of Nazi Germany.*

fore·short·ened /fɔrˈʃɔrtˈnd/ *adj.* objects, places etc. that are foreshortened appear to be smaller, shorter, or closer together than they really are —**foreshorten** *v.* [T]

fore·sight /ˈfɔrsaɪt/ *n.* [U] the ability to imagine what will probably happen, and to consider this in your plans for the future: *With foresight and planning, the drive to your vacation spot can be as enjoyable as your vacation.* | *City planners were criticized for not **having the foresight to** build bus lanes.*

fore·skin /ˈfɔrˌskɪn/ *n.* [C] a loose fold of skin covering the end of a man's PENIS

for·est /ˈfɔrɪst, ˈfɑr-/ *n.* [C,U] **1** a very large area of land that is covered with trees: *Much of Scandinavia is covered in dense pine forest.* | *a forest fire* —see picture on page 428 **2 not see the forest for the trees** to not notice what is important about something because you give too much of your attention to small details

fore·stall /fɔrˈstɔl/ *v.* [T] FORMAL to prevent an action or situation by doing something first: *The National Guard was sent in, to forestall any trouble.*

for·est·er /ˈfɔrəstɚ/ *n.* [C] someone who works in a forest taking care of, planting, and cutting down the trees

forest rang·er /ˈ.. ˌ../ *n.* [C] someone whose job is to protect or manage a forest owned by the government

for·est·ry /ˈfɔrəstri/ *n.* [U] the science and skill of taking care of and managing the use of forests

For·est Ser·vice, the /ˈ.. ˌ../ *n.* an organization that is responsible for taking care of forests in the U.S.

fore·taste /ˈfɔrteɪst/ *n.* **be a foretaste of sth** FORMAL to be a sign of something that is likely to happen in the future: *The violence on the streets was only a foretaste of what was to come.*

fore·tell /fɔrˈtɛl/ *v. past tense and past participle* **foretold** [T] to say what will happen in the future, especially by using special magic powers: *The end of the world is foretold in the biblical book of Revelations.*

fore·thought /ˈfɔrθɔt/ *n.* [U] careful thought or planning before you do something: *A long backpacking trip requires a lot of forethought.*

fore·told /fɔrˈtoʊld/ *v.* the past tense and past participle of FORETELL

for·ev·er /fəˈrɛvɚ, fɔ-/ *adv.* **1** for all future time; ALWAYS: *I'll remember you forever.* | *You can't avoid him forever, you know.* | *Many valuable works of art were lost forever.* **2** SPOKEN for a very long time: *Those Popsicles have been in the freezer forever.* | *She **takes forever** (=takes a very long time) to get ready to go anywhere.* | *It's going to take me **forever and a day** (=a very long time) to pay for the trip, but it will be worth it.* **3 go on forever** to be extremely long or large: *The train just seemed to go on forever.* **4 be forever doing sth** LITERARY to do something often or without stopping: *Science is forever trying to pinpoint the truth.* **5 forever and ever** a phrase meaning "forever," used especially in stories

for·ev·er·more /fəˌrɛvɚˈmɔr/ *adv.* LITERARY forever

fore·warn /fɔrˈwɔrn/ *v.* [T often passive] **1** to warn someone about something dangerous or bad that will happen: [+ of/about/against] *We'd been forewarned about the dangers of traveling at night.* | *Be forewarned that you should wear warm clothing and bring an umbrella.* **2 forewarned is forearmed** SPOKEN used to say that if you know about something before it happens, you can prepare for it —**fore·warning** *n.* [C,U]

fore·went, forwent /fɔrˈwɛnt/ *v.* past tense of FORGO

fore·wom·an /ˈfɔrˌwʊmən/ *n.* [C] **1** a woman who is in charge of a group of other workers, for example in a factory **2** a woman who is the leader of a JURY and who announces the jury's decision in court

F

fore·word /ˈfɔrwəd/ *n.* [C] a short piece of writing at the beginning of a book that introduces the book or the person who wrote it —compare AFTERWORD

for·feit¹ /ˈfɔrfɪt/ *v.* [T] to give something up or have it taken away from you, because of a law or rule: *Pregnant teenage girls will have to live with their parents or forfeit their benefits.* | *If a team does not show up with enough players, they forfeit the game.* —**forfeiture** /ˈfɔrfɪtʃə/ *n.* [U]

forfeit² *n.* [C,U] something that is taken away from you or that that you give up, because you have broken a law or rule: *The Dorsey High football team was declared the winner by forfeit* (=the other team broke a rule and had to give up the game).

forfeit³ *adj.* **be forfeit** LAW to be legally or officially taken away from you as a punishment

for·gave /fəˈgeɪv/ *v.* the past tense of FORGIVE

forge¹ /fɔrdʒ/ *v.* [T] **1** to illegally copy something, for example a document, a painting, or money, to make people think that it is real: *Someone stole my credit card and forged my signature.* | *He was carrying a forged passport.* **2 forge a relationship/alliance/ links etc.** to develop a strong relationship with other people, groups, or countries: *The European Community said it would forge diplomatic ties with Croatia.* **3** to produce something, especially after a lot of discussion: *The administration will forge new policies on environmental issues in the next few months.* **4** to make something from a piece of metal by heating the metal and shaping it

forge ahead *phr. v.* [I] **1** to make progress, especially quickly: *The company has forged ahead with its plans to build a new office building.* **2** to move forward in a strong and powerful way

forge² *n.* [C] a large piece of equipment that produces high temperatures and is used for heating and shaping metal objects, or the building where this is done

forg·er /ˈfɔrdʒə/ *n.* [C] someone who illegally copies documents, money, paintings etc., to try to make people think they are real

for·ger·y /ˈfɔrdʒəri/ *n. plural* **forgeries 1** [C] a document, painting, or piece of paper money that has been forged: *An art dealer insisted that the portrait is a forgery.* **2** [U] the crime or act of forging official documents, money etc.: *Special marks on the paper are intended to deter forgery.*

ˢ ᵂ
¹ ¹ **for·get** /fəˈgɛt/ *past tense* **forgot** *past participle* **forgotten** *v.*

1 facts/information [I,T] to not remember facts, information, or something that happened in the past: *I've forgotten her name.* | *Unless you make some notes, you'll forget it before the next class.* | [+ **(that)**] *Don't forget that Linda's birthday is on Tuesday.* | [+ **about**] *I'd completely forgotten about our bet until Bill reminded me.* | [+ **how/what/when/why etc.**] *Most adults seem to forget what it's like to be a teenager.*

2 sth you should do to not remember to do something that you should do: *I'd better put that on the calendar so I don't forget.* | [**forget to do sth**] *Maria forgot to close the door and the cat got out.* | [+ **about**] *He said he'd call me, but he forgot about it.* | [**forget (that)**] *Dan forgot that he was supposed to pick up the kids after school.* | *Let me get your sister's address, before I forget, so I can send her a thank-you note.* | *I was supposed to meet them there at six, but I forgot all about it.*

3 leave sth behind [T] to not remember to bring something with you that you intended to bring: *"Why did Carol come back?" "She forgot her purse."* | *Don't let me forget my sunglasses* (=remind me to bring my sunglasses).

4 stop thinking about [I,T] to stop thinking or worrying about someone or something: *Forget him, he's not worth it.* | *After a while, you forget you're wearing contact lenses.* | [+ **about**] *I hated high school; I just want to forget about it.*

5 stop a plan [I,T] to stop planning to do or get something, because it is not possible anymore: *If you don't finish your homework, you can forget going*

skiing this weekend. | *If we can't get any funding, we might as well forget the whole thing.* | [+ **about**] *You can forget about finding a hotel downtown – they're all full.*

6 not care about [I,T] to not care about someone or something anymore: *Thanks for everything; I'll never forget you guys.* | [+ **about**] *Once they have money, some people forget about all their old friends.*

7 forget yourself LITERARY **a)** to do something stupid or embarrassing, especially by losing control of your emotions: *Veronica was worried that she might forget herself and confess her true feelings.* **b)** to not worry about what others think of you, because you are thinking about doing something for other people: *When I was growing up, I was told to forget myself and pay attention to others.*

SPOKEN PHRASES

8 don't forget a) used to remind someone to do something: *Don't forget that the car needs gas.* | *Don't forget, we have to be there by five o'clock.* | [**don't forget to do sth**] *Don't forget to call Steve today, okay?* **b)** used to remind someone about an important fact or detail that they should consider: *Your grandparents have plenty of money now, but don't forget they worked hard to get it.* **c)** used to remind someone to take something with them: *Don't forget your lunch – it's on the counter.*

9 forget it a) used to tell someone that something is not important and they do not need to worry about it: *"I'm sorry, I can't fix this thing." "Forget it. I'll get someone at work to do it."* | *"Here, let me pay you back." "No, just forget it."* **b)** used to tell someone to stop asking or talking about something, because it is annoying you: *I'm not buying you that bike, so just forget it.* **c)** used when someone asks you what you just said and you do not want to repeat it: *"What'd you say?" "Nothing, just forget it."*

10 I forget NONSTANDARD used when you cannot remember a particular detail about something: *How old is Kristen again? I forget.* | *You know that guy we met last week – I forget his name.* | *I forget what he said, but she got really embarrassed.*

11 forget it/that used to tell someone that you refuse to do something: *Drive to the airport in this snow? Forget that!* | *He wanted me to work for minimum wage, so I said forget it.*

12 forget (about) sth to not consider doing or using something any longer: *The Mac's best for this job; you can forget about any other machine.* | *I'm ready to forget fashion and just try to keep warm.* | *If you're in a bad mood, forget it; don't try and train your dog then.*

13 I'll never forget used to say that you will always remember something from the past, because it was sad, funny, enjoyable etc.: *I'll never forget the look on Ben's face after the Lancers won the title.* | *I'll never forget that summer.*

14 ...and don't you forget it used to remind someone angrily about something important that should make them behave differently: *I'm your father, and don't you forget it!*

15 Aren't you forgetting (to do) sth? an annoying expression used to tell someone that they have not remembered something important: *Wait a minute – aren't you forgetting something? You were supposed to help me clean the house today.*

16 forget that used to tell someone to ignore what you have just said because it is not correct, important etc.: *Then mix a cup of milk, no, forget that, half a cup of milk.*

for·get·ful /fəˈgɛtfəl/ *adj.* often forgetting things: *My grandfather is getting more forgetful.* —**forgetfully** *adv.* —**forgetfulness** *n.* [U]

forget-me-not /.ˈ.. ˌ./ *n.* [C] a small plant with pale blue flowers

for·get·ta·ble /fəˈgɛtəbəl/ *adj.* not very interesting or good: *a completely forgettable movie*

for·giv·a·ble /fəˈgɪvəbəl/ *adj.* something that is forgivable is not seriously bad and you can easily

F

forgive it: *These are a few forgivable flaws in an otherwise important novel.*

for·give /fəˈgɪv/ v. *past tense* **forgave** *past participle* **forgiven** /-ˈgɪvən/ [I,T] **1** to decide not to blame someone or be angry with them, although they have done something wrong: *After several years of therapy, Deanna was finally able to forgive her father.* | [**forgive sb for sth**] *I made the mistake of saying what I thought, and he won't forgive me for it.* | [**forgive sb sth**] *Lord, please forgive us our sins.* | *If anything happened to the kids* **I'd never forgive myself.** | *"I'm sorry." "That's okay,* **you're forgiven."** | *Maybe you can* **forgive and forget** (=forgive someone and behave as if they had never done anything wrong), *but I can't.* **2 forgive a loan/debt** if a country or organization forgives a LOAN, it says that the person or country that borrowed the money does not have to pay it back: *The U.S. has forgiven Senegal's $42 million debt.* **3 forgive me** SPOKEN used when you are going to say or ask something that might seem impolite or offensive: *Forgive me, but that's not exactly a new idea.* | *Forgive me for saying so, but yellow doesn't look good on you.* **4 sb can/could/may be forgiven for sth** used to say that it is easy to understand why someone would think, believe, or do something: *You could be forgiven for being skeptical.*

for·give·ness /fəˈgɪvnɪs/ n. [U] the act of forgiving someone: *He's never admitted he was wrong or* **asked for forgiveness.**

for·giv·ing /fəˈgɪvɪŋ/ adj. **1** willing to forgive: *My father was a kind and forgiving man.* **2** if something is forgiving, it does not matter if you make small mistakes with it: *This recipe is very forgiving.*

for·go, forego /fɔrˈgoʊ/ v. *past tense* **forwent** *past participle* **forgone** /-ˈgɔn/ [T] FORMAL to decide to not do or have something: *Council members were asked to forgo their pay raises.*

for·got /fəˈgɑt/ v. the past tense of FORGET

for·got·ten[1] /fəˈgɑtn/ v. the past participle of FORGET

forgotten[2] adj. [usually before noun] that people have forgotten about or do not pay much attention to anymore: *Rural California is definitely the forgotten part of the state.*

fork[1] /fɔrk/ n. [C] **1** a tool used for picking up and eating food, with a handle and three or four points: *knives, forks, and spoons* **2** a place where a road or river divides into two parts, or one of the parts it divides into: *Turn left at the fork in the road.* | *the middle fork of the Klamath River* **3** a PITCHFORK **4** the parallel metal bars between which the front wheel of a bicycle or MOTORCYCLE is attached —see picture at BICYCLE[1] —see also TUNING FORK

fork[2] v. **1** [I] if a road, path, or river forks, it divides into two parts **2** [T] to pick up, carry, or turn something over using a fork: *Anna forked some more potatoes onto her plate.* **3 fork left/right** to travel toward the left or right part of a road when it divides into two parts

fork sth ↔ **over/out/up** phr. v. [I,T] INFORMAL to spend a lot of money on something because you have to: *He threatened to publish the photos unless she forked over $60,000.* | [**+ for/on**] *The crop has been badly affected, and consumers may have to fork over $2 or more for a head of lettuce.*

forked /fɔrkt/ adj. **1** having one end divided into two or more parts: *Snakes have forked tongues.* **2 speak with forked tongue** also **have a forked tongue** an expression meaning to "tell lies," which may be considered offensive: *The governor has been known to speak with forked tongue.*

forked light·ning /ˌ. ˈ../ n. [U] lightning that looks like a line of light that divides into several smaller lines near the bottom —compare HEAT LIGHTNING

fork·lift /ˈfɔrklɪft/ also **forklift truck** /ˈ.. ˌ./ n. [C] a small vehicle with special equipment on the front for lifting and moving heavy things, for example in a factory

for·lorn /fəˈlɔrn, fɔr-/ adj. LITERARY **1** sad and lonely: *A forlorn line of refugees stood near the truck.* **2** a place or thing that is forlorn seems empty and sad, and is often in bad condition: *The banners and ribbons looked forlorn in the rain.* **3 a forlorn hope** something you hope for that is very unlikely to happen: *We continued negotiating in the forlorn hope of finding a peace formula.*

form[1] /fɔrm/ n.

1 type [C] a particular type of something that exists in many different types: [**+ of**] *I think she died of some form of cancer.* | *Please bring two forms of identification, such as a passport or driver's license.*

2 way sth is/appears [C] the way in which something exists or appears: *You can buy Vitamin C in tablet or liquid form.* | *Children should make regular contributions to the family in the form of chores.* | *In the past, payments usually took the form of cattle, sheep, and goats, rather than money.*

3 document [C] an official document with spaces where you write information, especially about yourself: *The nurse asked her to sign the consent form.* | *a college application form* | **Fill out the** order **form** (=write your address etc. on the form) *and send it with your check to the address below.* —see picture at FILL[1]

4 shape [C] a shape: *The book discusses what the ideal female form has been for different centuries and cultures.* | *Dark forms seemed to hide behind the trees.* | *Pour the cement into the wooden form.* | *The main staircase was in the form of a large "S."*

5 art/literature [U] the structure of a work of art or piece of writing, rather than the ideas it expresses or events it describes: *Writers such as Henry James are concerned with form as well as content.* | *The story is told in the form of a ship's log.*

6 performance [U] how well a sports person, team, musician etc. is performing: *Johnson is far from his past form* (=he is not playing, running etc. as well as he did in the past) *and may not make the Olympic team.* | **in good/fine form** *The band was in good form that night.*

7 bad form FORMAL OR HUMOROUS behavior that is not socially acceptable: *It's bad form to say "I told you so" when a friend ignores your advice and makes a fool of himself.*

8 grammar [C] a way of writing or saying a word that shows its number, tense etc. For example, "was" is a past form of the verb "to be." —see also **not in any way, shape, or form** (WAY[1] (46))

form[2] v.

1 start to exist [I,T often passive] to start to exist, or make something start to exist, especially as the result of a natural process: *The rocks were formed more than 4 billion years ago.* | *Aspirin stops heart attacks by preventing blood clots from forming.* | [**+ on**] *Ice was already forming on the roads.*

2 shape/line [I,T] to come together in a particular shape or a line, or to make something have a particular shape: *Long lines formed outside the ticket offices.* | *Our house and the barn form a big "L."* | [**form sth into sth**] *Form the dough into a circle, then roll it out.*

3 establish [T] to start a new organization, government, country etc.: *The United Nations was formed in 1945.* | *IBM formed an alliance with Lotus, a software maker.*

4 be part of [linking verb] to be the thing, or one of the things, that makes up something else: *Newton's theories form the basis of modern mathematics.* | *Rice forms the most important part of their diet.* | *The Rio Grande forms the boundary between Texas and Mexico.*

5 form an opinion/impression/idea to use the information that you have in order to develop or reach an opinion or idea: *Members of the jury must not have formed opinions from publicity before the trial.*

6 form a relationship/attachment/bond etc. to establish and develop a relationship with someone: *Autistic children have difficulty forming close relationships.*

7 make/produce [T] to make something by combining two or more parts: *In English the past tense is* *usually formed by adding "ed."* | *The ions combine with proteins to form a reddish-colored complex.*

8 develop [T] to make someone develop into a particular type of person: *Events in early childhood help to form our personalities in later life.*

for·mal /ˈfɔrməl/ *adj.*

1 official made or done officially or publicly: *On July 19th a formal declaration of war was made.* | *They filed a formal complaint.* | *a formal announcement*

2 behavior formal behavior is very polite, and is used in official or important situations, or with people you do not know well: *His parents are very formal.* | *It's time for formal manners to be used again in the workplace.*

3 language formal language or writing is used for official or serious situations: *She wrote a formal letter of application for the job.* | *What should I call your mom? "Mrs. Dunlap" seems too formal.*

4 event/occasion a formal event is important, and people who go to it wear special clothes and behave very politely: *A formal ceremony was held to celebrate the anniversary of his death.* | *a formal dance*

5 clothes formal clothes, such as a TUXEDO or long dress, are worn to formal events: *men's formal wear* —see picture at CASUAL

6 formal education/training/qualification education in a subject or skill that you get in school rather than by practical experience: *Many priests have no formal training in counseling.*

7 organized done in a very organized way: *The class includes formal lectures as well as field trips.*

8 garden/park a formal garden, park, or room is arranged in a very orderly way: *Paris has a number of beautiful formal parks.* —see also FORMALLY

formal² *n.* [C] **1** a dance at which you have to wear formal clothes: *The school is holding a winter formal.* **2** an expensive and usually long dress that women wear on formal occasions

for·mal·de·hyde /fərˈmældəˌhaɪd, fɔr-/ *n.* [U] a strong-smelling gas that can be mixed with water and used for preserving things such as dead animals to be used in science etc.

formal dress /ˌ.. ˈ./ *n.* [U] clothes worn for formal social occasions, especially TUXEDOs for men, or long dresses for women

for·ma·lin /ˈfɔrmələn/ *n.* [U] a liquid made by mixing formaldehyde and water, used for preserving things such as dead animals to be used in science etc.

form·al·ism /ˈfɔrməˌlɪzəm/ *n.* [U] a style or method in art, religion, or science that pays too much attention to established rules —**formalist** *n., adj.*

for·mal·i·ty /fɔrˈmæləti/ *n. plural* **formalities 1** [C] something formal or official that you must do as part of an activity or process: *Jean and Fred will complete the adoption formalities this weekend* | *We've already decided to hire you; the interview is just a formality.* **2** [U] careful attention to polite behavior and language in formal situations: *The after-class meetings didn't have the formality of a classroom.*

for·mal·ize /ˈfɔrməˌlaɪz/ *v.* [T] to make a plan, decision, or idea official, especially by deciding and clearly describing all the details: *The contracts must be formalized within a month.* —**formalization** /ˌfɔrmələˈzeɪʃən/ *n.* [U]

for·mal·ly /ˈfɔrməli/ *adv.* **1** officially: *Taiwan formally calls itself the Republic of China.* | *The drug has been formally approved to treat chicken pox.* **2** in a polite way: *Mr. Takaki bowed formally to each guest in turn.*

for·mat¹ /ˈfɔrmæt/ *n.* [C] **1** the way in which something such as a computer document, television show, or meeting is organized or arranged: *The interview was written in a question and answer format.* **2** the size, shape, design etc. in which something such as a book or magazine is produced: *a large-format book of photographs* **3** the type of equipment that a VIDEO, music recording, or piece of computer SOFTWARE is designed to use: *Most compact camcorders operate in the 8mm format.*

format² *v.* **formatted, formatting** [T] **1** TECHNICAL to organize the space on a computer DISK so that

information can be stored on it **2** to arrange a book, page etc. according to a particular design or plan —**formatted** *adj.* —**formatting** *n.* [U]

for·ma·tion /fɔrˈmeɪʃən/ *n.* **1** [U] the process of starting a new organization or group: *Yeltsin organized the formation of the Commonwealth of Independent States.* **2** [U] the process by which something develops into a particular thing or shape: *Astronomers were able to observe a galaxy still in the process of formation.* | *[+ of] Burning plastics were responsible for the formation of toxic smoke.* **3** [C] the way in which a group of things are arranged to form a pattern or shape: *The players lined up in a T formation.* **4** in formation if a group of planes, ships, soldiers etc. are moving in formation, they are marching, flying etc. in a particular order or pattern: *The planes traveled 30 feet off the ground, flying in formation.* **5** [C] something that is formed in a particular shape, or the shape in which it is formed: *the natural rock formations of Bryce Canyon*

form·a·tive /ˈfɔrmətɪv/ *adj.* [only before noun] having an important influence on the way something or someone develops: *The plan is still in a formative stage.* | *The Marines were a formative experience for Bernie.* | *Weiss spent her formative years* (=the time she was growing up) *in Italy.*

for·mer¹ /ˈfɔrmɚ/ *adj.* [only before noun] **1** having a particular position before, but not now: *Her former husband now lives in Houston.* | *He was an adviser to former President Reagan.* **2** happening or existing before, but not now: *Canada is a former British colony.* | *Civil war raged for years in the former Yugoslavia.* **3** sb's/sth's former self what someone or something was like before they were changed by age, illness, trouble etc.: *She seems more like her former self.* | *So many people had moved away that the town was just a shadow of its former self* (=much less lively, exciting etc. than it used to be).

former² *n.* **the former** FORMAL the first of two people or things that are mentioned: *Of the two possibilities, the former seems more likely.* —opposite LATTER¹

for·mer·ly /ˈfɔrmɚli/ *adv.* in earlier times: *Peru was formerly ruled by the Spanish.* | *Churkin, 43, was formerly a deputy foreign minister.* | *Clark County's major employer is Navistar International, formerly International Harvester Co.* | *"Voyagers" is a 70-year-old program formerly known as "Indian Guides".*

form-fit·ting /ˈ. ˌ../ *adj.* form-fitting clothes fit closely around the body: *Crawford wore a sexy red form-fitting dress.*

For·mi·ca /fɔrˈmaɪkə/ *n.* [U] TRADEMARK strong plastic made in thin sheets and fastened to the top of tables, COUNTERS etc.

for·mic ac·id /ˌfɔrmɪk ˈæsɪd/ *n.* [U] an acid used especially for coloring cloth and making leather

for·mi·da·ble /ˈfɔrmədəbəl, fɔrˈmɪdə-/ *adj.* **1** very powerful or impressive: *The team faces some formidable opponents in the next week.* | *Russia still has a formidable nuclear arsenal.* **2** difficult to deal with and needing a lot of effort or skill: *They face the formidable task of working out a peace plan.* —**formidably** *adv.*

form·less /ˈfɔrmlɪs/ *adj.* without a definite shape: *Early myths described the Primal Being as a nameless, formless power.* —**formlessly** *adv.* —**formlessness** *n.* [U]

form let·ter /ˈ. ˌ../ *n.* [C] a standard letter that is sent to a number of people

for·mu·la /ˈfɔrmyələ/ *n. plural* **formulas** or **formulae** /-li/ **1** [C, usually singular] a method or set of principles that you use to solve a problem or to make sure that something is successful: *Juanita's plan is based on the proven formula of investing money to make money.* | *[+ for] A sensible diet and plenty of exercise is the formula for weight loss.* | *O'Brien has no magic formula* (=a method that is certain to work) *for success, other than hard work.* **2** [C] a series of numbers or letters that represent a mathematical or scientific rule: *[+ for] the formula for* *calculating distance* **3** [C] a list of the substances used to make a medicine, FUEL, drink etc., showing the amounts of each substance that should be used: *Coca-Cola's patented formula* **4** [U] a liquid food for babies that is similar to a woman's breast milk **5** [C] a set of words that is familiar to everyone and that seems meaningless or insincere: *Tobin's speech was full of the usual formulas and clichés.*

for·mu·la·ic /ˌfɔrmjəˈleɪ·ɪk/ *adj.* FORMAL, DISAPPROVING containing or made from ideas or expressions that have been used many times before and are therefore not very new or interesting: *a formulaic mystery novel*

Formula One /ˌ... ˈ./ *n.* [U] a type of car racing in very fast cars with powerful engines

for·mu·late /ˈfɔrmjəˌleɪt/ *v.* [T] **1** to develop something such as a plan or set of rules, and decide all the details of how it will be done: *The city is currently formulating policies on new road expansions.* **2** to think carefully about what you want to say, and say it clearly: *Jackie paused to formulate her reply.* **3** to make something using particular amounts of different substances: *The gasoline is formulated to burn more cleanly, producing less pollution.* —**formulation** /ˌfɔrmjəˈleɪʃən/ *n.* [C,U]

for·ni·cate /ˈfɔrnəˌkeɪt/ *v.* [I] LITERARY, DISAPPROVING to have sex with someone you are not married to —**fornication** /ˌfɔrnəˈkeɪʃən/ *n.* [U]

for·sake /fəˈseɪk, fɔr-/ *v. past tense* **forsook** /-ˈsʊk/ *past participle* **forsaken** /-ˈseɪkən/ [T] **1** FORMAL to stop doing or leave something that you have or enjoy: *More than 80 older men and women have forsaken retirement to help at local schools.* **2** LITERARY to leave someone, especially when you should stay because they need you: *Gwendolyn begged Hugo not to forsake her.* —see also GODFORSAKEN

for·sooth /fəˈsuθ/ *adv.* OLD USE certainly

For·ster /ˈfɔrstɚ/, **E.M.** /i ɛm/ (1879–1970) a British writer of NOVELs

for·swear /fɔrˈswɛr/ *v. past tense* **forswore** /-ˈswɔr/ *past participle* **forsworn** /-ˈswɔrn/ [T] LITERARY to stop doing something, or to promise that you will stop doing something: *Both sides agreed to forswear all acts of terrorism.*

for·syth·i·a /fɚˈsɪθiə/ *n.* [C,U] a bush that is covered with bright yellow flowers in early spring

fort /fɔrt/ *n.* [C] **1** a strong building or group of buildings used by soldiers or an army for defending an important place: *The Civil War began when Southern troops fired on Fort Sumter.* **2** a permanent place where an army lives or trains: *soldiers from Fort Bragg* —see also **hold the fort** (HOLD¹ (29))

forte¹ /fɔrt, ˈfɔrteɪ/ *n.* [C] **1 be sb's forte** to be something that someone is good at doing: *Cooking has never been Chelsea's forte.* **2** a note or line of music played or sung loudly

for·te² /ˈfɔrteɪ/ *adj., adv.* music that is forte is played or sung loudly

for·te·pi·an·o /ˌfɔrteɪpiˈænoʊ/ *n. plural* **fortepianos** [C] an old-fashioned musical instrument like a piano that was popular in the 18th century

S W 1 2 **forth** /fɔrθ/ *adv.* LITERARY **1 from this/that day/time/moment forth** LITERARY beginning on that day or at that time: *From this day forth you shall speak to no one.* **2** [only after verb] LITERARY going out or away from where you are: *They marched forth into battle.* —see also **back and forth** (BACK¹ (10)), **hold forth** (HOLD¹), **put forth** (PUT), **and so on/forth** (SO¹ (5))

forth·com·ing /ˌfɔrθˈkʌmɪŋ◂/ *adj.* **1** [only before noun] happening or coming soon: *She has a part in Steven Spielberg's forthcoming film.* **2** [not before noun] given or offered when needed: *If more money is not forthcoming, the theater will have to close.* **3** [not before noun] be willing to give information about something: [+ about] *The charity has not been forthcoming about its finances.*

forth·right /ˈfɔrθraɪt/ *adj.* saying honestly what you think, in a way that may seem impolite: [+ in] *He has been forthright in his criticism.*

forth·with /fɔrθˈwɪθ/ *adv.* FORMAL immediately: *Sanctions will take effect forthwith.*

for·ti·eth¹ /ˈfɔrtiɪθ/ *adj.* 40th; next after the thirty-ninth: *It's our fortieth anniversary next week.*

fortieth² *pron.* **the fortieth** the 40th thing in a series

fortieth³ *n.* [C] one of forty equal parts of something

for·ti·fi·ca·tion /ˌfɔrtəfəˈkeɪʃən/ *n.* **1** [U] the process of making something stronger or more effective **2 fortifications** [plural] towers, walls etc. built around a place in order to protect it or defend it: *battlefield fortifications*

for·ti·fied /ˈfɔrtəˌfaɪd/ *adj.* **1** made stronger and easier to defend: *The border is the most heavily fortified in the world.* **2** if food or drinks are fortified, they have VITAMINs added to them to make them more healthy: *vitamin-fortified cereals*

fortified wine /ˌ... ˈ./ *n.* [C,U] wine such as SHERRY that has strong alcohol added

for·ti·fy /ˈfɔrtəˌfaɪ/ *v.* **fortifies, fortified, fortifying** [T] **1** to make an area easier to protect or defend, especially by putting soldiers there or by building walls, towers etc.: *Concrete blocks were piled high to fortify the government center.* **2** to encourage an attitude or feeling and make it stronger: [**fortify sb with sth**] *His mother was a heroic woman who fortified her children with faith in the future.* **3** [usually passive] to make food or drinks more healthy by adding VITAMINs to them: [+ **with**] *orange juice fortified with calcium* **4** to make someone feel physically or mentally stronger: *Several performers fortified themselves at the bar* (=drank alcohol to make themselves feel stronger) *before going on stage.*

for·tis·si·mo /fɔrˈtɪsəˌmoʊ/ *adj., adv.* music that is fortissimo is played or sung very loudly —compare FORTE²

for·ti·tude /ˈfɔrtəˌtud/ *n.* [U] courage shown when you are in pain or having a lot of trouble: *Janet met each challenge with fortitude and a wry good humor.* —see also **intestinal fortitude** (INTESTINAL (2))

fort·night /ˈfɔrtˌnaɪt/ *n.* [C usually singular] LITERARY two weeks

for·tress /ˈfɔrtrɪs/ *n.* [C] a large, strong building used for defending an important place

Fort Sum·ter /ˌfɔrt ˈsʌmtɚ/ a FORT in Charleston, South Carolina, where the first battle of the American Civil War was fought in 1861

for·tu·i·tous /fɔrˈtuətəs/ *adj.* FORMAL lucky and happening by chance: *a fortuitous meeting* —**fortuitously** *adv.*

for·tu·nate /ˈfɔrtʃənɪt/ *adj.* **1** [not before noun] someone who is fortunate has something good happen to them, or is in a good situation; LUCKY: *People have been very helpful – I'm very fortunate.* | [**fortunate to do sth**] *I've been fortunate to have done a lot of traveling.* | [**fortunate that**] *We were very fortunate that there were no serious injuries.* | *We were fortunate enough to get tickets for Saturday's playoff game.* **2 the less fortunate** people who are poor: *The organization is collecting canned food to help the less fortunate.* **3** [only before noun] a fortunate event is one in which something good happens by chance, especially when this saves you from trouble or danger: *It was a fortunate coincidence that the police were passing by just then.* —opposite UNFORTUNATE

for·tu·nate·ly /ˈfɔrtʃənɪtli/ *adv.* [sentence adverb] happening because of good luck: *We were late getting to the airport, but fortunately our plane was delayed.* —opposite UNFORTUNATELY

for·tune /ˈfɔrtʃən/ *n.* S W 3
1 money [C,U] a very large amount of money: *He lost much of his $1.4 billion fortune in the stock market crash.* | *To a four-year-old, $10 seems like a fortune.* | *Julia must have spent a fortune on her wedding dress.* | *A car like that costs a fortune.* | *The guy who invented Post-It notes must have made a fortune* (=earned a lot of money). | *Mrs. Foy made a small fortune* (=a lot of money, but not a very large amount) *buying and selling real estate.*
2 chance [U] chance, and the good or bad influence that it has on your life: *It is useless to*

struggle against fortune. | Elizabeth told me of their **good fortune** to find jobs right away. | I consider myself privileged to **have the good fortune to** know him. | She felt that not stopping to pray was to **risk bad fortune.**
3 what happens to you [C usually plural] the good or bad things that happen in life: This defeat marked a change in the team's fortunes. | **sinking/declining/ slumping fortunes** Alfonso's drinking got worse during the years of the family's declining fortunes.
4 sb's fortune [C,U] what is supposed to happen to someone in the future: A woman at the fair was **telling** people's **fortunes** (=using special cards or looking at people's hands to tell them what will happen to them).
5 fortune smiles on sth/sb LITERARY used to say that someone or something is lucky —see also **fame and fortune** (FAME), **seek your fortune** (SEEK (4)), SOLDIER OF FORTUNE

fortune cook·ie /'.. ,../ n. [C] a cookie with a piece of paper inside it that tells you what is supposed to happen in your future, often served after a meal in Chinese restaurants in the U.S.

fortune hunt·er /'.. ,../ n. [C] someone who wants to make a lot of money quickly and easily: Fortune hunters went to the hills in search of gold.

fortune tell·er /'.. ,../ n. [C] someone who uses cards or looks at people's hands in order to tell them what will happen to them in the future —**fortune telling** n. [U]

Fort Worth /,fɔrt 'wɔθ/ a city in the U.S. state of Texas

for·ty /'fɔrti/ number **1** 40 **2 the forties** also **the '40s a)** the years from 1940 through 1949 **3 sb's forties** the time when someone is 40 to 49 years old | **in your early/mid/late forties** a man in his mid forties **4 in the forties** if the temperature is in the forties, it is between 40° and 49° Fahrenheit: **in the high/low forties** The temperature was in the low forties. **5 forty winks** a very short sleep: Mr. Carzy lay down on the sofa for forty winks.

forty-five /,.. '.ˎ/ n. [C] INFORMAL **1** also **45** a small record with one song on each side **2** also **.45, Colt 45** TRADEMARK a small gun

fo·rum /'fɔrəm/ n. [C] **1** an organization, meeting, report etc. in which people have a chance to publicly discuss an important subject: [+ **for**] The United Nations should be a forum for solving international problems. | [+ **on**] A large number of mayors attended the forum on crime. **2** a group of computer users who are interested in a subject and discuss it through an ONLINE SERVICE (=company that provides computer connections) or a BULLETIN BOARD SYSTEM —see also NEWSGROUP **3** a large outdoor public place in ancient Rome used for business and discussion

for·ward¹ /'fɔrwəd/ adv. **1** also **forwards** toward a place or position that is in front of you: Greg leaned forward to hear what they were saying. | The truck was moving forwards into the road. **2** toward more progress, improvement, or development: Negotiators are trying to find a way forward in the peace talks. | NASA's project cannot **go forward** without more money. **3** toward the future in a way that is hopeful: Companies must **look forward** (=make plans for the future) and invest in new technologies. **4 from this/that day/time/moment etc. forward** beginning on that day or at that time: They never met again from that day forward. **5** in or toward the front part of a ship —see also **backward and forward** (BACKWARD¹ (5)), FAST FORWARD, **look forward to** sth (LOOK¹) —opposite BACKWARD¹

forward² adj. **1** [only before noun] closer to a person, place, or position that is in front of you: Army roadblocks prevented any further forward movement. | Troops were moved to a forward position on the battlefield. **2 forward planning/thinking/ progress etc.** plans, ideas etc. that are helpful in a way that prepares you for the future: The company is suffering from a lack of forward planning. **3 no further forward** not having made much progress, especially compared to what was expected: The talks are no further forward than they were two weeks ago. **4** [only before noun] at the front part of a ship, vehicle, plane etc.: We got a forward cabin. **5** too

confident and friendly in dealing with people you do not know very well: Kirstie did not wish to sound too forward. —compare BACKWARD²

forward³ v. **1** [T] to send a letter, message etc. that you have received to another person: You can use an anonymous e-mail service that forwards your messages but removes the address. | [**forward sth to sb**] The Post Office will be forwarding my mail to my new address. | Bernie's complaint was forwarded to the city manager. **2** [T] FORMAL to help something to develop so that it becomes successful: This new responsibility is a good chance to forward my career.

forward⁴ n. [C] in basketball, one of two players whose main job is to SHOOT the ball at the other team's BASKET

for·ward·ing ad·dress /,... '.., ,... .'./ n. [C] an address that you give to someone when you move so that they can send your mail to you: Unfortunately, Francine didn't **leave a forwarding address**.

forward-look·ing /'.. ,../ adj. planning for and thinking about the future in a positive way, especially by being willing to try new ideas: Assistance with childcare costs is offered by some forward-looking companies.

for·ward·ness /'fɔrwəd-nɪs/ n. [U] behavior that is too confident or friendly

for·wards /'fɔrwədz/ adv. FORWARD¹

forward-think·ing /,.. '..ˎ/ adj. FORWARD-LOOKING

for·went /fɔr'wɛnt/ v. another spelling of FORE-WENT

Fos·sey /'fɔsi/, **Di·an** /daɪ'æn/ (1932–1985) a U.S. ZOOLOGIST who lived near GORILLAS in Africa and studied them for many years

Dian Fossey

fos·sil /'fɑsəl/ n. [C] **1** part of an animal or plant that lived millions of years ago and that has been preserved, or the shape of one of these plants or animals that is preserved in rock: Several dinosaur fossils were found in Montana. **2** INFORMAL an insulting word for an old person

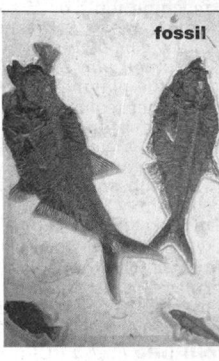
fossil

fossil fu·el /,.. '../ n. [C,U] a FUEL such as coal or oil that is formed from decayed animals and plants that lived millions of years ago

fos·sil·ize /'fɑsə,laɪz/ v. [I,T usually passive] **1** to become or form a FOSSIL by being preserved in rock: fossilized dinosaur bones **2** if people, ideas, systems etc. fossilize or are fossilized, they never change or develop, even though there are good reasons why they should change: The Soviets were unwilling to support the fossilized East German regime. —**fossilization** /,fɑsələ'zeɪʃən/ n. [U]

fos·ter¹ /'fɔstə, 'fɑ-/ v. **1** [T] FORMAL to help to develop a skill, feeling, idea etc. over a period of time: The workshops can foster better communication between husbands and wives. **2** [I,T] to take care of someone else's child for a period of time and have them live with you, without becoming their legal parent: The Hammonds fostered a little Romanian boy for a few months. —compare ADOPT (1)

foster² adj. **1 foster mother/father/parents/family** the person or people who foster a child **2 foster brother/sister** someone who has different parents than you, but who is fostered in the same family

3 foster child a child who is fostered **4 foster home** a person's or family's home where a child is fostered

Fou·cault /fuˈkou/, **Jean Ber·nard Lé·on** /ʒɑn bɛrˈnɑr leɪˈɑn/ (1819–1868) a French scientist who studied the speed of light

fought /fɔt/ *v.* the past tense and past participle of FIGHT[1]

foul[1] /faʊl/ *adj.*
1 smell/taste a foul smell or taste is very bad: *Residents have complained of foul odors from the factory.* | *a pile of foul-smelling garbage*
2 foul language impolite and offensive words; SWEAR WORDS: *Never use foul language to a customer.*
3 have a foul mouth INFORMAL to use a lot of SWEAR WORDS and offensive language
4 sports not within the rules of a sport or not within the limits of the playing field or COURT: *Sanchez hit three foul balls before connecting with a line drive to right field.*
5 air/water very dirty: *The foul haze of pollution has meant an increase in asthma cases.*
6 in a foul mood in a very bad mood and likely to get angry: *Leave Marge alone; she's in a foul mood and you're not helping.*
7 weather foul weather is stormy and windy, with a lot of rain or snow: *As beds are provided at the camps, you only need to carry clothing and foul-weather gear in your packs.*
8 evil LITERARY evil or cruel: *foul deeds* —**foully** *adv.* —**foulness** *n.* [U] —see also **cry foul** (CRY[1] (5)), **by fair means or foul** (FAIR[1] (19)), **fall foul of sb/sth** (FALL[1] (36))

foul[2] *v.* **1** [I,T] **a)** if a sports player fouls or is fouled, they do something that is not allowed by the rules of the sport: *Hardaway was fouled trying to make a three-point shot.* **b)** to hit a ball outside the limit of the playing area in BASEBALL: *On average, most batters foul at least one ball in each at bat.* **2** [T] to make something very dirty, especially with waste: *The oil spill has fouled at least four beaches.* **3** [I,T] also **foul up** TECHNICAL if a rope, chain, or part of a machine fouls or if something fouls it, it twists or cannot move as it should: *Check that nothing can foul the moving parts.*
foul out *phr. v.* [I] **a)** in baseball, to hit a ball outside the playing area that is caught by a player on the other team, so that your turn to try to hit the ball is over **b)** in basketball, to make more than five fouls in a game, so that you are not allowed to play in that game anymore
foul up *phr. v.* INFORMAL [I,T **foul sth ↔ up**] to do something wrong or to ruin something by making a mistake: *Ellen's suing her doctor for fouling up her operation.* | *You've totally fouled up this time.*

foul[3] *n.* [C] **1** an action in a sport that is against the rules: *He'd committed three fouls by half-time.* **2** in baseball, a ball that has been hit outside the playing area —compare STRIKE[2] (4)

foul line /ˈ. ./ *n.* [C] a line marked on a sports field, outside of which a ball cannot be legally played

foul-mouthed /ˈ. ./ *adj.* swearing too much: *a foul-mouthed man*

foul play /ˌ. ˈ./ *n.* [U] **1** if the police think someone's death was caused by foul play, they think that person was murdered: *The autopsy report showed no evidence of foul play.* **2** an action that is dishonest, unfair, or illegal: *There have been rumors of foul play in the last election.*

foul-up /ˈ. ./ *n.* [C] INFORMAL a problem caused by a stupid or careless mistake: *I had to retake my driver's test because of some clerical foul-up.*

found[1] /faʊnd/ *v.* the past tense and past participle of FIND[1]

found[2] *v.* [T] **1** to start something such as an organization, institution, company or city: *Founded in 1935 in Ohio, Alcoholics Anonymous is now a worldwide organization.* | *Mr. Packard was instrumental in founding the Stanford Industrial Park in the 1950s.*
2 be founded on/upon sth a) to base your ideas, beliefs etc. on something: *Racism is not founded on rational thought, but on fear.* | *The Soviet Union was originally founded on Socialism.* **b)** to be the solid layer of CEMENT, stones etc. that a building is built on: *The castle is founded on solid rock.* **3** TECHNICAL to melt metal and pour it into a MOLD (=a hollow shape), to make things such as tools, parts for machines etc. —**founding** *n.* [U] *the founding of the University of Chicago* —see also FOUNDATION, WELL-FOUNDED

foun·da·tion /faʊnˈdeɪʃən/ *n.*
1 building [C] the solid layer of CEMENT, bricks, stones etc. that is under a building to support it: *After the earthquake, I noticed several cracks in the foundation of the house.* | *It should take them about three weeks to lay the foundation* (=build it).
2 basic idea [C] a basic idea, principle, situation etc. that something develops from: *Reading, writing, and arithmetic provide a solid foundation for a child's education.* | *The Chinese diet is built on a foundation of rice, with only small amounts of meat.*
3 organization [C] an organization that gives or collects money to be used for special purposes, especially for CHARITY, or research: *The Heritage Foundation is a conservative political research organization.* | *the National Foundation for the Arts*
4 be without foundation also **have no foundation** FORMAL if a statement, idea etc. is without foundation, there is no proof that it is true: *I believe that claims of "psychic powers" are without foundation.*
5 establishment [C,U] the establishment of an organization, business, school etc.: *This school has served the community since its foundation in 1835.*
6 lay/provide the foundation(s) for sth to provide the conditions that will make it possible for something to be successful: *Tests on healthy people may lay the foundation for a vaccine to prevent AIDS.*
7 skin [U] a cream in the same color as your skin that you put on before the rest of your MAKEUP —see picture at MAKEUP
8 shake/rock sth to its foundations to completely change the way something is done or the way people think by having a completely new idea: *Darwin's theory rocked the scientific establishment to its foundations.*

foundation gar·ment /ˈ.. ˌ../ *n.* [C] OLD-FASHIONED a piece of clothing worn by women under their clothes to give shape to their bodies

foundation stone /ˈ.. ˌ./ *n.* [C] **1** a large stone placed at the bottom of an important building, usually as part of a ceremony **2** the facts, ideas, principles etc. that form the base from which something else develops or begins: *The creation of a world at peace is one of the foundation stones of Judaism and Christianity.*

found·er[1] /ˈfaʊndɚ/ *n.* [C] someone who establishes a business, organization, school etc.: *The shop is still run by the founder and his two sons.*

found·er[2] *v.* [I] FORMAL **1** if a ship or boat founders, it fills with water and sinks **2** to fail after a period of time because something has gone wrong or a new problem has caused difficulties: *According to court records, Dubroff's business was foundering and he was facing eviction.* —compare FLOUNDER[1] (2)

found·ing fa·ther /ˌ.. ˈ../ *n.* [C] **1** someone who begins something such as a new way of thinking or a new organization: [+ of] *Brooks Stevens was a founding father of industrial design.* **2 the Founding Fathers** [plural] the group of men who wrote the American Constitution and Bill of Rights and started the U.S. as a country

found·ling /ˈfaʊndlɪŋ/ *n.* [C] OLD-FASHIONED a baby who has been left by its parents, and is found and taken care of by other people

found·ry /ˈfaʊndri/ *n. plural* **foundries** [C] a place where metals are melted and made into new parts for machines, tools etc.

fount /faʊnt/ *n.* [C usually singular] a place, person, idea etc. that provides a large supply of something; SOURCE: **a fount of information/knowledge** *The telephone hotline is a fount of information for busy parents.*

foun·tain /'faʊn˺n/ n. [C] **1** a small pool with a structure from which water is pushed up into the air, used as a decoration **2** also **water fountain** a piece of equipment in a public place that produces a stream of water for you to drink from **3** a flow of liquid, or of something bright and colorful, that goes straight up into the air: [+ of] *A dazzling fountain of lava burst from the volcano.* —see also DRINKING FOUNTAIN, SODA FOUNTAIN

foun·tain·head /'faʊn˺n,hɛd/ n. [singular + of] the origin of something; SOURCE[1] (1)

fountain of youth /,.. '.'./ n. [C usually singular] something that many people believe will keep you young

fountain pen /'.. ,./ n. [C] a pen that you fill with liquid ink

four /fɔr/ number **1** 4 **2** 4 o'clock: *I get off work at four.* **3 on all fours** supporting your body with your hands and knees: *Billy was down on all fours playing with the puppy.* **4 the four corners of the Earth/world** LITERARY places or countries that are very far away from each other: *For centuries, the Spanish traveled to the four corners of the Earth in search of new lands.* **5 four on the floor** INFORMAL if a car has four on the floor, it has four GEARs that you change using a GEAR SHIFT —**fourth** adj. —see also **be scattered to the four winds** (SCATTER (3)), TWO-BY-FOUR

four-by-four /'.. ,./ usually written as **4 x 4** n. [C] a vehicle that has four wheels and FOUR-WHEEL DRIVE

four eyes /'. ./ n. [singular, not with **the**] an insulting word for someone who wears glasses, used especially by children —**four-eyed** adj.

4-H /,fɔr 'eɪtʃ/ n. [U] an organization that teaches modern methods of farming and other skills to young people

four-leaf clo·ver /,. '.'./ n. [C] a CLOVER plant that has four leaves instead of the usual three, and that people consider to be lucky

four-let·ter word /,.. .. '.'./ n. [C] **1** a word that is considered very offensive, especially one relating to sex or body wastes: *No four-letter words, please – this is a family show.* **2** [usually singular] HUMOROUS a word that expresses an idea that people do not like or agree with: *"Diet" has become a four-letter word in the commercial weight-loss business; now they're called "foodplans."*

four-one-one /,. .. ./ n. **the 411** SLANG information: *What's the 411 on that show Friday night?*

401K /,fɔr oʊ wʌn 'keɪ/ n. [U] a way of saving money for your RETIREMENT that is handled through the company where you work

four-post·er bed /,. .. './ also **four-poster** /,. '../ n. [C] a bed with four tall posts at the corners, usually with a cover attached at the top of the posts and curtains around the sides

four·some /'fɔrsəm/ n. [C] a group of four people who are together to play a game such as BRIDGE or GOLF

four·square[1] /fɔr'skwɛr/ adj. a building that is foursquare is solidly and plainly built, and square in shape

foursquare[2] adv. firmly and completely: *Seymour said he would stand foursquare behind* (=strongly supporting) *the President's policies in the Middle East.*

four-star gen·e·ral /,fɔrstar 'dʒɛnərəl/ n. [C] an officer with a very high rank in the army

four-stroke en·gine /,. .. '.'./ n. [C] an engine that works with two up and two down movements of a PISTON

four·teen /,fɔr'tin˹/ number 14

four·teenth[1] /,fɔr'tinθ˹/ adj. 14th; next after the thirteenth: *the fourteenth century*

fourteenth[2] pron. **the fourteenth** the 14th thing in a series: *Let's have dinner on the fourteenth* (=the 14th day of the month).

fourth[1] /fɔrθ/ adj. 4th; after the third: *Her apartment was on the fourth floor.* | *Mark is starting fourth grade in the fall.*

fourth[2] pron. **the fourth** the 4th thing in a series: *Does your flight leave on the fourth* (=the 4th day of the month)?

fractal

fourth[3] n. [C] 1/4; one of four equal parts: **one-fourth/three-fourths** *Three-fourths of the adults with this heart condition are not receiving the medicine.* —see also QUARTER[3]

fourth di·men·sion /,. .'../ n. **a)** **the fourth dimension** an expression meaning "time," used especially by scientists and writers of SCIENCE FICTION **b)** [singular] a type of experience that is outside normal human experience: *"I think there's a fourth dimension, and taking drugs allows you to explore it," said Streminski.*

fourth es·tate /,. .'../ n. **the fourth estate** newspapers, news magazines, television and radio news, the people who work for them, and the political influence that they have; the PRESS[2] (1)

Fourth of Ju·ly /,. . .'./ n. **the Fourth of July** Independence Day: *a Fourth of July picnic*

four-wheel drive /,. .' ./ written abbreviation **4WD** n. [C,U] a system in a vehicle that gives the power of the engine to all four wheels to make it easier to drive, or a vehicle that has this type of system —**four-wheel drive** adj.

four-wheel·er /,. '../ n. [C] **1** a small vehicle, a little bit like a MOTORCYCLE but with four fat wheels, that people ride for fun **2** INFORMAL a vehicle with four-wheel drive —**four-wheeling** n. [U]

fowl /faʊl/ n. plural **fowls** or **fowl** [C,U] a bird, especially a chicken, that is kept for its meat and eggs —see also **neither fish nor fowl** (FISH[1] (8))

Fox /faks/ a Native American tribe from the northeastern area of the U.S.

fox /faks/ n. **1** [C] a wild animal like a dog, with reddish-brown fur, a pointed face, and a thick tail **2** [C] INFORMAL someone who is sexually attractive: *She's such a fox!* **3** [C] someone who is intelligent and good at deceiving people: *He was a sly old fox.* **4 crazy like a fox** an expression used to describe someone who behaves in a way that makes people think they are strange or crazy, in order to get something **5** [U] the skin and fur of a fox, used to make clothes

fox·glove /'faksglʌv/ n. [C] a tall plant with many bell-shaped flowers, whose leaves are used to make a medicine for heart problems

fox·hole /'fakshoʊl/ n. [C] **1** a hole in the ground that soldiers dig for protection **2** a hole in the ground where a fox lives

fox·hound /'fakshaʊnd/ n. [C] a dog with a very good sense of smell, trained to hunt and kill FOXes

fox·hunt·ing /'faks,hʌntɪŋ/ n. [U] the sport of hunting FOXes with dogs while riding on a horse —**foxhunt** n. [C]

fox ter·ri·er /,. '.../ n. [C] a small dog with short hair

fox·trot /'fakstrat/ n. [C] a type of formal dance which combines short, quick steps with long slow steps, or a piece of music for this dance —**foxtrot** v. [I]

fox·y /'faksi/ adj. **foxier, foxiest 1** INFORMAL sexually attractive: *Regina is a truly foxy lady.* **2** skillful at deceiving people: *The foxy old monk decided to play one last trick on Chu.* **3** like a FOX in appearance

foy·er /'fɔɪɚ/ n. [C] **1** a large room or hall at the entrance to a public building; LOBBY: *About 200 tourists were gathered in the main foyer of the White House.* **2** a room or hall at the entrance to a house or apartment

FPO n. [C] an abbreviation of "fleet post office" or "field post office," used as part of the address of someone in the navy or army

Fr. **1** a written abbreviation of "Father", used in front of the name of a priest: *Fr. Edmond Lavalle* **2 fr.** a written abbreviation of "from" **3** a written abbreviation of "French" or "France"

frac·as /'frækəs, 'freɪ-/ n. [singular] a short, noisy fight involving several people: *Eight people were injured in the fracas.*

frac·tal /'fræktl/ n. [C] TECHNICAL a pattern, usually produced by a computer, that is made by repeating the same shape many times at smaller and smaller sizes —**fractal** *adj.*: *fractal geometry*

frac·tion /ˈfrækʃən/ *n.* [C] **1** a very small amount of something: [+ **of**] *I got these shoes at a fraction of the original price.* **2** a part of a whole number in mathematics, such as ¹/₂ or ³/₄ —see also COMMON FRACTION, IMPROPER FRACTION, PROPER FRACTION

frac·tion·al /ˈfrækʃənl/ *adj.* **1** very small in amount: *The report shows a fractional sales increase for the month of December.* **2** relating to fractions, in mathematics **3** TECHNICAL happening or done in a series of steps: *fractional distillation* —**fractionally** *adv.*

frac·tious /ˈfrækʃəs/ *adj.* someone who is fractious gets angry very easily and tends to start fights: *Maggie grew up in a large, fractious family.* —**fractiousness** *n.* [U]

frac·ture¹ /ˈfræktʃɚ/ *v.* **1** [I,T] if a bone or other hard substance fractures or is fractured, it breaks or cracks: *Ron fractured his finger in the first half of the game.* **2** [I,T] if a group, organization etc. fractures or is fractured, the people in it disagree and do not work well together anymore: *The country has already been fractured by bitter ethnic and political clashes.* | *Lithuania fractured the Soviet Union by declaring its independence.* **3** [T usually passive] to use something such as language in a way that is not correct, or to do something without following the correct rules: **fractured syntax/English etc.** *The announcer boomed out anti-American propaganda in fractured English.*

fracture² *n.* [C] a crack or broken part in a bone or other hard substance: *X-rays showed no fractures in his leg.* | *a hairline fracture* (=very thin crack)

frag /fræg/ *v.* **fragged, fragging** [T] SLANG a word meaning "to completely destroy an enemy," used especially by people in the army, or when talking about computer games

frag·ile /ˈfrædʒəl/ *adj.* **1** easily broken, damaged or ruined: *Be careful with that vase – it's very fragile.* **2** easily harmed: *Ed's already fragile health deteriorated after he left the hospital.* | *Sandra knew just what to say to protect Mike's fragile ego.* | *This is an environmentally fragile area.* —compare FRAIL —**fragility** /frəˈdʒɪləti/ *n.* [U]

frag·ment¹ /ˈfrægmənt/ *n.* [C] a small piece of something that has broken off or that comes from something larger: *Some glass fragments hit me when the window was smashed.* | [+ **of**] *Doctors found fragments of metal embedded in his legs.*

frag·ment² /ˈfrægˌment/ *v.* [I,T] to break something, or be broken into a lot of small, separate parts: *His day was fragmented by interruptions and phone calls.* —**fragmentation** /ˌfrægmənˈteɪʃən/ *n.* [U]

frag·men·tar·y /ˈfrægmənˌteri/ *adj.* consisting of many different small parts: *I have only a fragmentary recollection of the house where I grew up.*

frag·ment·ed /ˈfrægˌmentɪd/ *adj.* separated into many parts, groups, or events, and not seeming to have a clear purpose: *Having such a wide variety of products has caused a fragmented corporate image.*

fra·grance /ˈfreɪgrəns/ *n.* **1** [C,U] a nice smell: *the rich fragrance of a garden flower* —compare AROMA, SCENT¹ (1), SMELL¹ (1) —see Usage Note at SMELL¹ **2** [C] a liquid that you put on your body to make it smell nice; PERFUME: *Would you like to try White Diamonds, the new fragrance from Elizabeth Taylor?*

fra·grant /ˈfreɪgrənt/ *adj.* having a nice smell: *Our bedroom window overlooks a fragrant rose garden.* —**fragrantly** *adv.*

fraid·y cat /ˈfreɪdi ˌkæt/ *n.* [C] INFORMAL a word meaning someone who is too afraid to do something, used especially by children; SCAREDY-CAT

frail /freɪl/ *adj.* **1** someone who is frail is thin and weak, especially because they are old: *Walter looked extremely frail and old as he stepped out of the car.* **2** not strongly made or built, and therefore easily damaged: *A fierce storm engulfed the frail ship.* —compare FRAGILE

frail·ty /ˈfreɪlti/ *n. plural* **frailties 1** [C,U] something bad or weak in your character: *I've had to come to terms with my deepest human frailties.* **2** [U] the lack of strength or health: *Mr. Zimmer is still alert, despite his age and the frailty of his body.* | *The recent riots are evidence of the frailty of the peace agreement.*

frame¹ /freɪm/ *n.*

1 border [C] a firm structure that holds something such as a picture or window, and provides a border for it: *That's a nice picture – you should put it in a frame.* | **a picture/door/window etc. frame** *The window frames were rotting and the paint was peeling in places.*

2 structure [C] the structure or main supporting parts of a piece of furniture, vehicle, or other object: *There's nothing wrong with the frame of the chair, but the upholstery needs replacing.* | *a bicycle frame*

3 body [C] the general shape formed by the bones of someone's body: *He bent his lanky frame into the small car.*

4 glasses [C usually plural] the metal or plastic part of a pair of GLASSES that holds the LENSes: *She wore sunglasses with pointy black frames.*

5 frame of mind the attitude you have at a particular time | **be in a good/bad etc. frame of mind** *You just need to be in the right frame of mind to win.*

6 main facts/ideas [C usually singular] the main ideas, facts etc. that something is based on: *A clear explanation of the subject provides a frame on which a deeper understanding can be built.* | *Some comments may or may not be understood as harassment, depending on your* **frame of reference** (=knowledge and beliefs that influence the way you think).

7 film [C] an area of film that contains one photograph, or one of the series of separate photographs that make up a movie: *Movies are shot at 24 frames per second.*

8 sports [C] a complete part in the game of BOWLING: *I won the next three frames.* —see also TIME FRAME

frame² *v.* [T] **1** to surround something with a border so that it looks nice, or so that you can see it clearly: *An arch of floral curtains frames the window.* | *Just look through the viewfinder to frame your subject and press the button.* **2** to put a picture in a structure that will hold it firmly: *I'm going to get the picture framed and give it to Mom for her birthday.* | **gold-framed/wood-framed etc.** *There was a gold-framed mirror on the wall.* **3** to deliberately make someone seem guilty of a crime when they are not guilty, by providing things that seem like proof: *Wanda claims she was framed by her ex-husband and his brother.* —see also FRAME-UP **4** FORMAL to carefully plan the way you are going to say a question, statement, etc.: *Suzanne paused for a moment, carefully framing her answer.*

frame house /ˌ. ˈ./ *n.* [C] a house whose main structure is made of wood

frame-up /ˈ. ./ *n.* [C] a plan to make someone seem guilty of a crime when they are not guilty

frame·work /ˈfreɪmwɚk/ *n.* [C] **1** [usually singular] a set of facts, ideas etc. from which more complicated ideas are developed, or on which decisions are based: [+ **of**] *We must act within the framework of the Constitution.* | [+ **for**] *The report could serve as the possible framework for a compromise.* **2** **political/legal/social etc. framework** the structure of a society, a legal or political system etc.: *We as residents have the right, within the legal framework, to decide what the city will look like.* **3** the main supporting parts of a building, vehicle, or object: *A rigid metal framework supported the sculpture.*

franc /fræŋk/ *n.* [C] the standard unit of money in various countries, including France and Belgium

France /fræns/ a country in western Europe

France /fræns, frɑns/**, An·a·tole** /ˈænəˌtoʊl/ (1844–1924) a French writer of short stories and NOVELs

fran·chise¹ /ˈfræntʃaɪz/ *n.* **1** [C] a business that sells a particular company's products or services under a special agreement: *Many towns were full of shopping malls and fast-food franchises.* **2** [C] a professional sports team: *This franchise will never have another* second baseman as talented as Roberto Alomar. **3** [C] permission that a company gives to a person or group so that they can sell the company's products or services: *The city was still negotiating with cable TV companies over who'd get the first franchise to beam programs into people's homes.* **4** [U] FORMAL the legal right to vote in your country's elections: *The constitution provided broad electoral franchise.*

franchise[2] *v.* [T] to give or sell a franchise to someone: *The corporation that owns the spa is hoping to franchise this treatment nationally.*

fran·chis·ee /ˌfræntʃaɪˈziː/ *n.* [C] someone who is given or sold a franchise to sell a company's products or services

fran·chis·er, **franchisor** /ˈfræntʃaɪzɚ/ *n.* [C] a company that gives people or businesses permission to sell its products or services to the public

Fran·cis·cans /frænˈsɪskənz/ *n.* [plural] a Christian religious group begun by St. Francis of Assisi in 1209, whose members live a holy life according to strict rules —**Franciscan** *adj.*

Fran·cis Fer·di·nand /ˈfrænsɪs ˈfɚdnˌænd/ (1863–1914) an Austrian ARCHDUKE who was killed by a Serbian ASSASSIN and whose death started World War I

Francis of As·si·si, St. /ˌfrænsɪs əv əˈsiːsi/ (1182–1226) an Italian Christian leader who started the Franciscan religious ORDER

Francis Xa·vi·er, St. /ˌfrænsɪs ˈzeɪviɚ/ —see XAVIER, ST. FRANCIS

Franck /frɑŋk/, **Cé·sar** /ˈseɪzɑr/ (1822–1890) a French musician, born in Belgium, who wrote CLASSICAL music

Franco- /ˈfræŋkoʊ, ˈfræŋkə/ *prefix* [in nouns and adjectives] **1** relating to France; FRENCH: *The area has a large francophone (=French-speaking) population.* **2** French and something else: *a Franco-German proposal*

Fran·co /ˈfræŋkoʊ/, **Fran·cis·co** /frænˈsɪskoʊ/ (1892–1975) a Spanish military leader and RIGHT-WING politician, who led the Nationalist side in the Spanish Civil War, and ruled Spain as a DICTATOR until his death

fran·co·phone /ˈfræŋkəˌfoʊn, -koʊ-/ *n.* [C] someone who speaks French as their first language —**francophone** *adj.*

Fran·glais /ˌfrɑŋˈɡleɪ/ *n.* [U] INFORMAL a mixture of the French and English languages

Frank /fræŋk/ *n.* one of the people that lived in Germany in the third century A.D. and ruled much of western Europe from the fifth century to the ninth century A.D.

frank[1] /fræŋk/ *adj.* **1** honest and truthful: *In an unusually frank speech, Glenn acknowledged the gravity of the economic situation.* | [+ **with**] *We've always tried to be frank with the kids.* **2 to be frank** SPOKEN used when you are saying something true that other people may not like: *To be absolutely frank, there is entirely too much speculation about my future with the company.* —**frankness** *n.* [U]

frank[2] *n.* [C] a long cooked SAUSAGE, usually eaten in a long piece of bread; HOT DOG[1] (1)

frank[3] *v.* [T] to print a sign on an envelope showing that the cost of sending it has been paid: *One morning a franked official letter from the state capitol arrived.*

Frank, Anne /æn/ (1929–1945) a Jewish girl who wrote a famous DIARY, in which she describes her life while she and her family were hiding from the Nazis in Amsterdam

Frank·fort /ˈfræŋkfɚt/ the capital city of the U.S. state of Kentucky

frank·fur·ter /ˈfræŋkˌfɚtɚ/ *n.* [C] FORMAL a FRANK[2]

frank·in·cense /ˈfræŋkənˌsɛns/ *n.* [U] a substance that is burnt to give a sweet smell, especially at religious ceremonies

franking ma·chine /ˈ.. .ˌ./ *n.* [C] a POSTAGE METER

Frank·lin /ˈfræŋklɪn/, **Benjamin** (1706–1790) a U.S. politician, writer, and scientist, who was involved in writing the Declaration of Independence and the U.S. Constitution —see picture on page 1329

frank·ly /ˈfræŋkli/ *adv.* **1** [sentence adverb] used to show that you are saying what you really think about something: *Frankly, I think the Internet is overrated.* | *Quite frankly, I'm very troubled by what you've told me.* **2** honestly and directly: *Stan admitted frankly that he needs help to fight his drug problem.*

fran·tic /ˈfræntɪk/ *adj.* **1** extremely worried and frightened about a situation, so that you cannot control your feelings: *A frantic note had crept into Jane's voice.* | *People were frantic, trying to call relatives after the earthquake.* **2** extremely hurried and using a lot of energy, but not very organized: *I spent three frantic days getting everything ready for Christmas.* —**frantically** /-kli/ *adv.* —see also FRENETIC

frap·pe /fræp/ *n.* [C] a thick kind of MILKSHAKE

frap·pé /fræˈpeɪ/ *n.* [C] a drink served over very thin pieces of ice

frat /fræt/ *n.* [C] INFORMAL a FRATERNITY (1): *a frat boy* (=a member of a fraternity)

fra·ter·nal /frəˈtɚnl/ *adj.* FORMAL **1** showing a special friendliness to other people because you share interests or ideas with them: *The fraternal spirit seems to be declining in relations between our churches.* **2** relating to brothers: *fraternal loyalty* —**fraternally** *adv.*

fraternal twin /.,.. '. / *n.* [C usually plural] one of a pair of babies born at the same time to the same mother, but who develop from different EGGS[1] (3) —compare IDENTICAL TWIN

fra·ter·ni·ty /frəˈtɚnəti/ *n. plural* **fraternities** **1** [C] a club at a college or university that has only male members: *The university's fraternities have a reputation for lively parties.* —compare SORORITY **2** [U] a feeling of friendship between members of a group: *The Nobel prize is awarded to someone who has worked to promote fraternity between nations.* **3 the educational/scientific etc. fraternity** all the people who work in a particular profession: *Even members of the economic fraternity are confused by the new policy.*

frat·er·nize /ˈfrætɚˌnaɪz/ *v.* [I] to be friendly with someone who is not allowed to be your friend: [+ **with**] *They have ordered the soldiers not to fraternize with the local residents* —**fraternization** /ˌfrætɚnəˈzeɪʃən/ *n.* [U]

frat·ri·cide /ˈfrætrəˌsaɪd/ *n.* [C,U] TECHNICAL the crime of murdering your brother or sister

fraud /frɔd/ *n.* **1** [C,U] the illegal action of deceiving people in order to gain money, power etc.: **election/tax/mail etc. fraud** *Companies have responded to widespread credit card fraud by issuing cards with photos on them.* **2** [C] someone who pretends to be someone else in order to gain money, friendship etc.: *It was weeks before they realized that the young man who had charmed them all was a fraud.* | *I was uncomfortable sitting behind that huge desk — I started to **feel like a fraud.***

fraud·u·lent /ˈfrɔdʒələnt/ *adj.* intended to deceive people in an illegal way, in order to gain money, power etc.: *She entered the country using a fraudulent passport.* | *a fraudulent insurance claim* —**fraudulently** *adv.* —**fraudulence** *n.* [U]

fraught /frɔt/ *adj.* full of something, especially problems or negative feelings: [+ **with**] *Theirs had been a marriage fraught with pain and frustration.* | *The voyage promised to be fraught with dangers.*

fray[1] /freɪ/ *n.* **1** [C] an argument or fight: *Three civilians were injured during the fray.* | **enter/join the fray** *Lewis entered the fray recently, telling reporters he would not change his vote.* | **jump/step/ leap into the fray** *Then Merton jumped into the fray and tried to persuade company bosses to lower prices.* **2 be/stay above the fray** to not be involved in a fight or argument: *Wigmore always tried to stay above the political fray and concentrate on her work.*

fray[2] *v.* **frays, frayed, fraying** [I] **1** if cloth or other material frays, the threads become loose because the material is old: *The collar had started to fray on*

Jack's trench coat. **2** if someone's temper or nerves fray, they become annoyed: *It was only three o'clock and tempers were already beginning to fray.* —**frayed** *adj.*

Fra·zier /ˈfreɪʒɚ/, **Joe** /dʒoʊ/ (1944–) a U.S. BOXER who was world CHAMPION in 1970–1973

fraz·zle /ˈfræzəl/ *n.* **be worn to a frazzle** to be extremely tired after doing something: *We were worn to a frazzle after our last-minute Christmas shopping.*

fraz·zled /ˈfræzəld/ *adj.* INFORMAL extremely tired and unable to deal with problems or difficulties, especially because you have been very busy: *Some parents say they feel frazzled most nights.*

FRB —see FEDERAL RESERVE BANK

freak[1] /frik/ *n.* [C] **1 computer/fitness/jazz etc. freak** INFORMAL someone who is very interested in a particular thing or activity, or likes something a lot: *I've been a huge health freak since my daughter was born.* **2 a control freak** INFORMAL someone who always wants to control situations and other people: *Some bosses are control freaks, while others are too unclear about what they want from you.* **3** someone who looks very strange or behaves in a very unusual way: *If people can't put you into a category, they tend to just think of you as a freak.* **4** something in nature, such as a strangely-shaped plant or animal, that is very unusual: *Nowadays twins are seen less as a freak of nature and more as a gift.*

freak[2] *adj.* [only before noun] **a freak accident/storm etc.** an accident, storm etc. that is unexpected and very unusual: *The first day of spring brought rain and freak weather across much of the state.*

freak[3] *v.* [I] SPOKEN, INFORMAL to become suddenly angry or afraid, especially so that you cannot control your behavior: *When I told Ben about the accident, he just freaked.*

freak out *phr. v.* [I,T] INFORMAL to become very anxious, upset, or afraid, or make someone very anxious, upset or afraid: *These actors would all completely freak out and panic in a real medical emergency.* | *Those people really freak me out.*

freak·ing /ˈfrikən, -kɪŋ/ *adj.* [only before noun], *adv.* VULGAR used instead of "fucking" to emphasize how angry or annoyed you are: *I told you, there is nothing wrong with my freaking leg!* | *That guy is just freaking nuts.*

freak·ish /ˈfrikɪʃ/ *adj.* very unusual and strange, and sometimes frightening: *One of the characters is Sheeva, a freakish eight-foot-tall woman with four arms.* —**freakishly** *adv.* —**freakishness** *n.* [U]

freak show /ˈ. ./ *n.* [C] **1** a place or occasion when people can look at people or animals that look strange or behave in an unusual way: *a circus freak show* **2** a very unusual and strange performance or event which people watch with interest

freak·y /ˈfriki/ *adj.* **freakier, freakiest** SPOKEN strange and slightly frightening: *It was kind of freaky to meet all of his old girlfriends.*

freck·le /ˈfrɛkəl/ *n.* [C usually plural] a small brown spot on someone's skin, especially the face, usually caused by the sun: *She had the same red hair and freckles as her mother.*

freck·led /ˈfrɛkəld/ *adj.* having freckles: *a lightly freckled face*

Fred·er·icks·burg /ˈfrɛdrɪksˌbɚg/ a city in the U.S. state of Virginia where the Confederate general Robert E Lee defeated a Union army in the American Civil War

-free /fri/ *suffix* [in adjectives and adverbs] without something that you do not want: *a salt-free diet* | *a trouble-free trip* | *a smoke-free restaurant* (=where you are not allowed to smoke)

free[1] /fri/ *adj.*
1 can do what you want allowed to live, exist, or happen without being controlled or restricted: *We are waiting for the day when our people's homeland is free.* | [**be free to do sth**] *As soon as her divorce is final, Helen will be free to marry Jim.*

2 no cost not costing any money: *A free bus service will be provided from the parking lot at the train station.* | *The soft drinks are free, but you have to pay for the beer.*

3 not busy if you are free, or have some free time, you have no work, and nothing else that you must do: *Are you free next weekend?* | *My husband and I never seem to have any free time together.* | *a free morning/afternoon etc. I'll give you a call if I have a free evening next week.*

4 not being used something that you want to use is free if no one else is using it: *There's a washing machine free, but you may have to wait for a dryer.* | *Excuse me, is this seat free?*

5 no restrictions without restrictions or controls: *The country is holding the first free elections in over sixty years.* | *a free exchange of information* | *The men were merely exercising their right of free speech* (=the right to say whatever you want). | *A season ticket provides free access to the health club and tennis courts.*

6 not a prisoner not a prisoner: *The rapist could be free in as little as three years.* | *Mandela was finally set free in 1990.*

7 free from/of sth without something that you do not want to have: *Lydia has been completely free from cancer since 1995.* | *free of obligations*

8 free of sth/sb away from something or someone, and happy about it: *I was glad to be free of that dismal office at last.*

9 break free to escape from someone or something, or not be influenced or affected by it: [+ **of/from**] *Kristy says her whole life changed when she broke free of drug addiction.*

10 loose and not fastened to anything or held by anything or anyone: *The free end of the flag has been torn by the wind.* | **work/pull/tear etc. free** *Ken grabbed her around the waist, but she managed to struggle free.* | *Mike screamed and shook himself free.*

11 feel free SPOKEN used to tell someone that they can do something: *If you have any questions, feel free to call me.* | *"Can I use the microwave?" "Oh, feel free."*

12 walk free if a criminal walks free, they are not put in prison: *Some prisons are so overcrowded that convicted felons are allowed to walk free.*

13 run free if an animal runs free, it is allowed to go where it wants to go, without being controlled: *All the animals in our zoo have space to run free.*

14 get a free ride to get something without having to pay for it, because someone else is paying for it: *The law is meant to ensure that illegal immigrants aren't getting a free ride at U.S. taxpayers' expense.*

15 there's no free lunch also **there's no such thing as a free lunch** HUMOROUS used to say that you should not expect to get something good or valuable without having to pay for it or make any effort: *As a country, we must face the fact that there is no free lunch for Social Security recipients.*

16 give sb a free hand/rein to let someone do whatever they want or need to do in a particular situation: *They've given me a free hand with the budget, as long as I stay under $10,000.*

17 your free hand/arm the arm or hand that you are not already using to do something: *I put my arm around Nina and with my free hand took off my hat.*

18 free and easy relaxed, friendly, and without many rules: *a free and easy lifestyle*

19 be free with sth to be generous with something, and possibly more generous than people think you should be: *She's always very free with praise for her employees.* | *Ken's a little too free with his money.*

20 it's a free country SPOKEN, HUMOROUS used to say that you are or should be allowed to do something, after someone has said that you should not do it: *"You can't say things like that!" "I can say whatever I want – it's a free country."*

21 translation a translation that is free gives a general idea of a piece of writing rather than translating every word exactly

22 not showing respect OLD-FASHIONED too friendly, in a way that does not show enough respect: *Your son's manner is rather free.*

23 chemistry TECHNICAL not combined with any

other chemical substance; pure: *free oxygen* —see also FREE RADICAL

s w **free²** v. [T] **1** to allow someone to leave prison or a place where they have been kept by force: *The kidnappers freed the last two hostages unharmed.* | *After being freed Tuesday, the whale swam toward the ocean.* **2** to move something or someone that is firmly fastened or trapped: *We're going to need some rope to help free the girl.* **3** also **free up** to make something available so that it can be used: *Try freeing some memory by shutting down a few applications.* | *Working from home will free up more time to spend with your family.* **4** to help someone by removing something bad or harmful, or something that restricts them in some way: [free sb from sth] *Treatment has freed Jenna from her drug addiction, allowing her to live a productive life.* **5** to help someone to do something, by removing restrictions or making them responsible for fewer things: [free sb to do sth] *The insurance settlement has freed her to travel to New Zealand.*

s w **free³** adv. without payment: *They will provide credit reports free to consumers once a year.* | *Gary told me he could do the ad for free.* | *Consumers who bought the faulty strollers will receive a new one free of charge.* —compare FREELY —see also SCOT-FREE

free a·gent /ˌ. ˈ../ n. [C] a professional sports player who does not have a contract with any team: *Dexter signed with the San Diego Chargers as a free agent in 1986.*

free as·so·ci·a·tion /ˌ. ...ˈ../ n. [U] a method of finding out about someone's mind by asking them to say the first word they think of when you say a particular word —**free-associate** v. [I]

free·base /ˈfriːbeɪs/ v. [I,T] to smoke the illegal drug COCAINE after heating it over a flame

free·bie /ˈfriːbi/ n. [C] INFORMAL something that you are given free, usually something small and not expensive: *Members of Congress are showered daily with parties, freebies and perks.*

free·boot·er /ˈfriːˌbuːtə/ n. [C] OLD USE someone who joins in a war in order to steal other people's goods and money —**freeboot** v. [I]

free·born /ˌfriːˈbɔːrn/ adj. OLD USE not born as a slave

freed·man /ˈfriːdmən, -mæn/ n. plural **freedmen** /-mən, -men/ [C] someone who was born a slave, but has been set free

s w **free·dom** /ˈfriːdəm/ n. **1** [C,U] the right to do what you want without being controlled or restricted by the government, police etc.: *People here like their freedom and privacy.* | *As children, they dreamed about the freedoms and riches they would enjoy in the U.S.* | [freedom to do sth] *After years of struggle, they finally gained the freedom to vote and speak freely.* **2** **freedom of speech/religion etc.** the legal right to say what you want, choose your own religion etc.: *The First Amendment guarantees freedom of expression.* **3** [U] the state of being free and allowed to do what you want: *Kids have too much freedom these days.* **4** [U] the state of being free because you are not in prison: *Davis celebrated his freedom with a steak and a beer.* **5** **freedom from sth** the state of not being affected by something that makes you worried, unhappy, afraid etc.: *Gandhi advocated nonviolence in India's struggle for freedom from British rule.* **6** **freedom of choice** the right or ability to choose whatever you want to do or have: *Health insurance plans that offer patients greater freedom of choice in selecting doctors are becoming too expensive for most people.* **7** **freedom of information** the availability to everyone of information that a government has about people and organizations —compare LIBERTY

freedom fight·er /ˈ.. ˌ../ n. [C] someone who fights in a war against an unfair or dishonest government, army etc. —compare GUERRILLA, TERRORIST

free en·ter·prise /ˌ. ˈ.../ n. [U] the principle and practice of allowing private business to operate without much government control —see also PRIVATE ENTERPRISE

free fall, freefall /ˈ. ./ n. [singular,U] **1** the time when something that has fallen or someone who has

---

577   **free-range**

jumped is only affected by the Earth's GRAVITY (=natural pulling force), for example when someone jumps out of an airplane before the PARACHUTE opens **2** a very fast and uncontrolled fall in the value of something: *The economy is in freefall and there are no signs that it will stop.* —**free-falling** adj.

free-float·ing /ˌ. ˈ..◂/ adj. not connected to or influenced by anything: *Mondale saw his role as more of a free-floating adviser to the President.*

free-for-all /ˈ. . ˌ./ n. [singular] **1** a noisy fight or argument that a lot of people join: *The sheer number of cars creates a free-for-all on the city's potholed roads.* **2** a situation in which there is total freedom and anything can happen: *the free-for-all of sexual activity in the 1970s* | *As the Internet free-for-all grows, it is becoming impossible for businesses to ignore.* —**free-for-all** adj. [only before noun]

free-form /ˈ. ./ adj. [only before noun] having a shape or structure that is not regular or fixed: *free-form designs*

free·hand /ˈfriːhænd/ adj. drawn without any special tools, by using just your hands and a pen or pencil: *a freehand sketch* —**freehand** adv.

free kick /ˌ. ˈ., ˈ. ./ n. [C] a chance for a player on a SOCCER team to kick the ball without opposition because the other team did something wrong

free·lance /ˈfriːlæns/ adj., adv. doing work for companies without being employed by a particular company: *a freelance journalist* | *Steve plans to start working freelance this year.* —**freelance** v. [I] *Fran freelances for several translation agencies.* —**freelance** also **freelancer** n. [C]

free·load·er /ˈfriːloʊdə/ n. [C] INFORMAL someone who regularly takes food or other things from other people, without giving anything in return, in a way that is annoying —**freeload** v. [I] *These days, Nicole is freeloading off her boyfriend.*

free love /ˌ. ˈ./ n. [U] an expression meaning the practice or principle of having sex with many different people without being married, used especially in the 1960s and 1970s

free·ly /ˈfriːli/ adv. **1** without any restrictions: *If your muscles are tense and tight, blood cannot circulate freely.* | *the country's first freely elected president* **2** if you can travel, speak, operate etc. freely, you can do it as much as you want and in whatever way you want: *Foreign tourists will be allowed to leave the country freely.* | *Thomas could not find anyone with whom he could speak freely.* **3** **freely available** very easy to obtain: *Contraceptives are freely available without prescription in pharmacies.* **4** **freely admit/acknowledge** to agree that something is true, especially when this is difficult: *He has freely admitted to using drugs.* **5** if a piece of writing is translated freely, the translation does not attempt to translate the original words exactly, but gives the general meaning **6** generously, or in large quantities: *Sugar is given away freely in restaurants.*

free·man /ˈfriːmən/ n. [C] someone who is not a slave

free mar·ket /ˌ. ˈ../ n. [C] an economic system in which prices are not controlled or limited by the government or any other powerful group: *a free-market economy*

free mar·ket·eer /ˌ. ..ˈ./ n. [C] someone who thinks that prices should be allowed to rise and fall naturally and should not be controlled by the government or any other powerful group

Free·ma·son /ˈfriːˌmeɪsən/ n. [C] FORMAL a Mason

Free·ma·son·ry /ˌfriːˈmeɪsənri/ n. [U] the system and practices of Masons

free port /ˌ. ˈ./ n. [C] a port where goods from all countries can be brought in and taken out without being taxed

free rad·i·cal /ˌ. ˈ.../ n. [C] TECHNICAL an atom or group of atoms with at least one free ELECTRON, which combines with other atoms very easily

free-range /ˌ. ˈ.◂/ adj. [only before noun] **1** free-range farm animals are not kept in small CAGES but

F

are allowed to move around in a large area: *free-range hens* **2** free-range meat or eggs come from these farm animals: *a free-range turkey*

free·sia /ˈfriʒə/ *n.* [C] a plant with nice-smelling flowers

free spir·it /ˌ. ˈ../ *n.* [C] someone who lives the way they want to rather than in the way that society considers normal: *Dan didn't like to wear a suit and wanted to be more of a free spirit.*

free·stand·ing /ˌfriˈstændɪŋ◂/ *adj.* standing alone without being fastened to a frame, wall, or other support: *a freestanding storage unit*

free·style /ˈfristaɪl/ *n.* **1** [singular] a swimming competition in which swimmers use the CRAWL (=fast style of swimming): *the 100-meter freestyle* **2** [singular] a sports competition, for example in SKIING, WRESTLING etc. in which all types of movement are allowed **3** [C] a RAP song in which the artist sings words directly from their imagination, without planning or writing them first

free·think·er /ˌfriˈθɪŋkə/ *n.* [C] someone who does not accept official opinions or ideas, especially about religion —**freethinking** *adj.*

free throw /ˈ. ./ *n.* [C] a chance for one player on a basketball team to throw the ball without any opposition, because a player on the other team did something wrong

Free·town /ˈfritaʊn/ the capital and largest city of Sierra Leone

free trade /ˌ. ˈ./ *n.* [U] a situation in which the goods coming into or going out of a country are not controlled or taxed

free verse /ˌ. ˈ./ *n.* [U] poetry that does not follow a definite structure and does not RHYME at the end of lines —compare BLANK VERSE

free·ware /ˈfriwɛr/ *n.* [U] free computer SOFTWARE, often available on the Internet —compare SHAREWARE

S W **free·way** /ˈfriweɪ/ *n. plural* **freeways** [C] a very wide
3 road in the U.S., built for fast travel: *the Ventura Freeway* —compare EXPRESSWAY, HIGHWAY (1), INTERSTATE

free·wheel /ˌfriˈwil/ *v.* [I] to ride a bicycle or drive a vehicle toward the bottom of a hill, without using power from your legs or the engine; COAST

free·wheel·ing /ˌfriˈwilɪŋ◂/ *adj.* [only before noun] without a lot of rules, or not worried about rules: *Brinkley made his comments during a freewheeling discussion with several colleagues.*

free will /ˌ. ˈ./ *n.* [U] **1 do sth of your own free will** to do something because you want to, not because someone else has forced you to: *Bronson gave us his confession of his own free will.* **2** human effort, which some people believe affects what happens in life more than God or FATE (2)

S W **freeze¹** /friz/ *v. past tense* **froze** *past participle* **frozen**
1 **make solid** [I,T] if a liquid or thing freezes, or something freezes it, it becomes hard and solid because it is very cold: *The lake had frozen overnight.* | *Run a thin stream of water to help keep the pipes from freezing.* | *The cold weather froze firefighters' hoses.* —compare MELT¹ (1), THAW¹ (1)
2 **food** [I,T] to make food extremely cold so that you can preserve it for a long time, or to be able to be preserved in this way: *You can freeze any leftover chili for another meal.* | *Tomatoes don't freeze well.*
3 **feel cold** [I] SPOKEN if someone freezes, they feel very cold: *You'll freeze if you don't put a coat on.* | *We almost froze to death* (=felt extremely cold) *at the football game.*
4 **wages/prices** [T] to officially stop something from happening in order to prevent money from being spent, or prevent prices, pay etc. from being increased: *Dole urged fellow Republicans to back his plan to freeze state spending and cut taxes.* | *The city may have to freeze the hiring of new police officers.*
5 **money/property** [T] to legally prevent money in a bank from being spent, property from being sold

etc.: *The court issued an order freezing the company's assets temporarily.*
6 **stop moving** [I] to stop moving suddenly and stay completely still and quiet: *I froze and listened; someone was in my apartment.* | *"Freeze! Drop your weapons!" shouted the policeman.*
7 **freeze to death** to become so cold that you die
freeze sb ↔ **out** *phr. v.* [T] to deliberately prevent someone from being involved in something by making it difficult for them, not being nice to them etc.: [+ **of**] *The program provides loans to buyers who would otherwise be frozen out of home ownership.*
freeze over *phr. v.* [I] **1** if an area or pool of water freezes over, its surface turns into ice: *We'll go skating tomorrow if the lake freezes over.* **2 until/when hell freezes over** OFFENSIVE used to say that something will continue forever, or will never happen: *We'll keep fighting until hell freezes over.*

freeze² *n.* **1** [C] an occasion when prices or pay are not allowed to be increased | **a price/wage freeze** *The orchestra asked musicians to agree to a wage freeze and a shorter season.* **2** [C usually singular] a short period of time, especially at night, when the temperature is extremely low: *My pansies didn't survive the first hard freeze of the season.* **3** [C] a stopping of some activity: [+ **on**] *He called for a freeze on hiring and a cut in all non-essential services.* —see also DEEP FREEZE

freeze-dry /ˈ. ./ *v. past tense and past participle* **freeze-dried** *present participle* **freeze-drying** [T usually passive] to preserve food by freezing and drying it very quickly: *freeze-dried instant coffee*

freeze-frame /ˈ. ˌ./ *n.* [C,U] the process of stopping the action on a VIDEO at one particular place, or the place where you stop the action —**freeze-frame** *v.* [T]

freez·er /ˈfrizə/ *n.* [C] a large piece of electrical **S W** equipment that is usually part of a REFRIGERATOR, in **3** which food can be stored at very low temperatures for a long time —compare DEEP FREEZE, REFRIGERATOR

freez·ing¹ /ˈfrizɪŋ/ *n.* [U] **above/below freezing** above or below 32°F or 0°C, the temperature at which water freezes: *Temperatures remained below freezing during the afternoon.*

freezing² *adj.* extremely cold, or feeling extremely cold: *Close the window – it's freezing in here.* | *My flimsy jacket was inadequate for the freezing Japanese weather.* | *We were **freezing cold** in the tent last night.*

freezing point /ˈ.. ˌ./ *n.* [C usually singular] **1** the temperature at which water turns into ice, 32°F or 0°C **2** the temperature at which a particular liquid freezes: *Alcohol has a lower freezing point than water.* —compare BOILING POINT

freight¹ /freɪt/ *n.* **1** [U] goods that are carried by train, airplane, or ship: *These trains haul freight between Grand Junction and Denver.* **2** [U] the money charged for sending goods by train, airplane, or ship: *The basic model is listed at $16,298 plus $500 freight.* **3** [C] a FREIGHT TRAIN

freight² *v.* [T] to send goods by train, airplane, or ship

freight·er /ˈfreɪtə/ *n.* [C] a large ship that carries goods

freight train /ˈ. ./ *n.* [C] a train that carries goods, not passengers

Fré·mont /ˈfrimɑnt/, **John C.** (1813–1890) a U.S. soldier, politician, and EXPLORER, who traveled across the western part of North America and made maps of this area. He encouraged U.S. citizens to move to these places, which are now the states of Idaho, Nevada, Washington, Oregon, and California.

French¹ /frɛntʃ/ *n.* **1** the language of France, and some other countries: *Patric's family speaks French at home.* | *How do you say "mushrooms" in French?* **2** the language and literature of France as a subject of study: *I had to take two years of French in high school.* **3 the French** the people of France: *The territory was originally colonized by the French.*

French² *adj.* **1** relating to France or its people: *French cuisine* | *I stayed with a French family in Paris.* **2** relating to the French language: *Aren't you*

F

in my French class? **3 pardon/excuse my French** SPOKEN, INFORMAL used to say that you are sorry that you just used an offensive word

French bread /ˌ. '.ˌ/ *n.* [U] white bread that is baked in a long narrow shape

French Ca·na·di·an /ˌ. .'....ˌ/ *n.* [C] a person from Canada whose first language is French —**French-Canadian** *adj.*

French doors /ˌ. '.ˌ/ *n.* [plural] a pair of doors with many pieces of glass in a frame

French dress·ing /ˌ. '..ˌ/ *n.* [U] a special SAUCE for SALADS that is reddish-orange in color and is sold in bottles

French fry /'. .ˌ/ *n. plural* **French fries** [C usually plural] a thin piece of potato that has been cooked in hot oil —**French-fry** *v.* [T usually passive] *French-fried onions*

French Gui·a·na /ˌfrɛntʃ giˈɑnə, -ˈænə/ a country in northeast South America that is ruled by France

French horn /ˌ. '.ˌ/ *n.* [C] a musical instrument that is shaped like a circle, with a wide bell-like opening

French kiss /ˌ. '.ˌ/ *n.* [C] a romantic kiss between two people with their mouths open and with their tongues touching —**French-kiss** *v.* [I,T]

French·man /'frɛntʃmən/ *n. plural* **Frenchmen** /-mən/ [C] a man born in France or one who has French parents

French toast /ˌ. '.ˌ/ *n.* [U] pieces of bread put into a mixture of eggs and milk and then cooked in hot oil

French win·dows /ˌ. ..ˌ/ *n.* [plural] FRENCH DOORS

French·wom·an /'frɛntʃˌwomən/ *n. plural* **French-women** /-ˌwimin/ [C] a woman born in France, or one who has French parents

fre·net·ic /frəˈnɛtɪk/ *adj.* frenetic activity is fast, exciting, and not very organized: *frenetic pace/activity/motion We're afraid that we won't adapt to the frenetic pace of life in the city.*

fren·zied /'frɛnzid/ *adj.* frenzied activity is done with a lot of anxiety or excitement and not much control: *It was at least five minutes before the crowd's frenzied applause died down.* —**frenziedly** *adv.*

fren·zy /'frɛnzi/ *n. plural* **frenzies** **1** [C,U] the state of being very anxious, excited, and unable to control your behavior: *Gaetz's last minute goal sent the crowd into a frenzy.* **2** [C usually singular] a period in which people do a lot of things very quickly: *Rumors of their divorce stirred up a frenzy of media attention.* | *a buying/selling/shopping etc. frenzy An initial price decline touched off a selling frenzy at the Chicago Board of Trade.* **3 a feeding frenzy a)** an occasion when a lot of people are being involved in an activity in a wild and uncontrolled way: *After the initial reports on CBS, this scene became a media feeding frenzy* **b)** an occasion when a lot of wild animals, especially SHARKS, come together to eat things in a very wild way

Fre·on /'friɑn/ *n.* [U] TRADEMARK a chemical that was used for cooling in equipment such as REFRIGERATORS and AIR CONDITIONERS until it was found to be harmful to the environment

freq. the written abbreviation of FREQUENCY or FREQUENTLY

fre·quen·cy /'frikwənsi/ *n. plural* **frequencies** **1** [C,U] the number of times that something happens within a particular period or within a particular group of people: *Divorces are being initiated with more frequency by women.* | *[+ of] There is a higher frequency of diabetes in older people.* **2** [U] the fact that something happens a lot: *[+ of] We are concerned about the frequency of crime in the area.* **3** [C] the number of radio waves broadcast per second by a particular station, used to express where to find a station on the radio **4** [C,U] the rate at which a sound WAVE[2] (8) moves up and down per second: *Women hear high frequency sounds better than men.*

fre·quent[1] /'frikwənt/ *adj.* happening or doing something often: *Gunshots are so frequent in the neighborhood that they rarely calls the police anymore.* | *a frequent flier/traveler/visitor etc. Shaw's Market is offering a discount to frequent shoppers.* —opposite INFREQUENT

frequent[2] *v.* [T usually passive] FORMAL to go to a particular place often: *The hotel is frequented by American tourists.*

frequent fli·er /ˌ.. '..ˌ/ *n.* [C] someone who is often a passenger on a particular AIRLINE, so that they receive free flight tickets, a more comfortable place to sit etc.: *frequent flier program/mileage/award* etc. *Hope has racked up 9 million miles on his frequent flier account.*

fre·quent·ly /'frikwəntli/ *adv.* very often or many times: *Stir the sauce frequently to avoid burning.* | *You see her pretty frequently, don't you?*

fres·co /'frɛskou/ *n. plural* **frescoes** or **frescos** [C] a painting made on a wall, on a surface of wet PLASTER[1] (1) —compare MURAL

fresh /frɛʃ/ *adj.*

1 |new| an amount or a thing that is fresh is added to or replaces what was there before: *Most houses on the street boast fresh paint.* | *Marly put fresh sheets (=clean sheets) on the beds in the guest room.*

2 |food/flowers| **a)** fresh food is very recently produced, picked, or prepared and tastes good: *fresh vegetables* | *You can use fresh or frozen strawberries.* | *The cookies were fresh out of the oven.* **b)** fresh flowers have recently been picked

3 fresh air air from outside, especially away from a city where the air is cleaner: *I leave the window open at night to get some fresh air.*

4 |interesting| good or interesting because it has not been done, seen, read etc. before: *Hill's vibrant singing style makes even the old songs sound fresh.* | *Ryan will bring a fresh approach and strong leadership skills to the job.* | *The movie business seems starved for fresh ideas.*

5 |not tired| full of energy because you are not tired: *Somehow Julia managed to seem fresh and lively even at the end of the day.* | *She woke up feeling fresh as a daisy (=not tired and ready to do things).*

6 fresh from sth/fresh out of sth having just finished something such as your education or training, and often not having a lot of experience: *Iacocca started in the auto industry fresh out of Princeton.*

7 be fresh out of sth SPOKEN to have just used your last supplies of something: *Sorry, we're fresh out of swordfish – perhaps you'd like to try the tuna?*

8 |cool/clean| looking, feeling, smelling, or tasting pleasantly clean or cool: *a fresh minty taste*

9 |weather| wind or weather that is fresh feels fairly cold: *a fresh breeze*

10 |water| fresh water contains no salt and comes from rivers and lakes

11 fresh-made/fresh-cut/fresh-grated etc. having just been made, cut, grated etc.: *fresh-squeezed orange juice* —see also FRESHLY

12 fresh in your mind recent enough to be remembered clearly: *It's a good idea to reread the notes you take in class while they are still fresh in your mind.*

13 a fresh start an act of starting something again in a completely new and different way after being unsuccessful: *Around six years ago, she departed for California to make a fresh start.*

14 |person| SLANG a person or thing that is fresh is very good or attractive; COOL[1] (2): *Will's a pretty fresh guy.*

15 get/be fresh with sb a) to behave or speak in a way that does not show respect for someone: *Don't you get fresh with me, son!* **b)** to show someone in a confident but impolite way that you think they are sexually attractive: *He started getting fresh with me.*

16 a fresh complexion healthy-looking skin on your face —**freshness** *n.* [U] —see also **new/fresh blood** (BLOOD (3))

fresh·en /'frɛʃən/ *v.* **1** [T] also **freshen up** to make something look clean, new, and attractive, or smell nice: *To freshen a celery stalk, trim the base and place in cold water.* | *Some new pastel curtains should freshen up the bedroom.* **2** [T] to make something feel cool: *Freshen your skin with avocado body lotion.* **3** [I] if wind or the weather freshens, it gets colder

F

freshen up *phr. v.* [I,T] to wash your hands and face in order to feel clean and comfortable: *Sara hurried into the bathroom to freshen up before the meeting.*

fresh-faced /'. ./ *adj.* having a young, healthy-looking face, and often seeming to have little experience or knowledge of the world: *Weir, 49, was a fresh-faced teen when he met up with Garcia.*

fresh·ly /'freʃli/ *adv.* [+ past participle] very recently: *freshly ground black pepper* | *The two girls were dressed in freshly pressed dresses.*

S W
2
fresh·man /'freʃmən/ *n. plural* **freshmen** /-mən/ [C] a student in the first year of HIGH SCHOOL or college —compare JUNIOR² (1), SENIOR² (1), SOPHOMORE

fresh·wa·ter /'freʃ,wɔtɚ/ *adj.* [only before noun] relating to or coming from rivers or lakes, rather than the ocean: *freshwater lakes* | *freshwater crabs* —compare SALTWATER²

fret¹ /fret/ *v.* **fretted, fretting** [I] to feel worried about small or unimportant things: *Don't fret – everything will be all right.* | [+ **about/over**] *Jolie spent her days fretting about boys and clothes.*

fret² *n.* [C] one of the raised lines on the NECK (=long straight part) of a GUITAR, BANJO etc.

fret·ful /'fretfəl/ *adj.* anxious and complaining, especially about small or unimportant things: *The baby was tired and fretful.* —**fretfully** *adv.* —**fretfulness** *n.* [U]

fret·ted /'fretɪd/ *adj.* TECHNICAL cut or shaped into complicated patterns as decoration

fret·work /'fretˌwɚk/ *n.* [U] patterns cut into thin wood, or the activity of making these patterns

F

Freud /frɔɪd/, **Sig·mund** /'sɪgmənd/ (1856–1939) an Austrian doctor who developed a new system for understanding the way that people's minds work, and a new way of treating mental illness called PSYCHOANALYSIS. His ideas have had a very great influence on the way that people think in the 20th century

Freud·i·an /'frɔɪdiən/ *adj.* **1** relating to Sigmund Freud's ideas about the way the mind works, and the way it can be studied **2** a Freudian remark or action is connected with the ideas about sex that people have in their minds but do not usually talk about

Freudian slip /,... './ *n.* [C] something which you say that is different from what you intended to say, and shows your true thoughts

Fri. a written abbreviation of Friday

fri·a·ble /'fraɪəbəl/ *adj.* TECHNICAL friable rocks or soil are easily broken into very small pieces or into powder

fri·ar /'fraɪɚ/ *n.* [C] a man who belongs to a Catholic group, whose members in past times traveled around teaching about religion and who were very poor —compare MONK

fric·as·see /'frɪkə,si/ *n.* [C,U] a dish made of small pieces of meat in a thick SAUCE (1) —**fricassee** *v.* [T]

fric·a·tive /'frɪkətɪv/ *n.* [C] TECHNICAL a sound, such as /f/ or/z/, made by forcing your breath through a narrow opening between your lips and teeth, or between your tongue and teeth

frick·ing /'frɪkən, -ɪŋ/ *adj.* [only before noun] *adv.* VULGAR used instead of "fucking" to emphasize how angry or annoyed you are: *I can't get this fricking pen to write.*

fric·tion /'frɪkʃən/ *n.* **1** [U,plural] disagreement or angry feelings between people: *Pay is a continuing source of friction with the workers.* | *Creative differences led to friction within the band.* **2** [U] the rubbing of one surface against another: *Check your rope frequently, as friction against the rock can wear it down.* **3** [U] TECHNICAL the natural force that prevents one surface from sliding easily over another surface: *Heat can be produced by chemical reactions or friction.*

Fri·day /'fraɪdi, -deɪ/ *written abbreviation* **Fri.** *n.* [C,U] the sixth day of the week, between Thursday and

Saturday: *Our Spanish class has a test Friday.* | *Richard's birthday is on Friday.* | *Mom said she mailed the letter last Friday.* | *We're having a huge party next Friday!* | *It is supposed to rain this Friday* (=the next Friday that is coming). | *Jody only works on Fridays* (=each Friday). | *Did you say Mike's getting married on a Friday?* | **Friday morning/afternoon/night etc.** *I've set aside a time for you on Friday morning.* —see Usage Note at SUNDAY

fridge /frɪdʒ/ *n.* [C] INFORMAL a REFRIGERATOR

S W
3

fried /fraɪd/ the PAST TENSE and PAST PARTICIPLE of FRY

Frie·dan /'fridn/, **Bet·ty** /'beti/ (1921–) a U.S. writer whose ideas were important in starting the modern WOMEN'S MOVEMENT

Fried·man /'fridmən/, **Milton** (1912–) a U.S. ECONOMIST who helped to develop the idea of MONETARISM

friend /frend/ *n.* [C]

S W
1 1

1 **person you like** someone who you like very much and like to spend time with: *Jerry, I'd like to introduce you to my friend Lucinda.* | [**be friends with sb**] *Billy's parents are friends with my dad.* | *I'm going to visit a friend of mine in Flagstaff.* | *Stuart is just my brother's best friend – I've known him since I was six.* | *I ran into an old friend* (=someone who has been your friend for a long time) *last night.* | **good/close friends** *Karen and I are getting a divorce, but we're still good friends.* | *I met Stephano through a friend of a friend.*

2 **make friends** to meet someone and become friendly with them: *Did you make any new friends at school today?* | [+ **with**] *A little boy came over and tried to make friends with Tommy.*

3 **be just (good) friends** SPOKEN used to say that you are friendly with someone but are not having a romantic relationship with them: *I'm not going out with Nathan, you know – we're just friends.*

4 **supporter** someone who supports a theater, arts organization, CHARITY (1) etc. by giving money or help: [+ **of**] *Carol is chairman of the Friends of the Library committee.*

5 **not an enemy** someone who is not an enemy and will not harm you or cause trouble for you: *Who goes there? Friend or foe?* | *Don't worry, you're among friends here.*

6 **have friends in high places** to know important people who can help you: *I just happened to have friends in high places, who could arrange things like meetings with the mayor.*

7 **With friends like that, who needs enemies?** SPOKEN, HUMOROUS used to say that someone who you thought was your friend has done something to you that was not nice

8 **be no friend of sth** to oppose someone or something: *I've never been a friend of Republicans.*

9 **our/your friend** SPOKEN used to talk about someone you do not know, who is doing something annoying: *Our friend with the loud voice is back.*

10 **at public occasion** SPOKEN used to address a group of people in a meeting or other formal public occasion: *Friends, we are gathered here today to witness the marriage of John and Beth.*

11 **Friend** a member of the Society of Friends; a Quaker

12 **a friend in need** FORMAL someone who helps you when you need it

friend·less /'frendlɪs/ *adj.* having no friends and no one to help you

friend·ly /'frendli/ *adj.* **friendlier, friendliest** **1** behaving toward someone in a way that shows you like them and are ready to talk to them or help them: *A friendly voice answered the phone.* | *Misha was being very friendly today.* | [+ **to/toward**] *People in Paris were really friendly to me.* **2** **be friendly with sb** to be friends with someone: *I recently moved into an apartment and became friendly with the mother of three young children.* **3** **environmentally friendly/ozone friendly etc.** not damaging to the environment, OZONE etc.: *All goods are shipped in environmentally friendly packaging.* —see also USER-FRIENDLY **4** **friendly fire** bombs, bullets etc. that accidentally kill people who are fighting on the same side **5** not at war with your own country, or not opposing you: *friendly nations* —**friendliness** *n.* [U]

S W
2 3

USAGE NOTE: FRIENDLY

GRAMMAR

Although **friendly** ends in "ly," it is an adjective and not an adverb: *Amy is a very friendly girl.* | *We aim to treat all our clients in a friendly, courteous manner.*

-friendly /frɛndli/ *suffix* [in adjectives] **1** not difficult for particular people to use: *user-friendly software* | *a customer-friendly shopping environment* **2** not harming something: *eco-friendly paper products* (=not harming the environment)

friend·ship /ˈfrɛndʃɪp/ *n.* **1** [C] a relationship between friends: *Our friendship developed quickly over the weeks that followed.* | [**form a friendship**] *The two boys formed a deep and lasting friendship.* **2** [U] the feelings and behavior that exist between friends: *In his speech, Irving talked about the importance of friendship and loyalty.*

fri·er /ˈfraɪɚ/ *n.* [C] another spelling of FRYER

fries /fraɪz/ **1** the plural of FRY **2** the third person singular form of the verb FRY

frieze /friz/ *n.* [C] a thin border along the top of the wall of a building or in a room, usually decorated with pictures, patterns etc.

frig·ate /ˈfrɪgɪt/ *n.* [C] a small, fast ship used in wars, especially for protecting other ships

frig·ging /ˈfrɪgən, -gɪŋ/ *adj.* [only before noun] *adv.* VULGAR used instead of "fucking" to emphasize how angry or annoyed you are: *These frigging shoes are killing me!*

fright /fraɪt/ *n.* **1** [singular,U] a sudden feeling of fear: *Darren was pale with fright.* | [**give sb a fright**] *The heart attack gave Dick quite a fright, but he's doing well.* **2** **look a fright** OLD-FASHIONED to look unattractive, or much worse than usual —see also STAGE FRIGHT

fright·en /ˈfraɪtn/ *v.* [T] **1** to make someone feel afraid: *Travis, you just frighten the dog when you play that music.* | *The driver was frightened by the shots.* **2 frighten sb into doing sth/frighten sb out of doing sth** to force someone to do something or not to do something by making them afraid: *Mrs. Fenn tried to frighten the boy into telling her who had broken her window.*

frighten sb ↔ **away** *phr. v.* [T] to make a person or animal go away by making them feel afraid: *Our yelling and screaming frightened the bear away.*

frighten sb/sth ↔ **off** *phr. v.* [T] to make a person or animal so nervous or afraid that they go away or do not do something they were going to do: *They believe that banging on pots will frighten off evil spirits.*

fright·ened /ˈfraɪtnd/ *adj.* feeling afraid: *a frightened animal* | [+ of] *He was very frightened of being alone.* | *She was too frightened to testify against the man that attacked her.* | *I was frightened to death* (=very scared) *when I saw a burglar in the house.* —see Usage Note at ADJECTIVE

fright·en·ing /ˈfraɪtnɪŋ/ *adj.* making you feel afraid or nervous: *The crime rate in this city is frightening.* | *Flying in an airplane can be a frightening prospect for some people.* | *It was frightening not to know what was happening.* —see Usage Note at ADJECTIVE —**frighteningly** *adv.*: *The attack was frighteningly similar to one that had occurred a week earlier.*

fright·ful /ˈfraɪtfəl/ *adj.* OLD-FASHIONED very bad, or not nice: *There's been a frightful accident.* —**frightfulness** *n.* [U]

fright·ful·ly /ˈfraɪtfəli/ *adv.* [+ adj.] OLD-FASHIONED very: *Lawrence was so frightfully strict with the children.*

frig·id /ˈfrɪdʒɪd/ *adj.* **1** very cold: *frigid winds* **2** a woman who is frigid does not like having sex **3** LITERARY not friendly or nice: *a frigid look* —**frigidly** *adv.* —**frigidity** /frɪˈdʒɪdəti/ *n.* [U]

frill /frɪl/ *n.* [C] **1** additional features that are nice but not necessary: *Some cheaper airlines offer few frills.* | *If you want to save money, choose a well-made, no-frills model.* **2** an edge on a piece of cloth that has many small folds in it and that is used as decoration: *Cindy's dress was covered with frills and bows.*

frill·y /ˈfrɪli/ *adj.* **frillier, frilliest** having many frills: *a frilly nightgown*

fringe[1] /frɪndʒ/ *n.* [C] **1** an edge of hanging threads on a curtain, piece of clothing etc. **2 on the fringes a)** not completely belonging to or accepted by a group of people who share the same job, activities etc.: [+ of] *a small group on the fringes of the art world* **b)** also **on the fringe** at the part of something that is farthest from the center: [+ of] *It was easier to move around on the fringe of the crowd.* **3 the nationalist/radical etc. fringe** a group of people within an organization or political party who have extreme ideas that most people do not agree with: *activists on the political fringe of the union* —see also **the lunatic fringe** (LUNATIC (3))

fringe[2] *adj.* [only before noun] different from the most usual or accepted way of thinking or doing things: **fringe activists/groups/movements etc.** *The government coalition included several smaller fringe parties.* —see also FRINGE BENEFIT

fringe[3] *v.* [T] to be around the edge of something; BORDER: *A line of trees fringed the pool.*

fringe ben·e·fit /ˈ. ,.../ *n.* [C usually plural] a service or advantage that you are given with a job, in addition to your pay, such as health insurance, a company car etc.

frip·per·y /ˈfrɪpəri/ *n. plural* **fripperies** [C usually plural] an unnecessary and useless object or decoration: *Hotel managers refused to install cable TV and other fripperies that would distract clients from gambling.*

Fris·bee, frisbee /ˈfrɪzbi/ *n.* [C,U] TRADEMARK a piece of plastic shaped like a plate that you throw to someone else to catch as a game

frisk /frɪsk/ *v.* **1** [T] to search someone for hidden weapons, drugs etc. by passing your hands over their body: *Visitors to the ceremony were frisked and asked to walk through metal detectors.* **2** [I] OLD-FASHIONED to run and jump in a playful way: *Barking and yelping, the puppy frisked at his heels.*

frisk·y /ˈfrɪski/ *adj.* **friskier, friskiest 1** full of energy, fun, and cheerfulness: *a frisky colt* **2** INFORMAL feeling sexually excited —**friskily** *adv.* —**friskiness** *n.* [U]

fris·son /friˈsoun/ *n.* [C usually singular] a sudden feeling of excitement or fear: [+ of] *A frisson of alarm went down my back.*

frit·ter[1] /ˈfrɪtɚ/ *n.* [C] a thin piece of fruit, vegetable, or meat covered with a mixture of eggs and flour and cooked in hot oil: *apple fritters*

fritter[2]

fritter sth ↔ **away** *phr. v.* [T] to waste time, money, or effort on something small or unimportant, so that you gradually have none left: [+ on] *He's just frittering away his money on booze and poker.*

fritz /frɪts/ *n.* **be/go on the fritz** INFORMAL if something is or goes on the fritz, it is not working correctly: *My TV is on the fritz.*

fri·vol·i·ty /frɪˈvɑləti/ *n. plural* **frivolities** [C,U] behavior or activities that are not serious or sensible: *Your frivolity is out of place on such a solemn occasion.*

friv·o·lous /ˈfrɪvələs/ *adj.* **1** not serious or sensible, especially in a way that is not appropriate for a particular occasion: *Work time is too valuable to waste on frivolous games.* | *New York is trying to limit the number of frivolous lawsuits.* **2** a frivolous person likes having fun rather than doing serious or sensible things: *It could hardly be said that Mrs. Bush had led a frivolous or unproductive life.* —**frivolously** *adv.*

frizz /frɪz/ *v.* [I,T] INFORMAL if your hair frizzes or you frizz it, it curls very tightly —**frizz** *n.* [U]

friz·zle /ˈfrɪzəl/ *v.* [I,T] INFORMAL also **frizzle up** to dry or burn something, or to be dried or burned, especially into a curly shape

F

frizz·y /ˈfrɪzi/ *adj.* **frizzier, frizziest** frizzy hair is tightly curled and looks a little messy

fro /froʊ/ *adv.* —see TO AND FRO[1]

frock /frɑk/ *n.* [C] **1** OLD-FASHIONED a woman's or girl's dress: *a party frock* **2** a long loose piece of clothing worn by some Christian MONKs

frock coat /ˈ. ./ *n.* [C] a knee-length coat for men, worn in the 19th century

frog /frɔg, frɑg/ *n.* [C] **1** a small green animal that lives near water and has long legs for jumping —compare TOAD **2 have a frog in your throat** INFORMAL to have difficulty speaking because of a sore throat **3 Frog** an insulting word for a French person

frog·man /ˈfrɔgmən/ *n. plural* **frogmen** /-mən/ [C] someone who swims under water using special equipment to help them breathe, especially as a job

frol·ic[1] /ˈfrɑlɪk/ *v.* **frolicked, frolicking** [I] to play in an active, happy way: [+ **around/about/over**] *The penguins waddle down to the shore and frolic in the icy waters.*

frolic[2] *n.* [C often plural] a cheerful, enjoyable game or activity: *The season of snow frolics, skiing and sledding got a later start than usual this year.*

frol·ic·some /ˈfrɑlɪksəm/ *adj.* LITERARY active and liking to play: *frolicsome kittens*

from /frəm; *strong* frʌm/ *prep.*
1 where sb/sth starts starting at a particular place, position, or condition: *They took a train from California when they came for the wedding.* | *Things have gone from bad to worse since Tara moved in.* | *He was grinning from ear to ear.* | *Reilly was encased from head to toe* (=all over his body) *in plaster and gauze.*
2 when sth starts starting at a particular time: *He'll be here tomorrow from about seven o'clock onward.* | *I was only there from 11:30 to 1 o'clock.* | *The TV was on constantly, from morning till night.* | *Christopher's a very long name – from now on* (=starting now and continuing into the future) *we'll call him Chris.* | *a week/2 months/5 years etc. from now I'll call you back about an hour from now.*
3 level of sth beginning at a particular limit or price: *The sizes range from small to extra-large.*
4 where you do sth if you see, watch, or do something from a place, this is where you are when you see, watch, or do it: *Sandi looked at me disapprovingly from behind her desk.* | *From the top of the hill, you can see for miles.*
5 distance used to express a distance: *We live about five miles from Boston.* | *It's about an hour and a half from San Jose.*
6 origin used to say what the origin of something is: *Tim gets his good looks from his mother.* | *Mr. Schultz poured himself a drink from a carton in the fridge.* | *Spot died of an infectious disease that he got from another dog.* | *I think they come from a pretty wealthy family.*
7 move/separate if something is moved or taken from a place or person, it is removed, taken away or taken out: *Diane pulled her chair away from her desk.* | *I had to take that new toy away from Corey.* | *Subtract three from fifteen.*
8 place someone who comes from a particular place was born there or lives, works, or belongs there. *Actually, Ron's from New Orleans.* | *Orders have come in from all fifty states.* | *Hi Dot, it's Marie from the Senior Center.*
9 sent/given by sb sent or given by someone: *We got a message from Fred yesterday.* | *You need to get permission from your parents.* | *The card was signed, "With lots of love, from Elaine and Marty."* | *Have you heard anything from Gary yet?*
10 reason for sth used to introduce the reason for, or origin of, an opinion or judgment: *I speak from experience.* | *From what I understand, you all did pretty well on the test.*
11 cause of sth used to state the cause of something: *I've gained a lot of weight this winter from not doing any exercise.* | *Death rates from accidents have declined.*
12 stop sth used after words such as "protect," "prevent," or "keep," to introduce the situation or action that is stopped, avoided, or prevented: *Winston's bad eyesight prevented him from driving.* | *The rope around Jan's waist kept her from falling into the shark-infested water.*
13 substance used to state the substance that is used to make something: *Our Christmas tree is made from recycled plastic.*
14 comparing used when you are comparing things, and saying how they are similar or different: *New York cheddar cheese is different from Wisconsin cheddar cheese.* | *Our two cats are so much alike, I can never tell one from the other.*

USAGE NOTE: FROM

WORD CHOICE: from and **since**
Use **from** when you want to say that something happened from a particular time in the past to another: *She lived in France from 1988 to 1995.* Use **since** when you want to say that something has been happening from a particular time in the past until now: *She's been living in France since 1995.*

Fromm /frɑm/, **Er·ich** /ˈɛrɪk/ (1900–1980) a U.S. PSYCHOLOGIST, born in Germany, who wrote about the way that social conditions and arrangements affect human behavior

frond /frɑnd/ *n.* [C] a leaf of a FERN or PALM[1] (2)

front

Sue ran in front of the bus.

Sue got a seat at the front of the bus.

front[1] /frʌnt/ *n.*
1 forward side/surface **the front** the side or surface of something that is in the direction that it faces or moves: [+ **of**] *Where did that scratch on the front of my car come from?* —compare REAR[1] (1)
2 group/line **the front** the front of a group or line of people or things is the position that is farthest forward in the direction that they are facing or moving: [+ **of**] *She always sits at the front of the class.* | *TV reporters shoved their way to the front of the crowd.*
3 in front of sth a) near the side of something that is in the direction that it faces or moves: *They've set up some food booths in front of the museum.* | *I parked in front of Paul's car.* —opposite BEHIND[1] **b)** near the entrance to a building: *He dropped me off right in front of Columbia Pictures in Hollywood.*
4 in front of sb a) ahead of someone, in the direction that they are facing or moving: *This really tall guy came and sat in front of me.* **b)** if you say or do something in front of someone, you do it where they can see or hear you: *I didn't want to say anything in front of the kids.* **c)** if you have problems or difficulties in front of you, you will need to deal with them soon
5 the front the most important side or surface of something, that you look at first: *The postcard had a picture of our hotel on the front.* | [+ **of**] *His picture is on the front of the book.* —opposite BACK[2] —compare REAR[1] (1)
6 in front a) in the most forward or leading position; ahead: *He drove straight into the car in front.* | *Shouldn't the class officers be sitting in front, leading the meeting?* —compare BEHIND[1] (1)
7 out front the area near the entrance to a building: *Now what's going on out front?*

8 in (the) front in the part of a car where the driver sits: *Can I sit in front, Mom?*

9 `weather` [C] TECHNICAL the place where two areas of air of different temperatures meet, often shown as a line on weather maps | **a warm/cold front** (=the edge of an area of warm or cold air)

10 up front INFORMAL **a)** money that is paid up front is paid for work is done, or before goods are supplied: *We've got to have the money up front before we can do anything.* **b)** directly and clearly from the start: *I told you up front that I didn't want to be in a relationship with anyone.* —see also UPFRONT

11 `type of activity` [C] a particular area or activity: **on the political/economic etc. front** *On the diplomatic front, the government has sent envoys to negotiate with the rebels.* | *After months of trouble on just about all fronts NASA officials were delighted to have such a smooth flight.*

12 `body` **your front** your chest, or the part of your body that faces forward: *I hoped I wouldn't embarrass myself by spilling my drink down my front.*

13 `illegal business` [C] something that hides a secret or an illegal activity: **[+ for]** *Inspectors found that the import/export business was just a front for a huge drug smuggling operation.*

14 `hide feelings` [C usually singular] a way of behaving that shows what you want people to see, rather than what you feel *I know you're scared, but you've got to* **put on a brave front.**

15 `organization` [singular] used in the name of a political party or unofficial military organization: *the People's Liberation Front*

16 `war` [C] the area where fighting happens in a war; FRONT LINE: *Trucks are heading toward the front with fresh supplies.* —see also HOME FRONT

USAGE NOTE: FRONT

WORD CHOICE: in front of, behind, in back of, at/in the front of, at/in the back of, face, across from, before
In front of (opposite **behind** or **in back of**) is used when one thing is separate from the other: *A boy ran out in front of the bus* (=in the street outside the bus). **At/in the front of** (opposite **at/in the back of**) is used when one thing is inside or part of the other: *The boy took a seat at/in the front of the bus* (=in the front part of the bus). If the front part of a building is in front of something, it **faces** it: *Our hotel faced the central square.* A person or place that faces another one exactly, with a space between, is **across from** it. If the bus stop is *across from the school,* it is not *in front of the school* but on the other side of the street. *I live across from Greg.* One event may happen **before** another: *Let's have a drink before dinner* (NOT *in front of dinner*).

_{S W}
_{1 2} **front**[2] *adj.* [only before noun] **1** at, on, or in the front of something: *There was a "For Sale" sign on the front lawn.* | *You only need one key for both the* **front door** *and the back door.* | *Six other girls beat me to the box office, but I did manage to get* **front row seats.** —opposite BACK[4] **2** a front man or organization acts legally in business as a way of hiding a secret or illegal activity: *a front organization for importing heroin* **3** TECHNICAL a front vowel sound is made by raising your tongue at the front of your mouth, such as the vowel sound in "see" —opposite BACK[4]

front[3] *v.* **1** [T usually passive] if a building fronts something, the front of the building faces it: *The stately mansion is fronted by a sweeping lawn.* | *The Hyatt hotel fronts a beach called Shipwreck.* **2** [T] to lead something such as a musical group or television program by being the person that the public see most: *Genesis was originally fronted by Peter Gabriel.* **3 glass-fronted/marble-fronted etc.** having a particular substance on the front surface of something: *glass-fronted cabinets*

  front for sb/sth *phr. v.* [T] INFORMAL to be the person or organization that hides the real nature of a secret or illegal activity: *Rep. Felando denied that he is fronting for the tobacco companies.*

front·age /ˈfrʌntɪdʒ/ *n.* [U] the part of a building or piece of land that is along a road, river etc.

frontage road /ˈ.. ˌ./ *n.* [C] a small road next to a large road such as a FREEWAY or EXPRESSWAY, that lets you drive to the buildings that are near the larger road but cannot be reached directly from it

fron·tal /ˈfrʌntəl/ *adj.* [only before noun] FORMAL **1** toward the front of something: *Washington is launching a frontal attack on the enemy.* | *a frontal collision* **2** relating to the front part of something: *A tumor had formed in the right frontal lobe of his brain.* **3 full frontal nudity** the fact of showing the front of people's bodies with no clothes on, in movies, pictures etc. —**frontally** *adv.*

frontal sys·tem /ˈ.. ˌ./ *n.* [C] TECHNICAL a weather FRONT[1] (9)

front and cen·ter /ˌ. . ˈ../ *adj., adv.* in a very important position, where it will receive attention: *Front and center in the school's mission statement is the goal that all students learn how they fit into society.*

front door /ˌ. ˈ./ *n.* [C usually singular] the main entrance door to a house, at the front —compare BACK DOOR —see picture on page 423

front-end load·er /ˌ. . ˈ../ *n.* [C] a large vehicle that is used for lifting and moving piles of dirt, rocks etc.

fron·tier /frʌnˈtɪr/ *n.* **1 the frontier** the area beyond the places that people know well or live in, especially in the western U.S. in the 19th century: *Wilder's novel is about a family's struggle on the American frontier.* | *Alaska is known as the last frontier.* **2** [C] the limit of what is known about something: *The study of the brain is often described as the next intellectual frontier.* | *In labs across the country, researchers and scientists are pushing back* **the frontiers of science. 3** [C] FORMAL the border of a country, or the area near the border: *They settled in Ronco, a picturesque village near the Italian frontier.* | **[+ between/with]** *The government closed the frontier between Lithuania and Poland.*

fron·tiers·man /frʌnˈtɪrzmən/ *n.* [C] a man who lived on the American frontier, especially in the 19th century

fron·tiers·wom·an /frʌnˈtɪrzˌwʊmən/ *n.* [C] a woman who lived on the American frontier, especially in the 19th century

fron·tis·piece /ˈfrʌntɪsˌpis/ *n.* [C] a picture or photograph at the beginning of a book, facing the page that has the title on it

front line /ˌ. ˈ./ *n.* [C] **1** the place where fighting happens in a war; FRONT[1] (16): *68% of people approve of women fighting on the front lines.* **2** a position in which you are doing something important or difficult that has not been done before: *Researchers concluded that the front line of HIV prevention had shifted to smaller cities.* —**front-line** *adj.* [only before noun] *front-line conditions*

front man /ˈ. ./ *n.* [C usually singular] **1** a person who speaks for an organization, often an illegal one, but is not the leader of it: *Giovanni was alleged to be the front man for a fascist movement.* **2** the leader, and usually the singer, of a musical group

front mon·ey /ˈ. ˌ./ *n.* [U] money that is paid for something before you get it

front of·fice /ˌ. ˈ../ *n.* [singular] the managers of a company

front page /ˌ. ˈ./ *n.* [C usually singular] the first page of a newspaper: *The story made the front page of the New York Times.*

front-page /ˈ. ./ *adj.* [only before noun] **front-page story/news/article etc.** something that is printed on the first page of a newspaper because it is very important or exciting

front room /ˌ. ˈ./ *n.* [C usually singular] a LIVING ROOM: *Maureen was lying on the sofa in the front room.*

front-run·ner, front-runner /ˈfrʌntˌrʌnɚ/ *n.* [C] the person or thing that is most likely to win a competition: *The Dolphins are the frontrunners in this year's Super Bowl.*

F

front-wheel drive /ˌ. . ˈ./ *n.* [C,U] a system in a vehicle which sends the power of the engine to the front wheels only —**front-wheel drive** *adj.*

frosh /frɑʃ/ *n. plural* **frosh** [C] OLD-FASHIONED a student who is in their first year at a high school, college, or university

frost¹ /frɔst/ *n.* **1** [U] ice that looks white and powdery and covers things outside when the temperature is very low: *There was frost on the windows and a chill in the air.* | *A frost warning was issued for most of South Carolina.* **2** [C] an occasion when the weather is so cold that water freezes: *The Ohio valley is expecting the first frost of the season by Monday morning.* | *The only thing that could hurt the crop now is an early frost.* —see also FROSTED, FROSTY

frost² *v.* **1** [T] to cover a cake with FROSTING **2** [I,T] to cover something with frost, or to become covered with frost: [+ **over/up**] *All the windowpanes had frosted over during the night.* **3** [T] to make some parts of your hair lighter than the rest by using chemicals

Frost /frɔst/**, Rob·ert** /ˈrɑbət/ (1874–1963) a U.S. poet

Frost Belt /ˈ. ./ *n.* **the Frost Belt** the northern or northeastern parts of the U.S., where the weather is very cold in the winter —compare SUN BELT

frost·bite /ˈfrɔstˌbaɪt/ *n.* [U] a condition caused by extreme cold, that makes your fingers, toes etc. swell, become darker and sometimes fall off —**frost-bitten** *adj.*

frost·ed /ˈfrɔstɪd/ *adj.* **1** covered with FROST¹ (1), or with something that looks like frost: *Alice poured her beer into a tall, frosted mug.* **2** covered with frosting: *chocolate frosted cookies* **3** frosted hair has parts that have been made much lighter than others by using chemicals

frosted glass /ˌ.. ˈ.◂/ *n.* [U] glass whose surface has been made rough, so that it is not transparent

frost-free /ˌ. ˈ.◂/ *adj.* a frost-free REFRIGERATOR or FREEZER gets slightly warm at times to make the frost inside it disappear, so that you do not have to remove the frost yourself

frost heave /ˈ. ./ *n.* [U] a situation in which the surface of a road breaks apart because water has entered it and then frozen

frost·ing /ˈfrɔstɪŋ/ *n.* [U] a sweet substance that is put on cakes, made from sugar and butter —compare ICING

frost line /ˈ. ./ *n.* [C usually singular] the lowest level under the Earth's surface that frost reaches

frost·y /ˈfrɔsti/ *adj.* **frostier, frostiest** **1** very cold, or covered with FROST¹ (1): *I tapped on the frosty window and said, "Anybody home?"* | *They were both shivering slightly from the frosty air.* **2** unfriendly: **a frosty stare/look/welcome** *Pat gave him a frosty, calculating stare.* —**frostily** *adv.* —**frostiness** *n.* [U]

froth¹ /frɔθ/ *n.* [U] **1** a mass of small BUBBLES that form on top of a liquid: *Skim the froth off the top of the melted butter.* **2** small, white BUBBLES of SALIVA around a person's or animal's mouth **3** [U] words or ideas that are attractive, but have no real value or meaning: *The play is an enjoyable bit of holiday froth.*

froth² *v.* [I] **1** if a liquid froths, it produces or contains a lot of small BUBBLES on top: *Cottonwoods and elm trees cast long shadows across the frothing creek.* **2 be frothing at the mouth** INFORMAL to be extremely angry or excited about something: *Baseball fans were frothing at the mouth about strikes and rising ticket prices.* **3** if someone's mouth froths, SALIVA comes out as a lot of small white BUBBLES: *Hal and his friends played Frisbee with the dog until she was frothing at the mouth.*

froth·y /ˈfrɔθi, -ði/ *adj.* **frothier, frothiest** **1** a liquid that is frothy has a lot of small BUBBLES on top: *Order a frothy cappuccino and sit back and relax.* **2** a frothy book, movie etc. is enjoyable but not serious or important: *It's not a superscientific exhibition, but kind of frothy and nice for summer.* —**frothily** *adv.*

frown¹ /fraʊn/ *v.* [I] to make an angry, unhappy, or confused expression by moving your EYEBROWS together: *Sheila saw Al frown as he read the letter.* | *Paul frowned but said nothing.* | [+ **at**] *Mattie stood frowning at the closed door for a long time.*

frown on/upon sb/sth *phr. v.* [T usually passive] to disapprove of something, especially someone's behavior: *Drinking is thoroughly frowned upon in many churches.* | *Unlike many math experts, Ms. Saxon frowns on students using calculators.*

fruit

seeds

pear　　figs　　bananas　　skin　　grapes

kiwi　　peach　　plum　　coconut

peel

segment

pith

orange　　melon　　apple　　lemon

stalk

flesh

watermelon　　pineapple　　cherries　　cantaloupe

F

frown[2] *n.* [C usually singular] the expression on your face when you frown: *Sarah shook her head, with a frown on her face.*

froze /frəʊz/ the past tense of FREEZE[1]

fro·zen[1] /ˈfrəʊzən/ the past participle of FREEZE[1]

frozen[2] *adj.* **1** frozen food has been stored at a very low temperature in order to preserve it: *We made a pizza last night with frozen bread dough.* | *frozen peas* **2** made very hard or turned to ice because of cold temperatures: *The ground was frozen beneath our feet.* | *I think the water in the dog's bowl is frozen.* | **frozen stiff/solid** *Rosen's body was found frozen stiff by the railroad tracks.* **3 be frozen** SPOKEN to feel very cold: *He went out without a jacket – he must be frozen.* **4 be frozen with fear/terror/fright** to be so afraid, shocked etc. that you cannot move

fruc·ti·fy /ˈfrʌktəˌfaɪ, ˈfrʊk-/ *v. past tense and past participle* **fructified** [I,T] TECHNICAL to produce fruit or to make a plant produce fruit —**fructification** /ˌfrʌktəfəˈkeɪʃən/ *n.* [U]

fruc·tose /ˈfrʊktoʊs, ˈfrʌk-/ *n.* [U] a type of natural sugar in fruit juices and HONEY (1)

fru·gal /ˈfruːgəl/ *adj.* **1** careful to only buy what is necessary: *Hidden hotel costs can be a source of frustration to the frugal traveler.* **2** a frugal meal is a small meal of plain food —**frugally** *adv.* —**frugality** /fruˈgæləti/ *n.* [U]

fruit[1] /fruːt/ *n. plural* **fruit** *or* **fruits** **1** [C,U] the part of a plant, tree, or bush that contains seeds and is often eaten as food: *We usually eat fresh fruit after dinner.* | *Jack grows a variety of fruits and vegetables in the garden.* | *You should eat a few pieces of fruit every day.* **2 the fruit/fruits of sth** the good results that you have from something, after you have worked very hard: *Bruce Thompson is holding a CD release party to celebrate the fruits of his labors.* **3 bear fruit** if a plan or activity bears fruit, it produces the good results that you intended: *The boys remained optimistic that their musical career might bear fruit.* **4 in fruit** TECHNICAL trees and plants that are in fruit are producing their fruit **5 the fruits of the Earth/nature** all the natural things that the Earth produces, such as fruit, vegetables, or minerals **6 the fruit of sb's loins** BIBLICAL OR HUMOROUS someone's children **7** [C] OFFENSIVE a HOMOSEXUAL man

fruit[2] *v.* [I] TECHNICAL if a tree or a plant fruits, it produces fruit

fruit bat /ˈ. ./ *n.* [C] a large BAT[1] (1) (=small animal like a flying mouse) that lives in hot countries and eats fruit

fruit·cake /ˈfruːtkeɪk/ *n.* **1** [C,U] a type of heavy cake that has pieces of dried fruit in it **2** [C] IN-FORMAL someone who seems to be mentally ill or who behaves in a strange way: *I figured he must have been a real fruitcake to write a letter like that.*

fruit cock·tail /ˌ. ˈ../ *n.* [U] a mixture of small pieces of fruit, sold in cans

fruit fly /ˈ. ./ *n. plural* **fruit flies** [C] a small fly that eats fruit or decaying plants

fruit·ful /ˈfruːtfəl/ *adj.* **1** producing good results: *Mr. Baker and I have had a very fruitful discussion.* —opposite FRUITLESS **2** LITERARY land that is fruitful produces a lot of grain, vegetables, fruit etc. —**fruitfully** *adv.* —**fruitfulness** *n.* [U]

fru·i·tion /fruˈɪʃən/ *n.* [U] FORMAL the successful result of a plan, idea etc.: *She died without seeing her plan come to fruition.*

fruit·less /ˈfruːtlɪs/ *adj.* FORMAL failing to achieve what was wanted, especially after much effort: *Rescue efforts have been called off after three days of fruitless searching.* —opposite FRUITFUL —**fruitlessly** *adv.* —**fruitlessness** *n.* [U]

fruit sal·ad /ˌ. ˈ../ *n.* [C,U] a mixture of many different types of fruit that have been cut into small pieces

fruit·y /ˈfruːti/ *adj.* **fruitier, fruitiest** **1** tasting or smelling strongly like fruit: *a fruity red wine* **2** INFORMAL silly or stupid: *This must be one of Mike's fruity ideas.*

frump /frʌmp/ *n.* [C] a woman who is frumpy

frump·y /ˈfrʌmpi/ *adj.* **frumpier, frumpiest** a woman who is frumpy looks unattractive because she dresses in old-fashioned clothes that do not fit her well: *a frumpy housewife*

frus·trate /ˈfrʌstreɪt/ *v.* [T] **1** [usually passive] if something frustrates you, it makes you feel annoyed or angry because you are unable to do what you want: *Klaas was frustrated by the frequent traffic delays and vowed to do something about it.* **2** to prevent someone's plans, efforts or attempts from succeeding: *Thick fog frustrated their attempt to land on the tiny island.*

frus·trat·ed /ˈfrʌstreɪtɪd/ *adj.* **1** feeling annoyed, upset, and impatient, because you cannot control or change a situation, or achieve something: *Stella got so frustrated that she stormed out of the office and didn't come back.* | [+ with/at] *He retired from politics because he was frustrated at being in the minority.* **2 sexually frustrated** not satisfied because you do not have any opportunity to have sex **3 a frustrated poet/actor/dancer etc.** someone who wants to develop a particular skill but has not been able to do this

frus·trat·ing /ˈfrʌstreɪtɪŋ/ *adj.* making you feel annoyed, upset, or impatient because you cannot do what you want to do: *It's so frustrating not to have a car to get around.* | *Many callers have had frustrating experiences with customer service lines.*

frus·tra·tion /frʌˈstreɪʃən/ *n.* **1** [C,U] the feeling of being annoyed, upset, or impatient, because you cannot control or change a situation, or achieve something: *Students have spoken of their growing frustration with school administrators.* | *Poetry helps me express some of the frustrations I feel.* **2** [U] the fact of being prevented from achieving what you are trying to achieve: [+ of] *Recession can lead to the frustration of entrepreneurial initiative.*

fry[1] /fraɪ/ *v. past tense and past participle* **fried** **1** [I,T] to cook something in hot oil or fat, or to be cooked in hot oil or fat: *Fry the pork for five minutes.* | *I could smell the onions frying.* **2** [I,T] SLANG to kill someone, or to be killed, as a punishment in the ELECTRIC CHAIR —**fried** *adj.* —see also DEEP-FRY, FRENCH FRY, STIR-FRY

fry[2] *n. plural* **fries** **1** [C usually plural] a long thin piece of potato that has been cooked in hot oil; FRENCH FRY **2** [C] an amount of fries that are served together, especially in a FAST FOOD restaurant: *I'll have a cheeseburger and a large fry.* **3 fry** [plural] very young fish —see also **small fry** (SMALL[1] (16))

fry·er /ˈfraɪə/ *n.* [C] **1** a special pan or piece of electrical equipment for frying food **2** a chicken that has been specially bred to be fried

fry·ing pan /ˈ.. ˌ./ *n.* [C] **1** a round flat pan with a long handle, used for frying food; SKILLET —see picture at PAN[1] **2 out of the frying pan (and) into the fire** SPOKEN from a bad situation to one that is even worse

FSLIC *n.* [singular] Federal Savings and Loan Insurance Corporation; an official government organization that insures the money you keep in a SAVINGS AND LOAN ASSOCIATION

f-stop /ˈɛf stɑp/ *n.* [C] a position of the opening in a camera LENS that controls how much light can enter the camera

ft. **1** the written abbreviation of FOOT[1] (1) or feet **2 Ft.** the written abbreviation of FORT, used in the names of places: *Ft. Lauderdale*

FTC *n.* [singular] Federal Trade Commission; an official government organization that makes sure that businesses do not do anything illegal or unfair

FTP *n.* [U] TECHNICAL File Transfer Protocol; a standard for sending information from one computer to another over the Internet

fuch·sia[1] /ˈfyuːʃə/ *n.* **1** [U] a bright pink color **2** [C,U] a type of bush with hanging bell-shaped flowers in red, pink, or white

F

fuchsia² *adj.* bright pink

fuck¹ /fʌk/ *v.* SPOKEN, TABOO **1 fuck you/it/them etc.** used to show that you are very angry at someone or something: *So fuck you and stay out of my life!* **2** [I,T] to have sex with someone **3 Fuck off!** a rude way of telling someone to go away: *I just slammed the door on them and told them to fuck off.* **4 fuck that shit!** used to say that you do not like something or are not interested in it at all: *Oh, fuck that shit! Just turn the TV off.*

fuck around *phr. v.* [I] to waste time or behave in a silly or careless way: *I don't have time to fuck around. Just answer the question.*

fuck sb ↔ **over** *phr. v.* [T] to treat someone very badly: *They'll just fuck you over if you let them.*

fuck up *phr. v.* **1** [I,T **fuck** sth ↔ **up**] to make a mistake or do something badly: *Troy's doing everything he can to fuck up that relationship.* **2** [T **fuck** sb **up**] to make someone very unhappy and confused so that they cannot control their life: *Heroin really fucks you up.*

fuck with sb/sth [T] *phr. v.* **1** [**fuck with** sb] to annoy someone or make them angry: *Don't fuck with me, man!* **2** [**fuck (around) with** sth] to try to fix or change something, especially so that it becomes damaged or stops working: *Quit fucking around with the TV and call a repairman.*

fuck² *interjection* SPOKEN, TABOO used when you are very annoyed about something: *Fuck! I hate it when the streets don't have signs on them.*

fuck³ *n.* SPOKEN, TABOO **1 the fuck** used when you are angry or surprised to emphasize what you are saying: *Shut the fuck up, Norman!* | *Get the fuck out of my backyard!* | *What/how/who etc. the fuck] What the fuck are you talking about?* **2** [C usually singular] the act of having sex **3 not give a (flying) fuck** to not care at all what happens: *I really don't give a fuck who comes to your party, Jack.*

fucked up /ˌ. ˈ.◂/ *adj.* SPOKEN, TABOO **1** damaged or not working correctly: *These speakers are fucked up.* | *Todd has kind of a fucked-up family.* **2** very unhappy and unable to control your life: *When I was with Mary, I was really fucked up.* **3** having drunk too much alcohol or taken illegal drugs: *I'm too fucked up to drive.*

fuck·er /ˈfʌkɚ/ also **fuck** *n.* [C] SPOKEN, TABOO someone who you dislike very much, think is stupid etc.: *You dumb fucker!*

fuck·ing /ˈfʌkɪŋ, -kɪn/ *adv.* SPOKEN, TABOO **1** used to emphasize that you are very angry or annoyed: *He fucking called me at three o'clock in the morning.* | *I fucking hate the smell of cigarettes.* | *It took a fucking long time.* **2** used to emphasize your opinion of something: *She makes fucking good coffee.* —**fucking** *adj.* [only before noun] *What a fucking idiot!*

fuck-up /ˈfʌkʌp/ *n.* [C] SPOKEN, TABOO **1** someone who is very confused and is not in control of their life: *Ted is such a fuckup.* **2** a situation that has been dealt with very badly: *It's just another one of the management's fuckups.*

fud·dy-dud·dy /ˈfʌdi ˌdʌdi/ *n. plural* **fuddy-duddies** [C] INFORMAL someone who has old-fashioned ideas and attitudes: *That dress makes you look like such a fuddy-duddy.*

fudge¹ /fʌdʒ/ *n.* [U] a type of soft candy, made with milk, butter, sugar, and usually chocolate

fudge² *v.* [I,T] **1** to change important figures or facts in order to deceive people: *Tom admitted to fudging the numbers to stay ahead of the competition.* **2** to avoid giving exact details or a clear answer about something: [+ on] *A lot of people fudged on their answers about exercise.*

fudge³ *interjection* used when you are angry, annoyed, or disappointed, instead of saying a more offensive word: *Oh, fudge! I forgot to mail Janet's birthday card.*

fudg·y /ˈfʌdʒi/ *adj.* slightly sticky with a strong sweet chocolate taste: *fudgy brownies*

fueh·rer /ˈfjʊrɚ/ *n.* another spelling of FUHRER

fuel¹ /fjul, ˈfjuəl/ *n.* [C,U] a substance such as coal, gas, or oil that can be burned to produce heat or energy: *The plane was running low on fuel.* | *The fuel tank holds 14 gallons.* —see also **add fuel to sth** (ADD (5)), FOSSIL FUEL

fuel² *v.* **1** [T] to make something happen, grow, increase etc., or to encourage someone to do something: *Easy credit terms helped fuel the economic expansion.* | **fuel fears/worry/speculation etc.** *Work continued slowly, fueling concern that the stadium would not be finished on time.* **2** [I,T] also **fuel up** to take fuel into a vehicle, or to provide a vehicle with fuel: *Workers began fueling the spaceship for liftoff.*

fuel-ef·fi·cient /ˈ. .ˌ.../ *adj.* a fuel-efficient engine or vehicle burns fuel in a more effective way than usual, so that it uses less fuel

fuel in·jec·tion /ˈ. .ˌ./ *n.* [U] a method of using pressure to put fuel such as gasoline directly into an engine, which allows a vehicle to burn the fuel in a more effective way —**fuel-injected** *adj.*

fuel oil /ˈ. ./ *n.* [U] a type of oil that is burned to produce heat or power

Fu·en·tes /fuˈɛnteɪs/, **Car·los** /ˈkɑrloʊs/ (1928–) a Mexican writer of NOVELS

fu·gi·tive¹ /ˈfjudʒətɪv/ *n.* [C] someone who is trying to avoid being caught, especially by the police: [+ from] *In the movie, the two women are fugitives from the law.*

fugitive² *adj.* [only before noun] **1** trying to avoid being caught, especially by the police: *The fugitive leader was captured last night.* **2** LITERARY continuing for a very short time: *They shared a fugitive embrace.*

fugue /fjug/ *n.* [C] a piece of serious music in which a tune is repeated regularly by different instruments, voices etc. with small changes each time

fuh·rer /ˈfjʊrɚ/ *n.* **the Fuhrer, the Führer** Adolf Hitler, the leader of the Nazi party in Germany in the 1930s and early 1940s during World War II

Fu·ji, Mount /ˈfudʒi/ also **Fu·ji·ya·ma** /ˌfudʒiˈɑmə/ a VOLCANO on the largest island in Japan, southwest of Tokyo, that is the highest mountain in Japan

-ful¹ /fəl/ *suffix* [in adjectives] **1** having a particular quality: *a beautiful girl* | *Is it painful?* | *Mick's a safe and skillful driver.* **2** full of something: *She gave me a gleeful wink.* | *an eventful day* —**-fully** /fəli, fli/ *suffix* [in adverbs] *a delightfully fruity wine*

-ful² /fʊl/ *suffix* [in nouns] **1** the amount of a substance needed to fill a particular container: *Add two cupfuls of milk.* **2** as much as can be carried by, or contained in, a particular part of the body: *Monica carried an armful of flowers.* | *a mouthful of water*

Ful·bright /ˈfʊlbraɪt/, **J. William** (1905–1995) a U.S. politician who established the Fulbright Scholarships

Fulbright Schol·ar·ship /ˈ.. ˌ.../ *n.* [C] money provided for U.S. university students and teachers so that they can study in other countries, and for students and teachers from other countries so that they can study in the U.S. —**Fulbright Scholar** *n.* [C]

ful·crum /ˈfʊlkrəm, ˈfʌl-/ *n.* [C] the point on which a LEVER turns, balances, or is supported when it is turning or lifting something

ful·fill /fʊlˈfɪl/ *v.* [T] **1** if you fulfill a hope, promise, wish etc., you achieve the thing that you had hoped for, promised, wanted etc.: *An Arizona couple fulfilled their dream of getting married in Tahiti.* | *Will the government fulfill its pledge to hold free elections?* | *He never fulfilled his potential as a basketball player.* **2** to provide something that is needed, or to reach a particular standard: *The housing commission chose the site because it fulfilled a need in the neighborhood.* | *Anne took Lederman's course to fulfill the science requirement.* | **fulfill a role/function/duty etc.** *Cintrat argued that France had never fulfilled its obligations under the 1787 treaty.* **3 fulfill yourself** to feel satisfied because you are using all your skills, qualities etc.: *She succeeded in fulfilling herself both as an actress and as a mother.* —see also SELF-FULFILLING PROPHECY

ful·filled /fʊlˈfɪld/ adj. satisfied with your life, job etc. because you feel that it is interesting, useful, or important, and you are using all your skills: *It's not necessary to have a boyfriend to enjoy yourself and be fulfilled.*

ful·fill·ing /fʊlˈfɪlɪŋ/ adj. a job, relationship etc. that is fulfilling makes you feel satisfied because it allows you to use all your skills and personal qualities: *Finding a fulfilling career may be the key to personal happiness.*

ful·fill·ment /fʊlˈfɪlmənt/ n. [U] **1** the feeling of being satisfied, especially in your job, because you are using all your skills and personal qualities: *I get a real **sense of fulfillment** when I go out and perform.* **2** the act or state of meeting a need, demand, or condition: *The government should make an effort to speed up the fulfillment of its promises.*

full¹ /fʊl/ adj.
1 container/room/place etc. holding or containing as much of something as possible, or as many things or people as possible: *a full box of cereal* | *The restaurant was already full when we got there.* | *Fill the muffin cups about half full.*
2 including everything [only before noun] including all parts or details; complete: *Please write your full name and address on the form.* | *Salcido gave a full confession to the police.* | *We are not being told **the full story** (=everything someone knows about something) by our political leaders.*
3 highest level [only before noun] being the highest level or greatest amount that is possible; total: *Wait until there's a sale so you don't have to pay full price.* | *After decades of nearly full employment, about 3000 local residents lost their jobs when the factory closed.* | *Please stay seated until the plane **comes to a full stop** (=stops completely).*
4 be full of sth a) to contain a large number of things, or a large amount of something: *Dan's garage is full of half-finished projects.* | *They sent us some brochures full of information about the park.* **b)** to feel or express a strong emotion, or have a lot of a particular quality: *Boston's streets are full of history.* | *We were full of admiration for Kim's ability to choose the right thing to say.*
5 food [not before noun] SPOKEN having eaten so much food that you cannot eat any more: *"Do you want more noodles?" "No, thanks. **I'm full.**"*
6 be full of it/crap etc. SPOKEN, IMPOLITE used to say that you think what someone is saying is wrong or stupid: *Don't listen to Wayne – he's so full of crap.*
7 be full of yourself to think or talk about yourself all the time, in a way that other people find annoying: *Tim is just so full of himself.*
8 time **a)** [only before noun] used to emphasize that something continues for a long time: *He sat on the witness stand for four full days.* **b)** filled with many things to do: *I've had a full week. I'm looking forward to staying home tonight.*
9 on a full stomach if you do something on a full stomach, you do it shortly after you have eaten a large meal: *It's not a good idea to go swimming on a full stomach.*
10 be in full swing if an event or process is in full swing it has reached its highest level of activity: *The college football season is now in full swing.*
11 rank [only before noun] having all the rights, duties etc. relating to a particular rank or position, because you have reached the necessary standard: *a full **professor/member/colonel etc.** Watson joined the club when he was 21 and has been a full member for six years.*
12 (at) full speed/tilt as fast or as strongly as possible: *Viola said he will go at full speed in spring training, despite his injuries.*
13 full speed/steam ahead with as much energy and eagerness as possible: *In the meantime, the three cruise lines are moving full speed ahead with major expansion plans.*
14 (at) full blast as strongly, loudly, or fast as possible: *The heating was on full blast, but it was still cold.*
15 sound/taste etc. a quality such as a sound, taste etc. that is full is pleasantly strong: *Cheddar cheese ages well to produce a full, rich aroma.*

16 clothing a full skirt, pair of pants etc. is made with a lot of material and fits loosely: *full sleeves* | *a dress with a full skirt*
17 body a full face, body etc. is rounded, large, or fat
18 come/go full circle to end in the same situation in which you began, even though there have been changes in the time in between: *After the experiments of the 1960s, education has come full circle in its methods of teaching reading.*
19 in full view of sb/sth so that everyone watching can see everything: *The fight occurred in full view of the fans who arrived early.*
20 to the fullest in the best or most complete way: *His disabilities don't stop him from enjoying life to the fullest.*
21 have/lead a full life to do many different and interesting things: *She had a very full life and enjoyed good health well into her 90s.*
22 draw yourself up to your full height also **rise to your full height** to stand up very straight
23 in full cry if someone is in full cry, they are criticizing someone or something strongly or loudly: *By that time, the press was in full cry, insisting that White House staff knew more than they were saying.*
—see also FULLY, **have your hands full** (HAND¹ (24))

full² n. **in full** if you pay an amount of money in full, you pay the whole amount: *The balance must be paid in full each month.*

full³ adv. directly: [+ in/on] *The door struck me full in the face.* —see also **know full well** (KNOW¹ (4))

full·back /ˈfʊlbæk/ n. [C] a player on a football team whose main duties are to run with the ball and to block players on the other team

full-blood·ed /ˌ. ˈ..⊲ / adj. [only before noun, no comparative] having parents, grandparents etc. from only one race of people, especially a race that is not the main one in a particular society: *There are very few full-blooded Cherokee Indians left.*

full-blown /ˌ. ˈ. / adj. [only before noun, no comparative] a full-blown illness, problem, bad situation etc. is in its most fully developed or advanced stage: *What began as a serious oil spill has become a full-blown environmental disaster.* | *full-blown AIDS*

full-bod·ied /ˌ. ˈ..⊲ / adj. tasting strong, in a pleasant way: *a full-bodied beer*

full bore /ˌ. ˈ. / adv. if someone or something is running, working etc. full bore, they are working as hard and as thoroughly as possible: *The Transit Authority plans to proceed full bore with building the airport extension.* —**full-bore** adj. [only before noun]

full-col·or /ˌ. ˈ..⊲ / adj. [only before noun] printed using colored inks, so that pictures and photographs look REALISTIC: *a 76-page, full-color brochure*

full-court press /ˌ. . ˈ. / n. [singular] **1** a method of defending in a fierce way across the whole COURT in basketball **2** the use of pressure or influence by several groups on someone: *The DEA and the Justice Department put a full-court press on the drug barons.*

full dress /ˌ. ˈ. / n. [U] special clothes that are worn for official occasions and ceremonies —**full-dress** adj.: *a full-dress military ceremony*

Ful·ler, Mar·garet /ˈfʊlɚ, ˈmɑrgrɪt/ (1810–1850) a U.S. writer and social REFORMER who supported women's rights and TRANSCENDENTALISM

Fuller, Mel·ville /ˈmɛlvɪl/ (1833–1910) a CHIEF JUSTICE on the U.S. Supreme Court

Fuller, R. Buck·min·ster /ɑr ˈbʌkmɪnstɚ/ (1895–1983) a U.S. ARCHITECT and engineer, famous for inventing the GEODESIC DOME

full-face /ˌ. ˈ.⊲ / adj. a full-face photograph or picture of someone shows their whole face —compare PROFILE¹ (1)

full-fig·ured /ˌ. ˈ..⊲ / adj. a polite way of describing a woman who is slightly fat and has large breasts

full-fledged /ˌfʊl ˈflɛdʒd⊲ / adj. completely developed, trained, or established: *At the age of 22, Davis became the youngest full-fledged member of the board of directors.*

F

F

full-grown /ˌ. '.ˌ / adj. a full-grown animal, plant, or person has developed to their full size and will not grow any bigger: *Full-grown female whales are about one-third the size of an average male.*

full house /ˌ. './ n. [C usually singular] **1** an occasion at a movie theater, concert hall, sports field etc. when every seat has someone sitting in it: *Organizers expect a full house for tonight's game.* **2** a combination of three cards of one value and a pair of another value in a game of POKER

full length /ˌ. '.ˌ / adv. [only after verb] someone who is lying full length is lying flat with their legs straight out: *Alison was stretched out full length on the couch.*

full-length /ˌ. '.ˌ / adj. **1 full-length mirror/photograph/portrait etc.** a mirror, photograph etc. that shows all of a person, from their head to their feet **2 full-length skirt/dress/coat etc.** a full-length skirt, dress, coat etc. reaches the ground, or is the longest possible for that particular type of clothing: *a full-length evening dress* **3 full-length play/book/movie etc.** a play, book, movie etc. of the normal length

full moon /ˌ. './ n. [singular] the moon when it looks completely round —compare HALF MOON, NEW MOON

full·ness /'fʊlnɪs/ n. [U] **1** the condition of being full: *People who diet no longer eat according to their natural feelings of hunger and fullness.* **2** satisfaction from doing different things: *He intends to enjoy the fullness of life until the day he dies.* **3 in the fullness of time** when the right time comes; EVENTUALLY: *I'm sure he'll tell us everything in the fullness of time.*

full-page /ˌ. '.ˌ / adj. [only before noun] covering all of one page, especially in a newspaper or magazine: *a full-page anti-smoking ad*

full pro·fes·sor /ˌ. .'..'../ n. [C] a teacher of the highest rank at a college or university

full-scale /ˌ. '.ˌ / adj. [only before noun] **1** as complete as possible, or to the greatest degree possible: *The country is on the brink of full-scale civil war.* **2** a full-scale drawing, model, copy etc. of something is the same size as the thing it represents

full-size also **full-sized** /ˌ. '.ˌ / adj. **1** of the normal, usual, or largest possible size: *The new IBM laptop features a full-size keyboard.* **2 a)** a full-size bed is 54 inches (=137 cm) wide and 75 inches (=191 cm) long **b)** full-size sheets, BLANKETS¹ (1) etc. are made to be used on a full-size bed —compare KING-SIZE, QUEEN-SIZE, TWIN-SIZE

full stop /ˌ. './ n. [C] BRITISH a PERIOD¹ (5)

full-term /ˌ. '.ˌ / adj. relating to a PREGNANCY of a normal length: **a full-term infant/pregnancy/birth etc.** *a full-term baby* —compare PREMATURE (2)

full-time /ˌ. '.ˌ / adj., adv. **1** working or studying for the number of hours that work is usually done: *Janine attends high school full-time and works part-time.* | *Only full-time employees get health coverage.* **2 a full-time job a)** a job that you do for all the normal working hours in a week **b)** INFORMAL hard work that you are not being paid for that takes a lot of your time: *I've got to raise my children, and that's a full-time job.* —compare PART-TIME

ful·ly /'fʊli/ adv. **1** completely: *The President is fully aware of the problem.* | *A fully equipped kitchen* | *Patients must fully understand the risks involved in this type of surgery.* **2** FORMAL used to emphasize how big a number is, and to say that it could possibly be even bigger: *Fully 75 percent of cultural articles were devoted to sports.*

fully-grown /ˌ.. '.ˌ / adj. FULL-GROWN

ful·mi·nate /'fʊlmə,neɪt, 'fʌl-/ v. [I] FORMAL to speak angrily against something: [+ against/about] *Politicians still fulminate against the war crimes.* —**fulmination** /ˌfʊlmə'neɪʃən/ n. [C,U]

ful·some /'fʊlsəm/ adj. FORMAL a fulsome piece of writing, speech etc. gives too much praise to be sincere: *Leading Hollywood actors were fulsome in their praise for the director at Thursday night's tribute.* —**fulsomely** adv. —**fulsomeness** n. [U]

Ful·ton /'fʊltⁿn/, **Rob·ert** /'rɑbət/ (1765–1815) a U.S. engineer and inventor who designed and built several STEAMSHIPS

Fu Man·chu mus·tache /ˌfu mæntʃu 'mʌstæʃ/ n. [C] a MUSTACHE whose ends hang down toward or below the chin

fum·ble¹ /'fʌmbəl/ v. **1** [I] to hold or try to move something with your hands carelessly or awkwardly: [+ for/with] *I fumbled in my pockets for a box of matches.* **2** [I,T] to drop the ball after catching it in a game of football **3** [I] if you fumble your words when you are speaking, you have difficulty saying something: [+ for/with] *The group fumbled for a response to Janet's accusations.*

fumble² n. [C] an act of dropping a football after catching it, or an occasion when this happens: *Scott's fumble gave Atlanta a last minute chance.*

fume /fyum/ v. [I] **1** to be angry, usually without saying anything: *A crucial document disappeared for years while frustrated investigators fumed.* | [+ over/about] *He stormed out, fuming over the department's inefficiency.* **2** to give off smoke or gases

fumes /fyumz/ n. [plural] strong-smelling gas or smoke that is bad to breathe in: *A strong smell of paint fumes filled the studio.*

fu·mi·gate /'fyumə,geɪt/ v. [I,T] to clear disease, BACTERIA, insects etc. from somewhere using smoke or chemical gases —**fumigation** /ˌfyumə'geɪʃən/ n. [U]

fun¹ /fʌn/ n. **1** [U] an experience or activity that is very enjoyable and exciting: *Did you have fun at Denny's the other night?* | *It's no fun to be sick when you're on vacation.* | *That sounds like fun. What kind of movie is it?* | *I decided to come out and join in the fun*, instead of just watching. **2 for fun** also **for the fun of it** if you do something for fun, you do it because you enjoy it and not for any other reason: *Encourage your child to read all kinds of books for fun.* **3 make fun of sb/sth** to make jokes about someone that are insulting or make them feel bad: *Stop it – I don't make fun of the way you talk, do I?* **4 fun and games** playful activities: *It started out as fun and games but became a successful business.* | *Of course, college is not all fun and games – you have to work hard too.* **5 in fun** if you make a joke or say something about someone in fun, you do not intend it to be insulting: *Carlin shook Bond's hand to show his act was all done in fun.* **6 sb's idea of fun** used to talk about an activity, situation etc. that is exciting or interesting to someone else, but not to you: *Larsen's idea of fun is to row a canoe around four nights a week.* | *Running in the August heat is not my idea of fun.* **7 like fun** OLD-FASHIONED used when you think something will not happen, or when something is not true: *"I'm going to Barbara's house." "Like fun you are! Come and finish your chores first."* —see also **figure of fun** (FIGURE¹ (13)), FUNNY, **poke fun at sb/sth** (POKE¹ (4)) —see Usage Note at FUNNY

fun² adj. **1** a fun activity or experience is enjoyable: *Have a fun Labor Day!* | *Boulder is a fun place to live.* | *This soccer class is really fun.* **2** someone who is fun is enjoyable to be with because they are cheerful and amusing: *Randy's really fun guy to be around.*

func·tion¹ /'fʌŋkʃən/ n. **1** [C] the purpose that something is made for, or the job that someone does: [+ of] *Until this century, little was known about the function of the ovaries.* | *The main function of a healthy family is to support one another.* **2** [C,U] the way in which something works or the way in which it is used: *Long term exercise changes the function of the heart, blood, and muscles.* | *Bauhaus architects thought that function was more important than form.* **3** [C] a large party or ceremonial event, especially for an important or official occasion: *The Great Hall is available for weddings and other social functions.* **4 a function of sth a)** if one thing is a function of another, it is produced by or changes according to the other thing: *The balance of calcium in the body is largely a function of its absorption in the intestines.* **b)** TECHNICAL a mathematical quantity that changes according to how another mathematical quantity changes: *In $x = 5y$, x is a function of y.* **5** [C] one of the basic operations performed by a computer

function[2] *v.* [I] **1** if something functions, it works correctly or in a particular way: *The alarm system was not functioning when the paintings were stolen.* | *Ancient Egyptians used herbs to help the stomach function naturally.* **2 not function** if someone cannot function, they cannot do the activities that people normally do: *You can't really function in society if you can't read.*

function as sth *phr. v.* [T] to be or work as something: *Busterback Ranch functions as a ski resort in winter.*

func·tion·al /'fʌŋkʃənəl/ *adj.* **1** designed to be useful: *These tin cookie cutters are both functional and decorative.* **2** working in the way that something is supposed to: *The 1100 FD model is a fully functional PC-compatible notebook computer.* **3** having a useful purpose: *The company was divided into four main functional areas.* —**functionally** *adv.*

functional ill·it·er·ate /,... '.../ *n.* [C] someone who may be able to read a little, but cannot read well enough to do many things in society, such as getting a good job

func·tion·al·ism /'fʌŋkʃənə,lɪzəm/ *n.* [U] the idea that the most important thing about a building, piece of furniture etc. is that it is useful —**functionalist** *n.* [C] —**functionalist** *adj.*

func·tion·a·ry /'fʌŋkʃə,nɛri/ *n. plural* **functionaries** [C] someone who has a job doing unimportant or boring official duties

function key /'.. ,./ *n.* [C] TECHNICAL a button on the KEYBOARD of a computer that tells the machine to perform a particular function

function word /'.. ,./ *n.* [C] a word such as a PRONOUN or PREPOSITION that is used in place of another word, or that shows the relationship between two words. For example, in the sentences "The cat is hungry. It hasn't been fed yet," "it" is a function word.

fund[1] /fʌnd/ *n.* **1** [C] an amount of money that is collected and kept for a particular purpose: *The government agreed to create a fund to help develop rural areas.* | *Carol wants to set up an investment fund.* —see also FUNDING, SLUSH FUND, TRUST FUND **2 funds** [plural] the money needed to do something: *To qualify for funds, organizations must be non-profit companies.* | *We didn't have enough funds to complete the project.* **3 be/run short of funds** to have little or no money: *Many federal programs are running short of funds.* **4** [C] an organization that is responsible for collecting and spending money for a particular purpose: *The New Children's Shelter Fund received a grant of $80,000.* —compare CHARITY (1) **5 a fund of** sth a large supply of something: *Ronny has a bottomless fund of anecdotes.*

fund[2] *v.* [T] **1** to provide money for an activity, organization, event etc.: *The women's shelter is funded entirely by the church.* **2** TECHNICAL to change the arrangements for paying a debt, so that you have more time to pay

fun·da·men·tal[1] /,fʌndə'mɛntl/ *adj.* **1** affecting the simplest and most important parts of something: *A lot of companies are making fundamental changes in their structure.* | *The Red Sox made a fundamental mistake in the sixth inning.* **2** very necessary and important as a part of something from which everything else develops: [+ **to**] *Competition is fundamental to keeping prices down.*

fundamental[2] *n.* [C usually plural] the most important ideas, rules etc. that something is based on: [+ **of**] *These two programs teach the fundamentals of keyboard use.*

fun·da·men·tal·ism /,fʌndə'mɛntl,ɪzəm/ *n.* [U] **1** the practice of following religious laws very strictly **2** a belief of some Christians that everything in the Bible is completely true

fun·da·men·tal·ist /,fʌndə'mɛntl-ɪst/ *n.* [C] **1** someone who follows religious laws very strictly: *Muslim fundamentalists* **2** a Christian who believes that everything in the Bible is completely true —**fundamentalist** *adj.*: *a fundamentalist religion*

fun·da·men·tal·ly /,fʌndə'mɛntl-i/ *adv.* **1** in every way that is important or basic: *Both sides remain fundamentally divided on key issues.* **2** [sentence

adverb] when you consider the most important or basic parts: *Fundamentally, we have a good safety program.*

fund·ing /'fʌndɪŋ/ *n.* [U] an amount of money for a specific purpose: *Were you able to get funding to finish your dissertation?*

fund·rais·er /'fʌnd,reɪzɚ/ *n.* [C] **1** an event that is held to collect money for a specific purpose such as a CHARITY or political party **2** a person who collects money for a specific purpose such as a CHARITY or a political party, for example by arranging social events that people pay to attend

fu·ner·al /'fyunərəl/ *n.* [C] a ceremony for burying or burning a dead person: *Don went to Boston to attend a friend's funeral.* | *Private funeral services are scheduled for Saturday.*

funeral di·rec·tor /'... ,../ *n.* [C] someone whose job is to organize funerals

funeral home /'... ,./ also **funeral par·lor** /'... ,../ *n.* [C] the place where a body is kept before a funeral and where the funeral is sometimes held

fu·ner·ar·y /'fyunə,rɛri/ *adj.* [only before noun] FORMAL relating to a funeral or a grave: *the funerary procession*

fu·ne·re·al /fyu'nɪriəl/ *adj.* FORMAL **1** [only before noun] sad, slow, and appropriate for a funeral: *funereal music* **2** making it difficult to feel hopeful or happy: *The local weather was always funereal.* —**funereally** *adv.*

fun·gal /'fʌŋgəl/ *adj.* TECHNICAL relating to or caused by a fungus: *a fungal infection*

fun·gi·ble /'fʌndʒɪbəl/ *adj.* TECHNICAL fungible things, money, BONDS, STOCKS etc. can be exchanged for another amount of the same thing, or used instead of another thing, especially because they are of the same type —**fungible** *n.* [C usually plural]

fun·gi·cide /'fʌngə,saɪd, 'fʌndʒə-/ *n.* [C,U] a chemical used for destroying fungus

fun·goid /'fʌŋgɔɪd/ *adj.* TECHNICAL like a fungus: *fungoid growths*

fun·gus /'fʌŋgəs/ *n. plural* **fungi** /-gaɪ, -dʒaɪ/ or **funguses 1** [C,U] a simple fast-growing living thing, such as a MUSHROOM or MOLD (1) **2** [U] this type of living thing, especially considered as a disease

fun house /'. ./ *n.* [C] a building at a FAIR in which there are things that amuse or shock people

fu·nic·u·lar /fyu'nɪkyələ, fə-/ also **funicular rail·way** /.,... '../ *n.* [C] a small vehicle that goes up a hill or a mountain, pulled by a thick metal rope

funk /fʌŋk/ *n.* [U] **1** a style of music with a strong RHYTHM that is based on JAZZ and African music **2 in a (blue) funk** INFORMAL very unhappy, worried, or afraid about something: *Sam drove off in a funk.* **3** INFORMAL a strong smell, especially one that comes from someone's body: *Well, that explains the strange funk in your room.*

funk·y /'fʌŋki/ *adj.* **funkier, funkiest** INFORMAL **1** fashionable and interesting, and often unusual: *All these people were wearing funky leather outfits.* **2** funky music is simple with a strong RHYTHM that is easy to dance to **3** having a bad, dirty smell or appearance: *This water looks a little funky.*

fun·nel[1] /'fʌnl/ *n.* [C] a tube that is wide at one end and narrow at the other end, used for pouring liquids or powders into a container with a narrow opening

funnel[2] *v.* **1** [I,T] to pass or be passed through a narrow opening, causing to pass a large amount of something into a small space: [+ **to/through/into**] *Solar cells collect and funnel energy to the batteries.* | *The four-lane highway funnels into a two-lane connector to Interstate 580.* **2** [T] to send a large number of things or money from different places to a particular place: *Economic aid from 24 countries will be funneled into the war zone.*

fun·nies /'fʌniz/ *n.* INFORMAL **the funnies** the part of a newspaper with many different CARTOONS

fun·ni·ly /'fʌnl-i/ *adv.* in an odd or unusual way: *Canseco's throw was straight, but wobbled funnily at* the last minute. —see also **strangely/oddly/funnily enough** (ENOUGH¹ (2))

S W **funny** /'fʌni/ adj. **funnier, funniest**
1 ~~amusing~~ making you laugh: *Come on, sit on my lap and I'll tell you a funny story.* | *You'll like Alan – he's really funny.*
2 ~~strange~~ unusual and difficult to explain: *I always thought that was a funny place to have a house.* | *There's a funny smell coming from Pete's room.*
3 ~~dishonest~~ seeming to be illegal or dishonest, although you are not exactly sure why: *There's something funny going on here.* | *I don't want any funny business going on while I'm gone.*
4 feel funny to feel slightly sick: *Nicole says her stomach feels funny.*
5 see the funny side of sth to be able to laugh in a difficult or bad situation: *Landon could always see the funny side of all the horrible gossip the media wrote about him.*

SPOKEN PHRASES

6 it's funny used to say that you do not really understand why something happens, but it does and you think it is strange, interesting, worrying etc.: *It's funny you mentioned that, because we were just talking about UFOs.* | [+ **how**] *It's funny how two sisters can be so different.* | [+ (**that**)] *It's funny that he and Gloria have never gotten married.*
7 that's funny used when you are surprised by something that has happened and you can not explain it: *That's funny. I'm sure I put my wallet down there, and now it's gone.*
8 the funny thing is used to say what the strangest or most amusing part of a story or situation is: *My uncle Dan taught us how to do a lot of illegal stuff. And the funny thing is, his son's a police officer.*
9 it's not funny used to tell someone not to laugh at or make jokes about something you think is very serious: *It's not funny to be making jokes about fat people all the time.*
10 very funny! used when someone is laughing at you or making a joke and you do not think it is funny: *Oh, that's very funny. I know you're in there.* | *Very funny! Who hid my car keys?*
11 what's so funny? used when someone is laughing and you want to know why: *"What's so funny?" "Marcia just spilled purple paint all over herself!"*
12 funny little... used to describe something or someone that is small and unusual: *I like the funny little way Maury has of smiling.*
13 funny old... used to describe something or someone that is strange but that you like or think is interesting: *Like they say, it's a funny old game.*
14 funny weird/strange or **funny ha ha?** used when someone has described something as funny, and you want to know if they mean that it is strange or amusing: *"Tim's a funny guy." "Funny weird or funny ha ha?"*

USAGE NOTE: FUNNY

WORD CHOICE: fun and funny
Use **fun** to talk about things or events that you enjoy: *We had a fun time at the dance.* | *That sounds like fun.*
Use **funny** to talk about people or things that make you laugh: *Mike Myers is a funny guy.* | *The skits were so funny last night.*

funny bone /'.. ,./ n. [singular] **1** the soft part of your elbow that hurts a lot when you hit it hard **2** your sense of humor: *Bennett's latest show is guaranteed to tickle your funny bone* (=make you laugh).

funny farm /'.. ,./ n. [C] INFORMAL an expression meaning a hospital for people who are mentally ill, that is usually considered offensive

funny-look·ing /'.. ,../ adj. INFORMAL having a strange or amusing appearance: *Jon was a really funny-looking little kid.*

fun·ny·man /'fʌni,mæn/ n. plural **funnymen** /-mɛn/ [C] a man who acts in funny movies or television shows, or works as a COMEDIAN

funny mon·ey /'.. ,../ n. [U] INFORMAL money that has been printed illegally —compare COUNTERFEIT¹

funny pa·pers /'.. ,../ n. [plural] INFORMAL another expression meaning FUNNIES

fun·ny·wom·an /'fʌni,wʊmən/ n. plural **funny-women** /-,wɪmɪn/ [C] a woman who acts in funny movies or television shows, or works as a COMEDIAN

fun run /'. ./ n. [C] an event in which people run a long distance in order to collect money, usually for CHARITY

fur /fɚ/ n. **1** [U] the thick soft hair that covers the bodies of some types of animal, for example cats or dogs: *There was cat fur all over the chair.* —compare HAIR (3) **2** [C,U] the fur-covered skin of an animal, especially used for making clothes: *Furs from the far north of Canada were exchanged for cotton and other goods.* | *the fur industry* | *a fur coat* | *Darcie came in wearing a **fake fur** jacket* (=one made of artificial material that looks like fur). **3** [C] a coat or piece of clothing made of fur: *In the hall, Mrs. Welland was putting on her fur.* **4 the fur flies** used to say that an angry argument or fight starts: *When Marcia found out where Keith was all night, that's when the fur really started to fly.* —see also FURRY

fu·ri·ous /'fyʊriəs/ adj. **1** extremely angry: *Tony was furious when Bobbie admitted the truth.* | *Williams got a call that day from a furious Larry Parnes.* | [+ **with/at/about etc.**] *They were furious at finding no doctors on duty at the hospital.* **2** [only before noun] done with a lot of energy, effort, or anger: *The Huskies made a furious comeback in the second half.* | *Darlene started heading through the woods **at a furious pace*** (=very fast and with a lot of energy). | *The following round of questions for the President was **fast and furious**.* —**furiously** adv.

furl /fɚl/ v. [T] LITERARY to roll or fold something such as a flag, UMBRELLA, or sail —**furled** adj. —compare UNFURL

fur·long /'fɚlɔŋ/ n. [C] a unit for measuring length used in horse racing, equal to 220 yards or 201 meters

fur·lough /'fɚloʊ/ n. [C,U] **1** a period of time when a soldier or someone working in another country can return to their own country: *Last time I saw Jenkins was when he was **on furlough** back in July.* **2** a temporary period of time when a worker is told not to work, especially because there is not enough work or not enough money to pay them: *The mayor has ordered a four-day furlough for 26,000 city employees.* —compare LAYOFF **3** a short period of time when a prisoner is allowed to leave prison before returning

fur·nace /'fɚnɪs/ n. [C] **1** a piece of equipment that is used to heat a house or building **2** a large container in which a very hot fire is made, to produce power or heat, or to melt metals —see also BLAST FURNACE **3 be (like) a furnace** to be extremely hot

fur·nish /'fɚnɪʃ/ v. [T] **1** [usually passive] to put furniture and other things into a house or room: *Nina's room was plainly furnished with a bed and a desk.* | *The house was furnished in the most beautiful taste.* **2** to supply or provide something: *Buyers of any gun must furnish two pieces of identification.* | [**furnish sb with sth**] *U.S. embassies can furnish you with a list of local hospitals and English-speaking doctors.* —**furnished** adj.: *a furnished apartment*

fur·nish·ing /'fɚnɪʃɪŋ/ n. [U,plural] the furniture and other things in a room, such as curtains, decorations etc.: *home furnishings*

fur·ni·ture /'fɚnɪtʃɚ/ n. [U] large movable objects such as chairs, tables, and beds that you use in a room to make it comfortable to live or work in: *The master bedroom is filled with antique furniture.* | *office furniture* | *Former tenants had left behind several pieces of furniture.* **S W**

fu·ror /'fyʊrɔr/ n. [singular] a sudden expression of anger or excitement among a large group of people about something that has happened: *Some say the furor over the artist's trial has drawn more people to his photo exhibit.*

F

fur·ri·er /ˈfɚiɚ, ˈfʌriɚ/ *n.* [C] someone who makes or sells fur clothing

fur·row[1] /ˈfɚoʊ, ˈfʌroʊ/ *n.* [C] **1** a long narrow cut made in the surface of a field with a PLOW **2** a deep line or fold in the skin of someone's face, especially on the top front part of their head **3** a long, narrow cut or hollow area in the surface of something: *The boat's propellers slashed dark furrows in the water.*

furrow[2] *v.* **1** [I,T] to make the skin on your face form deep lines or folds, especially because you are worried, angry, or thinking very hard: *Ralph **furrowed his brow**, trying to work everything out.* **2** [T] to make a deep cut or hollow area in something —**furrowed** *adj.*: *a furrowed brow*

fur·ry /ˈfɚi/ *adj.* **furrier, furriest** covered with fur, or looking or feeling as if covered with fur: *a furry puppy* | *a furry cap*

S W 2 2 **fur·ther**[1] /ˈfɚðɚ/ *adv.*

1 more if you do something further you do it more, or to a greater degree: *Moving to a new location further hurt Tanya's business.* | *The cheese's flavor and texture may be further improved during the aging period.* | [+ **into/away etc.**] *Our educational system continues to slide **further and further** into mediocrity.*

2 distance used to say that a place is a long way from, or more distant than, another place: *They've never been further south than San Diego.* | [+ **up/away/along etc.**] *The lodge is several hundred feet further up the mountain.*

3 take sth further to take action at a more serious or higher level, especially in order to punish someone or to get the result that you want: *We take it further than just explaining drug abuse and saying "Don't do it."* | *If we do not receive payment by May 5, we will **take the matter further**.*

4 go (one step) further to do or say more than before: *A few days later the department went one step further and filed a lawsuit.*

5 time further back/on/ahead etc. a longer way in the past or future: *Five years further on, a cure has still not been found.* | *These papers go back further than that, all the way to 1970.* | *He'll come up with a different idea **further down the road*** (=in the future).

6 in addition [sentence adverb] FORMAL used to introduce something additional that you want to talk about; FURTHERMORE: *It is possible to make good movies cheaply. Further, "low-budget" doesn't have to mean "bad."*

7 nothing could be further from the truth used when you want to say that something is completely untrue: *A lot of people think soufflés are hard to make. Nothing could be further from the truth.* —see Usage Note at FARTHER

S W 2 **further**[2] *adj.* [only before noun] **1** more or additional: *For further information, travelers may contact the consulate.* | *Add the sesame seeds, and bake for **a further** 20 minutes.* **2 until further notice** until you are told that something has changed: *All three schools were closed until further notice.*

further[3] *v.* [T] to help something succeed or be achieved: *Rodney had no opportunities to further his education.*

fur·ther·ance /ˈfɚðərəns/ *n.* [U] FORMAL **1 the furtherance of sth** the development or progress of something: *the furtherance of human rights* **2 in furtherance of sth** in order to help something progress or become complete: *What steps will you take in furtherance of that resolution?*

fur·ther·more /ˈfɚðɚˌmɔr/ *adv.* [sentence adverb] FORMAL in addition to what has already been said: *Most Americans increased their wealth in the past decade. Furthermore, the gains were substantial.*

fur·thest /ˈfɚðɪst/ *adj., adv.* **1** at the greatest distance from a place or point in time: *The telescope is designed to study the furthest reaches of the universe.* | [+ **away/from etc.**] *The cheapest apartments tend to be the ones furthest away from urban centers.* **2** to the greatest degree or amount, or more than before: *Croatia and Slovenia have moved **the furthest** toward free-market economics.* | *Selling records was **the furthest thing from my mind** when I started singing.*

fur·tive /ˈfɚt̬ɪv/ *adj.* behaving as if you want to keep something secret: *She was having a furtive affair with a cameraman.* | *Tim and Joanie exchanged **furtive glances** across the room.* —**furtively** *adv.* —**furtiveness** *n.* [U]

fu·ry /ˈfyʊri/ *n.* **1** [singular,U] a state or feeling of extreme, often uncontrolled anger: *Shaking with uncontrollable fury, she stood up to confront him.* | *A gunman shot seven people **in a fury** over rejection by his girlfriend.* **2 a fury of sth** a state of very busy activity or strong feeling: *She drove down the road in a fury of emotion.* **3 the fury of the wind/sea/waves etc.** LITERARY used to describe bad weather conditions: *No one was prepared for the devastating fury of Mt. Pinatubo.* **4 the Furies** [plural] the three GODDESSES in ancient Greek stories, who have snakes in their hair and who punish crime

fuse[1] /fyuz/ *n.* [C] **1** a short thin piece of wire that is inside electrical equipment and prevents damage by melting and stopping the electricity when there is too much power: *Suddenly, **a fuse blew** and the whole house went dark.* | *The electronic scoreboard **blew a fuse** and the display disappeared.* **2** also **fuze** a part of a bomb, FIREWORK etc. that delays the explosion until you are a safe distance away, or makes it explode at a particular time: *Be sure all safety measures have been taken before lighting the fuse.* **3 have a short fuse** to get angry very easily —see also **blow a fuse** (BLOW[1] (8))

fuse[2] *v.* [I,T] **1** to join together, or to make things join together, to become a single thing: *Getz was one of the first musicians to fuse jazz and Latin rhythms.* | *King sought to fuse the civil rights movement with anti-war activists.* **2** if metals, rocks etc. fuse or if you fuse them, they become joined together by being heated: *The radio's wires had been fused by the heat.* **3** TECHNICAL if a rock or metal fuses or if you fuse it, it becomes liquid by being heated: *Lead fuses at a fairly low temperature.*

fuse box /ˈ. ./ *n.* [C] a box that contains the fuses of the electrical system of a house or other building

fu·se·lage /ˈfyusəˌlɑʒ, -lɪdʒ, -zə-/ *n.* [C] the main part of an airplane, in which people sit or goods are carried

fu·sil·lade /ˈfyuzəˌleɪd/ *n.* [C usually singular] **1** a rapid series of loud noises, especially shots from a gun: [+ **of**] *The first officers who burst into the house were met with a fusillade of bullets.* **2** a rapid series of questions or remarks: [+ **of**] *Ms. Hills ran into a fusillade of hostile questions at Tuesday's committee meeting.*

fu·sion /ˈfyuʒən/ *n.* **1** [singular,U] the combination or joining together of separate things, ideas, or groups: *The Cherry Blossom restaurant serves a fusion of Japanese and Californian cooking.* **2** [U] the joining together of separate things by heating them **3** also **fusion jazz** [U] a style of music that combines JAZZ and ROCK —compare FISSION —see also NUCLEAR FUSION

fusion bomb /ˈ.. ˌ./ *n.* [C] another word for a HYDROGEN BOMB

fuss[1] /fʌs/ *n.* **1** [singular,U] attention or excitement that makes something seem more serious or important than it is: *Passengers strained to see what all the fuss was about.* | *The current fuss about San Jose's proposed downtown arena has been noticed in other parts of the state.* **2 make a fuss/kick up a fuss** also **raise a fuss** to complain or become angry about something, especially in a way that is stronger than necessary: *Davis kicked up a fuss when the waiter forgot her order.* **3 make a fuss over sb/sth** to pay too much attention to someone or something that you like: *People always make such a fuss over babies when they're little and cute.*

fuss[2] *v.* [I] **1** to behave in a nervous or unhappy way: *Mary Alice fussed and squirmed until she got her bottle.* **2** to pay too much attention to small, unimportant details: *The girls **fussed with** their hair and put on makeup.*

fuss over sb/sth *phr. v.* [T] **1** to pay a lot of, or too much, attention to someone or something that you like: *Mrs. Wilson fussed over the little dog in her lap.* **2** to worry a lot about things that may not be very important: *Mom's still fussing over the seating plans.*

fuss·budg·et /ˈfʌsˌbʌdʒɪt/ *n.* [C] OLD-FASHIONED someone who is always too concerned or worried about small, unimportant details

fuss·y /ˈfʌsi/ *adj.* **fussier, fussiest 1** too concerned or worried about small, usually unimportant details: *I've become much more fussy about how I draw the characters.* —compare FASTIDIOUS **2** unhappy or difficult to please: *a fussy baby* | *Children nowadays are very fussy eaters.* **3 not be fussy** SPOKEN used to say that you do not mind what decision is made, where you go etc.: *"What would you like to eat?" "Oh, whatever – I'm not fussy."* **4** fussy clothes, objects, buildings etc. are too detailed and decorated: *fussy wallpaper* —**fussily** *adv.* —**fussiness** *n.* [U]

fus·tian /ˈfʌstʃən/ *n.* [U] **1** a type of rough heavy cotton cloth, worn especially in past times **2** LITERARY words that sound important but have very little meaning —**fustian** *adj.*

fus·ty /ˈfʌsti/ *adj.* **1** OLD-FASHIONED if rooms, clothes, buildings etc. are fusty, they have a bad smell, because they have not been used for a long time **2** ideas or people that are fusty are old-fashioned: *A number of young economists, impatient with such fusty arguments, began searching for new models.* —**fustiness** *n.* [U]

fu·tile /ˈfyutl/ *adj.* actions that are futile are useless because they have no chance of being successful: *Rescue workers made a **futile attempt** to save the people trapped in the collapsed building.* —**futility** /fyuˈtɪləti/ *n.* [U]

fu·ton /ˈfutɑn/ *n.* [C] a type of bed that you can roll up when you are not using it, originally from Japan —see picture at BED[1]

fu·ture[1] /ˈfyutʃɚ/ *n.*
1 the future the time after the present: *Buckley won't make plans for the future until the charges are dropped.* | *We need to provide boys and girls with career opportunities for the future.* | *In the future, this kind of business will be very lucrative.* | *in the near/foreseeable future It is unlikely that we will achieve any profits in the near future.*
2 what will happen to you [C usually singular] what someone or something will do or what will happen to them in the future: *At issue is the future of six U.S. military bases.* | *Gabby assured me that she is confident about her future.*
3 possibility of success [singular,U] a chance or possibility of success at a later time: *I'd like to discuss my future in the company.* | *Myles is optimistic about the future of electric cars.* | *I think Trisha definitely **has a future** in the newspaper business.* | *have a great/promising/bright future (=to seem likely to do well in a job, sport etc.)*
4 futures [plural] goods, money, land etc. that are bought and sold for an agreed price but supplied or exchanged at a later date, even though the value of the goods may have changed
5 the future also **the future tense** TECHNICAL in grammar, the form of a verb that shows that an action or state will happen or exist at a later time. In the sentence "I will leave tomorrow," "will leave" is in the future.

future[2] *adj.* [only before noun] **1** likely to happen, become, or exist at a time after the present: *The time and place for future meetings has not been revealed.* | *We're getting together to talk about future plans for the show.* | *sb's future wife/husband/son-in-law etc. (=someone who will be your wife, husband, son-in-law etc.)* **2** TECHNICAL in grammar, being the form of a verb used to show an action or state that will happen or exist in the future: *the future tense* **3 for future reference** something kept for future reference is kept in order to be used or looked at in the future

future per·fect /ˌ.. ˈ../ *n.* TECHNICAL **the future per-**fect in grammar, the form of a verb that shows that an action will be complete before a particular time in the future, formed in English by "will have." In the sentence, "I will have finished my finals by next Friday," "will have finished" is in the future perfect. —**future perfect** *adj.*

fu·tur·ism /ˈfyutʃəˌrɪzəm/ *n.* [U] **1** a style of painting, music, and literature from the early 20th century that expresses the violent, active qualities of modern life, machines, science etc. **2** the act of imagining what may happen in the future, especially through scientific developments or politics: *Gingrich's lectures contain clear evidence of his interest in futurism and technology.* —**futurist** *n.* [C]

fu·tur·is·tic /ˌfyutʃəˈrɪstɪk/ *adj.* **1** a futuristic building/movie/design etc. a building, movie, design etc. that is so unusual and modern in appearance that it looks as if it belongs in the future instead of the present time: *The remote control for the TV looks like a futuristic pistol.* **2** futuristic ideas, books etc. imagine what may happen in the future, especially through scientific developments

fu·tu·ri·ty /fyuˈtʊrəti, -ˈtʃʊr-/ *n. plural* **futurities** **1** [U] FORMAL the time after the present; the FUTURE **2** [C] a type of horse race in which the horses are entered in the competition at the time they are born

futz /fʌts/ *v.*
futz around *phr. v.* [I] INFORMAL **1** to waste time, especially by doing small, unimportant jobs slowly: *Yolanda futzed around in the supermarket while the rest of us were ready to go.* **2** to make changes or move things around without knowing exactly what needs to be done, especially in a way that is annoying or dangerous: [+ with] *Brad spent a couple of hours futzing around with the speaker connections.*

fuze /fyuz/ *n.* [C] another spelling of FUSE

fuzz[1] /fʌz/ *n.* [U] **1** thin soft hair or a hairlike substance that covers something: *There's some green fuzz growing on the leftovers in the fridge.* **2** a small amount of soft material that has come from clothing etc.: *You wouldn't believe all the dust and fuzz that gathers behind the computer.* **3 the fuzz** SLANG an insulting word for the police, used especially in the 1960s and 1970s

fuzz[2] *v.* [T usually passive] to make something fuzzy

Fuzz·Bust·er /ˈfʌzˌbʌstɚ/ *n.* [C] TRADEMARK a machine in your car that warns you when there are any police cars nearby, so that you know that you should not drive too fast

fuzz·y /ˈfʌzi/ *adj.* **fuzzier, fuzziest 1** unclear or confused and lacking details: *Clarence had only a few fuzzy memories of his grandparents.* **2** having a lot of very small thin hairs, fur etc. that look very soft: *a fuzzy hat* **3** if a picture or sound is fuzzy, it is unclear: *Police have only a fuzzy videotape of the bank robbery.* **4 warm (and) fuzzy** used to describe something that gives you a good feeling, especially relating to love or caring: *What do you think of all these warm and fuzzy campaign commercials?* —**fuzzily** *adv.* —**fuzziness** *n.* [U]

fuzzy log·ic /ˌ.. ˈ../ *n.* [U] a machine, computer, or piece of equipment that uses fuzzy logic is able to change for particular situations in order to do a job better, rather than always doing things in exactly the same way

FWIW, fwiw a written abbreviation of "for what it's worth," used in EMAIL, or by people communicating in CHAT ROOMs on the Internet

f-word /ˈɛf wɚd/ *n.* **the f-word** a word used when you are talking about the word "FUCK" but do not want to say it because it is offensive: *I don't want to hear anyone using the f-word in this house, all right?*

fwy. the written abbreviation of FREEWAY

FX 1 an abbreviation of SPECIAL EFFECTS **2** an abbreviation of FOREIGN EXCHANGE

FY the abbreviation of FISCAL YEAR

-fy /faɪ/ *suffix* [in verbs] to affect or change someone or something in a particular way: *to stupefy (=make you feel very surprised or bored)* —see also -IFY

FYI the abbreviation of "for your information," used especially in short business notes and EMAILs

G, g /dʒi/ *plural* **G's, g's** *n.* **1** [C] the seventh letter of the English alphabet **2** [C,U] **a)** the fifth note in the musical SCALE[1] (9) of C MAJOR[1] (3) **b)** the musical KEY[1] (4) based on this note

g the written abbreviation of GRAM

G[1] /dʒi/ *n.* **1** [C] TECHNICAL the amount of force caused by GRAVITY (1) on an object that is lying on the Earth: *The MiG-29 fighter jet can take nine G's* (=nine times the force of gravity). **2** [C,U] SPOKEN a GRAND (=$1000)

G[2] /dʒi/ *adj.* an abbreviation of "General", used to show that a movie is appropriate for people of any age —compare PG

G8 /dʒi 'eɪt/ *n.* **the G8** eight of the most important industrial nations in the world (Canada, France, Germany, Britain, Italy, Japan, Russia, and the U.S.) who meet to discuss world political and economic problems

GA the written abbreviation of Georgia

gab /ɡæb/ *v.* **gabbed, gabbing** [I] INFORMAL to talk continuously, usually about things that are not important: *They spend way too much time gabbing when they should be working.* —see also **the gift of gab** (GIFT[1] (4)) —**gab** *n.* [U] —**gabby** *adj.*

gab·ar·dine /ˈɡæbəˌdin/ *n.* [U] a type of cloth that is made of tightly woven wool, cotton, or POLYESTER, especially used for making clothes

gab·ble[1] /ˈɡæbəl/ *v.* **gabbled, gabbling** [I,T] to say something so quickly that people cannot hear you or understand you well

gabble[2] *n.* [singular,U] **1** a lot of talking that is difficult to understand, especially when several people are talking at the same time: *the gabble of the audience before the show* **2** the sound that a group of geese or ducks make

gab·er·dine /ˈɡæbəˌdin/ *n.* [U] another spelling of GABARDINE

ga·ble /ˈɡeɪbəl/ *n.* [C] the top part of a wall of a house where it joins with a sloping roof and makes a shape like a TRIANGLE

ga·bled /ˈɡeɪbəld/ *adj.* having one or more gables: *a gabled roof*

Ga·bon /ɡæˈboʊn/ a country in west central Africa on the Atlantic Ocean —**Gabonese** /ˌɡæbəˈniz◂, -ˈnis◂/ *n., adj.*

Ga·bo·ro·ne /ˌɡabəˈroʊni/ the capital city of Botswana

Ga·bri·el /ˈɡeɪbriəl/ in the Bible an ARCHANGEL who brings messages from God to people on Earth. In the Muslim religion, Gabriel gave Muhammad the messages from Allah which form THE KORAN.

Gad /ɡæd/ *interjection* a word used instead of "God" to emphasize what you are saying: *Gad, what was I doing so far from home?*

gad /ɡæd/ *v.* **gadded, gadding**
  gad around *phr. v.* [I] INFORMAL to go out and enjoy yourself, going to many different places, especially when you should be doing something else

gad·a·bout /ˈɡædəˌbaʊt/ *n.* [C] INFORMAL someone who goes out a lot or travels a lot in order to enjoy themselves

Gad·da·fi /ɡəˈdɑfi/, **Colonel Mu·am·mar al-** /ˈmoʊəmɑr æl/ —see QADDAFI

gad·fly /ˈɡædflaɪ/ *n. plural* **gadflies** [C] **1** someone who annoys other people by criticizing them: *Hirschfield, a wealthy political gadfly, spoke at the conference.* **2** a fly that bites cattle and HORSES

gad·get /ˈɡædʒɪt/ *n.* [C] a word meaning a small, useful, and well-designed machine or tool, sometimes used when you think the tool is not necessary: *kitchen gadgets such as avocado peelers* —see Usage Note at MACHINE[1]

gadg·et·ry /ˈɡædʒɪtri/ *n.* [U] a word meaning small machines and tools considered as a group, sometimes used when you think the machines are complicated or not necessary: *high-tech medical gadgetry*

gad·zooks /ɡædˈzuks/ *interjection* OLD-FASHIONED used to show that you are surprised about something

Gae·a, Gaia /ˈɡaɪə, ˈdʒiə/ in Greek MYTHOLOGY, the goddess of the Earth

Gael·ic[1] /ˈɡeɪlɪk, ˈɡælɪk/ *n.* [U] one of the Celtic languages, especially spoken in parts of Scotland and in Ireland

Gael·ic[2] *adj.* speaking Gaelic, or relating to Gaelic

gaff[1] /ɡæf/ *n.* [C] a stick with a hook at the end, used to pull big fish out of the water

gaff[2] *v.* [T] to pull big fish out of the water with a gaff

gaffe /ɡæf/ *n.* [C] an embarrassing mistake, especially in something you say, that is made in a social situation or in public: *In France, using the familiar form "tu" ("you") in a business setting would be a major gaffe.*

gaf·fer /ˈɡæfə/ *n.* [C] **1** the person who is in charge of the lighting in making a movie **2** INFORMAL, HUMOROUS an old man

gag[1] /ɡæɡ/ *v.* **gagged, gagging** **1** [I] to feel sick in a way that makes you feel as though you might VOMIT (=bring food from your stomach back through your mouth): *I heard him gagging and coughing.* | [+ on] *A customer gagged on a piece of meat.* **2** [T] to put a piece of cloth over someone's mouth to stop them making a noise: *Five of the occupants were bound and gagged (=tied and gagged) by the robbers.* **3** [T] to stop people saying what they want to say and expressing their opinions: *The mayor was accused of trying to gag the media.* **4** [I] INFORMAL to feel surprised and annoyed about something you think is not fair: *The price of these tickets is enough to make anyone gag.* **5 gag me (with a spoon)!** SPOKEN used especially by older children and TEENAGERS in the 1980s to express a strong feeling of dislike

gag[2] *n.* [C] **1** INFORMAL a joke, funny story, or trick that is done to make someone look silly: *He wrote gags for the Jack Benny show.* | *The movie has some good sight gags* (=things that are funny because of what happens rather than what is said). **2** a piece of cloth put over someone's mouth to stop them making a noise

ga·ga /ˈɡɑɡɑ/ *adj.* [not before noun] INFORMAL having a strong but often temporary feeling of love for someone, or having a strong liking for something: *Customers have gone gaga over the restaurant's cheese steak sandwiches.* | *I can't understand why Susan's so gaga about him.* **2** used to describe someone who is acting confused: *Staying home with the kids is making me a little gaga.*

Ga·ga·rin, Yu·ri /ɡəˈɡɑrɪn, ˈyʊri/ (1934–1968) a Soviet ASTRONAUT who became the first man in space when he traveled round the Earth in 1961

gage /ɡeɪdʒ/ *n.* another spelling of GAUGE

gag·gle /ˈɡæɡəl/ *n.* **1 a gaggle of tourists/children** etc. HUMOROUS a noisy group of people **2 a gaggle of geese** a group of geese (GOOSE)

gag or·der /ˈ. ˌ../ *n.* [C] an order made by a court of law that stops people from reporting on what is happening in a TRIAL that is still being considered by the court

gag rule /ˈ. ./ *n.* [C] a rule or law that stops people from talking about a subject during a particular time or in a particular place

gai·e·ty /ˈɡeɪəti/ *n.* OLD-FASHIONED **1** [U] a feeling of cheerfulness and fun: *the warmth and gaiety of a family reunion* **2 gaieties** enjoyable events or activities: *Elaine missed the gaieties of life in Paris.* —see also GAY[1] (3)

gai·ly /ˈɡeɪli/ *adv.* OLD-FASHIONED **1 gaily colored/painted/decorated etc.** having bright cheerful colors: *a gaily wrapped package* **2** in a happy cheerful way: *Marge waved gaily at us.*

S W **gain**[1] /geɪn/ v.
1 `get sth` [T] to get, win, or achieve something important or valuable: *Detroit gained a spot in the finals with a 4-0 victory over Toronto.* | *Hawaii gained statehood in 1959.*
2 `get gradually` [I,T] to gradually get more and more of a useful or valuable quality, skill etc.: *Democrats hope to gain more voter support for their budget plan.* | *Taylor has gained a reputation* (=become known) *for making quick and profitable business decisions.* | **gain in popularity/confidence/efficiency** etc. *Iced coffee has gained in popularity over the last three years.* —opposite LOSE
3 `get an advantage` [I,T] to get an advantage from a situation, opportunity, or event: [**gain (sth) from sth**] *People with higher incomes clearly gained the most from the tax cuts.* | *Larger airlines stand to gain* (=are likely to get) *a larger market share if the new regulations are passed.* | *There's nothing to be gained* (=it will not help you) *by losing your temper.* —opposite LOSE
4 gain weight/speed/height to increase in weight, speed, or height: *Witnesses said the train was gaining speed before the collision.* —opposite LOSE
5 gain access (to sth) a) to be able to enter a building or place: *Prison officials wouldn't say how the inmates gained access to the roof.* **b)** to be allowed to see someone or use something: *Crancer says the court is trying to gain access to the confidential files.*
6 gain entrance/entry a) to enter a building that is locked: *Police had to break the door down to gain entry into the building.* **b)** to join or become part of a system or organization: *The company is trying hard to gain entry to the Japanese market.* **c)** to be allowed to come into a country: *The two men used fake passports to gain entry into Germany.*
7 gain ground make steady progress and become more popular, more successful etc.: *In the currency markets, the dollar gained ground in Japan and Europe.*
8 gain time to deliberately do something to give yourself more time to think or to do something: *"Well, let me see," he said slowly, trying to gain time before answering the question.*
9 gain currency FORMAL to become more popular or more accepted: *Legalizing marijuana is a concept that has gained currency in recent years.*
10 `clock` [I,T] if a clock or watch gains or gains time, it goes too fast
11 `arrive` [T] FORMAL OR LITERARY to reach a place after a lot of effort or difficulty: *The swimmer finally gained the river bank.* —see also **nothing ventured, nothing gained** (VENTURE[2] (3))
gain on/upon sb/sth *phr. v.* [T] **1** to gradually get closer to a person, car etc. that you are chasing: *Gant began to gain on Allison in the final few laps.* **2** to gradually become almost as successful as someone or something else: *Right now we're the best Internet service provider, but the competition is gaining on us.*

USAGE NOTE: GAIN

WORD CHOICE: gain, earn, win, make, get
Use **gain** to talk about gradually getting more of something, such as an ability or quality: *You'll gain a lot of management experience working here.* Use **earn** to talk about getting money by working. *She earns about $50,000 a year.* Use **win** to say that someone has gotten a prize in a contest or game: *Carla won $1,000 in Las Vegas!* You can also **win** new friends. Use **make** to talk about getting money from your own business or in a way that does not involve working. *Wayne made over five million dollars on the stock market last week.* **Gain** is a more formal word than **get**.

S W **gain**[2] n. **1** [C,U] an increase in the amount or level of something: [+ **in**] *Producers were delighted by the show's gain in popularity.* | *Older children should be on a low-fat diet to prevent weight gain.* | *Women have made economic, legal, and social gains.* **2** [C,U]

financial profit: *Many stocks showed gains in heavy trading.* | *Unfortunately, many companies are only concerned about short-term gains.* | *He hopes the economic reforms will bring the country gain.* **3** [C] an advantage or improvement, especially one achieved by planning or effort: *Since World War II, there have been significant gains in medical technology.* **4 ill-gotten gains** HUMOROUS money or advantages obtained dishonestly —see also CAPITAL GAINS

gain·ful /'geɪnfəl/ adj. **gainful employment/work/activity** FORMAL work or activity for which you are paid —**gainfully** adv.

gain·say /ˌgeɪn'seɪ/ v. past tense and past participle **gainsaid** /-'sɛd/ [T usually in negatives] FORMAL to say that something is not true, or to disagree with someone: *It may be very difficult to gainsay the claim.*

Gains·bor·ough /'geɪnzbərə/, **Thomas** (1727–1788) a British artist best known for his PORTRAITS (=pictures of people) and LANDSCAPES (=pictures of the countryside)

gait /geɪt/ n. [singular] the way someone walks: *His gait is slow and he tires easily.*

gai·ter /'geɪtər/ n. [C usually plural] a cloth or leather covering that covers your lower leg and ANKLE, or sometimes just your ANKLE

gal /gæl/ n. [C] INFORMAL a girl or woman: *She's a great gal.* S W

gal. the written abbreviation of "gallon"

ga·la /'gælə, 'geɪlə/ n. [C] an event at which a lot of people are entertained and celebrate a special occasion

ga·lac·tic /gə'læktɪk/ adj. relating to a galaxy

Ga·lap·a·gos Islands, the /gə'læpəgoʊs, -'lɑ-/ a group of islands in the east Pacific Ocean that belong to Ecuador

Ga·la·tians /gə'leɪʃənz/ a book in the New Testament of the Christian Bible

gal·ax·y /'gæləksi/ n. plural **galaxies** [C] **1** any of the large groups of stars that make up the universe **2 the Galaxy** the large group of stars that the Earth's sun and stars are a part of **3** [singular] a large number of things that are similar: *Lane was awarded a galaxy of medals for her bravery.*

Gal·braith /'gælbreɪθ/, **John Ken·neth** /dʒɑr 'kɛnɪθ/ (1908–) an American ECONOMIST, born in Canada, who has written several books about the way society is developing and changing

gale /geɪl/ n. [C] **1** a very strong wind: *The ship sank in the gale.* **2 gales of laughter** a lot of loud laughter: *Her comments brought the audience to its feet in gales of laughter.*

gale-force /'. ./ adj. a gale-force wind is strong enough to be dangerous or cause damage —**gale-force** adv.

Ga·len /'geɪlən/ (?130–?201) a Greek doctor and writer whose ideas had a great influence on doctors in Europe until the Renaissance

Ga·li·le·o /ˌgælə'lioʊ, -'leɪ-/ also **Galileo Gal·i·lei** /-'leɪi/ (1564–1642) an Italian ASTRONOMER, mathematician, and PHYSICIST whose many discoveries had a great influence on modern science. He was punished by the Catholic Church because he believed that the Sun, not the Earth, was the center of the universe.

gall[1] /gɔl/ n. **1 have the gall to do sth** to do something impolite and unreasonable that most people would be too embarrassed to do: *Congress actually had the gall to vote for a pay raise for themselves.* **2** [U] OLD-FASHIONED anger and hate that will not go away **3** [U] OLD USE: —see BILE (1) **4** [C] a swelling on a tree or plant caused by damage from insects or infection **5** [C] a painful place on an animal's skin, caused by something rubbing against it

gall[2] v. [T] to make someone feel upset and angry because of something that is unfair: [**it galls sb (that)**] *It galls me that tax dollars are so carelessly spent.*

gal·lant[1] /'gælənt/ adj. **1** brave: *gallant deeds* **2** OLD-FASHIONED a man who is gallant is kind and polite toward women —**gallantly** adv.

gal·lant² /gə'lænt, 'gælənt/ *n.* [C] OLD USE a well-dressed young man who is kind and polite toward women

gal·lant·ry /'gæləntri/ *n.* [U] FORMAL **1** courage, especially in a battle: *a medal for gallantry* **2** polite attention given to women by men

gall blad·der /'. ,../ *n.* [C] the organ in your body in which BILE (1) is stored —see picture at DIGESTIVE SYSTEM

gal·le·on /'gæliən/ *n.* [C] a sailing ship used mainly by the Spanish from the 15th to the 17th century

gal·ler·y /'gæləri/ *n. plural* **galleries** [C] **1 a)** a room, hall, or building where people can see famous pieces of art: *the National Portrait Gallery in Washington | The museum's new gallery will be named after the Andersons.* **b)** [C] a small store or STUDIO where you can see and buy pieces of art: *a craft gallery downtown* **2** [C] an upper floor like a BALCONY in an AUDITORIUM, theater, or church, from which people can watch a performance, DEBATE etc.: *the public gallery in Congress* **3 the gallery** the people sitting in a gallery **4 play to the gallery** to do or say something just because you think it will please people and make you popular **5** [C] a level passage under the ground in a mine or CAVE —see also PRESS GALLERY, SHOOTING GALLERY

gal·ley /'gæli/ *n. plural* **galleys** [C] **1** a kitchen on a ship **2** a long low Greek or Roman ship with sails that was rowed by SLAVES in past times **3 a)** a TRAY used by printers that holds TYPE¹ (4) **b)** also **galley proof** a sheet of paper on which a PRINTER prints a book so that mistakes can be corrected before it is printed to be sold

Gal·lic /'gælɪk/ *adj.* relating to France or French people

gall·ing /'gɔlɪŋ/ *adj.* making you feel upset and angry because of something that is unfair: *It's always galling when people blame the victim for being careless.*

gal·li·vant /'gælə,vænt/ *v.* [I] INFORMAL OR HUMOROUS to spend time enjoying yourself and going from place to place for pleasure: [+ **around**] *She spent six months gallivanting around Europe.*

gal·lon /'gælən/ *n.* [C] a unit for measuring liquids, equal to 4 QUARTS or 3.785 liters *a gallon of water | The car gets about 47 **miles to the gallon** (=you can drive 47 miles with each gallon of gas).*

gal·lop¹ /'gæləp/ *v.* **1** [I,T] if a horse gallops, it runs as fast as it can, with all its feet leaving the ground together: *A thoroughbred can gallop a mile in about 90 seconds.* | [+ **along/across/toward etc.**] *Wild horses galloped through the canyon.* **2** [I,T] if you gallop or gallop a horse, you ride very fast on a horse or you make it run very fast: [+ **along/across/ toward etc.**] *Mounted police galloped down Main Street with drawn pistols.* **3** [I always + adv./prep.] to move or do something very quickly: [+ **through/ past etc.**] *This is a bill that will gallop through Congress.*

gallop² *n.* **1 a)** [singular] the movement of a horse running as fast as it can, with all four feet leaving the ground together **b)** [C] a ride on a horse when it is galloping **2 in full gallop a)** a horse in full gallop is running as fast as it can **b)** INFORMAL running very quickly

gal·lop·ing /'gæləpɪŋ/ *adj.* [only before noun] increasing or developing very quickly: *the galloping cost of health care*

gal·lows /'gælouz/ *n. plural* **gallows** [C] a structure used for killing criminals by hanging them from a rope

gallows hu·mor /'.. ,../ *n.* [U] humor that makes very bad or serious things seem funny: *In medicine, gallows humor is common, as doctors deal with death every day.*

gall·stone /'gɔlstoun/ *n.* [C] a hard stone that can form in your GALL BLADDER

Gal·lup /'gæləp/, **George** (1901–1984) a U.S. public opinion ANALYST who developed the Gallup poll

Gal·lup poll /'.. ,./ *n.* [C] TRADEMARK a POLL (=COUNT)

---

of what people think about a subject, often done to find out how they will vote in an election

ga·loot /gə'lut/ *n.* [C] OLD-FASHIONED someone who is not graceful at all, and does not dress neatly

ga·lore /gə'lɔr/ *adj.* [only after noun] in large amounts or numbers: *At the flea market, there were quilts, furniture, and books galore.*

ga·losh·es /gə'lɑʃɪz/ *n.* [plural] OLD-FASHIONED rubber shoes worn over ordinary shoes when it rains or snows

ga·lumph /gə'lʌmf/ *v.* [I always + adv./prep.] INFORMAL to move in a noisy, heavy, and awkward way: *Children were galumphing around the stage.*

gal·van·ic /gæl'vænɪk/ *adj.* **1** FORMAL making people react suddenly with strong feelings or actions: *Stage director Tozzi has produced a particularly galvanic version of "Lucia."* **2** TECHNICAL relating to the production of electricity by the action of acid on metal

gal·va·nism /'gælvə,nɪzəm/ *n.* [U] TECHNICAL the production of electricity by the use of chemicals, especially as in a BATTERY

gal·va·nize /'gælvə,naɪz/ *v.* [T] to shock or surprise someone so that they do something to solve a problem, improve a situation etc.: *The girl's disappearance has galvanized residents to begin a neighborhood watch program.*

gal·va·nized /'gælvə,naɪzd/ *adj.* **galvanized iron/ metal etc.** galvanized iron etc. has a covering of ZINC so that it does not RUST

gal·va·nom·e·ter /,gælvə'nɑmətər/ *n.* [C] an instrument that measures small electrical currents

Gam·bi·a, the /'gæmbiə/ a country on the coast of West Africa next to Senegal —**Gambian** *n., adj.*

gam·bit /'gæmbɪt/ *n.* [C] **1** something that you do or say that you hope will give you an advantage in an argument, conversation, or meeting: *a political gambit | This may be **the opening gambit** (=the first thing that is said or done) of working out a trade agreement.* **2** a planned series of moves at the beginning of a game of CHESS

gam·ble¹ /'gæmbəl/ *v.* **1** [I] to risk money or possessions because you might win more if a card game, race etc. has the result you want: *We won $700 gambling in Las Vegas.* | [+ **on**] *He is on probation for illegally gambling on a college basketball game.* **2** [I,T] to do something risky because you hope a particular result will happen: *At the trial, defense attorney Neal gambled by calling no defense witnesses.* | [+ **on**] *We're gambling on the weather being nice for our outdoor wedding.* | [+ **with**] *Doctors shouldn't gamble with their patients' lives just to test new drugs.*

gamble sth ↔ **away** *phr. v.* [T] to lose money by gambling: *Nielsen gambled his inheritance away.*

gamble² *n.* [singular] an action or plan that is risky but that you hope will succeed: *The city's decision to not ration water during the summer was a gamble that paid off.* | *Gaetz had little experience, but they **took a gamble** and hired him.*

gam·bler /'gæmblər/ *n.* [C] someone who gambles

gam·bling /'gæmblɪŋ/ *n.* [U] **1** the practice of risking money or possessions because you might win a lot more if a card game, race etc. has the result you want *Gambling is still illegal in Arkansas.* **2 gambling den** a place where people go to gamble illegally

gam·bol /'gæmbəl/ *v.* [I always + adv./prep.] to jump or run around in an excited active way: *lambs gamboling in the fields* —**gambol** *n.* [C]

game¹ /geɪm/ *n.*
1 activity or sport [C] an activity or sport in which people compete with each other according to agreed rules: *Evansville will play Maryland in the championship game.* | *Board games are still popular gifts.* | *a video game*
2 particular occasion [C] an occasion when a game is played: *They've lost 4 of their last 6 games.* | *Let's have a game of chess.*

3 `part of a competition` [C] one of the parts into which a single competition is divided, for example in tennis: *Sampras leads, two games to one.* —compare MATCH¹ (2)

4 `children's play` [C] a children's activity in which they play with toys, pretend to be someone else etc.: *Children at the language school even **play games** in French.*

5 `sports event` **games** [plural] a large organized sports event that includes many different sports: *the Olympic Games*

6 be (just) a game (to sb) if something is just a game, you do not consider it to be serious or important: *War is not a game, and should never be treated as one.*

7 play games (with sb) a) to behave in a dishonest or unfair way in order to get what you want: *Many taxpayers try to play games on their tax returns.* **b)** to not be serious about doing something: *We want an agreement. We're not interested in playing games.*

8 `animals/birds` [U] wild animals, birds, and fish that are hunted for food, especially as a sport —see also BIG GAME

9 be the only game in town used to say that something is the only possible choice in a situation: *Before long, HMOs will be the only game in town.*

10 your game how well you play a particular game: *Lisa's taking lessons to improve her tennis game.*

11 beat sb at their own game to beat someone or fight back against them by using the same methods that they use

12 a game of chance a game in which you risk money on the result: *Poker is a game of chance.*

13 the advertising/public relations etc. game INFORMAL the profession of advertising etc.

14 sb got game SPOKEN NONSTANDARD used to say that someone is very skillful at doing something, especially playing a sport —see also **away game/match** (AWAY²), FAIR GAME, **fun and games** (FUN¹ (4)), **the name of the game** (NAME¹ (8))

game² *adj.* willing to try something new, difficult, or dangerous: [**game to do sth**] *Are you game to go rock climbing with us?* —**gamely** *adv.*

game³ *v.* **game the system** to use rules or laws to your advantage in an unfair but legal way so that you get what you want: *Linder accused insurance companies of gaming the system to increase profits.*

game cock /'. ./ *n.* [C] a ROOSTER (=male chicken) that is trained to fight other roosters

game·keep·er /'geɪmˌkipɚ/ *n.* [C] someone whose job is to take care of the wild animals and birds that are kept to be hunted on private land

game park /'. ./ *n.* [C] a GAME RESERVE

game plan /'. ./ *n.* [C] **1** a plan for winning a game in sports: *If we stick to the game plan, there's no way we'll lose.* **2** a plan for achieving success in business or politics

game point /'. ,./ *n.* [C,U] the situation in a game such as tennis in which one player will win the game if they win the next point —compare MATCH POINT

game pre·serve /'. .,./ *n.* [C] a game reserve

gam·er /'geɪmɚ/ *n.* [C] **1** SLANG someone who likes to play VIDEO GAMES **2** INFORMAL a person who plays a sport very well, and can help a team win games

game re·serve /'. .,./ *n.* [C] a large area of land where wild animals can live safely

game show /'. ./ *n.* [C] a television program in which people play games or answer questions to win money and prizes

games·man·ship /'geɪmzmənˌʃɪp/ *n.* [U] **1** the ability to influence events or people so that you gain an advantage: *political gamesmanship* **2** the ability to succeed by using the rules of a game to your own advantage

gam·ete /'gæmit/ *n.* [C] a type of cell that joins with another cell, starting the development of a baby or other young creature

game war·den /'. ,./ *n.* [C] someone whose job is to take care of wild animals in a GAME RESERVE

gam·ey /'geɪmi/ *adj.* another spelling of GAMY

gam·in /'gæmɪn/ *n.* [C] OLD USE a young boy who lives on the streets

ga·mine /gæ'min, 'gæmin/ *n.* [C] **1** a small thin girl or woman who looks like a boy **2** OLD USE a young girl who lives on the streets —**gamine** *adj.*: *a gamine hairstyle*

gam·ing /'geɪmɪŋ/ *n.* [U] playing cards or other games of chance for money; GAMBLING: *gaming tables*

gam·ma /'gæmə/ *n.* [C] the third letter of the Greek alphabet

gamma glob·u·lin /ˌ.. '.../ *n.* [U] a natural substance in your body that is a type of ANTIBODY and gives protection against some diseases

gamma ray /'.. ,./ *n.* [C usually plural] a beam of light with a short WAVELENGTH, that can pass through solid objects

gam·ut /'gæmət/ *n.* **the gamut** the complete range of possibilities: [+ **of**] *The movie uses the gamut of traditional and computerized special effects.* | *Riesling wines **run the gamut from** dry **to** sweet* (=include the complete range of possibilities).

gam·y, gamey /'geɪmi/ *adj.* **gamier, gamiest** having the strong taste or smell of wild animals

-gamy /gəmi/ *suffix* [in U nouns] marriage to a particular number or type of people: *monogamy* (=marriage to one person) | *bigamy* (=marriage to two people) —**-gamous** *suffix* [in adjectives]

gan·der /'gændɚ/ *n.* [C] **1** a male GOOSE **2 have/take a gander at sth** SPOKEN to look at something: *Take a gander at this letter I just got from Janet.* —see also **what's good/sauce for the goose is good/sauce for the gander** (GOOSE¹ (3))

Gan·dhi /'gɑndi/**, In·di·ra** /'ɪndɪrə/ (1917–1984) a PRIME MINISTER of India

Gandhi, Mo·han·das (Ma·hat·ma) /ˌmouhən'dɑs mə'hɑtmə/ (1869–1948) an Indian leader who helped India gain its independence from Great Britain

gang¹ /gæŋ/ *n.* **1** a group of young people who spend time together, and often cause trouble and fight against other groups: *a motorcycle gang* | *Several gang members have been questioned about the shooting.* | [+ **of**] *a gang of teenage boys* **2** [C] a group of criminals who work together: *Several gangs were operating in the area.* | [+ **of**] *a gang of thieves* **3** INFORMAL a group of friends, especially young people: *She went with Sarah and Jacquie and the gang.* **4** a group of workers or prisoners doing physical work together —see also CHAIN GANG

gang² *v.*

gang up on sb *phr. v.* [T] to join together into a group to attack or criticize someone: *You two stop ganging up on your sister!*

gang-bang /'. ,./ *n.* [C] **1** IMPOLITE an occasion when several people have sex with each other at the same time **2** a GANG RAPE —**gang-bang** *v.* [I,T]

gang-bang·ing /'. ,../ *n.* [U] the activity of gangs fighting with other gangs —**gang-banger** *n.* [C]

gang·bust·ers /'gæŋˌbʌstɚz/ *n.* **like gangbusters** INFORMAL doing something very eagerly and with a lot of energy, or happening very quickly: *Fraser's historical novels are selling like gangbusters.*

Gan·ges, the /'gændʒiz/ a long river that flows through northern India and Bangladesh. To the Hindus the Ganges is a holy river.

gang·land /'gæŋlænd/ *adj.* **a gangland killing/murder/shooting etc.** a killing etc. that is related to the activities of violent gangs or ORGANIZED CRIME

gan·gling /'gæŋglɪŋ/ *adj.* gangly

gan·gli·on /'gæŋgliən/ *n.* [C] TECHNICAL **1** a painful raised area of skin that is full of liquid, often on the back of your wrist **2** a mass of nerve cells

gan·gly /'gæŋgli/ *adj.* **ganglier, gangliest** unusually tall and thin, and not able to move gracefully: *a gangly sixteen-year-old boy*

gang·plank /'gæŋplæŋk/ n. [C] a board for walking on between a boat and the shore, or between one boat and another

gang rape /ˌ. './ n. [C] a criminal act when several men attack a woman or man to force her or him to have sex with them —**gang-rape** v. [T]

gan·grene /'gæŋgrin, gæŋ'grin/ n. [U] the decay of the flesh on part of your body because blood has stopped-flowing there as a result of illness or injury —**gangrenous** /'gæŋgrənəs/ adj.: a gangrenous foot

gang·sta /'gæŋstə/ n. [C] SLANG someone who is a member of a gang

gangsta rap /'. ˌ./ n. [U] a type of RAP music with words about drugs, violence, and life in poor areas of cities

gang·ster /'gæŋstə/ n. [C] a member of a group of violent criminals

gang·way /'gæŋweɪ/ n. [C] 1 a large GANGPLANK 2 gangway! SPOKEN used to tell people in a crowd to let someone go through 3 a narrow path between two things such as rooms or rows of seats

gan·ja /'gɑndʒə, 'gæn-/ n. [U] SLANG: see MARIJUANA

gan·net /'gænɪt/ n. [C] a large sea bird that lives in large groups on cliffs

gan·try /'gæntri/ n. plural **gantries** [C] a large metal frame that is used to support heavy machinery or railroad signals

s w 3 **gap** /gæp/ n. [C]
1 a space an empty space between two objects or two parts of an object: [+ in] There was an 18 minute gap in the tape recordings (=nothing was recorded for 18 minutes). | [+ between] The caulk has to cover the gap between the tub and the wall.
2 difference a big difference between two situations, amounts, groups of people etc.: [+ between] The gap between the rich and the poor is widening. | This program exists to **bridge the gap** (=reduce the amount or importance of a difference) between environmentalists and businesses. —see also **the generation gap** (GENERATION (5))
3 sth missing something that is missing that stops something else from being good or complete: [+ in] Inner-city hospitals are being crippled by a serious gap in medical technology. | There are huge gaps in my knowledge of history. | Venezuela has stepped up oil production to help **fill the gap** in world supplies.
4 in time a period of time when nothing is happening, that exists between two other periods of time: an uncomfortable gap in the conversation
5 in a mountain a low place between two higher parts of a mountain
6 **a gap in the market** a product or service that does not exist, so that there is an opportunity to develop that product or service and sell it

gape /geɪp/ v. [I] **1** to look at something for a long time, especially with your mouth open, because you are very surprised or shocked: A small boy pressed his face against the window and gaped in awe. —compare GAZE[1] —see Usage Note at GAZE[1] **2** also **gape open** to come apart or to open widely: The wound on his neck gaped open 2 inches. —**gape** n. [C]

gap·ing /'geɪpɪŋ/ adj. [only before noun] a gaping hole, wound, or mouth is very wide and open

gap-toothed /ˌ. './ adj. having wide spaces between your teeth

s w 2 **ga·rage** /gə'rɑʒ, gə'rɑdʒ/ n. [C] **1** a building for keeping a car in, usually next to or attached to a house —compare CARPORT —see picture on page 423 **2** a place where cars are repaired: My car's at the garage.

garage band /'. ˌ./ n. [C] a group of musicians who play loud ROCK music and practice in a garage

garage sale /'. ˌ./ n. [C] a sale of used furniture, clothes etc. from people's houses, usually done in someone's garage or yard

garb[1] /gɑrb/ n. [U] FORMAL OR LITERARY a particular style of clothing, especially clothes that show your type of work or that look unusual: green surgical garb

garb[2] v. **be garbed in sth** LITERARY to be dressed in a particular type of clothes: The men were garbed in Army uniforms.

gar·bage /'gɑrbɪdʒ/ n. **1** [singular,U] waste material that is thrown away, such as paper, empty containers, and old food; TRASH: Can you **take out the garbage** when you go? **2** [singular] the container this is put in: The garbage is under the sink. **3** [U] stupid words, ideas etc.: You're talking garbage. **4** **garbage in, garbage out** used to say that if you put bad information into a computer, you will get bad results s w 2

garbage bag /'. ˌ./ n. [C] a large plastic bag for holding waste material

garbage can /'. ˌ./ n. [C] a plastic or metal container with a lid that is used for holding waste until it can be taken away —see picture on page 423

garbage col·lec·tion /'.. ˌˌ../ n. [U] the act of taking waste from houses and businesses

garbage col·lec·tor /'.. ˌˌ./ n. [C] someone whose job is to remove waste from garbage cans

garbage dis·pos·al /'.. ˌˌ../ n. [C] a small machine in the kitchen SINK that cuts food waste into small pieces so that it can be washed down the DRAIN of the sink

garbage dump /'.. ˌ./ n. [C] a place where waste is taken and stored

garbage man /'.. ˌ./ n. [C] a garbage collector

garbage truck /'.. ˌ./ n. [C] a large vehicle that goes from house to house to collect the garbage from garbage cans

gar·ban·zo /gɑr'bɑnzou/ also **garbanzo bean** /.'.. ˌ./ n. plural **garbanzos** another word for CHICKPEA, used especially in the western U.S.

gar·bled /'gɑrbəld/ adj. **1** very unclear and confusing, and often not giving correct information: The newspapers had some garbled version of the story. **2** difficult to hear or understand: The voice on the tape was too garbled to understand.

Gar·cí·a Lor·ca /gɑrˌsiə 'lɔrkə/, **Fed·e·ri·co** /fɛdə'rikou/ (1898–1936) a Spanish poet and writer of plays

García Már·quez /gɑrˌsiə 'mɑrkɛs/, **Gabriel** (1928–) a Colombian writer of NOVELS

gar·çon /gɑr'soun/ n. [C] a WAITER, especially in a French restaurant

gar·den[1] /'gɑrdn/ n. **1** [C] the part of a piece of land around or next to your house that has flowers and plants in it: a vegetable garden —see picture on page 423 **2** **gardens** [plural] a public park where a lot of unusual plants and flowers are grown: the Brooklyn Botanical Gardens s w 2 2

garden[2] v. [I] to work in a garden, keeping it clean, making plants grow etc.: Stephen's mom loves to garden in her spare time. —**gardening** n. [U]

gar·den·er /'gɑrdnə/ n. [C] **1** someone whose job is to work in gardens **2** someone who enjoys growing flowers and plants

gar·de·nia /gɑr'dinyə/ n. [C] a large white nice-smelling flower that grows on a bush

garden-va·ri·e·ty /'.. ˌˌ../ adj. [only before noun] very ordinary and not very interesting: This is not your garden-variety case of fraud.

Gar·field /'gɑrfild/, **James** (1831–1881) the 20th President of the U.S.

gar·gan·tu·an /gɑr'gæntʃuən/ adj. extremely large: a gargantuan task

gar·gle[1] /'gɑrgəl/ v. [I,T] to clean the inside of your mouth and throat by blowing air through water or medicine in the back of your throat: The ad promises that gargling mouthwash will freshen your breath and kill germs. | [+ with] Gargle with salt water to help your sore throat.

gargle[2] n. **1** [C,U] liquid that you gargle with **2** [singular] the act of gargling

gar·goyle /'gɑrgɔɪl/ n. [C] a stone figure with the face of a strange and ugly creature, that carries rain

G

water from the roof of an old building, especially a church

Gar·i·bal·di /ˌgærəˈbɔːldi/, **Giu·sep·pe** /dʒuˈsɛpi/ (1807–1882) an Italian military leader who helped Italy to become a united independent country by taking control of Sicily and Naples in 1860

gar·ish /ˈgærɪʃ, ˈgɛr-/ adj. very brightly colored in a way that is annoying to look at: *a garish necktie* —**garishly** adv. —**garishness** n. [U]

gar·land[1] /ˈgɑrlənd/ n. [C] a ring of flowers or leaves, worn on your head or around your neck for decoration or for a special ceremony

garland[2] v. [T] LITERARY to decorate someone or something, especially with flowers

s w **gar·lic** /ˈgɑrlɪk/ n. [U] a plant like a small onion with a very strong taste, used in cooking: *a clove of garlic* (=a single section of it) —**garlicky** adj.

garlic press /ˈ.. ˌ./ n. [C] a kitchen tool used to crush garlic

gar·ment /ˈgɑrmənt/ n. [C] FORMAL a piece of clothing —see Usage Note at CLOTHING

garment bag /ˈ.. ˌ./ n. [C] a special SUITCASE (=bag) used to carry clothes such as suits and dresses

gar·ner /ˈgɑrnɚ/ v. [T] FORMAL to take or get something, especially information or support: *The party garnered 70 percent of the vote.*

gar·net /ˈgɑrnɪt/ n. **1** [C] a dark red stone used as a jewel **2** [U] a dark red color

gar·nish[1] /ˈgɑrnɪʃ/ v. [T] **1** to add something to food in order to decorate it: [garnish sth with sth] *Place the turkey on a large platter and garnish it with parsley and orange sections.* **2** also **garnishee** TECHNICAL to take money from someone's salary because they have not paid their debts: *The state began garnishing my wages to pay for the parking tickets.*

garnish[2] n. [C] something that you add to food to decorate it

gar·ret /ˈgærɪt/ n. [C] a small room at the top of a house —compare ATTIC

gar·ri·son[1] /ˈgærəsən/ n. [C] a group of soldiers living in a town or FORT in order to defend it

garrison[2] v. [T] to send a group of soldiers to defend or guard a place

Gar·ri·son /ˈgærɪsən/, **William** (1805–1879) a U.S. newspaper writer and PUBLISHER famous for working to end SLAVERY in the U.S.

gar·rotte /gəˈrɑt/ v. [T] to kill someone using a metal collar or wire that is pulled tightly around their neck —**garrotte** n. [C]

gar·ru·lous /ˈgærələs/ adj. always talking a lot: *a garrulous young man*

gar·ter /ˈgɑrtɚ/ n. [C] **1** one of four pieces of ELASTIC attached to a woman's underwear and to her STOCKINGS to hold them up, used especially in past times **2** a band of ELASTIC (=material that stretches) worn around your leg to keep a sock or STOCKING up

garter belt /ˈ.. ˌ./ n. [C] a piece of women's underwear with garters hanging down from it that fasten onto STOCKINGS and hold them up, used especially in past times

garter snake /ˈ.. ˌ./ n. [C] a harmless snake with colored lines along its back, which lives in North and Central America

Gar·vey /ˈgɑrvi/, **Mar·cus** /ˈmɑrkəs/ (1887–1940) an African-American who started the "Back to Africa" movement to encourage other African-Americans to establish a society of their own in Africa

s w **gas**[1] /gæs/ n. **1** [U] also **gasoline** a liquid made from PETROLEUM, used mainly for producing power in the engines of cars, trucks etc.: *I probably spend over $200 a month on gas.* | *The mechanic found a hole in the gas tank.* **2** plural **gases** or **gasses** [C,U] a substance like air that is not solid or liquid, and that usually cannot be seen: *hydrogen gas* **3** [U] a clear substance like air that is burned for heating or cooking: *a gas stove* **4** [U] INFORMAL the condition of having a lot of air in your stomach **5 the gas** the

gas PEDAL of a car; ACCELERATOR: *The driver stepped on the gas* (=pushed down the gas pedal and made the car go faster) *and tried to escape.* **6** [singular] OLD-FASHIONED something that is fun and makes you laugh a lot

gas[2] v. **gassed, gassing 1** [T] to poison or kill someone with gas: *5000 civilians were gassed to death by the army.* **2** [I] OLD-FASHIONED to talk for a long time about unimportant or boring things

gas sth ↔ **up** phr. v. [I,T] to put gas in a car: *I need to gas up the car before we go.*

gas·bag /ˈgæsbæg/ n. [C] INFORMAL someone who talks too much

gas cham·ber /ˈ. ˌ../ n. [C] a large room in which people or animals are killed with poisonous gas

gas·e·ous /ˈgæsiəs, ˈgæʃəs/ adj. like gas or in the form of gas

gas-fired /ˈ. ./ adj. OLD-FASHIONED using gas as a FUEL: *a gas-fired heater*

gas-guz·zler /ˈ. ˌ../ n. [C] INFORMAL a car that uses a lot of gas —**gas-guzzling** adj.

gash /gæʃ/ n. [C] **1** a large deep wound from a cut: *Thomas suffered a gash above his left eye.* **2** a long deep hole in something: *a gash in the sidewall of a tire* —**gash** v. [T]

gas·i·fy /ˈgæsəˌfaɪ/ v. **gasifies, gasified, gasifying** [I,T] to change into a gas, or to make something do this —**gasification** /ˌgæsəfəˈkeɪʃən/ n. [U]

gas·ket /ˈgæskɪt/ n. [C] **1** a flat piece of rubber placed between two surfaces of a machine, especially an engine, that prevents steam, oil, gas etc. from escaping **2 blow a gasket a)** if a vehicle blows a gasket, the gasket breaks and steam or gas escapes from the machine **b)** INFORMAL to become very angry

gas·light /ˈgæs-laɪt/ n. **1** [U] the light produced from burning GAS[1] (3) **2** also **gas lamp** [C] a lamp in a house or on the street that gives light from burning GAS[1] (3)

gas main /ˈ. ./ n. [C] a pipe that supplies GAS[1] (3) to buildings and houses, and is buried under the ground

gas mask /ˈ. ./ n. [C] a piece of equipment worn over your face to protect you from poisonous gases, especially during a war

gas me·ter /ˈ. ˌ../ n. [C] a piece of equipment that measures how much GAS[1] (3) is used in a building or house

gas·o·hol /ˈgæsəhɔl/ n. [U] gas with a small amount of alcohol in it, which can be used in special cars and is cheaper than regular gas

gas·o·line /ˌgæsəˈlin, ˈgæsəˌlin/ n. [U] GAS[1] (1)

gasp[1] /gæsp/ v. [I,T] **1** to breathe in suddenly in a way that can be heard, especially because you are surprised or shocked: *Most people gasp when they hear how much money Patsy makes.* | [+ in/with] *Len gasped in astonishment as the man pulled out a gun.* | [+ at] *Everyone gasped at the sight of a two-headed dog.* **2** [I] to breathe quickly because you are having difficulty breathing: **gasp for air/breath** *She was rushed to the hospital, gasping for breath.*

gasp[2] n. [C] **1** an act of taking in your breath suddenly in a way that can be heard, especially because you are surprised or shocked: *The announcement that he was guilty brought gasps and sobs in the packed courtroom.* | [+ of] *a gasp of pain* **2** an act of taking in air quickly because you are having difficulty breathing: *Between gasps Michael said that he was allergic to cats.* **3 sb's/sth's last gasp** about to die, or about to stop happening or existing: *This cold spell appears to be winter's last gasp for the year.*

gas ped·al /ˈ. ˌ../ n. [C] the thing that you press with your foot to make a car go faster; ACCELERATOR —see picture on page 427

gas per·me·a·ble lens /ˌ. ˌ..... ˈ./ n. [C] a type of CONTACT LENS that allows oxygen to reach your eyes

gas pump /ˈ. ./ n. [C] a machine at a GAS STATION that is used to put gasoline into cars

gas sta·tion /ˈ. ˌ../ n. [C] a place where you can buy gas and oil for cars, trucks etc.

gas·sy /ˈgæsi/ adj. **gassier, gassiest** INFORMAL having a lot of air in your stomach

gas·tric /ˈgæstrɪk/ *adj.* [only before noun] TECHNICAL
1 relating to your stomach: *gastric ulcers* **2 gastric juices** the acids in your stomach that break food into smaller parts

gas·tri·tis /gæˈstraɪtɪs/ *n.* [U] an illness that makes the inside of your stomach become swollen, so that you feel a burning pain

gas·tro·en·ter·i·tis /ˌgæstrooˌentəˈraɪtɪs/ *n.* [U] an illness that makes your stomach and INTESTINES become swollen

gas·tro·in·tes·ti·nal /ˌgæstrooɪnˈtestɪnl/ *adj.* of or relating to the stomach and INTESTINES

gas·tro·nom·ic /ˌgæstrəˈnɑmɪk/ *adj.* [only before noun] relating to the art of cooking good food or the pleasure of eating it: *a gastronomic tour of European restaurants*

gas·tron·o·my /gæˈstrɑnəmi/ *n.* [U] the art and science of cooking and eating good food

gas tur·bine /ˌ. ˈ../ *n.* [C] an engine in which a wheel of special blades is pushed around at high speed by hot gases

gas·works /ˈgæswɜks/ *n.* *plural* **gasworks** [C] a place where gas is made from coal

gat /gæt/ *n.* [C] SLANG a gun

S W
2 3
gate /geɪt/ *n.* [C] **1** the part of a fence or outside wall that you can open and close like a door: *a garden gate* —compare DOOR (1) —see picture on page 423 **2** the place where you leave an airport building to get on an airplane: *Air France flight 76 leaves from gate 6A.* **3 -gate** INFORMAL used with the name of a place or a person to give a name to an event involving dishonest behavior by a politician or other public official: *the Irangate scandal* **4 a)** the number of people who go in to see a sports event or concert: *This game should get the biggest gate ever.* **b)** the amount of money that is made from a sports event, concert, movie etc.: *The new Disney movie took a gate of $4.6 million.*

gate·crash·er /ˈgeɪtˌkræʃə/ *n.* [C] someone who goes to a party or event that they have not been invited to or do not have a ticket to —**gatecrash** *v.* [I,T]

gated com·mu·ni·ty /ˌ.. .ˈ.../ *n.* *plural* **gated communities** [C] an area of expensive houses, stores, tennis courts etc. with a fence or wall around it and an entrance that is guarded

gate·house /ˈgeɪthaus/ *n.* [C] **1** a small building next to the gate of a park, castle, large house etc. **2** the building where the controls for a DAM or CANAL are

gate·keep·er /ˈgeɪtˌkipə/ *n.* [C] **1** someone whose job is to open and close a gate and control who comes in or out **2** a person or organization with the power to make decisions about which people get certain jobs or opportunities in a company or profession: *Law schools are the gatekeepers of the profession.*

gate-leg ta·ble /ˌ. . ˈ../ *n.* [C] a table that can be made larger by moving a leg out to support a folding part

gate·post /ˈgeɪtˌpoust/ *n.* [C] one of two strong upright poles set in the ground to support a gate —see picture on page 423

Gates /geɪts/**, Bill** /bɪl/ (1955–) a U.S. computer programmer and businessman, who started the Microsoft computer company and is famous for being the richest man in the world

gate·way /ˈgeɪtweɪ/ *n.* *plural* **gateways** [C] **1** the opening in a fence, wall etc. that can be closed by a gate **2 the gateway to sth a)** a place, especially a city, that you can go through in order to reach another place: *St. Louis was once the gateway to the West.* **b)** a way of achieving something: *Hard work is the gateway to success.*

3 a way of connecting two different computer NETWORKS that helps them to work together **4** an airport that people fly into in order to fly on to other places: *London's Heathrow Airport is the dominant gateway in Europe.*

gath·er¹ /ˈgæðə/ *v.*
S W
1 2 3
1 **come together** [I,T] to come together and form a group: *A group of elderly folks gather daily at the senior center to sing songs.* | **[+ around]** *A crowd gathered around to watch the fight.* | **[+ together]** *This is the first time these groups have gathered together to speak out for sensible gun laws.* | **[be gathered]** *Around fifty protesters were gathered in the park.*

2 **know/think** [T not in progressive] to believe that something is true, because of what you have seen or heard: *Jack was not happy about the news, I gather.* | **[gather (that)]** *I gather that you really don't want to be here.* | **from what I can gather/as far as I can gather** (=from the information you have heard)

3 **gather speed/force/momentum etc.** to move faster, become stronger, get more support etc.: *The plane gathered speed down the runway with an ear-splitting roar.* | *The international relief effort appears to be gathering momentum.*

4 **collect** [I,T] to get things from different places and put them together in one place: *Some hospitals are using twins to gather information on a variety of diseases.* | **[+ together/up]** *Debbie gathered up the clothes and got in line to pay for them.*

5 **gather yourself (together)** also **gather your thoughts/strength etc.** to prepare yourself for something you are going to do, especially something difficult: *I took a few moments to gather my thoughts before going into the meeting.*

6 **gather dust a)** if something useful gathers dust, it is not being used: *We sold our piano because it was just gathering dust.* **b)** if something gathers dust, dust sticks to it easily: *The biggest disadvantage to having silk flowers is that they gather dust.*

7 **cloth** [T] **a)** to pull cloth into small folds at the edge: *Gather the material and baste it.* **b)** to pull cloth or a piece of clothing closer to you: *Grandma gathered her scarf around her neck as she went out the door.*

8 **the gathering darkness/dusk/shadows etc.** LITERARY the time in the evening when it is getting dark

9 **gather sb to you/gather sb up** OLD-FASHIONED to take someone into your arms and hold them in order to protect them or show them love

gather² *n.* [C] a small fold produced by pulling cloth together at the edge

gath·ered /ˈgæðəd/ *adj.* having small folds produced by pulling the edge of a piece of cloth together: *a skirt gathered at the waist.*

gath·er·ing /ˈgæðərɪŋ/ *n.* [C] **1** a meeting of a group of people: *a large gathering of war veterans* **2** a fold or group of folds in cloth

ga·tor /ˈgeɪtə/ *n.* [C] INFORMAL an ALLIGATOR

GATT /gæt/ General Agreement on Tariffs and Trade; an organization of about 80 countries whose aim is to make agreements that will encourage international trade and remove rules or restrictions that make trade more difficult. GATT was replaced in 1995 by a new organization with similar aims, called WTO (=the World Trade Organization).

gauche /gouʃ/ *adj.* INFORMAL doing or saying wrong or impolite things, especially because you do not know the right way to behave: *I never discuss money. It's gauche.*

gau·cho /ˈgautʃou/ *n.* *plural* **gauchos** [C] a South American COWBOY

gaud·y /ˈgɔdi/ *adj.* **gaudier, gaudiest** clothes, decorations, colors etc. that are gaudy are too bright and look cheap: *a gaudy neon sign* —**gaudily** *adv.* —**gaudiness** *n.* [U]

gauge¹, gage /geɪdʒ/ *n.* [C]
1 **instrument** an instrument for measuring the

G

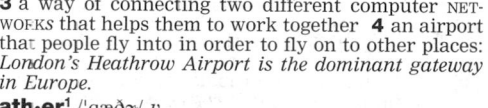
Bill Gates

amount or size of something: *the car's gas gauge* | *an oil pressure gauge*
2 width/thickness **a)** the width of thin metal objects such as wire or screws: *a narrow-gauge screw* **b)** the thickness of thin material such as metal or plastic sheets: *heavy gauge black polythene*
3 standard a standard by which something is measured: [+ of] *Looking at statistics is not always the best gauge of who really is playing good football.*
4 gun the width of the BARREL of a gun: *a 12-gauge shotgun*
5 railroad the distance between the lines of a railroad or between the wheels of a train: *a narrow-gauge track*

gauge[2] *v.* [T] **1** to judge how people feel about something or what they are likely to do: [+ **what/how** etc.] *It's difficult to gauge how the public will respond to this product.* **2** to judge or calculate something by using a particular method or instrument: *They hope to find ways to gauge the effectiveness of drug rehab programs.*

Gau·guin /gouˈgæn/, **Paul** (1848–1903) a French PAINTER famous for his brightly colored paintings of the people of Tahiti

gaunt /gɔnt, gɑnt/ *adj.* **1** very thin and pale, especially because of sickness or worry: *He has lost his hair and some teeth and appeared quite gaunt.* **2** a building, mountain etc. that is gaunt looks very plain and ugly: *a gaunt cathedral*

gaunt·let /ˈgɔntˈlɪt, ˈgɑntˈ-/ *n.* **1 throw down the gauntlet** to invite someone to fight or compete over a disagreement **2 take up the gauntlet** to accept the invitation to fight or compete over a disagreement **3 run the gauntlet** to go through a difficult process: *A defendant should be required to run the gauntlet of the criminal court system only once.* **4** two lines of people who are facing each other: *Our players have to go through a gauntlet of fans to get to their cars.* **5** [C] a long GLOVE that covers someone's wrist and protects their hand, worn for example by workers in a factory **6** [C] a GLOVE covered in metal, used for protection by soldiers in past times

Gau·ta·ma Bud·dha /ˌgautəmə ˈbudə, ˌgou-/ the Buddha

gauze /gɔz/ *n.* [U] **1** also **gauze bandage** thin cotton with very small holes in it that is used for wrapping around a wound **2** very thin transparent cloth with very small holes in it, often used for curtains —**gauzy** *adj.*: *a gauzy blouse*

gave /geɪv/ *v.* the past tense of GIVE[1]

gav·el /ˈgævəl/ *n.* [C] a small hammer that the person in charge of a meeting, court of law, AUCTION etc. hits on a table in order to get people's attention

ga·votte /gəˈvɑt/ *n.* [C] a fast, cheerful French dance, or the music for this dance

gawd /gɔd/ *interjection* NONSTANDARD another spelling and pronunciation of the word "God," which is said when you are surprised, upset etc.

gawk /gɔk/ *v.* [I] to look at something for a long time, in a way that seems stupid: [+ **at**] *Drivers slowed to gawk at the accident.*

gawk·y /ˈgɔki/ *adj.* **gawkier, gawkiest** moving in a nervous and awkward way, as if you cannot control your arms and legs: *a gawky, long-legged teenager* —**gawkiness** *n.* [U]

gay[1] /geɪ/ *adj.* **1** sexually attracted to people of the same sex as yourself; HOMOSEXUAL: *the gay community* **2** OLD-FASHIONED bright or attractive **3** OLD-FASHIONED cheerful and excited **4 with gay abandon** in a careless and thoughtless way —see also GAILY, GAIETY —**gayness** *n.* [U]

gay[2] *n. plural* **gays** [C] someone who is HOMOSEXUAL, especially a man —compare LESBIAN

gay·dar /ˈgeɪdɑr/ *n.* [U] SPOKEN, HUMOROUS an ability that some people think they have to recognize someone who is HOMOSEXUAL

gaze[1] /geɪz/ *v.* [I always + adv./prep.] to look at someone or something for a long time, especially without

realizing you are doing it: [+ **into/at** etc.] *He sat for hours gazing out kitchen window.* | *We gazed up at the stars.*

USAGE NOTE: GAZE

WORD CHOICE: look, gaze, stare, gape
These words all describe **looking** at someone or something for a long time. You may **gaze** at something interesting or beautiful without realizing you are doing it: *Len stood gazing up at the sky.* If you **stare** at someone or something, you look directly at them for a long time without moving your eyes, for example because you are angry, very interested, or are thinking hard about something: *She stared at the page for several minutes, and then began to write.* You **gape** at something with your mouth open when you are very surprised or shocked: *He just stood and gaped as the two cars ran into each other.*

gaze[2] *n.* [singular] a long steady look: *a small man with a shrewd gaze* | *His eyes **met the gaze** (=looked directly at someone who was looking at him) of a young man who looked familiar*

ga·ze·bo /gəˈzibou/ *n. plural* **gazebos** [C] a small building in a garden or park, where you can sit

ga·zelle /gəˈzɛl/ *n.* [C] an animal like a small DEER, which moves and jumps very quickly and gracefully

ga·zette /gəˈzɛt/ *n.* [C] a newspaper or magazine

gaz·et·teer /ˌgæzəˈtɪr/ *n.* [C] a list of names of places, printed for example in a dictionary or as a list at the end of a book of maps

GB the written abbreviation of Great Britain

Gb the written abbreviation of GIGABYTE

GDP GROSS DOMESTIC PRODUCT —compare GNP

gear[1] /gɪr/ *n.* **1** in cars etc. [C,U] the machinery in a vehicle that turns power from the engine into movement: *Put the car **in gear** (=connect the engine to the gear that turns the wheels) and slowly release the clutch.* | *It's a good habit to take the car **out of gear** (=stop the connection between the engine and the gear that turns the wheels) while you're at a stoplight.* | **low/ high gear** (=the gear used for going slowly or going fast)

2 equipment/clothes etc. equipment, clothes, tools etc. that you need for a particular activity: *He's crazy about photography – he's got all the gear.* | *camping gear* | *You'll probably need to bring your **rain gear** (=special clothes that keep you dry when it rains).*

3 in high gear a) using the gear for high speeds **b)** doing something with the greatest possible effort and energy: *The first session of the 102nd Congress swings into high gear this week.*

4 change/shift gears a) to move a vehicle into a different gear **b)** to quickly change to doing something in a different way, or to change to doing something different: *We changed gears and decided to play more aggressively in the second half.*

5 machinery a piece of machinery that performs a particular job: *the landing gear of a plane*

6 drugs [U] SLANG a word meaning "illegal drugs," used by people who take drugs

gear[2] *v.* [T] **be geared to sb/sth** to be organized in a way that is appropriate for a particular purpose or situation: *The new air fares are geared to business travelers.* | [**be geared to do sth**] *Oil refineries generally are geared to take only a certain type of oil.*

gear up *phr. v.* [I,T] to prepare for something, or prepare to do something: [**gear up to do sth**] *Taxi companies geared up to give free rides home to New Year's Eve party-goers.* | [+ **for**] *The National Education Association is gearing up for its four-day convention in Boston.* | [**be geared up to do sth/for sth**] *The McDonald's restaurant in Moscow is geared up to serve 17,000 people daily.*

gear·box /ˈgɪrbɑks/ *n.* [C] a metal box containing the gears of a vehicle

gear lev·er /ˈ. ˌ../ *n.* [C] a gear shift —see picture at BICYCLE[1]

gear shift /ˈ. ./ *n.* [C] a metal ROD that you move in

order to control the gears of a vehicle —see picture on page 427

geck·o /ˈgɛkoʊ/ *n. plural* **geckos** or **geckoes** [C] a type of small LIZARD

GED *n.* [C] General Equivalency Diploma; a DIPLOMA (=piece of paper that shows you have finished a particular level of education) that people who did not finish high school can obtain by taking a test

s w
1 **gee** /dʒi/ *interjection* used to show that you are surprised or annoyed: *Aw, gee, Mom, do we have to go?*

gee-gaw /ˈdʒigɔ, ˈgi-/ *n.* [C] another spelling of GEWGAW

geek /gik/ *n.* [C] SLANG someone who is not popular because they wear clothes that are not fashionable, do not know how to behave in social situations, or do strange things: *a computer geek* —**geeky** *adj.*

geese /gis/ *n.* the plural of GOOSE[1]

gee-whiz /ˈdʒi wɪz/ *adj.* INFORMAL very good, in a way that is surprising and exciting: *the gee-whiz graphics of a computer game*

gee whiz /ˌdʒi ˈwɪz/ *interjection* OLD-FASHIONED used to show that you are surprised or annoyed

geez /dʒiz/ *interjection* another spelling of JEEZ

gee·zer /ˈgizɚ/ *n.* [C] INFORMAL an old man

Geh·rig /ˈgɛrɪg/, **Lou** /lu/ (1903–1941) a baseball player famous for playing in more CONSECUTIVE games than any other player before him, and who died of a serious muscle disease which is now called "Lou Gehrig's Disease"

Gei·ger count·er /ˈgaɪgɚ ˌkaʊntɚ/ *n.* [C] an instrument for finding and measuring RADIOACTIVITY

gei·sha /ˈgeɪʃə, ˈgiʃə/ also **geisha girl** /ˈ.. ˌ./ *n.* [C] a Japanese woman who is trained in the art of dancing, singing, and providing entertainment, especially for men

gel[1] /dʒɛl/ *n.* [C,U] a thick, wet substance that is used in beauty or cleaning products: *hair gel* | *a gel toothpaste*

gel[2] *v.* **gelled, gelling 1** [I] another spelling of JELL **2** [T] to put hair gel into your hair: *a handsome man with short, gelled hair*

gel·a·tin, gelatine /ˈdʒɛlətən, -lətˌn/ *n.* **1** [U] a clear substance obtained from boiled animal bones, used for making liquid food more solid and in sweet foods such as JELL-O **2** [C] a piece of colored plastic that is put over a light to change its color

ge·lat·i·nous /dʒəˈlætˌn-əs/ *adj.* in a state between solid and liquid, like a gel

geld /gɛld/ *v.* [T] to remove the TESTICLES of a horse

geld·ing /ˈgɛldɪŋ/ *n.* [C] a horse that has been gelded

gel·id /ˈdʒɛlɪd/ *adj.* very cold

gel·ig·nite /ˈdʒɛlɪgˌnaɪt/ *n.* [U] a very powerful explosive

gem /dʒɛm/ *n.* [C] **1** also **gem stone** a beautiful stone that has been cut into a special shape: *a precious gem* **2** something that is very special or beautiful: *Dubrovnik was a Renaissance gem not only of Croatia but of all Europe.* **3** a very helpful or special person: *Ben, you're a real gem!*

Gem·i·ni /ˈdʒɛməˌnaɪ/ *n.* **1** [singular] the third sign of the ZODIAC, represented by TWINS and believed to affect the character and life of people born between May 21 and June 21 **2** [C] someone who was born between May 21 and June 21: *Bob's a Gemini.*

gem·ol·o·gy /dʒɛˈmɑlədʒi/ *n.* [U] the study of gems —**gemologist** *n.* [C]

Gen. a written abbreviation of General

-ge·nar·i·an /dʒɛnɛriən/ *suffix* [in nouns and adjectives] someone who is a particular number of DECADES (=periods of 10 years) old: *an octogenarian* (=between 80 and 89 years old) | *a septuagenarian* (=between 70 and 79 years old)

gen·darme /ˈʒɑndɑrm/ *n.* [C] a French police officer

s w
3 **gen·der** /ˈdʒɛndɚ/ *n.* **1** [C,U] FORMAL the fact of being male or female: *Hiring employees on the basis of gender or race is not permitted.* **2 a)** [U] TECHNICAL the system in some languages of marking words such as nouns, adjectives, and PRONOUNS as being MASCULINE, FEMININE, or NEUTER **b)** [C] TECHNICAL a

---

group such as FEMININE, into which words are divided in this system

gender bend·er /ˈ.. ˌ../ *n.* [C] INFORMAL someone who dresses or behaves in a way typical of the opposite sex

gender dis·crim·i·na·tion /ˈ.. ...ˌ../ *n.* [U] SEX DISCRIMINATION

gender-neu·tral /ˌ.. ˈ..◂/ *adj.* [usually before noun] gender-neutral language or words do not specifically mention men or women, and so can be understood to include everyone: *Instead of using "he" all the time, try to choose a gender-neutral term such as "they."* —compare GENDER-SPECIFIC

gender-spe·cif·ic /ˌ.. .ˈ..◂/ *adj.* [usually before noun] relating to or for males only, or relating to or for females only: *Try to avoid gender-specific language such as "mankind," which seems to refer only to men.* —compare GENDER-NEUTRAL

gene /dʒin/ *n.* [C] a small part of a cell that controls the development of the qualities that have been passed on to a living thing from its parents: *Some women may carry a gene that increases the risk of breast cancer.* s w
3

ge·ne·al·o·gy /ˌdʒini ˈɑlədʒi/ *n. plural* **genealogies 1** [U] the study of the history of families **2** [C] an account of the history of a family, especially one that shows how each person is related to the others —**genealogist** *n.* [C] —**genealogical** /ˌdʒiniəˈlɑdʒɪkəl/ *adj.*

gene pool /ˈ. ./ *n.* [C] all of the genes available to a particular SPECIES

gen·er·a /ˈdʒɛnərə/ *n.* the plural of GENUS

gen·er·al[1] /ˈdʒɛnərəl, ˈdʒɛnrəl/ *adj.*

1 most important features describing only the main features or parts of something, not the details: *This course is a general introduction to banking and finance.* | *I've got **a general idea** of how I want the room to look.* | *The two companies described their agreement only **in general terms** (=without describing specific details).* s w
1

2 in general a) usually or in most situations: *In general, the cost of these cameras ranges from $200 to $300.* **b)** as a whole: *For our little store, business in general has been very good this year.*

3 as a whole considering the whole of a situation, group, thing etc., rather than specific parts or details of it: *There has been a general decline in standards.* | *Your voice reveals much about your general health.*

4 most people shared by or affecting most people, or most of the people in a group: *How soon can the drug be made available for general use?* | *On his radio show, Bill Gordon answers questions of **general interest** (=what most people are interested in) on automotive topics.* —see Usage Note at COMMON[1]

5 the general area/neighborhood/location etc. not the exact place or direction, but somewhere near: *We think that these criminals are still in the general vicinity of Chicago.*

6 job used in the name of a job to show that the person who does this job has complete responsibility: *the general manager* | *the Attorney General*

7 the general public/population ordinary people, who do not have important positions or belong to specific groups: *The cave is closed to the general public.*

8 not limited not limited to one subject, service, product etc.: *It's a good general fertilizer.* | *Twenty years ago, most children got a good general education in public schools.* —opposite SPECIALIZED —see also GENERALLY, **as a (general) rule** (RULE[1] (3))

gen·er·al[2] *n.* [C] an officer of very high rank in the Army, Marines, or Air Force s w
3

General Ac·count·ing Of·fice, the /ˌ.. .ˈ.. ˌ../ a U.S. government department that checks and examines all records of U.S. government spending

general an·es·thet·ic /ˌ... .ˈ../ *n.* [C] a medicine that makes you unconscious and keeps you from feeling any pain, used during a medical operation

G

General As·sem·bly /ˌ... .'../ *n.* [C] **1 the General Assembly** the group of countries that make up the United Nations **2** the group of people who make laws in a state LEGISLATURE

general coun·sel /ˌ... '../ *n.* [C] **1** the chief legal officer of a company **2** a firm of lawyers that gives general legal advice

general de·liv·er·y /ˌ... .'.../ *n.* [U] a post office department that keeps someone's letters until that person comes to get them

general e·lec·tion /ˌ... .'../ *n.* [C] an election in which all the people in a country who can vote elect a president, GOVERNOR, SENATOR etc.

general head·quar·ters /ˌ... '.../ *n.* [plural] the place from which the actions of an organization, especially a military one, are controlled

gen·er·al·ist /'dʒɛnərəlɪst/ *n.* [C] a person who knows about many different things and can do many things well

gen·er·al·i·ty /ˌdʒɛnə'ræləti/ *n. plural* **generalities** **1** [C often plural] a very general statement that avoids mentioning details or specific cases: *When asked about the new plan, Strock would talk only in generalities.* **2** [U] FORMAL the quality of being true or useful in most situations

gen·er·al·i·za·tion /ˌdʒɛnərələ'zeɪʃən/ *n.* **1** [C] a statement that may be true in some or many situations but is not true all of the time: *You can't make generalizations about what men or women are like.* | **broad/sweeping/gross generalization** (=a statement that says something is always true, when it is not true in every case) **2** [U] the act of making generalizations: *Those who reject generalization insist that history consists of unique and separate events.*

gen·er·al·ize /'dʒɛnərəˌlaɪz/ *v.* **1** [I,T] to form a general principle or opinion after considering only a small number of facts or examples: *She's always quick to generalize and put people into categories.* | [+ about] *It has always been difficult to generalize about China because it's such a huge country.* | [+ from] *We can generalize from the samples and conclude that nitrogen levels have increased.* **2** [I] to make a statement about a number of different things or people without mentioning any details: [+ about] *It's difficult to generalize about a subject as broad as world history.* **3** [T] FORMAL to put a principle, statement, or rule into a more general form so that it covers a larger number of examples: *Physicians are still debating whether to generalize the data on aspirin to women.*

general knowl·edge /ˌ... '../ *n.* [U] knowledge of facts about many different subjects that most people know about

sw **gen·er·al·ly** /'dʒɛnərəli/ *adv.* **1** considering some-
2|2 thing as a whole, without details or specific cases: *It was generally a positive conversation.* | [sentence adverb] *Generally, the team has been more successful at home.* **2** by or to most people: *Morrison is generally regarded as New York's best defensive player.* **3** usually or most of the time: *The quality of the food here is generally good.* **4 generally speaking** used to introduce a statement that is true in most cases but not always: *Generally speaking, older people are less able to speak up for their rights.*

general part·ner /ˌ... '../ *n.* [C] someone who controls a company along with one or more other people

general prac·tice /ˌ... '../ *n.* **1** [U] the work of a doctor or lawyer who deals with all the ordinary types of illnesses or legal cases, rather than one specific type **2** [C] a group of lawyers or doctors who do all types of work rather than one specific type

general prac·ti·tion·er /ˌ... .'.../ *n.* [C] a doctor who is trained in general medicine

general-pur·pose /ˌ... '..◂/ *adj.* [only before noun] a general-purpose product, vehicle etc. is appropriate for most situations or jobs that such things are normally used for: *a general-purpose computer*

gen·er·al·ship /'dʒɛnərəlˌʃɪp/ *n.* [U] the skill of leading an army and developing plans for battle

general staff /ˌ... '../ *n.* the general staff the group of military officers who work for a commanding officer

general store /ˌ... '../ *n.* [C] a shop that sells a wide variety of goods, especially one in a small town

general strike /ˌ... '../ *n.* [C] a situation when most of the workers in a country refuse to work in order to protest about working conditions, salary etc.

gen·er·ate /'dʒɛnəˌreɪt/ *v.* [T] **1** to produce or make sw something: *The computer industry has generated* 2
3 *hundreds of new jobs in the area.* | **generate revenue/profits/income etc.** *Lottery officials said the plan should generate enough revenue to build several new schools.* | *Their success at the Olympics has generated quite a bit of interest in women's team sports.* **2** to produce heat, electricity, or another form of energy: *The 2.4-liter four-cylinder engine generates 138 horsepower.*

gen·er·a·tion /ˌdʒɛnə'reɪʃən/ *n.* **1** [C] all people of sw about the same age: *Over half of the people in my* 2|2 *generation have parents who are divorced.* | **the older/ younger generation** *The older generation still recalls the horrors of World War II.* **2** [C] all the members of a family of about the same age: *Three generations of Monroes have lived in this house.* **3** [C] the average period of time between the birth of a person and the birth of that person's children: *One generation ago, most families could afford a house on one salary.* **4** [C] all the members of a group of things which have been developed from a previous group: *a new generation of TV technology* **5 the generation gap** the lack of understanding between generations or people, caused by their different attitudes and experiences **6** [U] the process of producing something or making something happen: *the generation of electricity* —see also -GENERATION

-generation /dʒɛnəreɪʃən/ [in adjectives] **first-generation/second-generation Canadian etc.** someone who is a first-generation Canadian etc. was born in Canada but their parents were not, and a second-generation Canadian has parents that were born in Canada, but their grandparents were not

Generation X /ˌdʒɛnəreɪʃən 'ɛks/ *n.* [U] the group of people who were born during the late 1960s and 1970s in the U.S.

gen·er·a·tive /'dʒɛnərətɪv/ *adj.* FORMAL able to produce something: *Knowledge gained from research is often dynamic and generative.*

generative gram·mar /ˌ.... '../ *n.* [C,U] the description of a language by rules that produce all the possible correct sentences of the language

gen·er·a·tor /'dʒɛnəˌreɪtə/ *n.* [C] a machine that produces electricity

ge·ner·ic /dʒə'nɛrɪk/ *adj.* **1** a generic product does not have a special name to show that it is made by a particular company: *generic drugs* **2** relating to a whole group of things rather than to one thing in particular: *Fine Arts is a generic term for subjects such as painting, music, and sculpture.* —**generically** /-kli/ *adv.*

gen·er·os·i·ty /ˌdʒɛnə'rɑsəti/ *n.* [C,U] willingness to give money, time etc. in order to help or please someone, or something you do that shows this quality: *The generosity of Mr. and Mrs. Kaplan made the museum project possible.*

gen·er·ous /'dʒɛnərəs/ *adj.* **1** willing to give more money, time etc. than is expected to help someone or give them pleasure: *Mrs. Flatch is a very generous woman.* | [+ to] *Ida is more generous to family and friends than her sister.* | [+ with] *My grandfather has always been very generous with his money.* | [it is generous of sb to do sth] *It's very generous of you to help.* **2** [usually before noun] larger or more than the usual or expected amount: *a generous slice of cake* | *a generous pension plan* **3** sympathetic in the way you deal with people, and tending not to criticize them, get angry, or treat them in a way that is not nice: *She is usually generous in her judgments of people.* —**generously** *adv.* —see also **generous/kind etc. to a fault** (FAULT[1] (7))

Gen·e·sis /ˈdʒenəsɪs/ the first book of the Bible

gen·e·sis /ˈdʒenəsɪs/ n. FORMAL **the genesis** the beginning or origin of something: [+ **cf**] *The company dates the genesis of its problems to the early 1980s.*

gene ther·a·py /ˌ. ˈ.../ n. [U] a way of treating certain diseases by using GENETIC ENGINEERING

ge·net·ic /dʒəˈnetɪk/ adj. relating to GENES or GENETICS: *They now have a genetic test for that disease.* | *genetic mutations* —**genetically** /-kli/ adv.: *Hair color is a genetically transmitted characteristic.*

genetic code /.,.. ˈ./ n. [C] the arrangement of GENES that controls the way a living thing develops

genetic en·gi·neer·ing /.,.. ..ˈ../ n. [U] the science of changing the structure of the GENES of an animal, plant, or human, usually to make them stronger or healthier —**genetic engineer** n. [C] —**genetically engineered** adj.

genetic fin·ger·print /.,.. ˈ.../ n. [C] the pattern of GENES that is different for each person or animal

genetic fin·ger·print·ing /.,.. ˈ..../ n. [U] the process of examining the pattern of someone's GENES, especially in order to find out if they are guilty of a crime

ge·net·ics /dʒəˈnetɪks/ n. [plural] the study of how the qualities of living things are affected and passed on by GENES —**geneticist** /dʒəˈnetəsɪst/ n. [C]

Ge·ne·va /dʒəˈnivə/ a city in Switzerland which is the main base for several important international organizations

Geneva, Lake a lake in southwest Switzerland that is the largest lake in central Europe

Gen·ghis Khan /ˌɡeŋɡɪs ˈkɑn, ˌdʒeŋ-/ (?1160–1227) the ruler of the Mongol tribe in China, who took control of northern India and sent his armies as far west as the Black Sea

ge·nial /ˈdʒiniəl, -niəl/ adj. cheerful, kind, and friendly: *Mr. Parker is a genial old man.* —**geniality** /ˌdʒiniˈæləti/ n. [C]

ge·nie /ˈdʒini/ n. [C] a magical spirit, especially in Arabian stories, that will do what you want when you call it

gen·i·tal /ˈdʒenətl/ adj. [only before noun] relating to or affecting the outer sex organs: *genital herpes* —**genitally** adv.

gen·i·tals /ˈdʒenətlz/ **gen·i·ta·li·a** /ˌdʒenəˈteɪlyə/ n. [plural] TECHNICAL the outer sex organs

gen·i·tive /ˈdʒenətɪv/ n. [C] TECHNICAL a form of the noun in some languages, which shows a relationship of possession or origin between one thing and another —**genitive** adj.

ge·nius /ˈdʒinyəs/ n. **1** [U] a very high level of intelligence, mental skill, or artistic ability, which only a few people have: *Sakharov was a man of genius.* | *Her teachers recognized her genius early on.* **2** [C] someone who has an unusually high level of intelligence, mental skill, or artistic ability: *a math genius* | [+ **at**] *Sandra's a genius at crossword puzzles.* **3 have a genius for (doing) sth** to be especially good at doing something: *Kimble has a genius for motivating his employees.* **4** [U] the special quality of a particular group of people, period of time etc.: *I admire the Japanese genius for improving ideas from other countries.* —see also **a stroke of genius/inspiration etc.** (STROKE[1] (6))

gen·o·cide /ˈdʒenəˌsaɪd/ n. [U] the deliberate murder of a whole group or race of people: *Several of the military leaders have been accused of genocide.* —**genocidal** /ˌdʒenəˈsaɪdl/ adj.

ge·nome /ˈdʒinoum/ n. [C] TECHNICAL the total of all the GENES that are found in one type of living thing: *the human genome*

gen·re /ˈʒɑnrə/ n. [C] FORMAL a particular type of art, writing, music etc., which has certain features that all examples of this type share: *This movie is much better than others of the horror genre.*

gent /dʒent/ n. [C] OLD-FASHIONED, INFORMAL a GENTLEMAN

gen·teel /dʒenˈtil/ adj. **1** polite, gentle, or graceful: *The downtown has a genteel southern charm.* **2** OLD-

FASHIONED from or relating to a good social class: *Dawson came from a genteel family.*

gen·tian /ˈdʒenʃən/ n. [C] a small plant with blue or purple flowers that grows in mountain areas

gen·tile /ˈdʒentaɪl/ n. [C] someone who is not Jewish —**gentile** adj.

gen·til·i·ty /dʒenˈtɪləti/ n. [U] FORMAL the quality of being polite, gentle, or graceful: *Beaufort, an old Southern town, is a picture of gentility.*

gen·tle /ˈdʒentl/ adj. **1** kind and careful in the way you behave, so that you do not hurt or damage anyone or anything: *Mia's such a gentle person.* | [+ **with**] *Be gentle with the baby.* **2** not strong, loud, forceful, or extreme: *The program contains nine gentle exercise routines set to music.* | *Her voice is gentle and warm.* | *the gentle warmth of the fire* **3** a gentle wind or rain is soft and light: *She lay on the beach enjoying the gentle breeze.* **4** a gentle hill or slope is not very steep or sharp —see also GENTLY —**gentleness** n. [U]

gen·tle·folk /ˈdʒentlˌfouk/ n. [plural] OLD USE people belonging to the higher social classes

gen·tle·man /ˈdʒentlmən/ n. plural **gentlemen** /-mən/ [C] **1** a polite word meaning a "man," used especially when talking to or about a man you do not know: *Please show this gentleman to his seat.* | *Ladies and gentlemen*, *please welcome tonight's guest speaker, Leo Brown.* **2** a man who is polite and behaves well toward other people: *Roland was a perfect gentleman last night.* **3** OLD-FASHIONED a man from a high social class, especially one whose family owns a lot of property **4 sb's gentleman friend** OLD-FASHIONED a woman's male friend; BOYFRIEND —**gentlemanly** adj.

gentleman farm·er /ˌ... ˈ../ n. [C] a man with a lot of money who owns and runs a farm for pleasure rather than as his job

gentleman's a·gree·ment /ˌ... .ˈ../ n. [C] an agreement that is not written down, made between people who trust each other

gen·tle·wom·an /ˈdʒentlˌwumən/ n. plural **gentlewomen** /-ˌwɪmɪn/ [C] OLD USE a woman who belongs to a high social class

gen·tly /ˈdʒentli/ adv. in a gentle way: *Don gently kissed her on the cheek.*

gen·tri·fi·ca·tion /ˌdʒentrəfəˈkeɪʃən/ n. [U] the gradual process of changing an area from an area in bad condition where poor people live, to one in better condition where people with more money want to live: *The rising housing costs are a result of gentrification.* —**gentrify** /ˈdʒentrəˌfaɪ/ v. [T usually passive]

gen·try /ˈdʒentri/ n. [plural] OLD-FASHIONED people who belong to a high social class: *the landed gentry* (=the gentry who own land)

gen·u·flect /ˈdʒenyəˌflekt/ v. [I] to bend one knee when in a church or a holy place, as a sign of respect —**genuflection** /ˌdʒenyəˈflekʃən/ n. [C,U]

gen·u·ine /ˈdʒenyuɪn/ adj. **1** a genuine feeling, desire etc. is one that you really have, not one that you pretend to have; SINCERE: *Mrs. Liu showed a genuine concern for Lisa's well-being.* **2** [no comparative] something genuine really is what it seems to be; real: *a genuine diamond* **3** someone who is genuine is honest and friendly and can be trusted **4 the genuine article** INFORMAL a person, or sometimes a thing, that is a true example of their type: *If you ever wanted to meet a real cowgirl, Katy was the genuine article.* —**genuinely** adv.: *He genuinely believes in what he sells.* —**genuineness** n. [U]

ge·nus /ˈdʒinəs/ n. plural **genera** /ˈdʒenərə/ [C] TECHNICAL a group of animals or plants that are closely related, but cannot BREED[1] (2) with each other

Gen X /ˌdʒen ˈeks/ n. [U] INFORMAL: see GENERATION X

geo- /dʒiou, dʒiə/ prefix TECHNICAL relating to the Earth or its surface: *geophysics* | *geopolitical*

ge·o·cen·tric /ˌdʒiouˈsentrɪk◂/ adj. having the Earth as the central point, or measured from the center of the Earth: *Ptolemy's model of the universe was geocentric.*

ge·ode /'dʒioud/ *n.* [C] a round stone that is hollow, and that often has CRYSTALS inside

ge·o·de·sic dome /,dʒiədizik 'doum/ *n.* [C] TECHNICAL a building shaped like half a ball, made from small flat pieces that are connected together to form POLYGONS

ge·o·gra·phi·cal /,dʒiə'græfikəl/ also **ge·o·graph·ic** /,dʒiə'græfik / *adj.* relating to geography: *geographical maps of the area* —**geographically** /-kli/ *adv.*

ge·og·ra·phy /dʒi'ɑgrəfi/ *n.* [U] **1** the study of the countries, oceans, rivers, mountains, cities etc. of the world: *a geography lesson* —see also PHYSICAL GEOGRAPHY, POLITICAL GEOGRAPHY **2** the way the parts of a place are arranged, such as where the streets, mountains, rivers etc. are: *What effects has geography had on the population?* | *The space probe is designed to study* **the geography of** *Venus.* —**geographer** *n.* [C]

ge·ol·o·gy /dʒi'ɑlədʒi/ *n.* [U] the study of materials such as rocks, soil, and minerals, and the way they have changed since the Earth was formed —**geologist** *n.* [C] —**geological** /,dʒiə'lɑdʒikəl/ also **geologic** *adj.*: *geological periods* —**geologically** /-kli/ *adv.*

ge·o·met·ric /,dʒiə'mɛtrik/ also **ge·o·met·ri·cal** /,dʒiə'mɛtrikəl/ *adj.* **1** having or using lines or shapes from GEOMETRY, such as circles or squares, especially when these are used in regular patterns: *a geometric design* **2** relating to GEOMETRY —**geometrically** /-kli/ *adv.*

geometric pro·gres·sion /,.... .'../ *n.* [U] a set of numbers in order, in which each is multiplied by a specific number to produce the next number in the series, for example as in 1, 2, 4, 8, 16,..., in which each is multiplied by two —compare ARITHMETIC PROGRESSION

ge·om·e·try /dʒi'ɑmətri/ *n.* [U] the study in MATHEMATICS of the form and relationships of angles, lines, curves, shapes, and solid objects

ge·o·phys·ics /,dʒiou'fiziks/ *n.* [U] the study of the movements of parts of the Earth, and the forces involved with this, including the weather, oceans etc. —**geophysical** *adj.* —**geophysicist** *n.* [C]

ge·o·pol·i·tics /,dʒiou'pɑlə,tiks/ *n.* [U] the study of the effects of a country's position, population etc. on its political character and development —**geopolitical** /,dʒioupə'litikəl/ *adj.*

George /dʒɔrdʒ/ *n.* **by George!** OLD-FASHIONED, SPOKEN used when you are pleasantly surprised: *By George, I think you're right!*

George III, King /,dʒɔrdʒ ðə 'θɜd/ (1738–1820) a king of Great Britain and Ireland, who is remembered as the British king at the time of the Revolutionary War

George·town /'dʒɔrdʒtaun/ **1** a fashionable area of the city of Washington, D.C. **2** the capital and largest city of Guyana **3** the capital and largest city of the Cayman Islands

geor·gette /dʒɔr'dʒɛt/ *n.* [U] a light strong material, used for making clothes

Geor·gia /'dʒɔrdʒə/ **1** *written abbreviation* **GA** a state in the southeastern U.S. **2** a country in western Asia, east of the Black Sea —**Georgian** *n. adj.*

ge·o·sta·tion·ar·y /,dʒiou'steiʃə,nɛri/ also **ge·o·syn·chro·nous** /,dʒiou'siŋkrənəs/ *adj.* a geostationary SPACECRAFT or SATELLITE (1) goes around the Earth at the same speed as the Earth moves, so that it is always above the same place on the Earth

ge·o·ther·mal /,dʒiou'θɜməl/ *adj.* relating to or coming from the heat inside the earth: *a geothermal energy plant*

ge·ra·ni·um /dʒə'reiniəm/ *n.* [C] a common house plant with colorful flowers and large round leaves

ger·bil /'dʒɜbəl/ *n.* [C] a small animal with soft fur and a long tail that is kept as a pet

ger·i·at·ric /,dʒɛri'ætrik/ *adj.* **1** [only before noun] relating to the medical care and treatment of old people: *a geriatric hospital* **2** INFORMAL too old to work well: *A geriatric truck had stalled near the highway.*

ger·i·at·rics /,dʒɛri'ætriks/ *n.* [U] the medical treatment and care of old people —compare GERONTOLOGY —**geriatrician** /,dʒɛriə'triʃən/ *n.* [C]

germ /dʒɜm/ *n.* [C] **1** NOT TECHNICAL a very small living thing that can make you sick; BACTERIA: *Cover your mouth when you cough so you won't spread germs.* **2 the germ of an idea/hope etc.** the beginning of an idea that may develop into something else: *The germ of the scandal was born during Carter's presidency.* —see also GERM WARFARE, WHEAT-GERM

Ger·man¹ /'dʒɜmən/ *adj.* **1** relating to or coming from Germany **2** relating to the German language

German² *n.* **1** [U] the language used in Germany, Austria, parts of Switzerland etc. **2** [C] someone from Germany

ger·mane /dʒɜ'mein/ *adj.* FORMAL an idea, remark etc. that is germane to something is related to it in an important and appropriate way; RELEVANT: [+ **to**] *He wanted to find anyone with information germane to the case.*

Ger·man·ic /dʒɜ'mænik/ *adj.* **1** relating to the language family that includes German, Dutch, Swedish, and English **2** typical of Germany or the Germans

German mea·sles /,.. '../ *n.* [U] an infectious disease that causes red spots on your body; RUBELLA

German shep·herd /,.. '../ *n.* [C] a large dog that looks like a WOLF, often used by the police, for guarding property etc.

Ger·ma·ny /'dʒɜməni/ a country in central Europe —**German** *n., adj.*

ger·mi·cide /'dʒɜmə,said/ *n.* [C,U] a substance that kills BACTERIA

ger·mi·nate /'dʒɜmə,neit/ *v.* **1** [I,T] if a seed germinates or is germinated, it begins to grow: *Most seeds germinate best between 85 and 95 degrees Fahrenheit.* **2** [I] if an idea, feeling etc. germinates, it begins to develop: *The idea of forming a business partnership began to germinate in his mind.* —**germination** /,dʒɜmə'neiʃən/ *n.* [U]

germ war·fare /,. '../ *n.* [U] the use of harmful BACTERIA in war to cause illness and death among the enemy

Ge·ron·i·mo /dʒə'rɑnə,mou/ (1829–1909) an Apache chief famous for fighting to keep his people on their own land in New Mexico and Arizona, until the U.S. army forced them to move to Oklahoma

ge·ron·i·mo /dʒə'rɑnə,mou/ *interjection* a shout used by U.S. PARATROOPERS when they jump out of airplanes and by children when jumping off a high place

ger·on·toc·ra·cy /,dʒɛrən'tɑkrəsi/ *n.* [C,U] government by old people, or a government that consists of old people

ger·on·tol·o·gy /,dʒɛrən'tɑlədʒi/ *n.* [U] the scientific study of old age and the changes it causes in the body —compare GERIATRICS —**gerontologist** *n.* [C] —**gerontological** /,dʒɛrəntə'lɑdʒikəl/ *adj.*

ger·ry·man·der·ing /'dʒɛri,mændəriŋ/ *n.* [U] the action of changing the borders of an area before an election so that one person, group, or party has an unfair advantage —**gerrymander** *v.* [I,T]

Gersh·win /'gɜʃwin/, **George** (1898–1937) a U.S. musician who wrote both CLASSICAL music and popular songs and tunes. His brother Ira Gershwin (1896–1983) wrote the words for many of his popular songs.

ger·und /'dʒɛrənd/ *n.* [C] TECHNICAL in grammar, a noun in the form of the PRESENT PARTICIPLE of a verb, such as "reading" in the sentence "He enjoys reading"

ge·stalt /gə'ʃtɑlt, -'stɑlt/ *n.* [C] TECHNICAL a whole thing that cannot easily be divided into its separate parts, and that has qualities that are not present in any of its parts by themselves: *gestalt psychology*

Ge·sta·po /gəˈstɑːpoʊ/ *n.* [U] the secret police force used by the state in Germany during the NAZI period

ges·ta·tion /dʒɛˈsteɪʃən/ *n.* [U] **1** TECHNICAL the process of a child or young animal developing inside its mother's body, or the period of time when this happens: *Humans have a nine-month gestation period.* **2** the process of developing a new idea, piece of work etc., or the period of time when this happens: *The gestation of the biotechnology industry has been rather short.*

ges·tic·u·late /dʒɛˈstɪkyəˌleɪt/ *v.* [I] to make movements with your arms and hands, usually while speaking, because you are excited, angry, or cannot think of the right words to use: *Jane gesticulated wildly and shouted "Stop! Stop!"* —**gesticulation** /dʒɛˌstɪkyəˈleɪʃən/ *n.* [C,U]

ges·ture¹ /ˈdʒɛstʃɚ, ˈdʒɛʃtʃɚ/ *n.* **1** [C,U] a movement of your arms, hands, or head that shows what you mean or how you feel: *He made a rude gesture at us as he drove by.* **2** [C] something that you do or say to show how you feel about someone or something: *The flowers were really a nice gesture.* | [+ of] *A flag was burned as a gesture of protest against the government.* —**gestural** *adj.*

gesture² *v.* [I always + adv./prep.] to move your arms, hands, or head to tell someone something: [+ to/toward etc.] *"This is how we think she escaped," he said, and gestured to the window behind him.* | [gesture for sb to do sth] *Robin gestured for me to move out of the way.*

ge·sund·heit /gəˈzʊnthaɪt/ *interjection* used to wish someone good health when they have just SNEEZED

s w **get** /gɛt/ *v.* past tense **got** past participle **gotten**
1 1 present participle **getting**
1 ▐buy/obtain▐ [T not in passive] to buy or obtain something: *What are you going to get for lunch?* | [get sb sth] *My parents got me this T-shirt in Switzerland.* | [get sth for sb/sth] *Jill knows a woman who can get the material for you.* | *I got these earrings for a dollar.* —see Usage Note at OBTAIN

2 ▐receive▐ [T not in passive] to receive or be given something: *We haven't gotten any mail for three days.* | *Did you get the job?* | *If you buy one, you get one free.* | [get sth from sb] *How much money did you get from Grandma?* | *I got a rude surprise when the bill arrived.*

3 ▐become▐ [linking verb] to change from one state, feeling etc. to another; BECOME: *Vicky got really mad at him.* | *If I wear wool, my skin gets all red.* | *Don't worry about me getting lost, I'll find it.* | *The weather had suddenly gotten cold.* | *Mom told you you'd get hurt if you did that!* —see Usage Note at BECOME

4 ▐move▐ [I always + adv./prep.] to move to a different place or position, often when this is difficult: [+ off/onto/into etc.] *How did the guy get into their house?* | *The gunman told everybody to get down on the floor.* | *Colleen got up slowly and went to the window.*

5 ▐make sth move▐ [T always – adv./prep. not in passive] to make something move to a different place or position, especially when this is difficult: *Can you get the bags out of the car?* | *I don't think we'll be able to get that through the door.*

6 ▐reach a place▐ [I always + adv./prep.] to reach a particular place, position, or stage: *What time will we get there?* | *She got downstairs and found that the room was full of smoke.* | [– to] *You might be disappointed when you get to the end of the book.*

7 ▐bring▐ [T not in passive] to bring someone or something back from somewhere: *Run upstairs and get my glasses.* | [get sb/sth from sth] *I'm going to go get the kids from the babysitter's.*

8 get sth to do sth [not in passive] to make someone or something do something: *Bonnie couldn't get the light to work.*

9 get sb to do sth [not in passive] to persuade someone to do something: *I tried to get Teresa to come out tonight, but she was too busy.*

10 get to do sth to have permission or an opportunity to do something that you want to do: *Tom gets to go to Disneyland this summer.* | *I didn't get to sit down all day.*

11 get sb upset/excited/mad etc. to make someone feel a particular way, or to make something happen to them: *Rhonda got me in trouble with the teacher.* | *Don't let the illness get you down* (=make you unhappy).

12 get sth fixed/done etc. a) to repair something, do something etc., especially when this is difficult: *She has to get two papers written by tomorrow afternoon.* | *I can't get this bag of potato chips open.* **b)** to have someone repair something, do something etc.: *We're going to get the house painted by professionals this time.* **c)** to have something happen to a part of your body or a piece of clothing: *She got her finger caught in the door.*

13 ▐illness▐ [T not in passive] to catch an illness, especially one that is not very serious: *I got the flu when we were on vacation.*

14 get the feeling/idea etc. to start to feel, think etc. something: *I get the feeling you don't like her very much.*

15 ▐money▐ [T not in passive] to earn a particular amount of money, or receive a particular amount of money by selling something: *Jennifer gets $19 an hour at her new job.* | [get sth for sth] *How much can you get for a house this size?* —see Usage Note at GAIN¹

16 ▐happen/exist▐ sb/sth gets sth INFORMAL used in order to say that something happens or exists: *We get a lot of rain around here in the summer.* | *Denver gets a lot of visitors for conferences.*

17 ▐understand▐ [T not in passive or progressive] INFORMAL to understand something: *Tracy didn't get the joke.* | [get what/how/who etc.] *He still doesn't get what we were trying to tell him.* | **get the message/hint** *Okay, I get the message – you want me to leave now.* | *Oh, now I get it – you have to divide 489 by 3.*

18 get going/moving/cracking to make yourself do something or move somewhere more quickly: *Get moving, or we're going to be late.*

19 get to know/like etc. sb/sth to gradually begin to know, like etc. someone or something: *As you get to know the city, I'm sure you'll like it better.*

20 ▐radio/television▐ [T not in passive or progressive] to be able to receive a particular radio signal or television station: *We don't get Channel 24.*

21 get sb/sth doing sth to make someone or something start doing something: *He got the engine running.* | *You know, our conversation last night got me thinking.*

22 get a bus/train etc. to leave on a bus or train, or to travel on it: *We need to get the four-twenty bus if we're going to be there by six.*

23 ▐call▐ [T not in passive] to call someone on the telephone and be able to talk to them: *Sarah, would you get me Mr. Jones, please?* | *Hi, I'm trying to get the customer services department.*

24 ▐meal▐ [T not in passive] to prepare a meal: *She gets breakfast for all four children before sending them to school.*

SPOKEN PHRASES

25 have got a) used to say that you have something: *Mike's got a wife and three kids.* **b)** used to say that you need to do something or you must do something: *I've got to go to the bathroom.*

26 get the phone/door to answer the telephone, or open the door to see who is there: *Val, can you get the phone, please – I'm making dinner.*

27 ▐punish▐ [T not in passive or progressive] to do something to harm or embarrass someone, especially because they have done something bad to you: [get sb for sth] *I'm going to get you for that, you little brat!*

28 get it to be punished for something bad you have done: *You're really going to get it when Dad gets home.*

29 get sth on/off to put a piece of clothing on or take it off: *Get your shoes on – it's time to go.*

30 ▐fool/surprise▐ [T not in passive or progressive] to trick or surprise someone: *I really got you good that time, didn't I?*

G

31 catch [T not in passive or progressive] to catch, hit, or kill someone or something: *That stupid dog tried to get me.*
32 you('ve) got me INFORMAL used to say you do not know the answer to something: *"Why did he attack him?" "You got me."*
33 hear to hear something, or to hear something clearly: *I'm sorry, I didn't get your name.*
34 it (really) gets me used to say that something really annoys you: *It really gets me the way he acts like he knows everything.*
35 get this said when telling someone something that is surprising: *And the whole thing only cost – get this – $12.95.*
36 pay for sth [T not in passive] to pay for something: *I'll get dinner if you get the movie.* | *That's okay, I'll get it.*
37 get some/any OFFENSIVE, SLANG to have sex
38 get you/him/her used to say that you think someone is trying to seem more important, intelligent etc. than they really are: *Get you, in that fancy suit.*

get sth ↔ **across** phr. v. [T] to be able to make someone understand an idea or piece of information: [**get** sth **across to** sb] *It was difficult to get my idea across to the committee.*

get ahead phr. v. [I] to be successful, especially in your job: *She lacks the business skills she'll need to get ahead.*

get along phr. v. [I] **1** to have a friendly relationship with someone or a group of people: *Dave and Vince have never gotten along.* | [+ **with**] *Rachel doesn't get along with Cyrus at all.* **2** to succeed in dealing with a situation, especially a difficult one, and be able to continue doing something: *I was able to get along pretty well in Spanish when I was in Mexico.* | [+ **without**] *We've had to get along without much help from the main office.* **3** SPOKEN to leave a place: *Well, I guess I'd better be getting along before it gets too late.*

get around phr. v. **1** [T **get around** sth] to find an unusual or intelligent way of dealing with a problem or a person, often by avoiding them: *They've hired an accountant to help them get around the new tax laws.* **2** [I] to move or travel to different places: *His new wheelchair lets him get around more easily.* **3** [I] if news or information gets around, a lot of people hear about it: *If this news gets around, we'll have reporters calling us all day.* | *We're expecting more business as word gets around* (=people hear about us). **4** [T **get around** sth] to avoid admitting that something is true: *You can't get around the fact there are very few stores left downtown.* **5** sb **gets around** SPOKEN used to say that someone has sex with a lot of people

get around to sth phr. v. [T] to do something that you have been intending to do for some time: *I meant to go to the bookstore, but I never got around to it.* | [**get around to doing** sth] *It was a year before he finally got around to unpacking his books.*

get at sth phr. v. [T] **1** to try to explain something, especially something difficult: *Did you understand what he was getting at?* **2 get at the meaning/facts** etc. to discover the meaning of something, the facts about someone or something etc.: *The judge asked a few questions to try to get at the truth.* **3** to be able to reach something: *I could see the ring stuck under there, but I couldn't get at it.*

get away phr. v. [I] **1** to leave a place, especially when this is difficult: *Barry had to work late and couldn't get away till 9:00.* **2** to escape from someone who is chasing you or trying to catch you: *The two men got away in a blue pickup truck.* | [+ **from**] *He climbed out of a window to get away from the attacker.* **3** INFORMAL to go on vacation: *Are you going to be able to get away this summer?*

get away from sth phr. v. [T] **1** to begin to talk about other things rather than the subject you are supposed to be discussing: *I think we're getting away from the main issue.* **2 get away from it all** to leave

behind your normal life or problems, especially on vacation: *Get away from it all in sunny Barbados.*

get away with sth phr. v. [T] **1** to not be noticed, caught, or punished when you have done something wrong: *Somehow the basketball team gets away with not going to class.* | *His parents let him get away with murder* (=do very bad things and not get caught or punished). **2** SPOKEN to be able to do something that other people cannot, because you have enough confidence or because you have the right kind of PERSONALITY, social position etc.: *Only Susan could get away with wearing a bikini like that.*

get sb **back** phr. v. [T] also **get back at** sb INFORMAL to do something to hurt or embarrass someone who has hurt or embarrassed you: [+ **for**] *Jerry's just trying to get back at her for leaving him.*

get back to phr. v. [T] **1** [**get back to** sth] to start doing something again after not doing it for a while: *Laura found it hard to get back to work after her maternity leave.* **2** [**get back to** sb] to talk or write to someone at a later time because you are busy, or do not know how to answer their question: *I'll try to get back to you later today.*

get by phr. v. [I] to have enough money to buy the things you need, but no more: *He only earns enough to barely get by.* | [+ **on**] *Somehow they manage to get by on $800 a month.*

get down phr. v. **1** [T **get** sth ↔ **down**] to write something down on paper, especially quickly: *Let me get your number down before I forget it.* **2** [T **get** sth **down**] to succeed in swallowing food or drink: *These pills are so big I can't get them down easily.* **3** [I] SLANG to dance in a skillful stylish way

get down to sth phr. v. [T] to finally start doing something that will take a lot of time or effort: *By the time we finally got down to work, it was already 10:00.*

get in phr. v. **1** [I,T **get** sb **in**] to be allowed or able to enter a place, or to make it possible for someone to do this: *The door was locked, and he couldn't get in.* | *I'd like to get in to see "The Tonight Show" in September.* | *Give me a few minutes, and I'm sure I can get you in.* **2** [I] to arrive at a particular place: *What time does your plane get in?* | *Steve just got in a few minutes ago.* **3** [T **get** sth **in**] to send or give something to a particular person, company etc.: *Make sure you get your homework in by Thursday.* **4** [I] to be elected to a position of political power: *It's unlikely Coogan will get in again.* **5** [T **get** sth ↔ **in**] to gather together something such as crops and bring them to a sheltered place: *They're trying to get the rest of the corn in before it rains.*

get (sb) **in on** sth phr. v. [T not in passive] INFORMAL to become involved in something that other people are doing or planning: *I wanted to make sure we get your department in on the planning.* | *Democrats want tax cuts – now Republicans want to get in on the act* (=get involved in doing something).

get into 1 [T **get into** sth] to be allowed to go to a school, college, or university: *Lori got into the graduate program at Cornell.* **2 what's/something's gotten into sb** SPOKEN used to express surprise that someone is behaving very differently from the way they usually behave: *I don't know what's gotten into him, but he's been really grouchy lately.* **3** [T **get into** sth] to begin to have a discussion about something: *Let's not get into it right now. I'm tired.* **4 get (sb) into trouble/difficulties etc** to do something that causes trouble for yourself or for someone else: *I was always getting into trouble at school.* **5** [T **get into** sth] to start doing something regularly | **get into the habit/way/routine etc of**: *He just could not get into the habit of walking to the office in the mornings.* **6** [T **get into** sth] to become very interested in an activity: *But what's interesting is how our young black customers are getting into older black music.* **7 cannot get into sth** if you cannot get into clothes, they are too small for you: *I can't get into these pants anymore.*

get off phr. v. **1** [I,T **get off** sth] to finish working at your work place: *What time do you get off work?* | *Shelly gets off at 5:30.* **2** [I,T **get** (sb) **off**] to get little or no punishment for a crime, or to help someone escape punishment: *I can't believe his lawyers managed to get him off.* [+ **with**] *He got off with just a*

small fine. **3 where does sb get off (doing sth)?**
SPOKEN said when you think someone has done something to you that they do not have a right to do:
Where does he get off telling me how to live my life?
4 get off on the wrong foot to start a job, relationship etc. badly by doing something that annoys people: *We just got off on the wrong foot the other day.* **5 get off it!** SPOKEN used to tell someone to stop talking about a particular subject because it is annoying you **6** [I] VULGAR to have an ORGASM

get off on sth *phr. v.* [T] VULGAR DISAPPROVING to enjoy doing something bad to someone, especially in a sexual way: *I think she gets off on hurting people.*

get off to *phr. v.* [T] to do something in a particular way | **get off to a good/bad start** *As far as school goes, Johnnie has gotten off to an extremely good start.*

get on *phr. v.* **1 be getting on (in years)** INFORMAL to be old: *Dad's getting on in years, but he's still healthy.* **2 get on the subject (of sth)** to start talking about something: *How did we get on the subject of eating habits?* **3 get it on** SLANG to have sex: *Do you think those two are ever going to get it on?*

get on with sth *phr. v.* [T] **1** to continue doing something after you have stopped doing it for a while: *Let's get on with the meeting, so we can go home on time.* **2 get on with it** used to tell someone to hurry: *Get on with it will you? I don't have all day!*

get onto sb/sth *phr. v.* [T] **1** to start talking about a particular subject after you have been talking about something else: *Then we got onto the subject of women in the military, and Craig wouldn't shut up.* **2** SPOKEN to criticize someone about something they have done [+ for/about] *Mrs. Prichett got onto me for turning my homework in late.*

get out *phr. v.* **1** [I,T get sb out] to be allowed to leave a place, or to make it possible for someone to do this: *He got out after serving a 12-year sentence for manslaughter.* | *They're starting a letter-writing campaign to help get the political prisoners out.* [+ of] *We got out of school early on Thursday.* **2** [I] to escape from a place: *The dog got out again.* **3** [I] if information gets out, a lot of people learn about it, even though it is meant to be secret: *If this gets out, we might lose our jobs.* [**get out that**] *Word got out that the band was staying at the Hilton, and a huge crowd of fans showed up.* **4** [T get sth ↔ out] to succeed in saying something, especially when this is very difficult: *I wanted to tell him I loved him, but couldn't get the words out.* **5** [T get sth ↔ out] to produce or PUBLISH something: *We plan to get the book out next month.*

get out of *phr. v.* [T] **1** [get out of sth] to avoid doing something you have promised to do or are supposed to do: *Dana couldn't get out of the meeting, so she canceled dinner.* [**get out of doing sth**] *Joe is always trying to get out of cleaning the bathroom.* **2** [get sb out of sth] to help someone avoid doing something they are supposed to do [**get sb out of doing sth**] *OK, I'll see if I can get you out of having to testify.* **3** [get sth out of sth] to feel a particular way, learn something etc. because of something you do: *Are you getting anything out of your classes?* [**get sth out of doing sth**] *She gets a lot of pleasure out of painting.* **4** [get sth out of sb] to force or persuade someone to tell you something or give you something

get over 1 [T get over sth] to start to feel better after an emotional experience that has caused a lot of sadness or disappointment: *The family still hadn't gotten over the shock of Jennifer's death.* | *Don't worry. I'm sure you'll get over it in time.* **2** [T get over sth] to become well again after you have been ill: *It took him a week to get over the flu.* **3 sb can't/couldn't get over sth** SPOKEN used to say that someone is very surprised, shocked, or amused by something: *I can't get over how thin you are!* **4 get over it!** SPOKEN used to tell someone to stop being so upset about something, because they are annoying you

get sth **over with** *phr. v.* [T] to finish doing something you do not like doing as quickly as possible: *"The shot should only hurt a little." "OK. Just get it over with."*

get through *phr. v.* **1** [T get through sth] to manage to deal with a difficult or bad experience until it ends: *I was so embarrassed, I don't know how I got through the rest of dinner.* **2** [I] to succeed in reaching someone by telephone: *When she finally got through, the manager wasn't there.* **3** [I,T get sth through] if a law gets through Congress or another official organization, or if someone gets it through, it is officially accepted **4** [T get sb through sth] to help someone manage to deal with a difficult or bad experience until it ends: *Are you willing to stand by him and get him through this difficult time?* | *The unemployment checks got him through November, but he needs to find a job soon.* **5 get sth through your head** to understand or believe something: *When are you going to get it through your head that I'm not interested in her?* **6** [T get through sth] to finish doing something: *I want to get through this chapter before I go to bed.*

get through to sb *phr. v.* [T] to be able to make someone understand something, especially when this is difficult: *Sometimes it's like I just can't get through to her.*

get to sb *phr. v.* [T] INFORMAL to upset or annoy someone: *Don't let him get to you, honey.*

get together *phr. v.* **1** [I] to meet with someone or with a group of people: *We should really get together for lunch sometime.* [+ with] *Every time he gets together with Murphy, they argue.* **2** [I] to start a romantic relationship with someone: *Those two should get together – they have a lot in common.* **3 get yourself together** also **get it together** SPOKEN to begin to be in control of your life, your emotions etc.: *After my husband left, it took a year for me to get myself together.*

get up *phr. v.* **1** [I,T get sb up] to wake up and get out of your bed, especially in the morning, or to make someone do this: *I have to get up early tomorrow.* | *Could you get me up at 8:00?* **2** [I] to stand up: *Tom got up to make some more coffee.*

get·a·way /'gɛtəˌweɪ/ *n.* [C] **1** an escape from a place or a bad situation, especially after you have done something illegal: *The bank robber made his getaway in a red truck.* | *a getaway car* (=a car used by criminals to escape after a crime) **2** a short trip that you take as a vacation, or the place where you go: *Big Bear Lake is a popular weekend getaway.*

get

cocktail

hammock

getting away from it all

get-go /'. ./ *n.* **from the get-go** INFORMAL from the beginning: *Harry's been involved in the project from the get-go.*

get-rich-quick /ˌ. . './ *adj.* [only before noun] relating to the desire to earn a lot of money quickly, or relating to a method of doing this: *a get-rich-quick scheme*

get·ter /'gɛtɚ/ *n.* [C usually singular] something or someone that gets or receives something: *Gilroy was*

G

the top vote-getter. | *It's fun to drive – it's an attention getter.* —see also GO-GETTER

get·to·geth·er /'. .,../ *n.* [C] a friendly informal meeting or party: *a family get-together*

Get·ty /'gɛti/, **J. Paul** /dʒeɪ pɔl/ (1892–1976) a U.S. businessman who owned an oil company and became one of the richest men in the world. He built the Getty Museum in Malibu, California.

Get·tys·burg /'gɛtiz,bɚg/ a town in the U.S. state of Pennsylvania where the Confederate general Robert E. Lee was defeated by a Union army in the American Civil War

Gettysburg Ad·dress, the /,... .'./ a famous speech made by Abraham Lincoln at Gettysburg in 1863, about the Union soldiers who had died in the Civil War

get·up /'gɛtʌp/ *n.* [C] INFORMAL strange or unusual clothes that someone is wearing: *Josh showed up at the party in a 1920s gangster getup.*

get-up-and-go /,. . .'./ *n.* [U] INFORMAL energy and determination to do things: *She had more get-up-and-go than the other job applicants.*

gew·gaw /'gyugɔ, 'gu-/ *n.* [C] a cheap brightly colored piece of jewelry or decoration

gey·ser /'gaizɚ/ *n.* [C] a natural spring that sends hot water and steam into the air from a hole in the ground

Gha·na /'gɑnə/ a country in west Africa east of Ivory Coast —**Ghanaian** /gɑ'neɪən/ *n. adj.*

ghast·ly /'gæstli/ *adj.* **ghastlier, ghastliest** **1** extremely bad, shocking, or upsetting: *They keep showing ghastly pictures of the accident on TV.* | *a ghastly mistake* **2** FORMAL looking or feeling very sick, upset, or unhappy: *She felt ghastly afterwards.*

Ghats, the /gɑts, gɔts/ two RANGES of mountains in central India

GHB *n.* [U] a chemical substance that is taken as a drug by some people, especially at parties and dance clubs

gher·kin /'gɚkɪn/ *n.* [C] a small type of CUCUMBER that is often made into a PICKLE[1] (1)

ghet·to /'gɛtoʊ/ *n. plural* **ghettos** or **ghettoes** [C] **1** a word that is often considered offensive, for a very poor part of a city, especially where most people come from MINORITY groups: *Rap music began in the ghettos of New York and Washington.* **2** a part of a city where people who belonged to a particular race were forced to live by the government, especially in the past: *the Jewish ghetto in Warsaw* **3** an area or environment that is limited to a particular group of people: *His office marked the edge of the executive ghetto.*

ghetto blast·er /'.. ,../ *n.* [C] OLD-FASHIONED a word for a BOOM BOX, now considered offensive

ghet·to·ize /'gɛtoʊ,aɪz/ *v.* [T] **1** to make a ghetto in a city, society etc.: *In the north part of the city, the neighborhoods were becoming ghettoized.* **2** to force someone to live in a ghetto: *Blacks coming from the South were ghettoized in high-rise housing projects.*

ghost[1] /goʊst/ *n.* [C]
1 spirit the spirit of a dead person, that some people believe they can see or feel: *They say the captain's ghost still haunts the waterfront.* —see also HOLY GHOST
2 memory/effect the memory or effect of someone or something bad that lived, existed, or happened in the past: *The ghost of Stalinism still affects life in Russia today.*
3 not a ghost of a chance not even a slight chance of doing something, or of something happening: *There's not a ghost of a chance that we'll get there on time now.*
4 give up the ghost HUMOROUS **a)** if a machine gives up the ghost, it does not work anymore and cannot be repaired: *My old car's finally given up the ghost.* **b)** to die

5 image on a screen a second image that is not clear on a television or computer screen
6 the ghost of a smile/sound etc. a smile, sound etc. that is so slight you are not sure it happened: *He had the ghost of a smile on his lips.*
7 a GHOST WRITER

ghost[2] *v.* [I,T] INFORMAL to write something as a GHOST WRITER: *The former reporter ghosted Reagan's autobiography.*

ghost·ly /'goʊstli/ *adj.* slightly frightening and seeming to be related to ghosts or spirits: *a ghostly voice* —**ghostly** *adv.*

ghost sto·ry /'. ,../ *n.* [C] a story told or written in order to frighten people, especially a story told late at night

ghost town /'. ./ *n.* [C] a town that is empty because most or all of its people have left

ghost writer, ghostwriter /'. ,../ *n.* [C] someone who writes a book or story for another person who then says it is their own work —**ghostwrite** *v.* [I,T]

ghoul /gul/ *n.* [C] **1** an evil spirit in stories, that takes bodies from graves and eats them **2** someone who gets pleasure from things that are bad or not nice, such as accidents that shock other people —**ghoulish** *adj.*

GHQ *n.* [U] General Headquarters; the place that a large military operation is controlled from

GI, G.I. *n.* [C] Government Issue; a soldier in the U.S. army

Gia·co·met·ti /,dʒɑkə'mɛti/, **Al·ber·to** /æl'bɛrtoʊ/ (1901–1966) a Swiss SCULPTOR and PAINTER, famous for his work in the style of SURREALISM

gi·ant[1] /'dʒaɪənt/ *adj.* extremely large and much bigger than other things of the same type: *a giant TV screen* s w

giant[2] *n.* [C] **1** a very tall, strong man who is often bad and cruel, in children's stories **2** a very successful or important person or company: *Clapton is one of the giants of the music industry.* **3** a very big man

gi·ant·ess /'dʒaɪəntɪs/ *n.* [C] an extremely tall or successful woman

giant pan·da /,.. '../ *n.* [C] a PANDA

gib·ber /'dʒɪbɚ/ *v.* [I] to speak quickly in a way that no one can understand, especially because you are frightened, shocked, or excited: *He was gibbering with rage.*

gib·ber·ish /'dʒɪbərɪʃ/ *n.* [U] something you write or say that has no meaning, or is very difficult to understand: *This manual is written in computer gibberish.*

gib·bet /'dʒɪbɪt/ *n.* [C] a wooden frame on which criminals were HANGed in past times using a rope around their neck

gib·bon /'gɪbən/ *n.* [C] a small animal like a monkey, with long arms and no tail, that lives in trees in Asia

gibe /dʒaɪb/ *n.* [C] another spelling of JIBE[2]

gib·lets /'dʒɪblɪts/ *n.* [plural] organs such as the heart and LIVER that you remove from a bird before cooking it

Gi·bral·tar /dʒɪ'brɔltɚ/ a town on the Rock of Gibraltar on the southern coast of Spain

Gibraltar, the Strait of a narrow piece of sea that connects the Mediterranean Sea at its western end with the Atlantic Ocean

Gib·ran /dʒʊ'brɑn/, **Kah·lil** /kɑ'lil/ (1883–1931) a Lebanese poet

gid·dy[1] /'gɪdi/ *adj.* **giddier, giddiest** **1** feeling silly, happy, and excited, or showing this feeling: *Drinking champagne always makes me giddy.* | *giddy optimism* | [+ with] *The children are giddy with excitement.* **2** feeling slightly sick and unable to balance, because everything seems to be moving; DIZZY: *Just watching those kids spinning makes me feel giddy.* **3** OLD-FASHIONED silly and not interested in serious things: *a giddy girl* —**giddily** *adv.* —**giddiness** *n.* [U]

giddy[2] *v.*
  giddy up *phr. v.* [I] used to command a horse to go faster

Gide /ʒid/, **An·dré** /'andreɪ/ (1869–1951) a French writer famous especially for his NOVELS

Gid·e·on Bi·ble /ˌɡɪdiən 'baɪbəl/ a Bible that is put in a hotel room by a Christian organization called Gideons International, so that people staying there can read it

GIF n. [C] TECHNICAL Graphics Interchange Format; a type of computer FILE¹ (3) used on the Internet that contains pictures, photographs, or other images

s w
1 2
gift¹ /ɡɪft/ n. [C] **1** something that you give someone you like, want to thank etc.; PRESENT: *The earrings were a gift for my birthday.* | *The Machon family made a substantial gift of land to the college.* | *You receive a free gift* (=something that you do not have to pay for) *with any purchase of $20 or more.* **2** a natural ability; TALENT: [+ for] *Elena sure has a gift for telling stories.* —see also GIFTED **3** a gift (from God) something good you receive or something good that happens to you, even though you might not deserve it: *It's definitely a gift from God to be home for the holidays.* **4** the gift of gab INFORMAL an ability to speak easily and confidently with other people: *Peter is known for his gift of gab.* **5** don't look a gift horse in the mouth SPOKEN used to tell someone to be thankful for something that has been given to them, instead of asking questions about it or finding something wrong with it —see also **God's gift to sb/sth etc.** (GOD (5))

gift² v. [T] INFORMAL to give someone something as a gift: [gift sb with sth] *He gifted us each with $100.*

USAGE NOTE: GIFT

WORD CHOICE: gift, give
Although some people use **gift** as a verb, especially in advertising and in some newspaper articles, most teachers think this is not correct. They prefer that you use **give** instead: *He gave us each $100.*

---

gift cer·tif·i·cate /'. .,..../ n. [C] a special piece of paper worth a particular amount of money that you buy for someone as a gift, so that they can exchange it for goods in a store

gift·ed /'ɡɪftɪd/ adj. **1** having a natural ability to do one or more things extremely well: *a gifted poet* | [be gifted with sth] *Elaine is gifted with a superb singing voice.* **2** very intelligent: *a special class for gifted children*

gift shop /'. ./ n. [C] a store that sells small things that are appropriate for giving as presents

gift wrap¹ /'. ./ also **gift wrapping** n. [U] attractive colored paper for wrapping presents in

gift wrap², **gift-wrap** v. **gift wrapped, gift wrapping** [T] to wrap a present with gift wrap at a store: *Would you like this gift wrapped?*

gig¹ /ɡɪɡ/ n. [C] **1** INFORMAL a performance by musicians, especially musicians who play popular music or JAZZ, a COMEDIAN etc. that they do to earn money: *Tom's band has a gig at the Blues Bar next week.* **2** INFORMAL a job, especially one that does not last for a long time: *Working for a TV show is a pretty good gig.* **3** INFORMAL a gigabyte **4** a small carriage with two wheels that is pulled by one horse

gig² v. **gigged, gigging** [I] to give a performance of modern popular music, JAZZ etc. for money

gig·a·byte /'ɡɪɡəˌbaɪt/ *written abbreviation* Gb n. [C] a unit for measuring the amount of information a computer can store or use, equal to about a BILLION BYTES

gi·gan·tic /dʒaɪˈɡæntɪk/ adj. [no comparative] extremely large: *a gigantic statue of Buddha*

gig·gle¹ /'ɡɪɡəl/ v. **giggled, giggling** [I] to laugh quickly and quietly in a high voice because you think something is very funny or because you are nervous: *What are you two girls giggling about?* —**giggly** adj.

giggle² n. [C] a quick quiet high-sounding laugh: *a nervous giggle* | *One of the other boys got the giggles* (=was unable to stop giggling) *during prayer time.* —**giggly** adj.

gig·o·lo /'dʒɪɡəˌloʊ/ n. *plural* **gigolos** [C] a man who has sex with women for money

Gi·la monster, gila monster /'hilə ˌmɑnstɚ/ n. [C] a large orange and black LIZARD that is poisonous and lives in the deserts of the southwestern U.S. and western Mexico

gild /ɡɪld/ v. [T] **1** to cover something with a thin layer of gold or gold paint: *a gilded picture frame* **2** LITERARY to make something look as if it is covered in gold: *The autumn sun gilded the lake.* **3** gild the lily to spoil something by trying to improve it when it is already good enough

gill¹ /ɡɪl/ n. [C] **1** one of the organs on the sides of a fish through which it breathes —see picture at BARRACUDA **2** one of the thin pale lines on the bottom of a MUSHROOM **3** to the gills completely or extremely: *The plane was packed to the gills with relief supplies.*

gill² /dʒɪl/ n. [C] a measure of liquid equal to ¹/₄ of a PINT or 0.118 liters

Gil·man /'ɡɪlmən/, **Char·lotte Per·kins** /'ʃarlət 'pɔkɪnz/ (1860–1935) a U.S. writer who supported women's rights, famous for her book on women and ECONOMICS

gilt¹ /ɡɪlt/ adj. [only before noun] covered with a thin layer of gold or gold-covered paint: *gilt lettering*

gilt² n. **1** [U] a thin layer of gold or gold-colored paint, used to cover objects for decoration **2** [C] a young female pig **3** [C] a STOCK¹ (2) or SHARE² (4) that is gilt-edged

gilt-edged /ˌ. '.⸱/ adj. **1** a gilt-edged book has gilt at the edges of its pages **2** extremely good or respected: *a gilt-edged credit history* **3** TECHNICAL gilt-edged STOCKS¹ (2) or SHARES² (4) do not give you much INTEREST (=additional money) but are considered very safe because they are sold mainly by governments

gim·let /'ɡɪmlɪt/ n. [C] **1** an alcoholic drink made with GIN or VODKA and LIME juice **2 gimlet-eyed** also **gimlet eyes** if someone is gimlet-eyed or has gimlet eyes, they look at things very closely and notice every detail **3** a tool that is used to make small holes in wood so that you can put screws in easily

gim·me¹ /'ɡɪmi/ NONSTANDARD a way of writing the spoken short form of "give me": *Gimme that ball back!*

gimme² n. [C] INFORMAL something that is so easy to do or succeed at that you do not even have to try: *The victory was a gimme for the New York Yankees.*

gim·mick /'ɡɪmɪk/ n. [C] DISAPPROVING a trick or something unusual that you do to make people notice someone or something: *advertising gimmicks* —**gimmicky** adj. DISAPPROVING —**gimmickry** n. [U] DISAPPROVING

gimp /ɡɪmp/ n. [C] OFFENSIVE someone who cannot walk normally, because one or both of their legs are hurt or they are physically unable to use them

gimp·y /'ɡɪmpi/ adj. INFORMAL **1** a gimpy leg or knee does not work normally, especially because it is hurt **2** a gimpy person cannot walk normally, either because one or both of their legs are hurt, or because they are physically unable to use them: *Even with a gimpy quarterback, we managed to win.*

gin /dʒɪn/ n. **1** [C,U] a strong alcoholic drink made mainly from grain —see also GIN AND TONIC **2** [U] the situation in the game of GIN RUMMY when all the cards in your hand are matched in sets and you win **3** [U] GIN RUMMY —see also COTTON GIN

gin and ton·ic /ˌ. . '../ n. [C,U] an alcoholic drink made with gin and TONIC (=a special type of water), served with ice and a thin piece of LEMON or LIME

gin·ger /'dʒɪndʒɚ/ n. [U] **1** a SPICY light brown root, or the powder made from this root, that is used in cooking **2** the plant that this root comes from

ginger ale /ˌ.. ,.. ,.. '../ n. [C,U] a SOFT DRINK with a ginger taste

gin·ger·bread[1] /'dʒɪndʒɚˌbrɛd/ *n.* [U] **1** a type of cookie with ginger and sweet SPICEs in it, that is usually cut into shapes before baking it: *a gingerbread house/man* (=a piece of gingerbread in the shape of a house or a person) **2** complicated decorations on the outside of a house: *a Victorian mansion decorated with gingerbread* **3** a heavy cake that has GINGER and MOLASSES in it

gingerbread[2] *adj.* decorated with gingerbread: *a house with gingerbread trim*

gin·ger·ly /'dʒɪndʒɚli/ *adv.* very slowly, carefully, and gently: *They gingerly loaded the patient into the ambulance.* —**gingerly** *adj.*

gin·ger snap /'.. ,./ *n.* [C] a hard cookie with GINGER in it

ging·ham /'ɡɪŋəm/ *n.* [U] cotton cloth that has a pattern of small white and colored squares on it: *a red and white gingham tablecloth*

gin·gi·vi·tis /ˌdʒɪndʒə'vaɪtɪs/ *n.* [U] a medical condition in which your GUMs are red, swollen, and painful

gink·go, gingko /'ɡɪŋkoʊ/ *n.* [C] a type of tree from China with leaves that are shaped like small FANS[1] (2)

gin rum·my /ˌ. '../ *n.* [U] a type of RUMMY (=card game)

Gins·berg /'ɡɪnzbɚɡ/, **Al·len** /'ælən/ (1926–1997) a U.S. poet and leader of the Beat Generation

gin·seng /'dʒɪnsɛn, -sɪŋ/ *n.* [U] medicine made from the root of a Chinese plant, that some people think keeps you young and healthy

Giot·to /'dʒɔtoʊ/ (?1266–1337) an Italian painter and ARCHITECT who was one of the most important painters of his time

gip·sy /'dʒɪpsi/ *n.* [C] OLD USE another spelling of GYPSY

gi·raffe /dʒə'ræf/ *n.* [C] a tall African animal with a very long neck and legs and dark spots on its yellow-brown fur

gird /ɡɚd/ *v. past tense and past participle* **girded** or **girt 1** [I,T] if you gird for something, or you gird yourself for something, especially something difficult, you prepare for it: [+ **for**] *District officials are girding for a tough campaign.* **2 gird (up) your loins** HUMOROUS OR BIBLICAL to get ready to do something, especially to fight: *I'm girding up my loins for battle on this tax issue.* **3** to surround something, especially to give it support or protection: *The Romans enclosed the town with walls that still gird the Old City.* **4** if you gird someone or something, you fasten something around them: [+ **with**] *Experts have decided to gird the medieval tower with steel rings.*

gird·er /'ɡɚdɚ/ *n.* [C] a strong beam, made of iron or steel, that supports a floor, roof, or bridge

gir·dle /'ɡɚdl/ *n.* [C] a piece of underwear that a woman wears tightly around her stomach, bottom, and HIPs to make her look thinner

girl /ɡɚl/ *n.* [C]
1 child a female child: *She's tall for a girl her age.* | *I used to live in Colorado when I was a little girl.* | *A small girl hugged her mother's legs.*
2 daughter a daughter: *They have two girls and a boy.*
3 woman a word meaning a woman, which is considered offensive by some people: *A nice girl like you needs a husband.*
4 the girls INFORMAL a woman's female friends: *I'm going out with the girls tonight.*
5 animal used to speak to a female animal, such as a horse, cat, or dog: *Bring me the stick. Good girl!*
6 girl SPOKEN used by a woman to address another woman that she knows well: *Come on, girls!*
7 (you) go, girl! SLANG used to encourage a girl or woman, or to say that you agree with what she is saying

8 relationship OLD-FASHIONED a word for a woman who you are having a romantic relationship with, now usually considered offensive: *She's my girl.*
9 employee OLD-FASHIONED a word for a female worker, especially in an office, now considered offensive by most people: *I'll have my girl send it over.*
10 servant OLD-FASHIONED a woman servant

girl Fri·day /ˌ. '../ *n.* [C] a girl or woman worker who does several different jobs in an office

girl·friend /'ɡɚlfrɛnd/ *n.* [C] **1** a girl or woman with whom you have a romantic relationship: *Seth is bringing his new girlfriend to Heidi's party.* | *an ex-girlfriend* (=a former girlfriend) **2** a woman's female friend: *She's out with one of her girlfriends.* —see also BOYFRIEND

girl·hood /'ɡɚlhʊd/ *n.* [U] the period of a woman's life when she is a girl —see also BOYHOOD

girl·ie[1], **girly** /'ɡɚli/ *adj.* **1** INFORMAL **a girlie magazine/calendar etc.** a magazine etc. with pictures of women with no clothes on **2** SPOKEN appropriate only for girls rather than men or boys: *Do you think this watch looks too girlie?* **3** DISAPPROVING a woman or a girl who is girlie behaves in a silly way, for example by pretending to be shy or always thinking about how she looks

girlie[2] *n.* [C] OLD-FASHIONED, OFFENSIVE used by men to talk to a woman who they think is less sensible or intelligent than a man

girl·ish /'ɡɚlɪʃ/ *adj.* behaving like a girl, or looking like a girl: *girlish laughter* —**girlishly** *adv.*

Girl Scout /'. ./ *n.* **1** [C] a member of the Girl Scouts **2 the Girl Scouts** an organization for girls that teaches them practical skills and helps to develop their character —compare BOY SCOUT

girl·y /'ɡɚli/ *adj.* another spelling of GIRLIE[1]

girt /ɡɚt/ *v.* a past participle of GIRD

girth /ɡɚθ/ *n.* **1** [C,U] the distance around the middle of someone or something: *the enormous girth of a redwood tree's trunk* | *She is a woman of substantial girth* (=she is fat). **2** [C] a band of leather that is passed tightly around the middle of a horse to keep a SADDLE or load firmly in position

gist /dʒɪst/ *n.* **the gist** the main idea or meaning of what someone has said or written: *I don't understand French very well, but I think I got the gist of* (=understood the main ideas of) *what she said.*

give[1] /ɡɪv/ *v. past tense* **gave** *past participle* **given**
1 put in sb's hand [T] to put something near someone or in their hand so that they can use it, hold it etc.: [**give sb sth**] *Here, give me your coat. I'll hang it up for you.* | [**give sth to sb**] *Give the keys to Daddy, Amanda.* | *I gave the money to her on Wednesday.*
2 provide [T] to provide or supply someone with a thing, a service etc.: [**give sb sth**] *Dan gave me a ride to work.* | *The doctor gave him something for the pain.* | *I wasn't given any help at all.* | [**give sth to sb**] *They gave the job to some guy from Texas.*
3 allow sb to have sth to allow someone to have an opportunity, a right, power etc.: [**give sb sth**] *They never gave me a chance to explain.* | *Women were given the right to vote in the early 1900s.* | [**give sth to sb**] *The plan gives control of the firm to an Indonesian company.*
4 present [T] to provide someone with something as a present: *What are you giving Mom for Christmas?* | [**give sb sth**] *Aunt Jo gave Alex a telescope.* | [**give sth to sb**] *He gave a dozen roses to his wife on their anniversary.* —see Usage Note at GIFT[2]
5 tell sb sth [T] to tell someone information or details about something: *The police asked him to give a description of the man.* | [**give sb sth**] *Would you give Kim a message for me?* | *Let me give you some advice.* | *He didn't give us any explanation for what he did.*
6 do an action a word used before some words that show action, meaning to do the action: *The boy gave Lynn a big smile.* | *Give me a call* (=telephone me) *at 8:00.* | *Come on, give Grandpa a hug.*
7 give sb trouble/problems etc. to do something that causes problems or makes a situation difficult for someone: *The machines in the lab are giving us*

trouble. | *Stop **giving** me **a hard time*** (=stop criticizing me).

8 **feeling** [T] to make someone have a particular physical or emotional feeling: [give sb sth] *The noise is giving me a headache.*

9 **illness** [T] to infect someone with the same illness you have: [give sb sth] *My husband gave me this cold.*

10 **give a speech/concert/performance etc.** to talk, play an instrument etc. in front of a group of people: *Yo Yo Ma gave a wonderful performance last night.*

11 **give sb/sth time** to allow a person or situation to have time to think, act, or develop: *Give her some time. She'll make the right decision.* | [give sb/sth time to do sth] *I need you to give me time to finish the report.*

12 **money** [I,T] to give money, food etc. in order to help others: *He gives generously to the church.* | [give sth to sb/sth] *They gave $25 to the Princess's memorial fund.*

13 **quality/shape etc.** [T not in progressive] to make someone have a particular quality, shape, look etc.: *The color of the room gives it a warm cozy feeling.* | *His new hairstyle gives him a youthful look.*

14 **give (sb) the impression/feeling etc.** to make someone have a particular idea or feeling about someone or something: *He gave me the impression that he wasn't happy with work.*

15 **pay** [T] to pay a particular amount of money for something: [give sb sth for sth] *I'll give you $75 for the oak desk.*

16 **bend/stretch** [I] if a material gives, it bends or stretches when you put pressure on it: *The leather will give slightly when you wear the boots.*

17 **give or take a few minutes/a mile/a penny etc.** used in order to show that a number or amount is not exact: *The show lasts about an hour, give or take five minutes.*

18 **give a party/dance etc.** to be the person who organizes a party, dance etc., especially at your own home: *Julie is giving a birthday party for Lori next Saturday.*

19 **give (sb/sth) credit/respect/priority etc.** to treat something or someone in a way that shows you think they have done something well, that they are important etc.: *You have to give him credit for taking charge of a difficult situation.* | *Top priority should be given to finishing on schedule.*

20 **produce an effect** [T] to produce a particular effect, solution, result etc.: *The field goal gave the team a two-point lead over Fullerton.*

21 **job** [T] to ask or tell someone to do a job or TASK: *Our English teacher always gives us a lot of homework.* | *If you're bored, I'll give you something to do.* | *Who **gave the order** to shoot?*

22 **give sth a try/shot/whirl** to try to do something: *Are you having trouble fixing the printer? Let me give it a shot.*

SPOKEN PHRASES

23 **not give a damn/shit etc.** INFORMAL an impolite phrase used to say that you do not care about something: *I don't give a damn what she thinks.*

24 **don't give me that!** INFORMAL said when you do not believe someone's excuse or explanation: *"I'm too tired." "Oh, don't give me that! You just don't want to come."*

25 **sb would give anything/a lot/their right arm etc.** said to emphasize that someone wants something very much: *I'd give anything to be able to get tickets to see the Rolling Stones.*

26 **give me sth (any day/time)** used to say that you like something much more than something else: *I don't like those fancy French desserts. Give me a bowl of chocolate ice cream any day.*

27 **I give it six weeks/a month etc.** used to say that you think that something is not going to continue successfully for very long: *They're moving in together? I give it about two months.*

28 **give it to sb** to angrily criticize or punish someone: *He's going to give it to you when he finds out.*

29 **change** [I] to be willing to change what you think or do in a situation according to what else

happens: *I'm willing to compromise somewhat, but he won't **give an inch** (=change what he thinks).*

30 **give it to me straight** used to ask someone to tell you something directly, even if it is upsetting or bad

31 **What gives?** used to ask someone what is happening when there is a problem: *"The security code I have for the gate doesn't work anymore." "What gives?"*

32 **give as good as you get** to fight or argue with someone, using the same amount of skill or force that they are using: *The youngest of three sons, Dave can give as good as he gets.*

33 **I'll give you that** used to say that you accept that something is true, even though you do not like it or disagree with other parts of it: *It's nice – I'll give you that – but I still wouldn't want to live there.*

34 **I give you the chairman/president/groom etc.** FORMAL used to introduce a special guest to an AUDIENCE

35 **give sb what for** OLD-FASHIONED, INFORMAL to tell someone angrily that you are annoyed with them

36 **give (sth) thought/attention/consideration etc.** to spend some time thinking about something carefully: *He is giving serious consideration to running again for president.* | *I'll give the matter some thought and let you know my decision next week.* | ***Don't give** it **a second thought** – I'll take care of everything.*

37 **judge** [T] to decide how much time a criminal will have to spend in prison: [give sb sth] *Jones was given thirty years for the murder.*

38 **be caring** [I] to be caring and generous, especially in a relationship: *She's looking for a man who knows how to give.*

39 **something has to give** used to say that a situation cannot remain as it is and that something must change: *With 800 refugees arriving every day, something has to give.*

40 **give (sb) a signal/sign etc.** to say or do something that tells someone what to do in a particular situation: *As he left the building, he gave the crowd a thumbs-up sign.*

41 **give sb a/the name** to name someone: *We gave him the nickname "Spanky."*

42 **telephone** [T] to make a telephone connection for someone: *Operator, could you give me extension 103, please?*

43 **have a baby** [T] OLD-FASHIONED to have a baby for a man: *She gave him three sons.*

44 **give sb to understand/believe that** FORMAL to make someone believe that something will happen or is true: *We never actually see the young woman in the play, but we are given to understand that she is unstable.*

45 **break** [I] also **give way** to break or fall down suddenly under pressure: *The branch suddenly gave beneath him.*

46 **sex** [T] OLD-FASHIONED if a woman gives herself to a man, she has sex with him

give away *phr. v.* [T] **1** [give sth ↔ away] to give something to someone instead of selling it: *I'm going to give some of these old clothes away.* | [give sth away to sb/sth] *The store is giving away a toaster to the first 50 customers.* **2** [give sb/sth ↔ away] to do or say something that shows thoughts or feelings that should be kept secret: *He said he hadn't told her, but his face gave him away* (=showed that he had told her). | *I was afraid the kids would give the surprise party away.* **3** [give sth ↔ away] to lose something in a competition by doing something silly or stupid: *Unfortunately, we did a lot of things to give the game away today.* | *I swear the Democrats are just giving away this election.* **4** [give sb ↔ away] when a man, especially the BRIDE's father, gives the bride away, he walks with her to the front of the church and formally gives permission for her to marry

give back *phr. v.* **1** [T give sth ↔ back] to return something to the person who owns it or who owned it before: [give sth back to sb] *Will you give this money back to Rich for me?* | [give sb back sth] *Give* me back my book. | [**give sb sth back**] *I want you to give her her dolls back.* **2** [I,T] to give something to someone or do something for them because they have helped you in the past: *Anytime you do volunteer work, you give back to the community.* | [**give** sth ↔ **back**] *I hope to give back to scouting what it has given me.* **3** [T **give** sth ↔ **back**] if you give someone back a quality or ability you make them have it again after they had lost it: *The operation gave him back his sight.*

give in *phr. v.* **1** [I] to agree to something you were unwilling to agree to before, especially after a long argument: *Randy asked her out for months before she finally gave in.* | [+ **to**] *We will never give in to terrorist demands.* **2** [I] to accept that you will be defeated and stop playing, fighting etc.: *Despite a bad first half, Iowa didn't give in and went on to win 85–65.*

give in to *phr. v.* [T] to stop being able to control a strong need, emotion, or desire: *They refuse to give in to despair.* | *Abby gave in to temptation and ate the ice cream.*

give of sth *phr. v.* [T] if you give of yourself, your time or money, you do things for other people without expecting them to do anything for you: *These professionals give of their free time to help poor children.*

give off sth *phr. v.* [T] to produce a smell, light, heat, a sound etc.: *People complain about the terrible smell that the factory gives off.*

give on/onto sth *phr. v.* [T not in passive] FORMAL if a window, door, building etc. gives on or onto a particular place, it leads to that place or you can see that place from it: *The door gave on a cement stairway leading down.*

give out

He gave out books to all the new students.

give out *phr. v.* **1** [T **give** sth ↔ **out**] to give something to a number of different people, especially to give them information: *She gave out copies of the report to the committee before the meeting.* | *You shouldn't have given my phone number out.* **2** [I] to stop working correctly: *My voice gave out halfway through the song.*

give over to *phr. v.* [T] **1 be given over to sth** to be used for a particular purpose: *The upstairs bedroom is given over to her collection of antique dolls.* **2 give yourself over to sth** also **give your life over to sth** to allow yourself or your life to be completely controlled by another person, a feeling, or an activity: *You have to give yourself over to football if you want to be good at it.* **3** [**give** sb/sth **over to** sb] to give the responsibility for something or someone to someone else: *His mother gave him over to his uncle's care when he was very small.*

give up *phr. v.*
1 stop trying [I,T] to stop trying to do something or work at something, especially something difficult, without completing it: *I looked everywhere for the keys – finally I just gave up.* | [**give up doing sth**] *Vladimir has given up trying to teach her Russian.*
2 stop doing [I,T **give** sth ↔ **up**] to stop doing or

having something, especially something that you do or have regularly: *She gave up her job, and started writing full time.* | *Ed has given up his dream of becoming a professional athlete.* | [**give up doing sth**] *I gave up smoking when I got pregnant.*
3 I give up SPOKEN used when you do not know the answer to a question or joke: *"Why did the chicken cross the road?" "I give up. Why?"*
4 to police [T **give** sb **up**] to allow yourself or someone else to be caught by the police or enemy soldiers: *One of the accomplices gave himself up to police on Thursday.*
5 let sb have [T **give** sb/sth ↔ **up**] to let someone else have something that is yours: *Peggy gave up her seat to an old woman on the bus.* | *She gave up her first child for adoption.*
6 give it up (for sb) SPOKEN, INFORMAL to APPLAUD (=hit your open hands together) for someone: *Come on everybody, let's give it up for Elton John!*
7 give time [T **give** sth **up**] to agree to use your free time to do something else: *Carol has generously given up two evenings a week to help us on this project.*
8 end a relationship [T **give** sb ↔ **up**] to end a relationship with someone, especially a romantic relationship: *He's started going out with Leslie, but he doesn't want to give up his old girlfriend.*
9 give sb up for dead/lost etc. to believe that someone is dead and stop looking for them: *The ship sank and the crew was given up for dead.* —see also **give up the ghost** (GHOST¹ (4))

give up on sb/sth *phr. v.* [T] to stop hoping that someone will change their behavior, that something will happen etc.: *I'd been in trouble so many times that my teachers had given up on me.*

give way *phr. v.* **1** [I] to break because of too much weight or pressure: *More than 50 homes were flooded when the dam gave way.* **2 give way to sth** to change to something newer, better, or different: *After television, many movie houses closed down, giving way to smaller theaters.* | *As the days grew shorter, October gave way to November.* **3** [I] to agree to do what someone else wants to do, instead of what you wanted to do: *It is unlikely that either side will give way in the dispute over the islands.* **4** [I] to YIELD¹ (4)

give² *n.* [U] the ability of a material to bend or stretch when it is under pressure: *This skirt doesn't have a lot of give to it.*

give-and-take, give and take /ˌ. . '. './ *n.* [U] a situation in which two people or groups are each willing to let the other have or do some of the things they want: *In every successful marriage there is a certain amount of give and take.*

give·a·way¹ /ˈgɪvəˌweɪ/ *n. plural* **giveaways 1** [C] an act of giving something away: *At the church they're having a holiday giveaway of clothes and toys.* **2** [C] something that is given away for free, especially a product, prize etc. that a store or company gives to its customers **3 be a dead giveaway** to be something that makes it easy for you to guess something: *Vince was lying. His red face was a dead giveaway.*

giveaway² *adj.* [only before noun] giveaway prices are extremely low

give·back /ˈgɪvbæk/ *n.* [C] a reduction of pay or other advantages that a union accepts for its members because the economic situation is bad or because they are given other advantages

giv·en¹ /ˈgɪvən/ *v.* the past participle of GIVE

given² *adj.* [only before noun] **1 any/a given...** any particular time, idea, thing etc. that is being used as an example: *On any given day in the Houston area, half the hospital beds are empty.* **2 a given time,** date, place etc. is one that has been determined or agreed on: *They didn't meet me at the given time.* **3 be given to (doing) sth** to tend to do something, especially something that you should not do: *Some adults are still given to temper tantrums.*

given³ *prep.* used to say that something is not surprising when you consider the situation it happened in; CONSIDERING¹: *Given the number of people we invited, I'm surprised so few came.* | [+ **that**] *I think*

G

I did all right, given that I didn't study much for the test.

given[4] *n.* **a given** a basic fact that you accept as being true: *Sandra will be at least 15 minutes late – that's a given.*

given name /'.. ,./ *n.* [C] your FIRST NAME

giv·ing /'gɪvɪŋ/ *adj.* kind, caring, and generous: *She's a very giving person.*

giz·mo, **gismo** /'gɪzmoʊ/ *n. plural* **gizmos** [C] INFORMAL a GADGET

giz·zard /'gɪzəd/ *n.* [C] an organ near a bird's stomach that helps it break down food

gla·cial /'gleɪʃəl/ *adj.* **1** relating to ice or glaciers or formed by glaciers: *a glacial valley* **2** a glacial look or expression is extremely unfriendly **3** extremely cold: *a glacial wind* —**glacially** *adv.*

gla·ci·a·tion /ˌgleɪʃi'eɪʃən, -si-/ *n.* [U] TECHNICAL the process in which land is covered by glaciers, or the effect this process has

gla·cier /'gleɪʃə/ *n.* [C] a large mass of ice that moves slowly over an area of land

s w
glad[1] /glæd/ *adj.* **gladder**, **gladdest 1** [not before noun] happy or satisfied about something: [glad (that)] *We're really glad that you kids could come home for Christmas.* | [glad to do sth] *I'm glad to hear that you're feeling better.* | [glad when] *We'll be glad when this is all over.* | [+ for/about] *He's glad for the opportunity to practice his English.* | **glad to be alive/healthy etc.** *I'm glad to be home.* **2 be glad to do sth** to be willing to do something: *He said he'd be glad to help me.* **3 be glad of sth** OLD-FASHIONED to be grateful for something: *The weather's been great, and I'm glad of that.* **4** making people feel happy: *It was a glad day for everyone.* **5 glad tidings** OLD-FASHIONED OR BIBLICAL good news —see also GLAD-HAND, GLADLY —see Usage Note at HAPPY —**gladness** *n.* [U]

glad[2] *n.* [C] INFORMAL a GLADIOLA

glad·den /'glædn/ *v.* [T] also **gladden sb's heart** OLD-FASHIONED to make someone feel pleased and happy: *It gladdens me to see young people doing volunteer work.*

glade /gleɪd/ *n.* [C] LITERARY a small open space inside a forest —compare MEADOW

glad-hand /'. ./ *v.* [I,T] to give someone a very friendly welcome or be nice to them, especially when this is not sincere: *Studio executives were busy glad-handing each other after the awards ceremony.*

glad·i·a·tor /'glædi,eɪtə/ *n.* [C] a strong man who fought other men or animals as a public event in ancient Rome —**gladiatorial** /ˌglædiə'tɔriəl/ *adj.*

glad·i·o·la /ˌglædi'oʊlə/ also **glad·i·o·lus** /ˌglædi'oʊləs/ *n. plural* **gladiolas** or **gladioli** /-laɪ/ [C] a garden plant with long leaves and many brightly colored flowers that grow on a long stem

glad·ly /'glædli/ *adv.* **1** willingly or eagerly: *My parents would gladly loan us the money.* **2** happily: *"Here's Michelle!" he said gladly*

glad rags /'. ./ *n.* [plural] OLD-FASHIONED your best clothes that you wear for special occasions

Glad·stone /'glædstoʊn/**, Wil·liam Ew·art** /'wɪlyəm 'yuərt/ (1809–1898) a British politician, who was Prime Minister four times (1868–74, 1880–85, 1836, 1892–94)

glam·or /'glæmə/ *n.* [U] another spelling of GLAMOUR

glam·or·ize /'glæmə,raɪz/ *v.* [T] to make something seem more attractive or exciting than it really is: *Hollywood has always glamorized drinking.* —**glamorization** /ˌglæmərə'zeɪʃən/ *n.* [U]

glam·or·ous /'glæmərəs/ *adj.* attractive, exciting, and relating to wealth and success: *On television she looks so beautiful and glamorous.* | *glamorous clothes*

glam·our, **glamor** /'glæmə/ *n.* **1** [U] the exciting attractive quality that is related to rich, famous, or fashionable people, places, jobs etc.: *Actress Marlene Dietrich was once the ultimate symbol of glamour and elegance.* | [+ of] *The thrill and glamour of traveling the world for tennis tournaments has faded for her.* **2 a glamour girl/boy** someone who is young, attractive, and wears glamorous clothes

glance[1] /glæns/ *v.* [I always + adv./prep.] **1** to quickly look at someone or something: [+ at/toward/up etc.] *He glanced at his watch.* | *Gary glanced over his shoulder to see if anyone was following him.* **2** to read something very quickly: [+ at/over etc.] *Susan glanced at the menu and ordered a ham sandwich.*

glance off *phr. v.* [I,T] **1** to hit a surface at an angle and then move away from it in another direction: *The bullet glanced off the side of the car.* **2** if light glances off something, it flashes or shines on it: *The beam of his flashlight glanced off something metallic in the water.*

USAGE NOTE: GLANCE

WORD CHOICE: glance, take a quick look, glimpse, catch/get a glimpse of

If you **glance** at something, you look at it quickly: *She glanced at the clock and saw it was five o'clock already.* In spoken English you often use **take a (quick) look**, especially to check if something is correct or working correctly: *Could you just take a quick look at the engine for me?* If you **glimpse** (or more commonly **catch/get a glimpse of**) someone or something, you see them by chance, for a very short time: *I'm not sure what he was wearing. I only caught a glimpse of him as he was leaving.*

---

glance[2] *n.* **1** [C] an occasion when you look quickly at someone or something: *He gave her a glance as she walked by.* | *The sisters exchanged glances* (=looked at each other quickly) *and started to laugh.* | **take/shoot/throw a glance at sb** *She shot a glance at the man behind her.* **2 at a glance a)** in a short form that is easy to see or read quickly: *Here are the weekend football scores at a glance.* **b)** as soon as you see or look at something: *I saw at a glance that the place was full of police.* **3 at first glance** when you see or think about something for the first time: *At first glance, the paintings all look the same.*

glanc·ing /'glænsɪŋ/ *adj.* **a glancing blow** a hit that partly misses, so that it does not have its full force

glanc·ing·ly /'glænsɪŋli/ *adv.* if you talk or write about something glancingly, you do not talk or write about it much, or you do so in an indirect way: *The main problem only glancingly mentioned in the article.*

gland /glænd/ *n.* [C] an organ of the body that produces a liquid substance that the body needs, for example HORMONES, SWEAT, or SALIVA: *The doctor noticed that the glands in my neck were swollen.* —**glandular** /'glændʒələ/ *adj.*

glare[1] /glɛr/ *v.* [I] **1** to angrily look at someone or something for a long time: [+ at] *Lilly just glared at me when I asked her what was wrong.* **2** [always + adv./prep.] to shine with such a strong light that it hurts your eyes: [+ through/in/off] *Sunlight glared off the shiny hood of the car.*

glare[2] *n.* **1** [singular,U] a light that is too bright and hurts your eyes: *the glare from the skylight* | *Polarized sunglasses reduce glare.* **2** [C] a long angry look: *She gave him an icy glare.* **3 the glare of publicity** also **the glare of the national/international etc. spotlight** the full attention of newspapers, television etc., especially when you do not want it: *Williams goes to trial under the glare of the national spotlight.*

glare screen /'. ./ *n.* [C] a piece of glass that is put in front of a computer screen to protect your eyes from the strong light that comes from it

glar·ing /'glɛrɪŋ/ *adj.* **1** very bad and very easy to notice: **a glaring mistake/error/omission etc.** *The report contained a number of glaring errors.* **2** too bright to look at: *the glaring sun*

glar·ing·ly /'glɛrɪŋli/ *adv.* in a way that is very clear and easy to notice: *Some of the clues were glaringly obvious.*

G

Glas·gow /ˈglæsgoʊ, ˈglæz-/ the largest city in Scotland

glas·nost /ˈglæznoʊst, ˈglɑz-/ n. [U] the POLICY begun by Mikhail Gorbachev during the 1980s in the former USSR that allowed discussion of the country's political, economic, and social problems

glasses

shot glass

snifter

glass

wine glass

s w **glass** /glæs/ n.
1 1

1 transparent material [U] a hard transparent material that is used for making windows, bottles etc.: *a glass bowl*

2 for drinking [C] a container without a handle that you use for drinking liquids and that is usually made out of glass: *wine glasses*

3 amount of liquid [C] the amount of a drink contained in a glass: [+ of] *Would you like a glass of milk?*

4 for eyes **glasses** [plural] two pieces of specially cut glass or plastic in a FRAME that you wear in front of your eyes to see better: *I need a new pair of glasses.* —see also DARK GLASSES, FIELD GLASSES, OPERA GLASSES, SUNGLASSES

5 glass objects [U] objects made of glass: *an impressive collection of Venetian glass*

6 people (who live) in glass houses shouldn't throw stones used to say that you should not criticize someone for having a fault if you have the same fault yourself

7 mirror [C] OLD USE a mirror —see also CUT GLASS, GROUND GLASS, LOOKING GLASS, MAGNIFYING GLASS, PLATE GLASS, **raise your glass (to sth)** (RAISE[1] (16)), SPY-GLASS, STAINED GLASS

Glass /glæs/**, Phil·ip** /ˈfɪlɪp/ (1937–) a U.S. musician who writes modern CLASSICAL music and is known for his MINIMALIST style

glass·blow·er /ˈglæsˌbloʊɚ/ n. [C] someone who shapes hot glass by blowing air through a tube

glass ceil·ing /ˌ. ˈ../ n. [singular] the attitudes and practices that prevent women or people from MINOR-ITY groups from getting high level jobs, even though there are no actual laws or rules to stop them

glassed-in /ˌglæst ˈɪn◂/ adj. surrounded by a glass structure: *a glassed-in back porch*

glass·ful /ˈglæsfʊl/ n. [C] the amount of liquid a glass will hold

glass·ware /ˈglæswɛr/ n. [U] glass objects, especially containers that you drink from

glass·y /ˈglæsi/ adj. **glassier, glassiest 1** smooth and shiny, like glass: *the glassy surface of the lake* **2** glassy eyes are shiny, do not move, and do not show any expression

glassy-eyed /ˈ.. ˌ./ adj. having eyes that do not move or show any expression, because you are tired, sick, or taking drugs: *Many of the students were glassy-eyed from studying all night.*

glau·co·ma /glaʊˈkoʊmə, glɔ-/ n. [U] an eye disease in which increased pressure inside your eye gradually makes you lose your ability to see

glaze[1] /gleɪz/ v. **1** [I] also **glaze over** if your eyes

glaze over, they show no expression because you are very bored or tired: *By the second chapter, your eyes begin to glaze.* **2** [T] to cover fruit, cake, or meat with a liquid that gives it an attractive shiny surface: *The rolls are glazed with egg before they are baked.* **3** [T] to cover clay pots, bowls etc. with a thin liquid that is then dried in a very hot OVEN, in order to give them a shiny surface: *We later learned that the dishes had not been properly glazed.* **4** [T] to cover something such as a road with a thin layer of ice: *Temperatures fell suddenly, glazing all highways in the region.* **5** [T] to put glass into window frames in a house, door etc.

glaze[2] n. **1** [C,U] a liquid that is put on clay pots, bowls etc. and then dried in a hot OVEN, in order to give them a shiny surface **2** [C,U] a liquid that is put on fruit, cake, or meat to give it an attractive shiny surface **3** [C] a thin layer of ice, for example on a road **4** [C,U] a transparent covering of oil paint spread over a painting

glazed /gleɪzd/ adj. **glazed look/eyes/expression etc.** if you have a glazed look, eyes etc., your eyes show no expression, usually because you are very bored or tired

gla·zier /ˈgleɪʒɚ, -ziɚ/ n. [C] someone whose job is to put glass into window frames

glaz·ing /ˈgleɪzɪŋ/ n. [U] glass that has been put into windows, or the activity of putting glass in windows

gleam[1] /glim/ v. [I] **1** if something gleams, it throws back light, especially because it is clean or has been polished: *The old walnut dining table gleamed under the chandelier.* | [+ with] *The engine gleamed with oil.* **2** if your eyes or face gleam, they show that something pleases you: *John's face gleamed as he thought of his plan for revenge.* | [+ with] *Her eyes gleamed with amusement.* —**gleaming** adj.: *gleaming new silverware*

gleam[2] n. **1** [C usually singular] the shiny quality that something, especially something polished, has when light shines on it: [+ of] *I noticed a gleam of gold from his watch.* **2** [C usually singular] an expression that appears for a moment on someone's face or in their eyes, or a sudden strong emotion that they feel: [+ of] *There was a gleam of happiness on his face.* | *I could tell by the gleam in her eyes that something good had happened.* | *Avis walked down the aisle with a gleam in his eye* (=showing that he was happy or amused). **3** [C usually singular] a small pale light, especially one that shines for a short time: [+ of] *They saw the gleam of the lighthouse in the distance.* **4 sth was (just) a gleam in sb's eye** SPOKEN used to say that at a particular time in the past something did not exist, or to emphasize how new something is: *Back then, CD-ROMs were just a gleam in the eye of some young engineer.* **5 sb was (just) a gleam in sb's father's/daddy's eye** SPOKEN used to say that at a particular time in the past someone was not yet born, or to emphasize how young they are: *You weren't even a gleam in your father's eye when I was out fighting a war.*

glean /glin/ v. **1** [T] to find out information, even though this is difficult and takes time: [glean sth from sb/sth] *Several lessons can be gleaned from our experience so far.* **2** [I,T] to collect grain that has been left behind in a field after the crops have been cut

glean·ings /ˈglinɪŋz/ n. [plural] **1** small pieces of information that you have found out, even though doing this was difficult **2** grain that is left behind in a field after the crops have been cut, which is then collected

glee /gli/ n. [U] a feeling of happy excitement and satisfaction: *The kids shouted with glee when they saw Santa.*

glee club /ˈ. ./ n. [C] a group of people who sing together for enjoyment

glee·ful /ˈglifəl/ adj. happily excited and satisfied: *A gleeful grin crossed his face.* —**gleefully** adv

glen /glɛn/ n. [C] LITERARY a deep narrow valley

Glenn /glɛn/**, John** (1921–) a U.S. ASTRONAUT who became the first American to make a journey in space in 1962 —see picture on page 1329

glib /glɪb/ adj. **glibber, glibbest 1** said without thinking about all the problems in something, or about how your remarks will affect someone: *The doctor made some glib comment about my headaches being "just stress."* **2** speaking easily and smoothly, but usually not sincerely, and without considering things carefully: *All of those glib egotistical talk show hosts annoy me.* —**glibly** adv.

glide[1] /glaɪd/ v. **1** [I always + adv./prep.] to move smoothly and quietly, as if no effort is being made: [+ across/over etc.] *We watched the sailboats glide across the lake.* **2** [I always + adv./prep.,T] to fly without engine power, or to make something fly in this way: *He glided the aircraft into a vacant field.* | *The plane glided through heavy clouds.* **3** [I always + adv./prep.] to smoothly move from one subject, activity, song etc. to another without stopping: *The pianist glided easily from a Billy Joel song into "Make Believe Rag."*

glide[2] n. [C] **1** a smooth, quiet movement that seems to take no effort: *They danced with sweeping gestures and romantic glides.* **2** the act of moving from one musical note to another without a break in sound **3** TECHNICAL a vowel sound which is made by moving your tongue from one position to another one, for example "i" /aɪ/ —see also DIPHTHONG

glid·er /ˈglaɪdɚ/ n. [C] a light airplane without an engine

glid·ing /ˈglaɪdɪŋ/ n. [U] the sport of flying in a glider —see also HANG GLIDING

glim·mer[1] /ˈglɪmɚ/ n. [U] **1 a glimmer of hope/doubt/recognition** a small sign of hope, doubt etc.: *There is a glimmer of hope that the war may be over soon.* **2** a light that does not shine very brightly: *the glimmer of a candle*

glimmer[2] v. [I] to shine weakly with a pale light: *A light glimmered at the end of the hall.*

glim·mer·ing /ˈglɪmərɪŋ/ n. [C often plural] a small sign of something such as a thought or feeling: *We are now witnessing the first glimmerings of democracy in that part of the world.*

glimpse[1] /glɪmps/ n. [C] **1** a quick look at someone or something that does not allow you to see them clearly: **get/catch a glimpse of** *Dad only caught a glimpse of the guy who stole our car.* —see Usage Note at GLANCE[2] **2** a short experience of understanding that helps you begin to understand it: *The exhibit gives us a glimpse of what life might be like in the future.*

glimpse[2] v. [T] **1** to see someone or something for a moment, without getting a complete view of them: *From the corner of my eye, I glimpsed a man running out of the store.* **2** to begin to understand something for a moment: *He glimpsed the despair that she must have felt.* —see Usage Note at GLANCE[1]

glint[1] /glɪnt/ v. [I] **1** if something that is shiny or smooth glints, it flashes or throws back a small amount of light: *His badge glinted in the evening sun.* **2** if your eyes glint, they shine and show an unfriendly feeling: *Derek's eyes glinted when he saw the money.* **3** if light glints off or on something shiny or smooth, it is thrown back off it and flashes: [+ off/on] *The full moon glints off the polished granite.*

glint[2] n. [C] **1** a small flash of light that shines or is thrown back off something smooth or shiny: *the glint of his gold watch* **2** a look in someone's eyes that shows a particular emotion: *I saw the glint of hope in her eyes.*

glis·san·do /glɪˈsɑndoʊ/ n. [C] TECHNICAL a smooth series of musical notes that is played, for example, by sliding a finger rapidly over the keys of a piano —**glissando** adj. adv.

glis·ten /ˈglɪsən/ v. [I] to shine and look wet or oily: *Blood glistened on the jaguar's shoulder.* | [+ with] *His chest was glistening with sweat.*

glitch /glɪtʃ/ n. [C] **1** a small problem that prevents something from working correctly: *Company records were lost due to a computer glitch.* **2** a sudden change or increase in the supply of electric power

glit·ter[1] /ˈglɪtɚ/ v. [I] to shine with a lot of small flashes of light: *Fresh snow glittered in the morning light.*

glitter[2] n. [U] **1** a lot of small flashes of light: *the glitter of her diamond necklace* **2** very small pieces of shiny plastic or metal that you glue onto paper, cards etc. for decoration **3** the exciting attractive quality of a place, way of life etc. that is related to rich, famous, or fashionable people, but is often false: *the glitter of L.A.* —**glittery** adj.

glit·te·ra·ti /ˌglɪtəˈrɑti/ n. [plural] rich, famous, and fashionable people whose activities are often reported in newspapers and magazines

glit·ter·ing /ˈglɪtərɪŋ/ adj. **1** giving off many small flashes of light: *glittering jewels* **2** very successful, and often relating to rich, important, or famous people: *a glittering career in the diplomatic service* —**glitteringly** adv.

glitz /glɪts/ n. [U] DISAPPROVING an exciting and attractive quality that something or someone rich, famous, or fashionable has, that there is too much of: *show business glitz* —**glitzy** adj.

gloam·ing /ˈgloʊmɪŋ/ n. [U] **the gloaming** POETIC the time in the early evening when it is becoming dark; DUSK

gloat /gloʊt/ v. [I] to show in an annoying way that you are proud of your success, or happy about someone else's failure: [+ over] *Jason's still gloating over beating me at chess.*

glob /glɑb/ n. [C] INFORMAL a small amount of a soft substance or thick liquid, that has a round shape: *a glob of ketchup*

glob·al /ˈgloʊbəl/ adj. **1** affecting the whole world, or relating to the whole world: *AIDS is a global problem which needs a global response.* **2** considering all parts of a problem or a situation together: *We've done a global study on the company's weaknesses.* **3** affecting a whole computer system, program, or FILE: *a global search* **4 global village** a word that means the world, which is used to say that the world is very small and we all must depend on each other: *In today's global village, events in Japan or Kuwait affect everyone.* —**globally** adv.

glob·al·i·za·tion /ˌgloʊbələˈzeɪʃən/ n. [U] the process of making something such as a business international, or the result of this: *the globalization of world markets* —**globalize** /ˈgloʊbəˌlaɪz/ v. [I,T]

global warm·ing /ˌ.. ˈ../ n. [U] a general increase in world temperatures caused by increased amounts of CARBON DIOXIDE around the Earth

globe /gloʊb/ n. [C] **1 the globe** the world: *Our company has offices all around the globe.* **2** a round object with a map of the Earth on it **3** an object shaped like a ball; SPHERE

globe·trot·ter /ˈgloʊbˌtrɑtɚ/ n. [C] INFORMAL someone who travels to many different countries —**globetrotting** adj.

glob·u·lar /ˈglɑbyəlɚ/ adj. in the shape of a globule or a globe

glob·ule /ˈglɑbyul/ n. [C] a small round drop of a liquid or a melted substance: *tiny globules of mercury*

glob·u·lin /ˈglɑbyəlɪn/ n. [U] TECHNICAL one of a type of PROTEINS that are found in blood, muscle, milk, and plants —see also GAMMA GLOBULIN

glock·en·spiel /ˈglɑkənˌspil, -ˌʃpil/ n. [C] a musical instrument consisting of many flat metal bars of different lengths, which is played with special hammers

glom /glɑm/ v. **glommed, glomming** INFORMAL
glom onto sb/sth phr. v. **1** to attach to someone or something in such a strong way that it is difficult to break the attachment: *Researchers found that the antibodies glom onto the virus and destroy it.* **2** to be very attracted to an idea, opinion, style etc. and give it a lot of importance: *College students have glommed onto the new African styles.*

gloom /glum/ n. [singular,U] **1** LITERARY darkness that you can hardly see through: *He couldn't read in the dim gloom of the warehouse.* **2** a feeling of great sadness and lack of hope: *There was a sense of gloom in the city after the team's loss.*

gloom·y /ˈglumi/ *adj.* **gloomier, gloomiest 1** making you feel sad because things will not improve: *a gloomy economic forecast* **2** dark, especially in a way that makes you feel sad **3** sad because you do not have a lot of hope: *Professor Vardell was a gloomy man who never smiled.* —**gloomily** *adv.* —**gloominess** *n.* [U]

glop /glɑp/ *n.* [U] INFORMAL a thick soft wet mass, especially of something disgusting: *We were served some lukewarm glop with tuna in it.* —**gloppy** *adj.*

glo·ri·fied /ˈglɔrəˌfaɪd/ *adj.* [only before noun] made to seem like something more important: *My title is "Editorial Assistant," but I'm really just a glorified secretary.*

glo·ri·fy /ˈglɔrəˌfaɪ/ *v.* **glorifies, glorified, glorifying** [T] **1** to make someone or something seem more important or better than they really are: *Movies that glorify violence may be responsible for some of the rise in crime.* **2** to praise someone or something important, especially God: *Everyone was on their knees glorifying and praising God.* —**glorification** /ˌglɔrəfəˈkeɪʃən/ *n.* [U] [+ of] *the glorification of war*

glo·ri·ous /ˈglɔriəs/ *adj.* **1** having or deserving great FAME, praise, or honor: *a glorious victory* **2** beautiful or extremely nice: *It was a glorious day* (=beautiful sunny weather)*!* | *We spent six glorious days in Acapulco.* | *glorious fall colors* —**gloriously** *adv.*

glo·ry¹ /ˈglɔri/ *n. plural* **glories 1** [U] the importance, praise, and honor that people give someone they admire: *At 19 he won glory as an Olympic champion.* | *Someone in the church shouted out, "Glory to God!"* **2** [C] something that is especially beautiful or admired, or that makes you feel proud: *The designs reflect the glories of French fashion.* | *Becoming a Supreme Court judge was the crowning glory* (=the final most successful part) *of her legal career.* **3** [U] a beautiful and impressive appearance: *They spent $10 million restoring the Grand Theater to its former glory.* | *The sun emerged from behind the clouds in all its glory.* **4 glory days** a time in the past when someone was admired: *I fondly remember our glory days on the high school football team.* **5 to the (greater) glory of sb/sth** FORMAL in order to increase the honor that is given to someone or something: *Bach composed to the greater glory of God.* **6 go to glory** OLD USE to die —see also **bask in sb's reflected glory** (BASK (2))

glo·ry² *v.* **glories, gloried, glorying**
glory in sth *phr. v.* [T not in passive] LITERARY to enjoy or be proud of the praise, attention, and success that you get: *The new mayor gloried in his win.*

gloss¹ /glɔs, glɑs/ *n.* **1** [singular,U] a shiny, attractive brightness on a surface: *This hair gel is guaranteed to add gloss even to the dullest hair.* | *walls painted gloss white* | **polish/shine to a high gloss** *The silverware had been polished to a high gloss.* **2** [C] an explanation of a piece of writing, especially in a note at the end of a page or book: *a helpful gloss on Shakespeare's sonnet* **3** [singular,U] a pleasant appearance of something, which is better than the truth: *The regime held elections in October, giving itself a gloss of democracy.* **4 gloss finish/print/paint etc.** a surface, photograph, paint etc. that is shiny —compare MATTE —see also LIP GLOSS

gloss² *v.* [T] to provide an explanation of a piece of writing, especially in a note at the end of a page or book
gloss over sth *phr. v.* [T] to deliberately avoid talking about unfavorable facts or say as little as possible about them: *The report glossed over the company's financial problems.*

glos·sa·ry /ˈglɔsəri, ˈglɑ-/ *n. plural* **glossaries** [C] a list of special words and explanations of what they mean, written at the end of the book

gloss·y¹ /ˈglɔsi/ *adj.* **glossier, glossiest 1** shiny and smooth: *glossy black hair* **2 a glossy magazine/brochure etc.** a magazine etc. that is printed on

good quality, shiny paper, usually with lots of color pictures **3** something is glossy if it is designed to look attractive or perfect, even though it is not really this way: *Film critics are calling the movie a glossy melodrama.* —**glossiness** *n.* [U]

glossy² *n. plural* **glossies** [C] a photograph printed on shiny paper: *an 8" by 10" glossy of Frank Sinatra*

glot·tal stop /ˌglɑtl ˈstɑp/ *n.* [C] TECHNICAL a speech sound made by completely closing and then opening your glottis, which in some forms of spoken English may take the place of a /t/ between vowel sounds or may be used before a vowel sound

glot·tis /ˈglɑtɪs/ *n.* [C] the space between your VOCAL CORDS, which produces the sound of your voice by movements in which this space is opened and closed —**glottal** *adj.*

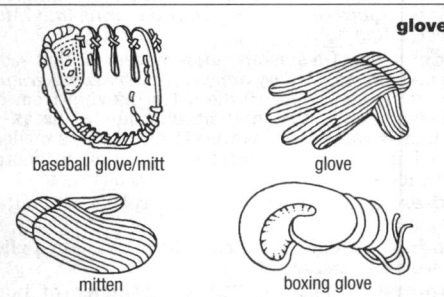

gloves

baseball glove/mitt   glove

mitten   boxing glove

glove /glʌv/ *n.* [C] **1** a piece of clothing worn on your hand, with separate parts to cover your thumb and each finger —compare MITTEN **2** a large leather glove used in BOXING, which does not have separate parts for your fingers **3** a large leather glove used to catch the ball in BASEBALL —see also **fit like a glove** (FIT¹ (1))

glove com·part·ment /ˈ. .,../ also **glove box** /ˈ. ./ *n.* [C] a small cupboard in a car in front of the passenger seat, where small things such as maps can be kept —see picture on page 427

gloved /glʌvd/ *adj.* wearing a glove or gloves

glow¹ /gloʊ/ *n.* [singular] **1** a soft steady light: *The golden glow of candlelight gives a room a romantic atmosphere.* | *the green glow of my computer monitor* **2** the bright color your face or body has because you are healthy, proud, or very happy: *She always had a healthy glow about her.* **3 a glow of pleasure/satisfaction/happiness etc.** a strong feeling of pleasure, satisfaction etc. **4** brightness of color, especially colors such as red and orange: *the glow of copper pans*

glow² *v.* [I] **1** to shine with, REFLECT, or produce a soft, steady light: *The church walls glowed in the candlelight.* **2 glow in the dark** if something glows in the dark, it produces a soft light in the dark: *The golfers will play the evening game with balls that glow in the dark.* **3 glow with pride/joy/pleasure etc.** to look very happy because you feel proud, good etc. **4** if your face or body glows, it is red or hot because of exercise or strong emotion —see also GLOW-IN-THE-DARK

glow·er /ˈglaʊɚ/ *v.* [I] to look at someone in an angry way: [+ at] *Mrs. Smith glowered at the boys until they were quiet.* —**gloweringly** *adv.*

glow·ing /ˈgloʊɪŋ/ *adj.* **1 glowing report/recommendation/description etc.** a report, RECOMMENDATION etc. that is full of praise: *The play has received glowing reviews in the local papers.* **2 in glowing terms** using a lot of praise: *The two men speak of their friendship in glowing terms.* —**glowingly** *adv.*

glow-in-the-dark /ˌ. . ˈ.◂/ *adj.* **a glow-in-the-dark ring/ball/toy etc.** a glow-in-the-dark ring, ball etc. can be seen in the dark because it produces a soft light

glow·worm /ˈgloʊwɚm/ *n.* [C] an insect that produces a small amount of light from its body

glu·cose /ˈglukoʊs/ *n.* [U] a natural form of sugar that exists in fruit

glue¹ /glu/ *n.* [C,U] a sticky substance used for joining things together

glue² *v. present participle* **gluing** *or* **glueing** [T] **1** to join two things together using a special sticky substance: [**glue sth (back) together**] *I think we can glue the lamp back together.* | [**glue sth to sth**] *Who glued my pen to the desk?* **2 be glued to sth** INFORMAL **a)** to look at something with all your attention: *Dad was glued to the TV all day long.* **b)** to not move because you are very interested, surprised, frightened etc.: *We were glued to our chairs and listening intently to every word.*

glue snif·fing /'. ,../ *n.* [U] the act or habit of breathing in dangerous gases from glues or similar substances in order to produce an artificial state of excitement or happiness —**glue sniffer** *n.* [C]

glu·ey /'glui/ *adj.* **1** sticky like glue **2** covered with glue

glum /glʌm/ *adj.* **glummer, glummest** sad and quiet, especially because you are upset about something; GLOOMY: *On the day of the funeral, the mood in the house was glum.*

glut¹ /glʌt/ *n.* [C usually singular] a supply of something that is more than you need: [+ **of**] *a glut of new cars on the market*

glut² *v. past tense and past participle* **glutted** *present participle* **glutting** [T] to make something have too much of something: [**be glutted with sth**] *Many downtown areas are glutted with half-empty office buildings.* | *Overproduction in Norway is glutting the market with fish.*

glu·ten /'glutⁿ/ *n.* [U] a sticky PROTEIN substance that is found in wheat flour

glu·ti·nous /'glutⁿ-əs/ *adj.* very sticky

glut·ton /'glʌtⁿ/ *n.* [C] **1** someone who eats too much **2 a glutton for punishment** someone who seems to enjoy working hard or doing something unenjoyable —**gluttonous** *adj.*

glut·ton·y /'glʌtⁿ-i/ *n.* [U] FORMAL the bad habit of eating and drinking too much

glyc·er·in, glycerine /'glɪsərɪn/ *n.* [U] a thick colorless liquid used in soaps, medicines, explosives, and foods

glyc·er·ol /'glɪsə,rɔl/ *n.* [U] TECHNICAL a chemical substance that is used to make foods sweeter and is used in products such as soap and explosives

GMAT *n.* [U] TRADEMARK Graduate Management Admissions Test; a test that you take when you APPLY to study in a business program at a university after you have finished your first degree

GMO *n.* [C] genetically modified organism; a plant or other living thing whose GENES have been changed by scientists in order to make it stronger, less likely to get diseases etc. —**GMO** *adj.* [only before noun] *GMO crops*

GMT *n.* [U] Greenwich Mean Time; the time as measured at Greenwich in London, England, that is used as an international standard for measuring time

gnarled /narld/ *adj.* **1** a gnarled tree or branch is rough and twisted **2** gnarled hands or fingers are twisted, rough, and difficult to move, usually because they are old

gnarl·y /'narli/ *adj.* SLANG **1** a word meaning "very good" or "excellent," used by young people: *"Look at the size of that wave." "Gnarly!"* **2** a word meaning "very bad," used by young people: *On the way home, there was a gnarly car wreck on the side of the road.*

gnash /næʃ/ *v.* [T] LITERARY **gnash your teeth** to move your teeth against each other so that they make a noise, especially because you are unhappy or angry

gnat /næt/ *n.* [C] a small flying insect that bites

gnaw /nɔ/ *v.* [I always + adv./prep.,T] to keep biting something hard: [+ **away/at/on**] *The puppy sat in the corner and gnawed on a bone.* | [**gnaw sth**] *A rat had gnawed a hole in the box.*

gnaw at sb *phr. v.* [T] to make someone feel worried or frightened: *The thought of being fired gnawed at him all day.*

gnaw·ing /'nɔ-ɪŋ/ *adj.* [only before noun] worrying or

painful, especially for a long time: *a gnawing dissatisfaction with day-to-day life*

gnome /noum/ *n.* [C] **1** a creature in children's stories who looks like a little old man and lives under the ground **2** a stone or plastic figure representing one of these creatures: *a garden gnome* **3** someone who helps decide financial plans in a country: *the gnomes who work in the U.S. Treasury*

gno·mic /'noumɪk/ *adj.* gnomic remarks are short, intelligent, and difficult to understand

GNP *n.* [singular] the abbreviation of GROSS NATIONAL PRODUCT

gnu /nu/ *n.* [C] a WILDEBEEST

go¹ /gou/ *v. past tense* **went** *past participle* **gone** *3rd person singular present tense* **goes**

1 leave somewhere [I] to leave the place where the speaker is in order to move to somewhere else; DEPART: *I wanted to go, but Anna wanted to stay.* | *Come on, Joe, it's time to go.* | **be/get going** *It's late – I should be going.*

2 visit *past participle* also **been** [I] to visit a place and then leave it: *Nancy has gone to Paris* (=she is in Paris now). | *Nancy has been to Paris* (=she has visited Paris in the past). | [+ **to**] *Are you going to the game this Saturday?* | **go (to) see/visit** *Has Elaine gone to see Mrs. Aamot yet?* | *I'll go visit Barbara when I'm in Los Angeles.*

3 move/travel [I always + adv./prep.] to travel or move in a particular way, to a particular place, or for a particular distance: *Where are you going?* | [+ **by**] *Several cars went by very quickly.* | [+ **to**] *We're going to my parents' for Christmas.* | *Jones went to prison for murder.* | *I want to* **go home.** | **go by car/bus/plane** etc. (=use a car etc. to travel somewhere)

4 be going to do sth a) to be certain or expected to happen in the future: *It looks like it's going to rain.* —see also GONNA **b)** to intend to do something: *Nancy's going to meet us at the airport.* —see Usage Note at WILL¹

5 go shopping/swimming/fishing etc. to go somewhere in order to shop, swim etc.: *Let's go jogging tomorrow.*

6 go for a walk/swim etc. to spend time walking, swimming etc.: *Do you want to go for a walk?*

7 reach [I always + adv./prep., not in progressive] to reach as far as a particular place, or lead to a particular place: [+ **to/from/down** etc.] *Does this road go to the station?* | *This belt won't go around my waist.* | *The trees go right up to the beach.* | *The pond doesn't go very deep.*

8 belong/fit [I always + adv./prep., not in progressive] to belong or fit in a particular place or position: *Where do these plates go?* | [+ **in/under/on** etc.] *The sofa can go against the wall.* | *I don't think all of this will go in the trunk.*

9 be sent [I] to be sent or passed on: [+ **by/through** etc.] *The package was late because it had to go through customs.* | *Plans for a new civic center will go before* (=be presented to) *the committee today.*

10 become [linking verb] to become something different, especially something not as good, either naturally or by changing deliberately: *The company went bankrupt last year.* | **go sour/bad** *The milk had gone sour.* | **go bald/deaf/blind** etc. (=lose your hair, hearing, sight etc.) | **go wild/red/white with sth** *She went white with fright.* —see Usage Note at BECOME

11 be in a state [linking verb] to be or remain in a particular state, especially a bad one: *Unfortunately, his cries for help went unheard.* | *The mother bird will often* **go hungry** (=have nothing to eat) *to keep her babies alive.*

12 go to church/school etc. to regularly attend church, school etc.: *Josh loves going to kindergarten.*

13 happen [I always + adv./prep.] to happen or develop in a particular way: **go well/fine/smoothly etc.** *The game was going great until Jerry twisted his knee.* | *As always, everything went wrong at the last minute.* | *Most people said they*

G

were satisfied with **the way things were going** *in the country today.*

14 song/story [I always + adv./prep.,T, not in progressive] to be said or sung in a particular way: *I don't exactly remember how the song goes.* | *The story* **goes that** *he was poisoned by his wife.*

15 make a sound [T] to make a particular sound: *Cats go "meow."*

16 to go a) still remaining before something happens: *We have only two weeks to go before our trip to Hawaii!* **b)** still to be dealt with before you have finished what you are doing: *I have ten more pages to go until I'm finished with the book.* **c)** still to travel before you reach the place you are going to: *We still have five more miles to go.* **d)** if you buy food from a restaurant to go, you buy it to take away and eat at home or somewhere else: *I'll have a burger and fries to go, please.* —compare TAKEOUT

17 disappear [I] to not exist anymore; disappear: *Is your headache gone yet?*

18 get rid of [I] if someone or something has to go, you have to get rid of them: *This ugly old couch has to go.* | *"Do you want to keep these records?" "No, they can go."*

19 work correctly [I] INFORMAL if a machine goes, it works in the way that it should: *I can't get the lawnmower to go.*

20 be spent [I] if money or time goes, it is spent or used up: *I don't know where all my money goes! Katherine is three already, the time goes so fast.* [+ **to**] *All the money goes to local charities.*

21 go out of your way to do sth to do something that you do not have to do and that involves making an effort: *They went out of their way to make me feel welcome.*

22 get worse [I] to get worse or be lost completely: *I think my hearing is starting to go.*

23 be sold [I] to be sold: [+ **to**] *The jewels will go to the highest bidder.* | [+ **for**] *The painting should go for about $200.* | *I bought some mugs that* **were going cheap** (=were being sold at a low price).

24 ready to go to be prepared to start doing something: *The builders are ready to go, but their boss hasn't arrived yet.*

25 make a movement [I always + adv./prep.] to make a particular movement: [+ **up/down etc.**] *When the teacher asked who wanted some candy, all of the children's hands went up.*

26 match [I] to look or taste good together: *Do you think this goes?* | [+ **with/together**] *Does red wine go with chicken?* | *Those colors don't go together well.* —see Usage Note at FIT[1]

SPOKEN PHRASES

27 how are things going?/how's it going?/how goes it? used to ask how someone's situation is or how things are developing, especially used as a greeting: *"Hey, Al, how's it going?" "Fine."*

28 go and do sth to go somewhere in order to do something: *I'll go and get the car for you.*

29 go like this/that used with body movements to describe how someone moves or how something is: *He went like this and knocked over the lamp.*

30 say [T] NONSTANDARD to say something: *Then she goes, "Sorry for interrupting your dinner."*

31 go (to the bathroom) to make waste come out of your body, especially to URINATE: *I drank three beers and now I really* **have to go.**

32 don't go doing sth used to tell someone not to do something, especially something that is wrong or bad: *It's a secret, so don't go telling everyone.*

33 it/this/which just goes to show used to say that something helps to prove that something is true: *It just goes to show, anything can happen in America.*

34 what sb says goes used to say that someone is in authority and other people must do as they say: *I'm in charge here and what I say goes.*

35 here/there sb goes (again) used when someone has annoyed you by continuing to do something they know you do not like: *There he goes again – telling those stupid jokes of his.*

36 not go there used to say that you do not want to talk or think about something: *"What if the two of them actually..." "Don't even go there."*

37 you go, girl! SLANG said to encourage a girl or a woman to continue doing or saying something you approve of

38 have gone and done sth used when you are surprised by what someone has done, especially when it is something bad: *Kay's gone and lost the car keys!* | *Tom's really* **gone and done it** (=made a really big mistake) *this time.*

39 go do sth used to tell someone to go away when you are angry: *Go fly a kite!*

40 go one better to do something better than someone else had done it, or get something better than they have: *Several small firms have gone one better in mass marketing than the big insurance companies.*

41 go too far to go beyond the limits of what is reasonable or acceptable: *Investors are concerned that real estate inflation has gone too far.*

42 go all the way (with sb) INFORMAL to have sex with someone

43 go far a) to succeed in whatever you choose to do: *Pat Falloon is so talented that he should go far as a professional hockey player.* **b)** if an amount of money does not go far, you cannot buy much with it: *$20 dollars doesn't go as far as it used to.*

44 going, going, gone used to say something has been sold at an AUCTION

45 go out of style/fashion to stop being popular: *Leisure suits went out of style over 20 years ago.*

46 anything goes used to say that anything someone says or does is acceptable: *With this season's fashions, anything goes.*

47 as sb/sth goes INFORMAL compared with the average person or thing of that type: *He's not bad, as politicians go.* | *$40 a ticket isn't bad as football tickets go.*

48 church-goer/theater-goer etc. someone who goes to church, the theater etc., especially regularly: *I didn't know you were much of an opera-goer.*

49 theater-going/church-going etc. the act of regularly going to the theater, to church etc.: *a church-going family*

50 go it alone to do something, especially start a business, alone: *Sayles hasn't regretted his decision to go it alone as a filmmaker.* —see also GOING[1], GOING[2], GONE[2], **here goes (nothing)/here we go** (HERE[1] (19)), **have a lot going for you** (LOT[1] (4)), **there goes sth** (THERE[2] (13)), **there (you go)** (THERE[2] (9)), **the way things are (going)** (WAY[1] (40))

go about sth *phr. v.* [T] to begin or begin working at something; TACKLE[1]: *What's the best way to go about it?* | [**go about (doing) sth**] *We think it's the wrong way to go about solving a very serious problem.*

go ahead *phr. v.* [I] **1** SPOKEN said in order to politely let someone move in front of you, give someone permission to do something, or to let someone speak first: *You can go ahead of me in line – I'm waiting for someone.* | *"Do you mind if I smoke?" "No, go right ahead."* | *Go ahead, I'm listening.* **2** to begin or continue with something: *Work on the new building will go ahead in May.* | *I guess I'll go ahead and ask her out on a date.* | [**go ahead with (doing) sth**] *Jeff and Thena decided to go ahead with the wedding.* | [**go ahead and do sth**] *The newspaper decided to go ahead and publish the story.* **3** also **go on ahead** to go somewhere before the other people in your group: *You can go ahead and we'll catch up with you later.*

go along *phr. v.* [I] **1** if you do something as you go along, you do it without preparing or planning it: *I just made up the story as I went along.* **2** to continue with a plan, activity etc.: [**go along doing sth**] *I went along making the same mistake for weeks.*

go along with sb/sth *phr. v.* [T] to agree with or support someone or something: *You'll never get Mom to go along with your idea.*

go around *phr. v.* **1 go around doing sth** if you go around doing something, especially something people do not approve of, you often do it: *You can't go around calling people liars.* **2** [I,T **go around** sth] to usually dress or behave in a particular way: *It's so*

G

embarrassing the way he goes around with his pants unzipped. | I can't believe how she goes around town in that funny hat. **3** [I] if an illness, some news etc. is going around, it is being passed from one person to another: *There's a rumor going around that Randy's having an affair.* | *Last week, I had that stomach virus that's being going around.* **4** [I] to be enough for everyone to have some: *There should be enough ice-cream bars to go around.* **5** [I] to move in a circular way: *The wheels went around faster and faster.* —see also **go/run around in circles** (CIRCLE[1] (6)) **6 what goes around comes around** an expression meaning that if you do something bad, something bad will happen to you some day

go at sth/sb *phr. v.* [T not in passive] INFORMAL to attack someone or start to fight: *The two dogs went at each other as soon as I opened the gate.* | *The boxers **went at it** until officials pulled them apart.*

go away *phr. v.* [I] **1** to leave a place or person: *Go away! Leave me alone!* **2** to spend some time somewhere else, especially on vacation: *We're going away for seven days.* **3** if a problem, bad feeling etc. goes away, it disappears or does not happen any longer: *Has your headache gone away yet?*

go back *phr. v.* [I] **1** to continue something you were doing before: *Once you've made the decision, I'm afraid there's no going back.* | [**go back to (doing) sth**] *I'll go back to studying after the news is over.* **2** to return to a place that you have just come from: *I think we ought to go back now.* | [+ **for**] *I had to go back for my passport.* | [+ **to/into/out** etc.] *It's cold out here – let's go back to the kitchen.* **3 go back a long way** INFORMAL also **go way back** if two people go back a long way, they have known each other for a long time: *Bill and I go back a long way.* **4** [always + adv./prep.] to have been made, built, or started at some time in the past: *Their family history goes back to the 16th century.*

go back on sth *phr. v.* [T] to not do what you said you would do: *Mollari went back on the agreement.* | **go back on your promise/word** *I have a hard time trusting Jack – he's gone back on his word too many times.*

go by *phr. v.* **1** [I] if time goes by, it passes: *Five years went by before they saw each other again.* **2** [T not in passive **go by** sth] to use the information or advice you get from a person, a book, a set of rules etc.: *Don't go by that old map – it's out of date.* | *Taylor is a tough, good cop who always **goes by the book*** (=obeys the rules very strictly). **3** [T not in passive **go by** sth] to form an opinion or judgment of someone or something from something else: *You can't always go by appearances.*

go down *phr. v.* [I]
1 to be prepared to start doing something to go to a lower floor of a building: *Are you going down for lunch anytime soon?*
2 become lower to not be as expensive, high etc. as it was before: *Coffee has gone down a lot recently* (=it costs less than before). | *The water level in the pool has gone down quite a bit.*
3 standard if something goes down, its quality or standard gets worse: *This neighborhood has really gone down in the last few years* | **go down in sb's estimation/opinion** (=someone is respected less)
4 go down well/badly etc. to get a particular sort of reaction from someone: *Marsha's joke about Canadians didn't go down well at the party.*
5 sun if the sun goes down, you cannot see it above the ground anymore, and it becomes night
6 sink to disappear from sight, or disappear below a surface: *Ten men died when the ship went down.*
7 become flatter to become less swollen or lose air: *Put some ice on your knee to make the swelling go down.*
8 be remembered [always + adv./prep.] to be recorded or remembered in a particular way: [+ **as/in**] *The talks went down as a landmark in the peace process.* | *This day will surely **go down in history*** (=be remembered for a long time)
9 computer to stop working for a short time: *My computer went down an hour ago.*
10 food/drink to pass down your throat: *My*

---

throat was so sore that I couldn't get the pill to go down.
11 lights if lights go down, they become less bright: *The lights went down and the curtain rose on an empty stage.*
12 sports **a)** to lose a game or competition: *Chang went down to Sampras in the third set.* **b)** to move down to a lower position in an official list of teams or players: [+ **to**] *Dallas has gone down to second place in the NFL.*

go down on sb *phr. v.* [T not in passive] VULGAR to touch someone's sex organs with the lips and tongue, in order to give sexual pleasure

go for sb/sth *phr. v.* [T] **1** to try to get or win something: *Biondi is going for his second gold medal in swimming.* —see also **go for broke** (BROKE[2] (3)) **2 go for it** SPOKEN said when you want to encourage someone to do something **3 I could/ would go for sth** SPOKEN to want to have something: *I could really go for a taco right now.* **4 that goes for you, too** SPOKEN to also be true about someone or something else: *Peter, you need to be quiet and listen, and that goes for you, too Steve* (=Steve needs to be quiet and listen also). **5** SPOKEN to usually like a particular type of person or thing, or to usually choose a particular type of person or thing: *I tend to go for bright colored ties.*

go in with sb *phr. v.* [T] to join someone in order to start a business etc.: *We've been thinking about going in with them on the time-share condo.*

go in for sth *phr. v.* [T] **1** to like something or become interested in something: *Bill has never gone in for transcendental meditation.* **2** to get medical treatment at a hospital or CLINIC: *He stayed in bed for three weeks after he went in for his back surgery.*

go into sth *phr. v.* [T]
1 job [not in passive] to enter a particular profession or business: *Vivian wants to go into politics.* | *I might **go into business*** (=begin a business) *with Brian.*
2 time/money/effort [not in passive] to be used in order make something work or happen: *It's obvious that a lot of money has gone into this house.*
3 explain/describe to explain, describe, or talk about something in detail: *I don't want to go into the matter now.* | *He went into a long speech about European politics.* | *Clare wouldn't **go into details** about her divorce.*
4 hit [not in passive] if a vehicle goes into a tree, wall, or another vehicle, it hits it: *The driver lost control and went into the median.*
5 divide [not in passive] INFORMAL if a number goes into another number, the second number can be divided by the first: *12 goes into 60 five times.*
6 consider to examine something thoroughly: *During this course, we'll go into the main causes of the French Revolution.*
7 begin a movement [not in passive] if something or someone goes into a particular movement, they start to do it: *After taking the medication, the muscles in my back went into spasms.*

go off *phr. v.* **1** [I] to explode: *Fireworks went off all over the city last night.* **2** [I] to make a loud noise: *I overslept because my alarm clock didn't go off.* **3** [I] if a machine goes off, it stops working: *Suddenly, all the lights went off.* **4 go off well/badly etc.** to happen in a particular way: *We hope the party goes off well.*

go off on sb/sth *phr. v.* INFORMAL to show your anger at someone or about something by saying what you really think: *Lisa called him a bad name, so Brett just went off on her.*

go off with sb/sth *phr. v.* [T] INFORMAL **1** to leave your husband, wife, partner etc. in order to have a relationship with someone else: *She's gone off with her husband's best friend.* **2** to take something away from a place without having permission: *Apparently someone's gone off with my notebook.*

go on *phr. v.*
1 continue an action [I] to continue without stopping or changing: [**go on doing sth**] *We can't go on*

fighting like this. | [**go on with sth**] *I just want to go on with my life and forget the whole experience.*

2 do sth next [I] to do something after you have finished doing something else: [**go on to do sth**] *After dropping out of Harvard, he went on to become one of the richest men in the world.* | [**go on to sth**] *Go on to question 5 when you're finished.*

3 happen to take place or happen: *The festival's been going on for about 15 years.* | **What's going on in there?** | *She didn't really understand what was going on.* | [**+ with**] *What's going on with Seth? I haven't heard from him in a while.* —see also GOINGS-ON

4 use as proof [T not in passive **go on** sth] to base an opinion or judgment on something: *Police haven't much to go on in their hunt for the killer.*

5 begin to work [I] if a machine goes on, it begins to operate: *Our coffeemaker is set to go on at 7 a.m.*

6 time [I] to pass: *As time went on, I began to like him more.*

7 continue with a story/explanation etc. [I] to continue talking, especially after stopping or changing to a different subject: *Go on, I'm listening.* | [**+ with**] *She paused for a moment to dry her eyes and then went on with her story.* | [**go on to do sth**] *I later went on to explain why I was so upset with them.*

8 be going on to be nearly a time, age, number etc.: *Aunt Cleda must be going on 65 by now.* | *Jenny's 16 going on 70* (=she behaves older than she is).

9 medicine [T not in passive **go on** sth] to begin to take a type of medicine: *Dani's too young to go on the pill.*

10 go in front of [I] to go somewhere before the other people you are with: [**+ ahead**] *Dad told me to go on ahead and he would meet me at the restaurant.*

11 talk too much [I] INFORMAL to talk or complain too much: [**+ about**] *I wish you'd stop going on about my haircut.* | *Grandpa went on and on about how good he was at golf.*

12 go on SPOKEN used to encourage someone to do something: *Go on, have another piece.*

go out *phr. v.* [I]

1 for entertainment to leave your house, especially in order to enjoy yourself: *Are you going out tonight?* | [**go out doing sth**] *She goes out partying every weekend.* | [**go out and do sth**] *Can I go out and play now?* | **go out for dinner/lunch etc.** *We went out for dinner a couple of times.*

2 with boy/girl to have a romantic relationship with someone: [**go out with sb**] *Leah's still going out with Colin.*

3 fire/light to stop burning or shining: *Our campfire went out while we were sleeping.*

4 **go out like a light** INFORMAL to go to sleep very quickly: *As soon as his head hit the pillow, he went out like a light.*

5 sea to go back to its lower level: *The tide's going out.* —opposite **come in** (COME¹)

6 **heart/thoughts go out to sb** to have a lot of sympathy for someone: *Our hearts go out to the victim's family.*

7 time [always + adv./prep.] LITERARY to end: *Spring went out with a bang as four tornadoes rolled through the state yesterday.*

8 travel to travel to a place that is far away, in order to live there: *They've gone out to Malaysia with his work.*

9 make public OLD-FASHIONED to officially let everyone know about something: *In a statement that just went out from the White House, it is reported that the Secretary of State has resigned.*

go over *phr. v.*

1 go near sb/sth [I] to go nearer to someone or something: *Brad went over and got a scotch and soda.* | [**+ to**] *We went over to the man to ask for directions.* | [**go over to do sth**] *I think I'll go over to thank them for the gift.*

2 examine [T **go over** sth] to look at something or think about something carefully: *Jake went over his notes again before the test.*

3 search [T **go over** sth] to search something or a place very carefully: *Investigators have gone over every square inch of the area looking for clues.*

4 repeat [T **go over** sth] to repeat something in order to learn it or understand it: *We went over the speech word by word.*

5 **go over well/badly etc.** if a speech, performance, type of behavior etc. goes over well, badly etc., people like it, do not like it etc.: [**+ with**] *That kind of racial humor doesn't go over well in New York.*

6 change [I] to change your beliefs, religion, habits, job etc.: [**+ to**] *Cribbs is going over to CJC Communications P.R. firm.*

7 clean [T] to clean something: *I went over the table twice with a wet rag, so it should be clean.*

8 TV/radio [I] to change from being broadcast from one place to being broadcast from another place: [**+ to**] *Now we'll go over to Bryant in Atlanta.*

go through *phr. v.*

1 experience sth [T **go through** sth] to suffer or experience something bad: *How does she keep smiling after all she's been through?*

2 use all of sth [T **go through** sth] to use something and have none left: *Jerry goes through at least a quart of milk every day.*

3 pass a law [I,T **go through** sth] if a law goes through, it is officially accepted: *The law finally went through with a lot of effort from the Democrats.* | *Everyone expects this bill to go through Congress quickly.*

4 approve officially [I] if a deal or agreement goes through, it is officially accepted: *We found out that our car loan application has gone through.*

5 practice sth [T **go through** sth] to practice something, for example a performance: *Let's go through the song one more time.*

6 look at/for sth [T **go through** sth] to look at or for something carefully: *I went through all of our closets and I still can't find my tennis racket.*

go through with sth *phr. v.* [T] to do something you had promised or planned to do, even though it causes problems or you are not sure you want to do it anymore: *Rich said he just wasn't ready to go through with the wedding.*

go to sth *phr. v.* [T not in passive] **1 go to great lengths/go to a lot of trouble** to use a lot of effort to get something or to do something: *Your dad went to a lot of trouble to get you these baseball cards.* **2 go to sleep/war etc.** to begin sleeping, fighting a war etc.: *Shh! The baby's trying to go to sleep.* **3 go to great expense** to spend a lot of money for something or to do something: *Some people go to great expense to decorate their homes with fresh flowers.*

go together *phr. v.* [I] OLD-FASHIONED if two people are going together, they are having a romantic relationship

go under *phr. v.* [I] **1** if a business goes under, it has serious problems and fails: *Paul's roofing business went under last year.* **2** if a ship or something that is floating goes under, it sinks beneath the surface: *The Titanic finally went under, watched by those survivors who had found a place in the lifeboats.*

go up *phr. v.* [I]

1 increase to increase in number or amount: *The price of gas has gone up twenty cents since August.*

2 be built to be built: *The new civic center went up last month.*

3 explode/burn to explode or be destroyed in a fire: *The factory went up in flames before the firemen arrived.* —see also **go up in smoke** (SMOKE¹ (5))

4 shout if a shout or a CHEER goes up, people start to shout or CHEER

go with *phr. v.* [T not in passive] **1** to be included as part of something: *The company car goes with the job.* | [**go with doing sth**] *They should accept the duties that go with being a member of the club.* **2** to choose something or choose to do something: *I think I'll go with the green tie instead.* **3** OLD-FASHIONED to have someone as your BOYFRIEND or GIRLFRIEND

go without *phr. v.* [I,T] **1** to be able to live without something or without doing something: *I help the homeless because I don't like to see people go without.* | [**go without (doing) sth**] *It is unhealthy to go without*

G

sleep for a long period of time. **2 it goes without saying** used to say that something is understood by everyone and that it does not need to be said: *It goes without saying that she has no talent.*

go² *n.* **1 make a go of sth** INFORMAL to try to make a business, marriage etc. succeed: *They both want to make a go of their relationship.* | *His family believes he might be able to* **make a go of it** *in the computer business.* **2 on the go** INFORMAL very busy or working all the time: *My kids keep me always on the go.* **3** [singular] INFORMAL an attempt to do something: [**have a go at (doing) sth**] *Steve Martin's going to have a go at the role Spencer Tracy made so memorable.* | [**give sth a go**] *Young children shouldn't worry too much about spelling, but just give it a go.* **4** [C] someone's turn in a game: *It's your go.*

SPOKEN PHRASES

5 sth is a go used to say that things are working correctly, or that you have permission to do something: *I just got word from our boss, and the trip to London is a go.* **6 sth is (a) no go** used to say that something has not happened or that it will not happen: *I asked for a raise but it was a no go.* **7 all systems are go** used to say that everything is working the way that it should

---

—see also GET-UP-AND-GO

goad¹ /good/ *v.* [T] **1** to make someone do something by annoying them or encouraging them until they do it: [**goad sb into (doing) sth**] *Several boys surrounded him and goaded him into a fight.* | [**goad sb on**] *The man mumbled something and they goaded him on with insults.* **2** to push animals ahead of you with a sharp stick

goad² *n.* [C] **1** a sharp stick for making animals, especially cattle, move forward **2** something that forces someone to do something

go·a·head¹ /'. .,./ *n.* **give (sb) the go-ahead/get the go-ahead** to give or be given permission to start doing something: *The state utilities commission gave the go-ahead for the water company to raise rates.*

go-ahead² *adj.* **a go-ahead goal/touchdown/basket etc.** a go-ahead goal, touchdown etc. in sports is one that puts a team ahead in points in a game

goal /goʊl/ *n.* [C] **1** something that you hope to achieve in the future: **achieve/reach a goal** *Our division reached its sales goal for the month.* | *My* **long-term goal** *is to make a million dollars by my 40th birthday.* **2** the action of making the ball go into a particular area to win a point in games such as football or SOCCER, or the point won by doing this: *Ronaldo* **scored** *three* **goals** *for Brazil.* **3** the area between two posts where the ball must go for a point to be won

goal·ie /'goʊli/ *n.* [C] INFORMAL a goalkeeper

goal·keep·er /'goʊl,kipɚ/ *n.* [C] the player on a sports team who tries to stop the ball from going into his team's goal

goal line /'. ./ *n.* [C] a line that marks the end of a playing area, where the goal is placed

goal·mouth /'goʊlmaʊθ/ *n.* [C] the area directly in front of the GOAL

goal·post /'goʊlpoʊst/ *n.* [C usually plural] one of the two posts, with a bar along the top or across the middle, that form the GOAL in games such as SOCCER or football

goal·ten·der /'goʊl,tɛndɚ/ *n.* [C] a GOALKEEPER

goat /goʊt/ *n.* [C] **1** an animal that has horns on top of its head and long hair under its chin, and that can climb steep hills and rocks **2 get sb's goat** SPOKEN to make someone very angry or annoyed: *Relax – don't let him get your goat.* **3** old *goat* INFORMAL an old man who is not nice, especially one who annoys women in a sexual way —see also BILLY-GOAT

goat·ee /goʊ'ti/ *n.* [C] a small pointed BEARD on the end of a man's chin

goat·herd /'goʊthɚd/ *n.* [C] someone who takes care of a group of goats

goat·skin /'goʊt,skin/ *n.* **1** [C,U] leather made from the skin of a goat, or a wine container made from this **2** [C] the skin of a goat

gob /gɑb/ *n.* [C] INFORMAL **1** a mass of something wet and sticky: [+ of] *There's a gob of gum on my chair.* **2 gobs** [plural] INFORMAL a large amount of something: [+ of] *The Johnsons must have gobs of money.*

gob·bet /'gɑbɪt/ *n.* [C] OLD USE a small piece of something, especially food

gob·ble /'gɑbəl/ *v.* INFORMAL **1** [I,T] also **gobble up** to eat something very quickly or in a way that people do not consider polite: *We gobbled up all of the cake in one evening.* **2** [T] also **gobble up** to use a supply of something quickly: *Housing costs gobble up almost half of our budget.* **3** [I] to make a sound like a TURKEY —**gobble** *n.* [C]

gob·ble·dy·gook, gobbledegook /'gɑbəldi,gʊk/ *n.* [U] INFORMAL complicated language that seems to have no meaning, especially language used in an official document

gob·bler /'gɑblɚ/ *n.* [C] INFORMAL a male TURKEY

go-be·tween /'. .,./ *n.* [C] someone who takes messages from one person or group to another, because the two places cannot meet or do not wish to meet: **act/serve as a go-between** *UN representative Charles Gaulkin will act as a go-between for leaders of the two countries.*

Go·bi Des·ert, the /,goʊbi 'dɛzɚt/ also **the Gobi** one of the largest deserts in the world. It is partly in northern China and partly in Mongolia.

gob·let /'gɑblɪt/ *n.* [C] a cup of glass or metal, with a base and a long stem but no handle

gob·lin /'gɑblɪn/ *n.* [C] a small ugly creature in children's stories that likes to trick people

go-cart /'. ./ *n.* [C] a small car made of an open frame on four wheels, that people race for fun

god /gɑd/ *n.* [C] **1 God** [singular, not with **the**] the spirit or BEING whom Christians, Jews, and Muslims believe created the universe, and to whom they pray **2** [C] a male spirit or BEING who is believed to control the world or part of it, or who represents a particular quality: *Mars, the god of war* —see also GODDESS **3 God-given** received from God: *She has a God-given talent for singing.* | *Many Jews believe they have a* **God-given right** *to live in Israel.* **4 play God** to behave as though you have the power to do whatever you like: *Bans on human cloning were called for by people afraid of scientists playing God.* **5 God's gift to sb/sth** someone who thinks they are perfect or extremely attractive: *John thinks he's God's gift to tennis.*

G

SPOKEN PHRASES

6 God/oh (my) God/my God/good God/God almighty used to emphasize what you are saying, when you are surprised, annoyed, or amused: *Oh God, I can't believe she said that!* **7 I swear/hope/pray etc. to God** used to emphasize that you promise, hope etc. that something is true or that something happens: *I hope to God that she'll make it home safely.* **8 God (only) knows a)** used to show that you are annoyed because you do not know something, or because you think that something is unreasonable: [**God (only) knows who/what/how etc.**] *God only knows where those kids are now!* **b)** used to emphasize what you are saying: *God knows she's had a hard life.* **9 what/how/where/who in God's name** used to emphasize a question when you are angry or surprised: *What in God's name is that noise?* **10 for God's sake** used to emphasize something you are saying, especially when you are telling someone to do something: *For God's sake, shut up!* **11 honest to God** used to emphasize that you are not lying or joking: *"Are you on drugs?" "No, honest to God, I'm not."* **12 God forbid** used when you very much hope that something will not happen: [+ that] *God forbid that he would get fired.* **13 God help you/him etc.** used to warn someone that something bad will happen: *Aunt Betsy's such a neat-freak – God help you if you spill anything on her carpet.* **14 God help sb (if...)** used when you think that something bad is going to happen: *God help us if they can't find a peaceful solution to the crisis.* **15 God bless** used to say that you hope someone will be safe and happy, used especially when you are saying goodbye: *Good night and God bless.* **16 there is no God** HUMOROUS said when something happens that seems very unfair and cannot be explained: *If a girl like Mindy can get a man like him, there is no God.* **17 God willing** used to say that you hope there will be no problems: *God willing, the war will end soon.* **18 by God** used for emphasis when you are expressing determination or surprise: *By God, that's good money!* **19 God give me strength!** used when you are becoming annoyed **20 God rest his/her soul** also **God rest him/her** OLD-FASHIONED used to show respect when speaking about someone who is dead

21 the gods [plural] the force that some people believe controls their lives, bringing them good or bad luck: *The gods are against me!* **22** [C] someone or something to which you give too much importance or respect: *Money was his god.* —see also **act of God** (ACT[1] (8)), **by the grace of God** (GRACE[1] (5)), **so help me (God)** (HELP[1] (13)), **thank God/goodness/heavens** (THANK (3))

USAGE NOTE: GOD

FORMALITY AND POLITENESS
In informal spoken English, using **God** in various phrases is very common. Although they are often used in a non-religious way, some people who are religious would consider these phrases offensive because they think that it is not respectful to God. Here is a list of some of these phrases: *God | oh (my) God | my God | good God | God knows | God almighty | thank God*

SPELLING
God is always written with a capital "G" in these expressions.

GRAMMAR
God is not used with *the*: *I pray to God* (NOT *the God*) *every night.*

Go·dard /gou'dar/, **Jean-Luc** /ʒɑn luk/ (1930–) a French movie writer and DIRECTOR who is known for using new and unusual methods of making films

god-aw·ful, God-awful, godawful /ˌ. '..ˌ/ adj. [only before noun] INFORMAL very bad or annoying: *What is that god-awful smell?*

god·child /'gɑdtʃaɪld/ n. plural **godchildren** /-ˌtʃɪldrən/ [C] a child that a GODPARENT promises to help and to teach Christian values to

god·dam·mit, God damn it /ˌgɑd'dæmɪt/ interjection a word used to express strong annoyance, anger etc., considered offensive by some Christians

god·damn, goddamn /ˌgɑd'dæm•/ also **god·damned, God damned** /ˌgɑd'dæmd•/ adj. [only before noun] SPOKEN a word used to show that you are very annoyed or angry, considered offensive by some Christians: *I hate filling out these goddamn forms.* —**goddamn goddam, goddamned** adv.: *You should not say something so goddamned stupid.* —compare DAMN[3]

God·dard /'gɑdəd/, **Rob·ert** /'rɑbət/ (1882–1945) a U.S. scientist who developed the first ROCKET that used liquid fuel

god·daugh·ter /'gɑdˌdɔtə/ n. [C] a girl that a GODPARENT promises to help and to teach Christian values to

god·dess /'gɑdɪs/ n. [C] a female spirit or BEING who is believed to control the world or part of it, or represents a particular quality: *Aphrodite, goddess of love* —see also GOD (2), SEX GODDESS

god·fa·ther /'gɑdˌfɑðə/ n. [C] **1** a man who promises to help a child and to teach him or her Christian values **2** SLANG the head of a criminal organization or MAFIA group

God-fear·ing /'. ˌ..ˌ/ adj. OLD-FASHIONED leading a good life and following the rules of the Christian religion: *God-fearing Christians*

god-for·sak·en, Godforsaken /'gɑdfəˌseɪkən/ adj. a godforsaken place is far away from where people live and contains nothing interesting, attractive, or cheerful in it: *Our car broke down in some godforsaken corner of the Pennsylvania backwoods.*

God·head /'gɑdhɛd/ n. **the Godhead** FORMAL a word that Christians use to mean the Father, the Son, and the Holy Spirit, whom they consider to be one God in three parts

god·hood, Godhood /'gɑdhʊd/ n. [U] the quality or state of being God or a god

god·less /'gɑdlɪs/ adj. OLD-FASHIONED not showing respect for God or not having a belief in a god: *godless Communists* —**godlessly** adv.

god·like /'gɑdlaɪk/ adj. having a quality like God or a god: *After World War II, Stalin had become a godlike figure in the Soviet Union.*

god·ly /'gɑdli/ adj. OLD-FASHIONED obeying God and leading a good life —**godliness** n. [U]

god·moth·er /'gɑdˌmʌðə/ n. [C] a woman who promises to help a child, and to teach him or her Christian values

god·par·ent /'gɑdˌpɛrənt/ n. [C] someone who promises to help a child, and to teach him or her Christian values

god·send /'gɑdsɛnd/ n. [singular] something good that happens to you when you really need it: *The good weather has been a real godsend for construction companies.*

god·son /'gɑdsʌn/ n. [C] a boy that a godparent promises to help and to teach Christian values to

god·speed, Godspeed /ˌgɑd'spid/ n. [U] OLD USE used to wish someone good luck, especially before a trip

God squad /'. ./ n. SPOKEN an insulting way of describing Christians who try to persuade other people to become Christians

go·er /'gouə/ n. [C] **movie-goer/concert-goer/ theater-goer** etc. someone who goes to movies, concerts etc.

Goe·the /'gətə/, **Jo·hann Wolf·gang von** /'youhɑn 'wʊlfgɑŋ vɑn/ (1749–1832) a German poet, scientist, and writer of plays and NOVELs

go·fer /'goufə/ n. [C] INFORMAL someone who carries messages or gets or takes things for their employer

go-get·ter /ˌ. '../ n. [C] someone who is likely to be successful because they are very determined and have a lot of energy: *She's a real go-getter.*

gog·gle /'gagəl/ v. [I] to look at something with your eyes wide open in surprise or shock: [+ **at**] *They were goggling at us as if we were freaks.*

gog·gle-eyed /'.. ./ adj. with your eyes wide open because you are surprised or shocked

gog·gles /'gagəlz/ n. [plural] something that protects your eyes, made of glass or plastic with a rubber or plastic edge that fits against your skin: *safety goggles*

go-go /'. ./ adj. INFORMAL **1** a go-go period of time is one in which prices and salaries increase very quickly: *Thousands of people became millionaires during the go-go 1980s.* **2** go-go STOCKS increase in value very quickly in a short period of time, but are risky: *We've invested in several go-go medical stocks.*

go-go danc·er /'.. ˌ../ n. [C] a woman who dances with sexy movements in a bar or NIGHTCLUB —**go-go dancing** n. [U]

Go·gol /'gougɑl/, **Nik·o·lai** /'nɪkəˌlaɪ/ (1809–1852) a Russian writer of plays and NOVELs

go·ing[1] /'gouɪŋ/ n. [U] **1 rough/hard/good etc. going** the difficulty or speed with which something is done: *The first two years of their marriage were tough going.* | *We climbed the mountain in three hours, which was pretty good going.* **2** the act of leaving a place: *His going will be no great loss to the company.* **3 while the going's good** before someone stops you from doing what you want or before something becomes difficult: *Let's get out while the going's good.* **4 heavy going** if a book, play etc. is heavy going, it is boring and difficult to understand —see also **sb's comings and goings** (COMING¹ (2))

going² *adj.* **1 the going rate** the usual cost of a service or job: *Thirty dollars an hour is the going rate for a math tutor.* **2** [not before noun] INFORMAL available, or able to be found: **the best/fastest/cheapest sth going** *We think we make the best computers going.* **3 a going concern** a business that is making a profit and is expected to continue to do so

going-o·ver /ˌ.. ˈ../ *n.* [singular] INFORMAL a thorough examination of something to make sure it is all right: *Our lawyers will give the contract a good going-over.*

goings-on /ˌ.. ˈ./ *n.* [plural] activities or events that are strange or interesting, especially ones that involve something illegal: *Kennedy was shocked at some of the goings-on at the school.*

goi·ter /ˈɡɔɪtɚ/ *n.* [C,U] a disease of the THYROID GLAND that makes your neck very swollen

S W **gold¹** /ɡoʊld/ *n.* **1** [U] *symbol* **Au** a valuable soft yellow metal that is an ELEMENT and is used for making coins, jewelry etc. —see also **strike gold/oil etc.** (STRIKE¹ (14)) **2** [U] coins, jewelry etc. made of this metal **3** [C,U] the color of this metal: *The flag's colors are red, gold, and blue.* **4** [C,U] INFORMAL a GOLD MEDAL: *Hanson won the gold in the 100-meter dash.* —see also **have a heart of gold** (HEART (28))

S W **gold²** *adj.* **1** made of gold: *a gold necklace* **2** having the color of gold: *gold nail polish* —compare GOLDEN

Gold·berg /ˈɡoʊldbɚg/, **Rube** /rub/ (1883–1970) a U.S. artist famous for his CARTOONs of strange and extremely complicated machines that are designed to do very simple jobs

gold·brick /ˈɡoʊldbrɪk/ also **gold·brick·er** /ˈɡoʊldˌbrɪkɚ/ *n.* [C] INFORMAL someone who stays away from their work, and especially uses the false excuse that they are sick —**goldbrick** *v* [I]

gold card /ˈ. ./ *n.* [C] a special CREDIT CARD that gives you additional advantages or services, such as a high spending limit

gold dig·ger /ˈ. ˌ../ *n.* [C] **1** SLANG a woman who tries to attract rich men in order to get their money **2** OLD-FASHIONED someone who dug for gold in past times

gold dust /ˈ. ./ *n.* [U] gold in the form of a fine powder

S W **gold·en** /ˈɡoʊldən/ *adj.* **1** having a bright rich yellow color, like gold: *golden sunlight | golden hair* **2** made of gold: *a golden statue* **3 a golden opportunity** a good chance to get something valuable or to be very successful: *By not buying that stock, I missed a golden opportunity to become a millionaire.* **4 sb is golden** SPOKEN, INFORMAL used to say that someone is in a very good situation: *If the right editor looks at your article, you're golden.* **5 golden years** old age *I want to enjoy my golden years.* **6 golden boy/girl** someone who is popular and successful: *She's Hollywood's current golden girl.*

golden age /ˈ.. ˌ./ *n.* [usually singular] the time when something was at its best: *the golden age of radio*

golden an·ni·ver·sa·ry /ˌ.. ˌ..ˈ...../ *n.* [C] the date that is exactly 50 years after the beginning of something, especially a marriage —compare DIAMOND ANNIVERSARY, SILVER ANNIVERSARY

golden brown /ˌ.. ˈ./ *adj.* a light brown color: *Bake the cookies for 12 minutes or until golden brown.*

golden ea·gle /ˌ.. ˈ../ *n.* [C] a large light brown bird that lives in northern parts of the world

Gold·en Gate, the /ˌ.. ˈ./ an area of water on the western coast of the U.S. that connects San Francisco Bay in California with the Pacific Ocean. It is crossed by the Golden Gate Bridge. —see picture on page 1331

golden hand·cuff /ˌ.. ˈ../ *n.* [C usually plural] INFORMAL something that companies give to important EMPLOYEES to make them less likely to leave their job for a different one, because they will not make as much money or receive as many advantages: *The stock is being used as a golden handcuff to keep him with the company.*

golden hand·shake /ˌ.. ˈ../ *n.* [C] a large amount of money given to someone when they leave their job

golden old·ie /ˌ.. ˈ../ *n.* [C] a song, movie etc. which is old but is still liked by many people: *a radio station that plays golden oldies*

golden par·a·chute /ˌ.. ˈ../ *n.* [C] part of a business person's contract that states that they will be paid a large amount of money when their contract ends or when they leave the company

golden rai·sin /ˌ.. ˈ../ *n.* [C] a RAISIN made from white GRAPEs

golden re·triev·er /ˌ.. ˈ../ *n.* [C] a large dog with light brown fur, especially used for hunting

gold·en·rod /ˈɡoʊldənˌrad/ *n.* **1** [C] a plant with small yellow flowers **2** [U] a yellow-orange color

golden rule /ˌ.. ˈ./ *n.* [usually singular] **1 the Golden Rule** a principle which states that you should treat others as you want them to treat you **2** a very important principle, way of behaving etc. that should be remembered: *My golden rule of cooking is to use the best of fresh ingredients.*

gold·field /ˈɡoʊldfild/ *n.* [C usually plural] an area of land where gold can be found

gold·finch /ˈɡoʊldˌfɪntʃ/ *n.* [C] a small singing bird with yellow feathers on its wings

gold·fish /ˈɡoʊldˌfɪʃ/ *n.* [C] a small shiny orange fish often kept as a pet

goldfish bowl /ˈ.. ˌ./ *n.* [C] **1** a round glass bowl in which fish are kept as pets **2 live in a goldfish bowl** to be in a situation in which people can know everything about your life: *Living in small towns can be like living in a goldfish bowl.*

Gold·ing /ˈɡoʊldɪŋ/, **William** (1911–1993) a British writer of NOVELs

gold leaf /ˌ. ˈ./ *n.* [U] gold that has been beaten into extremely thin sheets and is used to cover things such as picture frames for decoration

Gold·man /ˈɡoʊldmən/, **Em·ma** /ˈɛmə/ (1869–1940) a U.S. political writer, speaker and organizer, born in Lithuania, who was an ANARCHIST, supported BIRTH CONTROL, and opposed military CONSCRIPTION

gold med·al /ˌ. ˈ../ *n.* [C] a prize made of gold that is given to someone for a special achievement, especially for winning a race or competition —see also BRONZE MEDAL, SILVER MEDAL

gold med·al·ist /ˌ. ˈ.../ *n.* [C] someone who has won a gold medal

gold·mine /ˈɡoʊldmaɪn/ *n.* [C] **1** INFORMAL a business or activity that produces large profits: *His printing business has turned out to be a real goldmine.* **2** a deep hole or system of holes under the ground from which rock containing gold is taken **3 be sitting on a goldmine** to own something very valuable, especially without realizing this

gold plate /ˌ. ˈ./ *n.* [U] **1** a layer of gold on top of another metal **2** dishes, spoons etc. made of gold —**gold-plated** *adj.*: *Is it solid gold or gold-plated?*

gold-rimmed /ˌ. ˈ.◂/ *adj.* having a gold edge or border: *gold-rimmed glasses*

The Golden Gate

G

gold rush /'. ./ *n.* [C] a situation when a lot of people hurry to a place where gold has just been discovered: *the California gold rush*

gold·smith /'gould,smɪθ/ *n.* [C] someone who makes things out of gold

gold stan·dard /'. ,../ *n.* **the gold standard** the use of the value of gold as a standard on which the value of money is based

Gold·wyn /'gouldwɪn/, **Samuel** /'sæmuəl/ (1882–1974) a U.S. movie PRODUCER, born in Poland, who started the company that became MGM and had an important part in the development of the Hollywood movie industry

go·lem /'gouləm/ *n.* [C] INFORMAL a stupid person

sw **golf** /gɑlf, gɔlf/ *n.* [U] a game in which the players hit a small white ball into holes in the ground with a set of golf clubs: *a round of golf* (=a complete game of golf) —**golfer** *n.* [C]

golf ball /'. ./ *n.* [C] **1** a small hard white ball used in the game of golf **2** a small ball in an electric TYPEWRITER that has the letters of the alphabet on it, and that moves to print them onto paper

golf cart /'. ./ *n.* [C] a small vehicle that people use to drive around a golf course when they are playing golf

golf club /'. ./ *n.* [C] **1** a long wooden or metal stick used for hitting the ball in the game of golf **2** an organization of people who play golf, or the land and buildings where a golf course is

golf course /'. ./ *n.* [C] an area of land that golf is played on

golf·ing /'gɑlfɪŋ/ *n.* [U] the activity of playing golf: *Holt loves to go golfing.*

golf links /'. ./ also **links** *n.* [plural] a golf course

Go·li·ath /gə'laɪəθ/ *n.* **1** in the Bible, a GIANT (=a very big strong man) who was killed by a boy who later became King David **2 goliath** [C] a person or organization that is very large and powerful: *How can a small computer company compete with the goliaths of the industry?*

gol·ly /'gɑli/ *interjection* OLD-FASHIONED said when you are surprised

-gon /gɑn, gən/ *suffix* [in nouns] a shape with a particular number of sides and angles: *a hexagon* (=with six sides) | *a polygon* (=with many sides)

go·nad /'gounæd/ *n.* [C] TECHNICAL the male or female sex organ in which the SPERM or eggs are produced

gon·do·la /'gɑndələ, gɑn'doulə/ *n.* [C] **1** a long narrow boat with a flat bottom and high points at each end, used on the CANALs in Venice in Italy **2** the place where passengers sit that hangs beneath an AIRSHIP or HOT-AIR BALLOON **3** the enclosed part of a CABLE CAR where the passengers sit

gon·do·lier /,gɑndə'lɪr/ *n.* [C] a man who rows a gondola in Venice

gone[1] /gɔn, gɑn/ *v.* the past participle of go —see GO[1]

gone[2] *adj.* INFORMAL **1** dead: *Now that his wife is gone, he doesn't get out very much.* **2 be gone** showing the effects of taking drugs or drinking alcohol: *Look at Michelle – she's totally gone!*

gon·er /'gɔnɚ/ *n.* [C] INFORMAL someone who will soon die, or who is in an impossible situation: *When one of the plane's engines went out, I thought I was a goner.*

gong /gɔŋ, gɑŋ/ *n.* [C] a round piece of metal that hangs in a frame and is hit with a stick to make a loud sound, especially as a signal

gon·na /'gɔnə, gənə/ NONSTANDARD a written form of the spoken short form of "going to": *What are you gonna do this weekend?*

gon·or·rhe·a /,gɑnə'riə/ *n.* [U] a disease of the sex organs that is passed on during sex

gon·zo jour·nal·ism /'gɑnzou ,dʒɚnl-ɪzəm/ *n.* [U] INFORMAL reporting in newspapers that is concerned with shocking or exciting the reader and not with giving true information —**gonzo journalist** *n.* [C]

goo /gu/ *n.* [U] INFORMAL **1** a disgusting sticky substance: *Crews are working day and night to clean up the goo from the oil tanker accident.* **2** words or feelings that are too emotional or romantic —see also GOOEY

goo·ber /'gubɚ/ *n.* [C] INFORMAL **1** also **goober pea** /'.. ./ a PEANUT **2** a stupid person

good[1] /gud/ *adj.* comparative **better** superlative **best** sv
1 of a high standard of a high standard or quality: *a good quality car* | *This book is not as good as her last one.* | *Terry's always been a good father to Denise.* | *Which restaurant is better?* | *I bought the best big-screen TV I could find.* | **very/pretty/extremely etc. good** *He's done a very good job of making the company profitable.* | *Your work's simply not good enough.* —opposite BAD[1] (2), POOR (3)
2 suitable **a)** useful or appropriate for a particular purpose: *Today's a good day for going to the beach.* | [be good for (doing) sth] *These shoes are supposed to be good for your feet.* **b)** convenient for someone: [be good for sb] *Ten o'clock is good for me.*
3 skillful smart or skillful: *Andrea is a good cook.* | [be good at (doing) sth] *Brice is good at crossword puzzles.* | *I'm no good at speaking in public.* | [+ with] *Mona is good with children* (=skillful at dealing with children). | *Is the new salesman any good?* —opposite BAD[1] (9), POOR (5)
4 no good/not much good/not any good **a)** not very useful or successful: [no good to do sth] *It does me no good to go on a diet – I just gain the weight right back later.* | [no good doing sth] *It's no good trying to adjust the radio, one of the speakers is broken.* | [be no good for sth] *This paper's no good for taking notes.* | [be no good to sb] *A car's not much good to me since I can't drive anymore.* **b)** bad: *That movie wasn't any good.*
5 nice enjoyable and pleasant: *good weather* | *Have a good weekend!* | [be good to do sth] *It's good to see you again.* —see also **good/big etc. old** (OLD (12))
6 healthy **a)** useful for your health: [be good for sb] *Eating junk food all the time isn't good for you.* **b)** healthy: *"How are you feeling?" "Better, thanks."* **c)** useful to your character: [be good for sb] *Watching so much TV isn't good for you.*
7 successful result likely to result in success or to help someone: *That's really good news!* | *Investing just for short-term profits is probably not a good idea.* | *The best method for removing the bricks is to use a hammer and chisel.*
8 well-behaved well-behaved, used especially about a child: *Be a good boy and eat your vegetables.* | *She's the author of five books on good manners.* | *Both children were on their best behavior* (=they were deliberately behaving well).
9 correct correct or true; ACCURATE: *I have a pretty good idea of what it will be like.* | *Many realty offices will give you a good estimate of local rents.* | *Nobody knows for sure what was said, but we can make some good guesses.* —see also **pay good money for sth** (MONEY (11))
10 in satisfactory condition in a satisfactory condition for use; not broken, damaged etc.: *Mom always made us wear our best clothes when we went to church.* | *There, now the table is as good as new* (=fixed so that it looks like new again).
11 sensible sensible or useful: *John has very good judgment.* | *The best reason to visit in wintertime is the lack of tourists.*
12 helpful helpful and useful: *The school district's plan is a good example of how to prepare for an emergency.* | *The best advice for new mothers is sleep when the baby sleeps.* —opposite BAD[1], POOR
13 able to be used able to be used for a particular period of time: [+ for] *The warranty for my stereo is good for one year.*
14 kind kind and concerned about what other people need or want: [+ about] *Mom's good about lending people money when they need it.* | [good of sb (to do sth)] *It was good of her to offer us a ride home.* | [good to sb] *Mrs. Russell has always been good to me.*
15 morally right morally right in what someone believes or does: *a good woman* | *Mr. Amos lived a good life.* | *That's my good deed* (=something you do

to help someone) *for the day.* | *The* **good guys** (=the people who behave in the morally right way, especially in movies) *often wear white hats in these old movies.* | *Stay away from Gerry. He's* **no good** (=a morally bad person). —opposite BAD¹ (4)

16 large/long large in amount, area, or range: *I'd walked a good distance that day.* | *a good-sized house* | *They've been gone* **a good while** (=a long time).

17 complete complete and thorough: *The dog definitely needs a good bath.* | *Take a good look at this picture.*

18 a good deal a lot: *I've spent a good deal of time preparing this report.*

19 a good deal larger/better etc. much larger, better etc.: *Your room is a good deal bigger than mine.*

20 as good as almost: **as good as done/finished** etc. *The work is as good as finished.* | **as good as dead/ruined/useless** etc. *The carpet's as good as ruined.*

21 likely to happen likely to happen; STRONG: *There's a good chance of rain tomorrow.* —opposite POOR, WEAK

22 believable likely to be believed or persuade people: *You'd better have a good explanation for being late.*

SPOKEN PHRASES

23 good a) used to say that you are pleased that something happens or is done: *"Everything's packed and we're ready to go." "Good." | "I brought my grade up to an A minus in Biology, Mom." "Oh, good."* **b)** used to tell someone that you think their work or what they are doing is of a high quality or standard: *Keep your eye on the ball and follow through on your swing. Good!*

24 good idea/point/question etc. used when someone says or suggests something interesting or important that you had not thought of before: *"Let's take some sandwiches with us." "Good idea." | Uh, good question. I'll have to find out for you.*

25 good luck used to say that you hope that someone is successful, or that something good will happen to them: *Good luck on your job interview tomorrow.*

26 that's good used to approve of something: *"We're going to buy a house." "Oh, that's good!" | The stove's brand new? That's good.*

27 good for you/her/him etc. used to say that you approve of or are pleased with what someone has done or decided: *"He told Sandy that his personal life was none of her business." "Well, good for him." | "I made the team!" "Good for you!"*

28 it's a good thing said when you are glad something has happened, because there would have been problems if it had not happened: *It's a good thing you remembered to bring napkins.*

29 good grief/God/Lord/heavens/gracious! used to express surprise, anger, or other strong feelings: *Good grief! I forgot my keys again.*

30 have a good one used to say goodbye and wish someone a nice day

31 good enough used when you are satisfied with something: *"Is that okay?" "Yeah, good enough." | He said six golf balls weren't good enough. He needed a minimum of nine.*

32 as good a time/place etc. as any used to say that although a time etc. is not perfect, there will not be a better one: *Well, I suppose this is as good a spot as any to set up camp.*

33 that's a good one used to tell someone that you do not believe something they have said and think it is a joke or a trick: *My car's on fire? Boy, that's a good one!*

34 what a good girl/boy/dog etc. used to tell a child or animal that it has behaved well or done something well: *You picked up all of your toys. What a good boy!*

35 good and ready completely prepared and willing to do something: *Don't rush me! I'll call her when I'm good and ready.*

36 that's no good used to say that something is not appropriate or convenient: *"Could you come over for dinner Thursday?" "That's no good. I'm busy that day."*

37 be good for a laugh to be enjoyable or amusing to do, although not useful, important etc.: *Let's go watch Brent play volleyball. That'll be good for a laugh.*

38 all in good time used when someone wants you to hurry but you are not going to: *"When are you going to pay me?" "All in good time."*

39 if you know what's good for you used to threaten someone and to say that something bad will happen to them if they do not do something: *If you know what's good for you, you'll do what I tell you.*

40 it's all good SLANG used to say that a situation is good or acceptable, or not a problem: *Don't worry about it man – it's all good.*

41 be good to go to be ready to do something: *I've got my shoes on and I'm good to go.*

42 would you be good enough to do sth also **would you be so good as to do sth** OLD-FASHIONED used to ask someone very politely to do something: *Would you be good enough to get my glasses for me?*

43 a good friend someone who you know very well and like very much

44 a good three miles/ten years etc. at least three miles, ten years etc., and probably more: *It's a good mile away. | He's a good ten years younger than her.*

45 be good for another three years/hundred miles etc. something that is good for a particular length of time will probably be able to be used for that length of time: *This old truck is good for another 100,000 miles.*

46 a good many INFORMAL a fairly large number of people or things: *A good many people are upset about the new gas tax.*

47 too much of a good thing if something becomes too much of a good thing, it stops being pleasant or enjoyable because you have too much of it or it continues for too long: *Spending an entire month at the beach was too much of a good thing.*

48 be too good for sb if someone is too good for someone, they have a better character than the other person: *David doesn't deserve to have a girlfriend like Kate. She's way too good for him!*

49 good old John/Karen etc. used to praise someone, especially because they have behaved in the way that you would expect them to: *Good old Jake! I knew he'd come.*

50 be too good to be true/to last INFORMAL to seem to be so good that you think something must be wrong, or expect something bad to happen: *"She found out he was married." "I knew he was too good to be true!"*

51 the good good people in general, or people who do what is right

52 in her/their etc. own good time INFORMAL someone who does something in their own good time does not do it when other people want them to, but only when they are completely ready to do it

53 good for nothing INFORMAL someone or something that is good for nothing is completely useless and worthless —see also GOOD-FOR-NOTHING

54 be in sb's good graces/book INFORMAL if you are in someone's good graces or book, they like you or approve of you more than they usually do: *I'll ask my boss for the day off – I'm in her good book at the moment.*

55 give as good as you get INFORMAL to react to someone who attacks or harms you by attacking or harming them in a way that is equally strong

56 have a good thing going to be doing something that is successful: *They've got a good thing going with that little business of theirs.*

57 be as good as your word to keep your promise

58 to be good for a meal/a few drinks etc. INFORMAL be likely to give you something: *My uncle should be good for a few bucks.*

59 good offices [plural] FORMAL services, especially services provided by someone in a position of power, that help someone out of a difficulty: *We hope to have*

G

use of the UN's good offices to find a peaceful solution to the crisis.
60 a good word for sb/sth a favorable remark about someone or something: *Stacey put in a good word for me at her company, so I might get a job there.*
61 the good life a simple, natural way of living —see also **so far so good** (FAR¹ (16)), **while the going's good** (GOING¹ (3)), **for good measure** (MEASURE¹ (6)), **that's/it's (all) well and good** (WELL³ (6))

USAGE NOTE: GOOD

WORD CHOICE: good, well
Use **good** as an adjective to talk about the quality of someone or something: *She's a good singer.* Use **well** as an adverb to talk about the way that something is done: *She sings very well.* In spoken English, **good** is sometimes used as an adverb instead of **well**: *You did good.* However, many people think this is incorrect English.

---

s w **good²** *n.*

1 advantage something that improves a situation or gives you an advantage: *It'll do you good* (=make you feel better) *to have a vacation.* | *For his own good, I told him he was completely wrong.* | *do/cause more harm than good Having the tumor removed may do more harm than good.* | *He's too ambitious for his own good* (=his ambition may cause him problems rather than being an advantage). | *Drunk-driving laws were made for the common good* (=the advantage of everyone in society). —see also **do sb a world of good** (WORLD¹ (13))
2 products goods [plural] things that are produced in order to be sold: *The cost of goods and services has soared.* | *fresh baked goods* (=bread, cake etc.) | *Organizers are collecting canned goods* (=food that is packaged in cans) *for the local homeless shelter.* | *The cost of many consumer goods* (=televisions, washing machines etc.) *has risen ten percent in the last five years.* —compare SERVICE¹
3 do no good, not do any good to not have any useful effect: *You can talk to him all you want, but I don't think it'll do any good.*
4 What's the good of...?, What good is...? INFORMAL used to say that having or doing something brings you no advantage: *What's the good of buying an expensive house if I'm always traveling?* | *People are asking, "What good is this democracy to me, when I've got nothing to eat?"*
5 good behavior [U] actions or behavior that are morally right or that follow religious principles: *In spite of his rudeness, there's a lot of good in him.* | *the battle between good and evil* —see also DO-GOODER
6 make good on a debt/promise/threat etc. to do what you say you are going to do or what you should do: *The company made good on its promise to support education by donating 100 computers to local schools.*
7 for good if something changes, stops etc. for good, or if you do something for good, the change etc. is permanent and will always be that way: *The injury may keep him out of football for good.* | *I'd like to stay in Colorado for good.*
8 be up to no good INFORMAL to be doing or planning something wrong or dishonest: *Those guys look like they're up to no good.*
9 make good to become successful after being poor: *Hsieh came to America as a poor teenager, but worked hard and made good.*
10 come up with the goods/deliver the goods to do what other people need or expect: *Neil Young's annual fall concert always delivers the goods with famous musicians and good music.*
11 be (all) to the good to have a positive result or a positive effect on something: *If the higher insurance rates means that drivers will be extra careful, then it's all to the good.*
12 have/get the goods on sb to have or find proof that someone is guilty of a crime: *The two detectives went undercover to get the goods on the Parducci family.*

13 make good your escape LITERARY to succeed in escaping —see also DRY GOODS, **sb's worldly goods/possessions** (WORLDLY (1))

good³ *adv.* SPOKEN, NONSTANDARD well: *Listen to me good!*

good af·ter·noon /ˌ.ˌ..'./ *interjection, n.* [C] FORMAL s w used to say hello when you are greeting someone in the afternoon, especially someone you do not know

Good Book /ˌ. './ *n.* OLD-FASHIONED **the Good Book** the Christian Bible

good·bye /gʊdˈbaɪ, gədˈbaɪ/ *interjection, n.* [C] said when you are leaving or being left by someone: *"Goodbye, Mrs. Anderson."* | *I just have to say goodbye to Erika.* | *We said our goodbyes and left.*

good day /ˌ. './ *interjection* **1** an expression meaning "hello," used when you are greeting someone, especially in the morning or afternoon **2** OLD-FASHIONED an expression used to say hello or goodbye

good eve·ning /ˌ. '../ *interjection, n.* [C] FORMAL used to say hello when you are greeting someone in the evening, especially someone you do not know —compare GOOD NIGHT

good faith /ˌ. './ *n.* **1 in good faith** if an agreement, deal etc. is made in good faith, it is made honestly with no intention to deceive anyone: *We bargained in good faith all the way through.* **2** acting or behaving honestly, with no intention to deceive anyone: *Many of the Democrats question the good faith of the Republicans in reaching a compromise.* —**good-faith** *adj.*: *a good-faith effort*

good-for-noth·ing /'. . ,..'./ *n.* [C] someone who is lazy or has no skills —**good-for-nothing** *adj.* [only before noun] *a lazy good-for-nothing brother*

Good Fri·day /ˌ. './ *n.* [C,U] the Friday before the Christian holiday of EASTER

good-heart·ed /ˌ. '..◂/ *adj.* kind and generous

good-hu·mored /ˌ. '..◂/ *adj.* naturally cheerful and friendly: *Karen is a good-humored, intelligent person.*

good·ie /'gʊdi/ *n.* [C] another spelling of GOODY

good-look·ing /ˌ. '..◂/ *adj.* someone who is good-looking is physically attractive, and especially has an attractive face: *Don't you think Dave is good-looking?* —**good-looker** *n.* [C] —see Usage Note at BEAUTIFUL

good looks /ˌ. './ *n.* [plural] the attractive appearance of someone's face: *Fans admire Dupond for his good looks, grace, and acting ability.*

good·ly /'gʊdli/ *adj.* [only before noun] **1 a goodly number/sum/amount etc.** OLD-FASHIONED a large amount: *a goodly number of people* **2** OLD USE pleasant in appearance or good in quality

good morn·ing /ˌ. '../ also **morning** *interjection, n.* s w [C] used to say hello when you are greeting someone in the morning

good-na·tured /ˌ. '..◂/ *adj.* naturally kind and helpful and not easily made angry: *She's a very good-natured child.* —**good-naturedly** *adv.*

good·ness /'gʊdnɪs/ *n.* [U] s w

SPOKEN PHRASES

1 my goodness/goodness (gracious) said when you are surprised or annoyed: *My goodness, this house is big.* **2 for goodness' sake** said when you are annoyed or surprised: *For goodness' sake, be quiet!* **3 goodness (only) knows** used to emphasize that you are not sure about something, or to make a statement stronger: *The last bridge cost $30 million, and goodness knows how much a new one will cost.*

---

4 the quality of being good: *Anne believes in the basic goodness of all people.* **5** the part of food that tastes good or is good for your health: *Walnuts add crunchy goodness to salads, soups, and desserts.* —see also **goodness gracious** (GRACIOUS²), HONEST-TO-GOODNESS, **thank God/goodness/heavens** (THANK (3))

good night /ˌ. './ *interjection, n.* [C] used to say good- s w bye when you are leaving or being left by someone at night, especially before going to bed or to sleep: *Good night. Sleep well.* —compare GOOD EVENING, **night, night** (NIGHT (6))

good old boy /ˌ. . './ also **good ol' boy** /ˌgʊd oʊl ˈbɔɪ/

n. [C] INFORMAL a white man from the southern U.S. who is loud, friendly, and has rough manners, often considered to be uneducated or RACIST by people who are not like this

Good Sa·mar·i·tan, good Samaritan /ˌɡʊd səˈmærət̬ n̩/ *n.* [C] a person who helps people who need help, especially strangers

good-tem·pered /ˌ. ˈ...•/ *adj.* cheerful and not easily made angry

good·will /ɡʊdˈwɪl/ *n.* [U] **1** kind feelings toward or between people and a willingness to be helpful: *The visit by the Eskimo dancers was made as a goodwill gesture.* **2** the success of a company, and its good relationship with its customers, considered as part of its value

good·y[1] /ˈɡʊdi/ *n. plural* **goodies** [C usually plural] INFORMAL **1** something that is nice to eat: *We brought lots of goodies for the picnic.* **2** something attractive, pleasant, or desirable: *The bank's giving away radios and other goodies when you open a new account.*

goody[2] *interjection* INFORMAL said especially by children to express pleasure or excitement: *Oh, goody – ice cream for dessert!*

Good·year /ˈɡʊdyɪr/, **Charles** (1800–1860) a U.S. inventor who discovered how to VULCANIZE rubber and make it strong enough for car tires

goody-goody /ˈ.. ,.., ,.. ˈ../ *also* **goody-two-shoes** /ˌ.. ˈ. ./ *n. plural* **goody-goodies** [C] DISAPPROVING someone who likes to seem very good and helpful in order to please their parents, teachers etc.

goo·ey / ɡui/ *adj.* **gooier, gooiest** INFORMAL **1** sticky, soft and often sweet: *gooey chocolate cakes* **2** expressing your love for someone in a way that other people think is silly; SENTIMENTAL: *Babies make her go all gooey.*

goof[1] /ɡuf/ *v.* [I] INFORMAL to make a silly mistake: *Somebody at the company goofed and entered the wrong check amount.*

goof around *phr. v.* [I] INFORMAL to spend time doing silly things or not doing very much: *We spent the afternoon just goofing around the mall.*

goof off *phr. v.* [I] INFORMAL to waste time or avoid doing any work: *If you hadn't been goofing off, you would have had your paper written by now.* —**goof-off** *n.* [C]

goof up *phr. v.* [I,T **goof sth ↔ up**] INFORMAL to make a silly mistake: *What can I say? I just goofed up.* | *The printer goofed up my business cards by spelling my name wrong.* —**goof-up** *n.* [C]

goof[2] *n.* [C] INFORMAL **1** a silly mistake: *The goof could cost the city $5 million.* **2** someone who is silly

goof·ball /ˈɡufbɔl/ *n.* [C] INFORMAL someone who is silly or stupid

goof·y /ˈɡufi/ *adj.* **goofier, goofiest** INFORMAL stupid or silly: *I look goofy in that picture.* —**goofily** *adv.* —**goofiness** *n.* [U]

goo·gol /ˈɡuɡɔl/ *n.* [C] TECHNICAL the number that is written as the number 1 followed by 100 zeros

goo·gol·plex /ˈɡuɡɔlˌplɛks/ *n.* [C] TECHNICAL the number that is written as the number 1 followed by a googol of zeros

goo goo /ˈ. ./ *n.* [C] a word used for a sound that babies make

goo-goo eyes /ˌ.. ˈ./ *n.* [plural] HUMOROUS a silly look that shows that you love someone: *Hey, Dave's making goo-goo eyes at Barbara.* —**goo-goo eyed** *adj.*

gook /ɡuk/ *n.* [C] TABOO someone from a country in Eastern Asia. Do not use this word.

goon /ɡun/ *n.* [C] INFORMAL **1** a violent criminal who is paid to frighten or attack people **2** a silly or stupid person

goop /ɡup/ *n.* [U] INFORMAL a thick, slightly sticky substance: *What's that goop you're putting on your hair?*

goose[1] /ɡus/ *n.* **1 a)** *plural* **geese** [C] a bird that is similar to a duck but larger and makes loud noises **b)** a female goose —compare GANDER (1) **2** [U] the cooked meat of this bird **3 what's good/sauce for**

the goose is good/sauce for the gander used to say that what is fair for one person is fair for other people too **4** OLD-FASHIONED a silly person —see also **kill the goose that lays the golden egg** (KILL[1] (13)), WILD GOOSE CHASE

goose[2] *v.* [T] INFORMAL to hit or press someone on their BUTTOCKS as an impolite joke

goose·ber·ry /ˈɡusˌbɛri/ *n. plural* **gooseberries** [C] a small round green fruit with a sour taste that grows on a bush

goose·bumps /ˈɡusbʌmps/ *n.* [plural] a condition in which your skin is raised up in small points because you are cold, afraid or excited

goose·down /ˈɡusdaʊn/ *n.* [U] the soft fine feathers of a GOOSE, often used between layers of material to make warm clothes and bed covers

goose egg /ˈ. ./ *n.* [singular] INFORMAL zero: *"What score did you get on your test?" "I got a big goose egg."*

goose·flesh /ˈɡusflɛʃ/ *n.* [U] goosebumps

goose pim·ples /ˈ. ,../ *n.* [plural] goosebumps

goose·step /ˈɡus-stɛp/ *n.* **the goosestep** a way of marching, used by soldiers in some countries, in which each step is taken without bending your knee —**goosestep** *v.* [I]

GOP *n.* **the GOP** the Grand Old Party; another name for the Republican Party in U.S. politics

go·pher /ˈɡoʊfɚ/ *n.* [C] **1** a North and Central American animal that looks similar to a large SQUIRREL and lives in holes in the ground, and that often damages crops **2** another spelling of GOFER **3** *also* **Gopher** TRADEMARK a program that helps computer users find and use FILES on the Internet

Gor·ba·chev /ˈɡɔrbəˌtʃɔf/, **Mi·khail** /mɪˈkaɪl/ (1931–) the President of the Soviet Union from 1985 to 1991, who started the process of economic and political change which improved his country's relationship with the West and resulted in the end of Communism in the Soviet Union and Eastern Europe

Gor·di·an knot /ˌɡɔrdiən ˈnɑt/ *n.* **cut the Gordian knot** to quickly solve a difficult problem by determined action

Gor·di·mer /ˈɡɔrdɪmɚ/, **Na·dine** /næˈdin/ (1923–) a South African writer of NOVELS

gore[1] /ɡɔr/ *v.* [T] if an animal gores someone, it wounds them with its horns or TUSKS

gore[2] *n.* **1** [U] LITERARY blood that has flowed from a wound and has become thicker and darker —see also GORY **2** [C] a piece of material that gets wider toward the bottom, used in making a skirt

Gore /ɡɔr/, **Al·bert** /ˈælbɚt/ **(Al)** /æl/ (1948–) a U.S. POLITICIAN who was Vice President under Bill Clinton and a CANDIDATE for U.S. President in 2000

gorge[1] /ɡɔrdʒ/ *n.* [C] a deep narrow valley with steep sides

gorge[2] *v.* **1 gorge yourself (on/with sth)** to eat until you are too full to eat any more: *We gorged ourselves on popcorn and hot dogs at the game.* **2 be gorged with sth a)** to be too full of something: *The Chari River is gorged with water during the rainy season, and often floods.* **b)** to have eaten so much of something that you are completely full: *Snakes were gorged with small rodents in preparation for their winter hibernation.*

gor·geous /ˈɡɔrdʒəs/ *adj.* INFORMAL **1** extremely beautiful or attractive: *Liz is absolutely gorgeous.* **2** extremely pleasant or enjoyable: *What a gorgeous day* (=a day with warm and sunny weather)! —**gorgeously** *adv.*

Gor·gon /ˈɡɔrɡən/ *n.* [C] one of the three sisters in ancient Greek stories, who had snakes on their heads that made anyone who looked at them change into stone

go·ril·la /ɡəˈrɪlə/ *n.* [C] **1** a very large African monkey that is the largest of the APES **2** SLANG an ugly strong man, especially one who is employed to protect an important person

Gor·ky /ˈgɔrki/**, Max·im** /ˈmæksɪm/ (1868–1936) a Russian writer of NOVELs, famous especially for his book about his own life

gorse /gɔrs/ *n.* [U] a bush with bright yellow flowers and sharp pointed parts on its stems, which grows in Europe

gor·y /ˈgɔri/ *adj.* **gorier, goriest 1** INFORMAL clearly describing or showing violence, blood, and killing: *a gory movie* **2 the gory details** HUMOROUS all the interesting details about an event, especially a bad one: *Come on, I want to hear all the gory details.* **3** LITERARY covered in blood —see also GORE² (1)

gosh /gɑʃ/ *interjection* INFORMAL used to express surprise: *Gosh, I didn't know that about Louis.*

gos·ling /ˈgɑzlɪŋ/ *n.* [C] a young GOOSE

gos·pel /ˈgɑspəl/ *n.* **1 Gospel** [C] one of the four stories of Jesus Christ's life in the Christian Bible **2** [C usually singular] a particular set of ideas that someone believes in very strongly and tries to persuade other people to accept: **preach/spread the gospel (of sth)** *Young is tireless in preaching his gospel of economic growth.* **3** [U] something that is completely true: *Don't take what Ellen says as gospel.* **4 the gospel truth** if you think or say that something is the gospel truth, you believe completely that it is true: *I've never met him before, and that's the gospel truth.* **5** [U] also **gospel music** a style of Christian music usually performed by black singers, in which religious songs are sung strongly and loudly: *a gospel singer*

gos·sa·mer /ˈgɑsəmɚ/ *n.* [U] **1** LITERARY a very light thin material: *a gossamer silk kimono* **2** something that is light and delicate **3** light silky thread which SPIDERs leave on grass and bushes

gos·sip¹ /ˈgɑsəp/ *n.* **1** [C,U] conversation or information about other people's behavior and private lives, often including remarks that are untrue or not nice: *Polly follows all the gossip about the royal family.* | *She always knows all the juicy gossip* (=interesting and often shocking information). | *idle gossip* (=gossip not based on facts) **2 the gossip mill** the people who start gossip **3** [C] someone who likes talking about other people's private lives

gossip² *v.* [I] to talk or write gossip about someone or something: *This is where the locals gather to gossip and talk politics.* | [+ about] *Employees were gossiping about the latest rumors.*

gossip col·umn /ˈ.. ˌ../ *n.* [C] a regular article in a newspaper or magazine about the behavior and private lives of famous people —**gossip columnist** *n.* [C]

gos·sip·y /ˈgɑsəpi/ *adj.* INFORMAL **1** talk or writing that is gossipy is informal and full of gossip: *a gossipy magazine* **2** a gossipy person likes to gossip

got /gɑt/ *v.* **1** the past tense of GET **2** a PAST PARTICIPLE of GET

USAGE NOTE: GOT

WORD CHOICE: got, gotten, have got, have
Use **gotten** as the past participle of **get**: *I have gotten up early every day this week.* You can use **got** as a past tense verb instead of "become": *Kim just got engaged.* You can use **have got** to mean "possess" or "own": *They've got three cars.* Usually, though, we use **have** instead for this: *They have three cars.*

---

got·cha /ˈgɑtʃə/ *interjection* INFORMAL **1** a short form of "I've got you," said when you catch someone or when you have gained an advantage over them: *"Did he really say that?" "Gotcha* (=I fooled you)*!" | Gotcha, Katie! Now I'm gonna tickle you!* **2** a word meaning "I understand" or "all right": *"Put used white paper in this box and used colored paper in that one." "Gotcha."*

Goth /gɑθ/ one of the people from central Europe, in what is now Germany, who attacked and moved into the Roman Empire several times between the 3rd and 5th centuries A.D.

goth /gɑθ/ *n.* **1** [U] a type of loud, slow, and sad popular music that is played on electric GUITARs and KEYBOARDs **2** [C] someone who likes goth music and dresses in a style that includes having very pale skin and wearing dark eye MAKEUP and black clothes

Goth·ic /ˈgɑθɪk/ *adj.* **1** the Gothic style of building was common in Western Europe between the 12th and 16th centuries. Its main features were pointed ARCHes, tall PILLARs, and tall thin pointed windows **2** a Gothic story, movie etc. is about frightening things that happen in mysterious old buildings and lonely places, especially stories that were popular in the early 19th century **3** Gothic writing, printing etc. has thick decorated letters

got·ta /ˈgɑtə/ SPOKEN, NONSTANDARD a short form of "got to," "have got to," "has got to," "have got a," or "has got": *I gotta go now.* | *Gotta keep this light off, okay?* | *Bob, you gotta minute to talk to Randy?* | *I've still gotta get traveler's checks.*

got·ten /ˈgɑtⁿn/ *v.* the past participle of GET: *You've gotten us into a lot of trouble.*

gou·ache /guˈɑʃ, gwɑʃ/ *n.* **1** [U] a method of painting using colors that are mixed with water and made thicker with a type of GUM¹ (3) **2** [C] a picture produced by this method

Gou·da /ˈgudə/ *n.* [U] a yellow Dutch cheese that does not have a very strong taste

gouge¹ /gaʊdʒ/ *v.* [T] **1** to make a deep hole or cut in the surface of something: *Bombs from the B-52s gouged huge craters in the downtown area.* **2** INFORMAL to make people spend too much money for something you are selling: *Hotels are ready to gouge Olympic visitors by raising room prices.*

gouge sth ↔ out *phr. v.* [T] **1** to make a hole in something such as rock etc. by removing material that is on the surface: *Gouge out the decay until the hole shows only sound wood.* **2 gouge sb's eyes out** to remove someone's eyes with a pointed weapon

gouge² *n.* [C] a hole or cut made in something, usually by a sharp tool or weapon

gou·lash /ˈgulɑʃ, -læʃ/ *n.* [C,U] a dish made of meat cooked in liquid with PAPRIKA (=hot tasting pepper)

Gou·nod /guˈnoʊ/**, Charles** (1818–1893) a French musician who wrote CLASSICAL music

gourd /gɔrd, gʊrd/ *n.* [C] **1** a round fruit with a hard outer shell that is sometimes used as a container **2** a container made from this fruit

gour·mand /ˈgʊrmɑnd/ *n.* [C] DISAPPROVING someone who likes to eat and drink a lot of food —compare GOURMET²

gour·met¹ /ʊrˈmeɪ, ˈgʊrmeɪ/ *adj.* [only before noun] producing or relating to very good food and drink: *a gourmet restaurant*

gourmet² *n.* [C] someone who knows a lot about food and wine and who enjoys good food and wine

gout /gaʊt/ *n.* [U] a disease that makes your toes, fingers, and knees swollen and painful —**gouty** *adj.*

gov·ern /ˈgʌvɚn/ *v.* **1** [I,T] to officially and legally control a country and make all the decisions about taxes, laws, public services etc.: *The same party has governed the country for thirty years.* **2** [T] if rules, principles etc. govern the way a system or situation works, they control how it happens or what happens: *Rules governing the distribution of legal drugs are likely to be changed.* **3** [T] OLD-FASHIONED to control a strong or dangerous emotion

gov·ern·ess /ˈgʌvənɪs/ *n.* [C] a female teacher who lives with a rich family and teaches their children at home

gov·ern·ing /ˈgʌvənɪŋ/ *adj.* **1** [only before noun] having the power to control an organization country etc.: *FIFA is the governing body* (=the group of people controlling an organization) *of world soccer.* | *Kaifu's two-year term as leader of the governing party* (=the political party that is governing a country) *has ended.* **2 governing principle** a principle that has the most important influence on something: *Freedom of speech for all is one of the governing principles in a democracy.* —see also SELF-GOVERNING

gov·ern·ment /'gʌvəmənt, 'gʌvənmənt/ *n.* **1** [C] also **Government** the group of people who govern a country or state: *the French government* | *The government said that Iceland has no plans to resume whaling.* | **government policies/funding/statistics** etc. *Government figures show that bankruptcies have increased this year.* **2** [C,U] a form or system of government: *The local government* (=the government of towns, cities etc.) *is unable to meet the demands for affordable housing.* | *It has been difficult for the central government* (=the government of a whole country) *to conduct elections in remote regions.* | *The federal government* (=the government of a whole country in which states make some laws) *will supply $10.1 million of the $15 million needed.* **3** [U] the process of governing, or the system used for governing: *The Liberal Democrats have been in government* (=governed) *for five years.* | *The voters just want good government and less taxes.* **4** [C,U] the degree to which the government controls economic and social activities: *Conservatives have protested against big government* (=when the government controls many activities) *and federal spending.* — **governmental** *adj.* /'gʌvəməntl/

S W
2

gov·er·nor, Governor /'gʌvənə, -və-/ *n.* [C] **1 a)** the person in charge of governing a state in the U.S.: *the governor of South Dakota* | *Governor Brown refused to answer the question.* **b)** the person in charge of governing a country that is under the political control of another country: *the former governor of Hong Kong* **2** a part of a machine that controls how the machine works, especially by limiting it in some way —see also GUBERNATORIAL

Governor-Gen·er·al /,... '.../ *n.* [C] someone who represents the King or Queen of Great Britain in other Commonwealth countries which are not REPUBLICS: *the Governor-General of Australia*

gov·er·nor·ship /'gʌvənəˌʃɪp/ *n* [U] the position of being governor, or the period during which someone is governor

govt. a written abbreviation of "government"

gown /gaʊn/ *n.* [C] **1** a long dress worn by a woman on formal occasions: *a silk evening gown* **2** a long loose piece of clothing worn by someone staying in a hospital **3** a long loose piece of clothing worn for special ceremonies by people such as judges or teachers at universities

goy /gɔɪ/ *n. plural* **goyim** /'gɔɪ-ɪm/ *or* **goys** [C] DISAPPROVING a word used by Jewish people to talk about someone who is not Jewish

Go·ya /'gɔɪə/, **Fran·cis·co de** /fran'sɪskoʊ dɪ/ (1746–1828) a Spanish artist famous for his pictures of members of the royal families of Spain

G.P. *n.* [C] the abbreviation of GENERAL PRACTITIONER

GPA *n.* [C] grade point average; a number representing the average of all a student's grades, in which an A is 4 points, a B is 3, a C is 2, a D is 1, and an F is 0: *Applicants need at least a 3.1 GPA.*

S W
1 **3**

grab¹ /græb/ *v.* **grabbed, grabbing** [T] **1** to take hold of someone or something with a sudden or violent movement: *Two men grabbed her and pushed her to the ground.* | [**grab sth from sb/sth**] *Stuart grabbed a flashlight from his car.* | *He quickly grabbed hold of the rope and saved the boat from floating out to sea.* **2** INFORMAL to get some food or sleep quickly because you are busy: *Do we have time to grab a bite to eat before the movie?* **3 grab a chance/opportunity** INFORMAL to take the opportunity to do or have something immediately: *Sylvia grabbed the chance to work in Italy for the summer.* **4** to take something for yourself, sometimes in an unfair way: *The firm is trying to grab a share of the market from competitors.* | *Could you get there early and grab some good seats for us?* | *Tompkins grabbed the lead* (=he took first place in a race) *from Barve.* **5 how does sth grab you?** SPOKEN used to ask someone if they would be interested in doing a particular thing: *How does going to Hawaii for Christmas grab you?*

grab at *phr. v.* [T] to quickly and suddenly put out your hand in order to take hold of something: *Tubbs grabbed at a camera lens and ripped the cover off.*

grab² *n.* **1 make a grab for/at sth** to suddenly try to

take hold of something: *He made a grab for the knife.* **2 be up for grabs** INFORMAL if a job, prize, opportunity etc. is up for grabs, it is available for anyone who wants to try to have it **3** [C] the act of getting something quickly, especially dishonestly: *Hamilton's actions were nothing more than a power grab within the company.*

grab bag /'. ,./ *n.* **1** [C] a container filled with small presents, in which you put your hand to pick one out **2** [singular] a mixture of different things or styles: *The treaty covers a grab bag of issues.* **3** [singular] INFORMAL a situation in which things are decided by chance

grab·by /'græbi/ *adj.* **grabbier, grabbiest** INFORMAL a word used when speaking to children, to say that they are being SELFISH and impolite by grabbing things: *Don't be so grabby! I have one for you too.*

grace¹ /greɪs/ *n.*

S W
3

1 way of moving [U] a smooth way of moving that seems natural, relaxed, and attractive: *She moved with the grace of a dancer.*

2 behavior **a)** [U] polite and pleasant behavior: *The princess always handled herself with grace and dignity.* | [**have the grace to do sth**] *At least he had the grace to admit he was wrong.* **b) graces** [plural] the skills needed to behave in a way that is considered polite and socially acceptable: *social graces*

3 more time [U] also **grace period** more time that is added to the period you are allowed for finishing a piece of work, paying a debt etc.: *I have a six-month grace period before I have to begin paying back my student loans.* | **a day's/week's** etc. **grace** *My professor gave me a few days' grace to finish my essay.*

4 with good/bad grace willingly and cheerfully, or in an unwilling and angry way: *Kevin smiled and accepted defeat with good grace.*

5 god's kindness [U] God's kindness, shown to people because he loves them: *You are saved by grace alone, not by good works.* | **By the grace of God** (=because of God's kindness), *Alan wasn't hurt in the accident.*

6 prayer [C,U] a prayer thanking God, said before a meal: *Frank, would you say grace for us?*

7 soul [U] the state of someone's soul when it has been freed from evil, according to Christian belief: *a state of grace* (=a state when you die in which you are forgiven by God for what you have done wrong)

8 Your/His etc. **Grace** used as a title for talking to or about a DUKE, DUCHESS, or ARCHBISHOP

9 the Graces three beautiful Greek GODDESSes who often appear in art —see also **fall from grace/favor** (FALL¹ (35)), **be in sb's good graces/book** (GOOD¹ (54)), **saving grace** (SAVE¹ (12))

grace² *v.* [T] **1 grace sb/sth with your presence** HUMOROUS an expression meaning to bring honor to an occasion or group of people by being present, said when someone arrives late, or when someone who does not often come to events arrives **2** to make a place or an object look more beautiful or attractive: *His portrait now graces the wall of the drawing room.*

grace·ful /'greɪsfəl/ *adj.* **1** moving in a smooth and attractive way, or having a smooth attractive shape: *a graceful dancer* | *graceful silk flowers* **2** polite and exactly right for a situation: *a graceful acceptance of defeat* —**gracefully** *adv.* —**gracefulness** *n.* [U]

grace·less /'greɪslɪs/ *adj.* moving or doing something in a way that seems awkward: *I managed a slow graceless turn as I skied down the hill for the first time.* —**gracelessness** *n.* [U]

gra·cious¹ /'greɪʃəs/ *adj.* **1** behaving in a polite, kind, and generous way: *a gracious hostess* **2** having the type of expensive style, comfort, and beauty that only wealthy people can afford: *a gracious Victorian country home* | *gracious living* (=an easy way of life enjoyed by rich people) **3** a word meaning "kind and forgiving," used to describe God —**graciously** *adv.* —**graciousness** *n.* [U]

gra·cious² *interjection* OLD-FASHIONED also **goodness**

G

gracious used to express surprise or to emphasize "yes" or "no"

grack·le /'grækəl/ *n.* [C] a type of bird with shiny black feathers

grad[1] /græd/ *n.* [C] INFORMAL **1** a GRADUATE[1] **2** CANADIAN, INFORMAL a dance to celebrate students' GRADUATION from high school

grad[2] *adj.* [only before noun] INFORMAL: see GRADUATE[3]

grad·a·ble /'greɪdəbəl/ *adj.* a gradable adjective or adverb can be used in the COMPARATIVE or SUPERLATIVE forms, or with words such as "very," "fairly," and "almost" —**gradability** /,greɪdə'bɪləti/ *n.* [U]

gra·da·tion /greɪ'deɪʃən, grə-/ *n.* [C] FORMAL a small change in a set of changes, or one level in a number of levels of development: *The film can display over 4000 gradations of color.*

grade[1] /greɪd/ *n.*
1 school year [C] one of the 12 years you are in school in the U.S., or the students in a particular year: *What grade are you in?* | *The seventh grade is taking a trip to Minneapolis next week.*
2 number/letter in school [C] a number or letter that shows how well you have done in school, college etc.: *Ellen always gets good grades.*
3 standard [C,U] a particular standard, measurement, or level of quality that a product, material etc. has: *Grade A beef* | *weapons-grade nuclear material* | *a low-grade fever* (=a fever with a slightly high temperature)
4 make the grade to succeed or reach the necessary standard: *Only a few athletes make the grade in professional sports.*
5 slope [C] how much slope something has, especially a road or railroad tracks; GRADIENT: *a steep grade*
6 company [C,U] the level of importance you have or the level of pay you receive in a company or organization: *The pay scale is based on grade and length of service.*

grade[2] *v.* [T] **1** to give a grade to a test or to a piece of school work: *I spent the weekend grading tests.* **2** to separate things, or arrange them in order according to their quality or rank: *Beef is graded on the basis of its fat content.* **3** to make something such as road or hill less steep: *The hillsides must be graded to prevent erosion.*

grade cross·ing /'. ,../ *n.* [C] a place where a road and railroad tracks cross each other at the same level, often with gates that close the road while the train passes

grad·ed /'greɪdɪd/ *adj.* **1** designed to suit different levels of learning: *graded textbooks* **2** made level or less steep: *graded highways*

grade point av·er·age /'. . ,../ *n.* [C] GPA

-grad·er /greɪdɚ/ *n.* [C] a student in a particular grade of school: *a cute little first-grader*

grade school /'. ./ *n.* [C] an ELEMENTARY SCHOOL

gra·di·ent /'greɪdiənt/ *n.* [C] **1** a GRADE[1] (5) **2** TECHNICAL the rate of change of pressure, temperature etc. in relation to something else, especially distance, or a curved line representing this

grad·ing /'greɪdɪŋ/ *n.* [U] the activity of checking students' written work and giving it a grade

grad school /'. ./ *n.* [C] INFORMAL a GRADUATE SCHOOL

grad·u·al /'grædʒuəl/ *adj.* **1** happening, developing, or changing slowly over a long time: *We're seeing gradual improvement in labor conditions.* | *Over the past year, her friends have noticed gradual changes in her behavior.* **2** a gradual slope is not steep

grad·u·al·ly /'grædʒuəli, -dʒəli/ *adv.* in a way that happens, develops, or changes slowly over a long time: *She gradually got sicker and sicker.*

grad·u·ate[1] /'grædʒuɪt/ *n.* [C] someone who has successfully completed their studies at a school, college, or university: *a high school graduate* | *[+ of]* a *graduate of Ohio State University* —compare UNDERGRADUATE

grad·u·ate[2] /'grædʒu,eɪt/ *v.* **1** [I] to obtain a DIPLOMA or a degree by completing your studies at a school, college, or university: *[+ from] Ruth graduated from Princeton.* **2 graduate (from sth) to sth** to start doing something that is better, more advanced, or more important: *Bob played college baseball but never graduated to the majors.* **3** [T] to give a DIPLOMA or a degree to someone who has completed a course of study: *We expect to graduate nearly 300 students this year.*

grad·u·ate[3] /'grædʒuɪt/ *adj.* [only before noun] relating to or involved in study for a MASTER'S DEGREE or a DOCTORATE, after receiving your first degree from a college or university: *a graduate student*

grad·u·at·ed /'grædʒu,eɪtɪd/ *adj.* **1** divided into different levels or GRADES[1] (3): *graduated rates of income tax* **2** a graduated tool or container has small marks on it showing measurements

graduate school /'grædʒuɪt ,skul/ *n.* [C] a college or university where you can study for a MASTER'S DEGREE or a DOCTORATE after receiving your first degree, or the period of time when you study for these degrees

grad·u·a·tion /,grædʒu'eɪʃən/ *n.* **1** [U] the time when you complete a college or university degree or high school education: *After graduation Jayne went to nursing school.* **2** [U] a ceremony at which you receive a DIPLOMA or degree: *We're going to Sarah's graduation today.* **3** [C] a mark showing measurement on an instrument or container for measuring

graf·fi·ti /grə'fiti/ *n.* [U] writing and pictures illegally drawn on the walls of buildings, trains etc., that usually say something impolite or funny or give a political opinion

graft[1] /græft/ *n.* **1** [C] a piece of healthy skin or bone taken from someone's body and put in or on another part of their body that has been damaged **2** [C] a piece cut from one plant and attached to another plant, so that it grows there **3** [U] the practice of dishonestly using your position or influence to get money or advantages: *Six politicians were accused of graft and corruption.*

graft[2] *v.* [T] **1** to put a piece of skin or bone from one part of someone's body onto another part that has been damaged: *[graft sth onto sth] Doctors grafted skin from Mike's arm onto his face where it was burned.* **2** to join a part of a flower, plant, or tree onto another flower, plant, or tree: *[graft sth onto sth] Clippings from the tree are being grafted onto existing seedlings.* **3** to try to combine an idea, style etc. with another idea or style: *[graft sth onto sth]* | *The political parade was grafted onto the Frontier Days celebration.*

graft off sb *phr. v.* [T] to get money or advantages from someone by dishonestly using your position or influence, especially political influence: *The bosses grafted off the men.*

Gra·ham /'greɪəm/, **Bil·ly** /'bɪli/ (1918–) a U.S. religious leader and EVANGELIST, who travels around the world and tries to persuade people to follow the Christian religion

Graham, Mar·tha /'mɑrθə/ (1894–1991) a U.S. dancer and CHOREOGRAPHER known especially for her work in MODERN DANCE

graham cracker /'greɪəm ,krækɚ/ *n.* [C] a type of sweet brown CRACKER that is made from WHOLE-WHEAT flour

Grail /greɪl/ *n.* the Grail —see HOLY GRAIL

grain /greɪn/ *n.*
1 food **a)** [U] the seeds of crops such as corn, wheat, or rice that are gathered for use as food, or the crops themselves: *fields of grain* | *five-grain cereal* **b)** [C] a single seed of wheat, rice etc.
2 small piece [C] a single, very small piece of a substance such as sand, salt etc.
3 the grain the lines or patterns you can see in things such as wood, rock, or flesh: *Split the wood along the grain.*
4 go/cut against the grain to do something or happen in a way that is different from what people expect and usually accept: *The song goes against the grain of the slick country music establishment.*

5 a grain of truth/doubt etc. a small amount of truth, doubt etc.: *There's more than a grain of truth in what Spencer said.*

6 take sth with a grain of salt to not completely believe what someone tells you because you know that they often lie or are wrong: *When Kevin talks sometimes you have to take it with a grain of salt.*

7 **measure** [C] TECHNICAL the smallest measure of weight, used for medicines, equal to 0.002285 OUNCES or 0.0648 grams

grain·y /'greɪni/ *adj.* **grainier, grainiest 1** a photograph that is grainy has a rough appearance, as if the images are made up of spots **2** a grainy substance feels rough when you touch it or eat it because it contains many small pieces, seeds, or grains: *grainy mustard*

gram, gramme /græm/ *written abbreviation* **g** or **gm** *n.* [C] a unit for measuring weight in the METRIC system, equal to 1/1000 of a kilogram or 0.035 OUNCES

-gram /græm/ *suffix* [in nouns] something that is written or drawn: *See the diagram on page 20.* | *I got the telegram this morning.*

gram·mar /'græmɚ/ *n.* **1** [U] the rules according to which the words of a language change their form and are combined into sentences, or the study or use of these rules: *English grammar is very different from Japanese grammar.* | *Students' essays will be graded for grammar and spelling.* **2** [C] a particular description of grammar, or a book that describes grammar rules: *a good French grammar*

gram·mar·ian /grə'mɛriən/ *n.* [C] someone who studies and knows about grammar

grammar school /'.. ,./ *n.* [C] OLD-FASHIONED an ELEMENTARY SCHOOL

gram·mat·i·cal /grə'mætɪkəl/ *adj.* **1** [only before noun] relating to the use of grammar: *grammatical errors* **2** correct according to the rules of grammar: *a grammatical sentence* —**grammatically** /-kli/ *adv.*

gramme /græm/ *n.* [C] another spelling of GRAM

Gram·my /'græmi/ *n. plural* **Grammys** or **Grammies** [C] a prize given in the U.S. every year to the best song, the best singer etc. in the music industry

gram·o·phone /'græmə,foʊn/ *n.* [C] OLD-FASHIONED a RECORD PLAYER

Gramps /græmps/ *n.* SPOKEN, INFORMAL a word meaning "grandfather," that is used when speaking to him: *Come on, Gramps. It's time for dinner.*

gra·na·ry /'greɪnəri, 'græ-/ *n. plural* **granaries** [C] **1** a place where grain is stored **2** an area that produces a lot of grain: *The U.S. is one of the world's leading granaries.*

grand[1] /grænd/ *adj.* **1** a word used with some expressions to mean bigger, more impressive, higher in rank etc. than others of the same kind: *The grand finale is the Handel's "Hallelujah" chorus.* | *Carne filmed the movie on a grand scale during World War II.* | *the grand prize* **2 grand total** the final total you get when you add up several numbers or amounts **3** a grand plan, idea etc. aims to achieve something very impressive: *the grand ideas of Gandhi* **4 the grand old man of sth** a man who has been involved in an activity or a profession for a long time and is highly respected: *the grand old man of Japanese design* **5** kind, impressive, and respected: *She was a grand lady loved by everyone.* **6** OLD-FASHIONED impressive, and done or made in a way that attracts attention **7** OLD-FASHIONED very good, pleasant, or enjoyable —**grandly** *adv.* —**grandness** *n.* [U]

grand[2] *n.* [C] **1** *plural* **grand** INFORMAL a thousand dollars: *She made 60 grand last year.* **2** INFORMAL a GRAND PIANO

Grand Can·yon, the /ˌ. '../ a very large, deep GORGE in the southwestern U.S., in the state of Arizona

grand·child /'græntʃaɪld/ *n. plural* **grandchildren** /-ˌtʃɪldrən/ [C] the child of your son or daughter

Grand Cou·lee Dam, the /ˌgrænd ˌkuli 'dæm/ a DAM built across the Columbia River in the U.S. state of Washington

grand·dad /'grændæd/ *n.* [C] INFORMAL grandfather

grand·dad·dy /'grænˌdædi/ *n. plural* **grandaddies** [C] INFORMAL **1** grandfather **2 the grandaddy of sth**

the first or greatest example of something: *Aspirin is the granddaddy of pain relievers.*

grand·daugh·ter /'grænˌdɔtɚ/ *n.* [C] the daughter of your son or daughter

grande dame /ˌgran 'dam/ *n. plural* **grandes dames** or **grande dames** /ˌgran 'dam/ [C] a respected older woman who has a lot of experience in a particular subject: *a grande dame of American theater*

gran·dee /græn'di/ *n.* [C] **1** a Spanish or Portuguese NOBLEMAN of the highest rank **2** someone who has a lot of influence or power, especially in politics

gran·deur /'grændʒɚ, -dʒʊr/ *n.* [U] impressive beauty, power, or size: *the grandeur of the Rocky Mountains* —see also **delusions of grandeur** (DELUSION (2))

grand·fa·ther[1] /'grænd,faðɚ/ *n.* [C] the father of your father or mother

grandfather[2] *v.* [T] also **grandfather sb/sth ↔ in** to give someone or something special permission to continue doing what they have been doing and not obey a new law or rule: *Even though the new owners banned pets, they grandfathered my cat so I could stay.*

grandfather clause /'... ,./ *n.* [C] a part of a new law or rule that gives people who were already doing something that is now against the law or rule special permission to continue doing it: *There's a grandfather clause that allows us to continue selling abroad even though we don't meet the new regulations.*

grandfather clock /'... ,./ *n.* [C] a tall clock in a wooden case that stands on the floor

grand fi·nal·e /ˌ. '..ˌ/ *n.* [C] the last and most impressive or exciting part of a show or performance

gran·dil·o·quent /græn'dɪləkwənt/ *adj.* FORMAL using words that are too long and formal in order to sound important; POMPOUS: *a grandiloquent prose style* —**grandiloquence** *n.* [U]

gran·di·ose /'grændi,oʊs, ˌgrændi'oʊs/ *adj.* grandiose plans, buildings, thoughts etc. seem very important or impressive but are not practical: *It's just another of Wheeler's grandiose schemes.*

grand ju·ry /ˌ. '../ *n.* [C] LAW a group of people who decide whether someone who may be guilty of a crime should be judged in a court of law —**grand juror** *n.* [C]

grand lar·ce·ny /ˌ. '..ˌ/ *n.* [U] LAW the crime of stealing very valuable goods

grand·ma /'grændma, 'græma/ *n.* [C] INFORMAL **1** grandmother **2** an insulting word for a woman who the person speaking considers to be old: *Hey, grandma, learn how to drive!*

grand mal /ˌgran mal, -mæl/ *n.* [U] TECHNICAL a serious form of EPILEPSY —compare PETIT MAL

grand mas·ter /ˌ. '..ˌ/ *n.* [C] a CHESS player who plays at a very high standard

grand·moth·er /'grænd,mʌðɚ/ *n.* [C] the mother of your mother or father

grand op·er·a /ˌ. '..ˌ/ *n.* [C,U] an OPERA with a serious subject, and in which all the words are sung

grand·pa /'grændpa, 'græmpa/ *n.* [C] INFORMAL **1** grandfather **2** an insulting word for a man who the person speaking considers to be old: *Watch what you're doing, grandpa.*

The Grand Canyon

grand·par·ent /ˈɡrændˌpɛrənt/ n. [C usually plural] one of the parents of your mother or father: *My grandparents live in Oregon.*

grand pi·an·o /ˌ. .ˈ../ n. [C] the type of large piano often used in concerts —compare UPRIGHT PIANO

grand prix /ˌɡrɑn ˈpri/ n. [C] one of a set of international races, especially a car race

grand slam /ˌ. ˈ./ n. [C] **1** a hit in baseball that gets four points because it is a HOME RUN and there are players on all the BASES **2** the act of winning all of a set of important sports competitions in the same year **3** the winning of all of the TRICKS possible in one game of cards, especially in BRIDGE

grand·son /ˈɡrændsʌn/ n. [C] the son of your son or daughter

grand·stand /ˈɡrændstænd/ n. [C] a large structure that has many rows of seats and a roof, where people sit and watch sports competitions, games, or races —compare BLEACHERS

grand·stand·ing /ˈɡrændˌstændɪŋ/ n. [U] actions that are intended to make people notice you or think you are important: *Critics feel that allowing television cameras into the courtroom will lead to grandstanding by lawyers.* —**grandstand** v. [I] —**grandstand** adj. [only before noun]

grand tour /ˌ. ˈ./ n. [C] **1** an occasion when someone takes you through all the rooms in a building to show it to you: *They took us on a grand tour of their new house.* **2 the grand tour** a trip around Europe made in past times by young English or American people from rich families as part of their education

grange /ɡreɪndʒ/ n. [C] OLD-FASHIONED a farm, including the main house and the buildings near it

gran·ite /ˈɡrænɪt/ n. [U] a very hard gray rock, often used in buildings

gran·ny¹, grannie /ˈɡræni/ n. plural **grannies** [C] INFORMAL **1** grandmother **2** an insulting word for a woman who the person speaking considers to be old

granny², grannie adj. [only before noun] having a style typically used by old women: *granny shoes*

granny glass·es /ˈ.. ˌ../ n. [plural] INFORMAL GLASSES that have two very small round pieces of glass for the eyes and a thin metal FRAME: *John Lennon's granny glasses*

granny knot /ˈ.. ˌ./ n. [C] a SQUARE KNOT in which the two pieces of string are crossed in the wrong way so that the knot does not hold well

gra·no·la¹ /ɡrəˈnoʊlə/ n. [U] breakfast food made from mixed nuts, grains, and seeds

granola² adj. [only before noun] INFORMAL, HUMOROUS a granola person eats healthy food, is concerned about the environment, and wears loose comfortable clothing

grant¹ /ɡrænt/ n. [C] an amount of money given to a person or organization, especially by the government, for a particular purpose: *The medical school has received a grant for cancer research.*

grant² v. **1 take sth for granted** to expect that the things or advantages that you have will always exist, and so not pay much attention to them: *Most people take their health for granted.* | *Television is so common now that we take it for granted.* **2 take it for granted (that)** to believe that something is true without making sure; ASSUME: *We just took it for granted that the $1000 was part of the normal fee for buying a house.* **3 take sb for granted** to expect that someone will always be there when you need them, and never show them any special attention or thank them: *He spends all his time at work and takes his wife for granted.* **4** [T] FORMAL to give someone something that they have asked for, especially official permission to do something: [**grant sb sth**] *Ching Hua was granted American citizenship last year.* | *She refused to **grant our request** for an interview.* **5** [I,T] to admit that something is true although it does not make much difference to your opinion: *Granted, he didn't practice much, but he*

still played well. | *I **grant you that** it's a nice-looking car, but I still don't understand why it's so popular.* —**grantor granter** n. [C]

Grant /ɡrænt/, **U·lys·ses** /yuˈlɪsiz/ (1822–1885) the 18th President of the U.S., who had commanded the army of the Union during the American Civil War.

grant·ee /ɡrænˈti/ n. [C] a person or organization that receives a grant

gran·u·lar /ˈɡrænyələ/ adj. consisting of or covered with granules: *granular fertilizer*

gran·u·lat·ed /ˈɡrænyəˌleɪtɪd/ adj. granulated sugar is in the form of small white grains

gran·ule /ˈɡrænyul/ n. [C] a small hard piece of something: *instant coffee granules*

grape /ɡreɪp/ n. [C] a small round green or purple fruit that grows in bunches on a VINE and is often used for making wine: *a bunch of grapes* —see picture at FRUIT¹

grape·fruit /ˈɡreɪpfrut/ n. [C] a round yellow or pink bitter-tasting CITRUS fruit with a thick skin, which looks like a large orange

grape·vine /ˈɡreɪpvaɪn/ n. [C] **1 hear sth through the grapevine** to hear news because it has been passed from one person to another in conversation: *Sarah had heard through the grapevine that Larry was getting the job.* **2** a climbing plant that produces grapes

graph /ɡræf/ n. [C] a drawing that that shows how two or more sets of measurements are related to each other: *The graph on page 6 shows population growth over the past 50 years.* —**graph** v. [T] —see picture at CHART¹

graph·ic¹ /ˈɡræfɪk/ adj. **1 a graphic account/description etc.** a very clear description of an event that gives a lot of details, especially bad ones: *a graphic report of sexual and physical abuse* **2** graphic language uses a lot of swearing and sexual words: *The movie contains graphic language and scenes of drug use.* **3** [only before noun] relating to drawing or printing: *a graphic artist* —compare GRAPHICAL

graphic² n. **1** [C] a drawing, graph etc., especially one that is used to help you understand something **2 graphics** [U] drawings or images that are designed to represent objects or facts, especially in a computer program, or the activity of drawing them: *The computer program allows you to combine text with graphics.*

graph·i·cal /ˈɡræfɪkəl/ adj. relating to or using GRAPHICS: *a graphical computer program* —compare GRAPHIC¹ (3)

graph·i·cal·ly /ˈɡræfɪkli/ adv. **1** clearly and with a lot of detail: *The videotape graphically depicted the accident.* **2** FORMAL using a graph or GRAPHICS: *Temperature changes are shown here graphically.*

graphic arts /ˌ.. ˈ./ n. [plural] the activity of drawing, painting, making prints etc.

graphic de·sign /ˌ.. .ˈ./ n. [U] the art of combining pictures, words, and decoration in the production of books, magazines etc. —**graphic designer** n. [C]

graph·ite /ˈɡræfaɪt/ n. [U] a soft black substance that is a type of CARBON and is used in pencils, paints, and electrical equipment

gra·phol·o·gy /ɡræˈfɑlədʒi/ n. [U] the study of HANDWRITING in order to understand people's characters —**graphologist** n. [C]

graph pa·per /ˈ. ˌ../ n. [U] paper with many squares printed on it, used for drawing GRAPHS

-graphy /ɡrəfi/ suffix [in nouns] the making of a copy, picture, or record of something: *photography* | *a complete bibliography* (=a list of books used in a report, study etc.)

grap·nel /ˈɡræpnəl/ n. [C] **1** an ANCHOR with three or more hooks **2** a GRAPPLING HOOK

grap·ple /ˈɡræpəl/ v. [I] **1** to try hard to deal with a difficult problem: [**+ with**] *He's never had to grapple with the issues that most principals deal with.* **2** to fight or struggle with someone, holding them tightly: [**+ with**] *A young man was grappling with the guard.*

grappling hook /ˈ.. ˌ./ also **grappling i·ron** /ˈ.. ˌ../ n. [C] an iron tool with several hooks on it, that you tie to a rope and use to hold a boat still, look for objects on the bottom of a river etc.

grasp[1] /græsp/ v. [T] **1** to take something and hold it firmly: *The handgrips should be shaped so that children can grasp them firmly.* **2** [not in progressive] to completely understand something, especially a complicated fact or idea: *Taylor manages to explain technical ideas in a way that non-specialists can grasp.* —see also **be grasping/clutching at straws** (STRAW (4))

grasp at sth *phr. v.* [T] **1** to eagerly try to use an opportunity: *I am worried that desperate patients will grasp at any experimental treatment.* **2** to try to reach something: *The crowd grasped at the money.*

grasp[2] *n.* [singular] **1** the ability to understand a complicated idea or situation **have a good/poor etc. grasp of** sth *MacMillan has a grasp of the issues facing the city.* | *I'm afraid that's **beyond my grasp** (=too difficult for me to understand).* **2** your ability to achieve or gain something: *Control of the whole program was now **within her grasp** (=achievable).* **3** a hold on something, or your ability to hold it: [+ **on/of**] *Take a firm grasp on the rope.* **4** control of a situation: *Recent moves have weakened his grasp on power.*

grasp·ing /ˈgræspɪŋ/ *adj.* too eager to get money and unwilling to give any of it away or spend it: *Hanson was a hard, grasping man.*

grass /græs/ *n.* **1** [U] a very common plant with thin green leaves that grows across yards, parks, fields etc., and which is often eaten by animals: *Please keep off the grass.* **2** [C] a particular type of grass: *wild grasses* **3** [U] SLANG: see MARIJUANA **4 the grass is always greener (on the other side)** used to say that other people's situations always seem better than yours, even when they really are not **5 not let the grass grow under your feet** to not waste time or delay starting something —see also GRASS-ROOTS, **snake in the grass** (SNAKE[1])

Grass /græs/, **Gün·ter** /ˈgʊntə/ (1927–) a German writer of NOVELS

grass·hop·per /ˈgræsˌhɒpə/ *n.* [C] an insect that has long back legs for jumping and that makes short loud noises —see also **knee-high to a grasshopper** (KNEE-HIGH[1] (2))

grass·land /ˈgræslænd/ *n.* [U] also **grasslands** [plural] large areas of land covered with wild grass —compare WETLAND, WOODLAND

grass roots /ˌ. './ *n.* **the grass roots** the ordinary people in an organization, rather than the leaders

grass-roots /ˌ. '.◂/ *adj.* relating to or involving the ordinary people in an organization, rather than the leaders: *a grass-roots campaign*

grass snake /'. ./ *n.* [C] a common snake that is not poisonous

gras·sy /ˈgræsi/ *adj.* **grassier, grassiest** covered with grass: *a grassy hill*

grate[1] /greɪt/ v. **1** [T] to rub cheese, fruit etc. against a rough or sharp surface in order to break it into small pieces: *The Parmesan cheese was freshly grated.* —see picture on page 425 **2** [I,T] to make an annoying sound by rubbing against another hard surface, or to make something do this: [+ **on/against**] *chalk grating against a blackboard* **3 grate on sb's nerves** INFORMAL to annoy someone: *My aunt really grates on my nerves.* —see also GRATING[2]

grate[2] *n.* [C] **1** the frame and metal bars that hold the wood, coal etc. in a FIREPLACE **2** a metal frame with bars across it that covers a hole, window etc.: *The homeless slept on subway grates to keep warm.*

grate·ful /ˈgreɪtfəl/ *adj.* **1** feeling that you want to thank someone because of something kind that they have done, or showing this feeling: *Fay is one of Dr. Scott's grateful patients.* | *a grateful sigh of relief* | [+ **for**] *He is grateful for the opportunity to help.* | [**grateful to sb for sth**] *Mona was grateful to Lorenzo for his support.* | [**grateful that**] *I'm grateful that I have a steady job that I enjoy.* | **be deeply/ eternally/extremely grateful** *Mr. Graham is deeply grateful for the cards and flowers he has received.* —opposite UNGRATEFUL **2 I/we would be grateful if...** used in formal situations or letters to

make a request: *I would be grateful if you would allow me to visit your school.* —**gratefully** *adv.*: *We gratefully accepted their offer.*

grat·er /ˈgreɪtə/ *n.* [C] a tool used for grating food: *a cheese grater*

grat·i·fy /ˈgrætɪˌfaɪ/ v. **past tense and past participle gratified** [T] FORMAL **1** to satisfy a desire, need etc.: *Too many men believe that women exist mainly to gratify their needs.* **2** [usually passive] to make someone feel pleased and satisfied: [+ **by**] *She is gratified by all the public support.* | [**be gratified (that)**] *We are gratified that the court has agreed to hear our case.* | [**be gratified to do sth**] *I was gratified to hear that they like my work.* —**gratification** /ˌgrætɪfɪˈkeɪʃən/ *n.* [C,U]

grat·i·fy·ing /ˈgrætɪˌfaɪ-ɪŋ/ *adj.* pleasing and satisfying: *It's gratifying to know that my work has helped so many people.*

grat·ing[1] /ˈgreɪtɪŋ/ *n.* [C] a GRATE[2] (2)

grating[2] *adj.* **1** a grating sound is annoying and not nice to listen to: *a grating voice* **2** tending to annoy people: *a grating personality* —**gratingly** *adv.*

gra·tis /ˈgrætɪs, ˈgrɑ-/ *adj. adv.* provided without payment; free: *Medical advice was provided gratis.*

grat·i·tude /ˈgrætɪˌtud/ *n.* [U] the feeling of being grateful: *I would like to express my gratitude to everyone that helped us.* | [+ **for**] *The first Thanksgiving was celebrated out of gratitude for survival.* —opposite INGRATITUDE —see also **owe a debt (of gratitude) to sb** (DEBT (3))

gra·tu·i·tous /grəˈtuətəs/ *adj.* said or done without a good reason, in a way that offends someone: *The gratuitous killing of dolphins must be stopped.* —**gratuitously** *adv.*

gra·tu·i·ty /grəˈtuəti/ *n. plural* **gratuities** [C] FORMAL a TIP[1] (2)

grave[1] /greɪv/ *n.* [C] **1** the place in the ground where a dead body is buried —compare TOMB **2 sb would turn/roll over in their grave** used to say that someone who is dead would strongly disapprove of something happening now: *Mozart would roll over in his grave if he heard this music.* **3 the grave** ESPECIALLY LITERARY death: *He took that secret with him to the grave.* —see also **from (the) cradle to (the) grave** (CRADLE[1] (3)), **dig your own grave** (DIG[1] (6)), **have one foot in the grave** (FOOT[1] (13)), **a watery grave** (WATERY (4))

grave[2] *adj.* FORMAL **1** very serious and worrying: *I have grave doubts that this new government will last.* | *a grave mistake* **2** looking or sounding very serious, especially because something important or worrying has happened: *Dr. Fromm looked grave. "I have some bad news," he said.* —**gravely** *adv.* —see also GRAVITY (2)

grave[3] *adj.* a grave ACCENT[1] (4) is a mark put above a letter in some languages, such as French, to show the pronunciation, for example è —compare ACUTE (7), CIRCUMFLEX

grave·dig·ger /ˈgreɪvˌdɪgə/ *n.* [C] someone whose job is to dig graves

grav·el /ˈgrævəl/ *n.* [U] small stones used to make a surface for paths, roads etc.: *a gravel driveway* | *a gravel pit* (=a place where gravel is dug out of the ground) —**gravel** *v.* [T]

grav·el·ly /ˈgrævəli/ *adj.* **1** a gravelly voice has a low, rough sound **2** covered with or mixed with gravel: *gravelly soil*

grav·en /ˈgreɪvən/ *adj.* **a graven image** LITERARY an image or figure that has been made out of stone, wood, or metal

grave rob·ber /'. ˌ../ *n.* [C] someone who digs up graves to steal valuable things or the dead bodies inside

grave·side /ˈgreɪvsaɪd/ *n.* **at the graveside** beside a grave, especially when someone is being buried there —**graveside** *adj.* [only before noun] *graveside services*

G

grave·stone /'greɪvstoʊn/ n. [C] TOMBSTONE

grave·yard /'greɪvyɑrd/ n. [C] **1** an area of ground where people are buried, often near a church —compare CEMETERY, CHURCHYARD **2** a place where things that are no longer wanted or useful are left: *a graveyard for old cars*

graveyard shift /'.. ,./ n. [C] a regular period of working time that begins late at night and continues until the early morning, or the people who work during this time: *I've been really tired since I started working the graveyard shift.*

grav·i·tate /'grævə,teɪt/ v. [I always + adv./prep.] FORMAL to be attracted to something and therefore move toward it or become involved with it: [+ to/toward] *Originally he wanted to be an actor, but gravitated toward singing after he moved to Nashville.*

grav·i·ta·tion /,grævə'teɪʃən/ n. [U] **1** TECHNICAL the force that makes two objects such as PLANETs move toward each other because of their MASS **2** the act of gravitating toward something

grav·i·ta·tion·al /,grævə'teɪʃənl/ adj. TECHNICAL relating to or resulting from the force of gravity: *the Earth's gravitational pull*

grav·i·ty /'grævəti/ n. [U] **1** TECHNICAL the force that causes something to fall to the ground or one PLANET to be attracted to another one: *Mars' gravity is only about 38% of Earth's.* **2** FORMAL the seriousness or importance of an event, situation etc.: *I don't think you quite understand the gravity of the situation.* **3** an extremely serious way of behaving, speaking etc.: *They speak with passion and gravity.* —see also CENTER OF GRAVITY

S W
3 **gra·vy** /'greɪvi/ n. plural **gravies** [C,U] **1** SAUCE made from the juice of cooked meat, flour, and water **2** INFORMAL something good that is more than you expected to get: *Once you've paid your debts, the rest of the money **is gravy**.*

G

gravy boat /'.. ,./ n. [C] a long bowl that you pour gravy from

gravy train /'.. ,./ n. **the gravy train** INFORMAL an organization, activity, or business from which many people can make money or profit without much effort

S W
2
3 **gray¹** /greɪ/ adj. **1** having a color of black mixed with white, like rain clouds: *the icy gray waters of the Atlantic* **2** having gray hair: **turn/go gray** *Ryan went gray when he was only 40.* **3** if the weather is gray, the sky is full of clouds and the sun is not bright: *The telegram came on a gray April day.* **4 a gray area** an area of a subject such as law or science that is hard to deal with or understand because it does not have clear rules or limits **5** looking pale because you are tired, frightened, or sick **6** boring and unattractive: *gray faceless bureaucrats*

gray² n. **1** [C,U] the color of smoke and rain clouds, between black and white **2** an animal, especially a horse or a WHALE, that is gray

gray³ v. [I] if someone grays or their hair grays, their hair becomes gray: *Jim's beginning to gray at the temples.*

gray·ing /'greɪ-ɪŋ/ n. **the graying of sth** the process by which a group of people becomes older, or the average age of a population increases: *the graying of America*

gray·ish /'greɪ-ɪʃ/ adj. slightly gray

gray mar·ket /,. '..◂/ n. [C] the system by which people buy and sell goods that are hard to find in a way that is legal, but not morally good or correct —compare BLACK MARKET

gray mat·ter /,. '../ n. [U] INFORMAL your intelligence, or your brain

Gray Pan·thers /,. '../ an organization of older and RETIRED people

graze¹ /greɪz/ v. **1** [I,T] if an animal grazes or if you graze it, it eats grass that is growing: *The sheep continued to graze.* | *Ranchers will have to pay more to graze their cattle on federal land.* **2** [T] to touch something lightly while passing it, sometimes

damaging it: *A bullet grazed his arm.* **3** [T] to break the surface of your skin by rubbing it against something rough: *Billy grazed his knee on the sidewalk when he fell.* **4** [I] INFORMAL to eat small amounts of food instead of having a full regular meal: *Here are some low-fat snacks for holiday grazing.*

graze² n. [C] a wound caused by rubbing, which slightly breaks the surface of your skin

GRE n. [C] TRADEMARK Graduate Record Examination; a test taken by students who have completed a first degree and want to go to GRADUATE SCHOOL

grease¹ /gris/ n. [U] **1** a thick oily substance that is put on the moving parts of a car, machine etc. to make it run or move smoothly **2** soft fat from animals or vegetables, especially after it has melted: *bacon grease*

grease² v. [T] **1** to put grease on something: *Grease the pan before you pour the batter in.* **2 grease sb's palm** to give someone money in a secret or dishonest way in order to persuade them to do something **3 like greased lightning** INFORMAL extremely fast: *They expect the bill to move through Congress like greased lightning.*

grease gun /'. ./ n. [C] a tool for forcing grease into machinery

grease mon·key /'. ,../ n. [C] INFORMAL someone who repairs car engines or other machinery; MECHANIC

grease·paint /'gris-peɪnt/ n. [U] a thick soft kind of paint that actors use on their face or body

greas·er /'grisɚ, -zɚ/ n. [C] **1** OLD-FASHIONED a young man who is very interested in MOTORCYCLEs and cars and behaves in a rough way **2** TABOO someone from Latin America, especially Mexico. Do not use this word.

greas·y /'grisi, -zi/ adj. **greasier, greasiest 1** covered in grease or oil, or full of grease: *greasy French fries* | *long greasy hair* **2** annoyingly friendly in order to get something for yourself: *a greasy gangster* —**greasiness** n. [U]

greasy spoon /,.. './ n. [C] INFORMAL a small cheap restaurant that mainly serves fried (FRY¹ (1)) food

great¹ /greɪt/ adj.
1 useful INFORMAL very useful or appropriate for something: [+ for] *This stuff's great for getting stains out of clothes.*
2 large very large in size, amount, or degree: *the Great Lakes* | *A great many people died.* —see Usage Note at BIG
3 important [only before noun] important, successful, or famous: *Ella Fitzgerald was the greatest jazz singer ever.* | *the Great Powers of Europe* (=the countries with the most power and influence)
4 a great deal a lot: *He's traveled a great deal.* | [+ of] *The explosion caused a great deal of damage.*
5 in good health feeling or looking well and happy: *I feel great this morning!* | *You look great! Have you lost weight?*

S W
1 1

SPOKEN PHRASES

6 very good very good; EXCELLENT: *That was a great dinner.* | *It'd be great if you could come.* | *"I'll see you tomorrow." "Great!"*
7 skillful able to do something well or deal with someone or something well: [+ at] *Candy's great at swimming.* | [+ with] *He's great with babies.*
8 not good said when you really think that something is not good, satisfactory, or enjoyable at all: *"Your car won't be ready until next week." "Oh, great! I need it tomorrow."*
9 the great thing about sth the most important advantage of something: *The great thing about eating out is that you don't have to wash dishes.*
10 it'd be great if... used to ask someone politely to do something to help you: *It'd be great if you could get here by 8:30 tomorrow.*
11 be no great shakes to not be very good or interesting, or not very skillful: *The food we got there was no great shakes.*
12 go great guns INFORMAL to do something very fast and successfully: *The Porters say their business is going great guns.*
13 Great Scott! OLD-FASHIONED used to express surprise

14 great care/pleasure/strength etc. a lot of care etc.: *These lies have caused me and my family great pain.* | *It gives me great pleasure to introduce my next guest.*

15 the Great used in the name or title of someone or something to show their importance: *Alexander the Great* | *the Great Houdini*

16 great-grandmother/great-uncle etc. the grandmother, uncle etc. of one of your parents

17 great-granddaughter/great-nephew etc. the GRANDDAUGHTER, NEPHEW etc. of your child

18 great friend/admirer etc. a very good friend, a serious admirer etc.: [+ **of**] *She is a great admirer of Barbara Bush.*

19 admirable good or generous in a way that should be admired: *Rebuilding the hospital was a great humanitarian gesture.* | *a great lady*

20 Greater used before the name of a city to mean the city and its outer areas: *Greater Los Angeles* —**greatness** *n.* [U] —see also **be heavy/great/big with child** (CHILD (7))

great² *adv.* INFORMAL **1** very well: *I can see great with these glasses.* **2 great big** very big: *a great big box of toys*

great³ *n.* [C usually plural] one of the most famous and successful performers, especially in sports or entertainment: *Jack Nicklaus is one of the all-time greats of golf.*

Great Bar·ri·er Reef, the /ˌ. ˌ... './ the largest CORAL REEF in the world, off the northeast coast of Australia

great·coat /'greɪtˌkoʊt/ *n.* [C] a long heavy coat

Great Di·vid·ing Range, the /ˌ. .'.. ˌ./ a system of mountain RANGEs in Australia that follows the line of the east coast through the states of Victoria, New South Wales, and Queensland

great-grand·child /ˌ. '../ *n.* [C] the GRANDCHILD of your child

Great Lakes, the /ˌ. './ a group of five lakes along the border between the U.S. and Canada, which consists of Lake Superior, Lake Michigan, Lake Huron, Lake Erie, and Lake Ontario

great·ly /'greɪtli/ *adv.* FORMAL [usually before verb or participle] extremely or very much: *The money you sent us was greatly appreciated.* *We greatly enjoyed the play.*

Great Plains /ˌ. './ *n.* **the Great Plains** the MIDWESTERN parts of the U.S. and Canada, where there is a lot of flat land that is used for farming

Great Salt Lake, the /ˌ. . './ a lake in the U.S. state of Utah which is about 70 miles long and has very salty water

Great Smok·y Moun·tains, the /ˌ. ˌ... '../ also **the Great Smokies** /ˌ. '.../ also **the Smokies** a range of mountains in the southeastern U.S. along the border between the states of North Carolina and Tennessee

Great War, the /ˌ. './ another name for WORLD WAR I

grebe /grib/ *n.* [C] a bird similar to a duck

Gre·cian /'griʃən/ *adj.* LITERARY from ancient Greece, or having a style or appearance that is considered typical of ancient Greece: *a Grecian urn*

Greco- /grɛkoʊ/ *prefix* **1** relating to ancient Greece; GREEK **2** ancient Greek and something else: *Greco-Roman art*

Gre·co, El /'grɛkoʊ, ɛl/ —see EL GRECO

Greece /gris/ a country in southeast Europe on the Mediterranean Sea

greed /grid/ *n.* [U] a strong desire for more money, power, possessions etc. than you need: *He is driven by greed and envy.*

greed·y /'gridi/ *adj.* **greedier, greediest** DISAPPROVING **1** always wanting more money, power, possessions etc.: *The fee limit is there to protect veterans from greedy lawyers.* **2** wanting more food or drink than you need: *One of the cats gets greedy and eats the other one's food.* —**greedily** *adv.* —**greediness** *n.* [U]

Greek¹ /grik/ *adj.* **1** relating to or coming from Greece **2** relating to the Greek language **3 Greek god** INFORMAL a very attractive man

Greek² *n.* **1** [U] the language of modern or ancient

Greece **2** [C] someone from Greece **3** [C] a member of a SORORITY or FRATERNITY at an American college or university **4 it's all Greek to me** INFORMAL used to say that you cannot understand something

Greek Or·tho·dox Church, the /ˌ. ˌ... './ a branch of the Christian Church in east Europe and southwest Asia, which split away from the western (now Catholic) church in the year 1054

Green /grin/ *n.* [C] someone who supports a political organization that is concerned about environmental problems —**Green** *adj.*: *Green politics*

green¹ /grin/ *adj.*

1 color having the color of grass or leaves: *Go! The light's green.* | *green eyes*

2 grassy covered with grass, trees, bushes etc.: *rolling green fields*

3 fruit/plant not ready to be eaten, or very young: *green bananas*

4 environment relating to or concerned about the environment: *There are lots of green groups in Portland and Seattle.*

5 be green with envy to want very much something that someone else has

6 without experience INFORMAL young and lacking experience: *The trainees are still pretty green.*

7 have a green thumb to be good at making plants grow

8 green around the gills INFORMAL looking or feeling sick

9 ill INFORMAL looking pale and unhealthy because you are sick: *George turned greener with each rock of the boat.*

10 the green-eyed monster HUMOROUS OR LITERARY: see JEALOUSY

11 the green stuff INFORMAL money

green² *n.* **1** [C,U] the color of grass and leaves **2** [C] a smooth flat area of grass around a hole on a GOLF COURSE **3 greens** [plural] **a)** vegetables with large green leaves: *Eat your greens, they're good for you.* **b)** leaves and branches used for decoration, especially at Christmas —compare GREENERY **4** [C] a level area of grass, especially in the middle of a small town —see also BOWLING GREEN

green³ *v.* [T] INFORMAL also **green up** to fill an area with growing plants in order to make it more attractive: *Earth Day advocates were busy greening up the city's parks.* —see also GREENING

green·back /'grinbæk/ *n.* [C] a dollar BILL

green bean /'. ., ˌ. './ *n.* [C] a long thin green vegetable which is picked before the beans inside it grow —see picture at VEGETABLE

green belt /'. ./ *n.* [C,U] an area of trees, fields etc. around a city, where no building is allowed

Green Be·ret /ˌgrin bə'reɪ/ *n.* [C] a member of the U.S. Special Army Forces

green card /'. ./ *n.* [C] an official document that shows that a non-citizen can legally live and work in the U.S.

Greene /grin/, **Gra·ham** /'greɪəm/ (1904–1991) a British writer of NOVELs and plays

green·er·y /'grinəri/ *n.* [U] green leaves and plants, often used as decoration

green·fly /'grinflaɪ/ *n. plural* **greenflies** [C] a very small green insect that feeds on and damages young plants

green·gro·cer /'grinˌgroʊsɚ, -ˌgroʊʃɚ/ *n.* [C] someone who sells fresh fruit and vegetables

green·horn /'grinhɔrn/ *n.* [C] INFORMAL someone who lacks experience and can be easily deceived: *The greenhorns headed out to the corral for their first ride.*

green·house /'grinhaʊs/ *n.* [C] a glass building used for growing plants that need warmth, light, and protection

greenhouse ef·fect /'. . ˌ./ *n.* **the greenhouse effect** the gradual warming of the air surrounding the Earth as a result of heat being trapped by POLLUTION —see also GLOBAL WARMING

greenhouse gas /'.. ,./ n. [C] a gas, especially CARBON DIOXIDE or METHANE, that is thought to trap heat above the Earth and cause the greenhouse effect

green·ing /'griniŋ/ n. INFORMAL **the greening of sb/ sth** the process of making a person or organization realize the importance of environmental problems: *the greening of corporate America*

green·ish /'grinɪʃ/ adj. slightly green: *a greenish tinge*

Green·land /'grinlənd, -lænd/ a large island in the North Atlantic Ocean, near northeast Canada, which belongs to Denmark but has its own government

Green·land·ic /grin'lændɪk/ n. [U] a language spoken by the Inuit people in Greenland —**Greenlandic** adj.

green light /,. './ n. [C] **1** the TRAFFIC LIGHT that shows cars they can go forward **2** give sb/sth the **green light** to allow a piece of work, plan etc. to begin: *The board just gave us the green light to begin research.*

green·mail /'grinmeɪl/ n. [U] the practice of buying STOCK in your own company, usually at a high price, from someone who is trying to take control of your company by owning a lot of STOCK, or the money paid to do this

Green Moun·tains, the /,. '../ a part of the northern Appalachians that runs from southeastern Canada to the U.S. state of Massachusetts

green on·ion /,. '../ n. [C] an onion with a small white round part and a long green stem, usually eaten raw

Green·peace /'grinpis/ an international organization whose members work to protect the environment from damage caused by industrial processes or military activities

green pep·per /,. '../ n. [C] a vegetable with green flesh and white seeds, that you can cook or eat raw

green rev·o·lu·tion /,. ..'../ n. [singular] **1** a large increase in the amount of crops, such as wheat or rice, that are produced because of improved scientific methods of farming **2** the interest in protecting the environment that has developed in many parts of the world

green room /'. ./ n. **the green room** the room in a theater, television STUDIO etc. in which performers wait when they are not on stage performing

green sal·ad /,. '../ n. [C] a SALAD made with LETTUCE and other raw green vegetables

green tea /,. './ n. [U] light-colored tea made from leaves that have been heated with steam, especially popular in eastern Asia

Green·wich Mean Time /,grɛnɪtʃ min 'taɪm, ,grɛnɪtʃ 'min ,taɪm/ *abbreviation* **GMT** n. [U] the time as measured at Greenwich in London, England, which is used as a standard to set times all over the world

Greenwich Vil·lage /,grɛnɪtʃ 'vɪlɪdʒ/ an area of New York City known for being the home of many artists

greet /grit/ v. [T] **1** to say hello to someone or welcome them: *The delegation was greeted by the President.* | [**greet sb with sth**] *Roz's mother greeted her with hugs and kisses.* **2** [always + adv./prep.] to react to something in a particular way: [**greet sth with/by sth**] *The proposal was greeted with loud laughter.* **3** to be the first thing you see or hear when you arrive somewhere: *As we entered, complete chaos greeted us.*

greet·ing /'gritɪŋ/ n. [C] **1** something you say or do when you meet someone: *The only acceptable form of greeting in business is a handshake.* | *The two men exchanged greetings* (=said hello to each other). **2** **birthday/Christmas etc. greetings** a message saying that you hope someone will be happy and healthy on their BIRTHDAY, at Christmas etc.

greeting card /'.. ,./ n. [C] a card that you send to someone on their BIRTHDAY, at Christmas etc.

greet·ings /'gritɪŋz/ *interjection* FORMAL OR HUMOROUS used to say hello to someone

gre·gar·i·ous /grɪ'gɛriəs/ adj. **1** someone who is gregarious is friendly and enjoys being with other people: *Kim is gregarious and fun-loving.* **2** TECHNICAL gregarious animals tend to live in a group

Gre·go·ri·an cal·en·dar /grɪ,gɔriən 'kæləndɚ/ n. **the Gregorian calendar** the system of arranging the 365 days of the year in months and giving numbers to the years from the birth of Jesus Christ, used in the West since 1582

Gregorian chant /,.... './ n. [C,U] a type of church music for voices alone

Greg·o·ry XIII, Pope /,grɛgəri ðə θɚ'tinθ/ (1502–1585) the POPE who introduced the Gregorian calendar

grem·lin /'grɛmlən/ n. [C] an imaginary evil spirit that is blamed for problems in machinery

Gre·na·da /grə'neɪdə/ a country in the Caribbean Sea consisting of the island of Grenada and some of a group of small islands called the Grenadines —**Grenadian** n. adj.

gre·nade /grə'neɪd/ n. [C] a small bomb that can be thrown by hand or fired from a gun: *a hand grenade*

gren·a·dier /,grɛnə'dɪr/ n. [C] a soldier in a particular part of the British army

gren·a·dine /'grɛnə,din, ,grɛnə'din/ n. [U] a sweet liquid made from POMEGRANATES that is used in drinks

Gretz·ky /'grɛtski/, **Wayne** /weɪn/ (1961–) a Canadian HOCKEY player

grew /gru/ v. the past tense of GROW

grey /greɪ/ adj. another spelling of GRAY

grey·hound /'greɪhaʊnd/ n. [C] a type of thin dog that can run very fast and is used in races

grid /grɪd/ n. **1** [C] a pattern of straight lines that cross each other and form squares: *In many U.S. cities, the streets are organized in a grid.* **2** [C] a system of numbered squares printed on a map so that the exact position of any place can be found **3** the network of electricity supply wires that connects POWER STATIONS and provides electricity to buildings in an area: *a power grid* **4** [C] a set of starting positions for all the cars in a motor race

grid·dle /'grɪdl/ n. [C] a flat metal plate that is used for cooking on top of a STOVE or over a fire

grid·dle·cake /'grɪdl,keɪk/ n. [C] a PANCAKE

grid·i·ron /'grɪdaɪɚn/ n. [C] **1** a football field **2** an open frame of metal bars for cooking meat or fish over a very hot fire

grid·lock /'grɪdlɑk/ n. [singular,U] **1** a situation in which streets in a city are so full of cars that they cannot move: *The average commuter spends the equivalent of 3.5 days in gridlock every year.* **2** a situation in which nothing can happen, usually because people disagree strongly: *Because of an increase in the number of lawsuits, the court system is in gridlock.* —**gridlocked** adj.

grief /grif/ n. **1** [U] extreme sadness, especially because someone you love has died: *We didn't say much, but his grief was obvious.* | [+ **at/over**] *Tagore's grief at losing his wife was so strong that he would often stay in bed all day.* **2** **give sb grief** INFORMAL to criticize someone in an annoying way: *Frank always gives me grief about my sloppy handwriting.* **3** **good grief!** SPOKEN used when you are slightly surprised or annoyed: *Good grief! Look the mess in here!*

grief-strick·en /'grif,strɪkən/ also **grief·struck** /'grif,strʌk/ adj. feeling very sad because of something that has happened

Grieg /grig/, **Ed·vard** /'ɛdvard/ (1843–1907) a Norwegian musician who wrote CLASSICAL music

griev·ance /'grivəns/ n. [C,U] something that you complain about because you feel you have been treated unfairly: [+ **against**] *a list of grievances against their employer* | *One woman filed a grievance* (=officially complained to the company) *last year after her supervisor refused to promote her.* | *Many Native Americans still feel a deep sense of grievance* (=a feeling that they were treated unfairly) *for what the government did to them in the past.*

grieve /griv/ v. **1** [I,T] to feel extremely sad, especially because someone you love has died: *It's healthy to take time to grieve after the death of a loved one.* | [+ over/for] *I felt like I would never stop grieving over my dead brother.* | [**grieve sth** *We are still grieving the death of our mother.* **2** [T] if something grieves you, it makes you feel very unhappy: **it grieves sb to think/say/see etc.** *It grieves me to see him wasting his talent like that.*

grieved /grivd/ *adj.* LITERARY very sad and upset: *The whole community is deeply grieved by her tragic death.*

griev·ous /ˈgrivəs/ *adj.* **1** FORMAL very serious and likely to be very harmful: *a grievous error* | *The Mormon Church considers abortion a grievous sin.* **2** ESPECIALLY LITERARY a grievous wound or pain is severe and hurts a lot —**grievously** *adv.*

grif·fin, **gryphon** /ˈgrɪfən/ *n.* [C] an imaginary animal in stories that has a lion's body and an EAGLE's wings and head

Grif·fith /ˈgrɪfɪθ/, **D.W.** /di ˈdʌbəlˌyu/ (1875–1948) a U.S. movie DIRECTOR, famous especially for inventing new ways of making movies and of using the camera

grift·er /ˈgrɪftə/ *n.* [C] INFORMAL someone who dishonestly obtains something, especially money —**grift** *v.* [T]

grill¹ /grɪl/ *v.* **1** [I,T] if you grill something, you cook it by putting it on a flat metal frame with bars across it, over very strong direct heat, or for something to cook this way: *The chicken is grilled over an open flame.* —compare BROIL (1) **2** [T] to ask someone a lot of difficult questions in order to make them explain their actions, opinions etc.: *She then grilled Smith about how he received the bruises and rib injury.*

grill² *n.* [C] **1** a flat metal frame with bars across it that can be put over strong direct heat, so that food can be cooked on it **2** a place where you can buy and eat grilled food: *Bennigan's Bar and Grill* **3** also **grille** a frame with metal bars or wire across it that is put in front of a window or door for protection **4** also **grille** the metal bars at the front of a car that protect the RADIATOR (2)

grilled /grɪld/ *adj.* something that is grilled has been cooked on a grill: *grilled chicken*

grill·ing /ˈgrɪlɪŋ/ *n.* the process of asking someone a lot of difficult questions in order to make them explain their actions or opinions: *Glaspie underwent a severe grilling before the Senate Foreign Relations Committee.*

grim /grɪm/ *adj.* **grimmer, grimmest 1** making you feel worried and unhappy: *a grim economic situation* | *The future of public schools in America looks pretty grim.* **2** ugly and unattractive: *a grim industrial town* | *the grim details of the war* **3** looking or sounding very serious because the situation is very bad: *a grim-faced policeman* | *It was their grim determination* (=serious determination in spite of difficulties or dangers) *that got them to the top of Mount Everest.* | *Rosen came out of the meeting looking grim* (=looking serious and worried). —**grimly** *adv.*: *a grimly realistic movie*

grim·ace¹ /ˈgrɪməs/ *v.* [I] to twist your face in an ugly way because you do not like something, because you are feeling pain, or because you are trying to be funny: [+ at] *Hannegan grimaced at the big black painting on the wall.* | *Duran bent over and grimaced in pain.*

grimace² *n.* [C] an expression you make by twisting your face because you do not like something or because you are feeling pain: *Bernie gave a grimace of disgust and left the room.*

grime /graɪm/ *n.* [U] oily dirt that forms a black layer on surfaces: *His hand were black with grime from working on the car.*

Grimm /grɪm/ the family name of two German brothers, Jakob Grimm (1785–1863) and Wilhelm Grimm (1786–1859) famous for writing GRIMM'S FAIRY TALES, a collection of nearly 200 stories

Grim Reap·er /ˌ. ˈ../ *n.* **the Grim Reaper** a figure, usually a SKELETON in a black ROBE holding a SCYTHE, who represents death, especially in stories and poems

grim·y /ˈgraɪmi/ *adj.* **grimier, grimiest** covered with black oily dirt: *grimy factories*

grin¹ /grɪn/ *v.* **grinned, grinning** [I] **1** to smile widely: *"I guess we'll soon find out who's better," she said with a grin.* | [+ at] *Every time I walk by him, he just grins at me.* | [+ with] *She grinned with delight.* | *Thomas was grinning from ear to ear* (=grinning very widely) *as he received the trophy.* **2 grin and bear it** to accept a bad or difficult situation without complaining, especially because you realize there is nothing you can do to make it better

grin² *n.* [C] a wide smile —see also **wipe the smile/ grin off sb's face** (WIPE¹ (4))

grind¹ /graɪnd/ *v. past tense and past participle* **ground 1** into small pieces [T] **a)** also **grind up** to break something such as corn or coffee beans into small pieces or powder, either in a machine or between two hard surfaces: *Could you grind up some coffee for me?* **b)** to cut food, especially raw meat, into very small pieces by putting it through a machine **2** smooth/sharp [T] to make something smooth or sharp by rubbing it on a hard surface or by using a machine: *The lenses are ground to a high standard of precision.* **3** press sth down [T always + adv./prep.] to press something down into a surface and rub it with a strong twisting movement: [**grind sth into/in sth**] *He paused and ground his cigarette butt into the ashtray.* **4 grind to a halt a)** if a vehicle grinds to a halt, it stops gradually: *Traffic ground to a halt as we got closer to the accident.* **b)** if a country, organization, or process grinds to a halt, it gradually stops working: *Production ground to a halt at five of the factories.* **5 grind your teeth a)** to rub your upper and lower teeth together, making a noise **b)** to be annoyed by something: *traffic problems that make us grind our teeth* —see also **have an ax to grind** (AX¹ (3))

grind sb ↔ **down** *phr. v.* [T] to make someone lose all courage, hope, or energy, especially by treating them badly: *The air attacks are grinding down the enemy's ability to fight.*

grind on *phr. v.* [I] to continue for a long time, which seems longer than necessary: *The trial has been grinding on for six months now.*

grind sth ↔ **out** *phr. v.* [T] **1** to produce information, writing, music etc. in such large amounts that it becomes boring: *Franklin just keeps grinding out detective stories.* **2** to do something with a lot of effort: *The Giants were only able to grind out one touchdown against the Lions.*

grind² *n.* [singular] something that is hard work and physically or mentally tiring or boring: *All the paperwork I have to do is a real grind.* | **the daily grind** (=things that you have to do every day that are tiring or boring)

grind·er /ˈgraɪndə/ *n.* [C] **1** a machine used to break up or cut food into small pieces: *a coffee grinder* **2** a HERO SANDWICH

grind·ing /ˈgraɪndɪŋ/ *adj.* [only before noun] **1 grinding poverty/work etc.** a bad situation that makes your life very difficult and unhappy, and never seems to improve **2** a grinding noise is the continuous annoying noise of machinery parts rubbing together

grind·stone /ˈgraɪndstoʊn/ *n.* [C] a large round stone that is turned like a wheel, used for making tools, knives etc. sharp —see also **keep your nose to the grindstone** (NOSE¹ (8))

grin·go /ˈgrɪŋgoʊ/ *n. plural* **gringos** [C] TABOO a word for someone from North America, especially someone who is white and speaks English, used by people in Latin American countries. Do not use this word.

grip¹ /grɪp/ *n.*

1 firm hold [C usually singular] the way you hold something tightly, or your ability to do this: *It's hard to get a good grip on this box.* | *Squeeze a tennis ball regularly to improve your grip.*

G

2 power [singular] power and control over someone or something | **have/keep a grip on sth** *They're not the biggest fruit grower in the world, but they do have a good grip on the market.*
3 come to grips with sth to understand and deal with a difficult problem or situation: *Eric still hasn't come to grips with his alcoholism.*
4 get/keep a grip (on sth) SPOKEN to start or continue controlling your emotions when you have been very upset: *Get a grip – you're overreacting.*
5 lose your grip INFORMAL to become less confident and less able to deal with a situation: *Unfortunately, her mother seems to have lost her grip on reality.*
6 be in the grip(s) of sth to be experiencing a very bad situation that cannot be controlled or stopped: *Our economy is deep in the grips of a recession.*
7 stop sth from slipping **a)** [C] a special part of a handle that has a rough surface so that you can hold it firmly without it slipping: *This pen has a rubber grip for your fingers.* **b)** [C,U] the ability of something to stay on a surface without slipping: *These tires assure good grip and a quiet, steady ride.*
8 cameraman [C] someone whose job is to move the cameras around while a television show or movie is being made
9 bag [C] OLD-FASHIONED a bag used for traveling; suitcase

grip² *v.* **gripped, gripping** [T] **1** to hold something very tightly: *He gripped the steering wheel firmly as he sped up to get on the freeway.* **2** to have a strong effect on someone or something: *Icy cold weather has gripped most of the East Coast.* | *The university's campus is gripped by fear due to the two recent murders.* **3** to hold someone's attention and interest: *I was gripped by the tragic stories of his childhood.* **4** if something grips a surface, it stays on it without slipping: *Radial tires grip the road well.* —see also GRIPPING

gripe¹ /graɪp/ *v.* [I] to complain about something continuously and in an annoying way: [+ about] *What are you griping about now?*

gripe² *n.* INFORMAL **1** [C] something unimportant that you complain about: *Students' main gripe is the poor quality of the dorm food.* **2 the gripes** OLD-FASHIONED sudden bad stomach pains

grippe, grip /grɪp/ *n.* [singular] OLD USE the FLU

grip·ping /ˈgrɪpɪŋ/ *adj.* a gripping movie, story etc. is very exciting and interesting and keeps your attention

gris·ly /ˈgrɪzli/ *adj.* **grislier, grisliest** extremely nasty and bad, especially because death or violence is involved: *a grisly murder*

grist /grɪst/ *n.* **grist for the mill** something that is useful in a particular situation: *For many years, the baseball star's love life has been grist for the tabloid mill.*

gris·tle /ˈgrɪsəl/ *n.* [U] the part of a piece of meat that is not soft enough to eat —**gristly** *adj.*

grit¹ /grɪt/ *n.* **1** [U] very small pieces of stone or sand, often scattered on frozen roads to make them less slippery **2** [U] INFORMAL determination and courage **3 grits** [plural] crushed HOMINY grain that is cooked and often eaten for breakfast **4 Grit** CANADIAN a member of the Liberal Party in Canada

grit² *v.* **gritted, gritting** [T] **1 grit your teeth** to use all your determination to continue in spite of difficulties: *I guess I'll have to just grit my teeth and wait for things to get better.* **2** to scatter grit on a frozen road to make it less slippery

grit·ty /ˈgrɪti/ *adj.* **grittier, grittiest 1** full of dirt, small stones, or sand: *a gritty dust storm* **2** having a lot of courage or determination: *a gritty football player*

griz·zled /ˈgrɪzəld/ *adj.* LITERARY having gray or grayish hair

griz·zly bear /ˈgrɪzli ˌbɛr/ also **grizzly** *n.* [C] a very large brown bear that lives in the Northwest of North America —see picture on page 429

groan¹ /groʊn/ *v.* [I] **1** to make a long deep sound because you are in pain or unhappy about something: *Everyone groaned as Scott began to tell another one of his stupid jokes.* **2** to bend slightly from carrying a heavy load: *The shelves groaned under the weight of hundreds of books.* **3** to make a sound similar to a groan **4** if a table groans with food, there is a very large amount of food on it

groan² *n.* [C] **1** a long deep sound that you make when you are in pain, are disappointed, or do not want to do something: *The crowd let out a groan when the ball was dropped and the other team scored.* **2** LITERARY a long low sound like someone groaning: *The door opened with a groan.*

groats /groʊts/ *n.* [plural] grain, especially OATS with the outer shell removed

gro·cer /ˈgroʊsɚ, -sɚ/ *n.* [C] someone who owns or works in a grocery store

gro·cer·ies /ˈgroʊsəriz, ˈgroʊʃriz/ *n.* [plural] food and other things used in the home that are sold at a grocery store or SUPERMARKET

grocery shop·ping /ˈ... ˌ../ *n.* [U] the activity of buying food and other things at a grocery store: *I do the grocery shopping and most of the other household chores.*

grocery store /ˈ... ˌ./ also **grocery** *n.* [C] a store that sells food and other things used in the home; SUPERMARKET

gro·dy /ˈgroʊdi/ *adj.* SPOKEN a word meaning "very bad" or "offensive," used especially by children

grog /grɑg/ *n.* [U] **1** a mixture of strong alcoholic drinks, especially RUM, and water **2** INFORMAL any alcoholic drink

grog·gy /ˈgrɑgi/ *adj.* **groggier, groggiest** weak and unable to walk steadily or think clearly because you are sick or very tired: *Bill looked groggy after studying all night.*

groin /grɔɪn/ *n.* [C] the place where the tops of your legs meet the front of your body —see picture at BODY

grom·met /ˈgrɑmɪt/ *n.* [C] a small metal ring used to make a hole in cloth or leather stronger

groom¹ /grum/ *v.* **1** [T] to prepare someone for an important job or position in society by training them over a long period: [groom sb to do sth] *Graham's son was being groomed to take over the business.* | [groom sb as/for sth] *By the time I was four, I had been groomed for a life of farming.* **2** [T] to take care of animals, especially horses, by cleaning and brushing them **3** [T] to prepare an area for a particular activity: *The resort has fifteen magnificently groomed ski runs.* **4** [I,T] if an animal grooms itself or another animal, it cleans its own fur and skin or that of the other animal **5** [I,T] to take care of your own appearance by keeping your hair and clothes clean and neat **6** [T] to take care of plants by cutting off leaves or branches —**grooming** *n.* [U] —see also WELL-GROOMED

groom² also **bridegroom** *n.* [C] **1** a man at the time he gets married, or just after he is married **2** someone whose job is to feed, clean, and take care of horses

grooms·man /ˈgrumzmən/ *n.* [C] a friend of a GROOM who has special duties at a wedding

groove¹ /gruv/ *n.* [C] **1** a thin line cut into a surface, especially to guide the movement of something: *The bolt slid easily into the groove.* **2 be/get in the groove** INFORMAL to begin to do an activity well and without much effort or thought, especially for a period of time: *After a while, I felt I got in a nice groove and threw the ball well.* **3** INFORMAL the beat of a piece of popular music, especially one that you can dance to: *As the lights went down and the groove got going, people started dancing.* **4 be in a groove** to be living or working in a comfortable situation that has been the same for a long time and that is unlikely to change, so that it is easy for you

groove² *v.* [T] to make a long narrow track in something —**grooved** *adj.*

groov·y /ˈgruvi/ *adj.* **groovier, grooviest** INFORMAL a word meaning "fashionable, modern, and fun," used especially in the 1960s

grope[1] /grōup/ v. **1** [I always + adv./prep.] to try to find something that you cannot see by feeling with your hands: [+ **for/through/around** etc.] *We groped around the dark room looking for the light switch.* **2 grope your way along/across** etc. to go somewhere by feeling the way with your hands, because you cannot see: *I groped my way down the hallway till I found my room.* **3** [I] to try hard to find the right words to say, or the right solution to a problem, but without any real idea of how to do this: [+ **for**] *He looked tired, and occasionally groped for words at the news conference.* **4** [T] INFORMAL to touch or GRAB someone's body in a sexual way, when they do not like it

grope[2] n. [C] INFORMAL an act of groping

Gro·pi·us /ˈgroʊpiəs/, **Wal·ter** /ˈwɔltə/ (1883–1969) a German-American ARCHITECT famous for starting and directing the Bauhaus style of design

gross[1] /grəʊs/ adj. **1** SPOKEN very disgusting to look at or think about: *Ooh, gross! The dog just threw up on the carpet!* **2** a gross amount of money is the total amount before any taxes or costs have been subtracted: *a gross income of $150,000* | **gross receipts/sales/revenues** etc. *The sporting goods chain had gross sales totaling $10 million.* —compare NET[2] (1) **3 gross negligence/misconduct/injustice** etc. wrong and unacceptable in a way that is very clear or extreme: *gross inequalities in salaries* **4** gross weight is the total weight of something, including its wrapping **5** extremely fat and unattractive —**grossly** adv.: *grossly overweight* —**grossness** n. [U]

gross[2] adv. **make/earn $25,000** etc. **gross** to earn a particular amount of money before taxes have been subtracted: *Henry makes more than $30,000 gross.*

gross[3] v. [T] to gain an amount as a total profit, or earn it as a total amount, before taxes have been subtracted: *The animated film "Jungle Book" grossed $7.7 million.*

gross sb **out** phr. v. [T] SPOKEN to make someone feel sick because of something you say or do: *Guys with hair all over their backs really gross me out.*

gross[4] determiner n. plural **gross** [C] **1** a total profit before taxes have been subtracted: *Cats has made a gross of over $460 million in the United States alone.* **2** a quantity of 144 of something *a gross of pencils*

gross do·mes·tic prod·uct /ˌ. .ˌ.. ˈ../ n. **the gross domestic product** TECHNICAL the GDP; the total value of all the goods and services produced in a country, except for income received from abroad —compare GROSS NATIONAL PRODUCT

gross mar·gin /ˌ. ˈ../ n. [C] TECHNICAL the financial difference between what something costs to produce and what it is sold for

gross na·tion·al prod·uct /ˌ. ˌ... ˈ../ n. **the gross national product** TECHNICAL the GNP; the total value of all the goods and services produced in a country, including income from abroad —compare GROSS DOMESTIC PRODUCT

gross prof·it /ˌ. ˈ../ n. [C] GROSS MARGIN

Gros Ventre /ˈgroʊ vɑnt/ another name for the Atsina and Hidatsa tribes of Native Americans

gro·tesque[1] /groʊˈtɛsk/ adj. **1** strange or unusual in a way that is shocking or offensive: *The news showed grotesque film clips of people being attacked by dogs.* **2** extremely ugly in a strange or unnatural way: *"The disease can also cause grotesque lumps under the skin," Ketch said.* —**grotesquely** adv.

gro·tesque[2] n. [C] an image in art of someone who is strangely ugly

grot·to /ˈgrɑtoʊ/ n. plural **grottoes** or **grottos** [C] a small natural CAVE, or one that someone has made

grouch[1] /graʊtʃ/ n. [C] INFORMAL someone who is always slightly angry or complaining: *Dad's such a grouch in the morning.*

grouch[2] v. [I + **about**] INFORMAL to complain in a slightly angry way; GRUMBLE

grouch·y /ˈgraʊtʃi/ adj. **grouchier, grouchiest** in a bad mood, especially because you are tired —**grouchiness** n. [U]

ground[1] /graʊnd/ n.

1 the ground a) the surface of the Earth: *The*

ground is too wet to sit on. | *The platform is at least four inches* **off the ground** (=above the ground). | **below/under ground** *Miners work 10-hour shifts below ground.* | *Residents went to* **higher ground** (=a hill, for example) *to escape the flood.* —compare FLOOR[1] (1) —see Usage Note at LAND[1] **b)** the soil on and under the surface of the earth: *The ground is too hard to plant trees now.* | *marshy ground*

2 area of land grounds [plural] **a)** a large area of land or ocean that is used for a particular activity or sport: *hunting grounds* | *burial grounds* **b)** the land or gardens around a building: *prison grounds*

3 area of knowledge [U] an area of knowledge, ideas, experience etc.: *Scientists are* **breaking new ground** (=discovering new ideas) *in surgical techniques.* | *Vaughn's book covers much of* **the same ground** (=the same things) *as Graham's.* | *Keith's* **on familiar ground** (=dealing with a subject he knows a lot about) *working with this type of computer.* | **cover a lot of ground/cover too much ground** (=to give a lot of information about many different parts of a subject)

4 lose ground to lose an advantage and become less successful: *American students lost ground in achievement levels in math and science between the 1970s and 1980s.*

5 gain ground a) to get an advantage and become more successful: *Stock prices gained ground in late trading today.* **b)** if an idea, belief etc. gains ground, it starts to become accepted or believed by more people: *The idea that environmental issues are also religious issues is gaining ground among churches in the U.S.*

6 reason grounds [U,plural] a reason, especially one that makes you think that something is true or correct: [+ **for**] *Jay's affair with his secretary was grounds for divorce.* | *My opposition of the war is based* **on moral grounds**. | *They have no* **legal grounds** *to file a lawsuit.* | *Zoe was awarded compensation* **on the grounds that** *the doctor had been negligent.*

7 common/middle ground an area of opinion that two people or groups share: *Bair said he believes the sides can find a middle ground.*

8 get off the ground if a plan, a business idea etc. gets off the ground, or if you get it off the ground, it starts to be successful: *Construction of the theme park never got off the ground.*

9 stand/hold your ground to refuse to change your opinion in spite of opposition: *Kessler vowed to stand his ground and fight for justice, even if it meant losing his job.*

10 give ground to change your opinion, or to agree that someone else is right about something: *Neither side gave ground in Maine's budget battle.*

11 cover a lot of ground to travel a very long distance: *For travelers in Europe who want to cover a lot of ground, the Eurail Pass is good value.*

12 be on dangerous ground to be expressing ideas that are likely to offend or embarrass someone or make them angry: *I'd be on dangerous ground if I told her that I didn't like her cooking.*

13 the moral high ground an opinion that is regarded as morally better than others: *Gorham has abandoned the moral high ground by involving himself in backroom deals.*

14 home ground in the place or situation that is most familiar to you, or where you feel the most comfortable: *I wouldn't dream of meeting my ex-husband again unless I was on home ground.*

15 work/drive yourself into the ground to work so hard that you become extremely tired: *Kay's working herself into the ground trying to meet her deadlines.*

16 fertile ground/breeding ground a situation in which it is easy for something to develop: *The housing projects are fertile ground for drug dealers.*

17 on the ground in the actual place where something, especially a war, is happening, rather than in another place where it is being discussed: *While the talks continue, the situation on the ground is worsening.*

G

18 small pieces **grounds** [plural] the small pieces of something such as coffee which sink to the bottom of a liquid: *coffee grounds*
19 electrical [singular] a wire that connects a piece of electrical equipment to the ground for safety
20 paint [C] the first covering of paint on a painting —see also **break fresh/new ground** (BREAK[1] (38)), **have/keep both feet on the ground** (FOOT[1] (18)), **hit the ground running** (HIT[1] (25))

ground[2] *v.* **1** [T usually passive] to stop an aircraft or pilot from flying: *All planes are grounded until the fog clears.* **2 be grounded in/on sth** to be based on something: *The group is committed to environmental policies that are grounded in science.* **3** [T] INFORMAL to stop a child from doing something they enjoy doing for a period of time, as a punishment for behaving badly: *You'll be grounded for a week if I catch you smoking again.* **4** [T] to make a piece of electrical equipment safe by connecting it to the ground with a wire: *Ground the black cable to the engine block, and then connect the red cable to the batteries.* **5** [I,T] if you ground a boat or if it grounds, it hits ground where the water is not very deep, so that it cannot move —see also WELL-GROUNDED

ground sb in sth *phr. v.* [T usually passive] to teach someone the basic things they should know in order to be able to do something: *Most parents want their children to be grounded in the basics of reading and writing.*

ground out *phr. v.* [I] to hit a ball in baseball so that it goes over the ground to a player who throws the ball to first base before you get there, so that you are OUT: *Santiago grounded out twice in yesterday's game.*

ground[3] *adj.* [only before noun] **1 ground beef/turkey/pork etc.** meat that has been cut up into very small pieces, often formed into a shape to be cooked, for example for HAMBURGERS **2** ground coffee or nuts have been broken up into powder or very small pieces, using a special machine

ground[4] *v.* the past tense and past participle of GRIND[1]

ground ball /ˈ. ˌ., ˈ. ./ *n.* [C] a GROUNDER

ground·break·ing /ˈ. ˌ../ *adj.* **1** groundbreaking work involves making new discoveries, using new methods etc.: *MacKinnon's groundbreaking legal work changed the way sexual harassment was viewed.* **2** the act of digging up the ground in order to start building something

ground cloth /ˈ. ./ *n.* [C] a piece of material that water cannot pass through, which people sleep on or put under a tent when they are camping

ground con·trol /ˈ. ˌ,./ *n.* [U] the people on the ground who are responsible for guiding the flight of SPACECRAFT or aircraft

ground cov·er /ˈ. ˌ../ *n.* [U] plants that cover the soil

ground crew /ˈ. ./ *n.* [C] the group of people who work at an airport and take care of the aircraft

ground·er /ˈɡraʊndɚ/ *n.* [C] a ball hit along the ground in baseball

ground floor /ˌ. ˈ.◂/ *n.* [C] **1** the first floor of a building that is at the same level as the ground **2 be/get in on the ground floor** to become involved in a plan, business activity etc. from the beginning

ground forc·es /ˈ. ˌ../ *n.* [plural] military groups that fight on the ground rather than at sea or in the air

ground glass /ˌ. ˈ.◂/ *n.* [U] **1** glass that has been made into a powder **2** glass that has been rubbed on the surface so that you cannot see through it, but light passes through it

ground·hog /ˈɡraʊndhɑɡ/ *n.* [C] a small North American animal that has thick brown fur and lives in holes in the ground; WOODCHUCK

Groundhog Day /ˈ.. ˌ./ *n.* [C] February 2; according to American stories, the first day of the year that a GROUNDHOG comes out of its hole. If it sees its shadow, there will be six more weeks of winter. If it does not, good weather will come early.

ground·ing /ˈɡraʊndɪŋ/ *n.* **1** [singular] training in the basic parts of a subject or skill: [+ **in**] *A thorough grounding in mathematics is essential for the economics course.* **2** [C] a punishment for a child's bad behavior in which they are not allowed to do something they enjoy doing for a period of time

ground·less /ˈɡraʊndlɪs/ *adj.* groundless fears, worries, claims etc. are unnecessary because there are no facts or reasons to base them on: *The charges against him are groundless.*

ground lev·el /ˈ. ˌ../ *n.* [singular] the same level as the surface of the earth, rather than above it or below it

ground·nut /ˈɡraʊndnʌt/ *n.* [C] TECHNICAL a PEANUT or PEANUT plant

ground plan /ˈ. ./ *n.* [C] **1** a drawing of how a building is arranged at ground level, showing the size, position, and shape of walls, rooms etc. **2** a basic plan for doing something in the future

ground rules /ˈ. ./ *n.* [plural] the basic rules or principles on which future actions or behavior should be based: *They first had to agree on the ground rules of the debate before they could get started.*

grounds·keep·er /ˈɡraʊndzˌkipɚ/ *n.* [C] a man whose job is to take care of an area of land such as a garden or sports field

ground squir·rel /ˈ. ˌ../ *n.* [C] a GOPHER

ground staff /ˈ. ./ *n.* [C] GROUND CREW

ground stroke /ˈ. ˌ./ *n.* [C] a way of hitting the ball after it has hit the ground in tennis and similar games

ground·swell /ˈɡraʊndswɛl/ *n.* **1 groundswell of support/enthusiasm etc.** a sudden increase in how strongly people feel about something: *a groundswell of interest in natural products* **2** [singular,U] the strong movement of the ocean that continues after a storm or strong winds

ground·wa·ter, ground water /ˈɡraʊndˌwɔtɚ/ *n.* [U] water that is under the ground that supplies water to WELLS, lakes, streams etc.

ground·work /ˈɡraʊndwɚk/ *n.* [U] important work that has to take place before another activity, plan etc. can be successful: *The groundwork for next year's conference has already begun.*

ground ze·ro /ˌ. ˈ../ *n.* [U] the place where a NUCLEAR bomb explodes, where the most severe damage happens

group[1] /ɡrup/ *n.* [C] **1** several people or things that are all together in the same place: *We got all the family together for a group photo.* | [+ **of**] *a group of tall trees* | *Get into groups of four.* **2** several people or things that are related to each other in some way: [+ **of**] *a group of investors* | **ethnic/religious/environmental etc. group** (=people with the same races, religion, interests etc.) **3** a number of musicians or singers who perform together, usually playing popular music: *a rock group* **4** several companies that all have the same owner: *The Pearson Group owns a diverse array of companies.* —see also AGE GROUP, INTEREST GROUP, PLAY GROUP

group[2] *v.* **1** [I,T] to come together to make a group, or to arrange people or things in a group: [+ **on/in/together etc.**] *Reporters were grouped on the steps below him.* | *The tourists grouped themselves around the statue.* **2** [T always + adv./prep.] to divide people or things into groups or types according to a system: *The plates were grouped according to color and size.*

group dy·nam·ics /ˌ. .ˈ../ *n.* [singular,U] the way in which the members of a group behave toward and react to each other

group·ie /ˈɡrupi/ *n.* [C] someone, especially a young woman, who likes a musician, movie star, or sports star and follows them around hoping to meet them

group·ing /ˈɡrupɪŋ/ *n.* [C] a set of people, things, or organizations that have the same interests, qualities, or features: *The Council of the African Synod is a grouping of bishops from 16 African nations.*

group prac·tice /ˌ. ˈ../ *n.* [C,U] a group of doctors who work together in the same building

group ther·a·py /ˌ. ˈ.../ *n.* [U] a method of treating people with emotional or PSYCHOLOGICAL problems by bringing them together in groups to talk about their problems

group·ware /ˈgrupwɛr/ *n.* [U] a special type of computer SOFTWARE that allows several computers on a network to work on the same computer DOCUMENT at the same time

grouse[1] /graʊs/ *v.* [I + about] INFORMAL to complain about something: *"Everything tastes the same,"* George groused.

grouse[2] *n.* [C,U] a small fat bird that is hunted and shot for food and sport, or the meat of this bird

grove /groʊv/ *n.* **1** [C] a group of trees: *the redwood groves of Northern California* **2** [C] an area of land planted with a particular type of fruit tree, especially LEMON or orange trees: *a lemon grove* —compare ORCHARD

grov·el /ˈgrɑvəl, ˈgrʌ-/ *v.* [I] **1** to behave with too much respect toward someone, because you are asking them to help or forgive you: *There's nothing worse than seeing a man grovel just to keep his job.* **2** to lie or move flat on the ground because you are afraid of someone, or as a way of showing that you will obey them: *That dog grovels every time you shout.*

grow /groʊ/ *v.* past tense **grew** past participle **grown**
1 `person/animal` [I] to become bigger and develop over a period of time: *It's hard to believe how much the kids have grown.* | *Jamie's grown three inches this year.* | **a growing boy/girl** *Of course he eats a lot. He's a growing boy!* | *Jerry's* **growing like a weed** (=growing very quickly).
2 `plants/crops` **a)** [I] to exist and develop somewhere in a natural way: *Our lawn has all kinds of weeds growing in it.* | *It's too cold for orchids to grow here.* **b)** [T] to make plants or crops grow by taking care of them: *We're trying to grow roses in our garden this year.* —see Usage Note at RAISE[1]
3 `hair/nails` **a)** [I] if hair, FINGERNAILS etc. grow, they become longer **b)** [T] if you grow your hair, FINGERNAILS etc., you do not cut them: *Are you growing a beard?* | **grow your hair out/grow out your hair** (=to not cut your hair because you want it to become longer)
4 `increase` [I] to increase in amount, size, or degree: *The town's population grew from about 34,000 to more than 42,000 in only five years.* | *Lower prices on inline skates have also contributed to their growing popularity.* | **A growing number of** *people are buying handguns for protection.* | **[+ in]** *The issue of security on the Internet has been growing in importance in the past few years.*
5 `become` [linking verb] to become old, hot, worse etc. over a period of time: *The crowd grew louder and more enthusiastic when the band came on the stage.*
6 **grow to like/fear/respect etc.** to gradually start to like etc. someone or something: *After three years here, I've grown to like Dallas.*
7 `improve` [I] to improve in ability or character: *Beth has grown quite a bit as an actress.*
8 `business` [T] to make something such as a business become larger or more successful: *The president revealed his plan to grow the economy by five percent.*
9 **money doesn't grow on trees** SPOKEN used to say that someone should not waste money because it is hard to get

grow apart *phr. v.* [I] if two people grow apart, their relationship becomes less close: *Several months ago, I realized that we had grown apart and I didn't love her anymore.*

grow away from sb *phr. v.* [T not in passive] **1** to begin gradually to have a less close relationship with someone that you loved: *My son began to grow away from me the year he left for college.* **2** to gradually become less closely related: *Rural economies have grown away from a reliance on agriculture.*

grow into sb/sth *phr. v.* [T not in passive] **1** to develop over a period of time and become a particular kind of person or thing: *Cable TV has grown into a multi-billion-dollar business.* **2** if a child grows into clothes, they become big enough to wear them: *His new jacket's a bit big for him now, but he'll soon*

grow into it. **3** to gradually learn how to do a job or deal with a situation successfully

grow on sb *phr. v.* [T] if someone or something grows on you, you like them more and more: *I didn't like blue cheese at first, but the taste has kind of grown on me.*

grow out of sth *phr. v.* [T] **1** if a child grows out of clothes, they become too big to wear them **2** if a child grows out of a habit, they stop doing it as they get older: *Jonathan still sucks his thumb, but we hope he'll grow out of it soon.* **3** to develop from something small or simple into something bigger or more complicated: *The push to organize in a union grew out of worker dissatisfaction.*

grow up *phr. v.* [I] **1** to develop from being a child to being an adult: *Chris said he wants to be a fireman when he grows up.* | *I grew up in Chicago.* **2 grow up!** SPOKEN said to tell someone to behave more like an adult, especially when they have been behaving in a childish way **3** to start to exist and become bigger or more important: *A large shopping area has grown up around the city's train station.*

grow·er /ˈgroʊɚ/ *n.* [C] a person or company that grows fruit, vegetables etc. in order to sell them: *potato growers*

grow·ing pains /ˈ.. ˌ./ *n.* [plural] **1** pain that children can sometimes feel in their arms and legs when they are growing **2** problems and difficulties that are experienced at the beginning of a new activity: *Any new show goes through a lot of growing pains.*

growl /graʊl/ *v.* **1** [I] if an animal growls, it makes a long deep angry sound: *Their dog growls at everyone.* **2** [I,T] to say something in a low angry voice: *"Leave that alone,"* she growled. —**growl** *n.* [C]

grown[1] /groʊn/ *adj.* [only before noun] **grown man/woman** an expression meaning an adult man or woman, used especially when you think someone is not behaving as an adult should: *Grown men in three-piece suits were playing video games.* —compare FULL-GROWN

grown[2] *v.* the past participle of GROW

grown-up[1] /ˌ. ˈ.◂/ *adj.* **1** a word meaning fully developed as an adult, used especially when you are comparing an adult to a child: *They have three grown-up children who live in other states.* **2** a word meaning behaving like an adult or typical of an adult, used when you are comparing what an adult does or can do with what a child does: *The movies deals with grown-up subjects such as sex and domestic violence.*

grown-up[2] /ˈ. ./ *n.* [C] a word meaning an "adult person," used especially by children or when speaking to children: *I wish my parents would treat me like a grown-up for a change.*

growth /groʊθ/ *n.*
1 `increase in amount` [U] an increase in amount, size, or degree: *population growth* | **[+ in]** *There's been tremendous growth in the health food industry.* | *Overall, the* **growth rate** (=the speed at which something increases or grows) *for manufacturing sales is expected to be two percent.* | **growth area/ industry** (=an area of business that is growing very quickly)
2 `person/animal/plant` [U] the development of the physical size, strength etc. of a person, animal, or plant over a period of time: *Eating nutritious food is important for healthy growth in children.*
3 `increase in importance` [singular,U] the gradual development and increase in the importance or influence of something: **[+ of]** *the growth of modern technology*
4 `personal development` [U] the development of someone's character, intelligence, emotions etc.: *a job that provides opportunities for personal growth* | *emotional growth*
5 `swelling` [C] a swelling on your body or under your skin, caused by disease: *a cancerous growth*
6 `growing thing` [C,U] something that is growing: *There are signs of new growth on the tree.*

G

Groz·ny /ˈgroʊzni/ the capital and largest city of Chechnya

grub¹ /grʌb/ n. **1** [U] INFORMAL food: *You can get good grub for less than $10 a person.* **2** [C] an insect when it is in the form of a small soft white worm

grub² [I always + adv./prep.] **1** INFORMAL to ask for something rather than buying it or working for it yourself: [+ **for**] *All the candidates are busy grubbing for money.* —see also MONEY-GRUBBING **2** INFORMAL to look for something, especially by moving things, looking under them etc.: [+ **for**] *The pigs are behind the barn grubbing for roots.*

    grub sth ↔ **up/out** *phr. v.* [T] to dig around something and then pull it out of the ground: *Farmers grubbed the sagebrush up by hand.*

grub·by /ˈgrʌbi/ adj. **grubbier, grubbiest 1** dirty: *grubby clothes* **2** not respectable, or morally unacceptable: *Her grubby studio boss just cared about money.* **3** sb's **grubby hands/mitts/paws etc.** used to talk about someone else's hands, when you are angry because you do not want them to touch something or someone: *Get your grubby mitts off my stuff.* —**grubbiness** *n.* [U]

grub·stake /ˈgrʌbˌsteɪk/ n. [U] INFORMAL money that someone gives to help develop a new business, in return for a share of the profits

grudge¹ /grʌdʒ/ n. [C] **1** a feeling of anger or dislike you have for someone who has harmed you: **have/carry/bear a grudge against sb** (=continue to be angry with someone) | *Diane doesn't hold grudges* (=continue to have a grudge). **2** a **grudge fight/match** a fight or competition in sports between two people who dislike each other very much

grudge² *v.* [T] **1** to do or give something in a very unwilling way: *I grudged the time I had to spend doing housework instead of playing.* **2** BEGRUDGE

grudg·ing /ˈgrʌdʒɪŋ/ adj. done or given in a very unwilling way: *a grudging apology* —**grudgingly** adv.

gru·el /ˈgruəl/ n. [U] thin OATMEAL that was eaten in the past by poor or sick people

gru·el·ing /ˈgruəlɪŋ/ adj. very tiring because you have to use a lot of effort for a long time: *a grueling three-hour climb* —**gruelingly** adv.

grue·some /ˈgrusəm/ adj. very upsetting or bad to look at or hear about, and usually involving death or injury: *a gruesome accident*

gruff /grʌf/ adj. **1** unfriendly or annoyed, especially in the way you speak: *Dad can be gruff and impatient at times.* **2** a gruff voice sounds low and rough, as if the speaker does not want to talk or is annoyed —**gruffly** adv.

grum·ble¹ /ˈgrʌmbəl/ v. [I] **1** to complain in a quiet but slightly angry way: [+ **about/at** etc.] *Our neighbors often grumble about the noise we make.* **2** to make a very low sound that continuously gets quieter then louder then quieter: *Thunder grumbled in the distance.* —**grumbler** *n.* [C]

grumble² *n.* [C] **1** a continuing complaint: *Consumer grumbles continue over cable TV rates.* **2** a low continuous sound that gets quieter then louder then quieter

grump·y /ˈgrʌmpi/ adj. **grumpier, grumpiest** easily annoyed and tending to complain: *a grumpy old man* —**grump** *n.* [C] —**grumpily** adv. —**grumpiness** *n.* [U]

grunge /grʌndʒ/ n. [U] **1** a type of loud music played with electric GUITARS, popular in the early 1990s **2** a style of fashion popular with young people in the early 1990s, in which they wore clothes that looked dirty and messy **3** INFORMAL dirt and GREASE; GRIME

grun·gy /ˈgrʌndʒi/ adj. **grungier, grungiest** INFORMAL dirty and sometimes smelling bad: *grungy jeans*

grunt¹ /grʌnt/ v. **1** [I,T] to make short sounds or say only a few words in a low rough voice, when you do not want to talk: *He just grunted "Hi" and kept walk-*

ing. **2** [I] if someone or an animal, especially a pig, grunts, they make a short low sound in their throat

grunt² *n.* [C] **1** a short low sound made in your throat, or a similar sound that an animal makes, especially a pig: *He stood up with a grunt.* **2** SLANG an INFANTRY soldier

grunt work /ˈ. ./ *n.* [U] INFORMAL the hard uninteresting part of a job or PROJECT

Gru·yère /gruˈyɛr/ n. [U] a type of hard Swiss cheese with holes in it

gryph·on /ˈgrɪfən/ n. [C] another spelling of GRIFFIN

g-spot /ˈdʒi spɑt/ n. [C] a place in a woman's VAGINA where some people think she feels the most sexual pleasure

G-string /ˈdʒi ˌstrɪŋ/ n. [C] very small underwear that does not cover the BUTTOCKS

gua·ca·mo·le /ˌgwɑkəˈmoʊleɪ/ n. [U] a Mexican dish made with crushed AVOCADOs

Gua·dal·ca·nal /ˌgwɑdlkəˈnæl/ the largest of the Solomon Islands in the western Pacific Ocean

Gua·de·loupe /ˌgwɑdəˈlup, ˈgwɑdəˌlup/ a country consisting of a group of islands in the Caribbean Sea, which is ruled by France

Guam /gwɑm/ a U.S. TERRITORY that is the largest of the Mariana Islands in the western Pacific Ocean

gua·no /ˈgwɑnoʊ/ n. [U] solid waste from sea birds that is often put on soil to help plants grow

guar·an·tee¹ /ˌgærənˈti/ v. [T]   **S W**   3 3
1 promise sth will happen to promise that something will happen or be done: [**guarantee (that)**] *She guarantees that she will be there on time.* | [**guarantee sth**] *The plan would guarantee health care to all Americans.* | [**guarantee sb sth**] *Even if you complete your training, I can't guarantee you a job.*
2 product to make a formal written promise to repair or replace a product if it has a fault within a specific period of time after you buy it: [**guarantee sth against sth**] *All stereo parts are guaranteed against failure for a year.*
3 make sth certain to make it certain that something will happen: *A good education doesn't guarantee a good job.*
4 be **guaranteed to do sth** to be certain to behave, work, or happen in a particular way: *Going out with friends is guaranteed to cheer you up.*
5 legal to make yourself legally responsible for the payment of money: *The loans are guaranteed by the government.*
6 protect to provide complete protection against harm or damage: [**guarantee sth against sth**] *This protective coating guarantees your car against corrosion.*

guarantee² *n.* [C] **1** a formal promise that some-   **S W**   3
thing will be done or will happen: [+ **of**] *The Constitution's guarantee of free speech does not apply in all cases.* | [**give sb a guarantee (that)**] *Can you give me a guarantee that the work will be finished on time?* | *There's no guarantee that the books will be delivered this week* (=it is not sure to happen). **2** a formal promise, especially in writing, that a product will please the customer or perform in a particular way for a specific length of time: *The microwave comes with a money-back guarantee* (=a promise to return your money if it does not work). —compare WARRANTY **3** an action, situation etc. that makes it certain that something else will happen: [+ **of**] *Hard work is no guarantee of success.* **4 a)** an agreement to be responsible for someone else's promise, especially a promise to pay a debt: *a loan guarantee* **b)** something valuable that is given to someone to keep until the owner has kept their promise, especially to pay a debt —compare SECURITY (6)

guar·an·tor /ˌgærənˈtɔr, ˈgærəntə/ n. [C] LAW someone who promises that they will pay for something if the person who should pay for it does not

guar·an·ty /ˈgærənti/ n. [C] LAW a GUARANTEE² (4)

guard¹ /gɑrd/ n.   **S W**   2 2
1 person [C] someone whose job is to guard people, places, or objects, so that they are not attacked or stolen: *The guards stopped us at the gate.* —see also BODYGUARD, SECURITY GUARD

2 `in a prison` [C] someone whose job is to prevent prisoners from escaping
3 be on guard to be responsible for guarding a place or person for a specific period of time: *Hogan was on guard the night the prisoners escaped.*
4 stand/keep guard (over sb/sth) to guard or watch a person or place: *Thousands of police stood guard over today's ceremony.*
5 be under (armed) guard to be guarded by a group of people with weapons: *City hall was under tight guard all night.*
6 catch/take/throw sb off guard to surprise someone by doing or saying something that they are not ready to deal with: *The sudden snowstorm caught weather forecasters off guard.*
7 sb's guard the state of paying careful attention to what is happening, in order to avoid being tricked or getting into danger: *Tina's not going to let down her guard* (=relax because a threat is gone). | *Hanson's dismissal has put others in the department on their guard.*
8 the old guard people who belong to a group which wants to do things the way they have always been done in the past: *the old guard of the Communist Party*
9 `equipment` [C] something that covers and protects someone or something: *All college hockey players must wear face guards on their helmets.*
10 `basketball` [C] one of two players on a basketball team who is responsible for moving the ball so that it is easy for their team to gain points
11 `football` [C] one of two players on a football team who play on either side of the CENTER
12 `fighting` [C] the position of holding your hands or arms up in fighting to defend yourself, or the position in which you hold a sword to defend yourself: *If you want to be a successful boxer, you have to keep your guard up.*
13 `group` **the guard** a group of people, especially soldiers, who guard someone or something.: *In London, we watched the changing of the guard.*

S W
3

guard[2] *v.* **1** [T] to protect a person, place, or valuable object by staying near them and watching them: *A dog guards the house.* | [guard sb/sth against sth] *There is no one to guard the area against possible attack.* **2** [T] to watch a prisoner and prevent them from escaping: *We've hired someone to guard the entrance.* **3 guard a secret** to not tell a secret to anyone: *It is a matter of honor to guard family secrets, no matter how bad.* **4** [T] to prevent a player from another sports team from gaining points or moving forward, or to defend a part of the playing field: *Byron will guard Jordan in tonight's game.* **5 guard your tongue** OLD-FASHIONED used to tell someone to be careful about what they say, so that they do not tell a secret
guard against *phr. v.* [T] **1** [guard against sth] to try to prevent something from happening by being careful: *Both countries must guard against a breakdown in communication.* **2** [guard (sb/sth) against sth] to provide protection from something bad, or to prevent it from happening: *Exercise can help guard against a number of serious illnesses.*

guard dog /'. ./ *n.* [C] a dog that is trained to guard a place

guard·ed /'gardɪd/ *adj.* careful not too say too much or show too much emotion: *Baker spoke about the project with guarded enthusiasm.* —**guardedly** *adv.*

guard·house /'gardhaʊs/ *n.* [C] a building for soldiers who are guarding the entrance to a military camp

guard·i·an /'gardiən/ *n.* [C] **1** someone who is legally responsible for someone else, especially a child **2** FORMAL a person or organization that tries to protect laws, moral principles, traditional ways of doing things etc.: [+ of] *Saudi Arabia sees itself as the guardian of Islam.*

guardian an·gel /,... '../ *n.* [C] **1** an ANGEL (=good spirit) who is believed to protect a person or place **2** someone who helps or protects someone else when they are in trouble

Guardian An·gels, the *n.* /,... '../ an organization whose members try to protect people from being

attacked or robbed, especially when they are traveling on SUBWAYS in big cities

guard·i·an·ship /'gardiən,ʃɪp/ *n.* [U] LAW the position of being legally responsible for someone else, especially a child, or the period during which you have this position

guard·rail /'gard-reɪl/ *n.* [C] a long metal bar that is intended to prevent cars or people from falling over the edge of a road, boat, or high structure

guards·man /'gardzmən/ *n.* [C] a member of the U.S. National Guard

Gua·te·ma·la /,gwatə'malə/ a country in Central America, between the Pacific and Atlantic Oceans —**Guatemalan** *n. adj.*

Guatemala Cit·y /,.... '../ the capital and largest city of Guatemala

gua·va /'gwavə/ *n.* [C] a small tropical fruit with pink flesh and many seeds inside

gu·ber·na·to·ri·al /,gubənə'təriəl/ *adj.* FORMAL relating to the position of being a GOVERNOR

guer·ril·la, guerilla /gə'rɪlə/ *n.* [C] a member of an independent fighting group that fights for political reasons, usually against their government, and attacks the enemy in small groups: *guerrilla warfare* —compare FREEDOM FIGHTER, TERRORIST

guess[1] /gɛs/ *v.*
S W
1
2
1 `without being sure` [I,T] to try to answer a question or make a judgment about something without knowing all the facts, so that you are not sure whether you are correct: *He guessed she was about 30.* | [guess who/what/why etc.] *Guess who I saw at the store today.* | [+ at] *Blumstein said she could only guess at the reasons for the change.* | *"On Friday?" "Well, I don't know, I'm just guessing."*
2 `guess correctly` [I,T] to guess something correctly: *"Don't tell me – you got the job." "How'd you guess?"* | [guess (that)] *I would never have guessed they were a couple.* | [guess sth] *Tom knew then that she hadn't guessed the answer.* | *They told us they were getting married, but we'd already guessed as much* (=guessed correctly before they told us).
3 keep sb guessing to not tell someone what is going to happen next: *Our supervisor likes to keep everyone guessing.*

G

SPOKEN PHRASES

4 I guess a) said when you think something is true or likely, but you are not completely sure: *His light's on, so I guess he's still up.* | *They live somewhere between Saginaw and Lansing, I guess.* **b)** said to show that you do not feel very strongly about what you are planning or agreeing to do: *I guess I'll stay home tonight.* **c)** said to show that you know about a situation, because someone else has told you about it rather than because you were there yourself: *I guess his dad had to work two jobs when they were little.*
5 I guess so/not used to say yes or no when you are not very sure, or when you are making your decision based on what someone else has told you: *"She wasn't happy?" "I guess not."*
6 guess what! also **you'll never guess who/what/where etc.** used when you are about to tell someone something that will surprise them: *Guess what! I won a free trip to Europe! | You'll never guess what she was wearing.*

guess[2] *n.* [C] **1** an attempt to guess something: *I'll give you three guesses. | Just take a guess. | It was a wild guess* (=made without much thought), *but I got the right answer.* **2** an opinion formed by guessing: *My guess is that Dan won't come today.* **3 be anybody's guess** to be something that no one knows: *It's anybody's guess where he's disappeared to.* **4 your guess is as good as mine** SPOKEN said to tell someone that you do not know any more than they do about something: *"When's the next bus coming?" "Your guess is as good as mine."*
S W
3

guess·ti·mate /'gɛstəmɪt/ *n.* [C] INFORMAL an attempt

to judge a quantity by guessing it —**guesstimate** /'gɛstə,meɪt/ v. [I,T]

guess·work /'gɛswɚk/ n. [U] the way of trying to find the answer to something by guessing: *Many of Carey's price estimates are based on guesswork.*

s w **guest¹** /gɛst/ n. [C]
2 2
1 at your house someone who is visiting or staying in someone else's home because they have been invited: *We're having guests this weekend.* | *a dinner guest*

2 at a hotel someone who is paying to stay in a hotel: *The hotel takes very good care of its guests.*

3 at a restaurant/club someone who is invited to a restaurant, theater, club etc. by someone else who pays for them: *Now you and Anna are our guests this evening, all right?*

4 be my guest SPOKEN said when giving someone permission to do what they have asked to do: *"Could I use your phone?" "Be my guest."*

5 on a show someone famous who is invited to take part in a show, concert etc., in addition to those who usually take part: *Tonight's special guest will be Mel Gibson.*

6 guest of honor the most important person who has been invited to a special occasion, especially a celebration that is given for them: *Ambassador Harris was the guest of honor at the ball.*

7 in a foreign country someone who visits another country for a short period of time: *We want our guests from Asia to feel welcome.* —compare HOST¹

guest² adj. **1 a guest speaker/star/artist etc.** someone who is invited to speak on a subject or take part in a performance, in addition to those who usually take part **2** [only before noun] for guests to use: *the guest room* | *guest towels* **3 a guest appearance** a performance that is given by someone who is invited to take part in a show, concert etc., in addition to those who usually take part: *Tom Arnold will make a guest appearance on the show this week.*

G

guest³ v. [I] to take part in a show, concert etc. as a guest performer: *Pearl Bailey also guested on a special for Bob Hope.*

guest book /'. ./ n. [C] a book in which everyone who comes to a formal occasion or stays at a hotel writes their name

guest·house /'gɛsthaʊs/ n. [C] a small building next to a main house that visitors can stay in

guest star, guest-star /'. ./ v. [I] to perform on a television show along with the people who normally take part in the show: *DeVito guest stars as Homer's long-lost half brother.*

guest work·er /'. ,../ n. [C] a foreign worker, usually from a poor country, working in another country for a particular period of time

Gue·va·ra /gɛ'vɑrə/, **Er·nes·to (Ché)** /ɚ'nɛstoʊ keɪ, tʃeɪ/ (1928–1967) a Marxist military leader, born in Argentina, who developed the method of fighting known as GUERRILLA warfare and helped Fidel Castro to gain control of Cuba

guff /gʌf/ n. [U] SPOKEN stupid or annoying behavior or talk: *Don't take any guff from those guys.*

guf·faw /gə'fɔ/ v. [I] to laugh loudly —**guffaw** n. [C]

Gug·gen·heim /'gʊgən,haɪm/, **Sol·o·mon** /'sɑləmən/ (1861–1949) a U.S. INDUSTRIALIST who started a FOUNDATION for modern art that later built the Guggenheim Museum in New York City

GUI /'gui/ n. [U] TECHNICAL Graphical User Interface; a way of arranging computer information on a screen using pictures, which makes it easier for users to tell the computer what to do

guid·ance /'gaɪdns/ n. [U] **1** helpful advice given to someone about their work, education, personal life etc.: *Dad has given me a lot of guidance on choosing a career.* **2** the activity of leading, influencing, or directing someone or something: *Spitz started training under the guidance of Coach Ballatore.* **3** the process of directing a MISSILE (1) in flight: *The missiles have an electronic guidance system.*

guidance coun·sel·or /'.. ,.../ n. [C] someone who works in a school, whose job is to give advice to students about what subjects to study and help them with personal problems

guide¹ /gaɪd/ n. [C] **1** someone whose job is to show **s w** tourists around a city, MUSEUM etc.: *a tour guide* **3 3** **2** someone who shows you the way to a place, especially a place that is difficult or dangerous to reach: *One of our guides helped me set up the tent.* **3 a)** a book, PAMPHLET etc. that provides information on a particular subject or explains how to do something; HANDBOOK: [+ **to**] *The Complete Guide to Computer Literacy* | [+ **for**] *a guide for new parents* **b)** a GUIDEBOOK **4** someone or something that helps you form opinions about something or helps you decide what to do or how to do it: *A friend's experience isn't always the best guide for you.*

guide² v. [T] **1** to take someone to or through a place **s w** that you know very well, showing them the way: **3** [+ **along/through/to** etc.] *Abdul guided us through the narrow streets to the central mosque.* **2** to help someone or something to move in a particular direction: *The pilot guided the plane to a safe landing.* **3** to strongly influence someone's behavior, thoughts etc.: *We were always guided by the belief that we would be rescued.* **4** to show someone the right way to do something, especially something difficult or complicated: [**guide sb through sth**] *Tax-preparation programs guide you through the tax form.* —see also GUIDING —see Usage Note at LEAD¹

guide·book /'gaɪdbʊk/ n. [C] a special book about a city, area etc. that gives details about the place and its history

guid·ed mis·sile /,.. '../ n. [C] a MISSILE that can be controlled electronically while it is flying

guide dog /'. ./ n. [C] a dog trained to guide a blind person

guided tour /,.. './ n. [C] a trip around a city, building etc., led by someone who tells people about the place: *We were given a guided tour of the palace.*

guide·lines /'gaɪdlaɪnz/ n. [plural] rules or instructions about the best way to do something: [+ **for/on**] *The FCC has set federal guidelines on TV violence.*

guide·post /'gaɪdpoʊst/ n. [C] **1** something that helps you decide what to do or the best way to do it: *History is an important guidepost for leaders.* **2** a sign beside a road, path etc. that tells people which way to go

guid·ing /'gaɪdɪŋ/ adj. **a guiding principle/star/light** a principle, idea, or person that you follow in order to help you decide what you should do in a difficult situation

guild /gɪld/ n. [C] an organization of people who share the same interests, skills, or profession: *the writer's guild*

guil·der /'gɪldɚ/ n. [C] the standard unit of money in the Netherlands

guild·hall /'gɪldhɔl/ n. [C] a large building in which members of a guild met in past times

guile /gaɪl/ n. [U] FORMAL the use of smart but dishonest methods to deceive someone: *By guile and skill, they managed to escape.* —**guileful** adj.

guile·less /'gaɪl-lɪs/ adj. behaving in an honest way, without trying to hide anything or deceive people

guil·lo·tine¹ /'gɪlə,tin, 'giə-, ,giə'tin/ n. [C] a piece of equipment used to cut off the heads of criminals in past times, especially in France

guillotine² v. [T] to cut off someone's head using a guillotine

guilt¹ /gɪlt/ n. [U] **1** a feeling of shame and sadness when you know or believe you have done something wrong: [+ **about/at/over**] *The guilt I felt over the way I had treated her was overwhelming.* | *Marta felt a sense of guilt about leaving home.* **2 a guilt trip** INFORMAL a feeling of guilt about something, when this is unreasonable: *I wish my parents would stop laying a guilt trip on me* (=stop trying to make me feel guilty) *about not going to college.* **3** the fact of having broken an official law or moral rule: *The juror was sure of the defendant's guilt.* **4** the state of being responsible for something bad that has happened: *Most of the guilt for his poor academic performance lies with him.* —opposite INNOCENCE

guilt² *v.* [T] INFORMAL, NONSTANDARD to try to make someone feel guilty, especially so they will do what you want: **[guilt sb into doing sth]** *Her parents guilted her into not going to the concert.*

guilt·less /'gɪltlɪs/ *adj.* not responsible for a crime or for having done something wrong; INNOCENT¹ —**guiltlessly** *adv.*

guilt-rid·den /'. ,../ *adj.* feeling so guilty about something that you cannot think about anything else: **[+ over/about]** *Barkowski was guilt-ridden over the way she had treated her son.*

s w
3 3
guilt·y /'gɪlti/ *adj.* **guiltier, guiltiest 1** ashamed and sad because you know or believe you have done something wrong: **[+ about]** *I feel guilty about not inviting her to the party.* | *It's just that I have a guilty conscience* (=feel guilty) *whenever I skip practice.* **2** having done something that is a crime: *The court found him guilty of* (=officially decided that he was guilty of) *fraud.* | *He plans to plead not guilty* (=say in a court of law that was not guilty) *to the murder charges.* | *Both defendants were found guilty as charged* (=guilty of the illegal action that someone said they did). —opposite INNOCENT¹ **3** responsible for behavior that is morally or socially unacceptable or for something bad that has happened: **[guilty of (doing) sth]** *These officials are guilty of arrogance and greed.* **4 the guilty party** the person who has done something illegal or wrong —**guiltily** *adv.* —**guiltiness** *n.* [U]

Guin·ea /'gɪni/ a country in west Africa north and east of Sierra Leone —**Guinean** *n. adj.*

Guinea-Bis·sau /,gɪni bɪ'saʊ/ a small country in west Africa between Guinea and Senegal —**Guinean** *n. adj.*

guinea fowl /'gɪni ,faʊl/ *n.* [C] a gray African bird that is often used for food

guin·ea pig /'gɪni ,pɪg/ *n.* [C] **1** INFORMAL someone who is used in a test to see how successful or safe a new product, system etc. is: *My guests are guinea pigs for all the new dishes I try out.* **2** a small animal like a large rat with long fur, short ears, and no tail, which is often kept as a pet

Guin·e·vere /'gwɪnə,vɪr, 'gwɛ-/ in old stories the wife of King Arthur, who had a sexual relationship with Sir LANCELOT

guise /gaɪz/ *n.* [C] FORMAL the way someone or something seems to be, which is meant to hide the truth: **in/under the guise of sth** *The four reporters passed the checkpoints in the guise of U.S. soldiers.*

s w
2
gui·tar /gɪ'tar/ *n.* [C] a musical instrument that has six or twelve strings, a long neck, and a wooden body, which is played by pulling on the strings with your fingers or a PICK² (5) —**guitarist** *n.* [C]

gu·lag /'gulag/ *n.* [C] one of a group of prison camps in the former U.S.S.R., where conditions were very bad

gulch /gʌltʃ/ *n.* [C] a narrow deep valley formed by flowing water, but that is usually dry

gulf /gʌlf/ *n.* [C] **1** a large area of ocean partly enclosed by land: *the Gulf of Mexico* **2** a great difference and lack of understanding between two groups of people, especially in their beliefs, opinions, and way of life: **[+ between]** *There is a wide gulf between the rich and poor in the country.* **3** a deep hollow place in the Earth's surface

Gulf of Mex·i·co, the /,. . '.../ an area of the Atlantic Ocean that is south of the U.S., east of Mexico, and west of Cuba

Gulf states /'. ./ *n.* **the Gulf States** the southern states of the U.S. that are next to the Gulf of Mexico

Gulf Stream /'. ./ *n.* **the Gulf Stream** a current of warm water that flows northeastward in the Atlantic Ocean from the Gulf of Mexico toward Europe

Gulf War, the /,. './ a war which began in 1991, after Iraq attacked Kuwait and took control of it. A United Nations force led by the U.S. attacked Iraq and forced the Iraqi army out of Kuwait.

gull¹ /gʌl/ *n.* [C] **1** a SEAGULL **2** LITERARY someone who is easily deceived

gull² *v.* [T] OLD USE to cheat or deceive someone

Gul·lah /'gʌlə/ *n.* [U] **1** a language spoken by the Gullah people in the southeastern U.S., which is a mixture of English and West African languages **2** a member of the group of African Americans who live on the Sea Islands and in the coastal areas of the southeastern U.S.

gul·let /'gʌlɪt/ *n.* [C] OLD-FASHIONED the tube through which food goes down your throat

gul·ley /'gʌli/ *n.* [C] another spelling of gully

gul·li·ble /'gʌləbəl/ *adj.* too ready to believe what other people say, and therefore easy to trick: *a group of gullible tourists* —**gullibility** /,gʌlə'bɪləti/ *n.* [U]

gul·ly /'gʌli/ *n. plural* **gullies** [C] **1** a small narrow valley, usually formed by a lot of rain flowing down the side of a hill **2** a deep DITCH¹

gulp¹ /gʌlp/ *v.* **1** [T] also **gulp sth ↔ down** to swallow something quickly: *She gulped her coffee and ran for the bus.* **2** [T] also **gulp sth ↔ in** to take in quick large breaths of air: *Steve swam up to the surface and gulped in air.* **3** [I] to swallow suddenly because you are surprised or nervous: *Mandy read the test questions and gulped.* **4 gulp back/down tears** to try to prevent yourself from crying: *Keenan gulped back tears as he talked about his childhood.*

gulp² *n.* [C] an act of swallowing something quickly, or the amount swallowed: *Rachel took a gulp of soda.* | *He drank the rest of the beer in one gulp.*

s w
2
gum¹ /gʌm/ *n.* **1** a sweet sticky type of candy that you chew for a long time but do not swallow **2** [C usually plural] the firm pink part inside your mouth that holds your teeth **3** [U] a sticky substance found in the stems of some trees **4** [C] a GUM TREE **5 by gum!** SPOKEN, OLD-FASHIONED used to express surprise

gum² *v.* **gummed, gumming**
gum sth ↔ up *phr. v.* [T] INFORMAL to prevent something from working correctly by covering it with a sticky substance: *How did this lock get so gummed up?*

gum·ball /'gʌmbɔl/ *n.* [C] gum in the form of a small brightly colored ball

gum·bo /'gʌmboʊ/ *n.* [U] **1** a thick soup made with meat, fish, and OKRA (=a small green vegetable) **2** another word for OKRA, used in some parts of the U.S.

gum·drop /'gʌmdrɑp/ *n.* [C] a small CHEWY candy

gum·my /'gʌmi/ *adj.* **gummier, gummiest 1** sticky, or covered in GUM: *a baby's gummy fingers* **2** a gummy smile shows the GUMS in your mouth

gump·tion /'gʌmpʃən/ *n.* [U] INFORMAL the ability and determination to decide what needs to be done and do it

gum·shoe /'gʌm,ʃu/ *n.* [C] OLD-FASHIONED a DETECTIVE

gum tree /'. ./ *n.* [C] a tall tree that produces a strong-smelling oil used in medicine

G

s w
2 2
gun¹ /gʌn/ *n.* [C]
1 weapon a weapon that fires bullets or SHELLS (=large metal objects), especially one that can be carried
2 the big/top gun INFORMAL someone who controls an organization, or who is the most successful person in a group: *All the big guns are sitting near the head table.*

3 [tool] a tool or object used to send out objects or a liquid by using pressure: *a paint gun* | *a nail gun* —see also FLASHGUN, SPRAY GUN

4 under the gun INFORMAL if someone is under the gun, they are in a difficult situation in which they must do something in order to prevent something bad from happening: **[be under the gun (to do sth)]** *To remain competitive, companies are under the gun to cut costs.*

5 a hired gun INFORMAL someone who is paid to shoot someone else or to protect someone

6 a **21-gun salute** an act of shooting guns as a sign of respect —see also **go great guns** (GREAT¹ (12)), **jump the gun** (JUMP¹ (9)), SON OF A GUN, **stick to your guns** at STICK to (STICK¹)

gun² v. **1** [T] INFORMAL to make a car go very fast by pressing the ACCELERATOR very hard: *Gun it* (=make the car go quickly)*!* **2 be gunning for sb** to be looking for an opportunity to criticize or harm someone: *As long as we're number 1, everybody will be gunning for us.* **3 be gunning for sth** to be trying very hard to obtain something: *Another officer is already gunning for his job.*

gun sb ↔ **down** *phr. v.* [T] to shoot someone and badly injure or kill them, especially someone who cannot defend themselves: *Two people were gunned down in a drive-by shooting Tuesday.*

gun·boat /ˈgʌnboʊt/ n. [C] **1** a small military ship that is used near a coast **2 gunboat diplomacy** the practice of threatening to use force against a smaller country in order to make it agree to your demands

gun car·riage /ˈ. ˌ../ n. [C] a frame with wheels on which a heavy gun is moved around

gun con·trol /ˈ. .ˌ./ n. [U] laws that restrict the possession and use of guns

gun·fight /ˈgʌnfaɪt/ n. [C] a fight between people using guns —**gunfighter** n. [C]

gun·fire /ˈgʌnfaɪr/ n. [U] the repeated firing of guns, or the noise made by this: *enemy gunfire*

gung-ho /ˌgʌŋ ˈhoʊ/ adj. INFORMAL very eager or too eager to do something: *Baxter is a gung-ho supporter of Senator Thompson.*

gunk¹ /gʌŋk/ n. [U] INFORMAL any substance that is thick, dirty, and sticky: *There's a bunch of gunk clogging the drain.* —**gunky** adj.

gunk² v. **be gunked up (with sth)** INFORMAL to be blocked with a dirty sticky substance

gun·man /ˈgʌnmən/ n. [C] a criminal or TERRORIST who uses a gun

gun·met·al /ˈgʌnˌmɛtl/ n. [U] **1** a dull gray-colored metal that is a mixture of COPPER, TIN, and ZINC **2** the dull gray color of gunmetal —**gunmetal** adj.: *gunmetal skies*

gun·ner /ˈgʌnər/ n. [C] a soldier, sailor etc. whose job is to aim or fire a large gun

gun·ner·y /ˈgʌnəri/ n. [U] the science and practice of shooting with heavy guns: *a gunnery officer*

gun·ny·sack /ˈgʌniˌsæk/ n. [C] INFORMAL a large BURLAP bag used for storing and sending grain, coffee etc.

gun·point /ˈgʌnpɔɪnt/ n. **at gunpoint** while threatening people with a gun, or while being threatened with a gun: *The storekeeper was robbed at gunpoint.*

gun·pow·der /ˈgʌnˌpaʊdər/ n. [U] an explosive substance in the form of powder

gun-run·ning /ˈ. ˌ../ n. [U] the activity of taking guns into a country secretly and illegally, especially so that they can be used to fight the government —**gun-runner** n. [C]

gun·ship /ˈgʌnˌʃɪp/ n. [C] a military aircraft such as a HELICOPTER, that is used to protect soldiers who are fighting and to destroy enemy guns

gun·shot /ˈgʌnʃɑt/ n. **1** [C] the action of shooting a gun, or the sound that this makes **2** [U] the bullets fired from a gun: *a gunshot wound*

gun-shy /ˈ. ./ adj. **1** very careful or frightened about doing something, because of a bad experience in the

past: *Cecile is still a little gun-shy about traveling alone.* **2** a hunting dog that is gun-shy is easily frightened by the noise of a gun

gun·sling·er /ˈgʌnˌslɪŋər/ n. [C] someone who is very skillful at using guns, especially a criminal in past times —**gun-slinging** adj. [only before noun]

gun·smith /ˈgʌnˌsmɪθ/ n. [C] someone who makes and repairs guns

gun·wale /ˈgʌnl/ n. [C] TECHNICAL the upper edge of the side of a boat or small ship

gup·py /ˈgʌpi/ n. plural **guppies** [C] a very small brightly-colored tropical fish

gur·gle /ˈgɜrgəl/ v. [I] **1** if something such as a stream gurgles, it makes a pleasant low sound, like water flowing through a pipe **2** if a baby gurgles, it makes this kind of sound in its throat —**gurgle** n. [C]

gur·ney /ˈgɜrni/ n. plural **gurneys** [C] a long narrow table with wheels, used for moving sick people in a hospital

gu·ru /ˈguru, ˈgʊru/ n. [C] **1** INFORMAL someone who knows a lot about a particular subject, and to whom people go for advice: *a nutrition guru* **2** a Hindu religious teacher or leader

gush¹ /gʌʃ/ v. **1** [I always + adv./prep.,T] if a liquid gushes from something, or if something gushes it, it flows or pours out quickly in large quantities: **[+ out/from/down etc.]** *Oil gushed from the broken pipeline.* | **[gush sth]** *His wound was gushing blood.* **2** [I,T] to express your admiration, pleasure etc. in a way that other people think is too strong: *"I just love your outfit," she gushed.*

gush² n. **1** a large quantity of liquid that suddenly flows from somewhere: *a gush of water* **2 a gush of relief/pride/ideas etc.** a sudden feeling or expression of emotion, ideas etc.

gush·er /ˈgʌʃər/ n. [C] INFORMAL an OIL WELL where the natural flow of oil out of the well is very strong, so that a pump is not needed

gush·ing /ˈgʌʃɪŋ/ also **gush·y** /ˈgʌʃi/ adj. INFORMAL expressing admiration, pleasure etc. in a way that other people think is too strong: *a gushing speech*

gus·set /ˈgʌsɪt/ n. [C] a small piece of material stitched into a piece of clothing to make it stronger, wider, or more comfortable in a particular place

gus·sy /ˈgʌsi/ v. **gussied, gussying**

gussy sb/sth ↔ **up** *phr. v.* [T] INFORMAL to make someone look attractive by dressing them in their best clothes, or to make something look attractive by decorating it etc.: *They got all gussied up for the performance.*

gust¹ /gʌst/ n. [C] **1** a sudden strong movement of wind, air, snow etc.: *A gust of wind blew our tent over.* **2** a sudden strong feeling or expression of anger, excitement etc.: *A gust of rage swept over him.* —**gusty** adj.

gust² v. [I] if the wind gusts, it blows strongly with sudden short movements: *Winds were gusting up to 46 miles per hour.*

gus·ta·to·ry /ˈgʌstəˌtɔri/ adj. [only before noun] FORMAL relating to taste or tasting: *Burritos are one of life's gustatory pleasures.*

gus·to /ˈgʌstoʊ/ n. [U] **with gusto** if you do something with gusto, you do it with a lot of eagerness and energy: *Elizabeth sang with gusto.*

gut¹ /gʌt/ n.

1 a gut reaction/feeling/instinct etc. INFORMAL a reaction or feeling that you are sure is right although you cannot give a reason for it: *My gut reaction is that it's a bad idea.*

2 [courage] **guts** [plural] INFORMAL the courage you need to do something difficult or something that you do not want to do: *Rich didn't have the guts to say what he really thought.*

3 [stomach] [C] INFORMAL your stomach: *He hit me right in the gut.* | *Phil has a huge beer gut* (=unattractive fat stomach caused by drinking too much beer).

4 [inside your body] NOT TECHNICAL **a) guts** [plural] the organs inside your body, especially the INTESTINES **b)** [C] the tube through which food passes when it leaves your stomach; INTESTINE

5 work/run etc. your guts out INFORMAL to work, run etc. very hard

6 machine/equipment guts [plural] INFORMAL the parts inside a machine, piece of equipment, factory etc.: *The guts of the answering machine were spread across his desk.*

7 at gut level if you know or feel something at gut level, you feel sure about it, although you can not give a reason for it: *She knew at gut level that he was lying.*

8 most important parts guts [plural] INFORMAL the most important or basic parts of something: *He took the guts of our songs and reworked them.*

9 string [U] a type of strong string made from the INTESTINE of an animal —see also BLOOD-AND-GUTS, **bust a gut** (BUST¹ (7)), CATGUT, **hate sb's guts** (HATE¹ (3)), **spill your guts** (SPILL¹ (4))

gut² v. **gutted, gutting** [T] **1** to completely destroy the inside of a building, especially by fire: *The Sunday night fire gutted St. Mary's church.* **2** to change something by removing some of the most important parts: *Democrats have gutted the anti-crime bill.* **3** to remove the organs from inside a fish or animal in order to prepare it for cooking: *Gut and clean all the fish before cooking.*

Gu·ten·berg /'gutn,bɔg/, **Jo·han·nes** /you'hɑnɪs/ (1397–1468) a German printer who is considered to have invented the method of printing that uses movable letters

Guth·rie /'gʌθri/, **Wood·y** /'wʊci/ (1912–1967) a singer and writer of FOLK MUSIC, known especially for his songs about working people

gut·less /'gʌtlɪs/ adj. INFORMAL lacking courage: *a gutless decision* | *He's been called a **gutless wonder** (=someone with no courage at all) for not running for governor.*

gut·sy /'gʌtsi/ adj. **gutsier, gutsiest** INFORMAL brave and taking risks: *Going to a start-up company was a gutsy career move.*

gut·ter¹ /'gʌtə/ n. **1** [C] the low place along the edge of a road, where water collects and flows away **2** [C] an open pipe at the edge of a roof for collecting and carrying away rain water —see picture on page 423 **3 the gutter** dirty and difficult conditions that you experience because of lack of care or money: *He was an alcoholic who had only recently gotten his life out of the gutter.* **4 gutter mouth/talk/language** someone who has a gutter mouth, or uses gutter talk, uses offensive words, especially relating to sex **5** the low area on both sides of a LANE (4) in a BOWLING ALLEY: *a gutter ball* (=a ball that goes in the gutter)

gutter² v. [I] LITERARY if a CANDLE gutters, it burns with an unsteady flame

gut·ter·snipe /'gʌtə,snaɪp/ n. [C] OLD-FASHIONED **1** a dirty, badly-behaved child who lives on the street **2** someone from the poorest social class

gut·tur·al /'gʌtərəl/ adj. a guttural sound is produced deep in the throat

s w
1 1
guy /gaɪ/ n. [C] **1** INFORMAL a man, especially a young man: *Dave's a nice guy when you get to know him.* | *There's some guy who wants to talk to you.* **2 (you/those) guys** SPOKEN said when talking to or about two or more people, male or female: *We'll see you guys Sunday, okay?* —compare Y'ALL **3** also **guy rope** a rope that stretches from the top or side of a tent, pole, or structure to the ground to keep it in the

647

gyroscope

right position —see also **no more Mr. Nice Guy!** (MR. (4)), **wise guy** (WISE¹ (4))

Guy·an·a /gaɪ'ɑnə/ a country in northeastern South America on the Atlantic Ocean, east of Venezuela —**Guyanese** /,gaɪə'niz◂ , -'niz◂/ n., adj.

guz·zle /'gʌzəl/ v. [I,T] INFORMAL to drink a lot of something, eagerly and quickly: *Chris has been guzzling beer all evening.* —see also GAS-GUZZLER

gym /dʒɪm/ n. INFORMAL **1** [C] a special building or room that has equipment for doing physical exercise or playing sports: *the boys' gym at the high school* **2** [U] exercises done indoors for physical development and as a sport, especially as a school subject: *a gym class* ⟨s w / 3⟩

gym·na·si·um /dʒɪm'neɪziəm/ n. [C] a GYM (1)

gym·nast /'dʒɪmnæst, -nəst/ n. [C] someone who does gymnastics as a sport, especially someone who competes against other people

gym·nas·tics /dʒɪm'næstɪks/ n. [U] **1** a sport involving physical exercises and movements that need skill, strength, and control, and that are often performed in competitions: *Korbut was a gymnastics gold medalist.* **2 mental/intellectual/verbal etc. gymnastics** thinking, speaking etc. that is very quick, complicated, and skillful **3** movements that are quick, complicated, and skillful —**gymnastic** adj.

gym shoe /'. ./ n. [C] a shoe that is appropriate to wear for playing sports

gyn- /gaɪn/ prefix TECHNICAL relating to women: *gynecology*

gy·ne·col·o·gy /,gaɪnə'kɑlədʒi/ n. [U] the study and treatment of medical conditions and illnesses affecting only women —**gynecologist** n. [C] —**gynecological** /,gaɪnəkə'lɑdʒɪkəl/ adj.

gyp¹ /dʒɪp/ v. **gypped, gypping** [T] SPOKEN to cheat or trick someone: *I got gypped out of $50!*

gyp² n. [singular] SPOKEN something that you were tricked into buying, or a situation in which you feel you have been cheated: *What a gyp!*

gyp·sum /'dʒɪpsəm/ n. [U] a soft white substance, usually in the form of powder, that is used to make PLASTER OF PARIS, which becomes hard after it has been mixed with water and has dried

gyp·sy /'dʒɪpsi/ n. plural **gypsies** [C] **1** a member of a group of people originally from northern India, who used to live and travel around in CARAVANs, and now live in many countries all over the world —see also ROMANY (1) **2** someone who does not like to stay in the same place for a long time

gypsy moth /'.. ,./ n. [C] a type of MOTH whose CATERPILLARs eat leaves and damage trees

gy·rate /'dʒaɪreɪt/ v. [I] to turn around fast in circles: *The dancers gyrated wildly to the beat of the music.* —**gyration** /dʒaɪ'reɪʃən/ n.

gy·ro¹ /'dʒaɪroʊ/ n. [C] INFORMAL a gyroscope

gy·ro² /'dʒaɪroʊ, 'yiroʊ/ n. plural **gyros** [C] a Greek SANDWICH usually made of lamb, onion, and TOMATO in PITA BREAD

gy·ro·scope /'dʒaɪrə,skoʊp/ n. [C] a wheel that spins inside a frame, and is used for keeping ships and aircraft steady —**gyroscopic** /,dʒaɪrə'skɑpɪk/ adj.

G

H

H, h /eɪtʃ/ *n. plural* **H's, h's** [C] the 8th letter of the English alphabet —see also H-BOMB

H₂O /ˌeɪtʃ tu ˈoʊ/ *n.* [U] TECHNICAL the chemical sign for water

ha, hah /hɑ/ *interjection* used when you are surprised or have discovered something interesting: *Ha! I told you it wouldn't work.* —see also AHA, HA HA

ha. the written abbreviation of HECTARES

Ha·bak·kuk /ˈhæbəˌkʌk, həˈbækək/ a book in the Old Testament of the Christian Bible

ha·be·as corpus /ˌheɪbiəs ˈkɔrpəs/ *n.* [U] LAW the right of someone in prison to come to a court of law so that the court can decide whether they should stay in prison

hab·er·dash·er /ˈhæbɚˌdæʃɚ/ *n.* [C] OLD-FASHIONED someone who works in or owns a store that sells men's clothes

hab·er·dash·er·y /ˈhæbɚˌdæʃəri/ *n.* [C,U] OLD-FASHIONED a store or part of a store that sells men's clothing, especially hats, or the clothes and hats sold there

hab·it /ˈhæbɪt/ *n.*

1 sth you do regularly [C,U] something that you do regularly, often without thinking about it because you have done it so many times before: *healthy eating habits* | [**be in the habit of doing sth**] *Liz is in the habit of going to lunch with them every day.* | *You should get into the habit of exercising when you're young.* | *I still shop at K mart out of habit, even though Wal-Mart is closer.*

2 annoying behavior [C] something that someone does regularly and that other people think is annoying: [**have a habit of doing sth**] *My teenage daughter has a habit of leaving home without her house key.* | *Biting your nails is a bad habit.*

3 drugs [C usually singular] a strong physical need to keep taking a drug regularly: *Many of them get into petty crime to support their habit.* | *Akira quit his four-pack-a-day cigarette habit.*

4 break/kick the habit to stop doing something that is annoying or bad for your health: *With the help of doctors, Louis was able to kick his drug habit* (=stop taking drugs).

5 clothes [C] a long loose piece of clothing worn by people in some religious groups: *a nun's habit*

SPOKEN PHRASES

6 don't make a habit of (doing) sth used to tell someone who has done something bad or wrong that they should not do it again: *You can turn your paper in late this time, but don't make a habit of it.*

7 I'm not in the habit of doing sth used when you are offended because someone has suggested that you have done something that you have not done: *I'm not in the habit of lying to my friends.*

8 old habits die hard used to say that it is difficult to make people change their attitudes or behavior

—see also **a creature of habit** (CREATURE (4)), **by/from force of habit** (FORCE¹ (11))

USAGE NOTE: HABIT

WORD CHOICE: habit, custom, tradition, practice, convention
A **habit** is something that someone does again and again, usually without thinking about it: *He has an irritating habit of picking his ears.* A **custom** is something which has been done for a long time by a society, and which happens or is done the same way every time: *According to Islamic custom, a woman must cover her hair.* A **tradition** is similar to a **custom,** but

may be older, and children usually learn about it from their parents: *There's a tradition in the Southwest that strings of red chilies bring good luck.* | *a family tradition.* A **practice** is the usual way of doing things in business, law etc.: *The normal practice in this company is to send the bill as soon as the job is done.* The **conventions** of a society are its generally accepted rules of behavior: *It is a matter of convention for people attending funerals to wear dark clothes.*

---

hab·it·a·ble /ˈhæbətəbəl/ *adj.* good enough for people to live in: *It would cost a fortune to make the place habitable.* —**habitability** /ˌhæbətəˈbɪləti/ *n.* [U]

hab·i·tat /ˈhæbəˌtæt/ *n.* [C] the natural environment of a plant or animal: *The owl's natural habitat is in the forests of the Northwest.*

Habitat for Hu·man·i·ty /ˌ... . .ˈ.../ an organization that helps poor people to build and own their own homes

hab·i·ta·tion /ˌhæbəˈteɪʃən/ *n.* FORMAL **1** [U] the act of living in a place: *What are the chances of achieving permanent habitation in space?* | *Many of the housing projects are unfit for human habitation* (=not safe or healthy for people to live in). **2** [C] LITERARY a house or place to live in

habit-form·ing /ˈ.. ˌ.../ *adj.* a drug or activity that is habit-forming makes you want to keep taking it, keep doing it etc.: *Video games can be habit-forming.*

ha·bit·u·al /həˈbɪtʃuəl/ *adj.* **1** done as a habit or doing something from habit: *Many of the prisoners are habitual liars.* **2** [only before noun] usual or typical of someone: *James took his habitual morning walk around the park.* —**habitually** *adv.*

ha·bit·u·ate /həˈbɪtʃuˌeɪt/ *v.* [T usually passive] FORMAL to be or gradually become used to something: [**be habituated to sth**] *Many bears in Yellowstone Park have become habituated to people feeding them.*

ha·bit·u·é /həˈbɪtʃuˌeɪ, həˌbɪtʃuˈeɪ/ *n.* [C] FORMAL someone who regularly goes to a particular place or event

ha·ci·en·da /ˌhɑsiˈɛndə/ *n.* [C] a large farm in Spanish-speaking countries

hack¹ /hæk/ *v.* **1** [I always + adv./prep.,T always + adv./prep.] to cut something into pieces roughly or violently: *The bodies of the five men had been hacked to pieces.* | [**+ away/at**] *She hacked at what little meat remained on the turkey.* | [**hack through/into sth**] *Explorers hacked their way through the jungle with machetes.* **2 can't hack it** SPOKEN to feel that you cannot do something that is difficult or boring: *Debbie just couldn't hack it in Mr. Temple's physics class.* **3** [I] to use a computer to enter someone else's computer system without their permission: [**+ into**] *A teenage boy managed to hack into military computer networks.* **4** [I] to cough very loudly and painfully: *I couldn't stop hacking last night.* —**hacking** *n.* [U]

hack² *n.* [C] **1** a writer who does a lot of low-quality work, especially writing newspaper articles: *the hacks who write TV movies* **2** someone who does whatever they need to in order to be an artist, musician, politician etc., even if this means doing low-quality or boring work: *Before the election Davies was considered just a political hack.* **3** INFORMAL a taxi, or a taxi driver **4** an old tired horse

hack·er /ˈhækɚ/ *n.* [C] someone who uses computers a lot, especially in order to secretly use or change the information in another person's computer system

hacking cough /ˌ.. ˈ./ *n.* [usually singular] a repeated painful cough with a loud sound

hack·les /ˈhækəlz/ *n.* [plural] **1 raise sb's hackles** to say or do something that makes someone very angry: *The proposal to build 135 new homes has raised environmentalists' hackles.* **2** the long feathers or hairs on the back of the neck of some animals and birds, which stand up straight when they are in danger

hack·neyed /ˈhæknid/ *adj.* a hackneyed phrase, statement etc. is boring and does not have much meaning, because it has been used so often

hack·saw /ˈhæksɔ/ n. [C] a type of SAW (=CUTTING TOOL) with small teeth on its blade, used especially for cutting metal —see picture at TOOL[1]

had /əd, həd; strong hæd/ v. **1** the past tense and past participle of HAVE **2 be had** INFORMAL to be tricked or cheated and made to look stupid: When they looked closely at the watch, they realized they'd been had. **3 have had it a)** to be very tired and not want to do something anymore: I've had it. Let's go home. **b)** to be very annoyed about something or what someone is doing, and not want it to continue: I've had it with you! You listen to me!

had·dock /ˈhædək/ n. plural **haddock** [C,U] a common fish that lives in northern oceans and is often used as food

Ha·des /ˈheɪdiz/ n. [U] the place where people went after they died in the stories of ancient Greece; HELL

had·n't /ˈhædnt/ v. the short form of "had not": I went to visit a friend I hadn't seen for years.

haft /hæft/ n. [C] TECHNICAL a long handle on an AX or on other weapons

hag /hæg/ n. [C] an ugly or mean woman, especially one who is old or looks like a WITCH

Hag·gai /ˈhægaɪ, -gi,aɪ/ a book in the Old Testament of the Christian Bible

hag·gard /ˈhægəd/ adj. having lines on your face and dark marks around your eyes, especially because you are sick, worried, or have not had enough sleep: The jurors looked haggard on their tenth day of deliberations.

hag·gle /ˈhægəl/ v. [I] to argue especially about the amount of money you will pay for something: [+ over] I hate having to haggle over prices. —**haggling** n. [U]

hag·i·og·ra·phy /ˌhægiˈɑgrəfi, ˌhædʒi-/ n. [C,U] **1** a book about the lives of SAINTS **2** a book about someone that describes them as better than they really are

Hague, The /heɪg/ a city in the Netherlands. The country's government is in The Hague, but its capital city is Amsterdam.

hah /hɑ/ interjection another spelling of HA

ha ha /hɑ ˈhɑ/ interjection **1** used in writing to represent a shout of laughter **2** SPOKEN used, sometimes angrily, to show that you do not think something is funny: Oh, very funny, John, ha ha. —see also **funny weird/strange or funny ha ha** (FUNNY (14))

Hai·da /ˈhaɪdə/ a Native American tribe from the coast of northwest Canada and Alaska

hai·ku /ˈhaɪku/ n. plural **haiku** [C] a type of Japanese poem with three lines consisting of five, seven, and five SYLLABLES

hail[1] /heɪl/ v. **1** [I] if it hails, small balls of ice fall from the clouds **2** [T] to call to someone in order to attract their attention: **hail a taxi/cab** The hotel doorman will hail a cab for you.
hail sb/sth **as** sth phr. v. [T often passive] to describe someone or something as being very good, especially in newspapers, magazines etc.: Lang's first film was immediately hailed as a masterpiece.
hail from sth phr. v. [T not in passive] OLD-FASHIONED to have been born in a particular place: What part of the world do you hail from?

hail[2] n. **1** [U] frozen rain that falls as balls of ice: Hail the size of golf balls fell in Andrews, Texas. **2 a hail of bullets/stones etc.** a large number of bullets, stones etc. thrown or fired at someone: A hail of enemy fire forced them back into the trenches. **3 a hail of criticism/abuse** a lot of criticism about something someone says or does

hail[3] interjection LITERARY used to greet someone: Hail to the King!

Hail Ma·ry /ˌheɪl ˈmɛri/ n. [C] a special Catholic prayer to Mary, the mother of Jesus Christ

hail·stone /ˈheɪlstoun/ n. [C] a small ball of frozen rain

hail·storm /ˈheɪlstɔrm/ n. [C] a storm when a lot of HAIL falls

hair /hɛr/ n.
1 on head [U] the things like thin threads that

grow on your head: Brandi has nice long hair. | a small boy with blond hair and blue eyes | **get/have your hair done** (=have it cut or given a particular style) —see picture at BODY

2 on body [U] the short thin things like thread that grow on some parts of your body, for example on your legs or under your arms: pubic hair

3 on animals [U] a word meaning hair that grows on the bodies of some animals, used especially when it is has come off the animal's body: The couch is covered in cat hair. —compare FUR (1)

4 one hair [C] one human or animal hair: Yuck! There's a hair in my sandwich.

5 tear/pull your hair out INFORMAL to be very anxious or angry about something: I was pulling my hair out trying to find someone to help me.

6 not harm/touch a hair on sb's head to not harm someone in any way: Our dog Benji wouldn't harm a hair on little Ron's head.

7 a hair a small amount: Larson won the race by a hair.

8 not have a hair out of place to have a very neat appearance: Joel never has a hair out of place.

9 let your hair down INFORMAL to enjoy yourself and start to relax, especially after working very hard: Playing softball is just a good way to let your hair down and have fun.

10 a bad hair day HUMOROUS a day on which your hair will not do what you want it to do

11 make sb's hair stand on end to make someone very frightened: The thought of a lawsuit was enough to make his hair stand on end.

12 make your hair curl INFORMAL if a story, experience etc. makes your hair curl, it is very surprising, frightening, or shocking: The stories they tell about him would make your hair curl.

13 a/the hair of the dog (that bit you) HUMOROUS an alcoholic drink that is supposed to make you feel better after drinking too much alcohol the night before —see also -HAIRED, **a head of hair** (HEAD[1] (33)), **not hide nor hair of sb** (HIDE[2] (3)), **split hairs** (SPLIT[1] (8))

hair·ball /ˈhɛrbɔl/ n. [C] a ball of hair that forms in the stomach of animals such as cats that LICK their fur

hair·breadth /ˈhɛrbrɛtθ, -brɛdθ/ n. [singular] another spelling of HAIR'S BREADTH

hair·brush /ˈhɛrbrʌʃ/ n. [C] a brush you use on your hair to make it look neat —see picture at BRUSH[1]

hair-care /ˈ. ./ adj. relating to the things people do and use to keep their hair clean, healthy, and attractive: children's hair-care products —**hair care, hair-care** n. [U]

hair·cloth /ˈhɛrklɔθ/ n. [U] rough material made from animal hair, especially from horses or CAMELS

hair·cut /ˈhɛrkʌt/ n. [C] **1** the act of having your hair cut by someone: I'm going to **get a haircut** later on today. **2** the style your hair has when it is cut: Do you like my new haircut?

hair·do /ˈhɛrdu/ n. plural **hairdos** [C] INFORMAL a woman's HAIRSTYLE

hair·dress·er /ˈhɛrˌdrɛsə/ n. [C] a person who washes, cuts, and arranges people's hair in particular styles: I'm going to the hairdresser after work. —compare BARBER —**hairdressing** n. [U]

hair·dryer, hairdrier /ˈhɛrˌdraɪə/ n. [C] **1** a BLOW DRYER **2** a machine that you sit under that blows out hot air, used for drying hair

-haired /hɛrd/ [in adjectives] **red-haired/curly-haired/long-haired etc.** having a particular type or color of hair: Miss Dykstra was a tall, red-haired woman.

hair·less /ˈhɛrlɪs/ adj. with no hair: his hairless chin

hair·line[1] /ˈhɛrlaɪn/ n. [C] the area around the top of you face where your hair starts growing: Bruce is embarrassed about his **receding hairline** (=used to say that he is losing hair).

H

hairline² *adj.* **a hairline crack/fracture** a very thin crack in something hard: *She had a hairline fracture in her leg.*

hair·net /'hɛrnɛt/ *n.* [C] a very thin net that stretches over your hair to keep it in place

hair·piece /'hɛrpis/ *n.* [C] a piece of false hair used to cover a BALD place on your head, or to make your own hair look thicker

hair·pin /'hɛr,pɪn/ *n.* [C] a pin used to hold hair in a particular position, that is made of wire bent into a U-shape —see picture at PIN¹

hairpin turn, hairpin curve /,. './ *n.* [C] a very sharp U-shaped curve in a road, especially on a steep hill

hair·rais·ing /'. ,../ *adj.* frightening in a way that is exciting: *Riding to work with Harry is usually a hair-raising experience.*

hair re·stor·er /'. .,../ *n.* [C,U] a substance or liquid that is supposed to make hair grow again

hair's breadth /'. ./ *n.* [singular] a very small amount or distance: *I came within a hair's breadth of losing my life.*

hair shirt /,. './ *n.* [C] a shirt made of rough uncomfortable cloth that contains hair, worn in past times by some religious people as a punishment

hair·split·ting /'. ,../ *n.* [U] the act of paying too much attention to small differences and unimportant details: *It is this kind of hair-splitting that gives politics a bad name.* —see also **split hairs** (SPLIT¹ (8))

hair spray, hairspray /'. ./ *n.* [U] a sticky liquid that you SPRAY on your hair to make it stay in place

hair·style /'hɛrstaɪl/ *n.* [C] the style in which someone's hair has been cut or shaped

hair ton·ic /'. ,../ *n.* [C,U] a liquid that is supposed to make hair grow on an area of your head that is BALD (=hairless)

hair·trig·ger¹ /,. '..◄ / *n.* [C] a TRIGGER on a gun that needs very little pressure to fire the gun

hair·trigger² *adj.* **a hair-trigger temper** someone who has a hair-trigger temper gets very angry easily: *Dirk is the guy with the shaved head and the hair-trigger temper.*

hair weave /'. ./ *n.* [C] a piece of artificial hair that is attached to your own hair to make it look longer or thicker

hair·y /'hɛri/ *adj.* **hairier, hairiest 1** having a lot of body hair: *Someone who is as hairy as he is should keep his shirt on.* | *a big hairy spider* **2** INFORMAL dangerous or frightening, often in a way that is exciting: *It got pretty hairy climbing down the cliff.* —**hairiness** *n.* [U]

Hai·ti /'heɪți/ a country in the Caribbean Sea on the island of Hispaniola, which it shares with the Dominican Republic —**Haitian** /'heɪʃən/ *n., adj.*

hajj, haj /hɑdʒ/ *n.* [C] a trip to Mecca for religious reasons, that all Muslims try to make at least once in their life

haj·ji, hadji /'hɑdʒi/ *n.* [C] used as a title for a Muslim who has made a hajj

hake /heɪk/ *n.* [C,U] an ocean fish, used as food

ha·lal, hallal /hə'lɑl/ *adj.* [U] halal meat is meat from an animal that has been killed in a way that is approved by Muslim law

hal·berd /'hɑlbɚd/ *n.* [C] a weapon with a blade on a long handle, used in past times

hal·cy·on /'hælsiən/ *adj.* [only before noun] **halcyon days/years/season etc.** LITERARY the happiest and most peaceful time of someone's life, or a company's most successful time: *She often recalled the halcyon days of her youth.*

hale /heɪl/ *adj.* LITERARY someone, especially an old person, who is hale is very healthy and active: *Horszowski, still hale and hearty at 98, will give a piano recital on May 28.*

Hale /heɪl/**, Na·than** /'neɪθən/ (1755–1776) a U.S. soldier who was caught by the British and hanged for being a SPY during the Revolutionary War

half¹ /hæf/ *quantifier adj.* [only before noun] **1** ½ of an amount, time, distance, number etc.: *All I had was half a bagel and some yogurt.* | *Only half the guests had arrived by seven o'clock.* | *I only drank* **half a bottle** *of beer.* | *I'll wait for another* **half hour** (=thirty minutes), *but then I have to go.* **2** if something is half one thing and half something else, it is a combination of those two things: *Lacey's mother is half Chinese and half Portuguese* **3 half a dozen a)** six: *half a dozen eggs* **b)** several or many: *He had rewritten the story half a dozen times.* **4 be half the battle** SPOKEN used to say that when you have done the most difficult part of an activity, everything else is easier: *Getting Jeff to listen to me is half the battle.* **5 half the time/people etc.** most of the time, people etc.: *The dog is the only character in the film who's not drunk half the time.* **6 only half the story** an explanation that is not complete, used especially to say that someone is trying to keep something secret: *How could you side with them after hearing only half the story?* **7 have half a mind to do sth** SPOKEN used to say that you would like to do something but you probably will not do it, especially when you want to show that you disapprove of what someone has done: *I have half a mind to tell her what I really think of her.* **8 half-measures** also **half measures** actions or methods that are not effective in dealing with a difficult problem: *Half-measures will not fix America's health-care crisis.*

half² *n., pron. plural* **halves** /hævz/ [C] **1** 50% either of the two equal parts into which something is divided or can be divided; ½: *Half of 50*

---

hairstyles

flattop   crew cut   bob   dreadlocks

ponytail   braid   bun   braids/pigtails

is 25. | *I talked to Susan about a week and a half ago.* | *You'll only be tested on the second half of the material.* | *Put the rice mixture into the squash halves.* | **cut/reduce sth by half** (=make something 50% smaller)

2 `sports event` either of the two parts into which a sports event is divided: *Johnson scored 15 points in the second half.*

3 in half a) into two equal pieces: *Divide the dough in half.* **b)** if you fold, bend etc. something in half, you fold it so that two equal pieces are on top of each other, next to each other etc.: *Fold the omelet in half and serve on a warm plate.*

4 `number` the number 1/2: *Four halves make 2.*

5 go halves (on sth) to share something, especially the cost of something, equally between two people: *Do you want to go halves on a pizza?*

6 half past one/two/three etc. thirty minutes after the hour mentioned: *Oh, my goodness, it's nearly half past twelve!*

7 and a half SPOKEN used to emphasize that someone has a quality very strongly: *He's a flirt and a half, isn't he?*

8 not do sth by halves OLD-FASHIONED to do something very eagerly and using a lot of care and effort: *I'm sure it will be a fantastic wedding. Eva never does anything by halves.*

9 your better/other half HUMOROUS your husband or wife

10 you don't know the half of it SPOKEN used to emphasize that a situation is more difficult, more complicated, or worse than people realize: *"It sounds like you had a really bad time." "Oh, you don't know the half of it."*

11 how the other half lives how people who are much richer or much poorer than you manage their lives, work, money etc.: *High-ranking officials should take the bus so they can see how the other half lives.*

half³ *adv.* **1** partly, but not completely: *Her first album is now half finished and is due out later this year.* | **half-filled/half-empty** etc. *A half-filled wine-glass stood on the table.* **2** used to emphasize something, especially when a situation is extremely bad: *I had been driven half out of my mind with worry.* | *The kitten looked half starved.* **3 half as good/interesting etc. (as)** much less good, less interesting etc. than someone or something else: *The movie wasn't half as entertaining as the book.* | *Homemade bread costs half as much as commercially baked bread.* **4 not half bad** an expression meaning "good," used especially when you are surprised that something is good: *The pizza here isn't half bad.* **5 half and half** partly one thing and partly another: *It looked like the crowd was about half and half, men and women.*

half-and-half /ˌ. . '. / *n.* [U] a mixture that is half milk and half cream, used in coffee

half·a·sleep, half asleep /ˌ. . '. / *adj.* almost asleep, but still partly awake: *I was half-asleep when I heard a knock on the door.*

half-assed /ˌhæf 'æst / also **half-ass** *adj.* VULGAR done or made without enough attention or effort, or in a way that seems stupid: *They did a half-assed job of planning.*

half·back /'hæfbæk/ *n.* [C] **1** one of two players in football who, at the start of play, are behind the front line of players and next to the FULLBACK **2** a player who plays in the middle part of the field, in SOCCER, RUGBY etc.

half-baked /ˌ. '. / *adj.* a half-baked idea, suggestion, plan etc. has not been thought about and planned carefully: *What we've got here is a half-baked proposal that still needs a great deal of work.*

half-breed /'. . / *n.* [C] TABOO someone whose parents are of different races, especially one white parent and one Native American parent. Do not use this word —**half-breed** *adj.*

half broth·er /'. ,../ *n.* [C] a brother who is the son of only one of your parents

half-caste /'. . / *n.* [C] TABOO someone whose parents are of different races. Do not use this word —**half-caste** *adj.*

half-cocked /ˌ. '. / *adj.* **go off half-cocked** to do

something without enough thought or preparation, so that it is not successful: *You ought to talk to her before you go off half-cocked.*

half-crazed, half crazed /ˌ. '. / *adj.* behaving in a slightly crazy, uncontrolled way: *a half-crazed old man* | [+ **with**] *We were surrounded by adults half crazed with terror and hunger.*

half-cup /ˌ. '. / *n.* [C] a small container used to measure an amount of food or liquid when cooking, or the amount that this holds: *Add a half-cup of sugar.*

half-day /'. . / *n.* [C] a day when you work or go to school either in the morning or the afternoon, but not all day: *I'm working only half-days now.*

half dol·lar /ˌ. '. / *n.* [C] a coin worth 50 cents

half-gal·lon /ˌ. '. / *n.* [C] one half of a GALLON, equal to two QUARTS: *a half-gallon of milk*

half-heart·ed /ˌ. '. / *adj.* done without much effort and without much interest in the result: *She made a half-hearted attempt to be friendly to the new girl.* —**half-heartedly** *adv.* —**half-heartedness** *n.* [U]

half-hour, half hour /ˌ. '. / *n.* [C] a period of time that is thirty minutes long: *I got off work a half-hour ago.* —**half-hour** *adj.*: *Buses arrive here at half-hour intervals.*

half-inch /ˌ. '. / *n.* [C] one half of an inch: *She's grown a half-inch this month.*

half-length /'. . / *adj.* a half-length painting or picture shows the top half of someone's body

half-life /'. . / *n.* [C] the half-life of a RADIOACTIVE substance is the length of time it takes to lose half of its RADIOACTIVITY

half-light /'. . / *n.* [U] the dull gray light you see when it is almost dark, but not completely dark: *the misty half-light of dawn*

half-mast /ˌ. '. / *n.* **be/fly at half-mast** a flag that is at half-mast has been raised only to the middle of the pole in order to show respect and sadness for someone important who has died

half-mile /'. . / *n.* [C] **1** one half of a mile: *There's a gas station about a half-mile down the road.* **2** a race in which you run this length

half moon /ˌ. '. / *n.* [C] the shape of the moon when only half of it can be seen —compare FULL MOON, NEW MOON

half nel·son /ˌhæf 'nɛlsən/ *n.* [C] a way of holding your opponent's arm behind their back in the sport of WRESTLING

half note /'. . / *n.* [C] TECHNICAL a musical note that continues for half the length of a WHOLE NOTE —see picture at MUSIC

half-pound /ˌ. '. / *n.* [C] one half of a pound in weight: *a half-pound of hamburger*

half price /ˌ. '. / *adv.* SPOKEN at half the usual price: *I got the stereo system half price.* —**half-price** *adj.*: *half-price tickets*

half-sis·ter /'. ,../ *n.* [C] a sister who is the daughter of only one of your parents

half step /'. . / *n.* [C] TECHNICAL the difference in PITCH¹ (3) between any two notes that are next to each other on a piano

half-tim·bered /ˌ. '.. / *adj.* a half-timbered house is usually old and shows the wooden structure of the building on the outside walls

half·time, half-time /'hæftaɪm/ *n.* [U] a short period of rest between two parts of a game, such as football or basketball: *The score at halftime was 34-7.*

half-time /'. . / *adj., adv.* PART-TIME: *Louisville Housing Services employs only one half-time consultant.*

half-tone /'hæftoʊn/ *n.* **1** [U] a method of printing black and white photographs that shows different shades of gray by changing the number of black DOTS in an area of the photograph **2** [C] a photograph printed by this method

half-truth /'. . / *n.* [C] a statement that is only partly true, especially one that is intended to keep something secret: *The article is full of lies and half-truths.*

H

half·way /ˌhæfˈweɪ‹/ *adj., adv.* [no comparative] **1** at the middle point in space or time between two things: *It's halfway between Baton Rouge and New Orleans.* | *I filled my glass only halfway with orange juice.* | **[+ across/through/up etc.]** *His voice cracked halfway through his speech.* | *They drove halfway across the country to visit us.* | **the halfway point/mark** *Fittspaldi was leading up until the halfway point of the race.* **2 be halfway there** to be half the way to achieving something: *Construction on the civic center is halfway there.* **3 halfway decent** fairly good: *This is really halfway decent coffee.* **4 be/ go halfway toward doing sth** to achieve something partly but not completely: *The Foundation is halfway toward its goal of raising $10,000.* —see also **meet sb halfway** (MEET¹ (14))

halfway house /ˌ.. ˌ./ *n.* [C] a place for people who have had mental illnesses or drug problems or who have been in prison, where they can live until they are ready to live on their own

half-wit, halfwit /ˈ. ./ *n.* [C] a stupid person or someone who has done something stupid —**half-witted** *adj.* —**half-wittedly** *adv.*

hal·i·but /ˈhæləbət/ *n.* [C] a large flat ocean fish used as food

Hal·i·fax /ˈhæləˌfæks/ the capital and largest city of the Canadian PROVINCE of Nova Scotia

hal·i·to·sis /ˌhæləˈtoʊsɪs/ *n.* [U] TECHNICAL a condition in which someone's breath smells very bad

^{s w} **hall** /hɔl/ *n.* [C] **1** a passage in a building or house
^{2 2} that leads to many of the rooms: *We heard the principal coming down the hall.* **2** a building or large room for public events such as meetings or dances —see also CITY HALL, DANCE HALL, TOWN HALL **3** used in the names of dormitories (DORMITORY (1)): *As a freshman, you can either live in West Bennet or Drummond Hall.* **4** a HALLWAY

hal·le·lu·jah /ˌhæləˈluyə/ *interjection* said in order to express thanks, JOY, or praise to God —**hallelujah** *n.* [C]

Hal·ley, Ed·mond /ˈheɪli, ˈɛdmənd/ (1656–1742) a British ASTRONOMER who was the first to calculate the time that a COMET would return and be seen again from Earth

H

hall·mark¹ /ˈhɔlmɑrk/ *n.* [C] **1** an idea, method, or quality that is typical of a particular person or thing: **[+ of]** *Clog dancing is a hallmark of Appalachian culture.* | **has/bears all the hallmarks of sth** *Oates's new novel has all the hallmarks of her earlier work.* **2** a mark put on silver, gold, or PLATINUM that shows the quality of the metal, and where and when it was made

hallmark² *v.* [T] to put a hallmark on silver, gold, or PLATINUM

Hall of Fame /ˌ. . ˈ./ *n.* [C] a list of famous sports players, or the building where their uniforms, sports equipment, and information about them are shown

hal·lowed /ˈhæloʊd/ *adj.* **1** holy or made holy: *For Muslims, Mecca is **hallowed ground** (=land that is holy).* **2** important and respected: *His first album was released on the hallowed Blue Note jazz label.*

Hal·low·een, Hallowe'en /ˌhæləˈwin, ˌhɑ-/ *n.* [U] a holiday on the night of October 31, when children wear COSTUMEs, play tricks, and walk from house to house asking for candy —see also TRICK OR TREAT

hal·lu·ci·nate /həˈlusəˌneɪt/ *v.* [I] to see, feel, or hear things that are not really there

hal·lu·ci·na·tion /həˌlusəˈneɪʃən/ *n.* [C,U] something you see, feel, or hear that is not really there, or the experience of this, usually caused by a drug or mental illness: *Doctors believe the medication was the cause of her hallucinations.*

hal·lu·ci·na·to·ry /həˈlusənəˌtɔri/ *adj.* FORMAL **1** causing hallucinations or resulting from hallucinations: *hallucinatory drugs* **2** using strange images, sounds etc. like those experienced in a hallucination: *It is, after all, a fairy tale, as the movie's hallucinatory ending proves.*

hal·lu·cin·o·gen /həˈlusənədʒɪn/ *n.* [C] something that causes hallucinations: *LSD is a dangerous hallucinogen.*

hal·lu·ci·no·gen·ic /həˌlusənəˈdʒɛnɪk/ *adj.* causing hallucinations: *hallucinogenic mushrooms*

hall·way /ˈhɔlweɪ/ *n. plural* **hallways** [C] **1** the area ^{s w} just inside the door of a house or other building that ³ leads to other rooms **2** a passage in a building or house that leads to many of the rooms; CORRIDOR (1)

ha·lo /ˈheɪloʊ/ *n. plural* **halos** [C] **1** a bright circle that is often shown above or around the heads of holy people in religious art **2** a bright circle of light around a person or thing, or something that looks similar: *A halo of wispy blonde curls capped her pretty face.*

hal·o·gen¹ /ˈhælədʒɪn/ *n.* [U] one of a group of five simple chemical substances that make compounds easily

halogen² *adj.* **a halogen lamp/light/bulb etc.** a type of lamp or LIGHT BULB that uses halogen gas to produce light

halt¹ /hɔlt/ *n.* [singular] a stop or pause | **come/grind to a halt** *The train came to a halt, and Mr. Thomas stepped out.* | *About 10,000 people **calling for a halt to** military aid marched in front of the White House today.*

halt² *v.* **1** [I,T] to stop or make something stop: *Heavy rain halted five railroad lines in the Tokyo area.* | *The taxi halted at the hotel's front door.* **2 halt!** used as a military command to order someone to stop moving or soldiers to stop marching: *Company halt!* | *Halt! Who goes there?*

hal·ter /ˈhɔltɚ/ *n.* [C] **1** also **halter top** a type of clothing for women that covers the chest and ties behind the neck and waist, so that the arms and back are not covered **2** a rope or leather band that fastens around a horse's head, usually used to lead the horse

halt·ing /ˈhɔltɪŋ/ *adj.* if your speech or movements are halting, you stop for a moment between words or movements, especially because you are not confident: *In halting English, he gave us directions to the museum.* —**haltingly** *adv.*

halve /hæv/ *v.* [T] **1** to cut or divide something into two equal pieces: *Halve the eggplant lengthwise and hollow out the center.* **2** to reduce something by a half: *His 13-year prison term was halved because of good behavior.*

halves /hævz/ *n.* the plural of HALF —see also **go halves (on sth)** (HALF² (5)), **not do sth by halves** (HALF² (8))

hal·yard /ˈhælyɚd/ *n.* [C] TECHNICAL a rope used to raise or lower a flag or sail

ham¹ /hæm/ *n.* **1** [C,U] the upper part of a pig's leg, ^{s w} or the meat from this that is preserved with salt or ³ smoke: *a ham sandwich* | *a ham for Easter dinner* **2** [C] INFORMAL an actor who performs with too much false emotion **3** [C] someone who receives and sends radio messages for fun rather than as their job

ham² *v.* **ham it up** INFORMAL to perform or behave with too much false emotion, especially in order to be funny: *Every year Dad puts on his Santa suit and hams it up for the kids.*

ham·burg·er /ˈhæmˌbɚgɚ/ *n.* **1** [C] a type of SAND- ^{s w} WICH made from BEEF that has been formed into a flat ³ circular shape and cooked, which is eaten between pieces of round bread **2** [U] BEEF that has been ground (GRIND (1)) into very small pieces: *Could you pick up a pound of hamburger on your way home?*

ham-fist·ed also **ham-hand·ed** /ˈ. ˌ../ *adj.* INFORMAL **1** not skillful or careful at all in the way that you do something: *Many fans are upset with the ham-handed way that Simmons was let go.* **2** not skillful at all with your hands; CLUMSY —**ham-fistedly** also **ham-handedly** *adv.*

Ham·ill, Do·ro·thy /ˈhæməl, ˈdɔrəθi, ˈdɑrθi/ (1956–) a U.S. FIGURE SKATEr who won a GOLD MEDAL at the 1976 Winter Olympics

Ham·il·ton /ˈhæməltən/ the capital city of Bermuda

Hamilton, Alexander (1755–1804) a U.S. politician

who helped to write the U.S. Constitution and became the first U.S. Secretary of the Treasury

ham·let /ˈhæmlɪt/ *n.* [C] a very small town

Ham·mar·skjöld /ˈhæmə.ʃəld/, **Dag** /dɑg/ (1905–1961) the Secretary General of the United Nations from 1953 until his death in 1961

ham·mer¹ /ˈhæmə/ *n.* [C]

1 tool **a)** a tool with a heavy metal part on a long handle, used for hitting nails into wood **b)** a tool like this with a wooden head, used to make something flat, make a noise etc.: *an auctioneer's hammer* —see picture at TOOL¹

2 come/go under the hammer to be offered for sale at an AUCTION: *Three Renoir paintings will come under the hammer at Sotheby's in New York.*

3 gun the part of a gun that hits the explosive CHARGE¹ (11) that fires a bullet

4 sport a heavy metal ball on a wire with a handle that is thrown as far as possible, as a sport

5 be/go at it hammer and tongs INFORMAL to fight or argue very loudly

6 piano a wooden part of a piano that hits the strings inside to make a musical sound

ham·mer² *v.*

1 hit with hammer [I,T] to hit something with a hammer in order to force it into a particular position or shape: *After a weekend of sawing and hammering nails into 2-by-4s, the dog house was finished.*

2 hit repeatedly [I] to hit something many times, especially making a loud noise: [+ against/on] *The rain was hammering against the window.*

3 hurt with problems [T] to hurt someone or something by causing them a lot of problems: *Investors have been hammered by a series of dismal economic reports.*

4 say sth repeatedly [I,T] to do or say something continuously until you are sure that people understand or accept what you mean: [+ away] *Brennan hammered away at the fact that the administration was to blame.* | *Senator O'Neil wanted to hammer home the point that he is opposed to the trade initiative.*

5 criticize [T] to strongly criticize or attack someone for something they have said or done: *The President has been hammered for his lack of leadership.*

6 defeat [T] INFORMAL to defeat someone completely in a war or at a sport: *Chicago hammered San Diego 13–2.*

7 heart [I] if your heart hammers, you feel it beating strongly and quickly: *She stood outside the door, her heart hammering.*

hammer sth **in/into** sb *phr. v.* [T] to repeat something continuously until people completely understand it: *The coach hammered the concept of teamwork into the squad.*

hammer sth ↔ **out** *phr. v.* [T] to decide on an agreement, contract etc. after a lot of discussion and disagreement: *Company officials spent Thursday hammering out the details.*

hammer and sick·le /ˌ.. . ˈ../ *n.* [singular] **1** the sign of a hammer crossing a SICKLE on a red background, used as a sign of COMMUNISM **2** the flag of the former Soviet Union

ham·mered /ˈhæməd/ *adj.* [only before noun] **1** hammered silver, gold etc. has a pattern of small hollow areas on its surface **2** SPOKEN very drunk

ham·mer·ing /ˈhæmərɪŋ/ *n.* **1 take a hammering** to be attacked very severely: *Dresden took a real hammering during the war.* **2** [U] the action or sound of someone hitting something with a hammer or with their FISTS (=closed hands): *I heard hammering outside the building.*

Ham·mer·stein /ˈhæməstaɪn/, **Os·car** /ˈɑskə/ (1895–1960) a U.S. writer who worked with the musician Richard Rodgers to produce many famous MUSICALS

ham·mock /ˈhæmək/ *n.* [C] a large piece of material or a net that you can sleep on, that hangs between two trees or poles —see pictures at GET and on page 423

ham·per¹ /ˈhæmpə/ *v.* [T] to restrict someone's movements, activities, or achievements by causing

difficulties for them: *Cousteau's expedition was hampered by bad weather.*

hamper² *n.* [C] **1** a large basket that you put dirty clothes in until they can be washed **2** a basket with a lid, often used for carrying food

ham·ster /ˈhæmstə/ *n.* [C] a small animal like a mouse, often kept as a pet

ham·string¹ /ˈhæm.strɪŋ/ *n.* [C] a TENDON behind your knee

hamstring² *v. past tense and past participle* **ham·strung** /-.strʌŋ/ [T] to cause a person or group to have difficulty doing or achieving something: *Excessive regulations tend to hamstring honest businesses.*

Han·cock /ˈhænkɑk/, **John** (1737–1793) a U.S. politician who was the president of the Continental Congress, and was the first person to write his name on the Declaration of Independence —see also JOHN HANCOCK

hand¹ /hænd/ *n.*

1 body part [C] the part at the end of a person's arm, including the fingers and thumb, used to pick up or keep hold of things: *Go wash your hands.* | *I saw them holding hands and kissing.* | *The old lady led me by the hand to the kitchen.* —see picture at BODY

2 a hand help with something you are doing, especially something that involves physical work: **give/lend sb a hand** *Can you give your brother a hand up in the attic?* | *She's always the first to volunteer to help when I need a hand.* —see Usage Note at HELP¹

3 (on the one hand...) on the other hand used when comparing two different or opposite facts or ideas: *Gary, on the other hand, used to be very thin.* | *On the one hand, they work slowly, but on the other hand they always finish the job.*

4 on hand close by and ready when needed: *Organizers of the fair have a nurse on hand in case of any injuries.*

5 get out of hand to become impossible to control: *Pull or spray garden weeds before they get out of hand.* | *It was a practical joke that got a little out of hand.*

6 in the hands of sb also **in sb's hands** being dealt with or controlled by someone: *The decision is in your hands.* | *The area is already in the hands of the rebels.*

7 be good with your hands to be skillful at making things

8 hand in hand holding each other's hand, especially to show love: *They strolled hand in hand through the flower garden.*

9 have a hand in sth to influence or be involved in something: *Thorpe has had a hand in restoring the 21 houses.*

10 in hand being dealt with and controlled: *Officer Rogers said he has the situation in hand.*

11 in good/safe/capable etc. hands being dealt with or taken care of by someone who can be trusted: *Every parent wants to make sure they're leaving their child in safe hands.*

12 by hand a) done or made by a person, not a machine: *The rug was made by hand.* **b)** delivered from one person to another, not sent through the mail: *They delivered their invitations by hand.*

13 off your hands if something or someone is off your hands, you are not responsible for them anymore: *Hiring a new foreman would take a lot of responsibility off my hands.*

14 have sb/sth on your hands to have a difficult job, problem, or responsibility that you must deal with: *I think you have enough trouble on your hands already.*

15 at hand FORMAL **a)** near in time or space: *Graduation day is close at hand.* | *Repent, the kingdom of God is at hand!* **b)** needing to be dealt with now: *Some of his comments had nothing to do with the topic at hand.*

16 worker [C] someone who does physical work on a farm, in a factory etc.: *a hired hand*

H

17 hands down easily: *Harry would have won hands down, if he hadn't hurt his ankle.*
18 (at) first hand by direct personal experience: *The school deals first hand with all the problems of today's society.*
19 do sth with one hand (tied) behind your back SPOKEN used to say that you can do something easily and well: *I could beat them with one hand tied behind my back.*
20 get your hands on sth to obtain something: *The best seats in the house are $150, if you can get your hands on a ticket.*
21 get your hands on sb to catch someone you are angry with: *I'd love to get my hands on the guy who slashed my tires.*
22 get/lay your hands on sth to find or obtain something: *I've read everything on the subject that I could lay my hands on.*
23 have time on your hands to have a lot of time because you have no work to do: *Since he's retired, he has plenty of time on his hands to see his grandkids.*
24 have your hands full to be very busy or too busy: *Diane has her hands full with housekeeping chores and a new baby.*
25 sb's hands are tied if someone's hands are tied, they cannot do what they want because of particular conditions, rules etc.: *We'd really like to help you, but I'm afraid our hands are tied.*
26 go hand in hand to be closely related, or happen together: *Gangs pretty much go hand in hand with drug problems.*
27 make/spend/lose money hand over fist INFORMAL to gain, spend, or lose money very quickly and in large amounts: *For years they were making money hand over fist.*
28 card game [C] **a)** a set of playing cards held by one person in a game: *a winning hand* **b)** a game of cards: *We played a couple of hands of poker.*
29 on a clock [C] one of the long thin pieces of metal that point at the numbers on a clock: *the hour hand*
30 give sb a (big) hand to CLAP[1] (1) loudly in order to show your approval of a performer or speaker
31 at the hands of sb if you suffer at the hands of someone, they treat you badly: *He told of the abuse he had suffered at the hands of prison guards.*
32 refuse/reject/dismiss etc. sth out of hand if you refuse, reject etc. something out of hand, you refuse, reject it immediately and completely: *My request for more vacation time was rejected out of hand.*
33 a firm hand strict control of someone: *Active kids need a firm hand (=they need to be controlled).*
34 sb's hand (in marriage) OLD-FASHIONED permission or agreement for a man to marry a particular woman: *He finally asked for her hand in marriage.*
35 turn your hand to sth to start doing something new or practicing a new skill: *After 25 years in broadcasting, Cynthia decided to turn her hand to writing novels.*
36 horse [C] a unit for measuring the height of a horse, equal to four inches
37 tie/bind sb hand and foot a) to tie someone's hands and feet **b)** to severely restrict someone's freedom to make decisions: *We're bound hand and foot by all these safety regulations.*
38 writing [singular] the way you write; HAND-WRITING: *The letter was written in a neat hand.*
39 keep your hand in (sth) to keep doing something so you do not lose your skill: *Schmidt will keep his hand in as batting instructor for Detroit.*
40 hand in glove LITERARY closely related to someone or something: *Temperamentally and ideologically, the two men fit hand in glove.* —see also **bite the hand that feeds you** (BITE[1] (6)), **force sb's hand** (FORCE[2] (6)), **FREEHAND, HANDS-ON, HANDS UP, LEFT-HAND, LEFT-HANDED, LEFT-HANDER, be an old hand (at sth)** (OLD (21)), **overplay your hand** (OVERPLAY (2)), RIGHT-HAND, RIGHT-HANDED, RIGHT-HANDER, **shake hands (with sb)** (SHAKE[1] (4)), **wash your hands of sth** (WASH[1] (5)), **win hands down** (WIN[1] (1))

hand[2] *v.* [T] **1** to pass something to someone else: [hand sb sth] *Hand me the newspaper, will you?* | [hand sth to sb] *I handed the package to the security guard.* **2 you have to hand it to sb** SPOKEN used to say that you admire someone: *You have to hand it to her. She's really made a success of that company.*

hand sth ↔ **back** *phr. v.* [T] **1** to pass something back to someone: *The guard looked at my papers and slowly handed them back to me.* **2** to give something back to someone it used to belong to: *Hong Kong was handed back to China in 1997.*

hand sth ↔ **down** *phr. v.* [T] **1 hand down a decision/ruling/sentence** etc. to officially announce a decision, a punishment etc.: *The sentence was handed down on Monday.* **2** to give or leave something to people who are younger than you or live after you: *The recipe was handed down to me by my grandmother.* —see also HAND-ME-DOWN **3** to pass something to someone who is below you: *Can you hand that box down to me?*

hand sth ↔ **in** *phr. v.* [T] to give something to a person in authority: *He handed in his essay three days late.*

hand sth ↔ **out** *phr. v.* [T] to give something to each member of a group of people; DISTRIBUTE: *A guy in a Santa Claus suit was handing out candy.* —see also HANDOUT

hand over *phr. v.* **1** [T **hand** sb/sth ↔ **over**] to give someone or something to someone else to take care of or to control: *After the teller handed over the money, the robber ran out of the bank.* **2** [I,T **hand** sth ↔ **over**] to give power or responsibility to someone else: *The captain was unwilling to hand over the command of his ship.*

hand·bag /ˈhændbæg/ *n.* [C] a PURSE[1] (1)

hand·ball /ˈhændbɔl/ *n.* **1** [U] a game in which you hit a ball against a wall with your hand **2** [C] the ball used in this game

hand·bas·ket /ˈhændˌbæskɪt/ *n.* [C] OLD-FASHIONED a small basket with a handle —see **go to hell in a handbasket** (HELL (21))

hand·bill /ˈhændˌbɪl/ *n.* [C] a small printed notice or advertisement that is usually given by one person to other people

hand·book /ˈhændbʊk/ *n.* [C] a short book giving information or instructions: *Healthcare coverage is explained in detail in the employee handbook.*

hand·brake /ˈhændbreɪk/ *n.* [C] EMERGENCY BRAKE

hand·car /ˈhændkɑr/ *n.* [C] a small railroad vehicle operated by pushing large handles up and down to make it move forward and back

hand·cart /ˈhændkɑrt/ *n.* [C] a small vehicle used for carrying goods, that is pushed or pulled by hand

hand·craft·ed /ˈhændˌkræftɪd/ *adj.* skillfully made by hand, not by machine: *handcrafted jewelry*

hand·cuff /ˈhændkʌf/ *v.* [T] to put handcuffs on someone: *The unidentified man was handcuffed and led away.*

hand·cuffs /ˈhændkʌfs/ *n.* [plural] a pair of metal rings joined by a chain or bar, used for holding a prisoner's wrists together

Han·del /ˈhændl/, **George Fred·e·rick** /ˈdʒɔrdʒ ˈfrɛdərɪk/ (1685–1759) a British musician, originally from Germany, who wrote CLASSICAL music

hand-eye co·or·di·na·tion /ˌ. . . . . ˈ. ./ *n.* [U] the way in which your hands and eyes work together to make you able to do things well, for example to make you able to catch, hit, kick etc. a ball or to write or draw

hand·ful /ˈhændfʊl/ *n.* **1** [C] an amount that you can hold in your hand: [+ of] *I scooped up a handful of dinner mints as we left the restaurant.* **2** a very small number of people or things: *They played a handful of tunes from their new album.* **3 a handful** INFORMAL someone, especially a child, who is difficult to control: *3-year-old Matilda is a handful.*

hand gre·nade /ˈ. .ˌ./ *n.* [C] a small bomb that is thrown by a person rather than shot from a machine

hand·gun /ˈhændgʌn/ *n.* [C] a small gun that you hold in one hand when you shoot

hand-held /ˌ. ˈ.◂/ *adj.* a hand-held machine or piece

of electronic equipment is small enough to hold in your hand when you use it: *a hand-held video game*

hand·hold /'hændhoʊld/ *n.* [C] a place where you can safely put your hand when climbing a rock or mountain —see also FOOTHOLD, TOEHOLD

hand·i·cap¹ /'hændi,kæp/ *n.* [C] **1** an inability to use part of your body or mind because it has been damaged: *Miss Geller's handicap is barely noticeable after three years of physical therapy.* **2** a condition or situation that makes it difficult for someone to do something: *His lack of experience on Wall Street may prove to be a handicap.* **3** in GOLF, an advantage given to someone who is not very good, in order to make the competition fair: *Dick is trying to get his handicap down to a 12.* **4** a handicap horse race is one in which some of the horses carry more weight in order to make the competition fair: *the California Jockey Club Handicap*

hand·i·cap² *v.* [T] **1** to make it difficult for someone to do something: [be handicapped by] *His business plans were handicapped by lack of money.* **2** to try to guess what the results of a competition such as a horse race will be: *He used a computer to handicap horse races.*

hand·i·capped /'hændi,kæpt/ *adj.* **1** not able to use part of your body or mind fully because it has been damaged: *The center provides arts programs for mentally and physically handicapped children.* **2 the handicapped** people who are physically or mentally handicapped: *Current law requires businesses to make their buildings accessible to the handicapped.* —compare DISABLED

USAGE NOTE: HANDICAPPED

POLITENESS

Using the word **handicapped** to talk about someone who cannot use part of their body or mind normally may be considered offensive by some people. The word **disabled** is commonly used, but some people consider it more polite to say **challenged** or **impaired**: *physically challenged | visually impaired.*

---

hand·i·cap·per /'hændi,kæpə/ *n.* [C] someone who tries to guess what the results of a competition such as a horse race will be, especially as a job

hand·i·craft /'hændi,kræft/ also **craft** *n.* [C usually plural] a skill needing careful use of your hands, such as SEWING, making baskets etc.

hand·i·ly /'hændəli/ *adv.* if you handily win something or defeat someone, you do it easily: *Feinstein handily defeated Davis in the election.*

hand·i·work /'hændi,wɜk/ *n.* [U] **1** something that someone does or makes: *I could see that her haircolor was the handiwork of an expert.* **2** work that needs skill in using your hands: *Examples of her handiwork were propped around the studio.*

hand job /'. ./ *n.* [C] VULGAR the act of touching or rubbing a man's PENIS to give him sexual pleasure

hand·ker·chief /'hæŋkətʃɪf, -,tʃif/ *n.* [C] a piece of cloth used for drying your nose or eyes

han·dle¹ /'hændl/ *v.*

1 deal with sth [T] to deal with a situation or problem: *She doesn't want anyone to think she can't handle the pressure. | You were very discreet about the whole thing – I appreciate the way you handled it.*

2 deal with sb [T] to deal with people or behave toward them in a particular way: *You'll receive specific training on how to handle angry customers. | I can only handle Bob for about fifteen minutes. | He can handle himself quite well in a crisis.*

3 hold [T] to pick up, touch, or feel something with your hands: *You should wash your hands after handling raw meat.*

4 control with your hands [I,T] to control the movement of a vehicle, tool etc.: *Carver handles the basketball with confidence and skill. | The car was easy to park, had good brakes, and handled well around curves and corners.*

5 in charge of [T] to organize or be in charge of something: *HPC Architects handled the architectural work. | Jones has handled a wide variety of criminal cases.*

6 machines/systems [T] to have the power, equipment, or systems that are necessary to deal with a particular amount of work, number of people etc.: *At one time, AT&T handled over 70% of the nation's long-distance calls.*

7 buy/sell [T] to buy, sell, or deal with goods or services in business or trade: *Bennet was charged with handling stolen goods.*

handle² *n.* [C] **1** the part of a door, drawer, window etc. that you use for opening it **2** the part of an object that you use for holding it: *a knife with an ivory handle* —see picture at TOOL¹ —see picture at BAG¹ **3 get a handle on sth** to start to understand a person, situation etc.: *At least they have a handle on what caused the power failure.* **4** INFORMAL a name used by someone, especially by a user of a CB radio —see also **fly off the handle** (FLY¹ (14))

handlebar mus·tache /,... '../ *n.* [C] a long thick MUSTACHE that curves up at both ends

han·dle·bars /'hændl,barz/ *n.* [plural] also **handle·bar** [singular] the bar above the front wheel of a bicycle or MOTORCYCLE that you hold and use to control the direction it goes in —see picture at BICYCLE¹

han·dler /'hændlə/ *n.* [C] **1** someone whose job is to deal with a particular type of object, especially to move it or lift it: *baggage handlers for the airline* **2** someone whose job is to protect, advise, and represent a famous person or politician: *He had been carefully coached by White House handlers before the press conference.* **3** someone who trains an animal, especially a dog

hand·let·tered /,. '..◂/ *adj.* written by hand in large letters or with carefully made letters: *a hand-lettered invitation*

han·dling /'hændlɪŋ/ *n.* [U] **1** the way in which a problem or person is treated or dealt with: *Police have been criticized for their handling of the Stuart murder case.* **2** the act of picking something up, or touching or feeling it with your hands: *Most of these chemicals require special handling.*

handling charge /'.. ,./ *n.* [C] the amount charged for dealing with goods or moving them from one place to another: *The handling charge for phone or mail orders is $2.50.*

hand·loom /'hændlum/ *n.* [C] a small machine for weaving by hand

hand lug·gage /'. ,../ *n.* [U] the small bags that you carry with you when you travel, especially on an airplane

hand·made /,hænd'meɪd◂/ *adj.* made by hand, not by machine: *The table is handmade.*

hand·maid·en /'hænd,meɪdn/ also **hand·maid** /'hænd,meɪd/ *n.* [C] **1** OLD USE a female servant **2** FORMAL an idea, principle etc. that has an important part in supporting or helping another idea etc.: *St. Thomas Aquinas believed that reason should serve as the handmaiden of faith.*

hand-me-down /'. ., ,./ *n.* [C usually plural] a piece of clothing that has been used by someone and then given to another person in the family: *I always had to wear my sister's hand-me-downs.*

hand·out /'hændaʊt/ *n.* [C] **1** money or goods that are given to someone, for example because they are poor: *My parents were too proud to take handouts from the government.* **2** a piece of paper with information on it that is given to people who are attending a class, meeting etc.: *There's a four-page handout that you can pick up as you leave.*

hand·o·ver /'hænd,oʊvə/ *n.* [C] the act of making someone else responsible for something: *Arrangements for the handover of prisoners have been made.* —see also **hand over** (HAND²)

hand·picked /,hænd'pɪkt◂/ *adj.* someone who is handpicked has been carefully chosen for a special purpose: *Dawson was Mayor Kelly's handpicked successor.* —**handpick** *v.* [T]

hand·rail /'hændreɪl/ *n.* [C] a long bar fastened to a

wall for people to hold while they walk, for example up the stairs

hand·saw /'hændsɔ/ n. [C] a small tool for cutting wood etc. that has a flat blade and sharp V-shaped parts on the edge of the blade

hand·set /'hændsɛt/ n. [C] the part of a telephone that you hold with your hand to your ear and mouth

hands·free /ˌhændz'fri◂/ adj. [only before noun] a handsfree machine is one that you operate without using your hands: *a handsfree tape recorder*

hand·shake /'hændʃeɪk/ n. [C] **a)** the act of taking someone's right hand and shaking it, which people do when they meet or leave each other or when they have made an agreement **b)** the way that someone does this: *Nancy has a nice firm handshake.* —see also GOLDEN HANDSHAKE

hands off¹ /ˌ. './ interjection used to warn someone not to touch something: *Hands off, that's my candy bar!*

hands off² /'. ./ adj. [only before noun] letting other people do what they want and make decisions, without telling them what to do: *Most employees prefer Kohler's hands-off style of management.*

hand·some /'hænsəm/ adj. **1 a)** a man who is handsome is attractive; GOOD-LOOKING: *Roy is still as handsome as ever.* **b)** a woman who is handsome is attractive in a strong healthy way: *a handsome gray-haired woman* —see Usage Note at BEAUTIFUL **2** an object, building etc. that is handsome is attractive and well made: *a handsome colonial house* **3 a handsome profit/salary/sum etc.** a large amount of money: *She inherited a handsome fortune.* **4 a handsome gift/offer etc.** a generous or valuable gift etc. —**handsomely** adv.

hands-on /'. ./ adj. [only before noun] providing practical experience of something by letting people do it themselves: *The program gives students hands-on experience in a hospital.*

hand·spring /'hænd,sprɪŋ/ n. [C] a movement in which you turn yourself over completely, so that your feet go up in the air as your hands touch the ground, and then your feet come back on the ground and your head is upright again

hand·stand /'hændstænd/ n. [C] a movement in which you put your hands on the ground and your legs into the air: *I used to be able to **do a handstand**.*

hands up /ˌ. './ interjection used when threatening someone with a gun

hand-to-hand, hand to hand /ˌ. . '.◂/ adj., adv. **hand-to-hand fighting/combat** a way of fighting in a war using hands, knives etc. rather than guns: *All of the troops were trained in hand-to-hand combat.*

hand to mouth /ˌ. . '.◂/ adv. with just barely enough money and food to live and nothing for the future: *For years, the Taylor family **lived hand to mouth**.* —**hand-to-mouth** adj.: *a hand-to-mouth existence*

hand tool /'. ./ n. [C] a tool that you can use with your hands, especially a tool that is not electric

hand tow·el /'. ˌ../ n. [C] a small TOWEL for drying your hands

hand-wring·ing /'. ˌ../ n. [U] the state or activity of worrying and feeling nervous: *The was a lot of hand-wringing among Democrats before the election.*

hand·writ·ing /'hænd,raɪtɪŋ/ n. [U] **1** the style of someone's writing: *I recognized her handwriting on the envelope.* **2 the handwriting is on the wall** also **see/read the handwriting on the wall** used to say that it seems very likely that something will not exist much longer or that someone will fail: *The leaders should have seen the handwriting on the wall and taken action sooner.*

hand·writ·ten /ˌhænd'rɪt˥n◂/ adj. written with a pen or pencil, not printed: *a handwritten letter*

hand·y /'hændi/ adj. **handier, handiest 1** useful and simple to use: *There's a handy cup holder under the car radio.* **2** INFORMAL near and easy to reach: *Add a rail to keep kitchen equipment handy.* **3 come in**

handy to be useful: *I'm saving the memo – it might come in handy someday.* **4** good at using something, especially a tool: [+ **with**] *He's handy with a screwdriver.*

handy-dan·dy /ˌ.. '..◂/ adj. [only before noun] SPOKEN, HUMOROUS very simple and easy to use: *Next, you take your handy-dandy screwdriver and tighten this screw here.*

hand·y·man /'hændiˌmæn/ n. [C] someone who is good at doing repairs and practical jobs in the house

hang¹ /hæŋ/ v. past tense and past participle **hung** **1** hang from above [I,T] to put something somewhere so that its top part is firmly fastened but its bottom part is free to move, or to be in this position: *Hang your coat on the hook.* | *His hair hung down in front of his eyes.* | [+ **from**] *A single bulb hung from the ceiling.*

2 picture/photograph **a)** [I always + adv./prep., T] to fasten a picture, photograph etc. to a wall, or to be fastened this way: [+ **on/over**] *A portrait of his mother hung on the wall over the fireplace.* **b)** [I always + adv./prep., T] to show a picture publicly, or to be shown publicly: *A small study for the painting hangs in the J. Paul Getty Museum.* **c) be hung with sth** if the walls of a room are hung with pictures or decorations, the pictures, decorations etc. are on the walls: *The theater was hung with the flags of the United States and France.*

3 hang in the balance to be in a situation in which the result is not certain, and something bad may happen: *World leaders are meeting to discuss the situation, with peace in the region hanging in the balance.*

SPOKEN PHRASES

4 hang in there also **hang tough** to remain determined to succeed, even in a difficult situation: *If it's worth doing, it's worth hanging in there.*

5 spend time [I] SLANG to spend a lot of time in a particular place or with particular people: *Most of the time we hang at my house.* | [+ **with**] *We saw Pamela hanging with Connie.* —see also **hang out** (HANG¹)

6 how's it hanging? VULGAR, HUMOROUS used as a greeting for a man you know very well

7 hang a right/left used to tell the driver of a car to turn right or left: *Go straight on Vista for two blocks then hang a left.*

8 hang loose used to tell someone to stay calm and relaxed: *I told everybody to just hang loose.*

---

9 paper [T] to put WALLPAPER on a wall

10 mist/smoke/smell [T] to stay in the air in the same place for a long time: *A cloud of smoky fog hung over the town.*

11 hang by a thread to be in a very dangerous situation: *For weeks after the accident, her life hung by a thread.*

12 hang your head to look ashamed and embarrassed: *Kevin hung his head and left the room in silence.*

13 door/window [T] to put a door or window in position —see also **leave sb/sth hanging** (LEAVE¹ (37))

hang around phr. v. INFORMAL **1** [I,T **hang around sb**] to wait or stay somewhere with no real purpose: *I really enjoy hanging around Stacy.* | *What are you going to do – just hang around until six thirty?* **2 hang around with sb** to spend a lot of time with someone: *He's been hanging around with Randy a lot lately.*

hang back phr. v. [I] to be unwilling to speak or do something, often because you are shy: *The villagers hung back at a safe distance.*

hang on phr. v. **1** [I] to hold something tightly [+ **to**] *Hang on to the rail or you'll fall.* **2 hang on** SPOKEN used to ask or tell someone to wait: **hang on a minute/second** *Hang on a second, let me ask the nurse what's happening.* **3 hang on sb's every word** to pay close attention to everything someone is saying: *The students hung on his every word.* **4** [I] to continue doing something in spite of difficulties: *She hung on for five weeks before her kidneys failed.* **5** [T **hang on sth**] to depend on something: *His fate hangs on the legal negotiations.*

hang on to sb/sth *phr. v.* [T] to keep something, or continue a relationship with someone: *Go ahead and hang on to the book until you're finished.* | *If that's the kind of person he is, he's not worth hanging on to.*

hang out *phr. v.* **1** [I always + adv./prep.] INFORMAL to spend a lot of time in a particular place or with particular people: *I just want to hang out, eat pizza, and watch TV.* | [+ **with**] *Who does she usually hang out with?* —see also HANGOUT, HANG¹ (5) **2** [T **hang** sth ↔ **out**] to hang clothes on a piece of string outside in order to dry them: *I like to hang out the sheets to get a fresh smell.* **3** **hang** sb **out to dry** to severely criticize someone for something they have said or done: *The press has really hung Smith out to dry.*

hang over sb/sth *phr. v.* [I] if something bad hangs over you, you are worried because it is likely to happen soon: *The prospect of famine hangs over the whole area.* | *He has a six-month jail sentence hanging over his head.*

hang together *phr. v.* [I] **1** to help each other and work together to achieve an aim: *The party leaders have managed to hang together for over ten years.* **2** if a plan, story, set of ideas etc. hangs together, it is well-organized and makes sense: *Make sure that your paragraphs hang together well.*

hang out/hang up

hanging out the laundry

hanging up her jacket

After arguing for ten minutes with her husband she hung up on him.

hang up *phr. v.* **1** [I] to finish a telephone conversation by putting the RECEIVER (=the part you speak into) down: *Please hang up and dial again.* | *Why did you hang up on me* (=put the phone down before I was finished speaking)? **2** [T **hang** sth → **up**] to put something such as clothes on a hook or HANGER: *Amanda, hang up your clothes before you go to bed.* **3** **be hung up on/about** sth SPOKEN to be nervous or worried about something when there is no reason to be: *He's still hung up on his ex-wife.* **4** **hang up your** cleats/badge/gear etc. to stop doing a job or activity after a long time: *Yamaguchi says she has no plans to hang up her skates yet.* —see also HANG-UP

hang² *v. past tense and past participle* **hanged** [I,T] to

kill someone by dropping them with a rope around their neck, or to die in this way: *During the Civil War, Milligan hanged for treason.*

hang³ *n.* **get the hang of something** INFORMAL to learn how to do something or use something: *I still haven't gotten the hang of being a salesman.*

hang·ar /ˈhæŋɚ, ˈhæŋgɚ/ *n.* [C] a very large building where aircraft are kept

hang·dog /ˈhændɔg/ *adj.* a hangdog expression on your face shows you feel sorry or ashamed about something: *Tortoni is a bald man with a hangdog face.*

hang·er /ˈhæŋɚ/ *n.* [C] a curved piece of wood, plastic, or metal with a hook on it, on which you hang clothes

hanger-on /ˌ.. ˈ./ *n. plural* **hangers-on** [C] someone who spends a lot of time with a person who is important, famous, or rich, because they hope to get some advantage: *Several of Warhol's friends and hangers-on were interviewed for the documentary.*

hang glid·er /ˈ. ˌ../ *n.* [C] a large frame covered with cloth, which you hang from in order to fly

hang glid·ing /ˈ. ˌ../ *n.* [U] the sport of flying using a hang glider —see picture on page 1332

hang·ing /ˈhæŋɪŋ/ *n.* **1** [C,U] the action of killing someone by putting a rope around their neck and dropping them, used as a punishment **2** [C] a large piece of cloth hung on a wall as a decoration: *wall hangings*

hang·man /ˈhæŋmən/ *n.* **1** [C] OLD-FASHIONED someone whose job is to kill criminals by hanging them **2** [U] a game in which one player tries to guess a word the other player has chosen, by guessing letters one by one

hang·nail /ˈhæŋneɪl/ *n.* [C] a piece of skin that has become loose on the bottom or sides of the FINGERNAIL

hang·out /ˈhæŋaʊt/ *n.* [C] INFORMAL a place someone likes to go to often, especially with a particular group of people: *The Embry home is the neighborhood hangout, with kids pouring in and out at all hours.*

hang·o·ver /ˈhæŋˌoʊvɚ/ *n.* [C] **1** the feeling of sickness and the HEADACHE that you get the day after you have drunk too much alcohol: *I have a really bad hangover.* **2** **a hangover from** sth an action, feeling, or idea that has continued from the past into the present time: *Huge business debt is the hangover from the buyout mania of the 1980s.*

hang-up /ˈ. ./ *n.* [C] **1** INFORMAL if you have a hang-up about something, you feel worried or embarrassed about it in an unreasonable way: *All the characters have some weird psychological hang-ups.* **2** a problem that delays something being done: *Richards had a few technical hang-ups bringing the script to the screen.* —see also **hang up** (HANG¹)

hank /hæŋk/ *n.* [C] an amount of YARN, thread, or hair that has been wound into a loose ball

hank·er /ˈhæŋkɚ/ *v.* [I,T] INFORMAL to have a strong desire for something over a period of time: [+ **for/after**] *Voters seem to be hankering for change.* | [**hanker to do** sth] *I've been hankering to visit my father's birthplace for years.* —**hankering** *n.* [singular]

han·kie, hanky /ˈhæŋki/ *n.* [C] INFORMAL a HANDKERCHIEF

han·ky-pan·ky /ˌhæŋki ˈpæŋki/ *n.* [U] HUMOROUS sexual or illegal activity that is not very serious: *Worth may have been involved in some financial hanky-panky.*

Han·ni·bal /ˈhænəbəl/ (247–183 B.C.) a GENERAL who led the army of Carthage in its war against the Romans

Ha·noi /hæˈnɔɪ, hə-/ the capital city of Vietnam

Han·o·ver /ˈhænoʊvɚ/ the name of a German royal family who were the kings of Britain from 1714 to 1901

han·som cab /ˈhænsəm ˌkæb/ also **hansom** *n.* [C] a

two-wheeled vehicle pulled by a horse, used in past times as a taxi

Ha·nuk·kah, Chanukah /ˈhɑnəkə/ n. an eight-day Jewish holiday in December

hap·haz·ard /ˌhæpˈhæzɚd/ adj. happening or done in a way that is not planned or organized: *New employees have to deal with a haphazard filing system.* —**haphazardly** adv.

hap·less /ˈhæplɪs/ adj. [only before noun] LITERARY unlucky: *Several hapless hikers got caught in the storm.*

hap·pen /ˈhæpən/ v. [I]
1 occur if an event or situation happens, it starts, exists, and continues for a period of time, usually without being planned: *The accident happened early on Tuesday morning.* | *I'm not sure what happened.*
2 result to be caused as the result of an event or action: *Look, when I turn the key, nothing happens.* | *What happens if your parents find out?*
3 happen to sb if an event happens to someone or something, they are involved in it and affected by it: *Kids often believe nothing bad could happen to them.*
4 whatever/what happened to...? **a)** used to complain that something good does not seem to exist anymore or has been forgotten: *Whatever happened to plain common courtesy?* **b)** used to ask where someone or something is or what someone is doing now: *Whatever happened to Jeanne, anyway?* | *What happened to my keys?*
5 happen to do sth to do or have something by chance: *I happened to see Hannah at the store today.*
6 as it happens used to say what really is true in a situation: *Sam thought he'd find a new job right away, but as it happened, he was unemployed for months.*

SPOKEN PHRASES

7 what happened? used to ask what people are doing, or what the situation is, especially when you are worried or annoyed about this: *Hey, what happened? Why did the lights go out?* | [+ **to**] *What happened to your food – didn't the waitress bring it out?* | *For heaven's sake, what happened to you?*
8 what's happening? SLANG used when you meet someone you know well, to ask them how they are and what they have been doing: *Hey Carl, what's happening, man?*
9 sb/sth happens to be SPOKEN said when you are angry or annoyed, to emphasize what you are saying: *That happens to be my foot you're standing on!*
10 what's going to happen if/when...? also **what happens if/when...?**, **what will happen if/when...?** used to ask what the result of something will be: *What happens if you push this button?* | *What's going to happen when she finds out?*
11 whatever happens used to say that no matter what else happens, one thing will certainly happen: *We'll be thinking about you, whatever happens.*
12 it (just) so happens that said when one thing you are about to mention is related to what someone else has said or something else that has happened, in a way that you did not expect: *They needed a bottle opener, and it just so happened that Tom had one on his Swiss Army knife.*
13 these things happen used to tell someone not to worry about a mistake they have made, an accident they have caused etc.: *It was a tough loss, but these things happen.*
14 anything can happen used to say that it is impossible to know what will happen: *Anything can happen when children are left alone in the house.*
15 see what happens used to say that if someone does not know what the result of doing something will be, they should try it and find out: *The new school program starts Monday, so we'll just have to wait and see what happens.*
16 you don't happen to...? also **do you happen to...?** used politely to ask someone if they have or know something: *You don't happen to know his address, do you?*

—see also **accidents happen** (ACCIDENT (6))

happen across sth phr. v. [T] to find something by chance: *Turner happened across a photo of his parents in an old magazine.*
happen by phr. v. [I,T] to find a place or thing by chance: *A naturalist on board the boat points out any sea animals that happen by.*
happen on/upon sb/sth phr. v. [T] to find something or meet someone by chance: *If you happen on a good sale, stock up.*

hap·pen·ing¹ /ˈhæpənɪŋ/ n. [C] **1** something that happens: *The paper has a listing of the day's happenings.* **2** OLD-FASHIONED an artistic event that takes place without much planning, and that the people watching or listening can PARTICIPATE in

happening² adj. SLANG fashionable and exciting: *a happening club*

hap·pen·stance /ˈhæpənˌstæns/ n. [U] FORMAL something that happens by chance: *The similarities between the two books could not have occurred by happenstance.*

hap·pi·ly /ˈhæpəli/ adv. **1** in a happy way: *The puppy wagged its tail happily.* | *a happily married couple* **2** [sentence adverb] fortunately: *Happily, Bruce's injuries were not serious.* **3** very willingly: *I'd happily go pick up the kids for you.* **4 happily ever after** used at the end of children's stories to say that the people in the story were happy for the rest of their lives: *The prince and princess got married and lived happily ever after.*

hap·pi·ness /ˈhæpɪnɪs/ n. [U] the state of being happy: *Money is not the key to happiness.*

hap·py /ˈhæpi/ adj. happier, happiest
1 feeling having feelings of pleasure, often because something good has happened to you: *a happy baby* | *You look a lot happier today.* | [+ **for**] *Congratulations, I'm really happy for you.* | [**happy that**] *We're happy that things have worked out so well.* | [**happy to do sth**] *Margo was really happy to see you.* | [**happy to be doing sth**] *Part of me is sad, but another part is happy to be leaving.* —opposite SAD (1)
2 be happy to do sth to be very willing to do something, especially to help someone: *I'd be happy to cook if you want me to.*
3 happy time a happy time, place, occasion etc. is one that makes you feel happy: *Those were the happiest years of my life.* | *Most fairy tales have a happy ending.*
4 satisfied satisfied or not worried: [+ **about**] *I'm not happy about Dave buying a motorcycle, but I can't stop him.* | [+ **with**] *Anne wasn't very happy with their decision.* | *The restaurant's staff is determined to keep its customers happy.*
5 Happy Birthday/New Year/Anniversary etc. used as a greeting, or to wish someone happiness on their BIRTHDAY or a special occasion: *Happy Thanksgiving, everyone.*
6 a happy medium a way of doing something that is somewhere between two possible choices and that satisfies everyone: *The design is a happy medium between very plain dishes and fancy ones.*
7 a happy camper HUMOROUS someone who is pleased about a situation: *I won't be a very happy camper if I have to do yard work all weekend.*
8 the happy event OLD-FASHIONED the time when a baby is born or when two people get married
9 as happy as a lark OLD-FASHIONED very happy

10 **appropriate** FORMAL appropriate for a particular situation: *His choice of words was not a very happy one.*

USAGE NOTE: HAPPY

WORD CHOICE: happy, content, glad, ecstatic
There are several different words you can use to talk about being **happy**. If you are **content**, you are feeling happy because you are satisfied: *They're content to live a simple life.* If you are **glad**, you are pleased about something that has happened: *I'm really glad you were able to come.* If you feel very excited as well as happy, you are **ecstatic**: *The kids were ecstatic when summer vacation began.*

happy-go-luck·y /ˌ... . '..◂/ *adj* not caring or worrying about what happens: *Jim's a happy-go-lucky kind of person.*

happy hour /'.. ˌ./ *n.* [U] a special time, usually in the evening, when a bar sells alcoholic drinks at low prices

Haps·burg /'hæpsbɚg/ the name of an important European royal family, who ruled in Austria from 1278 to 1918 and in Spain from 1516 to 1700. The German spelling of the name is Habsburg. —**Haps·burg** *adj.*

har /hɑr/ *interjection* used to represent the sound of laughter, especially when you do not really think something is funny

har·a·kiri /ˌhærɪˈkɪri/ *n.* [U] a way of killing yourself by cutting open your stomach, used in past times in Japan to avoid losing honor

ha·rangue¹ /həˈræŋ/ *v.* [T] to speak in an angry way, often for a long time, in order to criticize someone or try to persuade them that you are right: *Teachers can't teach when they have to harangue the kids about good behavior.*

harangue² *n.* [C] an angry speech that criticizes or blames people, or tries to persuade them that you are right: *Women waiting at the clinic were forced to listen to anti-abortion harangues*

Ha·ra·re /həˈrɑreɪ/ the capital and largest city of Zimbabwe

ha·rass /həˈræs, ˈhærəs/ *v.* [T] **1** to annoy or threaten someone again and again: *Black teenagers are being constantly harassed by the police.* **2** to annoy someone by interrupting them again and again over a long period of time **3** to attack an enemy many times —**harasser** *n.* [C]

ha·rass·ment /həˈræsmənt, ˈhærəs-/ *n.* [U] behavior that is threatening or offensive to other people: *There have been inquiries into **sexual harassment** at the academy.*

har·bin·ger /'hɑrbɪndʒɚ/ *n.* [C] LITERARY a sign that something is going to happen soon: [+ of] *The increase in homes prices may be a harbinger of better economic times.*

har·bor¹ /'hɑrbɚ/ *n.* [C] an area of water next to the land where the water is calm, so that ships are safe when they are inside it, and can be left there

harbor² *v.* [T] **1** to keep bad thoughts, fears, or hopes in your mind for a long time: *Ralph harbors no bitterness toward his ex-wife.* **2** to hide something for a long time, especially something dangerous: *Dirty towels can harbor dangerous germs.* **3** to protect someone by hiding them from the police

har·bour /'hɑrbɚ/ the British spelling of harbor

s w
1 1
hard¹ /hɑrd/ *adj.*

1 **firm to touch** firm and stiff, and difficult to press down, break, or cut: *Diamond is the hardest substance known to man.* | *a piece of hard candy* | *a hard mattress* —opposite SOFT (1)

2 **difficult** difficult to do or understand: *Chemistry was one of the hardest classes I've ever taken.* | [be hard for sb] *It was hard for him, living in Berlin without speaking any German.* | [be hard to do sth] *The print was very small and hard to read.* | *The hard part is going to be getting the freezer down into the basement.* | *We lost the game in the last few seconds; that was really hard to take* (=difficult to accept or believe). | *I find it extremely hard to*

believe that no one saw the accident. | *Jobs were hard to come by* (=difficult to find) *then.* —opposite EASY¹ (1)

3 **a lot of effort** using or involving a lot of mental or physical effort: *Give the door a hard push.* | *Mowing the lawn is hard work.* | *She had a really hard day at work.*

4 **be hard on sb a)** to treat someone in a way that is unfair or too strict: *You're harder on Donald than you are on Monica.* **b)** to cause someone a lot of problems: *It's going to be hard on the kids if you move away.*

5 **be hard on sth** to have a bad effect on something: *Aspirin can be hard on your stomach.*

6 **problems** full of problems, especially not having enough money: *Times were hard, and we were forced to sell our home.* | *She's **had a hard life**, but she managed to bring up her kids right.*

7 **hard to tell/say** difficult to know: *It was hard to tell whether Katie really wanted to go.*

8 **not nice** showing no feelings of kindness or sympathy: *He's a hard man to work for, but he's fair.*

9 **hard facts/information/evidence etc.** facts, information etc. that are definitely true and can be proven: *Scientists have hard evidence that the hole in the ozone layer affects human health.*

10 **hard news** news stories that are about important events, politics etc., rather than about movie stars, animals, social events etc.

11 **learn/do sth the hard way** INFORMAL to learn about something by a bad experience or by making mistakes: *Dana found out the hard way that some medical tests are inaccurate.*

12 **give sb a hard time** INFORMAL **a)** to deliberately make someone feel uncomfortable or embarrassed, especially by joking: [+ about] *Bob was giving her a hard time about her new boyfriend.* **b)** to criticize someone a lot: *It's not my fault, John. Don't give me a hard time.*

13 **hard-earned/hard-won** achieved after a lot of effort: *your hard-earned dollars*

14 **hard cash** paper money and coins, not checks or CREDIT CARDS

15 **hard feelings a)** anger between people because of something that has happened: *Lori's sarcasm can lead to arguments and hard feelings.* **b) No hard feelings** SPOKEN used to tell someone whom you have been arguing with that you do not feel anger toward them anymore

16 **water** hard water contains a lot of minerals and does not mix easily with soap

17 **drugs/alcohol** very strong, difficult to stop using, and sometimes illegal: *It's all right if I drink a beer, but the doctor said to stay away from the hard stuff* (=strong alcohol). | *Mr. Beecher said he never drank hard liquor.*

18 **baked/set hard** made firm and stiff by being heated, glued etc.

19 **hard winter** a very cold winter —opposite MILD (3)

20 **take a (long) hard look at sth** to think about something without being influenced by your feelings: *We need to take a long hard look at the whole system of welfare payments.*

21 **hard-luck story** if someone tells you a hard-luck story, they tell you about all the bad things that have happened to them in order to make you feel sorry for them

22 **hard-luck kids/town etc.** someone or something that has had a lot of bad things happen to them

23 **hard left/right** a sharp turn to the left or right: *Make a hard left just after crossing Lindley Avenue.*

24 **take a hard line (on sth)** to deal with something in a very strict way: *They've taken a hard line in contract negotiations.*

25 **pronunciation** a hard "c" is pronounced /k/ rather than /s/; a hard "g" is pronounced /g/ rather than /dʒ/ —**hardness** *n.* [U] —see also **drive a hard bargain** (DRIVE¹ (14))

H

hard² *adv.*

1 using energy/effort using a lot of effort, energy, or attention: *Elaine had been working hard all morning.* | *We try hard to keep our customers happy.*

2 with force with a lot of force: *It's raining hard.* | *Tyson hit him hard on the chin.* | *She ran all that way and she wasn't even breathing hard.*

3 be hard hit also **be hit hard** to be badly affected by something that has happened: *Bridgeport was hard hit by economic troubles.*

4 be hard pressed/put/pushed (to do sth) INFORMAL to have difficulty doing something: *Small companies are hard pressed to provide health insurance for their employees.*

5 laugh/cry etc. hard to laugh, cry etc. a lot and loudly: *We were laughing so hard we could hardly breathe.*

6 take sth hard INFORMAL to feel upset about something, especially bad news: *Dad didn't say much, but I could tell he took it hard.*

7 hard on the heels of sth happening soon after something: *The warm weather has come hard on the heels of the coldest December on record.*

8 be hard on sb's heels to follow close behind or soon after someone —see also HARD UP, **play hard to get** (PLAY¹ (18))

USAGE NOTE: HARD

WORD CHOICE: hard, hardly
Use **hard** as an adverb to say that something is done using a lot of effort or force: *We studied hard for the test.* | *You have to push hard or the door won't open.* Use **hardly** to mean "almost not": *I could hardly believe it.* | *Laura hardly studied for the test, so it was no big surprise that she failed.*

---

hard-and-fast /ˌ. . ˈ. ./ *adj.* not able to be changed: *The school doesn't have any hard-and-fast rules about what children should wear.*

hard ass /ˈ. ./ *n.* [C usually singular] VULGAR someone who is very strict and difficult to deal with, often in a way that is unfair —**hard-ass** *adj.*

hard·back /ˈhɑrdbæk/ *n.* [C] a HARDCOVER —**hardback** *adj.*

hard·ball /ˈhɑrdbɔl/ *n.* [U] **play hardball** INFORMAL to be very determined to get what you want, especially in business or politics: *It is clear that the company is ready to play hardball with the unions.*

hard-bit·ten /ˌ. ˈ. .ˌ/ *adj.* not easily shocked or upset, because you have had a lot of experience: *a hard-bitten detective*

hard·board /ˈhɑrdbɔrd/ *n.* [U] a building material made from small pieces of wood pressed together to form a board

hard-boiled /ˌ. ˈ.ˌ/ *adj.* **1** a hard-boiled egg has been boiled until it becomes solid —compare SOFT-BOILED **2** INFORMAL **a)** not showing your emotions or influenced by your feelings in what you do; TOUGH: *a hard-boiled businesswoman* **b)** dealing with people who do not show their emotions: *hard-boiled detective novels*

hard·bound /ˈhɑrdbaʊnd/ *adj.* a hardbound book has a strong stiff cover

hard cop·y /ˌ. ˈ. ./ *n.* [C,U] information from a computer that is printed onto paper

hard·core, hard-core /ˈhɑrdkɔr/ *adj.* **1** [only before noun] having an extremely strong belief, opinion, or behavior that is unlikely to change: *We need to prevent juvenile offenders from becoming hardcore criminals.* | *hard-core Republicans* **2** hardcore **pornography** magazines, movies etc. that show the details of sexual behavior, often in a way that people think is too violent or shocking **3** hardcore PUNK or ROCK music is played very fast and loudly

hard·cov·er /ˈhɑrdˌkʌvər/ *n.* [C] a book that has a strong stiff cover —**hardcover** *adj.* —compare PAPERBACK

hard cur·ren·cy /ˌ. ˈ... ./ *n.* [C,U] money that can be used in any country because it is from a country that has a strong ECONOMY

hard disk /ˌ. ˈ. ./ *n.* [C] a stiff DISK inside a computer's hard DISK drive, used for permanently storing a large amount of information —compare FLOPPY DISK

hard-drink·ing /ˌ. ˈ..ˌ/ *adj.* drinking a lot of alcohol: *a hard-drinking man*

hard drive /ˈ. ./ *n.* [C] the part of a computer where information and PROGRAMs are stored, consisting of HARD DISKs and the electronic equipment that reads what is stored on them

hard-edged /ˌ. ˈ.ˌ/ *adj.* dealing with difficult subjects or criticizing someone severely in a way that may offend some people: *hard-edged, realistic stories*

hard·en /ˈhɑrdn/ *v.* **1** [I,T] to become firm or stiff, or to make something firm or stiff: *The clay needs to harden before it can be painted.* | *Harden the chocolates by putting them in the fridge.* **2** [I,T] to become or sound more strict and determined and less sympathetic, or to make someone become this way: *Opposition to the peace talks has hardened since the attack.* | *The death of a parent can harden young people, making them bitter.* **3 harden your heart** to make yourself not feel pity or sympathy for someone —opposite SOFTEN

hard·ened /ˈhɑrdnd/ *adj.* **1 hardened criminal/ police officer etc.** a criminal, officer etc. who has had a lot of experience with things that are shocking and is therefore less affected by them: *a combat-hardened soldier* **2 become hardened toward/to sth** to become used to something shocking because you have seen it many times: *Many inner-city residents have become almost hardened to the violence.*

hard hat /ˈ. ./ *n.* [C] a protective hat, worn especially by workers in places where buildings are being built —see picture at HAT

hard-head·ed /ˌ. ˈ.. ./ *adj.* practical and able to make difficult decisions without being influenced by your emotions: *a hard-headed manager* —**hard-headedness** *n.* [U]

hard-heart·ed /ˌ. ˈ.. ./ *adj.* not caring about other people's feelings —**hard-heartedness** *n.* [U]

hard-hit·ting /ˌ. ˈ.. ./ *adj.* criticizing someone or something in a strong and effective way: *a hard-hitting TV documentary*

har·di·ness /ˈhɑrdinɪs/ *n.* [U] the ability to bear difficult or severe conditions: *This type of wheat is noted for its hardiness.*

Hard·ing /ˈhɑrdɪŋ/**, War·ren** /ˈwɔrən/ (1865–1923) the 29th President of the U.S.

hard la·bor /ˌ. ˈ.. ./ *n.* [U] punishment in prison that consists of hard physical work

hard-line /ˌ. ˈ.ˌ/ *adj.* having extreme political beliefs, and refusing to change them: *a hard-line Communist country* —see also **take a hard line (on sth)** (HARD¹ (24))

hard-lin·er /ˌhɑrdˈlaɪnəˌ/ *n.* [C] a member of a political group who has strong political beliefs and wants political problems to be dealt with in a strong and extreme way

hard·ly /ˈhɑrdli/ *adv.* **1** almost not: *I hardly know the people I'm working with.* | *I was so tired I could hardly walk.* | *I don't know why we grow the zucchini* – **hardly anyone** (=almost no one) *likes it.* | *It isn't that much cheaper – there's **hardly any** (=very little) difference in price.* | *What do you mean? I **hardly even** (=almost not at all) know the guy!* | *We **hardly ever** (=almost never) go out to eat.* —see Usage Notes at ALMOST and HARDLY **2** used to say that something is not true, appropriate, possible etc. at all: *This is hardly the ideal time to buy a house.* | *The results of the survey were **hardly surprising**.* | *You can **hardly** blame her for being angry.* | *The program **could hardly be** easier to use.* **3** used to say that something had just happened or someone had just done something when something else happened: *The day had hardly begun, and he felt exhausted already.*

USAGE NOTE: HARDLY
GRAMMAR
Do not use **hardly** with "not" or "no" or other negative words. Say *The city has hardly any pollution* or *I could hardly believe they were sisters*, NOT *The city has hardly no pollution* and NOT *I couldn't hardly believe they were sisters*. **Hardly** usually comes just before the main verb: *I could hardly hear her* (NOT *I hardly could hear her*). **Hardly** is used at the beginning of sentences only in very formal or old-fashioned writing. People usually say *The game had hardly begun when it started to rain* rather than *Hardly had the game begun wher. it began to rain*, which sounds old-fashioned and literary. **Hardly** is not the adverb of **hard**. Say *She works very hard* (NOT *She works very hardly*).

hard mon·ey /'. ,../ *n.* [U] money that is given to a politician, which is limited by the government —compare SOFT MONEY

hard-nosed /, '.◂/ *adj.* [usually before noun] not affected by emotions, and determined to get what you want: *a hard-nosed negotiator*

hard of hear·ing /, . '../ *adj.* [not before noun] **1** unable to hear very well **2 the hard of hearing** people who are not able to hear very well

hard-on /'. ./ *n.* [C] VULGAR an ERECTION (1)

hard pal·ate /, '../ *n.* [C] the hard part of the top of your mouth that is at the front behind your teeth —compare SOFT PALATE

hard-pressed /, '.◂/ *adj.* having a lot of problems and not enough money or time: *The clinic provides help for hard-pressed families with young children.* —see also **be hard pressed/put/pushed (to do sth)** (HARD² (4))

hard rock /, './ *n.* [U] a type of ROCK MUSIC that is played loudly, has a strong beat, and uses electric instruments

hard-scrabble /'hard,skræbəl/ *adj.* **1** hardscrabble land is difficult to grow crops on **2** working hard without earning much money, especially by working on bad land: *Dole described his hardscrabble childhood in Kansas during the Great Depression.*

hard sell /, './ *n.* [singular] **1** a way of selling something in which you try very hard to persuade someone to buy it: *Brittan was giving the hard sell to a farmer.* **2** difficult to sell: *Fifteen years ago, California wines were a hard sell; everyone wanted French wines.* **3 sb is a hard sell** used to say that it is difficult to persuade someone to buy or do something: *I was a hard sell at first, but now I'm glad we moved.* —compare SOFT SELL

hard·ship /'hard,ʃɪp/ *n.* [C,U] something that makes your life very difficult, especially not having enough money or food: *economic hardships* | *The new taxes are creating extreme hardship for poor families.*

hard·tack /'hardtæk/ *n.* [U] a hard CRACKER, eaten especially in past times on ships

hard·top /'hardtap/ *n.* [C] a car's metal roof, which cannot be removed, or a car with this type of roof —compare CONVERTIBLE¹

hard up /, '.◂/ *adj.* not having something that you want or need, especially something involving money or sex: *Scott was pretty hard up, so I lent him $20.* | [+ for] *We were so hard up for entertainment we sat outside counting the cars go by.*

hard·ware /'hardwɛr/ *n.* [U] **1** computer equipment and machinery —compare SOFTWARE **2** equipment and tools, such as a hammer and nails, that you use in your home and yard **3** the machinery and equipment needed to do something: *tanks and other military hardware*

hard-wired /, '.◂/ *adj.* TECHNICAL computer systems that are hard-wired are controlled by HARDWARE rather than SOFTWARE and therefore cannot be easily changed by the user

hard·wood /'hardwod/ *n.* **1** [C,U] strong heavy wood from trees such as OAKs, used for making furniture **2** [C] a tree that takes a long time to grow and that produces this kind of wood —compare SOFTWOOD

hard-work·ing /, '.◂/ *adj.* working seriously and with a lot of effort, and not wasting time: *a hard-working teacher*

har·dy /'hardi/ *adj.* **hardier, hardiest 1** strong and healthy, and able to deal with difficult living conditions: *Red deer are hardy, adaptable animals.* | *A few hardy joggers were out running in the cold.* **2** a hardy plant is able to live through the winter

hare /hɛr/ *n.* [C] an animal like a rabbit, but larger and with longer ears and longer back legs, that can run very quickly

hare·brained /'hɛrbreɪnd/ *adj.* not sensible or practical: *a harebrained scheme*

Ha·re Krish·na /,hɛri 'krɪʃnə/ **1** a branch of the HINDU religion worshiping the god Krishna **2** [C] a member of Hare Krishna

hare·lip /'hɛr,lɪp/ *n.* [singular] the condition of having a top lip that is divided into two parts, because it did not develop correctly before birth —**harelipped** *adj.*

har·em /'hɛrəm, 'hærəm/ *n.* [C] **1** the group of wives or women who lived with a rich or powerful man in some Muslim societies in past times **2** the rooms in a Muslim home where the women live

harem pants /'.. ,./ *n.* [plural] loose-fitting women's pants made from thin cloth

Haring /'hærɪŋ/, **Keith** /kiθ/ (1958–1990) a modern U.S. PAINTER who used the style of GRAFFITI art

hark¹ /hark/ *v.*
hark back *phr. v.* [I] to harken back
hark to sth *phr. v.* [T] LITERARY to listen or pay attention to something

hark² *interjection* OLD USE used to tell someone to listen

har·ken /'harkən/ *v.* [I]
harken back to sth *phr. v.* [T] to remind people of something that happened in the past: *The band's songs harken back to a simpler time.*

har·le·quin /'harlə,kwɪn/ *n.* [C] **1** a harlequin pattern is made up of DIAMOND shapes **2** a character in a type of traditional Italian play who wears brightly colored clothes and plays tricks

har·lot /'harlət/ *n.* [C] LITERARY a PROSTITUTE

harm¹ /harm/ *n.* [U] **1** damage, injury, or trouble caused by someone's actions or by an event: *Several people were injured, but most escaped harm.* | **do/cause harm** *A little wine won't do you any harm.* | *Some types of diets do more harm than good* (=cause more problems than they solve). —see Usage Note at DAMAGE² **2 mean no harm** also **not mean any harm** to have no intention of hurting, offending, or upsetting anyone: *I know he meant no harm, but it was a very personal question.*

SPOKEN PHRASES
3 there's no harm in doing sth also **it does no harm to do sth** used to suggest that someone should do something: *There's no harm in trying.* | *It does no harm to ask.* **4 it wouldn't do sb any harm to do sth** SPOKEN used to suggest that it would be helpful or useful to someone if they did something: *It wouldn't do you any harm to get some experience first.* **5 no harm done** said in order to tell someone that you are not upset by something they have done or said, or that no damage or trouble was caused: *Don't worry, I'll clean it up. No harm done.* **6 what's the harm in (doing) sth?** used to ask what problems would be caused by something, especially after someone has criticized you: *What's the harm in letting a child watch a little TV?*

7 in harm's way in a place where something dangerous can happen: *Employees should never be put in harm's way.* **8 out of harm's way** in a safe place: *Move valuable objects out of harm's way when children are visiting.* **9 come to no harm** also **not come to any harm** to not be hurt or damaged: *With relief, she saw that none of the children had come to any harm.* —compare HURT³

harm² *v.* [T] **1** to damage something: *There are fears that a trade agreement will harm the economy.* **2** to

H

hurt someone or an animal: *These companies fish for tuna using methods that do not harm dolphins.* **3 harm sb's image/reputation** to make people have a worse opinion of a person or group: *The report has harmed the town's reputation as a health spa.*

harm·ful /'harmfəl/ *adj.* causing harm, or likely to cause harm: *Doctors have warned against the harmful effects of smoking.* | [+ **to**] *Some pesticides are harmful to the environment.* —**harmfully** *adv.* —**harmfulness** *n.* [U]

harm·less /'harmlɪs/ *adj.* **1** unable or unlikely to hurt anyone or cause damage: *Male mosquitoes are completely harmless – it's only the females that bite.* **2** not likely to upset or offend anyone: *harmless fun* —**harmlessly** *adv.* —**harmlessness** *n.* [U]

har·mon·ic /har'manɪk/ *adj.* TECHNICAL relating to the way notes are played or sung together to give a pleasing sound: *harmonic scales*

har·mon·i·ca /har'manɪkə/ *n.* [C] a small musical instrument that you play by blowing into it and moving it from side to side

har·mo·ni·ous /har'moʊniəs/ *adj.* **1** harmonious relationships, agreements etc. are ones in which people are friendly and helpful to one another **2** looking good or working well together: *The building is a harmonious blend of structure and the surrounding land.* | *harmonious flavors* **3** sounds that are harmonious sound good together and are pleasant —**harmoniously** *adv.* —**harmoniousness** *n.* [U]

har·mo·ni·um /har'moʊniəm/ *n.* [C] a musical instrument like a small ORGAN worked by pumped air

har·mo·nize /'harmə,naɪz/ *v.* **1** [I] if two or more things harmonize, they work well together or look good together: [+ **with**] *Buildings should harmonize with their natural surroundings.* **2** [T] to make two or more sets of rules, taxes etc. the same: *Countries need to work to harmonize standards on pesticides.* **3** [I] to sing or play music in HARMONY

har·mo·ny /'harməni/ *n. plural* **harmonies 1** [C usually plural,U] notes of music combined together in a pleasant way: *four-part harmony* | *We listened to the choir singing **in perfect harmony**.* —opposite DISSONANCE **2 be/work/live in harmony** FORMAL to work well together or be similar to each other: [+ **with**] *His religious ideas are in harmony with Hinduism.* | *In the movie, the Indians are seen as **living in harmony with** nature.* **3** [U] a situation in which people are friendly and peaceful, and agree with each other: *We sat down and talked in an effort to restore family harmony.* | *The mayor appealed for people to **live in** racial harmony.* **4** [U] the pleasant effect made by different things that form an attractive whole: *the harmony of sea and sky* | *The buildings are **in harmony with** the natural surroundings.* —compare DISCORD

har·ness[1] /'harnɪs/ *n.* [C,U] **1** a set of leather bands used to control a horse or to attach it to a vehicle the horse is pulling **2** a set of bands used to hold someone in a place or to stop them from falling: *An essential piece of rock-climbing equipment is a climbing harness.* **3 in harness** HUMOROUS working at a job: *Morin's book is a helpful guide to surviving the first few months in harness.*

harness[2] *v.* [T] **1** to control and use the natural force or power of something: *The Missouri River is harnessed for hydroelectric power.* **2** to fasten two animals together, or to fasten an animal to something using a harness **3** to put a harness on a horse

harp[1] /harp/ *n.* [C] a large musical instrument with strings that are stretched on a frame with three corners —**harpist** *n.* [C]

harp[2] *v.*

harp on sb/sth *phr. v.* INFORMAL [T] to complain or talk about something a lot: *My parents are always harping on my boyfriend's faults.*

Har·per's Fer·ry /,harpɚz 'fɛri/ a place in the U.S. state of West Virginia where the ABOLITIONIST John Brown took over a government weapons establishment in 1859

har·poon /har'pun/ *n.* [C] a weapon used for hunting WHALES or large fish —**harpoon** *v.* [T]

harp·si·chord /'harpsɪ,kɔrd/ *n.* [C] a musical instrument like a PIANO, used especially in CLASSICAL MUSIC

har·py /'harpi/ *n. plural* **harpies** [C] LITERARY a cruel woman

har·ri·dan /'hærɪdən/ *n.* [C] OLD-FASHIONED a woman who is not nice and is always in a bad mood

har·ried /'hærid/ *adj.* very busy and worried, especially because other people keep asking you to do things: *Robinson's harried secretary was on the phone.*

Har·ris /'hærɪs/**, Joel Chan·dler** /dʒoʊl 'tʃændlɚ/ (1848–1908) a U.S. writer famous for his books for children in which Uncle Remus tells stories about Brer Rabbit

Har·ris·burg /'hærɪs,bɚg/ the capital city of the U.S. state of Pennsylvania

Har·ris·on /'hærɪsən/**, Benjamin** (1833–1901) the 23rd President of the U.S.

Harrison, William (1773–1841) the ninth President of the U.S.

har·row /'hæroʊ/ *n.* [C] a farming machine with sharp round metal blades, used to break up the soil before planting crops —**harrow** *v.* [I,T]

har·rowed /'hæroʊd/ *adj.* a harrowed look or expression shows that you are very worried or afraid

har·row·ing /'hæroʊɪŋ/ *adj.* very frightening or shocking and making you feel very upset: *The book is a harrowing account of his stepfather's abuse.*

har·rumph /hə'rʌmf/ *v.* [I,T] to make a sound that shows you are annoyed or that you disapprove of something: [+ **that**] *Sawyer harrumphed that children ought to be seen and not heard.* —**harrumph** *interjection*

har·ry /'hæri/ *v.* **harried, harries, harrying** [T] LITERARY **1** to keep asking someone for something in a way that is upsetting or annoying **2** to attack an enemy again and again

harsh[1] /harʃ/ *adj.* **1** harsh conditions are difficult to live in and very uncomfortable: *the harsh Canadian winters* | *War toys make children less sensitive to the harsh realities of war.* **2** cruel, or strict, or not nice: *They suspended him? That seems pretty harsh.* | *The movie has received harsh criticism from the press.* **3** too loud or bright, making an effect that is not nice: *The stage lighting is harsh.* | *a harsh voice* **4** ugly and not nice to look at: *the harsh outline of the factories against the sky* **5** a cleaning substance that is harsh is too strong and likely to damage the thing you are cleaning —**harshly** *adv.* —**harshness** *n.* [U]

harsh[2] *v.*

harsh on sb *phr. v.* [T] SLANG to criticize someone or say things to them that are not nice

hart /hart/ *n.* [C] OLD USE a male DEER

Hart /hart/**, Lor·enz Mil·ton** /'lɔrənts 'mɪltⁿn/ (1895–1943) a U.S. SONGWRITER famous for writing MUSICALS with Richard Rodgers

Hart, Moss /mɔs/ (1904–1961) a U.S. writer and DIRECTOR of plays and MUSICALS

Hart·ford /'hartfɚd/ the capital city of the U.S. state of Connecticut

har·um-scar·um /,hɛrəm 'skɛrəm/ *adj.* OLD-FASHIONED someone who is harum-scarum does things without thinking about what the results might be: *a pair of harum-scarum boys* —**harum-scarum** *adv.*

har·vest[1] /'harvɪst/ *n.* **1** [C,U] the time when crops are gathered from the fields, or the act of gathering them: *September is usually harvest time.* | *the wheat harvest* **2** [C] the size or quality of the crops that have been gathered: *It should be a good harvest this year.* **3 reap a rich/bitter etc. harvest** to get good or bad results: *Fathers who ignore their children will reap a bitter harvest.*

harvest[2] *v.* [I,T] to gather crops from the fields

har·vest·er /'harvɪstɚ/ *n.* [C] **1** a farm machine that gathers crops **2** someone who gathers crops, fruit etc.

harvest moon /,.. './ *n.* [usually singular] the FULL MOON in the fall

beret

top hat

panama hat

baseball cap

bonnet

mortarboard

cowboy hat

hard hat

sun hat

has /əz, həz; *strong* hæz/ *v.* the third person singular of the present tense of HAVE[1]

has-been /'. ./ *n.* [C] INFORMAL someone who was important or popular, but who has now been forgotten

hash[1] /hæʃ/ *n.* [U] **1** a dish made with cooked meat and potatoes: *corned-beef hash* **2** INFORMAL hashish **3 make hash (out) of sth** to do something very badly: *The scriptwriters have made hash out of the story.* —see also REHASH, **sling hash** (SLING[1] (3))

hash[2] *v.*

hash sth ↔ out *phr. v.* [T] INFORMAL to discuss something very thoroughly and carefully, especially until you reach an agreement: *They spent hundreds of hours hashing out a compromise.*

hash sth ↔ over *phr. v.* [T] INFORMAL to talk a lot about something that has happened: *We watched a video of the game as the coach hashed over our mistakes.* —see also REHASH

hash browns /'. ./ *n.* [plural] potatoes that are cut into very small pieces, pressed together, and cooked in oil

hash·ish /'hæʃiʃ, hæ'ʃiʃ/ *n.* [U] the strongest form of the illegal drug MARIJUANA

hash mark /'. ./ *n.* [C] **1** one of the lines on a football field that marks a YARD (2) **2** a mark that shows rank that is put on a soldier's uniform SLEEVE

Ha·sid /'hæsid/ *n. plural* **Hasidim** /hæ'sidim/ a member of a Jewish religious group who wear special clothes and believe in coming close to God through prayer —**Hasidism** *n.*

has·n't /'hæzənt/ *v.* the short form of "has not": *She hasn't seen Bruce in five years.*

hasp /hæsp/ *n.* [C] a flat piece of metal used to fasten a door, lid etc.

has·sle[1] /'hæsəl/ *n.* **1** [C,U] something that is annoying, because it causes problems or is difficult to do: *Driving downtown is just too much hassle.* | *Buy Christmas presents early, and avoid the hassles of December shopping.* **2** [C] INFORMAL an argument between two people or groups: *An experienced real estate agent will be able to avoid legal hassles.*

hassle[2] *v.* INFORMAL [T] **1** to argue with someone or annoy them: *A homeless man was hassling motorists at the traffic lights.* **2** to ask someone again and again to do something, in a way that annoys them: [**hassle sb to do sth**] *I got tired of my parents hassling me to do my homework.*

has·sock /'hæsək/ *n.* [C] **1** a soft round piece of furniture used as a seat or for resting your feet on **2** a small CUSHION that you kneel on in a church

hast /həst; *strong* hæst/ **thou hast** OLD USE a way of saying "you have"

haste /heist/ *n.* [U] **1** great speed in doing something, especially because you do not have enough time: *In her haste to get to the airport, Mindy forgot the tickets.* **2 in haste** FORMAL quickly or in a hurry:

The army retreated in haste. **3 make haste** OLD-FASHIONED to hurry or do something quickly **4 haste makes waste** used to say that if you do something too quickly it does not turn out well

has·ten /'heisən/ *v.* **1** [T] to make something happen faster or sooner: *The agency hoped to hasten the approval process for new drugs.* **2 hasten to do sth** to do or say something quickly or without delay: *Barbara hastened to tell him that she was all right.* | *"Just kidding," Mullins hastened to add, saying that he is happily married.* **3** [I always + adv./prep.] FORMAL to go somewhere quickly: *We hastened toward shelter.*

hast·y /'heisti/ *adj.* **hastier, hastiest** done in a hurry, especially with bad results: *The mayor said he wouldn't be pressured into making a hasty decision.* —**hastily** *adv.* —**hastiness** *n.* [U]

hat /hæt/ *n.* [C] **1** a piece of clothing that you wear on your head: *a big straw hat* | *a cowboy hat* **2 hats off to sb** also **take your hat off to sb** INFORMAL used when you want to praise someone for their achievement: *Hats off to Bill Monroe, the man who made this town famous.* | *I take my hat off to the person who figured out a way to reduce crime here.* **3 throw/toss your hat into the ring** to officially announce that you will compete or take part in something: *He threw his hat into the ring for the job of chief officer.* **4 keep something under your hat** INFORMAL to keep information secret: *I decided to keep it under my hat for a while.* **5 be wearing your manager's/teacher's etc. hat** also **have your manager's/teacher's etc. hat on** INFORMAL to be doing your work as a manager etc., which is not your only work: *He made some bad decisions while wearing his business hat.* **6 my hat!** OLD-FASHIONED used to express great surprise —see also **at the drop of a hat** (DROP[2] (8)), HARD HAT, -HATTED

hat·box /'hætbaks/ *n.* [C] a special round box in which you keep a hat to protect it

hatch[1] /hætʃ/ *v.* **1** [I,T] if an egg hatches or is hatched, it breaks and a baby bird, fish, or insect is born: *The eggs should hatch any day now.* **2** [I,T] also **hatch out** to break through an egg in order to be born: *Millions of mosquito eggs will have hatched out by May.* **3 hatch a plot/plan/idea etc.** to think of a plan, idea etc., often secretly: *The idea for the dressed-up teddy bears was hatched when Mary needed a gift for a friend.*

hatch[2] *n.* [C] **1** a hole in a ship or aircraft, used for loading goods, or the door that covers it: *The astronauts were fixing a hatch aboard the Mir space station.* **2** a hatchback **3 escape hatch a)** a door on a ship or aircraft that you can leave from if there is an accident **b)** something that allows you to avoid a bad situation: *Kids are looking for an escape hatch from the pressures of home.* **4** the act of hatching eggs, or the animals that have hatched, considered as a group: *The oil spill will affect next spring's hatch.* **5 down the hatch** SPOKEN used when you are eating or drinking something **6** a HATCHWAY —see also BOOBY HATCH

hatch·back /'hætʃbæk/ *n.* [C] a car with a door at the back that opens up

hat·check /'hæt-tʃɛk/ *n.* [C] OLD-FASHIONED the place in a restaurant, theater etc. where you can leave your coat

hatch·er·y /'hætʃəri/ *n. plural* **hatcheries** [C] a place for hatching eggs, especially fish eggs

hatch·et /'hætʃit/ *n.* [C] **1** a small AX with a short handle **2 do a hatchet job on sb** INFORMAL to criticize someone severely and unfairly in a newspaper or on television: *Mangell said the paper had done a hatchet job on him.* —see also **bury the hatchet** (BURY (9))

hatchet-faced /'.. ,./ *adj.* having a thin ugly face with sharp features

hatchet man /'.. ,./ *n.* [C] INFORMAL someone who is employed to make unpopular changes in an organization

H

hatch·ing /'hætʃɪŋ/ *n.* [U] fine lines drawn on or cut into a surface

hatch·way /'hætʃweɪ/ *n. plural* **hatchways** [C] a small hole in the wall, floor, or ceiling of a room, or the door that covers it: *the hatchway into the attic*

hate[1] /heɪt/ *v.* [T not in progressive] **1** INFORMAL to dislike something very much: *It's the kind of movie you either love or hate.* | *Pat hates her job.* | [**hate doing sth**] *Paul hates having his picture taken.* | [**hate to do sth**] *I hate to just leave stuff here.* | [**hate sb doing sth**] *Jenny's mother hates her staying out late.* | *I hate it when she calls me at work.* **2** to dislike someone very much and feel angry toward them: *Jill really hates her stepfather.* **3** **hate sb's guts** to dislike someone very much: *The two of them hate each other's guts.*

SPOKEN PHRASES

4 I hate to say sth also **I hate to tell you...** used when saying something that is slightly embarrassing or not polite: *I hate to say it, but I think he's really boring.* **5 I'd hate (for) sb/sth to do sth** used to emphasize that you really do not want something to happen: *I'd hate all that food to spoil.* | *I'd hate for my child to grow up in such a violent city.* **6 I hate to...but...** used to show that you are sorry that you have to say something, interrupt someone etc.: *I hate to bother you, but could you answer a question?* | *I hate to disappoint you, but Jamie won't be there.* **7 I hate to think...** used when you feel sure that something would have a bad result, or when an idea is not nice to think about: [**I hate to think what/how/where etc.**] *I hate to think what would happen if he dropped out of school.* | [+ of] *I hate to think of the struggles ahead of me.* **8 I'd/I would hate to think (that)...** used to say that you hope that something is not true or that it will not happen: *I'd hate to think someone set the fire on purpose.* —**hated** *adj.: the hated dictator*

—opposite LOVE[1]

hate[2] *n.* [U] an angry feeling of wanting to harm someone you dislike a lot: *a look of hate* —opposite LOVE[2]

hate crime /'. ./ *n.* [U] a crime that is COMMITted against someone only because they belong to a particular race, religion etc.

hate·ful /'heɪtfəl/ *adj.* very bad or expressing a lot of hate: *a hateful letter* —**hatefully** *adv.*

hate·mon·ger /'heɪt ͵mʌŋgɚ, -͵maŋ-/ *n.* [C] someone who tries to make other people fear or hate other groups of people

hath /həθ; *strong* hæθ/ *v.* OLD USE has

hat·pin /'hæt ͵pɪn/ *n.* [C] a long pin that is used to make a woman's hat stay on her head —see picture at PIN[1]

ha·tred /'heɪtrɪd/ *n.* [U] an angry feeling of extreme dislike for someone or something: [+ of] *The group's hatred of foreigners has led to riots.* | [+ for/toward] *Price's hatred for police led to his attack on an officer.* | *Ellis was a sick young man with a deep hatred of women.*

hat stand also **hat rack** /'. ./ *n.* [C] a tall pole with hooks at the top that you can hang coats and hats on

-hatted /hætɪd/ [in adjectives] **fur-hatted/top-hatted etc.** wearing a particular type of hat

hat·ter /'hætɚ/ *n.* [C] OLD-FASHIONED **1** someone who makes or sells hats **2 as mad as a hatter** INFORMAL behaving in a way that is crazy or very strange

hat trick /'. ./ *n.* [C] three GOALs made by the same person in a single game of SOCCER or HOCKEY

haugh·ty /'hɔti/ *adj.* **haughtier, haughtiest** proud and unfriendly: *a haughty laugh* —**haughtily** *adv.* —**haughtiness** *n.* [U]

haul[1] /hɔl/ *v.* [I always + adv./prep., T] **1** to carry or pull something heavy: [**haul sth along/in/across etc.**] *I spent the morning hauling boxes into the new house.* **2** to carry a large amount of something in a

truck or ship: *The ship was hauling a load of iron ore.* | [**haul sth ↔ away/in/off etc.**] *Trucks haul away garbage to the landfill.* **3 haul yourself up/out of etc.** to pull yourself up, out of something etc.: *Welles hauled himself up the rock face using only his arms.* **4 haul ass** SLANG to hurry

haul sth ↔ in *phr. v.* [T] INFORMAL to earn a lot of money: *The movie hauled in $2 million in just one weekend.*

haul off *phr. v.* **1** [T **haul sb ↔ off**] to take someone somewhere they do not want to go, especially to prison: *Mahoney was hauled off for questioning in the murder.* **2 haul off and hit/punch/kick sb** INFORMAL to try to hit someone very hard

haul[2] *n.* [C] **1** a large amount of illegal or stolen goods: *San Antonio police seized their largest haul ever of crack cocaine.* **2 the long/short haul** the long or short time that it takes to achieve something: *They offer guaranteed savings over the short haul.* | *In the long haul, these changes will improve our children's education.* **3 a long haul** a long distance to travel: *It's a long haul from here to Boise.* **4** the amount of fish caught when fishing with a net —see also LONG-HAUL, SHORT-HAUL

haul·age /'hɔlɪdʒ/ *n.* [U] the business of carrying goods in trucks or trains

haul·er /'hɔlɚ/ *n.* [C] a company that carries goods in trucks or trains

haunch /hɔntʃ, hɑntʃ/ *n.* [C usually plural] **1** one of the back legs of a four-legged animal, especially when it is used as meat —see picture on page 429 **2 sb's haunches** the part of your body at the back between your waist and legs: *The kids were sitting on their haunches listening to Judy tell stories.*

haunt[1] /hɔnt, hɑnt/ *v.* [T not in progressive] **1** if the spirit of a dead person haunts a place, it appears there often: *People say the house is haunted by a former slave.* **2** if something haunts you, you keep remembering it and it makes you worry and feel sad: *Memories of the war still haunt her.* **3** to cause problems for someone over a long period of time: *All your mistakes will come back to haunt you.*

haunt[2] *n.* [C] a place that someone likes to go to often: *a local writers' haunt*

haunt·ed /'hɔntɪd/ *adj.* **1** a haunted place is one where the spirits of dead people are believed to live: *a haunted house* **2 haunted expression/look etc.** a worried or frightened expression

haunt·ing /'hɔntɪŋ/ *adj.* sad but also beautiful and staying in your thoughts for a long time: *a haunting melody* —**hauntingly** *adv.*

haute cou·ture /͵out ku'tur/ *n.* [U] the business of making and selling very expensive and fashionable clothes for women

haute cui·sine /͵out kwɪ'zin/ *n.* [U] cooking of a very high standard, especially French cooking

hau·teur /ho'tɚ, ou'tɚ/ *n.* [U] LITERARY a proud very unfriendly manner

Ha·van·a[1] /hə'vænə/ the capital and largest city of Cuba

Havana[2] *n.* a type of CIGAR made in Cuba

Ha·va·su·pai /͵havə'supaɪ/ a Native American tribe from the southwestern area of the U.S.

have[1] /əv, həv; *strong* hæv/ *auxiliary verb, past tense* **had** *third person singular present tense* **has** *negative short forms* **haven't, hadn't, hasn't** **1** used with the PAST PARTICIPLE of another verb to make the perfect tense of that verb: *I've read the book already.* | *She had lived in Peru for 30 years.* | *I don't think you've been telling me the truth.* **2** used with some MODAL VERBS and a PAST PARTICIPLE to make a past MODAL: *I must have left my wallet at home.* | *You should've been nicer to her.* **3 had better** used to give advice, or to say what is the best thing to do: *You'd better phone Julie to say you'll be late.* | *I'd better not go out tonight; I'm really tired.* **4 have had it** SPOKEN **a)** said when something is so old or damaged that it cannot be used anymore: *It looks like your stereo's had it.* **b)** used to say that someone is tired: *We'd better find a motel – the kids have just about had it.* **c)** used to say that if someone does something, it will cause problems or cause them trouble: *If you press the wrong button, you've had it.* **d) I've had it with sb/sth** said when you are so annoyed by someone or something that you do not want to deal with them any longer: *I've just about had it with you two – be quiet!* **5 had sb done sth** if someone had done something: *Had we known they were going to build a road right there, we would never have bought the house.*

have² /hæv/ *v.* [T not usually in passive]

1 [features/qualities] [not in progressive] used when saying what someone or something looks like, or what qualities or features they possess.: *Ruby has dark hair and brown eyes.* | *The stereo doesn't have a CD player.* | *Teachers need to have a lot of patience.*

2 [own or use] [not in progressive] to own something or to be able to use something: *They used to have three dogs.* | *The school doesn't have room for any more students.* | *Can I have the car tonight, Mom?*

3 have got used instead of "have" to mean "possess": *I've got four tickets to the Twins game on Saturday.*

4 [include/contain] [not in progressive] to include or contain something or a particular number of things or people: *Japan has a population of over 120 million.* | *Our old apartment had a huge kitchen.* | *How many pages does it have?*

5 [eat/drink/smoke] to eat, drink, or smoke: *Why don't you come out and have a beer with us?* | *We had steak for dinner last night.* | *I usually **have lunch** around noon.*

6 [experience/do] to experience something, do something, or be affected by something: *I have a meeting in fifteen minutes.* | *We went to Florida on our vacation and **had a great time**.* | *We've been **having** a lot of **problems** with the new computer system.*

7 [receive] to receive something: *Jenny! You have a phone call!* | *I had three letters from credit card companies this morning.*

8 [in a position/state] [not in progressive] to put or keep something in a particular position or state: *I had my eyes half-closed.* | *Why do you always **have** the TV **on** so loud?*

9 may I have, can I have, I'll have SPOKEN said when politely asking for something: *I'll have two hot dogs to go, please.* | *May I have your name, please?* | *Could we have our ball back?*

10 [sell/make available] [not in progressive] to sell something, or make it available for people to use: *Do you have any single rooms?* | *They didn't have the sweater I liked in my size.*

11 [family/friends etc.] [not in progressive] to know someone, or to be related to someone: *She has an uncle who lives in Wisconsin.* | *Chris has a friend who knows Randy Travis.*

12 [amount of time] [not in progressive] to be allowed a particular amount of time to do something: *You have 30 minutes to finish the test.* | *I wish I had more time to talk to you.*

13 have time if you have time to do something, there is nothing else that you must do at that particular time: *Will you vacuum if you have time?* | [have time to do sth] *Do you have time to come and have a cup of coffee with us?*

14 [disease/injury/pain] [not in progressive] to be sick with a particular illness, or be injured in a particular way: *Sarah has a broken leg.* | *Many older men have high cholesterol.*

15 [idea/thought/feeling] [not in progressive] to think of something, realize something, or experience a particular feeling: *If you have any good ideas for presents, let me know.* | *Survivors have a deep feeling of guilt.*

16 have your hair cut/have your car repaired etc. to employ someone to cut your hair, fix your car etc.: *We're having the house painted this week.* | *I just had it fixed.*

17 have sth ready/done/finished etc. to make something ready to be used, or to finish something: *They should have the car ready by Monday.* | *I'll have it done soon.*

18 [carry with you] [not in progressive] to be carrying something with you: *Do you have your purse?* | *I thought I **had** my keys **with me**, but I must have left them at home.* | *How much cash do you **have on you?***

19 [offer] used in the IMPERATIVE to offer someone something: *Here, Tina, have some popcorn.* | *Please **have a seat** (=sit down), and the doctor will be right with you.*

20 [guests] to be with someone, or be visited by someone: *I'll call back later – I didn't realize you had guests.* | [have sb with you] *Barry had an Australian guy with him.* | *It looks like the Hammills **have company** tonight.*

21 have an effect/influence/result etc. to influence someone or something, or cause a particular effect: *The fall in stock prices could have a disastrous effect.* | [have an effect etc. on sth] *Hungarian folk songs had a great influence on Bartok's music.*

22 have a baby/twins etc. to give birth: *Anna had a healthy baby boy on Tuesday.*

23 [medicine] **have an operation/treatment etc.** to be given an operation, treatment etc. for a medical problem: *She had to have chemotherapy for about nine months.*

24 have a job/position/role etc. if you have a particular job, position etc., it is yours and you are the one who does it: *She has a job as a manager for a printing company.*

25 have a duty/responsibility etc. to be responsible for doing something: *We have a duty to the public to ensure safe food preparation.*

26 have sth stolen/broken/taken etc. if you have something stolen, broken etc., someone steals it etc.: *She had her bike stolen from outside the house.* | *Coffey had his nose broken in the fight.*

27 have a party/concert etc. to hold an event such as a party: *We're having a party on Saturday – do you think you can come?*

28 have the chance/opportunity/honor etc. to be able to do something: *Go see the new Coen brothers movie if you have a chance.* | [have the chance to do sth] *I had the opportunity to work with some of the nation's top designers.* | [have the chance of doing sth] *My mother had the honor of meeting the President when she was in college.*

29 [employ/be in charge of] [not in progressive] to employ or be in charge of a group of workers: *Ahmad has five employees under him.*

30 [hold sb] **have sb by sth** to hold someone violently by a part of their body: *They had him by the throat.*

31 [make sb do sth] [not in progressive] **a)** to make someone start doing something: [have sb doing sth] *Within minutes he had the whole audience laughing and clapping.* **b)** to persuade or order someone to do something: [have sb doing sth] *She had me doing all kinds of jobs for her.* | [have sb do sth] *I'll have the bellboy take up your bags.*

H

SPOKEN PHRASES

32 have nothing against sb/sth, not have anything against sb/sth SPOKEN used to say that you do not dislike someone or something: *I have nothing against Jack personally, I just don't like his line of work.*

33 have it coming used to say someone deserved the bad thing that happened to them: *Tom got grounded for a week, but I guess he had it coming.*

34 have it in for sb/sth to want to harm someone or something: *I swear the garbage collectors have it in for my trash cans.*

35 I've got it used to say you have suddenly thought of the solution to a problem or understand

36 [not allow] **sb can't/won't have sth** used to say that you do not want something to happen or that it would not be good for something to happen: [can't/won't have sb doing sth] *We can't have you walking home alone, it's too late at night.* | *I won't have any kid leaving my class thinking he's stupid.*

37 you have me there also **you've got me there** used to say that you do not know the answer to a question

38 I'll have you know used to start to tell someone something when you are annoyed with them: *I'll have you know I speak six languages.*

39 have sth/sb (all) to yourself to be the only person or people in a place, using something, talking to someone else etc.: *For once I had the house to myself.*

40 have it (that) to say or be told that something is true: *Rumor has it he's going out with Michele.* | *I have it on good authority that Congress will soon debate the issue.*

41 have something against sb to dislike someone for something they have done: *I don't know what it is, but Roger has something against women.*

42 have it in you to have a particular quality, skill, or ability: *Look at Steve dance – I didn't know he had it in him!*

43 do sth a word meaning to do something: *He said it was interesting, so I had a look.* | *Don't worry, I had a shower this morning.*

44 sex [not in progressive] INFORMAL to have sex with someone: *Roy's had more women than he can count.*

45 have done with sth to finish or settle an argument or a difficult situation

  have on [T] **1** [have sth ↔ on] to be wearing a piece of clothing or type of clothing: *Bo had a blue shirt on.* | *Jimmy had nothing on* (=was wearing no clothes) *but his socks.* **2** [have sth on sb] to know about something bad that someone has done: *Do the cops have anything on Jen?* **3 have nothing on sb/sth** to not be nearly as good as someone or something else: *This fried chicken has nothing on my mother's.*

  have sth out *phr. v.* [T] **1 have a tooth/appendix etc. out** to have a tooth etc. removed in a medical operation: *Gwen had her tonsils out when she was nine.* **2 have it out with sb** INFORMAL to settle a disagreement or difficult situation by talking to the person involved, especially when you are angry with them

ha·ven /ˈheɪvən/ *n.* [C] **1** a place where people go to be safe: [+ for] *a haven for refugees* **2** a place where people go because it helps them feel happy: [+ for] *The town is a haven for artists and hippies.*

have-nots /ˈ. ./ *n.* **the have-nots** the poor people in a country or society —see also HAVES

have·n't /ˈhævənt/ *v.* the short form of "have not": *I haven't seen her in five years.*

hav·er·sack /ˈhævɚˌsæk/ *n.* [C] OLD-FASHIONED a bag that you carry on your back

haves /hævz/ *n.* **the haves** the rich people in a country or society: *In America, there is a huge gap between the haves and the have-nots.* —see also HAVE-NOTS

have to /ˈhæftə; *strong* ˈhæftu/ also **have got to** *modal verb* **1** to be forced to do something because someone makes you do it, or because a situation makes it necessary: *You don't have to answer that question.* | *We had to put her in a nursing home.* | *I hate having to get up early.* **2** used when saying that it is important that something happens: *There has to be an end to the violence.* | *You've got to believe me!* | *You'll have to be nice to Aunt Lynn.* **3** used when telling someone how to do something: *First of all, you have to mix the sugar and the butter.* **4** used when saying that you are sure that something will happen or is true: *The price of houses has to go up sooner or later.* | *Mark has to be stuck in traffic – he wouldn't be late otherwise.*

SPOKEN PHRASES

5 used when talking about an annoying event which caused you problems: *Of course it had to happen on a Sunday, when the veterinarian's office is closed.* **6** used when talking about something annoying or surprising that someone does: *Wanda has to have the best.* | *Bobby, do you have to* (=used to ask someone to stop doing something annoying) *keep making that noise?* **7 I have to say/admit/confess** used when speaking honestly about something awkward or embarrassing: *I have to say I don't know anything about computers.*

—see also MUST¹

WORD CHOICE: have to, have got to, must
You can use all of these phrases to talk about what it is necessary to do. Use **have to** to say that something is necessary, and you do not have a choice about it: *I have to study for my test.* | *We have to visit Grandma on Sunday.* **Must** is usually used in more formal writing about something that a government, law, or person in authority says is necessary: *All visitors must report to the office.* | *Children under 16 must be accompanied by a parent or guardian.* Use **have got to** instead of **have to** or **must** in order to emphasize how important something is: *I've got to talk to him today.* In informal speech, we often say **gotta** instead of **have got to**: *I gotta talk to him today.* Don't use **gotta** in written or formal English. The past tense of **have to**, **have got to**, and **must** is **had to**: *I had to talk to him.*

hav·oc /ˈhævək/ *n.* [U] a situation in which there is a lot of confusion or damage: *A strike will cause havoc for thousands of commuters.* | *The whiteflies have been wreaking havoc on* (=causing a lot of damage to) *crops.* | *A poor sugar harvest could play havoc with* (=cause great harm to) *the country's shaky economy.* | *When my sisters visit, their children absolutely create havoc* (=cause confusion and damage).

haw /hɔ/ *interjection* another spelling of HA¹

Ha·wai·i /həˈwaɪ-i/ **1** *written abbreviation* **HI** a U.S. state which consists of eight main islands in the central Pacific Ocean **2** the largest of the islands in the Pacific Ocean that form the U.S. state of Hawaii

Hawaii Stan·dard Time /ˌ..ˌ.. ˈ./ *abbreviation* **HST** *n.* [U] the time that is used in Hawaii

Hawaii Time /ˈ.. ˌ./ *abbreviation* **HT** *n.* [U] another word for HAWAII STANDARD TIME

hawk¹ /hɔk/ *n.* [C] **1** a large wild bird that eats small birds and animals **2** a politician who believes in using military force: *the hawks in the President's cabinet* —opposite DOVE¹ (2) **3 watch sb like a hawk** to watch someone very carefully: *Parents should watch their kids like a hawk for sunburns.* **4 news hawk** a REPORTER **5 have eyes like a hawk** to be quick to notice things, especially small details

hawk² *v.* **1** [T] to try to sell goods by talking about them and usually by carrying them from place to place: *A man on the corner was hawking T-shirts, caps and other souvenirs.* **2 hawk a loogie** SLANG to bring up an amount of PHLEGM (=thick sticky liquid) from your throat with a loud noise, and then SPIT it out

hawk·er /ˈhɔkɚ/ *n.* [C] someone who carries goods from place to place and tries to sell them

hawk-eyed /ˈ. ./ *adj.* quick to notice small details: *hawk-eyed customs officers*

hawk·ish /ˈhɔkɪʃ/ *adj.* supporting the use of military force —**hawkishness** *n.* [U] —opposite DOVISH

hawk-nosed /ˈ. ./ *adj.* having a nose that is large and curves down at the end

Hawks /hɔks/**, How·ard** /ˈhaʊɚd/ (1896–1977) a U.S. movie DIRECTOR

haw·ser /ˈhɔzɚ/ *n.* [C] TECHNICAL a thick rope or steel CABLE used on a ship

haw·thorn /ˈhɔθɔrn/ *n.* [C,U] a small tree that has small white flowers and red berries

Haw·thorne /ˈhɔθɔrn/**, Na·than·iel** /nəˈθænyəl/ (1804–1864) a U.S. writer of NOVELs and short stories

hay /heɪ/ *n.* [U] **1** a type of long grass that has been cut and dried, often used as food for cattle and horses: *a bale of hay* **2 make hay (while the sun shines)** to do something while the conditions are good: *The tourists won't be here forever, so we'd better make hay while the sun shines.* **3 hit the hay** INFORMAL to go to bed **4 sth isn't/ain't hay** HUMOROUS used to say that an amount is large and noticeable, and should not be ignored: *Earning 1 to 2 percent on a $17 billion investment sure ain't hay.* —see also **a roll in the hay** (ROLL² (10))

Hay·dn /ˈhaɪdn/, **Joseph** (1732–1809) an Austrian musician who wrote CLASSICAL music

Hayes /heɪz/, **Helen** /ˈhelən/ (1900–1993) a U.S. actress, famous for appearing in plays and movies

Hayes, Ruth·er·ford /ˈrʌðəfəd/ (1822–1893) the 19th President of the U.S.

hay fe·ver, hayfever /ˈ. ˌ../ n. [U] a medical condition, like a bad COLD, that is caused by breathing in POLLEN (=dust from plants)

hay·loft /ˈheɪlɔft/ n. [C] the top part of a farm building where hay is stored

hay·mak·ing /ˈheɪˌmeɪkɪŋ/ n. [U] the process of cutting and drying hay

hay·ride /ˈheɪraɪd/ n. [C] a ride in a CART filled with hay, usually as part of a social event

hay·seed /ˈheɪsid/ n. [C] INFORMAL someone from a country area, who does not know how to behave in the city —hayseed adj.

hay·stack /ˈheɪstæk/ n. [C] a large, firmly built pile of hay —see also **sth is like looking for a needle in a haystack** (NEEDLE¹ (7))

hay·wire /ˈheɪwaɪə/ adj. **go haywire** INFORMAL to start working in completely the wrong way: *My computer has gone haywire again.*

haz·ard¹ /ˈhæzəd/ n. [C] **1** something that may be dangerous or cause accidents, problems etc.: *Ice on the road is a major hazard at this time of the year.* | [+ **for**] *The small parts pose a choking hazard for small children.* | [**be a hazard to sth**] *Polluted water sources are a hazard to wildlife.* | *The leaves are a* **fire hazard** (=something that may cause a fire). | **health/safety hazard** *The lead in old paints is a real health hazard.* **2** a risk that cannot be avoided: [+ **of**] *One hazard of falling at such high speeds is a friction burn.* | *Burnout seems to be an* **occupational hazard** (=a danger that exists in a job) *for teachers.*

hazard² v. [T] **1** to say something that is only a suggestion or guess: *I don't really know, but I could* **hazard a guess.** **2** FORMAL to risk losing your money, property etc. in an attempt to gain something

hazard light /ˈ.. ˌ./ n. [C usually plural] a special light on a vehicle that flashes to warn other drivers of danger

haz·ard·ous /ˈhæzədəs/ adj. **1** dangerous and likely to harm people's health: [+ **to**] *Smoking is hazardous to your health.* | *Hazardous waste was going into the bay through the sewage system.* **2** involving danger: *a hazardous occupation*

hazard pay /ˈ.. ˌ./ n. [U] the money you are paid for doing dangerous work

haze¹ /heɪz/ n. [singular,U] **1** smoke, dust, or MIST in the air that is difficult to see through: *a haze of cigarette smoke* **2** the feeling of being very confused and unable to think clearly: *The family is in a haze of shock and grief.*

haze² v. [T] to play tricks on a new student or to make them do silly or dangerous things, as part of joining the school or a club at the school —hazing n. [U]

ha·zel¹ /ˈheɪzəl/ adj. hazel eyes are green-brown

hazel² n. **1** [C,U] a small tree that produces nuts **2** [U] the green-brown color of some people's eyes

ha·zel·nut /ˈheɪzəl,nʌt/ n. [C] the nut of the hazel tree

haz·y /ˈheɪzi/ adj. hazier, haziest **1** air that is hazy is not clear because there is a lot of smoke, dust, or mist in it: *Sunny but hazy weather is predicted for the weekend.* **2** not sure or not knowing a lot about something: *The origins of the word are a little hazy.* | [+ **about**] *At City Hall, officials were hazy about the details.* **3** an idea, memory etc. that is hazy is not clear or exact: *Greg's memory of the accident is a little hazy.* —hazily adv. —haziness n. [U]

HBO n. TRADEMARK Home Box Office; a CABLE television company that shows mainly movies

H-bomb /ˈeɪtʃ bɑm/ n. [C] INFORMAL a HYDROGEN BOMB

HCF TECHNICAL the abbreviation of HIGHEST COMMON FACTOR

he /i; strong hi/ pron. [used as subject of a verb] **1** a male person or animal that has already been mentioned or is already known about: *"Does Josh still live in New York?" "No, he moved to Ohio."* | *How old is he?* | *He's* (=he is) *my brother.* **2** used to talk about anyone, everyone, or an unknown person who may be either male or female: *Everyone should do what he considers best.* **3** **He** used when writing about God

---

USAGE NOTE: HE

POLITENESS

He can be used to mean either a man or a woman when the sex of the person in the sentence is not known or does not matter, for example in the sentence *Each person should do what he thinks is best.* Some people, however, do not like using **he** in this way because it seems unfair to women, and they prefer to use **he or she** or, in writing only, **s/he**: *Each person should do what he or she thinks is best.* | *Each person should do what s/he thinks is best.* Many people use **they** instead of **he**, especially in speech and less formal writing: *Each person should do what they think is best.* But other people do not think this is correct, because *each person* is singular and *they* is plural. Often you can avoid the problem by writing the sentence in a different way: *People should all do what they think is best.*

---

he- /hi/ prefix [in nouns] OLD-FASHIONED a male, especially a male animal: *a he-goat*

head¹ /hed/ n.

1 **top of body** [C] the top part of your body that has your eyes, mouth, brain etc. in it: *He turned his head to kiss her.* | *Collins suffered severe head injuries in the accident.* —see picture at BODY

2 **mind** [C] your mind: *Troy's head is just full of ideas* | *I have a picture of what it should be like* **in my head.** | *I can* **do the addition in my head.** | **have a head for figures/facts/business etc.** (=to be good at doing calculations, remembering facts etc.)

3 **leader** [C] the leader or person in charge of a group or organization, or the most important person in a group: *Professor Calder is the department head.* | [+ **of**] *Eileen is head of the family now.* | *The article is about the former head of the FBI, J. Edgar Hoover.*

4 **position** **the head** the top or front of something, or the most important part of it: [+ **of**] *Stuffed animals were lined up at the head of the bed.* | *The bride and groom sat at* **the head of the table.**

5 **on a tool** [C] the widest or top part of something such as a piece of equipment or a tool: *a shower head* | [+ **of**] *the head of a hammer*

6 **plant** [C] the top of a plant where its leaves and flowers grow: *a head of lettuce*

7 **(from) head to foot/toe** over your whole body: *The kids were covered head to foot in mud.*

8 **keep your head above water** to be just barely able to live or keep your business working when you are having money problems: *I work full time, but we're still just keeping our heads above water.*

9 **use your head** to think about something in a sensible or practical way: *If you don't have a splint, use your head and make one.*

10 **come/pop into sb's head** to have an idea suddenly: *The name just popped into my head.*

11 **come to a head** also **bring sth to a head** if a problem or difficult situation comes to a head, or if something brings it to a head, it suddenly becomes worse and you have to do something about it immediately: *The situation came to a head when the workers went out on strike.*

12 **laugh/shout/scream your head off** INFORMAL to laugh, shout etc. very loudly: *Fans were screaming their heads off.*

13 **put your heads together** INFORMAL to discuss a difficult problem together: *The challenge is to put our heads together and think of a new way of working.*

14 **a clear/cool head** the ability to think clearly or calmly in a difficult or dangerous situation: *The situation is tense, and cool heads are needed.*

H

15 can't get sth out of your head INFORMAL to be unable to stop thinking about something: *I couldn't get the tune out of my head.*

16 get/be in over your head to be doing something that is more difficult or risky than you are prepared to do: *New kayakers can easily get in over their heads.*

17 go over sb's head a) to be too difficult for someone to understand: *The more emotional scenes go right over the kids' heads.* **b)** to ask a more important person to deal with something than the person you would normally ask

18 keep/lose your head to remain calm in a difficult or dangerous situation, or to be unable to remain calm: *I just lost my head and started shouting.*

19 can't make head(s) nor tail(s) of sth to be completely unable to understand something: *I couldn't make heads or tails out of the book.*

20 go to sb's head INFORMAL **a)** if success goes to someone's head, it makes them feel more important than they really are: *Dave really let his promotion go to his head.* **b)** to make someone quickly feel slightly drunk: *The wine went straight to my head.*

SPOKEN PHRASES

21 heads up! used to warn people that something is falling from above, or that something is being thrown to them

22 not be right in the head to be mentally ill or crazy: *I think Lizzie's not quite right in the head.*

23 have a good head on your shoulders to be sensible or intelligent

24 get your head together to start behaving in a sensible and responsible way: *I got off drugs and started to get my head together.*

25 have your head screwed on (right/straight) also **keep your head on straight** to be sensible: *Even as a kid, Yolanda had her head screwed on right.*

26 get sth into your head to understand and realize something: *I wish he'd get it into his head that school is important.*

27 sth never entered sb's head used to say that you never thought of something: *It never entered my head that Bruce could steal from the company.*

28 need your head examined to be crazy: *Anybody who believes in UFOs needs their head examined.*

29 heads will roll used to say that some people will be punished severely for something that has happened

30 on your own head be it used to tell someone that they will be blamed if the thing they are planning to do has bad results

31 not bother/trouble your head about sth to not worry about something, because you think it is unimportant or too difficult to understand: *Hale doesn't bother his head about the opinions of strangers.*

32 heads the side of a coin that has a picture of a person's head on it

33 a head of hair a lot of hair on your head: *Roy's full head of hair is mostly gray.*

34 a head/per head for each person: *The meal will cost $7 a head.*

35 keep/put your head down a) to work in a steady and quiet way: *Back then, you didn't complain – you just put your head down and worked.* **b)** to try not to be noticed or not to get involved in something: *When Ali's parents are fighting, he just tries to keep his head down.*

36 have your head in the clouds to not be thinking in a practical or sensible way

37 be head over heels in love to love someone very much: *Sam was obviously head over heels in love with his new bride.*

38 go head to head with sb to deal with someone in a very direct and determined way: *Jim finally went head to head with his boss.*

39 have no head for heights to be unable to look down from high places without feeling nervous

40 beer [C usually singular] the layer of small white BUBBLES on the top of a glass of beer

41 electronics [C] a piece of equipment that changes information on something MAGNETIC, such as a recording TAPE or a computer HARD DISK, into electrical messages that electronic equipment can use

42 head of cattle/sheep etc. a particular number of cows, sheep etc.: *a small farm with 20 head of cattle*

43 be out of your head INFORMAL to not know what you are doing because you have taken illegal drugs or drunk too much alcohol

44 be banging your head against a brick wall to keep trying to do something which seems impossible: *I feel like I'm banging my head against a brick wall.*

45 take it into your head to do sth to suddenly decide to do something that does not seem sensible: *Neil suddenly took it into his head to go to Japan.*

46 turn/stand sth on its head to consider a statement or idea in the opposite way from the way in which it was intended: *"You stand logic on its head when you use arms control as an argument for a larger defense budget,"* Aspin said.

47 be head and shoulders above the rest/others to be much better at something than everyone else

48 give (sb) head VULGAR to perform ORAL SEX on someone

49 infection [C] the white center of a swollen spot on your skin

50 head of water/steam pressure that is made when water or steam is kept in an enclosed space

51 river/stream [C] the beginning of a river or stream —see also **bite sb's head off** (BITE[1] (5)), **bury your head in the sand** (BURY (11)), **eyes pop out (of your head)** (EYE[1] (27)), **hang your head** (HANG[1] (12)), **hold your head up/high** (HOLD[1] (35)), **nod your head** (NOD[1]), **a roof over your head** (ROOF[1] (2)), **shake your head** (SHAKE[1] (3)), **do sth standing on your head** (STAND[1] (16)), **off the top of your head** (TOP[1] (13)), **turn sb's head** (TURN[1] (23))

head[2] *v.*

1 go toward [I,T] to go or make something go in a particular direction: [be headed] *Where are you guys headed?* | [+ for/toward/across etc.] *The boys were headed toward the river.* | *A line of trucks were heading out of town.* | *We were just heading home.* | **head north/south** etc. | *They were going up the hill, heading west.*

2 be in charge [T] also **head up** to be in charge of a government, organization, or group of people: *Most single-parent families are headed by women.* | *The commission was headed up by Barry Kerr.*

3 be heading for sth also **be headed for sth** if you are heading for a situation, it is likely to happen: *You're heading for trouble.*

4 be at the top [T] **a)** to be at the top of a list or group of people or things: *The movie heads the list of Oscar nominations.* **b) be headed** if a page is headed with a particular word or sentence, it has it on the top: *The page was headed "Expenses."*

5 be at the front [T usually passive] to be at the front of a line of people: *The march was headed by the Reverend Martin Luther King.*

6 soccer [T] to hit the ball with your head, especially in SOCCER

head off *phr. v.* **1** [I] to leave to go to another place: *Where are you heading off to?* **2** [T **head** sth ↔ **off**] to prevent something from happening: *The budget agreement headed off some painful spending cuts.* **3** [T **head** sb ↔ **off**] to stop someone from moving in a particular direction by moving in front of them: *The police were able to head off the rioters at a cross street.* **4 head sb off at the pass** HUMOROUS to take action quickly in order to prevent someone from doing something that you do not want them to do: *Evans said her parents tried to head her off at the pass when she dreamed of becoming a star.*

head[3] *adj.* [only before noun, no comparative] most important, or highest in rank: *Knox was head coach of the Seahawks for nine years.* | *Athenour was named manager of the bank's head office in Pleasanton.*

-head /hɛd/ *suffix* [in nouns] **1** the top of something: *a letterhead* (=name and address printed at the top of a letter) **2** the place where something begins; SOURCE: *a fountainhead* (=source of a river or stream)

head·ache /'hɛdeɪk/ n. [C] **1** a pain in your head: *I had a really bad headache and couldn't eat anything.* | **a splitting/pounding headache** (=a very bad headache) **2** INFORMAL an annoying or worrying problem: *Police departments say the new bill will be a headache to enforce.*

head·band /'hɛdbænd/ n. [C] a band that you wear around your head to keep your hair off your face or as a decoration

head·bang·er /'hɛd,bæŋə/ n. [C] INFORMAL someone who enjoys HEAVY METAL music and moves their head around violently to the beat of the music —**headbang** v. [I] —**headbanging** n. [U]

head·board /'hɛdbɔrd/ n. [C] the upright board at the end of a bed where your head is

head·butt /'hɛdbʌt/ v. [T] to deliberately hit someone with your head

head·cheese /'hɛdtʃiz/ n. [U] a food made from pieces of meat from the head of a pig that are boiled and put in GELATIN, then served in thin pieces

head cold /'. ./ n. [C] a COLD that makes it very difficult for you to breathe

head count, headcount /'. ./ n. a count of how many people are present in a particular place at one time

head·dress /'hɛd-drɛs/ n. [C] something that someone wears on their head for decoration on a special occasion: *a feathered headdress*

-headed /hɛdɪd/ [in adjectives] **1** red-headed/gray-headed etc. having red hair, gray hair etc. **2** two-headed/three-headed etc. having two heads, three heads etc.

head·er /'hɛdə/ n. [C] **1** information at the top of a page, especially things such as page numbers that appear on each page in a document **2** information at the beginning of an EMAIL message that shows when it was written or sent, who wrote or sent it etc. **3** a shot in SOCCER made by hitting the ball with your head —see also DOUBLE-HEADER

head·first, head-first /,hɛd'fəst/ adv. **1** moving forward with the rest of your body following your head: *He jumped headfirst through a window.* **2** to start doing something too quickly, without thinking carefully: *Coe dove into the problem headfirst.*

head game /'. ./ n. [C usually plural] INFORMAL something you say or do that makes someone confused and annoyed, because it does not seem sensible to them: *Parlova's advice to women was, "Don't play head games to try to find out the other person's motives."*

head·gear /'hɛdgɪr/ n. [U] hats and other things that you wear on your head

head·hunt·er /'hɛd,hʌntə/ n. [C] **1** someone who finds people with the right skills and experience to do particular jobs **2** a member of a tribe of people who cut off and keep the heads of their enemies —**headhunt** v. [T]

head·ing /'hɛdɪŋ/ n. [C] **1** the title written at the top of a piece of writing **2** a particular direction on a COMPASS, toward which someone is traveling

head·land /'hɛdlənd, -lænd/ n. [C] an area of land that sticks out from the coast into the ocean

head·less /'hɛdlɪs/ adj. without a head: *a headless corpse*

head·light /'hɛdlaɪt/ also **head·lamp** /-læmp/ n. [C usually plural] one of the large lights at the front of a vehicle —see picture on page 427

head·line[1] /'hɛdlaɪn/ n. [C] **1** the title of a newspaper article, printed in large letters above the article: *A supermarket tabloid newspaper had the headline "Space Aliens Meet with the President."* **2** **in the headlines** widely reported in newspapers and on television and radio: *Computer viruses have not been in the headlines lately, but that does not mean they have gone away.* **3** **make/grab (the) headlines** to be widely reported in newspapers and on television and radio: *Woods' success has made headlines nationwide.*

headline[2] v. **1** [T usually passive] to give a headline to an article or story: *The report was headlined "Big Changes at City Hall."* **2** [I,T] to appear as the main

performer in a show: *Frank Sinatra headlined at the Sands Hotel for three consecutive seasons.*

head·lin·er /'hɛdlaɪnə/ n. [C] someone who is the main performer at a show

head·lock /'hɛdlɑk/ n. [C] a way of holding someone around their neck so that they cannot move: *Within seconds, Mangun had immobilized his opponent in a headlock.*

head·long /'hɛdlɔŋ, ,hɛd'lɔŋ/ adv. **1** **rush/plunge headlong into sth** to start doing something too quickly, without thinking carefully about it first: *Stockbrokers should prevent their clients from plunging headlong into trouble.* **2** falling with your head going first and the rest of your body following: *McGuire slid headlong into second base.* —**headlong** adj.

head·man /,hɛd'mæn, 'hɛdmæn/ n. plural **headmen** /-mɛn/ [C] a chief of a small town where a tribe lives

head·mas·ter /'hɛd,mæstə/ n. [C] a PRINCIPAL[2] (1) in a private school

head·mis·tress /'hɛd,mɪstrɪs/ n. [C] a female PRINCIPAL[2] (1) in a private school

head of state /,. . './ n. plural **heads of state** [C] the main representative of a country, such as a queen, king, or president

head-on /,. '. / adv. **1** **meet/crash etc. head-on** if two vehicles meet or hit head-on, the front part of one vehicle comes toward or hits the front part of the other vehicle: *The drivers were killed when their cars crashed head-on in one of the northbound lanes.* **2** if someone deals with a problem head-on, they deal with it in a direct and determined way: *Even companies that had family policies did not address the ethical issues head-on.* —**head-on** adj.: *a head-on collision*

head·phones /'hɛdfoʊnz/ n. [plural] a piece of equipment that you wear over your ears to listen to a radio or recording

headphones

head·piece /'hɛdpis/ n. [C] something you wear on your head

head·quar·tered /'hɛd,kwɔrtəd/ adj. **be headquartered** to have your headquarters at a particular place: *Many top companies are headquartered in northern California.*

head·quar·ters /'hɛd,kwɔrtəz/ n. plural **headquarters** [C] **1** the main building or offices used by a large organization **2** abbreviation **HQ** the place from which military operations are controlled

head·rest /'hɛdrɛst/ n. [C] the top part of a chair or of a seat in a car, airplane etc. that supports the back of your head —see picture on page 427

head·room /'hɛd-rum/ n. [U] the amount of space above your head inside a car or room, in a DOORWAY etc.

head·scarf /'hɛdskɑrf/ n. [C] a square piece of cloth that women wear on their heads, tied under their chin

head·set /'hɛdsɛt/ n. [C] a set of HEADPHONES, often with a MICROPHONE attached

head shop /'. ./ n. [C] INFORMAL a store that sells things that are used for taking illegal drugs, such as pipes

head·stand, head stand /'hɛdstænd/ n. [C] a position in which you turn your body upside down, with your head and hands on the floor and your legs and feet in the air: *Black admitted that he was unable to do a headstand.*

Head Start /,. './ n. a government program for poor children, that helps prepare them to start school

head start /,. './ n. [C usually singular] **1** an advantage that helps you to be successful: *The class gives kids a head start in learning a foreign language.* **2** a

H

start in a race in which you begin earlier or further ahead than someone else

head·stone /'hɛdstoʊn/ n. [C] a TOMBSTONE

head·strong /'hɛdstrɔŋ/ adj. very determined to do what you want, even when other people advise you not to do it: *a headstrong child*

head ta·ble /ˌ. '../ n. [C] a table at a formal meal where the most important people or the people who are going to give speeches sit

head-to-head /ˌ. . '.◂/ adv. directly competing with another person or group: *Courier companies are going head-to-head with the Post Office.* —head-to-head adj.: *head-to-head competition*

head trip /'. ./ n. [C] SLANG an experience that has a strong effect on your mind, as if you had taken a drug: *If Greenaway's last movie had been released in the '60s, it would have been considered the biggest head trip by hippies everywhere.*

head·wait·er, head waiter /ˌhɛd'weɪtɚ/ n. [C] the WAITER who is in charge of the other WAITERS in a restaurant

head·wa·ters /'hɛdˌwɔtɚz/ n. [plural] the place where a stream starts before it flows into a river

head·way /'hɛdweɪ/ n. **make headway a)** to make progress toward achieving something even when it is difficult: [+ toward/in/with etc.] *Foreign firms have made little headway in the U.S. market.* **b)** to move forward: *The ship had trouble making headway because of the storms.*

head·wind /'hɛdˌwɪnd/ n. [C,U] a wind that blows directly toward you when you are moving

head·word /'hɛdˌwɚd/ n. [C] TECHNICAL one of the words whose meaning is explained in a dictionary

head·y /'hɛdi/ adj. **headier, headiest** [usually before noun] **1** very exciting in a way that makes you feel you can do anything: *the heady years of fame* **2** a heady smell, drink etc. is pleasantly strong and seems to affect your senses: *a heady aroma*

heal /hil/ v. **1** [I,T] also **heal up** to make a wound or a broken bone healthy again, or to become healthy again: *A sprain usually takes longer to heal than a broken bone.* **2** [T] to cure someone who is sick: *They believe they have healed themselves using the "power of the mind."* —see Usage Note at CURE[1] **3** [I,T] to return or help someone return to a healthy mental and emotional state after a bad or shocking experience: *We've seen dozens of marriages failed and families healed here at the center.* | *Cassandra says the only way to heal after a rape is to talk about it.* **4 heal the wounds/breach/divisions** to make people stop being angry with each other

    heal over phr. v. [I] if a wound or an area of broken skin heals over, new skin grows over it and it becomes healthy again

heal·er /'hilɚ/ n. [C] someone who is able to have the natural ability to cure people

heal·ing /'hilɪŋ/ n. [U] the process of returning to a healthy mental and emotional state after a bad or shocking experience, or helping someone to do this: *Studies have shown that laughter enhances healing and protects against disease.* | *All I'm doing is sending energy to wake up your own internal processes of healing.* —see also FAITH HEALING

health /hɛlθ/ n. [U] **1** the general condition of your body, and how healthy you are: *Betty's worried about her husband's health.* | *Tyler has some serious health problems.* | *She's 92, but she's in good health.* | *My parents are not in the best of health* (=they are not very healthy). | *Fletcher's so overweight, it can't be good for his health.* **2** the work of providing medical services to keep people healthy: *Most Americans listed unemployment, health, and education as the most important issues.* | *Are you entitled to health insurance at your company?* **3** the state of being without illness or disease: *I wish you health and happiness.* **4** how successful an ECONOMY, business, or organization is: *Nasdaq stocks fell amid*

concerns about the health of dot-com companies. —see also **a clean bill of health** (CLEAN[1] (8))

health care, healthcare /'. ˌ./ n. [U] the service of taking care of people's health and giving them medical treatment: *a health-care plan*

health cen·ter /'. ˌ../ n. [C] **1** a place where college students go to get medical treatment or advice **2** a place where several doctors have their offices, and people can go for medical treatment or advice

health club /'. ./ n. [C] a place where people who have paid to become members can go to exercise

health food /'. ./ n. [C,U] food that contains only natural substances, and that is healthy to eat

health·ful /'hɛlθfəl/ adj. likely to make you healthy: *healthful mountain air*

health main·te·nance or·ga·ni·za·tion /ˌ. '... ...ˌ./ n. [C] an HMO

health spa /'. ./ n. [C] a SPA

health·y /'hɛlθi/ adj. **healthier, healthiest** **1** `person/animal` physically strong and not likely to become sick: *a healthy baby boy* | *I saw Hazel Phillips the other day, and she didn't look very healthy.* **2** `making you healthy` good for your body or your mind: *a healthy diet* | *It's not healthy for Donna to depend on Wayne so much.* | *We need to work toward a healthier environment.* **3** `company/relationship etc.` a healthy company, society, relationship etc. is working effectively and successfully: *Currently, there's a healthy climate for businesses.* | *a healthy marriage* **4** `amount` fairly large or noticeable: *All of our kids have healthy appetites.* | *a healthy profit* **5 a healthy respect/attitude/curiosity etc.** a natural and sensible feeling: *Hikers in the desert need to have a healthy respect for rattlesnakes.* **6** `showing good health` showing that you are healthy: *Her face had a healthy glow.* | *healthy skin* —healthily adv. —healthiness n. [U]

heap[1] /hip/ n. [C] **1** a large messy pile of things: *a compost heap* | [+ of] *a heap of newspapers* | *His clothes lay in a heap on the floor.* —see picture at PILE[1] **2 bottom of the heap** the lowest position in a competition or in the order of something: *MacPherson's excellent playing has lifted the team from the bottom of the heap.* —opposite **top of the heap 3 a heap of sth** also **heaps of sth** SPOKEN a lot of something: *You're going to be in a heap of trouble.* | *Plenty of parents suffer heaps of stress.* **4 fall/collapse/lie etc. in a heap** to fall down and lie without moving: *Mullin was crumpled in a heap after being pushed by Campbell.* **5** HUMOROUS an old car that is in bad condition

heap[2] v. [T] **1** also **heap up** to put a lot of things on top of each other in a messy way: *Piles of garbage were heaped everywhere.* | [heap sth on/onto sth] *Heap the blueberries on top of the filling.* | [be heaped with sth] *The bedroom was heaped with clothes, books, and toys.* **2 heap praise/abuse/criticism etc. on sb** to praise, criticize etc. someone a lot: *School board officials have heaped praise on the school's anti-drug program.* **3 be heaped with sth** if a plate is heaped with food, it has a lot on it

heap[3] adv. **heap big** [only before noun] INFORMAL a phrase meaning "very big" or "a lot of," considered offensive because it is supposed to IMITATE the way some people believed Native Americans spoke English: *We're in heap big trouble.*

heap·ing /'hipɪŋ/ adj. [only before noun] a heaping measurement of food is slightly more than the tool it is being measured with can hold: *Add two heaping tablespoons of cocoa.*

hear /hɪr/ v. past tense and past participle **heard** /hɚd/ **1** `hear sounds/words etc.` [I,T not in progressive] to know that a sound is being made, using your ears: *I love to hear a baby laugh like that.* | *You'll hear a click, and that means it's locked.* | *Sorry, Mary, but I couldn't hear a word you said.* | *Didn't you hear when I called you?* | *Grandma doesn't hear as well as she used to.* | [hear sb/sth doing sth] *I can hear their dog howling.* | [hear sb/sth do sth] *Jill heard him come in after midnight.* | *Williams was heard to say that he thought it would never work.*

Joe can't hear the phone ringing
because he's listening to music.

2 listen to sb/sth [T not usually in progressive] to listen to what someone is saying, the music they are playing etc.: *I heard a great new song on the radio.* | *Jeff, did you hear what I said?* | [hear sb do sth] *We went to hear Todd's band play at Mr. B's.*

3 be told sth [I,T not usually in progressive] to be told or find out a piece of information: *I heard a rumor that Katya was coming back.* | [hear (that)] *I heard they did a lousy job on the roof.* | [+ about] *How did you hear about it?* | hear sth about sb] *It's nice to meet you. I've heard a lot about you.* | [hear what/how/who etc.] *Did you hear what Sammy's latest idea is?* | *I'm glad to hear (that) your mother's feeling better.* | *'Nina quit her job.' "Yeah, so I heard."* (=I was told this information before) | *Hammell said he heard through/on the grapevine* (=found out about something in conversation) *that Payne had had a heart attack.* | *I've heard it said* (=heard people say) *that animals love you unconditionally.*

4 in court hear a case to listen to what is said in a court of law, and make a decision: *The case will be heard on July 16.*

SPOKEN PHRASES

5 (do) you hear (me)? said when you are giving someone an order and want to be certain that they will obey you: *Be home by ten, you hear?*

6 I hear you a) used to say that you understand what someone has told you to do and you will obey them: *"The bottom line is we have to finish on time." "Okay, I hear you."* **b)** used to say that you agree strongly with what someone just said: *"There's just too much junk on TV these days." "Yeah, I hear you."*

7 sb won't hear of it used to say that someone will not do something, even though you think it would be safer or better for them: *I think Clarence should stop driving, but he won't hear of it.*

8 have not heard the last of so used to say that someone or something will cause more problems for you: *I'm going to sue him. He hasn't heard the last of me.*

9 sb will never hear the end of it used to say that someone will criticize or make jokes about something you have done: *Marva cried at the wedding, and her brothers will never let her hear the end of it.*

10 be hearing things to imagine you can hear a sound when really there is no sound: *Oh, you are there. Good, for a second I thought I was hearing things.*

11 I can't hear myself think said when the place where you are is too noisy: *The boys were being so loud I could hardly hear myself think.*

12 you could hear a pin drop used to say that a place was extremely quiet: *You could hear a pin drop in the auditorium during Norvell's speech.*

13 have you heard the one/joke/story about... used when asking someone if they know a joke: *Have you heard the one about the Norwegian and the Swede at the doctor's office?*

14 I heard that! SPOKEN used to say that you strongly agree with what someone has just said: *"Sneakers have sure gotten expensive." "I heard that!'*

15 now hear this! OLD USE used to introduce an important official announcement

16 Hear! Hear! said after a speech or in a meeting when you agree with the person who is speaking

hear from sb *phr. v.* [T not in progressive] **1** to get news or information from someone: *Have you heard from Francis at all?* **2** to listen to someone giving their opinion: *We'll be hearing from the new Vice President for finance at the meeting.*

hear of sb/sth *phr. v.* [T] **have heard of sb/sth** to know that someone or something exists because you have been told about them: *I've heard of Louis de Bernieres, but I've never read anything by him.* | *Have you ever heard of a band called Big Star?* —see also UNHEARD OF

hear sb **out** *phr. v.* [T not in passive] to listen to all of what someone wants to tell you, without interrupting them: *Look, I know you're mad, but at least hear me out.*

USAGE NOTE: HEAR

WORD CHOICE: hear, listen

Use **hear** when you mean that a sound comes to your ears: *I heard loud music coming from the room next door.* Use **listen** when you mean you want to hear something and pay attention to it: *I was listening to music when the phone rang.*

---

hear·er /'hɪrɚ/ *n.* [C] someone who hears something

hear·ing /'hɪrɪŋ/ *n.* **1** [U] the sense which you use to hear sounds: *My hearing isn't as good as it used to be.* —see also HARD OF HEARING **2** [C] a meeting of a court or special committee to find out the facts about a case: *a public hearing* **3 give sb a (fair) hearing** to give someone an opportunity to explain their actions, ideas, or opinions: *Korb was given a fair hearing by the committee.* **4 in sb's hearing** FORMAL if you say something in someone's hearing, you say it where they can hear you: *Don't scold your child in his friends' hearing.*

hearing aid /'.. ../ *n.* [C] a small piece of equipment that you put in or behind your ear to make sounds louder if you cannot hear well

hearing-im·paired /'.. .,./ *adj.* **1** unable to hear well **2 the hearing-impaired** people who are unable to hear well

hear·ken, harken /'hɑrkən/ *v.* [I + to] LITERARY to listen

hear·say /'hɪrseɪ/ *n.* [U] something that you have heard about from other people, but do not know to be true: *Hearsay is not allowed as evidence in court.*

hearse /hɚs/ *n.* [C] a large car used to carry a dead body in a CASKET at a funeral

Hearst /hɚst/**, William Ran·dolph** /'wɪlyəm 'rændɔlf/ (1863–1951) a U.S. businessman who owned many popular newspapers

heart /hɑrt/ *n.*
1 body [C] the part of your body in your chest that pumps blood through your body: *Eating too many fatty foods is bad for the heart.* | *My heart was beating so fast I thought it would burst.* | *He's had heart trouble for years.* —see picture at RESPIRATORY
2 emotions/love [C] the part of you that is able to feel strong emotions such as love: *I knew in my heart that I wouldn't see him again.* | *I was hoping with all my heart that you would win.* | *It would break his heart* (=make him very sad) *to move out of his own home.* | *It broke her heart when Doug left her.* | *The novel takes a dark look at affairs of the heart* (=matters relating to love). | *I believe with my heart and soul that we will overcome this* (=I believe it completely).
3 your chest [C usually singular] the part of your chest near your heart: *Put your hand on your heart and repeat after me.*
4 shape [C] a shape used to represent love —see picture at SHAPE[1]
5 the heart of sth a) the main or most important part of something: *The issue is at the heart of Reddin's campaign.* | *Eckert wants to get to the heart of the problem, so it can be prevented in the*

H

future. **b)** the middle or the busiest part of an area: *The hotel is **in the heart of** the downtown area.*

6 know/learn something by heart to know or learn something so that you can remember all of it correctly: *Tony's watched "Star Wars" so many times he knows all the lines by heart.*

7 at heart if you are a particular kind of person at heart, that is the type of person you really are: *I guess I'm just a kid at heart.* —see also **have sb's (best) interests at heart** (INTEREST¹ (5)), **young at heart** (YOUNG¹ (6))

8 card games **a)** [C] a playing card with one or more red heart shapes on it **b) hearts** [plural] the set of playing cards that have these shapes on them: *the ace of hearts*

9 sing/dance/play etc. your heart out INFORMAL to sing, dance etc. with all your energy

10 tear/rip sb's heart out to make someone feel extremely upset: *It just tears your heart out to see how they live.*

11 from the heart if you say or do something from the heart, you feel it very strongly: *He spoke simply but from the heart.* | *It was a gift from the heart.* | *I want to thank you **from the bottom of my heart**. What she said came **straight from the heart**.*

12 sb's heart sank used to say that someone suddenly lost hope and began to feel sad: *My heart sank when I saw the mess the house was in.*

13 take heart to feel encouraged or have more hope: *Take heart – there are plenty of good vacation spots very close to home.* —opposite **lose hope** (HOPE²)

14 take sth to heart to be listen carefully to what someone says to you, and try to do what they say: *Jack took his father's advice to heart.*

15 do sth to your heart's content/desire to do something as much as you want to: *You can reorganize data files to your heart's content, but don't move the programs around.*

SPOKEN PHRASES

16 not have the heart to do something to be unable to do something because you do not want to make someone unhappy: *I didn't have the heart to tell my daughter we couldn't keep the puppy.*

17 my heart goes out to sb used to say that you feels a lot of sympathy for someone: *My heart just went out to those poor children.*

18 a man/woman after my own heart said when you like someone because they are similar to you: *She loves eating out in restaurants – a woman after my own heart.*

19 my heart stopped also **my heart was in my mouth** used to say that you suddenly felt very afraid: *My heart stopped when I got that phone call.*

20 sb's heart isn't in it used to say that someone does not really want to do something or does not care about what they are doing: *She was doing the best she could, but her heart just wasn't it it.*

21 have a heart! used to tell someone to be nicer or not to be too strict: *Have a heart! I'll never get all that done.*

22 it does sb's heart good to see/hear sth used to say that something makes you feel happy: *It does my heart good to see him running around again.*

23 with all your heart with all your strength, energy, or emotion: *I believed that with all my heart.*

24 sb's heart skips a beat used to say that someone is very excited, surprised, or afraid: *Frank's heart skipped a beat when he heard someone come in.*

25 the heart and soul of sth the most important part of something: *Miller is the heart and soul of the team.*

26 in your heart of hearts if you know, feel, or believe something in your heart of hearts, you are sure about it although you may not admit it: *I know in my heart of hearts that what we're doing is right.*

27 sb's heart is in the right place INFORMAL used to say that someone is really a kind person, even though they may not appear to be: *Mike's a little grouchy sometimes, but his heart's in the right place.*

28 have a heart of gold to have a very nice, generous character, though not seeming nice on the outside: *Watling is a tough guy with a heart of gold.*

29 set your heart on sth also **have your heart set on sth** to want something very much: *He's set his heart on a new bike for Christmas.*

30 have a heart of stone to be very cruel or unsympathetic

31 close/dear to sb's heart very important to someone

32 sb's heart leaped LITERARY used to say that someone suddenly felt happy and full of hope

33 know the way to sb's heart HUMOROUS to know the way to please someone: *What a great meal! You certainly know the way to a man's heart!*

34 vegetable [C] the firm middle part of some vegetables: *artichoke hearts*

35 your heart's desire also **everything your heart could desire** something that someone wants very much —see also **a broken heart** (BROKEN² (9)), **have a change of heart** (CHANGE² (1)), **cross my heart (and hope to die)** (CROSS¹ (10)), **eat your heart out** (EAT (4)), **with a heavy heart** (HEAVY¹ (28)), **sick at heart** (SICK¹ (8)), **strike at the heart of sth** (STRIKE¹ (22)), **wear your heart on your sleeve** (WEAR¹ (8)), **win sb's heart** (WIN¹ (4))

heart·ache /'hɑrteɪk/ *n.* [U] a strong feeling of sadness

heart at·tack /'. .,./ *n.* [C] **1** a serious medical condition in which someone's heart suddenly stops working, either for a short time or permanently: *Marv recently suffered his second heart attack.* **2** SPOKEN a sudden feeling of shock or a frightening experience: *I almost **had a heart attack** when they called my name.* | *You just about **gave me a heart attack** there, Dave.*

heart·beat /'hɑrt˩bit/ *n.* [C,U] **1** the action or sound of your heart as it pumps blood through your body: *A baby's heartbeat is nearly twice as fast as an adult's.* **2 be a heartbeat away from sth** to be very close to a particular position or condition: *The Red Sox are a heartbeat away from the American League championship.* **3 in a heartbeat** very quickly, or without thinking about something first: *If he asked me to marry him, I'd accept in a heartbeat.* **4 the heartbeat of sth** the main origin of activity, interest, or excitement in a place or organization: *Broadway has long been the heartbeat of popular music and the source of countless classics.*

heart·break /'hɑrt˩breɪk/ *n.* [U] a strong feeling of sadness or disappointment: *I still remember the heartbreak of watching my dad suffer from lung cancer.*

heart·break·ing /'hɑrt˩breɪkɪŋ/ *adj.* making you feel very upset, sad, or disappointed: *The story brought back some heartbreaking memories for me.* —**heartbreakingly** *adv.*

heart·bro·ken /'hɑrt˩broʊkən/ *adj.* very sad because someone or something has disappointed you: *Amy was heartbroken when her puppy was lost.*

heart·burn /'hɑrt˩bən/ *n.* [U] a slightly painful burning feeling in your stomach or chest caused by INDIGESTION

heart di·sease /'. .,./ *n.* [U] a medical condition in which a person's heart has difficulty pumping blood

-hearted /hɑrtɪd/ [in adjectives] **kind-/cold-/light-hearted etc.** having a particular type of character: *a kind-hearted woman*

heart·en /'hɑrt˩n/ *v.* [T usually passive] to make someone feel happier and more hopeful: *The administration was heartened by the U.N. vote* —**heartening** *adj.*: *It's very heartening to see more jobs coming to our area.* —**hearteningly** *adv.* —compare DISHEARTENING

heart fail·ure /'. ,../ *n.* [U] the failure of the heart to continue working, which causes death

heart·felt /'hɑrtfɛlt/ *adj.* very strongly felt and sincere: *a heartfelt apology*

hearth /hɑrθ/ *n.* [C] **1** the area of floor around a FIREPLACE in a house **2 hearth and home** LITERARY your home and family: *the joys of hearth and home*

heart·i·ly /ˈhɑrtl-i/ *adv.* **1** loudly and cheerfully: *Ryan laughed heartily.* **2** completely or very much: *I heartily agree with those who say raising children is a demanding job.* **3 eat/drink heartily** to eat or drink a large amount

heart·land /ˈhɑrtlænd/ *n.* [C] **1 the heartland** the central part of a country or area, usually considered to be the place where people live in a way that represents the basic values of that country: *Growing up in the Indiana heartland provided me with a clear sense of what was right and wrong.* **2** the most important part of a country or area for a particular activity, or the part where a political group has most support: *America's industrial heartland*

heart·less /ˈhɑrtlɪs/ *adj.* cruel or not feeling any pity: *Todd's father was cold and heartless.* —**heartlessly** *adv.* —**heartlessness** *n.* [U]

heart-lung ma·chine /ˌ. ˈ. ./ *n.* [C] a machine that pumps blood and oxygen around someone's body during a medical operation

heart rate /ˈ. ./ *n.* [C] the speed at which your heart beats

heart·rend·ing /ˈhɑrtˌrɛndɪŋ/ *adj.* making you feel great pity: *a heartrending sob*

heart·sick /ˈhɑrtˌsɪk/ *adj.* very unhappy or disappointed

heart·strings /ˈhɑrtˌstrɪŋz/ *n.* [plural] **tug/pull at sb's heartstrings** also **play on sb's heartstrings** to make someone feel a lot of pity or love: *Ramona's story of her escape clearly pulled at the heartstrings of many Mexicans.*

heart·throb /ˈhɑrtθrɑb/ *n.* [C] a famous person who many young people feel romantic love for: *teenage heartthrobs*

heart-to-heart /ˌ. . ˈ. ./ *n.* [C] a conversation in which two people honestly express their feelings or opinions about something: *It was time for a heart-to-heart with my daughter.* —**heart-to-heart** *adj.* [only before noun] *a heart-to-heart conversation*

heart·warm·ing /ˈhɑrtˌwɔrmɪŋ/ *adj.* making you feel happy, calm, and hopeful: *a heartwarming holiday story* —**heartwarmingly** *adv.*

heart·wood /ˈhɑrtwʊd/ *n.* [U] the older harder wood at the center of a tree

heart·worm /ˈhɑrtwɔrm/ *n.* [C,U] a type of WORM that lives in the heart of dogs and some other animals, or the condition of having these worms

heart·y /ˈhɑrti/ *adj.* **heartier, heartiest 1** cheerful and friendly, and usually loud: *Garofalo has a hearty, deep voice.* | *a hearty laugh* | *We received a hearty welcome.* **2** a hearty meal or food is satisfying and large: *a hearty split-pea soup* **3** if someone is a hearty EATER or if they have a hearty APPETITE, they eat a lot **4** complete or strong: *Board members expressed their hearty approval for Meyer's plan.* **5** OLD-FASHIONED strong and healthy —**heartiness** *n.* [U] —see also **hale and hearty** (HALE), HEARTILY

heat¹ /hit/ *n.*
1 system in house/building [U] the system in a house or other building that keeps it warm: *The classrooms lack heat and air conditioning.* | *She didn't pay her bills, so they turned off the heat.*
2 the heat the heat that comes from a system to keep a house warm, or from an OVEN or STOVE: *Lower the heat to 250°.* | **Turn the heat up** – *it's too cold in here.*
3 weather [U] very hot weather: *I'm just not used to this kind of heat.* | *The heat in the desert was incredible.*
4 warmth [U] warmth or hotness: *I'm worried the heat from the lamp will melt the cord.* | *Black surfaces absorb heat from the sun.*
5 food [U] a SPICY taste from food, that makes your mouth feel hot: *The chilies gave the sauce some heat.*
6 in the heat of the moment/argument/battle etc. while feeling angry or excited: *In the heat of the moment, I said some things I didn't mean.*
7 take the heat to deal with difficulties in a situation, especially by saying that you are responsible for them: *The coach took the heat from the press over the loss to the Spartans.*

8 take the heat off sb SPOKEN used to say that a situation that was very difficult is not so bad anymore: *I finally finished that project, so that took some of the heat off me.* —opposite **put the heat on sb**
9 be packing heat SLANG to be carrying a gun: *Most everybody around here has been packing heat for years even though the law says you can't.*
10 in heat if a female animal is in heat, her body is ready to have sex with a male
11 in a race [C] one of the parts of a race or competition from which the winners are chosen to compete against each other in the next part
12 if you can't stand the heat, get out of the kitchen used to say that if you cannot deal with problems, criticism, or other difficult things, then you should not become involved —see also DEAD HEAT, WHITE HEAT

heat² *v.* [I,T] to make something become warm or hot: *Heat the milk until it boils.*
heat up *phr. v.* **1** [I,T **heat sth ↔ up**] to become warm or hot, or to make something become warm or hot: *I heated up some leftover spaghetti sauce.* | *An electric stove takes a while to heat up.* **2** [I] if a situation heats up, it becomes more exciting or dangerous, with a lot more activity: *Police and social workers say gang activity is heating up.*
heat sth through *phr. v.* [T] to heat food thoroughly

heat·ed /ˈhitɪd/ *adj.* **1** kept warm by a heater: *a heated swimming pool* **2 heated argument/debate/discussion etc.** an argument etc. in which people become very angry and excited —**heatedly** *adv.*

heat·er /ˈhitɚ/ *n.* [C] a machine that makes air or water hotter: *Did you turn the heater off?* —see picture on page 427

heat ex·haus·tion /ˈ. .ˌ../ *n.* [U] weakness and sickness caused by doing too much work, exercise etc. when it is hot

heath /hiθ/ *n.* [C] an area of open land where grass, bushes, and other small plants grow

hea·then¹ /ˈhiðən/ *adj.* OLD-FASHIONED not related or belonging to the Christian religion or any of the large established religions

heathen² *n.* plural **heathen** [C] **1** OLD-FASHIONED someone who is not a member of the Christian religion or any of the large established religions **2** HUMOROUS someone who refuses to believe in something, or does not know about art, literature etc.

heath·er /ˈhɛðɚ/ *n.* [U] a low plant with small purple, pink, or white flowers, that grows on hills

heat in·dex /ˈ. .ˌ../ *n.* **the heat index** the combination of hot weather and HUMIDITY that makes the weather feel hotter: *The heat index was forecast in the range of 105 to 110 degrees in central Indiana.*

heat·ing /ˈhitɪŋ/ *n.* [U] a system for making a room or building warm: *the heating and air conditioning system*

heat light·ning /ˈ. ˌ../ *n.* [U] LIGHTNING without THUNDER or rain, usually seen in the evenings during hot weather

heat·proof /ˈhitpruf/ *adj.* heatproof material cannot be damaged by heat

heat pump /ˈ. ./ *n.* [C] a piece of equipment that can make a building warmer or cooler by taking heat from one place to another

heat rash /ˈ. ./ *n.* [C,U] painful or ITCHY red marks on someone's skin that are caused by heat

heat-re·sis·tant /ˈ. .ˌ../ *adj.* not easily damaged by heat

heat-seek·ing /ˈ. ˌ../ *adj.* a heat-seeking weapon is able to find and move toward the hot gases from an aircraft or ROCKET and destroy it

heat·stroke /ˈhitstrook/ *n.* [U] fever and weakness caused by being outside in the heat of the sun for too long —compare SUNSTROKE

heat wave /ˈ. ./ *n.* [C usually singular] a period of unusually hot weather, especially one that continues for a long time

heave¹ /hiv/ v.

1 pull/lift [I,T] to pull or lift something very heavy with a lot of effort: [**heave sth onto/into/toward etc. sth**] *Liz heaved the box onto the back of the truck.* | [**heave at/on sth**] *He heaved at the rope.*

2 throw [T] to throw something heavy using a lot of effort: *Joe heaved it over the fence into the alley.*

3 heave a sigh to breathe out loudly, especially because you have stopped worrying about something: *We **heaved a sigh of relief** when it was over.*

4 vomit [I] SLANG to VOMIT: *I think I'm gonna heave.*

5 ocean/ground [I] if the ocean or the ground heaves, it moves up and down with very strong movements: *Suddenly the ground heaved under their feet.*

6 chest [I] if someone's chest heaves, they are breathing very hard: *My chest was heaving with the effort.*

7 heave into sight/view past tense and past participle **hove** LITERARY to appear, especially by getting closer from a distance: *A few moments later a barge hove into view.*

heave to phr. v. past tense **hove to** [I] TECHNICAL if a ship heaves to, it stops moving

heave² n. **1** [C] a strong pulling, pushing, or lifting movement: *With one giant heave, they loaded the sack onto the trailer.* **2 the heaves** an occasion when you are VOMITing: *Shelly had **the dry heaves** (=vomiting with nothing coming out of her mouth).* **3** [U] LITERARY a strong rising or falling movement

heave-ho /ˌ. '.ˌ/ n. [singular] **1 give someone the (old) heave-ho** INFORMAL to end a relationship with someone, or to make someone leave their job **2** OLD-FASHIONED used as an encouragement to people who are pulling something, especially on ships

heav·en /ˈhɛvən/ n. **1** also **Heaven** [singular, not with **the**] according to some religions, the place where God or the gods live and where good people go after they die **2** [U] INFORMAL a very good thing, situation, or place: *The new kitchen is heaven compared to the old one.* | *Star Trek fans were **in heaven** today at the Science Fiction Convention.* | *The fresh crab was so good **I thought I'd died and gone to heaven**.* **3 the heavens** LITERARY the sky

---
SPOKEN PHRASES

4 for heaven's sake also **for heaven sakes a)** said when you are annoyed or angry: *Where was the kid's mother, for heaven's sake?* **b)** used to emphasize a question or request: *For heaven's sake, don't tell him my age!* **5 (Good) Heavens!** also **Heavens above, Heavens to Betsy!** OLD-FASHIONED said when you are surprised or slightly annoyed: *Good Heavens, what a mess!* **6 heaven forbid** used to emphasize that you hope something will not happen: *Heaven forbid you should have an accident!* **7 heaven knows** SPOKEN **a)** used to say that you do not know and cannot imagine what is happening or what will happen: *Heaven knows what the true unemployment rate is.* **b)** used to emphasize what you are saying: *Heaven knows, plenty of children need more attention.* **8 heaven help sb** used to say that something will cause problems or be dangerous if it happens: *Heaven help us if it snows again.* **9 what/how/why etc. in heaven's name...?** used when asking a surprised and angry question: *Where in heaven's name have you been?*
---

10 the heavens opened LITERARY it started to rain very hard **11 move heaven and earth** to try very hard to achieve something —see also **be in seventh heaven** (SEVENTH¹ (2)), **thank God/goodness/heaven(s)** (THANK (3))

heav·en·ly /ˈhɛvənli/ adj. **1** OLD-FASHIONED very beautiful or enjoyable: *What a heavenly sound!* **2** [only before noun] BIBLICAL existing in or belonging to heaven: *a heavenly choir of angels* | *Pray to our **heavenly Father** (=God).* | *The **Heavenly Host** (=all the angels) were praising God.* **3** LITERARY existing in or relating to the sky or stars

heavenly bod·y /ˌ... '..ˌ/ n. [C] LITERARY a star, PLANET, or the moon

heaven-sent /'.. ,./ adj. happening luckily at exactly the right time: *a heaven-sent opportunity*

heav·en·ward /ˈhɛvənwəd/ also **heavenwards** adv. LITERARY toward the sky

heav·i·ly /ˈhɛvəli/ adv. **1** a lot or in large amounts: *It's been raining heavily all day.* | *She's been drinking heavily recently.* | *Street gangs are often **heavily armed** (=they have a lot of guns).* **2** very or very much: *The air is heavily polluted.* | *Fifty houses were heavily damaged in the hurricane.* | *The southern region is heavily dependent on tourism.* **3** if you sleep heavily, you cannot be woken easily: *Joe slept heavily for eight hours.* **4 breathe heavily** to breathe slowly and loudly **5 heavily built** having a large broad body that looks strong **6** if you do or say something heavily, you do it slowly and with a lot of effort, especially because you are sad or bored: *He was walking heavily, his head down.*

heav·y¹ /ˈhɛvi/ adj. **heavier, heaviest**

1 weight weighing a lot: *My hiking boots are too heavy.* | *This camera is heavier, but the quality of the lens is worth the weight.* | ***How heavy** is the package?* (=how much does it weigh?) —opposite LIGHT² (2)

2 fat person used to politely describe someone who is fat: *Brian's gotten very heavy since we last saw him.* | *Myra's at least fifty pounds heavier than she used to be.* —see Usage Note at FAT¹

3 a lot unusually large in amount or quantity: *The traffic was heavier than normal and I was late for work.* | *Roads were closed due to the **heavy snow**.* | *Illegal parking carries a **heavy fine** (=you will have to pay a lot of money).* | *Most insurance companies suffered **heavy losses** (=they lost a lot of money) last year.*

4 heavy smoker/drinker someone who smokes a lot or drinks a lot of alcohol

5 heavy accent if someone speaks with a heavy accent, it is difficult to understand what they say because they use the sounds of their own language when they are speaking a different language: *Ricky's mother has a heavy Spanish accent.*

6 a heavy load/burden/responsibility etc. a problem or situation that is large or difficult to deal with: *Stephanie has a heavy load at school this quarter.* | *Food and rent put a heavy burden on a needy family's budget.*

7 clothes etc. clothes, jewelry, or shoes that are heavy are large, thick, and solid: *a heavy winter coat*

8 needing physical effort needing a lot of physical strength and effort: *heavy manual work*

9 needing mental effort very complicated or serious and needing a lot of mental effort: *I want something to read on vacation – nothing too heavy.* | *a heavy discussion*

10 be heavy on sth INFORMAL to use a lot or too much of something: *The car's pretty heavy on oil.*

11 busy a day etc. in which you have a lot to do in a short time: *I had a pretty **heavy day** at the office.*

12 heavy sleeper someone who does not wake easily

13 heavy breathing a) breathing that is slow and loud: *I could hear Carl's heavy breathing coming from the bedroom.* **b)** the act of breathing loudly while on the telephone, in order to frighten someone: *The calls were filled with heavy breathing and dirty language.*

14 food solid or containing a lot of fat, and making your stomach feel full and uncomfortable: *a heavy meal* | *heavy bread* | *heavy cream*

15 body/face having a large, broad, or thick appearance that is unattractive: *a large, heavy-featured woman* | *Kyle is a tall man with a **heavy build** (=a large broad body).*

16 heavy sky/clouds LITERARY looking dark and gray, as though it will rain soon

17 with force hitting something or falling with a lot of force or weight: *There was a sound of heavy footsteps in the hall.* | *Ali caught him with a heavy blow to the jaw.*

18 ground soil that is heavy is thick and solid

19 air too warm and with no wind: *the damp heavy atmosphere of the rainforest*

20 **smell** strong and usually sweet: *a heavy fragrance* | [+ **with**] *The garden was heavy with the scent of summer.*

21 **guns/equipment** [only before noun] large and powerful: *tanks and heavy weaponry* | *The ship was carrying a lot of heavy equipment to Alaska.*

22 **relationship** INFORMAL involving serious or strong emotions: *She didn't want things to get too heavy at such an early stage in their relationship*

23 **heavy date** a very important DATE that is likely to involve romantic or sexual activity

24 **heavy silence/atmosphere** a situation in which people feel sad, anxious, or embarrassed: *A heavy silence fell upon the room.*

25 **heavy seas** big waves on the surface of the ocean: *The ship went down in heavy seas off the coast of Scotland.*

26 **a heavy cold** a very bad cold

27 **be heavy with fruit/blossom etc.** LITERARY if trees are heavy with fruit etc. they have a lot of fruit etc. on them

28 **with a heavy heart** LITERARY feeling very sad: *It was with a heavy heart that Kate kissed her children goodbye.*

29 **heavy irony/sarcasm** remarks that very clearly say the opposite of what you really feel

30 **have a heavy foot** INFORMAL to drive too fast

31 **serious/worrying** SLANG a situation that is heavy makes you feel that people are very angry or have very strong feelings: *It was a pretty heavy scene.* —**heaviness** *n.* [U]

heavy² *adv.* **1** **time hangs/lies heavy on your hands** if time hangs or lies heavy on your hands, it seems to pass slowly because you are bored or have nothing to do **2** **be heavy into sth** SPOKEN, NONSTANDARD to be very involved in an activity, especially one that is not good for you: *Eric was real heavy into drugs for a while.*

heavy³ *n.* plural **heavies** [C] **1** a bad male character in a play or movie; VILLAIN **2** INFORMAL [usually plural] a large strong man who is paid to protect someone or to threaten other people

heavy-du·ty /ˌ.. '..◂/ *adj.* [no comparative] **1** heavy-duty materials are strong and thick and not easily damaged: *heavy-duty plastic garbage bags* **2** heavy-duty machines or equipment are designed to be used for very hard work **3** INFORMAL said when you want to emphasize how complicated, serious etc. someone or something is: *The bathroom needs a heavy-duty cleaning job.* | *a heavy-duty conversation*

heavy-hand·ed /ˌ.. '..◂/ *adj.* **1** strict, unfair, and not considering other people's feelings: *Penn has been criticized for his heavy-handed style of management.* **2** done in an awkward way: *Irving's new novel contains too much heavy-handed symbolism.* —**heavy-handedly** *adv.* —**heavy-handedness** *n.* [U]

heavy-heart·ed /ˌ.. '..◂/ *adj.* LITERARY very sad

heavy hit·ter /ˌ.. '../ *n.* [C] INFORMAL **1** someone or a company that has a lot of power, especially in business or politics: *The issue has drawn the attention of some of Hollywood's heavy hitters.* **2** a baseball player who hits the ball very hard —**heavy-hitting** *adj.*

heavy in·dus·try /ˌ.. '../ *n.* [C,U] industry that produces large goods such as cars and machines, or materials such as coal, steel, or chemicals —compare LIGHT INDUSTRY

heavy-lad·en /ˌ.. '..◂/ *adj.* LITERARY **1** carrying or supporting something very heavy **2** having many worries or problems

heavy-lid·ded /ˌ.. '..◂/ *adj.* [only before noun] having EYELIDS that seem to hang down over the eyes: *heavy-lidded eyes*

heavy met·al /ˌ.. '../ *n.* **1** [U] a type of ROCK music with a strong beat that is played very loudly on electric GUITARS **2** [C] TECHNICAL a very DENSE metal, especially one that is poisonous, such as MERCURY or LEAD³ (1)

heavy pet·ting /ˌ.. '../ *n.* [U] OLD-FASHIONED sexual activities that do not involve actually having sex

heavy-set /ˌ.. '..◂/ *adj.* someone who is heavy-set is large and looks strong or fat

H

heavy wa·ter /ˌ.. ˌ../ *n.* [U] a special type of water that is used in NUCLEAR REACTORS

heav·y·weight /ˈhɛviˌweɪt/ *n.* [C] **1** someone or a company that is important and that has a lot of power and experience in a particular business or job: *He was compared to Proust and other literary heavyweights.* | *political heavyweights* **2** someone who BOXES or WRESTLES in the heaviest weight group —**heavyweight** *adj.* [only before noun] *a heavyweight boxer*

He·bra·ic /hɪˈbreɪ-ɪk/ *adj.* relating to the Hebrew language or people: *Hebraic literature*

He·brew /ˈhibru/ *n.* **1** [U] the language traditionally used by the Jewish people **2** [C] a member of the Jewish people, especially in ancient times —**Hebrew** *adj.*

He·brews /ˈhibruz/ a book in the New Testament of the Christian Bible

heck /hɛk/ *interjection* INFORMAL **1** said to emphasize a question or statement: *It was **a heck of a** story.* | **who/what/where etc. the heck** *Who the heck was that?* | *What the heck was the name of that street?* **2** said when you are annoyed: *Aw, heck, I can't do this.* | *I had **a heck of a** time finding Jay's house.* **3** **what the heck!** said when you do something you probably should not do: *"Want another piece of pie?" "Sure, what the heck."* **4** **hard/funny/cold etc. as heck** said to emphasize what you are saying: *It was August, so of course it was as hot as heck outside.* **5** **for the heck of it** for no particular reason or purpose, or only for fun: *Let's go in and take a look around just for the heck of it.* **6** **run/work/hurt etc. like heck** to run, work etc. very quickly or very much: *We just shut the door and ran like heck.*

USAGE NOTE: HECK, HELL

POLITENESS
Heck is used in many of the same expressions as **hell** and means the same thing, but it is less strong. People often use **heck** in these expressions when they do not like to swear or when they do not want to offend anyone: *My back hurts like heck.* | *What the heck is going on here?*

---

heck·le /ˈhɛkəl/ *v.* [I,T] to interrupt and try to embarrass someone who is speaking or performing in public —**heckler** *n.* [C] —**heckling** *n.* [U]

heck·uv·a /ˈhɛkəvə/ *adj.* INFORMAL a way of spelling "heck of a" to show how it sounds when it is spoken; used to emphasize how big, good, bad etc. something is: *That was a heckuva storm last night.*

hec·tare /ˈhɛktɛr/ *n.* [C] a unit for measuring an area of land, equal to 10,000 square meters or 2.471 ACRES

hec·tic /ˈhɛktɪk/ *adj.* very busy or full of activity, and often slightly exciting: *It's been a pretty hectic week.* | *a hectic social life* —**hectically** /-kli/ *adv.*

hecto- /ˈhɛktoʊ, hɛktə/ *prefix* 100 times a particular unit of measurement: *a hectometer* (=100 meters)

hec·tor /ˈhɛktɚ/ *v.* [I,T] FORMAL to speak to someone in an angry, threatening way: *Brooks had hectored employees who refused to work overtime.* —**hectoring** *adj.*: *Several people were upset by Lubetkin's hectoring tone.*

he'd /id; *strong* hid/ **1** the short form of "he had": *He'd never been a very good dancer.* **2** the short form of "he would": *I'm sure he'd drive you there.*

hedge¹ /hɛdʒ/ *n.* [C] **1** a row of small bushes or trees growing close together, used as a border around a yard or between two yards —see picture on page 423 **2** something that helps avoid problems, losing a lot of money etc.: [+ **against**] *In the 1970s, officials kept water in storage as a hedge against droughts.*

hedge² *v.* **1** to avoid giving a direct answer to a question: [+ **of**] *Nunn hedged on the question of whether he might run for the presidency.* **2** **hedge your bets** to reduce your chances of failing or losing money by trying several different possibilities instead of one: *It's a good idea to hedge your bets by applying to more than one college.*

hedge against sth *phr. v.* [T] to try to protect yourself against possible problems, especially financial loss: *Any well-managed business will hedge against financial loss.*

hedge sb/sth **in** *phr. v.* **be hedged in a)** to be surrounded or enclosed by something: *They had a beautiful yard hedged in by hydrangeas.* **b)** if you feel hedged in by something, you feel that your freedom is restricted by it

hedge·hog /'hɛdʒhɑg, -hɔg/ *n.* [C] a small brown European animal whose body is round and covered with sharp needle-like hairs

hedge·row /'hɛdʒroʊ/ *n.* [C] LITERARY a line of bushes or small trees growing along the edge of a field or road

hed·on·ist /'hɛdn-ɪst/ *n.* [C] someone who believes that pleasure is the most important thing in life —**hedonism** *n.* [U] —**hedonistic** /ˌhɛdn'ɪstɪk/ *adj.*

hee·bie-jee·bies /ˌhibi 'dʒibiz/ *n.* **give sb the heebie-jeebies** INFORMAL to make someone feel nervous

heed[1] /hid/ *v.* [T] FORMAL to pay attention to someone's advice or warning: *Homeowners are heeding the advice of mortgage lenders.*

heed[2] *n.* [U] FORMAL **pay/take heed** to pay attention to something and seriously consider it: *Until Hoover, American presidents paid no heed to economic crises.* | *Congress has taken heed of voter dissatisfaction.*

heed·less /'hidlɪs/ *adj.* FORMAL not paying attention to something important: [+ of] *The country's leaders seem heedless of the possible consequences.*

hee-haw /'hi hɔ/ *n.* [C] the sound made by a DONKEY

s w
3
heel[1] /hil/ *n.* [C]
1 [foot] the back part of your foot —see picture at BODY
2 [shoe] the raised part of a shoe that is under the back of your foot: *Mary found a pair of black pumps with three-inch heels and silver buckles.* —see picture at SHOE[1]
3 heels [plural] a pair of women's shoes with high heels: *I just can't walk in heels.*
4 [hand] the raised part of your hand, near your wrist: *Using the heel of your hand, press the dough firmly into shape.*
5 [sock] the part of a sock that covers your heel
6 on the heels of sth very soon after something: *Often one storm will come on the heels of another.*
7 be on/at sb's heels a) to be following closely behind someone: *The dog trotted happily at Troy's heels.* **b)** to be close behind someone in a competition, election, race etc.: *Canseco is close on Fielder's heels, with 35 home runs this season to Fielder's 36.*
8 bring sb to heel FORMAL to force someone to behave in the way that you want them to: *Snelling's aim was to bring politicians to heel by limiting their ability to impose taxes.*
9 take to your heels LITERARY to start running as fast as possible: *The boys jumped down and took to their heels.*
10 turn/spin on your heel to suddenly turn away from someone, especially in an angry or impolite way: *Seifert turned on his heels and stomped away in anger.*
11 under the heel of sb/sth completely controlled by a government or group: *The country is once more under the heel of a dictator.*
12 [bad man] OLD-FASHIONED a man who behaves badly toward other people —see also ACHILLES' HEEL, **cool your heels** (COOL[1] (4)), **dig in your heels** at **dig in** (DIG[1]), **be hard on sb's heels** (HARD[2] (8)), **be head over heels in love** (HEAD[1] (37)), **be hot on sb's heels** (HOT (21)), **kick up your heels** at **kick up** (KICK[1]), WELL-HEELED

heel[2] *v.* **1 heel!** SPOKEN used to tell your dog to walk next to you **2** [T] to put a heel on a shoe

heel over *phr. v.* [I] LITERARY if something heels over, it leans to one side as if it is going to fall: *The ship was heeling over in the wind.*

-heeled /hild/ [in adjectives] **high-heeled/low-heeled** etc. high-heeled or low-heeled shoes have high or low heels —see also WELL-HEELED

heft[1] /hɛft/ *n.* [U] **1** someone or something's weight, or how heavy they are: *The glasses have more heft than an ordinary glass.* **2** someone's influence or power: *Schwarzenegger lent his heft to help open Planet Hollywood.*

heft[2] *v.* [T] **1** to lift something heavy: *Young men hefted the 110-pound sacks of potatoes into a truck.* **2** to lift something or hold it in your hand in order to judge how heavy it is

heft·y /'hɛfti/ *adj.* **heftier, heftiest 1** big, heavy, or strong: *a hefty slice of apple pie* | *Ivers is a big woman, six feet tall and hefty.* **2** a hefty amount of something such as money is very large: *He gets paid a pretty hefty salary.* | *a hefty fine* —**heftily** *adv.*

He·gel /'heɪgəl/, **Ge·org Wil·helm Frie·drich** /ˈgeɪɔrg ˈvɪlhɛlm ˈfridrɪk/ (1770–1831) a German PHILOSOPHER

he·gem·o·ny /hɪ'dʒɛməni, -'gɛ-, 'hɛdʒə,moʊni/ *n.* [U] a situation in which one state or country controls others

He·gi·ra, Hejira /'hɛdʒərə, hɪ'dʒaɪrə/ *n.* **the Hegira** the escape of Mohammed from Mecca to Medina in A.D. 622

Hegira cal·en·dar /ˌ... '..., ˌ... '.../ *n.* [singular] the Muslim system of dividing a year of 354 days into 12 months and starting to count the years from the Hegira

Hei·deg·ger /'haɪdɪgɚ/, **Mar·tin** /'mɑrt⌐n/ (1889–1976) a German PHILOSOPHER

heif·er /'hɛfɚ/ *n.* [C] a young cow that has not yet given birth to a CALF (=baby cow) —compare OX, STEER[2]

heigh-ho /ˌhaɪ 'hoʊ, ˌheɪ-/ *interjection* OLD-FASHIONED used when you have to accept something that is boring, or to show that you are surprised or excited

height /haɪt/ *n.* **1** [C,U] **a)** how tall someone is: s w
Sam's about my height, I guess. | *You have to be a* ⊟
certain height to get on some of the rides. | *When I'm* 3 3
wearing heels I'm the same height as he is. **b)** the distance between the base and the top of something: *Sunflowers can grow to a height of fifteen feet.* | *Some of the pyramids are over 200 feet in height.* —see picture at LENGTH **2** [C] a particular distance above the ground: *It's a miracle she didn't break her neck falling from that height.* | *A small plane can fly at a height of about 10,000 feet.* **3 heights** [plural] places that are a long way above the ground: *I'm afraid of heights.* | *You have to have a head for heights* (=not be afraid of high places) *to be a rock climber.* **4 heights** [plural] a particular high place: *the Golan Heights* **5 the height of** sth the part of a period of time that is the busiest, hottest etc., or when there is the most activity: *We wanted to avoid the height of the tourist season.* | *The defense budget is higher than it was at the height of the Cold War.* **6 new heights a)** a higher level of achievement or success than anyone has ever reached before: *Jones has reached new heights in the world of music.* | *The restaurant takes the humble meatloaf to new heights.* **b)** a greater level or degree than anyone has ever reached before: *Stock market prices jumped to new heights Tuesday.* **7 be at the height of your success/fame/powers etc.** to be at the time when you are most successful, famous etc.: *What a tragedy that Kennedy was killed at the height of his political career.* **8 be the height of fashion/stupidity/luxury etc.** to be extremely fashionable, stupid etc.: *Baseball caps, especially worn backwards, are the height of fashion on college campuses.* **9 gain/lose height** if an aircraft gains height or loses height, it moves higher in the sky or drops lower in the sky: *The plane was rapidly losing height.*

height·en /'haɪt⌐n/ *v.* [I,T] to increase or make something become increased, especially a feeling or effect; INTENSIFY: *Increased levels of fat in the diet could heighten the risk of cancer.* | *Trade tends to be protected when international tensions heighten.* | *This case should heighten the nation's awareness of the problem of sexual harassment.*

H

Heim·lich ma·neu·ver /ˈhaɪmlɪk məˌnuvɚ/ *n.* [C usually singular] a method of stopping someone from choking (CHOKE¹ (1)) or food, in which you stand behind them, put both your hands on the upper part of their stomach, and press suddenly toward a higher position in order to force the food out of their throat

hei·nie /ˈhaɪni/ *n.* [C] HUMOROUS the part of your body that you sit on; BUTT

hei·nous /ˈheɪnəs/ *adj.* **1** FORMAL very shocking and immoral: *a heinous crime* **2** SLANG extremely bad: *The food in the cafeteria is pretty heinous.* —**heinously** *adv.* —**heinousness** *n.* [U]

Heinz /haɪnz/**, Henry** (1844–1919) a U.S. food MANUFACTURER who started the H.J. Heinz Company

heir /ɛr/ *n.* [C] **1** someone who will legally receive or has received money, property etc. from someone else after that person's death: *Henry died a year ago, and his heirs sold the ranch.* | *[+ to] She's the heir to a department store fortune* (=her family made a lot of money running department stores). **2** the person who will take over a position or job after you, or who does things or thinks in a similar way: *Reagan's political heirs*

heir ap·par·ent /ˌ. .ˈ.../ *n.* [C] **1** an heir whose right to receive the family property, money, or title cannot be taken away **2** someone who seems very likely to take over a job, position etc after a particular person: *Huston is considered the governor's political heir apparent.*

heir·ess /ˈɛrɪs/ *n.* [C] a woman who will legally receive or has received a lot of money, property, etc. after the death of an older member of her family

heir·loom /ˈɛrlum/ *n.* [C] a valuable object that has been owned by a family for many years and that is passed from the older members to the younger members

Hei·sen·berg /ˈhaɪzənˌbɚg/**, Wer·ner** /ˈvɛrnɚ/ (1901–1976) a German PHYSICIST who studied the behavior of atoms, and is best known for developing the UNCERTAINTY PRINCIPLE

heist /haɪst/ *n.* [C] an act of robbing something very valuable from a store, bank etc.: *a jewelry heist* —**heist** *v.* [T]

He·ji·ra /ˈhɛdʒərə, hɪˈdʒaɪrə/ *n.* another spelling of HEGIRA

held /hɛld/ *v.* the past tense and past participle of HOLD¹

Hel·e·na /ˈhɛlənə/ the capital city of the U.S. state of Montana

Hel·en of Troy /ˌhɛlən əv ˈtrɔɪ/ the wife of the Menelaus, the king of Sparta, in ancient Greek stories, who was famous for her great beauty

hel·i·cop·ter /ˈhɛlɪˌkɑptɚ/ *n.* [C] a type of aircraft with large metal blades on top that spin very fast to make it fly —**helicopter** *v.* [I,T]

helicopter pad /ˈ.... ˌ./ *n.* [C] a helipad

he·li·o·trope /ˈhiliəˌtroup/ *n.* **1** [C] a plant that has nice-smelling pale purple flowers **2** [U] a pale purple color

hel·i·pad /ˈhɛləˌpæd/ *n.* [C] an area where HELICOPTERS can land, either on the ground or on top of a building

hel·i·port /ˈhɛləˌpɔrt/ *n.* [C] a small airport for HELICOPTERS

hel·i·ski·ing /ˈhɛliˌskiɪŋ/ *n.* [U] the sport of flying a HELICOPTER to a place in the mountains where you can SKI on deep snow that no one else has skied on

he·li·um /ˈhiliəm/ *n.* [U] *symbol* **He** a gas that is an ELEMENT and that is lighter than air, often used in order to make BALLOONS float

he·lix /ˈhiliks/ *n.* [C] TECHNICAL a line that curves and rises around a central line; SPIRAL —see also DOUBLE HELIX

he'll /ɪl, il, hɪl; *strong* hil/ the short form of "he will": *Mike called to say he'll be late this morning.* | *He'll do it, don't worry.*

hell /hɛl/ *n.*
1 when you die also **Hell** [singular, not with *the*] the place where bad people will be punished after death, according to some religions

2 bad situation [singular,U] INFORMAL, IMPOLITE a situation, experience, or place that is very bad: *Traffic was hell this morning.* | *The prison was like hell on earth.*

3 suffering [singular,U] INFORMAL, IMPOLITE a place or situation in which people suffer very much, either physically or emotionally: *War is hell.* | *My dad had a drinking problem that put my mother through hell.* | *The last two and a half weeks have been a living hell.* | *There are some wonderful mothers-in-law, but others can make your life hell.*

4 the sth from hell INFORMAL, IMPOLITE something that is the worst you can imagine: *At the time, she was going through the divorce from hell.* | *It was the vacation from hell.*

5 all hell broke loose INFORMAL, IMPOLITE used to say that a situation suddenly becomes very bad, disorganized, or violent: *When a fan jumped onto the stage, all hell broke loose.*

SPOKEN PHRASES

6 how/what/where etc. the hell? IMPOLITE used to emphasize your question, especially when you are very surprised or angry: *Where the hell have you been? You were supposed to be home two hours ago!* | *What the hell are you talking about?*

7 emphasize IMPOLITE used to emphasize a statement: *Well, hell, I don't know.* | *We lost every game, but hell, I slept well anyway.* | "*Are you working late tonight?*" "*Hell, no!*"

8 a/one hell of a sth IMPOLITE said to emphasize that something or someone is very big, very good, very bad etc.: *Ray's a hell of a salesman.* | *She's drinking a hell of a lot these days.* | *It was one hell of a party.*

9 to/the hell with sb/sth IMPOLITE an impolite way of saying that you do not care about something or someone any longer: *The hell with the rules, I'm going to do it anyway.* | *If he's going to be mean, to hell with it, I'm going home.*

10 go to hell! IMPOLITE an impolite phrase said when you are very angry with someone: *Don't answer the phone – he can go to hell!*

11 hard/funny/cold etc. as hell IMPOLITE said to emphasize what you are saying: *It was hard as hell to hear anything he was saying.*

12 for the hell of it IMPOLITE for no particular reason or purpose, or only for fun: *There's nobody out there, those dogs are barking just for the hell of it.*

13 run/work/hurt etc. like hell IMPOLITE to run, work etc. very quickly or very much: *My foot hurt like hell – it was all I could do to stand up.*

14 give sb hell IMPOLITE **a)** to tell someone angrily that they should not have done something: *My mom gave him hell, told me to never say things like that in front of us again.* **b)** Give him/them/'em hell! used to tell someone to use a lot of effort and try very hard to defeat an opponent

15 get the hell out (of somewhere) IMPOLITE to leave a place quickly and suddenly: *Tell Amy to get the hell out of my house.*

16 look/feel like hell IMPOLITE to feel or look very sick or tired: *I had a fever and I looked like hell.*

17 beat/irritate/scare etc. the hell out of sb IMPOLITE to beat, irritate etc. someone very much: *Dylan got lost in the woods, and it scared the hell out of him.*

18 what the hell! IMPOLITE said when you decide to do something and not worry about any problems it causes: *Okay, I'll bet $10 on the Cowboys, what the hell.*

19 the/like hell IMPOLITE said when you do not believe what someone has said, or when you disagree with it: "*I won't tell, I swear.*" "*The hell you won't.*" (=I think you will tell someone)

20 raise hell IMPOLITE to have fun in a loud and annoying way: *The kids can go in the den and raise hell without bothering us.*

21 go to hell in a handbasket IMPOLITE if a system or organization is going to hell in a handbasket, it does not work well anymore and is getting worse:

The education system in this state has gone to hell in a handbasket.

22 come hell or high water IMPOLITE in spite of any problems or difficulties: *I said I'd do it, so I will, come hell or high water.*

23 there'll be hell to pay IMPOLITE used to say that someone will be very angry: *If he doesn't do it on time, there'll be hell to pay.*

24 catch hell IMPOLITE to be blamed or punished: *That boy's going to catch hell when he gets home.*

25 hell on wheels IMPOLITE someone who does exactly what they want and does not care what happens as a result: *Sean is an angelic little baby, but Sara is hell on wheels.*

26 when/until hell freezes over IMPOLITE used to say that something will never happen, or will continue forever: *Jeff can keep waiting until hell freezes over, but I won't go back to him.*

27 run/go hell for leather OLD-FASHIONED to run as fast as possible

28 hell's bells OLD-FASHIONED said to express annoyance or surprise —see also **like a bat out of hell** (BAT¹ (3)), **not have a snowball's chance in hell** (SNOWBALL¹ (2)) —see Usage Note at HECK

hel·la /ˈhɛlə/ *adv.* SPOKEN, SLANG very or really: *That movie was hella cool.*

hel·la·cious /hɛˈleɪʃəs/ *adj.* SPOKEN used to emphasize that something is very good, bad etc.: *He used to have some hellacious parties out there.*

hell-bent /ˌ ˈ ◂/ *adj.* INFORMAL **be hell-bent on (doing) sth** very determined to do something without worrying about what happens to you: *Carlos is hell-bent on becoming a star.*

hell·cat /ˈhɛlkæt/ *n.* [C] INFORMAL a woman who becomes angry or violent very easily

Hel·lene /ˈhɛlin/ *n.* [C] LITERARY a Greek, especially an ancient Greek

Hel·len·ic /hɛˈlɛnɪk, hə-/ *adj.* relating to the history, society, art etc. of the ancient Greeks

Hel·ler /ˈhɛlɚ/, **Joseph** (1923–1999) a U.S. writer of NOVELS

hell·hole, hell hole /ˈhɛlhoʊl/ *n.* [C] a very dirty, ugly, and disgusting place: *How did you survive for so long in that hell hole of an apartment?*

hell·ish /ˈhɛlɪʃ/ *adj.* INFORMAL extremely bad or difficult: *five hellish months in the prison* —**hellishly** *adv.*

Hell·man /ˈhɛlmən/, **Lil·li·an** /ˈlɪliən/ (1905–84) a U.S. writer of plays

hel·lo /həˈloʊ, hɛˈloʊ, ˈhɛloʊ/ *interjection* **1** used when meeting or greeting someone: *Hello! How are you doing?* | *Tonight when Sarah calls I'll tell her you said hello.* | *Well, hello there Mr. Walker.* **2** used when answering the telephone or starting a telephone conversation: *Hello, may I speak to Terry, please?* **3** used when calling to get someone's attention: *Hello! Is anybody home?* **4** used when you think someone is not acting sensibly or has said something stupid: *You really thought she would just give you the money? Hello?* **5 say hello** to have a quick conversation with someone: *She just called to say hello.*

hell·uv·a /ˈhɛləvə/ *adj.* SPOKEN, IMPOLITE **a/one helluva...** used to emphasize that someone or something is very good, bad, big etc.: *a helluva nice guy* | *We gave them one helluva fight.*

helm /hɛlm/ *n.* **1 at the helm a)** in charge of something: *In a decade and a half at the helm, O'Neil transformed the company's image.* **b)** guiding a ship or boat **2** [C] the wheel or TILLER which guides a ship or boat **3** [C] OLD USE a helmet

hel·met /ˈhɛlmɪt/ *n.* [C] a hard hat that covers and protects your head —see also CRASH HELMET, PITH HELMET

hel·met·ed /ˈhɛlmɪtɪd/ *adj.* wearing a helmet

helms·man /ˈhɛlmzmən/ *n. plural* **helmsmen** /-mən/ [C] someone who guides a ship or boat

help¹ /hɛlp/ *v.*
1 people [I,T] to make it possible or easier for someone to do something: *If there's anything I can do to help, just give me a call.* | [help sb] *Don't you think we should all try to help each other?* | [help sb (to) do sth] *Les is going to come and help us set up the computer.* | [help (to) do sth] *Would you mind staying afterward to help clean up?* | [help (sb) with sth] *I'm helping with the Mardi Gras Ball this weekend.*
2 situations [I,T] to make a situation better, easier, or less painful: *Crying's not going to help.* | [it helps to do sth] *It helps to have some knowledge of the terms used.* | [help sth] *The money from increased tourism would help the economy.*
3 sb can't help (doing) sth also **sb can't help but do sth** used to say that someone is unable to change their behavior or feelings, or to prevent themselves from doing something: *I can't help it. I hear that song and I have to dance.* | *Ron can't help the way he feels about her.* | *I can't help wondering what happened to that little girl.* | *You talk to the guy for five minutes, and you can't help but like him.*
4 help sb move [T always + adv./prep.] to help someone move to a particular place, especially because they are old, sick, or hurt: [help sb into/up/across/off etc.] *Can you help me up, please?*
5 help sb on/off with sth to help someone put on or take off a piece of clothing: *Let me help you on with your coat.*

SPOKEN PHRASES

6 Help (me)! used to call people and ask them to help you when you are in danger
7 sb can't help it (if) used to say that someone is not responsible for something bad, difficult, or annoying: *I can't help it if Bill doesn't like me.*
8 I can't help thinking (that) said when giving an opinion that you are not happy about: *I can't help thinking I've made a very big mistake.*
9 sb can't help themselves to be unable to stop yourself from doing something you should not do: *I can't help myself – I've become obsessed with the man.*
10 help yourself (to sth) a) a phrase meaning to take something that you want, such as food, without asking permission, used especially in commands: *Go ahead and help yourselves to a drink.* **b)** INFORMAL to steal something: *She helped herself to some money she found lying around.*
11 it can't be helped used to say that there is nothing you can do to change a bad situation: *It's not an ideal solution, but it can't be helped.*
12 not if I can help it used to say that you will try very hard to avoid doing something or to prevent something from happening: *"Are you going to stay very long?" "Not if I can help it."*
13 so help me (God) used when making a serious promise, especially in a court of law —see also **God help sb (if...)** (GOD (14))

help out *phr. v.* **1** [I,T] to help someone who is busy by doing some of their work for them: *We're thinking of hiring a couple of people to help out in the store.* | [help sb ↔ out] *Carol started helping Mom out when I moved away.* **2** [T help sb ↔ out] to give help and support to someone who has problems: *It's an organization that helps out people in need.*

USAGE NOTE: HELP (v.)

WORD CHOICE: help, assist, give sb a hand
Help and **assist** are both used about what someone does to make it easier for someone else to do a job. However, **assist** is a more formal word, and suggests that the person assisting is doing the easier or less important parts: *I was employed to assist the manager in his duties.* If you **give somebody a hand**, you help them do something, especially by using your hands: *Can you give me a hand with the drinks?* This is an informal use.
GRAMMAR
Help can be followed by a verb in the *to* form or the basic form: *Ollie helps his brothers milk the cows* (or *...to milk the cows*). But after **can't help...** meaning "cannot stop yourself," the following verb is in the *-ing* form: *I couldn't help laughing* (NOT *to laugh*).

help² n. **1** [U] things you do to make it easier or possible for someone to do something: *I really want to thank you for all your help.* | [+ **with**] *Do you need some help with the stroller?* | *Ted's always willing to* **give help** *even without being asked.* | *She screamed at them to go and* **get help. 2** [singular,U] the fact of being useful or making something easier to do: *Kelly hasn't been much help either.* | *We got it open* **with the help of** *a knife.* | **be a big/great/real help** *I think those picture dictionaries are a real help.* **3** [U] a part of a computer program that helps someone using it by giving additional information **4** [U] advice, treatment, information, or money which is given to people who need it: *a plea for help* | *A lot of these children need professional help.* **5** [singular] also **the help** someone's servant or servants: *It's hard to get good help these days.*

USAGE NOTE: HELP (n.)

WORD CHOICE: help, assistance, aid
If you give **help** to someone, you do something or give them something that makes a job easier for them, improves their situation etc.: *Do you want some help moving those boxes?* **Assistance** is a more formal word, used especially to talk about help that is the easier or less important part of a job: *The governor has called for federal assistance to deal with flood damage.* | *Let me know if I can be of further assistance.* **Aid** is used to talk about food, money, medicine etc. given to countries or people that need them because they are poor or have serious problems: *Government aid cannot solve all the area's problems.*

---

help desk /'. ./ n. [C] a department of a company that other workers call for help with computer problems they are having

help·er /'helpɚ/ n. [C] someone who helps another person or does this as a job: *We have three student helpers in the office this semester.*

help·ful /'helpfəl/ adj. **1** providing useful help in making a situation better or easier: [**it is helpful to do sth**] *Sometimes it's helpful to make a list of everything you have to do.* | *Here's a* **helpful hint** *for how to chop onions without crying.* **2** willing to help *a helpful child* | *I'm sure Mr. Gleason was only trying to be helpful.* —**helpfully** adv. —**helpfulness** n. [U]

help·ing¹ /'helpɪŋ/ n. [C] the amount of food that you are given or that you take; SERVING: *He took a huge helping of potatoes.*

helping² adj. **a helping hand** help that you give to someone, especially someone who really needs it: **lend/give/extend a helping hand** *He's always ready to lend a helping hand to those in need.*

helping verb /'.. ,./ n. [C] TECHNICAL an AUXILIARY VERB

help·less /'helplɪs/ adj. **1** unable to take care of yourself or to do anything to help yourself: *I hate the thought of helpless animals being killed.* | *Doctors are rendered helpless by the lack of supplies.* | [**helpless to do sth**] *He feels helpless to change his behavior.* **2** unable to control a strong feeling that you have: [+ **with**] *We rolled on the floor, helpless with laughter.* —**helplessly** adv. —**helplessness** n. [U]

help·line /'helplaɪn/ n. [C] a telephone number that you can call if you need advice or information

help·mate /'helpmeɪt/ also **help·meet** /'helpmit/ n. [C] LITERARY a helpful partner, usually a wife

Hel·sin·ki /hel'sɪŋki, 'helsɪŋki/ the capital and largest city of Finland

hel·ter-skel·ter /ˌheltɚ'skeltɚ/ adj. adv. done in a disorganized, confusing, and hurried way: *a helter-skelter production system* | *The pillows were piled helter-skelter on the unmade bed.*

hem¹ /hem/ n. [C] the edge of a piece of a cloth that is turned under and sewn down, especially the lower edge of a skirt, pants etc.

hem² v. **hemmed, hemming 1** [T] to turn under the edge of a piece of material or clothing and sew it in place **2 hem and haw** to keep pausing before saying something, and avoid saying it directly: *Floyd hemmed and hawed when he was asked to introduce himself.*

---

hem sb ↔ **in** phr. v. [T usually passive] **1** to surround someone closely, in a way that prevents them from moving: *They were hemmed in by steep mountains on all sides.* **2** to make someone feel that they are not free to do what they want to do: *Employees don't want to be hemmed in by a bunch of regulations.*

he-man /'. ./ n. [C] HUMOROUS a strong man with powerful muscles

he·ma·tol·o·gy /ˌhimə'tɑlədʒi/ n. [U] the scientific study of blood

Hem·ing·way /'hemɪŋ-ˌweɪ/, **Er·nest** /'ɚnɪst/ (1899–1961) a U.S. writer famous for his NOVELs and short stories that are written in a simple and direct style

Ernest Hemingway

hem·i·sphere /'hemə,sfɪr/ n. [C] **1** one of the halves of the Earth, especially the northern or southern parts above and below the EQUATOR: *the Northern hemisphere* —see also WESTERN HEMISPHERE **2** TECHNICAL one of the two halves of your brain **3** TECHNICAL half of a SPHERE (=an object which is round like a ball)

hem·line /'hemlaɪn/ n. [C] the bottom edge of a dress, skirt, or pants, used especially when talking about their length: *The knee-length hemline has become very popular this fall.*

hem·lock /'hemlɑk/ n. [C,U] a very poisonous plant, or the poison that is made from it

hemo- /himoʊ, himə/ prefix relating to blood: *hemorrhage* (=an occasion when you bleed too much)

he·mo·glo·bin /'himə,gloʊbɪn/ n. [U] a red substance in the blood that contains iron and carries oxygen

he·mo·phil·i·a /ˌhimə'fɪliə, -'filyə/ n. [U] a serious disease that usually affects only men, which prevents the blood from becoming thick, so that they lose too much blood after being cut or wounded

he·mo·phil·i·ac /ˌhimə'fɪliæk/ n. [C] someone who suffers from hemophilia

hem·or·rhage /'hemərɪdʒ/ n. [C,U] a serious medical condition in which a person bleeds a lot, often inside the body

hem·or·rhoid /'hemə,rɔɪdz/ n. [C usually plural] a painfully swollen BLOOD VESSEL at the ANUS

hemp /hemp/ n. [U] a type of plant that is used to make rope, strong cloth, and the drug CANNABIS

hen /hen/ n. [C] **1** an adult female chicken **2** a fully grown female bird

hence /hens/ adv. FORMAL **1** [sentence adverb] used to show that what you are about to say is a result of what you have just said: *In "The Young Slave" the jealous stepmother turns the main character into a slave, hence the story's title.* **2 ten days/two weeks/ six months etc. hence** ten days, two weeks etc. from now: *The concert will be broadcast two months hence.* **3** OLD USE from this place

hence·forth /'hensfɔrθ, ,hens'fɔrθ/ also **hence·for·ward** /hens'fɔrwɚd/ adv. FORMAL from this time on: *Henceforth, death row inmates will have an automatic right to appeal.*

Jimi Hendrix

hench·man /'hentʃmən/ n. plural **henchmen** /-mən/ [C] DISAPPROVING someone who faithfully obeys a powerful person such as a politician or a criminal

Hen·drix /'hendrɪks/, **Jim·i** /'dʒɪmi/ (1942–1970) a U.S. musician and singer who played the GUITAR in a completely new way, and was known for his exciting performances

hen·house /'hɛnhaʊs/ n. [C] a small building where chickens are kept

hen·na /'hɛnə/ n. [U] a reddish-brown substance used to change the color of hair or to DYE the skin —**henna** v. [T]

hen·pecked /'hɛnpɛkt/ adj. a man who is henpecked is always being told what to do by his wife, and is afraid to disagree with her: a henpecked husband

Hen·ry /'hɛnri/, **John** a character in American stories and FOLK SONGS who worked on railways and was very strong

Henry, O. (1862–1910) a U.S. writer of short stories, whose real name was William Sydney Porter

Henry, Pat·rick /'pætrɪk/ (1736–1799) a U.S. politician who was one of the leaders of the fight for independence during the Revolutionary War

Henry V, King /ˌhɛnri ðə 'fɪfθ/ (1387–1422) a king of England who is remembered especially for defeating the French at the Battle of Agincourt

Henry VIII, King /ˌhɛnri ði 'eɪtθ/ (1491–1547) a king of England, who had six wives and made himself the head of the Church in England. This started the Reformation in England, in which the Protestant Church was established.

hep /hɛp/ adj. OLD-FASHIONED: see HIP[3]

he·pat·ic /hɪ'pætɪk/ adj. [only before noun] TECHNICAL relating to your LIVER

hep·a·ti·tis /ˌhɛpə'taɪtɪs/ n. [U] a disease of the LIVER that causes fever and makes the skin yellow. There are several types of hepatitis: hepatitis A, which is less severe, and hepatitis B and C which are much more serious

Hep·burn /'hɛpbən/, **Kath·arine** /'kæθrɪn/ (1907–) a U.S. movie and theater actress, known for appearing as strong, brave, and determined characters

He·phaes·tus /hɪ'fɛstəs/ in Greek MYTHOLOGY, the god of fire and METALWORK, who made weapons for the gods

hep·ta·gon /'hɛptəˌgɑn/ n. [C] a shape with seven sides —**heptagonal** /hɛp'tægənl/ adj.

Katharine Hepburn

hep·tath·lon /hɛp'tæθlɑn, -lən/ n. [singular] a women's sports competition involving seven running, jumping, and throwing events —compare DECATHLON, PENTATHLON

her[1] /ə; strong hə/ possessive adj. [possessive form of "she"] **1** belonging to or relating to a woman, girl, or female animal that has been mentioned or is known about: Maria locked her keys in the car. | This will be her first appearance on Broadway. **2** OLD-FASHIONED relating to a country, ship, or car that has been mentioned: Her top speed is about 110 miles an hour.

her[2] pron. [object form of "she"] **1** a woman, girl, or female animal that has been mentioned or is known about: Where did you meet her? | There's a picture of her in here. | I owe her $25. **2** OLD-FASHIONED a country, ship, or car that has been mentioned: God bless this ship and all who sail in her.

He·ra /'hɛrə, 'hɪrə/ in Greek MYTHOLOGY, the goddess of women and marriage. She was the wife of Zeus.

Her·a·cli·tus /ˌhɛrə'klaɪtəs/ (6th–5th century B.C.) a Greek PHILOSOPHER

Her·a·kles /'hɛrəˌkliz/ the Greek name for the HERO Hercules

her·ald[1] /'hɛrəld/ v. [T] FORMAL **1** to be a sign of something that is going to come or happen soon: The sound of bagpipes heralded the return of the hometown hero. **2** to be heralded as sth to be publicly called good or important: She has been heralded as one of the country's finest musicians. —see also MUCH-HERALDED

herald[2] n. [C] **1** someone who carried messages from a ruler in past times **2** a sign that something is soon going to happen: [+ of] The tiny green shoots are a herald of spring.

he·ral·dic /hɛ'rældɪk, hə-/ adj. relating to heraldry: heraldic banners

her·aid·ry /'hɛrəldri/ n. [U] COATS OF ARMS and other family SYMBOLS, or the study or skill of making them

herb /əb/ n. [C] a small plant that is used to improve the taste of food, or to make medicine

her·ba·ceous /hə'beɪʃəs, ə'beɪ-/ adj. TECHNICAL herbaceous plants have soft stems rather than wood-like stems

herb·al /'əbəl/ adj. made of or relating to herbs: herbal tea | herbal remedies

herb·al·ist /'əbəlɪst, 'hə-/ n. [C] someone who grows, sells, or uses herbs to treat illness

herbal med·i·cine /ˌ.. '.../ n. **1** [U] the practice of treating illness using plants **2** [C,U] medicine made from plants

herb gar·den /'. ˌ../ n. [C] a garden in which only HERBS are grown

her·bi·cide /'həbəˌsaɪd, 'ə-/ n. [C,U] TECHNICAL a substance used to kill unwanted plants

herb·i·vore /'həbəˌvɔr, 'əbə-/ n. [C] TECHNICAL an animal that eats only plants —**herbivorous** /hə'bɪvərəs/ adj. —compare CARNIVORE, OMNIVORE

Her·cu·le·an, herculean /ˌhəkyu'liən‹, hə'kyuliən/ adj. needing great strength or determination: The company closed despite Herculean efforts to keep going.

Her·cu·les /'həkyəˌliz/ in Roman MYTHOLOGY a HERO known for his very great strength and for performing twelve very difficult and dangerous jobs known as the Labors of Hercules

herd[1] /həd/ n. [C] **1** a group of animals of one kind that lives and feeds together: [+ of] a herd of elephants —compare FLOCK[1] (1) **2** DISAPPROVING a group of people that do the same thing or go to the same place: Most economists and investment advisers run in a herd.

herd[2] v. **1** [T always + adv./prep.] to move people together in a large group, especially roughly: [herd sb into/through etc.] Police officers herded the protesters onto the school football field. **2** [T] to make animals move together in a group: Cowboys rounded up the steers and herded them north.

herd men·tal·i·ty /'. .ˌ.../ n. [C usually singular] an attitude or way of thinking in which people decide to do things because other people are doing them

herds·man /'hədzmən/ n. plural **herdsmen** /-mən/ [C] a man who takes care of a herd of animals

here[1] /hɪr/ adv. **1** in or to the place where you are or where you are pointing: Ken was supposed to be here at ten. | Let's eat here. | Come here for a minute. | How far is Denver from here? | I'm afraid I'm not from around here. | We're over here! | Show me your evidence right here and now. | out/in here It's so cold in here. —compare THERE[2] (1) **2** at this point in time: If we win this game, it should be pretty easy from here. | Spring is here! **3** at this point in a situation or discussion: The real question here is whether he is qualified for the job. **4** here and there scattered around in several different places: Sprigs of parsley were tucked here and there around the chicken. **5** the here and now the present time: You need to live in the here and now and stop worrying about the future. **6** here to stay if something is here to stay, it has become a part of life and will continue to be so: Are video games a fad, or are they here to stay? **7** sb/sth is here to do sth used to say what someone or something's duty or purpose is: We're here to serve you.

8 here is sth also **here it is a)** said when you are giving something to someone, or showing something to them: Here's your twenty dollars. | Here are some pictures of our trip to Utah. **b)** said when you have found something you were looking for: *Have you seen my glasses? Oh, here they are.* **9 sb/sth is here** used to say that someone or something has arrived: *Mr. Nichols, your client is here to see you.* | *Is the mail here yet?* **10 here we go a)** also **here we go again** said when something bad or annoying is beginning to happen again: *"I still don't see why you blame me!" "Oh great, here we go again."* **b)** said when you are starting to do something or move in a particular direction: *Let's do that again. Ready? Here we go.* **11 here I am** said to tell someone where you are when they are looking for you: *"Mindy, where are you?" "Here I am, Mommy!"* **12 here you go/are** said when you are giving something to someone: *Here you go – four cappuccinos and a hot chocolate.* **13 here he/she etc. is** said when you have found someone you were looking for, or when someone you were waiting for arrives: *Here you are! We've been looking all over for you.* **14 here comes sb** also **here he/she etc. comes** said when you can see something or someone arriving: *Here comes your mother – be quiet!* **15 here he/she etc. is (doing sth)** used to describe the present situation, especially one you did not expect to happen: *A year ago we didn't know anything about business, and now here we are running our own company.* | *Here I am, 69 years old with no money in the bank.* **16 here we are a)** said when you have finally arrived somewhere you were traveling: *Here we are home again!* **b)** also **here we go** said when you have found something that you were looking for: *I know I read it somewhere... Here we go! It's at the bottom of page 78.* **17 here's to sb** said when you are going to drink something to wish someone good luck, show your respect for them etc.: *Here's to the happy couple.* **18 this book here/these shoes here etc.** used to talk about the book, shoes etc. that you are pointing at: *This little switch here controls the lights.* **19 here goes (nothing)** also **here we go** said when you are going to try something that is exciting or dangerous and you do not know what will happen: *O.K. Here goes. Stand back everyone.*

—see also **be neither here nor there** (NEITHER³ (3))

here² *interjection* used when you are giving or offering something to someone: *Here, have some more pineapple.* | *Here, let me help you with that.*

here·a·bouts /ˈhɪrəˌbaʊts, ˌhɪrəˈbaʊts/ *adv.* INFORMAL somewhere near the place where you are: *Where can a person get a good pastrami sandwich hereabouts?*

here·af·ter¹ /ˌhɪrˈæftɚ/ *adv.* **1** [sentence adverb] FORMAL from this time or in the future: *I have a feeling that life for me in Japan hereafter will be quite different.* **2** LAW in a later part of a legal document

hereafter² *n.* **the hereafter** a life after death: *They believed they would meet again in the hereafter.*

here·by /ˌhɪrˈbaɪ, ˈhɪrbaɪ/ *adv.* LAW as a result of this statement: *I hereby submit my resignation, effective immediately.*

he·red·i·tar·y /həˈrɛdəˌtɛri/ *adj.* **1** a hereditary mental or physical quality, or disease is passed to a child from the GENES of their parents: *Some forms of deafness are hereditary.* **2** a hereditary position, rank, or title can be passed from an older to a younger person in the same family, usually when the older one dies

he·red·i·ty /həˈrɛdəti/ *n.* [U] the process of passing on mental and physical qualities from a parent's GENES to a child

here·in /ˌhɪrˈɪn/ *adv.* FORMAL in this place, situation, document etc.: *Certain events and characters portrayed herein have been fictionalized.* —compare THEREIN

here·in·af·ter /ˌhɪrɪnˈæftɚ/ *adv.* LAW later in this official statement, document etc.: *Any license granted may be revoked as hereinafter provided.*

here·of /ˌhɪrˈʌv/ *adv.* FORMAL OR LAW relating to this —compare THEREOF

her·e·sy /ˈhɛrəsi/ *n. plural* **heresies** [C,U] **1** a belief that disagrees with the official principles of a particular religion: *He spent his life defending the Catholic faith against heresy.* **2** HUMOROUS a belief, statement etc. that disagrees with what a group of

people believe to be right: *It's heresy to consider changing the rules of baseball.*

her·e·tic /ˈhɛrəˌtɪk/ *n.* [C] someone who is guilty of heresy: *Joan of Arc was condemned as a heretic and burned at the stake.* —**heretical** /həˈrɛtɪkəl/ *adj.*

here·to /ˌhɪrˈtu/ *adv.* FORMAL to this: *My notes are attached hereto for the use of the reader.*

here·to·fore /ˌhɪrtəˈfɔr, ˈhɪrtəˌfɔr/ *adv.* FORMAL before this time: *The four-volume set includes old favorites as well as heretofore unreleased material.*

here·up·on /ˌhɪrəˈpɑn, ˈhɪrəˌpɑn/ *adv.* FORMAL at or after this moment

here·with /ˌhɪrˈwɪθ, -ˈwɪð/ *adv.* FORMAL with this letter or document: *I enclose herewith two copies of the contract.*

her·it·age /ˈhɛrətɪdʒ/ *n.* [singular,U] the traditional beliefs, values, customs, etc. of a family, country, or society: *Looking at these paintings makes people proud of their Latin heritage.*

her·maph·ro·dite /hɚˈmæfrəˌdaɪt/ *n.* [C] a living thing that has both male and female sexual organs —**hermaphrodite** *adj.* —**hermaphroditic** /hɚˌmæfrəˈdɪtɪk/ *adj.*

Her·mes /ˈhɚmiz/ in Greek MYTHOLOGY, the god who is the MESSENGER of the gods. He is usually shown in pictures with wings on his shoes and on his HELMET

her·met·i·cally /hɚˈmɛtɪkli/ *adv.* TECHNICAL **hermetically sealed** very tightly closed so that air cannot get in or out —**hermetic** *adj.*

her·mit /ˈhɚmɪt/ *n.* [C] someone who prefers to live far away from other people, usually for religious reasons —compare RECLUSE

her·mit·age /ˈhɚmɪtɪdʒ/ *n.* [C] a place where a hermit lives or has lived

hermit crab /ˈ.. ˌ./ *n.* [C] a type of CRAB that lives in the empty shells of other sea creatures

her·ni·a /ˈhɚniə/ *n.* [C,U] a medical condition in which an organ pushes through the skin or muscles that cover it

he·ro /ˈhɪroʊ/ *n. plural* **heroes** [C] **1** someone who is admired for doing something extremely brave: *Conway returned home, hailed as a hero of the war.* | *one of America's national heroes* **2** someone, especially a man or boy, who is the main character in a book, movie, play etc.: *The hero of the story is a young soldier.* **3** someone who is admired very much for a particular skill or quality etc.: *sports heroes* | **your/my/her etc. hero** *The convention gave Mike a chance to meet his political hero in person.* **4** a SANDWICH made of a long LOAF of bread filled with meat, cheese etc. —see also HEROINE

He·rod·o·tus /hɪˈrɑdətəs/ (485?–425 B.C.) a Greek writer of history

he·ro·ic /hɪˈroʊɪk/ *adj.* **1** extremely brave or determined, and admired by many people: *Soldiers made heroic efforts to get all the civilians out of the city.* | *Mandela grew to heroic stature as he remained in prison.* **2** a heroic story, poem etc. has a hero in it, usually from ancient LEGENDS **3 on a heroic scale** or **of heroic proportions** very large or great: *a battle on a heroic scale* | *The story of Ennis' life was a drama of heroic proportions.* —**heroically** /-kli/ *adv.*

heroic cou·plet /ˌ... ˈ../ *n.* [C] TECHNICAL a pair of lines in poetry which end with the same sound and have five main beats in each line

he·ro·ics /hɪˈroʊɪks/ *n.* [plural] brave actions or words, often ones that are meant to seem impressive to other people: *The Bears' last-minute heroics energized the crowd of 57,000.*

her·o·in /ˈhɛroʊɪn/ *n.* [U] a powerful illegal drug that people usually take by putting it into their arms with a special needle: *a heroin addict*

her·o·ine /ˈhɛroʊɪn/ *n.* [C] **1** the woman or girl who is the main character in a book, movie, play etc.: *The novel's heroine, Kate Lee, is born in the South at the turn of the century.* **2** a woman who is extremely brave and is admired by many people: *a heroine of the French Resistance* **3** a woman you admire very much for her intelligence, skill etc. —see also HERO

her·o·ism /'hɛroʊˌɪzəm/ *n.* [U] very great courage: *He won the Medal of Honor for heroism in Vietnam.*

her·on /'hɛrən/ *n.* [C] a large bird with very long legs and a long beak, that lives near water

hero wor·ship /'.. ,../ *n.* [U] DISAPPROVING great admiration for someone you think is very brave, good, skillful etc., when other people think that the person does not deserve so much admiration —**hero-worship** *v.* [T]

her·pes /'hɚpiz/ *n.* [U] a very infectious disease that causes spots on the skin, for example on the sexual organs or face

her·ring /'hɛrɪŋ/ *n. plural* **herrings** *or* **herring** [C,U] a long thin silver ocean fish, or the meat from this fish —see also RED HERRING

her·ring·bone /'hɛrɪŋˌboʊn/ *n.* [U] a pattern consisting of a continuous line of V shapes, used on cloth, or a type of cloth with this pattern on it

hers /hɚz/ *possessive pron.* [possessive form of "she"] the thing or things belonging to or relating to a female person or animal that has been mentioned or is known about: *This is my coat. Hers (=her coat) is over there.* | *My shoes are brown, and hers are red.* | *Paul is a friend of hers.*

her·self /ɚ'sɛlf; *strong* hɚ'sɛlf/ **1** the REFLEXIVE form of "she": *She hurt herself.* | *I think she really enjoyed herself.* **2** the strong form of "she," used to emphasize the subject or object of a sentence: *Bridget made her dress herself.* | *Sandy just got back herself.* **3** (all) by herself **a)** alone: *She was sitting at a table by herself.* **b)** without help from anyone else: *She raised her daughter by herself.* **4** have sth (all) to herself if a woman or girl has something to herself, she does not have to share it with anyone: *She had the house to herself while her parents were gone.* **5** not feel/look/seem like herself if a woman or girl is not feeling like herself, she does not feel or behave in the way that she usually does because she is nervous, upset, or sick: *Charlotte just doesn't look like herself today.*

hertz /hɚts/ *n. plural* **hertz** [C] a unit used to measure the FREQUENCY of SOUND WAVES

Herzl /'hɛrtsəl/, **The·o·dor** /'teɪədɔr/ (1860–1904) an Austrian politician who started Zionism

he's /iz; *strong* hiz/ **1** the short form of "he is": *He's in kindergarten already.* | *He's from Spain.* **2** the short form of "he has": *He's had three months of training.*

He·si·od /'hisiəd, 'hɛ-/ (8th century B.C.) a Greek poet

hes·i·tan·cy /'hɛzətənsi/ *also* **hes·i·tance** /'hɛzətəns/ *n.* [U] the quality of being uncertain or slow in doing or saying something: *Sensing Ann's hesitancy, Louella added quickly, "We won't stay long."*

hes·i·tant /'hɛzətənt/ *adj.* uncertain about what to do or say because you are nervous or unwilling: *He answered in his usual shy, hesitant manner.* | [be hesitant to do sth] *She is hesitant to draw conclusions until the study is over.* —**hesitantly** *adv.*

hes·i·tate /'hɛzəˌteɪt/ *v.* **1** [I] to pause before saying or doing something because you are nervous or not sure: *Paul started to speak but hesitated, searching for just the right words.* **2** not hesitate to do sth to be willing to do something because you are sure that it is right: *He does not hesitate to criticize the country's ruling party.* **3** don't hesitate to do sth used to tell someone that they can do something without worrying about it: *Don't hesitate to call me if you need any help.* —**hesitatingly** *adv.*

hes·i·ta·tion /ˌhɛzəˈteɪʃən/ *n.* [C,U] a pause before someone says or does something because they are nervous or not sure: *After some hesitation, one of them began to speak.* | *Ice cream is one food that most kids will eat **without hesitation**.* | *She **had no hesitation** in accepting their job offer.*

Hes·se /'hɛsə/, **Her·man** /'hɚmən/ (1877–1962) a German writer and poet famous for his NOVELS

Hes·ti·a /'hɛstiə, 'hɛstʃə/ in Greek MYTHOLOGY, the goddess of the HEARTH who protects people's homes

het·er·o /'hɛtəroʊ/ *n.* [C] SLANG someone who is attracted to people of the opposite sex —**hetero** *adj.* —compare HOMO

hetero- /hɛtəroʊ, -rə/ *prefix* FORMAL OR TECHNICAL the opposite of something, or different from something: *heterosexual* (=attracted to someone of the opposite sex) | *a heterogeneous mixture* (=a mixture of things that are not alike)

het·er·o·ge·ne·ous /ˌhɛtərəˈdʒiniəs, -nyəs/ *also* **het·e·rog·e·nous** /ˌhɛtəˈrɑdʒənəs/ *adj.* FORMAL consisting of parts or members that are very different from each other: *The U.S. has a very heterogeneous population.* —**heterogeneity** /ˌhɛtəroʊdʒɪˈniət/ *n.* [U] —**heterogeneously** /ˌhɛtərəˈdʒiniəsli/ *adv.* —compare HOMOGENEOUS

het·er·o·sex·u·al /ˌhɛtərəˈsɛkʃuəl/ *adj.* FORMAL sexually attracted to people of the opposite sex —**heterosexual** *n.* [C] —**heterosexuality** /ˌhɛtərəˌsɛkʃuˈæləti/ *n.* [U] —**heterosexually** /ˌhɛtərəˈsɛkʃuəl/ *adv.* —compare BISEXUAL, HOMOSEXUAL, STRAIGHT[2] (**5**)

heu·ris·tic /hyuˈrɪstɪk/ *adj.* TECHNICAL **1** heuristic education is based on discovering and experiencing things for yourself **2** helping you in the process of learning or discovery —**heuristically** /-kli/ *adv.*

heu·ris·tics /hyuˈrɪstɪks/ *n.* [U] TECHNICAL the study of how people use their experience to find answers to questions or to improve performance

hew /hyu/ *v. past tense* **hewed** *past participle* **hewed** *or* **hewn** LITERARY [I,T] to cut something with a cutting tool: *hewn stone* | *They hewed a huge cross from a tree.*

hew to sth *phr. v.* [T] FORMAL to obey someone, or to do something according to the rules or instructions: *She hews closely to tradition in her artwork.* —see also ROUGH-HEWN

hewn /hyun/ the past participle of HEW

hex[1] /hɛks/ *n.* [C] an evil CURSE[1] that brings trouble: *I think he's trying to put a hex on me.*

hex[2] *v.* [T] to use magic powers to make bad things happen to someone; CURSE[2] (2)

hex·a·dec·i·mal /ˌhɛksəˈdɛsəməl/ *also* **hex** *adj.* TECHNICAL hexadecimal numbers are based on the number 16 and are mainly used on computers

hex·a·gon /'hɛksəˌgɑn/ *n.* [C] a flat shape with six sides —**hexagonal** /hɛkˈsægənl/ *adj.*

hex·a·gram /'hɛksəˌgræm/ *n.* [C] a star shape with six points, made from two TRIANGLES

hex·am·e·ter /hɛkˈsæmətɚ/ *n.* [C] a line of poetry with six main beats

hey /heɪ/ *interjection* **1** a shout used to get someone's attention or to express surprise, interest, or annoyance: *Hey, wait a minute!* | *Hey, those are mine.* **2** INFORMAL hello: *Hey, girl, what's up?*

hey·day /'heɪdeɪ/ *n.* [C usually singular] the time when someone or something was most popular, successful, or powerful: *In the heyday of disco, we'd have 30 or 40 students in each of our dance classes.*

Hey·er·dahl /'haɪɚˌdɑl/, **Thor** /θɔr/ (1914–) a Norwegian ANTHROPOLOGIST famous for crossing the Pacific on a RAFT, the Kon-Tiki, to prove that people might have come to Polynesia from Peru

HI the written abbreviation of Hawaii

hi /haɪ/ *interjection* hello: *Hi! How are you?* | *Hi there, Charlie.*

hi·a·tus /haɪˈeɪtəs/ *n.* [singular,U] a break in an activity, or a time when something does not happen or exist for a while: *MacDowell is enjoying a long hiatus from moviemaking.* | *Gless' show is currently on hiatus and may return for the fall season.*

Hi·a·wa·tha /ˌhaɪəˈwɑθə/ a Native American chief who, in the 16th century, helped to unite the Iroquois into a single group called the Five Nations

hi·ba·chi /hɪˈbɑtʃi/ *n.* [C] a small piece of equipment for cooking food outdoors, over burning CHARCOAL

hi·ber·nate /ˈhaɪbəˌneɪt/ v. [I] if an animal hibernates, it sleeps all the time during the winter —**hibernation** /ˌhaɪbəˈneɪʃən/ n. [U]

hi·bis·cus /hɪˈbɪskəs, haɪ-/ n. [C,U] a tropical plant with large brightly colored flowers

hic·cough /ˈhɪkʌp/ n. [C usually plural] OLD-FASHIONED another spelling of HICCUP (1)

hic·cup[1] /ˈhɪkʌp/ n. [C] **1** [usually plural] a sudden repeated stopping of the breath, usually caused by eating or drinking too fast: *Do you have the hiccups?* **2** a small problem or delay: *There were a few minor hiccups in the space shuttle launch.*

hiccup[2] v. **hiccupped, hiccupping** [I] to have the hiccups

hick /hɪk/ n. [C] DISAPPROVING someone who lives in the country and is thought to be uneducated or stupid

hick·ey /ˈhɪki/ n. plural **hickeys** or **hickies** [C] INFORMAL a dark red or purple mark on someone's skin, especially on their neck, caused by someone else sucking it as a sexual act

Hick·ok /ˈhɪkɑk/**, Wild Bill** /waɪld bɪl/ (1837–1876) a U.S. soldier who was one of the first white Americans to live in the western U.S. where he became a MARSHAL

hick·o·ry /ˈhɪkəri/ n. plural **hickories** [C,U] a North American tree that produces nuts, or the wood that comes from this tree

hid /hɪd/ the past tense of HIDE[1]

Hi·dat·sa /hɪˈdɑtsə/ a Native American tribe from the northern central area of the U.S

hid·den[1] /ˈhɪdn/ the past participle of HIDE[1]

hidden[2] adj. **1** difficult to see or find: *Hidden video cameras were used to improve security.* **2** not easy to notice or realize: *Be on the lookout for hidden costs in hotel bills.*

hidden a·gen·da /ˌ... .ˈ../ n. [C] an intended result of a plan or activity that you do not tell other people about: *The mayor was a very straightforward guy who didn't have a hidden agenda.*

S W
2 2
hide[1] /haɪd/ v. past tense **hid** past participle **hidden 1** [T] to deliberately put or keep something in a place where it cannot easily be seen or found: [**hide sth in/under/behind etc.**] *Marcia hid the pictures in her desk drawer.* | *She keeps a bottle of gin hidden behind a stack of books.* **2** also **hide out** [I] to go or stay in a place where no one will see or find you: *She's coming – we'd better hide!* | [**+ in/under/behind etc.**] *The cat was hiding among the plants.* | *Weiss spent two years hiding from the Nazis.* **3** [T] to keep someone in a place where other people will not find them: *The old woman hid him in her cellar for three days.* | [**hide sb from sb**] *We'll have to hide him from the soldiers.* **4** [T] to not show your feelings to people: *José was unable to hide his embarrassment.* **5** [T] to deliberately not tell people facts or information: *He took off his ring to hide the fact that he was married.* | [**hide sth from sb**] *Don't try to hide anything from me.* **6 have nothing to hide** to be willing to tell people about everything you have done, because you have done nothing dishonest, illegal, or immoral: *He denied the charges against him and said he had nothing to hide.*

hide[2] n. **1** [C] an animal's skin, especially when it is removed to be used for leather: *a buffalo hide* **2 have/tan sb's hide** SPOKEN, HUMOROUS to punish someone severely **3 not see hide nor hair of sb** SPOKEN to not see someone anywhere for a fairly long time: *I haven't seen hide nor hair of him in months.*

hide-and-seek /ˌ.. .ˈ./ also **hide-and-go-seek** /ˌ.. .ˈ./ n. [U] a children's game in which one player shuts their eyes while the others hide, and then goes to look for them

hide·a·way /ˈhaɪdəˌweɪ/ n. [C] **1** a place where you can go to hide; HIDEOUT **2** a place where you can go to be alone and relax, for example on vacation: *a romantic hideaway in the mountains*

hide·bound /ˈhaɪdbaʊnd/ adj. DISAPPROVING having old-fashioned attitudes and ideas: *hidebound bureaucrats*

hid·e·ous /ˈhɪdiəs/ adj. extremely ugly or bad: *a hideous dress* | *a hideous crime* —**hideously** adv. —**hideousness** n. [U]

hide·out /ˈhaɪdaʊt/ n. [C] a place where someone goes because they do not want anyone to find them

hid·ing /ˈhaɪdɪŋ/ n. **1** [U] the state of staying somewhere in secret because you have done something illegal or are in danger: *He is believed to be in hiding somewhere in Mexico.* | *He went into hiding in 1973.* **2 a hiding** OLD-FASHIONED a severe physical punishment

hiding place /ˈ.. ˌ./ n. [C] a place where you can hide, or where you can hide something

hie /haɪ/ v. [I,T] OLD USE to make yourself hurry, or go quickly

hi·er·ar·chy /ˈhaɪəˌrɑrki/ n. plural **hierarchies 1** [C,U] a system of organization in which people or things are divided into levels of importance: *The caste system categorized Hindus into a social hierarchy.* | *Tatawi worked her way up through the corporate hierarchy to become President.* **2** [C] the most important and powerful members of an organization: *Smith has the backing of the Republican hierarchy.* —**hierarchical** /ˌhaɪəˈrɑrkɪkəl/ adj. —**hierarchically** /-kli/ adv.

hi·er·o·glyph·ics /ˌhaɪərəˈglɪfɪks/ n. [U,plural] a system of writing, especially one from ancient Egypt, that uses pictures to represent words —**hieroglyphic** adj.

hi-fi[1] /ˈhaɪ ˈfaɪ/ n. plural **hi-fis** [C] OLD-FASHIONED a STEREO[1] (1)

hi-fi[2] adj. [only before noun] HIGH FIDELITY

hig·gle·dy-pig·gle·dy /ˌhɪgəldi ˈpɪgəldi/ adj. things that are higgledy-piggledy are mixed together in a way that is not very neat —**higgledy-piggledy** adv.

high

a high shelf

a tall building

S W
1 1
high[1] /haɪ/ adj.
1 from bottom to top something that is high measures a long distance from its bottom to its top: *How high is the Eiffel Tower?* | *The palace is surrounded by a high concrete wall.* | *Mount St. Alban is Washington's highest point.* | [**10 feet/5 yards etc. high**] *The fountain shot a stream of water 15 feet high.*
2 above the ground being a long way, or a longer way than usual, above the ground, floor etc.: *Your apartment has such high ceilings.* | *There was a squirrel high up in the tree.* | *a high shelf*
3 large number a high amount, number, or level is large, or greater than normal or usual: *the high cost of living in the city* | *You got the highest score in the class.* | *Paul has extremely high blood pressure.* | *A high percentage/proportion of high school graduates have not learned geography.* | *Cable TV*

companies have received complaints about **high prices** and bad service. | Police chased the car at **high speeds** through town.

4 `containing a lot` containing a lot of a particular substance, or having a lot of a particular quality: It's hard to know which products have high lead levels. | [**high in sth**] Foods that are high in fat are also high in calories.

5 `rank/position` having an important or powerful position in society or in an organization: people in the highest levels of management | I know a guy who's **high up** in the Greenpeace organization. They've been trying to get into **high office** for years now. —see also **have friends in high places** (FRIEND (6))

6 high quality/standard/caliber etc. very good quality etc.: We provide our clients with investment advice of the highest caliber. | They're known for the high quality of their work.

7 be high on the list/agenda to be important, or need to be dealt with quickly: Democracy in the region will be high on the agenda of both meetings.

8 `sound` near the top of the range of sounds that humans can hear: Donna had some trouble reaching the high notes. —see also HIGH-PITCHED

9 high opinion/praise/regard etc. strong approval, or an expression of strong approval: Welch is **held in high regard** by his teammates. | I have a very high opinion of him.

10 have high standards/principles to always behave in a way that is correct and honest, and believe that other people should do the same: Mrs. Miller had high standards of dress and manners.

11 have high hopes/expectations to hope for or expect very good results or great success: Teachers should have high expectations for their students.

12 the high point/spot the best part of an activity or occasion: The dance is considered the high point of the social season.

13 `drugs` [not before noun] behaving in an unusually excited or relaxed way because of taking drugs: [+ **on**] He was arrested for driving while high on marijuana. | I got so **high** last night. | They were both as **high as a kite** (=greatly affected by drugs).

14 high spirits feelings of happiness and energy, especially when you are having fun: Peter could not hide his high spirits. | Despite the rain, everyone was in high spirits.

15 `happy/excited` OLD-FASHIONED happy and excited

16 it is high time sb did sth used to say that something should have been done already: It's high time we pulled together and got the job done right.

17 `time` [only before noun] the middle or the most important part of a particular period of time: high summer | The game starts at **high noon** (=exactly 12 o'clock in the middle of the day). —see also HIGH SEASON

18 be/get on your high horse to behave or talk as if you are better than other people

19 high and mighty talking or behaving as if you think you are more important than other people

20 leave sb high and dry INFORMAL to leave someone without any help or without the things that they need: Michael quit, leaving Elliot high and dry to run the new company.

21 a high wind a strong wind

22 high drama/adventure events or situations that are very exciting: The movie is full of grandeur and high adventure.

23 on the high seas traveling in a ship or boat on the ocean

24 high finance the business of dealing with very large sums of money —see also HIGH GEAR, HIGHLY, **in high dudgeon** (DUDGEON)

USAGE NOTE: HIGH

WORD CHOICE: high, tall
High (opposite **low**) is used of most things, especially when you are thinking of how far something, or the top of something, is from the ground: a high mountain |

The shelf's too high – I can't reach it. Many things which you cannot touch may also be **high**: a high standard | a high degree of sophistication | high technology. **Tall** (opposite **short**) is used for people and animals: Your son's getting really tall. **Tall** is also used for things that are high and narrow, especially when you are thinking of the complete distance from top to bottom: a tall building like the Sears Tower | a tall tree

high² adv.
1 `above the ground` at or to a level high above the ground: Garbage had been **piled high** on the sidewalk. | [+ **into/above etc.**] Paula threw the ball high into the air. | He held the trophy high above his head.
2 `value/cost/amount` at or to a high value, cost, amount etc.: Tom scored higher than anyone else in the class. | The dollar climbed higher against the yen today.
3 `sound` with a high sound: The girl's voice rang high above everyone else's.
4 `achievement` to a high rank or level of achievement, especially in an organization, business etc.: Sandy continued to rise higher in Zefco's ranks.
5 hold your head high to behave in a proud confident way, especially in a difficult situation: Jackie held her head high and ignored her husband's behavior.
6 look/search high and low to try to find someone or something by looking everywhere: We looked high and low for Sandy but couldn't find her.
7 live high on the hog INFORMAL to enjoy expensive food, clothes etc. without worrying about the cost: They've been living high on the hog since Jim got the money from his aunt. —see also **be riding high** (RIDE¹ (4)), **be running high** (RUN¹ (39))

high³ n. [C]
1 `number/amount` the highest price, number, temperature etc. that has ever been recorded: The price of oil reached a new high this week.
2 `weather` **a)** the highest temperature in a particular day, week, month etc.: Highs today were in the mid-90's. **b)** an area of HIGH PRESSURE that affects the weather
3 `drugs` a feeling of pleasure or excitement produced by some drugs: The high she got from cocaine never lasted.
4 `excitement` [usually singular] a feeling of happiness or excitement you get from doing something you enjoy: John **was on a** week-long **high** after getting the promotion.
5 High a short form of "high school," used in the name of a school: She graduated from Reseda High in 1989.
6 from on high FORMAL from someone in a position of authority: The advice from on high convinced Dustin to stay in school.
7 on high BIBLICAL in, to, or from heaven or a high place

high·ball /ˈhaɪbɔl/ n. [C] an alcoholic drink, especially WHISKEY or BRANDY mixed with water or SODA

high beam /ˈ. ./ n. **1 high beams** [plural] the HEADLIGHTS of a vehicle that shine higher and brighter than the regular lights in order to help you see things far away **2 on high beam** if your car lights are on high beam, they are brighter than the normal lights, so that you can see farther —compare **on low beam** (LOW BEAM)

high blood pres·sure /ˌ. ˈ. ˌ../ n. [U] a serious medical condition in which your BLOOD PRESSURE is too high: The drug could help people who have high blood pressure.

high-born /ˌ. ˈ. ˌ/ adj. FORMAL born into the highest social class

high·boy /ˈhaɪbɔɪ/ n. [C] a piece of wooden furniture with drawers and tall thin legs

high·brow /ˈhaɪbraʊ/ adj. **1** a highbrow book, movie etc. is very serious and may be difficult to understand **2** someone who is highbrow is interested in serious or complicated ideas and subjects; INTELLECTUAL —**highbrow** n. [C] —compare LOWBROW

high·chair /ˈhaɪtʃer/ n. [C] a special tall chair that a young child sits in to eat —see picture at CHAIR¹

High Church /ˌ. ˈ./ *n.* **the High Church** used to describe some Christian churches that have very traditional formal ceremonies

high-class /ˌ. ˈ./ *adj.* [usually before noun] of good quality and style, and usually expensive: *a high-class hotel* —compare LOW-CLASS

high com·mand /ˌ. .ˈ./ *n.* [singular] the most important leaders of a country's army, navy etc.: *the Army High Command*

high com·mis·sion /ˌ. .ˈ./ *n.* [C] a group of people working for a government or an international organization to deal with a specific problem: *the UN High Commission for Refugees* —**High Commissioner** *n.* [C]

high-def·i·ni·tion /ˌ. ..ˈ..◂/ *adj.* [only before noun] a high-definition television or computer MONITOR shows images very clearly

high-end /ˈ. ./ *adj.* [usually before noun] relating to products or services that are more expensive and of better quality than other products of the same type: *high-end computer memory chips* —compare LOW-END

high·er /ˈhaɪɚ/ *adj.* the COMPARATIVE of HIGH

higher ed·u·ca·tion /ˌ... ..ˈ../ *n.* [U] education at a college or university, after leaving HIGH SCHOOL

higher-end /ˈ. ./ *adj.* [usually before noun] HIGH-END

higher-up /ˌ.. ˈ.◂/ *n.* [C usually plural] INFORMAL someone who has a high rank in an organization: *Shelton was ordered by company higher-ups to reduce costs.*

highest com·mon fac·tor /ˌ... .. ˈ../ *n.* [C] TECHNICAL the largest number that a set of numbers can all be divided by exactly: *The highest common factor of 12, 24 and 30 is 6.*

high ex·plo·sive /ˌ. .ˈ..◂/ *n.* [C,U] a substance that explodes with great power and violence

high·fa·lu·tin, highfalutin' /ˌhaɪfəˈlutⁿ◂/ *adj.* INFORMAL, DISAPPROVING highfalutin language, things, ideas etc. seem silly although they are meant to be impressive: *I hate it when people use highfalutin' words when regular ones will do.*

high fi·del·i·ty /ˌ. .ˈ.../ *adj.* [usually before noun] high fidelity recording equipment produces sound that is very clear —see also HI-FI²

high-five /ˌ. ˈ./ *n.* [singular] the action of hitting someone's open hand with your own above your heads to show that you are pleased about something: *Gilbert ran over and gave him a high-five after hitting a home run.*

high-fli·er /ˌ. ˈ../ *n.* [C] a person or organization that is extremely successful, especially in business, work, or school: *The company was once a high-flier in the disk drive business.* —**high-flying** *adj.*

high-flown /ˌ. ˈ.◂/ *adj.* high-flown language, behavior etc. is meant to make you seem more important, intelligent etc. than you really are: *Clark never developed high-flown ideas about saving the world.*

high fre·quen·cy /ˌ. ˈ...◂/ *n.* [U] a radio FREQUENCY in the range of 3 to 30 MEGAHERTZ —compare LOW FREQUENCY —**high-frequency** *adj.*: *high-frequency broadcasts*

high gear /ˈ. ./ *n.* [U] **1** one of a vehicle's GEARS that you use when you are driving at fast speeds **2 in high gear** if a situation is in high gear, it is happening or changing very quickly or people are working very hard | **kick/move/swing into high gear** *The flu season usually swings into high gear in November.*

high-grade /ˌ. ˈ.◂/ *adj.* [only before noun] of the best quality: *high-grade oil*

high ground /ˌ. ˈ./ *n.* [U] **1** an area of land that is higher than the land around it: *Farmers moved livestock to high ground just ahead of rising flood waters.* **2** if someone or a group has the high ground in an argument, they have the advantage: *Workers have regained the high ground in the negotiations.* —see also **take/claim/seize etc. the moral high ground** (MORAL¹ (4))

high-hand·ed /ˌ. ˈ..◂/ *adj.* using your authority in an unreasonable way: *The company has a reputation for being high-handed in its treatment of clients.* —**high-handedly** *adv.* —**high-handedness** *n.* [U]

high heels /ˌ. ˈ./ *n.* [plural] women's shoes with high heels —**high-heeled** *adj.*

high jinks, hijinks /ˈhaɪ dʒɪŋks/ *n.* [U] noisy, silly, or excited behavior or activities which happen when people are having fun, and especially involve playing tricks on someone

high jump /ˈ. ./ *n.* **the high jump** a sports event in which someone runs and jumps over a bar that is raised higher each time they jump —**high jumper** *n.* [C]

high·land /ˈhaɪlənd/ *adj.* [only before noun] **1** relating to an area with a lot of mountains: *the highland city of Puno* **2** coming from or relating to the Scottish Highlands: *highland dancing*

High·land·er /ˈhaɪləndɚ/ *n.* [C] someone from the Scottish Highlands

high·lands /ˈhaɪləndz/ *n.* [plural] an area of a country where there are a lot of mountains: *the Andean highlands* —compare LOWLANDS

high-lev·el /ˌ. ˈ..◂/ *adj.* [only before noun] **1** in a powerful position or job, or involving people who are in powerful positions or jobs: *a high-level attorney* | *low-level positions in the company* **2** at a high degree or strength: *The virus has shown high-level resistance to penicillin.* | *a high-level philosophical discussion* **3** involving very technical or complicated ideas **4** a high-level computer language is similar to human language rather than machine language —compare LOW-LEVEL

high life /ˈ. ./ *n.* **the high life** a way of life that involves a lot of parties, and expensive food, wine, travel etc.

high·light¹ /ˈhaɪlaɪt/ *v.* [T] **1** to make something easy to notice so that people pay attention to it: *Your resumé should highlight your skills and achievements.* **2** to mark written words with a special colored pen, or in a different color on a computer, so that you can see them easily: *Highlight the desired file using the arrow keys.* **3** to make some parts of your hair a lighter color than the rest —**highlighting** *n.* [U]

highlight² *n.* [C] **1** the most important, interesting, or enjoyable part of an activity, movie, sports event etc.: *The weekend in Venice was definitely the highlight of our trip.* | *Before the game, fans were shown highlights of the season on a large video screen.* **2 highlights** [plural] areas of hair that have been made a lighter color than the rest **3** TECHNICAL a light bright area on a painting or photograph

high·light·er /ˈhaɪlaɪtɚ/ *n.* [C] a special light-colored pen used for marking words in a book, article etc.

high·ly /ˈhaɪli/ *adv.* **1** [+ adj./adv.] very: *a highly flammable liquid* | *He's a highly gifted young singer.* **2** [+ adj./adv.] to a high level or standard: *The demand for highly educated workers is still increasing.* **3 speak/think highly of sb** to tell other people how good someone is at doing something or to think they are very good at doing something: *Mr. Lloyd speaks highly of you.* **4 highly placed** in an important or powerful position: *It is not the first time Cole has investigated highly placed public figures.*

High Mass /ˌ. ˈ./ *n.* [C,U] a very formal church ceremony in the Catholic Church

high-mind·ed /ˌ. ˈ..◂/ *adj.* having very high moral standards or principles: *Taylor's made a high-minded pledge to clean up American politics.* —**high-mindedly** *adv.* —**high-mindedness** *n.* [U]

High·ness /ˈhaɪnɪs/ *n.* [C] **Your/Her/His Highness** used to speak to or about a king, queen, prince etc.

high-oc·tane /ˌ. ˈ..◂/ *adj.* high-octane GASOLINE is of a very high quality —**high-octane** *n.* [U] —compare OCTANE

high-per·form·ance /ˌ. .ˈ..◂/ *adj.* **high-performance cars/computers/tires etc.** cars, computers etc. that are able to go faster, do more work etc. than normal ones

high-pitched /ˌ. '.‹ / adj. a high-pitched voice or sound is higher than usual: *a high-pitched scream*

high-pow·ered /ˌ. '..‹ / adj. [usually before noun] **1** a high-powered machine, vehicle, or piece of equipment is very powerful: *a high-powered rifle* —compare LOW-POWER **2** very important or successful: *a high-powered law firm*

high pres·sure /ˌ. '..‹ / n. [U] **a layer/area of high pressure** a condition of the air over a large area that affects the weather

high-pres·sure /ˌ. '..‹ / adj. [only before noun] **1** a high-pressure job or situation is one in which you need to work very hard: *She decided to give up her high-pressure job on Wall Street.* **2** containing or using a very high pressure or force of water, gas, air etc.: *Workers used high-pressure hoses to clean the rocks after the oil spill.* **3 high-pressure sales pitches/tactics** very direct and often successful ways of persuading people to buy something **4 a high-pressure system** HIGH PRESSURE

high-priced /ˌ. '.‹ / adj. costing a lot of money: *high-priced apartments | high-priced lawyers*

high priest /ˌ. './ n. [C] **1** INFORMAL a man who is famous for being the best at something such as a type of art or music: *Age hasn't mellowed the high priest of punk, Iggy Pop.* **2** the most important PRIEST in some religions

high priest·ess /ˌ. '../ n. [C] **1** INFORMAL a woman who is famous for being the best at something such as a type of art or music **2** the most important PRIESTESS in some religions

high-prin·ci·pled /ˌ. '...‹ / adj. having high moral standards: *Drew's a high-principled man who lives for his family.*

high-pro·file /ˌ. '..‹ / adj. [only before noun] attracting a lot of public attention: *a high-profile trial* —**high profile** n. [singular]

high-rank·ing /ˌ. '..‹ / adj. [only before noun] having a high position in a government or other organization

high re·lief /ˌ. '.'./ n. [U] **1** a form of art in which figures cut in stone or wood stand out from the surface —compare BAS-RELIEF **2 throw/bring sth into high relief** to make something very clear and easy to notice

high-rise, highrise /'. ./ n. [C] a tall building, for example an office building or an apartment building —**high-rise** adj. [only before noun] —compare LOW-RISE

high-risk /ˌ. '.‹ / adj. [only before noun] involving a risk of death, injury, failure etc.: *The drug may help to reduce strokes in high-risk patients. | Buying a restaurant is a high-risk investment.*

high road /'. ./ n. **1 take the (moral) high road** to do what you believe is right according to your beliefs: *Daley has taken the high road in his campaign, trying to ignore Merriam's attacks.* **2** [C] OLD-FASHIONED a main road

high roll·er /ˌ. '../ n. [C] INFORMAL someone who spends a lot of money, especially by BETting¹ (1) on games, horse races etc.

high school /'. ./ n. [C,U] a school for students over the age of 14 which usually includes grades 9 or 10 through 12

high seas /ˌ. './ n. **the high seas a)** the areas of ocean around the world that do not belong to any particular country **b)** LITERARY the ocean

high sea·son /ˌ. '../ n. [singular,U] the time of year when businesses make a lot of money and prices are high, especially in the tourist industry

high-sound·ing /ˌ. '..‹ / adj. [only before noun] high-sounding statements, principles etc. seem very impressive, but are often insincere

high-speed /ˌ. '.‹ / adj. [only before noun] **1** designed to travel or operate very fast: *a high-speed train* **2 a high-speed chase** a situation when the police drive very fast to try to catch someone who is in a car

high-spir·it·ed /ˌ. '...‹ / adj. **1** someone who is high-spirited has a lot of energy and enjoys fun and adventure: *Sophie's a high-spirited young girl.* **2** a horse that is high-spirited is nervous and difficult to control

high-strung /ˌ. '.‹ / adj. nervous and easily upset or excited: *Kurt's a little high-strung, but otherwise a fine lawyer.*

high·tail /'haɪteɪl/ v. INFORMAL **hightail it** to leave a place quickly: *They ended up hightailing it across the border.*

high-tech /ˌhaɪ 'tɛk‹ / adj. [usually before noun] using the most modern information, machines, methods etc.: *high-tech weapons* —compare LOW-TECH —see Usage Note at TECHNIQUE

high tech·nol·o·gy /ˌ. .'...‹ / n. [U] also **high tech** INFORMAL the use of the most modern machines and methods in industry, business etc.

high-ten·sion /ˌ. '..‹ / adj. **high-tension wires/lines etc.** wires, lines etc. that have a powerful electric current going through them

high tide /ˌ. './ n. [C,U] the point or time at which the ocean reaches its highest level

high-toned /ˌ. '.‹ / adj. trying to seem more important, intelligent etc. than you really are: *high-toned English teachers*

high-tops, hightops /'. ./ n. [plural] INFORMAL sports shoes that cover your ANKLES —**high-top** adj.: *high-top basketball shoes*

high trea·son /ˌ. '../ n. [U] LAW the crime of putting your country's government or leader in great danger, for example by giving military secrets to an enemy

high-volt·age /ˌ. '../ adj. [only before noun] **1** containing a lot of electrical force: *high-voltage power lines* **2** having or showing a lot of energy: *a high-voltage performer*

high wa·ter /ˌ. '../ n. [U] the time when the water in a river, lake etc. is at its highest level —compare LOW WATER —see also **come hell or high water** (HELL (22))

high-water mark /ˌ. '.. ˌ./ n. [singular] **1** the mark that shows the highest level that the ocean or a river reaches **2** the time when someone or something is most successful: *Many think the '70s were the high-water mark of American journalism.*

high·way /'haɪweɪ/ n. plural **highways** [C] **1** a wide fast road that connects cities or towns together —compare FREEWAY, EXPRESSWAY **2 highway robbery** INFORMAL a situation in which something costs you a lot more than it should: *Sixty dollars for a textbook? That's highway robbery.*

high·way·man /'haɪweɪmən/ n. plural **highwaymen** /-mən/ [C] OLD USE someone who stopped people and carriages on the roads and robbed them

highway pa·trol /'.. .ˌ./ n. **the highway patrol** the police who make sure that people obey the rules on HIGHWAYS in the U.S.

high wire /'. ./ n. [C] a tightly stretched rope or wire high above the ground that someone walks along, usually as part of a CIRCUS performance

hi·jack /'haɪdʒæk/ v. [T] **1** to use violence or threats to take control of an airplane, vehicle, or ship: *The ship was hijacked by four young terrorists.* **2** to take control of something and use it for your own purposes: *We're not going to let a handful of radical students hijack our school.* —**hijacker** n. [C]

hi·jack·ing /'haɪdʒækɪŋ/ n. **1** [C,U] the use of violence or threats to take control of an airplane or vehicle: *One person was killed during the hijacking.* —see also CARJACKING **2** [U] the act of stealing goods from vehicles in this way

hi·jinks /'haɪdʒɪŋks/ n. [plural] another spelling of HIGH JINKS

hike¹ /haɪk/ n. [C] **1** a long walk in the country, mountains etc.: *It was a bright, warm fall weekend, perfect for a hike in the hills.* **2** a large increase in something: [+ **in**] *Last month saw another hike in the price of gasoline. | price/rate/tax etc. hikes Several airlines have announced fare hikes, effective October 1.*

3 take a hike SPOKEN an impolite way of telling someone to go away: *Take a hike, jerk.*

hike² *v.* **1** [I,T] to take a long walk in the country, mountains etc.: *I've hiked the canyon four times.* —see also HIKING **2** also **hike** sth ↔ **up** [T] to increase the price of something by a large amount: *The President wants to hike spending for foreign aid.*

hike sth ↔ **up** to pull or lift up a piece of your clothing: *She hiked her skirt up to climb the stairs.*

hik·er /ˈhaɪkə/ *n.* [C] someone who takes long walks in the country, mountains etc. for pleasure or exercise

hik·ing /ˈhaɪkɪŋ/ *n.* [U] an outdoor activity in which you take long walks in the mountains or country: *We're going to do some hiking this summer. | Southeast Utah is a great place to go hiking and mountain biking.*

hi·lar·i·ous /hɪˈlɛriəs, -ˈlær-/ *adj.* extremely funny: *You should read this book – it's hilarious.* —**hilariously** *adv.*

hi·lar·i·ty /hɪˈlærəti/ *n.* [U] laughter, or a feeling of fun: *Gloria's costume caused a good deal of hilarity.*

hill /hɪl/ *n.* [C] **1** an area of land that is higher than the land around it, like a mountain but smaller: *The hotel is up on the hill, overlooking the town.* —see picture on page 428 **2 the Hill** CAPITOL HILL **3 over the hill** INFORMAL too old for something or too old to do something well: *At 32, many considered Ali to be over the hill as a professional boxer.* **4 it doesn't amount to a hill of beans** it is not important **5 over hill and dale** OLD-FASHIONED for a long distance, up and down hills

Hil·la·ry /ˈhɪləri/**, Sir Ed·mund** /ˈɛdmənd/ (1919–) a New Zealand mountain climber known for being the first person, with Tenzing Norgay, to reach the top of Mount Everest in 1953

hill·bil·ly /ˈhɪlˌbɪli/ *n. plural* **hillbillies** [C] OFFENSIVE someone who lives in the mountains and is thought to be uneducated or stupid

hill·ock /ˈhɪlək/ *n.* [C] a small hill

hill·side /ˈhɪlsaɪd/ *n.* [C] the sloping side of a hill: *Her house was built on a hillside overlooking the ocean.*

hill·y /ˈhɪli/ *adj.* **hillier, hilliest** having a lot of hills: *hilly roads*

hilt /hɪlt/ *n.* [C] **1** the handle of a sword or knife that is used as a weapon **2 (up) to the hilt** as fully or as much as possible: *Everything I have is mortgaged to the hilt. | Troy lived each day to the hilt.*

him /ɪm; *strong* hɪm/ *pron.* the object form of "he": *I took him to lunch yesterday. | She's in love with him. | Why don't you just ask him yourself?*

Him·a·la·yas, the /ˌhɪməˈleɪəz/ a long range of mountains in southern Asia, northeast of India, that includes the highest mountain in the world, Mount Everest

him·self /ɪmˈsɛlf; *strong* hɪmˈsɛlf/ *pron.* **1 a)** the REFLEXIVE form of "he": *I don't think he hurt himself when he fell | Mikey calls himself Michael these days. | Peter considers himself a poet.* **b)** the REFLEXIVE form of "he," used after words like "everyone," "anyone," "no one" etc.: *Everyone here should decide for himself.* **2** the strong form of "he," used to emphasize the subject or object of a sentence: *Steve himself is just recovering from surgery. | He built the closets himself.* **3 (all) by himself a)** alone: *Don's traveling by himself.* **b)** without help from anyone else: *He's standing up by himself already.* **4 have sth (all) to himself** if a man or boy has something to himself, he does not have to share it with anyone: *Jerry wanted to have the company all to himself.* **5 not feel/look/ seem like himself** if a man or boy is not feeling, looking etc. like himself, he does not feel or behave in the way that he usually does because he is nervous, upset, or sick: *I think there's something on Doug's mind – he hasn't been himself lately.* —see also YOURSELF

hind /haɪnd/ *adj.* **hind legs/feet** the back legs or feet of an animal with four legs

hin·der /ˈhɪndə/ *v.* [T] to make it difficult for someone to do something or for something to develop: *The high cost of the vaccine has severely hindered its use.*

Hin·di /ˈhɪndi/ *n.* [U] one of the official languages of India

hind·most /ˈhaɪndmoʊst/ *adj.* OLD USE farthest behind

hind·quar·ters /ˈhaɪndˌkwɔrtəz/ *n.* [plural] the back part of an animal, including the back legs

hin·drance /ˈhɪndrəns/ *n.* **1** [C] something or someone that makes it difficult for you to do something successfully: *He feels marriage would be a hindrance to his career.* **2** [U] FORMAL the act of making it difficult for someone to do something: *They should be allowed to do their job without hindrance.*

hind·sight /ˈhaɪndsaɪt/ *n.* [U] the ability to understand facts about a situation after it has happened: *It's easy to say in hindsight that I should have done things differently.* —see also **20/20 hindsight** (TWENTY-TWENTY (2))

Hin·du /ˈhɪndu/ *n. plural* **Hindus** [C] someone who believes in Hinduism —**Hindu** *adj.*: *a Hindu temple*

Hin·du·ism /ˈhɪnduˌɪzəm/ *n.* [U] the main religion in India, which includes belief in many gods and in REINCARNATION

hinge¹ /hɪndʒ/ *n.* [C] a metal part used to fasten a door to its frame, a lid to a box etc., so that it can swing open and closed

hinge² *v.*

hinge on/upon sth *phr. v.* [T not in progressive] if a result hinges on something happening, it depends on it completely: *The case hinges on whether the jury believed the defendants.*

hinged /hɪndʒd/ *adj.* joined by a hinge: *a hinged lid*

hint¹ /hɪnt/ *n.* [C] **1** something that you say or do that helps someone guess what you really want or mean: *Come on, just give me a hint. | He's been dropping hints* (=giving hints indirectly) *that he might not return next year.* **2** a very small amount or sign of something: [+ of] *There was a hint of anger in his voice. | It's a well-balanced wine with a hint of sweetness.* **3** a useful piece of advice about how to do something: [+ on] *The article offers hints on how to avoid injuring your back.*

hint² *v.* [I,T] to say something in an indirect way, but so that someone can guess what you mean: [+ at] *What are you hinting at? |* [hint (that)] *I think she was hinting that I might be offered a contract.*

hin·ter·land /ˈhɪntəˌlænd/ *n.* [C] **1** [usually plural] an area of land far away from a city **2** an area of land away from a coast or large river

hip¹ /hɪp/ *n.* [C] **1** one of the two parts on each side of your body between the top of your leg and your waist —see picture at BODY **2** [usually plural] the red fruit of some kinds of ROSE bushes; ROSE HIP —see also **shoot from the hip** (SHOOT¹ (16))

hip² *interjection* **hip, hip, hooray!** used as a shout of approval

hip³ *adj.* **hipper, hippest** INFORMAL doing things or done according to the latest fashion: *It's really funny when Dad tries to be hip.*

hip flask /ˈ. ./ *n.* [C] a small container for strong alcoholic drinks, made to fit in your pocket

hip-hop /ˈ. ./ *n.* [U] **1** a type of dance music with a strong regular BEAT and spoken words **2** a type of popular CULTURE among young people in big cities which includes RAP music, dancing, and GRAFFITI art, especially popular among African-American young people

hip·hug·gers /ˈhɪpˌhʌgəz/ *n.* [plural] pants that fit tightly around your HIPs and do not cover your waist

hip·pie, hippy /ˈhɪpi/ *n.* [C] someone opposed to the traditional standards of society who wears unusual clothes, has long hair, and usually takes drugs for pleasure —see picture on page 1330

hip·po /ˈhɪpoʊ/ *n. plural* **hippos** [C] INFORMAL a hippopotamus

hip pock·et /ˌ. ˈ../ *n.* [C] a back pocket in a pair of pants or a skirt

Hip·poc·ra·tes /hɪˈpɑkrəˌtiz/ (?460–?377 B.C.) a doctor in ancient Greece who is considered to have begun the study of modern medicine

Hip·po·crat·ic oath /ˌhɪpəkrætɪk ˈoʊθ/ n. [singular] the promise made by doctors that they will obey the principles of the medical profession

hip·po·pot·a·mus /ˌhɪpəˈpɑtəməs/ n. [C] a large African animal with a large head, a wide mouth, and thick gray skin, that lives in and near water

hip·py /ˈhɪpi/ n. [C] another spelling of HIPPIE

hip·ster /ˈhɪpstɚ/ n. [C] INFORMAL someone who is very HIP³

hire¹ /haɪɚ/ v. [T] **1** to employ someone to start to work for you: *The Herald newspaper hired her in 1968.* | *Parker falsified his credentials to get hired.* **2** BRITISH: see RENT¹ (2)
   hire on phr. v. [I] to start to work somewhere or for someone: *These firefighters hire on only for the wildfire season.*

hire² n. **for hire** done for money or employment: *Gobie was operating a sex-for-hire business in the apartment.* —see also **murder-for-hire** (MURDER¹ (5))

hired hand /ˌ. ˈ./ n. [C] someone who is employed to help on a farm

hire·ling /ˈhaɪɚlɪŋ/ n. [C] DISAPPROVING someone who will work for anyone who is willing to pay

Hi·ro·hi·to /ˌhɪroʊˈhitoʊ/ (1901–1989) the EMPEROR of Japan from 1926 to 1989

hir·sute /ˈhɚsut, ˈhɪr-, hɚˈsut/ adj. LITERARY having a lot of hair on your body and face

his¹ /ɪz; strong hɪz/ possessive adj. [possessive form of "he"] **1** belonging to or relating to a man, boy, or male animal that has been mentioned or is known about: *His parents were born in Russia.* | *I think his name is Greg.* **2** FORMAL used after singular PRONOUNS such as "everyone," "anyone," "no one," "each" etc. to show the POSSESSIVE: *No one wants his family to be threatened.* —compare THEIR

USAGE NOTE: HIS

WORD CHOICE: his or their/theirs
Some people still use **his** as a singular pronoun or determiner with pronouns like **everyone**, especially in formal writing: *Everyone has his own ideas about what is important.* However, it is more common now to use the plural determiner **their** or the plural pronoun **theirs** instead: *Everyone has their own ideas about what is important.* In formal English, it is best to use "his or her": *Everyone has his or her own ideas about what is important.*

his² possessive pron. [possessive form of "he"] **1** the thing or things belonging to or relating to a male person or animal that has been mentioned or is known about: *I think he has my suitcase and I have his.* | *Martin's a friend of his.* **2** FORMAL used after singular PRONOUNS like "everyone," "anyone," "no one," "each" etc. to show the POSSESSIVE: *Everyone just wants what is his by right.* —compare THEIRS

His·pan·ic /hɪˈspænɪk/ adj. from or relating to a country where Spanish or Portuguese is spoken —**Hispanic** n. [C]

hiss /hɪs/ v. **1** [I] to make a noise which sounds like "ssss": *a snake hissing* **2** [T + at] to make this noise when you do not like a performer or speaker **3** [T] to say something in a loud whisper: *"Are you crazy?" he hissed.* —**hiss** n. [C]

his·self /ɪˈsɛlf; strong hɪˈsɛlf/ pron. NONSTANDARD himself

his·ta·mine /ˈhɪstəˌmin/ n. [C] a chemical compound that increases the flow of blood in your body and is involved in ALLERGIC reactions

his·to·ri·an /hɪˈstɔriən/ n. [C] someone who studies or writes about history

his·tor·ic /hɪˈstɔrɪk, -ˈstɑr-/ adj. [usually before noun] **1** a historic event, time, or place is or will be remembered as part of history, because important things happened in that time or place: *a historic building* | *historic developments in Eastern Europe* | *a historic voyage* **2** historic times are the periods of time whose history has been recorded —compare PREHISTORIC

his·tor·i·cal /hɪˈstɔrɪkəl/ adj. [usually before noun] **1** relating to the study of history: *the Historical Library in Springfield* **2** describing or based on events in the past: *a historical novel* **3** historical events, facts, people etc. happened or existed in the past: *The legend of John Henry is based on a real, historical figure.* —**historically** /-kli/ adv.

his·to·ry /ˈhɪstəri/ n. plural **histories**
1 `past events` [U] all the things that happened in the past, especially the political, social, or economic development of a nation: *Lincoln was one of the greatest presidents in America's history.* | *Throughout history, most societies have been governed by men.*
2 `subject of study` [U] the study of history, especially as a subject in school or college: *I got an 84 on my history test.*
3 `development of sth` [singular,U] the development of a subject, activity, institution etc. since it started: *the history of jazz music* | *Chernobyl was the worst accident in the history of nuclear power.*
4 `book` [C] a book about past events: *a history of World War II*
5 **have a history of sth** to have had an illness, problems etc. in the past: *Mr. Krasso has a history of heart problems.*
6 **make history** to do something important that will be recorded and remembered: *Lindbergh made history when he flew across the Atlantic in 1927.*
7 **sth will go down in history** used to say that something is important enough to be remembered and recorded: *1989 will go down in history as the year in which Stalinist Communism ended.*
8 **...and the rest is history** used to say that everyone knows the rest of a story you have been telling
9 **that's past/ancient history** SPOKEN used to say that something is not important anymore
10 **history repeats itself** used to say that things often happen in the same way as they happened before —see also NATURAL HISTORY, CASE HISTORY

his·tri·on·ics /ˌhɪstriˈɑnɪks/ n. [plural] loud extremely emotional behavior that is intended to get people's sympathy and attention —**histrionic** adj.

hit¹ /hɪt/ v. past tense and past participle **hit** present participle **hitting**
1 `strike` [I,T] to touch someone or something hard and quickly with your hand, a stick etc.: [hit sb with sth] *One woman died after a soldier hit her with a club.* | *No hitting, Eli. It's not nice.* | **hit sb on the head/on the nose/in the stomach etc.** (=hit a particular part of someone's body) —compare PUNCH¹ (1), SLAP¹ (1)
2 `crash into sb/sth` [T] to fall or crash into someone or something quickly and hard: *I guess he was crossing a busy street and got hit by a car.* | *There's a cut on his arm where he hit the pavement.*
3 `accidentally` [T] to move a part of your body quickly and hard against something by accident: *Careful, don't hit your head.* | [hit sth on/against etc.] *I kept hitting my knees on the seat in front.*
4 `affect badly` [T] to have a bad effect on someone or something: *Georgia and Alabama were hardest hit by the bad weather.*
5 `in sports` [T] to make something such as a ball move by hitting it with a BAT, stick etc.: *Sam's only three and he's already hitting baseballs really well.*
6 `bullets/bombs` [I,T] to attack, wound, or damage someone or something with bullets, bombs etc.: *Several missiles hit the city at dawn today.*
7 `reach sth` [T] to reach a particular level or number: *The temperature hit 100 degrees today.* | *The President's approval rating has hit a new low.*
8 `problem/trouble` [T] to experience trouble, a problem etc.: *I had hit a few snags in my work.*
9 `realize` [T] INFORMAL if a fact, idea etc. hits you, you suddenly realize its importance and feel surprised or shocked: *Suddenly it hit me: my granddaughter wasn't a baby any more.*

10 **arrive** [T] INFORMAL to arrive somewhere: *The Bolshoi Opera will hit New York on June 25.* | *Turn left at the first stop light you hit.*
11 **press sth** [T] INFORMAL to press a part in a machine, car etc. to make it work: *Hit the brakes!* | *Oops, I hit the wrong button.*

SPOKEN PHRASES

12 **do sth** [T] used in some expressions to show that you will do a particular thing: *It's time to hit the shower* (=go wash in one). | *We'll stay up north and hit Mount Rushmore* (=visit it). | *I have to hit the books* (=study).
13 **you've hit the nail on the head** used to say that what someone has said is exactly right
14 **hit the roof/the ceiling** to become extremely angry: *Nicole hit the ceiling when her flight got canceled.*
15 **hit the sack/hay** to go to bed: *It's getting late – I think I'll hit the sack.*
16 **hit the spot** if a food or drink hits the spot, it tastes good and is exactly what you want: *A cold beer sure would hit the spot.*

---

17 **not know what hit you** INFORMAL to be so surprised or shocked by something that you cannot think clearly
18 **hit sb where it hurts** also **hit sb where they live** INFORMAL to do something that damages or hurts someone a lot: *Instead of locking up drug offenders, hit them where it really hurts – in the wallet.*
19 **hit the road** INFORMAL to leave a place, especially to start on a trip: *She's planning to hit the road again in the morning.*
20 **hit it off (with sb)** INFORMAL if two people hit it off with each other, they like each other as soon as they meet: *Aliy's jealous that Matt and Ceara hit it off.*
21 **hit bottom** INFORMAL to be as unsuccessful or sad as you can be: *I had to hit bottom before I decided to kick the drugs.*
22 **hit it big** also **hit the big time** INFORMAL to suddenly become very famous, successful, and rich: *Swayze hit it big in the 1987 movie "Dirty Dancing."*
23 **tell sb sth** [T] INFORMAL if you hit someone with some information or news, you tell them something surprising or entertaining: *Once you've hit the customer with the price you want to close the deal quickly.*
24 **hit the ground/deck/dirt** INFORMAL to fall to the ground to avoid something dangerous: *"If gunfire starts, hit the ground!" a colonel barked at them.*
25 **hit the ground running** to start doing something successfully without any delay: *If we can hit the ground running, we'll stay ahead of the competition.*
26 **hit the jackpot a)** to win a lot of money **b)** INFORMAL to be very lucky or suddenly successful: *He really hit the jackpot when he married Cindy.*
27 **hit the bottle** INFORMAL to drink a lot of alcohol regularly
28 **hit a brick wall** INFORMAL to suddenly be unable to make any more progress in a situation —see also **hit/strike home** (HOME² (5)), **hit pay dirt** (PAY DIRT)

hit back *phr. v.* [I] to attack or criticize a person or group that has attacked or criticized you: *We had no choice but to hit back in defense of our people.*

hit on *phr. v.* [T] **1** [**hit on sb**] INFORMAL to talk to someone in a way that shows you are sexually attracted to them: *He's hit on every woman in the department.* **2** [**hit on/upon** sth] to have a good idea about something, often by chance: *Yes, Cargill, I think you've hit on something.*

hit out *phr. v.* [I] to express strong disapproval or disagreement of someone or something: [+ **at**] *Why try to hit out at people when this can be resolved peacefully?*

hit sb up for sth *phr. v.* [T] SPOKEN to ask someone for something: *Did he hit you up for cash again?*

hit² *n.* [C]
1 **popular** something such as a movie, song, play etc. that is extremely popular or successful: *an album of the Beatles' greatest hits* | *We didn't think the new album would be such a big hit.* | *a hit show/record/song Irving Berlin wrote dozens of hit songs.*

2 **hit sth** an occasion when something that is aimed at something else touches it, reaches it, or damages it: *One bomb scored a **direct hit** on the aircraft carrier.*
3 **computer** an occasion when someone uses a WEB-SITE: *Our site had 2000 hits in the first month.*
4 **search** a result of a computer search that you do for something on the Internet, a DATABASE etc.: *You may get thousands of hits that are irrelevant to your question.*
5 **baseball** an occasion when a baseball player hits the ball and successfully runs to a BASE
6 **be a hit (with sb)** to be liked very much by a person or group: *Since the museum opened, it has been a hit with the kids.*
7 **drug** SLANG an amount of a drug that you smoke, swallow etc.
8 **murder** SLANG a murder, especially one that is arranged to happen —see also HIT MAN

hit-and-miss also **hit-or-miss** /ˌ. . '. ◂/ *adj.* INFORMAL done in a way that is not planned or organized well: *a hit-and-miss advertising campaign*

hit-and-run /ˌ. . '. ◂/ *adj.* [only before noun] **1** a hit-and-run accident is one in which the driver of a car hits a person or another car and then drives away without stopping to help **2** a hit-and-run military attack is one in which the attackers arrive suddenly and without warning and leave quickly

hitch¹ /hɪtʃ/ *v.* **1** [I,T] INFORMAL to hitchhike: [+ **across/around/to**] *They spent the summer hitching around Europe.* **2** **hitch a ride a)** INFORMAL to get a ride from someone by hitchhiking: *We managed to hitch a ride in the back of a pickup truck.* **b)** SPOKEN to travel somewhere by asking someone such as a friend if you can go in their car: *I hitched a ride to school with Jamie.* **3** [T always + adv./prep.] to fasten something such as a TRAILER (1) to the back of a car so that it can be pulled **4** **get hitched** OLD-FASHIONED, INFORMAL to get married **5** [T always + adv./prep.] to tie a horse to something

hitch sth ↔ **up** *phr. v.* [T] **1** INFORMAL to pull a piece of clothing up, especially your pants **2** **hitch up a horse/wagon/team** to tie a horse to something, so that the horse can pull it

hitch² *n. plural* **hitches** [C] **1** a problem, especially one that delays something for a short time: *Thank goodness, the ceremony **went off without a hitch**.* **2** a part on a vehicle that is used to connect it to something it is pulling: *a trailer hitch* **3** INFORMAL a period of time you spend in the Army, Navy etc. **4** a type of loosely tied knot **5** a short sudden pull toward a higher position

Hitch·cock /ˈhɪtʃkɑk/**, Sir Al·fred** /ˈælfrɪd/ (1899–1980) a British movie DIRECTOR who is famous for his THRILLERS

H

hitchhike

hitch·hike /ˈhɪtʃhaɪk/ *v.* [I] to travel by standing beside a road and holding out your thumb to ask for free rides from passing cars; HITCH¹ (1) —**hitchhiker** *n.* [C]

hi-tech /ˌhaɪ ˈtɛk ◂/ *adj.* another spelling of HIGH-TECH

hith·er /ˈhɪðɚ/ *adv.* **1** **hither and thither/yon** LITERARY in many directions **2** a **come-hither look/voice** a way of looking at someone or saying something that is meant to attract someone **3** OLD USE here, to this place

hith·er·to /ˌhɪðəˈtu, ˈhɪðəˌtu/ adv. FORMAL until this time: *French astronomers have found a hitherto unknown galaxy.*

Hit·ler /ˈhɪtlə/, **A·dolf** /ˈeɪdɔlf/ (1889–1945) a German politician who was leader of the Nazi Party in Germany from 1921, and "Führer" (=leader) of Germany from the mid-1930s until his death. Hitler tried to establish a pure race of German people through a policy of ANTI-SEMITISM and started World War II by ordering his armies to enter Poland in 1939.

hit list /'. ./ n. [C] INFORMAL the names of people, organizations etc. whom you would like to damage or hurt: *Detective Bobby Caruso was at the top of his hit list.*

hit man /'. ./ n. [C] a criminal who is employed to kill someone

hit pa·rade /'. .,./ n. OLD-FASHIONED **the hit parade** a list of popular records or songs that shows which ones have sold the most copies

Hit·tite /ˈhɪtaɪt/ one of the people that lived in Turkey and Syria from the twentieth century to the eleventh century B.C.

HIV n. [U] Human Immunodeficiency Virus; a type of VIRUS that enters the body through the blood or sexual activity, and can cause AIDS: *Jeanie was HIV positive* (=has HIV in her body).

hive /haɪv/ n. **1** [C] **a)** also **beehive** a place where BEES live **b)** the group of bees that live together in a hive **2 a hive of activity/industry etc.** a place that is full of people who are very busy **3** [plural] **hives** a condition in which someone's skin swells and becomes red, usually because they are ALLERGIC to something

hi·ya /ˈhaɪyə/ interjection SPOKEN, INFORMAL hello

h'm, hmm /hm, hmh/ interjection a sound that you make to express doubt, a pause, or disagreement, or when you are thinking about what someone has said

HMO n. [C] Health Maintenance Organization; a type of health insurance in which members can only go to doctors and hospitals within the organization —compare PPO

hmph /hmf/ interjection used especially in writing to show that you do not approve of something

ho¹ /hoʊ/ interjection **1** also **ho ho** or **ho ho ho** used in writing to represent a shout of laughter in a deep voice **2 land/westward etc. ho** used to get someone's attention, in order to tell them that you can see land from a ship, that you are leaving to travel westward etc.

ho² n. plural **ho's** [C] SLANG **1** a PROSTITUTE **2** OFFENSIVE a woman or girl who you do not respect because she is too willing to have sex with many different people

hoa·gie /ˈhoʊgi/ n. [C] a SUBMARINE SANDWICH

hoard¹ /hɔrd/ v. [T] also **hoard up** to collect and hide large amounts of food, money etc., so you can use it later: *Some gasoline dealers began hoarding supplies.* —**hoarder** n. [C]

hoard² n. [C] a collection of things that someone keeps hidden, especially so that they can be used later: [+ of] *a hoard of weapons*

hoar·frost /ˈhɔrfrɔst/ n. [U] FROST¹ (1)

hoarse /hɔrs/ adj. someone who is hoarse has a voice that sounds rough, often because they have a sore throat: *His voice dropped to a hoarse whisper.* —**hoarsely** adv. —**hoarseness** n. [U]

hoar·y /ˈhɔri/ OLD-FASHIONED adj. **hoarier, hoariest** **1** old and not very interesting or original: *a hoary 1940s musical* **2** hoary hair is gray or white **3** having gray or white hair —**hoariness** n. [U]

hoax¹ /hoʊks/ n. [C] an attempt to make people believe something that is not true: *The UFO sightings were revealed to be a hoax.*

hoax² v. [T] to trick someone by using a hoax —**hoaxer** n. [C]

hob /hɑb/ n. OLD-FASHIONED **1** [C] a flat surface where you cook food or keep it warm, such as a shelf in a FIREPLACE or the top of a STOVE **2 play hob with sth** to do something that damages or spoils something

Hobbes /hɑbz/, **Thomas** (1588–1679) a British political PHILOSOPHER

hob·ble /ˈhɑbəl/ v. **1** [I] to walk with difficulty, taking small steps, usually because you are injured: *Laurel hobbled out of the taxi on crutches.* **2** [T] if an injury hobbles someone, it makes it difficult for them to walk: *A sprained toe hobbled Clemons for most of the week.* **3** [T] to make it difficult for a plan, system etc. to work successfully: *Mistakes can hobble a deal from the start.* **4** [T] to loosely fasten two of an animal's legs together, to stop it from running away

hob·by /ˈhɑbi/ n. plural **hobbies** [C] an activity that you enjoy doing in your free time: *My hobby is repairing antiques.* —**hobbyist** n. [C]

hob·by·horse /ˈhɑbi,hɔrs/ n. **1** [C] a child's toy like a horse's head on a stick, which the child pretends to ride on **2 be/get on your hobbyhorse** to talk for a long time about a subject you think is very interesting or important

hob·gob·lin /ˈhɑb,gɑblən/ n. [C] a GOBLIN that plays tricks on people

hob·nail /ˈhɑbneɪl/ n. [C] a large nail with a big flat top, used to make the bottom part of heavy boots and shoes stronger —**hobnailed** adj.

hob·nob /ˈhɑbnɑb/ v. [I] INFORMAL to spend time talking to people who are in a higher social position than you: [+ with] *Benech liked to hobnob with local politicians.*

ho·bo /ˈhoʊboʊ/ n. plural **hobos** [C] someone who travels around and has no home or regular job

Hob·son's choice /ˌhɑbsənz ˈtʃɔɪs/ n. [U] a situation in which there is only one thing you can do, that is, you have no choice at all

Ho Chi Minh /ˌhoʊ tʃi ˈmɪn/ (1890–1969) the President of North Vietnam during the first part of the Vietnam War

Ho Chi Minh Cit·y /ˌ. . . '../ a city in the southern part of Vietnam. It was formerly known as Saigon, and was the capital of South Vietnam when the country was divided.

hock¹ /hɑk/ n. **1 in hock** INFORMAL **a)** in debt: *I'm not going to put myself in hock for the rest of my life.* **b)** something that is in hock has been sold temporarily because you need money; PAWNed² **2** [C] a piece of meat from above the foot of an animal, especially a pig: *ham hocks* **3** [C] the middle joint of an animal's back leg

hock² v. [T] INFORMAL to sell something valuable to a PAWNBROKER in order to get some money, while hoping you can buy it back later; PAWNed²

hock·ey /ˈhɑki/ n. [U] **1** also **ice hockey** a sport played on ice, in which players use long curved sticks to hit a hard flat round object into a GOAL **2** FIELD HOCKEY

hock·shop /ˈhɑkʃɑp/ n. [C] INFORMAL a PAWNSHOP

ho·cus-po·cus /ˌhoʊkəs ˈpoʊkəs/ n. [U] a word meaning "magic," used about methods or beliefs that you think are meant to trick you or are based on false ideas: *Corporate executives should recognize financial hocus-pocus by now.*

hod /hɑd/ n. [C] a container shaped like a box with a long handle, used for carrying bricks

hodge·podge /ˈhɑdʒpɑdʒ/ n. [singular] INFORMAL a lot of things mixed up together with no order or arrangement: [+ of] *The album is a hodgepodge of folk, pop, soul, and jazz.*

hoe¹ /hoʊ/ n. [C] a garden tool with a long handle, used for making the soil loose and removing unwanted wild plants

hoe² v. **hoed, hoeing** [I,T] to make soil loose using a hoe —see also **a hard/tough row to hoe** (ROW¹ (4))

hoe·down /ˈhoʊdaʊn/ n. [C] a party where there is SQUARE-DANCING

hog¹ /hɑg, hɔg/ n. [C] **1** a large pig that is kept for its meat —compare BOAR, SOW² **2** INFORMAL someone who eats, keeps, or uses so much of something that there is not much left for other people: *Don't be such a hog.* **3 go (the) whole hog** INFORMAL to do something thoroughly: *We decided to go whole hog and stay in the Honeymoon suite.* **4 go hog wild** INFORMAL to suddenly do an activity in an uncontrolled and excited way —**hoggish** *adj.* —see also **live high on the hog** (HIGH² (7)), ROAD HOG

hog² *v.* **hogged, hogging** [T] INFORMAL to keep or use all of something so that other people cannot share it: *Mom, Pam's hogging the bathroom again!*

ho·gan /ˈhoʊɡən/ *n.* [C] a traditional Navajo house made of branches covered with mud or soil

Ho·gan /ˈhoʊɡən/, **Ben** /bɛn/ (1912–) a U.S. GOLF player

hogs·head /ˈhɑɡzhɛd, ˈhɔɡz-/ *n.* [C] a large container for holding beer, or the amount that it holds

hog-tie /ˈ. ./ *v.* **hog-tied, hog-tying** [T] to tie someone's hands and feet together in the way an animal's legs are sometimes tied after it is killed

hog·wash /ˈhɑɡwɑʃ, ˈhɔɡwɔʃ/ *n* [U] talk that you think is full of lies or is wrong: *That stuff is just a bunch of hogwash.*

ho ho ho /ˌhoʊ hoʊ ˈhoʊ/ *interjection* used to represent the sound of laughter

ho-hum /ˌhoʊ ˈhʌm/ *adj.* [no comparative] INFORMAL boring and ordinary: *a ho-hum performance*

hoi pol·loi /ˌhɔɪ pəˈlɔɪ/ *n.* **the hoi polloi** an insulting phrase for ordinary people

hoist¹ /hɔɪst/ also **hoist up** *v.* [T] **1** to raise, lift, or pull up something heavy or something that needs ropes to be raised: *A school custodian hoisted the American flag every morning.* | *Fathers hoisted sons on their shoulders to see Mr. Mandela.* **2 hoist a glass** to raise a glass of a drink in the air before you drink it to celebrate something **3 be hoisted by your own petard** to be harmed or embarrassed by something that you planned or said yourself

hoist² *n.* **1** [C] a piece of equipment for lifting heavy objects with ropes **2** [C usually singular] a pull toward a higher position

hoi-ty-toi-ty /ˌhɔɪti ˈtɔɪti/ *adj.* OLD-FASHIONED behaving in a proud way, as if you are important

ho·key /ˈhoʊki/ *adj.* **hokier, hokiest** INFORMAL expressing emotions in a way that is too simple, old-fashioned, or silly: *It may sound hokey, but county fairs are still great entertainment.*

ho·kum /ˈhoʊkəm/ *n.* [U] something that seems to be true or impressive but is actually wrong or not sincere: *Jackson said the entire plan was hokum.*

Hol·bein /ˈhoʊlbaɪn/, **Hans** /hɑns/ **1 Hans Holbein the Elder** (?1464–1524) a German PAINTER who painted pictures for churches and was the father of Hans Holbein the Younger **2 Hans Holbein the Younger** (1497–1543) a German PAINTER famous for his pictures of people

hold¹ /hoʊld/ *v. past tense and past participle* **held**
1 in your hands/arms to have something firmly in your hand or arms: *What a cute baby. Can I hold her?* | [hold sth in sth] *Sherman stood there, holding a gun in his hand.* | [hold sth up/toward/out etc.] *He sat down, still holding the newspaper in front of him.* | *Two little girls walked by, holding hands* (=each other's hands).
2 hold sb close [T] to put your arms around someone in order to comfort them, show you love them etc.: *That night, we slept in the truck, and Terry held me tight.*
3 keep sth in position [T always + adv./prep.] to make something stay in a particular position: [hold sth down/up/open etc.] *Martin held the door open for her.* | *Short posts will hold the rails in place.*
4 have space for [T not in progressive] to have the space to contain a particular amount of something: *Heat the stock in a pot large enough to hold the fish.* | *Each carton holds 113 oranges.*
5 hold a position/rank/job to have a particular job or position, especially one that shows you have succeeded in something: *Less than 4% of top business jobs are held by women.* | *Birnbaum holds a doctorate in physics.*
6 event [T] to have a meeting, party etc. in a

particular place or at a particular time: *The International Ballet Competition is held in Jackson every four years.* | *Vicki doesn't know where her class is being held.*
7 own sth [T] to own or possess something, especially money or land: *IBM still holds shares in the new company.*
8 keep sb somewhere [T] to keep a person or animal somewhere, and not allow them to leave: *Nobody will be held against their will* (=made to stay when they do not want to). | **held hostage/captive** (=kept as a prisoner)
9 arm/leg/back etc. [T always + adv./prep.] to put or keep a part of your body in a particular position: [hold sth up/out/straight etc.] *She held her hands out to keep from bumping into anything.*
10 hold a place/seat/room etc. to save a place, room etc. for someone until they want to use it: *I've asked them to hold a table for twelve people, okay?*
11 be strong enough [I,T] to support the weight of something: *I just want a shelf that will hold some plants.* | *The branch held, and Nick climbed higher up the tree.*
12 keep/contain [T] to keep or contain something so it can be used or gotten later: *Lost items will be held for thirty days.*
13 amount/level [I,T] to continue at a particular amount, level, or rate, or to make something do this: *Traders thought gold would hold at $350 an ounce.*
14 hold sb's interest/attention to make someone continue being interested in something: *Storytellers held the children's interest.*
15 believe [T not in progressive, usually passive] FORMAL to believe something to be true: [+ that] *Buddhism holds that the state of existence is suffering.*
16 hold sb responsible/accountable to consider someone to be responsible for something, so that they will be blamed if anything bad happens: [+ for] *I can't be held responsible for what Floyd does.*

SPOKEN PHRASES

17 hold it! also **hold everything! a)** used to interrupt someone: *Hold it a minute! I've just had a really good idea.* **b)** used to tell someone to wait or to stop what they are doing: *Hold it! Sara just lost a contact lens.*
18 [I] also **hold the line** to wait until the person you have telephoned is ready to answer: *Thank you for calling Society Bank – can you hold please?*
19 hold your horses! used to tell someone they are being impatient and should wait before doing something
20 hold your fire! a military order used to tell soldiers to stop shooting

---

21 hold true/good if a statement, fact, or promise holds true or holds good, it is still true or continues to have an effect: *If past experience holds true, about 10% of the injured will need immediate surgery.*
22 hold good if a law, rule, reason etc. holds good, it is or remains effective or true in different situations: *The President said that the promise will hold good no matter what the North Korean government does.*
23 music [T] to make a musical note continue for a long time
24 army [T] if an army holds a place, it either defends it from attack, or controls it by using force: *The French army held the town for three days.*
25 hold your own to defend yourself, or to succeed, in a difficult situation: *Colman held his own against Miller, one of the league's toughest players.*
26 hold fast to sth FORMAL to keep believing strongly in an idea or principle, or keep doing something in spite of difficulties: *Jackson urged the Democrats to hold fast to their traditions.*
27 weather/luck [I] if good weather or good luck holds, it continues without changing: *As long as the mild weather holds, you can keep planting.*
28 be left holding the bag to become responsible for something that someone else has started, whether you want to be or not

29 hold the fort to be responsible for taking care of something, while the person usually responsible is not there: *The three of you will be holding the fort in the kitchen tonight.*

30 the future [T] FORMAL used to talk about what will happen in the future or a particular situation in the future: *Who knows what the future holds?*

31 hold sth dear to feel that something is very important: *Everything I held dear was destroyed in the war.*

32 hold interest/appeal etc. FORMAL to have a particular quality: *Such an emphasis on religion may hold little appeal for modern tastes.*

33 not hold water if an argument, statement etc. does not hold water, it is not true or reasonable: *It may seem logical, but his argument doesn't hold water.*

34 hold a conversation to have a conversation

35 hold your head up/high to show pride or confidence in a difficult situation: *I can hold my head high because I know that I am innocent.*

36 not hold a candle to sb/sth INFORMAL to be much worse than someone or something else: *Dry herbs don't hold a candle to fresh ones.*

37 hold all the cards to have a strong advantage in a situation: *Politically, the logging industry holds all the cards.*

38 hold the road if a car holds the road well, you can drive it quickly around bends without losing control

39 hold your alcohol/liquor to be able to drink a lot of alcohol without becoming drunk

40 there's no holding sb (back) used to say that someone is so eager to do something that you cannot prevent them from doing it: *For Casey, there was no holding back when it came to music.*

41 hold a course if an aircraft, ship, storm etc. holds a course, it continues to move in a particular direction —see also **hold your breath** (BREATH (2)), **hold court** (COURT¹ (5)), **hold your tongue** (TONGUE (16))

hold sth **against** sb *phr. v.* [T] to allow something that someone has done to make you dislike them or want to harm them: *Patterson said he didn't hold the judgment against the jury.*

hold back *phr. v.* **1** [T **hold** sb/sth ↔ **back**] to make someone or something stop moving forward: *Police in riot gear held back the demonstrators.* **2** [T **hold** sth ↔ **back**] to stop yourself from feeling or showing a particular emotion: *Nancy tried to hold back a sob.* | *They don't hold anything back when they're on stage.* **3** [T **hold** sb/sth ↔ **back**] to prevent someone or something from developing or improving: *The housing market is still being held back by a weak economy.* **4** [I] to be slow or unwilling to do something, especially because you are being careful: *Trading was light as many investors held back.* **5** [I,T **hold** sth ↔ **back**] to keep something secret: *He held back important information about his background.*

hold down *phr. v.* [T] **1** [**hold** sth ↔ **down**] to prevent something such as prices from rising: *Hallmark has asked its employees to help hold down costs.* **2 hold down a job** to succeed in keeping a job for a period of time: *Clarke holds down two jobs to support his family.* **3** [**hold** sb ↔ **down**] to keep people under control or limit their freedom: *The treaty is meant to help people, not hold them down.*

hold forth *phr. v.* [I] give your opinion on a subject, especially for a long time: [+ **on**] *David Lean held forth on the disastrous state of the movie industry.*

hold off *phr. v.* **1** [I,T **hold** sth ↔ **off**] to delay something: [**hold off (on) doing sth**] *Businesses are holding off on hiring new employees.* **2** [T **hold** sb ↔ **off**] to prevent someone who is trying to attack you or defeat you from managing to do this: *The Pittsburgh Pirates held off New York 10–8.* **3** [I] if rain or snow holds off, none of it falls, although you thought it would

hold on *phr. v.* [I] **1 hold on!** SPOKEN **a)** said when you want someone to wait or stop talking for a short time, for example during a telephone call: *Could you hold on, please, while I transfer you.* | *Hold on a minute. Let me put this in the car.* **b)** used when you have just noticed something surprising: *Hold on, who's that in the picture?* **2** to hold something tightly with your hand or arms: [+ **to**] *She can walk now without holding on to anything.* **3** to continue doing something when it is very difficult to do so: *How long will good teachers like her hold on?*

hold on to *phr. v.* [T] **1** [**hold on to** sth] to keep something and not lose it, sell it, or have it taken from you: *Can you hold on to those tickets for me?* **2** [**hold on to** sb] to not lose someone who is important to you: *Stanford tries to hold on to all students until graduation.*

hold out *phr. v.* **1** [I] if something such as a supply of something holds out, there is still some left: *We stayed as long as the wine held out.* **2** [I] to continue to defend a place that is being attacked: *For ten weeks the troops have held out against mortar attacks.* **3 hold out little hope** also **not hold out much hope** to think that something is not likely to be possible or have a good result: *Authorities held out little hope of finding more survivors.*

hold out for sth *phr. v.* [T] to not accept anything less than what you have asked for: *Some house sellers are still holding out for higher offers.*

hold out on sb *phr. v.* [T] INFORMAL to refuse to give someone information or an answer that they need: *Why didn't you tell me right away instead of holding out on me?*

hold over *phr. v.* **1 be held over** if a play, movie, concert etc. is held over, it is shown for longer than planned, because it is very popular **2** [T **hold** sth **over** sb] to threaten to do something to someone if they do not do something you want: *The Coca Cola Company gives money to schools without holding anything over their heads* (=without making them promise to do anything in particular). **3** [T **hold** sth **over**] to do or deal with something at a later date: *The House committee plans to hold the bill over until next week.* —see also HOLDOVER

hold sb **to** sth *phr. v.* [T] **1** to make someone do what they have promised: *"I'll ask him tomorrow." "All right, but I'm going to hold you to that."* **2** to prevent your opponent in a sports game from getting more than a particular number of points: *Louisiana Tech held the Cougars to a 3–3 tie in the first quarter.*

hold together *phr. v.* **1** [I,T **hold** sth **together**] if a group or organization holds together or you hold it together, it stays strong and does not break apart: *It's love that holds this family together.* **2** [I] to remain whole, without breaking or separating: *Stir in milk just until the dough holds together.*

hold up *phr. v.* **1** [T **hold** sb/sth ↔ **up**] to support someone or something and stop them from falling down: *The crumbling arch is held up by scaffolding.* **2** [T **hold** sb/sth ↔ **up**] to delay someone or something: *The cotton harvest has been held up by rain.* | *Sorry I'm late – I was held up at work.* **3** [T **hold up** sth] to rob or try to rob a place while using a weapon: *Preston held up a jewelry store downtown.* —see also HOLDUP **4** [I] to remain strong or in good condition: *I'm surprised by how well this car has held up.*

hold sb/sth **up as** sth *phr. v.* [T] to use someone or something as an example: *Over the years, IBM has been held up as a model employer.*

hold² n.

1 action of holding sth [singular] the action of holding something tightly: *Kara tightened her hold on the bat.* | **have/keep hold of sth** *Keep hold of my hand when we cross the road.* —see also GRIP¹ (1)

2 get/take/grab/seize hold of sth to take something and hold it with one hand or both hands: *Grab hold of the rope and pull yourself up.* | *I took hold of her hand and gently led her away.*

3 get (a) hold of sb SPOKEN to manage to speak to someone for a particular reason: *Four-thirty would be the best time to get a hold of me.*

4 get (a) hold of sth SPOKEN to find or borrow something: *I need to get hold of a car.* | *We don't know how he got hold of our trade secrets.*

5 on hold waiting to speak or be spoken to on the telephone: *Do you mind if I put you on hold?*

6 put sth on hold to delay doing or starting something

7 take hold to start to have an effect: *The fever was beginning to take hold.*

8 sports [C] a particular position that you hold an opponent in, in a sport such as WRESTLING or JUDO

9 climbing [C] somewhere you can put your hands or feet when you are climbing: *The cliff is steep and it's difficult to find a hold.*

10 ship [C] the part of a ship below the DECK¹ where goods are stored

11 get hold of an idea/impression/story etc. INFORMAL to learn or begin to believe something: *Where on earth did you get hold of that idea?*

12 have a hold over/on to have power or influence over a person, group, or area: *Yeltsin's hold over the Russian parliament is weak.*

13 no holds barred used to say that there are no rules or limits in a situation: *There are no holds barred when it comes to making a profit.*

hold·er /'houldə/ n. [C] **1** someone who possesses or has control of a place, position, or thing: *Credit card holders can order tickets by phone.* **2** something that holds or contains something else: *a cigarette holder | candle holders*

hold·ing /'houldɪŋ/ n. [C] something that you own or rent, especially land or STOCK in a company

holding com·pa·ny /'.. ,.../ n. [C] a company that owns a controlling number of the SHARES in other companies

holding pat·tern /'.. ,.../ n. [C usually singular] **1** the path that an aircraft follows as it flies over a place while it is waiting for permission to go down to the ground **2** a situation in which you cannot do anything more until you know the results of someone else's decision or action: *The court case has been in a holding pattern, waiting for new charges.*

hold·o·ver /'hould,ouvə/ n. [C] a feeling, idea, fashion etc. from the past that has continued into the present: [+ from] *Abe, with his long hair and beard, looks like a holdover from the 1960s.* —see also **hold over** (HOLD¹)

hold·up /'houldʌp/ n. [C] **1** INFORMAL an attempt to rob a person or place, using a weapon: *a supermarket holdup* **2** INFORMAL a delay: *What's the holdup?* —see also **hold up** (HOLD¹)

hole¹ /houl/ n. [C]

1 space in sth solid an empty space in something that should be solid or whole: [+ in] *All my jeans have holes in the knees. | How can I fill the holes in my driveway cheaply? | a bullet hole* (=made by a bullet)

2 animal's home the home of a small animal: *a rabbit hole*

3 weak part a part of an idea, plan, story etc. that is weak or wrong: *Levitt concluded that the article was full of holes.*

4 be in the hole SPOKEN to owe money: *We're already $140 in the hole.*

5 unpleasant place INFORMAL a place for living in, working in etc. that is dirty, small, or in bad condition: *I have to get out of this hole.*

6 golf a hole in the ground that you try to get the ball into in the game of GOLF, or the area around one of these holes

7 hole in one an occasion when you hit the ball in GOLF from the starting place into the hole with only one hit

8 I need sth like a hole in the head SPOKEN used to say that you definitely do not need or want something: *I need a new girlfriend like I need a hole in the head.*

9 make a hole in sth INFORMAL to reduce an amount of money, food etc.: *The cost of the house repairs made a big hole in my savings.* —see also BLACK HOLE, WATERING HOLE

hole² v. **1 be holed** if an aircraft or ship is holed, it has a hole in it **2** [T] also **hole out** [I] to hit the ball into the hole in GOLF

hole up phr. v. [I always + adv./prep.] INFORMAL to hide or stay somewhere for a period of time: [+ at/in] *Nine Cuban refugees were holed up in the embassy.*

hole in the heart /,. . . . '. / n. [singular,U] a medical condition in which the two sides of someone's heart are not correctly separated

hole-in-the-wall /,. . . . '. / n. [C] INFORMAL a small dark store or restaurant: *We ended up at this hole-in-the-wall biker bar.*

hol·i·day /'halə,deɪ/ n. plural **holidays** [C] **1** a day set by law on which people do not have to go to work or school: *July 1 is a national holiday in Canada.* **2** the holiday season also the holidays the period of time between Thanksgiving and New Year's Day in the U.S.: *Sales were up during the holiday season. | We'll get together after the holidays.* **3** BRITISH a VACATION¹ —see Usage Note at VACATION¹

Hol·i·day, /'halə,deɪ/, **Bil·lie** /'bɪli/ (1915–59) a JAZZ and BLUES singer, who is considered one of the greatest jazz and blues singers ever

Billie Holiday

holier-than-thou /,. . . '. / adj. showing that you think you are morally better than other people: *a holier-than-thou attitude*

ho·li·ness /'houlinɪs/ n. **1** [U] the quality of being pure and good in a religious way: *God's holiness* **2 Your/His Holiness** used as a title for speaking to or talking about the Pope

ho·lis·tic /hou'lɪstɪk/ adj. **1** based on the principle that a person or thing needs to be dealt with as a whole, because they are more than just their many small parts added together: *a holistic approach to education* **2 holistic medicine** medical treatment based on the belief that the whole person must be treated, not just the part of their body that has a disease —**holistically** /-kli/ adv.

Hol·land /'halənd/ another name for the Netherlands

hol·lan·daise sauce /,halən'deɪz ,sɔs/ n. [U] a creamy SAUCE made of butter, eggs, and LEMON

hol·ler /'halə/ v. [I,T] INFORMAL to shout loudly: *If you need anything, just holler. | [+ at] Hollering at me isn't going to find us a parking place.* —**holler** n. [C]

hol·low¹ /'halou/ adj. **1** having an empty space inside: *The walls are made of hollow concrete blocks. | a hollow tree* **2** feelings or words that are hollow are not sincere or important: *hollow threats* **3 hollow-eyed/hollow-cheeked etc.** having eyes, cheeks etc. where the skin sinks in: *A hollow-cheeked POW climbed into the back of the truck.* **4** a sound that is hollow is low and clear like the sound made when you hit something empty: *The bread should sound hollow when you tap the bottom.* **5 hollow laugh/voice etc.** a hollow laugh or voice is one that makes a weak sound and is without emotion —**hollowly** adv. —**hollowness** n. [U]

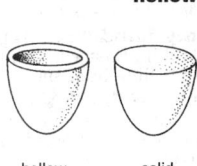

hollow

hollow   solid

hollow² n. a place in something that is at a slightly lower level than its surface: *Fill the hollow with the cream cheese mixture.*

hollow³ v.

hollow sth ↔ out phr. v. [T] to make a hole or empty space by removing the inside part of something: *Hollow out the pumpkin before you carve your jack-o-lantern.*

hol·ly /'hali/ n. [U] a small tree with sharp dark green leaves and red berries (BERRY), or the leaves and berries of this tree used as a decoration at Christmas

Hol·ly, /'hali/, **Bud·dy** /'bʌdi/ (1936–1959) a U.S. singer,

H

GUITAR player, and SONGWRITER who helped to make ROCK 'N' ROLL music popular in the 1950s

hol·ly·hock /'hɑli,hɑk/ *n.* [C] a tall thin garden plant with many flowers growing together

Hol·ly·wood /'hɑli,wʊd/ *n.* a part of Los Angeles, California, where movies are made, often used to mean the movie industry itself: *Beatty is wise and wary about his position in Hollywood.*

Holmes /hoʊmz, hoʊlmz/**, Ol·i·ver Wen·dell**[1] /'ɑlɔvɚ 'wɛndl/ (1809–1894) a U.S. doctor and writer

Holmes, Oliver Wendell[2] (1841–1935) a judge on the U.S. Supreme Court

hol·o·caust /'hɑlɔ,kɔst, 'hoʊ-/ *n.* [C] **1** an event that kills many people and destroys many things: *a nuclear holocaust* **2 the Holocaust** the killing of millions of Jews by the Nazis in World War II

hol·o·gram /'hoʊlɔ,græm, 'hɑ-/ *n.* [C] a type of photograph made with a LASER, that looks as if it is not flat when you look at it from an angle

ho·log·ra·phy /hoʊ'lɑgrɔfi/ *n.* [U] the process and science of making holograms —**holographic** /,hoʊlɔ-'græfɪk, ,hɑ-/ *adj.*

Holst /hoʊlst/**, Gus·tav** /'gʊstɑv/ (1874–1934) a British composer who wrote CLASSICAL music

Hol·stein /'hoʊlstin, -staɪn/ *n.* [C] a type of cow that is black and white

hol·ster /'hoʊlstɚ/ *n.* [C] a leather object in which a gun is carried, that is worn on a belt

ho·ly /'hoʊli/ *adj.* **holier, holiest 1** relating to God and religion; SACRED: *the holy city of Jerusalem* | *The Koran is the Islamic holy book.* **2** very religious: *a holy man* **3 holy cow/mackerel/moly etc.** SPOKEN used to express surprise, admiration, or fear **4 a holy terror** INFORMAL a child who causes a lot of trouble, especially because they are very active —see also **take (holy) orders** (ORDER[1] (17))

Holy Bi·ble /,.. '../ *n.* [singular] the BIBLE (1)

Holy Fam·i·ly /,.. '../ *n.* **the Holy Family** Jesus Christ, his mother Mary, and her husband Joseph

Holy Fa·ther /,.. '../ *n.* [singular] a phrase used when speaking to or about the Pope

Holy Ghost /,.. './ *n.* [singular] the HOLY SPIRIT

Holy Grail /,hoʊli 'greɪl/ *n.* [singular] **1** something that you try very hard to get or achieve: *A vaccine for malaria has become something of a scientific holy grail.* **2 the Holy Grail** the cup believed to have been used by Jesus Christ before his death

Holy Land /'.. ,./ *n.* **the Holy Land** the parts of the Middle East where most of the events mentioned in the Bible happened

holy of ho·lies /,... . '../ *n.* **a) the holy of holies** HUMOROUS a room in a building where only important people are allowed to go **b)** the most holy part of a Jewish TEMPLE

holy roll·er /,.. '../ *n.* [C] an insulting word for a member of a PENTECOSTAL church

Holy See /,.. './ *n.* FORMAL **the Holy See** the authority the Pope has, and everything he is responsible for

Holy Spir·it /,.. '../ *n.* **the Holy Spirit** God in the form of a spirit, according to the Christian religion

holy war /'.. ,./ *n.* [C] a war that is fought to defend the beliefs of a religion

holy wa·ter /,.. '../ *n.* [U] water that has been BLESSed by a priest

Holy Week /'.. ,./ *n.* [singular, not with **the**] the week before Easter in the Christian Church

Holy Writ /,.. './ *n.* [U] OLD-FASHIONED the Bible, considered as a book that is true in every detail

hom·age /'hɑmɪdʒ, 'ɑ-/ *n.* [U] FORMAL something that you say or do to show respect for a person or thing that you think is important: *Memorial Day is when Americans pay homage to those killed in the nation's wars.*

hom·bre /'ɑmbreɪ/ *n.* [C] a man, especially one who is strong: *He's one tough hombre.*

hom·burg /'hɑmbɔg/ *n.* [C] a soft hat for men with a wide edge around it

home[1] /hoʊm/ *n.*

1 `place where you live` [C,U] the house, apartment, or place where you live: *The restaurant isn't far from our home, so it's convenient.* | *I spent the evening* **at home** *watching TV.* | *Gene had to* **go home** *and feed the dog.* | *A family of swallows had* **made their home** *under the roof.*

2 `family` [C,U] the place where a child and his or her family live: *I think she still lives at home with her parents.* | *Neil wants to* **leave home** *as soon as he turns 18.* | *Are you* **going home** *for Christmas?*

3 `where you lived/belong` [C,U] where you lived as a child or where you usually live, especially when this is the place where you feel happy and comfortable: *She was born in Italy, but she's made Charleston her home.*

4 `in your country` in the country where you live, as opposed to foreign countries: *There may be a crisis abroad, but we also have problems* **here at home**. | *Be sure to notify your relatives* **back home** *if you change your travel plans.*

5 be/feel at home a) to feel happy or confident about doing or using something: [+ with/in] *I feel more at home in blue jeans than in a suit.* | *Takazauckas is* **equally at home** *directing theater and opera.* **b)** to feel comfortable in a place or with a person: [+ in] *I'm already feeling at home in the new apartment.* | *Helen always* **makes people feel at home** *(=makes people comfortable by being friendly).*

6 `property` [C] a house, apartment etc., considered as property that you can buy or sell: *The tax rate depends on when the home was purchased.*

7 `for taking care of sb` [C] a place where people who are very old or sick, or where children who have no family are taken care of: *They grew up in a children's home in Ohio.* | *I never wanted to put my mother in a home.* —see also NURSING HOME

8 make yourself at home SPOKEN used to tell someone who is visiting you that they should relax: *Make yourselves at home. Would you like a cup of coffee?*

9 be the home of sth a) to be the place where something was first made, discovered, or developed: *America is the home of baseball.* **b)** to be the place where a person, animal, or plant lives

10 be home to sth a) to be the place where a person, animal, or plant lives: *Paris was home to some of this century's most important artists.* **b)** to be the place where something is or where something typically happens: *North Carolina is home to the Green River Narrows.*

11 `sports team` **at home** if a sports team plays at home, it plays at its own sports field: *The Jets lost 6–3 at home to New England.* —opposite AWAY[2]

12 `in baseball` HOME PLATE

13 home away from home a place that you think is as pleasant and comfortable as your own house: *For many people, the office has become a home away from home.*

14 home sweet home used to say that you think it is very pleasant to be in your home —see also HOME RUN

home[2] *adv.* **1** to or at the place where you live: *Is Sue home from work yet?* | *I need to* **go home** *and try and get some sleep.* | *You should* **stay home** *until you're feeling better.* | **come/get home** *(=arrive at your home)* **2 take home** to earn a certain amount of money after tax has been taken off: *Diane takes home about $140 a week.* **3 hit/drive/hammer sth home a)** to do or say something in an extremely direct and determined way, to make sure that someone understands what you mean: *Children do have rights, and this week's report drives that point home.* **b)** to hit or push something firmly into the correct position **4 bring sth home to sb** to make you realize how serious, difficult, or dangerous something is: *The Christmas holidays can really bring home what it means to be out of work.* **5 hit/strike home** if a comment, situation, experience etc. hits or strikes home, it has a makes someone realize how serious, difficult, or dangerous something is: *The reality of* the war didn't hit home until someone from the neighborhood was killed. **6 be home free** INFORMAL to have succeeded in doing the most difficult part of something: *He's lost a lot of weight, but he's not home free yet.* —see also **hit/strike close to home** (CLOSE³ (4))

home³ *adj.* [only before noun] **1** done at home or intended for use in a home: *I'm looking forward to some **home** cooking* (=food that is cooked at home). | *a home computer* | *home appliances* **2** relating to or belonging to your home or family: **home address/number** (=the address at your house or the telephone number there) —see also HOMETOWN **3** played or playing at a team's own sports field, rather than an opponent's field: *a home game* | *the home team* (=from the place where the game is being played)

home⁴ *v.*

home in on *phr. v.* [T] to aim exactly at something and move directly toward it: *A rescue plane homed in on the location of the crash.*

home base /ˌ. './ *n.* **1** [C usually singular] the place that someone returns to in order to rest, learn new things, or exchange information, for example a soldier or someone who travels for their job: *the astronauts' home base at Johnson Space Center* **2** [C usually singular] a company's HEADQUARTERS **3** [U] HOME PLATE

home·bod·y /'hoʊmˌbɑdi/ *n.* [C] someone who enjoys being at home

home·boy /'hoʊmbɔɪ/ *n.* [C] SLANG a male HOMEY

home brew /ˌ. './ *n.* [U] beer made at home —**home brewed** *adj.*

home·com·ing /'hoʊmˌkʌmɪŋ/ *n.* **1** [C] an occasion when someone comes back to their home after a long absence **2** [C,U] a special occasion every year when former students return to their high school or college: **homecoming game/dance** (=special sports game or dance that happens at homecoming) **3** homecoming **king/queen** a boy and girl who are chosen by other students to represent them at homecoming events

home-court ad·van·tage also **home-field advantage** /ˌ. '. ˌ../ *n.* [singular,U] an advantage that a sports team has because it is playing a game on its own sports field or court

home ec·o·nom·ics /ˌ. ..'../ *n.* [U] the study of cooking, SEWING, and other skills used in the home, taught as a subject at school

home fries /'. ./ *n.* [plural] boiled potatoes that have been cut and fried in butter or oil

home front /'. ./ *n.* [singular] the people who stay and work in their own country while others go abroad to fight in a war: *The President also praised the families **on the home front**.*

home·grown /ˌhoʊm'groʊn◂/ *adj.* **1** born, made, or produced in your own country, town etc.: *homegrown entertainment* **2** vegetables and fruit that are homegrown are grown in your own garden

home·land /'hoʊmlænd/ *n.* [C] **1** the country where someone was born **2** an area of land made by or for a particular group of people to live in: *the creation of a Jewish homeland*

home·less /'hoʊmlɪs/ *adj.* **1 the homeless** people who do not have a place to live, and who often live on the streets **2** without a home: *Recent floods have left thousands homeless.* —**homelessness** *n.* [U]

home·ly /'hoʊmli/ *adj.* **homelier, homeliest 1** a homely person is not very attractive **2** simple and ordinary: *a homely tune*

home·made /ˌhoʊm'meɪd◂/ *adj.* made at home rather than bought in a store: *homemade ice cream*

home·mak·er /'hoʊmˌmeɪkɚ/ *n.* [C] APPROVING a woman who works at home cleaning, cooking etc. and does not have another job; HOUSEWIFE

home mov·ie /ˌ. '../ *n.* [C] a movie you make, often of a family occasion, that is intended to be shown at home rather than in a movie theater

home of·fice /ˌ. '../ *n.* [C] an office you have in your house so that you can do your job at home

ho·me·o·path /'hoʊmiəˌpæθ/ *n.* [C] someone who treats diseases using homeopathy

ho·me·op·a·thy /ˌhoʊmi'ɑpəθi/ *n.* [U] a system of medicine in which a disease is treated by giving extremely small amounts of a substance that makes healthy people show signs of the disease —**homeopathic** /ˌhoʊmiə'pæθɪk/ *adj.* —**homeopathically** /-kli/ *adv.*

home·own·er /'hoʊmˌoʊnɚ/ *n.* [C] someone who owns their house

home page /ˌ. './ *n.* [C] the place on a WEB SITE that appears first when you connect to it, that tells you how to find the information you want on that WEB SITE

home plate /ˌ. './ *n.* [singular, not with **the**] the place where you stand to hit the ball in baseball, which is also the last place the player who is running must touch in order to get a point —see picture at BASEBALL

Ho·mer /'hoʊmɚ/ a Greek poet who probably lived between 800 and 700 B.C. He is known for his two EPIC poems, the ILLIAD and the ODYSSEY which have had great influence on European literature —**Homeric** /hoʊ'mɛrɪk/ *adj.*

hom·er /'hoʊmɚ/ *n.* [C] INFORMAL a HOME RUN —**homer** *v.* [I]

Homer, Wins·low /'wɪnzloʊ/ (1836–1910) a U.S. painter, known especially for his paintings of the sea and people connected with the sea

home room /'. ./ *n.* [C] a CLASSROOM where students go at the beginning of every school day, or at the beginning of each SEMESTER, to get information that is given to all students

home rule /ˌ. './ *n.* [U] the right of the people in a country to control their own affairs, after previously being controlled by another country

home run /ˌ. './ *n.* [C] a long hit in baseball that lets the player who hit the ball run around all the bases and get a point

home-school /'. ./ *v.* [T] to teach children at home instead of sending them to school —**home-school** *adj.* [only before noun] *home-school programs* —**home schooling** *n.* [U]

home shop·ping net·work /ˌ. '.. ˌ../ *n.* [singular] a television company that shows products that you can order and buy by telephone

home·sick /'hoʊmˌsɪk/ *adj.* feeling unhappy because you are a long way from your home: [+ **for**] *Do you ever get homesick for Japan?* —**homesickness** *n.* [U]

home·spun /'hoʊmspʌn/ *adj.* **1** homespun ideas are simple and ordinary: *homespun wisdom* **2** homespun cloth is woven at home

home·stead¹ /'hoʊmstɛd/ *n.* [C] **1** a farm and the area of land around it **2** a piece of land, usually for farming, that was given to people by the U.S. government in past times

homestead² *v.* [I,T] to live and work on a homestead: *The McLeods homesteaded along the river in 1858.* —**homesteader** *n.* [C]

home stretch /ˌ. './ *n.* **a) the home stretch** the last part of a race where horses, runners etc. go straight to the finish **b)** the last part of an activity or trip: *New York's mayoral campaign hits the home stretch this week.*

home·town /'hoʊmtaʊn/ *n.* [C] the place where you were born and lived when you were a child: *Jeffers has contributed to many community projects in his hometown of Columbus, Ohio.*

home vis·it /'. ˌ../ *n.* [C] an occasion when a nurse, doctor etc. comes to see you at your home when you are sick —**home visitor** *n.* [C]

home·ward /'hoʊmwɚd/ *adv.* **1** toward home: *Frances made her way homeward along the old sea wall.* **2 homeward bound** LITERARY traveling or going toward home —**homeward** *adj.*: *the homeward journey* —opposite OUTWARD¹ (2)

home·work /'hoʊmwɚk/ *n.* [U] **1** work for school that a student does at home —compare CLASSWORK **2** something you do to prepare for an important

H

activity: *Do your homework and look at the company's record before investing.*

home·y¹ /'hoʊmi/ *adj.* **homier, homiest** pleasant, like home: *We stayed at a homey bed and breakfast inn.*

homey² *n. plural* **homeys** [C] SLANG a friend, or someone who comes from your area or GANG¹ (1): *What's up, homey?*

hom·i·ci·dal /ˌhɑməˈsaɪdl, ˌhoʊ-/ *adj.* likely to murder someone

hom·i·cide /'hɑməˌsaɪd/ *n.* **1** [C,U] the crime of murder **2** [U] the police department that deals with murders

hom·i·ly /'hɑməli/ *n. plural* **homilies** [C] FORMAL **1** a short speech given as part of a Christian church ceremony —compare SERMON **2** advice about how to behave that is often unwanted: *LaRussa spouted his usual homily about winning games.*

hom·ing /'hoʊmɪŋ/ *adj.* a bird or animal that has a homing instinct has a special ability that helps it find its way home over long distances

homing de·vice /'.. ˌ../ *n.* [C usually singular] a special part of a weapon that helps it to find the place that it is aimed at

homing pi·geon /'.. ˌ../ *n.* [C] a PIGEON that is able to find its way home over long distances

hom·i·ny /'hɑməni/ *n.* [U] a food made from dried corn

ho·mo /'hoʊmoʊ/ *n. plural* **homos** [C] OFFENSIVE a HOMOSEXUAL person, especially a man —see also HETERO

homo- /hoʊmoʊ, -mə, hɑmə/ *prefix* FORMAL OR TECHNICAL the same as something else: *homosexual* (=attracted to someone of your own sex) | *homographs* (=words spelled the same way)

ho·mo·ge·ne·ous /ˌhoʊməˈdʒiniəs, -nyəs/, **ho·mo·ge·nous** /həˈmɑdʒənəs/ *adj.* consisting of people or things that are all of the same kind: *an ethnically homogeneous country* —compare HETEROGENEOUS —**homogeneously** *adv.*

ho·mo·ge·nize /həˈmɑdʒəˌnaɪz/ *v.* [T] to change something so that its parts become similar or the same: *The American landscape is being homogenized by malls and fast-food restaurants.*

ho·mo·ge·nized milk /ˌ..... './ *n.* [U] milk that has had the cream on top mixed with the milk

hom·o·graph /'hɑməɡræf, 'hoʊ-/ *n.* [C] TECHNICAL a word that is spelled the same as another, but is different in meaning, origin, grammar, or pronunciation. For example, the noun "record" is a homograph of the verb "record."

homo milk /'.. ˌ./ *n.* [C] CANADIAN, INFORMAL: see WHOLE MILK

hom·o·nym /'hɑməˌnɪm/ *n.* [C] TECHNICAL a word that is spelled the same and sounds the same as another, but is different in meaning or origin. For example, the noun "bear" and the verb "bear" are homonyms.

ho·mo·pho·bi·a /ˌhoʊməˈfoʊbiə/ *n.* [U] hatred and fear of HOMOSEXUALs —**homophobic** *adj.*

hom·o·phone /'hɑməˌfoʊn, 'hoʊ-/ *n.* [C] TECHNICAL a word that sounds the same as another but is different in spelling, meaning, or origin. For example, the verb "knew" and the adjective "new" are homophones.

Ho·mo sa·pi·ens /ˌhoʊmoʊ ˈseɪpiənz/ *n.* [U] the type of human being that exists now

ho·mo·sex·u·al /ˌhoʊməˈsɛkʃuəl/ *adj.* sexually attracted to people of the same sex —**homosexual** *n.* [C] —**homosexuality** /ˌhoʊməˌsɛkʃuˈæləti/ *n.* [U] —compare BISEXUAL, HETEROSEXUAL —see also GAY¹ (1), LESBIAN

hon /hʌn/ *pron.* SPOKEN a short form of HONEY, used to address someone you love: *Are you going to eat those fries, hon?*

Hon. 1 the written abbreviation of HONORABLE **2** the written abbreviation of HONORARY, used in official job titles

hon·cho /'hɑntʃoʊ/ *n. plural* **honchos** [C] INFORMAL an important person who controls something: *The head honchos are flying in from Tokyo for the meeting.*

Hon·du·ras /hɑnˈdʊrəs/ a country in Central America, north of Nicaragua —**Honduran** *n., adj.*

hone /hoʊn/ *v.* [T] **1** to improve your skill at doing something, especially when you are already good at it: *It was during this period that Bush honed his diplomatic skills.* | **finely honed** *surgical techniques* **2** to make knives, swords etc. sharp

hon·est /'ɑnɪst/ *adj.*
1 character someone who is honest does not lie, cheat, or steal: *a fair and honest businessman* | [+ with] *Well, at least I was honest with him.* | [+ about] *She always been honest about her drug problems.*
2 statement/answer not hiding the truth or the facts about something: *an honest answer* | *Shannon, tell me the honest truth.* | *You need to have an honest opinion of yourself.*
3 ordinary/good people honest people are not famous or special, but behave in a good socially acceptable way: *They were good, honest, hard-working people.*
4 work honest work is done without cheating, using your own efforts
5 **make an honest woman (out) of sb** OLD-FASHIONED to marry a woman because she is going to have a baby

---

SPOKEN PHRASES

6 to be honest used when you tell someone what you really think: *To be honest, I'm glad she broke up with me.*
7 honest! used to try to make someone believe you: *I didn't mean to hurt him, honest!*
8 honest to God used to emphasize that something you say is really true: *Honest to God, I wasn't there.*

---

hon·est·ly /'ɑnɪstli/ *adv.* **1** in an honest way: *Please fill out the questionnaire as honestly as possible.* | *He needs to talk honestly with Billie.* **2** SPOKEN used to try to make someone believe that what you are saying is true: *Honestly, they didn't hear that from me.* | *I honestly don't know.* **3** SPOKEN used when you are surprised or annoyed, or to emphasize that you are shocked that something could be true: *I can't believe people honestly teased you about that.* | *Oh honestly! I don't know why I even bother.*

honest-to-good·ness /ˌ... './ also **honest-to-God** /ˌ... './ *adj.* [only before noun] exactly the way something is meant to be; GENUINE: *They specialize in honest-to-goodness homemade desserts.*

hon·es·ty /'ɑnəsti/ *n.* [U] **1** the quality of being honest: *He has a reputation for honesty and decency.* **2** the quality of being what you appear to be, so that you say what you think, show what you feel, etc.: *"There's such an honesty about kids," says Eastin.* | *the honesty of the song's lyrics* **3** in all honesty SPOKEN used to say that what you are saying is completely true: *In all honesty, I'm thinking of taking another year off.*

hon·ey /'hʌni/ *n.* [U] **1** a sweet sticky substance produced by BEES, used as food **2** also **honey bun/bunch** SPOKEN used to address someone you love: *Do you have a pen, honey?*

hon·ey·bee /'hʌnibi/ *n.* [C] a BEE that makes honey

hon·ey·comb /'hʌniˌkoʊm/ *n.* [C] **1** a structure made by BEES, which consists of many six-sided cells in which honey is stored **2** something that is arranged or shaped in this pattern

hon·ey·combed /'hʌniˌkoʊmd/ *adj.* [not before noun] filled with many holes, hollow passages etc.: *The region is honeycombed by mines.*

hon·ey·dew mel·on /'hʌnidu ˌmɛlən/ *n.* [C] a type of MELON with sweet green flesh

hon·eyed /'hʌnid/ *adj.* **1** honeyed words or honeyed voices sound soft and pleasant, but are often insincere: *Miss Verrett sang in a honeyed, seductive tone.* **2** tasting like HONEY, or covered in honey: *honeyed yams*

hon·ey·moon[1] /'hʌni,mun/ *n.* [C] **1** a vacation taken by two people who have just been married: *Mom and Dad went to Italy* **on their honeymoon.** **2 honeymoon period** the period of time when a new government, leader etc. has just started and no one criticizes them

honeymoon[2] *v.* [I always + adv./prep.] to go somewhere for your honeymoon: *They're honeymooning in Vermont.* —**honeymooner** *n.* [C]

hon·ey·suck·le /'hʌni,sʌkəl/ *n.* [C] a climbing plant with nice-smelling yellow or pink flowers

Hong Kong /,haŋ 'kaŋ‹/ an area on the south coast of China, consisting of several islands and a small part of the Chinese MAINLAND which is part of China but has its own government and financial system

Ho·ni·a·ra /,houni'arə/ the capital city of the Solomon Islands

honk[1] /haŋk, hɔŋk/ *n.* **1** a loud noise made by a car horn **2** a loud noise made by a GOOSE

honk[2] *v.* [I,T] if a car horn or a GOOSE honks, it makes a loud noise: *I saw you guys and honked, but you didn't see me.*

honk·ing /'haŋkɪŋ, 'hɔŋ-/ *adj.* SPOKEN used to emphasize that something is very large: *He was eating this big, honking corn dog.*

hon·ky, honkie /'haŋki, 'hɔŋ-/ *n.* [C] TABOO a word for a white person, used by African-Americans. Do not use this word.

hon·ky-tonk[1] /'haŋki taŋk/ *n.* [C] a cheap bar where COUNTRY MUSIC is played

honky-tonk[2] *adj.* [only before a noun] **1 honky-tonk music/piano** a type of piano music which is played in a loud cheerful way **2** cheap, brightly colored, and not good quality

Hon·o·lu·lu /,hanə'lulu/ the capital and largest city of the U.S. state of Hawaii

s w
3 3
hon·or[1] /'anə/ *n.*

1 respect [U] the respect that someone or something receives from other people: *Winning tomorrow's game is a matter of national honor.* | *His trophies hold a* **place of honor** *on the mantelpiece.*
2 sth that makes you proud [singular] FORMAL something that makes you feel very proud: [**have the honor of doing sth**] *Earlier this year I had the honor of meeting Mrs. Edelman.* | [**be an honor to do sth**] *It's an honor to serve your country.* | [**do sb the honor of doing sth**] *Sylvia has done me the honor of agreeing to be my wife.* | *I will always* **count it an honor** *to be his friend.*
3 moral principles [U] strong moral beliefs and standards of behavior that make people respect and trust you: *a soldier's honor* | *Gangs can provide a strong identity and a* **code of honor** (=rules about how to behave) *for their members.* | *I know Bob to be* *a man of honor.*
4 in honor of sb in order to show how much you admire and respect someone: *A rally in honor of Mandela will be held on Saturday.* | *Beth is giving a party in his honor.*
5 given to sb [C] something that is given to someone to show them that people respect and admire what they have done: *He's won an Academy Award and a host of other honors.*
6 Your Honor used when speaking to a judge
7 be an honor to sb/sth to bring admiration and respect to your country, school, family etc. because of your behavior or achievements: *In this culture, children are expected to be an honor to their parents.*
8 with honors if you finish high school or college with honors, you get one of the highest grades
9 with full military honors if someone is buried with full military honors, there is a military ceremony at their funeral
10 be/feel honor bound to feel that it is your moral duty to do something: *We felt honor bound to attend their wedding.*
11 do the honors SPOKEN to pour the drinks, serve food etc. at a social occasion: *Would you do the honors?*
12 on your/my honor if you swear on your honor to do something, you promise very seriously to do it
13 be on your honor OLD-FASHIONED if you are on

your honor to do something, you are being trusted to do it
14 sex [U] OLD USE if a woman loses her honor, she has sex with a man she is not married to —see also **guest of honor** (GUEST[1] (6)), MAID OF HONOR

honor[2] *v.* **1** [T] to treat someone with special s w respect: *We remember and honor the soldiers who* —— *didn't return from the Gulf.* **2 be/feel honored** to 3 feel very proud and pleased: *I am* **deeply honored** *to be chosen to head the campaign.* **3** [T] FORMAL to show publicly that someone is respected and admired, especially by praising them or giving them a special title: [**+ with**] *Vincent Price was honored with a lifetime achievement award.* **4 honor a contract/agreement/request etc.** to do what you have agreed to do: *We have honored the family's request to keep the details confidential.* **5 honor a check/coupon/card etc.** to accept something besides CASH as payment **6 sb has decided to honor us with their presence** SPOKEN, HUMOROUS said when someone arrives late, or to someone who rarely comes to a meeting, class etc. —see also TIME-HONORED

Hon·or·a·ble /'anərəbəl/ *adj.* used when writing to or about a judge or an important person in the government: *The Honorable James A. Baker*

hon·or·a·ble /'anərəbəl/ *adj.* **1** behaving in a way that is morally correct and shows you have high moral standards: *Dunne was an honorable and conscientious public servant.* **2** an honorable action or activity deserves respect and admiration: *Military service was considered an honorable career choice.* **3** an honorable agreement is fair to everyone who is involved in it

honorable dis·charge /,... '../ *n.* [C] if you leave the Army with an honorable discharge, your behavior and work have been very good

honorable men·tion /,... '../ *n.* [C] a special honor in a competition, for work that was of high quality but did not get a prize

hon·o·rar·i·um /,anə'reriəm/ *n.* [C] FORMAL a sum of money offered to a professional for a piece of advice, a speech etc.

hon·or·ar·y /'anə,reri/ *adj.* [no comparative] **1** an honorary title, rank, or college degree is given to someone as an honor, although the person did not earn the title etc. in the usual way **2** an honorary position in an organization is held without receiving any payment: *Montalban is the commission's honorary chairman.* **3** an honorary member of a group is treated like a member of that group but does not belong to it: *She was made an honorary citizen of Oklahoma that year.*

hon·or·if·ic /,anə'rɪfɪk/ *n.* [C] an expression or title that is used to show respect for the person you are speaking to —**honorific** *adj.*

honor roll /'.. ,./ *n.* [C] a list of the best students in a school or college

honor sys·tem /'.. ,../ *n.* [C] **1** an agreement between members of a group to obey rules, although no one checks to make sure they are being followed: *Ticket buying is on the honor system.* **2** a way of recording the fact that a student has achieved a high standard of work

hon·our /'anə/ *n. v.* the British and Canadian spelling of HONOR

hooch, hootch /hutʃ/ *n.* [U] strong alcohol, especially alcohol that has been made illegally

hood /hud/ *n.* [C]
1 car the metal covering over the engine on a car: *Shanae opened up the hood to check the oil.* | *Dan got out to take a look under the hood.* —see pictures at ENGINE and on page 427
2 cover for head **a)** a part of a coat, shirt etc. that you can pull up to cover your head: *Sandvik put his hood up against the cold.* **b)** a cover that goes over someone's face and head, used especially to prevent them from being recognized: *A black hood covered Gilbert's face.*

H

3 neighborhood [usually singular] also **'hood** SLANG a NEIGHBORHOOD: *Most of our relatives still live in the 'hood.*

4 equipment **a)** a piece of equipment with a FAN that is used above a STOVE to remove the smell of cooking from the kitchen **b)** an enclosed area in a scientific LABORATORY with a FAN that removes dangerous gases from the room

5 criminal INFORMAL a hoodlum: *A group of hoods mugged Tyler on Park Avenue.*

-hood /hʊd/ *suffix* [in nouns] **1** used to show a period of time or a state: *a happy childhood* (=time when you were a child) | *parenthood* (=state of being a parent) **2** the people who belong to a particular group: *the priesthood* (=all people who are priests) | *my neighborhood* (=the place where I live and the people in it)

Hood, Mount /hʊd/ a mountain in the Cascade Range that is the highest mountain in the U.S. state of Oregon

hood·ed /'hʊdɪd/ *adj.* having or wearing a hood: *a hooded sweatshirt*

hood·lum /'hʊdləm, 'hʊd-/ *n.* [C] a criminal, often a young person, who does violent or illegal things

hoo·doo /'hudu/ *n.* [U] a type of VOODOO (=magic)

hood·wink /'hʊd,wɪŋk/ *v.* [T] to trick someone so that you can get an advantage for yourself: [**hoodwink sb into doing sth**] *Dukell is a racist who is trying to hoodwink the voters into electing him.*

hoo·ey /'hui/ *n.* [U] SPOKEN stupid or untrue talk; NONSENSE: *That's just a bunch of hooey.*

hoof¹ /hʊf/ *n. plural* **hoofs** or **hooves** /huvz, hʊvz/ [C] the hard foot of an animal such as a horse, cow etc. —see picture at MOOSE

hoof² *v.* **1 hoof it** SPOKEN to run or walk, especially quickly **2** [I] INFORMAL to dance, especially in the theater as a job: *Romero acts and sings, and even hoofs a little.*

hoof·er /'hʊfɚ/ *n.* [C] INFORMAL a dancer, especially one who works in the theater

hoo·ha /'hu hɑ/ *n.* [U] INFORMAL noisy talk or excitement that seems too much for the thing it is about: *Today marks the start of three days of hoo-ha surrounding the governor's inauguration.*

hook¹ /hʊk/ *n.* [C]

1 for hanging things a curved piece of metal or plastic that you use for hanging things on: *The helmet hung from a hook next to Turner's jersey.*

2 fish a curved piece of thin metal with a sharp point for catching fish: *a fish hook*

3 let/get sb off the hook to allow someone or help someone to get out of a difficult situation: *People will think they let Charmaine off the hook because she's a woman.*

4 leave/take the phone off the hook to leave or take the telephone RECEIVER (=the part you speak into) off the part where it is usually placed so that no one can call you

5 be ringing off the hook if your telephone is ringing off the hook, a lot of people are calling you

6 way of hitting sb a way of hitting your opponent with your elbow bent in BOXING: *Jackson knocked Cooper down with a left hook to the body.*

7 by hook or by crook if you are going to do something by hook or by crook, you are determined to do it: *The police are going to get these guys, by hook or by crook.*

8 sth to get attention something that is attractive and gets people's attention and interest: *You have to find a hook to sell a new show.*

9 tune a part of the tune in a song that makes it very easy to remember

10 ball a way of hitting or throwing a ball, or an occasion when a ball is hit or thrown so that it moves in a curve

11 get your hooks into sb to succeed in taking control of someone, especially by deceiving them: *Six years ago, Deborah had gotten her hooks into me.*

12 hook, line, and sinker if someone believes something hook, line, and sinker, they completely believe a lie: *The media bought Stuart's story hook, line, and sinker.*

hook² *v.*

1 fish [T] to catch a fish with a hook: *I hooked a 14-inch rainbow trout.*

2 fasten [T always + adv./prep.] to attach or hang something onto something else: *Only one strap of his overalls was hooked.* | *Gorman stood there holding his hat, his umbrella hooked on his wrist.*

3 interest/attract [T] INFORMAL to succeed in making someone interested in something or attracted to something: *Banks used to give away toasters and stuff to hook new customers.*

4 [T always + adv./prep.] also **hook up** to connect a piece of electronic equipment to another piece of equipment or to an electricity supply: *We have a CD player, but it's not hooked up yet.* | *All the computers in the office are hooked together.*

5 bend your finger/arm etc. [T always + adv./prep.] to bend your finger, arm, or leg, especially so that you can pull or hold something else: [**hook sth in/around/through sth**] *Morrisey hooked his thumbs in his belt.*

6 ball [I,T] to throw or kick a ball so that it moves in a curve, or to move or curve in this way: *The ball just hooked a little bit to the left.*

7 rug [T] to make a RUG or decoration using short pieces of YARN that are pulled through special material with wide holes, using a special tool

hook up with sb *phr. v.* [T] **1** SLANG to start having a sexual relationship with someone: *You should hook up with Dee Dee, bro.* **2** SPOKEN to meet someone and become friendly with them: *Did you ever hook up with Maisy while you were there?* **3** INFORMAL to agree to work together with another person or organization for a particular purpose: *Mueller hooked up with Pirner to form the band Soul Asylum.*

hook·ah /'hukə/ *n.* [C] a pipe for smoking tobacco or drugs, that consists of a long tube and a container of water

hook and eye /ˌ. . '. / *n.* [U] a small metal hook and ring used for fastening clothes —see picture at FASTENER

hook-and-lad·der truck /ˌ. . '.. ˌ. / *n.* [C] a FIRE ENGINE with long LADDERS attached to it

hooked /hʊkt/ *adj.* **1** curved out or shaped like a hook: *a hooked nose* **2** [not before noun] INFORMAL if you are hooked on a drug, you feel a strong need for it and you cannot stop taking it; ADDICTED: [+ **on**] *Jada was hooked on crack for three years in the early '90s.* **3** [not before noun] if you are hooked on something, you enjoy it very much and you want to do it as often as possible: *Some parents who are concerned about computer games believe their children are hooked.* | [+ **on**] *Tim got hooked on the show after watching the first episode.*

hook·er /'hʊkɚ/ *n.* [C] INFORMAL a PROSTITUTE

hook-nosed /'. ˌ./ *adj.* having a large nose that curves out in the middle

hook·up /'. ./ *n.* [C] a temporary connection between two pieces of equipment such as computers, or between a piece of equipment and an electricity or water supply: *a satellite hook-up* | *As well as campsites, there are hook-ups for RVs.*

hook·y /'hʊki/ *n.* OLD-FASHIONED **play hooky** to stay away from school without permission

hoo·li·gan /'huligən/ *n.* [C] a noisy violent person who causes trouble by fighting, shouting etc. —**hooliganism** *n.* [U]

hoop /hup/ *n.* [C] **1** a circular piece of wood, metal, plastic etc.: *an embroidery hoop* **2 jump/go through hoops** to have to do a lot of difficult things as part of a process: *We had to jump through a lot of hoops in order to get the play on stage.* **3 hoops** [plural] the game of basketball: *Tom's at the park shooting hoops* (=playing basketball) *with some friends.* —see picture on page 423 **4** an EARRING that is shaped like a ring **5** a large ring that CIRCUS animals are made to jump through, or that children used to play with in the past **6** one of the circular bands of metal or wood around a BARREL **7 hoop skirt/dress** an old-fashioned skirt or dress with a long full bottom part that is supported by metal rings —see also HULA-HOOP

hoop·la /'hupla, 'hup-/ n. [U] INFORMAL excitement about something that attracts a lot of public attention: *The new casino opened amid much hoopla.*

hoo·ray /hʊˈreɪ/ interjection shouted when you are very glad about something: *Hooray! No more work 'til Monday!* —**hooray** n. [C] *Let's have a big hooray for everybody who helped.* —see also **hip hip hooray** (HIP²)

hoose·gow /'husgaʊ/ n. [C usually singular] HUMOROUS a prison: *Wayne ended up in the hoosegow on drunk-driving charges.*

hoot¹ /hut/ n. [C] **1** a shout or laugh that shows you think something is funny or stupid: *Leary's speech drew hoots from the crowd.* **2 not give a hoot** also **not give two hoots** SPOKEN to not care or be interested in something: *Nobody seems to give a hoot about recycling.* **3 be a hoot** SPOKEN to be very funny or amusing: *I thought Judy's performance was a real hoot.* **4 not be worth a hoot** SPOKEN to be completely worthless or useless: *We started playing in 1974, but we weren't worth a hoot until 1982.* **5** the sound that an OWL makes **6** a short clear sound made by a boat or ship, as a warning

hoot² v. **1** [I,T] to laugh loudly because you think something is funny or stupid: [+ at] *The audience hooted at the actors' mistakes.* **2** [I] if an OWL hoots, it makes a long "oo" sound **3** [I,T] if a boat or ship hoots, it makes a loud clear noise as a warning: *Ships hooted their horns as the flag went up.*

hoot·en·an·ny /'hutˈnˌæni/ n. [C] an event at which musicians play FOLK MUSIC or COUNTRY MUSIC, and the people listening often sing with them or dance to the music

hoot·ers /'hutɚz/ n. [plural] SLANG a word meaning a woman's large breasts, usually considered offensive

Hoo·ver /'huvɚ/, **Her·bert** /'hɚbɚt/ (1874–1964) the 31st President of the U.S.

Hoover, J. Ed·gar /dʒɛ ˈɛdgɚ/ (1895–1972) the director of the FBI from 1924 until his death

Hoover Dam, the /ˌ.. ˈ./ a DAM on the Colorado River on the border between the U.S. states of Arizona and Nevada

hooves /huvz, hʊvz/ n. the plural of HOOF

hop¹ /hɑp/ v. **hopped, hopping 1** [I] to move by jumping on one foot or by making short quick jumps on both feet: *Lorna hopped over to a bench to put on her shoes.* | *A wide-eyed little girl hopped into Santa's lap.* **2** [I always + adv./prep.] INFORMAL to get into, onto, or out of something, especially a vehicle: [+ in/out/on etc.] *Charley hopped in his car and drove down to the beach.* **3 hop a plane/bus/train etc.** INFORMAL to get on an airplane, bus, train etc., especially after suddenly deciding to do so: *Wilson hopped a plane and arrived in time for the auction.* **4** [I] if a bird, an insect, or a small animal hops, it moves by making quick short jumps **5 hop to it!** SPOKEN used to order someone to do something immediately **6 hopping mad** INFORMAL very angry

hop² n. **1** [C] a short jump: *The bird took another hop toward Kyle's outstretched hand.* **2** [C] a single short trip, especially by airplane: *It's just a short hop from Cleveland to Detroit.* **3** [C] an occasion when a ball falls on the ground, goes back into the air, and then falls again a short distance away *The ball got past the shortstop on a bad hop.* **4 a) hops** [U,plural] parts of dried flowers used in making beer, which give the beer a bitter taste **b)** [C] the tall plant on which these flowers grow **5** [C] OLD-FASHIONED a social event at which people dance **6 a hop, skip, and a jump** INFORMAL a very short distance: *My place is just a hop, skip, and a jump from here.* —see also HIP-HOP

SW 1 1 **hope¹** /hoʊp/ v. [I,T] **1** to want something to happen or be true, and to believe it is possible: [+ (that)] *Jo was hoping that Jamal would come tonight.* | *I hope everything is okay.* | [hope to do sth] *Allison is hoping to be a high-school teacher.* | [+ for] *The U.S. hopes for a peaceful end to the conflict.* | *Mrs. Leung had to decide whether to undergo treatment or wait*

and **hope for the best** (=hope that things end well when a lot may go wrong). | *Daniel waited all day, hoping against hope* (=hoping for something that is unlikely to happen) *that Annie would change her mind.*

SPOKEN PHRASES

2 I hope so used to say that you hope something that has been mentioned happens or is true: *"So you're going to the Amazon?" "I hope so."* **3 I hope not** used to say that you hope something that has been mentioned does not happen or is not true: *"Will it rain any more?" "I hope not."* **4 I'm hoping...** used to say that you hope something will happen, especially because you are depending on it: [+ (that)] *I'm hoping that the package will come today while I'm here.* | [+ to] *Jake's hoping to come in on the twentieth, unless Santo is busy.* **5 I hope...** used when you want to be polite and not offend someone: *I'm recording this conversation. I hope that's okay with you.* | *I hope you don't mind if Kathy comes too.* **6 let's hope (that)** used to tell someone that you hope something will happen or will not happen: *Let's hope that he will check his voice mail.* **7 I hope to God (that)** used to say that you hope very much that something will happen or will not happen, because of the serious problems that could happen: *I just hope to God there aren't any stalls or breakdowns.*

hope² n. S W 2 3

1 feeling [U] a feeling of wanting something to happen, and a belief that it is likely to happen: [+ for] *Sykes' letter provides hope for other women in similar situations.* | *Their initial success gave hope to Cecilia and her friends.* | *People are losing hope of an early peace settlement.* | *We will keep searching in the hope that a miracle might happen.* | *Frustrated Raiders fans found a glimmer of hope* (=a little hope) *in the team's new quarterback.* | *Panetta held out little hope* (=had very little hope) *that the decision would be reversed.*

2 sth you hope for [C] something that you hope will happen: *Your donation can fulfill the hopes and dreams of a child this Christmas.* | [+ of] *Grant was forced to abandon the hope of re-election.* | [hopes of doing sth] *I moved to the city with hopes of finding a job.* | *Tina had high hopes* (=hopes that something will be successful) *for her team at the beginning of the season.* | *The search for survivors continues, but hopes are fading* (=people are losing hope) *fast.*

3 get/build sb's hopes up to make what someone wants seem more likely to happen, or to feel that your hopes are more likely to happen: *Libby, don't get your hopes up, because you may not get the job.*

4 be sb's last/only hope to be someone's last or only chance of getting the result they want: *A bone marrow transplant is Marta's only hope for survival.*

5 chance [C,U] a chance of succeeding or of something good happening: [+ of] *Hine realized there was no hope of reaching the mountaintop before dark.* | [+ that] *There is every hope that he's going to recover.* | *Joe has no hope of getting into Yale.* | *We don't have a hope in hell* (=do not have even the smallest chance of success) *if Dave doesn't get here by noon.*

6 hope springs eternal LITERARY used to say that people will always hope that things will get better, even after something bad has happened

7 be beyond hope if a situation is beyond hope, it is so bad that there is no chance of any improvement: *It may be tempting to describe urban centers in the developing world as almost beyond hope.* —see also **dash (sb's) hopes/dreams** (DASH¹ (2)), **pin your hopes on sb/sth** (PIN² (2))

hope chest /'. ./ n. [C] a large wooden box containing things needed to start a new home, such as SILVERWARE and bed sheets, which young women used to collect before getting married

hope·ful¹ /'hoʊpfəl/ adj. **1** believing that what you hope for is likely to happen: [+ that] *We remain hopeful that her health will continue to improve.* |

H

[+ **about**] *Lakeisha is hopeful about the future.* **2** making you feel that what you hope for is likely to happen: *The peace talks concluded on a hopeful note.* | *Todd broke into a hopeful smile every time the phone rang.* —**hopefulness** *n.* [U]

hope·ful² *n.* [C] someone who is hoping to be successful, especially in politics, sports etc.: *a presidential hopeful*

S W 1 **hope·ful·ly** /'houpfəli/ *adv.* **1** [sentence adverb] SPOKEN a word used when you are saying what you hope will happen, which some people consider nonstandard: *Hopefully I'll be home by nine tonight.* | *This exercise should give you a good review for the test, hopefully.* | *We're hopefully going to keep practicing once a month.* **2** in a way that shows that you are hopeful: *"But," Tim added hopefully, "there's always tomorrow."*

hope·less /'houp-lɪs/ *adj.* **1** a hopeless situation is so bad that there is no chance of success or improvement: *Although Helga's condition appeared hopeless, her husband refused to give up.* | *The lawyers must have known their lawsuit was hopeless.* | *It's hopeless; I'm the only one who's really interested in getting anything done.* **2** INFORMAL very bad at doing something: *Doug was hopeless at waiting tables.* **3** feeling or showing no hope: *I had this hopeless feeling as I approached the hospital.* **4 hopeless case** someone who cannot be helped: *Doctors can now help people who were once considered hopeless cases.* —**hopelessness** *n.* [U]

hope·less·ly /'houp-lɪsli/ *adv.* **1** used when emphasizing how bad a situation is, and saying that it will not get better: *We're hopelessly behind schedule.* | *Sanders said that Congress was hopelessly out of touch with the needs of ordinary citizens.* **2 be/fall hopelessly in love** to have very strong feelings of love for someone **3** feeling that you have no hope: *"I feel like quitting," she said hopelessly.*

Ho·pi /'houpi/ *n.* a Native American tribe from Arizona in the U.S.

Hop·kins /'hɑpkɪnz/, **Mark** (1802–1887) a U.S. educator and THEOLOGIAN

hopped up /ˌ. './ *adj.* SLANG **1** happy and excited, especially because of the effects of drugs: [+ **on**] *I could tell Domingo was hopped up on speed.* **2** a hopped-up car, engine etc. has been made much more powerful: *a hopped-up Ford Mustang*

hop·per /'hɑpɚ/ *n.* [C] **1** a large container that is wide at the top, with a narrow opening at the bottom, in which things can be stored before being put into another container: *a grain hopper* **2 in/into the hopper** if someone's name, a proposal, an idea etc. is put or goes into the hopper, it is considered for something: *Another name in the hopper for the director's position is Kathleen Stocker.* **3** a box that proposals for new laws are put into before they are discussed in Congress **4** something that BOUNCES or HOPS: *Reed hit a one-hopper (=a ball that bounces once) to Gaetti.* —see also CLODHOPPER

Hop·per /'hɑpɚ/, **Ed·ward** /'ɛdwɚd/ (1882–1967) a U.S. painter known for his REALISTIC paintings of life

hop·scotch /'hɑpskɑtʃ/ *n.* [U] a children's game in which each child has to jump from one numbered square to another in a pattern marked on the ground

ho·ra /'hɔrə/ *n.* [C usually singular] a traditional Jewish dance in which a group of people hold hands and stand in a circle

Hor·ace /'hɔrəs, 'hɑr-/ (65–8 B.C.) a Roman poet whose work greatly influenced English poetry

horde /hɔrd/ *n.* [C usually plural] a large crowd moving in a noisy uncontrolled way: [+ **of**] *New York is overrun by hordes of tourists in the summer.*

ho·ri·zon /hə'raɪzən/ *n.* **1 the horizon** the line far away where the land or ocean seems to meet the sky: *Slowly, a full moon came up over the horizon.* **2 horizons** [plural] the limits of your ideas, knowledge, and experience: *Gorbachev opened new horizons of diplomacy and trade.* | *Takayo came to the U.S. to*

broaden her cultural horizons. **3 be on the horizon** to seem likely to happen in the future: *Companies don't see any improvement on the horizon.*

hor·i·zon·tal¹ /ˌhɔrə'zɑntəl, ˌhar-/ *adj.* flat and level, from left to right: *a horizontal line* | *Time is graphed along the horizontal axis.* | *horizontal layers of rock* —**horizontally** *adv.* —opposite VERTICAL¹ —compare DIAGONAL —see picture at VERTICAL¹

horizontal² *n.* **1 the horizontal** TECHNICAL a horizontal position: *The ramp was angled at 12 degrees below the horizontal.* **2** [C] a horizontal line or surface

hor·mone /'hɔrmoun/ *n.* [C] a chemical substance produced by your body that influences your body's growth, development, and condition: *growth hormone* | *teenagers with raging hormones (=changing levels of hormones, which are believed to make them act in ways that are not sensible)* —**hormonal** /hɔr'mounl/ *adj.*

hormone re·place·ment ther·a·py /ˌ.. .'.. ˌ..,../ *n.* [U] a medical treatment for women during or after MENOPAUSE (=the time when they stop having monthly PERIODS), which involves adding hormones to the body

horn¹ /hɔrn/ *n.*
1 [car] [C] the piece of equipment in a car, bus etc. that is used to make a loud sound as a signal or warning: *Someone behind me honked his horn when the light changed.* —see picture on page 427
2 [animal] [C] **a)** one of the pair of hard pointed parts that grow on the heads of cows, goats, and other animals **b)** a part of an animal's head that stands out like a horn, for example on a DEER; ANTLER —see picture on page 429
3 [musical instrument] [C] **a)** one of several musical instruments that consist of a long metal tube, wide at one end, that you play by blowing **b)** a FRENCH HORN **c)** INFORMAL a TRUMPET **d)** a musical instrument made from an animal's horn —see also ENGLISH HORN
4 get/be on the horn SPOKEN to use the telephone: *Su got on the horn and spoke to somebody in Design.*
5 [substance] [U] the substance that animals' horns are made of: *horn-rimmed glasses*
6 drinking horn/powder horn etc. a container in the shape of an animal's horn or made from an animal's horn, used in the past for drinking from, carrying GUNPOWDER etc.
7 pull in your horns to reduce the amount of money you spend: *Businesses are starting to pull in their horns.*
8 be on the horns of a dilemma to be in a situation in which you have to choose between two bad or difficult situations —see also **blow your own horn** (BLOW¹ (12)), **take the bull by the horns** (BULL¹ (3)), **lock horns with sb (over sth)** (LOCK¹ (9))

horn² *v.*
horn in *phr. v.* [I] to interrupt or try to take part in something when you are not wanted: [+ **on**] *Several companies have tried to horn in on the market for computer chips like Intel's.*

horn·bill /'hɔrnˌbɪl/ *n.* [C] a tropical bird with a very large beak

horned /hɔrnd/ *adj.* having horns or something that looks like horns: *a horned owl*

hor·net /'hɔrnɪt/ *n.* [C] **1** a large black and yellow insect that can sting **2 a hornet's nest** a situation in which there are a lot of problems and arguments, usually one that someone does not want to enter: *Hersh's book stirred up a hornet's nest (=created a lot of problems and arguments) in the media.*

horn of plen·ty /ˌ. . '../ *n.* [C] a CORNUCOPIA (1)

horn·pipe /'hɔrnpaɪp/ *n.* [C] a traditional dance performed by SAILORS, or the music for this dance

horn-rimmed /ˌ. './ *adj.* horn-rimmed GLASSES have frames made of dark-colored plastic

horn·y /'hɔrni/ *adj.* **hornier, horniest 1** VULGAR sexually excited: *It's another movie about horny teenagers.* **2** skin that is horny is hard and rough

hor·o·scope /'hɔrəˌskoup, 'har-/ *n.* [C] a description of your character and the things that will happen to you, based on the position of the stars and PLANETS at the time of your birth —see also ASTROLOGY, ZODIAC

hor·ren·dous /həˈrɛndəs, hɔ-/ *adj.* **1** frightening and terrible: *Pit bull dogs can inflict horrendous wounds on people.* **2** INFORMAL extremely unreasonable or bad: *horrendous medical costs* | *Traffic in the downtown Boston area is horrendous.* —**horrendously** *adv.*

hor·ri·ble /ˈhɔrəbəl, ˈhɑr-/ *adj.* **1** very bad and often frightening or upsetting: *The pain was horrible.* | *a horrible crime* **2** very bad: *She got some horrible kind of stomach flu.* | *This stuff tastes horrible!* **3** impolite and unfriendly: *Danny's such a horrible little brat.* —**horribly** *adv.*

hor·rid /ˈhɔrɪd, ˈhɑrɪd/ *adj.* **1** very bad and shocking: *The dogs were raised in horrid conditions.* **2** OLD-FASHIONED behaving in a way that is not nice at all: *a horrid little boy* —**horridly** *adv.*

hor·rif·ic /həˈrɪfɪk, hɔ-/ *adj.* extremely bad, especially in a way that is frightening, shocking, or upsetting: *He lost his legs in a horrific car crash.* —**horrifically** /-kli/ *adv.*

hor·ri·fy /ˈhɔrəˌfaɪ, ˈhɑ-/ *v.* **horrifies, horrified, horrifying** [T] to make someone feel very shocked and upset or afraid: *Some of the students wept, horrified by the Holocaust survivor's stories.* —**horrifying** *adj.* —**horrifyingly** *adv.*

hor·ror /ˈhɔrɚ, ˈhɑrɚ/ *n.* **1** [U] a strong feeling of shock and fear: *The neighbors watched in horror as the fire swept through the trailer where the children were sleeping.* | *I realized, to my horror, that I didn't have enough money to pay the bill.* **2 the horror of sth** the quality of being frightening and very shocking: *the horror of the Holocaust* **3** [C] something that is very terrible, shocking, or frightening: *The old cop spoke about the horrors of Alcatraz prison.* **4 have a horror of sth** LITERARY to be very frightened of something or dislike it very much: *I had long had a horror of alcohol.* **5** [C] something that is extremely ugly: *That dress is a horror.*

horror mov·ie /ˈ.. ˌ../ also **horror film** /ˈ.. ˌ./ *n.* [C] a movie in which strange and frightening things happen

horror sto·ry /ˈ.. ˌ../ *n.* [C] **1** a report about bad experiences, bad conditions etc.: *You hear a lot of horror stories when you're out looking for a job.* **2** a story in which strange and frightening things happen

horror-strick·en /ˈ.. ˌ../ also **horror-struck** /ˈ.. ./ *adj.* suddenly very shocked and frightened: *A horror-stricken Ronald raced to his brother's side.*

hors d'oeu·vre /ɔr ˈdɚv/ *plural* **hors d'oeuvres** *n.* [C] food that is served in small amounts before the main part of the meal

horse¹ /hɔrs/ *n.* **1** [C] a large strong animal that people ride on and use for pulling heavy things **2 (straight/right) from the horse's mouth** if you hear something straight from the horse's mouth, you are told it by someone who has direct knowledge of it **3 change/switch horses in midstream** to stop supporting or working with one person or set of ideas and start supporting or working with another, while you are in the middle of doing something: *It's not wise to change horses in midstream at this point in time.* **4 a horse of a different color** also **a horse of another color** something that is completely different from another thing or situation: *Accounting was a horse of a different color, although the Bureau tended to use the words "planning" and "accounting" to mean the same thing.* **5** [C] a piece of sports equipment in a GYMNASIUM that people jump over **6** [U] SLANG: see HEROIN —see also **put the cart before the horse** (CART¹ (4)), **choke a horse** (CHOKE¹ (7)), DARK HORSE, **beat/flog a dead horse** (DEAD¹ (8)), **I could eat a horse** (EAT (11)), **don't look a gift horse in the mouth** (GIFT¹ (5)), **be/get on your high horse** (HIGH (18)), **hold your horses!** (HOLD¹ (19)), STALKING HORSE

horse² *v.*

horse around *phr. v.* [I] INFORMAL to play roughly: *Some kids were horsing around on the playground.*

horse·back /ˈhɔrsbæk/ *n.* **1 on horseback** riding a horse **2 horseback riding** the activity of riding a horse for pleasure —**horseback** *adv.*

horse chest·nut /ˈ. ˌ../ *n.* [C] **1** a large tree that produces shiny brown nuts and has white and pink flowers **2** a nut from this tree

horse-drawn /ˈ. ./ *adj.* [only before noun] pulled by a horse: *a horse-drawn carriage*

horse·fly /ˈhɔrsflaɪ/ *n. plural* **horseflies** [C] a large fly that bites horses and cattle

horse·hair /ˈhɔrshɛr/ *n.* [U] the hair from a horse's MANE and tail, sometimes used to fill the inside of furniture

horseless car·riage /ˌ.. ˈ../ *n.* [C] a word for a car, used in the early 1900s when cars were very new and unusual

horse·man /ˈhɔrsmən/ *n. plural* **horsemen** /-mən/ [C] **1** someone who rides horses **2 the four horsemen of the Apocalypse** a phrase from the Christian Bible meaning war, FAMINE (=a severe lack of food), disease, and death, which the Bible says will affect the Earth just before the end of the world

horse·man·ship /ˈhɔrsmənˌʃɪp/ *n.* [U] the practice or skill of riding horses

horse·play /ˈhɔrs-pleɪ/ *n.* [U] rough noisy behavior in which children play by pushing or hitting each other for fun: *Horseplay on the school bus is not allowed.*

horse·pow·er /ˈhɔrsˌpaʊɚ/ written abbreviation **hp** *n. plural* **horsepower** [C,U] a unit for measuring the power of an engine

horse·puck·ey /ˈhɔrsˌpʌki/ *n.* [U] SPOKEN, OLD-FASHIONED nonsense; HORSESHIT

horse race /ˈ. ./ *n.* [C] **1** a race in which people ride horses around an OVAL track **2** a competition, especially in politics, in which all the competitors seem to have equal chances of succeeding and are trying very hard to win using every possible means, so that it is difficult to guess who will win

horse·rad·ish /ˈhɔrsˌrædɪʃ/ *n.* [U] **1** a strong-tasting white SAUCE made from the root of a plant, which is usually eaten with meat **2** the plant whose root is used in making this SAUCE

horse sense /ˈ. ./ *n.* [U] OLD-FASHIONED sensible judgment gained from experience; COMMON SENSE

horse·shit /ˈhɔrʃ-ʃɪt/ *n.* [U] VULGAR nonsense; BULLSHIT

horse·shoe /ˈhɔrʃ-ʃu, ˈhɔrs-/ *n.* **1** [C] a U-shaped piece of iron that is nailed onto the bottom of a horse's foot to protect it **2** [C] a U-shaped object which is used as a sign of good luck **3 horseshoes** [U] an outdoor game in which horseshoes are thrown at a post

horse show /ˈ. ./ *n.* [C] a sports event in which people riding horses compete to show their skill in riding

horse-trad·ing /ˈ. ˌ../ *n.* [U] discussions in which everyone tries hard to gain advantages for their own side, especially in politics or business: *political horse-trading*

horse trail·er /ˈ. ˌ../ *n.* [C] a large vehicle for carrying horses, pulled by another vehicle

horse·whip /ˈhɔrsˌwɪp/ *v.* [T] to beat someone hard with a whip —**horsewhip** *n.* [C]

horse·wom·an /ˈhɔrsˌwʊmən/ *n. plural* **horsewomen** /-ˌwɪmɪn/ [C] a woman who rides horses

hors·ey, horsy /ˈhɔrsi/ *adj.* **1** very interested in horses and events that involve horses **2** looking like a horse

hor·ti·cul·ture /ˈhɔrtəˌkʌltʃɚ/ *n.* [U] the practice or science of growing flowers, fruit, and vegetables —**horticultural** /ˌhɔrtəˈkʌltʃərəl/ *adj.* —**horticulturalist** *n.* [C] —compare AGRICULTURE

ho·san·na /hoʊˈzænə/ *n.* [C] a shout of praise to God —**hosanna** *interjection*

hose¹ /hoʊz/ *n.* **1** [C] a long rubber or plastic tube that can be moved and bent to put water onto fires, gardens etc. or to take air or a gas from one place to another **2** [U] PANTYHOSE **3** [U] tight-fitting pants worn by men in past times

hose² *v.* [T] **1** to cover something with water using

H

a hose: *You don't have to hose the car before washing it.* **2** SLANG to cheat or deceive someone: *Marcus tried to hose someone on a drug deal.*

hose sth/sb ⟷ **down** also **hose** sth/sb ⟷ **off** *phr. v.* [T] to use a hose to put water on something, for example in order to clean it or to make it completely wet: *They came in every week to hose down the floors of the prison cells.*

Ho·se·a /hoʊˈzeɪə, -ˈziə/ a book in the Old Testament of the Christian Bible

hosed /hoʊzd/ *adj.* [not before noun] SPOKEN, SLANG in a lot of trouble or in a very difficult situation: *If we don't finish this tonight, we're hosed.*

hos·er /ˈhoʊzɚ/ *n.* [C] SPOKEN, SLANG someone who you do not respect because you think they are stupid, unfashionable etc.

ho·sier·y /ˈhoʊʒəri/ *n.* [U] a word meaning clothing such as "socks" and STOCKINGs, used in stores and in the clothing industry

hos·pice /ˈhɑspɪs/ *n.* [C] a special hospital where people who are dying are taken care of

hos·pi·ta·ble /hɑˈspɪtəbəl, ˈhɑspɪ-/ *adj.* **1** friendly, welcoming, and generous to visitors: *Southerners are some of the most hospitable people we've ever met.* **2** favorable and allowing things to grow or develop: *a hospitable climate* —**hospitably** *adv.* —opposite INHOSPITABLE

hos·pi·tal /ˈhɑspɪtl/ *n.* [C,U] a large building where sick or injured people are taken care of and receive medical treatment: *Elena had the surgery on Friday and was **in the hospital** for a week.* | *Ramon **was admitted to the hospital** on Tuesday.*

hos·pi·tal·i·ty /ˌhɑspəˈtæləti/ *n.* [U] friendly behavior toward visitors: *Samoans are renowned for their hospitality.* —see also **corporate hospitality** (CORPORATE (3))

hos·pi·tal·ize /ˈhɑspɪtlˌaɪz/ *v.* [T usually passive] to put someone in a hospital for treatment: *Roger was hospitalized after a severe asthma attack.* —**hospitalization** /ˌhɑspɪtl-əˈzeɪʃən/ *n.* [U]

host[1] /hoʊst/ *n.* [C]
1 at a party the person at a party, meal etc. who has invited the guests and who gives them food, drinks etc.: *The President and his wife served as hosts at the concert.* | *The host got drunk and threw up on one of the guests.*
2 on television someone who introduces the guests on a television or radio show: *Leno replaced Johnny Carson as host of "The Tonight Show."*
3 country/organization a country, government, or organization that provides the necessary space, equipment etc. for a special event: *Baltimore beat the hosts, the Detroit Tigers, 9–7.* | *Helsinki **was host to** the 1938 Olympics.*
4 a (whole) host of sth FORMAL a large number of things: *A host of problems beset the family.*
5 animal/plant TECHNICAL an animal or plant on which a smaller animal or plant is living as a PARASITE
6 the Host TECHNICAL the bread that is used in the Christian ceremony of Communion

host[2] *v.* [T] **1** to provide the place and everything that is needed for an organized event: *The college will host an open house for prospective students.* **2** to be the host on a television or radio show: *Did Walter Cronkite once host a game show on TV?*

hos·tage /ˈhɑstɪdʒ/ *n.* [C] **1** someone who is kept as a prisoner by an enemy so that the other side will do what the enemy demands: *Four U.S. citizens are still being **held hostage** by the guerrillas.* | *The hijackers **took** a crew member **hostage.*** **2 be (held) hostage to** sth to be influenced or controlled by something, so that you are not free to do what you want: *Mondale was hostage to radical forces demanding special treatment.*

hos·tel /ˈhɑstl/ *n.* [C] **1** a place where people, especially people who have no homes or who are working in a place far from their home, can stay and eat fairly cheaply: *a hostel for migrant workers* **2** a YOUTH HOSTEL

hos·tel·er /ˈhɑstələ/ *n.* [C] someone who is traveling from one YOUTH HOSTEL to another

hos·tel·ry /ˈhɑstəlri/ *n. plural* **hostelries** [C] FORMAL a hotel

host·ess /ˈhoʊstɪs/ *n.* [C] **1** the woman at a party, meal etc. who has invited all the guests and provides them with food, drink etc. **2** the woman who introduces the guests on a television or radio show **3** a woman who takes people to their table in a restaurant **4 the hostess with the mostest** SPOKEN, HUMOROUS a woman who gives many parties and is considered very beautiful and fashionable

hos·tile /ˈhɑstl, ˈhɑstaɪl/ *adj.* **1** angry and deliberately unfriendly toward someone, and ready to argue with them: *A hostile audience refused to listen to Senator Jones' reply.* **2** opposing a plan or idea very strongly: [+ **to/toward**] *They tend to be hostile to anything they don't understand.* **3** belonging to an enemy: *Civilians had to flee through **hostile territory**.* **4 hostile takeover/bid/buyout** a situation in which one company starts to control a smaller one, or tries to start controlling it, because the smaller one does not have enough power or money to stop the larger company **5 hostile environment** conditions that are difficult to live in or exist in **6 hostile witness** LAW someone who is asked to answer questions in a court of law, but who is considered unlikely to give answers that are favorable to the side that asked them

hos·til·i·ty /hɑˈstɪləti/ *n.* **1** [U] a feeling or attitude that is extremely unfriendly: *The verdict may worsen racial hostility.* | [+ **toward/to/between**] *Long after World War II, many Poles still expressed hostility toward Germans.* **2** [U] strong or angry opposition to a plan or idea: *The reform program was greeted with hostility by conservatives.* | [+ **to**] *Specter questioned Judge Reichert on his hostility to affirmative-action programs.* **3 hostilities** [plural] FORMAL acts of fighting: *The hostilities in the south appear to be spreading toward the capital.*

hot /hɑt/ *adj.* **hotter, hottest**
1 weather/food/liquid etc. having a high temperature: *It was hot and humid in the Caribbean.* | *It's too hot to go for a bike ride.* | *a pot of hot coffee* | **boiling/scalding hot** (=used to describe liquid that is extremely hot) | *Heat waves rose off the **burning hot** desert sands.* | *Pour the sauce over the pasta and serve **piping hot**.* | *a **red-hot** (=very hot) furnace* | *Man, it's **hot as hell** (=extremely hot) in here.*
2 body [not before noun] if you feel hot, your body feels warm in a way that is uncomfortable: *Bea was hot and tired from the long walk home.*
3 food food that tastes hot contains pepper, CHILI etc. and has a burning taste that makes your mouth feel warm; SPICY: *hot salsa* —compare MEDIUM[1] (3), MILD (2)
4 popular INFORMAL popular at a particular point in time: *Levi's 501 jeans continue to be a hot item.* | *Films like "Say Anything" have made Cusack a **hot property** (=an actor, singer etc. that many companies want).*
5 sexually exciting a movie, book, relationship etc. that is hot is sexually exciting: *a **red-hot** love affair*
6 successful INFORMAL very successful or very lucky at doing something: *The Penguins are still hot, beating the Rangers 5–3.* | *Jimbo had a hot night in Las Vegas and won $430.*
7 causing trouble likely to cause problems, trouble, or arguments: *Studio bosses decided her video was **too hot to handle**.*
8 difficult situation [not before noun] INFORMAL if a situation or place becomes too hot for someone, it is because other people are angry with them: *When things got too hot for Derek, he sold up and left town.*
9 sexually attractive a person who is hot is sexually attractive: *Then this really hot Italian guy sat down at the next table.*

SPOKEN PHRASES
10 not so hot not very good or well: *"How's the sound quality of those new microphones?" "Not so hot."*
11 be hot on sth to know a lot about something: *I'm not too hot on sports.*

12 be hot at sth to be very good at doing something: *Brian was never too hot at math.*

13 (is it) hot enough for you? HUMOROUS used to say that the weather is very hot

14 be hot stuff a) to be sexually attractive **b)** to be very good at a particular activity: *You should see Doug on the tennis court – he's really hot stuff.*

15 be hot for sb to be sexually attracted to someone: *Everybody is hot for the new guy at the gym.*

16 Hot damn! IMPOLITE said when you are very pleased or excited about something: *"Hot damn! I never rode in a convertible before," said the grinning boy as he climbed in.*

17 hot shit VULGAR something or someone that is very good or popular: *You think you're such hot shit, but just wait until next week.*

18 hot temper someone who has a hot temper becomes angry very easily —see also HOT-TEMPERED

19 in hot pursuit following someone quickly and closely because you want to catch them: *The cops and the dogs set out after them in hot pursuit.*

20 be hot on sb's trail/tail/track to have been close to and likely to catch someone you have been chasing: *Dente said police are hot on the thief's trail.*

21 be hot on sb's heels to be very close behind someone: *The bullfighter showed his best moves with the bull hot on his heels.*

22 come hot on the heels of sth to happen very soon after another event: *The album comes hot on the heels of Martin's first movie.*

23 news hot news is about very recent events and therefore is interesting or exciting

24 be hot off the presses/press if a newspaper, report etc. is hot off the presses, it is very new and has just been printed

25 hot air INFORMAL things someone says that sound important or impressive, but really are not: *All this "new Democrat" talk is just a bunch of hot air.*

26 be in hot water to be in a difficult situation because you have done something wrong: *Cabral was in hot water over his job performance.*

27 hot under the collar angry and ready to argue

28 be in the hot seat to be forced to deal with a difficult or bad situation, especially in politics

29 hot spot a) a place where there is likely to be trouble, fighting etc.: *There are many hot spots of unrest in the area.* | *a traffic hot spot* **b)** an area that is popular for a particular activity or type of entertainment: *We visited a few downtown hot spots.* **c)** a HOTSPOT **d)** a place where a fire can spread from

30 competition competition that is hot is between people or companies that are trying very hard to win or succeed: *Competition for the best jobs is getting hotter all the time.*

31 stolen SLANG goods that are hot have been stolen: *The boss's new Ferrari turned out to be hot.*

32 music having a strong exciting RHYTHM

33 hot ticket an event that is very popular and fashionable: *One of the hottest tickets in Paris is a revival of "West Side Story."*

34 be hot and bothered INFORMAL **a)** to be so worried and confused by something that you cannot think clearly **b)** to be sexually excited

35 hot money money that is frequently moved from one country, bank, account etc. to another in order to make a quick profit

36 hot to trot INFORMAL feeling sexually excited and interested in finding someone to have sex with —see also HOTS, RED-HOT

hot-air bal·loon /. '. ,./ *n.* [C] a very large BALLOON made of cloth and filled with hot air with a large basket attached to the bottom, used for carrying people in the air

hot·bed /'hat'bɛd/ *n.* **be a hotbed of sth** a place where a lot of a particular type of activity, especially bad or violent activity, happens: *The troubled province is a hotbed of ethnic violence.*

hot-blood·ed /,. '..ʌ/ *adj.* having very strong emotions such as anger or love, that are difficult to control; PASSIONATE

hot but·ton /'. ,./ *n.* [C] a problem or subject that causes a lot of arguments or strong feelings between

people: *Your letter certainly hit a hot button.* —**hot-button** *adj.*: *hot-button issues*

hot·cake /'hatkeɪk/ *n.* [C] **1 be selling/going like hotcakes** INFORMAL to be sold very quickly and in large amounts **2** a PANCAKE

hot choc·o·late /,. '../ *n.* [C,U] a hot drink made with chocolate powder and milk or water; COCOA

hot-cross bun /,. . './ *n.* [C] a small round sweet bread roll, with a cross-shaped mark on top, eaten just before Easter

hot dish, hotdish /,. './ *n.* [C,U] hot food, usually a mixture of meat and vegetables, sometimes with PASTA, cooked and served in a deep covered dish

hot dog¹ /'. ./ *n.* [C] **1** a long type of SAUSAGE, cooked and eaten in a long BUN (=round piece of bread) **2** INFORMAL someone who does risky and exciting things in a sport, especially SKIing, in a way that attracts people's attention

hot dog² /,. './ *interjection* OLD-FASHIONED used to express pleasure or surprise

hot-dog /'. ./ *v.* [I] INFORMAL to do something in a sport, especially SKIing, in a fast, risky, and exciting way that attracts a lot of attention and admiration: *We were both hot-dogging down the hill.*

ho·tel /hoʊ'tɛl/ *n.* [C] a building where people pay to spend the night | **stay in/at a hotel** *The dancers were impressed to learn that Hughes was staying at their hotel.*

ho·te·lier /hoʊ'tɛlyɚ, ,oʊtl'yeɪ/ *n.* [C] FORMAL someone who owns or manages a hotel

hot flash /'. ./ *n.* [C] a sudden hot feeling, which women have during the MENOPAUSE (=the time when they stop having monthly PERIODS)

hot·foot /'hɑt'fʊt/ *v.* **hotfoot it** INFORMAL to walk or run quickly

hot·head /'hathɛd/ *n.* [C] INFORMAL someone who does things too quickly and without thinking about them before doing them —**hotheaded** *adj.*

hot·house /'hat,haʊs/ *n.* [C] **1** a heated building, usually made of glass, where flowers and plants can grow *hothouse flowers* (=grown in a hothouse) —compare GREENHOUSE **2** a place or situation where a lot of people are interested in particular ideas or activities: [+ of] *The campus was once a hothouse of political protest.* **3 hothouse atmosphere/environment** a situation or place with conditions that encourage a particular activity or attitude

hot key /'. ./ *n.* [C] a button or set of buttons that you can press on a computer KEYBOARD as a quick way of making it do a particular job

hot·line, hot line /'hat-laɪn/ *n.* [C] **1** a special telephone line for people to find out about or talk about something: *Call our special hotline to voice your opinion.* **2** [usually singular] a direct telephone line between government leaders in different countries, which is only used in serious situations

hot link /'. ,./ *n.* [C] INFORMAL a HYPERTEXT LINK

hot·ly /'hatli/ *adv.* **1 hotly debated/contested/disputed etc.** discussed etc. very angrily or with very strong feelings: *Increases in defense spending are always hotly contested.* **2 hotly pursued** chased closely by someone: *The BMW was hotly pursued by an unmarked police car.*

hot pad /'. ./ *n.* [C] a small piece of thick cloth, wood, plastic etc. that you put under a hot dish or plate

hot pants /'. ./ *n.* [plural] very short tight women's SHORTS

hot pink /,. './ *n.* [U] a very bright pink color —**hot pink** *adj.*

hot·plate, hot plate /'hat'pleɪt/ *n.* [C] a small piece of equipment with a flat heated top, used for cooking food

hot pot, hotpot /'. ./ *n.* [C] a piece of electrical equipment with a small container, used to boil water

hot po·ta·to /,. .'./ *n. plural* **hot potatoes** [C usually singular] a subject or problem that no one wants to deal with, because it is difficult and any decision will make people angry: *Euthanasia for terminally ill patients is a political hot potato.*

hot rod /'. ./ *n.* [C] INFORMAL an old car into which a more powerful engine has been put, to make it go very fast —**hot rodder** *n.* [C] —**hot rodding** *n.* [U]

hots /hɑts/ *n.* **have/get the hots for sb** INFORMAL to be sexually attracted to someone: *I think he's got the hots for you, Elaine.*

hot shot, hotshot /'. ./ *n.* [C] INFORMAL someone who is very successful and confident —**hotshot** *adj.*: *a hotshot lawyer*

hot·spot, hot spot /'hɑtspɑt/ *n.* [C] a part of a computer image on the screen that you can CLICK on or point to in order to make other pictures, words etc. appear —see also **hot spot** (HOT (29))

hot spring /ˌ. './ *n.* [C] a place where hot water comes up naturally from the ground

hot-tem·pered /ˌ. '..◂/ *adj.* tending to become angry easily

hot tod·dy /ˌhɑt 'tɑdi/ *n. plural* **hot toddies** [C] a hot drink made with WHISKEY, sugar, SPICES, and hot water

hot tub /'. ./ *n.* [C] a heated bathtub or large wooden container that several people can sit in —compare JACUZZI

hot·ty /'hɑti/ *n. plural* **hotties** [C] SLANG someone who is very sexually attractive

hot-wa·ter bot·tle /ˌ. '.. ˌ../ *n.* [C] a rubber container that you put hot water in, used to keep yourself warm or to make sore muscles feel better

hot-wire /'hɑt¯waɪɚ/ *v.* [T] INFORMAL to start the engine of a vehicle by using the wires of the IGNITION system, and not using the key

hound[1] /haʊnd/ *n.* [C] **1** INFORMAL a dog **2** a dog used for hunting —see also NEWS HOUND

hound[2] *v.* [T] to keep following someone and asking them questions in an annoying or threatening way: *She had been hounded by her ex-boyfriend for months.*

hound sb **out** *phr. v.* [T] to make things so bad for someone that they are forced to leave: [+ **of**] *It would be better for him to retire gracefully than be hounded out of office.*

hour /aʊɚ/ *n.* [C]
1 60 minutes a period of 60 minutes or 1/24 of a day: *We serve meals 24 hours a day, seven days a week.* | **$10/$4.50 etc. an hour** *A lot of attorneys charge about $175 an hour.* | *You can come back for us* **in an hour** (=an hour from now).
2 distance the distance you can travel in an hour: *We're still about* **three hours** *from Amarillo.* | *It's only about* **an hour's drive** *from here.*
3 time of day a particular period or point of time during the day or night: *Nicole goes biking during her* **lunch hour.** | *We danced until the* **small hours** (=between midnight and 2 or 3 o'clock) *of the morning.* | *Sir, I'm sorry to bother you* **at this hour** (=very late at night or early in the morning). | *My wife got me out of bed* **at some ungodly hour** *to go antique shopping.* | *Anonymous female admirers call Dylan's house* **at all hours.** | *He was out* **till all hours** (=until an unreasonably late time) *last night.* | **keep late/regular etc. hours** (=go to bed and get up at late, regular etc. times) —see also **waking hours/ life/day etc.** (WAKING)
4 hours [plural] a certain period of time in the day when a particular activity, business etc. happens: **office/opening/business hours** (=when an office, store etc. is open) | *Our telephone hotline is open* **during** *regular* **business hours.** | *You can come back tomorrow during* **visiting hours** (=when you can visit someone in a hospital). | **After hours** (=after an office, store etc. is closed), *callers can leave a voice mail message.* —see also RUSH HOUR, HAPPY HOUR
5 (work) long hours if you work long hours, the period that you work is longer than usual: *Long hours are the rule for most top executives.*

6 hours [plural] INFORMAL a long time or a time that seems long: *I've been trying to call you for* **hours.** | *I could spend* **hours and hours** (=a very long time) *telling you all the stories.*
7 within hours of sth only a few hours after doing something or after something happened: *Within hours of landing, troops had started to advance inland.*
8 o'clock the time of the day when a new hour starts, for example one o'clock, two o'clock etc.: *Carriage tours of the town depart* **every hour on the hour** (=every hour at nine o'clock, ten o'clock etc.). | **strike/sound the hour** (=if a clock strikes or sounds the hour, it rings to show that it is one o'clock, seven o'clock etc.)
9 by the hour also **from hour to hour** if a situation is changing by the hour or from hour to hour, it is changing very quickly and very often: *The number of casualties is mounting by the hour.*
10 important moment an important moment or period in history or in your life: *It was his* **finest hour** *as coach of the Detroit Lions.* | *Ahab neared* **his hour of destiny** *with Moby Dick.*
11 10/20/25 etc. minutes before/after the hour SPOKEN used by broadcasters on national programs in order to give the time without saying which hour it is, because the broadcast may be coming from a different TIME ZONE: *It's twelve minutes before the hour, and you're listening to Morning Edition on NPR.*
12 the sth of the hour something that is very popular or famous at the present time: *World security is the* **question of the hour** (=the problem being dealt with at a particular time). | *He was once hailed as the country's* **man of the hour** (=he had done something important at that particular time).
13 1300/1530/1805 hours used to give the time in official or military reports and orders, and in some airports, train stations etc. The system is based on numbering the hours from 0100 (1 a.m.) to 2400 (12 midnight).
14 in your hour of need FORMAL when you are in trouble: *He helped others in their hour of need.* —see also **at the eleventh hour** (ELEVENTH[1] (2)), HOURLY, ZERO HOUR

hour·glass /'aʊɚglæs/ *n.* [C] **1** a glass container for measuring time, in which sand moves slowly from the top half to the bottom in exactly one hour **2 hourglass figure** a woman who has an hourglass figure has a narrow waist in comparison with her chest and HIPS

hour hand /'. ˌ./ *n.* [C] the shorter of the two pieces on a clock or watch that show you what time it is —compare MINUTE HAND

hour·ly /'aʊɚli/ *adj.* **1** happening or done every hour: *The shuttle offers hourly flights linking New York and Washington.* **2 hourly pay/earnings/fees etc.** the amount you earn or charge for every hour you work —**hourly** *adv.*: *The database is updated hourly.*

house[1] /haʊs/ *n. plural* **houses** /'haʊzɪz/
1 where you live [C] **a)** a building that you live in and is intended to be used by one family: *My parents have a five-bedroom house.* | *I'm going to Bethany's house after school.* **b)** all the people who live in a house: *Be quiet or you'll wake the whole house!*
2 opera/court house etc. a large public building used for a particular purpose
3 government [C] **a)** one of the groups of people who make the laws of a state or country: *The bill has the backing of both houses of Congress.* **b) the House** the HOUSE OF REPRESENTATIVES
4 company [C] a company, especially one that produces books, lends money, or designs clothes: *America's oldest publishing house* | *the House of Dior*
5 keep house to do all the cooking, cleaning etc. in a house: *Owen's wife, Lauren, keeps house and looks after the children.*
6 be on the house if drinks or food are on the house, you do not have to pay for them because they are provided free by the owner of the bar, restaurant etc.
7 house of God also **house of worship** a church
8 theater [C] **a)** the part of a theater where people

sit: *Houston's recent concert tour played to* **packed houses** *across the nation.* | *The* **house lights** (=lights in the part where people sit) *came up, and we knew the show was finally over.* **b)** the people who have come to watch a performance: AUDIENCE
9 hen/coach/store house etc. a building in which animals, goods, equipment etc. are kept
10 house wine/white/red ordinary wine that is provided by a restaurant to be drunk with meals: *Dorothy ordered a glass of the house white with her fish.*
11 music [U] HOUSE MUSIC
12 do sth like a house on fire INFORMAL to do something very well and with a lot of eagerness and enjoyment: *McEntire can play guitar like a house on fire.*
13 the big house HUMOROUS prison
14 bring the house down to do something while performing in a play, concert etc. that the people watching enjoy a lot: *Sinatra brought the house down when he sang "New York, New York."*
15 royal family [C] an important family, especially a royal family: *the House of Windsor* —see also **eat sb out of house and home** (EAT (7)), HOUSE ARREST, IN-HOUSE, OPEN HOUSE

house² /haʊz/ v. [T] **1** to provide someone with a place to live: *Last year, the Tri-City Homeless Coalition housed 800 people.* **2** if a building houses something, it is in that building: *The plush hotel once housed a casino and several restaurants.*

house ar·rest /ˌ. .ˈ./ n. **be under house arrest** to be told by the government that you must stay inside your house, or you will go to prison

house·boat /ˈhaʊsboʊt/ n. [C] a boat that you can live in

house·bound /ˈhaʊsbaʊnd/ adj. unable to leave your house, especially because you are sick or old

house·boy /ˈhaʊsbɔɪ/ n. [C] a young man who works as a servant in someone's house, especially in past times

house·break /ˈhaʊsbreɪk/ v. [T] to train an animal, especially a dog, not to make the house dirty with its URINE and FECES (=body waste)

house·break·er /ˈhaʊsˌbreɪkə/ n. [C] a thief who enters someone else's house by breaking locks, windows etc.; BURGLAR —**housebreaking** n. [U]

house·bro·ken /ˈhaʊsˌbroʊkən/ adj. an animal that is housebroken has been trained not to make the house dirty with its URINE and FECES (=body waste)

house call /ˈ. ./ n. [C] a visit that someone, especially a doctor, makes to someone in their home as part of their job: *Where can you find a doctor who makes house calls nowadays?*

house·coat /ˈhaʊs-koʊt/ n. [C] a long loose coat worn at home to cover your clothes or PAJAMAS

house·fly /ˈhaʊsflaɪ/ n. plural **houseflies** [C] a common type of fly that often lives in houses

house·ful /ˈhaʊsfʊl/ n. **a houseful of sth** a large number of people or things in your house: *Having a houseful of relatives can be pretty stressful.*

house guest /ˈ. ./ n. [C] a friend or relative who is staying in your house for a short time

house·hold¹ /ˈhaʊshoʊld, ˈhaʊsoʊld/ n. [C] all the people who live together in one house: *a two-income household*

household² adj. [only before noun] **1** relating to taking care of a house and the people in it; DOMESTIC: *household cleaning products* | *household appliances* **2 be a household name/word** to be very well known: *Apple computers became a household word in the late '80s.*

house·hold·er /ˈhaʊsˌhoʊldə/ n. [C] FORMAL someone who owns or is in charge of a house

house hus·band /ˈ. ˌ../ n. [C] a husband who works at home doing the cooking, cleaning etc., but who does not have a job outside the house —compare HOUSEWIFE

house·keep·er /ˈhaʊsˌkipə/ n. [C] **1** someone who is employed to manage the cleaning, cooking etc. in a house or hotel **2** someone who is employed to clean your house, do the cooking etc.

house·keep·ing /ˈhaʊsˌkipɪŋ/ n. [U] **1** the work and organization of things that need to be done in a house, for example cooking and buying food **2** jobs that need to be done to keep a system working correctly **3** the department in a large building such as a hotel or a hospital that is RESPONSIBLE for cleaning the inside of the building

house·maid /ˈhaʊsmeɪd/ n. [C] OLD-FASHIONED a female servant who cleans someone's house

house·man /ˈhaʊsmən/ n. plural **housemen** /-mən/ [C] a man who is employed to do general work, especially cleaning work, in someone's house or in a hotel

house·mas·ter /ˈhaʊsˌmæstə/ n. [C] a male teacher who is in charge of a DORMITORY at a private school

house·moth·er /ˈhaʊsˌmʌðə/ n. [C] a woman employed to be in charge of a house or a DORMITORY where students or young people live at a private school

house mu·sic /ˈ. ˌ../ n. [U] a type of popular music played on electronic instruments, with a strong fast beat

house of cards /ˌ. . ˈ./ n. [singular] **1** a plan that is so badly arranged that is likely to fail **2** an arrangement of PLAYING CARDS built carefully but easily knocked over

House of Com·mons /ˌ. . ˈ../ n. **the House of Commons** the part of the British or Canadian PARLIAMENT whose members are elected by the people

House of Lords /ˌ. . ˈ./ n. **the House of Lords** the part of the British PARLIAMENT whose members are not elected but have positions because of their rank or title

House of Rep·re·sent·a·tives /ˌ. . . .ˈ.../ n. **the House of Representatives** the larger of the two parts of the U.S. Congress or of the PARLIAMENT of Australia or New Zealand —compare SENATE (1)

house par·ty /ˈ. ˌ../ n. [C] an occasion when a group of people stay as guests at someone's house

house phone /ˈ. ./ n. [C] a telephone that can only be used to make calls within a building, especially a hotel

house·plant /ˈhaʊsplænt/ n. [C] a plant that you grow indoors for decoration

house-sit, house sit /ˈ. ./ v. [I + for] to take care of someone's house while they are away —**house-sitter** n. [C]

house-to-house /ˌ. . ˈ./ adj. [only before noun] **house-to-house search/survey etc.** a search, SURVEY etc. made by visiting each house in a particular area: *Firefighters and police went on a house-to-house search for victims.*

house·top /ˈhaʊs-tɑp/ n. **1** [C usually plural] the ROOF of a house **2 shout/proclaim etc. sth from the housetops** to say something publicly so that everyone will hear or know about it

house·wares /ˈhaʊswɛrz/ n. [plural] small things used in the home, for example kitchen utensils, lamps etc., or the department of a large store that sells these things

house·warm·ing /ˈhaʊsˌwɔrmɪŋ/ also **housewarming par·ty** /ˈ... ˌ../ n. [C] a party that you give to celebrate when you have just moved into a new house: *Julie and Dean invited us to their housewarming.*

house·wife /ˈhaʊswaɪf/ n. plural **housewives** /-waɪvz/ [C] a married woman who works at home doing the cooking etc. but does not have a job outside the house; HOMEMAKER —**housewifely** adj. —compare HOUSE HUSBAND

house·work /ˈhaʊswək/ n. [U] work that you do to take care of a house, such as washing, cleaning etc.: *We encourage our kids to help with the housework.* —compare HOMEWORK

hous·ing /ˈhaʊzɪŋ/ n. **1** [U] the houses or conditions that people live in: *Hundreds of students are still looking for housing near campus.* | *Any plan that can provide affordable housing would be a plus.* | *public* *housing* (=provided by the government for poor people to live in) **2** [U] the work of providing houses for people to live in: *the housing authority* **3** [C] a protective cover for a machine: *the engine housing*

housing de·vel·op·ment /'.. .,.../ *n.* [C] a large number of houses that have been built together in a planned way

housing proj·ect /'.. ,../ *n.* [C] a group of houses or apartments, usually built with government money, for poor people to rent

Hous·ton /'hyustən/ a city and port in the U.S. state of Texas

Houston, Sam /sæm/ (1793–1863) a U.S. soldier and politician who fought to make Texas independent from Mexico and was President of the Republic of Texas from 1836 until it became a state of the U.S. in 1845

hove /hoʊv/ *v.* a past tense and past participle of HEAVE[1]

hov·el /'hʌvəl, 'hɑ-/ *n.* [C] a small dirty place where someone lives, especially a very poor person

hov·er /'hʌvɚ/ *v.* [I] **1** if a bird, insect, or HELICOPTER hovers, it stays in one place in the air **2** to stay nervously in the same place, especially because you are waiting for something or are uncertain what to do: [+ **around/over** etc.] *Jake hovered around anxiously in the kitchen, peeking at the turkey again and again.* **3** [always + adv./prep.] if something such as a price, temperature, or rate that can go up or down hovers, it remains at around a particular level for a period of time: [+ **around/between** etc.] *Temperatures hover around 100 degrees daily.*

hov·er·craft /'hʌvɚˌkræft/ *n. plural* **hovercraft** or **hovercrafts** [C] a vehicle that travels just above the surface of land or water using a strong current of air forced out beneath it —compare HYDROFOIL

HOV lane /ˌeɪtʃ oʊ 'vi leɪn/ *n.* [C] high-occupancy vehicle lane; a LANE on main roads that can only be used by vehicles carrying three or more passengers during the time of day when there is a lot of traffic

how[1] /haʊ/ *adv.*

1 questions **a)** used to ask about what way or what method you should use to do something, find out about something, go somewhere etc.: *How do you turn the printer on?* | *How should I dress for this job interview?* | *How are the kids going to get home?* | *How do I get to North Bend?* **b)** used to ask about the amount, size, degree etc. of something: *How much do they charge for a haircut?* | *How many people does each cabin sleep?* | *How long are you going to be here?* **c)** used to ask about someone's health or about their feelings: *How are you feeling this morning?* **d)** used to ask about someone's opinion of something or about their experience of something: *How do you like the painting, Chuck?* | *How was your trip?* **e)** used to ask about the way something looks, behaves, or is expressed: *How do I look in glasses?* | *How does American English differ from British?*

2 emphasize used before an adjective or adverb to emphasize the quality you are mentioning: *Everyone was talking about how great the workshop was.* | *He was surprised at how bitter Sabina sounded.* | *Have you seen how incredibly messy Fong's room is?*

SPOKEN PHRASES

3 how are you? used when you meet someone, to ask if they are well: *"How are you, Fumiko? "Fine, thank you."*

4 how's it going? also **how are you doing?, how are things? a)** used when you meet someone, to ask if they are well, happy etc.: *"How's it going, Joyce?" "Oh, okay, I guess."* | *"How are things at work?" "Just fine."* **b)** used to ask if someone is happy with what they are doing: *Hey, John, how is your work going?*

5 how about...? a) used to make a suggestion about what to do: *How about some iced tea?* | *How about if I read you and Mia a story?* | [**how about doing sth?**] *How about visiting the Smithsonian on the Web?* **b)** used to introduce a new idea, fact etc.

that has not yet been discussed: *"I couldn't get Missy to babysit." "How about Rebekah?"*

6 how about you? used to ask someone what they want or what their opinion is, after you have said what you want or what your opinion is: *I like to play tennis – how about you?*

7 how come? used to ask why something has happened or been said, especially when you are surprised by it: *"I didn't even eat lunch today." "Really? How come?"* | *How come you got back so early?*

8 how's that? also **how about that?** used to ask someone whether something is satisfactory: *We can use the leftover roast beef for sandwiches. How's that?* | *I'll just take half an inch off your bangs. How about that?*

9 how do you mean? used to ask someone to explain something they just said: *"You want to keep your knees straight." "How do you mean, straight?"*

10 how do you know? used to ask in a slightly impolite way how someone found out about something or why they are sure about something: *"I don't think Sherry's working tonight." "How do you know?"*

11 how can/could you...? used when you are very surprised by something or disapprove strongly of something: *How can you say that about your own parents?* | *How could you be so rude as to walk in here in the middle of my class?*

12 how about that! also **how do you like that!** used to ask what someone thinks of something that you think is surprising, impolite, very good etc.: *He's going to pay our mortgage for us. How about that!*

13 how so? used to ask someone to explain an opinion they have given: *"The scriptures make it perfectly clear." "Oh, how so?"*

14 and how! OLD-FASHIONED an expression meaning "yes, very much," used to strongly emphasize your reply to a question: *"Did you like your hot dog?" "And how!"*

15 how do you do? OLD-FASHIONED, FORMAL a polite expression used when you meet someone for the first time

how[2] *conjunction* **1** used at the beginning of a CLAUSE in which you explain the method of doing something: *The way you create a table depends on how you prefer to enter the data.* | [**how to do sth**] *I'll teach you how to tie your shoes.* **2** used at the beginning of a CLAUSE in which you introduce a fact or statement: *We were both traveling across Europe, and that's how we first met.* | *She was curious about how Jill came to be living in this house.* **3** SPOKEN in whatever way: *In your own house you can act how you want.*

how·dy /'haʊdi/ *interjection* used to say hello in an informal, usually humorous, way: *Howdy, folks!*

Howe /haʊ/, **E·li·as** /əˈlaɪəs/ (1819–1867) the U.S. inventor of the SEWING MACHINE —see picture on page 1329

Howe, Ju·li·a Ward /'dʒuliə wɔrd/ (1819–1910) a U.S. writer who supported women's rights and worked against SLAVERY

how·ev·er[1] /haʊˈɛvɚ/ *adv.* **1** [sentence adverb] used when you are adding a fact or piece of information that seems surprising, or seems to disagree with what you have just said: *Wyman stressed, however, that the main function of this church is to serve the needs of the poor.* | *Cotton production was on the increase. However, it was still a small industry compared to hemp and canvas production.* —see Usage Note at BUT[1] **2 however hard/serious/long** etc. used before adjectives and adverbs to show that it does not matter how long, serious etc. something is or how slowly etc. it happens: *You should report all accidents, however minor.* | *However much other people contradict him, he still thinks he's right.* **3** OLD-FASHIONED used to mean how, when you want to show that you find something very surprising: *My goodness, this room is so interesting. However did you think to decorate it in purple and green?*

however[2] *conjunction* in whatever way: *You guys can split up the driving however you want.*

how·it·zer /'haʊɪtsɚ/ *n.* [C] a heavy gun that fires SHELLS high into the air so that they travel a short distance

howl[1] /haʊl/ v. **1** [I] if a dog, WOLF, or other animal howls, it makes a long loud sound **2** [I,T] to shout or demand something angrily: *Many businesses are howling that they will not be able to operate efficiently under the new regulations.* **3** [I] to make a long loud cry because you are unhappy, in pain, or angry: *Dave howled in pain as Ranzel beat him.* **4** [I] if the wind howls, it makes a loud high sound as it blows: *Strong winds howled across the region.* **5 howl with laughter** to laugh very loudly

howl[2] n. [C] **1** a long loud sound made by a dog, WOLF, or other animal **2** a loud cry of pain or anger **3 howl of laughter** a very loud laugh **4 howl of protest** a statement or opinion that criticizes something very strongly or protests against it: *The suggestion provoked howls of protest from Republican senators.*

howl·er /ˈhaʊlə/ n. [C] INFORMAL a stupid mistake that makes people laugh

howl·ing /ˈhaʊlɪŋ/ adj. **1** making a long loud sound: *howling winds* **2 a howling success** something that is very successful: *The movie has been a howling success.*

how·so·ev·er /ˌhaʊsoʊˈɛvə/ adv. LITERARY: see HOWEVER

how-to /ˌ. ˈ./ adj. [only before noun] a how-to book, magazine etc. gives instructions on what you need to do to make something, fix something etc. —**how-to** n. [C] *Rather than the usual video gifts such as golf how-tos and sports tapes, why not try something a little different?*

HP the abbreviation of HORSEPOWER

HQ the abbreviation of HEADQUARTERS

HR **1** the written abbreviation of HOME RUN **2** the abbreviation of HUMAN RESOURCES

hr. plural **hrs.** the written abbreviation of "hour"

H.S. the written abbreviation of "high school"

HST the written abbreviation of HAWAII STANDARD TIME

HT the written abbreviation of HAWAII TIME

ht. the written abbreviation of "height"

HTML n. [U] TECHNICAL Hypertext Markup Language; a special computer language used to make documents that can connect to other documents and FILES even if they have very different forms. It is used especially for documents on the Internet

HTTP n. [U] TECHNICAL Hypertext Transfer Protocol; a set of standards that controls how computer DOCUMENTS written in HTML connect to each other

hub /hʌb/ n. [C] **1** the central part of an area, system etc., that all the other parts are connected to: *Flights to South America pass through the airline's hub airport in Rio de Janeiro, Brazil.* | [+ of] *Downtown St. Paul is a hub of culture and entertainment.* **2** the most important part of something, that all the other parts are related to: [+ of] *Vienna was then the hub of the multinational Hapsburg empire.* **3** the central part of a wheel to which the AXLE is joined —see picture at BICYCLE[1]

hub·ba-hub·ba /ˌhʌbə ˈhʌbə/ interjection OLD-FASHIONED, SPOKEN said when you think someone is very attractive

Hub·ble /ˈhʌbəl/, **Ed·win** /ˈɛdwɪn/ (1889–1953) a U.S. ASTRONOMER who made an important discovery that shows that the universe is EXPANDing

hub·bub /ˈhʌbʌb/ n. [singular,U] a mixture of loud noises, especially the noise of a lot of people talking at the same time

hub·by /ˈhʌbi/ n. plural **hubbies** [C] INFORMAL husband

hub·cap /ˈhʌbkæp/ n. [C] a metal cover for the center of a wheel on a car or truck

hu·bris /ˈhyubrɪs/ n. [U] LITERARY too much pride

huck·le·ber·ry /ˈhʌkəlˌbɛri/ n. plural **huckleberries** [C] a small dark-blue North American fruit that grows on a bush

huck·ster /ˈhʌkstə/ n. [C] **1** someone who sells things, especially in a way that seems dishonest or too direct **2** someone in past times who sold small things in the street or to people in their houses

huck·ster·ism /ˈhʌkstəˌrɪzm/ n. [U] the use of very strong, direct, and sometimes dishonest methods to try to persuade someone to buy something

HUD /hʌd/ Housing and Urban Development; a U.S. government department that is responsible for providing houses for people to live in, and the way cities are developed

hud·dle[1] /ˈhʌdl/ v. **1** [I,T] also **huddle together/up** if a group of people huddle together, they gather closely together in a group: *We lay huddled together for warmth.* | [+ around] *People huddled around their radios and TVs, waiting for news.* **2** [I always + adv./prep.] to lie or sit with your arms and legs close to your body, especially because you are cold or frightened: *Homeless men huddled beneath flimsy blankets on the sidewalk.* **3** [I] to sit or stand with a small group of people in order to discuss something or make a decision privately: *This week, the union's executive board huddled to discuss how to keep workers from competing against each other.* **4** [I] if football players huddle, they gather around one player who tells them the plan for the next part of the game

hud·dle[2] n. [C] **1** a group of players in football who gather around one player who tells them the plan for the next part of the game **2** a group of people standing or sitting close together, especially in order to discuss something **3** a group of things that are close together: [+ of] *Botwood was a huddle of small houses around a small harbor.*

Hud·son /ˈhʌdsən/, **Henry** (?1550–1611) an English EXPLORER who was the first European to discover the Hudson River

Hudson Bay /ˌ.. ˈ./ a large area of sea in northern Canada which is frozen for most of the year

Hudson Riv·er, the /ˌ.. ˈ../ a river in New York State in the northeastern U.S. that meets the Atlantic Ocean in New York City

hue /hyu/ n. [C] LITERARY a color or type of color: *In the fall, Boston ivy vines take on red hues.*

hue and cry /ˌ. . ˈ./ n. [singular,U] angry protests about something: *The bill has raised a hue and cry from the gay community.*

huff[1] /hʌf/ n. **in a huff** feeling angry or in a bad mood, especially because someone has offended you: *Michelle got mad and left in a huff.*

huff[2] v. [I] INFORMAL **1 huff and puff** to breathe out in a noisy way, especially because you are tired: *A couple of pudgy joggers were huffing and puffing along the path.* **2** [T] to say something in a way that shows you are angry, often because you have been offended: *"That was unbelievably irresponsible," huffed one teacher.*

huff·y /ˈhʌfi/ adj. **huffier, huffiest** INFORMAL in a bad mood, especially because someone has offended you: *Some customers get huffy when you ask them for their ID.* —**huffily** adv.

hug[1] /hʌg/ v. **hugged, hugging** **1** [I,T] to put your arms around someone and hold them tightly to show love or friendship: *We stood there crying and hugging each other.* | *They hugged one last time before Renata got into the car and drove off.* **2** [T] to move along the side, edge, top etc. of something, staying very close to it: *Gray whales hug the west coast as they move south.* **3** [T] if clothes hug your body, they fit closely | **body-/figure-hugging** *Surfers wear body-hugging wetsuits.* **4** [T] to hold something in your arms, close to your chest: *He was hugging a big pile of books.*

hug[2] n. [C] the act of hugging someone: *Come on, Kelly, give Grandma a hug.* —see also BEAR HUG

huge /hyudʒ/ adj. **1** extremely large: *Thelma baked a huge chocolate cake for me.* | *These shoes make my feet look huge.* **2** to a very great degree: *King's new novel will undoubtedly be a huge success.* | *The new system has made a huge difference.* —**hugely** adv.: *hugely successful* —**hugeness** n. [U]

Hughes /hyuz/, **Charles S.** (1862–1948) a CHIEF JUSTICE on the U.S. Supreme Court

H

Hughes, How·ard /ˈhaʊəd/ (1905–1976) a U.S. BUSI-
NESSMAN, aircraft designer, pilot, and film PRODUCER

Hughes, Lang·ston /ˈlæŋstən/ (1902–1967) a U.S.
poet and writer

Hu·go/ /ˈhyugoʊ/, **Vic·tor** /ˈvɪktə/ (1802–1885) a
French writer of poems, plays, and NOVELS

Hu·gue·nots /ˈhyugəˌnɑts/ a group of French Protes-
tants during the 16th and 17th centuries, when
Protestants were often treated very badly in France
—**Huguenot** adj.

huh /hʌ/ interjection **1** said when you have not heard
or understood a question: *It should work, don't you
think?" "Huh?"* **2** said at the end of a question, to
ask for agreement: *Not a bad restaurant, huh?*

huh-uh /ˈhʌ ʌ/ interjection a sound you make that
means "no": *"Did he lose that money?" "Huh-uh."*
—see also UH HUH

hu·la /ˈhulə/ n. [C] a Polynesian dance done by women
using gentle movements of the HIPS

Hula-Hoop, hula hoop /ˈ.. ˌ./ n. [C] TRADEMARK a
large ring which you make swing around your waist
by moving your HIPS

hula skirt /ˈ.. ˌ./ n. [C] a skirt made of many long thin
pieces of material or tropical grass that are fastened
together around the waist and hang loosely at the
bottom

hulk /hʌlk/ n. [C] **1** an old ship, plane, or vehicle that
is not used anymore: *The rusty hulks of old tractors
sit on the hill.* **2** a large heavy person or thing

hulk·ing /ˈhʌlkɪŋ/ adj. [only before noun] very big
and often awkward: *Two hulking guards stood at
attention.*

hull¹ /hʌl/ n. [C] **1** the main part of a ship **2** the
outer covering of seeds, rice, grain etc.

hull² v. [T] to take off the outer part of seeds, rice,
grain etc.

hul·la·ba·loo /ˈhʌləbəˌlu, ˌhʌləbəˈlu/ n. [C usually
singular,U] **1** excited talk, newspaper stories etc.,
especially about something surprising or shocking:
There's been a huge hullabaloo over Collins' new book.
2 a lot of noise, especially made by people shouting

hum¹ /hʌm/ v. hummed, humming **1** [I,T] to sing a
tune by making a continuous sound with your lips
closed: *Carol hummed along to the song on the
radio.* **2** [I] to make a low continuous sound: *Sewing
machines hummed on the factory floor.* **3** [I usually
in progressive] to be very busy and full of activity:
By nine o'clock, the restaurant was humming. | *Low
interest rates make borrowing easier and keep the
economy humming.*

hum² n. [singular,U] **1** a low continuous sound: *the
distant hum of traffic* **2** the sound made when you
hum

hu·man¹ /ˈhyumən/ adj. **1** belonging to or relating to
people, especially as opposed to animals or
machines: *human behavior* | *No two **human beings**
(=people) are exactly alike.* | *NASA said the accident
was a result of **human error** (=a mistake made by a
person, not a machine).* **2** human weaknesses, emotions etc. are typical of ordinary people: *The humor
springs from basic human emotions like love and fear
of failure.* **3** sb is only human used to say that someone should not be blamed for what they have done,
because they could not have done anything more:
*The Supreme Court's nine justices are only human –
sometimes they make mistakes.* **4** human shield
someone who is taken and kept as a prisoner by a
criminal in order to protect the criminal from being
killed, injured, or caught **5** someone who seems
human shows that they have the same feelings and
emotions as ordinary people: *The incident made
Herman seem more human to his fans.* —opposite
INHUMAN **6** human interest the quality of being
about people's lives, relationships etc. and therefore
interesting to other people: *human interest stories*
7 put a human face on sth to make the public think
differently about an event, political situation etc. by
directing their attention to a particular person

human² also **human be·ing** /ˌ.. ˈ../ n. [C] a person

hu·mane /hyuˈmeɪn/ adj. treating people or animals
in a way that is kind, not cruel: *Animals are now
raised in more humane conditions.* —**humanely** adv.
—opposite INHUMANE

Humane So·ci·e·ty /ˌ. .ˌ.../ a U.S. organization that
takes care of unwanted pets, especially ones that
were treated cruelly, and encourages people to treat
animals better

hu·man·ism /ˈhyumənˌnɪzəm/ n. [U] **1** a system of
beliefs that tries to solve human problems through
science rather than religion **2** Humanism the study
during the Renaissance of the ideas of the ancient
Greeks and Romans —**humanist** n. [C] —**humanistic**
/ˌhyuməˈnɪstɪk/ adj.

hu·man·i·tar·i·an /hyuˌmænəˈtɛriən/ adj. [only before
noun] concerned with improving bad living conditions and preventing unfair treatment of people:
Humanitarian aid is being sent to the refugees.
—**humanitarian** n. [C] —**humanitarianism** n. [U]

hu·man·i·ty /hyuˈmænəṭi/ n. **1** [U] kindness, respect,
and sympathy toward other people: *a man of deep
humanity* **2** [U] people in general: *The Nobel
committee said Gordimer's writing had benefited
humanity.* **3** humanities [plural] subjects of study
such as literature, history, art PHILOSOPHY etc., rather
than subjects relating to science or mathematics
4 [U] the state of being human and having qualities
and rights that all people have: *The medical course
stresses each patient's humanity.*

hu·man·ize /ˈhyuməˌnaɪz/ v. [T] to make a place or
system nicer or more appropriate for people: *The
administration has made attempts to humanize the
prison.*

hu·man·kind /ˈhyumənˌkaɪnd/ n. [U] people in general: *The telephone network is one of the greatest
engineering feats in the history of humankind.*

hu·man·ly /ˈhyumənli/ adv. **1 humanly possible
a)** as much as anyone could possibly do: *Firefighters
did everything humanly possible to save lives.* **b)** if
something is humanly possible, it can be done using
a great deal of effort: *The report was as fair as is
humanly possible.* **2** relating to humans: *The poor
animal's eyes seemed humanly expressive.*

human na·ture /ˌ.. ˈ../ n. [U] **1** the qualities or ways
of behaving that are natural and common to most
people: *What does the novel reveal about human
nature?* **2** it's (only/just) human nature used to say
that a particular feeling or way of behaving is
normal and natural: *It's human nature to put off
doing things you don't like to do.*

hu·man·oid /ˈhyuməˌnɔɪd/ adj. something that is
humanoid has a human shape and qualities
—**humanoid** n. [C]

human race /ˌ.. ˈ./ n. the human race all people,
considered together as a single group

human re·sourc·es /ˌ.. ˈ.../ n. **1** [U] the department
in a company that deals with employing, training,
and helping people; PERSONNEL **2** [plural] the abilities
and skills of people

human rights /ˌ.. ˈ./ n. [plural] the basic rights
which every person has to be treated in a fair equal
way without cruelty, especially by their government

hum·ble¹ /ˈhʌmbəl/ adj. **1** not considering yourself
or your ideas to be as important as other people's:
*Taylor's students describe him as a humble and
modest man.* —opposite PROUD **2** relating to a low
social class or position: *a humble house on a back
street* | **humble beginnings/origins** *The senator
rose from humble beginnings on an Iowa farm.* **3** in
my humble opinion SPOKEN used to give your opinion about something in a slightly humorous way
4 sb's humble abode HUMOROUS someone's house or
apartment which they are very proud of and think is
very nice: *Welcome to our humble abode.* **5** [only
before noun] simple, ordinary, and not special:
*Scientists say the humble potato may be the key to
feeding the world's fast-growing population.* **6** eat
humble pie to admit that you were wrong about
something —**humbly** adv. —see also HUMILITY

humble² *v.* **1 be humbled** if you are humbled, you realize that you are not as important, good, kind etc. as you thought you were: *You can't help but be humbled when you walk into this magnificent cathedral.* **2** [T] to easily defeat someone who is much stronger than you are: *The mighty U.S. army was humbled by a small South East Asian country.* **3 humble yourself** FORMAL to show that you are not too proud to ask for something, admit you are wrong etc. —**humbling** *adj.*: *a humbling experience*

hum·bug /'hʌmbʌg/ *n.* **1 bah, humbug** SPOKEN, HUMOROUS used when you do not believe something is true, or when you think something is insincere and silly: *Are you so depressed you're saying "Bah, humbug" to Christmas this year?* **2** [U] FORMAL something that is intended to trick or deceive people: *Barnum's original circus was little more than humbug and hype.* **3** [U] FORMAL insincere words or behavior: *All this talk of love and compassion is humbug when people are hungry and homeless.* **4** [U] OLD-FASHIONED someone who pretends to be someone they are not, or to have qualities or opinions they do not have

hum·ding·er /ˌhʌm'dɪŋə/ *n.* [singular] INFORMAL a very exciting or impressive game, performance, or event: *a humdinger of a party*

hum·drum /'hʌmdrʌm/ *adj.* boring and ordinary, and having very little variety or interest: *a humdrum job*

Hume /hyum/, **Da·vid** /'deɪvɪd/ (1711–1776) a Scottish writer on PHILOSOPHY and history, known for his belief in EMPIRICISM

hu·mer·us /'hyumərəs/ [C] *n.* TECHNICAL the bone between your shoulder and elbow —see picture at SKELETON

hu·mid /'hyumɪd/ *adj.* weather that is humid makes you feel uncomfortable because the air feels very hot and wet: *The forecast is for another hot and humid afternoon today.* —see Usage Note at DAMP¹

hu·mi·dex /'hyumɪˌdɛks/ *n.* [singular] CANADIAN: see HEAT INDEX

hu·mid·i·fi·er /hyu'mɪdəˌfaɪə/ *n.* [C] a machine that makes the air in a room less dry

hu·mid·i·fy /hyu'mɪdəˌfaɪ/ *v.* **humidifies, humidified, humidifying** [T] to add very small drops of water to the air in a room etc. because the air is too dry

hu·mid·i·ty /hyu'mɪdəti/ *n.* [U] the amount of water contained in the air: *Some plants need warmth and high humidity.*

hu·mi·dor /'hyumɪˌdor/ *n.* [C] OLD-FASHIONED a box that CIGARS are kept in

hu·mil·i·ate /hyu'mɪliˌeɪt/ *v.* [T] to make someone feel ashamed and upset, especially by making them seem stupid or weak: *Lewis says her son was humiliated by his teacher in front of his fifth-grade class.* —**humiliated** *adj.* —**humiliating** *adj.*: *a humiliating defeat*

hu·mil·i·a·tion /hyuˌmɪli'eɪʃən/ *n.* **1** [U] a feeling of shame and great embarrassment, because you have been made to look stupid or weak: *Rape is an act of violence and humiliation.* **2** [C] a situation that makes you feel humiliated

hu·mil·i·ty /hyu'mɪləti/ *n.* [U] APPROVING the quality of not being too proud about yourself: *Humility and discipline are important in the martial arts.* —see also HUMBLE¹

hum·ming·bird /'hʌmɪŋˌbəd/ *n.* [C] a very small brightly-colored bird whose wings move very quickly

hum·mus /'hʊməs, 'hu-/ *n.* [U] a type of Middle Eastern food made from a soft mixture of CHICKPEAS, oil, and GARLIC

hu·mon·gous, humungous /hyu'mʌŋgəs/ *adj.* INFORMAL very large: *They have a humongous dog.*

hu·mor¹ /'hyumə/ *n.* **1** [U] the quality in something that makes it funny and makes people laugh: *I just don't see the humor in racist jokes.* | *Be careful using humor in a job interview – it can easily be misunderstood.* **2** [U] the ability to laugh at things and think that they are funny: *Mr. Cohen is a man of great humor and charm.* | *Vicki has a really zany sense of*

humor. **3** [U] the way that a particular person or group find certain things amusing: *Jewish-American humor often emphasizes the extent to which ethnic traditions merge in the United States.* **4 good humor** a cheerful friendly attitude, even in situations that would annoy or upset most people: *Walsh took all the teasing in good humor.* **5 in a good humor** FORMAL in a good mood —opposite IN A BAD HUMOR —see also GOOD-HUMORED **6** [C] TECHNICAL one of the liquids that is naturally present in the body **7** [C] one of the four liquids that in the past were thought to be present in the body and to influence someone's character

humor² *v.* [T] to do what someone wants so they will not become angry or upset: *Just humor me and listen.*

hu·mor·ist /'hyumərɪst/ *n.* [C] someone, especially a writer, who tells funny stories

hu·mor·less /'hyuməlɪs/ *adj.* too serious and not able to laugh at things that are funny —**humorlessly** *adv.* —**humorlessness** *n.* [U]

hu·mor·ous /'hyumərəs/ *adj.* funny and enjoyable: *The book is a humorous account of Glover's travels in South America.* —**humorously** *adv.*

hu·mour /'hyumə/ the British and Canadian spelling of HUMOR, also used in the word "humourless"

hump¹ /hʌmp/ *n.* [C] **1** a large round shape that rises above the surface of the ground or a surface: *The car has a big hump in the middle of the rear floor, because of the rear-wheel drive mechanism.* **2** a raised part on the back of a CAMEL and some other animals **3 be over the hump** to have finished the most difficult part of something: *With this win, the coach feels the team is over the hump.* **4** a raised part on someone's back that is caused by an unusually curved SPINE

hump² *v.* [I,T] VULGAR to have sex with someone

hump·back /'hʌmpbæk/ *n.* [C] another form of HUNCHBACK

humpback whale /ˌ.. './ *n.* [C] a large type of WHALE

humph /hʌmf, hmh, hm/ *interjection* a sound you make to show that you do not believe something or do not approve of something

hu·mus /'hyuməs/ *n.* [U] soil made of decayed plants, leaves etc., which is good for growing plants

hum·vee /ˌhʌm'vi/ *n.* [C] a military car that can climb hills and drive through sand

Hun /hʌn/ *n.* [C] a member of a group of people from central Asia who attacked and controlled parts of Europe during the 4th and 5th centuries A.D.

hunch¹ /hʌntʃ/ *n.* [C] a feeling that something is true or that something will happen, even if you do not have any facts of proof about it: *I had a hunch you'd call this morning.* | *On a hunch that prices would go down, Laura sold her stocks.*

hunch² *v.* **1** [I always + adv./prep.] to bend down and forward so that your back forms a curve: [+ over] *Lori hunched over to keep the wind out of her face.* **2 hunch your shoulders** to raise your shoulders into a rounded shape, especially because you are cold, anxious etc. —**hunched** *adj.*

hunch·back /'hʌntʃbæk/ *n.* [C] OFFENSIVE someone who has a large raised part on their back because their SPINE curves in an unusual way

hun·dred¹ /'hʌndrɪd/ *number* **1** 100: *a hundred years* | *two hundred miles* **2 hundreds of sth** a very large number of things or people: *Hundreds of people marched in protest.* **3 a hundred times** SPOKEN a phrase meaning "many times," used when you are annoyed: *I've told you a hundred times to turn off the lights!* **4 a/one hundred percent** SPOKEN completely: *I'm not a hundred percent sure where she lives.* **5 give a hundred percent** also **give a hundred and ten percent** to do everything you can in order to achieve something: *Everyone on the team gave a hundred percent.*

USAGE NOTE: HUNDRED

GRAMMAR

Singular and plural forms of the number words **dozen, hundred, thousand, million,** and **billion** are all used in the same ways. When one of these words follows a word showing a number or amount, it is not put in the plural and does not have *of* after it: *a/three/several hundred years* (NOT *three hundreds of years*) | *ten million people* | *a few dozen eggs* | *about fifty thousand miles.* Where there is no other word showing a number or amount, the plural is used: *He has hundreds of books* (NOT *He has hundred of books*).| *It will cost thousands of dollars* (=I do not know how many thousand exactly).

hundred[2] *n.* [C] a piece of paper money worth $100

hun·dredth[1] /'hʌndrɪdθ/ *adj.* 100th; next after the ninety-ninth: *It's my great-grandmother's hundredth birthday tomorrow.*

hundredth[2] *pron.* **the hundredth** the 100th thing in a series

hundredth[3] *n.* [C] $^1/_{100}$; one of one hundred equal parts

hun·dred·weight /'hʌndrɪd,weɪt/ written abbreviation **cwt.** *n.* [C] a unit for measuring weight equal to 100 pounds or 45.36 kilograms

hung[1] /hʌŋ/ *v.* the past tense and past participle of HANG

hung[2] *adj.* **1 hung jury** a JURY that cannot agree about whether someone is guilty of a crime **2** SLANG WELL-HUNG —see also HUNG OVER

Hun·ga·ry /'hʌŋgəri/ a country in central Europe, east of Austria and west of Romania —**Hungarian** /hʌŋ'gɛriən/ *n., adj.*

hun·ger[1] /'hʌŋgə/ *n.* **1** [U] lack of food, especially for a long period of time, that can cause illness or death; STARVATION: *Thousands of people are dying from hunger every day.* **2** [U] the feeling that you need to eat: *Try to satisfy your hunger with raw veggies and fruit.* **3** [C,U] a strong need or desire for something: [+ **for**] *From birth, every child has a hunger for learning.*

hunger[2] *v.*

hunger for sth *phr. v.* [T] LITERARY to want something very much: *Many of these people are hungering for a better life.*

hunger strike /'.. ,./ *n.* [C] a situation in which someone refuses to eat for a long time, in order to protest about something: *In 1986, Snyder went on a hunger strike.* —**hunger striker** *n.* [C]

hung o·ver /,. '../ *adj.* feeling sick because you drank too much alcohol the previous day —see also HANGOVER

hun·gri·ly /'hʌŋgrəli/ *adv.* **1** in a way that shows you want to eat something very much: *The two little girls ate hungrily.* **2** in a way that shows you want something very much: *Developers have been eyeing the land hungrily.*

hun·gry /'hʌŋgri/ *adj.* **hungrier, hungriest 1** wanting to eat something: *I'm hungry – I didn't get any lunch today.* | *a hungry baby* | *There's some cold chicken in the fridge if you get hungry.* **2** sick or weak as a result of not having enough to eat for a long time: *America's cities have hundreds of hungry and homeless people.* **3 go hungry** to not have enough to eat: *Thousands of families go hungry every day.* **4 be hungry for** sth also **be hungry to do** sth to want or need something very much: *These kids are hungry to learn.* | *People are hungry for good music.* **5 the hungry** people who do not have enough food to eat

-hungry /hʌŋgri/ [in adjectives] **power-hungry/ news-hungry etc.** wanting power, news etc. very much

hung up /,. './ *adj.* INFORMAL **1** thinking or worrying too much about someone or something: [+ **on**] *People get hung up on the idea of talking to a computer, but*

they shouldn't. **2** liking someone very much and thinking about them all the time: [+ **on**] *Sally is still hung up on Andrew.*

hunk /hʌŋk/ *n.* [C] **1** a thick piece of something that has been taken from a bigger piece: [+ **of**] *a hunk of bread* **2** INFORMAL a sexually attractive man with a big strong body

hun·ker /'hʌŋkə/ *v.*

hunker down *phr. v.* [I] **1** to not do things that may be risky, so that you are safe and protected: *People are hunkering down and waiting for the economy to get better.* **2** to sit on your heels with your knees bent in front of you; SQUAT: *They hunkered down by the fire.*

hunk·y /'hʌŋki/ *adj.* **hunkier, hunkiest** a man who is hunky is sexually attractive and strong-looking

hun·ky-dor·y /,hʌŋki 'dɔri/ *adj.* [not before noun] INFORMAL a situation that is hunky-dory is one in which everyone feels happy and there are no problems

hunt[1] /hʌnt/ *v.* [I,T] **1** to chase or look for animals and birds in order to kill them: *The leopard hunts at night.* | *This isn't the season for hunting deer.* **2** to look for someone or something very carefully: *Darrell needs to improve his job-hunting skills.* | [+ **for**] *The kids were hunting for shells on the beach.* **3** [I,T] to search for and try to catch someone, especially a criminal: [+ **for**] *Police in three counties are hunting for the killer.* **4 hunt and peck** a method of typing by which you must look for every letter on the KEYBOARD before you type it

hunt sb/sth **↔ down** *phr. v.* [T] to find an enemy or a criminal after searching hard: *Army troops are hunting down the guerrillas.*

hunt sb/sth **↔ out** *phr. v.* [T] **1** to search for someone in order to catch or get rid of them: *The Pope at that time decided to hunt out those who did not support him.* **2** to look for something that is difficult to find: *Whenever they stopped, Converse would hunt out a shady spot where he could sit and read.*

hunt[2] *n.* [C] **1** [usually singular] a careful search for someone or something that is difficult to find: [+ **for**] *The hunt for the missing child continues today.* **2** an occasion when people look for or chase animals in order to kill them

hunt·er /'hʌntə/ *n.* **1** [C] a person or animal that hunts wild animals: *deer hunters* **2 bargain/job/ treasure etc. hunter** someone who looks for or collects a particular type of thing —see also BOUNTY HUNTER, FORTUNE HUNTER

hunt·ing /'hʌntɪŋ/ *n.* [U] **1** the act of chasing and killing animals for food or for sport **2 job-hunting/ house-hunting etc.** the activity of looking for a job, house etc. **3 go hunting** to hunt for animals, especially as a sport —**hunting** *adj.* [only before noun] *a hunting rifle*

hunting ground /'.. ,./ *n.* [C] **1** [usually plural] an area of land where animals are hunted **2** a place where people who are interested in a particular thing can easily find what they want: *The edges of the road are an ideal hunting ground for recyclable bottles and cans.*

Hun·ting·ton /'hʌntɪŋtən/, **Henry** (1850–1927) a U.S. businessman who helped in the development of towns, roads, etc. in southern California

hunt·ress /'hʌntrɪs/ *n.* [C] LITERARY a female hunter

hunts·man /'hʌntsmən/ *n.* [C] LITERARY a man who hunts animals

hur·dle[1] /'hɜdl/ *n.* **1** [C] a problem or difficulty that you must deal with before you can achieve something: *Women face a number of legal hurdles in trying to prove sexual harassment.* | *Even if the plan clears the money hurdle* (=deals successfully with it), *other problems exist.* **2** [C] a type of small fence that a person or horse has to jump over during a race **3 the 100/400 meter etc. hurdles** a race in which the runners have to jump over hurdles

hurdle[2] *v.* **1** [T] to jump over something while you are running: *Barrett hurdled the fence and ran down the street.* **2** [I] to run in hurdle races —**hurdler** *n.* [C] —**hurdling** *n.* [U]

hur·dy-gur·dy /ˌhɝdi ˈgɝdi/ *n. plural* **hurdy-gurdies** [C] a small musical instrument that you operate by turning a handle

hurl /hɝl/ *v.* **1** [T always + adv./prep.] to throw something violently and with a lot of force, especially because you are angry: [**hurl sth through/across/over etc. sth**] *Vandals hurled rocks through the windows at the school.* | *The accident hurled some of the railroad cars more than 40 yards from the tracks.* **2 hurl abuse/insults/accusations etc. at sb** to shout at someone in a loud and angry way: *Tran heard the man hurl a racial slur at him.* **3 hurl yourself at/against etc. something** to throw yourself at someone or something with a lot of force: *Occasionally, the whales hurl themselves completely out of the water.* **4** [I] SLANG to VOMIT

hur·ly-bur·ly /ˌhɝli ˈbɝli/ *n.* [U] a lot of busy noisy activity: *the hurly-burly of city life*

Hu·ron /ˈhyʊrən, -ɑn/ a group of Native American tribes who lived near the Great Lakes in North America in the 16th and 17th centuries

Huron, Lake the second largest of the five Great Lakes on the border between the U.S. and Canada

hur·ray /həˈreɪ, hʊˈreɪ/, **hur·rah** /həˈrɑ, hʊ-/ *interjection* OLD-FASHIONED another spelling of HOORAY

hur·ri·cane /ˈhɝɪˌkeɪn, ˈhʌr-/ *n.* [C] a storm that has very strong, fast winds and that usually moves over water —compare CYCLONE, TORNADO, TYPHOON —see picture on page 1333

hurricane lamp /ˈ... ˌ./ *n.* [C] a lamp that has a cover to protect the flame inside from the wind

hur·ried /ˈhɝid, ˈhʌrid/ *adj.* [usually before noun] done more quickly than usual; RUSHED: *The day was a blur of hurried meetings and brief telephone calls.* —**hurriedly** *adv.*

hur·ry¹ /ˈhɝi, ˈhʌri/ *v.* **hurries, hurried, hurrying** **1** [I,T] to do something or go somewhere more quickly than usual, especially because there is not much time: *If we hurry, we'll get there in time* | *I hate having to hurry a meal.* | *We'll have to hurry if we don't want to miss the start of the movie.* | [**hurry through/along/down etc.**] *While hurrying down the stairs, Tim fell and broke his left arm.* | [**hurry after sb**] *John looked apologetic, and hurried after his girlfriend.* | [**hurry to do sth**] *Congress hurried to enact a $151 billion highways bill.* **2** [T] to make someone do something more quickly: *Their mother hurried the children across the street.* **3** [T always + adv./prep.] to take someone or something quickly to a place: [**hurry sth to/through/across etc.**] *Emergency supplies have been hurried to the areas worst hit by the hurricane.*

hurry up *phr. v.* **1 hurry up!** SPOKEN used to tell someone to do something more quickly: *Hurry up – we're late!* **2** [I,T **hurry sb/sth up**] to make someone do something more quickly or to make something happen more quickly: *I'm trying to hurry up and get this done.* | *See if you can hurry things up a little in there.*

hur·ry² *n.* **1 in a hurry** more quickly than usual: *I was kind of in a hurry.* | *He needs to get that mailed off in a hurry.* | [**be in a hurry to do sth**] *Eva was in a hurry to get back to Albuquerque.* | *Anita looked like she was in a big hurry when she drove off.* **2 (there's) no hurry** SPOKEN said in order to tell someone that they do not have to do something quickly or soon: *You can get it sometime when you visit – there's no hurry.* **3 be in no hurry to do sth** also **not be in any hurry to do sth** to be unwilling to do something or not want to do it soon: *Jerry's in no hurry to sell that house.* **4 be in no hurry** also **not be in any hurry** to be able to wait because you have a lot of time in which to do something: *Take your time. I'm not in any hurry.* **5 what's (all) the hurry?** SPOKEN said when you think someone is doing something too quickly: *What's the hurry? It will still be there tomorrow.* **6 in sb's hurry to do sth** while someone is trying to do something too quickly: *In his hurry to leave, Carlos tripped over a chair.*

hurt¹ /hɝt/ *v. past tense and past participle* **hurt** **1** **feel pain** [I,T] to feel pain in a part of your body:

My feet hurt. | *It won't hurt, I promise.* | *I wanted to sit down, 'cause my leg was really hurting me.* **2** **injure sb** [T] to injure yourself or someone else: *Was anyone hurt in the accident?* | *Sammy! Don't throw stones, you'll hurt someone.* | *Watch you don't hurt your back.* | *Be careful you don't fall and hurt yourself.* —see Usage Note at DAMAGE² **3** **cause pain** [T] to cause pain in a part of your body: *The sun's hurting my eyes.* | *It hurts my knees to run.* **4** **upset sb** [I,T] to make someone feel very upset, unhappy, sad etc.: *It really hurt me that Troy didn't even bother to introduce me.* | *Michelle, I'm sorry. I didn't mean to hurt your feelings.* **5 be (only/just) hurting yourself** to be making yourself feel even more unhappy, upset, sad etc., or to be putting yourself in a bad situation: *You're only hurting yourself if you don't stay in school.* **6** **bad effect** [T] to have a bad effect on someone or something, especially by making them less successful or powerful: *The weak economy has hurt business for many retailers.* **7 be hurting a)** INFORMAL to feel very upset or unhappy about something: *Martha's going through a divorce and really hurting right now.* **b)** to not have something important that you need, for example money: *Tony has a car, a country club membership – he's not hurting.* | [+ **for**] *The team is hurting for quarterbacks.* **8 sth won't/doesn't hurt** SPOKEN said when you think someone should do something or that something is a good idea: *The house looks pretty good, but a fresh paint job wouldn't hurt either.* | [**it won't/doesn't hurt (sb) to do sth**] *It won't hurt Kyle to clean up his room.* | *It doesn't hurt to keep that personal contact in a sales relationship.* —compare HARM²

hurt² *adj.* **1** [not usually before noun] suffering pain or injury: *It's okay; nobody got hurt.* | *You could have been badly hurt!* **2** very upset or unhappy because someone has said or done something that is dishonest, unfair, or not nice: *a hurt expression* | *Alice was very hurt that she wasn't included in the invitation.*

hurt³ *n.* [C,U] a feeling of great unhappiness because someone, especially someone you trust, has treated you badly or unfairly: *I cannot describe the hurt and anger I feel.* —compare HARM¹

hurt·ful /ˈhɝtfəl/ *adj.* making you feel very upset or offended: *a hurtful remark* —**hurtfully** *adv.* —**hurtfulness** *n.* [U]

hur·tle /ˈhɝtl/ *v.* [I always + adv./prep.] if something, especially something big or heavy, hurtles somewhere, it moves or falls very fast: [**hurtle down/through/along etc.**] *Imagine an asteroid hurtling through space toward the Earth.*

hus·band¹ /ˈhʌzbənd/ *n.* [C] the man that a woman is married to: *Have you met my husband Roy?*

husband² *v.* [T] FORMAL to be very careful in the way you use your money, supplies etc., and not waste any: *Families have been husbanding their small reserves of food.*

hus·band·ry /ˈhʌzbəndri/ *n.* **1** [U] TECHNICAL farming: *animal husbandry* **2** [U] OLD-FASHIONED careful management of money and supplies

hush¹ /hʌʃ/ *v.* SPOKEN **hush** also **hush up** said in order to tell someone to be quiet, or to comfort a child who is crying or upset: *Hush, now. Try to get to sleep.* | *Hush, Darby, stop it.*

hush sth ↔ up *phr. v.* [T] to prevent the public from knowing about something dishonest or immoral: *According to one source, the Army has hushed up the theft of military guns.*

hush² *n.* [singular] a peaceful silence, especially one that happens when people are expecting something to happen: *The tension mounted as a hush fell over the crowd (=everyone became quiet).*

hushed /hʌʃt/ *adj.* [usually before noun] quiet because people are listening, waiting to hear something, or talking quietly: *A hushed courtroom awaited the verdict.* | *Visitors to the museum spoke in **hushed tones*** (=spoke quietly).

hush-hush /ˌ. '.◂/ *adj.* INFORMAL very secret: *The date and location of the operation were very hush-hush.*

hush mon·ey /'. ˌ../ *n.* [U] money that is paid to someone not to tell other people about something embarrassing

hush pup·py /'. ˌ../ *n. plural* **hush puppies** [C] a small round type of bread made of corn flour that is cooked in oil or fat and usually eaten in the southern states of the U.S.

husk[1] /hʌsk/ *n.* **1** [C,U] the dry outer part of corn, some grains, nuts, etc. **2** the useless outer part of something that remains after the important or useful part is gone or has been used: *Winwood's concert showed that he is just an empty husk of what he once was.*

husk[2] *v.* [T] to remove the husks from corn, grains, seeds etc.

husk·y[1] /'hʌski/ *adj.* **1** a husky voice is deep, quiet, and rough-sounding, often in an attractive way **2** a husky boy or man is big and strong —**huskily** *adv.* —**huskiness** *n.* [U]

husky

sled

husky[2] *n. plural* **huskies** [C] a large dog with thick hair, used in Canada and Alaska to pull SLEDs over the snow

Huss /hʌs/, **John** (?1372–1415) a Czech religious leader who criticized the Catholic Church

Hus·sein /huˈseɪn/, **Sad·dam** /sæˈdæm/ —see SADDAM HUSSEIN

hus·sy /'hʌsi, 'hʌzi/ *n. plural* **hussies** [C] OLD-FASHIONED a woman who is sexually immoral

hust·ings /'hʌstɪŋz/ *n.* **on the hustings** trying to persuade people to vote for you by traveling around to different towns and making speeches etc.: *Graham has been on the hustings with his message of tax cuts and education reform.*

hus·tle[1] /'hʌsəl/ *v.* **hustled, hustling 1** [T] to make someone move quickly, especially by pushing them: [**hustle sb out/into/through etc.**] *Jackson was hustled into his car by his bodyguards.* **2** [I] to do something with a lot of energy and determination: *Cindy's not a great player, but she really hustles.* | *Come on, guys, let's hustle.* **3** [I] to hurry in doing something or going somewhere: *We hustled back to the car.* **4** [I,T] to cheat someone, especially by selling them something: *I don't like answering the phone during dinner just to be hustled by some stranger.* **5** [I,T] SLANG to work as a PROSTITUTE, or to be in charge of PROSTITUTES

hustle[2] *n.* [U] **1** busy and noisy activity: *I was tired of the **hustle and bustle** of New York.* **2** ways of getting money that involve cheating or deceiving people **3** a quick and very active way of doing something: *Hey, good hustle, Paul!* | *Williams brings a lot of spirit and hustle to the team.*

hus·tler /'hʌslɚ/ *n.* [C] **1** someone who cheats or deceives people to get money **2** a PROSTITUTE

Hus·ton /'hyustən/, **John** (1906–1987) a U.S. movie DIRECTOR, writer, and actor

hut /hʌt/ *n.* [C] a small, simple building with only one or two rooms: *a wooden hut*

hutch /hʌtʃ/ *n.* [C] **1** a wooden box that small animals are kept in, especially rabbits **2** a piece of furniture used for storing and showing dishes

Hut·ter·ite /'hʌtəˌraɪt, 'hu-/ a member of a Christian religious group who live a simple life with strict rules, separate from other people, in Canada and the northwestern U.S.

Hux·ley /'hʌksli/, **Al·dous** /'ɔldəs/ (1894–1963) a British writer of NOVELs

Huxley, Thomas (1825–1895) a British BIOLOGIST who supported Darwin's ideas about EVOLUTION

hwy. *n.* the written abbreviation of HIGHWAY

hy·a·cinth /'haɪəˌsɪnθ/ *n.* [C] a garden plant with blue, pink, or white bell-shaped flowers and a sweet smell

hy·brid /'haɪbrɪd/ *n.* [C] **1** an animal or plant produced from parents of different breeds or types: *Eco-Foam is made of corn starch from a special corn hybrid.* | [**+ of**] *Triticale is a hybrid of wheat and rye.* **2** something that is a mixture of two or more other things: *a public/private hybrid company* | [**+ of**] *The cartridge is essentially a hybrid of a floppy disk and a hard disk.*

hy·dra /'haɪdrə/ *n.* [C] **1 Hydra** a snake in ancient Greek stories that has many heads which grow again when they are cut off **2** FORMAL a problem very difficult to get rid of because it keeps returning when you try to get rid of it

hy·drant /'haɪdrənt/ *n.* [C] a FIRE HYDRANT

hy·drate[1] /'haɪdreɪt/ *n.* [C] TECHNICAL a chemical substance that contains water

hydrate[2] *v.* [T usually passive] to supply someone or something with water to keep them healthy and in good condition: *Many of the rescued birds are being hydrated with electrolytes and kept warm on a heating pad.* —**hydration** /haɪˈdreɪʃən/ *n.* [U]

hy·drau·lic /haɪˈdrɔlɪk/ *adj.* [usually before noun] moved or operated by the pressure of water or other liquids: *a hydraulic pump* | *hydraulic brakes* —**hydraulically** /-kli/ *adv.*

hy·drau·lics /haɪˈdrɔlɪks/ *n.* **1** [plural] parts of a machine or system that use the pressure of water or other liquids to move or lift things: *A U-shaped cover enclosed the transmission and hydraulics under the mast.* **2** [U] the study of how to use the pressure of water or other liquids to produce power

hy·dro /'haɪdroʊ/ *n.* [U] CANADIAN, INFORMAL the supply of electricity, especially from water power

hydro- /'haɪdroʊ, -drə/ *prefix* **1** relating to water, or using water: *hydroelectricity* (=produced by water power) | *hydrotherapy* (=treatment of disease using water) **2** relating to HYDROGEN, or containing it: *hydrocarbons*

hy·dro·car·bon /'haɪdroʊˌkɑrbən/ *n.* [C usually plural] TECHNICAL a chemical compound that consists of HYDROGEN and CARBON, such as coal or NATURAL GAS

hy·dro·ceph·a·ly /ˌhaɪdroʊˈsɛfəli/ also **hy·dro·ceph·a·lus** /'-'sɛfələs/ *n.* [U] a serious medical condition, usually happening before someone is born, in which liquid becomes trapped inside their head, making their SKULL (=bones around their brain) very large and putting pressure on their brain —**hydrocephalic** /ˌhaɪdroʊsəˈfælɪk/ *adj.*

hy·dro·chlo·ric ac·id /ˌhaɪdrəklɔrɪk 'æsɪd/ *abbreviation* **HCl** *n.* [U] a strong acid used especially in industry

hy·dro·cor·ti·sone /ˌhaɪdroʊˈkɔrtɪˌsoʊn/ *n.* [U] a chemical substance that is used in skin creams and other medicines, and is also produced naturally in the body

hy·dro·e·lec·tric /ˌhaɪdroʊɪˈlɛktrɪk/ *adj.* using water power to produce electricity: *a hydroelectric power plant* —**hydroelectrically** /-kli/ *adv.* —**hydroelectricity** /ˌhaɪdroʊɪlɛkˈtrɪsəti/ *n.* [U]

hy·dro·foil /'haɪdrəˌfɔɪl/ *n.* [C] a large boat that raises itself above the surface of the water when it travels at high speeds —compare HOVERCRAFT

hy·dro·gen /'haɪdrədʒən/ *n.* [U] *symbol* **H** a gas that is an ELEMENT and that is lighter than air, and that forms water when it combines with OXYGEN

hy·dro·gen·at·ed /haɪˈdrɑdʒə,neɪtɪd/ *adj.* hydrogenated oils or fats, such as MARGARINE, have been through a process in which HYDROGEN is added to them, so that they become harder

hydrogen bomb /ˈ... ,./ *n.* [C] an extremely powerful NUCLEAR bomb

hydrogen per·ox·ide /,... .ˈ../ *n.* [U] a chemical liquid used for killing BACTERIA and for making hair and other substances lighter in color

hy·drol·o·gy /haɪˈdrɑlədʒi/ *n.* [U] the scientific study of water —**hydrologist** *n.* [C]

hy·dro·pho·bi·a /,haɪdrəˈfoubiə/ *n.* **1** [U] a technical word for RABIES **2** fear of water

hy·dro·plane[1] /ˈhaɪdrə,pleɪn/ *n.* **1** [C] an airplane that can take off from and land on water; SEAPLANE **2** [C] a HYDROFOIL

hydroplane[2] *v.* [I] **1** if a car hydroplanes, it slides out of control on a wet road **2** if a boat hydroplanes, it travels very quickly, just touching the surface of the water

hy·dro·pon·ics /,haɪdrəˈpɑnɪks/ *n.* [U] the practice of growing plants in special liquids, rather than in dirt —**hydroponic** *adj.* —**hydroponically** /-kli/ *adv.*

hy·e·na /haɪˈinə/ *n.* [C] a wild animal like a dog that makes a loud sound like a laugh

hy·giene /ˈhaɪdʒin/ *n.* [U] **1** the practice of keeping yourself and the things around you clean in order to prevent diseases: *Schools should have policies to ensure good hygiene in kitchen areas.* **2** the study and practice of preventing illness or stopping it from spreading, especially by keeping things clean: *public hygiene*

hy·gi·en·ic /haɪˈdʒɛnɪk, -ˈdʒinɪk/ *adj.* clean and likely to prevent BACTERIA, infections, or diseases from spreading: *Hygienic conditions are poor at hospitals in the war zone.* —**hygienically** /-kli/ *adv.*

hy·gien·ist /haɪˈdʒinɪst/ *n.* [C] a DENTAL HYGIENIST

hy·men /ˈhaɪmən/ *n.* [C] a piece of skin that partly covers the entrance to the VAGINA of some girls or women who have not had sex

hymn /hɪm/ *n.* [C] a song of praise to God: *a hymn book*

hym·nal /ˈhɪmnəl/ also **hymn book** /ˈ. ./ *n.* [C] a book of hymns

hype[1] /haɪp/ *n.* [U] attempts to make people think something is good or important by talking about it a lot on television, the radio etc.: *There's already been a lot of media hype about Murphy's book.*

hype[2] *v.* [T] also **hype sth ↔ up** to try to make people think something is good or important by talking about it a lot on television, the radio etc.: *The director is just using the controversy to hype his movie.*

hyped up /, ˈ./ *adj.* INFORMAL very excited or nervous, and unable to keep still: *He was as hyped up as a kid on Christmas Eve.*

hy·per /ˈhaɪpə/ *adj.* INFORMAL extremely excited and active: *No, don't give Luke any candy – it'll make him hyper.*

hyper- /haɪpə/ *prefix* **1** more than usual, especially too much: *hypersensitive* (=too sensitive) | *hyperextension* (=bending something too far) | *a hyperintelligent person* (=much smarter than normal people) **2** beyond the usual size or limits: *a hyperlink* (=from one WEB-SITE to another)

hy·per·ac·tive /,haɪpəˈæktɪv/ *adj.* TECHNICAL someone, especially a child, who is hyperactive is too active, and is not able keep still or be quiet for very long —**hyperactivity** /,haɪpəæktˈtɪvəti/ *n.* [U]

hy·per·bo·le /hɪˈpəbəli/ *n.* [U] a way of describing something by saying it is much bigger, smaller, worse etc. than it really is: *Rick said, with a touch of hyperbole, that it was the best movie he'd ever seen.* —**hyperbolic** /,haɪpəˈbɑlɪk/ *adj.* —see also EXAGGERATE

hy·per·crit·i·cal /,haɪpəˈkrɪtɪkəl◂/ *adj.* too eager to criticize other people and things, especially about small details —**hypercritically** /-kli/ *adv.*

hy·per·in·fla·tion /,haɪpərɪnˈfleɪʃən/ *n.* [U] a rapid

rise in prices that seriously damages a country's ECONOMY

hy·per·link /ˈhaɪpə,lɪŋk/ *n.* [C] TECHNICAL a LINK[2] (7) between two computer documents

hy·per·sen·si·tive /,haɪpəˈsɛnsətɪv/ *adj.* **1** if someone is hypersensitive to a drug, substance etc., their body reacts very badly to it: [+ **to**] *Jen's doctors found that she was hypersensitive to smoke.* **2** very easily offended or upset: [+ **to/about**] *Tad's hypersensitive to criticism.* —**hypersensitivity** /,haɪpə,sɛnsəˈtɪvəti/ *n.* [U]

hy·per·ten·sion /,haɪpəˈtɛnʃən, ˈhaɪpə,tɛnʃən/ *n.* [U] TECHNICAL a medical condition in which your BLOOD PRESSURE is too high

hy·per·text /ˈhaɪpə,tɛkst/ *n.* [U] a way of writing computer documents that makes it possible to move from one document to another by CLICKing on words or pictures, especially on the Internet

hy·per·ven·ti·late /,haɪpəˈvɛntl,eɪt/ *v.* [I] to breathe too quickly or too deeply, so that you get too much OXYGEN and feel DIZZY —**hyperventilation** /,haɪpə,vɛntlˈeɪʃən/ *n.* [U]

hy·phen /ˈhaɪfən/ *n.* [C] a short written or printed line (-) that joins words or SYLLABLES —compare DASH[2] (4)

USAGE NOTE: HYPHEN

SPELLING

Use a **hyphen** (-) to join two or more words that are used as an adjective in front of a noun: *a two-car garage* | *a ten-year-old boy.* You can also say *a garage for two cars* | *a boy who is ten years old* without using hyphens.

---

hy·phen·ate /ˈhaɪfə,neɪt/ *v.* [T] to join words or SYLLABLES with a HYPHEN —**hyphenated** *adj.* —**hyphenation** /,haɪfəˈneɪʃən/ *n.* [U]

Hyp·nos /ˈhɪpnəs, -nous/ in Greek MYTHOLOGY, the god of sleep

hyp·no·sis /hɪpˈnousɪs/ *n.* [U] **1** a state similar to sleep, in which someone's thoughts and actions can be influenced by someone else, or in which they can remember things they cannot remember when they are awake: *Seligson was able to remember details from his childhood while **under hypnosis**.* **2** the act of producing this state

hyp·no·ther·a·py /,hɪpnouˈθɛrəpi/ *n.* [U] the use of hypnosis to treat emotional or physical problems —**hypnotherapist** *n.* [C]

hyp·not·ic[1] /hɪpˈnɑtɪk/ *adj.* **1** making you feel sleepy or unable to pay attention to anything else, especially because a sound or movement is repeated: *The swaying of the dancers was hypnotic.* **2** [only before noun] relating to HYPNOSIS: *a hypnotic trance* —**hypnotically** /-kli/ *adv.*

hypnotic[2] *n.* [C] TECHNICAL a drug that helps you to sleep

hyp·no·tism /ˈhɪpnə,tɪzəm/ *n.* [U] the practice of hypnotizing people

hyp·no·tist /ˈhɪpnətɪst/ *n.* [C] someone who hypnotizes people, especially in public for entertainment, or in order to help them

hyp·no·tize /ˈhɪpnə,taɪz/ *v.* [T] **1** to produce a sleep-like state in someone, so that you can ask questions about things they do not remember while they are awake, or so that you can influence their thoughts or actions: *Nazan agreed to be hypnotized to help him stop smoking.* **2** [usually passive] to be so interesting or exciting that people cannot think of anything else: *The crowd was hypnotized by Parker's effortless sax playing.*

hy·po /ˈhaɪpou/ *n. plural* **hypos** [C] INFORMAL a HYPODERMIC needle

hypo- /haɪpou, -pə/ *prefix* TECHNICAL under or below something: *hypothermia* (=condition in which your body temperature is too low) | *a hypodermic injection* (=given under the skin)

H

hy·po·al·ler·gen·ic /ˌhaɪpoʊˌælə˞ˈdʒɛnɪk/ *adj.* hypo-allergenic MAKEUP, jewelry, soaps etc. are made so that they do not cause an ALLERGIC reaction when they are put on your skin

hy·po·chon·dri·a /ˌhaɪpəˈkɑndriə/ *n.* [U] a condition in which someone worries that there is something wrong with their health, even when they are not sick

hy·po·chon·dri·ac /ˌhaɪpəˈkɑndriˌæk/ *n.* [C] someone who worries all the time about their health, even when they are not sick —**hypochondriac** *adj.*

hy·poc·ri·sy /hɪˈpɑkrəsi/ *n.* [U] the act of saying that you have particular beliefs, feelings etc., but behaving in a way that shows you do not really have these beliefs: *It would be **sheer hypocrisy** to pray for success, since I've never believed in God.*

hyp·o·crite /ˈhɪpəˌkrɪt/ *n.* [C] someone who pretends to believe something or behave in a good way when really they do not

hy·po·crit·i·cal /ˌhɪpəˈkrɪṭɪkəl◂/ *adj.* behaving in a way that shows you do not really believe something or do not behave in a good way, when you have said that you do: *Several senators said it was hypocritical to ban imported weapons but not U.S.-made ones.*

hy·po·der·mic[1] /ˌhaɪpəˈdə˞mɪk/ *adj.* used in an INJECTION beneath the skin: *a hypodermic needle* —**hypodermically** /-kli/ *adv.*

hypodermic[2] *n.* [C] an instrument with a very thin hollow needle, used for putting drugs into someone's body through the skin; SYRINGE

hy·po·gly·ce·mi·a /ˌhaɪpoʊglaɪˈsimiə/ *n.* [U] a medical condition in which someone does not have enough sugar in their blood —**hypoglycemic** *adj.*

hy·pot·e·nuse /haɪˈpɑtˀnˌus/ *n.* [C] TECHNICAL the longest side in a RIGHT TRIANGLE

hy·po·thal·a·mus /ˌhaɪpoʊˈθæləməs/ *n.* [C usually singular] a small part of the brain that controls body temperature and some other FUNCTIONS

hy·po·ther·mi·a /ˌhaɪpəˈθə˞miə/ *n.* [U] a serious medical condition in which someone's body temperature becomes very low, caused by extreme cold

hy·poth·e·sis /haɪˈpɑθəsɪs/ *n.* plural **hypotheses** /-siz/ [C] an idea that is suggested as an explanation for something, but that has not yet been proven to be true: *Our hypothesis is that the dolphins ate contaminated fish, and this affected the dolphins' immune system.*

hy·poth·e·size /haɪˈpɑθəˌsaɪz/ *v.* [I,T] to suggest a possible explanation that has not yet been proven to be true: [**hypothesize that**] *Scientists have hypothesized that the dinosaurs were killed by a giant meteor.*

hy·po·thet·i·cal /ˌhaɪpəˈθɛṭɪkəl/ *adj.* based on a situation that is not real, but that might happen: *The car insurance for a hypothetical family with two cars and three drivers would be $3,200 a year.* —compare IMAGINARY —**hypothetically** /-kli/ *adv.*

hys·ter·ec·to·my /ˌhɪstəˈrɛktəmi/ *n.* plural **hysterectomies** [C] a medical operation to remove a woman's UTERUS

hys·te·ri·a /hɪˈstɛriə, -ˈstɪriə/ *n.* [U] **1** a situation in which a lot of people feel fear, anger, or excitement, which makes them behave in an unreasonable way: *During the 1950s, the U.S. was gripped by anti-Communist hysteria.* **2** TECHNICAL a medical condition in which someone suddenly feels very nervous, excited, anxious etc. and is not able to control their emotions —**hysteric** *adj.*

hys·ter·i·cal /hɪˈstɛrɪkəl/ *adj.* **1** unable to control your behavior or emotions because you are very upset, afraid, excited etc.: *Hysterical parents were calling the school for details of the accident.* **2** INFORMAL extremely funny: *It's a hysterical movie.* —**hysterically** /-kli/ *adv.*

hys·ter·ics /hɪˈstɛrɪks/ *n.* [plural] **1** a state of being unable to control your behavior or emotions because you are very upset, afraid, excited etc.: *She **went into hysterics** when she heard about her husband.* **2 in hysterics** if someone is in hysterics, they are laughing and not able to stop: *The audience was in hysterics.*

Hz *n.* [C] the written abbreviation of HERTZ

H

I

I, i /aɪ/ *n. plural* **I's, i's** [C] **1** the ninth letter of the English alphabet **2** the ROMAN NUMERAL representing the number one

-i /-i/ *suffix plural* **-is 1** [in nouns] a person from a particular country or place, or their language: *two Pakistanis* | *speakers of Nepali* **2** [in adjectives] relating to a particular place or country: *Bengali food* | *the Israeli Army*

I¹ /aɪ/ *pron.* used as the subject of a verb when you are the person speaking: *I saw Mike yesterday.* | *I'm going to Mexico next month.* | *I've been playing soft-ball every week.*

S W
1 | 1

I² /aɪ/ the abbreviation of INTERSTATE (=an important road between states in the U.S.): *To get to Memphis, take I-40 East from Little Rock.*

IA the written abbreviation of Iowa

I·a·coc·ca /ˌaɪəˈkoʊkə/, **Lee** /liː/ (1924–) a U.S. BUSI-NESSMAN who was President of the Ford car company and CHAIRMAN of the Chrysler car company

-ial /iəl/ *suffix* [in adjectives] relating to something, or like something: *a managerial job* (=with the duties of a manager) | *financial* (=relating to money) | *colonial style furniture* (=like the style used when America was a COLONY) —see also -AL

i·amb /ˈaɪ-æmb/ also **i·am·bus** /aɪˈæmbəs/ *n.* [C] TECH-NICAL a unit of RHYTHM in poetry that has one short or weak beat followed by a long or strong beat, as in the word "alive" —**iambic** /aɪˈæmbɪk/ *adj.*

iambic pen·tam·e·ter /ˌ.. ˈ...ˌ/ *n.* [C,U] a common pattern of beats in English poetry, in which each line consists of five iambs, used more commonly in the past

-ian /iən/ *suffix* **1** [in adjectives and nouns] someone or something from a place, or relating to a place: *a librarian* (=someone who works in a library) | *an old Bostonian* (=someone from Boston) **2** [in adjectives and nouns] relating to the ideas of a particular person or group, or someone who follows these ideas: *Jacksonian democracy* (=the ideas of Andrew Jackson) | *a Freudian* (=someone who follows the ideas of Sigmund Freud) **3** [in adjectives] relating to or similar to a person, thing, or period of time: *the Victorian era* —see also -AN, -EAN

-iana /iænə/ *suffix* [in U nouns] a collection of objects, papers etc., relating to someone or something: *Shakespeariana* —see also -ANA

I-beam /ˈaɪ biːm/ *n.* [C] a long piece of steel shaped like the letter "I," used in the CONSTRUCTION of buildings

I·be·ri·an /aɪˈbɪriən/ *adj.* relating to Spain or Portugal: *the Iberian peninsula*

i·bex /ˈaɪbɛks/ *n. plural* **ibexes** or **ibex** [C] a wild goat that lives in the mountains of Europe, Asia, and North Africa

ibid. *adv.* used in formal writing to mean from the same book, writer, or article as the one that has just been mentioned

-ibility /əˈbɪləti/ *suffix* [in nouns] used with adjectives that end in -IBLE to form nouns: *invincibility* | *flex-ibility* —see also -ABILITY

i·bis /ˈaɪbɪs/ *n. plural* **ibises** [C] a large bird with a long beak and long legs that is related to the STORK

-ible /əbəl/ *suffix* [in adjectives] used to show that someone or something has a particular quality or condition: *visible* (=able to be seen) | *irresistible* (=difficult to resist) —see also -ABLE

IBM-com·pat·i·ble /ˌaɪ biː ɛm kəmˈpætəbəl/ *adj.* an IBM-compatible computer is designed to work in the same way as a type of computer made by the IBM company, and can use the same computer PROGRAMS; PC —**IBM-compatible** *n.* [C]

Ib·sen /ˈɪbsən/, **Hen·rik** /ˈhɛnrɪk/ (1828–1906) a Nor-wegian writer of plays known especially for writing

about MIDDLE CLASS society and criticizing social attitudes and behavior

i·bu·pro·fen /ˌaɪbyuˈproufən/ *n.* [U] a drug used for reducing pain and swelling that contains no ASPIRIN

-ic /ɪk/ *suffix* **1** [in adjectives] relating to something, or similar to it: *an alcoholic drink* (=containing alco-hol) | *an Islamic country* (=where the laws follow the rules of Islam) | *pelvic pain* (=in your PELVIS) | *Byronic poetry* (=similar to the poems of Byron) **2** [in nouns] someone who is affected by a particular con-dition, for example a mental illness: *an alcoholic* (=someone who cannot stop drinking alcohol) —**-ically** /ɪkli/ *suffix* [in adverbs] *photographically*

-ical /ɪkəl/ *suffix* [in adjectives] another form of the SUFFIX -IC (1): *historical* (=relating to history) | *a satirical play* —**-ically** /ɪkli/ [in adverbs] *historically*

ICBM *n.* [C] Intercontinental Ballistic Missile; a MISSILE that can travel very long distances

ice¹ /aɪs/ *n.* [U] **1** water that has frozen into a solid state: *Drive carefully – there's ice on the road.* | *There was hardly any ice in my Coke.* **2** put/keep something on ice to do nothing about a plan or suggestion for a period of time: *Negotiations between the union and Chrysler have been put on ice for now.* **3** be (skating) on thin ice to be in a situation in which you do something risky that is likely to upset someone or cause trouble: *Legally, the company is on very thin ice with its actions.* **4** OLD-FASHIONED: see DIA-MONDS —see also BLACK ICE, **break the ice** (BREAK¹ (32)), **cut no ice** (CUT¹ (25)), DRY ICE, ICY

ice

S W
1 | 2

ice cubes

ice² *v.* [T] **1** to cover a cake with ICING (=a mixture made of liquid and sugar) —compare FROST² **2** when you ice a game, you put your team in a strong posi-tion to win: *Kemp iced the game in the final five seconds by scoring two free throws.*

ice sth ↔ **down** *phr. v.* [T] **a)** to cover an injury in ice to stop it from swelling: *Drabek iced down his sore shoulder after the game.* **b)** to put something in or on ice to make it cold: *Harry iced down a bottle of champagne to celebrate my promotion.*

ice over/up also **be iced over/up** [I] *phr. v.* to become covered with ice: *The windows of my car were iced over.* | *Thousands of workers were sent home early as roads iced up.*

Ice Age /ˈ. ./ *n.* [C] one of the long periods of time, thousands of years ago, when ice covered many northern countries

ice ax, ice axe /ˈ. ./ *n.* [C] a metal tool used by mountain climbers to cut into ice —see also ICE PICK

ice bag /ˈ. ./ *n.* [C] a bag containing ice that is put on an injured part of your body to reduce swelling or pain

ice·berg /ˈaɪsbərg/ *n.* [C] a very large mass of ice float-ing in the ocean, most of which is under the surface of the water —see also **the tip of the iceberg** (TIP¹ (6))

iceberg let·tuce /ˌ.. ˈ../ *n.* [C,U] a type of LETTUCE that is firm, round, pale, and green

ice·bound /ˈaɪsbaʊnd/ *adj.* surrounded by ice, espe-cially so that it is impossible to move: *Eight of the ships remain icebound.*

ice·box /ˈaɪsbɑks/ *n.* [C] **1** OLD-FASHIONED a REFRIGER-ATOR **2** a special cupboard in which you put ice in order to keep food cold, in past times

ice·break·er /ˈaɪsˌbreɪkər/ *n.* [C] **1** a ship that cuts a passage through floating ice **2** something that you say or do to make people less nervous when they first meet: *This game is an effective icebreaker at the beginning of a semester.* —see also **break the ice** (BREAK¹ (32))

ice buck·et /ˈ. ˌ../ *n.* [C] **1** a container filled with ice to keep bottles of wine cold **2** a container in which pieces of ice for putting in drinks are kept

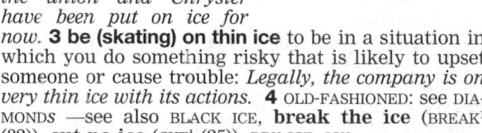

ice cap /'. ./ *n.* [C] an area of thick ice that permanently covers the North and South Poles

ice chest /'. ./ *n.* [C] a special box that you put ice in to keep food and drinks cold

ice-cold /,. '.◄/ *adj.* **1** extremely cold: *ice-cold beer* | *Her hands were ice-cold.* **2** unable to be successful, especially in making points in a game: *The Dallas Cowboys' offense was ice-cold in the first half.*

ice cream /'. ./ *n.* **1** [U] a frozen sweet food made of milk, cream, and sugar, with fruit, nuts, chocolate etc. sometimes added to it **2** [C] a small amount of this food for one person: *Let's stop here and get an ice cream.*

ice cream cone /'. ,./ *n.* [C] a hard thin cookie shaped like a CONE, that you put ice cream in, or one of these with ice cream in it: *In those days, a dime bought two ice cream cones.*

ice-cream par·lor /'. ,../ *n.* [C] a restaurant that only sells ice cream

ice-cream so·cial /,. '.'./ *n.* [C] a social event where people come together to eat ice cream

ice cream so·da /,. '../ *n.* [C] a mixture of ice cream, sweet SYRUP, and SODA WATER, served in a tall glass

ice cube /'. ./ *n.* [C] a small block of ice that is put in a drink to make it cold —see picture at ICE[1]

iced cof·fee also **ice coffee** /,. '../ *n.* [C,U] cold coffee with ice, milk, and sometimes sugar, or a glass of this drink

iced tea also **ice tea** /,. './ *n.* [C,U] cold tea with ice, and sometimes LEMON or sugar, or a glass of this drink

ice fish·ing /'. ,../ *n.* [U] the sport of catching fish through a hole in the ice on a lake or river

ice floe /'. ./ *n.* [C] an area of ice floating in the ocean, that has broken off from a larger mass

ice hock·ey /'. ,../ *n.* [U] HOCKEY

Ice·land /'aisland, -lænd/ an island country in the Atlantic Ocean just south of the Arctic Circle —**Icelandic** /ais'lændik/ *adj.*

Ice·land·er /'aislanda/ *n.* [C] someone from Iceland

ice·man /'ais-mæn/ *n. plural* **icemen** /-men/ [C] a man who delivered ice to people's houses in past times, so that they could keep food cold

ice milk /'. ./ *n.* [U] a frozen sweet food that is similar to ICE CREAM, but has less fat in it

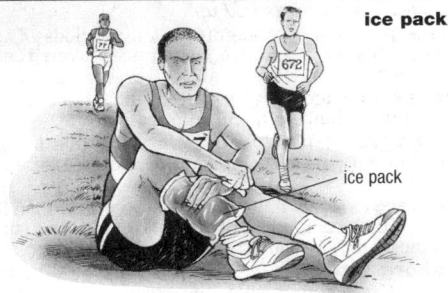

ice pack

ice pack

ice pack /'. ./ *n.* [C] **1** a bag containing ice that is put on an injured part of your body to reduce swelling or pain **2** a large area of crushed ice floating in the ocean —compare PACK ICE

ice pick /'. ./ *n.* [C] a sharp tool used for cutting or breaking ice

ice rink /'. ./ *n.* [C] a specially prepared surface of ice where you can ICE SKATE

ice sheet /'. ./ *n.* [C] an ICE CAP

ice skate[1] /'. ./ *n.* [C usually plural] a special boot with a metal blade on the bottom, that allows you to move quickly on ice —compare ROLLER SKATE

ice skate[2], **ice-skate** *v.* [I] to move on ice wearing ice skates —**ice skater** *n.* [C] —**ice skating** *n.* [U]

ice wa·ter /'. ,../ *n.* [C,U] very cold water with pieces of ice in it, or a glass of this

-ician /ɪʃən/ *suffix* [in nouns] a skilled worker who deals with a particular thing: *a beautician* (=someone who gives beauty treatments) | *a technician* (=someone with technical or scientific skills)

i·ci·cle /'aisikəl/ *n.* [C] a long thin pointed stick of ice hanging from a roof or other surface

-icide /ɪsaɪd/ *suffix* [in nouns] someone or something that kills a particular person or thing, or the act of killing: *insecticide* (=chemical substance for killing insects) | *fratricide* (=act of killing your brother or sister) —**-icidal** /ɪsaɪdl/ *suffix* [in adjectives] —**-icidally** /ɪsaɪdl-i/ [in adverbs] —see also -CIDE

i·ci·ly /'aisəli/ *adv.* if you say something icily or look at someone icily, you do it in an angry or very unfriendly way

ic·ing /'aisiŋ/ *n.* [U] **1** a mixture made from sugar, a liquid, and sometimes a fat such as butter, which is used to cover cakes —compare FROSTING **2 (the) icing on the cake** something that makes a good situation even better: *The raise was great, but getting a corner office was the icing on the cake.*

ick·y /'ɪki/ *adj.* SPOKEN very bad, especially to look at, taste, or feel: *What's this icky black stuff on the tree?*

i·con /'aikɑn/ *n.* [C] **1** someone famous who is admired by many people and is thought to represent an important idea: *a Swedish pop icon* **2** a small sign or picture on a computer screen that is used to start a particular operation: *Click on the report icon to open the program.* **3** also **ikon** a picture or figure of a holy person that is used in WORSHIP in the Greek or Russian Orthodox Church —**iconic** /ai'kɑnik/ *adj.*

i·con·o·clast /ai'kɑnə,klæst/ *n.* [C] someone who attacks established ideas and customs

i·con·o·clas·tic /ai,kɑnə'klæstik/ *adj.* iconoclastic ideas, opinions, writings etc. attack established beliefs and customs: *Wolfe's theories were revolutionary and iconoclastic.*

i·co·nog·ra·phy /,aikə'nɑgrəfi/ *n.* [U] the way that a particular people, religious, or political group etc. represent ideas in pictures or images

-ics /ɪks/ *suffix* [in nouns] **1** the scientific study of a subject, or the use of our knowledge about it: *linguistics* (=the study of language) | *electronics* (=the study or making of electronic equipment) | *genetics* (=the study of GENEs) **2** the actions typically done by someone with particular skills: *acrobatics* **3** used to make nouns out of words ending in -ICAL or -IC: *the acoustics* (=sound qualities) *of the hall*

ICU /,ai si 'yu/ *n.* [C] TECHNICAL Intensive Care Unit; a department in a hospital that gives special attention and treatment to people who are very sick or badly injured

ic·y /'aisi/ *adj.* **icier, iciest 1** extremely cold: *an icy wind* **2** covered in ice: *The sidewalks were icy and slippery.* **3** an icy remark, look etc. shows that you feel annoyed with someone or feel unfriendly toward them: *Her question got an icy response from the chairman.* —**iciness** *n.* [U] —see also ICILY

I'd /aid/ **1** the short form of "I would": *I'd love to go out for dinner.* **2** the short form of "I had": *I'd hoped to finish everything before the trip.*

ID[1] *n.* [C,U] a document or card that shows your name, date of birth etc., usually with a photograph; IDENTIFICATION: *Do you have any ID?* | *a fake ID*

ID[2] *v. past tense* **ID'd** *present participle* **ID'ing** [T] SPOKEN to IDENTIFY a criminal or dead body: *The police were able to ID the body quickly.*

ID[3] the written abbreviation of Idaho

id /id/ *n.* [singular] TECHNICAL according to Freudian PSYCHOLOGY, the part of your mind that is completely unconscious, but that has hidden desires and needs that you try to meet —compare EGO (3), SUPEREGO

I·da·ho /'aidə,hou/ *written abbreviation* **ID** a state in the northwestern U.S.

ID card /,ai 'di kɑrd/ *n.* [C] a card with your name, date of birth, photograph, SIGNATURE etc. on it, that proves who you are

-ide /aɪd/ *suffix* [in nouns] TECHNICAL a chemical compound: *cyanide* | *sulphide*

i·de·a /aɪˈdiə/ *n.*

1 plan/suggestion [C] a plan or suggestion for a possible course of action, especially one that you think of suddenly: *That's a good idea!* | [+ of] *I like Louis's idea of meeting on Saturday mornings.* | [+ for] *Ellen got the idea for the business ten years ago.* | *It was Pete's idea to have the wedding in December.* | *Laura always has great ideas for gifts.* | *Rob came up with the idea* (=thought of the idea) *of renting out a room in our house.* | *My son gave me the idea for the game* (=something he said or did helped her think of it).

2 information [C,U] some information or knowledge about something, that is not very exact: *Could you give me an idea of how bad his injuries are?* | *You must have some idea* (=have at least a little information) *of when Joyce will be home.* | *I have no idea* (=no knowledge about) *whose jacket that is.* | *a rough/general idea* (=one that is not very exact)

3 goal/purpose [C,U] the GOAL or purpose of doing something: *The idea is to teach children to save money.* | [+ of/behind] *The idea of the recycling campaign is to preserve the environment.* | *Everyone wanted Joe to take over the family business, but he had other ideas* (=had different plans). | *Weber was never at a loss for big ideas* (=plans to become important, successful etc.).

4 image [C,U] an image in your mind of what something is like or should be like: [+ of] *Mowing the lawn is not my idea of fun.* | *I only have a vague idea of the kind of work I'll be doing.*

5 belief [C usually plural] an opinion or belief that someone has that other people think is wrong or strange: [+ about] *Her ideas about marriage are very old-fashioned.* | *Somehow Ken's gotten the idea that* (=wrongly begun to believe) *I'm in love with him.*

6 principle [C] a principle or belief about how something is or should be: [+ of] *the Christian idea of an eternal soul* | [idea that] *This concept is based on Rousseau's idea that men are born morally neutral.*

7 it is (not) a good idea to do sth used to give someone advice about what to do, or what not to do: *It's a good idea to drink lots of water on hot days.* | *In general, it's not a good idea to turn away potential customers.*

SPOKEN PHRASES

8 have no idea also not have the faintest/slightest/foggiest idea to not know at all: *I have no idea how to fix this watch.* | *I don't have the foggiest idea where Liz is.*

9 get the idea to begin to understand something or be able to do something: *By now I'm sure you get the idea that this survey was not scientific.*

10 get the wrong idea to think that something is true when it is not: *Don't get the wrong idea – the Dixons aren't as arrogant as they sound.*

11 where did you get that idea? used to say that what someone thinks is completely wrong: *No, I didn't get fired. Where did you get that idea?*

12 that's/there's an idea! used to say that you like what someone has just suggested: *"Maybe you could do some babysitting." "Yeah, that's an idea."*

13 that's the idea a) used to tell someone who is learning to do something that they are doing it the right way, in order to encourage them: *Now push the button on the left to set the time. That's the idea!* b) used to emphasize what the main point of something is, or to say that someone understands that point: *"You're going to meet them there?" "Yeah, that's the idea."*

14 have an idea (that) to be fairly sure that something is true, without being completely sure: *I had a pretty good idea that this was going to happen.*

15 the idea! OLD-FASHIONED used to express surprise or disapproval when someone has said something stupid, strange, or shocking

16 have the right idea to act or think in a way that will probably lead to the correct result: *The new superintendent has the right idea about attacking illiteracy, but the wrong method.*

17 bright idea a very smart idea, often used in a joking way to mean a very stupid idea or action: *Whose bright idea was it to give the cat a bath?*

18 sb's idea of a joke INFORMAL something that is intended to be a joke but makes you angry: *Is this your idea of a joke?*

19 put ideas into sb's head INFORMAL to make someone think of doing something that they had not thought of before, especially something stupid or impossible

i·de·al¹ /aɪˈdiəl/ *adj.* **1** something that is ideal is the most appropriate for someone or for a specific job: *My new office is in an ideal location.* | [ideal for sb/sth] *The game is ideal for pre-school children.* **2** the best that something could possibly be: *I realize this isn't an ideal situation.* | *The weather was ideal for the whole vacation.* **3** [only before noun] an ideal world, job, system etc. is one that you imagine to be perfect, but that is not likely to exist: *In an ideal world, no one would ever get sick.*

ideal² *n.* [C] **1** a principle or standard that you would like to achieve or that you want to behave according to: *Many Southerners have deeply held ideals about honor.* **2** a perfect example of what something would be like if it had no faults or problems: [+ of] *the American ideal of the nuclear family*

i·de·al·ism /aɪˈdiəˌlɪzəm/ *n.* [U] **1** the belief that you should live your life according to high standards or principles, even when they are very difficult to achieve **2** TECHNICAL a way of using art or literature to show the world as a perfect place, even though it is not —compare REALISM, NATURALISM

i·de·al·ist /aɪˈdiəlɪst/ *n.* [C] someone who tries to live according to high standards or principles, especially in a way that is not practical or possible

i·de·al·ist·ic /ˌaɪdiəˈlɪstɪk/ *adj.* believing that you should live according to high standards or principles, even if they cannot really be achieved —**idealistically** *adv.*

i·de·al·ize /aɪˈdiəˌlaɪz/ *v.* [T] to imagine or represent something or someone as being perfect or better than they really are: *The movie idealizes life in the 1600s.* —**idealization** /aɪˌdiələˈzeɪʃən/ *n.* [U]

i·de·al·ly /aɪˈdiəli/ *adv.* **1** [sentence adverb] used to describe the way you would like things to be, even though this may not be possible: *Ideally, we should be saving money every month.* **2** ideally suited/placed/qualified etc. having the best qualities, experience, knowledge etc. for a particular situation: *Robertson is ideally suited for the job.*

i·den·ti·cal /aɪˈdɛntɪkəl, ɪ-/ *adj.* exactly the same: *three identical statues* | [+ to] *My work hours are almost identical to my daughters' school hours.* —**identically** /-kli/ *adv.*

identical twin /.,... './ *n.* [C usually plural] one of a pair of brothers or sisters born at the same time, who develop from the same EGG and look almost exactly alike —compare FRATERNAL TWIN

i·den·ti·fi·a·ble /aɪˌdɛntəˈfaɪəbəl, ɪ-/ *adj.* able to be recognized: *The fingerprint on the door was not identifiable.*

i·den·ti·fi·ca·tion /aɪˌdɛntəfəˈkeɪʃən/ *n.* [U] **1** official papers or cards, such as your PASSPORT, that prove who you are: *You need two pieces of identification to write a check here.* —see also ID¹ **2** the act or process of saying officially that you know who someone is, especially a criminal or a dead person: *The bodies were brought to the hospital for identification.* **3** the act or process of recognizing something or discovering exactly what it is, what its nature or origin is etc.: [+ of] *Correct identification of customer needs is vital.* **4** a strong feeling that you are like someone or something, and share the same qualities or feelings: [+ with] *Hales' success as editor of the Almanac is explained by his identification with readers.*

i·den·ti·fy /aɪˈdɛntəˌfaɪ/ *v.* **identifies, identified, identifying** [T] **1** to recognize and correctly name someone or something: *Can you identify the man who robbed you?* | [identify sb/sth as sb/sth] *The suspect* *was identified as Daniel Hargraves.* **2** to recognize something or discover exactly what it is, what its nature or origin is etc.: *Researchers have identified the substances which can cause allergies.* **3** if a particular thing identifies someone, it makes it clear to other people who that person is: [**identify sb as sb**] *Workers will wear badges to identify them as park employees.*

identify with sb/sth *phr. v.* [T] **1** [**identify with** sb] to be able to share or understand the feelings of someone else: *Young boys, especially, identify with the novel's main character.* **2** [**identify sth with** sb/sth] to think or show that something has a relationship or connection with something else: *Ad agencies glamorize drinking and identify it with social status.* | *Polo is a sport that is identified with the upper class.*

SW i·den·ti·ty /aɪˈdɛntəti, ɪ-/ *n. plural* **identities 1** [C,U] who someone is or the name of someone: *We still don't know the identity of the other man in the picture.* | *Wong was jailed overnight in* **a case of mistaken identity** (=someone thought that Wong was someone else). **2** [U] the qualities and attitudes a person or group of people have that make them different from other people: *Some fear the community is losing its Hispanic-Indian identity.* | *Many men get their* **sense of identity** *from their careers.* | *The city has been suffering a kind of* **identity crisis** (=a feeling of uncertainty about what its basic qualities are and what its purpose is). **3** [U] TECHNICAL an exact SIMILARITY between two things

id·e·o·gram /ˈɪdiəˌgræm, ˈaɪdiə-/ also **id·e·o·graph** /ˈɪdiəˌgræf, ˈaɪdiə-/ *n.* [C] a written sign, for example in Chinese, that represents an idea or thing rather than the sound of a word

i·de·o·log·i·cal /ˌaɪdiəˈlɑdʒɪkəl, ˌɪdiə-/ *adj.* based on a particular set of beliefs or ideas, especially political ideas: *The two Communist powers split over ideological differences in the late 1950s.* —**ideologically** /-kli/ *adv.*

i·de·o·logue /ˈaɪdiəˌlɑg, -ˌlɔg/ *n.* [C] someone whose actions are influenced too much by an ideology

i·de·ol·o·gy /ˌaɪdiˈɑlədʒi, ˌɪdi-/ *n. plural* **ideologies** [C,U] **1** a set of ideas on which a political or economic system is based: *democratic ideology* **2** a set of ideas and attitudes that strongly influence the way people behave: *a group with a racist ideology*

ides /aɪdz/ *n.* [plural] a date or period of time around the middle of the month in the ancient Roman CALENDAR

id·i·o·cy /ˈɪdiəsi/ *n.* **1** [U] extreme stupidity or silliness **2** [C] a very stupid remark or action

id·i·o·lect /ˈɪdiəˌlɛkt/ *n.* [C,U] TECHNICAL the way in which a particular person uses language —compare DIALECT

id·i·om /ˈɪdiəm/ *n.* **1** [C] a group of words that has a special meaning that is different from the ordinary meaning of each separate word: *"To be on top of the world" is an idiom that means to be very happy.* **2** [C,U] TECHNICAL a style of expression in writing, speech, or music, that is typical of a particular group of people

id·i·o·mat·ic /ˌɪdiəˈmætɪk◄/ *adj.* **1 an idiomatic phrase/expression** an idiom **2** typical of the natural way in which someone using their own language speaks or writes: *Their books are translated into idiomatic English.* —**idiomatically** /-kli/ *adv.*

id·i·o·syn·cra·sy /ˌɪdiəˈsɪŋkrəsi/ *n. plural* **idiosyncrasies** [C] **1** an unusual habit or way of behaving that someone has: *She's easy to work for, and her employees don't mind her idiosyncrasies.* **2** an unusual or unexpected feature that something has: *Flight crews must become familiar with each airplane's idiosyncrasies.* —**idiosyncratic** /ˌɪdiousɪŋˈkrætɪk/ *adj.*

SW id·i·ot /ˈɪdiət/ *n.* [C] **1** a stupid person, or someone who has done something stupid: *You idiot! What did you do that for?* **2** OLD USE a word meaning someone who is mentally ill or has a very low level of

intelligence, now considered offensive —**idiotic** /ˌɪdiˈɑtɪk/ *adj.* —**idiotically** /-kli/ *adv.*

idiot box /ˈ... ˌ./ *n.* [C usually singular] OLD-FASHIONED, INFORMAL a television

idiot light /ˈ... ˌ./ *n.* [C] NOT TECHNICAL one of the lights in a car that warns you when something is wrong

idiot-proof /ˈ... ˌ./ *adj.* HUMOROUS so easy to use or do that even stupid people will not break it or make a mistake: *We need to make copiers that are cheap and idiot-proof.*

i·dle¹ /ˈaɪdl/ *adj.* **1** not working or being used: *The factory has been idle since May.* | *Tractors were* **sitting idle** *in the fields.* **2** having no useful purpose: *idle gossip* | *Haley said he'd quit, and it wasn't an* **idle threat** (=a threat he did not mean). **3** OLD-FASHIONED lazy —**idly** *adv.*

i·dle² *v.* **idled, idling 1** [I,T] if an engine idles or if you idle it, it runs slowly while the vehicle, machine etc. is not moving: *My car starts easily, but it sounds rough when it idles.* **2** [T] to stop using a factory or stop providing work for your workers, especially temporarily: *GM announced it would idle four assembly plants.* **3** [I always + adv./prep.] to spend time doing nothing

idle sth ↔ **away** *phr. v.* [T] to spend time in a relaxed way, doing nothing: *I idled away the afternoon among the reference books in the library.*

i·dle³ *n.* [U] the idle of an engine is when it is running slowly while the vehicle, machine etc. is not moving

i·dler /ˈaɪdlə/ *n.* [C] OLD-FASHIONED someone who is lazy and does not work

i·dol /ˈaɪdl/ *n.* [C] **1** someone or something that you love or admire very much: *Muhammad Ali was my idol when I was a boy.* **2** a picture or STATUE that is WORSHIPped as a god

i·dol·a·try /aɪˈdɑlətri/ *n.* [U] **1** the practice of WOR-SHIPping IDOLS **2** too much admiration for someone or something —**idolatrous** *adj.*

i·dol·ize /ˈaɪdlˌaɪz/ *v.* [T] to admire and love someone so much that you think they are perfect: *Susan idolizes her mother.*

i·dyll /ˈaɪdl/ *n.* [singular] LITERARY a place or experience in which everything is peaceful and everyone is perfectly happy

i·dyl·lic /aɪˈdɪlɪk/ *adj.* very happy and peaceful, with no problems or dangers: *an idyllic vacation resort* —**idyllically** /-kli/ *adv.*

i.e. FORMAL an expression written before a word or phrase that gives the exact meaning of something you have just written or said: *The proposal could fail because of "real world" (i.e. economic) considerations.*

-ie /i/ *suffix* [in nouns] INFORMAL used to make a word or name less formal, and often to show that you care about someone: *Hi Eddie!* | *Come on, sweetie, put your sweater on.* —see also -Y² (1)

-ier /iə/ *suffix* [in nouns] **1** someone who does something, or someone who is in charge of something: *a cashier* (=someone who receives and pays out money) | *a hotelier* (=someone in charge of a hotel) **2** used instead of -ER after the letter "y": *a mail carrier* | *dry, drier*

-iest /iɪst/ *suffix* [in adjectives] used instead of -EST after the letter "y": *pretty, prettier, prettiest*

if¹ /ɪf/ *conjunction* **1** used to introduce a phrase when **SW** something else depends on that action and situation: *If you call Ann now, she should still be home.* | *We'll have to leave Monday if it snows today.* | *I might see them on Saturday.* **If not**, *then I definitely will on Sunday.* —see Usage Note at UNLESS **2** used to mean "whether" when you are asking or deciding whether something is true or will happen: *Do you know if we have to work on Christmas Eve?* | *I wonder if Matt's home yet.* —see Usage Note at WHETHER **3** used when you are talking about something that always happens in a particular situation: *If I drink too much coffee, I have to run to the bathroom all day long.* | *The plastic will melt if it gets too hot.* **4** said when you are surprised, upset, angry etc. that something has happened or is true: *I'm sorry if I upset you.* | *I don't care if my boss fires me – I'm still going to tell* him what I think. **5** used when making a polite request or saying you are sorry: *Would you mind if I used your phone?* | *I'm sorry if I disturbed you.* **6 if only a)** used to give a reason for something, although you think it is not a good one: *Just call her, if only to say you're sorry.* **b)** used to express a strong wish, especially when you know what you want cannot happen: *If only I could be 15 again!* **7 if I were you** SPOKEN used when giving advice and telling someone what you think they should do: *If I were you, I'd sell that car.* **8 if sb's... (then) I'm...** SPOKEN used to say that you do not believe what someone has said about themselves: *If Harry's a professional ice skater, I'm the Pope.* **9** used to mean "though" when you are describing someone or something that you like: *It's a really fast car, if a little expensive.* —see also **as if.../as though** (AS² (4)), **even if** (EVEN¹ (4))

if² *n.* [C usually plural] INFORMAL **1** a possibility or condition: *There are still too many ifs to know if our product will be successful.* **2 no ifs, ands, or buts** used to say that something is completely true, and there is no possibility to disagree: *No ifs, ands, or buts – you have to take a bath tonight.*

if·fy /'ɪfi/ *adj.* INFORMAL an iffy situation is one in which you do not know what will happen, but you think the result will probably not be good: *Your chances of finding a better job are iffy.*

-iform /ɪfɔrm/ *suffix* [in adjectives] TECHNICAL having a particular shape: *cruciform* (=cross-shaped)

-ify /əfaɪ/ *suffix* [in verbs] **1** to make something be in a particular state or condition: *to purify something* (=make it pure) | *to clarify a situation* (=make it clear) | *to amplify sound* (=make it louder) **2** to make someone have a particular feeling: *Spiders terrify me* (=make me very afraid). | *to stultify someone* (=make them extremely bored) **3** INFORMAL to do something in a silly or annoying way: *to speechify* (=make annoying speeches) —see also -FY

ig·loo /'ɪglu/ *n. plural* **igloos** [C] a house made from blocks of hard snow or ice

Ig·na·tius of Loy·o·la /ɪg'neɪʃəs əv lɔɪ'oʊlə/**, St.** also **St. Ignatius Loyola** (1491–1556) a Spanish priest who started the religious ORDER of Jesuits, also called the Society of Jesus

ig·ne·ous /'ɪgniəs/ *adj.* TECHNICAL igneous rocks are formed from LAVA (=hot liquid rock)

ig·nite /ɪg'naɪt/ *v.* **1** [T] to start a dangerous situation, angry argument etc.: *A shortage of bread ignited the 1917 riots.* **2** [I,T] FORMAL to start burning, or to make something start burning: *The firebomb did not ignite and caused only minor damage.*

ig·ni·tion /ɪg'nɪʃən/ *n.* **1** [C, usually singular] the place in a car where you put in a key to start the engine: *Phil left his key in the ignition again.* —see pictures at ENGINE and on page 427 **2** [singular] the electrical part of a vehicle's engine that makes it start working **3** [U] FORMAL the act of starting to burn, or of making something do this

ig·no·ble /ɪg'noʊbəl/ *adj.* FORMAL ignoble thoughts, feelings, or actions are ones that you should feel ashamed or embarrassed about —**ignobly** *adv.*

ig·no·min·i·ous /ˌɪgnə'mɪniəs/ *adj.* FORMAL making you feel ashamed or embarrassed: *an ignominious defeat* —**ignominiously** *adv.*

ig·no·min·y /'ɪgnəˌmɪni/ *n.* [C,U] FORMAL an event or situation that makes you feel ashamed or embarrassed, especially in public, or the state of feeling ashamed or embarrassed

ig·no·ra·mus /ˌɪgnə'reɪməs/ *n.* [C] someone who does not know about things that most people know about

ig·no·rance /'ɪgnərəns/ *n.* [U] **1** lack of knowledge or information about something: [+ of] *The average American's ignorance of geography is shocking.* **2 ignorance is bliss** used to say that if you do not know about a problem, you cannot worry about it

ig·no·rant /'ɪgnərənt/ *adj.* **1** not knowing facts or information that you ought to know: *a crude and ignorant man* | [+ of] *Many young people are ignorant of recent history.* | [+ about] *People are just amazingly ignorant about the Middle East.* **2** caused

by a lack of knowledge and understanding: *That was an ignorant joke!* —see Usage Note at IGNORE

ig·nore /ɪg'nɔr/ *v.* [T] **1** to behave as if you had not heard or seen someone or something: *Just ignore him and he'll stop pestering you.* **2** to deliberately pay no attention to something that you have been told or that you know about: *The school board has continually ignored the complaints of parents.*

USAGE NOTE: IGNORE

WORD CHOICE: ignore, be ignorant of
If you **ignore** something, you know about it or have seen or heard it, but choose not to take notice of it: *Some drivers simply ignore speed limits.* If you are **ignorant** of something, you do not know about it: *No driver can pretend to be ignorant of speed limits.*

I·gua·çu Falls /ˌigwəsu 'fɔlz/ a very large WATERFALL on the border between Argentina and Brazil in South America

i·gua·na /ɪ'gwɑnə/ *n.* [C] a large tropical American LIZARD

IIRC, iirc a written abbreviation of "if I remember correctly," used in EMAIL, or by people communicating in CHAT ROOMS on the Internet

IL a written abbreviation of Illinois

il- /ɪl/ *prefix* used instead of IN- (1) before the letter "l"; not: *illogical* (=not logical)

ILGWU International Ladies' Garment Workers' Union; a UNION of women in the clothing industry

ilk /ɪlk/ *n.* FORMAL **of that/his/their ilk** of that type, his type etc.: *Irving Berlin and composers of his ilk*

I'll /aɪl/ the short form of "I will": *I'll see you later.*

ill¹ /ɪl/ *adj.* **1** [not usually before noun] suffering from a disease or not feeling well; sick: *Several people became ill after eating the clams.* | *People who were mentally ill* (=with a disease of the mind) *were left to take care of themselves on the streets.* | *She is seriously ill with tuberculosis.* | *Mountain View Hospital is seeking volunteers to care for terminally ill* (=sick with something that they will die from) *patients.* | *Ill health forced Mr. Cacitti to retire in 1980.* —see also ILLNESS **2** [only before noun] bad or harmful: *The patient seems to be suffering no ill effects from the treatments.* **3 ill at ease** nervous, uncomfortable, or embarrassed: *Rehnquist sometimes can appear ill at ease in public.* **4 house/place of ill repute** a place where men can pay to have sex with PROSTITUTES —see also ILL WILL

ill² *adv.* **1** not well or not enough; BADLY: *We were ill-prepared to camp out in the snow.* **2** badly or cruelly: *The animals had been ill-treated by their owner.* **3 sb can ill afford (to do) sth** to be unable to do or have something without making the situation you are in very difficult: *The senator can ill afford another scandal.* **4 think/speak ill of sb** FORMAL to think or say bad things about someone: *The candidates clearly did not want to speak ill of each other during the campaign.*

ill³ *n.* **1** [U] FORMAL harm, evil, or bad luck: *Even though I don't agree with him, I do not wish Baxter any ill.* **2 ills** [plural] problems and difficulties: *Voters are looking for fresh solutions to the nation's ills.*

ill-ad·vised /ˌ. .'. / *adj.* FORMAL not sensible or not wise and likely to cause problems in the future: *an ill-advised decision* | [be ill-advised to do sth] *You would be ill-advised to discuss your salary with others in the company.* —**ill-advisedly** *adv.*

ill-con·ceived /ˌ. .'./ *adj.* not planned well and not having an aim that is likely to be achieved: *an ill-conceived scheme*

ill-con·sid·ered /ˌ. .'../ *adj.* FORMAL decisions, actions, ideas etc. that are ill-considered have not been carefully thought about: *an ill-considered business venture*

ill-de·fined /ˌ. .'. / *adj.* FORMAL **1** not described clearly enough: *The procedures are ill-defined and completely untested.* **2** not clearly marked, or not having a clear shape: *an ill-defined border*

il·le·gal¹ /ɪˈliːgəl/ *adj.* not allowed by the law: *It's illegal to make copies of computer programs.* | *illegal drugs* —**illegally** *adv.* —opposite LEGAL

illegal² *n.* [C] INFORMAL an illegal alien

illegal a·li·en also **illegal immigrant** /ˌ...ˈ..., ˌ... ˈ.../ *n.* [C] someone who comes into a country to live or work without official permission

il·le·gal·i·ty /ˌɪlɪˈgæləti/ *n. plural* **illegalities 1** [U] the state of being illegal **2** [C] an action that is illegal

il·leg·i·ble /ɪˈlɛdʒəbəl/ *adj.* difficult or impossible to read: *Ron's handwriting is completely illegible.* —**illegibly** *adv.* —**illegibility** /ɪˌlɛdʒəˈbɪləti/ *n.* [U] —opposite LEGIBLE

il·le·git·i·mate /ˌɪləˈdʒɪtəmɪt/ *adj.* **1** born to parents who are not married: *an illegitimate child* **2** not allowed or acceptable according to established rules or agreements: *Many of these insurance claims are illegitimate.* —**illegitimately** *adv.* —**illegitimacy** *n.* [U]

ill-e·quipped /ˌ. .ˈ.◂/ *adj.* FORMAL not having the necessary equipment or skills for a particular situation or activity: *These rural hospitals are ill-equipped to handle such emergencies.*

ill-fat·ed /ˌ. ˈ..◂/ *adj.* LITERARY unlucky and leading to serious problems or death: *an ill-fated journey*

ill-fa·vored /ˌ. ˈ..◂/ *adj.* **1** FORMAL not lucky **2** LITERARY OR OLD-FASHIONED having an unattractive face; ugly

ill feel·ing /ˌ. ˈ../ *n.* [U] angry feelings toward someone: *There's no ill feeling toward our rivals.*

ill-fit·ting /ˌ. ˈ..◂/ *adj.* ill-fitting clothes do not fit the person who is wearing them: *an ill-fitting suit*

ill-found·ed /ˌ. ˈ..◂/ *adj.* FORMAL based on something that is untrue: *ill-founded worries*

ill-got·ten /ˌ. ˈ..◂/ *adj.* **ill-gotten gains/wealth etc.** ESPECIALLY HUMOROUS money that was obtained in an unfair or dishonest way

il·lib·er·al /ɪˈlɪbərəl/ *adj.* FORMAL **1** not supporting freedom of expression or of personal behavior: *By necessity, the armed forces are illiberal and undemocratic.* **2** not generous

il·lic·it /ɪˈlɪsɪt/ *adj.* not allowed by laws or rules, or strongly disapproved of by society: *an illicit love affair* | *illicit drugs* —**illicitly** *adv.*

Il·li·nois /ˌɪləˈnɔɪ/ **1** *written abbreviation* **IL** a state in the Midwestern area of the U.S. **2** a group of Native American tribes who formerly lived in the northeastern central area of the U.S.

il·lit·er·ate /ɪˈlɪtərɪt/ *adj.* **1** someone who is illiterate has not learned to read or write **2** badly written, in an uneducated way: *an illiterate composition* **3 culturally/politically etc. illiterate** knowing very little about CULTURE, politics etc. —**illiteracy** *n.* [U] —**illiterate** *n.* [C usually plural]

ill-man·nered /ˌ. ˈ..◂/ *adj.* FORMAL not polite and behaving badly in social situations —opposite WELL-MANNERED

ill·ness /ˈɪlnɪs/ *n.* [C,U] a disease of the body or mind: *Most childhood illnesses can now be easily prevented.* | *mental illness* —compare DISEASE —see Usage Note at DISEASE

il·log·i·cal /ɪˈlɑdʒɪkəl/ *adj.* **1** not sensible or reasonable: *The current rules are illogical and unnecessary.* —opposite LOGICAL (1) **2** not based on the principles of LOGIC: *English has plenty of illogical spelling rules.* —**illogically** /-kli/ *adv.*

ill-served /ˌ. ˈ.◂/ *adj.* not helped by something or not represented well: *Lee believes women have been ill-served by the medical system.*

ill-starred /ˌ. ˈ.◂/ *adj.* LITERARY unlucky and likely to cause or experience a lot of problems or unhappiness: *Hawkins had an ill-starred career in football, with one injury after another.*

ill-suit·ed /ˌ. ˈ.◂/ *adj.* not useful for a particular purpose: [+ **for**] *an environment ill-suited to learning*

ill-tem·pered /ˌ. ˈ..◂/ *adj.* FORMAL **1** easily made angry or impatient **2** an ill-tempered meeting, argument etc. is one in which people are angry and often impolite to each other

ill-timed /ˌ. ˈ.◂/ *adj.* happening, done, or said at the wrong time: *His remarks are ill-timed and inappropriate.*

ill-treat /ˌ. ˈ./ *v.* [T usually passive] to treat someone in a cruel way: *Webb said the three men had not been ill-treated in any way.* —**ill-treatment** *n.* [U]

il·lu·mi·nate /ɪˈluːməˌneɪt/ *v.* [T] **1** to make a light shine on something, or fill a place with light: *The room was illuminated by candles.* **2** FORMAL to make something much clearer and easier to understand: *Newly discovered artifacts may help illuminate the culture of the Aztecs.* **3 illuminate sb's face** LITERARY to make someone look happy or excited: *A sudden smile illuminated her face.*

il·lu·mi·nat·ed /ɪˈluːməˌneɪtɪd/ *adj.* **1** lit up by lights: *an illuminated billboard* **2 an illuminated book/Bible/manuscript etc.** a book of a type produced by hand in the Middle Ages, whose pages are decorated with gold paint and other bright colors

il·lu·mi·nat·ing /ɪˈluːməˌneɪtɪŋ/ *adj.* making things much clearer and easier to understand: *The film proves many illuminating insights into Chinese culture.*

il·lu·mi·na·tion /ɪˌluːməˈneɪʃən/ *n.* **1** [U] FORMAL lighting provided by a lamp, light etc.: *The only illumination came from emergency lights over the doors.* **2** [U] FORMAL a clear explanation of a particular subject: *Among Clark's more important illuminations are his thoughts on Lewis' mysterious death.* **3** [C usually plural] a picture or pattern painted on a page of a book, especially in past times

il·lu·sion /ɪˈluːʒən/ *n.* [C] **1** an idea or opinion that is wrong, especially about yourself: *Jeff's **under the illusion that** (=believes wrongly that) he can afford to buy a house.* | *They **have no illusions about** (=realize the unpleasant truth about) how difficult the first year of marriage will be.* **2** something that seems to be different from the way it really is: **create/give an illusion** *A mirror gives the illusion that the room is much larger.* —see also OPTICAL ILLUSION

il·lu·sion·ist /ɪˈluːʒənɪst/ *n.* [C] someone who does surprising tricks that make things seem to appear or happen

il·lu·so·ry /ɪˈluːsəri, -zəri/ also **il·lu·sive** /ɪˈluːsɪv/ *adj.* FORMAL false but seeming to be real or true: *Signs of economic recovery may be illusory.*

il·lus·trate /ˈɪləˌstreɪt/ *v.* [T] **1** to make the meaning of something clearer by giving examples: *Pictures illustrate some of the ways in which rocks are formed.* **2** to be an example that shows that something is true or that a fact exists: *This story illustrates how important the family is in Latin American culture.* **3** [usually passive] to put pictures in a book, article etc.: *The book was illustrated by Robert May.*

il·lus·tra·tion /ˌɪləˈstreɪʃən/ *n.* **1** [C] a picture in a book, article etc., especially one that helps you to understand it **2** [C,U] an example that shows the truth or existence of something very clearly: [+ **of**] *The wrecked car was a graphic illustration of the dangers of being hit from the side.* **3** [U] the act or process of illustrating something

il·lus·tra·tive /ɪˈlʌstrətɪv, ˈɪləˌstreɪtɪv/ *adj.* **1** helping to explain the meaning of something: *His lectures are full of illustrative stories.* **2** having pictures, especially to help you understand something: *illustrative diagrams of home repairs* —compare ILLUSTRATE

il·lus·tra·tor /ˈɪləˌstreɪtɚ/ *n.* [C] someone who draws pictures, especially for books

il·lus·tri·ous /ɪˈlʌstriəs/ *adj.* FORMAL famous and admired because of what you have achieved: *The illustrious director Sir Richard Attenborough also attended the ceremony.*

ill will /ˌ. ˈ./ *n.* [U] a feeling of strong dislike or anger toward someone: *Jon's arrogance created a lot of ill* will within the company. | **bear/hold/harbor no ill will toward sb** (=feel no anger toward someone)

I'm /aɪm/ the short form of 'I am': *I'm a lawyer.* | *Hello, I'm Donna.*

im- /ɪm/ *prefix* **1** used instead of IN- (1) before the letters "b," "m," or "p"; not: *impossible* | *immobilize* (=not allow something to move) **2** used instead of IN- (2) before the letters "b," "m," or "p": *to implode* (=explode inward)

im·age /ˈɪmɪdʒ/ *n.* [C] **1** the way a person, organization, product etc. presents themselves to the public: *This latest scandal has severely hurt his image as a leader.* | *The company needs to* **improve** *its image among young people.* | *Attorneys want to* **project** *the best image possible for their clients* (=they want to make people see them in a good way). **2** a picture that you have in your mind, especially about what someone or something is like or the way they look: *At forty-six, Burnett hardly fits most people's image of an American college student.* | *People have this image of me as some kind of monster.* **3 a)** a picture of an object in a mirror or in the LENS of a camera: *When he stared at his image in the mirror, Smith saw a middle-aged man.* **b)** a picture on the screen of a television, movie theater, or computer: *The images of starving people on the news was what motivated us to send money.* **c)** a picture or shape of a person or thing that is copied onto paper or cut in wood or stone: *Mickey Mouse's image was plastered on billboards all over town.* **4** a word, phrase, or picture that describes an idea in a poem, book, movie etc.: *The image of the tree in "Cinderella" is particularly important because it symbolizes personal growth.* **5 in the image of sb/sth** LITERARY in the same form or shape as someone or something else: *According to the Bible, man was made in the image of God.* —see also MIRROR IMAGE, SPITTING IMAGE

image-mak·er, image maker /ˈ.. ˌ../ *n.* [C] someone whose job is to use newspapers, television, radio etc. to change people's opinion of a product, company, or famous person so that it is favorable

im·age·ry /ˈɪmɪdʒri/ *n.* [U] the use of words or pictures to describe ideas or actions in poems, books, movies etc.: *religious imagery*

i·mag·i·na·ble /ɪˈmædʒənəbəl/ *adj.* able to be imagined: *We had the best vacation imaginable.* | *Doctors have tried every imaginable treatment for her skin disease.*

i·mag·i·nar·y /ɪˈmædʒəˌnɛri/ *adj.* not real, but produced from pictures or ideas in your mind: *Many young children have imaginary playmates.* | *The events described in the book are imaginary.* —compare IMAGINATIVE

i·mag·i·na·tion /ɪˌmædʒəˈneɪʃən/ *n.* **1** [C,U] the ability to form pictures or ideas in your mind: *Debbie has a very good imagination.* **2** [U] something that is caused only by your mind, and does not really exist or did not really happen: *Maybe it was just my imagination, but he seemed really hostile.* **3 in your imagination** only existing or happening in your mind, not in real life: *Her fears of being followed were all in her imagination.* **4 leave sth to sb's imagination** to deliberately not describe something because you think someone can guess or imagine it: *The production successfully leaves much of the detail to the audience's imagination.* **5 leave nothing to the imagination a)** if someone is wearing clothes that leave nothing to the imagination, the clothes are very thin or are worn in a way that shows the person's body: *Her blouse left nothing to the imagination.* **b)** if something, especially something violent or sexual, is described in a way that leaves nothing to the imagination, it is explained in too much detail: *The description of the murders left nothing to the imagination.* **6 capture/catch sb's imagination** to make people feel very interested and excited: *The story of a boy raised by monkeys has caught the imagination of millions.* **7 use your imagination!** SPOKEN used to tell someone that you should not need to tell them the answer to their own question because they can easily guess the answer —see also **by any stretch (of the imagination)** (STRETCH[2] (3))

i·mag·i·na·tive /ɪˈmædʒənətɪv/ *adj.* **1** good at thinking of new and interesting ideas: *an imaginative novelist* **2** containing new and interesting ideas: *an imaginative Halloween costume* | *imaginative storytelling* —compare IMAGINARY —**imaginatively** *adv.*

i·mag·ine /ɪˈmædʒɪn/ *v.* [T] **1** [not usually in progressive] to form a picture or idea in your mind about what something could be like: [**imagine (that)**] *Imagine that you just won six million dollars.* | [**imagine what/how/why etc.**] *I can't imagine how it would feel to have so much influence.* | [**imagine sb doing sth**] *Can you imagine Becky going to the Olympics?* | [**imagine doing sth**] *It's hard to imagine living anywhere else but here.* | [**imagine sb/sth as sth**] *I never knew my grandmother, but I always imagine her as a kind, gentle person.* | [**imagine sb in/with/without etc. sth**] *Can you imagine Ted in a suit and tie?* **2** to have a false or wrong idea about something: *The lake is much prettier than I had imagined.* | *No, there's no one at the door. You're* **just imagining things**. **3** [not in progressive] SPOKEN to think that something is true or may happen, but without being sure or having proof: [**imagine (that)**] *I imagine you're feeling pretty homesick.* **4 you can imagine** SPOKEN used to emphasize how good, bad etc. something is: *You can imagine how mad I was when I found out our car was stolen.* **5 (just) imagine!** SPOKEN, OLD-FASHIONED used to show surprise, shock, or disapproval

i·mag·in·ings /ɪˈmædʒənɪŋz/ *n.* [plural] LITERARY situations or ideas that you imagine, but which are not real or true

i·mam /ɪˈmɑm, ˈɪmæm/ *n.* [C] a Muslim religious leader or priest

im·bal·ance /ɪmˈbæləns/ *n.* [C,U] a lack of a fair or correct balance between two things, which causes problems or results in an unfair situation: *a hormonal imbalance* | [+ **in/between**] *There has long been a trade imbalance between the two countries.*

im·be·cile /ˈɪmbəsəl/ *n.* [C] **1** someone who behaves very stupidly or who you think is stupid **2** OLD USE a word meaning someone who is not intelligent, now considered offensive

im·be·cil·i·ty /ˌɪmbəˈsɪləti/ *n.* [U] very stupid behavior

im·bed /ɪmˈbɛd/ *v.* **imbedded, imbedding** [T] another spelling of EMBED

im·bibe /ɪmˈbaɪb/ *v.* [I,T] FORMAL OR HUMOROUS to drink something, especially alcohol: *Light beer lets drinkers imbibe without taking in extra calories.*

im·bro·glio /ɪmˈbroulyoʊ/ *n. plural* **imbroglios** [C] FORMAL a difficult, embarrassing, or confusing situation, especially in politics or public life

im·bue /ɪmˈbyu/ *v.*
imbue sb/sth **with** sth *phr. v.* [T usually passive] **1** to make someone feel an emotion very strongly: *He was imbued with a deep love for his country.* **2** to give something a particular quality, especially strong emotion: *His songs are imbued with romantic tenderness.*

IMF *n.* **the IMF** the International Monetary Fund; an international organization that tries to encourage trade between countries and to help poorer countries develop economically

IMHO, imho a written abbreviation of "in my humble opinion," used in EMAIL, or by people communicating in CHAT ROOMs on the Internet when they are expressing their opinion

im·i·tate /ˈɪməˌteɪt/ *v.* [T] **1** to copy the way someone behaves, speaks, moves etc., especially in order to make people laugh: *He has a unique ability to imitate any sound he has heard.* **2** to copy something because you think it is good: *Our methods have been imitated all over the world.* —**imitator** *n.* [C]

im·i·ta·tion[1] /ˌɪməˈteɪʃən/ *n.* **1** [C,U] an attempt to imitate someone or something, or the act of doing this: *Children learn through imitation.* | [+ **of**] *Ed does a good imitation of Elvis.* **2** [C] a copy of something:

[+ **of**] *Chevy's is a good imitation of one of those good-time restaurants on Mexico's coast.*

imitation² *adj.* made to look and seem like something else: *Those shoes are made of imitation leather.*

im·i·ta·tive /ˈɪməˌteɪtɪv/ *adj.* FORMAL copying someone or something, especially in a way that shows you do not have any ideas of your own

im·mac·u·late /ɪˈmækyəlɪt/ *adj.* **1** very clean and neat: *an immaculate house* **2** exactly correct or perfect in every detail: *They dance with immaculate precision.* —**immaculately** *adv.*

Immaculate Con·cep·tion /..ˌ... ..ˈ../ *n.* **the Immaculate Conception** the Catholic belief that Jesus Christ's mother Mary was born without SIN

im·ma·nent /ˈɪmənənt/ *adj.* FORMAL **1** a quality that is immanent seems to be naturally present: *Hope seems immanent in human nature.* **2** God or another spiritual power that is immanent is present everywhere —**immanence, immanency** *n.* [U] —compare EMINENT, IMMINENT

im·ma·te·ri·al /ˌɪməˈtɪriəl/ *adj.* **1** not important in a particular situation: *The difference in our ages was immaterial.* **2** FORMAL not having a real physical form

im·ma·ture /ˌɪməˈtʃʊr, -ˈtʊr/ *adj.* **1** someone who is immature behaves or thinks in a way that is typical of someone much younger: *I think Jim's too immature to live on his own.* **2** not fully formed or developed: *an immature plant* —**immaturity** *n.* [U]

im·meas·ur·a·ble /ɪˈmɛʒərəbəl/ *adj.* FORMAL too big or too extreme to be measured: *The war has caused immeasurable suffering.* —**immeasurably** *adv.*

im·me·di·a·cy /ɪˈmidiəsi/ *n.* [U] the quality of something being important or urgent, and directly relating to what is happening now: *They approached the peace talks with a sense of immediacy.*

s w 3 **im·me·di·ate** /ɪˈmidiɪt/ *adj.* **1** happening or done without delay: *The benefits of the program have been neither immediate nor obvious.* | *The UN demanded the immediate release of the hostages.* **2** [only before noun] existing now, and needing to be dealt with quickly: *Our immediate concern was to stop the fire spreading.* **3** [only before noun] happening just before or just after someone or something else: *We have no plans in* **the immediate future** *to lay off workers.* **4** [only before noun] next to, or very near to, a particular place: *Several homes in the immediate area of the volcano were evacuated.* **5 immediate family** the people who are very closely related to you, such as your parents, children, brothers, and sisters: *Pierre was the first person in his immediate family to go to college.*

s w 2 **im·me·di·ate·ly** /ɪˈmidiɪtli/ *adv.* **1** without delay: *The Steelers will immediately begin the search for a new head coach.* | **not immediately available/ known/clear etc.** *The victims' identities were not immediately available.* **2** [+ adj./adv.] very soon before or after something: *I went home immediately after I heard the news.* **3** [+ adj./adv.] very near to something: *Our house is immediately across from the post office.* **4 immediately involved/concerned/ affected etc.** very closely involved etc. in a particular situation: *Ukraine was the republic immediately affected by the nuclear reactor's accident.*

im·me·mo·ri·al /ˌɪməˈmɔriəl/ *adj.* FORMAL starting longer ago than people can remember, or than written history shows: *an immemorial custom* | **from/ since time immemorial** *People have been gambling since time immemorial.*

im·mense /ɪˈmɛns/ *adj.* extremely large: *an immense palace*

im·mense·ly /ɪˈmɛnsli/ *adv.* very much; EXTREMELY: *Counseling has helped their relationship immensely.* | *They are immensely wealthy.*

im·men·si·ty /ɪˈmɛnsəti/ *n.* **1** [U] the great size and seriousness of something such as a problem you have to deal with or a job you have to do: *The immensity of the budget crisis was a surprise to*

everyone. **2** [C] something that is very great in size, especially something that cannot be measured: *the immensities of outer space*

im·merse /ɪˈmɚs/ *v.* [T] **1** FORMAL OR TECHNICAL to put someone or something deep into a liquid so that it is completely covered: [**immerse sb/sth in sth**] *If you immerse the mushrooms in water, they'll become soggy.* **2 immerse yourself in sth** to become completely involved in an activity: *Jarrod completely immersed himself in his work.* —**immersed** *adj.*: *Dan's totally immersed in his studies.*

im·mer·sion /ɪˈmɚʒən/ *n.* [U] **1** the fact of being completely involved in something you are doing: [+ **in**] *Fran discussed her total immersion in campus political activities.* **2** [+ **in**] the action of immersing something in liquid, or the state of being immersed **3** the language teaching method in which people are put in situations where they have to use the new language: *Spanish immersion classes* **4** a type of BAPTISM (=a ceremony to show that you belong to the Christian faith) in which someone's whole body is put into water

im·mi·grant /ˈɪməgrənt/ *n.* [C] someone who enters another country to live there permanently: *Santa Clara was a mesh of Italian, Mexican and German immigrants in the 1800s.* —compare EMIGRANT

im·mi·grate /ˈɪməˌgreɪt/ *v.* [I] to enter a country in order to live there permanently: [+ **from/to**] *Yatsu immigrated from Japan when he was 13.* —compare EMIGRATE —see Usage Note at EMIGRATE

im·mi·gra·tion /ˌɪməˈgreɪʃən/ *n.* [U] **1** the process of entering another country in order to live there permanently **2** the total number of people who immigrate: *Immigration fell in the 1980s.* **3** the place at an airport, border etc. where officials check the documents of everyone entering the country

Immigration and Nat·u·ral·i·za·tion Ser·vice, the /..ˌ.. ...ˈ.. ˌ../ the INS

im·mi·nent /ˈɪmənənt/ *adj.* an event that is imminent will happen very soon: *Ferreira says a deal with Jackson is imminent.* | *There appears to be no* **imminent danger** *of the hurricane hitting the coast.* —**imminently** *adv.* —**imminence** *n.* [U] —compare IMMANENT, EMINENT

im·mo·bile /ɪˈmoʊbəl/ *adj.* **1** not moving at all: *I stood there immobile with terror.* **2** unable to move or walk normally: *The disease can leave victims completely immobile.* —**immobility** /ˌɪmoʊˈbɪləti/ *n.* [U]

im·mo·bi·lize /ɪˈmoʊbəˌlaɪz/ *v.* [T] **1** to prevent someone or something from moving: *Doctors put on a cast to immobilize her ankle.* **2** to completely stop something from working: *The virus has immobilized around 6,000 computers linked to the Internet.* —**immobilization** /ɪˌmoʊbələˈzeɪʃən/ *n.* [U]

im·mod·er·ate /ɪˈmɑdərɪt/ *adj.* FORMAL not within reasonable and sensible limits; EXCESSIVE: *Management called the union's wage demand "immoderate."*

im·mod·est /ɪˈmɑdɪst/ *adj.* **1** having a very high opinion of yourself and your abilities, and not embarrassed about telling people how smart you are etc.: *I don't mean to sound immodest, but I graduated from high school when I was 15.* —opposite MODEST **2** behavior, especially sexual behavior, that is immodest may embarrass or offend people because it does not follow the usual social rules **3** clothes that are immodest show too much of someone's body —**immodestly** *adv.* —**immodesty** *n.* [U]

im·mo·late /ˈɪməˌleɪt/ *v.* [T] FORMAL to kill someone or destroy something by burning them —**immolation** /ˌɪməˈleɪʃən/ *n.* [U]

im·mor·al /ɪˈmɔrəl, ɪˈmɑr-/ *adj.* **1** morally wrong: *Their church believes that dancing is sinful and immoral.* **2** not following accepted standards of sexual behavior —**immorality** /ˌɪməˈræləti/ *n.* [U] —**immorally** /ɪˈmɔrəli, ɪˈmɑr-/ *adv.* —compare AMORAL

im·mor·tal /ɪˈmɔrtl/ *adj.* **1** an immortal line, play, song etc. is so famous that it will never be forgotten: *In the immortal words of James Brown, "I feel good!"* **2** living or continuing forever: *Christians believe that the soul is immortal.* —**immortal** *n.* [C]

im·mor·tal·i·ty /ˌɪmɔrˈtæləti/ n. [U] the state of living forever or being remembered forever

im·mor·tal·ize /ɪˈmɔrtlˌaɪz/ v. [T usually passive] to make someone or something famous for a long time, especially by writing about them, painting a picture of them etc.: *The Choptank is the river immortalized in James Michener's novel "Chesapeake."*

im·mov·a·ble /ɪˈmuvəbəl/ adj. **1** impossible to move: *Always lock your bicycle to something immovable like a railing.* **2** impossible to change or persuade: *Wilson refused their offer with immovable firmness.*

im·mune /ɪˈmyun/ adj. **1** someone who is immune to a particular disease cannot be affected or harmed by it: [+ to] *Some people are immune to the virus.* **2** not affected by something such as criticism, bad treatment etc.: [+ to] *The dictatorship seems immune to economic pressures.* **3** specially protected from something bad: [+ from] *The governor is popular, but not immune from criticism.*

immune sys·tem /.ˈ. ˌ../ n. [C usually singular] the system by which your body protects itself against disease

im·mu·ni·ty /ɪˈmyunəti/ n. [U] **1** the state or right of being protected from laws or bad things: *Both men were granted immunity* (=given immunity) *from prosecution.* **2** the state of being immune to a disease: *The patient's immunity is low.* | [+ to] *Babies fed on breast milk have more immunity to infection.*

im·mu·nize /ˈɪmyəˌnaɪz/ v. [T] to protect someone from a particular disease by giving them a VACCINE: [immunize sb against sth] *The money will be spent on immunizing children against measles.* —**immunization** /ˌɪmyənəˈzeɪʃən/ n. [C,U] —compare INOCULATE, VACCINATE

im·mu·no·de·fi·cien·cy /ˌɪmyənoʊdɪˈfɪʃənsi, ˌɪmyə-noʊ-/ n. [U] TECHNICAL a medical condition in which your body is unable to fight infection in the usual way —**immunodeficient** adj.

im·mu·nol·o·gy /ˌɪmyəˈnɑlədʒi/ n. [U] the scientific study of the prevention of disease and how the body reacts to disease

im·mu·ta·ble /ɪˈmyutəbəl/ adj. FORMAL never changing or impossible to change: *an immutable fact* —**immutability** /ɪˌmyutəˈbɪləti/ n. [U]

imp /ɪmp/ n. [C] OLD-FASHIONED **1** a child who behaves badly, but in a way that is funny **2** a small creature in stories, who has magic powers and behaves very badly —see also IMPISH

im·pact¹ /ˈɪmpækt/ n. **1** [C] the effect or influence that an event, situation etc. has on someone or something: *The change in leadership will have a huge impact on government policy.* | *Logging companies must prepare an environmental impact report.* **2** [C,U] the force of one object hitting another: *The aircraft was traveling at about 155 mph before impact.* **3 on impact** at the moment when one things hits another: *Their car burst into flames on impact.*

im·pact² /ɪmˈpækt/ v. **1** [I,T] to have an important or noticeable effect on someone or something: *It's still unclear how the new law will impact health care.* | [+ on] *How will this impact on our profits?* **2** FORMAL to hit something with a lot of force: *In September a second Luna spacecraft impacted on the near side of the moon.*

im·pact·ed /ɪmˈpæktɪd/ adj. a tooth that is impacted is growing under another tooth so that it cannot develop correctly

im·pair /ɪmˈpɛr/ v. [T] to damage something or make it not as good as it should be: *The amount of alcohol he had drunk seriously impaired his ability to drive.*

im·paired /ɪmˈpɛrd/ adj. **1** damaged, less strong, or not as good as it should be: *impaired vision* **2 hearing/visually/speech etc. impaired** someone who is hearing impaired, VISUALly impaired etc. cannot hear, see etc. well

im·pair·ment /ɪmˈpɛrmənt/ n. [C,U] **1 mental/hearing/ visual etc. impairment** a condition in which a part of a person's mind or body is damaged or does not work well **2** the condition of being damaged, or weaker or worse than usual: *The changes resulted in an impairment of the firm's ability to borrow money.*

---

im·pa·la /ɪmˈpælə, -ˈpɑ-/ n. [C] a large brown graceful African animal; ANTELOPE

im·pale /ɪmˈpeɪl/ v. [T often passive] if someone or something is impaled, a sharp pointed object goes through them: [+ on] *Evans was almost impaled on a spear as he slid into the hole.*

im·pal·pa·ble /ɪmˈpælpəbəl/ adj. FORMAL **1** impossible to touch or feel physically —opposite PALPABLE (2) **2** very difficult to understand

im·pan·el /ɪmˈpænl/ also **empanel** v. [T] to choose the people to serve on a JURY: *A new grand jury is to be impaneled Wednesday.*

im·part /ɪmˈpɑrt/ v. [T] FORMAL **1** to give a particular quality to something: [impart sth to sth] *French oak barrels impart a slight nut-like flavor to this chardonnay.* **2** to give information, knowledge, wisdom etc. to someone: [impart sth to sb] *The class teaches parents how to impart values to their children.*

im·par·tial /ɪmˈpɑrʃəl/ adj. not giving special FAVOR¹ (2) or support to any one person or group; FAIR: *The bureau provides impartial advice.* | *an impartial judge* —**impartiality** /ɪmˌpɑrʃiˈæləti/ n. [U] —**impartially** /ɪmˈpɑrʃəli/ adv.

im·pass·a·ble /ɪmˈpæsəbəl/ adj. impossible to travel along or through: *The flooding made many streets impassable Sunday.*

im·passe /ˈɪmpæs/ n. [C usually singular] a situation in which it is impossible to continue with a discussion or plan because the people involved cannot agree: *The two groups have reached an impasse in their talks.*

im·pas·sioned /ɪmˈpæʃənd/ adj. full of strong feeling and emotion: *an impassioned speech*

im·pas·sive /ɪmˈpæsɪv/ adj. not showing or feeling any emotions: *Ramirez's face was impassive as the judge spoke.* —**impassively** adv. —**impassivity** /ˌɪmpæˈsɪvəti/ n. [U]

im·pa·tience /ɪmˈpeɪʃəns/ n. [U] **1** annoyance at having to accept delays, other people's weaknesses etc.: [+ with] *There is growing impatience with delays in court and long trials.* **2** great eagerness for something to happen, especially something that is going to happen soon: [impatience to do sth] *Some troops expressed impatience to get home.*

im·pa·tiens /ɪmˈpeɪʃəns/ n. plural **impatiens** [C,U] a garden plant with brightly colored flowers

im·pa·tient /ɪmˈpeɪʃənt/ adj. **1** annoyed because of delays, someone else's mistakes etc.: *Roy gets impatient when people drive too slow in front of him.* | [+ with] *Citizens are growing impatient with the slow pace of reform.* **2** very eager for something to happen and not wanting to wait: [be impatient to do sth] *Trent was hungry and impatient to sit down to lunch.* | [+ for] *Business groups are impatient for change.* —**impatiently** adv.

im·peach /ɪmˈpitʃ/ v. [T] LAW **1** if a government official is impeached, they are formally ACCUSED of a serious crime in a special government court: *The governor was impeached for using state funds improperly.* **2** FORMAL if you impeach someone's honesty, you say that you think they are not telling the truth —**impeachment** n. [U]

im·pec·ca·ble /ɪmˈpɛkəbəl/ adj. completely perfect and impossible to criticize: *Audrey has impeccable taste in clothes.* —**impeccably** adv.

im·pe·cu·ni·ous /ˌɪmpɪˈkyuniəs/ adj. FORMAL OR HUMOROUS having very little money, especially over a long period of time: *a gifted but impecunious painter*

im·pe·dance /ɪmˈpidns/ n. [singular,U] TECHNICAL a measure of the power of a piece of electrical equipment to stop the flow of an ALTERNATING CURRENT

im·pede /ɪmˈpid/ v. [T] FORMAL to make it difficult for someone or something to make progress: *Rescue attempts were impeded by the storm.*

im·ped·i·ment /ɪmˈpɛdəmənt/ n. [C] **1** a fact or event that makes it difficult or impossible for someone or something to succeed or make progress: [+ to]

The country's debt has been an impediment to development. **2** a physical problem that makes speaking, hearing, or moving difficult: *a speech impediment*

im·ped·i·men·ta /ɪmˌpɛdəˈmɛntə/ *n.* [plural] FORMAL things that you think you need to have or do, but which can slow your progress

im·pel /ɪmˈpɛl/ *v.* [T] FORMAL to make you feel very strongly that you must do something: [**impel sb to do sth**] *Children feel impelled to fit in at school.* —compare COMPEL

im·pend·ing /ɪmˈpɛndɪŋ/ *adj.* likely to happen soon: *She met with her husband to discuss their impending divorce.*

im·pen·e·tra·ble /ɪmˈpɛnətrəbəl/ *adj.* **1** impossible to get through, see through, or get into: *An impenetrable fog halted traffic.* **2** very difficult or impossible to understand: *an impenetrable 25-page memo*

im·pen·i·tent /ɪmˈpɛnətənt/ *adj.* FORMAL not feeling sorry for something bad or wrong that you have done —**impenitence** *n.* [U]

im·per·a·tive[1] /ɪmˈpɛrətɪv/ *adj.* **1** extremely important, necessary, and urgent: [**it is imperative that**] *It's imperative that you leave immediately.* | [**it is imperative (for sb) to do sth**] *It is even more imperative to keep good records.* **2** TECHNICAL an imperative verb expresses a command, for example "Stand up!"

imperative[2] *n.* [C] **1** something that must be done urgently: *Reducing air pollution has become an imperative.* **2** TECHNICAL the form of a verb that expresses a command. In the sentence "Do it now!" the verb "do" is in the imperative —compare INDICATIVE[2], SUBJUNCTIVE **3** FORMAL an idea, belief, or emotion that strongly influences people to behave in a particular way: *Having children is a biological imperative.*

im·per·cep·ti·ble /ˌɪmpɚˈsɛptəbəl/ *adj.* impossible to see or notice: *an almost imperceptible earthquake* —**imperceptibly** *adv.*

im·per·fect[1] /ɪmˈpɚfɪkt/ *adj.* not completely perfect: *The conversation was limited by my imperfect Spanish.* | *Democracy, no matter how imperfect, is still the best method of government.* —**imperfectly** *adv.*

imperfect[2] *n.* TECHNICAL **the imperfect** also **the imperfect tense** the form of a verb that shows an incomplete action in the past, that is formed with "be" and the PAST PARTICIPLE. In the sentence "We were walking down the road," the phrase "were walking" is in the imperfect

im·per·fec·tion /ˌɪmpɚˈfɛkʃən/ *n.* [C,U] the state of being imperfect, or something that is imperfect: *human imperfection* | *There are slight imperfections in the cloth.*

im·pe·ri·al /ɪmˈpɪriəl/ *adj.* **1** relating to an EMPIRE or to the person who rules it: *History is full of attempts at imperial domination.* | *the imperial jewels* **2** [only before noun] relating to the British Imperial System of weights and measurements

im·pe·ri·al·ism /ɪmˈpɪriəˌlɪzəm/ *n.* [U] **1** a political system in which one country rules a lot of other countries **2** the desire of one country to rule or control other countries **3** DISAPPROVING methods by which a rich or powerful country can influence poorer countries or get political or trade advantages over them: *Small nations resent Western cultural imperialism.* —compare COLONIALISM —**imperialist**, **imperialistic** /ɪmˌpɪriəˈlɪstɪk/ *adj.* —**imperialist** *n.* —compare COLONIALISM

im·per·il /ɪmˈpɛrəl/ *v.* FORMAL [T] to put something or someone in danger: *Putting off the surgery would imperil the girl's life.*

im·pe·ri·ous /ɪmˈpɪriəs/ *adj.* giving orders and expecting to be obeyed, in a way that seems too proud: *His manner was abrupt and imperious.* —**imperiously** *adv.*

im·per·ish·a·ble /ɪmˈpɛrɪʃəbəl/ *adj.* FORMAL existing or continuing to be in good condition for a long time or forever

im·per·ma·nent /ɪmˈpɚmənənt/ *adj.* FORMAL not staying the same forever; TEMPORARY: *Buddhism stresses that life is impermanent and full of suffering.* —**impermanence** *n.* [U]

im·per·me·a·ble /ɪmˈpɚmiəbəl/ *adj.* TECHNICAL not allowing something, especially a liquid or gas, to pass through: *The layer of clay acts as an impermeable barrier against some chemicals.*

im·per·mis·si·ble /ˌɪmpɚˈmɪsəbəl/ *adj.* FORMAL not allowable: *The conduct of the officers in this case was impermissible.*

im·per·son·al /ɪmˈpɚsənəl/ *adj.* **1** not showing any feelings of sympathy, friendliness etc.: *Just signing your name on a Christmas card seems too impersonal.* **2** a place or situation that is impersonal does not make people feel that they are important: *The Church has been criticized for being too big and impersonal.* **3** TECHNICAL an impersonal sentence or verb is one where the subject is represented by a word such as "it," as in the sentence "It rained all day." —**impersonally** *adv.* —compare PERSONAL

im·per·so·nate /ɪmˈpɚsəˌneɪt/ *v.* [T] **1** to pretend to be someone else by copying their appearance, voice etc., in order to deceive people: *Daniels faces charges of impersonating a Navy officer.* **2** to copy someone's voice and behavior, especially to make people laugh: *Little became very famous impersonating President Nixon.* —**impersonation** /ɪmˌpɚsəˈneɪʃən/ *n.* [C,U]

im·per·son·at·or /ɪmˈpɚsəˌneɪtɚ/ *n.* [C] someone who copies the way that other people look, speak, and behave, as part of a performance or to deceive people

im·per·ti·nent /ɪmˈpɚtn̩-ənt/ *adj.* impolite and not respectful, especially to someone who is older or more important: *an impertinent child* | *impertinent questions* —**impertinence** *n.* [U]

im·per·turb·a·ble /ˌɪmpɚˈtɚbəbəl/ *adj.* remaining calm and unworried in spite of problems or difficulties: *Tom responded to the crisis in a steady, imperturbable manner.* —**imperturbably** *adv.*

im·per·vi·ous /ɪmˈpɚviəs/ *adj.* FORMAL **1** not affected or influenced by something and seeming not to notice it: [+ **to**] *The college administration seemed impervious to criticism.* **2** not allowing anything to enter or pass through: [+ **to**] *The brass table top is impervious to liquids.*

im·pe·ti·go /ˌɪmpəˈtigoʊ, -ˈtaɪgoʊ/ *n.* [U] an infectious skin disease

im·pet·u·ous /ɪmˈpɛtʃuəs/ *adj.* tending to do things very quickly and without thinking carefully first, or showing this quality: *Williams was wild and impetuous.* | *an impetuous decision to get married* —**impetuously** *adv.* —**impetuousness** *n.* [U] —**impetuosity** /ɪmˌpɛtʃuˈɑsəti/ *n.* [U]

im·pe·tus /ˈɪmpətəs/ *n.* [U] **1** an influence that makes something happen, or happen more quickly: [+ **for**] *The Surgeon General has provided the impetus for health prevention programs.* **2** TECHNICAL the force that makes an object start moving, or keeps it moving

im·pi·e·ty /ɪmˈpaɪəti/ *n. plural* **impieties** FORMAL [C,U] lack of respect for religion or God, or an action that shows this

im·pinge /ɪmˈpɪndʒ/ *v.*
   impinge on/upon sb/sth *phr. v.* [T] **1** FORMAL to have an effect, often an unwanted one, on someone or something: *Wilson denied that the helmet law would impinge on motorcyclists' freedom of choice.* **2** TECHNICAL if light, sound etc. impinges on something such as a surface, it hits it —**impingement** *n.* [U]

im·pi·ous /ɪmˈpaɪəs, ˈɪmpiəs/ *adj.* FORMAL lacking respect for religion or God —**impiously** *adv.*

imp·ish /ˈɪmpɪʃ/ *adj.* tending to behave badly, but in a way that is amusing rather than serious or annoying; MISCHIEVOUS: *an impish grin* —**impishly** *adv.*

im·plac·a·ble /ɪmˈplækəbəl/ *adj.* impossible to please and very determined to continue doing something, especially to continue opposing someone or something: *Iraq is one of Israel's most implacable enemies.* —**implacably** *adv.* —**implacability** /ɪmˌplækəˈbɪləti/ *n.* [U]

im·plant[1] /ɪmˈplænt/ v. [T] **1** to put something into someone's body by doing a medical operation: *Dr. DeVries implanted the artificial heart in Clark in 1982.* **2** to influence someone into strongly remembering, believing, or feeling an idea, emotion, or way of behaving: *Most people need to read something several times before it is implanted in their memory.* —**implantation** /ˌɪmplænˈteɪʃən/ n. [U]

im·plant[2] /ˈɪmplænt/ n. [C] something that has been implanted in someone's body in a medical operation: *Some actresses have had their breasts enlarged with implants for career reasons.* —compare TRANSPLANT[2]

im·plau·si·ble /ɪmˈplɔzəbəl/ adj. difficult to believe and not likely to be true: *Miss Harris's experience of healing, however implausible it seems, is common in religious meetings.* —**implausibly** adv. —**implausibility** /ɪmˌplɔzəˈbɪləti/ n. [U]

im·ple·ment[1] /ˈɪmpləˌmɛnt/ v. [T] if you implement a plan, process etc., you begin to make it happen: *Cost-cutting measures have been implemented in most hospitals.*

im·ple·ment[2] /ˈɪmpləmənt/ n. [C] a tool or instrument, especially one used in farming or building: *agricultural implements*

im·ple·men·ta·tion /ˌɪmpləmənˈteɪʃən/ n. [U] the act of implementing a plan, policy etc.

im·pli·cate /ˈɪmpliˌkeɪt/ v. [T] **1** if you implicate someone, you show or claim that they are involved in something wrong or illegal: **[implicate sb in sth]** *The suspect implicated two other men in the robbery.* **2** if something is implicated in something bad or harmful, it is shown to be its cause: **[implicate sth in sth]** *The gene has been implicated in many types of human cancer.*

im·pli·ca·tion /ˌɪmpliˈkeɪʃən/ n. **1** [C usually plural] a possible future effect or result of a plan, action, or event: **[+ of]** *What are the implications of life existing on other planets?* | *The new admissions policy could have serious implications for ethnic balances on campus.* **2** [C,U] something that is not directly said or shown, but that is suggested or understood: **[+ that]** *The implication that "time" meant "a long time" was clearly understood by patients.* | *The airline is among the youngest – and by implication the safest – in the air.* **3** [U] a situation in which it is shown or claimed that someone or something is involved in something wrong, illegal, or dangerous: **[+ of]** *Sales of butter have declined since the implication of fat in cases of heart disease.* —see also IMPLICATE

im·plic·it /ɪmˈplɪsɪt/ adj. **1** suggested or understood without being stated directly: *Levy's statement could be understood as an implicit admission of guilt.* | **[+ in]** *Implicit in the article is the message that single mothers are responsible for poverty.* —compare EXPLICIT **2 be implicit in sth** FORMAL to be a central part of something without being stated: *Risk is implicit in owning a business.* **3 implicit trust/faith** trust etc. that is complete and contains no doubts —**implicitly** adv.

im·plode /ɪmˈploʊd/ v. [I,T] to explode toward the inside, or to make something do this: *The jet's engine may have imploded.* —**implosion** /ɪmˈploʊʒən/ n. [C,U] —compare EXPLODE (1)

im·plore /ɪmˈplɔr/ v. [T] FORMAL to ask for something in an emotional way; BEG (1): **[implore sb to do sth]** *The human rights organization implored both groups to end the violence.*

im·ply /ɪmˈplaɪ/ v. past tense and past participle **implied** [T] **1** to suggest that something is true without saying or showing it directly: *an implied threat* | **[imply (that)]** *The salesmen only implied that the cars were safe.* | *Many prisoners' arms and legs have been broken, implying torture.* | *The wildlife refuge, as the name implies, is a peaceful natural area full of animals.* —compare INFER —see Usage Note at INFER **2** if a principle, action, idea etc. implies something, it makes other actions or conditions necessary: *Free trade implies shared values.*

im·po·lite /ˌɪmpəˈlaɪt/ adj. not polite; RUDE: *It is impolite not to eat what you are served at a dinner party.* —**impolitely** adv.

im·pol·i·tic /ɪmˈpɑləˌtɪk/ adj. FORMAL not sensible or not behaving in a way that is likely to bring you advantage: *an impolitic remark about people "deserving" AIDS*

im·pon·der·a·ble /ɪmˈpɑndərəbəl/ adj. FORMAL something that is imponderable cannot be exactly measured, judged, or calculated —**imponderable** n. [C usually plural]

im·port[1] /ˈɪmpɔrt/ n. **1** [C,U] the action or business of bringing goods into one country from another to be sold: *Oil imports have risen recently.* | **[+ of]** *The U.S. banned the import of African elephant ivory in 1989.* —opposite EXPORT[1] **2** [C] something that is brought into one country from another in order to be sold, especially a car: *California small-car buyers tend to buy imports.* **3** [U] FORMAL importance or meaning: *a matter of little import*

im·port[2] /ɪmˈpɔrt/ v. [T] **1** to bring something into a country from abroad in order to sell it: *Wood for the project will be imported from China.* **2** TECHNICAL to move computer information from one computer to the one you are working on, or from one computer DOCUMENT to the document you are working on —opposite EXPORT[2]

im·por·tance /ɪmˈpɔrtns, -pɔrtns/ n. [U] **1** the quality of being important: **[+ of]** *His story illustrates the importance of staying in school.* | *The government attaches great importance to human rights.* | *This is an issue of great importance to everyone in the region.* **2** the reason why something is important: *Explain the importance of the Monroe Doctrine in a 750-word essay.*

im·por·tant /ɪmˈpɔrtnt/ adj. **1** having a big effect or influence on people or events, or having a lot of value or meaning to someone or something: *She asked some important questions.* | *an important meeting* | **[+ for]** *Regular exercise is important for everyone.* | **[+ to]** *Money and possessions aren't very important to me.* | **[it is important (for sb) to do sth]** *It is important to tell your children that you are proud of them.* | **[it is important that sb/sth do sth]** *It's important that the community sees their tax dollars at work.* **2** having a lot of power or influence: *a very important customer* | *J. S. Bach is the most important Baroque composer.* —opposite UNIMPORTANT

im·por·tant·ly /ɪmˈpɔrtntli/ adv. **1 more/equally/less etc. importantly** [sentence adverb] used to show that the next statement or question is more, equally etc. important than what you said before it: *I enjoy my job, but more importantly, it pays the bills.* **2** in a way that shows you think that what you are saying or doing is important: *She walked importantly into the boss's office.*

im·por·ta·tion /ˌɪmpɔrˈteɪʃən/ n. **1** [U] the process of bringing goods into one country from another to be sold: *A 1930 U.S. law forbids importation of items made in prisons.* **2** [U] the act of bringing into a country something new or different such as a new plant, custom, or idea: *In the 9th century, the importation of ideas from Iran and India was enriched by original scholarship.* **3** [C] something that is brought into a country in this way

import du·ty /ˈ.. ˌ../ n. plural import duties [C,U] a tax on goods that are brought into one country from another country

im·port·er /ɪmˈpɔrtə/ n. [C] a person, company, or country that buys goods from another country, to be sold or used in their own country —compare EXPORTER

import li·cense /ˈ.. ˌ../ n. [C] a document that gives permission for goods to be brought into one country from another country

im·por·tu·nate /ɪmˈpɔrtʃənɪt, -tyunɪt/ adj. FORMAL continuously asking for things in an annoying or unreasonable way —**importunity** /ˌɪmpɔrˈtunəti/ n. [U]

im·por·tune /ˌɪmpɚˈtun/ v. [T] FORMAL to ask some-one for something continuously, especially in an annoying or unreasonable way; BEG

im·pose /ɪmˈpouz/ v. **1** [T] if you impose a rule, tax, punishment etc., you force people to accept it: *Thousands of troops were sent to the region to impose order before the election.* | [**impose sth on sb**] *Many countries imposed economic sanctions on South Africa during apartheid.* **2** [T] to force someone to have the same ideas, beliefs etc. as you: [**impose sth on sb**] *Churches are not allowed to impose their beliefs on people, but they are allowed to practice their faith freely.* **3** [I] to expect or ask someone to do something for you when this is not convenient for them: *No, we'll find a motel – we don't want to impose.* | [**+ on/upon**] *I'm sorry if I imposed on you.* **4 impose a burden/hardship etc. (on/upon sb/sth)** to have a bad effect on someone or something by causing them problems: *A higher sales tax would impose an unfair burden on poorer Americans.*

im·pos·ing /ɪmˈpouzɪŋ/ adj. large, important-looking, and impressive: *an imposing building*

im·po·si·tion /ˌɪmpəˈzɪʃən/ n. **1** [U] the introduction of something such as a rule, tax, or punishment: *the imposition of martial law* **2** [C usually singular] something that someone expects or asks you to do for them, when this is not convenient for you: *Some professors seem to feel that teaching is an imposition keeping them from their research.*

im·pos·si·ble[1] /ɪmˈpɑsəbəl/ adj. **1** not able to be done or to happen: *Many fear that peace is now impossible.* | *an impossible task* | [**it is impossible (for sb) to do sth**] *Pavarotti's sore throat made it impossible for him to sing.* | *The reading assignment put **impossible demands** (=demands for something that is not possible) on the young students.* **2** an impossible situation is extremely difficult to deal with: *Sometimes an abortion seems like the only way out of an impossible situation.* **3** behaving in unreasonable and annoying way: *You're impossible!* **4 an impossible dream** something that you hope for that is not likely to happen —**impossibility** /ɪmˌpɑsəˈbɪləti/ n. [C,U]

impossible[2] n. **the impossible** something that cannot be easily done: *We're asking our goalies to **do the impossible**, by making up for the poor playing of the rest of the team.*

im·pos·si·bly /ɪmˈpɑsəbli/ adv. [+ adj./adv.] extremely, in a way that is difficult to believe: *The French fashions were impossibly expensive.*

im·pos·tor, imposter /ɪmˈpɑstɚ/ n. [C] someone who pretends to be someone else in order to trick people: *The President had a telephone conversation with an impostor claiming to be Iran's president.*

im·pos·ture /ɪmˈpɑstʃɚ/ n. [U] FORMAL a situation in which someone tricks people by pretending to be someone else

im·po·tent /ˈɪmpətənt/ adj. **1** a man who is impotent is unable to have sex because he cannot get an ERECTION **2** unable to take effective action because you do not have enough power, strength, or control: *The U.S. seems impotent to influence events in the region.* —**impotently** adv. —**impotence** n. [U]

im·pound /ɪmˈpaʊnd/ v. [T] LAW if the police or a court of law impounds your possessions, they take them because you have broken a rule or law: *After the rally several bikes were impounded by police.*

im·pov·er·ish /ɪmˈpɑvərɪʃ/ v. [T] **1** [often passive] to make someone very poor: *Many patients worry that paying for treatments will impoverish them.* **2** to make something worse in quality: *Crop rotation has not impoverished the soil.* —**impoverishment** n. [U]

im·pov·er·ished /ɪmˈpɑvərɪʃt/ adj. **1** very poor: *an impoverished student* | *Brazil's impoverished northeast region* **2** worse in quality: *Our lives would be impoverished without music.*

im·prac·ti·ca·ble /ɪmˈpræktɪkəbəl/ adj. FORMAL impossible to do: *Thatcher called the plan for a single European currency impracticable.*

im·prac·ti·cal /ɪmˈpræktɪkəl/ adj. **1** an impractical plan, suggestion etc. is not sensible because it would be too difficult, too expensive etc.: *Ritter plans to tear down the building, saying restoration would be impractical.* **2** not useful, or not appropriate for a particular situation: *Short skirts are impractical if you want to sit down once in awhile.* **3** not good at dealing with ordinary practical matters —**impracticality** /ɪmˌpræktɪˈkæləti/ n. [C,U]

im·pre·ca·tion /ˌɪmprɪˈkeɪʃən/ n. [C] FORMAL an offensive word or phrase that you say when you are very angry, or the act of saying this to someone; a CURSE

im·pre·cise /ˌɪmprɪˈsaɪs/ adj. not exact: *imprecise estimates* | *His use of language is vague and imprecise.* —**imprecision** /ˌɪmprɪˈsɪʒən/ n. [U]

im·preg·na·ble /ɪmˈprɛgnəbəl/ adj. **1** very strong and unable to be broken through, entered, or defeated: *an impregnable fortress* **2** FORMAL impregnable attitudes, opinions etc. cannot be changed, influenced, or shown to be wrong

im·preg·nate /ɪmˈprɛgˌneɪt/ v. [T] **1** to make a woman or female animal PREGNANT **2** to make a substance spread completely through something, or to spread completely through something: [**+ with**] *The insulation is impregnated with insect repellent.*

im·pre·sa·ri·o /ˌɪmprəˈsɑrioʊ/ n. [C] someone who organizes performances in OPERA HOUSES, concert halls etc.

im·press[1] /ɪmˈprɛs/ v. [T] **1** [not in progressive] to affect someone, especially by making them feel admiration and respect for you: *You don't need to make fancy foods to impress guests – something simple but good will do.* | *He always impressed us as being very bright.* **2** to make the importance of something clear to someone: [**impress sth on/upon sb**] *The idea is to impress the importance of nature upon children early in life.* **3** to press something into or onto a surface, especially a soft surface, in order to make a mark or pattern

im·press[2] /ˈɪmprɛs/ n. [C] FORMAL OR LITERARY a mark or pattern made by pressing something into a surface

im·pressed /ɪmˈprɛst/ adj. feeling admiration and respect for someone or something: [**be impressed by/with**] *Dimas was impressed with the students' knowledge and insight.* | *The whole group was favorably impressed by the friendliness of the people.*

im·pres·sion /ɪmˈprɛʃən/ n. [C] **1** the opinion, belief, or feeling you have about someone or something because of the way they seem: [**+ of**] *My impression of Hal was that he was a solid, professional guy.* | *It's easy to get the impression that wine has to be expensive to be worth drinking.* | *It's important to make a good impression at your interview.* | *My first impression (=my opinion when I first saw something) was that the car was fun to drive.* **2 be under the impression that...** to believe that something is true, especially when it is not true: *People are under the impression that eating this plant can cause death.* **3** the act of copying the speech or behavior of a famous person in order to make people laugh: [**+ of**] *Sandy does a pretty good impression of Madonna.* **4** a mark left by pressing something into a soft surface: *An impression of a heel was left in the mud.* **5** all the copies of a book printed at one time —compare EDITION

im·pres·sion·a·ble /ɪmˈprɛʃənəbəl/ adj. easy to influence, especially because you are young: *What kind of impact will this movie have on impressionable kids?*

im·pres·sion·ism /ɪmˈprɛʃəˌnɪzəm/ n. [U] **1** a style of painting used especially in France in the 19th century, which uses color instead of details of form to produce effects of light or feeling **2** a style of music or literature from the late 19th and early 20th centuries that emphasizes feelings and images —**impressionist** adj.: *impressionist painters*

im·pres·sion·ist /ɪmˈprɛʃənɪst/ n. [C] **1** someone who uses impressionism in the paintings, music, or literature that they produce **2** someone who copies the speech or behavior of famous people in order to entertain other people

im·pres·sion·is·tic /ɪm,preʃəˈnɪstɪk/ *adj.* based on a general feeling of what something is like, rather than on specific facts or details: *The show is an impressionistic look at the sights and sounds of America.*

im·pres·sive /ɪmˈpresɪv/ *adj.* something that is impressive makes you admire it because it is very good, large, important etc.: *The Bruins have been impressive in their last five games.* | *Lexi was an impressive dramatic actress.* —**impressively** *adv.* —**impressiveness** *n.* [U]

im·pri·ma·tur /,ɪmprəˈmeɪtʊr, ɪmˈprɪməˌtʊr/ *n.* [singular] **1** approval of something, especially from an important person: *The New England Journal of Medicine put its imprimatur on the two studies.* **2** official permission to print a book, especially when this is given by the Catholic Church

im·print¹ /ˈɪmˌprɪnt/ *n.* [C] **1** the mark left by an object being pressed into or onto something: [+ of] *a rock with a fossil imprint of algae* **2** an effect or influence that something has on a place, person, event etc.: [+ on] *Simmons wants to put his own imprint on the firm.* **3** TECHNICAL the name of a PUBLISHER as it appears on a book: *This dictionary is published under the Longman imprint.*

im·print² /ɪmˈprɪnt, ˈɪmˌprɪnt/ *v.* **1** [T usually passive] to print or press the mark of an object on something: [**imprint sth with sth**] *The golf balls are imprinted with Nixon's signature.* | [**imprint sth on sth**] *Deep purple bruises were imprinted on her neck.* **2 be imprinted on your mind/memory** if something is imprinted on your mind or memory, you can never forget it: *The image of Helen's sad face was imprinted on his mind.*

im·pris·on /ɪmˈprɪzən/ *v.* [T] **1** to put someone in prison, or to keep them somewhere and prevent them from leaving: *If convicted she will be imprisoned for at least six years.* **2** if a situation or feeling imprisons people, it restricts what they can do: *Many elderly people felt imprisoned in their own homes.*

im·pris·on·ment /ɪmˈprɪzənmənt/ *n.* [U] the state of being in prison, or the time someone spends there: *Corelli could face life imprisonment* (=imprisonment for the rest of his life).

im·prob·a·ble /ɪmˈprɑbəbəl/ *adj.* **1** not likely to happen or be true: *It is highly improbable that mining would be allowed in the national parks.* **2** surprising and slightly strange: *The ladies were dressed in improbable combinations of colors.* —**improbably** *adv.* —**improbability** /ɪm,prɑbəˈbɪləti/ *n.* [C,U]

im·promp·tu /ɪmˈprɑmptu/ *adj.* done or said without any preparation or planning: *an impromptu performance* —**impromptu** *adv.*

im·prop·er /ɪmˈprɑpə/ *adj.* **1** unacceptable according to professional, moral, or social standards of behavior: *Displaying alcohol ads at the conference was improper, in my opinion.* | [**it is improper (for sb) to do sth**] *It would be improper for me to discuss the case at this point.* **2** illegal or dishonest: *It was a mistake, not an effort to seek improper financial gain.* **3** not correct according to certain rules: *Many cases of stomach flu result from improper cooking of food.* —**improperly** *adv.*

improper frac·tion /,.. '../ *n.* [C] TECHNICAL a FRACTION such as 107/8, in which the top number is larger than the bottom number —compare PROPER FRACTION

im·pro·pri·e·ty /,ɪmprəˈpraɪəti/ *n.* *plural* **improprieties** [C,U] FORMAL behavior or an action that is unacceptable according to moral, social, or professional standards: *Smith has denied any sexual impropriety with his former employees.*

im·prove /ɪmˈpruv/ *v.* [I,T] to become better, or to make something or yourself better: *Changes will be made if the situation doesn't improve.* | *Let's hope the weather improves before Saturday.* | [**improve sth**] *Lifting weights will improve your muscle strength.* | *The government hopes to improve relations with the West.*

improve on/ upon sth *phr. v.* [T] to do something

better than before, or to make it better than before: *Lemson wants to improve on last year's third-place finish.* —see Usage Note at RAISE¹

im·proved /ɪmˈpruvd/ *adj.* better than before: *They're the most improved team in the league.* | *a detergent with a new improved formula*

im·prove·ment /ɪmˈpruvmənt/ *n.* **1** [C,U] an act of improving or a state of being improved: [+ in] *There has been much improvement in air quality.* | [+ to] *At least $2 million is needed for improvements to the arena.* | *His condition has shown some improvement.* | *The campus looks better, but there's still room for improvement* (=the need for more improvement). **2** [C] a change or addition that improves something: *home improvements* **3 be an improvement over/on sth** to be better than something similar that existed before: *The new version of the software is a big improvement over the old one.*

im·prov·i·dent /ɪmˈprɑvədənt/ *adj.* FORMAL too careless to save any money or to plan for the future

im·pro·vise /ˈɪmprəˌvaɪz/ *v.* [I,T] **1** to do something without any preparation, especially because you are forced to do this by unexpected events: *I left my lesson plans at home, so I'll have to improvise.* **2** to make something using whatever you can find, because you do not have the equipment or materials that you need: *Use these recipes as a guideline, but feel free to improvise!* | *Kids were improvising games with a ball and some string.* **3** to perform music, sing etc. from your imagination, without preparing first: *Jazz musicians are good at improvising.* | *Robin Williams likes to improvise his comedy.* —**improvisation** /ɪm,prɑvəˈzeɪʃən/ *n.* [C,U]

im·pru·dent /ɪmˈprudnt/ *adj.* FORMAL not sensible or wise: *Banks are suffering the results of imprudent lending policies.* —**imprudence** *n.* [C,U]

im·pu·dent /ˈɪmpyədənt/ *adj.* impolite and not showing respect: *an impudent child* —**impudence** *n.* [U]

im·pugn /ɪmˈpyun/ *v.* [T] FORMAL to attack someone's honesty, courage, ability etc. or express doubts about them: *Gerlick has filed a complaint impugning the judge's integrity.*

im·pulse /ˈɪmpʌls/ *n.* **1** [C,U] a sudden strong desire to do something without thinking about the results: [**an impulse to do sth**] *The impulse to blame someone else is strong.* | *The bill will prevent people from buying and using a gun on impulse.* | *Last-minute shopping results in impulse buying* (=buying things without planning or choosing carefully). **2** [C] TECHNICAL a short electrical signal sent in one direction along a wire or nerve, or through the air **3** [C] a reason, feeling, or aim that causes a particular kind of activity or behavior: *The impulse of government all over the world is to control information.*

im·pul·sive /ɪmˈpʌlsɪv/ *adj.* tending to do things without thinking about the results, or showing this quality: *an impulsive decision* | *These children tend to be impulsive and restless.* —**impulsively** *adv.* —**impulsiveness** *n.* [U]

im·pu·ni·ty /ɪmˈpyunəti/ *n.* **with impunity** without punishment or risk of punishment: *People are more likely to steal if they see others breaking the law with impunity.*

im·pure /ɪmˈpyʊr/ *adj.* **1** mixed with other substances: *impure drugs* —opposite PURE (1) **2** OLD-FASHIONED morally bad, especially when relating to sex —opposite PURE (6)

im·pu·ri·ty /ɪmˈpyʊrəti/ *n.* *plural* **impurities 1** [C usually plural] a part of an almost pure substance that is of a lower quality: *All natural minerals contain impurities.* **2** [U] the state of being impure

im·pute /ɪmˈpyut/ *v.* [T] FORMAL if you impute a quality, blame, power etc. to someone or something, you say that they are responsible for it or that they have it: [**impute sth to sb/sth**] *The improper conduct of the company must be imputed to the top officials.* —**imputation** /,ɪmpyəˈteɪʃən/ *n.* [C,U]

IN the written abbreviation of Indiana

S W 1 1 **in¹** /ɪn/ prep. **1** used with the name of a container, place, or area to show where something is: *The scissors are in the top drawer.* | *I was still in bed at 11:30.* | *Bob's out working in the yard.* | *There's a hole in my sock.* | *He lived in Boston for four years.* | *Grandpa's in the hospital.* **2** from the outside to the inside of a container, a building etc.; into: *She went in the house.* | *Put your clothes in the closet.* **3** happening in a particular month, year, season etc.: *We bought our car in April.* | *In 1969 the first astronauts landed on the moon.* | *We use the furnace all the time in the winter.* **4** during a period of time: *We finished the whole project in a week.* **5** at the end of a period of time: *Gerry should be home in an hour.* | *I wonder if they'll still be married in a year.* **6** included as part of something: *One of the guys in the story is a doctor.* | *In the first part of the speech he talked about the environment.* **7** experiencing a particular state or situation: *I can't talk now. I'm kind of in a hurry.* | *You're in big trouble.* **8** taking part in a situation, activity, or organization: *I spent three years in the marching band.* | *He died in the war.* **9 sb has not done sth in years/months/weeks etc.** if you have not done something in years, months etc., you have not done it for that amount of time: *I haven't talked to him in months.* **10** using a particular kind of voice or way of speaking, writing, making art etc.: *Roger spoke in a low whisper.* | *I had to speak to him in French.* | *Do not write in pen on this test.* | *His early comedies were filmed in black and white.* **11** working at a particular type of job: *Wendy's in advertising.* **12** used to show what person or thing has the quality you are mentioning: *There's a hint of fall in the air.* | *She's everything I'd want in a wife.* **13** arranged in a particular way, often to form a particular shape or group: *Everybody stand against the wall in a straight line.* | *He made a bowl in the shape of a heart.* | *Put the files in alphabetical order.* **14** wearing a particular color or piece of clothing: *She was dressed in black.* | *He looked very handsome in his uniform.* **15** used to show the connection or relationship between two ideas or subjects: *That dessert looks awfully high in calories.* | *an expert in nuclear physics* | *strong growth in exports* **16** with a particular color: *The china is trimmed in blue.* **17** used before numbers or amounts to say how many people or things are involved with something: *Mourners lined the streets in the thousands to pay their respects.* **18 be in your 20s/30s/40s etc.** to be between the ages of 20 and 29, 30 and 39 etc.: *I'd say she's in her mid 40s.* **19** used before the bigger number when you are talking about a relationship between two numbers: *One in every ten children now suffers from asthma.* **20 in shock/horror etc.** used to describe a strong feeling someone has when they do something: *Lily looked at me in shock.* **21 in all** used when giving a total number or amount: *I think there were about 25 of us in all.* **22 in two/half/pieces/thirds etc.** used to say how many pieces something is divided into: *She ripped the sheet of paper in two.* **23 have sth in you** INFORMAL to have a particular quality, feeling, or ability: *The old girl still has a lot of fight in her.* **24 in doing sth** used to say that something else happens at the same time as what you are doing, or as a result of it: *In reading the story, I felt nothing but sympathy for the victims.* —see also **the ins and outs (of sth)** (INS)

S W 1 1 **in²** adv. **1** from the outside to the inside of a container, building etc.: *She pushed the box toward me so that I could put my money in.* | *Should we wait out here, or should we go in?* **2** inside a building, especially the building where you live or work: *Ms. Shaewitz isn't in yet this morning.* | *You're never in when I call.* **3** if a bus, train, airplane etc. gets in or is in, it arrives or has arrived at a station, airport etc.: *What time does his bus get in?* | *Her flight's not in yet.* **4** given or sent to a particular place to be read or looked at: *Your final papers have to be in by Friday.* | *Letters have been pouring in from all over the country.* **5** if you write, paint, or draw something

in, you write it, paint it etc. in the correct place: *Write in your name and address at the bottom.* **6** if someone is in or is voted in, they have been elected to be part of the government: *The Republicans are in now, but for how long?* **7** if you color, paint, fill etc. in a shape or space, you cover the area inside its borders with color, paint etc.: *Can you color in this picture of a teddy bear for me?* **8** if a ball is in during a game, it is inside the area where the game is being played: *Her second serve was just in.* **9** if clothes, colors etc. are in, they are fashionable: *Long hair is in again.* **10 be in for sth** if someone is in for something bad, it is going to happen to them: *She's in for a surprise if she thinks we're going to help her pay for it.* | *You're really in for it now!* (=you are going to be punished) **11 be in on sth** to be involved in something, especially something secret: *The movie asks questions about who was in on the plan to kill Kennedy.* —compare **get** (sb) **in on** sth (GET) **12 in joke** an in joke is one that is only understood by a small group of people **13** if the TIDE comes in or is in, the ocean water moves toward the shore, or is at its highest level **14** if you are in, you agree to take part in a plan, particular job etc.: *We need to make plans for next week, so are you in or out?* **15 sb has (got) it in for sb** INFORMAL if someone has it in for you, they do not like you and want to cause problems or difficulties for you: *I think the P.E. teacher has it in for me.* **16** if something falls or turns in, it falls or turns toward the center: *The map had started to curl in at the edges.* **17 be/get in with sb** INFORMAL to be friendly with someone, or to become friendly with them: *She's in with the theatrical crowd.* **18 in that** FORMAL used before a phrase that gives more information about the limited way in which the rest of the sentence is true: *The new system is similar to the old one in that there is still a strong central government.*

in- /ɪn/ prefix **1** the opposite of something, or the lack of something; not: *insensitive* (=not sensitive) | *inattention* (=lack of attention) —compare UN- —see also IL-, IM-, IR- **2** in or into something: *income* (=money that you receive) | *inward* (=toward the inside) | *to insert something* (=put it in something else) —see also IM-

-in /ɪn/ suffix [in nouns] an activity organized by a group of people as a protest against something: *a sit-in* (=where people sit in a place to prevent its usual activity)

in·a·bil·i·ty /ˌɪnəˈbɪləti/ [singular,U] a lack of the ability, skill etc. to do something: *An inability to concentrate affects these children's schoolwork.*

in ab·sen·tia /ˌɪn æbˈsɛnʃə/ adv. without being present: *The ten men were tried and convicted in absentia.*

in·ac·ces·si·ble /ˌɪnɪkˈsɛsəbəl/ adj. **1** difficult or impossible to reach: *These mountain villages are completely inaccessible in winter.* **2** difficult or impossible to understand or afford: *This textbook would be inaccessible to my students.* —**inaccessibility** /ˌɪnɪkˌsɛsəˈbɪləti/ n. [U]

in·ac·cu·ra·cy /ɪnˈækyərəsi/ n. plural **inaccuracies 1** [C] a mistake: *The ad contained several inaccuracies regarding the computer.* **2** [U] a lack of correctness: *the inaccuracy of a weather forecast*

in·ac·cu·rate /ɪnˈækyərɪt/ adj. **1** not completely correct: *Some of the information provided was inaccurate or incomplete.* **2** not aimed correctly, or not reaching the place aimed for: *an inaccurate pass* —**inaccurately** adv.

in·ac·tion /ɪnˈækʃən/ n. [U] lack of action: *Continued pollution of the lake shows the state government's inaction.*

in·ac·tive /ɪnˈæktɪv/ adj. **1** not doing anything, not working, or not moving: *The fault, which scientists had believed was inactive, caused a 6.5 earthquake.* | *Children whose parents are inactive* (=do not exercise) *are less likely to be active themselves.* | *The virus can be inactive in the body for more than ten years.* **2** not taking part in something or working, especially when you used to take part or usually take part: *Haley was inactive for Saturday's game because of a knee injury.* **3** TECHNICAL an inactive substance does not react chemically with other substances —**inactivity** /ˌɪnæk'tɪvəti/ *n.* [U]

in·ad·e·qua·cy /ɪn'ædəkwəsi/ *n. plural* **inadequacies** **1** [U] the fact of not being good enough in quality, ability, size etc. for a particular purpose: [+ of] *the inadequacy of America's health-care system* **2** [U] the feeling that you are unable to deal with situations because you are not as good as other people: *My father teased me mercilessly to compensate for his own feelings of inadequacy.* **3** [C] something that is not good enough: *Parents were complaining about the school's inadequacies.*

in·ad·e·quate /ɪn'ædəkwɪt/ *adj.* not good enough, big enough, skilled enough etc. for a particular purpose: *An inadequate supply of vitamin A can lead to blindness.* | [+ for] *The highways are inadequate for the number of cars that pass through here.* —**inadequately** *adv.*

in·ad·mis·si·ble /ˌɪnəd'mɪsəbəl/ *adj.* FORMAL not allowed, especially in a court of law: *Lie detector tests are inadmissible in criminal trials.* —**inadmissibility** /ˌɪnədˌmɪsə'bɪləti/ *n.* [U]

in·ad·vert·ent·ly /ˌɪnəd'vət˺ntli/ *adv.* without intending to do something: *The construction crew inadvertently cut through a telephone cable.* —**inadvertent** *adj.*

in·ad·vis·a·ble /ˌɪnəd'vaɪzəbəl/ *adj.* an inadvisable action, decision etc. is not sensible: *Bad weather made the trip inadvisable at this time.*

in·al·ien·a·ble /ɪn'eɪlyənəbəl/ *adj.* FORMAL an inalienable right cannot be taken away from you

in·ane /ɪ'neɪn/ *adj.* extremely stupid or without much meaning: *an inane movie* —**inanity** /ɪ'nænəti/ *n.* [C,U]

in·an·i·mate /ɪn'ænəmɪt/ *adj.* not living: *an inanimate object*

in·ap·pli·ca·ble /ɪn'æplɪkəbəl, ˌɪnə'plɪkəbəl/ *adj.* a description, question, or rule that is inapplicable to a particular situation cannot sensibly be used about it: [+ to] *His model of how disease spreads is inapplicable to the AIDS epidemic.* —**inapplicability** /ɪnˌæplɪkə'bɪləti/ *n.* [U]

in·ap·pro·pri·ate /ˌɪnə'proupriɪt/ *adj.* not appropriate or correct for a particular purpose or situation: *A poster showing a nude woman is wholly inappropriate for the office.* | [be inappropriate (for sb) to do sth] *Vano said it would be inappropriate to comment on the report.* | [+ for] *The movie is inappropriate for children.* —**inappropriately** *adv.*

in·ar·tic·u·late /ˌɪnɑr'tɪkyəlɪt/ *adj.* **1** not able to express yourself or speak clearly: *He is a shy and inarticulate man.* **2** speech that is inarticulate is not clearly expressed or pronounced: *young and inarticulate children*

in·as·much /ˌɪnəz'mʌtʃ/ *adv.* FORMAL **inasmuch as** used to begin a phrase that explains the rest of your sentence by showing the limited way that it is true: *He gave up running for football, a difficult decision inasmuch as he was the 100-meter champion last year.*

in·at·ten·tion /ˌɪnə'tɛnʃən/ *n.* [U] lack of attention: [+ to] *Several workers were fired for inattention to their duties.*

in·at·ten·tive /ˌɪnə'tɛntɪv/ *adj.* not giving enough attention to someone or something: *inattentive students* —**inattentively** *adv.* —**inattentiveness** *n.* [U]

in·au·di·ble /ɪn'ɔdəbəl/ *adj.* if something is inaudible, it is not able to be heard, usually because it is too quiet: *The whistle is inaudible to most humans.* —**inaudibly** *adv.* —**inaudibility** /ɪnˌɔdə'bɪləti/ *n.* [U]

in·au·gu·ral /ɪ'nɔgyərəl/ *adj.* [only before noun] **1** relating to a ceremony that inaugurates a President, governor etc.: *Over 500 people attended the inaugural ball.* | *the governor's inaugural speech* **2** inaugural game/show/flight etc. the first in a series of games, shows etc.

in·au·gu·rate /ɪ'nɔgyəˌreɪt/ *v.* [T] **1** to have an official ceremony in order to show that someone is beginning an important job: *The new President will be inaugurated in January.* **2** to open a new building or start a new service or public event with a ceremony: *In 1960, Brazil inaugurated its new capital, Brasilia.* **3** if an event inaugurates an important

change or period of time, it comes at the beginning of it: *The International Trade Agreement inaugurated a period of high economic growth.* —**inauguration** /ɪˌnɔgyə'reɪʃən/ *n.* [C,U] *a presidential inauguration*

in·aus·pi·cious /ˌɪnɔ'spɪʃəs/ *adj.* FORMAL seeming to show that the future will be unlucky: *The loss was an inauspicious beginning to Darling's baseball career.* —**inauspiciously** *adv.*

in·be·tween /ˌ. .'./ *adj.* INFORMAL in the middle between two points, sizes, periods of time etc.: *She's at that in-between age, neither a girl nor a woman.*

in·board /'ɪnbɔrd/ *adj.* inside a boat or an airplane: *an inboard motor* —compare OUTBOARD MOTOR

in·born /ˌɪn'bɔrn/ *adj.* an inborn quality or ability is one that you have had naturally since birth: *Some people seem to have an inborn talent for cooking.*

in·bound[1] /'ɪnbaʊnd/ *adj.* an inbound flight, train etc. is coming toward the place where you are

inbound[2] *v.* [T] to return the ball to the playing area in a sport such as basketball: *The Lakers called time out and tried to inbound the ball.*

in·bounds /ˌ. '.٠/ *adv.* if the ball is in-bounds in a sport, it is in the playing area

in box, inbox /'. ./ *n.* [C] **1** a container on an office desk to hold work and letters that need to be dealt with **2** a place on a computer where the EMAIL messages you have received are kept —compare OUT BOX

in·bred /ˌɪn'brɛd/ *adj.* **1** DISAPPROVING an inbred quality or attitude develops as a natural part of someone's character, because of the beliefs or attitudes of the people they grew up with: *There is an inbred racism in some parts of the country.* **2** produced by inbreeding: *an inbred genetic defect*

in·breed·ing /'ɪnˌbridɪŋ/ *n.* [U] the producing of children, animals, or new plants from closely related members of the same family

Inc. /ɪŋk, ɪn'kɔrpəˌreɪtɪd/ the written abbreviation of INCORPORATED: *Pizza Hut Inc.*

In·ca /'ɪŋkə/ *n.* one of the people who lived in and controlled a large area of the Andes mountains in South America until the 16th century —**Inca** *adj.*: *the Inca priesthood*

in·cal·cu·la·ble /ɪn'kælkyələbəl/ *adj.* too many or too great to be measured: *The ash from the volcano has caused incalculable damage to crops.*

in·can·des·cent /ˌɪnkən'dɛsənt/ *adj.* giving a bright light when heated: *an incandescent light bulb* —**incandescence** *n.* [U] —compare FLUORESCENT

in·can·ta·tion /ˌɪnkæn'teɪʃən/ *n.* [C,U] a set of special words that someone uses in magic, or the act of saying these words

in·ca·pa·ble /ɪn'keɪpəbəl/ *adj.* unable to do something or to feel a particular emotion: [+ of] *The present leaders seem incapable of improving the situation.* | *She is an elderly woman who is physically incapable of caring for herself.*

in·ca·pac·i·tate /ˌɪnkə'pæsəˌteɪt/ *v.* [T often passive] **1** to make someone too sick or weak to live and work normally: *The volunteers shop, drive, and cook for people incapacitated by cancer.* **2** to make something unable to work normally, especially by damaging it: *Last year, severe storms incapacitated the whole town.* —**incapacitation** /ˌɪnkəˌpæsə'teɪʃən/ *n.* [U]

in·ca·pac·i·ty /ˌɪnkə'pæsəti/ *n.* [singular,U] lack of ability, strength, or power to do something, especially because you are sick: *mental incapacity*

in·car·cer·ate /ɪn'kɑrsəˌreɪt/ *v.* [T usually passive] FORMAL to put someone in prison, or keep them there: *He was incarcerated for 240 days.* —**incarceration** /ɪnˌkɑrsə'reɪʃən/ *n.* [U]

in·car·nate[1] /ɪn'kɑrnɪt, -ˌneɪt/ *adj.* [usually after noun] **evil/beauty/greed etc. incarnate** someone who is considered to be the human form of evil, beauty etc.

in·car·nate[2] /ɪn'kɑrˌneɪt/ *v.* [T] FORMAL **1** to show a particular quality so much that you seem to be the human form of that quality: *She incarnates the innocence that makes "Don Giovanni" such a moving story.* **2** to make something appear in a human form

in·car·na·tion /ˌɪnkɑrˈneɪʃən/ *n.* [C] **1** the form of something that can exist, appear, or be available in different forms: *Supporters hope that the party in its new incarnation will be more popular with the voters.* **2** the state of being alive in the form of a particular person or animal, or the period during which this happens, according to some religions: *In Hindu lore, Rama is an incarnation of the god Vishnu.* **3 be the incarnation of goodness/evil/sweetness** to perfectly represent goodness etc. in the way you live: *She is the incarnation of perfect femininity.* **4 the Incarnation** the act of God coming to Earth in the human form of Jesus Christ, according to the Christian religion

in·cau·tious /ɪnˈkɔʃəs/ *adj.* done or said without thinking about the possible effects, and therefore causing problems: *Incautious investors may lose money.*

in·cen·di·ar·y¹ /ɪnˈsɛndiˌɛri/ *adj.* [only before noun] **1** incendiary **bomb/device etc.** a bomb, piece of equipment etc. designed to cause a fire **2** an incendiary speech or piece of writing is intended to make people angry and is likely to cause trouble

incendiary² *n. plural* **incendiaries** [C] a bomb designed to cause a fire

in·cense¹ /ˈɪnsɛns/ *n.* [U] a substance that has a pleasant smell when you burn it, which is often used in religious ceremonies

in·cense² /ɪnˈsɛns/ *v.* [T] to make someone extremely angry: *The zoning changes incensed nearby residents.*

in·censed /ɪnˈsɛnst/ *adj.* extremely angry: [+ **by/at**] *Perry was incensed at the accusations.* | [**incensed that**] *Marks became incensed that the children did not treat him with respect.*

in·cen·tive /ɪnˈsɛntɪv/ *n.* [C,U] something that encourages you to work harder, start new activities etc.: *Low prices give the farmers little incentive.* | [**incentive to do sth**] *Not winning this year gives us an incentive to work harder next year.* | *The city offers financial incentives to homeowners to fix up their homes.* | *The high-tech industry was lured here by tax incentives* (=offers of reduced taxes).

in·cep·tion /ɪnˈsɛpʃən/ *n.* [singular] FORMAL the start of an organization or institution: *Graham danced with the company since its inception in 1976.*

in·ces·sant /ɪnˈsɛsənt/ *adj.* without stopping, in an annoying way: *The incessant buzzing of helicopters filled the evening sky.* —**incessantly** *adv.*

in·cest /ˈɪnsɛst/ *n.* [U] illegal sex between people who are closely related, for example between a brother and sister, or a father and daughter

in·ces·tu·ous /ɪnˈsɛstʃuəs/ *adj.* **1** relating to a sexual relationship between people who are closely related in a family **2** relating to a relationship in which a small group of people or organizations only help each other, in a way that is unfair to other people: *an incestuous relationship among city officials*

inch¹ /ɪntʃ/ *written abbreviation* **in.** *n.* [C] **1** a unit for measuring length, equal to 1/12 of a FOOT or 2.54 centimeters **2** [usually plural] a very small distance: *The next bullet missed Billy's kneecaps by inches* (=almost hit them). **3 every inch a)** all of something or someone: [+ **of**] *Every inch of the apartment was filled with boxes.* **b)** completely or in every way like something: *She looks every inch the high-powered businesswoman.* **4** enough rain or snow to cover an area an inch deep: *Storms have dumped nine inches on San Antonio since Wednesday.* **5 inch by inch** very slowly or by a small amount at a time: *The old buses moved inch by inch toward the pyramids.* **6 not budge/give an inch** to refuse to change your opinions at all: *Schmidt said she would not budge an inch on abortion rights.* **7 give sb an inch and they'll take a mile** used to say that if you allow someone a little freedom or power, they will try to

take a lot more **8 within an inch of sth** very near someone, something, or a result: *He was beaten within an inch of his life* (=hit so much that he almost died).

inch² *v.* [I always + adv./prep., T always + adv./prep.] to move or do something very slowly and carefully, or to move something in this way: [+ **along/ toward/around etc.**] *The two sides are inching toward agreement.* | *Several buses inched their way toward the exit.* | [**inch sth along/toward etc.**] *We inched our luggage forward as we waited in line.*

in·cho·ate /ɪnˈkoʊɪt/ *adj.* FORMAL inchoate ideas, plans, attitudes etc. are just starting to develop or are not well-formed

in·ci·dence /ˈɪnsədəns/ *n.* [C usually singular,U] FORMAL the number of times something happens, especially something bad: *There is a higher incidence of suicide among women than men.*

in·ci·dent¹ /ˈɪnsədənt/ *n.* [C] something unusual, serious, or violent that happens: *Three people were arrested in connection with the rock-throwing incident.* | *The plane took off without incident* (=without anything unusual or bad happening). ⟦S W 2⟧

incident² *adj.* **1** FORMAL [not before noun] happening or likely to happen as the result of something else: [+ **to**] *injuries incident to military service* **2** TECHNICAL incident light hits a surface

in·ci·den·tal¹ /ˌɪnsəˈdɛntl/ *adj.* **1** if something is incidental, it is less important than something else it happens or exists in connection with: [+ **to**] *The subject of the story became incidental to his great story-telling ability.* **2** FORMAL happening or existing as a result of something in a way that is not planned: *Tuition and incidental fees for students total $21,975.* | [+ **to**] *The dolphin catch was incidental to the fishing operation.*

incidental² *n.* [C usually plural] small ITEMS, EXPENSES etc. that are less important than others: *After paying rent, she has very little money for food, clothing, and incidentals.*

in·ci·den·tally /ˌɪnsəˈdɛntli/ *adv.* **1** [sentence adverb] used when giving additional information, or when changing the subject: *The symphony, incidentally, will perform outdoors for its final concert.* **2** happening or existing as a result of something else, but in a less important way or in a way that is not planned: *The moon landing was only incidentally about science.*

incidental mu·sic /ˌ.... ˈ../ *n.* [U] music played during a play, movie etc. in order to give the right feeling

in·cin·er·ate /ɪnˈsɪnəˌreɪt/ *v.* [T] to burn something completely so that it is destroyed: *The entire neighborhood was incinerated in the first half hour of the fire.* —**incineration** /ɪnˌsɪnəˈreɪʃən/ *n.* [U]

in·cin·er·a·tor /ɪnˈsɪnəˌreɪtɚ/ *n.* [C] a machine that burns things at a very high temperature in order to destroy them

in·cip·i·ent /ɪnˈsɪpiənt/ *adj.* [only before noun] FORMAL starting to happen or exist: *an incipient drinking problem*

in·cise /ɪnˈsaɪz/ *v.* [T] **1** FORMAL to cut a pattern or mark into a surface: [+ **in/into**] *Someone had incised their initials in the tree.* **2** TECHNICAL to cut carefully into something with a sharp knife

in·ci·sion /ɪnˈsɪʒən/ *n.* [C,U] a cut that a doctor makes in someone's body during an operation, or the act of making this cut

in·ci·sive /ɪnˈsaɪsɪv/ *adj.* very clear, direct, and dealing with the most important part of a subject: *an incisive critique of American politics*

in·ci·sor /ɪnˈsaɪzɚ/ *n.* [C] one of the eight teeth at the front of your mouth that have sharp edges and are used for biting food —compare CANINE TOOTH, MOLAR

in·cite /ɪnˈsaɪt/ *v.* [T] to deliberately encourage people to cause trouble, fight, argue etc.: *Holland denied that he was inciting a riot.* | [**incite sb to do sth**] *In 1962, Mandela was arrested for inciting black workers to break the law by striking.* | [**incite (sb) to sth**] *Three men were arrested for inciting the crowd to violence.* —**incitement** *n.* [U]

in·ci·vil·i·ty /ˌɪnsəˈvɪləti/ n. [U] FORMAL impolite behavior

incl. the written abbreviation of "including"

in·clem·ent /ɪnˈklɛmənt/ adj. FORMAL inclement weather is bad because it is cold, rainy etc. —**inclemency** n. [U]

in·cli·na·tion /ˌɪnkləˈneɪʃən/ n. **1** [C,U] the desire to do something: [**inclination to do sth**] Neither side has shown any inclination to compromise. **2** [C,U] tendency to think or behave in a particular way: [**inclination to do sth**] If something is hot, your natural inclination is to stay away from it. **3** [C,U] FORMAL a slope or the angle at which something slopes: a 62-degree inclination **4 inclination of sb's head** the movement of bending your neck so that your head is lowered: With a slight inclination of his head, he indicated that he understood.

in·cline¹ /ɪnˈklaɪn/ v. [not in progressive] **1** [T] FORMAL if a situation, fact etc. inclines you to do or think something, it influences you toward a particular action or opinion: [**incline sb to do sth**] Nothing has happened that would incline us to agree to the proposal. **2** [I,T] to slope at a particular angle or to make something do this **3** [I,T] FORMAL to think that a particular belief or opinion is most likely to be right: [**incline to do sth**] I incline to trust the Harrises. **4** [I] FORMAL to tend to behave in a particular way or show a particular quality: [+ **to/toward**] Men who incline toward violence don't make good husbands. **5 incline your head** to bend your neck so that your head is lowered

in·cline² /ˈɪnklaɪn/ n. [C] a slope: a steep incline

in·clined /ɪnˈklaɪnd/ adj. **1** [not before noun] wanting to do something: [**inclined to do sth**] I'm not inclined to give them any more money at all. | Car lovers can visit the showroom if they are so inclined. **2 be inclined to agree/think/believe etc.** to have a particular opinion, but to not hold it very strongly: I'm inclined to believe her story. **3** [not before noun] likely or tending to do something: [**inclined to do sth**] My mother is inclined to overreact. **4 mathematically/linguistically/musically inclined** naturally interested in or good at mathematics, languages etc.: My son is not mechanically inclined. **5** sloping or leaning in a particular direction

in·close /ɪnˈkloʊz/ v. [T] another spelling of ENCLOSE

in·clos·ure /ɪnˈkloʊʒɚ/ n. [C,U] another spelling of ENCLOSURE

in·clude /ɪnˈklud/ v. [T] **1** [not in progressive] if a set or a group includes something or someone, it has that thing or person as one of its parts: The price for the hotel includes breakfast. **2** to make something or someone part of a larger set or group: [**include sth in/on sth**] Why did they include Baltimore on the list? **3** to allow someone to take part in an activity, or to pay attention to them: Could we maybe include Wendell in the game? —opposite EXCLUDE —see Usage Note at COMPRISE

in·clud·ed /ɪnˈkludɪd/ adj. [only after noun] including someone or something: Everyone's going to church, you included.

in·clud·ing /ɪnˈkludɪŋ/ prep. used to show that someone or something is part of the larger group that you are talking about: They stole everything in my purse, including my credit cards. | There's about twenty of us, including the instructors. —opposite EXCLUDING

in·clu·sion /ɪnˈkluʒən/ n. **1** [C,U] the act of including someone or something in a larger group or set, or the fact of being included in one: Madison opposed the inclusion of a Bill of Rights in the Constitution. | [+ **in/into**] Shaeffer had proposed Miller's inclusion in the committee. | The old business district has been selected for inclusion in the National Register of Historic Places. **2** [C] someone or something that has been included in a larger group or set

in·clu·sive /ɪnˈklusɪv/ adj. including all the possible information, parts, numbers etc.: The list is not **all-inclusive**. | [+ **of**] Church leaders adopted standards that would be more inclusive of women. —opposite EXCLUSIVE¹

in·cog·ni·to /ˌɪnkɑgˈnitoʊ/ adv. if a person, especially

a famous person, does something incognito, they are hiding who they really are

in·co·her·ent /ˌɪnkoʊˈhɪrənt/ adj. **1** badly explained, or unable to be understood: Rawlings gave rambling, incoherent answers. **2** not talking clearly, or not able to express yourself clearly: One man was incoherent with grief. —**incoherently** adv. —**incoherence** n. [U]

in·come /ˈɪnkʌm, ˈɪŋ-/ n. [C,U] **1** the money that you earn from working or that you receive from INVESTMENTS: The amount you have to pay depends on your income. | She's **on a fixed income** (=an income that cannot be made larger) and barely getting by. —see Usage Note at PAY² **2 low-/middle-/high-income** having a small, large etc. income: help for low-income families

income tax /ˈ.. ˌ./ n. [U] tax paid on the money that you earn

in·com·ing /ˈɪnˌkʌmɪŋ/ adj. [only before noun] **1** incoming call/letter/fax a telephone call, letter etc. that you receive: Please hold all my incoming calls. **2** coming toward a place or about to arrive: incoming flights | the incoming tide **3** an incoming president, government, class etc. is just beginning a period of time in that position: Women made up 40% of the incoming freshman class this year.

in·com·mo·di·ous /ˌɪnkəˈmoʊdiəs/ adj. FORMAL inconvenient, difficult, or uncomfortable

in·com·mu·ni·ca·do /ˌɪnkəˌmyuniˈkɑdoʊ/ adj. adv. not allowed or not wanting to communicate with anyone: The opposition leader has been held incommunicado for two years.

in·com·pa·ra·ble /ɪnˈkɑmpərəbəl/ adj. so impressive beautiful, unusual etc. that nothing or no one is similar or better: His singing voice is incomparable. | incomparable views of the mountains

in·com·pat·i·ble /ˌɪnkəmˈpætəbəl/ adj. **1** too different to be able to have a good relationship with each other: Diane and I are completely incompatible. **2** incompatible beliefs, statements, actions etc. are too different to exist or be accepted together: [+ **with**] Such violent attacks are incompatible with a civilized society. **3** too different to be used together or to work together: [+ **with**] The software is incompatible with the operating system. —**incompatibly** adv. —**incompatibility** /ˌɪnkəmˌpætəˈbɪləti/ n. [U]

in·com·pe·tence /ɪnˈkɑmpətəns/ n. [U] lack of the ability or skill to do your job correctly or well: City money is being wasted through governmental incompetence.

in·com·pe·tent /ɪnˈkɑmpətənt/ adj. **1** not having the ability or skill to do your job correctly or well: Incompetent teachers should be fired. | Some drivers are just plain incompetent. **2** not able to understand something, because you are very sick, have a mental illness, or are not intelligent enough: Price was found mentally incompetent to stand trial. —**incompetent** n. [C]

in·com·plete /ˌɪnkəmˈplit/ adj. **1** not having all its parts: Historical records for this time are incomplete. | an incomplete job application **2** not completely finished: incomplete drawings **3** an incomplete pass a ball thrown in football that is not caught by the player you are throwing to —**incompletely** adv.

in·com·pre·hen·si·ble /ˌɪnkɑmprɪˈhɛnsəbəl/ adj. difficult or impossible to understand: The logic of that agreement is completely incomprehensible. | thick, incomprehensible legal documents

in·com·pre·hen·sion /ˌɪnˌkɑmprɪˈhɛnʃən/ n. [U] the state of not being able to understand something: He stared at her with annoyed incomprehension.

in·con·ceiv·a·ble /ˌɪnkənˈsivəbəl/ adj. too strange or unusual to be thought real or possible: [**it is inconceivable that**] It is inconceivable that anyone would choose to live here.

in·con·clu·sive /ˌɪnkənˈklusɪv/ adj. not leading to a clear decision or result: Jurors often have to make decisions based on inconclusive evidence. | Studies on *the benefits of year-round schools are inconclusive.* —**inconclusively** *adv.*

in·con·gru·ous /ɪnˈkɑŋgruəs/ *adj.* seeming to be wrong, not appropriate, strange, or unexpected in a particular situation: [+ **with**] *The high-tech building is incongruous with its rural surroundings.* —**incongruity** /ˌɪnkənˈgruəti/ *n.* [C,U] —**incongruously** /ɪnˈkɑŋgruəsli/ *adv.*

in·con·se·quen·tial /ˌɪnkɑnsəˈkwɛnʃəl/ *adj.* not important; INSIGNIFICANT: *an inconsequential little lie* —**inconsequentially** *adv.*

in·con·sid·er·a·ble /ˌɪnkənˈsɪdərəbəl/ *adj.* **not inconsiderable** FORMAL fairly large or important: *Anyone in the region faces a not inconsiderable risk of getting the disease.*

in·con·sid·er·ate /ˌɪnkənˈsɪdərɪt/ *adj.* not caring about the feelings or needs of other people: *It was really inconsiderate of him not to even leave a message.*

in·con·sist·en·cy /ˌɪnkənˈsɪstənsi/ *n. plural* **inconsistencies** **1** [U] the quality of changing your ideas too often or of doing something differently each time: *The team's inconsistency on defense has lost them three games.* **2** [C,U] information or a statement that cannot be true if the rest of the information or statement is true, or the state of being inconsistent in this way: *There appear to be some inconsistencies in the witnesses' statements.*

in·con·sist·ent /ˌɪnkənˈsɪstənt/ *adj.* **1** ideas, statements, or actions that are inconsistent cannot be accepted or believed together because they are different when they should be the same: *Students are rightfully upset by the college's inconsistent grading policy.* **2 be inconsistent with sth** behavior that is inconsistent with a particular set of principles or standards is not right according to those principles etc.: [+ **with**] *Warren's conservative views seem inconsistent with his upbringing in a poor neighborhood.* | *For her, believing in God is not inconsistent with marveling at scientific discoveries.* **3** inconsistent behavior, work etc. changes too often from good to bad or from situation to situation: *The team's performance has been extremely inconsistent this season.*

in·con·sol·a·ble /ˌɪnkənˈsoʊləbəl/ *adj.* so sad that it is impossible for anyone to comfort you: *During the funeral, Doris was inconsolable.* —**inconsolably** *adv.*

in·con·spic·u·ous /ˌɪnkənˈspɪkyuəs/ *adj.* not easily seen or noticed: *Saunder's studio is in an inconspicuous red-brick building on a quiet side street.* —**inconspicuously** *adv.*

in·con·stant /ɪnˈkɑnstənt/ *adj.* FORMAL **1** unfaithful in love or friendship: *an inconstant and unreliable friend* **2** not happening all the time: *inconstant winds* —**inconstancy** *n.* [U]

in·con·test·a·ble /ˌɪnkənˈtɛstəbəl/ *adj.* clearly true and impossible to disagree with; INDISPUTABLE: *Proof of the harmful effects of smoking is incontestable.*

in·con·ti·nent /ɪnˈkɑntᵊn-ənt, -tənənt/ *adj.* **1** unable to control your BLADDER or BOWELS **2** OLD USE unable to control your sexual urges —**incontinence** *n.* [U]

in·con·tro·vert·i·ble /ˌɪnkɑntrəˈvɚtəbəl/ *adj.* a fact that is incontrovertible is definitely true and no one can prove it to be false; INDISPUTABLE: *There is incontrovertible evidence that Wallenberg did not die in 1947.* —**incontrovertibly** *adv.*

in·con·ven·ience¹ /ˌɪnkənˈvinyəns/ *n.* **1** [C] something that causes you problems or difficulty: *Having to go downtown to pay the parking ticket was a major inconvenience.* **2** [U] the state of having problems or difficulty: *We apologize for any inconvenience the strike has caused to our customers.*

inconvenience² *v.* [T] to cause someone problems or difficulty: *Budget cuts in bus and train services will greatly inconvenience commuters.*

in·con·ven·ient /ˌɪnkənˈvinyənt/ *adj.* causing problems or difficulty, often in a way that is annoying: *Not having a visa can cause inconvenient and expensive delays.* | *Computer breakdowns are annoying and inconvenient.* —**inconveniently** *adv.*

in·cor·po·rate /ɪnˈkɔrpəˌreɪt/ *v.* [T] to include something as part of a group, system, plan etc.: *Karate is a martial art that incorporates kicking, striking, and punching techniques.* | [**incorporate sth into/in sth**] *Several schools are trying to incorporate ethnic foods into their menus.* —**incorporation** /ɪnˌkɔrpəˈreɪʃən/ *n.* [U]

in·cor·po·rat·ed /ɪnˈkɔrpəˌreɪtɪd/ *written abbreviation* **Inc.** *adj.* used after the name of a company in the U.S. to show that it has become a CORPORATION

in·cor·po·re·al /ˌɪnkɔrˈpɔriəl/ *adj.* FORMAL not existing in any physical form but only as a spirit

in·cor·rect /ˌɪnkəˈrɛkt/ *adj.* **1** not correct or true; wrong: *an incorrect answer* **2** not following the rules of polite behavior —**incorrectly** *adv.* —**incorrectness** *n.* [U]

in·cor·ri·gi·ble /ɪnˈkɔrədʒəbəl, -ˈkɑr-/ *adj.* FORMAL OR HUMOROUS someone who is incorrigible is bad in a way that cannot be changed or improved, or has bad habits that they do not change: *an incorrigible criminal* —**incorrigibly** *adv.*

in·cor·rupt·i·ble /ˌɪnkəˈrʌptəbəl/ *adj.* **1** too honest to be persuaded to do anything that is illegal or morally wrong: *Costner is believable in the role of the incorruptible defense lawyer.* **2** FORMAL material that is incorruptible will never decay: *Gold was precious because it was incorruptible.* —**incorruptibly** *adv.* —see also CORRUPT¹

in·crease¹ /ɪnˈkris/ *v.* [I,T] to become larger in amount, number, or degree, or to make something do this: *The city plans to increase the number of public housing units.* | *The telephone company has had to increase its workforce by 10 percent.* | [+ **by**] *Sales of automobiles have increased by 7 percent over last year.* | [+ **in**] *Investments in real estate are certain to increase in value.* —**increasing** *adj.*: *There have been an increasing number of work-related accidents.* —opposite DECREASE¹ —compare REDUCE (1)

in·crease² /ˈɪnkris, -ɪŋ/ *n.* [C,U] a rise in amount, number, or degree: *Recent wage increases have boosted morale in the company.* | [+ **in**] *a sharp increase in housing prices* | *Hate crimes are on the increase* (=increasing) *around the nation.* —see Usage Note at RAISE¹

in·creased /ɪnˈkrist/ *adj.* larger or more than before: *Men as well as women are at increased risk for cancer from X-rays.*

in·creas·ing /ɪnˈkrisɪŋ/ *adj.* becoming larger in size, amount, or number: *An increasing number of teenagers are working at part-time jobs.*

in·creas·ing·ly /ɪnˈkrisɪŋli/ *adv.* more and more all the time: [+ adj./adv.] *The rebel group's actions have become increasingly violent.* [sentence adverb] *Increasingly, humans and animals are in competition for the same land.*

in·cred·i·ble /ɪnˈkrɛdəbəl/ *adj.* **1** extremely good, large, or impressive: *Winning the championship was an incredible feeling.* | *She's an incredible dancer.* **2** too strange to be believed or very difficult to believe: *The divorce rate in the U.S. is pretty incredible.* | *an incredible story of survival* —**incredibility** /ɪnˌkrɛdəˈbɪləti/ *n.* [U]

in·cred·i·bly /ɪnˈkrɛdəbli/ *adv.* **1** [+ adj./adv.] extremely: *Raising money for the homeless has been incredibly difficult.* **2** [sentence adverb] used when something is hard to believe: *Incredibly, six men ran the 100-meter final in less than 10 seconds.*

in·cre·du·li·ty /ˌɪnkrɪˈduləti/ *n.* [U] a feeling that you cannot believe something; DISBELIEF: *Workers expressed incredulity and anger at being laid off.*

in·cred·u·lous /ɪnˈkrɛdʒələs/ *adj.* unable or unwilling to believe something, or showing this: *"You don't have a car?" asked one incredulous woman.* —**incredulously** *adv.*

in·cre·ment /ˈɪnkrəmənt, -ɪŋ-/ *n.* [C] an amount by which a number, value, or amount increases: *Annenberg donated $150 million to be paid in increments of $10 million for 15 years.* —**incremental** /ˌɪnkrəˈmɛntl/ *adj.*

in·crim·i·nate /ɪnˈkrɪməˌneɪt/ *v.* [T] to make someone seem guilty of a crime: *You have the right not to say* *anything that would incriminate you.* | *incriminating documents* —**incrimination** /ɪn,krɪmə'neɪʃən/ *n.* [U]

in·crim·i·na·to·ry /ɪn'krɪmənə,tɔri/ *adj.* making someone seem to be guilty

in-crowd /'. ./ *n.* **the in-crowd** a small group of people in an organization or activity who are popular and have influence, and who are friendly with each other but do not want other people to join them: *We were never part of the in-crowd in high school.*

in·crust·a·tion /,ɪnkrʌ'steɪʃən/ *n.* [C] an amount of dirt, salt etc. that forms a hard layer on a surface

in·cu·bate /'ɪŋkyə,beɪt/ *v.* [I,T] **1** if an animal such as a bird incubates its eggs or if they incubate, they are kept warm under the animal's body until the young animals come out **2** TECHNICAL if a disease incubates, or if you incubate it, it develops in your body until you show physical signs of it

in·cu·ba·tion /,ɪŋkyə'beɪʃən/ *n.* [U] **1** the period between becoming infected with a disease and showing the first physical signs of it **2** the period of time that an egg is kept warm before it HATCHES[1] (1)

in·cu·ba·tor /'ɪŋkyə,beɪtə/ *n.* [C] **1** a piece of hospital equipment like a clear box that is used for keeping very small or weak babies alive by keeping them warm, giving them the right amount of oxygen to breathe etc. **2** a heated container for keeping eggs warm until the young birds etc. come out, and for protecting very young birds or animals

in·cu·bus /'ɪŋkyəbəs/ *n.* [C] a male DEVIL that in past times was believed to have sex with a sleeping woman —compare SUCCUBUS

in·cul·cate /'ɪnkʌl,keɪt, ɪn'kʌl,keɪt/ *v.* [T] FORMAL to make someone accept an idea by repeating it to them often: [inculcate sth ↔ in/into sb] *Dad had inculcated in us a strong sense of family loyalty.* | [inculcate sb with sth] *The Army inculcates its recruits with a strong patriotism.* —**inculcation** /,ɪnkʌl'keɪʃən/ *n.* [U]

in·cul·pa·ble /ɪn'kʌlpəbəl/ *adj.* FORMAL not guilty; BLAMELESS

in·cul·pate /ɪn'kʌlpeɪt, 'ɪnkʌl,peɪt/ *v.* [T] FORMAL to show that someone is guilty of a crime

in·cum·ben·cy /ɪn'kʌmbənsi/ *n. plural* **incumbencies** [C] FORMAL the period of time during which someone is an incumbent

in·cum·bent[1] /ɪn'kʌmbənt/ *n.* [C] FORMAL someone who has been elected to an official position, and who is doing that job at the present time: *Steiner easily beat the incumbent to become governor.*

incumbent[2] *adj.* FORMAL **1 the incumbent President/Senator etc.** the president, governor etc. at the present time, especially in or near the time of an election **2 it is incumbent upon sb to do sth** used to say that it is someone's duty or responsibility to do something: *It is incumbent upon parents to control what their children watch on TV.*

in·cur /ɪn'kə/ *v.* **incurred, incurring** [T] **1** to have something bad happen to you, such as a punishment or debt, because of something you have done: *The auto manufacturer incurred a $843.6 million loss in 1990.* | *Crowder's comments incurred the wrath of the board of directors.* **2 incur expenses** to have to spend money on something

in·cur·a·ble /ɪn'kyurəbəl/ *adj.* **1** impossible to cure: *an incurable disease* **2** incurable attitudes or behavior are impossible to change or stop: *Jane is an incurable gossip.* —**incurably** *adv.* —**incurable** *n.* [C]

in·cu·ri·ous /ɪn'kyuriəs/ *adj.* FORMAL not naturally interested in finding out about the things around you

in·cur·sion /ɪn'kəʒən/ *n.* [C] FORMAL **1** a sudden attack into an area of land that belongs to other people: *Government forces were able to halt the rebel incursion.* **2** the unwanted arrival of something in a place where it does not belong: *The incursion of whiteflies into the area could damage crops.*

in·debt·ed /ɪn'dɛtɪd/ *adj.* **1 be (greatly/deeply) indebted to sb/sth** to be very grateful to someone for the help they have given you: *Marcus feels indebted to the school for giving him a scholarship.*

2 owing money to someone: *a heavily indebted hotel chain* —**indebtedness** *n.* [U]

in·de·cen·cy /ɪn'disənsi/ *n.* [U] LAW behavior that is sexually offensive, especially INDECENT EXPOSURE

in·de·cent /ɪn'disənt/ *adj.* **1** indecent behavior, movements, clothes etc. are likely to shock or offend people, because they involve sex or because they show parts of the body that are usually covered: *Woodall said the man also took an indecent photo of the child.* **2** completely unacceptable: *The prices they charge for this food are indecent.* —**indecently** *adv.*: *indecently dressed*

indecent as·sault /.,... .'./ *n.* [C,U] LAW an attack on someone that includes sexual violence

indecent ex·po·sure /.,... .'../ *n.* [U] LAW the crime of deliberately showing your sex organs in a public place —see also FLASHER

in·de·ci·pher·a·ble /,ɪndɪ'saɪfrəbəl/ *adj.* impossible to read or understand: *an indecipherable signature*

in·de·ci·sion /,ɪndɪ'sɪʒən/ *n.* [U] the state of being unable to decide what to do: *We finally bought the house after months of indecision.*

in·de·ci·sive /,ɪndɪ'saɪsɪv/ *adj.* **1** unable to make clear decisions or choices: *a weak and indecisive leader* **2** not having a clear result: *an indecisive debate* —**indecisiveness** *n.* [U]

in·dec·o·rous /ɪn'dɛkərəs/ *adj.* FORMAL behaving in a way that is not polite or socially acceptable

in·deed /ɪn'did/ *adv.* **1** [sentence adverb] FORMAL used when adding more information to emphasize what you have just said: *Minorities are not well represented. Indeed, the city has only one black city council member.* **2** used to emphasize a statement or answer: *The blood tests prove that Vince is indeed the father.* **S W 1**

in·de·fat·i·ga·ble /,ɪndɪ'fætɪgəbəl/ *adj.* FORMAL determined and never becoming tired: *an indefatigable worker*

in·de·fen·si·ble /,ɪndɪ'fɛnsəbəl/ *adj.* **1** too bad to be excused or defended: *It is indefensible that in such a rich country so many people are poor.* **2** impossible or very difficult to defend from military attack

in·de·fin·a·ble /,ɪndɪ'faɪnəbəl/ *adj.* an indefinable feeling, quality etc. is difficult to describe or explain: *She felt a sudden indefinable sadness.*

in·def·i·nite /ɪn'dɛfənɪt/ *adj.* **1** an indefinite action or period of time has no definite end arranged for it: *The refugees will be housed and fed here for an indefinite period.* **2** not clear or definite; VAGUE: *Our plans for traveling are deliberately indefinite.*

indefinite ar·ti·cle /.,... '.../ *n.* [C] the words "a" and "an" —compare DEFINITE ARTICLE —see also ARTICLE (4)

in·def·i·nite·ly /ɪn'dɛfənɪtli/ *adv.* for a period of time for which no definite end has been arranged: *Pete Rose was barred indefinitely from baseball in 1989 for gambling.*

indefinite pro·noun /.,... '../ *n.* [C] TECHNICAL a word that is used in place of a noun, but that does not say exactly which person or thing is meant, such as "some," "any," or "either"

in·del·i·ble /ɪn'dɛləbəl/ *adj.* **1** impossible to remove or forget; PERMANENT: *His death left an indelible impression on my life.* **2 indelible ink/markers etc.** ink, pens etc. that make a permanent mark which cannot be removed —**indelibly** *adv.*: *The book indelibly shaped my political views.*

in·del·i·cate /ɪn'dɛlɪkɪt/ *adj.* impolite or offensive: *an indelicate and tasteless comment* —**indelicacy** *n.* [U]

in·dem·ni·fi·ca·tion /ɪn,dɛmnɪfə'keɪʃən/ *n.* LAW **1** [U + for/against] the act of paying or promising to pay someone for loss, injury, or damage **2** [C + for] a payment made to someone for loss, injury, or damage

in·dem·ni·fy /ɪn'dɛmnə,faɪ/ *v.* [T] LAW [indemnify sb against/for sth] to promise to pay someone if something they own is damaged or lost or if they are injured

I

in·dem·ni·ty /ɪnˈdɛmnəti/ n. LAW **1** [U] protection against loss, damage, or injury, especially in the form of a promise to pay you if these things happen **2** [C] a payment for injury or the loss of money, goods etc.

in·dent /ɪnˈdɛnt/ v. [T] to start a line of writing closer to the middle of the page than other lines

in·den·ta·tion /ˌɪndɛnˈteɪʃən/ n. **1** [C] a space at the beginning of a line of writing **2** [C] a space or cut which goes into the surface or edge of something: *Gently make a small, shallow indentation in the center of each cookie.* **3** [U] the act of indenting

in·dent·ed /ɪnˈdɛntɪd/ adj. an indented edge or surface has cuts or spaces that go into the surface of it: *Don't buy sweet potatoes that appear bruised or have indented areas.*

in·den·tured /ɪnˈdɛntʃɚd/ adj. an indentured servant or worker was in past times forced to work for their employer for a particular number of years —**indenture** n. [C,U]

s w **in·de·pend·ence** /ˌɪndɪˈpɛndəns/ n. [U] **1** political freedom from control by the government of another country: [+ from] *Algeria won independence from France more than thirty years ago.* | *The U.S.A. declared independence* (=officially stated their independence) *in 1776.* **2** the time when a country becomes politically independent: *Since independence, the country has had high unemployment.* **3** the freedom and ability to make your own decisions and take care of yourself, without having to ask other people for permission, help, or money: *The apartments allow older people to keep their independence, while having medical care available.* | *financial independence*

Independence Day /ˌ..ˈ.. ˌ./ n. [C,U] **1** the day in which a country celebrates its independence from another country that controlled it in the past **2** this day in the U.S., celebrated on July 4th

In·de·pend·ent /ˌɪndɪˈpɛndənt/ n. [C] a politician who does not belong to a political party

s w **in·de·pend·ent** /ˌɪndɪˈpɛndənt‹/ adj. **1** confident and able to do things by yourself in your own way, without needing help or advice from other people: *a strong independent woman* **2** [no comparative] existing separately and not influenced or controlled by other people, organizations or the government: *Independent legal experts have been studying the case.* | *Yonkers has several independent bus lines* (=it has buses that are not owned by the government). | [+ of] *The research center is on Harvard's campus, but is independent of the university.* **3** [no comparative] an independent country is not governed or controlled by another country: *Croatia became an independent nation in 1991.* **4** [no comparative] done or given by people who are not involved in a particular situation and who can therefore be trusted to be fair in judging it: *The blood samples are being sent out for independent analysis.* **5** having enough money to live without having to ask for help from other people: *She is financially independent.* **6 a man/woman of independent means** someone who has their own income, especially so that they do not have to work or depend on anyone —**independently** adv.: *The two departments operate independently of each other.*

independent clause /ˌ.... ˈ./ n. [C] TECHNICAL a CLAUSE that can make a sentence by itself; for example, "He woke up" in the sentence "He woke up when he heard the bell."; MAIN CLAUSE

in-depth /ˌ. ˈ.‹/ adj. [only before noun] **an in-depth study/report/investigation etc.** a study, report etc. of something that is thorough and complete and considers all the details

in·de·scrib·a·ble /ˌɪndɪˈskraɪbəbəl/ adj. too good, strange, frightening etc. to be described, or very difficult to describe: *Fresh salmon has an indescribable flavor.* —**indescribably** adv.

in·de·struct·i·ble /ˌɪndɪˈstrʌktəbəl/ adj. impossible

to destroy: *Diamonds are practically indestructible.* —**indestructibility** /ˌɪndɪˌstrʌktəˈbɪləti/ n. [U]

in·de·ter·min·a·ble /ˌɪndɪˈtəmənəbəl/ adj. impossible to find out or calculate exactly

in·de·ter·mi·nate /ˌɪndɪˈtəmənɪt/ adj. impossible to know about definitely or exactly: *an indeterminate length of time*

in·dex[1] /ˈɪndɛks/ n. plural **indices** /-dɪˌsiz/ or **indexes** [C] **1** an alphabetical list of names, subjects etc. at the back of a book, with the numbers of the pages where they can be found **2** a set of cards or a DATABASE containing information, usually arranged in alphabetical order and used especially in a library **3** a standard by which the level of something can be judged or measured: *The changing size of an infant's head is considered an index of brain growth.* **4** TECHNICAL a system by which prices, costs etc. can be compared to those of a previous date

index[2] v. [T] to make an index for something

in·dex·a·tion /ˌɪndɛkˈseɪʃən/ n. [U] TECHNICAL the practice of increasing salaries or SOCIAL SECURITY at the same rate as prices increase, according to the CONSUMER PRICE INDEX

index card /ˈ.. ˌ./ n. [C] a small card for writing information on, used especially in an index

index fin·ger /ˈ.. ˌ../ n. [C] the finger next to your thumb; FOREFINGER

In·di·a /ˈɪndiə/ a large country in south Asia —**Indian** n., adj.

India ink /ˈ... ˌ./ n. [U] black ink used especially for Chinese or Japanese writing with a brush

In·di·an[1] /ˈɪndiən/ n. **1** [C] a word for a Native American person, which may be considered offensive **2** [C] someone from India

Indian[2] adj. **1** relating to NATIVE AMERICANS **2** from or relating to India

In·di·an·a /ˌɪndiˈænə/ written abbreviation **IN** a state in the Midwestern area of the U.S.

In·di·a·nap·o·lis /ˌɪndiəˈnæpəlɪs/ the capital city of the U.S. state of Indiana

Indian corn /ˈ... ˌ./ n. [U] **1** corn with KERNELs of different colors **2** OLD USE corn

Indian file /ˈ... ˌ./ n. [singular, not with the] OLD-FASHIONED a straight line in which one person walks behind another person; SINGLE FILE

Indian giv·er /ˈ... ˌ../ n. [C] INFORMAL a word for someone who gives you something and then wants it back, considered offensive by many people

Indian O·cean, the /ˌ... ˈ../ the ocean between Africa and Australia

Indian res·er·va·tion /ˌ.... ..ˈ../ n. [C] OLD-FASHIONED a RESERVATION (3)

Indian sum·mer /ˌ... ˈ../ n. [C] **1** a period of warm weather in the fall **2** a happy or successful time, especially near the end of your life or CAREER

Indian wres·tling /ˌ... ˈ../ n. [U] a game in which you stand facing someone with your foot touching theirs, and try to push them over by pushing one of their hands

india rub·ber /ˌ... ˈ.‹/ n. [U] a type of ERASER made from rubber

in·di·cate /ˈɪndəˌkeɪt/ v. [T] **1** to show that a particular situation exists, or that something is likely to be true: *The study indicates a strong connection between poverty and crime.* | [**indicate that**] *Reports from hospitals indicated that over thirteen people died in the storm.* **2** to direct someone's attention to something, for example by pointing: *He indicated the chair near his desk and I sat down.* **3** to say or do something to make your wishes, intentions, meaning etc. clear: *As many as 10 women have indicated they may run for the Senate in Texas.* | [**indicate that**] *He nodded several times to indicate that he understood.* **4** to represent something: *On this scale, one indicates poor quality and four indicates excellent quality.*

in·di·ca·tion /ˌɪndəˈkeɪʃən/ n. [C,U] a sign that something is probably happening or that something is probably true: [+ of] *Dark green leaves are a good indication of healthy roots.* | [**indication that**] *Police said there was no indication that the two* robberies were related. | *Collier* **gave every indication** (=gave very clear signs) *that he was ready to compromise.*

in·dic·a·tive[1] /ɪnˈdɪkətɪv/ *adj.* **be indicative of sth** to be a clear sign that a particular situation exists or that something is likely to be true: *Yesterday's win was indicative of the U.S. team's talent.*

indicative[2] *n.* [C,U] TECHNICAL the form of a verb that is used to make ordinary statements. For example, in the sentences "Penny passed her test," and "Michael likes cake," the verbs "passed" and "like" are in the indicative —compare IMPERATIVE[2] (2), SUBJUNCTIVE

in·di·ca·tor /ˈɪndəˌkeɪtər/ *n.* [C] **1** something that can be regarded as a sign of something else: *High levels of cholesterol may be an important indicator of heart disease risk.* **2** a POINTER on a machine that shows the temperature, speed etc.

in·di·ces /ˈɪndəˌsiz/ *n.* the plural of INDEX

in·dict /ɪnˈdaɪt/ *v.* [I,T] LAW to officially charge someone with a crime: [indict sb for sth] *Three of the men were indicted for kidnapping.*

in·dict·a·ble /ɪnˈdaɪtəbəl/ *adj.* LAW an indictable offense is one for which you can be indicted

in·dict·ment /ɪnˈdaɪtmənt/ *n.* **1** [U] LAW the act of officially charging someone with a crime: *Owners of the city's biggest casino are under indictment* (=charged with a crime). **2 be an indictment of sth** to show clearly that a system, method etc. is very bad or very wrong: *Steinbeck's novel "The Grapes of Wrath" was an indictment of agricultural labor relations.* **3** [C] LAW an official written statement charging someone with a crime

in·die /ˈɪndi/ *n.* [C] a small independent company, especially one that produces popular music or movies

indie mu·sic /ˈ.. ˌ../ *n.* [U] popular music that is recorded, produced, and sold by a small independent company

in·dif·fer·ence /ɪnˈdɪfrəns/ *n.* [U] lack of interest or concern: [+ to] *America has a history of indifference to racial discrimination.*

in·dif·fer·ent /ɪnˈdɪfrənt/ *adj.* **1** not interested in someone or something, or not having any feelings or opinions about a person, thing event etc.: [+ to] *Politicians were seen as indifferent to the hardworking middle class.* **2** not particularly good: *The service at the restaurant was indifferent at best.*

in·dig·e·nous /ɪnˈdɪdʒənəs/ *adj.* **1** indigenous people, customs, CULTURES etc. are the people, customs etc. that have always been in a place, before other people or customs arrived **2** indigenous animals, plants etc. have always lived or grown naturally in the place where they are, as opposed to others that were brought there: [+ to] *Red foxes are indigenous to the East and Midwest parts of the U.S.*

in·di·gent /ˈɪndɪdʒənt/ *adj.* FORMAL not having much money or many possessions; POOR —**indigent** *n.* [C] —**indigence** *n.* [U]

in·di·gest·i·ble /ˌɪndɪˈdʒɛstəbəl, -daɪ-/ *adj.* **1** food that is indigestible cannot easily be broken down in the stomach into substances that the body can use **2** facts that are indigestible are not easy to understand: *indigestible statistics*

in·di·ges·tion /ˌɪndɪˈdʒɛstʃən/ *n.* [U] pain that you get when it is difficult for your stomach to break down the food that you have eaten: *Spicy food always gives me indigestion.*

in·dig·nant /ɪnˈdɪgnənt/ *adj.* angry and surprised, because you feel insulted or unfairly treated: [+ at/over] *Eric was indignant over being made to wait for 20 minutes.* —**indignantly** *adv.*

in·dig·na·tion /ˌɪndɪgˈneɪʃən/ *n.* [U] feelings of anger and surprise because you feel insulted or unfairly treated: [+ at] *I certainly understand the public's indignation at the loss of public services.* | *His voice rose in indignation as he talked about the beating he suffered.*

in·dig·ni·ty /ɪnˈdɪgnəti/ *n. plural* **indignities** [C,U] a situation that makes you feel very ashamed, unimportant, and not respected: *Many women have suffered the indignity of being sexually harassed.*

in·di·go /ˈɪndɪgoʊ/ *n.* [U] a dark purplish blue color —**indigo** *adj.*

in·di·rect /ˌɪndəˈrɛkt, -daɪ-/ *adj.* **1** not directly caused by or related to something: *Losing weight seems to be an indirect result of smoking cigarettes.* **2** not coming directly from a particular thing or place: *indirect lighting* **3** not using the fastest, easiest, or straightest way to get to a place: *The cab driver obviously took the indirect route to the hotel.* **4** suggesting something without saying it directly: *George's comments were an indirect way of blaming me for the situation.* —**indirectly** *adv.*

indirect dis·course /ˌ... '../ *n.* [U] TECHNICAL: see REPORTED SPEECH

indirect ob·ject /ˌ... '../ *n.* [C] TECHNICAL in grammar, the person or thing that receives something as the result of the action of the verb in a sentence. In the sentence "Ryan gave me a gift," the indirect object is "me." —compare DIRECT OBJECT

indirect speech /ˌ... './ *n.* [U] TECHNICAL: see REPORTED SPEECH

indirect tax·a·tion /ˌ... ˌ../ *n.* [U] a system of collecting taxes by adding an amount of tax to the price of goods and services that people buy

in·dis·cern·i·ble /ˌɪndɪˈsɜrnəbəl/ *adj.* very difficult to see, hear, or notice: *The crack in the windshield was almost indiscernible.*

in·dis·ci·pline /ɪnˈdɪsəplɪn/ *n.* [U] a lack of control over a group of people, so that they behave badly —see also DISCIPLINE[1] (2)

in·dis·creet /ˌɪndɪˈskrit/ *adj.* careless about what you say or do, especially by talking about things that should be kept secret —**indiscreetly** *adv.*

in·dis·cre·tion /ˌɪndɪˈskrɛʃən/ *n.* [C,U] an action, remark or behavior that shows bad judgment and a lack of careful thought, and is usually considered socially or morally unacceptable: *sexual indiscretions* | *Dodd says his involvement in the racist group was just youthful indiscretion.*

in·dis·crim·i·nate /ˌɪndɪˈskrɪmənɪt/ *adj.* **1** indiscriminate killing, violence, damage etc. is done without any thought about who is harmed or what is damaged: *Troops were accused of indiscriminate killings of civilians.* **2** not thinking carefully before you make a choice —**indiscriminately** *adv.*

in·dis·pen·sa·ble /ˌɪndɪˈspɛnsəbəl/ *adj.* someone or something that is indispensable is so important or useful that it is impossible to manage without them: *Police dogs have proved indispensable in the war on drugs.* —**indispensably** *adv.* —**indispensability** /ˌɪndɪˌspɛnsəˈbɪləti/ *n.* [U]

in·dis·posed /ˌɪndɪˈspoʊzd/ *adj.* FORMAL [not before noun] **1** sick and therefore unable to be present: *Because Skarowsky was indisposed, Karajan stepped in to conduct the Salzburg Festival.* **2 be indisposed to do sth** to not be willing to do something

in·dis·po·si·tion /ˌɪnˌdɪspəˈzɪʃən/ *n.* FORMAL **1** [C,U] a slight illness: *the actor's sudden indisposition* **2** [U] an unwilling attitude

in·dis·pu·ta·ble /ˌɪndɪˈspyutəbəl/ *adj.* an indisputable fact must be accepted because it is definitely true: *The evidence was indisputable.* —**indisputably** *adv.*

in·dis·sol·u·ble /ˌɪndɪˈsɑlyəbəl/ *adj.* FORMAL an indissoluble relationship cannot be destroyed —**indissolubility** /ˌɪndɪˌsɑlyəˈbɪləti/ *n.* [U]

in·dis·tinct /ˌɪndɪˈstɪŋkt/ *adj.* an indistinct sound, image, or memory cannot be seen, heard, or remembered clearly: *He spoke in a raspy, indistinct voice.*

in·dis·tin·guish·a·ble /ˌɪndɪˈstɪŋgwɪʃəbəl/ *adj.* things that are indistinguishable are so similar that you cannot see any difference between them: [+ from] *Africanized bees appear indistinguishable from European bees.*

in·di·vid·u·al[1] /ˌɪndəˈvɪdʒuəl/ *adj.* **1** [only before noun] considered separately from other people or things in the same group: *Individual tickets for Red*

I

Sox games go on sale this morning. | *Each individual employee was given a bonus.* **2** [only before noun] belonging to or intended for one person rather than a group: *The children get far more individual attention in these small classes.* | *an individual serving of mashed potatoes* **3** an individual style, way of doing things etc. is different from anyone else's: *He has his own individual method of organizing his work.*

in·di·vid·u·al² *n.* [C] **1** one person, considered separately from the rest of the group or society that they live in: *the rights of the individual* | *Effects of the drug vary from individual to individual.* **2** INFORMAL a particular person, especially one who is unusual in some way: *Mandy's a real individual.*

in·di·vid·u·al·ism /ˌɪndəˈvɪdʒuə,lɪzəm/ *n.* [U] **1** the belief that the rights and freedom of individual people are the most important rights in a society **2** the practice of allowing someone to do things in their own way, without being influenced by other people

in·di·vid·u·al·ist /ˌɪndəˈvɪdʒuəlɪst/ *n.* [C] someone who does things in their own way and has different opinions from most other people —**individualistic** /ˌɪndə,vɪdʒuəˈlɪstɪk/ *adj.*

in·di·vid·u·al·i·ty /ˌɪndə,vɪdʒuˈæləti/ *n.* [U] the quality that makes someone or something different from all other things or people: *Changing the color of his hair was his way of expressing his individuality.*

in·di·vid·u·al·ize /ˌɪndəˈvɪdʒuə,laɪz/ *v.* [T] to make something different so that it fits the special needs of a particular person or place: *an individualized approach to weight loss*

in·di·vid·u·al·ly /ˌɪndəˈvɪdʒuəli, -dʒəli/ *adv.* separately, not together in a group: *Wrap cupcakes individually in plastic wrap.*

in·di·vid·u·ate /ˌɪndəˈvɪdʒu,eɪt/ *v.* **1** [T] to make someone or something clearly different from others of the same kind: *The characters are beautifully individuated in the play.* **2** [I] to have an idea of yourself as an independent person, separate from other people

in·di·vis·i·ble /ˌɪndəˈvɪzəbəl/ *adj.* something that is indivisible cannot be separated or divided into parts —**indivisibly** *adv.* —**indivisibility** /ˌɪndə,vɪzəˈbɪləti/ *n.* [U]

Indo- /ɪndoʊ/ *prefix* INDIAN¹ (2) and something else: *Indo-European languages*

In·do·chi·na /ˌɪndoʊˈtʃaɪnə/ a former name given to part of southeast Asia by Europeans. During the 19th century, Indochina included Vietnam, Cambodia, Myanmar (Burma), Thailand, Malaysia, and Laos, but in the 20th century Indochina came to mean the countries ruled by France: Vietnam, Cambodia, and Laos.

in·doc·tri·nate /ɪnˈdɑktrə,neɪt/ *v.* [T] to train someone to accept a particular set of beliefs, especially political or religious ones, and not consider any others: *Training seminars and retreats are held to indoctrinate recruits.* —**indoctrination** /ɪn,dɑktrə-ˈneɪʃən/ *n.* [U]

Indo-Eu·ro·pe·an /ˌ... ...ˈ...ˌ/ *adj.* the Indo-European group of languages includes languages spoken in the past in Europe and central southwest and southern Asia

in·do·lent /ˈɪndələnt/ *adj.* FORMAL lazy —**indolently** *adv.* —**indolence** *n.* [U]

in·dom·i·ta·ble /ɪnˈdɑmətəbəl/ *adj.* having determination, courage, or other qualities that can never be defeated: *an indomitable will to succeed*

In·do·ne·si·a /ˌɪndəˈniʒə/ a country in the southeastern Pacific Ocean consisting of more than 13,000 islands, including Java, Sumatra, most of Borneo, Sulawesi, and Bali —**Indonesian** *n., adj.*

in·door /ˈɪndɔr/ *adj.* [only before noun] used or happening inside a building: *indoor lighting* | *indoor soccer* —opposite OUTDOOR

in·doors /ˌɪnˈdɔrz/ *adv.* into or inside a building: *Let's stay indoors where it's nice and warm.* —opposite OUTDOORS²

in·du·bi·ta·ble /ɪnˈdubɪtəbəl/ *adj.* FORMAL definitely true without any possible doubt —**indubitably** *adv.*

in·duce /ɪnˈdus/ *v.* [T] **1** to make someone decide to do something, especially something that does not seem wise: [induce sb to do sth] *Many activists say that beer advertisements play a strong role in inducing teenagers to drink.* **2** FORMAL to cause a particular physical condition: *The drug can induce anything from stomach cramps to comas.* | *a stress-induced allergy* **3** to make a woman give birth to her baby, by giving her a special drug: *She had to be induced because the baby was four weeks late.*

in·duce·ment /ɪnˈdusmənt/ *n.* [C,U] something such as money or a gift that you are offered to persuade you to do something: *The company is offering discounts on long-distance calls as an inducement to customers.*

in·duct /ɪnˈdʌkt/ *v.* [T often passive] FORMAL **1** to introduce someone into an important official position: [+ to] *Nabbani was inducted to the post of foreign minister late last year.* **2** to introduce someone into an important place of honor in a special ceremony: [+ into] *Rick Barry was inducted into the Basketball Hall of Fame in 1987.* **3** to officially make someone a member of a group, club, organization etc. in a special ceremony: *On Sunday, the fraternity inducts the new pledges.* **4** to take someone into a military organization such as the Army or Navy

in·duct·ee /ˌɪndʌkˈti/ *n.* [C] someone who is being taken into the Army, Navy, or another organization

in·duc·tion /ɪnˈdʌkʃən/ *n.* **1** [C,U] the act of officially introducing someone into an official position or place of honor, or the ceremony in which this is done **2** [U] a process of thought that uses known facts to produce general rules or principles —compare DEDUCTION (1) **3** [C,U] TECHNICAL the act or process of making a woman give birth to her baby by giving her a special drug **4** [U] TECHNICAL the production of electricity in one object by another that already has electrical or MAGNETIC power

induction coil /.'.. ,.ˈ/ *n.* [C] TECHNICAL a piece of electrical equipment that changes a low VOLTAGE to a higher one

in·duct·ive /ɪnˈdʌktɪv/ *adj.* TECHNICAL **1** using known facts to produce general principles: *inductive reasoning* **2** relating to electrical or MAGNETIC induction

in·dulge /ɪnˈdʌldʒ/ *v.* **1** [I,T] to let yourself do or have something that you enjoy, especially something that is considered bad for you: [+ in] *A funeral is not an appropriate time to indulge in gossip.* | [indulge yourself] *If you're dieting, indulge yourself once in a while* (=eat what you want). | [indulge sth] *I have to indulge my craving for chocolate at least a few times a week.* **2** [T] to let someone have or do whatever they want, even if it is bad for them: *Katie's a spoiled brat because her parents indulge her too much.*

in·dul·gence /ɪnˈdʌldʒəns/ *n.* **1** [U] the habit of eating too much, drinking too much etc. **2** [C] something that you do or have for pleasure, not because you need it: *Swiss chocolate is my only indulgence.* **3** [C,U] freedom from punishment by God, or a promise of this, which was sold by priests in the Middle Ages. **4** [U] OLD USE permission

in·dul·gent /ɪnˈdʌldʒənt/ *adj.* willing to allow someone, especially a child, to do what they want, even if this is not good for them: [+ with] *Billy's parents are too indulgent with him.* —**indulgently** *adv.* —see also SELF-INDULGENT

in·dus·tri·al /ɪnˈdʌstriəl/ *adj.* **1** relating to industry or the people working in it: *modern industrial practices* | *The factory has developed an ingenious way of dealing with industrial waste.* **2** of the type used in industry: *The cleaner is for industrial use* (=not to be used at home) *only.* **3** having many industries, or industries that are well developed: *an industrial nation* —**industrially** *adv.* —compare INDUSTRIOUS

industrial arts /.,... '../ *n.* [U] a subject taught in school about how to use tools, machinery etc.

industrial es·pi·o·nage /.,... '..../ *n.* [U] stealing secret information from one company in order to help a different company

in·dus·tri·al·ism /ɪnˈdʌstriəˌlɪzəm/ n. [U] the system by which a society gets its wealth through industries and machinery

in·dus·tri·al·ist /ɪnˈdʌstriəlɪst/ n. [C] the owner or manager of a factory, industrial company etc.

in·dus·tri·al·ize /ɪnˈdʌstriəˌlaɪz/ v. [I,T] if a country or place is industrialized or if it industrializes, it develops a lot of industry —**industrialization** /ɪnˌdʌstriələˈzeɪʃən/ n. [U]

in·dus·tri·al·ized /ɪnˈdʌstriəˌlaɪzd/ adj. having factories, mines, industrial companies etc. on a very wide scale: an industrialized nation

industrial park /.ˌ.. './ n. [C] an area of land that has offices, businesses, small factories etc. on it

industrial re·la·tions /.ˌ.. .'../ n. [plural] the relationship between workers and employers

industrial rev·o·lu·tion /.ˌ.. ... ../ n. [singular] **1 the Industrial Revolution** the period in the 18th and 19th centuries in Europe, when machines and factories began to be used to produce goods in large quantities **2** a period of time in other countries when more machines are being used to produce goods

industrial-strength /.'... ,./ adj. [only before noun] very strong or effective, and appropriate for use in factories: an industrial-strength detergent

in·dus·tri·ous /ɪnˈdʌstriəs/ adj. someone who is industrious tends to work hard —**industriousness** n. [U] —compare INDUSTRIAL

in·dus·try /ˈɪndəstri/ n. plural industries **1** [U] the production of goods, especially in factories: The chemicals are widely used in industry as refrigerants. | The government encourages the development of industry with tax breaks. **2** [C] a particular type of trade or service: the airline industry | Miami's tourist industry **3** FORMAL the energy and willingness to work very hard: She has demonstrated a great deal of industry in finishing the project on time. —see also HEAVY INDUSTRY, LIGHT INDUSTRY, SERVICE INDUSTRY

-ine /aɪn, ɪn/ suffix FORMAL OR TECHNICAL **1** relating to a particular thing: equine (=relating to horses) **2** made of something, or similar to it: a crystalline substance

in·e·bri·ate /ɪˈnibriɪt/ n. [C] OLD-FASHIONED someone who is often drunk —**inebriate** adj.

in·e·bri·at·ed /ɪˈnibriˌeɪtɪd/ adj. FORMAL drunk

in·ed·i·ble /ɪnˈɛdəbəl/ adj. not good enough to eat, or not appropriate for eating: The meat had been cooked so long that it was inedible.

in·ed·u·ca·ble /ɪnˈɛdʒəkəbəl/ adj. FORMAL impossible or very difficult to educate

in·ef·fa·ble /ɪnˈɛfəbəl/ adj. FORMAL too great to be described in words: ineffable satisfaction —**ineffably** adv.

in·ef·fec·tive /ˌɪnəˈfɛktɪv/ adj. something that is ineffective does not achieve what it is intended to achieve: Efforts to get homeless people off the streets have been largely ineffective. —**ineffectively** adv. —**ineffectiveness** n. [U]

in·ef·fec·tu·al /ˌɪnəˈfɛktʃuəl/ adj. not having the ability, confidence, or personal authority to get things done: an ineffectual leader | All of their attempts to come to an agreement has been ineffectual. —**ineffectually** adv.

in·ef·fi·cient /ˌɪnəˈfɪʃənt/ adj. a worker, organization, or system that is inefficient does not work well and wastes time, money, or energy: an inefficient banking system | The army was inefficient and poorly equipped. —**inefficiently** adv. —**inefficiency** n. [C,U]

in·el·e·gant /ɪnˈɛləgənt/ adj. not graceful or well done: His manners are somewhat inelegant. | inelegant architecture

in·el·i·gi·ble /ɪnˈɛlɪdʒəbəl/ adj. not allowed to do or have something: [+ for] His dishonorable discharge from the Navy makes him ineligible for military benefits. | [ineligible to do sth] Since he was born in England, he's ineligible to run for president in this country. —**ineligibility** /ɪnˌɛlɪdʒəˈbɪləti/ n. [U]

in·e·luc·ta·ble /ˌɪnɪˈlʌktəbəl/ adj. LITERARY impossible to escape from; UNAVOIDABLE

in·ept /ɪˈnɛpt/ adj. having no skill: When it comes to girls, Isaac is socially inept and awkward. | the inept management of the team —**ineptly** adv. —**ineptitude, ineptness** n. [U]

in·e·qual·i·ty /ˌɪnɪˈkwɑləti/ n. plural inequalities [C,U] an unfair situation, in which some groups in society have less money, influence, or opportunity than others: The statistics show the growing inequality of income in America.

in·eq·ui·ta·ble /ɪnˈɛkwɪtəbəl/ adj. FORMAL not equally fair to everyone; UNJUST: an inequitable distribution of wealth —**inequitably** adv.

in·eq·ui·ty /ɪnˈɛkwɪti/ n. plural inequities [C,U] FORMAL lack of fairness, or something that is unfair: There are many inequities in our health-care system.

in·e·rad·i·ca·ble /ˌɪnɪˈrædɪkəbəl/ adj. FORMAL a fact, quality, or situation that is ineradicable is permanent and cannot be changed: Poverty seems an ineradicable fact of the human condition.

in·ert /ɪˈnɝt/ adj. **1** TECHNICAL not producing a chemical reaction when combined with other substances: inert gases **2** not moving or not having the strength or power to move: She lay there, inert. **3** very slow and unwilling to take any action: School officials remained inert on the issue of bullying. —**inertly** adv. —**inertness** n. [U]

in·er·tia /ɪˈnɝʃə/ n. [U] **1** a tendency for a situation to stay unchanged for a long time: the inertia and bureaucracy of large companies **2** lack of energy and a feeling that you do not want to do anything: The group helped me overcome my inertia and lose weight. **3** TECHNICAL the force that keeps an object in the same position, or keeps it moving until it is moved or stopped by another force —**inertial** adj.

in·es·cap·a·ble /ˌɪnəˈskeɪpəbəl/ adj. impossible to avoid: The conclusion is inescapable. This was an accidental drug overdose and not a suicide. —**inescapably** adv.

in·es·sen·tial /ˌɪnəˈsɛnʃəl/ adj. FORMAL not needed; UNNECESSARY: Many people consider air conditioning inessential here. —**inessentials** n. [plural]

in·es·ti·ma·ble /ɪnˈɛstəməbəl/ adj. FORMAL too much or too great to be calculated: Carey has been an inestimable help in my life. —**inestimably** adv.

in·ev·i·ta·ble /ɪˈnɛvətəbəl/ adj. **1** certain to happen and impossible to avoid: Since the leaders can't agree, more fighting is inevitable. | Payton handled the inevitable questions about his past with great dignity. **2 the inevitable** a situation that is certain to happen: One day the inevitable happened and I got a speeding ticket. —**inevitability** /ɪˌnɛvətəˈbɪləti/ n. [U]

in·ev·i·ta·bly /ɪˈnɛvətəbli/ adv. if something will inevitably happen, it is sure to happen and cannot be prevented: Such bad economic conditions inevitably lead to more crime.

in·ex·act /ˌɪnɪgˈzækt/ adj. not exact: the inexact science of earthquake prediction —**inexactness** n. [U]

in·ex·cus·a·ble /ˌɪnɪkˈskyuzəbəl/ adj. inexcusable behavior is too bad to be excused: Being late for your own wedding is inexcusable. —**inexcusably** adv.

in·ex·haust·i·ble /ˌɪnɪgˈzɔstəbəl/ adj. existing in such large amounts that it can never be finished or used up: Cold fusion would be a cheap and virtually inexhaustible energy source. | the public's inexhaustible fascination with crime —**inexhaustibly** adv.

in·ex·o·ra·ble /ɪnˈɛksərəbəl/ adj. FORMAL an inexorable process cannot be stopped: the inexorable progress of rain forest destruction —**inexorably** adv.

in·ex·pe·di·ent /ˌɪnɪkˈspidiənt/ adj. FORMAL not quick or effective in helping to solve a problem —**inexpedience** also **inexpediency** n. [U]

in·ex·pen·sive /ˌɪnɪkˈspɛnsɪv/ adj. APPROVING cheap and of good quality for the price you pay: an inexpensive meal —**inexpensively** adv. —see Usage Note at CHEAP[1]

I

in·ex·pe·ri·ence /ˌɪnɪkˈspɪriəns/ *n.* [U] lack of experience or knowledge: *His political inexperience often shows.*

in·ex·pe·ri·enced /ˌɪnɪkˈspɪriənst/ *adj.* not having much experience or knowledge: *inexperienced drivers*

in·ex·pert /ɪnˈɛkspət/ *adj.* not having the skill to do something —**inexpertly** *adv.*

in·ex·pli·ca·ble /ˌɪnɪkˈsplɪkəbəl/ *adj.* too unusual or strange to be explained or understood: *For some inexplicable reason, some rooms of the mansion will suddenly turn very cold.* —**inexplicably** *adv.*

in·ex·press·i·ble /ˌɪnɪkˈsprɛsəbəl/ *adj.* **inexpressible joy/bitterness/grief etc.** a feeling or condition that is too strong to be described in words —**inexpressibly** *adv.*

in·ex·pres·sive /ˌɪnɪkˈsprɛsɪv/ *adj.* a face that is inexpressive shows no emotion at all

in·ex·tin·guish·a·ble /ˌɪnɪkˈstɪŋwɪʃəbəl/ *adj.* LITERARY **inextinguishable hope/love/passion etc.** hope, love etc. that is so strong that it cannot be destroyed

in ex·tre·mis /ˌɪn ɪkˈstrimɪs/ *adv.* FORMAL **1** in a very difficult and urgent situation when very strong action is needed **2** at the moment of death

in·ex·tric·a·ble /ˌɪnɪkˈstrɪkəbəl, ɪnˈɛkstrɪk-/ *adj.* FORMAL two or more things that are inextricable cannot be separated from each other: *There is an inextricable link between language and culture.*

in·ex·tric·a·bly /ˌɪnɪkˈstrɪkəbli/ *adv.* **be inextricably linked/connected/mixed etc.** if two or more things are inextricably LINKed, connected etc., they are very closely connected and cannot be separated: *The racism in our culture today is inextricably tied to our past.*

in·fal·li·ble /ɪnˈfæləbəl/ *adj.* **1** always right and never making mistakes: *Having been divorced three times, Aden admits he's far from infallible.* **2** something that is infallible always works or has the intended effect: *DNA testing is an almost infallible method of identification.* —**infallibly** *adv.* —**infallibility** /ɪnˌfæləˈbɪləti/ *n.* [U]

in·fa·mous /ˈɪnfəməs/ *adj.* well known for being bad or morally evil: *an infamous crime* | *infamous killer* —**infamously** *adv.* —see Usage Note at FAMOUS[1]

in·fa·my /ˈɪnfəmi/ *n.* **1** [U] the state of being evil or well known for evil things **2** [C usually plural] an evil action

in·fan·cy /ˈɪnfənsi/ *n.* [singular,U] **1** the period of a child's life before they can walk or talk: *John's twin brother died in infancy* (=during infancy). **2 in its infancy** also **during/in the infancy of sth** something that is in its infancy is just starting to be developed: *In 1891, football on the West Coast was still in its infancy.*

s w **in·fant**[1] /ˈɪnfənt/ *n.* [C] FORMAL a baby, especially one ┌─┐ that has not yet learned to walk or talk —see Usage └─┘ Note at CHILD
3

infant[2] *adj.* [only before noun] an infant company, organization etc. has just started to exist or be developed

in·fan·ti·cide /ɪnˈfæntəˌsaɪd/ *n.* [U] TECHNICAL the crime of killing a young child

in·fan·tile /ˈɪnfənˌtaɪl, -təl/ *adj.* **1** infantile behavior seems silly in an adult because it is typical of a child: *an infantile temper tantrum* **2** [only before noun] TECHNICAL affecting very young children: *infantile development*

infantile pa·ral·y·sis /ˌ... .ˈ.../ *n.* [U] OLD-FASHIONED: see POLIO

infant mor·tal·i·ty rate /ˌ... .ˈ... ˌ./ *n.* [C] the number of deaths of babies under one year old, expressed as the number out of each 1,000 babies born alive in a year

in·fan·try /ˈɪnfəntri/ *n.* [U] soldiers who fight on foot —compare CAVALRY

in·fan·try·man /ˈɪnfəntrimən/ *n. plural* **infantrymen** /-mən/ [C] a soldier who fights on foot

in·farc·tion /ɪnˈfɑrkʃən/ *n.* [C] TECHNICAL a medical condition in which a blood VESSEL becomes blocked

in·fat·u·at·ed /ɪnˈfætʃuˌeɪtɪd/ *adj.* having strong unreasonable feelings of love for someone or interest in something: [+ **with**] *Sheppard was infatuated with his friend's fiancee.* | *a country infatuated with TV violence*

in·fat·u·a·tion /ɪnˌfætʃuˈeɪʃən/ *n.* [C,U] strong unreasonable feelings of love for someone or interest in something: [+ **with**] *Bardo said his infatuation with Schaeffer dominated his life.* | *an infatuation with sex*

in·fect /ɪnˈfɛkt/ *v.* [T usually passive] **1** to give someone a disease: [+ **with**] *Twenty people were infected with tuberculosis by one sick employee.* **2** to make food, water, the air etc. dangerous and able to spread disease: *The fruits were infected by a fungus disease called brown rot.* **3** if a feeling or interest that you have infects other people, it makes them begin to feel the same way: *The book may infect you with a passion for mountain climbing.* **4** if a computer VIRUS infects your computer or DISKs, it changes or destroys the information in them

in·fect·ed /ɪnˈfɛktɪd/ *adj.* **1** a part of your body or a wound that is infected has harmful BACTERIA in it that prevents it from HEALing: *The cut on my foot became infected.* | *an infected finger* **2** food, water etc. that is infected contains BACTERIA that spread disease: *The water here is infected with cholera.* **3** if a computer or DISK is infected, the information in it has been changed or destroyed by a computer VIRUS

in·fec·tion /ɪnˈfɛkʃən/ *n.* [C,U] a disease caused by s w BACTERIA or a VIRUS that affects a particular part of ┌─┐ your body: *an ear infection* | *The antibiotic ointment* └─┘ *will prevent infection.* 3 3

in·fec·tious /ɪnˈfɛkʃəs/ *adj.* **1** an infectious disease can be passed from one person to another, especially through the air you breathe: *Doctors say that the disease is most infectious in the first twenty-four hours.* **2** someone who is infectious has an illness and could pass it to other people **3** infectious feelings or laughter spread quickly from one person to another: *Sheila has an infectious smile.*

in·fe·lic·i·ty /ˌɪnfɪˈlɪsəti/ *n. plural* **infelicities** [C,U] FORMAL **1** the quality of not being happy **2** something such as a remark, way of writing or speaking etc. that is not appropriate or not correct for a particular situation: *Despite some infelicities, Sohmer has written a wonderful thriller.* —**infelicitous** *adj.*

in·fer /ɪnˈfə/ *v.* **inferred, inferring** [T] to form an opinion that something is probably true because of other information that you already know: [+ **from**] *The judge told the jury not to infer anything from the defendant's refusal to testify.* | [**infer that**] *It can be inferred that Gilbert supplemented his income with his profits from drug sales.* —compare IMPLY

USAGE NOTE: INFER

WORD CHOICE: infer, imply
A speaker or writer can **imply** something, and the listener or reader can **infer** it. *Jeanie implied that she was mad at me.* This means that Jeanie indirectly said that she was mad, but did not say those words specifically. *I inferred from what Jeanie said that she was mad at me.* This means that this is what I thought she meant.

---

in·fer·ence /ˈɪnfərəns/ *n.* **1** [C] something that you think is probably true, based on information that you already know: *Previously, scientists had to* **draw inferences** (=decide what to think) *about genes from the chemicals that are part of them, rather than studying them directly.* **2** [U] the act of inferring something: *They portrayed her as the hero, and* **by inference,** *Mr. Thompson as the villain.* —**inferential** /ˌɪnfəˈrɛnʃəl/ *adj.* —**inferentially** *adv.*

in·fe·ri·or[1] /ɪnˈfɪriɚ/ *adj.* **1** not good, or worse in quality, value, or skill than someone or something else: *Shockingly, they still perceive women as inferior.* | *inferior health-care facilities* | [+ **to**] *Some people view American wines as inferior in quality to European wines.* **2** FORMAL lower in rank: *an inferior court of law* —**inferiority** /ɪnˌfɪriˈɔrəti, -ˈɑr-/ *n.* [U] —compare SUPERIOR[1]

inferior[2] *n.* [C] someone who has a lower position or rank than you in an organization —compare SUPE-RIOR[2]

inferiority com·plex /...'...,../ *n.* [C] a continuous feeling that you are much less important, smart etc. than other people

in·fer·nal /ɪnˈfɜ·nl/ *adj.* **1** [only before noun] OLD-FASHIONED used to express anger or annoyance about something: *I can't get this infernal machine to work.* **2** LITERARY relating to HELL and evil

in·fer·no /ɪnˈfɜ·noʊ/ *n. plural* **infernos** [C] LITERARY an extremely large and dangerous fire: *High winds quickly turned the fire into a deadly inferno.*

in·fer·tile /ɪnˈfɜ·tl/ *adj.* **1** an infertile person or animal is unable to have babies or unable to produce eggs or SPERM **2** infertile land or soil is not good enough to grow plants in —**infertility** /ˌɪnfəˈtɪləti/ *n.* [U]

in·fest /ɪnˈfɛst/ *v.* [T] if insects, rats etc. infest a place, they are there in large numbers and usually cause damage: *mosquito-infested swamps* | [+ **with**] *The trees are infested with bark beetles.* —**infestation** /ˌɪnfɛsˈteɪʃən/ *n.* [C,U]

in·fi·del /ˈɪnfədl, -ˌdɛl/ *n.* [C] OLD-FASHIONED used by people from one religion to talk with strong disapproval about someone who believes in a different religion

in·fi·del·i·ty /ˌɪnfəˈdɛləti/ *n. plural* **infidelities** [C,U] when one person has a sexual relationship with someone who is not their wife, husband, or partner: *a marriage destroyed by infidelity*

in·field /ˈɪnfild/ *n.* [singular] **1** the part of a baseball field inside the four bases —see picture at BASEBALL **2** the group of players who play in this part of the field —**infielder** *n.* [C] —compare OUTFIELD

in·fight·ing /ˈɪnˌfaɪtɪŋ/ *n.* [U] unfriendly competition and disagreement among members of the same group or organization: *political infighting*

in·fil·trate /ɪnˈfɪlˌtreɪt, ˈɪnfɪl-/ *v.* **1** [I always + adv./prep., T] to secretly join an organization or enter a place in order to find out information about it or to harm it: *Federal undercover agents infiltrated a Miami drug ring.* | [+ **into**] *Intelligence reports confirm that terrorists have infiltrated into the region.* **2** [T] to put people into an organization or place to find out information about it or to harm it: [**infiltrate sb into sth**] *They repeatedly tried to infiltrate assassins into the palace.* —**infiltrator** *n.* [C] —**infiltration** /ˌɪnfɪlˈtreɪʃən/ *n.* [U]

in·fi·nite /ˈɪnfənɪt/ *adj.* **1** very great: *One of Keyes' gifts is her infinite patience.* | *Different types of sausage are available in infinite variety.* **2** without limits in space or time: *The universe is infinite.* —compare FINITE (1)

in·fi·nite·ly /ˈɪnfənɪtli/ *adv.* [+ adj./adv.] very much: *Our new office building is infinitely better than the old one.*

in·fin·i·tes·i·mal /ˌɪnfɪnəˈtɛsəməl/ *adj.* extremely small: *The risk of getting AIDS from a health-care worker is infinitesimal.* —**infinitesimally** *adv.*

in·fin·i·tive /ɪnˈfɪnətɪv/ *n.* [C] TECHNICAL in grammar, the basic form of a verb, used with "to." In the sentence "I want to watch TV," "to watch" is an infinitive —see also SPLIT INFINITIVE

in·fin·i·tude /ɪnˈfɪnəˌtud/ *n.* [singular,U] FORMAL a number or amount without limit

in·fin·i·ty /ɪnˈfɪnəti/ *n.* **1** [U] a space or distance without limits or an end: *the infinity of space* **2** [singular] a number that is too large to be calculated: *an infinity of possible solutions*

in·firm /ɪnˈfɜ·m/ *adj.* **1** weak or sick, especially because you are old: *He was too infirm to hold a steady job.* **2 the infirm** all the people who are weak or sick

in·fir·ma·ry /ɪnˈfɜ·məri/ *n. plural* **infirmaries** [C] **1** a room in a school or other institution where people can get medical treatment **2** a hospital, especially in the military

in·fir·mi·ty /ɪnˈfɜ·məti/ *n. plural* **infirmities** [C,U] FORMAL bad health or a particular illness

in fla·gran·te de·lic·to /ɪn fləˌɡrænteɪ dɪˈlɪktoʊ/ *adv.* FORMAL OR HUMOROUS during the act of having sex, especially with someone else's husband or wife

in·flame /ɪnˈfleɪm/ *v.* [T] to make someone's feelings of anger, excitement etc. much stronger: *The shooting inflamed ethnic tensions.*

in·flamed /ɪnˈfleɪmd/ *adj.* a part of your body that is inflamed is red and swollen, because it is hurt or infected: *an inflamed left knee*

in·flam·ma·ble /ɪnˈflæməbəl/ *adj.* **1** inflammable materials or substances will start to burn very easily; FLAMMABLE: *an inflammable liquid* —opposite NONFLAMMABLE —see Usage Note at FLAMMABLE **2** easily becoming angry or violent, or easily making people angry or violent: *an inflammable political issue*

in·flam·ma·tion /ˌɪnfləˈmeɪʃən/ *n.* [C,U] swelling and soreness on or in part of your body, which is often red and feels hot: *The disease causes inflammation of the brain.*

in·flam·ma·to·ry /ɪnˈflæməˌtɔri/ *adj.* **1** an inflammatory speech, piece of writing etc. is likely to make people feel angry: *inflammatory news accounts of the trial* **2** TECHNICAL an inflammatory disease, condition etc. causes inflammation

in·flat·a·ble /ɪnˈfleɪtəbəl/ *adj.* an inflatable object has to be filled with air before you can use it: *an inflatable life boat*

inflate

in·flate /ɪnˈfleɪt/ *v.* **1** [I,T] if you inflate something, or if it inflates, it fills with air or gas so that it becomes larger: *We inflated the balloons with helium.* | *The raft inflates automatically.* **2** [T] to make something seem more important or impressive than it is: *Beauty, money, and popularity can all inflate a person's ego.* **3** [T] TECHNICAL to make prices increase, or to tell someone that the amount or price of something is higher than it really is: *Axe says that the management pressured him to inflate cost estimates on repairs.* —opposite DEFLATE

in·flat·ed /ɪnˈfleɪtɪd/ *adj.* **1** inflated prices, sums etc. are high and unreasonable: *an inflated budget estimate* **2** inflated ideas or opinions about something make it seem more important than it really is: *All this attention has given Carla an inflated opinion of herself.* **3** filled with air or gas

in·fla·tion /ɪnˈfleɪʃən/ *n.* [U] **1** a continuing increase in prices, or the rate at which prices increase: *Inflation is now running at over 16%.* **2** the process of filling something with air

in·fla·tion·a·ry /ɪnˈfleɪʃəˌnɛri/ *adj.* [usually before noun] relating to or causing price increases: *inflationary pressures in the economy* | *an inflationary spiral* (=the continuing rise in wages and prices because an increase in one causes an increase in the other)

inflation-proof /.'...,./ *adj.* protected against price increases: *inflation-proof stocks*

in·flect /ɪnˈflɛkt/ *v.* **1** [I] TECHNICAL if a word inflects, its form changes according to its meaning or use **2** [I,T] if your voice inflects or if you inflect it, the sound of it becomes higher or lower as you are speaking

in·flect·ed /ɪnˈflɛktɪd/ adj. TECHNICAL an inflected language contains many words that change their form according to their meaning or use: *German is an inflected language.*

in·flec·tion /ɪnˈflɛkʃən/ n. **1** [U] TECHNICAL the way in which a word changes its form to show difference in its meaning or use **2** [C] TECHNICAL one of the forms of a word that changes in this way, or one of the parts that is added to it **3** [C,U] the way the sound of your voice goes up and down when you are speaking —**inflectional** adj.

in·flex·i·ble /ɪnˈflɛksəbəl/ adj. **1** inflexible rules, arrangements etc. are impossible to change: *The proposed law is poorly written and inflexible.* **2** unwilling to make even the slightest change in your attitudes or plans etc.: *Some of his employees find him inflexible.* **3** inflexible material is stiff and will not bend —**inflexibility** /ɪnˌflɛksəˈbɪləti/ n. [U]

in·flict /ɪnˈflɪkt/ v. **1** [T] to make someone suffer something bad or painful: [**inflict sth on sb/sth**] *Parents in these difficult situations may inflict emotional and physical abuse on their children.* | *Hurricanes often inflict severe damage on South Florida.* **2 inflict yourself on sb** HUMOROUS to visit or be with someone when they do not want you: *Frank's parents are inflicting themselves on us for the weekend.* —**infliction** /ɪnˈflɪkʃən/ n. [U]

in-flight /ˈ. ./ adj. [only before a noun] provided or happening during an airplane flight: *in-flight movies*

in·flow /ˈɪnfloʊ/ n. **1** [C] the movement of people, money, goods etc. into a place: *the inflow of foreign investments* **2** [singular,U] the flow of water into a place —opposite OUTFLOW

S W
2
in·flu·ence[1] /ˈɪnfluəns/ n. **1** [C,U] power to have an effect on the way someone or something develops, behaves, or thinks without using direct force or commands: [**+ with**] *Broderick used his influence with city hall to cover up the crime.* | *No individual has had a more positive influence on world politics than Gorbachev.* | *They had come under the influence of* (=controlled by the influence of) *a strange religious sect.* **2** [C] someone or something that has an effect on other people or things | **be a bad/good/negative etc. influence (on/in sb/sth)** *Her grandmother has been such a good influence in her life.* | *Basically, both sides want to limit any outside influence* (=influence from other groups or people) *on the negotiations.* **3 under the influence of sth** drunk or feeling the effects of a drug

influence[2] v. [T] to have an effect on the way someone or something develops, behaves, thinks etc. without directly forcing or commanding them: *Some of the romantic painters were very much influenced by Goya's work.* | *Don't let me influence your decision.* | [**influence sb to do sth**] *What influenced you to study philosophy?*

influence-ped·dling /ˈ... ˌ../ n. [U] when a politician agrees illegally to help someone, support their plans etc. in exchange for money

in·flu·en·tial /ˌɪnfluˈɛnʃəl/ adj. having a lot of influence and therefore changing the way people think and behave: *an influential religious leader* | [**influential in (doing) sth**] *Chavez was influential in improving working conditions for farm workers.*

in·flu·en·za /ˌɪnfluˈɛnzə/ n. [U] FORMAL the FLU

in·flux /ˈɪnflʌks/ n. [C] the arrival of large numbers of people or large amounts of money, goods etc., especially suddenly: [**+ of**] *Tourism has brought a huge influx of wealth into the region.*

in·fo /ˈɪnfoʊ/ n. [U] INFORMAL information

in·fo·mer·cial /ˈɪnfoʊˌmɜʃəl/ n. [C] a long television advertisement that provides a lot of information about a product and seems like a normal program

S W
3
in·form /ɪnˈfɔrm/ v. [T] **1** to formally or officially tell someone about something or give them information: [**inform sb about/of sth**] *The bank never informed us of how the money was being invested.* | [**inform sb (that)**] *Then the doctors informed the family that* there was no hope for his recovery. **2** [usually passive] FORMAL to influence someone's attitude, opinion, or way of doing something: *Her style is informed by the writings of Kafka, Artaud, and Beckett.*

inform on sb phr. v. [T] to tell the police information about what someone has done, especially something illegal: *Robard is now informing on others, hoping to reduce his jail sentence.*

in·for·mal /ɪnˈfɔrməl/ adj. **1** relaxed and friendly without being restricted by rules of correct behavior: *The atmosphere at work is fairly informal.* | *The two groups met for informal talks.* **2** informal clothes are appropriate for wearing at home or in ordinary situations; CASUAL (1) **3** an informal style of writing or speaking is appropriate for ordinary conversations or letters to friends —**informally** adv. —**informality** /ˌɪnfərˈmæləti/ n. [U]

in·form·ant /ɪnˈfɔrmənt/ n. [C] someone who secretly tells the police, the army, the government etc. about criminal activities, especially in return for money: *Working as an informant, Johnson provided the FBI with details on the Mafia's criminal activities*

in·for·ma·tion /ˌɪnfərˈmeɪʃən/ n. **1** [U] facts or details that tell you something about a situation, person, event etc.: *Harrington was arrested for selling government information to other countries.* | [**+ about/on**] *You can find more information on the Civil War at the library.* | **Additional information** *can be obtained by writing or faxing your questions.* | *Your travel agent can provide you with more information about visas.* | **gather/collect information** *Surveys are good for gathering information about your customers.* | *The most important piece of information in a cab is the driver's number.* **2** [U] the telephone service that you can call to get someone's telephone number **3 for your information** SPOKEN used when you are telling someone that they are wrong about a particular fact: *For your information, he really was sick yesterday.* —compare FYI —**informational** adj. —see also **inside information** (INSIDE[4] (2))

S W
11

information cen·ter /ˈ..ˈ. ˌ../ n. [C] a place where you can get information about an area, event etc.

information re·triev·al /ˈ..ˈ. ˌ../ n. [U] the process of finding stored information, especially on a computer

information sci·ence /ˌ.... ˈ. ./ n. [U] the science of collecting, arranging, storing, and sending out information

information su·per·high·way /ˌ..ˌ.. ..ˈ. / n. the **information superhighway** the system of computer connections that people anywhere in the world can use to electronically send or obtain information, pictures, sounds etc.

information tech·nol·o·gy /ˌ..ˌ.. .ˈ.../ abbreviation **IT** n. [U] the study or use of electronic processes for gathering information, storing it, and making it available, using computers

information the·o·ry /ˈ..ˈ. ˌ../ n. [U] TECHNICAL the mathematical principles relating to sending and storing information

in·form·a·tive /ɪnˈfɔrmətɪv/ adj. providing many useful facts or ideas: *She gave an informative talk on various aspects of child care.* —**informatively** adv. —**informativeness** n. [U]

in·formed /ɪnˈfɔrmd/ adj. **1** [usually before noun] having a lot of knowledge or information about a particular subject or situation: *an informed public* | *The report was confirmed by informed sources within the government.* **2 an informed decision/choice/recommendation etc.** a decision, choice etc. that is based on knowledge of a subject or situation: *Women need to be able to make an informed choice about contraception.* **3 keep sb informed** to give someone the latest news and details about a situation: *Please keep me fully informed of any new developments.*

-informed /ɪnˈfɔrmd/ [in adjectives] **well-informed/ill-informed/badly-informed** knowing a lot or not knowing much about what is happening in the world: *The new data will help biologists make well-informed decisions about management of species.*

in·form·er /ɪnˈfɔrmə/ n. [C] someone who secretly

tells the police, the army etc. about criminal activities, especially in return for money

in·fo·tain·ment /ˌɪnfoʊˈteɪnmənt/ *n.* [U] television programs that deal with important subjects in a way that people can enjoy

infra- /ˈɪnfrə/ *prefix* TECHNICAL below and beyond something in a range: *an infrared camera* (=that can see things below red in the color range) —compare ULTRA- (1)

in·frac·tion /ɪnˈfrækʃən/ *n.* [C,U + **of**] FORMAL an act of breaking a rule or law

in·fra·red /ˌɪnfrəˈrɛd◂/ *adj.* infrared light gives out heat but cannot be seen —compare ULTRAVIOLET

in·fra·struc·ture /ˈɪnfrəˌstrʌktʃə/ *n.* [C] the basic systems and structures that a country or organization needs in order to work well, for example roads, communications, and banking systems —**infrastructural** *adj.*

in·fre·quent /ɪnˈfrikwənt/ *adj.* not happening often; RARE: *Rain is infrequent in this normally hot, dry region of the world.* —**infrequently** *adv.* —**infrequency** *n.* [U]

in·fringe /ɪnˈfrɪndʒ/ *v.* [T] to do something that is against a law or that limits someone's legal rights: *The court ruled that he had infringed the company's patent.* —**infringement** *n.* [C,U]
infringe on/upon sth *phr. v.* [T] to limit someone's freedom in some way: *The smoking ban in public buildings infringes on the rights of smokers.*

in·fu·ri·ate /ɪnˈfyʊriˌeɪt/ *v.* [T] to make someone extremely angry: *Her racist attitudes infuriated her co-workers.*

in·fu·ri·at·ing /ɪnˈfyʊriˌeɪtɪŋ/ *adj.* extremely annoying: *a whining and infuriating two-year-old boy* —**infuriatingly** *adv.*

in·fuse /ɪnˈfyuz/ *v.* **1** [T] FORMAL to fill something or someone with a particular feeling or quality: *Knowles' Christian beliefs continue to infuse both his personal life and his politics.* | [**be infused with** sth] *The novel is infused with humor, irony, and grief.* | [**infuse** sb **with** sth] *The program has infused kids with new hope.* **2** [I,T] if you infuse tea or HERBS or if they infuse, you leave them in very hot water while their taste passes into the water

in·fu·sion /ɪnˈfyuʒən/ *n.* **1** [C,U] the act of putting a new feeling or quality into something: *What the department needs is an infusion of new ideas.* **2** [C] a medicine made with HERBS in hot water and usually taken as a drink

-ing /ɪŋ/ *suffix* **1** [in verbs] used to form the present participle of verbs: *They're dancing.* | *to go dancing* | *a dancing bear* **2** [in U nouns] the action or process of doing something: *She hates swimming.* | *No parking.* **3** [in U nouns] **a)** an example of doing something: *a meeting* **b)** a product or result of doing something: *a beautiful painting* **4** [in nouns] something used for making something or used to do something: *a silk lining* (=fabric for the inside of clothes) | *underground piping* (=pipes used to carry water away)

Inge /ɪndʒ/, **William** (1913–1973) a U.S. writer of plays

in·ge·nious /ɪnˈdʒinyəs/ *adj.* **1** an ingenious plan, idea, INVENTION etc. works well and is the result of intelligent thinking and new ideas: *an ingenious marketing strategy* **2** someone who is ingenious is very good at inventing things or thinking of new ideas —**ingeniously** *adv.*

in·gé·nue /ˈændʒənu, ˈɑnʒə-/ *n.* [C] a young inexperienced girl especially in a movie or play

in·ge·nu·i·ty /ˌɪndʒəˈnuəti/ *n.* [U] skill at inventing things and thinking of new ideas

in·gen·u·ous /ɪnˈdʒɛnyuəs/ *adj.* FORMAL an ingenuous person trusts people too much and is honest, especially because they do not have experience in how badly people can behave —**ingenuously** *adv.* —**ingenuousness** *n.* [U] —opposite DISINGENUOUS

in·gest /ɪnˈdʒɛst/ *v.* [T] TECHNICAL to take food into your body —**ingestion** /ɪnˈdʒɛstʃən/ *n.* [U] —compare DIGEST¹ (1)

in·gle·nook /ˈɪŋgəlˌnʊk/ *n.* [C] a seat by the side of a large open FIREPLACE, or the space that it is in

in·glo·ri·ous /ɪnˈglɔriəs/ *adj.* LITERARY causing shame and dishonor: *an inglorious defeat* —**ingloriously** *adv.*

in·got /ˈɪŋgət/ *n.* [C] a LUMP of pure metal in a regular shape, usually shaped like a brick

in·grained /ɪnˈgreɪnd, ˈɪngreɪnd/ *adj.* **1** ingrained attitudes or behavior are firmly established and therefore difficult to change: *deeply ingrained religious beliefs* **2** ingrained dirt is under the surface of something and very difficult to remove

in·grate /ˈɪngreɪt/ *n.* [C] FORMAL someone who is ungrateful

in·gra·ti·ate /ɪnˈgreɪʃiˌeɪt/ *v.* DISAPPROVING **ingratiate yourself (with** sb) to try hard to get someone's approval, by doing things to please them, expressing admiration etc.: *Isn't it sickening how Daniela tries to ingratiate herself with Harriet?*

in·gra·ti·at·ing /ɪnˈgreɪʃiˌeɪtɪŋ/ *adj.* DISAPPROVING trying too hard to get someone's approval: *Durning's character is both ingratiating and calculating.* —**ingratiatingly** *adv.*

in·grat·i·tude /ɪnˈgrætəˌtud/ *n.* [U] the quality of not being grateful for something: *He regularly accuses his children of ingratitude and selfishness.*

in·gre·di·ent /ɪnˈgridiənt/ *n.* [C] **1** one of the different types of foods that you use to make a particular dish: *The main ingredient was spicy ground pork.* | *Add the **dry ingredients** (=flour, SPICES etc.) to the egg mixture.* **2** a quality you need to achieve something: *Imagination and hard work are the **key ingredients** (=most important qualities) of success.*

In·gres /ˈæŋgrə/, **Jean Au·guste Dom·i·nique** /ʒɑn oʊˈgust dɑmɪˈnik/ (1780–1867) a French PAINTER famous for his pictures of people

in·gress /ˈɪngrɛs/ *n.* [U] LITERARY the right to enter a place or the act of entering it

in·group /ˈ. ./ *n.* [C] a small group of people in an organization or activity who are popular or have influence, and who are friendly with each other but do not want other people to join them; CLIQUE —**ingroup** *adj.*

in·grown /ˈɪngroʊn/ *adj.* [no comparative] an ingrown TOENAIL or FINGERNAIL grows inwards, cutting into the surrounding skin

in·hab·it /ɪnˈhæbɪt/ *v.* [T] if animals or people inhabit an area or place, they live there: *The site once was inhabited by the Ohlone Indians.* —**inhabitable** *adj.*

in·hab·it·ant /ɪnˈhæbətənt/ *n.* [C] one of the people who live in a particular place: *a city of six million inhabitants*

in·ha·lant /ɪnˈheɪlənt/ *n.* [C,U] a medicine or drug that you breathe in, for example when you have a cold

in·hale /ɪnˈheɪl/ *v.* [I,T] to breathe in air, smoke, or gas: *It was later determined that Burke had inhaled poisonous fumes.* | *Myra lit another cigarette and **inhaled deeply** (=inhaled a lot of smoke).* —opposite EXHALE —**inhalation** /ˌɪnhəˈleɪʃən/ *n.* [C,U]

in·hal·er /ɪnˈheɪlə/ *n.* [C] a small plastic tube containing medicine that you inhale in order to make breathing easier

in·here /ɪnˈhɪr/ *v.*
inhere in sth *phr. v.* [T] TECHNICAL to be a natural part of something

in·her·ent /ɪnˈhɪrənt, -ˈhɛr-/ *adj.* a quality that is inherent in something is a natural part of it and cannot be separated from it: *Dance is also an inherent part of the culture.* | [+ **in**] *They discussed the risks inherent in starting a small business.* —**inherently** *adv.*

in·her·it /ɪnˈhɛrɪt/ *v.* **1** [I,T] to receive money, property etc. from someone after they have died: [**inherit** sth **from** sb] *Jones inherited $2 million from an elderly woman he had once helped.* —compare DISINHERIT **2** [T] to get a quality, type of behavior, appearance etc. from one of your parents: [**inherit** sth **from** sb] *Janice inherited her good looks from her mom.* **3** [T] to have a problem that was caused by mistakes that other people have made in the past: [**inherit sth from sb**] *I inherited this mess from my supervisor who got fired.* **4** [T] INFORMAL to get something from someone else who does not want it any longer: [**inherit sth from sb**] *We inherited the furniture from the previous tenants.*

in·her·i·tance /ɪnˈhɛrɪtəns/ *n.* **1** [C,U] money, property etc. that you receive from someone after they have died: *Garth doesn't work; he just lives off his inheritance.* **2** [U] FORMAL ideas, beliefs, skills, literature, music etc. from the past that influence people in the present: *our literary inheritance*

inheritance tax /.ˈ… ˌ./ *n.* [U] a tax on the money or property that you receive from someone after they die

in·her·i·tor /ɪnˈhɛrɪtə/ *n.* [C] someone who receives money, property etc. from someone else after that person has died

in·hib·it /ɪnˈhɪbɪt/ *v.* [T] **1** to prevent something from growing or developing as much as it might have: *We're doing all we can to inhibit urban sprawl and maintain the city's identity.* **2** to make someone feel embarrassed or less confident so that they cannot do or say what they want to: [**inhibit sb from doing sth**] *Taping the meeting would inhibit people from expressing their opinions.*

in·hib·it·ed /ɪnˈhɪbɪtɪd/ *adj.* not confident or relaxed enough to do or say what you want to: *Girls in all-female science classes **feel** less **inhibited** about asking questions.*

in·hi·bi·tion /ˌɪnhɪˈbɪʃən, ˌɪnə-/ *n.* [C,U] a feeling of worry or embarrassment that stops you from doing or saying what you really want to: *People seem to **lose their inhibitions** (=stop feeling worry or embarrassment) when talking with each other on the Internet.*

in·hos·pi·ta·ble /ˌɪnhɑˈspɪtəbəl/ *adj.* **1** an inhospitable place is difficult to live or stay in because of severe weather conditions or lack of shelter: *inhospitable climate* **2** unfriendly to a visitor, especially by not welcoming them, not offering them food etc.

in-house /ˌ. ˈ.ˌ/ *adj. adv.* within a company or organization rather than outside it: *All of our product design is done in-house.* | *an in-house training program*

in·hu·man /ɪnˈhyumən/ **1** very cruel without any normal feelings of pity: *To send these people back to their war-torn country is cruel and inhuman.* | *inhuman living conditions* **2** lacking any human qualities in a way that seems strange or frightening: *The interviewer had a cold, almost inhuman, manner.*

in·hu·mane /ˌɪnhyuˈmeɪn/ *adj.* treating people or animals in a cruel and unacceptable way: *the inhumane treatment of prisoners* —**inhumanely** *adv.*

in·hu·man·i·ty /ˌɪnhyuˈmænəti/ *n.* [C usually plural, U] cruel behavior or acts of extreme cruelty: *Amnesty International protests against injustice and inhumanity.*

in·im·i·cal /ɪˈnɪmɪkəl/ *adj.* making it difficult for something to exist or happen: *a cold, inimical climate* | [+ **to**] *Price controls are inimical to economic growth.*

in·im·i·ta·ble /ɪˈnɪmɪtəbəl/ *adj.* too good or skillful for anyone else to copy with the same high standard: *the inimitable comedian, Charlie Chaplin* —compare IMITATE

in·iq·ui·tous /ɪˈnɪkwətəs/ *adj.* FORMAL very unfair and morally wrong: *an iniquitous system of taxes*

in·iq·ui·ty /ɪˈnɪkwəti/ *n. plural* **iniquities** [C,U] FORMAL the quality of being very unfair or evil, or something that is very unfair —see also **den of iniquity** (DEN (5))

s w
3 3 **i·ni·tial¹** /ɪˈnɪʃəl/ *adj.* [only before noun] happening at the beginning of a plan, process, situation etc.; FIRST: *Initial sales figures have been very good.* | *the initial stages of the disease*

initial² *n.* [C] the first letter of someone's or something's name: *Ed is known as Easy, because of his initials, E.C.*

initial³ *v.* [T] to write your initials on a document to make it official or to show that you have seen it or agree with it: *You have to initial any corrections you make to the form.*

in·i·tial·ly /ɪˈnɪʃəli/ *adv.* at the beginning of a plan, s w
3 process, situation etc.: *Stan initially wanted to go to medical school.*

i·ni·ti·ate¹ /ɪˈnɪʃiˌeɪt/ *v.* [T] **1** FORMAL to arrange for something to start, such as an official process or a new plan: *A large number of companies have initiated recycling programs.* **2** to introduce someone to special knowledge or skills that they did not know about before: [**initiate sb into sth**] *My grandmother initiated me into the mysteries of quilting.* **3** to introduce someone into an organization, club, group etc., usually with a special ceremony: [**initiate sb**] *Sororities and fraternities are initiating new members this week.*

i·ni·ti·ate² /ɪˈnɪʃiɪt/ *n.* [C] someone who has been allowed to join a particular group and has been taught its secrets

in·i·ti·a·tion /ɪˌnɪʃiˈeɪʃən/ *n.* [C,U] **1** the process of officially introducing someone into a club or group, or of introducing a young person to adult life, often with a special ceremony: *the group's secret initiation rite* **2** the act of starting something such as an official process, a new plan etc.

i·ni·tia·tive /ɪˈnɪʃətɪv/ *n.* **1** [U] the ability to make s w
2 decisions and take action without waiting for someone to tell you what to do: *Employers look for workers who **show initiative**.* | *Greyhound banned smoking on buses **on its own initiative** (=without being told to do it), before it became law.* | *Don't keep asking me for advice. **Use your initiative**.* **2** [C] an important new plan or process that has been started in order to achieve a particular aim or to solve a particular problem: *a government initiative to help exporters* **3** [C] LAW a process by which ordinary citizens can suggest a change in the law by signing a PETITION asking for the change to be voted on **4** **the initiative** if you have or take the initiative, you are able to take actions that will influence events or a situation, especially in order to change a situation or gain an advantage for yourself: *Parents at the school **took the initiative** to raise money for a music program.* | *Zhukov was quick to **seize the initiative** and launched a massive counter attack.*

in·ject /ɪnˈdʒɛkt/ *v.* [T] **1** to put liquid, especially a drug, into someone's body by using a special needle: [**inject sth into sb/sth**] *A pain-killer was injected into his foot before the operation.* | [**inject sb/yourself with sth**] *She purposely injected herself with a fatal drug dose.* **2** to improve something by adding excitement, interest etc. to it [**inject sth into sth**] *They hoped that the adoption of a child would inject new life into their marriage.* **3** [**inject sth into sth**] to provide more money, equipment etc. for something: *Hastings Corporation has injected huge amounts of money into the venture.*

in·jec·tion /ɪnˈdʒɛkʃən/ *n.* **1** [C,U] an act of giving a drug by using a special needle: [**give sb/sth an injection (of sth)**] *The zookeeper gave the tiger an injection of morphine.* **2** [C,U] the act of forcing a liquid into something: *a fuel-injection engine* **3** [C] an addition of money to something in order to improve it: [+ **of**] *The oil company is counting on a $1 billion injection of capital from the government for research.*

in-joke /ˈ. ./ *n.* [C] a joke that is only understood by a particular group of people

in·ju·di·cious /ˌɪndʒuˈdɪʃəs/ *adj.* FORMAL an injudicious action, remark etc. is not sensible and is likely to have bad results: *an injudicious investment* —**injudiciously** *adv.*

In·jun /ˈɪndʒən/ *n.* OLD-FASHIONED **1** a word for a Native American, now considered offensive **2** **honest Injun** an expression used especially by children to make someone believe they are telling the truth, now considered offensive

in·junc·tion /ɪnˈdʒʌŋkʃən/ *n.* [C] **1** LAW an order given by a court which forbids someone to do something: *The environmental group is seeking an* *injunction to stop the sale of public land.* | [+ **against**] *Judge Atkins issued an injunction against the deportation of the refugees.* **2** FORMAL a piece of advice or a command from someone in authority

in·jure /ˈɪndʒə/ v. [T] **1** to hurt someone or yourself, for example in an accident or an attack: *Dad injured his back lifting some heavy boxes.* | *Two men were severely injured trying to save a 5-year-old girl from a pit bull.* **2 injure sb's pride/self-esteem etc.** to upset someone by damaging their confidence —compare WOUND³ —see Usage Note at DAMAGE²

in·jured /ˈɪndʒəd/ adj. **1** having an injury: *an injured bird* | *Runners should not run while injured.* **2 the injured** injured people: *Eight of the injured are still in serious condition.* **3 an njured look/expression etc.** LITERARY a look that shows you feel you have been treated unfairly **4 injured pride/feelings etc.** a feeling of being upset or offended because you think you have been unfairly treated **5 the injured party** FORMAL the person who has been unfairly treated in a particular situation

injured list /ˈ.. ../ n. the DISABLED LIST

in·ju·ri·ous /ɪnˈdʒʊriəs/ adj. FORMAL causing injury, harm, or damage: *Sniffing glue is injurious to your health.*

in·ju·ry /ˈɪndʒəri/ n. plural **injuries 1** [C] a wound or damage to part of your body caused by an accident or attack | **suffer/sustain injury** *Rasmussen sustained head and neck injuries in the crash.* | *Three of the passengers have **internal injuries** (=injuries inside their bodies).* **2** [U] physical harm that is caused by an accident or attack: *The policy covers injury suffered on the job.* —see also **add insult to injury** (ADD (6))

in·jus·tice /ɪnˈdʒʌstɪs/ n. **1** [C,U] a situation in which people are treated very unfairly and not given their rights: *The movie deals with injustices suffered by Native Americans.* | *racial injustice* **2 do sb an injustice** to do something bad to someone: *Cutting the benefits of war veterans would be doing them a great injustice.*

ink¹ /ɪŋk/ n. **1** [C,U] colored liquid used for writing, printing, or drawing **2** [U] the black liquid in an ocean creature such as an OCTOPUS or SQUID —see also RED INK

ink² v. [T] **1** to put ink on something: *The number was inked on the side of his helmet.* **2** OLD-FASHIONED to write something in ink, especially your SIGNATURE on a contract etc.

ink sth in phr. v. [T] to complete something done in pencil by drawing over it in ink

ink·blot /ˈɪŋkblɑt/ n. [C] a pattern made by a drop of ink on a piece of paper, especially used in PSYCHOLOGICAL tests

ink·jet print·er /ˈɪŋkdʒɛt ˌprɪntə/ n. [C] a type of electronic PRINTER, usually connected to a small computer

ink·ling /ˈɪŋklɪŋ/ n. **have an inkling** to have a slight idea about something: *I had an inkling that he would change jobs.*

ink pad /ˈ. ./ n. [C] a small box containing ink on a thick piece of cloth, used for putting ink onto a STAMP¹ (2) that is then pressed onto paper

ink·stand /ˈɪŋkstænd/ n. [C] a container used for holding pens and pots of ink, kept on a desk

ink·well /ˈɪŋk-wɛl/ n. [C] a container that holds ink and fits into a hole in a desk, used especially in past times

ink·y /ˈɪŋki/ adj. **inkier, inkiest 1** very dark: *clouds of inky black smoke* **2** marked with ink: *inky fingers*

in·laid /ˈɪnleɪd, ɪnˈleɪd/ adj. **1** an inlaid box, table, floor etc. has a thin layer of another material set into its surface for decoration: [+ **with**] *a belt inlaid with diamonds and rubies* **2** [+ **in/into**] metal, stone etc. that is inlaid into the surface of another material is set into its surface as decoration

in·land¹ /ˈɪnlənd/ adj. [only before noun] an inland area, city etc. is not near the coast

in·land² /ɪnˈlænd, ˈɪnlænd/ adv. in a direction away from the coast and toward the center of a country: *The mountains are five miles inland.*

in-laws /ˈ. ./ n. [plural] INFORMAL your relatives by marriage, especially the father and mother of your husband or wife: *My in-laws are coming to visit next week.*

in·lay /ˈɪnleɪ/ n. **1** [C,U] a material that has been set into the surface of furniture, floors etc. for decoration, or the pattern made by this: *The guitar has a mother-of-pearl inlay on its fret board.* **2** [C] a substance used by a DENTIST to fill a hole in a decayed tooth

in·let /ˈɪnlɛt, ˈɪnlət/ n. [C] **1** a narrow area of water reaching from an ocean or a lake into the land or between islands **2** the part of a machine through which liquid or gas flows in

in-line skate /ˌ. ˈ. ./ n. [C usually plural] a special boot with a single row of wheels attached under it; —compare ROLLER SKATE —see picture at SKATE¹

in-line ska·ting /ˌ. ˈ.. ./ n. [U] the sport of using in-line skates to move quickly over roads, streets etc. —see picture on page 430

in lo·co pa·ren·tis /ɪn ˌloʊkoʊ pəˈrɛntɪs/ adv. LAW having the responsibilities of a parent for someone else's child

in·mate /ˈɪnmeɪt/ n. [C] someone who is kept in a prison or MENTAL HOSPITAL

in me·mo·ri·am /ɪn məˈmɔriəm/ prep. an expression meaning "in memory of," used especially on the stone above a grave

in·most /ˈɪnmoʊst/ also **innermost** adj. [only before noun] **1** your inmost feelings, desires etc. are the ones you feel most strongly about and usually do not talk about **2** FORMAL farthest inside —opposite OUTERMOST

inn /ɪn/ n. [C] **1** a word used in the names of some hotels and restaurants: *We're staying at the Ramada Inn.* **2** a small hotel, especially one in the country

in·nards /ˈɪnədz/ n. [plural] INFORMAL **1** the parts inside your body, especially your stomach **2** the parts inside a machine

in·nate /ˌɪˈneɪt/ adj. an innate quality is part of a person's character from the time they are born: *Children have an innate curiosity about the physical world* —**innately** adv.

in·ner /ˈɪnə/ adj. [only before noun]

1 inside on the inside or close to the center of something: *My wallet is in the inner breast pocket of my jacket.* | *Carefully remove the inner skin of the chestnuts.* —opposite OUTER

2 inner workings/meanings/thoughts etc. meanings, thoughts etc. are either secret or not well known: *His book provides a vivid picture of the inner workings of the bank.*

3 inner circle the few people in an organization, political party etc. who control it or share power with its leader: *Hollywood's inner circle*

4 relating to your soul or deepest feelings or coming from there: *I've had to rely on my inner strength to weather the rumors.*

5 sb's inner voice thoughts or feelings that someone does not express but which seem to warn or advise them: *My inner voice told me to be cautious.*

6 sb's inner child the part of someone's character that still feels like a child even though they are an adult

7 the inner man/woman the soul

inner cit·y /ˌ. ˈ.. ./ n. plural **inner cities** [C] the part of a city near the middle, where usually the buildings are in a bad condition and the people are poor —**inner-city** adj.: *inner-city schools*

inner ear /ˌ.. ˈ./ n. [C] TECHNICAL the part of your ear inside your head that you use for hearing and balance

inner·most /ˈɪnəmoʊst/ adj. INMOST

inner tube /ˈ.. ˌ./ n. [C] the rubber tube filled with air that is inside a tire

inner-tub·ing /ˈ.. ˌ.. ./ n. [U] **go inner-tubing** to ride on an inner tube either on water or down a snow-covered hill

in·nie /ˈɪni/ *n.* [C] INFORMAL a BELLY BUTTON that does not stick out —compare OUTIE

in·ning /ˈɪnɪŋ/ *n.* [C] one of the nine playing periods in a game of baseball or SOFTBALL

inn·keep·er /ˈɪnˌkipɚ/ *n.* [C] OLD USE someone who owns or manages an INN

in·no·cence /ˈɪnəsəns/ *n.* [U] **1** the fact of being not guilty of a crime: *Lawyers are trying to prove their client's innocence.* | *Both defendants maintained their innocence* (=continued to say they were not guilty). —opposite GUILT¹ **2** the state of not having much experience of life or knowledge about evil in the world: *In our innocence, we believed everything we were told.* | *the innocence of childhood*

in·no·cent¹ /ˈɪnəsənt/ *adj.* **1** not guilty of a crime: *Nobody believes that she's innocent.* | [+ **of**] *Nathan's lawyer says his client is innocent of any wrongdoing.* | *The jury found him innocent of dealing drugs.* —opposite GUILTY (2) **2** innocent victims/bystanders/people etc. people who get hurt or killed in a war or as a result of a crime, though they are not involved in it **3** done or said without intending to harm or offend anyone: *I'm sorry. It was just an innocent mistake.* **4** not having much experience of life, so that you are easily deceived; NAIVE: *I was thirteen years old and very innocent.* —**innocently** *adv.*

innocent² *n.* [C] someone who does not have much experience about life or knowledge about evil in the world: *He's such an innocent; anyone can take advantage of him.*

in·noc·u·ous /ɪˈnɑkyuəs/ *adj.* not offensive, dangerous, or harmful: *The interviewer only asked boring, innocuous questions.* | *innocuous chemicals* —**innocuously** *adv.*

in·no·vate /ˈɪnəˌveɪt/ *v.* [I] to begin to use new ideas, methods, or inventions: *Their ability to innovate has allowed them to compete in world markets.*

in·no·va·tion /ˌɪnəˈveɪʃən/ *n.* **1** [C] a new idea, method, or invention: *Anti-lock brakes have been a major safety innovation.* **2** [U] the introduction of new ideas, methods, or inventions: *Innovation and hard work are the cornerstones of this company.*

in·no·va·tive /ˈɪnəˌveɪtɪv/ *adj.* **1** an innovative process, method, plan etc. is new, different, and better than those that existed before **2** using or inventing good new ideas and methods: *an innovative young man*

in·no·va·tor /ˈɪnəˌveɪtɚ/ *n.* [C] someone who introduces changes and new ideas

in·nu·en·do /ˌɪnyuˈɛndoʊ/ *n. plural* **innuendoes** or **innuendos 1** [C] an indirect remark about sex or about something bad that someone has done: *The dialogue is full of sexual innuendoes.* **2** [U] the act of making this type of negative remark: *The family is being torn apart by rumor and innuendo.*

In·nu·it /ˈɪnuɪt/ *n.* another spelling of INUIT

in·nu·mer·a·ble /ɪˈnumərəbəl/ *adj.* very many, or too many to be counted: *She has received innumerable get-well cards and flowers.*

in·nu·mer·a·cy /ɪˈnumərəsi/ *n.* [U] the inability to do calculations or understand basic mathematics —**innumerate** *adj.*

in·oc·u·late /ɪˈnɑkyəˌleɪt/ *v.* [T] to protect someone against a disease, usually by INJECTing them with a weak form of it: [+ **against**] *None of the children had been inoculated against measles.* —**inoculation** /ɪˌnɑkyəˈleɪʃən/ *n.* [C,U] —compare IMMUNIZE, VACCINATE

in·of·fen·sive /ˌɪnəˈfɛnsɪv/ *adj.* unlikely to offend anyone: *His first campaign ads were bland and inoffensive.* —**inoffensively** *adv.*

in·op·er·a·ble /ɪnˈɑpərəbəl/ *adj.* **1** an inoperable illness or TUMOR (=lump) cannot be treated or removed by a medical operation: *an inoperable brain tumor*

2 an inoperable system or method does not work or cannot be used because it is broken or not practical

in·op·er·a·tive /ɪnˈɑpərətɪv/ *adj.* **1** a machine that is inoperative is not working, or is not in working condition **2** a system or a law that is inoperative is not working or cannot be made to work

in·op·por·tune /ɪnˌɑpɚˈtun, ˌɪnɑ-/ *adj.* happening at a time that is not appropriate or good for something: *Telemarketers always seem to call at the most inopportune moments.*

in·or·di·nate /ɪnˈɔrdn̩-ɪt/ *adj.* much more than you expect or think is reasonable or normal: *an inordinate number of meetings* —**inordinately** *adv.*

in·or·gan·ic /ˌɪnɔrˈgænɪk◂/ *adj.* **1** not containing any HYDROCARBONS, or not consisting of anything that is living **2** not produced or allowed to develop in a natural way —**inorganically** /-kli/ *adv.*

inorganic chem·is·try /ˌ.... ˈ.../ *n.* [U] TECHNICAL the science and study of substances that do not contain HYDROCARBONS —compare ORGANIC CHEMISTRY

in·pa·tient /ˈɪnˌpeɪʃənt/ *n.* [C] someone who stays in a hospital for treatment, rather than coming in for treatment from home —compare OUTPATIENT

in·put¹ /ˈɪnpʊt/ *n.* [C,U] **1** information that is put into a computer **2** ideas, advice, money, or effort that you put into a job, meeting etc. in order to help it succeed: *We value the input of everyone who answered the questionnaire.* **3** electrical power that is put into a machine for it to use —compare OUTPUT

input² *v. past tense and participle* **inputted** or **input** [T] to put information into a computer

in·quest /ˈɪnkwɛst/ *n.* [C] **1** a legal process to find out the cause of a sudden or unexpected death, especially if there is a possibility that the death is the result of a crime: *The inquest ruled the cause of death was suicide.* **2** an unofficial discussion about the reasons for someone's defeat or failure to do something

in·qui·e·tude /ɪnˈkwaɪəˌtud/ *n.* [U] LITERARY anxiety

in·quire, enquire /ɪnˈkwaɪɚ/ *v.* [I,T] to ask someone for information: *"Did you ever raise money illegally?" the interviewer inquired.* | [+ **about**] *I am writing to inquire about subscribing to your magazine.* | [+ **of**] *The committee will inquire of Millhouse about his involvement with the bank.* | [**inquire why/whether/how etc.**] *It's just human nature to inquire why things went wrong.* | *I inquired as to whether I could call back later.* —**inquirer** *n.* [C] —see Usage Note at ASK

inquire into sth *phr. v.* [T] to ask questions in order to get more information about something or to find out why something happened: *Inspectors also inquire into nursing home residents' quality of life.*

in·quir·ing, enquiring /ɪnˈkwaɪərɪŋ/ *adj.* [only before noun] **1** an inquiring mind/reader/reporter etc. someone who has an inquiring mind or is an inquiring reader, REPORTER etc. is naturally very interested in finding out more information or gaining more knowledge **2** an inquiring look or expression shows that you want to ask about something —**inquiringly** *adv.*

in·quir·y, enquiry /ɪnˈkwaɪəri, ˈɪŋkwəri/ *n. plural* **inquiries 1** [C] a question you ask in order to get information: [+ **about**] *The Internet is useful for making inquiries about flights and hotel accommodations.* **2** [C] an official process intended to get information about something or find out why something happened: *The chancellor must convince students that the inquiry was thorough and fair.* | [+ **into**] *An inquiry into the killings of six priests has still not revealed any new evidence.* **3** [U] the act or process of asking questions in order to get information or find out about something: *On further inquiry, it became clear that Walters had not been involved.* **4** scientific/scholarly/intellectual etc. inquiry a process of trying to discover facts by scientific, SCHOLARLY etc. methods

in·qui·si·tion /ˌɪnkwəˈzɪʃən/ *n.* **1 the Inquisition** the Catholic organization in past times whose purpose was to find and punish people who had unacceptable religious beliefs **2** [singular] a series of questions that someone asks you in a way that seems threatening or not nice: *The detectives have turned the investigation into an inquisition.*

in·quis·i·tive /ɪnˈkwɪzətɪv/ *adj.* **1** interested in a lot of different things and wanting to find out more about them: *a bright, inquisitive child* **2** asking too many questions and trying to find out too many details about something or someone: *Don't be so inquisitive – it makes people uncomfortable.* —**inquisitively** *adv.*

in·quis·i·tor /ɪnˈkwɪzətɚ/ *n.* [C] **1** someone who asks you a lot of difficult questions and makes you feel very uncomfortable **2** an official of the INQUISITION —**inquisitorial** /ɪnˌkwɪzəˈtɔriəl/ *adj.* —**inquisitorially** *adv.*

in re /ɪn ˈri, -ˈreɪ/ *prep.* an expression used especially in business letters that means "concerning" —see also RE[1]

in·roads /ˈɪnroʊdz/ *n.* **make inroads 1** to become more and more successful, powerful, or popular and so take away power, trade, votes etc. from a competitor or enemy: [+ **in/into/on**] *Many banks have made inroads into the insurance business.* **2** to make steady progress toward achieving something difficult: *The program can make inroads by helping students to see how what they are learning relates to life.*

INS *n.* **the INS** the Immigration and Naturalization Service; the U.S. government department that deals with people who come to live in the U.S. from other countries

ins /ɪnz/ *n.* **the ins and outs (of sth)** all of the details of something such as a system, profession etc.: *I'm still learning the ins and outs of the import/export business.*

in·sa·lu·bri·ous /ˌɪnsəˈlubriəs/ *adj.* FORMAL insalubrious conditions or places are dirty or not nice, and are bad for your health

in·sane /ɪnˈseɪn/ *adj.* **1** INFORMAL completely stupid or crazy, often in a way that is dangerous: *Paul must be insane, spending all that money on a boat.* **2** someone who is insane is permanently and seriously mentally ill so that they cannot live in normal society: *The killer was declared criminally insane.* **3 drive sb insane** INFORMAL to make someone feel more and more annoyed or angry, usually over a long period of time: *The noise from the construction project is driving us completely insane.* —**insanely** *adv.: insanely jealous*

in·san·i·tar·y /ɪnˈsænəˌteri/ *adj.* UNSANITARY

in·san·i·ty /ɪnˈsænəţi/ *n.* [U] **1** the state of being seriously mentally ill, so that you cannot live normally in society: *Brennan blames her actions on temporary insanity.* **2** very stupid actions that may cause you serious harm: *It was sheer insanity to try to drive through the mountains in that thunderstorm.*

in·sa·tia·ble /ɪnˈseɪʃəbəl/ *adj.* always wanting more and more of something: *an insatiable appetite for attention* —**insatiably** *adv.*

in·scribe /ɪnˈskraɪb/ *v.* [T] to carefully cut, print, or write words on something, especially on the surface of a stone or coin: [**inscribe sth on/in sth**] *Fittingly, Martin Luther King's words are inscribed on the Civil Rights Memorial's granite wall.* | [**be inscribed with**] *The box was inscribed with the name "Judy."*

in·scrip·tion /ɪnˈskrɪpʃən/ *n.* [C] a piece of writing inscribed on a stone, in the front of a book etc.

in·scru·ta·ble /ɪnˈskruţəbəl/ *adj.* if someone is inscrutable, it is very difficult to know what they are feeling or thinking, because they do not show their feelings or reactions: *He handled the questions with the inscrutable face of a diplomat.* —**inscrutability** /ɪnˌskruţəˈbɪləţi/ *n.* [U]

in·seam /ˈɪnsim/ *n.* [C] a SEAM on the part of a pair of pants that covers the inside of your legs

in·sect /ˈɪnsɛkt/ *n.* [C] a small creature such as a fly or ANT, that has six legs, and sometimes wings

in·sec·ti·cide /ɪnˈsɛktəˌsaɪd/ *n.* [U] a chemical substance used for killing insects —**insecticidal** /ɪnˌsɛktəˈsaɪdl/ *adj.* —compare PESTICIDE

in·sec·ti·vore /ɪnˈsɛktəˌvɔr/ *n.* [C] a creature that eats insects —**insectivorous** /ˌɪnsɛkˈtɪvərəs/ *adj.*

in·se·cure /ˌɪnsɪˈkyʊr/ *adj.* **1** not feeling confident about yourself, your abilities, your relationships etc.: *Meeting new people always makes me feel insecure.* | [+ **about**] *Most teenagers are insecure about their looks.* **2** a job, situation etc. that is insecure does not give you a feeling of safety, because it is likely to change or be taken away at any time: *The U.S needs to reduce its dependence on insecure foreign oil supplies.* **3** a building or structure that is insecure is not safe, because it is likely to fall down —**insecurity** *n.* [U] —**insecurely** *adv.*

in·sem·i·nate /ɪnˈsɛməˌneɪt/ *v.* [T] TECHNICAL to put SPERM into a woman or female animal in order to make her have a baby —**insemination** /ɪnˌsɛməˈneɪʃən/ *n.* [U] —see also ARTIFICIAL INSEMINATION

in·sen·sate /ɪnˈsɛnseɪt, -sɪt/ *adj.* FORMAL **1** not able to feel things **2** unreasonable and crazy: *insensate rage*

in·sen·si·bil·i·ty /ɪnˌsɛnsəˈbɪləţi/ *n.* [U] **1** FORMAL the state of being unconscious **2** OLD USE inability to experience feelings such as love, sympathy, anger etc.

in·sen·si·ble /ɪnˈsɛnsəbəl/ *adj.* FORMAL **1** not knowing about something that could happen to you; UNAWARE: [+ **of**] *She remained insensible of the dangers that lay ahead.* **2** unable to feel something or be affected by it: [+ **to/of**] *Doug seemed insensible to the cold.*

in·sen·si·tive /ɪnˈsɛnsəţɪv/ *adj.* **1** not noticing other people's feelings, especially not realizing when something that you do upsets them: *Kelsey denies making racially insensitive statements.* | [+ **to**] *She's totally insensitive to Jack's feelings.* **2** not paying attention to what is happening or to what people are saying, and therefore not changing your behavior because of it: [+ **to**] *The state government is insensitive to the needs of the poor and minorities.* **3** not affected by physical effects or changes: [+ **to**] *Some people are more insensitive to pain than others.* | *The material is insensitive to light.* —**insensitively** *adv.* —**insensitivity** /ɪnˌsɛnsəˈtɪvəţi/ *n.* [U]

in·sen·tient /ɪnˈsɛnʃənt/ *adj.* FORMAL not feeling or not being conscious —**insentience** *n.* [U]

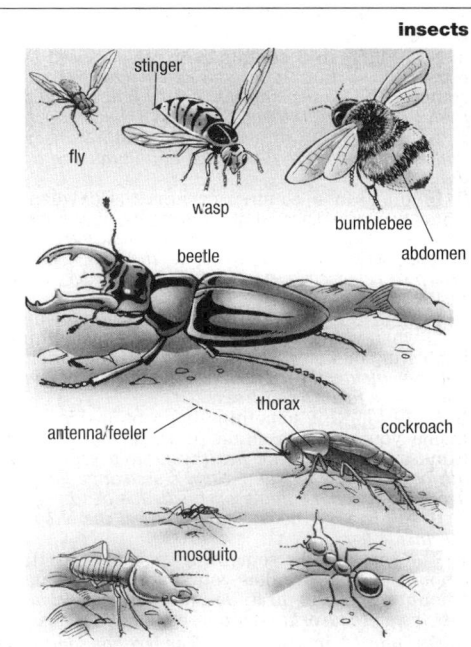

insects

stinger

fly

wasp

bumblebee

beetle

abdomen

thorax

cockroach

antenna/feeler

mosquito

termite

ant

in·sep·a·ra·ble /ɪnˈsɛpərəbəl/ *adj.* **1** people who are inseparable are always together and are very friendly with each other: *Ever since they met those two have been inseparable.* **2** things that are inseparable cannot be separated or cannot be considered separately: *Work and ongoing education are becoming inseparable in our society.* | [+ **from**] *Kelly considers equality to be inseparable from true liberty.* —**inseparably** *adv.*

in·sert¹ /ɪnˈsɚt/ *v.* [T] **1** to put something inside or into something else: [**insert sth in/into/between sth**] *Insert two quarters into the machine.* | *A pin was inserted in Pollard's leg to speed the healing process.* **2** to add something to a document or piece of writing: *A clause was inserted in the contract that gives him 30% of any future earnings.*

insert

in·sert² /ˈɪnsɚt/ *n.* [C] **1** a printed page that is put inside a newspaper or magazine in order to advertise something: *Look for the coupon inserts in Sunday's paper.* **2** something that is designed to be put inside something else: *The Tri-X table comes with glass, granite, or steel inserts.*

in·ser·tion /ɪnˈsɚʃən/ *n.* **1** [U] the act of putting something inside something else **2** [C] something that is added to the middle of a document or piece of writing

in·serv·ice /ˌ. ˈ..ˌ/ *adj.* **in-service training/courses etc.** training etc. that you do while you are working in a job

in·set¹ /ˈɪnsɛt/ *n.* [C] a small picture, map etc. on a page or larger picture, that shows more detail or information: *The inset on the following page shows more detail of the downtown area.*

in·set² /ˈɪnsɛt, ɪnˈsɛt/ *v. past tense and past participle* **inset** [T] **1** to put something in as an inset on a printed page **2 be inset with sth** if something is inset with decorations, jewels etc., it has them set in its surface

in·shore /ˌɪnˈʃɔr/ *adv.* near, toward, or to the shore: *A couple of fishermen had sighted the boat close inshore.* —**inshore** *adj.*: *inshore currents*

in·side¹ /ɪnˈsaɪd, ˈɪnsaɪd/ *prep.*
1 container in a container or other closed space, especially so that it is completely covered or surrounded: *Inside the mailbox, a bird had built a small nest.* | *Try to guess what I'm holding inside my hand.*
2 building/room in a room or building: *Inside the house, police officers found two handguns and a shotgun.*
3 country in a country or area, used when you want to emphasize that something is happening there and not outside it: *The guerrillas were said to be operating from bases inside the war zone.* | *A group of reporters were stopped at a border crossing inside France.*
4 organization in an organization or company, used when you want to emphasize that something is happening or known about there, but not outside it: *Sources inside the company said that they plan to move more factories overseas.*
5 head/mind if something happens inside you, or inside your head or mind, it is part of what you think and feel: *It's not healthy to keep your feelings all locked inside of you.* | *Steve's a strange guy – you never know what's going on inside his head.*
6 body in your body: *She could feel the baby kicking inside her.*
7 time if you do something inside a particular amount of time, it takes you slightly less than that amount of time to do it: *Jonson's finishing time was just inside the world record.* —opposite OUTSIDE¹

in·side² *adv.* **1** in something: *The box has some letters inside.* **2** in a house or other building: *I'm getting cold. Let's go inside.* | *When we got to the window, we saw that there were already people inside.* | [+ **of**] *There were more than 20 people packed inside of her dorm room.* **3** if you have a feeling inside, you have the feeling but do not show it to other people: *Gabby cringed a little inside when Peter showed up drunk.* **4 inside of sth** SPOKEN if you do something inside of a particular amount of time, it takes you slightly less than that amount of time to do it: *I should be back inside of an hour.*

inside³ *n.* **1 the inside** the inner part of something, which is surrounded or hidden by the outer part: *The inside of the cup was stained.* | *The door had been locked from the inside.* —opposite OUTSIDE⁴ **2 inside out** with the usual outside parts on the inside: *She had her shirt on inside out.* | *Before I hung up my jeans, I turned the pockets inside out to dry.* —see picture at UPSIDE DOWN¹ **3 sb's insides** INFORMAL someone's stomach: *My insides are telling me I need to eat.* **4 on the inside** someone who is on the inside is a member of a group or an organization: *To have such accurate information, they must have someone on the inside.* —see also **know sth inside (and) out** (KNOW¹ (14)), **turn sth inside out** (TURN¹ (16))

inside⁴ *adj.* **1** on or facing the inside of something: *The tulip's inside petals are canary yellow on ivory white.* **2 inside information/story etc.** information that is available only to people who are part of a particular group or organization: *A newspaper bought his inside story of the inner workings of the Chicago Bulls.* —opposite OUTSIDE³

in·sid·er /ɪnˈsaɪdɚ/ *n.* [C] someone who has a special knowledge of a particular organization because they are part of it: *a White House insider* —compare OUTSIDER

insider trad·ing also **insider deal·ing** /.ˌ.. ˈ../ *n.* [U] the illegal buying and selling of a company's STOCK that involves the use of secret information known only by people who work with the company

inside track /ˌ.. ˈ./ *n.* [C] **1** a position that gives someone an advantage over the people they are competing against: *Johnston appears to have the inside track on directing the movie.* **2** the part of a circular track for racing that is nearest to the center of the circle and is therefore shorter

in·sid·i·ous /ɪnˈsɪdiəs/ *adj.* an insidious change or problem happens gradually without being noticed, and causes serious harm: *A more insidious form of water pollution is chemicals used on farms that get into the water supply.* —**insidiously** *adv.* —**insidiousness** *n.* [U]

in·sight /ˈɪnsaɪt/ *n.* **1** [C,U] a sudden clear understanding of something, especially something complicated: [+ **into**] *Her research has given us some insight into what sparks a teenager's curiosity.* | [+ **about**] *The reports provided little insight about the economy's condition.* **2** [U] the ability to understand and realize what people or situations are really like: *a woman of great insight*

in·sig·ni·a /ɪnˈsɪɡniə/ *n. plural* **insignia** [C] a PATCH or other object that shows what official or military rank someone has, or which group or organization they belong to

in·sig·nif·i·cant /ˌɪnsɪɡˈnɪfəkənt/ *adj.* too small or unimportant to consider or worry about: *The cost of the software is insignificant compared with the cost of training employees to use it.* | *an insignificant detail* —**insignificantly** *adv.* —**insignificance** *n.* [U]

in·sin·cere /ˌɪnsɪnˈsɪr/ *adj.* pretending to be pleased, sympathetic etc., especially by saying nice things, but not really meaning what you say: *The mayor's sympathy seemed insincere.* | *an insincere smile* —**insincerely** *adv.* —**insincerity** /ˌɪnsɪnˈsɛrəti/ *n.* [U]

in·sin·u·ate /ɪnˈsɪnyuˌeɪt/ *v.* [T] **1** to say something that seems to mean something negative, without saying it directly: [**insinuate that**] *He insinuated that Harkham was lying about the accounts.* **2 insinuate yourself into sth** to gradually gain someone's love, trust etc. by pretending to be friendly and sincere: *Carolyn tried to insinuate herself into the rich Solomon family.*

in·sin·u·a·tion /ɪnˌsɪnyuˈeɪʃən/ n. **1** [C] something that someone insinuates: *an insinuation of sexual harassment* **2** [U] the act of insinuating something

in·sip·id /ɪnˈsɪpɪd/ adj. **1** food or drink that is insipid does not have much taste: *Canned coffees taste either harsh or insipid.* **2** not interesting, exciting, or attractive: *insipid commercials* —**insipidly** adv. —**insipidness** n. [U]

in·sist /ɪnˈsɪst/ v. [I,T] **1** to say firmly and often that something is true, especially when other people think it may not be true: [**insist (that)**] *Tomita insisted that the changes would not affect most tax-payers.* | *Experts insist there is no chance of a reces-sion in the near future.* **2** to demand that something should happen and refuse to let anyone say no: *Let me pay this time. I insist.* | [**insist (that)**] *I'm glad my parents insisted that we speak Spanish at home.* | *Bud insisted he drive us home.* **3 if you insist** SPOKEN used when agreeing to do something that you do not really want to do: *"Let's invite them over for dinner." "OK, if you insist."*

insist on sth phr. v. [T] **1** to think that something is very important, and demand that you have it or do it: *The chef insists on the best and freshest ingredi-ents.* | *He insists on calling me by my first name.* **2** to keep doing something, especially something that is inconvenient or annoying: *Tim insists on watching those stupid action movies.*

in·sist·ence /ɪnˈsɪstəns/ n. [U] an act of demanding that something should happen and refusing to let anyone say no: [**insistence that**] *Espinosa backed off from his insistence that employees use time cards when they began and left work.* | [**+ on**] *Their insis-tence on a formal apology created tension between the two countries.* | *At Ms. Taylor's insistence, (=because she insisted) an ambulance was called to the store.*

in·sist·ent /ɪnˈsɪstənt/ adj. **1** demanding firmly and often that something should happen or that some-thing is true: [**insistent that**] *The mechanic was insistent that repairing the car was hopeless.* | [**+ on**] *Grandma was always insistent on going to church on Sunday.* **2** continuing in a way that is difficult to ignore: *the insistent pressure of fear* —**insistently** adv.

in si·tu /ɪn ˈsaɪtu, -ˈsɪtu/ adv. if something remains in situ, it remains in its usual place

in·so·far as, in so far as /ˌɪnsəˈfar əz/ conjunction FORMAL to the degree that: *He agreed to assist us with moving and other expenses, insofar as he was able to do so.*

in·sole /ˈɪnsoʊl/ n. [C] a flat piece of cloth, leather etc. cut in the shape of your foot that is inside your shoe

in·so·lent /ˈɪnsələnt/ adj. impolite and not showing any respect: *The band is known for their insolent atti-tude.* | *Joe was disciplined for being insolent toward the teacher.* —**insolently** adv. —**insolence** n. [U]

in·sol·u·ble /ɪnˈsalyəbəl/ adj. **1** an insoluble prob-lem is or seems impossible to solve: *At this point, the crisis appears insoluble.* **2** an insoluble substance does not become a liquid when you put it into liquid —compare DISSOLVE (1)

in·solv·a·ble /ɪnˈsalvəbəl, -ˈsɔl-/ adj. INSOLUBLE (1)

in·sol·vent /ɪnˈsalvənt/ adj. not having enough money to pay what you owe; BANKRUPT: *insolvent businesses* —**insolvency** n. [U]

in·som·ni·a /ɪnˈsamniə/ n. [U] the condition of not being able to sleep

in·som·ni·ac /ɪnˈsamniˌæk/ n. [C] someone who cannot sleep easily —**insomniac** adj.

in·so·much /ˌɪnsoʊˈmʌtʃ/ adv. FORMAL **1 insomuch that** to such a degree that **2** another form of the word INASMUCH

in·sou·ci·ance /ɪnˈsusiəns/ n. [U] FORMAL a cheerful feeling of not caring or worrying about anything *For all her apparent insouciance, she was desperately unhappy.* —**insouciant** adj. —**insouciantly** adv.

in·spect /ɪnˈspɛkt/ v. [T] **1** to examine something carefully in order to find out more about it or check that it is satisfactory: *At the airport, Customs officials inspected my purse and hand luggage.* | [**inspect sth**

for sth] *We hired someone to inspect our roof for leaks.* **2** to make an official visit to a building, orga-nization etc. to check that everything is satisfactory and that rules are being obeyed: *Restaurants are inspected at least once a year by Health Department officials.* | *General Allen arrived to inspect the troops.* —see Usage Note at CONTROL[2]

in·spec·tion /ɪnˈspɛkʃən/ n. [C,U] **1** an official visit to a building or organization to check that every-thing is satisfactory and that rules are being obeyed: *Federal inspection is required for all meat and poultry products.* | [**+ of**] *an inspection of the facility* **2** a careful examination of something to find out more about it: *Federal investigators conducted a five-day inspection of the crash site.* | **On closer inspection** (=when she looked more closely), *she realized they were baby rats.*

in·spec·tor /ɪnˈspɛktɚ/ n. [C] **1** an official whose job is to check that something is satisfactory and that rules are being obeyed: *the building inspectors* | *a Health Department inspector* **2** a police officer of middle rank: *Inspector Blake*

in·spi·ra·tion /ˌɪnspəˈreɪʃən/ n. **1** [C] the place, person etc. that you get ideas from or that encour-ages you to do something: [**+ for**] *Turner uses his childhood in rural Alabama as the inspiration for his stories.* | *Sam Walton is an inspiration to business students everywhere.* **2** [U] a feeling of encourage-ment that you get from someone or something, which gives you ideas about what you should do: *The pyramids and other ancient monuments often provide inspiration for modern architects.* | *The preacher claimed divine inspiration (=inspiration from God) for his ministry.* **3** [C] a sudden good idea about what you should do or say

in·spi·ra·tion·al /ˌɪnspəˈreɪʃənəl/ adj. providing inspiration: *an inspirational speech*

in·spire /ɪnˈspaɪɚ/ v. [T] **1** to encourage someone by making them feel confident and eager to achieve something great: *The country needs a leader who can inspire its citizens.* | [**inspire sb to do sth**] *My two daughters were inspired to take violin lessons when a friend played for them.* | [**inspire sb to sth**] *The coach inspired them to victory.* **2** to make someone have a particular feeling or react in a particular way: *Mrs. Pianto was the kind of woman who inspired kindness.* | [**inspire sth in sb**] *Elway is so gifted he inspires wonder in those who see him play.* **3** to give someone the idea for a story, painting, poem etc.: *The movie was inspired by real events.* **4** TECHNICAL to breathe in

in·spired /ɪnˈspaɪɚd/ adj. **1** having very exciting spe-cial qualities that are better than anyone or any-thing else: *an inspired leader* | *Dickinson wrote some very inspired poems.* **2 politically/divinely/religiously etc. inspired** started for political, divine, religious etc. reasons: *John Byne's court-martial was politi-cally inspired.*

in·spir·ing /ɪnˈspaɪrɪŋ/ adj. giving people energy, a feeling of excitement, and a desire to do something great: *an inspiring success story*

in·sta·bil·i·ty /ˌɪnstəˈbɪləti/ n. [U] **1** UNCERTAINTY in a situation that is caused by the possibility of sudden change: *the instability of the market* | *There are fears that political instability in the region will lead to civil war.* **2** mental problems that are likely to cause sudden changes of behavior: *Her mental instability led her to commit these crimes.*

in·stall /ɪnˈstɔl/ v. [T] **1** to put a piece of equipment somewhere and connect it so that it is ready to be used: *Lights were installed under the upper cabinets to illuminate the counter tops.* **2** to put someone in an important job or position, especially with a cere-mony: [**install sb as sth**] *The military installed Cher-ington as president.*

in·stal·la·tion /ˌɪnstəˈleɪʃən/ n. **1** [C,U] the act of fit-ting a piece of equipment somewhere: *the installa-tion of a security system* **2** [C] a place where industrial or military equipment, machinery etc. has been put: *The bombing raids targeted military installations.* **3** [U] FORMAL the ceremony of putting someone in an important job or position: *the installation of the new government* **4** [C] a piece of equipment that has been fitted in its place: *Surround-sound capabilities can be added to older video installations.*

in·stall·ment /ɪnˈstɔlmənt/ n. [C] **1** one of a series of regular payments, especially ones that you make until you have paid all the money you owe: *We just paid the last installment of our car loan.* | *The Rotary Club will make its annual donation in two installments of $2,000 to the shelter.* **2** one of the parts of a story that appears as a series in a magazine, newspaper, movie etc.; EPISODE: *"The Gambler Returns" is the fourth installment of Rogers' western movie series.*

installment plan /.ˈ.. ˌ./ n. [singular,U] a system of paying for goods by making a series of small regular payments

in·stance /ˈɪnstəns/ n. **1 for instance** for example: *Old English was in many ways similar to Modern German. For instance, the nouns, adjectives, and verbs were highly inflected.* **2** [C] an example of a particular type of situation: [+ of] *The group cited several instances of injustice.* | *In this instance, I have decided there is not enough evidence to bring the case to court.* **3 in the first instance** at the beginning of a series of actions: *We must act to prevent pollution in the first instance.*

in·stant¹ /ˈɪnstənt/ adj. **1** happening or produced immediately: *He took an instant dislike to LeRoy.* | *Underwater cables permitted instant communication between the continents.* **2** [only before noun] instant food, coffee etc. is in the form of powder and is prepared by adding hot water

instant² n. **1** [C usually singular] a moment: *It took me an instant to recognize who he was.* | *In the desert, dust storms can rise up in an instant* (=immediately). **2 the instant (that)** as soon as something happens: *The instant I saw the place, I knew it was the right house for us.* **3 this instant** SPOKEN used when telling someone, especially a child, to do something immediately: *Come here this instant!*

in·stan·ta·ne·ous /ˌɪnstənˈteɪniəs/ adj. happening immediately: *Fortunately for him, his death was instantaneous.* —**instantaneously** adv.

in·stant·ly /ˈɪnstəntli/ adv. immediately: *They recognized him instantly.* | *He knew instantly something was wrong.*

instant mes·sag·ing /ˌ.. ˈ.../ n. [U] the activity of sending messages to someone and receiving messages from them very quickly while you are both using the Internet —**instant message** n. [C]

instant re·play /ˌ.. ˈ../ n. [C] the immediate repeating of an important moment in a sports game by showing the film or VIDEOTAPE again

in·stead /ɪnˈstɛd/ adv. **1 instead of sth** if you do one thing instead of another thing, you choose to do the first and not the second: *We should do something instead of just talking about it.* | *You must have picked up my keys instead of yours.* | *Could I have tuna instead of ham?* **2** in place of something or someone that has just been mentioned: *If Joe can't attend the meeting, I could go instead.* | *We didn't have enough money for a movie, so we went to the park instead.* | [sentence adverb] *Cardew did not join the navy. Instead, he decided to join the theater and become an actor.*

in·step /ˈɪnstɛp/ n. [C] **1** the raised part of the bottom of your foot between your toes and your HEEL **2** the part of a shoe or sock that covers this part

in·sti·gate /ˈɪnstəˌgeɪt/ v. [T] **1** to start trouble by persuading someone to do something bad: *Both sides accuse each other of instigating the fighting.* **2** to start something such as a legal process or an official INQUIRY: *Vidovich instigated an investigation into the charges of police brutality.* —**instigator** n. [C]

in·sti·ga·tion /ˌɪnstəˈgeɪʃən/ n. **1 at sb's instigation** also **at the instigation of sb** FORMAL because of

someone's suggestion, request, or demand: *Shepard lied to investigators at the instigation of his direct superior officer.* **2** [U] the act of starting something

in·still /ɪnˈstɪl/ v. [T] to teach someone a way of thinking or behaving over a long period of time: [**instill sth in sb**] *She tried to instill responsibility in her sons.* —**instillation** /ˌɪnstɪˈleɪʃən/ n. [U]

in·stinct /ˈɪnstɪŋkt/ n. [C,U] a natural tendency or ability to behave or react in a particular way, without having to learn it or think about it: *My instincts tell me that she's not the right woman for you.* | [+ **for**] *an instinct for self-preservation* | [**instinct to do sth**] *a lion's instinct to hunt* —compare INTUITION

in·stinc·tive /ɪnˈstɪŋktɪv/ adj. based on instinct: *an instinctive sense of style* —**instinctively** adv.: *I instinctively moved away from his punch.*

in·sti·tute¹ /ˈɪnstəˌtut/ n. [C] an organization that has a particular purpose such as scientific or educational work, or the building where this organization is based: *the Academy of Arts Institute* | *research institutes*

institute² v. [T] FORMAL to introduce or start a system, rule, legal process etc.: *Marchand wants to institute reforms by the end of the year.*

in·sti·tu·tion /ˌɪnstəˈtuʃən/ n. [C] **1** a large establishment or organization that has a particular type of work or purpose, such as scientific, educational, or medical work: *Tokyo University is the most important educational institution in Japan.* | *a financial institution* **2** a large building where old people, ORPHANS, prisoners, people who are mentally ill etc. live and are taken care of by an official organization: *Children in these institutions do not receive good care because the government cannot afford it.* **3** an established system or custom in society: *the institution of marriage* **4** the act of starting or introducing a system, rule etc.: [+ **of**] *They approved the institution of a new law.* **5 be an institution** HUMOROUS if a person, place, or event is an institution, they or it are so well known or liked that they seem to be a permanent part of a place: *The Sea Dolphin Café is not just a restaurant; it's an institution.* —**institutional** adj.

in·sti·tu·tion·al·ize /ˌɪnstəˈtuʃənlˌaɪz/ v. [T] **1** to put someone in a mental hospital or institution for old people etc. **2** to make something a part of a system or organization: *What NAFTA did was institutionalize the economic reforms.*

in·sti·tu·tion·al·ized /ˌɪnstəˈtuʃənlˌaɪzd/ adj. **1 institutionalized violence/racism/corruption etc.** violence etc. that has happened for so long in an organization or society that it has become accepted as normal **2** FORMAL someone who has become institutionalized has lived for a long time in a prison, mental hospital etc. and now cannot easily live outside one

in·store /ˌ. ˈ./ adj. happening within a large store, especially a DEPARTMENT STORE: *an in-store bakery*

in·struct /ɪnˈstrʌkt/ v. [T] **1** to officially tell someone what to do: [**instruct sb to do sth**] *Tourists are instructed to not take pictures inside the building.* | *We got there at 11:55 a.m. and rang the bell as instructed* (=in the way that we were instructed). **2** to teach or show someone how to do something: [**instruct sb in sth**] *In flight school, we were instructed in the basics of aerial combat.* —see Usage Note at TEACH

in·struc·tion /ɪnˈstrʌkʃən/ n. **1 instructions** the printed information that tells you how to use a piece of equipment, product etc.: [+ **on/about**] *Some stores selling wine are posting instructions on how to open wine bottles.* | *Follow the instructions printed on the back of the box.* **2** [C usually plural] a statement telling someone what they must do: [**instruction to do sth**] *The guards were given instructions to watch the prisoner's every move.* | [**instruction that**] *The teacher had left instructions that no one was to talk during the test.* | *I gave strict instructions that we were not to be disturbed during the meeting* | *A stewardess gave safety instructions in both English and Spanish.* | *The bank transfers were made on the instructions of Mrs. Noland's personal secretary*

(=she told the bank to do it). | **My instructions** (=ones that were given to me by someone in authority) *are to give the package to him personally.* **3** [U] FORMAL teaching that you are given in a particular skill or subject: *All the children receive religious instruction.* | [+ **in**] *basic instruction in chemistry* | **Under Stewart's instruction** (=while being taught by him), *I slowly mastered the art of glass blowing.*

in·struc·tion·al /ɪnˈstrʌkʃənl/ *adj.* providing instruction: *He learned by watching an instructional videotape on how to play the guitar.*

instruction man·u·al /.ˈ.. ˌ../ *n.* [C] a book that gives you instructions on how to use or take care of a machine, piece of equipment etc.

in·struc·tive /ɪnˈstrʌktɪv/ *adj.* providing a lot of useful information: *The book is filled with instructive drawings.*

S W **in·struc·tor** /ɪnˈstrʌktə/ *n.* [C] **1** someone who teaches a particular subject, sport, or skill: *ski instructors* **2** someone who teaches at a college or university and who has a rank below ASSISTANT PROFESSOR: *Who is your chemistry instructor?* —see Usage Note at PROFESSOR

S W **in·stru·ment** /ˈɪnstrəmənt/ *n.* [C]

1 tool a small tool used in work such as science or medicine: *surgical instruments*

2 music an object such as a piano, horn, VIOLIN etc., used for producing musical sounds; MUSICAL INSTRUMENT: *The instrument produces a sound similar to a violin.*

3 for measuring a piece of equipment for measuring and showing distance, speed, temperature etc.: *The instrument measures breathing and blood pressure.* | *The crew attempted **an instrument landing** (=bringing an airplane to the ground using only instruments) during the storm.*

4 method [usually singular] something such as system, method, or law that is used to achieve a particular result: *Spending was once considered the most powerful instrument of government policy.* | *The army is an instrument of the government.*

5 instrument of torture a piece of equipment used to make people suffer pain

6 LITERARY **instrument of fate/God** someone or something that is used by an unseen power which is beyond our control

7 document FORMAL a legal document

in·stru·men·tal¹ /ˌɪnstrəˈmɛntl/ *adj.* **1 be instrumental in (doing) sth** to be important in making something possible: *Siegel was instrumental in erecting the Las Vegas as it is today.* **2** instrumental music is for instruments, not for voices

instrumental² *n.* [C] a piece of music or a part of a piece of music where no voices are used, only instruments

in·stru·men·tal·ist /ˌɪnstrəˈmɛntl-ɪst/ *n.* [C] someone who plays a musical instrument —compare VOCALIST

in·stru·men·ta·tion /ˌɪnstrəmɛnˈteɪʃən/ *n.* [U] **1** the way in which a piece of music is arranged to be played by several different instruments **2** the set of INSTRUMENTS (3) used to control a machine: *The company produces electronic instrumentation systems.*

instrument pan·el /.ˈ.. ˌ../ *n.* [C] the board in front of the pilot of an aircraft, where all the INSTRUMENTS (INSTRUMENT (3)) are

in·sub·or·di·na·tion /ˌɪnsəˌbɔrdnˈeɪʃən/ *n.* [U] the act of refusing to obey someone who has a higher rank than you: *Shores was fired for insubordination.* —**insubordinate** /ˌɪnsəˈbɔrdn-ɪt/ *adj.*

in·sub·stan·tial /ˌɪnsəbˈstænʃəl/ *adj.* **1** FORMAL not solid, large, strong, or satisfying: *Epstein called the evidence insubstantial (=not good enough).* **2** LITERARY not existing as a real object or person: *insubstantial ghosts* —**insubstantiality** /ˌɪnsəbˌstænʃiˈæləti/ *n.* [U]

in·suf·fer·a·ble /ɪnˈsʌfərəbəl/ *adj.* extremely annoying or bad: *Churchill complained of his insufferable rudeness.* *The heat was insufferable.* —**insufferably** *adv.*

in·suf·fi·cient /ˌɪnsəˈfɪʃənt/ *adj.* not enough: *an insufficient source of water* | [+ **for**] *The planes had an insufficient fuel supply for a return flight.* |

[**insufficient to do sth**] *There was insufficient evidence to convict them.* —**insufficiently** *adv.* —**insufficiency** *n.* [singular,U]

in·su·lar /ˈɪnsələ/ *adj.* **1** DISAPPROVING not interested in anything except your own group, country, way of life etc.: *Landres is a small, insular community in the Midwest.* **2** FORMAL relating to or like an island —**insularity** /ˌɪnsəˈlærəti/ *n.* [U]

in·su·late /ˈɪnsəˌleɪt/ *v.* [T] **1** to cover or protect something so that electricity, sound, heat etc. cannot get in or out: *She spent $10,000 insulating her home to try to keep the highway noise out.* | *insulated containers for cold drinks* **2** to protect someone from bad experiences or unwanted influences: [**insulate sb/sth from sth**] *Her family's money insulated her from the pressures of the real world.*

in·su·lat·ing tape /ˈ.... ˌ./ *n.* [U] narrow material used for wrapping around electric wires to insulate them

in·su·la·tion /ˌɪnsəˈleɪʃən/ *n.* [U] **1** material used to insulate something, especially a building **2** the act of insulating something or the state of being insulated: *Blankets provided insulation against the cold.*

in·su·la·tor /ˈɪnsəˌleɪtə/ *n.* [C] an object or material that insulates, especially one that does not allow electricity to pass through it

in·su·lin /ˈɪnsələn/ *n.* [U] a substance produced naturally by your body that allows sugar to be used for energy —see also DIABETES

in·sult¹ /ˈɪnsʌlt/ *n.* [C] **1** an impolite or offensive remark or action: *The longer he talked, the more insults the crowd yelled at him.* | *We **took** his low offer for the car **as an insult**.* **2 be an insult to sb's intelligence** if something such as a book, class, or television program is an insult to your intelligence, it offends you by being too simple or stupid —see also **add insult to injury** (ADD (6))

in·sult² /ɪnˈsʌlt/ *v.* [T] to say or do something that offends someone by showing that you do not respect them: *Maybe I'm old-fashioned, but I **feel insulted** when a young person calls me by my first name.* | [**insult sb by doing sth**] *He insulted the delegates by refusing to shake their hands.*

in·sult·ing /ɪnˈsʌltɪŋ/ *adj.* very impolite or offensive to someone, and showing a lack of respect: *Patting a woman on the head can be insulting.*

in·su·per·a·ble /ɪnˈsupərəbəl/ *adj.* FORMAL an insuperable difficulty or problem is impossible to deal with: *The legal barriers are presently insuperable.*

in·sup·port·a·ble /ˌɪnsəˈpɔrtəbəl/ *adj.* FORMAL **1** not acceptable or not able to be proved needed or useful: *Staffing levels are currently insupportable.* **2** too annoying or bad for you to accept or deal with: *insupportable pain*

in·sur·ance /ɪnˈʃʊrəns/ *n.* **1** [U] an arrangement with a company in which you pay them money each year and they pay the costs if anything bad happens to you or your house, things etc., such as having an illness or an accident: *Many Americans cannot afford health insurance.* | [+ **on/for**] *Do you have insurance on your car?* | *The Osaka club **took out insurance** for all its members (=started paying for insurance protection).* —see also LIFE INSURANCE **2** [U] the business of providing insurance: *My uncle works in insurance.* **3** [singular,U] protection against something bad happening: [+ **against**] *An underground water supply is good insurance against drought.*

insurance ad·jus·ter /.ˈ.. .ˌ../ *n.* [C] someone who works for an insurance company and decides how much to pay people who have had an accident, had something stolen etc.

insurance a·gent also **insurance brok·er** /.ˈ.. ˌ../ *n.* [C] someone who arranges and sells insurance as their job

insurance pol·i·cy /.ˈ.. ˌ../ *n. plural* **insurance policies** [C] a written agreement for insurance with an insurance company

insurance pre·mi·um /.'.. ,.../ *n.* [C] the money that you pay regularly to an insurance company

in·sure /ɪnˈʃʊr/ *v.* [T] **1** to buy insurance to protect yourself against something bad happening to you, your family, your possessions etc.: *We insured all our valuables before the move.* | [**insure sb/sth against sth**] *Purchases made with the card are insured against theft.* | [**insure sb/sth for sth**] *The planes are insured for $3.1 million.* **2** to provide insurance for something or someone: *No one will insure him because of his heart condition.* **3** another spelling of ENSURE

USAGE NOTE: INSURE

WORD CHOICE: assure, reassure, insure, ensure, make sure

If you **assure** someone of something, you tell them that it is really true or will happen: *Adam assured me that he would call.* You **reassure** someone who is worried by telling them that there is nothing to worry about: *The government needs to reassure the people that the food supply is safe.* You may **insure** someone or something against something bad happening to them by paying money to an insurance company: *The apartment building is insured against earthquakes.* If you **insure** (or, more formally, **ensure**) that something happens, that means you make certain or **make sure** (less formal) it does happen: *Anything that prevents surprises will help insure our success.* | *Make sure you lock the door when you leave.*

---

in·sured /ɪnˈʃʊrd/ *n.* **the insured** LAW the person or people who are insured: *The insured is required to pay a portion of all medical bills.*

in·sur·er /ɪnˈʃʊrɚ/ *n.* [C] a person or company that provides insurance: *The full cost of storm damage will be paid by the insurer.*

in·sur·gen·cy /ɪnˈsɚdʒənsi/ *n. plural* **insurgencies** [C] an attempt by a large group of people to take control of their government using force and violence: *A communist group is waging a 21-year insurgency against the national government.* —see also COUNTER-INSURGENCY

in·sur·gent /ɪnˈsɚdʒənt/ *n.* [C usually plural] **1** one of a large group of people who are fighting against the government of their own country **2** someone, especially a member of a political party, who opposes or fights against authority —**insurgent** *adj.*: *insurgent forces*

in·sur·mount·a·ble /ˌɪnsɚˈmaʊntəbəl/ *adj.* an insurmountable difficulty or problem is too large or too difficult to deal with: *Graham overcame seemingly insurmountable transportation barriers to complete his tour.*

in·sur·rec·tion /ˌɪnsəˈrɛkʃən/ *n.* [C,U] an attempt by a large group of people within a country to take control of their government using force and violence: *Rebel members of the army staged an insurrection against the Argentinean president in the 1980s.* —**insurrectionist** *n.* [C]

in·tact /ɪnˈtækt/ *adj.* [not before noun] not broken, damaged, or spoiled, usually after something bad has happened: *The package arrived intact.* | *Somehow his reputation survived the scandal intact.*

in·ta·glio /ɪnˈtælyoʊ, -ˈtɑl-/ *n.* [C,U] the art of cutting patterns into a hard substance, or the pattern that you get by doing this

in·take /ˈɪnteɪk/ *n.* FORMAL **1** [singular] the amount of food, FUEL etc. that is eaten by someone or put into something: *Pregnant women should reduce their intake of caffeine.* **2** [C] a tube, pipe, etc. through which air, gas, or liquid is taken in: *air intakes on a jet engine* **3** [singular,U] the number of people allowed to enter a school, profession etc., or the process of someone entering a school, profession etc.: *the yearly intake of students* | *Eberson is the intake officer for the prison.* **4 an intake of breath** a sudden act of breathing in, showing that you are shocked, surprised etc.

in·tan·gi·ble /ɪnˈtændʒəbəl/ *adj.* an intangible quality or feeling cannot be clearly felt or described, although you know it exists: *Customer goodwill is an important intangible asset of any business.* —**intangible** *n.* [C]

in·te·ger /ˈɪntədʒɚ/ *n.* [C] TECHNICAL a whole number, for example 6 is an integer, but 6.4 is not

in·te·gral /ˈɪntəɡrəl, ɪnˈtɛɡrəl/ *adj.* **1** forming a necessary part of something: *Music should be an integral part of children's education.* | [+ **to**] *Cooperation is integral to the success of the program.* **2** relating to integers

in·te·grate /ˈɪntəˌɡreɪt/ *v.* **1** [I,T] to end the practice of separating people of different races in a place or institution, usually by making the separation illegal; DESEGREGATE: *Many cities have given up trying to integrate the schools.* —compare SEGREGATE **2** [T] to combine two or more things in order to make an effective system: *Bus and subway services have been fully integrated.* | [**integrate sth with/into sth**] *Using computers, students are able to integrate text with graphics.* **3** [I,T] to join in the life and customs of a group or society, or to help someone do this: *Disabled students are integrated in regular classrooms.* | [+ **into/with**] *After we moved, I just wanted to integrate into the neighborhood.*

in·te·grat·ed /ˈɪntəˌɡreɪtɪd/ *adj.* an integrated system, institution etc. combines many different groups, ideas, or parts in a way that works well: *integrated information systems* | *a racially integrated neighborhood* —compare SEGREGATED

integrated cir·cuit /ˌ.... '../ *n.* [C] TECHNICAL a very small set of electronic connections printed on a single piece of SEMICONDUCTOR material instead of being made from separate parts

in·te·gra·tion /ˌɪntəˈɡreɪʃən/ *n.* [U] **1** the combining of two or more things so that they work together effectively: *the integration of European economies* **2** the process of making or allowing people of different races to live, work etc. together instead of separately: *Integration of the public schools is still a goal.* **3** the acceptance of someone or something into a group or society: *There is a need for Cuba's integration into the Latin American community.*

in·teg·ri·ty /ɪnˈtɛɡrəti/ *n.* [U] **1** the quality of being honest and of always having high moral principles: *Rooney brought dignity and integrity to the profession.* **2** FORMAL the state of being united as one complete thing: *They have vowed to protect the country's territorial integrity.*

in·teg·u·ment /ɪnˈtɛɡyəmənt/ *n.* [C] TECHNICAL something such as a shell that covers something else

in·tel·lect /ˈɪntəlˌɛkt/ *n.* **1** [C,U] the ability to understand things and to think intelligently: *Schools should nurture a child's intellect.* | *Her friendliness hides a shrewd intellect.* **2** [C] someone who is very intelligent: *Corning wasn't a great intellect, but he knew how to get things done.*

in·tel·lec·tu·al¹ /ˌɪntəlˈɛktʃuəl/ *adj.* **1** relating to the ability to understand things and to think intelligently: *the intellectual development of children* **2** an intellectual person is well-educated and interested in serious ideas and subjects such as science, literature etc. —see Usage Note at INTELLIGENT **3** involving or needing serious thinking to be understood: *an intellectual film* —**intellectually** *adv.*

intellectual² *n.* [C] someone who is intelligent and well educated, and who thinks about complicated ideas: *Soviet intellectuals helped change the political climate of the country.*

in·tel·lec·tu·al·ize /ˌɪntəlˈɛktʃuəˌlaɪz/ *v.* [I,T] to think or talk about a problem carefully, especially in order to avoid dealing with your feelings about it

intellectual prop·er·ty /ˌ..... '.../ *n.* [U] LAW something that someone has invented or has the right to make or sell, especially something protected by a PATENT, TRADEMARK, or COPYRIGHT

in·tel·li·gence /ɪnˈtɛlədʒəns/ *n.* [C,U] **1 a)** the ability to learn, understand, and think about things: *Researchers were looking for ways to increase children's intelligence.* **b)** a high level of this ability: *a* *leader with intelligence* **2** information about the secret activities of foreign governments, the military plans of an enemy etc.: *New global problems have changed the kinds of intelligence we need to gather.* **3** a group of people or an organization that gathers secret information for their government: *Don hopes to get a job in military intelligence.*

intelligence quo·tient /.'... ,. .'. / n. [C] IQ

in·tel·li·gent /ɪn'tɛlədʒənt/ adj. **1** having a high level of ability to learn, understand, and think about things, or showing this ability: *Vlasic is a very intelligent player.* | *an intelligent decision* **2** an intelligent creature is able to think, understand, and communicate: *Do you think there are intelligent life forms on other planets?* —**intelligently** adv.

USAGE NOTE: INTELLIGENT

WORD CHOICE: intelligent, intellectual
An **intelligent** person is someone who is smart with a quick mind, but an **intellectual** person is someone who is well educated and interested in subjects that need a lot of study. A small child, or even a dog, can be **intelligent** but cannot be called **intellectual**. Intelligent and **intellectual** are both adjectives, but **intellectual** can also be a noun: *The movement was led by students and intellectuals.*

---

in·tel·li·gent·si·a /ɪn,tɛlə'dʒɛntsiə/ n. **the intelligentsia** the people in a society who are most highly educated and who are most interested in new ideas and developments, especially in art, literature, or politics

intelligent ter·mi·nal /.'... ,.../ n. [C] a type of computer that is connected to another computer, but which can still perform certain operations without using the other computer —compare DUMB TERMINAL

in·tel·li·gi·ble /ɪn'tɛlədʒəbəl/ adj. intelligible speech, writing, or ideas can be easily understood: *It is rare to find a singer who can make every word fully intelligible.* | [+ to] *The book makes Eastern culture intelligible to Westerners.* —**intelligibly** adv. —**intelligibility** /ɪn,tɛlədʒə'bɪləti/ n. [U] —opposite UNINTELLIGIBLE

in·tem·per·ate /ɪn'tɛmpərɪt/ adj. FORMAL **1** not having enough control over your feelings, so that you behave in a way that is unacceptable to other people: *Haskell's intemperate remarks led to a suspension from the team.* **2** regularly drinking too much alcohol —**intemperance** n. [U]

in·tend /ɪn'tɛnd/ v. [T] **1** to have something in your mind as a plan or purpose: [intend to do sth] *The laws were intended to protect wildlife.* | *Miss Stein fully intended to make the painting a gift.* | [intend sb/sth to do sth] *The music is different from how we intended it to sound.* | [intend that] *It was never intended that Ford pay the money back.* | [intend doing sth] *Kristen intends staying in Rome for three days.* **2 be intended for sb/sth** to be provided or designed for a particular purpose or person: *The movie is intended for adults.* **3 intended target/victim/destination etc.** the person, thing, result etc. that an action is intended to affect or reach, especially when it does not actually affect or reach them: *The bomb hit a hillside some distance away from the intended target.*

in·tend·ed /ɪn'tɛndɪd/ n. sb's intended OLD-FASHIONED OR HUMOROUS the person that someone is going to marry

in·tense /ɪn'tɛns/ adj. **1** having a very strong effect or felt very strongly: *Some of these young people are under intense pressure to succeed.* | *the intense heat of the desert* **2** making you do a lot of work, think hard etc.: *Very intense exercise may actually be bad for you.* **3** serious and having very strong feelings or opinions: *He's a little too intense for me.* **4** serious and making you feel strong emotions or opinions: *an intense conversation* —**intensely** adv.

in·ten·si·fi·er /ɪn'tɛnsə,faɪɚ/ n. [C] TECHNICAL a word, usually an adverb, that is used to emphasize an adjective, adverb, or verb, for example the word "badly" in the phrase "badly needed changes"

in·ten·si·fy /ɪn'tɛnsə,faɪ/ v. past tense and past participle **intensified** [I,T] to increase in strength, size, amount etc., or to make something do this: *Winds intensified during the afternoon.* | *Police have now intensified the search for the lost child.* —**intensification** /ɪn,tɛnsəfə'keɪʃən/ n. [U]

in·ten·si·ty /ɪn'tɛnsəti/ n. [U] **1** the quality of being felt very strongly or having a strong effect: *The intensity of the hurricane was frightening.* **2** the brightness or strength of light or of a color: *Light intensity is very important for plants.* **3** the quality of being serious and having very strong feelings or opinions, or making you feel this way: *He spoke with great intensity.*

in·ten·sive /ɪn'tɛnsɪv/ adj. **1** involving a lot of activity, effort, or careful attention in a short period of time: *The program includes intensive instruction in English.* | *intensive diplomatic efforts to gain a cease-fire* **2 intensive farming/agriculture** farming that produces a lot of food from a small area of land —**intensively** adv.

-intensive /ɪntɛnsɪv/ [in adjectives] **labor-intensive/paper-intensive etc.** involving or needing a lot of workers, paper etc.: *He works in a highly information-intensive environment.*

intensive care /.,.. '. / n. [U] the department in a hospital that treats people who are very sick or badly injured, or the treatment that they receive there: *She was in critical condition and was being treated in intensive care.* | *an intensive care nurse*

in·tent¹ /ɪn'tɛnt/ n. [U] **1** FORMAL what you intend to do; intention: [intent to do sth] *Wilder announced his intent to seek reelection.* **2** LAW the intention to do something illegal: *The gun was fired with intent.* | [intent to do sth] *Lars was arrested for possession of cocaine with intent to sell it.* **3 for/to all intents and purposes** almost completely, or very nearly: *For all intents and purposes, Lee's surrender ended the Civil War.*

intent² adj. **1 be intent on/upon (doing) sth** to be determined to do something or achieve something: *Abortion foes are intent on changing the laws allowing abortion.* **2** paying careful attention to something so that you think about nothing else: *an intent gaze* | [+ on/upon] *Band members were intent on their instruments as they played.* —**intently** adv.: *Jurors listened intently to the testimony.*

in·ten·tion /ɪn'tɛnʃən/ n. [C,U] **1** a plan or desire to do something: [intention of doing sth] *I have no intention of moving again anytime soon.* | *Perez bought the house with the intention of fixing it up and reselling it.* | *They have good intentions* (=a desire to do something good or kind, especially when you do not succeed in doing it), *but they never get things done.* **2 what are your intentions (toward sb)?** OLD-FASHIONED OR HUMOROUS used to ask someone whether or not they plan to marry someone else —see also WELL-INTENTIONED

in·ten·tion·al /ɪn'tɛnʃənəl/ adj. done deliberately: *an intentional violation of the tax laws* —opposite UNINTENTIONAL

in·ten·tion·al·ly /ɪn'tɛnʃənəli/ adv. in a way that is intended or planned DELIBERATELY: *Employees may have intentionally broken the law.*

in·ter /ɪn'tɚ/ v. **interred, interring** [T] FORMAL to bury a dead person —opposite DISINTER —see also INTERMENT

inter- /ɪntɚ/ prefix between or among a group of things or people: *to intermarry* (=marry someone of another race, religion etc.) | *the Internet* (=connection among computers) —compare INTRA-, INTRO-

in·ter·act /,ɪntɚ'rækt/ v. [I] **1** if people interact with each other, they talk to each other, work together etc.: *Playing a game is a way for a family to interact.* | [+ with] *Desks are arranged in a U-shape, so the teacher can interact easily with the students.* **2** if two or more things interact, they have an effect on each other and work together: *We learned about how people and their environment interact.* [+ with] *How will the drug interact with other medications?*

in·ter·ac·tion /ˌɪntɚ'rækʃən/ *n.* [C,U] **1** the activity of talking to other people, working together with them etc.: [+ with/between/among] *Families need to encourage activities that promote interaction between parent and child.* **2** a process by which two or more things have an effect on each other and work together: [+ of] *the interaction of carbon and hydrogen* | [+ with/between] *Iran's interaction with the West*

in·ter·ac·tive /ˌɪntɚ'ræktɪv/ *adj.* **1** something such as a computer PROGRAM or system that is interactive does things in reaction to the actions of the person who is using it: *an interactive software program* | *The museum features interactive exhibits.* **2** involving talking and working together: *Our school encourages interactive teaching methods.* —**interactivity** /ˌɪntɚæk'tɪvəti/ *n.* [U]

in·ter·a·gen·cy /ˌɪntɚ'eɪdʒənsi/ *adj.* between or involving different organizations or departments, especially within a government: *an interagency committee*

in·ter a·li·a /ˌɪntɚ 'eɪliə, 'ɑliə/ *adv.* FORMAL among other things: *The paper discussed, inter alia, recent political issues.*

in·ter·breed /ˌɪntɚ'brid/ *v. past tense and past participle* **interbred** /-'brɛd/ [I,T] to produce young animals from parents of different breeds or groups: [+ with] *The bees are unable to interbreed with native species.* —compare CROSSBREED[1], INBREEDING

in·ter·cede /ˌɪntɚ'sid/ *v.* [I] **1** to talk to someone in authority in order to prevent something bad from happening to someone else: [+ with] *Johnson interceded with the authorities on Kelly's behalf.* | [+ for] *The prison chaplain would often intercede for inmates.* **2** to try to help two or more people, groups etc. end a disagreement, war etc.: [+ in] *The President may intercede in the strike if it threatens the national economy.* —see also INTERCESSION

in·ter·cept /ˌɪntɚ'sɛpt/ *v.* [T] to stop or catch something or someone that is going from one place to another: *Clay intercepted nine passes during the game.* | *The boat carrying 653 refugees was intercepted at sea.* —**interception** /ˌɪntɚ'sɛpʃən/ *n.* [C,U]

in·ter·cep·tor /ˌɪntɚ'sɛptɚ/ *n.* [C] **1** a light fast military aircraft **2** a MISSILE (1) designed to intercept enemy MISSILES

in·ter·ces·sion /ˌɪntɚ'sɛʃən/ *n.* **1** [U] an act of interceding **2** [C,U] a prayer asking for someone to be helped or cured

in·ter·change[1] /'ɪntɚˌtʃeɪndʒ/ *n.* **1** [C] a place where two or more HIGHWAYS or FREEWAYS meet **2** [singular,U] an exchange, especially of ideas or thoughts: *a friendly interchange of greetings* | *The Internet is a forum for the interchange of ideas, images, and information.*

in·ter·change[2] /ˌɪntɚ'tʃeɪndʒ/ *v.* [I,T] to put or use each of two things in the place of the other, or to be exchanged in this way: *The two spices can be easily interchanged.*

in·ter·change·a·ble /ˌɪntɚ'tʃeɪndʒəbəl/ *adj.* things that are interchangeable can be used instead of each other: *The camera has two interchangeable lenses.* | *The terms "sociopath" and "psychopath" are interchangeable.* —**interchangeably** *adv.* —**interchangeability** /ˌɪntɚˌtʃeɪndʒə'bɪləti/ *n.* [U]

in·ter·cit·y /ˌɪntɚ'sɪti/ *adj.* [only before noun] going from one city to another, or happening between different cities: *intercity bus service*

in·ter·col·le·giate /ˌɪntɚkə'lidʒɪt/ *adj.* intercollegiate competitions are between members of different colleges: *an intercollegiate golf tournament*

intercom

in·ter·com /'ɪntɚˌkɑm/ *n.* [C] a communication system by which people in different parts of a building, aircraft etc. can speak to each other, especially so that everyone can hear at the same time: *"Welcome to St. Petersburg," said a voice over the intercom.*

in·ter·con·nect·ed /ˌɪntɚkə'nɛktɪd/ *adj.* interconnected problems, systems etc. relate to each other, influence each other, or are connected to each other: *The Earth and its various parts should be studied as one complete, interconnected system.* | *a book with three interconnected themes* —**interconnectedness** *n.* [U] —**interconnect** *v.* [I,T] —**interconnection** /ˌɪntɚkə'nɛkʃən/ *n.* [C]

in·ter·con·ti·nen·tal /ˌɪntɚˌkɑntə'nɛntl, -ˌkɑnt̚n-'ɛntl/ *adj.* happening between two CONTINENTS, or going from one CONTINENT to another: *Intercontinental trade between North and South America has increased.* | *an intercontinental flight*

in·ter·course /'ɪntɚˌkɔrs/ *n.* [U] FORMAL **1** the act of having sex; SEXUAL INTERCOURSE **2** an exchange of ideas, feelings etc. that make people or groups understand each other better: *She seemed tired and unable to keep up with ordinary social intercourse.*

in·ter·cul·tur·al /ˌɪntɚ'kʌltʃərəl/ *adj.* between or involving two or more countries or societies: *Kim attended a training seminar on intercultural communication.*

in·ter·cut /ˌɪntɚ'kʌt/ *v.* [T] if a movie, song etc. is intercut with pictures, words, sounds etc., the pictures or words appear in different places in the movie or song: *The score is intercut with bits of Mexican music.*

in·ter·de·nom·i·na·tion·al /ˌɪntɚdɪˌnɑmə'neɪʃənl/ *adj.* between or involving Christians from different groups or churches: *Please join us for an interdenominational prayer service at 10:00 on Sundays.*

in·ter·de·part·men·tal /ˌɪntɚdɪpɑrt̚'mɛntl/ *adj.* between or involving different departments of a company, government etc.: *The college's interdepartmental mail system is extremely efficient.*

in·ter·de·pend·ent /ˌɪntɚdɪ'pɛndənt/ *adj.* depending on or necessary to each other: *Ecosystems are interdependent networks of plants and animals.* —**interdependence** *n.* [U]

in·ter·dict /'ɪntɚˌdɪkt/ *n.* [C] **1** LAW an official order from a court telling someone not to do something **2** TECHNICAL a punishment in the Catholic Church, by which someone is not allowed to take part in church ceremonies —**interdict** /ˌɪntɚ'dɪkt/ *v.* [T] —**interdiction** /ˌɪntɚ'dɪkʃən/ *n.* [C,U]

in·ter·dis·ci·pli·nar·y /ˌɪntɚ'dɪsəpləˌnɛri/ *adj.* involving ideas, information, or people from different subjects or areas of study: *An interdisciplinary team of researchers are examining the disease.*

in·ter·est[1] /'ɪntrɪst/ *n.*

1 feeling [singular,U] a feeling that makes you want to pay attention to someone or something and find out more about them: [+ in] *Mark and his father have a common interest in soccer.* | *He was looking at me with interest.* | *Kids who aren't challenged in school soon lose interest.* | *No one at home took an interest in the children's welfare.* | *Lori has shown interest in learning to dance.* | *Other cities have expressed an interest in the school program.*

2 activity [C] a subject or activity that you enjoy studying or doing: *In retirement, Nelson added personal computing to his interests.* | *Ms. Walters has many outside interests* (=interests other than her work).

3 money [U] **a)** money that you must pay for borrowing money: [+ on] *The foundation has been paying 8.5% interest on the loan.* **b)** money that a bank pays you when you keep money there: *This* *savings account **earns interest** even if the balance is very low.* —see also COMPOUND INTEREST, SIMPLE INTEREST

4 quality [U] a quality or feature of something that attracts your attention or makes you want to know more about it: *A job like selling shoes **holds no interest** for me whatsoever.* | *This report might be of **interest to** your students.* | *A needlepoint rug **adds interest** to the dark wood floor* | *Questions of general interest* (=that everyone wants to know about) *can be sent to him at the newspaper.* | *of special/particular interest to sb Today's guest will be of particular interest to hunters.*

5 advantage [C] the things or situations that gives someone an advantage or are favorable to them: *The President should be doing more to advance U.S. interests abroad.* | *I don't think it **was in his best interest** to resign.* | *I've always **had my children's best interests at heart*** (=been concerned about what is best for them).* | *the national/public interest The commission's aim is to protect the public interest.*

6 have no interest in doing sth not to want to do something: *I have no interest in continuing this conversation.*

7 share in company [C,U] TECHNICAL a share in a company, business etc.: *He is expected to concentrate on developing his hotel interests.* | *The government sold its **controlling interest** in the national phone company.*

8 powerful group [C] TECHNICAL a group of people in the same business who share aims or ideas and often try to influence people in authority: *Agricultural and environmental interests have both been influential in water policy.* | ***Special interests*** (=groups who are concerned about particular subjects) *may have too much power in American politics.*

9 in the interest(s) of justice/efficiency etc. in order to make a situation or system fair, EFFICIENT etc.: *The judge dismissed the case in the interest of justice.*

10 pay sb back, with interest INFORMAL to harm or offend someone in an even worse way than they have harmed you —see also CONFLICT OF INTEREST, **human interest** (HUMAN[1] (6)), **sb's love interest** (LOVE[2] (6)), SELF-INTEREST, SPECIAL INTEREST GROUP, **vested interest** (VESTED).

interest[2] v. [T] **1** to make someone want to pay attention to something and find out more about it: *The book doesn't really interest me that much.* | *It may interest you to know that Bob and Rachel are getting a divorce.* **2 could I interest you in a drink/dessert etc.?** SPOKEN used as a polite way of offering someone something

S W **in·terest·ed** /ˈɪntrɪstɪd, ˈɪntəˌrestɪd/ adj. **1** giving a lot of attention to something, because you want to find out more about it or because you enjoy it: [+ **in**] *Zack is only interested in girls and skateboarding. It was great that they were interested in our opinions.* | **be interested to hear/know/see etc.** *I'd be interested to find out what really happened.* —opposite UNINTERESTED **2** eager to do or have something *I offered to help, but they weren't interested.* | [**interested in doing sth**] *Michelle is interested in joining the tennis club.* | [+ **in**] *Would you be interested in a second-hand Volvo?* **3 interested party/group** a person or group that is directly or personally concerned with a situation and is likely to be affected by its results: *All interested parties are invited to attend the meeting.* —see also DISINTERESTED —see Usage Note at ADJECTIVE

interest-free /ˈ.. ./ adj. an interest-free LOAN has no interest charged on it: *interest-free credit*

interest group /ˈ.. ˌ./ n. [C] a group of people who join together to try to influence the government in order to protect their own particular rights, advantages, concerns etc.

S W **in·terest·ing** /ˈɪntrɪstɪŋ, ˈɪntəˌrestɪŋ/ adj. unusual or exciting in a way that keeps your attention or makes you think: *an interesting man* | *I got an interesting letter in the mail today.* | [**it is interesting that**] *It's interesting that so few men are involved in early childhood education.* | **it is interesting to see/know** etc. *It will be interesting to see how the team plays*

this week. —opposite BORING —see Usage Note at ADJECTIVE

in·terest·ing·ly /ˈɪntrɪstɪŋli, ˈɪntəˌrestɪŋli/ adv. **1** [sentence adverb] used to introduce a fact that you think is interesting: ***Interestingly enough,** many of the writers were Vietnamese immigrants.* **2** in an interesting way: *She was interestingly pretty.*

interest rate /ˈ.. ˌ./ n. [C] the PERCENTAGE amount that is charged by a bank etc. when you borrow money, or that is paid to you by a bank when you keep money in an account there: *Interest rates are pretty low right now.*

in·ter·face[1] /ˈɪntəˌfeɪs/ n. [C] **1** something that helps a computer or a PROGRAM work with another program, another piece of electronic equipment, or the person who is using the computer **2** the way in which two subjects, events etc. affect each other: *the interface between labor and management* **3** TECHNICAL the surface where two things touch each other

in·ter·face[2] /ˈɪntəˌfeɪs/ v. TECHNICAL **1** [I,T + **with**] if you interface two parts of a computer system, or if they interface, you connect them **2** [I + **with**] if two people or groups interface with each other, they communicate with each other and work together

in·ter·faith /ˈɪntəˌfeɪθ/ adj. between or involving people from different religions: *an interfaith Thanksgiving service*

in·ter·fere /ˌɪntəˈfɪr/ v. [I] to deliberately get involved in a situation where you are not wanted or needed: *Schools should be managed by teachers, not interfering bureaucrats.* | [+ **in**] *Rollings said her mother interfered in her adult life and treated her like a child.*

interfere with sth/sb phr. v. [T] **1** to prevent something from succeeding or from happening in the way that is normal or planned: *Aspirin interferes with the body's ability to form blood clots.* **2** if something interferes with a television or radio broadcast, it spoils the sound or picture that you receive

in·ter·fer·ence /ˌɪntəˈfɪrəns/ n. [U] **1** an act of interfering: [+ **in**] *China protested the outside interference in its internal affairs.* **2** unwanted noise on television, the radio, or the telephone, or problems in the television picture: *There's a lot of interference on my car radio.* **3** the act of blocking or touching another player in a sports game, for example by standing in front of them or holding on to them, when you are not supposed to **4 run interference a)** to protect a player who has the ball in football by blocking players from the opposing team **b)** to help someone achieve something by dealing with people or problems that might cause them trouble: *Truscati's job is to run interference for troubled kids with their parents, schools, and the courts.*

in·ter·fer·on /ˌɪntəˈfɪrɑn/ n. [U] a chemical substance that is produced by your body to fight against VIRUSes that cause disease

in·ter·ga·lac·tic /ˌɪntəgəˈlæktɪk/ adj. happening or existing between the galaxies (GALAXY (1) (=large groups of stars)) in space: *intergalactic travel*

in·ter·gen·er·a·tion·al /ˌɪntəˌdʒɛnəˈreɪʃənl/ adj. between or involving people from different age groups: *School officials say the intergenerational programs help both the children and retired people.*

in·ter·gov·ern·men·tal /ˌɪntəgʌvəˈmɛntl/ adj. between or involving governments of different countries: *An intergovernmental conference is being held in Geneva today.*

in·ter·im[1] /ˈɪntərəm/ adj. [only before noun] an interim arrangement, report, director etc. is used or accepted for a short time, until a final one is made or found; PROVISIONAL: *An interim director was appointed until the end of the year.*

interim[2] n. **in the interim** in the period of time between two events: *A new police chief will be chosen, but Keyter will be acting chief in the interim.*

in·te·ri·or[1] /ɪnˈtɪriə/ n. **1** [C usually singular] the inner part or inside of something: *Almost no engine* noise enters the car's interior. | Heat is trapped in the Earth's interior. —opposite EXTERIOR¹ **2 the interior** the part of a country or area that is farthest away from the coast or its borders: *Nearly 100 forest fires continued in the vast interior of Alaska.*

interior² adj. [only before noun] inside or indoors: *The interior walls are all painted white.* —opposite EXTERIOR²

interior dec·o·ra·tor /.,... '..../ n. [C] an interior designer —**interior decorating** also **interior decoration** n. [U]

interior de·sign·er /.,... .'../ n. [C] someone whose job is to plan and choose the colors, materials, furniture etc. for the inside of buildings, especially people's houses —**interior design** n. [U]

in·ter·ject /,ɪntɚˈdʒɛkt/ v. [I,T] to interrupt what someone else is saying with a sudden remark: *"Of course not!" Garland interjected.*

in·ter·jec·tion /,ɪntɚˈdʒɛkʃən/ n. **1** [C] TECHNICAL a word or phrase used to express surprise, shock, pain etc. In the sentence "Ouch! That hurt!," "Ouch!" is an interjection **2** [C,U] the act of making a sudden remark while someone else is speaking, or this remark itself

in·ter·lace /,ɪntɚˈleɪs/ v. **1** [I,T] to join things together by weaving and twisting them over and under each other, or to be joined in this way: *He sat with his fingers interlaced.* **2** [T] to mix or combine two things: [**interlace sth with sth**] *The economies of the two countries are becoming tightly interlaced with each other.*

in·ter·leu·kin /,ɪntɚˈlukɪn/ n. [U] a type of PROTEIN (=a substance the body produces) that helps the body fight disease

in·ter·link /,ɪntɚˈlɪŋk/ v. [I,T] to connect or be connected with something else: *Such forces will interlink the economies of both parts of Ireland.*

in·ter·lock /,ɪntɚˈlɑk/ v. [I,T] if two or more things interlock or are interlocked, they fit firmly together: *The path is paved with interlocking stones.*

in·ter·loc·u·tor /,ɪntɚˈlɑkyətɚ/ n. [C] FORMAL the person someone is speaking with

in·ter·lop·er /ˈɪntɚˌloʊpɚ/ n. [C] someone who enters a place or group where they should not be: *They were treated as interlopers in their new country.*

in·ter·lude /ˈɪntɚˌlud/ n. [C] **1** a short period of time, an event, an activity etc. that comes between other events, activities etc.: *the brief interlude of peace between the world wars* **2** a short romantic or sexual meeting or relationship: *a romantic interlude* **3** a short piece of music that comes between parts of a longer piece of music, between parts of a play etc.

in·ter·mar·ry /,ɪntɚˈmæri/ v. past tense and past participle **intermarried** [I] **1** to marry someone from a different group or race: [+ **with**] *In the late 18th century, Spaniards and Mexicans began to intermarry with the Indians.* **2** to marry someone within your own group or family: *It is not unusual for royal cousins to intermarry.* —**intermarriage** n. [U]

in·ter·me·di·a·ry¹ /,ɪntɚˈmidiˌɛri/ n. plural **intermediaries** [C] **1** a person or organization that tries to help two other people or groups to agree with each other: *Switzerland's foreign minister served as an intermediary between the two countries.* **2** someone who represents someone else and does things for them: *The King responded to the questions through an intermediary.*

intermediary² adj. **1** involving an intermediary or relating to being an intermediary: *Larsen had an intermediary role in the negotiations.* **2** coming between two other stages, levels etc.: *This is an intermediary step on the way to full national elections.*

in·ter·me·di·ate /,ɪntɚˈmidɪt/ adj. **1** existing between the beginning skill level and the most advanced level, or made for someone at this level: *intermediate skiers* | *an intermediate Japanese class* **2** existing, happening, or done between two other stages, levels etc.: *an intermediate step in the problem-*

solving process **3** existing or happening in the middle of a range of amounts, qualities etc.: *One intermediate estimate put the cost at $3,500.*

intermediate school /.'... ,./ n. [C] a JUNIOR HIGH SCHOOL or MIDDLE SCHOOL

in·ter·ment /ɪnˈtɚmənt/ n. [C,U] FORMAL the act of burying a dead body —see also INTER

in·ter·mez·zo /,ɪntɚˈmɛtsoʊ, -ˈmɛdʒoʊ/ n. [C] a short piece of music, especially one that is played between the main parts of a concert, OPERA etc.

in·ter·mi·na·ble /ɪnˈtɚmənəbəl/ adj. very long and boring: *We watched an interminable documentary on rice production.* —**interminably** adv.

in·ter·min·gle /,ɪntɚˈmɪŋgəl/ v. [I,T usually passive] to mix together, or to mix something with something else: *The movie intermingles danger and humor.*

in·ter·mis·sion /,ɪntɚˈmɪʃən/ n. [C] a short period of time between the parts of a play, concert etc.

in·ter·mit·tent /,ɪntɚˈmɪtˈnt/ adj. starting and stopping again and again: *There were clouds and intermittent rain during the festival.* —**intermittently** adv.

in·ter·mix /,ɪntɚˈmɪks/ v. [I,T] to mix together, or to mix things together: *Heavy rain was intermixed with snow and ice.*

in·tern¹ /ɪnˈtɚn/ v. [T] to put someone in prison or limit their ability to go places without charging them with a crime, for political reasons or during a war: *Seven hundred men were interned in the camps.* —see also INTERNMENT

in·tern² /ˈɪntɚn/ n. [C] **1** someone who has nearly finished training as a doctor and is working in a hospital **2** someone, especially a student, who works for a short time in a particular job in order to gain experience

in·ter·nal /ɪnˈtɚnl/ adj. **1** within a particular country, company, organization etc., rather than outside it: *Guest ordered an internal investigation into the money transfers.* | *The internal affairs of other nations should not be of concern to us.* | *an internal memo* **2** inside your body: *internal organs such as the heart or liver* **3** [only before noun] inside something rather than outside: *They took him into the internal corridor.* | *a computer's internal hard drive* **4** existing in your mind: *an internal dialogue with himself* —opposite EXTERNAL

internal-com·bus·tion en·gine /.,.. .'.. ,../ n. [C] an engine that produces power by burning GASOLINE

in·ter·nal·ize /ɪnˈtɚnlˌaɪz/ v. [T] **1** if you internalize a particular belief, attitude, way of behaving etc. it becomes part of your character: *At the end of colonial rule, many of the people had internalized foreign values.* **2** if you internalize emotions, you do not express them but think about them: *Girls tend to internalize their fears, sometimes to the point of making themselves sick.* —**internalization** /ɪn,tɚnələˈzeɪʃən/ n. [U]

in·ter·nal·ly /ɪnˈtɚnl-i/ adv. **1** inside your body: *She was bleeding internally.* **2** within a particular company, country, organization etc.: *Two of the men were fired when they complained internally about the harassment.*

internal med·i·cine /.,.. '.../ n. [U] a type of medical work in which doctors treat illnesses that do not need operations

Internal Rev·e·nue Serv·ice /.,.. '... ,../ n. [singular] the IRS

in·ter·na·tion·al¹ /,ɪntɚˈnæʃənəl/ adj. **1** concerning more than one nation or people from more than one nation: *The restaurant serves international cuisine.* | *international trade* **2** thinking or behaving in a way that shows that you know about other countries: *someone with an international perspective*

international² n. [C] **1** an international sports game **2** a company or organization that exists, works, or has members in more than one country

international date line /.,... '. ./ n. the international date line an imaginary line that goes from the NORTH POLE to the SOUTH POLE in the Pacific Ocean, to the east of which the date is one day earlier than it is to the west

in·ter·na·tion·al·ism /ˌɪntɚˈnæʃənlˌɪzəm/ *n.* [U] the belief that nations should work together and help each other —**internationalist** *n.*

in·ter·na·tion·al·ize /ˌɪntɚˈnæʃənlˌaɪz/ *v.* [T] to make something international or bring it under international control: *The crisis has become internationalized.* —**internationalization** *n.* [C]

in·ter·na·tion·al·ly /ˌɪntɚˈnæʃɚl i-/ *adv.* in many different parts of the world: *Wagner's opera will be telecast internationally.* | **internationally known/famous** *Urban is an internationally known cancer surgeon.*

International Mon·e·tar·y Fund /..ˌ... '.... ˌ./ *n.* the IMF

International PEN /..ˌ... './ an international organization of writers

International Pho·net·ic Al·pha·bet /..ˌ... .'.. ˌ ../ *n.* [singular] the IPA

international re·la·tions /..ˌ.. .'../ *n.* [plural] the political relationships between countries, or the study of this

in·ter·nec·ine /ˌɪntɚˈnɛsin/ *adj.* FORMAL internecine fighting, DISPUTEs etc. happen between members of the same group or nation: *internecine warfare in the Balkans*

in·tern·ee /ˌɪntɚˈni/ *n.* [C] someone who is put into prison during a war or for political reasons, usually without a TRIAL

s w **In·ter·net** /ˈɪntɚˌnɛt/ *n.* **the Internet** a network of computer connections that allows millions of computer users around the world to exchange information

in·ter·nist /ɪnˈtɚnɪst/ *n.* [C] a doctor who has a general knowledge about illnesses and medical conditions of organs inside your body, and who treats illnesses that do not need operations

in·tern·ment /ɪnˈtɚnmənt/ *n.* [C,U] the act of keeping people in prison or in special camps for political reasons, without charging them with a crime, or the period of time during which someone is kept this way: *Mandela was released after 27 years' internment.*

internment camp /.'.. ˌ./ *n.* [C] a special place where people are kept as prisoners, often for political reasons

in·ter·of·fice /ˈɪntɚˌɔfɪs/ *adj.* between or involving different offices of the same organization or company: *interoffice mail*

in·ter·per·son·al /ˌɪntɚˈpɚsənl/ *adj.* involving relationships between people: *interpersonal communication*

in·ter·plan·e·tar·y /ˌɪntɚˈplænəˌtɛri/ *adj.* [only before noun] happening or existing between the PLANETs: *interplanetary exploration*

in·ter·play /ˈɪntɚˌpleɪ/ *n.* [U] the way in which two people or things react to one another or affect each other: *There's a lot of wonderful interplay between the writer and his characters.*

In·ter·pol /ˈɪntɚˌpoul/ *n.* [singular not with **the**] an international police organization that helps national police forces catch criminals

in·ter·po·late /ɪnˈtɚpəˌleɪt/ *v.* [T] FORMAL **1** to put additional words, ideas, information etc. into something such as a piece of writing: *Some of the writing seems to have been interpolated at a later date.* **2** to interrupt someone by saying something **3** TECHNICAL to find or guess the middle of a range of amounts: *The bonds yield 42 points above the interpolated bond curve.* —**interpolation** /ɪnˌtɚpəˈleɪʃən/ *n.* [C,U]

in·ter·pose /ˌɪntɚˈpouz/ *v.* [T] FORMAL **1** to put yourself or something else between two other things: *She interposed herself between the general and his wife.* **2** to introduce something between the parts of a conversation or argument: *"That might be difficult,"* interposed Mrs. Flavell.

s w **in·ter·pret** /ɪnˈtɚprɪt/ *v.* **1** [I,T] to change words spoken in one language into another: *For the school's deaf students, she interpreted the entire play in American Sign Language.* —compare TRANSLATE (1) **2** [T] to consider someone's actions or behavior or an event as having a particular meaning: [**interpret**

sth as sth] *Differences in the way people are treated can be interpreted as evidence of discrimination.* **3** [T] to understand or explain the meaning of something: *An artist has as much right to interpret history as a historian.* | *The data has not yet been interpreted.* **4** [T] to perform a part in a play, a piece of music etc. in a way that shows your feelings about it or what you think it means

in·ter·pre·ta·tion /ɪnˌtɚprəˈteɪʃən/ *n.* [C,U] **1** the way in which someone explains or understands an event, information, someone's actions etc.: *Lawyers called the police department's interpretation of the law "ridiculous."* | **open/subject to interpretation** (=able to be explained or understood in different ways) **2** the way in which someone performs a play, a piece of music etc.: *Leonard won for his skillful interpretation of a piece by Mozart.*

in·ter·pre·ta·tive /ɪnˈtɚprəˌteɪtɪv/ *adj.* interpretive

in·ter·pret·er /ɪnˈtɚprətɚ/ *n.* [C] **1** someone who changes spoken words from one language into another, especially as their job —compare TRANSLATOR **2** a computer PROGRAM that changes an instruction into a form that can be understood directly by the computer

in·ter·pre·tive /ɪnˈtɚprətɪv/ *adj.* **1** relating to, explaining, or understanding the meaning of something: *Reading is an interpretive process.* **2** relating to how feelings are expressed through music, dance, art etc.: *interpretive dance*

interpretive cen·ter /.'... ˌ../ *n.* [C] a room or building where tourists can receive information about the place they are visiting, for example information about its history or about the animals and plants there

in·ter·ra·cial /ˌɪntɚˈreɪʃəl/ *adj.* between different races of people: *Interracial marriage is more common today*

in·ter·reg·num /ˌɪntɚˈrɛgnəm/ *n.* plural **interregnums** or **interregna** /-nə/ [C] **1** a period of time when a country has no king or queen, because the new ruler has not yet started to rule **2** a period of time when a company, organization etc. has no leader, because the new leader has not started their job

in·ter·re·late /ˌɪntɚrɪˈleɪt/ *v.* [I,T] if two or more things interrelate or you interrelate them, they are connected and have an effect on each other: *The diagram interrelates population and natural resources.*

in·ter·re·lat·ed /ˌɪntɚrɪˈleɪtɪd/ *adj.* things that are interrelated are connected and have an effect on each other: *The book consists of four interrelated stories.*

in·ter·re·la·tion·ship /ˌɪntɚrɪˈleɪʃənˌʃɪp/ *n.* [C,U] a connection between two things that makes them affect each other: *the interrelationship of the world economy*

in·ter·ro·gate /ɪnˈtɛrəˌgeɪt/ *v.* [T] to ask someone a lot of questions for a long time in order to get information, sometimes in a threatening way: *During the war, he interrogated more than 150 prisoners of war.* —**interrogation** /ɪnˌtɛrəˈgeɪʃən/ *n.* [C,U] —**interrogator** /ɪnˈtɛrəˌgeɪtɚ/ *n.* [C] —see Usage Note at ASK

in·ter·rog·a·tive[1] /ˌɪntɚˈrɑgətɪv/ *adj.* TECHNICAL an interrogative sentence, PRONOUN etc. asks a question or has the form of a question. For example, "who" and "what" are interrogative PRONOUNs.

interrogative[2] *n.* TECHNICAL **1** the interrogative the form of a sentence or verb that is used for asking questions **2** [C] a word such as "who" or "what" that is used to ask questions

in·ter·rog·a·to·ry /ˌɪntɚˈrɑgəˌtɔri/ *n.* [C] LAW a formal or written question that a WITNESS[1] (2) must answer —**interrogatory** *adj.*

s w **in·ter·rupt** /ˌɪntəˈrʌpt/ *v.* **1** [I,T] to stop someone from continuing what they are saying or doing by suddenly saying or doing something yourself: *Can I interrupt for a second?* | *Sorry. I didn't mean to interrupt you.* **2** [T] to make a process or activity stop for a short time: *Train service was interrupted for about* *ten minutes.* **3** [T] LITERARY if something interrupts a line, surface, view etc. it stops it from being continuous

in·ter·rup·tion /ˌɪntəˈrʌpʃən/ *n.* [C,U] **1** the act of stopping someone from speaking or doing something by suddenly saying or doing something yourself, or the things that you say or do: *Frequent interruptions by the kids make conversation difficult.* **2** the act of stopping a process or activity for a short time, or the things that make it stop: *The fire at the communications center caused no interruption in telephone service.*

in·ter·scho·las·tic /ˌɪntəskəˈlæstɪk/ *adj.* between or involving different schools: *interscholastic athletics*

in·ter·sect /ˌɪntəˈsɛkt/ *v.* **1** [I,T] if two lines or roads intersect, they go across each other **2** [T usually passive] to divide an area with several lines, roads etc.: *Venus's surface is intersected by a network of ridges and valleys.*

in·ter·sec·tion /ˈɪntəˌsɛkʃən, ˌɪntəˈsɛkʃən/ *n.* [C] **1** the place where two or more roads, lines etc. meet and go across each other: *Turn left at the intersection onto Mohawken Avenue.* **2** [U] the act of intersecting something

in·ter·ses·sion /ˈɪntəˌsɛʃən/ *n.* [C,U] the time between two parts of a college year, when ordinary classes are not taught

in·ter·sperse /ˌɪntəˈspəs/ *v.* [T usually passive] to mix one group of things together with another group, or to put parts of one group between parts of the other group: [**intersperse sth between/among sth**] *New homes are interspersed among the apple trees.* | [**intersperse sth with sth**] *The 12-minute program was interspersed with 30-second commercials.*

in·ter·state¹ /ˈɪntəˌsteɪt/ *n.* [C] a wide road that goes between states, on which cars can travel very fast

interstate² *adj.* [only before noun] between or involving different states in the U.S.: *interstate commerce* —**interstate** *adv.*

in·ter·stel·lar /ˌɪntəˈstɛlə/ *adj.* [only before noun] happening or existing between the stars: *interstellar gas and dust*

in·ter·stice /ɪnˈtəstɪs/ *n.* [C usually plural] FORMAL a small space or crack between things placed close together: *Small plants were growing in the interstices of the rock.*

in·ter·twined /ˌɪntəˈtwaɪnd/ *adj.* **1** closely related: *Research and teaching are intertwined.* **2** twisted together: *intertwined arms and legs* —**interwine** *v.* [I,T]

in·ter·val /ˈɪntəvəl/ *n.* [C] **1** a period of time or distance between two events, activities etc.: *After a five-minute interval, if the baby is still crying, go back and check on her.* | [**+ between**] *The intervals between the passing cars increased.* **2 at daily/weekly/monthly etc. intervals** every day, week, month etc.: *The train runs at seven-minute intervals throughout the day.* **3 at regular intervals** with the same amount of time or distance between each thing, activity etc.: *Feed your puppy at the same regular intervals each day.* **4 at intervals of 3 minutes/five feet etc.** with a particular amount of time or distance between things, activities etc.: *Tests were given at intervals of three or six months.* **5** TECHNICAL the amount of difference in PITCH between two musical notes

in·ter·vene /ˌɪntəˈvin/ *v.* [I] **1** to do something to try and stop an argument, war etc. or to deal with a problem, especially one that you are not directly involved in: *The UN has not yet decided whether to intervene militarily.* | [**+ in**] *So far the high court has refused to intervene in the case.* **2** if an event intervenes, it happens in a way that prevents something else: *The country was on its way to an economic renewal, but then an earthquake intervened.* **3** if a period of time intervenes, it comes between two events

in·ter·ven·ing /ˌɪntəˈvinɪŋ/ *adj.* **the intervening years/months/decades etc.** FORMAL the amount of time between two events: *I hadn't seen him since 1980, and he had aged a lot in the intervening years.*

in·ter·ven·tion /ˌɪntəˈvɛnʃən/ *n.* [C,U] the act of intervening in something such as an argument or activity to influence what happens, or the things you do to intervene: *He opposed U.S. military intervention overseas.* | *Early intervention can save the lives of many women who get breast cancer.*

in·ter·ven·tion·ism /ˌɪntəˈvɛnʃəˌnɪzəm/ *n.* [U] **1** the belief that a government should try to influence trade by spending government money **2** the belief that a government should try to influence what happens in foreign countries —**interventionist** *adj.*

in·ter·view¹ /ˈɪntəˌvyu/ *n.* **1** [C] an occasion when a famous person is asked questions about their life, experiences, or opinions for a newspaper, magazine, television program etc.: *Elton John gave an interview to Barbara Walters* (=he answered her questions). | [**+ with**] *an interview with several sports stars* **2** [C,U] a formal meeting at which someone is asked questions, for example to find out if they are good enough for a job: *Can you come in for an interview?* | [**+ for**] *He has an interview next Thursday for a job at the Dallas Tribune.*

interview² *v.* **1** [T] to ask someone questions during an interview: *We interviewed 12 candidates in three days.* **2** [I] to go to a job interview in order to try to get a job: [**+ with/at**] *I've only interviewed with two other companies so far.*

in·ter·view·ee /ˌɪntəvyuˈi/ *n.* [C] the person who answers the questions in an interview

in·ter·view·er /ˈɪntəˌvyuə/ *n.* [C] the person who asks the questions in an interview

in·ter·weave /ˌɪntəˈwiv/ *v.* past tense **interwove** /-ˈwoʊv/ past participle **interwoven** /-ˈwoʊvən/ **1** [I,T usually passive] if two or more lives, problems etc. interweave or are interwoven, they are closely related in a complicated way: *"Poison" is three interwoven stories in one.* | [**+ with**] *The American economy is being more interwoven with the world economy.* **2** [T usually passive] to weave two or more things together: *The silk is interwoven with gold and silver threads.* **3** [T] to mix together different styles or methods: *The modern music is interwoven with hits from the 1920s.*

in·tes·tate /ɪnˈtɛˌsteɪt/ *adj.* LAW **die intestate** to die without having made a WILL (=an official statement about who you want to have your property after you die)

in·tes·ti·nal /ɪnˈtɛstənl/ *adj.* **1** relating to or existing in the intestines: *intestinal disease* **2 intestinal fortitude** HUMOROUS courage or the determination to continue something even when it is very difficult: *This stock is only recommended for investors with intestinal fortitude.*

in·tes·tine /ɪnˈtɛstɪn/ *n.* [C usually plural] the long tube, consisting of two parts, that takes food from your stomach out of your body —see also LARGE INTESTINE, SMALL INTESTINE —see picture at DIGESTIVE SYSTEM

in-thing /ˌ. ˈ./ *n.* **be the in-thing** INFORMAL to be very fashionable and popular at the present time

in·ti·ma·cy /ˈɪntəməsi/ *n. plural* **intimacies** **1** [U] a state of having a close personal relationship with someone: *Building houses far apart reduces intimacy among neighbors.* **2** [C,U] a situation that is private and personal: *the intimacy of the bedroom* **3** [C usually plural] remarks or actions of a type that happen only between people who know each other very well: *the whispered intimacies of lovers* **4** [U] a word meaning "sex," used when you want to avoid saying this directly: *Intimacy took place on several occasions.*

in·ti·mate¹ /ˈɪntəmɪt/ *adj.*

1 restaurant/meal/place private and friendly, so that you feel comfortable: *Dinner was served in an intimate room with just two other tables.*

2 private relating to very private or personal matters: *She was asked about the most intimate details of her life.*

3 friends having an extremely close relationship: *He knew Monet as an associate, if not an intimate friend.* | *an intimate relationship*

4 `sexual` physically very close and personal, especially in a sexual way: *The virus can only be transmitted through intimate contact.* | *intimate apparel* (=clothes such as underwear)
5 an intimate knowledge of sth very detailed knowledge of something, as a result of careful study or a lot of experience: *Goldston has an intimate knowledge of the footwear industry.*
6 `connection` a very close connection between two things **intimate link/connection etc.** *There is an intimate connection between war and male power.*
7 be intimate with sb FORMAL to have sex with someone
8 be on intimate terms with sth to know a lot about something: *Sailors used to be on intimate terms with the stars.* —**intimately** *adv.*

in·ti·mate² /ˈɪntəˌmeɪt/ *v.* [T] FORMAL to make people understand what you mean without saying it directly: [intimate that] *Cuevas intimated that a compromise might be reached soon.*

in·ti·mate³ /ˈɪntəmɪt/ *n.* [C] a close personal friend

in·ti·ma·tion /ˌɪntəˈmeɪʃən/ *n.* [C,U] FORMAL an indirect or unclear sign that something is true or may happen: *There are strong intimations that the company is having financial problems.*

in·tim·i·date /ɪnˈtɪməˌdeɪt/ *v.* [T] **1** to frighten someone by behaving in a threatening way, especially in order to make them do what you want: *In the former Soviet Union, the KGB was used to intimidate those who disagreed with the Communist Party.* **2** to make someone feel worried and less confident: *Large audiences don't intimidate him.* —**intimidation** /ɪnˌtɪməˈdeɪʃən/ *n.* [U]

in·tim·i·dat·ed /ɪnˈtɪməˌdeɪtɪd/ *adj.* feeling worried and less confident, for example because you are in a difficult situation or other people seem better than you: *Springer says she doesn't feel intimidated by coaching a boys' team.*

in·tim·i·dat·ing /ɪnˈtɪməˌdeɪtɪŋ/ *adj.* making you feel worried and less confident: *Cawley received an intimidating letter from her ex-husband's lawyer.*

in·to /ˈɪntə; *before vowels* ˈɪntu; *strong* ˈɪntu/ *prep.*
1 from the outside to the inside of a container, substance, place, area etc.: *The child had fallen into the water.* | *Jeff went into the living room.* | *I've got to go into town this morning and do some shopping.*
2 involved in a situation or activity: *They decided to go into business together.* | *Don't get into any trouble.*
3 from one situation or physical form to a different one: *Ellen is going into fifth grade next year.* | *Roll the cookie dough into balls.* **4** to a point where you hit something, usually causing damage: *Maggie bumped into the dessert cart and knocked it over.* | *The other car just backed into me.* **5** in a particular direction: *They rode off into the sunset.* | *Make sure you're speaking directly into the microphone.* **6 be/get into sth** SPOKEN to like and be interested in something, or to become interested in it: *I was really into ice skating when I was 10.* **7** at or until a certain time: *We talked into the night.* **8** SPOKEN used to say that a second number is divided by the first number: *Six goes into thirty five times.* | *Eight into twenty-four is three.* **9 be into sb** SLANG to owe someone money: *He's into me for $25.*

in·tol·er·a·ble /ɪnˈtɑlərəbəl/ *adj.* too difficult, bad, annoying etc. for you to accept or deal with: *Living conditions at the farm worker's camp were intolerable.*

in·tol·er·ant /ɪnˈtɑlərənt/ *adj.* **1** not willing to accept ways of thinking and behaving that are different from your own: *Their position on homosexuality is intolerant and ignorant.* | [+ of] *He admitted being intolerant of blacks and Jews in his youth.* **2** not physically able to accept or deal with something: *Her son is gluten-intolerant* (=he cannot eat bread etc. with GLUTEN in it). | [+ of] *She became increasingly intolerant of various foods.* —**intolerance** *n.* [U] *racial intolerance*

in·to·na·tion /ˌɪntəˈneɪʃən, -toʊ-/ *n.* [C,U] **1** the way in which the level of your voice changes in order to add meaning to what you are saying, for example by going up at the end of a question **2** [U] the act of intoning something

in·tone /ɪnˈtoʊn/ *v.* [T] say something slowly and clearly without making your voice rise and fall much as you speak: *Uncle Danny intoned the prayer in Hebrew.*

in to·to /ɪn ˈtoʊtoʊ/ *adv.* as a whole; totally: *The paper reprinted the article in toto.*

in·tox·i·cant /ɪnˈtɑksəkənt/ *n.* [C] TECHNICAL something that makes you drunk, especially an alcoholic drink

in·tox·i·cat·ed /ɪnˈtɑksəˌkeɪtɪd/ *adj.* **1** FORMAL drunk: *The driver was clearly intoxicated.* **2** happy, excited, and unable to think clearly, especially as a result of love, success, power etc.: *We were intoxicated by victory.* —**intoxicate** *v.* [T]

in·tox·i·cat·ing /ɪnˈtɑksəˌkeɪtɪŋ/ *adj.* **1** intoxicating drinks can make you drunk **2** making you feel happy, excited, and unable to think clearly: *an intoxicating aroma from the oven*

in·tox·i·ca·tion /ɪnˌtɑksəˈkeɪʃən/ *n.* [U] the state of being drunk

intra- /ɪntrə/ *prefix* FORMAL OR TECHNICAL into, inside or within something: *intra-departmental* (=within a department) | *an intranet* (=connection for computers inside a company) | *an intravenous injection* (=into a VEIN) —compare INTER-, INTRO-

in·trac·ta·ble /ɪnˈtræktəbəl/ *adj.* FORMAL **1** an intractable problem is very difficult to deal with or solve: *Even rich nations often have intractable poverty.* **2** having a strong will and difficult to control: *intractable enemies* —**intractability** /ɪnˌtræktəˈbɪləti/ *n.* [U]

in·tra·mu·ral /ˌɪntrəˈmyʊrəl/ *adj.* happening within one school, or intended for the students of one school: *intramural sports* —compare EXTRAMURAL

in·tra·net /ˈɪntrəˌnɛt/ *n.* [C] a computer system within a company or organization that allows its computer users around the world to exchange information

in·tran·si·gent /ɪnˈtrænsədʒənt, -zə-/ *adj.* FORMAL unwilling to change your ideas or behavior in a way that seems unreasonable, or showing this quality: *Conservatives have maintained an intransigent position on the war.* —**intransigence** *n.* [U] —**intransigently** *adv.*

in·tran·si·tive /ɪnˈtrænsətɪv, -zə-/ *adj.* TECHNICAL an intransitive verb has a subject but no object. For example, in the sentence "They arrived," "arrive" is an intransitive verb. Intransitive verbs are marked [I] in this dictionary. —compare TRANSITIVE

in·tra·pre·neur /ˌɪntrəprəˈnɚ/ *n.* [C] TECHNICAL someone who helps the company they work for by working to develop new products or ways of working —**intrapreneurial** *adj.* —compare ENTREPRENEUR

in·tra·state /ˈɪntrəˌsteɪt/ *adj.* [only before noun] within one state in the U.S.: *intrastate phone calls* —compare INTERSTATE²

in·tra·u·ter·ine /ˌɪntrəˈyutərɪn, -raɪn/ *n.* [C] an IUD

in·tra·ve·nous /ˌɪntrəˈvinəs/ *adj.* **1** within or into a VEIN (=a tube that takes blood to your heart): *an intravenous injection* **2** intravenous drugs/fluids etc. drugs, liquids etc. that are put directly into the blood in a VEIN —**intravenously** *adv.*

in·trep·id /ɪnˈtrɛpɪd/ *adj.* FORMAL willing to do dangerous things or go to dangerous places: *Intrepid pioneers came to California by wagon train.*

in·tri·ca·cy /ˈɪntrɪkəsi/ *n.* **1 the intricacies of sth** the complicated details of something: *She knew very little about the intricacies of running a city when she was elected.* **2** [U] the state of containing a large number of parts or details: *The song has a jazz-like intricacy of rhythm.*

in·tri·cate /ˈɪntrɪkɪt/ *adj.* containing many small parts or details: *a pair of intricate beaded earrings*

in·trigue¹ /ɪnˈtrig/ *v.* **1** [T] to interest someone a lot, especially by being strange or mysterious: *Specialists were intrigued by a woman who writes upside-down.* **2** [I] LITERARY to make secret plans to harm someone or make them lose their position of power: *While King Richard was abroad, the barons had been intriguing against him.*

in·trigue² /ˈɪntriɡ, ɪnˈtriɡ/ *n.* **1** [U] the act or practice of secretly planning to harm someone or make them lose their position of power: *Silver is caught in a web of political intrigue.* **2** [C] a secret plan to harm someone or make them lose their position of power

in·tri·gu·ing /ɪnˈtriɡɪŋ/ *adj.* something that is intriguing is very interesting because it is strange, mysterious, or unexpected: *a strong story, with intriguing, realistic characters* —**intriguingly** *adv.*

in·trin·sic /ɪnˈtrɪnzɪk, -sɪk/ *adj.* being part of the nature or character of someone or something: *Parents need to teach children the intrinsic value of good behavior.* | [+ **to**] *Flexibility is intrinsic to creative management.* —**intrinsically** /-kli/ *adv.*

in·tro /ˈɪntroʊ/ *n.* [C] INFORMAL the introduction to a song, piece of writing etc.

intro- /ɪntrə/ *prefix* inside or within something: *intro-spection* (=examining your own feelings and thoughts) —compare INTER-, INTRA-

s w **in·tro·duce** /ˌɪntrəˈdus/ *v.* [T]
2 2 **1** ‖ when people meet ‖ if you introduce someone to another person, you tell them each other's names for the first time: *I don't think we've been introduced yet.* | [**introduce sb to sb**] *Russell, let me introduce you to Katie.* | *We'll go around the room, and each of you can **introduce yourself**.* **2** ‖ make sth happen/exist ‖ to make a change, plan, system, product etc. happen, exist, or be available for the first time: *Nearly 60 notebook computer models were introduced in 1991.* | *Slovenia introduced its own currency shortly after independence.* **3** **introduce sb to sth** to show someone something or tell them about it for the first time: *I was introduced to the African holiday of Kwanzaa at the Museum of Natural History.* **4** ‖ bring to a place ‖ to take or bring something to a place or put it in a place for the first time from somewhere else: [**introduce sth to/into sth**] *The technique was introduced to this country from Australia.* **5** ‖ present ‖ to formally present or announce someone or something in public: *Jim will introduce tonight's speaker.* **6** ‖ law ‖ to formally present something such as a BILL (=possible law) or facts to be discussed and considered: *The judge ruled that the evidence could not be introduced in court.* | *Several senators introduced legislation aimed at sexual harassment.* **7** ‖ be the start of ‖ if an event introduces a particular period or time or a change, it is the beginning of it: *The bank merger introduced a period of uncertainty in the financial markets.* **8** ‖ put sth into sth ‖ TECHNICAL to put something carefully into something else: *Fuel was introduced into the jet pipe.*

in·tro·duc·tion /ˌɪntrəˈdʌkʃən/ *n.*
1 ‖ making sth available ‖ [U] the act of making something exist, happen, or be available for the first time: *Since its introduction two years ago, the game has outsold all its competitors.* | [+ **of**] *the introduction of new drugs to fight AIDS* **2** ‖ book/speech ‖ [C] a written or spoken explanation at the beginning of a book, speech etc.: *The introduction was written by Colin Powell.* **3** ‖ learn about sth ‖ [C] something that provides a way of learning about something or trying something for the first time: [+ **to**] *an introduction to poetry class* | *The story provides a wonderful introduction to Jewish spirituality.* **4** ‖ bringing sth to a place ‖ [C,U] **a)** the act of bringing something to a place or putting it in a place for the first time from somewhere else: [+ **of**] *The bird's habitat was destroyed by the introduction of rice fields along the Louisiana coast.* **b)** something that is brought into a place for the first time from somewhere else: *The potato was a 16th century introduction.* **5** ‖ when people meet ‖ [C often plural] the act of

formally telling two people each other's names when they first meet: *I'll **make the introductions**.* **6** ‖ letter ‖ [C] an official letter that explains who you are, given to someone you have not met before: *a letter of introduction*

in·tro·duc·to·ry /ˌɪntrəˈdʌktəri/ *adj.* [usually before noun] **1** said or written at the beginning of a book, speech etc. in order to explain what it is about: *Singer wrote an introductory essay to the book of photographs.* **2** intended for people who do not know a lot about a particular subject or activity: *an introductory course on "Understanding Computers"* | *an introductory psychology textbook* **3** designed or arranged to encourage people to buy a new product: *The introductory subscription rate is $165 per year.*

in·tro·spec·tion /ˌɪntrəˈspɛkʃən/ *n.* [U] the process of thinking deeply about your own thoughts and feelings to find out their real meaning

in·tro·spec·tive /ˌɪntrəˈspɛktɪv/ *adj.* tending to think deeply about your own thoughts, feelings etc.: *a quiet, introspective woman* —**introspectively** *adv.*

in·tro·vert /ˈɪntrəˌvɜrt/ *n.* [C] someone who is quiet and shy, and does not enjoy being with other people —opposite EXTROVERT

in·tro·vert·ed /ˈɪntrəˌvɜrtɪd/ *adj.* quiet and shy, and not enjoying being with other people: *Nolan describes himself as introverted and serious.* —**introversion** /ˌɪntrəˈvɜrʒən/ *n.* [U] —opposite EXTROVERTED

in·trude /ɪnˈtrud/ *v.* **1** [I] to interrupt someone or become involved in their private affairs in an annoying and unwanted way: *Would I be intruding if I came with you?* | [+ **on/upon/into**] *Employers should not have the right to intrude on employees personal situations.* **2** [I] to have an unwanted effect on a situation: [+ **on**] *Gas stations and fast food places intrude on the city's sense of history.*

in·trud·er /ɪnˈtrudər/ *n.* [C] **1** someone who illegally enters a building or area, usually in order to steal something: *Along with other equipment, intruders took a computer that was used by handicapped kids.* **2** someone who is in a place where they are not wanted: *At first, I felt like an intruder in their family.*

in·tru·sion /ɪnˈtruʒən/ *n.* **1** [C,U] an unwanted action or person in a situation that is private: *Are you sure that my staying here won't be an intrusion?* | [+ **into/on/upon**] *government intrusion into business* **2** [C,U] something that has an unwanted effect on a situation, on people's lives etc.: *Some players resent the intrusion of religion into sports.*

in·tru·sive /ɪnˈtrusɪv/ *adj.* affecting someone's private life or interrupting them in an unwanted and annoying way: *intrusive questions* | *The photographers were pushy and intrusive.*

in·tu·it /ɪnˈtuɪt/ *v.* [I,T] FORMAL to understand that something is true through your feelings rather than through thinking about it

in·tu·i·tion /ˌɪntuˈɪʃən/ *n.* **1** [U] the ability to understand or know something by using your feelings rather than by carefully considering the facts: *women's intuition* | *Much of what doctors do is based largely on intuition.* **2** [C] an idea about what is true in a particular situation, based on strong feelings rather than facts: *People had an intuition that something was not right.*

in·tu·i·tive /ɪnˈtuɪtɪv/ *adj.* **1** based on feelings rather than on knowledge or facts: *Macelo's style of management is intuitive and informal.* **2** someone who is intuitive is able to understand situations using their feelings, without being told what is happening or having any proof —**intuitively** *adv.* —**intuitiveness** *n.* [U]

In·u·it /ˈɪnuɪt/ *n. plural* **Inuits** or **Inuit** [C] a word often used to mean Inuk

I·nuk /ˈɪnuk/ *n. plural* **Inuit** [C] a member of a race of people living in the very cold northern areas of North America —compare ESKIMO

I·nuk·ti·tut /ɪˈnuktəˌtut/ *n.* [U] the language of the Inuits

in·un·date /ˈɪnənˌdeɪt/ *v.* **1** **be inundated with sth** to receive so much of something that you cannot easily deal with it all: *During the power outage, Metro*

Power and Light was inundated with complaints.
2 [T] to cover an area with a large amount of water: *Floodwaters periodically inundate the lowlands of the state.* —**inundation** /ˌɪnənˈdeɪʃən/ *n.* [C,U]

in·ure /ɪˈnʊr/ *v.*

    inure sb **to** sth *phr. v.* [T usually passive] to make someone become used to something bad, upsetting, or difficult, so that they do not get upset by it anymore: *As a politician, he's inured to the criticism.*

in·urn·ment /ɪˈnɜnmənt/ *n.* [C] FORMAL the act of putting a dead person's ashes into an URN in order to bury them —**inurn** *v.* [T]

in·vade /ɪnˈveɪd/ *v.* **1** [I,T] to enter a country, town, or area using military force, in order to take control of it: *Hitler invaded Poland in 1939.* **2** [T] to go into a place in large numbers or amounts, when this is not wanted: *Every summer the town is invaded by tourists.* | *A virus has invaded most of their computers.* **3** [T] to affect someone in an unwanted and annoying way: *He claims investigators invaded his privacy by searching his garage.* —see also INVASION

in·vad·er /ɪnˈveɪdɚ/ *n.* [C usually plural] someone who is part of an army that enters a country or town by force in order to take control of it

in·val·id[1] /ɪnˈvælɪd/ *adj.* **1** a contract, ticket, claim etc. that is invalid is not legally or officially acceptable: *Do not detach the coupon or your ticket will be invalid.* **2** reasons, opinions etc. that are invalid are not based on clear thoughts or facts: *Ackerman said the argument was invalid.* —**invalidity** /ˌɪnvəˈlɪdəti/ *n.* [U]

in·va·lid[2] /ˈɪnvələd/ *n.* [C] someone who cannot take care of themselves because of illness, old age, or injury —**invalid** *adj.*: *her invalid father*

in·val·i·date /ɪnˈvæləˌdeɪt/ *v.* [T] **1** to make a document, ticket, claim etc. not legally or officially acceptable anymore: *The Educational Testing Service invalidated the scores of 18 students.* **2** to show that something such as a belief or explanation is wrong: *The elements of Christianity that come from older beliefs do not necessarily invalidate the religion.*

in·val·u·a·ble /ɪnˈvælyəbəl, -yuəbəl/ *adj.* extremely useful: *Martin's marketing expertise has been invaluable to our project.*

in·var·i·a·ble /ɪnˈvɛriəbəl, -ˈvær-/ *adj.* **1** always happening in the same way, at the same time etc.: *Mrs. Van der Luyden's invariable reply was, "I'll have to discuss it with my husband."* **2** TECHNICAL never changing: *the invariable rules of mathematics*

in·var·i·a·bly /ɪnˈvɛriəbli/ *adv.* if something invariably happens or is invariably true, it almost always happens or is true, so that you expect it: *The trains here are invariably punctual.*

in·va·sion /ɪnˈveɪʒən/ *n.* **1** [C,U] an occasion when one country's army enters another country by force, in order to take control of it: *the invasion of Normandy* **2** [C] the arrival in a place of a lot of people or things, often where they are not wanted: *an invasion of cheap imports* **3 invasion of privacy** a situation in which someone tries to find out personal details about another person's private affairs in a way that is upsetting and often illegal

in·va·sive /ɪnˈveɪsɪv/ *adj.* invasive medical treatment involves cutting into someone's body

in·vec·tive /ɪnˈvɛktɪv/ *n.* [U] FORMAL impolite and insulting words that someone says when they are very angry

in·veigh /ɪnˈveɪ/ *v.*

    inveigh against sb/sth *phr. v.* [T] FORMAL to criticize someone or something strongly

in·vei·gle /ɪnˈveɪgəl/ *v.*

    inveigle sb **into** sth *phr. v.* [T] FORMAL to persuade someone to do what you want, especially in a dishonest way

in·vent /ɪnˈvɛnt/ *v.* [T] **1** to make, design, or produce something new for the first time: *The geodesic dome was invented by R. Buckminster Fuller in 1947.* **2** to think of an idea, story etc. that is not true, usually in order to deceive people: *Kai invented some excuse about having a headache.*

USAGE NOTE: INVENT

WORD CHOICE: invent, discover
You **invent** something that did not exist before, such as a machine or a method: *Abner Doubleday invented baseball in 1839.* You **discover** something that existed before but was not known, such as a place, thing, or fact: *Gold was discovered in California in the 19th century.*

in·ven·tion /ɪnˈvɛnʃən/ *n.* **1** [C] a useful machine, tool, instrument etc. that has been invented: *The dishwasher is surely a wonderful invention.* **2** [U] the act of inventing something: *the invention of the wheel* **3** [C,U] a story, explanation etc. that is not true: *Accounts of Koritz's involvement in the crime are pure invention.* **4** [U] the ability to think of new and smart ideas: *Let's apply America's special genius for invention to our schools.*

in·ven·tive /ɪnˈvɛntɪv/ *adj.* able to think of new, different, or interesting ideas: *Carrington is also an inventive writer.* —**inventively** *adv.* —**inventiveness** *n.* [U]

in·ven·tor /ɪnˈvɛntɚ/ *n.* [C] someone who has invented something, or whose job is to invent things

in·ven·to·ry /ˈɪnvənˌtɔri/ *n. plural* **inventories** **1** [C,U] a list of all the things in a place: *My job was to take inventory* (=make a list of everything in a store) *at the end of each month.* **2** [U] all the goods in a store; STOCK[1] (1): *Our store has the largest inventory in the mattress business.*

in·verse[1] /ɪnˈvɚs, ˈɪnvɚs/ *adj.* **1 in inverse proportion to** sth getting bigger at the same rate as something else gets smaller, or getting smaller at the same rate as something else gets bigger: *The usefulness of a meeting is in inverse proportion to the attendance.* **2** [only before noun] FORMAL exactly opposite, especially in order or position: *The list of winners will be read in inverse order.* —**inversely** *adv.*

in·verse[2] /ˈɪnvɚs, ɪnˈvɚs/ *n.* [singular] TECHNICAL the complete opposite of something: *The inverse is also true.*

in·ver·sion /ɪnˈvɚʒən/ *n.* [C,U] **1** also **inversion lay·er** /.ˈ.. ˌ../ TECHNICAL a type of weather condition in which the air nearest the ground is cooler than the air above it **2** FORMAL the act of changing something so that it is the opposite of what it was before, or of turning something upside down

in·vert /ɪnˈvɚt/ *v.* [T] FORMAL to put something in the opposite position to the one it was in before, especially by turning it upside down —**inverted** *adj.*: *an inverted triangle*

in·ver·te·brate /ɪnˈvɚtəˌbrɪt, -breɪt/ *n.* [C] a living creature that does not have a BACKBONE —**invertebrate** *adj.* —compare VERTEBRATE

in·vest /ɪnˈvɛst/ *v.* **1** [I,T] to give money to a company, business, or bank, in order to get a profit back: [**invest** (sth) **in** sth] *Rowntree then invested $70,000 of his savings in a new store.* | *Many of us had invested heavily* (=invested a lot of money) *in high-tech stocks.* **2** [T] to use a lot of time, effort etc. in order to make something succeed: [**invest** sth **in** sth] *It's a chance for students to invest time in non-profit work.*

    invest in sth *phr. v.* [T] **1** to buy something in order to sell it again when the value increases, and so make a profit: *Oliver invested in antique furniture.* **2** to buy something or spend more money or time on something, because it will be useful for you: *We decided it was finally time to invest in a new car.* | *Everyone here has a lot invested in their careers.*

    invest sb/sth **with** sth *phr. v.* [T often passive] FORMAL **1** to officially give someone power to do something: *Later that year, the Congress invested Gorbachev with broader powers.* **2** to make someone or something seem to have a particular quality or character: *Richard's heavy-rimmed glasses invested him with an air of dignity.*

in·ves·ti·gate /ɪnˈvɛstəˌgeɪt/ *v.* **1** [I,T] to try to find out the truth about something such as a crime, accident, or scientific problem: *The FBI has been called in to investigate the murder.* | *I heard a noise and went downstairs to investigate.* **2** [T] to try to find out more about someone's character, actions etc., because you think they may have been involved in a crime: *Hunt was investigated for more than a year before he was arrested.*

in·ves·ti·ga·tion /ɪnˌvɛstəˈgeɪʃən/ *n.* **1** [C] an official attempt to find out the reasons for something such as a crime, accident, or scientific problem: *a criminal investigation* | [+ **into**] *an investigation into the accident* **2** [U] the act of investigating something: *the investigation of drug smuggling* | *Dodd is still under investigation* (=being investigated).

in·ves·ti·ga·tive /ɪnˈvɛstəˌgeɪtɪv/ *adj.* **investigative journalism/report/work** work or activities that involve investigating something

in·ves·ti·ga·tor /ɪnˈvɛstəˌgeɪtə/ *n.* [C] someone who investigates things, especially crimes

in·ves·ti·ga·to·ry /ɪnˈvɛstəgəˌtɔri/ *adj.* relating to investigation

in·ves·ti·ture /ɪnˈvɛstəˌtʃʊr, -tʃə/ *n.* [C] FORMAL a ceremony at which someone is given an official title: *the investiture of the new County Supervisor*

in·vest·ment /ɪnˈvɛstmənt/ *n.* **1** [C,U] the money that people or organizations have put into a company, business, or bank, in order to get a profit or to make a business activity successful: [+ **in**] *In 1990, Japanese investment in U.S. real estate totaled $13.06 billion.* | *A Certificate of Deposit remains one of the safest investments.* | **short-term/long-term investment** (=one that will give you results in a short time, or only after a long time) **2** something that you buy or do because it will be useful later: *Going back to college was a good investment.* **3** [C,U] a large amount of time, energy, emotion etc. that you spend on something: *Raising kids requires a huge investment of time and energy.*

investment bank /.ˈ.. ˌ./ *n.* [C] a bank that buys and sells securities (SECURITY (3)) such as STOCKS[1] (2) or BONDS[1] (2) —**investment banker** *n.* [C] —**investment banking** *n.* [U]

in·ves·tor /ɪnˈvɛstə/ *n.* [C] someone who gives money to a company, business, or bank in order to get a profit back

in·vet·er·ate /ɪnˈvɛtərɪt/ *adj.* [only before noun] **1 inveterate liar/smoker/womanizer etc.** someone who smokes a lot, lies a lot etc. and cannot stop **2 inveterate fondness/distrust/hatred etc.** an attitude or feeling that you have had for a long time and cannot change —**inveterately** *adv.*

in·vid·i·ous /ɪnˈvɪdiəs/ *adj.* bad or unfair, especially because it is likely to offend people or make you unpopular: *The ruling may create an invidious distinction in the way the courts treat the rich and the poor.*

in·vig·or·ate /ɪnˈvɪgəˌreɪt/ *v.* [T usually passive] to make the people in an organization or group feel excited again, so that they want to make something successful: *Carey's hope was that the church would be renewed and invigorated.*

in·vig·or·at·ed /ɪnˈvɪgəˌreɪtɪd/ *adj.* [not before noun] feeling healthier and stronger, and having more energy than you did before: *A weekend in the mountains always makes me feel invigorated.*

in·vig·o·rat·ing /ɪnˈvɪgəˌreɪtɪŋ/ *adj.* making you feel like you have more energy: *cold, invigorating air*

in·vin·ci·ble /ɪnˈvɪnsəbəl/ *adj.* **1** too strong to be destroyed or defeated: *an invincible army* | *"Kids think they're invincible," said the school's drug counselor.* **2** an invincible belief, attitude etc. is extremely strong and cannot be changed —**invincibly** *adv.* —**invincibility** /ɪnˌvɪnsəˈbɪləti/ *n.* [U]

in·vi·o·la·ble /ɪnˈvaɪələbəl/ *adj.* FORMAL an inviolable right, law, principle etc. is extremely important and should not be gotten rid of —**inviolability** /ɪnˌvaɪələˈbɪləti/ *n.* [U]

in·vi·o·late /ɪnˈvaɪəlɪt/ *adj.* FORMAL something that is inviolate cannot be attacked, changed, or destroyed

in·vis·i·ble /ɪnˈvɪzəbəl/ *adj.* **1** something that is invisible cannot be seen: *The house was surrounded by trees and was invisible from the road.* | [+ **to**] *The Stealth bomber is meant to be invisible to radar.* **2** not noticed, or not talked about: *There's an invisible barrier that keeps women out of top jobs.* **3 invisible trade/earnings/exports etc.** money that is made from services and TOURISM rather than from products —**invisibly** *adv.* —**invisibility** /ɪnˌvɪzəˈbɪləti/ *n.* [U]

invisible ink /.ˌ... ˈ./ *n.* [U] ink that cannot be seen on paper until it is heated, treated with chemicals etc., used for writing secret messages

in·vi·ta·tion /ˌɪnvəˈteɪʃən/ *n.* **1** [C] a card asking someone to attend a party, wedding, meal etc.: [+ **to**] *Did you get an invitation to Keri's party?* **2** [C,U] a written or spoken request to someone, asking them to go somewhere or do something: [**an invitation to do sth**] *Kirkham accepted an invitation to teach at Harvard this summer.* | *Attendance at the dinner is by invitation only* (=only people who are invited can attend). | *Dukakis declined an invitation* (=did not accept an invitation) *to speak at the conference.* **3** [singular,U] encouragement to do something: *He took my silence as an invitation to talk.* **4 open/standing invitation** an invitation to do something, especially to visit someone, at any time you like: *You have a standing invitation to use our hot tub, you know that.* **5 be an open invitation for/to sb** to make it very easy for someone to rob you or harm you: *Leaving the car unlocked is just an open invitation to thieves.* **6 at sb's invitation** also **at the invitation of sb** if you go somewhere or do something at someone's invitation, you go there or do it because they have invited you to

in·vite[1] /ɪnˈvaɪt/ *v.* [T] **1** to ask someone to come to a party, wedding, meal etc.: [**invite sb to sth**] *Oh, about a hundred people were invited to the wedding.* | [**invite sb to do sth**] *You want to invite Randy to come to dinner with us?* | [**invite sb for sth**] *We've been invited for drinks on Friday at the Thompson's.* | [**be invited**] *No, I wasn't invited.* **2** to politely offer someone the chance to do something: [**invite sb to do sth**] *Mr. Quinn was invited to sing a song he had written.* **3** to encourage something bad such as trouble or criticism to happen to you, especially without intending to: *Allowing a sixteen-year-old to stay out all night is just inviting trouble.*

invite sb **along** *phr. v.* [T] to ask someone if they would like to come with you when you are going somewhere: *Why don't you invite Barbara along?*

invite sb **back** *phr. v.* [T] to ask someone to come to your home, your office etc. again: *If you keep arguing with Gerry, they won't invite us back.*

invite sb **in** *phr. v.* [T] to ask someone to come into your home: *Can I invite you in for coffee?*

invite sb **out** *phr. v.* to ask someone to go somewhere with you, especially to a restaurant or movie: *Josh called and invited her out for Saturday night.*

invite sb **over** *phr. v.* [T] to ask someone to come to your home for a drink, a meal, a party etc.: *Marian invited a bunch of people over to watch a movie.*

in·vite[2] /ˈɪnvaɪt/ *n.* [C] SPOKEN, INFORMAL an invitation to a party, meal etc.

in·vit·ing /ɪnˈvaɪtɪŋ/ *adj.* an inviting object, place, smell, offer etc. is very attractive and makes you want to go somewhere or do something: *Nothing's more inviting than a plump sofa or chair.* —**invitingly** *adv.*

in vi·tro fer·til·i·za·tion /ɪn ˌvitroʊ fətl-əˈzeɪʃən/ *n.* [U] TECHNICAL a process in which a human egg is FERTILIZED outside a woman's body

in·vo·ca·tion /ˌɪnvəˈkeɪʃən/ *n.* LITERARY **1** the invocation a speech or prayer at the beginning of a ceremony or meeting: *Rabbi Gutterman gave the invocation at the graduation ceremony.* **2** [C,U] a request for help, especially from God or a god

in·voice[1] /ˈɪnvɔɪs/ *n.* [C] a list of goods that have been supplied or work that has been done, showing how much you owe for them

invoice² v. [T] **1** to send someone an invoice **2** to prepare an invoice for goods that have been supplied or work that has been done

in·voke /ɪnˈvoʊk/ v. [T] FORMAL **1** if you invoke a law, rule etc., you say that you are doing something because the law allows or forces you to: *The UN threatened to invoke economic sanctions if the talks were broken off.* **2** to make a particular idea, image or feeling appear in people's minds: *During his speech, he invoked the memory of Harry Truman.* **3** to use a law, principle, or THEORY to support your views: *Judge Pregerson, in his dissent, invoked an individual's right to be left alone.* **4** to ask for help from someone more powerful than you, especially God or a god: *Rev. Moran invoked a blessing.* **5** to make spirits appear by using magic

in·vol·un·tar·y /ɪnˈvɑlənˌtɛri/ adj. an involuntary movement, sound, reaction etc. is one that you make suddenly and without intending to because you cannot control yourself: *an involuntary muscle contraction* —**involuntarily** adv. —**involuntariness** n. [U]

s w **in·volve** /ɪnˈvɑlv/ v. [T] **1** to include something as a necessary part or result: *What will the job involve?* | [**involve doing sth**] *Running your own business usually involves working long hours.* **2** to include or affect someone or something: *A study involving long-distance runners is being done at the Medical Center.* **3** to ask or allow someone to take part in something: [**involve sb in sth**] *The city is making an effort to involve the public in these discussions.* **4 involve yourself** to take part actively in a particular activity: [**+ in**] *The U.S. has so far been extremely unwilling to involve itself in the crisis.*

s w **in·volved** /ɪnˈvɑlvd/ adj. **1 be/get involved** to take part in an activity or event, or be connected with it in some way: [**+ in**] *More than 30 software firms were involved in the project.* | [**+ with**] *Landel is one of the professors who was involved with the Hercules program.* | *I don't want to **get involved in** another nasty argument with him.* | **deeply/heavily involved** (=involved very much) **2 be involved in an accident/fight/crash etc.** to be one of the people in an accident, crash etc.: *As many as 10 vehicles were involved in the collision.* **3 the work/effort/money etc. involved in doing sth** the amount of work, effort, money etc. that is needed in order to make something succeed: *A tremendous amount of planning is involved in putting on a concert.* **4 be involved with sb a)** to be having a sexual relationship with someone, especially someone you should not have a relationship with: *Matt's involved with a married woman at work.* **b)** to spend time with someone that you have a relationship with: *He's a father who wants to be more involved with his family.* **5** having so many different parts that it is difficult to understand; complicated: *The plot was so involved that very few people knew what was going on.*

s w **in·volve·ment** /ɪnˈvɑlvmənt/ n. [U] **1** the act of taking part in an activity or event, or the way in which you take part in it: *School officials say they welcome parental involvement.* | [**+ in**] *Bittman could not discuss any aspect of his involvement in the case.* **2** the feeling of excitement and satisfaction that you get from an activity: *There was very little emotional involvement in their marriage.* **3** a romantic relationship between two people, especially when they are not married to each other: *He denied ever having any involvement with her.*

in·vul·ner·a·ble /ɪnˈvʌlnərəbəl/ adj. someone or something that is invulnerable cannot be harmed or damaged if you attack or criticize them: [**+ to**] *Malaria that is invulnerable to drugs is spreading across the world.* —**invulnerably** adv. —**invulnerability** /ɪnˌvʌlnərəˈbɪləti/ n. [U] —compare VULNERABLE

in·ward /ˈɪnwɚd/ adj. **1** [only before noun] felt or experienced in your own mind but not expressed to other people: *As we talked, I felt a sudden inward tension.* **2** toward the inside or center of something: *The middle of the car door was bent inward.* —**inwardly** adv.: *Inwardly, I was furious.* —opposite OUTWARD¹

inward-look·ing /ˈ.. ˌ../ adj. an inward-looking person or group is more interested in themselves than in other people: *an inward-looking society*

i·o·dine /ˈaɪəˌdaɪn, -ˌdɪn/ n. [U] symbol **I** a dark red chemical substance that is an ELEMENT and is used on wounds to prevent infection

i·o·dized /ˈaɪəˌdaɪzd/ adj. iodized salt has had iodine added to it to help your body stay healthy

i·on /ˈaɪən, ˈaɪɑn/ n. [C] TECHNICAL an atom that has been given a positive or negative force by adding or taking away an ELECTRON

-ion /ən/ suffix [in nouns] used to make nouns that show actions, results, or states: *the completion of a task* (=act of finishing it) | *an election* (=when someone is elected) | *complete exhaustion* (=state of being extremely tired)

I·o·nes·co /ˌiəˈnɛskoʊ/, **Eu·gène** /yuˈdʒɪn, uˈʒɛn/ (1912–1994) a French writer of plays, born in Romania

I·o·ni·an /aɪˈoʊniən/ **1** one of the people that lived in ancient Greece from the twentieth century B.C. **2** one of the people from ancient Greece that lived on the northeast coast of the Mediterranean from the tenth century B.C.

Ionian Sea, the /ˌ..ˈ./ a part of the Mediterranean Sea that is between southern Italy and southern Greece

I·on·ic /aɪˈɑnɪk/ adj. made in the simply decorated style of ancient Greek buildings: *an Ionic column*

i·on·ize /ˈaɪəˌnaɪz/ v. [I,T] to form ions or make them form —**ionization** /ˌaɪənəˈzeɪʃən/ n. [U]

i·on·iz·er /ˈaɪəˌnaɪzɚ/ n. [C] a machine used to make the air in a room more healthy by producing negative IONS

i·on·o·sphere /aɪˈɑnəˌsfɪr/ n. **the ionosphere** the part of the ATMOSPHERE (2) that is used to help send radio waves around the Earth

i·o·ta /aɪˈoʊtə/ n. [singular] **1 not one iota** not even a small amount: *Your eyesight has not changed one iota.* **2** the Greek letter "I"

IOU n. [C] INFORMAL a note that you sign to say that you owe someone some money

-ious /iəs/ suffix [in adjectives] used to make adjectives; -OUS: *furious* (=extremely angry) —see also -EOUS

I·o·wa¹ /ˈaɪəwə/ written abbreviation **IA** a state in the Midwestern area of the U.S. —**Iowan** n., adj.

Iowa² a Native American tribe from the northern central area of the U.S.

IPA n. [singular] the International Phonetic Alphabet; a system of special signs that are used to represent the sounds made in speech

IPO n. [C] initial public offering; the first time that STOCK in a company is available to be bought by people in general

ip·so fac·to /ˌɪpsoʊ ˈfæktoʊ/ adv. FORMAL used to say that something is known from or proved by the facts

IQ, I.Q. n. [C] Intelligence Quotient; your level of intelligence, measured by a special test, with 100 being the average result: *Lead can cause slowed growth and reduced IQ.*

ir- /ɪr/ prefix used instead of IN- (1) before the letter "r"; not: *irregular* (=not regular)

IRA n. Individual Retirement Account; a special bank account in which you can save money for your RETIREMENT without paying tax on it until later

I·ran /ɪˈræn, ɪˈrɑn/ a country in southwest Asia, east of Iraq and west of Afghanistan —**Iranian** /ɪˈreɪniən/ n., adj.

I·raq /ɪˈræk, ɪˈrɑk/ a country in southwest Asia, west of Iran and north of Saudi Arabia —**Iraqi** n., adj.

i·ras·ci·ble /ɪˈræsəbəl/ adj. FORMAL easily becoming angry: *an irascible actress* —**irascibly** adv.

i·rate /ˌaɪˈreɪt/ adj. extremely angry, especially because you think you have been treated unfairly: *an irate customer* —**irately** adv.

ire /aɪə/ n. [U] FORMAL anger: **raise/draw sb's ire** (=make someone angry)

Ire·land /'aɪələnd/ a large island to the west of Great Britain, from which it is separated by the Irish Sea. It is divided politically into Northern Ireland and the Republic of Ireland. Northern Ireland is part of the U.K.

ir·i·des·cent /ˌɪrə'dɛsənt/ adj. showing colors that seem to change in different lights: *an iridescent silk suit* —**iridescence** n. [U]

i·rid·i·um /ɪ'rɪdiəm/ n. [U] *symbol* **Ir** a rare metal that is an ELEMENT and is used in medicine

i·ris /'aɪrɪs/ n. [C] **1** a tall plant with long thin leaves and large purple, yellow, or white flowers **2** the round colored part of your eye, that surrounds the black PUPIL (2)

I·rish[1] /'aɪrɪʃ/ n. **the Irish** people from Ireland

Irish[2] adj. from or relating to Ireland

Irish cof·fee /ˌ.. '../ n. [C,U] coffee with cream and WHISKEY added

I·rish·man /'aɪrɪʃmən/ n. [C] a man from Ireland

Irish set·ter /ˌ.. '../ n. [C] a type of large dog with long hair

I·rish·wom·an /'aɪrɪʃˌwʊmən/ n. [C] a woman from Ireland

irk /ɚk/ v. [T] if something irks you, it makes you feel annoyed, especially because you feel you cannot change the situation: *The increased traffic noise has irked many residents.*

irk·some /'ɚksəm/ adj. FORMAL annoying: *an irksome habit*

i·ron[1] /'aɪɚn/ n. **1** [U] *symbol* **Fe** a common hard metal that is an ELEMENT, is used to make steel, is MAGNETIC, and is found in very small quantities in food and blood: *iron ore | a window with iron bars on it | My doctor said I need more iron in my diet.* **2** [C] a thing used for making clothes smooth, which has a heated flat metal base **3 have several irons in the fire** to be involved in several different activities or have several plans **4** [C] a GOLF CLUB made of metal rather than wood **5 irons** [plural] LITERARY a set of chains used to prevent a prisoner from moving —see also **pump iron** (PUMP[2] (8)), **rule sb/sth with an iron fist/hand** (RULE[2] (4)), **strike while the iron is hot** (STRIKE[1] (29)), **have a will of iron** (WILL[2] (6))

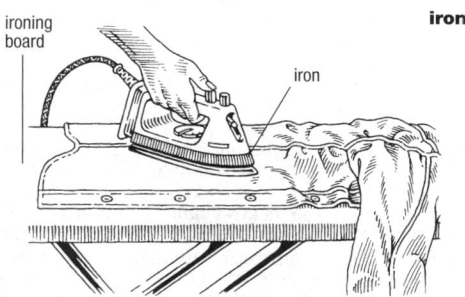
ironing board

iron

iron

iron[2] v. [T] to make clothes smooth using an iron: *I need to iron a few shirts for my trip.* —see also IRONING

iron sth ↔ **out** *phr. v.* [T] **1** to solve or get rid of problems or difficulties, especially small ones: *We're meeting tomorrow to iron out the details of the contract.* **2** to remove the folds from your clothes by ironing them

iron[3] adj. [only before noun] very firm and strong or determined: *iron discipline*

Iron Age /'.. ˌ./ **the Iron Age** the period of time about 3000 years ago when iron was first used for making tools, weapons etc. —compare BRONZE AGE, STONE AGE

i·ron·clad /'aɪɚnˌklæd/ adj. **1** an ironclad agreement, proof, defense etc. is so strong and sure that it cannot be changed or argued against: *an ironclad*

---

guarantee **2** covered with iron: *an ironclad battleship*

Iron Cur·tain /ˌ.. '../ **the Iron Curtain** the name that was used for the border between the Communist countries of Eastern Europe and the rest of Europe

iron-gray /ˌ.. '.ˌ/ adj. iron-gray hair is a dark gray color

i·ron·ic /aɪ'rɑnɪk/ also **i·ron·i·cal** /aɪ'rɑnɪkəl/ adj. **1** an ironic situation is one that is unusual or amusing because something strange happens or the opposite of what is expected happens or is true: *In a strange and ironic way, many Americans profited from the war.* | *It's ironic that the largest state in the union has such a small Legislature.* **2** using words that are the opposite of what you really mean, often in a joking way: *ironic comments* —compare SARCASTIC

i·ron·i·cal·ly /aɪ'rɑnɪkli/ adv. **1** [sentence adverb] used to say that a situation is one in which the opposite of what you expected happens or is true: *Ironically, he had decided not to install a burglar alarm before the break-in occurred.* **2** in a way that shows you really mean the opposite of what you are saying

i·ron·ing /'aɪɚnɪŋ/ n. [U] **1** the activity of making clothes smooth with an iron: *I do the laundry and Sharon does the ironing.* **2** clothes that are waiting to be ironed or have just been ironed

ironing board /'... ˌ./ n. [C] a small narrow table used for ironing clothes —see picture at IRON[2]

iron lung /ˌ.. './ n. [C] a large machine with a metal case that fits around your body and helps you to breathe, used especially for people who had POLIO

iron-on /'.. ˌ./ also **iron-on patch** /ˌ.. '.ˌ/ n. [C] a PATCH[1] (2) that you can stick to your clothes using a hot iron

i·ron·stone /'aɪɚnˌstoʊn/ n. [U] a type of rock that contains a lot of iron

i·ron·ware /'aɪɚnˌwɛr/ n. [U] things made of iron, especially for cooking

i·ron·work /'aɪɚnˌwɚk/ n. [U] fences, gates etc. that are made of iron bent into attractive shapes

i·ro·ny /'aɪrəni/ n. [U] **1** the use of words that are the opposite of what you really mean, often in order to be amusing: *Through irony and humor, James dilutes the seriousness of the novel.* —compare SARCASM **2** a situation that is unusual or amusing because something strange happens, or the opposite of what is expected happens or is true: *The tragic irony is that the drug was supposed to save lives.* —see also DRAMATIC IRONY

ir·ra·di·ate /ɪ'reɪdiˌeɪt/ v. [T] **1** TECHNICAL to treat someone or something with X-RAYS or other kinds of RADIATION: *The flies were irradiated to make them sterile.* **2** LITERARY to make something look bright by shining light onto it —**irradiated** adj.: *irradiated meat* —**irradiation** /ɪˌreɪdi'eɪʃən/ n. [U]

ir·ra·tion·al /ɪ'ræʃənəl/ adj. **1** irrational behavior, feelings etc. seem strange because they are not based on clear thought or reasons: *an irrational fear of flying* **2** someone who is irrational tends to behave or do things without thinking clearly or without good reasons: *Vance is becoming increasingly irrational.* —**irrationally** adv. —**irrationality** /ɪˌræʃə'næləti/ n. [U]

ir·rec·on·cil·a·ble /ɪˌrɛkən'saɪləbəl/ adj. **1** irreconcilable opinions, positions etc. are so strongly opposed to each other that it is not possible for them to reach an agreement: [+ **with**] *Fighting in a war was irreconcilable with his religious beliefs.* **2 irreconcilable differences** strong disagreements between two people who are married, given as a legal reason that they can give for getting a DIVORCE —**irreconcilably** adv.

ir·re·cov·er·a·ble /ˌɪrɪ'kʌvərəbəl/ adj. something that is irrecoverable is lost or has gone and you cannot get it back: *irrecoverable costs* —**irrecoverably** adv.

ir·re·deem·a·ble /ˌɪrɪ'diməbəl/ adj. **1** FORMAL too bad to be CORRECTed or repaired **2** TECHNICAL irredeemable STOCK[1] (2) cannot be exchanged for money —**irredeemably** adv.

ir·re·duc·i·ble /ˌɪrɪ'dusəbəl/ adj. an irreducible sum,

level etc. cannot be made smaller or simpler —**irreducibly** *adv.*

ir·re·fut·a·ble /ˌɪrɪˈfyutəbəl, ɪˈrɛfyətəbəl/ *adj.* an irrefutable statement, argument etc. cannot be disagreed with and must be accepted: *There was irrefutable evidence of his guilt.* —**irrefutably** *adv.*

ir·re·gard·less /ˌɪrɪˈgɑrdlɪs/ *adv.* irregardless of sth NONSTANDARD a word meaning REGARDLESS, which many people consider incorrect

ir·reg·u·lar¹ /ɪˈrɛgyələ/ *adj.* **1** having a shape, surface, pattern etc. that is not even, smooth, or balanced: *a jagged, irregular coastline* **2** not happening at times that are an equal distance from each other: *an irregular heartbeat* **3** not doing something or happening at the expected time every day, week etc.: *Some weeks, I work long, irregular hours.* | *irregular meals* **4** FORMAL not obeying the usually accepted legal or moral rules: *There was nothing irregular about the loan.* **5** an irregular verb/form/plural etc. a verb or a form of a word that does not follow the usual pattern of grammar, such as the verb "go" or the plural "deer" **6** a word meaning CONSTIPATED (=unable to easily pass solid waste from your body), used in order to be polite —**irregularly** *adv.*

irregular² *n.* [C] a soldier who is not an official member of a country's army

ir·reg·u·lar·i·ty /ˌɪˌrɛgyəˈlærəti/ *n. plural* **irregularities** **1** [C usually plural] a situation in which something has not been done according to rules: *None of the U.N. observers had reported any irregularities in the voting.* | **financial/accounting irregularities** (=when rules for dealing with money have not been followed) **2** [C,U] a situation in which something does not happen regularly in the way it should or at the time it normally does: *Heart irregularities can lead to sudden death.* | *menstrual irregularity* **3** [U] a word meaning CONSTIPATION, used in order to be polite

ir·rel·e·vance /ɪˈrɛləvəns/ also **ir·rel·e·van·cy** /ɪˈrɛləvənsi/ *n.* **1** [U] a lack of importance in a particular situation **2** [C] someone or something that is not important in a particular situation: *Age is an irrelevance for most jobs.*

ir·rel·e·vant /ɪˈrɛləvənt/ *adj.* not useful in or not relating to a particular situation, and therefore not important: *Students viewed Latin as boring and irrelevant.* | [+ to] *Her comments seemed irrelevant to the real issue.* —**irrelevantly** *adv.*

ir·re·lig·ious /ˌɪrɪˈlɪdʒəs/ *adj.* FORMAL opposed to religion, or not having any religious feeling

ir·re·me·di·a·ble /ˌɪrɪˈmidiəbəl/ *adj.* FORMAL so bad that it is impossible to make it better —**irremediably** *adv.*

ir·rep·a·ra·ble /ɪˈrɛpərəbəl/ *adj.* irreparable damage, harm etc. is so bad that it can never be repaired or made better: *Boxing can cause irreparable damage to the brain.* —**irreparably** *adv.*

ir·re·place·a·ble /ˌɪrɪˈpleɪsəbəl/ *adj.* too special, valuable, or unusual for anything else to be used instead: *Several works of art were lost, many of them irreplaceable.*

ir·re·press·i·ble /ˌɪrɪˈprɛsəbəl/ *adj.* full of energy, confidence, and happiness, so that you never seem unhappy: *an irrepressible optimist* —**irrepressibly** *adv.*

ir·re·proach·a·ble /ˌɪrɪˈproutʃəbəl/ *adj.* FORMAL something such as someone's behavior that is irreproachable is so good that you cannot criticize it —**irreproachably** *adv.*

ir·re·sist·i·ble /ˌɪrɪˈzɪstəbəl/ *adj.* **1** so attractive, desirable etc. that you cannot prevent yourself from wanting it: *the irresistible aroma of fresh bread* | *Tax-cutting proposals could prove irresistible to lawmakers.* | *Men find Natalie irresistible.* **2** too strong or powerful to be stopped or prevented: *Roth was possessed by an irresistible urge to fix things up.* —**irresistibly** *adv.*

ir·res·o·lute /ɪˈrɛzəˌlut/ *adj.* FORMAL unable to decide what to do; uncertain —**irresolutely** *adv.* —**irresolution** /ˌɪˌrɛzəˈluʃən/ *n.* [U]

ir·re·spec·tive /ˌɪrɪˈspɛktɪv/ *adv.* **irrespective of sth** used when saying that a particular fact has no effect on a situation and is not important: *Every adult pays the same amount of tax, irrespective of income.*

ir·re·spon·si·ble /ˌɪrɪˈspɑnsəbəl/ *adj.* doing careless things without thinking or worrying about the possible bad results: *When it comes to money, Dan is completely irresponsible.* | **[be irresponsible to do sth]** *It's irresponsible to have a debt that large.* | **[be irresponsible for/of sb to do sth]** *Smith admitted it was irresponsible of him to have unprotected sex.* —**irresponsibly** *adv.* —**irresponsibility** /ˌɪrɪˌspɑnsəˈbɪləti/ *n.* [U]

ir·re·triev·a·ble /ˌɪrɪˈtrivəbəl/ *adj.* FORMAL **1** an irretrievable situation cannot be made right again: *the irretrievable breakdown of their marriage* **2** the loss of something that you can never get back: *After money is transferred out of the U.S., it's practically irretrievable.* —**irretrievably** *adv.*

ir·rev·er·ent /ɪˈrɛvərənt/ *adj.* showing a lack of respect for organizations, customs, beliefs etc.: *an irreverent sense of humor* —**irreverently** *adv.* —**irreverence** *n.* [U]

ir·re·vers·i·ble /ˌɪrɪˈvəsəbəl/ *adj.* unable to be changed back to how something was before, because the change is so serious or so great: *an irreversible decision* | *Miller is in an irreversible coma.* —**irreversibly** *adv.*

ir·rev·o·ca·ble /ɪˈrɛvəkəbəl/ *adj.* an irrevocable decision, action etc. cannot be changed or stopped —**irrevocably** *adv.*: *Computers have irrevocably changed our society.*

ir·ri·gate /ˈɪrəˌgeɪt/ *v.* [T] **1** to supply land or crops with water **2** TECHNICAL to wash a wound with a flow of liquid —**irrigation** /ˌɪrəˈgeɪʃən/ *n.* [U] *an irrigation system*

ir·ri·ta·ble /ˈɪrətəbəl/ *adj.* **1** getting annoyed quickly or easily: *Since Steve quit smoking, he's been really irritable.* **2** TECHNICAL very sensitive and sore —**irritably** *adv.* —**irritability** /ˌɪrətəˈbɪləti/ *n.* [U]

ir·ri·tant /ˈɪrətənt/ *n.* [C] **1** something that makes you feel annoyed over a period of time: *Drug smuggling has been a major irritant in U.S.–Mexican relations.* **2** a substance that can make a part of your body painful and sore: *Caution: the contents of this container are an irritant to eyes.*

ir·ri·tate /ˈɪrəˌteɪt/ *v.* [T] **1** to make someone feel annoyed and impatient: *I don't want to listen to muzak in stores – it irritates me.* **2** to make a part of your body painful and sore: *Perfumes in soap can irritate skin.*

ir·ri·tat·ed /ˈɪrəˌteɪtɪd/ *adj.* **1** feeling annoyed and impatient about something: [+ about/at/with/by] *Now he was irritated with himself for making such a stupid comment.* **2** painful and sore: *Her skin looked really irritated.*

ir·ri·tat·ing /ˈɪrəˌteɪtɪŋ/ *adj.* making you feel annoyed and impatient: *a dog with an irritating, high-pitched bark* —**irritatingly** *adv.*

ir·ri·ta·tion /ˌɪrəˈteɪʃən/ *n.* **1** [U] the feeling of being annoyed about something, especially something that happens again and again: *The heavy traffic is a constant source of irritation.* | [+ about/with] *Professor Allison expressed irritation with inaccurate reports in the media.* **2** [C] something that makes you annoyed: *Attwood's metallic music was an irritation.* **3** [C,U] a painful sore feeling on a part of your body: *Exposure to the fertilizer can cause irritation to the skin or eyes.* | *a throat irritation*

IRS *n.* **the IRS** the Internal Revenue Service; the department of the U.S. government that collects national taxes

Ir·ving /ˈəvɪŋ/**, John** (1942–) a U.S. writer of NOVELS

Irving, Washington (1783–1859) a U.S. writer known especially for his stories

is /z, s, əz; *strong* ɪz/ *v.* the third person singular of the present tense of BE

I·sa·iah /aɪˈzeɪə/ **1** (8th century B.C.) in the Jewish and Christian religions, a Hebrew PROPHET who said that God would send a MESSIAH to save the Jews. **2** a book in the OLD TESTAMENT in the Bible

ISBN *n.* International Standard Book Number; a number that is given to every book that is PUBLISHed

ISDN *n.* [U] TECHNICAL Integrated Services Digital Network; a special telephone network through which computers can send information much faster than usual

-ish /ıʃ/ *suffix* **1** [in nouns] the people or language of a particular country or place: *I'm trying to learn Turkish* (=the language of Turkey). | *the British* (=people from Britain) **2** [in adjectives] relating to a particular place: *Spanish food* (=from Spain) **3** [in adjectives] similar to a particular type of person or thing, or having qualities of that person or thing: *foolish behavior* (=typical of a fool) | *Don't be so childish* (=don't behave like a child)! | *a cartoonish live-action movie* **4** [in adjectives] used in some adjectives that show disapproval: *selfish* | *childish* **5** [in adjectives] a little; SLIGHTLY: *tallish* (=slightly tall) | *youngish* (=still a little young) | *reddish hair* **6** [in adjectives] SPOKEN about; APPROXIMATELY: *We'll expect you around eightish* (=at about 8 o'clock). | *He's fortyish* (=about 40 years old). **7** [in adjectives and nouns] having a particular set of beliefs, or being a member of a religious group: *Jewish traditions* | *the Amish people* **8** SPOKEN, INFORMAL used as an answer to mean "slightly" or "not exactly": *"Oh, are you feeling sick?" "Ish."* (=slightly)

I·sis /'aısıs/ in ancient Egyptian MYTHOLOGY, the most important goddess. She was the goddess of nature and was also the wife and sister of Osiris.

Is·lam /'ızlɑm, ız'lɑm, 'ıslɑm/ *n.* [U] **1** the Muslim religion, which was started by Mohammed and whose holy book is the Koran **2** the people and countries that follow this religion —**Islamic** /ız'lɑmık, ıs'lɑmık/ *adj.*

Is·lam·a·bad /ıs'lɑmə,bɑd/ the capital city of Pakistan

sw 2|2 **is·land** /'aılənd/ *n.* [C] **1** a piece of land completely surrounded by water: *the island of Trinidad* | *the Hawaiian Islands* —see also DESERT ISLAND **2** a place that is different in some way from the area that surrounds it: *For centuries, Switzerland was an island of peace in troubled Europe.* —see also TRAFFIC ISLAND

island

is·land·er /'aıləndɚ/ *n.* [C] someone who lives on an island

isle /aıl/ *n.* [C] a word for an island, used in poetry or in names of islands: *the Isle of Cozumel*

is·let /'aılıt/ *n.* [C] a very small island

ism /'ızəm/ *n.* [C] INFORMAL used to describe a set of ideas or beliefs whose name ends in "ism," especially when you think that they are not reasonable or practical

-ism /ızəm/ *suffix* [in nouns] **1** a religion, political belief, or style of art based on a particular principle or the teachings of a particular person: *Buddhism* | *socialism* | *cubism* (=a style of modern art) | *Darwinism* (=based on the work of Charles Darwin) **2** the state of being like someone or something, or of having a particular quality: *heroism* (=being a HERO) | *magnetism* (=being MAGNETIC) **3** the practice of treating people unfairly because of something: *racism* (=against people of a different race) | *classism* (=against people in a different social class) **4** the action or process of doing something: *his criticism of my work* (=he criticizes it) **5** an action or remark that has a particular quality: *witticisms* (=smart funny remarks) **6** illness caused by too much of something: *Alcoholism is an all too common feature of affluent* (=wealthy) *societies.*

is·n't /'ızənt/ *v.* the short form of "is not": *Lisa isn't home.*

iso- /aısou, -sə/ *prefix* TECHNICAL the same all through or in every part of something; EQUAL: *an isosceles triangle* (=that has two sides that are the same length)

i·so·bar /'aısə,bɑr/ *n.* TECHNICAL a line on a weather map joining places where the air pressure is the same

i·so·late /'aısə,leıt/ *v.* [T] **1** to prevent a country, political group etc. from getting support from other countries or groups etc., so that it becomes weaker: *The U.S. has tried to isolate Cuba both economically and politically.* **2** TECHNICAL to separate a substance, disease etc. from other substances, so that it can be studied: *We've succeeded in isolating the gene that determines a person's weight.* **3** to separate an idea, word, problem etc., so that it can be examined or dealt with by itself: [isolate sth from sth] *It is impossible to isolate political responsibility from moral responsibility.* **4** to make someone feel separate from other people in a society or group, and make them feel lonely or unhappy: [isolate sb from sb] *Presley's early success isolated him from his friends.* **5** to make a place separate from other places so that people cannot enter it: *Their goal is to surround and isolate the town.* **6** to keep someone separate from other people, especially because they have a disease: [isolate sb from sb] *Tuberculosis patients are isolated from the other patients.*

i·so·lat·ed /'aısə,leıtıd/ *adj.* **1** an isolated place is far away from where there are other buildings, towns etc.: *The balloon had landed in an isolated area of the Northwest Territories.* | *an isolated mountain village* **2** an isolated action, event, example etc. happens only once or in only one place, and is not related to other things that happen: *Abram believes the five recent shootings are isolated incidents.* | *isolated thunderstorms* **3** feeling alone and unable to meet or speak to other people: *During my first month here, I felt terribly isolated.*

i·so·la·tion /,aısə'leıʃən/ *n.* [U] **1** a feeling of being lonely and unable to meet or speak to other people: *First-year college students often experience feelings of isolation.* **2** the act of deliberately separating one group, person, or thing from others, or the state of being separate: *After the transplant, Shannon will remain in isolation* (=alone in a special hospital room) *for up to six weeks.* | *Jones is being held in isolation* (=away from other prisoners) *until the trial.* | *The island's isolation has been a major factor in preserving its beauty.* **3 in isolation** if something exists or is considered in isolation, it exists or is considered separately from other things that are related to it: *Environmental issues can't be dealt with in isolation.*

i·so·la·tion·is·m /,aısə'leıʃə,nızəm/ *n.* [U] DISAPPROVING beliefs or actions that are based on the political principle that your country should not be involved in the affairs of other countries —**isolationist** *n.* [C] —**isolationist** *adj.*

isolation pe·ri·od /..'.. ,.../ *n.* [C] the period of time that someone with an infectious illness needs to be kept apart from other people

i·so·met·rics /,aısə'mɛtrıks/ *n.* [plural] exercises that make your muscles stronger, done by making the muscles work against each other —**isometric** *adj.*

i·sos·ce·les /aı'sɑsəliz/ *adj.* an isosceles TRIANGLE is a three-sided shape in which two of the sides are the same length —compare EQUILATERAL, SCALENE

i·so·therm /'aısə,θɚm/ *n.* [C] TECHNICAL a line on a weather map joining places where the temperature is the same

i·so·tope /'aısə,toup/ *n.* [C] TECHNICAL one of the possible different forms of an atom of a particular ELEMENT (4)

ISP *n.* [C] Internet Service Provider; a business that connects the computers of single users to the Internet

Is·ra·el /'ızriəl/ **1** a country on the eastern side of the Mediterranean Sea, north of Egypt, west of Jordan, and south of Lebanon **2** in the Bible, another name for Jacob, which is sometimes used to mean all the Jewish people —**Israeli** /ız'reıli/ *n., adj.*

Is·ra·el·ite /ˈɪzriəˌlaɪt, ˈɪzrə-/ n. someone who lived in the ancient KINGDOM of Israel —**Israelite** adj.

Is·sa·char /ˈɪsəˌkɑr/ in the Bible, the head of one of the 12 tribes of Israel

is·sue[1] /ˈɪʃu/ n.

1 subject/problem [C] a problem or subject that people discuss: *Racial discrimination is a* **sensitive issue**. | *the immigration issue* | *If I had known it would cause so much trouble, I wouldn't have* **raised the issue** (=said that a problem should be discussed). | *My coming home late* **is not the issue** (=is not what is important) – *you just don't trust me.* | *With my new job, affording a house is* **no longer an issue** (=is not a problem). | **avoid/dodge/duck/evade the issue** (=avoid discussing a problem or subject) | **confuse/cloud the issue** (=make a problem or subject more difficult by talking about things that are not directly related to it)

2 magazine [C] a magazine or newspaper printed for a particular day, week, or month: *this week's issue of "Newsweek"*

3 take issue with sth to disagree with a report, a statement, someone's behavior etc.: *Critics, including Senator Biden, took issue with the survey.*

4 what's the big issue? SPOKEN said when you do not think that something is a problem and you cannot understand why people are worried or arguing

5 at issue the problem or subject at issue is the most important part of what you are discussing or considering: *At issue are the moral questions raised by cloning.*

6 make an issue (out) of sth to argue about something, especially in a way that annoys other people because they do not think it is important: *There's nothing wrong with your hair, so stop making an issue out of it.*

7 have issues (with sth) INFORMAL to have problems dealing with something because of something that happened in your past: *There's a self-help group for people who have issues with money.*

8 act of giving sth [U] the act of officially giving someone something to use: *the issue of a driver's license*

9 set of things for sale [C] a new set of something such as STOCKS or stamps, made available for people to buy: *a new issue of bonds* —see also **die without issue** (DIE[1] (8)), -ISSUE

issue[2] v. [T] **1** to officially make a statement, give an order, warning etc.: *The State Department will issue a statement at noon.* | *a warning issued by the Surgeon General* **2** to provide something for each member of a group: *Every soldier is issued a rifle.* **3** to officially produce something such as new stamps, coins, or STOCKS and make them available for people to buy

issue forth phr. v. [I] FORMAL OR LITERARY to come out of a place: *Three or four reports issue forth each year from the Institute.*

issue from phr. v. [T] FORMAL if something such as a sound or liquid issues from somewhere, it comes out of that place: *Shots issued from the hillside.*

-issue /ɪʃu/ [in adjectives] **army-issue/military-issue/government-issue** given to someone by an official government organization: *black, army-issue glasses*

-ist /ɪst/ suffix **1** [in nouns] someone who believes in or practices a particular religion, set of principles or ideas, or style of art: *a Baptist* | *an Impressionist painter* **2** [in adjectives] relating to a particular set of political or religious beliefs, or to the ideas of a particular person: *her feminist views* | *the Communist party* | *Marxist theory* **3** [in nouns] someone who studies a particular subject, plays a particular instrument, or does a particular type of work: *a linguist* (=who studies or learns languages) | *a guitarist* (=who plays the GUITAR) | *a novelist* (=who writes NOVELS) —see also -OLOGIST **4** [in adjectives and nouns] treating people unfairly because of something, or someone who does this: *a very sexist remark* (=unfair to someone because of their sex) | *They're a bunch of racists.*

Is·tan·bul /ˈɪstænˌbʊl, -stɑn-/ the largest city in Turkey, which is at the point where Europe joins Asia

isth·mus /ˈɪsməs/ n. [C] a narrow piece of land with water on both sides, that connects two larger areas of land: *the Isthmus of Panama*

IT n. [U] the abbreviation of INFORMATION TECHNOLOGY

it /ɪt/ pron. [used as subject or object] **1** used to talk about the thing, situation, idea etc. that has already been mentioned or that the person you are talking to already knows about: *Do you like my tie? It was on sale.* | *In the summer, it must be beautiful there.* | *With the new stereo in the car, it makes a big difference.* **2** used as the subject or object of a verb when the real subject or object is later in the sentence: *It's a nice camera.* | *What's it like living in Miami?* | *It costs $12 just to get in the door.* **3** used with the verb "be" to make statements about the weather, the time, distances etc.: *It's a three-hour drive to Boston.* | *It was 4 o'clock and the mail still hadn't come.* | *It was sprinkling when we came in.* **4** the situation that someone is in now: *I can't stand it any longer. I'm resigning.* | *How's it going, Bob?* | *And that's the end of it?* **5** used to emphasize that one piece of information in a sentence is more important than the rest: *It was Jane who paid for the meal yesterday* (=it was Jane and not another person). | *It was the meal that Jane paid for yesterday* (=it was a meal and not something else). | *It was yesterday that Jane paid for the meal* (=it was yesterday and not at another time). **6** used as the subject of "seem," "appear," "look," and "happen": *It looks like they've left without us.* | *Since it happened to be such a nice day, they went to the beach.* **7 if it weren't for sth** also **if it hadn't been for sth** if something had not happened: *If it hadn't been for our cat getting sick, we we'd have come.* **8 a)** INFORMAL a particular ability or quality: *I'm sorry, but you just don't have it as a singer.* **9** used to talk about a child or an animal when you do not know what sex they are: *What will you call it if it's a boy?*

SPOKEN PHRASES

10 it's... used to give the name of a person or thing when it is not already known: *"What was that noise?" "It's just the heater." | "Who's that over there?" "It's Ann Palmer."* **11 it's me/John etc.** used to say who is speaking on a telephone: *Hi, Scott. It's Mark.* **12** SLANG: see SEXUAL INTERCOURSE *So, did you two do it last night?* **13 That's it! a)** used to say that a particular situation has finished: *That's it! I want both of you to be quiet!* **b)** used to praise someone because they have done something correctly: *That's it! Just keep your eye on the ball.* **14 this is it!** used to say that something you expected to happen is actually going to happen

I·tal·ian[1] /ɪˈtælyən/ adj. **1** relating to or coming from Italy **2** relating to the Italian language

Italian[2] n. **1** [U] the language used in Italy **2** [C] someone from Italy

I·tal·ian·ate /ɪˈtælyəˌneɪt, -nɪt/ adj. having an Italian style or appearance: *an Italianate villa*

i·tal·i·cize /ɪˈtæləˌsaɪz/ v. [T] to put or print something in italics: *Check in the writer's manual to see if you should italicize a foreign word.* —**italicized** adj.

i·tal·ics /ɪˈtælɪks, aɪ-/ n. [plural] TECHNICAL a type of printed letters that lean to the right, often used to emphasize particular words: **in italics** (=printed this way) —**italic** adj.: *italic script* —compare ROMAN

Italo- /ɪˈtæloʊ/ prefix Italian and something else: *the Italo-Austrian border*

It·a·ly /ˈɪtli/ a country in southern Europe, surrounded on three sides by the Mediterranean Sea

itch[1] /ɪtʃ/ v. **1** [I,T] if part of your body or your clothes itch, you have an annoying feeling on your skin that makes you want to SCRATCH it: *My back itches.* | *These pants itch me.* **2 be itching to do sth** INFORMAL to want to do something very much, as soon as possible: *Chris is itching to get back to work.*

itch[2] n. **1** [C usually singular] an uncomfortable feeling on your skin that makes you want to rub it with your nails **2** INFORMAL a strong desire to do or have something: [**itch to do sth**] *My old itch to travel was coming back.*

itch·y /'ɪtʃi/ *adj.* **itchier, itchiest 1** part of your body that is itchy has an annoying feeling that makes you want to rub it with your nails: *I feel terrible and my eyes are itchy.* **2** clothes that are itchy make you have this feeling on your skin: *an itchy sweater* **3** wanting to go somewhere new or do something different: *With election day approaching, Congressmen are getting itchy to get out and speak to the voters.* | *This cold weather is giving me itchy feet* (=the desire to travel or go somewhere new). **4 itchy fingers** INFORMAL someone with itchy fingers is likely to steal things: *I tucked the money deep in my pocket, away from itchy fingers.* **5 have an itchy trigger finger** to be likely to shoot a gun in a situation in which you are afraid or nervous —**itchiness** *n.* [U]

it'd /'ɪtəd/ USUALLY SPOKEN **1** the short form of "it would": *It'd be nice if you could come.* **2** the short form of "it had": *It'd been raining since Sunday.*

-ite /aɪt/ *suffix* **1** [in nouns] a follower or supporter of a particular idea or person: *a group of Trotskyites* (=followers of Trotsky) **2** [in adjectives] relating to a particular set of political or religious ideas, or to the ideas of a particular person: *a Mennonite woman* **3** [in nouns] someone who lives in a particular place or belongs to a particular group: *a suburbanite* (=someone who lives just outside a city) | *the Israelites* (=the people of Israel, in the Bible) **4** [in U nouns] a substance such as a mineral, a compound, or an explosive: *graphite* | *dynamite*

i·tem /'aɪtəm/ *n.* [C] **1** a single thing in a set, group, or list: *We moved on to the next item on the agenda.* | *an item of clothing* **2** a single, usually short, piece of news in a newspaper or magazine, or on TV: *Irene read quickly over the short news item.* **3 be an item** INFORMAL to be having a sexual or romantic relationship: *They're not an item any more.*

i·tem·ize /'aɪtə,maɪz/ *v.* [T] to write down information about all the parts of something in a list: *I don't need to itemize my tax deductions.* —**itemized** *adj.: an itemized bill*

it·er·ate /'ɪtə,reɪt/ *v.* **1** [I,T] if a computer iterates, it goes through a set of instructions once before going through it again **2** [T] FORMAL to say or do something again —**iteration** /,ɪtə'reɪʃən/ *n.* [C,U] —**iterative** /'ɪtə,reɪtɪv, -rə-/ *adj.*

i·tin·er·ant /aɪ'tɪnərənt/ *adj.* [only before noun] FORMAL traveling from place to place, especially to work: *itinerant farm workers*

i·tin·er·ar·y /aɪ'tɪnə,reri/ *n. plural* **itineraries** [C] a plan or list of the places you will visit on a trip

-itis /aɪtɪs/ *suffix* [in U nouns] **1** a disease or INFLAMMATION that affects a particular part of the body: *tonsilitis* (=infection of the TONSILs) **2** HUMOROUS the condition of having too much of something or of liking something too much: *televisionitis* (=watching too much television)

it'll /'ɪtl/ USUALLY SPOKEN the short form of "it will": *It'll be hard to go back to work after two weeks of vacation.*

it's /ɪts/ **1** the short form of "it is": *It's all over now.* **2** a short form of "it has": *It's been snowing all day.*

its /ɪts/ *possessive adj.* [possessive form of "it"] belonging or relating to a thing, situation, person, or idea that has been mentioned or is known about: *By November the tree had lost all its leaves.*

it·self /ɪt'sɛlf/ *pron.* **1** the REFLEXIVE form of "it": *The tape player shuts itself off when it's done.* | *The bird was looking at itself in the mirror.* **2** used to emphasize a thing, situation, animal, or idea that has already been mentioned: *The meeting itself was quite interesting.* **3 in itself** also **in and of itself** considered

without other related ideas or situations: *Housework is a full-time job in itself.* **4 (all) by itself a)** alone: *Will the dog be safe left in the car by itself?* **b)** without help: *The door's not going to close by itself.* **5 (all) to itself** if something has something else to itself, it does not have to share that thing with others: *This idea deserves a chapter to itself.*

itty-bitty /,ɪti 'bɪti◂/ also **it·sy-bit·sy** /,ɪtsi 'bɪtsi/ *adj.* [only before noun] SPOKEN, HUMOROUS very small: *itty-bitty mice*

-itude /ətud/ *suffix* [in nouns] FORMAL the state of having a particular quality: *certitude* (=being certain) | *exactitude* (=being exact) —see also -TUDE

-ity /əti/ *suffix* [in nouns] the state of having a particular quality, or something that has that quality: *Floods happen here with great regularity* (=regularly). | *stupidities* (=stupid actions or remarks) —see also -TY

IUD *n.* [C] a small plastic or metal object placed inside a woman's UTERUS (=place where a baby develops) *to prevent her from being able to have a baby* —see also COIL² (4)

IV *n.* [C] the abbreviation of INTRAVENOUS; a piece of medical equipment that is used to put liquid directly into your blood; DRIP² (4)

I·van IV /,aɪvən ðə 'fɔrθ/ also **Ivan the Terrible** (1530–1584) the ruler of Russia from 1547 to 1584, who made many changes to Russia's laws and system of government

I've /aɪv/ the short form of "I have": *I've seen him somewhere before.*

-ive /ɪv/ *suffix* [in nouns and adjectives] someone or something that does something or is able to do something: *a detective* | *the adoptive parents* (=who ADOPT a child) | *an explosive* (=substance that can explode)

Ives /aɪvz/**, Charles** (1874–1954) a U.S. musician who wrote CLASSICAL music

IVF TECHNICAL: see IN VITRO FERTILIZATION

i·vied /'aɪvid/ *adj.* LITERARY covered with ivy: *an ivied campus*

i·vo·ry /'aɪvəri/ *n. plural* **ivories 1** [U] the hard smooth yellowish-white substance from the TUSKs (=long teeth) of an ELEPHANT **2** [U] a yellowish white color **3 ivory tower** a place or situation where you are separated from the difficulties of ordinary life and so are unable to understand them, used especially to describe a college or university or someone who teaches there: *Scientists are coming out of the ivory tower and starting businesses.* **4 the ivories** INFORMAL the KEYs (=parts you press down) of a piano —see also **tickle the ivories** (TICKLE¹ (5)) **5** [C often plural] something made of ivory, especially a small figure of a person or animal: *a collection of Chinese ivories* **6 ivories** [plural] HUMOROUS someone's teeth

I·vo·ry Coast /,... './ a country on the coast of West Africa, between Ghana and Liberia. It is sometimes called Côte d'Ivoire. —**Ivorian** /aɪ'vɔriən/ also **Ivoirian** /i'vwɑriən/ *n., adj.*

i·vy /'aɪvi/ *n. plural* **ivies** [C,U] a climbing plant with dark-green shiny leaves —see also POISON IVY

Ivy League /,.. './ *adj.* relating to a group of eight old respected universities in the northeastern U.S.: *an Ivy League college* —**Ivy League** *n.* [singular]

-ization /əzeɪʃən/ *suffix* [in nouns] used to make nouns from verbs that end in -IZE: *civilization* | *industrialization*

-ize /aɪz/ *suffix* [in verbs] **1** to do something to a thing or a person so that they change or have a particular quality: *a computerized phone system* (=that has been changed so that computers control it) | *Diamonds are crystallized carbon* (=that has turned into CRYSTALs). **2** to put someone or something into a particular place or condition: *She was hospitalized after the accident.* | *This may jeopardize our chances of winning* (=make it less likely). **3** to speak in a particular way: *his endless sermonizing* (=talking in a boring way about morals)

J

J, j /dʒeɪ/ *plural* **J's, j's** *n.* [C] **1** the tenth letter of the English alphabet **2** the written abbreviation of JOULE

jab¹ /dʒæb/ *v.* **jabbed, jabbing** [I,T] to quickly push or hit something into or toward something else: *Connors jabbed his finger in the umpire's face.* | [+ *at*] *She jabbed at the buttons on the remote control.*

jab² *n.* [C] **1** something you say to criticize someone or something else: *White House officials took a sharp jab at the Democrats' plan.* **2** a sudden hard push or hit, especially with a pointed object or your FIST (=closed hand) | **right/left jab** (=a push made with your right or left hand)

jab·ber /'dʒæbə/ *v.* [I,T] to talk quickly, in an excited way, and not very clearly: *a pair of jabbering parrots* —**jabber** *n.* [singular,U]

jac·a·ran·da /,dʒækə'rændə/ *n.* [C] a type of tropical American tree with purple flowers

jack¹ /dʒæk/ *n.* [C] **1** a piece of equipment used to lift a heavy weight off the ground, such as a car, and support it while it is in the air: *a hydraulic jack* **2** a card used in card games that has a man's picture on it and is worth less than a QUEEN and more than a ten **3** an electronic connection for a telephone or other electric machine: *a phone jack* **4** **jacks** [U] a children's game in which the players try to pick up small objects (=jacks) while bouncing (BOUNCE) and catching a ball **5** [C] a small metal or plastic object that has six points, used in the game of JACKS **6 jack (shit)** VULGAR an impolite expression meaning "nothing at all": *It doesn't look like they did jack shit.* —see also JUMPING JACK, UNION JACK

jack² *v.* **be jacked (up)** SPOKEN to be excited and nervous: *I didn't expect Theo to be jacked about it.*

jack sb around *phr. v.* [T] SLANG to waste someone's time by deliberately making things difficult for them: *Quit jacking me around, and just tell me!*

jack off *phr. v.* [I,T **jack sb ↔ off**] SLANG if a man jacks off or jacks himself off, he MASTURBATES

jack sb/sth up *phr. v.* [T] **1** to lift something heavy such as a car off the ground using a jack **2** INFORMAL to increase prices, sales etc. by a large amount: *It's the local sales tax that really jacks the prices up.*

jack·al /'dʒækəl/ *n.* [C] **1** a wild animal like a dog that lives in Asia and Africa and eats the remaining parts of dead animals **2** someone who does things for their own advantage, without caring if it harms someone else: *the jackals of Wall Street*

jack·ass /'dʒækæs/ *n.* [C] **1** VULGAR an annoying or stupid person **2** a male DONKEY (=animal similar to a horse)

jack·boot /'dʒækbut/ *n.* [C] a boot worn by soldiers that covers their leg up to the knee —**jackbooted** *adj.*

jack·daw /'dʒækdɔ/ *n.* [C] a type of small European CROW

jack·et /'dʒækɪt/ *n.* [C] **1** a short light coat: *a denim jacket* **2** the part of a SUIT that covers the top part of your body: *a jacket and tie* **3** a DUST JACKET **4** a stiff paper cover that protects a record **5** a cover that surrounds and protects some types of equipment, machines etc. —see also DINNER JACKET, LIFE JACKET, STRAITJACKET

Jack Frost /,dʒæk 'frɔst/ *n.* a name used to describe FROST¹ (1) as a person, especially when talking to children

jack·ham·mer /'dʒæk,hæmə/ *n.* [C] a large powerful tool used to break hard materials such as the surface of a road

jack-in-the-box /'. . . ,./ *n.* [C] a children's toy shaped like a box with a figure inside that jumps out when the box is opened

jack-in-the-pul·pit /'. . . ,./ *n.* [C] a type of wild flower in the northeastern U.S.

jack·knife¹ /'dʒæknaɪf/ *n. plural* **jackknives** /-naɪvz/ [C] **1** a knife with a blade that folds into its handle —see picture at KNIFE¹ **2** a DIVE² (4) in which you bend at the waist while in the air and then make your body straight again before you go into the water

jackknife² *v.* **jackknifed, jackknifing** [I] **1** if a large vehicle with two parts jackknifes, the back part swings toward the front part: *A big-rig jackknifed and spilled diesel fuel.* **2** to perform a jackknife DIVE into water

jack-of-all-trades /,. . ,. './ *n.* [singular] someone who can do many different types of work

jack-o'-lan·tern /'dʒæk ə ,læntən/ *n.* [C] a PUMPKIN used at Halloween that has a design cut through it, usually of a face, and that usually has a light inside

jack·pot /'dʒækpɑt/ *n.* [C] a large amount of money that you can win in a game that is decided by chance —see also **hit the jackpot** (HIT¹ (26))

jack·rab·bit /'dʒæk,ræbɪt/ *n.* [C] a large North American HARE (=animal like a large rabbit) with very long ears

Jack·son /'dʒæksən/ the capital city of the U.S. state of Mississippi

Jackson, Bo /bou/ (1962–) a U.S. baseball and football player

Jackson, Reg·gie /'rɛdʒi/ (1946–) a baseball player famous for hitting HOME RUNS, especially during the World Series

Jackson, the Reverend Jes·se /'dʒɛsi/ (1941–) a U.S. politician in the Democratic Party, who was a leader in the U.S. CIVIL RIGHTS movement

Jackson, Thomas "Stone·wall" /'stounwɔl/ (1824–1863) a general in the Confederate army during the U.S. Civil War

Jack the Rip·per /,dʒæk ðə 'rɪpə/ the name given to a British criminal who killed and cut up the bodies of several PROSTITUTES, and was never caught

Ja·cob /'dʒeɪkəb/ in the Bible, the son of Isaac whose 12 sons were the ANCESTORS of the 12 tribes of Israel

Jac·o·be·an /,dʒækə'biən/ *adj.* relating to or typical of the period between 1603 and 1623 in Britain, when James I was king: *a Jacobean play*

Ja·cuz·zi /dʒə'kuzi/ *n.* [C] TRADEMARK a large bathtub that makes hot water move in strong currents around your body —compare HOT TUB, SPA

jade /dʒeɪd/ *n.* [U] **1** a hard, usually green, stone often used to make jewelry **2** also **jade green** the light green color of this stone

jad·ed /'dʒeɪdɪd/ *adj.* not interested in or excited by life anymore, because you have experienced too many things: *New York musicians are jaded and tough.*

jade plant /'. ./ *n.* [C] a plant with thick dark green leaves that can be kept in a house or grown outside in hot places

Jag /dʒæg/ *n.* [C] SPOKEN a Jaguar car

jag /dʒæg/ *n.* [C] INFORMAL **crying/shopping/talking etc. jag** a short period of time when you suddenly do something without controlling how much you do it

jag·ged /'dʒægɪd/ *adj.* having a rough uneven edge or surface, often with sharp points on it: *jagged mountain peaks*

jag·uar /'dʒægwɑr/ *n.* [C] a large South American wild cat with brown and yellow fur and black spots

jai a·lai /'haɪ laɪ/ *n.* [U] a game played by two, four, or six people in which they use an object like a basket on a stick to throw a ball against a wall

jail¹ /dʒeɪl/ *n.* [C,U] a place where criminals are kept as part of their punishment, or where people who have been charged with a crime are kept before they are judged in a court of law; PRISON: *Konrad's been in jail for nine years.*

jail² *v.* [T] to put someone in jail: *Two brothers were jailed for robbery.*

jail·bait /'dʒeɪlbeɪt/ n. [U] INFORMAL a girl who is too young to legally have sex, so that a boy or man who has sex with her can be charged with RAPE

jail·bird /'dʒeɪlbɜːd/ n. [C] INFORMAL someone who has spent a lot of time in prison

jail·break /'dʒeɪlbreɪk/ n. [C] an escape or an attempt to escape from prison, especially by several people

jail·er /'dʒeɪlə/ n. [C] someone whose job is to guard a prison or prisoners

jail·house /'dʒeɪlhaʊs/ n. [C] **1** a building that has a jail in it **2 jailhouse confession/clothes/interview etc.** something that is related to prisons or prisoners, or happens in a prison **3 jailhouse lawyer** a lawyer who deals with prisoners

Jain /dʒaɪn, dʒeɪn/ n. [C] someone whose religion is Jainism —**Jain** adj.

Jain·ism /'dʒaɪ,nɪzəm/ n. [C] a religion from India that is against violence toward any living things

Ja·kar·ta /dʒə'kɑrtə/ the capital and largest city of Indonesia, which is in northwest Java

ja·la·pe·ño /,hælə'peɪnyoʊ, ,hɑ-, -'pi-/ n. plural **jalapeños** [C] a small very hot green PEPPER, used especially in Mexican food

ja·lop·y /dʒə'lɑpi/ n. plural **jalopies** [C] INFORMAL a very old car in bad condition

jal·ou·sie /'dʒæləsi/ n. [C] a covering for a window that is made of a set of HORIZONTAL flat pieces of wood, metal, or plastic that can be moved to let in sun or air

s w **jam¹** /dʒæm/ v.
1 push hard [I,T] to push something somewhere using a lot of force, or to push too many things into a small place: *All five boys jammed happily into the back seat.* | [jam sth into/under/on sth] *Mr. Braithe jammed the letters into his pocket and left.*
2 block [T] also **jam up** if a lot of people or vehicles jam a place, they block it so that it is difficult to move: *Crowds of supporters jammed the lobby.*
3 machine [I,T] also **jam up** if a machine jams or you jam it, it stops working because part of it is stuck: *One pilot reported that his controls had jammed.*
4 music [I] to play music in an informal way with others for fun, without practicing first: *We were jamming with J.D. and Rich last night.* —see also JAM SESSION
5 jam on the brakes to suddenly put your foot down hard on the BRAKE to stop a car
6 jam a switchboard if telephone calls jam a SWITCHBOARD, so many people are telephoning the same organization that its telephone system cannot work correctly
7 radio/television [T] to deliberately prevent broadcasts or other electronic signals from being received, by sending out noise on the same WAVELENGTH: *The electronic equipment jams enemy radar signals.*
8 sb is jamming SLANG said when someone is doing something very quickly or well —see also JAMMED

s w **jam²** n. **1** [C,U] a thick sweet sticky substance made from boiled fruit and sugar and eaten especially on bread: *strawberry jam* **2** [C] a situation in which it is difficult or impossible to move because there are so many people, things, cars etc. close together: *Sorry we're late. We got stuck in a traffic jam.* **3 be/get in a jam** INFORMAL to be or become involved in a difficult or uncomfortable situation: *Mindy, can you help me out? I'm kind of in a jam.* **4** a situation in which something is stuck somewhere: *a jam in the copy machine* **5** a JAM SESSION

Ja·mai·ca /dʒə'meɪkə/ a country which is an island in the Caribbean Sea —**Jamaican** n., adj.

jamb /dʒæm/ n. [C] a side post of a door or window

jam·ba·lay·a /,dʒʌmbə'laɪə/ n. [U] a dish from the southern U.S. containing rice and SEAFOOD

jam·bo·ree /,dʒæmbə'ri/ n. [C] **1** a big noisy party or celebration **2** a large meeting of SCOUTs

James /dʒeɪmz/ a book in the New Testament of the Christian Bible

James, Henry (1843–1916) an American writer of NOVELS

James, Jes·se /'dʒɛsi/ (1847–1882) a famous bank and train robber

James, Saint in the Bible, a brother or close relation of Jesus who was important in the early Church

James, William (1842–1910) an American PHILOSOPHER and PSYCHOLOGIST

James the Great, Saint /,. . './ in the Bible, one of the 12 APOSTLEs, a son of Zebedee and brother of Saint John

James the Less, Saint /,. . './ in the Bible, one of the 12 APOSTLEs, son of Alpheus

James·town /'dʒeɪmztaʊn/ a town, established in 1607, in the U.S. state of Virginia which was the first town built by English people who went to live in North America

jammed /dʒæmd/ adj. **1** full of people, vehicles, or other things: *The place was already jammed an hour before the game.* **2** [not before noun] impossible to move or use because of being stuck in a particular position: *The stupid lock's jammed again.*

jam·mies /'dʒæmiz/ n. [plural] INFORMAL: see PAJAMAS

jam-packed /,. '. / adj. INFORMAL full of people or things that are very close together: [+ with] *Gloria's closet is jam-packed with designer clothes.*

jam ses·sion /'. ,../ n. [C] an occasion when JAZZ or ROCK musicians play music together in an informal way for fun

Jan. the written abbreviation of January

Jane Doe /,dʒeɪn 'doʊ/ n. [C,U] a name used especially by the police for a woman whose name is not known —compare JOHN DOE

jan·gle /'dʒæŋgəl/ v. **1** [I,T] if metal objects or bells jangle or if you jangle them, they make a sharp sound when they hit each other: *He kept jangling the coins in his pocket* **2 jangle sb's nerves** to make someone feel nervous or upset —**jangle** n. [C,U]

jan·i·tor /'dʒænətə/ n. [C] someone whose job is to clean and take care of a large building: *the school janitor* —**janitorial** /,dʒænə'tɔriəl/ adj.

Jan·u·ar·y /'dʒænyu,ɛri/ written abbreviation **Jan.** n. [C,U] the first month of the year, between December and February: *She wanted to go to Texas in January.* | *On January 19, Kelley's brother will be here.* | *I haven't seen Julio since last January.* | *Next January Ben will be three years old.* | *We leave January 1st and return January 29th.*

USAGE NOTE: JANUARY

GRAMMAR: January, February, March, April etc.
When you use a month without a date, say "in January," "in February," etc. If you use it with a date, write "on January 9" or "on January 9th," "on February 22" or "on February 22nd" etc., but always say "on January ninth," "on February twenty-second" etc. The preposition "on" does not always have to be included before the month.

JAP /dʒæp/ n. [C] SPOKEN, OFFENSIVE Jewish American Princess; a Jewish girl or woman who has a lot of money and behaves in a SPOILED way —**jappy** adj.

Jap /dʒæp/ n. [C] TABOO someone from Japan or whose family was originally from Japan. Do not use this word.

Ja·pan /dʒə'pæn/ a country in East Asia consisting of four large islands, Hokkaido, Honshu, Shikoku, and Kyushu, and many smaller ones

Jap·a·nese¹ /,dʒæpə'niz◂/ adj. **1** relating to or coming from Japan **2** relating to the Japanese language

Japanese² n. **1** [U] the language used in Japan **2 the Japanese** [plural] people from Japan

Japanese lan·tern /,... '../ n. [C] a paper decoration, usually with a light inside

jar¹ /dʒɑr/ n. **1** [C] a round glass container with a s w wide lid, used for storing food: *a honey jar* —see picture at CONTAINER **2** [C] the amount of food, drink etc. contained in a jar: *half a jar of peanut butter* **3** [C] a round container made of clay, stone etc. that you keep food in: *a cookie jar* **4** [singular] the shock of two things hitting each other, or a sudden pain from something hitting you

jar² *v.* **jarred, jarring 1** [I,T] to shock a person or group, or make them feel nervous or upset: *Their laughter jarred and confused me.* | **[jar sb into sth]** *What the crisis has done is to jar rich nations into realizing their risk if war breaks out.* **2** [I,T] to shake or hit something with enough force to damage it or make it become loose: *Alice landed badly, jarring her ankle.* | *O'Neal jarred the ball loose from Marino.* **3** [I + with] to be different in style or appearance from something else and therefore look strange —**jarring** *adj.*

jar·gon /ˈdʒɑrgən/ *n.* [U] TECHNICAL words and expressions that are used mainly by people who belong to the same professional group, and that are difficult for others to understand: *military jargon*

jas·mine /ˈdʒæzmɪn/ *n.* [C,U] a climbing plant with small sweet-smelling white or yellow flowers

jas·per /ˈdʒæspər/ *n.* [U] a red, yellow, or brown stone that is not very valuable

jaun·dice /ˈdʒɔndɪs, ˈdʒɑn-/ *n.* [U] a medical condition in which your skin and the white part of your eyes become yellow

jaun·diced /ˈdʒɔndɪst/ *adj.* **1** suffering from jaundice **2** tending to judge people and things in an unfavorable way, often because you have had disappointing experiences yourself: *a jaundiced view of the world* | **with a jaundiced eye** (=thinking of people and situations in a jaundiced way)

jaunt /dʒɔnt, dʒɑnt/ *n.* [C] a short trip for pleasure: *a weekend jaunt* —**jaunt** *v.* [I]

jaun·ty /ˈdʒɔnti, ˈdʒɑnti/ *adj.* **jauntier, jauntiest** jaunty actions, clothes etc. show that you are confident and cheerful: *a jaunty pink shirt* —**jauntily** *adv.*

Ja·va¹ /ˈdʒɑvə/ an island which is part of Indonesia

Ja·va² /ˈdʒɑvə, ˈdʒæ-/ *n.* [U] TRADEMARK a computer language used especially to write computer programs for the Internet

ja·va /ˈdʒɑvə/ *n.* [U] INFORMAL coffee: *a cup of java*

jav·e·lin /ˈdʒævəlɪn, -vlɪn/ *n.* **1** [C] a light SPEAR for throwing, now used mostly in sports **2 the javelin** a sports event in which competitors throw a javelin to see who can throw it the farthest

jaw¹ /dʒɔ/ *n.*

1 bones/face one of the two bones that your teeth are connected to, or the lower part of your face that covers these bones: *a broken jaw*

2 set your jaw to hold your jaw in a firm position to show that you are determined: *Tom set his jaw and stared at the officer.*

3 sb's jaw dropped used to say that someone looked surprised or shocked: *Conley's jaw dropped, and she left without saying anything.*

4 mouth jaws [plural] the mouth of a person or animal, especially a dangerous animal

5 tool jaws [plural] the two parts of a machine or tool that move together to hold something tightly

6 the jaws of death/defeat/despair LITERARY a situation in which you almost die, are almost defeated etc.: **snatch victory from the jaws of defeat** (=manage to win or succeed after you have nearly failed)

7 shape of jaw [C usually singular] the shape of someone's jaw, especially when it shows something about their character: *a strong jaw* —see also JAWS OF LIFE, -JAWED

jaw² *v.* [I] INFORMAL to talk

jaw·bone /ˈdʒɔboʊn/ *n.* [C] one of the two big bones of the jaw, especially the lower jaw —see picture at SKELETON

jaw·break·er /ˈdʒɔˌbreɪkər/ *n.* [C] **1** a type of round very hard candy **2** a word that is difficult to say

-jawed /dʒɔd/ *adj.* [in adjectives] **square-jawed/fine-jawed/strong-jawed etc.** having a jaw that has a particular shape or appearance —see also SLACK-JAWED

jaw·line /ˈdʒɔlaɪn/ *n.* [C usually singular] the shape of someone's JAW

Jaws of Life /ˌ. . ˈ./ *n.* [plural] TRADEMARK **the Jaws of Life** a tool used to make a hole in a vehicle after an accident, so the people inside can be taken out

jay /dʒeɪ/ *n.* [C] a type of noisy bird —see also BLUEJAY

Jay /dʒeɪ/**, John** (1745–1829) the first CHIEF JUSTICE of the U.S. Supreme Court

jay·bird /ˈdʒeɪbərd/ *n.* —see **naked as a jaybird** (NAKED (5))

Jay·cee /ˌdʒeɪˈsi/ a member of the Junior Chamber of Commerce, a local organization in the U.S. that encourages useful and interesting activities for young people

jay·walk·ing /ˈdʒeɪˌwɔkɪŋ/ *n.* [U] the act of walking across a street in an area that is not marked for walking —**jaywalker** *n.* [C] —**jaywalk** *v.* [I]

jazz¹ /dʒæz/ *n.* [U] **1** a type of popular music that usually has a strong beat and parts for performers to play alone: *a jazz festival* **2 and all that jazz** SPOKEN and things like that: *Yeah, bring in the candy bars, the cookies, and all that jazz.*

jazz² *v.*

jazz sth up *phr. v.* [T] INFORMAL to make something more attractive or exciting: *You could jazz up that jacket with some rhinestones.* —**jazzed-up** *adj.*

jazzed /dʒæzd/ *adj.* [not before noun] SPOKEN excited: *Amanda's really jazzed about her new class.*

jazz·y /ˈdʒæzi/ *adj.* **jazzier, jazziest** INFORMAL **1** bright, colorful, and easily noticed: *a jazzy tie* **2** similar to the style of jazz music: *a jazzy version of the song*

jct. the written abbreviation of JUNCTION

jeal·ous /ˈdʒɛləs/ *adj.* **1** feeling angry and unhappy because someone has a quality, thing, or ability that you wish you had: [+ of] *Jerome is definitely jealous of his brother's success.* **2** feeling angry and unhappy because someone you like or love is showing interest in another person, or another person is showing interest in them: *a jealous husband* | *She's just using him to make her old boyfriend jealous.* **3 jealous of sth** FORMAL wanting to keep or protect something that you have because you are proud of it: *a country jealous of its heritage* —**jealously** *adv.*

USAGE NOTE: JEALOUS

WORD CHOICE: jealous, envious
If you feel **jealous**, you feel angry or unhappy because you cannot have something that someone else has: *Eric was jealous of his sister's success.* | *Older siblings can sometimes be jealous of the attention given to the new baby.* If you are **envious**, you want to have the things or qualities that someone else has: *Hank was envious of his neighbor's fancy new lawnmower.*

---

jeal·ous·y /ˈdʒɛləsi/ *n.* *plural* **jealousies 1** [U] the feeling of being jealous **2** [C] an act of being jealous, or something you are jealous about: *He quit last week, citing office politics and petty jealousies.*

jeans /dʒinz/ *n.* [plural] a popular type of pants made from DENIM (=a strong, usually blue, cotton cloth)

jeep, Jeep /dʒip/ *n.* [C] TRADEMARK a type of car made to travel over rough ground

J

jeep

jeer /dʒɪr/ v. [I,T] to laugh at someone in a way that is not nice, to show that you strongly disapprove of them or do not respect them: *About 5,000 teachers jeered Gov. Gardner on Friday.* | [+ at] *Richardson was jeered at during a parade in his New Mexico district.* —**jeer** n. [C]

jeer·ing /'dʒɪrɪŋ/ adj. a jeering remark or sound is not nice and shows disapproval: *jeering laughter*

jeez /dʒiz/ interjection used to express feelings such as surprise, anger, annoyance etc.: *Give me a break, man, jeez.*

Jef·fer·son /'dʒɛfɚsən/, **Thomas** (1743–1826) the third President of the U.S. and writer of most of the Declaration of Independence

Jefferson Ci·ty /ˌ... '../ the capital city of the U.S. state of Missouri

Je·ho·vah /dʒɪ'hoʊvə/ n. a name given to God in the OLD TESTAMENT (=first part of the Bible)

Jehovah's Wit·ness /.ˌ.. '../ n. [C] a member of a religious organization that believes the end of the world will happen soon and sends its members to people's houses to try to persuade them to join

je·june /dʒɪ'dʒun/ adj. FORMAL **1** ideas and behavior that are jejune are childish: *jejune political opinions* **2** writing or speech that is jejune is boring

Jek·yll and Hyde /ˌdʒɛkəl ənd 'haɪd/ n. [C] someone who is sometimes nice but at other times is nasty or violent

jell /dʒɛl/ v. [I] **1** if a thought, plan etc. jells, it becomes clearer or more definite: *The ideas have been around for a while, but nothing really jelled until recently.* **2** if two or more people jell, they start working well together as a group: *It will take some time for the team to jell.* **3** if a liquid jells, it becomes firmer or thicker

jel·lied /'dʒɛlid/ adj. [only before noun] cooked or served in GELATIN or jelly, or in the form of GELATIN or jelly: *jellied cranberry sauce*

Jell-O, jello /'dʒɛloʊ/ n. [U] TRADEMARK a soft sweet food made from GELATIN and fruit juice

jel·ly /'dʒɛli/ n. plural **jellies** **1** [U] a very thick sweet substance made from boiled fruit and sugar with no pieces of fruit in it, that is usually eaten on bread: *a peanut butter and jelly sandwich* **2** [U] a thick soft substance that can be spread easily: *petroleum jelly* **3 feel like jelly** also **turn to jelly** if your legs, knees etc. feel like jelly, they start to shake because you are frightened or nervous: *When the boss called me into her office, my legs felt like jelly.* **4** [C] a substance that is solid but very soft, and moves easily when you touch it: *The frogs' eggs are in a protective jelly.* —compare GELATIN

jelly bean /'.. ˌ./ n. [C] a type of small soft candy that is shaped like a bean, each piece having a different color and taste

jel·ly·fish /'dʒɛliˌfɪʃ/ n. [C] a round transparent animal that lives in the ocean, that has long parts that hang down from its body

jelly roll /'.. ˌ./ n. [C] a long thin cake that is rolled up with JAM or cream inside

je ne sais quoi /ˌʒə nə seɪ 'kwɑ/ n. OFTEN HUMOROUS a good quality that you cannot easily describe: *Being a New Yorker, she had a certain je ne sais quoi.*

Jen·ner /'dʒɛnɚ/, **Ed·ward** /'ɛdwɚd/ (1749–1823) a British doctor who developed the prevention of SMALLPOX by VACCINATION

jeop·ard·ize /'dʒɛpɚˌdaɪz/ v. [T] to risk losing or spoiling something important or valuable: *Three women refused to testify, fearing it would jeopardize their careers.*

jeop·ard·y /'dʒɛpɚdi/ n. **in jeopardy** in danger of being lost or harmed: *The killings could put the whole peace process in jeopardy.*

jer·e·mi·ad /ˌdʒɛrə'maɪəd/ n. [C] FORMAL a long speech or piece of writing that complains about a situation, or says that bad things will happen

Jer·e·mi·ah /ˌdʒɛrə'maɪə/ (6th century B.C.) in the Bible, a Hebrew PROPHET who said that God would become angry with the Jews and punish them

Jer·i·cho /'dʒɛrɪˌkoʊ/ a city in Israel, north of the Dead Sea, thought to be the oldest city in the world

jerk¹ /dʒɚk/ v. [I,T] **1** to move with a quick sudden movement, or to make part of your body move in this way: *Sue jerked her thumb toward the garage.* **2** to pull something suddenly and roughly: *Mark jerked the phone away from the girl.* —see also TEARJERKER

jerk sb around phr. v. [T] INFORMAL to waste someone's time or deliberately make things difficult for them: *Consumers get jerked around by advertisers all the time.*

jerk off phr. v. [I,T **jerk sb ↔ off**] SLANG if a man jerks off or jerks himself off, he MASTURBATES

jerk² n. [C] **1** INFORMAL someone, especially a man, who is stupid or who does things that annoy or hurt other people: *Why do you put up with a jerk like that?* **2** a sudden quick pulling movement: *Sherman gave the leash a real jerk* (=pulled it hard). —see also KNEE-JERK

jer·kin /'dʒɚkɪn/ n. [C] a short JACKET that covers your body but not your arms, worn in past times

jerk·wa·ter /'dʒɚkˌwɔtɚ/ adj. [only before noun] SPOKEN a jerkwater town, organization etc. is small and uninteresting

jerk·y¹ /'dʒɚki/ adj. **jerkier, jerkiest** **1** jerky movements are rough, with many start and stops: *the jerky motion of old movies* —opposite SMOOTH¹ (6) **2** SPOKEN annoying or stupid: *jerky guys* —**jerkily** adv.

jerk·y² n. [U] meat that has been cut into thin pieces and dried in the sun or with smoke

Jer·ry /'dʒɛri/ n. plural **Jerries** [C] OFFENSIVE someone from Germany

jerry-built /'dʒɛriˌbɪlt/ adj. [no comparative] built cheaply, quickly, and badly: *jerry-built structures*

jer·sey /'dʒɚzi/ n. plural **jerseys** **1** [C] a shirt worn as part of a sports uniform: *a football jersey* **2** [U] a soft material that stretches easily, used for clothing **3** [C] a shirt or SWEATER that is made out of this material

Je·ru·sa·lem /dʒə'rusələm/ a city in Israel, which is of great historical importance to Jews, Christians, and Muslims, and is regarded by Israel as its capital city

Jerusalem ar·ti·choke /.ˌ... '../ n. [C] a plant that has a TUBER (=part like a root) that you can eat

jest¹ /dʒɛst/ n. **1 in jest** something you say in jest is intended to be funny, not serious **2** [C] OLD-FASHIONED something that you say or do to amuse people; JOKE

jest² v. [I + about] OLD-FASHIONED OR HUMOROUS to say things that you do not really mean in order to amuse people | **Surely you jest** (=said when you do not believe what someone is saying)

jest·er /'dʒɛstɚ/ n. [C] a man employed in past times by a king or ruler to entertain people with jokes, stories etc.

Jes·u·it /'dʒɛzuɪt, -ʒuɪt/ n. [C] a man who is a member of the Catholic religious Society of Jesus —**Jesuit** adj.

Je·sus¹ /'dʒizəs/ also **Jesus Christ** /ˌ... '../ the person who Christians believe was the son of God, and whose life and teaching Christianity is based on

Jesus² also **Jesus Christ** interjection an expression used to express anger or surprise, considered offensive by many Christians: *Oh Jesus! That was scary.*

USAGE NOTE: JESUS

FORMALITY AND POLITENESS
Jesus!, **Christ!**, and **Jesus Christ!** are all used in a non-religious way in informal spoken English. They have the same uses as **God**, but are even stronger: *Jesus, that hurts!* Some people, especially those who believe in the Christian religion, are very offended by these uses of these expressions.

Jesus freak /ˈ.. ˌ./ *n.* [C] SPOKEN, OFFENSIVE someone who is too involved with the Christian religion

jet¹ /dʒɛt/ *n.* **1** [C] a fast airplane with a jet engine: *a jet fighter* **2** [C] a narrow stream of liquid or gas that comes quickly out of a small hole, or the hole itself: *strong jets of water* **3** [U] a hard black stone that is used for making jewelry

jet² *v.* **jetted, jetting** [I always + adv./prep.] **1** INFORMAL to travel by airplane, especially when you go to many different places: *Martinez greeted supporters in Tampa, then jetted to Miami.* **2** if a liquid or gas jets from somewhere, it comes quickly out of a small hole

jet-black, jet black /ˌ. ˈ.◂/ *adj.* very dark black: *jet-black eyebrows*

jet en·gine /ˌ. ˈ../ *n.* [C] an engine that pushes out a stream of hot air and gases behind it, used in aircraft

jet foil /ˈ. ./ *n.* [C] a boat that rises out of the water on structures that look like legs when it is traveling fast

jet lag /ˈ. ./ *n.* [U] the tired and confused feeling that you can get after flying a long distance, because of the difference in time between the place you left and the place you arrived at —**jet-lagged** *adj.*

jet-pro·pelled /ˌ. .ˈ.◂/ *adj.* using a jet engine for power

jet pro·pul·sion /ˌ. .ˈ../ *n.* [U] the use of a JET ENGINE for power

jet·sam /ˈdʒɛtsəm/ *n.* [U] things that are thrown from a ship and float on the ocean toward the shore —see also **flotsam and jetsam** (FLOTSAM (2))

jet set /ˈ. ./ *n.* **the jet set** rich and fashionable people who travel a lot —**jet-setter** *n.* [C] —**jet set** *v.* [I]

jet-ski /ˈ. ./ *n.* [C] a small fast vehicle on which one or two people can ride over water for fun

jet stream /ˈ. ./ *n.* [singular,U] a current of very strong winds high above the Earth's surface

jet·ti·son /ˈdʒɛtəsən, -zən/ *v.* [T] **1** to get rid of something or decide not to do something anymore: *Berger jettisoned much of the original movie plot.* **2** to throw things away, especially from a moving airplane or ship: *One crew member accidentally jettisoned half of the plane's fuel.*

jet·ty /ˈdʒɛti/ *n. plural* **jetties** [C] **1** a wide wall built out into the water as protection against large waves **2** a PIER —compare WHARF

Jew /dʒu/ *n.* [C] a member of a group of people whose religion is Judaism, who lived in ancient times in the land of Israel, some of whom now live in the modern state of Israel and others in various countries of the world

jew /dʒu/ *v.*
jew sb/sth ↔ **down** *phr. v.* a word meaning "to persuade someone to lower the price for something," considered offensive by many people

jew·el /ˈdʒuəl/ *n.* [C] **1** a small valuable stone, such as a DIAMOND **2** jewels [plural] jewelry or other objects made with valuable stones and used for decoration **3** INFORMAL someone or something that is very valuable, attractive, or important: *Sarasota is a jewel of a city.* **4** the jewel in the crown the best or most valuable part of something **5** a very small stone used in the machinery of a watch —see also CROWN JEWEL, FAMILY JEWELS

jew·eled /ˈdʒuəld/ *adj.* decorated with jewels

jew·el·er /ˈdʒuələ/ *n.* [C] someone who buys, sells, makes, or repairs jewelry

jew·el·ry /ˈdʒuəlri/ *n.* [U] small decorations you wear that are usually made from gold, silver, or jewels such as rings and NECKLACES: *a piece of jewelry* —see also COSTUME JEWELRY

Jew·ess /ˈdʒuɪs/ *n.* [C] OLD-FASHIONED a word meaning "a Jewish woman," now usually considered offensive

Jew·ish /ˈdʒuɪʃ/ *adj.* relating to Jews or Judaism: *Kate's husband is Jewish.* | *the Jewish community*

Jewish Com·mu·ni·ty Cen·ters As·so·ci·a·tion /ˌ.. .ˈ.. ˌ. ..ˌ./ an organization that provides activities for Jewish communities in sports, education, and other areas

Jew·ry /ˈdʒuri/ *n.* [U] FORMAL Jewish people as a group

jib /dʒɪb/ *n.* [C] **1** a small sail —compare MAINSAIL **2** the long part of a CRANE —see also **like the cut of sb's jib** (LIKE² (7))

jibe¹ /dʒaɪb/ *v.* [I] **1** if two statements, reports etc. jibe with each other, the information in them matches: [+ **with**] *What you see in movies doesn't always jibe with reality.* **2** also **gibe** to say something that is intended to make someone seem stupid or that criticizes them

jibe², gibe *n.* [C] a remark that is not nice and is intended to make someone seem stupid or criticize them: *For two hours, legislators traded jibes over the bill.*

ji·ca·ma /ˈhikəmə/ *n.* [C] a type of root that is often eaten raw in SALADS

jif·fy /ˈdʒɪfi/ also **jiff** /dʒɪf/ *n.* SPOKEN **in a jiffy** very soon: *I'll be with you in a jiffy.*

jig¹ /dʒɪg/ *n.* **1** [C] a type of quick dance, or a piece of music for this dance **2 the jig is up** used to say that something wrong or illegal that someone has been doing has been discovered and will have to stop

jig² *v.* **jigged, jigging 1** [I] to dance a jig **2** [I always + adv./prep.] to move up and down with quick short movements

jig·ger¹ /ˈdʒɪgə/ *n.* [C] a unit for measuring alcohol, equal to 1.5 OUNCES, or the small glass this is measured with

jigger² *v.* [T] to slightly change something for illegal or dishonest purposes

jig·gle /ˈdʒɪgəl/ *v.* **jiggled, jiggling** [I,T] to move with short small quick movements, or to make something do this: *The video camera lets you shoot from a moving car without jiggling the picture.*

jig·gy /ˈdʒɪgi/ *adj.* **get jiggy** SLANG to dance with a lot of energy to popular music

jig·saw /ˈdʒɪgsɔ/ *n.* [C] a special SAW (=cutting tool) for cutting out shapes in thin pieces of wood —see picture at TOOL¹

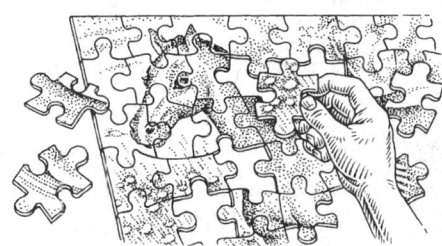

jigsaw puzzle

jigsaw puz·zle /ˈ.. ˌ../ also **jigsaw** *n.* [C] a picture cut up into many pieces that you try to fit together for fun

ji·had /dʒɪˈhɑd/ *n.* [C] a holy war fought by Muslims

jilt /dʒɪlt/ *v.* [T] to suddenly end a relationship with someone —**jilted** *adj.*: *a jilted lover*

Jim Crow /ˌdʒɪm ˈkroʊ/ *n.* a system of laws and practices used in the U.S. until the 1960s, that treated African-American people unfairly and separated them from white people

jim-dan·dy /ˌdʒɪm ˈdændi/ *adj.* SPOKEN, OLD-FASHIONED very good or of high quality

jim·my¹ /ˈdʒɪmi/ *v.* **jimmied, jimmying** [T] to force a door, window, lock etc. open by using a metal bar: *Angela jimmied the lock on Craig's desk drawer.*

jimmy² *n.* [C] a small metal bar used especially by thieves to break open doors, windows etc.

jin·gle¹ /ˈdʒɪŋgəl/ *v.* **jingled, jingling** [I,T] to shake small metal things together so that they produce a sound, or to make this sound: *Noah was jingling his keys in his pocket.*

J

jingle² *n.* **1** [C] a short song used in advertisements **2** [singular] the sound of small metal objects being shaken together **3** [singular] SPOKEN a telephone call

jin·go·ism /ˈdʒɪŋɡoʊˌɪzəm/ *n.* [U] DISAPPROVING a strong belief that your own country is better than others —**jingoistic** /ˌdʒɪŋɡoʊˈɪstɪk/ *adj.*

jinks /dʒɪŋks/ *n.* —see HIGH JINKS

jinn /dʒɪn/ *n.* [C] a DJINN

jinx¹ /dʒɪŋks/ *n. plural* **jinxes** [C usually singular] someone or something that brings bad luck, or a period of bad luck that results from this: [+ **on**] *B.J. is convinced there's a jinx on the building.*

jinx² *v.* [T] to make someone or something have bad luck: *It's better not to jinx the project by talking about it.* —**jinxed** *adj.*

jinx³ *interjection* INFORMAL said, especially by children, when you have just said the same thing at the same time as someone else

jit·ter·bug /ˈdʒɪtɚˌbʌɡ/ *n.* [singular] a popular fast JAZZ dance in the 1940s

jit·ters /ˈdʒɪtɚz/ *n.* [plural] INFORMAL the feeling of being nervous and worried, especially before an important event: *The scandal gave Wall Street traders* **the jitters**.

jit·ter·y /ˈdʒɪtɚri/ *adj.* INFORMAL anxious or nervous: *jittery investors*

jive¹ /dʒaɪv/ *n.* **1** [C,U] a very fast dance, popular especially in the 1930s and 1940s, performed to fast JAZZ music **2** [U] SLANG statements that you do not believe are true: *Don't you give me any of that jive.* —**jive** *adj.*

jive² *v.* **1** [I] to dance a jive **2** [T] SLANG to try to make someone believe something that is not true: *Come on, Laura, don't jive me.* —compare JIBE¹

Joan of Arc /ˌdʒoʊn əv ˈɑrk/ also **St. Joan** (?1412–1431) the PATRON SAINT of France, who led a French army which defeated the English at Orléans. Later she was made a prisoner by the English and burned to death as a WITCH.

Job¹ /dʒoʊb/ **1** in the Bible, a man who continued to have faith in God even though God destroyed his property and his family **2** a book in the OLD TESTAMENT in the Bible

Job² *n.* **1** have the patience of Job to be extremely patient **2** Job's comforter someone who tries to make you feel more cheerful, but actually makes you feel worse

s w **job** /dʒɑb/ *n.*
1 1

1 work [C] the regular paid work that you do for an employer: *Jennifer* **got a job as** *a receptionist.* | *Pat* **took a job** (=accepted a job) *up in Albany.* | *More than 40 workers* **lost their jobs.** | *I was* **offered** *a job at BYU, but I turned it down.* | *Twelve other people were* **applying for** *the same job* (=trying to get it). | *She just* **quit her job** *because she was having a baby.* | *Maybe it's time for you to* **change jobs** (=get a different job). | *Kelly wants to prove to his father that he can* **hold down a job** (=keep a job). | *If we don't get this account, we'll all* **be out of a job** (=no longer have a job). | *He hasn't held* **a steady job** (=a job that is likely to continue) *in eight years.* | a **part-time/full-time job** (=a job in which you work less than 40 hours per week, or one that you work 40 hours per week) —see also JOB DESCRIPTION

2 on the job while doing work, or at work: *on-the-job training* | *Today's my first day on the job.*

3 duty [C usually singular] a particular duty or responsibility that you have: *At our house,* **it's my job** *to make sure the bills are paid on time.*

4 a nose/face/boob etc. job SURGERY to change the shape of a part of your body

5 sth you must do [C] something that you have to do which involves working or making an effort: *Moving all this stuff is going to be a big job.* | *I've got a lot of* **odd jobs** (=different things) *to do on Saturday.* | *Pay attention to* **the job at hand** (=the work you are doing now).

6 do a good/great/bad etc. job to do something well or badly

7 do the job INFORMAL to have the effect or produce the result that you want or need: *A little more glue should do the job.*

8 job security the state of being sure that your job is permanent: *Strikers are asking for better pay and job security.*

9 do a job on sb/sth INFORMAL to have a damaging effect on someone or something: *The sun does quite a job on people's skin.*

10 crime [C] INFORMAL a crime in which money is stolen from a bank, company etc.: *a bank job* | **an inside job** (=a crime done by a member of the organization in which it happens)

11 job satisfaction how much you like or enjoy your job: *I'm earning less, but I get more job satisfaction.*

12 computer [C] an action for a computer to do: *a print job*

SPOKEN PHRASES

13 type of thing [C] also **jobby** used to say that something is of a particular type: *His new computer's one of those little portable jobs.*

14 good job used to tell someone they have done something well: *That looks a lot better, Betty Ann. Good job.*

15 I'm just/only doing my job used to say that it is not your fault if you have to do something in your work that other people do not like

16 if you want a job done right (you've got to do it yourself) said when you are going to do something, especially after someone else has done it in an incorrect way

17 any job worth doing is worth doing right used to say that if you are going to do something, you should do it carefully and correctly

—see also BLOW JOB, HAND JOB, PAINT JOB

USAGE NOTE: JOB

WORD CHOICE: job, work, post, position, line of work/business, occupation, trade, profession, vocation, career
Use **work** as a general word to talk about what you do every day in order to earn money: *I have to go to work.* It can also be used when there is no payment or you are not working for someone else: *volunteer work.* Your **job** is the particular type of work that you do to earn money: *James is looking for a job in marketing.* **Occupation** is a formal word for **job** that is used on official forms: *Please state your name, address, and occupation.* **Position** is a formal word for a particular job in a company, at a university etc.: *Parker took the position of Director in 1987.* **Position** is also used for a job that is advertised in the newspaper or by the person who is answering the advertisement: *I am writing to apply for the position of Assistant Manager.* **Post** is used mainly for very important jobs, especially ones in the government: *a senior post at the State Department.* In informal use, the type of work or job you do may be called your **line of work/business**: *It's not so easy to get into this line of work.* A **trade** is skilled work in which you make or do things with your hands: *Anderson is a carpenter by trade.* A **profession** is a type of work such as that of a doctor or lawyer, for which you need many years of education. Some **professions**, such as teaching and nursing, are also called **vocations**, which suggests that people do them in order to help others rather than to earn a lot of money. A **career** is the type of work that you do for most of your life or for a long time: *She started her acting career on the stage in New York.*

---

job ac·tion /ˈ. ˌ../ *n.* [C] an action such as a STRIKE² (1) that does not continue for very long, done by workers who are asking for more money or better working conditions

job·ber /ˈdʒɑbɚ/ *n.* [C] **1** someone whose job is buying and selling STOCKS and SHARES **2** someone who buys a product from a company at a WHOLESALE price and then sells it to a customer, usually another company, at a higher price

job de·scrip·tion /ˈ. .,../ *n.* [C] an official list of the work and responsibilities that you have in your job

job·less /ˈdʒɑblɪs/ *adj.* **1** for or relating to people without jobs: *the jobless rate* (=number of people who do not have jobs) **2** without a job; UNEMPLOYED: *jobless workers*

job lock /ˈ. ./ *n.* [C] INFORMAL a situation in which you are afraid to leave your job because you will lose your medical insurance

job lot /ˈ. ./ *n.* [C] a large mixed group of things that are sold together: *a job lot of furniture*

Jobs /dʒɑbz/**, Steve** /stiv/ (1955–) a U.S. computer designer and BUSINESSMAN who together with Steve Wozniak, designed the first personal computer and started the Apple computer company

job-shar·ing /ˈ. .,../ *n.* [U] an arrangement by which two people both work PART-TIME doing the same job —**jobshare** *n.* [C]

job shop /ˈ. ./ *n.* [C] a factory that only produces goods which have already been ordered by its customers

jock /dʒɑk/ *n.* [C] **1** INFORMAL, DISAPPROVING someone, especially a student, who plays a lot of sports and is often considered to be stupid **2** INFORMAL a JOCK-STRAP

jock·ey[1] /ˈdʒɑki/ *n. plural* **jockeys** [C] someone who rides horses in races —see also COMPUTER JOCKEY, DESK JOCKEY, DISC JOCKEY

jockey[2] *v.* **jockeyed, jockeying 1** [I always + adv./ prep.] to compete strongly to get into the best position or situation, or to get the most power: *Two airlines are jockeying for position in the trans-Atlantic market.* **2** [I,T] to ride a horse as a jockey **3** [T] to skillfully make something move in a particular direction or fit somewhere: *Camera operators jockey the cameras around as instructed by the director.* —**jockeying** *n.* [U]

Jockey shorts /ˈ.. ,./ *n.* [plural] TRADEMARK a type of men's cotton underwear that fits tightly —compare BOXER SHORTS

jock itch /ˈ. ./ *n.* [U] NOT TECHNICAL a medical condition in which the skin cracks and starts to ITCH near a man's sex organs

jock·strap /ˈdʒɑkstræp/ *n.* [C] a piece of underwear that men wear to support their sex organs when playing sports

jo·cose /dʒəˈkoʊs, dʒoʊ-/ *adj.* LITERARY joking or humorous —**jocoseness, jocosity** /dʒəˈkɑsəti/ *n.* [U]

joc·u·lar /ˈdʒɑkyələ/ *adj.* FORMAL joking or humorous: *a jocular tone* —**jocularity** /,dʒɑkyəˈlærəti/ *n.* [C,U]

joc·und /ˈdʒɑkənd, ˈdʒoʊ-, dʒoʊˈkʌnd/ *adj.* LITERARY cheerful and happy —**jocundly** *adv.* —**jocundity** /dʒoʊˈkʌndəti, dʒɑ-/ *n.* [U]

jodh·purs /ˈdʒɑdpɚz/ *n.* [plural] a special type of pants that you wear when riding horses

Joe /dʒoʊ/ *n.* INFORMAL **1** [C usually singular] also **Joe Blow/Schmo** an ordinary average man: *a regular Joe* **2 Joe College/Citizen** etc. someone who is a typical example of people in a particular situation or involved in a particular activity: *He was your average Joe Businessman – nothing special to look at.* **3 Joe Six-Pack** a man who is a typical example of someone who does physical work, and who has the same political, moral etc. ideas as most people in this social class —see also JOHN Q. PUBLIC

joe /dʒoʊ/ *n.* [U] INFORMAL **a cup of joe** a cup of coffee

Jo·el /ˈdʒoʊəl/ a book in the Old Testament of the Christian Bible

Jof·frey /ˈdʒɑfri/**, Rob·ert** /ˈrɑbɚt/ (1930–1988) an American dancer and CHOREOGRAPHER of modern dance and BALLET

jog[1] /dʒɑg/ *v.* **jogged, jogging 1** [I] to run slowly and in a steady way, especially as a way of exercising: *Kathy and her husband jog together every morning.* **2 jog sb's memory** to make someone remember something: *Maybe this picture will help jog your memory.* **3** [T] to knock or push something lightly by mistake: *I accidentally jogged her elbow.*

jog[2] *n.* [singular] **1** a slow steady run, especially done as a way of exercising: *I'm going for a jog in the park.* **2** a light knock or push done by accident

jog·ger /ˈdʒɑgɚ/ *n.* [C] someone who runs slowly and in a steady way as a way of exercising

jog·ging /ˈdʒɑgɪŋ/ *n.* [U] the activity of running slowly and in a steady way as a way of exercising: *There was too much rain to go jogging.*

jogging suit /ˈ.. ,./ *n.* [C] loose clothes that you wear when you are running for exercise, or to keep warm after exercise —compare SWEAT SUIT

jog·gle /ˈdʒɑgəl/ *v.* [I,T] INFORMAL to shake or move up and down, or to make something move this way

Jo·han·nes·burg /dʒoʊˈhænɪs,bɚg, -ˈhɑ-/ also **Jo'burg** /ˈdʒoʊbɚg/ INFORMAL the largest city in South Africa

John /dʒɑn/ **1** also **The Gospel according to St. John** one of the four books in the New Testament of the Christian Bible that describe the life and teaching of Jesus **2 1 John, 2 John, 3 John** three short books in the New Testament of the Christian Bible

john /dʒɑn/ *n.* [C] **1** INFORMAL a toilet or BATHROOM **2** SLANG the customer of a PROSTITUTE —see also LONG JOHNS

John, King (1167–1216) a king of England, remembered especially for signing the Magna Carta which put limits on his power as king

John, Saint in the Bible, one of the 12 APOSTLEs who is believed to have written several of the books of the New Testament of the Bible

John Birch So·ci·e·ty, the /,. ˈ. .,..../ a very RIGHT-WING organization started in the U.S. during the 1950s to fight Communism

John Doe /,dʒɑn ˈdoʊ/ *n.* [C,U] a name used especially by the police for a man whose name is not known —compare JANE DOE

John Han·cock /,dʒɑn ˈhænkɑk/ *n.* [C] INFORMAL your SIGNATURE[1] (1)

John·ny-come-late·ly /,dʒɑni kʌm ˈleɪtli/ *n.* [singular] someone who has only recently started doing something, supporting something etc.: *I've worked as an engineer for 25 years – I'm not some Johnny-come-lately.*

Johnny-on-the-spot /,.... ˈ./ *n.* [singular] INFORMAL someone who immediately offers to help, takes an opportunity etc.

John Paul II, Pope /,dʒɑn pɔl ðə ˈsɛkənd/ (1920–) a Polish priest who became the first Polish POPE

John Q. Pub·lic /,dʒɑn kyu ˈpʌblɪk/ *n.* [C,U] INFORMAL a name that is used to mean an average person or people in general —see also JOE

Johns /dʒɑnz/**, Jas·per** /ˈdʒæspɚ/ (1930–) a U.S. PAINTER famous for his paintings of ordinary things like letters, numbers, and flags, in the style of POP ART

john·son /ˈdʒɑnsən/ *n.* [C] SLANG a PENIS

John·son /ˈdʒɑnsən/**, An·drew** /ˈændru/ (1808–1875) the 17th President of the U.S.

Johnson, Lyn·don /ˈlɪndən/ (1908–1973) the 36th President of the U.S.

Johnson, Mag·ic /ˈmædʒɪk/ (1959–) a U.S. basketball player

Johnson, Samuel (1709–1784) known as **Dr. Johnson**, a British CRITIC and dictionary writer, famous for his "Dictionary of the English Language"

John XXIII, Pope /,dʒɑn ðə ,twɛnti ˈθɚd/ (1881–1963) the POPE who called together the Second Vatican Council, a meeting of church leaders from all over the world

joie de vi·vre /,ʒwɑ də ˈvivrə/ *n.* [U] a feeling of pleasure and excitement because you are alive

join /dʒɔɪn/ *v.*

1 group/organization [I,T] to become a member or part of an organization, group etc.: *During the war he joined the Air Corps and became a pilot.* | *Eight new members are expected to join.*

2 activity [T] to begin to take part in an activity that other people are involved in: *It is not known if the other parties will join the peace talks.* | *Merigan urged everyone to join the fight against AIDS.*

3 do sth together [I,T] to do something together with someone else: [join (with) sb in doing sth] *Please join with me in welcoming tonight's speaker.* | [join (with) sb to do sth] *Two Republicans joined the Democrats to pass the law.* | *Everyone is invited to join in the fun.*

4 go/be with sb [T] to go somewhere with someone, or to go to where they are in order to be with them: [join sb (for sth)] *Are you going to join us for dinner?*

5 connect **a)** [T] to connect or fasten things together: *The wooden buildings are joined by ivy-covered walkways.* **b)** [I,T] also join up to come together and become connected: *They met at the spot where the creek joins the river.* | *The pipes join right over here.*

6 join the club SPOKEN used to say that you and a lot of other people are in the same situation: *Your office is either too hot or too cold? Join the club.*

7 join hands if people join hands, they hold each other's hands

8 join voices to sing or speak together

9 be joined in marriage also be joined in holy matrimony FORMAL to be married

10 join battle FORMAL to begin fighting —see also join/combine forces (FORCE¹ (8)), if you can't beat 'em, join 'em (BEAT¹ (13))

join in *phr. v.* [I] to take part in an activity as part of a group of two or more people: *Now, when Steve starts talking about sports, I can join in.*

join up *phr. v.* [I] to become a member of an organization, especially the military —compare CARPENTER

join up with sb/sth *phr. v.* [T] INFORMAL to begin to do something with other people so that you form one group: *Employers have joined up with insurance companies to collect information on employee's medical experiences.*

join·er /'dʒɔɪnɚ/ *n.* [C] **1** someone who makes wooden doors, window frames etc. —compare CARPENTER **2** someone who is always eager to join different clubs or organizations in order to do things with other people

join·er·y /'dʒɔɪnəri/ *n.* [U] the trade and work of a joiner —compare CARPENTRY

SW **joint¹** /dʒɔɪnt/ *adj.* [only before noun] involving two or more people or groups, or owned or shared by them: *a joint bank account* | *Eight northeastern states will take joint action on air pollution issues.* | *The mission is a joint effort of NASA and the European Space Agency.* —jointly *adv.*

SW **joint²** *n.*

1 body part [C] a part of your body where two bones meet, that can bend: *an elbow joint*

2 place [C] INFORMAL a place, especially a BAR, club, or restaurant: *a fast-food joint*

3 drugs [C] SLANG a MARIJUANA cigarette

4 join together [C] a place where two things or parts of an object are joined together: *the joints of a chair*

5 out of joint **a)** if a bone in your body is out of joint, it has been pushed out of its correct position **b)** if a system, group etc. is out of joint, it is not working correctly: *The climate seems out of joint.* —see also put sb's nose out of joint (NOSE¹ (10))

6 the joint SLANG prison

7 meat a large piece of meat for cooking, usually containing a bone: *a joint of beef* —see also case the joint (CASE² (2))

Joint Chiefs of Staff /ˌ. '. ˌ. . '. / *n.* [plural] the Joint Chiefs of Staff the group consisting of the leaders of the Army, Navy, Air Force, and Marines, that gives the U.S. President advice

joint cus·to·dy /ˌ. '.../ *n.* [U] LAW a situation in which DIVORCED parents share the responsibility for taking care of their child and share the right to spend time with their child

joint·ed /'dʒɔɪntɪd/ *adj.* having joints and able to move and bend: *a jointed puppet* —see also DOUBLE-JOINTED

joint res·o·lu·tion /ˌ. ..'..'../ *n.* [C] LAW a decision or law agreed by both houses of the U.S. Congress and signed by the President

joint-stock com·pa·ny /ˌ. '. ˌ.../ *n.* [C] TECHNICAL a company that is owned by all the people with STOCK in it

joint ven·ture /ˌ. '../ *n.* [C] a business PROJECT begun by two or more people or companies working together

joist /dʒɔɪst/ *n.* [C] one of the beams that support a floor or ceiling

joke¹ /dʒouk/ *n.* [C] SW

1 sth funny something that you say or do to make people laugh, especially a funny story or trick: *Do you want to hear a good joke?* | *We stayed up telling jokes until 2 a.m.* | *The lady thought we were playing a joke on her* (=tricking her or making her look stupid). | *It's not funny to make jokes about other people all the time.* | *I don't think he gets the joke* (=understands why a joke is funny). | *She's always cracking jokes* (=saying something funny). | dirty/sick joke (=a joke about sex or something disgusting)

2 sth stupid INFORMAL a situation or event that is so stupid or unreasonable that you do not consider it seriously: *What a joke that meeting was.*

3 take a joke to be able to laugh at a joke about yourself: *What's wrong? Can't you take a joke?*

4 sth is no joke used to emphasize that a situation is serious or that someone really means what they say: *These bills are no joke.*

5 make a joke (out) of sth to treat something serious as if it was intended to be funny: *My mother always makes a joke of everything.*

6 sb's idea of a joke SPOKEN a situation that someone else thinks is funny but you do not: *Is this your idea of a joke?*

7 the joke's on sb used to say that something has happened to make someone seem stupid, especially when they were trying to make other people seem stupid —see also IN-JOKE, PRACTICAL JOKE, standing joke (STANDING¹ (4))

joke² *v.* [I] **1** to say things that are intended to be funny: [+ about/with] *I can joke with my boss about anything.* **2** you must be joking! also you've got to be joking! SPOKEN used to tell someone that what they are suggesting is so strange or stupid that you cannot believe that they are serious: *Marry him? You must be joking.* **3** all joking aside SPOKEN used before you say something serious after you have been joking: *All joking aside, you did a really nice job tonight.* —jokingly *adv.* SW

joke around *phr. v.* [I] INFORMAL to behave or speak in a silly way: *Sometimes guys joke around to get rid of tension.*

jok·er /'dʒoukɚ/ *n.* [C] **1** SPOKEN someone who behaves in a way you think is stupid: *Some joker had nailed the bench to the floor.* **2** a PLAYING card that has no particular value and is only used in some card games **3** someone who makes a lot of jokes

jok·ey, joky /'dʒouki/ *adj.* jokier, jokiest INFORMAL not serious and tending to make people laugh: *a jokey TV show*

Jo·li·et /ʒoul'yeɪ, 'dʒouliˌɛt/, **Lou·is** /'lui/ (1645–1700) a French-Canadian EXPLORER who, with Jacques Marquette, discovered the upper Mississippi River in 1673

Jo·li·ot-Cu·rie /ˌʒoulyou kyu'ri/, **I·rène** /i'rɛn/ (1897–1956) a French scientist, daughter of Pierre and Marie Curie, who discovered how to produce new RADIOACTIVE substances with her husband Frédéric Joliot-Curie (1900–1958)

jol·lies /'dʒɑliz/ *n.* [plural] get your jollies SPOKEN, DISAPPROVING to get pleasure from a particular experience or activity, especially when the activity is strange: *What kind of sick person gets his jollies out of setting fires?*

jol·li·ty /'dʒɑləti/ *n.* [U] FORMAL the state or quality of being happy and cheerful

jol·ly¹ /'dʒɑli/ *adj.* jollier, jolliest **1** happy and cheerful: *a jolly Santa Claus* **2** OLD-FASHIONED very pleasant and enjoyable: *a very jolly occasion*

J

jolly² v. jollied, jollying [T] INFORMAL to try to make someone happy so that they will do something for you or give you something: [jolly sb into (doing) sth] *Mr. Finsand could jolly anybody into doing anything.*

Jol·ly Rog·er /ˌdʒɑli ˈrɑdʒɚ/ n. a black flag with a picture of a SKULL and bones on it, used in past times by PIRATES —see also SKULL AND CROSSBONES (1)

jolt¹ /dʒoʊlt/ n. [C] **1** a sudden rough shaking movement: *Residents felt the first jolt of the earthquake at about 8 a.m.* **2** a sudden shock or surprise: *The news of his resignation gave even critics a jolt.* **3** a sudden burst of energy: *electric jolts* **4** something that has a sudden strong effect: *The tax laws may be a severe jolt to the economy.* | *a jolt of caffeine*

jolt² v. **1** [I,T] to move suddenly and roughly, or to make someone or something move in this way: *Their house had been jolted right off its foundation.* **2** [T] to give someone a sudden shock or surprise: *Vic was jolted awake by at least five explosions.*

Jo·nah /ˈdʒoʊnə/ **1** in the Bible, a PROPHET who tried to escape from God by getting on a ship, and was then swallowed by a WHALE **2** a book in the OLD TESTAMENT of the Bible

Jones /dʒoʊnz/, **John Paul** (1747–1792) an American navy officer who fought the British in the American Revolutionary War

Jones, Le·Roi /ˈlɪrɔɪ/ the original name of the African-American writer Amiri Baraka

Jones·es /ˈdʒoʊnzɪz/ n. —see keep up with the Joneses at keep up (KEEP¹)

jon·quil /ˈdʒɑŋkwəl/ n. [C] a small common spring flower that is bright yellow

Jon·son /ˈdʒɑnsən/, **Ben** /bɛn/ (1572–1637) an English writer of plays

Jop·lin /ˈdʒɑplɪn/, **Scott** /skɑt/ (1868–1917) a U.S. JAZZ musician who played the piano and wrote RAGTIME music

Jor·dan¹ /ˈdʒɔrdn/ an Arab country in the Middle East, which is east of Israel and west of Iraq —**Jordanian** /dʒɔrˈdeɪniən/ n., adj.

Jordan² a river in Israel and Jordan, that flows into the Dead Sea

Jordan, Mi·chael /ˈmaɪkəl/ (1963–) a U.S. basketball player who is considered the best player of the 1980s and 1990s

Michael Jordan

Jo·seph¹ /ˈdʒoʊzəf/ in the Bible, a son of Abraham who was sent to Egypt as a slave, became powerful there, and brought his people to live in Egypt

Joseph² in the Bible, the husband of Mary, the mother of Jesus

Joseph, Chief (?1840–1904) the chief of a Native American tribe who fought against the U.S. army in 1870

Jo·se·phine /ˈdʒoʊzəˌfin/ (1763–1814) the EMPRESS of France from 1804 to 1809 and the wife of Napoleon

josh /dʒɑʃ/ v. OLD-FASHIONED [I,T] to talk to someone or in a gentle joking way: [+ with] *The secretary-general joshed with reporters as they yelled questions at him.*

Josh·u·a /ˈdʒɑʃuə/ **1** in the Bible, a man who led the Jews to the "Promised Land" **2** a book in the OLD TESTAMENT of the Bible

joss stick /ˈdʒɑs ˌstɪk/ n. [C] a stick of INCENSE¹

jos·tle /ˈdʒɑsəl/ v. [I,T] to push or knock against someone, especially in a crowd: *Three people were hurt as the crowd jostled for a better view.*

jot¹ /dʒɑt/ v. **jotted, jotting** [T] to write something quickly: *O'Reilly sat there while the officer jotted notes.*

jot sth ↔ down phr. v. [T] to write a short piece of information quickly: *Let me jot down your number.*

jot² n. **not a jot** OLD-FASHIONED not at all, or none at all

jot·tings /ˈdʒɑtɪŋz/ n. [plural] INFORMAL short notes, usually written to remind yourself about something

joule /dʒul, dʒaʊl/ n. [C] TECHNICAL a measure of energy or work

jour·nal /ˈdʒɚnl/ n. [C] **1** a written record that you make of the things that happen to you each day; DIARY **2** a serious magazine produced for professional people or those with a particular interest: *The New England Journal of Medicine*

jour·nal·ese /ˌdʒɚnlˈiz/ n. [U] DISAPPROVING language that is typical of newspapers

jour·nal·is·m /ˈdʒɚnlˌɪzəm/ n. [U] the job or activity of writing reports for newspapers, magazines, television, or radio

jour·nal·ist /ˈdʒɚnlˌɪst/ n. [C] someone who writes s w reports for newspapers, magazines, television, or radio —compare REPORTER

jour·ney¹ /ˈdʒɚni/ n. plural journeys [C] **1** a trip s w from one place to another, especially a long one: *The journey will take the President to Japan, China, and Australia.* —see Usage Note at TRAVEL¹ **2** a long and often difficult process by which someone or something changes or develops: *an alcoholic's journey to recovery* **3** a time when you think about things that happened in the past: *Walking through historic New Almaden is a journey into the past.*

journey² v. **journeyed, journeying** [I always + adv./prep.] LITERARY to travel

jour·ney·man /ˈdʒɚnimən/ n. [C] OLD-FASHIONED **1** a trained worker who works for the person who owns the business **2** an experienced worker whose work is acceptable but not excellent

joust·ing /ˈdʒaʊstɪŋ/ n. [U] **1** fighting or arguing: *verbal jousting* **2** the activity of fighting with LANCEs (=long sticks) while riding a horse —**joust** v. [I] —**joust** n. [C]

Jove /dʒoʊv/ n. **by Jove!** OLD-FASHIONED used to express surprise or to emphasize something

jo·vi·al /ˈdʒoʊviəl/ adj. friendly and cheerful: *jovial laughter* —**joviality** /ˌdʒoʊviˈæləti/ n. [U]

jowl /dʒaʊl/ n. [C] **1** [usually plural] the skin that covers your lower jaw on either side of your face **2** **heavy-jowled** having large jowls that hang down slightly —see also **cheek by jowl** (CHEEK (5))

joy¹ /dʒɔɪ/ n. plural joys **1** [U] great happiness and s w pleasure: *Christmas is a time of joy.* | **with/for joy** *I yelled for joy as we drove into Colorado.* **2** [C] something or someone that gives you happiness and pleasure: *Everyone who knew her said she was a joy and an inspiration.* | [be a joy to do] *His stories are always a joy to read.* —see also **jump for joy** (JUMP¹ (14))

joy² v. **joyed, joying**

joy in sth phr. v. [T] LITERARY to be happy because of something

Joyce /dʒɔɪs/, **James** (1882–1941) an Irish writer of NOVELS, famous for his use of unusual and invented words, and new styles of writing

joy·ful /ˈdʒɔɪfəl/ adj. very happy, or likely to make people very happy: *a joyful celebration* —**joyfully** adv.

joy·less /ˈdʒɔɪlɪs/ adj. without any happiness or pleasure at all: *a joyless task*

Joy·ner /ˈdʒɔɪnɚ/, **Flor·ence Grif·fith** /ˈflɔrəns, ˈflɑ- ˈɡrɪfɪθ/ (1955–1998) a U.S. runner who won three GOLD MEDALS at the Olympic Games in 1988

joy·ous /ˈdʒɔɪəs/ adj. LITERARY very happy, or likely to make people very happy: *a joyous occasion* —**joyously** adv.

joy·rid·ing /ˈdʒɔɪˌraɪdɪŋ/ n. [U] the crime of stealing a car and driving it in a fast and dangerous way for fun —**joyride** n. [I] —**joyrider** n. [C]

joy·stick /ˈdʒɔɪˌstɪk/ n. [C] an upright handle that you use to control something such as an aircraft or a computer game

J.P. n. [C] a JUSTICE OF THE PEACE

J

JPEG also **JPG** n. [C] TECHNICAL Joint Photographic Experts Group; a type of computer FILE¹ (3) used on the Internet that contains pictures, photographs, or other images

Jr. the written abbreviation of JUNIOR; used after the name of a man who has the same name as his father: *Donald McGee, Jr.*

Juan Car·los /wɑn ˈkɑrloʊs/ (1938–) the King of Spain since 1975, who had an important part in helping Spain to become a DEMOCRATIC country after Franco's DICTATORSHIP

Juá·rez /ˈwɑrɛz/, **Be·ni·to** /beɪˈnitoʊ/ (1806–1872) a Mexican politician who was President of Mexico, introduced changes that gave more people wealth and political power, and tried to stop foreign countries having influence over Mexico

ju·bi·lant /ˈdʒubələnt/ adj. extremely happy and pleased, or showing this emotion: *a jubilant smile* —**jubilantly** adv.

ju·bi·la·tion /ˌdʒubəˈleɪʃən/ n. [U] FORMAL extreme happiness and pleasure: *Shouts of jubilation rose from the crowd.*

ju·bi·lee /ˌdʒubəˈli, ˈdʒubəli/ n. [C] a date that is celebrated because it is exactly 25 years, 50 years etc. after the beginning of something

Ju·dah /ˈdʒudə/ in the Bible, one of Jacob's sons

Ju·da·ism /ˈdʒudiˌɪzəm, -deɪ-, -də-/ n. [U] the Jewish religion based on the Old Testament of the Bible, the Talmud, and the later teachings of the RABBIS —**Judaic** /dʒuˈdeɪɪk/ adj.

Ju·das¹ /ˈdʒudəs/ also **Judas Is·car·i·ot** /ɪˈskæriət/ in the Bible, one of the 12 APOSTLES, who BETRAYed Jesus to the Jewish authorities

Judas² n. [C] someone who is disloyal to a friend; TRAITOR

Jude /dʒud/ **1** in the Bible, one of the 12 APOSTLES, also called Thaddeus **2** a book in the New Testament of the Bible

judge¹ /dʒʌdʒ/ n. [C] **1** the official in control of a court who decides how criminals should be punished: *Judge Pamela Gifford* | *a judge's controversial decision* | **federal judge/high court judge** (=a judge in a particular court) **2** someone who decides on the result of a competition: *The panel of judges included several well-known writers.* **3 a good/bad judge of sth** someone whose opinion on something is usually right or wrong: *Sarah's not a very good judge of character.* **4 let me be the judge of that** also **I'll be the judge of that** SPOKEN used to tell someone angrily that you do not need their advice

judge² v. judged, judging
1 opinion [I,T] to form or give an opinion about someone or something after thinking carefully about all the information you know about them: *He seems like a nice guy, but it's too early to judge.* | [judge sb/sth by sth] *Her leadership will be judged by how she deals with difficult problems.* | [judge sb/sth on sth] *A public library is judged on how well it serves people.* | [judge sb/sth (to be) sth] *We believe the experiment will be judged a success.*
2 judging by/from sth used to say that you are making a guess based on what you have just seen, heard, or learned: *I'd say she's pretty rich, judging from her clothes.*
3 competition [I,T] to decide on the result of a competition: *Who's judging the talent contest?* | [judge sb on sth] *The gymnasts are judged on skill and strength.*
4 criticize [I,T] to form an opinion about someone, especially in an unfair or criticizing way: *Bridget, you shouldn't judge people like that.*
5 law [T] to decide whether someone is guilty of a crime in court: *I think they're waiting to see if he's judged guilty.*
6 guess [I,T] to guess an amount, distance, height, weight etc.; ESTIMATE: *I have a hard time judging ages, but the baby looked about six months old.*

7 don't judge a book by its cover used to say that you should not form an opinion based only on the way someone or something looks

8 it's not for me to judge also **who am I to judge?** used to say that you do not think you have the right to give your opinion about something

Judg·es /ˈdʒʌdʒɪz/ a book in the Old Testament of the Christian Bible

judg·ment, judgement /ˈdʒʌdʒmənt/ n.
1 opinion [C,U] an opinion that you form, especially after thinking carefully about something: *They basically made a judgment without knowing all the facts.* | **In our judgment** (=according to our opinion), *the very poor would benefit most from the program.* | *I'm not passing judgment on any lifestyle* (=giving an opinion about it or criticizing it).
2 ability to decide [U] the ability to make decisions about situations or people: *I trust your judgment, Phyllis.* | **have good/bad judgment** (=usually make good or bad decisions)
3 suspend/reserve judgment FORMAL to not make a decision about something until you know more about it: *The Chinese government has reserved judgment on the plan.*
4 law [C,U] an official decision given by a judge or a court of law: *The court did not alter the $2,500 judgment.*
5 a judgment call INFORMAL a decision you have to make yourself because there are no certain rules in a situation
6 against sb's better judgment if you do something against your better judgment, you do it even though you do not think it is the right thing to do: *I lent her the money against my better judgment.*
7 sit in judgment (over sb) to criticize someone's behavior, especially unfairly —see also LAST JUDGMENT, VALUE JUDGMENT

judg·ment·al /dʒʌdʒˈmɛntl/ adj. too quick and willing to criticize people: *You're being too judgmental.*

judgment day /ˈ.. ˌ./ n. [singular, not with the] also **the day of judgment** the time after death when everyone is judged by God for what they have done in life, according to Christianity and some other religions

ju·di·ca·ture /ˈdʒudɪkətʃɚ/ n. the judicature FORMAL judges and the organization, power etc. of the law

ju·di·cial /dʒuˈdɪʃəl/ adj. [only before noun] **1** relating to a court of law, judges, or their decisions: *the judicial system* **2 the judicial branch** the part of a government that decides whether laws are good and whether people have disobeyed these laws —compare **the executive branch** (EXECUTIVE² (3)), **the legislative branch** (LEGISLATIVE (3)) **3** FORMAL relating to the way judges are meant to behave, especially in being sensible and fair

ju·di·ci·ar·y /dʒuˈdɪʃiˌɛri, -ʃəri/ n. **the judiciary** FORMAL all the judges in a country who, as a group, form part of the system of government

ju·di·cious /dʒuˈdɪʃəs/ adj. FORMAL sensible and careful: *You have to be very judicious about how you spend the taxpayers' money.* —**judiciously** adv.

Ju·dith /ˈdʒudɪθ/ a book in the Apocrypha of the Protestant Bible and in the Old Testament of the Catholic Bible

ju·do /ˈdʒudoʊ/ n. [U] a Japanese method of defending yourself, in which you try to throw your opponent onto the ground, usually done as a sport

jug /dʒʌg/ n. [C] **1** a large deep container for liquids that has a narrow opening and a handle **2** also **jugful** the amount of liquid that a jug will hold: *a two-gallon jug of wine*

jug-eared /ˈdʒʌg ɪrd/ adj. having large ears that stick out

jug·ger·naut /ˈdʒʌgɚˌnɔt, -ˌnɑt/ n. [C] something powerful that is very hard to defeat, or that destroys everything it meets: *the former East German sports juggernaut*

jug·gle /ˈdʒʌɡəl/ v. **1** [I,T] to keep three or more objects moving through the air by throwing and catching them very quickly **2** [I,T] to try to fit two or more jobs, activities etc. into your life: *It's hard trying to juggle a job, kids, and housework.* **3** [T] to arrange numbers, information etc. in the way that you want: *By juggling the figures, Taylor can make the data say anything he wants.* —**juggler** n. [C] —see also **balancing/juggling act** (ACT¹ (10))

juggle

jug·u·lar /ˈdʒʌɡyələ/ n. [C] **1** a jugular vein **2** go for the jugular INFORMAL to criticize or attack someone very strongly, especially in order to harm them

jugular vein /ˈ... ˌ./ n. [C usually singular] the large VEIN (=tube) in your neck that takes blood from your head back to your heart

juice¹ /dʒus/ n. **1** [C,U] the liquid that comes from fruit and vegetables, or a drink that is made from this: *orange juice* **2** [U] the liquid that comes out of meat when it is cooked **3** gastric/digestive juice(s) the liquid inside your stomach that helps you to DIGEST food **4** [U] INFORMAL something that produces power, such as electricity or gasoline: *Give it a little more juice.* —see also **stew (in your own juices)** (STEW² (2))

juice² v. [T] to get the juice out of fruit or vegetables; SQUEEZE (2)

juice sth up phr. v. [T] INFORMAL to make something more interesting or exciting: *They juiced up the movie as much as they could.*

juice box /ˈ. ./ n. [C] a small box filled with enough juice for one person, that comes with a STRAW to drink from

juiced /dʒust/ adj. [not before noun] **1** also **juiced up** INFORMAL excited: *If I'm nervous and juiced up I pitch better.* **2** OLD-FASHIONED drunk

juic·er /ˈdʒusə/ n. [C] a small kitchen tool used for getting juice out of fruit, or an electric machine for doing this

juic·y /ˈdʒusi/ adj. juicier, juiciest **1** containing a lot of juice: *a juicy steak* **2** juicy gossip/details/stories etc. INFORMAL interesting or shocking information, especially about people's sexual behavior **3** INFORMAL giving you work to do that will lead to a feeling of satisfaction: *She's been waiting for years to get a really juicy role.* **4** INFORMAL involving a lot of money: *a big juicy contract* —**juiciness** n. [U]

ju·jit·su /ˌdʒuˈdʒɪtsu/ n. [U] a Japanese method of defending yourself, in which you hold, throw, and hit your opponent

ju·ju /ˈdʒudʒu/ n. [C,U] a type of West African magic involving objects with special powers, or one of these objects

ju·ju·be /ˈdʒudʒuˌbi/ n. [C] a small soft CHEWY candy that tastes like fruit

juke /dʒuk/ v. [I,T] INFORMAL to pretend to run in one direction, then quickly change directions, in order to trick an opponent in games such as football and SOCCER

juke box /ˈ. ./ n. [C] a machine in restaurants, BARS etc. that plays music when you put money in it

juke joint /ˈ. ./ n. [C] INFORMAL a place, popular in the middle 20th century, where people could eat inexpensive food, drink alcohol, and dance

ju·lep /ˈdʒuləp/ n. —see MINT JULEP

ju·li·enne /ˌdʒuliˈɛn/ adj. cut in very thin pieces: *julienne strips of ham* —**julienne** v. [T]

Ju·ly /dʒʊˈlaɪ, dʒə-/ written abbreviation **Jul.** n. [C,U] the seventh month of the year, between June and August: *"When do you go to Greece?" "In July." | I know three people who were born on July 14th. | Last July my parents drove to Santa Fe. | I hope to finish this project by next July. | A ceremony was*

held July 7 to honor the Gulf War veterans. —see Usage Note at JANUARY

jum·ble¹ /ˈdʒʌmbəl/ n. [singular] a mixture of things that are in no particular order: [+ **of**] *The business district is a crowded jumble of shops and restaurants.*

jumble² also **jumble up** v. [T often passive] to mix things together so that they are not in a neat order: *Jewelry, belts and scarves were jumbled in the bottom drawer.*

jum·bo /ˈdʒʌmboʊ/ adj. [only before noun] INFORMAL larger than other things of the same type: *jumbo shrimp* —see also MUMBO-JUMBO

jumbo jet /ˈ.. ˌ./ also **jumbo** n. [C] a very large aircraft for carrying passengers

Jum·bo·Tron /ˈdʒʌmboʊˌtrɑn/ n. [C] TRADEMARK a very large screen similar to a television screen, which is used at sports STADIUMs for showing points, VIDEOs, pictures etc.

jump¹ /dʒʌmp/ v.
1 upward [I] to push yourself suddenly up in the air using your legs: [+ **on/across** etc.] *One dog actually jumped onto the hood of my car. | Boy, it's hot – I feel like jumping in the pool right now. | Fans were jumping up and down and cheering.*
2 over/across [T] to go over or across something by jumping: *A couple of kids had jumped the fence and were playing around inside.*
3 downward [I] to let yourself drop from a place that is above the ground: [+ **out/down** etc.] *The worst moment was jumping out of the plane.*
4 move fast [I always + adv./prep.] to move quickly or suddenly in a particular direction, or to do something quickly: [+ **out/away/up** etc.] *Joe jumped up to answer the telephone. | Flames jumped across treetops, setting roofs on fire. | I'll be ready soon. I'm about to jump in the shower.*
5 in fear/surprise [I] to make a sudden movement because you are surprised or frightened: *Sorry, I didn't mean to make you jump. | She just about jumped out of her skin* (=she moved suddenly because she was very surprised).
6 increase [I] to increase suddenly and by a large amount: [+ **to**] *The number of employees is expected to jump to 35,000 by next year.*
7 jump down sb's throat INFORMAL to suddenly speak angrily to someone: *I was just asking a question. You don't have to jump down my throat!*
8 jump to conclusions to form an opinion about something before you have all the facts: *Right now it doesn't look very good, but let's not jump to any conclusions.*
9 jump the gun to start doing something too soon, especially without thinking about it carefully: *Miller is young, and comparing him to the great quarterbacks is jumping the gun.*
10 keep changing [I] to change quickly from one place, position, idea etc. to another, often missing something that comes in between: *Cathy's conversation jumped wildly from one topic to another. |* [+ **ahead**] *The second part of the story jumps ahead to 20 years in the future.*
11 attack [T] INFORMAL to attack someone suddenly: *Somebody jumped her from an alley as she was walking home.*
12 jump all over sb to criticize or punish someone severely, especially in an unfair way: *I tried to tell her about it, but she jumped all over me.*
13 car [T] INFORMAL to JUMP-START¹ (1) a car
14 jump for joy to be extremely happy and pleased: *The unions should be jumping for joy after the deal they got.*
15 jump through hoops to do a series of things that are difficult or annoying, but that are usually necessary in order to achieve something: *They'll have to jump through a lot of hoops to prove we can trust them.*
16 jump rope to jump over a rope as you swing it over your head and under your feet, as a game or for exercise
17 jump bail to leave a town, city, or country where

J

a court of law has ordered you to stay until your TRIAL¹

SPOKEN PHRASES

18 (go) jump in the lake! used to tell someone in an impolite way to go away
19 sex [T] also **jump sb's bones** VULGAR to have sex with someone
20 be jumping to be full of activity: *The place was really jumping last night.*
21 jump to it! SPOKEN used to order someone to do something immediately

---

22 jump the tracks if a train jumps the tracks, it falls off its tracks
23 jump ship a) INFORMAL to stop doing a job, activity etc.: *Many workers will jump ship if their employers try to limit their bonus.* **b)** to leave a ship on which you are working as a sailor, without permission
24 jump in line to join a line of people by moving in front of others who were already waiting; CUT¹ (12)
25 jump a train to travel on a train, especially a train carrying goods, without paying
26 jump a claim an expression meaning "to claim someone else's land as your own," used especially in the 19th century in the U.S. —see also **a hop, skip, and a jump** (HOP² (6))

jump at sth *phr. v.* [T] to eagerly accept an opportunity to do something: *Michael jumped at the chance to teach in Barcelona.*
jump in *phr. v.* [I] to interrupt someone or suddenly join a conversation: *I was trying to talk to Connie, but Ted kept jumping in.*
jump on sb *phr. v.* [T] INFORMAL to criticize or punish someone, especially unfairly: [+ **for**] *Dad jumps on Jeff for every little mistake.*
jump out at sb *phr. v.* [T] if something jumps out at you, it is extremely easy to notice: *For me to like a picture, it has to jump out at me.*

jump² *n.* **1** [C] an act of pushing yourself suddenly up into the air using your legs: *That was his best jump of the competition.* **2** [C] an act of letting yourself drop from a place that is above the ground: *a parachute jump* **3** [C] a sudden large increase in an amount or value: [+ **in**] *a jump in real estate prices* **4 get a jump on sb/sth** INFORMAL to gain an advantage, especially by doing something earlier than usual or earlier than someone else: *I want to get a jump on my Christmas shopping.* **5** [C] a fence, gate, or wall for jumping over in a race or competition —see also HIGH JUMP, **a hop, skip, and a jump** (HOP² (6)), LONG JUMP, RUNNING JUMP, SKI JUMP

jump ball /'. ./ *n.* [C] the act of throwing the ball up in a game of basketball, so that one player from each team can try to gain control of it
jump·er /'dʒʌmpɚ/ *n.* [C] **1** a dress without SLEEVES, usually worn over a shirt **2** a person or animal that jumps **3** a JUMP SHOT
jumper ca·bles /'.. ,./ *n.* [plural] thick wires used to connect the batteries (BATTERY (1)) of two cars in order to start one that has lost power
jumping bean /'.. ,./ *n.* [C] a MEXICAN JUMPING BEAN
jumping jack /'.. ,./ *n.* [C] a jump in which you start from a standing position and then move your arms and legs out to the side
jumping-off point /,.. '. ,./ *n.* [C] a place to start from, especially at the beginning of a trip: *The tiny town is the jumping-off point for most Milford trail hikers.*
jump jet /'. ./ *n.* [C] an aircraft that can take off and land by going straight up and down
jump rope /'. ./ *n.* [C] a long piece of rope that you pass over your head and under your feet as you jump, either as a game or for exercise —**jump rope** *v.* [I]
jump seat /'. ./ *n.* [C] a small seat in a car, airplane etc. that folds down
jump shot /'. ./ *n.* [C] an action in basketball in which you throw the ball toward the basket as you jump in the air

jump-start /'. ./ *v.* [T] **1** to start a car whose BATTERY has lost power by connecting it to the battery of another car **2** to help a process or activity start or become more successful: *Congress hopes the tax cut will jump-start the economy.* —**jump start** *n.* [C]
jump·suit /'dʒʌmpsut/ *n.* [C] a single piece of clothing like a shirt attached to a pair of pants, worn especially by women
jump·y /'dʒʌmpi/ *adj.* **jumpier, jumpiest** worried, nervous, or excited, especially because you are expecting something bad to happen: *The recent violence is over, but it's left people feeling jumpy.*
junc·tion /'dʒʌŋkʃən/ *n.* [C] a place where one road, railroad track etc. joins another: *a highway junction*
junc·ture /'dʒʌŋktʃɚ/ *n.* FORMAL **1** a particular point in an activity or period of time: *At this juncture, I'd like to suggest we take a short break.* | *"We stand at a critical juncture in our history," Baker said.* **2** [C] a place where two things join: *the juncture of the Mississippi and Arkansas rivers*
June /dʒun/ *written abbreviation* **Jun.** *n.* [C,U] the sixth month of the year, between May and July: *In June, the kids are going to visit their grandmother.* | *We get paid on June 24th.* | *Tim and Debra got divorced last June.* | *I hope to move to California next June.* | *His birthday's June 21.* —see Usage Note at JANUARY
Ju·neau /'dʒunoʊ/ the capital city of the U.S. state of Alaska
June·teenth /,dʒun'tinθ/ *n.* [singular] an African-American celebration on June 19 that celebrates the time when slaves in Texas learned that they had been set free
Jung /yʊŋ/, **Carl Gus·tav** /karl 'gʊstaf/ (1875–1961) a Swiss PSYCHIATRIST who studied the importance of dreams and religion in problems of the mind, and developed the idea of the COLLECTIVE UNCONSCIOUS —**Jungian** *adj.*
jun·gle /'dʒʌŋgəl/ *n.* **1** [C,U] a thick tropical forest with many large plants growing very close together: *the Amazon jungle* **2** [singular] a situation or place in which it is difficult to become successful or get what you want, especially because a lot of people are competing with each other: *I don't see New York as some awful jungle.* **3** [singular] something that is very messy, complicated, and confusing: *a jungle of freeways and highways* —see also CONCRETE JUNGLE, **the law of the jungle** (LAW (8))
jungle gym /,.. './ *n.* [C] a large frame made of metal bars for children to climb on
Jun·ior /'dʒunyɚ/ *n.* [singular] **1** —see JR. **2** SPOKEN, HUMOROUS a name used when speaking to or about a boy or younger man, especially your son: *Where's Junior?*
junior¹ /'dʒunyɚ/ *adj.* [only before noun] younger or of a lower rank: *a junior partner* —opposite SENIOR¹
junior² *n.* **1** [C] a student in the third year of HIGH SCHOOL or college —compare FRESHMAN, SENIOR² (1), SOPHOMORE **2 be two/five/ten etc. years sb's junior** to be two, five, ten etc. years younger than someone: *She married a man seven years her junior.* **3** [C,U] also **junior miss** a range of clothing sizes for girls and young women **4** [C] someone who has a low rank in an organization or profession —see also SENIOR¹
junior col·lege /,.. '../ *n.* [C,U] a college where students take a course of study that continues for two years; COMMUNITY COLLEGE
junior high school /,.. '. ,./ also **junior high** *n.* [C,U] a school in the U.S. and Canada for students aged between 12 and 14 or 15 —compare MIDDLE SCHOOL, SENIOR HIGH SCHOOL
junior var·si·ty /,.. '.../ *n.* [C,U] JV
ju·ni·per /'dʒunəpɚ/ *n.* [C,U] a small bush that produces berries and has leaves that are green all year
junk¹ /dʒʌŋk/ *n.* **1** [U] old or unwanted objects that have no use or value: *a garage filled with junk* **2** [U] SPOKEN: see JUNK FOOD: *Don't fill yourself up with junk – dinner's in an hour.* **3** [C] a Chinese sailing boat **4** [U] SLANG a dangerous drug, especially HEROIN

junk² *v.* [T] to get rid of something because it is old or useless: *It would have been too expensive to fix the car, so we junked it.*

junk bond /'. ./ *n.* [C] a BOND that has a high risk and is often sold to pay for a TAKEOVER

junk·er /'dʒʌŋkɚ/ *n.* [C] INFORMAL an old car in bad condition

jun·ket /'dʒʌŋkɪt/ *n.* [C] INFORMAL a free trip that is paid for by government money or by a business that hopes to gain some advantage by paying for people to go on this trip —**junket** *v.* [I]

junk food /'. ./ *n.* [U] INFORMAL food that is not healthy because it contains a lot of oil or sugar

junk·ie, junky /'dʒʌŋki/ *n.* [C] SLANG **1** someone who takes dangerous drugs and is physically dependent on them **2** HUMOROUS someone who likes something so much that they seem to be dependent on it: *My dad's a TV junkie.*

junk mail /'. ./ *n.* [U] letters that advertisers send to people

junk shop /'. ./ *n.* [C] a small store that buys and sells old things

junk yard /'. ./ *n.* [C] a business that buys old cars, broken furniture etc. and sells the parts of them that can be used again, or the place where this business keeps these things —compare DUMP² (1)

Ju·no /'dʒunoʊ/ the Roman name for the goddess Hera

jun·ta /'hʊntə, 'dʒʌntə/ *n.* [C] a military government that has gained power by using force

Ju·pi·ter /'dʒupɪtɚ/ **1** the largest PLANET, fifth in order from the sun **2** the Roman name for the god Zeus

ju·rid·i·cal /dʒʊ'rɪdɪkəl/ *adj.* FORMAL relating to judges or the law

jur·is·dic·tion /ˌdʒʊrɪs'dɪkʃən/ *n.* [U] the right to use an official power to make legal decisions, or the area where this right exists: *Kansas has no jurisdiction over inspectors licensed in other states.*

ju·ris·pru·dence /ˌdʒʊrɪs'prudns/ *n.* [U] FORMAL the science or study of law

ju·rist /'dʒʊrɪst/ *n.* [C] FORMAL someone who has a very detailed knowledge of law

ju·ror /'dʒʊrɚ/ *n.* [C] a member of a jury

ju·ry /'dʒʊri/ *n. plural* **juries** [C] **1** a group of twelve people who listen to details of a case in court and decide whether someone is guilty or not: *People with criminal records may not sit on a jury* (=be part of a jury). **2** a group of people chosen to judge a competition **3 the jury is out on sth** used to say that something is still not yet certain: *The jury is still out on whether children are better off with their mother or father when their parents divorce.* —see also GRAND JURY

jury box /'.. ˌ./ *n.* [C usually singular] the place where the jury sits in a court

jury du·ty /'.. ˌ../ *n.* [U] a period of time during which you must be ready to be part of a jury if necessary

jury-rig /'.. ˌ./ *v.* **jury-rigged, jury-rigging** [T] INFORMAL to put something together quickly for temporary use, using whatever is available: *We jury-rigged a shower from water bottles.* —**jury-rigged** *adj.*

just¹ /dʒʌst/ *adv.* **1** exactly: *My brother looks just like my dad.* | *Thank you! That's just what I wanted.* | *You got the sauce just right.* **2** only: *She's not dating Zack – they're just friends.* | *He's just a kid. Don't be so hard on him.* | *Can you wait five minutes? I just have to iron this* (=it is the last thing I have to do). **3** if something has just happened, it happened only a short time ago: *I just got off the phone with Mrs. Kravitz.* | *Myra just saw him yesterday.* **4 just about** almost: *It's just about time to leave.* | *I'm just about finished.* **5 be just about to do sth** to be going to do something soon: *I was just about to say the same thing.* **6 be just doing sth** to be doing something now: *We're just sitting down to eat – can I call you later?* **7** used to emphasize a statement: *She just kept eating and eating.* | *I just can't believe it.* **8 just before/after/over etc.** only a short time before, after etc.: *I got there just before Aaron.* | *Coby's just over two months old now.* **9 just as good/strong/nice etc. (as sth)** equally as good, strong etc. as something else:

The $250 TV is just as good as the $300 one. **10 just around the corner a)** very near: *I live just around the corner.* **b)** used to say that something will happen or arrive soon: *Summer is just around the corner.* **11 just then** at exactly that moment: *Just then Mr. Struthers walked in.* **12 (only) just** if something just happens or is just possible, it does happen or is possible, but it almost did not happen or almost was not possible: *Kurt only just made it home before it started to rain.* **13 just the thing** INFORMAL exactly the right thing: *A cup of hot chocolate would be just the thing right now.*

SPOKEN PHRASES

14 used when politely asking something or telling someone to do something: *Could I just use your phone for a minute?* **15** used when firmly telling someone to do something: *Just sit down and shut up!* **16 a) just a minute/second/moment** used to ask someone to wait for a short time while you do something: *Just a minute. Let me see if he's here.* **b)** used to interrupt someone in order to ask them something, disagree with them etc.: *Just a minute, that's not what she told us.* **17** used to pause while you think what to say next or think how to describe something: *Yeah, so I just, uh, I went to the doctor.* **18 it's just that** used when explaining the reason for something, especially when someone thinks there is a different reason: *He's not ugly or anything. It's just that he's too short for me.* **19 just now** a moment ago or at the moment: *I'm not sure what show it is. I just now turned the TV on.* | *He's in the shower just now.* **20 would just as soon** if you would just as soon do something, you are saying in a polite way that you would prefer to do it: *I'd just as soon ride with you, if that's okay.* **21 it's just as well** used to say that it is lucky that something has happened in the way it did, because if it had not happened that way there might have been problems: *It's just as well Scott didn't go to the party, because Lisa was there.* **22 just because ... doesn't mean** used to say that although one thing is true, another thing is not necessarily true: *Just because you're older than me doesn't mean you can tell me what to do.* **23 just because** said when you do not want to explain your reasons for something: *"Why'd you leave so early?" "Just because."* **24 may/might just** might possibly: *I might just ask for next weekend off and take a trip.* **25 not just yet** not quite yet: *I can't leave just yet. I've still got a couple of e-mails to send.* **26 be just looking** to be looking at things in a store without intending to buy anything: *"Can I help you?" "No thanks, I'm just looking."* **27 just kidding** used to tell someone that you were not serious about something you have just said, especially when you think you may have upset them: *Oh, no, I left the tickets at home! ... Just kidding.* **28 just think/look/listen** used to tell someone to imagine, look at, or listen to the same thing that you are imagining, looking at, or listening to: *Just think – in a couple of hours we'll be home.* **29 might just as well** if you might just as well do something, it would be sensible or a good idea to do it: *I don't think they're going to show up. We might just as well leave.* **30 just the same** used to say that one fact or argument does not change a situation or your opinion: *It doesn't matter what kind of bike it is – they'll steal it just the same.* **31 just testing** said when you have made a mistake, to pretend that you only did it to see if someone would notice: *"He's from Idaho, not Iowa." "I know – just testing."* **32 just checking** used to tell someone not to be offended when you ask if they have done something yet: *"Did you remember to lock the front door?" "Of course I did." "Just checking."* **33 just so** with everything arranged very neatly: *Her house always has to be just so.* —see also **just my luck!** (LUCK¹ (10))

just² *adj.* **1** morally right and fair: *a just reward* —opposite UNJUST **2 just deserts** the punishment that other people think you deserve: *The defendant got his just deserts.* —**justly** *adv.*

USAGE NOTE: JUST

GRAMMAR: just, already, yet
In formal or written English, these words are usually used with the present perfect tense: *He's just gotten here.* | *I've already read it.* | *Have you eaten yet?* However, in speech and less formal writing, we often use these words, especially **just**, with the simple past tense: *He just got here.* | *I already read it.* | *Did you eat yet?*

s w jus·tice /'dʒʌstɪs/ *n.*
1 system of judgment [U] the system by which people are judged in courts of law and criminals are punished: *Many people no longer have confidence in the criminal justice system.*
2 fairness [U] fairness in the way people are treated: *Children have a strong sense of justice.* —opposite INJUSTICE —see also POETIC JUSTICE
3 bring sb to justice to catch someone whom you think is guilty of a crime and arrange for them to go to court: *The killers will be brought to justice.*
4 escape justice to avoid being punished for a crime: *Drug traffickers have escaped justice by bribing court workers.*
5 justice has been done/served used to say that someone has been treated fairly or has been given a punishment they deserve
6 do justice to sb/sth also **do sb/sth justice** to treat or represent someone or something in a way that is fair and shows their best qualities: *TV doesn't do the excitement of the game justice.*
7 judge [C] also **Justice** a judge in a law court
8 being right [U] the quality of being right and deserving fair treatment: *No one doubts the justice of our cause.* —see also **rough justice** (ROUGH¹ (14))

Justice of the Peace /ˌ.... '../ *abbreviation* **J.P.** *n.* [C] someone who judges less serious cases in small law courts and can perform marriage ceremonies

jus·ti·fi·a·ble /ˌdʒʌstə'faɪəbəl/ *adj.* actions, reactions, decisions etc. that are justifiable are done for good reasons: *justifiable anger* —**justifiably** *adv.*

justifiable hom·i·cide /ˌ..... '../ *n.* [U] LAW a situation in which you are not punished for killing someone, usually because you did it to defend yourself

jus·ti·fi·ca·tion /ˌdʒʌstəfə'keɪʃən/ *n.* [C,U] a good and acceptable reason for doing something: *There is no justification for holding her in jail.*

jus·ti·fied /'dʒʌstə,faɪd/ *adj.* **1** having an acceptable explanation or reason: *A few of his complaints were justified.* | [justified in doing sth] *Do you think I'm justified in refusing?* **2 right/left justified** TECHNICAL printed material that is right or left justified has a straight edge where all the words line up on the right or left of a page

jus·ti·fy /'dʒʌstə,faɪ/ *v.* **justified, justifying** [T] **1** to give an acceptable explanation for something that other people think is unreasonable: *Torcuato is a murderer, but his crime can be justified.* | [justify doing sth] *How can you justify spending so much money on shoes?* **2** to be a good and acceptable reason for something: *The issue is whether the benefits justify the costs.* **3 justify yourself (to sb)** to prove that what you are doing is reasonable: *I don't have to justify myself to you or anyone.* **4 justify the margins** to type or print TEXT so that the words form a straight line on the right and left sides of the page

jut /dʒʌt/ *v.* **jutted, jutting** [I always + adv./prep.] also **jut out** something that juts in a particular direction sticks up or out further than the other things around it: *Tall jagged rocks jutted out over the beach.*

jute /dʒut/ *n.* [U] a natural substance that is used for making rope and rough cloth

ju·ve·nile /'dʒuvənl, -,naɪl/ *adj.* **1** [only before noun] LAW relating to young people who are not yet adults: *juvenile crime* **2** silly and typical of a child rather than an adult: *a juvenile desire to shock people* —**juvenile** *n.* [C]

juvenile de·lin·quent /ˌ... .'../ *n.* [C] a child or young person who behaves in a criminal way —**juvenile delinquency** *n.* [U]

jux·ta·pose /'dʒʌkstə,poʊz, ˌdʒʌkstə'poʊz/ *v.* [T] FORMAL to put things together, especially things that are not normally together, in order to compare them or make something new: *Saladino's bedroom juxtaposes antiques with modern furniture.* —**juxtaposition** /ˌdʒʌkstəpə'zɪʃən/ *n.* [C,U]

JV *n.* [U] SPOKEN junior varsity; the younger and less experienced of two teams of sports players who represent a school or college —compare VARSITY

K

K, k /keɪ/ *plural* **K's, k's** *n*. [C] **1** the eleventh letter of the alphabet **2** INFORMAL an abbreviation of "one thousand": *a salary of $30k a year* **3** an abbreviation of KILOBYTE (=a measurement of computer information)

K2 /ˌkeɪ 'tu/ also **Mount Goodwin Austen** a mountain in the Himalayas, on the border between Kashmir and China, that is the second highest mountain in the world

K-12 /ˌkeɪ 'twelv/ *adj*. [only before noun] relating to education in schools from KINDERGARTEN through twelfth grade: *increases in funding for K-12 education*

ka·bob /kə'bɑb/ *n*. [C] small pieces of meat and vegetables cooked on a stick

ka·boom /kə'bum/ *interjection* INFORMAL used to represent the sound of an explosion: *The whole thing will probably go "Kaboom!" and we'll go flying across the room.*

ka·bu·ki /kə'buki/ *n*. [U] a traditional type of Japanese theater plays in which men wear decorated clothes and use strictly controlled movements and dances

Ka·bul /'kɑbəl, kə'bʊl/ the capital and largest city of Afghanistan

Kad·dish /'kɑdɪʃ/ *n*. [singular,U] a Jewish prayer for the dead: *say/read (the) Kaddish Fiedler says there will be no one to say Kaddish for him when he dies.*

kaf·fee·klatsch /'kɔfi,klætʃ/ *n*. [C] another spelling of COFFEE KLATCH

Kaf·ka /kɑfkə/, **Franz** /frɑnz/ (1883–1924) a Czech writer who wrote in German, known for his NOVELs and stories about ordinary people trying to deal with large organizations and strange events

Kaf·ka·esque /ˌkɑfkɑ'ɛsk/ *adj*. a Kafkaesque situation is one in which everyone seems to be against you, and which is impossible to change because society and organizations are not working in the usual or expected ways, commonly found in the writing of Franz Kafka

kaf·tan /'kæftæn/ *n*. [C] another spelling of CAFTAN

Kah·lo /'kɑloʊ/, **Fri·da** /'fridə/ (1907–1954) a Mexican PAINTER famous for her paintings of herself that express strong feelings in the style of SURREALISM

ka·hu·na /kə'hunə/ *n*. **1 the big kahuna** SPOKEN, HUMOROUS someone who has a very important powerful position **2** [C usually singular] a traditional priest or leader from Hawaii

Ka·lash·ni·kov /kə'lɑʃnɪ,kɑf/ *n*. [C] a type of RIFLE (=long gun) that can fire very quickly

kale /keɪl/ *n*. [U] a dark green vegetable with curled leaves

ka·lei·do·scope /kə'laɪdə,skoʊp/ *n*. [C] **1** a pattern, situation, or scene that is always changing and has many details or bright colors: [+ of] *a kaleidoscope of cultures* **2** a tube with mirrors and pieces of colored glass at one end, that shows colored patterns when you look into the tube and turn it

ka·lei·do·scop·ic /kə,laɪdə'skɑpɪk/ *adj*. kaleidoscopic scenes, colors, or patterns change often and quickly

ka·mi·ka·ze[1] /ˌkɑmɪ'kɑzi/ *n*. [C] **1** a pilot, especially one from Japan during World War II, who deliberately crashes his airplane on enemy camps, ships etc., knowing he will be killed **2** a strong alcoholic drink containing VODKA and LIME juice

kamikaze[2] *adj*. kamikaze pilot/criver/fighter etc. someone who deliberately takes risks and behaves dangerously, without caring about their own safety

Kam·pa·la /kɑm'pɑlə/ the capital and largest city of Uganda, on Lake Victoria

Kan·din·sky /kæn'dɪnski/, **Was·si·ly** /'vɑsɪli/ (1866–

1944) a Russian PAINTER famous for his ABSTRACT paintings

kan·ga·roo /ˌkæŋgə'ru/ *n*. *plural* **kangaroos** [C] an Australian animal that has strong back legs for jumping and carries its babies in a POUCH (=a special pocket of skin) on its stomach —see picture at MARSUPIAL

kangaroo court /'... ,./ *n*. [C] an unofficial court that punishes people unfairly

Ka·no Ei·to·ku /'kɑnoʊ 'eɪtoʊku/ (1543–1590) a Japanese PAINTER who was the best artist of the Kano family of Japanese court painters, and introduced many important new ideas into Japanese art

Kan·sas /'kænzəs/ *written abbreviation* **KS** a state in the Great Plains area of the central U.S. —**Kansan** *n., adj.*

Kansas Cit·y /ˌ.. '../ *written abbreviation* **KC** a city and port on the Mississippi River in the U.S. state of Missouri

Kant /kɑnt/, **Im·man·u·el** /ɪ'mænuəl/ (1724–1804) a German PHILOSOPHER who believed that moral decisions must be based on reason

ka·o·lin /'keɪəlɪn/ *n*. [U] a type of white clay used for making cups, plates etc., and also in medicine and beauty products

ka·put /kə'pʊt/ *adj*. [not before noun] SPOKEN broken: *All three phones were kaput.*

Ka·ra·ko·ram Range, the /ˌkærə'kɔrəm/ a system of mountain RANGEs that runs from northern Pakistan through India to southwest China and includes K2, the world's second highest mountain

kar·a·o·ke /ˌkæri'oʊki/ *n*. [U] the activity of singing to specially recorded music for fun

kar·at /'kærət/ *n*. [C] a measurement used for showing how pure gold is, on a scale from 1 to 24, which is pure gold —compare CARAT

ka·ra·te /kə'rɑti/ *n*. [U] a Japanese fighting sport, in which you use your hands and feet to hit and kick

kar·ma /'kɑrmə/ *n*. [U] **1** the force that is produced by the things you do in your life and that will influence you in the future, according to the Hindu and Buddhist religions **2** FATE: *Some might call it karma, saying that Artie had it coming.* **3** INFORMAL the feeling that you get from a person, place, or action | **good/bad karma** *The house had a lot of bad karma.* —**karmic** *adj*.

Kar·ok /kə'rɑk/ a Native American tribe from the southwestern area of the U.S.

Kas·kas·ki·a /kæs'kæskiə/ a Native American tribe from the northeastern central area of the U.S.

Kath·man·du, **Katmandu** /ˌkætmæn'du, ˌkɑtmən-/ the capital and largest city of Nepal

ka·ty·did /'keɪti,dɪd/ *n*. [C] a type of large GRASSHOPPER (=insect) that makes a noise like the sound of the words "katy did"

Kau·ai /'kaʊi/ an island in the Pacific Ocean that is part of the U.S. state of Hawaii

Kauf·man /'kɔfmən/, **George** (1889–1961) a U.S. writer of plays and MUSICALs

kay·ak[1] /'kaɪæk/ *n*. [C] a type of light boat usually for one person, that has a hole in the top for that person to sit in, and that is moved using a PADDLE

kayak[2] *v*. [I] to travel in a kayak —**kayaking** *n*. [U] —**kayaker** *n*. [C]

Ka·zakh·stan /'kæzæk,stæn, 'kɑzɑk,stɑn/ a country in central Asia, between Russia and China, which was part of the former Soviet Union, and is now an independent country —**Kazakh** *n., adj.*

Ka·zan /kə'zæn/, **E·lia** /'ilyə/ (1909–) a U.S. movie and theater DIRECTOR, who helped to start the Actors' Studio in New York City

ka·zoo /kə'zu/ *n*. [C] a simple musical instrument that you play by holding it to your lips and making sounds into it

Kb an abbreviation of KILOBYTE

K

Keats /kits/, **John** (1795–1821) a British poet and a leading figure in the Romantic movement

ke·bab /kə'bab/ *n.* [C] another spelling of KABOB —see also SHISH KEBAB

keel[1] /kil/ *n.* [C] **1** a bar along the bottom of a boat that keeps it steady in the water **2 stay/remain on an even keel** also **keep an even keel** to continue doing the things you always do or feeling the way you always feel, without any sudden changes: *The prescription drugs allow Sonia to remain on an even keel.*

keel[2] *v.*

keel over *phr. v.* [I] to fall over sideways: *Ed just keeled over on the floor.*

keel·haul /'kilhɔl/ *v.* [T] to pull someone under the keel of a ship with a rope as a punishment

keen /kin/ *adj.* **1** very interested in something or very eager to do it: *a keen interest in science* | *keen golfers* | [not be keen on sth] *Margaret wasn't keen on moving so far away.* | [keen to do sth] *Airlines will be keen to lease more aircraft in coming years.* **2** intelligent and quick to understand things: *Greg has a keen mind.* | *a keen understanding of finance* **3** a keen sense of smell, sight, or hearing etc. is an extremely good ability to smell etc.: *Dogs have a very keen sense of smell.* | *a keen eye for detail* **4 keen competition** a situation in which people compete strongly: *We won the contest in the face of keen competition.* **5** LITERARY a keen knife or blade is extremely sharp —**keenness** *n.* [U]

keen·er /'kinɚ/ *n.* [C] CANADIAN, INFORMAL someone who BROWN-NOSES

keen·ly /'kinli/ *adj.* **keenly aware/interested/felt etc.** extremely or strongly AWARE, interested etc.

S W
1 1 **keep**[1] /kip/ *v. past tense and past participle* **kept**
1 not give back [T] to have something and not give it back to the person who had it before: *Mom and Dad said we could keep the puppy.* | *You ought to keep those old coins – they might be valuable.*
2 not lose [T] to continue to have something and not lose it or get rid of it: *We decided to keep our old car instead of selling it.* | *I kept his letters for years.* | *In spite of the difficulties, Roby's kept his sense of humor.*
3 not change/move [I,linking verb] to continue to be in a particular state, condition, or place and not change or move: *We huddled around the fire to keep warm.* | *Keep still. I need to put a bandage on your finger.* | *It's best to **keep on** Kevin's **good side** (=not annoy him) if you want him to help you.* | ***Keep right*** (=stay on the right side) *as you stand on the moving walkway.*
4 make sb/sth not change or move [T] **a)** to make someone stay in a place: *Steve was kept in the hospital overnight.* **b)** to make someone or something continue being in a particular state or situation: *My job keeps me really busy.* | *It's hard to keep the house clean with three kids.* | [keep sb/sth doing sth] *You kept me waiting for more than an hour!* | *Keep the water running until it gets hot.* | *Don't keep me in suspense any longer!*
5 do sth repeatedly [T] to continue doing an activity or repeat the same action several times: [keep (on) doing sth] *I keep making the same mistake over and over.* | *Don just kept on talking like nothing happened.*
6 delay sb [T] to delay someone or stop someone from doing something: *Mac should be here by now. What's keeping him?* | *Don't let me keep you.*
7 store sth [T always + adv./prep.] to leave something in one particular place so that you can find it easily: [keep sth in/on/under etc. sth] *I keep a flashlight in the drawer in case the power goes out.*
8 keep a record/account/diary etc. to regularly write down information in a particular place: *Keep a record of the food you eat for one week.*
9 keep your promise/word etc. to do what you have promised to do: *You can rely on Kurt – he always keeps his word.*

10 keep sth quiet also **keep quiet (about sth)** to not say anything in order to avoid complaining, telling a secret, or causing problems: *My brothers knew what I was doing, but they kept it quiet.*
11 keep to yourself to live a very quiet private life and not do many things that involve other people
12 keep sb posted to continue to tell someone the most recent news about someone or something: *Keep me posted – I'd like to know of any changes.*
13 keep guard/watch to guard a place or watch around you all the time
14 fresh food [I] if food keeps, it stays fresh enough to be eaten: *Potato salad doesn't keep very well in the summertime.*
15 animals [T] to own and take care of animals: *We keep chickens and a couple of pigs.*
16 provide food/clothes etc. [T] to provide someone with money, food etc.: [keep sb in sth] *Zach's growing so fast we can hardly keep him in jeans.*
17 keep sb going to give someone the necessary hope or energy they need to continue living or doing something: *Her letters were the only things that kept me going while I was a prisoner.*
18 god [T] FORMAL to guard or protect someone: *May the Lord bless you and keep you.*
19 celebrate [T] OLD-FASHIONED to do the things that are traditionally done to celebrate something such as Christmas: *People don't keep Christmas the way they used to.*

SPOKEN PHRASES

20 keep going used to encourage someone who is doing something and to tell them to continue: *Keep going! You can break the record!*
21 keep it used to tell someone that they can keep something you have given them or lent them: *Keep it. It's a gift.*
22 keep quiet used to tell someone not to say anything or make any noise: *Keep quiet! I'm trying to hear what your brother has to say.*
23 keep away/back! used to tell someone not to go near something or to move away from something: *Keep back! He needs some air.*
24 keep down! used to tell someone to keep near the ground so they cannot be seen, shot etc.
25 keep it down used to tell someone to be quieter: *Keep it down, will you? We're trying to sleep.*
26 keep the change used when paying someone, to tell them they can keep the additional amount of money you have given them: *"That's $18." "Here's $20. Keep the change."*
27 keep your shirt/hair on! used to tell someone to be more calm, patient etc.
28 it'll keep used to say that you can tell someone something or do something later: *"I don't have time to listen now." "Don't worry, it'll keep."*

—see also **keep/lose your head** (HEAD[1] (18)), **keep house** (HOUSE[1] (5)), **keep pace (with sb/sth)** (PACE[1] (5)), **keep track of sb/sth** (TRACK[1] (1))

keep at sth/sb *phr. v.* [T] **1** to continue working hard at something: *Keep at it! You're almost done.* **2** SPOKEN to continue asking, attacking etc. someone, so that they become less determined or stop opposing you: *We kept at them and finally wore them down.*

keep away *phr. v.* [I,T **keep** sb/sth ↔ **away**] to avoid going somewhere or seeing someone, or to make someone or something do this [keep (sb/sth) away from sb/sth] *Just keep away from my daughter!* | *Mom kept us away from school for a week.* —see also KEEP-AWAY

keep back *phr. v.* **1** [T **keep** sth ↔ **back**] to not tell someone something that you know: *I couldn't live with the knowledge that I had kept something back from her.* **2** [T **keep** sb **back**] to prevent someone from being as successful as someone else: *Falletti said that fear and stereotypes have kept women back for centuries.*

keep down *phr. v.* [T] **1** [keep sth ↔ **down**] to control something in order to prevent it from increasing: *The new regulations should help keep rents down.* **2** [keep sth ↔ **down**] to succeed in keeping food in your stomach, without VOMITing: *I just couldn't keep anything down yesterday.* **3** [keep sb ↔ **down**] to prevent someone from achieving something, usually by not letting them do things other people are allowed to do: *One way plantation owners kept slaves down was by refusing them an education.*

keep from sth/sb *phr. v.* [T] **1** [keep sth **from** sb] to not tell someone something that you know: *You won't be able to keep the truth from Emily's father.* **2 keep (sb/sth) from doing sth** to prevent someone from doing something or prevent something from happening: *She had to cover her mouth to keep from laughing.* | *Put the pizza on the bottom rack of the oven to keep the cheese from burning.* | *The play was so boring I could hardly keep myself from falling asleep.*

keep sth ↔ **off** *phr. v.* [T] to prevent something from affecting or damaging something else: *Spray pesticide every 10 days to keep the fungus off new leaves.*

keep on *phr. v.* **1 keep on (doing sth)** to continue doing something: *They reached the edge of the woods but kept on until they found a suitable place to stay.* | *Why do you keep on calling Brad?* **2** [T keep sb ↔ on] to continue to employ someone: *They might keep me on until next summer.*

keep out *phr. v.* **1 Keep out!** used on signs to tell people to stay away from a place or not enter it **2** [T keep sth ↔ out] to prevent someone or something from getting into a place: *You ought to close the lid to keep the ants out.*

keep out of sth *phr. v.* [T] to try not to become involved in something: *You should keep out of other people's business.* | *Andy! Keep out of trouble, okay?*

keep to sth *phr. v.* [T] **1** [keep to sth] to stay on a particular road, course, piece of ground etc.: *It's best to keep to the paved roads.* **2** [keep to sth] to continue to do or use something, and not change: *Mullin kept to the same strategy through most of the game.* **3** [keep to sth] to do what you have promised or agreed to do: *Keep strictly to the terms of the contract.* **4 keep sth to yourself** to keep something secret: *I've got cancer, but I would appreciate if you would keep this to yourself.* **5 keep to the point/subject etc.** to talk or write only about the subject you are supposed to be talking about **6** [keep sth to sth] to prevent an amount, degree, or level from going higher than it should: *Can you please keep costs to a minimum?*

keep up *phr. v.*
1 stay at high level [T keep sth ↔ up] to prevent something from falling or going to a lower level: *The shortage of supplies is keeping the price up.*
2 continue [I,T keep sth ↔ up] to continue doing something, or to make something continue: *Keep up the good work!* | *It's unlikely either runner will be able to keep this quick pace up.* | [+ **with**] *Edie was finding it hard to keep up with her rent payments.*
3 move as fast [I] to move as fast as someone else: *Slow down – Davey can't keep up.* | [+ **with**] *Janir struggled to keep up with the bigger kids.*
4 learn as fast [I] to learn as fast or do as much as other people: [+ **with**] *I'm having trouble keeping up with the rest of the class.*
5 continue to read/learn [I] to continue to read and learn about a particular subject: [+ **with/on**] *I read the newspaper every morning to keep up with current events.*
6 stop from sleeping [T keep sb up] INFORMAL to prevent someone from going to sleep: *The baby kept us up all night.*
7 talk/write to friend [I] to continue to talk or write to someone, especially a friend, so that know what they are doing: [+ **with**] *How is Jody? I haven't kept up with her since college.*
8 keep your spirits/strength/morale etc. up to try to stay happy, strong, confident etc.: *We sang as we marched, to keep our spirits up.*
9 keep up appearances to pretend that everything in your life is normal and happy even though you are in trouble, especially financial trouble
10 keep up with the Joneses to try to have all the possessions that your friends or NEIGHBORS have, because you want people to think that you are as good as they are

keep² *n.* **1 for keeps** INFORMAL forever: *Marriage ought to be for keeps.* **2** [U] all the things such as food, clothing etc. that you need to keep you alive, or the cost of providing this: *It's time you got a job and started earning your keep* (=making money to help

buy your food, clothing etc.). **3** [C] a large strong tower, usually in the middle of a castle

keep-a-way /'. .,./ *n.* [U] a children's game in which you try to catch a ball that is being thrown between two other people

keep·er /'kipɚ/ *n.* [C] **1** someone who cares for or protects animals: *Demitros is the zoo's head gorilla keeper.* —see also GAMEKEEPER **2** someone whose job is to take care of a particular place or thing: *a lighthouse keeper* | [+ **of**] *The CEO could be considered the keeper of the company's assets.* —see also STORE-KEEPER **3** [usually singular] INFORMAL something you have found or caught, especially a fish, that is worth keeping: *This one's a keeper.* **4 I am not sb's keeper** SPOKEN used to say that you are not responsible for someone else's actions: *I'm not Janey's keeper.* **5 keeper of the flame** someone who considers it their duty to continue supporting an idea, belief etc. **6** a GOALKEEPER in SOCCER

keep·ing /'kipɪŋ/ *n.* [U] **1 in keeping with sth** appropriate for a particular occasion or purpose: *In keeping with tradition, everyone wore black.* —opposite **out of keeping with sth 2 in sb's keeping** being taken care of or guarded by someone —see also SAFEKEEPING

keep·sake /'kipseɪk/ *n.* [C] a small object that reminds you of someone or something

keg /kɛg/ *n.* [C] a large round container, used especially for storing beer

keg·ger /'kɛgɚ/ also **keg par·ty** /'. ,../ *n.* [C] SLANG a big party, usually outside, where beer is served from KEGS

keis·ter /'kistɚ, 'kaɪstɚ/ *n.* [C] SPOKEN your BUTTOCKS (=part of your body that you sit on): *Barry fell off his chair and landed on his keister.*

Kel·ler /'kɛlɚ/, **Hel·en** /'hɛlən/ (1880–1968) a U.S. writer known especially for the way she learned to speak and write after becoming blind and DEAF as a baby

Helen Keller

Kel·logg /'kɛlɑg, -lɔg/, **Will K.** /wɪl keɪ/ (1860–1951) a U.S. maker of CEREALS who started the Kellogg Company

Kel·ly /'kɛli/, **Gene** /dʒin/ (1912–96) a U.S. dancer, singer, actor, and DIRECTOR who appeared in many movies that were MUSICALS

kelp /kɛlp/ *n.* [U] a type of large brown SEAWEED (=plant that grows in the ocean)

kel·vin /'kɛlvɪn/ *n.* [U] a unit for measuring temperature, used in science

Kel·vin /'kɛlvɪn/, **William** (1824–1907) a British scientist who discovered the second law of THERMO-DYNAMICS and invented the Kelvin scale for measuring temperature

Kem·pis /'kɛmpɪs/, **Thom·as à** /'tɑməs ə/ (?1380–1471) a German MONK who is believed to be the writer of a book, THE IMITATION OF CHRIST, which has influenced many Christians

ken /kɛn/ *n.* **beyond your ken** OLD-FASHIONED outside your knowledge or understanding

Ken·ne·dy /'kɛnədi/, **Jack·ie** /'dʒæki/ —see ONASSIS, JACQUELINE KENNEDY

Kennedy, John Fitz·ger·ald /dʒɑn fɪtz'dʒɛrəld/ (1917–1963) the 35th President of the U.S., who was shot in Dallas, Texas in 1963 —see picture on page 1330

John Fitzgerald Kennedy

K

Kennedy, Joseph (1888–1969) a U.S. businessman and government official who was the father of President Kennedy

Kennedy, Rob·ert Fran·cis (Bob·by) /'rabət 'frænsıs, 'babi/ (1925–1968) a U.S. politician in the Democratic Party who was the brother of John F. Kennedy. He was shot in 1968, when he was trying to become elected President of the U.S.

ken·nel /'kɛnl/ n. [C] **1** a place where dogs are bred (BREED[1] (1)) or can stay while their owners are away **2** a small building with an enclosed space around it, where a dog sleeps

Ken·ny, Elizabeth (1886–1952) an Australian nurse who developed new ways of treating people with POLIO

ke·no /'kinoʊ/ n. [U] a game, played especially in CASINOS, in which you try to guess which numbers a computer will choose

Ken·tuck·y /kən'tʌki/ written abbreviation **KY** a state in the south-central U.S.

Ken·ya /'kɛnyə, 'ki-/ a country in east Africa which is south of Ethiopia and north of Tanzania —**Kenyan** n., adj.

Kenya, Mount a mountain in Kenya that is the second highest mountain in Africa

Kep·ler /'kɛplə/, **Jo·han·nes** /yoʊ'hanəs/ (1571–1630) a German ASTRONOMER who discovered how the PLANETS move around the sun

kept /kɛpt/ v. **1** the past tense and past participle of KEEP[1] **2 a kept woman** OLD-FASHIONED a woman who is given a place to live, money, and clothes by a man who visits her regularly for sex

ker·a·tin /'kɛrətɪn/ n. [U] a type of PROTEIN that exists in hair, skin, the NAILS on your fingers and toes etc.

kerb /kəb/ n. the British spelling of CURB[1] (1)

ker·chief /'kətʃɪf/ n. [C] **1** a square piece of cloth, worn especially by women in past times around their head or neck **2** OLD-FASHIONED a HANDKERCHIEF

Ke·ren·sky /kə'rɛnski/, **A·lek·san·dr** /ˌælɪg'zændə/ (1881–1970) a leader of the Russian government after the Russian Revolution, who was removed from power by the Bolsheviks

ker·nel /'kənl/ n. [C] **1** one of the small yellow parts that you eat on a COB of corn **2** the center part of a nut or seed, usually the part you can eat **3** something that forms a small but important part of a statement, idea, plan etc.: This history is too simplified, but it contains a **kernel of truth**.

ker·o·sene /'kɛrəˌsin, ˌkɛrə'sin/ n. [U] a type of oil that is burned for heat and used in lamps for lighting

Ker·ou·ac /'kɛroʊˌæk/, **Jack** /dʒæk/ (1922–1969) a U.S. writer famous as one of the 1950s BEAT GENERATION

Jack Kerouac

kes·trel /'kɛstrəl/ n. [C] a type of small FALCON

ketch /kɛtʃ/ n. [C] a small sailing ship with two MASTS (=poles)

ketch·up /'kɛtʃəp, 'kæ-/ n. [U] a thick red SAUCE made from TOMATOes, eaten with food

ket·tle /'kɛtl/ n. [C] **1** also **teakettle** a special metal pot with a handle and SPOUT, used for boiling and pouring water **2** a large pot, used especially for making soup

ket·tle·drum /'kɛtlˌdrʌm/ n. [C] a large metal drum with a round bottom, used in an ORCHESTRA —compare TIMPANI

Kev·lar /'kɛvlar/ n. [U] TRADEMARK an extremely strong material used in clothing that protects people from being shot

kew·pie doll /'kyupi ˌdal/ also **kewpie** n. [C] a type of plastic DOLL with a fat body and a curl of hair on its head

key[1] /ki/ n. plural **keys** [C] ⌗S ⌗W
1 ‖lock‖ a small specially shaped piece of metal that you put into a lock and turn in order to lock or unlock a door, start a car etc.
2 the key the part of a plan, action, etc., that everything else depends on: [+ to] Hard work is the key to success.
3 ‖machine/musical instrument‖ the part of a machine, computer, or musical instrument that you press with your fingers to make it work: Type in your PIN code, then press the ENTER key. | piano keys
4 ‖musical notes‖ a set of musical notes with a particular base note, or the quality of sound that they have: a minor key | The song is played **in the key of** G.
5 ‖map/drawing‖ the part of a map, technical drawing etc. that explains the signs or SYMBOLs on it
6 ‖test answers‖ the printed answers to a test or to the questions in a TEXTBOOK that are used to check your work
7 ‖island‖ a small flat island, especially one near the coast of Florida: the Florida Keys —see also LOW-KEY

key[2] adj. [no comparative] very important and necessary for success or to understand something: the area's key businesses | Communication is key for the newspaper team. | key points/questions/issues etc. This outline helps me remember the key points of my speech. | key mover/player etc. (=the most important person in achieving a result, change etc.) ⌗S ⌗W

key[3] v. [T] **1 key a car** to pull a key along the side of a car to SCRATCH it because you are angry at its owner **2** INFORMAL if you key a win for your team, you help your team win a game by playing better than anyone else: Rollins keyed a 98–89 victory for the Hawks. —see also KEYED UP
   key sth ↔ **in** phr. v. [T] to put information into a computer by using a KEYBOARD
   key on sth also **key in on** sth phr. v. INFORMAL to direct your energy or attention toward one particular thing: The 49ers keyed on stopping Sanders.
   key sth **to** sth phr. v. [T usually passive] if something is keyed to something else in a system or plan, a change in one thing is designed to directly affect the other: Pension adjustments are keyed to the rate of inflation (=as prices increase through inflation, pensions are also increased).

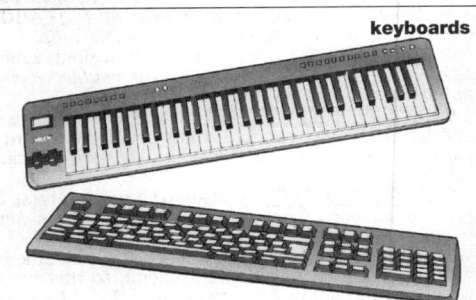

keyboards

key·board[1] /'kibɔrd/ n. [C] **1** a row or several rows of keys on a musical instrument such as a piano or a machine such as a computer: a computer keyboard —see picture on page 426 **2** an electronic musical instrument with a keyboard similar to a piano, that can sound like a piano, drums etc.

keyboard[2] v. [I] to put information into a computer using a KEYBOARD —**keyboarder** n. [C] —**keyboarding** n. [U]

key card /'. ./ n. [C] a special plastic card that you put in an electronic lock to open a door, gate etc.

key chain /'. ./ n. [C] a KEY RING with some type of decoration attached to it

keyed up /ˌ. './ adj. [not before noun] INFORMAL

worried or excited: [+ **about**] *I can tell Mike's already really keyed up about the tournament.*

key·hole /ˈkihoʊl/ *n.* [C] the hole that you put a key in to open a lock

Keynes /keɪnz/, **John May·nard** /dʒɑn ˈmeɪnard/ (1883–1946) a British ECONOMIST whose ideas greatly influenced economic thinking in the 20th century, and who believed that governments should use public money to control the level of employment —**Keynsian** *adj.*

key·note¹ /ˈkinoʊt/ *n.* [C] **1 keynote address/speech** the most important speech at an official event **2 keynote speaker** the person who gives the most important speech at an official event **3** the main point in a piece of writing, system of beliefs, activity etc., that influences everything else: [+ **of**] *Creating jobs was the keynote of Dyson's campaign.*

keynote² *v.* [T] to give a keynote speech at a ceremony, meeting etc.: *Mr. Graham is expected to keynote the conference.*

key·pad /ˈkipæd/ *n.* [C] **1** a small KEYBOARD on a piece of electronic equipment such as a CALCULATOR **2** the part of a computer KEYBOARD that has the number and command keys on it

key·punch /ˈkipʌntʃ/ *n.* [C] a machine that puts holes in special cards which are read by computers

key ring /ˈ. ./ *n.* [C] a metal ring that you keep keys on

key sig·na·ture /ˈ. ,.../ *n.* [C] a set of marks at the beginning of a line of written music to show which KEY¹ (4) it is in

key·stone /ˈkistoʊn/ *n.* [C usually singular] **1** the large central stone in an ARCH that keeps the other stones in position **2** the most important part of an idea, belief, event etc., often one that other parts depend on: [+ **of**] *A high level of production has become a keystone of economic security.*

key·stroke /ˈkistroʊk/ *n.* [C] the action of pressing a key on a TYPEWRITER or computer KEYBOARD

kg the written abbreviation of KILOGRAM

KGB *n.* **the KGB** the secret police of the former U.S.S.R.

kha·ki /ˈkæki/ *n.* [U] **1** a dull brown or green-brown color **2** strong cloth of this color, especially when worn by soldiers **3 khakis** [plural] pants made of strong cotton cloth, usually dull brown in color —**khaki** *adj.*

khan /kɑn/ *n.* [C] a ruler or official in India or central Asia, or their title

Khar·toum /kɑrˈtum/ the capital and largest city of Sudan

Khru·shchev /ˈkrustʃɔf, -tʃɛf/, **Ni·ki·ta** /nɪˈkitə/ (1894–1971) a Russian politician who was leader of the former Soviet Union from 1953 to 1964, and publicly criticized Stalin and his policies after Stalin's death in 1953

kHz the written abbreviation of KILOHERTZ

KIA *n.* [C] killed in action; a soldier who is killed in a battle

kib·ble /ˈkɪbəl/ *n.* [U] small round pieces of dry food for dogs or cats

kib·butz /kɪˈbʊts/ *n. plural* **kibbutzes** or **kibbutzim** /ˌkɪbʊtˈsim/ [C] a type of farm in Israel where many people live and work together

kib·itz /ˈkɪbɪts/ *v.* [I] INFORMAL **1** to make unhelpful remarks while someone is doing something **2** to talk in an informal way about things that are not important —**kibitzer** *n.* [C]

ki·bosh /ˈkaɪbɑʃ, kɪˈbɑʃ/ *n.* **put the kibosh on sth** INFORMAL to stop a plan, idea etc. from developing

kick¹ /kɪk/ *v.*

1 hit with your foot [T] to hit something with your foot: *Some jerk was kicking the back of my seat the entire flight.* | [**kick sth in/down/over etc.**] *The ball bounced in front of Harris, who kicked it into the goal.* | [**kick sb in the head/face/stomach etc.**] *That kid over there just kicked me in the shin!*

2 move your legs [I,T] to move your legs as if you were kicking something: *One boy lay on the floor, kicking and screaming.* | **kick your legs/feet** *Casey was waving her arms and kicking her feet in the air.*

3 kick a habit to stop doing something, such as smoking or taking drugs, that is a harmful habit: *After nearly 60 years, it's hard to **kick the habit** (=stop smoking).*

SPOKEN PHRASES

4 kick yourself said when you are annoyed with yourself because you realize that you have made a mistake or missed a chance: *I could have kicked myself for getting her name wrong.*

5 sth/sb kicks ass also **sb kicks ass at (doing) sth** VULGAR an impolite expression meaning that something is very good, or that someone is very good at doing something

6 kick (sb's) ass/butt VULGAR to punish or defeat someone: *Don't even think about it, 'cause I will kick your sorry ass.*

7 be kicking (it) to be relaxing and having a good time: *Victor and his friends were kicking it on the porch.*

8 kick sb when they are down to criticize or attack someone who is already in a weak position or having difficulties: *The newspapers cannot resist kicking a man when he is down.*

9 kick sb in the teeth/stomach/pants etc. INFORMAL to disappoint or upset someone very much, especially when they need support or hope: *Then Laura kicks me in the teeth and says she's leaving.*

10 kick sb upstairs to move someone to a job that seems to be more important than their present one, but that actually has less influence or power

11 kick the bucket HUMOROUS to die

kick around *phr. v.* INFORMAL **1** [T **kick sb ↔ around**] to treat someone badly and unfairly: *Don't let your sister kick you around like that!* **2** [T **kick sth ↔ around**] to think about something a lot or ask other people's opinions about it before making a decision: *Mom's been kicking around the idea of moving to Florida.* **3** [I,T **kick around** sth] to move around a place without having a plan of what to do or where to go: *We kicked around downtown all morning.* | *Romero has been kicking around the minor leagues for ten years.*

kick back *phr. v.* [I] INFORMAL to relax and not worry about your problems: *I'm just going to kick back and wait for the end of the semester.*

kick in *phr. v.* **1** [I] INFORMAL to begin to have an effect or come into operation: *Around noon, my cold medicine kicked in.* | *When your income reaches $85,500, the 31% tax kicks in.* **2** [I,T **kick in** sth] INFORMAL to join with others in giving money or help; CONTRIBUTE: *Our company kicked in $5000 for the school's music program.* **3 kick sb's face/head in** INFORMAL to severely hurt someone by kicking them: *If Jared says one more thing, I'm going to kick his head in.* **4** [T **kick sth ↔ in**] to kick something such as a door so hard that it breaks open: *Firemen kicked in the door and rescued three children.*

kick off *phr. v.* **1** [I] INFORMAL when a game of football kicks off, it starts: *The Jets–Lions game kicks off at 1 o'clock.* **2** [I,T **kick sth ↔ off**] INFORMAL if you kick off a meeting, event etc., or if it kicks off, it starts: *Cinco de Mayo celebrations will kick off around noon.* | *The Poetry Center kicks off its fall reading series at 8 p.m. Wednesday.* [+ **with**] *Our annual conference kicked off with a speech from the President.* **3 kick your shoes off** also **kick off your shoes** to remove your shoes by shaking them off your feet: *I slumped into the armchair and kicked off my shoes.* **4 kick sb off the team** to make someone leave a sports team **5** [I] SPOKEN to die: *It's only been about a month since Joe kicked off.*

kick sb out *phr. v.* [T] to make someone leave or dismiss them: *I can't believe that Glen's wife kicked him out.* | [+ **of**] *What did you do to get kicked out of the restaurant?*

kick up sth *phr. v.* [T] **1 kick up a fuss/controversy/debate etc.** to cause people to start complaining or arguing about something: *Mom kicked up a fuss when Dad told her how much the car cost.* **2 kick**

K

up your heels to dance with a lot of energy and enjoyment: *Women in cowgirl outfits kicked up their heels before an audience of 24,000.* **3** to make something, especially dust, go up into the air by walking or moving: *The bulldozers moved in, kicking up so much dust that you could hardly see.*

kick² *n.* [C] **1** an act of hitting something with your foot: *Just give the lawnmower a good kick and it'll start up.* **2** an act of kicking a ball in a sports game, or the ball that is kicked and the direction in which it goes: *Bahr's kick went just to the left of the goal post.* **3 a kick in the teeth/stomach/pants etc.** INFORMAL something that is very disappointing or upsetting, especially when you need support or hope: *Finding out that Roger lied to me was a real kick in the pants.* **4 a kick in the pants/butt/rear etc.** INFORMAL criticism or strong words of encouragement that make someone start doing something they should do, work faster etc.: *Somebody needs to give the staff a good, swift kick in the pants.* **5 get a kick out of sth** also **get a kick from sth** INFORMAL to enjoy doing something very much: *I get a real kick out of watching my two cats play.* **6 do sth (just) for kicks** also **get your kicks (from) doing sth** INFORMAL to do something, especially something dangerous or harmful, in order to get a feeling of excitement: *Kent blew up things just for kicks.* **7 have a kick (to it)** SPOKEN if something such as alcohol or food has a kick, it has a strong effect or taste **8 be on a health/decorating/dieting etc. kick** INFORMAL to have a strong new interest in something

Kick·a·poo /'kɪkə,pu/ a Native American tribe from the northeastern central area of the U.S.

kick-ass /'. ./ *adj.* [only before noun] VULGAR, SLANG very good, strong, or impressive: *a kick-ass sports car*

kick·back /'kɪkbæk/ *n.* [C usually plural] money that you pay someone for secretly or dishonestly helping you to make money, especially by using their political or professional influence: *The Director said that administrators at her clinic accepted kickbacks from suppliers.*

kick·ball /'kɪkbɔl/ *n.* [U] a children's game, similar to baseball, in which you kick a large rubber ball that is rolled along the ground

kick·box·ing /'kɪk,baksɪŋ/ *n.* [U] a form of BOXING in which you kick as well as hit —**kickboxer** *n.* [C]

kick·off /'kɪk-ɔf/ *n.* [C usually singular] **1** the time when a game of football starts, or the first kick in a SOCCER game: *Kickoff is at 3:00.* **2** the beginning of a new activity: *Visitors poured into Washington for the kickoff activities for the Presidential inauguration.*

kick·stand /'kɪkstænd/ *n.* [C] a metal bar that supports a bicycle or MOTORCYCLE when it is not moving, and keeps it in an upright position

kick start /'. ./ *n.* **1** [C] also **kick starter** the part of a MOTORCYCLE that you press with your foot to start it **2** [singular] something that helps a process or activity to start or develop more quickly: *The deal is likely to give the Web TV market a kick start.*

kick-start /'. ./ *v.* [T] **1** to start a MOTORCYCLE using your foot **2** to do something to help a process or activity start or develop more quickly: *Interest rates were lowered to kick-start the economy.*

kick·y /'kɪki/ *adj.* INFORMAL kicky clothes, designs, songs etc. are interesting and fun in an exciting way

kid¹ /kɪd/ *n.* **1** [C] a child: *Tell the kids next door to turn down their music.* | *Who's the kid in the blue jacket over there?* —see Usage Note at CHILD **2** [C] a son or daughter: *We have two kids in high school now.* | *Billy is Paul O'Brien's kid, isn't he?* **3** [C] a young person: *college kids* **4 kid stuff** also **kids' stuff** INFORMAL something that is very easy, boring, or not very serious: *Baseball cards aren't just kid stuff anymore – there's serious money involved.* **5** [C,U] a young goat, or the leather made from its skin —see also **the new kid on the block** (NEW (14))

kid² *v.* **kidded, kidding** INFORMAL **1** [I,T] to say something that is not true, especially as a joke: *You've got to be kidding me! What do you mean you lost the tickets?* | *"Did you really go to China?" "No, I'm just kidding."* | *"A movie there costs $15." " You're kidding, right?"* | **[kid sb about sth]** *Uncle Gene always kids me about my long hair.* **2 kid yourself** to make yourself believe something that is not true or not likely: *You're kidding yourself if you think the test's going to be easy.* **3 no kidding** SPOKEN **a)** used when you do not completely believe someone, or are surprised by what they say: *No kidding? You mean Becky's actually going to Princeton?* **b)** used to agree with what someone has said: *"Man, physics class is hard!" "No kidding!"* **4 I kid you not** SPOKEN, HUMOROUS used to emphasize that you are telling the truth —**kidder** *n.* [C] —**kidding** *n.* [U]

kid around *phr. v.* [I] to behave in a silly way: *Hey, don't get mad! I was just kidding around.*

kid³ *adj.* **1 sb's kid sister/brother** INFORMAL your sister or brother who is younger than you **2 treat/ handle someone with kid gloves** to treat someone very carefully because they easily become upset

Kidd /kɪd/, **William** (?1645–1701) a British PIRATE

kid·die¹ /'kɪdi/ *n.* [C] INFORMAL a young child

kiddie², kiddy *adj.* [only before noun] made or intended for young children: *a kiddie pool*

kid·do /'kɪdoʊ/ *n.* [C usually singular] SPOKEN said when talking to a child or friend: *Cheer up, kiddo – there'll be other games.*

kid·nap /'kɪdnæp/ *v.* **kidnapped, kidnapping** also **kidnaped, kidnaping** [T] to take someone away illegally, usually by force, and demand money for returning them: *Ten tourists were kidnapped by militants in a remote southern area.* —**kidnapper** *n.* [C]

kid·nap·ping /'kɪdnæpɪŋ/ also **kidnap** [C,U] the crime of kidnapping someone: *the recent series of kidnappings* | *a kidnap attempt*

kid·ney /'kɪdni/ *n. plural* **kidneys 1** [C] one of the two organs in your lower back that separate waste liquid from your blood and make URINE **2** [C,U] one or more of these organs from an animal, used as food

kidney bean /'.. ,./ *n.* [C] a dark red bean that has a wide curved shape slightly like the letter "C"

kidney-shaped /'.. ,./ *adj.* [usually before noun] having a wide curved shape that looks slightly like the letter "C"

kidney stone /'.. ,./ *n.* [C] a small hard piece of minerals that can form in your kidney, causing a lot of pain

kiel·ba·sa /kɪl'basə/ *n.* [U] a type of SAUSAGE originally from Poland, that is eaten hot

Kier·ke·gaard /'kɪrkə,gard/, **Sör·en Aa·bye** /'sɔən 'abi/ (1813–1855) a Danish PHILOSOPHER

Ki·ev /'kiɛv, -ɛf/ the capital city of Ukraine

Ki·ga·li /kɪ'gali/ the capital city of Rwanda

kike /kaɪk/ *n.* [C] TABOO a Jewish person. Do not use this word.

Kil·i·man·ja·ro /,kɪlɪmən'dʒaroʊ/ **Mount Kiliman·jaro** a mountain in Tanzania that is the highest mountain in Africa

kill¹ /kɪl/ *v.*

1 `make sb/sth die` [I,T] to make a person or living thing die: *Noland is accused of killing her stepfather.* | *You'll kill your plants if you water them too much.* | *Smoking kills.* | *It's such a shock; I can't believe Neil killed himself.*

2 `make sth stop/fail` [T] to make something stop or fail, or turn off the power to something: *Give me something to kill the pain* | *Quick! Kill the lights.*

3 `angry` [T] INFORMAL to be very angry with someone: *Carrie will kill me if I forget her birthday.*

4 `annoyed/sad` [T] INFORMAL to make someone feel extremely unhappy, angry etc.: *It kills her to have to be nice to Randy.*

5 kill time to do something that is not very useful or interesting while you are waiting for something to happen

6 my head/back etc. is killing me used to say that a part of your body is hurting a lot: *I can't go with you tonight. My head is killing me.*

7 it won't/wouldn't kill sb (to do something) used when saying that someone could easily do something, and ought to do it: *It wouldn't kill you to do the dishes.*

8 make sb laugh [T] to make someone laugh a lot at something: *Alan wore a dress to the party? That kills me!*

9 (even) if it kills me said when you want to show that you are determined to do something, even if it is very difficult: *I'm going to finish this even if it kills me.*

10 kill a beer/a bottle of wine etc. to drink something quickly or to finish what is left of a drink: *Let's kill these beers and go.*

11 kill yourself to do sth to work very hard to achieve something, but in a way that is likely to make you sick or very tired: *He's spent the past two years killing himself to make the business go.*

12 kill two birds with one stone to achieve two things with one action: *Deedee killed two birds with one stone, both shopping and looking for a shop of her own to rent.*

13 kill the goose that lays the golden egg to destroy the thing that brings you profit or success

14 kill sb with kindness to be too kind to someone who does not like or approve of you —see also **dressed to kill** (DRESSED (4)), **if looks could kill** (LOOK² (7))

kill sth/sb ↔ **off** *phr. v.* [T] **1** to cause the death of a lot of living things: *Some scientists think an asteroid killed off the dinosaurs.* **2** used to say that a character in a story dies: *For some reason, the main character's dog gets killed off in the first chapter.*

USAGE NOTE: KILL

WORD CHOICE: kill, murder, execute, put to death, kill yourself, commit suicide, slaughter, assassinate, massacre

Kill is the general word meaning to make someone or something die: *My uncle was killed in a plane crash.* | *A hard frost can kill young plants.* **Murder** means to kill someone deliberately and illegally: *Gerard admitted to killing his brother.* If someone is killed legally as a punishment for a crime, they are **executed** or **put to death**: *Should serial killers be executed?* | *At 10 p.m., Jones was put to death by lethal injection.* If someone **kills** himself or herself, they **commit suicide**. **Slaughter** is the technical word for killing animals for food, leather etc. but it is also used to describe the violent and unnecessary killing of a large number of people: *Thousands of people were slaughtered in the civil war.* To **assassinate** someone means to murder an important, famous, and usually powerful person for political reasons: *Who really assassinated President Kennedy?* To **massacre** means to kill large numbers of ordinary people, especially people who cannot defend themselves: *Hundreds of men, women, and children were massacred in the attack.*

---

kill² *n.* **1** [C usually singular] the act of killing a hunted animal: *Shoot only if you are confident of a kill.* **2 move/go/close in for the kill** to come nearer to something and prepare to kill, defeat, or destroy it: *Enemy submarines were moving in for the kill.* **3** [singular] an animal killed by another animal, especially for food **4** [C] the act of gaining a point by hitting the ball very hard down to the ground in VOLLEYBALL: *The winning point came on a kill by Amy Earle.*

kill·deer /ˈkɪlˌdɪr/ *n.* [C] a type of bird with two black rings across its breast

kill·er¹ /ˈkɪlɚ/ *n.* [C] **1** a person, animal, or thing that kills: *Police are still searching for the killer.* | *Heart disease is America's number one killer.* —see also SERIAL KILLER **2** something that is very difficult and tiring, or very boring: *Tracy's schedule is a real killer.* —see also LADY-KILLER

---

killer² *adj.* **1** SPOKEN very attractive or very good: *The concert was killer.* | *If you guys like garlic, this pickled garlic is killer stuff.* **2** very harmful or likely to kill you: *a killer cyclone* **3 killer instinct** a desire to succeed that is so strong that you are willing to harm other people

killer app /ˈ.. ˌ./ also **killer ap·pli·ca·tion** /ˈ.. ..ˌ../ *n.* [C] a piece of computer SOFTWARE that many people want to buy, especially one that works so well on a particular type of machine that people also want to buy the machine

killer whale

killer whale /ˈ.. ˌ./ *n.* [C] a black and white WHALE that eats meat

kill·ing /ˈkɪlɪŋ/ *n.* [C] **1** a murder: *a gang-related killing* **2 make a killing** to make a lot of money in a short time: *Alexander recalled making a killing in the stock market in the '80s.*

kill·joy /ˈkɪldʒɔɪ/ *n. plural* **killjoys** [C] someone who spoils other people's pleasure

kill switch /ˈ. ./ *n.* [C] a part of a machine or piece of electrical equipment that immediately stops the flow of electricity so that the machine stops working

kiln /kɪln/ *n.* [C] a special OVEN for baking clay pots, bricks etc.

ki·lo /ˈkiloʊ, ˈkɪ-/ *n. plural* **kilos** [C] a word meaning KILOGRAM, used especially when talking about illegal drugs: *One case in Louisiana involved the seizure of 275 kilos of cocaine.*

kilo- /ˈkɪlə/ *prefix* 1000 times a particular unit of measurement: *a kilogram* (=1000 grams)

ki·lo·byte /ˈkɪləˌbaɪt/ *abbreviation* **K** *n.* [C] a unit for measuring computer information, equal to 1024 BYTES

ki·lo·gram /ˈkɪləˌgræm/ *written abbreviation* **kg** *n.* [C] a unit for measuring weight, equal to 1000 grams

ki·lo·hertz /ˈkɪləˌhɚts/ *written abbreviation* **kHz** *n.* [C] a unit for measuring wave lengths, especially of radio signals, equal to 1000 HERTZ

ki·lom·e·ter /kɪˈlɑmətɚ, ˈkɪləˌmitɚ/ *written abbreviation* **km** *n.* [C] a unit for measuring length, equal to 1000 meters

ki·lom·e·tre /kɪˈlɑmətɚ, ˈkɪləˌmitɚ/ the British and Canadian spelling of kilometer

kil·o·ton /ˈkɪləˌtʌn/ *n.* [C] **1** a unit of weight equal to 1000 TONS **2** the force of an explosion which is equal to that of 1000 TONS of TNT

kil·o·watt /ˈkɪləˌwɑt/ *written abbreviation* **kW** *n.* [C] a unit for measuring electrical power, equal to 1000 WATTS

kil·o·watt hour /ˈ... ˌ./ *written abbreviation* **kWh** *n.* [C] a unit for measuring electrical power, equal to the amount of work produced by a KILOWATT in one hour

kilt /kɪlt/ *n.* [C] a type of wool skirt with a pattern of lines and squares on it, traditionally worn by Scottish men

kil·ter /ˈkɪltɚ/ *n.* **out of kilter** if something is out of kilter, it is not working the way it should be or not doing what it should: *The district's budget was $9 million out of kilter.* —see also OFF-KILTER

K

kim·chee, kimchi /'kɪmtʃi/ *n.* [U] a SPICY Korean food made from CABBAGE in sour-tasting liquid

ki·mo·no /kə'moʊnoʊ/ *n. plural* **kimonos** [C] **1** a traditional piece of Japanese clothing like a long coat, that is worn at special ceremonies **2** a long loose piece of clothing like a ROBE worn indoors, especially by women

kin /kɪn/ *n.* [plural] OLD-FASHIONED also **kinfolk** your family, including your grandparents, AUNTs, uncles, COUSINs etc. —see also KITH AND KIN, NEXT OF KIN

s w **kind¹** /kaɪnd/ *n.*
1 1

1 type [C] a type or sort of person or thing: *They had a few bags in the store, but they weren't the right kind.* | *corruption of the worst kind* | *Ben's not the marrying kind* (=he is unlikely to want to get married). | *[+ of] What kind of car is that?* | *Are you in some kind of trouble?* | *All kinds of people live here.* | *Disasters of this kind take everyone by surprise.* | *It's the best sports shoe of its kind.* | **be the kind (of person/man etc.) to do sth** *Martha's not the kind of woman to make quick decisions.*

SPOKEN PHRASES
---

2 kind of also **kinda a)** slightly or in some ways: *I'm kind of disappointed Grandma didn't come.* **b)** used when you are explaining something and want to avoid being exact or giving details: *I kind of borrowed the money from your wallet.*
3 a kind of (a) used to say that your description of something is not exact: *It's a kind of circular-shaped thing.*
4 something of that kind something similar to what has been mentioned: *"Did he really say that he was sorry?" "Yeah, something of that kind."*

5 nothing of the kind also **not anything of the kind** used to emphasize that something or someone is completely different from the way they have been described: *Golding denied saying anything of the kind.* | *He has been portrayed as quiet and polite, but he is nothing of the kind.*
6 group [U] people or things that are similar in some way or belong to the same group: *New immigrants tend to cling to their own kind* (=people who are like them).
7 two/three etc. of a kind two or three people or things that are of the same type: *Three of a kind* (=three playing cards with the same number on them) *beats two pairs.*
8 one of a kind the only one of a particular type of something: *This Persian carpet is one of a kind.* —see also ONE-OF-A-KIND
9 sth of a kind used to say that something is not as good as it should be: *Elections of a kind are held, but there is only one party to vote for.*
10 in kind reacting by doing the same thing as someone else has just done: *Other airlines responded in kind to United's lowering of prices.* —see also **payment in kind** (PAYMENT (4))

USAGE NOTE: KIND

WORD CHOICE: kind of, sort of
Kind of and **sort of** mean that something is uncertain or partly true (mainly before adjectives and verbs) and are used only in informal contexts: *I kind of like getting up early.* | *"Did you enjoy the movie?" "Sort of* (=not as much as I hoped)."
FORMALITY
Kind of and **sort of** are sometimes used in informal speech to make a serious statement sound weaker or amusing: *He sort of came up to me and pushed me. So I kind of hit him in the face.* Some people do not consider this to be good English.
GRAMMAR
Kind of and **sort of** are regularly used in the singular before singular and uncountable nouns: *one kind of flower/person/bread.* The plural forms **kinds of/sorts of** are used before plural nouns in more informal English: *these kinds of flowers/programs/people* (but NOT *this kind/sort of programs*, though you can more formally

---

say *programs of this kind/sort*). Remember that whether **kind** or **sort** itself is singular or plural also relates to the word used just before: *this/one/each/every kind of...* | *another kind of soft drink* | *these/ten/many/all/a few kinds of...* | *in other kinds of schools* | *toys of all sorts.* In informal speech, people do say things like: *Those kind/sort of questions are very difficult*, but some people think this is incorrect.

kind² *adj.* **1** saying or doing things that show that you care about other people and want to help them or make them happy: *That was such a kind thing to say.* | *Your great-aunt Olga was a very kind woman.* | *[+ to] It's so kind of the Olsens to let us borrow their car.*
2 would you be so kind as to do sth FORMAL used to make a polite request: *I wonder if you would be so kind as to check these figures for me.* —opposite UNKIND —see also KINDLY¹, KINDNESS and see Usage Notes at KINDLY¹ and RATHER

kind·a /'kaɪndə/ SPOKEN, NONSTANDARD a short form of "kind of": *I'm kinda tired.*

kin·der·gar·ten /'kɪndɚ‚gɑrt‾n, -‚gɑrdn/ *n.* [C,U] a school or class for young children, usually aged five to six, that prepares them for later school years —compare NURSERY SCHOOL

kin·der·gart·ner /'kɪndɚ‚gɑrt‾nɚ, -‚gɑrd-/ *n.* [C] a child who is in kindergarten

kind-heart·ed /‚. '..◂/ *adj.* kind and generous —**kind-heartedly** *adv.* —**kind-heartedness** *n.* [U]

kin·dle /'kɪndl/ *v.* **1** [T] to make something start burning **2 kindle interest/excitement etc.** to make someone interested, excited etc.: *Recent events have kindled hope for an end to the violence.* —see also REKINDLE

kin·dling /'kɪndlɪŋ/ *n.* [U] small pieces of dry wood, leaves etc. that you use for starting a fire

kind·ly¹ /'kaɪndli/ *adv.* **1** in a kind way; GENEROUSLY: *Jason kindly offered to give me a ride home.* **2 not take kindly to sth** to be annoyed or upset by something that someone does or says: *Nancy doesn't take kindly to being corrected.* **3 to put it kindly** used to say that the way you are describing something or someone may not seem very nice, but it is more favorable than the situation really is: *The scandal was caused by managers' greed and, to put it kindly, poor financial decisions.* **4 look kindly on/upon sb/ sth** to approve of someone or something: *The leaders did not look kindly on those who spoke out for freedom.* **5** SPOKEN, FORMAL a word meaning "please," which is sometimes used when you are annoyed: *Would you kindly stop kicking the back of my seat?* **6 think kindly of sb** FORMAL to remember how nice someone was: *I hope people will think kindly of me when I die.*

USAGE NOTE: KINDLY

FORMALITY
A request like **would you kindly...?** or **kindly shut the door!** is formal and polite as well as somewhat old-fashioned. In informal contexts, it sounds as though you are annoyed, so **could you please...?** is better to use since it is more commonly used.
WORD CHOICE: kindly, kind
Kindly is either the adverb of **kind**: *He kindly opened the door for me,* or an adjective with a slightly different meaning from **kind** which is much less common: *She is a kindly person.* The adjective **kindly** describes a person's general character, and is not commonly used. Use **kind** to describe a person's general character or their behavior at one particular moment: *Betsy is a kind person.* | *It was kind of you to help me.* | *She's often kind to me* (NOT *kindly*).

---

kindly² *adj.* OLD-FASHIONED kind and caring for other people: *a kindly old man* —**kindliness** *n.* [C]

kind·ness /'kaɪndnɪs/ *n.* **1** [U] kind behavior toward someone: *We were overwhelmed by the kindness of the people there.* **2** [C usually singular] FORMAL a kind action: *It would be doing him a kindness to tell him the truth.*

K

kin·dred¹ /'kɪndrɪd/ adj. [only before noun] FORMAL **1 a kindred spirit/soul** someone who thinks and feels the way you do **2** belonging to the same group or family

kindred² n. [U + with] LITERARY a family relationship; KINSHIP

ki·net·ic /kɪ'netɪk/ adj. **1** TECHNICAL relating to movement **2 kinetic art/sculpture etc.** art that has moving parts

kinetic en·er·gy /...,.. '.../ n. [U] TECHNICAL the power that something moving has, such as the power of running water

ki·net·ics /kɪ'netɪks/ n. [U] TECHNICAL the science that studies the action or force of movement

kin·folk /'kɪnfoʊk/ n. [plural] OLD-FASHIONED your KIN

king /kɪŋ/ n. [C]

1 ☐ruler a man who is the ruler of a country because he is from a royal family: [+ of] *the king of Norway* —compare QUEEN¹

2 ☐the best **a)** someone who is considered to be the most important or best member of a group: [+ of] *Elvis was widely called the king of Rock 'n' Roll.* **b)** something that is the best of its type: [+ of] *the king of luxury cars*

3 ☐chess the most important piece in CHESS

4 ☐cards a playing card with a picture of a king on it

5 be king if something is king at a particular time, it has a big influence on people: *During the middle 1800s, cotton production was king in the South.*

6 the king of the jungle a lion

7 a king's ransom a very large amount of money

8 live like a king to have a very good quality of life

9 the King of Kings a name used for Jesus Christ

King /kɪŋ/, **B.B.** /bi bi/ (1925–) a U.S. JAZZ musician and singer who plays the GUITAR

King, Bil·lie Jean /'bɪli dʒin/ (1943–) a U.S. tennis player famous for winning many women's tennis CHAMPIONSHIPS

Martin Luther King

King, Mar·tin Lu·ther /'martn 'luθər/ (1929–1968) an African-American religious leader who became the most important leader of the CIVIL RIGHTS MOVEMENT and worked hard to achieve social changes for African-Americans —see picture on page 1330

king·dom /'kɪŋdəm/ n. [C] **1** a country governed by a king or queen: *the kingdom of Jordan* **2 the kingdom of God/heaven** heaven **3 the animal/plant/mineral kingdom** one of the three parts into which the natural world is divided **4 blow sb/sth to kingdom come** INFORMAL to completely destroy someone or something **5 wait till kingdom come** INFORMAL to wait forever

king·fish·er /'kɪŋˌfɪʃər/ n. [C] a small brightly colored bird with a blue body that eats fish in rivers

king·ly /'kɪŋli/ adj. good enough for a king, or typical of a king: *a kingly sum of money*

king·mak·er /'kɪŋˌmeɪkər/ n. [C] someone who chooses people for important jobs, or who influences the choice of people for important jobs

king·pin /'kɪŋˌpɪn/ n. [C] the most important person or thing in a group: **drug/cocaine etc. kingpin** (=someone who has a lot of power related to selling illegal drugs)

Kings /kɪŋz/ **1 Kings, 2 Kings** two books in the Old Testament of the Christian Bible

king·ship /'kɪŋʃɪp/ n. [U] the official position or condition of being a king: *the responsibilities of kingship*

king-size also **king-sized** /'. ./ adj. **1** very large, and usually the largest size of something: *a king-size bed* **2** INFORMAL very big or strong: *a king-size thirst*

King·ston /'kɪŋstən/ the capital and largest city of Jamaica

Kings·town /'kɪŋztaʊn/ the capital city of St. Vincent and the Grenadines

kink¹ /kɪŋk/ n. [C] **1** a twist or uneven part in something that is normally straight or smooth: [+ in] *If there's a kink in the hose, you won't get any water.* **2** a problem or something you do not agree about: *There's only one minor kink remaining to be discussed in the contract.* **3 work/iron out the kinks** to solve all the problems in a plan, situation etc.: *A few more weeks and the play's production should have all the kinks worked out.* **4** a painful tight place in a muscle, especially in your neck or back **5** something strange or dangerous in your character

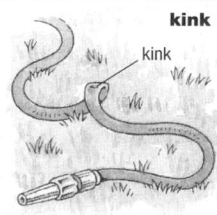

kink

kink

kink² v. [I,T] to get or give something a kink

kink·y /'kɪŋki/ adj. kinkier, kinkiest **1** INFORMAL someone who is kinky, or does kinky things, has strange ways of getting sexual excitement **2** kinky hair has a lot of tight curls —**kinkily** adv. —**kinkiness** n. [U]

Kin·sey /'kɪnzi/, **Al·fred Charles** /'ælfrɪd tʃɑrlz/ (1894–1956) a U.S. scientist who studied human sexual behavior

Kin·sha·sa /kɪn'ʃɑsə/ the capital and largest city of the Democratic Republic of Congo

kin·ship /'kɪnʃɪp/ n. **1** [U] LITERARY a family relationship: *the ties of kinship* **2** [singular,U] a strong relationship between people who are not part of the same family: [+ with/for] *We felt a strong kinship with the people of China.*

kins·man /'kɪnzmən/ n. [C] OLD USE a male relative

kins·wo·man /'kɪnzˌwʊmən/ n. [C] OLD USE a female relative

ki·osk /'kiask/ n. [C] a small building near a street where newspapers, candy etc. are sold

Ki·o·wa /'kaɪəwə, -ˌweɪ/ a Native American tribe from the southern central area of the U.S.

Kiowa A·pach·e /,... '../ a Native American group that lived as part of the Kiowa tribe but had a different language

Kip·ling /'kɪplɪŋ/, **Rud·yard** /'rʌdyərd/ (1865–1936) a British writer born in India, known for his NOVELS, poems, and short stories set in that country

kip·per /'kɪpər/ n. [C] a type of fish that has been preserved using smoke and salt

Kir·i·bati /'kɪrəˌbæs, -ˌbɑs/ a country in the Pacific Ocean consisting of 33 islands

kirsch /kɪrʃ/ n. [U] a strong alcoholic drink made from CHERRY juice

Ki·shi·nev /'kɪʃəˌnɛf, -ˌnɛv/ —see CHISINAU

kis·met /'kɪzmɛt/ n. [U] LITERARY the things that will happen to you in your life; FATE (1)

kiss¹ /kɪs/ v.

1 ☐show love/greeting [I,T] to touch someone with your lips as a greeting or to show them love: *Terry and I gazed at the stars together and kissed.* | *Will you kiss Daddy goodnight?* | *He kissed her gently on the cheek.*

2 ☐show respect [T] to touch something with your lips as a sign of respect: *Each person knelt before the Pope and kissed his ring.*

3 kiss sth goodbye INFORMAL used when you think it is certain that someone will lose their chance of getting or doing something: *After a stupid mistake like that, you can kiss your promotion goodbye.*

4 kiss (sb's) ass VULGAR, DISAPPROVING to be very nice to someone in order to get an advantage for

K

yourself: *Boyd will kiss anybody's ass if he thinks it'll get him promoted.* —see also KISS-ASS

5 kiss my ass VULGAR used to show that you do not respect someone or that you are angry with them

6 kiss sth away/better SPOKEN an expression meaning to take away the pain of something by kissing someone, used especially with children: *Here, let Mommy kiss it better.*

7 sun/rain etc. [T] LITERARY if the sun, rain etc. kisses something, it gently touches or moves it

kiss up to sb *phr. v.* [T] SPOKEN to try to please someone in order to get them to do something for you: *It makes me sick the way Chuck kisses up to the teacher.*

kiss² *n.* [C] **1** an act of kissing: *Do you remember your first kiss?* | *I leaned over and **gave** her **a kiss**.* **2 the kiss of death** HUMOROUS something that spoils or ruins a plan, activity etc.: *An "X" rating can be the kiss of death at the box office for a big-budget movie.* —see also AIR KISS, **blow sb a kiss** (BLOW¹ (19)), FRENCH KISS

kiss-and-tell /ˌ. . . '.◂/ *adj.* INFORMAL a kiss-and-tell story, book etc. is one in which someone publicly tells the secret details of a romantic or business relationship: *kiss-and-tell memoirs*

kiss-ass /'. ./ *adj.* [only before noun] VULGAR used to describe the behavior of someone who tries too hard to please other people

kiss·er /'kɪsɚ/ *n.* [C usually singular] INFORMAL your mouth: *Janice **hit** him **right in the kisser**.*

kissing cous·in /ˌ.. '../ *n.* [C] OLD-FASHIONED someone you are not closely related to, but whom you know well

kiss·off /'kɪsɔf/ *n.* [C] SLANG **give sb the kissoff** to suddenly end a romantic relationship with someone, without caring about their feelings: *Lisa gave Ed the big kissoff.*

kit /kɪt/ *n.* **1** shaving/sewing/repair etc. kit a set of tools, equipment etc. that you use for a particular purpose or activity **2** [C] something that you buy in parts and put together yourself: *a model airplane kit* **3 the whole kit and caboodle** OLD-FASHIONED everything —see also FIRST-AID KIT, TOOL KIT

kitch·en /'kɪtʃən/ *n.* [C] **1** the room where you prepare and cook food: *Jay's in the kitchen washing the dishes.* | *the kitchen table* —see picture on page 423 **2 everything but the kitchen sink** HUMOROUS a phrase meaning "everything": *Burglars broke in and took everything but the kitchen sink.*

kitch·en·ette /ˌkɪtʃə'nɛt/ *n.* [C] a small area, especially in a hotel room or office building, where you can cook food

kitch·en·ware /'kɪtʃən,wɛr/ *n.* [U] pots, pans, and other things used for cooking

kite¹ /kaɪt/ *n.* [C] **1** a toy that you fly in the air on the end of a long string, made from a light frame covered in paper or plastic **2** a type of HAWK (=bird that eats small animals) **3** INFORMAL an illegal CHECK¹ (2) —see also **go fly a kite** (FLY¹ (20)), **fly a kite** (FLY¹ (21)), **high as a kite** (HIGH¹ (13))

kite² *v.* [I,T] INFORMAL to obtain money using an illegal check —see also CHECK-KITING

kith and kin /ˌkɪθ ən 'kɪn/ *n.* [plural] OLD-FASHIONED family and friends

kitsch /kɪtʃ/ *n.* [U] **1** decorations, movies etc. that seem to be cheap and unfashionable, and often amuse people because of this: *The local stone was made into key rings and other tourist kitsch.* **2** the quality of being cheap and unfashionable, and often amusing because of this —**kitsch, kitschy** *adj.*

kit·ten /'kɪtn/ *n.* [C] a young cat —see also SEX KITTEN

kit·ten·ish /'kɪtⁿn-ɪʃ/ *adj.* OLD-FASHIONED a kittenish woman behaves in a silly way in order to attract men

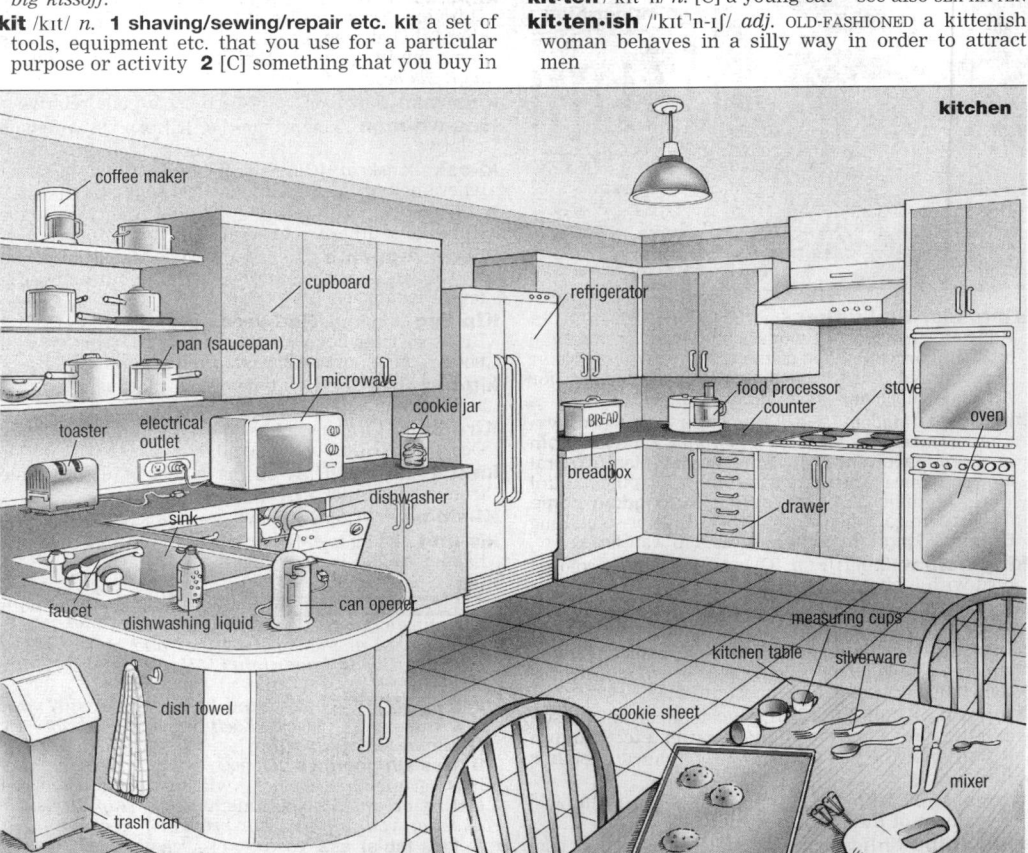

kitchen

coffee maker | cupboard | refrigerator | food processor | stove | oven | pan (saucepan) | microwave | cookie jar | toaster | electrical outlet | dishwasher | BREAD breadbox | drawer | sink | can opener | faucet | dishwashing liquid | measuring cups | kitchen table | silverware | dish towel | cookie sheet | mixer | trash can

K

kit·ty /'kɪti/ *n. plural* **kitties** [C] **1** a word for a cat, used especially by children or when calling the cat: *Here, kitty, nice kitty.* **2** [usually singular] the money that people have collected for a particular purpose: *The funds go into the kitty, to be used for special school projects.* **3** [usually singular] the money that all the players in a game of cards have BET, which is given to the winner

kitty-cor·ner /'.. ,../ *adv.* **kitty-corner from sth** on the other side of a street from a particular place, and slightly to the left or right; DIAGONALLY across from a particular place: *The drugstore is kitty-corner from the bank.*

Kitty Lit·ter, *kitty litter* /'.. ,../ *n.* [U] TRADEMARK small grains of a special substance that people put into an open container where a pet cat gets rid of its body wastes

Ki·wa·nis /kə'wɑnɪs/ an organization of business people in a town who work together to raise money for people who are poor or sick, or to help the town

ki·wi /'kiwi/ *n.* [C] **1** also **kiwi fruit** a soft green fruit with small black seeds and a thin brown skin covered in many short hairs —see picture at FRUIT¹ **2** a New Zealand bird that has very short wings and cannot fly **3 Kiwi** INFORMAL someone from New Zealand

KKK *n.* the abbreviation of Ku Klux Klan

Klam·ath /'klæməθ/ a Native American tribe from the western area of the U.S.

klans·man /'klænzmən/ *n.* [C] a member of the Ku Klux Klan

klax·on /'klæksən/ *n.* [C] a loud horn that was attached to police cars and other official vehicles in past times

Klee /kleɪ, kli/, **Paul** (1879–1940) a Swiss PAINTER famous for his ABSTRACT paintings

Kleen·ex /'klinɛks/ *n.* [C,U] TRADEMARK a paper TISSUE (1)

klep·to·ma·ni·a /,klɛptə'meɪniə/ *n.* [U] a mental illness in which you have a desire to steal things

klep·to·ma·ni·ac /,klɛptə'meɪni æk/ also **klep·to** /'klɛptoʊ/ *n.* [C] INFORMAL someone who is suffering from kleptomania

klez·mer /'klɛzmə/ *adj.* **klezmer music/band/ orchestra etc.** a type of traditional Jewish music or group that plays this music

Klimt /klɪmt/, **Gus·tav** /'gʊstɑv/ (1862–1918) an Austrian PAINTER famous for his work in the ART NOUVEAU style

Klon·dike, the /'klɑndaɪk/ an area in northwest Canada, in the Yukon, where gold was discovered in the 1890s

kluge /kludʒ/ *adj.* SLANG a kluge solution to a computer problem is not a good or intelligent solution

klutz /klʌts/ *n.* [C] INFORMAL someone who often drops things and falls easily —**klutzy** *adj.*

km *n.* the written abbreviation of KILOMETER

knack /næk/ *n.* [singular] INFORMAL a natural skill or ability that you have to do something well: [**a knack for (doing) sth**] *a knack for languages* | *Tomlin's knack for creating believable characters makes her a popular writer.* | *Keller has a knack for explaining technical concepts in an understandable way.*

knap·sack /'næpsæk/ *n.* [C] a small bag that you carry on your shoulders; BACKPACK

knave /neɪv/ *n.* [C] OLD USE a dishonest boy or man —**knavish** *adj.*

knav·er·y /'neɪvəri/ *n.* [U] OLD USE dishonest behavior

knead /nid/ *v.* [T] **1** to press DOUGH (=a mixture of flour, water, and fat for making bread etc.) many times with your hands —see picture on page 425 **2** to press, rub, and SQUEEZE something many times with your fingers or hands: *He began kneading my sore shoulder muscles.*

knee¹ /ni/ *n.* [C]
1 body part the joint that bends in the middle of your leg: *The only thing I remember from my ski lessons was "keep your knees bent."* | *Diaz's leg had to be amputated at the knee.* —see picture at BODY
2 clothes the part of your clothes that covers your knee: *Billy's jeans had holes in both knees.*

3 on sb's knee on the top part of your legs when you are sitting down: *I used to sit on Grandpa's knee and ask him read to me.*
4 at sb's knee if you learn something at someone's knee, you learn it directly from them when you are young: *I learned Polish at my mother's knee.*
5 bring sb/sth to their knees a) to defeat a country or group of people in a war **b)** to have such a bad effect on an organization, activity etc. that it cannot continue: *The recession has brought many companies to their knees.*
6 on your knees in a way that shows respect or that you are very sorry: *Eric got on his knees and asked me to marry him.*
7 drop/fall to your knees to quickly move to a position where your body is resting on your knees
8 put/take sb over your knee OLD-FASHIONED to punish a child by hitting them on their BUTTOCKS —see also **be the bee's knees** (BEE (4)), **on bended knee** (BEND¹ (6)), **knee/elbow/shoulder pad** (PAD¹ (1)), **weak at the knees** (WEAK (12))

knee² *v.* [T] to hit someone with your knee: *I kneed him in the groin.*

knee·cap /'nikæp/ *n.* [C] the bone at the front of your knee —see picture at SKELETON

knee-deep /,. '. ‹/ *adj.* **1 a)** deep enough to reach your knees **b)** in something that is deep enough to reach your knees: [+ **in**] *knee-deep in water* **2 knee-deep in sth** INFORMAL very involved in something, or greatly affected by something you cannot avoid: *We ended up knee-deep in debt.*

knee-high¹ /,. '. ‹/ *adj.* **1** tall enough to reach your knees: *knee-high grass* **2 knee-high to a grasshopper** OLD-FASHIONED used when talking about the past to say that someone was a very small child then

knee-high² *n.* [C usually plural] a sock that ends just below your knee

knee-jerk /'. ./ *adj.* [only before noun] a knee-jerk reaction, opinion etc. is what you feel or say about a situation from habit, without thinking about it

kneel /nil/ also **kneel down** *v. past tense and past participle* **knelt** also **kneeled** [I] to be in or move into a position where your body is resting on your knees: *Five members of the family **knelt in prayer** at the front of the church.*

knee-length /'. ./ *adj.* long enough to reach your knees *a knee-length skirt*

knell /nɛl/ *n.* [C] LITERARY the sound of a bell being rung slowly because someone has died —see also DEATH KNELL

knelt /nɛlt/ *v.* a past participle of kneel

knew /nu/ *v.* the past tense of KNOW¹

knick·er·bock·ers /'nɪkəˌbɑkəz/ *n.* [plural] OLD-FASHIONED knickers

knick·ers /'nɪkəz/ *n.* [plural] short loose pants that fit tightly at your knees, worn especially in past times

knick·knack /'nɪkˌnæk/ *n.* [C usually plural] a small object used as a decoration in the home

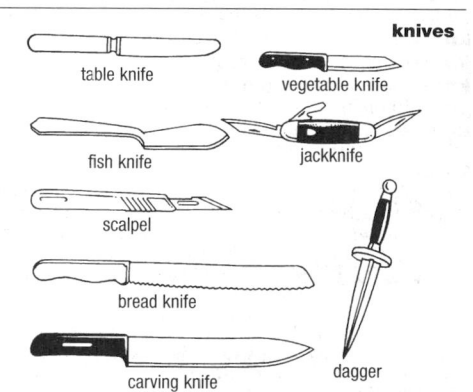

knives

table knife

vegetable knife

fish knife

jackknife

scalpel

bread knife

carving knife

dagger

K

S W
knife[1] /naɪf/ *n. plural* **knives** /naɪvz/ [C] **1** a tool used for cutting or as a weapon, consisting of a metal blade attached to a handle: *a knife and fork* | **kitchen/bread/vegetable etc. knife** (=a knife used in the kitchen, for cutting bread etc.) **2 you could cut the atmosphere/air/tension etc. with a knife** used to say that you felt the people in a room were angry with each other **3 go under the knife** HUMOROUS to have a medical operation **4 pull a knife** to take a knife out of your clothes, where it had been hidden, and threaten someone with it: [+ on] *Lyons claimed that Bessemer pulled a knife on him.* **5 twist/turn the knife** to say something that makes someone more upset about a subject they are already unhappy about

knife[2] *v.* **knifes, knifed, knifing** [T + in] to put a knife into someone's body; STAB[1] (1)

knight[1] /naɪt/ *n.* [C] **1** a European man with a high rank in past times, who was trained to fight while riding a horse —see also WHITE KNIGHT **2** the CHESS piece with a horse's head on it **3** a man who has received a knighthood and has the title "SIR (2)" before his name **4 a knight in shining armor** a brave man who saves someone from a dangerous situation

knight[2] *v.* [T usually passive] to give someone the rank of knight

knight·hood /'naɪthʊd/ *n.* [C,U] a special rank or title that is given to someone by the British king or queen

knight·ly /'naɪtli/ *adj.* LITERARY relating to being a knight or typical of a knight, especially by behaving with courage and honor

Knights of Co·lum·bus, the /ˌ. . .'../ an organization of Catholic men in a town who work together to raise money for people who are poor or sick, or to help the town

knit[1] /nɪt/ *v. past tense and past participle* **knit** or **knitted, knitting** [I,T] **1** to make clothing out of thread or YARN (=thick thread) using two KNITTING NEEDLES or a special machine: [knit sb sth] *Mom knit me a pair of socks.* —compare CROCHET **2** to join people, things, or ideas more closely, or to be closely related: [+ together] *The trade agreement will attempt to knit together three vastly different economies.* | *a closely knit family* (=a family that has a close relationship) **3 knit your brows** LITERARY to show you are worried, thinking hard etc. by moving your EYEBROWS together **4** a bone that knits after being broken grows into one piece again: [+ together] *A pin holds the bones in place while they knit together.* **5** TECHNICAL to use a PLAIN (=basic) knitting stitch —compare PURL[1] —**knitter** *n.* [C] —see also CLOSE-KNIT, LOOSE-KNIT, TIGHT-KNIT

knit[2] *adj.* [only before noun] made by knitting: *a black knit cap*

knit[3] *n.* [C] a type of cloth made by knitting, or clothing made by knitting: *a collection of bright knits*

knit·ting /'nɪtɪŋ/ *n.* [U] something that is being knitted: *Penny sat down with her knitting.*

knitting nee·dle /'.. ,../ *n.* [C] one of the two long sticks with round ends that you use to knit something

knit·wear /'nɪtˌwɛr/ *n.* [U] clothing made by knitting

knives /naɪvz/ *n.* the plural of KNIFE[1]

K

knob /nɑb/ *n.* [C] a round handle or thing that you turn to open a door, turn on a radio etc.

knob·by /'nɑbi/ *adj.* with hard parts that stick out from under the surface of something: *knobby knees*

S W
knock[1] /nɑk/ *v.*
1 door [I] to hit a door or window with your closed hand to attract the attention of the people inside: *You should knock before you come in.* | [+ at/on] *I think Al's knocking at the door.* —compare TAP[2] (1)
2 hit/make sth move [I always + adv./prep.,T] to hit someone or something with a short quick action, so that it moves, falls down etc.: [knock sth down/over etc.] *I accidentally knocked over the pitcher of water.* | [knock (sb) against/into sth] *Stewart's car knocked into a pole.* | *The man then knocked Bailey against a wall and shot him.* | *Jason*

was so mad that he **knocked a hole in** (=made a hole in) *the wall with his fist.* | *Huge boulders were knocked loose by the earthquake.*
3 hit sb hard **a) knock sb to the ground** also **knock sb on their butt/rear etc.** to hit someone so hard that they fall down: *Everyone panicked and I got knocked to the ground.* **b) knock sb unconscious/senseless/silly** to hit someone so hard that they become unconscious: *The blast from the explosion knocked him unconscious.* **c) knock the living daylights out of sb** also **knock the hell/stuffing/shit out of sb** INFORMAL to hit someone many times or very hard **d) knock the wind out of sb** to hit someone in the stomach so that they cannot breathe for a moment

SPOKEN PHRASES

4 knock it off used to tell someone to stop doing something, because it is annoying you: *You kids, knock it off in there!*
5 knock on wood an expression that is used after a statement about something good, in order to prevent your luck from becoming bad: *I haven't had a cold all winter, knock on wood.*
6 knock some sense into sb/into sb's head INFORMAL to make someone learn to behave in a more sensible way: *Maybe getting arrested will knock some sense into him.*
7 knock sb's socks off also **knock 'em dead** to surprise and please someone by doing something in a way that is very impressive: *Cierra's performance knocked my socks off!*
8 knock sb's block off to hit someone hard in the head or face: *If you touch it, I'll knock your block off!*
9 knock (sb's) heads together used to threaten punishment to people who are arguing or behaving stupidly in order to make them stop: *If you two don't stop yelling at each other, I'll knock your heads together!*

10 criticize [T] to criticize someone or their work, especially in an unfair or annoying way: *Some movie reviewers seem to knock every picture they see.* | *"I'd never eat sushi." "Hey, don't knock it till you've tried it."* (=used to tell someone not to criticize something they have not tried)
11 make a noise [I] if an engine or pipes etc. knock, they make a noise like something hard being hit, usually because something is wrong with them: *Cheap gasoline will make your engine knock.*
12 knock the bottom out of sth to make something such as a price much lower or weaker: *A recession would knock the bottom out of corporate profits.*
13 you could have knocked me over with a feather OLD-FASHIONED used to emphasize how surprised you were by something: *You could have knocked us over with a feather when we saw Brooke on stage.*

knock around *phr. v.* INFORMAL **1** [T knock around] to hit someone several times: *Maggie's ex-husband used to knock her around.* **2** [I,T knock sth ↔ around] to discuss and think about an idea, plan etc. with other people: *I've been knocking around the idea of changing jobs.* **3** [I,T knock around sth] to travel to different places, especially without doing anything very important: *Jeff spent three years just knocking around Europe.*

knock sth ↔ back *phr. v.* [T] INFORMAL to drink a large amount of alcohol very quickly: *Grace knocked back three shots of whiskey before dinner.*

knock sb/sth ↔ down *phr. v.* [T] **1** to hit or push someone so that they fall to the ground: *Mercer was knocked down by the burglar.* | *I got knocked down by the crowd at the concert.* **2** to destroy a building or part of a building: *My elementary school was knocked down so a mall could be built.* **3** INFORMAL to reduce the price of something by a large amount: *The price of the sofa was knocked down to $300.* —see also KNOCKDOWN

knock off *phr. v.* INFORMAL **1** [I] to stop working at the end of the day: *I'm going to knock off early today.* **2** [T knock sth ↔ off] to reduce the price of something by a particular amount: *We finally got the car dealer to knock a hundred dollars off the price.* **3** [T knock sth ↔ off] to produce something quickly and easily: *Could you knock off a couple of copies of the report?* **4** [T knock sb ↔ off] INFORMAL to murder someone

knock sb/sth ↔ **out** *phr. v.* [T] **1** to make someone become unconscious: *Paulina was knocked out when she smashed the car into the garage.* **2** if a team or player is knocked out of a competition, they cannot take part anymore, especially because they were defeated: [+ **of**] *Seattle's Kelly Stouffer was knocked out of the game with a strained knee.* | *The Bulls knocked Boston out of the playoffs.* —see also KNOCK-OUT¹ (3) **3** to stop the supply of electricity to an area: *Lightning knocked out power in the North Chicago area.* **4** INFORMAL to produce something easily and quickly, especially so that it is not of very good quality: *The factory can knock out 400 cars a week* **5** INFORMAL to make you feel surprised and full of admiration: *I was knocked out the first time I heard the song.* **6 knock yourself out** INFORMAL to work very hard in order to do something well, especially so that you are very tired when you finish: *This project isn't that important, so don't knock yourself out trying to get it done.*

knock over

knock sth ↔ **over** *phr. v.* [T] **1** to hit or push something so that it falls to the ground: *Who knocked over the vase?* **2** INFORMAL to rob a place such as a store or bank and threaten or attack the people who work there

knock sb ↔ **up** *phr. v.* [T usually passive] INFORMAL to make a woman PREGNANT

knock² *n.* [C] **1** the sound of something hard hitting a hard surface: *a loud knock at the door* | *a knock in the engine* **2** the action of something hard hitting your body: [+ **on**] *She got a knock on the head.* **3** a criticism of someone or something: *The only knock against Whitney is his defensive playing.* **4 take/have a knock** INFORMAL to have some bad luck or trouble: *Kathy's had a few hard knocks in her lifetime.* —see also **the school of hard knocks** (SCHOOL¹ (11))

knock·down /ˈnɑkdaʊn/ *adj.* [only before noun] a knockdown price is very cheap —see also **knock down** (KNOCK¹)

knock-down-drag-out /ˌ. . ˈ. ./ *adj.* [only before noun] a knock-down-drag-out argument or fight is an extremely angry or violent one

knock·er /ˈnɑkɚ/ *n.* **1** [C] a piece of metal on an outside door that you use to knock loudly **2 knockers** [plural] OFFENSIVE, SLANG a woman's breasts

knock-kneed /ˈ. ./ *adj.* having knees that point in slightly —compare BOW-LEGGED

knock-knock joke /ˈ. . ˌ. ./ *n.* [C] a type of joke that begins with one person saying, "Knock knock," and another person asking, "Who's there?"

knock-off /ˈnɑk-ɔf/ *n.* [C] a cheap copy of something expensive

knock·out¹ /ˈnɑk-aʊt/ *n.* [C] **1** an act of hitting your opponent in BOXING so hard that he falls down and cannot get up again **2** INFORMAL someone or something that is very attractive or exciting: *Leslie's a real knockout.* | *Sunday's concert was a knockout.* **3** a defeat in a competition, in which winning players or teams continue playing until there is only one winner

knockout² *adj.* **1 knockout pills/drops etc.** PILLS

etc. that make someone unconscious **2 a knockout punch/blow a)** a hard hit that causes someone to fall down and be unable to get up again —see also **knock out** (KNOCK¹) **b)** an action or event that causes defeat or failure: *A change in consumer tastes was the knockout blow to the retail chain.*

knoll /noʊl/ *n.* [C] a small round hill

knot¹ /nɑt/ *n.* [C]

1 **tied string** a place where two ends or pieces of rope, string etc. have been tied together, or where a rope, string etc. is tightly twisted together: *There's a knot in my shoelace.* | *Next, **tie a knot** with the two threads.* | *I can't get **this knot undone** (*=remove it).* **2** **hair a)** many hairs, threads etc. that are accidentally twisted together: *I can't get the comb through all of these knots in your hair.* **b)** a way of arranging your hair into a tight round shape at the back of your head **3** **wood** a hard round place in a piece of wood where a branch once joined the tree **4** **stomach** a tight uncomfortable feeling in your stomach etc., caused by a strong emotion such as fear or anger: *My stomach was in knots, not knowing what I would find.* | *Tara felt **a knot in her stomach** as she waited to go on stage.* **5** **muscle** a tight painful place in a muscle: [+ **in**] *a knot in my shoulder muscle* **6** **ship's speed** a measure of speed used for ships and aircraft that is about 1853 meters per hour **7** **people** a small group of people standing close together: [+ **of**] *Tathir emerged from a knot of players.* **8** **swollen skin** an area of skin that is swollen because you have hit it on something —see also GORDIAN KNOT, **tie the knot** (TIE¹ (4)), **tie yourself (up) in knots** (TIE¹ (5))

knot² *v.* **knotted, knotting 1** [T] to tie together two ends of rope, cloth, string etc. **2** [I,T] if hair or threads knot, they become twisted together **3** [I,T] if a muscle or other part of your body knots or is knotted, it feels hard and uncomfortable: *Fear and anxiety knotted her stomach.*

knot·hole /ˈnɑthoʊl/ *n.* [C] a hole in a piece of wood that is caused by a knot that fell out when the wood was cut

knot·ted /ˈnɑtɪd/ *adj.* **1** containing a lot of knots, or tied with a knot: *pieces of knotted string* **2** if a muscle or other part of your body is knotted, it feels hard and uncomfortable: *knotted shoulder muscles* **3** if the SCORE of a game is knotted, both teams or players have the same number of points: *At halftime, Iowa and Kansas were knotted at 21–21.* **4** knotted hands or fingers are twisted because of old age or too much work

knot·ty /ˈnɑti/ *adj.* **1** difficult to solve: *a knotty problem* **2** knotty wood contains a lot of knots

know¹ /noʊ/ *v.* past tense **knew** past participle **known** [not in progressive]

1 **have information** [I,T] to have information about something: *Who knows the answer?* | *Nobody knows anything about the case.* | *I asked several people where Paul was, but no one knew.* | **[know (that)]** *We didn't know that Martin was coming.* | **[know what/where/when etc.]** *Do you know when Dad will get home?* | *I don't know what I'm supposed to be doing.* | **[+ about]** *The police are trying to find out what Samantha knows about the murder.* | *Solly **knows all about** (*=has a lot of information about) *Jewish history.* | ***Let me know*** *(*=tell me) *when she gets here.* | *Mom **wants to know** (*=wants to be told) *who broke the vase.* | *Wayne snuck out of the house **without** his parents **knowing**.* | ***How did** he **know*** *(*=how did he find information about) *our names?*

2 **be certain** [I,T] to be sure about something: *"Are you going home for Christmas?" "I don't know yet."* | **[know (that)]** *I knew they wouldn't get along.* | **[know what/how/who etc.]** *Mark knew exactly what he wanted.* | **[know if/whether]** *They didn't know if they could do it.* | **[know sth/sb to be sth]** *We know this story to be true.* | *I think it starts at*

K

S W
1 1

8:00, but I don't know for sure. | *How do you know it won't happen again?*

3 be familiar with [T] to be familiar with a person, place, system etc.: *Carol doesn't know the city very well yet.* | *Ask Eric about your brakes – he knows cars.* | [**know sb from somewhere**] *We know each other from church.* | [**know sb as sth**] *I had first known Ann as a little girl.* | *Working here, you really get to know your customers* (=you become familiar with who they are, what they like etc.). | *The new laws promise to end welfare as we know it.* | *Kelly is one of the few candidates who knows the issues backward and forward* (=knows them very well).

4 realize [I,T] to realize that something exists or is true, or to understand something: [**know how/ what/ why etc.**] *She didn't know how difficult it would really be.* | *I know exactly what you mean.* | [**know (that)**] *Lennon's son, Julian, knew that going into music wouldn't be easy.* | [**+ about**] *More women need to know about this program.* | [**know to do sth**] *Will people know to return the forms?* | *Bunton knew full well* (=understood very well) *that he was breaking the law.* | *You should have known he'd forget the bread.* | *I might have known you'd do something like this.* | *I didn't say that, and you know it!* | *If I had known you were so sick, I would have asked somebody else to help.*

5 recognize [T] to be able to recognize someone or something: [**know sb by sth**] *She knew it was Gail by her voice.* | *I don't recognize the name, but I'd know him by sight* (=recognize him if I saw him).

6 skill/experience [T] to have learned a lot about something or be skillful and experienced at doing something: *I don't know anything about football.* | [**know how to do sth**] *Some of the kids don't know how to read yet.* | *She knows from experience that they won't want to hear the truth.* | *Are you sure you know what you are doing* (=have enough skill and experience to deal with something properly)? | *You listen to Aunt Kate, she knows what she's talking about.*

7 know a language to be able to speak and understand a foreign language: *I know a little Indonesian.*

8 know a song/a tune/a poem etc. to be able to sing a song, play a tune, say a poem etc. because you have learned it: *Do you know all the words to "The Star-Spangled Banner?"* | *Gabriela knew the whole piece by heart* (=had learned it and could play it from memory).

9 know your way around a) to be familiar with a place, organization, system etc. so that you can use it effectively: *Children should know how to use the appliances in a kitchen – it helps give them self-confidence.* **b)** to be familiar with a place, city etc., so that you can easily move from one place to another and know where buildings, restaurants etc. are: *Local people are hired to do the census, because they know their way around.*

10 know the way to know how to get to a place: [**+ to**] *Does she know the way to our house?*

11 know sth from sth to understand the difference between one thing and another: *I wouldn't know a French wine from a California wine.*

12 know a thing or two INFORMAL to have a lot of useful information gained from experience: *Coach Anderson knows a thing or two about winning.*

13 know better a) to be wise or experienced enough to avoid making mistakes: *Parents should know better than their children, but they don't always necessarily do.* **b)** to know or think you know more than someone else: *The man said it was an 18 carat diamond, but Dina knew better.*

14 know sth inside (and) out to know something in great detail: *Kirstie knows marketing inside out.*

15 sb knows best used to say that someone should be obeyed or that their way of doing things should be accepted because they are experienced

16 know the ropes INFORMAL to know all the things you need to know in order to do a job or deal with a system: *Nathan knows the ropes – he's been with the company for ten years.*

17 know the score INFORMAL to know the real facts of a situation, including any unfavorable ones: *Just so you know the score, Walt, Ann's going to be working with me from now on.*

18 not know what hit you INFORMAL to be so surprised or shocked by something that you cannot think clearly

19 sb has been known to do sth used to say that someone does something sometimes, especially something unusual: *She has been known to eat an entire box of cookies by herself.*

20 sb/sth is not known to be sth also **sb/sth is not known to do sth** used to say that there is no information that says that a person or animal behaves in a particular way: *This species is not known to be vicious.*

21 know your place OFTEN HUMOROUS to behave in a way that shows that you know which people are more important than you: *I'll get back to the kitchen then – I know my place!*

22 not know your own strength to not realize how strong you are

23 know no bounds FORMAL if someone's honesty, kindness etc. knows no BOUNDS, they are extremely honest, kind etc.: *Paul's love for her knew no bounds.*

24 not know sb from Adam INFORMAL to not know who someone is at all: *Why should he help me? He doesn't know me from Adam.*

25 you will be delighted/pleased/happy etc. to know that FORMAL used before you give someone information that they will be happy to hear: *You will be pleased to know that we have accepted your offer.*

SPOKEN PHRASES

26 you know a) said when you need to keep someone's attention, but cannot quickly think of what to say next: *So I, you know, spent some time cleaning up afterward.* **b)** said when you are explaining or describing something and want to give more information: *We saw Nick, you know, Melissa's husband, downtown.* **c)** said when you begin talking about a subject: *You know what I was going to do? Go over and see Barbara.* **d)** said in order to check if someone understands what you are saying: *Bob looks exactly like him, you know? Could be his son.*

27 I know a) used to agree with someone or to say that you feel the same way: *"It is really hot out there today." "I know. It's miserable."* **b)** said when you suddenly know the score, or think of the answer to a problem: *I know! Let's turn the couch this way and then the table will fit.* **c)** said to prevent someone from OBJECTing to what you say by saying the OBJECTION first: *I know, I know, we should have called and made reservations.*

28 I don't know a) used to say that you do not have the answer to a question: *"Where's the nearest restroom?" "I don't know."* **b)** used to show that you disagree slightly with what has just been said: *"I couldn't live there." "Oh, I don't know. It might not be so bad."* **c)** used when you are not sure about something, or it does not matter to you: *Oh, I don't know, we could meet at 3 or 4 o'clock.* | [**+ if/whether/ that**] *I don't know if I work that hard.*

29 you know what? a) used to introduce new information in a conversation: *You know what? George finally got a job.* **b)** used to emphasize what you are about to say: *Management is talking about layoffs again. And you know what? I don't even care.*

30 as far as I know said when you think something is true, but you are not sure: *As far as I know, those dishes have never been used.*

31 let sb know to tell someone about something: *If you need any help, just let me know.*

32 you never know used to say that you are not sure what will happen: *He might say yes. You never know.*

33 as you know used when saying something that you and your listener already know: *As you know, sales have not been good this year.*

34 you know sb/sth? used to start talking about someone or something: *You know your cousin? You'll never guess what she did!*

35 (you) know what I'm saying? INFORMAL said to check that someone has understood what you are saying. *You shouldn't try to tell other people what's good for them – know what I'm saying?*

36 (do) you know what I mean? also **if you know what I mean** used when checking that someone has understood what you are saying: *People in this town are so weird, you know what I mean?*

37 I know what you mean used to tell someone that you understand what they are talking about, because you have had the same experience yourself: *He's cute, but I know what you mean about his personality.*

38 I don't know about you, but... used to give an opinion, suggestion, or decision of your own that might be different from that of the person listening: *I don't know about you, but I'm getting tired of this band.*

39 for all I know used to emphasize that you do not know anything about a particular subject: *It cost millions. It could be billions for all I know.*

40 who knows! also **Heaven/God/goodness (only) knows! a)** used to say that you do not have any idea what an answer might be, and do not expect to know: *"What's Roger going to do once he gets there?" "Who knows?"* **b)** used to emphasize a statement: *I haven't seen her for goodness knows how long.*

41 wouldn't you know (it) used to say that something bad or funny that has happened could have been expected because you usually have bad luck, because someone usually behaves in that way etc.: *"He showed up late again." "Wouldn't you know it."*

42 you don't know used to emphasize how strong your feelings are about what you are saying: *You don't know how long I've waited to hear you say that!*

43 I don't know how to thank you/repay you FORMAL used to emphasize that you are very grateful to someone for doing something for you

44 I wouldn't know used to say that you do not know and you are not the person who should be asked: *"When's he coming back?" "I wouldn't know."*

45 how should/would I know? also **how do I know?** used to say that it is not reasonable to expect that you should know something: *How should I know where she lives? I just met her.*

46 what does sb know? used to angrily say that you do not think someone else's opinion is important or correct: *I'm not going to listen to Martha. What does she know?*

47 knowing sb... used to say that you expect someone to behave in a particular way because you know what they are like: *Knowing Michelle, she'll probably make her father pay for it.*

48 (well,) what do you know! used to express surprise: *Well, what do you know – look who's here!*

49 I've never known sb/sth to do sth used to say that you do not think someone or something has ever behaved in a particular way: *I've never known him to make any kind of trouble.*

50 know your stuff to be good at and know all you should know about a job or subject: *When it comes to math, he really knows his stuff.*

51 if you know what's good for you used to tell someone that they should do something, or you will harm them in some way: *You'll just keep your mouth shut about this if you know what's good for you!*

52 I ought to know also **I should know** used to emphasize that you know about something because you made it, experienced it etc.: *"Are you sure there's no salt in it?" "Of course. I ought to know, I made it."*

53 how did/could I know? also **how was I to know?** used to say that something is not your fault because you could not have known about it: *Don't get mad at me – how could I know the train would leave early?* —see also YOU-KNOW-WHAT, YOU-KNOW-WHO

know of sb/sth *phr. v.* **1** [T] to have been told or to have read about someone or something, but not know much about them: *I only know of him – I've never actually met him.* **2** used to ask for or give advice: *Do you know of any good restaurants in Chinatown? | I know of one or two people who could help you out with this.* **3 not that I know of** used when answering a question to say that you believe that the answer is "no," but there may be facts that you do not know about: *"Did anyone call for me?" "Not that I know of."*

USAGE NOTE: KNOW

WORD CHOICE: know, find out, hear/read about, learn, study

If you **know** a fact, person, or place, or how to speak a language, drive a car etc., you have information about it in your mind, or the skills to do it. Often you **know** something only after you have **heard** or **read about** it, or if you have **found** it **out**: *I read about the accident in the paper. | Right now they're trying to find out what happened* (NOT know). After you meet someone, you **get to know** them before you really **know** them. In formal English, you can use **learn** to mean **find out**: *We were sorry to learn that your father had died.* But **learn** usually means to make an effort to remember something you have found out or been taught, or to practice a skill, so that you then **know** it: *I'm trying to learn the names of all the students in my class* (NOT know). | *She is learning English. | I learned to drive when I was 14.* If you spend time learning about something, especially in a school, college etc. you **study** it: *I can't go out with you tonight – I have to study* (NOT learn). | *She's studying art history.*

know² *n.* **in the know** INFORMAL having more information about something than most people: *People in the know say Sikma will get the position.*

know-how /'. ./ *n.* [U] INFORMAL knowledge, practical ability, or skill to do something: *We have the know-how to prevent accidents from happening.*

know·ing /'noʊɪŋ/ *adj.* [not before noun] showing that you know all about something, even if it has not been discussed directly: *"I heard what you were saying," Maya said with a knowing smile.*

know·ing·ly /'noʊɪŋli/ *adv.* **1** deliberately: *He would never knowingly upset people.* **2** in a way that shows you know about something secret or embarrassing: *J.D. laughed softly and knowingly.*

know-it-all /'. . ,./ *n.* [C] INFORMAL, DISAPPROVING someone who behaves as if they know everything: *a twelve-year-old know-it-all*

knowl·edge /'nɑlɪdʒ/ *n.* [U] **1** the information and understanding that you have gained through learning or experience: *scientific knowledge | [+ of] She has impressed people with her knowledge of mathematics. | [+ about] American students have been accused of a lack of knowledge about geography.* **2** information that you have about a particular situation, event etc.: [+ about] *Few parents have enough knowledge about college entry requirements to help their children. | **To the best of our knowledge**, the young men are not part of a gang* (=we think this is true although we may not have all the facts). *| She opened two checking accounts in my name **without my knowledge*** (=without my knowing about it). *| "Is he planning to leave?" "**Not to my knowledge*** (=I do not think this is true, based on what I know)." *| Nelson **denied any knowledge of** the bribe. | The agency had approved the contract **with full knowledge of** its terms* (=knowing all the details about them). *We rejoiced **in the knowledge that** the hostage crisis was over* (=knowing that it was over). —see also **common knowledge** (COMMON¹ (8)), GENERAL KNOWLEDGE, **a working knowledge (of sth)** (WORKING¹ (4))

knowl·edge·a·ble /'nɑlɪdʒəbəl/ *adj.* knowing a lot: [+ about] *Mike's quite knowledgeable about jazz.* —**knowledgeably** *adv.*

known¹ /noʊn/ *v.* the past participle of KNOW¹

known² *adj.* [only before noun] **1** known about, especially by many people: *a known drug dealer | [+ to] The actress is not known to many people outside Britain.* **2 a known quantity** someone or something that you are sure will behave in the way you expect them to —see also WELL-KNOWN

Knox /nɑks/**, John** (?1505–1572) a Scottish Protestant religious leader, who started the Presbyterian religion in Scotland, and established the Church of Scotland

K

knuck·le¹ /'nʌkəl/ n. [C] **1** one of the joints in your fingers, including the ones where your fingers join your hands **2** a piece of meat around the lowest leg joint: *a knuckle of pork* **3 give sb a knuckle sandwich** SPOKEN to hit someone with your FIST —see also **a rap on/over the knuckles** (RAP¹ (7)), BRASS KNUCKLES

knuckle² v.

knuckle down *phr. v.* [I] INFORMAL to suddenly start working or studying hard: *You're going to have to knuckle down if you want to pass.*

knuckle under *phr. v.* [I] INFORMAL to accept someone's authority or orders without wanting to: [+ **to**] *She refused to knuckle under to company regulations regarding dress.*

knuckle ball /'nʌkəl,bɔl/ n. [C] a ball in baseball that is thrown so that it moves slowly and slightly up and down

knuck·le·head /'nʌkəl,hɛd/ n. [C] SPOKEN, INFORMAL a word meaning someone who has done something stupid, used when you are not angry about it: *Don't be such a knucklehead.*

KO¹ /keɪ 'oʊ, 'keɪ oʊ/ v. **KO'd, KO'ing** [T] to make someone become unconscious by hitting them: *Joe Louis KO'd Billy Conn in the eighth round.*

KO² n. the abbreviation of KNOCKOUT

ko·a·la /koʊ'ɑlə/ also **koala bear** /.'.. ,./ n. [C] an Australian animal like a small bear with no tail that climbs trees and eats leaves —see picture at MARSUPIAL

Ko·dak mo·ment /'koʊdæk ,moʊmənt/ n. [C] TRADE-MARK a special time when you want to take a photograph so that you can remember the situation later, used humorously

kohl /koʊl/ n. [U] a black pencil used to draw around women's eyes to make them more attractive

Kohl /koʊl/, **Hel·mut** /'hɛlmʊt/ (1930–) a German politician who was Chancellor of West Germany from 1982 to 1990 and was elected Chancellor of the united Germany in 1990

kook /kuk/ n. [C] INFORMAL someone who is silly or crazy: *Some kook at the post office makes you sing for your packages.* —**kooky** adj.

Ko·ran /kə'ræn, -'rɑn/ n. **1 the Koran** the holy book of the Muslims **2** [C] a copy of this book —**Koranic** adj.

Ko·re·a /kə'riə/ a country in East Asia which, in 1948, was divided into two countries, North Korea and South Korea —**Korean** n., adj.

Ko·re·an War, the /.,.. './ a war between Chinese and North Korean forces on one side and UN and South Korean forces on the other. The war began in 1950 and ended in 1953, with neither side having won.

Kor·or /'kɔrɔr/ the capital city of Palau

ko·sher /'koʊʃə/ adj. **1** kosher food is prepared according to Jewish law: *kosher meats* **2** kosher stores, restaurants, or kitchens obey Jewish food laws and sell or prepare kosher food **3 keep kosher** obey Jewish food laws **4** INFORMAL honest and legal, or socially acceptable: *This deal doesn't sound quite kosher to me.*

kosher salt /'.. ,./ n. [U] a type of salt which is in large grains and is prepared according to Jewish law

kow·tow /'kaʊtaʊ/ v. [I] to be too eager to obey or be polite to someone who has more power than you or who has something you want: [+ **to**] *Members of Congress shouldn't be kowtowing to special interest groups.*

KP n. [U] work that soldiers or children at a camp have to do in a kitchen, such as cleaning or cooking

kph the written abbreviation of "kilometers per hour"

Kra·ka·tau, Krakatoa /,krækə'toʊə/ an island in Indonesia that is an active VOLCANO

Kraut /kraʊt/ n. [C] OFFENSIVE someone from Germany —see also SAUERKRAUT

Krem·lin /'krɛmlɪn/ n. **the Kremlin 1** the government of Russia and the former U.S.S.R. **2** the buildings in Moscow where this government's offices are

krill /krɪl/ n. [U] small SHELLFISH

Kris Krin·gle, Kriss Kringle /,krɪs 'krɪŋgəl/ n. another name for SANTA CLAUS

kro·na /'kroʊnə/ n. plural **kronor** or **kronur** /-nə/ [C] the standard unit of money in Sweden and Iceland

kro·ne /'kroʊnə/ n. plural **kroner** /-nə/ [C] the standard unit of money in Denmark and Norway

Kru·ger·rand /'krugə,rænd, -,rɑnd/ n. [C] a South African gold coin

kryp·ton /'krɪptɑn/ n. [U] symbol **Kr** a gas that is an ELEMENT, found in very small quantities in the air

KS the written abbreviation of Kansas

kt the written abbreviation of KNOT¹ (1)

Kua·la Lum·pur /,kwɑlə lʊm'pʊr/ the capital and largest city of Malaysia

Ku·blai Khan /,kublə 'kɑn/ (1212–1294) a Mongol emperor from China from 1259 until his death, who moved the capital of China to Peking

Ku·brick /'kubrɪk/, **Stanley** /'stænli/ (1928–1999) a U.S. movie DIRECTOR, PRODUCER, and writer

Stanley Kubrick

ku·dos /'kudoʊs, -doʊz/ n. [U] admiration and respect that you get for being important or for doing something important: *Kudos to Ms. Peters for her hard work on tonight's program.*

kud·zu /'kʊdzu, 'kʌd-/ n. [U] a type of VINE used for animal food that grows very quickly and is common in the Southern U.S.

Ku Klux Klan /,ku klʌks 'klæn, ,klu-/ abbreviation **KKK** n. **the Ku Klux Klan** a U.S. political organization whose members are Protestant white people, and who believe that people of other races or religions should not have any power or influence in American society

kum·quat /'kʌm,kwɑt/ n. [C,U] a fruit that looks like a very small orange, or the tree on which this fruit grows

kung fu /,kʌŋ 'fu/ n. [U] an ancient Chinese fighting art in which you attack people with your hands and feet

Kun·lun Mountains /'kunlun/ also **Kunlun Shan** /'kunlun ʃɑn/ a RANGE of high mountains in western China, north of Tibet

Kurd /kəd/ n. [C] a member of a group of people that live in Iran, Iraq, Turkey etc. and speak a Kurdish language —**Kurdish** adj.

Ku·ro·sa·wa /,kʊrə'saʊə/, **A·ki·ra** /æ'kɪrə/ (1910–1998) a Japanese movie DIRECTOR

Ku·wait /kʊ'weɪt/ a country in the Middle East, north of Saudi Arabia and south of Iraq —**Kuwaiti** n., adj.

Kuwait City /.,. '../ the capital city of Kuwait

kvetch /kvɛtʃ, kfɛtʃ/ v. [I] INFORMAL to continue to complain about something: *You can either kvetch, or actually do something about it.* —**kvetch** n. [C]

kW the written abbreviation of KILOWATT

Kwa·ki·u·tl /,kwɑki'yutḷ/ a Native American tribe from western Canada

Kwan·zaa, Kwanza /'kwɑnzə/ n. [C,U] a holiday celebrated by some African-Americans between December 26 and January 1

kWh the written abbreviation of KILOWATT HOUR

KY the written abbreviation of Kentucky

K-Y also **K-Y Jel·ly** /,. . '../ n. [U] TRADEMARK a type of LUBRICANT for your body

Kyr·gy·zstan /'kɪrgɪ,stæn, -,stɑn/ a country in central Asia that is west of China and east of Uzbekistan —**Kyrgyz** /kɪr'giz/ n., adj.

K

L

L, l /ɛl/ *n. plural* **L's, l's** [C] **1** the twelfth letter of the English alphabet **2** the number 50 in the system of ROMAN NUMERALS **3** the written abbreviation of "lake"

L /ɛl/ used to warn people that a television show uses words that may offend some people

l 1 the written abbreviation of LITER **2** the written abbreviation of "line"

L1 /ɛl 'wʌn/ *n.* [C usually singular] TECHNICAL someone's first language: *In a bilingual class, parts of the lesson can be done in L1 and others in L2.*

L2 /ɛl 'tu/ *n.* [C usually singular] TECHNICAL someone's second language, or another language that they are learning

LA 1 the written abbreviation of Louisiana **2** also **L.A.** the abbreviation of Los Angeles

la /lɑ/ *n.* [singular] the sixth note in a musical SCALE, according to the SOL-FA system

lab /læb/ *n.* [C] **1** INFORMAL a LABORATORY **2** INFORMAL a Labrador

labels

label

label

label

la·bel[1] /'leɪbəl/ *n.* [C] **1** a piece of paper or other material that is attached to something and has information about that thing printed on it: *Use a liquid fertilizer, following the directions on the label.* | *Labels on clothes should be removed for kids with sensitive skin.* —compare STICKER **2** a famous name that represents a company that is selling a product, especially a record company: *The group has just produced their new album on the Warner label.* **3** a word or phrase which is used to describe a person, group, or thing, but which is often unfair or not correct: *Stacy blushes at the label "father" of the institution, but admits he likes it.*

label[2] *v.* **labeled, labeling** also **labelled, labelling** [T] **1** to attach a label to something or write information on something: *She carefully labeled each jar with its contents and the date.* | [**label sth poison/secret etc.**] *The file was labeled "Top Secret."* **2** to use a particular word or phrase to describe someone or something, often unfairly or in an incorrect way: [**label sb/sth (as) sth**] *None of the candidates wants to be labeled as "soft" on crime.*

la·bi·a /'leɪbiə/ *n.* [plural] TECHNICAL the outer folds of the female sex organ

la·bi·al /'leɪbiəl/ *adj.* **1** TECHNICAL a labial speech sound is made using one or both lips **2** FORMAL relating to the lips —**labial** *n.* [C] —see also BILABIAL

la·bor[1] /'leɪbə/ *n.* **1** [U] work, especially work using a lot of physical effort: *The repairs cost $25 for parts and $60 for labor.* | *The cleanup will take several days and a lot of **manual labor** (=physical work).* —see also HARD LABOR **2** [U] all the people who work for a company or in a country: *Much of Harkin's* support comes from organized labor. | **Labor costs** (=the amount of money you must pay workers) *are increasing very slowly all over the country.* | *a shortage of **skilled labor*** | *Companies have gone around the world in search of **cheap labor*** (=people who are paid low wages). —see also LABOR FORCE **3** [singular, U] the process in which a baby is born by being pushed from its mother's body, or the period of time during which this happens: *Meg was **in labor** for 18 hours.* | *Doreen **went into labor** at 5:30.* | *The **labor pains** were incredible.* **4 a labor of love** something that is hard work but that you do because you want to very much **5 sb's labors** FORMAL a period of hard work: *Their labors produced a fabulous evening of entertainment.*

labor[2] *v.* [I] **1** to work very hard, especially with your hands: [**labor to do sth**] *Workers were laboring to fix the three-foot hole in the boat.* **2** to work at doing something that is difficult: [**+ over**] *Mozart labored over these two works during the last weeks of his life.* **3 labor under a delusion/misconception/misapprehension etc.** to believe something that is not true **4** if a car, train, engine, person etc. labors, they work or move slowly and with difficulty: *The train shook as it labored up the steep hill.*

lab·o·ra·to·ry /'læbrə,tɔri/ *n. plural* **laboratories** [C] a special room or building in which scientists do tests and RESEARCH: *a research laboratory* | *The facility uses animals in laboratory tests for some of its drugs.* —see also LANGUAGE LABORATORY

labor camp /'.. ,./ *n.* [C] a prison camp where prisoners have to do hard physical work

Labor Day /'.. ,./ *n.* a public holiday in the U.S. and Canada on the first Monday in September

la·bored /'leɪbəd/ *adj.* showing signs of effort and difficulty: *the patient's labored breathing*

la·bor·er /'leɪbərə/ *n.* [C] someone whose job involves a lot of physical work: *a farm laborer*

labor force /'.. ,./ *n.* **the labor force** all the people who work for a company or in a country

labor-in·ten·sive /,.. '..</ *adj.* an industry, type of work, or product that is labor-intensive needs a lot of workers or a lot of work: *a labor-intensive industry such as cloth manufacturing* —see also CAPITAL-INTENSIVE

la·bo·ri·ous /lə'bɔriəs/ *adj.* needing to be done slowly, and with a lot of effort: *For Perry, writing is a laborious process.* —**laboriously** *adv.*

labor mar·ket /'.. ,./ *n.* [C] the combination of the workers available and the jobs available in one place at one time: *Minorities make up a large part of the labor market in the city.*

labor move·ment /'.. ,./ *n.* **the labor movement** the organizations, political parties etc. that represent working people

labor re·la·tions /'.. ,../ *n.* [plural] the relationship between employers and workers

labor-sav·ing /'.. ,./ *adj.* [only before noun] **labor-saving device/gadget etc.** something that makes it easier for you to do a particular job

labor u·nion /'.. ,./ *n.* [C] an organization that represents the ordinary workers in a particular trade or profession, especially in meetings with employers

la·bour /'leɪbə/ the British and Canadian spelling of LABOR

Lab·ra·dor /'læbrə,dɔr/ also **labrador re·triev·er** /,... '../ *n.* [C] a large dog with fairly short black or yellow hair, often used in hunting wild animals and birds, or for guiding blind people

lab·y·rinth /'læbə,rɪnθ/ *n.* [C] **1** a large network of paths or passages that cross each other, making it very difficult to find your way; MAZE (4): [**+ of**] *a labyrinth of underground tunnels* **2** something that is very complicated and difficult to understand: *a bureaucratic labyrinth* —**labyrinthine** /,læbə'rɪnθən, -'rɪnθaɪn/ *adj.*

lace[1] /leɪs/ *n.* **1** [U] a type of fine cloth made with

L

patterns of very small holes: *a lace wedding veil* —see also LACY **2** [C usually plural] a string that is pulled through special holes in shoes or clothing and tied, in order to pull the edges together and fasten them —see also SHOELACE

lace² v. [T] **1** also **lace up** to pull something together or fasten something by tying a lace: *Dave laced up his running shoes and ran off.* **2** to pass a string or lace through holes in something such as a pair of shoes **3** to add a small amount of something such as alcohol, a SPICE, a drug, or poison to a drink or food: **[lace sth with sth]** *A woman was poisoned with a soft drink laced with rat poison.* | *hot chocolate laced with cinnamon* **4** **be laced with sth** if a book, lesson, speech etc. is laced with something, it has a lot of a particular quality all through it: *Their conversations are laced with swearing.* **5** to weave or twist something together: *Hannah laced her fingers together.*

lac·er·ate /ˈlæsəˌreɪt/ v. [T] to badly cut or tear the skin or flesh: *The rope lacerated his forehead and scalp.*

lac·er·a·tion /ˌlæsəˈreɪʃən/ n. [C,U] TECHNICAL a serious cut in your skin or flesh: **[+ to]** *multiple lacerations to the upper arms*

lace-up /ˈ. ./ adj. lace-up shoes are fastened with LACES —**lace-up** n. [C usually plural]

lace·work /ˈleɪswɜːk/ n. [U] **1** something that is made out of lace **2** something that forms a complicated pattern: *the delicate lacework of feathers*

lach·ry·mal /ˈlækrəməl/ adj. TECHNICAL relating to tears: *lachrymal glands*

lach·ry·mose /ˈlækrəˌmoʊs/ adj. FORMAL **1** often crying **2** making you feel sad: *a lachrymose drama*

S W **lack**¹ /læk/ n. [singular,U] **1** the state of not having 2 something, or of not having enough of it: **[+ of]** *a lack of affordable housing* | *Robbery charges were dropped for lack of evidence* (=because there was not enough). | **a total/complete/distinct etc. lack of sth** *a total lack of interest* | *There's no lack of holiday spirit around the high school* (=there is a lot of it). **2** **for lack of a better word/phrase/term etc.** SPOKEN said when you are using a word or expression that you do not think is completely appropriate: *City employees will receive training in – for lack of a better term – customer relations.*

S W **lack**² v. **1** [T] to not have something, or to not have 2 enough of it: *Kevin lacks a willingness to try new things.* **2** **not lack for sth** to have a lot of something: *The resistance movement will not lack for funds.*

lack·a·dai·si·cal /ˌlækəˈdeɪzɪkəl/ adj. not showing enough interest in something or not putting enough effort into it: *a lackadaisical approach to security*

lack·ey /ˈlæki/ n. plural **lackeys** [C] someone who, like a servant, always does what someone else wants them to

lack·ing /ˈlækɪŋ/ adj. [not before noun] **1** not having enough of a particular quality, skill etc.: *Porter said his golf game is definitely lacking.* | **[+ in]** *She certainly is not lacking in determination.* **2** not existing or available: *Financial backing for the project is still lacking.*

lack·lus·ter /ˈlækˌlʌstə/ adj. not very exciting, impressive etc.; DULL: *lackluster economic growth* | *The food was okay, but the service was lackluster.*

la·con·ic /ləˈkɑnɪk/ adj. FORMAL tending to use only a few words when you talk

lac·quer¹ /ˈlækə/ n. [U] a clear liquid painted onto metal or wood to form a hard shiny surface

lacquer² v. [T] to cover something with lacquer: *black lacquered chopsticks*

la·crosse /ləˈkrɔs/ n. [U] a game played on a field by two teams of ten players, in which each player has a long stick with a net on the end of it and uses this to throw, catch, and carry a small ball

lac·tate /ˈlækteɪt/ v. [I] TECHNICAL if a woman or animal lactates, milk is produced in her breasts or comes out of her breasts —**lactation** /lækˈteɪʃən/ n. [U]

lac·tic /ˈlæktɪk/ adj. TECHNICAL relating to milk

lactic ac·id /ˌ.. ˈ../ n. [U] an acid produced by muscles after exercising or found in sour milk, wine, and some other foods

lac·tose /ˈlæktoʊs/ n. [U] a type of sugar found in milk

la·cu·na /ləˈkunə/ n. plural **lacunae** /-ni/ or **lacunas** [C] FORMAL an empty space where something is missing, especially in a piece of writing

lac·y /ˈleɪsi/ adj. **lacier, laciest** made of LACE¹ (1), or looking like LACE: *lacy underwear* | *trees with lacy leaves*

lad /læd/ n. [C] OLD-FASHIONED a boy or young man —compare LASS

lad·der /ˈlædə/ n. [C] **1** a piece of equipment used for S W climbing up to high places, consisting of two long 3 pieces of wood, metal, or rope, joined to each other by RUNGs (=steps)—see also ROPE LADDER, STEPLADDER **2** a series of activities or jobs you have to do in order to gradually become more powerful or important: *Stevens worked his way to the top of the corporate ladder.*

lad·en /ˈleɪdn/ adj. **1** LITERARY heavily loaded with something, or containing a lot of something: *the copper-laden earth* (=soil that has a lot of copper in it) | **[+ with]** *cakes and pastries laden with cream and chocolate* **2** **laden with troubles/emotion etc.** having a lot of a particular quality, thing etc.: *For both nations, rice farming is laden with historical and cultural meaning.* —see also -LADEN

-laden /leɪdn/ [in adjectives] **debt-laden/detail-laden/value-laden etc.** having a lot of a particular quality, thing etc.: *a debt-laden publishing company*

la-di-da¹, **lah-di-dah** /ˌlɑ di ˈdɑ / adj., adv. INFORMAL talking and behaving as if you think you are better than other people: *a la-di-da attitude*

la-di-da², **lah-di-dah** interjection INFORMAL said when you think someone else is trying to make themselves seem more important or impressive than they really are: *"I'm going to the opera tonight." "Well, la-di-da."*

ladies' man /ˈ.. ˌ./ n. [C] a man who likes to spend time with women and thinks they enjoy being with him

la·dies' room /ˈ.. ˌ./ n. [C] a women's toilet

lad·ing /ˈleɪdɪŋ/ n. [C,U] —see BILL OF LADING

la·dle¹ /ˈleɪdl/ n. [C] a large deep spoon with a long handle, used for lifting liquid out of a container: *a soup ladle* —see picture at SPOON¹

ladle² v. [T] to serve soup or other food onto plates or bowls, especially using a ladle: *Ladle the soup over rice.*

la·dy /ˈleɪdi/ n. plural **ladies** [C] S W
1 woman **a)** a word meaning a "woman," used in 1 2 order to be polite, especially when you do not know the woman: *The young lady behind the counter asked if I needed any help.* | *It was a present from a lady I worked for.* | *the International Ladies' Garment Workers Union* —see also CLEANING LADY **b)** APPROVING a woman, especially one with a strong character: *Sharon can be a tough lady to negotiate with.* **c)** SPOKEN, IMPOLITE said when talking directly to a woman you do not know, when you are angry or annoyed with her: *Hey, lady, would you mind getting out of my way?*
2 polite woman a woman who behaves in a polite and formal way: *Sheila always tries to be a lady.*
3 lady friend OFTEN HUMOROUS a woman that a man is having a romantic relationship with; GIRLFRIEND: *Henry had just come in with his new lady friend.*
4 Lady used as the title of the wife or daughter of a British NOBLEMAN or the wife of a KNIGHT¹ (1): *Lady Macbeth*
5 lady of the evening a polite expression meaning a PROSTITUTE, used to avoid saying this directly
6 the lady of the house OLD-FASHIONED the most important woman in a house, usually the mother of a family
7 lady of leisure OFTEN HUMOROUS a woman who does not work and has a lot of free time: *So you're a lady of leisure now that the kids are at school?*

la·dy·bug /'leɪdi,bʌg/ *n.* [C] a small round BEETLE (=a type of insect) that is usually red with black spots

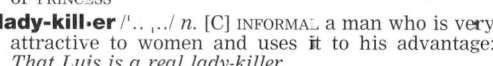

ladybug

la·dy·fin·ger /'leɪdi,fɪŋgə/ *n.* [C] a small cake shaped like a finger, used in some DESSERTS

lady-in-wait·ing /,.. . '../ *n.* [C] a woman who takes care of and serves a queen or PRINCESS

lady-kill·er /'.. ,../ *n.* [C] INFORMAL a man who is very attractive to women and uses it to his advantage: *That Luis is a real lady-killer.*

la·dy·like /'leɪdi,laɪk/ *adj.* OLD-FASHIONED behaving in the polite, quiet way that was once believed to be typical of or appropriate for women: *Jill is a ladylike child who doesn't like to play in the dirt.*

la·dy·ship /'leɪdi,ʃɪp/ *n.* your/her ladyship used as a way of speaking to or talking about a woman with the title of Lady

La·fa·yette /,lafɛɪ'ɛt/, **Mar·quis de** /mar'ki də/ (1757–1834) a French politician who supported the Americans in the American Revolutionary War and was active as a MODERATE in the French Revolution

La·fitte /lə'fit/, **Jean** /ʒɑn/ (?1780–?1826) a French PIRATE

la Fon·taine /lɑ fɑn'tɛn/, **Jean de** /ʒɑn də/ (1621–1695) a French poet

lag[1] /læg/ *v.* **lagged, lagging** [I] to move or develop more slowly than other things, people, situations etc.: *This year, private fund-raising for the museum has lagged.* | [+ behind] *Sales figures are lagging behind last year's by 40 percent.*

lag[2] *n.* [C] a delay or period of waiting between one event and a second event —see also JET LAG

la·ger /'lagə/ *n.* [U] a type of light-colored beer

lag·gard /'læg(ə)d/ *n.* [C] someone or something that is very slow or late —**laggardly** *adj.*

la·goon /lə'gun/ *n.* [C] an area of ocean that is not very deep, and that is almost completely separated from the ocean by rocks, sand, or CORAL

laid /leɪd/ *v.* the past tense and past participle of LAY

laid-back /,. '.../ *adj.* relaxed and seeming not to be worried about anything: *I think Morris is too laid-back to run the company.* | *Colorado's laid-back lifestyle*

lain /leɪn/ *v.* the past participle of LIE[1]

lair /lɛr/ *n.* [C] **1** a secret place where you can hide: *the smugglers' lair* **2** the place where a wild animal hides and sleeps

lais·sez-faire, laisser-faire /,lɛseɪ 'fɛr/ *n.* [U] **1** the principle that the government should not control or INTERFERE with businesses or the ECONOMY: *laissez-faire policies* **2** the attitude that you should not become involved in other people's personal affairs

la·i·ty /'leɪəti/ *n.* **the laity** all the members of a religious group apart from the priests

lake /leɪk/ *n.* [C] a large area of water surrounded by land: *In the summer, we go water skiing on the lake.* | *Lake Erie* —see picture on page 428

lake·bed /'leɪkbɛd/ *n.* [C] the bottom of a lake

lake·front /'leɪkfrʌnt/ *n.* [singular] the land along the edge of a lake: *lakefront property*

lake·side /'leɪksaɪd/ also **lake·shore** /'leɪkʃɔr/ *n.* [singular] the land beside a lake or the edge of a lake: *a lakeside resort*

La·lique /lɑ'lik/, **Re·né** /rə'neɪ/ (1860–1945) a French designer famous for his jewelry and glass objects in the ART NOUVEAU style

lam /læm/ *n.* **on the lam** INFORMAL escaping or hiding from someone, especially the police: *While on the lam, Benek worked as a waitress at a small diner.*

la·ma /'lɑmə/ *n.* [C] a Buddhist priest in Tibet or Mongolia

---

La·ma·ism /'lɑmə,ɪzəm/ *n.* [U] a form of the Buddhist religion common in Tibet or Mongolia

La·marck /lə'mɑrk/, **Jean** /ʒɑn/ (1744–1829) a French scientist who developed a system of ideas about EVOLUTION

La·maze /lə'mɛiz/ *n.* [U] a method of controlling pain by breathing in a special way, used by women who want to give birth to a baby without using drugs

lamb[1] /læm/ *n.* **1** [C] a young sheep **2** [U] the meat of a young sheep: *lamb stew* **3** [C] SPOKEN someone gentle and lovable, especially a child: *In spite of his bad temper, Norman can sometimes be a lamb.* **4 like a lamb** quietly and without any argument: *Suzie went off to school like a lamb today.* **5 like a lamb to the slaughter** used when someone is going to do something dangerous because they do not realize it or have no choice

lamb[2] *v.* [I] to give birth to lambs: *The ewes are lambing this week.*

lam·ba·da /lɑm'bɑdə/ *n.* [singular,U] a DISCO dance from Brazil in which two people hold each other closely and move their bodies at the same time

lam·baste, lambast /læm'beɪst, 'læmbeɪst/ *v.* [T] to attack or criticize someone very strongly, usually in public: *The organization lambasted officials for overcrowing in the prisons.*

lamb·skin /'læm,skɪn/ *n.* **1** [C,U] the skin of a lamb, with the wool still on it: *a lambskin jacket* **2** [U] leather made from the skin of lambs

lambs·wool, lamb's wool /'læmz,wʊl/ *n.* [U] very soft wool that comes from lambs: *a lambswool sweater*

la·mé /lɑ'meɪ, læ-/ *n.* [U] cloth containing gold or silver threads: *a gold lamé dress*

lame[1] /leɪm/ *adj.* **1** unable to walk well because your leg or foot is injured or weak: *a lame dog* | **go lame** (=become lame) *Filago went lame with an injury in his lower right leg.* **2** INFORMAL a lame explanation or excuse does not sound very believable: *I don't want to hear any of your lame excuses for being late.* —see also LAMELY **3** SLANG boring or not very good: *The party was lame.* —**lameness** *n.* [U]

lame[2] *v.* [T usually passive] to make a person or animal unable to walk well

lame·brain /'leɪmbreɪn/ *n.* [C] INFORMAL someone you think is stupid —**lamebrained** *adj.*

lame duck /,. '../ *n.* [C] **lame duck president/governor/legislature etc.** a president, governor, legislature etc. with no real power because their period in office will soon end

lame·ly /'leɪmli/ *adv.* if you say something lamely, you do not sound confident and other people find it difficult to believe you: *"It wasn't my responsibility,"* he lamely explained.

la·ment[1] /lə'mɛnt/ *v.* [I,T] **1** to express feelings of sadness about something: *A gathering of family and friends lamented the deaths of the two pilots.* **2** to express annoyance or disappointment about something you think is unsatisfactory or unfair: *"I can remember my first day of school," Grandpa lamented, "but I can't remember what I had for lunch."*

lament[2] *n.* [C] a song, poem, or something that you say, that expresses a feeling of sadness: *A lone piper played a lament.*

la·ment·a·ble /lə'mɛntəbəl/ *adj.* FORMAL very unsatisfactory or disappointing: *It is lamentable that Cassidy will not get to coach his team next season.* —**lamentably** *adv.*

lam·en·ta·tion /,læmən'teɪʃən/ *n.* [C,U] FORMAL deep sadness, or something that expresses it: *Buchman's lamentation about the state of American democracy is not justified.*

Lam·en·ta·tions /,læmən'teɪʃənz/ a book in the Old Testament of the Christian Bible

lame-o /'leɪm oʊ/ *n.* [C] SLANG someone who is boring and not very good at doing anything

L

lam·i·nate /ˈlæməˌneɪt, -nɪt/ *n.* [C,U] laminated material

lam·i·nat·ed /ˈlæməˌneɪtɪd/ *adj.* **1** covered with a layer of thin plastic: *a laminated ID card* **2** laminated material has several thin sheets joined on top of each other: *a laminated wood table top* —**laminate** /ˈlæməˌneɪt/ *v.* [T]

lamp /læmp/ *n.* [C] **1** an object that produces light by using electricity, oil, or gas: *a desk lamp* —see also FLOOR LAMP, SAFETY LAMP, STREETLAMP **2** a piece of electrical equipment used to provide a special type of heat, especially as a medical treatment: *an infrared lamp* —see also SUNLAMP

lamp·black /ˈlæmpˌblæk/ *n.* [U] a fine black substance made from SOOT (=the black powder made by burning something) that is used in making matches, bombs etc. and in coloring things

lamp·light /ˈlæmp-laɪt/ *n.* [U] the soft light produced by a lamp: *Check the carpet's appearance in lamplight and daylight.*

lamp·light·er /ˈlæmpˌlaɪtɚ/ *n.* [C] someone whose job was to light lamps in the street in past times

lam·poon /læmˈpun/ *v.* [T] to criticize someone such as a politician in a humorous way that makes them seem stupid or silly, in a piece of writing, a play etc.; SATIRIZE: *Trudeau regularly lampoons the president in his comic strip.* —**lampoon** *n.* [C]

lamp·post, lamp post /ˈlæmp-poʊst/ *n.* [C] a pole supporting a light over a street: *Two people were injured when the car struck a lamppost.* —see also STREETLIGHT

lam·prey /ˈlæmpri, -preɪ/ *n.* [C] a type of small fish that attaches itself to larger fish

lamp·shade /ˈlæmpʃeɪd/ *n.* [C] a cover put over a lamp to reduce or direct its light

LAN /læn, ˌɛl eɪ ˈɛn/ *n.* [C] TECHNICAL local area network; a system for communicating by computer in a large place such as an office building

lance¹ /læns/ *n.* [C] a long thin pointed weapon that was used in past times by soldiers riding on horses

lance² *v.* [T] to cut a small hole in someone's flesh with a sharp instrument to let out PUS (=yellow liquid produced by infection): *A doctor carefully lanced the boil.*

lance cor·po·ral /ˌ. ˈ...ˑ/ *n.* [C] a low rank in the Marines, or someone who has this rank

Lan·ce·lot, Sir /ˈlænsəˌlɑt/ in old European stories, the most famous of King Arthur's knights, who had a romantic relationship with Arthur's wife, Guinevere

lan·cet /ˈlænsɪt/ *n.* [C] **1** a small very sharp pointed knife with two cutting edges, used by doctors to cut flesh **2 lancet arch/window** TECHNICAL a tall narrow ARCH or window that is pointed at the top

land¹ /lænd/ *n.*

1 ground [U] ground, especially when used for farming or building: *A mall is being built on the land near the lake.* | *500 acres of land* | *high land prices*

2 not ocean [U] the solid dry part of the Earth's surface: *After 21 days at sea, we sighted land.* | *Frogs live on land and in water.* | *Rebel forces attacked the port city by land* (=they went over the land rather than using a boat or plane).

3 country [C] LITERARY a country or place: *Their journey took them to many foreign lands.* | *He had almost given up hope of returning to his native land* (=the land where he was born).

4 not city the land the countryside thought of as a place where people grow food: *The peasants live off the land* (=grow or catch the food they need) *with little left to sell for money.* | *In the U.S., about 4 percent of the population works the land* (=grows crops).

5 property [U] the area of land that someone owns: *It was our dream to have our own land to raise cattle on.*

6 land of milk and honey an imaginary place where life is easy and pleasant

7 in the land of the living SPOKEN, HUMOROUS awake, or not sick anymore

8 the land of nod OLD-FASHIONED an expression meaning "sleep," used especially when talking to children

USAGE NOTE: LAND

WORD CHOICE: earth, land, ground, floor, soil, country

The hard surface of the Earth, when it is compared with the area covered by water, is called **land** [U], but when you are comparing it with the air you say **the ground** or, on a larger scale, **(the) earth**: *After three weeks of crossing the ocean, we spotted land.* | *The horse fell to the ground.* | *The balloon landed gently on the ground.* | *Once a meteor from outer space fell to earth here.* | *The earth shook and huge cracks appeared.* Inside a building the surface you walk on is called the **floor** (but it is called **the ground** outside): *The dishes crashed to the kitchen floor.* | *We sat on the ground around the campfire.* An area thought of as property is a piece of **land** [U]: *the high price of land in Tokyo* | *He owns a lot of land in New Mexico* (NOT **earth** or **ground** or **big land**). Also, when you are talking about large areas, especially when it is used for a particular purpose, you say **land**: *The land isn't much good for growing corn.* | *Much of the land here is used for industry.* The substance that plants grow in is **soil** [U] or **dirt** [U]: *The soil here is good for growing tomatoes.* | *When I was little, I loved to play in the dirt.* Land that is not part of a town or city is **the country**: *I don't think I would be happy living in the country* (NOT *land*). You call a country a **land** [C] if you are using it in a literary way: *He visited many foreign lands* (=strange and mysterious countries). Compare: *He visited many foreign countries* (this sounds like a report of simple facts).

land² *v.*

1 airplane [I,T] if an airplane lands or if a pilot lands it, it moves down onto the ground: *Flight 846 from Cleveland landed five minutes ago.*

2 arrive by boat/plane [I always + adv./prep.] to arrive somewhere in an airplane, boat etc.: [+ on/ in/at etc.] *In 1969, the first men landed on the moon.* | *When did the Pilgrims land in America?*

3 fall/come down [I always + adv./prep.] to come down through the air and stop moving: [+ in/on/ under etc.] *A large branch landed on the hood of my car.* | *Louis fell out of the tree and landed in a holly bush.*

4 job/contract etc. [T] INFORMAL to succeed in getting a job, contract etc. that was difficult to get: *Luckily, I managed to land a great job with a law firm.* | [**land yourself sth**] *Bill's just landed himself a part in a Broadway show.*

5 land sb in trouble/court/debt etc. to do something that causes someone to have serious problems or be in a difficult situation: *Elaine's reckless driving landed her in the hospital.*

6 fish [T] to catch a fish: *You mean Rich landed an 18-pound fish by himself?*

7 land on your feet to get into a good situation again, after having problems: *Capra lost his job, but landed on his feet when Columbia Pictures hired him.*

8 land a punch/blow etc. to succeed in hitting someone: *In the third round, Lopez landed a right hook to Bettis' jaw.*

9 get sth unexpectedly [I always + adv./prep.] to arrive UNEXPECTEDly, and cause problems: [+ in/on/ under etc.] *Just when I thought my problems were over, this letter landed on my desk.*

10 goods/people [T] to put something or someone on land from an airplane or boat: *Fishermen were landing their catch at the harbor.*

Land /lænd/, **Ed·win Her·bert** /ˈɛdwɪn ˈhɚbɚt/ (1909–1991) a U.S. scientist who invented the Polaroid treatment of glass and the Polaroid camera

land·ed /ˈlændɪd/ *adj.* [only before noun] OLD-FASHIONED **1 landed gentry/family/nobility** a family or group that has owned a lot of land for a long time **2** including a lot of land: *landed estates*

land·fall /ˈlændfɔl/ *n.* [C usually singular] the first land that you see or arrive at after a long trip by ocean or air: *Columbus made landfall* (=arrived) *on San Salvador Island in the Bahamas.*

land·fill /'lændfɪl/ *n.* **1** [C] a place where waste is buried under the ground **2** [U] the practice of burying waste under the ground, or the waste buried in this way

land grab /'. ./ *n.* [C] the act of someone powerful, such as the government, taking land, especially in an unfair or illegal way

land·hold·er /'lænd,hoʊldə/ *n.* [C] the person who owns a particular piece of land

land hold·ings, landholdings /'. ,../ *n.* [plural] the land that is owned by someone

land·ing /'lændɪŋ/ *n.* [C] **1** the action of arriving on land, or of making something such as an airplane or boat come onto land: *the first landing of settlers in America* | **crash/emergency landing** (=a sudden landing made by an airplane because it is having trouble) —compare TAKEOFF (1) **2** the floor at the top of a set of stairs or between two sets of stairs

landing charge /'.. ,./ *n.* [C] TECHNICAL money that you have to pay when goods are unloaded at a port

landing craft /'.. ,./ *n.* [C] a flat-bottomed boat that opens at one end to allow soldiers and equipment to come directly onto a shore

landing gear /'.. ,./ *n.* [U] an aircraft's wheels and wheel supports

landing pad /'.. ,./ *n.* [C] a special area where a HELICOPTER can come down

landing strip /'.. ,./ *n.* [C] a level piece of ground that has been prepared for airplanes to use

land·la·dy /'lænd,leɪdi/ *n. plural* **landladies** [C] the woman that you rent a room, building, or piece of land from

land·less /'lændləs/ *adj.* owning no land —**landless** *n.* [plural]

land·locked /'lændlɑkt/ *adj.* a landlocked country, state etc. is surrounded by other countries, states etc. and has no coast

land·lord /'lændlɔrd/ *n.* [C] someone that you rent a room, building, or piece of land from

land·lub·ber /'lænd,lʌbə/ *n.* [C] OLD-FASHIONED someone who does not have much experience of the ocean or ships

land·mark /'lændmɑrk/ *n.* [C] **1** something that is easy to recognize, such as a tall tree or building, and that helps you know where you are: *The Washington Monument is a popular historical landmark.* **2** one of the most important events, changes, or discoveries that influences someone or something: *a landmark court victory*

land·mass /'lændmæs/ *n.* [C] TECHNICAL a large area of land

land·mine /'lændmaɪn/ *n.* [C] a type of bomb hidden in the ground that explodes when someone walks or drives over it

land of·fice /'. ,../ *n.* [C] **1** a government office in the U.S. that records the sales of all public land **2 do (a) land-office business** to be very busy and make a lot of money: *Moore, manager of a Florida-based travel company, said her agency is doing a land-office business.*

land·own·er /'lænd,oʊnə/ *n.* [C] someone who owns land, especially a large amount —**landowning** *adj.* —**landownership** *n.* [U]

land re·form /'. .,./ *n.* [C,U] the political principle of sharing farm land so that more people own some of it

Lan·dry /'lændri/**, Tom** /tɑm/ (1924– 2000) a U.S. football COACH

land·scape[1] /'lændskeɪp/ *n.* **1** [C] an area of COUNTRYSIDE or land, considered in terms of how attractive it is to look at: *the rugged landscape of the West* | *The island's landscape is similar to Hawaii's.* **2** [C] a photograph or painting showing an area of COUNTRYSIDE or land: *Adams is best know for his landscapes of Yosemite National Park.* **3** [U] the painting or drawing of landscapes in art: *Landscape, in a blend of Eastern and Western styles, is his main subject.* **4 the political/intellectual etc. landscape** the general

situation in which a particular activity takes place: *O'Neil was a fixture of the political landscape of Washington.* **5** [U] TECHNICAL —see LANDSCAPE MODE

landscape[2] *v.* [T often passive] to make a park, garden etc. look attractive and interesting by planting trees, bushes, flowers etc. —**landscaping** *n.* [U]

landscape ar·chi·tec·ture /,.. '..../ *n.* [U] the profession or art of planning the way an area of land looks, including the roads, buildings, and planted areas —**landscape architect** *n.* [C]

landscape gar·den·ing /'.. ,../ *n.* [U] the profession or art of arranging gardens and parks so that they look attractive and interesting —**landscape gardener** *n.* [C]

landscape mode /'.. ,./ *n.* [C] TECHNICAL a piece of paper, a picture etc. that has the longer edge at the top and bottom —opposite PORTRAIT MODE

land·scap·er /'lænd,skeɪpə/ *n.* [C] someone whose job is to arrange plants, paths etc. in gardens and parks

land·slide /'lændslaɪd/ *n.* [C] **1** a victory in an election in which one person or party gets a lot more votes than all the others: *a landslide election victory* | *Lang won by a landslide.* **2** the sudden falling of a lot of earth or rocks down the side of a hill: *Flooding caused landslides and serious property damage.*

Land·stei·ner /'lænd,staɪnə/**, Karl** /kɑrl/ (1868–1943) a U.S. scientist who discovered the four main human BLOOD TYPES

land·ward /'lændwəd/ *adj.* facing toward the land and away from the ocean: *the landward side of the hill* —**landward** *adv.*

lane /leɪn/ *n.* [C] **1** one of the parts of a main road that are divided by painted lines to keep traffic apart: *That idiot changed lanes without signaling.* | *Cars in the fast lane were traveling at over 80 miles an hour.* | **the inside lane** (=the lane near the edge of a road) | **the outside lane** (=the lane near the center of a road) **2** one of the narrow parallel areas marked for each competitor in a running or swimming race: *The Russian swimmer in lane 6 is in the lead.* **3** a line or course along which ships or aircraft regularly travel between ports or airports: *busy shipping lanes* **4** a wooden path on which a BOWLING BALL is rolled in a BOWLING ALLEY **5** a narrow road between fields or houses, especially in the COUNTRYSIDE —see also **life in the fast lane** (FAST[1] (5)), **a walk/trip down memory lane** (MEMORY (10))

Lange /lændʒ/**, Dor·o·the·a** /,dɔrə'θiə/ (1895–1965) a U.S. PHOTOGRAPHER

Lang·ley /'læŋli/**, Samuel** (1834–1906) a U.S. scientist who built the first model aircraft that could fly successfully

lan·guage /'læŋgwɪdʒ/ *n.*
1 English/French/Arabic etc. [C,U] a system of communication by written or spoken words, which is used by the people of a particular country or area: *the Japanese language* | *How many languages do you speak?* *Kim's native language* (=the first language she learned) *is Korean.* | *Latin is a dead language* (=language that is no longer spoken). | *Urbach helped convert ancient Hebrew into a modern language* (=a language that is spoken today).
2 communication [U] the use of written or spoken words to communicate: *language skills*
3 computers [C,U] TECHNICAL a system of instructions and commands for operating a computer: *the programming language C++*
4 style/type of words [U] the type of words and the style used in a particular type of writing or by people in a particular job or activity: *Confused by the legal language of the letter, Patterson called his attorney.* | *poetic language* | *Unfortunately, Jimmy was introduced to street language* (=impolite words that some people find offensive) *at an early age.*
5 swearing [U] INFORMAL words that most people think are offensive: *You never heard such language! It was disgusting.* | *Ben! Watch your language* (=stop swearing)!

L

6 strong language a) angry words used to tell people exactly what you mean **b)** words that most people think are offensive; SWEARING

7 speak the same language if two people speak the same language, they have similar attitudes and opinions

8 sounds/signs/actions [U] the way that something such as poetry or music expresses feelings: *the language of music* —see also BODY LANGUAGE, SIGN LANGUAGE

lan·guage lab·o·ra·to·ry /ˈ.. ,..../ *n.* [C] a room in a school or college where you can learn to speak a foreign language by listening to TAPEs and recording your own voice

lan·guid /ˈlæŋgwɪd/ *adj.* **1** moving slowly and making very little effort: *Another couple began turning languid circles on the tiny dance floor.* **2** slow and peaceful: *We spent a languid summer afternoon by the pool.* —**languidly** *adv.*

lan·guish /ˈlæŋgwɪʃ/ *v.* [I] FORMAL **1** to remain in a condition without improving or developing: *The housing market continues to languish.* | [+ **in**] *The case has languished in the courts for years.* **2** to be forced to stay somewhere where you are unhappy: [+ **in**] *Tran spend five long years languishing in refugee camps.* **3** [+ **for**] LITERARY to become sick and unhappy because you want someone or something very much

lan·guor /ˈlæŋgɚ/ *n.* LITERARY **1** [C,U] a pleasant feeling of tiredness or lack of strength **2** [U] pleasant or heavy stillness of the air: *the languor of a hot afternoon* **3** [U] a feeling of sadness because you want someone or something very much —**languorous** *adj.* —**languorously** *adv.*

lank /læŋk/ *adj.* **1** lank hair is thin, straight, and unattractive **2** lanky

lank·y /ˈlæŋki/ *adj.* tall and thin in an awkward way: *a tall lanky young man* —**lankiness** *n.* [U]

lan·o·lin /ˈlænl-ɪn/ *n.* [U] an oil that is in sheep's wool and is used in skin creams

Lan·sing /ˈlænsɪŋ/ the capital city of the U.S. state of Michigan

lan·tern /ˈlæntɚn/ *n.* [C] **1** a lamp that you can carry, consisting of a metal or glass container surrounding a flame or light **2** TECHNICAL a structure at the top of a tower or LIGHTHOUSE that has windows on all sides —see also CHINESE LANTERN, MAGIC LANTERN

lantern-jawed /,.. ˈ.ᐠ/ *adj.* having a long narrow jaw and cheeks that sink in

lan·yard /ˈlænyɚd/ *n.* [C] **1** a short piece of rope or steel, used on a ship to tie things **2** a thick string that you can hang around your neck to carry something on, such as a WHISTLE

La·os /laʊs, ˈlɑoʊs, ˈleɪɑs/ a country in southeastern Asia that is south of China and north of Cambodia

La·o·tian /leɪˈoʊʃən, ˈlaʊʃən/ *adj.* **1** relating to or coming from Laos **2** relating to the language of Laos —**Laotian** *n.* [C]

Lao-tzu /lau ˈdzʌ/ (6th century B.C.) a Chinese religious leader who is believed to have started Taoism

lap¹ /læp/ *n.* [C] **1** the upper part of your legs when you are sitting down: *Shannon sat on her mother's lap and smiled for the camera.* **2** a single trip around a race track or between the two ends of a pool: *With one lap to go in the race, Petty's car blew a tire.* | *Every morning she swims fifty laps in the pool.* | *Afterward, he took a victory lap* (=a lap to celebrate winning). **3 drop/dump sth in sb's lap** SPOKEN to make someone else deal with something difficult that is your responsibility: *How will Reno deal with the political problem that's been dumped in her lap?* **4 in the lap of luxury** having a very easy and comfortable life with a lot of money, expensive possessions etc.

lap² *v.* **lapped, lapping 1** [I,T] if water laps something or laps against something such as the shore or a boat, it moves against it or hits it in small waves: [+ **at/over/against** etc.] *We sat on the shore and let the warm water lap over our feet.* **2** [I,T] also **lap up**

if an animal laps something, it drinks it by making small tongue movements **3 a)** [T] to pass a competitor in a race after having completed a whole lap more than they have: *Senna lapped everyone in the San Marino Grand Prix.* **b)** [I,T] to make a single trip around a track, race course etc. in a particular time: *Patrese lapped the 2.7-mile circuit at 128 mph.* **4** [I,T] TECHNICAL if one thing laps another, a part of one covers part of the other; OVERLAP² **5** [T always + adv./prep.] LITERARY to fold or wrap something around something else —**lapping** *n.* [U]

lap ↔ **sth up** *phr. v.* [T] **1** to enjoy or believe something without criticizing or doubting it at all: *We sat there lapping up Uncle Gene's stories of his childhood.* **2** to drink all of something eagerly

lap·a·ro·scope /ˈlæpərəˌskoʊp/ *n.* [C] TECHNICAL a piece of equipment like a tube with a light on it that a doctor can use to look inside someone's body, or that the doctor can pass a small knife down to do an operation

lap·a·ros·cop·y /,læpəˈrɑskəpi/ *n.* [C,U] TECHNICAL an examination or medical operation done using a laparoscope

La Paz /lə ˈpɑz/ the capital and largest city of Bolivia

lap belt /ˈ. ./ *n.* [C] a type of safety belt that fits across your waist when you are sitting in the back of a car —see also SEAT BELT

lap danc·er /ˈ. ,../ *n.* [C] a dancer in a bar who sits on customers' laps and moves in a sexually exciting way as part of their performance —**lap dancing** *n.* [U]

lap·dog, lap dog /ˈlæpdɔg/ *n.* [C] **1** a small pet dog **2** someone who is completely under the control of someone else and will do anything they say

la·pel /ləˈpɛl/ *n.* [C] the part of the front of a coat or JACKET that is joined to the collar and folded back on each side

lap·i·dar·y¹ /ˈlæpəˌdɛri/ *adj.* [only before noun] TECHNICAL relating to the cutting or polishing of valuable stones or jewels

lapidary² *n.* [C] TECHNICAL someone who is skilled at cutting and polishing jewels and valuable stones

lap·is laz·u·li /,læpɪs ˈlæzəli/ *n.* [C,U] a valuable bright blue stone

La·place, Pierre Si·mon de /pyɛr siˈmoʊn də/ (1749–1827) a French ASTRONOMER who did important work on GRAVITY and the SOLAR SYSTEM

lap robe /ˈ. ./ *n.* [C] a small thick BLANKET used to cover your legs when you are traveling

lapse¹ /læps/ *n.* [C] **1** a short time when you forget something, do not pay attention, or fail to do something you should: [+ **in**] *The company admitted a lapse in its standards and apologized to customers in a newspaper ad.* | [+ **of**] *A single lapse of concentration cost Becker the game.* | *After taking the drug, several patients suffered memory lapses* (=they were unable to remember some things for short periods of time). | *Children shouldn't be harshly punished for a lapse of judgment* (=a time when they chose the wrong thing to do). **2** a period of time in which something is allowed to become worse: [+ **in**] *a lapse in building quality* **3** [usually singular] a period of time between two events: [+ **of**] *There was a lapse of five seconds before another round of shots was fired.* **4** a failure to do something you should do, especially a failure to behave correctly: *He didn't offer Darren a drink, and Marie did not appear to notice the lapse.*

lapse² *v.* [I] **1** if a contract, agreement, legal right etc. lapses, it comes to an end, for example because an agreed time limit has passed: *Crockett wishes he hadn't let his insurance policies lapse last year.* **2** to gradually come to an end or to stop for a period of time: *I let the conversation lapse and Kelly finally spoke up.*

lapse into sth *phr. v.* [T] **1 lapse into silence/a coma/sleep etc.** to go into a quiet or less active state: *He lapsed into a coma and died two days later.* **2** to return to behaving or speaking in a way that you did before, especially a way that is less good or acceptable: *Following his death, the Empire lapsed into chaos.* | *Gerhardt frequently lapses into German.*

L

lapsed /læpst/ adj. [only before noun] **1** no longer having the beliefs you used to have, especially religious beliefs: *a lapsed Catholic* **2** LAW not used anymore

laptop

lap·top /'læptɑp/ n. [C] a small computer that you can carry with you —**lap-top** adj. —see picture on page 426

lar·board /'lɑrbəd/ n. [U] OLD-FASHIONED the left side of a ship; PORT (4)

lar·ce·nist /'lɑrsənɪst/ n. [C] LAW a thief

lar·ce·ny /'lɑrsəni/ n. plural **larcenies** [C,U] LAW the act or crime of stealing —**larcenous** adj. —see also PETTY LARCENY

larch /lɑrtʃ/ n. [C,U] a tree that looks like a PINE tree but drops its leaves in winter

lard¹ /lɑrd/ n. [U] white fat from pigs that is used in cooking

lard² v. [T] **1 be larded with sth a)** if a speech, piece of writing etc. is larded with particular types of words or phrases, there are a lot of them in it: *The chairman's speech was larded with criticisms of the governor.* **b)** to include a lot of things that are not related or necessary: *The bill has become larded with pet spending projects of lawmakers.* **2** to put small pieces of BACON onto meat before cooking it

lard-ass /'. ./ n. [C] OFFENSIVE someone who is fat

lar·der /'lɑrdə/ n. [C] a small room or large cupboard for storing food in a house

large /lɑrdʒ/ adj.
1 big bigger or more than usual in number, amount, or size: *What size shirt do you wear? Medium or Large?* | *A large population of homeless people live in the park.* | *I bought the largest TV I could find.*
2 person a large person is tall and often fat: *Aunt Betsy was a very large woman.* —see Usage Note at FAT¹
3 be at large if a dangerous person or animal is at large, they have escaped from somewhere and may cause harm or damage: *Two of the escaped prisoners are still at large.*
4 the world/country/public etc. at large people in general: *We appeal to members of the community at large to help in cleaning up our city.*
5 larger than life someone who is larger than life attracts a lot of attention because they are more amusing, attractive, or exciting than most people: *Graham was one of the larger-than-life legends of the rock era.*
6 in large part/measure FORMAL mostly
7 the larger issues/picture/view the important general facts and questions about a situation, problem etc.: *Let's focus our discussion of the environment on the larger issues first.* —**largeness** n. [U] —see also **by and large** (BY (4)), **loom large** (LOOM¹ (3)), **writ large** (WRIT²) —see Usage Notes at BIG and WIDE¹

large in·tes·tine /ˌ. .'../ n. [singular] the lower part of the INTESTINES, in which food is changed into waste matter —compare SMALL INTESTINE —see picture at DIGESTIVE SYSTEM

large·ly /'lɑrdʒli/ adv. mostly or mainly: *Our church's congregation is largely made up of young families with children.* | *Most of the cities depend largely on hydroelectric power.*

large-scale /ˌ. '. ◂/ adj. [only before noun] **1** using or involving a lot of effort, people, supplies etc.: *a*

large-scale rescue operation **2** a large-scale map, model etc. is drawn or made bigger than usual, so that more details can be shown

lar·gesse, largess /lɑr'dʒɛs, -'ʒɛs/ n. [U] FORMAL the quality or act of being generous and giving money or gifts to people who have less than you, or the money or gifts that you give

larg·ish /'lɑrdʒɪʃ/ adj. INFORMAL fairly big

lar·go /'lɑrgoʊ/ adj. adv. TECHNICAL played or sung slowly and seriously —**largo** n. [C]

lar·i·at /'læriət/ n. [C] a LASSO¹

lark /lɑrk/ n. [C] **1** INFORMAL something that you do to amuse yourself or as a joke: *The trip to Dresden was a lark.* | **on/as/for a lark** *Grisham began writing as a lark, a break from his law practice.* **2** a small brown singing bird with long pointed wings; SKYLARK —see also **as happy as a lark** (HAPPY (9))

lark·spur /'lɑrkspə/ n. [C] a type of flower

lar·va /'lɑrvə/ n. plural **larvae** /-vi/ [C] a young insect with a soft tube-shaped body, that will become an insect with wings —**larval** adj. —see picture at METAMORPHOSIS

lar·yn·gi·tis /ˌlærən'dʒaɪtɪs/ n. [U] an illness which makes talking difficult because your larynx and throat are swollen

lar·ynx /'lærɪŋks/ n. [C] TECHNICAL the part of your throat where your voice is produced

la·sa·gna, lasagne /lə'zɑnyə/ n. [C,U] a type of Italian food made with flat pieces of PASTA, meat or vegetables, and cheese

las·civ·i·ous /lə'sɪviəs/ adj. DISAPPROVING showing strong sexual desire, or making someone feel this way: *lascivious paintings of nude women* —**lasciviousness** n. [U]

la·ser /'leɪzə/ n. [C] **1** a piece of equipment that produces a powerful narrow beam of light which can be used in medical operations, to cut metals etc.: *laser surgery* **2** a beam of light produced by this machine

laser disc, laser disk /'.. ,./ n. [C] a flat round object like a CD that can be read by laser light, used in computers or to watch movies

laser print·er /'.. ,../ n. [C] a machine connected to a computer system, that prints by using laser light

lash¹ /læʃ/ v.
1 tie [T always + adv./prep.] to tie something tightly to something else with a rope, or tie two things together: [**lash sth to/onto sth**] *With our luggage lashed to the car's roof, we set out for Utah.*
2 wind/rain etc. [I always + adv./prep.,T] to hit against something with violent force: *Giant waves continuously lashed the shore.* | [+ **against/down/across**] *The wind lashed violently against the door.*
3 hit [T] to hit someone very hard with a whip, stick etc.: *Several of the men were lashed for falling asleep on guard duty.*
4 tail [I,T] if an animal lashes its tail or its tail lashes, it moves it from side to side quickly and strongly, especially because it is angry
5 criticize [I,T] a word meaning "to criticize someone angrily," used especially in newspapers: *One politician lashed Bush as being the president of the wealthy.* | [+ **back**] *Gallins lashed back at those who accused him of corruption* (=he angrily criticized people who criticized him).
6 lash sb into a fury/rage/frenzy etc. to deliberately make a group of people have strong violent feelings: *The crowd was being lashed into a frenzy by the speaker.*
lash out phr. v. [I] **1** to suddenly speak angrily to someone: [+ **at**] *Judge Atkins lashed out at the defense attorneys for talking to the press.* **2** to try to hit someone, with a series of violent, uncontrolled movements: *In its panic, the bear started to lash out.*

lash² n. [C] **1** [usually plural] one of the hairs that grow around the edge of your eyes; EYELASH **2** a hit with a whip, given especially as a punishment: *They were each given 50 lashes.* **3** a sudden or violent

L

movement like that of a whip: *With a lash of its tail, the lion sprang at its prey.* **4** the thin piece of leather at the end of a whip

lash·ing /ˈlæʃɪŋ/ *n.* [C] **1** a punishment of hitting someone with a whip **2** a rope that fastens something tightly to something else

lass /læs/ also **las·sie** /ˈlæsi/ *n.* [C] OLD-FASHIONED a girl or young woman —compare LAD

Las·sen Peak /ˌlæsən ˈpik/ a mountain in the Cascade Range that is in the U.S. state of California and is an active VOLCANO

las·si·tude /ˈlæsɪˌtud/ *n.* [U] FORMAL **1** tiredness and lack of energy **2** laziness or lack of interest: *The candidates have been trying to lift voters out of their lassitude.*

lasso

las·so¹ /ˈlæsou/ *n. plural* **lassos** [C] a rope with one end tied in a circle, used to catch cattle and horses, especially in the western U.S.

lasso² *v.* [T] to catch an animal using a lasso

last¹ /læst/ *determiner, adj.* **1** most recent, or the nearest one to the present time: *Did you go to Tulsa last week?* | *You spoke at the last conference, didn't you?* | *The last time I ate there, I got sick.* —compare NEXT¹ (1) **2** happening or existing at the end, after everything and everyone else: *The last page contains all of the answers.* | *"I love you" was the last thing he said before he died.* **3** remaining after all others have gone, been used etc.: *Go ahead and take the last piece of cake.* | *We were the last ones to leave the party.* **4 the last person/thing** someone or something that you do not want at all, that is most inappropriate, that you did not expect etc.: *The last thing we wanted was to go into debt.* | *Chad's the last person I would ask for advice.* **5 last thing (at night)** at the very end of the day: *Take a couple of these pills last thing at night to help you get to sleep.* **6 the last straw** the final thing in a series of annoying things that makes a person very angry: *Suzy lying to me about the money was the last straw.* **7 have the last laugh** to finally be successful, win an argument etc., after other people have earlier criticized you, defeated you etc. **8 have the last word a)** to make the last statement in an argument, which gives you an advantage: *Erin always has to have the last word!* **b)** to be the person who makes the final decision on something: *Of course, the manager has the last word on any price.* **9 on its last legs** INFORMAL old or in bad condition, and likely to stop working soon: *Your car sounds like it's on its last legs.* **10 on your last legs** INFORMAL **a)** very tired: *Sarah looks as if she's on her last legs.* **b)** very sick and likely to die soon **11 last hurrah** a final effort, event etc. at the end of a long period of work, a CAREER, a life etc.: *"Star Trek – Generations" was the original cast's last hurrah.* **12 sb's last will and testament** OLD-FASHIONED a WILL² (2) **13 be the last word in sth** to be the best, most modern, or most comfortable example of something: *It's the last word in luxury resorts.* —see Usage Note at LASTLY

last² *adv.* **1** most recently before now: *When I saw her last, she was pregnant.* **2** after everything or everyone else: *I was told I'll be speaking last.* | *Connect the red wires first and the black ones last.* **3 last of all** used when giving a final point or statement: *Last of all, I'd like to say that everyone has done a wonderful job.* **4 last but not least** used when mentioning the last person or thing in a list, to emphasize that they are still important: *Last but not least, I would like to thank my wife for her support.*

last³ *n., pron.* **1 the last** the person or thing that comes after all the others: *Joel was the last of nine kids.* | *I was the last to go to bed that night.* **2 at (long) last** if something happens at last, it happens after you have waited a long time: *At last, we were able to afford a house.* **3 the day/week/year etc. before last** the day, week etc. before the one that has just finished: *We got our new car the week before last.* **4 the last of sth** the remaining part of something: *Dennis ate the last of the bread at lunchtime.* **5 haven't heard the last of sb/sth** if you have not heard the last of someone or something, they or it have caused problems for you in the past and may cause problems for you in the future: *I'll leave now, but you haven't heard the last of this.* **6 the last I/we...** SPOKEN used to tell someone the most recent news that you know about a person or situation: *The last I heard, Paul was in Cuba.* | *The last we talked to Shelly, she seemed fine.* **7 to the last** FORMAL until the end of an event or the end of someone's life: *Brown died in 1987, insisting to the last he was innocent.*

last⁴ *v.* [I] **1** [I always + adv./prep., linking verb] to continue for a particular length of time: *Her operation lasted around three hours.* | *The ceasefire didn't last long.* | [+ **for/until/through** etc.] *The rainy season lasts until March.* **2** [I] to continue to be effective, useful, or in good condition for a long time, or to continue to exist: *Most batteries last for about 8 hours.* | *The good weather won't last.* **3** [I] to manage to remain in the same situation, even when this is difficult: *It's hard to say how much longer the astronauts will last without fresh supplies.* **4** [linking verb] to be enough for someone to use | **last (sb) a week/month/year etc.** *I have enough paper to last me a lifetime.* | *The money should last the rest of the month.*

last⁵ *n.* [C] a piece of wood or metal shaped like a human foot, used by someone who makes shoes

last call /ˌ. ˈ./ *n.* [U] the time when the person who is in charge of a bar tells customers they can order just one more set of drinks because the bar is going to close

last-ditch /ˌ. ˈ.◂/ *adj.* **a last-ditch attempt/effort etc.** a final attempt to achieve something before it is too late: *The negotiators made a last-ditch effort to reach an agreement.*

last·ing /ˈlæstɪŋ/ *adj.* strong enough, well enough planned etc. to continue for a very long time: *The committee's decision could have a lasting effect on the community.* | *a lasting peace settlement* | *Our first meeting left a lasting impression on me.*

Last Judg·ment /ˌ. ˈ../ *n.* **the Last Judgment** the time after the end of the world when everyone is judged by God for what they have done in life, according to Christianity and some other religions

last·ly /ˈlæstli/ *adv.* [sentence adverb] used when telling someone the last thing at the end of a list or series of statements: *Lastly, the course trains students to think logically.*

USAGE NOTE: LASTLY

WORD CHOICE: lastly, last of all, finally, in the end, at last

Lastly, **last of all**, and **finally** are often used to end a set of points where time is not involved: *There are three reasons why I hate him: first(ly) he's rude, second(ly) he's a liar, and lastly/last of all/finally he owes me money* (NOT *at last*). **Last (of all)** and **finally** also end a set of actions, often at points of time: *First I get dressed, next I bring in the paper, then I feed the cat, and last/finally I fix my breakfast* (NOT *at last*). **Finally** is also used, like **in the end**, just to mark something as

L

happening after a long period of time: *I finally was able to convince Albert that I was telling the truth.* | *In the end, he turned out to be a liar and a cheat.* Remember that **in the end** usually has a more literary use. **At last** has a similar use, but only when something good happens after a period of time: *We were able to get married at last.* | *At last I have a good dictionary (=I have waited a long time to find one)!*

last-min·ute /ˌ. ˈ.◂/ *adj.* [only before noun] happening or done as late as possible within a process, event, or activity: *a last-minute decision*

S W
2
last name /ˌ. ˈ./ *n.* [C] your family's name, which in English comes after your other names —compare FIRST NAME, MIDDLE NAME

last rites /ˌ. ˈ./ *n.* [plural] the ceremony performed in some religions, especially the Catholic religion, for people who are dying

Las Ve·gas /lɑs ˈveɪgəs/ a city in the desert of the U.S. state of Nevada

lat. the written abbreviation of LATITUDE

latch[1] /lætʃ/ *n.* [C] a small metal or plastic object used to keep doors, gates, windows etc. closed: *Put childproof latches on cabinet doors and drawers.*

latch

latch[2] *v.* [T] to fasten a door, window etc. with a latch
latch onto sb/sth also **latch on to** sb/sth *phr. v.* [T] INFORMAL **1** if you latch onto an idea, style, phrase etc., you think it is so good, important etc. that you start using it too: *In recent years, doctors have latched onto the idea of using natural medicines.* **2** to follow someone and keep trying to talk to them, get their attention etc., especially when they would prefer to be left alone: *He latched onto Sandy at the party and wouldn't go away.* **3** to bite or suck and not let go of someone or something: *The big black dog then latched on to my ankle.*

latch·key /ˈlætʃki/ *n.* [C] a key that opens a lock on an outside door of a house or apartment

latchkey kid also **latchkey child** /ˌ. ˈ./ *n.* [C] a child whose parents both work and who spends time alone in the house after school

S W
1 1
late[1] /leɪt/ *adj.*
1 ‹after expected time› arriving, happening, or done after the time that was expected, agreed, or arranged: *Sorry I'm late – I overslept.* | *The bus is late again.* | [+ for] *Peggy was late for school.* | [be too late to do sth] *Is it too late to apply for next semester?*
2 ‹near the end› [only before noun] near the end of a period of time: *a house built in the late 19th century* | *Paul's in his late forties.*
3 ‹after usual time› happening or done after the usual or normal time: *a late breakfast* | *The harvest was late this year because of the rains.*
4 ‹payments etc.› **a)** paid, given back etc. after the arranged time: *Oh, no, my library books are late.* **b)** be late with sth to pay something, bring something back etc. after the arranged time: *I've never been late with a payment before.*
5 ‹evening› [only before noun] happening at the end of the day, especially at night when most people are asleep: *I watched the late show on TV.*
6 as late as used to express surprise that something considered old-fashioned was still happening so recently: *As late as the 1960s, about 20 states had laws against interracial marriage.*
7 ‹dead› [only before noun] FORMAL dead: *Mrs. Moody's late husband*
8 a late bloomer/developer **a)** a child who develops socially, emotionally, or physically at a later age than other children **b)** someone who does not become successful until later in life
9 ‹women› if a woman is late, she has not had her PERIOD (=the monthly flow of blood) when she expected it

10 late of sth FORMAL having lived in a place, worked in a place etc. until fairly recently: *Julia Loukyanov, late of Moscow*
11 it's (a little) late in the day used to show disapproval because someone has done something too late for it to be effective: *It's a little late in the day to say you're sorry!* —see also LATER[2], LATEST[1]

S W
2
3
late[2] *adv.* **1** after or later than the usual time: *All the stores in the mall are open late for the sale.* | *I stayed late at work last night.* **2** after the arranged or expected time: *The bus came ten minutes late.* **3** near to the end of a period of time or an event: [+ in] *late in the afternoon* | *We took a walk late at night.* **4** of late FORMAL recently: *He's taken to mountain climbing of late.* **5** late in life if you do something late in life, you do it at an older age than most people do it **6** better late than never used to say that you are glad someone has done something, or that they should do something, even though they are late —see also LATER[1], **run late/early/on time** (RUN[1] (10))

late-break·ing /ˈ. ˌ./ *adj.* late-breaking news concerns events that happen just before a news broadcast or just before a newspaper is printed

late·com·er /ˈleɪtˌkʌmɚ/ *n.* [C] someone who arrives late

S W
2
late·ly /ˈleɪtli/ *adv.* recently: *I've been really tired lately.*

USAGE NOTE: LATELY

GRAMMAR: lately, recently
Use both these words with the present perfect tenses to talk about something that began in the recent past and continues until now: *Lately I've been thinking about changing jobs.* | *You've been going to a lot of parties recently.* You can also use **recently** (but NOT **lately**) with the past tense to talk about a particular action in the recent past: *She got married recently* (NOT *lately*).

---

late-night /ˌ. ˈ.◂/ *adj.* [only before noun] happening late at night: *a late-night TV talk show*

la·tent /ˈleɪtⁿnt/ *adj.* something that is latent is present but hidden, and may develop or become more noticeable in the future: *The virus remains latent in the body for many years.* | *Police experts found latent fingerprints on the glass.* —**latency** *n.* [U]

latent heat /ˌ. ˈ./ *n.* [U] TECHNICAL the additional heat necessary to change a solid into a liquid, or a liquid into a gas

S W
1 1
lat·er[1] /ˈleɪtɚ/ *adv.* **1** after the present time or a time you are talking about: *They reached the edge of the city half an hour later.* | *Later that night Bernstein visited her in her apartment.* | *Okay, talk to you later, Mom.* **2** see you later, later SPOKEN used to say goodbye to someone you will see again soon: *Later, Wayne.* | *All right. I'll see you later.* **3** later on at some time later or in the future: *She took notes so she could remember it all later on.* **4** no/not later than used when saying that something must be done by a particular time in the future: *Applications must be received no later than April 21.* —see Usage Note at AFTER[1]

lat·er[2] *adj.* [only before noun] **1** coming in the future or after something else: *You'll find that information in a later chapter.* | *The weapons will be destroyed at a later date.* **2** more recent: *The Hartmans traded in their '92 VW for a later model.* **3** in sb's later years also in later life when someone is older: *In her later years, Alva came to regret many of the mistakes she had made.*

lat·er·al[1] /ˈlætərəl/ *adj.* **1** FORMAL relating to the sides of something or movement to or from the side: *The wall is weak and requires lateral support.* | *a lateral pass* **2** a lateral move a change of jobs within a company or between companies in which you stay at a similar level or rank **3** TECHNICAL a lateral speech sound is made by using the sides of the tongue —**laterally** *adv.*

lat·er·al[2] *n.* [C] TECHNICAL **1** something that is at the side or comes from the side **2** a lateral speech sound

L

lat·est[1] /'leɪtɪst/ *adj.* [only before noun] the most recent or the newest: *Have you heard the latest news?* | *the latest fashion* —see Usage Note at NEW

latest[2] *n.* **1 the latest** INFORMAL the most recent news, fashion, or technical improvement: *Every hospital wants the latest in high-tech equipment.* **2 at the latest** no later than the time mentioned: *I want you home by 11 at the latest.*

la·tex /'leɪtɛks/ *n.* [U] **1** a thick whitish liquid produced by some plants, especially the rubber tree, and used in making rubber, paint, glue etc. **2** an artificial substance similar to this

lath /læθ/ *n.* [C] a long flat narrow piece of wood used in building to support PLASTER (=material used to cover walls)

lathe /leɪð/ *n.* [C] a machine that shapes wood or metal, by turning it around and around against a sharp tool

lath·er[1] /'læðɚ/ *n.* [singular,U] **1** a white mass of BUBBLEs produced by mixing soap in water **2** a white mass that forms on a horse's skin when it has been SWEATing[1] (1) **3 in a lather** INFORMAL very anxious or upset: *The mayor's supporters get in a lather over those kinds of accusation.* —**lathery** *adv.*

lather[2] *v.* also **lather up 1** [I] to produce a lather: *This soap lathers really well.* **2** [I,T] to cover something, especially your body, with lather: *I turn the water off while I'm lathering up in the shower.*

Lat·in[1] /'læt'n/ *n.* **1** [U] the language of the ancient Romans, now used mostly for legal, scientific, or medical words **2** [C] someone from Mexico, Central America, or South America **3** [C] someone from a country in southwestern Europe

Latin[2] *adj.* **1** relating to or coming from Mexico, Central America, or South America: *Latin music* **2** relating to the Latin language: *a Latin inscription* **3** relating to a nation that speaks a language such as Italian, Spanish, or Portuguese, that developed from Latin

La·ti·na /lə'tinə/ *n.* [C] a woman in the U.S. whose family comes from a country in Latin America

Latin A·mer·i·ca /ˌ.. .'.../ *n.* the land including Mexico, Central America, and South America —**Latin American** *adj.*

La·ti·no /lə'tinoʊ/ *n. plural* **Latinos** [C] a man in the U.S. whose family comes from a country in Latin America. In the plural, Latinos can mean a group of men and women, or just men. —**Latino** *adj.*: *Latino culture*

lat·i·tude /'lætəˌtud/ *n.* **1** [C,U] TECHNICAL the distance north or south of the EQUATOR (=the imaginary line around the middle of the world) measured in degrees —compare LONGITUDE **2** [U] FORMAL freedom to do or say what you like: *Having his own show gives Williams wide latitude to discuss controversial topics.* **3 latitudes** [plural] an area at a particular latitude: *The mission will explore the planet's southernmost latitudes.* —**latitudinal** /ˌlætə'tudn-əl/ *adj.*

la·trine /lə'trin/ *n.* [C] a toilet that is outdoors in a camp or military area

lat·te /'lɑteɪ/ *n.* [C,U] coffee with STEAMed milk in it, or a cup of this

lat·ter[1] /'lætɚ/ *n.* **the latter** FORMAL the second of two people or things just mentioned: *Both the oatmeal cookie and the granola bar were good, but I preferred the latter* (=the granola bar). —opposite FORMER[2]

latter[2] *adj.* [only before noun] FORMAL **1** being the second of two people or things, or the last in a list just mentioned: *Of the phrases "go crazy" and "go nuts," the latter term is used less frequently.* **2** the latter part of a period of time is nearest to the end of it: *Crandall served in Italy during the latter part of the war.*

latter-day /'.. ˌ../ *adj.* [only before noun] **a latter-day Versailles/Czar etc.** something or someone that exists now but is like a famous thing or person that existed in the past: *Romer portrayed himself as a latter-day Robin Hood.*

Latter-Day Saints /ˌ.. . '../ *n.* [plural] the MORMONs

lat·tice /'lætɪs/ *n.* [C] **1** also **lat·tice·work** /'lætɪsˌwɚk/ a pattern or structure made of long flat narrow pieces of wood, plastic etc. that are arranged so that they cross each other and the spaces between them are shaped like DIAMONDs: *cherry pie with a lattice crust* **2** TECHNICAL a regular arrangement of things over an area or in space: *a crystal lattice*

Lat·vi·a /'lætviə/ a country in northeastern Europe on the Baltic Sea, that is south of Estonia and north of Lithuania —**Latvian** *n., adj.*

laud /lɔd/ *v.* [T] FORMAL to praise someone or something: *Honig lauded his wife's charity work.*

laud·a·ble /'lɔdəbəl/ *adj.* FORMAL deserving praise or admiration, even if not completely successful: *Preserving our natural environment is a laudable goal.* —**laudably** *adv.*

lau·da·num /'lɔdn-əm, -nəm/ *n.* [U] a substance containing the drug OPIUM, used in the past to control pain and help people to sleep

laud·a·to·ry /'lɔdəˌtɔri/ *adj.* FORMAL expressing praise or admiration: *a laudatory book review*

laugh[1] /læf/ *v.* S W
1 1

1 make sound [I] to make sounds with your voice, usually while you are smiling, because you think something is funny: *We were laughing so hard we couldn't stop.* | [+ at/about] *Everybody laughed at the joke.* | *When we saw what had happened to the cake we burst out laughing* (=suddenly started laughing). | *When I first heard the idea, I almost laughed out loud* (=laughed so that other people could hear). | *Joe's probably outside someplace laughing his head off* (=laughing a lot).

2 no laughing matter something serious that should not be joked about: *Dole and his staff know that age discrimination is no laughing matter.*

3 don't make me laugh SPOKEN used when someone has just told you something that is completely untrue, has asked for something impossible etc.: *"Could you finish this by tomorrow?" "Don't make me laugh."*

4 be laughing all the way to the bank INFORMAL to be in a good situation because you have made a lot of money without making much effort

5 not know whether to laugh or cry to feel upset or annoyed by something bad or unlucky that has happened, but to also be able to see that there is something funny about it: *When the whole cake fell off the table, I didn't know whether to laugh or cry.*

6 laugh in sb's face to show that you do not respect someone or care about what they think: *I confronted my daughter, but she just laughed in my face.*

7 be laughed out of court/out of City Hall etc. if a person or idea is laughed out of a place, the idea is not accepted because people there think it is completely stupid: *When Clements introduced the drug bill, he got laughed out of Congress.*

8 speak [T] to say something in a voice that shows you are amused: *"It won't even be cold when we get there," Sabina laughed.*

9 you have to laugh SPOKEN used to say that, even though a situation is annoying or disappointing, you can also see that there is something funny about it

10 laugh up your sleeve to be secretly happy, especially because you have played a trick on someone or criticized them without their knowing

11 sb will be laughing out of the other side of their mouth SPOKEN an unkind expression meaning that although someone is happy or confident now, they will be in trouble or in difficulty later

laugh at sb/sth *phr. v.* [T] **1** to make unkind or funny remarks about someone, because they have done or said something you think is stupid: *Kids hate to be laughed at.* | *When Briggs predicted that the Berlin wall would come down, people laughed at him.* | *He's the kind of person who laughs at people behind their backs* (=is unkind about someone when they are not there). **2 laugh at yourself** to not be serious about what you are doing all the time, and be able to understand that other people might think it is funny **3** to seem not to care about something that most people would worry about: *Criminals just laugh at the gun control laws.*

laugh sth ↔ **off** *phr. v.* [T] to pretend that something is less serious than it really is by laughing or joking about it: *Palin laughed off rumors that she was going to change jobs.*

laugh[2] *n.* [C] **1** an act of laughing, or the sound you make when you laugh: *a nervous laugh* | *"I guess I'm a comedian at heart," she said* ***with a laugh***. **2** INFORMAL a person, thing, or idea that cannot be considered seriously because it is so silly, stupid, or difficult to believe: *"She says she'll be here early to help." "That's a laugh."* **3 be a laugh riot** also **be a laugh a minute** INFORMAL to be very funny, amusing, and enjoyable: *Bridges' performance is a laugh riot.* **4 for laughs a)** if you do something for laughs, you do it in a particular way so that other people will laugh: *Williams plays the part for laughs.* **b)** for fun: *We took the helicopter ride just for laughs.* **5 get/have a laugh (out of sth)** to enjoy something and think it is funny: *The ads are fun to do; we get a lot of laughs from the process.*

laugh·a·ble /ˈlæfəbəl/ *adj.* impossible to be treated seriously because of being so silly, bad, or difficult to believe: *The price of the house was almost laughable.* —**laughably** *adv.*

laughing gas /ˈ.. ˌ./ *n.* [U] INFORMAL a gas that is sometimes used to stop you from feeling pain during an operation

laugh·ing·ly /ˈlæfɪŋli/ *adv.* **1** if you do something laughingly, you are laughing while you do it: *Several other women laughingly agreed.* **2** if something is laughingly called something or described in a particular way, it is done in a joking, often unkind, way: *Critics laughingly called CNN "Chicken Noodle News."*

laugh·ing·stock /ˈlæfɪŋˌstɑk/ *n.* [C] someone who has done something so silly or stupid that people laugh at them in a way that is not nice: *He has become the laughingstock of the election.*

laugh lines /ˈ. ./ *n.* [plural] lines on your skin around your eyes that are made when you laugh

laugh·ter /ˈlæftɚ/ *n.* [U] the action of laughing or sound of people laughing: *She stared at me for a moment, then* ***burst into laughter*** (=suddenly started laughing). | *The audience* ***roared with laughter.***

laugh track /ˈ. ./ *n.* [C] recorded laughter that is used during a humorous television show to make it sound as if people are laughing during the performance

launch[1] /lɔntʃ, lɑntʃ/ *v.* [T] **1** to start something new, such as an activity, plan, or profession: *The book launched his career as a novelist.* | *Wysling has launched a campaign to raise $7000 to restore the monument.* | *Rebels launched another attack late Sunday.* **2** to send a weapon or SPACECRAFT into the sky or into space: *NASA will try to launch the space shuttle again on Sunday.* **3** to put a boat or ship into the water **4** to make a new product, book etc. available for sale for the first time: *Fiat has launched the smaller car model for city driving.* **5** INFORMAL to throw something into the air with a lot of force **6 launch (yourself) forward/up/from etc.** to jump up and forward into the air with a lot of energy

launch into sth *phr. v.* [T] to suddenly start a description, story, or activity, or suddenly start criticizing something: *Powell launched into a ten-minute summary of the plan.*

launch[2] *n.* [C] **1** an act of launching something: *the West Coast launch of his new cologne* | *the launch of nuclear weapons* **2** a large boat with a motor

launch·er /ˈlɔntʃɚ, ˈlɑn-/ *n.* [C] a structure from which a weapon, ROCKET, or SPACECRAFT is sent into the sky

launch pad /ˈ. ./ also **launching pad** /ˈ.. ˌ./ *n.* [C] a special place from which a ROCKET or MISSILE is sent up into the sky

laun·der /ˈlɔndɚ, ˈlɑn-/ *v.* [T] **1** to put money that has been obtained illegally into legal businesses and bank accounts, so that you can hide it or use it: *Norio worked with foreign banks to launder drug profit.* **2** FORMAL to wash and sometimes IRON clothes, sheets etc. —**laundered** *adj.*

Laun·dro·mat, laundromat /ˈlɔndrəˌmæt/ *n.* [C] TRADEMARK a place where you pay money to wash your clothes in machines

laun·dry /ˈlɔndri/ *n. plural* **laundries 1** [U] clothes, sheets etc. that need to be washed or have just been washed: *I have to pack and* ***do the laundry*** (=wash clothes, sheets etc.). **2** [C] a place or business where clothes etc. are washed and IRONed[2]

laundry bas·ket /ˈ.. ˌ../ *n.* [C] a basket used for carrying clothes that have been washed or need to be washed

laundry list /ˈ.. ˌ./ *n.* [C] INFORMAL a list of a lot of different things: *a laundry list of complaints*

laundry room /ˈ.. ˌ./ *n.* [C] a room in a house or apartment building where there are machines so that you can wash and dry clothes, sheets etc.

lau·re·ate /ˈlɔriɪt, ˈlɑr-/ *n.* [C] someone who has been given an important prize or honor: *a Nobel laureate* —see also POET LAUREATE

lau·rel /ˈlɔrəl, ˈlɑr-/ *n.* **1** [C,U] a small tree with smooth shiny dark green leaves that do not fall off in winter **2 laurels** [plural] honors that you receive for something you have achieved: *academic laurels* **3 rest/sit on your laurels** to be satisfied with what you have achieved and therefore stop trying to achieve anything new **4 look to your laurels** to work hard in order not to lose the success that you have achieved

la·va /ˈlɑvə, ˈlævə/ *n.* [U] **1** hot liquid rock that flows from a VOLCANO **2** this rock when it has become cold and solid —see picture at VOLCANO

lava lamp /ˈ.. ˌ./ *n.* [C] a type of lamp that has a colored liquid substance inside that moves up and down, used as a decoration

lav·a·to·ry /ˈlævəˌtɔri/ *n. plural* **lavatories** [C] FORMAL a room containing a toilet, especially in a school, hospital etc.

lav·en·der /ˈlævəndɚ/ *n.* **1** [C,U] a plant that has purple flowers with a nice smell **2** [U] the dried flowers of this plant, often used to make things smell nice **3** [U] a pale purple color

lavender wa·ter /ˈ... ˌ../ *n.* [U] a PERFUME made from lavender oil and alcohol, used in past times

lav·ish[1] /ˈlævɪʃ/ *adj.* **1** [usually before noun] large, generous, or expensive: *The restaurant has a lavish dessert menu.* | *a lavish apartment* **2 be lavish with sth** to give something very generously: *He's never very lavish with his praise.* —**lavishly** *adv.*: *a lavishly illustrated book* —**lavishness** *n.* [U]

lavish[2] *v.* [T] to give someone a lot of something such as expensive presents, love, or praise: [**lavish sth on/upon sb**] *McGlinn lavished praise on the winners.* | [**lavish sb with sth**] *His followers lavished him with riches.*

La·voi·si·er /ləˌvwɑziˈeɪ/, **An·toine** /ɑnˈtwɑn/ (1743–1794) a French scientist whose work is considered to be the beginning of modern chemistry

law /lɔ/ *n.*

1 system of rules [singular,U] the system of rules that citizens of a country, city, state etc. must obey: *Public drunkenness is* ***against the law*** *in Mexico.* | *It is* ***against the law*** *to sell cigarettes to minors.* | *He* ***broke the law*** (=did something illegal) *and deserves to be punished.* | *The bill may* ***become law*** *without the President's signature* (=be officially made a law). | *Candidates are required* ***by law*** *to file financial reports.* | *The court has ruled that the adult theater was operating* ***within the law*** (=not doing anything illegal). | ***tax/divorce/libel etc. law*** (=all the laws relating to tax etc.) —see also CRIMINAL, LAW FIRM

2 a rule [C] a rule that people in a particular country, city, state etc. must obey: ***Under the new law,*** *all drivers over the age of 18 are required to have insurance.* | [**– against**] *Michigan had no law against assisted suicide.* | [**+ on**] *the law on prescription drug advertising*

3 study/profession [U] the study of law, or the profession involving laws: *She practices law in New York.*

L

4 the law INFORMAL the police: *He's in trouble with the law again.*

5 law and order a situation in which people respect the law, and crime is controlled by the police, the prison system etc.: *The new government is gradually restoring law and order.*

6 description/explanation [C] a statement that describes and explains how something works: *the economic law of supply and demand | the law of gravity*

7 sports [C] one of the rules that say how a sport should be played: *the laws of football*

8 the law of the jungle a) the idea that people should only take care of themselves and not care about other people, if they want to succeed **b)** the principle that only the strongest creatures will stay alive

9 take the law into your own hands to do something illegal in order to correct a situation that you think is not fair or not being dealt with correctly by the authorities, for example by violently punishing someone instead of informing the police: *Citizens should not be expected to take the law into their own hands.*

10 have the law on your side to be legally right in what you are doing

11 the law of averages the PROBABILITY that one result will happen as often as another if you try something often enough: *The law of averages says we're due for a win.*

12 there's no law against it SPOKEN used to tell someone who is criticizing you that you are not doing anything wrong

13 there ought to be a law (against sth) SPOKEN used to say that you think something should not be accepted or allowed

14 be a law unto yourself to behave in an independent way and not worry about the usual rules of behavior or what other people do or think —see also CIVIL LAW, COMMON LAW, **lay down the law** at **lay down** (LAY¹), MURPHY'S LAW, ROMAN LAW, **unwritten law** (UNWRITTEN)

law·a·bid·ing /'. .,.../ *adj.* respectful of the law and obeying it: *a law-abiding citizen*

law·break·er /'lɔ,breɪkɚ/ *n.* [C] someone who does something illegal —**law-breaking** *n.* [U]

law en·force·ment /'. .,.../ *n.* [U] the job of making sure that the law is obeyed

law enforcement a·gent /'. .,.. ,../ *n.* [C] a police officer

law firm /'. ./ *n.* [C] a company that provides legal services and employs many lawyers

law·ful /'lɔfəl/ *adj.* FORMAL OR LAW **1** considered by the government or law courts to be legal and correct: *a lawful marriage* **2** allowed by law: *The police may not interfere in lawful demonstrations.* —**lawfully** *adv.*

law·less /'lɔlɪs/ *adj.* not obeying the law, or not controlled by the law: *lawless terrorists | a lawless war zone* —**lawlessness** *n.* [U]

law·mak·er /'lɔ,meɪkɚ/ *n.* [C] any elected official responsible for making laws; LEGISLATOR

law·man /'lɔmən/ *n. plural* **lawmen** /-mən/ [C] INFORMAL any professional officer who is responsible for making sure that the law is obeyed

lawn /lɔn/ *n.* **1** [C] an area of ground in a yard or park, that is covered with short grass: *The boy next door mows the lawn* (=cuts the grass) *for us.* —see picture on page 423 **2** [U] a fine cloth made from cotton or LINEN

lawn bowl·ing /'. ,../ *n.* [U] an outdoor game played on grass in which you try to roll a big ball as near as possible to a smaller ball

lawn chair /'. ./ *n.* [C] a light chair that you use outside, especially one that folds up —see picture at CHAIR¹

lawn mow·er /'. ,../ *n.* [C] a machine that you use to cut grass

lawn par·ty /'. ,../ *n. plural* **lawn parties** [C] a formal party held outside in the afternoon, especially in a large yard

lawn ten·nis /'. ,../ *n.* [U] FORMAL: see TENNIS

Law·rence /'lɔrəns, 'lɑr-/, **D.H.** /di eɪtʃ/ (1885–1930) a British writer of NOVELS

Lawrence, Jacob (1917–) a U.S. PAINTER and educator, famous for his paintings of people and events from African-American history

law school /'. ./ *n.* [C,U] a part of a university or a special school where you study to become a lawyer after you get your BACHELOR'S DEGREE

law·suit /'lɔsut/ *n.* [C] a problem or complaint that someone brings to a court of law to be settled, especially for money: *Neighbors have filed a lawsuit to stop development.*

law·yer /'lɔyɚ/ *n.* [C] someone whose job is to advise people about laws, write formal agreements, or represent people in court —compare ATTORNEY, COUNSEL¹

lax /læks/ *adj.* **1** not strict or careful about standards of behavior, work, safety etc.: *lax security for the building* **2** not firm, stiff, or tight: *The weakness in her legs made her go lax in Adrienne's arms.* —**laxly** *adv.* —**laxity, laxness** *n.* [U]

lax·a·tive /'læksətɪv/ *n.* [C] a medicine or something that you eat that makes your BOWELS empty easily —**laxative** *adj.*

lay

laying a dress on the bed   lying on the bed

lay¹ /leɪ/ *v. past tense and past participle* **laid**

1 put sb/sth down [T always + adv./prep.] to put someone or something down carefully into a flat position: [lay sth/sb down] *Nancy laid the baby down to change it.* | [lay sth in/on/under etc. sth] *"Do you love me?" she asked, laying a hand on his thigh.* | *He sank into the chair and laid his gloves on the floor.*

2 lay bricks/carpet/cables etc. to put or attach something in the correct place, especially onto something flat or under the ground: *Workers spent most of the day laying carpet in the new office building.*

3 eggs [I,T] if an animal, insect etc. lays eggs, it produces them from its body: *Turtles lay their eggs on the beach at night.*

4 lie NONSTANDARD [I] to LIE¹ (1)

5 lay a finger/hand on sb to touch someone, or to hurt them, especially by hitting them: *If you lay a hand on her, I'll kill you!*

6 lay (the) blame on sb also **lay the blame at sb's feet/doorstep** to blame someone for something: *The President is laying the blame on Congress.*

7 lay bare/open sth also **lay sth bare/open a)** to remove what covers, hides, or shelters something: *New bricks were removed, laying bare the old foundations.* **b)** to stop hiding something, or to show what the truth about something really is: *Krushchev laid bare Stalin's crimes.*

8 lay waste (to sth) to destroy or damage everything in a place, especially in a war: *The 1990 fire laid waste to the area.*

9 lay sth to rest to stop arguing about, worrying about, or discussing something, or to make people stop doing this: *He is anxious to lay all the rumors to rest.*

10 get laid VULGAR to have sex with someone: *Some guys are just looking to get laid* (=have sex).

11 lay sth on the line a) to state something, especially a threat, demand, or criticism, in a very clear way **b)** to risk losing your life, your job etc., especially in order to help someone

12 lay plans/a trap etc. to carefully prepare something, especially something that will harm someone else: *A group of business leaders is laying plans to raise money for the stadium.*

13 lay tracks/rubber SLANG to start driving a car very quickly from a stop, so that rubber from the tire is left on the road

14 make a statement [T] to make a statement, give information etc. in an official or public way: *Moyers laid his case before the public.*

15 lay sb open to blame/criticism/ridicule etc. FORMAL to do something that makes it possible for other people to blame you, criticize you etc.: *Remarks such as these laid him open to charges of sexual harassment.*

16 even the best-laid plans can go awry used to say that even if you plan carefully, you may still have problems

17 lay sb to rest FORMAL to bury someone

18 lay sth at sb's door to say that something is someone's fault

19 lay an egg INFORMAL to fail or be unsuccessful at something that you are trying to do: *The first episode of the series laid an egg.*

20 lay hands (on sb) to pray for someone while touching them

21 risk money [T] to risk an amount of money on the result of a race, sports game etc.: *She laid $10 on the favorite, Golden Boy.*

22 lay sb/sth flat to hit someone or something and knock them down: *Jones laid him flat with a single punch!*

23 lay sb low a) if an illness lays someone low, they are unable to do their normal activities for a period of time: *The infection laid her low for a month.* **b)** LITERARY to knock someone down or injure them seriously

24 lay stress/emphasis on sth FORMAL to emphasize something because you regard it as very important

25 OLD-FASHIONED **lay a table** to put the cloth, plates knives, forks etc. on a table, ready for a meal; set the table —see also **put/lay your cards on the table** (CARD¹ (10)), **lay/provide the foundation(s) for sth** (FOUNDATION (6)), **get/lay your hands on sth** (HAND¹ (22))

lay sth ↔ **aside** *phr. v.* [T] **1** to stop using, doing, or preparing something, especially for a short time: *Yolanda laid aside the baby blanket she was sewing.* **2** to stop behaving in a particular way or showing a particular emotion, even if you still feel that way, so that you can achieve something: *Taylor and Herrera laid aside their personal differences in the interest of national defense.* **3** to store something to use in the future: *I've laid aside a little money for next summer.*

lay back *phr. v.* [I] to relax or avoid doing something: *We're not going to lay back and let them close our business.*

lay sth ↔ **down** *phr. v.* [T] **1 lay down your weapons/arms etc.** to stop fighting in a war, battle etc. when you realize that you cannot win: *The Prime Minister urged the rebels to lay down their arms.* **2** to officially state rules that must be obeyed, systems that must be used etc., or to state something officially or firmly: *Members greet newcomers and lay down the ground rules.* **3 lay down your life** FORMAL to lose your life, for example in a war, in order to help other people: *He considered it a privilege to lay down his life for his country.* **4 lay down the law** to tell other people what to do, how they should think etc., in a strong, annoying, and impolite way: *Parents need to lay down the law regarding how much TV their children watch.* **5** to store something, especially wine, to use in the future

lay sth ↔ **in** *phr. v.* [T] FORMAL to obtain and store a large supply of something to use in the future: *Squirrels laid in plenty of nuts for the winter.*

lay into sb *phr. v.* [T] to attack someone physically or with words: *As soon as he got home, she laid into him.*

lay off *phr. v.* **1** [T **lay** sb ↔ **off**] to stop employing a worker, especially for a period in which there is

not much work to do: *The company closed and laid off 40 employees.* **2** [I,T **lay off** sth] INFORMAL to stop doing, having, or using something: *I think you should lay off coffee for a while.* **3** [I,T **lay off** sb] to stop annoying someone: *Just lay off, would you? I'm tired of arguing.*

lay on *phr. v.* **1** [**lay** sth ↔ **on**] to provide food, entertainment etc. in a very generous way: *Lola really laid on a great meal for us.* **2** [**lay** sth **on** sb] to give someone something such as a responsibility or problem that is hard to deal with: *Sorry to lay this on you now, but we really need the final report finished by Friday.* **3 lay it on thick** INFORMAL to do or say something in a way that makes something seem better, more amusing, bigger etc. than it really is; EXAGGERATE: *She flattered him like crazy, really laid it on thick, and he thought it was great.*

lay out *phr. v.*

1 spread [T **lay** sth ↔ **out**] to spread something out: *Lay out the map on the table and we'll take a look.*

2 arrange [T **lay** sth ↔ **out**] to arrange or plan a building, town, garden etc.: *May's home is laid out in a U-shape.*

3 describe [T **lay** sth ↔ **out**] to officially tell about or describe a plan, idea etc.: *The letter laid out the administration's plans for economic reform.*

4 lie [I] SPOKEN, NONSTANDARD to lie in the sun: *If the weather's good this afternoon, I'm going to lay out.*

5 spend [T **lay** sth ↔ **out**] INFORMAL to spend money, especially a lot of money: [+ **on**] *We had to lay out $800 on car repairs.* —see also OUTLAY

6 hit [T **lay** sb ↔ **out**] to knock someone down, especially hard enough to make them unconscious: *Hal's solid punch laid him out on the ground.*

7 body [T **lay** sb ↔ **out**] FORMAL to prepare a dead body so that it can be buried

lay over *phr. v.* [I] to stay somewhere for a short time before continuing your trip

lay sb/sth ↔ **up** *phr. v.* [T] **1** [usually passive] if an injury or illness lays you up, you have to stay in bed: [**be laid up with sth**] *Jeff is laid up with a broken leg.* **2** OLD-FASHIONED to collect and store something to use in the future

USAGE NOTE: LAY

WORD CHOICE: lay, lie, lie
Lay means "to put something in a particular position": *Just lay the papers on the desk.* The other forms of this verb are **laid**, **laid**, and **laying**. **Lie** has two different meanings. Use one meaning of **lie** to talk about someone or something that is flat on a surface: *He was lying face down on the bathroom floor.* | *Don't leave your stuff lying all over the house.* The other forms of this verb are **lay**, **lain**, and **lying**. In spoken English you will also sometimes hear things like: *I need to lay down* (instead of *I need to lie down*) but this is generally considered incorrect. The other meaning of **lie** is "to say something that is not true": *Are you lying to me?* The other forms of this verb are **lied** and **lying**.

lay² *v.* the past tense of LIE¹

lay³ *n.* [C] **1 the lay of the land a)** the situation that exists at a particular time: *He's got to get the lay of the land before he makes any decisions.* **b)** the appearance of an area of land, the way it slopes etc. **2 be a good/lousy etc. lay** VULGAR to be good or bad to have sex with **3** LITERARY a poem or song

lay⁴ *adj.* [only before noun] **1** not in an official position in the church: *a lay minister* **2** not trained or knowing much about a particular profession or subject: *To the lay observer, these technical terms are incomprehensible.*

lay·a·way /ˈleɪəˌweɪ/ *n.* [U] a method of buying goods in which you give the seller of the goods a small amount of money to keep the goods until you can pay the full price: *I put the dress on layaway.* —**layaway** *adj.: a layaway plan*

L

lay·er¹ /'leɪə/ n. [C] **1** an amount of a substance that covers all of a surface: [+ **of**] *The road was covered by a thin layer of ice.* **2** something that is placed on or between other things, or that exists on or between other things: [+ **of**] *Separate the layers of cookies with wax paper.* | *Several layers of clothing are warmer than one thick layer.* | *a layer of volcanic rock* —see also OZONE LAYER **3** one of several different levels in a complicated organization, system, set of ideas etc.: [+ **of**] *There are many layers of meaning to be discovered in the poem.* | *layers of bureaucracy* —see also -LAYERED

layer² v. [T] **1** to make a layer of something, or to put something down in layers: *The cliffs are layered with fossil remains.* **2** to cut someone's hair in layers of different length rather than all the same length

-layered /leɪəd/ [in adjectives] **multi-layered/single-layered** etc. having a lot of layers, one layer etc.

lay·ette /leɪ'ɛt/ n. [C] a complete set of clothing and other things that a new baby needs

lay·man /'leɪmən/ n. plural **laymen** /-mən/ [C] **1** someone who is not trained in a particular subject or type of work, especially when they are being compared with someone who is: *The report was readable and understandable to **the layman** (=laymen in general).* | *a technical report written **in layman's terms** (=in simple language anyone can understand).* **2** someone who is not a priest but is a member of a church

lay·off /'leɪɔf/ n. [C] the act of stopping a worker's employment because there is not enough work: *Some of the layoffs were caused by the weak economy.* —see also **lay off** (LAY¹)

lay·out /'leɪaʊt/ n. [C] **1** the way in which something such as a town or building is arranged **2** the way in which writing and pictures are arranged on a page —see also **lay out** (LAY¹)

lay·o·ver /'leɪˌoʊvə/ n. [C] a short stay somewhere between parts of a trip, especially a long airplane trip

lay·per·son /'leɪˌpɚsən/ n. plural **laypeople** /-ˌpipəl/ [C] a word for a LAYMAN, used when the person could be a woman or a man

lay read·er /ˌ. '../ n. [C] someone in the Episcopal or Catholic Church who is not a priest but who has been given authority to read part of the religious service

lay·up, lay-up /'leɪʌp/ n. [C] a throw in basketball made from very close to the basket or from under it

lay·wom·an /'leɪˌwʊmən/ n. [C] **1** a woman not trained in a particular subject or type of work, especially when she is being compared with someone who is **2** a woman who is not a priest but is a member of a church

Laz·a·rus /'læzərəs/, **Em·ma** /'ɛmə/ (1849–1887) a U.S. writer famous for her poem that is written at the base of the Statue of Liberty

laze /leɪz/ v. [I always + adv./prep.] to relax and enjoy yourself in a lazy way: *I'm just going to laze around and watch TV.* —**laze** n. [singular]

la·zy /'leɪzi/ adj. **lazier, laziest 1** disliking work or physical activity, and never making any effort: *He's too lazy to cook himself dinner.* | *She's the laziest girl I know.* **2** a lazy period of time is spent doing nothing except relaxing: *a lazy afternoon* **3** moving slowly: *a lazy river* —**lazily** adv. —**laziness** n. [U]

la·zy·bones /'leɪziˌboʊnz/ n. [C] INFORMAL a word for a lazy person, often used in a friendly way to someone you like: *Come on, lazybones! Get out of bed.*

lazy eye /ˌ.. '../ n. [singular] NOT TECHNICAL a medical condition in which one eye does not move with the other one

lazy Su·san /ˌleɪzi 'suzən/ n. [C] a shelf or TRAY for food, that turns around in a circle

lb. plural **lbs.** the written abbreviation of POUND¹ (1)

LCD n. [C] Liquid Crystal Display; the part of a WATCH, CALCULATOR, or small computer where numbers and letters are shown by means of an electric current that is passed through a special liquid

lea /li/ n. [C] POETIC an area of land with grass

leach /litʃ/ also **leach out** v. [I,T] TECHNICAL if a substance leaches or is leached from a larger mass such as the soil, it is removed from it by water passing through the larger mass: *Nitrates from fertilizers leached into the rivers* (=they passed from the soil into the rivers).

lead¹ /lid/ v. past tense and past participle **led**

1 **guide a)** [T always + adv./prep.] to take someone to a place by going with them or in front of them: [**lead sb through/to/along etc. sth**] *Dale led us down a dirt path to the farmhouse.* **b)** [T] to take a person or animal somewhere while holding the person's arm or hand, or pulling a rope tied to the animal: [**lead sb up/down/through etc. sth**] *She was so nearsighted I had to take her hand and lead her to the table.* | *We led the horses along the river.*

2 **go in front** [I,T] to go in front of a group of people or vehicles: *The high school band is leading the parade.*

3 **road/wire** [I] if a path, pipe, wire etc. leads somewhere or leads in a particular direction, it goes there or goes in that direction: [+ **down/into/toward** etc.] *The two sets of footprints led off in different directions.* | *Someone cut the wires leading to the surveillance cameras.* | *Where does this road lead?*

4 **door** [I] if a door or passage leads to a particular room or place, you can get there by going through it: [+ **to/into**] *A court officer opened the door that led to the jury room.*

5 **be in charge of** [T] to be in charge of something such as an important activity, a group of people, or an organization, and therefore influence what people do: *Who is leading the investigation?* | *The government, led by conservatives, has been unwilling to join the talks.* | *UN-led hostage negotiations*

6 **win** [I,T] to be winning a game or competition: *With two minutes to play, the Lakers are still leading.* | [+ **by**] *The Cowboys led by 19 points midway through the second half.* | [**lead sb/sth**] *Mayor Davis leads his opponent by 28 points.*

7 **make sb do sth** [T] to be the thing that makes someone decide to do something: [**lead sb to do sth**] *Several factors led us to choose Austria for our study.*

8 **lead sb to believe/expect/understand** to make someone think something is true, especially when it is not: *He led me to believe that he'd never been married before.*

9 **lead a normal/exciting/dull etc. life** to have a normal, exciting etc. type of life: *You kids have led such an easy life.*

10 **success** [I,T] to be more successful than other people, companies, or countries in a particular activity or area of business or study: [**lead (sb/sth) in sth**] *Japan leads the world in life expectancy.* | *Cameron's new movie led the field* (=was most successful in a particular group) *with seven Oscar nominations.*

11 **lead the way a)** to guide someone in a particular direction: *Gluck led the way to the science lab.* **b)** to be the first or best at doing something, which is likely to encourage others to do the same thing: *New York has led the way in protection of freedom of the press.*

12 **conversation** [I,T] to direct a conversation or discussion, especially so that it develops in the way you want: *Debbie always leads the conversation back around to herself.*

13 **lead sb astray** to deceive someone and encourage them to do bad or immoral things that they would not normally do: *Claudio is the false friend who leads Leonardo astray into drinking and gambling.*

14 **lead sb by the nose** INFORMAL to make someone do anything you want them to

15 **you can lead a horse to water (but you can't make him drink)** used to say that you cannot force anyone to do what they do not want to do

16 **this leads me to...** SPOKEN used in a speech or discussion to introduce a new subject and connect it with what you have just said: *This leads me to our sales targets for next year.*

17 lead sb down the garden/primrose path IN-FORMAL to deceive someone

18 `cards` [I,T] to play a particular card as your first card in one part of a game of cards: [+ with] *He led with the eight of hearts.*

19 `dancing` [I,T] to be the one of two people that are dancing together who decides which direction they will move: *Juan led her slowly around the dance floor.*

20 lead with your left/right to hit someone mainly with your left or right hand in BOXING

lead into sth *phr. v.* [T not in passive] if one subject, discussion etc. leads into another, the second one follows naturally from the first because there is a clear relationship between them: *Some teachers use the history lesson to lead into discussions of modern-day problems.*

lead off *phr. v.* **1** [I,T **lead** sth → **off**] to start something such as a meeting, discussion, or performance by saying or doing something: *I'd like to lead off by thanking Dr. Jacobs for finding the time to be with us today.* | *A group of three jets led off the parade.* | [+ with] *He led off with a few jokes.* **2** [I] to be the first player to try to hit the ball in an INNING (=period of play) in a game of baseball

lead sb → **on** *phr. v.* [T] to deceive someone, especially by making them think that you are romantically interested in them when you really are not: *I don't want to lead her on, but I don't want to hurt her feelings either.*

lead to sth *phr. v.* [T not in passive] to make something happen or exist as a result of something else: *A reward has been offered for information leading to the arrest of the thieves.* | **One thing led to another** (=a series of events happened), *and we got in another big fight.*

lead up to sth *phr. v.* [T not in passive] **1** to come before something and often cause it: *Baker's popularity dropped in the last few days leading up to the election.* | *the events leading up to the war* **2** to gradually introduce a subject into a conversation, especially a subject that may be embarrassing or upsetting for you or the person you are talking to: *I guess what I'm leading up to is that I think we need to rewrite the proposal.*

USAGE NOTE: LEAD

WORD CHOICE: lead, take, guide, direct
Lead means "to show the way by going first": *He led us around to the back door.* **Take** means "to go with someone to a place, often because they cannot get there by themselves": *Will you take me home? I'm not feeling very well.* **Guide** means "to show the way and explain things": *She guides tourists around the White House.* **Direct** is a formal word that means "to explain to someone how to get somewhere": *Could you direct me to the station?*

ˢ ʷ **lead²** *n.*
²

1 `races` **the lead** the position or situation of being in front of or better than everyone else in a race or competition: *Lewis is still in the lead.*

2 take the lead a) to go ahead of the other competitors in a race or competition: *Kent took the lead in the fifth lap.* **b)** to take the responsibility for doing something: *It's up to the U.S. and Russia to take the lead in solving the crisis.* **c)** to be the first to do something, hoping that others will copy you: *Germany took the lead in recognizing the new republics.*

3 `winning amount` [singular] the distance, number of points etc. by which one competitor is ahead of another: [+ over] *Virginia holds a 12-game lead over Kentucky.* | [+ of] *In March the Republican candidate had a lead of 35%.*

4 follow sb's lead to copy what someone else has done, or to do what they tell you to do: *Toyota is following Nissan's lead in building factories in Britain.*

5 `information` [C] a piece of information that may help you to make a discovery or help find the answer to a problem: *The police have no leads in the murder investigation.*

6 `performer` [C] the main acting part in a play, movie etc.: *Who's playing the lead in the school play?*

7 `news` [C] the first or most important story in a television news program, newspaper etc., or the first part of such a story

8 be sb's lead if it is your lead in a game of cards, you have the right to play your card first

9 `for dog` a LEASH¹ (1)

10 `electric wire` TECHNICAL a wire that is used to connect parts of a piece of electrical equipment

lead³ /lɛd/ *n.* **1** [U] *symbol* **Pb** a soft heavy gray metal that is an ELEMENT, that melts easily, and is poisonous, which was used for water pipes, covering roofs etc.: *High levels of lead were discovered in the soil in Skagway.* **2** [C,U] the middle part of a pencil that makes the marks when you write **3 a lead foot** if someone has a lead foot, they always drive their car very fast **4 go down like a lead balloon** if a suggestion or joke goes down like a lead BALLOON, people do not like it at all **5** [U] OLD-FASHIONED bullets: *Tucker got a belly full of lead.*

lead⁴ /lid/ *adj.* [only before noun] **1 lead guitarist/singer/attorney etc.** the first or most important person in a group **2 lead story/editorial** a very important or interesting article that is given the first or most important place in a newspaper **3 lead runner/car etc.** the person, car etc. that is in front of a group: *The lead car was less than a lap ahead.* **4 lead time** the period of time between when something is started and when it is finished or happens: *There's a four-year lead time required to produce new automobiles.*

lead·ed gas /ˌlɛdɪd ˈgæs/ *n.* also **leaded gas·o·line** /ˌ... ...ˈ./ [U] gasoline containing LEAD³ (1)

lead·en /ˈlɛdn/ *adj.* **1** LITERARY dark gray: *leaden skies* **2** without happiness, excitement, or energy: *a leaden speaking style*

lead·er /ˈlidɚ/ *n.* [C] **1** the person who directs or controls a team, organization, country etc., or someone who has the ability to do this: *our national political leaders* | *a Boy Scout leader* | [+ of] *The leader of the revolt was Antonio Miranda.* | **a religious/military/community etc. leader** (=with an important position in a particular type of group) **2** the person, organization etc. that is in front of all the others in a race or competition: *The Detroit Tigers are now the American League division leaders.* **3** the product or company that is the best or most successful in a particular area: [+ in] *a leader in the field of genetic research* —see also MARKET LEADER **4** someone who directs the playing of a musical group: *a band leader* ˢ ʷ / ² ¹ / ² □

lead·er·ship /ˈlidɚˌʃɪp/ *n.* **1** [U] the position of being the leader of a team, organization etc.: *Assistant Coach Contanzo was given full leadership of the team.* | *The Mormons moved to Utah under the leadership of Brigham Young* (=while Young was their leader). | *Due to his experience, Eckhart has an important leadership role in the company.* **2** [U] the quality of being good at leading a team, organization, country etc.: *It was Gorbachev's leadership which helped reform the country.* **3** [C] all the people who lead a group, organization, country etc.: *the Chinese leadership* **4** [U] the position of being better than your competitors: *the company's leadership in robot technology* ˢ ʷ / ² / ³ □

lead-free /ˌlɛd ˈfri/ *adj.* containing no LEAD³ (1); UNLEADED

lead-in /ˈlid ɪn/ *n.* [C] remarks made by someone to introduce a television or radio show

lead·ing /ˈlidɪŋ/ *adj.* [only before noun] **1** best, most important, or most successful: *CCI is a leading provider of cellular phone service in Ohio.* | *the leading scorer in college basketball* **2 leading edge a)** the part of an activity in which the most modern and advanced equipment and methods are used: *To survive, companies must stay on the leading edge of technology.* —see also LEADING-EDGE **b)** TECHNICAL the part of something that is at the front of it when it

L

moves: *the leading edge of a plane's wing* **3 leading light** a respected person who leads a group or organization, or is important in a particular area of knowledge or activity **4 a leading question** a question that deliberately tricks someone into giving the answer you want **5 leading lady/man** the woman or man who acts the most important female or male part in a movie, play etc.

lead·ing² /'lɛdɪŋ/ *n.* [U] TECHNICAL **1** the space left between lines of print on a page **2** LEAD³ (1) used for window frames

leading-edge /ˌlidɪŋ 'ɛdʒ/ *adj.* [only before noun] leading-edge machines, systems etc. are the most modern and advanced ones that exist: *leading-edge communication devices* —see also **leading edge** (LEADING¹ (2))

lead-off /'lid ɔf/ *adj.* happening or going first or before others: *Perez will be the lead-off batter for the Pirates.*

lead time /'lid taɪm/ *n.* [C] the time it takes to prepare, make, and deliver something to someone who has ordered it

SW **leaf¹** /lif/ *n. plural* **leaves** /livz/ **1** [C] one of the flat green parts of a plant that are joined to its stem or branches: *the leaves of a maple tree* | **be in leaf/ come into leaf** (=grow leaves in the spring) —see pictures at ROSE¹ and OAK **2** [C] a part of the top of a table that can be taken out to make the table smaller **3** [U] metal, especially gold or silver, in a very thin sheet **4** [C] TECHNICAL a thin sheet of paper, especially a page in a book —see also LOOSE-LEAF, **turn over a new leaf** at **turn over** (TURN¹)

leaf² *v.*

leaf through sth *phr. v.* [T] to turn the pages of a book quickly, without reading it thoroughly or carefully: *We spent the evening leafing through my old scrapbook.*

leaf·age /'lifɪdʒ/ *n.* [U] the leaves on a tree or plant; FOLIAGE

leaf·let¹ /'liflɪt/ *n.* [C] a piece of printed paper with information, political statements, or advertising on it: **pass/hand out leaflets** (=give them to people in a public place)

leaflet² *v.* [I,T] to give leaflets to people in a particular area, usually a public place: *Miller's group will continue leafleting the area around City Hall.*

leaf mold /'. ./ *n.* [U] dead decaying leaves that form a rich surface on soil

leaf·y /'lifi/ *adj.* **leafier, leafiest 1** having a lot of leaves: *Spinach, chard, and other leafy greens are excellent in salads.* **2** having a lot of trees and plants: *a leafy town*

SW **league¹** /lig/ *n.* [C] **1** a group of sports teams or players who play games against each other to see who is best: *the National Football League* —compare CONFERENCE (3) **2 not be in the same league (as/with sb/sth)** to be not nearly as good or important as someone or something else: *American beers are just not in the same league as South American ones.* **3 sb is out of their league** if someone is out of their league, they are not skilled or experienced enough to do something: *Kendall's out of his league when it comes to marketing.* **4 be in league (with sb)** to be working together secretly, especially for a bad purpose: *Union leaders were accused of being in league with the Mafia.* **5** a group of people or countries who have joined together because they have similar aims, political beliefs etc.: *the League of Women Voters* **6** an old unit for measuring, equal to about five kilometers

league² *v.* [I,T] FORMAL to join together with other people, especially in order to fight for or against something

League of Wom·en Vot·ers /ˌ. . ˌ.. '../ a U.S. organization that encourages women to vote, and makes sure that laws or government plans that affect women are properly discussed and thought about

leak¹ /lik/ *v.* **1** [I,T] if a container, pipe, roof etc. leaks, or if it leaks gas, liquid etc., there is a small hole or crack in it that lets the gas or liquid flow out or flow through: *The roof always leaks when it rains.* | *They found the pipe that was leaking chlorine.* **2** [I] if a gas or liquid leaks, it gets in or through a hole in something: [+ **into/through/ from** etc.] *Water was leaking out of the radiator.* **3** [T] to deliberately give secret information to a newspaper, television company etc.: [**leak** sth **to** sb] *Details of the contract were leaked to the press.* **4 leak like a sieve** to leak very badly

leak

leak out *phr. v.* [I] if secret information leaks out, a lot of people find out about it: *News of the deal leaked out three weeks ago.*

leak² *n.* [C] **1** a small hole that lets liquid or gas flow into or out of something: *A leak was discovered in the cooling system.* **2 a gas/oil/water leak** an escape of gas or liquid through a hole in something **3** a situation in which secret information is deliberately given to a newspaper, television company etc.: *White House officials are anxious to find the person responsible for the leak.* **4 take a leak** SLANG to pass water from your body; URINATE —see also **spring a leak** (SPRING² (7))

leak·age /'likɪdʒ/ *n.* **1** [C,U] an occasion when gas, water etc. leaks, or the amount of gas or liquid that has leaked **2** [U] the deliberate spreading of information that should be kept secret

leak·y /'liki/ *adj.* **leakier, leakiest** a container, roof etc. that is leaky has a hole or other fault in it, so that liquid or gas passes through it: *a leaky faucet* —**leakiness** *n.* [U]

lean¹ /lin/ *v.* **1** [I always + adv./prep.] to move or bend your body in a particular direction: [+ **for- ward/back/over** etc.] *Celia leaned forward to pick up her pencil.* | *Then the man leaned over and kissed his wife.* **2** [I always + adv./prep.,T always + adv./prep.] to support yourself or an object in a sloping position against a wall or other surface, or to put something in a sloping position in which it is supported: [+ **on/against**] *Don't lean on the fence. It's not very sturdy.* | *Lou leaned against the wall as he talked.* | [**lean** sth **on/against** sth] *Dad leaned the ladder against the house.* **3** [I] to slope or bend from an upright position: *All of the trees were leaning in the wind.*

lean

leaning against a wall

lean on sb/sth *phr. v.* [T] **1** to depend on someone or something for support or help, especially at a difficult time: *The Lakers have leaned heavily on O'Neill's talent all season.* **2** INFORMAL to try to influence someone, especially by threatening them: [**lean on** sb **to do** sth] *Apparently, Roberts leaned on the family to give him money.*

lean toward sth *phr. v.* [T] to be likely to make a particular decision or support a particular set of opinions, beliefs etc.: *I'm leaning toward taking the job in Miami.*

lean² *adj.* **1** thin in a healthy and attractive way: *a lean and athletic man* **2** lean meat does not have much fat on it **3** a lean organization, company etc. uses only as much money and as many people as it needs, so that nothing is wasted: *a **lean and mean** (=very competitive) corporation* **4** a lean period is a very difficult time because there is not enough money, business etc.: *a lean year for business* —**lean-ness** *n.* [U]

lean³ *n.* [U] OLD-FASHIONED the part of meat that you eat, but not the bone or fat

lean·ing /'liːnɪŋ/ *n.* [C] a tendency to prefer or agree with a particular set of beliefs, opinions etc.: *Fran has Communist leanings.* | [+ **toward**] *a leaning toward the Left* —**leaning** *adj.*: *the conservative-leaning court*

lean-to /'. ./ *n.* [C] a small roughly made building that rests against the side of a larger building

leap¹ /liːp/ *v. past tense and past participle* **leapt** *or* **leaped** **1 a)** [I always + adv./prep.] to jump high into the air, or to jump in order to land in a different place: [+ **over/across**] *A deer leapt over the fence.* **b)** [T] LITERARY to jump over something: *Brenda leaped the gate and ran across the field.* **2** [I always + adv./prep.] to move very quickly and with a lot of energy: [+ **up/out/into etc.**] *I leapt up the stairs three at a time.* | *Fraser leaped to his feet* (=quickly stood up) *and protested.* | **leap to sb's defense/assistance** (=quickly defend or help someone) **3** [I] to increase quickly and by a large amount: *The price of gas leapt 15% overnight.* **4 sth leaps out at you** if something you are looking at leaps out at you, it is very easy for you to notice because it is unusual or unexpected **5** [I] LITERARY if your heart leaps, you feel sudden surprise, happiness, or excitement —see also **look before you leap** (LOOK¹ (7))

leap at sth *phr. v.* to accept a chance, opportunity, or offer very eagerly: *I leapt at the chance of going to India.*

leap² *n.* [C] **1** a big jump: *Powell won with a leap of 27 feet, 10 inches.* **2 by leaps and bounds** if someone or something increases, develops, grows etc. by leaps and BOUNDS, they do it very quickly: *The Hispanic population of the county has grown by leaps and bounds.* **3** a sudden large increase in the number or amount of something: [+ **in**] *a leap in prices* **4 a leap of faith** something you do even though it involves a risk, hoping that it will have a good result: *It took a huge leap of faith to open the restaurant during a slow economy.* **5** a mental process that is needed to understand something difficult or to see the connection between two very different ideas: *It takes quite a leap of the imagination to see John as a teacher.* **6 a leap in the dark** something you do, or a risk that you take, without knowing what will happen as a result

leap·frog¹ /'liːpfrɑːɡ/ *n.* [U] a children's game in which someone bends over and someone else jumps over them

leapfrog² *v.* [I,T] to achieve something more quickly than usual, especially by missing some of the usual stages: *The Cubs knew a win would leapfrog them into second place.*

leapt /lɛpt/ *v.* a past tense and past participle of LEAP¹

leap year /'. ./ *n.* [C] a year when February has 29 days instead of 28, which happens every four years

Lear·jet /'lɪrdʒɛt/ *n.* [C] TRADEMARK a type of airplane that is fast and comfortable

learn /lɜːrn/ *v.*

1 subject/skill [I,T] to gain knowledge of a subject or skill in an activity, by experience, by studying it, or by being taught: *When did you begin learning Spanish?* | *Sarah is a student who is eager to learn.* | [**learn (how) to do sth**] *Didn't you learn to drive when you were 15?* | [+ **about**] *We're learning about the Civil War in history class.* | [**learn how/what/who etc.**] *Learning how to read is a long process.* —compare TEACH —see also KNOW¹

2 find out [I,T] FORMAL to find out information, news etc. by hearing it from someone else: [+ **of/about**] *I learned of her death yesterday.* | [**learn sth**] *Where did you learn the news?* | [**learn (that)**] *Several months ago McNaughtan learned that he had cancer.* | [**learn who/what/whether etc.**] *By the end of the week, we'll learn whether we'll get a bonus.*

3 remember [T] to get to know something so well that you can easily remember it; MEMORIZE: *As an actor, she always had trouble learning her lines.*

4 change your behavior [I,T] to gradually understand a situation and start behaving in the way that you should: [**learn to do sth**] *Both of us have learned to treat each other with respect.* | [**learn (that)**] *I learned that being a good father means being a good husband first.*

5 learn your lesson to suffer so much because you did something wrong or stupid that you will not do it again: *I hope Pereira has learned his lesson about how to treat employees.*

6 learn from your mistakes to improve the way you do things because of mistakes you have made

7 learn (sth) the hard way to understand a situation or develop a skill by learning from your mistakes and bad experiences: *I learned the hard way that drugs weren't an answer to my problems.*

8 that'll learn sb! SPOKEN, NONSTANDARD used when something bad has just happened to someone, especially because they ignored your warning —see also **live and learn** (LIVE¹ (28)) —see Usage Note at KNOW¹

USAGE NOTE: LEARN

WORD CHOICE: learn, teach, show
Both **teach** and **learn** are used about things that take time to be able to do. **Learn** means to study or practice so that you can know facts or know how to do something: *Ron's learning how to drive.* **Teach** means to explain to someone what to do or how to do it, over a period of time: *Who taught you how to play the guitar?* **Show** means to use actions to explain how to do something: *Here, I'll show you how to unlock the door.*

---

learn·ed /'lɜːrnɪd/ *adj.* FORMAL **1** having a lot of knowledge because you have read and studied a lot: *a learned professor* **2 learned books/works etc.** books or other materials that are written by people who have a lot of knowledge —**learnedly** *adv.*

learn·er /'lɜːrnɚ/ *n.* [C] someone who is learning to do something: **slow/quick/fast learner** *Jill's a very quick learner.* | [+ **of**] *a grammar book for learners of English*

learner's per·mit /'.. ,../ *n.* [C] an official document that gives you permission to learn to drive

learn·ing /'lɜːrnɪŋ/ *n.* [U] knowledge gained through reading and study: *a woman of great learning*

learning curve /'.. ,./ *n.* [C] the rate at which you learn a new skill

learning dis·a·bil·i·ty /'.. ..,.../ *n.* [C] a mental problem that affects a child's ability to learn

learnt /lɜːrnt/ *v.* OLD-FASHIONED a past tense and past participle of LEARN

leas·a·ble /'liːsəbəl/ *adj.* available to be leased: *112,000 square feet of leasable office space*

lease¹ /liːs/ *n.* [C] **1** a legal agreement that allows you to use a car, building etc. for a period of time, in return for rent: *a six-month lease on an apartment* | *I decided to take out a lease* (=get one) *on a BMW.* **2 give sb/sth a new lease on life a)** to make someone feel healthy, active, or happy again after being weak, sick, or tired: *Changing jobs has given me a new lease on life.* **b)** to change or improve a thing or a situation so that something will continue to work longer: *Rising oil prices could give atomic energy a new lease on life.*

lease² *v.* [T] **1** also **lease out** to use or let someone use buildings, property etc. on a lease: [**lease sth to sb**] *They decided to lease the building to another company.* **2** to pay to use expensive machinery or equipment for a long period, instead of buying it: *We lease all our computers.*

lease·back /'liːsbæk/ *n.* [C,U] TECHNICAL an arrangement in which you sell or give something to someone, but continue to use it by paying them rent

lease·hold /'liːshoʊld/ *n.* [C] LAW an agreement by which you lease a building or piece of land for a particular, usually long, period of time

lease·hold·er /'liːs,hoʊldɚ/ *n.* [C] LAW someone who has leased a building or piece of land

S W
3
leash[1] /liʃ/ n. [C] **1** a piece of rope, leather etc. attached to a dog's collar in order to control it: *All dogs must be kept on a leash at all times in the park.* **2 have sb on a leash** HUMOROUS to be able to control someone: *Jerry's wife has him on a tight leash.*

leash[2] v. [T] to put a leash on a dog —**leashed** adj.

S W
1 1
least[1] /list/ quantifier **1 at least a)** not less than a particular number or amount: *At least fifty people were waiting in line.* | *It will take a year at the very least* (=not less than a year, and probably much more) *to build the stadium.* **b)** even if nothing else is true, or even if nothing else happens: *At least you should listen to his explanation.* | *His parents should at least go to his graduation.* **c)** used when you are mentioning an advantage that makes particular problems or disadvantages seem less serious: *The food was terrible, but at least we had a nice view.* **d)** used when you are correcting or changing something that you have just said: *His name is Kevin. At least that's what he told me.* | *The law has changed, at least as far as I know.* **2 the least** the smallest in number, amount, or importance: *Which jacket costs the least?* | *$10,000 is the least we'll need to repair the roof.* **3 least of all** especially not a particular person or thing: *Dave doesn't take anything seriously, least of all himself.* **4 the least sb could do** used when saying what you think someone should or could do to help someone else: *The least he could do is help you with the housework.* **5 not in the least** also **not the least (bit)** none at all, or not at all: *Neither of them is adventurous in the least.* | *She didn't seem the least bit worried.* **6 to say the least** used to show that something is worse or more serious than you are actually saying: *Mrs. Russel was upset, to say the least.* **7 the least of your worries** something you are not worried about because there are other more important problems: *Figuring out where to go eat is the least of my worries right now.* **8 not least** FORMAL used to emphasize that something is important: *There are many factors which limit productivity; not least is employee education.*

least[2] adv. less than anything or anyone else: *Car problems happen when you least expect them.* | *I was the least experienced member of the expedition.* | *The tax hits those who can least afford it.*

least·wise /'listwaɪz/ also **least·ways** /'listweɪz/ adv. INFORMAL at least; ANYWAY: *He was there a minute ago, leastwise that's what Sue said.*

S W
3
leath·er /'lɛðɚ/ n. **1** [U] animal skin, especially from cows, that has been treated to preserve it, and is used for making shoes, bags etc.: *The belt is made of fine calfskin leather.* | *a pair of leather gloves* **2 leathers** [plural] special leather clothes worn for protection by someone riding a MOTORCYCLE —see also **run/go hell for leather** (HELL (27))

Leath·er·ette /ˌlɛθɚˈɛt/ n. [U] TRADEMARK a cheap material made to look like leather

leath·er·neck /'lɛðɚˌnɛk/ n. [C] SLANG a U.S. Marine

leath·er·y /'lɛðəri/ adj. thick and stiff like leather rather than soft or smooth: *leathery skin*

S W
1 1
leave[1] /liv/ v. past tense and past participle **left**
1 go away [I,T] to go away from a place or a person: *I usually leave the house at six in the morning.* | [+ for] *We're leaving for Tokyo next week.* | [leave to do sth] *I have to leave to pick up the kids at school.*
2 let sth remain [T always + adv./prep.] to let something or someone stay where they are when you go away: [leave sth in/on etc.] *We're leaving the kids with Debbie tonight.* | *Your toys will get ruined if you leave them in the yard.*
3 for sb to find [T] to put something in a place where someone else can find it and use it: [leave sth for sb] *We left $20 on the table for you to go get a pizza.* | [leave sb sth] *Why didn't you leave me any bread?*
4 letter/message [T] to leave a letter, package, message etc. somewhere for someone: *Please leave your name and number and I'll get back to you.* |

[leave sth for sb] *Lucy left a note for you.* | [leave sb sth] *If I'm not home, you can leave me a message.* | **Leave word with** (=leave a message with) *my secretary if you can't come.*
5 be left also **have sth left** to remain after everything else has been taken away or used: *Is there any coffee left?* | *By 5 o'clock there was hardly anyone left in the office.* | *I still have three chapters left to read.* | *If there's any money left over* (=remaining after the rest is used or spent), *you can keep it for yourself.*
6 in a state/position [T] to make something stay or let something stay in a particular state or position: *I wish you'd stop leaving the door open.* | *The trial left a lot of questions unanswered.* | [leave sth on/off/out etc.] *Leave the kitchen light on when you leave.* | [leave sth doing sth] *Don't leave the water running while you brush your teeth.*
7 forget sth [T always + adv./prep.] to forget to take something with you when you leave a place: [leave sth in/on/at etc.] *I think I left my umbrella at the store.*
8 let sb decide/take responsibility [T] to let someone decide something or take responsibility for something: [leave sth to sb] *I've always left financial decisions to my wife.* | [leave doing sth to sb] *Nancy left shopping for groceries to me.* | [leave it (up) to sb to do sth] *You shouldn't leave it up to Ryan to get the packing done.* | *He would leave it to the jury to decide whether the pictures were obscene* (=it will be their responsibility to decide).
9 in a condition [T] if something leaves you in a particular condition, you are in that condition as a result of it: *The tornado left many people homeless.* | *Nate's generosity left me speechless.* | [leave sb doing sth] *Carla's narrow escape left her shaking with terror.*
10 husband/wife etc. [I,T] to stop living with someone you had a close relationship with: *It was the constant arguing that made Pam leave.* | *I'm surprised that Kent left her.* | [leave sb for sb] *Jan's husband left her for another woman.*
11 country/place [I,T] to stop living in a country, town etc. and go somewhere else: *They're leaving Minneapolis to live in Santa Fe.*
12 job/group [I,T] to stop working for a company, or stop being a member of a group: *After 30 years, Paige is leaving the company.* | *Church officials are concerned about all the people who have left.*
13 home/school etc. [I,T] to stop living at your parents' home, stop going to school etc.: *I left home when I was 14.* | *Brian's parents talked him out of leaving college.*
14 train/ship etc. [T] to get off a train, ship etc.: *Please take all your belongings with you when you leave the plane.*
15 delay [T] to not do something until later: *Let's leave the ironing for tomorrow.* | *I left the dishes until the morning.*
16 when you die [T] **a)** to give something to someone after you die: [leave sb sth] *Uncle Gene left us his house.* | [leave sth to sb/sth] *He had left all his money to charity.* **b)** FORMAL to have members of your family still alive when you die: *Collins leaves a wife and three children.*
17 not eat/drink [T] if you leave food or drink, you do not eat it because you do not like it or you have had enough: *If you don't like the stew, just leave it.*
18 leave something/nothing to chance to take no action and wait to see what happens, or to make sure you have done everything to make something happen the way you want: *The producers of the show left nothing to chance.*
19 leave sb with no choice/option etc. to force someone to do something because there is nothing else they can do: *I was left with no alternative other than to take out a loan.*
20 leave a mark/stain/scar etc. to make a mark that cannot be removed: *The cut left a scar on my left hand.* | *Red wine can leave terrible stains on clothes.*
21 leave a space/gap etc. to deliberately leave a space or room for something when you are doing something: *Leave two spaces between each sentence.* | *Leave room in the trunk for my suitcase.*

L

22 leave sb in the lurch to put someone in a difficult situation because you did not do something, especially something you promised to do: *The strike leaves hundreds of customers in the lurch.*
23 leave well (enough) alone to not try to change a situation because you might make it worse than it was before: *If I were you, I would leave well enough alone.*
24 leave something/a lot/much to be desired to be very unsatisfactory: *Your grades leave a lot to be desired.*
25 leave sb cold to not interest or excite someone at all: *Opera leaves me cold.*

SPOKEN PHRASES

26 leave sb alone to stop annoying or upsetting someone: *Just leave me alone and let me sleep!*
27 leave sth alone to stop touching something: *Leave it alone or you'll break it.*
28 leave it at that used to say that you have said or done enough about something: *We're not moving, so let's leave it at that.*
29 leave it to sb used to say that no one should be surprised if someone does something, because it is typical of them: *Leave it to you to have your whole year planned already!*
30 leave sb/sth be OLD-FASHIONED to not DISTURB or annoy someone, or not touch or move something: *Leave me be! I've got a lot of things to think about.*

31 leave sb to sth to go away and let someone continue what they are doing: *I'll leave you to your work.*
32 leave yourself open to blame/criticism/ridicule etc. to do something that makes it possible that you will be blamed, criticized, ridiculed etc.: *Expressing your true opinions can leave you open to criticism.*
33 not leave sb's side to always be with someone and take care of them: *Walter never left his wife's side in the hospital.*
34 leave sb to themselves to go away from someone so that they are alone
35 leave sb to their own devices to not tell someone what to do or offer them help, but let them do what they decide to do
36 leave sb in the dust to be more successful, smarter, better etc. than someone else, especially someone you are competing with: *Japanese students leave American kids in the dust.*
37 leave sb/sth hanging to fail to finish something, or not to tell someone your decision about something: *The investigation should not be left hanging.*
38 leave a bad taste in your mouth if an experience leaves a bad taste in your mouth, remembering it upsets you or makes you feel uncomfortable
39 leave no stone unturned to do everything that you can in order to find something or solve a problem —see also **take it or leave it** (TAKE¹ (24))
leave sth ↔ **aside** *phr. v.* [T] to not think about or consider something for a time, so that you can think about something else: *Leaving aside the issue of whether it's legal, is it even possible?*
leave sb/sth **behind** *phr. v.* **1** [T] to not take something or someone with you when you leave a place or go somewhere: *Oh no, I left my wallet behind in the kitchen.* | *I always got left behind when everyone else went to the movies.* **2** [T] to move far ahead of someone who cannot run, walk, or drive as fast as you can: *Slow down, we're leaving Jim behind.* | **leave** sb **far/way behind** (=move very far ahead of someone) **3 be/get left behind** to not work as well or as quickly as someone else, so that you make less progress than they do: *You'll have to put in some extra work if you don't want to get left behind.*
leave off *phr. v.* INFORMAL **1** [I] to stop doing something: *Let's start again from where we left off.* **2** [T **leave** sb/sth **off** sth] to not include someone or something in a group, list, activity etc.: *Why was my name left off the honor roll?*
leave sb/sth ↔ **out** *phr. v.* [T] **1** to not include someone or something: *It's fine with me if you leave out the chili powder.* | *Leave her out of this.* **2 be/feel left out** to feel as if you are not wanted or welcome in a social group: *The whole time I went to the youth group I felt completely left out.*

leave² *n.* **1** [U] time that you are allowed to spend away from your work, especially in the military or for a particular reason: *They're giving me five days' leave.* | *Carter is in charge of the office while I'm on leave.* | **sick/maternity/disability etc. leave** (=leave that you take because you are sick, having a baby, disabled etc.) | *Mrs. Deming is on maternity leave.* —see Usage Note at VACATION¹ **2 leave of absence** a period of time that you are allowed to spend away from work for a particular purpose: *Arienne is taking a leave of absence to do a Master's degree.* **3 take leave of your senses** to suddenly start behaving in a crazy way: *You want to marry him? Have you taken leave of your senses?* **4 take leave of sb** also **take your leave** FORMAL to say goodbye to someone **5 by your leave** OLD USE used when asking permission to do something

leav·en¹ /ˈlɛvən/ *v.* [T] **1** FORMAL to make something less boring and more interesting or cheerful: [+ with/by] *Snyder's travel guide is leavened with a sense of humor.* **2** OLD-FASHIONED to add leavening to a mixture of flour and water —see also UNLEAVENED

leaven² also **leavening** *n.* **1** [C,U] LITERARY a small amount of a quality that makes an event or situation less boring and more interesting or cheerful **2** [U] another word for LEAVENING

leav·en·ing /ˈlɛvənɪŋ/ *n.* [U] also **leavening agent** a substance such as YEAST that is added to a mixture of flour and water so that it will swell and can be baked into bread

leaves /livz/ *n.* the plural of LEAF

leave-tak·ing /ˈ. ˌ../ *n.* [C] LITERARY an act of saying goodbye when you go away

leav·ings /ˈlivɪŋz/ *n.* [plural] OLD-FASHIONED things that are left because they are not wanted, especially food —compare LEFTOVERS

Leb·a·non /ˈlɛbə nɑn, -nən/ a country in the Middle East on the Mediterranean Sea, that is north of Israel and west of Syria —**Lebanese** /ˌlɛbəˈniz/ *adj.*

lech /lɛtʃ/ *n.* [C] INFORMAL a lecher

lech·er /ˈlɛtʃə/ *n.* [C] DISAPPROVING a man who is always thinking about sex or trying to get sexual pleasure —**lecherous** *adj.* —**lecherously** *adv.*

lech·er·y /ˈlɛtʃəri/ *n.* [U] too much interest in or desire for sex

Le Cor·bu·si·er /lə ˌkɔrbuˈzyeɪ/ (1887–1965) a French ARCHITECT who built many important modern buildings, and planned the city of Chandigarh in India

lec·tern /ˈlɛktən/ *n.* [C] a piece of furniture that you stand behind when giving a speech, teaching a class etc., that is like a tall desk with a sloping surface for putting an open book or notes on

lec·ture¹ /ˈlɛktʃə/ *n.* **1** [C] a long talk given to a group of people on a particular subject, especially as a method of teaching in colleges or universities: [+ on/about] *a lecture on economics* | *Professor Dunn will give a lecture on the art exhibit.* **2** [C] an act of criticizing someone or warning them about something in a long, serious talk, in a way that they think is unfair or unnecessary: [+ on/ about] *Look, I don't need lectures on how to use my own camera.* **3 the lecture circuit** the activity of giving speeches about a subject in a number of different cities

lecture² *v.* **1** [T] to talk seriously or angrily to someone in order to criticize or warn them, in a way that they think is unfair or unnecessary: *I wish you'd stop lecturing me!* | [**lecture sb about/on sth**] *Barry often lectured schoolchildren about the dangers of drugs.* **2** [I] to talk to a group of people on a particular subject, especially as a method of teaching at a college or university

lec·tur·er /ˈlɛktʃərə/ *n.* [C] **1** someone who gives a lecture **2** someone who teaches at a college or university, who has a rank below that of an ASSISTANT PROFESSOR

LED *n.* [C] TECHNICAL Light Emitting Diode; a small piece of equipment on a watch, computer screen etc. that produces light when electricity passes through it

L

led /lɛd/ v. the past tense and past participle of LEAD[1]

-led /lɛd/ suffix [in adjectives] having a particular thing as the most important or effective cause, influence etc.: an export-led economic recovery

ledge /lɛdʒ/ n. [C] **1** a flat narrow shelf or surface that sticks out from a building or wall on the outside: Flags hung from the **window ledges**. **2** a flat narrow surface of rock that is parallel to the ground

ledg·er /ˈlɛdʒə/ n. [C] **1** a book recording the money received and spent by a business, bank etc. **2** a ledger line

ledger line /ˈ.. ˌ./ n. [C] a line on which you write musical notes that are too high or low to be recorded on a STAFF[1] (4)

lee /li/ n. **1 the lee of sth** the side of something that is away from the wind or provides shelter from it: a cabin in the lee of the hills **2 the lees** [plural] the substance that collects at the bottom of a bottle of wine —compare DREGS (1)

Lee /li/, **Har·per** /ˈhɑrpə/ (1926–) a U.S. writer famous for her NOVEL "To Kill a Mockingbird"

Lee, Rob·ert E. /ˈrɑbət i/ (1807–1870) a general in the Confederate army during the U.S. Civil War

leech /litʃ/ n. [C] **1** a small soft creature that attaches itself to the skin of animals in order to drink their blood **2** someone who takes advantage of other people, usually by taking their money, food etc. **3** OLD USE a doctor

leek /lik/ n. [C] a vegetable with a long white stem and long flat green leaves, which tastes a little like an onion

leer /lɪr/ v. [I] to look at someone in a way that upsets or offends them because it shows that you find them sexually attractive: [+ at] The man leered at her from the other end of the bar. —**leer** n. [C] a disgusting leer

leer·y /ˈlɪri/ adj. [not before noun] INFORMAL careful in the way that you deal with something or someone, because you are worried something bad may happen; WARY: [+ of] Landlords are often leery of renting to large families.

lee shore /ˈ. ./ n. [singular] TECHNICAL a shore which the wind from the ocean is blowing onto

Leeu·wen·hoek /ˈleɪvənˌhʊk/, **An·ton van** /ˈæntən væn/ (1632–1723) a Dutch scientist who developed MICROSCOPEs with which he could see blood cells and BACTERIA

lee·ward /ˈliwəd, ˈluəd/ adj. TECHNICAL **1** the leeward side of something is the side that is sheltered from the wind **2** a leeward direction is the same direction as the wind is blowing —**leeward** adv. —opposite WINDWARD

Lee·ward Is·lands, the /ˌliwəd ˈaɪləndz/ a group of islands in the Caribbean Sea, between Puerto Rico and Martinique, which includes the islands of Antigua, Montserrat, and Guadeloupe, and the Virgin Islands

lee·way /ˈliweɪ/ n. [U] **1** freedom to do things in the way you want to: States now have more leeway to restrict the sale of guns. **2** TECHNICAL the sideways movement of a ship, caused by strong wind

left[1] /lɛft/ v. the past tense and past participle of LEAVE[1]

left[2] adj. [only before noun] **1** on the side of your body that contains your heart: my left foot —opposite RIGHT[1] (3) **2** on, by, or in the direction of your left side: the left side of the page | a left turn **3** [never before noun] if something is left, that is what remains after the other things are gone or have been used: Joe only had $8 left. | How much milk is left in the fridge? | There were a few sandwiches left over from the party. —see also LEFTOVER **4 have two left feet** INFORMAL to be very awkward in the way you move **5 the left hand doesn't know what the right hand is doing** used to say that the people in one part of a group or organization do not know what is happening in the other parts of it —opposite RIGHT[1] —see also LEFT-OF-CENTER

left[3] adv. toward the left side: Turn left at the stop light. —opposite RIGHT[2] (4)

left[4] n. **1** [singular] the left side or direction: The entrance to the freeway is on the left. | You can get a ticket at the booths on your left. | To the left of the church is an old shoe factory. **2 the left/Left** political parties or groups, such as Socialists and Communists, that want money and property to be divided more fairly, and generally support workers rather than employers **3** [C] a hit made with your left hand

left field /ˌ. ˈ./ n. **1** [singular, not with the] a position in baseball in the left side of the OUTFIELD **2 be (way) out in left field** INFORMAL strange or unusual: Some of his ideas are way out in left field. **3 come (from) out of left field** INFORMAL to be very surprising or unexpected: Winning an Oscar was something that came out of left field for us.

left field·er /ˌ. ˈ../ n. [C] a baseball player who plays in left field

left-hand /ˈ. ./ adj. [only before noun] **1** on the left side of something: Write your name in the upper left-hand corner of the test. | Our house is on the left-hand side of the street. | a left-hand turn **2** using your left hand to do a particular thing: a left-hand piano concerto —opposite RIGHT-HAND

left-handed

Dad is left-handed.

a left-handed catch

left-hand·ed /ˌ. ˈ.◂/ adj. **1** someone who is left-handed uses their left hand for most things, especially writing **2** done with the left hand: a left-handed punch **3** made to be used by left-handed people: left-handed scissors **4 a left-handed compliment** a statement that seems to express admiration or praise, but at the same time is insulting —**left-handed** adv. —**left-handedness** n. [U] —opposite RIGHT-HANDED

left-hand·er /ˌ. ˈ../ n. [C] someone who uses their left hand, especially for throwing a ball —opposite RIGHT-HANDER

left·ie /ˈlɛfti/ n. another spelling of LEFTY

left·ist /ˈlɛftɪst/ adj. supporting LEFT-WING politics, groups, or ideas: leftist views | a leftist human rights group —**leftism** n. [U] —**leftist** n. [C]

left-of-cen·ter /ˌ. . ˈ.◂/ adj. having ideas or opinions that agree more with the LEFT[4] (2) in politics than with the RIGHT[3] (4), but not being extreme in those ideas

left·o·ver /ˈlɛftˌoʊvə/ adj. [only before noun] remaining after all the rest has been used, eaten etc.: There's some leftover soup.

left·o·vers /ˈlɛftˌoʊvəz/ n. [plural] food that has not been eaten at the end of a meal, and that was not on anyone's plate: You can have the leftovers for lunch tomorrow.

left·ward /ˈlɛftwəd/ adj., adv. **1** tending to support the LEFT[4] (2) in politics: Seymour is intent on moving the Republican Party leftward on social issues. **2** on or toward the left: a leftward bend —opposite RIGHTWARD

left wing /ˌ. ˈ./ n. [singular] **1** a group of people whose ideas are more left-wing than those of other members of the same political group: the left wing of the Democratic Party **2** the left side of a playing area in sports such as SOCCER and HOCKEY, or a player who plays on this side

left-wing /ˌ. ˈ.ˌ/ adj. supporting the political aims of groups such as Socialists and Communists, such as the idea that money and property should be divided more fairly: a left-wing newspaper —**left-winger** n. [C] —opposite RIGHT-WING

left·y /ˈlɛfti/ n. [C] INFORMAL someone who uses their left hand to write, throw etc.

leg /lɛg/ n.

1 body part [C] either of the two long parts of your body that your feet are joined to and that you use for walking, or a similar part on an animal or insect: Angie broke her leg skiing. | A spider has 8 legs. —see picture at BODY

2 furniture [C] one of the upright parts that supports a piece of furniture: a table leg

3 pants [C, usually plural] the part of your pants that covers your leg: Here, pull up your pant legs and let me see if your knees are hurt.

4 food [C,U] the leg of an animal when eaten as food: roast leg of lamb

5 trip/race etc. [C] a part of a long trip, race, process etc. that is done one part at a time: the second leg of the Rolling Stones' U.S. tour

6 leg room space in which to put your legs comfortably when you are sitting in a car, aircraft etc.: Sports cars just don't provide enough leg room for me.

7 a leg up an advantage over a person or group of people: This new technology should give GE a leg up on their competition.

8 sth is on its last legs INFORMAL used to say that something is in very bad condition and about to stop working: Our printer acts like it's on its last legs.

9 sth has legs INFORMAL if a movie, television show, piece of news etc. has legs, people continue to be interested in it: Everybody knows Arnold Schwarzenegger movies have legs.

10 not have a leg to stand on INFORMAL to be in a situation where you cannot prove or legally support what you say: If you didn't sign a contract, you won't have a leg to stand on. —see also **break a leg!** (BREAK (20)), -LEGGED, PEG LEG, **pull sb's leg** (PULL[1] (11)), SEA LEGS, **shake a leg** (SHAKE[1] (14)), **stretch your legs** (STRETCH[1] (11))

leg·a·cy /ˈlɛgəsi/ n. plural legacies [C] **1** a situation that exists as a result of things that happened at an earlier time: [+ of] Racial tension in the country is a legacy of slavery. **2** money or property that you receive from someone after they die: The house was a legacy from her aunt. **3** someone who joins an organization or attends a college or university that someone in their family used to belong to or attend

le·gal /ˈligəl/ adj. **1** allowed, ordered, or approved by law: Mitchell won a $700 legal award against her ex-landlord. | Office betting pools are not legal. **2** [only before noun] relating to the law: the legal system | a long legal battle **3 take legal action** to use the legal system to settle an argument, put right an unfair situation etc.: Citizens' groups are taking legal action to prevent the expansion of the freeway. **4 make it legal** INFORMAL to get married: When are you two going to make it legal? —opposite ILLEGAL[1] —see also LEGALLY

legal age /ˌ.. ˈ./ n. **1** [U] the age at which a person is legally considered an adult, usually 18 or 21: Since your daughter's **of legal age**, she can marry anyone she wishes. **2** [singular] the age at which someone is legally allowed to do something: The legal age for gambling in Nevada is 21. | **the legal driving/drinking age** (=when someone is allowed drive a car or buy alcoholic drinks)

legal aid /ˌ.. ˈ./ n. [U] legal help that is given free to people who cannot pay for it

le·gal·ese /ˌligəlˈiz/ n. [U] INFORMAL language used by lawyers that is difficult for most people to understand

legal hol·i·day /ˌ.. ˈ.../ n. [C] a holiday that the government has established and on which most government offices and banks are closed

le·gal·is·tic /ˌligəˈlɪstɪk/ adj. too concerned about small rules or details, and not concerned enough about what is really important —**legalistically** /-kli/ adv. —**legalism** /ˈligəˌlɪzəm/ n. [U]

le·gal·i·ty /lɪˈgæləti/ n. [U] the fact of being allowed by

law: The legality of testing employees for drugs is questionable.

le·gal·ize /ˈligəˌlaɪz/ v. [T] to make a law that allows people to do something that was not allowed before: Gambling has recently been legalized in three towns in Colorado. —**legalization** /ˌligələˈzeɪʃən/ n. [U]

le·gal·ly /ˈligəli/ adv. **1** according to the law: Government employees cannot legally go on strike. | The school could be **held legally responsible** for the accident. | **legally blind/dead/drunk etc.** (=declared to be in a particular condition according to the law) **2 legally binding** an agreement or document that is legally BINDING must be obeyed, because it is illegal not to obey it

legal pad /ˈ.. ˌ./ n. [C] a long PAD[1] (2) of yellow writing paper with lines on it

legal pro·fes·sion /ˈ.. .ˌ../ n. **the legal profession** lawyers, judges, and other people who work in courts of law or advise people about legal problems

legal-size /ˈ.. ˌ./ adj. legal-size paper is 14 INCHes long and 8 inches wide

legal sys·tem /ˈ.. ˌ../ n. [C] the laws and the way they work through the police, courts etc. in a particular country

legal ten·der /ˌ.. ˈ./ n. [U] coins or paper money that are officially allowed to be used as money

leg·ate /ˈlɛgət/ n. [C] an important official representative, especially one sent by the POPE

leg·a·tee /ˌlɛgəˈti/ n. [C] someone who has received money or property from someone who has died because they were mentioned in that person's WILL[2] (2)

le·ga·tion /lɪˈgeɪʃən/ n. [C] **1** an office that represents a government in a foreign country but that is lower in rank than an EMBASSY: the Cuban legation **2** the people who work in this office

le·ga·to /lɪˈgɑtoʊ/ adj., adv. TECHNICAL played or sung so that each note connects to the next one without pauses between them —compare STACCATO

le·ga·tor /lɪˈgeɪtɚ/ n. [C] LAW someone who gives money or property to someone else after they die by making a WILL[2] (4)

leg·end /ˈlɛdʒənd/ n. **1** [C,U] an old, well-known story, often about brave people, adventures, or magical events: The Legend of Prince Valiant | **Legend has it that** an ape-like man lives in the woods around here. **2** [U] all stories of this kind: Dr. John's music is **the stuff of legend** (=so good that stories are told about it). **3** [C] someone who is famous and admired for being extremely good at doing something: the rock and roll legend Elvis Presley —see also **living legend** (LIVING[1] (5)) **4** [C usually singular] the words that explain a picture, map etc., or that explain the SYMBOLS used on a map, CHART etc.; KEY[1] (5) **5** LITERARY words that have been written somewhere, for example on a sign —see also URBAN LEGEND

leg·end·ar·y /ˈlɛdʒənˌdɛri/ adj. **1** famous and admired: the legendary guitarist Jimi Hendrix **2** talked or read about in legends: the legendary palace of Kublai Khan

Lé·ger /leɪˈʒeɪ, Fer·nand /fɛrˈnɑn/ (1881–1955) a French PAINTER famous for his work in the style of Cubism

leg·er·de·main /ˌlɛdʒɚdəˈmeɪn/ n. [U] OLD-FASHIONED skillful use of your hands when performing tricks

-legged /lɛgɪd/ [in adjectives] **four-legged/two-legged/long-legged etc.** having four legs, two legs, long legs etc.: a four-legged animal —see also BOW-LEGGED, CROSS-LEGGED

leg·gings /ˈlɛgɪŋz/ n. **1** [plural] women's tight pants that stretch to fit the shape of the body, and that have no ZIPPER **2** [C usually plural] a piece of clothing worn to protect your legs, especially the lower part of your legs

leg·gy /ˈlɛgi/ adj. leggier, leggiest a woman or child who is leggy has long legs: a leggy blonde —**legginess** n. [U]

L

leg·i·ble /ˈlɛdʒəbəl/ adj. written or printed clearly enough for you to read: *The letter was torn and dirty but still legible.* —**legibly** adv. —**legibility** /ˌlɛdʒə-ˈbɪləti/ n. [U] —opposite ILLEGIBLE

le·gion[1] /ˈlidʒən/ n. [C] **1** a large group of soldiers, especially in the army of ancient Rome **2** LITERARY a large number of people

legion[2] adj. [not before noun] LITERARY very many; NUMEROUS: *Accounts of Ali's kindness and generosity are legion.*

le·gion·ar·y /ˈlidʒəˌnɛri/ n. [C] a member of a legion

le·gion·naire /ˌlidʒəˈnɛr/ n. [C] a member of a legion, especially the French Foreign Legion

legionnaire's dis·ease /ˌ...ˈ. .ˌ./ n. [U] NOT TECHNICAL a serious lung disease

leg i·rons /ˈ. ˌ../ n. [plural] metal circles or chains that are put around a prisoner's legs

leg·is·late /ˈlɛdʒəˌsleɪt/ v. [I,T] **1** to make a law about something: *Congress failed to legislate effective handgun controls.* | [+ **against**] *It's useless to try to legislate against something that people want to do.* **2 legislate from the bench** DISAPPROVING if a judge or court of law legislates from the BENCH, they make an official decision that has the effect of a new law

leg·is·la·tion /ˌlɛdʒəˈsleɪʃən/ n. [U] **1** a law or set of laws: *civil rights legislation* **2** the act of making laws

leg·is·la·tive /ˈlɛdʒəˌsleɪtɪv/ adj. **1** a legislative institution has the power to make laws: *a legislative committee* **2** relating to laws or to making laws: *The governor has shown in the legislative process.* **3 the legislative branch** the part of a government that makes laws —compare **the executive branch** (EXECUTIVE[2] (3)) **the judicial branch** (JUDICIAL (2))

leg·is·la·tor /ˈlɛdʒɪˌsleɪtɚ/ n. [C] someone who has the power to make laws or who belongs to an institution that makes laws, and has usually been elected

leg·is·la·ture /ˈlɛdʒəˌsleɪtʃɚ/ n. [C] an institution that has the power to make or change laws, and whose members are usually elected: *the Florida State Legislature* —compare CONGRESS (1)

leg·it /lɪˈdʒɪt/ adj. [not before noun] SPOKEN **1** legal or following official rules; LEGITIMATE: *The win was strictly legit.* | *The Corleone family has gone legit.* **2** honest and not trying to deceive people: *Are you sure he's legit?*

le·git·i·mate /lɪˈdʒɪtəmɪt/ adj. **1** correct, allowable, or operating according to the law: *legitimate business operations* | *The legitimate government was overthrown in a coup.* **2** fair, correct, or reasonable according to accepted standards of behavior: *Safety is an obvious and legitimate concern.* | *a legitimate reason* **3** LAW legitimate children are born to parents who are legally married to each other —**legitimately** adv. —**legitimacy** n. [U] —opposite ILLEGITIMATE

le·git·i·mize /lɪˈdʒɪtəˌmaɪz/ v. [T] **1** to make something, especially something that is unfair or morally wrong, seem acceptable and right: *The news media helped to legitimize the use of force by government troops.* **2** to make something official or legal that had not been before: *Elections will be held to legitimize the current regime.* **3** LAW to make a child LEGITIMATE (3)

leg·man /ˈlɛgmæn/ n. plural **legmen** /-mɛn/ [C] someone who works for someone else and does things for them such as collecting information which involves a lot of walking or traveling around

Leg·o /ˈlɛgoʊ/ n. plural **Legos** [C usually plural] TRADEMARK a toy consisting of plastic pieces of various sizes that can be put together to build things

leg room /ˈ. ./ n. [U] space for your legs in front of the seats in a car, theater etc.

leg·ume /ˈlɛgyum, lɪˈgyum/ n. [C] **1** a plant from the family that includes beans, PEAS, LENTILS etc. that has seeds in a POD (=a long thin case) **2** a bean, seed, or POD from one of these plants that people eat —**leguminous** /lɪˈgyumɪnəs/ adj. TECHNICAL

leg warm·er /ˈ. ˌ../ n. [C usually plural] a cover made from YARN, for the lower part of your leg, usually worn by dancers while practicing

leg·work /ˈlɛgwɚk/ n. [U] work, such as collecting information for a PROJECT, which involves a lot of walking or traveling around

lei /leɪ/ n. [C] a circle made of flowers that you put around someone's neck as a greeting, especially in Hawaii

Leib·niz /ˈlaɪbnɪts/**, Gott·fried Wil·helm, Baron von** /ˈgɑtfrid ˈvɪlhɛlm/ (1646–1716) a German PHILOSOPHER and mathematician

lei·sure /ˈliʒɚ/ n. [U] **1** time when you are not working or studying, and can relax and do things you enjoy: *leisure activities* | *The average person who travels for business or leisure probably has an e-mail account.* | *A lot of people seem to have less **leisure time** these days.* **2 at sb's leisure** as slowly as someone wants, and when they want: *Return the forms to me at your leisure.* **3 at leisure** not working, and having time to relax: *James spent the summer at leisure.* **4 a gentleman/lady of leisure** HUMOROUS someone who does not have to work

lei·sured /ˈliʒɚd/ adj. [only before noun] FORMAL not needing to work and having a lot of leisure time, especially because you are rich: *At 50, Larry won the lottery and became a member of the leisured class.*

lei·sure·ly /ˈliʒɚli/ adj. moving or done in a relaxed way, without hurrying: *After church we usually take a leisurely drive through the country.* | *a leisurely pace* —**leisurely** adv.: *The Colonel moved leisurely across the room.*

leisure suit /ˈ.. ˌ./ n. [C] an informal suit popular during the 1970s, consisting of a shirt-like JACKET and pants made of the same material

leisure wear /ˈ.. ˌ./ n. [U] a word meaning clothes that are made to be worn when relaxing or playing sports, used especially by stores or by the companies that make these clothes

leit·mo·tif, leitmotiv /ˈlaɪtmoʊˌtif/ n. [C] **1** a musical phrase that is played at various times during an OPERA or similar musical work to represent a particular character or idea —compare MOTIF **2** a feature that appears often in something such as a book, a speech, or an artist's work

lem·ming /ˈlɛmɪŋ/ n. [C] **1** a small rat-like animal that many people believe kills itself by following other lemmings and jumping into the ocean in large numbers **2 like lemmings** if people do something like lemmings, a large number of them copy other people's actions and ideas without thinking about it: *Companies may rush like lemmings into buying technology with a short lifespan.*

lem·on /ˈlɛmən/ n. **1** [C,U] a fruit with hard yellow skin and sour juice: *a slice of lemon* —see picture at FRUIT[1] **2** [U] also **lemon yellow** a bright yellow color **3** [C] something, especially a car, that is useless because it fails to work correctly: *Our van turned out to be a real lemon.*

lem·on·ade /ˌlɛməˈneɪd/ n. [U] a drink made from lemon juice, sugar, and water

Le·Mond /ləˈmɑnd/**, Greg** /grɛg/ (1961–) a U.S. bicycle racer who was the first American to win the Tour de France bicycle race

lem·on grass, lemongrass /ˈ.. ˌ./ n. [U] a tropical grass that is used in cooking to give food a taste similar to lemons

lemon law /ˈ.. ˌ./ n. [C] a law that forces companies to give money to people who have bought a car that does not work from them, or to repair the car so that it works

lemon sole /ˌ.. ˈ./ n. [C,U] a flat fish, or the meat of this fish

lem·on·y /ˈlɛməni/ adj. tasting, smelling, or looking like lemon: *The cake had a tart, lemony flavor.*

lemon yel·low /ˌ.. ˈ..◂/ n. [U] a bright yellow color

le·mur /ˈlimɚ/ n. [C] a small animal like a monkey with large eyes and a long tail, that lives mainly in Madagascar

I borrowed $20

My friend lent me $20

I paid her back the next day

lend /lɛnd/ *v. past tense and past participle* **lent**
1 **bank** [I,T] if a bank or financial institution lends money, it lets someone borrow it if they pay it back with an additional amount of money: [+ **to**] *I doubt they'll lend to us, with our credit histories.* | [**lend sth to sb**] *U.S. banks lent billions of dollars to developing countries in the 1970s.*
2 **let sb borrow** [T] to let someone borrow money from you or use something that you own, which they will give back later: [**lend sb sth**] *Could you lend me $5 until tomorrow?* | [**lend sth to sb**] *"Where'd you get the car, Mimi?" "A friend lent it to me."*
3 **lend (sb) a hand** to help someone do something, especially something that needs physical effort: *Lend me a hand with this box.*
4 **sth lends itself to sth** used to say that something is appropriate for being used in a particular way: *Fish does not lend itself well to reheating.*
5 **give a quality** [T] FORMAL to give something, especially an event, a particular quality: [**lend sth to sth**] *Whisky lends an interesting flavor to the sauce.*
6 **lend an ear** to listen to someone in a sympathetic way
7 **lend support/assistance** to support or help someone
8 **lend weight/credibility/credence to sth** to make an opinion, belief etc. seem more likely to be correct: *The new evidence lends weight to the theory that the killer was a man.*
9 **lend your name to sth** to allow your name to be used to support something, sell something etc.: *Nintendo lends its name to new games developed by about 60 companies.* —**lender** *n.* [C] —see Usage Note at BORROW

USAGE NOTE: LEND

WORD CHOICE: lend, borrow, loan
Use **lend** for a situation in which you let someone use something that they will give back to you: *Heidi lent me this sweatshirt.* We can use **loan** with the same meaning: *We loaned them our car for the weekend.* However, some teachers believe that this use of **loan** is not correct, and that it should only be used for situations in which a bank or a person is lending money to someone: *Bankers loaned him $245 million to buy the airline.* Use **borrow** for a situation in which you use something that belongs to someone else and will give it back to them: *Could I borrow your pen for a minute?*

lending li·brar·y /'.. ,.../ *n. plural* **lending libraries** [C] a library that lends books, records etc. for people to use at home —compare REFERENCE LIBRARY
lending rate /'.. ,./ *n.* [C] the rate of INTEREST[1] (3) that you have to pay to a bank or other financial institution when you borrow money from them
Len·dl /'lɛndl/, **I·van** /'aɪvən/ (1960–) a Czech-American tennis player considered one of the best players of the 1980s
L'En·fant /'lɑnfɑn/, **Pierre** /pyɛr/ (1754–1825) a French-American ARCHITECT famous for designing the plans for the city of Washington D.C.

length /lɛŋkθ, lɛnθ/ *n.*
1 **size** [C,U] the measurement of something from one end to the other: *I like the length of this skirt.* | [+ **of**] *The leaves reach a length of about 4 inches.* | *Each board measures 3 feet in length.* —compare BREADTH (1), HEIGHT (1), WIDTH (1)
2 **time** [C,U] the amount of time that you spend doing something, or that something continues for: *The average length of a stay in the hospital has dropped sharply.* | *Anyone who has lived here for any length of time is familiar with the housing problem.*
3 **books/writing etc.** [C,U] the amount of writing in a book, article etc.: *Greene's book is less than half the length of most novels.*
4 **go to great lengths to do sth a)** to try very hard and use many different methods to achieve something: *Most companies go to great lengths to avoid controversy.* **b)** also **go to any lengths to do sth** to be very determined and willing to use any methods to achieve something, often in a way that seems unreasonable: *Many people will go to great lengths to avoid math problems.*
5 **at length a)** for a long time: *She spoke at great length about the dangers of smoking.* **b)** LITERARY after a long time: *"Yes," she answered at length.*
6 **piece** [C] a piece of something long and thin: [+ **of**] *a length of rope*
7 **in races** [C] the measurement from one end of a horse, boat etc. to the other, used when saying how far one is ahead of another: *Aksar won by three lengths.*
8 **walk/drive/run etc. the length of sth** to walk, drive, run etc. the whole distance from one end of an object, room, area etc. to the other: *Highway 25 stretches the length of the state.*
9 **swimming** [C] the distance from one end of a swimming pool to the other: *Ron swims several lengths every morning.*
10 **the length and breadth of sth** in or through every part of a large area: *We need to unite our people across the length and breadth of the country.* —see also **at arm's length** (ARM[1] (8)), FULL-LENGTH, SHOULDER-LENGTH

length·en /'lɛŋkθən/ *v.* [I,T] to make something longer, or to become longer: *Can you lengthen these pants for me?* | *Shadows began to lengthen as the sun sank in the sky.* —opposite SHORTEN
length·wise /'lɛŋkθwaɪz/ *adv.* in the direction or position of the longest side: *Slice each banana lengthwise.* —**lengthwise** *adj.* [only before noun] *a lengthwise cut* —compare CROSSWISE
length·y /'lɛŋkθi/ *adj.* **lengthier, lengthiest 1** continuing for a long time, often too long: *Paul should expect a lengthy period of recovery from surgery.* **2** a speech, piece of writing etc. that is lengthy is long and often contains too many details: *a lengthy two-volume book*
le·ni·ent /'liniənt, 'linyənt/ *adj.* not strict in the way you punish someone or control their behavior: *His parents are too lenient with him.* | *a very lenient sentence* —**leniency** also **lenience** *n.* [U] *Ross asked the judge for leniency in his sentencing.* —**leniently** *adv.*
Len·in /'lɛnɪn/, **Vlad·i·mir Il·yich** /'vlædɪmɪr 'ɪlɪtʃ/ (1870–1924) a Russian Marxist REVOLUTIONARY and writer who was leader of the Bolshevik party and first leader of the Soviet Union
lens /lɛnz/ *n.* [C] **1** a piece of curved glass or plastic which makes things look bigger or smaller, for example in a pair of GLASSes or in a TELESCOPE: *Jan wears glasses with thick lenses.* **2** the part of a camera through which the light travels before it reaches the film: *a 115mm zoom lens* **3** the clear part inside your eye that FOCUSes so you can see things clearly **4** a CONTACT LENS

Lent /lɛnt/ *n.* [U] the 40 days before Easter when some Christians stop eating particular things or stop particular habits —**Lenten** *adj.* [only before noun]

lent /lɛnt/ *v.* the past tense and past participle of
LEND

len·til /'lɛntəl/ *n.* [C usually plural] a small round
seed like a bean, which has been dried and can be
cooked

Le·o /'lioʊ/ *n.* **1** [U] the fifth sign of the ZODIAC, represented by a lion, and believed to affect the character and life of people born between July 23 and
August 22 **2** [C] someone who was born between
July 23 and August 22: *Ernie's a Leo.*

Le·o·nar·do da Vin·ci /liə,nɑrdoʊ də 'vɪntʃi, leɪə-/
(1452–1519) an Italian painter, inventor, and scientist
of the Renaissance period, who is generally regarded
as one of the greatest artists and GENIUSes who ever
lived

le·o·nine /'liə,naɪn/ *adj.* LITERARY relating to lions, or
like a lion in character or appearance: *a leonine
mane of hair*

leop·ard /'lɛpəd/ *n.* [C] **1** a large animal of the cat
family, with yellow fur and black spots, which lives
in Africa and South Asia **2 a leopard can't change
its spots** used to say that people cannot change their
character

le·o·tard /'liə,tɑrd/ *n.* [C] a tight-fitting piece of
women's clothing that covers your whole body from
your neck to the top of your legs, and is worn for
exercise or dancing

lep·er /'lɛpə/ *n.* [C] **1** someone who has leprosy
2 someone that people avoid because they have done
something that people disapprove of: *They treated me
like some kind of leper.*

lep·re·chaun /'lɛprə,kɑn/ *n.* [C] an imaginary creature in the form of a little man, in old Irish stories,
who will show hidden gold to anyone who can catch
him

lep·ro·sy /'lɛprəsi/ *n.* [U] an infectious disease in
which someone's skin and nerves are gradually
destroyed —**leprous** *adj.*

Ler·ner /'lɜnə/**, A·lan Jay** /'ælən dʒeɪ/ (1918–1983) a
U.S. SONGWRITER famous for writing MUSICALs with
Frederick Loewe

les·bi·an /'lɛzbiən/ *n.* [C] a woman who is sexually
attracted to other women —**lesbian** *adj.* —**lesbian-
ism** *n.* [U] —compare GAY[2], HOMOSEXUAL

les·bo /'lɛzboʊ/ *n. plural* **lesbos** [C] SLANG, OFFENSIVE
a lesbian

le·sion /'liʒən/ *n.* [C] TECHNICAL **1** a wound or injury:
multiple lesions to the skin **2** a sore red area on the
skin, caused by an infection or disease **3** a dangerous change in part of someone's body such as their
lungs or brain, caused by injury or illness: *a spinal
cord lesion*

Le·so·tho /lə'soʊtoʊ/ a country in southern Africa
that is completely surrounded by the Republic of
South Africa —**Sotho** *adj.*

S W **less**[1] /lɛs/ *quantifier pron.* [the comparative of "little"]
2 **1 a)** [with uncountable nouns] a smaller amount:
Skim milk has less fat than whole milk. | *He said he
would accept $30,000 and no less.* | *I can finish it in
less than an hour.* |[+ of] *She spends less of her time
playing tennis now.* **b)** NONSTANDARD used to mean
"fewer" or "not as many," but often considered
incorrect in this meaning: *There were less people
there than we expected.* **2 less and less** gradually
becoming smaller in amount: *They began spending
less and less time with each other.* —see also **the
less... the better** (BETTER[3] (5))

> **USAGE NOTE: LESS**
>
> **GRAMMAR: less, fewer**
> Use **less** before an uncountable noun: *We've had a lot
> less rain this year than last year.* Use **fewer** before a
> countable noun: *There are fewer kids in our neighbor-
> hood now.*

S W **less**[2] *adv.* [the comparative of "little"] **1** not so
1 1 much, or to a smaller degree: *You should drive less*

and walk more often. | *Tickets were less expensive
than I expected.* | *We go to movies less often than we
used to.* —opposite MORE[1] **2 nothing less than sth**
used to emphasize how important or serious something really is: *The change in Bob's behavior has
been nothing less than a miracle.* **3 less and less**
gradually becoming smaller in amount or degree:
The fighting has become less and less frequent.
4 much/still less used to say that because one thing
does not happen, is not true etc., another thing
cannot possibly happen or be true: *The average
person is unlikely to pick up this type of book, much
less read it.* **5 no less a)** used to emphasize that an
amount or number is large: [+ than] *No less than six
people claim to have written the song.* **b)** used to
emphasize that the person or thing you are talking
about is very important or impressive: *Our awards
were presented by the mayor, no less.* | *The notes were
written by no less a personage than Thomas Jefferson himself.* —see also **I/he/they etc. couldn't care
less** (CARE[1] (6)), **think less/badly of sb (for doing
sth)** (THINK (16))

less[3] *adj.* [not before noun] **less than helpful/per-
fect/friendly etc.** not helpful, perfect, friendly etc. at
all: *The marketing department seemed less than
enthusiastic about our newest product.*

less[4] *prep.* taking away or not counting a particular
amount: *He gave us our money back, less the $2
service charge.*

-less /lɪs/ *suffix* [in adjectives] **1** not having something; without: *a childless couple* (=without chil-
dren) | *He was shirtless* (=wore no shirt). **2** never
doing something: *ceaseless complaints* (=that never
end) | *It's perfectly harmless* (=will not harm you).
3 unable to be treated in a particular way, or never
becoming a particular way: *She spent countless hours
volunteering* (=too many hours to be counted). | *a
tireless helper* (=who never gets tired)

les·see /lɛ'si/ *n.* [C] LAW someone who is legally
allowed to use a house, building, land etc. for a particular period of time in return for payment to the
owner —compare LESSOR

less·en /'lɛsən/ *v.* [I,T] to become smaller in size,
amount, importance, or value, or to make something
do this: *Peace talks have lessened the tension between
the two countries.* | *By Thursday, smoke in the valley
had considerably lessened.*

less·er /'lɛsə/ *adj.* **1** [only before noun] FORMAL not
as large, as important, or as much as something else:
*The jury found him innocent of murder, but could not
decide on the lesser charges.* | *In the 1980s, the drug
was popular in Hawaii and to a lesser extent on the
West Coast.* | *A lesser man* (=someone not as strong
or brave) *would have quit before now.* **2 the lesser
of two evils** the less bad or harmful of two bad
choices **3 lesser-known** not well known, or not as
well known as others: *a lesser-known French poet*
4 TECHNICAL used in the names of some types of
animal, bird, or plant that are slightly smaller than
the main type

les·son /'lɛsən/ *n.* [C]
1 learning a skill a period of time in which someone is taught a particular skill, for example how to
play a musical instrument or drive a car: [+ in/on]
lessons in fire safety | *Geraldine is taking piano
lessons.*
2 warning an experience, especially a bad one,
that makes you more careful in the future: *Our experience with the fire will serve as a lesson to the entire
state.*
3 let that be a lesson to you SPOKEN used to warn
someone that they must be more careful, in order to
avoid having the same bad experience happen again
4 book a part of a book that is used for learning a
particular subject, especially in school: *Turn to
lesson 25.*
5 church a short piece that is read from the Bible
during a Christian religious ceremony
6 in school OLD-FASHIONED a period of time in
which students in a school are taught a particular
subject; CLASS —see also **learn your lesson** (LEARN
(5)), **teach sb a lesson** (TEACH (6))

L

les·sor /ˈlɛsɔr, lɛˈsɔr/ *n.* [C] LAW someone who allows someone else to use their house, building, land etc. for a period of time for payment —compare LESSEE

lest /lɛst/ *conjunction* LITERARY **1** in order to make sure that something will not happen: *She pulled away from the window lest anyone see them.* **2** used to show that someone is afraid or worried that a particular thing might happen: *He paused, afraid lest he say too much.*

let /lɛt/ *v. past tense and past participle* **let** *present participle* **letting**
1 **allow** [T not in passive] **a)** to allow someone to do something: *I want to go to Europe this summer, but my parents won't let me.* | [let sb do sth] *His wife won't let him watch football on TV.* | *Let me show you how to do it.* **b)** to allow something to happen: *It'll drive you crazy if you let it.* | [let sth do sth] *Don't let the door slam shut.* —see Usage Note at FORBID
2 **let go a)** to stop holding someone or something: *Just let go and jump.* | [+ of] *Mommy, make him let go of my toes!* **b)** to stop worrying or thinking about a person or a problem: *I know he's grown up now, but it's hard for me to let go.*
3 **let sb go a)** to allow a person or animal to leave a place where they have been kept: *The police let her go after a night in jail.* **b)** a phrase meaning "to dismiss someone from their job," used to avoid saying this directly: *We've had to let three people go this month.*
4 **let sb know** to tell someone some information: *Could you let me know by Thursday?* | [let sb know if/whether] *Let us know if you need anything else.* | [let sb know what/when/where etc.] *Let me know what time your plane lands and I'll meet you at the airport.*
5 **let sb have sth** to give or sell something to someone: *Let your brother have the remote control for a while.* | *I can let you have both chairs for $75.*
6 **let alone** used to say that because one thing does not happen, is not true etc., another thing cannot possibly happen or be true: *I wouldn't work with my mom, let alone my whole family.*
7 **let sth go/pass** to decide not to react to something bad or annoying that someone has done or said: *I'll let it go this time, but don't let it happen again.*
8 **let sb/sth be** also **let sb/sth alone** to stop annoying someone, or asking questions, or trying to change things: *Kate, let her be right now. You two are getting on my nerves.*
9 **let yourself go a)** to allow yourself to relax completely in a social situation, and not worry about what other people think **b)** to take less care of your appearance than usual: *She's really let herself go since she had the baby.*
10 **let sth drop/rest** to stop discussing something or trying to deal with something that has been annoying you or worrying you: *After the way they treated me, there's no way I'm going to let the matter drop.*
11 **let sth go for $2/$25 etc.** INFORMAL to sell something for a low price
12 **wish** LITERARY used to express a wish that something will happen or will not happen: *Let him come home safely, she prayed.*
13 **let yourself be bullied/mistreated etc.** to allow other people to treat you badly: *Don't let yourself be pushed around like that.*
14 **let us do sth** FORMAL **a)** used to suggest to a group of people that you all do something together: *Let us pray.* **b)** used to ask a reader or listener to do something, as a way of helping them understand what you are talking about: *Let us consider a few examples of how man and the environment interact.*
15 **let sth be/equal/represent sth** FORMAL used in mathematics or science to mean that one thing can be imagined as representing another: *Let c equal 6.*
16 **let sb have it** INFORMAL **a)** to shout at someone because they are angry with them: *Mrs. Kramer really let him have it for spilling the paint.* **b)** to attack or punish someone severely
17 **room/building** [T] BRITISH to allow someone to use a room or building in return for money every week or month: *Interhome has over 20,000 houses to let across Europe.* —compare RENT[1] (1)

SPOKEN PHRASES
18 **let me see/think** said when pausing to think of some information or think what to do next: *He was eating a...let me think...an apple muffin.*
19 **let me do sth a)** used to politely offer to do something for someone: *Here, let me get the door for you.* **b)** used to tell someone what you are going to do next: *Let me take this phone call and then I can help you.*
20 **let sb (do sth) a)** used to say that you do not care whether someone does something or not: *Well, if he wants to go and kill himself, let him.* **b)** used to say that someone else should do something instead of you: *Let them clean up the mess – they made it.*
21 **let me tell you** used to emphasize that a feeling you had was very strong: *It was pretty early in the morning too, let me tell you!*
22 **I'll/we'll let it go at that** used to tell someone that you will not punish or criticize them anymore for something bad they have done: *If you give me $25, we'll just let it go at that.*

—see also **let the cat out of the bag** (CAT[1] (2)), **let fly** (FLY[1] (18)), LET's, **live and let live** (LIVE[1] (25)), **let sth ride** (RIDE[1] (6)), **let her/it rip** (RIP[1] (5)), **let (it) slip that** (SLIP[1] (10))

let down *phr. v.* **1** [T let sb ↔ down] to make someone feel disappointed because you have not behaved well or not done what you said you would do: *I'm counting on you to be there – don't let me down!* **2** [T let sth ↔ down] to give something to someone who is in a lower position, or to move something that is on a string, rope etc. down: *Let the basket down gently.* **3** **let your hair down** INFORMAL to relax and enjoy yourself, especially after working hard: *You can really let your hair down and do what you want at the club.* **4** **let sb down easy** to end a romantic relationship with someone in a way that will not upset them too much **5** to make a piece of clothing longer: *I'm going to let down this old dress for my daughter.*

let in *phr. v.* **1** [T let sb ↔ in] to open the door of a room, building etc. so that someone can come in: *I unlocked the door and let him in.* | *If I'm not there, just let yourself in.* **2** [T let sth ↔ in] to allow light, water, air etc. to enter a place: *These curtains let in too much light.* **3** **let sb in on sth** to tell someone about a secret plan, idea etc., and trust them not to tell other people: *I'm going to let you in on a little secret.* **4** **let yourself in for something** INFORMAL to do something or become involved with something that will cause you trouble later: *I don't think Jamie knows what he's letting himself in for.*

let sb/sth into sth *phr. v.* [T] to allow someone to come into a room or building: *Maria wouldn't let Billy into her house.*

let sb off *phr. v.* [T] **1** to not punish someone, or to not make them do something they should do: *Our teacher let us off with no homework tonight.* | *You're lucky that she let you off so easy.* **2** to allow someone to get out of a car, off an airplane etc.: *You can let me off at the next corner.* **3** to allow someone to leave work: *They let me off work to come to this class.* —see also **let/get sb off the hook** (HOOK[1] (3)), **let/blow off steam** (STEAM[1] (4))

let on *phr. v.* [I,T] INFORMAL to tell someone something that was meant to be a secret: *I think he knows more about it than he's letting on.* | [let on (that)] *Don't let on that I told you.*

let out *phr. v.* **1** [T let sb ↔ out] to allow someone to leave a room, building etc.: *Who let the cat out?* | [+ of] *I'm not going to let you out of there until you say you're sorry.* **2** [I] if a school, college, movie etc. lets out, it ends, so that the people attending it can leave: *School lets out at 3:15.* **3** [T let sth ↔ out] to allow light, water, air etc. to leave a place: *Close the door – you're letting all the heat out.* **4** **let out a scream/cry/roar etc.** to make a sound, especially a loud sound: *Anita let out a sob.* **5** [T let sth ↔ out] to make a piece of clothing wider or looser, especially because the person it

L

belongs to has become fatter: *I'm going to have to let this dress out again.*

let up *phr. v.* [I] **1** if something, such as bad weather or a bad situation, lets up, it stops or becomes less serious: *I wish this rain would let up.* **2** to treat someone less strictly, or to stop doing something, especially something that is annoying someone else: *They kept banging on the door and they wouldn't let up.* | [+ **on**] *America must not let up on its criticism of the dictatorship.*

-let /lɪt/ *suffix* [in nouns] **1** a smaller type of something: *a booklet* (=small book with a thin cover) | *a piglet* (=young pig) **2** a band worn on a particular part of your body: *an anklet* (=worn on the ankle)

letch /lɛtʃ/ *n.* [C] another spelling of LECH

let·down /'lɛtdaʊn/ *n.* [singular] INFORMAL something that makes you feel disappointed because it is not as good as you expected; DISAPPOINTMENT: *It will be a major letdown if we lose the game to Kansas.* —see also **let down** (LET)

le·thal /'liθəl/ *adj.* **1** causing death, or able to cause death: *a lethal dose of heroin* **2** HUMOROUS likely to be powerful, dangerous, or dangerously effective: *That cocktail looks pretty lethal.*

le·thar·gic /lə'θɑrdʒɪk/ *adj.* feeling as if you have no energy and no interest in doing anything: *Problems at home were making Will feel lethargic.* —**lethargy** /'lɛθərdʒi/ *n.* [U]

let's /lɛts/ SPOKEN **1** the short form of "let us," used to suggest to someone or a group of people that you all do something together: *I'm hungry. Let's eat!* | *Let's buy a present for Grandma together.* | *Let's not talk about work tonight.* —see Usage Note at PROPOSE **2 let's see a)** said when you are going to try to do something: [**let's see if/whether**] *Let's see if I can get this window open.* **b)** said when pausing because you cannot remember or find something: *Now, let's see, where did I leave my glass?* **c)** used to ask someone to show you something: *"I got some new shoes." "Really? Let's see."* **3 let's say** said to ask someone to imagine something in order to discuss it or understand it better: *If you found some money on the street – let's say $100 – what would you do?* | [**let's say (that)**] *Okay, let's say it's a year from now. Do think you'll still feel the same way?* **4 let's hope (that)** said when you hope something is true or will happen: *Let's hope they remembered to bring the tickets.* **5 let's just say** used to say that you are not going to tell someone all the details about something: *"So who was she with?" "Let's just say it wasn't Ted."* **6 let's face it/let's be honest** used to say that you must accept a fact that is difficult or unfavorable: *Let's face it, Scott. We're not as young as we used to be.*

let·ter¹ /'lɛtər/ *n.* [C] **1** a written or printed message that is usually put in an envelope and sent through the mail: *Jim wrote a letter to his Congressman.* | *Could you mail these letters for me?* **2** any of the signs in writing or printing that represent a speech sound: *There are 26 letters in the English alphabet.* **3 to the letter** exactly: *She thinks recipes must be followed to the letter.* **4 the letter of the law** the exact words of a law or agreement, rather than the intended or general meaning: *The builders may have adhered to the letter of the law, but not its spirit.* **5** a large cloth letter that you sew onto a JACKET, given as a reward for playing on a school or college sports team: *Mark got a letter in soccer.* **6 English/American/German etc. letters** FORMAL the study of the literature of a particular country or language —see also CHAIN LETTER, COVER LETTER, DEAD LETTER, DEAR JOHN LETTER, LETTER OF CREDIT, MAN OF LETTERS, OPEN LETTER

letter² *v.* **1** [I,T] to write, draw, or paint letters or words on something: *He makes signs and letters business vans.* | **badly/beautifully/carefully etc. lettered** *a plainly lettered sign* —see also HAND-LETTERED, LETTERED **2** [I] to earn a LETTER¹ (5) in a sport in school or college: [+ **in**] *I lettered in track my senior year.*

letter bomb /'.. ,./ *n.* [C] a small bomb hidden in a package and sent to someone in order to hurt or kill them

let·ter·box /'lɛtərbɑks/ *n.* **1** [U] a way of showing movies on television with a black band across the top and bottom of the screen, so that the whole width of the picture can be shown: *Kubrick's masterpiece is available in letterbox format for $19.95.* **2** [C] BRITISH a narrow hole in a door, or a special box where letters, packages etc. are delivered; MAILBOX

letter car·ri·er /'.. ,.../ *n.* [C] a MAIL CARRIER

let·tered /'lɛtərd/ *adj.* FORMAL well educated

let·ter·head /'lɛtərhɛd/ *n.* **1** [U] paper that has the name and address of a person or business printed at the top of it: *References should be submitted on company letterhead.* **2** [C] the name and address of a person or business printed at the top of a sheet of paper

let·ter·ing /'lɛtərɪŋ/ *n.* [U] **1** written or drawn letters, especially of a special type, size, color etc.: *two scrolls in Chinese lettering* **2** the art of writing or drawing letters or words

let·ter·man /'lɛtərmən/ *n.* [C] OLD-FASHIONED someone who earns a LETTER¹ (5) in sports in high school or college

letter of cred·it /,.. '../ *n.* [C] an official letter from a bank allowing a particular person to take money from another bank

letter of in·tent /,.. .'./ *n.* [C] an official document that says what someone plans to do, such as join a sports team, buy a company etc.

letter-per·fect /,.. '..·/ *adj.* correct in every detail: *The ballet production was letter-perfect.*

letter-qual·i·ty /'.. ,../ *adj.* a letter-quality PRINTER (1) produces print that is good enough to be used for business letters, reports etc.

letter-size /'.. ,./ *adj.* letter-size paper is 8½ inches wide and 11 inches long and is the standard size used for business letters and in computers in the U.S.

let·tuce /'lɛtɪs/ *n.* [C,U] a vegetable with thin green leaves which are used raw in SALADs: *a head of lettuce*

let·up /'lɛtʌp/ *n.* [singular,U] a pause or a reduction in a difficult, dangerous, or tiring activity: *There is no sign of a letup in the crisis.* —see also **let up** (LET)

leu·ke·mi·a /lu'kimiə/ *n.* [U] a type of CANCER in which the blood contains too many WHITE BLOOD CELLS, causing weakness and sometimes death

leu·ko·cyte /'lukəˌsaɪt/ *n.* [C] TECHNICAL one of the cells in your blood which fight against infection; WHITE BLOOD CELL

lev·ee /'lɛvi/ *n.* [C] a special wall built to stop a river from flooding

level

The parking garage has four levels.

lev·el¹ /'lɛvəl/ *n.* [C]
1 amount the amount, degree, or number of something, as compared to another amount, degree, or number: [+ **of**] *There appears to be a low level of interest in the conference.* | *We can expect the temperature to stay at these levels until Friday.* | *Stock prices were at their highest level since June.*

2 [height] the height or position of something in relation to the ground or to another thing: *Check the water level in the car radiator.* | *Do not raise the weight above shoulder level.* —see also EYE LEVEL, SEA LEVEL

3 [standard] a particular standard of skill or ability in a subject, sport etc.: *Few athletes can compete at the international level.* | *higher-level math courses*

4 [floor/ground] a floor or piece of ground, especially when considered in relation to another floor or piece of ground that is higher or lower: *Didn't we park the car on Level 2?*

5 [rank] a particular position in a system that has different ranks: *We have seen an increase in minority groups at all levels of the company.* | *high-level talks* (=discussions between important people)

6 [way of understanding] a way of considering or understanding something: *We can find meaning in the story on many different levels.* | **on a practical/personal etc. level** *They never got along on either a personal or a professional level.*

7 a level playing field a situation in which different companies, countries etc. can all compete fairly with each other because no one has special advantages: *We just want our exports to compete on a level playing field.*

8 [tool] a tool used for checking that a surface is flat

9 at local/state/national etc. level happening within a small area, or the whole area of a state, country etc.: *No research was being done at the federal level.*

10 be on the level INFORMAL to be honest: *Do you think his offer is on the level?*

level² *adj.* **1** flat and not sloping, with no surface higher than the rest: *The floor was level, but the walls sloped inward.* **2 be level** two things that are level are at the same height as each other: [+ with] *Your eyes should be level with the top of the computer screen.* **3 do your level best** to try as hard as possible to do something: *I'll do my level best to help you.* **4 a level voice/look/gaze** a steady voice, look etc., that shows you are calm or determined **5 level spoonful/teaspoon etc.** an amount of a substance, that is just enough to fill a spoon, used as a measure in cooking

level³ *v.* [T] **1** to knock down or completely destroy a building or area: *The storm leveled hundreds of houses, but left some untouched.* **2 level a charge/accusation/criticism etc.** to publicly criticize someone or say they are responsible for a crime, mistake etc.: [+ at/against] *Outrageous accusations were leveled against some of Hollywood's most famous stars.* **3** to make something flat and even: *Workers leveled the wet concrete with a piece of wood.* **4** to aim something such as a weapon: [+ at] *A gun was immediately leveled at Ron's head.*

level off/out *phr. v.* **1** [I] to stop going up or down, and continue at the same height or amount: *The plane climbed to 20,000 feet, then leveled off.* | *There is evidence that the murder rate has begun to level off.* **2** [T **level** sth ↔ **off/out**] to make something flat and smooth

level with sb *phr. v.* [T] INFORMAL to speak honestly to someone, after hiding some facts from them for a period of time: *I wish the President would level with the American people.* —see also **be on the level** (LEVEL¹ (10))

lev·el·er /ˈlɛvələ/ *n.* [C] something that makes people of all classes and ranks seem equal, because they can all use it or because it affects them all equally: *Public school was viewed as the great leveler.*

level-head·ed /ˌ... ˈ...ˑ/ *adj.* calm and sensible in making judgments or decisions, or showing this quality: *a level-headed solution*

lev·er /ˈlɛvɚ, ˈliː-/ *n.* [C] **1** a stick or handle attached to a machine, that you move to make the machine work **2** a long thin piece of metal, wood etc. that you use to lift something heavy by putting one end under the object and pushing the other end down **3** something that you use to influence a situation in order to get the result that you want: *Many nations used sanctions as an economic lever to help end apartheid in South Africa.* —**lever** *v.* [T]

lev·er·age¹ /ˈlɛvərɪdʒ, ˈliː-/ *n.* [U] **1** influence that you can use to make people do what you want: *Turkey has promised not to use its control of the rivers for political leverage.* **2** the action, power, or use of a lever **3** borrowed money that is used to INVEST or buy something such as a company

leverage² *v.* [T] TECHNICAL to make money available to someone in order to INVEST or buy something such as a company: *Development programs often use public funds to leverage private investment.*

leveraged buy·out /ˌ... ˈ.../ *n.* [C] TECHNICAL a situation in which someone gets a LOAN to buy most or all of the STOCK in a company by promising to pay the bank back by selling the company's ASSETS if they cannot pay back the money they borrowed

Le·vi /ˈliːvaɪ/ in the Bible, the head of one of the 12 tribes of Israel

le·vi·a·than /lɪˈvaɪəθən/ *n.* [C] **1** something very large and strong: *a leviathan of a ship* **2** LITERARY any very large and frightening sea animal, especially a WHALE

Lé·vi-Strauss /ˌlɛvi ˈstraʊs, ˌleɪ-/, **Claude** /kloʊd/ (1908–) a French teacher and writer in the area of ANTHROPOLOGY who helped to develop important ideas in STRUCTURALISM

lev·i·tate /ˈlɛvəˌteɪt/ *v.* [I,T] to rise and float in the air as if by magic, or to make someone do this: *Followers claim that she has levitated frequently during prayer.* —**levitation** /ˌlɛvəˈteɪʃən/ *n.* [U]

Le·vit·i·cus /ləˈvɪtɪkəs/ a book in the Old Testament of the Christian Bible

lev·i·ty /ˈlɛvəti/ *n.* [U] FORMAL the quality of telling jokes and having fun instead of being serious: *Dr. Watkins brought some much-needed levity into his lecture on economic theory.*

lev·y¹ /ˈlɛvi/ *v.* past tense and past participle **levied** [T] **levy a tax/charge etc.** to officially make someone pay a tax etc.: [+ on] *A 15% tax is levied on most hotel services.*

levy² *n.* plural **levies** [C] an additional sum of money, usually paid as a tax

lewd /luːd/ *adj.* **1** using OBSCENE words or behaving in a way that makes someone think of sex: *a lewd gesture* **2 lewd and lascivious behavior/acts/conduct etc.** LAW sexual behavior that is illegal and morally unacceptable: *Hankins was arrested for lewd and lascivious conduct with a minor.* —**lewdly** *adv.* —**lewdness** *n.* [U]

Lew·is /ˈluːɪs/, **Carl** /kɑrl/ (1961–) a U.S. ATHLETE who won several GOLD MEDALs in the Olympic Games for the LONG JUMP and for running races

Lewis, C.S. (1898–1963) a British writer and university professor, known especially for his children's stories with a SPIRITUAL meaning

Lewis, Sin·clair /ˈsɪnklɛr/ (1885–1951) a U.S. writer of NOVELs, known for writing about life in small U.S. towns

lex·i·cal /ˈlɛksɪkəl/ *adj.* TECHNICAL dealing with words, or related to words

lex·i·cog·ra·phy /ˌlɛksɪˈkɑgrəfi/ *n.* [U] the skill, practice, or profession of writing dictionaries —**lexicographer** *n.* [C] —**lexicographical** /ˌlɛksɪkəˈgræfɪkəl/ *adj.*

lex·i·con /ˈlɛksɪˌkɑn/ *n.* [C] **1** all the words used in a language, a particular group, a particular profession etc.: *the political lexicon* **2** a book containing lists of words with their meanings

lex·is /ˈlɛksɪs/ *n.* [U] TECHNICAL all the words in a language

lg. the written abbreviation of "large"

li·a·bil·i·ty /ˌlaɪəˈbɪləti/ *n.* plural **liabilities** **1** [U] legal responsibility for something, especially for paying money that is owed, or for damage or injury: [+ for] *Ford did not admit any liability for the misleading advertising.* **2 liabilities** [plural] TECHNICAL the amount of debt that a company owes —compare ASSET (1) **3** [C] someone or something that is likely

L

to cause problems for someone: [+ to] *In his letter of resignation, the General admitted he was a liability to the president.* **4** [U] LITERARY the quality of being likely —compare ASSET —see also LIMITED LIABILITY

li·a·ble /ˈlaɪəbəl/ *adj.* **1 be liable to do sth** to be likely to do something, behave in a particular way, or be treated in a particular way: *Protests are liable to occur throughout the prime minister's visit.* | *She's liable to start crying if you start talking about Mike.* | *Refugees are liable to be shot if they return.* **2** [not before noun] legally responsible for something, especially for the cost of something: *Executives at the company are being* **held** *personally* **liable for** *investors' losses.* **3** [not before noun] likely to be affected by a particular kind of problem, illness etc.: [+ to] *Prostitutes are particularly liable to infection.*

li·aise /liˈeɪz/ *v.* [I + **with**] FORMAL to exchange information with someone who works in another organization or department so that you can both be more effective

li·ai·son /liˈeɪˌzɑn/ *n.* **1** [C] also **liaison officer** someone whose job is to talk to different departments, groups, organizations etc. and to tell each of them about what the others are doing: [+ **between**] *Turner serves as a liaison between management and staff.* **2** [C] a sexual relationship between two people who are not married **3** [U] a working relationship between two groups, companies etc.

li·ar /ˈlaɪɚ/ *n.* [C] someone who tells lies

lib /lɪb/ *n.* —see AD-LIB, WOMEN'S LIB

li·ba·tion /laɪˈbeɪʃən/ *n.* [C] **1** LITERARY a gift of wine to a god **2** HUMOROUS an alcoholic drink

lib·ber /ˈlɪbɚ/ *n.* **women's libber** –see WOMEN'S LIB

li·bel¹ /ˈlaɪbəl/ *n.* [C,U] an act of writing or printing untrue statements about someone so that other people are likely to have a bad opinion of them: *Holt sued the newspaper for libel.* | *a libel suit* (=a court case against someone for libel) —compare SLANDER¹ (1)

li·bel² *v.* [T] to write or print untrue statements about someone so that other people are likely to have a bad opinion of them: *Kandell contends he was libeled by the Journal.*

li·bel·ous /ˈlaɪbələs/ *adj.* containing untrue written statements about someone which could make other people have a bad opinion of them: *libelous statements*

S W 3 **lib·er·al¹** /ˈlɪbrəl, -bərəl/ *adj.* **1** willing to understand or respect the different behavior, ideas etc. of other people: *a liberal view of homosexuality* —compare CONSERVATIVE¹ (1) **2** supporting political ideas that include more involvement by the government in business and in people's lives, and willing to respect the different behaviors of other people in their private lives: *Some liberal Democrats want to introduce stricter price controls.* —compare CONSERVATIVE¹ (2) **3** supporting or allowing changes in political, social, or religious systems that give people more freedom: *liberal immigration policies* **4** generous, or given in large amounts: *a liberal supply of drinks* **5** not exact: *a liberal interpretation of the original play* **6 liberal education** a type of education that encourages you to develop a large range of interests and knowledge and respect for other people's opinions, rather than learning specific technical skills

lib·er·al² *n.* [C] someone with liberal opinions or principles —compare CONSERVATIVE²

liberal arts /ˌ.. ˈ./ *n.* [plural] the areas of learning which develop someone's ability to think and increase their general knowledge, rather than developing technical skills: *a liberal arts college*

liberal de·moc·ra·cy /ˌ.. .ˈ../ *n. plural* **liberal democracies** [C,U] a political system in which everyone can vote to elect the government, and in which people have a lot of freedom and the government does not influence trade very much

lib·er·al·is·m /ˈlɪbrəˌlɪzəm/ *n.* [U] LIBERAL¹ (1) opinions and principles, especially on social and political subjects —compare CONSERVATISM

lib·er·al·i·ty /ˌlɪbəˈræləti/ *n.* [U] FORMAL **1** understanding of, and respect for, other people's opinions: *a spirit of liberality and fairness* **2** the quality of being generous

lib·er·al·ize /ˈlɪbrəˌlaɪz/ *v.* [T] to make a system, laws, or moral attitudes less strict: *Both candidates promised to liberalize trade laws to allow for more imports.* —**liberalization** /ˌlɪbrələˈzeɪʃən/ *n.* [U]

lib·er·al·ly /ˈlɪbrəli/ *adv.* in large amounts: *Apply sunscreen liberally to all exposed skin.*

liberal stud·ies /ˌ.. ˈ../ *n.* [plural] a subject of study at a college or university that includes a little of many different subjects such as history, literature, and politics: *a liberal studies major* —compare LIBERAL ARTS

lib·er·ate /ˈlɪbəˌreɪt/ *v.* [T] **1** to free someone from feelings or conditions that make their life unhappy or difficult: [**liberate sb from sth**] *In the 1930s, electricity liberated farmers from many hard chores.* **2** to free prisoners, a city, a country etc. from someone's control: *The city was liberated by the Allies in 1944.* —**liberating** *adj.*: *a liberating experience* —**liberator** *n.* [C]

lib·er·at·ed /ˈlɪbəˌreɪt̮ɪd/ *adj.* free to behave in the way you want, and not restricted by old rules of social and sexual behavior: *a liberated woman*

lib·er·a·tion /ˌlɪbəˈreɪʃən/ *n.* [U] **1** the act of freeing prisoners, a city, a country etc.: [+ **of**] *the liberation of Kuwait* **2** the state of being liberated: *the sexual liberation movement*

Li·be·ri·a /laɪˈbɪriə/ a country in west Africa on the Atlantic Ocean, to the southeast of Sierra Leone —**Liberian** *n., adj.*

lib·er·tar·i·an /ˌlɪbɚˈtɛriən/ *n.* [C] someone who believes strongly that people should be free to do and think what they want to, and not be influenced by the government —**libertarian** *adj.*

lib·er·tine /ˈlɪbɚˌtin/ *n.* [C] someone who leads an immoral life and always looks for pleasure, especially sexual pleasure —**libertine** *adj.*

lib·er·ty /ˈlɪbɚt̮i/ *n. plural* **liberties**
1 freedom [U] the freedom and the right to do whatever you want without asking permission or being afraid of authority: *The Constitution promises liberty and justice to all citizens.*
2 legal right [C usually plural] a particular legal right: *civil liberties*
3 be at liberty to do sth FORMAL to have the right or permission to do something: *We are not at liberty to discuss our hiring practices.*
4 take the liberty of doing sth to do something without asking permission because you do not think it will upset or offend anyone: *I took the liberty of helping myself to a piece of cake.*
5 take liberties with sth to make unreasonable changes in something such as a piece of writing: *The media seems too willing to take liberties with facts.*
6 take liberties with sb OLD-FASHIONED to treat someone without respect by being too friendly too quickly, especially in a sexual way

li·bi·do /lɪˈbidoʊ/ *n. plural* **libidos** [C,U] TECHNICAL someone's desire to have sex —**libidinous** /lɪˈbɪdn-əs/ *adj.*

Li·bra /ˈlibrə/ *n.* **1** [U] the seventh sign of the ZODIAC, represented by a pair of SCALEs, and believed to affect the character and life of people born between September 23 and October 23 **2** [C] someone who was born between September 23 and October 23: *Steve's a Libra.*

li·brar·i·an /laɪˈbrɛriən/ *n.* [C] someone who works in a library —**librarianship** *n.* [U]

li·brar·y /ˈlaɪˌbrɛri/ *n. plural* **libraries** [C] **1** a room or building containing books that you can read there or borrow: *a public library* | *library books* —compare BOOKSTORE **2** a group of books, records etc., collected by one person **3** a set of books, records etc. that are produced by the same company and have the same general appearance: *a library of modern classics* **4** a room in a large house where most of the books are kept

a library

a bookstore

library sci·ence /ˌ... ˈ../ *n.* [U] the study of the skills that are necessary to organize and work in a library

li·bret·tist /lɪˈbrɛtɪst/ *n.* [C] someone who writes librettos

li·bret·to /lɪˈbrɛtoʊ/ *n. plural* **librettos** [C] the words of an OPERA or musical play

Li·bre·ville /ˈlibrəvɪl/ the capital city of Gabon

Lib·y·a /ˈlɪbiə/ a country in north Africa on the Mediterranean Sea, that is east of Algeria and west of Egypt —**Libyan** *n., adj.*

lice /laɪs/ *n.* the plural of LOUSE[2]

li·cense[1] /ˈlaɪsəns/ *n.* **1** [C] an official document giving you permission to own something or do something for a period of time: *How much does a driver's license cost?* | *a fishing license* **2 lose your license** to have your driver's license taken by the police as punishment **3** [U] freedom to do or say whatever you think is best: *Teachers should be given greater license in the classroom.* **4 artistic/poetic/creative license** the way in which a writer or painter changes the facts of the real world to make their story, description, or picture of events more interesting or more beautiful **5** [C,U] the right to behave in a way that is wrong, disgusting, or immoral: *Being old does not give someone license to be rude.* **6 under license** if something is sold, made etc. under license, it is sold, made etc with the official permission of a company or organization **7 a license to print money** INFORMAL an officially approved plan in which there is no control over how much money is spent

license[2] *v.* [T usually passive] to give official permission for someone to do something or for an activity to take place: [**license sb to do sth**] *He is licensed to carry a gun.*

li·censed /ˈlaɪsənst/ *adj.* **1** having been given official permission to do something: *a licensed private investigator* | *licensed drivers* **2** a licensed car, gun etc. is one that someone has official permission to own or use

licensed prac·ti·cal nurse /ˌ.. ˌ... ˈ./ *abbreviation* **LPN** *n.* [C] someone who has been trained and is officially allowed to work as a nurse if a doctor or REGISTERED NURSE works with them

licensed vo·ca·tion·al nurse /ˌ.. ˌ... ˈ./ *abbreviation* **LVN** *n.* [C] a licensed practical nurse in California or Texas

li·cen·see /ˌlaɪsənˈsi/ *n.* [C] someone who has official permission to do something

license plate /ˈ.. ˌ./ *n.* [C] one of the signs with numbers and letters on it at the front and back of a car —see picture on page 427

li·cen·tious /laɪˈsɛnʃəs/ *adj.* LITERARY sexually immoral or uncontrolled: *licentious behavior* —**licentiousness** *n.* [U]

li·chee /ˈlitʃi/ *n.* [C] another spelling of LYCHEE

li·chen /ˈlaɪkən/ *n.* [C,U] a gray, green, or yellow plant that spreads over the surface of stones and trees —compare MOSS

Lich·ten·stein /ˈlɪktən-ˌstaɪn, -ˌstin/, **Roy** /rɔɪ/ (1923–1997) a U.S. PAINTER and SCULPTOR famous for his work in POP ART, especially paintings in the style of COMIC STRIPS

Roy Lichtenstein

lic·it /ˈlɪsɪt/ *adj.* FORMAL legal: *licit drugs* —opposite ILLICIT

lick[1] /lɪk/ *v.*
1 **tongue** [T] to move your tongue across the surface of something in order to eat it, clean it etc.: *Paul put down the chicken and licked his fingers.*
2 **defeat** [T] INFORMAL to defeat an opponent or solve a problem: *Manley has been unable to lick his drinking problem*
3 **flames/waves** [I,T] LITERARY if flames or waves lick something, they touch it again and again with quick movements: [+ **at/against**] *Flames licked at the top story of the eight-floor building.*
4 lick your lips/chops INFORMAL to feel eager and excited because you are expecting something good: *Executives were licking their chops at the prospect of the merger.*
5 lick your wounds to quietly think about the defeat or disappointment you have just suffered: *The day after the election, many defeated conservatives were licking their wounds.*
6 lick sb's boots DISAPPROVING to obey someone completely or do things to please them —see also BOOTLICKING

lick sth ↔ **up** *phr. v.* [T] to drink or eat something by licking it: *The dog licked up the puddle of melting ice cream.*

lick[2] *n.* **1** [C usually singular] an act of licking something with your tongue: *Can I have a lick of your ice cream cone?* **2 not a lick of sth** OLD-FASHIONED not even a small amount of something: *Those kids don't have a lick of common sense.* **3** [C] INFORMAL an act of hitting someone: *Ellis landed a few licks early in the third round.* **4 give sth a lick and a promise a)** to do a job quickly and carelessly **b)** to wash or clean something quickly and carelessly

lick·e·ty-split /ˌlɪkəti ˈsplɪt/ *adv.* OLD-FASHIONED very quickly

lick·ing /ˈlɪkɪŋ/ *n.* [singular] INFORMAL **1** a severe beating as a punishment **2** a defeat in a sports competition: *The Reds took a licking in the first two games.*

lic·o·rice /ˈlɪkərɪʃ/ *n.* [U] **1** a type of strong-tasting black candy made with a substance from the root of a plant **2** a strong-tasting sweet black substance from the root of a plant, used in candy and medicine

lid /lɪd/ *n.*
1 **cover** [C] a cover for the open part of a pot, box, or other container: *Where's the lid for this jar?*
2 keep a lid on sth to control a situation or to keep something secret, especially so that the situation does not become worse: *The slow economy kept a lid on inflation last month.* | *Company officials are keeping a tight lid on their plans.*
3 **eye** [C] an EYELID
4 put a lid on sth to do something that stops a bad situation from getting worse: *New laws could put a lid on the rising cost of insurance.*
5 take the lid off sth/lift the lid on sth to let people know the true facts about a bad or shocking situation

lid·ded /ˈlɪdɪd/ *adj.* a lidded container, pot etc. has a lid —see also HEAVY-LIDDED

L

S W
2 1

lie¹ /laɪ/ *v. past tense* **lay** *past participle* **lain** *present participle* **lying**

1 **flat position** [I always + adv./prep.] **a)** to be in a position in which your body is flat on the floor, on a bed etc.: [+ **on/in/there etc.**] *We lay on the beach for a couple of hours.* | *Almost every night I lie awake in bed worrying about my family.* **b)** also **lie down** to put yourself in a position in which your body is flat on the floor, on a bed etc.: [+ **on/in/ there etc.**] *He lies on the floor to stretch his back.* **c)** to be in a flat position on a surface: [+ **on/in/ there etc.**] *The train is still lying on its side after falling off the tracks Tuesday.*

2 **be in a place** [I always + adv./prep.] to be in a particular place: [+ **in/on/below etc.**] *The town lies in a small wooded valley.*

3 **exist** [I always + adv./prep.] used to say where something such as a reason or answer can be found: [+ **in/within/outside etc.**] *The solution lies in alternative sources of power.* | *China's future lies with the world community* (=it will be an important part of China's future).

4 **be in a condition** [I] to be or remain in a particular condition or position: *Now the town lay in ruins.* | *Recent storms destroyed a wall that had lain undisturbed underwater for thousands of years.*

5 **lie low** to remain hidden because someone is trying to find you or catch you: *Brown seems to be lying low until the controversy passes.*

6 **lie ahead** also **lie in store (for sb)** if something lies ahead, it is going to happen in the future: *It's clear to us that many difficult tasks still lie ahead.*

7 **lie in wait (for sb/sth) a)** to remain hidden in a place and wait for someone so that you can attack them: *Mulder has not determined if the robber lay in wait for the victim.* **b)** if something bad lies in wait for you, it is going to happen to you

8 **lie at the heart of sth** to be the most important part of something: *Oil and tourism lie at the heart of the dispute between the two nations.*

9 **lie heavy on sb** FORMAL if something lies heavy on you, it makes you feel responsible and unhappy: *The duties of leadership lay heavy on him.*

10 **lie in state** FORMAL if an important person who has died lies in state, their body is put in a public place so that people can go and show their respect for them

11 **here lies sb** written on the stone above someone's grave, especially in the past, to say that they are buried there: *Here lies Edgar Fuller, 1834–1912.* —see also **let sleeping dogs lie** (SLEEP¹ (7)) —see Usage Note at LIE¹

lie around *phr. v.* [I] **1** to be left out of the correct place, so that things look messy: *Books and papers were lying around everywhere.* **2** to spend time being lazy and not doing anything useful: *When I got home, he'd been lying around the house all day.* **3** **be lying around** INFORMAL if something is lying around, it has been left in a place where it would not usually be, in a messy or careless way: *You shouldn't leave your keys lying around like that.*

lie behind sth *phr. v.* [T] to be the true reason for an action, decision etc.: *It is still unclear what lay behind the sudden resignation of the two officials.*

lie down *phr. v.* **1** [I] to put yourself in a position in which your body is flat on the floor or on a bed: *I'm really sleepy – I'm going to go lie down for a little while.* **2** **take sth lying down** INFORMAL to accept bad treatment without complaining: *We are not going to take this verdict lying down. There will be protests.* **3** **lie down on the job** to be lazy at work and not work as hard as you should **4** **if you lie down with dogs, you get up with fleas** used to say that if you become involved with bad people, bad things will happen to you

lie with sb *phr. v.* [T] **1** if a power, duty etc. lies with someone, they are responsible for it: *Much of the responsibility for the city's current problems lies with the mayor.* **2** OLD USE OR BIBLICAL to have sex with someone

L

lie² *v. past tense and past participle* **lied** *present participle* **lying** **1** [I] to deliberately tell someone something that is not true: *I was pretty sure she was lying about where she was.* | [**lie to sb**] *I wish you wouldn't lie to me.* **2** [I not in progressive] if a picture, numbers etc. lie, they do not show the true facts or the true situation: *The camera doesn't lie.* **3** **lie through your teeth** to deliberately say something that is completely untrue, in a way that makes other people angry or upset —see Usage Note at LAY¹

S W
1

lie³ *n.* **1** [C] something that you say or write that you know is untrue: *Tina got in trouble for telling lies.* | *White calls her accusations "a pack of lies* (=a set of statements that is completely untrue)." | *I knew it was a bald-faced lie* (=a clear and shocking lie). **2** **give the lie to sth** FORMAL to show that something is untrue: *Their success gives the lie to predictions of the city's economic doom.* —see also WHITE LIE

S W
3

Liech·ten·stein /ˈlɪktən.ʃtaɪn, -.staɪn/ a very small country in Europe that is west of Austria and east of Switzerland —**Liechtensteiner** *n.*

lie de·tec·tor /ˈ. .,../ *n.* [C] a piece of equipment used especially by the police to check whether someone is lying, by measuring sudden changes in their heart rate

lien /lin, ˈliən/ *n.* [C + **against/on**] LAW the legal right to keep something that belongs to someone who owes you money, until the debt has been paid

lieu /lu/ *n.* **in lieu (of sth) a)** FORMAL instead of something else: *In some cases, a telephone interview will be held in lieu of a personal visit.* **b)** LAW if you are held in lieu of a particular amount of money, you will be kept in prison until someone pays that money to the police: *She was being held in lieu of $40,000 bail.*

lieu·ten·ant /luˈtɛnənt/ *n.* **1** *written abbreviation* **Lt.** [C] an officer who has a middle rank in the Army, Navy, Air Force, Marines, police etc. **2** **lieutenant colonel/general etc.** an officer with the rank below COLONEL, GENERAL² etc. **3** [C] someone who does work for, or in place of, someone in a higher position; DEPUTY (1)

lieutenant gov·er·nor /.,.. '.../ *n.* [C] the person who is next in rank to the GOVERNOR of a U.S. state and who is responsible for the Governor's duties if he or she is unable to do them

life /laɪf/ *n. plural* **lives** /laɪvz/ **1** **period of being alive** [C,U] the period between a person's birth and death, during which they are alive: *Learning goes on throughout life.* | *My mother worked hard all her life.* | *This is one of the happiest days of my life.* | *I'd only seen her maybe three times in my life.* | *He deserves to spend his life in prison for what he's done.* | *The accident left him crippled for life* (=for the rest of his life). | *It is hard to get reliable information about St. Catherine's early life* (=the part of her life when she was young). | *Arlene's father took up painting in later life* (=when he was older). | *She didn't have children until relatively late in life* (=when she was fairly old).

S W
1 1

2 **state of being alive** [C] the state of being alive: *A heart transplant could save his life.* | *Chuen risked his life* (=did something during which he could have been killed) *to save Sammler.* | *Over 2000 Americans lost their lives* (=died) *in the attack.* | *When she discovered Carl was dead, Anna decided to take her own life* (=kill herself). | *Every time you cross this highway you take your life in your hands* (=put yourself in a dangerous situation).

3 **living things** [U] **a)** the quality that people, animals, and plants have that rocks, machines, dead bodies etc. do not have: *a baby's first moments of life* (=immediately after it is born) **b)** living things, such as people, animals, or plants: *Do you think there is life on other planets?* | **animal/plant/bird life** (=living animals, plants, or birds)

4 **way of living** [C,U] all the experiences and activities that are typical of a particular way of living: *Life in L.A. is exciting.* | *He started his working life as an urban planner.* | *Married life isn't everything we expected.* | *the American way of life* | *This is the life* (=what we are doing is the most enjoyable way to live)!

5 experiences [C usually singular] the type of experience that someone has during their life: *At least Aunt Edith had a happy life.* | *I'm hoping to win the lottery and live a life of luxury!* | *He hasn't led a very easy life, you know.* —see also LIFE STORY

6 private/sex/social etc. life activities in your life that are private, relate to sex, are done with friends etc.: *Max studied all the time and had no social life.*

7 real life what really happens as opposed to what happens in people's imaginations or in stories: *a real-life drama* | *In real life it's not so easy to catch a criminal.*

8 prison [U] also life imprisonment the punishment of being put in prison for the rest of your life: *Pratt was sentenced to life for the 1968 murder.* —see also LIFE SENTENCE

9 [U] activity or movement: *There were a few tiny signs of life in the river.* | *Eddie is 70, but he's still full of life* (=very cheerful and active).

10 human existence [U] human existence, considered as a variety of activities and experiences: *Life can be hard sometimes.* | *Cindy still doesn't know much about life.*

11 working/existing [singular] **a)** the period of time during which something happens or exists: [+ of] *The interest rate varies over the life of the loan.* **b)** the period of time during which something is still good enough to use: [+ of] *What's the average life of a passenger airplane?* —see also SHELF LIFE

12 bring sb/sth to life **a)** to make someone or something live: *The rescue team brought the baby back to life.* **b)** to make something more exciting or interesting: *Maps, drawings, and photos bring the subject matter to life.*

13 come to life **a)** to suddenly start living, start working, or become more active: *The children stared in amazement as the stone elephants came to life.* | *After a week of not working, the computer suddenly came to life.* **b)** to become exciting or interesting: *Printed words come to life as the authors read them aloud.* **c)** if a dream, idea etc., especially a bad one, comes to life, it becomes real: *Wednesday was a commuter nightmare come to life.*

14 be sb's (whole) life to be the most important thing or person in someone's life: *Music is Laura's life*

15 be the life of the party to be the person who brings fun and excitement to a social group or occasion

16 make life difficult/easier etc. to make it difficult, easier etc. to do something: *It would make life easier for me if the two of you would cooperate.*

17 the race/surprise/game etc. of sb's life the best race someone has ever run, the biggest surprise they have ever had etc. —see also have the time of your life (TIME¹ (50))

18 start/make a new life to completely change your life, for example by moving to another place: *They moved out West to start a new life there.*

19 the woman/man in your life the woman or man with whom you have a sexual or romantic relationship

20 paint/draw from life to paint or draw something that you are looking at directly, not from another picture

21 book/movie [C] the story of someone's life; BIOGRAPHY: *A Life of Christopher Columbus*

22 the next life/the life to come a continued existence that is expected after death

SPOKEN PHRASES

23 not on your life! used to say that you definitely will not do something

24 Get a life! used to tell someone you think they are boring

25 for the life of me said when you cannot do something, even when you try very hard: *I can't remember her name for the life of me!*

26 that's life used when you are disappointed or upset that something has happened, but realize that you must accept it: *Oh well, that's life!*

27 life is too short (to do sth) said when telling someone that something is not important enough to worry about: *Life's too short to spend time thinking about the color of your curtains.*

—see also for dear life (DEAR³ (3)), HIGH LIFE, larger than life (LARGE (5)), give sb/sth a new lease on life (LEASE¹ (2)), LOW LIFE, sth is a matter of life and death (MATTER¹ (27))

USAGE NOTE: LIFE

WORD CHOICE: life, living, lifestyle

Use **life** to talk about the whole experience of living: *Muriel had a long and happy life.* Use **living** to talk about the physical needs of living, especially how much money you need: *You can make a pretty good living* (=earn enough money) *in this town as a waiter.* Use **living conditions** (NOT *life conditions*) to talk about the kind of houses people live in and whether they have things like water, heat etc. Use **standard of living** (NOT *standard of life*) to talk about how comfortable someone's life is, how much money they have etc. But use **quality of life** (NOT *quality of living*) to talk about how enjoyable their life is. The **cost of living** (NOT *the cost of life*) is how much money people need to spend in order to buy necessary things: *The cost of living keeps going up, but my salary stays the same.* A **lifestyle** or **way of life** is the way someone lives, for example what they eat, how often they exercise, what they do in their free time etc.: *He doesn't have a very healthy lifestyle.*

GRAMMAR

When talking about **life** [U] in general, do not use *the*: *Life is full of surprises* (NOT *The life...*).

---

life-af·firm·ing /ˈ. .ˌ.../ *adj.* giving you a positive and happy attitude about life: *a life-affirming celebration of African-Americans' contribution to U.S. culture*

life belt /ˈ. ./ *n.* [C] a special belt you wear in the water to prevent you from sinking

life·blood, **life-blood** /ˈlaɪfblʌd/ *n.* [U] **1** [singular] the most important thing needed by an organization, relationship etc. for it to continue to exist or develop successfully: *Advertising is the lifeblood of newspapers.* **2** LITERARY your blood

life·boat /ˈlaɪfboʊt/ *n.* [C] **1** a small boat carried by ships in order to save people if the ship sinks **2** a boat that is sent out to help people who are in danger on the ocean

life buoy /ˈ. ./ *n.* [C] a large ring made of material that floats, that you throw to someone who has fallen in the water, to prevent them from DROWNING

life cy·cle /ˈ. ˌ.../ *n.* [C] all the different levels of development that an animal or plant goes through during its life

life ex·pect·an·cy /ˈ. .ˌ.../ *n.* [C] **1** the length of time that a person or animal is expected to live **2** the length of time that something is expected to continue to work, be useful etc.: *CDs have a life expectancy of at least 20 years.* —compare LIFESPAN

life form /ˈ. ./ *n.* [C] a living thing such as a plant or animal

life guard /ˈ. ./ *n.* [C] someone who works at a beach or swimming pool to help swimmers who are in danger

life his·to·ry /ˌ. ˈ.../ *n.* [C] all the events and changes that happen during the life of a living thing

life in·sur·ance /ˈ. .ˌ../ *n.* [U] a type of insurance that someone makes regular payments into so that when they die their family will receive money

life jack·et /ˈ. ˌ../ *n.* [C] a piece of clothing that you wear around your upper body to prevent you from sinking in the water

life·less /ˈlaɪflɪs/ *adj.* **1** LITERARY dead or appearing to be dead: *Anton's lifeless body was found floating in the lake.* **2** lacking the positive qualities that make something or someone interesting, exciting, or active: *a lifeless performance* **3** not living, or not having living things on it: *The surface of the moon is dry and lifeless.* —**lifelessly** *adv.* —**lifelessness** *n.* [U]

life·like /ˈlaɪflaɪk/ *adj.* a lifelike picture, model etc. looks exactly like a real person or thing: *a lifelike doll*

L

life·line /'laɪflaɪn/ n. [C] **1** something that someone depends on completely: *Because I work at home, the telephone is like a lifeline to me.* **2** a rope used for saving people in danger, especially on the ocean

life·long /'laɪflɒŋ/ adj. [usually before noun] continuing or existing all through your life: *a lifelong relationship*

life pre·serv·er /'. .,../ n. [C] something such as a LIFE BELT or LIFE JACKET that can be worn in the water to prevent you from sinking

lif·er /'laɪfə/ n. [C] INFORMAL **1** someone who has been sent to prison for the rest of their life **2** someone who spends their whole working life in the military or in a profession

life raft /'. ./ n. [C] a small rubber boat that can be filled with air and used by passengers on a sinking ship

life·sav·er /'laɪf,seɪvə/ n. [C] **1** someone or something that helps you avoid a difficult or bad situation: *The company's day care service has been a lifesaver for many parents.* **2** someone or something that prevents you from dying: *The seat belt is the biggest single lifesaver in cars.* **3** a LIFE GUARD

life·sav·ing /'laɪf,seɪvɪŋ/ n. [U] the skills necessary to save a person from DROWNing: *All of the staff have been trained in lifesaving.*

life-saving, lifesaving /'. ,../ adj. [only before noun] a life-saving drug, action, piece of equipment etc. has saved someone's life, or makes it possible to save people's lives: *a life-saving operation*

life sci·enc·es /,. '../ n. [plural] subjects such as BIOLOGY that are concerned with the study of humans, plants, and animals

life sen·tence /,. '../ n. [C] the punishment of sending someone to prison for the rest of their life

life-size also **life-sized** /'. ./ adj. a picture or model of something or someone that is life-size is the same size as they really are: *a life-sized statue of Elvis*

life·span /'laɪfspæn/ n. [C] the average length of time that someone will live or that something will continue to work: *Men have a shorter lifespan than women.* —compare LIFE EXPECTANCY, LIFETIME

life sto·ry /,. '../ n. [C] the story of someone's whole life: *Karinna can't resist telling her life story to anyone who will listen.*

life·style /'. ./ n. [C] the way someone lives, including the place they live in, the things they own, the type of job they have, and the activities they enjoy: *an urban lifestyle* —see Usage Note at LIFE

life sup·port sys·tem /'. . . ,../ n. [U] machines or methods that keep someone alive when they are extremely sick or in conditions where they would not normally be able to live, such as in space: *She spent 12 days on life support in the hospital.* | *the life support systems of the space shuttle*

life-threat·en·ing /'. ,.../ adj. a life-threatening situation or injury could cause a person to die

sw **life·time** /'laɪftaɪm/ n. [C usually singular] **1** the period of time during which someone is alive or something exists: *In our lifetime, ordinary people will travel to the moon.* **2 the chance/experience etc. of a lifetime** the best opportunity, experience etc. that you will ever have —compare LIFESPAN

life vest /'. ./ n. [C] a LIFE JACKET

life·work /laɪf'wɜːk/ n. [U] the main work that someone does during their life, especially work that is very important to them: *Simon Rodia began his lifework as a sculptor in about 1921.*

lift¹ /lɪft/ v.

sw **1** move sth with your hands [T] to take something in your hands and raise it, move it, or carry it somewhere: *Can you help me lift the big boxes?* | **lift sth up/off/onto etc.** *Brendan lifted Gilbert out of the wheelchair.*

2 raise [I,T] also **lift up** to move something up, into the air, or to move up into the air: *I'm so tired I can't even lift up my arms.* | *Blown by a sudden breeze, the balloon lifted just beyond his reach.* —see Usage Note at RAISE¹

3 head/eyes [T] to move your head or eyes up so that you can look at someone or something: *He lifted his head to see who was at the door.*

4 controls/laws [T] to remove a rule or a law that says that something is not allowed: *The government plans to lift its ban on cigar imports.*

5 clouds/mist [I] if cloud or mist lifts, it disappears

6 increase [T] to increase the amount or level of something: *Lower prices should eventually lift corporate profits.*

7 not lift a finger INFORMAL to do nothing to help: *He never even lifted a finger to help me with the kids.*

8 lift sb's spirits to make someone feel more cheerful and hopeful

9 use sb's ideas/words [T] to copy words, ideas, music etc. that someone else has written: *The movie's ending was lifted from Frankenheimer's "Black Sunday."*

10 steal [T] INFORMAL to steal something

11 lift (up) your voice LITERARY to speak, shout, or sing more loudly

lift off phr. v. [I] if an aircraft or space vehicle lifts off, it leaves the ground and rises into the air

lift sb past sb phr. v. [T] to gain enough points in a game to defeat another team: *Messier's goal was enough to lift New York past Washington.*

lift² n. **1** [C usually singular] if you give someone a lift, you take them somewhere in your car; RIDE: *Sheri gave me a lift home.* **2 give sb/sth a lift a)** to make someone feel more cheerful and more hopeful: *If I'm feeling down, buying makeup always gives me a lift.* **b)** to make something such as a business, the ECONOMY etc. operate better: *Good deals in auto stock prices gave the stock market a lift today.* **3** a piece of equipment used to lift heavy objects, especially one for helping injured or DISABLED (1) people go up stairs **4** [U] the pressure of air that keeps something up in the air or lifts it higher **5** INFORMAL a CHAIRLIFT —see also SKI LIFT **6** [C] BRITISH an ELEVATOR

lift-off /'. ./ n. [C,U] the moment when a vehicle that is about to travel in space leaves the ground: *Lift-off is set for 10:55 a.m.* —compare TAKEOFF (1)

lig·a·ment /'lɪgəmənt/ n. [C] a band of strong material in your body, similar to muscle, that joins bones or holds an organ in its place

light¹ /laɪt/ n.

sw **1** natural/artificial light **a)** [U] the energy from the sun, a flame, a lamp etc. that allows you to see things: *We could see light coming from under the door.* | *That light's really bright.* | *Lincoln studied by the light of* (=using light produced by) *a fire.* | *Come into the light* (=out of the shadows to a place with more light) *where I can see you.* | *Suddenly the grounds were bathed in a harsh light* (=one that is too strong). | *A beam of light* (=a thin line of light) *shone through a crack in the door.* | **soft/warm light** (=light that is not too strong) | **blinding/dazzling light** (=extremely bright light) **b)** [U] a particular type of light, with its own particular color, level of brightness etc.: *I enjoy sitting on my steps in the morning light.* —see also NORTHERN LIGHTS

2 the light the light produced by the sun during the day: *We worked for as long as the light lasted.*

3 lamp/electric light etc. [C] **a)** an electric light: *The 5-inch model of the starship came complete with blinking lights.* | **turn the light on/off** *Please turn on the light.* | **switch on/off the light** *Could you switch off all the lights?* | *Suddenly all the lights in the house went out.* | **turn the lights down/dim the lights** (=make lights less bright) | *The audience cheered as the house lights* (=the lights in a theater, movie theater etc.) *came up.* —see also **the bright lights (of sth)** (BRIGHT (8)) **b)** something such as a lamp or a FLASHLIGHT: *Shine a light over here, will you?*

4 traffic control [C usually plural] one of a set of red, green, and yellow lights used for controlling traffic: *I can't believe you just ran a red light* (=drove past a red light). | **the light turns red/green/yellow** (=the light becomes red, green, yellow) —see also GREEN LIGHT, TRAFFIC LIGHTS

5 on a vehicle [C, usually plural] one of the lights on a car, bicycle etc., especially the HEADLIGHTS: *You've left your lights on.* —see also BRAKE LIGHT, PARKING LIGHT

6 be/stand in sb's light to prevent someone from getting all the light they need to see or do something: *Could you move to the left a little? You're standing in my light.*

7 for a cigarette **a light** a match or CIGARETTE LIGHTER to light a cigarette: *Do you have a light?*

8 in a new/different/bad etc. light if you see or show someone or something in a new, different etc. light, you begin to understand them in a particular way, or make someone else do this: *Baltz is trying present the sales figures in a positive light.*

9 in light of sth if you do or decide something in light of a new situation or new information, you do it because of that situation or information: *Investors are being more cautious in light of the recent drop in stock prices.*

10 come to light also **be brought to light** if new information comes to light, it becomes known: *It eventually came to light that the CIA had information about a security problem.*

11 throw/shed/cast light on sth to provide new information that makes a difficult subject or problem easier to understand: *Newly found Aztec artifacts may shed some light on their mysterious culture.*

12 see the light of day a) if an object sees the light of day, it is taken from the place where it has been hidden, and becomes publicly known: *Business contracts go through armies of lawyers before they see the light of day.* **b)** if a law, decision etc. sees the light of day, it begins to exist

13 light at the end of the tunnel something that gives you hope for the future after a long and difficult period: *After a year of declining profits, there's finally a light at the end of the tunnel.*

14 see the light a) OFTEN HUMOROUS to suddenly understand something: *Danny finally saw the light and bought me flowers on Valentine's Day.* **b)** INFORMAL to begin to believe in a religion very strongly

15 go/be out like a light INFORMAL to go to sleep very quickly because you are very tired: *She was out like a light, as soon as we put her in bed.*

16 the light of sb's life the person whom someone loves the most: *We have a four-year-old son who is the light of my life.*

17 first light LITERARY the time when light first appears in the morning sky; DAWN[1]: *The search continued at first light.*

18 in your eyes [singular] LITERARY an expression in your eyes that shows an emotion or intention

19 have your name in lights INFORMAL to be successful and famous in theater or movies

20 a leading light in/of sth INFORMAL someone who is important in a particular group: *Mrs. Shaewitz is a leading light in the local drama society.*

21 the lights are on, but nobody's home SPOKEN, HUMOROUS used to say that someone is stupid or not paying attention

22 window [C] TECHNICAL a window or other opening in a roof or wall that allows light into a room

23 light and shade brightness and darkness in a painting or photograph —see also **in the cold light of day** (COLD[1] (16)), **be all sweetness and light** (SWEETNESS (2))

light² s w adj. ¹⁄₂

1 color a light color or light skin is pale and not dark: *a light blue shirt* | *She has light brown hair.* —compare DARK[1] (2), DEEP[1] (5)

2 weight not weighing very much, or weighing less than you expect: *Why is your suitcase lighter than mine?* | *You can carry this – it's light.* | **as light as air/as light as a feather** (=extremely light) —opposite HEAVY[1] (1) —see also LIGHTEN (3), LIGHTWEIGHT² (3)

3 clothes light clothes are thin and not very warm: *You'll need at least a light jacket.* —opposite THICK[1]

4 it is/gets light used to say that there is enough natural light outside to see by, or that the light outside increases because the sun rises: *It gets light before 6 a.m.*

5 room a room that is light has plenty of light in it, especially from the sun: *The studio was light and spacious.* —opposite DARK[1]

6 wind blowing without much force: *a light breeze* —opposite STRONG

7 touch very gentle and soft: *She gave him a light kiss on the cheek.* —see also LIGHTLY (1)

8 small in amount, or less than you expected: *The traffic's much lighter than usual.* | **a light meal/lunch etc.** (=a meal in which you only eat a small amount)

9 a) not containing much fat or having fewer CALORIES: *light yogurt* —see also LITE **b)** food or an alcoholic drink that is light either does not have a strong taste or is easy to DIGEST[1] (1): *a light white wine* | *a light dessert* —compare HEAVY[1] (14)

10 punishment not very severe: *Jones received only a light punishment.* —opposite HARSH[1] (2)

11 be a pound/two ounces etc. (too) light if something is a pound etc. light, it weighs that amount less than it should weigh

12 work/exercise not very tiring: *I try to have a light workout every day.*

13 a light smoker/drinker/eater etc. someone who does not smoke, drink, eat etc. very much

14 make light of sth to joke about something or treat it as not being very serious, especially when it is important: *It is shocking that anyone could make light of child abuse.*

15 entertainment not serious in meaning, style, or manner, and only intended for entertainment: *an evening of light music* | *I picked up a romance novel for some light reading on the flight.* | *In her book, Rose handles these difficult questions with a light touch* (=a relaxed and pleasant style). | **on a lighter note/in a lighter vein** (=used to introduce a joke, funny story etc. after you have been speaking about something serious) —see also LIGHTLY (3)

16 a light sleeper someone who wakes up easily if there is any noise etc.

17 light sleep sleep from which you wake up easily

18 be light on your feet to be able to move quickly and gracefully

19 make light work of sth to finish a job quickly and easily

20 soil easy to break into small pieces —opposite HEAVY[1] (18)

21 heart LITERARY someone who has a light heart feels happy and not worried —see also LIGHT-HEADED, LIGHT-HEARTED —**lightness** n. [U]

light³ v. past tense and past participle **lit** or **lighted** s w ²⁄₂

1 [I,T] to start to burn, or to deliberately make something start to burn: *The old man lit a cigarette and took a puff.* | *The fire won't light.* —see picture at FIRE[1] —see Usage Note at FIRE[1] **2** [T usually passive] to give light to something: *Osborn's Christmas display is lighted by some 30,000 colored bulbs.* | **well/poorly lit** also **well/poorly lighted** *a well lit room* —see also LIGHTEN (2) **3 light sb's way** also **light sb into/along** OLD-FASHIONED to provide light for someone while they are going somewhere

light on/upon sth *phr. v.* [T] **1** to fly to something and sit on it: *The dragonfly had lighted on her arm.* **2** LITERARY if your eyes light on something, you see something interesting or pleasant: *His eye lit on the wedding ring on her finger.*

light out *phr. v.* [I] INFORMAL to go or run somewhere as quickly as you can: *The boys lit out for home.*

light up *phr. v.* **1** [T **light** sth ↔ **up**] to give light to a place or to shine light on something: *Fireworks lit up the sky.* **2 a)** [I] if someone's face or eyes light up, they show pleasure, excitement etc.: *Sue's face lit up when Sean walked in.* | [+ **with**] *The boy's face lit up with delight.* **b)** [T **light** sth ↔ **up**] to make someone's face or eyes show pleasure or excitement: *Suddenly a smile lit up her face.* **3** [I] to become bright with light or color: *All the buttons on his phone were lit up.* **4** [I] INFORMAL to light a cigarette: *Before you light up in the house, think about how it affects your family.*

L

light⁴ *adv.* —see **travel light** (TRAVEL¹ (1))

light air·craft /ˌ. '../ *n.* [C] a small airplane

light bulb /'. ./ *n.* [C] the glass object inside a lamp that produces light

light·en /'laɪt⁻n/ *v.* **1** [T] to reduce the amount of work, worry, debt etc. that someone has: *School administrators are looking at ways to lighten teachers' workloads.* **2** [I,T] to become brighter or less dark, or to make something brighter etc.: *As the sky lightened, we could see the distant mountains.* —opposite DARKEN (1) **3** [I,T] to reduce the weight of something or become less heavy **4 lighten up!** SPOKEN used to tell someone not to be so serious about something: *Lighten up, dude! Let's not argue about this.*

light·er /'laɪtɚ/ *n.* [C] a small object that produces a flame for lighting cigarettes etc.

light-fin·gered /'. ˌ../ *adj.* **1** likely to steal things **2** able to move your fingers easily and quickly, especially when you play a musical instrument

light-foot·ed /'. ˌ../ *adj.* able to move quickly and gracefully

light-head·ed /'. ˌ../ *adj.* [not before noun] unable to think clearly or move steadily because you are sick or have drunk alcohol; DIZZY: *The wine had made him a little light-headed.* —**light-headedness** *n.* [U]

light-heart·ed /'. ˌ../ *adj.* **1** not intended to be serious: *a light-hearted comedy* **2** cheerful and not worried about anything: *a happy, light-hearted girl* —**light-heartedly** *adv.* —**light-heartedness** *n.* [U]

light heav·y·weight /ˌ. '.../ *n.* [C] a BOXER (1) who weighs between 160 and 175 pounds (72.5 and 79.5 kilograms) —**light heavyweight** *adj.*

light·house /'laɪthaʊs/ *n.* [C] a tower with a powerful flashing light that guides ships away from danger near the shore —see picture on page 428

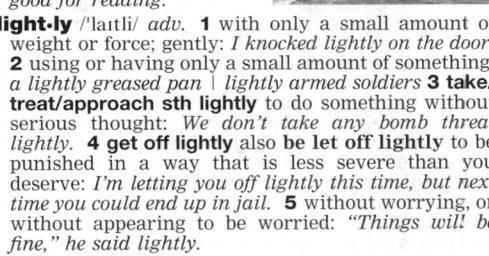
lighthouse

light in·dus·try /ˌ. '.../ *n.* [U] the part of industry that produces small goods, such as things used in the house

light·ing /'laɪtɪŋ/ *n.* [U] the lights that light a room, building, or street, or the quality of the light produced: *The lighting isn't good for reading.*

light·ly /'laɪtli/ *adv.* **1** with only a small amount of weight or force; gently: *I knocked lightly on the door.* **2** using or having only a small amount of something: *a lightly greased pan* | *lightly armed soldiers* **3 take/treat/approach sth lightly** to do something without serious thought: *We don't take any bomb threat lightly.* **4 get off lightly** also **be let off lightly** to be punished in a way that is less severe than you deserve: *I'm letting you off lightly this time, but next time you could end up in jail.* **5** without worrying, or without appearing to be worried: *"Things will be fine," he said lightly.*

light me·ter /'. ˌ../ *n.* [C] an instrument used by a photographer to measure how much light there is

light·ning¹ /'laɪt⁻nɪŋ/ *n.* [U] **1** a powerful flash of light in the sky caused by electricity and usually followed by THUNDER: *Two farmworkers were struck by lightning* (=hit by lightning). **2 like lightning** extremely quickly: *The cat ran up the tree like lightning.*

lightning² *adj., adv.* [only before noun] very fast, and often without warning: *In his prime, Brown was a lightning quick running back.* | **at/with lightning speed** (=extremely quickly)

lightning bug /'.. ˌ./ *n.* [C] an insect with a tail that shines in the dark; FIREFLY

lightning rod /'.. ˌ./ *n.* [C] **1** a metal ROD or wire on a building or structure that gives lightning a direct path to the ground, so that it does not cause damage **2 a lightning rod (for sth)** someone or something who gets most of the criticism, blame, or public attention when there is a problem, although they may not be responsible for it: *Women's Health Services has become the lightning rod for the battle over abortion.*

lightning strike /'.. ˌ./ *n.* [C] a situation in which LIGHTNING hits something

light op·era /ˌ. '../ *n.* [C,U] an OPERETTA, or this type of entertainment

light pen /'. ./ *n.* [C] a piece of equipment like a pen, used to draw or write on a computer screen

light rail /ˌ. '.◂/ *n.* [C] an electric railroad system that uses light trains and usually carries only passengers, not goods —**light-rail** *adj.*

light·ship /'laɪtˌʃɪp/ *n.* [C] a small ship that stays near a dangerous place in the ocean and guides other ships using a powerful flashing light

light show /'. ./ *n.* [C] a type of entertainment that uses a series of moving colored lights, especially at a POP concert

lights-out /ˌ. './ *n.* [U] the time at night when a group of people who are in a school, the army etc. must turn the lights off and go to sleep

light·weight¹ /'laɪt⁻weɪt/ *adj.* **1** weighing less than average: *a lightweight computer* **2** lightweight clothing or material is thin enough to be worn in warm weather: *a lightweight jacket* **3** showing a lack of serious thought: *lightweight novels*

lightweight² *n.* [C] **1** DISAPPROVING someone who you do not think has the ability to think about serious or difficult subjects: *Call me a lightweight, but I like movies with happy endings.* **2** DISAPPROVING someone who has no importance or influence: *a political lightweight* **3** a BOXER (1) who weighs between 126 and 135 pounds (59 and 61 kilograms)

light year /'. ./ *n.* [C] **1** the distance that light travels in one year, about 9,500,000,000,000 kilometers (5.88 trillion miles), used for measuring distances between stars **2 light years ahead/better etc. than sth** INFORMAL much more advanced, much better etc. than someone or something else: *The show's weird vision of the world was light years ahead of its competition.* **3 light years ago** a long time ago

lig·nite /'lɪgnaɪt/ *n.* [U] a soft substance such as coal, used as FUEL¹

lik·a·ble, likeable /'laɪkəbəl/ *adj.* likable people are nice and easy to like

like¹ /laɪk/ *prep.*

1 similar in some way to something else: *The lamp was round, like a ball.* | *You two are behaving like children.* | **look/sound/taste/smell like sth** *Ken looks like his brother.* | *This candy tastes like peppermint.* | *I have some shoes* **just like** (=exactly like) *yours.* | *A new paint job made the car look* **like new**.

2 nothing like sth, anything like sth used to say that something is not similar at all to something else, or to ask whether it is similar: *Being married is nothing like I imagined.* | *Was the movie anything like the book?*

3 like this/so SPOKEN said when you are showing someone how to do something: *Cut the paper diagonally, like this.*

4 typical of a particular person: *It's not like Emily to lie.*

5 what is sb/sth like? used when asking someone to describe or give their opinion of a person or thing: *What's the new teacher like?* | *What's it like living in Spain?*

6 for example a word meaning "for example" or "such as," which some people consider incorrect: *Fruits like oranges and kiwis have lots of vitamin C.*

7 something like not much more or less than a particular amount; about: *The project will take us something like three weeks.*

8 more like used when giving an amount or number that you think is more correct than one that has been mentioned: *Brian said he'll be here at 7, but it'll probably be more like 8 or 9.*

9 there's nothing like SPOKEN used to say that a particular thing is the best: *There's nothing like Mom's chicken soup.*

L

10 that's more like it SPOKEN used to tell someone that what they are doing or suggesting is more satisfactory than what they did or suggested before: *"I said 400, but I meant 200." "Oh OK, that's more like it."*

s w **like²** *v.* [T not usually in progressive]
1 like sth to enjoy something or think that it is nice: *I like your new car.* | *My daughter doesn't like lima beans.* | [like doing sth] *My mother likes working in her vegetable garden.* | [like to do sth] *I like to go mountain biking on the weekends.* | [like sth about sb/sth] *She's very independent – I like that about her.* | *I like the blue one best* (=prefer it). | *Linda doesn't like it when we talk about politics.* | *I don't like the look of that black cloud over there. We'd better go in.* | *I don't think I'll ever get to like flying.* | **like the idea/thought of (doing) sth** *Paul doesn't like the idea of borrowing money.*
2 like sb to think that someone is nice or enjoy being with them: *I liked her, but I was afraid to ask her to go out with me.* | *I don't think Professor Riker likes me.*
3 prefer to prefer that something is done in one particular way or at one particular time rather than another: *I like to put lots of ketchup on my fries.* | *How do you like your steak cooked?*
4 think sth is good to do to think that it is good to do something, so that you do it regularly or so that you want other people to do it regularly: [like to do sth] *I like to try to eat well and keep myself healthy.* | [like sb to do sth] *They like their children to be involved in sports.*
5 not like to do sth also **not like doing sth** to not want to do something because you do not feel it is polite, fair, nice etc.: *I don't like calling her at work.*
6 approve to approve of something or have a good opinion of it: *I like the way she interacts with children.* | [like sb doing sth] *Dad doesn't like anyone disagreeing with him.* | [like sb to do sth] *I like people to be polite to each other.*
7 like the cut of sb's jib HUMOROUS OR OLD-FASHIONED to like the way someone appears or behaves: *I guess Pauline's father didn't like the cut of my jib.*

SPOKEN PHRASES

8 I'd like used to say what you want | *I'd like sth I'd like a vanilla milkshake.* | [I'd like you/John etc. to do sth] *I'd like you kids to clean up your rooms.*
9 would you like...? used to ask someone if they want something: *Would you like a glass of wine?* | [would you like to do sth?] *Would you like to go shopping with me?* | [would you like sb to do sth?] *Would you like me to babysit for you?*
10 would like used to express politely what you want to happen or do: *We'd really like a new washing machine.* | [would like to do sth] *I'd like to know how much it'll cost.* | [would like sb to do sth] *Grandma would like you to be there if you can.* | [would like (to have) sth done] *I'd like to have the report finished by tomorrow.*
11 if you'd like also **if you like a)** used to suggest or offer something: *If you'd like, I'll do the dishes.* **b)** used to agree to something, even if it is not what you want yourself: *"Can we have spaghetti tonight?" "If you'd like."*
12 whatever/anything etc. you like whatever you want: *You can wear whatever you like.* | *Eat as much as you like – there's plenty.*
13 how would you like...? a) used to ask someone if they want something, especially when you already know they want it | **how would you like sth?** *How would you like a big plate of pancakes?* | **how would you like to do sth?** *How would you like to go to Hawaii this December?* **b)** used to ask someone to imagine how they would feel if something bad happened to them instead of to you or someone else: *How would you like it if someone made fun of you?* | **how would you like sb doing sth?** *How would you like your boss calling you an idiot?*
14 how do you like sth? a) used to ask someone for their opinion of something: *How did you like the movie?* **b)** used to ask someone whether they want something added to a drink or how they want

---

something cooked: *"How do you like your coffee?" "Black, thanks."*
15 how do you like that? said when you are annoyed by something that has just happened or that you have just heard about: *Well, how do you like that? He didn't even say thank you.*
16 (whether you) like it or not used to emphasize that something bad is true or will happen and cannot be changed: *You're going to the dentist, whether you like it or not.*
17 I'd like to see sb do sth used to say that you do not believe someone can do something: *I'd like to see you run that fast.*
18 I'd like to think/believe (that) a) used to say that you wish or hope something is true, when you are not sure that it is: *I'd like to believe that he's telling the truth.* **b)** used to say that you think you do something well, especially when you do not want to make yourself seem better than other people: *I'd like to think I know a little about airplanes.*
19 like it or lump it used to say that someone must accept a situation or decision they do not like because it cannot be changed

like³ *adv.* SPOKEN, NONSTANDARD **1 I'm/he's/she's** s w **like... a)** used in order to tell someone the exact words someone used: *I asked him if he thought Liz was cute, and he's like, yeah, definitely.* **b)** used to describe an event, feeling, or person, when it is difficult to describe or when you use a noise instead of a word: *He was like, huh* (=he was really surprised)? | *We were like, oh no* (=we realized something was wrong)! **2** said when you pause because you do not know what to say, because you are embarrassed etc.: *Do you think you could, like, not tell anyone what happened?* **3** said in order to give an example: *That is a scary intersection. Like yesterday I saw two cars go straight through a red light.* **4** said when what you are saying is not exact: *It was like 9 o'clock when I got home.*

like⁴ *n.* **1 sb's likes and dislikes** all the things you like and do not like: *Don't let personal likes and dislikes get in the way of the job.* **2 and the like** similar things: *Most of the cash was spent on gold chains, bracelets and the like.* **3 the like(s) of sb/sth** also **sb's/sth's like** something similar to someone or to a particular person or thing, or of equal importance or value: *Our country enjoys peace and wealth the likes of which no civilization has ever seen.* | *Arlins is a lying politician, and we have seen his like before.* **4 the likes of him/her/us etc.** SPOKEN **a)** used to talk about someone you do not like: *I'd never vote for the likes of him!* **b)** used to talk about people of a particular type or social class: *Those expensive restaurants with fancy food aren't for the likes of us.*

like⁵ *adj.* [only before noun] FORMAL similar in some way: *I'm glad we're of like minds about the project.*

like⁶ *conjunction* ESPECIALLY SPOKEN **1** as if: *He acted* s w *like he owned the place.* **2 like I say/said** used when you are repeating something that you have already said: *Like I said, I really appreciate your help.* **3** in the same way as: *I don't want him treating me like Jim treated me.*

-like /laɪk/ *suffix* [in adjectives] like something, typical of something, or appropriate for something: *a jelly-like substance* | *childlike simplicity*

like·a·ble /ˈlaɪkəbəl/ *adj.* another spelling of LIKABLE

like·li·hood /ˈlaɪkliˌhʊd/ *n.* [U] **1** the degree to which something can reasonably be expected to happen; PROBABILITY: *The likelihood of food riots this winter will increase as shortages spread.* | *They must face the likelihood that the newspaper might go bankrupt.* **2 in all likelihood** almost certainly: *In all likelihood, Davis will be traded to the Dallas Cowboys.*

like·ly¹ /ˈlaɪkli/ *adj.* **likelier, likeliest 1** something s w that is likely will probably happen or is probably true: *Showers and thunderstorms are likely in the afternoon.* | [likely to do/be sth] *Children who live in rural areas are likely to be poor.* | *It is more than likely* (=almost certain) *the votes will have to be*

L

counted again. | **more/most/very likely** *The conference will most likely take place in Washington.* **2** [only before noun] appropriate, or almost certain to produce good results: *a list of likely candidates* | **most/least likely** *I finally found some path in the least likely place you could imagine.* **3 a likely story** SPOKEN used to tell someone you do not believe what they have just said

like·ly² *adv.* probably | **most/very likely** *I'd most likely have done the same thing in your situation.*

like-mind·ed /ˌ. ˈ..◂/ *adj.* having similar interests and opinions —**like-mindedness** *n.* [U]

lik·en /ˈlaɪkən/ *v.*
liken sb/sth **to** sb/sth *phr. v.* [T usually passive] FORMAL to describe something or someone as being similar to another person or thing: *Critics have likened the new theater to a barn.*

like·ness /ˈlaɪknɪs/ *n.* **1** [C] the image of someone in a painting or photograph: [+ **of**] *The red pins bore the likeness of Lenin.* **2** [C,U] the quality of being similar in appearance to someone or something else; RESEMBLANCE: [+ **to**] *They joked about Phillip's likeness to his father.*

like·wise /ˈlaɪk-waɪz/ *adv.* **1** FORMAL in the same way; similarly: *I put on my life jacket and told the children to do likewise.* | [sentence adverb] *The clams were delicious. Likewise, the eggplant was excellent.* **2** SPOKEN used to return someone's greeting or polite remark: *"It's great to see you." "Likewise."*

lik·ing /ˈlaɪkɪŋ/ *n.* **1 liking for sb/sth** FORMAL the feeling when you like someone or something: *She'd tried to hide her liking for him.* | *I'd developed a liking for afternoon talk shows.* **2 take a liking to sb/sth** to begin to like someone or something: *He immediately took a liking to Malden.* **3 to your liking** FORMAL being just what you wanted: *I hope everything in the suite was to your liking, sir.*

li·lac /ˈlaɪlək, -læk, -lɑk/ *n.* **1** [C] a small tree with pale purple or white flowers **2** [U] a pale purple color —**lilac** *adj.: a lilac dress*

lil·li·pu·tian /ˌlɪləˈpjuʃən◂/ *adj.* extremely small compared to normal things

Li·long·we /lɪˈlɔŋweɪ/ the capital and largest city of Malawi

lilt /lɪlt/ *n.* [singular] a pleasant pattern of rising and falling sound in someone's voice or in music: *Michelle spoke with a soothing Southern lilt.* —**lilting** *adj.: a lilting melody*

lil·y /ˈlɪli/ *n. plural* **lilies** [C] one of several types of plants with large bell-shaped flowers of various colors, especially white —see also **gild the lily** (GILD (3)), WATER LILY

lily-liv·ered /ˈ.. ˌ../ *adj.* OLD-FASHIONED lacking courage

lily of the val·ley /ˌ.. . . . ˈ../ *n.* [C] a plant with several small white bell-shaped flowers

lily pad /ˈ.. ˌ./ *n.* [C] the round leaf of the WATER LILY, that you can see on the surface of the water

lily-white /ˌ.. ˈ.◂/ *adj.* **1** LITERARY pure white: *lily-white skin* **2** INFORMAL morally perfect: *You're not so lily-white yourself!*

Li·ma /ˈlimə/ the capital and largest city of Peru

li·ma bean /ˈlaɪmə ˌbin/ *n.* [C] a flat bean that grows in tropical America, or the plant that produces it

limb /lɪm/ *n.* [C] **1** a large branch of a tree **2 go/be out on a limb** to do something risky or uncertain, or be in a situation that is risky or uncertain: *I thought, I'll hate myself if I don't try this – sometimes you have to go out on a limb.* **3** an arm or leg —see also **risk life and limb** (RISK² (1)), **tear** sb **limb from limb** (TEAR² (6))

-limbed /lɪmd/ [in adjectives] **strong-limbed/long-limbed etc.** having strong, long etc. arms and legs

lim·ber¹ /ˈlɪmbə/ *v.*
limber up *phr. v.* [I] to do gentle exercises in order to make your muscles stretch and move easily, especially when preparing for a race, competition etc.

limber² *adj.* able to move and bend easily: *I'm not even limber enough to touch my toes.*

lim·bo /ˈlɪmboʊ/ *n.* **1** to be in an uncertain situation in which it is difficult to know what to do: *$900 million worth of grain sales is in limbo while the two countries negotiate a new trade deal.* **2 the limbo** a Caribbean dance in which the dancer leans backward and goes under a stick that is lowered gradually each time the dancer goes under

lime¹ /laɪm/ *n.* **1** [C] a small juicy green fruit with a sour taste, or the tree this fruit grows on **2** [U] a white substance used for making CEMENT, marking sports fields etc. **3** [C] LITERARY a LINDEN tree

lime² *v.* [T] TECHNICAL to add lime to soil to control acid

lime·ade /ˌlaɪmˈeɪd, ˈlaɪmeɪd/ *n.* [U] a drink made from the juice of limes

lime green /ˌ. ˈ.◂/ *n.* [U] a light yellowish green color —**lime-green** *adj.*

lime·light /ˈlaɪmlaɪt/ *n.* **the limelight** the attention someone gets from newspapers and television: *"I'm not used to being in the limelight,"* Hargrove told reporters.

lim·er·ick /ˈlɪmərɪk/ *n.* [C] a humorous short poem, with two long lines, two short lines, and then one more long line

lime·stone /ˈlaɪmstoʊn/ *n.* [U] a type of rock that contains CALCIUM

li·mey /ˈlaɪmi/ *n.* [C] OLD-FASHIONED an insulting word for a British person

lim·it¹ /ˈlɪmɪt/ *n.* [C]
1 greatest/least allowed the greatest or least amount, number, speed etc. that is allowed: *The speed limit is 65 mph.* | [+ **to/on**] *There's a limit on the time you have to take the test.* | *My wife and I set a limit on how much we spend on clothes.* | **the lower/upper limit** *The amount of protein he prescribes is the upper limit suggested in the government's Dietary Guidelines.*
2 greatest amount possible also **limits** [plural] the greatest possible amount or degree of something that can exist or be obtained: [+ **of**] *the limits of human knowledge* | *Our finances are stretched to the limit* (=we do not having any extra money). | *There's no limit to what you can do if you try.*
3 place also **limits** [plural] the furthest point or edge of a place, that must not be passed: *He had not been outside the limits of the prison walls for 23 years.* | *The public is not allowed within a 2-mile limit of the missile site.*
4 within limits within the time, level, amount etc. considered acceptable: *You can decorate the apartment yourself – within limits, of course.*
5 off limits beyond the area where someone is allowed to go: *The basement was always off limits to us kids.*
6 be over the limit to have drunk more alcohol than is legal or safe for driving
7 know your limits INFORMAL to know what you are good at doing and what you are not good at: *I know my limits, and I'm not a great runner.*
8 have your limits INFORMAL to have a set of ideas about what is reasonable to do, and to not accept behavior that does not follow those ideas: *I have my limits. You will not use that kind of nasty language in my class.*
9 there are limits! SPOKEN used to express shock or disapproval of someone's behavior

limit² *v.* [T] **1** to stop an amount or number from increasing beyond a particular point: *The higher toll should limit the number of cars on the bridge.* | [**limit** sth **to** sth] *Seating is limited to 500.* **2** to stop someone from using as much of something as they want or from behaving in the way they want: *A lack of formal education will limit your job opportunities.* | [**limit yourself to** sth] *I limit myself to two cups of coffee a day.* **3 be limited to** sth to exist or happen only in a particular place, group, or area of activity: *The damage was limited to the roof.*

lim·i·ta·tion /ˌlɪməˈteɪʃən/ *n.* **1** [U] the act or process of limiting something: *a nuclear limitation treaty* | [+ **on**] *The city's current height limitation on residential*

L

buildings is 26 feet. —see also STATUTE OF LIMITATIONS
2 [C usually plural] a limit on how good someone or something can be, what they are able to do etc.: *Computers definitely have their limitations.*

lim·it·ed /ˈlɪmɪtɪd/ *adj.* **1** not very great in amount, number, ability etc.: *Open space for new businesses is limited.* | *Her family lives on a limited income* (=they do not have much money). | *a person of limited intelligence* **2** a limited train or bus only makes a few stops: *Take the number 38 limited to downtown.* **3** restricted by law in what you are allowed to do or what you are responsible for: *Police departments enjoy a limited immunity from lawsuits.* **4** **Limited** written abbreviation **Ltd.** used after the name of British or Canadian companies that have limited LIABILITY —compare INCORPORATED

limited e·di·tion /ˌ... .ˈ.../ *n.* [C] a small number of special copies of a book, picture etc. which are produced at one time only —**limited-edition** *adj.*

limited li·a·bil·i·ty /ˌ... ..ˈ.../ *n.* [U] TECHNICAL the legal position of being responsible for paying only a limited amount of debt if something bad happens to yourself or your company

limited part·ner·ship /ˌ... ˈ.../ *n.* [C] a business relationship formed by two or more people, in which some of the people have less power in the company

lim·it·ing /ˈlɪmɪtɪŋ/ *adj.* **1** preventing any improvement or increase in something: *A limiting factor in the health care system is the way money and resources are distributed.* **2** INFORMAL preventing someone from developing and doing what they are interested in: *I found staying at home with the kids very limiting.*

lim·it·less /ˈlɪmɪtlɪs/ *adj.* without a limit or end: *limitless possibilities* —**limitlessly** *adv.* —**limitlessness** *n.* [U]

lim·o /ˈlɪmoʊ/ *n. plural* **limos** [C] INFORMAL a limousine

lim·ou·sine /ˈlɪməˌzin, ˌlɪməˈzin/ *n.* [C] **1** a very large, expensive, and comfortable car, driven by someone who is paid to drive **2** a small bus that people take to and from airports in the U.S.

limp¹ /lɪmp/ *adj.* something that is limp is soft or weak when it should be firm or strong: *a limp handshake* | *The green beans were limp from overcooking.* —**limply** *adv.* —**limpness** *n.* [U]

limp² *v.* [I] **1** to walk slowly and with difficulty because one leg is hurt or injured **2** if a vehicle, airplane etc. limps somewhere, it goes there slowly, because it has been damaged
limp along *phr. v.* [I] if a company, vehicle, process etc. limps along, it does not work well at all: *The team is limping along in fifth place.*

limp³ *n.* [C] the way someone walks when they are limping: *Young had a slight limp.*

lim·pet /ˈlɪmpɪt/ *n.* [C] a small sea animal with a cone-shaped shell, which usually attaches itself to a rock

lim·pid /ˈlɪmpɪd/ *adj.* LITERARY clear or transparent: *limpid blue eyes* —**limpidly** *adv.* —**limpidness** *n.* [U] —**limpidity** /lɪmˈpɪdəti/ *n.* [U]

limp-wrist·ed /ˈ. ˌ.../ *adj.* OFFENSIVE used about a man who is or may be HOMOSEXUAL

lin·age /ˈlaɪnɪdʒ/ *n.* [U] another spelling of LINEAGE²

linch·pin /ˈlɪntʃˌpɪn/ *n.* **the linchpin of sth** the person or thing in a group, system etc. that is most important, because everything depends on them: *My mother had always been the linchpin of our family.*

Lin·coln /ˈlɪŋkən/ the capital city of the U.S. state of Nebraska

Lincoln, Abraham (1809–65) the 16th President of the U.S., famous especially for the Emancipation Proclamation in 1863 by which all SLAVES in the U.S. became free people, and for his speech known as the Gettysburg Address

Lind·bergh /ˈlɪndbɚg/, **Charles** (1902–1974) a U.S. pilot who in 1927 became the first person to fly alone across the Atlantic Ocean without stopping —see picture on page 1330

lin·den /ˈlɪndən/ *n.* [C,U] a tree which has heart-shaped leaves and light yellow flowers, or the wood of this tree

Lind·say /ˈlɪnzi/, **Va·chel** /ˈveɪtʃəl, ˈvæ-/ (1879–1931) a U.S. poet

drawing a line   **line**

standing in line

line¹ /laɪn/ *n.*

S W
1 1

1 ‖long thin mark‖ [C] a long thin, usually continuous mark on a surface: *a straight line* | *If you make a mistake, draw a line through the word and go on.* | *Sign your name on the dotted line* (=a broken straight line drawn or printed on paper).

2 ‖limit/end‖ [C] a long thin mark used to show a limit or end of something: *You're supposed to park between the white lines.* —see also FINISH LINE

3 **on line** able to work or communicate using a computer: *All the classrooms are now on line.* —see also ONLINE

4 **along the lines of sth** also **along the same/similar etc. lines** used to say that something is similar to or done in a similar way to what you are talking about: *The band's musical style is along the lines of the Beatles.* | *They're organizing a trip to the beach or something along those lines* (=something like that).

5 ‖attitude/belief‖ [C usually singular] an attitude or belief, especially one that is stated publicly: [+ on] *What's the candidate's line on abortion?* | *There is a fear of expressing views contrary to the party line* (=the official opinion of a political party or other group).

6 **take a firm/hard/strict etc. line on sth** to have a very strict attitude toward something: *The governor has taken a hard line on illegal immigration.*

7 **line of action/thought/reasoning etc.** a way or method of doing something or thinking about something: *Cowie's line of thinking is in direct opposition to the First Amendment.*

8 **do sth along religious/party/ethnic etc. lines a)** if people's opinions are divided along religious, party etc. lines, they make a decision or vote according to the beliefs of the religion, political party etc. they belong to: *The vote was 35–24, almost strictly along party lines.* **b)** to organize something according to a particular method or idea: *The party was reformed along socialist lines in 1992.*

9 **be/stand/wait in line** to stand in a row of people who are standing behind each other while waiting for something: *I waited in line for over an hour to get my license.*

10 ‖on sb's face‖ [C] a line on the skin of someone's face or skin; WRINKLE¹: *I'm getting little lines around my eyes.*

11 ‖shape‖ [C usually plural] the outer shape of something long or tall: *the car's smooth elegant lines*

12 ‖telephone‖ [C] a telephone wire, or the wires that connect a system of telephones: *We're thinking about getting a second line installed for the computer.* | *The lines were down* (=they were not working) *for days after the storm.* | *There's a lot of static on the line.* | *We got a bad line* (=one that is not working well so that it is difficult to hear) *last time we tried to call Poland.*

L

13 county/state etc. line a border between two counties (COUNTY), states etc.: *The escaped prisoners went across state lines from Arizona into Nevada.*

14 land [C] an imaginary line, for example one that shows the limits of an area of land: *The 38th parallel is the line that divides North and South Korea.* | *lines of longitude*

15 the line a piece of string or rope that you hang wet clothes on outside in order to dry them; CLOTHES-LINE: *Towels hung on the line.*

16 fishing [C] a strong thin string with a hook on the end, used for catching fish

17 words [C] a line of words on a page from a poem, story, song etc.: *Read the first two lines of the poem.*

18 actor's speech [C usually plural] the words of a play or performance that an actor learns: *After 30 years on the stage, I still forget my lines.*

19 people/things [C] a row of people or things next to each other: [+ of] *a line of bushes* | *The toys were arranged in a line on the shelf.*

20 give sb a line if someone gives you a line, they tell you something that you know is not true: *"We just haven't had enough time to..." "Don't give me that line."*

21 railroad a track that a train travels along: *A train had broken down further along the line.* | *a railroad line* | **the Richmond/Freemont etc. line** (=the line that goes to Richmond, Freemont etc.)

22 direction [C usually singular] the direction or the imaginary line along which something travels between two points in space: *Light travels in a straight line.* | **line of fire/attack/movement etc.** (=the direction in which someone shoots, attacks, moves etc.)

23 sb's line of vision in the area that someone can see at a particular time: *He froze where he stood, trying to stay out of Sabine's line of vision.*

24 job [C usually singular] the kind of work someone does: *What line of work are you in?*

25 in the line of duty if something happens in the line of duty, it happens while you are doing your job: *Officer Choi was killed in the line of duty.*

26 fall into line INFORMAL to start to do something in the way that a company, organization etc. wants you to: *All the Republicans except Elton and Carson fell into line and voted yes.*

27 bring sb into line INFORMAL to make someone behave the way you want them to: *The right wing of the party has got to be brought into line.*

28 be out of line if someone's behavior is out of line, it is not appropriate in a particular situation: *I thought what Kenny said was way out of line.*

29 war [C usually plural] a row of military defenses in front of the area that an army controls during a war: *The base was stationed 100 miles inside enemy lines.*

30 be in line with sth also **be brought into line with sth** if one thing is in line with another, they are similar to each other, or they happen or work in similar ways: *Your debts must be brought into line with the money you have coming in.*

31 a thin/fine line between only a slight difference between two things, one of which is something bad: *There's a fine line between arrogance and an awareness of self-worth.*

32 be in line for sth to be very likely to get or be given something: *Claire's in line for a promotion.* | **be first/second/next etc. in line for sth** (=to be the first, second, next etc. person to be likely to get something)

33 be on the line if your job, position etc. is on the line, there is a possibility you might lose it: *With the game on the line, Kansas City scored two touchdowns in five minutes.*

34 somewhere along the line INFORMAL during the time that you are involved in an activity or process: *Somewhere along the line, we just stopped talking to each other.*

35 product [C] a type of goods for sale in a store:

a new line of clothes for winter | *Sears has discontinued a line of* (=stopped selling) *stuffed animals.*

36 company [C] a company that provides a system for moving goods by sea, air, road etc.: *a shipping line*

37 be in the line of fire also **be on the firing line** **a)** to be one of the people who could be criticized or blamed for something: *Bradley's been on the firing line in industry – he knows the problems that managers face.* **b)** to be in a place where a bullet etc. might hit you

38 sports [C] a row of players in a game such as football or RUGBY that is formed when they move into position before play starts again

39 line of scrimmage the place where the football is put immediately before play begins

40 get a line on sb/sth INFORMAL to get information about someone or something: *Have we got any kind of line on that guy Marston?*

41 drug [C] INFORMAL an amount of an illegal drug in powder form, arranged in a line before it is taken: [+ of] *a line of coke*

42 family [singular] the people that came or existed before you in your family: *She comes from a long line of actors.* —see also **draw the line (at sth)** (DRAW¹ (6)), **hook, line, and sinker** (HOOK¹ (12)), **lay sth on the line** (LAY¹ (11)), **picket line** (PICKET¹ (1)), **the poverty line/level** (POVERTY (2)), **read between the lines** (READ¹ (9))

line² *v.* **1** [T] to cover the inside or inner surface of something with something else, or to make something do this: *Use wax paper to line the baking pan.* | **[line sth with sth]** *The jacket is lined with fur.* | *We lined the box with newspaper.* **2** [T] to form rows along something, especially along the edge of something: *Fans lined the street just to get a glimpse of the band.* **3 line your own pockets** to make yourself richer by doing something dishonest **4** [I,T] to hit a ball straight with a lot of force in baseball: *Harbin lined the ball into right field.*

line up *phr. v.* **1** [I,T] to form a row or arrange people or things in a row: *At 7:45, there were more than 100 people lined up in front of the store.* | **[line sb/sth up]** *The teacher lined the students up to go to the playground.* **2** [I,T] to make arrangements so that something will happen or that someone will be available for an event: **[line up sb/sth]** *I've already lined up a job for January.* —see also LINE-UP

lin·e·age¹ /ˈlɪnɪɪdʒ/ *n.* [C,U] FORMAL the way in which members of a family are DESCENDed from other members: *Jean de la Moussaye can trace his lineage back to Louis XIV.*

line·age², linage /ˈlaɪnɪdʒ/ *n.* [U] the number of printed lines in a newspaper, magazine etc. or a particular part of a newspaper etc., used as a measurement of space: *Advertising lineage at the Journal has declined 16 percent.*

lin·e·al /ˈlɪnɪəl/ *adj.* **1** FORMAL related directly to someone who lived a long time before you: *lineal descendants* **2** another form of LINEAR —**lineally** *adv.*

lin·e·a·ment /ˈlɪnɪəmənt/ *n.* [C usually plural] FORMAL **1** the basic shape of the physical features of a person or GEOGRAPHICAL area **2** a typical quality or feature that makes someone or something different from others of the same kind

lin·e·ar /ˈlɪnɪɚ/ *adj.* **1** consisting of lines, or in the form of a straight line: *a linear diagram* **2** [only before noun] concerning length: *linear measurements* **3** involving a series of directly connected events, ideas etc.: *linear thinking* —compare LATERAL¹ —**linearly** *adv.* —**linearity** /ˌlɪniˈærəti/ *n.* [U]

linear ac·cel·er·a·tor /ˌ... ˈ..../ *n.* [C] TECHNICAL a piece of equipment that makes PARTICLES (=small pieces of atoms) travel in a straight line at increasing speed

line·back·er /ˈlaɪnˌbækɚ/ *n.* [C] a player in football who tries to TACKLE¹ (2) the member of the other team who has the ball

lined /laɪnd/ *adj.* **1** a coat, skirt etc. that is lined has a piece of thin material covering the inside: *cashmere-lined gloves* **2** paper that is lined has straight lines printed or drawn across it **3** skin that is lined has WRINKLEs on it

line dance /'. ./ *n.* [C] a dance that is done, especially to COUNTRY MUSIC, by a group of people standing together in a line —**line dance** *v.* [I] —**line dancing** *n.* [U]

line draw·ing /'. ,../ *n.* [C] a DRAWING consisting only of lines

line drive /'. ./ *n.* [C] a BASEBALL hit with great force in a straight line fairly near the ground

line·man /'laɪnmən/ *n. plural* **linemen** /-mən/ [C] **1** a player who plays in the front line of a football team **2** someone whose job is to take care of railroad lines or telephone wires

lin·en /'lɪnən/ *n.* [U] **1** sheets, TABLECLOTHS etc.: *bed linen* | *table linen* **2** cloth made from the FLAX plant, used to make high quality clothes, home decorations etc.: *a linen jacket* **3** OLD USE underwear

linen clos·et /'.. ,../ *n.* [C] a special CLOSET in which sheets, TOWELS etc. are kept

line of scrim·mage /, . '../ *n.* [C] a line in American football where the ball is placed at the beginning of a particular PLAY[2] (3)

lin·er /'laɪnə/ *n.* **1** [C] a piece of material used inside something in order to protect it: *a trash can liner* **2** [C] a large passenger ship especially one of several owned by a company: *an ocean liner* —see also AIRLINER, CRUISE LINER **3** [C,U] INFORMAL: see EYELINER

lin·er notes /'.. ,./ *n.* [plural] printed information about a CD or record that appears on its cover

lines·man /'laɪnzmən/ *n. plural* **linesmen** /-mən/ [C] an official in a sport who decides when a ball has gone out of the playing area

line-up /'. ./ *n.* [C usually singular] **1** the players in a sports team who play in a particular game: *Cordell may not be in the line-up for tonight's game.* | **the starting line-up** (=the players who begin the game) **2** a group of people, especially performers, who have agreed to be involved in an event: *The line-up of performers includes Cher and Garth Brooks.* **3** a set of events or programs arranged to follow each other: *CBS has a great Wednesday night line-up.* **4** a row of people examined by a WITNESS to a crime in order to try to recognize a criminal

-ling /lɪŋ/ *suffix* [in nouns] a smaller, younger, or less important type of something: *a duckling* (=young duck) | *Prussian princelings* (=young princes)

lin·ger /'lɪŋgə/ *v.* [I] **1** also **linger on** to be slow to go, end, or decrease: *Summer weather has lingered longer than usual.* | *Doubts about Manzi's honesty still linger on.* **2** to stay somewhere a little longer, especially because you do not want to leave: *I lingered on the sidewalk outside the old house, wondering who lived there now.* **3** [always + adv./prep.] to continue looking at or dealing with something for longer than is usual: [+ on/over etc.] *The camera lingered over the man's old wrinkled face.* **4** also **linger on** to die slowly so that you stay alive for a long time although you are extremely weak: *Uncle Gene lingered on a year longer than doctors expected* —**lingerer** *n.* [C]

lin·ge·rie /,lɑnʒə'reɪ, ,lɑndʒə-/ *n.* [U] women's underwear

lin·ger·ing /'lɪŋgərɪŋ/ *adj.* slow to finish or disappear: *Dad suffers from the lingering effects of radiation treatments* | *lingering questions about the assassination* | **a lingering death** (=a slow and often painful death) —**lingeringly** *adv.*

lin·go /'lɪŋgoʊ/ *n.* [C usually singular] INFORMAL **1** words used only by a group of people who do a particular job or activity: *"Deliver the package" is pilot lingo for dropping a bomb on a target.* **2** SPOKEN, INFORMAL a language, especially a foreign one: *I'd like to go to Greece, but I don't speak the lingo.*

lin·gua fran·ca /,lɪŋgwə 'fræŋkə/ *n.* [C] a language used between people whose main languages are different: *Swahili is the lingua franca of East Africa.*

lin·gual /'lɪŋgwəl/ *adj.* **1** related to the tongue **2** a lingual sound is made by the movement of the tongue —see also BILINGUAL

lin·gui·ni /lɪŋ'gwini/ *n.* [U] long thin flat pieces of PASTA

lin·guist /'lɪŋgwɪst/ *n.* [C] **1** someone who studies and is good at foreign languages **2** someone who studies or teaches linguistics

lin·guis·tic /lɪŋ'gwɪstɪk/ *adj.* related to language, words, or linguistics: *linguistic skills* —**linguistically** /-kli/ *adv.*

lin·guis·tics /lɪŋ'gwɪstɪks/ *n.* [U] the study of language in general and of particular languages, their structure, grammar, and history —compare PHILOLOGY

lin·i·ment /'lɪnəmənt/ *n.* [U] a liquid containing oil, that you rub on your skin to cure soreness and stiffness

lin·ing /'laɪnɪŋ/ *n.* [C,U] a piece of material covering the inside of a box, piece of clothing etc.: *The coat has a silk lining.* —see picture at SHOE[1]

link[1] /lɪŋk/ *v.* [T]
1 be linked if two things are linked, they are related often because one strongly affects or causes the other: *The author explains clearly how these types of economic and military issue are linked.* | *Power and personality are closely linked.* | [+ to/with] *Many believe that the rise in gangs is directly linked to poor living conditions.*
2 [make connection] to make a connection between people, groups, situations etc.: *An intense concern for human rights links the two poets.* | [link sb to/with sth] *Her last unhappy marriage had linked her to the crazy McGovern family.* | [link sb/sth together] *The institution links Jews from all communities and all nations together.*
3 [prove connection] if scientists, officials etc. link two people, situations, or things, they say or prove that there is a connection between them: [link sth to/with sth] *The study links the gene to an increased risk of cancer.* | *He was charged after investigators linked him to more than $100 million in cash in European banks.*
4 [make sth depend on sth] to make one action or situation dependent on another action or situation: [link sth to sth] *Congress may link a country's trade status to its human rights policy.*
5 [computers] also **link up** to connect computers, broadcast systems etc., so that electronic messages can be sent between them: [link sth to/with sth] *All our computer workstations are linked to a main server.*
6 [places] also **link up** to connect one place to another: *The Brooklyn Bridge links Brooklyn and Manhattan.*
7 link arms to bend your arm and put it through someone else's bent arm
8 [put together] to connect two or more things by putting them through or around each other, such as pieces of a chain
link up *phr. v.* [I,T] **1** to make a connection with something: [+ with] *Southern Pacific Railway laid tracks to link up with Union Pacific's in the East.* **2** to connect computers, broadcast systems etc., so that electronic messages can be sent between them: *Gilligan's job entailed linking up computers to networks.* **3** to meet with someone to begin a relationship or to work with them: *European leaders will link up again on Monday to discuss trade issues.* | [+ with] *The UPS strategy has been to buy or link up with foreign companies.* —see also LINKUP

link[2] *n.* [C]
1 [things or ideas] a relationship between two things or ideas, in which one is caused or affected by the other: [+ between] *the link between drug use and crime*
2 [people, countries etc.] a connection between two or more people, countries, organizations etc.: [+ with/ between] *Schools are looking to find new ways to forge links with families.*
3 a satellite/telephone/rail etc. **link** something that makes communication or travel between two places possible
4 [chain] one of the rings in a chain
5 link in the chain one of a series of things, facts, people involved in the process of achieving or

finishing something: *The new witness is just one of many links in the chain of evidence against Murphy.*
6 a/the weak link (in sth) the weakest part of a plan or the weakest member of a team: *The 26-year-old forward has been criticized as the team's weak link.*
7 computer a special picture or word in a computer DOCUMENT that you CLICK on to move quickly to a place where you can find more information, or the connection that makes this possible
8 the links GOLF LINKS —see also CUFF LINK, MISSING LINK

link·age /'lɪŋkɪdʒ/ *n.* **1** [singular,U] a condition in a political or business agreement, by which one country or company agrees to do something, only if the other promises to do something in return **2** [singular, U] a LINK² (1) **3** [C] a system of links or connections

link·ing verb /'.. ˌ./ *n.* [C] a verb that connects the subject of a sentence to a word or phrase that describes it. In the sentence, "She seems friendly," "seems" is the linking verb

link·up /'lɪŋk-ʌp/ *n.* [C] a connection between computers, broadcasting systems etc. that sends electronic messages between them

Lin·nae·us /lɪ'niəs, -'neɪ-/, **Ca·rol·lus** /'kærələs/ (1707–1778) a Swedish BOTANIST who invented the Linnean System, by which plants and animals are put into groups according to their GENUS (=general type) and SPECIES (=particular type)

li·no·cut /'laɪnoʊˌkʌt/ *n.* **1** [U] the art of cutting a pattern on a block of linoleum **2** [C] a picture printed from such a block

li·no·le·um /lɪ'noʊliəm/ *n.* [U] smooth shiny material in flat sheets used to cover a floor

Li·no·type /'laɪnəˌtaɪp/ *n.* [U] TRADEMARK a system for arranging TYPE¹ (4) in the form of solid metal lines

lin·seed /'lɪnsid/ *n.* [U] the seed of the FLAX (1) plant

linseed oil /'.. ˌ./ *n.* [U] the oil from linseed used in some paints, inks etc.

lint /lɪnt/ *n.* [U] soft light pieces of thread or wool that come off cotton, wool, or other material

lin·tel /'lɪntl/ *n.* [C] a piece of stone or wood across the top of a window or door, forming part of the frame

li·on /'laɪən/ *n.* [C] **1** a large yellowish-brown animal of the cat family that eats meat, and lives in Africa and parts of Southern Asia —see also LIONESS **2 the lion's share (of sth)** the largest part of something: *The Lopez family owns the lion's share of the country's farmland.* **3** ESPECIALLY LITERARY someone who is very important, powerful, or famous **4 in the lion's den** among people who are your enemies **5 be thrown/tossed to the lions** to be put in a dangerous or difficult situation

li·on·ess /'laɪənɪs/ *n.* [C] a female lion

li·on·heart·ed /'laɪənˌhɑrtɪd/ *adj.* LITERARY very brave

li·on·ize /'laɪəˌnaɪz/ *v.* [T] to treat someone as being important or famous —**lionization** /ˌlaɪənəˈzeɪʃən/ *n.* [U]

Lions Club /'.. ˌ./ *n.* an international organization whose members work together to help their local areas by doing CHARITY WORK

s w
2 2
lip /lɪp/ *n.* **1** [C] one of the two edges of your mouth where your skin is redder or darker: *Her lower lip was red and swollen.* | *Marty kissed me right on the lips!* **2** [U] INFORMAL a word meaning impolite, angry talking, used especially by adults to children: *Don't give me any of your lip!* **3** [C usually singular] the top edge of something such as a bowl or cup which sticks out **4** [C] the edge of a hollow or deep place in the land, usually one made out of rock: [+ of] *the lip of the canyon* **5 my lips are sealed** SPOKEN used to say that you are not going to tell anyone about a secret **6 on everyone's lips** being talked about by everyone: *News of the divorce seems to be on everyone's lips.* —see also **lick your lips/ chops** (LICK¹ (4)), **thin-lipped/full-lipped etc.** (-LIPPED), **never/not pass sb's lips** (PASS¹ (24)), **pay**

lip service to sth (PAY¹ (16)), **read sb's lips** (READ¹ (16)), **keep a stiff upper lip** (STIFF¹ (9))

lip balm /'. ./ *n.* [C,U] a substance used to protect dry lips

lip gloss /'. ./ *n.* [C,U] a substance used to make lips look very shiny

lip·id /'lɪpɪd/ *n.* [C] TECHNICAL one of several types of FATTY substance in living things, such as fat, oil, or WAX¹ (1)

lip·o·suc·tion /'lɪpoʊ, sʌkʃən/ *n.* [U] a type of medical operation in which fat is removed from someone's body using SUCTION

-lipped /lɪpt/ [in adjectives] **thin-lipped/full-lipped etc.** with lips that are thin, round etc.

lip-read /'lɪp rid/ *v.* [I,T] to understand what someone is saying by watching the way their lips move, especially because you cannot hear —**lip-reading** *n.* [U]

lip·stick /'lɪpˌstɪk/ *n.* [C,U] a piece of a substance shaped like a small stick, used for adding color to your lips —see picture at MAKEUP

lipstick les·bi·an /ˌ.. '.../ *n.* [C] INFORMAL a word, which may be considered offensive, for a LESBIAN who dresses in a FEMININE way, as opposed to one who dresses like a man

lip synch /'lɪp ˌsɪŋk/ *n.* [U] the action of moving your lips at the same time as a recording is being played, to give the appearance that you are singing —**lip-synch** *v.* [I]

liq·ue·fy /'lɪkwəˌfaɪ/ *v.* **liquefies, liquefied, liquefying** [I,T] FORMAL to become liquid, or make something become liquid: *Some gases liquefy at cold temperatures.* —**liquefaction** /ˌlɪkwəˈfækʃən/ *n.* [U]

li·queur /lɪ'kɚ, lɪ'kʊɚ/ *n.* [C,U] a sweet and very strong alcoholic drink, drunk in small quantities after a meal —compare LIQUOR

liq·uid¹ /'lɪkwɪd/ *n.* **1** [C,U] a substance that is not a solid or a gas, and which flows, is wet, and has no particular shape: *Cook the rice until all the liquid is absorbed.* **2** [C] TECHNICAL either of the CONSONANT sounds /l/ and /r/ —see also DISHWASHING LIQUID

liquid² *adj.* **1 liquid oxygen/soap etc.** oxygen, soap etc. in the form of a liquid, instead of its usual gas or solid form **2** easily exchanged or sold to pay debts: *Certificates of deposit are not as liquid as money in a passbook account.* —see also LIQUID ASSETS **3 liquid refreshment** HUMOROUS something you drink, especially alcoholic drink **4 liquid lunch** HUMOROUS a lunch in which you mainly have alcoholic drinks rather than eating food **5** clear and shiny, like water: *liquid green eyes* **6** LITERARY liquid sounds are very clear

liquid as·sets /ˌ.. '../ *n.* [plural] TECHNICAL the money that a company or person has, and the property they can easily exchange for money

liq·ui·date /'lɪkwəˌdeɪt/ *v.* **1** [I,T] to close a business or company in order to pay its debts by selling everything, especially at very low prices **2** [T] TECHNICAL to pay a debt: *The stock will be sold to liquidate the loan.* **3** [T] INFORMAL to kill someone

liq·ui·da·tion /ˌlɪkwəˈdeɪʃən/ *n.* [C,U] **1** the act of closing down a company in order to pay its debts by selling its ASSETS: *The department chain has gone into liquidation.* **2** the act of paying a debt

liq·ui·da·tor /'lɪkwəˌdeɪtɚ/ *n.* [C] a person or company that sells everything that another company owns, so that its debts can be paid

li·quid·i·ty /lɪ'kwɪdəti/ *n.* [U] TECHNICAL **1** a situation in which you have money or goods that can be sold to pay debts **2** the state of being LIQUID¹ (1)

liq·ui·dize /'lɪkwəˌdaɪz/ *v.* [T] to turn something into liquid by crushing or melting it

liquid meas·ure /ˌ.. '../ *n.* [U] the system of measuring the VOLUME of liquids

Liquid Pa·per /ˌ.. '../ *n.* [U] TRADEMARK white liquid that is used to cover mistakes in writing, typing etc.

liq·uor /'lɪkɚ/ *n.* [U] a strong alcoholic drink, such as WHISKEY —compare LIQUEUR

liquor store /'.. ˌ./ *n.* [C] a shop where alcohol is sold

li·ra /'lɪrə/ *n. plural* **lire** /'lɪreɪ/ or **liras** [C] the standard unit of money in various countries including Italy, Syria, and Turkey

Lis·bon /ˈlɪzbən/ the capital and largest city of Portugal

lisle /laɪl/ n. [U] cotton material, used in the past for GLOVES and STOCKINGS

lisp[1] /lɪsp/ v. [I,T] to speak, pronouncing "s" sounds as "th"

lisp[2] n. [C, usually singular] if someone has a lisp, they lisp when they speak: *She speaks with a slight lisp.*

lis·som, lissome /ˈlɪsəm/ adj. LITERARY a body that is lissom is thin and graceful: *the girl's lissom figure*

list[1] /lɪst/ n. [C] a set of words, numbers etc. written one below the other, so that you can remember them or keep them in order: *an alphabetical list of students* | *Baking soda wasn't on the shopping list.* | [+ of] *Make a list of the things you have to do.* | **at the top/bottom of the list** (=regarded as most or least important) —see also HIT LIST, MAILING LIST, SHORT LIST, WAITING LIST

list[2] v. **1** [T] to write a list, or mention things one after the other: *A new 30-page Hong Kong guide lists more than 100 budget hotels.* **2 list sb in fair/stable/critical etc. condition** if a hospital lists someone who is sick or injured in a fair STABLE, critical etc. condition, it says officially that they are in that condition: *Two of the shooting victims were listed in stable condition.* **3** [I] if a ship lists, it leans to one side **4** [I] OLD USE to listen

listed se·cu·ri·ty /ˌ...ˈ....../ n. [C] TECHNICAL a BOND or STOCK in a large company that you can buy or sell on the STOCK EXCHANGE

lis·ten /ˈlɪsən/ v. [I] **1** to pay attention to what someone is saying or to a sound that you can hear: *You had better be listening because I'm not going to repeat myself.* | [+ to] *I like listening to the radio.* | *You have to **listen hard** (=try to hear something that is quiet) to hear what he's saying.* | *His students **listened intently** (=listened carefully and with interest) to his war stories.* —see picture at HEAR —see Usage Note at HEAR **2** SPOKEN used to tell someone to pay attention to what you are about to say: *Listen, don't panic. I'm sure we can get your money back.* | *Now **listen here** (=used to emphasize, especially when you are angry), you two. You know I can't break my promises.* **3** to consider carefully what someone says to you: *I told him not to go, but he wouldn't listen.* | [+ to] *I wish I'd listened to your advice.*

listen for sb/sth phr. v. [T] to pay attention so that you are sure you will hear a sound if it OCCURS: *I listened for any sound from the baby's room, but it was quiet.*

listen in phr. v. [I] to listen to someone's conversation without them knowing it: [+ on] *The FBI had been listening in on their conversations for months.*

listen up phr. v. [I] SPOKEN used to get people's attention so they can hear what you are going to say: *Listen up! Pat's got something to say.*

USAGE NOTE: LISTEN

GRAMMAR
Remember you can only **listen to** (or sometimes **for**) something: *He's listening to music* (NOT *He's listening music*).

---

lis·ten·a·ble /ˈlɪsənəbəl/ adj. INFORMAL pleasant to hear

lis·ten·er /ˈlɪsənə/ n. [C] **1** someone who listens, especially to the radio: *Some of our regular listeners have complained about the new program schedule.* —compare VIEWER (1) **2 a good listener** someone who listens patiently and sympathetically to other people

lis·ten·ing de·vice /ˈ... .ˌ../ n. [C] a piece of equipment that allows you to listen secretly to other people's conversations; a BUG[1] (5) —compare HEARING AID

Lis·ter /ˈlɪstə/, **Joseph** (1827–1912) a British doctor who was the first person to use ANTISEPTICS during operations

lis·te·ri·a /lɪˈstɪriə/ n. [U] a type of BACTERIA that makes you sick

list·ing /ˈlɪstɪŋ/ n. **1** [C] something that is on a list **2 listings** [plural] lists of films, plays, and other events with the times and places at which they will happen

list·less /ˈlɪstlɪs/ adj. feeling tired and not interested in things: *Her performance was dull and listless.* —listlessly adv. —listlessness n. [U]

list price /ˌ. ˈ./ n. [C] a price that is suggested for a product by the people who make it

list·serv /ˈlɪstˌsɜv/ n. [C] a computer program that allows a group of people to send and receive EMAIL from each other about a particular subject

Liszt /lɪst/, **Franz** /frænz/ (1811–1886) a Hungarian musician who wrote CLASSICAL music and was considered the greatest PIANIST of the 19th century

lit /lɪt/ the past tense and past participle of LIGHT[3]

lit. an abbreviation of LITERATURE or LITERARY

lit·a·ny /ˈlɪtn-i/ n. plural **litanies** [C] **1** a long prayer in the Christian church in which the priest says a sentence and the people reply **2** something that takes a long time to say, that repeats phrases, or sounds like a list: *an endless litany of rules*

li·tchi /ˈlɪtʃi/ n. [C] another spelling of LYCHEE

lite /laɪt/ adj. used in the names of some food and drink products to mean that they have fewer CALORIES or less fat than normal food or drinks: *lite beer* | *lite sour cream*

li·ter /ˈlitə/ n. [C] **1** the basic unit for measuring an amount of liquid, in the METRIC system, equal to 2.12 PINTS or 0.26 GALLONS **2 1.3/2.4 etc. liter engine** a measurement that shows the size and power of a vehicle's engine

lit·er·a·cy /ˈlɪtərəsi/ n. [U] **1** the state of being able to read and write: *The program is designed to promote literacy in the community.* **2 computer literacy** the ability to understand and use computers

lit·er·al /ˈlɪtərəl/ adj. **1** the literal meaning of a word or expression is its basic or original meaning: *A trade war is not a war in the literal sense.* —compare FIGURATIVE (1) **2 literal translation** a translation that gives a single word for each original word instead of giving the meaning of the whole sentence in a natural way **3 literal-minded** not showing much imagination —literalness n. [U]

lit·er·al·ly /ˈlɪtərəli/ adv. **1** according to the most basic or original meaning of a word or expression: *The word "polygraph" literally means "many writings."* | *I know I said I felt like quitting, but I didn't **mean it literally** (=mean exactly what you say).* **2** used to emphasize that something is actually true: *Literally thousands of people lost their life savings in the market crash.* **3 take sb/sth literally** to only understand the most basic meaning of words, phrases etc., often with the result that you do not understand what someone really means: *A lot of what they said on the tapes was damaging if you took it literally.* **4** SPOKEN used to emphasize something you say that is already expressed strongly: *Jan and I have literally nothing in common.*

lit·er·a·ry /ˈlɪtəˌrɛri/ adj. **1** relating to LITERATURE: *a literary prize* | *literary criticism* **2** typical of the style of writing used in literature rather than in ordinary writing and talking: *a very literary style of writing* **3** liking literature very much, and studying or producing it: *a literary woman* —literariness n. [U]

lit·er·ate /ˈlɪtərɪt/ adj. **1** able to read and write —compare NUMERATE **2 computer literate/musically literate etc.** having enough knowledge to use a computer, play a musical instrument etc. **3** well educated —opposite ILLITERATE —see also LITERACY —literately adv. —literateness n. [U]

lit·e·ra·ti /ˌlɪtəˈrɑti/ n. **the literati** FORMAL a small group of people in a society who know a lot about literature

lit·er·a·ture /ˈlɪtərətʃə, ˈlɪtrə-/ n. [U] **1** books, plays, poems etc. that people think have value: *"The Sun Also Rises" is a classic of American literature.* **2** works such as these that are studied as a subject: *a master's degree in Asian literature* **3** all the books, articles etc. on a particular subject: *medical literature* **4** printed information produced by organizations that want to sell something or tell people about something: *sales literature*

lithe /laɪð/ adj. having a body that moves easily and gracefully: *the dancer's lithe body* —**lithely** adv.

lith·i·um /ˈlɪθiəm/ n. [U] *symbol* **Li** a soft silvery ELEMENT that is the lightest known metal

lith·o·graph¹ /ˈlɪθəˌgræf/ n. [C] a printed picture made by lithography

lithograph² v. [T] to print a picture by lithography

li·thog·ra·phy /lɪˈθɑgrəfi/ n. [U] a process for printing patterns, pictures etc. from something that has been cut into a piece of stone or metal —**lithographic** /ˌlɪθəˈgræfɪk/ adj.

Lith·u·a·ni·a /ˌlɪθəˈweɪniə/ a country in northeastern Europe on the Baltic Sea, which is south of Latvia and north of Poland —**Lithuanian** n., adj.

lit·i·gant /ˈlɪtəgənt/ n. [C] LAW someone who is making a claim against someone or defending themselves against a claim in a court of law

lit·i·gate /ˈlɪtəˌgeɪt/ v. [I,T] LAW to take a claim or complaint against someone to a court of law

lit·i·ga·tion /ˌlɪtəˈgeɪʃən/ n. [U] LAW the process of taking claims to a court of law, in a non-criminal case

li·ti·gious /lɪˈtɪdʒəs/ adj. FORMAL too willing to take any disagreements to a court of law —**litigiousness** n. [U]

lit·mus /ˈlɪtˌməs/ n. [U] a chemical that turns red when touched by acid, and blue when touched by an ALKALI

litmus pa·per /ˈ.. ˌ../ n. [U] paper containing litmus used to test whether a chemical is an acid or an ALKALI

lit·mus test /ˈ.. ˌ./ n. **1** [singular] something that makes it clear what someone's attitude, intentions etc. are: *Personal loyalty seems to be the litmus test for the mayor's new appointees.* **2** [C] a test using litmus paper

li·to·tes /ˈlaɪtəˌtiz, ˈlɪ-, laɪˈtoutiz/ n. [U] TECHNICAL a way of expressing your meaning by using a word that has the opposite meaning with a negative word such as "not," for example by saying "not bad" when you mean "good"

li·tre /ˈlitə/ n. [C] the British and Canadian spelling of LITER

lit·ter¹ /ˈlɪtə/ n. **1** [U] waste paper, containers etc. that people have thrown away and left on the ground in a public place: *The vacant lot across the street is filled with litter.* —see also GARBAGE (1), TRASH¹ (1) **2** [C] a group of baby animals such as dogs or cats which one mother gives birth to at the same time **3 a litter of sth** a group of things arranged in a messy way: *A litter of cocaine bags and razor blades was found in the room.* **4** [U] STRAW (1) that a farm animal sleeps on **5** [C] a very low bed for carrying important people on, used in past times —see also CAT LITTER

litter² v. **1** also **litter up** [I,T] if things litter an area, there are a lot of them in that place, scattered in a messy way: *Dirty plates littered the kitchen.* | **be littered with sth**] *The streets were littered with smashed vehicles and glass.* **2** [I,T] to leave pieces of waste paper etc. on the ground in a public place: *The sign says, "Please do not litter."* **3 be littered with sth** if something is littered with things, there are a lot of those things in it: *The guide book is littered with bits of wisdom and humor.* **4** [I] TECHNICAL if an animal such as a dog or cat litters, it gives birth to babies

lit·ter bag /ˈ.. ˌ./ n. [C] a small bag used to put waste in, especially kept in a car

lit·ter·bug /ˈlɪtəˌbʌg/ n. [C] INFORMAL someone who leaves waste on the ground in public places

lit·tle¹ /ˈlɪtl/ adj.

1 a little bit not very much: *This will only hurt a little bit.* | *Could I have **a little bit of** (=a small amount of) milk in my coffee?*

2 size small in size: *a little farm on the hill* | *I always bring Maggie **a little something** (=a small present) when I come back from business trips.*

3 time/distance short in time or distance: *a little nap* | *He had climbed a little way up the tree and gotten scared.* | *I waited **a little while** (=a short period of time) before I called back.*

4 young young and small: *a cute little puppy* | *I loved playing with blocks when I was little.* | **a little boy/girl** (=a young boy or girl) | **your little boy/girl** (=your son or daughter who is still a child) | **little brother/sister** (=a younger brother or sister who is still a child)

5 used to emphasize used between an adjective and the noun it describes to emphasize that you like or dislike something small or unimportant: *a nice little house* | *a useful little gadget* | *Todd's stupid little jokes* | *a boring little man* | *a poor little bird*

6 unimportant **a)** not important: *Alice gets angry over little things.* **b)** used humorously when you really think that something is important: *There's just that little matter of the $5000 you owe me.*

7 slight done in a way that is not very strong or noticeable; slight: *a little laugh*

8 (just) that little bit extra/harder/better etc. a small amount that will have an important effect: *I should be able to pay all my bills this month, because I've got that little bit extra in my paycheck.*

9 a little bird told me SPOKEN, HUMOROUS used to say that someone who you are not going to name has told you something about another person: *A little bird told me there's a new man in your life.*

10 the little woman SPOKEN an expression meaning "someone's wife," considered offensive by many women

11 (the) little people a) all the people in a country or organization who have no power: *The real victims of the bank failure will be the little people.* **b)** fairies (FAIRY (1)), especially LEPRECHAUNS —see also LITTLE FINGER, LITTLE TOE —see Usage Note at FEW

USAGE NOTE: LITTLE

WORD CHOICE: little, small
Little usually expresses an emotional attitude you have about someone or something such as whether you like or dislike someone or something: *We rented a cozy little cottage in the mountains.* | *Shawn's little laugh is getting on my nerves.* **Small** generally describes the size of something: *This jacket's too small for me.* | *He packed his things into a small bag.*

---

little² quantifier, pron., n. **1** only a small amount or hardly any of something: *Little is known about the Etruscan language.* | *There's less gold in this ring than in the more expensive one.* | **very/so/too little sth** *Scott has very little time these days.* | *The government does little to help single working mothers.* | *Little or no attention is paid to the rights of victims.* | *Little of the food shipment has made it past the army.* | *I've spent my life doing **as little as possible** (=the smallest amount that I have to do).* | *We've got **precious little** (=very little) in the budget for travel expenses.* —see also LEAST¹, LESS¹ **2 a little** also **a little bit** a small amount: *I know only a little bit of Korean.* | *Sara's already told me a little about the accident.* | *A little over half the class can swim.* | *Would you like **a little more** cake?* **3** a short time or distance: *Mr. Jones must be **a little over** (=a few years older than) fifty.* | *Phoenix is **a little under** 100 miles from here.* **4 what little** also **the little (that)** the small amount that there is, that is possible etc.: *They spent what little money they had on a new stereo.* | *Constant logging threatens to wipe out the little that is left of the rain forest.* **5 a little (of sth) goes a long way** SPOKEN used to say you do not need much of something: *A little ketchup goes a long way.*

s w **little**³ *adv.* **1 a little** also **a little bit** to a small
degree: *The table had been moved a little closer to the
wall. | I'm a little upset with you right now. | Pull the
rope a little more to your right.* **2** not much or only
slightly: *The pattern of life here has changed little
since I was a boy. | a little known* (=not known by
many people) *corner of the world | With little more
than three minutes left in the half, Chicago scored a
touchdown. | Kendall's condition has improved very
little since last week. | Callahan interferes as little
as possible with the running of the business.* **3 little
did sb know/think/realize** used to mean that someone did not know, think, realize etc. that something
was true: *Little did she know that her phone conversations were being monitored.* **4 little by little** gradually: *Little by little I became more fluent in German.*

Little Big·horn, the /ˌlɪtl ˈbɪghorn/ a river in the
U.S. state of Montana, where General Custer fought
against and was killed by Native Americans led by
Sitting Bull and Crazy Horse in the Battle of the
Little Bighorn

Little Dip·per /ˌ.. ˈ../ *n.* **the Little Dipper** a group of
stars which is thought to look like a bowl with a
handle, seen in the sky near the BIG DIPPER

little fin·ger /ˌ.. ˈ../ *n.* [C] the smallest finger on your
hand

Little League /ˈ.. ˌ./ *n.* a baseball LEAGUE for children

Little Rock /ˈ.. ˌ./ the capital and largest city of the
U.S. state of Arkansas

little toe /ˌ.. ˈ./ *n.* [C] the smallest toe on your foot

lit·to·ral /ˈlɪtərəl, ˌlɪtəˈræl, -ˈrɑl/ *n.* [C] TECHNICAL an
area of land near the coast —**littoral** *adj.*

li·tur·gi·cal /lɪˈtɜːdʒɪkəl/ *adj.* [only before noun] related
to church services and ceremonies —**liturgically** /-kli/
adv.

lit·ur·gy /ˈlɪtərdʒi/ *n. plural* **liturgies 1** [C,U] a way of
praying in a religious service using a particular
order of words, prayers etc. **2 the Liturgy** the written form of these services

liv·a·bil·i·ty /ˌlɪvəˈbɪləti/ *n.* [U] the degree to which a
place is comfortable, attractive, and easy to live in:
*The church and ten other local groups will receive an
award for enhancing the city's beauty and livability.*

liv·a·ble /ˈlɪvəbəl/ *adj.* **1 a)** good enough to live in,
but not very good; HABITABLE: *The area is poor, but
livable.* **b)** nice to live in: *Bisbee has recently been
voted one of the most livable towns in the country.* **2 a
livable wage/salary** an amount of money that you
are paid for work that is enough to buy the necessary things for life, such as food and housing **3** a
situation that is livable is satisfactory, but not very
good: *livable working conditions*

s w **live**¹ /lɪv/ *v.*
1 be/stay alive [I] to be alive or continue to stay
alive: *Females live longer on average than males. |
St. Patrick probably lived in the 5th century. | Plants
can't live without water. |* [**live to be sth**] *Why do
some people live to be 100? | They never thought
they'd live to see their grandchildren graduate from
college. | The doctors only give him a year to live*
(=they only expect him to live a year).
2 in a place/home [I always + adv./prep.] to have
your home in a particular place: *Where do you live? |
Is Pete still looking for a place to live* (=a house, apart-
ment etc. to live in)? *| Kitty still lives at home*
(=lives with her parents).
3 live in a particular way [I always + adv./prep.,T]
to have a particular type of life, or live in a particu-
lar way: *Those guys live like pigs. | The number of
children living in poverty is increasing. | Villagers
lived in fear of another attack. | People with the
virus can live normal productive lives. | Keenan has
lived the life of a nomad.*
4 live from day to day to deal with each day as it
comes without making plans
5 live by doing sth to keep yourself alive by doing
a particular thing: *Walt lives by selling aluminum
cans and other stuff he finds on the street.*
6 live by your wits to get money, food etc. in some
way other than having a job: *The city's homeless live
completely by their wits.*

7 live a lie to pretend all the time that you feel or
believe something when actually you do not: *Betts
said he announced his homosexuality because he
couldn't go on living a lie.*
8 still have influence also **live on** [I] if someone's
idea or work lives, it continues to influence people:
Elvis lives.
9 live happily ever after a phrase that means to live
a happy life until you die, used especially at the end
of children's stories
10 live out of a suitcase to travel a lot, especially
as part of your work
11 live it up INFORMAL to do things that you enjoy
and spend a lot of money: *Lisa was living it up like
she didn't have a care in the world.*
12 live beyond your means to spend more money
than you earn
13 live in a dream/fantasy/imaginary world also
live in a world of your own to have strange ideas
about life that are not practical or are not like those
of other people: *She's a sweet woman, but she lives in
a dream world.*
14 the best/greatest/worst ... that ever lived someone who was better, greater etc. at doing something
than anyone else in the past or present: *Olivier was
one of the greatest actors that ever lived.*
15 exciting life [I] to have an exciting life: *At 40,
you really start to live!*
16 live in sin OLD-FASHIONED, DISAPPROVING to live
together and have a sexual relationship without
being married
17 live from hand to mouth to have very little
money and never be sure if you will have enough to
eat
18 live and breathe sth to enjoy doing something
so much that you spend most of your time on it: *Residents of the city live and breathe high school football.*
19 be living on borrowed time to be still alive after
the time that you were expected to die
20 live in the past to think too much about the past,
or to have old-fashioned ideas and attitudes: *You've
got to stop living in the past.*
21 live by a principle/rule etc. to always behave
according to a particular set of rules or ideas: *My
daughters are going to live by my rules, or else.*
22 sb will live to regret sth used to say that someone will wish that they had not done something: *If
we don't do something about Paul's drug problem
now, we'll live to regret it.*
23 live to fight/see another day to continue to live
or work after a failure or after you have dealt with
a difficult situation

SPOKEN PHRASES

24 as long as I live used to emphasize that you will
always do or feel something: *I'll never forget this day
as long as I live.*
25 live and let live used to say that you should accept
other people's behavior, even if it seems strange
26 you haven't lived until... used to say that someone's life will not be complete unless they do or experience a particular thing, often used humorously: *You
haven't lived until you've tried my mom's apple pie.*
27 sb'll live used to say that you do not think someone should get too upset about something: *"Dad's
going to be mad we're late." "He'll live."*
28 live and learn used to say that you have learned
something from a bad experience you have had and
you will not make the same mistake again —see also
long live sb/sth (LONG² (10))

---

live sth down *phr. v.* [T] **not live sth down** to not
be able to make people forget about something bad
or embarrassing you have done: *You'll never live this
evening down.*

live for sb/sth *phr. v.* [T] **1** to consider someone or
something very important, or the most important
thing in your life: *Some men seem to live for football.* **2 live for the day when...** to want something to
happen very much: *Lilly lives for the day when she
can have an apartment of her own.*

L

live off sb/sth *phr. v.* [T] to depend on someone or something as your main SOURCE of food or money: *Dave's been living off his girlfriend for a year.* | *I was living off bagels and TV dinners.* | *They wanted to have a simple life and* **live off the land** (=get food from growing vegetables, hunting etc.).

live on *phr. v.* **1** [T **live on** sth] to keep yourself alive by eating a particular food: *These chickens from Peru live on ants.* **2** [T **live on** sth] to buy your food, pay bills etc. with a particular amount of money, especially a small amount: *The whole family lives on just $900 a month.* **3** [I] to continue to exist: *She will live on in our memories.* —see also LIVE[1] (8)

live out *phr. v.* **1 live out a dream/fantasy etc.** to experience or do something that you have planned or hoped for: *The adult sports league gives many people a chance to live out their childhood dreams.* **2 live out your life/days** to continue to live in a particular way or place until you die: [+ **in/on/along** etc.] *Polly married Bemis and lived out her days in the mining camp.*

live through sth *phr. v.* [T] to still be alive after experiencing difficult or dangerous conditions, during which you thought you might die: *Don didn't expect to live through the war.*

live together *phr. v.* [I] to live in the same house or apartment with another person in a sexual relationship, without being married: *Lori and her boyfriend have been living together for two years.*

live up to sth *phr. v.* [T] if something or someone lives up to a standard, REPUTATION, or promise, they do as well as they were expected to, do what they promised etc.: *Most fathers live up to their responsibilities.* | *The movie didn't really* **live up to my expectations.**

live with sb/sth *phr. v.* [T] **1** to live in the same house, apartment etc. with another person, especially in a sexual relationship without being married: *Tim is living with a woman he met in college.* **2** to accept a difficult situation that is likely to continue for a long time: *She's had to learn to live with the pain.*

s w live² /laɪv/ *adj.*

⅓ **1** living [only before noun] not dead or artificial; LIVING: *They are campaigning against experiments on live animals.* —compare DEAD[1] (1) —see also **real live...** (REAL[1] (9))
2 music/concert etc. performed for people who are watching, rather than for a movie, record etc.: *Café du Nord has live music every Saturday.* | *Weber released a* **live recording** (=a recording made of a live performance) *of his New York concert.* | *Episodes are recorded before a* **live** *studio* **audience** (=people who are watching the performance in person, not on television etc.).
3 a live broadcast/report etc. a concert, sports event etc. that is seen or heard on television or radio at the same time as it is happening —compare DELAYED BROADCAST
4 electric equipment or a wire that is live has electricity flowing through it —see also LIVE WIRE (2)
5 bullets/bombs a live bullet, bomb etc. still has the power to explode because it has not been used: *live ammunition*
6 a live ball a ball that is being played with inside the area allowed by the rules of some sports —compare DEAD[1] (11)
7 live coals pieces of coal or other material that are burning
8 a live issue/concern an ISSUE that still interests or worries people

live³ /laɪv/ *adv.* **1 broadcast/show sth live** to broadcast something such as a concert, speech etc. at the same time as it actually happens: *We'll be broadcasting the program live from Washington.* **2 perform live** to perform in front of people who have come to watch, rather than for a movie, record etc.

live·a·ble /ˈlɪvəbəl/ *adj.* another spelling of LIVABLE

lived-in /ˈ. ./ *adj.* a place that looks lived-in has been used often by people, so that it does not seem too new or neat: *Sally's apartment had that comfortable lived-in look.*

live-in /ˈlɪv ɪn/ *adj.* [only before noun] **1 live-in maid/nanny etc.** a worker who lives in the house belonging to the family they work for **2 live-in lover/boyfriend etc.** a phrase meaning someone who lives with their sexual partner without being married to them, used especially by people who do not approve of this

live·li·hood /ˈlaɪvliˌhʊd/ *n.* [C,U] the way you earn money in order to live: *Farmers depend on the weather for their livelihood.*

live·long /ˈlɪvlɔŋ/ *adj.* **all the livelong day** OLD-FASHIONED a phrase meaning "all day," used when this seems like a long time to you

live·ly /ˈlaɪvli/ *adj.* **livelier, liveliest**
1 people very active, full of energy, and cheerful: *Her face was lively and animated as she acted out the scene.* | *a lively kid*
2 movements/music involving a lot of movement, happening quickly etc.: *a lively dance* | *the lively swirls of the stream* | *lively Latin rhythms*
3 place/situation a place or situation that is lively is exciting because a lot of things are happening, or things are happening quickly: *It was a lively and happy celebration.*
4 discussion/conversation etc. exciting because people are speaking quickly, have a lot of interesting ideas etc.: *Garvy's novels have interesting characters and lively dialogue.* | *a lively debate*
5 taste strong but pleasant: *The wine has a lively, fruity flavor.*
6 a lively imagination someone with a lively imagination often invents stories, descriptions etc. that are not true
7 color very bright: *a lively combination of colors*
8 Step lively! SPOKEN, HUMOROUS used to tell someone to hurry —**liveliness** *n.* [U]

li·ven /ˈlaɪvən/ *v.*
liven up *phr. v.* **1** [I,T **liven** sth ↔ **up**] to become more exciting, or to make an event become more exciting: *Things have livened up around here since Diane was hired.* | *Better music might liven the party up.* **2** [T **liven** sth ↔ **up**] to make something look, taste etc. more interesting or colorful: *A colorful shawl can liven up a trench coat.* **3** [I,T **liven** sb ↔ **up**] to become more interested or excited, or to make someone feel like this: *After a few drinks, she livened up a little.*

liv·er /ˈlɪvɚ/ *n.* **1** [C] a large organ in your body which produces BILE (1) and cleans your blood —see picture at DIGESTIVE SYSTEM **2** [U] the liver of an animal, used as food

liv·er·ied /ˈlɪvərid/ *adj.* wearing LIVERY (1): *a liveried servant*

liver spot /ˈ.. ˌ./ *n.* [C usually plural] a small round brown spot that appears on someone's skin, especially their hands, as they get older

liv·er·wurst /ˈlɪvɚˌwɚst/ *n.* [U] a type of cooked soft SAUSAGE, made mainly of LIVER (2)

liv·er·y /ˈlɪvəri/ *n. plural* **liveries** **1** [C,U] a type of old-fashioned uniform for servants **2** [C] a company that rents out vehicles, or drives people where they want to go for money: *a livery cab* **3** [U] the business of keeping and taking care of horses for money, especially in the past **4** a livery stable —see also LIVERIED

livery sta·ble /ˈ... ˌ../ *n.* [C] a place where people pay to have their horses kept, fed etc. or where horses can be rented, especially in past times

lives /laɪvz/ the plural of LIFE

live·stock /ˈlaɪvstɑk/ *n.* [plural, U] the animals that are kept on a farm

live wire /ˌlaɪv ˈwaɪɚ/ *n.* [C] **1** INFORMAL someone who is very active and has a lot of energy **2** a wire that has electricity passing through it

liv·id /ˈlɪvɪd/ *adj.* **1** extremely angry; FURIOUS: *I was so livid I just ripped up the letter.* **2** a mark on your skin that is livid is dark blue and gray: *livid bruises* **3** LITERARY a face that is livid is very pale

liv·ing¹ /ˈlɪvɪŋ/ *adj.* **1** [only before noun] alive now:

one of the greatest living composers | **Ecology** is the study of how **living things** (=plants, animals, and people) *relate to their environment.* **2 living proof** if someone is living proof of a particular fact, they are a good example of how true it is: *I'm living proof that people can make their dreams come true.* **3 in living memory** for as long as anyone can remember: *The famine is worse than any disaster in living memory.* **4 living language** a language that is still spoken today **5 living legend** someone who is famous for being extremely good at something: *one of the living legends of rhythm and blues* **6 a living hell** a situation that causes you a lot of suffering for a long time: *My life has been a living hell since the attack.* **7 living wage** money that you earn from your work that is enough to allow you to buy the things that you need to live: *A lot of people around here don't even earn a living wage.* **8 a living death** a life that is so bad that it would seem better to be dead —see also **beat/knock/pound the (living) daylights out of sb/sth** (DAYLIGHT (4)), **scare/frighten the (living) daylights out of sb** (DAYLIGHT (3)) —see Usage Note at LIFE

living² *n.* **1** [C usually singular] the way that you earn money, or the money that you earn: *It's not a great job, but it's a living.* | *So what do you do for a living?* | *I want to make a living* (=earn enough money to live) *being creative.* **2 the living** [plural] all the people who are alive as opposed to dead people: *Funeral needs are meant to address the needs of the living.* **3** [U] the way in which someone lives their life: *the harsh realities of city living* —see also COST OF LIVING, **in the land of the living** (LAND¹ (7)), **scratch (out) a living** (SCRATCH¹ (12)), STANDARD OF LIVING

living quar·ters /ˈ.. ˌ../ *n.* [plural] the part of an army or industrial camp etc. or a large official building where the soldiers or workers live and sleep

living room /ˈ.. ˌ../ *n.* [C] the main room in a house where people relax, watch television etc. —compare FAMILY ROOM —see picture on page 423

living stan·dard /ˈ.. ˌ../ *n.* [C usually plural] the level of comfort and wealth that people have; STANDARD OF LIVING: *a decline in the country's living standards*

Liv·ing·stone /ˈlɪvɪŋstən/, **Dr. Da·vid** /ˈdeɪvɪd/ (1813–1873) a Scottish MISSIONARY and EXPLORER of Africa, who was the first European to see the Zambezi River and the Victoria Falls

living will /ˌ.. ˈ./ *n.* [C] a document explaining what medical or legal decisions should be made if you become so sick that you cannot make those decisions yourself

Liv·y /ˈlɪvi/ (59 B.C.–A.D. 17) a Roman HISTORIAN known for his history of Rome, which greatly influenced historical writing. His Latin name was Titus Livius.

liz·ard /ˈlɪzəd/ *n.* [C] a type of REPTILE that has four legs and a long tail

Ljub·lja·na /ˌlyublɪˈanə/ the capital and largest city of Slovenia

'll /əl, l/ *v.* the short form of "will": *She'll be gone until Wednesday.*

lla·ma /ˈlamə/ *n.* [C] a South American animal with thick hair like wool and a long neck

LL.B. *n.* [C] Bachelor of Laws; a first college or university degree in law

LL.D. *n.* [C] Doctor of Laws; a DOCTORATE in law

LL.M. *n.* [C] Master of Laws; a MASTER'S DEGREE in law

Ln. the written abbreviation of LANE

lo /loʊ/ *interjection* **lo and behold** HUMOROUS said before mentioning something funny or surprising that has happened: *When we arrived, lo and behold, there was Dave sitting in the front row.*

s w **load¹** /loʊd/ *n.* [C]
³ **1** **amount of sth** a large quantity of something that is carried by a person, a vehicle etc.: [+ of] *The young boy struggled to carry his load of bananas up the hill.*
2 truckload/carload etc. the largest amount or number of something that a car, truck etc. can carry: [+ of] *a busload of tourists*

3 **work** the amount of work that a person or machine has to do: *Leslie has a light teaching load* (=not much work) *this semester.*
4 **washing clothes** a quantity of clothes that are washed together in a washing machine: *I did two loads of laundry this morning.*
5 a responsibility or worry that is difficult to deal with: *a $1.2 billion debt load* | *Working three jobs is a heavy load to bear.*
6 **weight** the amount of weight that the frame of a building or structure can support: *a load-bearing wall*
7 **money** TECHNICAL an amount of money that someone pays a company in order to let them INVEST (=put their money) in a particular FUND: *a no-load mutual fund*
8 **electricity** TECHNICAL an amount of electrical power that is produced by a GENERATOR or a POWER PLANT: *Load demand can exceed 66 percent during peak periods.* —see also **be a load/weight off your mind** (MIND¹ (19))

SPOKEN PHRASES

9 a load of sth also **loads of sth** a lot of something: *We ate loads of French fries.*
10 a load of crap/bull etc. IMPOLITE used to say that something is untrue, wrong, or stupid: *That's the biggest load of bunk I ever heard!*
11 get a load of sb/sth used to tell someone to look at or listen to something surprising or funny: *Get a load of Ted's new haircut!*
12 take a load off used to invite someone to sit down

—see also **drop a load** (DROP¹ (34))

load² *v.* **1** also **load up** [I,T] to put a load of something on or into a vehicle: *Trucks may not stop on city streets to load or unload between 11 and 6.* | *I took an hour to load the van.* | [load sth with sth] *He loaded up the car with camping gear.* | [load sth into/onto sth] *Coast Guard officials loaded the marijuana onto a plane.* **2** [T] to put a necessary part into something so that it will work, such as bullets into a gun, film into a camera etc.: *Wait a minute — I need to load my camera.* **3** [I,T] to put a program into a computer, or to be put into a computer: *This program takes a while to load.* **4 load the bases** to get players in a baseball game on all the BASES, so that they are in a position to be able to gain points
s w
2
3

load sb/sth down *phr. v.* [T usually passive] to make someone or something carry too many things or do too much work: [+ with] *Cora was loaded down with two 70-pound suitcases.*

load up on sth *phr. v.* [T] to get a lot of something, so that you are sure that you will have enough available: *People were loading up on bottled water.*

load sb (up) with sth *phr. v.* [T] to give someone a lot of things to carry: *I see Dick's loaded you up with boxes.*

load·ed /ˈloʊdɪd/ *adj.*
1 **gun/camera etc.** containing bullets, film etc.: *That gun's not loaded, is it?* | *a loaded camera*
2 **full vehicle** carrying a load of something: *a loaded truck*
3 **rich** [not before noun] INFORMAL very rich: *Carter's family is loaded.*
4 loaded question a question containing a word or words which are intended to have a strong emotional effect on someone and influence the answer they give —compare **leading question** (LEADING¹ (4))
5 **word/statement** having more meanings than you first think, or having a strong emotional effect: *politically loaded words*
6 be loaded with sth INFORMAL to be full of a particular quality, or containing a lot of something: *The library is loaded with interesting books.* | *Linda's fruitcake is loaded with fruit and nuts.*
7 **drunk** INFORMAL very drunk
8 loaded dice DICE¹ (1) that have weights in them so that they always fall with the same side on top, used to influence games in an unfair way

L

9 baseball if the BASES are loaded, there are players on all three bases so that they are in a position to be able to gain points

load·ing dock /'.. ,./ n. [C] a structure from which goods are taken off or put onto trucks, trains etc.

load·mas·ter /'loud,mæstə/ n. [C] someone who is responsible for loading heavy equipment, weapons etc. on or off an aircraft

loaf¹ /louf/ n. plural **loaves** /louvz/ [C] **1** bread that is shaped and baked in one piece and can be cut into SLICES: *a loaf of bread* **2** food that has been cut into very small pieces, pressed together, and baked in the shape of a loaf of bread: *a nut loaf* —see also MEAT-LOAF

loaf² v. **loafs, loafed, loafing** [I] to waste time in a lazy way when you should be working: *He spent all summer loafing around the house.*

loaf·er /'loufə/ n. [C] **1** also **Loafer** TRADEMARK a flat leather shoe without LACES that you slide onto your foot —see picture at SHOE¹ **2** someone who wastes time in a lazy way when they should be working

loam /loum/ n. [U] good-quality soil consisting of sand, clay, and decayed plants —**loamy** adj.

S W **loan¹** /loun/ n. **1** [C] an amount of money that you borrow from a bank, financial institution etc.: [+ of] *a loan of $175,000* | *I had to take out a loan* (=borrow money) *to buy my car.* | **pay off/back a loan** *Liz is still paying off her student loans* (=money lent to students to pay for college). | *Krebs needed more time to pay back the loan.* **2 on loan** if something such as a painting or book is on loan, someone is borrowing it: [+ from] *The gems in the display are on loan from the Academy of Science.* **3** [U] the act of lending something: [+ of] *The committee asked at least 20 companies for the loan of a private jet.* —see Usage Notes at BORROW and LEND

loan² v. [T] **1** to let someone borrow something: [loan sb sth] *Can you loan me $5?* | *Jeff loaned us his car for the weekend.* **2** to lend something valuable, such as a painting, to an organization: *The family loaned their collection of paintings for the exhibition.*

loan cap·i·tal /'. ,../ n. [U] the part of a company's money that was borrowed to help start it

loan·er /'lounə/ n. [C] INFORMAL something such as a car, piece of equipment etc. that someone is allowed to use while theirs is being repaired

loan shark /'. ./ n. [C] DISAPPROVING someone who lends money at a very high rate of INTEREST¹ (3) and will often use threats or violence to get the money back —**loansharking** n. [U]

loan word, loanword /'. ./ n. [C] a word taken into one language from another and sometimes changed to fit the rules of the new language

loath /louθ, louð/ adj. **be loath to do sth** FORMAL to be unwilling to do something: *He seemed loath to raise the subject.*

loathe /louð/ v. [T not in progressive] FORMAL to hate someone or something very much: *Many conservatives loathe the current president.*

loath·ing /'louðɪŋ/ n. [singular,U] FORMAL a very strong feeling of hatred: [+ for] *The more he called me "Sugar," the more my loathing for him increased.*

loath·some /'louθsəm, 'louð-/ adj. FORMAL very bad or cruel: *He is a loathsome disgusting creature.*

loaves /louvz/ the plural of LOAF¹

lob /lab/ v. **lobbed, lobbing** [T] **1** to throw something somewhere in a high curve, especially over a wall, fence etc.: [lob sth into/at/over etc. sth] *About 40 demonstrators lobbed eggs over police barricades.* **2** to throw or hit a ball in a slow high curve, especially in a game of tennis: *Sampras lobbed the ball high over Chang's head.* —**lob** n. [C]

lob·by¹ /'labi/ n. plural **lobbies** [C] **1** a wide area or large hall just inside the entrance to a public building: *a hotel lobby* —compare FOYER (1) **2** a group of people or companies who try to influence the government so that a particular law or situation will be changed, to make it more favorable to them: *The law has the support of the gun-control lobby.*

lobby² v. **lobbies, lobbied, lobbying** [I,T] to try to influence the government or someone with political power so that they change a law to make it more favorable to you: [+ for/against] *Price lobbied hard for passage of the helmet law.* | [lobby sb to do sth] *Alquist is lobbying the governor to sign the controversial bill.*

lob·by·ist /'labiɪst/ n. [C] someone whose job is to try to influence or persuade the government to change a law so that it is more favorable to them

lobe /loub/ n. [C] **1** the soft piece of flesh at the bottom of your ear; EAR LOBE **2** TECHNICAL a round part of an organ in your body, especially in your brain or lungs

lo·bot·o·my /lə'baṭəmi, lou-/ n. plural **lobotomies** [C] a medical operation to remove part of someone's brain in order to treat mental problems, which was done more commonly in the past —**lobotomize** v. [T]

lob·ster /'labstə/ n. **1** [C] an ocean animal with eight legs, a shell, and two large CLAWS —see picture at CRUSTACEAN **2** [U] the meat of this animal

S W 3

lob·ster·man /'labstəmən/ n. [C] someone whose job is to catch lobsters

lobster pot /'. ,./ n. [C] a trap shaped like a basket, in which lobsters are caught

lo·cal /,lou 'kæl/ adj. INFORMAL another spelling of LOW-CAL

lo·cal¹ /'loukəl/ adj. **1** connected with a particular place or area, especially the place you live in: *The fire was reported in the local newspaper.* | *Government control was primarily local until the early part of the century.* | *I don't think the hotel charges guests for local calls* (=telephone calls to someone in the same area as you). **2 local train/bus** a train or bus that stops at all regular stopping places —compare **express train/bus** (EXPRESS² (3)) **3** TECHNICAL affecting or limited to one part of your body: *a local anesthetic*

S W 1 2

local² n. [C] **1** [usually plural] someone who lives in the place where you are, or the place that you are talking about: *The new theaters are attracting crowds of tourists and locals alike.* **2** a branch of a UNION (1): *Local 54 of the Hotel Employees' Union* **3** a bus, train etc. that stops at all regular stopping places —compare EXPRESS³ (1)

local ar·e·a net·work /,.. ,... '../ n. [C] TECHNICAL: see LAN

local call /'.. ,./ n. [C] a telephone call to someone in a place near you —compare **long-distance call** (LONG-DISTANCE (2))

local col·or /,.. '../ n. [U] the unusual or additional details about a place or in a story that give you a better idea of what it is like, and that make it special or interesting: *The old covered bridges provide local color.*

lo·cale /lou'kæl/ n. [C] the place where an event happens, or where the action takes place in a book or a movie: *Malta is the perfect locale for the conference.*

local gov·ern·ment /,.. '.../ n. [C,U] the government of cities, towns etc. rather than of a whole country

local his·to·ry /,.. '.../ n. [U] the history of a particular area in a country, state etc. —**local historian** n. [C]

lo·cal·i·ty /lou'kæləti/ n. plural **localities** [C] a small area of a country, city etc.: *Police officers are generally expected to live in the same locality in which they work.*

lo·cal·ize /'loukə,laɪz/ v. [T] FORMAL **1** to limit the effect that something has, or the size of area it covers, or to be limited in this way: *Croft plans to localize his campaign to each state.* **2** to find out exactly where something is —**localization** /,loukələ-'zeɪʃən/ n. [U]

lo·cal·ized /'loukə,laɪzd/ adj. FORMAL only within a small area: *localized flooding* | *localized cancer*

lo·cal·ly /'loukəli/ adv. **1** in or near the area where you are or the area you are talking about: *Microtech employs 1300 workers locally.* **2** in particular small areas: *locally elected governments*

local pa·per /ˌ.. ˈ../ n. [C] a newspaper that contains local news in addition to national and international news

local time /ˈ.. ˌ./ n. [U] the time of day in a particular part of the world: *We'll arrive in Boston at 4:00 local time.*

lo·cate /ˈloʊkeɪt/ v. **1** [T] to find the exact position of someone or something: *Whales use low-frequency calls to locate each other.* **2 be located in/by/near etc. sth** to be in a particular place or position: *Ski Apache is located in southern New Mexico.* **3** [I always + adv./prep.] to come to a place and start a business, company etc. there: [+ **in/at** etc.] *Several discount stores have located in nearby communities.*

lo·ca·tion /loʊˈkeɪʃən/ n. **1** [C] a particular place or position, especially in relation to other areas, buildings etc.: *His apartment is in a really good location.* | [+ **of**] *The map shows the location of the crash.* —see Usage Note at POSITION¹ **2** [C,U] a place where a movie is filmed, away from the STUDIO: *The film was shot on location in Hungary.* **3** [U] the act of locating something

loch /lɑk/ n. [C] a word meaning a lake or a part of the ocean partly enclosed by land, used in Scotland: *Loch Ness*

lo·ci /ˈloʊsaɪ, -kaɪ/ n. the plural of LOCUS

lock¹ /lɑk/ v.
1 fasten [I,T] to fasten something with a lock, or to be fastened with a lock: *Lock the door when you go.* | *I can't get this drawer to lock.* —opposite UNLOCK
2 in a safe place [T always – adv./prep.] to put something in a safe place and lock the door, lid etc., or to attach it to something using a lock: [**lock sth in/to sth**] *Always lock valuables in the trunk of your car while shopping.* | *We locked our bikes to the fence.*
3 prevent sb from entering/leaving [T always + adv./prep.] to prevent a person or animal from entering or leaving a place by locking a door, lid etc.: [**lock sb/sth in sth**] *She locked herself in her room.* | [**lock sb/sth out of sth**] *I accidentally locked myself out of the house.*
4 machine/body part [I,T] to become set in one position and impossible to move, or to set a wheel, a part of a machine etc. in this way: *She was just chewing her dinner and her jaw locked.* | *Lock the brakes before you take him out of the stroller.*
5 not change [I,T] to be unable to change a situation, especially a bad one, or to make someone unable to change a situation: [+ **in**] *Some families are locked in a cycle of poverty.*
6 be locked in an embrace if two people are locked in an EMBRACE, they are holding each other very tightly
7 lock arms to join your arms tightly together with someone else: *Fifty students locked arms to block the entrance to the building.*
8 be locked in battle/combat/dispute etc. to be involved in a serious argument, fight etc. with someone: *The two law firms have been locked in struggle for months.*
9 lock horns with sb (over sth) to argue or fight with someone —**lockable** adj.
lock sb/sth away phr. v. [T] **1** to put something in a safe place and lock the door, lid etc.: *He locked his money away in the safe.* **2** to put someone in prison
3 lock yourself away to keep yourself separate from other people by staying in your room, office etc.
lock in phr. v. [T] **1** [**lock sb in**] to prevent someone from leaving a room or building by locking the door: *Prisoners are only locked in at night.* **2** [**lock sth ↔ in**] to do something so that a price, offer, agreement etc. cannot be changed: *Sell your stocks now to lock in some of the gains of recent months.*
lock into sth phr. v. [T] **be locked into sth** to be unable to change a situation: *The company is locked into a three-year contract with PARCO.*
lock onto sth phr. v. [T] if something such as a MISSILE or SATELLITE locks onto a TARGET or signal, it finds it and follows it closely
lock sb ↔ out phr. v. [T] **1** to prevent someone from entering a place by locking the door: *Oh no, I locked myself out!* **2** if employers lock workers out, they do not let them enter their place of work until they accept the employers' conditions for settling a disagreement —see also LOCKOUT

lock up phr. v. **1** [T **lock sb ↔ up**] INFORMAL to put someone in prison or in a place that they cannot escape from: *He was repeatedly locked up for drug dealing.* **2** [I,T **lock sth ↔ up**] to make a building safe by locking the doors, especially at night: *I have to lock up and turn on the alarm before I go.* **3** [T **lock sth ↔ up**] to put something in a safe place and lock the door, lid etc., or to attach it to something using a lock: *I have all my stuff locked up downstairs.* **4** [I] if a wheel, a part of a machine etc. locks up, it becomes set in one position and impossible to move: *The steering wheel locked up and we drove into a ditch.* **5 be locked up (in sth)** if your money is locked up, you have put it into a business, INVESTMENT etc. and cannot easily move it or change it into CASH **6 lock sb up and throw away the key** INFORMAL to put someone in prison permanently

lock² n. [C]
1 on a door a thing that keeps a door, drawer etc. fastened or shut and is usually opened with a key: *There's no lock on the door.* | *Kelly patiently picked the lock on the desk drawer* (=he used something such as a pin to open it).
2 lock, stock, and barrel including every part of something: *They sold everything lock, stock, and barrel.*
3 under lock and key a) kept safely in something that is locked: *Oswald's FBI file has been kept under lock and key.* **b)** kept in a place such as a prison
4 hair a small number of hairs on your head that grow and hang together: *She kept a lock of his baby hair in a book.*
5 locks [plural] POETIC someone's hair: *long flowing locks*
6 on a river a part of a CANAL or river that is closed off by gates on either end so that the water level can be increased or decreased to raise or lower boats
7 in a fight a HOLD² (8) that a WRESTLER uses to prevent their opponent from moving: *a head lock*
8 gun the part of a gun that makes the bullet explode out of the gun
9 result a result that you know will be a good one, for example in a competition or election: *Parnell has a lock on the Republican nomination.*

Locke /lɑk/, **John** (1632–1704) an English PHILOSOPHER who developed the idea of EMPIRICISM and believed that a government received the right to rule from the people

lock·er /ˈlɑkɚ/ n. [C] **1** a type of large box or container attached to a wall, that can be locked so that you can leave your books, clothes etc. there while you do something else **2** a very cold room used for storing food in a restaurant or factory: *a meat locker*

locker room /ˈ.. ˌ./ n. [C] a room where people change their clothes and leave them in lockers, especially in places where they are playing sports

locker-room hu·mor /ˌ... ˈ../ n. [U] jokes that men tell, especially about sex

lock·et /ˈlɑkɪt/ n. [C] a piece of jewelry like a small round box that you can put a picture, piece of hair etc. in, that you wear around your neck on a chain

locket

lock·jaw /ˈlɑkdʒɔ/ n. [U] NOT TECHNICAL: see TETANUS

lock·out /ˈlɑk-aʊt/ n. [C] a period of time when a company does not allow workers to go back to work, especially in a factory, until they accept its working conditions —see also **lock sb out** (LOCK¹) —compare STRIKE¹ (4)

L

lock·smith /ˈlɑkˌsmɪθ/ *n.* [C] someone who makes and repairs locks

lock·step /ˈlɑkstɛp/ *n.* **in lockstep** agreeing with someone completely, or doing something in exactly the same way as them, often without thinking: [+ **with**] *Romania marched in lockstep with China on many issues.*

lock·up /ˈlɑk-ʌp/ *n.* [C] **1** a small prison where a criminal can be kept for a short time **2** a situation in which a wheel, part of a machine, body part etc. becomes set in one position and is impossible to move **3** an act of locking someone in prison or in a place they cannot escape from

Lock·wood /ˈlɑkwʊd/, **Bel·va** /ˈbɛlvə/ (1830–1917) a U.S. lawyer who supported women's rights and was the first woman lawyer to appear before the U.S. Supreme Court

lo·co /ˈloʊkoʊ/ *adj.* INFORMAL crazy —see also IN LOCO PARENTIS

lo·co·mo·tion /ˌloʊkəˈmoʊʃən/ *n.* [U] FORMAL OR TECHNICAL movement or the ability to move

lo·co·mo·tive¹ /ˌloʊkəˈmoʊtɪv/ *n.* [C] **1** a train engine **2** a powerful force that makes other things happen or succeed: *Few expect the EU to take over as the locomotive of the world economy.*

locomotive² *adj.* TECHNICAL relating to movement

lo·co·weed /ˈloʊkoʊˌwid/ *n.* [C] a plant that makes animals very sick if they eat it

lo·cus /ˈloʊkəs/ *n. plural* **loci** /ˈloʊkaɪ, -ki/ [C] **1** FORMAL a place or position where something is particularly known to exist or happen: [+ **of**] *The Politburo was the locus of all power in the Soviet Union.* **2** TECHNICAL the set of all points given by a particular rule in mathematics

lo·cust /ˈloʊkəst/ *n.* [C] an insect similar to a GRASSHOPPER that flies in large groups and often destroys crops: *a swarm of locusts*

lo·cu·tion /loʊˈkyuʃən/ *n.* TECHNICAL **1** [U] a style of speaking **2** [C] a phrase, especially one used in a particular area or by a particular group of people: *a Yiddish locution*

lode /loʊd/ *n.* [C usually singular] an amount of ORE (=metal in its natural form) found in a layer between stones —see also MOTHER LODE (1)

lodge¹ /lɑdʒ/ *n.* [C] **1** a building or hotel in the country or in the mountains where people can stay for a short time, especially to do a particular activity: *a ski lodge | Lake Star Lodge has rooms for a reasonable price.* **2** a local meeting place for some organizations, or the group of people who belong to one of these organizations: *a Masonic lodge* **3** a traditional structure such as a LONGHOUSE or a WIGWAM that Native Americans live in, or the group of people that live in it **4** the home of a BEAVER

lodge² *v.* **1** [I always + adv./prep.,T usually passive] to become firmly stuck somewhere, or make something become stuck: [+ **in/down** etc.] *A piece of meat lodged in her throat.* | [**be lodged in/down** etc.] *The bullet is still lodged in his chest.* —opposite DISLODGE **2 lodge a complaint/protest/appeal etc.** to make a formal or official complaint, protest etc.: *Officials say the country will lodge a complaint with the United Nations Security Council.* **3** [T] to give or find someone a place to stay for a short time: *This building was used to lodge prisoners of war.* | [**lodge sb in/at etc. sth**] *The refugees were lodged in old army barracks.* **4** [I always + adv./prep.] to pay someone rent so you can live in a room in their house: *Kim lodged with a local family the summer she studied in Paris.*

lodg·er /ˈlɑdʒɚ/ *n.* [C] OLD-FASHIONED someone who pays to live in a room or rooms in someone else's house

lodg·ing /ˈlɑdʒɪŋ/ *n.* [C,U] a place to stay: *The tourist office will send you information on lodging.*

Loewe /loʊ/, **Fred·erick** /ˈfrɛdrɪk/ (1904–1988) a U.S.

COMPOSER famous for writing MUSICALs with Alan Jay Lerner

loft¹ /lɔft/ *n.* [C] **1** a raised area in a BARN used for storing HAY or other crops: *a hay loft* **2** a raised area above the main part of a room, usually used for sleeping **3** a space above a business, factory etc. that was once used for storing goods, but has been changed into living space or work space for artists: *Marris lives in a loft in lower Manhattan.* **4** the raised place in a church where the ORGAN or CHOIR is: *the choir loft* **5** a set of CAGES used to keep PIGEONS in

loft² *v.* [T] to hit, kick, or throw a ball in a high gentle curve, especially in some sports such as GOLF

loft·y /ˈlɔfti/ *adj.* **loftier, loftiest 1** lofty ideas, beliefs, attitudes etc. show high standards or high moral qualities: *lofty ideals of equality and social justice* **2** LITERARY lofty mountains, buildings etc. are very high **3** seeming to think you are better than other people, or showing this quality —**loftily** *adv.*

log¹ /lɔg, lɑg/ *n.* [C] **1** a thick piece of wood cut from a tree **2** an official recorded or written record of something, especially a trip in a ship or airplane **3** a LOGARITHM —see also **it's as easy as falling off a log** (EASY¹ (12)), **sleep like a log** (SLEEP¹ (2))

log² *v.* **logged, logging 1** [T] to make an official record of events, facts etc.: *By mid-July the INS had logged only 72 applications.* **2** [T] to travel a particular distance or to work for a particular length of time, especially in an airplane or ship: *The pilot had logged over 150 hours of flying time.* **3** [I,T] to cut down large numbers of trees to be sold

log in/on *phr. v.* [I] to enter a computer system by typing (TYPE² (2)) a special word or giving it a particular command

log off/out *phr. v.* [I] to stop using a computer system by giving it a particular command or typing (TYPE² (2)) a special word

-log /lɔg, lɑg/ *suffix* [in nouns] something that is written or spoken: *a sportswear catalog* (=a book with pictures and information) —see also -LOGUE

Lo·gan, Mount /ˈloʊgən/ the highest mountain in Canada

lo·gan·ber·ry /ˈloʊgənˌbɛri/ *n. plural* **loganberries** [C] a soft dark red berry, similar to a RASPBERRY

log·a·rithm /ˈlɔgəˌrɪðəm/ *also* **log** *n.* [C] TECHNICAL the number of times a number, usually 10, must be multiplied by itself to equal another number

log book /ˈ. ./ *n.* [C] a LOG¹ (2)

log cab·in /ˌ. ˈ../ *n.* [C] a small house made of LOGS¹ (1)

log·ger /ˈlɔgɚ/ *n.* [C] someone whose job is to cut down trees

log·ger·heads /ˈlɔgɚˌhɛdz, ˈlɑ-/ *n.* **be at loggerheads** if two people are at loggerheads they disagree very strongly with each other about something: [+ **over sth**] *Officials are at loggerheads over energy policy.*

log·ging /ˈlɔgɪŋ/ *n.* [U] the work of cutting down trees in a forest: *the logging industry*

log·ic /ˈlɑdʒɪk/ *n.* **1** [singular,U] a set of sensible and correct reasons, or reasonable thinking: [+ **of/in**] *She examined the logic of his plan and found it flawless.* | [+ **behind**] *We just don't see the logic behind the decision.* **2** [U] the science or study of careful REASONING using formal methods **3** [U] TECHNICAL a set of choices that a computer uses to solve a problem

log·i·cal /ˈlɑdʒɪkəl/ *adj.* **1** seeming reasonable and sensible: *Taking the job seemed like the logical thing to do at the time.* | *a logical explanation* —opposite ILLOGICAL **2** a logical step/conclusion/extension etc. a part of a process, a result etc. that you expect or think should happen because it seems sensible: *The next logical step would be to open your own business.* **3** relating to or obeying the rules of logic: *a logical error* —**logically** /-kli/ *adv.*

lo·gi·cian /loʊˈdʒɪʃən/ *n.* [C] someone who studies or is skilled in logic

-logist /lədʒɪst/ *suffix* [in nouns] someone who studies or does work in a particular type of science: *a genealogist* (=who studies the history of families) | *a biologist* (=who studies biology) —see also -OLOGIST

lo·gis·tics /loʊˈdʒɪstɪks, lə-/ *n.* **1 the logistics** the practical arrangements that are needed in order to make a plan or activity successful: [**the logistics of (doing) sth**] *The logistics of educating the state's 3.6 million pre-school children remain complex.* **2** [U] the study or skill of moving soldiers, supplying them with food etc. —**logistical** *also* **logistic** *adj.* —**logistically** /-kli/ *adv.*

log·jam /ˈlɔgdʒæm/ *n.* [C] **1** a lot of problems that are preventing something from being done: *If we don't* **break the** *budget* **logjam** *soon* (=solve the problems), *Congress won't accomplish anything this session.* **2** a tightly packed mass of floating LOGS on a river

lo·go /ˈloʊgoʊ/ *n. plural* **logos** [C] a small design or way of writing a name that is the official sign of a company or organization

log·roll·ing /ˈlɔgˌroʊlɪŋ/ *n.* [U] **1** INFORMAL the practice in the U.S. Congress of helping a member to pass a BILL, so that they will do the same for you later **2** INFORMAL the practice of praising or helping someone, so that they will do the same for you later **3** a sport in which two people stand on a LOG floating on water and roll it, each person trying to make the other fall off

-logue /lɔg, lɑg/ *suffix* [in nouns] something that is written or spoken: *a monologue* (=speech by one person) | *the book's prologue* (=the introduction to it)

-logy /ləˈdʒi/ *suffix* [in nouns] a spelling of -OLOGY used if there is already a sound like "a" or "o" before this SUFFIX: *mineralogy* (=the study of minerals) | *geology* (=the study of rocks and the Earth)

loin /lɔɪn/ *n.* **1 loins** [plural] LITERARY the part of your body below your waist and above your legs, which includes your sexual organs **2** [C,U] a piece of meat from the lower part of an animal's back —see also **the fruit of sb's loins** (FRUIT[1] (6)), **gird (up) your loins** (GIRD (2))

loin·cloth /ˈlɔɪnklɔθ/ *n.* [C] a piece of cloth that men in some hot countries wear around their loins

Loire, the /lwɑr/ a river in central France that flows into the Bay of Biscay

loi·ter /ˈlɔɪtɚ/ *v.* [I] **1** to stand or wait somewhere, especially in a public place, without any clear reason: *Teens were loitering in the parking lot.* **2** to move or do something slowly, or to keep stopping when you should keep moving: *No one has time to loiter over a meal these days.* —**loiterer** *n.* [C]

loi·ter·ing /ˈlɔɪtərɪŋ/ *n.* [U] the crime of staying in a place for a long time without having any reason to be there, so that it seems as if you are going to do something illegal: *Towne was arrested for loitering and prowling.*

LOL, lol a written abbreviation of "laughing out loud," used by people communicating in CHAT ROOMS on the Internet to say that they are laughing at something that someone else has written

loll /lɑl/ *v.* **1** *also* **loll around** to sit or lie in a very lazy and relaxed way: *He lolled around in the Florida sunshine.* **2** [I,T] if your head or tongue lolls or if you loll your head, you allow it to hang in a relaxed uncontrolled way

lol·li·pop /ˈlɑliˌpɑp/ *n.* [C] a hard candy made of boiled sugar on the end of a stick

lol·lop /ˈlɑləp/ *v.* [I + around/across/about] to run with long awkward steps: *Rick's dog came lolloping across the yard.*

lol·ly·gag /ˈlɑliˌgæg/ *v.* [I] INFORMAL to waste time, or move or work very slowly: *Quit lollygagging and get back to work!*

lol·ly·pop /ˈlɑliˌpɑp/ *n.* [C] another spelling of LOLLIPOP

Lom·bar·di /ləmˈbɑrdi/, **Vince** /vɪns/ (1913–1970) a U.S. football COACH whose team won the first two Super Bowls in 1967 and 1968

Lo·mé /loʊˈmeɪ/ the capital and largest city of Togo

Lon·don /ˈlʌndən/ the capital and largest city of the U.K.

London, Jack /dʒæk/ (1876–1916) a U.S writer of adventure NOVELS

Jack London

London broil /ˌ.. ˈ./ *n.* [C,U] BEEF that is cooked under direct heat and cut into thin pieces

lone /loʊn/ *adj.* [only before noun] LITERARY being the only person or thing in a place, or the only person or thing that does something: *Councilman Dexter cast the lone "no" vote.* | *a lone figure in the snow* —see Usage Note at ALONE

lone·ly /ˈloʊnli/ *adj.* **lonelier, loneliest** **1** unhappy because you are alone and feel that you do not have anyone to talk to, or making you feel this way: *Jay was never lonely with Nurse Dees nearby.* | *a lonely journey* **2** ESPECIALLY LITERARY a lonely place is a long way from where people live and very few people go there: *She left me at a lonely crossroads.* —**loneliness** *n.* [U] —see also LONESOME, ALONE (5) —see Usage Note at ALONE

lonely hearts /ˌ.. ˈ./ *n.* **lonely hearts club/page/column** a club or an advertisement page of a newspaper that is used by people who want to meet a friend or a lover

lon·er /ˈloʊnɚ/ *n.* [C] someone who prefers to be alone or someone who has no friends

lone·some /ˈloʊnsəm/ *adj.* **1** very unhappy because you are alone or have no friends, or making you feel this way: *Beth is lonesome without the kids around.* | *a lonesome song* **2** a lonesome place is a long way from where people live and very few people go there: *a lonesome desert highway* **3** **on/by your lonesome** INFORMAL alone: *Are you by your lonesome this weekend?* —see also LONELY —see Usage Note at ALONE

lone wolf /ˌ. ˈ./ *n.* [C] a loner

long¹ /lɔŋ/ *adj.*

1 [great length/distance] measuring a great length or distance, or a greater length or distance than usual, from one end to the other: *I don't like long hair on guys.* | *We went for a long drive in the country.* | *Springfield is* **a long way** *from Chicago.* —opposite SHORT[1] (1)

2 [large amount of time] continuing for a large amount of time, or for a larger amount of time than usual: *The meeting was too long.* | *Exercise can help people live longer, healthier lives.* | *Writing a novel* **takes a long time.** | *It took me* **the longest time** (=a very long time) *to figure out how to open the windows.* | *I can't wait for the days to start* **getting longer.** —opposite SHORT[1] (2)

3 [a particular length/time] [usually after noun] having a particular length or continuing for a particular amount of time: *How long is the movie?* | *The sofa is six feet long.*

4 [seeming long] INFORMAL seeming to continue for a longer time or distance than is usual, especially because you are bored, tired etc.: *It's been* **a long day.**

5 **long hours** **a)** if you work long hours, you work for more time than is usual: *The worst thing about this job is the long hours.* **b)** a large amount of time: *He spent long hours just thinking in his cabin.*

6 [book/list/name etc.] a long book, list etc. has a lot of pages, details etc.: *"Gone With the Wind" is a really long book.* | *He has a long last name that nobody can pronounce.* —opposite SHORT[1] (4)

7 **a long weekend** three or more days, including Saturday and Sunday, when you do not have to go to work or school

8 **in the long run** when something is finished, or at a later time: *All our hard work will be worth it in the long run.*

L

9 clothing long dresses, pants, SLEEVES etc. cover all of your arms or legs: *a long ballgown*
10 all day/year/summer etc. long during all of the day, year etc.
11 at long last after a long period of time; FINALLY: *At long last, change may be coming.*
12 long time no see SPOKEN used to say hello when you have not seen someone for a long time
13 not by a long shot not at all, or not even close or similar to something: *The report isn't finished yet – not by a long shot.*
14 long odds if there are long ODDS against something happening, it is very unlikely that it will happen
15 take the long view (of sth) to think about the effect that something will have in the future rather than what happens now
16 a long look a situation in which you consider something carefully for a long time: *We need to take a long look at how the office is organized.*
17 have come a long way to have developed or changed a lot: *Psychiatry has come a long way since the 1920s.*
18 be a long way from sth to be very different from what is true or from a particular standard or level of development: *Art's hair may be thinning, but he's a long way from being bald.*
19 the long and the short of it SPOKEN used to tell someone that you are telling them everything or the most important information about something: *The long and the short of it is, he just didn't do the work.*
20 go a long way toward doing sth to help greatly in achieving something: *Your contributions will go a long way toward helping children in need.*
21 a long face an expression on someone's face that shows they are unhappy or worried
22 not long for this world likely to die or stop existing soon: *The old corner drugstore is not long for this world.*
23 a long memory an ability to remember things that happened a long time ago
24 long on sth having a lot of a quality, especially a good one: *DeSantos was long on hope, but his team lost anyway.*
25 vowel a long vowel in a word is pronounced for a longer time than a short vowel with the same sound, or it is pronounced as part of a DIPHTHONG
26 long in the tooth INFORMAL too old: *Some of our vehicles are getting a bit long in the tooth.*
27 long drink a) a large cold drink, containing little or no alcohol, served in a tall glass **b)** if you take a long drink, you drink a large amount of liquid at one time —see also **as long as your arm** (ARM[1] (10)), **a long/short haul** (HAUL[2] (2)), **a little (of sth) goes a long way** (LITTLE[2] (5)), LONG SHOT, **it's a long story** (STORY (9)), **make/cut a long story short** (STORY (12)), **in the long/short/near etc. term** (TERM[1] (7)), **have a (long) way to go** (WAY[1] (25))

long² *adv.* **1** for a long time: *I haven't been waiting long.* | *It took me longer to finish than I thought.* **2** at a time that is a long time before or after a particular time: *We met again long after she had gotten married.* | *Your grandfather sold the farm long before you were born.* | *Life was different long ago.* | *It wasn't long before* (=a short time later) *everyone was laughing and having a good time.* **3 for long** [usually in questions and negatives] for a long time: *Have you known the Garretts for very long?* **4 as/so long as a)** used to say that one thing can happen or be true only if another thing happens or is true: *You can go as long as you're home for dinner.* **b)** used to say one thing can continue happening for the same amount of time that another thing is happening or is true: *Pam stayed awake as long as she could.* **c)** used to say that because one thing is true, something else can or should happen or be true: *As long as you're just sitting there, come help me with the groceries.* **5 no longer** also **not any longer** FORMAL used when something used to happen or exist in the past but does not happen or exist now: *The Robins Company is no longer in business.* **6 so long** SPOKEN goodbye

7 before long soon: *The school year will be over before long.* **8 sb/sth won't be long** SPOKEN used to say that someone or something will be ready, will be back, will happen etc. soon: *Wait here. I won't be long.* | *Dinner won't be long – we'll eat in five minutes.* **9 long since** if something has long since happened, it happened a long time ago: *I've long since stopped caring about him.* **10 long live sb/sth** used to show support for a person, idea, principle, or nation: *Long live the King!*

long³ *v.* [I] FORMAL to want something very much, especially when it seems unlikely to happen soon: [+ for] *We longed for a bed after several days of camping.* | [long to do/have sth] *Kyoto is a city I have always longed to visit.* | *a longed-for vacation* —see also LONGING, LONGINGLY

long⁴ *n.* **1 the long and (the) short of it** the most important part or main idea of something: *The long and short of it is that I had too much to drink and said something I shouldn't have.* **2** used in the sizes of clothing for men who are taller than average: *38/42/44 etc. long I think Jim wears a 44 long.*

long. the written abbreviation of LONGITUDE

long-a·wait·ed /ˌ. .'.. ◄/ *adj.* [only before noun] a long-awaited event, moment etc. is one that you have been waiting for a long time: *the long-awaited sequel to her first novel*

long·bow /'lɒŋboʊ/ *n.* [C] a large BOW² (2) made from a long thin curved piece of wood, used in the past for hunting or fighting

long-dis·tance /ˌ. '.. ◄/ *adj.* [only before noun] **1 long-distance runner/driver etc.** someone who runs, travels etc. a long distance **2 long-distance call** a telephone call to someone in a place that is far away —**long-distance** *adv.* —compare LOCAL CALL

long di·vi·sion /ˌ. .'../ *n.* [C,U] a method of dividing one large number by another

long-drawn-out /ˌ. ˌ. '. ◄/ *adj.* [only before noun] continuing for a longer time than necessary: *a long-drawn-out court battle*

lon·gev·i·ty /lɑnˈdʒɛvəṭi, lɔn-/ *n.* [U] **1** FORMAL long life: *The inhabitants enjoy good health and longevity.* **2** TECHNICAL the length of a person or animal's life

long-ex·pect·ed /ˌ. .'.. ◄/ *adj.* [only before noun] a long-expected event, moment etc. is one that you have been expecting for a long time: *Carr announced his long-expected resignation Tuesday.*

Long·fel·low /'lɔŋˌfɛloʊ/, **Hen·ry Wads·worth** /'hɛnri 'wɑdzwəθ/ (1807–1882) a U.S. poet

long-hair /'lɔŋhɛr/ *n.* [C] someone with long hair, especially a HIPPIE

long·hand /'lɔŋhænd/ *n.* [U] writing full words by hand rather than using a machine such as a computer —compare SHORTHAND (1)

long-haul /'. ./ *adj.* a long-haul aircraft or flight goes a very long distance without stopping —compare SHORT-HAUL —see also **the long/short haul** (HAUL² (2))

long·horn /'lɔŋhɔrn/ *n.* **1** [C] a type of cow with long horns that is raised for meat **2** [U] a type of CHEDDAR cheese

long·house /'lɔŋhaʊs/ *n.* [C] a type of house, about 100 feet long, that was used by some Native American tribes

long·ing /'lɔŋɪŋ/ *n.* [singular,U] a strong feeling of wanting something or someone: *The piece lacks the desperate longing of the composer's other works.* | [+ for] *a longing for home*

long·ing·ly /'lɔŋɪŋli/ *adv.* in a way that shows that you want someone or something very much: *Jack looked longingly at the cookies.* —**longing** *adj.*

long·ish /'lɔŋɪʃ/ *adj.* INFORMAL fairly long: *an artist with longish red hair*

Long Is·land /ˌ. '../ an island in the U.S. that contains the New York City BOROUGHs of Queens and Brooklyn, and many other towns

lon·gi·tude /'lɑndʒəˌtud/ *n.* [C,U] a position on the Earth that is measured in degrees east or west of a MERIDIAN (=an imaginary line drawn from the top part of the Earth to the bottom): *The town is at longitude 21° east.* —compare LATITUDE (1)

L

lon·gi·tu·di·nal /ˌlɑndʒəˈtudn-əl/ *adj.* **1** FORMAL relating to the development of something over a period of time: *a longitudinal study of unemployed workers* **2** going from top to bottom, not across: *longitudinal muscles* **3** TECHNICAL measured according to longitude —**longitudinally** *adv.*

long johns /ˈ. ./ *n.* [plural] warm underwear that covers your legs

long jump /ˈ. ./ *n.* **the long jump** a sport in which each competitor tries to jump as far as possible —**long jumper** *n.* [C]

long-last·ing /ˌ. ˈ.-/ *adj.* existing or continuing to work for a long time: *The impact of divorce on children can be long-lasting.* | *long-lasting razor blades*

long-life /ˌ. ˈ.-/ *adj.* long-life batteries (BATTERY (1)), LIGHT BULBS etc. are made so that they continue working for a long time

long-lived /ˌlɔŋ ˈlɪvd-/ *adj.* living or existing a long time: *Ostriches are long-lived birds.* | *the band's long-lived appeal* —compare SHORT-LIVED

long-lost /ˈ. ./ *adj.* [only before noun] lost or not seen for a long time: *long-lost treasures* | *a long-lost uncle*

long-play·ing rec·ord /ˌ. .. ˈ../ *n.* [C] an LP

long-range /ˌ. ˈ./ *adj.* [usually before noun] **1** relating to a time that continues far into the future: *the city's long-range development plans* **2** a long-range missile, bomb etc. is able to hit something that is a long way away

long-run·ning /ˌ. ˈ.-/ *adj.* [usually before noun] a long-running battle, show etc. has been happening for a long time: *a long-running FBI investigation*

long·shore·man /ˌlɔŋˈʃɔrmən, lɔŋˌʃɔrmən/ *n.* [C] someone whose job is to load and unload ships at a DOCK

long shot /ˈ. ./ *n.* [C] INFORMAL **1** someone or something with very little chance of success: *Murphy is a long shot for the position.* **2 not by a long shot** not at all, or not nearly: *This isn't over, not by a long shot.*

long-stand·ing /ˌ. ˈ.-/ *adj.* having continued or existed for a long time: *a long-standing agreement between the two countries* | *a tradition of long-standing*

long-suf·fer·ing /ˌ. ˈ.-/ *adj.* [usually before noun] patient in spite of problems, other people's annoying behavior, or unhappiness: *a long-suffering wife*

long-term /ˌ. ˈ. / *adj.* continuing for a long period of time into the future, or relating to what will happen in the distant future: *long-term investments* | *People need to think long-term.* —see also **in the long/short/near etc. term** (TERM¹ (7)) —opposite SHORT-TERM

long·time, long-time /ˈlɔŋtaɪm/ *adj.* [only before noun] having existed or continued to be a particular thing for a long time: *a longtime member of the Democratic Party*

long wave /ˌ. ˈ./ *written abbreviation* **LW** *n.* [U] radio broadcasting or receiving on waves of 1000 meters or more in length —compare MEDIUM WAVE, SHORTWAVE

long·ways /ˈlɔŋweɪz/ *adv.* LONGWISE

long-wearing /ˌlɔŋˈwɛrɪŋ-/ *adj.* long-wearing clothes, shoes etc. remain in good condition for a long time even when they are used a lot

long-wind·ed /ˌ. ˈ.-/ *adj.* continuing to talk for too long or using too many words in a way that is boring: *long-winded politicians*

long·wise /ˈlɔŋwaɪz/ *adv.* in the direction of the longest side; LENGTHWISE: *Cut the cucumber in half longwise and scoop out the seeds.*

loo·fah, loofa /ˈlufə/ *n.* [C] a rough type of SPONGE¹ (1), made from the dried inner part of a tropical fruit

loo·gie /ˈlugi/ *n.* [C] SLANG, PHLEGM (=thick sticky liquid from your throat) that you SPIT (=force) out of your mouth —see also **hawk a loogie** (HAWK² (2))

look up

He looked the word up in his dictionary.

look¹ /lʊk/ *v.*
1 see [I] to deliberately turn your eyes so that you can see something: *If you look closely, you can see ducks at the edge of the lake.* | [+ **at**] *"I have to go," Mel said, looking at his watch.* | [+ **through/toward/across etc.**] *The children looked sadly through the locked gates.* | [**look away/up/down** etc.] *She smiled sadly then looked away.* —see picture at SEE¹ —see Usage Notes at GAZE¹ and SEE¹
2 search [I] to try and find someone or something that is hidden or lost, using your eyes: *I've looked everywhere, but I can't find my gloves.* | *Did you look under the bed?* | [**look for sth**] *Could you help me look for my notebook?*
3 seem [linking verb] to seem to be something, especially by having a particular appearance: *Do these jeans make me look fat?* | *When I saw him last week he didn't look very good.* | *She looks just like someone I used to work with.* | **look as if/though** *This car looks as if it could cost more.* | *With all the commotion it looked as if the circus had come to town.*
4 strange-looking/good-looking/smooth-looking etc. having a particular type of appearance: *a funny-looking dog*
5 look over your shoulder to be nervous or worried that something bad is going to happen to you: *Since half of the staff was laid off, we're all looking over our shoulders.*
6 be looking to do sth INFORMAL to be planning or expecting to do something: *We're not just looking to make money.*
7 look before you leap used to say that it is wise to think about possible dangers or difficulties before doing something

SPOKEN PHRASES

8 look a) used to tell someone to look at something that you think is interesting, surprising etc.: *Look! There's a bluejay!* | [+ **at**] *Look at me, Mommy!* | [**look what/how/where** etc.] *Look how tall he's gotten!* **b)** said to get someone's attention so that you can tell them something, or to emphasize what you are saying when you are annoyed: *Look, I'm very serious about this.*
9 look at that! used to tell someone to look at something that you think is interesting, bad etc.: *Wow, look at that! It's huge!*
10 (I'm) just looking used when you are in a store, to say that you are only looking at things, and do not intend to buy anything now: *"Do you need help with anything?" "No thanks. We're just looking."*
11 look the other way a) to deliberately ignore a problem or something bad that someone else is doing: *Politicians have looked the other way while children go hungry.* **b)** to turn your head and look in the opposite direction, especially to avoid looking at someone or something
12 look out! used to tell someone to pay attention or warn them that they are in danger: *Look out! You almost hit that cat!*

L

13 it looks like... used to say that it is likely that someone will do something or something will happen: *If this rain keeps up, it looks like we'll have to cancel the picnic.*

14 look sb in the eye/face to look directly at someone when you are speaking to them, especially to show that you are not afraid of them or that you are telling the truth: *Timmy, look me in the eye and tell me that you didn't take that money.*

15 look who's here! said when someone arrives without being expected: *Well, look who's here! It's Jill and Paul!*

16 don't look now used when you see someone you want to avoid: *Don't look now – here comes Kristen.*

17 look at you! said especially to a child when you want them to pay attention to how they look: *Look at you! You're filthy!*

18 look what you've done! used to angrily tell someone to look at the result of a mistake they have made or something bad they have done: *Now look what you've done! You'll have to clean it up.*

19 lookin' good! SLANG used to tell someone that they look attractive

20 not be looking yourself to appear tired, unhappy, sick etc., when you are not this way usually: *Are you okay? You haven't been looking yourself lately.*

21 look what the cat dragged in! said when someone comes into a room or building late or in a worse than normal condition

22 look here OLD-FASHIONED used to get someone's attention in order to tell them something, especially when you are annoyed with them: *Look here, you can't say things like that to me!*

23 look sb up and down to look at someone, examining them carefully from their head to their feet, as if you are judging their appearance

24 look down your nose at sb/sth INFORMAL to behave as if you think that someone or something is not good enough for you: *I can go in a shirt and jeans and no one looks down his nose at me.*

25 never/don't look a gift horse in the mouth INFORMAL used to tell someone to be grateful for something that has been given to them, instead of asking questions about it or finding something wrong with it

26 face a direction [I] if a building looks in a particular direction, it faces that direction: *The cabin looks east, so we get the sun first thing in the morning.*

27 look daggers at sb to look at someone with a very angry expression on your face

look after sb/sth *phr. v.* [T] **1** to take care of someone by helping them, giving them what they need, or keeping them safe: *Will you look after the cat while we're gone?* **2** to be responsible for dealing with something and making sure nothing bad happens to it: *Clayton has a manager who looks after his business interests.*

look ahead *phr. v.* [I] to plan future situations, events etc., or to think about the future: *It's been a rough year, but the Joneses are looking ahead to the future.*

look around *phr. v.* **1** [I,T look around sth] to look at what is in a place such as a building, store, town etc., especially when you are walking: *We have about three hours to look around the downtown.* **2** [I] to search for something: *"Have you found a house yet?" "No, we're still looking around."* | [+ for] *She got the bread out and looked around for a plate.*

look at sb/sth *phr. v.* [T] **1** to read something quickly, but not thoroughly: *I haven't had a chance to look at the report yet.* **2** if someone with a special skill, such as a doctor, looks at something that is damaged or broken, they examine it and try to find out what is wrong with it: *You should get the doctor to look at that cut.* **3** to study and consider something, especially in order to decide what to do: *Wildlife experts are looking at ways to protect the animals.* **4 look at sb** SPOKEN used to tell someone to consider someone else as an example of something: *Look at Eric. He didn't go to college, and he's doing*

all right. **5 not much to look at** INFORMAL if someone is not much to look at, they are not attractive

look back *phr. v.* [I] **1** to think about something that happened in the past: [+ on/to/at] *Looking back at the '80s isn't much fun for Cole.* | ***Looking back on it***, *I'm glad I was not offered the position.* **2 never look back** to not think about what has happened in the past, especially because you are very successful and are thinking about the future: *After Berg left baseball in 1978, he never looked back.*

look down on sb/sth *phr. v.* [T] to think that you are better than someone else: *Many of the natives looked down on the new immigrants.*

look for sb/sth *phr. v.* [T] **1** to try to find someone who is not where they should be: *Brad was looking for you last night.* **2** to try to find a particular type of thing or person that you need or want: *How long have you been looking for a job?* | *Leslie, you're **just the person I was looking for**! Come help me with this.* **3 be looking for trouble** INFORMAL to be behaving in a way that makes it likely that problems will happen: *The kid with the knife was looking for trouble.*

look forward to sth *phr. v.* [T] to be excited and pleased about something that is going to happen: *I'm looking forward to Halloween this year.* | [**look forward to doing sth**] *We're really looking forward to skiing in Aspen.*

look in *phr. v.* [I] INFORMAL to make a short visit to someone, while you are going somewhere else, especially if they are sick or need help: [+ on] *Could you go up and look in on Granny for a minute?*

look into sth *phr. v.* [T] to try to find out the truth about a problem, crime etc. in order to solve it: *A special investigator will look into the murders.*

look on *phr. v.* **1** [I] to watch something happening, without being involved in it or trying to stop it: *The crowd looked on as the two men fought.* **2** [T **look on/upon** sth] to consider something in a particular way, or as a particular thing: [**look on/upon sth as sth**] *My family looks on divorce as a sin.* | [**look on/upon sth with sth**] *Others in the community looked upon them with contempt.*

look out for sb/sth *phr. v.* [T] **1** to pay attention to what is happening around you so you will notice a particular person or thing if you see them, or you will be prepared for anything dangerous that might happen: *In this section of the river, you have to look out for snakes.* **2** to try to protect someone or something from anything bad that might happen, or to try to give them advantages: *Residents must look out for each other.* **3 look out for yourself/for number one** to think only about what will bring you an advantage, and not think about other people

look out on sth *phr. v.* [T] to face a particular direction, so that you can see things in that direction: *My apartment window looks out on the park.*

look sth/sb ↔ **over** *phr. v.* [T] to examine something quickly, without paying much attention to detail: *Can you look this letter over before I send it?* —see also OVERLOOK[1]

look through sb/sth *phr. v.* [T] **1** to look for something among a pile of papers, in a drawer, in someone's pockets etc.: *I caught my mother looking through my stuff.* **2** to not notice someone or pretend that you do not see them: *I said hello to Paige, but she just **looked right through** me.*

look to/toward sb/sth *phr. v.* [T] **1** to depend on someone to provide help, advice etc.: [+ for] *Cities are looking to state governments for aid.* **2** to pay attention to something or consider it, especially in order to improve it: *It is doubtful that any company would look to this site for development.* **3** to think about something in the future and plan for it, instead of thinking about the past: *The ballet company is looking toward the 21st century.*

look up *phr. v.* **1** [T **look** sth ↔ **up**] to try to find information in a book, on a computer etc.: *If you don't know the word, look it up in the dictionary.* **2** [I] if a situation is looking up, it is improving: ***Things are looking up*** *for downtown businesses.* **3** [T **look** ↔ **sb up**] to visit someone you know, especially when you have come to the place where they live for a different reason: *If you ever get to Nashville, look me up.*

look up to sb phr. v. [T] to admire or respect someone: *Kids need role models to look up to.*

look² n.

1 **looking at sth** [C usually singular] an act of looking at something: *Wow! Take a look at that moon. It's huge! | If you take a good look* (=look carefully) *I think you'll see it's a raccoon. | I'm not sure. I didn't get a look at his face. | Take a look around and see if you like the place.*

2 **considering sth** [C] an act of reading something quickly or considering it, especially in order to decide what to do: *Let me take a look at this tonight, and I'll discuss it with you tomorrow.*

3 **expression** [C] an expression that you make with your eyes or face to show how you feel: *Heather gave him an angry look. | I swear the cat gave me a dirty look* (=an unfriendly look) *when I pushed him off the sofa.*

4 **description** [C] a short explanation or description of something: *Here's a brief look at some of the problems we'll be facing in the coming year.*

5 **looks** [plural] someone's physical attractiveness: *Most actors are afraid of losing their looks* (=becoming less attractive). *| She gets her good looks* (=attractive appearance) *from her mother.*

6 **appearance** [C usually singular] the appearance of something or someone: *Computer graphics gave the creature a watery look. | I don't like the look of that bruise – maybe you should see a doctor. | By the looks on their faces, I don't think they had a very good time.*

7 **if looks could kill** used to say that someone looked at someone else in a very angry way: *If looks could kill, Barlowe would have dropped dead right there.*

8 **fashion** [singular] a fashionable style in clothes, hair, furniture etc.: *He's trying for a '70s disco look.*

look·a·like, lookalike /'.. .,./ n. [C] INFORMAL someone who looks very similar to someone else, especially someone famous: *an Elvis look-alike*

look·er /'lokə/ n. [C] INFORMAL someone who is attractive, usually a woman

looker-on /,.. './ n. plural **lookers-on** [C] an ONLOOKER

look·ing glass /'.. ,./ n. [C] OLD-FASHIONED a MIRROR

look·it /'lokɪt/ interjection NONSTANDARD **1** used to get someone's attention so that you can tell them something, especially when you are annoyed: *Lookit, there are only three of us, so we all have to help.* **2** used to tell someone to look at something that you think is interesting, surprising etc.: *Lookit! I think he's going to throw up.*

look·out /'lok-aot/ n. **1 be on the lookout for sth** to continuously watch a place or pay attention in order to find something you want or to be ready for problems or opportunities: *You've got to be on the lookout for snakes around here.* **2 keep a lookout** to keep watching carefully for something or someone, especially for danger: *Soldiers kept a lookout for enemy planes through the night.* **3** [C] someone whose duty is to watch carefully for something, especially danger **4** [C] a place for a lookout to watch from

look-see /,. './ n. [C] INFORMAL a quick look at something: *We moved in closer for a look-see.*

loom¹ /lum/ v. [I] **1** [always + adv./prep.] to appear as a large, unclear shape, especially in a threatening way: *The mountain loomed in front of us.* **2** if a problem or difficulty looms, it is likely to happen very soon: *The two countries believe that a crisis is looming.* **3 loom large** to seem important, worrying, and difficult to avoid: *My 40th birthday has loomed larger in my mind with each passing day.*

loom² n. [C] a frame or machine on which thread is woven into cloth

loon /lun/ n. [C] **1** a large North American bird that eats fish and that makes a long wild sound **2** a silly or strange person —see also **crazy as a loon** (CRASY¹ (8))

loon·y¹ /'luni/ n. plural **loonies** [C] **1** SPOKEN someone who behaves in a crazy or silly way: *Janet's brother is a complete loony.* **2** CANADIAN also **loonie** a Canadian one-dollar coin

loony² adj. also **loony tunes** /'.. ./ **loonier, looniest** INFORMAL silly, crazy, or strange: *a loony idea*

loony bin /'.. ,./ n. [C] INFORMAL an expression meaning a hospital for people who are mentally ill, that is usually considered offensive

loop¹ /lup/ n. [C]
1 **shape or line** a shape like a curve or a circle made by a line curving back toward itself, or a piece of wire, string etc. that has this shape: *A loop of wire held the gate shut. | belt loops* (=cloth loops used for holding a belt on pants)

2 **knock/throw sb for a loop** INFORMAL to surprise and upset someone: *His response really threw me for a loop.*

3 **be out of the loop** to not be part of a group of people that makes decisions or gets information: *The Vice President insists that he was out of the loop at the time the arms scandal was taking place.* —opposite **be in/inside the loop**

4 **computer** a set of operations in a computer PROGRAM that repeats constantly

5 **film/tape** a film or TAPE¹ (1) loop contains images or sounds that are repeated again and again

6 **plane** also **loop-the-loop** a pattern like a circle made by an airplane flying up, upside down, and then down

loop² v. **1** [I,T] to make a loop or make something into a loop: *A man in the next car was looping a tie around his neck.* **2** [I] to move in a circular direction that forms the shape of a loop: *The space probe looped toward Jupiter.* **3 loop the loop** to fly an airplane in a loop

loop·hole /'luphool/ n. [C] a small mistake in a law that makes it possible to avoid doing something that the law is supposed to make you do: *tax loopholes*

loop·y /'lupi/ adj. **loopier, loopiest** INFORMAL crazy or strange: *a loopy sense of humor*

loose¹ /lus/ adj.
1 **not fastened** not firmly attached or fastened in place: *a loose screw | One of Sean's front teeth is loose. | One of my buttons came loose.*

2 **not tied tightly** not tied or fastened very tightly: *My shoelaces are loose. | a loose knot*

3 **clothes** loose clothes are big and do not fit your body tightly: *a loose sweatshirt*

4 **free** free from being controlled or held in a CAGE, prison, or institution: *A 34-year-old inmate broke loose from the sheriff's office Saturday. | In 1882 pigs were turned loose on the streets of New York City to eat garbage. | Don't let your dog loose on the beach.*

a loose pair of pants

5 **not attached** not tied together, fastened to anything else etc.: *loose papers | The boat broke loose from the dock.*

6 **cloth** woven in a way that is not tight, so that there are small holes between the threads: *linen cloth with a loose weave*

7 **not exact** [usually before noun] not exact or thoroughly done: *The title is a loose translation of the Korean original. | a loose interpretation of the law*

8 **not controlled** [only before noun] not strictly controlled or organized: *a loose group of local organizations*

9 loose change coins that you have in your bag or pocket

10 loose cannon someone who cannot be trusted because they say or do things you do not want them to

11 loose ends parts of something that have not been completed or correctly done: *His new movie will tie up some of the loose ends from the last one.*

L

12 cut loose INFORMAL to start enjoying yourself in a happy, noisy way after a period of controlled behavior: *I'm ready to cut loose and enjoy the weekend.*

13 let loose (sth) to relax and speak or behave in an uncontrolled way: *She let loose a string of four-letter words that shocked everyone.*

14 be at loose ends to have nothing to do

15 loose bowels/stools NOT TECHNICAL having a problem in which the waste from your BOWELs has too much liquid in it

16 turn sb loose on sth to allow someone to deal with something in the way they want to: *He had a lot of ability, so his boss decided to turn him loose on the project.*

17 turn sb loose on sb to get someone to argue, fight, criticize etc. someone else for you: *Shapiro turned his assistant loose on his critics.*

18 hang/stay loose SPOKEN used to tell someone to stay calm, or not to worry about something

19 talk OLD-FASHIONED not careful about what you say or who is listening

20 immoral OLD-FASHIONED behaving in a way that is considered to be sexually immoral: *a loose woman*

21 loose lips sink ships OLD-FASHIONED used to say that if you tell other people's secrets you will cause problems for them —**loosely** *adv.*: *A towel was loosely wrapped around his neck.* | *The film is loosely based on the novel.* —**looseness** *n.* [U]

loose² *v.* [T] **1** to untie someone or something, especially an animal: *Police fired tear gas and loosed police dogs.* **2** to make something bad or negative begin to happen: *The recent court case has loosed a number of racist attacks.* **3** to let a substance escape or flow out of something: *The tanker loosed 13,000 gallons of pesticide into the river.* **4** LITERARY to shoot an ARROW (1), a bullet from a gun etc.

loose sth on/upon sb/sth *phr. v.* [T] to allow something dangerous or harmful to begin to affect a situation or other people: *Many of the evils loosed upon humanity in World War II might have been avoided.*

loose³ *n.* **be on the loose** if a criminal or dangerous animal is on the loose, they have escaped from prison or from their CAGE

loose⁴ *adv.* NONSTANDARD loosely —see also **play fast and loose with sb/sth** (PLAY¹ (24))

loose-fit·ting /ˌ. ˈ.. / *adj.* loose-fitting clothes are big and do not fit your body closely, so that they are comfortable

loose-knit /ˌ. ˈ.◂ / *adj.* [only before noun] a loose-knit group of people are not closely related to each other: *a loose-knit coalition of human rights groups*

loose-leaf /ˈluslif/ *adj.* [only before noun] having pages that can be put in and removed easily: *a loose-leaf binder*

loos·en /ˈlusən/ *v.* **1** [I,T] to make something less tight or less firmly fastened, or to become less tight or less firmly fastened: *After the meal we all had to loosen our belts.* | *The screws in this shelf have loosened.* **2** [T] to make laws, rules etc. less strict: *Congress has loosened some of the restrictions on immigration.* **3 loosen your grip/hold a)** to reduce the control or power you have over someone or something: [+ on] *The government has loosened its hold on the media considerably.* **b)** to start holding someone less tightly than you were before: *When the policeman loosened his grip, Biff ran away.* **4 loosen sb's tongue** to make someone talk more than usual, especially about things they should not talk about

loosen up *phr. v.* **1** [I,T **loosen** sb ↔ **up**] to become more relaxed and feel less worried or serious: *We used to fight a lot, but Dad has loosened up a little lately.* **2** [I,T **loosen** sth ↔ **up**] if your muscles loosen up, or if you loosen them up, they stop feeling stiff

loos·ey-goos·ey /ˌlusi ˈgusi/ *adj.* SPOKEN, INFORMAL very relaxed, informal, and not well organized

loot¹ /lut/ *v.* [I,T] to steal things, especially from stores or homes that have been damaged in a war or

RIOT: *Rioters looted stores and set fires.* —**looter** *n.* [C] —**looting** *n.* [U]

loot² *n.* [U] **1** INFORMAL goods or money that have been stolen **2** goods taken by soldiers from a place where they have won a battle **3** SLANG money: *I'd love to win the lottery and take home all that loot.* **4** INFORMAL, HUMOROUS things that you have bought or been given in large amounts: *Jodie came home from the mall with bags of loot.*

lop /lɑp/ *v.* **lopped, lopping** [T] to cut branches from a tree, especially with a single strong movement

lop sth off *phr. v.* [T] **1** to cut a part of something off **2** to remove a particular amount from a price or charge: *The judge lopped $1.1 million off the $4.2 million award.*

lope /loʊp/ *v.* [I always + adv./prep.] to run easily with long steps: [+ along/across/up etc.] *Karen loped up two flights of stairs.* —**lope** *n.* [singular]

lop-eared /ˈ. ./ *adj.* a lop-eared animal such as a rabbit has long ears that hang down

lop·sid·ed /ˈlɑpˌsaɪdɪd/ *adj.* **1** having one side that is lower, larger, or heavier than the other: *a lopsided grin* **2** unequal or uneven, especially in a way that seems unfair: *a lopsided vote on the abortion bill*

lo·qua·cious /loʊˈkweɪʃəs/ *adj.* FORMAL liking to talk a lot, sometimes too much: *The normally loquacious Simpson had nothing to say.* —**loquaciousness** also **loquacity** /loʊˈkwæsəti/ *n.* [U]

Lord /lɔrd/ *n.* **1 a)** a title of God or Jesus Christ, used when praying to God: *Thank you, Lord, for your blessings.* **b) the Lord** God or Jesus Christ, used when talking about God: *The Lord helps and guides us.* **2 the Lord's Day** Sunday, considered as the holy day of the Christian religion

---

SPOKEN PHRASES

3 Lord knows a) used to emphasize that something is true: *Lord knows I used to stay out late when I was in high school.* **b)** also **Lord only knows** used when you do not know the answer to something: *Lord knows how old she is now.* **4 (Good) Lord!/Oh Lord!** said when you are suddenly surprised, annoyed, or worried about something: *Good Lord, Tom! What are you doing?* **5 Lord willing** OLD-FASHIONED used to say that you hope nothing will prevent something from happening: *We'll finally be able to take that trip this year, Lord willing.*

---

lord¹ /lɔrd/ *n.* [C] **1** also **Lord** a man who has a particular position in the ARISTOCRACY, especially in Britain, or his title: *Lord Tennyson* —compare LADY (4) **2** a man in MEDIEVAL Europe who was very powerful and owned a lot of land: *the feudal lords* **3 sb's lord and master** HUMOROUS someone who must be obeyed because they have power over someone else

lord² *v.* **lord it over sb** to behave in a way that shows you think you are better or more powerful than someone else: *He didn't use his position on the council to lord it over people.*

lord·ly /ˈlɔrdli/ *adj.* **1** behaving in a way that shows you think you are better or more important than other people: *a lordly disdain for the common man* **2** very grand or impressive: *a lordly feast*

Lord's Prayer /ˌ. ˈ./ *n.* **the Lord's Prayer** the most important prayer of the Christian religion

Lor·dy, lordy /ˈlɔrdi/ *interjection* SPOKEN, OLD-FASHIONED used when you are suddenly surprised, annoyed, or worried about something: *Lordy, there are a lot of people here.*

lore /lɔr/ *n.* [U] knowledge or information about a subject, for example nature or magic, that is not written down but that one person tells to another person: *According to local lore, a ghost still haunts the castle.*

lor·gnette /lɔrˈnyɛt/ *n.* [C] a pair of GLASSES with a long handle at the side that you hold in front of your eyes

lor·ry /ˈlɔri, ˈlɑri/ *n. plural* **lorries** [C] BRITISH a TRUCK

Los Al·a·mos /lɔs ˈæləmoʊs, lɑs/ a town in the U.S. state of New Mexico where the first ATOM BOMB and HYDROGEN BOMB were developed

Los An·ge·les /lɔs ˈændʒələs, -liz/ the largest city in the U.S. state of California

lose /luz/ *v. past tense and past participle* **lost**

1 `not have anymore` [T] to stop having something that is important to you or that you need: *Michelle lost her job again.* | *Tim's brother **lost everything** in the earthquake.* —opposite GAIN[1]

2 `cannot find` [T] to be unable to find someone or something: *Stephen keeps losing his gloves.* | *Oh there you are – I thought I'd lost you.*

3 `not win` [I,T] to not win a game, argument, war etc.: *I'm not playing tennis with her any more – I always lose.* | *Noel lost the argument.* | [+ **to/against**] *The Vikings lost to the Packers 27–7.* | [+ **by**] *Mr. Ewing lost by at least 39,000 votes.* | [**lose sth by sth**] *Penn State lost the game by only one basket.* | [**lose sth to/against sb**] *Reseda High lost the homecoming game to Birmingham.* —opposite WIN[1]

4 `money` **a)** if a business loses money, it earns less than it spends: *NRT Corporation lost $2.2 million in the most recent quarter on sales of $6.3 million.* **b)** if a person loses money, they have less money than they had before, often because of a bad INVESTMENT: *Investors lost several million dollars on the project.*

5 `weight` [T] to get rid of weight and become thinner: *You look different. Have you lost weight?* | *I need to lose 10 pounds before the wedding.*

6 lose your memory/sight/voice etc. to stop having a particular ability or sense: *McGarrity lost his sight in the Vietnam war.* | *She lost her voice* (=was temporarily unable to speak) *and had to cancel her performance.*

7 `stop having a quality` [T] to not have a particular quality, belief, attitude etc. anymore: *The kids were losing interest in the game* | *He was going to go talk to her, but he lost his nerve* (=stopped being confident). | *Don't lose heart* (=become disappointed and unhappy) *– you'll do better next time.* | *He lost his head* (=stopped being calm) *and, in a state of panic, started running.* | **lose your temper/cool** (=to become angry)

8 lose an arm/leg etc. to have an arm, leg etc. cut off after an injury in an accident or in a war: *He lost his right arm in a motorcycle accident.*

9 lose sb sth to make someone stop having something that is important, or to make them not win a game, argument etc.: *Allegations of corruption lost Wilson the election.*

10 lose your balance/footing to become unsteady or fall: *Sam lost his footing on the rocks and fell in the stream.*

11 lose sb a) INFORMAL to confuse someone when you are trying to explain something to them: *You've lost me. Can you repeat that?* **b)** used to say that someone has died, especially when you do not want to upset anyone by saying it directly: *Fern lost her husband six years ago.* | *Oh, I didn't know she'd lost the baby* (=the baby died before being born). **c)** to escape from someone who is chasing or following you: *Whew! I think we lost him.* **d)** to stop being able to follow someone: *He tried to follow her on foot but lost her in the crowd.*

12 lose your life to die: *Over 100 soldiers lost their lives.*

13 `waste` [T] to waste time or opportunities etc.: *We lose time whenever we have to make a change.* | *Sorry, you lost your chance.* | *Hurry – there's no time to lose.* | *Johnson lost no time in applying for the grant* (=she did it immediately).

14 lose touch (with sb/sth) a) to not speak to, write to, or see someone for a long time, so that you do not know where they are: *Over the years we just lost touch with each other.* **b)** to not know the most recent or important information about something and therefore be unable to understand it correctly: *A lot of producers have lost touch with what makes good music.* | *Sometimes I think Darrin's lost touch with reality.*

15 lose your touch INFORMAL to stop having a special ability or skill: *Goldman's script is excellent, proving he hasn't lost his touch.*

16 lose it SPOKEN **a)** to suddenly start shouting, laughing, crying etc. a lot because you think something is very bad, funny, or wrong: *Whatever Brad said must have made her angry because she totally*

lost it. **b)** to become crazy: *After her mom and dad were killed in the car accident, Ginny just seemed to lose it.*

17 lose sight of sb/sth a) to stop being able to see someone or something: *He lost sight of the car as it went around the curve.* **b)** to forget about the most important part of something you are doing: *We can't lose sight of our goals.*

18 lose your way/bearings a) to not know where you are or which direction you should go: *I completely lose my bearings when I go outside the city.* **b)** to not know what you should do or what you believe in: *The Congressional black caucus has lost its way since Republicans took over Congress.* | *When my wife left me, I kind of lost my bearings for a while.*

19 lose your mind to become crazy or to stop behaving sensibly: *What are you doing on the roof? Have you lost your mind?*

20 lose your heart to sb to start to love someone very much

21 `clock/watch` [T] if a clock or watch loses time, it works too slowly: *That clock loses about 2 minutes a day.* —opposite GAIN[1] (10)

22 sth loses sth in (the) translation used to say that something is not exactly the same when it is done in a new or different way or when it is said in a different language: *The joke loses something in the translation.*

23 lose yourself in sth to be so involved in something that you do not notice anything else: *Small children have the ability to lose themselves in imaginary worlds.*

24 lose face to not be trusted or respected anymore, especially in a public situation, because of something you have done

25 lose altitude if an aircraft loses ALTITUDE it drops to a lower height in the sky

lose out *phr. v.* [I] to not get something such as a job, business contract, or profit because someone else gets it instead: *The union lost out in this round of negotiations.* | [+ **to**] *Tierney was nominated for the Oscar, but lost out to Joan Crawford.* | [+ **on**] *If you don't act soon, you'll lose out on the low interest rates.*

USAGE NOTE: LOSE

WORD CHOICE: lose, miss, lost, missing, disappear
Use **lose** if you cannot find something: *I lost my favorite pen.* Use **miss** if you do not attend a class, meeting etc. that you regularly go to or that you intended to go to: *You've been missing a lot of school lately.* Use **lost** to describe someone who does not know where they are, or someone or something that you cannot find: *We have a lost little boy at the customer service desk.* Use **missing** to describe someone or something that you have been looking for, especially when the situation is serious: *a missing Rembrandt* | *Police continue to search for the missing children.* Use **disappear** when the way in which someone or something has been lost seems very strange: *Five planes disappeared off the coast of Florida.* | *The seven-year-old girl disappeared on her way home from school* (But don't say: *the disappeared planes* or *the disappeared girl*).

---

los·er /ˈluzɚ/ *n.* [C] **1** someone who has lost a competition or game: *My dad taught us to be **good losers** (=someone who behaves well after losing).* | *a **bad/sore/poor loser** (=someone who behaves badly after losing)* **2** someone who is in a worse situation than they were, because of something that has happened: *If these budget cuts are made, the big losers will be the poor and minorities.* **3** someone who is never successful in life, work, or relationships: *I swear Joe's **a born loser**.*

loss /lɒs/ *n.*

1 `no longer having sth` [C,U] the fact of not having something anymore that you used to have, or the action of losing something: *About 35,000 job losses are expected.* | *Weight loss should be gradual.* | [+ **of**] *the loss of innocence*

L

2 [money] [C,U] money that a business, person, government etc. had before, but that it does not have anymore: [+ of] *The company reported losses of $82 million for the third quarter.* | *She had to sell her house at a loss* (=for less money than she paid for it).

3 [game] [C] an occasion when you do not win a game or a competition; DEFEAT[1]: [+ to] *a 52–14 loss to Georgia Tech* | *three wins and four losses*

4 [life] [C,U] the death of someone: *I was sorry to hear about the loss of your mother.* | *U.S. forces withdrew after **suffering heavy losses**.* | *The war has led to a tragic **loss of life**.*

5 [feeling] [U] a feeling of being sad or lonely because someone or something is not there anymore: *He looks back on his youth with an overwhelming **sense of loss**.*

6 be at a loss a) to be confused and uncertain about what to do or say: *State officials are **at a loss to explain** the sudden rise in unemployment.* | *When she won the award, she seemed **at a loss for words*** (=she could not think of what to say). **b)** to not have enough of something: [+ for] *I was never at a loss for female companionship.*

7 [problem] [singular] a disadvantage caused by someone or something leaving or being removed: *His retirement is **a great loss** to the entire community.*

8 it's sb's loss SPOKEN said when you think someone is stupid for not taking a good opportunity: *Well, if he doesn't want to come it's his loss.* —see also **cut your losses** (CUT[1] (11)), **a dead stop/silence/hush/loss etc.** (DEAD[1] (12))

loss lead·er /ˈ. ˌ../ *n.* [C] something that is sold at a very low price to make people go into a store

lost[1] /lɔst/ *adj.*

1 [cannot be found] something that is lost is something you had but cannot now find: *a lost dog* | *My keys are lost again.*

2 [cannot find your way] not knowing where you are or which way to go: *a lost tourist* | *We **got lost** driving around the city.*

3 [wasted] not used in the right way; WASTED: *New computer systems could save us millions of dollars in lost time.* | *Several good business opportunities have been lost.*

4 feel/be lost to not feel confident or able to take care of yourself: *I'd be lost without all your help.*

5 [destroyed/killed] destroyed, ruined, or killed: *Several ships were **lost at sea** in the storm.* | *More than 250 troops were **lost in battle*** (=killed in the war).

6 be lost on sb if something is lost on someone, they do not understand or want to accept it: *The joke was lost on Chris.* | *All my warnings were completely lost on Beth.*

7 Get lost! SPOKEN used to tell someone in an impolite way to go away or stop annoying you

8 a lost cause something that has no chance of succeeding: *Trying to make it to the playoffs at this point is a lost cause.*

9 [not won] a lost game, battle etc. was not won

10 [not noticing] [not before noun] thinking so hard about something or being so interested in something that you do not notice what is happening around you: *For a moment she seemed **lost in thought**.*

11 get lost (in sth) to be forgotten or not noticed in a complicated process or busy time: *It's easy for your main points to get lost in the middle of a long essay.* | **lost in the crowd/shuffle** (=not noticed in a large group or busy situation)

12 [confused] completely confused by a complicated explanation: *"Did you understand him?" "No, I'm completely lost."*

13 [not existing] not existing or owned anymore: *the lost dreams of her youth*

14 lost soul OFTEN HUMOROUS someone who does not seem to know what they should do —see also **give sb up for dead/lost etc.** at **give up** (GIVE[1]), **there is no love lost between sb and sb** (LOVE[2] (10)), **make up for lost time** at **make up for** sth (MAKE[1]) —see Usage Note at LOSE

lost[2] *v.* the past tense and past participle of LOSE

lost-and-found /ˌ. . ˈ./ *n.* **the lost-and-found** a place where things that are lost are kept until someone comes to claim them

lot[1] /lɑt/ *quantifier, pron.* INFORMAL **1 a lot a)** a large amount, quantity, or number: *Wow, Nancy, you really wrote a lot.* | [+ of] *A hundred dollars was a lot of money in 1901.* | *There's **an awful lot** (=a very large amount) of cake left.* | *A lot of times* (=usually or very often) *we just sat around and talked.* | **a lot to do/see/eat etc.** *There's still a lot to do before we're ready.* **b)** [+ comparative] much: *You'll get there a lot quicker if you drive.* | *This is a lot more work than I thought it would be.* **c)** very often: *He gets drunk a lot with his friends.* —see also LOTS

2 have a lot on your mind to have a lot of problems that you are worried about: *Stacy didn't go to the party on Saturday because she had a lot on her mind.*

3 have a lot on your plate INFORMAL to have many problems to deal with or work to do: *Harris has a lot on his plate at the moment. Why don't we give the project to Melinda?* **4 have a lot going for you** to have many advantages and good qualities that will bring success: *With her brains and good looks, she certainly has a lot going for her.* —opposite **not have much going for you 5 have a lot of explaining to do** to be responsible for a bad situation, or to seem to be responsible: *Jacobs has a lot of explaining to do for the company's losses.* —see also **a fat lot of good/use** (FAT[1] (9)), **thanks a lot** (THANKS[1] (2)) —see Usage Note at MUCH[1]

lot[2] *n.* [C]

1 [land] an area of land used for building on or for another particular purpose: *We used to play baseball in the vacant lot.* | *a used-car lot* —see also PARKING LOT

2 [sb's lot] the work, responsibilities, social position etc. that you have, especially when they could be better: *She seems happy enough with her lot in life.*

3 [movie] a building and the land surrounding it where movies are made: *the Universal Studios lot*

4 [group] a group of people or objects considered together: *Keeler is the best player of the lot.*

5 [to be sold] something that is sold, especially at an AUCTION[1]: *Lot fifteen was a box of old books.*

6 throw in your lot with sb also **cast your lot with sb** to join or support someone, so that what happens to you depends on what happens to them: *The new government has cast its lot with the West.*

7 by lot if someone or something is decided on by lot, it is decided on by choosing one piece of paper, object etc. from among many —see also **draw lots** (DRAW[1] (28))

loth /louθ/ *adj.* another spelling of LOATH

lo·tion /ˈlouʃən/ *n.* [C,U] a liquid mixture that you put on your skin to make it soft or protect it: *suntan lotion*

lots /lɑts/ *quantifier, pron.* INFORMAL a large quantity or number: *"Do you have any cigarettes?" "Yeah, I have lots."* | [+ of] *There are lots of fun things to do there.* | *It saves **lots and lots of** time.*

lot·sa /ˈlɑtsə/ *quantifier, pron.* a way of writing "lots of" to show how it sounds when it is spoken

lot·ter·y /ˈlɑtəri/ *n. plural* **lotteries 1** [C] a game used to make money for a state or a CHARITY (1) in which people buy numbered tickets, so that if their number is picked by chance, they win money or a prize: *a lottery ticket* | *Well, if I **win the lottery** I'll buy it for you.* —compare RAFFLE[1], DRAWING (3) **2** [C,U] a system of choosing who will get something by choosing people's names by chance: *the NFL draft lottery* | *The State Department issues 55,000 visas each year **by lottery*** (=using a lottery system). **3** [singular] a situation in which what happens depends on chance and is risky: *A baby's sex is a genetic lottery. It all depends on the chromosomes the baby receives from its parents.*

lo·tus /ˈloutəs/ *n.* [C] **1** a flower that grows on the surface of lakes in Asia, or the shape of this flower used in decorations **2** a fruit that gives you a pleasant dreamy feeling after you eat it, according to ancient Greek stories

sw **loud¹** /laʊd/ *adj.* **1** making a lot of noise: *a loud explosion* | *The TV's too loud.* **2** someone who is loud talks too loudly and confidently: *Bloom is loud and aggressive.* **3** loud clothes are too bright or have too many bright patterns: *a loud purple jacket* **4 loud and clear** very easily understood: *The play's message is loud and clear.* **5 be loud in your praise/opposition etc.** to express your approval, disapproval etc. very strongly: *Administration officials have been loud in their urgings to the Fed to cut rates.* —**loudly** *adv.* —**loudness** *n.* [U]

sw **loud²** *adv.* **1** SPOKEN in a way that makes a lot of noise; loudly: *Could you speak a little louder?* | *The band was playing so loud, we couldn't hear each other.* **1** used in such a way that people can hear you; ALOUD: *Could you read the passage out loud for us?* | *When I saw what he was wearing, I couldn't help laughing out loud.* | *Sorry. I was just thinking out loud* (=saying what you are thinking, without planning it first or intending other people to listen). —see also **actions speak louder than words** (ACTION (15)), **for crying out loud** (CRY¹ (3))

loud·mouth /'laʊdmaʊθ/ *n.* [C] someone who talks too much and says offensive or stupid things —**loud-mouthed** *adj.*

loud·speak·er /'laʊd,spikɚ/ *n.* [C] **1** a piece of equipment used to make sounds louder: *The voice over the loudspeaker said the flight was delayed.* **2** a SPEAKER (3)

Lou Geh·rig's dis·ease /,lu 'gɛr gz dɪ,ziz/ *n.* [U] NOT TECHNICAL a serious disease in which your muscles become weaker and weaker until you cannot move anymore

Lou·is /'luɪs/, **Joe** /dʒoʊ/ (1914–1981) a U.S. BOXER famous for being the world HEAVYWEIGHT CHAMPION for 11 years, the longest time that any BOXER held this title

Lou·i·si·a·na /lu,izi'ænə/ *written abbreviation* LA a state in the southern U.S.

Louisiana Pur·chase, the /..... '../ also **the Louisiana Territory** /..... '..../ the area of land which the U.S. bought from France in 1803, that covered the land between the Mississippi River and the Rocky Mountains and between Canada and the Gulf of Mexico

Lou·is·ville /'luivɪl/ the largest city in the U.S. state of Kentucky

Lou·is XIV, King /,lui ðə fɔr'tin/ (1638–1715) a king of France who was called the "Sun King," built the PALACE at Versailles, and supported important artists and writers

Louis XV, King /,lui ðə fɪf'tin/ (1710–1774) the king of France at the time when it lost power in Canada to England

Louis XVI, King /,lui ðə sɪks'tin/ (1754–1793) the king of France from 1774 to 1792. He and his wife Marie Antoinette were put in prison and killed during the French Revolution.

lounge¹ /laʊndʒ/ *n.* [C] **1** a public room in a hotel, airport, or other building where people can relax, sit down, or drink: *the airport's departure lounge* **2** a COCKTAIL LOUNGE

lounge² *v.* [I] [always + adv./prep.] to stand or sit in a lazy way: [+ in/on etc.] *We spent the weekend lounging on the beach.*
lounge around *phr. v.* [I] to spend time doing nothing: *James does nothing but lounge around the apartment.*

lounge chair /'. ./ *n.* [C] a comfortable chair made for relaxing in, such as an EASY CHAIR —see picture at CHAIR¹

lounge liz·ard /'. ,../ *n.* [C] INFORMAL, DISAPPROVING a man who spends a lot of his time at COCKTAIL LOUNGES, drinks too much, and thinks he is stylish and attractive to women

lounge mu·sic /'. ,../ *n.* [U] a relaxed style of music from the 1940s and 1950s, usually songs, piano music, or JAZZ

louse¹ /laʊs/ *n.* [C] **1** *plural* **lice** /laɪs/ a small wingless insect that lives on people's or animals' skin and hair **2** *plural* **louses** INFORMAL someone who is mean and treats people very badly: *"You louse!" she yelled.*

louse² *v.*
louse up *phr. v.* INFORMAL **1** [T **louse** sth ↔ **up**] to make something that is good become worse; spoil: *I don't want to louse things up in our relationship.* **2** [I] to do something badly: [+ **on**] *Chris really loused up on his finals.*

lous·y /'laʊzi/ *adj.* **lousier, lousiest 1** ESPECIALLY SPOKEN very bad: *What lousy weather!* | *I feel lousy.* **2** SPOKEN small, useless, or unimportant: *He left me a lousy fifty cent tip.* **3** SPOKEN not very good at doing something: [+ **at/with**] *I'm lousy at tennis.* | *Brenda's lousy with kids.* **4 be lousy with sth** OLD-FASHIONED **a)** a place that is lousy with people of a particular kind is too full of them: *The town was lousy with tourists.* **b)** someone who is lousy with money has a lot more of it than they need **5** covered with lice (LOUSE¹ (1))

lout /laʊt/ *n.* [C] FORMAL a man who is very impolite or offensive

lou·ver, louvre /'luvɚ/ *n.* [C] a narrow piece of wood, glass etc., in a door or window, that slopes out to let some light in and keep rain or strong sun out —**louvered** *adj.*: *a louvered window*

lov·a·ble /'lʌvəbəl/ *adj.* friendly and attractive: *a sweet lovable child*

sw **love¹** /lʌv/ *v.* [T not in progressive]
1 ⬛care about⬛ to care very much about someone, especially a member of your family or a close friend: *It's incredible how much she loves those two kids.* | *a much-loved author* | *The group was founded to help cancer patients and their loved ones* (=people they love).
2 ⬛romantic attraction⬛ to have a strong feeling of caring for and liking someone, combined with sexual attraction: *I love you, Betty.* | *Tom was the only man she had ever loved.*
3 ⬛like/enjoy⬛ [not in passive] to like something very much or enjoy doing something very much: [**love doing sth**] *Katie loves playing tennis.* | [**love sth**] *I love chocolate.* | *Don't you just love the way she dresses?* | [**love to do sth**] *We all love to talk about ourselves.*
4 ⬛loyalty⬛ to have a strong feeling of loyalty to your country, an institution etc.: *Dad's always loved the Navy.*

SPOKEN PHRASES
5 I'd love to (do sth) used to say that you want to do something very much: *"Would you like to go out to dinner?" "I'd love to."* | *I'd have loved to have gone to Italy with them.* | *I'd love to know just what she's really thinking.*
6 I love it! also **don't you just love it?** used when you are amused by something, especially by someone else's mistake or bad luck: *"So then Susan had to explain how the dishes got broken." "Oh, I love it!"*
7 she's/he's etc. going to love sth used to say that someone will enjoy something or be amused by it: *Listen guys, you're going to love this.*
8 you (have) got to love sth used to say that you are amused by something because it is so bad, good, or unusual that it is funny: *You've got to love the way she always lies about her age when she meets men.*

—see also LOVER —opposite HATE¹

love² *n.*
1 ⬛for family/friends⬛ [U] a strong feeling of caring about someone, especially a member of your family or a close friend: *What these kids need is love and support.* | [+ **for**] *a mother's love for her child* —opposite HATE², HATRED
2 ⬛romantic⬛ [U] a strong feeling of liking and caring about someone, especially combined with sexual attraction: *He is so in love with Mary.* | *We fell in love on our first date.* | *When you met your husband, was it love at first sight* (=when you love someone the first time you see them)? | *Teenage girls dream of finding true love* (=strong romantic love that remains for ever). —see also **head over**

L

heels in love (HEAD¹ (37)), **madly in love (with sb)** (MADLY (2))

3 person you love [C] someone that you feel a strong romantic and sexual attraction to: *Jack was her first love.* | *I think of her as the love of my life* (=the person that you feel or felt the most love for).

4 pleasure/enjoyment **a)** [singular,U] a strong feeling of pleasure and enjoyment that something gives you: [+ of/for] *Jerrod has a love for the game of chess.* **b)** [C] something that gives you a lot of pleasure and enjoyment: *Sailing was her great love.*

5 **make love (to/with sb) a)** to have sex with someone that you love: *We made love all afternoon.* **b)** OLD USE to say loving things to someone, to kiss them etc.

6 **sb's love interest** the person that someone is in love with in a movie, book etc.

7 **send your love (to sb)** to ask someone to give your loving greetings to someone else when they see them, write to them etc.: *Aunt Mary sends her love.*

8 **give my love to sb** SPOKEN used to ask someone to give your loving greetings to someone else: *Bye! Give my love to Jackie.*

9 **love** also **lots of love** used at the end of a letter to a friend, a member of your family, or someone you love: *See you soon. Lots of love, Clare.*

10 **there is no love lost between sb and sb** if there is no love lost between two people, they dislike each other: *There's no love lost between Bart and Stephen.*

11 tennis [U] an expression meaning "no points," used in the game of tennis

12 **not for love or/nor money** INFORMAL if you cannot get something or do something for love or money, it is impossible to obtain or to do: *I can't get a hold of that book for love nor money.*

13 **for the love of God/Mike etc.** OLD-FASHIONED, SPOKEN used to show that you are extremely angry, disappointed etc.

14 **love nest** HUMOROUS a place where two people who are having a romantic relationship live or go to see each other —see also **a labor of love** (LABOR¹ (4))

love af·fair /'. .,./ *n.* [C] **1** a romantic sexual relationship, usually between two people who are not married to each other: *a passionate love affair* —see also AFFAIR (3) **2** a strong enjoyment of something: *America's love affair with the automobile*

love·bird /'lʌvbɚd/ *n.* [C] **1** lovebirds HUMOROUS two people who show by their behavior that they love each other very much **2** a small brightly colored PARROT¹

love·child /'lʌvtʃaɪld/ *n.* [C] a word meaning a child whose parents are not married, used especially in newspapers

love·fest /'lʌv,fɛst/ *n.* [C] INFORMAL, HUMOROUS a situation in which everyone is very friendly, says nice things to each other etc.

love·less /'lʌvlɪs/ *adj.* without love: *a loveless marriage*

love let·ter /'. ,../ *n.* [C] a letter that someone writes to tell someone else how much they love them

love life /'. ./ *n.* [C,U] the part of your life that involves your romantic relationships, especially sexual ones

love·lorn /'lʌvlɔrn/ *adj.* LITERARY sad because the person you love does not love you

s w **love·ly** /'lʌvli/ *adj.* lovelier, loveliest **1** beautiful or
² attractive: *What a lovely baby!* | *Her hair's a lovely shade of red.* | *You look lovely in blue.* **2** SPOKEN very pleasant, enjoyable, or good: *Thank you for a lovely evening.* **3** INFORMAL friendly and pleasant: *Rita's a lovely young girl.* —**loveliness** *n.* [U]

love·mak·ing /'lʌv,meɪkɪŋ/ *n.* [U] the act of having sex —see also **make love (to/with sb)** (LOVE² (5))

s w **lov·er** /'lʌvɚ/ *n.* [C] **1** someone who has a sexual rela-
³ ³ tionship with someone they are not married to: *Arabella has had many lovers.* **2** someone who enjoys doing a particular thing very much or is very interested in it: *an opera lover*

love·seat /'lʌvsit/ *n.* [C] a small SOFA for two people

love·sick /'lʌv,sɪk/ *adj.* spending all your time thinking about someone you love, especially someone who does not love you: *You're acting like a lovesick teenager!*

love tri·an·gle /'. ,.../ *n.* [C] INFORMAL a situation in which one person is having a romantic relationship with two other people

lov·ey-dov·ey /,lʌvi 'dʌvi◂/ *adj.* INFORMAL behavior that is lovey-dovey is too romantic: *The newlyweds were acting all lovey-dovey.*

lov·ing /'lʌvɪŋ/ *adj.* [only before noun] behaving in a way that shows you love someone: *a loving husband* | *Right now I just need some **tender loving care**.* —**lovingly** *adv.*

-loving /lʌvɪŋ/ [in adjectives] **peace-loving/fun-loving etc.** thinking that peace, having fun etc. is very important: *a peace-loving nation* | *a music-loving family*

loving cup /'.. ,./ *n.* [C] a very large cup with two handles that was passed around at formal meals in past times

low

a low wall

shallow water

low¹ /loʊ/ *adj.*
1 height **a)** having a top that is not far above the ground: *a low fence* | *a low building* **b)** at a point that is not far above the ground: *low clouds* | *I'm going to trim some of the low branches.* **c)** below the usual height: *a low ceiling* | *The reservoir's water level has been low for weeks now.*
2 amount **a)** small, or smaller than usual, in amount, value etc.: *a low income* | *low-cost housing* | *The price of oil is at its lowest in 10 years.* **b)** having less than the usual amount of a substance or chemical: [+ in] *Do they really make eggs that are low in cholesterol?* | *a low-salt diet*
3 number **in the low 20s/30s/40s etc.** a number, temperature etc. in the low 20s, 30s etc. is no higher than 23, 33 etc.: *Tonight's temperatures will be in the low 50s.*
4 level/degree small, or smaller than usual, in level or degree: *Morale has been low since the latest round of job-cuts.* | *a low-risk investment*
5 standards/quality bad, or below an acceptable or usual level or quality: *low quality goods* | *My class's scores on the test were quite low.*
6 supply if a supply of something is low, you have used almost all of it | **be/get/run low (on sth)** *We're running low on gas.* | *The medical supplies were getting low.*
7 sound a low voice, sound etc. is quiet or deep:

The volume is too low. Turn it up please. | You could hear Dan's low voice in the other room.

8 light a light that is low is not bright, especially so that it makes a room feel more relaxing: *The lights in the restaurant were low.*

9 heat if you cook something on a low heat, you use only a small amount of heat

10 unhappy unhappy and without much hope for the future: *I've been feeling pretty low since he left.* | *Carol looks like she's in low spirits* (=unhappy and not hopeful) *today.*

11 battery a BATTERY that is low does not have much power left in it

12 dishonest behavior that is low is unfair or not nice: *I can't believe you said that. That's a low blow* (=that is an unfair or mean thing to say)*!*

13 of low birth/breeding OLD-FASHIONED not from a high social class —**lowness** n. [U] —compare HIGH¹ —see also **be at a low ebb** (EBB¹ (2)), LOW GEAR

^{S W} **low²** adv. **1** in or to a low position or level: *The sun sank low on the horizon.* | *Turn lights down low.* **2** near the ground: *That plane's flying too low.* **3** if you play or sing musical notes low, you play or sing them with quiet deep notes: *She sang low and sweetly.* **4 be brought low** OLD-FASHIONED to become much less rich or important —see also **look/search high and low** (HIGH² (6)), **lay sb low** (LAY¹ (23)), **lie low** (LIE¹ (5)), LOWLY

low³ n. [C] **1** the smallest or least amount or level that has happened at a particular time: *The pound has fallen to a new low* (=is worth less than ever before) *against the dollar.* | *Prices on homes have dropped to an all-time low* (=much lower than ever before). **2** a very bad situation in someone's personal life: *The 1920s marked an all-time low* (=the worst situation that had happened) *in the U.S. economy.* | *the highs and lows* (=good times and bad times) *of parenting* **3** [usually singular] **a)** the lowest point that the temperature reaches during a particular time: *The overnight low will be 25° F.* **b)** a large area of air where there is very little pressure, which affects the weather in a particular area: *A low is making its way over the Mid-Atlantic states.* **4** the **lowest of the low** INFORMAL **a)** someone you think is completely unfair, cruel, immoral etc. **b)** someone from a low social class

low⁴ v. [I] LITERARY if cattle low, they make a deep sound

low beam /'. ./ n. **1 low beams** [plural] the regular HEADLIGHTS of a vehicle, as opposed to the brighter HIGH BEAMS **2 on low beam** if your car lights are on low beam, they are shining at the normal level of brightness —compare **on high beam** (HIGH BEAM

low-born /ˌloʊˈbɔrn◂/ adj. OLD-FASHIONED coming from a low social class

low-brow, low-brow /'loʊbraʊ/ adj. not complicated or serious, or not of good quality: *lowbrow entertainment* —compare HIGHBROW

low-cal, lo-cal /ˌloʊ ˈkæl◂/ adj. INFORMAL low-cal food or drink does not contain many CALORIES

low-class /ˌ. ˈ.◂/ adj. INFORMAL, DISAPPROVING **1** not having a lot of money and behaving in a way that is not socially acceptable: *a low-class woman* **2** having or showing qualities that are not desirable or attractive: *a low-class street in the downtown area* —compare HIGH-CLASS

Low Coun-tries, the /'. ˌ../ an area of northwest Europe that includes Belgium, Luxembourg, and the Netherlands, and is also known as Benelux

low-cut /ˌ. ˈ.◂/ adj. a low-cut dress, BLOUSE etc. is shaped so that it shows a woman's neck and the top of her chest

low-down /'loʊdaʊn/ n. **the lowdown (on sth)** INFORMAL the most important facts about something or someone: *Ryan called and gave me the lowdown on the merger.*

low-down /'. ./ adj. [only before noun] INFORMAL dishonest and not nice: *What a low-down, dirty trick.*

Low-ell /'loʊəl/, **A-my** /'eɪmi/ (1874–1925) a U.S. poet

Lowell, James Rus-sell /ˌdʒeɪmz ˈrʌsəl/ (1819–1891) a U.S. poet and newspaper EDITOR

Lowell, Rob-ert /'rɑbət/ (1917–1977) a U.S. poet and writer of plays

low-end /'. ./ adj. [usually before noun] relating to products or services that are less expensive and of lower quality than other products of the same type: *low-end electronics* —compare HIGH-END

low-er¹ /'loʊə/ adj. [only before noun] **1** below something else, especially beneath something of the same type: *your lower lip* | *muscles of the lower leg* **2** at or near the bottom of something: *the lower deck of the stadium* **3** [only before noun] less important than something else of the same type: *the lower levels of the organization* **4** the **lower forty-eight (states)** also the **lower 48 (states)** all the states of the U.S. except for Alaska and Hawaii: *Unfortunately, the number of grizzly bears in the lower forty-eight can only be counted in the hundreds.* —opposite UPPER¹ ^{S W}

lower² v. **1** [I,T] to reduce something in amount, degree, strength etc., or to become less: *We're lowering prices on all of our trucks.* | *Houses have lowered in value recently.* | *Graham lowered his voice* (=made it quieter) *to a near whisper.* **2** [T] to move something down from a higher position: *The flags were lowered to half-mast.* | *We had our kitchen cabinets lowered to be more accessible.* | **[lower sth down/into/between etc. sth]** *The workers carefully lowered the box onto the cart.* **3 lower yourself** [usually in negatives] to behave in a way that makes people respect you less: *I'd like to tell these creeps off, but I don't want to lower myself to their level.* **4 lower your eyes** to look down: *Mike lowered his eyes as Adrianne came into the room.* —**lowered** adj. ^{S W}

lower³ v. [I] **1** when the sky or the weather lowers, it becomes dark because there is going to be a storm: *lowering clouds* **2** LITERARY to look threatening or annoyed; FROWN: *The old man just lowered at us as we walked by.*

lower case /ˌ.. ˈ.◂/ n. [U] letters in their small forms, such as a, b, c etc. —**lower case** adj. —compare CAPITAL¹ (4) —opposite UPPER CASE

lower cham-ber /ˌ.. ˈ../ n. [C usually singular] the LOWER HOUSE

lower class /ˌ.. ˈ.◂/ also **lower classes** n. [C] OLD-FASHIONED the social class that has less money, power, or education than anyone else —**lower-class** adj. —see also WORKING CLASS —compare MIDDLE CLASS, UPPER CLASS

lower-end /ˌ.. ˈ.◂/ adj. [usually before noun] LOW-END

lower house /ˌ.. ˈ./ n. [C usually singular] the larger of two elected groups of government officials that make laws, usually more REPRESENTATIVE¹ (2) and made up of less experienced officials than the smaller group —compare UPPER HOUSE

lower or-ders /ˌ.. ˈ../ n. OLD-FASHIONED **the lower orders** an expression meaning "people of a low social CLASS," used especially by people who consider themselves to be more important

lowest com-mon de-nom-i-na-tor /ˌ... ˌ... .ˈ..../ n. [U] **1** the biggest possible number of people, including those who are very easily influenced or are willing to accept low standards: *The band's vulgar lyrics appeal to the lowest common denominator.* **2** TECHNICAL the smallest number that the bottom numbers of a group of FRACTIONS can be divided into exactly

low-fat /ˌ. ˈ.◂/ adj. containing or using only a small amount of fat: *low-fat cottage cheese*

low-fly-ing /. ˈ..◂/ adj. flying close to the ground

low fre-quen-cy /ˌ. ˈ.../ n. [U] a radio FREQUENCY in the range of 30 to 300 KILOHERTZ —**low-frequency** adj.: *a low-frequency radio antenna* —compare HIGH FREQUENCY

low gear /ˌ. ˈ./ n. [C,U] one of a vehicle's GEARs that you use when you are driving at a slow speed

low-key /ˌ. ˈ.◂/ adj. not intended to attract a lot of attention to an event, subject, person, or thing: *This year's campaign was low-key and quiet.* | *a low-key approach to management*

L

low·lands /'loʊləndz/ n. [plural] an area of land that is lower than the land around it: *the Bolivian lowlands* —**lowland** adj. [only before noun] —**lowlander** n. [C] —compare HIGHLANDS

low-lev·el /ˌ. '..‹/ adj. **1** not in a powerful position or job, or involving people who are not in powerful positions or jobs: *a low-level manager* | *low-level positions in the company* **2** at a low degree or strength: *a low-level tension headache* **3** a low-level computer language is used to give instructions to a computer and is similar to the language that the computer operates in —compare HIGH-LEVEL

low life /'. ./ n. **1** [C] also **lowlife** INFORMAL someone who is involved in crime or who is bad: *Venuto is a lowlife who can't be trusted.* **2** [U] the life and behavior of people from a low social class, especially those who are involved in criminal activities: *De Beauvoir was fascinated with brothels, prostitutes and other forms of low life.* —**low-life** adj. INFORMAL

low·ly /'loʊli/ adj. not high in rank, importance, or social class: *a lowly trainee* —**lowliness** n. [U]

low-ly·ing /ˌ. '..‹/ adj. **1** low-lying land is not far above the level of the ocean **2** below the usual level: *low-lying fog*

low-paid /ˌ. '.‹/ adj. providing or earning only a small amount of money: *low-paid workers*

low-pay·ing /ˌ. '..‹/ adj. providing only a small amount of money: *low-paying jobs*

low-pitched /ˌ. '.‹/ adj. **1** a low-pitched musical note or sound is deep: *She heard a familiar low-pitched "good morning."* **2** a low-pitched roof is not steep

low point /'. ./ n. [C usually singular] the worst moment of a situation or activity: *Being arrested was the low point of my life.*

low-pow·er /ˌ. '..‹/ adj. **1** relating to television or radio stations that do not have a powerful broadcasting signal: *a low-power AM radio station* **2** also **low-powered** a low-powered machine, vehicle, or piece of equipment is not very powerful: *a low-powered telescope* —compare HIGH-POWERED

low-pres·sure /ˌ. '..‹/ n. [U] a condition of the air over a large area, that affects the weather

low·rid·er /'loʊraɪdɚ/ n. [C] a big car that has its bottom very close to the ground, or a young man who drives this type of car

low-rise /'. ./ adj. [only before noun] a low-rise office building or apartment building does not have as many stories (STORY (4)) as a HIGH-RISE building

low-risk /ˌ. '.‹/ adj. [only before noun] likely to be safe or without difficulties: *a low-risk investment*

low-slung /ˌ. '.‹/ adj. built or made to be closer to the ground than usual: *A low-slung gray Chevy pulled into the lot.*

low-spir·it·ed /ˌ. '...‹/ adj. unhappy; DEPRESSED (1): *He was a dull, low-spirited companion.*

low-tech /ˌloʊ 'tɛk‹/ adj. not using the most modern machines or methods in business or industry —opposite HIGH-TECH

low tide /ˌ. '.‹/ n. [C,U] the time when ocean water is at its lowest level: *You can walk across to the island at low tide.* —opposite HIGH TIDE

low wa·ter /ˌ. '../ n. [U] the time when the water in a river, lake etc. is at its lowest level

low water mark /ˌ. '.. ˌ./ n. [C] a mark showing the lowest level reached by a river or other area of water

lox /lɑks/ n. [U] SALMON that has been treated with smoke in order to preserve it

loy·al /'lɔɪəl/ adj. always supporting your friends, principles, country etc., and never changing your feelings about them: *Their fans remain loyal.* | *loyal customers* | [+ to] *Most corporate executives do not feel loyal to their firms.* —**loyally** adv.

loy·al·ist /'lɔɪəlɪst/ n. [C] someone who continues to support a government or country, when a lot of people want to change it —**loyalist** adj.

loy·al·ty /'lɔɪəlti/ n. plural **loyalties** **1** [singular,U] the quality of remaining faithful to your friends, principles, country etc.: *a family with a strong sense of loyalty* | [+ to/toward] *Readers feel a strong loyalty to their local newspaper.* **2** [C usually plural] a feeling of support for someone or something: *political loyalties* | *During World War II, many families in the region had divided loyalties* (=loyalty to two different or opposing people, groups etc.).

Loy·o·la /lɔɪ'oʊlə/, **St. Ignatius (of)** /ɪg'neɪʃəs/ —see IGNATIUS OF LOYOLA, ST.

loz·enge /'lɑzəndʒ/ n. [C] **1** a small flat candy, especially one that contains medicine: *a cough lozenge* **2** a shape similar to a square, with two angles of less than 90° opposite each other and two angles of more than 90° opposite each other

LP n. [C] long playing record; a record that turns 33 times per minute, and usually plays for between 20 and 25 minutes on each side

LPN n. [C] a LICENSED PRACTICAL NURSE

LSAT /'ɛlsæt/ n. [C] TRADEMARK Law School Admission Test; an examination taken by students who have completed a first degree and want to go to LAW SCHOOL

LSD n. [U] an illegal drug that makes you see things as more beautiful, strange, frightening etc. than usual, or see things that do not exist

Lt. the written abbreviation of LIEUTENANT

Ltd. the written abbreviation of LIMITED (4), used in the names of companies or businesses: *M. Dixon & Son Ltd.* —compare INC.

Lu·an·da /lu'ɑndə/ the capital city of Angola

lu·au /'luaʊ/ n. [C] an outdoor party at which Hawaiian food is cooked and served outdoors, and to which people often wear LEIS (=circles of flowers worn around your neck)

lube /lub/ n. INFORMAL **1** [singular] also **lube job** [C] the service of lubricating the parts of a car's engine **2** [C,U] INFORMAL a lubricant —**lube** v. [T]

lu·bri·cant /'lubrəkənt/ n. [C,U] a substance such as oil that you put on surfaces that rub together, especially parts of a machine, in order to make them move smoothly and easily

lu·bri·cate /'lubrəˌkeɪt/ v. [T] to put a lubricant on something in order to make it move more smoothly: *Lubricate all moving parts with grease.* —**lubrication** /ˌlubrə'keɪʃən/ n. [U]

lu·bri·cious /lu'brɪʃəs/ adj. FORMAL too interested in sex, in a way that seems disgusting or unacceptable —**lubriciously** adv.

Luce /lus/, **Henry** (1898–1967) a U.S. EDITOR and PUBLISHER who started "Time" magazine

lu·cid /'lusɪd/ adj. **1** expressed in a way that is clear and easy to understand: *a lucid analysis of the situation* **2** a word meaning "able to understand and think clearly," used especially about someone who is not always able to do this: *At the moment, Peter is lucid and quite talkative, but his condition is becoming worse.* —**lucidly** adv. —**lucidity** /lu'sɪdəti/ n. [U]

Lu·ci·fer /'lusɪfɚ/ n. the DEVIL

luck[1] /lʌk/ n. [U]
1 success also **good luck** the good things that happen to someone by chance, not through their work or effort: *I've always had good luck meeting nice people in this apartment building.* | *It was sheer luck* (=used to emphasize that something happened only by luck) *that we happened to see each other in the crowd.* | *It was a stroke of luck* (=used to say that someone has very good luck) *that the Australian actress happened to get the part. She hadn't even intended to go to the audition.*
2 bad luck the bad things that happen to someone by chance, not because of something they did: *It was just bad luck that she happened to get sick that day.* | *I've always had bad luck with women.* | *The team has had a run of bad luck* (=had a series of bad things happen) *with all this rain.*
3 it's good/bad luck to do sth used to say that doing, seeing, finding etc. something makes good or bad things happen to someone: *It's bad luck to walk under a ladder.*

4 be in luck INFORMAL to be able to do or get something, especially when you did not expect to: *You're in luck. There's one ticket left.*

5 be out of luck INFORMAL to be prevented from getting or doing something by bad luck: *We're out of luck. The store's closed.*

6 wish sb luck to tell someone that you hope they will be successful in something they are about to do: *Mom came over to wish me luck before the race.*

SPOKEN PHRASES

7 Good luck! used to tell someone that you hope they will be successful in something they are about to do: *Good luck in the interview.*

8 any/no luck used in questions and negatives to say whether or not someone has been able to do something: *Did you have any luck getting into the show?* | *"Any luck?" "Yes, I got a flight on Friday."* | *I'm having no luck reaching Julie at home.* | *"No luck?"* (=said when you think someone has not been able to do something) *"No, the guy said they left yesterday."*

9 no such luck! used to say you are disappointed, because something good that could have happened did not happen: *"Will we get there on time?" "No such luck!"*

10 just my luck! used to say that you are not surprised something bad has happened to you, because you are usually unlucky: *Just my luck! They've already gone home.*

11 with/knowing sb's luck used to say that you expect something bad will happen to someone because bad things often do happen to them: *Knowing his luck, he'll get hit with a golf ball or something.*

12 some people/guys have all the luck! used to say that you wish you had what someone else has

13 better luck next time! used to say that you hope someone will be more successful the next time they try to do something

14 (one) for luck used when you take, add, or do something for no particular reason, or in order to say that you hope good things happen: *You get three kisses for your birthday, and one for luck.*

15 with any luck INFORMAL if things happen in the way you want; HOPEFULLY: *With any luck, the old music hall will never be torn down.*

16 chance the fact of good or bad things happening to people by chance: *Dice is a game of luck.* | *You never know who you'll get as a roommate. It's just a matter of luck.*

17 the luck of the draw the result of chance rather than something you can control: *It was by the luck of the draw that I got a corner office.*

18 as luck would have it INFORMAL used to say that something happened by chance: *As luck would have it, there were two seats left on the last flight.*

19 do sth for luck to do something because you think it might bring you good luck: *John always carried a rabbit's foot for luck.*

20 be down on your luck INFORMAL to have no money because you have had a lot of bad luck over a period of time: *The program is for motivated people who are temporarily down on their luck.*

21 luck is on sb's side if luck is on someone's side, things go well for them: *With two kids and a beautiful wife, luck was on his side.* —see also **hard-luck story** (HARD¹ (21)), **push your luck** (PUSH¹ (11)), **tough luck** (TOUGH¹ (7)), **trust sth to luck/chance/fate etc.** (TRUST¹ (5)), **try your luck** (TRY¹ (10))

USAGE NOTE: LUCK

WORD CHOICE: luck, lucky
Use the noun **luck** without an adjective to mean the good things that happen to you by chance: *It was just luck that there were two seats left.* | *With luck, you'll find the right job.* You can use the verb "have" with the word **luck**, but only if a word such as an adjective or determiner comes before **luck**: *Ted's had a lot of bad luck recently.* *Did you have any luck* (NOT "did you have luck") *reaching Tina on the phone?* Use **lucky** to describe a situation that is good by chance, or someone who has good luck: *You're lucky you didn't lose any money in Fran's business venture.*

---

luck² *v.*

luck out *phr. v.* [I] INFORMAL to be lucky: *We lucked out and found someone who spoke English.*

luck·i·ly /ˈlʌkəli/ *adv.* as a result of good luck: [sentence adverb] *Luckily, no one was injured in the accident.* | [+ **for**] *Luckily for me, I had kind and caring parents.*

luck·less /ˈlʌklɪs/ *adj.* LITERARY having no luck in something you are trying to do: *William Holden stars as a luckless scriptwriter in "Sunset Boulevard."*

luck·y /ˈlʌki/ *adj.* **luckier, luckiest 1** having good luck; FORTUNATE: [**be lucky to do/be sth**] *He's lucky to be alive.* | *We were lucky to find a parking spot right in front of the store.* | *John was lucky enough to be selected for the team.* | [**lucky (that)**] *Janet's lucky the car didn't hit her.* | [+ **with**] *Our school district has been very lucky with our superintendents.* | **consider/count yourself lucky** *William considers himself lucky to have married Leonora.* **2** resulting from good luck: *In the second half, the Red Wings scored a very lucky goal.* | *That was just a lucky guess. I had no idea what the answer was.* **3** bringing good luck: *a lucky rabbit's foot*

^{s w}

SPOKEN PHRASES

4 lucky you/me etc.! used to say that someone is fortunate to be able to do something: *"I've got free tickets to the game!" "Lucky you."* **5 be sb's lucky day** used to say that something good and often unexpected has happened to someone: *"Look at the size of the fish I caught!" "It must be your lucky day!"* **6 I'll be lucky if...** used to say that you think something is very unlikely: *I'll be lucky if I get even half of my money back.* **7 I/you should be so lucky!** used to say that someone wants something that is not likely to happen, especially because it is unreasonable: *Sleep past 6 a.m.? I should be so lucky!* **8 (you) lucky dog!** used to say that someone is very lucky and that you wish you had what they have: *You didn't have to pay for the tickets? You lucky dog!*

—see also **thank your lucky stars** (THANK (4)) —see Usage Note at LUCK¹

lu·cra·tive /ˈlukrətɪv/ *adj.* a job or activity that is lucrative lets you earn a lot of money; PROFITABLE: *a lucrative business*

lu·cre /ˈlukə/ *n.* [U] DISAPPROVING money or wealth: *filthy lucre*

Lud·dite /ˈlʌdaɪt/ *n.* [C] DISAPPROVING someone who is strongly opposed to using modern machines and methods

lude /lud/ *n.* [C] SLANG a QUAALUDE

lu·di·crous /ˈludɪkrəs/ *adj.* completely unreasonable, stupid, or wrong; RIDICULOUS: *They want two million dollars for the house? That's ludicrous!* —**ludicrously** *adv.*: *The test was ludicrously easy.* —**ludicrousness** *n.* [U]

lug¹ /lʌg/ *v.* **lugged, lugging** [T] to pull or carry something heavy with difficulty: [**lug sth up/down/around etc. sth**] *We had to lug the sofa up four flights of stairs.* —see also **chug-a-lug** (CHUG (3))

lug² *n.* [C] a big, stupid, slow-moving man: *I can't figure out why Penelope's so attracted to the big lug.*

luge /luʒ/ *n.* [C] a vehicle with blades instead of wheels, on which you slide down a track made of ice

lug·gage /ˈlʌgɪdʒ/ *n.* [U] the suitcases, bags etc. carried by someone who is traveling

luggage rack /ˈ.. ˌ./ *n.* [C] **1** a special frame on top of a car that you tie luggage, boxes etc. onto **2** a shelf in a train, bus etc. for putting luggage on

lug nut /ˈ. ./ *n.* [C] a small rounded NUT (2) that is screwed onto a BOLT¹ (2)

lu·gu·bri·ous /ləˈgubriəs/ *adj.* LITERARY OR HUMOROUS very sad and serious: *a lugubrious voice* —**lugubriously** *adv.* —**lugubriousness** *n.* [U]

Luke /luk/ also **the Gospel according to St. Luke**

L

one of the four books in the New Testament of the Christian Bible that describe the life and teaching of Jesus

Luke, Saint in the Bible, one of the 12 APOSTLES, who is believed to have written the Gospel according to St. Luke

luke·warm /ˌlukˈwɔrmˑ/ *adj.* **1** food, liquid etc. that is lukewarm is slightly warm, often when it should be or is usually hot: *a lukewarm bath* | *The meal was only lukewarm.* **2** not showing much interest or excitement: *Sikes' new movie received a lukewarm reaction from critics.*

lull¹ /lʌl/ *v.* [T] **1** to make someone feel calm or sleepy: *The soft music lulled me to sleep.* **2** to make someone feel safe and confident so that they are completely surprised when something bad happens: [**lull sb into (doing) sth**] *The tests have lulled the public into believing the water is safe to drink.* | *The disease is not common, but tourists should not be **lulled into a false sense of security** (=made to think they are safe when they are not).*

lull² *n.* [C] **1** a short period of time when there is less activity or less noise than usual: [+ **in**] *a brief lull in the conversation* | *a lull in the fighting* **2 the lull before the storm** a short period of time when things are calm that is followed by a lot of activity, noise, or trouble

lul·la·by /ˈlʌləˌbaɪ/ *n. plural* **lullabies** [C] a slow, quiet song sung to children to make them go to sleep

lu·lu /ˈlulu/ *n.* [C] INFORMAL **1** something very good or exciting: *The roller coaster at Magic Mountain is a **real lulu**.* **2** something extremely stupid, bad, embarrassing etc.: *She's said some stupid things in her life, but that one was a lulu!*

lum·ba·go /lʌmˈbeɪgoʊ/ *n.* [U] OLD-FASHIONED pain in the lower part of the back

lum·bar /ˈlʌmbɑr, -bɚ/ *adj.* TECHNICAL relating to the lower part of the back: *The seats have built-in lumbar supports.*

lum·ber¹ /ˈlʌmbɚ/ *v.* [I] **1** [always + adv./prep.] to move in a slow, awkward way: [+ **after/into/along** etc.] *The bear lumbered over to our campsite.* **2** to cut down trees in a large area and prepare them to be sold

lumber² *n.* [U] pieces of wood used for building, that have been cut to specific lengths and widths

lum·ber·jack /ˈlʌmbɚˌdʒæk/ *n.* [C] OLD-FASHIONED someone whose job is cutting down trees for wood

lum·ber·man /ˈlʌmbɚmən/ *n.* [C] someone in the business of cutting down large areas of trees and selling them for wood

lum·ber·yard /ˈlʌmbɚˌyɑrd/ *n.* [C] a place where wood is kept before it is sold

lu·mi·nar·y /ˈluməˌnɛri/ *n. plural* **luminaries** [C] someone who is very famous or highly respected for their skill at doing something or their knowledge of a particular subject: *Guests included show business luminaries such as Bob Hope.*

lu·mi·nous /ˈlumənəs/ *adj.* **1** made of a substance or material that shines in the dark: *luminous paint* | *luminous road signs* **2** very brightly colored, especially in green, pink, or yellow: *luminous socks* —**luminously** *adv.* —**luminosity** /ˌluməˈnɑsəṭi/ *n.* [U]

lum·mox /ˈlʌməks/ *n.* [C] LITERARY a large, stupid, slow-moving man

lump¹ /lʌmp/ *n.* [C] **1** a small piece of something solid, that does not have a definite shape: *Stir the mixture until all the lumps are gone.* | [+ **of**] *a lump of clay* **2** a small hard swollen area that sticks out from someone's skin or grows in their body, usually because of an illness: *The lump in Kay's breast turned out to be cancerous.* **3 bring a lump to sb's throat** to make someone feel as if they want to cry: *Martin's speech at the funeral brought a lump to my throat.* **4** a small square block of sugar, used to sweeten coffee or tea: *One lump or two?* **5 take your lumps** INFORMAL to accept the bad things that happen to you and not let them affect you: *Our team took its*

lumps this season, but still finished with a winning record.

lump² *v.* [T] [always + adv./prep.] to put two or more different people or things together and consider them as a single group: [**lump sth together**] *The statistics lump all minority students together.* | [**lump sth with sth**] *Investors often lump venture capital with other types of investment.* | [**lump sb in with sb**] *Marijuana is often lumped in with more dangerous drugs.*

lump·ec·to·my /lʌmˈpɛktəmi/ *n.* [C] an operation in which a TUMOR is removed from someone's body, especially from a woman's breast

lum·pen /ˈlʌmpən, ˈlʊm-/ *adj.* [only before noun] unintelligent and rude

lump·ish /ˈlʌmpɪʃ/ *adj.* **1** awkward or stupid: *lumpish dialogue* **2** like a lump: *lumpish food*

lump sum /ˌ. ˈ./ *n.* [C] an amount of money given in a single payment: *At retirement, your pension money can be taken out as a lump sum.*

lump·y /ˈlʌmpi/ *adj.* **lumpier, lumpiest** covered with or containing small solid pieces: *lumpy mashed potatoes*

lu·na·cy /ˈlunəsi/ *n.* [U] **1** a situation or behavior that is completely crazy: *It would be **sheer lunacy** to turn down a great offer like that.* **2** OLD-FASHIONED mental illness —see also LUNATIC

lu·nar /ˈlunɚ/ *adj.* relating to the moon or with travel to the moon: *the lunar landscape*

lunar e·clipse /ˌ.. .ˈ./ *n.* [C] an occasion when the sun and the moon are on the opposite sides of the Earth, so that the moon is hidden by the Earth's shadow for a short time

lunar month /ˌ.. ˈ./ *n.* [C] a period of 28 or 29 days between one NEW MOON and the next

lu·na·tic /ˈlunəˌtɪk/ *n.* [C] **1** someone who behaves in a crazy or very stupid way: *Some lunatic came into the store and shot him.* **2** OLD-FASHIONED, TECHNICAL someone who is mentally ill **3 the lunatic fringe** the people in a political group or organization who have the most extreme opinions or ideas —**lunatic** *adj.*

lunatic a·sy·lum /ˈ... .ˌ../ *n.* [C] OLD-FASHIONED a word for a hospital where people who are mentally ill are cared for, now considered offensive

lunch¹ /lʌntʃ/ *n.* [C,U] **1** a meal eaten in the middle of the day, or that time of day: *We've already had lunch.* | *I'm starved. Let's have some lunch.* | *What did you bring for lunch?* | *Anna said something at lunch about leaving.* | *She came last week and took my parents out to lunch* (=paid for their lunch at a restaurant). | *What time are we going to **go to lunch** (=go somewhere to eat lunch)?* | *The restaurant's atmosphere is well-suited for a **working lunch** (=a lunch during which you discuss business).* | **bag/sack lunch** (=food, usually sandwiches, that you take with you to work, school etc.) **2 sb's out to lunch** INFORMAL used to say that someone is behaving in a strange and confused way, or that they do not know what they are talking about —see also **there's no free lunch** (FREE¹ (15))

lunch² *v.* FORMAL [I] to eat lunch

lunch·box /ˈlʌntʃbɑks/ *n.* [C] a box in which food is carried to school, work etc.

lunch break /ˈ. ./ *n.* [C] the time in the middle of the day when people at work or at school stop working to eat lunch

lunch coun·ter /ˈ. ˌ../ *n.* [C] a place in a building or store in the past that served quick, simple meals for lunch, or a small restaurant that was open only for lunch

lunch·eon /ˈlʌntʃən/ *n.* [C,U] FORMAL lunch

lunch·eon·ette /ˌlʌntʃəˈnɛt/ *n.* [C] a place in a building or store in the past that served quick, simple food for lunch

lunch meat /ˈ. ./ also **luncheon meat** /ˈ.. ˌ./ *n.* [U] meat that has been cooked, pressed down, and sold in SLICES in a package

lunch pail /ˈ. ./ *n.* [C] a PAIL (=metal container) that children or workers carried their lunch in in past times

lunch·room /'lʌntʃrum/ n. [C] a large room in a school or office where people can eat —compare CAFETERIA

lunch·time /'lʌntʃtaɪm/ n. [U] the time in the middle of the day when people usually eat their LUNCH

lung /lʌŋ/ n. [C] one of the two organs in your body that you breathe with: *Smoking can cause lung cancer.* —see also IRON LUNG, **sing/shout/yell etc. at the top of your lungs** (TOP¹ (14))

lunge /lʌndʒ/ v. [I] to make a sudden forceful movement toward someone or something, especially to attack them: [+ at] *The man lunged at them with a knife.* | [+ forward/toward etc.] *Turner lunged toward the goal line.* —**lunge** n. [C]

lunk·head /'lʌŋkhɛd/ n. [C] INFORMAL someone who is very stupid

lu·pine /'lupɪn/ n. [C] a plant with a tall stem and many small flowers

lu·pus /'lupəs/ n. [U] any of several diseases that affect the skin and joints

lurch¹ /lɜtʃ/ v. [I] **1** to walk or move suddenly in an uncontrolled or unsteady way: [+ across/into/along etc.] *The train suddenly lurched forward.* | *Jill lurched into me drunkenly.* **2 your heart/stomach lurches** used to say that your heart or stomach seems to move suddenly because you feel shocked, frightened etc. **3 lurch from one crisis/extreme etc. to the next** also **lurch from one crisis etc. to another** to seem to have no plan and no control over what you are doing: *From the day it opened last April, the theater seemed to lurch from one problem, one scandal to the next.*

lurch² n. [C] **1** a sudden movement: *"I felt a lurch and then a big bump," one resident said of the earthquake.* **2 leave sb in the lurch** to leave someone at a time when they need your help: *The pager company shut down Tuesday, leaving 2000 customers in the lurch.*

lure¹ /lʊr/ v. [T] to persuade someone to do something, often something wrong or dangerous, by making it seem attractive or exciting: [lure sb into/to/away etc. sth] *Sanders was nearly lured into pro baseball right after high school.*

lure² n. [C] **1** [usually singular] something that attracts people, or the quality of being able to do this: [+ of] *the lure of power and money* —compare TEMPTATION (2) **2** an object used to attract animals or fish so that they can be caught —compare DECOY (2)

lu·rid /'lʊrɪd/ adj. **1** a description, story etc. that is lurid is deliberately shocking and involves sex or violence: *lurid headlines* | *details of lurid sexual misconduct* **2** too brightly colored: *lurid red nail polish* —**luridly** adv. —**luridness** n. [U]

lurk /lɜk/ v. [I always + adv./prep.] **1** to wait somewhere quietly and secretly, usually because you are going to do something bad: [+ around/in/beneath etc.] *Witnesses said they saw a man lurking near the woman's home.* **2** if something such as danger, a feeling etc. lurks, it exists, but you are not fully AWARE of it: *Racism continues to lurk in the heart of American society.*

Lu·sa·ka /lu'sɑkə/ the capital and largest city of Zambia

lus·cious /'lʌʃəs/ adj. **1** extremely good to eat or drink: *luscious ripe strawberries* **2** INFORMAL a word meaning "very sexually attractive"

lush¹ /lʌʃ/ adj. **1** plants that are lush grow many leaves and look healthy and strong: *a lush garden* **2** very beautiful, comfortable, and expensive: *lush fabrics*

lush² n. [C] INFORMAL an ALCOHOLIC

lust¹ /lʌst/ n. **1** [C,U] very strong sexual desire, especially when it does not include liking or love: *There was a mixture of lust and guilt in his eyes.* **2** [singular,U] a very strong desire to have something, usually power or money: [+ for] *Stalin's unbridled lust for power* **3 (a) lust for life** a strong determination to enjoy life as much as possible: *Quinn's lust for life is contagious.*

lust² v.

lust after sb/sth phr. v. [T] INFORMAL, OFTEN HUMOROUS **1** to be strongly sexually attracted to someone, and think about having sex with them: *Andy's been lusting after Marla for years.* **2** to want something very much, especially something that you do not really need: *Every day I would go there and lust after the 1357 Chevy Bel Air in the window.*

lus·ter /'lʌstə/ n. [singular,U] **1** the quality that makes something interesting or exciting: *Beverly Hills has not lost its luster.* | **add/give/lose luster to sth** *Hei-Kyung Hong's soprano adds luster to the role of the lead Rhinemaiden.* **2** an attractive shiny appearance: *Wax is sprayed on the apples to give them more luster.*

lust·ful /'lʌstfəl/ adj. feeling or showing strong sexual desire: *Club Med is the renowned retreat for lustful yuppies.* —**lustfully** adv.

lus·trous /'lʌstrəs/ adj. shining in a soft, gentle way: *lustrous black hair*

lust·y /'lʌsti/ adj. **lustier, lustiest** strong and healthy; POWERFUL: *The baby gave a lusty cry.* | *lusty young men* —**lustily** adv. —**lustiness** n. [U]

lute /lut/ n. [C] a musical instrument similar to a GUITAR with a round body, played especially in past times

Lu·ther /'luθə/, **Mar·tin** /'mɑrt'n/ (1483–1546) a German religious leader whose ideas helped to start the Reformation, and who translated the Bible from Latin into German

Lu·ther·an /'luθərən/ n. [C] a member of a Protestant Christian church that follows the teachings and ideas of Martin Luther —**Lutheran** adj.

Lux·em·bourg /'lʌksəm,bɔg/ **1** a small country in western Europe, between Germany and France **2** the capital city of Luxembourg —**Luxembourger** n.

Lux·em·burg /'lʌksəm,bɔg/, **Ro·sa** /'roʊzə/ (1871–1919) a German SOCIALIST leader, born in Poland

lux·u·ri·ant /lʌg'ʒʊriənt, lʌk'ʃʊ-/ adj. **1** growing strongly and thickly: *a luxuriant black beard* | *luxuriant vegetation* **2** beautiful and pleasing to your senses: *luxuriant prose* —**luxuriantly** adv. —**luxuriance** n. [U]

lux·u·ri·ate /lʌg'ʒʊri,eɪt/ v.

luxuriate in sth phr. v. [T] to relax and consciously enjoy something: *Luxuriating in a bubble bath can help reduce stress.*

lux·u·ri·ous /lʌg'ʒʊriəs/ adj. very expensive, beautiful, and comfortable: *a luxurious brown leather sofa* —**luxuriously** adv. —**luxuriousness** n. [C]

lux·u·ry /'lʌkʃəri, 'lʌgʒəri/ n. plural **luxuries 1** [U] very great comfort and pleasure, such as you get from expensive food, beautiful houses, cars etc.: *In this society, a few enjoy luxury while others endure grinding poverty.* | **a luxury home/vacation/car etc.** (=expensive and of the highest standard) | *They led a life of luxury, in a huge house in the country.* **2 have/enjoy the luxury of sth** to have something that is very helpful or convenient, that you are not always able to have: *This was the first time I'd ever enjoyed the luxury of a regular paycheck.* | *Unfortunately, we don't have the luxury of waiting until next week for a decision.* **3** [C] something expensive that you do not need, but that you buy for pleasure and enjoyment: *We can't afford luxuries like piano lessons any more.* —compare NECESSITY (1) —see also **in the lap of luxury** (LAP¹ (4))

LVN n. [C] a LICENSED VOCATIONAL NURSE

LW the written abbreviation of LONG WAVE

-ly /li/ suffix **1** [in adverbs] in a particular way: *walking slowly* | *Everything was done secretly.* **2** [in adverbs] considered in a particular way: *Politically, it's a bad idea.* | *We're doing all right financially.* **3** [in adjectives and adverbs] happening at regular periods of time: *an hourly check* (=done every hour) | *They visit monthly* (=once a month). **4** [in adjectives] like a particular thing or person in manner, type, or appearance: *a cowardly act* | *a*

L

motherly woman (=showing the love, kindness etc. of a mother)

ly·ce·um /laɪˈsiəm, -ˈseɪəm/ *n.* [C] OLD-FASHIONED a building used for public meetings, concerts, speeches etc.

ly·chee /ˈlitʃi/ *n.* [C] a small round fruit with a rough pink-brown shell outside and sweet white flesh inside

Ly·cra /ˈlaɪkrə/ *n.* [U] TRADEMARK a material that stretches, used especially for making tight-fitting sports clothes

lye /laɪ/ *n.* [U] a substance using for making soap in past times

ly·ing /ˈlaɪ-ɪŋ/ *v.* the present participle of LIE

lying-in /ˌ.. ˈ./ *n.* [singular] OLD-FASHIONED the period of time during which a woman stays in bed before and after the birth of a child

Lyme dis·ease /ˈlaɪm dɪˌziz/ *n.* [U] a serious illness that is caused by a bite from a TICK[1] (2)

lymph /lɪmf/ *n.* [U] a clear liquid that is formed in your body and passes into your blood system to fight against infection —**lymphatic** /lɪmˈfætɪk/ *adj.*

lymph node also **lymph gland** /ˈ. ./ *n.* [C] a small rounded GLAND in your body through which lymph passes to be made pure before entering your blood system

lynch /lɪntʃ/ *v.* [T] if a crowd of people lynches someone, they kill them, especially by HANG*ing* (HANG[2]) them, without using the usual legal process: *One of*

the city leaders was nearly lynched on Nov. 27 by a mob. —**lynching** *n.* [C]

lynch mob /ˈ. ./ *n.* [C] a group of people that kills someone by HANG*ing*[2] them, without a legal TRIAL (1)

lynch·pin /ˈlɪntʃˌpɪn/ *n.* [C] another spelling of LINCH-PIN

Lynn /lɪn/, **Lo·ret·ta** /ləˈrɛtə/ (1935–) a U.S. COUNTRY AND WESTERN singer

lynx /lɪŋks/ *n.* [C] a large wild cat that has no tail and lives in forests

lyre /laɪə/ *n.* [C] a musical instrument with strings across a U-shaped frame, used especially in ancient Greece

lyr·ic[1] /ˈlɪrɪk/ *n.* **1** [C] TECHNICAL a poem, usually a short one, written in a lyric style **2 lyrics** [plural] the words of a song, especially a modern popular song: *the sophisticated brilliance of Sondheim's lyrics*

lyric[2] *adj.* [only before noun] **1** expressing strong personal emotions such as love, in a way that is similar to music in its sounds and RHYTHM: *lyric poetry* **2** TECHNICAL a lyric singing voice is high and not very loud: *a lyric soprano*

lyr·i·cal /ˈlɪrɪkəl/ *adj.* **1** beautifully expressed in words, poetry, or music: *Cynthia Kadohota's lyrical first novel* **2 wax lyrical** to talk about and praise something in a very eager way: *Krzyzewski waxed lyrical on his team's winning effort.* —**lyrically** /-kli/ *adv.*

lyr·i·cism /ˈlɪrəˌsɪzəm/ *n.* [U] the romantic or song-like expression of something in writing or music

lyr·i·cist /ˈlɪrəsɪst/ *n.* [C] someone who writes the words for songs, especially modern popular songs

L

M

M, m /ɛm/ *n. plural* **M's, m's** [C] **1** the 13th letter of the English alphabet **2** the number 1000 in the system of ROMAN NUMERALS **3** [singular,U] TECHNICAL **M0/M1/M2/M3** etc. different measures of a country's supply of money

m., m or **M** the written abbreviation of **a)** meter **b)** mile **c)** million **d)** male **e)** married **f)** MEDIUM

M.A. *n.* [C] Master of Arts; a university degree in a subject such as history or literature that you can get after you have your first degree: *Mrs. Wilding has an M.A. in education.* —compare M.S.

MA the written abbreviation of Massachusetts

Ma, ma /mɑ/ *n.* [C] INFORMAL **1** mother: *Hey Ma, can I go out with Billy?* **2** OLD-FASHIONED a word meaning "Mrs.," used in some country areas of the U.S.: *old Ma Harris*

ma'am /mæm/ *n.* SPOKEN **1** used to address a woman in order to be polite or show respect: *Can I help you today, ma'am?* | *"Are you done with that?" "Yes, ma'am."* **2** used to get the attention of a woman whose name you do not know: *Oh ma'am, are these keys yours?* —see also MADAM, SIR

Mac /mæk/ *n.* **1** [C] TRADEMARK Macintosh; a type of PERSONAL COMPUTER: *My roommate just got a Mac.* **2** SPOKEN used to talk to a man whose name you do not know, in a way that is often considered impolite: *Hey, Mac, get out of the way.*

ma·ca·bre /məˈkɑbrə, məˈkɑb/ *adj.* very strange and unpleasant, and relating to death, serious accidents etc.: *a macabre sense of humor* | *These drawings of the dead are moving rather than macabre.*

mac·ad·am /məˈkædəm/ *n.* [U] a road surface made of layers of broken stones and TAR or ASPHALT

mac·a·da·mi·a /ˌmækəˈdeɪmiə/ *n.* [C] **1** also **macadamia nut** a sweet nut that grows on a tropical tree **2** a tree that produces this type of nut

Ma·cao, Macau /məˈkaʊ/ a small area in southeast China, which was a Portuguese PROVINCE but became part of China in 1999

mac·a·ro·ni /ˌmækəˈroʊni/ *n.* [U] a type of PASTA in the shape of small tubes, which is cooked in boiling water: *a good recipe for **macaroni and cheese*** (=macaroni baked with a cheese sauce)

mac·a·roon /ˌmækəˈrun/ *n.* [C] a small round cookie made of sugar, eggs, and crushed ALMONDs or COCONUT

Mac·Ar·thur /məˈkɑrθɚ/, **Doug·las** /ˈdʌgləs/ (1880–1964) the leader of the U.S. Army in the Pacific area during World War II

ma·caw /məˈkɔ/ *n.* [C] a large brightly colored bird like a PARROT, with a long tail

Mac·ca·bees /ˈmækəˌbiz/ **1 Maccabees, 2 Maccabees** two books in the Apocrypha of the Protestant Bible and in the Old Testament of the Catholic Bible

Mace /meɪs/ *n.* [U] TRADEMARK a chemical that makes your eyes and skin sting painfully, which some women carry to defend themselves

mace /meɪs/ *n.* **1** [U] powder made from the dried shell of a NUTMEG, used to give food a special taste **2** [C] a heavy ball with sharp points that is attached to a short metal stick, used in past times as a weapon **3** [C] a decorated stick that is carried by an official in some ceremonies as a sign of power

Ma·ce·do·nia /ˌmæsɪˈdoʊnyə/ **1** a country in southeast Europe, north of Greece and south of Serbia, that was formerly part of Yugoslavia and is officially called the Former Yugoslav Republic of Macedonia (FYROM) **2** a PROVINCE of northern Greece —**Macedonian** *n. adj.*

mac·er·ate /ˈmæsəˌreɪt/ *v.* [I,T] TECHNICAL to make something soft by leaving it in water, or to become

---

soft in this way —**maceration** /ˌmæsəˈreɪʃən/ *n.* [U]

Mach, mach /mɑk/ *n.* [U] a number showing the speed of an airplane in relation to the speed of sound: *The plane can sustain a speed of Mach 3, or three times the speed of sound.*

ma·che·te /məˈʃɛti, -ˈtʃɛ-/ *n.* [C] a large knife with a broad heavy blade, used as a weapon or a tool

Mach·i·a·vel·li /ˌmækiəˈvɛli/, **Nic·co·lò** /ˈnɪkəloʊ/ (1469–1527) an Italian political PHILOSOPHER famous for his book THE PRINCE, in which he explains how political leaders can gain power and keep it

Mach·i·a·vel·li·an /ˌmækiəˈvɛliən/ *adj.* using smart but immoral methods to get what you want: *a Machiavellian conspiracy*

mach·i·na·tions /ˌmækəˈneɪʃənz, ˌmæʃə-/ *n.* [plural] secret and intelligent plans: *political machinations*

ma·chine¹ /məˈʃin/ *n.* [C] **1** a piece of equipment that uses power such as electricity to do a particular job: *Just hit that button to stop the machine.* | *Our soft-serve ice cream machine isn't working.* | **sewing/washing etc. machine** (=a machine that can sew, wash clothes etc.) **2** a computer: *You need a machine with 64 kilobytes of memory to run the program.* **3** INFORMAL an ANSWERING MACHINE: *Whenever she calls and the machine is on, she hangs up.* **4** a group of people who control an organization, especially a political party: *the party machine* | *the government's propaganda machine* **5 a well-oiled machine** something that works very smoothly and effectively: *If you're trained correctly you become like a well-oiled machine.* **6** someone who does something without stopping, or who seems to have no feelings or independent thoughts: *He's like an eating machine.* —see also CASH MACHINE, SLOT MACHINE, TIME MACHINE

USAGE NOTE: MACHINE

WORD CHOICE: machine, appliance, device, gadget, and tool

Machine is a general word for a piece of equipment that does a particular type of work, using power from an engine or electricity: *a vending machine* | *metal cutting machines*. An **appliance** is a large machine that is used to do something in people's homes: *They carry household appliances such as dishwashers and stoves*. A **device** is a piece of equipment that is usually small and has been designed to do a particular job: *A transponder is a device used to signal an airplane's identity* | *a birth control device*. A **gadget** is a small well-designed piece of equipment that makes a particular job easier to do: *kitchen gadgets* | *It's a gadget for cooking bacon in the microwave*. A **tool** is a small object used for making and repairing things, that usually does not use electricity: *a carpenter's tools* | *a small tool for cutting wire*.

---

machine² *v.* [T] **1** to fasten pieces of cloth together using a SEWING MACHINE **2** to make or shape something using a machine

machine code /.ˈ. ˌ./ *n.* [C,U] TECHNICAL instructions in the form of numbers that are understood by a computer

ma·chine gun /.ˈ. ˌ./ *n.* [C] a gun that fires a lot of bullets very quickly —**machinegun** *v.* [T]

machine lan·guage /.ˈ. ˌ../ *n.* [C,U] instructions in a form such as numbers that can be used by a computer

machine-made /.ˈ. ˌ./ *adj.* made using a machine: *machine-made candles* —compare HANDMADE

machine read·a·ble /.ˌ. ˈ...ˌ/ *adj.* in a form that can be understood and used by a computer

ma·chin·er·y /məˈʃinəri/ *n.* [U] **1** machines, especially large ones: *farm machinery* | *We've come to depend on labor-saving machinery.* **2** the parts inside a machine that make it work: *Loose clothing and jewelry can easily get caught in the machinery.* **3** system or set of processes for doing something: *the machinery of government*

M

machine tool /'. ,./ n. [C] a tool used for cutting and shaping metal, wood etc., usually run by electricity

machine trans·la·tion /.,. .'../ n. [U] translation done by a computer

machine-wash·a·ble /.,. '.../ adj. able to be washed in a WASHING MACHINE, rather than washed in water by a person —**machine wash** v. [T usually passive]

ma·chin·ist /mə'ʃɪnɪst/ n. [C] someone who operates a machine, especially in a factory

ma·chis·mo /mɑ'tʃɪzmoʊ/ n. [U] traditional male behavior that emphasizes how brave, strong, and sexually attractive a man is

ma·cho /'mɑtʃoʊ/ adj. INFORMAL macho behavior emphasizes a man's physical strength, lack of sensitive feelings, and other qualities considered to be typical of men: *All the guys that go to the gym are being macho and showing off.* | *Allen's show is based on tool-crazy macho men* (=men who are always trying to show that they are macho).

Mac·ken·zie /mə'kɛnzi/, **Alexander** (1764–1820) a Scottish EXPLORER who discovered the Mackenzie River in Canada and was the first European to cross the North American CONTINENT

mack·er·el /'mækərəl/ n. plural **mackerel** [C] an ocean fish that has oily flesh and a strong taste

mack·in·tosh /'mækɪn,tɑʃ/ n. [C] OLD-FASHIONED a RAINCOAT

Mack truck /'mæk trʌk/ n. [C] TRADEMARK **1** a type of large truck used to carry goods **2** INFORMAL a big strong man

mac·ra·mé /,mækrə'meɪ/ n. [U] the art of knotting string together in patterns for decoration

mac·ro /'mækroʊ/ n. plural **macros** [C] a set of instructions for a computer, stored and used as a unit

macro- /mækroʊ, -krə/ prefix TECHNICAL dealing with large systems as a single unit, rather than with the particular parts of them: *macroeconomics* (=the study of large money systems) —compare MICRO-

mac·ro·bi·ot·ic /,mækroʊbaɪ'ɑtɪk/ adj. macrobiotic food consists mainly of grains and vegetables, with no added chemicals

mac·ro·cosm /'mækrə,kɑzəm/ n. [C] a large, complicated system such as the whole universe or a society, considered as a single unit —compare MICROCOSM

mac·ro·ec·o·nom·ics /,mækroʊ,ɛkə'nɑmɪks/ n. [U] the study of large economic systems such as those of a whole country or area of the world —**macroeconomic** adj. —compare MICROECONOMICS

sw **mad** /mæd/ adj. **madder, maddest**
1 angry [not before noun] angry: *Was he mad?* | [+ about] *Local residents are mad about the new arena.* | [+ at] *Why are you so mad at me? I didn't do anything.* | *Mom got really mad.* | *I'm mad as hell and I'm not going to take it anymore!* | **hopping/ boiling mad** (=very angry)
2 do sth like mad INFORMAL to do something quickly or as well as you can: *I ran like mad to catch up to his car.*
3 wild/uncontrolled behaving in a wild, uncontrolled way, without thinking about what you are doing: *We made a mad dash for the departing boat.* | *They became the voice of reason in a region gone mad* (=where everyone seems to be doing crazy things).
4 mentally ill OLD-FASHIONED OR LITERARY mentally ill; INSANE: *There was a mad gleam in his bloodshot eyes.* | *He looked at me as if I had gone mad.*
5 be mad about sb/sth OLD-FASHIONED to love someone or be very interested in something, in a strong, uncontrolled way: *"I have been mad about trains since I was 5," said Smith.*
6 crazy BRITISH crazy or silly

-mad /mæd/ [in adjectives] **power-mad/money-mad/sex-mad etc.** only interested in power, money etc.: *This country is publicity-mad.*

Mad·a·gas·car /,mædə'gæskər/ an island in the Indian Ocean near the coast of southeast Africa that is an independent country —**Madagascan** n. adj.

mad·am /'mædəm/ n. **1 Madam President/Ambassador etc.** used to address a woman who has an important official position **2 Dear Madam** used at the beginning of a business letter to a woman whose name you do not know **3** [C] a woman who is in charge of a BROTHEL (=place where women are paid to have sex with men) **4** OLD-FASHIONED used to address a woman in order to be polite, especially someone you do not know: *How do you do, Madam?*

Ma·dame /mə'dɑm, mɑ-/ n. plural **Mesdames** /meɪ'dɑm/ [C] a title used to address a woman who speaks French, especially a married one: *Madame Lefevre*

mad·cap /'mædkæp/ adj. [no comparative] done or behaving in a wild or silly way that is often amusing or entertaining: *a madcap adventure*

mad cow dis·ease /,. '. .,./ n. [U] NOT TECHNICAL: see BSE

mad·den /'mædn/ v. [T usually passive] to make someone extremely angry or annoyed

mad·den·ing /'mædn-ɪŋ, 'mædnɪŋ/ adj. extremely annoying: *Golf can be a maddening game.* —**maddeningly** adv.

made /meɪd/ v. **1** the past tense and past participle of MAKE[1] **2 be made of sth** to be produced from a particular substance or material: *I bet this table is made of mahogany.* | *a doll made of cloth* **3 be made for each other** INFORMAL if two people, groups, organizations etc. were made for each other, they are completely appropriate for each other: *Television and the Muppets were made for each other.* **4 sb has (got) it made** INFORMAL to have everything that you need for a happy life or to be successful: *Get three more contracts, and you've got it made.* **5 what sb is (really) made of** INFORMAL how strong, brave etc. someone is: *People really show what they're made of when things are toughest for them.* **6 I'm not made of money** SPOKEN used to say that you cannot afford to buy whatever you want: *I can't buy you shoes as well – I'm not made of money!*

Ma·dei·ra /mə'dɪrə, -'dɛr-/ n. [U] a strong sweet wine

Mad·e·moi·selle /,mædəmwə'zɛl/ n. plural **Mesdemoiselles** /,meɪdəmwə'zɛl/ [C] a title used to address a young unmarried woman who speaks French: *Mademoiselle Dubois*

made-to-meas·ure /,. . '..◂/ adj. made-to-measure clothes are specially made to fit you

made-to-or·der /,. . '..◂/ adj. [only before noun] made specially for one particular customer: *Even better are their made-to-order omelets.* —**made to order** adv.: *I got a rug made to order at a good price.*

made-up /,. '.◂/ adj. **1** something that is made-up is not true or real: *a made-up name* **2** wearing MAKEUP on your face: *Do I look too made-up?*

mad·house /'mædhaʊs/ n. [C] **1** a place with lot of people, noise, and activity: *The police station is a madhouse most of the time.* **2** OLD USE a MENTAL HOSPITAL

Mad·i·son /'mædɪsən/ the capital city of the U.S. state of Wisconsin

Mad·i·son, James (1751–1836) the 4th President of the U.S.

mad·ly /'mædli/ adv. **1** in a wild, uncontrolled way: *As soon as the train stops, passengers push madly toward the doors.* **2 madly in love (with sb)** very much in love with someone

mad·man /'mædmæn, -mən/ n. plural **madmen** /-mɛn, -mən/ [C] **1** NOT TECHNICAL a man who is mentally ill **2 like a madman** in a wild, uncontrolled way: *The fans cheered like madmen when he scored a touchdown.*

mad mon·ey /'. ,./ n. [U] INFORMAL money that you have saved in order to spend it when you suddenly see something you want

mad·ness /'mædnɪs/ n. [U] **1** NOT TECHNICAL serious mental illness **2** stupid or uncontrolled behavior, especially behavior that could be dangerous: *Smith's photographs reflect the madness of our times.* | *Stores are preparing for the annual holiday shopping madness.* —see also **there's a method to sb's madness** (METHOD (3))

Ma·don·na /məˈdɑnə/ n. **1 the Madonna** Mary, the mother of Jesus Christ, in the Christian religion **2** [C] a picture or figure of Mary

mad·ras /ˈmædrəs, məˈdræs/ n. [U] a type of cotton cloth with a brightly colored PLAID pattern

Ma·drid /məˈdrɪd/ the capital and largest city of Spain

mad·ri·gal /ˈmædrɪgəl/ n. [C] a song for several singers without musical instruments, popular in the 16th and 17th centuries

mad·wom·an /ˈmæd,wʊmən/ n. plural **madwomen** /-ˌwɪmɪn/ [C] NOT TECHNICAL a woman who is mentally ill

mael·strom /ˈmeɪlstrəm/ n. [C] **1** a situation full of activity, confusion, or violence: [+ of] *A maelstrom of criticism surrounded Simon's last album.* **2** a violent storm

mae·stro /ˈmaɪstrou/ n. plural **maestros** [C] someone who can do something very well, especially a musician or CONDUCTOR (1)

ma·fi·a /ˈmɑfiə/ n. [singular] **1 the Mafia** a large organized group of criminals who control many illegal activities, especially in Italy and the U.S. **2** a powerful group of people within an organization or profession who support and protect each other: *the legal mafia*

ma·fi·o·so /ˌmɑfiˈousou/ n. plural **mafiosi** /-si/ [C] a member of the Mafia

mag /mæg/ n. [C] INFORMAL a magazine

mag·a·zine /ˌmægəˈzin, ˈmægəˌzin/ n. [C] **1** a large thin book with a paper cover that contains news stories, articles, photographs etc., and is sold weekly or monthly: *travel magazines | a photographic magazine* **2** the part of a gun that holds the bullets **3** the container that holds the film in a camera or PROJECTOR **4** a room or building for storing weapons, explosives etc.

Ma·gel·lan /məˈdʒɛlən/, **Fer·di·nand** /ˈfɔdn,ænd/ (?1480–1521) a Portuguese sailor who led the first EXPEDITION to sail around the world

ma·gen·ta /məˈdʒɛntə/ n. [U] a bright purple-red color —**magenta** adj.

mag·got /ˈmægət/ n. [C] a small creature like a WORM that is the young form of a FLY and lives in decaying food, flesh etc.

Ma·gi /ˈmædʒaɪ/ n. [plural] **the Magi** the three wise men who brought gifts to the baby Jesus Christ, according to the Christian religion

mag·ic¹ /ˈmædʒɪk/ n. **1** [U] a secret power used to control events or do impossible things, by saying special words or performing special actions: *a wizard who can do magic* —see also BLACK MAGIC, WHITE MAGIC **2** [U] a special, attractive, or exciting quality: *Christmas has a magic that appeals to young and old. | The band's guitars* **worked their magic** *on the crowd.* **3** [U] the skill of doing tricks to entertain people that are used by MAGICIANs, for example making something disappear, or the tricks a magician does **4 like magic** also **as if by magic** in a surprising way that seems impossible to explain: *The two cats vanished from the roof as if by magic. | His law enforcement methods have* **worked like magic** *in Charleston.*

magic² adj. **1** [only before noun] having special powers that are not normal or natural, so that you can do impossible things: *Brien has no magic formula for success, other than lots of practice. |* **magic spell/charm/hat** etc. (=something that lets you do things which seem impossible) **2** relating to the tricks or performance of a magician: *The kids will learn how to perform* **magic tricks**. *| a magic act* **3** very special, attractive, or exciting: *When I was a kid and television arrived, it was magic.* **4 magic number/word** a number or word that is very important or that has a powerful effect on people: *The Maharishi's followers say that 7000 is a magic number.* **5 magic bullet** INFORMAL a quick, painless cure for illness, or something that solves a difficult problem in an easy way: *There is no magic bullet for reducing cholesterol.* **6 the magic touch** a special ability to make things work well or to make people happy: *At the height of his career, he suddenly lost his magic touch.* **7 the magic word** SPOKEN the word

"please," said to remind a child to be polite: *What's the magic word, then, Katie?*

mag·i·cal /ˈmædʒɪkəl/ adj. **1** very enjoyable, exciting, or romantic, in a strange or special way: *Candles have a magical quality that transforms a room.* **2** containing magic, or done using magic: *Some people think garlic has magical powers.* —**magically** /-kli/ adv.

magical re·al·ism /ˌ... ˈ..../ also **magic realism** n. [U] a style in literature that combines REALISM (2) with magic, imagination, dreams, etc.

magic car·pet /ˌ... ˈ../ n. [C] a CARPET that people use to travel through the air, according to children's stories

ma·gi·cian /məˈdʒɪʃən/ n. [C] **1** someone in stories who can use magic **2** an entertainer who performs magic tricks

magic lan·tern /ˌ.. ˈ../ n. [C] a piece of equipment used in past times to make pictures shine onto a white wall or surface

Magic Mark·er /ˌ.. ˈ../ n. [C] TRADEMARK a large pen with a thick soft point: *a sign written in red magic marker*

magic mush·room /ˌ.. ˈ../ n. [C] INFORMAL a type of MUSHROOM that has an effect like some drugs, and makes you see things that are not really there

magic wand /ˌ.. ˈ./ n. [C] **1** a small stick used by a MAGICIAN **2 wave a magic wand** to solve problems or difficulties immediately: *The city council can't wave a magic wand and make taxes disappear.*

mag·is·te·ri·al /ˌmædʒəˈstɪriəl/ adj. **1** a magisterial way of behaving or speaking shows that you think you have authority: *In a magisterial tone he announced the Chaplain's arrival.* **2** a magisterial book is written by someone who has very great knowledge about a subject: *Finkelstein wrote a magisterial essay on the subject.* **3** relating to or done by a magistrate: *Magisterial permission is necessary for any public gathering.* —**magisterially** adv.

mag·is·tra·cy /ˈmædʒəstrəsi/ n. [U] **1** the official position of a magistrate, or the time during which someone has this position **2 the magistracy** magistrates considered together as a group

mag·is·trate /ˈmædʒɪˌstreɪt, -strɪt/ n. [C] someone who judges less serious crimes in a court of law

magistrates' court /ˈ... ˌ./ n. [C] a court of law that deals with less serious crimes

mag·ma /ˈmægmə/ n. [U] TECHNICAL hot melted rock below the surface of the Earth

mag·na cum lau·de /ˌmægnə kʊm ˈlaudeɪ, -də, -ˈlɔ-/ adj., adv. with high honor; used to show that you have finished high school or college at the second of the three highest levels of achievement that students can reach —compare CUM LAUDE, SUMMA CUM LAUDE

mag·nan·i·mous /mægˈnænəməs/ adj. kind and generous toward other people, especially people who are not in as good a position as you are: *It was a magnanimous gesture on their part.* —**magnanimously** adv. —**magnanimity** /ˌmægnəˈnɪməti/ n. [U]

mag·nate /ˈmægneɪt, -nɪt/ n. [C] a rich and powerful person in a particular industry: *newspaper magnate William Randolph Hearst*

mag·ne·sia /mægˈniʒə/ n. [U] a light white powder used in medicine and in industry —see also MILK OF MAGNESIA

mag·ne·si·um /mægˈniziəm, -ʒəm/ n. [U] symbol **Mg** a common silver-white metal that is an ELEMENT and that burns with a bright yellow light

mag·net /ˈmægnɪt/ n. [C] **1** a piece of iron or steel that can make other metal objects move toward it **2** a person or place that attracts many other people or things: [+ for] *Comaneci's gym is a magnet for*

magnet

M

young gymnasts from around the country. **3** a MAGNET SCHOOL

mag·net·ic /mæg'nɛtɪk/ *adj.* **1** relating to or produced by MAGNETISM: *A compass needle points to the magnetic north pole.* | *magnetic forces* **2 magnetic personality** a quality that someone has that makes other people feel strongly attracted toward them **3** having the power of a magnet: *a magnetic bulletin board* —**magnetically** /-kli/ *adv.*

magnetic field /.,.. '.,/ *n.* [U] an area around an object that has magnetic power

magnetic head /.,.. './ *n.* [C] **1** the part of a TAPE RECORDER that records sound **2** the part of a computer that reads and writes DATA

magnetic me·di·a /.,.. '.../ *n.* [plural,U] magnetic methods of storing information for computers, for example FLOPPY DISKs or MAGNETIC TAPE

magnetic north /.,.. './ *n.* [U] the northern direction shown by the needle on a COMPASS —compare TRUE NORTH

magnetic pole /.,.. './ *n.* [C] **1** one of the two points near the North and South Poles of the Earth, toward which the needle on a COMPASS points **2** a POLE¹ (5a)

magnetic res·o·nance im·ag·ing /.,.. '... ,.../ *abbreviation* **MRI** *n.* [U] the process of using strong MAGNETIC FIELDs to make an image of the inside of the body

magnetic tape /.,.. './ *n.* [U] a type of TAPE on which sound, pictures, or computer information can be recorded using magnetism

mag·net·ism /'mægnə,tɪzəm/ *n.* [U] **1** the physical force by which a MAGNET attracts metal, or which is produced when an electric current is passed through iron or steel **2** a quality that makes other people feel attracted to you: *She was overcome by his animal magnetism* (=his physical qualities).

mag·net·ize /'mægnə,taɪz/ *v.* [T] **1** to make iron or steel able to attract other pieces of metal **2** to have a powerful effect on people, so that they feel strongly attracted to you: *Students are always magnetized by her teaching.*

mag·ne·to /mæg'niṭoʊ/ *n.* [C] a piece of equipment containing one or more MAGNETs that is used for producing electricity

magnet school /'.. ,./ *n.* [C] a school that has more classes in a particular subject than usual, or special equipment to teach that subject, and so attracts students from a wide area: *a math magnet school*

mag·ni·fi·ca·tion /,mægnəfə'keɪʃən/ *n.* **1** [U] the act of magnifying: *High-power magnification is needed to see the crystals.* **2** [C] the degree to which something is able to magnify things: *The mirror has triple magnification and a light.*

mag·nif·i·cent /mæg'nɪfəsənt/ *adj.* extremely impressive because of being very big, beautiful etc.: *Wolves are magnificent and beautiful animals.* | *a magnificent art deco building* —**magnificently** *adv.* —**magnificence** *n.* [U]

mag·ni·fy /'mægnə,faɪ/ *v.* **magnified, magnifying** [T] **1** to make something look bigger than it is, especially using special equipment: *Her eyes were magnified by her thick glasses.* | *Binoculars magnify far-off objects.* **2** to make a problem much worse or more serious: *Our lack of information magnified our mistakes.* **3** to make something seem more important than it really is: *This report tends to magnify the risks involved.* **4** BIBLICAL to praise God —**magnifier** *n.* [C]

magnifying glass /'.... ,./ *n.* [C] a round piece of glass with a handle, used to make objects or print look bigger

mag·ni·tude /'mægnə,tud/ *n.* **1** [U] greatness of size or importance: *We've never dealt with a problem of this magnitude before.* **2** [U] TECHNICAL how strong an EARTHQUAKE is **3** [C] TECHNICAL the degree of brightness of a star

mag·no·lia /mæg'noʊlyə/ *n.* [C] a tree with large white, pink, yellow, or purple flowers that smell sweet

mag·num /'mægnəm/ *n.* [C] **1** a large bottle containing about 1.5 liters of wine, CHAMPAGNE etc. **2** a type of large PISTOL (=hand-held gun): *a .44 magnum*

magnum o·pus /,.. '../ *n.* [singular] the most important piece of work by a writer or artist

mag·pie /'mægpaɪ/ *n.* [C] **1** a bird with black and white feathers and a long tail **2** INFORMAL someone who talks a lot

Ma·gritte /mə'grit/, **Re·né** /rə'neɪ/ (1898–1967) a Belgian PAINTER famous for his pictures in the style of SURREALISM that combine familiar objects that are not usually seen together

ma·ha·ra·jah, maharaja /,mɑhə'rɑdʒə/ *n.* [C] an Indian PRINCE or king

ma·ha·ra·ni, maharanee /,mɑhə'rɑni/ *n.* [C] an Indian PRINCESS or queen

ma·ha·ri·shi /,mɑhə'riʃi/ *n.* [C] a HINDU holy teacher

Ma·hi·can, Mohican /mə'hikən/ a Native American tribe that formerly lived in the northeastern area of the U.S.

mah·jong, mahjongg /'mɑʒɑŋ, mɑ'ʒɑŋ/ *n.* [U] a Chinese game played with small pieces of wood or bone with pictures on them

Mah·ler /'mɑlɚ/, **Gus·tav** /'gʊstɑv/ (1860–1911) an Austrian musician who wrote CLASSICAL music

ma·hog·a·ny /mə'hɑgəni/ *n.* **1** [C,U] a type of hard reddish brown wood used for making furniture, or the tree that produces this wood **2** [U] a dark, reddish-brown color —**mahogany** *adj.*

maid /meɪd/ *n.* [C] **1** someone who cleans houses as their job **2** a female servant, especially in a large house: *a kitchen maid* **3** LITERARY a woman or girl who is not married —see also OLD MAID

maid·en¹ /'meɪdn/ *n.* [C] LITERARY a girl who is not married

maiden² *adj.* **maiden flight/voyage** the first trip that an airplane or ship makes

maiden aunt /,.. './ *n.* [C] an AUNT who has never married

maid·en·hair /'meɪdn,hɛr/ *n.* [U] a type of FERN

maid·en·head /'meɪdn,hɛd/ *n.* LITERARY **1** [U] the state of being a female VIRGIN **2** [C] a HYMEN

maid·en·ly /'meɪdnli/ *adj.* LITERARY typical of a girl or young woman: *maidenly modesty*

maiden name /,.. './ *n.* [C] the family name that a woman had before she got married

maid of hon·or /,.. '../ *n.* [C] **1** the main BRIDESMAID at a wedding **2** an unmarried lady who serves a queen or a PRINCESS

maid·ser·vant /'meɪd,sɚvənt/ *n.* [C] OLD USE a female servant —compare MANSERVANT

mail¹ /meɪl/ *n.* [singular,U] **1** the system of collecting and delivering letters, packages etc.: *You'll get your room assignment in the mail.* | *More people than ever shop by mail.* —see also ELECTRONIC MAIL, SNAIL MAIL **2** the letters, packages etc. that are delivered to a particular person or at a particular time: *Is that all the mail that came today?* | *Sarah brought your mail over.* | *Did you show Dad what you got in the mail?* —see also JUNK MAIL **3** [U] ARMOR made of metal, worn in the Middle Ages

mail² *v.* [T] to send a letter, package etc. to someone: **[mail sb sth]** *They're going to mail me a check.* | **[mail sth to sb]** *We'll just mail the flyers to all the people on the list.*

mail sth ↔ out *phr. v.* [T] to send letters, packages etc. to a lot of people at the same time: *The department has just mailed out 300,000 notices.*

mail·bag /'meɪlbæg/ *n.* **1** a large, strong bag used for carrying mail by train, truck etc. **2** a bag used by mail carriers to deliver letters to people's houses

mail·box /'meɪlbɑks/ *n.* [C] **1** a box, usually outside a house, where someone's letters are delivered or picked up —see picture on page 423 **2** a special box in the street or at a POST OFFICE where you mail letters —compare P.O. BOX

mail car·ri·er /'. ,.../ *n.* [C] someone who delivers mail to people's houses

mail drop /'. ./ *n.* [C] **1** an address where someone's mail is delivered, but which is not where they live **2** a box in a post office where your mail can be left

mail·er /'meɪlɚ/ *n.* [C] a container or envelope used for sending something small by mail

Mai·ler /'meɪlɚ/, **Nor·man** /'nɔrmən/ (1923–) a U.S. writer and JOURNALIST, known for his NOVELS

mail·ing list /'.. ,./ *n.* [C] **1** a list of names and addresses kept by an organization, so that it can send information or advertising material by mail **2** a list of names and EMAIL addresses kept on a computer so that you can send the same message to the same group of people at the same time

mail·man /'meɪlmæn, -mən/ *n.* plural **mailmen** /-mɛn, -mən/ [C] a man who delivers mail to people's houses

mail or·der /'. ,./ *n.* [U] A method of buying and selling in which the buyer chooses goods at home and orders them from a company that sends them by mail: *Our software is available by mail order.* —**mail-order** *adj.: a mail-order catalog*

mail train /'. ./ *n.* [C] a train that carries mail

maim /meɪm/ *v.* [T] to wound or injure someone very seriously and often permanently: *A five-year-old girl was maimed in the bombing.*

Mai·mon·i·des /maɪˈmɑnəˌdiz/ (1135–1204) a Jewish PHILOSOPHER

main[1] /meɪn/ *adj.* [only before noun] **1** more important or bigger than all other things, ideas, influences etc. of the same kind: *Well, that's the main reason I was calling. | I think the next main road is where we have to turn left. | Our main concern was "What did we do wrong?" | Gigi will be working the main cash register. | The **main character** in "The Big Picture" is Max Popper.* **2 the main thing** SPOKEN used to say what is the most important thing in a situation: *Saving the peace plan is the main thing right now. | The main thing is to impress Bora and get on the team.*

main[2] *n.* **1** [C] a large pipe or wire carrying the public supply of water, electricity, or gas: *A broken water main flooded the building's garage.* **2 in the main** mostly: *Their track record has, in the main, been a positive one.*

main clause /, './ *n.* [C] TECHNICAL in grammar, a CLAUSE that can form a sentence on its own

main course also **main dish** /, './ *n.* [C] the largest part of a meal: *We're having appetizers, a main course, a dessert, drinks, everything.*

main drag /, './ *n.* INFORMAL **the main drag** the most important street in a town or city, where big stores and businesses are: *We went into this restaurant called Cooter's, right there on the main drag.*

Maine /meɪn/ *written abbreviation* **ME** a state in the northeastern U.S. next to the Atlantic coast

main·frame /'meɪnfreɪm/ *n.* [C] a large computer that can work very fast and that a lot of people can use at the same time

main·land /'meɪnlænd, -lənd/ *n.* **the mainland** the main area of land that forms a country, as compared to islands near it that are also part of that country: *There are no direct flights from the mainland to Molokai.* —**mainland** *adj.: mainland China*

main·line[1] /'meɪnlaɪn/ *adj.* [only before noun] belonging to the normal, accepted part of a group, business, tradition etc., and therefore having a position that is fairly important: *mainline Protestant churches | a mainline news network*

mainline[2] *v.* [I,T] SLANG to INJECT illegal drugs into your blood: *By that time he was mainlining heroin.*

main·ly /'meɪnli/ *adv.* as the largest or most important reason, thing, part of something etc.: *Is Idaho where you grew up, mainly? | I joined the club **mainly because** it has a basketball court. | AIDS is transmitted mainly through sexual contact. | We cater mainly to small businesses.*

main·mast /'meɪnmæst, -məst/ *n.* [C] the largest or

most important of the MASTS that hold up the sails on a ship

main·sail /'meɪnseɪl, -səl/ *n.* [C] NOT TECHNICAL the largest and most important sail on a ship

main·spring /'meɪnsprɪŋ/ *n.* **1 the mainspring of sth** FORMAL the most important reason or influence that makes something happen: *The villagers' fierce independence formed the mainspring of revolt.* **2** [C] the most important spring in a watch or clock

main·stay /'meɪnsteɪ/ *n. plural* **mainstays** [C] **1** an important part of something that makes it possible for it to work correctly or continue to exist: *Tourism has long been the economic mainstay of Kashmir.* **2** someone whom a group or organization depends on to do important work: *Another mainstay of the opera company is Tatiana Troyanos.*

main·stream[1] /'meɪnstrim/ *n.* **the mainstream** the beliefs and opinions that represent the most usual way of thinking about or doing something, or the people who have these beliefs: *Tamayo brought Mexican themes into the mainstream of international art.* —**mainstream** *adj.: mainstream American politics*

mainstream[2] *v.* [T] to include a child with physical or mental problems in an ordinary class

Main Street /'. ./ *n.* **1** [C] the most important street in many small towns in the U.S., with many stores and businesses on it **2** [U] ordinary people who believe in traditional American values: *The President's new tax hikes won't be too popular on Main Street.*

main·tain /meɪnˈteɪn/ *v.*

1 | make sth continue | [T] to make something continue in the same way or at the same standard as before; KEEP: *Our main wish is to help maintain world peace. | Volkswagen has maintained close business ties with them for over 20 years. | King lives in Chicago but maintains an apartment in New York.*

2 | level/rate | [T] to make a level or rate of activity, movement etc. stay the same: *They're finding it difficult to maintain such high interest rates. | Dieters should try to reach and maintain a reasonable weight.*

3 | take care of sth | [T] to take care of something so that it stays in good condition: *His first job was installing and maintaining computers. | It's hard to do this job and still maintain a marriage.*

4 | say | [T] to strongly express your belief that something is true: [**maintain (that)**] *Sautter maintains writers do get respect in the film and TV business. | During their trial, the brothers **maintained their innocence** (=continued to say they were not guilty).*

5 maintain your silence/opposition etc. to continue to be silent, to oppose something etc.: *The smaller unions have maintained their independence within the organization.*

6 | support life | to provide people, animals, plants etc. with the things they need in order to exist: *The goal is to build a space station that can **maintain life** on a faraway planet like Mars.*

7 | not lose control | [I] SPOKEN to deal with a difficult situation without losing control: *Cox said he and his wife, Chrissy, were "trying to just maintain."*

main·te·nance /'meɪntn̩-əns/ *n.* [U] **1** the repairs, painting etc. that are necessary to keep something in good condition: [+ **of**] *Do you know how much the maintenance of city buildings costs?* | **home/car/building etc. maintenance** *the state's highway maintenance department* | **maintenance man/worker/persons** (=someone who looks after buildings and equipment for a school or company) **2** the act of making a state or situation continue: *Our primary concern is the maintenance of discipline in the school.*

maintenance fee /'... ,./ *n.* [C] money that you pay for your share of the cleaning and repairs of the building that your CONDOMINIUM is part of

mai·tre d' /ˌmeɪtrə ˈdi, ˌmɛ-, ˌmeɪtɚ-/ also **maître d'hôtel** /-douˈtɛl/ *n.* [C] someone who is in charge of a restaurant, and who welcomes guests, gives orders to the WAITERS etc.

M

maize /meɪz/ *n.* [U] CORN

Maj. the written abbreviation of MAJOR² (1)

ma·jes·tic /məˈdʒɛstɪk/ *adj.* very big, impressive, and beautiful: *the majestic coast around Big Sur* —**majestically** /-kli/ *adv.*

maj·es·ty /ˈmædʒəsti/ *n.* **1** [U] the quality that something big has of being impressive, powerful, and beautiful: *the majesty of the Rocky Mountains* **2 Your/Her/His Majesty** used when talking to or about a king or queen: *His Majesty, King Juan Carlos I | How do you like the White House, Your Majesty?*

ma·jor¹ /ˈmeɪdʒɚ/ *adj.* [no comparative] **1** [usually before noun] very large, serious, or important, when compared to other things or people of a similar kind: *Confidence is a major part of leadership. | She's had major surgery, but she's doing fine. | Most major credit cards are accepted. | Everybody had a good time and there were no **major problems**.* —opposite MINOR¹ (1) **2** [not before noun] SPOKEN used to emphasize that something is very large, important, bad etc.: *I have to go on a major shopping trip before I start this job.* **3** a major KEY is based on a musical SCALE in which there are HALF STEPS between the third and fourth and the seventh and eighth notes: *a symphony in D major* —compare MINOR¹ (2)

ma·jor² *n.* [C] **1** also **Major** a rank in the Army, Marines, or Air Force, or someone who has this rank —see also DRUM MAJOR **2** the main subject that a student studies at a college or university: *I'm changing my major to political science.* —compare MINOR² (2) **3** someone studying a particular subject as their main subject at a college or university: *Greg is a philosophy major.*

major³ *v.*
major in sth *phr. v.* [T] to study something as your main subject at a college or university: *What do you want to major in?*

ma·jor·do·mo /ˌmeɪdʒɚˈdoʊmoʊ/ *n.* [C] OLD-FASHIONED a man who is in charge of the servants in a large house

ma·jor·ette /ˌmeɪdʒəˈrɛt/ *n.* [C] a girl who spins a BATON while marching with a band

major gen·er·al, **Major General** /ˌ.. ˈ...ˌ/ *n.* [C] a high rank in the Army or the Air Force, or someone who has this rank

ma·jor·i·ty /məˈdʒɔrəti, -ˈdʒɑr-/ *n. plural* **majorities 1 the majority** most of the people or things in a particular group: [+ of] *Hispanics make up a majority of the city's residents.* | **the great/vast majority of sth** (=almost all of a group) | **a majority decision/ruling** (=a decision made by more people voting for it than against it) **2** [C] the difference between the number of votes gained by the winning party or person in an election and the number of votes gained by other parties or people: *A two-thirds majority is needed to override a veto.* | *He won the seat with a majority of 71 percent.* **3 be in the majority** to form the largest part of a group: *Each tribe claims to be in the majority.* **4** [U] LAW the age when someone legally becomes a responsible adult —opposite MINORITY¹

majority lead·er /.ˈ...ˌ.../ *n.* [C] the person who organizes the members of the political party that has the most people elected, in either the House of Representatives or the Senate —compare MINORITY LEADER

major league, **major-league** /ˌ.. ˈ.ˌ/ *adj.* [usually before noun] **1** relating to the Major Leagues: *a major league pitcher* **2** important, large, or having a lot of influence: *Some of the new Gallo wines come with major-league price tags.*

Major Leagues /ˌ.. ˈ./ *n.* [plural] **the Major Leagues** the group of teams that make up the highest level of American professional baseball —**major leaguer** *n.* [C] —compare MINOR LEAGUE

Ma·ju·ro /məˈdʒʊroʊ/ the island that is the capital of the Marshall Islands

make¹ /meɪk/ *v. past tense and past participle* **made**
1 produce sth [T] to produce something by

working or doing something: *Carol's making carrot cake for dessert. | Did you make that dress yourself? | a car made in Japan | He made two small holes in the wood. | Mark made a video of his daughter's wedding.* | [**make sth out of sth**] *You can make some bookcases out of those crates.* | [**make sth from sth**] *We made a shelter from leaves and branches.* | [**make sb sth**] *Can you make me a copy of those receipts?* —see also **be made of sth** (MADE) —see Usage Note at COOK¹

2 do sth [T] used with some nouns to say that you do the actions relating to the noun: *Lt. Richards will try to **make a decision** by Friday. | Can I use your cell phone to **make a call** ? | I really feel she's **making a mistake**. | Can I **make a suggestion** ? | Did you **make an appointment** to see the doctor? | Would you like to **make a statement**, Mr. Rojack? | You need to **make reservations** at least six weeks in advance. | People have to **make a commitment** to be in the program.* | **make a contribution/donation** etc. (=give money for a particular purpose) | *The budget plan **makes a start** (=begins something) at reducing the debt. | My car's **making** that weird **noise** again. | Eric **made** the biggest **mess** in the kitchen.* | **make an appearance/entrance** etc. (=to suddenly appear somewhere, enter a room etc.)

3 cause sth [T] to cause a particular state or situation, or cause something to happen: *The song was made famous by the Andrews Sisters.* | [**make sb/sth do sth**] *What made you think of that? | This cold medicine makes me fall asleep. | Drink this – it'll **make you feel better**.* | **make sb happy/sad/mad** etc. (=cause a particular feeling) | *Make certain that scuba equipment meets safety standards. | He's **making himself sick** worrying about the trial. | Earlier this year, Reid **made it known** that he was thinking of retiring. | Do these jeans **make me look fat**?* | **make sth the best/worst/most expensive** etc. *What makes humans the most successful animal species on earth?*

4 force [T] to force someone to do something, or force something to happen: [**make sb do sth**] *Mom made him wear a hat because of the wind. | You can't make someone stop smoking. They have to want to do it.*

5 earn money [T] to earn or get money: *Who's that baseball player that makes seven million dollars a year? | Do you **make** decent **money** in that line of work? | Betty **makes a living** (=makes enough money to buy the things she needs) growing organic vegetables. | They could sell CDs for three bucks each and still **make a profit** (=earn money in a trade or business).* —see Usage Note at GAIN¹

6 make a difference to cause a change in a situation, especially an improvement: *Printing your résumé on nice paper makes a big difference. | All the extra hours we put in made no real difference. | A positive attitude **makes all the difference**.*

7 make it a) INFORMAL to arrive somewhere in time for something, when you were not sure you would: *It's only ten till seven – we'll make it.* | [+ **to**] *We just made it to the hospital before the baby arrived.* **b)** INFORMAL to manage to continue doing something difficult until it is finished: [+ **to**] *Three of my students didn't make it to the midterm.* | [+ **through**] *I'm so tired, I'm not sure I can make it through the 11 o'clock news.* **c)** SPOKEN to be at an event, meeting etc. that has been arranged, when there was a possibility that you might not be: *I'm glad you could make it, Nancy.* | [+ **to**] *Eric won't be able to make it to the meeting tomorrow.* **d)** INFORMAL to live after a serious illness or accident, or manage to deal with a difficult experience: *Children with the disease rarely make it past their tenth birthday.* | [+ **through**] *Would $50 help you to make it through the rest of the week? | New antifreeze will help the car make it through the winter.* **e)** INFORMAL to be successful in a particular activity or profession, when this is difficult: *He was starting to wonder if he would ever make it in the Major Leagues. | We had two flop records before we **made it big** (=became very successful).*

8 make the meeting/the party/Tuesday etc. to be able to go to something that has been arranged for a particular date or time, even though you are busy: *I* *can make eight thirty on Tuesday. | Will you be able to make the next meeting?*

9 make a deadline/target/rate to succeed in doing something by a particular time, producing a particular amount etc.: *We'll never make the deadline.*

10 have a quality [linking verb] to have the qualities, character etc. necessary for a particular job, use, or purpose: *Cooper's going to make a good doctor one day. | Don't they make a cute couple? | An old cardboard box makes a comfortable bed for a kitten.*

11 make your way (to/through/back etc.) a) to move toward something, especially slowly or with difficulty: *Lisac eventually made his way to Canada and settled there.* **b)** to slowly become successful in a particular job, activity, or profession: *A number of firms are unable to make their way in the new capitalist system.*

12 make way (for sb/sth) a) to move to one side so that someone or something can pass: *She made way for him, pushing back her chair.* **b)** to remove something so that something newer or better can be used or made instead: *Stores are clearing winter goods to make way for spring merchandise.*

13 make the papers/headlines/front page to be interesting or important enough to be printed in the newspaper: *Stories about the couple's split continue to make the papers.*

14 make the team/squad etc. to be good enough to be chosen to play on a sports team: *Heidi is sure to make the varsity basketball team.*

15 make the bed to pull the sheets and covers over a bed so that it is neat after someone has slept in it

16 make time (for sb/sth) to find enough time to do something, even though you are busy: *We always made time to see Sam when we were in San Francisco.*

17 adding numbers [linking verb] if two or more numbers make another number, they equal a particular amount when added together: *Two plus two makes four. | There are nine people coming, plus me, which makes ten.*

SPOKEN PHRASES

18 make it quick/snappy used to tell someone to do something as quickly as possible: *Okay, have a Coke, but make it quick.*

19 make that/it used when correcting something you have just said: *And an order of onion rings. No, better make it two orders. | His employees think he's a hero. Make that a god.*

20 make it 10/20/100 etc. [T] to decide that a particular amount, especially an amount of money, is acceptable, even if it is not the exact amount owed or needed: *I think it was $19.50, but let's just make it an even $20.*

21 that makes two of us used to agree with someone's opinion or to say that something that happened to them has also happened to you: *"I'd like to work in Hawaii." "That makes two of us."*

22 make it up to sb to do something good for someone because you feel responsible for something bad or disappointing that happened to them: *I'm sorry I couldn't get away from the office last night. I'll make it up to you this weekend.*

---

23 make do (with/without sth) INFORMAL to manage with or without something, even though this is not completely satisfactory: *Until our furniture arrives we're making do with a couple of card tables.*

24 make sb captain/leader etc. to give someone a new job or position in a group, organization etc., that is higher than the one they had before: *She's just been made a full partner.*

25 make or break sb/sth to cause either great success or complete failure: *A review by Rich can make or break a show on Broadway.*

26 make believe to pretend that something is true or exists: *You can't go on making believe that nothing is wrong.* —see also MAKE-BELIEVE

27 make as if to do sth to move in such a way that it seems that you are going to do something, although you do not do it: *Hardin made as if to rise from his seat.*

28 make sth perfect [T] INFORMAL to provide the qualities that make something complete or successful:

The hat really makes the outfit. | Your letter really made my day (=made the day seem good)!

29 make it with sb OLD-FASHIONED to have sex with someone

30 arrive at a place [T] OLD-FASHIONED to arrive at a particular place after a long or difficult trip: *We'll never make town before nightfall.* —see also **make friends** (FRIEND (2)), **make good on a debt/promise/threat etc.** (GOOD² (6)), **make love (to/with sb)** (LOVE² (5)), MADE, **make sense** (SENSE¹ (2))

make away with sb/sth *phr. v.* [T] INFORMAL to steal something and take it away from a place: *Thieves made away with over $20,000 in yesterday's robbery.*

make for sth *phr. v.* [T] **1** to move toward something, or move in a particular direction: *Sue made for the snack bar while Brian bought tickets.* **2** to be likely to have a particular result or make something possible: *New chrome trim on the car makes for a modern, sporty look.* —see also **be made for each other** (MADE (3))

make sb/sth **into** sth *phr. v.* [T] **1** to change something so that it has a different form or purpose: *NBC wants to make Judd's story into a miniseries.* **2** to change someone's character, job, or position in society: *Good new players have made the Steelers into a great team.*

make sth **of** sb/sth *phr. v.* [T] **1** to understand something in a particular way, or have a particular opinion about something: *He smiled, not quite sure what to make of my comments. | Come, Watson, and tell me what you make of this gentleman.* **2** to use the chances, opportunities etc. you have in a way that achieves a good result: *Their dream was to get jobs and make something of themselves. | Danville **makes the most of** the snow by holding an annual winter carnival (=they do something really good with the situation).* **3 make (too) much of sth** to treat something as if it is more important than it really is: *Much is being made of the number of women serving in the army.* **4 make a day/night/evening of it** to decide to spend a whole day, night etc. doing something: *Why don't you make a day of it and have lunch with us?* **5 do you want to make sth (out) of it?** SPOKEN used in an angry way to say that you are willing to have a fight or argument with someone —see also **make the best of** (BEST³ (7)), **what sb is (really) made of** (MADE (5))

make off with sth *phr. v.* [T] to take something that does not belong to you: *Someone tried to make off with the red and white pole from the barber shop.*

make out *phr. v.* **1** [T **make** sth ↔ **out**] to be just barely able to hear, see, or understand something: *Many in the crowd could hardly make out what he was saying, as he spoke without a microphone.* **2 make out a check (to sb)** to write a check: *Who do I make the check out to?* **3** [T **make** sb ↔ **out**] INFORMAL to understand someone's character, or what they think, feel, want etc.: *I couldn't make him out at all.* **4** [T] INFORMAL to claim or pretend that something is true when it is not: [**make out that**] *To make out that people are oppressed here is just insane. | [**make sb out to be sth**] Norm's not the big bad guy that some people make him out to be.* **5** [I] to succeed or progress in a particular way: *How did your parents make out in Las Vegas?* **6** [I] INFORMAL to kiss and touch someone in a sexual way: *Several kids were making out in the hallway.* **7 make out like a bandit** INFORMAL to get a lot of money or gifts, win a lot etc.: *Insurance companies always make out like bandits.*

make sth ↔ **over** *phr. v.* [T] to change something so that it looks different or has a different use: *Redgrave has made herself over completely for the movie role.* —see also MAKEOVER

make up *phr. v.*

1 excuse/explanation [T **make** sth ↔ **up**] to invent a story, explanation etc. in order to deceive someone: *Oh, she wouldn't make up a story like that.* —see also MADE-UP

2 song/poem [T **make** sth ↔ **up**] to invent the words or music for a new song, story, poem etc.: *In*

M

an improvisation, I get the rhymes first and then make up the rest.

3 form/be [T **make** sth ↔ **up**] to combine together to form a particular system, group, result etc.: *In Los Angeles, minority groups make up 64% of the population.* | *Protons and neutrons are made up of smaller components called quarks.* —see Usage Note at COMPRISE

4 prepare/arrange [T **make** sth ↔ **up**] to prepare or arrange something by putting things together: *Why don't you make up a list of what we need from the store?* | *I made up a batch of cookies for the church social.*

5 sb's face [I,T **make** sb ↔ **up**] to put special paint, color etc. on someone's face to change the way they look: *They made him up to look like he was dead.* —see also MADE-UP, MAKEUP

6 time/work [T **make** sth ↔ **up**] to work at times when you do not usually work, so that you do all the work that you should have done: *I'm trying to make up the time I lost while I was sick.* | *Is it OK if I make the work up next week?*

7 friends [I] to become friendly with someone again after you have had an argument: *Have you two made up yet?* | *I think they just fight because they like to kiss and make up.*

8 [T **make up** sth] to complete an amount or number to the level that is needed: *If you don't have it, we can make up the fifteen dollar difference.*

9 from cloth [T **make** sth ↔ **up**] to produce something from cloth by cutting and sewing: [+ **into**] *I'm going to make that material up into a dress.* —see also **make up your mind** (MIND¹ (3))

make up for sth *phr. v.* **1** [T] to make a bad situation seem better, by providing something nice; COMPENSATE: *What the airline lacks in frills it makes up for in service.* **2 make up for lost time a)** to work more quickly, or at times when you do not usually work, because something has prevented you from working before: *The bus driver was speeding to make up for lost time.* **b)** to become involved in an activity very eagerly, because you wish you could have done it earlier in your life: *He's girl crazy! He went to a boys' school and now he's making up for lost time.* **3** [T] to have so much of one quality that it does not matter that you do not have enough of something else: *She's not particularly bright, but she so nice that that makes up for it.*

USAGE NOTE: MAKE

WORD CHOICE: make or do
There is no simple rule for when to use **make** or **do.** Generally, we tend to use **make** to talk about producing things that did not exist before: *I made a blueberry pie.* | *John made a good point.* | *You're making a mess there.* We also use **make** when someone or something is changed in some way: *That should make him happy.* | *You'll have to make the picture bigger.* | *They've really made a name for themselves.* We usually use **do** to talk about actions: *My kids don't have to do chores in the summer.* | *Could you do a favor for me?* | *Have you done your homework?*

---

make² *n.* **1** a particular type of product, made by one company: *What make is your car?* | [+ **of**] *They use a different make of computer.* **2 be on the make** INFORMAL **a)** to be always trying to get an advantage for yourself **b)** to be trying to have a sexual relationship with someone

make-be·lieve /ˌ. .'. ◂/ *adj.* not real, but imagined or pretended: *Many small children have make-believe friends.* —**make-believe** *n.* [U]

make-or-break /ˌ. . '. / *adj.* causing either great success or complete failure: *The last couple of games were make-or-break.*

make·o·ver /'meɪkˌoʊvɚ/ *n.* [C] **1** a process of improving your own or someone else's appearance with new clothes, a new HAIRCUT, MAKEUP etc.: *He picks a guest from the audience and gives them a*

makeover, right on TV. **2** a process of changing the way a place looks: *a kitchen makeover*

mak·er /'meɪkɚ/ *n.* [C] **1** a person or company that makes or produces something: *Daimler-Benz AG is the maker of Mercedes-Benz automobiles.* | *wine makers* **2 decision/policy etc. maker** someone who is good at or responsible for making decisions: *U.S. policy makers must address a number of tough issues.* —see also PEACEMAKER, TROUBLEMAKER **3 ice cream/popcorn/coffee etc. maker** a machine used to make a particular thing —see also **meet your maker** (MEET¹ (19))

make·shift /'meɪkˌʃɪft/ *adj.* [only before noun] made for temporary use when you need something and there is nothing better available: *Thousands have tried to flee in makeshift boats.*

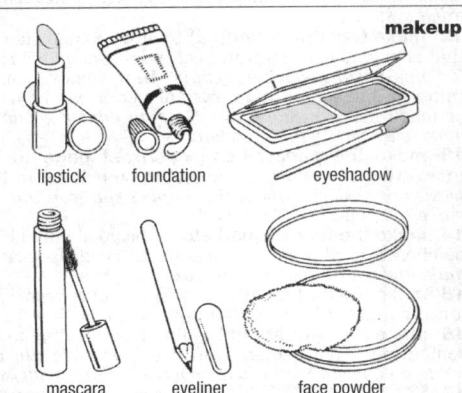

makeup

lipstick   foundation   eyeshadow

mascara   eyeliner   face powder

---

make·up, make-up /'meɪk-ʌp/ *n.* **1** [U] substances such as powders, creams, and LIPSTICK that people, especially women or actors, put on their faces to improve or change their appearance: *She never wears makeup.* | *Give me a minute to put on my makeup.* —see also **make up** (MAKE¹), PANCAKE MAKEUP **2** [singular] a particular combination of people or things that form a group or whole: *Our workforce reflects the multicultural makeup of the area.* **3 sb's makeup** the qualities, attitudes etc. in someone's character: *Jeff seems to have the emotional makeup of a 13-year-old.* **4** [C] also **makeup test/exam** a test taken in school because you were not able to take a previous test

make-work /'. ./ *n.* [U] work that is not important but is given to people to keep them busy: *Another 1.8 million people are in what amounts to make-work jobs.*

mak·ing /'meɪkɪŋ/ *n.* **1** [U] the process or business of making or producing something: *Eleanor Coppola wrote a book about the making of "Apocalypse Now."* | *Many things can interfere with effective decision making.* | *quilt-making* **2 in the making** in the process of being made or produced: *This is not just news – this is history in the making.* **3 have the makings of sth** to have the qualities or skills needed to become a particular kind of person or thing: *We've got the makings of a winning team.* **4 of your own making** problems or difficulties that are of your own making have been caused by you and no one else: *He found himself caught in a dilemma of his own making.*

mal- /mæl/ *prefix* bad or badly: *a malodorous room* (=that smells bad) | *a computer malfunction* (=it doesn't work the way it should)

Mal·a·bo /'mæləboʊ, mɑ'lɑboʊ/ the capital city of Equatorial Guinea

Mal·a·chi /'mæləˌkaɪ/ a book in the Old Testament of the Christian Bible

mal·ad·just·ed /ˌmælə'dʒʌstɪd◂/ *adj.* unable to form good relationships with people because of problems in your character and attitudes —**maladjustment** *n.* [U]

mal·ad·min·is·tra·tion /ˌmæləd mɪnə'streɪʃən/ *n.* [U] FORMAL careless or dishonest management

mal·a·droit /ˌmæləˈdrɔɪt/ *adj.* FORMAL not good at dealing with people or problems —**maladroitly** *adv.* —**maladroitness** *n.* [U]

mal·a·dy /ˈmælədi/ *n. plural* **maladies** [C,U] FORMAL **1** an illness: *Some doctors still regard menopause as a malady.* **2** something that is wrong with a system or organization: *The airline suffers from a common malady – lack of cash.*

mal·aise /mæˈleɪz/ *n.* [singular,U] **1** a feeling of anxiety, DISSATISFACTION, and lack of confidence within a group of people that is not clearly expressed or understood: *There is a restlessness, a malaise, among the workers.* | *economic malaise* **2** a feeling of being slightly sick that usually does not continue for very long

Mal·a·mud /ˈmæləˌmʌd/, **Ber·nard** /bəˈnɑrd/ (1914–1986) a U.S. writer of NOVELs

mal·a·prop·ism /ˈmæləˌprɑpɪzəm/ *n.* [C] an amusing mistake that is made when someone uses a word that sounds similar to the word they intended to say, but that means something completely different

ma·lar·i·a /məˈlɛriə/ *n.* [U] a disease common in hot countries that is caused when an infected MOSQUITO bites you —**malarial** *adj.*: *malarial fever*

ma·lar·key /məˈlɑrki/ *n.* [U] INFORMAL talk that is meant to be impressive or deceive you but does not mean anything; nonsense: *Serious scientists say that's malarkey.*

Ma·la·wi /məˈlɑwi/ a country in east Africa between Zambia and Mozambique —**Malawian** *n., adj.*

Ma·lay[1] /məˈleɪ, ˈmeɪleɪ/ *n.* **1** [C] someone from the largest population group in Malaysia **2** [U] the language of these people

Malay[2] *adj.* relating to Malaysia: *the Malay peninsula*

Ma·lay·si·a /məˈleɪʒə/ a country in southeast Asia made up of 13 states on the Malay PENINSULA and on the island of Borneo —**Malaysian** *n., adj.*

Mal·colm X /ˌmælkəm ˈɛks/ (1925–1965) an African-American political leader who worked to improve the social and economic position of African-Americans

Malcolm X

mal·con·tent /ˌmælkənˈtɛnt/ *n.* [C] FORMAL someone who is likely to cause trouble because they are not satisfied with existing conditions *political malcontents*

Mal·dives, the /ˈmɔldaɪvz/ a country that consists of a group of small islands in the Indian Ocean southwest of Sri Lanka —**Maldivian** /mɔlˈdɪviən/ *n., adj.*

male[1] /meɪl/ *adj.* **1** belonging to the sex that cannot have babies: *A rooster is a male chicken.* | *All the selected texts are written by male philosophers.* **2** typical of or relating to this sex: *male sexuality* | *a survey of male and female attitudes* **3** male **plant/flower etc.** a plant, flower etc. that cannot produce fruit **4** TECHNICAL a male PLUG[1] (1a) fits into a hole or SOCKET (2) —**maleness** *n.* [U] —opposite FEMALE[2] —see Usage Note at MASCULINE

male[2] *n.* [C] **1** a male animal: *The male uses its light to find receptive female fireflies.* **2** a man, especially a typical man: *Males under 25 have a higher accident rate.* —opposite FEMALE[1]

Ma·lé /ˈmɑli, -leɪ/ the capital city of the Maldives

male bond·ing /ˌ. ˈ../ *n.* [U] OFTEN HUMOROUS the forming of strong friendship between men: *Yeah, they went away over the weekend to do some male bonding.*

male chau·vin·ist /ˌmeɪl ˈʃoʊvənɪst/ *n.* [C] a man who believes that men are better than women and who has strict, traditional ideas about the way men and women should behave and is not willing to change his ideas: *That's Joe all right – the biggest male chauvinist pig in the world.*

mal·e·dic·tion /ˌmæləˈdɪkʃən/ *n.* [C] FORMAL a wish or prayer that something bad will happen to someone; CURSE[2]

mal·e·fac·tor /ˈmæləˌfæktɚ/ *n.* [C] FORMAL someone who does evil things

ma·lef·i·cent /məˈlɛfəsənt/ *adj.* FORMAL doing evil things, or able to do them —**maleficence** *n.* [U]

male men·o·pause /ˌ. ˈ.../ *n.* [singular] HUMOROUS a period in the middle of a man's life when he feels anxious and unhappy —compare MIDLIFE CRISIS

ma·lev·o·lent /məˈlɛvələnt/ *adj.* showing a desire to harm other people: *the story of a malevolent ghost* —**malevolence** *n.* [U] —**malevolently** *adv.*

mal·fea·sance /ˌmælˈfizəns/ *n.* [U] LAW illegal activity, especially by a government official

mal·for·ma·tion /ˌmælfɔrˈmeɪʃən/ *n.* **1** [C] a part of the body that is badly formed: *a malformation of the brain* **2** [U] the state of being badly formed: *organ malformation*

mal·formed /ˌmælˈfɔrmd/ *adj.* badly formed: *a malformed spinal cord*

mal·func·tion /mælˈfʌŋkʃən/ *n.* [C] a fault in the way a machine or computer operates —**malfunction** *v.* [I]

Ma·li /ˈmɑli/ a large country in west Africa, south of Algeria —**Malian** *n., adj.*

mal·ice /ˈmælɪs/ *n.* **1** [U] the desire or intention to deliberately harm someone: *Hagen's voice brims with malice as he plots his revenge.* | *I bare no malice against this man whatsoever.* **2 with malice afore-thought** LAW a criminal act that is done with malice aforethought is done in a carefully planned and deliberate way

ma·li·cious /məˈlɪʃəs/ *adj.* showing a desire to harm or hurt someone: *malicious rumors* —**maliciously** *adv.* —**maliciousness** *n.* [U]

ma·lign[1] /məˈlaɪn/ *v.* [T usually passive] to say or write bad things about someone that are untrue: *Schools have been maligned by politicians and newspapers.* | **much-maligned/oft-maligned/often-maligned** (=criticized by a lot of people, often unfairly)

malign[2] *adj.* FORMAL harmful: *malign spirits* —**malignly** *adv.* —**malignity** /məˈlɪgnəti/ *n.* [U]

ma·lig·nan·cy /məˈlɪgnənsi/ *n. plural* **malignancies** **1** [C] TECHNICAL a TUMOR **2** [U] FORMAL feelings of great hatred

ma·lig·nant /məˈlɪgnənt/ *adj.* **1** TECHNICAL a malignant TUMOR, disease etc. is one that develops quickly and cannot be easily controlled and is likely to cause death **2** FORMAL showing hatred and a strong desire to harm someone: *Moby Dick is used as a symbol of all the malignant forces in the world.* —**malignantly** *adv.* —compare BENIGN

ma·lin·ger /məˈlɪŋgɚ/ *v.* [I] to avoid work by pretending to be sick —**malingerer** *n.* [C]

mall /mɔl/ *n.* [C] a very large building with a lot of stores in it: *Maybe we can meet at the mall and go see a movie.* | *a huge new shopping mall*

mal·lard /ˈmælɚd/ *n.* [C] a type of wild duck

Mal·lar·mé /ˌmælɑrˈmeɪ/, **Sté·phane** /stɛˈfɑn/ (1842–1898) a French poet

mal·le·a·ble /ˈmæliəbəl, -ləbəl/ *adj.* **1** something that is malleable is able to be pressed or pulled into a new shape: *malleable steel* **2** someone who is malleable is easily influenced, changed, or trained —**malleability** /ˌmæliəˈbɪləti/ *n.* [U]

mal·let /ˈmælɪt/ *n.* [C] **1** a wooden hammer with a large end: *Use a mallet to hammer in the tent pegs.* —see picture at TOOL[1] **2** a wooden hammer with a long handle used when playing CROQUET or POLO

mal·low /ˈmæloʊ/ *n.* [C,U] a plant with pink or purple flowers and long stems —see also MARSHMALLOW

mal·nour·ished /ˌmælˈnɚɪʃt, -ˈnʌrɪʃt/ *adj.* sick or weak because of not having enough food to eat, or because of not eating good food: *a pale, malnourished child*

M

mal·nu·tri·tion /ˌmælnuˈtrɪʃən/ *n.* [U] sickness or weakness caused by not having enough food to eat, or by not eating good food

mal·o·dor·ous /mælˈoʊdərəs/ *adj.* LITERARY smelling bad: *Skunks repel attackers with a malodorous spray.*

mal·prac·tice /ˌmælˈpræktɪs/ *n.* [C,U] the act of failing to do a professional duty correctly, or of making a mistake while doing it: *Hospitals are always concerned about malpractice suits.*

Mal·raux /mælˈroʊ/, **An·dré** /ɑnˈdreɪ/ (1901–1976) a French politician and writer of NOVELS

malt¹ /mɔlt/ *n.* **1** [U] grain, usually BARLEY, that has been kept in water for a time and then dried, used for making beer, WHISKEY etc. **2** [C] a drink made from milk, malt, and ICE CREAM, that usually has something else such as chocolate added: *a cheeseburger and a chocolate malt* **3** [C,U] also **malt whiskey** a type of high-quality WHISKEY from Scotland

malt² *v.* [T] to make grain into malt

Mal·ta /ˈmɔltə/ a country which consists of a group of small islands in the Mediterranean Sea —**Maltese** /ˌmɔlˈtiz◂/ *n., adj.*

malt·ed /ˈmɔltɪd/ also **malted milk** /ˌ.. ˈ./ *n.* [C] a MALT¹ (2)

Maltese Cross /ˌ.. ˈ./ *n.* [C] a cross with four pieces that become wider as they go out from the center

Mal·thus /ˈmælθəs/, **Thomas** (1766–1834) a British ECONOMIST who studied population growth —**Malthusian** /mælˈθuʒən/ *adj.*

malt liq·uor /ˌ. ˈ../ *n.* [U] a type of beer

mal·treat /mælˈtrit/ *v.* [T] to treat a person or animal cruelly: *Several of the prisoners had been maltreated.* —**maltreatment** *n.* [U]

S W **ma·ma, mamma, momma** /ˈmɑmə/ *n.* [C] a word
2   meaning "mother," used by or to children

ma·ma's boy /ˈ.. ˌ./ *n.* [C] a man or boy who people think is weak, because his mother protects him too much and always does what his mother says

mam·ba /ˈmɑmbə, ˈmæmbə/ *n.* [C] a poisonous African snake that is black or green

Mam·et /ˈmæmɪt/, **Da·vid** /ˈdeɪvɪd/ (1947–) a U.S. writer of plays and writer and director of movies

mam·ma /ˈmɑmə/ *n.* [C] another spelling of MAMA

mam·mal /ˈmæməl/ *n.* [C] one of the class of animals that drinks milk from its mother's body when it is young —**mammalian** /məˈmeɪliən/ *adj.*

mam·ma·ry /ˈmæməri/ *adj.* TECHNICAL [only before noun] relating to the breasts: *mammary cancer*

mammary gland /ˈ... ˌ./ *n.* [C] TECHNICAL the part of a woman's breast that produces milk, or a similar part of a female animal

mam·mo·gram /ˈmæməˌgræm/ *n.* [C] an X-RAY picture of a woman's breast, used to check for CANCER: *Women over the age of fifty should have yearly mammograms.* —**mammography** /mæˈmɑgrəfi/ *n.* [U]

mam·mon /ˈmæmən/ *n.* [U] FORMAL, DISAPPROVING money, wealth, and profit, regarded as something that people want or think about too much

mam·moth¹ /ˈmæməθ/ *adj.* [only before noun] extremely large: *This country has a mammoth drug problem.* | *a mammoth corporation*

mammoth² *n.* [C] a large hairy ELEPHANT that lived on Earth thousands of years ago

mam·my /ˈmæmi/ *n.* [C] OLD-FASHIONED a mother

S W **man¹** /mæn/ *n. plural* **men** /mɛn/
1 1 **1** male person [C] an adult male person: *He's a smart man.* | *There were two men and a woman in the car.* | *a man's watch*
2 all people **a)** [U] all people, both male and female, considered as a group: *the evolution of man* | *This is one of the worst diseases known to man.* **b)** [C] OLD-FASHIONED a person, either male or female: *All men are equal in the eyes of the law.*
3 worker [C] **a)** [usually plural] a man who works for an employer, especially someone who works

using their hands: *Many of the men said they would vote for the strike.* **b)** a man who comes to your house to do a job for you, especially to repair something: *The gas man came by to read the meter.*
4 soldier [C usually plural] a soldier or SAILOR, police officer etc. who has a low rank: *Ask the men to meet here at 11:00 for a briefing.*
5 game [C] one of the pieces you use in a game such as CHESS
6 strong/brave man [C usually singular] a man who has the qualities that people think a man should have, such as being brave, strong etc.: *If you're going to say something, be a man and put your name on it.* | *Would you be man enough to* (=be strong or brave enough) *stand up for your beliefs?* | *The Army will make a man of him.* (=make a boy or young man start behaving in a strong, confident way)
7 what sb likes [C] a man who likes, or likes doing, a particular thing: *He's a meat-and-potatoes man.* | *If I were a gambling man, I'd put money on the Saints.*
8 man from particular place/work etc. [C] a man who belongs to a particular organization, comes from a particular place, does a particular type of work etc.: *Bush was a Yale man.* (=he went to Yale University) | *You never see Fuller Brush men any more.*

SPOKEN PHRASES

9 used to speak to sb [singular] used in order to speak to someone, especially an adult male: *Hey, what's happening, man?*
10 the man a) used to talk about a particular man in a negative or insulting way: *I can't stand the man.* | *Come on, the man weighs over three hundred pounds!* **b) The Man** OLD-FASHIONED someone who has authority over you, especially a white man or police officer: *This record deal could free them all from working for The Man.*
11 you the/da man! also **you're the man!** SLANG used to praise someone for having done something well
12 my man used by some men when talking to a male friend
13 sb's your/our/the man used to say that a man is the best person for a particular job, situation etc.: *If you want someone to give you the juicy gossip, I'm not your man.*
14 a man OLD-FASHIONED used by a man to mean himself: *Can't a man read his paper in peace?*

15 husband/partner [C] INFORMAL a woman's husband, or the man she is having a romantic relationship with: *Tania was at the party with her new man.*
16 take sth like a man to accept a difficult situation or bad treatment without showing any emotion: *Stop whining and take it like a man.*
17 the man on the street the average man or the average person, who represents the opinion of many people: *He remains a hero to the man on the street.*
18 a man of his word a man you can trust, who will do what he has promised to do: *He was a man of his word, and I had great respect for his intellect.*
19 a man of few words a man who does not talk very much: *He was a man of few words except when he mounted the stage to recite his poetry.*
20 a man of the people a man who understands and expresses the views and opinions of ordinary people: *Springsteen is still a man of the people.*

mammoth

trunk

tusk

M

21 be your own man to behave and think independently without worrying about what other people think: *Do you want to be your own man and run your own business?*

22 it's every man for himself INFORMAL used to say that people will not help each other: *In journalism it's every man for himself.*

23 a man of God a religious man, especially a priest or minister

24 a man of letters a very well-educated man who studies literature or writes

25 man about town also **man-about-town** a rich man who spends a lot of time at parties, restaurants, theaters etc.: *Thompson's a man-about-town, a leading figure at the Rotary Club.*

26 man's best friend a dog

27 a man's man a man who other men admire and like, because he is strong and likes the kinds of activities that men usually do: *He was a Vietnam veteran, a man's man who liked to hunt and ride his motorcycle.*

28 to a man also **to the last man** used to say that all the men in a group do something or have a particular quality: *To a man, they all credit their success to an influential teacher.*

29 be/become man and wife FORMAL to be or become married: *I now pronounce you man and wife.*

30 live as man and wife to live together as though you are married, although you are not

31 servant [C] OLD-FASHIONED a male servant —see also BEST MAN, LADIES' MAN, MAN-TO-MAN, OLD MAN, a **man/woman of the world** (WORLD[1] (20))

man[2] *v.* **manned, manning** [T] to use or operate a vehicle, system, piece of equipment etc.: *The booths are manned by customs officials.* | *the first manned spacecraft*

man[3] *interjection* **1** used to emphasize what you are saying: *Man, your refrigerator makes a lot of noise.* **2 oh, man** used when you are disappointed, annoyed, or surprised, in order to emphasize what you are saying: *Oh, man, it's snowing.*

man·a·cle /ˈmænəkəl/ *n.* [C usually plural] an iron ring on a chain that is put around the hands or feet of prisoners —**manacled** *adj.*

man·age /ˈmænɪdʒ/ *v.*

1 do sth difficult [I,T] to succeed in doing something difficult, especially after trying very hard: *I even managed a few slow turns the first time I went skiing.* | *There isn't really anything that Ann can't manage.* | [manage to do sth] *Did you manage to get any sleep on the plane?* | *He managed to arrange a loan through a finance company.*

2 business [T] to direct or control a business and the people who work in it: *Turpin manages a staff of six employees.* | *The Marriot company manages fifteen retirement complexes.* | *a badly managed company*

3 without much money [I] to succeed in buying the things you need even though you do not have very much money: *I guess we'll manage somehow.* | [+ on] *We are trying to manage on a limited budget.*

4 living with problems [I] to succeed in living in a difficult situation: *It's hard to see sometimes how single parents manage.* | [+ without] *How do you manage without a phone?*

5 not need help [I,T] SPOKEN to be able to do something or carry something without help: *"Can I help you with that?" "That's OK, I can manage."*

6 control/organize [T] to control or organize something: *The Director of Admissions manages the process of recruiting and admitting students.* | *The teacher was incapable of managing such a large number of students.* —see also MANAGEABLE —see Usage Note at CONTROL[2]

7 property/land [T] to have the job of taking care of a building, piece of land etc., often including the financial matters connected with it: *A few companies encourage tenants to form their own corporations and manage the property themselves.* | *The Forestry Service manages all the land in the area.*

8 manage your time/money to use your time or money effectively, without wasting them: *Jack was completely unable to manage his money.*

9 be strong enough [T] to be able to do something because you are strong enough or healthy enough: *Grandma can't manage the stairs by herself any more.* | *I could only manage three sit-ups.*

10 eat/drink [T] to be able to eat or drink something: *I think I could manage another glass of wine.*

11 manage a smile/a few words etc. to make yourself say or do something when you do not really want to: *Smith managed a smile after her defeat.*

12 cause problems [T] SPOKEN to do something that causes problems: [manage to do sth] *The kids managed to spill paint all over the carpet.*

13 sb can manage (to do) sth SPOKEN used to say that someone has enough time to do something, even though they are busy: *I can probably manage a couple of hours on Wednesday afternoon, if that's okay with you.*

man·age·a·ble /ˈmænɪdʒəbəl/ *adj.* easy to control or deal with: *My hair's more manageable since I had it cut.* —opposite UNMANAGEABLE —**manageability** /ˌmænɪdʒəˈbɪləti/ *n.* [U]

managed care /ˌ.. ˈ./ *n.* [U] a system of health care in which people have health insurance that allows them only to use particular doctors or hospitals

man·age·ment /ˈmænɪdʒmənt/ *n.* **1** [U] the act or process of controlling and organizing the work of a company or organization and the people who work for it: *Ueberroth won praise for his management of the Los Angeles Olympics.* | *Franklin runs a management consulting firm.* | *The timber mill closed largely because of bad management.* **2** [C,U] the people who are in charge of a company or organization: *The management felt this was the right decision.* | *There has been a recent change in management at the restaurant.* | *A management decision* | *Miller spent 27 years in management at a pharmaceutical company.* | *Gannet Co. has announced five senior/upper management* (=people at the highest levels in a company) *appointments.* | *Many middle management* (=people in charge of small groups within a company) *jobs have been cut.* **3** [U] the act or process of dealing with a situation that needs to be controlled in some way: *traffic management* | *The Forest Service is preparing a new forest management plan.*

management buy·out /ˌ... ˈ../ *n.* [C] an occasion when the management of a company buys a lot of STOCK in that company so that they control it

management con·sult·ant /ˈ... .ˌ./ *n.* [C] someone who is paid to advise the management of a company about how to improve their organization and working methods

man·ag·er /ˈmænɪdʒɚ/ *n.* [C] **1** someone whose job is to manage part or all of a company or other organization: *White was later a store manager for Safeway Stores.* | *He is general manager of operations for three health clubs.* | *I'd like to speak to the manager, please.* **2** someone who is in charge of the business affairs of a singer, an actor etc. **3** someone who is in charge of training and organizing a sports team: *the manager of the Boston Red Sox*

man·a·ge·ri·al /ˌmænəˈdʒɪriəl/ *adj.* relating to the job of a manager: *a managerial decision*

managing di·rec·tor /ˌ... .ˈ../ *n.* [C] someone who is in charge of a large company or organization, or of a part of a large company

Ma·nag·ua /məˈnɑgwə/ the capital and largest city of Nicaragua

Ma·na·ma /məˈnæmə/ the capital city of Bahrain

ma·ña·na /mənˈyɑnə, mɑn-/ *adv., adj., n.* a word meaning 'tomorrow," often used when talking about someone who delays doing things: *a mañana attitude*

Ma·nas·seh /məˈnæsə/ in the Bible, the head of one of the 12 tribes of Israel

man·a·tee /ˈmænəˌti/ *n.* [C] a large plant-eating sea animal with FLIPPERS and a large flat tail

Man·chu·ri·a /mænˈtʃʊriə/ an area of northeast China that is south of Russia and west of Japan

man·da·la /ˈmændələ/ *n.* [C] a picture of a circle

M

around a square, that represents the universe in Hindu and Buddhist religions

Man·dan /'mændæn, -dən/ a Native American tribe from the northern central area of the U.S.

Man·da·rin /'mændərɪn/ n. [U] the official language of China, spoken by most educated Chinese people

man·da·rin /'mændərɪn/ n. [C] **1** also **mandarin orange** a type of small orange with skin that is easy to remove **2** an important official in an organization or government **3** an important government official in the former Chinese EMPIRE

man·date¹ /'mændeɪt/ n. **1** [C] an official command given to a person or organization to do something: [mandate to do sth] *The UN gave him a mandate to seek information on the conflict.* | *She was hired as the Tribune's editor with a mandate to change the newspaper's coverage.* **2** [C] the right and power that a government or elected official has to do something, as a result of winning an election or vote: [mandate to do sth] *The organization's leadership now has a mandate to pursue its eco-policies.* | *The administration was clearly **given a mandate** to tackle economic problems.* **3** [C,U] the power given to one country to govern another country, or the country that is being governed: *Lebanon became a French mandate after World War I.*

man·date² v. [T] **1** to give an official command that something must be done: *The state mandates that high school students take three years of English.* **2** [often passive] to give someone the right or power to do something: *The topic being debated was whether a doctor is mandated to stop life-sustaining treatment at the patient's request.*

man·dat·ed /'mæn,deɪtɪd/ adj. a mandated country has been placed under the control of another country: *mandated territories*

man·da·to·ry /'mændə,tɔri/ adj. something that is mandatory must be done, especially because a law or rule says it must be done; COMPULSORY: *Wearing a helmet when riding a motorcycle is mandatory.* | *The company's mandatory retirement age is 65.*

Man·del·a /mæn'dɛlə/, **Nelson** (1918–) the first black President of South Africa

man·di·ble /'mændəbəl/ n. [C] TECHNICAL **1** the jaw of an animal or fish, especially the lower jaw —see picture at SKELETON **2** the upper or lower part of a bird's beak **3** a part like a jaw at the front of an insect's mouth

man·do·lin /,mændə'lɪn, 'mændl-ən/ n. [C] a musical instrument with eight metal strings and a rounded back

mane /meɪn/ n. [C] **1** the long hair on the back of a horse's neck, or around the face and neck of a lion **2** INFORMAL a person's long thick hair

man-eat·er /'. ,../ n. [C] an animal that eats human flesh —**man-eating** adj.: *a man-eating tiger*

Ma·net /mæ'neɪ/, **Éd·ouard** /ɛ'dwɑr/ (1832–1883) a French PAINTER who greatly influenced the development of the style of IMPRESSIONISM

ma·neu·ver¹ /mə'nuvɚ/ n. **1** [C] a skillful or careful movement that you make, for example in order to avoid something or go through a narrow space: *basic skiing maneuvers* **2** [C,U] a skillful or carefully planned action intended to achieve something or avoid something: *The defense has tried a number of legal maneuvers to reduce the charges.* **3** **room to maneuver** the possibility of changing your plans or decisions: *The guidelines are written in a way that gives managers room to maneuver.* **4 maneuvers** [plural] a military exercise like a battle used for training soldiers: *Two ships are **on maneuvers** in the Atlantic.* —see also HEIMLICH MANEUVER

maneuver² v. [I,T] **1** to move or turn skillfully or to move or turn something skillfully, especially something large and heavy: *Officials doubted that the aircraft could maneuver along the main departure route.* | [maneuver sth along/into/through etc.] *The driver skillfully maneuvered the limo through the*

heavy traffic. **2** to use carefully planned and often dishonest methods to get what you want: *James maneuvered her into the bedroom.*

ma·neu·ver·a·ble /mə'nuvərəbəl/ adj. easy to move or turn within small spaces: *In-line skates are more maneuverable than regular roller skates.* —**maneuverability** /mə,nuvərə'bɪləţi/ n. [U]

ma·neu·ver·ing /mə'nuvərɪŋ/ n. [C,U] the use of carefully planned and sometimes dishonest methods to get what you want: *diplomatic maneuverings*

man·ful·ly /'mænfəli/ adv. in a brave and determined way —**manful** adj.

man·ga /'mɑŋgə/ n. [U] a Japanese COMIC BOOK for adults

man·ga·nese /'mæŋgə,niz/ n. [U] *symbol* **Mn** a grayish-white metal that is an ELEMENT and is used for making glass, steel etc.

mange /meɪndʒ/ n. [U] a skin disease that some animals get which makes them lose small areas of fur

man·ger /'meɪndʒɚ/ n. [C] a long open container that horses, cattle etc. eat from —see also **dog in the manger** (DOG¹ (12))

man·gle¹ /'mæŋgəl/ v. [T] **1** [often passive] to damage or injure something badly by crushing or twisting it: *A mangled bicycle lay by the railroad tracks.* **2** to spoil something, especially what someone has said or written: *People joke about Branston's ability to mangle the English language.*

mangle² n. [C] a machine with two ROLLERs, used in the past to remove water from washed clothes

man·go /'mæŋgoʊ/ n. *plural* **mangoes** or **mangos** [C] a tropical fruit with a thin skin, sweet yellow flesh, and a large seed

man·grove /'mæŋgroʊv/ n. [C] a tropical tree that grows in or near water and grows new roots from its branches: *a mangrove swamp*

mang·y /'meɪndʒi/ adj. **mangier, mangiest 1** suffering from MANGE **2** looking old, dirty, and in bad condition: *He wore a mangy fur hat and a ragged coat.*

man·han·dle /'mæn,hændl/ v. [T] **1** to push or move someone roughly, using force: *Rivera claimed he was kicked and manhandled by police.* **2** to move a heavy object using force

Manhattan

Man·hat·tan /mæn'hæt⁀n/ a BOROUGH of new York City that is an island between the Hudson River and the East River

man·hole /'mænhoʊl/ n. [C] a hole in the road covered by a lid, that people go down to examine pipes, wires etc.

man·hood /'mænhʊd/ n. **1** [U] qualities such as strength, courage, and especially sexual power, that people think a man should have **2** [U] the state of being a man and not a boy anymore: *Many societies have a special ceremony when a boy has reached manhood.* **3** [singular] LITERARY OR HUMOROUS a PENIS **4** [U] LITERARY all the men of a particular nation: *America's manhood* —compare WOMANHOOD

man-hour /'. ./ n. [C] the amount of work done by one person in one hour, used as a measurement

man·hunt /'mænhʌnt/ n. [C] an organized search, especially for a criminal or a prisoner who has escaped

ma·ni·a /'meɪniə/ n. [C,U] **1** a very strong desire for something or interest in something, especially one

M

that affects a lot of people at the same time: *Lottery mania is sweeping the state.* | [+ **for**] *The book is about the 1980s mania for mergers and takeovers.* **2** TECHNICAL a serious mental illness

ma·ni·ac /ˈmeɪniˌæk/ *n.* [C] **1** INFORMAL someone who behaves in a stupid or dangerous way: *He drives like a maniac.* **2 a religious/sex/computer etc. maniac** INFORMAL someone who thinks about religion, sex etc. all the time **3** OLD-FASHIONED someone who is mentally ill: *a homicidal maniac* (=a mentally ill person who kills people)

ma·ni·a·cal /məˈnaɪəkəl/ *adj.* behaving as if you are crazy: *maniacal laughter* —**maniacally** /-kli/ *adv.*

man·ic /ˈmænɪk/ *adj.* **1** INFORMAL behaving in a very anxious or excited way: *Williams is a comedian with a lot of manic energy.* **2** TECHNICAL relating to the feeling of great happiness and excitement that is part of manic depression

manic de·pres·sion /ˌ... .ˈ../ *n.* [U] a mental illness that makes people sometimes feel extremely happy and excited and sometimes extremely sad and hopeless

manic de·pres·sive /ˌ... .ˈ../ *n.* [C] someone who suffers from manic depression —**manic-depressive** *adj.*

man·i·cure /ˈmænɪˌkyʊr/ *n.* [C,U] a treatment for the hands and FINGERNAILs that includes cutting, cleaning, polishing etc. —**manicure** *v.* [T] —**manicurist** *n.* [C]

man·i·cured /ˈmænɪˌkyʊrd/ *adj.* **1** manicured hands have FINGERNAILs that are neatly cut and polished **2** manicured gardens or LAWNs are very neat, and the grass is cut very short

man·i·fest¹ /ˈmænəˌfɛst/ *v.* [T] FORMAL to clearly show a feeling, attitude, disease etc., so that it is easy to see: *Mountain sickness is usually manifested as headache and tiredness.* | *The stress of her job often manifests itself in anger instead of tears.*

manifest² *adj.* [no comparative] FORMAL **1** plain and easy to see; OBVIOUS: *The educational system is a manifest failure.* | *The event's full importance only became manifest much later.* **2 manifest destiny** the idea in the 19th century that the U.S. was clearly intended by God to spread over all the land between the Atlantic and Pacific Oceans —**manifestly** *adv.*: *manifestly untrue*

manifest³ *n.* [C] a list of all the goods or people carried on a ship, airplane, or train: *the flight's passenger manifest*

man·i·fes·ta·tion /ˌmænəfəˈsteɪʃən/ *n.* FORMAL **1** [C] a very clear sign that a particular situation or feeling exists: *The riots are a clear manifestation of growing discontent.* **2** [U] the act of appearing or becoming clear: *Manifestation of the disease often does not occur until middle age.* **3** [C] the appearance of a GHOST

man·i·fes·to /ˌmænəˈfɛstoʊ/ *n. plural* **manifestoes** or **manifestos** [C] a written statement by a group, especially a political group, saying what they believe in and what they intend to do: *the Communist manifesto*

man·i·fold¹ /ˈmænəˌfoʊld/ *adj.* FORMAL many and of different kinds: *the manifold possibilities in life*

manifold² *n.* [C] TECHNICAL an arrangement of pipes through which gases enter or leave a car engine: *an exhaust manifold*

Ma·nil·a /məˈnɪlə/ the capital and largest city of the Philippines

ma·nil·a /məˈnɪlə/ *adj.* made of a strong brown paper: *a manila envelope*

man·i·oc /ˈmæniˌɑk/ *n.* [U] CASSAVA

ma·nip·u·late /məˈnɪpyəˌleɪt/ *v.* [T] **1** DISAPPROVING to make someone do what you want by deceiving or influencing them: *Students were outraged that someone could use their newspaper to manipulate them.* **2** DISAPPROVING to dishonestly change information or influence an event or situation: *Local people were unwilling to believe that police had manipulated evidence.* **3** to work with or change information, systems etc. to achieve the result that you want: *The images can be manipulated and stored on disk.* |

Developing a budget involves manipulating numbers and requires strong analytical skills. **4** to make something move or turn in the way that you want, especially using your hands: *Babies investigate their world by manipulating objects.* | *Players manipulate characters on the screen using a joystick.* **5** TECHNICAL to skillfully move and press a joint or bone into the correct position —**manipulation** /məˌnɪpyəˈleɪʃən/ *n.* [U]

ma·nip·u·la·tive /məˈnɪpyələtɪv/ *adj.* **1** DISAPPROVING good at controlling or deceiving people to get what you want: *She was charming and manipulative.* **2** TECHNICAL relating to the skill of moving bones and joints into the correct position: *manipulative treatment* **3** TECHNICAL relating to the ability to handle objects in a skillful way: *manipulative techniques* —**manipulatively** *adv.*

ma·nip·u·la·tor /məˈnɪpyəˌleɪtɚ/ *n.* [C] DISAPPROVING someone who is good at controlling or deceiving other people in order to get what they want

Man·i·to·ba /ˌmænɪˈtoʊbə/ a PROVINCE in central Canada

man·kind /ˌmænˈkaɪnd/ *n.* [U] all humans considered as a group: *If the Earth's temperature rises, it will be a disaster for all mankind.* —compare WOMANKIND

man·ly /ˈmænli/ *adj.* having qualities that people expect and admire in a man, such as being brave and strong: *a manly name* —**manliness** *n.* [U]

man-made

natural lake

man-made lake

man-made, manmade /ˌ. ˈ.ˌ/ *adj.* **1** made of substances such as plastic that are not natural: *man-made fibers* **2** made by people, rather than by natural processes: *a man-made lake* —compare ARTIFICIAL, NATURAL¹ (2)

Mann /mæn/, **Hor·ace** /ˈhɔrəs, ˈhɑr-/ (1796–1859) a U.S. educator who made many important changes in public education

Mann /mɑn/, **Thomas** (1875–1955) a German writer of NOVELs

man·na /ˈmænə/ *n.* **1 manna from heaven** something that you need, which you suddenly get or are given **2** [U] the food which, according to the Bible, was provided by God for the Israelites in the desert after their escape from Egypt

man·ne·quin /ˈmænɪkən/ *n.* [C] **1** a model of the human body used for showing clothes in stores **2** OLD-FASHIONED a woman whose job is to wear fashionable clothes and show them to people; MODEL¹

man·ner /ˈmænɚ/ *n.*
1 way [singular] FORMAL the way in which something is done or happens: *The police were unable to determine the manner of Allen's death.* | *The issue should be resolved in a manner fair to both parties.*

M
S W
2

2 way of behaving/speaking [singular] the way in which someone behaves toward or talks to other people: *She has a very pleasant manner.* | *Greet the customer in a friendly and courteous manner.*

3 manners [plural] polite ways of behaving in social situations: *Thank-you notes are important – it's just basic manners.* | *Her kids have such good manners.* | *Jack, mind your manners.* (=used to tell a child to behave politely) | *It's bad manners to chew with your mouth open.* (=used when telling a child how to behave politely) | *I have to admit my table manners* (=how to eat politely) *aren't as good at home as when I'm at a restaurant.* **b)** FORMAL the customs of a particular group of people: *The book is about the life and manners of Victorian London.*

4 in a manner of speaking in some ways, though not exactly: *The illustrations make dinosaurs come alive, in a manner of speaking.*

5 all manner of sth FORMAL many different kinds of things or people: *This small portable oven is capable of cooking all manner of baked goods.*

6 [singular] in the style that is typical of a particular person or thing: *The house is built in the Victorian manner.* | *a painting in the manner of the early Impressionists*

7 what manner of...? LITERARY what kind of: *What manner of son would treat his mother in such a way?* —see also **a comedy of manners** (COMEDY (4)), -MANNERED

man·nered /ˈmænəd/ *adj.* DISAPPROVING relating to behavior that seems unnatural because it is only done to make people admire you: *a mannered way of speaking*

-mannered /mænəd/ [in adjectives] **well-mannered/bad-mannered/mild-mannered etc.** polite, impolite etc. in the way you behave in social situations: *He is arrogant and ill-mannered.*

man·ner·ism /ˈmænəˌrɪzəm/ *n.* **1** [C,U] a way of speaking or moving that is typical of a particular person: *He has the same mannerisms as his father.* **2** [U] the use of a style in art that does not look natural

man·ni·kin, manikin /ˈmænɪkən/ *n.* [C] another spelling of MANNEQUIN

man·nish /ˈmænɪʃ/ *adj.* a woman who is mannish or whose clothes look mannish behaves or looks like a man, especially when this is considered unattractive: *She was wearing a mannish-looking jacket.* —**mannishly** *adv.*

man of let·ters /ˌ. . ˈ.ˌ./ *n.* [C] a male writer, especially one who writes NOVELs or writes about literature

man-of-war /ˌ. . ˈ./ also **man-o'-war** /ˌmænə ˈwɔr/ *n.* [C] OLD USE a fighting ship in the Navy

man·or /ˈmænə/ *n.* [C] **1** also **manor house** a large house in the COUNTRYSIDE, especially in Europe, with a large area of land around it **2** the land that belonged to an important man, under the FEUDAL system —**manorial** /məˈnɔriəl/ *adj.*

man·pow·er /ˈmænˌpauə/ *n.* [U] all the workers available to do a particular kind of work: *The country has a large pool of skilled manpower.*

man·qué /mɑ̃ˈkeɪ/ *adj.* **artist/actor/teacher manqué** someone who could have been successful as an artist etc., but never became one

man·sard roof /ˈmænsɑrd ˌrʌf/ also **mansard** *n.* [C] a roof whose lower part slopes more steeply than its upper part

manse /mæns/ *n.* [C] a house that the minister of certain Christian churches lives in

man·ser·vant /ˈmænˌsəvənt/ *n.* [C] OLD-FASHIONED a male servant, especially a man's personal servant

-manship /mənʃɪp/ *suffix* [in U nouns] a particular skill or art: *horsemanship* (=skill at horse riding) | *salesmanship* (=the ability to sell things to people) —see also -SHIP (2)

man·sion /ˈmænʃən/ *n.* [C] a very large house

man-size also **man-sized** /ˈ. ./ *adj.* [only before noun] **1** about the same size as a man: *In the story, Gregor changes into a man-size cockroach.* **2** large and considered appropriate for, or typical of, a man: *Between man-size bites of a sandwich, Bly explained his theories.*

man·slaugh·ter /ˈmænˌslɔtə/ *n.* [U] LAW the crime of killing someone illegally but not deliberately —compare MURDER[1] (1)

manta ray /ˈmæntə ˌreɪ/ *n.* [C] a type of ocean fish with a flat body and two FINs that look like wings

man·tel /ˈmæntl/ also **man·tel·piece** /ˈmæntlˌpis/ *n.* [C] a frame surrounding a FIREPLACE, especially the top part that can be used as a shelf

man·til·la /mænˈtiyə, -ˈtɪlə/ *n.* [C] a piece of thin pretty material that covers the head and shoulders, traditionally worn by Spanish women

man·tis /ˈmæntɪs/ *n.* [C] a PRAYING MANTIS

man·tle[1] /ˈmæntl/ *n.* [C] **1 take on/assume/inherit etc. the mantle of sb** FORMAL to accept or have a particular duty or responsibility: *Yeltsin inherited Gorbachev's mantle as the leader of a superpower.* **2 a mantle of snow/darkness etc.** LITERARY something such as snow or darkness that covers a surface or area: *A mantle of snow lay on the trees.* **3** a loose piece of outer clothing without SLEEVEs, worn in past times **4** a cover put over the flame of a gas or oil lamp to make it shine more brightly **5** TECHNICAL the part of the Earth around the central CORE[1] (6)

man·tle[2] *v.* [T] LITERARY to cover the surface of something

Man·tle /ˈmæntl/, **Mick·ey** /ˈmɪki/ (1931–1995) a baseball player, known especially for his skill as a BATTER

man-to-man /ˌ. . ˈ.ˌ./ *adj.* [only before noun] INFORMAL **1** playing a game, especially basketball, in such a way that one person on your team tries to stay near one person on the other team: *man-to-man defense* **2** if two men have a man-to-man talk or discussion, they discuss something in an honest direct way —**man-to-man** *adv.*

man·tra /ˈmɑntrə/ *n.* [C] **1** a repeated word or sound used as a prayer or to help people MEDITATE, in the Hindu and Buddhist religions **2** INFORMAL a frequently used word or phrase that represents a rule or principle that someone believes is important: *The Treasury Secretary has stuck to his mantra that "a strong dollar is in America's interest."* **3** a piece of holy writing in the Hindu religion

man·u·al[1] /ˈmænyuəl/ *adj.* **1** involving the use of the hands: *manual work* | *manual skills* **2** using human power or skill, not electricity, machines etc.: *a manual typewriter* | *The car has a five-speed manual transmission.* —**manually** *adv.*

manual[2] *n.* [C] **1** a book that gives instructions about how to use a machine: *an instruction manual* **2 on manual** if a machine is on manual it can only be operated by using your hands and not by AUTOMATIC means

manual la·bor /ˌ... ˈ.ˌ./ *n.* [U] physical, often difficult, work that does not need a lot of skill —**manual laborer** *n.* [C]

manual work·er /ˌ... ˈ.ˌ./ *n.* [C] someone whose work involves using their hands —**manual work** *n.* [U]

man·u·fac·ture[1] /ˌmænyəˈfæktʃə/ *v.* [T] **1** to use machines to make goods or materials, usually in large numbers or amounts: *The car was manufactured in Germany until 1961.* **2** to invent an untrue story, excuse etc.: *If the media can manufacture stories like this, then who are we supposed to believe?* **3** TECHNICAL if your body manufactures a particular substance, it produces it: *Bile is manufactured by the liver.*

manufacture[2] *n.* [U] FORMAL **1** the process of making goods using machines, usually in large numbers: *During World War II, steel supplies were used in the manufacture of weapons.* **2 manufactures** [plural] TECHNICAL goods that are produced in large quantities using machinery

man·u·fac·tur·er /ˌmænyəˈfæktʃərə/ *n.* [C] a company or industry that makes large quantities of goods: *Contact the manufacturer of your washing machine for a replacement part.* | *a soft-drinks manufacturer*

man·u·fac·tur·ing /ˌmænjəˈfæktʃərɪŋ/ n. [U] the process or business of making goods in factories: *Thousands of jobs were lost in manufacturing.*

man·u·mis·sion /ˌmænjəˈmɪʃən/ n. [U] the act of allowing a SLAVE or SERVANT to become free —**manu·mit** /ˌmænjəˈmɪt/ v. [T]

ma·nure /məˈnʊɚ/ n. [U] waste matter from animals that is put into the soil to produce better crops —**manure** v. [T]

man·u·script /ˈmænjəˌskrɪpt/ n. [C] **1** a book or piece of writing before it is printed: *All Kingston's original manuscripts were lost in the fire.* **2** a book or document written by hand before printing was invented: *ancient manuscripts*

Manx /mæŋks/ adj. **1** a Manx cat is a type of cat that has no tail **2** related to the Isle of Man

man·y /ˈmɛni/ quantifier, pron. **1** used in formal English and in questions or negatives to mean a large number of people or things: *Many animals do not eat meat.* | *Does she have many friends?* | *How many people are coming to the party?* | "Have another donut." "No thanks, I've eaten too many already! (=more than I should).* | *We were behind by so many points I thought there was no chance of winning.* | *There aren't many (=are not many) tickets left.* | *Many of these old baseball cards are worth a lot of money.* | *Many of them do not speak any English.* | *For many, these have been very difficult years.* | *The many illustrations and photographs in the book are a delight.* | *I've baked many a cake since that first disastrous one.* —compare LOT¹ (1) **2 as many** the same number: *There weren't as many people at the meeting as we had hoped.* | *Print as many as you think you'll need.* | *Ressa made four free throws in as many attempts.* (=he tried four times and made it four times) | *The company now employs four times as many women as men.* **3 a good many** a fairly large number of people or things: *A good many guests brought along their children.* **4 a great many** a very large number of people or things: *The country has a great many problems that need urgent attention.* **5 have had one too many** INFORMAL to be drunk: *Ron looked like he'd had one too many.* **6 the many** FORMAL used to mean a large group of people who all have a particular disadvantage, usually to compare it with a smaller group who do not: *These economic policies have resulted in less for the many and more for the few.* **7 many a time** OLD-FASHIONED often: *I've sat here many a time and wondered about her.* **8 many's the time/day** OLD-FASHIONED used to say that a particular thing happens often: *Many's the time we had to borrow money to get through the year.* —opposite FEW —compare MORE², MOST² —see also MUCH², **in so many words** (WORD¹ (17)) —see Usage Note at MUCH²

man-year /ˈ. ./ n. [C] the amount of work done by one person in one year, used as a measurement

many-sid·ed /ˌ.. ˈ..◂/ adj. **1** consisting of many different qualities or features: *Johnson had a many-sided personality.* **2** having many sides

Mao·ism /ˈmaʊˌɪzəm/ n. [U] the system of political thinking invented by Mao Zedong —**Maoist** n., adj.

Mao·ri /ˈmaʊri/ n. **1** [C] someone who belongs to the race of people that first lived in New Zealand **2** [U] the language of the Maori people —**Maori** adj.: *a Maori tradition*

Mao Ze·dong /ˌmaʊ dzi ˈdʊŋ, -tsi ˈtʊŋ/ also **Chairman Mao** (1893–1976) a Chinese politician who helped to start the Chinese Communist Party in 1921 and became its leader in 1935. In 1949 he gained control of the government and established the People's Republic of China.

map¹ /mæp/ n. [C] **1** a drawing of an area of country showing rivers, roads, mountains, towns etc., or of a whole country or several countries: *Let me show you how to get there on the map.* | *a street map* | *[+ of]* *a map of Texas* | *He must be the only cab driver in the city who can't read a map* (=understand a map). **2 put sth on the map** to make a place, person, organization etc. famous, so that everyone knows it and talks about it: *It was Ray Kroc that really put McDonald's restaurants on the map.* | *The French town of Albertville hoped the winter Olympics would*

put the town on the map. —see also **wipe sth off the map** (WIPE¹ (6))

map² v. mapped, mapping [T] **1** to make a map of a particular area: *The Magellan spacecraft has mapped the surface of Venus.* **2** also **map sth ↔ out** to carefully plan how something will happen: *A number of senators are already mapping their campaigns for the presidency.* | *Polson has already mapped out a 20-week book promotion tour.* **3** TECHNICAL to find and record information about where a particular type of GENETIC information is on a CHROMOSOME

ma·ple /ˈmeɪpəl/ n. **1** [C] a tree that grows in northern countries, that has pointed leaves that turn red or yellow in the fall **2** [U] the wood from this tree

maple sug·ar /ˌ.. ˈ../ n. [U] a type of sugar made by boiling maple syrup, used to make candy

maple syr·up /ˌ.. ˈ../ n. [U] a sweet sticky liquid eaten especially with PANCAKES, obtained from some kinds of maple trees

map·ping /ˈmæpɪŋ/ n. **1** [U] the act or process of making a map **2** [C] TECHNICAL a relationship between two mathematical sets in which a member of the first set is matched by a member of the second

map-read·ing /ˈ. ˌ../ n. [U] the practice of using a map to find which way you should go: *Map-reading skills are essential for hikers.* —**map-reader** n. [C]

Ma·pu·to /məˈputoʊ/ the capital and largest city of Mozambique

mar /mɑr/ v. marred, marring [T often passive] to make something less attractive or enjoyable; SPOIL: *The movie's premiere was marred by gang-related violence.* | *The table was marred by cigarette burns.*

Mar. n. the written abbreviation of March

mar·a·bou /ˈmærəˌbu/ n. [C] a large African STORK (=a long-legged bird)

ma·ra·cas /məˈrɑkəz/ n. [plural] a PERCUSSION instrument consisting of a pair of hollow balls, filled with small objects such as stones, that are shaken

mar·a·schi·no /ˌmærəˈʃinoʊ, -ˈski-/ n. [U] a sweet alcoholic drink made from a type of CHERRY

maraschino cher·ry /ˌ...ˌ. ˈ../ n. [C] a CHERRY that has been colored bright red and kept in sweet liquid, and that is used for decorating cakes, drinks etc.

Ma·rat /məˈrɑ/, **Jean Paul** /ʒɑn pɔl/ (1743–1793) a political leader and writer in the French Revolution

mar·a·thon¹ /ˈmærəˌθɑn/ n. [C] **1** a long race in which competitors run 26 miles and 385 yards: *the Boston Marathon* | *Garcia ran the marathon in just under three hours.* **2** an activity that continues for a long time and needs a lot of energy, patience, or determination: *The movie theater is holding its annual horror film marathon.*

marathon² adj. [only before noun] continuing for a very long time: *a marathon game of Monopoly*

mar·a·thon·er /ˈmærəˌθɑnɚ/ n. [C] someone who runs in a marathon

ma·raud·ing /məˈrɔdɪŋ/ adj. [only before noun] a marauding person or animal moves around looking for something to destroy or kill: *A woman was left for dead in Central Park by a marauding gang of youths.* —**marauder** n. [C]

mar·ble /ˈmɑrbəl/ n. **1** [U] a type of hard rock that becomes smooth when polished, and is used for making buildings, STATUES etc.: *The columns were of white marble.* | *a marble statue* **2** [C] a small colored glass ball that children roll along the ground as part of a game **3** [C] TECHNICAL a STATUE or SCULPTURE made of marble **4 marbles** [U] a children's game played with marbles **5 lose your marbles** INFORMAL to start behaving in a crazy way

marble cake /ˈ.. ˌ./ n. [C] a cake made with two different colors of BATTER that form curved lines in the cake

mar·bled /ˈmɑrbəld/ adj. **1** having an irregular pattern of lines and colors: *a marbled silk scarf* **2** made of marble: *a marbled floor* **3** marbled meat contains lines of fat

M

March /mɑrtʃ/ *written abbreviation* **Mar.** *n.* [C,U] the third month of the year, between February and April —see Usage Note at JANUARY

march[1] /mɑrtʃ/ *v.* **1** [I] to walk quickly and with firm, regular steps like a soldier: *The 555th Battalion marched in the parade.* | [+ across/along/through] *The Union Army marched through Georgia.* **2** [I] to walk somewhere in a large group to protest about something: *Several hundred students marched across campus to protest.* | [+ on] *Outraged citizens marched on City Hall, demanding the police chief's resignation.* | [+ for/against] *The suffragettes marched for women's right to vote early in the century.* **3** [I always + adv./prep.] to walk somewhere quickly and with determination, often because you are angry: [+ down/off etc.] *One angry woman marched out, dragging her daughters behind her.* **4** [T always + adv./prep.] to force someone to walk somewhere with you, often pushing or pulling them roughly: *The prisoners of war were marched around the compound.* **5 marching orders** the instructions someone has been given by the people who have authority over them: *Barnett has given the department heads their marching orders: cut the budget, or else.* —**marcher** *n.* [C]

s w **march**[2] *n.* [C] **1** an organized event in which many people walk together to protest about something: *a Civil Rights march in Washington* **2** the act of walking with firm regular steps like a soldier: *The soldiers did a march around the parade ground.* **3** a piece of music with a regular beat for soldiers to march to **4 on the march a)** an army that is on the march is marching somewhere **b)** a belief, idea etc. that is on the march is becoming stronger and more popular: *Fascism is on the march again in some parts of Europe.* **5 the march of time/history/events etc.** FORMAL the progress of time and of things happening that cannot be stopped: *Too many trees are being lost in the constant march of development.* —see also **steal a march on sb** (STEAL[1] (10))

march·ing band /'.. ,./ *n.* [C] a group of musicians who march while they play musical instruments

March of Dimes, the /,. . './ a U.S. CHARITY organization that collects money for children, especially those with serious mental or physical disabilities (DISABILITY)

Mar·ci·a·no /,mɑrsi'ɑnoʊ/, **Rock·y** /'rɑki/ (1923–1969) a BOXER who was world HEAVYWEIGHT CHAMPION from 1952 to 1956

Mar·co·ni /mɑr'koʊni/, **Gu·gliel·mo** /gʊ'lyɛlmoʊ/ (1874–1937) an Italian electrical engineer who invented the first method of sending messages by radio

Mar·cus Au·re·li·us /,mɑrkəs ɔ'riliəs/ (121–180) a Roman EMPEROR and PHILOSOPHER

Mar·cu·se /mɑr'kuzə/, **Her·bert** /'hɔbət/ (1898–1979) a U.S. PHILOSOPHER and writer on politics

Mar·di Gras /'mɑrdi ,grɑ, -,grɔ/ *n.* [C,U] the day before Lent, or the music, dancing etc. that celebrate this day

mare /mɛr/ *n.* [C] a female horse or DONKEY —compare STALLION

mar·ga·rine /'mɑrdʒərɪn/ *n.* [U] a yellow substance that is similar to butter but is made from oil, which you eat with bread or use for cooking

mar·ga·ri·ta /,mɑrgə'ritə/ *n.* [C] an alcoholic drink made with TEQUILA and LIME juice

s w **mar·gin** /'mɑrdʒɪn/ *n.* [C] **1** the empty space at the side of a printed page: *The program sets the margins automatically.* | *There were some penciled notes in the margin.* **2** the difference in the number of votes, points etc. that exists between the winners and the losers of an election or competition: *an eight-goal margin of defeat* | *The mayor was voted out of office by a wide margin* (=by a lot of votes). **3** the difference between what a business pays for something and what they sell it for; PROFIT MARGIN **4 margin of error** the degree to which a calculation can be wrong without affecting the final results: *The poll has a margin of error of three percent.* **5 on the margin(s)** a person on the margins of a situation or group is one of the least important, powerful, or typical parts of that situation or group: *Many mentally ill people have been forced to live on the margins of society.* **6** the edge of something, especially an area of land

mar·gin·al /'mɑrdʒənl/ *adj.* **1** a marginal change or difference is too small to be important: *There has been only a marginal increase in sales.* **2** marginal people, things etc. are the least powerful, important, or typical ones in a particular group or situation: *Large cities in America had become the home of the poor and socially marginal groups.* **3** TECHNICAL relating to a change in cost, value etc. when one more thing is produced, one more dollar is earned etc.: *marginal revenue* **4 marginal land** land that cannot produce good crops **5** written in a margin: *marginal notes* —**marginality** /,mɑrdʒə'næləti/ *n.* [U] —see also MARGINALLY

mar·gin·al·ize /'mɑrdʒənə,laɪz/ *v.* [T] to make a group of people unimportant and powerless: *Year after year, the political system further marginalizes average citizens while empowering those with money.* —**marginalized** *adj.* —**marginalization** /,mɑrdʒə-nələ'zeɪʃən/ *n.* [U]

mar·gin·al·ly /'mɑrdʒənl-i/ *adv.* not enough to make an important difference: *Stock prices rose marginally in early trading today.* | [+ adj./adv.] *The population of New Hampshire is only marginally larger than that of the city of Detroit.*

ma·ri·a·chi /,mɑri'ɑtʃi/ *n.* [U] a type of Mexican dance music

Mar·i·an·as Trench, the /,mæri'ænəs, -'ɑnəs/ a very deep part of the western Pacific Ocean that is the deepest part of all the oceans in the world

Ma·rie An·toi·nette /mə,ri æntwɑ'nɛt/ (1755–1793) the Queen of France from 1774 to 1792, and the wife of Louis XVI. She and Louis XVI were killed in the French Revolution.

mar·i·gold /'mærə,goʊld, 'mɛr-/ *n.* [C] a plant with golden-yellow flowers

mar·i·jua·na, marihuana /,mærə'wɑnə/ *n.* [U] an illegal drug in the form of dried leaves that people smoke

ma·rim·ba /mə'rɪmbə/ *n.* [C] a musical instrument like a XYLOPHONE

ma·ri·na /mə'rinə/ *n.* [C] a small area of water where people keep boats that are used for pleasure

mar·i·nade /,mærə'neɪd/ *n.* [C,U] a mixture of oil, wine, and SPICEs in which meat or fish is put before it is cooked

mar·i·nate /'mærə,neɪt/ also **marinade** *v.* [I,T] to leave meat or fish in a marinade, or to be left in a marinade for a period of time

ma·rine /mə'rin/ *adj.* [only before noun] **1** relating to the ocean and the animals and plants that live there: *marine biology* **2** relating to ships or the Navy

mar·i·ner /'mærənə/ *n.* [C] LITERARY a SAILOR

Ma·rines /mə'rinz/ *n.* **1 the Marines** also **the Marine Corps** the military organization of the U.S. consisting of soldiers who work from ships **2 tell it to the Marines!** SPOKEN used to say that you do not believe what someone has told you —compare AIR FORCE, ARMY, NAVY[1] (1)

Ma·ri·no /mə'rinoʊ/, **Dan** /dæn/ (1961–) a U.S. football player who is considered one of the best QUARTER-BACKs in the NFL

mar·i·o·nette /,mæriə'nɛt/ *n.* [C] a toy that looks like a person, animal etc., that is moved by pulling strings attached to its body —compare PUPPET (1)

Mar·is /'mæris/, **Ro·ger** /'rɑdʒə/ (1934–1985) a U.S. baseball player famous for hitting 61 HOME RUNs in 1961, which broke the record of Babe Ruth

mar·i·tal /'mærətl/ *adj.* relating to marriage: *The stress of the job causes marital problems for many police officers.* | *What is your marital status* (=are you married or unmarried?)?

mar·i·time /'mærə,taɪm/ *adj.* **1** relating to ships that

M

sail on the ocean **2** near the ocean: *the Canadian maritime provinces*

mar·jo·ram /'mɑrdʒərəm/ *n.* [U] an HERB that smells sweet and is used in cooking

Mark /mɑrk/ also **The Gospel according to St. Mark** one of the four books in the New Testament of the Christian Bible that describe the life and teaching of Jesus

mark¹ /mɑrk/ *v.*

1 `write on sth` [T] to make a sign, shape, or word using a pen or pencil: *I'll just mark the one I want in the catalog.* | [mark sth with sth] *Joe's boxes were marked with a blue triangle.* | [mark sth on sth] *She's marked on the calendar that you're taking care of Lucy on Tuesday.* | *Five children were marked absent that day* (=the teacher wrote down that they were not there). | **mark sth personal/fragile/urgent** etc. *The letter was marked "personal."*

2 `show position` [T] to show where something is or was: *Two shiny bronze plaques marked the former entrance to the palace.* | *He had marked the route in red.* | *I folded the page to mark my place.*

3 `show a change` [T] to show that an important change has happened, or show the beginning of a new period in the development of something: *The album marks a change in Young's musical style.*

4 `quality/feature` [T often passive] if a particular quality or feature marks something, it is a typical or important part of that thing: *The meeting was marked by bitter exchanges between the two sides.* | *It is a potentially fatal illness, marked by internal bleeding.*

5 **mark sb/sth (as sth)** if a quality or feature marks someone or something as something, it shows that they are that type of person or thing: *Flashy clothes may mark you as a tourist.*

6 `celebrate` to celebrate an important event in a particular way: [mark sth with sth] *The last day of the holidays is marked with a lavish feast.*

7 `year/month/week` if a particular year, month, or week marks an important event, the event happens during that time: *This year marks the company's 50th anniversary.*

8 `spoil sth` [I,T] to make a mark on something in a way that spoils its appearance or damages it, or to become spoiled in this way: *Her shoes marked the floor.* | *The linoleum marks easily.*

9 `student's work` [T] to grade a student's work

10 mark time a) INFORMAL to spend time doing very little because you are waiting for something else to happen: *Investors are marking time, waiting for evidence that the market is growing.* **b)** if soldiers mark time, they move their legs as if they were marching, but remain in the same place.

11 (you) mark my words! OLD-FASHIONED used to tell someone that they should pay attention to what you are saying: *Mark my words, that relationship won't last.* —see also MARKED

mark sb/sth ↔ **down** *phr. v.* [T] **1** to reduce the price of things that are being sold: *All our merchandise has been marked down by at least 30%!* **2** to write something down, especially in order to keep a record: *Mark down everything you eat on the chart.* **3** to give a student a lower grade on a test, paper etc. because they have made mistakes: *You'll be marked down five points for each spelling mistake.*

mark sb/sth ↔ **off** *phr. v.* [T] **1** to make an area separate by drawing a line around it, putting a rope around it etc.: *Police marked off the area with white lines.* **2** to make a mark on something such as a list to show that something has been done or completed: *We marked off the days on the calendar.*

mark sb/sth ↔ **out** *phr. v.* [T] **1** to show the shape or position of something by drawing lines around it: *A volleyball court had been marked out on the grass.* **2** to make someone or something seem different from or better than other similar people or things: [mark sb/sth out as sth] *The red carpeting everywhere marks the Concert Hall out as a typical Ogilvy and Ogilvy building.*

mark sb/sth ↔ **up** *phr. v.* [T] **1** to increase the price of something, so that you sell it for more than you paid for it: *The retailers mark up the goods by 3 to 10 percent.* —see also MARK-UP **2** to write notes or

instructions on a piece of writing, music etc.: *Someone had already marked up the alto part.*

mark² *n.* [C]

1 `dirt` a spot or small dirty area on something that spoils its appearance: *The tape left a mark on the paint* | *Police said the skid marks* (=marks left by a car's tires) *were over 30 feet long.*

2 `writing` a shape or sign that is written or printed: *Put a check mark beside each person's name as they come in.* | *Rose made a mark on the map to show where her house was.*

3 `damaged area` a cut, hole, or other small damaged area: *Check the power cord for any burn marks.* | *Garvin had scratch marks on the side of her face.*

4 `level/number` a particular level, number, amount, or time: *The city's population has passed the million mark.*

5 make/leave your mark to become successful or famous: [+ as] *Ivins made her mark as the managing editor of the Texas Observer.* | [+ in] *Graduates of Stuyvesant High have made their marks in many different fields.* | [+ on] *Ruth has left his mark on baseball history.*

6 be off the mark also **be wide of the mark** to be incorrect: *Our estimate was way off the mark.*

7 hit the mark a) to be correct and exact, or to have the effect that you intended: *Their economic predictions for the coming year hit the mark.* | *Most of the acting in her latest movie hits the mark.* **b)** to hit the thing that you were aiming at —opposite **miss the mark**

8 a mark of respect/prestige/affection etc. a sign that something exists or is true: *Being a priest is a mark of prestige in Poland.* | *Everyone brought gifts as a mark of respect for the old man.*

9 be a mark of sth if a particular quality or feature is a mark of something, it is typical of that thing: *This hopefulness in the face of difficulties is a mark of Humphrey's novels.*

10 leave/make its mark on sb to affect someone or something so that they change in a permanent or very noticeable way: *Growing up during the Depression left its mark on Schreier.*

11 be quick/slow/first etc. **off the mark** INFORMAL to be quick, slow, first etc. to understand things or react to situations: *The country has been slow off the mark with its reforms.*

12 on your mark(s), get set, go! SPOKEN said in order to start a race

13 `student's work` a GRADE

14 `crime` someone that a criminal has chosen to steal from or trick

15 Mark 1/2/3 etc. used to show the type or VERSION of a car, machine etc.: *the Lincoln Mark 5*

16 `money` the standard unit of money in Germany

17 `signature` OLD USE a sign in the form of a cross, used by someone who is not able to write their name —see also BIRTHMARK, **a black mark (against sb)** (BLACK¹ (5)), **halfway point/mark** (HALFWAY), MARKING, PUNCTUATION MARK, QUESTION MARK, QUOTATION MARK

Mark, Saint one of Jesus Christ's DISCIPLES. He is believed to have written "The Gospel according to St. Mark,' which describes the life and teaching of Jesus.

mark·down /'mɑrkdaʊn/ *n.* [C] a reduction in the price of something: [+ of] *a markdown of 20%*

marked /mɑrkt/ *adj.* **1** very easy to notice: *Doctors noted a marked improvement in the patient's condition.* | *The blue-green office tower is in marked contrast to the traditional brick buildings that line the street.* **2 a marked man/woman** someone who is in danger because someone wants to harm him or her —**markedly** /'mɑrkɪdli/ *adv.*: *They have a markedly different approach to the problem.*

mark·er /'mɑrkə/ *n.* [C] **1** an object, sign etc. that shows the position of something: *A granite marker shows where the battle took place.* **2** a large pen with a thick point, used for marking or drawing: [continues]

M

The card was signed with a silver marker. —see picture at PEN¹ **3 put/lay/set down a marker** to say or do something that clearly shows what you will do in the future

sw **mar·ket¹** /'markıt/ n.
1 ‾place to buy things‾ [C] **a)** an area outside where people buy and sell goods, food etc.: *I went down to the flower market to get these – aren't they gorgeous?* | *Every Sunday there's a farmer's market in the park.* **b)** a GROCERY STORE
2 the market a) the STOCK MARKET: *Most analysts think the market will continue to rise.* | *Investors are currently reluctant to **play the market** (=risk money on the stock market).* | *A sharp decline in the Dow Jones average rocked the markets (=all the stock markets in the world) Friday.* **b)** the total amount of trade in a particular kind of goods: *They've captured about 60% of the market.* | *There have been dramatic changes in the real estate market.* | *[+ in] the world market in aluminum* **c)** the system in which all prices and pay depend on what goods people want to buy, how many they buy etc.: *Capitalism is based on a belief in the market.*
3 on the market available for people to buy: *There are thousands of different computer games on the market.* | *The Paynes are putting their house on the market (=offering it for sale).* | *A clean-burning diesel fuel came onto the market (=began being sold) in 1993.* | *Handguns are freely available on the open market (=for anyone to buy).*
4 ‾country/area‾ [C] a particular country or area where a company sells its goods or where a particular type of goods is sold: *Japanese cars account for about 30% of the U.S. car market.* | *[+ for] The main market for computer software is still the U.S.* | *Some major overseas markets (=markets in other countries) have been having economic problems.*
5 ‾people who buy‾ [singular] the number of people who want to buy something, or the kind of people who want to buy it: *[+ for] a growth in the urban market for dairy products* | *There is a major market for Californian designs in Asia.*
6 be in the market for sth to be interested in buying something: *If you're in the market for a mobile home, this is a good time to buy.*
7 the job/labor market the people looking for work, and the number of jobs that are available: *Half of the teenagers entering the job market in Los Angeles are Latino.* | *competitive/tough/tight job market (=one in which many people are looking for the same jobs)*
8 a buyer's/seller's market a time that is better for buyers because prices are low, or better for sellers because prices are high —see also BLACK MARKET, **corner the market** (CORNER² (2)), FLEA MARKET, FREE MARKET, **price yourself out of the market** (PRICE² (4))

sw **market²** v. [T] **1** to try to persuade people to buy a product by advertising it in a particular way, using attractive packages etc.: *The toy is marketed for children aged 2 to 6.* | *[market sth as sth] The noodles are being marketed as a health food.* **2** to make a product available in stores: *Most turkeys are marketed at a young age.*

mar·ket·a·ble /'markıtəbəl/ adj. marketable goods, skills etc. can be sold easily because people want them: *Too many graduates lack marketable skills.* —**marketability** /ˌmarkıtə'bıləti/ n. [U]

market-driv·en /'.. ,../ adj. MARKET-LED

market e·con·o·my /ˌ.. '../ n. [C] a system of producing wealth based on the free operation of business and trade without government controls

mar·ket·eer /ˌmarkə'tır/ n. [C] someone who sells goods or services into a MARKET¹ (1a) —**marketeering** n. [U] —see also BLACK MARKETEER, FREE MARKETEER

M **market forc·es** /ˌ.. '.., '.. ,../ n. [plural] the free operation of business and trade without any government controls, which decides the level of prices and pay at a particular time

mar·ket·ing /'markıtıŋ/ n. [U] **1** the activity of deciding how to advertise a product, what price to charge for it etc., or the type of job in which you do this: *Car safety is a hot marketing topic.* | *Holbrook has a position in marketing for a large department store.* **2 do the marketing** OLD-FASHIONED to go to the store to buy food

market lead·er /ˌ.. '../ n. [C] the company that sells the most of a particular kind of product, or the product that is the most successful one of its kind: *Kodak is still the market leader.*

market-led /ˌ.. '.◂/ adj. market-led products, developments etc. are a result of public demand for a particular product, service, or skill

market mak·er /'.. ,../ n. [C] TECHNICAL someone who works on the STOCK MARKET buying and selling STOCKS and SHARES

mar·ket·place /'markıt,pleıs/ n. **1 the marketplace** the part of business activities that is concerned with buying and selling goods in competition with other companies: *The changes should increase our ability to achieve a strong position in the marketplace.* **2** [C] an open area in a town where a market is held

market price /'.. ,.., ,.. './ n. [singular] the price of something on a MARKET¹ (2b) at a particular time

market re·search /ˌ.. '.., ,.. .'./ n. [U] a business activity that involves collecting information about what goods people buy and why they buy them

market share /'.. ,../ n. [C,U] the PERCENTAGE (=amount measured as parts out of 100) of sales in a MARKET¹ (2b) that a company or product has

market val·ue /'.. ,../ n. [C,U] **1** the value of a product, building etc. based on the price that people are willing to pay for it rather than the cost of producing it or building it **2** the total value of all the SHARES on a STOCK MARKET, or the value of the stock of a particular company

mark·ing /'markıŋ/ n. **1** [C usually plural,U] things written or painted on something, especially something such as an aircraft, road, vehicle etc.: *The markings on the road are unclear.* | *a black box with no markings* **2** [C usually plural,U] the colored patterns and shapes on an animal's fur, on leaves etc.: *Minnie is a Holstein cow with black markings that look like Mickey Mouse on her side.* **3** [U] GRADING

mark·ka /'marka/ n. [C] the basic unit of money in Finland

marks·man /'marksmən/ n. plural **marksmen** /-mən/ [C] someone who can shoot very well

marks·man·ship /'marksmən,ʃıp/ n. [U] the ability to shoot very well

mark-up /'. ./ n. [C] an increase in the price of something, especially from the price a store pays for something to the price it sells it for: *The retailer's mark-up is 50%.*

Mar·ley /'marli/, **Bob** /bab/ (1945–1981) a Jamaican singer and SONGWRITER who helped to make REGGAE music popular

marlin

mar·lin /'marlın/ n. [C] a large ocean fish with a long sharp nose, which people hunt as a sport

Mar·lowe /'marloʊ/, **Christopher** (1564–1593) an English poet and writer of plays

mar·ma·lade /'marmə,leıd/ n. [U] a JAM made from fruit such as oranges, usually eaten at breakfast

A preposition is a word which is used to show the way in which other words are connected. Prepositions may be single words such as: **by, from, over, under,** or they may be more complex and composed of several words such as: **apart from, in front of, in spite of, instead of.**

Where are prepositions used?

Prepositions are usually followed by a noun or pronoun, a verb with **-ing**, or a **wh-** clause. In the following sentences, **in** is a preposition:

*Write your name **in** the book.*
*This soup's terrible. There's too much salt **in** it.*
*There's just no point **in** complaining.*
*I'm very interested **in** what you said.*

Note that prepositions are NOT used in front of infinitives or clauses beginning with **that**:

*I was astonished **at/by** the news.*
I was astonished to hear the news/to hear what she said.
*I was astonished (**by** the fact) that she had left her job.*

What do prepositions mean?

Unlike some other languages, English uses many prepositions to express basic relationships between words. Relationships of time and place, for example, are usually expressed by the use of a preposition:

*I can see you **on Monday/in August/at 8 o'clock/for half an hour/over the weekend** etc.*
*I'll meet you **at the bus stop/in Boston/on the corner/outside the theater** etc.*

Prepositions are used to express many other different kinds of relationships, such as:

reason	– *I did it **because of** my father/**for** my mother/**out of** a sense of duty.*
manner	– *She spoke **with** a smile/**in** a soft voice.*
means	– *I came **by** bus/**on** foot/**in** a taxi etc.*
reaction	– *I was surprised **at** his attitude/**by** his refusal etc.*

Note that a particular preposition can often be used to express more than one kind of relationship. For example, **by** can be used for relationships of:

time	– **by** *next week*
place	– **by** *the window*
means	– **by** *working very hard*

The entries for prepositions in this dictionary will show you which relationships they can be used to express.

Prepositions in fixed phrases

Prepositions are often part of fixed phrases in phrasal verbs, collocations, and idioms.

Phrasal verbs

Sometimes a combination of a verb and a preposition has its own particular meaning: **call on, look out for, send for.** In this dictionary, these combinations are treated as phrasal verbs. They are listed in a separate section at the end of the entry for the main verb.

Collocating prepositions

Some nouns, verbs, and adjectives are often followed by particular prepositions: **example (of), prohibit (from), afraid (of).** The prepositions which can be used with particular words are shown at the entries for these words.

Idioms and typical collocations

Typical collocations (groups of words which "naturally" go together, through common usage) are shown in **bold** in the dictionary entries. These collocations often show a fixed use of prepositions:

by the name of | **be out of your mind** | **be on a diet** | **in safe hands**

Word order

In some situations it is possible for a preposition to come at the end of a clause or sentence. This happens especially with **wh-** questions, relative clauses, exclamations, passive verbs, and some infinitive clauses:

*Who are you talking **to**?*
*Is this the book you're interested **in**?*
*Let me **in**!*
*Don't worry. He's being taken care **of**.*
*She's really interesting to talk **to**.*

This use is very common in everyday informal English, and especially in spoken English. Some people feel that in formal English it is better to avoid putting the prepositions at the end, by using sentences like this:

To whom *are you speaking?* | *Is this the book* **in which** *you are interested?*

However, sentences like these can sometimes sound too formal and old-fashioned, especially in spoken English.

See LANGUAGE NOTES: **Collocations, Phrasal verbs, Words followed by prepositions**

In English many nouns, verbs, and adjectives are commonly followed by prepositions. If you do not know whether to use a preposition with a particular word or if you are not sure which preposition to use, look up the word in this dictionary. At each entry, you will be given the prepositions which are commonly used with that word. These are printed in **bold** before an example showing how the word is used in context with a preposition.

Below are some sample entries for nouns, verbs, and adjectives.

Prepositions with nouns

This entry tells you that **candidate** can be used with the preposition **for**.

can·di·date /ˈkændə,deɪt, -dɪt/ n. [C] **1** someone who is being considered for a job or is competing to be elected: *One candidate must receive a majority of the vote.* | [+ **for**] *Parcells seemed to be the leading candidate for the coaching job at Tampa Bay.* | *Zimmerman is the **prime candidate** (=most likely candidate) to take over the position of conductor.* **2** a person, group, or idea that is appropriate for something or likely to get something: [+ **for**] *His obvious intelligence makes him a strong candidate for a school for the gifted.*

This entry tells you that **article** can be used with either **about** or **on**. The examples show you that the prepositions are used with the same meaning.

ar·ti·cle /ˈɑrtɪkəl/ n. [C] **1** a piece of writing about a particular subject in a newspaper, magazine etc.: [+ **about/on**] *an article about the Hubble telescope*

This entry shows you that in its first meaning, **bias** can be used with either **against**, **toward**, or **in favor of**. The choice of preposition will depend on the meaning of the sentence in which the word is used.

bi·as[1] /ˈbaɪəs/ n. **1** [singular,U] an opinion about whether a person, group, idea is good or bad, that influences how you deal with it: *Conservatives say the press has a liberal bias.* | [+ **against/toward/ in favor of**] *Investigators found a pattern of bias against women and minorities among police officers.* **2** [singular] a natural skill or interest in one particular area: *Lydia has a strong artistic bias.* **3 on the bias** in a DIAGONAL direction: *cloth cut on the bias*

Prepositions with verbs

This entry tells you that in its first meaning, **balk** is used with the preposition **at**. The first example shows that you usually **balk at** something.

balk /bɔk/ v. **1** [I] to not want to or refuse to do something that is difficult, or frightening: [+ **at**] *Several of the managers balked at enforcing the decision.* **2** [I] in baseball, to stop in the middle of the action of throwing the ball to the player who is trying to hit it

This entry tells you that **argue** can be used with the prepositions **with**, **about**, and **over**. The choice of preposition will depend on the meaning of the sentence in which the word is used.

ar·gue /ˈɑrgyu/ v. **1** [I] to disagree with someone in words, often in an angry way: *We could hear the neighbors arguing.* | [+ **with**] *He was sent off the court for arguing with a referee.* | [+ **about**] *They were arguing about how to spend the money.* | [+ **over**] *The kids were arguing over which TV program to watch.*

This entry tells you that in its first meaning, **chat** can be used with either **with** or **to**. The example shows you that these two prepositions are used with the same meaning.

chat[1] /tʃæt/ v. **chatted, chatting** [I] **1** to talk in a friendly informal way, especially about things that are not important: *The two women chatted all evening.* | [+ **about**] *Charlie and Kevin sat in the corner, chatting about life in the city.* | [+ **with/to**] *Dad really enjoys chatting with people from other countries.*

Prepositions with adjectives

This entry tells you that when **confused** means "unable to understand," it can be followed by the preposition **about**. Note that in its second meaning, it is used without a preposition.

con·fused /kənˈfyuzd/ *adj.* **1** unable to understand clearly what someone is saying or what is happening, or to think clearly about something: *Now I'm totally confused. Can you explain that again?* | [+ **about**] *If you're confused about anything, phone my office.* **2** not clear, or not easy to understand: *a lot of confused ideas* | *confused political thinking* —**confusedly** /kənˈfyuzɪdli/ *adv.*

This entry tells you that in its first meaning, **concerned** can be used with the prepositions **about** or **for**, but in its second meaning it is used with the prepositions **in** or **with**.

con·cerned /kənˈsɚnd/ *adj.* **1** worried worried about something important: *Concerned parents approached the school about the problem.* | [+ **about**] *Zoo officials are concerned about the mother elephant.* | [+ **for**] *Rescuers are concerned for the safety of two men trapped in the cave.* | [**concerned that**] *The police are concerned that the protests may lead to violence.* —see Usage Note at NERVOUS
2 involved [not before noun] involved in something or affected by it: *Divorce is very painful, especially when children are concerned.* | [+ **in**] *Everyone concerned in the incident was questioned by the police.* | [+ **with**] *Businesses concerned with the oil industry do not support solar energy research.* | *The company's closure was a shock to **all concerned***

Summary

Some words can be followed by different prepositions without changing their meaning (see **article**).

Some words are followed by different prepositions according to their different meanings (see **concerned**).

Some words can be followed by more than one preposition, but these are used in different ways (see **bias**, **argue**).

Some words can be used either with or without a preposition (see **confused**).

Prepositions can be followed by verbs in the **-ing** form (see **balk**). They cannot be followed by infinitives.

Phrasal verbs

The examples in this Language Note show words which can be used with a preposition but have a complete meaning in themselves. There are also many verbs where a word which looks like a preposition makes up part of the meaning, for example **come across** (=discover), **look into** (=investigate) etc. These are considered to be phrasal verbs and are listed in this dictionary under the main verb in a separate section at the end of the entry.

See LANGUAGE NOTES: **Collocations, Phrasal verbs**

You can use many different adjectives to ta k about large physical size: **big**, **large**, **enormous**, **huge**, **tall** etc. But which adjectives can you use to intensify a noun (to express the idea of great degree or strength) when you are talking about something which is not physical?

Below are some of the mos: common intensifying adjectives. Note that nouns can have different intensifying adjectives without really changing their meaning:

a great/large *quantity* | a **big/bitter/great** *disappointment* | **a big/definite/distinct/ marked** *improvement*

However, the choice of adjective depends on the noun: different nouns need different adjectives to intens fy them. Below, you will find some of the most common examples.

Great

Great s used in front of uncountable nouns which express feelings or qualities: *She takes* **great pride** *in her work.* | *His handling of the problem showed* **great sensitivity**. With uncountable nouns, **great** can be replaced by **a lot of** which is more informal, but very common: *I have* **a lot of admiration** *for her.* | *It takes* **a lot of skill** *to pilot a plane.* When used with countable nouns, **great** is more formal than **big**: *a* **big/great surprise**. **Great** can often be replaced by stronger adjectives, such as **enormous** and **tremendous**: **enormous enjoyment** | **tremendous admiration**. **Great** is commonly used with these nouns:

great admiration	great excitement	great power
great danger	great happiness	great pride
(in) great demand	(a) great honor	a great quantity (of sth)
in great detail	great importance	great respect
great difficulty	great joy	great skill
(a) great disappointment	at great length	great strength
great effort	a great number (of sth)	(a) great success
great enjoyment	great pleasure	great understanding

Total

Total, **complete**, **absolute**, ar d **utter** are used more frequently than **great** in front of words which express very strong feelirgs (such as **ecstasy** or **amazement**), or extreme situations, happenings etc., especially bad ones (such as **chaos** or **disaster**):

She stared at him in **utter amazement**. | *The trip was* **a complete disaster**.

In the examples below, **complete and absolute** could all be used in place of **total**:

total agony	total despair	a total idiot
total astonishment	total destruction	a total lack of sth
a total catastrophe	total ecstasy	total silence
a total collapse	total failure	a total stranger
total darkness		

Big

Big is mostly used when talking about physical size, but it can also be used as an intensifying adjective. Note that it is not usually used with countable nouns:

a big decision
a big disappointment
a big eater (=someone who eats a lot)

a big improvement
a big mistake

a big spender (=someone who spends a lot)
a big surprise

Large

Large is mostly used to express physical size. It is also commonly used with nouns which are connected with numbers or measurements, as in the examples below. Note that it is not usually used with uncountable nouns:

a large amount
a large number (of sth)

a large population
a large proportion

a large quantity
a large scale

Deep/heavy/high/strong

Deep, **heavy**, **high**, and **strong** are also commonly used as intensifying adjectives, as in these examples:

deep
deep depression
deep devotion

deep distrust
a deep feeling (=emotion)

(a) deep sleep
in deep thought

heavy
a heavy drinker
  heavy rain

a heavy sleeper
a heavy smoker

heavy snow
heavy traffic

high
high cost
high density
high energy
high esteem

a high expectation (of sth)
a high level (of sth)
a high opinion (of sb/sth)
  high pressure

a high price
high quality
high speed

strong
  strong demand
a strong denial
a strong feeling (that) (=idea)

a strong opinion (about sth)
a strong sense (of humor/fun etc.)
a strong smell

a strong taste

Other intensifying adjectives

The examples above show some of the most common intensifying adjectives, but many other adjectives are used to express the idea of great degree, size, or strength. When deciding which adjective to use, remember that it usually depends on the noun. Particular nouns need particular adjectives:

a **fierce/heated argument**
a **close connection**

a **distinct/marked improvement**
a **hard worker**

Note that different adjectives are used with different meanings of a noun:

*He has a very **high opinion** of her work* (=he thinks it is very good). | *She has **strong opinions** about politics.*

See LANGUAGE NOTE: **Collocations**

What is an idiom?

An idiom is a particular group of words with a special meaning which is different from the meanings of the individual words.

Idioms usually have a fixed word order

Although certain small changes can be made in idiomatic expressions (see below: **Using idioms**) you cannot usually change the words, the word order, or the grammatical forms in the same way as you can change a non-idiomatic expression. For example:

The answer's easy can be changed to *The answer's simple*. But in the expression *It's* **(as) easy as pie**, the word **simple** cannot be used.

She likes cats and dogs can be changed to *She likes dogs and cats*. But in the expression *It's* **raining cats and dogs** (=raining hard), the word order is unchangeable.

He almost bought the farm can be a literal expression meaning, for example, "he almost purchased some land for farming." In this case, **the farm** can be replaced by a pronoun: *He almost bought it*, or the verb can be used in the passive form: *The farm* **was** *almost* **bought**. However, *He almost* **bought the farm** can also be a fixed idiomatic expression meaning "he almost died." When this expression is used as an idiom, no word changes are possible.

Idioms have a special meaning

Sometimes the meaning of an idiom can be guessed from the meaning of one of the words:

to **rack your brains** (=to think hard; something to do with **brains**)
to live **in the lap of luxury** (=to have a lot of very expensive things; something to do with **luxury**)

Usually, however, the meaning of an idiom is completely different from any of the separate words:

She was **over the moon** *about her new job* (=she was extremely happy).
The test was a **piece of cake** (=the test was very easy).

Sometimes an expression can have two meanings, one literal and one idiomatic. This happens most often when the idiomatic expression is based on a physical image:

a slap in the face (=a physical hit to the face; an insult or an action which seems to be aimed directly at somebody)
to **keep your head above water** (=to prevent yourself from sinking into the water; to be just barely able to live on your income, or to be just barely able to go on with life, work etc.)

Recognizing idioms

How do you recognize an idiom? It is sometimes difficult to know whether an expression is literal or idiomatic, so it is useful to remember some of the most common types of idioms.

Pairs of words

touch-and-go | **high and dry** | **in black and white** | **the birds and the bees**

(Note that the word order in these pairs is unchangeable.)

Similes

(as) blind as a bat I **(as) large as life** I **(as) mad as a hatter** I **(as) old as the hills**

Phrasal verbs

chicken out of sth I **come across** sb/sth I **nod off** I **put up with** sb/sth

Actions which represent feelings

look down your nose (in scorn or dislike) I **raise your eyebrows** (in surprise, doubt, displeasure, or disapproval)

These idioms can be used by themselves to express feelings even when the feeling is not stated. For example *There were a lot of raised eyebrows at the news of the governor's resignation* just means "everyone was very surprised."

Sayings

Many sayings are complete sentences. Remember, however, that sayings are not always given in full:

> *We'll probably win the tournament, but we shouldn't* **count our chickens** *yet*. (The speaker is warning that people should not be too confident about what will happen.) The full saying is: **Don't count your chickens before they hatch**.

> *They may never accept our proposal*. **You can lead a horse to water**, *you know*. (The speaker says that no matter how much effort they put in, they may not get the results they want.) The full saying is: **You can lead a horse to water, but you can't make him drink**.

> *I didn't say you were a liar, but hey*, **if the shoe fits**. (The hearer previously thought the speaker had accused him of being a liar. The speaker had not said this, but believes that the hearer is a liar.) The full saying is: **If the shoe fits, wear it**.

Using idioms

Before using an idiom, ask yourself the following questions:

How fixed is the expression?

Sometimes certain parts of an idiom can be changed.

Verbs, for example, can often be used in different forms. (Note, however, that they are rarely used in the passive form.)

> *He* **caught** *her eye*. I **Catching** *the waiter's eye, he asked for the bill*.

In many expressions, it is possible to change the **subject pronoun**:

> **He** *swallowed his pride*. I **They** *swallowed their pride*. I **Janet** *swallowed her pride*.

Someone can usually be replaced by other nouns or pronouns:

> *jog* **someone's** *memory* I *She jogged* **my** *memory*. I *This photo might jog* **your** *memory*.

Remember, however, that most idioms are far more fixed than literal expressions, and many cannot be changed at all. (See the *Longman American Idioms Dictionary* for full details.)

Is the style right for the situation?

Many idiomatic expressions are informal or slang, and are only used in informal (usually spoken) language. Compare:

He said the wrong thing and *He* **put his foot in his mouth**. (INFORMAL)
They all felt very depressed and *They were all* **down in the dumps**. (INFORMAL)

Some expressions are literary or old-fashioned and are not often used in everyday language except possibly as a joke:

I guess Jen's parents didn't **like the cut of my jib**. (humorous use of an old-fashioned idiom)

You will find all the common English idioms in this dictionary. Look them up at the entry for the first main word in the idiom. Idioms are shown in bold, and each idiom has its own number.

> See LANGUAGE NOTES: **Collocations, Phrasal verbs**

Language Note: Modal verbs

Modal verbs are a small group of verbs which are used with other verbs to change their meaning in some way. The table below shows you some of the many meanings which can be expressed by the modal verbs: **can, could, may, might, must, have to, ought, shall, should, will,** and **would**. The examples show you some of the ways in which these verbs are commonly used:

prediction of future events	*He'll (=will) forget his umbrella if you don't remind him.* *What will the world be like in 50 years?* *Stop crying! It won't make things any better, you know.*	Remember that the negative form of **will** is **won't**.
personal intention, willingness, wish	*I'll (= will) be back in a minute.* *I won't ever speak to him again.* **Will/would** *you help me with my homework?* (request) *No, I* **won't** (refusal) *I'll (=will) do it for you if you like.* (offer) **Shall I** *give you a hand with the dishes?* (offer) **Shall we** *buy her a present?* (suggestion)	**Shall** can be used in questions with **I** and **we**, but is only used in statements in very formal or official English.
ability	*I* **can** *speak Chinese, but I* **can't** *write it.* *She could swim when she was younger.* **Can/Could** *you close the window, please?* (request)	**Could** is used to talk about ability, NOT about particular events which actually happened in the past. Other expressions like **manage to** or **be able to** can be used instead: *She finally* **managed to** *pass the test.* Or no other verb is needed: *She finally passed the test.* Polite requests are often made with **can** and **could**.
permission	**Can/may** *I have another piece of cake, Dad?* (request) *No, you* **can't**. *You'll make yourself sick.*	**Can** is commonly used to ask for or give permission. **May** is very formal.

	Do you think I **could** *leave early tonight?* (request) *You* **can/may** *leave at 5:30 if you want.* *No, you* **can't** *leave until you're finished with that work.*	**Could** is used to ask for (NOT to give) permission. It is more tentative than **can**.
unreality, hypothesis	*I* **would** *love to travel around the world* (if I had the chance). *What* **would** *you do if you won a million dollars?* *I* **wouldn't have** *gone, if I'd known he was going to be there.* **Would** *you like some coffee?* (offer) **Should** *you have any questions* (if you have any questions), *please give us a call.* (formal)	**Would** is commonly used in the main clause of conditional sentences to show that a situation is unreal or uncertain. Because it can express uncertainty, **would** is also used in polite invitations, offers, and requests.
possibility	*She* **may/might** *(not) go to Denver tomorrow.* *They* **may/might** *(not) be meeting her.* *Joe* **may have/might have** *missed the flight.* *Where* **can/could** *they be?* *Learning English* **can** *be fun* (=is sometimes fun). *Don't touch that wire. It* **could** *be dangerous.* *They* **could have** *had an accident, I suppose.*	**Could** suggests that something is less likely than **may** or **might**. **Can't**, **couldn't**, and **couldn't have** are used to show that there is no possibility. (See **certainty** below.)
certainty	*Joe* **must** *be at least 45* (=I'm sure he's at least 45). *No, he* **can't** *be over 40* (=I'm sure he isn't over 40). *He* **must have** *started working 20 years ago* (=I'm sure he started working 20 years ago). *We* **couldn't have** *been at college together* (=I'm sure we weren't at college together). *They'd be back by now* (=I'm sure they're back). *No, they* **wouldn't** *be there yet* (=I'm sure they are not there yet). *Mary* **would have** *landed already* (=I'm sure she's landed already). *No, she* **wouldn't have** *left home yet* (=I'm sure she hasn't left home yet).	**Must have** (+ past participle) is the form of **must** that is used to express certainty about things in the past. **Must** and **must have** express stronger certainty than **would** and **would have**. **Couldn't** and **couldn't have** express stronger certainty than **wouldn't** and **wouldn't have**.
obligation, requirement	*All visitors* **must** *report to the office.* *I* **have to** *finish this job by tomorrow.* *He* **had to** *finish the job by the next day.* *You* **don't have to** *do it until next week* (=it is not necessary).	**Must** and **must not** are used mainly in formal or official writing. **Have to** is usually used instead of **must** in more informal writing and speech. **Had to** is the past form of **must** when it is used to express obligation.

	You **must not** smoke in the theater (=it is forbidden). I **didn't have to** get up early this morning (=either **a** the speaker did not get up early, or **b** the speaker did, in fact, get up early).	**Don't have to** is used to show that there is no obligation. **Must not** is used in official language to show that something is not allowed.
desirability	You **should/ought to** quit smoking. (advice) We **should/ought to** go to that new Japanese restaurant sometime. (suggest on) The residents **should have/ought to have** been consulted (but they were not consulted). You **shouldn't** work so hard, you know.	The contracted form **oughtn't** is rarely used.
probability	Their meeting **should/ought to** be over now (=I think it probably is). He **should/ought to** be home at 5 o'clock today (=I think he probably will be). They **should have/ought to have** received our letter by now (=I think they probably have).	In this meaning, **should** and **ought to** are not as strong as **will** and **must**. (See **certainty** above.)

Grammatical behavior of modal verbs

Grammatically, modal verbs behave in a different way from ordinary verbs.

They have no **-s** in the third person singular.

Most modal verbs, except for **ought**, are followed by the infinitive of other verbs without **to**.

Modal verbs have no infinitive or **-ing** form. They can be replaced by other expressions if necessary: She **can** leave work early if she wants. | She likes **being able to** leave work early.

They make questions and negative forms without using **do/did**: **May** I see that? | You **shouldn't** shout.

Note that some modal verbs appear to have past tense forms (**could, should, might**), but these are not usually used with a past meaning. One exception is **could** which, when talking about ability, is used as a past form of **can**: I **could** run a long way when I was younger.

Most modal verbs can be used in some of their meanings with another verb in the present perfect to talk about the past: I **may have** seen him yesterday. | You **should have** told me last week. (See the table for more examples.)

In past indirect speech, the following modals usually change their form:

can	"You **can't** leave until tomorrow."	They said she **couldn't** leave until the next day.
have to	"You **have to** finish your work first."	"Dad said I **had to** finish my work first."
may	"They **may** have missed the bus."	He suggested that they **might** have missed the bus.
will	"I'll do that tomorrow."	She said she **would** do it the next day.

Other modals usually remain the same:

She said she **would** like some coffee (her words were, "I'd like some coffee."). | She told me I **ought to** stop smoking (her words were, "You **ought to** stop smoking.").

Why do you **drive** a car but **ride** a bicycle, **do** your best but **make** a mistake, **give** a performance but **play** a part? There is often no real reason except that a particular noun needs a particular verb to express what is done to it.

In order to speak or write English well, it is important to know which nouns take **make** and which take **do**. There are some general rules to help you decide (see Usage Note at MAKE) but often it has to be learned through practice.

Some typical uses of Make and Do

You can **make**		You can **do**	
an accusation	a meal (=prepare	your best	the ironing
an arrangement	a meal)	business (with	a job
an attempt	a mistake	someone)	the laundry
a change	money	the cleaning	research
a comment	a movement	a course (of study)	(some) work
a deal	a noise	(some) damage	
a decision	an offer	a dance	
a demand	progress	the dishes	
an effort	a promise	your duty	
an estimate	a recommendation	(someone) a favor	
a fuss	a remark	harm	
a gesture	a request	your homework	
an impression (on	a statement	the housework	
someone)			

Other verbs commonly used with particular nouns

You can **give**	You can **take**	You can **have**
(someone) a chance	action	an accident
a command	advantage (of something	a fit
details	or someone)	a headache
evidence	a bath	an idea
information	a course	an illness (a cold, cancer)
a performance	a guess	a meal (=eat a meal)
permission	a look	an operation (if you are sick)
an opinion	medicine	a party
an order	a picture/photo	a thought
a talk/speech/lecture	a pill	
	responsibility (for something)	
	risks	
	a test	
	a walk	

You can **play**		You can **perform**
cards	a trick (on someone)	a duty
a game	a tune	a function
a musical instrument		an operation (if you are
music		a doctor)
a part		a piece of music
a CD, cassette, tape etc		a play
a role		a task

Using more than one word with a noun

Using different verbs with a similar meaning

Sometimes it is possible to use more than one verb with a noun to express a similar meaning. For example, you can **arrive at/come to/make/reach a decision**. Usually, however, the choice is limited.

Using different verbs for different actions

Of course there are usually several different things which can be done to a noun, and different verbs are used to describe these actions.

Compare:

You **take** a test.
  (if you are a student)
You **give** a test.
  (if you are a teacher)
You **pass** a test.
  (if you are successful)
You **fail** a test.
  (if you are not successfu)

You **drive** a bus.
  (if you are the driver)
You **ride/take** a bus.
  (to travel from one place to another)
You **catch** a bus.
  (if you arrive on time)
You **miss** a bus.
  (if you are too late)

Using different verbs for different senses

If a noun has more than one sense, different verbs may be used for the different senses.

Compare:

He **played** a trick on his brother.
  (trick = a joke)
She **performed/did** some tricks at the party.
  (tricks = card tricks or magic tricks)

He **placed** an order for some new office furniture.
  (order = a list of things to be bought)
The captain **gave** orders to advance.
  (orders = military commands)

When you look up a word in this dictionary, remember to read the examples! They will often help you to choose a verb to go with a noun.

> See LANGUAGE NOTE: **Collocations**

Language Note: Phrasal verbs

In this dictionary, a verb is considered to be a phrasal verb if it consists of two or more words. One of these words is always a verb; the other may be an adverb as in **throw away**, a preposition as in **look into**, or both an adverb and a preposition as in **put up with**. The meaning of a phrasal verb is often very different from the meaning of the verb on its own. For example, **look into** (=investigate) and **look after** (=take care of) have completely different meanings from **look**. In fact, many phrasal verbs are idiomatic (see Language Note: **Idioms**).

How are phrasal verbs listed?

Phrasal verbs are listed in alphabetical order at the end of the entry for the main verb. They are marked *phr. v.* In this sample entry, **polish off** and **polish up** are phrasal verbs listed after the entry for **polish**.

> **polish** sb ↔ **off** *phr. v.* [T] INFORMAL to kill or defeat someone: *Miami has polished off eleven teams in a row this season.*
>   **polish** sth ↔ **up** *phr. v.* [T] **1** also **polish up on sth** to improve a skill or an ability by practicing it: *I need to polish up on my writing skills.*

Sometimes the main verb of a phrasal verb is not used alone. In these cases, the verb is shown as a headword but the phrasal verb is listed immediately underneath the headword. This sample entry tells you that the verb **gad** is not used alone but only as part of the phrasal verb **gad around**.

> **gad** /gæd/ v. **gadded, gadding**
> **gad around** phr. v. [I] INFORMAL to go out and enjoy yourself, going to many different places, especially when you should be doing something else

With or without an object?

As with all other verbs, some phrasal verbs are used with an object and some are not used with an object. In this dictionary, phrasal verbs are marked [T] (transitive – takes an object) or [I] (intransitive – no object) accordingly. These sample entries show that **grow out of** takes an object and **grow up** does not.

> **grow out of** sth phr. v. [T] **1** if a child grows out of clothes, they become too big to wear them **2** if a child grows out of a habit, they stop doing it as they get older: *Jonathan still sucks his thumb, but we hope he'll grow out of it soon.* **3** to develop from something small or simple into something bigger or more complicated: *The push to organize in a union grew out of worker dissatisfaction.*

> **grow up** phr. v. [I] **1** to develop from being a child to being an adult: *Chris said he wants to be a fireman when he grows up.* | *I grew up in Chicago.* **2 grow up!** SPOKEN said to tell someone to behave more like an adult, especially when they have been behaving in a childish way **3** to start to exist and become bigger or more important: *A large shopping area has grown up around the city's train station.*

Position of the object

When a phrasal verb takes an object, it is important to know where to put the object. Sometimes it comes after the adverb or preposition. This entry tells you that the direct object, which can be a person (sb) or a thing (sth), is always placed after the complete phrasal verb **plow into**.

> **plow into** sb/sth phr. v. [T] to crash into something or someone, causing damage or harm: *A train derailed and plowed into two houses.*

Sometimes the direct object can appear in either position. This is shown by the use of the symbol ↔ . This entry tells you that you can say **hand in** *your papers* or **hand** *your papers* **in**.

> **hand** sth ↔ **in** phr. v. [T] to give something to a person in authority: *He handed in his essay three days late.*

Note, however, that with verbs of this type, when the direct object is a pronoun it MUST be put between the verb and the adverb or preposition:

> **Hand in** *your papers* or **Hand** *your papers* **in** but only **Hand** *them* **in** (NOT "**Hand in** *them*").
> They **knocked down** *the building* or They **knocked** *the building* **down** but only They **knocked** *it* **down** (NOT "They **knocked down** *it*").

Some phrasal verbs can have more than one object. The dictionary will help you decide where to put these objects. This entry tells you that **take out on** has two objects; the first always follows the verb and the second always follows **on**.

> **take** sth **out on** sb phr. v. [T] to treat someone badly because you are feeling angry, tired etc.: *Don't take it out on me! It's not my fault.*

Finally, note that some phrasal verbs can be used with or without an object. This entry shows you that **lead off** is one of these verbs. It also tells you that when it is transitive, the direct object comes either before or after **off**.

lead off *phr. v.* **1** [I,T **lead** sth ↔ **off**] to start something such as a meeting, discussion, or performance by saying or doing something: *I'd like to lead off by thanking Dr. Jacobs for finding the time to be with us today.* | *A group of three jets led off the parade.* | [+ **with**] *He led off with a few jokes.*

Passives

In passive forms, phrasal verbs follow the usual pattern of word order with the grammatical subject coming in front of the main verb:

> When's this problem going to be **looked into**?
> He says he**'s** always **being picked on** by the boss.
> Papers **must be handed in** before the end of the week.
> Hackett's proposal **was put to** the board last week.

See LANGUAGE NOTES: **Idioms, Prepositions**

Language Note: Articles

In English, it is often necessary to use an article in front of a noun. There are two kinds of article: the definite article **the**, and the indefinite article **a** or **an**. In order to speak or write English well, it is important to know how articles are used. When deciding whether or not to use an article, and which kind of article to use, you should ask the following questions:

Is the noun countable or uncountable?

Singular countable nouns always need an article or another determiner like **my**, **this** etc. Other nouns can sometimes be used alone. The chart below tells you which articles can be used with which type of noun:

the	+ { singular countable nouns	the bag, the apple
	plural countable nouns	the bags, the apples
	uncountable nouns	the water, the information
a/an	+ singular countable nouns	a bag, an apple
no article or **some**	+ { plural countable nouns	(some) bags, (some) apples
	uncountable nouns	(some) water, (some) information

The dictionary shows you when nouns are countable [C] or uncountable [U]. Nouns which are labeled [C,U] can be either countable or uncountable, depending on the context. The examples below show how articles can be used with countable and uncountable nouns:

countable/uncountable noun	examples
butterfly [C]	**The butterfly** *is an insect.*
	The butterflies *on that bush are very rare.*
	She caught **a butterfly** *in her net.*
	There were **some butterflies** *in the tree.*
	The park was full of **butterflies.**

countable/uncountable noun	examples
pizza [C,U]	The **pizza** [C] *we ordered was delivered two hours later.* The **pizzas** [C] *were cold when they arrived.* The *piece of* **pizza** [U] *that's still in the box is stale.* *We'd like* **a pizza** [C] *with pepperoni and extra cheese.* *There are still* **some pizzas** [C] *in the freezer.* *I'll just make* **some pizza** [U] *for supper.* *They make really good* **pizzas** [C] *at Gino's.* *I could eat* **pizza** [U] *every day.*
information [U]	The **information** *they gave us was wrong.* *We'd like* **some information** *about hotels.* *What we really need is* **information**.

Note that most proper nouns, like **Susan**, **Boston**, and **Canada**, do not usually have an article:

Susan's *traveling through* **Boston** *next week, on her way to Canada.* However, **the** is usually used with names of rivers (**the Colorado River**), oceans (**the Pacific**), groups of mountains (**the Andes**), deserts (**the Gobi Desert**), museums and theaters (**the Playhouse**), and hotels (**the Ritz Hotel**). It is also used with the names of a few countries, especially those whose names contain a common countable noun, such as **the People's Republic of China**.

Are you talking about things or people in general?

When nouns appear in general statements, they can be used with different articles, depending on whether they are countable or uncountable.

In general statements, countable nouns can be used

in the plural without an article:

Elephants have tusks. | *I like elephants.*

in the singular with **the**:

The *elephant is a magnificent animal.* | *He is studying* **the** *elephant in its natural habitat.*

in the singular with **a/an**:

An *elephant can live for a very long time.*

Note that **a/an** can only be used in this way if the noun is the grammatical subject of the sentence.

In general statements, uncountable nouns are always used

without an article:

Photography is a popular hobby. | *She's interested in photography.* |
Water is essential to life.

Are you talking about particular things or people?

Nouns are more often used with a particular meaning. Particular meanings can be **definite** or **indefinite**, and they need different articles accordingly.

Definite

Both countable and uncountable nouns are definite in meaning when the speaker and the hearer know exactly which people or things are being referred to. For example, the definite article **the** is used

when the noun has already been mentioned:

> I saw a man and a woman in the street. **The man** looked very cold. | I took her some paper and a pencil, but she said she didn't need **the paper**.

when it is clear from the situation which noun you mean:

> Can you pass me **the salt**, please? (=the salt on the table) | I'm going to **the store** for some fruit (=the store I always go to).

when the words following the noun explain exactly which noun you mean:

> I just talked to **the man from across the street** (=not just any man). | **The information that you gave me** was wrong (=not just any information).

when the person or thing is the only one that exists:

> I'm going to travel around **the world** (=there is only one world).

Indefinite

Nouns can also be used with a particular meaning without being definite. For example, in the sentence I met **a man** in a bar, the speaker is talking about one particular man (not all men in general), but we do not know exactly which man.

Singular countable nouns with an indefinite meaning are used with the indefinite article, **a/an**:

> Would you like **a cup** of coffee?
> She's **an engineer**.

When their meaning is indefinite, plural countable nouns and uncountable nouns are used with **some** or **any**, or sometimes with no article:

> I think you owe me **some money**.   We don't have **any milk**.
> Do you have **any money** on you?   Would you like **some coffee**?
> We need **some matches**.   Would you like **coffee, tea, or orange juice**?

(For more information about the uses of **some** and **any**, see Usage Note at SOME.)

Does the noun follow a special rule for the use of articles?

The dictionary will tell you if a noun is always used with a particular article. For example:

Nouns describing people or things which are considered to be the only ones of their kind are used with **the**.

> **Big Ap·ple** /ˌ. '../ n. INFORMAL **the Big Apple** a name for New York City

Some nouns are used with different articles when they have different meanings. (The entry tells you that **backbone** in its first meaning is always used with **the**.)

> **back·bone** /'bækboʊn/ n. **1 the backbone of sth** the most important part of an organization, set of ideas etc.: The cocoa industry is the backbone of Ghana's economy. **2** [C] the row of connected bones that go down the middle of your back; SPINE **3** [U] courage and determination: Stuart doesn't have the backbone to be a good manager.

Some nouns are never used with **the**.

> **god** /gɑd/ n. **1 God** [singular, not with **the**] the spirit or BEING whom Christians, Jews, and Muslims believe created the universe, and to whom they pray

Nouns in some common expressions, such as **in/to the hospital**, use **the**.

hos·pi·tal /'hɑspɪtl/ *n.* [C,U] a large building where sick or injured people are taken care of and receive medical treatment: *Elena had the surgery on Friday and was* **in the hospital** *for a week.* | *Ramon was* **admitted to the hospital** *on Tuesday.*

In some common expressions with prepositions, such as **on foot**, **go home**, **go to school**, **by plane**, **at noon**, the nouns do not use the article.

car /kɑr/ *n.* [C] **1** a vehicle with four wheels and an engine, that you use to travel from one place to another: *Cars were parked on both sides of the road.* | *You can take my car to work today if you need to.* | *We decided to go across the U.S.* **by car**.

When you look up a word in this dictionary, check the entry and read the examples to see whether there is any special information about the use of the article.

> See Usage Notes at SOME and THE

Language Note: Collocations

A collocation is a group of words which "naturally" go together through common usage. Unlike idioms, their meaning can usually be understood from the individual words. In order to speak natural English, you need to be familiar with collocations. You need to know, for example, that you say a "heavy smoker" because **heavy** (NOT **big**) collocates with **smoker**, and that you say "free of charge" because **free of** collocates with **charge** (NOT **cost**, **payment** etc.). If you do not choose the right collocation, you will probably be understood by native English speakers, but you will not sound natural. This dictionary will help you with the most common collocations.

Common fixed collocations

When you look up a word, read the examples carefully. Common collocations are shown in **bold**:

These entries show you that **take an exam, final exams, in fashion, go out of fashion, come into fashion, draw a picture, paint a picture,** and **take a picture** are all common collocations.

ex·am /ɪɡ'zæm/ *n.* [C] **1** a spoken or written test of knowledge, especially an important one at the end of a school year or course of study: *a chemistry exam* | *Do you have to* **take an exam** *in French?* | *When are your* **final exams**? —compare TEST¹ (1) **2** a set of medical tests: *an eye exam*

Note that you cannot change the word order in these phrases and that you cannot use other words even if they have similar meanings. We say **final exams** (NOT **tests**), **take** (NOT **make**) a picture.

fash·ion¹ /'fæʃən/ *n.* **1** [singular,U] the popular style of clothes, hair, behavior etc. at a particular time, that is likely to change: *The color black is always* **in fashion**. | *Harper carries classic styles that never* **go out of fashion** (=stop being popular). | *His ideas are* **coming back into fashion**. | *Our typical customer is very* **fashion conscious** (=always wanting to wear the newest fashions). | *Bottled mineral water was* **the fashion** *in the late 1980s.* **2** [C] a style of clothes, hair etc. that is popular at a particular time: *This year's men's fashions are brighter and more casual than ever before.* | *Platform sandals are this summer's fashion.* | *She always buys* **the latest fashions**. | *Nightclubbers and teenagers prompted* **the fashion of** *body piercing.*

Note that other examples in the entries show natural patterns of language.

pic·ture¹ /'pɪktʃɚ/ *n.*
1 image [C] a painting, drawing, or photograph: *Pictures of her family covered the coffee table.* | *Leo's* **picture** (=a photograph of Leo) *is in the paper today.* | **draw/paint a picture** *The children drew pictures of their houses.* | *Excuse me, could you* **take a picture** *of us* (=use a camera to take a photograph)?

Collocating prepositions

When you look up a word, the entry will show you if there is a particular preposition which collocates with it:

These entries show that you say:

graduate from:
She graduated from Yale.

> **grad·u·ate**[2] /ˈɡrædʒuˌeɪt/ *v.* **1** [I] to obtain a DIPLOMA or a degree by completing your studies at a school, college, or university: [+ **from**] *Ruth graduated from Princeton.* **2 graduate (from sth) to sth** to start doing something that is better, more advanced, or more important: *Bob played college baseball but never graduated to the majors.* **3** [T] to give a DIPLOMA or a degree to someone who has completed a course of study: *We expect to graduate nearly 300 students this year.*

admiration for:
I have a lot of admiration for Martha's courage.

> **ad·mi·ra·tion** /ˌædməˈreɪʃən/ *n.* [U] a feeling of admiring something or someone: *Carlos has earned our respect and admiration.* | [+ **for**] *Ms. Wright expressed her admiration for Albright's political abilities.*

harmful to:
Smoking is harmful to health.

> **harm·ful** /ˈhɑrmfəl/ *adj.* causing harm, or likely to cause harm: *Doctors have warned against the harmful effects of smoking.* | [+ **to**] *Some pesticides are harmful to the environment.* —**harmfully** *adv.* —**harmfulness** *n.* [U]

> See LANGUAGE NOTES: **Idioms, Identifying adjectives, Make and Do**

Language Note: Synonyms

You will often find that several words share a similar general meaning. But be careful – their meanings are almost always different in one way or another. When comparing two words in the dictionary, look at the definitions and examples and any Usage Notes. Then ask yourself these questions:

Is the meaning exactly the same?

Compare:

hurt/wound   Both words can mean "to damage part of someone's body," but **wound** is used to suggest that there is a hole or tear in the skin, especially if this has been done on purpose with a weapon:

> *He was seriously **hurt** in a car accident.* | *Two people were killed and forty **wounded** when fighting broke out last night.*

kill/murder   To murder means "to kill" but always has the additional meaning of "illegally and on purpose":

> *She was sent to prison for **killing/murdering** her brother.* | *Fifty people were **killed** (NOT **murdered**) on the state's highways last weekend.*

smell *n.*/**stink** *n.*   A **smell** can be good or bad but a **stink** is always a bad smell, especially a very strong one:

> *the **smell** of roses/the **smell** of rotten eggs/the **stink** of burning rubber*

Sometimes the words are different in degree

adore is a stronger word than **love**	**furious** is a stronger word than **angry**
astonishment is a stronger word than **surprise**	**soaking** is a stronger word than **wet**
filthy is a stronger word than **dirty**	**terror** is a stronger word than **fear**

Sometimes the words express a different attitude

You can say someone is **slim** if they are thin and you like the way they look. If you think they are too thin, you might say they are **skinny**, or if they are too thin in a way that looks ugly, **scrawny**.

You say something is **newfangled** if you disapprove of it because it is too modern, in a way that seems unnecessary. If you do not feel disapproval, you use words like **new** or **modern**.

Are the words used in the same situations?

Words with a similar meaning are often used in very different situations.

Sometimes the words have a different style

In these pairs, one of the words has a particular style which means that it is not usually used in an ordinary situation. Compare:

brainy (INFORMAL)/**intelligent**	**kick the bucket** (HUMOROUS)/**die**
comely (LITERARY)/**beautiful**	**crap** (IMPOLITE)/**nonsense**
cop (INFORMAL)/**policeman**	**seek** (FORMAL)/**look for**

Sometimes the words are used by particular people

Some words are normally used by specialists, such as doctors, lawyers, or scientists. Other people will use another word for the same thing: Compare:

demise (FORMAL OR LAW)/**death**	**cardiac arrest** (TECHNICAL)/**heart attack**

Do the words have the same grammar?

Sometimes words with a similar meaning are used in different grammatical patterns. Compare:

rob/steal	You **rob** a bank or **rob** somebody (of something):
	*He **robbed** the old couple (of all their savings).*
	You **steal** something (from somebody or from a place):
	*He **stole** a glass from the restaurant. I She **stole** some money from her sister.*
answer *v./* **reply** *v.*	**Answer** can be both transitive and intransitive:
	*I called him, but he didn't **answer**. I They never **answer** our letters.*
	Reply is always intransitive:
	*I wrote to her, but she didn't **reply**. I They never **reply** to our letters.*
advise/ recommend	Both verbs can mean "to tell someone what you think should be done," but are followed by different verb patterns:
	*The doctor **advised** me to stay in bed. I The doctor **recommended** that I stay in bed.*

Notice that even when words appear to be synonyms, they are rarely the same in all the ways discussed here. The entries in this dictionary will help you decide how they are different.

See Usage Note at THIN

mar·mo·re·al /mɑr'mɔriəl/ adj. LITERARY like MARBLE

mar·mo·set /'mɑrmə,sɛt, -,zɛt/ n. [C] a type of small monkey with long hair and large eyes that lives in Central and South America

mar·mot /'mɑrmət/ n. [C] a small animal like a large rat that lives in North America, especially in the mountains

ma·roon¹ /mə'run/ n. [U] a very dark red-brown color —**maroon** adj.

maroon² v. [T usually passive] to be left in a place where there are no other people or from which you cannot escape: *The car broke down and left us marooned in the middle of nowhere.*

mar·quee¹ /mɑr'ki/ n. [C] a large sign on a theater that gives the name of the play or movie

marquee² adj. a marquee player, actor etc. is someone who people want to see because they are good or famous

Mar·quette, **Jacques** /ʒɑk/ (1637–1675) a French MISSIONARY and EXPLORER in North America. He and Louis Joliet were the first Europeans to discover the Mississippi River.

mar·quis /'mɑrkwəs, mɑr'ki/ n. [C] a man who, in the British system of NOBLE titles, has a rank between DUKE and EARL

s w
2 ¹ **mar·riage** /'mærɪdʒ/ n. **1** [C] the relationship between two people who are married: *My folks have had a long and happy marriage.* | *One in three marriages ends in divorce.* **2** [U] the state of being married: *Many people still disapprove of sex before marriage.* **3** [C] the ceremony in which two people get married; WEDDING: *The marriage took place at Bethel Lutheran church.* **4 by marriage** if you are related to someone by marriage, they are married to someone in your family or you are married to someone in theirs

mar·riage·a·ble /'mærɪdʒəbəl/ adj. OLD-FASHIONED appropriate for marriage: *a young woman of marriageable age* —**marriageability** /,mærɪdʒə'bɪləti/ n. [U]

marriage cer·tif·i·cate /'.. .., ../ n. [C] an official document that proves that two people are married

marriage li·cense /'.. ,../ n. [C] an official written document saying that two people are allowed to marry

marriage of con·ven·ience /,.. . .'../ n. [C] a marriage that is made for political or economic reasons, not for love

marriage vows /'.. ,./ n. [plural] the promises that you make during the marriage ceremony

s w
2 ² **mar·ried** /'mærid/ adj. **1** having a husband or a wife: *Are you married or single?* | *More and more married women were returning to the workplace.* | *Tony is married to my sister.* | *Newlyweds often started married life by living with one set of in-laws.* **2 be married to sth** to give most of your time and attention to a job or activity —see also MARRY

mar·row /'mæroʊ/ n. **1** [U] the soft substance in the hollow center of bones **2 chilled/frozen/shocked etc. to the marrow** extremely cold, shocked etc.

s w
1 ¹
· ²
mar·ry /'mæri/ v. **marries, married, marrying**
1 [I,T] to become someone's husband or wife: *He converted to Catholicism so he could marry her.* | *When are you going to get married?* | *Tina married young* (=she was young when she got married). | *She always said she'd marry money* (=marry someone who is rich). —see also MARRIED **2** [T] to perform the ceremony at which two people get married: *Rabbi Feingold will marry us.* **3** [T] FORMAL to combine two different ideas, styles, tastes etc. together: [**marry sth with sth**] *The design marries traditional styles with modern materials.* **4 not the marrying kind** not the kind of person who wants to get married

marry into sth phr. v. [T] to join a family or social group by marrying someone who belongs to it: *In 1821, he married into the Ortega family.*

marry sb ↔ **off** phr. v. [T] to find a husband or wife for someone: [+ **to**] *Calla was married off to a prosperous local farmer.*

USAGE NOTE: MARRY

GRAMMAR
You *marry someone* or *get/are married to someone*, not *with* them. But you can be *married with four children.*

SPOKEN-WRITTEN
Get married is more informal and more common in spoken English than **marry**: *Ann is getting married to Chris next week* (compare *Ann is marrying Chris next week*). In spoken English, speakers often avoid using the word *to* with **married** by saying, for example: *Chris and Ann got married/are married.*

Mars /mɑrz/ n. **1** the small red PLANET that is fourth in order from the sun and is the first planet outside the Earth's orbit **2** the Roman name for the god ARES

Mar·seil·laise /,mɑrseɪ'ɛz/ n. [singular] the national song of France

marsh /mɑrʃ/ n. [C,U] an area of low wet ground, often between the ocean and land, in which grasses or bushes may grow —compare BOG¹, SWAMP¹ —**marshy** adj.: *marshy ground*

mar·shal¹ /'mɑrʃəl/ n. [C] **1** a police officer in the U.S. employed by the national or city government to make sure people do what a COURT ORDERS says they must do: *a federal marshal* **2** the officer in charge of a fire-fighting department in the U.S.: *the fire marshal* **3** an officer of the highest rank in an Army or Airforce: *Marshal Zhukov* **4** someone famous who is chosen to lead a PARADE: *Charlton Heston was the grand marshal of the Hollywood Christmas Parade.*

marshal² v. **marshaled, marshaling** [T] **1** to organize all the people and things that you need in order to be ready for a battle, election etc.: *Raia is a city police officer who marshaled support for the bill.* | *Walensa marshaled the forces that ended Communist rule in Poland.* **2 marshal your arguments/ideas/facts etc.** to organize your arguments, ideas etc. so that they are effective or easy to understand: *In a letter to customers, the company marshaled its arguments for higher prices.*

Mar·shall /'mɑrʃəl/, **George** (1880–1959) a general in the U.S. Army during World War II who later organized the Marshall Plan by which the U.S. helped Europe after the war

Marshall, John (1755–1835) a CHIEF JUSTICE on the U.S. Supreme Court

Marshall, Thur·good /'θɜˌgʊd/ (1908–1993) a U.S. lawyer who became the first African-American member of the Supreme Court in 1967

Marshall Is·lands, the /,.. '../ a country consisting of a group of islands in the central Pacific Ocean

marsh gas /'. ./ n. [U] gas formed from decaying plants under water in a MARSH; METHANE

marsh·land /'mɑrʃlænd/ n. [U] an area of land where there is a lot of MARSH

marsh·mal·low /'mɑrʃ,mɛloʊ/ n. [C,U] a very soft light white candy that is made of sugar and EGG WHITES

mar·su·pi·al /mɑr'supiəl/ n. [C] a type of animal that carries its babies in a pocket of skin on its body

Mart, -Mart /mɑrt/ n. [C] used in the names of stores, markets, or MALLS —see also MINI-MART

mar·ten /'mɑrt⁻n/ n. [C] a small flesh-eating animal that lives mainly in trees

mar·tial /'mɑrʃəl/ adj. [only before noun] relating to war and fighting: *martial music*

martial art /,.. './ n. [C usually plural] a sport such as JUDO or KARATE, in which you fight with your hands and feet, and which was developed in Eastern countries

martial law /,.. './ n. [U] a situation in which the army controls a city, country etc.: *Kuwait declared martial law after the Persian Gulf War.*

Mar·tian /'mɑrʃən/ n. [C] an imaginary creature from the PLANET Mars —**Martian** adj.

M

marsupials

opossum

koala

kangaroo

pouch

mar·tin /'mɑrt⌐n/ n. [C] a small bird like a SWALLOW

mar·ti·net /ˌmɑrt⌐n'ɛt/ n. [C] FORMAL someone who is very strict and makes people obey rules exactly

mar·ti·ni /mɑr'tini/ n. plural **martinis** [C,U] an alcoholic drink made by mixing GIN or VODKA with VERMOUTH

Mar·ti·nique /ˌmɑrtɪ'nik, -tn'ik/ an island in the Caribbean Sea that is controlled by France

Mar·tin Lu·ther King Day /ˌmɑrt⌐n ˌluθɚ 'kɪŋ ˌdeɪ/ n. an American holiday on the third Monday in January to remember the day that Martin Luther King Jr. was born

mar·tyr[1] /'mɑrtɚ/ n. [C] **1** someone who dies for their religious or political beliefs, and whose death makes people believe more strongly in those beliefs **2** someone who tries to get other people's sympathy by talking about how hard their life is: It sounds to me like she has a little bit of a martyr mentality. —**martyred** adj. [only before noun]

martyr[2] v. **be martyred** to become a martyr by dying for your religious or political beliefs

mar·tyr·dom /'mɑrtɚdəm/ n. [U] the death or suffering of a martyr

mar·vel[1] /'mɑrvəl/ v. marveled, marveling [I,T] to feel great surprise or admiration for the quality of something: [+ at] Listeners marveled at the speed and precision of his drumming. | [**marvel that**] We sat there marveling that anyone could be so stupid.

marvel[2] n. [C] something or someone that is extremely impressive: The bridge is an engineering marvel. | [+ of] His solo was a marvel of sound, subtlety, and musicality.

mar·vel·lous /'mɑrvələs/ the British and Canadian spelling of MARVELOUS

mar·vel·ous /'mɑrvələs/ adj. extremely good, enjoyable, or impressive: The food was absolutely marvelous. | It's really a marvelous place. —**marvelously** adv.

Marx /mɑrks/**, Karl** /kɑrl/ (1818–1883) a German writer and political PHILOSOPHER who established the principles of COMMUNISM with Friedrich Engels

Marx Broth·ers, the /'. ˌ../ three American actors, Groucho Marx (1890–1977), Harpo Marx (1888–1964) and Chico Marx (1891–1961), famous for performing in many humorous movies

Marx·ism /'mɑrkˌsɪzəm/ n. [U] a political system based on Karl Marx's ideas, that explains changes in history as the result of a struggle between social classes —**Marxist** n. [C]

Mar·y /'mɛri/ also **the Virgin Mary** in the Christian religion, the mother of Jesus Christ, and the most important of all the saints

Mar·y·land /'mɛrələnd/ written abbreviation **MD** a state on the east coast of the U.S.

Mary Mag·da·lene, Saint /ˌmɛri 'mægdələn, -lin/ in the Bible, a woman who was the first person to see Jesus Christ when he returned to life after his death

mar·zi·pan /'mɑrzɪˌpæn, 'mɑrtsəˌpɑn/ n. [U] a sweet food made from ALMONDs, sugar, and eggs, used in candies, cakes etc.

masc. the written abbreviation of MASCULINE

mas·car·a /mæ'skærə/ n. [U] a dark substance that you use to color your EYELASHes and make them look thicker —see picture at MAKEUP

mas·cot /'mæskɑt/ n. [C] an animal, toy etc. that represents a team or organization, and is thought to bring them good luck: Hammer dressed as the school's mascot, Leo the Lion, for the big game.

mas·cu·line /'mæskyəlɪn/ adj. **1** having qualities that are considered to be typical of men or of what men do: Even today, men tend to do such masculine tasks as car maintenance and yard work. **2** if a woman's appearance or voice is masculine, it is like a man's **3** in English grammar, a masculine noun or PRONOUN has a form that means it REFERs to a male, such as "widower": The word for "book" is masculine in French. —compare FEMININE

USAGE NOTE: MASCULINE

WORD CHOICE: masculine, feminine, male, female
Use **masculine** to talk about things that people think are typical of men: a masculine voice. Use **feminine** to talk about things that people think are typical of women: a feminine voice. Use **male** and **female** to describe the sex of a person or animal: a female rabbit.

---

mas·cu·lin·i·ty /ˌmæskyə'lɪnəti/ n. [U] the qualities that are considered to be typical of men: Children's ideas of masculinity tend to come from their fathers. —compare FEMININITY

ma·ser /'meɪzɚ/ n. [C] a piece of equipment that produces a very powerful electric force —compare LASER

Mas·er·u /'mæsəˌru/ the capital and largest city of Lesotho

mash[1] /mæʃ/ also **mash up** v. [T] to crush something, especially a food that has been cooked, until it is soft and smooth: Mash the banana and add it to the batter. —**masher** n. [C] —see picture on page 425

mash[2] n. [U] **1** a mixture of grain cooked with water to make a food for animals **2** a mixture of MALT or crushed grain and hot water, used to make beer or WHISKEY —see also MISHMASH

mashed po·ta·toes also **mashed potato** /ˌ. .'../ n. [U] potatoes that have been boiled and then mashed with butter and milk

mash note /'. ./ n. [C] OLD-FASHIONED a note to someone of the opposite sex in which you tell them that you like them and think they are attractive

mask[1] /mæsk/ n. [C] **1** something that covers all or part of your face, to protect or to hide it: a surgical face mask **2** something that covers your face, and has another face painted on it: In Japanese Kabuki theater, the actors wear special masks. | a Halloween mask **3** [usually singular] an expression or way of behaving that hides your real emotions or character **4** also **masque** a substance that you put on your face and leave there for a short time to clean the skin or make it softer: a facial mask —see also DEATH MASK, GAS MASK

mask[2] v. [T] **1** to hide the truth about a situation, about how you feel etc.: Small children find it hard to mask their emotions. | His public image masked a history of divorce and family problems. **2** a smell, taste, sound etc. that is masked by a stronger one cannot be noticed because of it: Throughout history, herbs and spices have masked odors and unpleasant flavors. **3** to cover something so that it cannot be clearly seen: The wall can be cleaned of graffiti and masked by vegetation.

masked /mæskt/ adj. wearing a mask: a masked gunman

M

masked ball /ˌ. './ n. [C] a formal dance at which everyone wears masks

mask·ing tape /'.. ˌ./ n. [U] narrow paper-like material that is sticky on one side, used especially for protecting the edge of something that you are painting

mas·och·ism /'mæsəˌkɪzəm/ n. [U] **1** sexual behavior in which you gain pleasure from being hurt **2** behavior that makes it seem that someone wants to suffer or have problems: *She's crazy, trying to work, bring up a kid, and go to school too – it's masochism.* —**masochist** n. [C] —**masochistic** /ˌmæsə'kɪstɪk/ adj. —compare SADISM

ma·son /'meɪsən/ n. [C] **1** someone who builds walls, buildings etc. with bricks, stones etc. **2 Mason** someone who belongs to a secret society, in which each member helps the other members to become successful

Ma·son-Dix·on line /ˌmeɪsən 'dɪksən ˌlaɪn/ n. **the Mason-Dixon line** the border between the states of Pennsylvania and Maryland, considered to be the dividing line between the northern and southern U.S.

Ma·son·ic /mə'sɑnɪk/ adj. relating to Masons: *a Masonic temple*

Mason jar /'.. ˌ./ n. [C] a glass container with a tight lid used for preserving fruit and vegetables

ma·son·ry /'meɪsənri/ n. [U] **1** brick or stone from which a building, wall etc. is made: *On the south side of the house the masonry had fallen off completely.* **2** the skill of building with stone **3** the system and practices of MASONS

masque /mæsk/ n. [C] **1** another spelling of MASK¹ (4) **2** a play written in poetry and including music, dancing, and songs, written and performed mainly in the 16th and 17th centuries

mas·quer·ade¹ /ˌmæskə'reɪd/ n. **1** [C] a formal dance or party where people wear MASKS and unusual clothes: *a masquerade ball* **2** [C,U] a way of behaving or speaking that hides your true thoughts or feelings: *She didn't really love him, but she kept up the masquerade for years.*

masquerade² v. [I] to pretend to be something or someone different: [+ as] *An FBI agent masqueraded as a member of the Mafia.* | *Some of these breakfast foods are really candy masquerading as cereal.*

s w **mass¹** /mæs/ n. **1** [C] **a)** a large amount or quantity of something: [+ of] *There is a huge mass of work to be done.* | *The table was heaped with masses of brilliant orange flowers.* **b)** a large amount of a substance, liquid or gas that does not have a definite or regular shape: [+ of] *I stood outside and saw a mass of black smoke to the south.* **2** [C] a large crowd: [+ of] *A mass of people marched before the White House.* **3 the mass of people/workers/the population** etc. most of the people in a group or society; the MAJORITY: *The mass of the American people are with us on this issue.* **4 the masses** [plural] all the ordinary people in society who do not have power or influence, and are thought of as not being very educated: *Henry Ford made automobiles affordable to the masses.* **5** also **Mass a)** [C,U] the main ceremony in some Christian churches, especially in the Catholic Church: *We go to Mass in the morning.* | say/**celebrate Mass** (=perform this ceremony as a priest) **b)** [C] a piece of music written to be played at this ceremony: *Mozart's Mass in C Minor* **6** [U] TECHNICAL the amount of material in something: *The sun makes up about 99.9% of the mass of the solar system.* —see also CRITICAL MASS

s w **mass²** adj. [only before noun] involving or intended for a very large number of people: *Annie has a degree in mass communications.* | *a mass grave* | *mass destruction*

mass³ v. [I,T] to come together in a large group, or to make people or things come together in a large group: *Large numbers of women massed behind a single women's rights issue.*

Mas·sa·chu·sett, Massachuset /ˌmæsə'tʃusɪt/ a Native American tribe who formerly lived in the northeastern area of the U.S.

Mas·sa·chu·setts /ˌmæsə'tʃusɪts/ *written abbreviation* **MA** a state on the northeast coast of the U.S.

mas·sa·cre¹ /'mæsəkə/ v. [T] to kill a lot of people, especially people who cannot defend themselves: *A family of eight was massacred by unidentified gunmen.* —see Usage Note at KILL¹

massacre² n. [C,U] the killing of a lot of people, especially people who cannot defend themselves: *The bombing of Dresden was one of the worst massacres in European history.*

mas·sage¹ /mə'sɑʒ, -'sɑdʒ/ n. [C,U] the action of pressing and rubbing someone's body with your hands, to help them relax or to reduce pain in their muscles *Once a month, Mary gets a massage and facial.* | *Massage can help relieve stress.*

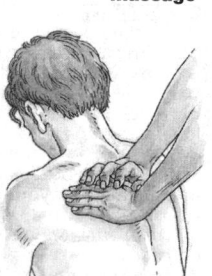
massage

massage² v. [T] **1** to press and rub someone's body with your hands, to help them relax or to reduce pain in their muscles: *Helen leaned over and massaged the back of her neck.* **2** to change official numbers or information in order to make them seem better than they are: *Speech writers were busy massaging the facts to be presented.* **3 massage sb's ego** to try to make someone feel that they are important, attractive, intelligent etc.: *This organization spends more time massaging egos than developing new products.*

massage par·lor /.'. ˌ../ n. [C] **1** a word meaning a BROTHEL (=place where people pay to have sex), used to pretend that it is not a brothel **2** a place where you pay to have a MASSAGE

massage ther·a·pist /.'. ˌ.../ n. [C] someone who has studied MASSAGE and whose job is to give massages —**massage therapy** n.

Mas·sa·soit /ˌmæsə'sɔɪt/ (?1580–1661) a Wampanoag chief who helped the Pilgrim Fathers after they landed in America

mas·se /mɑs/ —see EN MASSE

mas·seur /mæ'sə, mə-/ n. [C] a man who gives MASSAGES

mas·seuse /mæ'suz, mə-/ n. [C] a woman who gives MASSAGES

mas·sif /mæ'sif/ n. [C] TECHNICAL a group of mountains forming one large solid shape

mas·sive /'mæsɪv/ adj. **1** very large, solid, and heavy: *The bell is massive, weighing over 40 tons.* | *the castle's massive walls* **2** unusually large, powerful, or damaging: *a massive tax bill* | *I had a massive argument with Vicky yesterday.* | **a massive stroke/heart attack** etc. *He suffered a massive hemorrhage.*

mass-mar·ket /'. ˌ../ adj. [only before noun] designed for sale to as wide a range of people as possible: *Crichton's novels are available in mass-market paperback editions.* —**mass market** n. [C]

mass me·di·a /ˌ. '.../ n. [used with singular or plural verb] all the organizations, such as television, radio and newspapers, that provide news and information for large numbers of people in a society

mass mur·der·er /ˌ. '.../ n. [C] someone who has murdered a lot of people —**mass murder** n.

mass-pro·duced /ˌ. .'.◂/ adj. produced in large numbers using machinery, so that each object is the same and can be sold cheaply: *mass-produced furniture* —**mass-produce** v. [T] —**mass production** n. [U]

mass tran·sit /ˌ. '../ n. [U] a system of TRANSPORTATION in a city which includes buses, SUBWAYS, etc.: *Today, Los Angeles has virtually no mass transit.* —**mass-transit** adj.

mast /mæst/ n. [C] **1** a tall pole on which the sails or

M

flags on a ship are hung **2** a tall pole on which a flag is hung —see also HALF-MAST

mas·tec·to·my /mæˈstɛktəmi/ n. plural **mastectomies** [C] a medical operation to remove a breast, usually done to remove CANCER

sw **mas·ter**[1] /ˈmæstə/ n. [C]
2 2 **1** skilled someone who is very skilled at something: Maxwell's soul-singing style has been compared to that of such masters as Stevie Wonder and Marvin Gaye. | [+ of] Hitchcock was the master of suspense movies. | [+ at] Aunt Sonia is a master at cooking everything from lobster to salmon.
2 authority **a)** a man who has control or authority over other people or groups of people, for example servants, SLAVES or workers: At one time, the French were the colonial masters of Vietnam. | As a writer, you are your own master (=you control your work). **b)** a person whose teachings others accept and follow: a Zen master
3 original a document, record etc. from which copies are made: I gave him the master to copy.
4 be master of your own fate to be in complete control of a situation: If Maura is to become master of her own fate, she has got to start making her own decisions.
5 be a past master to be very good at doing something because you have done it a lot: [+ at] Duvall is a past master at playing this kind of role.
6 dog owner OLD-FASHIONED the owner of a dog
7 ship someone who commands a ship —see also GRAND MASTER, OLD MASTER, WEBMASTER

master[2] v. [T] **1** to learn a skill or a language so well that you understand it completely and have no difficulty with it: Nguyen helps Vietnamese students who haven't mastered English. **2 master your fear/weakness etc.** to manage to control a strong emotion: Rickey is where he is today because he has mastered the fear of failure.

master[3] adj. [only before noun] **1 master list/tape etc.** the original thing from which copies are made: the master list of telephone numbers **2 master craftsman/mechanic/chef etc.** someone who is very skilled at a particular job, especially a job that involves working with your hands **3** most important or main: All the information is gathered in the master file.

master-at-arms /ˌ.. . ˈ./ n. [C] an officer with police duties on a ship

master bed·room /ˌ.. ˈ../ n. [C] the largest BEDROOM in a house or apartment, that usually has its own BATHROOM

master class /ˈ.. ˌ./ n. [C] a lesson, especially in music, given to very skillful students by someone famous

mas·ter·ful /ˈmæstəfəl/ adj. **1** controlling people or situations in a skillful and confident way: Jenkins was masterful at maintaining his complicated life. **2** done with great skill and understanding: Rembrandt is famous for his masterful contrast of light and darkness. —**masterfully** adv.

master key /ˈ.. ˌ./ n. [C] a key that will open all the door locks in a building

mas·ter·ly /ˈmæstəli/ adj. done or made very skillfully: McGinniss writes in a masterly fashion.

mas·ter·mind[1] /ˈmæstəˌmaɪnd/ n. [C usually singular] someone who plans and organizes a complicated operation, especially a criminal operation: Duarte is thought to be the mastermind behind the kidnapping.

mastermind[2] v. [T] to think of, plan, and organize a large, important, and difficult operation: Manson was convicted of masterminding the murder of Tate and six others.

Master of Arts /ˌ.. . ˈ./ n. [C] an M.A.

master of cer·e·mo·nies /ˌ.. . ˈ..../ n. [C] someone who introduces speakers or performers at a social or public occasion

Master of Sci·ence /ˌ.. . ˈ../ n. [C] an M.S.

mas·ter·piece /ˈmæstəˌpis/ n. [C] a work of art, piece of writing, or music etc. that is of very high quality or that is the best that a particular artist, writer etc. has produced: Channel 6 is showing Orson Welles's masterpiece "Citizen Kane." | The painting is **a masterpiece of** (=a very good example of) Picasso's blue period.

master plan /ˈ.. ˌ./ n. [C usually singular] a detailed plan for controlling everything that happens in a complicated situation: The state recently unveiled its master plan for higher education.

mas·ter's /ˈmæstəz/ n. [C] INFORMAL a MASTER'S sw
DEGREE: [+ in] Eve has a master's in English. 3

Mas·ters and John·son /ˌmæstəz ən ˈdʒɑnsən/ two U.S. scientists, William Howell Masters (1915–) and Virginia Eshelman Johnson (1925–), who have studied and written about human sexual behavior

master's de·gree /ˈ.. ˌ./ n. [C] a university degree that you get by studying for one or two years after your first degree; an M.A. or M.S.

mas·ter·stroke /ˈmæstəˌstroʊk/ n. [C] a very intelligent, skillful, and often unexpected action that is completely successful: Politically, it was a masterstroke that rivaled Nixon's visit to China.

master switch /ˈ.. ˌ./ n. [C] the SWITCH that controls the supply of electricity to the whole of a building or area

mas·ter·work /ˈmæstəˌwərk/ n. [C] a painting, SCULPTURE, piece of music etc. that is the best that someone has done; MASTERPIECE

mas·ter·y /ˈmæstəri/ n. [U] **1** complete control or power over someone or something: [+ of/over] They have battled for years for mastery of the region. **2** thorough understanding or great skill: [+ of/over] Selection to the team is based on mastery of specified gymnastic skills.

mast·head /ˈmæsthɛd/ n. [C] **1** the name of a newspaper, magazine etc. printed in a special design at the top of the first page **2** the top of a MAST on a ship

mas·tic /ˈmæstɪk/ n. [U] a type of glue that does not crack or break when it is bent

mas·ti·cate /ˈmæstəˌkeɪt/ v. [I,T] TECHNICAL to CHEW (=crush food between the teeth) —**mastication** /ˌmæstəˈkeɪʃən/ n. [U]

mas·tiff /ˈmæstɪf/ n. [C] a large strong dog often used to guard houses

mas·tur·bate /ˈmæstəˌbeɪt/ v. [I,T] to make yourself or someone else sexually excited by touching or rubbing sexual organs —**masturbation** /ˌmæstəˈbeɪʃən/ n. [U]

mat[1] /mæt/ n. **1** a small piece of thick rough material that covers part of a floor: You can leave the key under the mat. **2** a small flat piece of wood, cloth etc. that protects a surface, especially on a table: a plastic place mat **3** a piece of thick soft material used in some sports for people to fall onto **4** a piece of thick paper that is put around a picture inside a frame **5 a mat of hair/fur/grass etc.** a thick mass of pieces of hair, fur etc. that are stuck together —see also MATTING

mat[2] adj. another spelling of MATTE

mat·a·dor /ˈmætəˌdɔr/ n. [C] a man who fights and kills BULLS during a BULLFIGHT

Ma·ta Ha·ri /ˌmɑtə ˈhɑri/ (1876–1917) a Dutch dancer famous for being a SPY for the Germans during World War I

match[1] /mætʃ/ n.
1 fire [C] a small wooden or paper stick with a special substance at the top, used to light a fire, cigarette etc.: a box of matches | **light/strike a match** (=rub a match against a surface to make it burn)
2 game [C] an organized sports event between two teams or people: a tennis match | Eric scored the only goal in the match against Albany.
3 appropriateness [singular] something that is appropriate for something else, so that the two things work together successfully: [+ for] Sauvignon blanc makes a perfect match for oysters. | Doctors failed to find a match for the bone marrow transplant.
4 colors/patterns [singular] something that is the same color or pattern as something else, or looks

M

attractive with it: *Stores will mix paints so you can get a good match for your curtains.*

5 be no match for sb to be much less strong, skilled, intelligent etc. than an opponent: *Washington was no match for the Spartans.*

6 be more than a match for sb to be much stronger, smarter etc. than an opponent

7 a shouting match a loud angry argument in which two people insult each other

8 be a perfect match if two people who love each other are a perfect match, they are appropriate for each other

9 make a good match OLD-FASHIONED to marry someone who is appropriate for you —see also **meet your match** (MEET[1] (13)), **mix and match** (MIX[1] (7)) —see Usage Note at FIT[1]

s w
2
3
match² *v.*

1 look good together [I,T] if one thing matches another, or if two things match, they look attractive together because they have a similar color, pattern etc.: *This lipstick matches your blouse exactly.* | *Teresa got everything to match for the baby's room.* —see also MATCHING —see picture at FIT[1]

2 look the same [I,T] if one thing matches another or if two things match, they look the same: *Your socks don't match.*

3 seem the same [I,T] if two reports or pieces of information match, or if one matches the other, there is no important difference between them: *Tom's description and mine matched.* | *Double check that you have an invoice to match every check.*

4 find sth/sb similar [T] to find something that is similar to or appropriate for something else: *Match the words on the left with the pictures on the right.* | *GMI tries to match students with companies that will hire them.*

5 be as good as [T] to be as good, skillful, intelligent etc. as something or someone else: *Nothing we have ever seen matches this moment.* | *Baltimore's economic performance has not matched that of comparable cities.*

6 give money [T] to give a sum of money equal to a sum given by someone else: *Anderson will receive a bonus that matches his base salary.*

7 make equal [T] to make something equal to or appropriate for something else: *Wages won't go up to match prices.* | [**match sth to sth**] *We have to match our ambitions to our resources.*

8 well-matched/ill-matched very appropriate or inappropriate for each other: *Beatty and Bening are well-matched in the movie.*

9 evenly matched if two competitors are evenly matched, they are equal in strength, skill, speed etc.

10 be matched with/against sb to be competing against someone else in a game or competition: *Stanford will be matched with Georgia Tech.*

match up *phr. v.* **1** [I] to be of a similar level or of similar quality as something else: *I'm really embarrassed that we didn't match up with Nebraska but they were too good for us.* **2** [I] if two reports or pieces of information match up, they seem the same **3 match up to your hopes/expectations/ideals etc.** to be as good as you expected, hoped etc. **4** [I,T **match** sth ↔ **up**] to belong with or fit together with something: *Do the two green circles match up?* | *The trick is to match up houseplants with similar growing needs.*

match·book /'mætʃbʊk/ *n.* [C] a small folded piece of thick paper containing paper matches

match·box /'mætʃbɑks/ *n.* [C] a small box containing matches

match·ing /'mætʃɪŋ/ *adj.* [only before noun] having the same color, style, or pattern as something else: *Keeshan wore a striped tie with a matching pocket handkerchief.*

match·less /'mætʃlɪs/ *adj.* FORMAL more intelligent, beautiful etc. than anyone or anything else: *We were dazzled by the matchless beauty of Antarctica.*

match·mak·er /'mætʃˌmeɪkɚ/ *n.* [C] someone who tries to find the right person for someone else to marry —**matchmaking** *n.* [U]

match point /'. './ *n.* **1** [U] a situation in tennis when the person who wins the next point will win

---

the match **2** [C] the point that a player must win in order to win the match —compare GAME POINT

match·stick /'mætʃˌstɪk/ *n.* [C] a wooden MATCH

mate¹ /meɪt/ *n.*
s w
3

1 office/band/locker etc. mate someone you do or share something with: *Myra and I were locker mates in high school.* —see also ROOMMATE, RUNNING MATE, SOUL MATE, TEAMMATE

2 animal [C] the sexual partner of an animal

3 husband/wife [C usually singular] a word meaning your "husband" or "wife," used especially in magazines: *Would you trade your mate for a million bucks?*

4 pair of objects [C] one of a pair of objects: *What happened to this sock's mate?*

5 sailor [C] a ship's officer who is one rank below the CAPTAIN: *the first mate*

6 navy officer [C] a U.S. Navy PETTY OFFICER

7 friend [C] BRITISH a male friend, or a friendly way of speaking to a man you do not know

mate² *v.* **1** [I + **with**] if animals mate, they have sex to produce babies **2** [T] to put animals together so that they will have sex and produce babies **3** [T] to achieve the CHECKMATE of your opponent in CHESS

ma·te·ri·al¹ /mə'tɪriəl/ *n.* **1** [C,U] cloth used for making clothes, curtains etc.; FABRIC: *T-shirt material* —see Usage Note at CLOTH **2** [C,U] a solid substance such as wood, plastic, or metal from which things can be made: *building materials* | *The chairs are made of recycled material.* **3** [U] also **materials** [plural] the things that are used for making or doing something: *There's a basket there with some books and writing materials.* | *art material* **4** [U] information or ideas used in books, movies etc.: *Menken is collaborating on the new material with Tim Rice.* | [+ **for**] *Kincaid finds raw material for her stories in her home life.* **5 officer material/executive material etc.** someone who is good enough for a particular job or position: *Do you think this guy is potential husband material?*
s w
1 1

material² *adj.* [usually before noun] **1** relating to people's money, possessions, living conditions etc., rather than the needs of their mind or soul: *Matt had little desire for **material possessions** but still worked hard.* | *Efforts have been made to improve the **material conditions** of the poor.* | *Many people lack **material comforts**.* **2** relating to the real world and physical objects: *Material damage to the ship was negligible.* **3** LAW important and needing to be considered when making a decision: *a material witness* | [+ **to**] *facts material to the investigation* **4** FORMAL important and having a noticeable effect: *material changes to the schedule* —see also MATERIALLY, RAW MATERIALS

ma·te·ri·al·ism /mə'tɪriəˌlɪzəm/ *n.* [U] DISAPPROVING **1** the belief that money and possessions are more important than art, religion, morality etc. **2** TECHNICAL the belief that only physical things really exist —**materialist** *adj., n.* [C]

ma·te·ri·al·is·tic /məˌtɪriə'lɪstɪk/ *adj.* DISAPPROVING caring only about money and possessions rather than things relating to the mind and soul, such as art or religion: *Christmas has become materialistic and commercial.* | *a materialistic person* —**materialistically** /-kli/ *adv.*

ma·te·ri·al·ize /mə'tɪriəˌlaɪz/ *v.* [I] **1** to happen or appear in the way that you planned or expected: *Officials were relieved that the predicted traffic nightmare never materialized.* **2** to appear in an unexpected and strange way: *A row of huts materialized out of the fog as we approached.* —**materialization** /məˌtɪriələ'zeɪʃən/ *n.* [U]

ma·te·ri·al·ly /mə'tɪriəli/ *adv.* **1** in a big enough or strong enough way to change a situation: *Our situation has gotten materially worse.* **2** in a way that concerns possessions and money, rather than the needs of a person's mind or soul: *Many people hunger for a materially better life.*

ma·té·ri·el, materiel /məˌtɪri'ɛl/ *n.* [U] supplies of weapons used by an army

M

ma•ter•nal /mə'tɝnl/ *adj.* **1** typical of the way a good mother behaves or feels: *I get sort of maternal when I'm around those kids.* | *Gertrude lacks any* ***maternal instinct*** (=desire to have and take care of babies). **2** [only before noun] relating to being a mother: *Maternal smoking increases the risk of low birth weight.* **3 maternal grandfather/aunt etc.** your mother's father, sister etc. —compare PATERNAL —**maternally** *adv.*

ma•ter•ni•ty¹ /mə'tɝnəṭi/ *adj.* [only before noun] relating to a woman who is PREGNANT, or who has had a baby, or to the time when she is PREGNANT: *maternity clothes* | *a maternity hospital*

maternity² *n.* [U] the state of being a mother

maternity leave /.'... ,./ *n.* [U] time that a mother is allowed to spend away from work when she has a baby

maternity ward /.'... ,./ *n.* [C] a department in a hospital where women who are having babies are cared for

S2 W3 **math** /mæθ/ *n.* [U] **1** mathematics: *Tina got a 95% on the math test.* | *I don't think Jim should major in math.* **2 do the math a)** to work with numbers and calculate amounts: *I've done the math, and I know we're losing money.* **b)** SPOKEN used to tell someone to consider the details of a situation, especially numbers, and guess their meaning: *She got married five months ago and just had a baby – you do the math.*

math•e•mat•i•cal /mæθ'mæṭɪkəl/ *adj.* **1** relating to or using mathematics: *a mathematical formula* | *mathematical calculations* **2** calculating things in a careful, exact way: *The whole trip was planned with mathematical precision.* **3 a mathematical certainty** something that is completely certain to happen **4 a mathematical chance (of sth)** a very small chance that something will happen —**mathematically** /-kli/ *adv.*

math•e•ma•ti•cian /ˌmæθmə'tɪʃən/ *n.* [C] someone who has special knowledge and training in mathematics

math•e•mat•ics /ˌmæθ'mæṭɪks, ˌmæθə-/ *n.* [U] the study or science of numbers and of the structure and measurement of shapes, including ALGEBRA, GEOMETRY, and ARITHMETIC

Math•er /'mæðɚ/**, Cot•ton** /'kɑtn/ (1663–1728) an American religious leader who was a PURITAN

Mather, In•crease /'ɪŋkris/ (1639–1723) an American political and religious leader who was the first President of Harvard University

mat•i•nee /ˌmæt˺n'eɪ/ *n.* [C] a performance of a play or movie in the afternoon

matinee i•dol /..'. ,../ *n.* [C] OLD-FASHIONED a movie actor who is very popular with women

mat•ing /'meɪṭɪŋ/ *n.* [U] sex between animals: *the mating season* | *mating rituals*

mat•ins /'mæt˺nz/ *n.* [U] the first prayers of the day in the Christian religion

Ma•tisse /mæ'tis/**, Hen•ri** /ɑn'ri/ (1869–1954) a French PAINTER and SCULPTOR famous for his paintings of ordinary places and objects that use pure bright colors and black lines

matri- /meɪtri, mætrə/ *prefix* **1** relating to mothers: *matricide* (=killing one's mother) **2** relating to women: *a matriarchal society* (=controlled by women) —compare PATRI-

ma•tri•arch /'meɪtriˌɑrk/ *n.* [C] a woman, especially an older woman, who controls a family or a social group —compare PATRIARCH

ma•tri•ar•chal /ˌmeɪtri'ɑrkəl◂/ *adj.* **1** ruled or controlled by women: *a matriarchal society* **2** relating to or typical of a matriarch —compare PATRIARCHAL

ma•tri•ar•chy /'meɪtriˌɑrki/ *n. plural* **matriarchies** [C,U] **1** a social system in which the oldest woman controls a family and its possessions **2** a society that is led or controlled by women —compare PATRIARCHY

mat•ri•cide /'mætrəˌsaɪd/ *n.* [U] FORMAL the crime of murdering your mother —compare PARRICIDE, PATRICIDE

ma•tric•u•late /mə'trɪkyəˌleɪt/ *v.* [I] FORMAL to officially begin studying at a school or college —**matriculation** /məˌtrɪkyə'leɪʃən/ *n.* [U]

mat•ri•mo•ny /'mætrəˌmoʊni/ *n.* [U] FORMAL the state of being married: *the institution of matrimony* —**matrimonial** /ˌmætrə'moʊniəl/ *adj.*

ma•trix /'meɪtrɪks/ *n. plural* **matrices** /-trəsiz/ or **matrixes** [C] TECHNICAL **1** an arrangement of numbers, letters, or signs on a GRID (=a background of regular crossed lines) used in mathematics, science etc. **2** a situation from which a person or society can grow and develop: *the cultural matrix* **3** a living part in which something is formed or developed, such as the substance out of which the FINGERNAILS grow **4** a MOLD into which melted metal, plastic, etc. is poured to form a shape **5** the rock in which hard stones or jewels have formed —see also DOT-MATRIX PRINTER

ma•tron /'meɪtrən/ *n.* [C] **1** LITERARY an older married woman: *At Café Europa, society matrons sip coffee after shopping.* **2** a woman who is in charge of women and children in a school or prison

ma•tron•ly /'meɪtrənli/ *adj.* a word to describe a woman who is fairly fat and not young anymore, used to avoid saying this directly

matron of hon•or /,... '../ *n.* [C] a married woman who helps the BRIDE on her wedding day and stands beside her during the wedding ceremony —compare MAID OF HONOR

matte, mat /mæt/ *adj.* matte paint, color, or photographs have a dull surface, not shiny: *matte paint* —compare GLOSS¹ (4)

mat•ted /'mæṭɪd/ *adj.* twisted or stuck together in a thick mass: *a messy, matted beard* | *Her hair was matted with blood.*

mat•ter¹ /'mæṭɚ/ *n.* S1 W1

1 subject/situation [C] a subject or situation that you have to think about or deal with: *We should discuss the matter ourselves.* | *Rick wasn't particularly interested in financial matters.* | *Wilson always consulted Landers on* ***matters of importance.*** | *The safety of Americans abroad is a* ***matter of*** *serious* ***concern.*** | *I think that's* ***a matter for*** *the voters to decide.* | *Woodbury had decided to* ***let the matter drop*** (=stop worrying about something), *but has since changed his mind.* | *He steered the conversation back to* ***the matter at hand.***

2 substance [U] TECHNICAL the material that everything in the universe is made of, including solids, liquids, and gases

3 it's (just) a matter of (doing) sth used to say that you only have to do a particular thing, or do something in a particular way, in order to be successful: *A lot of things in life are just a matter of believing it's going to happen.*

4 matters [plural] a situation that you are in or have been describing and that you have to deal with: *Herrera still hoped to settle matters peaceably.* | ***It didn't help matters*** *when the promised teaching material failed to arrive.*

5 it's no laughing/small matter used to say that something must be treated seriously: *People make jokes about snorers, but it's no laughing matter.*

SPOKEN PHRASES

6 what's the matter? used when someone seems upset, unhappy, or sick and you are asking them why: *What's the matter, Mark? Are you getting sleepy?*

7 what's the matter with sb/sth? used to ask why something is not working normally, someone seems upset or sick, or something looks wrong: *Honey, what's the matter with you? Don't you feel well?* | *What's the matter with the telephone?*

8 what's the matter with sb? used to emphasize that you are surprised by or angry about what someone says or does: *What's the matter with Mrs. Lowenstein, renting the house to a woman like that?* | *Don't be so rude! What's the matter with you?*

9 something's the matter (with sb/sth) used to say that something is not working normally, someone is

M

upset or sick, or something looks wrong: *Tom's been acting guilty – there must be something the matter.*

10 there's nothing the matter (with sb/sth) used to say that someone is not sick or upset, or that something is working correctly or looks good: *There was nothing the matter with the ladder until he left it out in the rain. | There's nothing the matter with your haircut – I really like it!*

11 as a matter of fact used when giving a surprising or unexpected answer to a question or statement: *Well, as a matter of fact, I heard he's still going out with Julie. | As a matter of fact, I have the woman's name written down somewhere.*

12 no matter how/where/what etc. used to say that something is always the same whatever happens, or in spite of someone's efforts to change it: *Vince tends to wake up at the same time, no matter what time he goes to bed. | No matter how hot it is outside, it's always cool in here.*

13 no matter what (happens) used to say that you will definitely do something: *I decided to leave at the end of six months, no matter what.*

14 no matter used to say that something you have asked about or said is not important: *No matter, I'll pick up the clothes at the cleaners tomorrow.*

15 or... for that matter used to say that what you are saying about one thing is also true about something else: *I've never seen the place this quiet on a Friday night, or any other night for that matter.*

16 be a different matter used to say that one situation or problem is much more serious than another: *Greta lets me borrow her scarves, but her jewelry is a different matter.*

17 the fact/truth of the matter (is) used to say what you think is really true: *The fact of the matter is we have a crisis on our hands.*

18 make matters worse to make a bad situation even worse: *Making matters worse, the family has received several death threats. | Tess just lost her job, and to make matters worse, her landlord is raising her rent.*

19 take matters into your own hands to deal with a problem yourself because other people have failed to deal with it: *The city council took matters into its own hands and set a date for the meeting.*

20 as a matter of course/routine as the usual thing that you do or that happens in a particular situation: *Voters expected as a matter of course that candidates would not keep all their promises.*

21 there's the little matter of sth used in a joking way to remind someone about something important that they would prefer not to think about: *Calder faces suspension, and there's that little matter of the bar fight in Houston.*

22 that's the end of the matter used to tell someone that you do not want to talk about something anymore: *You're not going out tonight, and that's the end of the matter.*

23 as a matter of principle/conscience/policy etc. because of your personal beliefs about what you should do: *As a matter of policy, the department refuses to comment on the investigation.*

24 as a matter of urgency FORMAL done as quickly as possible because it is very important: *The level of crime in our town is unhealthy and must be eliminated as a matter of urgency.*

25 sth is a matter of opinion used to say that people have different opinions about a subject: *Beauty is all a matter of opinion.*

26 sth is only/just a matter of time used to say that something will definitely happen at some time in the future: [+ until/before] *It's just a matter of time until Tony and Lisa get back together.*

27 sth is a matter of life and death used to say that a situation is extremely serious or dangerous and something must be done immediately: *Call the police immediately – this is a matter of life and death.*

28 sth is a matter of taste/cost/luck etc. used to say that what happens or what you decide depends on your judgment, how much something costs, how lucky you are etc.: *Whether to peel asparagus is a matter of taste.*

29 a matter of days/hours/months etc. only a few

days, hours etc.: *His whole life had come apart in a matter of days.*

30 reading/printed matter things that are written for people to read

31 waste/solid/organic/vegetable etc. matter a substance that consists of waste material, solid material etc.

32 body substance [U] a yellow or white substance that is found in wounds or next to your eye —see also GRAY MATTER, **mind over matter** (MIND[1] (44))

USAGE NOTE: MATTER

GRAMMAR
We use **the matter** to mean trouble or a problem only in questions or negative sentences: *What's the matter, Audrey? | There's nothing the matter with it.*

---

matter[2] *v.* [I] **1** to be important, especially to be important to you personally, or to have a big effect on what happens: *Does it matter if I bring my own car? | [+ to] Do you think what I say will matter to him? | It calls for brown sugar, but it doesn't matter – you can use white. |* [**matter who/why/what** etc.] *It doesn't matter how much suntan lotion I put on, I still burn. | Mom, does it matter which potatoes I use? | As long as it serves the community, that's **all that matters**. | That's **the only thing that matters** to them – if the product sells. | **What matters** is how the food tastes, not how it looks. | Her obsession with Farley was so powerful that **nothing else mattered**.* **2 it doesn't matter** SPOKEN **a)** used to say that you do not care which one of two things you have: *"Do you want white or dark meat?" "Oh, it doesn't matter."* **b)** used to tell someone that you are not angry or upset about something, especially something that they have done: *"I think I taped over your show." "It doesn't matter – I already watched it."* **3 what does it matter?** SPOKEN used to say that something is not very important: *We'll do it tomorrow or the next day. What does it matter?*

Mat·ter·horn, the /'mætəˌhɔrn/ a high mountain in the Alps near the border between Italy and Switzerland

matter-of-fact /ˌ.. . '. ./ *adj.* showing no emotion when you are talking about something exciting, frightening, upsetting etc.: *She spoke of death in a calm, matter-of-fact way.* —**matter-of-factly** *adv.* —**matter-of-factness** *n.* [U]

Mat·thew /'mæθyu/ also **The Gospel according to St. Matthew** one of the four books in the New Testament of the Christian Bible that describe the life and teaching of Jesus Christ

Matthew, Saint one of Jesus Christ's DISCIPLES, who is believed to have written "The Gospel according to St. Matthew," which describes the life and teaching of Jesus Christ

mat·ting /'mætɪŋ/ *n.* [U] strong rough material, used for making MATS

mat·tress /'mætrɪs/ *n.* [C] the soft part of a bed that you lie on: *It's important to have a good firm mattress.*

mat·u·ra·tion /ˌmætʃə'reɪʃən/ *n.* [U] FORMAL the period during which something grows and develops

ma·ture[1] /mə'tʃur, mə'tur/ *adj.*
1 sensible someone, especially a child or young person, who is mature behaves in a sensible and reasonable way, as you would expect an older person to behave: *Penny seemed more mature than most of the other students. | Mel's developed into a mature, hardworking person.* —opposite IMMATURE
2 fully grown fully grown and developed: *Mature violets reach a height of about 12 inches. | Eagles aren't sexually mature until age five.*
3 wine/cheese etc. mature cheese, wine etc. has a good strong taste that has developed during a long period of time
4 older a polite or humorous way of describing someone who is not young anymore; MIDDLE-AGED:

M

The magazine features wedding ideas for the mature bride.

5 novel/painting etc. a mature piece of work by a writer or an artist shows a high level of understanding or skill

6 financial TECHNICAL a mature financial arrangement, such as a BOND or POLICY, is ready to be paid —**maturely** *adv.*

mature² *v.* **1** [I] to become sensible and start to behave like an adult: *John's really matured in the last two years.* **2** [I] to become fully grown or developed: *Corn needs longer to mature than soybeans.* **3** [I,T] if a cheese, wine, WHISKEY etc. matures or is matured, it develops a good strong taste over a period of time **4** [I] TECHNICAL if a financial arrangement such as a BOND or POLICY matures, it becomes ready to be paid: *These bonds mature in 12 years.*

ma·tur·i·ty /məˈtʃʊrəti, -ˈtʊr-/ *n.* [U] **1** the quality of behaving in a sensible way and like an adult: *There's a real difference in the maturity level of a 13- and a 15-year-old.* **2** the time when a person, animal, or plant is fully grown or developed: *At maturity, a gray whale will reach a length of 40 to 50 feet.* **3** TECHNICAL the time when a financial arrangement such as a BOND or POLICY becomes ready to be paid

mat·zo, **matzoh** /ˈmɑtsə/ *n.* [C] a type of flat bread eaten especially by Jewish people during PASSOVER

maud·lin /ˈmɔdlɪn/ *adj.* **1** a maudlin song, story, movie etc. tries too hard to make people cry or feel emotions such as love or sadness so that it seems silly: *a song that is tender without being maudlin* **2** someone who is maudlin is talking or behaving in a sad, silly, and SENTIMENTAL way, especially because they are drunk

Maugham /mɔm/, **Som·er·set** /ˈsʌmɚˌsɛt/ (1874–1965) a British writer of NOVELs and short stories

Mau·i /ˈmaʊi/ an island in the Pacific Ocean that is part of the U.S. state of Hawaii

maul /mɔl/ *v.* [T] **1** to injure someone badly by tearing their flesh: *A six-year-old boy was mauled by a mountain lion.* **2** to badly defeat someone in a game or competition, or to severely criticize someone or something: *Cincinnati mauled the Oilers 41–14 at Riverfront Stadium.* **3** to touch someone in a rough sexual way

Mau·na Ke·a /ˌmaʊnə ˈkeɪə, ˌmɔ-/ a mountain on the island of Hawaii that is an active VOLCANO

Mauna Lo·a /ˌmaʊnə ˈloʊə, ˌmɔ-/ a mountain on the island of Hawaii that is an active VOLCANO

maun·der /ˈmɔndɚ, ˈmɑn-/ *v.* [I] LITERARY to talk or complain about something for a long time in a boring way

Maun·dy Thurs·day /ˌmɔndi ˈθɚzdi, ˌmɑn-/ *n.* [U] the Thursday before Easter

Mau·pas·sant /ˌmoʊpæˈsɑn/, **Guy de** /gi də/ (1850–1893) a French writer of short stories

Mau·riac /mɔriˈɑk/, **Fran·çois** /frɑnˈswɑ/ (1885–1970) a French writer of NOVELs

Mau·ri·ta·nia /ˌmɔrəˈteɪnyə/ a country in northwest Africa on the Atlantic coast and west of Mali —**Mauritanian** *n., adj.*

Mau·ri·tius /mɔˈrɪʃiəs, -ʃəs/ a country which is an island in the Indian Ocean —**Mauritian** *n., adj.*

mau·so·le·um /ˌmɔsəˈliəm, -zə-/ *n.* [C] **1** a large stone building containing many graves or built over a grave **2** a large building that seems very dark and empty and makes you feel sad

mauve /moʊv/ *n.* [U] a pale purple color —**mauve** *adj.*

ma·ven /ˈmeɪvən/ *n.* [C] someone who knows a lot about a particular subject: **food/fashion/media etc. maven** *Solly, my plant maven, says most people overwater their plants.*

mav·er·ick /ˈmævərɪk/ *n.* [C] someone who does not follow accepted rules of behavior or ways of doing things and who is confident and able to do things alone: *Programmers are often thought of as the*

mavericks of the computer business. —**maverick** *adj.*: *a maverick cop*

maw /mɔ/ *n.* [C] LITERARY **1** something that seems to swallow things or people completely: *They were about to enter the maw of the criminal justice system.* **2** an animal's mouth or throat

mawk·ish /ˈmɔkɪʃ/ *adj.* showing too much emotion in a way that is embarrassing; SENTIMENTAL: *The movie is set to a mawkish score.* —**mawkishly** *adv.* —**mawkishness** *n.* [U]

max¹ /mæks/ *n.* [U] **1** INFORMAL an abbreviation of MAXIMUM: *You can drive 65 miles per hour on this highway, but that's the max.* | *This credit card has a max of $2000.* **2** to the max INFORMAL to the greatest degree possible: *We had the air conditioner turned up to the max.* —**max** *adj., adv.*: *Let's say two hours to get there, max.*

max² *v.*

max out *phr. v.* INFORMAL **1** [T **max** sth ↔ **out**] to use something such as money or supplies so that there is none left: *We maxed out the credit card last weekend at Oakland Mall.* **2** [I] to do too much, eat too much etc.: [+ **on**] *Not turkey again – I maxed out on it at Thanksgiving.* **3** [I] to do something with as much effort and determination as you can: *Erickson has been maxing out every game.* —**maxed out** *adj.*

max·im /ˈmæksɪm/ *n.* [C] a well-known phrase or saying, especially one that gives a rule for sensible behavior

max·i·mal /ˈmæksɪməl/ *adj.* TECHNICAL as much or as large as possible: *The visitors' seats are angled strategically for maximal view.* —**maximally** *adv.*

max·i·mize /ˈmæksəˌmaɪz/ *v.* [T] **1** to increase something as much as possible: *We need to look at how to maximize our cash flow.* | *Diamonds are cut to maximize the stone's beauty.* **2** to CLICK on a special part of a WINDOW on a computer screen so that it becomes as big as the screen —**maximization** /ˌmæksəmə-ˈzeɪʃən/ *n.* [U] —compare MINIMIZE

max·i·mum¹ /ˈmæksəməm/ *adj.* [only before noun] the maximum amount, quantity, speed etc. is the largest that is possible or allowed: *Under new guidelines, hamburgers will have a maximum fat content of 22%.* | *Let's try to make maximum use of this opportunity.* | *She was posed and photographed for maximum effect.* —**maximum** *adv.* —compare MINIMUM¹

maximum² *n.* [C usually singular] the largest number or amount that is possible or is allowed: *Because he's under 18, he's facing a maximum of ten years in prison.* | *Tell them it'll take 45 minutes – that's the maximum.*

May /meɪ/ *n.* [C,U] the fifth month of the year, between April and June: *Memorial Day is always in May.* | *On May 8 I have a doctor's appointment.* | *My grandmother died last May.* | *Brian plans to move to San Francisco next May.* | *His court date is May 31st.* —see Usage Note at JANUARY

may /meɪ/ *modal verb* ⌐S W⌐
1 possibility if something may happen or may be true, there is a possibility that it will happen or be true but this is not certain: *Well, I may have been wrong.* | *Seven thirty may be too late.* | *We may not have class the last week of February, but I'll let you know for sure as the time approaches.* | *Altering a passport in any way may make it invalid.* | *They may have called when she was in Anaheim.* —compare MIGHT¹ (1)

2 may I...? a) SPOKEN used to ask politely if you can do something: *Hi, may I speak to Valerie, please?* | *Thank you for calling, how may I help you?* | *May I have the car on Saturday?* **b) may I say/ask/suggest etc.** FORMAL used to say, ask, or suggest something politely: *Sir, may I respectfully ask three things of you?* —compare CAN¹, MIGHT¹ (6)

3 allowed FORMAL used to say that someone is allowed to do something: *Thank you, you may go now.* | *You may now kiss the bride.* | *Travelers to Qatar may not bring in narcotics or weapons.*

4 may... but... used to say that although one thing is true, something else which seems very different is also true: *Roseanne may be fat, but she's pretty.* |

John's facts may be correct, but his conclusions are unprovable. —compare MIGHT[1] (12)

5 may as well SPOKEN used to say that you will do something that you do not really want to do, because you cannot think of anything better: *Since we're just sitting here, we may as well have a drink.* | *You may as well not turn it on, Cooper, until after the game.*

6 may well if something may well happen or may well be true, it is fairly likely to happen or be true: *It may well change forever the way you look at Greek art.* —compare **might well** (MIGHT[1] (11))

7 may you/he/they etc. do sth LITERARY used to say that you hope that a particular thing will happen to someone: *May the sun shine warm upon your face and the wind be always at your back.*

8 purpose FORMAL used after "so that" to say that someone does something in order to make something else possible: *The king has ordered a festival so that his son may select a bride.*

9 possible to do sth FORMAL if something may be done, completed etc. in a particular way, that is how it is possible to do it: *The Commission may then take one of three actions.*

Ma·ya /ˈmaɪə/ also **Ma·yan** /ˈmaɪən/ one of the tribes of the Yucatan area in central America, who had a very advanced society in the 4th–10th centuries A.D. —**Maya, Mayan** *adj.*

may·be /ˈmeɪbi/ *adv.* [sentence adverb] **1** used like "perhaps" to say that something may happen or may be true, but you are not certain: *Maybe I'll buy myself a new dress.* | *"Want to go shoot some pool?" "Maybe tomorrow night, Gaby."* | *Maybe this wasn't such a good idea.* **2** SPOKEN used to reply to a suggestion or idea when either you are not sure if you agree with it, or you do not want to say "yes" or "no": *"Mom, can I go to Kelly's after dinner?" "Maybe."* | *"Well, are you going to take the job or not?" "Maybe..."* **3** used to show that you are not sure of an amount or number: *Kovitsky earned maybe $45,000, after taxes.* **4** SPOKEN used to make a suggestion you are not very sure about: *Maybe you should hire a bodyguard.* | *I thought maybe you could give Eddy's mom a call for me.*

USAGE NOTE: MAYBE

FORMALITY
Maybe and **perhaps** mean the same thing, but **maybe** is more informal. To a friend you might say or write: *Maybe you could help, Joe.* In a report or a story you could write: *It was a large office containing perhaps twenty desks.*

May Day /ˈ. ./ *n.* [C,U] the first day of May when people traditionally celebrate the arrival of spring

may·day /ˈmeɪdeɪ/ *n.* [C, usually singular] a radio signal used to ask for help when a ship or an airplane is in serious danger —compare SOS

May·er /ˈmeɪə/, **Louis B.** /ˈluɪs bi/ (1885–1957) a U.S. movie PRODUCER, born in Russia, who started the company that became MGM with Samuel Goldwyn

may·est /ˈmeɪəst/ *v.* OLD USE **thou mayest** you may

may·fly /ˈmeɪflaɪ/ *n. plural* **mayflies** [C] a small insect that lives near water, and only lives for a short time

may·hem /ˈmeɪhɛm/ *n.* [U] an extremely confused situation in which people are very frightened or excited; CHAOS: *The new rules are meant to prevent mayhem on school enrollment days.*

May·o /ˈmeɪoʊ/ a COUNTY in the west of the Republic of Ireland

may·o /ˈmeɪyoʊ/ *n.* [U] SPOKEN mayonnaise

Ma·yo, Charles (1865–1939) a U.S. doctor who started the Mayo Clinic with his brother William Mayo (1861–1939)

Mayo Clin·ic, the /ˌ.. ˈ../ a medical institution and hospital in Rochester, Minnesota, famous for its modern equipment and successful treatments

may·on·naise /ˈmeɪəˌneɪz, ˌmeɪəˈneɪz/ *n.* [U] a thick white SAUCE made of egg and oil, often eaten on SANDWICHes

may·or /ˈmeɪə, mɛr/ *n.* [C] someone who is elected to

lead the government of a town or city —**mayoral** *adj.*: *mayoral candidates*

may·or·al·ty /ˈmeɪərəlti, ˈmɛrəlti/ *n.* [U] FORMAL the position of mayor, or the period when someone is mayor

may·pole /ˈmeɪpoʊl/ *n.* [C] a tall decorated pole around which people danced on May Day in past times

Mays /meɪz/, **Wil·lie** /ˈwɪli/ (1931–) a U.S. baseball player who is considered one of the greatest players ever

mayst /meɪst/ *v.* OLD USE **thou mayst** you may

may've /ˈmeɪəv/ *v.* the short form of "may have": *She may've already phoned him.*

maze /meɪz/ *n.* [C] **1 a maze of streets/paths/wires etc.** a complicated and confusing arrangement of streets etc. that it is difficult to find your way through: *We got completely lost in the maze of city streets.* **2 a maze of rules/regulations/details etc.** a large number of rules etc. that are complicated and difficult to understand **3** a game consisting of a complicated pattern of lines that you are supposed to draw a line through without crossing any of them, played especially by children **4** a specially designed system of paths, usually surrounded by tall plants and made in a park or public garden, that is difficult to find your way through

ma·zur·ka /məˈzɜkə/ *n.* [C] a fast Polish dance, or the music for this dance

Mb the written abbreviation of MEGABYTE

M.B.A., MBA *n.* [C] **1** Master of Business Administration; a university degree in the skills needed to be in charge of a business **2** a person who has this degree: *Rick is a 32-year-old MBA from Harvard.*

Mba·ba·ne /əmbaˈbanɛ, -ˈban/ the capital and largest town of Swaziland

MC the abbreviation of Master of Ceremonies —see also EMCEE

MCAT /ˈɛmkæt/ *n.* [C] TRADEMARK Medical College Admission Test; an examination taken by students who have completed a first degree and want to go to MEDICAL SCHOOL

McCain /məˈkeɪn/, **John** (1936–) a U.S. politician who was a CANDIDATE for U.S. President in 2000

Mc·Car·thy /məˈkɑrθi/, **Joseph** (1909–1957) a U.S. politician famous for saying officially that many important people were COMMUNISTS, and therefore enemies of the U.S.

Mc·Cor·mick /məˈkɔrmɪk/, **Cy·rus** /ˈsaɪrəs/ (1809–1884) the U.S. inventor of a machine to REAP crops

Mc·Coy /məˈkɔɪ/ *n.* **the real McCoy** INFORMAL something that is real and is not a copy, especially something valuable: *"Is it a Rolex watch?" "Yes, it's the real McCoy."*

Mount McKinley

Mc·Kin·ley, Mount /məˈkɪnli/ —see DENALI —see picture on page 1331

McKinley, William (1843–1901) the 25th President of the U.S.

M.D. 1 the written abbreviation of Doctor of Medicine **2** the abbreviation of MUSCULAR DYSTROPHY

MD the written abbreviation of Maryland

M

MDT the abbreviation of Mountain Daylight Time

ME the written abbreviation of Maine

s w **me** /mi/ *pron.* **1** the object form of "I": *You guys go without me.* | *He reminds me of David Bowie.* | *Bud was sitting across from me.* | *Kiki gave it to me for Christmas.* | *Judy, bring me that book.* **2 me too** SPOKEN said when you agree with someone, are in a similar situation, or are going to do the same thing as they are: *"I'll have a chocolate shake." "Me too."* **3 me neither** SPOKEN also **me either** NONSTANDARD said when you agree with a negative statement someone has just made: *"I can't believe he's fifty." "Me neither."*

me·a cul·pa /ˌmeɪə ˈkʊlpə/ *n.* [C] FORMAL a phrase used to admit that something is your fault: *A number of companies issued a public mea culpa for insurance industry abuses.*

mead /mid/ *n.* **1** [U] an alcoholic drink made from HONEY **2** [C] POETIC a meadow

Mead, Lake /mid/ the largest RESERVOIR in the U.S. on the Colorado River behind the Hoover Dam

Mead, Mar·ga·ret /ˈmɑrgrɪt/ (1901–1978) a U.S. ANTHROPOLOGIST who studied the ways in which parents on the islands of Samoa, Bali, and New Guinea taught their children

Margaret Mead

mead·ow /ˈmɛdoʊ/ *n.* [C] a field with wild grass and flowers

mead·ow·lark /ˈmɛdoʊˌlɑrk/ *n.* [C] a brown North American bird with a yellow front

mea·ger /ˈmigɚ/ *adj.* a meager amount of food, money etc. is too small and is much less than you need: *Maria's meager income doesn't always last through the month.* | *The prisoners were kept on meager rations.* —**meagerly** *adv.* —**meagerness** *n.* [U]

s w **meal** /mil/ *n.* **1** [C] an occasion when you eat food, for example breakfast or dinner: *I usually have one meal a day with Mom and Dad.* **2** [C] the food that you eat on a particular occasion: *It's eight dollars for my meal, without the tip.* | *a five-course gourmet meal* —see also **square meal** (SQUARE¹ (5)) **3** [U] grain that has been crushed into a powder, used for making flour or animal food —see also BONE MEAL, CORNMEAL

meal tick·et /ˈ. ˌ../ *n.* [C] **1** INFORMAL something or someone that you depend on to give you money or food: *My M.B.A. has not been the meal ticket I had hoped.* **2** a card that you use to get meals at school or work

meal·time /ˈmiltaɪm/ *n.* [C,U] a time during the day when you have a meal: *At mealtimes, the campers gather in a large dining hall.*

meal·y /ˈmili/ *adj.* **1** fruit or vegetables that are mealy are dry and do not taste good: *mealy apples* **2** containing MEAL (3)

mealy-mouthed /ˌmili ˈmaʊðd◂/ *adj.* not brave enough or honest enough to say clearly and directly what you really think

s w **mean¹** /min/ *v.* [T] *past tense and past participle* **meant**

1 have a particular meaning [not in progressive] to have or represent a particular meaning: *What does "patronizing" mean?* | *Do you know what "ambidextrous" means?* | *Just because it's red doesn't mean it's cherry-flavored.* | *What is meant by "essential" in this case?*

2 intend to say sth [not in progressive] to intend a particular meaning when you say something: [mean (that)] *It's not a problem, it just means that we can't use this information.* | *You may want to ask her later what she meant by that.*

3 intend to do sth to intend to do something or intend that someone else should do something: [mean to do sth] *Sorry, I didn't mean to pull your hair.* | *I've been meaning to ask you about this Federal Express bill.* | [mean for sb to do sth] *I didn't mean for Tina to get hurt.* —see also **mean no harm** (HARM¹ (2))

4 result in sth [not in progressive] to have a particular result: *Does this mean I can't go to the wedding?* | *The curfews meant that about 250,000 people were confined to their homes.*

5 say sth seriously [not in progressive] to have a serious purpose in something you say or write: *At first they laughed when we said we were getting married, but then they saw we meant it.* | *You don't really mean that, do you?*

6 I mean a) used when explaining or giving an example of something, or when pausing to think about what you are going to say next: *My father was a heavy drinker, I mean, he used to drink a quart of scotch a day.* | *I mean, he was nice and everything, but I just didn't find him attractive.* **b)** used to quickly correct something you have just said: *I just bought some apricots, no, I mean peaches.*

7 (do) you mean...? used when checking that you have understood what someone has said: *You mean I could make money off this?*

8 I see what you mean used to tell someone that you now understand what they have been saying: *Oh, I see what you mean about Jane's accent being strong.*

9 that's what I mean used when someone is saying the same thing that you were trying to say earlier: *"You've got to think about later on in life, too." "That's what I mean. It's getting closer."*

10 what do you mean...? a) used when you do not understand what someone is trying to say: *What do you mean by speech events?* **b)** used when you are very surprised or annoyed by what someone has just said: *I hit the ball in first! What do you mean I lost? | What do you mean the airplane's not moving?*

11 see what I mean? used when checking that someone has understood something you have said, often by showing them an example of it: *See what I mean, Dad, about this camera being difficult to use?*

12 how do you mean? used to ask someone to explain what they have just said or tell you more about it: *Straight? How do you mean, straight?*

13 say which person/thing [not in progressive] used to say that a particular person or thing is the one that you are talking about, pointing to etc.: *Oh, you mean the blue shorts.* | *What's her name, I mean the lady who gave the party?*

14 I didn't mean it used to say that you did not intend to upset or hurt someone: *I'm sure Suzy didn't really mean it.*

15 (that) doesn't mean used to say that something is not definitely true, or is not definitely going to happen, even though it may seem to be true because of something else you have mentioned: *For heaven's sake, just because we went out for coffee doesn't mean we're getting married.*

16 he/she means well used to say that someone intends to be helpful or kind, but often makes a situation worse: *The doctor meant well, I'm sure, but he should have checked the drug's side effects.* —see also **(do) you know what I mean?** (KNOW¹ (36)), **I know what you mean** (KNOW¹ (37))

17 involve doing sth [not in progressive] to involve having to do a particular thing: *Frank's surgery residency means staying in Albuquerque another five years.*

18 show sth is true/will happen [not in progressive] to be a sign that something is true or will happen: *The presence of HIV in the blood means a person may develop AIDS.*

19 sth means sth to sb used to say something is very important to someone: *It means a lot to me to do a good job.* | *The farm meant everything to Dad.* | *Hank, I love you so much, and you mean the world to me.*

20 mean nothing to sb a) to be unfamiliar to

someone or impossible for them to understand: *Until recently, global warming and acid rain meant nothing to most Americans.* **b)** to not be important to someone: *Democracy means nothing to those who do not have enough to eat.*

21 sth means trouble if something means trouble, it will cause you problems: *A lack of discipline in a child's life can mean trouble later on.*

22 sb means business to be determined to succeed in getting the result you want: *Stop fighting with your brother. Now, I mean business.*

23 mean something/anything to sb a) to be familiar to someone: *Does the name Blackman mean anything to you?* **b)** to be important to someone: *You say you love me, but you act like I don't mean anything to you.*

24 be meant to do sth a) to be intended to do something: *Christmas time is meant to bring people together.* **b)** if you are meant to do something, you should do it, especially because someone has told you to or because it is your responsibility: *Jenny is convinced she was meant to stay with Zev.*

25 be meant for sb/sth to be intended for a particular person or purpose: *I think this fork is meant for barbecuing.*

26 be meant to do/be sth to have the appropriate qualities to do a particular job or activity: *Perhaps she is meant to be a teacher.*

27 be meant for each other if two people are meant for each other, they are very good partners for each other: *Judith and Eric were meant for each other*

28 sth was meant to be used to say that you think a situation was certain to happen and that no one had any power to prevent it: *'He hasn't called yet.' 'Maybe it just wasn't meant to be.'*

29 know/understand/see what it means to be sth to have experienced a particular situation, so that you know what it is like: *Now they see what it means to be a Native American.* —see also WELL-MEANING, WELL-MEANT

S W **mean²** *n.*
2

1 **method** means [plural] a method, system, object etc. that you use as a way of achieving a result: [+ **of**] *The administration is looking for new means of financing highways.* | *Millions of Chinese rely on bicycles as their only means of transportation.* | *His political opponents sought to defeat him by illegal means.*

2 **money** means [plural] the money or income that you have: *Frequently we lack the means to pay guest conductors and soloists.* | *Spending beyond your means* (=more money than you have) *is a disadvantage of credit cards.* | *We're living within very minimal means, but we're happy.*

3 by means of sth using a particular method or system: *Critics were silenced by means of torture and unfair trials.*

4 by all means SPOKEN used to mean "of course" when politely allowing someone to do something or agreeing with a suggestion: *If you have binoculars, by all means take them along.* | *By all means, drink plenty of water while exercising.*

5 by no means also **not by any means** not at all: *The game is by no means over.* | *This is not murder, by any means.*

6 a means to an end something that you do only to achieve a result, not because you want to do it: *Technology is not a magic wand, but only a means to an end.*

7 man/woman of means LITERARY someone who is rich

8 the means of production TECHNICAL the materials, tools, and equipment that are used in the production of goods: *It would be foolish to nationalize all the means of production.*

9 the mean TECHNICAL the average amount, figure, or value: *The mean of 6, 9, and 12 is 9.*

10 the/a mean between sth and sth a method or way of doing something that is between two very different methods, and better than either of them: *It's a case of finding the mean between firmness and compassion.* —see also **by fair means or foul** (FAIR¹ (19)), **ways and means** (WAY¹ (35))

mean³ *adj.* **meaner, meanest**   S W
3

1 **not nice** cruel or not nice: *There's no reason to be mean.* | *That was a mean trick.* | [+ **to**] *Mom, Laverne is being mean to me.* | *She has a mean streak* (=a tendency to be mean) *that she doesn't bother to hide.* | *Clay doesn't have a mean bone in his body* (=he's not mean at all).

2 no mean feat/trick something that is very difficult to do, so that someone who does it deserves to be admired: *Charlie located a notepad, no mean feat given the state of his desk.*

3 no mean performer/player etc. someone who is very good at doing something: *The competition was judged by William Styron, no mean novelist himself.*

4 a mean sth INFORMAL used to say that something is very good or someone is very skillful at doing something: *Stritch plays a mean piano.* | *They always put on a mean Sunday brunch.*

5 **average** [only before noun] TECHNICAL average: *The mean length of stay in the hospital is 11 days.*

6 **poor** [only before noun] LITERARY poor or looking poor: *Howe captured forever the mean streets of New York.* —**meanly** *adv.* —**meanness** *n.* [U]

meander

The river meandered through the forest.

me·an·der /mi'ændə/ *v.* [I] **1** if a river, stream, road etc. meanders, it has a lot of curves in it: *From Mission Peak, the trail meanders eastward into Sunol Park.* **2** [always + adv./prep.] to move in a slow, relaxed way, not in any particular direction: *Ari and I meandered around the shops in Innsbruck.* **3** also **meander on** if a conversation, book, movie etc. meanders or meanders on, it is long and says things in a way that is unclear or boring: *The movie's plot meanders on and on.* —**meanderings** *n.* [plural] —**meander** *n.* [C]

mean·ie, meany /'mini/ *n.* [C] SPOKEN a word meaning a person who is cruel or not nice, used especially by children: *You meany!*

mean·ing /'minɪŋ/ *n.*   S W
2   2

1 **of a word/sign etc.** [C,U] the thing or idea that a word, expression, or sign represents: *The same symbol can have more than one meaning, depending on the context in which it is used.* | [+ **of**] *Use the examples to figure out the meaning of the word.*

2 **ideas in speech/book/movie etc.** [U] the things or ideas that someone intends to express when they say something, write a book, make a movie etc.: [+ **of**] *The exact meaning of the king's statement was not clear.*

3 what's the meaning of this? SPOKEN used to demand an explanation: *What's the meaning of this? I asked you to be here an hour ago!*

4 **purpose/special quality** [U] the quality that makes something seem important and makes people feel that their life, work etc. has a purpose and value: *Taking care of her family gave meaning to Bessy's life.* | *Because the song had no meaning to me, I didn't want to sing it.*

5 **true nature** [U] the true nature and importance of something: [+ **of**] *We want children to remember the true meaning of Christmas.*

6 (not) know the meaning of sth to have experience and understanding of a particular situation or feeling, or to not have this: *Mike Hardware was the kind of private eye who didn't know the meaning of fear.*

M

mean·ing·ful /ˈminɪŋfəl/ *adj.* **1** serious, important, or useful: *My father showed us that life is not meaningful without work.* | *She longs for a* **meaningful relationship** *with Lowell.* | *a meaningful conversation* **2** having a meaning that is easy to understand and makes sense: *The data isn't very meaningful to anyone but a scientist.* **3 a meaningful look/glance/ smile etc.** a look that clearly expresses the way someone feels, even though nothing is said: *Sam and Barbara exchanged a meaningful glance.* —**meaningfully** *adv.*

mean·ing·less /ˈminɪŋlɪs/ *adj.* **1** something that is meaningless has no purpose or importance and does not seem worth doing or having: *They had a brief, meaningless relationship a few years ago.* | *a meaningless ritual* **2** not having a meaning that you can understand or explain: *If he can't read it, then it will be meaningless to him.* —**meaninglessness** *n.* [U]

mean-spir·it·ed /ˌ. ˈ...ˌ/ *adj.* not generous or sympathetic: *Jordan is portrayed as mean-spirited and manipulative in the book.*

means test /ˈ. ./ *n.* [C] an official check in order to find out whether someone is poor enough to need money from the government —**means-tested** *adj.*: *means-tested programs* —**means testing** *n.* [U]

meant /mɛnt/ *v.* the past tense and past participle of MEAN[1]

mean·time /ˈmintaɪm/ *adv.* **1 in the meantime** in the period of time between now and a future event, or between two events in the past: *The doctor will be here soon. In the meantime, try and relax.* | *I didn't see Laura for another five years, and in the meantime she had gotten married and had a couple of kids.* **2 for the meantime** for the present time, until something happens: *The power supply should be back soon – for the meantime we'll have to use candles.*

mean·while /ˈminwaɪl/ also **in the meanwhile** *adv.* [sentence adverb] **1** in the period of time between two events: *The flight will be announced soon. Meanwhile, please remain seated.* | *I knew I wouldn't get my test results for several weeks, and I wasn't sure what to do in the meanwhile.* **2** while something else is happening: *Jim went to answer the phone. Meanwhile, Pete started to prepare lunch.* **3** used to compare two things that are happening at the same time: *The incomes of male professionals went up by almost 80%. Meanwhile, part-time women workers saw their earnings fall.*

mean·y /ˈmini/ *n.* [C] another spelling of MEANIE

mea·sles /ˈmizəlz/ also **the measles** *n.* [U] an infectious illness in which you have a fever and small red spots on your face and body —see also GERMAN MEASLES

mea·sly /ˈmizli/ *adj.* **measlier, measliest** [only before noun] INFORMAL very small and disappointing in size, quantity, or value: *That measly little paycheck barely covered the rent.*

meas·ur·a·ble /ˈmɛʒərəbəl/ *adj.* **1** large or important enough to have a definite effect: *He's made no measurable progress toward his accomplishing his goals.* **2** able to be measured: *measurable rainfall* —**measurably** *adv.*

meas·ure[1] /ˈmɛʒɚ/ *n.*
1 official action [C] an official action that is intended to deal with a particular problem, especially one that people vote on: *Voters in Montana rejected a measure to increase cigarette tax.*
2 take measures to do whatever is officially necessary to achieve a particular aim: *Measures are being taken to reduce crime in the city.*
3 a measure of sth a) something that shows how much there is of a quality, feeling etc.: [+ **of**] *The flowers and tears at the funeral were a measure of the people's love for her.* | *Profits are often used as a measure of a company's success.* **b)** a small amount of a quality, feeling etc., but enough of it to be noticed: *Jones simply wanted a measure of respect from her co-workers.*
4 unit of measurement [C,U] an amount or unit in

a measuring system, or the system for measuring amount, size, length etc.: *An inch is a measure of length.* | *a table of U.S. standard weights and measures*
5 half measures things done to deal with a difficult situation that are not effective or firm enough: *Half measures will not fix America's health-care problems.*
6 for good measure in addition to what you have already done or given: *Why don't you try calling them one more time, for good measure.*
7 in large/some measure to a great degree or to some degree: *Parents were in large measure responsible for getting the school a new library.*
8 beyond measure FORMAL very great or very much: *Burton and his wife had suffered beyond measure.*
9 alcohol a standard amount of an alcoholic drink: *a measure of bourbon*
10 the full measure of sth FORMAL the whole of something: *His poetry beautifully expresses the full measure of his joy.*
11 in full measure if someone gives something back in full measure, they give back as much as they received
12 thing used for measuring [C] something such as a piece of wood or a container used for measuring —see also TAPE MEASURE
13 music [C] one of a group of notes and RESTS[1] (10), separated by VERTICAL[1] (1) lines, into which a line of written music is divided —see also MADE-TO-MEASURE

measure[2] *v.* **1** [T] to find the size, length, or amount of something using standard units: *We should measure the wall before we buy new shelves.* | *The nurse weighed me and measured my height.* | [**measure sb for sth**] *She had to be measured for her prom dress.* **2** [T] to judge the importance, value, or true nature of something: *Doctors say it is too early to measure the effectiveness of the drug.* | [**measure sth by sth**] *You can't measure someone by the clothes they wear.* **3** [linking verb] to be a particular size, length, or amount: *When full grown, the Blue Whale measures 110 feet in length.* | *The earthquake measured 6.5 on the Richter scale.* **4** [T] to show or record a particular type of measurement: *An odometer measures the number of miles your car travels.*

measure sb/sth **against** sth *phr. v.* [T] to judge someone or something by comparing them with another person or thing: *Measured against our budget last year, $2.7 million seems small.*

measure sth ↔ **off** *phr. v.* [T] to measure a particular length or distance, and make a mark so that you can see the beginning and end: *He measured off three yards of rope.*

measure sth ↔ **out** *phr. v.* [T] to take a particular amount of liquid, powder etc. from a larger amount: *Measure out 1³/₄ cups of flour.*

measure up *phr. v.* **1** [I] to be good enough to do a particular job or to reach a particular standard: *We'll give you a week's trial in the job to see how you measure up.* | [+ **to**] *How will the Secretary General measure up to his new responsibilities?* **2** [I,T **measure sth ↔ up**] to measure something: *I'd better measure up before I start laying the carpet.*

meas·ured /ˈmɛʒɚd/ *adj.* careful and slow or steady: *a calm and measured response* | *She spoke in* **measured tones** (=a slow, deliberate way of speaking).

meas·ure·less /ˈmɛʒɚlɪs/ *adj.* LITERARY too big or too much to be measured

meas·ure·ment /ˈmɛʒɚmənt/ *n.* **1** [C usually plural] the length, height etc. of something: *What are his measurements?* | **take/make measurements of sth** *Take measurements of the room before you buy any new furniture.* | *The tailor* **took** *his* **measurements** *for a new suit.* **2** [U] the act of measuring something: *progress measurement*

measuring cup /ˈ... ˌ./ *n.* [C] a special cup used for measuring food or liquid when cooking —see picture at KITCHEN

measuring tape /ˈ... ˌ./ *n.* [C] a TAPE MEASURE

meat /mit/ *n.* **1** [C,U] the flesh of animals and birds eaten as food: *I stopped eating meat when I was 14.* | *spaghetti and meat sauce* | *cold meats* —see also DELI MEAT, LUNCH MEAT **2** [U] the main part of a talk, book etc. that includes all the interesting and important ideas and facts: *Finally we got down to the real meat of the debate.* | *There's* **no meat** *to their arguments.* **3 meat and potatoes** INFORMAL the most important or basic parts of a discussion, decision, piece of work etc.: [+ **of**] *Parks, crime and traffic are the meat and potatoes of council elections.* —see also MEAT-AND-POTATOES **4 need some (more) meat on your bones** INFORMAL used to say that someone looks too thin: *Matt, you need some more meat on your bones!* **5 meat and drink to sb** something that someone enjoys doing or finds very easy to do: *Most people can't deal with that much stress, but it's meat and drink to Rob.* **6 one man's meat is another man's poison** used to say that something that one person likes may not be liked by someone else —see also MEAT MARKET

meat-and-po·ta·toes /ˌ. . .'../ *adj.* [only before noun] **1** basic, simple, and ordinary: *meat-and-potatoes language* | *meat-and-potatoes voters* **2** a meat-and-potatoes person likes to eat basic meals that consist of traditional foods such as meat and vegetables: *My husband is a meat-and-potatoes man.*

meat·ball /'mitˌbɔl/ *n.* [C] a small round ball made from very small pieces of meat pressed together

meat grind·er /'. ˌ../ *n.* [C] a machine that cuts meat into very small pieces by forcing it through small holes

meat·less /'mitləs/ *adj.* food that is meatless contains no meat: *The menu has several meatless options.*

meat·loaf /'mitlouf/ *n.* [C,U] a dish made from GROUND meats (=meat cut into very small pieces) mixed with egg and bread, and then baked in the shape of a LOAF

meat mar·ket /'. ˌ../ *n.* [C] **1 be a meat market** INFORMAL used about a situation or place in which people are only interested in finding someone to have sex with **2** a place, often outside, where people go to sell or buy meats

meat·pack·ing /'. ˌ../ *n.* [U] the preparation of dead animals so that they can be sold as meat: *the meatpacking industry* —**meat-packer** *n.* [C]

meat·y /'miti/ *adj.* **meatier, meatiest 1** containing a lot of meat or having a strong meat taste: *a meaty bean stew* | *big, meaty barbecued ribs* **2** INFORMAL big and fat, with a lot of flesh: *ripe, meaty tomatoes* **3** INFORMAL large enough, powerful enough, or interesting enough to be important: *"Joan of Arc" was her first meaty role as an actress.* **4** having a strong, pleasant taste: *a meaty red wine*

mec·ca /'mɛkə/ **1** Mecca a city in Saudi Arabia that many Muslims want to visit because it is the holiest city of Islam **2** [singular] a place that many people want to visit for a particular reason: [+ **for**] *Florida is a mecca for students during spring break.*

me·chan·ic /mɪˈkænɪk/ *n.* **1** [C] someone who is skilled at repairing motor vehicles and machinery **2 the mechanics of (doing) sth** the way in which something works or is done: *He may not understand the mechanics of cooking, but he certainly enjoys fine food.* **3 mechanics** [U] the science that deals with the effects of forces on objects —see also QUANTUM MECHANICS

me·chan·i·cal /mɪˈkænɪkəl/ *adj.* **1** affecting or involving a machine: *The flight has been canceled due to mechanical failure.* *the space shuttle's mechanical arm* **2** using power from an engine or machine to do a particular type of work: *A mechanical Santa made toys in the store window.* **3** a mechanical action, reply etc. is done without thinking, and has been done many times before: *He was asked the same question so many times that the answer became mechanical.* **4** INFORMAL someone who is mechanical understands how machines work **5** TECHNICAL relating to or produced by physical forces: *the mechanical properties of solids* —**mechanically** /-kli/ *adv.*

mechanical en·gi·neer·ing /.ˌ... ..'../ *n.* [U] the study of the design and production of machines and tools —**mechanical engineer** *n.* [C]

mechanical pen·cil /.ˌ... '../ *n.* [C] a pencil made of metal or plastic, with a thin piece of LEAD (=the part that you write with) inside that comes out when you press a button on the pencil

mech·a·nism /'mɛkəˌnɪzəm/ *n.* [C] **1** part of a machine that does a particular job: *The locking mechanism on the car door is broken.* **2** a system that is intended to achieve something or deal with a problem: *The Army has set up mechanisms to help jobless ex-soldiers get work.* | [+ **for**] *The law sets out the mechanism for establishing tax rates.* **3** the way that something works: *the mechanism of the brain* **4 defense/survival/escape mechanism** a way of behaving that helps you to avoid or deal with something that is difficult or dangerous: *The odor is part of the bee's defense mechanism.*

mech·a·nis·tic /ˌmɛkəˈnɪstɪk◂/ *adj.* tending to explain the actions and behavior of living things as if they were machines: *a mechanistic view of nature* —**mechanistically** /-kli/ *adj.*

mech·a·nized /'mɛkəˌnaɪzd/ *adj.* **1** if a building, job, or tool is mechanized, it has been changed so that it uses machines instead of using people or animals: *a highly mechanized factory* | *mechanized farming* **2** a mechanized army uses TANKS and other ARMORED (=protected) military vehicles —**mechanize** *v.* [I,T] —**mechanization** /ˌmɛkənəˈzeɪʃən/ *n.* [U]

med·al /'mɛdl/ *n.* [C] a round flat piece of metal given to someone who has won a competition or who has done something brave: *an Olympic gold medal* —see also **sb deserves a medal** (DESERVE (3))

med·al·ist /'mɛdl-ɪst/ *n.* [C] someone who has won a medal in a competition: **gold/silver/bronze medalist** *an Olympic silver medalist*

me·dal·lion /məˈdælyən/ *n.* [C] a piece of metal shaped like a large coin, worn as jewelry on a chain around the neck

Medal of Hon·or /.ˌ... '../ *n.* [C] the highest award given by Congress to a soldier, sailor etc. who has done something extremely brave

med·dle /'mɛdl/ *v.* [I] to deliberately try to influence a situation that does not concern you, or change something that should not be changed: [+ **in/with**] *The legislation prevents the Catholic Church from meddling in state affairs.* | *Why meddle with the Constitution? It has served us well all these years.* —**meddler** *n.* [C]

med·dle·some /'mɛdlsəm/ *adj.* tending to become involved in situations that do not concern you, in a way that annoys people: *meddlesome neighbors*

Med·e·vac /'mɛdiˌvæk/ *n.* [C,U] air TRANSPORTATION provided for injured or very sick people who are far from a hospital or need to get there quickly, or the airplanes or HELICOPTERS used for this

Med·fly, medfly /'mɛdflaɪ/ *n.* [C] a type of fly that destroys CITRUS fruit trees

me·di·a /'midiə/ *n.* **1** [used with singular or plural verb] all the organizations, such as television, radio, and newspapers, that provide news and information for the public, or the people who report the news stories: ***The media** have reported two more arrests since Monday's riots.* | *Colson believes **the media** is overly critical since the Stanford game.* | *Pearson is wary of facing **the media** after last year's scandal.* | *There are not enough positive images of black males **in the media**.* | *The case received massive amounts of **media coverage** (=the way something is reported in the media).* | *The Superbowl is the NFL **media event** (=an event the media give a lot of attention to) of the year!* **2** the plural of MEDIUM —see also MASS MEDIA

me·di·an¹ /'midiən/ *n.* [C] **1** also **median strip** something that divides a road or HIGHWAY, such as a thin piece of land or a fence **2** the middle measurement in a set of measurements that are arranged in order **3** a line passing from one of the points of a TRIANGLE to the opposite side

median² *adj.* [only before noun] TECHNICAL **1** in or passing through the middle **2** TECHNICAL relating to a line passing from one of the points of a TRIANGLE to the opposite side

M

me·dia stud·ies /'... ,../ n. [U] a subject that you study at college, that deals with how newspapers, television, radio etc. work and how they affect society

me·di·ate /'midi,eɪt/ v. **1** [I,T] to try to help two people, groups, countries etc. to stop arguing and make an agreement: *Former President Jimmy Carter agreed to mediate the peace talks.* | [+ **between**] *U.N. officials mediated between the rebel fighters and the government.* **2** [T] to change the effect or influence of something, especially to make the effect less bad: *Exercise may mediate the effects of a bad diet.* —**mediator** n. [C] —**mediation** /,midi'eɪʃən/ n. [U]

med·ic /'mɛdɪk/ n. [C] someone who is trained to give medical treatment, but who is not a doctor —compare PARAMEDIC

Med·i·caid /'mɛdɪ,keɪd/ n. [U] a system in the U.S. by which the government helps to pay the cost of medical treatment for poor people —compare MEDICARE

med·i·cal /'mɛdɪkəl/ adj. relating to the treatment of disease or injury: *As many as 30,000 refugees died of hunger and a lack of medical care.* | *Most companies offer medical and dental benefits to their employees.* | *medical insurance* | *Is there still sexism within the medical profession* (=all the people who work as doctors, nurses etc.)? —**medically** /-kli/ adv.

medical cer·tif·i·cate /'... ,..../ n. [C] an official piece of paper signed by a doctor saying that you are too sick to work or that you are completely healthy

medical ex·am·in·er /'... ,..../ n. [C] a doctor who checks dead people's bodies in order to find out how they died, especially if they died in a sudden or unusual way

medical school /'... ,../ n. [C,U] a college or university where people study to become doctors

medical stu·dent /'... ,../ n. [C] someone who is studying to become a doctor

me·dic·a·ment /mɪ'dɪkəmənt, 'mɛdɪ-/ n. [C] FORMAL a substance used on or in the body to treat a disease

Med·i·care /'mɛdɪ,kɛr/ n. [U] a system by which the U.S. government helps to pay for the medical treatment of old people —compare MEDICAID

med·i·cate /'mɛdɪ,keɪt/ v. [T] to treat someone by giving them medicine or drugs: *Is she being medicated for her pain?*

med·i·cat·ed /'mɛdɪ,keɪtɪd/ adj. medicated products such as soap, powder, or SHAMPOO contain a small amount of medicine to treat medical problems of your skin that are not serious

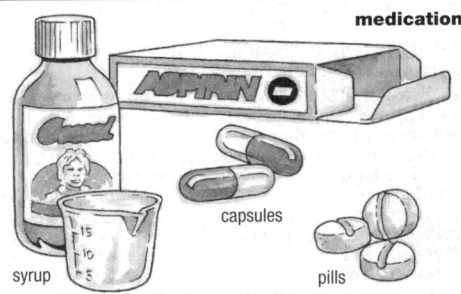

medication

capsules

syrup

pills

med·i·ca·tion /,mɛdɪ'keɪʃən/ n. [C,U] medicine or drugs given to people who are sick: **be on medication (for sth)** *He's on medication for high blood pressure.*

Med·i·ci, the /'mɛdɪtʃi/ a rich and powerful Italian family of bankers who ruled Florence, Italy, from the 15th to 18th centuries, and spent much of their money on art and on providing financial support to artists

me·dic·i·nal /mə'dɪsənəl/ adj. a medicinal substance can cure illness or disease: *Garlic is believed to have medicinal properties.* | *Marijuana was legalized*

for medicinal purposes (=for use as a medicine). —compare MEDICAL —**medicinally** adv.

med·i·cine /'mɛdəsən/ n. **1** [C,U] a substance used for treating illness: *Medicines should be kept out of children's reach.* | *Have you been **taking** your heart medicine?* **2** [U] the treatment and study of illnesses and injuries: *She was a professor of medicine at John Hopkins University.* | *Chinese herbal medicine* **3 the best medicine** the best way of making you feel better when you are sad: *Laughter is the best medicine.* **4 give someone a taste/dose of their own medicine** to treat someone as badly as they have treated you: *Just ignore him, Judy. That'll give him a taste of his own medicine.* **5 take your medicine** to accept an bad situation or a punishment that you deserve, without complaining —see also ALTERNATIVE MEDICINE, **strong medicine** (STRONG (26))

medicine chest /'... ,./ n. [C] a small cupboard used to store medicines, usually in the BATHROOM

medicine man /'... ,./ n. [C] a man in a Native American tribe who is considered to have the ability to cure illness and disease

medicine wom·an /'... ,../ n. [C] a woman in a Native American tribe who is considered to have the ability to cure illness and disease

me·die·val /mɪ'divəl, mɛ-, mi-/ adj. **1** relating to the Middle Ages (=the period between about AD 1100 and 1400): *medieval art* | *medieval Europe* **2** old-fashioned and not acceptable or not useful: *Civil rights groups complained that the law was "racist and medieval."*

me·di·o·cre /,midi'oʊkə/ adj. not very good: *The team is hoping to start winning again after last year's mediocre performance.* | *mediocre songs* —**mediocrity** /,midi'ɑkrəti/ n. [U]

med·i·tate /'mɛdə,teɪt/ v. **1** [I] to practice meditation: *Every morning I like to meditate for 20 minutes.* **2** [I] to think seriously and deeply about something: [+ **on/upon**] *She sat quietly, meditating on the day's events.* **3** [T] FORMAL to plan to do something, usually something bad: *Silently she meditated revenge.*

med·i·ta·tion /,mɛdə'teɪʃən/ n. **1** [U] a way of emptying your mind of thoughts and feelings, in order to relax completely or for religious reasons: *Yoga involves breathing exercises, stretching and meditation.* **2** [C usually plural,U] the act of thinking deeply and seriously about something: *Priests perform daily meditations at the temple.* | *a peaceful place for reading and quiet meditation* **3** [C usually plural] serious thoughts or writing about a particular subject: [+ **on**] *meditations on death and loss*

med·i·ta·tive /'mɛdə,teɪtɪv/ adj. thinking deeply and seriously about something: *Dr. Wijk contemplated the picture in meditative silence.* —**meditatively** adv.

Med·i·ter·ra·ne·an¹ /,mɛdətə'reɪniən/ n. **the Mediterranean** the sea that is surrounded by the countries of southern Europe, North Africa, and the Middle East

Mediterranean² adj. relating to or coming from the Mediterranean Sea, or typical of the area of Southern Europe around it: *a cruise along the Mediterranean coast* | *Mediterranean cuisine*

me·di·um¹ /'midiəm/ adj. **1** of middle size, level, or amount that is between the biggest and smallest or highest and lowest sizes, levels etc.: *What size shirt does he wear – medium or large?* | *two medium potatoes, peeled and sliced* | **medium height/length/build** etc. *Police are looking for a white man in his late 20s with dark hair and a medium build.* | *medium length brown hair* | *Fry the onions over **medium heat** (=a temperature that is not too hot or cold) until they are golden.* **2** also **medium rare** meat that is medium or medium rare is partly cooked but still slightly pink inside —compare RARE (2), WELL-DONE **3** having a slightly SPICY taste: *medium salsa* —compare MILD (2), HOT (3) **4 medium brown/blue** etc. a color that is neither light nor dark: *a medium gray sweater*

medium² n. plural **media** /-diə/ or **mediums** [C] **1** a particular way of communicating information and news to people, such as a newspaper, television broadcast etc.: [+ **of**] *Politicians prefer to use the*

M

medium of television. —see also MEDIA **2** a way of expressing your ideas, especially as a writer or an artist: [+ for] *The novel has always been an excellent medium for satire.* | *the visual media* **3** plural **mediums** someone who claims to have the power to receive messages from the spirits of the dead **4 medium of exchange** money or other ways of paying for things **5** TECHNICAL a substance or material in which things grow or exist **6** TECHNICAL a substance through which a force travels —see also **a happy medium** (HAPPY (6)), MAGNETIC MEDIA

medium-sized also **medium-size** /'... ,./ *adj.* not small, but not large either: *a medium-sized business*

medium term /'... ,./ *n.* [singular] the period of time that is a few weeks or months ahead of the present: *The company's prospects look good in the medium term.* —**medium-term** *adj.* —compare SHORT-TERM, LONG-TERM

medium wave /,... '../ *written abbreviation* **MW** *n.* [U] a system of radio broadcasting that uses radio WAVES that are between 100 and 1000 meters in length

med·ley /'medli/ *n. plural* **medleys** [C] **1** a group of songs or tunes sung or played one after the other as a single piece of music: *a medley of popular Christmas carols* **2** a swimming race in which the competitors swim using four different STROKES¹ (2) **3** [usually singular] a mixture of different types of something, which produces an interesting or unusual effect: *a delicately prepared medley of vegetables*

med school /'med skul/ *n.* [C] INFORMAL a MEDICAL SCHOOL

med stu·dent /'med ,studnt/ *n.* [C] INFORMAL a MEDICAL STUDENT

meek /mik/ *adj.* very quiet and gentle and unwilling to argue or express an opinion: *a shy, meek little child* | *This movie, with its violent scenes, is definitely not for the meek* (=people who are meek). —**meekly** *adv.: She smiled meekly.* —**meekness** *n.* [U]

S W | 1 1 |
meet¹ /mit/ *v. past tense and past participle* **met**
1 be in the same place [I,T not in passive] **a)** to come to the same place as someone else because you have arranged to find them there: *We're going to meet at her house at 11:00.* | *Why don't I meet you guys downtown?* | [+ for] *Kerry and I are meeting for coffee tonight.* **b)** to see someone you know by chance and talk to them: *I met him in the street, and we decided to go out for lunch.*
2 sb you do not know [I,T not in passive] to see and be introduced to someone you do not know, especially for the first time: *Did you ever get to meet her boyfriend?* | *Jim and I met when I was a freshman at NYU.* | *I met this really nice lady on the bus yesterday.* | *I'd met him a couple of times before.*
3 nice/pleased/good to meet you SPOKEN **a)** a polite phrase used to greet someone when you meet them for the first time, especially when another person has introduced you: *"This is my friend Betty." "Hi. Nice to meet you."* **b)** used when you are about to stop talking with someone you have just met: *Well, it was good to finally meet you, Joan.*
4 (it was) nice/good meeting you SPOKEN a polite phrase used when you say goodbye to someone you have met for the first time: *Nice meeting you, Karla.*
5 airport/station etc. [T] to be at an airport, station etc. when someone arrives: *Dad said he'd meet our flight.* | *I was met by a company representative at the bus station.*
6 committee/group etc. [I] to be together in the same place, usually in order to discuss something: *Officials of both sides have agreed to meet in North Korea's capital.*
7 opponent [I,T not in passive] to play against another person or team in a competition, or to fight another army in a war: *The Yankees and the Orioles will meet next week to fight for the American League pennant.*
8 rivers/roads/lines etc. [I,T not in passive] to join together at a particular place: *There's a stop sign where the two roads meet.* | *Wilmington is situated on the point where the river meets the ocean.*
9 meet a need/challenge/condition etc. to provide, do, or have all of the things that are necessary for

something to happen: *Customers who meet certain conditions will be given a 20% discount.*
10 meet a goal/target/aim etc. to achieve an aim etc.: *The Red Cross met their goal of raising $1.6 million for food supplies.*
11 meet debts/costs/expenses etc. to pay debts etc.: *Without public support, the community center will not be able to meet its costs.*
12 there's more to sb/sth than meets the eye used to say that someone or something is more interesting, intelligent etc. than they seem to be
13 meet your match to have an opponent who is as strong or as skillful as you are and therefore might be able to defeat you: *It seems Connoly's finally met her political match.*
14 meet sb halfway to do or give some of the things that someone wants or needs, in order to reach an agreement with them: *Parents will be unable to afford their children's education unless colleges are prepared to meet them halfway.*
15 meet (sth) head-on if you meet a problem head-on, you deal with it directly without trying to avoid it: *With its new factories, the company intends to meet the competition head-on.*
16 our/their eyes meet if two people's eyes meet, they look at each other, because they are attracted to each other or because they are thinking the same thing: *Their eyes met across the crowded room.*
17 touch/hit [I,T] to touch or hit another object: *Their hands met under the table.*
18 meet your death/end/fate/destiny to die in a particular way: *Two brothers met their tragic fate in the icy waters.*
19 meet your maker HUMOROUS to die —see also **make ends meet** (END¹ (7))
meet up *phr. v.* [I] to meet someone in an informal way in order to do something together: *Why don't we meet up for dinner in the city?* | [meet up with sb] *Molly's going to meet up with us after basketball practice.*
meet with sb/sth *phr. v.* [T] **1** to have a meeting with someone: *Dodd will fly to Washington, D.C. to meet with the Secretary of State.* **2** to get a particular reaction or result: **meet with approval/disapproval/criticism** *The company's decision was met with sharp criticism.* | **meet with success/failure** *Their efforts to save the Victorian theater have met with little success.* **3 meet with danger/death/disaster etc.** FORMAL to experience something by chance, usually something bad: *Five teens met with disaster when their stolen vehicle crashed into a wall.*

meet² *n.* [C] a sports competition, especially a competition between people who are racing: *a swim meet*

meet³ *adj.* OLD USE right or appropriate

meet·ing /'mitɪŋ/ *n.* [C] **1** an organized event at which people gather to talk and decide things: *Over a hundred people attended the meeting.* | *Can you call back later? She's in a meeting right now.* | *I have a meeting at 3 o'clock.* | *In July 1991, a meeting was held by the United Nations to discuss global warming.* **2 the meeting** FORMAL all the people who attend a meeting: *The meeting was asked to address the problem of unemployment.* **3** [usually singular] an occasion when two or more people meet each other by chance or because they have arranged to do this: *After a chance meeting at the airport, Annie was reunited with her brother.* **4** a game that is part of a larger competition in a particular sport: *San Diego won their first meeting this season 21–13.* **5 meeting of (the) minds** a situation in which two people agree with each other: *There is still no meeting of the minds between Congress and the White House.* **6** an event at which a group of Quakers (=a Christian religious group) worship together

meeting-house /'.. ,./ *n.* [C] a building where Quakers WORSHIP

mega- /mɛgə/ *prefix* **1** a million times a particular unit of something: *a 100-megaton bomb* | *You'll need at least 8 megabytes of RAM* (=computer memory space). **2** INFORMAL much larger than usual in amount,

M

importance, or size: *Hollywood megastars* | *She's got a megarich new boyfriend.*

meg·a·bit /'mɛgə,bɪt/ *n.* [C] TECHNICAL a million BITS[1] (5)

meg·a·bucks /'mɛgə,bʌks/ *n.* [plural] INFORMAL a very large amount of money: *It's costing me megabucks to get the car fixed.*

meg·a·byte /'mɛgə,baɪt/ *written abbreviation* **Mb** *n.* [C] a unit for measuring the amount of information a computer can use, equal to about a million BYTES

meg·a·hertz /'mɛgə,hɚts/ *written abbreviation* **MHz** *n.* [U] a million HERTZ

meg·a·lith /'mɛgə,lɪθ/ *n.* [C] **1** a very large company or business: *Hewlett Packard, one of the computer megaliths, is producing a new range of printers.* **2** a tall stone put outside in an open place, by people in ancient times —**megalithic** /,mɛgə'lɪθɪk/ *adj.*

meg·a·lo·ma·ni·a /,mɛgəloʊ'meɪniə/ *n.* [U] the belief that you are extremely important and powerful, which makes you want to control other people's lives, and is often a type of mental illness

meg·a·lo·ma·ni·ac /,mɛgəloʊ'meɪniæk/ *n.* [C] someone who believes they are extremely important or powerful and tries to control other people's lives —**megalomaniac** *adj.*

meg·a·phone /'mɛgə,foʊn/ *n.* [C] a piece of equipment like a large horn, that you talk through to make your voice sound louder when you are speaking to a crowd

meg·a·plex /'mɛgə,plɛks/ *n.* [C] a building with a very large number of movie theaters in it

meg·a·star /'mɛgə,stɑr/ *n.* [C] INFORMAL a very famous singer or actor: *country megastar Garth Brooks*

meg·a·ton /'mɛgə,tʌn/ *n.* [C] a measure of the power of an explosive that is equal to that of a million TONs of TNT (=a powerful explosive): *a 17-megaton nuclear warhead*

Me·ir /mɛ'ɪr/, **Gol·da** /'goʊldə/ (1898–1978) an Israeli politician who was Israel's first female Prime Minister, from 1969 to 1974

Me·kong, the /'meɪkɑŋ, -kɔŋ/ a river in southeast Asia that flows from Tibet through Cambodia and Laos to Vietnam

mel·a·mine /'mɛlə,min/ *n.* [U] a material like plastic used to make hard smooth surfaces on tables and shelves

mel·an·cho·li·a /,mɛlən'koʊliə/ *n.* [U] OLD-FASHIONED a feeling of great sadness and lack of energy, often caused by mental illness; DEPRESSION

mel·an·chol·ic /,mɛlən'kɑlɪk◂/ *adj.* FORMAL suffering from melancholia, or expressing great sadness and lack of hope

mel·an·chol·y[1] /'mɛlən,kɑli/ *adj.* sad or making you feel sad: *a secretive, melancholy man* | *the melancholy tone of the poem*

melancholy[2] *n.* [U] FORMAL a feeling of sadness: *Goya struggled with his feelings of deep melancholy.*

me·lange /meɪ'lɑnʒ/ *n.* [singular] a mixture of different things: *a melange of fresh berries served with a warm chocolate sauce*

mel·a·nin /'mɛlənɪn/ *n.* [U] a natural dark brown color in human skin, hair, and eyes

mel·a·no·ma /,mɛlə'noʊmə/ *n.* [C] TECHNICAL a TUMOR on the skin which causes CANCER

mel·a·to·nin /,mɛlə'toʊnɪn/ *n.* [U] a HORMONE that can be taken as a drug to help people who have problems sleeping, for example because of JET LAG

Mel·ba toast /'mɛlbə ,toʊst/ *n.* [U] a type of thin hard TOAST that breaks easily into small pieces

Mel·bourne /'mɛlbɚn/ the capital city of the state of Victoria in Australia

me·lée /'meɪleɪ, meɪ'leɪ/ *n.* [usually singular] a situation in which people rush around in a confused way: *Eight people were arrested after a melée broke out at the conference.*

mel·lif·lu·ous /mə'lɪfluəs/ *adj.* FORMAL having a

pleasant musical sound: *a mellifluous voice* —**mellifluously** *adv.*

Mel·lon /'mɛlən/, **An·drew** /'ændru/ (1855–1937) a U.S. FINANCIER who was Secretary of the Treasury for 11 years and gave the National Gallery of Art in Washington, D.C., to the nation

mel·low[1] /'mɛloʊ/ *adj.* **1** gentle, calm, and sympathetic because of age or experience: *She seems a little more mellow now that she's gotten married.* **2** friendly and relaxed, or feeling friendly and relaxed: *He's a totally mellow guy.* | *After a few drinks, everyone was pretty mellow.* **3** a mellow sound is pleasant and smooth: *the mellow sound of a trombone* | *a deep, mellow voice* **4** a mellow color or light looks soft, warm, and not too bright: *the mellow golden light of autumn sunsets* **5** a food or drink that is mellow has a smooth taste that is not too strong: *a rich, mellow blend of coffee* —**mellowness** *n.* [U]

mellow[2] *v.* [I,T] **1** also **mellow (sb) out** to become relaxed and calm, or make someone feel relaxed and calm: *Grandpa's mellowed over the last few years.* | *She's mellowed him out, and she seems to make him happy.* **2** if colors mellow or are mellowed, they begin to look warm and soft **3** if a food or drink mellows, or if it is mellowed, it gets a smoother taste that is not as strong

me·lod·ic /mə'lɑdɪk/ *adj.* **1** TECHNICAL relating to the main tune in a piece of music: *the melodic structure of Beethoven's symphonies* **2** having a pleasant tune or a pleasant sound like music: *a sweet melodic voice*

me·lo·di·ous /mə'loʊdiəs/ *adj.* FORMAL having a pleasant tune or a pleasant sound like music: *melodious temple bells* —**melodiously** *adv.* —**melodiousness** *n.* [U]

mel·o·dra·ma /'mɛlə,drɑmə/ *n.* [C,U] **1** a story or play with many sudden exciting events, and very good or bad characters, who show feelings that are too strong or simple to seem real, or this style of writing **2** a situation in which people behave with too much emotion and excitement: *Why does she have to turn everything into a melodrama?*

mel·o·dra·mat·ic /,mɛlədrə'mætɪk/ *adj.* **1** having or showing emotions that are too strong or not appropriate for the situation: *a melodramatic musical score* | *It sounds melodramatic, but I felt like someone was watching me.* **2** relating to melodrama: *a melodramatic play* —**melodramatically** /-kli/ *adv.*

mel·o·dy /'mɛlədi/ *n. plural* **melodies 1** [C,U] a song or tune: *a sad, haunting melody* **2** [C] the main tune in a complicated piece of music: *"Deutschlandlied" is based on the melody from a work by Haydn.* **3** [U] the arrangement of musical notes in a way that is pleasant to listen to

mel·on /'mɛlən/ *n.* [C,U] one of several types of large sweet juicy fruits that have hard skins and flat seeds —see picture at FRUIT[1]

melt[1] /mɛlt/ *v.* [I,T] **1** if something solid melts or if heat melts it, it becomes liquid: *It was not very cold, and some snow had melted.* | *Melt 2 tablespoons of butter in a small frying pan.* | *melted cheese* —compare FREEZE[1] (1), THAW[1] (1) —see picture on page 424 **2** to feel or to make someone feel more love, sympathy etc. than before: *I just melt whenever I see him.* | *Just seeing those little kids smile would melt your heart* (=make you suddenly feel very sympathetic). **3 melt in your mouth** if food melts in your mouth, it is soft and tastes good

melt away *phr. v.* [I,T **melt sth ↔ away**] to disappear quickly and easily, or to make something do this: *Exercise will help those pounds melt away.*

melt sth ↔ down *phr. v.* [T] to heat a metal object until it becomes a liquid, especially so that you can use the metal again: *The metal from the weapons will be melted down and used for a monument to peace.*

melt (sth) into sth *phr. v.* [T] to gradually become a part of something, until there is no difference between things: *Some ethnic groups quickly melted into the general American population.*

melt[2] *n.* [C] **1** a type of SANDWICH that has melted cheese on it: **patty/tuna/veggie melt** | *a turkey melt and french fries* **2** the water that flows out of an area as snow melts, or the time when this happens

melt·down /'mɛltdaʊn/ n. [C,U] **1** a very dangerous situation in which the material in a NUCLEAR REACTOR melts and burns through its container, allowing RADIOACTIVITY to escape **2** a situation in which an important system, process, way of living etc. fails completely: *a global moral meltdown*

melting point /'.. ,./ n. [singular] the temperature at which a solid substance becomes a liquid

melting pot /'.. ,./ n. [C usually singular] **1** a place where people from different races, countries, or social classes come to live together: *America has been a melting pot since the beginning of European immigration.* **2** a situation or place in which many different ideas are discussed: *Paris remains a melting pot for fashion.*

Mel·ville /'mɛlvɪl/, **Her·man** /ˈhɜːmən/ (1819–1891) a U.S. writer famous for his book MOBY DICK, one of the most famous American NOVELS

mem·ber /'mɛmbə/ n. [C] **1** someone who has joined a particular club, group, or organization: *Tickets are $7 for members, and $10 for non-members.* | *St. Joseph's church welcomes all new members.* | **club/party/committee etc. members** *Two gang members were arrested for the shooting of three children.* | **member states/countries/organizations etc.** (=the states etc. that have joined a particular group) **2** one of a particular group of people or things: *Dogs and wolves are both members of the same species.* | *Sarah's the first member of her family to graduate from college.* | *A staff member* (=worker at a particular company) *will return your call as soon as possible.* **3** TECHNICAL OR HUMOROUS the male sex organ; PENIS **4** OLD USE a part of the body, especially an arm or leg

Member of Par·lia·ment /,.. '../ n. [C] an MP (2)

mem·ber·ship /'mɛmbəʃɪp/ n. **1** [U] the state of being a member of a club, group, organization, or system, and receiving the advantages of belonging to that group: *To qualify for membership, you must be 55 or older.* | **[+ in]** *Membership in the country club is free to all Bellevue residents.* | *Present your membership card at the door.* | *The annual membership fee* (=money you must pay to be a member) *is $55.* **2** [C usually singular] all the members of a club, group, or organization: **[+ of]** *Half the entire membership of the UN voted against sending troops.* **3** [U] the number of people who belong to a club, group, or organization: *Membership has dropped by 500,000 since 1986.*

mem·brane /'mɛmbreɪn/ n. [C U] **1** a very thin piece of skin that covers or connects parts of the body: *The injury caused bleeding beneath the membrane of the brain.* **2** a very thin piece of material that covers or connects something —**membranous** /'mɛmbrənəs/ adj.

me·men·to /mə'mɛntoʊ/ n. plural **mementos** [C] a small thing that you keep to remind you of someone or something: **[+ of]** *One corner of his spacious office is full of mementos of his childhood.*

mem·o /'mɛmoʊ/ n. plural **memos** [C] a short official note to another person in the same company or organization: *A memo went around the office, reminding staff of the new dress code.*

mem·oir /'mɛmwɑr/ n. **1** [C] FORMAL a short piece of writing about someone or something that you know well **2** **sb's memoirs** a book written by a famous person about their life and experiences: *Nixon describes in his memoirs the first time he met Pat Ryan.*

mem·o·ra·bil·i·a /,mɛmərə'bɪliə, -'bɪl-/ n. [plural] things that you keep or collect because they relate to a famous person, event, or time: *Elvis memorabilia.*

mem·o·ra·ble /'mɛmrəbəl/ adj. very good, enjoyable, or unusual, and worth remembering: *The Tyson-Douglas fight was one of the most memorable events in boxing history.* —**memorably** adv.

mem·o·ran·dum /,mɛmə'rændəm/ n. plural **memoranda** /-də/ or **memorandums** [C] **1** FORMAL a MEMO **2** LAW a short legal document recording the conditions of an agreement

me·mo·ri·al[1] /mə'mɔriəl/ adj. [only before noun]

---

made, happening, or done in order to remind people of someone who has died: *Jackson Memorial Hospital* | *A **memorial service** will be held at Saratoga Presbyterian Church.* | **memorial prize/scholarship/fund etc.** *the Nobel Memorial Prize in Economic Science*

memorial[2] n. [C] something, especially something made of stone with writing on it, to remind people of someone who has died: *the Lincoln Memorial in Washington, D.C.* | **[+ to]** *a memorial to black Americans who fought in the Civil War* —see also WAR MEMORIAL

Memorial Day /.'... ,./ n. [U] a U.S. national holiday on the last Monday in May, to remember soldiers killed in wars

me·mo·ri·a·lize /mə'mɔriə,laɪz/ v. [T] to do something in order to remind people of someone who has died: *A sculpture memorializing the fall of the Berlin Wall was dedicated on December 18, 1992.*

mem·o·rize /'mɛmə,raɪz/ v. [T] to learn and remember words, music, or other information in detail: *There's no way I can memorize all these formulas before the test.* —**memorization** /,mɛmərə'zeɪʃən/ n. [U]

mem·o·ry /'mɛmri, -məri/ n. plural **memories** **1** ability to remember [C,U] the ability to remember things, places, experiences etc.: *Grandpa was getting old and his memory wasn't so good.* | *Marshall recited Martin Luther King Jr.'s famous speech from memory* (=without using anything written to help). | **have a good/bad/terrible etc. memory** *I have such a terrible memory.* **2** sth you remember [C usually plural] something that you remember from the past about a person, place, or experience: **[+ of]** *memories of her years at college* | **happy/good/bad etc. memories** *One of my fondest memories is going up to the lake to stay with my cousins.* | *Events of the past week have **brought back memories** of the Vietnam War.* | *Douglass recalls **childhood memories*** (=memories of the time when you were a child) *of long summers spent outside.* **3** computer **a)** [C] the part of a computer in which information can be stored **b)** [U] the amount of space that can be used for storing information on a computer or DISK: *16 megabytes of memory* **4** **in recent memory** during the recent past: *It was the first time in recent memory that American specialists were allowed in the country.* **5** **in memory of sb** also **in sb's memory** for the purpose of remembering someone and reminding other people of them after they have died: *The group lit candles in memory of Laura and her brother.* **6** **sb's memory** also **the memory of sb** the way you think about someone who has died, who you love, respect, or admire: *a rose garden dedicated to his memory* | *Janitz said her intention was to honor the memory of her mother.* **7** **sb's memory lives on** used to say that people still remember someone after they have died or gone away **8** **in living memory** since the earliest time that people now alive can remember: *the worst war in living memory* **9** **if memory serves** used when you are almost sure that you have remembered something correctly: *If memory serves, Steve Winterson joined the marketing team in 1983.* **10** **a walk/trip down memory lane** an occasion when you spend time remembering the past —see also **commit sth to memory** (COMMIT (5)), **jog sb's memory** (JOG[1] (2)), **lose your memory/sight/voice etc.** (LOSE (6)), **a photographic memory** (PHOTOGRAPHIC (2)), **refresh sb's memory/recollection** (REFRESH (2))

memory bank /'.. ,./ n. [C] the part of a large computer system that stores information

memory hog /'... ,./ n. [C] INFORMAL **1** a computer program that uses a lot of MEMORY (3) **2** someone who uses computer programs that use a lot of the

M

power available on a network, so that other people have trouble using their programs on the same network —**memory-hogging** adj. [only before noun]

Mem·phis /'mɛmfɪs/ the largest city in the U.S. state of Tennessee

men /mɛn/ n. the plural of MAN

men·ace¹ /'mɛnɪs/ n. **1** [C] something or someone that is dangerous: [+ to] *Psychologists believe he could still be a menace to society.* **2** [C] a person, especially a child, that is annoying or causes trouble **3** [U] a threatening quality or manner: *His eyes blazed with menace.*

menace² v. [T] FORMAL to threaten

men·ac·ing /'mɛnɪsɪŋ/ adj. making you expect something bad; THREATENING: *the dark, menacing sky* | *a deep, menacing voice* —**menacingly** adv.

mé·nage /meɪ'nɑʒ/ n. [C] FORMAL OR HUMOROUS all the people who live in a particular house; HOUSEHOLD¹

ménage à trois /meɪˌnɑʒ ɑ 'trwɑ/ n. [singular] a sexual relationship involving three people who live together

me·nag·er·ie /mə'nædʒəri, -ʒə-/ n. [C] **1** a collection of wild animals kept privately or for the public to see **2** a group of people or characters that seems strange because they are all very different: *Isadora arrived with her menagerie of admirers.*

Men·ci·us /'mɛnʃiəs, -ʃəs/ also **Meng·zi** /'mʌŋzi/ (?371–?289 B.C.) a Chinese PHILOSOPHER

Menck·en /'mɛŋkɪn/, **H.L.** /eɪtʃ ɛl/ (1880–1956) a U.S. JOURNALIST famous for his criticism of the American MIDDLE CLASS

mend¹ /mɛnd/ v.

1 repair [T] **a)** to repair a hole or tear, especially in a piece of clothing: *I need to get my sleeve mended.* **2** become healthy [I,T] to make a broken bone become whole and healthy again, or to become better after a bone injury: *Walters was off the team for a year while his ribs mended.* | *A pin was inserted to mend the fracture in his foot.* **3** **mend your ways** to improve the way you behave after behaving badly for a long time: *The Communist Party committees tried to 're-educate' him but he refused to mend his ways.* **4** **mend (your) fences** to talk to someone you have offended or argued with, and try to persuade them to be friendly with you again **5** **mend relations/ties etc.** if two people or groups mend their relations etc., they start to be friendly with each other again: *Whether McCain and the committee can mend their relationship is still uncertain.* **6** end a problem [T] to end a problem by dealing with its causes: *Mending this problem will take more than money.*

mend² n. [C] **be on the mend** to be getting better after an illness or after a difficult period: *Ron's still taking medication, but he's on the mend.* | *Increased sales are a sign that the housing market is on the mend.*

men·da·cious /mɛn'deɪʃəs/ adj. FORMAL not truthful: *a secretive and mendacious government* —**mendaciously** adv.

men·dac·i·ty /mɛn'dæsəti/ n. [U] FORMAL the quality of being false or not truthful

Men·del /'mɛndl/, **Greg·or Jo·hann** /'grɛgɔr 'youhɑn/ (1822–1884) an Austrian MONK whose studies of plants later provided some of the basic ideas of the new science of GENETICS

Men·de·ley·ev /ˌmɛndə'leɪəf/, **D·mi·tri** /də'mitri/ (1834–1907) a Russian scientist who discovered the rules about the structure of ELEMENTs that made possible the PERIODIC TABLE

Men·dels·sohn /'mɛndlsən/, **Fe·lix** /'filɪks/ (1809–1847) a German musician who wrote CLASSICAL music

men·di·cant /'mɛndɪkənt/ n. [C] FORMAL someone who asks people for money in order to live, usually for religious reasons —**mendicant** adj.: *mendicant monks*

mend·ing /'mɛndɪŋ/ n. [U] clothes that need to be mended

men·folk /'mɛnfoʊk/ n. [plural] OLD-FASHIONED a word for men, especially the male relatives of a family

me·ni·al¹ /'miniəl, -nyəl/ adj. menial work is boring and needs no skill, and is usually done using your hands rather than your mind: *Belknap was unable to find anything but menial labor.* —**menially** adv.

menial² n. [C] a servant who works in a house

men·in·gi·tis /ˌmɛnən'dʒaɪtɪs/ n. [U] a serious illness in which the outer part of the brain becomes swollen

Men·non·ites /'mɛnəˌnaɪts/ a Protestant religious group that refuses to join the armed forces or to hold official public positions, and does not BAPTIZE its children —**Mennonite** adj.

Men·no Si·mons /ˌmɛnoʊ 'simoʊnz, 'saɪ-/ (1496–1561) a Dutch religious leader who started the Mennonite religious group of Protestants

Me·nom·i·nee /mə'nɑməˌni/ a Native American tribe from the northeastern central area of the U.S.

men·o·pause /'mɛnəˌpɔz/ n. [U] the time when a woman stops menstruating (MENSTRUATE), which usually happens around age 50 —**menopausal** /ˌmɛnə'pɔzəl/ adj.

me·no·rah /mə'nɔrə/ n. [C] a special CANDLESTICK that holds seven CANDLEs, used in Jewish ceremonies

MENSA /'mɛnsə/ an international organization for people who are very intelligent

mensch /mɛnʃ/ n. [C] SPOKEN someone that you like and admire, especially because they have done something good for you: *You've been a real mensch.*

men·ses /'mɛnsiz/ n. [plural] TECHNICAL the blood that flows out of a woman's body each month

men's room /'. ./ n. [C] a room in a public place with toilets for men

men·stru·al /'mɛnstruəl, -strəl/ adj. relating to the time each month when a woman menstruates

menstrual pe·ri·od /ˌ... '.../ n. [C] FORMAL the time each month when a woman menstruates; PERIOD¹

men·stru·ate /'mɛnstruˌeɪt, -streɪt/ v. [I] TECHNICAL when a woman menstruates, blood flows from her body —**menstruation** /ˌmɛnstru'eɪʃən/ n. [C,U]

mens·wear /'mɛnzwɛr/ n. [U] a word meaning "clothing for men," used especially in stores: *the menswear department at Macy's*

-ment /mənt/ suffix [in nouns] **1** used to form nouns that show actions, the people who do them, and their results: *entertainment* (=activity of entertaining people) | *the company's management* (=people who manage it) | *an arrangement* (=result of arranging something) | *some interesting new developments* (=results from something that develops) **2** used to form nouns that show conditions that are the result of an action: *the unemployment rate* (=number of people who do not have jobs) —**-mental** /mɛntl/ suffix [in adjectives] *governmental*

men·tal /'mɛntəl/ adj. **1** affecting the mind or happening in the mind: *mental health* | *a child's mental development* | **mental picture/image** (=a picture that you form in your mind) **2** [only before noun] relating to illnesses of the mind, or to treating illnesses of the mind: *Violent mental patients were kept in a separate ward.* | *a mental institution* | *He was tested for brain damage and mental disorders* (=illnesses of the mind). —see also MENTAL HOSPITAL **3** **make a mental note** to make a special effort to remember something: *She made a mental note to call Marcia when she got home.* **4** **mental block** a difficulty in remembering something or in understanding something: *I have a complete mental block when it comes to computers.* **5** INFORMAL crazy: *That guy's mental!* —**mentally** adv.: *mentally ill*

mental age /ˌ.. './ n. [C] a measure of someone's ability to think, obtained by comparing their ability with the average ability of children at various ages: *a 25-year-old man with a mental age of seven*

mental a·rith·me·tic /ˌ.. '.../ n. [U] the act of adding numbers together, multiplying them etc. in your mind, without writing them down

M

S W
2
3

mental hos·pi·tal /'.. ,.../ also **mental in·sti·tu·tion** /'.. ..,../ n. [C] a hospital where people with mental illnesses are treated; PSYCHIATRIC HOSPITAL

men·tal·i·ty /men'tæləti/ n. plural **mentalities** [C] a particular type of attitude or way of thinking, often one that you think is wrong or stupid: *Marston weaves facts into the story about slave-trading and shows the sick mentality of the slavery system.*

mentally han·di·capped /,.. '.../ adj. **1** a mentally handicapped person has a problem with their brain, often from the time they are born, that affects their ability to think or control their body movements **2** [plural] **the mentally handicapped** people who are mentally handicapping

men·thol /'menθɔl, -θɑl/ n. [U] a substance that has a strong MINT smell and taste, used in cough medicines and cigarettes to give them a special taste

men·tho·lat·ed /'menθə,leɪtɪd/ adj. containing menthol

men·tion¹ /'menʃən/ v. [T] **1** to talk about something or someone in a conversation, piece of writing etc., especially without saying very much or giving details: *Did I mention I saw Lee and John yesterday? | As I mentioned earlier, sales this year have been lower than expected.* | **mention sth to sb** *Don't mention this to Larry, but I'm thinking of quitting my job.* | [+ **that**] *Sue mentioned that you might be moving to Florida.* | **It's worth mentioning that** (=this is a useful or important piece of information) *only 20% of all applicants are accepted each year.* **2 not to mention** used to introduce an additional thing that makes a situation even more difficult, surprising, interesting etc.: *There will be live music and food, not to mention games and prizes for the whole family!* **3 don't mention it** SPOKEN used to say politely that there is no need for someone to thank you for helping them: *"Thanks for the ride home!" "Don't mention it."* **4 above-mentioned/mentioned above** mentioned earlier in a piece of writing —see also **mention/say/note sth in passing** (PASSING² (1))

mention² n. [C usually singular,U] the act of mentioning something or someone in a conversation, piece of writing etc.: *Joe gets anxious **at the mention of** (=when people talk about) flying.* | *The President **made no mention of** (=did not say anything about) the bill in his speech to Congress.* | *There was no mention of profit losses in the Langeren report.* | *I didn't even **get a mention** (=I was not mentioned) in the list of contributors.* —see also HONORABLE MENTION

men·tor /'mentɔr, -tɔ/ n. [C] an experienced person who advises, encourages, and helps a less experienced person

men·tor·ing /'mentɔrɪŋ/ n. [U] a system of using people with a lot of experience, knowledge etc. to advise other people and give them encouragement to succeed at school or work: *mentoring programs for students at State colleges*

men·u /'menyu/ n. [C] **1** a list of all the types of food that are available for a meal, especially in a restaurant: *Could we have the menu, please?* | *Also **on the menu** are mesquite-grilled chicken and black bean chili.* **2** a list of things that you can choose from or ask a computer to do, that is shown on the SCREEN of the computer: **menu-driven** (=operated by using a menu)

me·ow /mi'aʊ/ n. [C] the crying sound that a cat makes —**meow** v. [I]

Meph·i·stoph·e·les /,mɛfɪ'stɑfə iz/ another name for the DEVIL, especially in the story of Faust —**Mephistophelean** /,mɛfɪstə'filiən, ,mɛfɪ,stɑfə'liən/ adj.

mer·can·tile /'mɜkən,til, -,taɪl/ adj. [only before noun] FORMAL relating to trade; COMMERCIAL¹: *mercantile law* —**mercantilism** /'mɜkənti,lɪzəm/ n. [U]

mer·ce·nar·y¹ /'mɜsə,nɛri/ n. plural **mercenaries** [C] a soldier who fights for any country or group that is willing to pay him: *Colombian police said the mercenaries were hired by drug traffickers.*

mercenary² adj. only interested in money, and not caring about whether your actions are right or wrong or about the effect of your actions on other

people: *Sponsors were criticized for their mercenary attitude toward the Olympic games.*

mer·cer·ized /'mɜsə,raɪzd/ adj. mercerized thread or cotton has been treated with chemicals to make it shiny and strong

mer·chan·dise¹ /'mɜtʃən,daɪz, -,daɪs/ n. [U] goods that are produced in order to be sold, especially goods that are shown in a store for people to buy: *The town has a tiny general store with wildly overpriced merchandise.*

merchandise² v. [T] to try to sell goods or services using methods such as advertising: *In the 1980s, he began merchandising his own hair care products.*

merchandise mix /'... ,./ n. [C] TECHNICAL the number and type of different products sold by a particular store: *The merchandise mix at supermarkets has increased.*

mer·chan·dis·ing /'mɜtʃən,daɪzɪŋ/ n. [U] the business of trying to sell products or services by using methods such as advertising: *the merchandising manager for Pontiac*

mer·chant /'mɜtʃənt/ n. [C] a person or store that buys and sells goods in large quantities: *Downtown merchants are stocking up for the Christmas shopping season.*

merchant bank /,.. './ n. [C] a bank that provides banking services for business

merchant ma·rine /,.. .'./ n. **the merchant marine** all of a country's ships that are used for trade, not war, and the people who work on these ships

merchant sea·man /,.. '../ n. [C] a sailor in the merchant marine

mer·ci·ful /'mɜsɪfəl/ adj. **1 merciful death/end/release** something that seems fortunate because it ends someone's suffering or difficulty: *With the Giants leading 28–7, half-time came as a merciful relief.* **2** being kind to people and forgiving them rather than punishing them or being cruel: *Merciful God*

mer·ci·ful·ly /'mɜsɪfəli/ adv. fortunately or luckily, because a situation could have been much worse: *Mercifully, the screaming ended.*

mer·ci·less /'mɜsɪləs/ adj. cruel and showing no kindness or forgiveness: *a merciless killer* —**mercilessly** adv. —**mercilessness** n. [U]

mer·cu·ri·al /mɜ'kyʊriəl/ adj. **1** LITERARY changing mood suddenly: *the actress's infamous mercurial nature* **2** LITERARY quick and lively: *her mercurial wit* **3** containing mercury

Mer·cu·ry /'mɜkyəri/ the Roman name for the god HERMES

mer·cu·ry /'mɜkyəri/ n. **1 Mercury** the PLANET that is nearest the sun **2** [U] symbol **Hg** a heavy silver-white metal that is an ELEMENT, is liquid at ordinary temperatures, and is used in THERMOMETERS **3 the mercury** the temperature outside: *The mercury dropped to 24° Thursday.*

mer·cy /'mɜsi/ n. **1** [U] kindness, pity, and a willingness to forgive, which you show toward someone that you have power over: *The terrorists **showed no mercy** to the hostages.* | *May God **have mercy on** their souls.* **2 at the mercy of sb/sth** unable to do anything to protect yourself from someone or something: *Having lost engine power, the boat's crew found themselves at the mercy of the wind.* | *Once again Oliver is separated from his friends and left at the mercy of strangers.* **3 leave sb to sb's (tender) mercies** OFTEN HUMOROUS to let someone be dealt with by another person, who may treat them very badly or strictly **4 mercy flight/mission etc.** a trip taken to bring help to people: *Helicopter ambulances were sent on a mercy mission in Honduras.* **5 throw yourself on the mercy of sb** to BEG someone to help you or not to punish you

mercy kill·ing /'.. ,../ n. [C,U] INFORMAL the act of killing someone who is very sick or old so that they do not have to suffer anymore; EUTHANASIA

M

mere¹ /mɪr/ adj. [only before noun, no comparative] **1** used to emphasize how small or unimportant something or someone is: *Admission costs a mere $5 for adults, and only $1 for children.* | *Most of the soldiers were mere boys.* **2** also **the merest** used when something small or unimportant has a big effect: *Stock prices dropped at the merest rumor of a company takeover.* | *The mere thought of drinking whiskey makes me feel sick.*

mere² n. [C] LITERARY a lake

mere·ly /ˈmɪrli/ adv. FORMAL used to emphasize that an action, person, or thing is very small, simple, or unimportant, especially when compared to what it could be; only; just: *Today people want more from working life than merely a paycheck.* | *He was merely a boy! I wouldn't have expected him to understand.* | *As Foreman became angrier and angrier, Paula merely smiled.*

mer·e·tri·cious /ˌmɛrəˈtrɪʃəs/ adj. FORMAL seeming attractive, interesting, or believable, but having no real value or not based on the truth: *a meretricious argument* —**meretriciously** adv. —**meretriciousness** n. [U]

merge /mədʒ/ v. **1** [I,T] to combine or join together to form one thing: [+ with] *The Atlanta-based telephone company had agreed to merge with GTI Corp.* | [merge sth] *Some of the district's high schools will be merged to cut costs.* | [+ into] *Once downloaded, the files are then merged into a single database.* **2 merge into sth** to seem to disappear in something by becoming part of it: *Kangi avoided reporters at the airport by merging into the crowd.* **3** if traffic merges, the cars from two roads come together onto the same road: *Expect delays where freeway traffic merges.*

merg·er /ˈmədʒər/ n. [C] the act of joining together two or more companies or organizations to form one larger one: [+ with] *Norton Co. has agreed to a $1.8 billion merger with the French firm.*

me·rid·i·an /məˈrɪdiən/ n. **1** [C] an imaginary line drawn from the North Pole to the South Pole over the surface of the Earth, used to show the position of places on a map **2 the meridian** TECHNICAL the highest point reached by the sun or another star, when seen from a point on the Earth's surface

me·ringue /məˈræŋ/ n. [C,U] a light sweet food made by baking a mixture of sugar and the white part of eggs: *lemon meringue pie*

me·ri·no /məˈrinoʊ/ n. [U] a type of sheep with long wool, or cloth made from this wool

mer·it¹ /ˈmɛrɪt/ n. **1** [C usually plural] one of the good features of something such as a plan or system: [+ of] *Board members met last week to discuss the merits of opening a new branch.* **2** [U] FORMAL a good quality that makes something deserve praise or admiration: *a merit scholarship* | **have merit/be of merit** *The arguments for legalizing marijuana have considerable merit.* | **artistic/literary merit** *a film lacking any kind of artistic merit* **3 judge/decide/accept sth on its merits** to judge something only by how good it is, without considering anything else: *Each application will be judged solely on its own merits.* —compare DEMERIT

merit² v. [T not in progressive] FORMAL to deserve something: *The committee will decide whether the case merits more serious attention.*

mer·i·toc·ra·cy /ˌmɛrəˈtɑkrəsi/ n. plural **meritocracies 1** [C] a social system that gives the greatest power and highest social positions to people with the most ability **2** [singular] the people who have power in this type of system

mer·i·to·ri·ous /ˌmɛrəˈtɔriəs/ adj. FORMAL very good and deserving praise —**meritoriously** adv.

Mer·lin /ˈmərlɪn/ in old stories, a MAGICIAN who helped King Arthur

mer·lot /mərˈloʊ/ n. [U] a type of red wine

mer·maid /ˈmərmeɪd/ n. [C] in stories, a woman who has a fish's tail instead of legs

mer·ri·ment /ˈmɛrɪmənt/ n. [U] FORMAL laughter, fun, and enjoyment: *The drinking and merriment were not enough to take his mind off Dinah.*

mer·ry /ˈmɛri/ adj. **merrier, merriest 1 Merry Christmas!** used to say that you hope someone will have a happy time at CHRISTMAS **2** cheerful and happy: *She smiled, her eyes bright and merry.* **3 the more the merrier** SPOKEN used to tell someone that you will be happy if they join you in something you are doing: *"Do you mind if I bring Tony?" "Nah, the more the merrier."* **4 make merry** LITERARY to enjoy yourself by drinking, singing etc. **5** OLD USE pleasant: *the merry month of June* —**merrily** adv. —**merriness** n. [U]

merry-go-round

merry-go-round /ˈ.. .ˌ./ n. **1** [C] a machine that children ride on for fun, which turns around and around and has seats in the shape of animals **2** [singular] a series of related events that happen very quickly one after another: *a merry-go-round of strikes, cash problems and closing banks*

mer·ry-mak·ing /ˈ.. .ˌ./ n. [U] LITERARY fun and enjoyment, especially drinking, dancing, and singing

me·sa /ˈmeɪsə/ n. [C] a hill with a flat top and steep sides, in the southwestern U.S.

mes·cal /ˈmɛskæl/ n. [U] an alcoholic drink made from a type of CACTUS

mes·ca·line /ˈmɛskəlin/ n. [U] an illegal drug made from a CACTUS plant that makes people imagine that they can see things that do not really exist

mesh¹ /mɛʃ/ n. [C,U] **1** a piece of material made of threads or wires that have been woven together like a net: *an iron mesh fence* **2** a combination of people, ideas, or things: [+ of] *In the 1880s the city was a mesh of Italian, Portuguese, Mexican and German immigrants.*

mesh² v. [I] **1** if two ideas or qualities mesh, they go well together and are appropriate for each other: [+ with] *Meshing Celtic folk with punk, the Pogues' music is sweet, strong and exciting.* **2** if two parts of an engine or machine mesh, they fit or connect correctly

me·shug·a /məˈʃʊgə/ adj. crazy

mes·mer·ize /ˈmɛzməˌraɪz/ v. [T often passive] to make someone feel that they cannot stop watching or listening to something or someone, because they are so interested in it or attracted by it: *Audiences will be mesmerized by the film's dazzling photography.* —**mesmerizing** adj.

mes·quite /mɛˈskit/ n. [C,U] a tree or bush from the northwest U.S., or the outer covering of this tree, used when cooking food on a BARBECUE to give it a special taste

mess¹ /mɛs/ n.
1 dirty/disorganized [singular,U] a place or group of things that looks dirty, or not neatly arranged: *Eric! Get in here and clean up this mess!* | *The house is a total mess.* | *My hair's a mess.* | *I hope the kids aren't making a mess in the living room.*
2 problems/difficulties [singular] INFORMAL a situation in which there are a lot of problems and difficulties, especially as a result of mistakes or people not being careful: *Dave's life was a mess.* | *The welfare system in this country is a mess.*
3 be in a mess to have a lot of problems: *If you'd paid the phone bill, we wouldn't be in this mess.*

4 make a mess of sth INFORMAL to do something badly and make a lot of mistakes: *I guess I've really made a mess of things* (=done everything wrong) *this time.*

5 a mess of sth INFORMAL a lot of something: *a mess of fresh fish*

6 army/navy [C] a room in which members of the army, navy etc. eat and drink together

7 waste matter [C,U] solid waste material from a baby or animal: *If the dog makes a mess, you clean it up!*

mess² *v.* [I] to have meals in a room where members of the army, navy etc. eat together

mess around *phr. v.* INFORMAL **1** [I] to play or do silly things instead of working or paying attention: *Stop messing around and get ready for school.* **2** to have a sexual relationship with someone whom you should not have a sexual relationship with: [+ **with**] *Sam's wife was caught messing around with another man.*

mess up *phr. v.* INFORMAL **1** [T **mess** sth ↔ **up**] to spoil or ruin something, especially something important or something that has been carefully planned: *I don't want to mess up my kids' chances at a good education.* | *His flight was canceled, which messed everybody's schedule up.* **2** [T **mess** sth ↔ **up**] to make something dirty or messy: *Stop it! You'll mess up my hair!* **3** [I,T **mess** sth ↔ **up**] to make a mistake and do something badly: *Don't worry if you mess it up the first time – just keep on practicing.* | [+ **on**] *I think I messed up on the last question.* —see also MESSED UP

mess (around) with sb/sth *phr. v.* [T] **1** [**mess (around) with** sb] to deal with someone you do not understand or should not become involved with, especially because they get angry easily or could harm you in some way: *You shouldn't mess around with Frank.* **2** [**mess (around) with** sth] to use something or make small changes to it: *Who's been messing with my computer?*

mes·sage /'mɛsɪdʒ/ *n.* [C] **1** a spoken or written piece of information that you send to another person: *Did you get my message?* | *Sarah called and left a message for you on the answering machine.* | *He's not at his desk.* **Can I take a message** for him (=used on the telephone when offering to give a message to someone)? **2** the main or most important idea that someone is trying to tell people: *The campaign sends a clear message that women do not have to tolerate violence.* **3 get the message** INFORMAL to understand what someone means or what they want you to do: *Hopefully he'll get the message and leave me alone.*

message² *v.* [T] to send a message using electronic equipment, for example EMAIL

mes·sag·ing /'mɛsɪdʒɪŋ/ *n.* [U] the system or process of sending messages using electronic equipment: *automated messaging*

messed up /ˌ. '.◂/ *adj.* INFORMAL someone who is messed up is very unhappy and has mental problems because of bad experiences: *Steve was pretty messed up in high school.*

mes·sen·ger /'mɛsəndʒɚ/ *n.* [C] **1** someone who takes messages to people **2 blame/shoot the messenger** to be angry with someone for telling you about something bad that has happened —see also BIKE MESSENGER

mess hall /'. ./ *n.* [C] a large room where soldiers eat

mes·si·ah /mə'saɪə/ *n.* [singular] **1 the Messiah a)** Jesus Christ, who is believed by Christians to be sent by God to save the world **b)** a great religious leader who, according to Jewish belief, will be sent by God to save the world **2** someone who people believe will save them from great social or economic problems: *The media made him out to be a political messiah.*

mes·si·an·ic /ˌmɛsi'ænɪk◂/ *adj.* FORMAL **1** someone who has messianic beliefs or feelings wants to make very big social or political changes: *The group works to preserve the environment with messianic zeal.* **2** relating to the Messiah

Messrs. /'mɛsɚz/ FORMAL the plural of MR.: *Messrs. Jacobson and Bates*

mess·y /'mɛsi/ *adj.* **messier, messiest 1** dirty, not organized, or not neatly arranged: *Their three-cheese pizza is excellent, but messy to eat.* | *Mom yells if my room is messy.* | *Does my hair look messy?* **2** INFORMAL a messy situation is complicated and not nice to deal with: *He's just been through a particularly messy divorce.* —**messily** *adv.* —**messiness** *n.* [U]

mes·ti·zo /mɛ'stizou/ *n. plural* **mestizos** [C] someone who has one Hispanic parent and one Native American parent

met /mɛt/ *v.* the past tense and past participle of MEET[1]

meta- /mɛtə/ *prefix* TECHNICAL beyond the ordinary or usual: *metaphysical* (=beyond ordinary physical things)

me·tab·o·lism /mə'tæbə,lɪzəm/ *n.* [C,U] the chemical activity in your body that changes food into the energy you need to work and grow: *After about age 30, your metabolism slows down and you start to gain weight.* —**metabolic** /ˌmɛtə'bɑlɪk/ *adj.*

me·tab·o·lize /mə'tæbə,laɪz/ *v.* [T] to change food into energy in the body by chemical activity

met·al /'mɛtl/ *n.* [C, U] **1** a hard, usually shiny substance such as iron, gold, or steel: *The frame is made of metal.* | *metal pipes* | *Jewels and **precious metals** (=expensive metals such as gold and silver) decorated the tombs.* **2** INFORMAL another word for HEAVY METAL music: *metal, punk, and folk bands* —see also METALLIC

met·a·lan·guage /'mɛtə,læŋgwɪdʒ/ *n.* [C,U] words used for talking about or describing language

metal de·tect·or /'.. .,../ *n.* [C] **1** a machine used to find pieces of metal that are buried under the ground **2** a special frame that you walk through at an airport used to check for weapons made of metal

metal fa·tigue /'.. .,./ *n.* [U] a weakness in metal that makes it likely to break

me·tal·lic /mə'tælɪk/ *adj.* **1** like metal in color, appearance, or taste: *a metallic blue jacket* **2** a metallic noise sounds like pieces of metal hitting each other: *a metallic, female voice* **3** made of or containing metal: *metallic minerals*

met·al·lur·gy /'mɛtl,ɚdʒi/ *n.* [U] the scientific study of metals and their uses —**metallurgical** /ˌmɛtl'ɚdʒɪkəl/ *adj.* —**metallurgist** /'mɛtl,ɚdʒɪst/ *n.* [C]

met·al·work /'mɛtl,wɚk/ *n.* [U] **1** the activity or skill of making metal objects: *metalwork classes* **2** objects made by shaping metal: *Art Nouveau metalwork* —**metalworker** *n.* [C]

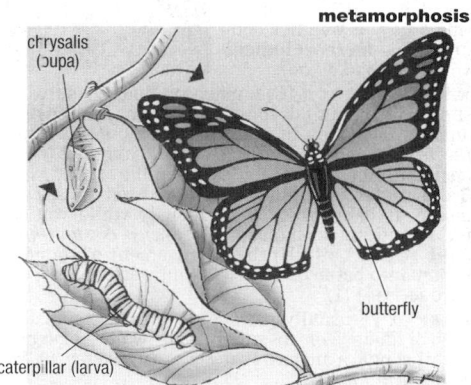

metamorphosis

chrysalis (pupa)

butterfly

caterpillar (larva)

met·a·mor·pho·sis /ˌmɛtə'mɔrfəsɪs/ *n. plural* **metamorphoses** /-siz/ [C,U] **1** FORMAL a process in which something changes completely into something very different: *Lewis has gradually **undergone a metamorphosis** into the state's best basketball player.* **2** a process in which a young insect, FROG etc. changes into another stage in its development —**metamorphose** /ˌmɛtə'mɔrfouz/ *v.* [I,T]

M

met·a·phor /'mɛtəˌfɔr/ n. [C,U] **1** a way of describing something by comparing it to something else that has similar qualities, without using the words "like" or "as": *She was a caged bird, to use her own metaphor, that had to break free.* | *Through metaphor and symbolism, Thoreau discusses the importance of nature.* —compare SIMILE **2 mixed metaphor** the use of two different metaphors at the same time to describe something, especially in a way that seems silly or funny **3** [C,U] something in a book, painting, movie etc. that is intended to represent a more general idea or quality: [+ **for**] *Dancing becomes a metaphor for marriage and life in "Shall We Dance."*

met·a·phor·i·cal /ˌmɛtəˈfɔrɪkəl/ adj. using words to mean something different from their ordinary meaning when describing something in order to achieve a particular effect —**metaphorically** /-kli/ adv.: *I was, metaphorically speaking, pushed over the edge.*

met·a·phys·i·cal /ˌmɛtəˈfɪzɪkəl/ adj. **1** relating to the study of metaphysics **2** using words or ideas that are so complicated that you cannot understand them —**metaphysically** /-kli/ adv.

met·a·phys·ics /ˌmɛtəˈfɪzɪks/ n. [U] the part of the study of PHILOSOPHY that tries to explain the nature of reality and discusses whether ideas, space, life, the world etc. really exist

mete /mit/ v.
  mete sth ↔ **out** phr. v. [T] FORMAL to give someone a punishment: *A life sentence was meted out to Collins, 33, for killing his infant son.*

me·te·or /'mitiə/ n. [C] a piece of rock or metal that floats in space, and makes a bright line in the night sky when it falls through the Earth's ATMOSPHERE (2)

me·te·or·ic /ˌmitiˈɔrɪk, -ˈar-/ adj. **1** happening very suddenly and quickly: **meteoric rise/career** *his meteoric rise in politics* **2** from a METEOR —**meteorically** /-kli/ adv.

me·te·or·ite /'mitiəˌraɪt/ n. [C] a piece of rock or metal that has come from space and landed on Earth

meteorite

me·te·or·ol·o·gist /ˌmitiəˈralədʒɪst/ n. [C] **1** someone who studies meteorology **2** someone on television or the radio who tells you what the weather will be like; WEATHER FORECASTER

me·te·or·ol·o·gy /ˌmitiəˈralədʒi/ n. [U] the scientific study of weather conditions —**meteorological** /ˌmitiərəˈladʒɪkəl/ adj.

meter¹ /'mitə/ n. **1** [C] a machine that measures and shows the amount of something you have used or the amount of money that you must pay: *a gas meter* | *the taxi meter* —see also PARKING METER **2** [C] the basic unit for measuring length in the METRIC SYSTEM **3 the meter is running (on sth)** used to say that money is being spent continuously while you wait for something to happen: *The meter is running on bank reform.* **4** [C,U] the arrangement of sounds in poetry into patterns of strong and weak beats —compare RHYTHM (1)

meter² v. [T usually passive] to measure something with a meter, or to supply gas, water, electricity etc. through a meter: *Water use is metered in most Sacramento homes.*

-meter /mətə, mitə/ suffix [in nouns] **1** part of a meter, or a particular number of meters: *a millimeter* (=1/1000th of a meter) | *a kilometer* (=1000 meters) **2** an instrument for measuring something: *an altimeter* (=measures the height at which an aircraft is flying)

meter maid /'.. ˌ./ n. [C] OLD-FASHIONED a woman whose job is to make sure that cars are not parked illegally

meth /mɛθ/ n. [U] INFORMAL: see METHAMPHETAMINE

meth·a·done /'mɛθəˌdoʊn/ n. [U] a drug that is often given to people who are trying to stop taking HEROIN

meth·am·phet·a·mine /ˌmɛθæmˈfɛtəˌmin/ n. [U] an illegal drug that makes you feel like you have more energy

meth·ane /'mɛθeɪn/ n. [U] a colorless gas with no smell that can be burned to give heat

meth·a·nol /'mɛθəˌnɔl, -ˌnoʊl/ n. [U] a poisonous alcohol that can be made from wood

me·thinks /mɪˈθɪŋks/ v. OLD USE OR HUMOROUS I think

meth·od /'mɛθəd/ n. **1** [C] a planned way of doing something, especially one that a lot of people know about and use: *I think we should try again using a different method.* | *traditional teaching methods* | [+ **of**] *The pill is one of the safest methods of birth control.* | [+ **for**] *a new method for the early detection of cancer* **2** [U] FORMAL a reasonable and effective way of planning something: *He didn't seem to have any method in the way he approached the problem.* **3 there's a method to sb's madness**, **there is method in sb's madness** used to say that even though someone seems to be behaving strangely, there is a sensible reason for what they are doing

me·thod·i·cal /məˈθadɪkəl/ adj. **1** always doing things carefully, using an ordered system: *a cautious, methodical killer* **2** done in a careful and well organized way: *methodical research* —**methodically** /-kli/ adv.

Meth·od·ist /'mɛθədɪst/ n. [C] someone who belongs to a Christian religious group that follows the teachings of John Wesley —**Methodist** adj. —**Methodism** n. [U]

meth·od·ol·o·gy /ˌmɛθəˈdalədʒi/ n. plural **methodologies** [C,U] the set of methods and principles that are used when studying a particular subject or doing a particular type of work: *scientific methodology* —**methodological** /ˌmɛθədəˈladʒɪkəl/ adj. —**methodologically** /-kli/ adv.

Me·thu·se·lah /məˈθuzələ/ n. **1** a name used for someone who is extremely old **2** in the Bible, a man who lived for 969 years

meth·yl al·co·hol /ˌmɛθəl ˈælkəhɔl/ n. [U] TECHNICAL: see METHANOL —compare ETHYL ALCOHOL

me·tic·u·lous /məˈtɪkyələs/ adj. very careful about small details, and always making sure that everything is done correctly: *He would listen to each reply, making meticulous notes as he went.* | *a meticulous manager* | [+ **in/about**] *Mother was meticulous in her housekeeping.* —**meticulously** adv. —**meticulousness** n. [U]

me·tier /mɛˈtyeɪ, ˈmɛtyeɪ/ n. [C usually singular] FORMAL a type of work or activity that you enjoy doing because you have a natural ability to do it well: *Modern music is not his metier.*

me·tre /'mitə/ n. [C,U] the British and Canadian spelling of METER

-metre /mətə, mitə/ suffix [in nouns] the British and Canadian spelling of -METER

met·ric /'mɛtrɪk/ adj. using or relating to the metric system of weights and measures: *2.3 metric tons* —compare IMPERIAL (2)

met·ri·cal /'mɛtrɪkəl/ adj. TECHNICAL written in the form of poetry, with regular beats —**metrically** /-kli/ adv.

metric sys·tem /'.. ˌ../ n. **the metric system** the system of weights and measures that is based on the meter and the kilogram —compare AVOIRDUPOIS

metric ton /ˌ.. '.'/ n. [C] a unit for measuring weight, equal to 1000 kilograms or about 2,205 pounds

me·tro /'mɛtroʊ/ n. [C] a railroad system that runs under the ground below a city; SUBWAY: *the Paris Metro*

met·ro·nome /'mɛtrəˌnoʊm/ n. [C] a piece of equipment that shows the speed at which music should be played, by making a short repeated sound

me·trop·o·lis /məˈtrapəlɪs/ n. [C] a very large city that is the most important city in a country or area

met·ro·pol·i·tan /ˌmɛtrəˈpalətˈn/ adj. relating or

belonging to a very large city: *the Miami metropolitan area*

met·tle /ˈmɛtl/ *n.* [U] **1** courage and determination to do something even when it is very difficult: **test/ prove/show your mettle** *It'll be a hard game, but it should give the team a chance to show their mettle.* **2 be on your mettle** to be ready to try as hard as possible because your abilities are being tested

mew /myu/ *v.* [I] to MEOW —**mew** *n.*

Mexican jump·ing bean /ˌ... ˈ.. ˌ./ *n.* [C] a seed of particular Mexican plants that has the LARVA (=young form) of a MOTH (=flying insect) inside it which makes the seed move

Mex·i·co /ˈmɛksɪˌkoʊ/ a country that is south of the U.S. and north of Guatemala —**Mexican** /ˈmɛksɪkən/ *n., adj.*

Mexico Cit·y /ˌ... ˈ../ the capital and largest city of Mexico

mez·za·nine /ˈmɛzəˌnin, ˌmɛzəˈnin/ *n.* [C] **1** the lowest BALCONY in a theater, or the first few rows of seats in that balcony **2** the floor just above the main floor in a hotel, store etc., which usually has a low ceiling

mez·zo[1] /ˈmɛtsoʊ, ˈmɛdzoʊ/ *adv.* **mezzo forte/piano etc.** TECHNICAL a word meaning not too loud, softly etc., used in instructions for performing music

mez·zo[2] *n. plural* **mezzos** [C] a mezzo-soprano

mez·zo-so·pran·o /ˌ... ˈ.../ *n.* [C] **1** a woman's voice that is lower than a SOPRANO but higher than an ALTO **2** a woman who sings with this kind of voice

mez·zo·tint /ˈmɛtsoʊˌtɪnt/ *n.* [C U] OLD-FASHIONED a picture printed from a metal plate that is polished in places to produce areas of light and shade

M.F.A. *n.* [C] Master of Fine Arts; a university degree in a subject such as painting or SCULPTURE

mfg. the written abbreviation of MANUFACTURING

mfr. the written abbreviation of MANUFACTURER

mg the written abbreviation of MILLIGRAM

mgr. *n.* the written abbreviation of "manager"

MHz the written abbreviation of MEGAHERTZ

MI 1 the written abbreviation of Michigan **2** also **M.I.** the written abbreviation of MIDDLE INITIAL (=first letter of your middle name), usually written on forms

mi /mi/ *n.* [singular] the third note in a musical SCALE according to the SOL-FA system

MIA *n. plural* **MIA's** [C] missing in action; a soldier who has disappeared in a battle and who may still be alive —**MIA** *adj.*

Mi·am·i /maɪˈæmi/ **1** a city in the southeast of the U.S. state of Florida **2** a Native American tribe from the northeastern central area of the U.S.

mi·as·ma /miˈæzmə, maɪ-/ *n.* [singular,U] LITERARY **1** an unhealthy and bad smell or mist: *An acrid miasma came from the sewage plant.* **2** an evil influence or feeling: *You feel the devastation of the war like a miasma over the battlefield.*

mi·ca /ˈmaɪkə/ *n.* [U] a mineral that separates easily into small flat transparent pieces of rock, often used to make electrical instruments

Mi·cah /ˈmaɪkə/ a book in the Old Testament of the Christian Bible

mice /maɪs/ *n.* the plural of mouse

Mi·chel·an·ge·lo /ˌmaɪkəlˈændʒəˌloʊ/ (1475–1564) an Italian painter, SCULPTOR, and ARCHITECT of the Renaissance period

Mich·i·gan /ˈmɪʃɪgən/ *written abbreviation* **MI 1** a state in the north of the U.S. **2 Lake Michigan** a large lake in the north of the U.S., which is one of the Great Lakes

mick·ey /ˈmɪki/ also **Mickey Finn** /ˌmɪki ˈfɪn/ *n.* [C] OLD-FASHIONED, INFORMAL a type of drug that you secretly put into someone's drink in order to make them unconscious: **slip/give sb a mickey** (=to secretly put a drug into someone's drink)

Mickey Mouse /ˌ... ˈ.ˌ/ *adj.* [only before noun] **1 a Mickey Mouse operation/organization/outfit** a company or organization that is usually very small and

that does not do things well **2** something that people do not take seriously, especially because it is too easy or simple: *a Mickey Mouse class* | *He had some Mickey Mouse excuse for being late.*

Mic·mac /ˈmɪkmæk/ a Native American tribe from eastern Canada

micro- /maɪkroʊ, -krə/ *prefix* **1** extremely small compared with others of the same type: *a microcomputer* | *microelectronics* (=using extremely small electrical parts) **2** dealing with the smaller parts that make up a large unit: *microeconomics* (=the study of all of the parts of a national economy) —compare MACRO-

mi·crobe /ˈmaɪkroʊb/ *n.* [C] an extremely small living creature that cannot be seen without a MICROSCOPE, and that can sometimes cause diseases —**microbial** *adj.*

mi·cro·bi·ol·o·gy /ˌmaɪkroʊbaɪˈɑlədʒi/ *n.* [U] the scientific study of very small living things such as BACTERIA —**microbiologist** *n.* [C] —**microbiological** /ˌmaɪkroʊˌbaɪəˈlɑdʒɪkəl/ *adj.*

mi·cro·brew /ˈmaɪkroʊˌbru/ *n.* [C] a type of beer that is produced only in small quantities

mi·cro·brew·er·y /ˈmaɪkroʊˌbruəri/ *n. plural* **microbreweries** [C] a small company that makes only a small amount of beer to sell, and often has a restaurant where its beer is served

mi·cro·chip /ˈmaɪkroʊˌtʃɪp/ *n.* [C] a computer CHIP

mi·cro·cli·mate /ˈmaɪkroʊˌklaɪmɪt/ *n.* [C] the general weather patterns in a small area, which are different from the weather patterns in the surrounding area

mi·cro·com·put·er /ˈmaɪkroʊkəmˌpyutɚ/ *n.* [C] TECHNICAL a small computer; PC

mi·cro·cosm /ˈmaɪkrəˌkazəm/ *n.* [C,U] a small group, society etc. that has the same qualities as a much larger one: [+ of] *New York's mix of people is a microcosm of America.* | *Harris' production company is starting to look like an empire **in microcosm**.* —**microcosmic** /ˌmaɪkrəˈkazmɪk/ *adj.* —compare MACROCOSM

mi·cro·dot /ˈmaɪkroʊˌdat, -krə-/ *n.* [C] a secret photograph of something such as a document, that is made as small as a DOT so that it can easily be hidden

mi·cro·ec·o·nom·ics /ˌmaɪkroʊɛkəˈnamɪks/ *n.* [U] the study of small economic systems that are part of national or international systems, such as those of particular companies, families etc. —**microeconomic** *adj.* —compare MACROECONOMICS

mi·cro·e·lec·tron·ics /ˌmaɪkroʊɪlɛkˈtraniks/ [U] the practice or study of designing very small PRINTED CIRCUITS that are used in computers —**microelectronic** *adj.*

mi·cro·fiche /ˈmaɪkroʊˌfiʃ/ *n.* [C,U] a sheet of microfilm that can be read using a special machine, especially in a library

mi·cro·film /ˈmaɪkrəˌfɪlm/ *n.* [C,U] a special film used for making very small photographs of important documents, newspapers, maps etc. —**microfilm** *v.* [T]

mi·cro·light /ˈmaɪkroʊˌlaɪt/ *n.* [C] a very light small airplane for one or two people —**microlight** *adj.* [only before noun]

mi·cro·man·age /ˈmaɪkroʊˌmænɪdʒ/ *v.* [T] to organize and control all the details of other people's work in a way that they find annoying: *Professors warned that students will suffer if the state legislature tries to micromanage public education.* —**micromanagement** *n.* [U]

mi·crom·e·ter /maɪˈkramətɚ/ *n.* [C] **1** an instrument for measuring very small distances **2** one millionth of a meter

mi·cron /ˈmaɪkran/ *n.* [C] a MICROMETER (2)

Mi·cro·ne·si·a /ˌmaɪkrəˈniʒə/ a group of more than 2000 small islands in the western Pacific Ocean, including the Caroline Islands, the Marshall Islands, and Kiribati —**Micronesian** *n., adj.*

mi·cro·or·ga·nism /ˌmaɪkroʊˈɔrgəˌnɪzəm/ *n.* [C] a

M

living thing that is so small that it cannot be seen without a microscope

mi·cro·phone /ˈmaɪkrəˌfoʊn/ *n.* [C] a piece of equipment that you hold in front of your mouth when you are singing, giving a speech etc. in order to make your voice sound louder or to record your voice

mi·cro·proc·es·sor /ˌmaɪkroʊˈprɑsɛsɚ/ *n.* [C] the central CHIP in a computer, that controls most of its operations

mi·cro·scope /ˈmaɪkrəˌskoʊp/ *n.* [C] **1** a scientific instrument that makes extremely small things appear large enough to be seen **2 under the microscope** being examined very closely and carefully: *The school district's finances were put under the microscope.* | *Jim felt like he was under the microscope whenever he was in Ted's presence.*

mi·cro·scop·ic /ˌmaɪkrəˈskɑpɪk/ *adj.* **1** extremely small and therefore very difficult to see: *Inspectors discovered microscopic cracks in the hull of the submarine.* **2** [only before noun] using a microscope: *The cells were identified through microscopic analysis.* —**microscopically** /-kli/ *adv.*

mi·cro·sec·ond /ˈmaɪkroʊˌsɛkənd/ *n.* [C] one millionth of a second

mi·cro·sur·ger·y /ˈmaɪkroʊˌsɚdʒəri/ *n.* [U] medical treatment in which very small instruments and LASERS are used

sw **mi·cro·wave**[1] /ˈmaɪkrəˌweɪv/ *n.* [C] **1** also **microwave oven** a type of OVEN that cooks food very quickly by using electric waves instead of heat —see picture at KITCHEN **2** a very short electric wave that is used in cooking food, sending messages by radio, and in RADAR

microwave[2] *v.* [T] to cook something in a microwave oven —**microwaveable, microwavable** /ˌmaɪkrəˈweɪvəbəl/ *adj.*

sw **mid-** /mɪd/ *prefix* in the middle of something: *She's in her mid-20s (=about 25 years old).* | *in mid-July* | *a cold midwinter night*

mid·air /ˌmɪdˈɛr/ *n.* **in midair** in the air or the sky, away from the ground: *These aircraft are able to refuel in midair.* —**midair** *adj.* [only before noun] *a midair collision*

Mi·das touch /ˈmaɪdəs ˌtʌtʃ/ *n.* **the Midas touch** if someone has the Midas touch, everything they do is successful and makes money for them: *Pavarotti is a unique performer with the Midas touch.*

mid-At·lan·tic /ˌ. .ˈ...◂/ *adj.* **mid-Atlantic states/region** the U.S. states that are on the Atlantic coast, for example Pennsylvania, Maryland, Delaware, and New Jersey, but that are not considered to be part of New England

mid·day /ˈmɪd-deɪ/ *n.* [U] the middle of the day, around 12:00 p.m.; NOON: *The wind was measured at 54 miles per hour at midday.* | *Details were to be given at a midday news conference.* —compare MIDNIGHT

sw **mid·dle**[1] /ˈmɪdl/ *n.* **1 the middle a)** the center part of a thing, place, or position: *Janet was on her knees in the middle of the floor.* | *Ken's in the middle, between Josie and Sue.* **b)** the part that is between the beginning and the end of an event, story, period of time etc.: *He was supposed to be back sometime in the middle of the week.* | *The furnace went out in the middle of winter.* **c)** the inside part of an object such as a ball, or piece of fruit: *The muffins have strawberry jam in the middle.* **d)** the position or rank that is between the highest and the lowest position in a list of people or things: *I guess I finished somewhere around the middle of my class.* **2 be in the middle of (doing) sth** to be busy doing something: *He's in the middle of a meeting.* | *I'm in the middle of fixing dinner – can I call you back?* **3** involved in a bad situation, especially an argument between two people: *Innocent people are caught in the middle of the war between the two factions.* **4 in the middle of nowhere** a long way from the nearest town or from any interesting places: *Michael lives way out in the middle of nowhere.* **5 divide/split sth down the middle** to divide something into equal halves or groups: *The vote was split right down the middle.* **6** [C usually singular] INFORMAL the waist and the part of the body around the stomach

---

USAGE NOTE: MIDDLE

WORD CHOICE: middle, center
Use both of these words to talk about where something is. The **middle** of something is the area or part that is farthest away from the sides or edges: *His clothes were in a heap in the middle of the floor.* The **center** cf something is exactly in the middle: *Put the vase in the center of the table.*

---

middle

Peter   Brad   Dwayne
Brad is in the middle.

middle[2] *adj.* [only before noun] **1** nearest to the center of something: *A white carpet ran down the middle aisle of the church.* | *It's in the middle drawer of the file cabinet.* **2** HALFWAY through an event or period of time: *I missed the middle part of the movie.* **3 middle brother/child/daughter etc.** the brother, child etc. who is between the oldest and the youngest **4 middle course/way/path etc.** a way of dealing with something that is between two opposite and often extreme ways: *Schoenfeld is steering a middle course between restoration and modernization of the building.* **5 Middle English/French etc.** an old form of English, French etc., used in the Middle Ages —see also MIDDLE FINGER, MIDDLE NAME

middle age /ˌ. ˈ./ *n.* [U] **1** the period of your life when you are not young anymore but are not yet old, from about age 40 to age 65: *The new technique allows women to have children well into middle age.* **2 the Middle Ages** the period in European history between the 5th and 15th centuries A.D.

middle-aged /ˌ. ˈ.◂/ *adj.* **1** not young anymore but not yet old, usually between the ages of around 40 to 65: *a middle-aged businessman* **2 middle-aged spread** an area of fat that many people develop around their waist as they grow older

Middle A·mer·i·ca /ˌ.. ˈ.../ *n.* [U] **1** the central part of the U.S.: *Asian immigrants have been moving into middle America in greater numbers.* **2** the part of American society that is neither rich nor poor, usually with traditional ideas and beliefs: *Car buyers in Middle America are looking for value and comfort.* —**middle American** *adj.*

mid·dle·brow, middle-brow /ˈmɪdlˌbraʊ/ *adj.* DISAPPROVING liked by ordinary people and not difficult to understand: *Yan's cooking program appeals to middlebrow cooks rather than gourmets.* —compare HIGHBROW, LOWBROW

middle C /ˌ.. ˈ./ *n.* [singular] the musical note C which is at the middle point of a piano KEYBOARD

middle class /ˌ.. ˈ.◂/ *n.* **the middle class** also **the middle classes** the social class that includes people who are neither rich nor poor: *Tuition increases will hit the middle class especially hard.* —compare LOWER CLASS, UPPER CLASS, WORKING CLASS

middle-class /ˌ.. ˈ.◂/ *adj.* **1** belonging to or typical of the middle class: *a middle-class neighborhood* | *The audience was mainly middle-class men.* **2** middle-class attitudes, values etc. are typical of middle-class people and are often concerned with work, education, and possessions: *a middle-class view of life*

middle dis·tance /ˌ.. '../ *n.* **the middle distance** the part of a picture or a view that is between the nearest part and the part that is farthest away: *Ezra leaned against the sink and stared off into the middle distance.*

middle-dis·tance /ˌ.. '..◂/ *adj.* [only before noun] a middle-distance race is neither very short nor very long, and a middle distance runner is someone who runs those races

middle ear /ˌ.. '../ *n.* [singular] the central part of the ear, between the outside part and the EARDRUM

Middle East /ˌ.. '..◂/ *n.* **the Middle East** the part of Asia that is between the Mediterranean Sea and the Arabian Sea, including countries such as Turkey and Iran —**Middle Eastern** *adj.* —compare FAR EAST

middle fin·ger /ˌ.. '../ *n.* [C] the longest finger, which is the middle one of the four fingers and thumb on your hand

middle ground /ˌ.. '../ *n.* [singular,U] something that two opposing groups can both agree about: *The two sides have shown no willingness to **find a middle ground.***

mid·dle·man /ˈmɪdlˌmæn/ *n. plural* **middlemen** /-ˌmɛn/ [C] someone who buys things in order to make a profit by selling them to someone else, or who helps to arrange business deals for other people: *Stanley worked as a middleman on U.S. and Soviet business deals.* | *Manufacturers are **cutting out the middleman** (=not using a middleman) and selling directly to customers.*

middle man·age·ment /ˌ.. '../ *n.* [U] managers who are in charge of small groups of people but do not make the most important decisions —**middle manager** *n.* [C]

middle name /ˌ.. '../ *n.* [C] **1** the name that, in English, comes between your first name and your family name **2 sth is sb's middle name** INFORMAL used to say that someone has a lot of a particular personal quality: *Don't worry – consistency is my middle name.* —compare FIRST NAME, LAST NAME

middle-of-the-road /ˌ.. . . . '.◂/ *adj.* middle-of-the-road ideas, opinions etc. are not extreme, so many people agree with them: *Wilson appealed to middle-of-the-road voters.*

middle school /ˈ.. ˌ./ *n.* [C,U] a school in the U.S. for children between the ages of 11 and 14, usually including grades 6 through 8th grade

middle-sized /ˌ.. '.◂/ *adj.* neither very large nor very small: *middle-sized cities*

mid·dle·weight /ˈmɪdlˌweɪt/ *n.* [C] a BOXER who weighs between 147 and 160 pounds (67 – 73 kilograms)

Middle West /ˌ.. '../ *n.* **the Middle West** another form of the Midwest

mid·dling /ˈmɪdlɪŋ/ *adj.* INFORMAL not very good or bad, not very big or small etc.; AVERAGE: *They've had only middling success.* | *Jonathan considers himself a **fair to middling** (=not very good) dessert maker.*

Mid·east /ˌmɪdˈist/ *n.* **the Mideast** another form of the Middle East

mid·field /ˈmɪdfild/ *n.* [U] the middle part of the area where a game such as football or SOCCER is played: *Jackson carried the ball out of bounds at midfield.*

mid·field·er /ˈmɪdˌfildɚ/ *n.* [C] a football or SOCCER player who usually plays in the midfield

midge /mɪdʒ/ *n.* [C] a small flying insect that bites people

midg·et¹ /ˈmɪdʒɪt/ *n.* [C] **1** OFFENSIVE a very small person who will never grow tall **2** someone or something that is very small: *The skyscraper is a midget by today's standards.*

midget² *adj.* **midget car/camera etc.** a very small car etc.

MIDI /ˈmɪdi/ *n.* [C] musical instrument digital interface; a system that allows computers to communicate with electronic musical instruments

mid·i /ˈmɪdi/ *adj.* **midi skirt/dress/coat** a skirt, dress etc. that comes to the middle of the lower leg

mid·life cri·sis /ˌmɪdlaɪf ˈkraɪsɪs/ *n.* [C] a period of

---

worry and lack of confidence that some people feel when they are about 40 or 50 years old: *Brook's latest film about a writer who's suffering a midlife crisis received poor reviews.*

mid·night /ˈmɪdnaɪt/ *n.* [U] 12 o'clock at night, or 12:00 a.m.: *The restaurant is open from 5 p.m. to midnight every day.* | *We always go to midnight mass on Christmas Eve.* —compare MIDDAY, NOON —see also **burn the midnight oil** (BURN¹ (14))

midnight sun /ˌ.. '../ *n.* **the midnight sun** the sun, seen in the middle of the night in summer in the far north or south of the world

mid·point /ˈmɪdpɔɪnt/ *n.* [C usually singular] a point that is HALFWAY through or along something: *The beach is about a mile long; at its midpoint are a snack bar and restrooms.*

mid·riff /ˈmɪdrɪf/ *n.* [C] the part of the body between your chest and your waist

mid·sec·tion /ˈmɪdˌsɛkʃən/ *n.* [C usually singular] the middle part of something or of someone's body: *There are 24 missiles in the submarine's midsection.*

mid·ship·man /mɪdˈʃɪpmən/ *n.* [C] someone who is training to become an officer in the Navy

mid·size /ˈmɪdsaɪz/ *adj.* [only before noun] of middle size; neither very large nor very small: *A midsize car rents for $35 a day.*

midst /mɪdst/ *n.* **1 in the midst of sth a)** in the middle of something such as a period, situation, or event: *Deb's in the midst of a messy divorce.* **b)** in the middle of a place or a group of things: *We stood in the midst of thousands of people.* **2 in sb's midst** FORMAL in a particular group of people: *They believe there are angels in our midst.*

mid·stream /ˌmɪdˈstrim◂/ *n.* [U] **1 in midstream** while something is happening or being done: *The employees found it difficult to adjust to changes in midstream.* —see also **change/switch horses in midstream** (HORSE¹ (3)) **2** the middle of a river or STREAM

mid·sum·mer /ˌmɪdˈsʌmɚ◂/ *n.* [U] the middle of summer: *Daylight hours are long in midsummer in Alaska.*

mid·term¹ /ˈmɪdtɚm/ *n.* **1** [C] a test that students take in the middle of a SEMESTER or QUARTER: *Alison has a history midterm next week.* **2** [U] the middle of the period when elected government officials are in power: *Nixon was the first president to resign in midterm.*

midterm² *adj.* [only before noun] **1** during or in the middle of a SEMESTER or QUARTER: *midterm exams* **2** during the middle of an elected government official's time in power: *midterm elections*

mid·town /ˈmɪdtaʊn/ *adj., adv.* in the area of a city that is near the center but is not the main business area: *a restaurant in midtown Manhattan* —**midtown** *n.* [U] —compare DOWNTOWN, UPTOWN

mid·way¹ /ˈmɪdˈweɪ◂/ *adj., adv.* **1** in the middle of a period of time or event: [+ **through**] *Shepherd scored six points midway through the second half of the game.* **2** at the middle point between two places or along a line: [+ **between/along**] *Both companies are located in a fast-growing area between Akron and Cleveland.*

mid·way² /ˈmɪdweɪ/ *n.* [C usually singular] the place where games, shows, and food are at a FAIR

Mid·way A·toll /ˌmɪdweɪ ˈætɔl/ two small islands in the Pacific Ocean northwest of Honolulu that are controlled by the U.S. and used as a U.S. military base

mid·week /ˌmɪdˈwik◂/ *adj., adv.* on one of the middle days of the week, such as Tuesday, Wednesday, or Thursday: *Many resorts offer midweek discounts.* | *A meeting is scheduled for midweek.*

Mid·west /ˌmɪdˈwɛst/ *n.* **the Midwest** the north-central area of the U.S., including states such as Iowa, Illinois, and Minnesota —**Midwestern** *adj.*

mid·wife /ˈmɪdwaɪf/ *n. plural* **midwives** /-waɪvz/ [C]

M

a specially trained nurse, usually a woman, whose job is to help women when they are having a baby

mid·wife·ry /ˈmɪd,waɪfəri, ˌmɪd'waɪ-/ n. [U] the skill or work of a midwife

mid·win·ter /ˌmɪd'wɪntə-/ n. [U] the middle of winter: *They crossed the Great Smoky Mountains in midwinter.* —**midwinter** adj. [only before noun] *a midwinter festival*

mid·year /ˈmɪdjɪr/ n. [U] the middle of the year: *Sales had improved by midyear.* —**midyear** adj. [only before noun] *a midyear review*

mien /min/ n. [singular,U] LITERARY someone's typical expression or way of behaving: *Endicott grew into a young man with a solemn mien.*

Mies van der Ro·he /ˌmis væn də 'roʊə, ˌmiz-/, **Lud·wig** /ˈlʊdwɪg/ (1886–1969) a U.S. architect, born in Germany, famous for his steel and glass buildings

miffed /mɪft/ adj. INFORMAL slightly annoyed or upset: *Tess was a little miffed that Sean didn't bother to call her.*

s w
1 1
might[1] /maɪt/ modal verb negative short form **mightn't** **1** used in order to talk about what is or was possible, when you cannot be certain: *Carrie might not be able to go.* | *This might help the pain a little bit.* | *He might have been outside.* **2** used instead of "may" when reporting what someone said or thought: *I thought it might rain, so I brought an umbrella.* | *She said she might call you tomorrow.* **3** used in CONDITIONAL sentences to show possibility: *If Hawaii is too expensive, we might go to Florida.* **4** used in order to give advice or make a suggestion: *You might try calling the store.* | *You **might want to** get your blood pressure checked.*

SPOKEN PHRASES

5 might as well a) used to say that you will do something even though you are not very interested in it or excited about it: *I might as well go with you – I don't have anything else to do.* **b)** used to suggest that someone should do something, because there will be no advantage in doing it differently: *By the time you've paid for postage, you **might as well** just buy it here.* **6 might I say/ask/ add etc.** also **I might say/add etc.** used to politely give more information, ask a question, interrupt etc.: *Whose underwear is that, might I ask?* | *I can't believe he would quit after three years of study – damn hard study, I might add.* **7** used when you are angry or surprised when someone did not do something that you think they should have done: *You might have at least said thank you.* **8 I might have known/ guessed etc.** used to say that you are not surprised at a situation: *I might have known you'd never finish.* **9** OLD-FASHIONED used to ask politely if you can do something: *Might I come in?* **10** OLD-FASHIONED, HUMOROUS used to politely ask for information: *And who might you be, young man?*

---

11 might well if something might well happen or might well be true you think it is fairly likely to happen or be true: *McCarthy might well have difficulty raising the money.* **12 might...but...** used to tell someone that although what they said is true, something else which seems very different is also a fact: *You might be a strong swimmer, but that doesn't mean you can win a triathlon.* **13** LITERARY used to say why something happens or the reason why someone does something: *Samuel left his children a letter, so that they might understand why he had to go away.* —compare MAY —see also **try as sb might** (TRY[1] (8))

might[2] n. [U] LITERARY **1** strength and power: *The full might of the army could not defeat them.* | *She tried **with all her might** to push him away.* **2 might makes right** used to say that powerful people and countries can do whatever they want

might-have-beens /ˈmaɪtə,bɪnz, -tʌv-/ n. [plural] things that you wish had happened in the past but which never did

M

might·i·ly /ˈmaɪtəli/ adv. **1** a lot or to a great degree: *The country has changed mightily in recent years.*

2 [+ adj./adv.] very: *Parkman was **mightily** impressed with the wildlife and open spaces of America's West.* **3** using great strength and determination: *Taylor has struggled mightily to help her daughter.*

might·n't /ˈmaɪtʰnt/ v. OLD-FASHIONED the short form of "might not": *He mightn't like it.*

might·y[1] /ˈmaɪti/ adj. **mightier, mightiest** ESPECIALLY LITERARY very strong and powerful, or very big and impressive: *the mighty Mississippi river* | *mighty warriors* —see also **high and mighty** (HIGH[1] (19))

mighty[2] adv. [+ adj./adv.] SPOKEN very: *You seem mighty sure of it.* | *That's a mighty big fish.* | *They got out of there mighty fast, I can tell you.*

mi·graine /ˈmaɪgreɪn/ n. [C] an extremely bad HEADACHE, during which you feel sick and have pain behind your eyes

mi·grant /ˈmaɪgrənt/ n. [C] **1** someone who goes to another area or country, especially in order to find work: *Historically, California has welcomed migrants from other states and nations.* | ***Migrant workers** still live in poor quality housing.* | *Officials said they did not know whether the people were **economic migrants** (=people who go to another country to find better jobs and living conditions) or political refugees.* —compare EMIGRANT, IMMIGRANT **2** TECHNICAL a bird or animal that travels from one part of the world to another, especially in the fall and spring

mi·grate /ˈmaɪgreɪt/ v. [I] **1** if birds or animals migrate, they travel from one part of the world to another, especially in the fall and spring: *More than 2 million ducks migrate to the lake each fall.* **2** to go to another area or country, usually in order to find a place to live or work: *The first Americans migrated across the Bering land bridge more than 10,000 years ago.* —see Usage Note at EMIGRATE

mi·gra·tion /maɪ'greɪʃən/ n. [C,U] the movement from one place to another of a large group of people, birds, animals etc.: *the yearly migration of geese*

Mik·a·su·ki, Miccosukee /ˌmɪkə'suki/ a Native American tribe from the southwestern area of the U.S.

mike[1] /maɪk/ n. [C] INFORMAL a MICROPHONE —see also OPEN MIKE

mike[2] v. [T] to attach a MICROPHONE to someone or something: *All the instruments are miked.*

mi·la·dy /mɪ'leɪdi/ n. [singular] LITERARY a way of politely speaking to a woman who is of a higher social class

mild /maɪld/ adj.
1 small effect not having a serious or severe effect: *"Damn" is now only a mild swear word.* | *a mild earthquake* | *The doctor thinks Geri has a mild concussion.* | *Steve had a **mild case of** food poisoning.*
2 food/taste not very strong-tasting or SPICY: *a mild salsa* | *Lentils have a mild nutty flavor.* —compare MEDIUM[1] (3), HOT (3)
3 weather not too cold or wet: *Sunny skies and mild temperatures are predicted.* | *We had a pretty mild winter last year.* —opposite HARD[1] (19)
4 punishment/criticism not severe or strict: *a mild rebuke*
5 soap etc. soft and gentle to your skin: *Use water and a mild detergent to scrub the mud off.*
6 character/manner OLD-FASHIONED having a gentle character and not easily getting angry: *Joe was a mild man who rarely raised his voice.* —see also MILDLY

mil·dew /ˈmɪldu/ n. [U] a white or gray FUNGUS (=simple type of plant without leaves) that grows on walls, leather, or other surfaces in warm, slightly wet places —**mildewed** adj.

mild·ly /ˈmaɪldli/ adv. **1** slightly: *McKee was only mildly interested.* **2 to put it mildly** SPOKEN said when you are saying something bad in the most polite way that you can: *He's a troubled youngster, **to put it mildly**.* **3** in a gentle way without being angry: *"Perhaps," she answered mildly.*

mild-man·nered /ˌ. '...·/ adj. gentle and polite: *a mild-mannered, kind man*

mile /maɪl/ *n.* [C] **1** a unit for measuring distance or length, equal to 1760 yards or 1609 meters: *Dane's father lives about a mile from here.* | *Mark jogs at least five miles a day.* | *The car gets about thirty miles to the gallon.* **2 miles** INFORMAL a very long distance: *The campsite is miles from anywhere.* | *The traffic was backed up for miles* (=for a very long distance). | *They finally found him, wandering around miles from home.* | *For some reason they decided to buy a house that's miles from nowhere* (=a long way from the nearest town). **3 talk a mile a minute** SPOKEN to talk very quickly without stopping **4 go the extra mile** to try a little harder in order to achieve something, after you have already used a lot of effort: *The President vowed to go the extra mile for peace in the region.* **5 miss/beat sth by a mile** to miss or be better than something by a large amount or distance: *This chocolate beats Hershey's by a mile.* **6 join the mile-high club** SPOKEN, HUMOROUS to have sex on an airplane **7 the mile** a race that is a mile in length: *He's the world record holder in the mile.* —see also NAUTICAL MILE

mile·age /ˈmaɪlɪdʒ/ *n.* [U] **1** the number of miles a vehicle has traveled since it was made or since another particular time: *a used car with low mileage* | *The rental car costs $35 a day, with unlimited mileage.* | *I set the mileage each time I get gas.* **2** also **gas mileage** the number of miles a vehicle can travel using each GALLON of gasoline: *The Geo gets pretty good mileage.* **3** the advantage or use that you get from something: *Mitchell was trying to decide which ideas still had some mileage left in them.* | *Perry got some good comic mileage out of a stuffed fish* (=he made several jokes about it) *in the opening scene.* **4** an amount of money paid for each mile that is traveled by someone using a car for work: *I get paid for mileage.* | *Varsity coaches' mileage allowance will be increased to 26¢.* **5** a distance in miles that is covered by something: *By adding another city to the network, we can actually decrease the mileage of cable needed.*

mile·post /ˈmaɪlpoʊst/ *n.* [C] **1** a small sign next to a road that marks distances by miles **2** a MILESTONE (1)

mil·er /ˈmaɪlə/ *n.* [C] a person or horse that competes in one-mile races

mile·stone /ˈmaɪlstoʊn/ *n.* [C] **1** a very important event in the development of something: *Graduation and marriage are important milestones in people's lives.* | *[+ in] The bill is an important milestone in preserving America's natural resources.* **2** a stone next to a road that shows the distance in miles to another town

mi·lieu /mil'yu, mil'yʊ/ *n.* [C] FORMAL the things and people that surround you and influence the way you live and think: *Lester lives and works in an academic milieu.*

mil·i·tant /ˈmɪlətənt/ *adj.* a militant organization or person is willing to use extreme methods in order to achieve political or social change: *militant nationalists* | *After the assassination of Martin Luther King, black leaders became more militant.* —**militant** *n.* [C] —**militancy** *n.* [U] —**militantly** *adv.*

mil·i·ta·rism /ˈmɪlɪtəˌrɪzəm/ *n.* [U] the belief that a country should increase its military forces and use them to get what it wants —**militarist** *n.* [C] —**militaristic** /ˌmɪlɪtəˈrɪstɪk/ *adj.*

mil·i·ta·rized /ˈmɪlɪtəˌraɪzd/ *adj.* a militarized area is one that has a lot of soldiers and weapons in it —compare DEMILITARIZE

mil·i·tar·y¹ /ˈmɪləˌteri/ *adj.* [only before noun, no comparative] relating to or used by the army, navy, air force, Marine Corps, or Coast Guard, or relating to war: *a military helicopter* | *German military power was restricted after World War II.* | *The government warned about the possibility of future military action.* | *Leaders are concerned about racism in the nation's military forces* (=the army, navy etc.). | **military school/academy** *We are going to send our 15-year-old son to military school.* —**militarily** *adv.*

military² *n.* **the military** the military organizations of a country, such as the army and navy: *The military*

took over when police were unable to stop the rioting. | *There have been many studies of women in the military* (=in the army, navy etc.).

military in·tel·li·gence /ˌ.... '.../ *n.* [U] information about what another country's military forces plan to do, which is usually obtained secretly

military po·lice /ˌ.... '.../ *n.* [plural] a police force in the military forces whose job is to deal with members of the army etc. who break the rules —see also MP (1)

mil·i·tate /ˈmɪləˌteɪt/ *v.*
militate against sth *phr. v.* [T] FORMAL to prevent something or make it less likely to happen: *Environmental factors militate against developments in this area.*
militate for sth *phr. v.* [T] FORMAL to make something possible or more likely to happen: *Conflicts between Indians and settlers in Ecuador militated for land reform laws in the 1950s.*

mi·li·tia /məˈlɪʃə/ *n.* [C] **1** a group of people trained as soldiers, who are not part of the permanent army **2** a group of people who disagree with some of the U.S. government's actions, and who often live as a group in a country area and practice fighting with guns and other weapons

mi·li·tia·man /məˈlɪʃəmən/ *n.* [C] a member of a militia

milk¹ /mɪlk/ *n.* [U] **1** a white liquid that people drink, usually produced by cows, goats, or sheep: *a glass of milk* | *We need more milk.* **2** a white liquid produced by female animals and women for feeding their babies **3** a liquid or juice produced by certain plants, especially the COCONUT **4 the milk of human kindness** LITERARY ordinary kindness and sympathy for other people —see also **cry over spilled milk** (CRY¹ (6)), EVAPORATED MILK, **land of milk and honey** (LAND¹ (6)), SKIM MILK

milk² *v.* [T] **1** to take milk from a cow or goat **2** INFORMAL to get all the money or advantages etc. that you can from a situation, person, or thing: **[milk sb for sth]** *Vacationers at state parks have been milked for cash for the last decade.* **3** to take the poison from a snake

milk choc·o·late /ˌ. '.../ *n.* [U] chocolate made with milk and sugar

milk cow /ˈ. ./ *n.* [C] a cow kept to give milk rather than for meat

milking ma·chine /ˈ.. ./ *n.* [C] a machine used for taking milk from cows

milking par·lor /ˈ.. ./ *n.* [C] a building on a farm where milk is taken from the cows

milk·maid /ˈmɪlkmeɪd/ *n.* [C] OLD USE a woman who gets milk from cows on a farm

milk·man /ˈmɪlkmæn/ *n.* plural **milkmen** /-mɛn/ [C] someone who delivers milk to houses each morning

milk of mag·ne·sia /ˌ. . ... ./ *n.* [U] a thick white liquid medicine used for stomach problems and CONSTIPATION

milk run /ˈ. ./ *n.* [C] INFORMAL a train trip or regular airplane flight that stops in many places

milk·shake /ˈmɪlkʃeɪk/ *n.* [C] a drink made of milk, ICE CREAM, and fruit or chocolate

milk·sop /ˈmɪlksɑp/ *n.* [C] OLD-FASHIONED a boy or man who is too gentle and weak, and who is afraid to do anything dangerous

milk·weed /ˈmɪlkwid/ *n.* [U] a common North American plant that produces a bitter white substance when its stem is broken

milk·y /ˈmɪlki/ *adj.* **1** a drink that is milky contains a lot of milk: *milky coffee* **2** water or other liquids that are milky are not clear and look like milk: *The tree has a milky sap.* **3** milky skin is white and smooth —**milkiness** *n.* [U]

Milky Way /ˌ. '. / *n.* **the Milky Way** the pale white band in space that consists of a large number of stars, that you can see across the sky at night

mill¹ /mɪl/ *n.* [C] **1** a building containing a large machine for crushing grain into flour, or the machine itself: *an old mill with a ruined water-wheel* **2** a factory where materials such as paper, steel, or cotton cloth are made: *a lumber mill* **3 coffee/ pepper mill** a small machine or tool for crushing coffee or pepper **4 go through the mill** to go through a time when you experience a lot of difficulties and problems, or to make someone go through such a time: *Busiack has been through the mill with these federal investigators.* **5 put sb through the mill** to make someone answer a lot of difficult questions or do a lot of difficult things in order to test them: *Candidates are put through the mill by the Senate.* **6** TECHNICAL a unit of money equal to $^1/_{10}$ of a cent, used in setting taxes and for other financial purposes **7** SPOKEN a short form of "million": *The movie has earned almost $2 mill in the first weekend.* —see also **grist for the mill** (GRIST), **the rumor mill** (RUMOR (2)), RUN-OF-THE-MILL

mill² *v.* [T] **1** to produce flour by crushing grain in a mill **2** to press, roll, or shape metal in a machine **3** TECHNICAL to mark the edge of a coin with regular lines **4** if a lot of people mill around, they move around a place in different directions without any particular purpose: *Harrison joined a crowd of about 5000 milling outside the radio station.* | [+ around/ about] *Neighborhood residents milled around and watched from front steps and balconies.*

Mill /mɪl/, **John Stu·art** /dʒɑn 'stuət/ (1806–1873) a British PHILOSOPHER and ECONOMIST

Mil·lay /mɪ'leɪ/, **Ed·na St. Vin·cent** /'ɛdnə seɪnt 'vɪnsənt/ (1892–1950) a U.S. poet

mil·len·ni·um /mə'lɛniəm/ *n. plural* **millennia** /-niə/ **1** [C] a period of 1000 years **2** [C usually singular] the time when a new 1000-year period begins, for example on January 1, 2000: *What did you do to celebrate the millennium?* **3 the millennium** the time in the future when Christians believe that Jesus Christ will return and rule on Earth for 1000 years —**millennial** *adj.*

mill·er /'mɪlɚ/ *n.* [C] OLD USE someone who owns or operates a mill that makes flour

Mil·ler /'mɪlɚ/, **Arthur** (1915–) a U.S. writer of plays that deal with political or moral problems

Miller, Henry (1891–1980) a U.S. writer of NOVELS

mil·let /'mɪlət/ *n.* [U] a plant similar to grass, with small seeds that are used as food

milli- /mɪlə/ *prefix* 1/1000th part of a particular unit: *a milliliter* (=1/1000th of a liter)

mil·li·bar /'mɪlə,bɑr/ *n.* [C] TECHNICAL a unit for measuring the pressure of air

mil·li·gram /'mɪlə,græm/ *written abbreviation* **mg** *n.* [C] a unit for measuring weight, equal to 1/1000th of a gram

mil·li·li·ter /'mɪlə,litɚ/ *written abbreviation* **ml** *n.* [C] a unit for measuring the amount of a liquid, equal to 1/1000th of a liter

mil·li·me·ter /'mɪlə,mitɚ/ *written abbreviation* **mm** *n.* [C] a unit for measuring length, equal to 1/1000th of a meter

mil·li·ner /'mɪlənɚ/ *n.* [C] someone who makes and sells women's hats

mil·li·ner·y /'mɪlə,nɛri/ *n.* [U] **1** a word meaning "hats," used in stores and in the fashion industry **2** the activity of making women's hats

mil·lion /'mɪlyən/ *plural* **million** *or* **millions** *number, quantifier* **1** 1,000,000: *three million dollars* | *a population of 12 million people* **2** also **millions** an extremely large number of people or things: *Millions of people will be affected by the tax changes.* | *He made millions* (=a lot of money) *on that deal.* | *I've heard that excuse a million times.* **3 not/never in a million years** SPOKEN said in order to emphasize how impossible or unlikely something is: *I never would have guessed in a million years!* **4 one in a million** INFORMAL **a)** the best of all possible people or things: *Sherry spent her life helping people – she was one in a million.* **b)** used to show how unlikely something

is: *Archaeology students made a one in a million find when they uncovered an ancient lost monument.* **5 feel/look like a million bucks/dollars** INFORMAL to look very attractive or feel very happy and healthy: *I felt like a million bucks in that tux.* —**millionth** *adj., pron., n.* —see Usage Note at HUNDRED[1]

mil·lion·aire /,mɪlyə'nɛr/ *n.* [C] someone who is very rich and has at least one million dollars

mil·lion·air·ess /,mɪlyə'nɛrɪs/ *n.* [C] OLD-FASHIONED a woman who is very rich and has at least one million dollars

mil·li·pede /'mɪlə,pid/ *n.* [C] a long thin insect with a lot of legs

mill·pond /'mɪlpɑnd/ *n.* [C] a very small lake that supplies water to turn the wheel of a WATER MILL

mill·stone /'mɪlstoʊn/ *n.* [C] **1** one of the two large circular stones that crush grain into flour in a MILL **2 a millstone (around your neck)** something that causes you a lot of problems and prevents you from doing what you would like to do: *The President's past has become a millstone around his neck.*

Milne /mɪln/, **A.A.** (1882–1956) a British writer best known for his books for children

milque·toast /'mɪlktoʊst/ *n.* [C] OLD-FASHIONED, HUMOROUS a weak, quiet man with no courage; WIMP

Mil·ton /'mɪlt'n/, **John** (1608–1674) an English poet who is best known for his EPIC poem "Paradise Lost"

Mil·wau·kee /mɪl'wɔki/ the largest city in the U.S. state of Wisconsin

mime¹ /maɪm/ *n.* **1** [C,U] the use of actions or movements to express what you want to say without using words: *Clark is wonderful in the role, which is mostly mime and dance.* **2** [C] an actor who performs without using words **3** [C] a performance in which no words are used: *One performer did a silly mime during the overture.*

mime² *v.* [I,T] to perform something using actions and movements without any words: *They mimed a tug of war.*

mim·e·o·graph /'mɪmiə,græf/ *v.* [T] to copy a letter, paper etc. on a special machine, using a special ink: *Students worked on mimeographed worksheets.* —**mimeograph** also **mimeograph ma·chine** /'.... ,.../ *n.* [C]

mi·met·ic /mɪ'mɛtɪk/ *adj.* TECHNICAL copying the movements or appearance of someone or something else

mim·ic¹ /'mɪmɪk/ *v. past tense and past participle* **mimicked** [T] **1** to copy the way someone speaks, moves, or behaves, especially in order to make people laugh: *Jackson mimicked a foreign accent to make his point.* **2** to behave or operate in exactly the same way as something or someone else: *The taste and texture mimic that of ice cream, without all the fat.* **3** if an animal mimics something, it tries to look or sound like something in order to protect itself: *This insect mimics the appearance of a wasp.* —**mimicry** *n.* [U]

mimic² *n.* [C] **1** a performer who copies the way famous people speak or behave **2** a person or animal that is good at copying the movements, sound, or appearance of someone or something else: *Parrots are excellent mimics.*

mi·mo·sa /mɪ'moʊsə/ *n.* [C,U] **1** a small tree that grows in hot countries and has small yellow flowers **2** a drink that is a mixture of CHAMPAGNE and orange juice

min. *n.* **1** the written abbreviation of MINIMUM **2** the written abbreviation of "minute" or "minutes"

min·a·ret /,mɪnə'rɛt, 'mɪnərɛt/ *n.* [C] a tall thin tower on a MOSQUE from which Muslims are called to prayer

min·a·to·ry /'mɪnə,tɔri/ *adj.* FORMAL threatening

mince /mɪns/ *v.* **1** [T] to cut food into extremely small pieces: *Mince the garlic and add to the onion.* **2 not mince words** to say exactly what you think, even if this may offend people: *If Sara doesn't like somebody, she doesn't mince words.* **3** [I always + adv./prep.] to walk in an unnatural way, taking short steps and moving your HIPS: [+ across/down/ along etc.] *Fashion models minced down the runway in the latest designs.*

mince·meat /ˈmɪnsmit/ *n.* [U] **1** a mixture of apples, dried fruit, and SPICEs, but no meat, used in PIES **2 make mincemeat (out) of sb** INFORMAL to completely defeat someone in an argument, fight, or game: *The mayor will make mincemeat of DeCarlini in the election.*

s w **mind**[1] /maɪnd/ *n.*

1 [C,U] your thoughts, or the part of your brain used for thinking and imagining thing: *Grandma's body is wearing out, but her mind is as sharp as ever.* | *It's hard to understand what's going on in Susanna's mind.*
2 change your mind to change your opinion or decision about something: *Use a pencil so you can erase it if you change your mind.* | [+ **about/on**] *Garcia changed his mind about attending after speaking to Williams.*
3 make up your mind a) to decide something, especially after thinking for a long time about your choices: *It was such a good offer, it only took me about 30 seconds to make up my mind.* | [+ **about/on**] *Chet hasn't made up his mind about running for Congress.* | [+ **whether/which/what**] *I can't make up my mind whether I want to drive or fly home for Christmas.* | *Have you made up your mind which college you want to go to?* **b)** to become very determined to do something, so that you will not change your decision: *I made up my mind I was going to retire.* | [**make up your mind to do sth**] *Once she made her mind up to go, there was no stopping her.* | [+ **that**] *We made up our minds that, if business didn't get better by June, we'd sell it.*
4 have sth/sb in mind to be thinking about or considering a particular person, plan etc. for a particular purpose: *If you have a major purchase in mind, wait for it to come on sale.*
5 keep/bear sth in mind to remember a fact or piece of information, especially because it will be useful to you or will affect you in the future: *It's a good idea – I'll keep it in mind.* | *Bear in mind that April 15th is the tax deadline.*
6 with sth/sb in mind while thinking about something or someone or considering them: *The hospital was designed with children in mind.*
7 on your mind a) if something is on your mind, you keep thinking about it and worrying about it: *You look worried, Sarah. Is there something on your mind?* | *He just found out his 15-year-old daughter is pregnant, so he has a lot on his mind* (=has a lot of problems to worry about). | *Her husband's illness was weighing on her mind* (=making her worry). **b)** if something is on your mind, that is what you are thinking about: *She just says what's on her mind.* | *I had a few questions on my mind when I went to see him.*
8 go out of your mind also **lose your mind** INFORMAL to start to become mentally ill or behave in a strange way: *If I have to wait in one more line, I'm going to go out of my mind.* | *I'm with the kids all day, and I'm starting to feel like I'm losing my mind.*
9 come/spring/leap to mind [not in progressive] if something comes or springs to mind, you think of it, especially suddenly: *When I was looking for a low-fat dessert, fruit compotes came to mind.*
10 bring/call sth to mind to remind you of something: *Each ornament on their Christmas tree brings to mind the friend or relative that gave it.* | *Wiesel's speech called to mind the victims of the Holocaust.*
11 cross/enter your mind (that) [not in progressive] if something crosses or enters your mind, you have a particular thought or idea, especially for a short time: *In her grief, thoughts of suicide crossed her mind.* | *It didn't enter my mind to ask for it.* | *The thought never crossed my mind that I could just not do anything to help.*
12 in your right mind sensible and making good decisions: *Who in their right mind would want to rock climb without a rope?* | *The place is falling apart – no one in their right mind would want to live here.*
13 intelligence [C usually singular] intelligence and ability to think rather than emotions; INTELLECT: *Peacher has an incredibly good mind.* | *I don't really have a scientific mind.* | [+ **for**] *Sandra has a good mind for numbers.*

14 intelligent person [C] someone who is very intelligent, especially in a particular area of study or activity: *Cuomo is one of our foremost political minds.*
15 character [C] a particular way of thinking that is part of someone's character: *O'Rourke has a very devious mind.*
16 keep your mind on sth to keep paying attention to something even if it is boring or if you want to think about something else: *With all the talk of job losses, I was having trouble keeping my mind on my work.*
17 sb's mind is not on sth to not be thinking about what you are doing, because you are thinking or worrying about something else: *I was trying to study, but my mind just wasn't on it.*
18 take/get/keep your mind off sth to make yourself stop thinking about something that is worrying you: *I was nervous on the day of the game and went to a movie to take my mind off it.*
19 be a load/weight off your mind to be something that you do not need to worry about anymore: *"Emotionally, it's a huge weight off my mind," said Hughes after the court judgment.*
20 get/push/block sb/sth out of your mind to stop thinking about someone or something, or try to forget them: *It's like when you have a crush on somebody and can't get them out of your mind.* | *Cary says he's trying to put the rumors out of his mind.*
21 be the last thing on sb's mind to be the thing that someone is least likely to be thinking about: *Marriage is the last thing on my mind right now.*
22 your mind goes blank if your mind goes blank, you suddenly cannot remember something: *As soon as Mr. Daiche asked me the question, my mind just went blank.*

SPOKEN PHRASES

23 be out of your mind to behave in a way that is crazy or stupid: *You'd be out of your mind to sell it now.* | *Are you out of your mind?*
24 bored out of your mind INFORMAL extremely bored: *The kids were bored out of their minds this summer.*
25 stoned/drunk etc. out of your mind affected by drugs or alcohol so that you do not really know what you are doing
26 there's no doubt/question in my mind used when you are very sure about something: *There's no doubt in my mind that she'll be high school All-American in her senior year.*
27 great minds think alike used to say in a joking way that you and someone else must be very intelligent because you both agree about something or you have both thought of something
28 have half a mind to do sth also **have a good mind to do sth a)** used as a not very serious threat when you want to show your disapproval of what someone has done: *I have a good mind to ground you for months, after what you've done.* **b)** used when you are considering doing something, but are not sure you will do it: *I have half a mind to just go home.*
29 in/to my mind used when you are giving your opinion about something: *In my mind, his actions amount to criminal fraud.*

30 at/in the back of your mind if something is at the back of your mind, you keep remembering it or feeling it, but you do not think about it directly: *I was hurt that she'd left, but I guess at the back of my mind I always knew she would.*
31 give sb a piece of your mind INFORMAL to tell someone how angry you are with them: *If one of the kids is being sassy, Inez gives them a piece of her mind.*
32 state/frame of mind the way someone is thinking and feeling at a particular time, such as how happy or sad they are: *What was his state of mind on the day of the shooting?* | *He went off to work in a pleasant frame of mind.*
33 keep/have an open mind (about sth) also **do**

M

sth **with an open mind** to be willing to think about and accept new ideas or ways of doing things: *Kypriani has an open mind on the subject of marijuana legalization.* —see also OPEN-MINDED

34 have a mind of your own a) to decide on your opinions and make your own decisions: *Joey's only two, but he has a mind of his own.* **b)** if you say that an object has a mind of its own, it seems as though that thing is moving or doing something that you do not want it to do: *My hair seems to have a mind of its own today.*

35 be of two minds about sth to be unable to make a decision about something, or to not be sure what you think of something: *Americans are of two minds about the proposed health care changes.*

36 be of sound mind LAW to have the ability to think clearly and be responsible for your actions

37 put/set sb's mind at ease/rest to make someone feel less worried or anxious: *Call your mom and tell her you're here, just to set her mind at rest.*

38 sth is all/just in sb's mind used to tell someone that they have imagined something and it does not really exist: *At first, doctors said the illness was all in her mind.*

39 your mind wanders if your mind WANDERS, you stop paying attention to something, especially because you are bored

40 be of one/the same/like mind FORMAL to agree with someone about something: *I think we're of one mind that the service should be maintained.* | [+ on/ about] *The seven European leaders are not of the same mind on the issue of trade.*

41 have a closed mind (about sth) to refuse to think about or accept new ideas or ways of doing things

42 know your own mind to be very clear about what your opinions or beliefs are and not be influenced by what other people think

43 in your mind's eye if you see something in your mind's eye, you can imagine what it looks like because you remember it: *I can't remember her name, but I can clearly see her in my mind's eye.*

44 mind over matter an expression used when someone uses their intelligence to control a difficult situation

45 have it in mind to do sth to intend to do something: *Bill said he had it in mind to drop out of school and see the world.*

46 put you in mind of sb/sth [not in progressive] to remind you of a person or thing: *Petra's orange hair will put you in mind of Little Orphan Annie.*

47 put/set your mind to sth to decide to do something, and use a lot of effort in order to succeed: *You can do anything if you just set your mind to it.*

48 pay sb/sth no mind OLD-FASHIONED to not pay any attention to someone or something or not care about what they are saying or doing: *Most people paid no mind to the marchers.* —see also **sth blows your mind** (BLOW[1] (7)), **the mind boggles** (BOGGLE), **sb/sth drives sb out of their mind** (DRIVE[1] (8)), **meeting of (the) minds** (MEETING (5)), -MINDED, ONE-TRACK MIND, **peace of mind** (PEACE (3)), PRESENCE OF MIND, **read sb's mind/thoughts** (READ[1] (10)), **out of sight, out of mind** (SIGHT[1] (14)), **slip your mind** (SLIP[1] (7)), **speak your mind** (SPEAK (6)), **stick in sb's mind** (STICK[1] (5)), **turn sth over in your mind** at turn over TURN[1]

s w **mind**[2] *v.*

1️⃣
2️⃣

1 feel annoyed [I,T not in progressive or passive, usually in questions and negatives] to feel annoyed, worried, or angry about something: *Are you sure your mother doesn't mind?* | *Of course I don't mind if you bring a few friends over.* | [mind sth] *I don't mind the winter – I like the snow.* | [mind sb doing sth] *I don't mind them coming as long as they behave.* | [mind that] *David says his parents don't mind that he spends so much time on his computer.*

M

SPOKEN PHRASES

2 would/do you mind used to ask someone something politely: [would/do you mind doing sth]

Would you mind opening the window, please? | [would/do you mind if] *Do you mind if I call my mom?*

3 never mind a) used in order to tell someone that something was not important or that you do not want to say something again: *"What did you say?" "Oh, never mind."* | *"I was already planning to have chicken tonight." "Oh, never mind, it was just an idea."* **b)** used to tell someone not to do something or to not pay attention to something you have said: *Oh, Dad, never mind, Cheryl's got them.* | *I need to get Miriam's number from Steve... oh, here it is, never mind.* | *Never mind the dishes – I'll do them later.* **c)** used to tell someone that something does not really matter: *This is food at its best. Never mind that the service still needs work.* **d)** used to emphasize that something is impossible, because something that should be easier or better is also impossible: *He was ashamed to tell his family, never mind a stranger.* **e)** used to say that something is much less important than something else: *I'll take it, never mind the cost!* | [+ about] *Never mind about baseball and football, say fans of soccer.*

4 not mind doing sth to be willing to do something: *San Diego's nice, I wouldn't mind living there.* | *I don't mind driving if you're tired.*

5 if you don't mind used when checking that someone is willing to do something or let you do something: *I'm going to close the window, if you don't mind.*

6 mind your own business/beeswax to not get involved in or ask questions about other people's lives or personal details: *I was just standing there minding my own business and this kid comes up and starts being a smart aleck.* | *Mom, mind your own beeswax.*

7 don't mind me used to tell someone not to pay any attention to you: *Oh, don't mind me, I was just thinking out loud.*

8 do you mind! used when you are annoyed at something that someone has done: *Do you mind! I just washed that floor!*

9 mind you used to say something that emphasizes what you are talking about: *It wasn't excellent, mind you, but it was a definite improvement.*

10 (I) don't mind if I do HUMOROUS used when politely accepting something such as food or drink that has been offered to you: *"Would you like another piece of cake?" "Thanks – don't mind if I do."*

11 mind your manners/p's and q's to be careful about how you behave so that you do not offend anyone: *If I want federal funding I'd better mind my p's and q's.* | *Corey, mind your manners.*

12 obey [T not in progressive] to obey someone's instructions or advice: *Some dogs will mind instructions better than others.*

13 mind the store to be in charge of something, especially while the person who is usually in charge is not there: *Congressmen, embarrassed that they had not been minding the store, moved to prevent future scandals.*

14 take care of [T] OLD-FASHIONED to take care of a child, especially for someone else; WATCH[1] (3): *He spends as much time as his wife minding the children.*

mind-bend·ing /'. ,../ *adj.* INFORMAL strange and difficult to understand: *The forms have a page of mind-bending charts to help you figure out your tax.*

mind-blow·ing /'. ,../ *adj.* INFORMAL very exciting, shocking, or strange: *The astronauts had mind-blowing views of planet Earth.* —see also **sth blows your mind** (BLOW[1] (7))

mind-bog·gling /'maɪndˌbɑgəlɪŋ/ *adj.* INFORMAL strange or complicated, and difficult to imagine or believe: *The amount of logging being done in national forests is mind-boggling.*

-minded /maɪndɪd/ [in adjectives] **1 safety-minded/ efficiency-minded etc.** believing in the importance of safety etc.: *a budget-minded traveler* **2 serious-minded/evil-minded etc.** having a particular attitude or way of thinking: *an independent-minded little girl* —see also ABSENT-MINDED, NARROW-MINDED, OPEN-MINDED, SIMPLEMINDED, SINGLE-MINDED

mind·ful /'maɪndfəl/ *adj.* FORMAL behaving in a way

that shows you remember a rule or fact: [+ **of**] *City officials said they were mindful of the neighborhood's needs.*

mind games /'. ./ *n.* [plural] words and actions that are intended to make someone feel confused, less confident, and unhappy: *Jamal likes to play mind games with all of his girlfriends.*

mind·less /'maɪndlɪs/ *adj.* **1** so simple that you do not have to think carefully about it: *Stuffing envelopes is mindless work.* **2** completely stupid and without any purpose: *The movie is full of mindless violence.* —**mindlessly** *adv.* —**mindlessness** *n.* [U]

mind read·er /'. ,../ *n.* [C] OFTEN HUMOROUS someone who knows what someone else is thinking without being told: *Your mother-in-law is no mind reader – tell her how you feel.*

mind·set /'maɪndsɛt/ *n.* [C usually singular] someone's way of thinking about things, which is often difficult to change: *The book accurately captures the mindset of a teenage girl.*

s w mine¹ /maɪn/ *possessive pron.* [possessive form of "I"] the thing or things belonging or relating to the person who is speaking: *"Whose coat is this?" "It's mine."* | *Louisa didn't have a pencil, so I let her borrow mine.* | *Tom's a good friend of mine.*

s w mine² *n.* [C] **1** a type of bomb that is hidden below the surface of the ground or in the water, which explodes when someone or something touches it: *Many countries have recently banned the production of land mines.* **2** a deep hole or series of holes in the ground from which coal, gold etc. is dug: *an old gold mine* —compare QUARRY¹ (1) —see also STRIP MINE **3 a mine of information/gossip etc.** someone who knows a lot about something or something that tells you a lot about a subject: *The letters are a mine of information about the period.* **4** TECHNICAL a passage dug beneath the place where an enemy army is

mine³ *v.* **1** [I,T] to dig into the ground in order to get gold, coal etc.: [+ **for**] *Explorers have been mining for gold in this area for several years.* **2** [T often passive] to hide bombs in the ocean or under the ground: *The border is heavily mined.* **3** [T] to get information, ideas etc. from something: *Simon mines his childhood experiences for his plays.*

mine⁴ *determiner* OLD USE a way of saying "my," before a vowel sound or "h," or after a noun: *mine host*

mine·field /'maɪnfild/ *n.* [C] **1** an area of land that has mines hidden on it **2** [usually singular] something that has hidden dangers or difficulties: *The subject of abortion is a political minefield.*

min·er /'maɪnɚ/ *n.* [C] someone who works in a mine, digging out coal, gold etc.: *a coal miner*

min·er·al /'mɪnərəl/ *n.* [C] **1** a substance that is formed naturally in the earth, especially a solid substance such as coal, salt, stone, or gold: *an area rich in minerals* **2** a natural substance such as CALCIUM or iron that is present in some foods and that is important for good health: *This cereal says it's fortified with 10 essential vitamins and minerals.*

min·er·al·o·gy /,mɪnə'rɑlədʒi/ *n.* [U] the scientific study of minerals —**mineralogist** *n.* [C]

mineral oil /'... ,./ *n.* [U] a clear oil that is made from PETROLEUM and can be used on wooden furniture, on your skin, or taken as a LAXATIVE

mineral wa·ter /'... ,../ *n.* [U] water that comes from under the ground and contains minerals

min·e·stro·ne /,mɪnə'strouni/ *n.* [U] an Italian soup containing vegetables and small pieces of PASTA

mine·sweep·er /'maɪn,swipɚ/ *n.* [C] a ship that has equipment for removing bombs from under water —**minesweeping** *n.* [U]

min·gle /'mɪŋgəl/ *v.* **1** [I,T] if two or more feelings, sounds, smells etc. mingle or are mingled, they combine with each other: *Playfulness and formality can mingle, even at a wedding.* | [+ **with**] *The scent of perfume mingled with sweat lingered in the air.* **2** [I] to meet and talk with a lot of different people at a social event: *Families mingled and enjoyed themselves at a block party.* | [+ **with**] *The cast came out to mingle with the audience.* —**mingled** *adj.*

min·i /'mɪni/ *n.* [C] a very short skirt or dress

mini- /mɪni/ *prefix* very small compared with others of the same type: *a miniskirt* (=very short skirt) | *a mini-market* (=a small food store) —compare MICRO-

min·i·a·ture¹ /'mɪniətʃɚ, 'mɪnɪtʃɚ/ *adj.* very small: *a miniature train*

miniature² *n.* **1** [C] something that has the same appearance as someone or something else, but is much smaller: *portrait miniatures* **2 in miniature** exactly like something or someone but much smaller: *She has her mother's face in miniature.*

miniature golf /,.... './ *n.* [U] a GOLF game, played for fun outdoors, in which you hit a small ball through passages, over small bridges and hills etc.

min·ia·tur·ist /'mɪnɪtʃərɪst/ *n.* [C] someone who paints very small pictures, or makes very small objects

min·i·a·tur·ize /'mɪniətʃə,raɪz, 'mɪnɪ-/ *v.* [T usually passive] to make something in a very small size —**miniaturized** *adj.* —**miniaturization** /,mɪniətʃərə'zeɪʃən/ *n.* [U]

min·i·bar /'mɪni,bɑr/ *n.* [C] a small REFRIGERATOR in a hotel room in which there are alcoholic drinks, juice etc.

min·i·bike /'mɪni,baɪk/ *n.* [C] a small MOTORCYCLE

min·i·bus /'mɪni,bʌs/ *n.* [C] a small bus with seats for six to twelve people

min·i·cam /'mɪni,kæm/ *n.* [C] a small movie camera, used especially by news programs

min·i·car /'mɪni,kɑr/ *n.* [C] a very small car

min·i·com·put·er /'mɪnikəm,pyutɚ/ *n.* [C] a computer that is larger than a PERSONAL COMPUTER and smaller than a MAINFRAME, used by businesses and other large organizations

mini·golf /'mɪni,gɑlf/ *n.* [U] MINIATURE GOLF

min·i·mal /'mɪnəməl/ *adj.* very small in degree or amount: *Desert plants will stay healthy even with minimal watering.* | *The effect on taxpayers will be minimal.* —**minimally** *adv.*

min·i·mal·ism /'mɪnəmə,lɪzəm/ *n.* [U] art, music etc. that uses very simple ideas or patterns that are repeated often —**minimalist** *n.* [C] —**minimalist** *adj.*

min·i·mart /'mɪni,mɑrt/ also **mini-mar·ket** /'.. ,../ *n.* [C] a small store that stays open very late and that sells food, cigarettes, etc. and sometimes gasoline

min·i·mize /'mɪnə,maɪz/ *v.* [T] **1** to make the degree or amount of something as small as possible: *The city is working on plans to minimize traffic problems.* **2** to make something seem less serious or important than it really is: *White House officials sought to minimize the importance of the meeting.* **3** to CLICK on a special part of a WINDOW on a computer screen so that it is represented as a small picture —compare MAXIMIZE

min·i·mum¹ /'mɪnəməm/ *adj.* [only before noun] the **s w** minimum number, amount or degree is the smallest that it is possible to have: *The minimum order is five hundred business cards.* —compare MAXIMUM¹

minimum² *n.* [C usually singular] **1** the smallest amount, number, or degree of something that is possible, allowed, or needed: *We'll need a minimum of* (=at least) *nine tables for that many people.* | *A lot of the students are just doing the bare minimum* (=the least amount they can) *of work.* | *Staffing levels are down to an absolute minimum.* **2 keep/reduce sth to a minimum** to limit something, especially something bad, to the smallest amount or degree possible: *Development in the hills has been kept to a minimum.*

minimum-se·cur·i·ty pris·on /,... ,... '../ *n.* [C] a prison that does not restrict prisoners' freedom as much as ordinary prisons

minimum wage /,... './ *n.* [C usually singular] the lowest amount of money that can legally be paid per hour to a worker: *Most of the new jobs in the area only pay the minimum wage.* —**minimum-wage** *adj.*: *a minimum-wage job*

M

min·ing /'maɪnɪŋ/ n. [U] the action or industry of getting metals and minerals out of the earth

min·ion /'mɪnyən/ n. [C] a very unimportant person in an organization, who just obeys other people's orders

min·is·cule /'mɪnə,skyul/ adj. another spelling of MINUSCULE

min·i·se·ries /'mɪni,sɪriz/ n. [C] a television DRAMA that is divided into several parts and shown on different nights, usually during one or two weeks

min·i·skirt /'mɪni,skɚt/ n. [C] a very short skirt

min·is·ter¹ /'mɪnəstɚ/ n. [C] **1** a religious leader in some Christian churches —compare PASTOR, PRIEST —see Usage Note at PRIEST **2** a politician who is in charge of a government department in some countries: *The Russian foreign minister was also present at the meeting.* —see also PRIME MINISTER **3** someone whose job is to represent their country in another country, but who is lower in rank than an AMBASSADOR

minister² v. [I] to be a minister: *Rev. Wilson spent 20 years ministering in New York's Hell's Kitchen.*
minister to sb/sth phr. v. [T] FORMAL to give help to someone or something who needs it: *Volunteers minister to the poor and sick.*

min·is·te·ri·al /,mɪnə'stɪriəl/ adj. relating to a minister, or done by a minister: *ministerial committees*

min·is·tra·tions /,mɪnə'streɪʃənz/ n. [plural] FORMAL the giving of help and service, especially to people who are sick or who need the help of a priest

min·is·try /'mɪnəstri/ n. plural **ministries 1 the ministry** the profession of being a church leader, especially in the Protestant church: *Nate felt called to the ministry.* **2** [C] a government department in some countries: *the Ministry of Agriculture* **3** [U] the work done by a priest or other religious person: *Allen has been involved with Lutheran music ministry for more than 20 years.*

min·i·van /'mɪni,væn/ n. [C] a large vehicle with seats for six or more people

mink /mɪŋk/ n. plural **mink** [C,U] a small animal with soft brown fur, or the valuable fur from this animal: *a mink coat*

Min·ne·ap·o·lis /,mɪni'æpəlɪs/ a city in the U.S. state of Minnesota, which is a port on the Mississippi River. The city Saint Paul is across the river, and together, Minneapolis and Saint Paul are known as the Twin Cities.

Min·ne·so·ta /,mɪnə'soʊtə/ written abbreviation **MN** a state in the northern central part of the U.S. —**Minnesotan** n., adj.

min·now /'mɪnoʊ/ n. [C] a very small fish that lives in rivers, lakes etc.

Min·o·an /mɪ'noʊən/ adj. of or about the civilization of ancient Crete (3000–1100 B.C.)

mi·nor¹ /'maɪnɚ/ adj. **1** small and not very important or serious, especially when compared with other things: *Williams suffered a minor stroke.* | *Most of the problems have been very minor.* | *a minor traffic violation* —opposite MAJOR¹ (1) **2** based on a musical SCALE in which the third note of the related MAJOR scale has been lowered by a half step: *a minor key* | *a symphony in D minor* —compare MAJOR¹ (3)

minor² n. [C] **1** LAW someone who is below the age at which they become legally responsible for their actions: *Thomas pleaded guilty to buying alcohol for a minor.* **2** the second main subject that you study in college for your degree: *"What's your minor?" "History."* —compare MAJOR² (2) **3 the minors** the MINOR LEAGUES

minor³ v.
minor in sth phr. v. [T] to study a second main subject as part of your college degree: *Nguyen minored in theater studies.* —opposite MAJOR³

mi·nor·i·ty¹ /mə'nɔrəti, maɪ-, -'nɑr-/ n. plural **minorities 1** [C usually plural] **a)** a group of people of a different race or religion than most people in a country:

Both republics have sizable Serbian minorities. **b)** someone in one of these groups: *The law prevents job discrimination against minorities and women.* | *minority-owned businesses* **2** [singular] a small part of a larger group of people or things: *Gaelic is still spoken in Ireland by a tiny minority.* | [+ of] *Mountain trails benefit only a small minority of the county's population.* **3 be in the minority** to be less in number than any other group: *Male teachers are in the minority in elementary schools.* **4 a minority of one** the only person in a group who has a particular opinion: *On policy votes, Marshall is often a minority of one.* **5** [U] LAW the period of time when someone is below the age at which they become legally responsible for their actions —opposite MAJORITY

minority² adj. [only before noun] **1** not belonging or relating to the race of people with white skin: *The GAO study showed that run-down schools are likely to be found in poor neighborhoods with large percentages of minority students.* | *Minority businesses contribute to both the local and national economies.* | *Failure to attract minority faculty limits students' exposure to multicultural diversity.* **2** relating to a group of people who do not have the same opinion, religion, race etc. as most of the larger group that they are in: *Sabdullayev is collecting money from other minority regions in Russia to rebuild Chechnya's heritage.*

minority lead·er /.'... ,../ n. [C usually singular] the leader of the political party that has fewer politicians in Congress than the leading party —compare MAJORITY LEADER

minor league /,.. '.◂/ n. **1 the Minor Leagues** also **the minor leagues** [plural] the groups of teams that form the lower levels of American professional baseball —compare MAJOR LEAGUES **2** [C] small businesses and organizations, rather than large powerful ones —**minor leaguer** n. [C]

minor-league /,.. ./ adj. [only before noun] **1** relating to the minor leagues in sports: *a minor-league catcher* **2** not very important, or large: *Collins and Reynolds were just minor-league crooks.*

Minsk /mɪnsk/ the capital and largest city of Belarus

min·strel /'mɪnstrəl/ n. [C] **1** a singer or musician in the Middle Ages **2** a white singer or dancer who pretended to be an African-American person and who performed in shows in the early part of the 20th century

mint¹ /mɪnt/ n. **1** [C,U] a candy that tastes like PEPPERMINT (=a strong fresh-tasting substance obtained from a plant) **2** [U] a small plant with leaves that have a strong fresh smell and taste and are used in cooking and making medicine —see also PEPPERMINT, SPEARMINT **3 a mint** a large amount of money: *Many young MBAs dream of making a mint on Wall Street.* **4** [C] a place where coins are officially made

mint² v. [T] **1** to make a coin **2** to invent new words, phrases, or ideas **3** [usually passive] to give someone a degree or give them the appropriate skills for a particular job etc.: *a newly minted engineering graduate*

mint³ adj. **in mint condition** looking new and in perfect condition: *Look – somebody's selling a 1968 Mustang in mint condition.*

mint ju·lep /,mɪnt 'dʒuləp/ n. [C] a drink in which alcohol and sugar are mixed with ice and mint leaves are added

mint·y /'mɪnti/ adj. tasting or smelling like mint

min·u·et /,mɪnyu'ɛt/ n. [C] a slow graceful dance of the 17th and 18th century, or a piece of music for this dance

mi·nus¹ /'maɪnəs/ prep. **1** used in mathematics when you SUBTRACT one number from another: *17 minus 5 is 12 (17 – 5 = 12)* **2** without something that would normally be there: *He came back from the fight minus a couple of front teeth.* —opposite PLUS¹

minus² n. [C] **1** a minus sign **2** something that is a disadvantage because it makes a situation bad: *There are both pluses and minuses to living in a big city.* —opposite PLUS⁴

minus³ adj. **1 minus 5/20/30 etc.** less than zero,

especially less than 0° in temperature: *At night the temperature can go as low as minus 30.* **2 A minus, B minus etc.** a grade used in a system of judging students' work. A minus is lower than A, but higher than B plus. —opposite PLUS[3]

min·us·cule /ˈmɪnəˌskyul/ *adj.* extremely small: *The chances of getting the disease are minuscule.* | *a minuscule amount of food*

minus sign /ˈ.. ˌ./ *n.* [C] a sign (–) showing that a number is less than zero, or that the second of two numbers is to be SUBTRACTed from the first

min·ute[1] /ˈmɪnɪt/ *n.* [C]

1 time a period of time equal to 60 seconds: *The power went out for about 15 minutes.* | *Set the wok over high heat for one minute.* | *It takes Paula about three minutes to swim a lap.* | [+ **to/after**] *It's ten minutes after two.*

2 last minute the last possible time, just before it is too late: *There were a few last minute changes to the program.* | *Ellen got some extra tickets* **at the last minute.** —see also LAST-MINUTE

3 love/enjoy/hate etc. every minute (of sth) INFORMAL to love, enjoy etc. all of something: *"I hear John is in Alaska." "Yes, and loving every minute of it."*

4 by the minute also **minute by minute** more and more as time passes: *Medical technology changes almost by the minute.*

5 within minutes very soon after something has happened: *Police responded to the alarm within minutes.*

6 not a minute too soon if something happens or you do something not a minute too soon, it happens almost too late

---

SPOKEN PHRASES

7 a minute a very short period of time; MOMENT: *Stay here a minute.* | *I just have to sit back* **for a minute** *and rest.*

8 in a minute a) very soon: *Tell him we'll be there* **in a minute.** | *I've got a meeting with Liz in a minute.* | *Your waiter will be here* **in just a minute.** **b)** used to say that you would do something without stopping to think about it: *I would have married her in a minute.*

9 wait/just a minute also **hold on a minute a)** used to tell someone you want them to wait for a short time while you do or say something else: *Just a minute, Margaret, I want to introduce you to Betty.* | *Wait a minute, let me see if I understand this correctly.* **b)** used to tell someone to stop speaking or doing something for a short time because they have said or done something wrong: *Hey, wait a minute, she wasn't supposed to tell you.*

10 any minute (now) used to say that something will happen extremely soon: *Oh, they're going to be here any minute!*

11 do you have a minute? used to ask someone if it is convenient for you to talk to them for a short time: *Do you have a minute? I have a couple of questions.*

12 one minute a) used to say that a situation suddenly changes: *How can you guys be so nice one minute, and then so mean the next?* **b)** used to ask someone to wait for a short time while you do something else: *One minute – I'll put your call through.*

13 the minute (that) sb does sth as soon as someone does something: *The minute I say something is cute, she'll hate it.*

14 not think/believe/etc. for one minute used to say that you certainly do not think something, believe something etc.: *I never for one minute believed in Santa Claus.*

15 this minute a) right now: *You don't have to tell me right this minute.* **b)** used to tell someone, often angrily, to do something immediately: *Get back in your room this minute.*

---

16 notes **minutes** [plural] an official written record of what is said and decided at a meeting: *The school board is required by law to* **keep minutes** *of closed-session discussions.*

17 mathematics TECHNICAL one of the 60 parts into which a degree of angle is divided —see also UP-TO-THE-MINUTE —see Usage Note at MOMENT

mi·nute[2] /maɪˈnut/ *adj.* **1** extremely small: *We used a*

microscope to look at the minute plant forms. | *The print was so minute I nearly went blind reading it.* **2** paying careful attention to the smallest details: *minute scrutiny* | *He remembers everything* **in minute detail.** —**minutely** *adv.* —**minuteness** *n.* [U]

minute hand /ˈmɪnɪt ˌhænd/ *n.* [C] the long thin piece of metal that points to the minutes on a clock or watch

min·ute·man /ˈmɪnɪtˌmæn/ *n. plural* **minutemen** /-ˌmɛn/ [C] one of a group of men who were not official soldiers but who were ready to fight at any time during the Revolutionary War in the U.S.

mi·nu·tiae /maɪˈnuʃə, mə-/ *n.* [plural] very small and exact but unimportant details

minx /mɪŋks/ *n.* [C] OLD-FASHIONED a girl who is FLIRTATIOUS, confident, and who does not show respect

mips /mɪps/ *n.* [plural] TECHNICAL millions of instructions per second; a way of measuring how fast a computer works

mir·a·cle /ˈmɪrəkəl/ *n.* [C] **1** something very good or lucky that you hope will happen, but that does not seem likely: *It'll be a miracle if we get to the airport in time.* | *Manley's hope for an economic miracle in Jamaica was not realized.* **2** something that you admire very much and that is a great example of a particular quality or skill: *Genetic testing is indeed a scientific miracle.* | [+ **of**] *The Golden Gate bridge is a miracle of engineering.* **3** an action or event that is impossible according to the ordinary laws of nature, and that some people believe was done by God: *She performed many miracles and had the gift of prophecy.* **4 work/perform miracles** to have a very good effect or result: *We're relying on Foster performing miracles out on the football field today.* **5 miracle cure a)** a very effective medical treatment that cures even serious diseases **b)** something that solves a very difficult problem: *a miracle cure for the educational crisis*

mi·rac·u·lous /mɪˈrækyələs/ *adj.* completely unexpected and usually resulting from extreme good luck: *Try to live as though every moment is miraculous.* | *Tricia was released from the hospital after her* **miraculous recovery.** —**miraculously** *adv.*

mi·rage /mɪˈrɑʒ/ *n.* [C] **1** a strange effect caused by hot air in a desert, in which you think you can see objects when they are not actually there **2** a dream, hope, or wish that cannot come true

mire[1] /maɪr/ *n.* [U] **1** deep mud **2** a situation that you do not want to be in but that is difficult to escape from: *It's a novel about innocent people sucked* **into the mire** *of international espionage.*

mire[2] *v.* **be mired (down) in sth a)** to be in a situation where you are not developing or making any progress at all: *The team continues to be mired in last place.* | *Let's try to consider our overall objectives and not get mired down in all of the details.* **b)** to be stuck in deep mud: *The plane was mired in mud and snow at the end of the runway.*

Mi·ró /miˈrou/, **Jo·án** /ʒoˈɑn/ (1893–1983) a Spanish PAINTER famous for his use of bright color and ABSTRACT shapes in the style of SURREALISM

mir·ror[1] /ˈmɪrə/ *n.* [C] **1** a piece of special flat glass that you can look at and see yourself in: *I examined my own face* **in the mirror.** —see picture at REFLECTION **2 a mirror of sth** something that gives a clear idea of what something else is like: *This is Chicago, mirror of all that's gruesome and glorious in America's urban experience.* —see also REARVIEW MIRROR

mir·ror[2] *v.* [T] to be very similar to something or a copy of it: *Victor's expression mirrored her own, both of them staring in amazement.*

mirror im·age /ˌ.. ˈ../ *n.* [C] **1** an image of something in which the right side appears on the left, and the left side appears on the right **2** something that is either very similar to something else or is the complete opposite of it: *The situation is a mirror image of the one Republicans faced 25 years ago.*

M

mirth /mɚθ/ *n.* [U] LITERARY happiness and laughter —**mirthful** *adj.* —**mirthfully** *adv.*

mirth·less /'mɚθlɪs/ *adj.* LITERARY mirthless laughter or a mirthless smile does not seem to be caused by real amusement or happiness —**mirthlessly** *adv.*

mis- /mɪs/ *prefix* **1** bad or badly: *misfortune* (=bad luck) | *He's been misbehaving* (=behaving badly). **2** wrong or wrongly: *a miscalculation* | *I misunderstood what you said.* **3** used to show an opposite or the lack of something: *I mistrust him* (=I don't trust him).

mis·ad·ven·ture /ˌmɪsəd'vɛntʃɚ/ *n.* [C,U] bad luck or an accident: *He survived a series of misadventures, including the loss of his boat and a stint in jail.*

mis·al·li·ance /ˌmɪsə'laɪəns/ *n.* [C] FORMAL a situation in which two people or organizations have agreed to work together, marry each other etc., but are not appropriate for each other

mis·an·thrope /'mɪsən,θroʊp, 'mɪz-/ also **mis·an·thro·pist** /mɪs'ænθrəpɪst, mɪz-/ *n.* [C] FORMAL someone who does not like other people and prefers to be alone —**misanthropic** /ˌmɪsən'θrɑpɪk/ *adj.* —**misanthropy** /mɪs'ænθrəpi/ *n.* [U]

mis·ap·ply /ˌmɪsə'plaɪ/ *v.* **misapplies, misapplied, misapplying** [T] to use a principle, rule, money etc. in an incorrect way or for a wrong purpose: *Ross was charged with misapplying public money.* —**misapplication** /ˌmɪsæplə'keɪʃən/ *n.* [U]

mis·ap·pre·hen·sion /ˌmɪsˌæprɪ'hɛnʃən/ *n.* [C] a belief that is not correct or that is based on a wrong understanding of something: *Mr. Roeper labors under the misapprehension that Jack is a millionaire.* —**misapprehend** *v.* [T]

mis·ap·pro·pri·ate /ˌmɪsə'proʊpri,eɪt/ *v.* [T] FORMAL to dishonestly take something that you have been trusted to keep safe, for example, to take money that belongs to your employer: *One professor had misappropriated research funds.* —**misappropriation** /ˌmɪsə,proʊpri'eɪʃən/ *n.* [U]

mis·be·got·ten /ˌmɪsbɪ'gɑt‾n‹ / *adj.* [only before noun] **1** a misbegotten plan, idea, etc. is not likely to succeed because it is badly planned or not sensible: *a misbegotten diplomatic mission* **2** FORMAL OR HUMOROUS a misbegotten person is completely stupid or useless

mis·be·have /ˌmɪsbɪ'heɪv/ *v.* [I] to behave badly, and cause trouble or annoy people: *Larry and Myesha have been misbehaving all day.*

mis·be·hav·ior /ˌmɪsbɪ'heɪvyɚ/ *n.* [U] behavior that is not acceptable to other people: *Yelling and screaming do little to stop children's misbehavior.*

mis·cal·cu·late /mɪs'kælkyə,leɪt/ *v.* [I,T] **1** to make a mistake when deciding how long something will take to do, how much money you will need etc.: *It is estimated that the IRS miscalculates interest charges 25% of the time.* **2** to make a wrong judgment about a situation: *I think we miscalculated how people would react to the scene.*

mis·cal·cu·la·tion /mɪs,kælkyə'leɪʃən/ *n.* [C] **1** a mistake made in deciding how long something will take to do, how much money you will need etc. **2** a wrong judgment about a situation

mis·car·riage /'mɪs,kærɪdʒ, ˌmɪs'kærɪdʒ/ *n.* [C,U] the act of accidentally giving birth too early for the baby to live: *She had a miscarriage but is now back at work.* —compare ABORTION STILLBIRTH

miscarriage of jus·tice /ˌ... . '../ *n.* [C,U] a situation in which someone is wrongly punished by a court of law for something they did not do

mis·car·ry /ˌmɪs'kæri/ *v.* **miscarries, miscarried, miscarrying** [I] **1** to give birth to a baby too early for it to live —compare ABORT (2) **2** FORMAL if a plan miscarries, it is not successful

mis·cast /ˌmɪs'kæst/ *v. past tense and past participle* **miscast** [T usually passive] to choose an actor who is not appropriate to play a particular character in a play or movie

mis·ceg·e·na·tion /mɪ,sɛdʒə'neɪʃən, ˌmɪsɪ-/ *n.* [U] FORMAL, DISAPPROVING OR OFFENSIVE a word which means the act of two parents of different races having children, especially when one of the parents is white

mis·cel·la·ne·ous /ˌmɪsə'leɪniəs/ *adj.* [usually before noun] consisting of many different things or people who do not seem to be related to each other: *List your miscellaneous expenses in the right-hand column.* | *It was in a box labeled "miscellaneous."*

mis·cel·la·ny /'mɪsə,leɪni/ *n. plural* **miscellanies** [C] a collection of different things: *a miscellany of travel writing*

mis·chance /ˌmɪs'tʃæns/ *n.* [C,U] LITERARY bad luck, or a situation that results from bad luck

mis·chief /'mɪstʃɪf/ *n.* [U] **1** bad behavior, especially by children, that causes trouble or damage, but no serious harm: *I can't stop the baby from getting into mischief.* | *Fred just loves to make mischief.* **2** enjoyment of playing tricks on people or embarrassing them: *Ann's light brown eyes glimmered with mischief.* **3** LAW damage or harm that may or may not have been intended: *criminal mischief*

mischief-mak·er /'.. ,../ *n.* [C] OLD-FASHIONED someone who deliberately causes trouble or arguments

mis·chie·vous /'mɪstʃəvəs/ *adj.* **1** liking to have fun, especially by playing tricks on people or doing things to annoy or embarrass them: *Will is a fun-loving, mischievous guy.* | *Gabby looked at me with a mischievous grin.* **2** causing trouble or arguments deliberately: *a mischievous remark* —**mischievously** *adv.* —**mischievousness** *n.* [U]

mis·con·ceived /ˌmɪskən'sivd‹ / *adj.* a misconceived plan or program will not succeed because it is stupid or has not been carefully thought about

mis·con·cep·tion /ˌmɪskən'sɛpʃən/ *n.* [C,U] an idea that is wrong or untrue, but that people believe because they do not understand it correctly: [**misconception that**] *It's a misconception that red meat cannot be part of a healthy diet.* | *There's a popular misconception that no humans live in the tropical rain forest.*

mis·con·duct /ˌmɪs'kɑndʌkt/ *n.* [U] FORMAL bad or dishonest behavior by someone in a position of authority or trust: *She faces eight charges of misconduct and abuse of power.*

mis·con·struc·tion /ˌmɪskən'strʌkʃən/ *n.* [C,U] FORMAL an incorrect understanding of something

mis·con·strue /ˌmɪskən'stru/ *v.* [T] FORMAL to fail to understand something that someone has said or done

mis·count /ˌmɪs'kaʊnt/ *v.* [I,T] to count wrongly: *They claim some ballots were miscounted.*

mis·cre·ant /'mɪskriənt/ *n.* [C] FORMAL a bad person who causes trouble, hurts people etc. —**miscreant** *adj.*

mis·cue /mɪs'kyu/ *n.* [C] **1** a mistake or MISUNDERSTANDING: *Several of the staff were out last week, which led to a series of delays and miscues in our department.* **2** a mistake in a games such as POOL¹ (2) where the stick does not hit the ball correctly —**miscue** *v.* [I,T]

mis·deed /ˌmɪs'did/ *n.* [C] FORMAL a wrong or illegal action: *A congressional committee is investigating the department's misdeeds.*

mis·de·mean·or /ˌmɪsdɪ'minɚ/ *n.* [C] LAW a crime that is not very serious —compare FELONY

mis·di·ag·nose /ˌmɪsdaɪəg'noʊs/ *v.* [T usually passive] to give an incorrect explanation of an illness, a problem in a machine etc.: *Roy's heart condition was originally misdiagnosed as pneumonia.* —**misdiagnosis** *n.* [C]

mis·di·rect /ˌmɪsdə'rɛkt/ *v.* [T usually passive] **1** FORMAL to use your efforts, energy, or abilities in a way that is wrong or inappropriate: *Wyche's ideas may be misdirected at times but we need people like him.* **2** FORMAL to send someone or something to the wrong place: *Our mail was misdirected to the wrong street.* **3** if a judge misdirects a JURY, he or she gives them incorrect information about the law —**misdirection** /ˌmɪsdə'rɛkʃən/ *n.* [U]

M

mise-en-scène /ˌmiz ɑn ˈsɛn, -ˈseɪn/ *n.* [C] **1** TECHNICAL the arrangement of furniture and other objects used on the stage in a play **2** FORMAL the environment in which an event takes place

mi·ser /ˈmaɪzə/ *n.* [C] someone who hates spending money and likes saving it

s w
3
mis·er·a·ble /ˈmɪzərəbəl/ *adj.* **1** extremely unhappy, for example because you feel lonely, sick, or badly treated: *Preston had a miserable childhood.* | *Dana was in the other day and she looked miserable.* | *John's lying and cheating are making his wife's life miserable.* **2** [usually before noun] making you feel very unhappy, uncomfortable etc.: *Jen has been stuck in a miserable job for the last two years.* | *Wear your coat, or you'll get sick in this miserable weather* **3** [only before noun] very bad or disappointing in size or quality: *I wish this city would do something about the miserable condition of the roads.* | *All that work for this miserable paycheck.* —**miserably** *adv.*

mi·ser·ly /ˈmaɪzəli/ *adj.* **1** a miserly amount, salary etc. is one that is much too small **2** a miserly person is one who hates spending money —**miserliness** *n.* [U]

mis·er·y /ˈmɪzəri/ *n. plural* **miseries 1** [C,U] great suffering, caused for example by being very poor or very sick: *It started with a sore throat and became a week of total misery.* | [+ of] *the miseries of war* **2** [C,U] great UNHAPPINESS: *You're just bringing all this misery on yourself.* **3 put sth/sb out of their misery** to kill a person or an animal that is sick or wounded in order to end their suffering

mis·fea·sance /mɪsˈfizəns/ *n.* [U] LAW a situation in which someone does not do something they are responsible for doing by law

mis·fire /ˌmɪsˈfaɪə/ *v.* [I] **1** if a plan or joke misfires, it does not have the result that you intended **2** if a gun misfires, the bullet does not come out **3** if an engine misfires, the gas mixture does not burn at the right time —**misfire** /ˈmɪsˌfaɪə, ˌmɪsˈfaɪə/, **misfiring** *n.* [C]

mis·fit /ˈmɪsˌfɪt/ *n.* [C] someone who does not seem to belong in a place because they are very different from the other people there: *I was a social misfit at school.*

mis·for·tune /mɪsˈfɔrtʃən/ *n.* [C,U] very bad luck, or something that happens to you as a result of bad luck: *These people are taking advantage of our misfortunes.* | *Truman had the misfortune to inherit the presidency from Roosevelt.*

mis·giv·ing /mɪsˈɡɪvɪŋ/ *n.* [C usually plural,U] a feeling of doubt, distrust, or fear about what might happen or about whether something is right: [+ about] *McKenna expressed serious misgivings about several of the officers.* | *Marcoux says she had misgivings about being in front of the camera.*

mis·guid·ed /mɪsˈɡaɪdɪd/ *adj.* **1** intended to be helpful but in fact making a situation worse: *The proposal is a misguided government effort to help the poor.* **2** a misguided idea or opinion is wrong because it is based on a wrong understanding of a situation: *Coleman was acting out of misguided jealousy.* —**misguidedly** *adv.*

mis·han·dle /ˌmɪsˈhændl/ *v.* [T] **1** to deal with a situation badly, because of a lack of skill or care: *He was arrested on suspicion of mishandling public funds.* **2** to treat something roughly, often causing damage: *mishandled baggage* —**mishandling** *n.* [U]

mis·hap /ˈmɪshæp/ *n.* [C,U] a small accident or mistake that does not have very serious results: *The fire began because of a mishap in the kitchen.* | *After many delays, the launch of the space shuttle Atlantis proceeded without mishap.*

mis·hear /mɪsˈhɪr/ *v. past tense and past participle* **misheard** /-ˈhɜːd/ [I,T] to not correctly hear what someone says, so that you think they said something different: *It seemed like a strange question; I wondered if I had misheard.*

mish·mash /ˈmɪʃmæʃ/ *n.* [singular] a mixture of things, ideas, styles etc. that are not in any particular order and are not similar to one another: *The dancers' costumes are a mishmash of fashion trends.*

mis·in·form /ˌmɪsɪnˈfɔrm/ *v.* [T usually passive] to give someone information that is incorrect or untrue: *He's either badly misinformed or willfully lying.*

mis·in·for·ma·tion /ˌmɪsɪnfəˈmeɪʃən/ *n.* [U] incorrect information, especially information that is deliberately intended to deceive people —compare DISINFORMATION

mis·in·ter·pret /ˌmɪsɪnˈtɜːprɪt/ *v.* [T] to not understand the correct meaning of something that someone says or does, or to explain something wrongly to other people: *Delgado badly misinterpreted the statistics of the survey.* —**misinterpretation** /ˌmɪsɪnˌtɜːprəˈteɪʃən/ *n.* [C,U]

mis·judge /ˌmɪsˈdʒʌdʒ/ *v.* [T] **1** to form a wrong or unfair opinion about a person or situation: *Automakers misjudged the American consumer when they stopped making convertibles.* **2** to guess an amount, distance etc. wrongly: *I misjudged the distance to the turnstile and slammed into it.* —**misjudgment** *n.* [C,U]

mis·lay /mɪsˈleɪ/ *v. past tense and past participle* **mislaid** [T] **1** to put something somewhere, then forget where you put it; MISPLACE: *Ben mislaid the tape he needed for his English class.* **2** to lay or place something wrongly: *mislaid linoleum*

mis·lead /mɪsˈlid/ *v. past tense and past participle* **misled** [T] to make someone believe something that is not true by giving them false or incomplete information: *Livingstone says there was no attempt to intentionally mislead the public.* | *Don't be misled by products with the word "fresh" on the label.*

mis·lead·ing /mɪsˈlidɪŋ/ *adj.* likely to make someone believe something that is not true: *Your diagram is a little misleading, Watson.* —**misleadingly** *adv.*

mis·led /mɪsˈlɛd/ the past tense and past participle of MISLEAD

mis·man·age /ˌmɪsˈmænɪdʒ/ *v.* [T] if someone mismanages something they are in charge of, they deal with it badly: *The department is understaffed and mismanaged.* —**mismanagement** *n.* [U]

mis·match /ˈmɪsmætʃ/ *n.* [C] a combination of things or people that do not work well together or are not appropriate for each other: *A mismatch between worker and work station can lead to repetitive strain injuries.* —**mismatched** /ˌmɪsˈmætʃt/ *adj.*: *mismatched socks*

mis·no·mer /ˌmɪsˈnoʊmə/ *n.* [C] a name that is wrong or inappropriate: *"Silent movie" is a misnomer since the movies usually had a musical accompaniment.*

mi·sog·y·nist·ic /mɪˌsɑdʒəˈnɪstɪk/ also **misogynist** /mɪˈsɑdʒənɪst/ *adj.* showing hate, strong dislike, or a complete lack of respect for women: *The group's misogynistic lyrics have outraged parents and women's groups.*

mi·sog·y·ny /mɪˈsɑdʒəni/ *n.* [U] hate, strong dislike, or complete lack of respect for women —**misogynist** *n.*

mis·place /ˌmɪsˈpleɪs/ *v.* [T] to lose something for a short time by putting it in the wrong place: *The papers arrived but were misplaced in the mailroom.*

mis·placed /ˌmɪsˈpleɪst/ *adj.* misplaced feelings of trust, love etc. are wrong and inappropriate, because the person that you have these feelings for does not deserve them: *Children must be warned against a misplaced trust of strangers.*

mis·print /ˈmɪsˌprɪnt/ *n.* [C] a mistake, especially a spelling mistake, in a book, magazine etc.

mis·pro·nounce /ˌmɪsprəˈnaʊns/ *v.* [T] to pronounce a word or name wrongly —**mispronunciation** /ˌmɪsprəˌnʌnsiˈeɪʃən/ *n.* [C,U]

mis·quote /ˌmɪsˈkwoʊt/ *v.* [T] to make a mistake in reporting what someone else has said: *All through the interview I took careful notes so as not to misquote him.* —**misquote** /ˈmɪskwoʊt/, **misquotation** /ˌmɪskwoʊˈteɪʃən/ *n.* [C]

M

mis·read /ˌmɪsˈrid/ v. past tense and past participle **misread** /-ˈrɛd/ [T] **1** to make a wrong judgment about a person or situation: *We misread the level of interest in the campaign.* **2** to read something in an incorrect way —**misreading** n. [C,U]

mis·re·port /ˌmɪsrɪˈpɔrt/ v. [T usually passive] to give an incorrect or untrue account of an event or situation: *Steber's age, widely misreported throughout her career, was 76.*

mis·rep·re·sent /ˌmɪsrɛprɪˈzɛnt/ v. [T] to deliberately give a wrong description of someone's opinions or of a situation: *Some sellers will attempt to misrepresent the condition of a house to buyers.* —**misrepresentation** /mɪsˌrɛprɪzɛnˈteɪʃən/ n. [C,U]

mis·rule /ˌmɪsˈrul/ n. [U] FORMAL bad government: *The country may now go hungry after years of communist misrule.*

miss

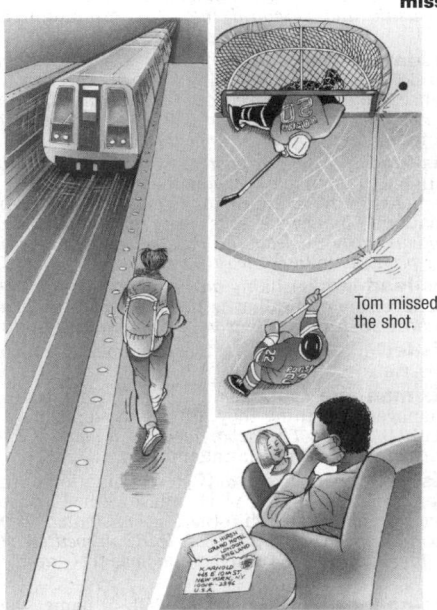

Tom missed the shot.

Lorna missed the train.   Kevin misses his girlfriend.

miss¹ /mɪs/ v.

1 not go/do [T] to not go somewhere or do something, especially when you want to but cannot: *Terry's illness caused him to miss a whole month of school.* | *Let's hurry back so we don't miss the start of the game.*

2 not hit/catch [I,T] to not hit something or catch something: *Darrow fired several shots at the receptionist but missed.* | *The Colts missed their first seven attempts at the goal.* —see picture at CATCH¹

3 feel sad about sb [T] to feel sad because someone you love is not with you: *I miss Mom, don't you?* | *Did you miss me when I was in Hawaii?*

4 feel sad about sth [T] to feel sad because you do not have something or cannot do something you had or did before: *I can think of so many things I'll really miss when I leave.* | [miss doing sth] *Michelle's going to miss living in New York.*

5 miss a chance/opportunity to fail to use an opportunity to do something: *It would be unforgivable to miss this opportunity to travel.*

6 I wouldn't miss it for the world SPOKEN used to say that you really want to go to an event, see something etc.

7 too late [T] to be too late for something: *By the time we got there we'd missed the beginning of the movie.* | *I think I've missed the last bus.* —opposite CATCH¹

8 not see/hear [T] to not see, hear, or notice something, especially when it is difficult to notice: *What did he say? I missed it.* | *Two inspections missed the fault in the engine that led to the crash.*

9 miss the point to not understand the main point of what someone is saying: *You're both missing the point, which is to get more people to use public transportation.*

10 you can't miss it/him etc. SPOKEN used to say that it is very easy to notice or recognize someone or something: *It's the house with the green windows – you can't miss it.*

11 miss the boat INFORMAL to fail to take an opportunity that will give you an advantage: *Customers were worried about missing the boat by not buying any stocks.*

12 sb doesn't miss a trick used to say that someone notices every opportunity to get an advantage: *Filmmaker Joe Ruben doesn't miss a trick in his new thriller.*

13 notice sth isn't there [T] to notice that something or someone is not in the place you expect them to be: *It tastes so great, you won't miss the fat.*

14 without missing a beat also not miss a beat if you do something without missing a beat, you do it without showing that you are surprised or shocked: *Cuomo answered the reporters' questions without missing a beat.*

15 sb's heart misses a beat used to say that someone is very excited, surprised, or frightened: *When Caroline smiled at Eddie, his heart missed a beat.*

16 engine [I] if an engine misses, it stops working for a very short time and then starts again —see Usage Note at LOSE

miss out phr. v. [I] to not have the chance to do something that you enjoy: *Sticking to a healthy diet always makes you feel that you're missing out.* | [+ on] *I feel I'm missing out on having fun with my kids.*

miss² n.

1 Miss Smith/Davis etc. used in front of the family name of a woman who is not married to speak to her politely, to write to her, or to talk about her —compare MRS., MS. —see Usage Note at MR.

2 Miss Italy/Ohio/World etc. used before the name of a country, city etc. that a woman represents in a beauty competition

3 not hit/catch [C] a failed attempt to hit, catch, or hold something: *Murphy scored 78 consecutive foul shots without a miss.*

4 young woman used as a polite way of speaking to a young woman when you do not know her name: *Excuse me, miss, could I have another glass of water?* —compare MA'AM, SIR (1)

5 a miss is as good as a mile used to say that although someone failed by only a small amount to do something, they were still unsuccessful —see also HIT-AND-MISS

mis·sal /ˈmɪsəl/ n. [C] a book containing all the prayers said during each Mass for a whole year in the Catholic Church

mis·shap·en /ˌmɪsˈʃeɪpən, ˌmɪˈʃeɪ-/ adj. not the normal or natural shape: *Ballerinas often have blunted, misshapen toes.*

mis·sile /ˈmɪsəl/ n. [C] **1** a weapon that can fly over long distances and that explodes when it hits the thing it has been aimed at: *a nuclear missile* **2** an object that is thrown at someone in order to hurt them

miss·ing /ˈmɪsɪŋ/ adj. **1** something that is missing is not in its usual place, often so that you cannot find it: *There's a screw missing.* | [+ from] *Three buttons were missing from his shirt.* **2** something that is missing should exist but does not, or should have been included but was not: *The baby was born with a finger missing.* | [+ from] *Are you sure you're registered? Your name is missing from the list.* **3** someone who is missing has disappeared, and no one knows where they are: *Two crew members survived, but two are still missing.* **4** missing in action a soldier who is missing in action has disappeared in a battle and may still be alive: *Approximately 58,000 soldiers were dead or missing in action.* —see Usage Note at LOSE

M

missing link /ˌ.. './ n. [C] **1** something that you need in order to solve a problem: *Police continue looking for missing links in the Stewart murder case.* **2 the missing link** an animal similar to humans that may have existed at the time when APES developed into humans

missing per·son /ˌ.. '../ n. plural **missing persons** [C] **1** someone who has disappeared and whose family has asked the police to try to find them **2 Missing Persons** the part of the police department responsible for trying to find people who have disappeared

s w **mis·sion** /ˈmɪʃən/ n. [C]
1 air force/army etc. an important job done by a member of the Air Force, Army etc., especially an attack on the enemy: *Bush flew bomber missions for the Navy in World War II.*
2 government group a group of important people who are sent by their government to another country to discuss something or collect information: *The Prime Minister of Canada will be leading a trade mission to India and Pakistan.*
3 purpose the purpose or the most important aim of an organization: *The mission of International House is to enable students of different cultures to live together and build life-long friendships.*
4 job an important job that someone has been given to do, especially when they are sent to another place: *Their mission is to go to the rainforest to study possible medicinal uses of the plants there.*
5 duty a duty or service that you have chosen to do and be responsible for: *My new mission in life is to help educate others.*
6 space a special trip made by a space vehicle: *the Galileo mission to Mars*
7 religion **a)** the work of a religious leader or organization that has gone to a foreign country in order to teach people about Christianity or to help poor people: *Longobardi headed up the Jesuit mission to China.* **b)** a building where this type of work is done
8 place for help a place that gives food, medical help etc. to people who need it: *The food missions in Pittsburgh usually serve 750 people per day.*
9 mission accomplished used when you have finished a job that someone has asked or told you to do

mis·sion·ar·y /ˈmɪʃəˌnɛri/ n. plural **missionaries** [C] someone who has been sent to a foreign country to teach people about Christianity and persuade them to become Christians: *Sister Courtney was a missionary in Nicaragua for 15 years.*

missionary po·si·tion /ˌ.... .ˌ../ n. [singular] the sexual position in which the woman lies on her back with the man on top of her and facing her

mission con·trol /ˌ.. .'./ n. [singular, not with **the**] the people on earth who control, communicate with, and guide a group of people on a space flight

mission state·ment /'.. ˌ../ n. [C] a clear statement about the aims of a company or organization

Mis·sis·sip·pi /ˌmɪsəˈsɪpi/ **1** *written abbreviation* **MS** a state in the southeastern U.S. **2 the Mississippi** the longest river in the U.S. which flows from Minnesota to the Gulf of Mexico

mis·sive /ˈmɪsɪv/ n. [C] FORMAL a letter

Mis·sou·ri /mɪˈzʊri/ **1** *written abbreviation* **MO** a state in the central U.S. **2 the Missouri** a long river in the U.S., which flows from the Rocky Mountains to join the Mississippi at St. Louis

mis·spell /ˌmɪsˈspɛl/ v. [T] to spell a word wrongly: *The bride's name was misspelled in the newspaper.* —**misspelling** n. [C,U]

mis·spend /ˌmɪsˈspɛnd/ v. past tense and past participle **misspent** /-ˈspɛnt/ [T] **1** to use time, money, etc. badly, and not carefully or effectively: *Their business manager misspent millions of the couple's money.* **2 misspent youth** HUMOROUS someone who had a misspent youth wasted their time or behaved badly when they were young

mis·step /ˈmɪs-stɛp/ n. [C] a mistake, especially one that is caused by not understanding a situation correctly: *A misstep here could cost millions of dollars.*

mis·sus /ˈmɪsɪz/ n. [singular] SPOKEN, HUMOROUS a man's wife: *How's the missus?*

mist¹ /mɪst/ n. **1** [C,U] a light cloud low over the ground that makes it difficult for you to see very far: *Within seconds he had completely vanished in the mist.* —compare FOG¹ (1) **2** [singular] air that is filled with very small drops of a particular liquid: *A murky mist of smog obscured the view of the city.* **3 lost in the mists of time** if something such as a fact or secret is lost in the mists of time, no one remembers it because it happened so long ago

mist² v. [T] to cover something with very small drops of liquid in order to keep it wet: *Mist the plant daily to keep it moist.*
mist over/up phr. v. [I] if someone's eyes mist over, they become filled with tears: *Dorothy's eyes misted over as she spoke of the young wounded soldier.*

mis·take¹ /mɪˈsteɪk/ n. [C] **s w** **2 2**
1 incorrect action/opinion etc. something that has been done in an incorrect way, or an opinion or statement that is incorrect: *I feel that what we did and the way we did it was a mistake.* | *The attorney admitted that she had made a mistake in writing the contract.* | *This can't be the right hotel – there must be some mistake.* | *We better start learning from our mistakes* (=understanding what we have done wrong and not do this again) *or this team will never win.*
2 by mistake if you do something by mistake, you do it without intending to: *Jodie opened the letter by mistake* —opposite **on purpose** (PURPOSE¹ (2))
3 stupid action something unwise or stupid that someone does, which they are sorry about later: *Buying the house seemed a great idea at the time, but now I can see it was a mistake.* | *Well, go ahead, but you're making a big mistake.* | *[make the mistake of doing sth]* *Kendra made the mistake of asking about Randy.* | *[it is a mistake to do sth]* *It is a mistake to rely on foreign supplies of oil.*
4 in speech or writing something that is said or written in an incorrect way, for example in a piece of school work: *There are a lot of mistakes in this – I'll print it out again.* | *She made four mistakes in grammar and punctuation.*

SPOKEN PHRASES

5 we all make mistakes used when telling someone not to be worried because they have made a mistake
6 make no mistake (about it) also **let there be no mistake (about it)** used to emphasize and show that you are very certain about what you are saying: *Make no mistake about it – I am not going to put up with this anymore.*

—see Usage Note at ERROR

mistake² past tense **mistook** past participle **mistaken** v. [T] **1** to understand something wrongly: *To her embarrassment, she mistook the date of the elections.* **2 there is no mistaking sb/sth** used to say that you are certain about something: *There is no mistaking Hall's books as anything other than romantic fiction.* **3 you can't mistake sb/sth** used to say that someone or something is very easy to recognize: *Their lies are so obvious, you can't mistake them.*
mistake sb/sth for sb/sth phr. v. [T] to think that one person or thing is someone or something else: *Ron mistook Phil's silence for indifference.* | *Lyme Disease is often mistaken for arthritis.*

mis·tak·en /mɪˈsteɪkən/ adj. **1** [not before noun] someone who is mistaken is wrong about something: *Schultz was afraid to say anything, fearing she might be mistaken.* | *I think there's mint in this sauce, if I'm not mistaken.* **2 mistaken idea/belief/impression etc.** a mistaken idea, belief etc. is not correct or is based on bad judgment: *There is a mistaken idea that begonias require a lot of water.* **3 a case of mistaken identity** a situation in which someone believes that they have seen a particular person, especially

M

taking part in a crime, when in fact it was someone else: *Lang was shot to death, apparently in a case of mistaken identity.* —**mistakenly** *adv.*

mis·ter /'mɪstə/ *n.* **1 Mister** the full form of Mr. **2** SPOKEN, OLD-FASHIONED used to speak to a man whose name you do not know: *You don't have any change, do you mister?* —compare SIR (1)

mis·time /ˌmɪs'taɪm/ *v.* [T usually passive] to do something at the wrong time or at a time that is not appropriate: *a mistimed pregnancy*

mis·tle·toe /'mɪsəl,toʊ/ *n.* [U] a plant with small white berries, which grows over other trees and is often used as a decoration at Christmas

mis·took /mɪ'stʊk/ *v.* the past tense of MISTAKE (2)

mis·tral /'mɪstrəl/ *n.* [singular] a strong cold dry wind that blows from the north into the south of France

mis·tress /'mɪstrɪs/ *n.* [C] **1** a woman that a man has a sexual relationship with, even though he is married to someone else: *Harris claims she was the millionaire's mistress.* **2** OLD-FASHIONED the female employer of a servant **3 be mistress of sth** OLD-FASHIONED if a woman is mistress of something she is in control of it, highly skilled at it etc.: *It was evident that she was mistress of her subject.* **4** OLD-FASHIONED the female owner of a dog, horse etc. **5 Mistress** OLD USE used with a woman's family name as a polite way of addressing her —compare MASTER[1]

mis·tri·al /'mɪstraɪl/ *n.* [C] a TRIAL during which a mistake in the law is made, so that a new trial has to be held: *Judge Garcia was forced to declare a mistrial.*

mis·trust[1] /mɪs'trʌst/ *n.* [U] the feeling that you cannot trust someone, especially because you think they may treat you unfairly or dishonestly [+ of] *She showed a great mistrust of doctors.*

mistrust[2] *v.* [T] to not trust someone, especially because you think they may treat you unfairly or dishonestly: *The motel clerk mistrusted Beattie because he didn't have any ID.* —**mistrustful** *adj.* —**mistrustfully** *adv.* —compare DISTRUST[2]

mist·y /'mɪsti/ *adj.* **mistier, mistiest 1** misty weather is weather with a lot of mist: *It was a gray and misty spring morning.* **2** LITERARY also **misty-eyed** sad and crying a little, or almost crying: *As we walked out of the house, we looked back one more time, a little misty-eyed* **3** not clear or bright: *Misty people in overcoats stood against the wall.*

mis·un·der·stand /ˌmɪsʌndə'stænd/ *v.* past tense and past participle **misunderstood** [I,T] to fail to understand correctly: *Oh, I must have misunderstood. I thought we were going to meet at 11:00.*

mis·un·der·stand·ing /ˌmɪsʌndə'stændɪŋ/ *n.* **1** [C, U] a problem caused by someone not understanding a question, situation, or instruction correctly: *Listening carefully reduces misunderstandings.* **2** [C] an argument or disagreement that is not very serious: *Misunderstandings can be caused by cultural differences between workers.*

mis·un·der·stood /ˌmɪsʌndə'stʊd/ *adj.* something or someone that is misunderstood does not receive enough sympathy and respect: *Some people think that Rodman is misunderstood, that he's really a sweet guy.*

mis·use[1] /ˌmɪs'yuz/ *v.* [T] **1** to use something in the wrong way or for the wrong purpose: *He misused public funds to build and furnish his home.* **2** to treat someone badly or unfairly

mis·use[2] /ˌmɪs'yus/ *n.* [C,U] the use of something in the wrong way or for the wrong purpose: *His career was ruined through the misuse of drugs.*

mite /maɪt/ *n.* **1** [C] a very small insect that lives in plants, CARPETs etc. **2 a mite** a little: [+ adj./adv.] *Diane looked a mite tired.* | *It's a mite too big for the box.* **3** [C] OLD-FASHIONED a small child, especially one that you feel sorry for

mi·ter /'maɪtə/ *n.* [C] a tall pointed hat worn by BISHOPs and ARCHBISHOPs

mit·i·gate /'mɪtə,geɪt/ *v.* [T] FORMAL to make a situation or the effects of something less bad, harmful, or serious: *We have to figure out a way to mitigate the costs.*

mit·i·gat·ing /'mɪtə,geɪtɪŋ/ *adj.* **mitigating circumstances/factors etc.** facts about a situation that make a crime or bad mistake seem less serious: *The jury was read a list of mitigating factors to consider.*

mit·i·ga·tion /ˌmɪtə'geɪʃən/ *n.* [U] **1** FORMAL a reduction in how bad, harmful, or serious a situation is **2 in mitigation** LAW if you say something in mitigation, you say something that makes someone's crime or mistake seem less serious or that shows that they were not completely responsible

mitt /mɪt/ *n.* [C] **1** a GLOVE made of thick material, worn to protect your hand: *an oven mitt* | *boxing mitts* **2** a type of leather GLOVE used to catch a ball in baseball **3** INFORMAL someone's hand: *Would you keep your grubby mitts to yourself!*

mit·ten /'mɪtn/ *n.* [C] a type of GLOVE that does not have separate parts for each finger —see picture at GLOVE

mix[1] /mɪks/ *v.*
1 combine substances [I,T] if you mix two or more substances or if they mix, they combine to become a single substance, and they cannot be easily separated: *In a large bowl mix the butter and flour.* | *Oil and water don't mix.* | [**mix sth together/in etc. (sth)**] *Mix the cheese into the spinach.* | [**mix sth with sth**] *Mix the beans thoroughly with the sauce.* —see picture on page 425
2 combine ideas/activities etc. [I,T] to combine two or more different activities, ideas, groups of things etc., or to be combined in this way: *Ferns mix well with other shade-loving plants.* | *Kellor enjoys mixing high and low culture.* | [**mix sth with sth**] *His books mix historical fact with fantasy.* | *I always tell patients that I never mix business with pleasure* (=do business and social activities at the same time).
3 not mix if two different ideas, activities etc. do not mix, they are not appropriate for each other and cause problems when they are combined *Safety and alcohol do not mix.*
4 prepare by mixing [T] to prepare something, especially food or drink, by mixing things together: *At the bar, she mixed a double scotch and water.*
5 meet people [I] to enjoy meeting, talking, and spending time with other people, especially people you do not know very well: [+ **with**] *It will help your career if you mix socially with successful people.*
6 sound [T] TECHNICAL to control the balance of sounds in a record or movie
7 mix and match to put different things, or parts of things, together to make something that looks good or works well: *You can mix and match this home-office furniture to fit your needs.* —**mix-and-match** *adj.*: *mix-and-match clothing*

mix up *phr. v.* [T] **1** [**mix sb/sth ↔ up**] to make the mistake of thinking that someone or something is another person or thing: *I think you've got the dates mixed up, dear.* | [+ **with**] *I keep mixing up this place with where she lived before she got married.* **2** [**mix sb up**] to make someone feel confused: *That's just going to mix everybody up.* **3** [**mix sth ↔ up**] to change the way things have been arranged, often by mistake, so that they are not in the same order anymore: *Gina panicked when she realized she had mixed up the sample test tubes.* **4 mix it up with sb** to argue or threaten to fight with someone: *The fans like it when they see a player mixing it up with the umpire.* —see also MIXED UP, MIX-UP

mix[2] *n.* **1** [singular] the particular combination of things or people that form a group: *There's a real ethnic mix in the city nowadays.* | [+ of] *Des Jardins' mix of cultures is reflected in the food she cooks.* **2** [C,U] a combination of substances that you mix together to make something such as a cake: *What cake mix did you use – it's really good.* | *lemonade mix*

mixed /mɪkst/ *adj.* **1** [only before noun] consisting of many different types of things or people: *a salad of mixed greens* | *a mixed-race family* **2 mixed reaction/response/reviews etc.** if something gets a mixed reaction etc., some people say they like it or agree with it, but others dislike it or disagree with it: *Bailey's play opened to mixed reviews in New York.* **3 have mixed emotions/feelings about sth** to be unsure about whether you like or agree with something or someone: *I had mixed feelings about moving.* **4 a mixed blessing** something that is good in some ways but bad in others: *Staying at home with the baby has been something of a mixed blessing for Pam.* **5 a mixed bag** INFORMAL **a)** something that has both good and bad points: *It's a mixed bag. The actors are fine, but the story is not very believable.* **b)** a group of things that are all very different from each other: [+ of] *The show is a mixed bag of songs and dances.* **6 in mixed company** when you are with people of both sexes: *Until recently, I would not have considered saying the word "penis" in mixed company.*

mixed dou·bles /ˌ. '../ *n.* [U] a game in a sport such as tennis in which a man and a woman play against another man and woman

mixed e·con·o·my /ˌ. .'.../ *n.* [C] TECHNICAL an economic system in which some industries are owned by the government and some are owned by private companies

mixed mar·riage /ˌ. '../ *n.* [C,U] a marriage between two people from different races or religions

mixed me·di·a /ˌ. '.../ *n.* [U] a combination of substances or materials that are used in a painting, SCULPTURE etc.

mixed up /ˌ. '.◂/ *adj.* **1** [not before noun] confused, for example because you have too many different details to remember or think about: *There was so much paperwork that Brian got mixed up and forgot to sign the check.* **2 be mixed up with sb** to be involved with someone who has a bad influence on you: *Conley got mixed up with Keating and lost millions of dollars.* **3 be mixed up in sth** to be involved in an illegal or dishonest activity: *I'd have to be crazy to get mixed up in something like this now.* **4** INFORMAL confused and suffering from emotional problems: *a mixed up college kid* —see also **mix up** (MIX[1]), **MIX-UP**

mix·er /ˈmɪksɚ/ *n.* [C] **1** a piece of kitchen equipment used to mix flour, sugar, butter etc. together: *Beat eggs and sugar with an electric mixer.* —see picture at KITCHEN **2** someone whose job is to control the sound when making a record or TAPE of a piece of music, or to control the quality of the picture when making a movie **3** OLD-FASHIONED a party held so that people who have just met can get to know each other better: *Are you going to the freshman mixer?*

mix·ing bowl /ˈ.. ,./ *n.* [C] a large bowl used for mixing things such as flour and sugar for making cakes

Mix·tec /ˈmɪstɛk/ a Native American tribe who lived in southern Mexico until they were defeated by the Aztecs in the 16th century

s w **mix·ture** /ˈmɪkstʃɚ/ *n.* **1** [C,U] a liquid or other substance made by mixing several substances together: *Paul marinated the chicken in a mixture of olive oil, lemon juice, and spices.* **2** [C] a combination of two or more people, things, feelings, or ideas that are different: *His work is a mixture of photography and painting.* | *A mixture of concern and anger invaded her.* **3** [C] TECHNICAL a combination of substances that are put together but do not mix with each other —compare COMPOUND[1] (2) **4** [U] FORMAL the action of mixing things or the state of being mixed

mix-up /ˈ. ./ *n.* [C] INFORMAL a mistake that causes confusion about details or arrangements: *A patient received the wrong drugs because of a hospital mix-up.*

ml the written abbreviation of MILLILITER

mm[1] /m/ *interjection* used when someone else is speaking and you want to show that you are listening or that you agree with them

mm[2] the written abbreviation of MILLIMETER

MN the written abbreviation of Minnesota

mne·mon·ic /nɪˈmɑnɪk/ *n.* [C] something such as a poem or a sentence, that you use to help you remember a rule, a name etc. —**mnemonic** *adj.* —**mnemonically** /-kli/ *adv.*

M.O. *n.* [singular] modus operandi; a way of doing something that is typical of one person or a group of people

MO the written abbreviation of Missouri

mo. the written abbreviation of "month"

moan[1] /moʊn/ *v.* [I] **1** to make a long low sound expressing pain, UNHAPPINESS, or sexual pleasure: *I lay in bed, moaning in pain.* **2** to complain in an annoying way, especially in an unhappy voice: *"But, Mom, there's nothing to do here," moaned Josh.* | *It's easy to **moan and groan** about salaries.* **3** LITERARY if the wind moans, it makes a long low sound —**moaner** *n.* [C]

moan[2] *n.* [C] **1** a long low sound expressing pain, UNHAPPINESS, or sexual pleasure: *He **gave a terrible moan** as he tried to stand up.* | *The announcement drew moans from the 150 people at Wednesday's meeting.* **2** LITERARY a low sound made by the wind

moat /moʊt/ *n.* [C] **1** a deep wide hole, usually filled with water, that was built around a castle as a defense **2** a deep wide hole dug around an area used for animals in a ZOO to stop them from escaping —**moated** *adj.*

mob[1] /mɑb/ *n.* [C] **1** a large, noisy crowd, especially one that is angry and violent: *In two recent incidents, police fired at mobs of unruly protesters.* **2** a group of people of the same type: *A mob of reporters surrounded the quarterback.* **3 the Mob** the MAFIA (=a powerful organization of criminals) **4 the mob** OLD USE an insulting expression meaning all the poorest and least educated people in society —see also LYNCH MOB

mob[2] *v.* **mobbed, mobbing** [T usually passive] **1** to form a crowd around someone in order to express admiration or to attack them: *The star was mobbed at the airport by photographers and reporters.* **2** if a place is mobbed with people, there is a big crowd of people in the place: *When we went to Disney World last spring, it was mobbed.*

mob cap /ˈ. ./ *n.* [C] a light cotton hat worn by women in the 18th and 19th centuries

Mo·bile /ˈmoʊbil, moʊˈbil/ a city in the U.S. state of Alabama

mo·bile[1] /ˈmoʊbəl/ *adj.* **1** able to move or travel easily: *It's important to keep the patient mobile during recovery.* | *Alligators are really mobile animals, used to moving from one body of water to another.* **2** tending to move or able to move from one social class, job, or place to another: *The population of the U.S. has become more geographically and socially mobile.* **3 mobile clinic/classroom/library etc.** a clinic etc. that is kept in a vehicle and driven from place to place: *The clinic operates a mobile medical van for area homeless* **4 mobile face/features** a face that can change its expression quickly —compare PORTABLE[1] (1) —see also IMMOBILE, UPWARDLY MOBILE

mo·bile[2] /ˈmoʊbil, moʊˈbil/ *n.* [C] a decoration made of small objects tied to wires or string and hung up so that the objects move when air blows around them

mobile home /ˌ.. './ *n.* [C] a type of house made of metal that can be pulled by a large vehicle and moved to another place —see picture on page 423

mobile phone /ˌ.. './ *n.* [C] a CELLULAR PHONE —see picture on page 426

mo·bil·i·ty /moʊˈbɪləti/ *n.* [U] **1** the ability to move easily from one job, place to live, or social class to another: *There is a large degree of mobility among public accountants.* | *New jobs would provide opportunities for **upward mobility**.* **2** the ability to move easily from place to place: *Pawlawksi will have to lose weight to improve his mobility.* | *Shuttles will give mobility to employees without cars.*

mo·bi·lize /ˈmoʊbəˌlaɪz/ *v.* **1** [T] to bring people together so that they can all work to achieve something important: *The shooting mobilized the community, which started several political action groups.* **2 mobilize support/resources etc.** to bring together

M

the supporters, resources etc. that you need and prepare them for action: *We need to mobilize public support to get results.* **3** [I,T] if a country mobilizes or mobilizes its army, it prepares to fight a war —see also DEMOBILIZE —**mobilization** /ˌmoubələˈzeɪʃən/ *n.* [C,U]

mob·ster /ˈmɑbstɚ/ *n.* [C] a member of an organized criminal group, especially the Mafia

moc·ca·sin /ˈmɑkəsɪn/ *n.* [C] a flat comfortable shoe made of soft leather —see picture at SHOE¹

mo·cha /ˈmoukə/ *n.* [U] **1** a type of coffee **2** a combination of coffee and chocolate

mock¹ /mɑk/ *v.* FORMAL **1** [I,T] to laugh at someone or something and try to make them look stupid by making bad remarks about them or by copying them: *Lillian was openly mocked for her skinny body.* **2** [T] to make something seem completely useless: *We are tired of criminals mocking our justice system with technicalities.* —**mockingly** *adv.* —see also **make fun of sb/sth** (FUN¹ (3))
   mock sth ↔ **up** *phr. v.* [T] to make a model of something that is going to be made or built, which shows how it will look

mock² *adj.* [only before noun] **1** not real, but intended to be very similar to a real situation, substance etc.: *Mock court sessions help people to understand the judicial process.* | *a mock combat mission* **2** mock **surprise/horror/indignation etc.** surprise etc. that you pretend to feel, especially as a joke: *"Who are these people?" Furst asked in mock despair.*

mock- /mɑk/ *prefix* pretending to be or feel something: *Sarah had a mock-serious expression on her face* (=she was only pretending to be serious).

mock·er·y /ˈmɑkəri/ *n.* **1 make a mockery of sth a)** to make something such as a plan, system, or organization seem completely useless or ineffective: *These endless appeals and delays make a mockery of justice.* **b)** to make something that is serious or important seem stupid or unimportant: *He had stolen the best months of her life and made a mockery of her love.* **2** [singular] something that is completely useless or ineffective: *An embargo without enforcement would be a mockery.* **3** [U] a feeling or attitude of laughing at someone or something, or of trying to make them seem stupid: *Kline's mockery of Palin's stuttering in the movie was offensive.*

mock·ing·bird /ˈmɑkɪŋˌbɚd/ *n.* [C] an American bird that copies the songs of other birds —see picture on page 429

mock tur·tle·neck /ˌ. ˈ.. ./ *n.* [C] a shirt or SWEATER with a high, close-fitting band around the neck

mock-up /ˈ. ./ *n.* [C] a full-size model of something that is going to be made or built, which shows how it will look: *Architects wanted the mock-up to be as near as possible to the final specifications of the building.* —see also **mock** sth **up** (MOCK¹)

mo·dal¹ /ˈmoudl/ *n.* [C] a modal verb

modal² *adj.* TECHNICAL [only before noun] relating to the MOOD (8) of a verb —**modally** *adv.*

modal aux·il·ia·ry /ˌ.. .ˈ.../ *n.* [C] a modal verb

modal verb /ˌ.. ˈ./ also **modal** *n.* [C] TECHNICAL in grammar, a verb that is used with other verbs to change their meaning by expressing ideas such as possibility, permission, or intention. In English, the modals are: can, could, may, might, shall, should, will, would, must, ought to, used to, need, had better, and dare —see also AUXILIARY VERB

mode /moud/ *n.* [C] **1** FORMAL a particular way or style of behaving, living or doing something: *Commercial airlines have the lowest accident rate of all transportation modes.* | *In the late 20th century, we have more choices about modes of living.* **2 be in work/survival/teaching etc. mode** INFORMAL to be thinking or behaving in a particular way at a particular time: *While in cost-cutting mode, he replaced the security officer with a guard dog.* **3** TECHNICAL a particular way in which a machine operates when it is doing a particular job: *To put the VCR in record*

mode you press record and play simultaneously. | *The car features an economy driving mode.* **4 be the mode** OLD-FASHIONED to be fashionable at a particular time —see also À LA MODE

model
runway

mod·el¹ /ˈmɑdl/ *n.* [C]
1 small copy a small copy of a building, vehicle, machine etc., especially one that can be put together from separate parts: *As children build models they learn about design and construction.* | [+ **of**] *He has a shelf full of models of airplanes that never got built.*
2 fashion someone whose job is to show clothes, hair styles etc. by wearing them and being photographed: *a top fashion model* —see also SUPERMODEL
3 type of car etc. a particular type or design of a vehicle or machine: *We also have a deluxe model for $125.* | *Ford Motor Co. will offer new features and new models this year.*
4 art someone who is employed by an artist or photographer to be painted or photographed
5 good/special person someone who has good qualities or behavior that you should copy: [+ **of**] *As a politician, she was a model of integrity and decency.* | *Brando's a **role model** for everybody in the business.*
6 good/successful thing a way of doing something that is successful or useful and therefore worth copying: [+ **of/for**] *The college is a recognized model of higher education.* | *IBM has long served as the model for American companies in Japan.*
7 description a simple description of a system or structure that is used to help people understand similar systems or structures: *Civil society is a classical economist's model of the free market.*

model² *adj.* **1 model airplane/train/car etc.** a small copy of an airplane, train etc., especially one that a child can play with or put together from separate parts **2 model wife/employee/student etc.** someone who behaves like a perfect wife, employee etc.: *We always thought she came from a model family.* **3 model city/school/farm etc.** a city, school etc. that has been specially designed or organized to be as good as possible, so that other cities, schools etc. can learn from them

model³ *v.* **1** [I,T] to wear clothes in order to show them to possible buyers: *Here we have a Kenar T-shirt modeled by Linda Evangelista.* **2** [I,T] to be employed by an artist or photographer to be painted or photographed: *She made a living modeling for art classes.* **3 model yourself after sb** to try to be like someone else because you admire them: *Byron says he models himself after Philadelphia player Charles Barkley.* **4 be modeled on sth** to be designed in a way that copies another system or way of doing something: *Mrs. Mingott's house is modeled on the private hotels of Paris.* **5** [T] to make small objects from materials such as wood or clay

mod·el·ing /ˈmɑdl-ɪŋ/ *n.* [U] **1** the work of a MODEL: *Johnson's looks got him modeling assignments.* **2** the activity of making model ships, airplanes, figures etc.

mo·dem /ˈmoudəm/ *n.* [C] a piece of electronic equipment that allows information from one computer to be sent along telephone lines to another computer —see picture on page 426

mod·er·ate¹ /ˈmɑdərɪt/ *adj.* **1** neither very big nor very small, very hot nor very cold, very fast nor very slow etc.: *The store suffered moderate damage before* firefighters arrived. | *Chrysanthemums do well in more moderate temperatures.* | *I'd rate the degree of difficulty as moderate.* **2** having opinions or beliefs, especially about politics, that are not extreme and that most people consider reasonable or sensible: *Fox surprised everyone by taking a moderate stance on government spending.* | *a group of moderate Republican senators* **3** staying within reasonable or sensible limits: *A moderate amount of exercise is good for the body.* | *Trading on the stock exchange was moderate Friday.* —see also MODERATELY

mod·e·rate² /'mɑdəˌreɪt/ v. **1** [T] to control a discussion or argument and to help people reach an agreement: *NBC's Tom Brokaw will moderate the debate.* **2** [I,T] FORMAL to make something less extreme or violent, or to become less extreme or violent: *Bloom has since moderated his position on low-income housing.*

mod·er·ate³ /'mɑdərɪt/ n. [C] someone whose opinions or beliefs, especially about politics, are not extreme and are considered reasonable by most people: *Cochrane considers himself a moderate on growth and open space issues.*

mod·er·ate·ly /'mɑdərɪtli/ adv. **1** fairly but not very: *The dollar rose moderately against the Japanese yen.* **2 moderately priced** not too expensive: *moderately priced homes*

mod·er·a·tion /ˌmɑdə'reɪʃən/ n. [U] **1 in moderation** if you do something in moderation, such as drinking alcohol or smoking, you do not do it too much: *Use sugar and salt in moderation.* **2** FORMAL control of your behavior, so that you keep your actions, feelings, habits etc. within reasonable or sensible limits: [+ **in**] *Matsuyama's secret to a long life is moderation in eating.* **3** FORMAL reduction in force, degree, speed etc.: [+ **in**] *Prospects for a moderation in labor costs are not favorable.*

mod·e·ra·to /ˌmɑdə'rɑtoʊ/ adj., adv. a word meaning "at an average speed," used as an instruction on how fast to play a piece of music

mod·er·at·or /'mɑdəˌreɪtə/ n. [C] **1** someone whose job is to control a discussion or argument and to help people reach an agreement **2** someone who asks questions and keeps the marks of competing teams in a spoken game or competition **3** a religious leader who is in charge of the council of the Presbyterian and United Reformed Churches

S W **mod·ern** /'mɑdən/ adj. **1** [only before noun] belonging to the present time or most recent time: *Doherty is a professor of modern European history.* | *Drugs have become the plague of the modern world.* | *Such long trips are rare for wooden ships in modern times.* **2** made or done using the most recent methods: *He'll receive the most modern medical treatment.* | *a modern computer network* **3** using or willing to use very recent ideas, fashions, or ways of thinking: *We want to create a modern and uncluttered look in the new kitchen.* **4** [only before noun] modern art, music, literature etc. uses styles that have been recently developed and are very different from traditional styles: *The prince is known for his critical views of modern architecture.* **5 Modern Greek/Hebrew/English** the form of the Greek etc. language that is used today —see Usage Note at NEW

modern-day /'.. ./ adj. [only before noun] existing in the present time, but considered in relation to someone or something else in the past: *Gilliam's movie is a modern-day fairy tale.*

mod·ern·ism /'mɑdəˌnɪzəm/ n. [U] a style of art, building etc. that was popular especially from the 1940s to the 1960s, in which artists used simple shapes and modern artificial materials —**modernist** adj. —**modernist** n. [C] —compare POSTMODERNISM

mod·ern·is·tic /ˌmɑdə'nɪstɪk / adj. designed in a way that looks very modern and very different from previous styles: *modernistic furniture*

mo·der·ni·ty /mɑ'dənəti, mə-/ n. [U] FORMAL the quality of being modern: *Another characteristic of good design is modernity.*

mod·ern·ize /'mɑdəˌnaɪz/ v. **1** [T] to change something so that it is more appropriate for the present time by using new equipment or methods: *Any money raised will be used to modernize classrooms.* |

Salinas pledged to modernize Mexico when he was elected. **2** [I] to start using more modern methods and equipment: *The business will lose money if it doesn't modernize.* —**modernization** /ˌmɑdənə'zeɪʃən/ n. [C,U]

modern pen·tath·lon /ˌ... .'../ n. [singular] a sports competition that involves running, swimming, riding horses, FENCING, and shooting guns

mod·est /'mɑdɪst/ adj. **1** APPROVING unwilling to talk **S W** proudly about your abilities and achievements: *Renzel remains one of the most sincere and modest men I know.* | *Don't be so modest!* | [+ **about**] *Jason, a scholarship winner, is modest about his achievements.* **2** not very big, expensive etc., especially less big, expensive etc. than you would expect: *Some new brands from South America are making terrific wines for modest prices.* | *Elliot's home in Ironwood is modest, but surrounded by beautiful forests.* **3** shy about showing your body or attracting sexual interest, because you are easily embarrassed **4** modest clothing covers the body in a way that does not attract sexual interest: *They're really very modest bathing suits.* —**modestly** adv. —opposite IMMODEST

mod·es·ty /'mɑdəsti/ n. [U] **1** APPROVING behaving or talking about your achievements in a way that is not proud: *He answers with modesty when asked about his role in the war.* | *Rod isn't known for his modesty.* **2 in all modesty** used to say that you do not want to seem too proud of something you have done, when in fact you are: *In all modesty, I think I've matured quite a bit since those days.* **3** the feeling of shyness about showing your body or doing anything that may attract sexual interest —see also **false modesty** (FALSE (4))

mod·i·cum /'mɑdɪkəm/ n. **a modicum of sth** FORMAL a small amount of something, especially a good quality: *Sometimes there is a modicum of truth within a cliché.*

mod·i·fi·ca·tion /ˌmɑdəfə'keɪʃən/ n. **1** [C] a small change made in something such as a design, plan, or system: *Volvo made modifications to the car to ensure passenger safety.* **2** [U] the act of modifying something, or the process of being modified: *The equipment can be used without modification.*

mod·i·fi·er /'mɑdəˌfaɪə/ n. [C] TECHNICAL a word or group of words that give additional information about another word. Modifiers can be adjectives (such as "fierce" in "the fierce dog"), adverbs (such as "loudly" in "the dog barked loudly"), or phrases (such as "with a short tail" in "the dog with a short tail").

mod·i·fy /'mɑdəˌfaɪ/ v. **modifies, modified, modifying** [T] **1** to make small changes to something in order to improve it and make it more appropriate or effective: *I modified the handlebars on my bike to make it more comfortable.* **2** TECHNICAL if an adjective, adverb etc. modifies another word, it describes it or limits its meaning. In the phrase "walk slowly," the adverb "slowly" modifies the verb "walk."

Mo·di·glia·ni /ˌmoʊdil'yɑni/, **Am·e·de·o** /ˌɑmə'deɪoʊ/ (1884–1920) an Italian PAINTER and SCULPTOR known especially for his pictures of people in which the bodies and faces are much longer than in real life

Mo·doc /'moʊdɑk/ a Native American tribe from the western U.S.

mod·u·lar /'mɑdʒələ/ adj. based on modules or made using modules: *a modular storage system* | *modular furniture*

mod·u·late /'mɑdʒəˌleɪt/ v. [T] **1** to change the sound of your voice or the strength of something: *During his speech, Joe's voice sounded as soft and well-modulated* (=carefully balanced) *as a professor's.* **2** TECHNICAL to change the form of a radio signal so that it can be broadcast more effectively —**modulation** /ˌmɑdʒə'leɪʃən/ n. [C]

mod·ule /'mɑdʒul/ n. [C] **1** a part of a SPACECRAFT that can be separated from the main part and used for a particular purpose **2** TECHNICAL one of several parts of a piece of computer SOFTWARE that does a

M

particular job: *a word processor module* **3** one of several separate parts that can be combined to form a larger object, such as a machine or building

mo·dus op·er·an·di /ˌmoʊdəs ˌɑpəˈrændi/ *n.* [singular] FORMAL: see M.O.

modus vi·ven·di /ˌmoʊdəs vɪˈvɛndi/ *n.* [singular] FORMAL an arrangement between people with very different opinions or habits that allows them to live or work together without fighting

mo·fo /ˈmoʊfoʊ/ *n.* [C] VULGAR a MOTHERFUCKER

Mog·a·dish·u /ˌmoʊɡəˈdɪʃu, ˌmɑ-/ the capital and largest city in Somalia

mo·gul /ˈmoʊɡəl/ *n.* **1** a movie/newspaper/record etc. mogul someone who has great power and influence in a particular industry or activity **2** [C] a pile of hard snow on a SKI SLOPE

mo·hair /ˈmoʊhɛr/ *n.* [U] expensive wool made from the hair of the ANGORA goat: *a mohair sweater*

Mo·ham·med /moʊˈhæməd/ also **Mu·ham·mad** /muˈhæməd/ (?570–632) an Arab religious leader, born in Mecca, who started the religion of Islam and is its most important PROPHET. According to Islam, God told him many things which were later written down to form the holy book called the Koran.

Mo·ham·med·an /moʊˈhæmədən/ *n.* [C] OLD-FASHIONED a MUSLIM —**Mohammedan** *adj.* —**Mohammedanism** *n.* [U]

Mo·ha·ve, Mojave /moʊˈhɑvi/ a Native American tribe from the southwestern area of the U.S.

Mo·hawk /ˈmoʊhɔk/ a Native American tribe from the northeast region of the U.S.

Mo·he·gan /moʊˈhiɡən/ a Native American tribe from the northeastern area of the U.S.

moi·e·ty /ˈmɔɪəti/ *n. plural* **moieties** [C + of] FORMAL a half of something

moi·ré /mwɑˈreɪ/ *n.* [U] a type of silk with a pattern that looks like waves: *a moiré bow*

moist /mɔɪst/ *adj.* **moister, moistest** slightly wet but not very wet, especially in a way that seems nice: *a moist chocolate cake* —**moistness** *n.* [U] —compare DAMP[1] —see Usage Note at MOIST

moist·en /ˈmɔɪsən/ *v.* [I,T] to become slightly wet, or to make something slightly wet

mois·ture /ˈmɔɪstʃər/ *n.* [U] small amounts of water that are present in the air, in a substance, or on a surface: *All plants require constant moisture when first planted.*

mois·tur·ize /ˈmɔɪstʃəˌraɪz/ *v.* [T] **1** to keep your skin soft by using a special liquid or cream **2** moisturizing cream/lotion/oil cream, oil etc. that you put on your skin to keep it soft

mois·tur·iz·er /ˈmɔɪstʃəˌraɪzər/ *n.* [C,U] a liquid or cream that you put on your skin to keep it soft

Mo·ja·ve Desert, the /moʊˈhɑvi/ also **the Mohave Desert** a large desert in southern California

mo·lar /ˈmoʊlər/ *n.* [C] one of the large teeth at the back of the mouth used for crushing food —compare INCISOR —**molar** *adj.*

mo·las·ses /məˈlæsɪz/ *n.* [U] a thick dark sweet liquid that is obtained from raw sugar plants when they are being made into sugar

mold[1] /moʊld/ *n.* **1** [U] a soft green or black substance that grows on food which has been kept too long, and on objects that are in warm, wet air: *You can cut the mold off the cheese and still eat it.* **2** [C] a hollow container that you pour liquid into, so that when the liquid becomes solid, it takes the shape of the container: *Cool the cake in the mold before serving.* **3** [singular] if someone is in a particular mold, or fits into one, they have all the attitudes and qualities typical of a certain type of person: *In a lot of ways he doesn't fit the mold of a typical politician.* **4 break the mold** to change a situation completely, by doing something that has not been done before: *He urged educators to break the mold and find new ways of teaching.*

mold[2] *v.* **1** [T] to shape a soft substance by pressing or rolling it or by putting it into a mold: *The cheeses are molded into distinctive shapes.* | *The toys are made of molded rubber.* **2** [T] to influence the way someone's character or attitudes develop: *I try to take young athletes and mold them into team players.* **3** [I,T] to fit closely to the shape of something: *The lining of the boot molds itself to the shape of your foot.*

mol·der /ˈmoʊldər/ *v.* [I] also **molder away** to decay slowly and gradually: *Decades-old medical supplies moldered in the warehouses.*

mold·ing /ˈmoʊldɪŋ/ *n.* **1** [C,U] a thin line of stone, wood, plastic etc. used as decoration around the edge of something such as a wall, car, or piece of furniture **2** [C] an object produced from a mold

Mol·do·va /mɑlˈdoʊvə/ a country in eastern Europe between Romania and the Ukraine, which used to be part of the former Soviet Union —**Moldovan** *n., adj.*

mold·y /ˈmoʊldi/ *adj.* **moldier, moldiest** covered with MOLD: *moldy bread* —**moldiness** *n.* [U]

mole[1] /moʊl/ *n.* [C] **1** a small dark brown mark on the skin that is often slightly higher than the skin around it **2** a small animal with brown fur that cannot see very well and usually lives in holes under the ground **3** someone who works for an organization, especially a government, while secretly giving information to its enemy: *FBI moles had infiltrated the company looking for evidence of fraud.* **4** TECHNICAL a scientific unit for measuring the quantity of a substance

mole[2] /ˈmoʊleɪ/ *n.* [U] a SPICY Mexican sauce that has chocolate in it and that you put on meat

mol·e·cule /ˈmɑləˌkyul/ *n.* [C] the smallest unit into which any substance can be divided without losing its own chemical nature, usually consisting of two or more atoms: *a nitrogen molecule* —**molecular** /məˈlɛkyələr/ *adj.*

mole·hill /ˈmoʊlˌhɪl/ *n.* [C] a small pile of earth made by a MOLE —see also **make a mountain out of a molehill** (MOUNTAIN (3))

mole·skin /ˈmoʊlˌskɪn/ *n.* [U] **1** the skin of a MOLE **2** a soft, thick material that you put on your feet to protect them from rubbing against your shoes: *I put a moleskin patch on my heel.* **3** thick dark cloth that feels like SUEDE

mo·lest /məˈlɛst/ *v.* [T] **1** to attack or harm someone, especially a child, by touching them in a sexual way or trying to have sex with them: *The boy told officers he had been molested several times.* —compare ABUSE[2] (1) **2** OLD-FASHIONED to attack and physically harm someone —**molester** *n.* [C] —**molestation** /ˌmɑləˈsteɪʃən, ˌmoʊ-, -lɛ-/ *n.* [U]

Mo·lière /moʊlˈyɛr/ (1622–1673) a French actor and writer of humorous plays whose real name was Jean-Baptiste Poquelin

moll /moʊl, mɑl/ *n.* [C] OLD-FASHIONED, SLANG a criminal's GIRLFRIEND: *a gangster's moll*

mol·li·fy /ˈmɑləˌfaɪ/ *v.* **mollifies, mollified, mollifying** [T] to make someone feel less angry and upset about something: *Mel appeared somewhat mollified by her words.* —**mollification** /ˌmɑləfəˈkeɪʃən/ *n.* [U]

mol·lusk /ˈmɑləsk/ *n.* [C] a type of sea or land animal that has a soft body covered by a hard shell

mol·ly·cod·dle /ˈmɑliˌkɑdl/ *v.* [T] to treat someone too kindly: *Stop mollycoddling those kids – they need to think for themselves.*

Mo·lo·kai /ˌmɑləˈkaɪ, moʊ-/ an island in the Pacific Ocean that is part of the U.S. state of Hawaii

Mo·lo·tov cock·tail /ˌmɑlətɔf ˈkɑkteɪl, ˌmɔl-/ *n.* [C] a simple bomb consisting of a bottle filled with gasoline, with a piece of cloth at the end that you light

molt /moʊlt/ *v.* [I] when a bird or animal molts, it loses hair, feathers, or skin so that new ones can grow

mol·ten /ˈmoʊltʰn/ *adj.* [usually before noun] molten metal or rock has been made into a liquid by being heated to a very high temperature: *molten lava*

mol·to /ˈmoʊltoʊ/ *adv.* a word used in music meaning "very"

mol·y /ˈmoʊli/ —see **holy cow/mackerel/moly etc.** (HOLY (3))

mo·lyb·de·num /məˈlɪbdənəm/ *n.* [U] *symbol* **Mo** a pale-colored metal that is an ELEMENT and is used especially to strengthen steel

mom /mɑm/ *n.* [C] INFORMAL mother: *Mom, can I go over to Barbara's house? | My mom says I have to stay home tonight.*

mom-and-pop /ˌ.. ˈ.◂/ *adj.* [only before noun] INFORMAL a mom-and-pop business is owned and operated by a family or a husband and wife: *a mom-and-pop restaurant*

mo·ment /ˈmoʊmənt/ *n.*
1 short time [C] a very short period of time: *He was here a moment ago. | Can you spare a few moments to answer some questions? | Just a moment* (=used to tell someone to wait a short time): *I'll see if Ms. Marciano is free. | We'll come to some examples of this in a moment* (=very soon). *| Could you hold the line for a moment? | One moment, please* (=used to tell someone to wait a short time, especially on the telephone). *| Arthur, do you have a moment* (=used to ask someone if they have time to speak to you or do something for you)*?*
2 point in time [C] a particular point in time: *I was just waiting for the right moment to tell her. | From the first moment I got on the ice I knew this wasn't the sport for me. | At that moment* (=used to emphasize when something happened) *she started to cry.*
3 at the moment now: *At the moment, the county is doing nothing with the property south of town.*
4 for the moment used to say that something is happening now but will probably change in the future: *For the moment, we will ignore the question of whether the costs are reasonable.*
5 the sth of the moment the job, person, event etc. of the moment is the one that is most important or famous at the present time: *The question of the moment is, will Bradley run again for the Senate?*
6 opportunity [C usually singular] a particular period of time when you have a chance to do something: *It was Tara's big moment* (=her chance to show her skill); *she breathed deeply and began to play.*
7 have its/your moments to have periods of being good or interesting: *The Saints had their moments, but they still lost.*
8 at a moment's notice without being given much time to prepare: *Hancock's staff is ready to deal with a variety of medical emergencies at a moment's notice.*
9 the moment of truth the time when you will find out if something will work correctly, be successful etc.: *The moment of truth came when I tasted the sauce.*
10 a moment of weakness a time when you can be persuaded more easily than usual
11 of great moment LITERARY important: *Barry is a good writer, even when he is not writing about things of great moment.*

USAGE NOTE: MOMENT

WORD CHOICE: moment, minute, second
Moment, **minute**, and **second** are used in many of the same phrases to mean exactly the same thing. **Minute** is probably the most commonly used word in these types of phrases. For example, you can say: *She'll call you the minute she gets home, She'll call you the moment she gets home,* or *She'll call you the second she gets home.*

---

mo·men·tar·i·ly /ˌmoʊmənˈtɛrəli/ *adv.* **1** FORMAL for a very short time: *Spoleto paused momentarily to speak with reporters.* **2** SPOKEN very soon: *I'll be with you momentarily.*

mo·men·tar·y /ˈmoʊmənˌtɛri/ *adj.* usually before noun continuing for a very short time: *Davis was surprised into a momentary silence.*

mo·men·tous /moʊˈmɛntəs, mə-/ *adj.* a momentous event, occasion, decision etc. is very important, especially because of the effects it will have in the future: *a momentous shift in policy | At the time, our department was going through some momentous changes.*

mo·men·tum /moʊˈmɛntəm, mə-/ *n.* [U] **1** the ability to keep increasing, developing, or being more

---

successful: *Leconte won the first match, then seemed to lose momentum* (=become weaker or stop being successful). *| The economic recovery is expected to gain momentum* (=become stronger or more successful) *soon.* **2** the force that makes a moving object keep moving: *Carey's momentum carried him past the base. | The hill got steeper and the sled gained momentum* (=moved faster). *| The train loses momentum* (=moves more slowly) *as it comes into the station.* **3** TECHNICAL the force or power contained in a moving object calculated by multiplying its weight by its speed

mom·ma /ˈmɑmə/ *n.* [C] another spelling of MAMA

mom·my, mommie /ˈmɑmi/ *n.* [C] a word meaning "mother," used by or to young children

mommy track /ˈ.. ˌ./ *n.* [C] INFORMAL a situation in which women with children have less opportunity to make large amounts of money or become very successful at their jobs, for example because they are not able to work as many hours as other people

Mon. the written abbreviation of Monday

Mon·a·co /ˈmɑnəˌkoʊ/ a small PRINCIPALITY (=country ruled by a prince) on the Mediterranean coast between France and Italy —**Monacan** /ˈmɑnəkən, məˈnɑkən/ also **Monégasque** *n., adj.*

Monaco-Ville /ˌmɑnəkoʊ ˈvil/ the capital city of Monaco

mon·arch /ˈmɑnək, ˈmɑnɑrk/ *n.* [C] FORMAL a king or queen —**monarchic** /məˈnɑrkɪk/ also **monarchical** *adj.: monarchic rule*

mon·ar·chist /ˈmɑnəkɪst/ *n.* [C] someone who supports the idea that their country should be ruled by a king or queen

mon·ar·chy /ˈmɑnəki/ *n. plural* **monarchies** **1** [U] the system in which a country is ruled by a king or queen **2** [C] a country that is ruled by a king or queen: *Burns hated European monarchies and helped lead the American Revolution.* —compare REPUBLIC

mon·as·ter·y /ˈmɑnəˌstɛri/ *n. plural* **monasteries** [C] a building or group of buildings where MONKs live —compare CONVENT

mo·nas·tic /məˈnæstɪk/ *adj.* **1** concerning or relating to MONKs or monasteries: *a monastic order* **2** someone who has a monastic way of life lives alone and very simply —**monastically** /-kli/ *adv.* —**monasticism** /məˈnæstəˌsɪzəm/ *n.* [U]

Mon·day /ˈmʌndi, -deɪ/ *written abbreviation* **Mon.** *n. plural* **Mondays** [C,U] the second day of the week, between Sunday and Tuesday: *Steve said he'd arrive Monday. | It was raining on Monday. | Jo had a doctor's appointment last Monday. | I'll see you next Monday. | The concert's going to be on the radio this Monday* (=the next Monday that is coming). *| The restaurant is usually closed on Mondays* (=each Monday). *| Labor Day is always on a Monday. | Monday morning/afternoon/night etc. I have a date Monday night.* —see Usage Note at SUNDAY

Monday morn·ing quar·ter·back /ˌ.. .. ˈ...../ *n.* [C] INFORMAL someone who gives advice on something only after it has happened —**Monday morning quarterbacking** *n.* [U]

mon·do /ˈmɑndoʊ/ *adj.* [only before noun] SLANG very large, strange, good etc.: *Jerry's sound system has some mondo speakers.*

Mon·dri·an /ˌmɑndriˈɑn/, **Piet** /pit/ (1872–1944) a Dutch painter famous for his ABSTRACT work

Mon·é·gasque /ˌmɑneɪˈgæsk/ *adj.* relating to or coming from Monaco —**Monégasque** *n.* [C]

Mon·et /moʊˈneɪ/, **Claude** /kloʊd, klɔd/ (1840–1926) a French painter who helped to start the IMPRESSIONIST movement

mon·e·ta·rism /ˈmɑnətəˌrɪzəm/ *n.* [U] the belief that the best way to manage and control a country's economic system is to limit the amount of money that is available and being used —**monetarist** *adj., n.* [C]

mon·e·tar·y /ˈmɑnəˌtɛri/ *adj.* [usually before noun] relating to money, especially all the money in a

M

particular country: *The country has a monetary system based on the value of gold.*

mon·e·tize /'mɑnə,taɪz/ v. [T] TECHNICAL to change government BONDS and debts into money —**monetization** /,mɑnətə'zeɪʃən/ n. [U]

S W
1 1
mon·ey /'mʌni/ n. [U] **1** what you earn by working and use in order to buy things, usually in the form of coins or pieces of paper with their value printed on them: *$250 is a lot of money.* | *Leon dropped all his money on the floor.* | *His stereo system cost a lot of money.* | *Do you have enough money* (=have money in the form coins or paper) *to pay for the sandwiches?* | *Ann really wanted to go to Yellowstone with us, but she didn't have the money* (=she had not saved enough). | *Asa's making a lot of money, but he's working eighteen-hour days.* | *Lynn's dad worked two jobs to earn extra money.* | *All the money was spent on special effects; the script wasn't very good at all.* | *They never seem to turn the heat on; I guess they're trying to save money.* | *The restaurant is losing money* (=spending more money than it earns). | *They charge a lot of money just to rent a video.* | *I didn't really want to have to borrow money to go to grad school.* | *The church is trying to raise money for a new carpet.* | *She's making about $40,000 a year, which is pretty good money* (=a good salary for your work). | *The state needs to put more money into* (=spend more money on) *the schools.* | *Just take it back to the store, they'll give you your money back.* **2** all the money that a person, organization, or country owns; WEALTH: *Money isn't everything.* | *In 1929, hundreds of rich men lost all their money when the stock market crashed.* | *Perot made his money in a successful computer business.* **3 get your money's worth** to get something worth the price that you paid: *Some publishers feel they haven't been getting their money's worth from the show.* **4 French/Japanese/Turkish etc. money** the money that is used in a particular country; CURRENCY: *I still have $10 in Canadian money left.* **5 have money to burn** INFORMAL to have a lot of money to spend on things, especially things that other people think are unnecessary or silly: *People who buy expensive cars have money to burn, and they want you to know it.* | *Adventure expeditions are growing in popularity, particularly among older Americans with money to burn.* **6 money is no object** used to say that you can spend as much money as you want to on something: *If money were no object, what kind of house would you want?* **7 there's money (to be made) in sth** used to say that you can get a lot of money from a particular activity or from buying and selling something: *Experts and city officials agree there's money to be made in the casino business.* **8 marry (into) money** to marry someone whose family is rich **9 money pit** something such as a boat or house that causes you to spend a lot of money very often in order to keep it working or repaired: *Critics have called the space station a money pit in the sky.*

SPOKEN PHRASES

10 that kind of money a phrase meaning "a lot of money," used when you think something costs too much, when someone earns a lot more than other people etc.: *If I had that kind of money, I guess I'd splurge too.* | *He wanted $5000 for the truck, and I just don't have that kind of money.* **11 pay good money for sth** to spend a lot of money on something: *I paid good money for that sofa, so it should last.* **12 be (right) on the money** used when something is perfect or exactly right for the situation: *Carson was right on the money when he said people are tired of big-shot politicians.* **13 for my money** used when giving your opinion about something, to emphasize that you believe it strongly: *For my money, it's one of the most romantic places in Hawaii.* **14 money talks** used to say that money is powerful, and people who have money can get what they want: *Money talks, and poor working people are ignored.* **15 my money's on sb/sth, the smart money is on sb/sth** used to say that you think is

very likely to happen in a situation: *The smart money is on the A's to win the series.* **16 put your money where your mouth is** to show by your actions that you really believe what you say: *It's time for the governor to put his money where his mouth is.* **17 I'd put money on it** used to emphasize that you are completely sure about something: *We're not going to lose. I'd put money on it.* **18 I'm not made of money** used to say that you do not have a lot of money when someone asks you for some **19 money doesn't grow on trees** used to tell someone that they should not waste money, or that there is not enough money to buy something expensive **20 be in the money** to have a lot of money, especially suddenly or when you did not expect to

—see also BLOOD MONEY, HUSH MONEY, POCKET MONEY, **give sb a (good) run for their money** (RUN² (16)), **smart money** (SMART¹ (3)), **throw money at sb/sth** (THROW¹ (18))

USAGE NOTE: MONEY

WORD CHOICE: money, cash, change, currency
Money is the most general word: *Do you have any money?* | *taxpayers' money.* **Cash** usually means money in coins or paper money, rather than checks or credit cards: *"Can I pay by check?" "Sorry, we only take cash."* | *He pays me in cash.* **Change** means the money that is given back to you when you have given more money for something than the amount it costs: *Here's your change, sir – three dollars and fifteen cents.* **Change** can also mean money in low-value coins or paper money: *Do you have change for five dollars?* | *two dollars in small change.* **Currency** is the unit of money used in a particular country: *You can use your credit card to obtain foreign currency when traveling abroad.*

---

mon·ey·bags /'mʌni,bægz/ n. [singular] INFORMAL someone who has a lot of money

money belt /'.. ,./ n. [C] a special belt that you can carry money in while you are traveling

money chang·er, moneychanger /'.. ,./ n. [C] someone whose business is to exchange one country's money for money from another country, sometimes without official approval

mon·eyed, monied /'mʌnid/ adj. [only before noun] FORMAL rich: *a resort for moneyed Floridians*

money-grub·bing /'mʌni,grʌbɪŋ/ adj. [only before noun] INFORMAL determined to get money, even by unfair or dishonest methods: *money-grubbing land developers* —**moneygrubber** n. [C]

mon·ey·lend·er, money lender /'mʌni,lɛndɚ/ n. [C] someone whose business is to lend money to people, especially at very high rates of INTEREST

mon·ey·mak·er, money-maker /'mʌni,meɪkɚ/ n. [C] a product or business that earns a lot of money: *Farrell's book will undoubtedly be a moneymaker.*

money mar·ket /'.. ,./ n. [C] the banks and other financial institutions that buy and sell BONDS, CURRENCY (=paper money) etc.

money or·der /'.. ,./ n. [C] a special type of check that you buy and send to someone so that they can exchange it for money

money sup·ply /'.. ,./ n. **the money supply** TECHNICAL all the money that exists in a country's economic system at a particular time

-mon·ger /mʌŋgɚ, mɑŋgɚ/ suffix [in nouns] **1** someone who says things that are not nice or encourages activities that are immoral or not nice: *rumor mongers* (=people who say untrue things about other people) | *warmongers* (=people who are eager to start wars) **2** OLD-FASHIONED someone who sells a particular thing: *a fishmonger*

Mon·gol /'mɑŋgəl, -goʊl/ **1** one of the people who live in Mongolia **2** one of the people from several related groups who live in central Asia

Mon·go·li·a /mɑŋ'goʊliə/ a country in north central Asia between Russia and China —**Mongolian** n., adj.

mon·goose /'mɑŋgus/ n. plural **mongooses** [C] a small furry tropical animal that kills snakes and rats

mon·grel /'mʌŋgrəl, 'mʌŋ-/ n. [C] a dog that is a mix of several different breeds —compare MUTT

mon·ied /'mʌnid/ adj. another spelling of MONEYED

mon·ies /'mʌniz/ n. [plural] LAW money: *All monies should appear in the budget, regardless of source.*

mon·i·ker /'mɑnɪkɚ/ n. [C] INFORMAL someone's name, SIGNATURE, or NICKNAME: *Burke still goes under the moniker of "the king of rock and soul."*

mon·i·tor¹ /'mɑnətɚ/ n. [C] **1** the part of a computer that looks like a television and that shows information: *a color monitor* —compare SCREEN¹ (1) **2** a television that shows a picture of what is happening in a particular place: *A security man was watching a row of monitors.* **3** a piece of equipment that receives and shows information about what is happening inside someone's body: *a monitor that shows the baby's heartbeat* **4** a child who has been chosen to help the teacher in some way: *milk monitors* **5** someone whose job is to listen to news, messages etc. from foreign radio stations and report on them

monitor² v. [T] **1** to carefully watch, listen to, or examine something over a period of time, to check for any changes or developments: *U.N. peacekeepers will be sent to monitor the ceasefire.* | *Nurses constantly monitor the patients' condition.* **2** to secretly listen to other people's telephone calls, foreign radio broadcasts etc.: *Army intelligence has been monitoring the enemy's radio broadcasts.* —see Usage Note at CONTROL¹

monk /mʌŋk/ n. [C] a man who is member of a group of religious men who live together in a MONASTERY —**monkish** adj.: *a monkish silence* —compare NUN

Monk /mʌŋk/, **The·lo·ni·ous** /θə'lounɪəs/ (1917–1982) a JAZZ musician who played the piano

mon·key¹ /'mʌŋki/ n. plural **monkeys** [C]
1 ▶animal◀ a small animal with a long tail, which uses its hands to climb trees and lives in hot countries
2 ▶child◀ INFORMAL a small child who is very active and likes to play tricks: *Stop that you little monkey!*
3 monkey business behavior that may cause trouble or may be dishonest: *The proposal had become the victim of political monkey business and deceit.*
4 a monkey on your back INFORMAL a serious problem that makes your life very difficult, especially being dependent on drugs or losing a lot of sports competitions
5 get a/the monkey off your back to get rid of or end a serious problem that has been making your life very difficult: *The win finally gets the monkey off our backs.*
6 I'll be a monkey's uncle! OLD-FASHIONED, SPOKEN said when you are very surprised about something
7 make a monkey (out) of sb to make someone appear stupid
8 monkey see, monkey do SPOKEN used to say that people will often do what they see other people doing, even if it is silly or stupid —see also GREASE MONKEY

monkey² v. monkeys, monkeyed, monkeying
monkey around phr. v. [I] INFORMAL to behave in a stupid or careless way: *The kids were monkeying around in the playground when Tad got hurt.*
monkey (around) with sth phr. v. [T] to touch or use something, usually when you do not know how to do it correctly: *You'll break the tape player if you don't stop monkeying with it.*

monkey bars /'.. ,./ n. [plural] a structure of metal bars for children to climb and play on

mon·key·shines /'mʌŋki,ʃaɪnz/ n. [plural] OLD-FASHIONED tricks or jokes

monkey suit /'.. ./ n. [C] OLD-FASHIONED, HUMOROUS a TUXEDO

monkey wrench /'.. ,./ n. [C] a tool that is used for holding and turning things of different widths, especially NUTS —see also **throw a (monkey) wrench in** sth (WRENCH² (2)) —see picture at TOOL¹

mon·o¹ /'mɑnou/ n. [U] INFORMAL **1** an infectious illness that makes your GLANDS swell and makes you feel weak and tired for a long time **2** a system of recording or broadcasting sound, in which the sound comes from only one direction

mono² adj. using a system of recording or broadcasting sound in which all the sound comes from only one direction: *a mono recording* —compare STEREO²

mono- /'mɑnou, -nə/ prefix one; SINGLE: *a monosyllabic word* (=a word that has only one SYLLABLE) | *a monolingual dictionary* (=dealing with only one language)

mon·o·chrome /'mɑnə,kroum/ adj. **1** a monochrome computer MONITOR uses one color as a background and only one other color for the letters on the screen **2** in shades of only one color, especially shades of gray: *a monochrome color scheme for the room*

mon·o·cle /'mɑnəkəl/ n. [C] a single LENS (=round piece of glass) that you hold in front of one eye to help you to see better

mon·o·cul·ture /'mɑnou,kʌltʃɚ/ n. [C,U] TECHNICAL the practice of growing only one type of crop on an area of land every year, which can be harmful to the soil

mo·nog·a·my /mə'nɑgəmi/ n. [U] the custom or practice of being married to only one person at a time —**monogamous** adj. —**monogamously** adv. —compare BIGAMY, POLYGAMY

mon·o·gram /'mɑnə,græm/ n. [C] a design made from the first letters of someone's names, that is put on things such as shirts or writing paper —**monogrammed** adj.: *monogrammed towels*

mon·o·graph /'mɑnəgræf/ n. [C + on] a serious article or short book about a subject

mon·o·lin·gual /,mɑnə'lɪŋgwəl/ adj. TECHNICAL speaking, using, or dealing with only one language: *a monolingual dictionary* —compare BILINGUAL, MULTILINGUAL

mon·o·lith /'mɑnl,ɪθ/ n. [C] **1** an organization, government etc. that is very large and powerful and difficult to change: *the collapse of the Communist monolith in Eastern Europe* **2** a very large, tall building that looks very solid and impressive: *The Hotel Dunbar was a pink and chocolate-colored brick monolith on 42nd Street.* **3** a large tall block of stone, especially one that was put in place in ancient times, possibly for religious reasons

mon·o·lith·ic /,mɑnl'ɪθɪk/ adj. **1** a monolithic organization, political system etc. is very large and powerful and difficult to change: *monolithic corporations* **2** very large, solid, and impressive: *monolithic office buildings*

mon·o·logue, monolog /'mɑnl,ɔg, -,ɑg/ n. [C] **1** a long speech by one character in a play, movie, or television show —compare DIALOGUE (1), SOLILOQUY **2** a long period of talking by one person that prevents other people from taking part in a conversation: *a rambling monologue*

mon·o·ma·ni·a /,mɑnou'meɪniə/ n. [U] TECHNICAL an unusually strong interest in a particular idea or subject —**monomaniac** adj., n. [C]

mon·o·nu·cle·o·sis /,mɑnou,nukli'ousɪs/ n. [U] TECHNICAL: see MONO¹ (1)

mon·o·plane /'mɑnəpleɪn, -nou-/ n. [C] TECHNICAL an airplane with only one wing on each side, like most modern airplanes —compare BIPLANE

mo·nop·o·lis·tic /mə,nɑpə'lɪstɪk/ adj. controlling or trying to control something completely, especially an industry or business activity: *monopolistic corporations*

mo·nop·o·lize /mə'nɑpə,laɪz/ v. [T] **1** to have complete control over something, especially a type of business, so that other people cannot get involved: *In Russia, Intourist no longer monopolizes the foreign tourism business.* | *The 49ers monopolized the ball in the third period.* **2** to demand or need a lot of someone's time and attention: *Susan's children monopolize her time and energy.* —**monopolization** /mə,nɑpələ'zeɪʃən/ n. [U]

mo·nop·o·ly /mə'nɑpəli/ n. plural **monopolies** **1** [C,U] the control of all or most of a business activity by a single company or by a government:

M

[**+ on/of**] *At the time, AT&T had a monopoly on telephone services.* **2** [C] a company that controls all or most of a business activity: *the De Beers diamond monopoly* **3** [singular] the state of having complete control or possession of something, so that other people cannot share it: *After all, no one person has a monopoly on hope.*

mon·o·rail /ˈmɑnəˌreɪl/ *n.* **1** [U] a type of railroad that uses a single RAIL, usually high above the ground **2** [C] a train that travels on this type of railroad

mon·o·so·di·um glu·ta·mate /ˌmɑnəˌsoʊdiəm ˈglutəˌmeɪt/ *n.* [U] TECHNICAL: see MSG

mon·o·syl·lab·ic /ˌmɑnəsɪˈlæbɪk◂/ *adj.* **1** someone who is monosyllabic or makes monosyllabic remarks seems impolite because they do not say much: *He grunted monosyllabic responses to questions.* **2** TECHNICAL a monosyllabic word has only one SYLLABLE

mon·o·syl·la·ble /ˈmɑnəˌsɪləbəl/ *n.* [C] TECHNICAL a word with one SYLLABLE

mon·o·the·ism /ˈmɑnəθiˌɪzəm/ *n.* [U] TECHNICAL the belief that there is only one God —**monotheist** *n.* [C] —**monotheistic** /ˌmɑnəθiˈɪstɪk/ *adj.* —compare POLYTHEISM

mon·o·tone /ˈmɑnəˌtoʊn/ *n.* [singular] a sound or way of speaking or singing that continues on the same note without getting any louder or softer, and therefore sounds very boring: *In a barely audible monotone, she gave her evidence.*

mo·not·o·nous /məˈnɑtˌn-əs/ *adj.* boring because there is no variety: *My job is monotonous, but at least I'm working.* | *a monotonous voice* —**monotonously** *adv.*

mo·not·o·ny /məˈnɑtˌn-i/ *n.* [U] a lack of variety that makes you feel bored: *the monotony of the prairie highways*

mon·o·un·sat·u·rat·ed /ˌmɑnoʊʌnˈsætʃəˌreɪt̮ɪd/ *adj.* TECHNICAL monounsaturated fats, such as OLIVE OIL, are better for your health than other types of fats, such as butter

mon·ox·ide /məˈnɑksaɪd/ *n.* [C,U] TECHNICAL a chemical compound containing one atom of oxygen to every atom of another substance: *carbon monoxide*

Mon·roe /mʌnˈroʊ/, **James** (1758–1831) the fifth President of the U.S.

Monroe, Mar·i·lyn /ˈmærəlɪn/ (1926–1962) a U.S. movie actress and singer, whose real name was Norma Jean Baker

Marilyn Monroe

Mon·ro·vi·a /mənˈroʊviə/ the capital and largest city of Liberia

Mon·si·gnor /mɑnˈsinyɚ/ *n.* [C] a way of addressing a priest of high rank in the Catholic Church

mon·soon /mɑnˈsun/ *n.* [C] **1** [usually singular] the season, from about April to October, when it rains a lot in India and other southern Asian countries **2** the rain that falls during this season, or the wind that brings the rain

mon·ster¹ /ˈmɑnstɚ/ *n.* [C]
1 in stories an imaginary large ugly frightening creature: *a sea monster*
2 cruel person someone who is very cruel and evil
3 child OFTEN HUMOROUS a small child, especially one who is behaving badly: *I hate taking the boys grocery shopping – they turn into monsters.*
4 sth large INFORMAL an object, animal etc. that is unusually large: *Their pumpkin this year was a monster.*
5 dangerous problem a dangerous or threatening problem, especially one that develops gradually: *The legislation will create a monster that will take years to correct.*

monster² *adj.* [only before noun] SLANG unusually large: *That's a monster tree!* | *a monster truck rally*

mon·stros·i·ty /mɑnˈstrɑsət̮i/ *n. plural* **monstrosities** [C] something large that is very ugly, especially a building: *a 275-room brick monstrosity*

mon·strous /ˈmɑnstrəs/ *adj.* **1** very wrong, immoral, or unfair: *a monstrous lie* **2** unusually large, and often frightening: *a monstrous 400-pound grizzly bear* —**monstrously** *adv.*

mon·tage /mɑnˈtɑʒ, moʊn-/ *n.* **1** [U] an art form in which a picture, movie, piece of writing etc. is made from parts of different pictures etc., that are combined to form a whole **2** [C] something made using this process: *a photo montage*

Mon·taigne /mɑnˈteɪn/, **Mi·chel Ey·quem de** /miˈʃɛl iˈkɛm də/ (1533–1592) a French writer of ESSAYS

Mon·ta·na /mɑnˈtænə/ *written abbreviation* **MT** a state in the northwestern U.S.

Mon·tauk /ˈmɑntɔk/ a Native American tribe from the northeastern area of the U.S.

Mont Blanc /mɔn ˈblɑŋ/ a mountain in the Alps on the border between France and Italy which is the highest mountain in western Europe

Mon·te·ne·gro /ˌmɑntɪˈnigroʊ, -ˈnɛ-/ a REPUBLIC that is part of the Federal Republic of Yugoslavia, which consists of Serbia and Montenegro

Mon·tes·quieu /ˌmɑntəsˈkyu/, **Charles, Baron de** (1689–1755) a French political PHILOSOPHER whose ideas about the separation of powers in government influenced the U.S. Constitution

Mon·tes·so·ri /ˌmɑntəˈsɔri/, **Ma·ri·a** /məˈriə/ (1870–1952) an Italian teacher and writer who developed a new way of teaching young children, which is used in children's schools in many countries

Mon·te·vi·de·o /ˌmɑntəvɪˈdeɪoʊ/ the capital and largest city of Uruguay

Mon·te·zu·ma /ˌmɑntəˈzumə/ (1466–1520) the last Aztec ruler of Mexico, who was taken prisoner by the Spaniards under Cortés, and later killed by his own people

Montezuma's re·venge /ˌ.ˌ.. .ˈ./ *n.* [U] HUMOROUS, DIARRHEA that you get from drinking water or eating food that is not very clean while traveling in poor countries

Mont·gol·fier /mɑntˈgɑlfiɚ, -fiˌeɪ/, **Jo·seph Mi·chel** /ˌʒoʊzɛf miˈʃɛl/ (1740–1810) a French inventor who made the first HOT-AIR BALLOON with his brother Jacques Etienne Montgolfier (1745–1799)

Mont·gom·er·y /mɑntˈgʌməri/ the capital city of the U.S. state of Alabama

month /mʌnθ/ *n.* [C] **1** one of the twelve periods of time that a year is divided into: *It snowed heavily during the month of January.* | *She'll be thirteen this month.* | *Phil is coming home for a visit next month.* | **once/twice etc. a month** *The magazine is published once a month.* **2** a period of about four weeks: *Tammy has an eight-month old daughter.* | *He'll be back a month from Friday.* **3 months** a long time, especially several months: *Redecorating the kitchen took months.* | *I haven't seen Sarah in months.* **4 month after month** used to emphasize that something happens regularly or continuously for several months: *I'm just doing the same old thing month after month.* **5 month by month** used when you are talking about a situation that develops over several months: *Unemployment figures are rising month by month.* **6 a month of Sundays** [usually with a negative] OLD-FASHIONED a very long time: *I haven't seen you in a month of Sundays, Percy.* —see also **that time of the month** (TIME¹ (36))

month·ly¹ /ˈmʌnθli/ *adj.* [only before noun] **1** happening or produced once a month: *a monthly magazine* | *a monthly meeting* **2** relating to a single month: *a monthly income of $3,750* | *a monthly credit card payment* | *a monthly commuter train ticket* —**monthly** *adv.*

monthly² *n. plural* **monthlies** [C] a magazine that is printed once a month

Mon·ti·cel·lo /ˌmɑntəˈtʃɛloʊ/ a large house and

ESTATE in the U.S. state of Virginia that was designed and lived in by U.S. President Thomas Jefferson

Mont·pel·ier /mɑntˈpilyɚ/ the capital city of the U.S. state of Vermont

Mon·tre·al /ˌmɑntriˈɔl/ a city in the PROVINCE of Quebec in eastern Canada

mon·u·ment /ˈmɑnyəmənt/ n. [C] **1** a building or other large structure that is built to remind people of an important event or famous person: [+ of/to] *The Vietnam memorial is a moving monument to the soldiers killed in the war.* **2** a building or place that is important, especially for historical reasons.: *Ellis Island is preserved as a historic monument.* **3 be a monument to sth** to be a very clear example of what can happen as a result of a particular quality: *The empty office buildings are a monument to bad planning.*

mon·u·men·tal /ˌmɑnyəˈmɛntl◂/ adj. **1** [only before noun] extremely large, bad, good, impressive etc.: *It was a monumental task.* | *The concert was a monumental embarrassment.* **2** [usually before noun] a monumental achievement, piece of work etc. is very important, and it is usually based on many years of work: *Darwin published his monumental work on evolution in 1859.* **3** [only before noun] appearing on a monument, or built as a monument: *a monumental temple*

mon·u·men·tal·ly /ˌmɑnyəˈmɛntl-i/ adv. extremely: *He would have to be monumentally stupid to do that.*

moo /mu/ n. [C] the sound that a cow makes —**moo** v. [I]

mooch /mutʃ/ v. [T] INFORMAL to get something by asking someone to give you it, instead of paying for it yourself: *Mom got sick of him mooching meals from us.*

mooch·ing /ˈmutʃɪŋ/ n. [U] a way of catching fish by leaving your hook still in the water and waiting for fish to come and eat the BAIT

s w 2 2 **mood** /mud/ n.
1 [way you feel] [C] the way you feel at a particular time: *Darla's a typical teenager – her moods change like lightning.* | **in a good/bad/rotten etc. mood** *Sorry – I'm just in a really bad mood today.* | *The traffic* **put me in a lousy mood** (=made me feel annoyed or angry).
2 be/feel in the mood to want to do something or feel that you enjoy doing something: [+ for] *I'm not really in the mood for Mexican food.*
3 [way people feel] [singular] the way a group of people feels about something or about life in general: *Back at the Fernandez house, the mood was glum.* | [+ of] *The bill appeals to the anti-government mood of the voters.*
4 be in no mood to not want to do something, or be determined not to do something: [+ for] *The boss is in no mood for compromise on this point.* | [**be in no mood to do sth**] *La Russo was in no mood to discuss the incident.*
5 mood swing an occasion when someone's feelings change very suddenly from one extreme to another: *Greg has been known to have occasional mood swings.*
6 [atmosphere] [C usually singular] the way that a place, book, movie etc. makes you feel: *The restaurant's decor aims at a romantic mood.*
7 be in a mood SPOKEN to feel unhappy or angry: *She's been in a mood all day.*
8 [grammar] [C,U] TECHNICAL one of the sets of verb forms in grammar such as the INDICATIVE (=expressing a fact or action), the IMPERATIVE (=expressing a command) or the SUBJUNCTIVE (=expressing a doubt or wish)

mood mu·sic /ˈ. ˌ../ n. [U] music that is supposed to make you feel particular emotions, especially romantic feelings

mood·y /ˈmudi/ adj. **moodier, moodiest 1** having moods that change often and quickly, especially angry or bad moods: *She's been really moody and emotional.* | *a moody teenager* **2** easily becoming annoyed or unhappy: *He became moody and unpredictable after his wife left him.* **3** making people feel particular moods: *a moody, black-and-white movie* —**moodily** adv. —**moodiness** n. [U]

moo·lah, **moola** /ˈmulə/ n. [U] SLANG money

moon¹ /mun/ n. **1 the moon** also **the Moon** the round object that you can see shining in the sky at night, and that moves around the Earth every 28 days **2** [singular] the appearance or shape of this object at a particular time: *There's no moon tonight* (=you cannot see it). | *a full moon* (=the moon appearing as a full circle) **3** [C] a round object that moves around PLANETS other than the Earth: *the moons of Saturn* **4 be asking for the moon** INFORMAL to ask for something that is difficult or impossible to obtain: *I don't think the employees are asking for the moon.* **5 many moons ago** POETIC a long time ago —see also FULL MOON, HALF MOON, NEW MOON, **once in a blue moon** (ONCE¹ (13)), **promise (sb) the moon/world** (PROMISE¹ (5))

moon² v. [T] INFORMAL to bend over and show someone your BARE BUTTOCKS as a joke or as a way of insulting someone: *One couple mooned the President's limousine as it drove past.*

moon over sb/sth phr. v. [T] OLD-FASHIONED to spend your time thinking and dreaming about someone or something that you love: *My father used to sit mooning over Doris Day.*

moon·beam /ˈmunbim/ n. [C] a beam of light from the moon

moon boot /ˈ. ./ n. [C usually plural] a thick warm cloth or plastic boot worn in snow and cold weather

moon-faced /ˈ. ./ adj. having a round face

Moon·ie /ˈmuni/ n. [C] a member of a religious group started by the Korean businessman Sun Myung Moon

moon·less /ˈmunlɪs/ adj. a moonless sky or night is dark because the moon cannot be seen: *a cloudy, moonless night*

moon·light¹ /ˈmunlaɪt/ n. [U] the light of the moon: *To the west was a panorama of lakes and peaks by moonlight.*

moonlight² v. past tense and past participle **moonlighted** [I] to have a second job in addition to your main job: *Some officers were moonlighting as security guards.* —**moonlighter** n. [C] —**moonlighting** n. [U] *The new rule prohibits inspectors from moonlighting in the construction profession.*

moon·lit /ˈmun,lɪt/ adj. [only before noun] made brighter by the light of the moon: *a moonlit garden*

moon·roof /ˈmunruf/ n. [C] a small window in the roof of a car that lets in light and can be opened a small amount —compare SUNROOF

moon·scape /ˈmunskeɪp/ n. [C] an empty area of land that looks like the surface of the moon

moon·shine /ˈmunʃaɪn/ n. [U] INFORMAL strong alcohol that is produced illegally

moon shot, moonshot /ˈ. ./ n. [C] OLD-FASHIONED a SPACECRAFT flight to the moon

moon·stone /ˈmunstoun/ n. [C,U] a milky-white stone used in making jewelry

moon·struck /ˈmunstrʌk/ adj. INFORMAL slightly crazy

moor¹ /mur/ v. [I,T] to fasten a ship or boat to the land or to the bottom of a body of water using ropes or an ANCHOR: *Two battleships were moored to the east of Ford Island.*

moor² n. [C] usually **moors** [plural] a wild open area of high land, covered with rough grass or low bushes, especially in Great Britain

Moor /mur/ one of the Muslim people from North Africa who entered Spain in the 8th century and ruled the southern part of the country until 1492

Moore /mɔr/, **Henry** (1898–1986) a British SCULPTOR who is considered by many people to be the most important British sculptor of the 20th century

Moore, Mar·i·anne /ˈmɛriˌæn/ (1887–1972) a U.S. poet and CRITIC

moor·ing /ˈmurɪŋ/ n. [C] **1** the place where a ship or boat is moored: *Stultz headed back to their mooring, a few hundred yards east of the Trepassey town dock.*

M

2 [usually plural] the ropes, chains, ANCHORS etc. used to moor a ship or boat: *Several ships had broken their moorings during the storm.*

Moor·ish /'mʊrɪʃ/ *adj.* relating to the Moors: *Moorish architecture in Spain*

moose /mus/ *n. plural* **moose** [C] a large wild brown animal that has very large flat ANTLERS (=horns that look like branches) and a head like a horse, that lives in North America, northern Europe, and also in parts of Asia

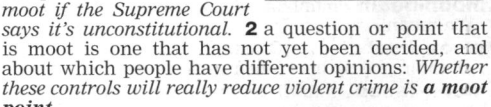

moose

antler

hoof

Moose In·ter·na·tion·al /ˌ. ..ˈ.../ an organization that does CHARITY work

moot¹ /mut/ *adj.* **1** a situation or possible action that is moot is not likely to happen or exist anymore, or is not important anymore: *Even if Proposition 559 passes, it will become moot if the Supreme Court says it's unconstitutional.* **2** a question or point that is moot is one that has not yet been decided, and about which people have different opinions: *Whether these controls will really reduce violent crime is a moot point.*

moot² *v.* [T] **be mooted** FORMAL to be suggested for people to consider: *Once the trip was mooted, there were weeks of indecision about who would go.*

moot court /ˌ. ˈ./ *n.* [C,U] a court in which law students practice holding TRIALS

mop¹ /mɑp/ *n.* [C] **1** a thing used for washing floors, made of a long stick with threads of thick string or a SPONGE fastened to one end **2** [usually singular] INFORMAL a large amount of thick, often messy hair: *There is some gray in Fred's unruly mop of hair now.*

mop² *v.* **mopping, mopped** **1** [I,T] to wash a floor with a wet mop: *I just mopped the kitchen floor.* **2** [T] to remove liquid from a surface, especially from your face, by rubbing it with a cloth: *A trainer mopped Norwood's face with a towel.* **3** **mop the floor with sb** INFORMAL to completely defeat someone, for example in a game or argument

mop up *phr. v.* [I,T] **1** to remove liquid with a mop, cloth, or something soft, especially in order to clean a surface: *People in Oregon were trying to mop up after more than a week of stormy weather and floods.* | [mop sth ↔ up] *Workers mopped up thousands of gallons of spilled crude oil.* | *A few more tortillas would have been good to mop up the sauce.* **2** to complete a piece of work or finish dealing with something or someone: [mop sth ↔ up] *Firefighters mopped up the few hot spots left from Saturday's brush fire.* **3** to deal with the remaining members of a defeated army by killing them or making them prisoners: [mop sth ↔ up] *A spokesman said the army was mopping up the last of the rebel forces.*

mope /moʊp/ *v.* [I] also **mope around** to pity yourself and feel sad, without making any effort to be more cheerful: *She's just been sitting around moping all day.*

mo·ped /'moʊpɛd/ *n.* [C] a small two-wheeled vehicle with an engine, which can also be PEDALed like a bicycle —compare MOTORCYCLE

mop·pet /'mɑpɪt/ *n.* [C] INFORMAL a small child

mor·al¹ /'mɔrəl, 'mɑrəl/ *adj.*
1 about right and wrong [only before noun] relating to the principles of what is right and wrong, and with the difference between good and evil: *Parents are responsible for giving their children moral guidance.* | *The company is managed according to strict moral and ethical principles.* | *Abortion is a moral dilemma for many people* (=people cannot easily decide whether it is right or wrong) *in America today.* | *Babies are born without a moral sense* (=the ability to understand the difference between right and wrong).

2 based on what is right [only before noun] based on your ideas about what is right, rather than on what is legal or practical: *Women have a moral right to work without being sexually harassed.* | *Public schools have a moral responsibility to accept all children.* | *Does the U.S. have the moral authority* (=influence that you have because people accept that your beliefs are right) *to demand free elections in other countries?* | *Protesting against the war was an act of moral courage* (=the courage to do what you believe is right).

3 **moral support** encouragement that you give by expressing approval or interest, rather than by giving practical help: *Steve went with her to provide moral support.*

4 **take/claim/seize etc. the moral high ground** USUALLY DISAPPROVING to be the only one who does what is morally right in a situation, with the intention of being noticed and considered morally good by the public: *Zentec Corp. has seized the moral high ground, and stopped doing business in countries with oppressive military regimes.*

5 **moral victory** a situation in which you show that your beliefs are right and fair, even if you do not win the argument: *The protesters have won at least a moral victory.*

6 person always behaving in a way that is based on strong principles about what is right and wrong: *As moral people, we cannot accept that so many children grow up in poverty.*

7 story a moral story, play etc. is one that teaches or shows good behavior —compare AMORAL, IMMORAL —see also MORALLY

moral² *n.* **1** [C] a practical lesson about what to do or how to behave, that you learn from a story or from something that happens to you: *The moral of the story is be careful when you're offered something for nothing.* | *Is there a moral to all this?* **2** **morals** [plural] principles or standards of good behavior, especially in matters of sex: *The novel reflects the morals and customs of the time.* | *The government has a right to protect public morals* (=the standards of behavior, especially sexual behavior, expected by society) *by prohibiting nude dancing.* | *loose morals* (=someone with loose morals has sex with many different people)

mo·rale /mə'ræl/ *n.* [U] the level of confidence and positive feelings that a person or group has, especially a group that works together, belong to the same team etc.: *Employees have complained about low morale.* | *Morale in the sales division is high.* | **improve/boost morale** *Anytime someone important comes over here, it really boosts the morale of the troops.* | *Archer's promotion caused morale problems in the department.*

mor·al·ist /'mɔrəlɪst/ *n.* [C] **1** someone who has very strong beliefs about what is right and wrong and how people should behave **2** a teacher of moral principles

mor·al·is·tic /ˌmɔrə'lɪstɪk/ *adj.* having strong beliefs about what is right and wrong and how people should behave: *We need practical approaches to preventing teen pregnancies, not moralistic ones.* —**moralistically** /-kli/ *adv.*

mo·ral·i·ty /mə'ræləti/ *n. plural* **moralities** **1** [U] beliefs or ideas about what is right and wrong and about how people should behave: *Some leaders have blamed television for the decline in standards of morality.* **2** [U] the degree to which something is right or acceptable: [+ of] *There was a heated discussion on the morality of abortion.* **3** [U] behavior which is considered acceptable according to someone's beliefs about what is right and wrong: *Monogamy and sexual morality are extremely important to conservatives in the age of AIDS.* **4** [C,U] a system of beliefs and values concerning how people should behave, which is accepted by a particular person or group: *Christian morality*

mor·al·ize /ˈmɔrəˌlaɪz/ v. [I] to tell other people your ideas about what is right and wrong and how people should behave, especially when they have not asked for your opinion: [+ about/on] *How can these people sit and moralize about the personal lifestyle of a famous celebrity?* —**moralizer** n. [C] —**moralizing** n. [U]

mor·al·ly /ˈmɔrəli/ adv. **1** according to moral principles about what is right and wrong: *He was morally opposed to the war.* | *My belief that abortion is morally wrong is not based on religion.* **2** in a way which is good or right: *It is often difficult to behave morally.*

mo·rass /məˈræs/ n. **1** [singular] a complicated and confusing situation that is very difficult to get out of: *the state's budget morass* **2** [singular] a complicated amount of information: [+ of] *a morass of detail* **3** [C] ESPECIALLY LITERARY a dangerous area of soft wet ground

mor·a·to·ri·um /ˌmɔrəˈtɔriəm, ˌmɑr-/ n. [C usually singular] **1** an official announcement stopping an activity for a period of time: [+ on] *The amendment would put a moratorium on offshore drilling for oil.* **2** a law or an agreement that gives people more time to pay their debts: *a one-year moratorium on interest payments*

mo·ray eel /ˌmɔreɪ ˈil/ n. [C] a type of EEL (=fish like a snake) that lives in the ocean in tropical areas

mor·bid /ˈmɔrbɪd/ adj. **1** having a strong and unhealthy interest in disgusting subjects, especially death: *Judging from the book's sales, people have a morbid fascination with murder.* **2** TECHNICAL relating to or caused by a disease: *a morbid gene*

mor·bid·i·ty /mɔrˈbɪdəți/ n. [U] **1** TECHNICAL the rate at which a disease or diseases affect a population **2** the quality of being MORBID (1)

mor·bid·ly /ˈmɔrbɪdli/ adv. **1 morbidly obese** extremely fat, in a way that is dangerous to your health **2** in a way that shows an unhealthy interest in subjects such as death

mor·dant /ˈmɔrdnt/ adj. **mordant humor/wit/insights etc.** FORMAL humor etc. that criticizes or insults someone or something

s w 1 1 **more¹** /mɔr/ adv. **1** used before many adjectives and adverbs that have two or more SYLLABLEs in order to make the COMPARATIVE form, which shows that something has a particular quality to a greater degree than something else: *Can it be done more quickly?* | *It was a lot more expensive than I had expected.* | *Many children feel much more confident if they work in groups.* **2** happening a greater number of times or for longer: *I promised Mom I'd help more with the housework.* | *You need to get out of the house more often.* | *We'd like to see our grand-daughter more than we do.* | *He goes out a lot more now than he has a car.* **3** used with verbs to say that something is true or happens to a greater degree *I couldn't agree more.* | *She cares more for her dogs than she does for me.* **4 more and more** happening or becoming more than before and becoming common: *I find myself thinking about it more and more.* | *People seem to be getting allergies more and more.* **5 more and more tired/angry etc.** tired, angry etc. to a greater and greater degree as time passes: *The runners were getting more and more tired.* **6 once more a)** if you do something once more, you do it again and usually for the last time: *Try calling her once more.* **b)** ESPECIALLY LITERARY again: *Once more the soldiers attacked.* **7 more often than not** used to say that something usually happens: *Cheap movies on video are, more often than not, of very poor quality.* **8 more or less a)** almost: *This report says more or less the same thing as the previous one.* **b)** APPROXIMATELY: *There were 50 people there, more or less.* **9 be more than pleased/sorry etc.** used to emphasize that you are very pleased, very sorry etc.: *I'd be more than happy to sit down and discuss this with you.* **10 be more than a little angry/strange/sloppy etc.** used to emphasize how angry you are, how strange something is etc.: *The beef was more than a little chewy* (=it was very chewy). | *I'm more than a little concerned* (=very concerned) *about Corey's behavior.*

11 no more than a) used to say that something is needed or appropriate: *It's no more than you deserve.* **b)** also **little more than** used to say that someone or something is less important than they seem: *It was little more than a scratch.* **12 (and) what's more** used to add more information that emphasizes what you are saying: *What's more, the price of a mobile home often includes appliances.* **13 no more...than...** used to emphasize that something is not true, not appropriate etc.: *He's no more capable of killing someone than a fly.* **14 no more** LITERARY used in order to show that something that used to happen or be true does not happen or is not true now: *The Lost Princess is lost no more.*

USAGE NOTE: MORE

GRAMMAR
Use **more** as the opposite of both "less" and "fewer": *I think I'll need more money.* | *There were more people there today.* Don't use the "-er" form of the adjective with **more**: *He's more intelligent than his brother* (NOT *"he is more intelligenter than"*). He is richer than his brother (NOT *"he is more richer than his brother"*).

---

s w 1 1 **more²** quantifier [the comparative of "many" and "much"] **1** a greater amount or number: *There were more accidents on the highways this year than last year.* | *They haven't been gone more than two or three days.* | *Today, more and more people commute long distances.* | *A lot more people have given up smoking.* | [+ of] *Did Missy buy some more of those tapes?* **2** an additional number or amount: *You'll have to pay more for a double room.* | *Can you tell me more about your previous job?* | *I need to get two more tickets.* | *It will be five minutes more before dinner's ready.* | *Can I have a little more time to finish?* | *Is there any more coffee?* | *Aaron will finally be earning some more money.* | *I'll just make a few more phone calls.* | [+ of] *There are more of those cinnamon rolls if you want one.* **3 more and more** an increasing number of things or people: *More and more people are taking early retirement.* **4 not/no more than sth** used to say that a price, distance etc. is only a particular number or amount: *The house is no more than ten minutes from the beach.* | *The insurance covers not more than five days in the hospital.* **5 the more.../ the more..., the less** used to say that when you do something or something happens, a particular situation will be the result of it: *It always seems like the more I earn, the more I spend.* | *The more studying you do now, the easier the test will be.* | *The more money you can save, the less you'll need to borrow to buy a car.* —see also **the more...the better** (BETTER³ (4)), **the more, the merrier** (MERRY (3))

More /mɔr/, **Sir Thomas** (1478–1535) an English politician and writer, famous for his book UTOPIA, which describes his idea of a perfect society

more·o·ver /mɔrˈoʊvər/ adv. [sentence adverb] s w 3 FORMAL a word meaning "in addition to this," that is used in order to add information to something that has just been said: *Using language is a very complex enterprise. Moreover, there is more to communication than merely putting sentences together.*

USAGE NOTE: MOREOVER

FORMALITY
Moreover is very formal and not common in spoken English. But you may see it used in a report: *News programs are cheaper to produce than dramas. Moreover, they can attract more money from commercials.* **Also** is a less formal way of adding a reason or idea. It can be used at the beginning of a sentence to link it to the previous one: *You can stay at our house. Also, I can give you a ride home tomorrow.* Or it can be used within a sentence: *I can also give you a ride home tomorrow.* **Besides (that)** is more informal and used especially to add a reason. *I've heard it's not a very good movie. Besides, I'd rather stay home tonight.*

M

mo·res /ˈmɔreɪz/ n. [plural] FORMAL the customs, social behavior, and moral values of a particular group: *middle-class mores*

Mor·gan /ˈmɔrɡən/, **John Pier·point** /dʒɑn ˈpɪrpɔɪnt/ (1837–1913) a very powerful U.S. FINANCIER who collected art and gave money to hospitals and churches

morgue /mɔrɡ/ n. [C] **1** a building or room where dead bodies are kept until they are buried or burned **2** a place where copies of old newspapers are kept, especially at a newspaper office. **3** OFTEN HUMOROUS a quiet place where not much happens, so that you feel sad or bored: *So many people had left that the place was like a morgue.*

mor·i·bund /ˈmɔrəˌbʌnd, ˈmɑr-/ adj. **1** a moribund industry, institution, custom etc. is not active or effective anymore: *The Board is trying to stimulate the moribund economy.* **2** LITERARY slowly dying

Mor·mon /ˈmɔrmən/ adj. relating to a religious organization called The Church of Jesus Christ of Latter-Day Saints, which has strict moral rules and does not allow its members to drink alcohol or coffee —**Mormon** n. [C] —**Mormonism** n. [U]

morn /mɔrn/ n. [C usually singular] POETIC morning

morn·ing¹ /ˈmɔrnɪŋ/ n. [C,U] **1** the early part of the day, from when the sun rises until the middle of the day: *a sunny morning* | *Nancy will bring your book back Friday morning.* | *Liz picks me up on her way to work* **in the morning**. | *I talked to her* **this morning**. | *Do you have time to meet* **tomorrow morning**? **2** the part of the day from MIDNIGHT until the middle of the day: **one/two/three etc. in the morning** *The phone rang at three in the morning.* **3 in the morning** tomorrow morning: *Grandma and Grandpa will be here in the morning.* **4 mornings** during the morning each day: *Linda just works mornings, but it helps.* **5 morning, noon, and night** used to emphasize that something happens a lot or continuously: *I've been going to meetings morning, noon, and night lately.*

morning² interjection **(Good) morning** said in order to greet someone in the morning: *Morning, Dave. How are you?*

morning-af·ter pill /ˌ.. ˈ.. ˌ./ n. [C] NOT TECHNICAL a drug that a woman can take after having sex to prevent her from having a baby

morning coat /ˈ.. ˌ./ n. [C] a formal black coat with a long back that men wear at formal ceremonies during the day

morning glo·ry /ˈ.. ˌ../ n. [C,U] a plant that has white, blue, or pink flowers that open in the morning and close in late afternoon

morning sick·ness /ˈ.. ˌ../ n. [U] a feeling of sickness that some women have when they are PREGNANT

morning star /ˌ.. ˈ./ n. **the morning star** a bright PLANET, usually Venus, that you can see in the eastern sky when the sun rises —compare EVENING STAR

morning suit /ˈ.. ˌ./ n. [C] a special man's suit that is worn at formal ceremonies during the day

Mo·roc·co /məˈrɑkoʊ/ a country in northwest Africa on the coast where the Mediterranean Sea meets the Atlantic Ocean —**Moroccan** n., adj.

mo·roc·co /məˈrɑkoʊ/ n. [U] fine soft leather used especially for covering books

mo·ron /ˈmɔrɑn/ n. [C] INFORMAL someone who is very stupid: *He's just an obnoxious moron.* | *Why'd you put it there, you moron?* —**moronic** /məˈrɑnɪk, mɔ-/ adj. —**moronically** /-kli/ adv.

Mo·ro·ni /mɔˈroʊni/ the capital city of Comoros

mo·rose /məˈroʊs/ adj. in a bad mood, unhappy, and silent: *a morose man* —**morosely** adv. —**moroseness** n. [U]

M

morph /mɔrf/ v. [I,T] to develop or make something develop a new appearance or change into something else: [+ into] *The Consumnes River flooded its banks and morphed into a giant sea that swamped homes and ranches.* —see also MORPHING

mor·pheme /ˈmɔrfim/ n. [C] TECHNICAL the smallest meaningful unit of language, consisting of a word or part of a word that cannot be divided without losing its meaning. For example, "gun" contains one morpheme, but "gunfighter" contains three: "gun," "fight," and "-er"

mor·phi·a /ˈmɔˌfiə/ n. [U] OLD-FASHIONED morphine

mor·phine /ˈmɔrfin/ n. [U] a powerful and ADDICTIVE drug used for stopping pain

morph·ing /ˈmɔrfɪŋ/ n. [U] a computer method that is used to make one image gradually change into a different one —see also MORPH

mor·phol·o·gy /mɔrˈfɑlədʒi/ n. TECHNICAL **1** [U] the study of the MORPHEMES of a language and of the way in which they are joined together to make words —compare SYNTAX (1) **2** [U] the scientific study of how animals, plants, and their parts are formed **3** [C,U] the structure of an object or system or the way it was formed —**morphological** /ˌmɔrfəˈlɑdʒɪkəl/ adj.

mor·row /ˈmɑroʊ, ˈmɔr-/ n. LITERARY **the morrow a)** the next day **b)** the future: *What will the morrow bring?*

Morse /mɔrs/, **Samuel** (1791–1872) a U.S. inventor who developed the first TELEGRAPH system —see picture on page 1329

Morse code /ˌ. ˈ./ n. [U] a system of sending messages in which the alphabet is represented by short and long signals of sound or light

mor·sel /ˈmɔrsəl/ n. [C] **1** a small piece of food: *milk chocolate morsels* | [+ of] *a morsel of bread* **2** a small amount of something such as information: [+ of] *My editors were hungry for every morsel of gossip.*

mor·tal¹ /ˈmɔrtl/ adj. **1** not living forever: *We are all mortal.* —opposite IMMORTAL **2 mortal blow/injuries/danger etc.** causing death or likely to cause death: *A sword fight leads to Tristan's mortal wound.* | **mortal combat** (=fighting until one person kills the other) —compare LETHAL (1) **3 mortal enemy/foe** an enemy that you hate very much and always will hate **4 mortal fear/terror/dread** extreme fear **5** POETIC belonging to a human: *a sight as yet unseen by mortal eyes* —see also MORTALLY

mortal² n. [C] **1 mere/ordinary/lesser mortal** HUMOROUS ordinary people, as compared with people who are more important or more powerful: *Why does Simmons need a limo instead of driving like the rest of us mere mortals?* **2** LITERARY a word meaning a "human," used especially when comparing humans with gods, spirits etc.

mor·tal·i·ty /mɔrˈtæləti/ n. [U] **1** also **mortality rate** the number of deaths during a certain period of time among a particular group of people or from a particular cause: *Cancer mortality among older people is high.* | **Infant mortality** (=the rate at which babies die) *has been on the increase in certain areas.* **2** the condition of being human and having to die: *Doctors are reminded of their mortality every day.* —opposite IMMORTALITY

mor·tal·ly /ˈmɔrtl-i/ adv. **1** in a way that will cause death: *Lincoln was shot and* **mortally wounded** *by Booth.* **2** FORMAL extremely or greatly: *Zenia was mortally offended.*

mortal sin /ˌ.. ˈ./ n. [C] something that you do that is so bad, according to the Catholic church, that it will bring punishment to your soul forever after death unless you ask to be forgiven

mor·tar /ˈmɔrtɚ/ n. **1** [U] a mixture used in building to hold bricks or stones together, made of LIME, sand, and water **2** [C] a heavy gun that fires bombs or SHELLs in a high curve **3** [C] a stone bowl in which substances are crushed with a PESTLE (=tool with a heavy round end) into very small pieces or powder

mor·tar·board /ˈmɔrtɚˌbɔrd/ n. [C] a cap with a flat square top, that you wear when you GRADUATE from high school or college —see picture at HAT

mort·gage¹ /ˈmɔrɡɪdʒ/ n. [C] **1** a legal arrangement in which you borrow money from a bank in order to buy a house, and pay back the money over a period of years: *The mortgage payment will be around six* hundred dollars a month. | *Bart and Joe have taken out a mortgage on their first house.* | *We paid off our mortgage* (=finished paying for the mortgage) *last September.* —see also SECOND MORTGAGE **2** the amount of money you owe on a mortgage: *We still have a $180,000 mortgage on the house.*

mortgage² *v.* [T] **1** to borrow money by giving someone, usually a bank, the right to own your house, land, or property if you do not pay back the money they lent you within a certain period of time: *We mortgaged our house to start Paul's business* | *Everything I own is mortgaged to the hilt* (=I have borrowed money by mortgaging everything I own). **2 mortgage sb's future** to do something that will make things very difficult for someone in the future: *Our lack of respect for the environment is mortgaging our children's future.*

mor·ti·cian /mɔrˈtɪʃən/ *n.* [C] someone whose job is to arrange funerals and prepare bodies to be buried

mor·ti·fy /ˈmɔrtəˌfaɪ/ *v.* **mortifies, mortified, mortifying** [T] **1** to cause someone to feel extremely embarrassed or ashamed: *As a teenager, making any mistake socially would have mortified me.* **2 mortify the flesh** also **mortify yourself** LITERARY to try to control your natural physical desires and needs by making your body suffer pain —**mortification** /ˌmɔrtəfəˈkeɪʃən/ *n.* [U]

mor·ti·fy·ing /ˈmɔrtəˌfaɪ-ɪŋ/ *adj.* extremely embarrassing

mor·tise /ˈmɔrtɪs/ *n.* [C] TECHNICAL a hole cut in a piece of wood or stone to receive the TENON (=the shaped end) of another piece and form a joint

mor·tu·ar·y¹ /ˈmɔrtʃuˌɛri/ *n. plural* **mortuaries** [C] a place where a body is kept before a funeral and where the funeral is sometimes held

mortuary² *adj.* [only before noun] FORMAL relating to death or funerals: *a mortuary urn*

mo·sa·ic /mouˈzeɪ-ɪk/ *n.* **1** [C,U] a pattern or picture made by fitting together small pieces of colored stone, glass, paper etc.: *a Roman stone mosaic floor.* **2** [C usually singular] a group of various things that are seen or considered together as a pattern: [+ of] *Planted last fall, the garden is a mosaic of colors.*

Mos·cow /ˈmɑskou, -kau/ the capital and largest city in Russia

Mo·ses /ˈmouzɪz/ in the Bible, a leader of the Jewish people who brought them out of Egypt and received the TEN COMMANDMENTS from God

Moses, Ed·win /ˈɛdwɪn/ (1955–) a U.S. ATHLETE who set a world record for the 400 meters HURDLES in 1977, set a new record three times, and was not beaten in any race until 1988

Moses, Grandma also **Anna Mary Moses** (1860–1961) a U.S. PAINTER famous for her pictures of American country life painted in a very simple style

mo·sey /ˈmouzi/ *v.* **moseyed, moseying** [I always + adv./prep.] INFORMAL, HUMOROUS to walk somewhere in a slow relaxed way: [+ around/down etc.] *I had time to mosey around town on my own.*
mosey along *phr. v.* [I] to leave a place: *I guess I'd better mosey along – it's getting late.*

mosh /mɑʃ/ *v.* [I] SLANG to dance very violently at a concert with loud ROCK or PUNK music —**moshing** *n.* [U]

mosh pit /ˈ. ./ *n.* [C] an area in front of the stage at a ROCK or PUNK concert where people dance very violently

Mos·lem /ˈmɑzləm, ˈmɑs-/ *n.* [C] *adj.* another spelling of MUSLIM, which is unacceptable to some Muslims

mosque /mɑsk/ *n.* [C] a building in which Muslims WORSHIP

mos·qui·to /məˈskitou/ *n. plural* **mosquitoes** or **mosquitos** [C] a small flying insect that sucks the blood of people and animals, making you ITCH and sometimes spreading diseases

mosquito net /ˈ.. ˌ./ *n.* [C] a net placed over a bed as a protection against mosquitoes

moss /mɔs/ *n.* [C,U] a small flat green or yellow plant that looks like fur and grows on trees and rocks —**mossy** *adj.* —compare LICHEN

most¹ /moust/ *adv.* **1** [+ adj./adv.] used before many adjectives and adverbs that have two or more SYLLABLES in order to make the SUPERLATIVE form: *It's most comfortable if I sit with my legs up.* | *That's the most important part!* | *This style of management is most frequently used in Japan.* **2** more than anything else: *I guess the food I eat most is pasta.* | *She liked the dark beer most.* | *Most of all, I just felt sad that it was over.* **3** SPOKEN, NONSTANDARD almost: *We eat out most every weekend.* **4** [+ adj./adv.] FORMAL very: *I was most surprised to hear of your engagement.* | *It was a most interesting experience.*

USAGE NOTE: MOST

GRAMMAR
Most meaning "almost all" is followed by a noun when you are talking about something in general: *Most cheese contains a lot of fat* (NOT "most of cheese"). | *Most Americans own cars.* You use **most of the** when you are talking about almost all of a particular thing, group etc.: *Most of the champagne we bought was drunk that night.* | *Most of the Americans we talked to owned cars.* Use **the most** in comparisons before an adjective: *Donna is the most beautiful of the girls.* Don't use the "-est" form of the adjective with **most**: *He's one of the richest men in the world* (NOT "the most rich" or "the most richest").

---

most² *quantifier* [the superlative of "many" and "much"] **1** almost all of a particular group of people or things: *Most places have air conditioning in Albuquerque.* | *I think most people hate hospitals.* | *The speed limit is 35 miles an hour in most areas.* | *Of the money donated, most is spent directly on the refugees.* | [+ of] *We get most of our snow in February.* | *Sara does most of the cooking.* **2** more than anyone or anything else: *Apparently, BMWs are stolen most.* | *Who has the most kids?* | *I'd say that in our family, Kelly talks the most.* **3** the largest number or amount possible: *Television commercials reach most people; newspaper ads reach fewer.* | [+ of] *He spends most of his time in New York.* | *How can we get the most power from the engine?* | *I think two or three responses might be the most you can expect.* **4 at (the) most** used to say that a number or amount will not be larger than you say: *It's about ten minutes down the road, fifteen at the most.* —compare **at (the) very least** (LEAST¹ (1)) **5 for the most part** used when a statement or fact is generally true, but not completely true: *For the most part, people seemed pretty friendly.* | *You can get good deals there, for the most part* **6 make the most of sth** to get the most advantage that is possible from a situation: *Guel made the most of her time on court.*

-most /moust/ *suffix* [in adjectives] nearest to something, or at the greatest extreme; most: *China's westernmost region* | *The children's safety should be the uppermost concern* (=what is most important).

most-fa·vored-na·tion stat·us /. ˌ.. ˈ.. ˌ../ *adj.* [C,U] official permission given by one country to another, which allows the second country to buy and sell goods and services without high taxes from the first country

most·ly /ˈmoustli/ *adv.* in most cases or most of the time: *I do mostly secretarial-type work.* | *The people at the theater were mostly college students.* | *Mostly, we talk about the kids.*

USAGE NOTE: MOSTLY

GRAMMAR
With "all/everyone/every etc.," use **almost** rather than **mostly**: *Almost everyone seems to have a cold.*

---

mote /mout/ *n.* [C] OLD-FASHIONED a very small piece of dust

mo·tel /mouˈtɛl/ *n.* [C] a hotel for people traveling by car, with a space for the car near each room

M

mo·tet /mouˈtɛt/ n. [C] a piece of music on a religious subject

moth /mɔθ/ n. [C] an insect similar to a BUTTERFLY that usually flies at night, especially toward lights

moth·ball¹ /ˈmɔθbɔl/ n. [C usually plural] **1** a small white ball made of a strong-smelling chemical, used for keeping moths away from clothes **2 in moth-balls** stored and not used for a long time: *Putting the nuclear power plant in mothballs will save the government money.* **3 bring/take sth out of moth-balls** to begin to use something that has not been used for a long time: *Four ships were brought out of mothballs starting in 1982.*

mothball² v. [T] to close a factory or to decide not to use plans or machinery for a long time: *The Defense Department plans to mothball a munitions plant.*

moth-eat·en /ˈ. ˌ./ adj. cloth that is moth-eaten has holes eaten in it by moths: *a moth-eaten sweater*

moth·er¹ /ˈmʌðɚ/ n. [C]

1 parent a female parent of a child or animal: *My mother says I have to be home by 9 o'clock.* | *Mother just loved crossword puzzles.* | *a mother hen and her chicks* | *a young mother of two* (=of two children)
2 big SPOKEN something that is very large: *a real mother of a car*
3 the mother of sth a) INFORMAL something that is a very good or very bad example of its type: *I woke up with the mother of all hangovers.* | *the mother of all battles* **b)** the origin or cause of something: *Necessity is the mother of invention.*
4 be (like) a mother to sb to care for someone as if you were their mother
5 mother hen someone who tries to protect her children too much and worries about them all the time
6 learn sth at your mother's knee to learn something as a very young child: *She had learned to flirt at her mother's knee.*
7 slang SPOKEN, TABOO: see MOTHERFUCKER
8 Mother used to address the woman who is head of a CONVENT
9 every mother's son OLD-FASHIONED an expression meaning "every man," used to emphasize something: *I'd jail every mother's son of them.*

mother² v. [T] to take care of and protect something in the way that a mother does: *Brenda just tries to mother everyone.*

moth·er·board /ˈmʌðɚˌbɔrd/ n. [C] TECHNICAL the main CIRCUIT BOARD inside a computer

mother coun·try /ˈ.. ˈ../ n. [C usually singular] the country where you were born

Mother Earth /ˌ.. ˈ./ n. [U] the world considered as the place or thing from which everything comes: *Environmentalists say they are defending Mother Earth.* —see also EARTH MOTHER

moth·er·fuck·er /ˈmʌðɚˌfʌkɚ/ n. [C] SPOKEN, TABOO someone who you dislike very much or with whom you are very angry —**motherfucking** adj.

moth·er·hood /ˈmʌðɚˌhʊd/ n. [U] the state of being a mother: *teenage motherhood* | *She's enjoying mother-hood.*

mother-in-law /ˈ.. ˌ./ n. plural **mothers-in-law** [C] the mother of your wife or husband

moth·er·land /ˈmʌðɚˌlænd/ n. [C usually singular] the country where you were born or that you feel you belong to —see also FATHERLAND, MOTHER COUNTRY

moth·er·less /ˈmʌðɚlɪs/ adj. a motherless child is one whose mother has died

mother lode /ˈ.. ˈ./ n. [C usually singular] **1** a mine that is full of gold, silver etc. **2** a place where you can find a lot of a particular type of object: *The region is a mother lode of potential support for his candidacy.*

moth·er·ly /ˈmʌðɚli/ adj. typical of a kind of or concerned mother: *a kind, motherly woman* | *motherly advice* —**motherliness** n. [U] —see also MATERNAL (1)

Mother Na·ture /ˌ.. ˈ../ n. [U] an expression used to talk about the force that controls and organized the Earth, its weather, and the living creatures and plants on it: *After floods and a drought, what else can Mother Nature do to us?*

Mother of God /ˌ.. . ˈ./ n. [singular] a title for Mary, the mother of Jesus Christ, used in the Catholic Church

mother-of-pearl /ˌ.. . ˈ./ n. [U] a pale-colored hard smooth shiny substance on the inside of some SHELLS, used for making buttons, jewelry etc.

Mother's Day /ˈ.. ˌ./ n. [C,U] a holiday in honor of mothers, on which people give cards and presents to their mother, celebrated in the U.S. and Canada on the second Sunday in May

mother ship /ˈ.. ˌ./ n. [C usually singular] a large ship or SPACECRAFT from which smaller boats or spacecraft are sent out

Mother Su·pe·ri·or /ˌ.. .ˈ.../ n. [C usually singular] the woman who is the leader of a CONVENT

Mother Te·re·sa /ˌmʌðɚ təˈrisə/ (1910–1997) an Albanian Catholic NUN who worked to help the poor and the sick in the city of Calcutta in India

mother-to-be /ˌ.. . ˈ./ n. plural **mothers-to-be** [C] a woman who is PREGNANT

mother tongue /ˌ.. ˈ./ n. [C] LITERARY the first and main language that you learn as a child; NATIVE language: *More than one-fifth of the population had German as their mother tongue.*

mo·tif /mouˈtif/ n. [C] **1** an idea, subject, or pattern that is regularly repeated and developed in a book, movie, work of art etc.: *an action movie with a revenge motif* **2** a small picture or pattern used to decorate something: *Sylvia chose a set of china with a floral motif.* **3** an arrangement of notes that is often repeated in a musical work

mo·tion¹ /ˈmouʃən/ n.

1 movement [U] the process of moving or the way that someone or something moves: *the gentle rolling motion of the ship* | *Pete injured his knee, and doesn't have the same range of motion* (=the ability to move in many different directions) *he used to.*
2 moving your body [C] a single movement of your body, especially your hand or head: *a smooth throwing motion* | *For any exercise with a bending motion, the knees must be slightly bent.*
3 suggestion at a meeting [C] a proposal that is made formally at a meeting and then decided on by voting: **[motion to do sth]** *Is there a motion to continue?* | *I make a motion that we continue the public hearing next week.* | *I second the motion* (=be the second person to make a proposal) *to approve the minutes.* | *A two-thirds majority vote was required for the motion to pass.* | *Judge Lupo denied Smith's motion to dismiss charges against him.*
4 set/put sth in motion to start a process or series of events that will continue for some time: *The discovery set in motion two days of searching for the bodies.*
5 in slow motion a) if something on television or in the movies is shown in slow motion, it is shown more slowly than usual so that all the actions can be clearly seen: *They show the most important parts of the game in slow motion.* **b)** if something seems to happen in slow motion, it happens more slowly than usual: *Marcie threw her arm around Tad's neck, but in slow motion, as if she were drunk.*
6 in motion moving from one place or position to another: *a photograph of a frog in motion*
7 go through the motions to do something because you have to do it, without being very interested in it: *The players seemed to be just going through the motions.* —see also TIME AND MOTION STUDY

motion² v. [I,T] to give someone directions or instructions by moving your head, hands etc.: **[motion (for) sb to do sth]** *Evans motioned for Guzman to throw.* | **[motion to sb]** *The teacher motioned to a boy in the front row.* | **[motion to sb to do sth]** *He motioned to her to be quiet.* | **[motion sb in/out etc.]** *A policeman motioned me through.*

mo·tion·less /ˈmouʃənlɪs/ adj. not moving at all: *Kemp sat motionless as the verdict was read.* —**motionlessly** adv.

motion pic·ture /,.. '../ *n.* [C] a movie: *a major motion picture from Tri-Star*

motion sick·ness /'.. ,../ *n.* [U] a feeling of sickness that some people get when traveling in cars, airplanes, boats etc.

mo·ti·vate /'mouṭə,veɪt/ *v.* [T] **1** to make someone want to achieve something and make them willing to work hard in order to do it: *What can we do to motivate the players?* | [**motivate sb to do sth**] *The program aims to motivate teenage mothers to stay in school.* **2** [often passive] to provide the reason why someone does something: [**be motivated by sth**] *The attack was apparently motivated by racial prejudice.*

mo·ti·vat·ed /'mouṭə,veɪṭɪd/ *adj.* **1** very eager to do or achieve something, especially because you find it interesting or exciting: *Older students are often* **highly motivated**. **2 politically/financially/racially etc. motivated** done for political, financial etc. reasons: *a politically-motivated decision* | *Police believe the attack was racially motivated*

mo·ti·va·tion /,mouṭə'veɪʃən/ *n.* **1** [U] eagerness and willingness to do something: *Enthusiasm and motivation aren't usually problems for this team.* **2** [C] the reason why you want to do something: [+ **for**] *Their prime motivation for leaving the country is economic.*

mo·ti·va·tor /'mouṭə,veɪṭɚ/ *n.* [C] something or someone that makes you want to do or achieve something: *Money is a good motivator.*

mo·tive¹ /'mouṭɪv/ *n.* [C] **1** the reason that makes someone do something, especially when this reason is kept hidden: *Police say the motive for the killing was an unpaid drug debt.* **2** a MOTIF —**motiveless** *adj.*

motive² *adj.* [only before noun] TECHNICAL a motive power or force is one that causes movement

mot juste /,mou 'ʒust/ *n. plural* **mots justes** /,mou 'ʒust/ [C] FORMAL exactly the right word or phrase

mot·ley /'mɑtli/ *adj.* [only before noun] **1 a motley crew/bunch/crowd etc.** a group of people who do not seem to belong together, especially people you do not approve of: *The rebels are a motley force who arm themselves with anything they can find.* **2** a motley group of things contains objects that are all different in shape, size etc. and that do not seem to belong together: *a motley fleet of aircraft* **3** LITERARY motley clothes have many different colors on them

mo·to·cross /'mouṭou,krɔs/ *n.* [U] the sport of racing MOTORCYCLES over rough land, up hills, through streams etc.

mo·tor¹ /'mouṭɚ/ *n.* [C] **1** the part of a machine that makes it work or move, by changing power into movement: *The fan's motor made a funny popping sound.* **2** an engine, especially a small one: *I got out of the car but left the motor running.*

motor² *adj.* [only before noun] **1** relating to cars or other vehicles with engines: *motor oil* **2** using power provided by an engine: *a motor vehicle* **3** TECHNICAL relating to a nerve that makes a muscle move: *The disease results in impaired motor function.*

motor³ *v.* [I] to drive a vehicle with an engine: *I motored out to deeper water.*

mo·tor·bike /'mouṭɚ,baɪk/ *n.* [C] a MOTORCYCLE, especially a small one

mo·tor·boat /'mouṭɚ,bout/ *n.* [C] a small fast boat with an engine

mo·tor·cade /'mouṭɚ,keɪd/ *n.* [C] a group of cars and other vehicles that travel together and surround a very important person's car: *the President's motorcade*

motor car /'.. ,./ *n.* [C] OLD-FASHIONED a car

mo·tor·cy·cle /'mouṭɚ,saɪkəl/ *n.* [C] a fast, usually large, two-wheeled vehicle with an engine

motor home /,.. './ *n.* [C] a large vehicle with beds, a kitchen etc. in it, used for traveling

mo·tor·ing /'mouṭɚɪŋ/ *n.* [U] OLD-FASHIONED the activity of driving a car

motor inn /'.. ,./ *n.* [C] an expression meaning a MOTEL, used especially in names

mo·tor·ist /'mouṭɚɪst/ *n.* [C] FORMAL someone who drives a car: *Motorists in the mountains will need tire chains this weekend.*

mo·tor·ized /'mouṭə,raɪzd/ *adj.* [only before noun] **1** having an engine, especially when something does not usually have an engine: *a motorized wheelchair* **2** a motorized army or group of soldiers is one that uses motor vehicles —**motorize** *v.* [T]

motor lodge /'.. ,./ *n.* [C] FORMAL a MOTEL

mo·tor·man /'mouṭɚmən/ *n.* [C] a man who drives a SUBWAY train, CABLE CAR etc.

mo·tor·mouth /'mouṭɚ,mauθ/ *n.* [C] INFORMAL someone who talks too much and too loudly

motor neu·rone dis·ease /,.. '.. .,./ *n.* [U] a disease that causes a gradual loss of control over the muscles and nerves of the body, resulting in death

motor pool /'.. ,./ *n.* [C] a group of cars, trucks, and other vehicles that are available for people in a particular part of the government or military to use

motor rac·ing /'.. ,../ *n.* [U] the sport of racing fast cars on a special track

motor scoot·er /'.. ,../ *n.* [C] a SCOOTER (1)

motor ve·hi·cle /,.. '.. .,./ *n.* [C] FORMAL a car, bus, truck etc.: *This road is closed to motor vehicles.*

Mott /mɑt/, **Lu·cre·tia** /lu'kriʃə/ (1793–1880) a U.S. woman who supported women's rights and worked against SLAVERY

mot·tled /'mɑtld/ *adj.* covered with patterns of light and dark colors of different shapes: *a mottled gray-and-white whale*

mot·to /'mɑtou/ *n. plural* **mottos** *also* **mottoes** [C] a short statement that expresses the aims or beliefs of a person, school, organization etc.: *"Be prepared" is the motto of the Boy Scouts.* | *Try before you buy is a good motto.*

mould /mould/ the British and Canadian spelling of MOLD

mound /maund/ *n.* [C] **1** a pile of dirt, sand, stones etc. that looks like a small hill: *a mound of gravel* | *a burial mound* **2** a large pile of something: [+ **of**] *a mound of garbage* | *The pie was topped with a mound of freshly whipped cream.* **3** the small hill that the PITCHER stands on in the game of baseball —see picture at BASEBALL

mount¹ /maunt/ *v.*
1 increase [I] also **mount up** if something bad mounts, it increases gradually in size, amount, strength etc.: *Farmers' anxiety over the drought has mounted.* | *Costs on the project have been mounting up steadily.* —see also MOUNTING¹
2 event/process [T] to plan, organize, and begin an event or a process: *Newlin is mounting a campaign against drunk drivers.* | *The Tokyo prosecutor's office rarely mounts a case it cannot win.*
3 climb sth [T] FORMAL to go up something such as a set of stairs: *Reporters shouted questions as Mayor Bradley mounted the steps of City Hall.*
4 attach [T] to attach one thing firmly to another larger thing that supports it: [**mount sth on sth**] *A compass was mounted on the dashboard.*
5 picture [T] to fasten a picture or photograph to a larger piece of stiff paper: [**mount sth on sth**] *Entries to the photography competition should be mounted on white paper.*
6 horse/bicycle [I,T] to get on a horse, bicycle etc.: *She mounted and rode off.* —opposite DISMOUNT¹

motorcycles

motorcycle   scooter

M

7 sex [T] TECHNICAL if a male animal mounts a female animal, he gets up onto her back to have sex

mount² *n.* [C] **1 Mount** used in the names of mountains: *Mount Everest* **2** LITERARY an animal, especially a horse, that you ride on **3** OLD USE a mountain

Moun·tain /'maʊntˀn/ *n.* **1** SPOKEN a short form of **Mountain Time 2** the TIME ZONE in the west-central part of the U.S.

moun·tain /'maʊntˀn/ *n.* [C] **1** a very high hill: *the Rocky Mountains* | *The lodge is in the mountains of southern Idaho.* **2** also **mountains** [plural] INFORMAL a very large pile or amount of something: [+ of] *We get mountains of junk mail in the mailbox every day.* **3 make a mountain out of a molehill** to treat a problem as if it was very serious when in fact it is not

mountain ash /ˌ.. './ *n.* [C] a type of tree with red or orange-red berries

mountain bike /'.. ˌ./ *n.* [C] a strong bicycle with a lot of GEARS and wide thick tires, designed for riding up hills and on rough ground —see picture on page 1332

Mountain Day·light Time /ˌ.. '.. ˌ./ *abbreviation* **MDT** *n.* [U] the time that is used in the west-central part of the U.S. for over half the year, including the summer, when clocks are one hour ahead of Mountain Standard Time

moun·tain·eer /ˌmaʊntˀn'ɪr/ *n.* [C] someone who climbs mountains as a sport

moun·tain·eer·ing /ˌmaʊntˀn'ɪrɪŋ/ *n.* [U] the sport of climbing mountains

mountain goat /'.. ˌ./ *n.* [C] an animal that looks like a goat with thick white fur and lives in the western mountains of North America

mountain lau·rel /'.. ˌ../ *n.* [C] a bush with shiny leaves and pink or white flowers that grows in North America

mountain li·on /'.. ˌ../ *n.* [C] a COUGAR —see picture on page 429

moun·tain·ous /'maʊntˀn-əs/ *adj.* **1** having a lot of mountains: *a mountainous region of Turkey* **2** very large in amount or size: *Mountainous waves pounded the coast.*

mountain range /'.. ˌ./ *n.* [C] a long row of mountains that covers a large area

moun·tain·side /'maʊntˀnˌsaɪd/ *n.* [C] the side of a mountain: *Some of the farms are on remote mountainsides.*

Mountain Stan·dard Time /ˌ.. ˌ.. '., ˌ.. '.. ˌ./ *abbreviation* **MST** *n.* [U] the time that is used in the west-central part of the U.S. for almost half the year, including the winter —compare MOUNTAIN DAYLIGHT TIME

Mountain Time /'.. ˌ./ *abbreviation* **MT** *n.* [U] the time that is used in the west-central part of the U.S.

moun·tain·top /'maʊntˀnˌtɑp/ *n.* [C] the top part of a mountain: *snow on the mountaintops*

moun·te·bank /'maʊntɪˌbæŋk/ *n.* [C] LITERARY a dishonest person who tricks and deceives people

mount·ed /'maʊntɪd/ *adj.* mounted soldiers or police officers ride on horses

Mount·ie /'maʊnti/ *n.* [C] INFORMAL a member of the Royal Canadian Mounted Police

mount·ing¹ /'maʊntɪŋ/ *adj.* [only before noun] if something bad is mounting, it is increasing and getting worse: *The fighting capped weeks of mounting tensions in the area.* | *the nation's mounting foreign debt*

mounting² *n.* [C] an object to which other things, especially parts of a machine, are fastened to keep them in place: *The engine is supported by four rubberized mountings.*

Mount St. Hel·ens /ˌmaʊnt seɪnt 'hɛlənz/ a VOLCANO in Washington State in the northwestern U.S. —see picture on page 1330

Mount Ver·non /maʊnt 'vɜrnən/ the home of George Washington between 1747 and 1799 and the place where he is buried. It is in the U.S. state of Virginia.

mourn /mɔrn/ *v.* [I,T] **1** to feel very sad because someone has died, and show this in the way you behave: *Hundreds of people gathered to mourn the slain president.* | [+ for] *Church services were held to mourn for the victims of the fire.* | *She still mourns her son's death.* **2** to feel very sad because something does not exist anymore or is not as good as it used to be: *Residents mourned the loss of the trees.*

mourn·er /'mɔrnɚ/ *n.* [C] someone who attends a funeral

mourn·ful /'mɔrnfəl/ *adj.* very sad: *slow, mournful music* —**mournfully** *adv.* —**mournfulness** *n.* [U]

mourn·ing /'mɔrnɪŋ/ *n.* [U] **1** great sadness because someone has died: *The Kaddish is a prayer of mourning.* | *The family is in mourning* (=feeling great sadness). **2** black clothes worn to show that you are very sad that someone has died, especially in past times: *The widow wore mourning.* | *Some of the people were in mourning.*

mouse /maʊs/ *n.* [C] **1** *plural* **mouses** a small object connected to a computer by a wire, that you move with your hand and press to give commands to the computer —see picture on page 426 **2** *plural* **mice** /maɪs/ a small animal like a rat with a long tail, smooth fur, and a pointed nose that lives houses or fields: *a field mouse* **3** [usually singular] INFORMAL a quiet, shy person —see also **cat and mouse** (CAT¹ (3))

mous·er /'maʊsɚ/ *n.* [C] a cat that catches mice

mouse·trap /'maʊs-træp/ *n.* [C] a trap for catching mice

mousse /mus/ *n.* [C,U] **1** a sweet food made from a mixture of cream, eggs, and fruit or chocolate, that is eaten when it is cold: *chocolate mousse* **2** a white slightly sticky substance that you put in your hair to make it look thicker or to hold it in place **3** a food that is mixed and cooked with cream or eggs so that it is very light: *salmon mousse*

mous·tache /'mʌstæʃ, mə'stæʃ/ *n.* [C] another spelling of MUSTACHE

mous·y /'maʊsi, -zi/ *adj.* **1** a mousy woman is quiet, shy, and unattractive **2** mousy hair is a dull brown color —**mousiness** *n.* [U]

mouth¹ /maʊθ/ *n.* *plural* **mouths** /maʊðz/ [C]
1 face the part of your face that you put food into, or that you use for speaking: *Babies put everything into their mouths.* —see picture at BODY
2 keep your mouth shut INFORMAL **a)** to not say anything because you might make a mistake, or annoy someone or upset them: *He just doesn't know when to keep his mouth shut.* **b)** to not tell other people about a secret: *You'd better keep your mouth shut about this.*
3 open your mouth to start to speak, especially in a situation where you feel you should not say anything: *If you can get people to relax, they're more likely to open their mouths and talk.* —opposite **shut your mouth** (SHUT¹ (2))
4 come out of sb's mouth SPOKEN to be said by someone: *You just never know what's going to come out of her mouth.*
5 opening a) the open part at the top of a bottle or container **b)** the entrance to a large hole or CAVE
6 river the part of a river where it joins the ocean
7 big mouth INFORMAL someone who says things that they should not say or tells secrets
8 make your mouth water if food makes your mouth water, it looks so good you want to eat it immediately —see also MOUTH-WATERING
9 me and my big mouth SPOKEN said when you are annoyed with yourself for telling other people a secret or saying something you should not say
10 mouth to feed someone who you must provide food for, especially one of your children: *Some children were abandoned by parents who could not afford another mouth to feed.*
11 down in the mouth INFORMAL very unhappy: *Why do you look so down in the mouth today?*
12 out of the mouths of babes (and sucklings) HUMOROUS used when a small child has just said

something intelligent or interesting —see also **foam at the mouth** (FOAM[2] (2)), **put your foot in your mouth** (FOOT[1] (12)), **have a foul mouth** (FOUL[1] (3)), FOUL-MOUTHED, HAND TO MOUTH, LOUDMOUTH, MEALY-MOUTHED, -MOUTHED, **shut your mouth/trap/face!** (SHUT[1] (2)), **shoot your mouth off** (SHOOT[1] (15)), **by word of mouth** (WORD[1] (23))

mouth² /maʊð/ v. [T] **1** to move your lips as if you are saying words, but without making any sound: *Dana rolled her eyes and mouthed, "I'm bored," from across the room.* **2** to say things that you do not really believe or that you don't understand: *These men spent years mouthing the Communist party line.*

mouth off phr. v. [I] INFORMAL to speak in an angry or impolite way to someone: *She was suspended for mouthing off to teachers.*

-mouthed /maʊðd, maʊθt/ [in adjectives] **open-mouthed/wide-mouthed etc.** with an open, wide etc. mouth: *a wide-mouthed bottle*

mouth·ful /'maʊθfʊl/ n. [C] **1** an amount of food or drink that you put into your mouth at one time: *Joey had a mouthful of cookies.* | *I'm stuffed. I couldn't eat another mouthful.* **2** something that fills your mouth: *a mouthful of sharp teeth* **3 a mouthful** INFORMAL a long word or phrase that is difficult to say: *Her last name is quite a mouthful.* **4 say a mouthful** INFORMAL to say a lot of true and important things about something in a few words

mouth or·gan /'. ,../ n. [C] a HARMONICA

mouth·piece /'maʊθpis/ n. [C] **1** the part of a musical instrument, telephone etc. that you put in your mouth or next to your mouth **2** [usually singular] a person, newspaper etc. that expresses the opinions of a government or a political organization, especially without ever criticizing these opinions: *Pravda formally was the mouthpiece of the Communist Party.*

mouth-to-mouth re·sus·ci·ta·tion /,. . ,. ...'../ also **mouth-to mouth** n. [U] a method used to make someone start breathing again by blowing air into their mouth

mouth·wash /'maʊθwɑʃ/ n. [C,U] a liquid used to make your mouth smell fresh or to get rid of an infection in your mouth

mouth-wa·ter·ing /'. ,.../ adj. food that is mouth-watering looks or smells extremely good: *the mouth-watering smell of freshly baked bread*

mouth·y /'maʊθi, -ði/ adj. INFORMAL someone who is mouthy says what they want to even when it is not polite: *a mouthy 13-year-old girl*

mov·a·ble¹, moveable /'muvəbəl/ adj. able to be moved, rather than being fastened in one place or position: *a teddy bear with movable arms and legs*

movable², moveable n. [C usually plural] LAW a personal possession such as a piece of furniture

s w
1 1

move¹ /muv/ v.

1 change place/position [I,T] to change from one place or position to another, or to make something do this: *It took three men to move the piano.* | *Don't move, there's a wasp on your shoulder.* | *When you move the knobs, animals pop up from the top.* | [+ away/out/down etc.] *Move out of the way, Denise.* | *If your foot moves around in the shoe, they're too big.* | *Laura yelled that she couldn't move* (=was unable to move).

2 new house [I] to go to live in a different place: *His dad was in the army, so they moved a lot as kids.* | [+ to/from] *When did you move to Albuquerque?* | *They moved from Burlington to Stowe.* | [+ into] *Are you moving into a bigger apartment?*

3 company [I,T] if a company moves, all of its workers and equipment go to a new place to work: *The Fresh Food Company is moving its sales center downtown.* | [+ into] *We're moving into new offices across town.*

4 change job/class etc. [I,T] to change to a different job, class etc., or to make someone do this: [move sb to/into] *Children who disrupt classes can be moved to different schools.* | [+ to/from] *It's a step up to move from hostess to waitress, because you make a lot more money.*

5 feel emotion [T often passive] to make someone feel a strong emotion, especially of sadness or

sympathy: *I was deeply moved by what I heard.* | *Many in the room were moved to tears by the documentary about the Holocaust.* —see also MOVING (1)

6 be/feel moved to do sth to want to do something as a result of an experience or a strong emotion: *As I learned more about the situation, I felt moved to get involved.*

7 progress [I] to progress in a particular way or at a particular rate: *Things moved quickly once the contract was signed.* | *It's essential that these budget talks get moving.*

8 get moving SPOKEN used in order to say that someone needs to hurry: *We'd better get moving if we don't want to miss the start of the movie.*

9 start doing sth [I] to start doing something, especially in order to achieve something or deal with a problem: [+ on/against etc.] *The governor has yet to move on any of the committee's suggestions.* | *The justices said they would move quickly to rule on the case.* | *You'll need to move fast if you want tickets.*

10 get/keep things moving INFORMAL to make a process or event start happening, or to keep it happening

11 change your opinion **a)** [I] to change from one opinion or way of thinking to another: *Neither side is willing to move on this issue.* | [+ toward/away from] *The government is moving toward democratization.* | *We need to move away from the idea of unlimited welfare assistance.* **b)** [T] to persuade someone to change their opinion: *Once she's made up her mind, you can't move her.*

12 change subject/activity [I] to change from one subject or activity to another: [+ away from] *The country has moved away from central economic planning.* | [+ off] *We seem to have moved off the subject.* —see also **move on** (MOVE¹)

13 change arrangements [T] to change the time or order of something: [move sth to/from sth] *Ms. Parry's appointment was moved to 10:30.*

14 games [I,T] to change the position of one of the pieces used to play a game such as CHESS

15 at a meeting [I,T] FORMAL to officially make a proposal at a meeting: [move that] *The chairman moved that the meeting be adjourned.* | [move to do sth] *I move to approve the minutes as read.*

16 be (really) moving INFORMAL to travel very fast: *That truck was really moving!*

17 sell sth [I] INFORMAL to sell something quickly: *They have a lot of stock that didn't move over the Christmas period.*

18 you can't move also **you can hardly move** SPOKEN used to say that a place is very full and there is not much space: *The bar was so crowded you could hardly move.*

19 not move a muscle to stay completely still: *I was so scared, I couldn't move a muscle.*

20 move with the times to change the way you think and behave, as society changes around you: *You move with the times, or you fail, in this business.*

21 move in a society/world/circle to spend a lot of time with a particular type of people and know them well: *Barone moves in a different social world than most normal people.* —see also **move heaven and earth** (HEAVEN (11)), **move/go/close in for the kill** (KILL² (2)), **when/as the spirit moves you** (SPIRIT¹ (16))

move away phr. v. [I] to go to live in a different area: *I thought Gayle's family moved away when you were in high school.*

move in phr. v. [I] **1** to start living in a new house: *We just moved in yesterday.* **2** to start living with someone in the same house [+ with] *She wants a roommate, and asked me to move in with her.* **3** to go toward a place or group of people, especially in order to attack them or take control of them: *The UN peacekeepers moved in to separate the combatants.* | [+ on] *Immigration agents moved in on a nursing home operator who hired illegal aliens.* **4** to start being involved in or gaining an advantage in an activity that someone else has always had control of: [+ on]

953 | **move**

M

Investors moved in on a tight-knit group of car enthusiasts and took over the market.

move off *phr. v.* [I] if a vehicle or group of people moves off, they start to leave a place

move on *phr. v.* [I] **1 a)** to develop in your life and gain more experience as you become older: *I enjoyed the job, but it was time to move on.* | [+ **from**] *She has long moved on from the roles of her youth.* **b)** to progress, improve, or become more modern as time passes: *The business has moved on since we opened our first bakery.* **2** to leave your present job, class, or activity and start doing another one: *Some of the people he met at the shelter have moved on to jobs and homes.* | *Move on to the next exercise.* **3** to start talking about a new subject in a discussion, book etc.: *Then the conversation moved on to happier topics.* **4** to leave the place where you have been staying in order to continue on a trip: *After three days we decided it was time to move on.* **5** if time moves on, the year moves on etc., the time passes

move out *phr. v.* [I] **1** to leave the house where you are living now in order to go and live somewhere else: *The landlord wants me to move out by the 14th.* | [+ **of**] *Lola moved out of her parents' house when she was 18.* **2** if a group of soldiers moves out, they leave a place **3** SPOKEN to leave: *Is everything ready? Then let's move out.*

move over *phr. v.* [I] **1** to change position so that there is more space for someone else: *Move over a little, so I can sit down.* **2** to change to a different system, opinion, group of people etc.: [+ **to**] *Most companies have moved over to computer-aided design systems.* **3** to change jobs, especially within the same organization or industry: *McMillan moved over from guard to forward when he began playing college basketball.* **4 move over, sb/sth** INFORMAL used when saying that one thing that has existed for a long time is not as popular as something new: *Move over, croissants. Rugelach, a Jewish pastry, is the new favorite.*

move up *phr. v.* [I] **1** to get a better job than the one you had before: *Secretaries often find it difficult to move up within the company.* **2** to improve your position or the quality of something you own: [+ **to**] *As his income grew, he moved up to a Porsche.* | *Texas A&M moved up to the No. 2 position.* **3 move up in the world** to get a better job or social position

move² *n.* [C]

1 decision something that you decide to do in order to achieve something or make progress: *What will his next move be?* | *Three board members have opposed these moves.* | *Doing some research before an expensive trip is a **smart move**.* | *I think it was a **good move** (=a good decision).* | *A company spokesman said it was **making the move** in an effort to speed up production.* | *The authorities have **made no move** to resolve the conflict.*

2 progress something that is done to improve a situation: [+ **toward/against**] *The White House called his statement a move toward peace.* | *This decision is definitely **a move in the right direction**.*

3 action an action in which someone moves in a particular direction, especially in order to attack someone or escape: *The coach has taught the players some basic defensive moves.* | *Grodin **made a move** toward the door.* | *They watched, and **made no move** to stop us.*

4 be on the move a) to be changing and developing a lot, especially in a way that improves things: *The economy is finally on the move.* **b)** to be going or traveling to another place: *Abbot lives in Manhattan, but he's usually on the move.* **c)** to be busy and active: *Those kids are always on the move.*

5 get a move on SPOKEN used to tell someone to hurry: *Get a move on or we'll be late!*

6 going to a new place the process of leaving one house, office etc., and going to live or work in a different one: *The move took three days.*

7 games an act of changing the position of one of the objects in a game such as CHESS, or the time when a particular player does this: *It's your move.*

8 make the first move to do something first, especially in order to end an argument or start a relationship: *Neither side is willing to make the first move in the trade talks.*

9 watch/follow sb's every move to carefully watch everything that someone does, especially because you think they are doing something illegal: *The KGB watched our every move.*

move·a·ble /'muvəbəl/ *adj.* another spelling of MOVABLE

move·ment /'muvmənt/ *n.*

1 people working together [C] a group of people who share the same ideas or beliefs and work together to achieve a particular aim: *the civil rights movement* | *The environmental movement has been trying to preserve our natural resources.*

2 position/place [C,U] an act of changing position or going from one place to another: *a dancer's graceful movements* | *the movement of the human heart* | *The slower you do sit-ups, the harder the movement is to do.* | *We watched for signs of movement in the trees.* | *the movement of goods across state borders*

3 change/development [C,U] a change or development in a situation or in people's attitudes: *There's been no movement in the dispute since Thursday.* | [+ **toward/away from etc.**] *Recently, there has been further movement toward centralized management.* | *There is a growing movement among consumers away from buying processed foods.*

4 military [C,U] a planned change in the position of a group of soldiers: *Soldiers were sent into the area to report on the enemy's movements.*

5 sb's movements all of a person's activities over a certain period: *Police are trying to trace Carter's movements.*

6 music [C] one of the main parts into which some pieces of CLASSICAL music are divided: *the first movement of Bach's A Minor Violin Concerto*

7 body waste [C] FORMAL an act of getting rid of waste matter from the BOWELs

8 clock/watch [C] the moving parts of a piece of machinery, especially a clock or watch

mov·er /'muvɚ/ *n.* [C] **1** someone whose job is to help people move from one house to another **2 mover and shaker** INFORMAL an important person who has power and influence over what happens in a situation: *McKee was one of the city's movers and shakers in the late 19th century.* **3** someone or something that moves in a particular way: *Pluto is the slowest mover of all the planets.* **4** a STOCK that people are buying and selling a lot of —see also **key mover/player etc.** (KEY²), PRIME MOVER

mov·ie /'muvi/ *n.* **1** [C] a story that is told using moving pictures on film and sound: *a Hollywood movie* **2 the movies a)** the place where you go to watch a movie: *Do you want to **go to the movies** on Saturday?* | *"Where were you this afternoon?" "We were **at the movies**."* **b)** the business of producing movies: *Grisham's new book is being developed for the movies.*

mov·ie·go·er /'muvi,gouɚ/ *n.* [C] someone who goes to see movies, especially regularly

mov·ie·mak·er /'muvi,meɪkɚ/ *n.* [C] someone who DIRECTs or does other things in order to make movies: *Moviemaker George Lucas is continuing his Star Wars saga.* —**moviemaking** *n.* [U]

movie star /'.. ,./ *n.* [C] a famous movie actor or actress

movie the·a·ter /'.. ,.../ *n.* [C] a place where you go to watch a movie —see picture on page 430

mov·ing /'muvɪŋ/ *adj.* **1** making you feel strong emotions, especially sadness or sympathy: *The occasion was deeply moving.* | *Soprano Teresa Stratas gave a moving performance.* **2** [only before noun] changing from one position to another: *a moving stage* | *These boats are not for use in **fast-moving** water.* **3 the moving spirit** someone who makes something start to happen: *Rittall is regarded as the moving spirit behind the project.* —**movingly** *adv.*

moving part /,.. './ *n.* [C] a part of a machine that moves when it is operating: *Keep the moving parts well oiled.*

moving pic·ture /ˌ.. '..◂/ *n.* [C] OLD-FASHIONED a movie

moving van /'.. ˌ./ *n.* [C] a large vehicle used for moving furniture from one house to another

mow /mou/ *v. past participle* **mowed** or **mown** /moun/ [I,T] **1** to cut grass using a special machine or tool: *The boy next door mows the lawn for us.* **2 new-mown hay/grass etc.** recently cut hay, grass etc.

mow sb/sth **↔ down** *phr. v.* [T] **1** to kill large numbers of people at the same time, especially by shooting them: *Machine guns mowed down retreating soldiers.* **2** to knock something or someone down: *Impatient drivers just mow down the traffic cones.*

mow·er /'mouɚ/ *n.* [C] **1** a machine or tool used for cutting grass; LAWN MOWER **2** OLD USE someone who mows

mox·ie /'maksi/ *n.* [U] INFORMAL courage and determination: *Campanis makes up for her small size with plenty of moxie.*

Mo·zam·bique /ˌmouzəm'bik, -zæm-/ a country in southeast Africa, between Tanzania and South Africa —**Mozambiquean** *n., adj.*

Mo·zart /'moutsart/, **Wolf·gang Am·a·de·us** /'wolfgɑn æmə'deɪəs/ (1756–1791) an Austrian musician who wrote CLASSICAL music

moz·za·rel·la /ˌmatsə'rɛlə/ *n.* [U] a white Italian cheese that is often used on PIZZA

MP *n.* [C] **1** a member of the MILITARY POLICE **2** Member of Parliament; someone who has been elected to represent the people in a government that has a PARLIAMENT

MP3 *n.* [C] TRADEMARK a recording of music that can be DOWNLOADed from the Internet

mpg the abbreviation of "miles per gallon," used to describe the amount of gasoline used by a car: *a car that gets 45 mpg*

mph the abbreviation of "miles per hour," used to describe the speed of a vehicle: *He was caught going 100 mph.*

Mr. /'mistɚ/ **1** used in front of the family name of a man to speak to him politely, to write to him, or to talk about him: *Mr. Mayhew teaches our first-graders.* | *Dear Mr. Smith,....* **2** a title used when speaking to a man in an official position: *Mr. Chairman* | *Mr. President* —compare MADAM (1) **3 Mr. Right** a man who would be the perfect husband for a particular woman: *She's spent years waiting for Mr. Right to come along.* **4 no more Mr. Nice Guy!** used to say that you will stop trying to behave honestly and fairly **5 Mr. Clean** INFORMAL someone who is honest and always obeys the law: *He has a reputation as Mr. Clean.* **6 Mr. Big** INFORMAL the leader or most important person in a group, especially a criminal group **7** SPOKEN used before the name of a personal quality or type of behavior as a humorous name for a man who has that quality: *We don't need any comments from Mr. Sarcasm here.*

USAGE NOTE: MR.

POLITENESS

Mr., Mrs., Miss, and **Ms.** are only used with family names or people's full names: *Hello, Mr. Gray.* | *Mrs. Betty Schwarz, 610 Murdock Rd.* Do not use **Mr., Mrs., Miss,** or **Ms.** with a first name alone or with someone's job. For example, do not say *Please, Miss teacher* or *Good morning, Mr. Jerry.* When you are talking or writing to someone directly, you do not usually use their full name. For example, say *Hello, Mr. Smith* not *Hello, Mr. Alan Smith.* If you do not know the name of the person you are writing to, address the letter *Dear Sir* or *Dear Madam,* not *Dear Mr.* or *Dear Mrs.* Many women, especially younger women, prefer to be addressed as **Ms.** rather than **Miss** or **Mrs.,** because **Ms.** does not draw attention to whether or not the woman is married.

MRI *n.* **1** [U] MAGNETIC RESONANCE IMAGING **2** [C] a picture of the inside of someone's body produced with MAGNETIC RESONANCE IMAGING equipment

Mrs. /'misiz/ **1** used in front of the family name of a married woman in order to speak to her politely, to write to her, or to talk about her *Mrs. Monahan is*

---

secretary to the Chairman. | *Dear Mrs. Wright, ...* —compare MISS[2], MS. —see Usage Note at MR. **2** SPOKEN used before the name of a personal quality or type of behavior as a humorous name for a married woman who has that quality: *Here comes Mrs. Efficiency – everybody get back to work!*

M.S. *n.* [C] Master of Science; a college degree in science that you get after your first degree —compare M.A.

MS 1 the written abbreviation of Mississippi **2** [U] MULTIPLE SCLEROSIS

ms *n. plural* **mss** [C] the written abbreviation of MANUSCRIPT

Ms. /miz/ used in front of the family name of a woman who does not want to be called "Mrs." or "Miss," or when you do not know whether she is married or not: *Ms. Ramirez called this morning.* | *Dear Ms. Roderick, ...* —compare MISS[2], MRS. —see Usage Note at MR.

MS-DOS /ˌɛm ɛs 'dɔs, 'dɑs/ *n.* [U] TRADEMARK one of the most common OPERATING SYSTEMS for a computer

MSG *n.* [U] MONOSODIUM GLUTAMATE; a chemical compound added to food to make it taste better

MST the written abbreviation of Mountain Standard Time

MT 1 the written abbreviation of Montana **2** the written abbreviation of Mountain Time

Mt. the written abbreviation of MOUNT[2]: *Mt. Everest*

MTV Music Television; a television company that broadcasts popular music and VIDEOS of the musicians

much[1] /mʌtʃ/ *adv.* **1** used especially before COMPARATIVES and SUPERLATIVES to mean a lot: *It was much easier doing the letter on the computer.* | *She's feeling much better now.* | *Wayne looked much older than the last time I saw him.* | *These shoes are much more comfortable.* | *Mrs. Clausen was much loved and will be sadly missed.* **2 too/so/very/how etc. much** used to show the degree which someone does something or something happens: *Thank you very much!* | *He drinks too much.* | *We're looking forward to it so much.* **3 not much a)** only a little, only to a small degree etc.: *She isn't much younger than me.* | *Tony hasn't changed much in twenty years.* | *I didn't like the movie very much.* **b)** used to say that something does not happen often: *We don't go out much since the baby was born.* | *Kids don't play outside as much as they used to.* **4 much less** used to say that one thing is even less true or less possible than another: *I doubt Clemson will even make the finals, much less win.* **5 much as sb does sth** used to mean that although one thing is true, something else is also true: *Much as I would have liked to be there, it just wasn't possible.* **6 much to sb's surprise/disgust etc.** FORMAL used to say that someone was very surprised, very disgusted etc.: *I decided not to go to college, much to my later regret.* **7 not be much good at something** to not be able to do something very well: *I'm not much good at tennis.* **8 sth is much like/as sth** used to say that something is much the same (as sth) used to say that something is very similar to something else: *The taste is much like butter.* | *The orchestra members have to wear clothes that are much the same.* —see also **sb/sth is not so much... as...** (SO[1] (8)), **so much for sb/sth** (SO[1] (20)), **so much the better** (SO[1] (13))

USAGE NOTE: MUCH

GRAMMAR/WORD CHOICE: much, very, a lot, many Use **much** with adjectives that come from the past participle of verbs: *Her work is much admired.* **Very** is used in the same way with ordinary adjectives: *The painting is very beautiful.* In negative sentences and in questions, use **much** with uncountable nouns and use **many** with countable nouns: *These plants aren't getting much sunlight.* | *How much money does it cost?* | *There weren't many cars on the road.* In affirmative statements with countable nouns, use **a lot**: *She knows a lot of people.*

M

s w **much²** *quantifier* **1** used to mean "a lot of" in spoken questions and negatives and in formal or written English: *Was there much traffic?* | *I didn't spend as much time on the report as I should have.* | *She helped as much as she could.* | *Much thought and deliberation preceded these decision.* | [+ of] *The storm will bring rain to much of the state.* **2 how much?** used in order to ask about the amount or cost of something: *How much time do you think it will take?* | *How much is this jacket?* **3 so much/too much** used to talk about an amount that is very large, especially one that is too large: *I have too much work and not enough time.* | *There's so much to learn.* | *Some TV programs have* **far too much** *sex and violence in them.* **4 not/nothing much** used to mean that something is not important, interesting, worthy etc.: *"Anything happening?" "Not much."* | *There was nothing much I could do to help.* | *Jan's better at softball than her sister, but* **that's not saying much** (=her sister is very bad at softball, and Jan is only a little better). **5 be too much for sb** to be too difficult for someone to do: *Climbing the stairs is too much for Maisie who is in her 90s.* **6 think/say etc. as much** used to say that someone thought or said the fact or idea that has just been mentioned: *Cuts will have to be made, and school trustees said as much at a recent meeting.* **7 not be much of a sth** to not be a typical example of something, or not be very good at something: *Despite the forecast, it wasn't much of a storm.* | *I'm not much of a dancer.* **8 I'll say this/that much for sb/sth** used to praise someone or something when they are being criticized a lot: *I'll say this much for him, he was consistent until the end.* **9 make much of sb/sth** FORMAL to treat information, a situation etc. as though you think it is very important or serious: *The company has made much of its environmental advances.*

much-her·ald·ed /ˌ. '...ᵈ/ *adj.* [only before noun] talked about a lot before it actually appears: *the President's much-heralded health reforms*

much-vaunt·ed /ˌ. '..ᵈ/ *adj.* [only before noun] a much-vaunted achievement, plan, quality etc. is one that people often say is very good, important etc., especially with too much pride —see also VAUNTED

muck¹ /mʌk/ *n.* [U] INFORMAL something such as dirt, mud, or another sticky substance that makes something dirty: *Clean out the leaves and other muck from your house gutters.*

muck² *v.*
    muck sth ↔ **up** *phr. v.* [T] to spoil something, especially an arrangement or plan: *The Sharks did a good job of mucking up the King's offensive plans.*

muckety-muck /ˈmʌkəti ˌmʌk/ *n.* [C] INFORMAL a word meaning someone who is important and powerful, used when you want to show that you do not feel respect for their power: *He was invited to dinner with some Washington muckety-mucks.*

muck·rak·ing /ˈmʌkˌreɪkɪŋ/ *n.* [U] the practice in newspapers, magazines etc. of telling or writing unfavorable and sometimes untrue stories about people's private lives, especially famous people: *a muckraking, gossipy magazine* —**muckraking** *adj.* —**muckraker** *n.* [C]

muck·y /ˈmʌki/ *adj.* INFORMAL dirty or MUDDY

mu·cous mem·brane /ˈmyukəs ˌmɛmbreɪn/ *n.* [C] the thin surface that covers some inner parts of the body, such as the inside of the nose, and produces mucus

mu·cus /ˈmyukəs/ *n.* [U] a liquid produced in parts of your body such as your nose —**mucous** *adj.*

mud /mʌd/ *n.* [U] **1** wet earth that has become soft and sticky: *Remove mud from your bike by spraying with a hose.* **2** earth used for building: *a mud hut* **3 your name is mud** SPOKEN if your name is mud, people are annoyed with you because you have caused trouble **4 here's mud in your eye** SPOKEN, OLD-FASHIONED used for expressing good wishes when having an alcoholic drink with someone —see also **as clear as mud** (CLEAR¹ (14)), **drag sb's name through the mud** (DRAG¹ (10))

mud·bath /ˈmʌdbæθ/ *n.* [C] a health treatment in which heated mud is put onto your body, used especially to reduce pain

mud·dle¹ /ˈmʌdl/ *v.* [T]
    muddle along/on *phr. v.* [I] INFORMAL to continue doing something without having any clear plan: *The bureaucracy just seems to muddle along.*
    muddle through *phr. v.* INFORMAL [I,T **muddle through** sth] to achieve something even though you do not have a clear plan or do not use the best methods or equipment: *The team managed to muddle through another season.*

muddle² *n.* [C usually singular] a state of confusion or a lack of order: *a legal muddle*

mud·dled /ˈmʌdld/ *adj.* INFORMAL confused and difficult to understand: *This formula movie is much too violent and muddled.*

mud·dy /ˈmʌdi/ *adj.* **muddier, muddiest 1** covered with mud or containing mud: *muddy water* | *Are your shoes muddy?* **2** confused and not clear: *On the tax issue, the difference between the two parties is muddy.* **3** sounds that are muddy are not clear **4** colors that are muddy are dull —**muddiness** *n.* [U]

muddy² *v.* **muddies, muddied, muddying** [T] **1** to make something dirty with mud: *The storm muddied the fields.* **2** to make things more complicated or confusing in a situation that was simple before: *The documentary, supposedly a true account, has only* **muddied the waters**.

mud flap /ˈ. ./ *n.* [C] a piece of rubber that hangs behind the wheel of a vehicle to prevent mud from flying up —see picture on page 427

mud·flat /ˈmʌdflæt/ *n.* [C often plural] **1** an area of muddy land, covered by the ocean when it comes up at HIGH TIDE and uncovered when it goes down at LOW TIDE **2** the muddy bottom of a dry lake

mud·pack /ˈmʌdpæk/ *n.* [C] a soft mixture containing clay that you spread over your face and leave there for a short time to improve your skin

mud pie /ˌ. ˈ./ *n.* [C] **1** a little ball of wet mud made by children as a game **2** a DESSERT made of ice cream and chocolate

mud·slide /ˈmʌdslaɪd/ *n.* [C] the sudden falling of a lot of wet earth down the side of a hill —see picture on page 1333

mud·sling·ing /ˈmʌdˌslɪŋɪŋ/ *n.* [U] the practice of saying bad and often untrue things about someone in order to make other people have a bad opinion of them: *Haze says he is angry about the mudslinging in the campaign.* —**mudslinger** *n.* [C]

mud·wrest·ling /ˈ. ˌ../ *n.* [U] a sport in which people WRESTLE in a box filled with mud —**mud-wrestle** *v.* [I]

Muen·ster /ˈmʌnstɚ/ *n.* [U] a fairly soft and mild-tasting cheese

mues·li /ˈmyusli, ˈmyuz-/ *n.* [U] GRANOLA

mu·ez·zin /muˈɛzən, ˈmwɛzən/ *n.* [C] a man who calls Muslims to prayer from a MOSQUE

muff¹ /mʌf/ *n.* [C] **1** a short tube of thick cloth or fur that you can put your hands into to keep them warm in cold weather **2** a mistake in a sport, such as failing to catch a ball **3** VULGAR the area of hair around a woman's sex organs —see also EARMUFFS

muff² *v.* [T] INFORMAL **1** to make a mistake or do something badly: *The waiter muffed the drink order.* **2** to fail to catch or hold a ball in a game or sport: *Clark muffed a routine groundball.*

muf·fin /ˈmʌfən/ *n.* [C] a small, slightly sweet type of bread that often has fruit in it: *blueberry muffins*

muf·fle /ˈmʌfəl/ *v.* [T] **1** to make a sound less loud and clear: *The falling snow muffled all sounds.* **2** [T usually passive] also **muffle up** to cover yourself with something thick and warm: *The children were muffled up in thick coats.*

muf·fled /ˈmʌfəld/ *adj.* muffled sounds or voices cannot be heard clearly, for example because they come from behind or under something: *the muffled yells of children at play*

muf·fler /ˈmʌflɚ/ n. [C] **1** a piece of equipment on a vehicle that makes the noise from the engine quieter **2** a thick long piece of cloth worn to keep your neck warm

muf·ti /ˈmʌfti/ n. [C] someone who officially explains Muslim law

mug¹ /mʌg/ n. [C] **1** a large cup with straight sides used for drinking coffee, tea etc. **2** a large glass with straight sides and a handle, used especially for drinking beer **3** also **mugful** a mug and the liquid inside it: *a mug of cocoa* **4** OLD-FASHIONED a face

mug² v. **mugged, mugging 1** [T] to attack someone and rob them in a public place: *Every New Yorker expects to be mugged sometime.* —see Usage Note at STEAL¹ **2** [I] INFORMAL to make silly expressions with your face or behave in a silly way, especially in a photograph or a play: *Kids were mugging for the camera.*

mug·ger /ˈmʌgɚ/ n. [C] someone who attacks people and robs them in a public place —see Usage Note at THIEF

mug·ging /ˈmʌgɪŋ/ n. [C,U] an attack on someone in which they are robbed in a public place: *Robberies and muggings are common in the area.*

mug·gy /ˈmʌgi/ adj. **muggier, muggiest** INFORMAL muggy weather is not nice because it is too warm and the air seems wet: *Summer is hot and muggy in the Deep South.* —**mugginess** n. [U]

mug shot /ˈmʌg ʃɑt/ n. [C] INFORMAL a photograph of a criminal's face, taken by the police: *Seven witnesses chose his picture from a book of mug shots.*

Mu·ham·mad /muˈhæməd/ —see MOHAMMED

Muhammad, El·i·jah /əˈlaɪdʒə/ (1897–1975) the leader of the Black Muslims from the late 1930s until his death

Mu·ham·mad·an /muˈhæmədən, -ˈhɑ-/ n. adj. OLD-FASHIONED a word meaning "Muslim," now considered to be the incorrect word by most Muslims —**Muhammadan** adj. —**Muhammadanism** n. [U]

Muir /myʊr/, **John** (1834–1914) a U.S. NATURALIST born in Scotland who encouraged the development of national parks

mu·ja·he·ddin /mu,dʒɑhiˈdin/ n. [plural] Muslim soldiers with strong religious beliefs

muk·luks /ˈmʌklʌks/ n. [plural] boots made of animal skin that have a thick bottom, used for walking in snow

mu·lat·to /məˈlɑtoʊ/ n. plural **mulattoes** [C] OLD-FASHIONED a word for someone with one Black parent and one white parent, now considered offensive

mul·ber·ry /ˈmʌl,bɛri/ n. plural **mulberries 1** [C] a dark purple fruit that can be eaten, or the tree on which this fruit grows **2** [U] the dark purple color of these fruit

mulch¹ /mʌltʃ/ n. [singular,U] decaying leaves that you put on the soil to improve its quality, to protect the roots of plants, and to stop WEEDs growing

mulch² v. [T] to cover the ground with a mulch

mule /myul/ n. [C] **1** an animal that has a DONKEY and a horse as parents **2** [usually plural] a shoe or SLIP-PER without a back, that has a piece of material across the toes to hold it on your foot **3** SLANG someone who brings illegal drugs into a country by hiding them on or in their body —see also **as stubborn as a mule** (STUBBORN (1))

mu·le·teer /ˌmyuləˈtɪr/ also **mule·skin·ner** /ˈmyul,skɪnɚ/ n. [C] someone who leads mules

mul·ish /ˈmyulɪʃ/ adj. refusing to do something or agree to something in an unreasonable way; STUBBORN: *mulish obstinacy* —**mulishly** adv. —**mulishness** n. [U]

mull /mʌl/ v. [T] **1** to heat wine or beer with sugar and SPICEs **2** also **mull sth ↔ over** to think about a problem, plan etc. and consider it for a long time: *He's mulling over an offer from NBC to star in his own series.*

mul·lah /ˈmʌlə/ n. [C] a Muslim teacher of law and religion

mulled wine /ˌ. ˈ./ n. [U] wine that has been heated with sugar and SPICEs: *mulled wine with lots of cloves and cinnamon*

mul·let /ˈmʌlɪt/ n. [C] a fairly small ocean fish that can be eaten

mul·li·gan stew /ˌmʌlɪgən ˈstu/ n. [U] a type of STEW that is made of anything that you have in the house

mul·li·ga·taw·ny /ˌmʌlɪgəˈtɔni, -ˈtɑni/ n. [U] a soup that tastes hot because it contains hot SPICEs

multi- /mʌlti, -tɪ, -taɪ/ prefix more than one; many: *a multicolored bird* (=with many colors) | *a multiracial society* (=having people of many races)

mul·ti·col·ored /ˈmʌltɪ,kʌlɚd/ adj. having many different colors: *a multicolored sweatshirt*

mul·ti·cul·tur·al /ˌmʌltɪˈkʌltʃərəl, -tɪ-/ adj. involving people or ideas from many different countries, races, or religions: *The radio station serves a multicultural community.*

mul·ti·cul·tu·ral·is·m /ˌmʌltɪˈkʌltʃərə,lɪzəm/ n. [U] the belief that it is important and good to include people or ideas from many different countries, races, or religions —**multiculturalist** n. [C]

mul·ti·fac·et·ed /ˌmʌltɪˈfæsɪtɪd/ adj. having many parts or sides: *a multifaceted campaign to control the disease*

multi-faith /ˌ.. ˈ./ adj. [only before noun] including or involving several different religious groups: *a multi-faith service of thanksgiving*

mul·ti·fam·i·ly /ˌmʌltɪˈfæmli/ adj. multifamily housing is houses that have separate areas for more than one family: *large multifamily dwellings*

mul·ti·far·i·ous /ˌmʌltɪˈfɛriəs/ adj. of very many different kinds: *her multifarious business activities* —**multifariously** adv. —**multifariousness** n. [U]

mul·ti·lat·er·al /ˌmʌltɪˈlætərəl/ adj. involving several different countries, companies etc.: *multilateral trade negotiations* —**multilaterally** adv. —compare BILATERAL, UNILATERAL

mul·ti·lin·gual /ˌmʌltɪˈlɪŋgwəl/ adj. **1** able to speak several different languages: *The hotel has a multilingual staff.* **2** written in several different languages: *a multilingual phrasebook* —**multilingualism** n. [U] —compare BILINGUAL, MONOLINGUAL

mul·ti·me·di·a /ˌmʌltɪˈmidiə, -ti-/ adj. [only before noun] **1** relating to computers and computer programs that use a mixture of sound, pictures, VIDEO and writing to give information **2** using several different methods of showing or advertising information, for example television, newspapers, books, and computers —**multimedia** n. [U]

mul·ti·mil·lion /ˌmʌltɪˈmɪlyən/ adj. worth or costing many millions of dollars etc.: *a multimillion-dollar deal*

mul·ti·mil·lio·naire /ˌmʌlti,mɪlyəˈnɛr, -ˈmɪlyə,nɛr/ n. [C] an extremely rich person, who has many millions of dollars

mul·ti·na·tion·al¹ /ˌmʌltɪˈnæʃənl/ adj. **1** a multinational company has factories, offices, and business activities in many different countries: *a multinational manufacturer* **2** involving people from several different countries: *a multinational force sponsored by the UN* —**multinationally** adv.

multinational² n. [C] a large company that has offices, factories etc. in many different countries: *a Connecticut-based multinational that produces chemicals*

mul·ti·par·ty /ˈmʌltɪ,plaɪ/ adj. involving or including more than one political party: *the nation's first multiparty elections*

mul·ti·ple¹ /ˈmʌltəpəl/ adj. including or involving many parts, people, events etc.: *Nakamura received multiple job offers.* | *He underwent surgery for multiple gunshot wounds.*

multiple² n. [C] a number that contains a smaller number an exact number of times: *20 is a multiple of 5.*

multiple choice /ˌ... ˈ./ adj. a multiple choice test or question shows several possible answers and you have to choose the correct one

M
S W
3

multiple per·son·a·li·ty disorder /,... ..'... .,../ n. [U] a PSYCHOLOGICAL condition in which a person has two or more completely separate personalities (PERSONALITY) and ways of behaving

multiple scle·ro·sis /,mʌltəpəl sklə'rousɪs/ also **MS** n. [U] a serious illness that gradually destroys your nerves, making you weak and unable to walk

mul·ti·plex /'mʌltɪ,plɛks/ n. [C] a building with several movie theaters in it —**multiplex** adj.: a multiplex cinema

mul·ti·plex·ing /'mʌltɪ,plɛksɪŋ/ n. [U] TECHNICAL a system used to send several electrical signals using only one connection, used especially with MODEMS —**multiplexer** n. [C] —**multiplex** v. [I,T]

mul·ti·pli·ca·tion /,mʌltəplə'keɪʃən/ n. [U] **1** a method of calculating in which you add the same number to itself a particular number of times —compare DIVISION (4) **2** a large increase in the size, amount, or number of something: *The drug slows the multiplication of cancer cells.*

multiplication sign /...'.. ,./ n. [C] a sign (x) showing that one number is multiplied by another

multiplication ta·ble /...'.. ,../ n. [C usually plural] a list showing the result of numbers between one and twelve that have been multiplied together, used by children in schools

mul·ti·plic·i·ty /,mʌltə'plɪsəti/ n. [U] a large number or great variety of things: [+ of] *a multiplicity of opinions*

mul·ti·ply /'mʌltə,plaɪ/ v. multiplies, multiplied, multiplying **1** [I,T] to increase greatly or make something increase greatly: *Environmental laws have multiplied.* | *Computers have multiplied the possibilities open to the artist.* **2** [I,T] to do a calculation in which you add a number to itself a particular number of times: [multiply sth by sth] *3 multiplied by 4 is 12.* —compare DIVIDE[1] (4) **3** [I] to breed: *The germs multiply quickly in the heat, and can produce food poisoning.*

mul·ti·pur·pose /,mʌltɪ'pɔpəs‹, -ti-/ adj. having many different uses or purposes: *a multipurpose room*

mul·ti·ra·cial /,mʌltɪ'reɪʃəl‹, -ti-/ adj. including or involving many different races of people: *a multiracial society*

mul·ti·task·ing /'mʌltɪ,tæskɪŋ/ n. [U] **1** a computer's ability to do more than one job at a time **2** the practice of doing different types of work at your job at the same time

mul·ti·tude /'mʌltə,tud/ n. [C] **1 a multitude of sth** a very large number of people or things: *I love a novel with a multitude of characters and lots of action.* | *a multitude of advertisements for ice cream* **2 the multitude(s)** LITERARY a very large number of ordinary people in a particular place or situation: *The rich got richer, while the multitude struggled just to survive.* **3 cover/hide a multitude of sins** HUMOROUS to make faults or problems seem less clear or noticeable: *Patterned carpet can hide a multitude of sins.*

mul·ti·tu·di·nous /,mʌltə'tudn-əs‹/ adj. FORMAL very many

mul·ti·vi·ta·min /'mʌltɪ,vaɪtəmɪn/ n. [C,U] a PILL or liquid containing many different VITAMINS

mum[1] /mʌm/ n. [C] **mum's the word** used to tell someone that they must not tell other people about a secret

mum[2] adj. INFORMAL not telling anyone about a secret: *Hammer knew about the decision, but kept mum.*

mum[3] n. [C] BRITISH, CANADIAN: see MOM

mum·ble /'mʌmbəl/ v. [I,T] to say something too quietly and not clearly enough, so that other people cannot understand you: *He mumbled a few words and lost consciousness.* | *Stop mumbling!* —**mumbler** n. [C] —**mumble** n. [C]

mum·bo-jum·bo /,mʌmbou 'dʒʌmbou/ n. [U] something that is difficult to understand or that makes no sense: *legal mumbo-jumbo*

Mum·ford /'mʌmfɚd/, **Lew·is** /'luɪs/ (1895–1990) a U.S. writer on social problems who believed that developments in TECHNOLOGY are spoiling people's lives

mum·mi·fy /'mʌmə,faɪ/ v. [T] to preserve a dead body as a mummy —**mummification** /,mʌməfə'keɪʃən/ n. [U] —**mummified** /'mʌmə,faɪd/ adj.: *a mummified body*

mum·my /'mʌmi/ n. plural **mummies** [C] a dead body that has been preserved and often wrapped in cloth, especially in ancient Egypt

mumps /mʌmps/ also **the mumps** n. [U] an infectious illness in which your throat swells and becomes painful

munch /mʌntʃ/ v. [I,T] to eat something, especially in a way that makes a lot of noise: *kids munching popcorn at the movies* | [+ on] *Fans were munching on hot dogs in the stands.*

Munch /muŋk/, **Ed·vard** /'ɛdvɑrd/ (1863–1944) a Norwegian painter

munch·ies /'mʌntʃiz/ n. [plural] INFORMAL **1** food such as cookies or POTATO CHIPS, especially eaten at a party: *The small snack shop serves sandwiches, munchies, and drinks.* **2 have the munchies** to feel hungry and want to eat unhealthy food

munch·kin /'mʌntʃ,kɪn/ n. [C] INFORMAL someone who is small, especially a child

mun·dane /mʌn'deɪn/ adj. **1** ordinary and not interesting or exciting: *The mundane task of setting the table can be fun at holidays.* | *Most of the law cases he deals with are pretty mundane.* **2** FORMAL relating to ordinary daily life rather than religious matters —**mundaneness** n. [U] —**mundanely** adv.

mung bean /'mʌŋ ,bin/ n. [C] a small green bean, usually eaten as a BEAN SPROUT

Mu·nich /'myunɪk/ the capital of the state of Bavaria in southern Germany

mu·nic·i·pal /myu'nɪsəpəl/ adj. relating to or belonging to the government of a town or city: *the municipal bus and rail systems* | *municipal authorities* —**municipally** adv.

mu·nic·i·pal·i·ty /myu,nɪsə'pæləti/ n. plural **municipalities** [C] **1** a town, city, or other small area, which has its own government that makes decisions about local affairs: *the municipality of Knoxville* **2** the government of a town, city etc., which makes decisions about local affairs: *In the proposal, each part of Jerusalem would have its own municipality.*

mu·nif·i·cent /myu'nɪfəsənt/ adj. FORMAL very generous: *a munificent gift* —**munificence** n. [U] —**munificently** adv.

mu·ni·tions /myu'nɪʃənz/ n. [plural] military supplies such as bombs and large guns: *the manufacture of munitions* —**munition** adj. [only before noun]

mu·ral /'myurəl/ also **mural paint·ing** /,.. '../ n. [C] a painting that is painted on a wall, either inside or outside a building: *a mural 72 feet long and 7 feet tall* —compare FRESCO —**muralist** n. [C]

mur·der[1] /'mɚdɚ/ n. [C,U] **1** the crime of deliberately killing someone: *Curtis's husband has been charged with her murder.* | *a five-month murder trial* | *4600 murders were committed in the U.S. in 1975.* —compare MANSLAUGHTER —see Usage Note at KILL[1] **2 get away with murder** INFORMAL to not be punished for doing something wrong, or to be allowed to do anything you want, even bad things: *She lets those kids get away with murder.* **3 be murder** SPOKEN used to say that something is very difficult or bad: *Traffic was murder this morning.* **4 it's murder on sb/sth** SPOKEN used to say that something harms or damages something else: *It's murder on the people who have to work in the smoking section.* **5 murder-for-hire** the crime of killing someone because you have been paid to do it

mur·der[2] v. [T] **1** to kill someone deliberately and illegally: *The girl had been raped and murdered.* | *On his order, a million people were brutally murdered.* | *the murdered man* **2** INFORMAL to spoil a song, play etc. completely by performing it very badly: *The opening act murdered "Love is All Around."*

mur·der·er /ˈmɔdərə/ n. [C] someone who murders another person: *a convicted murderer*

mur·der·ous /ˈmɔdərəs/ adj. **1** very dangerous or violent and likely to kill someone: *Stalin's murderous regime* | *a murderous attack* **2 murderous glance/stare/expression** an expression that shows that someone is very angry —**murderously** adv. —**murderousness** n. [U]

murk /mɔk/ n. [U] LITERARY darkness caused by smoke, dirt, or clouds

murk·y /ˈmɔki/ adj. **murkier, murkiest 1** dark and difficult to see through: *murky water* **2** complicated and difficult to understand: *The committee is struggling to sort out the facts on a number of murky issues.* **3** involving dishonest or illegal activities that are kept secret: *the murky and ambiguous world of spying* —**murkily** adv. —**murkiness** n. [U]

mur·mur¹ /ˈmɔmɔ/ v. **1** [I,T] to say something in a soft quiet voice that is difficult to hear clearly: *I murmured a prayer of thanks.* **2** [I] to complain to friends and people you work with, but not officially: *He didn't murmur a single word of protest.* **3** [I] to make a soft, low sound: *The wind murmured through the trees* —**murmuring** n. [C,U]

murmur² n. [C] **1** a soft low sound made by people speaking quietly or from a long way away: *Wagner spoke in a barely audible murmur.* **2 murmur of agreement/pleasure/opposition etc.** a quiet statement that expresses agreement, pleasure etc.: *Reverend Van Dyke rose and left the room with a murmur of thanks.* **3** the soft low sound made by a stream, the wind etc.: *the murmur of the little brook* **4** [usually singular] an unusual sound made by the heart that shows there may be something wrong with it: *a heart murmur* **5** something that is talked about but is not official: [+ of/about] *There have been murmurs of an international boycott.* **6 do sth without a murmur** to do something without complaining, especially when this is surprising: *Students paid their tuition fees without a murmur, despite the raise.*

Mur·phy bed /ˈmɔfi ˌbɛd/ n. [C] a type of bed that can be stored upright in a large cupboard when it is not being used

Mur·phy's law /ˌmɔfiz ˈlɔ/ n. [singular] HUMOROUS an informal rule that says that bad things will happen whenever it is possible for them to do so

Mur·row /ˈmɔou, ˈmɑrou/, **Ed·ward R.** /ˈɛdwəd ɑr/ (1908–1965) a U.S. television news reporter known for dealing with political subjects

Mus·cat /ˈmʌskæt/ the capital and largest city of Oman

mus·ca·tel /ˌmʌskəˈtɛl/ n. [C,U] a sweet light-colored wine, or the type of GRAPE that is used to make it

mus·cle¹ /ˈmʌsəl/ n. **1** [C,U] one of the pieces of flesh inside your body that join bones together and make your body move: *This exercise works the muscles of your leg.* | **arm/chest/stomach etc. muscles** | *Weight lifting will improve your muscle tone* (=will make you stronger). | *I think I've just pulled a muscle* (=injured a muscle). **2** [U] military, political, or financial power or influence: *Panetta used his muscle to keep the budget agreement intact.* | *U.S. military muscle* **3** [U] physical strength and power: *It took some muscle to work in an old-fashioned kitchen, with its iron pots.* **4 not move a muscle** to remain completely still: *The performers didn't move a muscle.* **5** [U] SLANG strong men who are paid to protect or attack someone, especially by criminals —see also **flex your muscles** (FLEX (2))

muscle² v. **muscled, muscling** [I,T] to use your strength to go somewhere: *About 10 guys, drunk, tried to muscle their way in.*

muscle in on sth phr. v. [T] to use your strength or power to control or influence someone else's business: *Another transit company tried to muscle in on the deal.*

mus·cle·bound /ˈmʌsəlˌbaʊnd/ adj. having large stiff muscles because of too much physical exercise: *a muscle-bound man*

mus·cle·man /ˈmʌsəlˌmæn/ n. plural **musclemen** /-ˌmɛn/ [C] **1** a man who has developed big strong muscles by doing exercises **2** a strong man who is employed to protect someone, usually a criminal

Mus·co·vite /ˈmʌskəˌvaɪt/ n. [C] someone from Moscow, Russia

mus·cu·lar /ˈmʌskyələ/ adj. **1** having a lot of big muscles: *a tall, muscular man* | *You should see him, he's really muscular.* **2** relating to or affecting the muscles: *muscular pain* | *It requires a lot of muscular control.* —**muscularly** adv. —**muscularity** /ˌmʌskyəˈlærəti/ n. [U]

muscular dys·tro·phy /ˌmʌskyələ ˈdɪstrəfi/ n. [U] a serious illness in which the muscles become weaker over a period of time

muse¹ /myuz/ v. **1** [I] to think carefully about something for a long time: [+ on/about] *Brown was musing about the possibility of his running for President.* **2** [T] to say something in a thoughtful way, especially a question that you are trying to find the answer to: *"I wonder why she was killed," mused Poiret.* —**musingly** adv.

muse² n. [C] **1** an artist's, musician's etc. muse is the force or person that makes them want to write, paint, or make music, and helps them to have good ideas: *Maud Gonne was the muse of W.B. Yeats, the Irish poet.* **2 the Muses** a group of ancient Greek GODDESSes, each of whom represented a particular art or a science

mu·se·um /myuˈziəm/ n. [C] a building where important CULTURAL, historical, or scientific objects are kept and shown to the public: *the Museum of Modern Art*

museum piece /.ˈ.. ˌ./ n. [C] **1** a very old-fashioned piece of equipment or person: *Some of the weapons used by the rebels are museum pieces.* **2** an object that is so valuable or interesting that it should be in a museum: *a museum piece encased in glass*

mush¹ /mʌʃ/ n. **1** [singular, U] a disgusting soft mass of a substance, especially food, which is partly liquid and partly solid: *Cook the squash until it's soft, but not mush.* | *The parking lot had turned to mush in the rain.* **2** [U] a thick soft food made from CORNMEAL (=a powder-like substance made from crushed corn) **3** [U] a book, movie etc. that contains too many silly expressions of love

mush² v. [T] **1** to crush something, especially food, so that it becomes a soft wet mass: *He won't eat his food unless I mush it all up first.* **2** to travel over snow in a SLED that is pulled by a team of dogs

mush³ interjection used to tell a team of dogs that pull a SLED over snow to start moving

mush·er /ˈmʌʃə/ n. [C] someone who drives a SLED over snow, controlling the dogs that pull it

mush·room¹ /ˈmʌʃrum/ n. [C] **1** one of several kinds of FUNGUS with stems and round tops, some of which can be eaten and some of which are poisonous: *mushroom soup* —see picture at VEGETABLE **2** also **magic mushroom** [usually plural] a type of mushroom that has an effect like some drugs, and makes you see things that are not really there —compare TOADSTOOL

mushroom² v. [I] **1** to grow and develop very quickly: *Bernstein's law practice had mushroomed in recent years.* **2** [+ adv./prep.] to spread up into the air in the shape of a mushroom

mushroom cloud /.. ˌ./ n. [C usually singular] a large cloud shaped like a mushroom, which is caused by a NUCLEAR explosion

mush·y /ˈmʌʃi/ adj. **mushier, mushiest 1** soft and wet, and feeling disgusting: *a mushy banana* **2** expressing love in a silly way: *Dave gets all mushy when he's around Gina.* —**mushiness** n. [U]

Mu·si·al /ˈmyuziəl/, **Stan** /stæn/ (1920–) a baseball player known for his skill at hitting the ball

mu·sic /ˈmyuzɪk/ n. [U] **1** the arrangement of sounds made by instruments or voices in a way that is pleasant or exciting: *Oh, what beautiful music!* | *What kind of music does your band play?* | *"Don't Cry for Me, Argentina" is the only* **piece of music** *I can play.* | *Chuck* **wrote the music** *for the song.* **2** the art of writing or playing music: *My daughter teaches music.* | *Lincoln High has a good music program.* **3** a set of written marks representing music, or paper with the written marks on it: *He arranged his music on the stand.* | **read/write music** *McCartney never learned to read music.* —see also SHEET MUSIC **4 be music to your ears** if someone's words are music to your ears, they make you very happy or pleased: *Johnson's decision was music to the ears of the Women's Center directors.* **5 set/put sth to music** to write music so that the words of a poem, play etc. can be sung —see also **face the music** (FACE² (7))

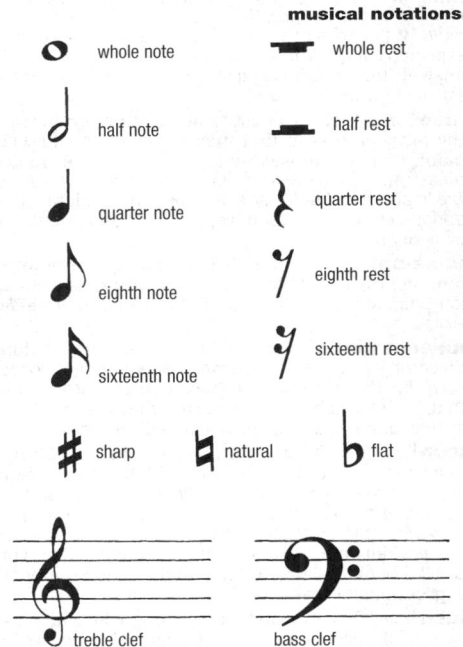

musical notations

○	whole note	▬	whole rest
♩	half note	▬	half rest
♩	quarter note	ξ	quarter rest
♪	eighth note	ϒ	eighth rest
♬	sixteenth note	ϒ	sixteenth rest
♯	sharp	♮	natural	♭	flat

𝄞 treble clef   𝄢 bass clef

mu·si·cal¹ /ˈmyuzɪkəl/ *adj.* **1** [only before noun] relating to music, or consisting of music: *DiFranco's musical skills keep winning her new fans.* | *a musical performance* **2** good at or interested in playing or singing music: *Amanda is so talented – she's musical and she can dance.* **3** having a pleasant sound like music: *a musical voice* —see also MUSICALLY

musical² *n.* [C] a play or movie that uses singing and dancing to tell a story: *a hit song from the 1940 musical "Pal Joey"* | *a Broadway musical* (=one that has been performed on Broadway, a famous street in New York)

musical chairs /ˌ... ˈ./ *n.* [U] **1** a children's game in which all the players must sit down when the music stops, but there is always one chair less than the number of people playing **2** a situation in which people change positions, jobs etc., for no good reason or with no useful result: *Buckley resigned in what was essentially a game of corporate musical chairs.*

musical in·stru·ment /ˌ... ˈ.../ *n.* [C] something that you use for playing music, such as a piano or GUITAR

mu·si·cal·ly /ˈmyuzɪkli/ *adv.* **1** in a way that is related to music: *The new album sees the band growing musically.* | *He's a genius, both intellectually and musically.* **2** in a way that sounds like music: *The birds twittered musically outside.*

music box /ˈ.. ./ *n.* [C] a box that plays a musical tune when you open it

mu·si·cian /myuˈzɪʃən/ *n.* [C] someone who plays a musical instrument, especially very well or as a job: *a talented young musician*

mu·si·cian·ship /myuˈzɪʃənʃɪp/ *n.* [U] skill in playing music: *It was the superb musicianship of the band that made this a memorable show.*

mu·si·col·o·gy /ˌmyuzɪˈkɑlədʒi/ *n.* [U] the study of music, especially the history of different types of music —**musicologist** *n.* [C] —**musicological** /ˌmyuzɪkəˈlɑdʒɪkəl/ *adj.*

music stand /ˈ.. ˌ./ *n.* [C] a metal or wooden object used for holding written music, so that you can read it while playing an instrument or singing

Music Tel·e·vi·sion /ˌ.. ˈ. ...../ MTV

music vid·e·o /ˈ.. ˌ.../ *n.* [C] a VIDEO¹ (2)

musk /mʌsk/ *n.* [U] a strong smelling substance used to make PERFUME

mus·ket /ˈmʌskɪt/ *n.* [C] a type of gun used in past times

mus·ket·eer /ˌmʌskəˈtɪr/ *n.* [C] a soldier in past times who used a musket

musk·mel·on /ˈmʌskˌmɛlən/ *n.* [C] a type of sweet MELON with orange colored flesh inside; CANTALOUPE

musk ox /ˈ. ./ *n. plural* **musk oxen** [C] a large animal with long brown or black hair and curved horns, that lives in northern Canada and Greenland

musk·rat /ˈmʌskræt/ *n.* [C] an animal that lives in water in North America and is hunted for its fur

musk·y /ˈmʌski/ *adj.* like MUSK: *a musky scent* —**muskiness** *n.* [U]

Mus·lim /ˈmʌzləm, ˈmʊz-, ˈmʊs-/ *n.* [C] someone whose religion is Islam —**Muslim** *adj.*

mus·lin /ˈmʌzlən/ *n.* [U] a type of strong cotton cloth used for making clothing, bed sheets, and curtains

muss¹ /mʌs/ *v.* [T] also **muss up** to make something messy, especially someone's hair: *A warm breeze mussed up her wispy hair.*

muss² *n.* **no muss, no fuss** HUMOROUS used to say that something is done easily and without problems: *It would be nice if income tax could be figured out in half an hour – no muss, no fuss.*

mus·sel /ˈmʌsəl/ *n.* [C] a small sea animal, with a soft body that can be eaten and a black shell that is divided into two parts

Mus·so·li·ni /ˌmusəˈlini/, **Be·ni·to** /bɛˈnitoʊ/ (1883–1945) an Italian leader who established the system of FASCISM and ruled Italy as a DICTATOR from 1925–1943

Mus·sorg·sky /məˈzɔrgski/, **Mo·dest** /noʊˈdɛst/ (1839–1881) a Russian musician who wrote CLASSICAL music

must¹ /məst; *strong* mʌst/ *modal verb negative short form* **mustn't 1** [past usually **had to**] used to say that something is necessary because the situation forces you, because of a rule or law, or because you feel that you should: *The $55 passport fee must accompany your application.* | *Identification must be carried at all times.* | *We must make every effort towards peace.* | *Production costs must not exceed $400,000.* | *I must admit, Mr. Klein, that I share your curiosity.* —compare HAVE TO —see Usage Note at HAVE TO **2** [past usually **must have**] used in order to say that something is very likely to be true or have happened: *Elsa must be furious with her.* | *This stereo must have cost a lot of money.* | *The plants must need watering by now.* | *Cox must have forgotten all about our appointment.* **3** SPOKEN, FORMAL **a)** used to suggest that someone do something, especially because you think they will enjoy it very much or you think it is a very good idea: *You must come and visit us in Houston.* **b)** used when you want to do something and hope to do it soon: *I must stop by sometime and thank her for all her help.* **4 if you must (do sth)** used to tell someone that they are allowed to do something, but that you do not approve or agree with it: *If you must travel at night in dangerous areas, turn on the interior light in your car.* | *"Who was that girl?" "Well, if you must know, her name is Mabel."*   S W 1 1

must² /mʌst/ *n.* **1** [C usually singular] something that you must do or must have: *Goggles are a must* *for skiing while it's snowing.* **2** [U] TECHNICAL the liquid from which wine is made; GRAPE juice

mus·tache, moustache /'mʌstæʃ, mə'stæʃ/ *n.* [C] hair that grows on a man's upper lip

mus·ta·chioed, moustachioed /mə'stæʃioud/ *adj.* HUMOROUS having a MUSTACHE

mus·tang /'mʌstæŋ/ *n.* [C] a small wild horse

mus·tard /'mʌstəd/ *n.* [U] **1** a yellow SAUCE with a strong taste, eaten especially with meat **2** a plant with yellow flowers whose seeds can be used to make the powder used to make mustard SAUCE **3 not cut the mustard** to not be good enough for a particular job: *When a director reaches a certain age, he just can't cut the mustard anymore.* **4** a yellow-brown color

mustard gas /'.. ,./ *n.* [U] a poisonous gas that burns the skin, which was used during World War I

mus·ter¹ /'mʌstə/ *v.* **1 muster (up) courage/support/energy etc.** to find as much courage, support etc. as you can in order to do something difficult: *Hill was able to muster dignity and grace under pressure.* | *Madge finally mustered up the courage to tell off her boss.* **2** [I,T] to gather a group of people, especially soldiers, together in one place, or to come together as a group: *Passengers were mustered to the lifeboats.*

muster² *n.* [C] LITERARY a group of people, especially soldiers, that have been gathered together —see also **pass muster** (PASS¹ (21))

must·n't /'mʌsnt/ *v.* the short form of "must not": *You mustn't touch the paintings.*

must-see /, '. './ *n.* [C] INFORMAL something that is so exciting, interesting, etc. that you think people should see it or visit: *The Brunelleschi exhibit is a must-see for anyone interested in Florence.* —**must-see** *adj.* [only before noun]

must·y /'mʌsti/ *adj.* a musty room, house, or object has a bad, wet smell, because it is old and has not had any fresh air for a long time: *a musty motel room* | *The furniture smelled musty and old.* —**mustiness** *n.* [U]

mu·ta·ble /'myutəbəl/ *adj.* FORMAL able or likely to change —**mutability** /,myutə'bɪləti/ *n.* [U] —opposite IMMUTABLE

mu·ta·gen /'myutədʒən/ *n.* [C] TECHNICAL a substance that causes a living thing to mutate

mu·tant /'myutnt/ *n.* [C] **1** an animal or plant that is different in some way from others of the same type, because of a change in its structure that happened by chance GENETIC structure **2** HUMOROUS something that is very different from others of the same type, in a way that is strange or bad: *It's supposed to be a papier-mâché ant, but it looks more like a mutant.* —**mutant** *adj.*

mu·tate /'myuteɪt/ *v.* [I] if a plant or animal mutates, it develops a feature that makes it different from other plants or animals of the same kind, because of a change in its GENETIC structure that happens by chance

mu·ta·tion /myu'teɪʃən/ *n.* [C,U] **1** a change in the GENETIC structure of an animal or plant, that happens by chance and makes it different from others of the same type **2** TECHNICAL a change in a speech sound, especially a vowel, because of the sound of the one next to it

mute¹ /myut/ *adj.* **1** not speaking, or refusing to speak: *The kid stared at me in a state of mute fear.* **2** unable to speak **3** TECHNICAL not pronounced: *a mute "e"* —**mutely** *adv.* —**muteness** *n.* [U]

mute² *v.* [T] **1** to make a sound quieter, or make it disappear completely: *I muted the TV sound to avoid the inane commentary.* **2** to make a musical instrument sound softer

mute³ *n.* [C] **1** something that is placed over or into a musical instrument to make it sound softer **2** someone who cannot speak —see also DEAF-MUTE

mut·ed /'myutɪd/ *adj.* **1 muted criticism/support/response etc.** criticism, support etc. that is not expressed strongly: *The atmosphere was one of muted optimism.* **2** quieter than usual: *He was awakened by a muted buzzer.* **3** a muted color is soft and gentle, not bright: *muted blues and purples*

mu·ti·late /'myutl,eɪt/ *v.* [T often passive] **1** to severely and violently damage someone's body, especially by removing part of it: *Blood poured down from her mutilated face.* **2** to damage or change something so much that it is completely spoiled or ruined —**mutilation** /,myutl'eɪʃən/ *n.* [C,U]

mu·ti·neer /,myutn'ɪr/ *n.* [C] someone who is involved in a mutiny

mu·ti·nous /'myutn-əs/ *adj.* **1** behaving in a way that shows you do not want to obey someone; REBELLIOUS: *There was a mutinous look in Rosie's eyes.* **2** involved in a mutiny: *mutinous soldiers* —**mutinously** *adv.*

mu·ti·ny /'myutn-i/ *n. plural* **mutinies** [C,U] a situation in which people, especially SAILORS or soldiers, refuse to obey the person who is in charge of them, and try to take control for themselves: *Captain Feener suspected the crew was planning a mutiny.* —**mutiny** *v.* [I]

mutt /mʌt/ *n.* [C] INFORMAL a dog that does not belong to any particular breed

mut·ter /'mʌtə/ *v.* **1** [I,T] to speak quietly or in a low voice, usually because you are annoyed about something, or because you do not want people to hear you: *"Sometimes she is such a pain," Jake muttered.* | *They both muttered something about homework and walked away.* **2** [I] to complain about something or express doubts about it, but without saying clearly and openly what you think: [+ about] *Some spoke of Saint Laurent's superb use of color, others muttered about vulgarity.* —**mutter** *n.* [C] *the mutters of players packing their bags* —**mutterer** *n.* [C] —**muttering** *n.* [C,U]

mut·ton /'mʌtn/ *n.* [U] the meat from an older sheep —compare LAMB¹ (2)

mutton chop /'.. ,./ *n.* [C] **1** a piece of meat containing a bone, that has been cut from the RIBS of a sheep **2** mutton chops also **mutton-chop sideburns** hair that grows only on the sides of a man's cheeks, not on his chin, in a style that was popular in the 19th century and again in the 1970s

mu·tu·al /'myutʃuəl/ *adj.* **1** [usually before noun] a feeling or action that is mutual is felt or done by two or more people toward one another: *We have mutual respect for each other's work.* | *Baker will leave the company shortly by mutual agreement.* —compare RECIPROCAL **2** [usually before noun] shared by two or more people: *They met years ago through a mutual friend* (=someone they both know). **3 mutual admiration society** HUMOROUS a situation in which two people praise each other a lot —**mutuality** /,myutʃu-'æləti/ *n.* [U] —see also **the feeling is mutual** (FEELING¹ (8)), MUTUALLY

mutual fund /'... ,./ *n.* [C] an arrangement managed by a company, in which you can buy STOCK in many different businesses

mu·tu·al·ly /'myutʃuəli, -tʃəli/ *adv.* **1** done or experienced equally by two people: *It was a mutually agreed upon decision.* **2 mutually exclusive/contradictory** two ideas or beliefs that are mutually exclusive cannot both exist or be true at the same time

muu-muu /'mu mu/ *n.* [C] a long loose dress, originally from Hawaii

Mu·zak /'myuzæk/ *n.* [U] TRADEMARK recorded music that is played continuously in airports, stores, hotels etc.

muz·zle¹ /'mʌzəl/ *n.* [C] **1** the nose and mouth of an animal such as a dog or horse: *The dog lifted his muzzle to pick up a scent.* —see picture on page 429 **2** something that you put over a dog's mouth to stop it from biting people **3** the end of the BARREL of a gun

muzzle² *v.* [T] **1** to prevent someone from speaking freely or expressing their opinions: *Frequently, employees are muzzled, threatened with dismissal or fired.* **2** to put a muzzle over a dog's mouth so that it cannot bite people

M

MVP *n.* [C] most valuable player; the player on a sports team who is chosen to receive an honor because they did the most to help the team win games

my[1] /maɪ/ *possessive adj.* [possessive form of "I"] **1** relating to or belonging to the person who is speaking: *I can't read without my glasses.* | *Mary Margaret is my godchild.* | *I won't have time to do my homework.* | *Why don't you take a nap in my room?* **2** used when you are shocked or angry about something: *Oh my goodness! What happened to your face?* | *My God, can't you kids shut up?* **3** used when addressing people who you love or like a lot: *All right, my dear, I'll see you tomorrow.*

my[2] *interjection* used when you are surprised about something: *My! Is all this yours, Tom?* | *"It's 3:30." "Oh my, I'm going to be late!"*

Myan·mar /'myɑnmɑr/ a country in southeast Asia, to the east of India and Bangladesh, and to the west of China and Thailand. It was called Burma until 1989.

My·lar /'maɪlɑr/ *n.* [U] TRADEMARK a thin strong shiny plastic-like material, used to cover windows, and many other things

my·nah bird /'maɪnə ˌbɚd/ also **mynah** *n.* [C] a large dark Asian bird that can copy human speech

my·o·car·di·al in·farc·tion /maɪoʊˌkɑrdiəl ɪn'fɑrk-ʃən/ *n.* [C] TECHNICAL a HEART ATTACK

my·o·pi·a /maɪ'oʊpiə/ *n.* [U] **1** the lack of ability to imagine what the results of your actions will be or how they will affect other people **2** TECHNICAL the lack of ability to see things clearly that are far away; NEARSIGHTEDNESS

my·op·ic /maɪ'ɑpɪk, -'oʊ-/ *adj.* **1** unwilling or unable to think about the future results of your actions: *Employees have suffered for management's myopic concentration on short-term goals.* **2** TECHNICAL unable to see things clearly that are far away; NEAR-SIGHTED —**myopically** /-kli/ *adv.*

myr·i·ad[1] /'mɪriəd/ *adj.* [only before noun] LITERARY too many to count: *There are myriad ways to help children learn to read.*

myriad[2] *n.* **a myriad of sth** LITERARY a very large number of things: *It's an area characterized by a myriad of cultural backgrounds.*

myrrh /mɚ/ *n.* [U] a sticky brown substance that is used for making PERFUME and INCENSE

myr·tle /'mɚtl/ *n.* [C] a small tree with shiny green leaves and sweet-smelling white flowers

my·self /maɪ'sɛlf/ *pron.* **1** the REFLEXIVE form of "me": *I looked at myself in the mirror.* | *I might make myself a sandwich.* | *Oh, I hurt myself.* **2** the strong form of "me," used to emphasize the subject or object of a sentence: *I myself would not recommend that restaurant.* | *I'll be flying in myself for the conference.* | *I'm not a very musical person myself.* **3 (all) by myself a)** alone: *Actually, I kind of wanted to be by myself tonight.* **b)** without help from anyone else: *I ate a whole gallon of ice cream by myself.* **4 have sth (all) to myself** to not have to share something with anyone: *I had a whole lane in the swimming pool to myself.* **5 not feel/look/seem like myself** to not feel or behave in the way you usually do because you are nervous, upset, or sick: *I finally started to feel like myself again last night.* —see also YOURSELF

mys·te·ri·ous /mɪ'stɪriəs/ *adj.* **1** mysterious events, behavior, or situations are difficult to explain or understand: *The General was killed in a mysterious plane crash.* | *a woman with a mysterious past* | *Five of his cows died under mysterious circumstances.* **2** a mysterious person is someone who you know very little about and who seems strange or interesting: *Who killed the mysterious visitor to Pine Valley?*

3 saying very little about what you are doing: [+ **about**] *Nelligan was mysterious about whom she modeled the character on.* —**mysteriously** *adv.* —**mysteriousness** *n.* [U]

mys·ter·y /'mɪstəri/ *n. plural* **mysteries 1** [C] something that is impossible to understand or explain or about which little is known: *The writer's identity is a mystery, but he is thought to be Spanish.* | *Scientists continue to unravel the mysteries of human genes.* | *Southern cooking remains a mystery to most people outside the region.* **2** [C] a story about a murder, in which you are not told who the murderer is until the end: *Sue Grafton's mysteries sell very well.* **3** [U] a quality that makes someone or something seem strange, secret, or difficult to explain: *From the beginning, an air of mystery has surrounded the case.* | *Even the origin of the name is shrouded in mystery.* **4 It's a mystery to me** SPOKEN used to say that you cannot understand something at all: *It's a mystery to me how you keep score in this game.* **5** [C] FORMAL a quality that something has that cannot be explained in any practical or scientific way, especially because it is related to God and religion: [+ **of**] *That may be one of the great mysteries of life.*

mystery play /'... ˌ./ *n.* [C] a religious play from the Middle Ages based on a story from the Bible

mys·tic[1] /'mɪstɪk/ *n.* [C] someone who practices MYSTICISM

mystic[2] *adj.* another word for MYSTICAL

mys·ti·cal /'mɪstɪkəl/ *adj.* **1** involving religious or magical powers that people cannot understand: *Few details of the mystical ceremony are known to the public.* | *McCann's book is a story of violence, hidden rooms, and mystical happenings.* **2** relating to mysticism: *mystical poetry* —**mystically** /-kli/ *adv.*

mys·ti·cism /'mɪstəˌsɪzəm/ *n.* [U] a religious practice in which people try to get knowledge of truth and to become united with God through prayer and MEDITATION

mys·ti·fy /'mɪstəˌfaɪ/ *v.* **mystifies, mystified, mystifying** [T] to be impossible for someone to understand or explain: *Her disappearance has mystified her friends and neighbors.* —**mystifying** *adj.* —**mystification** /ˌmɪstəfə'keɪʃən/ *n.* [U]

mys·tique /mɪ'stik/ *n.* [singular,U] a quality that makes someone or something seem different, mysterious, or special: *Alice's mystique was enhanced by her height and good looks.*

myth /mɪθ/ *n.* **1** [C,U] an idea or story that many people believe, but which is not true: *It's just a myth that divorced dads don't care about their kids.* | [+ **of**] *This exhibition explores the myths and realities of sharks.* | *dispel/debunk/explode a myth* (=prove that a myth is not true) **2** [C] an ancient story, especially one invented in order to explain natural or historical events: [+ **of**] *the Greek myth of Medea* **3** [U] this type of ancient story in general: *Opera combines myth, music, and drama.*

myth·ic /'mɪθɪk/ *adj.* **1** like something or someone in a myth: *The stories contained mythic visions of riches in the Middle East.* | *the mythic West* **2 mythic proportions** very great size or importance: *a feat of mythic proportions*

myth·i·cal /'mɪθɪkəl/ *adj.* **1** relating to or only existing in an ancient story: *the mythical hero Hercules* **2** imagined or invented: *Faulkner set his novels in the mythical Yoknapatawpha County.*

my·thol·o·gy /mɪ'θɑlədʒi/ *n. plural* **mythologies** [C,U] **1** ancient myths in general, and the beliefs they represent: *Greek mythology holds that the gods lived on Mt. Olympus.* **2** ideas or opinions that many people believe, but that are wrong or not true: *There's a lot of mythology surrounding tapeworms.* —**mythological** /ˌmɪθə'lɑdʒɪkəl/ *adj.* —**mythologist** /mɪ'θɑlədʒɪst/ *n.* [C]

M

N

N, n /εn/ *n. plural* **N's, n's** [C] the 14th letter of the English alphabet

N. the written abbreviation of "north" or "northern"

n. the written abbreviation of "noun"

'n' /n, ən/ INFORMAL a short form of "and": *rock 'n' roll*

N/A not applicable; written on a form to show that you do not need to answer a question

NAACP *n.* **the NAACP** the National Association for the Advancement of Colored People; an organization that works for the rights of African-American people

nab /næb/ *v.* **nabbed, nabbing** [T] INFORMAL **1** to catch someone doing something illegal or wrong: *A truck driver nabbed the suspected mugger.* **2** to get something quickly: *Bridget Fonda nabbed the starring role in the new movie.*

na·bob /'neɪbɑb/ *n.* [C] a rich, important or powerful person

Na·bo·kov /nə'bɔkɔf, -kəf/, **Vlad·i·mir** /'vlædɪmɪr/ (1899–1977) a U.S. writer of NOVELs, who was born in Russia

na·cho /'nɑtʃoʊ/ *n. plural* **nachos** [C usually plural] a small piece of TORTILLA usually covered with cheese, CHILIs etc.

nacho cheese /'.. ,./ *n.* [U] a type of cheese with SPICES and CHILIS added

Na·der /'neɪdɚ/, **Ralph** /rælf/ (1934–) a U.S. lawyer known for criticizing the government and big companies

na·dir /'neɪdɚ/ *n.* [singular] LITERARY the time when a situation is at its worst, or when something is at its lowest level: *The personal savings rate reached a nadir of less than 3 percent.* —opposite ZENITH

nads /nædz/ *n.* [plural] SPOKEN, SLANG the TESTICLES (=male sexual organs)

NAFTA /'ræftə/ North American Free Trade Agreement; an agreement between the U.S., Canada, and Mexico to remove restrictions and taxes on trade between them

nag¹ /næg/ *v.* **nagged, nagging** [I,T] **1** to keep complaining to someone about their behavior or asking them to do something, in a way that is very annoying: *Ben never picks up his dirty clothes, but nagging doesn't help.* | [+ **at**] *Mom is always nagging at us about finding the right man.* | [**nag sb to do sth**] *My family's been nagging me for years to write down my recipes.* **2** to make someone feel continuously worried or uncomfortable: [+ **at**] *The question that most nagged at me was what kind of wine to serve.* | [**be nagged by sth**] *Whelson has been nagged by injuries all season.*

nag² *n.* [C] INFORMAL **1** a person who nags continuously: *I don't want to be a nag, but do you have that ten bucks you owe me?* **2** a horse, especially one that is old or in bad condition: *Two old nags dragged a cart filled with hay.*

nag·ging /'nægɪŋ/ *adj.* [only before noun] making you worry or feel pain all the time: *There are still some nagging doubts about the future of the company.* | *I can't seem to shake off this nagging cold.*

Na·hum /'neɪəm/ a book in the Old Testament of the Christian Bible

nai·ad /'naɪæd/ *n.* [C] a female spirit who, according to ancient Greek stories, lived in a lake, stream, or river

na·if, naïf /nɑ'if/ *n.* [C] LITERARY someone who does not have much experience of how complicated life is, so they trust people too much and believe that good things will always happen

nail¹ /neɪl/ *n.* [C] **1** a thin pointed piece of metal that you force into a piece of wood with a hammer to fasten the wood to something else **2** the hard smooth layer on the ends of your fingers and toes: *Nurse Duckett sat buffing her nails.* **3** **a nail in sb's/sth's coffin** something bad that will help to destroy someone's success or hopes: *The report is likely to be the final nail in the coffin of the prosecution's case.* **4** **as tough/hard as nails** extremely determined or strict: *Jewson's lawyers are as tough as nails.* —see also **you've hit the nail on the head** (HIT¹ (13))

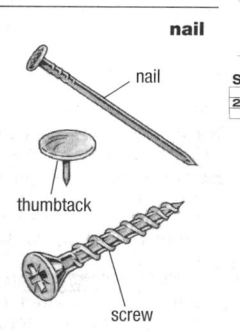

nail

nail

thumbtack

screw

nail² *v.* [T] **1** to fasten something to something else with a nail or nails: *Someone nailed the kitchen cabinets shut.* | [**nail sth down**] *Just nail that wire down along the wall.* | [**nail sth to sth**] *A letter of protest had been nailed to the post.* **2** INFORMAL to catch someone and prove that they are guilty of a crime or something bad: *Police use radar to nail speeding drivers.* | [**nail sb for sth**] *Williams was nailed for burglary.* **3** INFORMAL to do something exactly right, or to be exactly correct: *Boitano nailed a superb triple axel jump.* **4** **nail sb to the wall/cross** to punish someone severely

nail sb/sth **down** *phr. v.* [T] INFORMAL **1** to reach a final and definite decision about something: *We're still trying to nail down how it's going to work when everyone arrives.* **2** to get something, especially something that takes a lot of effort: *Vince finally nailed down that all-important college degree.*

nail-bit·ing /'. ,../ *adj.* [only before noun] extremely exciting because you do not know what is going to happen next: *The World Series provided a number of nail-biting moments.* —**nail-biter** *n.* [C]

nail-brush /'neɪlbrʌʃ/ *n.* [C] a small, stiff brush for cleaning the nails on your fingers —see picture at BRUSH¹

nail clip·pers /'. ,../ *n.* [plural] a small object with two sharp blades, used for cutting the nails on your fingers and toes

nail file /'. ./ *n.* [C] a thin piece of metal with a rough surface used for making the nails on your fingers a nice shape

nail pol·ish /'. ,../ also **nail e·nam·el** /'. .,../, **nail varnish** *n.* [U] colored or transparent liquid which women paint on the nails of their fingers or toes to make them look attractive

nail scis·sors /'. ,../ *n.* [plural] a small pair of scissors for cutting the nails on your fingers or toes —see picture at SCISSORS

Nai·ro·bi /naɪ'roubi/ the capital city of Kenya

Nai·smith /'neɪsmɪθ/, **James** (1861–1939) a Canadian sports teacher who invented the game of basketball

na·ive, naïve /nɑ'iv/ *adj.* not having much experience of how complicated life is, so that you trust people too much and believe that good things will always happen: *We're not naive anymore like we were in the 60s.* | *Stewart plays the naive new senator.* —**naively** *adv.* —**naiveté** /nɑ,iv'teɪ/ *n.* [U]

na·ked /'neɪkɪd/ *adj.* **1** not wearing clothes or not covered by clothes; NUDE: *Claire walks around naked all the time.* | *a picture of a naked man* | **stark/buck/butt naked** (=completely naked) **2** **the naked eye** if you can see something with the naked eye, you can see it without using anything to help you such as a TELESCOPE: *The tail of the comet is not visible to the naked eye.* **3** **naked truth/self-interest/aggression etc.** truth, self-interest, aggression etc. that is not hidden and is shocking: *The President*

N

condemned the invasion as an act of naked aggression. **4 naked light/flame etc.** a light, flame etc. that is not enclosed by a cover: Inside, a naked light-bulb dangled from a wire. **5 naked as a jaybird** OLD-FASHIONED, INFORMAL completely naked —**nakedly** adv. —**nakedness** n. [U]

Na·math /'neɪməθ/, **Joe** /dʒoʊ/ (1943–) a U.S. football player famous for his skill as a QUARTERBACK

nam·by-pam·by /ˌnæmbi 'pæmbi/ adj. HUMOROUS too weak, gentle, and lacking determination: In the end, the Beast turns back into a namby-pamby prince. —**namby-pamby** n. [C]

sw **name¹** /neɪm/ n.
1 1 **1** word known by [C] the word that someone or something is called or known by: Her name was Martha. | I can't remember the name of the island. | It seems disrespectful when some young kid calls me by my **first name**. | Sue didn't change her **last name** (=family name) when she got married. | O'Connor did not mention any politicians **by name**. | I just got off the phone with a guy **by the name of** (=whose name is) Tom Kaser. | Police say the suspect may **go by the name of** (=call himself a name that may not be his real one) Anthony. | Viett lived in Madgeburg **under the name of** (=using a name different from her real name) Eva Schnell.
2 big/famous/household name INFORMAL someone who is famous: The biggest names in golf are gathering for the national championship.
3 opinion [singular] the opinion that people have about a person or organization; REPUTATION: This kind of behavior **gives** hockey **a bad name** (=makes people have a bad opinion of it). | I just want the opportunity to restore my **good name**. | He spent the rest of his life trying to **clear his name** (=show that he had not done anything wrong, so that people should have a good opinion of him). | Kinski **made a name for himself** (=became known and admired by many people) in low-budget Westerns.
4 in sb's name if an official document, a hotel room etc. is in someone's name, it officially belongs to them or is for them: Walters reserved the boat ticket in Greenleaf's name. | The house is in my wife's name (=she owns it legally).
5 do sth in the name of science/religion etc. to use science, religion etc. as the reason for doing something, even if it is wrong: These violent demonstrations in the name of peace are pure hypocrisy.
6 in the name of sb doing something as someone else's representative: Neither of us has the right to attack the other in the name of God.
7 call sb names to say something insulting to someone
8 the name of the game INFORMAL the most important thing or quality needed for a particular activity: Popularity is the name of the game in television.
9 sb's name is mud INFORMAL used to say that people are angry with someone because of something he or she has done
10 in name only officially called something even though the name does not seem appropriate: The Black Hills are hills in name only.
11 take the name of the Lord in vain also **take the Lord's name in vain** OLD-FASHIONED OR BIBLICAL to swear using the words "God," "Jesus" etc.
12 in all but name if a situation exists in all but name, it is the real situation but has not been officially recognized: She was his wife in all but name.
13 I can't put a name to sb/sth SPOKEN used when you cannot remember what someone or something is called: I can't put a name to you, but I'm sure I've met you before. —see also **clear sb's name** (CLEAR² (3)), PEN NAME, **not have a penny to your name** (PENNY (6))

sw **name²** v. [T]
1 1 **1** give sb a name to give someone or something a particular name: Ron has a cat named Chicken. | [name sb John/Ann etc.] Joel and his wife named their daughter Paris. | [name sb/sth for sb] Thomas named Wendy's restaurants for his daughter. | [name

sb/sth after sb] We named the baby Sarah, after her grandmother.
2 say sb's or sth's name to say what the name of someone or something is: Can you name this tune? | Our sources spoke on condition that they not be named. | He would not name his clients.
3 name names to give the names of people who are involved in something, especially something wrong or something they want to hide: I won't name names, but there are many gay people in the music industry.
4 choose sb to officially choose someone or something: [name sb (as) sth] Trombetta was named as director of international marketing. | [name sb to sth] Brown named him to the Supreme Court in 1981.
5 to name (but) a few used after a short list of things or people to say that there are many more you could mention: The whole area is filled with orchard blooms – almonds, plums, peaches, to name a few.
6 you name it SPOKEN used after a list of things to mean that there are many more you could mention: We used axes, shovels, you name it.
7 name your price SPOKEN used to mean that you can decide how much money you want to buy or sell something for

name brand /'. ./ n. [C] a popular and well-known product name —**name-brand** adj. [only before noun] —compare BRAND NAME

name-cal·ling /'. ˌ./ n. [U] the act of saying things that are not nice about someone: There will be no profanity or name-calling in this classroom.

name day /'. ./ n. [C] the day each year when the Christian church gives honor to the particular SAINT (=holy person) who has the same name as you

name·drop /'neɪmdrɑp/ v. **namedropped name-dropping** [I] INFORMAL to mention famous or important people's names to make it seem that you know them personally —**namedropping** n. [U]

name·less /'neɪmlɪs/ adj. **1 sb/sth who/that/which shall remain nameless** SPOKEN used when you want to say that someone has done something wrong, but without mentioning their name: I work for a large food company which shall remain nameless. **2** not known by name: The information was supplied by a nameless source. **3** having no name: There's a land where the mountains are nameless. **4 a)** [only before noun] LITERARY difficult to describe: Nameless fears made her tremble. **b)** too terrible to name or describe: nameless crimes

name·ly /'neɪmli/ adv. [sentence adverb] used to introduce additional information that makes it clear exactly who or what you are talking about: Storni used earlier poetic movements, namely Romanticism and modernism, as models for her poetry.

name·plate /'neɪmpleɪt/ n. [C] a piece of metal or plastic that is attached to something, showing the name of the owner or maker, or the person who lives or works in a place

name·sake /'neɪmseɪk/ n. [C] sb/sth's namesake someone or something that has the same name as someone or something else: Isaac often read the story of his biblical namesake (=the character in the Bible who was also named Isaac).

name tag /'. ./ n. [C] a small sign with your name on it that you wear

Na·mib·i·a /nə'mɪbiə/ a country in southwest Africa, west of Botswana and north of South Africa —**Namibian** n., adj.

Na·nak /'nɑnək/, **Guru** (1469–?1539) an Indian religious leader who started the Sikh religion

nan·ny /'næni/ n. plural **nannies** [C] a woman whose job is to take care of the children in a family, usually in the children's own home

nanny goat /'. ˌ./ n. [C] a female goat

nano- /nænoʊ/ prefix one BILLIONth (=1/1,000,000,000) of a particular unit: a nanometer (=one billionth of a meter)

nan·o·sec·ond /'nænoʊˌsɛkənd/ n. [C] a unit for measuring time. There are one BILLION nanoseconds in a second.

nap¹ /næp/ n. **1** [C] a short sleep, especially during the day: Why don't you lie down and **take a nap**?

2 [singular] the soft surface on some cloth and leather, made by brushing the short, fine threads or hairs in one direction —compare PILE[1] (4)

nap[2] v. **napped, napping 1** [I] to sleep for a short time during the day **2 be caught napping** INFORMAL to not be ready to deal with something when it happens, although you should be ready for it

na·palm /'neɪpɑm/ n. [U] a thick liquid made from GASOLINE, that is used in bombs

nape /neɪp/ n. [singular] the back of your neck: *He nuzzled the soft, warm nape of her neck.*

Naph·ta·li /'næftə,laɪ/ in the Bible, the head of one of the 12 tribes of Israel

naph·tha /'næfθə/ n. [U] a chemical compound similar to GASOLINE

nap·kin /'næpkɪn/ n. [C] **1** a square piece of cloth or paper used for protecting your clothes and for cleaning your hands and lips during a meal **2** a SANITARY NAPKIN

napkin ring /'.. ,./ n. [C] a small ring in which a napkin is put for someone to use at a meal

Na·po·le·on /nə'poʊliən/ **Napoleon Bo·na·parte** /'boʊnə,pɑrt/ (1769–1821) the EMPEROR of France 1804–1815. His armies took control of many European countries, but he failed in his attack on Russia in 1812, and was finally defeated at the Battle of Waterloo in 1815.

nap·py /'næpi/ adj. INFORMAL nappy hair is short and has very tight curls, such as Black people's hair

narc[1] /nɑrk/ n. [C] SLANG a police officer who deals with the problem of illegal drugs

narc[2] v. [I + on] SLANG to secretly tell the police about someone else's criminal activities, especially activities involving illegal drugs

nar·cis·sism /'nɑrsə,sɪzəm/ n. [U] a tendency to admire your own physical appearance or abilities: *Luis went to the gym every day driven purely by narcissism.* —**narcissist** n. [C] —**narcissistic** /,nɑrsə'sɪstɪk/ adj.

nar·cis·sus /nɑr'sɪsəs/ n. [C] a white or yellow spring flower with a cup-shaped central part

nar·co·lep·sy /'nɑrkə,lɛpsi/ n. [U] an illness which makes you suddenly fall asleep for short periods of time during the day —**narcoleptic** /,nɑrkə'lɛptɪk/ adj.

nar·co·sis /nɑr'koʊsɪs/ n. [C usually singular,U] TECHNICAL a condition in which you cannot think, speak, or see clearly, usually because of drugs

nar·cot·ic[1] /nɑr'kɑtɪk/ n. [C usually plural] a type of drug that takes away pain and makes you feel sleepy, which may be used in hospitals but is usually illegal: *He died from an overdose of narcotics.* | **narcotics agent/officer** (=a police officer who deals with the problems of illegal drugs)

narcotic[2] adj. **1** [only before noun] relating to illegal drugs: *narcotic addiction* **2** a narcotic drug takes away pain or makes you sleep

Nar·ra·gan·sett, Narraganset /,nærə'gænsɪt/ a Native American tribe from the northeastern area of the U.S.

nar·rate /'næreɪt, næ'reɪt/ v. [T] to tell a story by describing all the events in order: *Omar Sharif narrated a documentary on the origins of Egypt's pyramids.*

nar·ra·tion /næ'reɪʃən/ n. [C,U] FORMAL **1** the act of telling a story: *The author combines narration, journal entries, and letters in the novel.* **2** a spoken description or explanation that someone gives during a movie, play etc.: *Gerson did the narration for Disney's "Cinderella."*

nar·ra·tive /'nærətɪv/ n. **1** [C,U] FORMAL something that is told as a story: *As the two narratives progress, the connections become evident.* **2** [U] the art of telling a story —**narrative** adj.: *a narrative poem*

nar·ra·tor /'næ,reɪtə/ n. [C] a person in some books, plays etc. who tells the story

nar·row[1] /'næroʊ/ adj.

1 not wide only measuring a small distance from side to side: *a narrow black tie* | *Columns that are too narrow are unattractive and difficult to read.* | *the*

narrow streets of Italian cities —compare BROAD[1] (2) —see picture at THIN[1]

2 narrow victory/defeat/majority etc. a win etc. that is just barely achieved or happens by only a small amount: *Defending champion Halsmer holds a narrow lead.*

3 by a narrow margin if you win or lose by a narrow margin, you do it by only a small amount

4 ideas/attitudes DISAPPROVING a narrow attitude or way of looking at a situation is too limited and does not consider enough possibilities: *Some teachers have a narrow vision of what art is.* | *Their interpretation of Christianity is narrow and limiting.* —see also NARROW-MINDED

5 narrow escape a situation in which you just barely avoid danger, difficulties, or trouble: *The family managed a narrow escape as fire consumed their apartment.*

6 careful FORMAL careful and thorough: *a narrow examination of events* —see also NARROWLY, NARROWS, **the straight and narrow** (STRAIGHT[3] (2)) —**narrowness** n. [U]

USAGE NOTE: NARROW

WORD CHOICE: narrow, thin

Thin means "not thick" and is used for objects if the distance through them from one side to the other is not very big: *a thin cookie* | *thin curtains* | *a thin book.* **Narrow** is usually used to describe a hole or something that is not very wide from side to side: *a narrow road* | *a narrow doorway* | *narrow shoulders.* But sometimes, especially when something is both long and narrow, **thin** can also be used with this meaning: *a thin stripe.*

---

narrow[2] v. [I,T] **1** to become narrower or make something narrower: *William's eyes narrowed as he looked toward the west.* | *Contractors will narrow the road to two lanes.* **2** also **narrow down** to become less or make something less in range, difference etc.: *The gap between the two candidates has narrowed, and they're starting to panic.* | *Levin and his editors then narrow down the list to 50 people.*

nar·row-gauge /,.. '../ adj. **narrow-gauge railroad/train/track etc.** a railroad train, track etc. that is narrower than the standard width

nar·row·ly /'næroʊli/ adv. **1** only by a small amount: *The bullet narrowly missed her.* | *Smith narrowly lost the election.* **2** looking at or considering only a small part of something: *A lot of workers have very narrowly focused job skills.* **3** FORMAL in a thorough way, looking for detail: *We will have to consider your proposal very narrowly.*

narrow-mind·ed /'.. ,../ adj. unwilling to accept or understand new or different ideas or customs; PREJUDICED —**narrow-mindedly** adv. —**narrow-mindedness** n. [U] —compare OPEN-MINDED

nar·rows /'næroʊz/ n. plural **narrows** [C] **1** also **Narrows** a narrow passage of water between two pieces of land that connects two larger areas of water **2** a narrow part of a river, lake etc.

nar·whal /'nɑrwəl/ n. [C] a type of WHALE that lives in cold northern oceans, the male of which has a long TUSK (=tooth-like part) on its head

nar·y /'nɛri/ adv. **nary a sth** LITERARY not even one thing: *The lawn is lush and green, with nary a brown spot* (=no brown spots) *to be seen.*

NASA /'næsə/ n. National Aeronautics and Space Administration; a U.S. government organization that controls space travel and the scientific study of space

na·sal[1] /'neɪzəl/ adj. **1** relating to the nose: *clogged nasal passages* **2** a sound or voice that is nasal comes mainly through your nose: *Miller's nasal country twang reveals his Georgia origins.* **3** TECHNICAL a nasal CONSONANT or vowel such as /n/ or /m/ is one that is produced wholly or partly through your nose —**nasally** adv.

nasal[2] n. [C] TECHNICAL a particular speech sound,

N

such as /m/, /n/, or /n/ that is made through your
nose

nas·cent /ˈnæsənt, ˈneɪ-/ *adj.* [only before noun]
FORMAL coming into existence or starting to develop:
*A nascent nationalist movement is emerging in the
Ukraine.*

NASDAQ /ˈnæzdæk/ *n.* [singular] TRADEMARK National
Association of Securities Dealers Automated Quotations; an official organization that provides prices
for STOCKs in U.S. companies that are not dealt with
on the NEW YORK STOCK EXCHANGE

Nash /næʃ/**, Og·den** /ˈɑgdən, ˈɔg-/ (1902–1971) a U.S.
writer famous for his humorous poems

Nash·ville /ˈnæʃvɪl/ the capital city of the U.S. state
of Tennessee

Nas·sau /ˈnæsɔ/ the capital city of the Bahamas

Nas·ser, Lake /ˈnæsɚ/ the RESERVOIR of water formed
by the Aswan High Dam in Egypt

nas·tur·tium /nəˈstɚʃəm/ *n.* [C] a garden plant with
orange, yellow, or red flowers and circular leaves

s w **nas·ty¹** /ˈnæsti/ *adj.* **nastier, nastiest** **1** cruel and
² not nice: *His mouth twisted into a nasty snarl.* | *I just
heard a nasty rumor about Jill.* | *Stacy said he was
really nasty to her.* **2** SPOKEN having a bad appearance, smell, taste etc.: *Don't let that nasty old dog
come up here.* | *This coffee tastes nasty!* **3** INFORMAL
very severe, painful, or bad: *I'm so glad you didn't
get that nasty flu, Joan.* | *A few days later, Brian had
a nasty case of poison oak.* **4** a nasty experience,
feeling, or situation is bad and not enjoyable at all:
Their marriage ended in a nasty divorce. | *It's pretty
nasty outside – they're expecting freezing rain.*
5 morally bad or offensive: *a nasty sense of humor* |
You've got a nasty mind. —**nastily** *adv.* —**nastiness**
n. [U]

nasty² *n.* **do the nasty** SLANG to have sex

na·tal /ˈneɪtl/ *adj.* TECHNICAL relating to birth: *All male
baboons eventually leave their natal group.* —see also
PRENATAL, POSTNATAL

natch /nætʃ/ *adv.* [sentence adverb] INFORMAL a short
form of "naturally," used to say that something is
exactly as you would expect: *Most of his clients are in
Southern California, natch.*

Natch·ez /ˈnætʃɪz/ a Native American tribe who formerly lived in the southeastern area of the U.S.

s w **na·tion** /ˈneɪʃən/ *n.* [C] **1** a country, considered espe-
¹ cially in relation to its people and its social or eco-
³ nomic structure: *The President's speech to the nation
lasted about ten minutes.* | *industrialized nations* **2** a
large group of people of the same race and language:
the Cherokee nation —see Usage Note at RACE¹

USAGE NOTE: NATION

WORD CHOICE: nation and country
Nation is a more formal word than **country** and is
usually used when talking about the political or
economic structures of a country: *Bolivia is a develop-
ing nation with a growing economy.* | *the member
nations of NATO.* Use **country** to talk about the place
where a person comes from, lives in etc.: *What part of
the country are you from?* | *He had left his country at
the age of 10.*

Na·tion /ˈneɪʃən/**, Car·ry** /ˈkæri/ (1846–1911) a U.S.
woman who tried to stop people from drinking alcohol by going into many bars and damaging them

s w **na·tion·al¹** /ˈnæʃənl/ *adj.* **1** relating to a whole
¹ nation, rather than to part of it: *Woodson appeared
² on national television.* | *The unemployment rate here
is much higher than the national average.* **2** relating
to a particular nation, rather than other nations: *our
national defense* | *Poles embrace Chopin as a
national hero.* **3** [only before noun] owned or controlled by the central government of a country:
Sabena, Belgium's national airline | *national
forests* | *Yosemite National Park* —see also NATION-
ALLY

national² *n.* [C] FORMAL someone who is a citizen of
a particular country, especially a citizen who lives
in another country: *About 4000 French nationals live
in Zaire.* —compare ALIEN² (1), CITIZEN (2), SUBJECT¹ (6)

national an·them /ˌ... ˈ../ *n.* [C] the official song of
a nation, that is sung or played on public occasions

**National As·so·ci·a·tion for the Ad·vance-
ment of Col·ored Peo·ple** /ˌ... ...,. . . .,.. ˈ.. ,./
—see NAACP

National Bas·ket·ball As·so·ci·a·tion, the /ˌ...
ˈ... ...,./ —see NBA

**National Col·le·giate Ath·let·ic As·so·ci·a·tion,
the** /ˌ... .,.. ˈ. ...,./

national debt /ˌ... ˈ./ *n.* [C] the total amount of
money owed by the government of a country

National En·dow·ment for the Arts, the /ˌ... .,..
. . ˈ./ a U.S. government organization which provides
money for artists

**National En·dow·ment for the Hu·man·i·ties,
the** /ˌ... .,.. . . . ˈ.,./ a U.S. government organization
which provides money for writers and other people
working in the HUMANITIES to help them with their
work

National Ge·o·graph·ic /ˌ... .. ˈ../ a U.S. monthly
magazine produced by the National Geographic Society which is known for its photographs, maps, and
articles about nature, wild animals, and people from
different societies all over the world

National Ge·o·graph·ic So·ci·e·ty, the /ˌ... ..ˈ.
.,.../ an organization that supports RESEARCH and education in GEOGRAPHY

National Guard /ˌ... ˈ./ *n.* **the National Guard** a military force in each U.S. state, that can be used when
it is needed by the state or the U.S. government

National In·sti·tutes of Health, the /ˌ... ,... ˈ./ a
U.S. government organization that supports medical
RESEARCH and gives information to doctors

na·tion·al·ism /ˈnæʃənlˌɪzəm/ *n.* [U] **1** the desire by
a group of people of the same race, origin, language
etc. to form an independent country: *Irish nationalism* **2** the belief that your own country is better
than any other country: *Europe can only live in peace
if nationalism is overcome.*

na·tion·al·ist¹ /ˈnæʃənl-ɪst/ *adj.* [only before noun] a
nationalist organization, party etc. wants to get or
keep political independence for their country and
people

nationalist² *n.* [C] someone who is involved in
trying to gain or keep political independence for
their country or people: *Serbian nationalists*

na·tion·al·is·tic /ˌnæʃnəˈlɪstɪk/ *adj.* someone who is
nationalistic believes that their country is better
than other countries, and often has no respect for
people from other countries —**nationalistically**
/-kli/ *adv.* —compare PATRIOTIC

na·tion·al·i·ty /ˌnæʃəˈnæləti/ *n.* plural **nationalities**
1 [C,U] the legal right of belonging to a particular
country: *What nationality are you?* | **American/
British etc. nationality** *Nguyen has had French
nationality since 1927.* **2** [C] a large group of people
with the same race, origin, language etc.: *Employers
cannot discriminate against someone's nationality.*

na·tion·al·ize /ˈnæʃənəˌlaɪz/ *v.* [T] if a government
nationalizes a very large industry or service such as
water, gas or electricity, it buys or takes control of
it: *Mexico's vast oil reserves were nationalized in 1938.*
—**nationalization** /ˌnæʃnələˈzeɪʃən, -ʃənl-ə-/ *n.* [C,U]
—compare PRIVATIZE

National League /ˌ... ˈ./ *n.* [singular] one of the two
groups that professional baseball teams in the U.S.
and Canada are divided into —see also AMERICAN
LEAGUE

na·tion·al·ly /ˈnæʃənl-i/ *adv.* by or to everyone in the
nation: *Saturday's Cal-UCLA game will be nationally
televised.*

national mon·u·ment /ˌ... ˈ.../ *n.* [C] a building,
special feature of the land etc. that is kept and protected by a national government for people to visit:
*The fossils were found in Dinosaur National Monu-
ment in Utah.*

National Or·gan·i·za·tion for Wom·en, the /ˌ... ...ˌ... '..'../ —see NOW

National Park Serv·ice, the /ˌ... '. ˌ../ a U.S. government organization that manages the national PARKs in the U.S.

National Ri·fle As·so·ci·a·tion, the /ˌ... '... ...ˌ../ a U.S. organization that supports people's rights to buy and keep guns, and opposes attempts to change the laws and introduce more strict controls on guns

national se·cu·ri·ty /ˌ... .'../ n. [U] the idea that a country must keep its secrets safe and its army strong in order to protect its citizens: *The investigation was done for reasons of national security.*

National Se·cu·ri·ty Coun·cil, the /ˌ... '... ˌ./ a powerful government COMMITTEE in the U.S. which controls the relationship between military and foreign POLICY

National Wild·life Fed·er·a·tion, the /ˌ... '. ...ˌ../ an organization that works to protect wild animals, birds etc. and the environment

Nation of Is·lam /ˌ... . '../ n. [singular] a Muslim group in the U.S. for African-American people who want to help and support people of their own race

nation-state /ˌ.. './ n. [C] a nation that is a politically independent country and whose citizens share the same language, origin etc.: *Since the fall of communism, old European nation-states have regained freedom.*

na·tion·wide /ˌneɪʃən'waɪd◂/ adj., adv. happening or existing in every part of the country: *The case got nationwide attention.* | *We have 350 sales outlets nationwide.*

na·tive¹ /'neɪtɪv/ adj.
1 [country] [only before noun] your native country, town etc. is the place where you were born: *Domingo has homes in Monte Carlo and in his native Madrid.* | *After a few years, she was sent back to her native country.*
2 native New Yorker/Californian etc. a person who has always lived in New York, California etc.
3 native language/tongue the language you spoke when you first learned to speak: *English is not his native language.*
4 [plant/animal] growing, living, produced etc. in one particular place: *the region's native birds* | [+ to] *Chilis are native to the New World.*
5 [art/custom] [only before noun] relating to the people of a country who were the earliest people to live there: *a blend of native culture and Christianity*
6 go native HUMOROUS to behave, dress, or speak like the people who live in the country where you have come to stay or work: *Austen has been living in Papua New Guinea so long he's gone native.*
7 native intelligence/wit etc. a quality that you have naturally from birth: *Mozart's native genius for music*

native² n. [C] **1** someone who was born in a particular place: [+ of] *Barber is a native of Arlington, Virginia.* **2** someone who lives in a place all the time or has lived there a long time: *It was easy to tell the natives from the tourists.* **3 the natives** a phrase used by white people in past times to mean one of the people who lived in America, Africa, southern Asia etc. before Europeans arrived, now considered offensive **4** a plant or animal that grows or lives naturally in a place: *Basil is a native of Thailand and India.* **5 the natives are (getting) restless** HUMOROUS used to say that a group of people are becoming impatient or angry

Native A·mer·i·can /ˌ... .'..'../ n. [C] someone from one of the races that lived in North, South, and Central America before Europeans arrived —**Native American** adj.

na·tive-born /'.. ./ adj. [only before noun] born in a particular place: *a native-born New Yorker*

native speak·er /ˌ.. '../ n. [C] someone who has learned a particular language as their first language, rather than as a foreign language: [+ of] *a native speaker of English*

Na·tiv·i·ty, nativity /nə'tɪvəti/ n. [singular] the birth of Jesus Christ: *the importance of the Nativity* | *At*

*Christmas, the church displays a **nativity scene** (=a model that shows Jesus and his parents just after his birth).* —compare CRÈCHE

Nativity play /.'... ,./ n. [C] a play telling the story of the birth of Jesus Christ, usually performed by children at Christmas

nat'l a written abbreviation of "national"

NATO /'neɪtoʊ/ n. [U] North Atlantic Treaty Organization; a group of countries including the U.S. and several European countries, which give military help to each other —see picture on page 1330

nat·ter /'nætə/ v. [I] OLD-FASHIONED to talk continuously about unimportant things

nat·ty /'næti/ adj. INFORMAL very neat and fashionable in appearance: *a natty tweed suit* —**nattily** adv.

nat·u·ral¹ /'nætʃərəl/ adj.
1 [normal] normal or usual, and what you would expect in a particular situation or at a particular time: *Death is a natural event, which you have to accept.* | *It's only natural to feel that way.* | [it is natural for sb to do sth] *It's natural for brothers to fight sometimes.* —opposite UNNATURAL, ABNORMAL
2 [not artificial] not caused, made, or controlled by people: *Laws are needed to preserve the state's natural beauty.* | *I can't even remember what my natural hair color is.* | *We use only natural fibers such as wool or cotton.* —compare ARTIFICIAL, MAN-MADE, SYNTHETIC —see picture at MAN-MADE
3 [tendency/ability] **a)** a natural tendency or type of behavior is part of your character when they are born, rather than one that you learn later: *Babies have a natural fear of falling.* **b)** [only before noun] having a particular quality or skill without needing to be taught and without needing to try hard: *Walsh was a natural leader.* | *a natural athlete*
4 [not pretending] behaving in a way that is normal and shows you are relaxed and not trying to pretend: *She was completely natural and unaffected by the attention.* | *a natural smile*
5 natural causes if someone dies of natural causes, they die because they were old or sick, not because they were killed by another person or in an accident etc.
6 natural parent/mother etc. the parent from whom a child is born, as opposed to an ADOPTIVE parent: *Eugene is obsessed with finding his natural mother.*
7 [food] with nothing added to change the taste: *all-natural snacks*
8 [not magic] not relating to gods, magic, or spirits: *I think we are dealing with a natural phenomenon here, not witchcraft.* —opposite SUPERNATURAL¹
9 [music] TECHNICAL a musical note that is natural has been raised from a FLAT³ (2) by one HALF STEP or lowered from a SHARP³ (1) by one half step —see picture at MUSIC —**naturalness** n. [U]

natural² n. [C] **1 be a natural** to be good at doing something without having to try hard or practice: *Schwartzkopf's a natural on TV.* **2** TECHNICAL **a)** a musical note that has been changed from a FLAT to a HALF STEP higher, or from a SHARP to a half step lower —compare FLAT³ (2), SHARP³ (1) **b)** the sign (♮) in written music that shows this

natural-born /ˌ... ,./ adj. **natural-born singer/storyteller etc.** INFORMAL someone who has always had a particular quality or skill without having to try hard

natural child·birth /ˌ... '../ n. [U] a method of giving birth to a baby in which a woman chooses not to use drugs

natural dis·as·ter /ˌ... .'../ n. [C] a sudden event that causes great damage or suffering, such as an EARTHQUAKE or flood

natural en·e·my /ˌ... '../ n. [C] an animal's natural enemy is another type of animal that eats animals of its type: *The whitefly has few natural enemies.*

natural gas /ˌ... './ n. [U] gas used for heating and lighting, taken from under the earth or under the ocean —compare COAL GAS

N

nat·u·ral his·to·ry /ˌ... ˈ.../ n. [U] the study of plants, animals, and minerals

nat·u·ral·ism /ˈnætʃərəˌlɪzəm, ˈnætʃrə-/ n. [U] a style of art or literature that tries to show the world and people exactly as they are —compare REALISM

nat·u·ral·ist /ˈnætʃərəlɪst/ n. [C] 1 someone who studies plants or animals, especially outdoors 2 someone who believes in naturalism in art or literature —compare NATURIST

nat·u·ral·is·tic /ˌnætʃərəˈlɪstɪk◂/ also **naturalist** adj. painted, written etc. according to the ideas of naturalism —**naturalistically** /-kli/ adv.

nat·u·ral·ize /ˈnætʃərəˌlaɪz/ v. [T usually passive] to make someone who was born outside of a particular country a citizen of that country: *naturalized U.S. citizens* —**naturalization** /ˌnætʃrələˈzeɪʃən/ n. [U]

nat·u·ral·ly /ˈnætʃərəli/ adv. 1 [sentence adverb] used to mean that the fact you are mentioning is exactly what you would have expected: *Naturally, Mike claims his barbecue is the best in the world.* | *My thoughts naturally centered on the difficult task at hand.* 2 as a natural feature or quality: *Dot had short, naturally blond hair.* | *Are you guys naturally weird, or do you have to work at it?* | *Bragging seems to* **come naturally** *to young men* (=they do it without being taught). 3 in a relaxed manner, without trying to look or sound different from usual: *She embraced Kenny and me as naturally as if we were family.* 4 SPOKEN, OLD-FASHIONED OR HUMOROUS used in order to agree with what someone has said, or to answer "of course" to a question: *"You bought this for me?" "Naturally."* —see Usage Note at CERTAINLY

natural phi·los·o·phy /ˌ... .ˈ.../ n. [U] OLD USE science

natural re·source /ˌ... .ˈ./ n. [C usually plural] something such as land, a mineral, natural energy etc. that exists in a country: *Water power is our country's most important natural resource.* | *Cambodia is very rich in natural resources.*

natural sci·ence /ˌ... .ˈ./ n. [C,U] chemistry, BIOLOGY, and PHYSICS considered together as subjects for study, or one of these subjects

natural se·lec·tion /ˌ... .ˈ../ n. [U] TECHNICAL the process by which only plants and animals that are naturally appropriate for life in their environment will continue to live, while all others will die

na·ture /ˈneɪtʃə/ n.
1 plants/animals etc. [U] everything in the physical world that is not controlled by humans, such as wild plants and animals, earth and rocks, and the weather: *I've always been a nature lover.* | *the laws of nature* —see also MOTHER NATURE
2 sb's character [C,U] someone's character or particular qualities: *Being distrustful had become a part of her nature.* | *It's* **human nature** (=the feelings and natural qualities that everyone has) *to get upset when things go wrong.* | *Murphy isn't a pessimist* **by nature.** | *He took advantage of people's* **better nature** (=feelings of kindness) *for his own gain.*
3 character of sth [C,U] a particular combination of qualities that makes something what it is and makes it different from other things: [+ of] *Information technology has changed the nature of work.* | *Fireworks* **by their very nature** *are dangerous.* | the **experimental/frightening etc. nature of sth** *Logging will harm the fragile nature of the area's plants.*
4 type [singular] a particular type of thing: | **of a personal/political/scientific etc. nature** *They're making arrangements of a legal nature.* | *He denies that any conversation* **of that nature** *ever occurred.* | *This letter is more* **in the nature of** (=similar to) *a personal attack than a scientific critique.*
5 **in the nature of things** according to the natural way things happen: *In the nature of things, a shrinking economy means less job security.*
6 **let nature take its course** to allow events to happen without doing anything to change the results:

With a cold, it's better to just let nature take its course.
7 **get/go back to nature** to start living in a simpler style, without many modern machines, and spending a lot of time outdoors
8 **the nature of the beast** the qualities that something has, that can make it difficult to deal with: *Running your own business can be exhausting, but that's just the nature of the beast.*
9 **in a state of nature** in a natural state, not having been affected by the modern world —see also **the call of nature** (CALL² (12)), SECOND NATURE

Nature Con·ser·van·cy, the /ˈ.. .ˌ.../ an organization that preserves and protects areas of the natural environment

nature re·serve /ˈ.. .ˌ./ n. [C] an area of land in which animals and plants, especially rare ones, are protected

na·tur·ist /ˈneɪtʃərɪst/ n. [C] FORMAL someone who enjoys not wearing any clothes because they believe it is natural and healthy; NUDIST —**naturism** n. [U]

na·tur·o·path /ˈneɪtʃərəˌpæθ/ n. [C] someone who tries to cure illness using natural things such as plants, rather than drugs —**naturopathy** /ˌneɪtʃəˈrɑpəθi/ n. [U] —**naturopathic** /ˌneɪtʃərəˈpæθɪk/ adj.

Nau·ga·hyde /ˈnɔɡəˌhaɪd, ˈnɑ-/ n. [U] TRADEMARK a type of material with plastic on one side that is made to look like leather: *a Naugahyde chair*

naught /nɔt/ n. [U] LITERARY nothing: *It appears all this work has been* **for naught.** | *Rourke's plans* **came to naught** (=did not happen or work)

naugh·ty /ˈnɔti/ adj. **naughtier, naughtiest 1** a naughty child behaves badly, is impolite, and does not obey adults: *a naughty little girl* **2** naughty behavior, language etc. is slightly offensive or inappropriate: *Betsy said a naughty word, Mom.* —**naughtily** adv. —**naughtiness** n. [U]

Na·u·ru /nɑˈuru/ an island in the southwestern Pacific Ocean near the Equator that is an independent REPUBLIC

nau·se·a /ˈnɔziə, ˈnɔʒə, ˈnɔʃə/ n. [U] FORMAL the feeling that you have when you think you are going to VOMIT (=bring food up from your stomach through your mouth): *Eating a poinsettia will cause nausea and even vomiting.* —see also AD NAUSEAM

nau·se·ate /ˈnɔziˌeɪt, -ʒi-/ v. [T] **1** FORMAL to make someone feel nausea: *Alcohol nauseates him, so he never drank.* **2** to make someone feel very angry and upset or offended: *It nauseates me to think that a person like that lived in this town.*

nau·se·at·ed /ˈnɔziˌeɪtɪd/ adj. feeling nausea: *He felt dizzy and nauseated from the fumes.*

nau·se·at·ing /ˈnɔziˌeɪtɪŋ/ adj. **1** making you feel nausea: *Nauseating odors wafted from the nearby sewage treatment plant.* **2** making you feel angry and upset or offended: *It's almost nauseating to think this could be true.* —**nauseatingly** adv. —compare DISGUSTING

nau·seous /ˈnɔʃəs, -ziəs/ adj. **1** feeling NAUSEA: *I'm a little nauseous from the medication.* **2** LITERARY making you feel NAUSEA, DISGUSTING: *She combined kitchen liquids into a nauseous potion.* —**nauseously** adv. —**nauseousness** n. [U]

nau·ti·cal /ˈnɔtɪkəl/ adj. relating to ships or sailing —**nautically** /-kli/ adv.

nautical mile /ˌ... ˈ./ n. [C] a measure of distance used on the ocean, equal to 1853 meters; SEA MILE

Nav·a·jo /ˈnævəˌhoʊ, ˈnɑ-/ n. **the Navajo** [plural] a Native American tribe from the southwest region of the U.S. —**Navajo** adj.

na·val /ˈneɪvəl/ adj. [only before noun] relating to or used by the navy: *a naval battle* | *Van Huygens began his naval career as a fighter pilot.*

nave /neɪv/ n. [C] the long central part of a church

na·vel /ˈneɪvəl/ n. [C] **1** FORMAL the small hollow or raised place in the middle of your stomach; BELLY BUTTON —see picture at BODY **2 contemplate your navel** also **gaze at your navel** HUMOROUS to spend too much time thinking about your own problems

navel gaz·ing /ˈ.. ˌ../ *n.* [U] HUMOROUS the act of spending too much time thinking about your own problems

navel o·range /ˌ.. ˈ../ *n.* [C] a type of orange with few or no seeds, and a small hole at the top

nav·i·ga·ble /ˈnævɪgəbəl/ *adj.* a river, lake etc. that is navigable is deep and wide enough for ships to travel on: *They're dredging the harbor to keep it navigable.* —**navigability** /ˌnævɪgəˈbɪləti/ *n.* [U]

nav·i·gate /ˈnævəˌgeɪt/ *v.* **1** [I,T] to find the way to or through a place, especially by using maps: *This time I'll drive and you navigate.* | **navigate by the stars/sun** (=use them to guide you) **2** [I,T] to find your way through a complicated system, set of rules etc.: *Americans may also have to navigate major changes in the housing market.* | *As a cadet, you'll have to navigate through the academy's internal politics.* **3** [T] FORMAL to sail all the way across or along an area of water: *The Elbe River is not as easy to navigate as the Rhine.*

nav·i·ga·tion /ˌnævəˈgeɪʃən/ *n.* [U] **1** the science of planning the way along which you travel from one place to another: *an electronic navigation system* **2** the act of sailing a ship or flying an airplane along a particular line of travel: *The voyage was an achievement of navigation and courage.* **3** the movement of ships or aircraft: *The channel is now open to navigation.* —**navigational** *adj.*

nav·i·ga·tor /ˈnævəˌgeɪtə/ *n.* [C] an officer on a ship or aircraft who plans the way along which it is traveling

Nav·ra·ti·lo·va /ˌnævræti ˈloʊvə/, **Mar·ti·na** /mɑr ˈtinə/ (1956–) a U.S. tennis player born in the former Czechoslovakia, who is regarded as one of the best players ever

na·vy¹ /ˈneɪvi/ *n. plural* **navies** **1** [C usually singular] also **Navy** the part of a country's military forces that is organized for fighting a war on the ocean: *Keating was a Navy fighter pilot.* | *Bruce joined the navy straight out of high school.* | *Koester served in the navy for eight years.* —compare AIR FORCE, ARMY, MARINES **2** [C] the war ships belonging to a country: *Their navies are no match for ours.* **3** [U] also **navy blue** a very dark blue color

navy² also **navy blue** /ˌ.. ˈ.◂/ *adj.* very dark blue: *a navy blue suit*

navy bean /ˈ.. ˌ./ *n.* [C] a small white bean which is cooked and eaten, especially in BAKED BEANS

nay¹ /neɪ/ *adv.* **1** [sentence adverb] LITERARY used when you are adding something to emphasize what you have just said: *You are permitted, nay, encouraged to come back as many times as you like.* **2** OLD USE no: *Boyd voted nay.*

nay² *n.* [C] a vote against something, or someone who votes against an idea, plan, etc. —opposite AYE YEA²

nay·say·er /ˈneɪˌseɪə/ *n.* [C] FORMAL someone who says that something cannot be done or that a plan will fail —**naysaying** *n.* [U]

Na·zi /ˈnɑtsi/ *n. plural* **Nazis** [C] **1** a member of the National Socialist Party of Adolf Hitler, which controlled Germany from 1933 to 1945 **2** SPOKEN someone who uses their authority in a way people think is cruel, unfair, or too strict —**Nazi** *adj.* —**Nazism** *n.* [U]

n.b., N.B. LITERARY used in formal writing to make a reader pay attention to an important piece of information

NBA *n.* National Basketball Association; the organization that arranges professional basketball games

NBC *n.* [U] National Broadcasting Company; one of the main U.S. television companies

NC the written abbreviation of North Carolina

NC-17 /ˌɛn si ˈsɛvənˈtin/ used to show that no one under the age of 17 is allowed to see a particular movie —compare G², PG, PG-13, R³, X (8)

NCO *n.* [C] noncommissioned officer; a soldier such as a CORPORAL or SERGEANT

ND the written abbreviation of North Dakota

-nd /nd/ *suffix* used with the number 2 to form ORDINAL numbers: *the 2nd* (=second) *of March* | *her 22nd birthday*

N'dja·mé·na /ˌɛndʒəˈmeɪnə/ the capital and largest city of Chad

N.E., NE the written abbreviation of "northeast": *N.E. Missouri*

NE the written abbreviation of Nebraska

NEA —see NATIONAL ENDOWMENT FOR THE ARTS, THE

ne·an·der·thal /niˈændəˌθɔl, -ˌtɔl, -ˌtɑl/ *n.* [C] **1** also **Neanderthal** a Neanderthal man **2** HUMOROUS a big, ugly, stupid man **3** someone who opposes all change without even thinking about it —**Neanderthal** *adj.*

Neanderthal man /.ˌ... ˈ./ *n.* [singular, not with **the**] an early type of human being who lived in Europe during the STONE AGE

Ne·a·pol·i·tan /ˌniəˈpɑlɪt⌐n/ *adj.* **1** relating to or coming from Naples, Italy: *a Neapolitan fisherman* **2** Neapolitan ICE CREAM has layers of different colors and tastes

near¹ /nɪr/ *adv. prep.* **1** only a short distance from a person or thing: *Asha's office is near the vending machines.* | *Sasha grew up on a farm near Ithaca, New York.* | **[near to sth]** *The company is trying to provide offices nearer to employees' homes.* | **go/ come/get etc. near sb/sth** (=move near someone or something) **2** close in time to a particular time or event, especially soon before it: *Add the cream near the end of the cooking time.* | **[+ to]** *Liza was near to turning 18 when the accident happened.* | *As Christmas draws near, shoppers start to panic.* **3 come/ be near (to) sth** to almost do something or almost be in a particular condition: *Larry was near death before a donor was found.* | **[come/be near to doing sth]** *With all that booze I came near to passing out.* **4 near perfect/impossible etc.** almost perfect, impossible etc.: *Road and rail travel are near impossible in winter.* **5 be near and dear to sb's heart** also **be near and dear to sb** to be very important or special to someone: *The President showed understanding of issues that are near and dear to valley residents.*

S W
1
2

USAGE NOTE: NEAR

WORD CHOICE: near, close
Use **near** and **close** to talk about short distances. **Close** is usually followed by the word "to," but **near** is not: *There's a public swimming pool near our house.* | *We live close to the swimming pool.* We also use **close** to talk about things that are not far away in time: *Kelly's birthday is close to Christmas.*

---

near² *adj.*

1 only a short distance away from someone or something: *Martha has to drive 20 miles to the nearest doctor.* | **[+ to]** *For information, call the library branch nearest to you.*

2 very close to having a particular quality or being a particular thing; SIMILAR: **[+ to]** *He seemed nearer to his old self on Wednesday.* | *The Algonquin Hotel is the nearest thing I have to a home away from home.*

3 a near miss a) a situation in which something almost hits something else: *For every serious accident there are dozens of near misses.* **b)** a situation in which something almost happens, or someone almost achieves something: *Nolte's performance was a near miss for the Oscar.*

4 in the near future soon: *I don't anticipate that happening in the near future.*

5 a near disaster/collapse etc. almost a DISASTER, a COLLAPSE etc.: *The concert was a near sellout.*

6 a near-death experience a situation in which you come close to dying because you are very sick, in an accident etc., but do not actually die

7 to the nearest $10/hundred etc. an amount to the nearest $10, hundred etc. is the number nearest to it that can be divided by $10, a hundred etc.: *Amounts are rounded to the nearest dollar.*

8 sb's nearest and dearest HUMOROUS someone's family

9 close to you [only before noun, no comparative]

S W
3

N

used to describe the side of something that is closest to where you are: *the near bank of the river* —**nearness** *n.* [U] —see also NEARLY, **nowhere (near)** (NOWHERE (4))

near³ *v.* **1** [T] to come closer to a particular place, time, or state: *Work is nearing completion.* | *Nevins is nearing 40 but still looks boyish.* **2** [I] FORMAL if a time nears, it gets closer and will come soon: *As the deadline neared, both sides agreed to continue talking.*

near beer /'. ./ *n.* [U] INFORMAL a drink that tastes similar to beer, but which contains almost no alcohol

s w **near·by** /'nɪrbaɪ/ *adj.* [only before noun] not far away: *Dinah lives in a nearby cottage.* —**nearby** /,nɪr'baɪ‹/ *adv.*: *Gabby hovered nearby.*

Near East /,. '. / *n.* **the Near East** the Middle East —**Near Eastern** *adj.*

s w **near·ly** /'nɪrli/ *adv.* almost, but not completely or exactly: *He's nearly six feet tall.* | *Oh, my goodness, it's nearly 12:30.* | *I nearly died from salmonella poisoning.* | [**not nearly as nice/good/tall etc.**] *I'm not nearly as busy as I used to be anymore.* —see Usage Note at ALMOST

near·sight·ed /'nɪr,saɪtɪd/ *adj.* unable to see things clearly unless they are close to you —**nearsightedly** *adv.* —**nearsightedness** *n.* [U] —opposite FARSIGHTED —compare SHORTSIGHTED (2)

s w **neat** /nit/ *adj.* **1** SPOKEN very good, enjoyable, interesting etc.: *What a neat idea!* | *Wow, that's pretty neat.* | *I met some really neat people at the conference.* **2** carefully arranged and not messy: *Chris looked neat and well shaven.* | *The firewood was stacked in a neat pile.* | *Their apartment was always neat and clean.* **3** someone who is neat does not like their things or house to be messy: *Neither of my sons is neat by nature.* **4** simple and effective: *I bought a neat tool for carving wood.* | *a neat software package* **5** neat alcoholic drinks have no ice or water or any other liquid added; STRAIGHT² (7): *Douglas drinks his scotch neat.* —**neatly** *adv.* —**neatness** *n.* [U]

neat freak /'. ./ *n.* [C] SPOKEN someone who always wants their things and their house to be neat and clean, in a way that other people find annoying

'neath /niθ/ *prep.* POETIC below: *'neath the stars*

Ne·bras·ka /nə'bræskə/ *written abbreviation* NE a state in the central U.S. —**Nebraskan** *n., adj.*

neb·u·la /'nɛbyələ/ *n. plural* **nebulas** or **nebulae** /-li/ [C] **1** a mass of gas and dust among the stars, often appearing as a bright cloud in the sky at night: *the Crab nebula* **2** a GALAXY (=mass of stars) that has this appearance —**nebular** *adj.*

neb·u·lous /'nɛbyələs/ *adj.* FORMAL **1** not clear or exact at all; VAGUE: *The rules are too nebulous to be applied consistently.* **2** a shape that is nebulous cannot be seen clearly and has no definite edges: *a nebulous ghostly figure* —**nebulously** *adv.* —**nebulousness** *n.* [U]

nec·es·sar·ies /'nɛsə,sɛriz/ *n.* [plural] things that you need, such as food or money, especially for a trip

s w **nec·es·sar·i·ly** /,nɛsə'sɛrəli/ *adv.* **1 not necessarily** used to say that something is not certain, even if it might be reasonable to expect it to be: *That is not necessarily true.* | *Bigger is not necessarily better.* | *"Are women getting better roles in movies?" "Not necessarily."* **2** FORMAL in a way that cannot be different or be avoided: *Income tax laws are necessarily complicated.*

s w **nec·es·sar·y** /'nɛsə,sɛri/ *adj.* **1** needed in order for you to do something or have something; ESSENTIAL: *Computers are as necessary as textbooks in schools.* | [**+ for**] *More data is necessary for improvement of the models.* | [**be necessary (for sb) to do sth**] *It's necessary to provide the same conditions under which the bulbs normally grow.* | [**make it necessary (for sb) to do sth**] *Recent violence made it necessary to take drastic measures.* | *Adjust seasoning with salt, pepper and lemon juice if necessary.* | *Ideally, they should fill out the form, but it's not absolutely necessary*

(=completely necessary). **2 a necessary evil** something bad that you have to accept in order to achieve what you want: *I, for one, consider yard work to be a necessary evil.* —see also NECESSARIES

ne·ces·si·tate /nə'sɛsə,teɪt/ *v.* [T] FORMAL to make it necessary for you to do something: *Sales have dropped dramatically, necessitating cuts in production and employment.* | [**necessitate doing sth**] *The Homecoming parade and street party will necessitate closing University Avenue.*

ne·ces·si·ty /nə'sɛsəti/ *n. plural* **necessities 1** [C] something that you need to have: *A car is an absolute necessity in this town.* | *Even basic necessities such as pencils and paper were lacking in the school.* | *We were forced to make do with just the **bare necessities*** (=basic things that you must have). —compare LUXURY (3) **2** [U] the fact of something being necessary: [**+ of**] *Eleanor stressed the necessity of punctuality at dinner.* | [**+ for**] *There is no real necessity for more parking.* | [**the necessity of doing sth**] *All members agreed about the necessity of repaving the street.* | [**necessity to do sth**] *There's no necessity to buy tickets in advance.* | *I learned to cook at a young age **out of necessity*** (=because I needed to). **3** [C] something that must happen, even if it is bad or not wanted: *Taxes are a regrettable necessity.* **4** [U] the condition of urgently needing something important, such as money or food: *The decision to sell the car was fueled by necessity.* **5 necessity is the mother of invention** used to say that if someone really needs to do something they will find a way of doing it **6 of necessity** FORMAL used when something happens in a particular way because that is the only possible way it can happen: *East–West relations have, of necessity, dominated the agenda for the past 45 years.*

neck¹ /nɛk/ *n.*

s w

1 part of the body [C] the part of your body that joins your head to your shoulders: *My neck is so sore.* | *Bud wrapped a scarf around his neck.* —compare THROAT (1) —see picture at BODY

2 clothing [C] the part of a piece of clothing that goes around your neck: *The neck's too low on this shirt.* —see also CREW NECK, SCOOP NECK, TURTLENECK, V-NECK

neck and neck

3 bottle [C] the narrow part of a bottle, near where the liquid comes out

4 be up to your neck in sth to be in a difficult situation, or to be very busy doing something: *We were up to our necks in problems with the Apollo program.*

5 I'll break/wring your neck SPOKEN used to tell someone that you are so angry with them you feel like hurting them

6 (hanging) around your neck if a problem or difficult situation is hanging around your neck, you are responsible for it, and this makes you worry —see also **an albatross (around your neck)** (ALBATROSS (2)), **a millstone (around your neck)** (MILLSTONE (2))

7 in this/sb's neck of the woods INFORMAL in this area or part of the country, or in the area where someone lives: *What are you doing in this neck of the woods?* | *We don't get much snow in our neck of the woods.*

8 neck and neck INFORMAL if two things or people are neck and neck in a competition or race, they each have an equal chance of winning

9 by a neck INFORMAL if a race is won by a neck, the winner is only a very short distance in front: *Our horse won by a neck.*

10 land [C] a narrow piece of land that comes out of a wider part —see also **be breathing down sb's neck** (BREATHE (4)), **-NECKED**, **be a pain (in the neck)** (PAIN¹ (4)), **stick your neck out** at **stick out** (STICK¹)

neck² *v.* [I] INFORMAL if two people neck, they kiss for a long time in a sexual way —**necking** *n.* [U]

-necked /nɛkt/ [in adjectives] **V-necked/open-necked etc.** also **V-neck/open-neck etc.** if a piece of clothing is V-necked, open-necked etc., it has that type of neck: *a navy V-necked sweater*

neck·er·chief /'nɛkətʃɪf, -tʃif/ *n.* [C] a square piece of cloth that is folded and worn tied around the neck

neck·lace /'nɛk-lɪs/ *n.* [C] a piece of jewelry that hangs around your neck: *a pearl necklace*

neck·line /'nɛk-laɪn/ *n.* [C usually singular] the shape made by the edge of a woman's dress, shirt etc. around or below the neck: *a black dress with a low neckline*

neck·tie /'nɛktaɪ/ *n.* [C] a TIE

nec·ro·man·cy /'nɛkrə,mænsi/ *n.* [U] LITERARY **1** magic, especially evil magic **2** the practice of claiming to talk with the dead —**necromancer** *n.* [C]

nec·ro·phil·i·a /,nɛkrə'fɪliə/ *n.* [U] sexual interest in dead bodies

nec·tar /'nɛktə/ *n.* [U] **1** thick juice made from some fruits: *apricot nectar* **2** the sweet liquid that BEES and some birds eat from flowers **3** the drink of the gods, in the stories of ancient Greece

nec·ta·rine /,nɛktə'rin/ *n.* [C] a round juicy yellow-red fruit that has a large rough seed and smooth skin, or the tree that produces this fruit

née /neɪ/ *adj.* OLD-FASHIONED used in order to show the family name that a woman had before she was married: *Mrs. Carol Cook, née Williams*

need¹ /nid/ *v.* [T not in progressive] **1** to feel that you must have or do something, or that something is necessary; REQUIRE: *I needed some sleep.* | *Nancy is going to the store – do we need any milk?* | [need to do sth] *Does anybody need to go to the bathroom?* | [need sth for sth] *We need some batteries for the camcorder.* | [need sb to do sth] *Peter needs you to take him to the airport.* | *Do you want some of these books? I don't need them anymore.* **2** to be without something that is necessary, or to lack something that would improve a situation; REQUIRE: *The front room needs a coat of paint.* | *I think Brad's car needs new tires.* **need cleaning/painting/replacing etc.** *My new watch never needs winding.* | *The Hamms bought a house in Napa that needs fixing up.* | *Rapid transit in the area is badly needed.* **3 need to do sth** to have to do something because you feel you should do it or because it is necessary: *You need to make reservations for Yosemite campgrounds.* | *The roof will probably need to be replaced next year.* | *Do I need to dress up for this party?* | *The pie doesn't need to be refrigerated.* **4 sb/sth need not do sth** FORMAL used to say that it is not necessary for someone to do something or for something to happen: *The nuclear family need not provide the only parenting a child gets.* | *As it turns out, he need not have worried.* | *Additional expenses need not be reported.* **5** if a job or activity needs a particular quality, you must have that quality in order to do it well: *A job like nursing needs patience and understanding.* **6 sb does not need sth** SPOKEN used in order to say that something is making someone's life more difficult: *I don't need this tension at the dinner table.* **7 need I do sth?** HUMOROUS used to say that it is not necessary to do something, because it is clear what someone would say, do etc.: *San Remo offers superb food, a nice atmosphere, and moderate prices. Need I say more?* | *The House of Representatives was responsible for $1.3 billion in labor costs – need I add that all of this was paid for by taxpayers?* **8 on a need-to-know basis** if information is given to people on a need-to-know basis, they are given only the details that they need at the time when they need them: *Access to the manufacturing process is on a strictly need-to-know basis.*

need² *n.* **1** sth that is necessary [singular,U] a situation in which something must be done, especially to improve the situation: [+ for] *There is a need for stricter safety regulations.* | [the need to do sth] *We recognize the need to improve teaching standards.* | *Our soldiers are ready to sacrifice their lives, if need be* (=if it is necessary), *to protect their country.* | *Strother can play defense if the need arises* (=whenever it is necessary).

2 be in need of sth a) to need help, advice, money etc., because you are in a difficult situation: *The project helps those who are in need of money, food, and clothing.* | *Many families are badly in need of medical help.* **b)** to need to be cleaned, repaired, or given attention in some way: *Some buildings damaged in the earthquake are still in need of repair.*

3 what you need [C usually plural] what someone needs to have in order to live a normal healthy life: *Prison programs should be tailored to the needs of offenders.* | *The charity serves the needs of the poor.* | *The school meets the educational needs of the deaf.* | *Ross was devoted to his wife and attended to her every need.*

4 no money [U] the state of not having enough food or money: *Thousands of people donated money and food to those in need.*

5 there's no need (for sb) to do sth a) used to say that someone does not have to do something: *There was no need for me to stay there.* **b)** SPOKEN used to tell someone to stop doing something: *There's no need to shout – I'm not deaf!* —see also **in your hour of need** (HOUR (14))

need·ful /'nidfəl/ *adj.* FORMAL needing things, help etc.

nee·dle¹ /'nidl/ *n.* [C]
1 sewing a small thin piece of steel used for sewing, that has a point at one end and a hole in the other end: *a needle and thread*
2 medicine the sharp hollow metal part on the end of a SYRINGE, which is pushed into your skin to put a drug or medicine into your body or to take out blood: *The AIDS virus can be transmitted by the use of dirty needles.*
3 tree a small thin pointed leaf, especially from a PINE or FIR tree: *The needles have dropped off the Christmas tree.*
4 knitting a long thin stick used in KNITTing
5 tool a long thin piece of metal on a scientific instrument, that moves backward and forward and points to numbers or directions: *a compass needle*
6 records the very small, pointed part in a RECORD PLAYER that picks up sound from the records: *There must be some dust on the needle.*
7 sth is like looking for a needle in a haystack INFORMAL used to say that something is almost impossible to find: *I don't know if we'll ever find the right gene – it's like looking for a needle in a haystack.*

needle² *v.* [T] to deliberately annoy someone by continuously making remarks that are not nice, or stupid jokes: *Paula kept needling him about getting a job, and so finally he hit her.*

Needle Park /'.. ,./ *n.* [U] SLANG a name given to a park in some cities where people who use illegal drugs spend time and leave their used NEEDLES (2)

nee·dle·point /'nidl,pɔɪnt/ *n.* [U] a method of making pictures by covering a piece of material with small stitches of colored thread, or something made in this way: *a needlepoint pillow*

need·less /'nid-lɪs/ *adj.* **1 needless to say** used when you are telling someone something that they probably already know or expect: *Needless to say, we're on a very tight budget.* **2** not necessary, and often easily avoided: *Why take needless risks?* —**needlessly** *adv.*: *Thousands of women die needlessly every year because of poor medical care.*

nee·dle·work /'nidl,wɜrk/ *n.* [U] the activity or art of sewing or decorating things using thread, or things made by sewing

need·n't /'nidnt/ *v.* the short form of "need not": *He needn't have worried.*

need·y /'nidi/ *adj.* **needier, neediest 1** having very little food or money: *a needy family* **2 the needy** needy people: *The soup kitchen serves the city's needy.* **3** someone who is needy has emotional problems in which they want people to love them and help them. —**neediness** *n.* [U]

ne'er /nɛr/ *adv.* POETIC never

N

ne'er-do-well /'nɛr du ˌwɛl/ n. [C] OLD-FASHIONED a lazy person who never works

ne·far·i·ous /nɪ'fɛriəs, -'fær-/ adj. FORMAL evil or criminal: *Many of the spies had been involved in murder, blackmail, or other nefarious activities.* —**nefariously** adv. —**nefariousness** n. [U]

neg. the written abbreviation of "negative"

ne·gate /nɪ'geɪt/ v. [T] FORMAL 1 to prevent something from having any effect: *The decision would negate last year's Supreme Court ruling.* 2 to state that something does not exist or is not true: *The witness's testimony negated what the defendant had claimed.* —**negation** /nɪ'geɪʃən/ n. [U]

s w
2 2
neg·a·tive¹ /'nɛgətɪv/ adj.
1 **effect** having a bad or harmful effect: *The agreement has had a negative impact on jobs.* | *Negative publicity has harmed the group's ability to get things done.* —opposite POSITIVE¹ (7)
2 **attitude** considering only the bad qualities of a situation, person etc. and not the good ones: *Tanya has a really negative self-image.* | *Critics said the article portrayed Latinos in negative way.* | [+ about] *Rick's hard to be with because he's so negative about everything.* —opposite POSITIVE¹ (2)
3 **no/not a)** saying or meaning "no": *Our request received a negative reply.* **b)** a negative word or sentence contains one of the words "no," "not," "nothing," "never" etc. For example, "cannot" or "can't" are negative forms of "can." —opposite AFFIRMATIVE²
4 **medical/scientific test** not showing any sign of the chemical or medical condition that is being looked for: *Anne's pregnancy test was negative.* —opposite POSITIVE¹ (6)
5 **number/quantity** less than zero: *negative numbers* | *There has been a negative return on our investment* (=we lost money).
6 **electricity** TECHNICAL having the type of electrical charge that is carried by ELECTRONS, shown by (–) on a BATTERY —opposite POSITIVE¹ (11)
7 **blood** TECHNICAL not having RHESUS FACTOR in your blood: *The Red Cross said it had virtually no stocks of type O negative blood available.* —opposite POSITIVE¹ (12) —**negatively** adv.

negative² n. [C] 1 a piece of film that shows dark areas as light and light areas as dark, from which a photograph is printed 2 a quality or feature of something that is not good or not useful: *Another negative was the increase in unemployment.* —opposite POSITIVE² 3 a statement or expression that means "no": *Griese responded in the negative to both requests.* —opposite AFFIRMATIVE²

ne·glect¹ /nɪ'glɛkt/ v. [T] 1 to not take care of someone or something very well: *Each year 700,000 children are abused or neglected.* | *Soon, Barker was neglecting the farm and spending most of his time in the casino.* 2 to not pay enough attention to someone or something: *My career was all-important, and my family got neglected.* | *The President had been criticized for neglecting domestic issues.* 3 to not do something or forget to do it, often because you are lazy or careless: *Four security guards were accused of neglecting their duties.* | [neglect to do sth] *Planners apparently neglected to consider future water and electricity requirements.*

neglect² n. [U] 1 failure to take care of something or someone well: *Cases of child abuse and neglect seem to be increasing in number.* | [+ of] *Employees complained of the company's neglect of safety standards.* | *Rangoon's buildings are crumbling from neglect.* 2 the condition that someone or something is in when they have not been taken care of: *The inner cities are in a state of neglect.* 3 the act of not doing something that you are supposed to do: *Lieutenant Bradley was demoted to sergeant for neglect of duty.*

ne·glect·ful /nɪ'glɛktfəl/ adj. FORMAL not taking care of something or someone very well, or not giving it enough attention: *neglectful parents*

neg·li·gee, negligée /ˌnɛglɪ'ʒeɪ, 'nɛglɪˌʒeɪ/ n. [C] a very thin, pretty coat, worn over a NIGHTGOWN

neg·li·gence /'nɛglɪdʒəns/ n. [U] failure to do something that you are responsible for in a careful enough way, so that something bad happens or could happen: *The jury found Dr. Cornwell guilty of negligence.*

neg·li·gent /'nɛglɪdʒənt/ adj. 1 not doing something that you are responsible for in a careful enough way, so that something bad happens or could happen: *Kitty was characterized as a negligent mother.* | [+ in] *The crew of the ship may have been negligent in following safety procedures.* 2 LITERARY careless, but in a pleasantly relaxed way: *The bartender set Tad's drink down with a negligent, easy grace* —**negligently** adv.

neg·li·gi·ble /'nɛglɪdʒəbəl/ adj. too slight or unimportant to have any effect: *Each piece of candy contains a negligible amount of fat.* | *The difference in cost would be negligible.* —**negligibly** adv.

ne·go·tia·ble /nɪ'goʊʃəbəl/ adj. 1 prices, agreements etc. that are negotiable can be discussed and changed before being agreed on: *Bank charges for loans are often negotiable.* 2 a road, path etc. that is negotiable is in a good enough condition to be traveled along: *The road is only negotiable in the dry season.* 3 TECHNICAL a check, BOND etc. that is negotiable can be exchanged for money —compare NON-NEGOTIABLE

s w
3
ne·go·ti·ate /nɪ'goʊʃiˌeɪt/ v. 1 [I,T] to discuss something in order to reach an agreement, especially in business or politics: *Teachers are under pressure to give up benefits negotiated by unions.* | *UN representatives are trying to negotiate a ceasefire.* | [+ with] *Skinner negotiated with several firms for the best offer.* | *The government and rebel leaders sat down at the negotiating table* (=started official discussions) *for the first time yesterday.* 2 [T] to succeed in getting past or over a difficult place on a path, road etc.: *Elderly people were carefully negotiating the hotel steps.* —**negotiator** n. [C]

s w
2
ne·go·ti·a·tion /nɪˌgoʊʃi'eɪʃən/ n. [C usually plural, U] official discussions between two or more groups who are trying to agree on something: *Negotiations involving 108 nations have been bogged down over the issue of refugees.* | *Any border changes will come about only by negotiation.* | [+ on] *Officials have refused to budge in negotiations on copyright laws.* | *Trade representatives have said the issue is open to negotiation* (=can be negotiated). | *The U.S. and Russia are likely to enter into negotiations* (=start negotiations) *on nuclear weapons next year.*

Ne·gro /'nigroʊ/ n. plural **Negroes** [C] OLD-FASHIONED a word used in the past for an African-American person, now considered offensive —**negro** adj.

Ne·groid /'nigrɔɪd/ adj. OLD-FASHIONED, TECHNICAL having the physical features of a black person from Africa

NEH —see NATIONAL ENDOWMENT FOR THE HUMANITIES, THE

Ne·he·mi·ah /ˌniə'maɪə/ a book in the Old Testament of the Protestant Bible

Neh·ru /'neɪru, 'nɛru/, **Ja·wa·har·lal** /dʒə'wɑhəˌlɑl/ (1889–1964) an Indian politician who was one of the leaders of India's fight for independence from the U.K. and became India's first Prime Minister from 1947 to 1964

neigh /neɪ/ v. [I] to make the long loud sound that a horse makes —**neigh** n. [C]

s w
2 2
neigh·bor /'neɪbə/ n. [C] 1 someone who lives in the house or apartment next to you or near you: *The neighbors invited us over for a Fourth of July party.* | *Our next-door neighbors* (=neighbors who live next to you) *are going to take care of the cat while we're on vacation.* | *The neighbor kids* (=kids who live near you) *were playing catch in the street.* 2 a country's neighbors are the countries that share a border with it: *Israel and its Arab neighbors* 3 someone who is standing or sitting next to you: *No visiting with your neighbor during the test, Billy.*

Rod and Ben are next-door neighbors.

s w **neigh·bor·hood** /'neɪbɚˌhʊd/ n. [C] **1** a small area of a town, or the people who live there: *I grew up in a quiet neighborhood of Boston.* | *a neighborhood school* | *Are there any good restaurants in the neighborhood?* **2 in the neighborhood of 5,000/$100 etc.** a little more or a little less than a particular amount: *Forstmann's bid for the company was in the neighborhood of $600 million.*

neighborhood watch /ˌ... './ n. [C] a system organized by the police, in which neighbors watch each other's houses to prevent crimes

neigh·bor·ing /'neɪbərɪŋ/ adj. [only before noun] near the place where you are or the place you are talking about; NEARBY: *Students are bused into the high school from neighboring towns.*

neigh·bor·ly /'neɪbɚli/ adj. friendly and helpful toward your neighbors: *All three men waved in a neighborly way.* —**neighborliness** n. [U]

neigh·bour /'neɪbɚ/ n. [C] the British and Canadian spelling of NEIGHBOR

s w **nei·ther¹** /'niðɚ, 'naɪ-/ determiner, pron. not one nor the other of two people or things: *Neither side is willing to compromise.* | *We saw a couple of houses, but neither was really what we wanted.* | *We asked both John and Jerry, but neither one could give us a satisfactory explanation.* | *Neither of them was interested in going to the concert.* —compare EITHER², NONE¹

neither² adv. used in order to agree with a negative statement that someone has just made, or to add a negative statement to your own that has just been made: *"I don't like herb tea." "Neither do I."* | *The Cowboys won't be playing in the Superbowl this year, and neither will the Falcons.* | *"I haven't seen Greg in a long time." "Me neither (=I also haven't)."* —compare EITHER⁴ —see Usage Note at ALSO

s w **neither³** conjunction **1 neither... nor...** used when mentioning two statements, facts, actions etc. that are not true or possible: *Neither Oleg's mother nor his father spoke English.* | *The equipment is neither accurate nor safe.* **2** FORMAL used in order to emphasize or add information to a negative statement: *If politics did not interest them, neither did they see it as affecting their lives.* **3 be neither here nor there** used when saying that something is not important because it does not affect or change a fact or situation: *What Cheng's intentions were is neither here nor there. What matters is what he did.*

Nel·son /'nɛlsən/, **Ho·ra·ti·o** /hə'reɪʃiˌoʊ/ (1758–1805) a famous leader of the British navy

nem·a·tode /'nɛməˌtoʊd/ n. [C] a type of small worm that can destroy crops

nem·e·sis /'nɛməsɪs/ n. [singular] **1** an opponent or enemy that it is very difficult for you to defeat: *The Warriors will face their old nemesis, the Phoenix Suns, tonight in the Coliseum Arena.* **2** LITERARY a punishment that is deserved and cannot be avoided

neo- /nioʊ, niə/ prefix [in nouns and adjectives] new, or more recent than something similar: *a neophyte (=someone who has just started learning something)* | *neonatal (=relating to newly born babies)* |

neoclassical architecture (=copying the style of ancient Greece and Rome)

ne·o·clas·si·cal /ˌnioʊ'klæsɪkəl/ adj. neoclassical art and ARCHITECTURE copy the style of ancient Greece or Rome

ne·o·co·lo·ni·al·ism /ˌnioʊkə'loʊniəˌlɪzəm/ n. [U] the economic and political influence that a powerful country uses to control another country —**neocolonialist** adj. —compare COLONIALISM

ne·o·con·ser·va·tive /ˌnioʊkən'sɚvəṭɪv/ adj. [usually before noun] supporting political ideas that include strict moral behavior and emphasizing each person's responsibility to work and take care of himself or herself, rather than depending on the government for help —**neoconservative** n. [C]

Ne·o·lith·ic /ˌniə'lɪθɪk/ adj. relating to the latest period of the STONE AGE, about 10,000 years ago, when people began to live together in small groups and make stone tools and weapons

ne·o·lo·gism /ni'ɑləˌdʒɪzəm/ n. [C] a new word or expression, or a word used with a new meaning

ne·on¹ /'niɑn/ n. [U] symbol **Ne** a gas that is an ELEMENT and that produces a bright light when electricity goes through it

neon² adj. [only before noun] **1** neon lights or signs use neon in glass tubes to produce brightly colored letters or pictures: *the neon lights of Las Vegas* | *a red neon martini glass on a bar sign* **2** neon colors are very bright: *neon pink shorts*

ne·o·na·tal /ˌnioʊ'neɪṭl/ adj. [only before noun] TECHNICAL relating to babies that have just been born: *the hospital's neonatal intensive care unit*

neo-Na·zi /ˌ... './ n. [C] a member of a group that supports the ideas of Adolf Hitler and expresses hatred of people who are not white or who come from other countries —**neo-Nazi** adj.

ne·o·phyte /'niəˌfaɪt/ n. [C] **1** someone who has just started to learn a particular skill, art, job etc.: *a political neophyte* **2** LITERARY a new member of a religious group —**neophyte** adj. [only before noun] *neophyte wine enthusiasts*

ne·o·prene /'niəˌprin/ n. [U] a type of artificial rubber

Ne·pal /nə'pɔl/ a country in south Asia, in the Himalaya mountains, north of India and south of China —**Nepalese** /ˌnɛpə'liz/ adj.

neph·ew /'nɛfyu/ n. [C] the son of your brother or **s w** sister, or the son of your husband's or wife's brother or sister

nep·o·tism /'nɛpəˌtɪzəm/ n. [U] the practice of unfairly giving the best jobs to members of your family when you are in a position of power —compare CRONYISM

Nep·tune¹ /'nɛptun/ n. the eighth PLANET from the sun

Nep·tune² the Roman name for the god Poseidon

nerd /nɚd/ n. [C] INFORMAL someone who is not fashionable and does not know how to act in social situations, and who studies hard in school and is often very interested in one subject: *a computer nerd (=someone who is very interested in computers)* | *Matt was such a nerd in high school.* —**nerdy** adj.

Nerf /nɚf/ adj. TRADEMARK Nerf balls and other toys are made of a soft FOAM RUBBER material

Ne·ro /'nɪroʊ/ (A.D. 37–68) a Roman EMPEROR, said to have killed his mother, his wives, and many other people

Ne·ru·da /neɪ'rudə/, **Pab·lo** /'pɑbloʊ/ (1904–1973) a Chilean poet

nerve¹ /nɚv/ n. **s w**
1 courage/confidence [U] courage and confidence in a dangerous, difficult, or frightening situation: *He would've won if he hadn't lost his nerve.* | *Reporting a colleague for sexual harassment takes a lot of nerve.* | *Not many people have the nerve to stand up and talk in front of a large audience.*
2 in the body [C] a long thin thread-like part of your body, along which feelings and messages are

N

sent to the brain: *I injured a nerve in my foot playing volleyball.*

3 nerves [plural] the feeling of being nervous because you are worried or a little frightened: *"What's wrong with Troy?" "It's just nerves. His driving test is tomorrow." | Carey had a drink to calm his nerves. | The constant noise frays people's nerves* (=makes them more nervous). *| The budget cuts are giving teachers a severe case of nerves* (=making them very nervous).

4 get on sb's nerves to annoy someone, especially by doing something repeatedly: *Nick's whining is really starting to get on my nerves.*

5 strike/touch/hit a (raw) nerve to mention something that people feel strongly about or that upsets people: *Ann Richards, the former Texas governor, found issues that struck a nerve with the voters.*

6 nerves of steel the ability to be brave and calm in a dangerous or difficult situation: *You need nerves of steel to be a race-car driver.*

7 **lack of respect** INFORMAL lack of respect for other people, which causes you to do impolite things: *You invited yourself? You have some nerve! | Parker had the nerve to take credit for work he hadn't done.*

nerve² *v.* [T] **nerve yourself** LITERARY to prepare yourself to be brave enough to do something difficult or dangerous

nerve cell /'. ./ *n.* [C] a NEURON

nerve cen·ter /'. ,../ *n.* [C] the place from which a system, activity, organization etc. is controlled: *The bridge is the ship's nerve center.*

nerve end·ings /'. ,../ *n.* [plural] the places in your skin and inside your body where your nerves receive information about temperature, pain etc.

nerve gas /'. ./ *n.* [C,U] a poisonous gas used in war, that damages your CENTRAL NERVOUS SYSTEM

nerve-rack·ing, nerve-wracking /'nɔv ˌrækɪŋ/ *adj.* a nerve-racking situation makes you feel very nervous because it is difficult or frightening: *Fran faced a nerve-racking wait for her medical test results.*

s w **nerv·ous** /'nɔvəs/ *adj.* **1** worried or afraid about
2 3 something, and unable to relax: *Sanders reassured nervous students that loans would be available this fall. | I didn't know him and was really nervous about having to work with him. | Job cuts are making auto workers very nervous about the future. | Chris gets nervous before speaking in public.* **2** often becoming worried or afraid, and easily upset: *a thin, nervous woman | The stress is making him into a nervous wreck* (=making him very worried and affecting his health and confidence). **3** relating to the nerves in your body: *a nervous disorder* **4 nervous exhaustion** OLD-FASHIONED a mental condition in which you feel very tired, usually caused by working too hard or a difficult emotional problem —**nervously** *adv.* —**nervousness** *n.* [U]

USAGE NOTE: NERVOUS

WORD CHOICE: nervous, worried, concerned, anxious, uneasy

Use **nervous** when you feel worried and frightened about something that is going to happen soon or that might happen, especially because you are not confident: *I was really nervous before the interview.* Use **worried** when you cannot stop thinking about a problem or about something bad that might happen, so that you feel very unhappy about it: *Tracy's parents were worried when she didn't come home after school.* Use **concerned** when you are worried about a particular problem: *We are concerned about the number of homeless people in our city.* Use **anxious** when you are very worried that something bad has happened or might happen, especially to someone you know: *The school tried to reassure anxious parents.* Use **uneasy** when you are a little worried because you think something bad may happen or may have already happened, but you do not know for sure: *When there is talk of layoffs, workers begin to feel uneasy.*

---

nervous break·down /ˌ.. '../ *n.* [C] NOT TECHNICAL a mental illness in which someone becomes extremely anxious and tired, and cannot deal with the things they usually do: **have/suffer a nervous breakdown** *Vonda came close to having a nervous breakdown last winter.*

nervous sys·tem /'.. ,../ *n.* [C] your nerves, brain, and SPINAL CORD, through which your body feels pain, heat etc. and controls your movements

-ness /nɪs/ *suffix* [in nouns] used to form nouns from adjectives and PARTICIPLES: *loudness | sadness | warm-heartedness* (=quality of being friendly and nice)

nest¹ /nɛst/ *n.* [C] **1** a hollow place made or chosen by a bird to lay its eggs in and to live in **2** a place where insects or small animals live: *a field mouse's nest* **3 leave/fly the nest** to leave your parents' home and start living somewhere else when you become an adult **4 a nest of spies/criminals/vice** etc. a place where there are many bad people or evil activities —see also **empty nest** (EMPTY¹ (7)), **feather your nest/bed** (FEATHER² (1)), **a hornet's nest** (HORNET (2)), **love nest** (LOVE² (14))

nest

nest² *v.* [I] to build or use a nest: *The birds stop briefly to nest and feed.*

nest egg /'. ./ *n.* [C] an amount of money that you have saved: *Eileen and Harry had to dip into their retirement nest egg to pay for their son's college fees.*

nes·tle /'nɛsəl/ *v.* **1** [I always + adv./prep. T always + adv./prep.] to move into a comfortable position, pressing your head or body against someone or against something soft: **[nestle against/beside/by etc.]** *The baby nestled against her mother's neck.* | **[nestle sth against/beside etc.]** *A young couple nestled a toddler between them.* **2** [I always + adv./prep.,T usually passive] LITERARY to be in a position that is protected from wind, rain etc.: **[+ among/between etc.]** *The many lakes nestled among the hills glowed like emeralds.*

nest·ling /'nɛstlɪŋ/ *n.* [C] a very young bird

net¹ /nɛt/ *n.* **1** [C,U] a material made of strings, threads, or wires woven across each other with regular spaces between them, or something made from this material: *a fishing net* **2** [usually singular] **a)** a long net used in games such as tennis that the players must hit the ball over **b)** a net used as a GOAL in some games such as basketball, SOCCER, or HOCKEY: *The puck went straight into the net.* **3** [U] very thin material made from fine threads woven together with very small spaces between the threads: *The bride wore a veil made of ivory net.* **4 the Net** also **the net** the Internet **5** [C] a communications or computer network —see also **cast your net wide** (CAST¹ (16)), HAIRNET, SAFETY NET

net² *adj.* [only before noun] **1** relating to the final s w
amount or number that remains when all the gains 3
and losses that affect the total have been calculated: **net profits/assets/gain/income etc.** (=what remains after taxes, costs etc. have been taken away) *| Vernon estimates the company's net worth at over $8 billion. | By comparison, there was a net loss of 164,000 jobs among workers older than 25. | Despite the increase in overseas sales, the United States is still a net importer of beef* (=it imports more than it exports). —compare GROSS¹ (2) **2 net result/effect** the final result of something: **[+ of]** *The net result of the plan will be higher costs to the consumer.* **3 net weight** the weight of something without its container **4 net price** the price of something, that cannot be reduced any more

net³ *v.* **netted, netting** [T] **1** to earn a particular amount of money as a profit after taxes have been

N

paid: *I was netting around $64,000 a year.* **2** to succeed in getting something, especially by using your skill: *An undercover drug sweep netted 22 suspects in one evening.* | *Measure A netted only 58 percent of the vote.* **3** INFORMAL to hit or kick the ball into the net in sport **4** to catch a fish in a net: *We netted three fish in under an hour.*

neth·er /ˈnɛðəʳ/ adj. [only before noun] LITERARY OR HUMOROUS lower down: *Had Jackson finally been banished to the **nether regions** of the gossip columns?*

Neth·er·lands, the /ˈnɛðəʳləndz/ a country in north-west Europe that is north of Belgium and east of Germany

neth·er·most /ˈnɛðəʳmoʊst/ adj. LITERARY lowest: *the nethermost fiery pit of hell*

neth·er·world, nether world /ˈnɛðəʳˌwɜʳld/ n. [C usually singular] LITERARY **1** the part of society that includes people who are involved in illegal activities: *The rest of the stolen pieces disappeared into the netherworld of the black market* **2** HELL

Net·i·quette /ˈnɛtɪkɪt/ n. [U] SLANG the commonly accepted rules for polite behavior when communicating with other people on the Internet

net·ting /ˈnɛtɪŋ/ n. [U] material consisting of string, wire etc. that has been woven into a net: *The crab traps are covered in wire netting.*

net·tle¹ /ˈnɛtl/ n. [C] a wild plant with rough leaves that sting you —see also **grasp the nettle** (GRASP¹)

nettle² v. [T] LITERARY to annoy someone: *The topic of a Midwestern identity has nettled writers for decades.*

net·tle·some /ˈnɛtlsəm/ adj. annoying or difficult: *nettlesome questions*

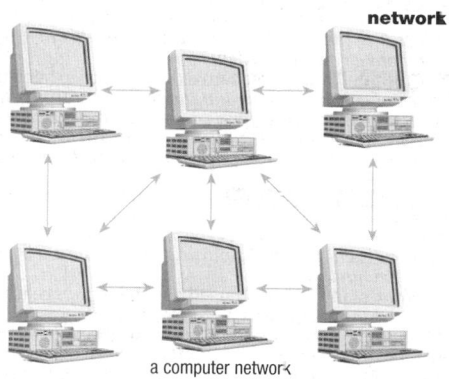

a computer network

s w **net·work¹** /ˈnɛtwɜʳk/ n. [C] **1** a group of radio or television stations, which broadcast many of the same programs in different parts of the country: *the four biggest TV networks* | *the network evening news* **2** a system of lines, tubes, wires, roads etc. that cross each other and are connected to each other: *the freeway network* | [+ of] *the network of blood vessels in the body* **3** a set of computers that are connected to each other so that they can share information: *Each user on the network will have his or her own private line to allow data to flow more smoothly.* **4** a group of people, organizations etc. that are connected or that work together: [+ of] *Tricia has built up a good network of professional contacts.*

network² v. **1** [I,T] to connect several computers together so that they can share information **2** [I] to meet other people who do the same type of work in order to share information, help each other etc.

net·work·ing /ˈnɛtwɜʳkɪŋ/ n. [U] the practice of meeting other people involved in the same type of work, in order to share information, support each other etc.

neur- /nʊr/ prefix TECHNICAL relating to the nerves: *neuralgia* (=pain in a nerve)

neu·ral /ˈnʊrəl/ adj. TECHNICAL relating to a nerve or the NERVOUS SYSTEM: *signs of neural activity*

neu·ral·gia /nʊˈrældʒə/ n. [U] a sharp pain along the length of a nerve —**neuralgic** adj.

neuro- /nʊroʊ, -rə/ prefix TECHNICAL relating to the nerves: *a neurosurgeon* (=who treats the body's nervous system)

neu·rol·o·gy /nʊˈrɑlədʒi/ n. [U] the scientific study of the NERVOUS SYSTEM and its diseases —**neurologist** n. [C] —**neurological** /ˌnʊrəˈlɑdʒɪkəl/ adj.

neu·ron /ˈnʊrɑn/ n. [C] a type of cell that makes up the NERVOUS SYSTEM and that sends messages to muscles and other parts of the body, and sends messages in the brain about feelings, sights, smells etc.; NERVE CELL

neu·ro·sis /nʊˈroʊsɪs/ n. plural **neuroses** /-siz/ [C,U] TECHNICAL a mental illness that makes someone very worried or afraid when they have no reason to be

neu·rot·ic /nʊˈrɑtɪk/ adj. **1** anxious or afraid in an unreasonable way: *I just got really neurotic about not wanting to spend any money.* **2** TECHNICAL relating to or affected by neurosis: *neurotic disorders* —**neurotic** n. [C] —**neurotically** /-kli/ adv.

neu·ro·trans·mit·ter /ˌnʊroʊˈtrænzmɪtəʳ/ n. [C] TECHNICAL a chemical in the NERVOUS SYSTEM that carries messages from one cell to another

neu·ter¹ /ˈnutəʳ/ v. [T] to remove part of the sex organs of an animal so that it cannot make babies: *a neutered tomcat* —compare SPAY

neuter² adj. **1** TECHNICAL in English grammar, a neuter PRONOUN such as "it" REFERS to something that is neither male nor female, or does not show the sex of the person or animal that it refers to **2** plants or animals that are neuter have undeveloped sex organs or no sex organs

neu·tral¹ /ˈnutrəl/ adj.

1 in an argument etc. not supporting any of the people or groups involved in an argument or disagreement: *The game will be held at a neutral site.* | *To avoid ugly scenes, choose neutral topics for discussion.*

2 in a war a country that is neutral does not support any of the countries involved in a war: *During World War II, Sweden was neutral.* | **neutral territory/waters** (=land or ocean that is not controlled by any of the countries involved in a war)

3 be/meet etc. on neutral ground if two opposing teams or representatives are on neutral ground, they are in a place that is not favorable to either of them: *The talks will be held on neutral ground.*

4 language language, words etc. that are neutral are deliberately chosen to avoid expressing any strong opinion or feeling: *Rather than describing Ross as her boyfriend, Claire preferred the neutral term "friend."*

5 color a neutral color is not very strong or bright, for example gray or light brown: *a dress in a neutral fabric*

6 wire TECHNICAL a neutral wire has no electrical CHARGE¹ (7)

7 chemical TECHNICAL a neutral substance is neither acid nor ALKALINE: *Gladioli prefer a neutral or slightly acidic soil.* —**neutrally** adv.

neutral² n. **1** [U] the position of the GEARS of a car or machine in which no power is being sent from the engine to the wheels or other moving parts: *Start the car in neutral.* **2** [C] a country or person that is not fighting for or helping any of the countries involved in a war **3** [C usually plural] a neutral color, such as gray or light brown: *Vera dresses mostly in neutrals.*

neu·tral·ist /ˈnutrəlɪst/ adj. tending not to support either side in a war, argument etc. —**neutralist** n. [C]

neu·tral·i·ty /nuˈtræləti/ n. [U] the state of not supporting either side in an argument or war: *After Pearl Harbor, U.S. neutrality ended.*

neu·tral·ize /ˈnutrəˌlaɪz/ v. [T] **1** to prevent something from having any effect: *The Oilers managed to neutralize the other team's defenses.* **2** TECHNICAL to make a substance chemically NEUTRAL: *This fertilizer neutralizes the salts in the soil.* **3** a word meaning to

N

kill someone, especially an enemy in a war, used when you do not want to say "kill" directly: *Government forces neutralized the rebels.* **4** to make a country or population NEUTRAL in war —**neutralization** /ˌnutrələˈzeɪʃən/ n. [U]

neu·tri·no /nuˈtrinoʊ/ n. plural **neutrinos** [C] a SUBATOMIC PARTICLE (=piece of matter that is smaller than an atom) that has little or no mass and a NEUTRAL electrical charge

neu·tron /ˈnutrɑn/ n. [C] a very small piece of matter with no electrical CHARGE, in the NUCLEUS (=CENTRAL PART) of an atom —compare ELECTRON, PROTON

neutron bomb /ˈ.. ./ n. [C] a type of NUCLEAR bomb which kills people but which does not cause much damage to buildings, roads etc.

Ne·va·da /nəˈvædə, -ˈvɑ-/ written abbreviation **NV** a state in the western U.S. —**Nevadan** n., adj.

nev·er /ˈnɛvɚ/ adv.
1 not at any time not at any time, or not once: *I've never been to Hawaii.* | *Theo was married twice, but he never had any children.* | *It never gets this hot in Vancouver.* | *I'll never make that mistake again.* | *I've never ever* (=used to emphasize that something has never happened) *heard Nina swear.* | *I always worked on Fridays, I never once* (=used to emphasize that something has never happened) *got to go to a high school basketball game.*

SPOKEN PHRASES

2 never mind a) used to tell someone that something is not important or serious, so that there is no need to worry or feel sorry: *"I forgot your books." "Oh, never mind, I'll get them another time."* **b)** used in order to say that you do not want to repeat something that you have said, or do not want to finish what you are saying: *"Hey, Debbie?" "What?" "Uh, never mind."*
3 you never know used to say that something that seems unlikely could happen: *You never know, Paul might love it.*
4 I never knew (that) used to mean that you did not know something until now: *I never knew you played the guitar!*
5 well, I never! OLD-FASHIONED used to say that you are very surprised
6 never fear OLD-FASHIONED used to tell someone not to worry

---

7 never so much as an expression meaning "not even," used to emphasize what you are saying: *I do everything for him, and he's never so much as made me a cup of coffee.*
8 never say never INFORMAL used to say that you should not say that you will never do something, because there is always a small possibility that you might do it: *I don't want to run for office, but I've learned to never say never. Who knows what will happen in 10 years?*
9 never say die INFORMAL used to encourage someone not to give up: *Kim Holtz is one athlete with a never-say-die attitude* (=she refuses to give up).

USAGE NOTE: NEVER

GRAMMAR
Don't use **never** with negative words such as "nobody," "no one," or "nothing." Instead, use **ever**: *Nobody will ever find me here.* You can use **never** with words such as "anybody," "anything," and "anywhere": *I never told anyone this before.* **Never** usually comes before the main verb: *I never go there.* If there is a modal or auxiliary verb (such as **have, will, should** etc.), **never** comes after this verb and before the main verb: *You should never talk to strangers.*

---

never-end·ing, neverending /ˌ.. ˈ..◂/ adj. seeming to continue for a very long time: *Keeping the house neat and clean is a never-ending battle.*

nev·er·more /ˌnɛvɚˈmɔr/ adv. POETIC never again

never-never land /ˌ.. ˈ.. ˌ./ n. [singular,U] INFORMAL an imaginary place where everything is perfect: *The play was set in a 1950s never-never land where everybody dresses like TV characters.*

nev·er·the·less /ˌnɛvɚðəˈlɛs◂/ adv. [sentence adverb] FORMAL in spite of what you have just mentioned: *Wagner was a Nazi supporter. Nevertheless, he is an important part of musical history.* | *The Sharks played with two men in the penalty box, but nevertheless managed to score.*

new /nu/ adj.
1 recently made recently made, built, or invented: *Can the new drugs help her?* | *Have you tried that new restaurant on Fourth Street?* | *We want to put a new bathroom in.* | *the new issue of "Time" magazine*
2 recently bought recently bought: *Hey, I like your jacket – is it new?* | *I had to buy a new refrigerator.*
3 not used before [no comparative] not used or owned by anyone before: *They sell both new and second hand books.* | *Denny just bought a brand new* (=completely new) *color printer.*
4 recently arrived having recently arrived in a place, or started a different job or activity: *Margo and Rod just had a new baby.* | *New students have priority in getting a room in the dorms.* | *Human Resources runs an orientation course for anyone who is new here.* | *[+ to] Since I'm new to the area, I was pleased to have the opportunity to meet people.* | *Las Vegas is America's fastest growing city, with 6000 new arrivals* (=someone who has just arrived in a place) *every month.*
5 recently changed recently changed, and replacing something that was there previously: *Have you met Keith's new girlfriend?* | *Do you have Christy's new address?* | *They just moved into a new apartment.*
6 not there before having recently developed: *new leaves on the trees* | *It's a new idea, very unusual, but it just may work.* | *This medical breakthrough offers new hope to cancer patients.*
7 unfamiliar not recognized or not experienced before: *Learning a new language is more difficult for adults.* | *Living in a foreign country for a while was a completely new experience.* | *[+ to] Remember, what is commonplace to you is wonderfully new to your child.*
8 recently discovered recently discovered: *Scientists were excited about the discovery of a new planet.* | *The company is looking for new oilfields in Alaska.* | *The gallery is putting on a show with works from new artists.*
9 what's new? SPOKEN used as a friendly greeting to ask what is happening in someone's life
10 like new also **as good as new** in excellent condition: *After cleaning, your pillows will be as good as new.* | *He's managed to keep the car looking like new for years.*
11 a new man/woman someone who feels much healthier and has a lot more energy than before, or who has a different attitude than before: *She came back from the experience a new woman.* | *I lost 19 pounds and felt like a new man.*
12 new life/day/era etc. a period of time that is just beginning and seems to offer better opportunities: *Dave convinced Connie to start a new life with him in South Carolina.* | *The agreement marks a new day for the national parks.*
13 new blood new members of a group or organization who will bring new ideas and be full of energy: *Every election brings a supply of new blood to the legislature.*
14 the new kid on the block the newest person in a job, school, place etc.: *I was the new kid on the block, and Ray helped me a lot.*
15 there's nothing new under the sun used to say that everything that happens now has happened before
16 new-made/new-formed etc. recently made, formed etc.
17 a new broom (sweeps clean) used about someone who has just become the leader or manager of an organization and is eager to make changes
18 the new unfamiliar ideas or changes in society: *A lot of people's anxiety is really just a fear of the new.* —**newness** n. [U] —see also **give sb/sth a new lease on life** (LEASE¹ (2)), **turn over a new leaf** at **turn over** (TURN¹)

USAGE NOTE: NEW

WORD CHOICE: new, recent, modern, current, up-to-date, latest

Use **new** to talk about something that has existed for only a short time: *Have you read Stephen King's new book?* Use **recent** to talk about something, especially an event, that happened a short time ago: *According to a recent survey, 45% of families owned one or more pets.* Use **modern** to describe things that exist now, especially in order to emphasize that they are different from earlier things of the same kind: *modern machinery | modern medical techniques.* Use **current** to describe something that exists now but that may change: *Home prices will continue to go down if the current real estate slump goes on.* Use **up-to-date** to describe the newest knowledge, information, way of doing things etc.: *an up-to-date computer system.* Use **latest** to talk about the newest thing in a series of similar things: *the latest issue of Newsweek magazine.*

New Age /ˌ. '.ˏ/ *n.* [U] **1** a set of beliefs about religion, medicine, and ways of life that are not part of traditional Western religions **2** a type of music that is meant to help you relax and feel calm —**New Age** *adj.*

New·ark /'nuək/ a large city in the U.S. state of New Jersey

new·bie /'nubi/ *n.* [C] SLANG someone who has just started doing something, especially using the Internet or computers

new·born /'nubɔrn/ *adj.* **newborn child/baby/son etc.** a child that has just been born —**newborn** *n.* [C]

New Bruns·wick /nu 'brʌnzwɪk/ a PROVINCE on the coast of western Canada

new·com·er /'nu,kʌmə/ *n.* [C] someone or something that has recently arrived somewhere or recently started a particular activity: *Also elected was council newcomer Mike Rowlinson.* | [– to] *Stair climbers are relative newcomers to the exercise scene.*

New Del·hi /nu 'dɛli/ the capital city of India

New Eng·land /nu 'ɪŋglənd/ *n.* [U] the northeastern part of the U.S. that includes the states of Maine, New Hampshire, Vermont, Massachusetts, Connecticut, and Rhode Island

new·fan·gled /'nu,fæŋgəld/ *adj.* DISAPPROVING newfangled ideas, machines etc. have been recently invented but seem complicated or unnecessary: *The regional companies rely on customer service rather than on marketing newfangled products.*

new-found /ˌ. '.ˏ/ *adj.* [only before noun] having only recently been gained: *McClellan had trouble dealing with her new-found fame.*

New·found·land /'nufənd,lænd, -lənd/ a PROVINCE of eastern Canada consisting of the island of Newfoundland and the coast of Labrador

New Hamp·shire /nu 'hæmpʃə/ *written abbreviation* **NH** a state in the northeastern U.S.

New Jer·sey /nu 'dʒɝzi/ *written abbreviation* **NJ** a state in the northeastern U.S.

new-look /ˈ. ./ *adj.* [only before noun] different from before, especially more modern or more attractive: *How will voters respond to the new-look presidential campaign?*

new·ly /'nuli/ *adv.* very recently: [+ past participle] *a newly built home | newly fallen snow | the newly appointed director*

new·ly·weds /'nuli,wɛdz/ *n.* [plural] a man and a woman who have recently gotten married —**newlywed** *adj.*

New Mex·i·co /nu 'mɛksɪ,kou/ *written abbreviation* **NM** a state in the southwestern U.S.

new mon·ey /ˌ. '../ *n.* [U] **1** people who have recently or suddenly become very rich: *In Chinatown, new money and old poverty live side by side.* **2** a large amount of money that someone has recently received or earned which makes them very rich: *Where did all of this astonishing new money come from?*

new moon /ˌ. '.ˈ/ *n.* **1** [C usually singular] the moon when it first appears in the sky as a thin CRESCENT **2** [C usually singular, U] the time of the month at which this is first seen **3** [C usually singular] TECHNICAL the time when the moon is between the Earth and the sun, and cannot be seen —compare FULL MOON, HALF MOON

New Or·le·ans /nu 'ɔrliənz, -lənz, ˌnu ɔr'linz/ a city in the U.S. state of Louisiana, which is regarded as the place where JAZZ music was originally developed

new po·ta·to /ˌ. .'../ *n.* [C] a small potato from one of the first crops of a year

new rich /ˌ. '.ˈ/ *n.* **the new rich** people who have recently or suddenly become very rich

news /nuz/ *n.* [U] **1** information about something that has happened recently: [+ about/of/on] *Is there any news on that job you applied for? | By the end of 1848, news about California gold reached South America.* | [+ that] *Brooks is thrilled at the news that his wife is pregnant. | They did a scan, and the cancer seems to be gone, so that's good news. | I have some bad news – I think the water heater's not working. | Have you heard the news that the dairy company is closing? | The space agency decision was a welcome piece of news. | The report has good news for middle-class renters. | Simmons broke the news (=told the bad news) to his 600 employees in a letter.* **2** reports of recent events in the newspapers or on television or the radio: [+ of/about] *There has been news of fighting in the area. | I was in a movie theater when I heard the news about Pearl Harbor.* | [news that] *The news came through that the Senate had ratified the treaty. | Walsh won an award for her news story on bilingual education. | What was the president's response to the latest news on unemployment? | Twenty years ago environmental issues rarely made the news (=were reported in newspapers etc.). | Crib death has been in the news (=been reported in newspapers etc.) lately, as scientists find out more about its causes. | Wallace's resignation was front-page news (=was important enough to be on the front page of a newspaper).* | **local/state/national/international news** *The Gazette covers mainly just local news.* **3 the news** a regular television or radio program that gives you reports of recent events: *I was watching the news last night and they were talking about it. | Channel 3 has the evening news. | The teachers' strike was on the news.* **4 be good/bad news for sb** if the facts about something are good or bad news for someone, they are likely to make life better or worse for them: *House prices are very low, which is good news for first-time buyers.* **5 sb/sth is bad news** INFORMAL used to say that someone or something is likely to cause trouble: *I don't want you hanging around with Tommy Crandall – that kid's nothing but bad news.*

SPOKEN PHRASES

6 I've got news for sb used to say that you are going to tell someone the facts about something, which they will probably not like to hear: *Everybody thinks they can drive wherever they want. But I've got news for them: I'm here to enforce the traffic laws.* **7 that's news to me!** said when you are surprised or annoyed because you have not been told something earlier: *The meeting's been canceled? That's news to me.* **8 no news is good news** used when you have not received any news about someone and you hope this means that nothing bad has happened

news a·gen·cy /ˈ. ˌ.../ *n.* [C] a company that supplies information to newspapers, radio, and television

news black·out /ˈ. ˌ../ *n.* [C] a period of time when particular pieces of news are not allowed to be reported

news bul·le·tin /ˈ. ˌ.../ *n.* [C] a short news announcement about something important that has just happened, that is broadcast suddenly in the middle of a television or radio program

news·cast /'nuzkæst/ *n.* [C] a news program on television

N

S W
3

news·cast·er /'nuz,kæstɚ/ *n.* [C] someone who reads the news on television

news con·ference /'. ,../ *n.* [C] a meeting at which someone, especially someone famous or important, makes official statements to people who write news reports: **have/hold/call a news conference** *Last week, the three executives held a news conference to announce the deal.*

news·group /'nuzgrup/ *n.* [C] a FORUM on the Internet

news·hawk /'nuzhɔk/ *n.* [C] INFORMAL a news hound

news hound, **newshound** /'. ./ *n.* [C] INFORMAL someone who writes for a newspaper

S W
3

news·let·ter /'nuz,lɛtɚ/ *n.* [C] a short written report of news about a club, organization, or particular subject that is sent regularly to people: *the church newsletter* | *They publish seven newsletters on investments.*

news·mak·er /'nuz,meɪkɚ/ *n.* [C] someone important, whose activities are reported in newspapers and on television

news·man /'nuzmən/ *n. plural* **newsmen** /-mən/ [C] a man who writes or reports news for a newspaper or for a television or radio broadcast

S W
2
1

news·pa·per /'nuz,peɪpɚ/ *n.* **1** [C] a set of large folded sheets of paper containing news, articles, pictures, advertisements etc. that is printed and sold daily or weekly: *a local newspaper* **2** [U] sheets of paper from old newspapers: *Wrap the plates in newspaper to stop them from breaking.* **3** [C] a company that produces a newspaper: *Hearst owned several newspapers.*

news·pa·per·man /'nuzpeɪpɚ,mæn/ *n.* [C] a newsman

newspaper stand /'... ,./ *n.* [C] a NEWSSTAND

news·pa·per·wom·an /'nuzpeɪpɚ,wumən/ *n.* [C] a NEWSWOMAN

news·print /'nuz,prɪnt/ *n.* [U] TECHNICAL cheap paper used mostly for printing newspapers

news·reel /'nuzril/ *n.* [C] a short movie containing news reports, seen in movie theaters in past times

news re·lease /'. .,./ *n.* [C] a PRESS RELEASE

news·room /'nuzrum/ *n.* [C] the office in a newspaper or broadcasting company where news is received and news reports are written

news·stand /'nuzstænd/ *n.* [C] a place on a street where newspapers and magazines are sold

news vend·or /'. ,../ *n.* [C] someone who sells newspapers

news·wom·an /'nuz,wumən/ *n. plural* **newswomen** /-,wɪmɪn/ [C] a woman who writes or reports news for a newspaper or for a television or radio broadcast

news·wor·thy /'nuz,wɚði/ *adj.* important or interesting enough to be reported as news: *Very little that was newsworthy was said at the conference.*

news·writ·er /'nuz,raɪtɚ/ *n.* [C] someone who writes news stories, especially to be read on television or radio news broadcasts

new·sy /'nuzi/ *adj.* a newsy letter is from a friend or relative and contains a lot of news about them

newt /nut/ *n.* [C] a small animal that lives in water and has a long body, four legs and a tail

New Tes·ta·ment /,. '...◂/ *n.* **the New Testament** the part of the Bible that is about the life of Jesus Christ and what he taught —compare OLD TESTAMENT

New·ton /'nut⁻n/, **Sir I·saac** /'aɪzək/ (1642–1727) a British PHYSICIST and MATHEMATICIAN who is best known for discovering GRAVITY and is considered one of the most important scientists who ever lived

New·to·ni·an /nu'tounian/ *adj.* relating to the laws of PHYSICS that were discovered by the scientist Isaac Newton: *Newtonian mechanics*

new wave /,. './ *n.* [C usually singular] a group of people who make an effort to introduce new ideas in music, movies, art, politics etc.: *Norris is considered part of the new wave of Native American participation in Arizona politics.* **2** [U] also **New Wave** a type of music that was popular in the late 1970s and the early 1980s, which uses SYNTHESIZERS and a strong

beat, and in which the words are sung without much emotion —**new wave** *adj.*: *new wave music*

New World /,. '.◂/ *n.* **the New World** North, Central, and South America: *Chili peppers are native to the New World.* —**New World** *adj.*: *New World civilizations* —compare OLD WORLD

New Year /'. ./ *n.* **1 New Year** also **New Year's** the time when you celebrate the beginning of the year: *We're spending New Year's at my parents' house.* | *Have a Merry Christmas and a **Happy New Year**!* | *Have you made any **New Year's resolutions** (=promises to improve yourself in the new year)?* **2 the new year** the year after the present year, especially the first few months of it: *The company plans to open several new stores in the new year.*

New Year's Day /,. . './ *n.* a holiday on January 1, the first day of the year in Western countries

New Year's Eve /,. . './ *n.* December 31, the last day of the year, when many people have parties to celebrate the beginning of the next year

New York /nu 'yɔrk/ **1** —see NEW YORK CITY **2** also **New York State** *written abbreviation* **NY** a state in the northeastern U.S.

New York Cit·y /,nu yɔrk 'sɪti/ also **New York** *written abbreviation* **NYC** the largest city in the U.S., which is divided into five BOROUGHs; Manhattan, the Bronx, Brooklyn, Queens, and Staten Island —**New Yorker** *n.* [C]

New York Stock Ex·change /,. . ' . .,./ *abbreviation* **NYSE** *n.* [singular] the main STOCK MARKET in the U.S., where STOCKs in large U.S. companies are bought and sold

New Zea·land /nu 'zilənd/ a country consisting of two main islands, North Island and South Island, and several smaller ones, in the Pacific Ocean southeast of Australia —**New Zealander** *n.*

S W
1 1

next¹ /nɛkst/ *determiner, adj.* **1** the next day, time, event etc. is the one that happens after the present one: *The next flight leaves in 45 minutes.* | *I'm going to be studying Spanish intensively for the next three months.* | *They went back to St. Louis the next day.* | *The staff picture will be taken next Wednesday.* | *Jill and I are going to go next weekend.* | *Next time (=when this happens again), be more careful.* —compare LAST¹ (1) **2** the next place is the one closest to where you are now: *Turn left at the next corner.* | *The walls were so thin you could hear everything from the next room.* **3** the next person or thing on a list, in a series etc. is the one that comes or is dealt with after the present one: *The letter continues on the next page.* | *Can I help the next person in line, please?* | *Read the next two chapters before Friday.* | *Do they have the next size up (=a slightly bigger size)?* | *The next biggest (=second-biggest) cost is fire protection.* **4 the next thing you know** SPOKEN used when talking about something that happened suddenly or was a surprise: *The next thing I knew he was trying to kiss me!* | *One minute everybody's laughing and the next thing you know, they're all arguing!* **5 the next best thing** the thing or situation that is almost as good as the one you really want: *If I can't be home for Christmas, this is the next best thing.* —see also NEXT OF KIN

S W
1 2

next² *adv.* **1** immediately after: *What do I do next?* | *Heat the chocolate until it melts. Next, pour it into the molds and leave to cool.* **2 next to sb/sth a)** very close to someone or something, with nothing in between: *There was a little girl sitting next to him.* | *Put it in the closet next to the bathroom.* **b)** used to say what is first of a list of things you like or prefer: *Next to volleyball, basketball is the sport I enjoy most.* **3 next to nothing** very little: *Phil earns next to nothing.* **4 next to impossible** very difficult: *It's next to impossible to get tickets to the game.* **5** LITERARY the next time: *When I next saw Sylvia, she completely ignored me.*

S W
3

next³ *pron.* **1** the person or thing in a list, series etc. that comes after the person or thing you are dealing with now: *Jamie was next in line.* | *What's next on the shopping list?* **2 the day/week etc. after next** the day, week etc. that follows the next one: *Joanie and her husband are coming to visit the week after*

next. 3 the next to last the one before the last one: *Stewart was assured of the championship in the next to last race of the year.* **4 next (please)** SPOKEN used to tell someone that it is now their turn to speak or their turn to do something **5 be next in line** to be the next person to become king, a leader etc.: *Prince Charles is next in line to become king of England.*

next door /ˌ. './ *adv.* in the house, room etc. next to yours or someone else's: *The boy next door cuts our grass for us.* | *Deanna's office is right next door.* | *The Garcias just bought the house next door to my mother's.*

next-door /ˌ. '. ◂/ *adj.* relating to the room, building etc. that is next to yours: *Our next-door neighbors will take care of the cat for us.*

next of kin /ˌ. . '. / *n.* [U] your most closely related family, including your husband or wife: *Social workers are still trying to find the victim's next of kin.*

nex·us /ˈnɛksəs/ *n. plural* **nexus** or **nexuses** [C] a connection or network of connections between a number of people, things, or ideas: *Many young Irish immigrants have made the East Village their social nexus.*

Nez Perce, Nez Percé /ˌnɛz ˈpɚs/ a Native American tribe from the northwestern area of the U.S.

NFC *n.* National Football Conference; a group of teams that is part of the NFL —see also AFC

NFL *n.* National Football League; the organization that is in charge of professional football in the U.S.

NH the written abbreviation of New Hampshire

NHL *n.* National Hockey League; the organization that is in charge of professional HOCKEY in the U.S. and Canada

ni·a·cin /ˈnaɪəsɪn/ *n.* [U] a type of VITAMIN

Niagara Falls

Ni·ag·a·ra Falls /naɪˌægrə ˈfɔz/ two very large WATERFALLs on the border between Canada and the U.S.

Ni·a·mey /niˈɑmeɪ/ the capital and largest city of Niger

nib /nɪb/ *n.* [C] the pointed metal part at the end of a pen

nib·ble¹ /ˈnɪbəl/ *v.* [I,T] **a)** to eat small amounts of food by taking very small bites: *Reyes puts out nuts and bread for squirrels to nibble.* | [+ at/on] *Guests were nibbling on hors d'oeuvres.* **b)** to gently bite something repeatedly: *Wally took her in his arms and began nibbling her ear.* —see picture at BITE¹

  nibble (away) at sth *phr. v.* [T] **1** to keep reducing something by taking smaller amounts from it: *House expenses are nibbling away at our savings.* **2** to begin to deal with something in a small way: *A few studies have begun to nibble at the issue of healthcare costs.*

nibble² *n.* **1** [C] a small bite of something: *One of the kids tried a nibble of the bread.* **2 nibbles** [plural] small things to eat, especially at a party: *a selection of cocktail nibbles* **3** [C] an expression of slight interest in an offer or suggestion: *We've had a few nibbles from potential buyers.*

Nic·a·rag·ua /ˌnɪkəˈrɑgwə/ **1** a country in Central America between the Caribbean Sea and the Pacific Ocean, and south of Honduras and north of Costa Rica **2 Lake Nicaragua** the largest lake in Central America —**Nicaraguan** *n., adj.*

nice /naɪs/ *adj.* **1** enjoyable/attractive good, pleasant, attractive, or enjoyable: *That's a nice dress.* | *Did you have a nice time?* | *I want a nice hot shower.* | *"Let's take a picnic lunch with us." "Yeah, that'd be nice."* | *You look nice*

today. | *It's really nice to see you again.* | *I had a nice long letter from Sara.* | **nice and cool/warm/big/ soft etc.** *Come back inside where it's nice and warm.* **2** friendly friendly or kind: *Dave's a really nice guy.* | *He had a lot of nice things to say about you.* | *Katherine! Be nice to the cat!* | *Thanks. It was nice of you to help.* **3** weather nice weather is warm and sunny: *What a nice day!* | *It's really nice out today.*

SPOKEN PHRASES

4 it is nice also **it would be nice** said when you think something is good or when you wish you could do something: *It's nice they're able to visit you so often.* | *It's so nice to sit down and rest for a while.* | *It would be nice if we could go to Thailand someday.* **5 have a nice day!** used to say goodbye to someone, especially to customers in stores and restaurants when they are leaving **6 nice try** used to say that what someone has done or guessed is very good, but not completely correct: *"I'd say you're about 35." "Nice try. I'm only 29."* **7 Nice going/move/one! a)** said as a joke when someone makes a mistake or does something wrong: *"Aargh, I just spilled my coffee!" "Nice move."* **b)** said when someone does something very well, especially when it is difficult: *In perfect condition, the baseball card Bryan bought for $12 is worth $2,200. Nice going, Bryan.* **8 it's nice to know (that)** used to mean that you feel happier when you know something: *Well, it's nice to know the ad is working.*

9 respectable OLD-FASHIONED having high standards of moral and social behavior: *It's the kind of place nice people don't go to.* | *Nice girls don't go out dressed like that.* **10** detail FORMAL involving a very small difference or detail: *a nice point of law* —**niceness** *n.* [U] —see also **nice/pleased/good to meet you** (MEET¹ (3)), **(it was) nice/good meeting you** (MEET¹ (4)), **no more Mr. Nice Guy!** (MR. (4))

USAGE NOTE: NICE

GRAMMAR

Nice is often used in two-part adjectival phrases such as *nice and quiet* or *nice and clean*. These phrases are always placed after the noun they modify, and usually follow a linking verb such as **is, seem** etc.: *Your new house looks nice and big.* Do not use "and" after **nice** when it comes in front of a noun: *This is a nice big house!*

SPOKEN-WRITTEN

Use **nice** in spoken English in order to show that you like someone or something: *We had a nice time at the party.* However, many teachers think it is better to use a more specific adjective in formal and written English: *They have a beautiful house.* | *She's a very thoughtful person.*

nice-look·ing /ˌ. '.. ◂/ *adj.* fairly attractive: *Ramon's a nice-looking boy.* | *a nice-looking salad*

nice·ly /ˈnaɪsli/ *adv.* **1** in a satisfactory, pleasing, or skillful way: *Ann dresses her children nicely.* | *His arm is healing nicely.* | *Turn the fillets and cook until nicely browned, 2 to 3 minutes longer.* **2** in a pleasant, polite, or friendly way: *If you ask Daddy nicely, I'm sure he'll give you some.* **3** FORMAL exactly or carefully: *a nicely calculated distance* | *Each new water molecule fits nicely into a space on the ice surface.*

ni·ce·ty /ˈnaɪsəti/ *n. plural* **niceties** [C usually plural] **1** something that is pleasant but not necessary: *The car includes such niceties as a cassette deck and bucket seats.* **2** FORMAL a small point of difference or detail: *legal niceties*

niche /nɪtʃ/ *n.* [C] **1** a job or activity that is perfect for the skills, abilities, and character that you have: *Rodgers found his niche as a high school baseball coach.* **2** also **niche market, market niche** a part of the population that buys a particular product or

N

uses a particular service, or is likely to do so: *Van Meer's magazines are aimed at two growing niche markets: Internet users and senior citizens.* **3** a small hollow place in a wall, often made to hold a STATUE

niche mar·ket·ing /ˌ. '.../ *n.* [U] the practice of trying to sell a product to a particular group of people

Nich·o·las /ˈnɪkələs/, **St.** a Christian BISHOP who lived in western Asia in the 4th century A.D. He became connected with the custom of giving gifts to children at Christmas and the imaginary character Santa Claus is based on stories about him. He is also the PATRON SAINT of Russia.

Nicholas II /ˌnɪkələs ðə ˈsɛkənd/ (1868–1918) the CZAR of Russia before the Russian Revolution of 1917, in which he was forced to ABDICATE and he and his family were killed

nick

just in the nick of time

nick¹ /nɪk/ *n.* **1 in the nick of time** just before it is too late or just before something bad happens: *The money came through just in the nick of time.* **3** [C] a very small cut made on the edge or surface of something

nick² *v.* [T] to make a small cut in the surface or edge of something, usually by accident: *I nicked myself shaving this morning.*

nick·el /ˈnɪkəl/ *n.* **1** [C] a coin that is worth five cents, used in the U.S. or Canada **2** [U] *symbol* **Ni** a hard silver-white metal that is an ELEMENT and is used in making other metals

nickel-and-dime¹ /ˌ... . '.../ *v.* [T] INFORMAL **1** to not give a problem or situation enough attention, money etc. to solve it effectively: *If we nickel-and-dime the problem now, we'll regret it later.* **2** to gradually ruin something or take away someone's money, especially by taking or not giving small amounts of money: *"Banks are trying to nickel-and-dime their customers with fees," said Cohn, an analyst.*

nickel-and-dime² *adj.* [only before noun] INFORMAL not large, important, or effective enough, especially not involving enough money: *We face big problems that can't be solved with nickel-and-dime solutions.*

nickel bag /ˈ.. ˌ./ *n.* [C] SLANG a small package of an illegal drug that costs five dollars —compare DIME BAG

Nick·laus /ˈnɪkləs/, **Jack** /dʒæk/ (1940–) a U.S. GOLFER

nick·name /ˈnɪkneɪm/ *n.* [C] a silly name or a shorter form of someone's real name, usually given by friends or family: *Johnson earned the nickname "Magic" while still in high school.* —**nickname** *v.* [T] *Monte-fusco was nicknamed "The Count" in his playing days.*

Nic·o·si·a /ˌnɪkəˈsiə/ the capital and largest city of Cyprus

nic·o·tine /ˈnɪkəˌtin/ *n.* [U] a substance in tobacco that makes it difficult for people to stop smoking

nicotine patch /ˈ... ˌ./ *n.* [C] a small piece of material containing nicotine, that you stick on your skin to help you stop smoking

niece /nis/ *n.* [C] the daughter of your brother or sister, or the daughter of your wife's or husband's brother or sister —compare NEPHEW

Nie·tzsche /ˈnitʃi, -tʃə/, **Fried·rich** /ˈfridrɪk/ (1844–1900) a German PHILOSOPHER —**Nietzschean** *adj.*

nif·ty /ˈnɪfti/ *adj.* **niftier, niftiest** INFORMAL very good, fast, effective, or attractive: *It's a nifty computer game that teaches math skills.* | *a nifty pair of sandals*

Ni·ger /ˈnaɪdʒɚ/ **1** a large country in west Africa, south of Algeria and north of Nigeria **2 the Niger** the third longest river in Africa, flowing through Mali, Niger, and Nigeria —**Nigerois** /ˌniʒɛrˈwɑ/ *n., adj.*

Ni·ge·ri·a /naɪˈdʒɪriə/ a country in west Africa, east of Benin and west Cameroon —**Nigerian** *n., adj.*

nig·gard·ly /ˈnɪgɚdli/ *adj.* FORMAL **1** unwilling to spend money or be generous; STINGY: *Banks have been niggardly in approving loans.* **2** a niggardly gift, amount, salary etc. is not worth very much and is not given willingly: *niggardly wages* —**niggardliness** *n.* [U]

nig·ger /ˈnɪgɚ/ *n.* [C] TABOO a black person. Do not use this word.

nig·gle /ˈnɪgəl/ *v.* [I,T] to annoy or worry you slightly, especially for a long time: *Doubts niggled at the back of her mind.*

nig·gling /ˈnɪglɪŋ/ *adj.* [only before noun] not very important, but continuing to annoy someone: *a niggling doubt*

nigh /naɪ/ *adv.* **1** LITERARY near: *The end of the world is nigh!* | *Winter is drawing nigh* (=coming soon). **2 well nigh** also **nigh on** FORMAL almost: *It is well nigh impossible to identify him after all this time.* —see also WELL-NIGH

night /naɪt/ *n.*

1 when it is dark [C,U] the dark part of each 24-hour period, when the sun cannot be seen: *a cold night* | *You can see the stars really clearly here at night.* | *The desert is summer by day and freezing winter by night.* | *I stayed up all night to finish my paper.* | *As night fell* (=it became dark)*, the Olympic flame was lit.*

2 evening [C,U] the time during the evening until you go to bed: *It was on the evening news a couple of nights ago.* | *I talked to Pat last night.* | *The plane leaves at 7:30 at night.* | *Are you going to be home tomorrow night?* | *I had dinner with Clay the other night* (=a few evenings ago)*.* | *The kids are normally in bed by eight on week nights* (=the evenings during the week, not weekends)*.* | *I don't want you walking home by yourself late at night.* | *Young people strolled with their dates on a night out* (=a night when you go to a party, restaurant etc.)*.* | **Tuesday/ Wednesday etc. night** *The school's open house is Thursday night.*

3 when you sleep the time when most people are sleeping: *I didn't sleep very well last night* (=the night just before this morning)*.* | *A lot of people work at night.* | *The baby cried all night.* | *We had to get up in the middle of the night to get to the airport.* | *All you need is a good night's sleep* (=to sleep well at night)*.* | *Katie still gets up in the night* (=during the night) *sometimes.* | *We'll spend the night* (=sleep) *at my parents' and come back Sunday.* | *I don't think she planned on staying the night* (=sleeping at someone's house)*.*

4 nights if you do something nights, you do it regularly or often at night: *Mom lies awake nights worrying about her.* | *Juan works nights.*

5 night! used to say goodbye to someone when it is late in the evening or when they are going to bed: *Night! Thanks again for dinner.*

6 night night! also **nighty night!** used to say goodbye to a child, when he or she is going to bed

7 at this time of night used when you are surprised because something happens late at night: *Who on earth could be calling at this time of night?*

8 night after night every night for a long period of time: *He sat up night after night to finish the game.*

9 night and day, **day and night** all the time: *My next door neighbor's dog barks day and night*

10 late night a night when you go to bed later than usual: *I can't manage late nights anymore, like I could in college.* —see also LATE-NIGHT

11 last thing at night just before you go to bed: *Lock the doors and turn off the lights last thing at night.*

12 first night also **opening night** the first performance of a play or show —see also NIGHTLY

night·cap /'naɪt‚kæp/ n. [C] **1** an alcoholic drink that you have just before you go to bed **2** a soft cap that people in past times used to wear in bed

night·clothes /'naɪt‚klouz/ n. [plural] FORMAL clothes that you wear in bed

night·club /'naɪt‚klʌb/ n. [C] a place where people can drink and dance, that is open late at night

night·crawl·er /'naɪt‚krɔlə/ n. [C] a type of worm that comes out of the ground at night, often used for fishing

night de·pos·i·to·ry /‚. .'..../ n. [C] a special hole in the outside wall of a bank, where a customer can put money or documents when the bank is closed

night·dress /'naɪt‚drɛs/ n. [C] a nightgown

night·fall /'naɪtfɔl/ n. [U] the time in the evening when it begins to get darker; DUSK: *There is a slight chance of showers by nightfall.*

night·gown /'naɪt‚gaun/ n. [C] a piece of loose clothing, like a dress, that women wear in bed

night·hawk /'naɪthɔk/ n. [C] someone who enjoys staying awake all night

night·ie /'naɪti/ n. [C] INFORMAL a NIGHTGOWN

night·in·gale /'naɪt‚n‚geɪl, 'naɪtɪŋ-/ n. [C] a small wild European bird that sings very beautifully, especially at night

Night·in·gale /'naɪt‚n‚geɪl, 'naɪtɪŋ-/, **Flor·ence** /'flɔrəns/ (1820–1910) an English nurse who set up a hospital for soldiers during the CRIMEAN WAR, and a school for nurses

night·life /'naɪt‚laɪf/ n. [U] entertainment in places where you can drink, dance etc. in the evening: *Smaller ski resorts have no crowds, but no nightlife, either.*

night light /'. ./ n. [C] a small, not very bright light, often used in a child's room at night so they will not be afraid of the dark

night·long /'naɪt‚lɔŋ/ adj. [only before noun] LITERARY continuing all night: *The protesters held a nightlong vigil.*

night·ly /'naɪtli/ adv. every night: *The band performs nightly.* —**nightly** adj.: *nightly news broadcasts*

night·mare /'naɪt‚mɛr/ n. [C] **1** a very frightening dream: *During the trial, she had nightmares.* **2** a person, thing, situation etc. that is very bad or very difficult to deal with: *It was a nightmare driving home in the snow.* | *Highway 17 is a commuter nightmare.* | *The winds are a firefighter's* **worst nightmare.** **3** something terrible that you are afraid may happen in the future: [+ of] *the nightmare of cancer* | *The government fears a* **nightmare scenario** (=the worst situation you can imagine) *of nuclear or chemical warfare.* —**nightmarish** adj.

night owl /'. ./ n. [C] INFORMAL someone who enjoys staying awake late at night

night school /'. ./ n. [U] classes taught in the evening, for adults who work during the day: *Kobayashi earned his degree in night school.*

night·shade /'naɪt‚ʃeɪd/ n. [U] a type of plant that has poisonous leaves

night shift /'. ./ n. [C usually singular] **1** a period of time at night during which people regularly work: *Kim's working the night shift at the hospital.* **2** the group of people who work at this time: *The night shift was just arriving.*

night·shirt /'naɪt‚ʃət/ n. [C] a long loose shirt that people, especially men, wear in bed

night spot /'. ./ n. [C] a place people go to at night for entertainment, such as drinking or dancing: *a popular Manhattan night spot*

night·stand /'naɪtstænd/ n. [C] a small table beside a bed

night·stick /'naɪtstɪk/ n. [C] a type of stick carried as a weapon by police officers

night ta·ble /'. ‚../ n. [C] a nightstand

night·time /'naɪt‚taɪm/ n. [U] the time during the night when the sky is dark: *Nighttime temperatures dipped below freezing.* —opposite DAYTIME

night watch·man /‚. '../ n. [C] someone whose job is to guard a building at night —**night watch** n. [singular,U]

night·wear /'naɪt‚wɛr/ n. [U] FORMAL clothes that people wear in bed at night

night·y night /‚naɪti 'naɪt/ interjection **1** used to say goodbye to a child, when he or she is going to bed **2 go nighty night** an expression meaning "to go to bed," used especially when speaking to children

ni·hil·ism /'niə‚lɪzəm, 'naɪ-/ n. [U] **1** the belief that nothing has any meaning or value **2** the idea that all social and political institutions should be destroyed —**nihilist** n. [C] —**nihilistic** /‚niə'lɪstɪk/ adj.

Ni·jin·sky /nɪ'dʒɪnski/, **Vas·lav** /'vatslaf/ (1890–1950) a Russian dancer and CHOREOGRAPHER of BALLET

-nik /nɪk/ suffix [in nouns] INFORMAL someone who belongs to a group of people that other people often disapprove of, because their ideas are extreme: *beatniks* (=young artists and writers in the 1950s) | *healthniks* (=people who are too concerned with their health)

nil /nɪl/ n. [U] nothing or zero: **almost/virtually nil** *The chances of that happening are almost nil.*

Nile, the /naɪl/ a river in northeast Africa that is the longest river in the world

nim·ble /'nɪmbəl/ adj. **1** able to move quickly, easily, and skillfully: *The vehicles need to be nimble and quick for city driving.* | *nimble fingers* **2** able to change or make decisions quickly: *Zirtech is a small, nimble company that is focused on innovation.* **3** a **nimble mind/wit etc.** an ability to think quickly or understand things easily —**nimbly** adv. —**nimbleness** n. [U]

nim·bus /'nɪmbəs/ n. **1** [C,U] a type of dark cloud that may bring rain or snow **2** [C] LITERARY a HALO

NIMBY /'nɪmbi/ n. plural NIMBYs [C] not in my back yard; someone who does not want a particular activity or building near their home —**nimby** adj.

Nim·itz /'nɪmɪts/, **Ches·ter** /'tʃɛstə/ (1885–1966) the leader of the U.S. Navy in the Pacific area during World War II

nim·rod /'nɪmrɑd/ n. [C] SPOKEN a stupid person: *What nimrod put this stuff here?*

nin·com·poop /'nɪŋkəm‚pup/ n. [C] OLD-FASHIONED a stupid person

nine /naɪn/ number **1** 9 **2** 9 o'clock: *I have a dentist's appointment at nine.* **3 nine times out of ten** almost always: *Nine times out of ten we can beat them, but last night they creamed us.* —see also **be on cloud nine** (CLOUD[1] (5)), **dressed to the nines** (DRESSED (5))

nine·teen /‚naɪn'tin/ number 19

nine·teenth[1] /‚naɪn'tinθ/ adj. 19th; next after the eighteenth: *the nineteenth century*

nineteenth[2] pron. **the nineteenth** the 19th thing in a series: *Let's have dinner on the nineteenth* (=the 19th day of the month).

nine·ti·eth[1] /'naɪntiɪθ/ adj. 90th; next after the eighty-ninth: *It's my grandmother's ninetieth birthday tomorrow.*

ninetieth[2] pron. **the ninetieth** the 90th thing in a series

nine-to-five /‚. . '.‚/ adv. from 9:00 a.m. until 5:00 p.m.; the hours that most people work in an office: *Derek usually works nine-to-five, unless there's a crisis.* —**nine-to-five** adj.: *a nine-to-five job*

nine·ty /'naɪnti/ number **1** 90 **2 the nineties** also **the '90s a)** the years from 1990 through 1999 **3 sb's nineties** the time when someone is 90 to 99 years old: **in your early/mid/late nineties** *My grandfather was in his mid nineties when he died.* **4 in the nineties** if the temperature is in the nineties, it is between 90° and 99° Fahrenheit: **in the high/low nineties** *It was hot – in the high nineties – most of the week.*

nin·ja /'nɪndʒə/ n. plural ninja or ninjas [C] a member of a Japanese class of professional killers in past times: *a ninja warrior*

N

nin·ny /ˈnɪni/ *n. plural* **ninnies** [C] OLD-FASHIONED a silly person

ninth[1] /naɪnθ/ *adj.* 9th; next after the eighth: *Sam is in ninth grade.*

ninth[2] *pron.* **the ninth** the 9th thing in a series: *Let's have dinner on the ninth* (=the 9th day of the month).

ninth[3] *n.* [C] 1/9; one of nine equal parts

nip[1] /nɪp/ *v.* **nipped, nipping 1** [I,T] to bite someone or something with small sharp bites, or to try to do this: *When I took the hamster out of his cage, he nipped me.* | [+ at] *This stupid dog keeps nipping at my ankles.* **2 nip sth in the bud** to prevent something from becoming a problem by stopping it as soon as it starts: *The idea is to nip minor school problems in the bud.* **3** [T] if cold weather nips something, it makes it very cold or damages it: *Keep the plants covered to keep frost from nipping them.* **4 be nipping at sb's heels** to be very close to defeating someone, or causing problems for them: *Creditors are nipping at EDJ's heels.*

nip sth ↔ **in** *phr. v.* [T usually passive] if a piece of clothing is nipped in at a particular place on the body, it fits more tightly there: *The skirt is nipped in at the knee.*

nip sth ↔ **off** *phr. v.* [T] to remove a small part of something, especially a plant, by pressing it tightly between your finger and thumb: *Nip off the growing tips of the plant.*

nip[2] *n.* [C] **1** a small sharp bite, or the action of biting someone or something: *The dog gave me a playful nip.* **2 nip and tuck** INFORMAL **a)** equally likely to happen or not happen, or to succeed or fail: *I made it to the airport, but it was nip and tuck.* **b)** if two competitors are nip and tuck in a race or competition, they are doing equally well: *The fourth quarter was nip and tuck, but the Bulls won 92–90.* **3** a small amount of a strong alcoholic drink: [+ of] *a nip of whiskey* **4 a nip in the air** coldness in the air

nip·per /ˈnɪpɚ/ *n.* [C] OLD-FASHIONED a child, especially a small boy

nip·ple /ˈnɪpəl/ *n.* [C] **1** the small dark raised circle on a woman's breast, that a baby sucks in order to get milk —see picture at BODY **2** one of the two small dark raised circles on a man's chest **3** the rubber part on a baby's bottle that a baby sucks milk through **4** something shaped like a nipple, for example on a machine

nip·py /ˈnɪpi/ *adj.* INFORMAL weather that is nippy is cold enough that you need a coat: *It still seems a little nippy out there.* —**nippiness** *n.* [U]

nir·va·na, Nirvana /nɚˈvɑnə, nɪr-/ *n.* **1** [singular,U] a condition or place of great happiness: *The West is a dam builder's nirvana, full of deep, narrow canyons.* **2** [U] TECHNICAL a state of knowledge or being that is beyond life and death, suffering, and change, and is the aim of believers in Buddhism

Ni·sei /ˈniseɪ/ *n. plural* **Nisei** [C] someone who is born in the U.S., but whose parents were born in Japan

nit /nɪt/ *n.* [C] an egg of a LOUSE (=a small insect), that is sometimes found in people's hair

nite /naɪt/ *n.* [C] INFORMAL an informal spelling of "night," used especially on signs

nit·pick·ing /ˈnɪtˌpɪkɪŋ/ *n.* [U] INFORMAL, DISAPPROVING the act of arguing about or criticizing unimportant details, especially in someone's work —**nitpick** *v.* [I] —**nitpicker** *n.* [C] —**nitpicking** *adj.*

ni·trate /ˈnaɪtreɪt/ *n.* [C,U] a chemical compound that is mainly used to improve the soil that crops are grown in

ni·tric ac·id /ˌnaɪtrɪk ˈæsɪd/ *n.* [U] a powerful acid that is used in explosives and other chemical products

ni·trite /ˈnaɪtraɪt/ *n.* [C,U] a chemical compound that is mainly used to preserve food, especially meat, and that may be harmful to people's health

ni·tro·gen /ˈnaɪtrədʒən/ *n.* [U] *symbol* **N** a gas that is an ELEMENT, has no color or smell, and is the main part of the Earth's air

ni·tro·glyc·er·in /ˌnaɪtroʊˈglɪsərɪn, -trəˈglɪsrən/ *n.* [U] a chemical compound that is used in explosives, and as a medicine to prevent HEART ATTACKS

ni·trous ox·ide /ˌnaɪtrəs ˈɑksaɪd/ *n.* [U] a type of gas used by DENTISTS to reduce pain; LAUGHING GAS

nit·ty-grit·ty /ˌnɪti ˈgrɪti, ˌnɪti ˈgrɪti/ *n.* **the nitty-gritty** INFORMAL the basic and practical facts of an agreement or activity: *It's time to get down to the nitty-gritty of how much this will cost.* —**nitty-gritty** *adj.*: *nitty-gritty contract talks*

nit·wit /ˈnɪtˌwɪt/ *n.* [C] INFORMAL a stupid or silly person

nix[1] /nɪks/ *v.* [T] INFORMAL to answer no to something or FORBID something: *The proposal was nixed by council members.*

nix[2] *adv.* OLD-FASHIONED no

Nix·on /ˈnɪksən/**, Richard** (1913–1994) the 37th President of the U.S.

NJ the written abbreviation of New Jersey

NM the written abbreviation of New Mexico

no[1] /noʊ/ *adv.* **1** used to give a negative reply to a question, offer, or request: *"Is Cindy married?" "No, she's not."* | *"Do you want a ride home?" "No, thanks, I have my car."* | *So, has evolution been proven true? Strictly speaking, no.* | *Neumann said he voted no because the management misled him.* | *I asked Dad if I could have a dog, but he said no.* —opposite YES[1] (1)

SW 11

SPOKEN PHRASES

2 used when you disagree with a statement: *"Ben's so weird." "No, he's just shy."* **3** said when you do not want someone to do something: *No, Jimmy, don't touch that.* **4** said to agree with a negative statement: *"Steve should never have left his job." "No, he shouldn't have."* **5** used to show that you are shocked, surprised, annoyed, or disappointed by what someone has just told you, or by what has just happened: *She's 45? No, you have to be kidding!* | *Oh no, you forgot to put the baking powder in!* **6 no can do** INFORMAL used to say that something is not possible: *"Why don't you just let us in?" "Sorry, no can do."*

---

7 sb won't take no for an answer if someone won't take no for an answer, they keep trying to do something or to get you to do something: *Lauren's the kind of person who just won't take no for an answer.* **8 no good/use etc.** not good, useful etc. at all: *The food's no good there.* | *These instructions were no use whatsoever.* **9 no better/more/less etc.** not better, not more etc.: *No more than three people were allowed in the room at one time.* **10** FORMAL used when you mean the opposite of what you are saying: *Linda played no small part in the orchestra's success* (=she was very important in making it succeed).

USAGE NOTE: NO and NOT

GRAMMAR
Use **no** before nouns to mean "not any": *It's no problem, really.* Use **not** in order to make a verb negative: *I decided not to go camping.* When the subject of a sentence is the word "all" or a word like "everyone," "everything," etc., use **not** to make the subject negative: *Not all of the students handed their papers in on time.* | *Not everyone likes horror movies.*

---

no[2] *determiner* **1** not any, or not at all: *There are no tickets available.* | *He has no control over his children.* | *There's no more milk.* | *There's no reason to get in an argument about this.* **2** used on a sign to say that something is not allowed: *No parking.* | *No smoking.* **3 there's no knowing/telling/saying etc.** SPOKEN used to say that it is impossible to guess what will happen or what is true: *There's just no telling what Sam'll do when he's mad.* **4 be no expert/scientist/idiot etc.** to not have a particular skill or quality: *I'm no expert, but global warming seems a real threat.*

SW 11

s w
no³ n. plural **noes** [C] **1** a negative answer or decision: *LeeAnn's answer was a definite no.* **2** [usually plural] votes against a proposal in a meeting: *The noes have it.* —opposite AYE

no. plural **nos.** the written abbreviation of "number": *Snoop's album entered the national charts at no. 1*

no-ac·count /ˈ. .ˌ./ adj. INFORMAL, OLD-FASHIONED someone who does not achieve very much because they are lazy: *Clem was a no-account drifter who died of drink.*

No·ah /ˈnoʊə/ in the Bible, a man chosen by God to build an ARK (=a large boat) so that he could save his family and every kind of animal from the flood which covered the Earth

No·bel /noʊˈbɛl/, **Al·fred** /ˈæfrɪd/ (1833–1896) a Swedish engineer and chemist who invented DYNAMITE and left all his money to establish the Nobel Prizes

No·bel Prize /ˌnoʊbɛl ˈpraɪz/ n. [C usually singular] a prize given in Sweden each year to people from any country for important work in science, medicine, literature, economics, or work toward world peace

no·bil·i·ty /noʊˈbɪləti/ n. **1 the nobility** the group of people in some countries who belong to the highest social class and use special titles with their names: *the Russian nobility* —compare ARISTOCRACY **2** [U] the quality of being noble in character or appearance: *Most of the pictures celebrate the nobility of working with one's hands.*

no·ble¹ /ˈnoʊbəl/ adj. **1** morally good or generous in a way that should be admired: *In the end, none of the characters are good or noble.* | *a noble purpose* **2** belonging to the nobility: *a man of noble birth* **3** something that is noble is very impressive and beautiful: *The Siberian tiger is regarded as a noble creature.* **4 noble savage** LITERARY someone, especially a character in a book or play, who comes from a society that is less developed than Western ones and is thought to be morally better than Westerners because of this

no·ble² n. [C] FORMAL a member of the highest social class in some countries, especially in past times: *a gathering of kings and nobles* —compare COMMONER

noble gas /ˌ.. ˈ./ n. [C] a gas, such as NEON or ARGON, that is an ELEMENT and that usually does not combine with other substances

no·ble·man /ˈnoʊbəlmən/ n. plural **noblemen** /-mən/ [C] a man who is a member of the NOBILITY

no·blesse o·blige /noʊˌblɛs əˈbliʒ/ n. FORMAL a phrase meaning that people who belong to a high social class should be generous and behave with honor

no·ble·wom·an /ˈnoʊbəlˌwʊmən/ n. plural **noblewomen** /-ˌwɪmɪn/ [C] a woman who is a member of the NOBILITY

no·bly /ˈnoʊbli/ adv. **1** in a morally good or generous way that should be admired: *Foreman sacrificed nobly for what he believed was right.* **2 nobly born** LITERARY having parents who are members of the NOBILITY

s w
no·bod·y¹ /ˈnoʊbɑdi, -ˌbɑdi/ pron. **1** no one, or not one person: *I knocked on the door, but nobody answered.* | *There's nobody home.* | *"Who was on the phone?" "Nobody you know."* **2 like nobody's business** SPOKEN very well, very much, or very fast: *People are buying Internet stocks like nobody's business.* —see also **be no fool/nobody's fool** (FOOL¹ (4))

nobody² n. plural **nobodies** [C] someone who is not important, successful, or famous: *Glazer went from being a nobody to being paid $2 million a year to play.*

no-brain·er /ˈ. ˌ... ˌ. ˈ./ n. [C usually singular] INFORMAL something that you do not need to think about, because it is easy to understand or do: *The movie is a complete no-brainer, but enjoyable.* | *If you ask me, it's a no-brainer. Of course you should accept the job.*

no-con·fi·dence vote /ˈ. ˌ... ˌ./ n. [C] a VOTE OF NO CONFIDENCE

no-count /ˈ. ./ adj. INFORMAL, OLD-FASHIONED another spelling of NO-ACCOUNT

noc·tur·nal /nɑkˈtɜnl/ adj. **1** TECHNICAL an animal that is nocturnal is active at night: *Hamsters are nocturnal creatures.* **2** FORMAL happening at night: *Al occasionally takes a nocturnal stroll.* —**nocturnally** adv.

noc·turne /ˈnɑktɜn/ n. [C] a soft beautiful piece of music, especially for the piano

s w
nod¹ /nɑd/ v. **nodded, nodding** **1** [I,T] to move your head up and down, especially in order to show that you agree with or understand something: *I asked her if she was OK, and she nodded.* | *When asked if he would come, he* **nodded yes.** | *Several women* **nodded in approval.** | *Casey was* **nodding his head** *in agreement.* **2** [I] to move your head up and down once toward someone or something, in order to greet them or give them a sign to do something: [+ at/to/toward etc.] *I nodded to the waiter and asked for the bill.* | *"She's in her room," Hans said, nodding toward the door.* **3 have a nodding acquaintance (with sb/sth)** to know someone slightly or know a little about a subject: *Hanley said she had only a nodding acquaintance with the retired Navy admiral.*
nod off phr. v. to begin to sleep, when you do not intend to: *I kept nodding off during the lecture.*

nod² n. [C usually singular] **1** an act of nodding: *Carlyle* **gave** *an approving* **nod.** **2** approval of something or someone: *Novels that* **got the nod** *from children included "Charlie and the Chocolate Factory"* —see also **the land of nod** (LAND¹ (8))

node /noʊd/ n. [C] **1** TECHNICAL a place where lines in a network, GRAPH etc. meet or join **2** the place on the stem of a plant from which a leaf or branch grows **3** a LYMPH NODE **4** TECHNICAL a computer that is part of a network —**nodal** adj.

nod·ule /ˈnɑdʒul/ n. [C] a small round raised part, especially a small swelling on a plant or someone's body —**nodular** adj.

No·el, Noël /noʊˈɛl/ n. [U] a word used in songs, on cards etc. meaning Christmas

noes /noʊz/ the plural of NO³

no-fault /ˌ. ˈ. ˌ/ adj. [only before noun] **1** no-fault car insurance will pay for the damage done in an accident, even if you caused the accident **2** a no-fault DIVORCE does not blame either the husband or the wife

no-fly zone /ˌ. ˈ. ˌ/ n. [C] an area that no airplane is allowed to enter, and in which it would be attacked

no-frills /ˌ. ˈ. ˌ/ adj. [only before noun] without any additional features that are not completely necessary; BASIC: *a no-frills airline*

nog·gin /ˈnɑgən/ n. [C] OLD-FASHIONED, INFORMAL your head or brain: *The stupid thing hit me right on the noggin.*

no-go /ˌ. ˈ./ n. **sth is (a) no-go** INFORMAL used to say that something does not work or does not happen: *I tried to trade with him, but it was no-go.*

no-good /ˌ. ˈ. ˌ/ adj. INFORMAL a no-good person causes trouble and does not behave in the way society expects them to: *Paula's no-good husband beat her up again last week.*

no-hit·ter /ˌ. ˈ./ n. [C] a baseball game in which one PITCHER (=player who throws the ball) prevents the other team from successfully hitting the ball through the whole game

no-holds-barred /ˌ. . ˈ./ adj. [only before noun] a no-holds-barred discussion, situation etc. is one in which there are no rules or limits: *Viewers had been promised a no-holds-barred interview with the former mayor.*

no·how, no how /ˈnoʊhaʊ/ adv. SPOKEN, NONSTANDARD not in any way or in any situation: *You don't have to do it, no way, nohow.*

s w
noise /nɔɪz/ n. **1** [C,U] a sound or sounds that are too loud, annoying, or not intended: *the noise of the traffic* | *What was that clunking noise?* | *Jerry's car*

N

started **making a weird noise.** | The kids were **making** too much **noise. 2 make (a) noise about sth** to talk about something a lot, so that people will notice it: They made a lot of noise about having improved graphics. | Now my 6-year-old is making noise about wanting a designer jacket. **3** [U] TECHNICAL unwanted signals produced by an electrical CIRCUIT **4** [U] TECHNICAL pieces of unwanted information that can prevent a computer from working effectively

---

USAGE NOTE: NOISE

WORD CHOICE: noise, sound
Use **sound** to talk about something that you hear: I love the sound of the ocean. | The sound of voices came from the next room. A **noise** is usually a loud unpleasant sound: They had to shout to make themselves heard above the noise of the machines. | Tell the kids to stop making so much noise.

---

noise·less·ly /ˈnɔɪzlɪsli/ adv. without making any sound: We crept noiselessly down the hall. —**noiseless** adj. —**noiselessness** n. [U]

noise·mak·er /ˈnɔɪzˌmeɪkɚ/ n. [C] something that you can use to make a loud noise, especially in order to celebrate something: People were shouting and rattling noisemakers at midnight.

noise pol·lu·tion /ˈ. .ˌ../ n. [U] very loud or continuous loud noise in the environment that is harmful to people

noi·some /ˈnɔɪsəm/ adj. LITERARY extremely bad, ugly etc.: noisome slums

nois·y /ˈnɔɪzi/ adj. **noisier, noisiest** making a lot of noise, or full of noise: The place was full of noisy teenagers. | Bars are too smoky and noisy. —**noisily** adv. —**noisiness** n. [U]

no-load /ˈ. ./ adj. **no-load fund/stock etc.** a FUND, stock etc. that does not charge people an additional amount of money when they INVEST in it

no·lo con·ten·de·re /ˌnoʊloʊ kənˈtɛndəri/ n. [U] LAW a statement by someone in a court of law that says that they will not admit that they are guilty but will also not fight against any punishment given by the court

no·mad /ˈnoʊmæd/ n. [C] **1** a member of a tribe that travels from place to place, especially to find fields for their animals **2** someone who often travels from place to place or who changes jobs, homes etc. often: A restless corporate nomad, Bollenbach has held jobs with five separate companies during the 1990s. —**nomadic** /noʊˈmædɪk/ adj.: nomadic tribes

no-man's-land /ˈ. .ˌ./ n. [singular,U] **1** an area of land that no one owns or controls, especially an area between two borders or opposing armies **2** an uncertain subject, situation etc. that does not clearly fit into a particular type because it is a combination of two or more types: Some of the most daring work was being done in that no-man's-land between painting and photography.

nom de guerre /ˌnɑm də ˈgɛr/ n. [C] LITERARY a name that someone uses instead of their real name, especially because they are fighting in a war

nom de plume /ˌnɑm də ˈplum/ n. [C] LITERARY a name used by a writer instead of their real name; a PSEUDONYM

no·men·cla·ture /ˈnoʊmənˌkleɪtʃɚ/ n. [C,U] FORMAL a system of naming things, especially in science: medical nomenclature

nom·i·nal /ˈnɑmənl/ adj. **1** **nominal head/leader etc.** someone who has the title of leader etc. but is not really doing that job: At the time, Gorbachev was still the nominal head of the armed forces. **2** **nominal fee/price/sum etc.** a small amount of money, especially when compared with the usual amount that would be paid for something: Most golf courses will rent clubs for a nominal fee. **3** TECHNICAL relating to or used as a noun. For example, "-ness" is a nominal ending because it forms a noun when added to another word.

nom·i·nal·ly /ˈnɑmənl-i/ adv. officially described as something, when this may not be really true: Eighty percent of the population is nominally Hindu.

nom·i·nate /ˈnɑməˌneɪt/ v. [T] **1** to officially choose someone or something to be one of the competitors in an election, competition etc.: The series has never won an Emmy, though it has been nominated repeatedly. | [nominate sb for sth] Ferraro was the first woman to be nominated for the job of vice president. **2** to choose someone for a particular job: [nominate sb sth] Meg was nominated club president. | [nominate sb as sth] Reagan nominated him as CIA director in 1987. | [nominate sb to sth] Souter was nominated to the Supreme Court.

nom·i·na·tion /ˌnɑməˈneɪʃən/ n. **1** [C,U] the act of officially choosing someone or something to be a competitor in an election, competition etc., or the official choice: [+ for] Who will get the Republican nomination for president? **2** [C,U] the act of choosing someone for a particular job, or the fact of being chosen: [+ to] O'Connor's nomination to the Supreme Court **3** [C] the name of a book, movie, actor etc. that has been suggested to receive an honor or prize: [+ for] The nominations for the Academy Awards were announced Tuesday.

nom·i·na·tive /ˈnɑmənətɪv, ˈnɑmnə-/ n. [singular] TECHNICAL a particular form of a noun in some languages, such as Latin and German, which shows that the noun is the SUBJECT of a verb —**nominative** adj.

nom·i·nee /ˌnɑməˈni/ n. [C] someone who has been suggested for a prize, duty, or honor: Speakers included former presidential nominee Bob Dole.

non- /nɑn/ prefix **1** [in adjectives and nouns] used to say that something does not have or do something: a nonalcoholic drink (=without alcohol in it) | a nonsmoker (=someone who does not smoke) | a nonstick frying pan (=that food does not stick to) **2** [in nouns] INFORMAL used to say that something does not deserve a particular name: a non-event (=something boring) | The book was filled with non-characters.

non·a·ge·nar·i·an /ˌnɑnədʒəˈnɛriən, ˌnoʊn-/ n. [C] someone between 90 and 99 years old

non-ag·gres·sion /ˌnɑn ..ˈ../ n. [U] the state of not fighting or attacking: a commitment to non-aggression | a non-aggression pact/treaty/agreement (=a promise not to attack another country)

non·al·co·hol·ic, **non-alcoholic** /ˌnɑnælkəˈhɔlɪk/ adj. a drink that is nonalcoholic does not contain alcohol: a nonalcoholic wine

non-a·ligned, **nonaligned** /ˌ. .ˈ.◂/ adj. a nonaligned country does not support, or is not dependent on, any of the powerful countries in the world —**non-alignment** n. [U]

no-name /ˈ. ./ adj. [only before noun] not famous, or not having a BRAND NAME: a no-name personal computer

non-bind·ing /ˌnɑnˈbaɪndɪ◂/ adj. a nonbinding vote, agreement, decision etc. expresses an opinion but does not have to be obeyed: a nonbinding resolution

nonce /nɑns/ adj. TECHNICAL **nonce word/phrase** a word or phrase that is invented and used only once for a particular occasion

non·cha·lant /ˌnɑnʃəˈlɑnt/ adj. behaving calmly and not seeming interested or worried about anything: Perkins was nonchalant about being chosen. —**nonchalance** n. [U] It would be abnormal to react with nonchalance in a situation like this. —**nonchalantly** adv.

non·com /ˈnɑnkɑm/ n. [C] INFORMAL an NCO

non-com·bat /nɑnˈkɑmbæt/ adj. [only before noun] belonging to the military, but not directly involved in fighting: Women were assigned to noncombat roles.

non-com·bat·ant /ˌnɑnkəmˈbætˈnt, -ˈkɑmbətˈnt/ n. [C] someone who is in the military during a war but does not actually fight, for example a doctor —**noncombatant** adj.

non-com·mis·sioned of·fi·cer /ˌ. ... ˈ.../ n. [C] an NCO

non-com·mit·tal /ˌnɑnkəˈmɪtl◂/ adj. not giving a definite answer, or not willing to express your opinions: [+ about/on] Baker was noncommittal on the question of economic aid. | a noncommittal answer —**noncommittally** adv.

non·com·pet·i·tive /ˌnɑnkəmˈpɛtətɪv/ adj. **1** not involving competition, or not liking competition: Valencia organized the Fun Games, a day of noncompetitive activities for the disabled. | The people in the art scene are noncompetitive and willing to help. **2** noncompetitive prices, salaries etc. are worse than prices etc. in other stores or companies: In addition to noncompetitive salaries, teachers have to cope with a poor public image of their profession. **3** TECHNICAL noncompetitive business activities, trading etc. are unfair and intended to restrict free competition between businesses: noncompetitive mergers

non·com·pli·ance /ˌnɑnkəmˈplaɪəns/ n. [U] FORMAL failure or refusal to do what you are officially supposed to do: [+ with] Noncompliance with these rules is a violation of federal law.

non com·pos men·tis /ˌnɑn ˌkɑmpəs ˈmɛntɪs/ adj. [not before noun] LAW unable to think clearly or be responsible for your actions

non·con·form·ist /ˌnɑnkənˈfɔrmɪst/ n. [C] someone who deliberately does not accept the beliefs and ways of behaving that most people in a society accept: a political nonconformist —**nonconformist** adj. —**nonconformity** n. [U]

non·co·op·er·a·tion /ˌnɑnkoʊˌɑpəˈreɪʃən/ n. [U] the refusal or failure to do something that you officially have to, especially as a protest: In this neighborhood, the noncooperation of witnesses was high.

non·count noun /nɑnˈkaʊnt ˌnaʊn/ n. [C] an UNCOUNTABLE noun

non·cus·to·di·al /ˌnɑnkəˈstoʊdiəl/ adj. a noncustodial parent does not have CUSTODY of his or her children (=his or her children do not live with him or her)

non·dair·y /ˌ. ˈ.../ adj. containing no milk, and used instead of a product that contains milk: non-dairy whipped topping

non·de·duct·i·ble /ˌnɑndɪˈdʌktəbəl/ adj. an amount of money that is nondeductible cannot be subtracted from the amount of money you must pay taxes on: nondeductible entertainment expenses

non·de·nom·i·na·tion·al /ˌnɑrdɪˌnɑməˈneɪʃənl/ adj. not relating to a particular religion or religious group: a nondenominational chapel

non·de·script /ˌnɑndɪˈskrɪpt◂/ adj. not having any special or interesting qualities: a nondescript gray suit

non·dis·clo·sure /ˌnɑndɪsˈkloʊʒə/ n. [U] **nondisclosure agreement/law etc.** an agreement, law etc. in which someone promises not to tell certain secret information to anyone else

none[1] /nʌn/ pron., quantifier **1** not any of something: "Can I have some more pie?" "Sorry, there's none left." | She had inherited none of her mother's beauty. | "Was there any mail?" "No, **none at all**." **2** not any of a number of people or things: None of my friends wanted to go. | None of the packages was for me. | Of all the issues in this campaign, none is more important to our future than the economy. **3** not one thing or person: Even an old car is better than none. | Any kind of decision is better than **none at all**. **4 none other than sb/sth** used to emphasize that someone or something is famous or well-known: "Star Trek" fans were happy to welcome none other than William Shatner to their convention. **5 sb will have none of sth** OLD-FASHIONED to not allow someone to do something, or to not allow someone to behave in a particular way: The school wanted Sarah to skip a grade, but her parents would have none of that. **6 none but sb/sth** LITERARY only someone or something: None but God knows all her pain. —see also **bar none** (BAR[3] (1)), NONETHELESS, **be second to none** (SECOND[1] (9))

USAGE NOTE: NONE

GRAMMAR

In spoken English, if **None of** is followed by a plural noun or pronoun, you can use a plural verb: None of the packages were for me. In written English, it is better to use a singular verb: None of my friends has a car.

---

none[2] adv. **1 none the worse/better etc.** not any worse, better etc. than before: She seems none the worse for her experience. | I've read the instructions, but I'm still **none the wiser** (=I don't know any more than I did before). | The car was **none the worse for wear** (=the use it got did not make it perform or look any worse), despite having been driven so recklessly. **2 none too soon/happy/likely etc.** not soon, happy etc. at all: The salad was none too fresh. | Harden's cousin was none too bright.

non·en·ti·ty /nɑnˈɛntəti/ n. plural **nonentities** [C] someone who has no importance, power, or ability: He's famous in Europe, but a nonentity in the U.S.

non·es·sen·tial /ˌnɑnɪˈsɛnʃəl◂/ adj. not completely necessary: Nonessential personnel were ordered to leave the embassy.

none·the·less /ˌnʌnðəˈlɛs◂/ adv. [sentence adverb] FORMAL in spite of what has just been mentioned; NEVERTHELESS: The paintings are complex, but have plenty of appeal nonetheless. | The substance may not affect humans. Nonetheless, the FDA is examining it closely.

non-e·vent /ˈnɑniˌvɛnt, ˌnɑniˈvɛnt/ n. [C usually singular] an event that is much less interesting and exciting than you expected: Carver's testimony turned out to be a non-event.

non·ex·ist·ent /ˌnɑnɪgˈzɪstənt◂/ adj. not existing at all, or not present in a particular place: Employment and job training for these young people is almost nonexistent. —**nonexistence** n. [U]

non·fat /ˌnɑnˈfæt◂/ adj. nonfat milk, YOGURT etc. has no fat in it

non·fic·tion /ˌnɑnˈfɪkʃən/ n. [U] books, articles etc. about real facts or events, not imagined ones —**nonfiction** adj.

non·fi·nite /ˌ. ˈ../ adj. TECHNICAL a non-finite verb is not marked to show a particular sense or subject, and is either the INFINITIVE or the PARTICIPLE form of the verb, for example "go" in the sentence "Do you want to go home?"

non·flam·ma·ble /ˌnɑnˈflæməbəl/ adj. nonflammable materials or substances do not burn easily or do not burn at all —opposite FLAMMABLE, INFLAMMABLE

non·gov·ern·men·tal /ˌnɑngʌvərnˈmɛntl/ adj. [only before noun] a nongovernmental organization provides useful services to the public, especially in EMERGENCY situations or to help improve social problems: The Red Cross and about 140 other nongovernmental aid agencies have been providing assistance.

non·im·mi·grant /ˌnɑnˈɪməgrənt/ n. [C] someone who is living in or visiting a foreign country, but is not planning to live there permanently —**nonimmigrant** adj.: a nonimmigrant student visa

non·in·ter·ven·tion /ˌ. ...ˈ../ n. [U] the refusal of a government to become involved in the affairs of other countries: a policy of non-intervention

non·judg·ment·al /ˌnɑndʒʌdʒˈmɛntl/ adj. not using your own standards or beliefs to judge or criticize other people: Express your concerns in a nonjudgmental way.

non·na·tive /ˌ. ˈ..◂/ adj. **1** a non-native plant does not originally come from the area it is growing in: Eucalyptus trees are a non-native species in the U.S. **2** someone who is a non-native speaker of a language did not learn it as their first language as a child: It is particularly difficult for a non-native English speaker to have a phone conversation. **3** someone who is non-native was not born in the place they are living in: Guam recently elected its first non-native governor.

non·ne·go·tia·ble /ˌ. .ˈ...◂/ adj. **1** not able to be discussed or changed: The price is non-negotiable. **2** a check, BOND etc. that is non-negotiable can only be exchanged for money by the person whose name is on it

no-no /ˈ. ./ n. plural **no-nos** [C] INFORMAL something that is not allowed, or is not socially acceptable: Handwritten signs in the restaurant are a no-no.

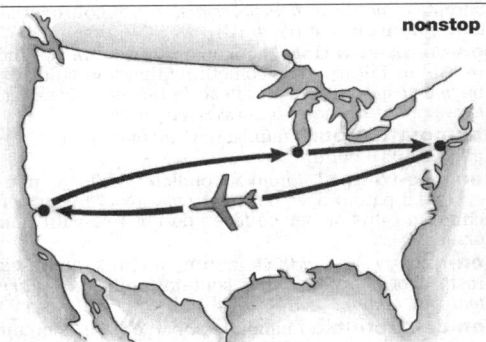

N

no·non·sense /ˌ. '..◂/ *adj.* [only before noun] **1** very practical, direct, and unwilling to waste time: *The commissioner was a hard-working, no-nonsense kind of guy.* **2** very practical: *no-nonsense black jeans*

non·pa·reil /ˌnɑnpəˈrɛl/ *n.* **1** [singular] LITERARY someone or something that is much better than all the others: *The nonpareil Lily Pons sang the role on tour.* **2** nonpareils [plural] very small balls of colored sugar used to decorate cakes, cookies etc. **3** [C] a chocolate candy covered with nonpareils —**nonpareil** *adj.*

non·par·ti·san, non-partisan /nɑnˈpɑrtəzən, -sən/ *adj.* not supporting the ideas of any political party or group: *The Council is a nonpartisan educational organization.*

non·pay·ment /nɑnˈpeɪmənt/ *n.* [U] failure to pay bills, taxes, or debts: [+ of] *The family was evicted for nonpayment of rent.*

non·plussed /ˌnɑnˈplʌst/ *adj.* so surprised that you do not know what to say or do: *"I don't know," he said, nonplussed at the question.*

non·pre·scrip·tion /ˌnɑnprɪˈskrɪpʃən◂/ *adj.* a non-prescription drug is one that you can buy in a store without a PRESCRIPTION (=written order) from a doctor

non·prof·it /nɑnˈprɑfɪt◂/ *adj.* a nonprofit organization, school, hospital etc. uses the money it earns to help people instead of making a profit, and therefore does not have to pay taxes —**nonprofit** *n.* [C]

non·pro·lif·er·a·tion /ˌ. ...'..ʃ/ *n.* [U] the act of limiting the number of NUCLEAR or chemical weapons that are being made around the world: *the nuclear nonproliferation treaty*

non·re·fund·a·ble /ˌnɑnrɪˈfʌndəbəl/ *adj.* if something you buy is nonrefundable, you cannot get your money back after you have paid for it: *nonrefundable airline tickets*

non·re·new·a·ble /ˌnɑnrɪˈnuəbəl/ *adj.* nonrenewable types of energy such as coal or gas cannot be replaced after they have been used: *The fibers are made from oil – a non-renewable resource.*

non·res·i·dent /nɑnˈrɛzədənt/ *n.* [C] someone who does not live permanently in a particular place or country: *Montana charges nonresidents more for hunting licenses.* —**nonresident** *adj.*: *About 3% of the college's degrees went to nonresident aliens.*

non·res·i·den·tial /ˌnɑnrɛzəˈdɛnʃəl◂/ *adj.* not relating to homes: *nonresidential buildings*

non·re·stric·tive /ˌ. '..◂/ *adj.* TECHNICAL a non-restrictive RELATIVE CLAUSE gives additional information about a particular person or thing rather than saying which person or thing is being mentioned. For example, in the sentence "Perry, who is 22, was arrested yesterday," the phrase "who is 22" is a nonrestrictive clause.

non·sec·tar·i·an /ˌnɑnsɛkˈtɛriən/ *adj.* not relating to a particular religion or religious group: *a nonsectarian charity*

non·sense /ˈnɑnsɛns, -səns/ *n.* [U] **1** [U] ideas, opinions, statements etc. that are not true or that seem very stupid: *"This dress makes me look fat." "Nonsense, you look great!"* | *Busch dismissed the accusations as nonsense.* | *You're just talking nonsense.* **2** behavior that is stupid and annoying: *No one should have to put up with that kind of nonsense.* | *She won't take any nonsense from the kids in her class.* **3** speech or writing that has no meaning or cannot be understood: *Dr. Seuss's nonsense words have delighted millions of children.* **4** nonsense poems/verse poetry that is humorous because it does not have a normal sensible meaning

non·sen·si·cal /nɑnˈsɛnsɪkəl/ *adj.* not reasonable or sensible: *nonsensical ideas* —**nonsensically** /-kli/ *adv.*

non se·qui·tur /nɑn ˈsɛkwɪtər/ *n.* [C] a statement that does not seem to be related to what was said before

non-shrink /ˌ. '.◂/ *adj.* non-shrink materials do not become smaller when they are washed

non·smok·er, non-smoker /nɑnˈsmoʊkər/ *n.* [C] someone who does not smoke

non·smok·ing /ˌnɑnˈsmoʊkɪŋ/ *adj.* a non-smoking area, building etc. is one where people are not allowed to smoke

non·spe·cif·ic /ˌnɑnspəˈsɪfɪk◂/ *adj.* **1** TECHNICAL a nonspecific medical condition could have one of several possible causes **2** not relating to or caused by one particular thing; general: *The fear may be nonspecific, perhaps a generalized dread of bad things.*

non·stan·dard /ˌnɑnˈstændərd/ *adj.* **1** not the usual size or type: *a nonstandard disk size* **2** TECHNICAL nonstandard words, expressions, or pronunciations are usually considered incorrect by educated speakers of a language —compare STANDARD², SUBSTANDARD

non·start·er /ˌnɑnˈstɑrtər/ *n.* [C usually singular] INFORMAL a person, idea, or plan that has no chance of success

non·stick, non-stick /ˌnɑnˈstɪk◂/ *adj.* non-stick pans have a special inside surface that food will not stick to

nonstop

He flew nonstop from New York to San Francisco with a three-hour stopover in Chicago on the return trip.

non·stop /ˌnɑnˈstɑp◂/ *adj. adv.* without stopping: *She talked nonstop for over an hour.* | *a nonstop flight to Los Angeles*

non·threat·en·ing /ˌnɑnˈθrɛtʰn-ɪŋ/ *adj.* not intended to threaten someone or cause them to feel afraid: *Conference time should be as nonthreatening to the student as possible.*

non·tox·ic, non-toxic /ˌnɑnˈtɑksɪk/ *adj.* not poisonous or harmful to your health: *All the paints are nontoxic and safe for children.*

non·tra·di·tion·al /ˌnɑntrəˈdɪʃənl/ *adj.* different from the way something happened or from what was considered typical in the past: *During the 1970s, older, nontraditional students fueled the growth of community colleges.*

non·un·ion, non-union /nɑnˈyunyən/ *adj.* [usually before noun] **1** not belonging to a UNION (=official organization for workers): *nonunion public employees* **2** not officially accepting UNIONs, or not employing their members: *nonunion factories* —**nonunionized** *adj.*

non·ver·bal, non-verbal /ˌnɑnˈvərbəl◂/ *adj.* not using words: *Nonverbal signals form an important part of communication.* —**nonverbally** *adv.*

non·vi·o·lence, non-violence /ˌnɑnˈvaɪələns/ *n.* [U] the practice of opposing a government without fighting, for example by not obeying laws

non·vi·o·lent /ˌnɑnˈvaɪələnt/ *adj.* not using or not involving violence: *nonviolent protests* —**nonviolently** *adv.*

non·white, non-white /ˌnɑnˈwaɪt◂/ *n.* [C] someone who does not belong to a white race —**nonwhite** *adj.*

noo·dle¹ /ˈnudl/ *n.* **1** [C usually plural] a long thin piece of soft food made from flour, water, and usually eggs, that is cooked in boiling water: *chicken noodle soup* **2** [C] OLD-FASHIONED your head or brain: *Just use your noodle.*

noo·dle² /'nudl/ v. [I + on/around] INFORMAL if someone noodles on an instrument or noodles around, they play music without planning the notes before

noo·gie /'nugi/ n. [C] INFORMAL the act of rubbing your KNUCKLES on someone's head while holding their head under your arm, usually as a joke: *If you couldn't answer, Mr. Regan would give you a noogie.*

nook /nʊk/ n. [C] **1** a small space in a corner of a room: *a breakfast nook* **2 nook and cranny** small parts of a place: *The grandkids love the house, with all its nooks and crannies.* | *We searched every nook and cranny.* **3** a small quiet place that is sheltered by a rock, a big tree etc.: *a shady nook*

noon /nun/ n. [U] 12 o'clock in the middle of the day: *Danny hardly ever gets up before noon.* | *The gallery is open from noon to 6 p.m.* | *the noon meal* | *Lunch will be at noon.* | *It is high noon* (=exactly noon) *and 108 degrees in the shade.* —see also **morning, noon, and night** (MORNING¹ (5))

noon·day /'nunde/ adj. [only before noun] LITERARY happening or appearing at noon: *the noonday sun*

no one /'. ./ pron. not anyone; NOBODY: *I tried calling last night, but no one was home.* | *No one could remember her name.*

noose /nus/ n. **1** [C] a circle of rope that becomes tighter as it is pulled, used especially for killing someone by hanging —compare LASSO¹ **2** [singular] an action that punishes or makes things difficult for a person, country etc.: *The U.S. tightened the economic noose around the dictatorship.* **3 the noose** punishment by hanging: *The outlaws managed to escape the hangman's noose.*

Noot·ka /'nʊtkə/ a Native American tribe from western Canada and the northwestern U.S.

nope /noʊp/ adv. SPOKEN no: *"Hungry?" "Nope, I just ate."*

no place /'. ./ adv. INFORMAL not any place; nowhere: *I had no place else to go.*

nor /nɔr, nə/ conjunction **1 neither... nor...** used in order to show that not one of a set of facts, people, qualities, actions etc. is true: *He can neither read nor write.* | *Neither Matt nor Julie said anything.* **2** FORMAL used after a negative statement, especially to add information, and meaning "and not," "or not," "neither," or "not either": *Worrall was not at the meeting, nor was he at work yesterday.* | *I am not, nor have I ever been, a Communist.*

Nor·dic /'nɔrdɪk/ adj. from or relating to the Northern European countries of Denmark, Norway, Sweden, Iceland, and Finland: *sailing in Nordic waters*

Nordic ski·ing /,.. '../ n. [U] CROSS-COUNTRY SKIING

nor'east·er /,nɔr'istə/ n. [C] a strong wind or storm coming from the northeast

norm /nɔrm/ n. **1** [C usually singular] the usual way of doing something etc.: *Working at home is becoming the norm for many employees.* | *Joyce's style of writing was a striking departure from the literary NORM.* **2** [C usually plural] a generally accepted way of behaving in society: *Traditional sexual norms have been called into question.*

nor·mal¹ /'nɔrməl/ adj. **1** usual, typical, or expected: *Under normal conditions, a number of plants grow well in aquariums.* | [be normal for sb/sth] *Temperatures in the mid-60s are normal for this time of year.* | [be normal (for sb) to do sth] *It's normal to feel nervous on your first interview.* **2** a normal person, especially a child, is physically and mentally healthy and does not behave strangely: *a normal healthy baby* | *Jerry seems like a perfectly normal guy, funny and nice.* —compare ABNORMAL

normal² n. [U] the usual level, amount, number etc.: *These patients will always be slightly shorter than normal.* | *His heart rate was back to normal by the time he reached the hospital.* | **above/below normal** *Rainfall has been below normal for this time of year.*

nor·mal·i·ty /nɔr'mæləti/ also **nor·mal·cy** /'nɔrməlsi/ n. [U] a situation in which things happen in the usual or expected way: *The war-torn area is returning to normality.*

N

nor·mal·ize /'nɔrmə,laɪz/ v. [I,T] to become normal again, or to make a situation become normal again: *In March 1944, Russia normalized relations* (=became friendly again after a period of disagreement) *with Italy.* —**normalization** /,nɔrmələ'zeɪʃən/ n. [U]

nor·mal·ly /'nɔrməli/ adv. **1** usually, or under normal conditions: *The flu normally lasts about a week or ten days.* | [sentence adverb] *Normally, it takes me twenty minutes to get to work.* **2** in the usual expected way: *Try to relax and breathe normally.*

nor·ma·tive /'nɔrmətɪv/ adj. FORMAL describing or establishing a set of rules or standards of behavior: *normative guidelines for senators*

Nor·plant /'nɔrplænt/ n. [singular] TRADEMARK a CONTRACEPTIVE (=way of keeping a woman from having babies) that is put under a woman's skin using SURGERY

Norse /nɔrs/ adj. relating to the people of ancient Scandinavia or their language: *Norse legends*

Norse·man /'nɔrsmən/ n. [C] LITERARY a Viking

north¹, North /nɔrθ/ n. [singular,U] **1** written abbreviation **N.** the direction toward the top of the world, that is on the left of someone facing the rising sun: *Which way is north?* | *A strong wind was blowing from the north.* | *The town is to the north of the lake.* **2 the north** the northern part of a country, state etc.: [+ of] *My relatives live in the north of the state.* **3 the North** the part of the U.S. that is east of the Mississippi River and north of Washington, D.C., especially the states that fought against the South in the U.S. Civil War **4 up North** in or to the north of a particular country, state etc.: *Brad's from somewhere up North.* —compare **down South** (SOUTH¹ (4))

USAGE NOTE: DIRECTIONS

WORD CHOICE: north, south, east, west
Use **north/south/east/west of** as a phrase to describe where a place is in relation to another place: *Chicago is south of Milwaukee.* Use **in the north/south/east/west of** as a noun phrase to say which part of a place you are talking about: *The mountains are in the north of the state.* You must use **northern, southern, eastern,** or **western** with the name of a place: *They have a cabin in northern Ontario.*

---

north² adj. **1** written abbreviation **N.** in, to, or facing north: *The north side of the building doesn't get much sun.* | [+ of] *The inn is about 20 miles north of Salem.* **2** a north wind comes from the north

north³ adv. toward the north: *The birds fly north in summer.* | *Go north on I-5 to Portland.* | *The window faces north.*

North Af·ri·ca /,. '../ the part of Africa that is on the coast of the Mediterranean Sea and west of Egypt, consisting of Morocco, Algeria, Tunisia, and Libya

North A·mer·i·ca /,. .'.../ n. one of the seven CONTINENTS, that includes land between the Arctic Ocean and the Caribbean Sea —**North American** n., adj.

north·bound /'nɔrθbaʊnd/ adj. traveling or leading toward the north: *northbound traffic* | *the northbound lanes of the freeway* —**northbound** adv.

North Car·o·li·na /,nɔrθ kærə'laɪnə/ written abbreviation **N.C.** a state on the eastern coast of the U.S.

North Da·ko·ta /,nɔrθ də'koʊtə/ written abbreviation **N.D.** a state in the northern central U.S. on the border with Canada

north·east¹ /,nɔrθ'ist◄/ n. [U] **1** written abbreviation **N.E.** the direction that is exactly between north and east **2 the Northeast a)** the part of a country, state etc. that is in the northeast **b)** the area of the U.S. that can include New England and the states of New Jersey, New York, and Pennsylvania

northeast² adj. **1** written abbreviation **N.E.** in or from the northeast: *the northeast outskirts of Las Vegas* **2** a northeast wind comes from the northeast

N

north·east[3] *adv.* toward the northeast: *The plane was traveling northeast.*

north·east·er /ˌnɔrθˈistɚ/ *n.* [C] a NOR'EASTER

north·east·er·ly /ˌnɔrθˈistɚli/ *adj.* **1** in or toward the northeast **2** a northeasterly wind comes from the northeast

north·east·ern /ˌnɔrθˈistɚn/ *adj.* in or from the northeast part of a country, state etc.: *the northeastern states of the U.S.*

Northeast Pas·sage, the /ˌ.. '../ a way by sea between the Atlantic and Pacific Oceans, going along the northern coasts of Europe and Asia

north·east·ward /ˌnɔrθˈistwɚd/ also **northeastwards** *adv.* toward the northeast —**northeastward** *adj.*

north·er·ly /ˈnɔrðɚli/ *adj.* **1** in or toward the north **2** a northerly wind comes from the north

north·ern /ˈnɔrðɚn/ *adj.* in or from the north of a country, state etc.: *northern Maryland*

north·ern·er, Northerner /ˈnɔrðɚnɚ/ *n.* [C] someone who comes from the northern part of a country

northern hem·i·sphere /ˌ.. '.../ *n.* the northern hemisphere the half of the world that is north of the EQUATOR

Northern Ire·land /ˌnɔrðɚn ˈaɪɚlənd/ the northern part of the island of Ireland, which is politically part of the United Kingdom

Northern Lights /ˌ.. './ *n.* [plural] the Northern Lights bands of colored light that are seen in the night sky in the most northern parts of the world

Northern Mar·i·an·a Islands, the /ˌnɔrðɚn ˌmæriˌænə ˈaɪləndz, -ˌ..ənə/ a U.S. TERRITORY with its own government that consists of all the Mariana Islands in the western Pacific Ocean except Guam

north·ern·most /ˈnɔrðɚnˌmoust/ *adj.* [only before noun] farthest north: *the northernmost tip of the island*

North Ko·re·a /ˌnɔrθ kəˈriə/ a country in East Asia, west of Japan and east of China, which is officially called the Democratic People's Republic of Korea —**North Korean** *n., adj.*

North Pole /ˌ. './ *n.* the North Pole the most northern point on the surface of the Earth, or the area around it —see also SOUTH POLE

North Sea, the /ˌ. './ part of the Atlantic Ocean that is between Great Britain and northwest Europe

North Star /ˈ. ˌ./ *n.* the North Star a star that is almost directly over the North Pole and that can be seen from the northern part of the world

north·ward /ˈnɔrθwɚd/ also **northwards** *adv.* toward the north: *We drove northward on country roads.* —**northward** *adj.*

north·west[1] /ˌnɔrθˈwɛst/ *n.* [U] **1** *written abbreviation* **N.W.** the direction that is exactly between north and west **2 the Northwest a)** the part of a country, state etc. that is in the northwest **b)** the area of the U.S. that can include the states of Idaho, Oregon, and Washington

northwest[2] *adj.* **1** *written abbreviation* **N.W.** in or from the northwest: *the northwest suburbs of the city* **2** a northwest wind comes from the northwest

northwest[3] *adv.* toward the northwest: *We drove northwest.*

north·west·er /ˌnɔrθˈwɛstɚ/ *n.* [C] a strong wind or storm coming from the northwest

north·west·er·ly /ˌnɔrθˈwɛstɚli/ *adj.* **1** in or toward the northwest **2** a northwesterly wind comes from the northwest

north·west·ern /ˌnɔrθˈwɛstɚn/ *adj.* in or from the northwest part of a country, state etc.: *northwestern Canada*

Northwest Pas·sage, the /ˌ.. '../ a way by sea between the Atlantic and Pacific Oceans, going along the northern coast of North America

Northwest Ter·ri·to·ries, the /ˌ... '..../ a very large area in northwest Canada east of the Yukon, whose capital is Yellowknife

Northwest Ter·ri·to·ry, the /ˌ.. '..../ an area of the northern central U.S. that reaches from the Ohio River and Mississippi River to the Great Lakes, and includes the states of Ohio, Indiana, Illinois, Michigan, and Wisconsin

north·west·ward /ˌnɔrθˈwɛstwɚd/ also **northwestwards** *adv.* going or leading toward the northwest —**northwestward** *adj.*

Nor·way /ˈnɔrweɪ/ a country in northern Europe that is west of Sweden and is part of Scandinavia —**Norwegian** /nɔrˈwidʒən/ *n., adj.*

nos. the written abbreviation of "numbers": *nos. 17–33*

nose[1] /nouz/ *n.*
1 on your face [C] the part of a person's or animal's face used for smelling or breathing: *Ripken's nose was broken when Hernandez accidentally hit him.* | *Here's a Kleenex – blow your nose* (=clear it by blowing). | *Robin has a sore throat and a runny nose* (=liquid is coming out of her nose because she has a cold). | *Davey, don't pick your nose* (=clean it with your finger)! —see picture at BODY
2 sb's nose is running if someone's nose is running, liquid is slowly coming out of it
3 (right) under sb's nose so close to someone that they should notice, but do not: *Pat's car was stolen, almost from under his nose.*
4 stick/poke your nose into sth to show too much interest in private matters that do not concern you: *No one wants the government sticking its nose into the personal business of citizens.* —see also NOSY
5 turn your nose up (at sth) INFORMAL to refuse to accept something because you do not think it is good enough for you: *Many professors turn their noses up at television.*
6 on the nose INFORMAL exactly: *He gets up at 6 a.m. on the nose every morning.*
7 have your nose in a book INFORMAL to be reading: *Celia always has her nose in a book.*
8 keep your nose to the grindstone INFORMAL to work very hard, without stopping to rest
9 by a nose if someone wins something by a nose, they win by only a very small amount
10 put sb's nose out of joint INFORMAL to annoy someone by attracting everyone's attention away from them
11 airplane [C] the pointed front end of an airplane, ROCKET etc.
12 have a (good) nose a) to be naturally good at finding and recognizing something: [+ for] *Some people have a nose for news.* **b)** to be good at recognizing smells: *Our dog has a very good nose, you know.*
13 keep your nose clean INFORMAL to make sure you do not get into trouble, or do anything wrong or illegal
14 keep your nose out (of sth) SPOKEN to stop showing too much interest in private matters that do not concern you: *Keep your nose out of my business!*
15 with your nose in the air behaving as if you are more important than other people and not talking to them: *She just walked past with her nose in the air.* —see also BROWN-NOSE, **cut off your nose to spite your face** at **cut off** (CUT[1]), **follow your nose** (FOLLOW (21)), HARD-NOSED, **look down your nose at sb/sth** (LOOK[1] (24)), NOSE JOB, **pay through the nose (for sth)** (PAY[1] (15)), **powder your nose** (POWDER[2] (2)), **thumb your nose at sb/sth** (THUMB[2] (2))

nose[2] *v.* [I always + adv./prep.,T always + adv./ prep.] if a vehicle, boat etc. noses forward, or if you nose it forward, it moves forward slowly: *The boat nosed out into the lake.*

nose around/into *phr. v.* [I,T] INFORMAL to try to find out private information about someone or something: *What were you doing nosing around my office?*

nose·bleed /ˈnouzblid/ *n.* **1** [C] blood that is coming out of your nose: *Chet has a nosebleed.* **2** nosebleed seats/section the seats or areas of a sports STADIUM or ARENA that are the highest and farthest away from the field or court

nose·cone /ˈnoʊzkoʊn/ *n.* [C] the pointed front part of a MISSILE or ROCKET

-nosed /noʊzd/ [in adjectives] **red-nosed/long-nosed etc.** having a nose that is red, long etc.

nose·dive[1] /ˈnoʊzdaɪv/ *n.* [C] **1** a sudden drop in amount, price, rate etc.: *The dollar took a nosedive early in trading today.* **2** a sudden steep drop made by an airplane, with its front end pointing toward the ground: *The plane suddenly went into a nosedive.*

nosedive[2] *v.* [I] **1** if a price, rate, amount etc. nosedives, it becomes smaller or reduces in value suddenly: *Sales have nosedived since January.* **2** if an airplane nosedives, it drops suddenly and steeply with its front end pointing toward the ground

nose·gay /ˈnoʊzɡeɪ/ *n.* [C] OLD-FASHIONED a small arrangement of flowers

nose job /ˈ. ./ *n.* [C] INFORMAL a medical operation on someone's nose to improve its appearance: *Natalie said she'd had a nose job.*

nos·ey /ˈnoʊzi/ *adj.* another spelling of NOSY

nosh[1] /nɑʃ/ *n.* [U] INFORMAL food, especially a small amount of food eaten between meals

nosh[2] *v.* [I] INFORMAL to eat

no-show /ˈ. ./ *n.* [C] someone who does not arrive somewhere they were expected to go, for example at a restaurant or airplane flight: *The weather meant that there were a lot of no-shows at the game.*

nos·tal·gia /nɑˈstældʒə, nə-/ *n.* [U] the slightly sad feeling you have when you remember happy events or experiences from the past: *Lamour remembers her first trip to Europe with warm nostalgia.* | [+ **for**] *Christmas often brings nostalgia for holidays past.*

nos·tal·gic /nɑˈstældʒɪk, nə-/ *adj.* feeling or expressing a slight sadness when remembering happy events or experiences from the past: *Many of these old newsreels will make people feel nostalgic.* | *"Radio Hour" is a nostalgic look at radio programs of the 1940s.* —**nostalgically** /-kli/ *adv.*

nos·tril /ˈnɑstrəl/ *n.* [C] one of the two openings at the end of your nose, through which you breathe and smell things

nos·trum /ˈnɑstrəm/ *n.* [C] **1** FORMAL an idea that someone thinks will solve a problem easily, but probably will not help at all: *an economic nostrum* **2** OLD-FASHIONED a medicine that is probably not effective and is not given by a doctor

nos·y /ˈnoʊzi/ *adj.* **nosier, nosiest** always trying to find out private information about someone or something: *Stop being so nosy!* | *a nosy neighbor* —**nosiness** *n.* [U]

not /nɑt/ *adv.* **1** used to make a word, statement, or question negative: *Most of the stores do not open until 10 a.m.* | *I don't smoke.* | *She's not a very nice person.* | *Is anyone not going to the party?* | *The changes were not at all surprising.* | *I do not like his attitude at all.* —compare NO[1] —see also -N'T **2** used in order to make a word or expression have the opposite meaning: *Des Moines isn't far now.* | *The food is not very good there.* | *Not much is known about the disease.* | *Most of the hotels are not that cheap* (=they are slightly expensive). | *Not many people have read it.* **3** used instead of a whole phrase, to mean the opposite of what has been mentioned before it: *No one knows if the story is true or not.* | *I should be home, but if not, leave me a message.* | *"Is Mark still sick?" "I hope not."* —compare SO[1] (4) **4 not only... (but) also** in addition to being or doing something: *Shakespeare was not only a writer but also an actor.* | *Not only do they want a pay increase, they also want reduced hours.* **5 not a** also **not one** not any person or thing: *Not one of the students knew the answer.* | *There wasn't a cloud in the sky.* | *Not a single person said thank you.* | *He had no criminal record, not even a parking ticket.* **6 not that...** used before a sentence or phrase to mean the opposite of what follows it, and to make the previous sentence seem less important: *Sarah has a new boyfriend - not that I care* (=I do not care). | *Janice had lost some weight, not that it mattered* (=it did not matter). **7 ...not!** SPOKEN, SLANG said when you mean the opposite of what you have just been saying: *She's*

really pretty - not! —see also **this/that is not to say** (SAY[1] (14))

USAGE NOTE: NOT

FORMAL/INFORMAL

In spoken English and informal writing **not** is usually shortened to **n't**: *Don't worry, it will be all right.* | *I won't go without you.* Don't use another negative word, for example, "nothing," "nobody," or "nowhere," in the same sentence as **not**. Use "anything," "anybody," "anywhere" etc. instead: *We didn't see anything.* | *Tom doesn't know anybody there.*

---

no·ta·ble /ˈnoʊtəbəl/ *adj.* [usually before noun] important, interesting, excellent, or unusual enough to be noticed: *a notable achievement* | *Schools have seen a notable increase in applications for free lunches.* | [+ **for**] *The music is notable for its complexity.* | *Most Western countries have rejected the refugees, with the notable exception of Germany* (=Germany has accepted them).

no·ta·bles /ˈnoʊtəbəlz/ *n.* [plural] important or famous people

no·ta·bly /ˈnoʊtəbli/ *adv.* **1** especially or particularly: *Some early doctors, notably Hippocrates, thought that diet and hygiene were important.* **2** FORMAL in a way that is clearly different, important, or unusual: *The project has been notably successful.*

no·ta·rize /ˈnoʊtəˌraɪz/ *v.* [T often passive] if a notary public notarizes a document, they make it official by putting an official stamp on it: *Enclose a notarized copy of your birth certificate*

no·ta·ry pub·lic /ˌnoʊtəri ˈpʌblɪk/ also **notary** *n.* [C] someone who has the legal power to make a signed statement or document official

no·ta·tion /noʊˈteɪʃən/ *n.* [C,U] a system of written marks or signs used for representing subjects such as music, mathematics, or scientific ideas

notch[1] /nɑtʃ/ *n.* [C] **1** a V-shaped cut or hole in a surface or edge: *Cut a notch near one end of the stick.* | *Move the broiler rack a notch lower.* **2** a level of achievement or social position: *Winning the game moved Virginia up a notch in the rankings.* **3 turn sth up a notch** to increase the amount of effort you are using, especially in order to win a competition, game etc.: *The Spartans turned it up a notch in the second half.* **4** a passage between two mountains or hills —see also TOP-NOTCH

notch[2] *v.* [T] **1** also **notch up** to achieve something, especially a victory or a particular total or SCORE: *Gooden notched the winning goal in a 1–0 win.* | *The Astros have notched up another win.* **2** to cut a V-shaped mark into something, especially as a way of showing the number of times something has been done

note[1] /noʊt/ *n.*

1 [short letter] [C] a short informal letter: *I was going to write Keisha a note, but I decided to call her instead.* | *Mom left a note on the counter telling us she'd gone to the store.* | *The kids are old enough now to write their own thank-you notes* (=a note to thank someone for a present etc.).

2 [to remind you] [C] something that you write down to remind you of something: *There were notes on little yellow Post-Its stuck all over the report.* | *Marina spoke without using any notes.* | *Tina made a note of their new address.*

3 [music] [C] **a)** a particular musical sound or PITCH | **high/low note** *Her singing, including lots of difficult high notes, was strong and beautiful.* **b)** a sign in written music that represents this

4 notes [plural] information that a student writes down during a class, from a book etc., so they will remember it: *Can I borrow your lecture notes?* | *I read the first three chapters and took notes* (=wrote notes).

5 [voice] [singular] if there is a particular note in someone's voice, they show what they are thinking or feeling by the way their voice sounds: *There was*

N

a strained note in Fischer's normally relaxed voice. | [+ of] *"Can you help me?" she asked, a note of hope in her voice.*

6 particular quality [singular] something that adds a particular quality to a situation, statement, or event: *She ended her speech on a personal note, telling how the war had affected her family.* | [+ of] *Councilman Buschman brought a note of realism to the debate.* | **strike/hit a note** *Burke struck a pessimistic note, saying the deadline may not be met.* | **the right/wrong note** (=an appropriate or inappropriate quality for a particular occasion)

7 take note to pay careful attention to something: *Saarela made the music world take note.* | [+ of] *Take note of how much water goes through your meter in 60 seconds.*

8 additional information [C] a short piece of writing at the bottom of a page or at the end of a book, that gives more information about something written in the main part: *Additional sources are listed in the notes at the back of the book.* —see also FOOTNOTE (1)

9 sb/sth of note important, interesting, or famous: *The school has produced several architects of note.*

10 worthy/deserving of note important or interesting and deserving to be noticed: *Three Latin American novels are especially worthy of note.*

11 government letter [C] TECHNICAL a formal letter between governments: *a diplomatic note*

12 money [C] a BILL (=piece of paper money) worth a particular amount of money —see also **compare notes (with sb)** (COMPARE[1] (4))

sw **note²** v. [T] FORMAL **1** to notice or pay careful attention to something: *Encourage the children to note the colors and textures of the fabrics.* | [note that] *Please note that the museum is closed on Mondays.* | [note who/what/how etc.] *Russell noted how animal research had led directly to some vaccines.* **2** to mention something because it is important or interesting: *The report noted a complete disregard for safety regulations.* | [note that] *A police spokesman noted that Miller had no previous criminal record.*

note down

3 also **note down** to write something down so that you will remember it: *Stuart noted the telephone number on a business card.*

sw **note·book** /ˈnoʊtˌbʊk/ n. [C] **1** a book of plain paper in which you can write notes **2** also **notebook computer** a small computer that you can carry with you

not·ed /ˈnoʊtɪd/ adj. well known or famous, especially because of some special quality or ability: *a noted author* | *Society Hill is noted for its 18th-century architecture.*

note·pad /ˈnoʊtˌpæd/ n. [C] a group of sheets of paper fastened together at the top, used for writing notes

note·pa·per /ˈnoʊtˌpeɪpɚ/ n. [U] paper used for writing letters or notes

note·wor·thy /ˈnoʊtˌwɚði/ adj. important or interesting enough to deserve your attention: *a noteworthy achievement*

not-for-prof·it /ˌ. . ˈ..ɪ/ adj. NONPROFIT

'noth·er /ˈnʌðɚ/ —see **a whole 'nother sth** (WHOLE[1] (8))

noth·ing¹ /ˈnʌθɪŋ/ pron. **1** not anything or no thing: *Nothing ever happens around here.* | *There's nothing in this box.* | *No, there's nothing wrong, I'm all right.* | *The kids were complaining there was nothing to do.* | *She had on socks and nothing else!* | *I have nothing against New York, I just wouldn't want to live there.* **2** not anything that you consider important or interesting: *I have nothing to wear to the wedding.* | *There's nothing on TV tonight.* | "What did you say?" "Oh, nothing." | *It's nothing, just a scratch.* **3** zero: *We beat them ten to nothing.* **4 for nothing a)** without paying for something or being paid for something: *My dad said he'd fix it for nothing.* | *You can't get something for nothing.* **b)** without having a good reason or purpose: *We drove all the way down there for nothing.* **5 have nothing to do with sb/sth** [not in progressive] **a)** if something has nothing to do with a fact or situation, it is not related to that fact or situation: *Forsman claimed that race had nothing to do with his hiring decisions.* **b)** if someone has nothing to do with a situation or person, he or she is not involved in it or with them: *I don't know why she's so worried about it; it has nothing to do with her.* **6 have/want nothing to do with sth** to not be involved in something, especially because you disapprove: *Joey said he wanted nothing to do with the stolen radios.* **7 nothing but sth** FORMAL only: *They wandered through the forest, eating nothing but fruits and berries.* **8 if nothing else** used when one thing will happen or be done even if something else does not: *If nothing else, the report points out the need for better math education.* **9 nothing special** having no very good or unusual qualities: *The food there is nothing special.* **10 there's nothing like sth** INFORMAL used to say that something is very good: *There's nothing like a nice hot bath to help you relax.* **11 sb has nothing to lose** used to say that someone should try to do something because the situation will not be worse if they fail: *You might as well apply for the job – you've got nothing to lose.* —opposite **have a lot to lose**

SPOKEN PHRASES

12 nothing much very little: "*What did you do last weekend?*" "*Oh, nothing much.*" **13 (there's) nothing to it/sth** used to say that something is easy to do: *Anyone can use a computer. There's nothing to it!* **14** [used with a negative] NONSTANDARD anything: *I never said nothing about taking you swimming.* **15 it was nothing** OLD-FASHIONED said when someone thanks you, in order to say that you did not mind helping: "*Thanks a lot!*" "*It was nothing.*" **16 nothing doing** OLD-FASHIONED used to refuse to do something: *Lend you $500? Nothing doing!*

17 there is nothing to sth used to say that what people are saying is not true: *An administration spokesman said there was nothing in the rumors.* —see also **nothing/ nowhere etc. on earth** (EARTH (4)), **to say nothing of sth** (SAY[1] (15)), **sweet nothings** (SWEET[1] (12)), **think nothing of (doing sth)** (THINK (7))

nothing² adv. **1 be nothing like sb/sth** to have no qualities or features that are similar to someone or something else: *We have hills at home, but they're nothing like the mountains here!* **2 be nothing less than sth** also **be nothing short of sth** used to emphasize that something or someone has a particular quality or seems to be something: *Japan's economic recovery was seen as nothing less than a miracle.* | *They way they treat their workers is nothing short of barbaric* (=it is very cruel). **3 be nothing if not sth** used to emphasize a particular quality that someone or something has: *That kid is nothing if not noisy* (=he is very noisy).

noth·ing·ness /ˈnʌθɪŋnɪs/ n. [U] **1** emptiness, or the absence of anything: *We stared into the black nothingness inside the cave.* **2** the state of not existing: *Is there only nothingness after death?*

sw **no·tice¹** /ˈnoʊtɪs/ v. [I,T not in progressive] **1** to see, hear, or feel someone or something: *I said "Hello,"* but she didn't notice. | You may *notice a numb feeling in your fingers.* | [notice (that)] *The lifeguard didn't notice that a boy was having trouble in the pool.* | [notice who/what/how etc.] *Have you noticed how often he interrupts people?* | [notice sb/sth doing sth] *I noticed them coming, and turned to my work.* 2 be/get noticed to get attention from someone: *The videotape résumé helped me get noticed.*

s w **notice**[2] *n.*

3 1 on paper [C] a written or printed statement that gives information or a warning to people: *I'll post a notice about it on the board.*
2 warning/time to prepare [U] information or a warning about something that will happen: *Prices are subject to change without notice.* | give/serve (sb) notice *Employees were given written notice of the layoffs* (=told they would have to leave their jobs) | *The election upset has served notice that voters want change now.* | *One of the players dropped out at short notice* (=without giving much warning). | *We were ready to leave at a moment's notice* (=without being given much warning).
3 take notice (of sb/sth) to pay attention to something or someone and let them affect or influence you: *The U.S. soccer team has finally made people take notice.* | *The recent success of women mystery writers has made publishers sit up and take notice* (=pay more attention). | *For years, employers took no notice of* (=paid no attention to) *the 1938 court decision.*
4 give notice also hand in your notice to inform your employer that you will be leaving your job soon, especially by writing a formal letter: *Ross gave notice yesterday.* | *We have to give three weeks' notice if we want to quit.*
5 until further notice from now until another change is announced: *The museum will be closed until further notice.*
6 attention FORMAL [U] if a fact, problem etc. comes or is brought to your notice, you pay attention to it or find out about it: *Unfortunately, an addiction to alcohol may escape the notice of friends and co-workers.* | *It came to our notice that the rules had been broken.* | *The letter brought the matter to Mr. Pearson's notice.*
7 book/play etc. [C usually plural] a statement of opinion, especially one written for a newspaper or magazine, about a new play, book, movie etc.; REVIEW: *The new play got mixed notices* (=some good, some bad) *in the newspapers.*

no·tice·a·ble /ˈnoʊtɪsəbəl/ *adj.* easy to notice: *Most people are not affected by the chemical in any noticeable way.* | *Don't worry; the stain is hardly noticeable.* | *We expect to see a noticeable improvement within three months.* —**noticeably** *adv.*

no·ti·fi·ca·tion /ˌnoʊtəfəˈkeɪʃən/ *n.* [C,U] FORMAL an act of officially informing someone about something: [+ of] *You should receive notification of the results within a week.*

no·ti·fy /ˈnoʊtəˌfaɪ/ *v.* notifies, notified, notifying [T] to formally or officially tell someone about something; INFORM: *Have you notified the police?* | [notify sb of sth] *The security company notified residents about the changes.*

s w **no·tion** /ˈnoʊʃən/ *n.* [C usually singular] 1 an idea, belief, or opinion about something, especially one that you think is wrong: [+ of] *The problem stems from an unrealistic notion of what teachers do.* [notion that] *We're trying to dispel the notion that it's cool to smoke or drink.* 2 a sudden desire to do something: [notion to do sth] *At midnight, Shelly had a sudden notion to go to the beach.* 3 notions [plural] small things, such as thread and buttons, used for sewing.

no·tion·al /ˈnoʊʃənl/ *adj.* existing only in the mind as an idea or plan, and not existing in reality: *Their calculations were based on a notional $3.50 per share.*

no·to·ri·e·ty /ˌnoʊtəˈraɪəti/ *n.* [U] 1 the state of being famous or well-known for doing something bad *Salem's tourist industry plays on its notoriety for the witchcraft trials.* 2 NONSTANDARD a word meaning the state of being famous for doing something good used especially by sports reporters: *Stewart, the new*

quarterback from Colorado, has gained a lot of notoriety for his versatility.

no·to·ri·ous /noʊˈtɔriəs/ *adj.* famous or well-known for something bad: *the notorious flaw in the Hubble Space Telescope* | [+ for] *Children are notorious for snacking, especially on high-fat foods.* —**notoriously** *adv.: The tests are notoriously unreliable.* —see Usage Note at FAMOUS[1]

not·with·stand·ing /ˌnɑtwɪθˈstændɪŋ/ *prep.* FORMAL if something is true notwithstanding something else, it is true even though the other thing has happened: *The end of the Cold War notwithstanding, the world is still a dangerous place.* —**notwithstanding** *adv.*

Nou·ak·chott /nuˈɑkʃɑt/ the capital and largest city of Mauritania

nou·gat /ˈnugət/ *n.* [U] a type of sticky soft candy with nuts and sometimes fruit

nought /nɔt, nɑt/ *n.* [U] OLD-FASHIONED nothing: *All my efforts were for nought.*

noun /naʊn/ *n.* [C] a word or group of words that represent a person, place, thing, quality, action, or idea. Nouns can be used as the subject or object of a verb, for example in "The teacher arrived" or "We like the teacher," or as the object of a PREPOSITION, for example in "He is good at football." —see also COMMON NOUN, COUNT NOUN, PROPER NOUN, UNCOUNT NOUN

nour·ish /ˈnɔɪʃ, ˈnʌrɪʃ/ *v.* [T] 1 to give a person, plant, or animal the food that is needed to live, grow, and stay healthy: *The roses bloom into November, nourished by lots of rain.* | *Crystal's children are well-nourished and wear decent clothes.* —see also UNDERNOURISHED 2 LITERARY to keep a feeling, idea, or belief strong or help it to grow stronger: *The Bill of Rights nourishes our freedom.*

nour·ish·ing /ˈnɔɪʃɪŋ/ *adj.* food that is nourishing makes you strong and healthy

nour·ish·ment /ˈnɔɪʃmənt/ *n.* [U] FORMAL 1 food that is needed to live, grow, and stay healthy: *The program provides basic nourishment to low-income families.* 2 something that helps a feeling, idea, or belief to grow stronger: *The retreat gives me a kind of spiritual nourishment.*

nou·veau riche /ˌnuvoʊ ˈriʃ/ *n. plural* **nouveaux riches** (SAME PRONUNCIATION) [C] someone who has only recently become rich and spends a lot of money, hoping that other people will notice and admire them —**nouveau riche** *adj.*

nou·velle cuisine /ˌnuvɛl kwɪˈzin/ *n.* [U] a style of cooking from France that uses fresh fruit and vegetables cooked in a simple way and attractively served

Nov. the written abbreviation of November

no·va /ˈnoʊvə/ *n.* [C] a star that explodes and suddenly becomes much brighter for a short time —see also SUPERNOVA

Nova Sco·tia /ˌnoʊvə ˈskoʊʃə/ a PROVINCE of southeast Canada

nov·el[1] /ˈnɑvəl/ *n.* [C] a long book in which the story and characters are usually imaginary: *a novel by John Irving* s w 2

novel[2] *adj.* new, different, and unusual: *a novel approach to the problem*

nov·el·ist /ˈnɑvəlɪst/ *n.* [C] someone who writes novels

nov·el·i·za·tion /ˌnɑvələˈzeɪʃən/ *n.* [C] a story that was originally written as a movie or television program before being written as a book

nov·el·la /noʊˈvɛlə/ *n.* [C] a story that is shorter than a novel, but longer than a SHORT STORY

nov·el·ty /ˈnɑvəlti/ *n. plural* **novelties** 1 [C] something new and unusual that attracts people's attention and interest: *In a few years, hand-held computers will not be novelties.* 2 [C often plural] an unusual, small, cheap object, often given as a present: *They sell a selection of crafts, novelties, and T-shirts.* | *a novelty key ring* 3 [U] the quality of being new, unusual, and interesting: *Modern art thrives on*

novelty. | *The **novelty** of video games **has worn off** for some kids* (=it no longer seems new and interesting).

No·vem·ber /nouˈvɛmbɚ, nə-/ *written abbreviation* **Nov.** *n.* [C,U] the eleventh month of the year, between October and December —see Usage Note at JANUARY

nov·ice /ˈnɑvɪs/ *n.* [C] **1** someone who has only begun learning a skill or activity; BEGINNER: *The computer program is easy for even a novice to master.* | *Knee and elbow pads are recommended for novice roller bladers.* **2** someone who has recently joined a religious group to become a MONK or NUN

no·vi·tiate /nouˈvɪʃət, nə-, -ʃiət/ *n.* [C] TECHNICAL the period of being a novice

No·vo·cain /ˈnouvəˌkeɪn/ *n.* [U] TRADEMARK a drug used for stopping pain during a small operation or treatment, especially on your teeth

NOW /nau/ National Organization for Women; an organization that works for legal, economic, and social equality between women and men

now¹ /nau/ *adv.* **1** at the present time: *Seattle is now one of the computer industry's major centers.* | ***Right now*** (=exactly now) *the weather is pretty hot.* | *Judy should have been home **by now** (=before now).* | *Mom says we have to be home by 9:00 on school nights **from now on*** (=starting now and continuing into the future). | *We'll just focus on strengthening your stomach muscles **for now*** (=for a short time). | *Multiple sclerosis, **as of now*** (=at the present time), *is an incurable disease.* | *I never really understood what she meant **until now**.* —see Usage Note at ACTUALLY **2** immediately: *Come on, Dave, if we don't leave now we'll be late.* | *Time's up – stop writing now.* | *Call her **right now**, before she leaves.*

SPOKEN PHRASES

3 said when you want to get someone's attention: *Now, how many people want cake?* | *Okay, now, watch me.* **4** said when you want some information: *Now who was Kathleen married to?* | *Let's see, now, he would have been about seven then?* **5** said when you pause because you are thinking about what to say next: *Okay, now, who's next?* **6 now then** said to get someone's attention before telling them to do something or asking them a question: *Now then, you'll be eighty-four in August – is that right?* **7** said when you are trying to comfort someone who is upset: *Don't cry, now, it'll be all right.* **8** used when you know or understand something because of something you have just seen, just been told etc.: *"I just went to see Jim." "So, now do you see why I'm worried about him?"* **9 now you tell me!** said when you are annoyed because someone has just told you something they should have told you before: *"Mom, I need to bring cookies for the whole class tomorrow." "Now you tell me!"* **10** said when telling or reminding someone to do something: *Call me when you get home from school – don't forget now!* **11 well now** said when giving your opinion or asking someone to tell you something: *Well now, do you agree or not?* **12 not now** said when you do not want to talk to someone or do something now, because you are busy, tired etc.: *"Tell me a story." "Not now, Daddy's working."* **13** said when you think a situation would have happened differently if some part of it were changed: *If I'd been there, now, I would've made sure it got done right.* **14 it's now or never** used to say that if someone does not do something now, they will not get another chance to do it **15 now's the time** used to say that someone should do something now, because it is the right time to do it: *Now's the time to buy a suit, while they're on sale.* **16 what is it now?** said when you are annoyed because someone keeps interrupting you or asking you things **17 now for sth** used when saying what you are going to do next: *Okay, now for the main point behind this meeting.* **18 and now** used when introducing the next activity, performer etc.: *And now, live from New York, it's "Saturday Night!"* **19 now, now** OLD-

---

FASHIONED **a)** said in order to try to make someone feel better when they are sad, upset, hurt etc.: *"Let me look at your leg." "Ow!" "Now, now, it's not that bad."* **b)** used when someone has just said something you think is not very nice: *"Peter's such an idiot sometimes." "Now, now." "It's true!"* **20 three weeks/two years etc. now** starting three weeks, two years etc. ago and continuing into the future: *They've been going out together for a long time now.* | *It's been over five years now since I started working here.* **21 any day/minute etc. now** very soon: *Peggy and Jack should get here any minute now.* **22 (every) now and then, now and again** used in order to say that something happens sometimes but not always: *I see Wanda every now and then at church.* **23 now...now...** LITERARY used to say that at one moment someone does one thing and immediately after, they do something else: *The eagle glided through the sky, now rising, now swooping.*

now², **now that** *conjunction* because of something or as a result of something: *My oldest son and I are getting along better now that he's getting ready to go to college.* | *I'm going to relax now the school year is over.*

NOW ac·count /ˈnau əˌkaunt/ *n.* [C] a CHECKING ACCOUNT that pays INTEREST¹ (3) on the money you have in it

now·a·days /ˈnauəˌdeɪz/ *adv.* in the present, compared with what happened in the past: *People are taller nowadays.*

no·where /ˈnouwɛr/ *adv.* **1** also **no place** not in any place or to any place: *When the cold hit, there was nowhere for them to go.* | *There was **nowhere else** to sit but the bed.* **2 get/go nowhere** to have no success or make no progress: *Flo has been looking for a job but has gotten nowhere.* | [+ with] *Police were getting nowhere with him and sent him back to his cell.* | *I can assure that threats will **get you nowhere**.* | *The negotiations are **going nowhere fast**.* **3 be nowhere to be found/seen** also **be nowhere in sight** to be not seen, found, or heard anywhere: *When her parents came into her room, Emma was nowhere to be found.* **4 nowhere (near) a)** far from a particular place or state: *I'm nowhere near the curb, am I?* | *They had nowhere near the number of people needed.* **b)** not at all: *She's **nowhere near as** pretty as you.* **5 out of nowhere** also **from nowhere** happening or appearing suddenly and without warning: *Owens came out of nowhere to block the shot.* | *Cinderella's fairy godmother appeared from nowhere.* —see also **in the middle of nowhere** (MIDDLE¹ (4))

no-win sit·u·a·tion /. ˈ. .,.../ *n.* [C] a situation that will end badly whatever you decide to do —compare WIN-WIN SITUATION

no·wise /ˈnouwaɪz/ *adv.* OLD USE not at all

nox·ious /ˈnɑkʃəs/ *adj.* FORMAL harmful or poisonous: *noxious fumes*

noz·zle /ˈnɑzəl/ *n.* [C] a short tube fitted to the end of a HOSE, pipe etc. to direct and control the liquid or gas pouring out

NPR *n.* National Public Radio: a national organization of radio stations in the U.S. that broadcasts without advertisements

NR *adj.* Not Rated; used to show that a particular movie has not been given an official rating and so only people older than 17 may see it

NRA —see NATIONAL RIFLE ASSOCIATION, THE

NRC —see NUCLEAR REGULATORY COMMISSION, THE

NSC —see NATIONAL SECURITY COUNCIL, THE

-n't /ənt/ the short form of "not": *Sorry, I hadn't realized you were busy.* | *She didn't see me.*

nth /ɛnθ/ *adj.* **1 to the nth degree** INFORMAL extremely, or as much as possible: *It's an exaggeration to the nth degree.* **2** [only before noun] INFORMAL the most recent of a long series of similar things that have happened: *Even after I'd reminded him for the nth time, he forgot.*

nu·ance /ˈnuɑns/ *n.* [C,U] a very slight, hardly noticeable difference in manner, color, meaning etc.: *There are layers of nuance and humor in her writing.* —**nuanced** *adj.*

nub /nʌb/ *n.* [C] **1** a small rounded piece of something, especially a piece that is left after it has been eaten, used etc.: *The baby clutched a nub of carrot.* **2** the central or main part of something: *I was just waiting for the discussion to get down to the real nub of things.*

nu·bile /'nubaɪl, -bəl/ *adj.* FORMAL a woman who is nubile is young and sexually attractive

nu·cle·ar /'nukliə/ *adj.* **1** using or relating to nuclear energy: *a nuclear power station* | *a nuclear-powered submarine* **2** relating to the NUCLEUS of an atom: *nuclear fission* **3** relating to or involving the use of NUCLEAR WEAPONS: *a nuclear testing area* | *the threat of nuclear war*

nuclear de·ter·rence /,... .'../ *n.* [U] the use of NUCLEAR WEAPONS as a threat to stop an enemy attacking

nuclear dis·ar·ma·ment /,... .'.../ *n.* [U] the process or activity of getting rid of NUCLEAR WEAPONS

nuclear en·er·gy /,... '.../ *n.* [U] the powerful force that is produced when the NUCLEUS of an atom is either split or joined to another atom

nuclear fam·i·ly /,... '../ *n.* [C] a family unit that consists only of husband, wife, and children —compare EXTENDED FAMILY

nuclear fis·sion /,... '../ *n.* [U] the splitting of the NUCLEUS of an atom, that results in a lot of power being produced

nuclear-free /,... '. / *adj.* places that are nuclear-free do not allow NUCLEAR materials to be carried, stored, or used in that area: *a nuclear-free zone*

nuclear fu·sion /,... '../ *n.* [U] a NUCLEAR reaction in which the nuclei (NUCLEUS (1)) of light atoms join with the nuclei of heavier atoms, which produces power without producing any waste

nuclear phys·ics /,... '../ *n.* [U] the area of PHYSICS that is concerned with the structure and features of the NUCLEUS of atoms

nuclear pow·er /,... '../ *n.* [U] power, usually in the form of electricity, from NUCLEAR ENERGY

nuclear re·ac·tion /,... .'../ *n.* [C] a process in which the parts of the NUCLEUS of an atom are arranged differently to form new substances

nuclear re·ac·tor /,... .'../ *n.* [C] a large machine that produces NUCLEAR ENERGY, especially as a means of producing electricity

Nuclear Reg·u·la·to·ry Com·mis·sion, the /,... '..... .,../ a U.S. government organization that checks on the safety of nuclear power PLANTS (PLANT[1] (2))

nuclear waste /,... '. / *n.* [U] waste material from NUCLEAR REACTORS, which is RADIOACTIVE

nuclear weap·on /,... '../ *n.* [C] a very powerful weapon that uses NUCLEAR ENERGY to destroy large areas

nu·cle·ic ac·id /nu,kliik 'æsɪd, -,klɛɪ-/ *n.* [C,U] one of the two acids, DNA and RNA, that exist in the cells of all living things

nu·cle·us /'nukliəs/ *n. plural* **nuclei** /-kliaɪ/ [C] **1** the central part of an atom, consisting of NEUTRONS, PROTONS, and other ELEMENTARY PARTICLES **2** the central part of almost all the cells of living things **3** a small important group at the center of a larger group or organization: *Doe and Cervenka were the nucleus of the great band "X."*

nude[1] /nud/ *adj.* **1** not wearing any clothes; NAKED **2** done by or involving people who are not wearing any clothes: *Rogers refuses to do nude scenes in movies.*

nude[2] *n.* **1** [C] a painting, STATUE etc. of someone not wearing clothes **2** **in the nude** not wearing any clothes: *He likes to swim in the nude.*

nudge /nʌdʒ/ *v.* **1** [T] to push someone gently, usually with your elbow, in order to get their attention: *They nudged each other as the principal called their names.* **2** [T always + adv./prep.] to move something or someone a short distance by gently pushing: *Southeast winds nudged the oil slick onto the shore.* **3** [I always + adv./prep.,T] also **nudge your way** to move forward slowly by pushing gently: *An old woman nudged her way to the back of the bus.* **4** [T always + adv./prep.] to gently persuade or encourage someone to take a particular decision or action: [**nudge sb into/toward sth**] *We're trying to nudge the city council into quicker action.* **5** [T usually in progressive] to almost reach a particular level or amount: *Temperatures were already nudging into the 80s before dawn today.* —**nudge** *n.* [C]

nud·ie /'nudi/ *adj.* [only before noun] INFORMAL involving people without any clothes on: *nudie magazines*

nu·dist /'nudɪst/ *n.* [C] someone who enjoys not wearing any clothes because they believe it is natural and healthy —**nudist** *adj.*: *a nudist camp* —**nudism** *n.* [U]

nu·di·ty /'nudəti/ *n.* [U] the state of not wearing any clothes: *The movie is rated R for nudity and violence.*

'nuff /nʌf/ *adj.* NONSTANDARD, SLANG a way of writing ENOUGH to represent its sound in informal spoken language

nug·get /'nʌgɪt/ *n.* [C] **1** a small rough piece of a valuable metal found in the earth: *gold nuggets* **2** a small round piece of food: *chicken nuggets* **3 nugget of information/wisdom etc.** a piece of interesting, good, or useful information, advice etc.: *It sounds ridiculous, but what he's saying contains a nugget of truth.*

nui·sance /'nusəns/ *n.* **1** [C usually singular] a person, thing, or situation that annoys you or causes problems: *Rabbits can be a nuisance to gardeners.* | *Billy made such a nuisance of himself no one wanted to eat lunch with him.* **2** [C,U] LAW the use of a place or property in a way that causes public annoyance: *The overgrown vacant lot was declared a public nuisance.*

nuke[1] /nuk/ *v.* [T] INFORMAL **1** to attack a place using NUCLEAR WEAPONS **2** to cook food in a MICROWAVE OVEN: *Will you nuke the pizza? It's not hot enough.*

nuke[2] *n.* [C] INFORMAL a NUCLEAR WEAPON

Nu·ku·'a·lo·fa /,nukuɑ'lɔfə/ the capital city of Tonga

null /nʌl/ *adj.* **1 null and void** LAW an agreement, contract etc. that is null and void has no legal effect; INVALID: *The elections were declared null and void.* **2 null result/effect etc.** TECHNICAL a result etc. that is zero or nothing

nul·li·fy /'nʌlə,faɪ/ *v.* **nullifies, nullified, nullifying** [T] **1** LAW to officially state that an agreement, contract etc. has no legal effect: *The judge nullified the sale of the property.* **2** FORMAL to make something lose its effect or value: *Hall's touchdown pass was nullified by the referee.* —**nullification** /,nʌləfə'keɪʃən/ *n.* [U]

nul·li·ty /'nʌləti/ *n.* [U] LAW the fact that an agreement, contract etc. does not have any legal force anymore

null set /'. ./ *n.* [C] TECHNICAL a mathematical set with no members, usually written { }

numb[1] /nʌm/ *adj.* **1** a part of your body that is numb is unable to feel anything, for example because you are very cold: *They gave me an injection to make my mouth go numb.* **2** unable to think, feel, or react in a normal way: *I went numb. I didn't know what to feel.* —**numbly** *adv.* —**numbness** *n.* [U]

numb[2] *v.* **1** to make someone unable to feel pain or other sensations: *The cold wind numbed my face and hands.* **2** to make someone unable to think, feel, or react in a normal way: *The prisoners were numbed by their years in jail.*

num·ber[1] /'nʌmbə/ *n.*

1 number [C] a word or sign that represents an amount or a quantity: *Pick a number between one and ten.* | *an even number* (=2, 4, 6, 8, 10 etc.) *of people* | *You can't play the game with an odd number* (=1, 3, 5, 7, 9 etc.) *of players.* | *It's easier to add it all up if you use round numbers* (=numbers ending in 0, such as 10, 20 etc.). —see also CARDINAL NUMBER, ORDINAL NUMBER, PRIME NUMBER, WHOLE NUMBER

N

2 telephone [C] a telephone number: *Ann's phone number is 555-3234.* | *We tried Phil's number but there was no answer.* | **sb's home/office/work number** *That's my home number.* | *I'm sorry, I think I have the wrong number.*

3 in a set/list [C] a number used to show the position of something in an ordered set or list: *We live in apartment number seven.* | *Take a look at question number three.* —see also NUMBER ONE[1]

4 for recognizing sb/sth [C] a set of numbers used to name or recognize someone or something: *May I please have your Social Security number?* | *Double check the account number to make sure it's right.* —see also PIN, SERIAL NUMBER

5 amount [C,U] an amount of something that can be counted: [+ of] *This year the number of houses for sale went up by 20%.* | *Rebels have amassed **large numbers of** tanks and weapons.* | *Expansion will **bring the number of** major league teams **to** (=make the number rise to) 30.* | *Hospital staff will be increased **in number** by 28%.* | *I've been to Greece **a number of** (=several) times.* | *We've gotten **a good number of** contributions for the campaign.* | *The sauce tastes great with **any number of** grilled dishes.*

6 music [C] a piece of popular music, a song, a dance etc. that forms part of a larger performance: *Cast members performed the new dance number.* —see also PRODUCTION NUMBER

7 the numbers [plural] **a)** information about something that is shown using numbers: *Get Charlie to look at the numbers and develop a business plan.* **b)** an illegal game in which people risk money on the appearance of a combination of numbers in a newspaper: *playing the numbers*

8 do a number on sb/sth INFORMAL to hurt or damage someone or something badly: *Danny did a real number on the car.*

9 have sb's number INFORMAL to understand something about someone that helps you deal with them: *You can tell Cara has his number. She knows exactly how to handle him when he's mad.*

10 red/sexy etc. little number INFORMAL a red, sexy etc. dress or suit, especially a woman's: *Houston appeared in a hot little sequined number.*

11 sb's number comes up someone has the winning number in a competition

12 sb's number is up also sb's number has come up INFORMAL **a)** someone will stop being lucky or successful: *This could be the year a lot of politicians find their number is up.* **b)** HUMOROUS to die: *When my number is up, I want it to be quick.*

13 one/some/20 etc. of sb's number FORMAL one, some etc. of a group of people: *The tribe says 400 of their number were killed.*

14 beyond/without number LITERARY if things are beyond number, there are so many of them that no one could count them all

15 grammar [U] TECHNICAL the form of a word, depending on whether one thing or more than one thing is being talked about. "Cats" is plural in number, "cat" is singular.

USAGE NOTE: NUMBER

GRAMMAR

When we use numbers such as one, 20, 214 etc. as the subject of a sentence, we usually use a plural verb: *500 people were invited to the wedding.* However, when we want to talk about the amount itself, we use a singular verb: *500 people is too many to invite.* The phrase **the number of sth** is always used with a singular verb: *The number of babies born in Japan is expected to fall this year.* However, the phrase **a number of sth** is always used with a plural verb: *A number of states are facing economic problems.*

---

number² *v.* **1** [T] to give a number to something that is part of an ordered set or list: *This function numbers all the pages in a document.* | *The streets in the Bronx are numbered.* | **[number sth (from) 1 to 10/100 etc.]** *Number the questions 1 to 25.* **2** if people or

things number a particular amount, that is how many there are: *Our student body numbered 400 last year.* | *Fifteen years ago, Kenya's elephant population numbered 65,000.* **3** sb's/sth's days are numbered used to say that someone or something cannot live or continue much longer: *I think Harry's days as a bachelor are numbered.* **4** number among sth FORMAL to be included as one of a particular group: *Numbered among the guests were models and movie stars.* **5** [T] LITERARY to count: *Who can number the stars?*

number crunch·er, number-cruncher /ˈ.. ˌ../ *n.* [C] INFORMAL **1** someone whose job involves working with numbers, such as an ACCOUNTANT **2** a computer program designed to work with numbers and calculate results

number crunch·ing, number-crunching /ˈ.. ˌ../ *n.* [U] INFORMAL the process of working with numbers and calculating results —**number-crunching** *adj.* —see also **crunch the numbers** (CRUNCH² (3))

num·ber·less /ˈnʌmbəlɪs/ *adj.* too many to be counted; INNUMERABLE: *numberless possibilities*

number one¹ /ˌ.. ˈ.◂/ *n.* **1** [singular] the best, most important, or most successful person or thing in a group: *Diana's children were always number one in her life.* | *Shearson is number one in the market this year.* **2** [singular] the musical record that is the most popular at a particular time: *The song was number one in the charts for two months.* **3** look out for number one INFORMAL to make sure that you get all the advantages, things etc. you want, and not worry about other people **4** [U] SPOKEN, INFORMAL a word meaning URINE, used especially with children to avoid saying this directly —compare NUMBER TWO

number one² *adj.* **1** most important or successful in a particular situation: *Safety is our number one concern.* | *California is the number one travel destination in the U.S.* **2** first on a list of several things to be considered, done etc.: *Number one – always lock doors and windows.*

Num·bers /ˈnʌmbəz/ a book in the Old Testament of the Christian Bible

number two /ˌ.. ˈ.◂/ *n.* [U] SPOKEN, INFORMAL a word meaning solid waste from your BOWELS, used especially with children to avoid saying this directly —compare NUMBER ONE¹ (4)

numb·skull /ˈnʌmskʌl/ *n.* [C] another spelling of NUMSKULL

nu·mer·al /ˈnumərəl, ˈnumrəl/ *n.* [C] a written sign that represents a number —**numeral** *adj.*

nu·mer·ate /ˈnumərət/ *adj.* able to do calculations and understand simple mathematics: *We need someone who's numerate for this job.* —**numeracy** *n.* [U] —compare LITERATE (1)

nu·mer·a·tion /ˌnuməˈreɪʃən/ *n.* [C,U] TECHNICAL a system of counting or the process of counting

nu·mer·a·tor /ˈnuməˌreɪtə/ *n.* [C] TECHNICAL the number above the line in a FRACTION (2), for example 5 is the numerator in $\frac{5}{6}$; —compare DENOMINATOR

nu·mer·i·cal /nuˈmɛrɪkəl/ *adj.* expressed or considered in numbers: *The Democrats still held a numerical advantage.* —**numerically** /-kli/ *adv.*

nu·mer·ol·o·gy /ˌnuməˈrɑlədʒi/ *n.* [U] the study of numbers and their influence on people and events

num·er·ous /ˈnumərəs/ *adj.* FORMAL many: *The advantages of the discount plan are numerous.* | *I've met Ron on numerous occasions.*

nu·mi·nous /ˈnumɪnəs/ *adj.* LITERARY having a mysterious and holy quality, which makes you feel that God is present

nu·mis·mat·ics /ˌnumɪzˈmætɪks/ *n.* [U] TECHNICAL the activity of collecting and studying coins and MEDALS —**numismatic** *adj.* —**numismatist** /nuˈmɪzmətɪst/ *n.* [C]

num·skull, numbskull /ˈnʌmskʌl/ *n.* [C] INFORMAL a very stupid person; IDIOT

nun /nʌn/ *n.* [C] someone who is a member of an all-female Christian religious group that lives together in a CONVENT —compare MONK

nun·cha·ku /nʌn'tʃɑku/ *n.* [C] also **nun·chucks** /'nʌntʃʌks/ a weapon that is made of two long sticks connected by a chain or rope

nun·ci·o /'nʌnsiou, 'nʊn-/ *n. plural* **nuncios** [C] a representative of the Pope in a foreign country

nun·ne·ry /'nʌnəri/ *n.* [C] LITERARY a CONVENT

nup·tial /'nʌpʃəl/ *adj.* FORMAL relating to marriage or the marriage ceremony: *nuptial vows | nuptial bliss*

nup·tials /'nʌpʃəlz/ *n.* [plural] FORMAL a wedding

Nu·re·yev /nʊ'reɪʏf/, **Ru·dolf** /'rudɔlf/ (1938–1993) a Russian ballet dancer who is regarded as one of the greatest male dancers ever

s w **nurse¹** /nɚs/ *n.* [C] **1** someone who is trained to take
2 care of people who are sick or injured, usually in a
3 hospital: *I asked the nurse what the problem was.* | *Josephine is a registered nurse.* **2** OLD-FASHIONED a woman employed to take care of a young child; NANNY —see also WET NURSE

nurse² *v.*

1 sick people [T] to take care of someone who is sick or injured: *Martha nursed Ted herself.* | *Cindy nursed the two puppies back to health.*

2 your illness/injury [T not in passive] to rest when you have an illness or injury so that it will get better: *Shaw has been nursing a sore ankle.*

3 feed a baby **a)** [I,T] if a woman nurses a baby, she feeds it with milk from her breasts; BREAST-FEED **b)** [I] if a baby nurses, it sucks milk from its mother's breast —compare BREAST-FEED, SUCKLE

4 your feelings [T not in passive] to secretly have a feeling or idea in your mind for a long time, especially an angry feeling: **nurse a grudge/griev-ance/ambition etc.** *I stayed at home, nursing my indignation.*

5 hold [T] to hold something carefully in your hands or arms close to your body: *Penelope sat on the couch nursing a scotch and soda.*

6 take care of sth [T] to take special care of something, especially during a difficult situation: [**nurse sth through/along etc.**] *Case nursed the hotel through the Depression and World War II.*

nurse·maid /'nɚsmeɪd/ *n.* [C] OLD-FASHIONED a woman employed to take care of young children

nurse prac·ti·tion·er /ˌ. .'.../ *n.* [C] a very highly trained NURSE, who is able to do some of the things that a doctor does, for example to PRESCRIBE medicine

nurs·er·y /'nɚsəri/ *n. plural* **nurseries** [C] **1** a place where plants and trees are grown and sold **2** a place where young children are taken care of during the day while their parents are at work, shopping etc. —see also DAY CARE CENTER **3** OLD-FASHIONED a baby's BEDROOM or a room where young children play

nurs·er·y·man /'nɚsərimən/ *n.* [C] someone who grows plants and trees in a nursery

nursery rhyme /'... ,./ *n.* [C] a short traditional song or poem for children

nursery school /'... ,./ *n.* [C] a school for children from three to five years old —compare KINDERGARTEN, PRESCHOOL

nurs·ing /'nɚsɪŋ/ *n.* [U] the job or skill of taking care of people who are sick, injured, or old: *I'd like to get into the nursing program.*

nursing home /'.. ,./ *n.* [C] a place where people who are too old or sick to take care of themselves can live —compare RETIREMENT HOME

nursing moth·er /ˌ.. '../ *n.* [C] a mother who is feeding her baby from her breast

nur·tur·ance /'nɚtʃərəns/ *n.* [U] FORMAL loving care and attention that you give to someone —**nurturant** *adj.*

nur·ture¹ /'nɚtʃɚ/ *v.* [T often passive] FORMAL **1** to help a plan, idea, feeling etc. to develop: *Reading aloud nurtures a love of books in children.* **2** to feed and take care of a child or a plant while it is growing

nurture² *n.* [U] FORMAL the education and care that you are given as a child, and the way it affects your later development and attitudes

nut /nʌt/ *n.* [C]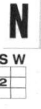

1 food a dry brown fruit inside a hard shell, that grows on a tree: *a selection of nuts | a cashew nut*

2 tool a small piece of metal with a hole through the middle, which is screwed onto a BOLT to fasten things together: *Use a wrench to tighten the nuts.*

3 crazy person INFORMAL someone who is crazy or behaves strangely: *Eleanor is such a nut.*

4 a golf/opera etc. nut INFORMAL someone who is very interested in GOLF etc.: *Theda is a real health nut – you wouldn't believe the things she eats.*

5 sexual organ SLANG one of a man's TESTICLES: *Hurry up, I'm freezing my nuts off out here.*

6 the nuts and bolts of sth INFORMAL the practical details of a subject or job: *They're good guys, but I'm not sure how familiar they are with the nuts and bolts of the banking system.*

7 a hard/tough nut to crack a difficult problem or situation: *Daytime television is a tough nut to crack. New shows have to be good enough to beat the old favorites.*

8 a tough/hard nut INFORMAL someone who is difficult to deal with: *The lawyers were worried because the circuit court judge was known to be a tough nut.* —see also NUTS¹

nut·case /'nʌtˌkeɪs/ *n.* [C] INFORMAL someone who behaves in a crazy way: *Tania is a major nutcase.*

nut·crack·er /'nʌtˌkrækɚ/ *n.* [C] a tool for cracking the shells of nuts

nut·house /'nʌthaʊs/ *n.* [C] INFORMAL an expression meaning a hospital for people who are mentally ill, that is usually considered offensive

nut·meg /'nʌtˌmɛg/ *n.* **1** [U] a brown powder used as a SPICE to give a particular taste to food **2** [C] the seed of a tropical tree from which this powder is made

nu·tri·ent /'nutriənt/ *n.* [C] a chemical or food that provides what is needed for plants or animals to live and grow: *Meat is rich in nutrients.* —**nutrient** *adj.*

nu·tri·ment /'nutrəmənt/ *n.* [C,U] FORMAL a substance that gives plants and animals what they need in order to live and grow

nu·tri·tion /nu'trɪʃən/ *n.* [U] the process of giving or getting the right type of food for good health and growth: *Women tend to be more conscious of good nutrition.* —**nutritional** *adj.* —**nutritionally** *adv.*

nu·tri·tious /nu'trɪʃəs/ *adj.* food that is nutritious is full of the natural substances that your body needs to stay healthy or to grow well: *Raw vegetable salads are very nutritious.*

nu·tri·tive /'nutrətɪv/ *adj.* **1** [no comparative] TECHNICAL relating to nutrition **2** FORMAL nutritious

nuts¹ /nʌts/ *adj.* [not before noun] INFORMAL **1** crazy: *Are you nuts or something?* | *I've been there for 12 years and I'm going nuts (=becoming crazy). | That phone's going to drive me nuts if it doesn't stop ring-ing.* **2 go nuts** SPOKEN **a)** to become very excited because something good has just happened: *The crowd went nuts after the third touchdown.* **b)** to become very angry about something: *Dad will go nuts if he finds out you took the car without asking.* **3 be nuts about/over sth** OLD-FASHIONED to like someone or something very much: *My dogs is nuts about popcorn.*

nuts² *interjection* OLD-FASHIONED used when you are angrily refusing to listen to someone: *"Nuts to that,"* he said, and left.

nut·shell /'nʌtˌʃɛl/ *n.* [C] **1 (to put it) in a nutshell** INFORMAL used when you are stating the main facts about something in a short, clear way: *The issue is, in a nutshell, who runs this organization?* **2** the hard outer part of a nut

nut·ty /'nʌti/ *adj.* **nuttier, nuttiest 1** tasting like nuts: *Grape leaves add a nutty taste to the rice.* **2** INFORMAL crazy: *We all got slightly nutty at times.* —**nuttiness** *n.* [C]

Nuuk /nuk/ the capital city of Greenland

N

nuz·zle /ˈnʌzəl/ v. [I always + adv./prep.,T] to gently rub or press your nose or head against someone to show you like them: *The kitten nuzzled her chin.*

NV the written abbreviation of Nevada

N.W. also **NW** the written abbreviation of NORTH-WEST

NY the written abbreviation of New York

ny·lon /ˈnaɪlɑn/ n. **1** [U] a strong artificial material that is used for making plastic, clothes, rope etc.: *a nylon backpack* | *nylon thread* **2 nylons** [plural] a piece of clothing that women wear on their legs, that is very thin and made of nylon

nymph /nɪmf/ n. [C] **1** one of the spirits of nature who, according to ancient Greek and Roman stories, appeared as young girls living in trees, mountains, streams etc. **2** POETIC a girl or young woman

nym·phet /nɪmˈfɛt/ n. [C] a young girl who is very sexually attractive

nym·pho·ma·ni·ac /ˌnɪmfəˈmeɪniˌæk/ also **nym·pho** /ˈnɪmfoʊ/ INFORMAL n. [C] a woman who wants to have sex often, usually with a lot of different men —**nymphomaniac** adj. —**nymphomania** /ˌnɪmfəˈmeɪniə/ n. [U]

NYSE n. [singular] the abbreviation of NEW YORK STOCK EXCHANGE

N.Z. also **NZ** the written abbreviation of New Zealand

O

O, o /oʊ/ *n. plural* **O's, o's** [C] **1** the 15th letter of the English alphabet **2** SPOKEN a zero

O¹ /oʊ/ *interjection* **1** POETIC used to show respect when speaking to someone or something: *O Lord, hear our prayer.* **2** another form of OH

O² /oʊ/ *n.* [U] a common human blood type

o' /ə/ *prep.* NONSTANDARD a way of writing "of" as it is usually said in speech: *a cup o' coffee*

oaf /oʊf/ *n.* [C] a stupid, awkward man or boy: *Watch it, you big oaf!* —**oafish** *adj.*

O·a·hu /oʊˈɑhu/ an island in the Pacific Ocean that is part of the U.S. state of Hawaii and contains its capital city, Honolulu

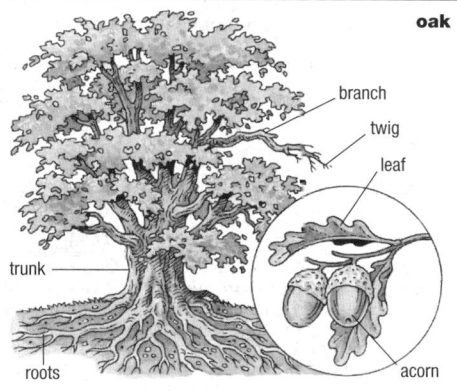

oak

branch
twig
leaf
trunk
roots
acorn

s w
3
oak /oʊk/ *n.* [C,U] a large tree that is common in northern countries, or the hard wood of this tree: *oak floors* —see also POISON OAK

oak·en /ˈoʊkən/ *adj.* ESPECIALLY LITERARY made of oak: *an oaken table*

Oak·ley /ˈoʊkli/**, An·nie** /ˈæni/ (1860–1926) a U.S. woman who was very skilled at shooting, and who performed in BUFFALO BILL's Wild West show

oa·kum /ˈoʊkəm/ *n.* [U] small pieces of old rope used for filling up small holes in the sides of wooden ships

oar /ɔr/ *n.* [C] a long pole with a wide flat blade at one end, used for rowing a boat —compare PADDLE¹ (1)

oar·lock /ˈɔrlɑk/ *n.* [C] one of the U-shaped pieces of metal on a boat that holds the oars

oars·man /ˈɔrzmən/ *n.* [C] someone who rows a boat, especially in races

oars·wom·an /ˈɔrzˌwʊmən/ *n.* [C] a woman who rows a boat, especially in races

OAS, the the Organization of American States; an organization whose members include the U.S. and Canada and most of the countries of Central and South America. Its aims are to preserve peace and to help the economic development of the area.

o·a·sis /oʊˈeɪsɪs/ *n. plural* **oases** /-siz/ [C] **1** a place with water and trees in a desert **2** a peaceful or pleasant place that is very different from everything around it: *The restaurant is a little oasis in the middle of downtown Los Angeles.*

oath /oʊθ/ *n. plural* **oaths** /oʊðz, oʊθs/ **1** [C] a formal and very serious promise, especially a promise to be loyal to someone: *He **swore an oath to** defend the Constitution.* **2** [singular] a formal promise to tell the truth in a court: *Lying **under oath** is a serious offense.* | *The first thing you will do as a witness in court is to **take the oath** (=make this promise).* **3 take the oath of office** to make an official promise to do your job well before taking an important government job: *Branstad took the oath of office of governor this afternoon.* **4** [C] an expression of strong

feeling that uses religious or sexual words in an offensive way: *He shouted oaths and curses as they took him away.*

oat·meal /ˈoʊtˌmil/ *n.* [U] crushed oats that are boiled and eaten for breakfast, or used in cooking

oats /oʊts/ *n.* [plural] **1** a grain that is eaten by people and animals **2** oatmeal —see also **sow your wild oats** (SOW¹ (3))

O·ba·di·ah /ˌoʊbəˈdaɪə/ a book in the Old Testament of the Christian Bible

ob·du·rate /ˈɑbdərət/ *adj.* FORMAL overly determined not to change your beliefs or feelings, or showing this quality: *She remained obdurate despite their pleas.* —**obduracy** *n.* [U]

o·be·di·ence /əˈbidiəns, oʊ-/ *n.* [U] obedient behavior or willingness to obey: [+ to] *Robin's obedience to her mother.* | *She **demands obedience** from all her staff.*

o·be·di·ent /əˈbidiənt, oʊ-/ *adj.* **1** always doing what you are told to do by your parents, by someone in authority etc.: *Edmund was a cheerful and obedient student.* **2 your obedient servant** OLD USE used to end a very formal letter —**obediently** *adv.* —opposite DISOBEDIENT

o·bei·sance /oʊˈbeɪsəns/ *n.* [C,U] FORMAL an act of showing respect and obedience, especially by bending your head or the upper part of your body: *Worshippers rang bells and **paid obeisance** to the gods.*

ob·e·lisk /ˈɑbəlɪsk/ *n.* [C] **1** a tall pointed stone PILLAR (1) **2** a DAGGER (1) sign used in printing

o·bese /oʊˈbis/ *adj.* very fat in a way that is unhealthy: *At least 25% of Americans are considered obese.* —see Usage Note at FAT¹

o·be·si·ty /oʊˈbisəti/ *n.* [U] the condition of being too fat in a way that is dangerous to your health

obey

COME HERE!

obey

COME HERE!

disobey

o·bey /əˈbeɪ, oʊ-/ *v.* [I,T] to do what someone in a position of authority tells you to do, or to do what a law or rule says you must do: *Look how well their dog obeys.* | *I expect my students to obey me.* | *Children should be taught to **obey the law**.* —opposite DISOBEY

ob·fus·cate /ˈɑbfəˌskeɪt/ *v.* [T] FORMAL to deliberately make something unclear or difficult to understand: *Politicians have once again obfuscated the issue.* —**obfuscation** /ˌɑbfəˈskeɪʃən/ *n.* [U]

ob/gyn also **ob-gyn** /ˌoʊ bi ˌdʒi waɪ ˈɛn/ *n.* **1** [U] the part of medical science that deals with OBSTETRICS and GYNECOLOGY **2** [C] a doctor who works in this part of medical science

o·bit /ˈoʊbɪt/ *n.* [C] INFORMAL an obituary

o·bit·u·ar·y /əˈbɪtʃuˌɛri, oʊ-/ *n. plural* **obituaries** [C] a report in a newspaper about the life of someone who has just died

ob·ject¹ /ˈɑbdʒɪkt, ˈɑbdʒɛkt/ *n.* [C]
1 **thing** a thing that you can hold, touch, or see, which is usually small: *a small metal object*
2 **purpose** [usually singular] the purpose of a plan, action, or activity: [+ of] *The object of the game is to score points by kicking the ball into the goal.* | *The*

s w
2 2

*changes will benefit the customer most, and that is, of course, **the object of the exercise** (=the purpose of what you are doing).*
3 an object of pity/desire/contempt etc. someone or something that is pitied, desired etc.: *He became an object of hatred and ridicule.* —see also SEX OBJECT
4 money/expense/cost is no object used to say that it does not matter to you if something cost a lot of money: *Pick out whatever you want – money is no object.*
5 grammar TECHNICAL a noun, noun phrase, or pronoun representing **a)** the person or thing that is directly affected by the action of a verb in a sentence. In the sentence "Sheila closed the door," "door" is a DIRECT OBJECT —compare SUBJECT[1] (5) **b)** the person or thing that is affected by an action in an indirect way. In the sentence "She gave Troy the book," "Troy" is an INDIRECT OBJECT **c)** the person or thing that is joined by a preposition to another word or phrase. In the sentence "He sat on the bench," "bench" is the object of the preposition
6 an object lesson an event or story that shows you the best or worst way of doing something: *Boilly was both artist and businessman, and his life is **an object lesson in** the handling of an artist's career.*

ob·ject[2] /əb'dʒɛkt/ *v.* **1** [I,T] to complain or protest about something, or to feel or say that you oppose it or disapprove of it: *His supporters will certainly object if he is fired.* | *"My name's not Sonny," the child objected.* | [+ **to**] *My boyfriend doesn't object to my job at the bar.* | *Rebecca objects to being asked out by people at work.* | [+ **that**] *A delegate rose to object that the vote was meaningless.* **2 I object** SPOKEN, FORMAL used in very formal meetings, discussions etc. to say that you disagree with what someone has said: *Mr. Chairman, I object. That is an unfair allegation.* —**objector** *n.* [C] —see also CONSCIENTIOUS OBJECTOR

object code /'.. ,./ *n.* [U] MACHINE CODE

ob·jec·tion /əb'dʒɛkʃən/ *n.* [C] **1** a reason against doing something, for not accepting something etc.: [+ **to**] *Her biggest objection to pets is that they're dirty.* | *CACP is an influential citizens group with **strong objections** to the death penalty.* | **raise/voice an objection** (=state an objection) **2** a feeling of opposing or disapproving of an action, idea etc.: *Beckler **had no objection** to the plan* (=was not annoyed or upset by it). **3 objection!** SPOKEN said by lawyers to a judge in a court when they do not think that what another lawyer has just said should be allowed

ob·jec·tion·a·ble /əb'dʒɛkʃənəbəl/ *adj.* immoral and likely to offend people; OFFENSIVE: *rock songs with objectionable words*

ob·jec·tive[1] /əb'dʒɛktɪv/ *n.* [C] **1** something that you are working hard to achieve: **main/primary/principal objective** *Our main objective is to win the tournament.* **2** a place that you are trying to reach, especially in a military attack: *The 4th Division's objective was a town 20 miles to the east.*

objective[2] *adj.* **1** based on facts, or making a decision based on facts rather than on personal feelings: *Originally, I went to the counselor because I needed an objective opinion about the whole situation.* | *Sometimes it's hard to be objective when the situation gets emotional.* —compare SUBJECTIVE (1) **2** FORMAL existing outside the mind as something real, rather than as just an idea; REAL: *There are no objective signs of injury on the body.* | *objective reality* **3** TECHNICAL relating to an OBJECT of a sentence: *the objective case* —**objectivity** /,ɑbdʒɛk'tɪvəti/ *n.* [U] *I'm not sure I have the objectivity to evaluate his work fairly.*

ob·jec·tive·ly /əb'dʒɛktɪvli/ *adv.* if you consider something objectively, you try to think about it without being influenced by your own feelings or opinions: *Try to look at your situation objectively.*

ob·jet d'art /,ɑbʒeɪ 'dɑr, ,ɔb-/ *n. plural* **objets d'art** /,ɑbʒeɪ 'dɑr, ,ɔb-/ [C] a small object, used for decoration, that has some value as art

ob·li·gate /'ɑblə,geɪt/ *v.* [T usually passive] **1** to make someone have to do something because it is right, a duty etc.: [**be obligated to do sth**] *Tenants are obligated to pay their rent on time.* **2 be/feel obligated** to feel that you have to do something because someone has done something nice for you: [**be/feel obligated to do sth**] *I don't want him to feel obligated to wear the shirt just because I gave it to him.* | [**feel obligated to sb**] *She felt obligated to Mr. Walters for the loan.*

ob·li·ga·tion /,ɑblə'geɪʃən/ *n.* [C,U] a moral or legal duty to do something: [**an obligation to do sth**] *I feel an obligation to tell the truth about what I know.* | [+ **to**] *We have an obligation to our customers.* | *The firm said it would continue to **meet** any legal **obligations** (=do what it should do) to the men.* | *You **are under no obligation** (=do not have to) answer these questions.* | *Russo said he stayed with the team out of a strong **sense of obligation** (=feeling that he should stay).*

o·blig·a·to·ry /ə'blɪgə,tɔri/ *adj.* **1** FORMAL something that is obligatory must be done because of a law, a rule etc.; MANDATORY: *Voting is obligatory for Brazilians aged 18 to 69.* **2 the obligatory hat/jokes/photo etc.** HUMOROUS used to describe something that must be done, worn, or included in a particular type of situation because it is always done in that way: *Who could enjoy a barbecue without the obligatory bottle of beer?*

o·blige /ə'blaɪdʒ/ *v.* FORMAL **1** [T usually passive] to make someone feel that it is necessary to do something: [**be/feel obliged to do sth**] *We feel obliged to respond to the inaccurate letters that have appeared in your paper.* **2** [I,T] to do something that someone has asked you to do: [**oblige sb**] *The brothers obliged police by turning down the music.* | *If you need a ride home, I'd **be happy to oblige**.* **3 I/we would be obliged if** used in formal letters to ask someone to do something for you: *I would be obliged if you could send me a copy of the contract as soon as possible.* **4 (I'm/we're) much obliged** SPOKEN, OLD-FASHIONED used to thank someone very politely

o·blig·ing /ə'blaɪdʒɪŋ/ *adj.* willing and eager to help: *an obliging landlord* —**obligingly** *adv.*

o·blique /ə'blik, oʊ-/ *adj.* **1** not expressed in a direct way: *Reneé made oblique references to his drinking problem.* **2** not straight or direct: *an oblique route* **3** sloping: *an oblique line* —**obliquely** *adv.* —**oblique** *n.* [C]

oblique an·gle /.,. '../ *n.* [C] TECHNICAL an angle that is not 90°, 180°, or 270°

ob·lit·er·ate /ə'blɪtə,reɪt/ *v.* [T] **1** to destroy something so completely that almost nothing remains: *Large areas of the city were obliterated during World War II.* **2** to cover something completely so that it cannot be seen: *The thick smog hung in the air, obliterating the hills from view.* **3** to remove a thought, feeling, or memory from someone's mind: *Nothing could obliterate the memory of those tragic events.* —**obliteration** /ə,blɪtə'reɪʃən/ *n.* [U]

ob·liv·i·on /ə'blɪviən/ *n.* [U] **1** the state of being completely forgotten: *CDs continue to push vinyl records toward oblivion.* **2** the state of being unconscious or of not noticing what is happening: *the oblivion of sleep*

ob·liv·i·ous /ə'blɪviəs/ *adj.* [not before noun] not knowing about or not noticing something that is happening around you; UNAWARE: [+ **to/of**] *Customers ate doughnuts at the counter, oblivious to the robbery taking place.* —**obliviousness** *n.* [U]

ob·long /'ɑblɔŋ/ *adj.* an oblong shape is much longer than it is wide: *an oblong pan* —**oblong** *n.* [C]

ob·lo·quy /'ɑbləkwi/ *n. plural* **obloquies** [U] FORMAL **1** very strong, offensive criticism **2** loss of respect and honor

ob·nox·ious /əb'nɑkʃəs/ *adj.* **1** very offensive or not nice: *Eddie is an obnoxious, insecure creep.* **2** extremely bad: *obnoxious sewage smells* —**obnoxiously** *adv.* —**obnoxiousness** *n.* [U]

o·boe /'oʊboʊ/ *n.* [C] a wooden musical instrument, shaped like a narrow tube, which you play by blowing air through a REED (2)

o·bo·ist /'oʊboʊɪst/ *n.* [C] someone who plays the oboe

ob·scene /əb'sin, ɑb-/ *adj.* **1** relating to sex in a shocking and offensive way: *The driver cursed at him and made an obscene gesture.* | *obscene photographs* | *She reported receiving several obscene phone calls* (=calls from an unknown person saying obscene things). **2** extremely immoral and unfair in a way that makes you angry: *You wouldn't believe the obscene profits these oil companies are making.* **3** SPOKEN extremely ugly in a way that shocks you: *This guy's thighs were so huge, it was obscene!* —**obscenely** *adv.*

ob·scen·i·ty /əb'sɛnəti/ *n. plural* **obscenities 1** [C usually plural] a sexually offensive word or action: *Protestors hurled rocks and screamed obscenities.* **2** [U] sexually offensive language or behavior, especially in a book, play, movie etc.: *laws against obscenity*

ob·scur·ant·is·m /əb'skyʊrən,tɪzəm/ *n.* [U] FORMAL the practice of deliberately stopping ideas and facts from being known —**obscurantist** *adj.*

ob·scure¹ /əb'skyʊr/ *adj.* **1** not well known at all, and usually not very important: *an obscure Flemish painter* | *obscure regulations* **2** difficult to understand: *The connection between the studies is somewhat obscure.*

obscure² *v.* [T] **1** to make something difficult to know or understand: *Recent successes obscure the fact that the company is still in trouble.* **2** to prevent something from being seen or heard clearly: *Parts of the coast were obscured by fog.*

ob·scur·i·ty /əb'skyʊrəti/ *n. plural* **obscurities 1** [U] the state of not being known or remembered: *Arbuckle died in obscurity in 1933.* **2** [C,U] something that is difficult to understand, or the quality of being difficult to understand: *obscurities in the text* **3** [U] LITERARY darkness

ob·se·quies /'ɑbsəkwiz/ *n.* [plural] FORMAL a funeral ceremony

ob·se·qui·ous /əb'sikwiəs/ *adj.* too eager to serve people and agree with them; SERVILE: *The salesman's obsequious manner was beginning to irritate me.* —**obsequiously** *adv.*

ob·serv·a·ble /əb'zɝvəbəl/ *adj.* able to be seen or noticed: *the observable universe* —**observably** *adv.*

ob·serv·ance /əb'zɝvəns/ *n.* **1** [C,U] a celebration of a religious or national event: *Most businesses are closed in observance of Christmas.* | *Veterans Day observances* **2** [U] the practice of obeying a law or a rule: [+ of] *the observance of human rights*

ob·serv·ant /əb'zɝvənt/ *adj.* **1** good or quick at noticing things: *Police are trained to be observant and to remember detail.* **2** obeying laws, religious rules etc.: *observant Muslims*

ob·ser·va·tion /,ɑbzɝ'veɪʃən, -sɝ-/ *n.* **1** [C,U] the process of watching something or someone carefully for a period of time: *a long-term observation of the solar system* | *The beached whale was under observation* (=being continuously watched) *throughout the night.* **2** [C] a spoken or written remark about something you have noticed: [+ on] *Friedan's observations on the women's movement today* | *Buñuel made some humorous observations about local politics.* **3 powers of observation** your natural ability to notice what is happening around you **4** [U] the act of obeying a law, rule etc.; OBSERVANCE (2) —**observational** *adj.*

observation post /.'.. ,./ *n.* [C] a position from which an enemy can be watched

observation tow·er /.'.. ,./ *n.* [C] a tall structure built so that you can see a long way, which is used, for example to watch prisoners, look for forest fires etc.

ob·serv·a·to·ry /əb'zɝvə,tɔri/ *n. plural* **observatories** [C] a special building from which scientists watch the moon, stars, weather etc.: *the Griffith Observatory*

ob·serve /əb'zɝv/ *v.* [T] **1** to watch something or someone carefully: *The space shuttle crew will observe the atmosphere, aurora, and stars.* | [observe

what/how/where] *Researchers are eager to observe how the change takes place.* **2** [not in progressive] FORMAL to see and notice something: [observe sb doing sth] *Officers observed Cox driving on the wrong side of the road.* | [observe that] *Doctors have observed that the disease only occurs in women over 50.* | [observe sth] *The car I had observed earlier was no longer there.* **3** to do what you are supposed to do according to a law, agreement, etc.: *Rebels continue to observe the truce.* **4** FORMAL to celebrate a holiday, a religious or national event etc.: *Zella and George observed their 55th wedding anniversary last August.* **5** FORMAL to say what you have noticed about a situation: [observe that] *Gresham, a noted culinary writer, observed that "cooking without herbs is not really cooking at all."*

ob·serv·er /əb'zɝvɚ/ *n.* [C] **1** someone who regularly watches or pays attention to particular things: *Political observers say Ball could still win the election.* | [+ of] *an observer of nature* **2** someone who is sent to meetings, classes, an area etc. to check what is happening and report any problems, changes, illegal actions etc.: *International observers criticized the use of military force in the region.* **3** someone who sees or notices something: *To the casual observer* (=someone who does not look carefully) *the old building may seem sturdy, but it is in great need of repair.*

ob·sess /əb'sɛs/ *v.* **1** [T usually passive] if something or someone obsesses you, you think about them all the time and you cannot think of anything else: [be obsessed with sb/sth] *Why are you so obsessed with your hair?* | *Jody has been obsessed with some life guard for months.* | [obsess sb] *The fact that much of our world is dying obsesses me.* **2** [I] INFORMAL to think about something or someone much more than is necessary or sensible: [+ over/ about] *Stop obsessing about your weight. You look fine.*

ob·ses·sion /əb'sɛʃən/ *n.* [C,U] an extreme, unhealthy interest in something, or worry about something, which stops you from thinking about anything else: *Freeing the hostages became his obsession.* | [+ with/about] *an obsession with sex* —**obsessional** *adj.*

ob·ses·sive /əb'sɛsɪv/ *adj.* thinking or worrying too much about someone or something so that you do not think about other things enough, or showing this quality: *She has an obsessive need to control everything.* | [obsessive about (doing) sth] *I tend to be a little obsessive about cleaning.* —**obsessively** *adv.*

obsessive-com·pul·sive /.,.. .'../ *adj.* TECHNICAL obsessive-compulsive behavior shows a tendency to think and worry too much, or repeat particular actions again and again as a result of strong anxiety, fear etc. —**obsessive-compulsive** *n.* [C]

ob·sid·i·an /əb'sɪdiən/ *n.* [U] a type of dark rock which looks like glass

ob·so·les·cence /,ɑbsə'lɛsəns/ *n.* [U] **1** the state of becoming old-fashioned and not useful anymore, because something else that is newer and better has been invented **2 planned/built-in obsolescence** the practice of making a product in such a way that it will soon become unfashionable or impossible to use

ob·so·les·cent /,ɑbsə'lɛsənt/ *adj.* becoming obsolete: *an obsolescent skill*

ob·so·lete /,ɑbsə'lit/ *adj.* not useful anymore because something newer and better has been invented: *obsolete technology* | *New computer developments have rendered our system obsolete.*

ob·sta·cle /'ɑbstɪkəl/ *n.* [C] **1** something that makes it difficult for you to succeed: [+ to] *There are no major environmental obstacles to building the golf course.* | *an obstacle in the way of economic recovery* **2** an object which blocks your way, so that you must go around it: *an obstacle in the road*

obstacle course /'... ,./ *n.* [C] **1** a line of objects that runners have to jump over, go under, climb through etc. in a race or as part of military training **2** a series of difficulties which must be dealt with to achieve a particular aim

ob·ste·tri·cian /ˌɑbstə'trɪʃən/ n. [C] a doctor who has special training in obstetrics

ob·stet·rics /əb'stɛtrɪks, ɑb-/ n. [U] the part of medical science that deals with the birth of children —**obstetric** adj.

ob·sti·nate /'ɑbstənɪt/ adj. DISAPPROVING determined not to change your opinions, ideas, behavior etc., or showing this quality; STUBBORN: *Ed is being obstinate again.* | *an obstinate refusal to face facts* —**obstinately** adv. —**obstinacy** n. [U]

ob·strep·er·ous /əb'strɛpərəs/ adj. noisy and refusing to agree or to do what someone else tells you to do, or showing this quality: *Some children placed on the drug became more subdued, less obstreperous.*

ob·struct /əb'strʌkt/ v. [T] **1** to block a road, passage etc.: *A wall of people in front of me were obstructing my view.* | *The truck was on its side, obstructing two lanes of traffic.* **2** to prevent someone from doing something by making it difficult for them: *Officials are hoping that none of these issues will obstruct progress in the peace talks.* | *Robbins was accused of obstructing the investigation.*

obstruction

ob·struc·tion /əb'strʌkʃən/ n. **1** [C,U] something that blocks a road, passage, tube etc., or the act of doing this: *They found an obstruction in one of the major arteries leading to the brain.* **2** [U] the act of trying to prevent or delay something from happening, especially a legal or political process: [+ of] *Kane could be charged with obstruction of justice for refusing to cooperate with authorities.* **3** [C] an offense in SOCCER, HOCKEY etc. in which a player gets between an opponent and the ball

ob·struc·tion·ism /əb'strʌkʃəˌnɪzəm/ n. [U] the practice of trying to prevent or delay a legal or political process —**obstructionist** n. [C]

ob·struc·tive /əb'strʌktɪv/ adj. **1** trying to prevent someone from doing something by deliberately making it difficult for them: *The socialists were accused of being obstructive and delaying the decision-making process.* **2** blocking a tube, passage etc.

s ᴡ **ob·tain** /əb'teɪn/ v. FORMAL **1** [T] to get something that you want, especially through your own effort, skill, or work: *Weisner is hoping to obtain funding for a follow-up study of the children.* | *Visitors must obtain a wilderness hiking permit to enter the park.* **2** [I not in progressive] if a situation, system, or rule obtains, it continues to exist: *These conditions no longer obtain.*

USAGE NOTE: OBTAIN

WORD CHOICE: get, obtain, achieve, receive
Get is the most common word in spoken English and informal writing meaning "to come to have something": *Where did you get that cup?* | *I only got $2500 for my car.* However, some people feel that **get** should not be used too often in writing. **Obtain** is a formal word that means to get something you want, especially by making an effort. It often sounds unnatural in spoken English or in a personal letter: *The agency obtained a $30 million loan.* | *We assumed the builders had obtained the proper permits.* If you get yourself into a better situation through your own efforts, you **achieve** something:

Abbot first achieved fame as a photographer in Paris in the 1920s. | *The conference will discuss the best ways to achieve job satisfaction.* You use the slightly formal word **receive** to mean get when you are given something, especially in an official situation: *The charity receives most of its money through private donations.*

---

ob·tain·a·ble /əb'teɪnəbəl/ adj. able to be obtained: *Radon gas can be detected using an easily obtainable device.*

ob·trude /əb'trud/ v. [I,T] FORMAL **1** if something obtrudes, or if you obtrude something, it becomes noticed where it is not wanted: [+ into/upon] *The author's personal taste is likely to obtrude into a book about wine.* **2** to stick out or make something stick out

ob·tru·sive /əb'trusɪv/ adj. noticeable in a way that is not nice: *Environmentalists are complaining that the amusement park is ugly and obtrusive.* | *Our waitress was friendly, but never obtrusive.*

ob·tuse /əb'tus, ɑb-/ adj. slow to understand things, in a way that is annoying: *Maybe I'm being obtuse, but I don't understand what you're so upset about.*

obtuse an·gle /ˌ.. '../ n. [C] TECHNICAL an angle between 90 and 180 degrees

ob·verse /'ɑbvɚs/ n. FORMAL **the obverse (of sth)** the opposite of a particular situation, feeling etc.: *She was the obverse of the devoted wife and mother.*

ob·vi·ate /'ɑbviˌeɪt/ v. [T] FORMAL to remove a difficulty: *New technologies have obviated the need for* (=made it unnecessary to do) *such extensive surgery.*

ob·vi·ous /'ɑbviəs/ adj. **1** easy to notice or understand: *an obvious mistake* | *There was no obvious reason for their behavior.* | [it is obvious (to sb) that] *It's obvious to everyone that he's unhappy.* | *Kyman is the obvious choice* (=the person who everyone would choose) *for team captain.* **2** be obvious (about sth) to behave in a way that shows you want something very badly, when other people think this behavior is not appropriate: *I know you want to go, but you don't have to be so obvious about it.* **3** state the obvious to say something that is already obvious and is therefore unnecessary: *Finally, at the risk of stating the obvious, I'd like to say that managers must manage better.* s ᴡ 2/2

ob·vi·ous·ly /'ɑbviəsli/ adv. used to mean that a fact can easily be noticed or understood: *He obviously likes you.* | *"Is she sorry?" "Obviously not, if she's still doing it."* | *The barber was obviously drunk.* —compare APPARENTLY, EVIDENTLY —see Usage Note at CERTAINLY s ᴡ 1/2

oc·a·ri·na /ˌɑkə'rinə/ n. [C] a small musical instrument shaped like an egg, that you blow through to play

O'Ca·sey /ou'keɪsi/, **Sean** /ʃɔn/ (1884–1964) an Irish writer of plays

oc·ca·sion¹ /ə'keɪʒən/ n. **1** [C] a time when something happens: *I've met with him on several occasions.* **2** [C] an important celebration, event, or ceremony: *I went out and bought a new dress just for the occasion.* | *We're saving the champagne for a special occasion.* **3** [singular,U] a good or appropriate time, reason or opportunity to do something: [+ for] *The summit is an occasion for different countries to exchange views.* | *I've never had occasion to dial 911 for emergency help.* **4** on occasion sometimes but not often: *Julie drops by my place on occasion.* **5** if/when the occasion arises if or when a particular action ever becomes necessary: *He could also be tough when the occasion arose.* —see also rise to the occasion/challenge (RISE¹ (14)), a sense of occasion (SENSE¹ (17)) s ᴡ 3/3

occasion² v. [T] FORMAL to cause something: *Milton's mismanagement of the company occasioned the loss of thousands of jobs.*

oc·ca·sion·al /ə'keɪʒənl/ adj. **1** happening sometimes but not often: *She still has occasional headaches.* | *I drink the occasional glass of wine, but not much else.* **2** doing something sometimes but not often: *an occasional smoker* **3** FORMAL written or intended for a special occasion: *occasional poems* s ᴡ

oc·ca·sion·al·ly /əˈkeɪʒənl-i/ *adv.* sometimes, but not regularly and not often: *He still occasionally goes out to bars.* | *We only see each other **very occasionally** (=rarely).*

occasional ta·ble /.ˈ... ,../ *n.* [C] a small light table that can be easily moved

Oc·ci·dent /ˈɑksədənt, -dɛnt/ *n.* **the Occident** LITERARY the western part of the world, especially Europe and the Americas —compare ORIENT²

oc·ci·den·tal /ˌɑksəˈdɛntl/ *n.* [C] FORMAL someone from the western part of the world —compare ORIENTAL¹ —**occidental** *adj.*

oc·clude /əˈklud/ *v.* [T] FORMAL to block an area or passage so that you cannot see or so that things cannot get through: *occluded arteries* —**occlusion** /əˈkluʒən/ *n.* [C]

oc·cult¹ /əˈkʌlt/ *n.* **the occult** mysterious practices and powers involving magic and spirits: *Dahmer's family feared he was involved in the occult.* —**occultist** *n.* [C]

occult² *adj.* mysterious and relating to magic and spirits: *occult beliefs*

oc·cu·pan·cy /ˈɑkyəpənsi/ *n.* [U] FORMAL **1** someone's use of a building, piece of land, or other space, for living or working in, or the period during which they live or work there: *The firm will **take occupancy** of the building October 1.* **2** the number of people allowed to stay, work, live, etc. in a room or building at the same time: *The new ordinance makes it illegal to limit occupancy to fewer than two people per bedroom.* | *The room was listed as $150 per night, **double occupancy** (=for two people).*

oc·cu·pant /ˈɑkyəpənt/ *n.* [C] FORMAL **1** someone who lives in a house, room etc.: *The letter was addressed to "Current Occupant."* **2** someone who is in a room, vehicle etc. at a particular time: *Neither of the car's two occupants was injured.*

oc·cu·pa·tion /ˌɑkyəˈpeɪʃən/ *n.* **1** [C] a job or profession: *The occupation of the third suspect is not known.* —see Usage Note at JOB **2** [U] the act of entering a place in a large group and taking control of it, especially by military force: *[- of] the German occupation of France* | *Union members are continuing their occupation of the factory.* **3** [C] FORMAL a way of spending your time; PASTIME: *One of my childhood occupations was collecting baseball cards.* **4** [U] the act of living or staying in a building or place: *When the first scientists came to the region they found little evidence of human occupation.*

oc·cu·pa·tion·al /ˌɑkyəˈpeɪʃənl/ *adj.* [only before noun] **1** relating to your job: *occupational training* **2 an occupational hazard** a risk that always exists in a particular job

occupational ther·a·py /..,... ˈ.../ *n.* [U] a form of treatment that helps people with physical or emotional problems do different activities —**occupational therapist** *n.* [U]

oc·cu·pi·er /ˈɑkyə,paɪɚ/ *n.* [C] someone who enters a place in a large group and takes control of it, especially by military force

oc·cu·py /ˈɑkyə,paɪ/ *v.* **occupies, occupied, occupying** [T]

1 stay in a place to live, exist, or stay in a particular place: *Movie stars occupy the large suites on the third floor.* | *The cafe occupies a single dimly lit room.*

2 fill time if something occupies you or your time, you are busy doing it: *Fishing occupies most of my spare time.* | *Glen **kept** the kids **occupied** by letting them drive the boat.* | *[be occupied with (doing) sth] Eisemann's time was occupied with ordering computer parts.*

3 seize and control to enter a place in a large group and take control of it, especially by military force: *Students occupied Sofia University on Monday.* | *an occupying army*

4 fill space to fill a particular amount of space: *Family photos occupied almost the entire wall.*

5 occupy sb's mind/thoughts/attention if something occupies your mind, thoughts, etc., you think about that thing more than anything else: *While she waited, she tried to occupy her mind with pleasant thoughts of the vacation.*

6 be occupied if a room, seat, or bed is occupied, someone is in it or using it

7 official position to have an official position or job: *All of the men occupied key supervisory positions for the state lottery.*

oc·cur /əˈkɚ/ *v.* **occurred, occurring** [I] FORMAL **1** to happen: *The explosion occurred at 5:30 a.m.* | *Giraldes claims he was with his wife when the killings occurred.* —see Usage Note at HAPPEN **2** [always + adv./prep.] to happen or exist in a particular place or situation: *[+ in/among etc.] Whooping cough occurs mainly in young children.*

occur to sb *phr. v.* [T not in passive] if an idea or thought occurs to you, it suddenly comes into your mind: *[it occurs to sb to do sth] I washed it in hot water – it never occurred to me to check the label.* | *[it occurs to sb that] Weird! It just occurred to me that that guy and your dog have the same name.*

oc·cur·rence /əˈkɚəns, -ˈkʌr-/ *n.* **1** [C] something that happens: *Rashes are **a common occurrence** among children.* | **a rare/unusual occurrence** (=something that does not happen often) **2** [U] the fact of something happening: *[+ of] You can reduce the occurrence of migraine headaches with aspirin.*

o·cean /ˈoʊʃən/ *n.* **1 the ocean** the great mass of salt water that covers most of the Earth's surface: *She stood on the beach, gazing at the ocean.* —see picture on page 428 **2** [C] one of the very large areas of water on the Earth's surface: *the Pacific Ocean* **3 oceans of sth** a great mass or amount of something: *oceans of collected data* —**oceanic** /ˌoʊʃiˈænɪk/ *adj.* —see also **a drop in the bucket/ocean** (DROP² (7))

o·cean·front /ˈoʊʃən,frʌnt/ *n.* [singular] the land along the edge of an ocean

o·cean-go·ing, ocean-going /ˈoʊʃən,goʊɪŋ/ *adj.* an oceangoing ship is designed to sail across the ocean: *an oceangoing tanker*

o·cean·og·ra·phy /ˌoʊʃəˈnɑgrəfi/ *n.* [U] the scientific study of the ocean —**oceanographer** *n.* [C]

oc·e·lot /ˈɑsə,lɑt/ *n.* [C] a large American wild cat that has a pattern of spots on its back

o·cher, ochre /ˈoʊkɚ/ *n.* [U] **1** a reddish-yellow earth used in paints **2** the color of ocher —**ochre** *adj.*

o'clock /əˈklɑk/ *adv.* **one/two/three etc. o'clock** one of the times when the clock shows the exact hour as a number from 1 to 12: *"It's already 5 o'clock."*

O'Con·nor /oʊˈkɑnɚ/, **Flan·ne·ry** /ˈflænəri/ (1925–1964) a U.S. writer of NOVELS

O'Connor, San·dra Day /ˈsændrə deɪ/ (1930–) a U.S. judge who became the first woman member of the SUPREME COURT in 1981

-ocracy /ɑkrəsi/ *suffix* [in nouns] a spelling of -CRACY used after CONSONANT sounds: *meritocracy* (=government by people with the most ability)

-ocrat /əkræt/ *suffix* [in nouns] a spelling of -CRAT used after CONSONANT sounds: *a technocrat* (=scientist who controls an organization or country) —**-ocratic** /əkrætɪk/ *suffix* —**-ocratically** /əkrætɪkli/ *suffix*

Oct. the written abbreviation of October

oc·ta·gon /ˈɑktə,gɑn/ *n.* [C] a flat shape with eight sides and eight angles —**octagonal** /ɑkˈtægənl/ *adj.*: *an octagonal room*

oc·tane /ˈɑkteɪn/ *n.* [U] a type of HYDROCARBON found in FUEL that is used as a measure of its quality: *high-octane gasoline*

oc·tave /ˈɑktəv/ *n.* [C] **1** the range of musical notes between the first note of a musical SCALE and the last one **2** the first and last notes of a musical SCALE played together

oc·tet /ɑkˈtɛt/ *n.* [C] **1** eight singers or musicians performing together **2** a piece of music for an octet

Oc·to·ber /ɑkˈtoʊbɚ/ *written abbreviation* **Oct.** *n.* [C,U] the tenth month of the year, between September and November —see Usage Note at JANUARY

oc·to·ge·nar·i·an /ˌɑktədʒəˈnɛriən/ *n.* [C] a person who is between 80 and 89 years old

oc·to·pus /'aktəpəs/ *n. plural* **octopuses** or **octopi** /-paɪ/ [C] an animal that lives in the ocean with eight TENTACLES (=arms)

octopus
tentacle

oc·u·lar /'akyələ/ *adj.* TECHNICAL relating to the eyes: *ocular movement*

oc·u·list /'akyəlɪst/ *n.* [C] OLD-FASHIONED a doctor who examines and treats people's eyes

OD /,oʊ 'di/ *v.* **OD'd, OD'ing** [I] SLANG **1** to take too much of a dangerous drug; OVERDOSE: [+ on] *"How did she die?" "She OD'd on heroin."* **2** to see, hear etc. too much of something —**OD** *n.* [C]

o·da·lisque /'oʊdl-ɪsk/ *n.* [C] LITERARY a beautiful female slave in former times

odd /ɑd/ *adj.*

1 strange different from what is normal or expected: *Timber? That's kind of an odd name for a kid.* | *Reynolds was an odd choice to host the show.* | *an odd combination* | [it is odd (that)] *It's odd that she can't remember more of it.*
2 **odd-looking/sounding** looking or sounding strange or unusual: *an odd-looking solar car*
3 **the odd moment/person/drink etc.** a few moments, people etc. that happen or appear at various times, but not often and not regularly: *I stopped writing down what he said, except for the odd phrase.* | *In addition to the odd horse or dog, there are always pigs on the road.*
4 various [only before noun] not specially chosen or collected: *Any odd scrap of paper will do.* | *The boys are earning money doing odd jobs* (=many different small pieces of work) *for neighbors.*
5 not in a pair/set [only before noun] separated from its pair or set: *an odd sock*
6 number an odd number cannot be divided exactly by two, for example 1, 3, 5, 7 —opposite EVEN² (5)
7 **20-odd/30-odd etc.** SPOKEN a little more than 20, 30 etc.: *None of the 30-odd passengers complained.*
8 **the odd man/one out** someone or something that is different or that is not included in the rest of a group: *I was always the odd man out in my class at school.* —see also ODDLY —**oddness** *n.* [U]

odd·ball /'ɑdbɔl/ *n.* [C] INFORMAL someone who behaves in a strange or unusual way —**oddball** *adj.*: *an oddball comedian*

Odd Fel·lows /'. ,../ an organization that gives its members help with medical costs, living in RETIREMENT, educating children etc.

odd·i·ty /'ɑdəti/ *n. plural* **oddities 1** [C] a strange or unusual person or thing: *A white buffalo is an animal oddity.* **2** [U] the quality of being strange or unusual: *The oddity of the situation didn't seem to bother her at all.* **3** [C] a strange quality in someone or something

odd lot /,. './ *n.* [C] an amount of something that is less than normal or usual: *To keep sales costs to a minimum, avoid trading in odd lots of less than 100 shares of stock.*

odd·ly /'ɑdli/ *adv.* **1** in a strange or unusual way: *Brenda's response was oddly reassuring.* | *an oddly dressed woman* **2** also **oddly enough** [sentence adverb] used to say that something seems strange or surprising: *Oddly enough, some of the best things about the broadcast were the commercials.* **3** **oddly matched/assorted** very different and looking strange together

odd·ments /'ɑdmənts/ *n.* [plural] small things of no value, or pieces of a material that were not used when something was made

odds /ɑdz/ *n.* [plural] **1** how likely it is that something will or will not happen, especially when this can be stated in numbers: [+ of] *Benton realized the odds of getting the position were not very good.* | **Odds are** (=it is likely) *they'll win, based on their past performance.* | **The odds against** *an alien landing on earth this century are 100–1.* | *Some scientists believe there are things you can do to change* **the odds in favor of** *giving birth to a girl or a boy.* **2** **be at odds a)** to disagree: [+ with/over] *The NAACP is at odds with some black parents who earn too much to qualify for the tax credit.* | *State lawmakers are at odds over* (=disagree about) *which experts to believe.* **b)** if two statements, descriptions, actions etc. are at odds with each other, they are different although they should be the same: [+ with] *Burt's latest evidence is at odds with his earlier statements.* **3** difficulties that make a good result seem very unlikely: *Assad overcame great odds to become commander of the air force.* | *Our team won the title* **against all odds** (=in spite of many difficulties). **4** **the odds are (stacked) against sb/sth** INFORMAL used to say that it will be very difficult for someone or something to succeed: *The odds are stacked against kids from poor families going to college.* **5** numbers based on the PROBABILITY of a horse winning a race, or a particular result in any competition, which show how much you can increase your money if you BET¹ (1) on the one that wins: *I bet $10 on Broadway Flyer with the* **odds at** *6–1.* | *I wouldn't* **lay odds on** (=be willing to risk your money on) *the outcome of that race.* | **long/short odds** (=odds based on a high or low risk of losing) | **set/offer (sb) odds** (=to officially say what the odds for a competition are)

odds and ends /,. . '. / *n.* [plural] small things of various kinds, without much value: *We packed just about everything, but probably left some odds and ends behind.*

odds-mak·er /'ɑdz,meɪkə/ *n.* [C] someone who decides what the chance of someone winning a race or game is, so that people can BET on it, especially in sports such as horse racing

odds-on /,. '. ◁ / *adj.* **the odds-on favorite** the competitor that is most likely to win a race, election, competition etc.

ode /oʊd/ *n.* [C] a poem or song that is written in order to praise a person or thing: *Beethoven's "Ode to Joy"*

O·dets /oʊ'dɛts/, **Clif·ford** /'klɪfəd/ (1903–1963) a U.S. writer of plays

O·din /'oʊdn/ in Norse MYTHOLOGY, the king of the gods

o·di·ous /'oʊdiəs/ *adj.* FORMAL making you feel strong dislike or DISGUST.: *The taking of hostages is an odious crime.* | *the odious task of scrubbing floors* —**odiously** *adv.*

o·dom·e·ter /oʊ'dɑmətə/ *n.* [C] an instrument in a vehicle that records the distance it has traveled —see picture on page 427

o·dor /'oʊdə/ *n.* [C] a smell, especially a bad one: *Neighbors had noticed a foul odor coming from the apartment.* —see also BODY ODOR —see Usage Note at SMELL¹

o·dor·if·er·ous /,oʊdə'rɪfərəs/ *adj.* LITERARY OR HUMOROUS odorous

o·dor·less /'oʊdəlɪs/ *adj.* having no smell: *an odorless gas*

o·dor·ous /'oʊdərəs/ *adj.* LITERARY having a smell, especially a pleasant one —compare MALODOROUS

O·dys·se·us /oʊ'dɪsiəs/ in ancient Greek stories, the King of Ithaca and husband of Penelope, whose trip home after the Trojan War is described in the poem "The Odyssey" by Homer

od·ys·sey /'ɑdəsi/ *n. plural* **odysseys** [C] **1** a long trip with many adventures or difficulties: *Clarke's cross-country odyssey began in South Carolina.* **2** a series of experiences that teach you something about yourself or about life in general: *a spiritual odyssey*

OECD *n.* **the OECD** the Organization for Economic Cooperation and Development; a group of rich countries who work together to develop trade and economic growth

oed·i·pal /'ɛdəpəl/ *adj.* related to an Oedipus complex: *oedipal longings*

Oe·di·pus /'ɛdɪpəs/ in ancient Greek stories, a man who did not know who his parents were, and killed his father and married his mother

Oedipus com·plex /'... ,../ *n.* [C] an unconscious sexual desire that a son feels for his mother, combined with a hatred for his father, according to Freudian PSYCHOLOGY —compare ELECTRA COMPLEX

o'er /ɔr/ *adv. prep.* POETIC over

oeu·vre /'uvrə/ *n.* [C] LITERARY all the works of an artist, such as a painter or writer, considered as a whole

of /əv, ə; *strong* ʌv/ *prep.* **1** used to show a feature or quality that something has: *the brightness of the sun | the smell of roses | the length of the driveway* **2** used to show that something is part of something else: *the first chapter of the book | I had a pain in the back of my leg | the ground floor of the building | all the details of the agreement* **3** used to show that something belongs to someone: *a cousin of mine | a friend of the family | a car of his own* **4** used to talk about a group or collection of people or things: *a flock of birds | a pack of cigarettes | a bunch of grapes* **5** used to talk about an amount or measurement of something: *a gallon of milk | ten pounds of cheese | a teaspoonful of baking soda | a cup of coffee* **6** used to talk about a particular person or thing from a larger group of the same people or things: *a member of the rock group | most of the students | That's one of her best poems.* **7** used in dates, before the name of a month: *the 12th of October* **8** used when giving the name of something or being more specific about something that is very general: *the game of chess | at the age of fifty | the city of New Orleans* **9 a)** used after nouns describing actions, to show who the action is done to: *the hiring of new workers* (=when new workers are hired) *| the introduction of a minimum wage* **b)** used after nouns describing actions, to show who does the action: *We could hear the barking of dogs.* **10** used to say which particular subject, person, thing etc. another subject, person, or thing is related to or deals with: *the president of the company | the difficulties of buying your own home | the decision of the city council* **11** used to describe a person or thing, showing what their main qualities or features are: *Albright was seen as a woman of great determination* (=as a very determined woman). *| The ring was an object of great beauty. | weapons of mass destruction* **12 a) the day/year etc. of sth** the day, year etc. that something happened: *the day of the accident | the week of the carnival* **b) ...of the day/year etc.** the best or most important person or thing during a particular period: *Midfielder Dennis Bergkamp was voted Player of the Month* **13** SPOKEN used in giving the time, to mean before: *a quarter of seven* (=6:45) **14** FORMAL used to say what substance or material something is made of: *a crown of gold and silver | The bride wore a dress of white silk.* **15** used to show that something is the result of something else: *He died of cancer. | the effects of overeating* **16** used to show where something is or how far it is from something else: *a small town to the west of Kansas City | The school is three blocks south of the park.* **17** used to say who writes a play, who paints a painting etc.: *the writings of a lunatic | the work of professional thieves* **18** used to show what a picture, story etc. is about or who is in it: *a map of the world | a photograph of my grandmother | a history of modern China* **19** about: *Have you ever heard of the poet T.S. Eliot? | News of Kirkland's arrest was all over town.* **20** used to say where someone comes from: *the people of Malaysia | Jesus of Nazareth* **21 it is kind/stupid/careless etc. of sb to do sth** used to say that something has done shows that they are kind, stupid etc.: *It was smart of you to bring extra food to the picnic.* —see also **of course** (COURSE¹ (1))

of course /. '../ *adv.* —see **of course** (COURSE¹ (1))

0

USAGE NOTE: OF

GRAMMAR
When you want to say that something belongs to someone, you usually use **'s** or plural **s'** rather than **of**: *her boyfriend's car | my parents' house.* But you can use **of** to say that something belongs to or is part of something else: *the corner of the street | the top of the mountain.* You also use **'s** and **s'** to talk about periods of time, for example: *a day's work | three weeks' vacation.* **'s** can also be used with the names of places, especially in newspapers: *America's most popular amusement park | China's recent history.* When you use words like **a, some, the, this** etc. with the word for something that belongs to someone, or the person you are talking about in connection with them, you can use both **of** and **'s** together: *an old boyfriend of Sarah's.*

off¹ /ɔf/ *adv.* **1** away or from where something is: *Nancy waved good-bye as she drove off. | The suspects quickly turned off onto a side road. | I saw him hurrying off to catch his plane. | We're off* (=we are leaving). *| It happened while his wife was off on a business trip.* **2** out of a bus, train, car etc.: *I'll get off at the next stop. | We need to stop and get gas soon.* **3** removed or not fastened to something anymore: *Can anyone get this lid off? | Take off your shoes.* **4** a machine, piece of equipment etc. that is off is not working or operating: *All the lights were off when I got home. | The engine shuts off automatically* (=makes itself stop working) *if it gets too hot. | Don't forget to turn off the oven.* —opposite ON² (5) **5** not at work, school etc. because you are sick or on vacation: *Carol is off for the whole week. | I'm going to take Thursday off to go to the dentist. | Do you get Christmas Eve off?* **6** lower in price by a particular amount: *Get 15% off on all winter coats in the store.* **7** an arranged event that is off will not happen: *I'm afraid the wedding's off. | Student leaders were asked to call off the protest march* (=arrange for it not to happen). **8** a particular distance away, or a particular amount of time away in the future: *Polly's wedding was still about six weeks off* (=it would happen six weeks in the future). *| I could see snow-capped mountains way off in the distance.* **9 off and on** also **on and off** for short periods but not regularly, over a long period of time: *Rachel and Alan have been dating off and on for five years.* **10** used in stage directions to mean that a sound or voice is not on the stage but still able to be heard in the theater; OFFSTAGE: *noises off* —see also BETTER OFF, WELL-OFF

off² *prep.* **1** not on something or someone, or not touching something or someone: *Get your feet off my couch. | Why are all of the lids off the paint cans? | Taking her hand off the steering wheel, Beth lit a cigarette.* —opposite ON¹ (1) **2** out of a bus, train, airplane etc.: *It was past midnight when I got off the bus in Cleveland.* **3** no longer held or supported by something: *One of the girls had fallen off her horse. | I finally took his picture off the wall.* **4** no longer connected or fastened to something: *Somehow my badge fell off my jacket. | James couldn't get the ring off his finger.* **5 off the subject/topic** not connected to a particular subject of conversation: *We're getting off the subject: Let's return to the Industrial Revolution. | Joe was clearly relieved to be off the topic of his ex-girlfriend* **6 a)** away from a particular place: *Three players had been sent off the field for fighting. | The other driver forced my car off the road.* **b)** near and connected to a path or road: *Oak Hills? Isn't that off Route 290? | The restrooms are just off* (=very near to) *the corridor, on the right.* **c)** in a body of water but near the land: *Coast Guard helicopters found the boat ten miles off Cape Cod. | an island off the coast of West Africa* **7** no longer taking something such as medicine or drugs: *He says he's been off cocaine for five months.* **8** taken or obtained from someone or something: *Mandy bought her T-shirt off some street vendor. | What do you plan to live off while you're studying?* **9** not in a particular

0

building, area etc.: *Our club had to meet off school grounds.*

off³ *adj.* **1** [not before noun] not as good as usual: *Sales figures for the third quarter are a little off compared to the second quarter.* **2** [not before noun] not exactly right or completely correct: *Our calculations were off.* | *Johnson's free throw shooting was off.* —see also **way off** (WAY² (1)) **3** [not before noun] TECHNICAL used to show that the STOCK EXCHANGE has fallen in value by a particular amount: *At the close of trading, the Dow Jones Index was off 28 points.* **4 an off day/week etc.** INFORMAL a day, week etc. when you are not doing something as well as you usually do it: *Everyone has an off day every now and then.* —see also OFF-SEASON

off⁴ *v.* [T] SLANG to kill someone

of·fal /ˈɔfəl, ˈɑ-/ *n.* [U] the inside organs of an animal, for example its heart, LIVER, and KIDNEYs, used as food

off-bal·ance /ˌ. ˈ..◂/ *adj.* **1** not prepared for something, so that it surprises you and you do not know what to do: *News of the merger caught us all off-balance.* **2** in an unsteady position so that you are likely to fall: *Tucker made a spectacular off-balance catch to end the game.* | **throw/knock/push sb off-balance** (=make someone fall or almost fall)

off·beat /ˌɔfˈbit◂/ *adj.* INFORMAL unusual and not what people normally expect, but in an interesting way: *an offbeat romance novel*

off-brand /ˌ. ˈ.◂/ *adj.* [only before noun] an off-brand product is made by a company that is not well known: *off-brand televisions* —**off-brand** *n.* [C] —compare NAME BRAND

off-Broad·way /ˌ. ˈ..◂/ *adj., adv.* an off-Broadway play is one that is performed outside the Broadway entertainment area in New York City and does not involve as much money as the famous plays on Broadway

off-cam·pus /ˌ. ˈ..◂/ *adj.* not on the CAMPUS (=the land and buildings) of a college or university: *off-campus housing for students*

off-cen·ter /ˌ. ˈ..◂/ *adj.* **1** not exactly in the center of something: *The picture is slightly off-center.* **2** INFORMAL different from other people, especially in a strange way: *Thompson's sense of humor was a little off-center.*

off-chance /ˈ. ./ *n.* **on the off-chance** hoping that something will happen, although it is unlikely: *I called on the off-chance that Patty might be home.*

off-col·or /ˌ. ˈ..◂/ *adj.* dealing with sex in a way that is not considered acceptable: *off-color jokes*

off-du·ty /ˌ. ˈ..◂/ *adj.* someone such as a police officer, nurse, or soldier is off-duty during the hours when they are not working: *The blaze was spotted by an off-duty fire-fighter.* | *Sorry, I'm off-duty now.*

of·fence /əˈfɛns/ the British and Canadian spelling of OFFENSE¹

of·fend /əˈfɛnd/ *v.* **1** [T] to make someone feel angry and upset, by doing or saying something that insults them or shows a lack of respect for them: *Some people are offended by swearing on television.* | *Jenny felt confused by Matt's behavior – had she done something to offend him?* | *The remarks deeply offended many in the African-American community.* **2** [I] to do something that is a crime: *The parole board felt that Harris was unlikely to offend again.* **3** [I,T] FORMAL to go against people's feelings of what is morally right: [+ against] *Broadcasters have a responsibility not to offend against good taste and decency.*

of·fend·er /əˈfɛndɚ/ *n.* [C] **1** someone who is guilty of a crime: *drug offenders* | *Prison officials announced a new program aimed at reducing the number of repeat offenders.* | **first-time offender** (=someone who has done a criminal action for the first time) —see also SEX OFFENDER **2** someone or something that is responsible for something bad that happens: *Among the causes of heart disease, smoking and high-fat foods are the worst offenders.*

of·fend·ing /əˈfɛndɪŋ/ *adj.* **the offending 1** causing people to feel angry or insulted: *NutriSystem pulled the offending ads from U.S. airwaves and publications.* **2** OFTEN HUMOROUS the thing that is causing a problem: *The offending food turned out to be spoiled potato salad.*

of·fense¹ /əˈfɛns/ *n.* **1** [C] an illegal action or a crime: *a parking offense that carries a $50 fine* | *Jones had committed two previous burglary offenses.* | *Cortese's bill would make it a criminal offense for minors to possess cigarettes.* | [+ against] *The military has committed numerous offenses against civilians.* | **first offense** (=the first illegal thing that someone has done) | **capital offense** (=a crime for which death is the punishment) | **federal offense** (=a very serious crime which the national government punishes) | **minor offense** (=one that is not very serious) **2** [U] hurt or angry feelings: *Briggs regrets that the book has caused offense* (=offended someone). | *Censorship laws ban anything that might give offense* (=offend someone). | *Rogers said he meant no offense* (=had no intention of offending) *to women.* **3 no offense** SPOKEN used to tell someone that you do not want to offend them by what you are about to say: *No offense, but could you put your shoes back on please.* **4 take offense** to feel angry and upset by what someone has said or done: *His jokes are mostly pretty harmless, though some people might take offense.*

of·fense² /ˈɔfɛns/ *n.* [U] **1** the part of a game such as football concerned with getting points, or the group of players who do this: *The Dallas Cowboys' offense is the best in the league.* | *The Lions need to be more aggressive on offense.* **2** FORMAL the act of attacking: *a weapon of offense* —compare DEFENSE²

of·fen·sive¹ /əˈfɛnsɪv/ *adj.* **1** very impolite or insulting, and likely to make people angry and upset: *Apparently some viewers found the show offensive.* | [+ to] *The novel has been criticized for being offensive to Muslims.* —opposite INOFFENSIVE **2** FORMAL disgusting: *an offensive smell* **3** [only before noun] related to the aim of getting points and winning a game, as opposed to stopping the other team from getting points: *the offensive player of the year* | *the Jets' offensive strategy* —compare DEFENSIVE¹ (3) **4** [only before noun] for attacking: *offensive weapons* | *Government troops took up offensive positions.* —compare DEFENSIVE¹ (1) —**offensively** *adv.*: *Government officials claimed that the planes would not be used offensively.* | *Rick's jokes were offensively sexist.* —**offensiveness** *n.* [U]

offensive² *n.* [C] **1** a planned military attack involving large forces over a long period: *Rebel forces have launched* (=started) *a major offensive to regain lost territory.* **2 be on the offensive** to be ready to attack or criticize people **3 take the offensive** also **go on the offensive** to be the first to make an attack or strong criticism: *He decided to go on the offensive before she could ask another question.* **4 sales/PR/diplomatic offensive** a planned set of actions intended to influence a lot of people

of·fer¹ /ˈɔfɚ, ˈɑfɚ/ *v.* **1** [T] to ask someone if they would like to have something, or to hold something out to them so that they can take it: [offer sb sth] *Can I offer you something to drink?* | *Sara has been offered a great part in a new movie.* | [offer sth to sb] *They are likely to offer the top job to someone from within the company.* **2** [T] to say that you are willing to pay a particular amount of money in exchange for something: [offer (sb) sth for sth] *Someone offered me $300 for the bike.* | *Robin is offering a reward for the return of her necklace.* **3** [I,T] to say that you are willing to do something for someone: *I'd like to offer help if you need it.* | [offer to do sth] *It was nice of Amy to offer to babysit this Friday.* **4** [T] to provide something that people need or want, such as information or services: *He offered no explanation for his actions.* | [offer sth to sb] *Both airlines offer a discount to travelers over 60.* **5 have much/plenty/a lot to offer** to have many qualities that people are likely to want or enjoy: *Mexico has a lot to offer in the way of great low-cost vacations.* **6 offer (up) a prayer/sacrifice etc.** to pray to God or give something to

God **7 offer your hand to sb** to hold out your hand in order to shake hands with someone **8 offer itself** FORMAL if an opportunity offers itself, it becomes available to you

offer² *n.* [C] **1** a statement that you are willing to give someone something or do something for them: [+ of] *an offer of employment* | [**offer to do sth**] *an offer to help* | **turn down/reject/refuse an offer** (=say "no" to an offer) **2** an amount of money that you are willing to pay for something: [**make (sb) an offer**] *McKrocklin made an offer of $43.5 million for the two properties.* | *We're prepared to make you a very generous offer.* | *Pan Am* **accepted an offer** *to sell its African and Asian routes.* **3** a reduction for a short time in the price of something that is for sale in a store: [+ on] *This special offer on GMC trucks is good for 30 days only.* **4 on offer** available to be bought or used: *We were disappointed by the standard of hotels on offer.*

of·fer·ing /ˈɔfrɪŋ, ˈɑ-/ *n.* [C] **1** something that has been produced for people to buy, see, read etc.: *the latest offering from Disney's Buena Vista studios* | *The lunch menu includes some tempting vegetarian offerings.* **2** STOCKS¹ (2) that are made available for people to buy: *Therapeutics Inc. is planning an offering of 2 million shares of common stock.* | *The* **offering price** (=the amount that a particular stock will cost) *is expected to be around $12 per share.* **3** money that is collected during a Christian religious service, or the part of a service when money is collected **4** something that is given to God or given as a present to please someone —see also PEACE OFFERING

of·fer·to·ry /ˈɔfətori, ˈɑ-/ *n.* [C] **1** the act of giving offerings to God in a Christian religious service **2** the music played in a Christian religious service while the offering is being collected

off guard /ˌ. ˈ.◂/ *adj.* **catch/throw/take sb off guard** to surprise someone by doing something they are not expecting and are not prepared to deal with: *The brief snow storm caught everyone off guard.*

off·hand¹ /ˌɔfˈhænd◂/ *adj.* **1** said or done without thinking or planning: *an offhand remark* **2** not caring or seeming not to care about something or someone: *I don't like his offhand manner.* —**offhandedness** *n.* [U]

offhand² *adv.* immediately, without time to think about it or find out about something: *I can't think offhand of anyone who'd be able to help you.*

of·fice /ˈɔfɪs, ˈɑ-/ *n.*
1 building [C] the building that belongs to a company or organization, with a lot of rooms where people work at desks: *The Department occupies an office just a mile from the White House.* | *I never really enjoyed working in an office.* | **main/head office** (=the most important office in a company) | *Did you go to the office* (=the office where you work) *today?* | *I must have left my keys at the office.*
2 room [C] a room where you do work that involves writing, calculating, or talking to people: *the supervisor's office* | *Frank shares an office with Shirley* (=they both work in the same room).
3 office hours a) the time between about nine in the morning and five in the afternoon, when the people in offices are working: *Call me back tomorrow during office hours.* **b)** the time during the day or week when students can meet with their teacher in the teacher's office: *Professor Lee's office hours are from 2 to 4 on Mondays and Thursdays.*
4 information/ticket etc. office a room or building where people go to ask for information, buy tickets etc. —see also BOX OFFICE, POST OFFICE
5 important job [C,U] an important job or position with power, especially in government: *the office of mayor* | *Brock has been* **in office** (=in an important position) *for three years now.* | *Mr. Christopher previously* **held office** *as Secretary of State.* | **take office** (=start an important job)
6 Office used in the names of some government departments: *the District Attorney's Office*
7 sb's good offices FORMAL help given by someone who has authority or can influence people: *The UN's good offices will be necessary in finding a peaceful solution to the crisis.*

office build·ing /ˈ.. ˌ../ *n.* [C] a large building with many offices in it

office hold·er /ˈ.. ˌ../ *n.* [C] someone who has an important official position, especially in the government

Office of Man·age·ment and Bud·get, the /ˌ... ˌ... . ˈ../ a U.S. government organization that provides help for the President in organizing the work of government departments and especially in preparing the BUDGET

office par·ty /ˈ.. ˌ../ *n.* [C] a party, usually just before Christmas, in the office of a company, government department etc. for the people who work there

of·fi·cer /ˈɔfəsə, ˈɑ-/ *n.* [C] **1** someone who is in a position of authority in the army, navy etc.: *a Marine officer* | *Cmdr. Gary G. Mahle is the commanding officer here.* **2** a police officer: *What's the problem, officer?* | *Crane has been an officer since 1966.* | *The investigation will be led by Officer Murdoch.* **3** someone who has an important position in an organization, such as a company or a government department: *the chief financial officer* | *the government contracting officer*

USAGE NOTE: OFFICER

WORD CHOICE: officer, official
An **officer** is someone in the police force or the military: *an army officer.* An **official** is someone in a government or business organization, in a position of authority: *Airline officials refused to comment to reporters while negotiations were continuing.*

---

of·fi·cial¹ /əˈfɪʃəl/ *adj.* **1** approved of or done by someone in authority, especially the government: *an official investigation into the causes of the explosion* | *Islam is the official religion of Saudi Arabia.* **2** done as part of your job and not for your own private purposes: *Senator Blake is here on official business.* | *The First Lady will make an official visit to Haiti.* **3** official information, reasons etc. are given formally and publicly, but may not always be true: *The official explanation for the crash was pilot error.* | *The news is not yet official.* (=has not been publicly announced) **4** [only before noun] chosen to represent a person or organization: *Visa is an official sponsor of the Winter Olympics.* | *The company's official logo* **5** [only before noun] an official event is a formal, public event: *the official opening of the new clinic*

official² *n.* [C] **1** someone who has a responsible position in an organization: *a union official* | *a government official* **2** a REFEREE —see Usage Note at OFFICER

of·fi·cial·dom /əˈfɪʃəldəm/ *n.* [U] a word meaning government departments or the people who work in them, used when you think they are unhelpful and have too many unnecessary rules

of·fi·cial·ly /əˈfɪʃəli/ *adv.* **1** publicly and formally: *Three players were officially reprimanded for fighting on the field.* | *At that stage, Britain and Germany were still not officially at war.* **2** [sentence adverb] according to what you say publicly, even though this may not be true: *Officially, Carter resigned, but everyone knows he was fired.*

of·fi·ci·ate /əˈfɪʃiˌeɪt/ *v.* [I + at] to do official duties, especially at a religious ceremony

of·fi·cious /əˈfɪʃəs/ *adj.* too eager to tell people what to do: *an officious guard at the security desk* —**officiously** *adv.* —**officiousness** *n.* [U]

off·ing /ˈɔfɪŋ/ *n.* **be in the offing** to be about to happen or to be possible: *Tighter airport security regulations could be in the offing.*

off-key /ˌ. ˈ.◂/ *adj.* music that is off-key does not sound good because it is played slightly above or below the correct PITCH¹ (3): *The lead singer was completely off-key.* —**off-key** *adv.*: *Harold always sings off-key.*

off·kil·ter /ˌ. '.·ˌ/ *adj.* **1** not completely straight or correctly balanced: *The paintings were slightly off-kilter.* **2** unusual, in a strange or interesting way: *her off-kilter sense of humor*

off lim·its /ˌ. '.·ˌ/ *adj.* **be off limits** if a place is off limits, you are not allowed to go there: [+ **to**] *The land is strictly off-limits to commercial developers.*

off·line /ˌɔf'laɪn·/ *adv.* when your computer is not connected to the Internet: *The software allows you to read and write email messages offline* —compare ONLINE —**offline** *adj.*

off·load /ˌɔf'loʊd/ *v.* [T] **1** to unload something from a truck or ship: *This is the part of the port where tankers offload their oil.* **2** to get rid of something that you do not need by giving it or selling it to someone else: [**offload sth onto sb**] *Some companies had offloaded substandard medicines onto Third World countries.*

off-off-Broad·way /ˌ. ˌ. '.ˌ/ *adj.* [only before noun] *adv.* off-off-Broadway plays, theater, events etc. are modern and often strange plays that do not cost a lot of money to make and are performed in New York City in places like churches and COFFEE HOUSES instead of in large theaters

off-peak /ˌ. '.·ˌ/ *adj.* **1** off-peak hours or periods are times when fewer people want to do something or use something: *Work on the highway will be done only during off-peak hours.* **2** off-peak travel is cheaper because it is done or used at these times

off-piste /ˌ. './ *adj.* not on a normal SKI SLOPE: *off-piste skiing* —**off-piste** *adv.*

off·print /'ɔfprɪnt/ *n.* [C] an article from a magazine that is printed and sold separately

off-ramp /'. ./ *n.* [C] a small road that leads from a HIGHWAY or FREEWAY to a street —compare ON-RAMP

off-road ve·hi·cle /ˌ. . '...ˌ/ *n.* [C] a vehicle that is built to be very strong so that it can be used on rough ground

off-screen /ˌ. '.·ˌ/ *adv.* when a movie actor is not acting: *Off-screen, Costner is a down-to-earth kind of guy.* —**off-screen** *adj.*: *off-screen romances*

off-sea·son /ˌ. '.·ˌ/ *n.* **the off-season a)** the time of the year when there is not much work or activity, especially in the tourist industry: *Travel packages to Hawaii are dirt cheap during the off-season.* **b)** the time in sports between the end one SEASON and the start of another, when teams do not play any games: *Mason works out everyday in the off-season.* —**off-season** *adj., adv.*: *off-season discounts*

off·set¹ /ˌɔf'sɛt, 'ɔfsɛt/ *v. past tense and past participle* **offset** *present participle* **offsetting** [T] **1** if something such as a cost or amount offsets another cost or amount, the two things have an opposite effect and so the situation remains the same: *Profits in GM's computer services were not enough to offset the huge losses in its automotive operations.* | [**be offset by**] *A fall in housing costs was offset by an increase in the cost of medical care.* **2** to make something look better by being close to it and different: *Streaks of blond in his hair offset his deep tan.*

off·shoot /'ɔfʃut/ *n.* [C] **1** an organization, system of beliefs etc. which has developed from a larger or earlier one: *the National Organization for Women and its offshoots* | [+ **of**] *The Samaritan religion is an offshoot of Judaism.* **2** a new stem or branch on a plant

off·shore /ˌɔf'ʃɔr·/ *adj.* **1** in the ocean, away from the shore: *offshore fishing* | *offshore oil reserves* **2 offshore bank/company/investment etc.** a bank etc. that is based abroad, in a country where you pay less tax than in your home country **3 offshore wind/current etc.** a wind etc. that is blowing or moving away from the land —compare INSHORE, ONSHORE —**offshore** *adv.*: *The ship was anchored half a mile offshore.*

off·side /ˌɔf'saɪd·/ *adj. adv.* in a position where you are not allowed to play the ball in sports such as SOCCER

off-site /ˌ. '.·ˌ/ *adj., adv.* happening away from a particular place, especially the place where someone works: *an off-site meeting*

off·spring /'ɔf,sprɪŋ/ *n. plural* **offspring** [C] **1** an animal's baby or babies **2** HUMOROUS someone's child or children

off·stage /ˌɔf'steɪdʒ·/ *adv.* **1** just behind or to the side of a stage in a theater, where the people watching a play cannot see: *There was a loud crash off-stage.* **2** when an actor is not acting: *Offstage, Peter always seemed a quiet, shy sort of person.* —**offstage** *adj.*

off-street /'. ./ *adj.* **off-street parking** places for parking that are not on main streets

off-the-cuff /ˌ. . '.·ˌ/ *adj.* [usually before noun] an off-the-cuff remark, reply etc. is one that you make without thinking about it first: *There were many hilarious discussions and off-the-cuff remarks.* —**off-the-cuff** *adv.*

off-the-rack /ˌ. . '.·ˌ/ *adj.* off-the-rack clothes are not specially made to fit one particular person, but are made in standard sizes —compare MADE-TO-MEASURE, MADE-TO-ORDER —**off the rack** *adv.*: *Like many tall women, Clare sometimes has problems buying clothes off the rack.*

off-the-rec·ord /ˌ. . '..·ˌ/ *adv.* if you say something off-the-record, your words are not official and are not supposed to be made public: *We were told off-the-record that the highway project would be canceled.* —**off-the-record** *adj.*: *an off-the-record briefing*

off-the-shelf /ˌ. . '.·ˌ/ *adj., adv.* already made and available in shops, not specially made for a particular customer: *off-the-shelf database software*

off-the-wall /ˌ. . '.·ˌ/ *adj.* INFORMAL a little strange or unusual, often in an amusing way: *Barkley was known for his sometimes outrageous and often off-the-wall commentary.*

off-track /ˌɔf'træk·/ *adj.* away from a place where horses race: *Few states allow offtrack betting.*

off-white /ˌ. '.·ˌ/ *n.* [U] a white that has some yellow or gray in it —**off-white** *adj.*: *an off-white blouse*

off-year /'. ./ *n.* [C usually singular] **1** a year when something is not as successful as usual: [+ **for**] *an off-year for car sales* **2** a year in which no elections happen

oft /ɔft/ *adv.* POETIC OR FORMAL often: *an oft-quoted author*

of·ten /'ɔfən, 'ɔftən/ *adv.* **1** if something happens often, or you do something often, it happens regularly or many times: *Rosi often works till 7 or 8 o'clock in the evening.* | *If you wash your hair too often, it can get too dry.* | *How often do you go out to dinner?* | *It's not often that a job like this comes along.* | *Lots of cars illegally park here, and quite often they are police cars.* | *I'm not home very often these days.* **2** [sentence adverb] if something happens often, it happens in many situations or cases: *The information is all there, but it's often difficult to find it.* | *Very often overweight children eat high-calorie foods that have little nutritional value.* **3 all too often** used to say that something sad, disappointing, or annoying happens too much: *I've seen cases of this kind of child abuse all too often.* **4 every so often** sometimes: *Every so often we go down to the beach.* **5 more often than not** also **as often as not** usually: *More often than not, low-paid service jobs are seen as just a short-term measure.*

of·ten·times /'ɔfən,taɪmz/ *adv.* often: *Oftentimes, these products are out of date almost as soon as they come on the market.*

o·gle /'oʊɡəl/ *v.* [I,T] to look at someone in an offensive way that shows you think they are sexually attractive: *The boys spent most of their time at the beach ogling girls in bikinis.*

o·gre /'oʊɡə/ *n.* [C] **1** a large ugly creature in children's stories who eats people **2** someone who seems cruel and frightening: *Her father was a real ogre.*

OH the written abbreviation of Ohio

oh /oʊ/ *interjection* **1** used to express a strong emotion or to emphasize what you think about something: *Oh, what a great idea!* | *Oh, be quiet!* | *Oh, no! My purse is gone!* **2** used to make a slight pause, especially before replying to a question or giving your opinion about something: *"What's the name of the person in tech support?" "Oh, I think it's Jim, isn't it?"* | *"Nick's kind of weird." "Oh, I don't know. I think he's really nice."* | *She's worked there for, oh, around twelve years.* **3** used to get or keep someone's attention so that you can ask them a question or continue what you are saying: *Oh, and don't forget to turn off the lights on your way out.* **4 oh, did he?/are you?/was she?/really? etc.** used to show that you did not previously know what someone has just told you: *"Did you hear that Kay and Mike are dating?" "Oh, really?"* **5 oh well** used to express that you accept something bad that has happened: *Oh well, I guess we can try to have our picnic next weekend.* **6** another form of O[1] (2)

O·hi·o /ouˈhaɪou/ *written abbreviation* **OH 1** a state in the Midwest of the U.S. **2 the Ohio** a long river in the central U.S.

ohm /oum/ *n.* [C] TECHNICAL a unit for measuring electrical RESISTANCE (5)

-oid /ɔɪd/ *suffix* [in adjectives] TECHNICAL similar to something, or shaped like something: *humanoid creatures* (=similar to humans) | *ovoid* (=egg shaped)

oil[1] /ɔɪl/ *n.* **1** [U] a smooth thick mineral liquid that is burned to produce heat, or used to make machines run easily: *You really should get the oil in your car changed more regularly.* | *an oil-burning heating system* **2** [U] the thick, dark liquid from under the ground from which oil and gasoline are produced; PETROLEUM: *Oil prices have dropped significantly since May.* **3** [C,U] a smooth, thick liquid made from plants or animals, used in cooking or for making beauty products: *olive oil* | *First fry the chicken in a little peanut oil.* **4 oils** [plural] paints that contain oil; OIL PAINTS: *Mostly I paint in oils.* —see also **burn the midnight oil** (BURN[1] (14))

oil[2] *v.* [T] to put oil into or onto something, such as a machine, in order to make it work more smoothly: *I need to oil the hinges on this door.*

oil-based /ˈ. ./ *adj.* made with oil as the main substance: *oil-based paint*

oil·bear·ing /ˈ. ˌ../ *adj.* oil-bearing rock contains oil

oil·cloth /ˈɔɪlklɔθ/ *n.* [U] cloth treated with oil to give it a smooth surface

oiled /ɔɪld/ *adj.* covered with oil: *an oiled frying pan* —see also WELL-OILED

oil·field /ˈɔɪlfild/ *n.* [C] an area of land or water under which there is oil

oil-fired /ˈ. ./ *adj.* an oil-fired heating system burns oil to produce heat

oil·man /ˈɔɪlmæn/ *n. plural* **oilmen** /-mən/ [C] someone who owns an oil company or works in the oil industry

oil paint /ˈ. ./ *n.* [C,U] paint that contains oil

oil paint·ing /ˈ. ˌ../ *n.* **1** [C] a picture painted with oil paint: *Above the bookcase hung an oil painting of a tall ship on the high seas.* **2** [U] the art of painting with oil paint

oil pan /ˈ. ./ *n.* [C] a part of an engine that holds the supply of oil

oil plat·form /ˈ. ˌ../ *n.* [C] an oil rig

oil rig /ˈ. ./ *n.* [C] a large structure with equipment for getting oil from under the ground, especially from under the bottom of the ocean

oil·skin /ˈɔɪl-skɪn/ *n.* **1** [U] cloth treated with oil so that water will not pass through it **2 oilskins** [plural] a coat and pants made of oilskin

oil slick /ˈ. ./ *n.* [C] a layer of oil floating on water, usually caused when oil accidentally pours out of a ship

oil strike /ˈ. ./ *n.* [C] a discovery of oil under the ground

oil tank·er /ˈ. ˌ../ *n.* [C] a ship that has large containers for carrying oil

oil well /ˈ. ./ *n.* [C] a hole that is dug in the ground to obtain oil

oil·y /ˈɔɪli/ *adj.* **oilier, oiliest 1** covered with oil or containing a lot of oil: *oily skin* | *oily fish* **2** looking or feeling like oil: *an oily liquid* **3** someone who is oily is polite and confident, but seems very insincere: *an oily used-car salesman* —**oiliness** *n.* [U]

oink /ɔɪŋk/ *interjection* used to represent the sound that a pig makes —**oink** *n.* [C]

oint·ment /ˈɔɪntmənt/ *n.* [C,U] a soft substance made of solid oil that you rub into your skin, especially as a medical treatment: *The ointment, made from plants, is applied directly to burned skin.* —see also **a fly in the ointment** (FLY[2] (8))

OJ *n.* [U] SPOKEN orange juice

O·jib·wa, Ojibway /ouˈdʒɪbweɪ/ CHIPPEWA

OK[1], **o·kay** /ouˈkeɪ/ *adj.* SPOKEN **1** [not before noun] not sick, injured, unhappy etc.: *Are you OK?* | *Is your stomach OK?* **2** acceptable or satisfactory: *Are these clothes OK for the opera?* | *"I couldn't find the shampoo you wanted." "That's okay."* | *I figure that 110 pounds is an OK weight for me to be.* **3 is it OK...?/...OK?** used to ask if you can do something or to tell someone they can do it: *Is it OK if I borrow your umbrella?* | *I'll call you tomorrow, OK?* | [it is OK for sb to do sth] *I see, so it's OK for Ben to stay out late, but not for me.* | [it is okay with/by sb] *It's OK with me if we just stay home tonight.* **4** [not before noun] fairly good, but not extremely good: *The movie was OK, but the book was better.* **5** nice, helpful, honest etc.: *Dwight's OK. You can trust him.* | *an OK kind of guy* —**OK** *adv.*: *I'm doing OK now. Is your car running OK?*

OK[2], **okay** *interjection* **1** used when you start talking about something else, or when you pause before continuing: *OK, now add the milk and eggs and then mix.* | *OK, let's begin chapter six.* **2** used to express agreement or give permission: *"Do you want to go to the mall later?" "Okay."* **3** used when you want to stop someone arguing with you or annoying you by being unreasonable: *OK, OK, It was just a mistake, and I've said I'm sorry. Look, I just can't walk any faster, OK?* **4** used as a question, to make sure that someone has understood you or that they agree with you: *Just don't tell anyone, OK?*

OK[3], **okay** *v.* **OK's, OK'd, OK'ing** or **okays, okayed, okaying** [T] INFORMAL to say officially that you will agree to something or allow it to happen: *Random drug testing has been OK'd for subway and bus drivers.*

OK[4], **okay** *n.* **give (sb) the okay/get the okay** INFORMAL to give or get permission to do something: *We just got the OK to buy new books.*

OK[5] the written abbreviation of Oklahoma

O'Keeffe /ouˈkif/, **Geor·gia** /ˈdʒɔrdʒə/ (1887–1986) a U.S. artist known especially for her paintings of flowers and animal bones

O·ke·fe·no·kee /ˌoukɪfəˈnouki/ a large area of SWAMP land in the U.S. states of Georgia and Florida

o·key-doke /ˌouki ˈdouk/ also **okey-do·key** /-ˈdouki/ *adj., adv.* SPOKEN used like "okay" to express agreement

o·kie /ˈouki/ *n.* [C] **a)** INFORMAL a person from Oklahoma **b)** OLD-FASHIONED an offensive word for someone from Oklahoma who moved to California during the 1930s to try to find work

O·kla·ho·ma /ˌoukləˈhoumə/ *written abbreviation* **OK** a state in the central part of the U.S.

Oklahoma Cit·y /ˌ.... ˈ../ the capital and largest city of the U.S. state of Oklahoma

o·kra /ˈoukrə/ *n.* [U] a green vegetable used in cooking, especially in Asia and the southern U.S.

old /ould/ *adj.* **older, oldest**
1 used or not new having existed for a long time, or having been used a lot before: *a pair of old shoes* | *a beat-up old car* | *It's one of the oldest buildings in San Francisco.* | *Well, you know the old saying – curiosity killed the cat.* | **(as) old as the hills** (=extremely old)
2 not young having lived for a long time: *an old woman* | *She wanted to have a baby before she was*

too old. | *a lovely old oak tree* | *I have two brothers, both older than me.* | **grow/get old** (=become old)

3 age used to talk about how long a person or thing has lived or existed: *How old is your cat?* | *Our house is 60 years old.* | *Police are looking for a 30-year-old woman with short blonde hair.* | *a six-week-old baby*

4 former [only before noun] used, known, or existing before, but not anymore: *I saw Phil with one of my old girlfriends.* | *The new stadium is much bigger than the old one.* | *We all liked the old teacher better.* | *Sikes got out of jail in 1983, and was soon back to his old habits.*

5 old friend/enemy etc. someone you have known for a long time: *Tom enjoys seeing his old army buddies.* | *Kara's an old friend of ours.*

6 old flame someone with whom you used to have a romantic relationship

7 the old days/times times in the past: *In the old days, most people never took vacations.*

8 the good old days an earlier time in your life or in history, when you think things were better than they are now: *Going to a movie only cost a five cents in the good old days.*

9 be/feel/look like your old self to feel or look better again after you have been sick or very unhappy: *After five months in the hospital, I'm feeling like my old self again.*

10 the same old boring because something has been experienced, heard, or seen many times before: *Network TV has nothing but the same old shows.* —see also **it's the same old story** (STORY (11))

11 good/poor/silly etc. old sb used to talk to or about someone you like: *Good old Debbie! She always brings cookies.* | *The poor old cat didn't like it when we moved to the city.*

12 good/big etc. old used with some adjectives, such as "big" and "old", to emphasize them: *We had a big old barbecue last weekend.*

13 the old... used to talk about something that you often use or are very familiar with: *I'll just turn off the old computer, and then I'll be ready.*

14 you old... used to show that you are surprised or amused by what someone has said or done: *You old coot! Let me do that for you.* | *Well you old devil! I didn't know you were dating her!*

15 old fool/bastard/idiot/grouch etc. used to talk about someone you do not like: *that old grouch who lives next door* | *silly old fool*

16 a good old sth used to talk about something you enjoy: *We had a good old time at the reunion.*

17 any old thing/hat/place etc. used to say that it does not matter which thing, place etc. you choose: *Any old restaurant will do.* | *Oh, just wear any old thing.*

18 any old way/how any way: *You can wrap the presents any old way you want.*

19 the old guard a group of people within an organization or club who have been there a long time and do not like changes or new ideas: *the old guard of the Republican Party*

20 of/from the old school old-fashioned and believing in old ideas and customs: *Harris was a newspaperman of the old school.*

21 be an old hand (at sth) to have a lot of experience of something: *Helms is an old hand at backroom politics.*

22 the old country the country that you were born in but do not live in anymore, used especially to mean Europe

23 the old old people: *Tax payers would have to pay health insurance premiums for the old and destitute.*

24 sb is old enough to know better used to say that you think someone should have behaved more sensibly

25 for old times' sake if you do something for old times' sake, you do it to remind yourself of a happy time in the past

26 sb's old enough to be your father/mother DISAPPROVING used to say that someone is too old for someone to have a sexual relationship with

27 old wives' tale a belief based on old ideas that are now considered to be untrue

28 be old before your time to look or behave like someone much older than you

29 of old LITERARY from a long ago in the past: *heroes and kings of old*

30 Old English/Icelandic etc. an early form of the English, Icelandic etc. language

---

USAGE NOTE: OLD

WORD CHOICE: older, elder, elderly, senior citizen
You can use **older** to describe either people or things. **Elder** (*adj.*) is a more formal word that means the same thing, but it is only used to talk about people and is used in more formal writing: *As the verdict was read, the defendant's elder brother stared silently ahead.* **Older** can be used with **than**, but **elder** cannot: *Shane is older than Mark* (NOT *"elder than"*). When you are talking about people, **elderly** (NOT *elder*) is a more polite word than **old**. Compare *an old church* and *an old/elderly lady*. Most elderly people, however, now prefer to be called **senior citizens**, and this is the most common, polite, and acceptable expression to use.

---

old age /ˌ. '.◂/ *n.* [U] the part of your life when you are old: *She's a little forgetful, but that comes with old age.* | *Even in his old age, Grandpa still used to mow the lawn himself.*

old-boy net·work /. '. ˌ../ *n.* **the old-boy network** USUALLY DISAPPROVING the system by which men from rich families, men who went to the same school, belong to the same club etc., use their influence to help each other

old·e /ˈoʊldi/ *adj.* an old-fashioned spelling of old, used in the names of shops, products etc. to make them seem traditional: *ye olde tea shoppe*

old·en /ˈoʊldən/ *adj.* **in (the) olden days** also **in olden times** a long time ago: *In the olden days, players didn't wear numbers on their jerseys.*

Ol·den·burg /ˈoʊldən,bɚg/, **Claes** /klɔs/ (1929–) a U.S. SCULPTOR, born in Sweden, famous for his large SCULPTUREs of ordinary objects, often made of soft materials

Old Eng·lish Sheep·dog /ˌ. .. '../ *n.* [C] a large dog with long thick gray and white hair

old-fash·ioned /ˌ. '.◂/ *adj.* **1** not modern, and not considered fashionable or interesting: *old-fashioned clothes* | *Most of the students found the course material boring and old-fashioned.* **2** an old-fashioned machine, object, method etc. is one that is not generally used anymore because it has been replaced by something newer: *The system uses fiber-optic cable instead of the old-fashioned copper wire.* | *Mandy was carrying a big old-fashioned leather briefcase.* **3** someone who is old-fashioned believes in ways of doing things that are not usual anymore: *her strict, old-fashioned father* | *old-fashioned ideas about sex* **4** not modern anymore, but in a way that people like because it is of good quality or it reminds them of the past: *Betty still bakes her own bread the old-fashioned way.* | *Her latest book is a good old-fashioned murder mystery.*

old fo·gey /ˌoʊld ˈfoʊgi/ *n. plural* **old fogeys** [C] INFORMAL someone who is boring and has old-fashioned ideas, especially someone old: *a conservative, bow-tied old fogey*

old folks /'. ./ *n.* [plural] INFORMAL an expression meaning "old people": *Most of the clinic's patients are women, babies, and old folks.*

old folks' home /ˌ. '. ./ *n.* [C] INFORMAL a word for a RETIREMENT HOME or a NURSING HOME that may now be considered insulting by some older people

Old Glo·ry /ˌ. '../ *n.* [U] the flag of the U.S.

old hat /ˌ. './ *adj.* [not before noun] familiar or old-fashioned, and therefore boring: *The movie's special effects now seem rather old hat.*

old·ie /ˈoʊldi/ *n.* [C] INFORMAL someone or something that is old, especially an old movie or an old song or record: *Now on video cassette, Joan Crawford's "Humoresque" is an oldie but goodie* (=old but good). —see also GOLDEN OLDIE

old la·dy /ˌ. ˈ./ *n.* SPOKEN **1** an expression for someone's wife or GIRLFRIEND, which many women think is offensive: *Did your old lady give you permission to go out with us tonight?* **2** an expression for someone's mother, which some women may find offensive

old maid /ˌ. ˈ./ *n.* [C] **1** an insulting expression meaning a woman who has never married and is not young anymore **2** INFORMAL someone who worries too much and has old-fashioned ideas

old man /ˌ. ˈ./ *n.* [C] SPOKEN **1** someone's father **2** someone's husband or BOYFRIEND

Old Mas·ter /ˌ. ˈ../ *n.* [C] a famous painter, especially from the 15th to 18th century, or a painting by one of these painters: *a priceless collection of Old Masters*

old mon·ey /ˈ. ˌ../ *n.* [U] money that has been in a family for years and that gives a family a high social position, or the families that have this type of money: *Most members of the Cleveland Country Club come from old money.* —**old-money** *adj.* —compare NOUVEAU RICHE

Old Tes·ta·ment /ˌ. ˈ...◂/ *n.* **the Old Testament** the first part of the Christian Bible, containing ancient Hebrew writings about the time before the birth of Jesus Christ —compare NEW TESTAMENT

old tim·er /ˌ. ˈ./ *n.* [C] INFORMAL **1** someone who has been in a particular job, place etc. for a long time and knows a lot about it **2** an old man

Old World /ˌ. ˈ./ *n.* **the Old World** the Eastern Hemisphere, especially Europe, Asia, and Africa —compare NEW WORLD

old-world /ˈ. ./ *adj.* [only before noun] an old-world place or quality is attractive because it is old or reminds you of the past: *Wittenberg has kept much of its old-world charm.*

ole /oʊl/ *adj.* a way of writing the word "old" to represent the way some people say it: *How's my ole friend Billy?*

o·le·ag·i·nous /ˌoʊliˈædʒənəs/ *adj.* **1** TECHNICAL containing, producing, or like oil **2** FORMAL behaving in a polite or friendly but very insincere way

o·le·an·der /ˈoʊliˌændə/ *n.* [C,U] a green bush with white, red, or pink flowers

ol·fac·to·ry /ɑlˈfæktəri, oʊl-/ *adj.* TECHNICAL relating to the sense of smell

ol·i·gar·chy /ˈɑləgɑrki/ *n. plural* **oligarchies 1** [U] government or control by a small group of people **2** [C usually singular] a state governed by a small group of people, or the group who govern such a state —**oligarch** *n.* [C]

ol·i·gop·o·ly /ˌɑləˈgɑpəli/ *n.* [C] TECHNICAL the control of all or most of a business activity by very few companies, so that other organizations cannot easily compete with them

ol·ive /ˈɑlɪv/ *n.* **1** [C] a small, bitter, egg-shaped black or green fruit, used as food and for making oil: *Greek black olives* **2** [C] a tree that produces this fruit, grown especially in Mediterranean countries **3** [U] a deep yellowish green color **4 olive skin/complexion** skin color that is typical in Mediterranean countries such as Greece, Italy and Turkey: *She had a long oval face and an olive complexion.* **5 extend/present/offer etc. an olive branch** to do something to show that you want to end an argument —**olive** *adj.*

olive drab /ˌ. ˈ./ *n.* [U] a grayish green color, used especially in military uniforms —**olive drab** *adj.*

olive oil /ˈ. ˌ./ *n.* [U] a pale yellow or green oil obtained from olives and used in cooking: *This salad is best with a vinegar and olive oil dressing.*

O·liv·i·er /əˈlɪviˌeɪ/, **Lau·rence** /ˈlɔrəns/ (1907–1989) a British actor famous for directing and acting in movies of plays by Shakespeare

Ol·mec /ˈoʊlmɛk/ one of the peoples that lived in southeast Mexico from the fifteenth to the tenth century B.C.

-ologist /ɑlədʒɪst/ *suffix* [in nouns] a person who

studies a particular science or subject: *a psychologist* | *a pathologist* (=who studies diseases) —see also -IST

-ology /ɑlədʒi/ *suffix* [in nouns] **1** the study of something, especially something scientific: *climatology* (=the study of CLIMATE) | *Egyptology* (=the study of ancient Egypt) **2** something that is being studied or described: *phraseology* (=the way someone uses words) | *a chronology of events* (=describing when, and in what order, things happened) —**-ological** /ɑlədʒɪkəl/ *suffix* [in adjectives] —**-ologically** /ɑlədʒɪkli/ *suffix* [in adverbs] —see also -LOGY

O·lym·pi·a /əˈlɪmpiə/ **1** the capital city of the U.S. state of Washington **2** an area of land and an ancient religious center in Greece, where the Olympic Games were held in ancient times

O·lym·pi·ad /əˈlɪmpiˌæd, oʊ-/ *n.* [C] **1** a particular occasion of the modern Olympic Games: *Barcelona was the site of the 25th Olympiad.* **2** an occasion when students compete against each other in subjects such as science, math, and knowledge: *the National Science Olympiad*

O·lym·pi·an¹ /əˈlɪmpiən/ *n.* [C] **1** someone who takes part in the Olympic Games: *former U.S. Olympian Pablo Morales* **2** one of the ancient Greek Gods

Olympian² *adj.* **1** like a god, especially by being calm or not concerned about ordinary things: *The college principal was an Olympian figure whom we hardly ever saw.* **2** relating to the ancient Greek gods

O·lym·pic /əˈlɪmpɪk/ *adj.* [only before noun] relating to or taking part in the Olympic Games: *the German Olympic team* | *the Olympic flag*

O·lym·pic Games /ˌ.ˌ. ˈ./ also **Olympics** *n.* [plural] **1** an international sports event held every four years in different countries **2** a sports event in ancient times, which was held at Olympia in Greece every four years

O·lym·pus /əˈlɪmpəs/, **Mount Olympus** the highest mountain in Greece and, in Greek MYTHOLOGY, the place where the gods lived

O·ma·ha¹ /ˈoʊməˌhɑ, -ˌhɔ/ a city in the U.S. state of Nebraska

Omaha² a Native American tribe from the central area of the U.S.

O·man /oʊˈmɑn/ a country in the Middle East, southeast of Saudi Arabia and northeast of Yemen —**Omani** *n., adj.*

O·mar Khay·yám /ˌoʊmɑr kaɪˈyɑm/ (?1048–?1123) a Persian mathematician and poet, famous in the West for his poem, the RUBAIYAT

OMB —see OFFICE OF MANAGEMENT AND BUDGET, THE

om·buds·man /ˈɑmbʊdzmən/ *n.* [C] someone who deals with complaints made by people against the government, banks, universities etc.

o·me·ga /oʊˈmeɪgə/ *n.* [C] the last letter of the Greek alphabet

ome·let, omelette /ˈɑmlɪt/ *n.* [C] eggs mixed together and cooked in a pan, and then folded over cheese, vegetables, etc..: *a cheese and mushroom omelet*

o·men /ˈoʊmən/ *n.* [C] a sign of what will happen in the future: **a good/bad/ill etc. omen (for)** *A sharp decline in consumer spending is seen as a bad omen for the economy.*

om·i·nous /ˈɑmənəs/ *adj.* making you feel that something bad is going to happen: *There was an ominous silence in the room.* —**ominously** *adv.*: *The sky looked ominously dark.*

o·mis·sion /oʊˈmɪʃən, ə-/ *n.* **1** [U] the act of not including or not doing something: *The omission of a warning on the product's label was the result of a printing error.* **2** [C] something that has been omitted: *Copies of the census lists were posted so omissions could be pointed out.* | **a glaring omission** (=one that is very bad and easily noticed)

0

o·mit /oʊˈmɪt, ə-/ v. **omitted, omitting** [T] **1** to not include someone or something, either deliberately or because you forget to do it; LEAVE out: *In his presentation of the theorem, Kelvin omitted many details.* | *Quady's name had been omitted from the list of honor students.* **2 omit to do sth** FORMAL to not do something, either because you forgot or deliberately: *Whittier omitted to mention exactly where he had gotten the money.*

omni- /ɑmni/ prefix [in nouns and adjectives] every possible thing or place; all: *an omniscient narrator* (=that knows everything) | *Goats are omnivores.* (=they eat all kinds of food)

om·ni·bus[1] /ˈɑmnɪbəs/ adj. [only before noun] an omnibus law contains several different laws collected together: *an omnibus civil rights bill*

omnibus[2] n. [C] **1** a book containing several stories, especially by one writer, which have already been printed separately **2** OLD USE a bus

om·nip·o·tent /ɑmˈnɪpətənt/ adj. able to do everything —**omnipotence** n. [U] *God's omnipotence*

om·ni·pres·ent /ˌɑmnɪˈprɛzənt◂/ adj. present or seeming to be present everywhere at all times: *Police were virtually omnipresent on the city streets.* —**omnipresence** n. [U]

om·ni·scient /ɑmˈnɪʃənt/ adj. knowing or seeming to know everything: *Even the botanical garden's omniscient botanist couldn't explain the meaning of the flower's name.* —**omniscience** n. [U]

om·ni·vore /ˈɑmnɪˌvɔr/ n. [C] TECHNICAL an animal that eats both meat and plants

om·niv·o·rous /ɑmˈnɪvərəs/ adj. **1** TECHNICAL an animal that is omnivorous eats both meat and plants **2** FORMAL interested in everything and trying to gather all kinds of information: *an omnivorous reporter*

on[1] /ɔn/ ɑn/ prep. **1** touching or supported by a particular surface: *Harry's the guy sitting on the sofa there.* | *You've got some tomato sauce on your shirt.* | *Don't put your feet on my desk!* —opposite OFF[2] (1) **2** hanging from, supported by, or connected to a particular thing: *Pictures of the family hung on the wall.* | *The men climbed down on a rope made of bed sheets.* | *It's not easy to skate on one foot.* **3** in a particular place, building, area of land etc.: *Our office is on the third floor.* | *Didn't Jim grow up on a farm?* | *The answers are on page 350.* **4** in a particular road: *Stephen lives on Crescent Drive.* | *Finding parking on Main Street is impossible.* **5** next to the side of something such as a road or river: *We stayed at a wonderful hotel on Lake Ouachita.* | *There's plenty of parking on the street.* | *El Paso is located on the U.S.-Mexico border.* **6** used to show the person or thing affected by an action or by something that happens: *a tax on gasoline* | *Mom's death has been hard on the family.* **7** used to show the day or date when something happens: *On Thursday, I'll go on vacation.* | *My birthday's on the 17th of June.* **8** in a particular direction: *On your left is the Lincoln Memorial.* **9** about a particular subject: *a book on China* | *Could you give some advice on what to wear?* **10** in a bus, train, aircraft etc.: *No one on the bus was injured in the wreck.* | *I got on the first flight to Chicago.* —see also **on foot** (FOOT[1] (3)), **on horseback** (HORSEBACK (1)) **11** used to say what has been used to do something: *I cut my hand on a piece of glass.* | *Did you make these graphs on a computer?* **12** used to say what food someone eats in order to live, what FUEL[1] something uses in order to operate etc.: *Granddad lives on meat and potatoes.* | *This new laptop runs on two AA batteries.* **13** used to say what money people use in order to live, or the amount of money that someone earns: *Things got so bad we had to go on welfare.* | *tax increases for workers on high salaries* **14** regularly taking a particular drug or medicine: *I'm now on a different antibiotic.* **15 on the phone** using a telephone: *Bridget's on the phone all day long.* **16 on television/on the radio** being broadcast by television or radio: *listening to the news*

on the radio | *The movie I want to watch is on Channel 9.* **17** during a trip, vacation etc.: *On the flight, I sat next to some guy with bad breath.* | *Could you stop by the store on your way home?* **18** FORMAL immediately after something has happened or after someone has done something: [**on doing sth**] *On hearing the news of the air attack most foreigners headed for the border.* | [**on sth**] *On arrival at reception, guests should sign the visitors' book.* **19** used to say that someone is a member of a team, organization etc.: *Hal's on the swim team and the basketball team.* **20 have/carry etc. sth on you** INFORMAL to have a particular thing in your pocket, your bag etc.: *Do you have a pen on you?* **21** SPOKEN used to say that someone will pay for something such as a drink or a meal: *Dinner's on me tonight.* **22** if you save money on something, you do not pay as much as you expected to: *You can save up to $100 on your ticket by booking early.* **23** INFORMAL used to show that someone or something causes you problems, for example if a machine stops working while you are using it: *Then the vacuum went dead on me.* | *You can't just quit on me before we finish the job.*

on[2] adj., adv. [not before noun] **1** used to show that someone continues to do something or something continues to happen: **go/carry on** (=continue what you are doing) *Go on. I'm listening.* | **go/keep/carry on doing sth** *The dog just kept on barking.* | *We can't go on spending money we don't have.* | **read/play/talk etc. on** *Read on. Maybe the answers are at the end of the page.* | *The peace talks have dragged on for months.* | *It seemed as if the war would go on forever.* **2** if you walk, drive etc. on, you continue on your journey or go toward a particular place: *Let's go on. I want to get home before it gets dark.* | *I sent Dan on ahead to find us seats at the theater.* **3** used to say that something happens at a time that is before or after another time: **earlier/later on** *He didn't realize how this would affect him later on in life.* | *You pay money into the fund until you are 65, and* **from then on** *you receive a monthly benefit check.* | **From that day on**, *we've never been apart.* **4** if you have something on, you are wearing it: *Put your shoes on, and let's go.* | *Rick was standing there with nothing on.* **5** a machine, piece of equipment etc. that is on is working or operating: *OK, who left the lights on?* | **Turn on** the radio. I want to hear the sports scores.* —opposite OFF[1] (4) **6** in a bus, train, aircraft etc.: *I usually get on at Irving Street.* **7** if a movie, TV program etc. is on, it is being broadcast or shown at a theater: *There's a good comedy on at eight.* **8** if an event is on, it has been arranged and it is happening or will happen: *As far as we know, the game is still on for tomorrow.* | *You should visit Chicago while the festival is on.* **9 go on about sth** INFORMAL to keep talking about something, in a way that is boring: *Carol started going on about how nobody liked her.* **10 on and off** also **off and on** for short periods but not regularly, over a long period of time: *It rained off and on for the whole afternoon.* **11 be on to something** to have discovered something very interesting or unusual that will bring you advantages: *We realized we were on to something when a newspaper offered us $1000 for the photos.* **12** if an actor is on, they are performing: *You're on in two minutes.* —see also HEAD-ON

on-air /ˌ. ˈ.◂/ adj. [only before noun] broadcast while actually happening: *an on-air interview*

O·nas·sis /oʊˈnæsɪs/, **Jac·que·line Ken·ne·dy** /ˈdʒækəlɪn ˈkɛnədi/ (1929–1994) the wife of President John Kennedy, and later of Aristotle Onassis, known for being very beautiful and fashionable

on-board /ˌɑnˈbɔrd◂/ adj. [only before noun] carried on a ship, in a car etc.: *an onboard motor* —**onboard** adv.

once[1] /wʌns/ adv.

1 one time on one occasion, or at one time: *I've only worn this dress once.* | *They'd met* **once before** *at a party.*

2 once a week/year etc. one time every week, year etc. as a regular activity: *Marlene says she washes her hair once a week.*

3 (every) once in a while sometimes, but not often: *I only see her every once in a while at school.*
4 once more/again a) one more time; again: *He kissed her once more and moved toward the door.* **b)** FORMAL used before you repeat something that you said before: *Once again, it must be stressed that the pilot was not to blame.*
5 at once a) at the same time, together: *I can't do two things at once!* **b)** FORMAL immediately, or without delay: *Everyone knew at once how serious the situation was.*
6 in the past at some time in the past, but not now: *Here's a picture of a convertible we had once.* | **once-great/beautiful/powerful etc.** *The once-elegant city was now a war zone.*
7 for once used to say that something which is happening is rare or unusual, especially if you think it should happen more often: *I see you've decided to help in the kitchen for once.* | *For once I agree with him.*
8 once and for all definitely and finally: *Let's settle this matter once and for all.*
9 (just) this once SPOKEN used to emphasize that this is the only time you will let someone do something, ask someone to do something etc.: *OK, you can stay up till 11, but just this once.*
10 all at once suddenly: *All at once the trailer started shaking.*
11 once upon a time a) a phrase meaning "a long time ago," used at the beginning of children's stories **b)** at a time in the past that you think was much better than now: *Once upon a time children did what they were told.*
12 once or twice a few times, but not often: *Once or twice, he thought about calling his parents, but then decided not to.*
13 once in a blue moon INFORMAL very rarely: *We go out to eat once in a blue moon.*
14 do sth once too often to do something until you make someone angry or until you are finally caught, hurt etc.: *The kids rang Brant's doorbell once too often, and he reported them to the police.*
15 once bitten, twice shy used to say that people will not do something again if it has been a bad experience
16 once is enough SPOKEN used to say that after you have done something one time you do not need or want to do it again

s w **once²** *conjunction* just after something happens, or from the moment that something happens: *I called Lara once he'd left.* | *Once in the US, the drugs are distributed to all the major cities.*

once-o·ver /ˈ. ˌ../ *n.* **give sb/sth a/the once-over** to look at someone or something quickly to check who they are or what they are like: *Give your car the once-over before you leave on your trip.*

on·col·o·gy /ɑnˈkɑlədʒi/ *n.* [U] the part of medical science that deals with TUMORs and CANCER (1) —**oncologist** *n.* [C]

on·com·ing /ˈɒn,kʌmɪŋ/ *adj.* **oncoming car/traffic etc.** a car etc. that is coming toward you

on-deck cir·cle /ˌ. . ˈ.. *n.* [C] the place where a baseball player stands when he or she is the next person who is going to try to hit the ball

s w **one¹** /wʌn/ *number* **1** 1 **2** one o'clock: *I have a meeting at one.* **3 one or two** INFORMAL a small number of people or things: *There are one or two things to sort out before I leave.* **4 one-armed/one-eyed/one-legged etc.** having only one arm, eye, leg etc.

s w **one²** *pron.* **1** used to mean someone or something that has already been mentioned or is known about: *We've been looking at houses but haven't found one we like yet.* | *"Do you know where those bowls are?" "Which ones?"* | *They're closing this factory but building two new ones in Atlanta.* | *I like all the pictures except* **this one**. | *Jane's* **the one** *with red hair.*
2 used to mean someone or something from a group or type that has been mentioned or is about to be mentioned: *The houses are all pretty similar, but one is a little bigger than the others.* | *[+ of] This is one of my favorite books.* **3 one by one** if people do something one by one, first one person does it, then the next, then the next etc.: *One by one, worshipers walked to the front of the church.* **4 one after the**

other also **one after another** if events or actions happen one after the other, they happen without much time between them: *One after another, tropical storms battered the Pacific coastline.* **5 (all) in one** if someone or something is many different things all in one, they are all of those things: *It's a TV, radio, and VCR all in one.* **6** FORMAL used to mean people in general, including yourself: *One can never be too careful.* **7 I, for one,...** used to emphasize that you are doing something, believe something etc. and hope others will do the same: *I, for one, am proud of the team's effort.* **8 ...for one** used to give an example of someone or something: *"Who's going to help you clean up?" "Well, you for one."* **9 be one up (on sb)** to have an advantage over someone —see also ONE-UPMANSHIP **10 the one that got away** someone or something good that you almost had or that almost happened, but did not **11 one and only a)** used to emphasize that someone is very special or admired *the one and only Frank Sinatra* **b)** used to emphasize that something is the only one of its kind *the architect's one and only significant achievement* **12 be/feel at one with sb/sth a)** to feel very calm or relaxed in the situation or environment you are in: *A spiritual journey helps you be at one with life.* **13 have had one too many** INFORMAL to have drunk too much alcohol **14 have one for the road** INFORMAL to have a last alcoholic drink before you leave a place **15 the one about...** SPOKEN a joke or humorous story: *Did you hear the one about the two-headed sailor?* **16 in ones and twos** if people do something in ones and twos, they do it on their own or in small groups: *Guests arrived in ones and twos.* **17 as one** if many people do something as one, they all do it at the same time.: *The whole team stood up as one and marched out of the room.* **18 a hard one/an easy one etc.** a particular kind of problem, question, story etc.: *213 divided by 12? That's a tricky one.* **19 one for the books** INFORMAL used to say that something that has happened is unusual, surprising, or special: *Spall's performance in "Life is Sweet" is one for the books.* **20 one and the same** the same person or thing: *Many of their supporters think of the two brothers as one and the same.* **21 not/never be one to do sth** INFORMAL to never do a particular thing, because it is not part of your character to do it: *Tom is not one to show his emotions.* **22 not/never be one for sth** INFORMAL to not enjoy a particular activity, subject etc.: *I've never really been one for lying around on beaches.* **23 one of the family** someone who is accepted as a member of a particular group of people: *They treat me like one of the family when I stay with them.* **24 one of us** SPOKEN used to say that someone belongs to the same group as you, or has the same ideas, beliefs etc.: *You can trust him – he's one of us.* **25 one and all** OLD-FASHIONED everyone: *The pastor is a friend to one and all.* **26 the little/young ones** OLD-FASHIONED children, especially young children —see also ONE-ON-ONE, ONE-TO-ONE

0

USAGE NOTE: ONE

FORMALITY
In informal spoken English, people often say **these ones** or **those ones**: *Give me those ones back, and I'll give you these ones.* But in more formal or written English, it is better not to use **ones**: *Give me those back, and I'll give you these.*

GRAMMAR
When **one** is the subject of the sentence, the verb is singular, even when a plural noun comes just before the verb: *One of the girls wants to be a doctor* (NOT *One of the girls want to be a doctor*).

---

one³ *determiner* **1** used before a noun to emphasize a particular person or thing: *One reason I like the house is because of the big kitchen.* **2 one day/afternoon etc. a)** a particular day, afternoon etc. in the past: *One morning Rick just decided he wasn't going to go to work anymore.* **b)** any day, afternoon etc. in **s w**

the future: *One day I hope to return the favor.* **3** only, or most important: *You're the one person I can trust.* | *My one worry is that she'll decide to leave college.* **4** used to talk about one person or thing in comparison with similar people or things: *Why does my card work in one cash machine and not in another?* | *It's one thing to see the plans on paper, but it's another thing to see the buildings completed.* **5 for one thing** INFORMAL used to introduce the first of several reasons: *No, of course you can't go. For one thing, you have too much homework to do.* **6** SPOKEN used to emphasize your description of someone or something: *That is one cute kid!* **7** FORMAL used before the name of someone who you do not know well: *The car belongs to one Joseph Nelson.*

one⁴ *n.* [C] a piece of paper money worth $1: *Do you have any ones?*

one an·oth·er /ˌ. .ˈ.ˌ/ *pron.* used to show that each of two or more people does something to the other or others: *Many witnesses contradicted one another.* —see Usage Note at EACH OTHER

one-armed ban·dit /ˌ. . ˈ.ˌ/ *n.* [C] a machine with a long handle, into which you put money in order to try to win more money; SLOT MACHINE

one-di·men·sion·al /ˌ. .ˈ.ˌ.ˌ/ *adj.* DISAPPROVING too simple and not considering or showing all the parts of something: *the novel's boring, one-dimensional characters*

one-horse /ˈ. ./ *adj.* **1 a one-horse town** INFORMAL a small and boring town **2** pulled by one horse: *a one-horse carriage*

O·nei·da /oʊˈnaɪdə/ a Native American tribe from the northeastern area of the U.S.

O'Neill /oʊˈnil/, **Eu·gene** /yuˈdʒin/ (1888–1953) a U.S. writer of plays

one-lin·er /ˌ. ˈ.ˌ/ *n.* [C] a very short joke or humorous remark

one-man /ˈ. ./ *adj.* [only before noun] performed, operated, done etc. by one man: *a one-man show* | *a one-man crusade to ban the film*

one-man band /ˌ. . ˈ./ *n.* [C] **1** a street musician who plays several instruments at the same time **2** INFORMAL an organization in which one person does everything: *It's a small local radio station, really just a one-man band.*

one·ness /ˈwʌnnɪs/ *n.* [U] a peaceful feeling of being part of a whole: [+ with] *oneness with nature*

one-night stand /ˌ. . ˈ./ *n.* [C] **1** INFORMAL **a)** an occasion when two people have sex, but do not intend to meet each other again **b)** a person that you have sex with once and do not see again **2** a performance that is given only once in a particular place: *The band was exhausted from playing a succession of one-night stands around the country.*

one-of-a-kind /ˌ. . . ˈ.ˌ/ *adj.* very special because there is nothing else or no one else like it, him, her etc.: *one-of-a-kind handmade carpets*

one-on-one /ˌ. . ˈ./ *adj.* between only two people: *Kids need one-on-one attention.* —**one-on-one** *adv.*: *He was speaking one-on-one with a member of the press.*

one-par·ent fam·i·ly /ˌ. .. ˈ.ˌ/ *n.* [C] a family in which there is only one parent who takes care of the children

one per·cent milk /ˈ. . ˌ.ˌ/ *n.* [U] milk that has had cream removed so that 1% of what remains is fat —compare SKIM MILK, TWO PERCENT MILK, WHOLE MILK

one-piece /ˈ. ./ *adj.* [only before noun] consisting of only one piece, not separate parts: *a one-piece bathing suit*

on·er·ous /ˈɑnərəs, ˈoʊ-/ *adj.* FORMAL work or responsibility that is onerous is difficult and worrying or makes you tired: *an onerous but necessary task*

one·self /wʌnˈsɛlf/ *pron.* FORMAL the REFLEXIVE form of ONE² (6): *Mandel stresses the importance of being able to defend oneself.*

one-shot /ˈ. ./ *adj.* [only before noun] happening or

done only once: *This is a one-shot deal. If it doesn't work, it's over.*

one-sid·ed /ˌ. ˈ.ˌ/ *adj.* **1** considering or showing only one side of a question, subject etc. in a way that is unfair: *I'm amazed the paper would print such one-sided views.* **2** an activity or competition that is one-sided is one in which one person or team is much stronger than the other: *a one-sided victory* —**one-sidedness** *n.* [U] —**one-sidedly** *adv.*

one-size-fits-all /ˌ. . . ˈ./ *adj.* **1** one-size-fits-all clothing is designed so that people of many different sizes can wear it: *one-size-fits all dresses* **2** designed to please or be appropriate for many different people, sometimes with the result that it is good for no one: *a one-size-fits-all public education program*

one-stop /ˈ. ./ *adj.* **1 one-stop shopping** a situation in which you can buy many different products and do many different activities all in one place **2 a one-stop shop/center etc.** a place where you can buy many different things, get many kinds of information etc.

one-time, one-time /ˈwʌntaɪm/ *adj.* [only before noun] **1** former: *Kearney, a onetime journalist, was elected to Congress in 1993.* **2** happening only once: *a one-time fee of $5*

one-to-one /ˌ. . ˈ.ˌ/ *adj.* [only before noun] **1** between only two people: *one-to-one counseling* **2** matching each other exactly: *The two currencies were exchanged on a one-to-one basis.*

one-track mind /ˌ. . ˈ./ *n.* **have a one-track mind** to be continuously thinking about one particular thing, especially sex: *That guy has a one-track mind.*

one-two /ˌ. ˈ./ *n.* [C] also **one-two punch** **1** a movement in which a BOXER hits his opponent with one hand and then quickly with the other: *Ali gives his opponent the old one-two, and it's all over.* **2** a combination of two bad things happening one after the other: *The arts center was defeated by a one-two punch: loss of funding and a steep hike in rents.*

one-up /ˌ. ˈ./ *v.* [T] INFORMAL to try to make yourself seem better than someone else: *Department stores try to one-up each other when it comes to cutting prices.*

one-up·man·ship /ˌwʌn ˈʌpmənˌʃɪp/ *n.* [U] attempts to make yourself seem better than other people, no matter what they do

one-way /ˌ. ˈ.ˌ/ *adj.* [usually before noun] **1** moving or allowing movement in only one direction: *one-way traffic* | *a one-way street* **2** a one-way ticket is for traveling from one place to another but not back again —compare ROUND-TRIP **3** a one-way process, relationship etc. is one in which only one person makes any effort

one-way mir·ror /ˌ. . ˈ.ˌ/ *n.* [C] a mirror that can be used as a window by people secretly watching from the other side of it

one-wom·an /ˈ. ˌ.ˌ/ *adj.* [only before a noun] performed, operated, done etc. by only one woman: *a one-woman show*

on·go·ing /ˈɔnˌɡoʊɪŋ/ *adj.* [usually before noun] continuing, or continuing to develop: *an ongoing partnership* | *ongoing negotiations* —see also **go on** (GO¹)

on·ion /ˈʌnyən/ *n.* [C,U] a round vegetable with brownish or reddish skin and many white layers inside, which has a strong taste and smell —see picture at VEGETABLE

onion dome /ˈ.. ˌ./ *n.* [C] a round pointed roof that is shaped like an onion, which is common on Russian churches

on·line, on-line /ˌɒnˈlaɪn/ *adj.* **1** connected to other computers through the Internet, or available through the Internet: *All the city's schools will be online by the end of the year.* | *online banking* **2** directly connected to or controlled by a computer: *an online printer* —compare OFFLINE —**online** *adv.*: *The reports are not available online yet.*

on·look·er /ˈɒnˌlʊkə/ *n.* [C] someone who watches something happening without being involved in it: *A crowd of onlookers gathered at the scene of the accident.*

on·ly¹ /ˈoʊnli/ *adv.* **1** not more than a particular

amount, number, age etc., especially when this is unusual: *Becky was only three when she started to read.* | *I was only gone 15 minutes.* **2** nothing or no one except the thing or person mentioned: *You're only wearing a T-shirt. No wonder you're cold.* | *Only Denny got all six answers right.* | *The restrooms are for customers only.* | **men-only/women-only etc.** *a women-only health club* **3** in one place, situation, or way and no other, or for one reason and no other: *These flowers grow only in Hawaii.* | *He says he'll come, but only if you promise not to tease him.* | *I only did it because I thought you wanted me to.* **4** not better, worse, or more important than someone or something: *She doesn't earn very much. She's only a cashier.* | *Oh, come on. I was only joking.* **5** no earlier than a particular time: *I only got here last night.* | *She heard her sister leave and only then* (=at that moment and not before) *did she open her eyes.* **6 only just a)** a very short time ago: *We've only just begun to understand how serious the situation is.* **7 if only a)** used to give a reason for something, although you think it is not a good one: *Just call her, if only to say you're sorry.* **b)** used to express a strong wish: *If only I could be 15 again!* **8 only too well/happy/willing etc.** very or completely well, happy etc.: *Scott was only too happy to tell the story.* **9 only to find/learn/discover etc.** used to say that someone did something, with a disappointing or surprising result: *Police arrived at Newhall's home at 6 a.m. only to find him gone.*

SPOKEN PHRASES

10 I only wish/hope used to express a strong wish or hope: *I only wish I knew what I could do to help.* **11 only so many/much** used to say that there is a limited amount or quantity of something: *There's only so much you can do with hair this fine.* **12 you'll only...** used to tell someone that what they want to do will have a bad effect: *Don't interfere; you'll only make things worse.* **13 you only have to read sth/look at sth etc.** used to say that it is easy to realize that something is true because you can see or hear things that prove it: *The effects of the recession are obvious – you only have to look at all the boarded-up shops.* **14 I can only assume/suppose etc.** used to say that you can think of one explanation for something surprising or disappointing and no other: *I can only assume that it was an accident.*

—see also **only have eyes for sb** (EYE¹ (36)), **not only...but (also)** (NOT (4)),

---

USAGE NOTE: ONLY

GRAMMAR
The meaning of a sentence can change depending on where you use **only**. To make the meaning of your sentence clear, it is best to put **only** directly before the word it describes: *Only Paul saw the lion* (=no one except Paul saw it). | *Paul only saw the lion* (=he saw it, but he did not do anything else to it, such as touch it). | *Paul saw only the lion* (=the lion was the only animal he saw).

---

only² *adj.* [only before noun] **1 the only thing/ person/way etc. a)** the one single thing, person etc. that there is when there are no others: *Vera's the only one that knows how to run the machine.* | *The only food in the house was a box of crackers.* **b)** the best: *She's the only person for this job.* | *Flying is really the only way to go.* **2 an only child** a child who has no brother or sisters **3 the only thing is...** SPOKEN used when you are going to mention a problem or disadvantage about something: *It's a great apartment. The only thing is it's a little expensive.* —see also **one and only** (ONE¹ (11))

only³ *conjunction* INFORMAL used like "but" to introduce the reason why something is not possible: *I'd offer to help, only I'm kind of busy right now.*

on·o·mat·o·poe·ia /ˌɑnəˌmætəˈpiə/ *n.* [U] TECHNICAL the use of words that sound like the thing that they are describing, like "hiss" or "boom" —**onomatopoeic** *adj.*

On·on·da·ga /ˌɑnənˈdɑgə, -ˈdɔgə/ a Native American tribe from the northeastern area of the U.S.

on-ramp /ˈ. ./ *n.* [C] a road for driving onto a HIGHWAY or FREEWAY —compare OFF-RAMP

on·rush /ˈɑnrʌʃ/ *n.* [singular] a strong fast movement forward: [+ of] *a sudden onrush of water* —**onrushing** *adj.*: *onrushing flames*

on-screen, onscreen /ˌ. ˈ.◂/ *adj.* **1** appearing, happening etc. in a movie or on television, rather than in real life: *Birch plays Bacall's on-screen granddaughter.* **2** appearing on the screen of a computer or television: *Use the remote control to call up an onscreen program menu.* —**on-screen** *adv.*

on·set /ˈɑnsɛt/ *n.* **the onset of sth** the beginning of something, especially something bad: *Doctors can slow the onset of the disease with drugs.*

on·shore /ˌɑnˈʃɔr/ *adj.* [only before noun] **1** on or near the land rather than in the ocean: *onshore oil reserves* **2** moving toward the land: *strong onshore winds* —**onshore** *adv.*

on-site, on·site /ˈ. ./ *adj.* [only before noun] done at the place where something happens: *on-site medical treatment for the accident victims* —see also **on site** (SITE¹ (3))

on·slaught /ˈɑnslɔt/ *n.* [C] **1** a very strong attack: *The city was in ruins after a prolonged onslaught by enemy warplanes.* **2** a lot of criticism, opposition etc. all at one time, which causes great problems for someone: *a massive propaganda onslaught* | [+ of] *The President faced an onslaught of accusations.*

on·stage /ˌɑnˈsteɪdʒ◂/ *adj., adv.* happening or performing on a stage in front of a group of people: *Seven bands performed onstage.*

on-stream /ˌ. ˈ.◂/ *adv.* in operation or ready to begin operation: *Another reactor is scheduled to go on-stream in January.* —**on-stream** *adj.*

On·ta·ri·o /ɑnˈtɛriˌoʊ/ a PROVINCE in the east of central Canada

Ontario, Lake the smallest of the five Great Lakes on the border between the U.S. and Canada

on-the-job /ˌ. . ˈ.◂/ *adj.* [only before noun] while working, or at work: *on-the-job training*

on-the-spot /ˌ. . ˈ.◂/ *adj.* [only before noun] happening or done where someone is at the time they are there: *on-the-spot repairs to the car* —see also **on the spot** (SPOT¹ (4))

on·to /ˈɑntə, ˈɑn-; *strong* ˈɑntu, ˈɑn-/ *prep.* **1** used to show movement to a position of being on a surface, area, or object: *I don't like it when the cat jumps onto my lap.* | *Sara stepped carefully onto the ice.* **2 be onto sb** INFORMAL to know who did something wrong or illegal: *He's scared. He knows we're onto him.* **3 be onto something** INFORMAL to have produced or discovered something interesting or unusual that will give you many advantages: *Analysts say Xerox is onto something with its new product.* **4 look/open onto sth** to face in a particular direction, or to allow movement through one place into another: *The sitting room looked out onto a beautiful view of the mountains.*

on·tol·o·gy /ɑnˈtɑlədʒi/ *n.* [U] a subject of study in PHILOSOPHY that is concerned with the nature of existence —**ontological** *adj.*

o·nus /ˈoʊnəs/ *n.* **the onus** the responsibility for something: [**the onus is on sb (to do sth)**] *The onus is on consumers to pay for these services.*

on·ward¹ /ˈɑnwərd/ also **onwards** *adv.* **1 from... onward** beginning at a particular time and continuing from then: *Farmers expect good crops from April onward.* **2** forward: *The ship sailed onward through the fog.* **3 onward and upward** used to describe a situation in which someone continues to succeed

onward² *adj.* [only before noun] **1** moving forward or continuing: *tickets for onward travel* **2** developing over a period of time: *the onward march of scientific progress*

O

0

on·yx /'aniks/ n. [U] a stone with lines of different colors in it, often used in jewelry

oo·dles /'udlz/ n. [plural] INFORMAL a large amount of something: [+ **of**] *They've got oodles of money.*

oof /uf/ interjection the sound that you make when you have been hit, especially in the stomach

ooh¹ /u/ interjection said when you think something is very beautiful, bad, surprising etc.: *Ooh. Nice dress, Carol.*

ooh² v. [I] INFORMAL to make the sound "ooh" when you think something is beautiful, surprising etc.: *The crowd oohed and aahed at the fireworks.*

ooh la la /ˌu lɑ 'lɑ/ interjection HUMOROUS said when you think that something or someone is surprising, unusual, or sexually attractive

oomph /umf/ n. [U] INFORMAL energy or excitement: *The campaign just didn't have any oomph.*

oops /ups, ups/ interjection said when you have fallen, dropped something, or made a small mistake: *Oops. I hit the wrong button.*

oops-a-dai·sy /'. . ,./ interjection said when someone has fallen, especially a child

ooze¹ /uz/ v. **1** [I always + adv./prep.,T] if a liquid oozes from something or if something oozes a liquid, the liquid flows out very slowly: *Volcanoes usually ooze rivers of lava rather than exploding.* | [+ **from/out**] *Melted cheese oozed from the ravioli.* **2** [I,T] to clearly show a particular quality or feeling, so that it is very easy to notice: *School spirit oozes from every hallway.* | [+ **with**] *Stewart was talking to a girl, his voice oozing with charm.*

ooze² n. **1** [U] very soft mud, especially at the bottom of a lake or the ocean **2** [singular] a very slow flow of liquid

ooz·y /'uzi/ adj. INFORMAL soft and wet like mud

Op. the written abbreviation of OPUS

o·pac·i·ty /ouˈpæsəti/ n. [U] **1** the quality of being difficult to understand **2** the quality of being difficult to see through

o·pal /'oupəl/ n. [C,U] a type of white stone with changing colors in it, or a piece of this stone used in jewelry

o·pal·es·cent /ˌoupəˈlɛsənt/ adj. having colors that shine and seem to change: *an opalescent blue-green* —**opalescence** n. [U]

o·paque /ouˈpeɪk/ adj. **1** glass, liquid, or other substances that are opaque are too thick or too dark to see through: *huge opaque clouds* **2** speech or writing that is opaque is difficult to understand: *a dry opaque writing style* —compare TRANSLUCENT, TRANSPARENT (1) —see also OPACITY —**opaqueness** n. [U]

op art /'ap art/ n. [U] a form of art using patterns that seem to move or to produce other shapes as you look at them

op. cit. /ˌap 'sɪt/ an abbreviation used in formal writing to REFER to a book that has been mentioned already

OPEC /'oupɛk/ n. [U] Organization of Petroleum Exporting Countries; an organization of countries that produce and sell oil, which sets the price of the oil

op-ed /ˌap 'ɛd/ adj. **op-ed page/article etc.** the page in a newspaper that has articles containing opinions on various interesting subjects, or one of these articles

s w **o·pen¹** /'oupən/ adj.
1 1
1 door/container **a)** not closed, so that you can go through, take things out, or put things in: *an open window* | *Why is that drawer open?* | *She left the door* **wide open** (=completely open). | **fly/blow/burst etc. open** *The two gates burst open and people started streaming through.* | **push/slide/force etc. sth open** *In the end, the police had to force the door open.* | **tear/rip sth open** *Mac took the envelope and tore it open.* **b)** not locked: *Come on in – it's open.*

2 eyes/mouth not closed: *The nurse held the child's mouth open.* | *Sherman stared at the man with*

his eyes **wide open** (=completely open, especially when you are surprised).

3 store/bank etc. [not before noun] ready for business and letting customers, visitors etc. come in: *The corner store stays open till midnight.*

4 public use ready or available to be used, visited etc. by the public: *We hope to have the new museum open by June.*

5 not restricted available to everyone in a particular group, so that they can all take part: *open admission to the college* | [+ **to**] *Few jobs were open to women then.* | *All conference events are* **open to the public** (=anyone can attend). | *Fascell* **threw** the meeting **open to** his colleagues for questions and comments.

6 not blocked if a road or line of communication is open, it is not blocked and it can be used: *Highway 5 is blocked by snow, but Route 35 remains open.*

7 not enclosed [only before noun] not enclosed or covered by buildings, walls etc.: *Increased development has led to a loss of open land in the county.* | *an open staircase* —see also OPEN SPACE

8 not covered without a roof or cover: *an open carriage* | *an open sewer* | **open to the sky/elements** (=without a roof)

9 an open wound/sore etc. a wound that has not HEALed and is not covered

10 clothes not fastened: *Bill's white shirt was open at the collar.*

11 not secret [only before noun] open actions, feelings, intentions etc. are not hidden or secret: *I am bothered by your open admiration of these criminals.* | *Some of the memos were shown* **in open court** (=in a court of law where everything is public). | *Hamel's marriage breakdown had been* **an open secret** (=something that is supposed to be secret, but which most people know about) *long before it was reported in the paper.*

12 honest honest and not wanting to hide any facts from other people: *frank and open discussions* | [+ **with**] *I've been very open with you, and I would appreciate your support.*

13 be open to suggestions/help/offers etc. to be ready to consider people's suggestions, help, or offers: *As far as the title of the movie goes, I'm still open to suggestions.*

14 be open to discussion/negotiation/dispute etc. if something is open to discussion, NEGOTIATION etc., it has not been finally decided, so you can still discuss it, suggest changes etc.: *I've made up my mind, and the matter is not open to discussion.*

15 be open to criticism/blame/suspicion etc. to be likely to be criticized, blamed etc.: *Nelson's behavior leaves him open to accusations of favoritism.*

16 be open to question/doubt if something is open to question or doubt, you are not sure if it is good, true, likely to succeed etc.: *The authenticity of the relics is open to doubt.* | *Their motives are open to question* (=they may not be honest).

17 keep/have an open mind to deliberately not make a decision or form a definite opinion about something: *We have to keep an open mind until we see how the treatment works.*

18 book a book that is open has its pages moved apart so that you can read it: *A book lay open on the table.*

19 be an open book to not have any secrets and be easily understood: *I'd always thought of Jeff as an open book.*

20 keep your eyes/ears open to keep looking or listening so that you will notice anything that is important, dangerous etc.

21 welcome/greet sb with open arms to show that you are very pleased to see someone: *Returning troops were welcomed with open arms.*

22 leave yourself (wide) open to say or do something that makes it very easy for someone to attack or criticize you: [+ **to**] *By accepting the money Bass has left himself wide open to criticism.*

23 be (wide) open for/to sth to be ready for a particular activity or willing to accept it: *Siberia is wide open for development.*

24 opportunity if an opportunity or possible action is open to someone, they have the chance to do it: [**+ to**] *She has a right to know about all the options open to her.*

25 `job` [not before noun] a job that is open is available: *Is the position still open?*

26 keep/leave your options open to delay any decision so that you can choose later: *We want to keep our options open until the last possible minute.*

27 an open invitation a) an invitation to visit someone whenever you like **b)** something that makes it easier for someone to do something illegal or bad: *An unlocked car is an open invitation to thieves.*

28 in the open air outdoors, especially without any shelter or protection: *Each summer, they perform a play in the open air.* —see also **in the open** (OPEN³ (1)), OPEN-AIR

29 the open road roads that you can travel on freely or quickly: *They spent the day out driving on the open road.*

30 `time` [not before noun] if a time is open, nothing has been planned for that time: *I'm sorry, but the doctor doesn't have anything open for this afternoon.*

31 the open sea part of the ocean that is far from any land

32 open weave/texture cloth with an open weave or TEXTURE has wide spaces between the threads —see also **keep an eye open/peeled** (EYE¹ (21)), OPEN-EYED

open² *v.*

1 `door/window etc.` [I,T] to move a door, window etc. so that people, things, air etc can pass through, or to be moved in this way: *Will you open the door for me?* | *That window doesn't open.*

2 `container/package` [T] to unfasten or remove the lid, top, or cover of a container, package etc.: *Don't open another Coke – you can have the rest of mine.* | *Did you open the mail?*

3 `business time` [I] if a store, bank, public building etc. opens at a particular time, it begins to let customers or visitors come in at that time: *What time does the bank open?*

4 `start a business` [I,T] if a new business such as a store or restaurant opens or is opened, it starts operating: *The Thai restaurant that just opened is supposed to be good.* | *Runyan plans to open a casino.*

5 `start an activity` **a)** [I,T] to start an event, series of actions etc., or to be started in a particular way: *Tonight's concert opens a two-week festival.* | *Hecht opened the news conference by announcing his retirement.* | [**+ with**] *The story opens with the family's arrival in Boston from another city.* **b) open an inquiry/investigation** to start a process of collecting information about something: *The Health Department will open an investigation into the causes of the epidemic.*

6 `spread` [I,T] to spread something out, or to become spread out: *How do you open this umbrella?* *The rosebuds are starting to open.* | *Open your books to page 63.*

7 `open a way through` [T] to make it possible for cars, goods etc. to pass through a place: *They're plowing the snow to open the road to Aspen.* | *There has been an increase in violence since the country opened its borders to the West.*

8 `eyes` **a) open your eyes** to raise your EYELIDS so that you can see **b) open sb's eyes (to sth)** to make someone realize something that they had not realized before: *His speech really opened my eyes to the way big corporations operate.*

9 open fire (on sb) to start shooting at someone or something: *Troops opened fire on the rioters.*

10 open your mouth to move your lips apart

11 `movie/play etc.` [I] to start being shown to people: *The movie opens locally on Friday.*

12 open sth to the public to let people come and visit a house, park etc.: *Remington plans to open the museum to the public later this year.*

13 open an account to start an account at a bank or other financial organization by putting money into it

14 open your arms a) to stretch your arms wide apart, especially to show that you want to hold someone **b)** to welcome someone or treat them very

kindly: *Local people opened their arms to the earthquake victims.*

15 open the door/way to provide an opportunity for something to happen: [**+ to/for**] *Today's ruling could open the way to a large number of new lawsuits.*

16 open doors (for/to sb) to give someone an opportunity to do something: *Working on the movie was exciting and it opened doors for me.*

17 `official ceremony` [T] to perform a ceremony in which you officially state that a building is ready to be used: *The new airport will be officially opened by the President himself.*

18 `computer` [T] to make a document or computer PROGRAM ready to use: *Click on this icon to open your File Manager.*

19 open your mind to sth to be ready to consider or accept new ideas

20 open your heart (to sb) to tell someone your real thoughts and feelings because you trust them

21 open old wounds to remind someone of bad things that happened in the past: *Seeing my ex-boyfriend opened some old wounds.*

22 the heavens/skies open used to say that it starts to rain heavily —see also **open the floodgates** (FLOODGATE (1))

open onto/into sth *phr. v.* [T] if a room, door etc. opens onto or into another place, you can enter the other place directly through it: *The kitchen opens onto a patio.*

open onto

The back door opened onto the patio.

open out *phr. v.* [I] if a road, path, or passage opens out, it becomes wider: [**+ into**] *The lane opened out into a large paved courtyard.*

open up *phr. v.*

1 `opportunity` [I,T **open** sth ↔ **up**] to become available or possible, or to make something available or possible: *Roger is worried that nothing seems to be opening up for him.* | *Education opens up all kinds of career choices.*

2 `land` [I,T **open** sth ↔ **up**] if someone opens up a country or area of land, or if it opens up, it becomes easier to reach and ready for development, trade etc.: *Eastern Europe continues to open up to the West.* | *Most voters won't be upset if politicians open the land up for development.* | *an explorer who helped to open up trade routes to China*

3 `talk` [I] to stop being shy, and talk freely about your thoughts or feelings: [**+ to**] *It took Martha several weeks to open up to her therapist.*

4 `start a business` [I,T **open** sth ↔ **up**] if a store, restaurant etc. opens up or is opened up, someone starts it: *There's a new supermarket opening up in our neighborhood.*

5 `door/box` [I,T **open** sth ↔ **up**] to open a door or something such as a box or case: *Open up, we know you're in there.* | *Could you open up the suitcase, please?*

6 `with a gun` [I] to start shooting: *All of a sudden the soldiers opened up with gunfire.*

0

USAGE NOTE: OPEN

WORD CHOICE: open, close, shut, turn on/off, shut off, switch on/off
Use **open** and **close** or **shut** to talk about your mouth and eyes and objects such as doors and windows: *Close the door – I'd like to talk to you in private.* Use **turn on** (NOT open) and **turn off** or **shut off** (NOT close) to talk about water or gas: *Did you remember to turn off the gas?* Use **turn on** or **switch on** (NOT open) and **turn off**, **shut off**, or **switch off** (NOT close) to talk about things that use electricity: *Shut that radio off.* | *He sat down and turned on the TV.*

open³ *n.* **1 in the open a)** outdoors without any shelter or protection: *Let the seeds lie in the open for a day before planting them.* **b)** not hidden or secret: *a noisy argument that **brought** a lot of problems **out into the open*** **2** [C usually singular] a sports competition that both professional players and AMATEURS can compete in: *the US Open*

open-air /ˌ.. ˈ.◂/ *adj.* [only before noun] happening or existing outdoors, not in a building: *open-air concerts* | *an open-air market*

open-and-shut case /ˌ... .ˌ. ˈ./ *n.* [C usually singular] something such as a law CASE¹ (2) that is very easy to prove and will not take long to solve

open bar /ˌ.. ˈ./ *n.* [C] a bar at an occasion such as a wedding, where drinks are served free

open door pol·i·cy /ˌ.. ˈ. ˌ.../ *n.* [C] **1** the principle of allowing people and goods to move freely into your country **2** the principle of allowing anyone to come and talk to you while you are working

open-end·ed /ˌ.. ˈ.◂/ *adj.* **1** without a definite ending: *an open-ended run at the theater* **2** not having a single, definite answer, result etc.: *an open-ended question*

o·pen·er /ˈoʊpənə/ *n.* [C] **1** a tool or machine used to open letters, bottles, or cans: *an electric can opener* **2** the first of a series of things such as sports competitions: *the Nuggets' season opener* **3 for openers** INFORMAL as a beginning or first stage: *For openers, why not put a special tax on cigarettes to fund health education?* —see also EYE-OPENER

open-eyed /ˌ.. ˈ.◂/ *adj. adv.* **1** awake, or with your eyes open **2** accepting or taking notice of all the facts of a situation: *clear, open-eyed reasoning*

open-faced sand·wich /ˌ.. ˈ..◂/ *n.* [C] a single piece of bread with meat, cheese etc. on top

open-hand·ed /ˌ.. ˈ..◂/ *adj.* **1** done with an open hand: *an open-handed slap* **2** generous and friendly: *Martha's a very open-handed, generous person.* —**openhandedness** *n.* [U]

open-heart·ed /ˌ.. ˈ..◂/ *adj.* kind and sympathetic

open-heart sur·gery /ˌ.. ˌ. ˈ.../ *n.* [U] a medical operation in which doctors operate on someone's heart, while a special machine keeps the person's blood flowing

open house /ˌ.. ˈ./ *n.* [C] **1** an occasion when a college, factory, or organization allows the public to come in and see the work that is done there **2** an occasion on which someone who is selling their house lets everyone who is interested in buying it come to see it **3** a party at someone's house that you can come to or leave at any time during a particular period: *Wanda's having an open house Saturday to show off her new condo.*

o·pen·ing¹ /ˈoʊpənɪŋ/ *n.* **1** [C] an occasion when a new business, building, road etc. starts working or being used: [+ of] *the opening of the new library* **2** [C] a hole or space in something through which air, light, objects etc. can pass: *There was a narrow opening, just big enough for us to squeeze through.* **3** [C] a job or position that is available: [+ for] *There are two openings at the university for financial aid counselors.* **4** [C usually singular] the beginning or first part of something: *the play's exciting opening* | [+ of] *the opening of the trial* **5** [C] a good chance for

someone to do or say something: [**opening to do sth**] *I waited for an opening to give my opinion.* **6** [U] the act of opening something: [+ **of**] *the opening of Christmas presents*

opening² *adj.* [only before noun] first or beginning: *the opening round of the tournament*

opening hours /ˈ... ˌ./ *n.* [plural] the hours during which a shop, office etc. is open to the public

opening night /ˌ... ˈ./ *n.* [C] the first night that a new play, movie etc. is shown to the public

opening time /ˈ... ˌ./ *n.* [C] the time when a shop, office etc. opens to the public

open let·ter /ˌ.. ˈ../ *n.* [C] a letter to an important person, which is printed in a newspaper or magazine so that everyone can read it, usually in order to protest about something

o·pen·ly /ˈoʊpənli/ *adv.* in a way that does not hide your feelings, opinions, or the facts: *At that time, people did not often talk openly about death.* | *an openly gay politician*

open mar·ket /ˌ.. ˈ../ *n.* **1** [C usually singular] a type of economic system in which there are few laws and controls restricting the buying and selling of goods with other countries: *efforts to establish a more competitive open market in the former Soviet Union* **2 on the open market** available for sale publicly, not privately or secretly: *The terrorists purchased high-powered weapons on the open market.* **3** [C] an outdoor area in a city where things can be bought and sold by anyone —**open-market** *adj.*: *the open-market price*

open marriage /ˌ.. ˈ../ *n.* [C] a marriage in which having sex with other people is allowed

open mike /ˌ.. ˈ./ *n.* [U] a time when anyone is allowed to tell jokes, sing etc. in a bar or NIGHTCLUB —**open-mike** *adj.* [only after noun] *open-mike night*

open-mind·ed /ˌ.. ˈ..◂/ *adj.* willing to consider and accept other people's ideas, opinions etc.: *Dr. Sutton is very open-minded about non-traditional treatments.* —**openmindedly** *adv.* —**openmindedness** *n.* [U] —compare NARROW-MINDED

open-mouthed /ˌ.. ˈ.◂/ *adj., adv.* with your mouth wide open, because you are very surprised or shocked: *We stared open-mouthed at the meteor shower.*

open-necked /ˌ.. ˈ.◂/ *adj.* an open-necked shirt is one on which the top button has not been fastened

o·pen·ness /ˈoʊpənnɪs/ *n.* [U] **1** the quality of being honest and not keeping things secret: *a relationship based on trust and openness* **2** the quality of being willing to accept new ideas or people: [**openness to sth**] *Improving public education will require openness to change and innovation.* **3** the quality of being open and not enclosed: [+ **of**] *the openness of the city's downtown area*

open-plan /ˌ.. ˈ./ *adj.* an open-plan office, school etc. does not have walls dividing it into separate rooms

open pri·mar·y /ˌ.. ˈ.../ *n.* [C] a PRIMARY ELECTION in the U.S. in which any voter may vote for someone from any party

open re·la·tion·ship /ˌ.. .ˈ.../ *n.* [C] a romantic relationship in which having sex with other people is allowed

open sea·son /ˌ.. ˈ../ *n.* [singular] **1** the period of time each year when it is legal to kill certain animals or fish as a sport: [+ **for/on**] *open season for ducks* **2 open season (on sb)** a time when a lot of people take the opportunity to criticize someone: *In the press, it seems to be open season on overpaid executives.*

open se·cret /ˌ.. ˈ../ *n.* [C] something that is supposed to be a secret but is actually known by everyone: [+ **that**] *It was an open secret in Washington that the Senator was having an affair.*

open ses·a·me /ˌ.. ˈ.../ *n.* [singular] a fast way to achieve something that is very difficult: [+ **to**] *He discovered that having wealth wasn't an open sesame to gaining respect.*

open shop /ˌ.. ˈ./ *n.* [C] a business such as a factory where EMPLOYEES do not have to be members of a UNION (1) in order to work there —compare CLOSED SHOP

open space /ˌ.. './ n. [C,U] land on which people are not allowed to build houses, buildings etc. because it is officially protected by a government, especially so that people can use it for outdoor activities

open sys·tem /ˌ.. '../ n. [C] TECHNICAL a computer system that is made so that it can be connected with similar computer systems or parts made by other companies —**open-system** adj.

open-toed /ˌ.. '.◄/ adj. **open-toed sandals/shoes** shoes that do not cover the top or end of your toes

open vow·el /ˌ.. '../ n. [C] TECHNICAL a vowel that is pronounced with your tongue flat on the bottom of your mouth

op·era /ˈɑprə, ˈɑpərə/ n. **1** [C] a musical play in which the words are sung rather than spoken: *one of Puccini's best-loved operas* | *We try to* **go to the opera** (=go to a performance of an opera) *a few times a year.* **2** [U] these plays considered as a form of art: *Do you enjoy opera?* —**operat·ic** /ˌɑpəˈrætɪk/ adj. —**operatically** /-kli/ adv. —see also COMIC OPERA, GRAND OPERA, SOAP OPERA —compare OPERETTA

op·er·a·ble /ˈɑprəbəl/ adj. a medical condition that is operable can be treated by an operation —compare INOPERABLE

opera glass·es /ˈ.. ˌ../ n. [plural] a pair of special small glasses used at the theater so that you can see the stage more clearly

opera house /ˈ.. ˌ./ n. [C] a theater where operas are performed

op·er·ate /ˈɑpəˌreɪt/ v. **1 a)** [T] to use and control a machine or piece of equipment: *A team of three men operate the dam.* | *It took me weeks to learn to operate the VCR.* **b)** [I always + adv./prep.] if a machine operates in a particular way, it works in that way; FUNCTION: *Our generator doesn't operate well in cold weather.* | [+ **at/on**] *The heating system operates on natural gas* (=it uses natural gas as fuel). | *a processor operating at 450MHz* **2** [I,T] to organize a business or activity, or to carry out your business or activities in a particular way: *The company operates fast-food restaurants in over 60 countries.* | [+ **in/within/from** etc.] *Pan Am Shuttle mainly operates between New York and Boston. They are seeking permission for the hospital to* **operate as** *a nursing home.* **3** [I] to cut open someone's body in order to remove or repair a part that is damaged: *They had operated on him six times before he was a year old.* | [+ **on**] *Doctors had to operate on his spine.* **4** [I] if a system or process operates in a particular way, it works in that way and has particular results: *The legislative system operates independently of the President.* **5** [I always + adv./prep.] to do your job or try to achieve things in a particular way: *Alice operates on her own time schedule.* | *Smith was accused of operating without the knowledge of his commanding officer.*

operating ex·pens·es /ˈ.... ˌ../ n. [plural] the money that you have to spend to keep a business going, such as paying for rent and office supplies

operating room /ˈ.... ˌ./ n. [C] a room in a hospital where operations are done

operating sys·tem /ˈ.... ˌ../ n. [C] a system in a computer that helps all the programs in it work together

operating ta·ble /ˈ.... ˌ../ n. [C] a special table that you lie on to have a medical operation

op·er·a·tion /ˌɑpəˈreɪʃən/ n.
1 medical [C] the process of cutting into someone's body to repair or remove a part that is damaged: *a throat operation* | [+ **on**] *Dan had an operation on his left hip.* | *It took three hours for doctors to* **perform the operation**.
2 business **a)** [C] a business, company, or organization, especially one with many parts: *a profitable data storage operation* | *She runs one of the most powerful lobbying operations in Washington.* **b)** [C U] the work or activities done by a business, organization etc., or the process of doing this work: *These are the lottery's worst results since its first year of operation.* | *Ross Discount Clothing has over 200 stores* **in operation**.
3 organized actions [C] a set of planned actions, especially done by a large group of people, to achieve

a particular purpose: *a big rescue operation* | *In a joint U.S.-Mexican operation, police arrested 28 people on charges of drug-smuggling.*
4 machine/equipment [U] the way the parts of a machine or piece of equipment work together, or the process of making a machine work: *Tell the mechanic to check the operation of the ignition system.* | *The nuclear reactor has been* **in operation** (=working) *since 1985.*
5 principle/law/plan etc. [U] the way that something such as a law, system, or process works and has an effect: *the operation of the laws of gravity* | *New immigration controls will be* **in operation** *by next January.* | *The U.S. Parcel Post system first* **went into operation** (=started operating) *in 1913.*
6 computers [C] TECHNICAL an action done by a computer: *The new chip can process millions of operations per second.*

op·er·a·tion·al /ˌɑpəˈreɪʃənl/ adj. **1** [usually after noun] working and ready to be used: *The satellite is expected to be operational by next week.* | *Denver's new airport is now* **fully operational**. **2** [only before noun] related to the operation of a business, government etc.: *the bank's operational budget* —**operationally** adv.

op·er·a·tive¹ /ˈɑprətɪv/ adj. **1** the **operative word** used when you repeat a word from a previous statement to emphasize its importance: *He's a kind of amateur psychologist, and amateur is the operative word here.* **2** working and having an effect: *Old trading restrictions are no longer operative.*

operative² n. [C] **1** someone who does secret work, especially for a government organization: *a CIA operative* **2** TECHNICAL a worker, especially one who has a practical skill: *factory workers and similar operatives*

op·er·a·tor /ˈɑpəˌreɪtə/ n. [C] **1** someone who works on a telephone SWITCHBOARD, who you can call to get information or to get help: *Dial "0" to get the operator.* **2** someone who operates a machine or piece of equipment: *an elevator operator* **3** a person or company that operates a particular business: *a day-care center operator.* | *a tour operator* **4** a disapproving word for someone who is good at getting what they want by persuading people: *a political operator* | *The former governor is seen* **a smooth operator** *who does favors for his friends.*

op·e·ret·ta /ˌɑpəˈrɛtə/ n. [C] a short or romantic musical play in which some of the words are spoken and some are sung: *Herbert's operetta "Babes in Toyland"* —compare OPERA

oph·thal·mi·a /ɑfˈθælmiə, ɑp-/ n. [U] TECHNICAL a disease that affects the eyes and makes them red and swollen

oph·thal·mic /ɑfˈθælmɪk, ɑp-/ adj. [only before noun] TECHNICAL related to the eyes and the diseases that affect them: *an ophthalmic surgeon*

oph·thal·mol·o·gist /ˌɑfθəˈmɑlədʒɪst, -θəlˈmɑ-, ˌɑp-/ n. [C] TECHNICAL a doctor who treats people's eyes and does operations on them —compare OPTOMETRIST

oph·thal·mol·o·gy /ˌɑfθəˈmɑlədʒi/ n. [U] TECHNICAL the study of the eyes and diseases that affect them

o·pi·ate /ˈoʊpiət, -eɪt/ n. [C] a type of drug that contains OPIUM and makes you sleepy

o·pine /oʊˈpaɪn/ v. [T + **that**] FORMAL to express your opinion: *"This project is great news for Tucson,"* opined the Mayor.

o·pin·ion /əˈpɪnyən/ n. **1** [C] your ideas or beliefs about a particular subject: [+ **about/on**] *He was asked for his opinion on the Arab-Israeli peace process.* | *Carol has some pretty strong opinions about the military.* | **give/express an opinion** (=say what you think about something) **2** [U] the general ideas or beliefs that a group of people have about something: *Opinion seemed to be moving in favor of the president's accusers.* | *a development plan that took no account of* **public opinion 3** [C] judgment or advice from a professional person about something:

0

an expert opinion | We got **a second opinion** (=advice from a second person to make sure the first was right) before we replaced our furnace. **4 have a high/low/bad etc. opinion of sb/sth** to think that someone or something is very good or very bad: I've always had a good opinion of Rick's artwork. **5 in my opinion** also **if you want my opinion** used to firmly tell someone what you think about a particular subject: In my opinion, Will and Martha should have never gotten married. **6 be of the opinion (that)** FORMAL to think that something is true: The committee is of the opinion that Barnes was wrongfully dismissed. —see also **difference of opinion** (DIFFERENCE (5)), **sth is a matter of opinion** (MATTER¹ (25))

o·pin·ion·at·ed /ə'pɪnyə,neɪtɪd/ adj. expressing very strong opinions, and sure that your opinions are always right: opinionated professors

opinion-mak·ers /.'.. ,../ n. [plural] people who have great influence over the way the public thinks

opinion poll /.'.. ,./ n. [C] —see POLL¹

o·pi·um /'oupiəm/ n. [U] a powerful illegal drug made from POPPY seeds, that used to be used legally to stop pain, and that is used for making HEROIN

o·pos·sum /ə'pɑsəm/ also **possum** n. [C] one of various small animals from America and Australia that has fur and climbs trees and often pretends it is dead when it is in danger —see picture at MARSUPIAL

opp. the written abbreviation of "opposite"

Op·pen·hei·mer /'ɑpən,haɪmɚ/, **J. Rob·ert** /dʒeɪ 'rɑbɚt/ (1904–1967) a U.S. PHYSICIST who led the Manhattan Project to develop the first ATOMIC BOMB

S W
2

op·po·nent /ə'pounənt/ n. [C] **1** a person or group who tries to defeat another person or group in a competition, game, fight, election etc.: Carson is Seymour's main opponent for the Republican Senate nomination. **2** someone who disagrees with a plan, idea etc., and wants to try and stop it: [+ of] Reed is an outspoken opponent of the death penalty.

op·por·tune /,ɑpɚ'tun/ adj. FORMAL **1 an opportune moment/time/place etc.** a time that is very appropriate for doing something: Now is not the most opportune time to discuss buying a home. **2** done or said at a very appropriate time: her opportune arrival —**opportunely** adv. —opposite INOPPORTUNE

op·por·tun·ism /,ɑpɚ'tunɪzəm/ n. [U] using every chance to gain power or advantages for yourself, without caring if you have to use dishonest methods: To her opponents, Goodright's support for minority rights looked like political opportunism.

op·por·tun·ist /,ɑpɚ'tunɪst/ n. [C] someone who uses every chance to gain power or advantages, even if they have to use dishonest methods: an unethical opportunist —**opportunist** adj.: the union's opportunist leadership

op·por·tun·is·tic /,ɑpɚtu'nɪstɪk/ adj. **1** typical of an opportunist: It was a typically opportunistic change of loyalties. **2 opportunistic infection/disease/virus** an illness that affects your body when it is weak and cannot fight diseases —**opportunistically** /-kli/ adv.

S W
2 1

op·por·tu·ni·ty /,ɑpɚ'tunəti/ n. plural **opportunities** **1** [C,U] a chance to do something, or an occasion when it is easy for you to do something: [opportunity to do sth] Maybe we'll have an opportunity to sit down and talk this weekend. | Project work gives students the opportunity to develop their language skills. | [+ for] It seemed like a great opportunity for making money. | I'd like to **take this opportunity to** (=use this chance to) thank my staff for their hard work.. | His children seem to get into trouble **at every opportunity** (=whenever they have the chance to do it). | **at the first/earliest opportunity** (=as soon as possible) **2** [C] a chance to get a job: Educators are worried about rapidly diminishing opportunities for graduates. —see also **equal opportunities** (EQUAL¹ (2))

opposable thumb /.,... './ n. [C] a thumb that

people, MONKEYS etc. have that can be used for holding things

op·pose /ə'pouz/ v. [T] **1** to disagree with something such as a plan or idea and try to prevent it from happening or succeeding: It is typical for local residents to oppose the building of a nuclear waste facility. **2** to fight or compete against another person or group in a battle, competition, or election: Gillmore will be opposed by former Councilman Tobkin for the post of mayor.

S W
2 2

op·posed /ə'pouzd/ adj. [not before noun] **1 be opposed to sth** disagreeing with a plan, a type of behavior etc., or feeling that it is wrong: Most company bosses say they are opposed to employees working a lot of overtime. | Senator Thomson is **bitterly opposed to** (=completely against) any form of gun control. **2 as opposed to sth** used to compare two different things and show that you mean one and not the other: The tax system favors the very rich as opposed to ordinary working people. —see also **diametrically opposed/opposite** (DIAMETRICALLY)

op·pos·ing /ə'pouzɪŋ/ adj. [only before noun] **1** opposing teams, groups, forces etc. are competing, arguing, or fighting against each other: Michigan's complex offense has kept opposing teams guessing. | a political group that split into two opposing factions **2** opposing ideas, opinions etc. are completely different from each other: Russia and the U.S. have opposing views on arms sales to the region.

op·po·site¹ /'ɑpəzɪt, -sɪt/ adj. **1** as different as possible from something else: two words with opposite meanings | Raising interest rates to slow the economy may have the opposite effect. | [+ to] a political philosophy that was opposite to everything she believed in **2** on the other side of the same area, often directly across from it: I think our hotel is **on the opposite side of** the street. | We live **at opposite ends** of the state (=on different sides of the state, very far apart) so we don't often see each other. **3** the opposite direction, way etc. is directly away from someone or something: Two suspects were seen running off **in the opposite direction**. **4 the opposite sex** people of the other sex: The magazine article's title was "How to become irresistible to the opposite sex." **5 opposite number** someone who has the same job in another similar organization: her opposite number in the Republican Party

opposite² prep. **1** if one thing or person is opposite another, they are facing each other: Put the piano opposite the sofa. **2 play/star/appear opposite sb** to act with another person in a movie or play as one of the main characters: Vivien Leigh played opposite Clark Gable in "Gone With The Wind."

opposite³ n. [C] **1** a person or thing that is as different as possible from someone or something else: The two sisters are complete opposites. | [the opposite (of sb/sth)] The results were the opposite of what we expected. | He says one thing and then does the opposite. | Eileen's parents are very formal, but mine are **just the opposite**. **2 opposites attract** said to explain the romantic attraction between two people who are very different from each other

S W
3

opposite⁴ adv. in a position on the other side of the same area: My cousin was sitting opposite.

op·po·si·tion /,ɑpə'zɪʃən/ n. [U] **1** strong disagreement with, or protest against, something such as a plan, law, or official decision: [opposition to sth] There continues to be overwhelming opposition to cutting school funding. | **strong/fierce opposition** The plan has met fierce opposition from environmentalists. | **meet/encounter opposition** The push for national school tests is encountering opposition from Republicans. [in opposition (to sth)] Restaurant owners jammed City Hall in opposition to the new regulations. **2** the people who you are competing against, especially in a sports game: In the last 17 games, the Red Wings have outscored the opposition 36–8.

S W
2

op·press /ə'prɛs/ v. [T often passive] **1** to treat a group of people unfairly or cruelly, and prevent them from having the same rights and opportunities as other people: "My people were oppressed by your people for three hundred years," Cavita commented.

2 to make someone feel unhappy by restricting their freedom in some way: *The loneliness of her little apartment oppressed her.*

op·pressed /ə'prɛst/ *adj.* **1** a group of people who are oppressed are treated unfairly or cruelly and prevented from having the same rights and opportunities as other people: *oppressed minorities* | **the oppressed** (=people who are oppressed) **2** someone who is oppressed feels their freedom has been restricted

op·pres·sion /ə'prɛʃən/ *n.* [U] the act of oppressing a group of people, or the state of being oppressed: *the oppression of women*

op·pres·sive /ə'prɛsɪv/ *adj.* **1** powerful, cruel, and unfair: *an oppressive dictatorship* **2** weather that is oppressive is very hot with no movement of air, which makes you feel uncomfortable: *Summers in Houston can be oppressive.* **3** a situation that is oppressive makes you feel too uncomfortable to do or say anything: *The silence in the meeting was becoming oppressive.* —**oppressively** *adv.* —**oppressiveness** *n.* [U]

op·pres·sor /ə'prɛsɚ/ *n.* [C] a person, group, or country that oppresses people: *Members of the minority community view the police department as their oppressor.*

op·pro·bri·ous /ə'proubriəs/ *adj.* FORMAL showing great disrespect —**opprobriously** *adv.*

op·pro·bri·um /ə'proubriəm/ *n.* [U] FORMAL strong public criticism, hatred, or shame: *Any country trading in these weapons would face international opprobrium.*

opt /ɑpt/ *v.* [I] to choose one thing or one course of action instead of another: [+ **for**] *About 40 percent of Mazda MX-3 buyers opted for the V-6 engine.* | [**opt to do sth**] *Many visitors opt to stay along the Costa Brava south of Barcelona.*

opt out *phr. v.* [I] **1** to decide not to do something, or to excuse yourself from doing something: [+ **of**] *David felt sick and opted out of going to his Uncle's house for dinner that night* **2** to decide not to join a group, system or action: [+ **of**] *Miller opted out of military service for religious reasons.*

op·tic /ɑptɪk/ *adj.* [only before noun] concerning the eyes: *optic nerves*

op·ti·cal /ɑptɪkəl/ *adj.* [only before noun] **1** used for seeing images and light: *They sell optical equipment such as cameras and telescopes.* **2** using light as a means of sending or storing information, especially for use in a computer system: *Optical bar-code scanners have revolutionized the postal system.* **3** relating to the way light is seen: *optical distortions caused by poor quality lenses* —**optically** /-kli/ *adv.*

optical fi·ber /ˌ... '../ *n.* [U] a thread-like material made of glass which is used for sending information for example in a telephone or computer system

optical il·lu·sion /ˌ... '../ *n.* [C] a picture or image that tricks your eyes and makes you see something that is not actually there

op·ti·cian /ɑp'tɪʃən/ *n.* [C] someone who makes and sells LENSes for GLASSes (GLASS (4)) —compare OPTOMETRIST

op·tics /ɑptɪks/ *n.* [U] the scientific study of light

op·ti·mal /ɑptəməl/ *adj.* FORMAL the best or most appropriate; OPTIMUM

op·ti·mism /ɑptə,mɪzəm/ *n.* [U] a tendency to believe that good things will always happen and the future will be good: *the optimism of the postwar years* —opposite PESSIMISM

op·ti·mist /ɑptə,mɪst/ *n.* [C] someone who is always hopeful and always believes that good things will happen: *You have to be an optimist to be in an occupation such as farming.* —opposite PESSIMIST

op·ti·mis·tic /ˌɑptə'mɪstɪk/ *adj.* believing that good things will happen in the future, or feeling confident that you will succeed: [**optimistic (that)**] *Authorities say they are optimistic the killer will be caught.* | [+ **about**] *Investment analysts seemed optimistic about the company's prospects.* | *She said she could be here by 7:30, but I think that's a little optimistic.* —**optimistically** /-kli/ *adv.* —opposite PESSIMISTIC —see also OVER-OPTIMISTIC

op·ti·mize /ɑptə,maɪz/ *v.* [T] to make the way that something operates as effective and successful as possible: *a software package that optimizes data storage on your hard disk* —**optimization** /ˌɑptəmə'zeɪʃən/ *n.* [U]

op·ti·mum /ɑptəməm/ *adj.* [only before noun] ESPECIALLY TECHNICAL the best or most appropriate that is possible: *Under optimum conditions, as many as 50 meteors per hour may be seen.* | *Winter squash needs plenty of moisture to reach the optimum size.*

op·tion /ɑpʃən/ *n.* **s w** **2 2**
1 a choice [C,U] something that you can chose to do in a particular situation: *Joining the military seemed like the best option at the time.* | [**the option of doing sth**] *We were given the option of canceling our insurance policy.* | *I had no option but to turn the documents over to the police* (=I had to do it, because there were no other choices).
2 keep/leave your options open to wait and consider all possibilities before making a decision: *The band is keeping its options open, and doesn't rule out the possibility of another tour.*
3 right to buy/sell [C] the right to buy or sell something in the future: [+ **on**] *After two years with the firm, employees are given an option on 100 shares of stock.*
4 sth that is additional [C] something that is offered in addition to the standard equipment when you buy something new, especially a car: *Leather seats are an option on the Toyota Camry.*
5 computers [C] one of the possible choices you can make when using a computer program: *Press "P" to select the print option.*
6 first option the chance to buy or get something before anyone else: *Local farmers will get first option to buy land when the military base closes.*

op·tion·al /ɑpʃənl/ *adj.* if something is optional, you **s w** do not have to do it or use it, but you can choose to **1** if you want to: *Attendance at the meeting is optional.*

op·tom·e·trist /ɑp'tɑmətrɪst/ *n.* [C] someone who tests people's eyes and orders GLASSes (4) for them

op·u·lence /ɑpyələns/ *n.* [U] wealth and LUXURY: *the opulence of Monte Carlo*

op·u·lent /ɑpyələnt/ *adj.* **1 a)** very beautiful, highly decorated, and made from expensive materials; LUXURIOUS: *the opulent Fontainebleau Hotel* **b)** very rich and spending a lot of money: *Morishita leads an opulent lifestyle.* **2** growing in a healthy way and in large amounts

o·pus /'oupəs/ *n.* [usually singular] **1** a piece of music by a great musician, numbered according to when it was written: *Beethoven's Sonata in E Major, Opus 109* **2** a piece of work by a well-known writer, painter etc.: *Woody Allen's latest opus is a musical comedy, shot on location in Venice.* —see also MAGNUM OPUS

OR 1 the written abbreviation of Oregon **2** the abbreviation of OPERATING ROOM

or /ɚ; *strong* ɔr/ [conjunction] **1** used between two **s w** things, ideas, actions etc., or before the last in a list **1 1** of possibilities: *Was it an accident, or did she do it on purpose?* | *dangerous sports, such as mountaineering or hang-gliding* | *Would you like your sandwich on white, wheat, or rye bread?* | *You can have either cherry or apple pie for dessert.* —compare EITHER[1] **2 or anything/or something** SPOKEN similar to what you have just mentioned: *Jeff plays the bongo drums or something.* | *Does it have chili peppers or anything in it?* **3** used after a negative verb when you mean not one thing and also not another thing: *Jody doesn't eat meat or dairy products.* | *I've never been to Africa or Asia.* **4** used to warn or advise someone that if they do not do something, something bad will happen: *Hurry up or you'll miss your flight.* | *They have to deliver the pizza in 30 minutes, or it's free.* | *Get me my money by next week or else* (=used as a threat). **5 or so** used with an amount, number, distance etc. to show that it is not exact: *There's a gas station a mile or so down the road.* **6 a minute/a**

0

dollar etc. or two a small amount or number of something: *It's been a week or two since we had lunch together.* **7** used to explain why something happens or to show that something must be true: *Josh must be very tired, or he wouldn't have yelled at us.* | *It must be important,* **or else** *he wouldn't have called at 3 a.m.* **8** used to correct something that you have said or to give more specific information: *She was born in Saigon, or Ho Chi Minh City as it is now called.* | *We used to tease Andy about his height,* **or rather** *his lack of height.*

-or /ə/ *suffix* [in nouns] someone who does something: *an actor* (=someone who acts) | *an inventor* (=someone who invents things) —see also -ER

or·a·cle /'ɔrəkəl, 'ɑr-/ *n.* [C] **1** someone the ancient Greeks believed could communicate with the gods, who gave advice to people or told them what would happen in the future **2** a message given by an oracle

o·rac·u·lar /ɔ'rækyələ, ə-/ *adj.* **1** said by an oracle **2** difficult to understand

o·ral[1] /'ɔrəl/ *adj.* **1** spoken, not written: *an oral report* | *oral history* **2** concerned with or involving the mouth: *oral cancer* | *oral hygiene* —**orally** *adv.*

oral[2] *n.* [C] a test in which questions and answers are spoken, rather than written

oral con·tra·cep·tive /ˌ.. ..'../ *n.* [C] a drug that a woman takes by mouth, so that she can have sex without having a baby; the pill (PILL (2))

oral ex·am /'.. .,.., ,.. './ *n.* [C] an ORAL

oral sex /ˌ.. './ *n.* [U] touching someone's sex organs with the lips and tongue to give sexual pleasure

oral sur·geon /ˌ.. '../ *n.* [C] a DENTIST who performs operations in the mouth

or·ange /'ɔrɪndʒ, 'ɑr-/ *n.* **1** [C] a round fruit that has a thick orange skin and is divided into parts inside: *Oranges are a good source of Vitamin C.* | *We had toast and orange juice for breakfast.* —see picture at FRUIT[1] **2** [U] a color that is between red and yellow: *They had painted the house in shades of orange, blue, and tan.* —**orange** *adj.: an orange cotton sweater*

or·ange·ade /ˌɑrəndʒ'eɪd, ˌɔr-/ *n.* [U] a drink that tastes like oranges

or·ange·ry /'ɑrəndʒri, 'ɔr-/ *n.* [C] a place where orange trees are grown

o·rang·u·tang, o·rang·u·tan /ə'ræŋə,tæŋ/ *n.* [C] a large APE[1] (1) with long arms and long orange hair

o·ra·tion /ə'reɪʃən, ɔ-/ *n.* [C] a formal public speech

or·a·tor /'ɔrətə, 'ɑr-/ *n.* [C] someone who is good at making speeches that can influence the way people think and feel

or·a·to·ri·o /ˌɔrə'tɔrioʊ, ˌɑr-/ *n.* [C] a long piece of music in which a large group of people sing

or·a·to·ry /'ɔrə,tɔri, 'ɑr-/ *n.* **1** [U] the skill of making powerful speeches that persuade others to believe you or do what you ask them: *Reverend Sonny Lara is well-known for his oratory.* **2** [C] a small building or part of a church where people can go to pray —**oratorical** /ˌɔrə'tɔrɪkəl, ˌɑr-/ *adj.: oratorical skills* —**oratorically** /-kli/ *adv.*

orb /ɔrb/ *n.* [C] LITERARY a bright ball-shaped object, especially the sun or the moon: *a bright orb on the horizon*

or·bit[1] /'ɔrbɪt/ *n.* [C] **1** the path traveled in space by an object which is moving around another much larger object, such as the Earth or the sun: *the Moon's orbit around the Earth* | *Two more satellites have since been* **put into orbit** (=into space, so that they are traveling in this kind of path). **2** an area of power and influence: *Diplomats want to draw the two republics into the West European orbit.*

orbit[2] *v.* [I,T] to travel in a circle in space around a much larger object, such as the Earth or the sun: *Venus orbits the sun once every 225 Earth days.*

or·bit·al /'ɔrbɪtl/ *adj.* concerned with the orbit of one object around another: *the Earth's orbital path*

or·chard /'ɔrtʃəd/ *n.* [C] a place where fruit trees are grown: *a peach orchard*

or·ches·tra /'ɔrkɪstrə/ *n.* [C] a large group of musicians playing many different kinds of instruments, usually CLASSICAL MUSIC, and led by a CONDUCTOR (1): *the Chicago Symphony Orchestra*

or·ches·tral /ɔr'kɛstrəl/ *adj.* concerned with or written for an orchestra: *orchestral music*

orchestra pit /'... ,./ *n.* [C] the space below the stage in a theater where the musicians sit

or·ches·trate /'ɔrkɪ,streɪt/ *v.* [T] **1** to carefully organize an event or a complicated plan, especially secretly: *Police believe Casey orchestrated the kidnapping.* **2** to arrange a piece of music so that it can be played by an orchestra —**orchestrated** *adj.* —**orchestration** /ˌɔrkɪ'streɪʃən/ *n.* [C,U]

or·chid /'ɔrkɪd/ *n.* [C] a plant that has flowers with three parts, the middle one being shaped like a lip

or·dain /ɔr'deɪn/ *v.* [T usually passive] **1** to officially make someone a priest or religious leader: *Kahan was ordained in Brooklyn in 1938.* | [**be ordained (as) sth**] *She is the first woman to be ordained as a bishop.* —see also ORDINATION **2** FORMAL to make the decision that something should happen: *King Henry VIII believed his role as ruler was ordained by God.* | [**ordain that**] *It was as if fate had ordained that they would marry.*

or·deal /ɔr'dil/ *n.* [C] a very bad or frightening experience: *The hostages described their terrifying six-week ordeal.* | [**+ of**] *His new movie is about the ordeal of a college student after she is raped.*

or·der[1] /'ɔrdə/ *n.*

1 [arrangement] [C,U] the way that several things, events etc. are arranged or put on a list, showing whether something is first, second, third etc.; SEQUENCE: *The program shows the order of events for the day.* | *Check that all the names are in the right order.* | *Could you put these pictures* **in order** (=so that they are arranged in the correct way)? | *What order are these notes supposed to be in?* | *Hey, you've got these forms* **out of order** (=in the wrong order). | **in order of importance/preference/appearance** etc. *Characters are listed in order of appearance.* | **in chronological/alphabetical/numerical order** *The names of contributing authors are listed in alphabetical order.* | **in reverse order** (=in the opposite order to what is usual) | **in ascending/descending order** (=starting with the lowest or highest number)

2 [for a purpose] **a) in order to do sth** for the purpose of doing something: *They need to raise $5 million in order to pay for the repairs.* | *In order to speed things up, we agreed to have another meeting tomorrow.* **b) in order for sb/sth to do sth** so that someone can do something, or something can happen: *In order for you to graduate this year, you'll need to go to summer school.* **c) in order that** FORMAL so that something can happen: *Judge Harris delayed the trial in order that the defendant could be given psychological tests.*

3 [well-organized condition] [U] a situation in which everything is well organized and correctly arranged: *You have some good ideas here, but you need to give them some order.* | *We desperately needed help in* **putting** *our finances* **in order** (=organizing them properly).

4 [no trouble or crime] [U] a situation in which rules and laws are obeyed, and authority is respected: *Neighborhood leaders are working with police to maintain* **law and order**. | *Strikes have caused a breakdown of* **public order** *in the capital.* | *With almost 40 students in the class, it's impossible to* **keep order** (=stop the students from talking, behaving badly etc.) | *They had to call in the National Guard to* **restore order**. | **call sb to order** (=order

order

alphabetical order

SW
1 1

someone in a formal meeting or court of law to obey the rules) | **Order in the court!** (=used in court to tell people to be quiet and obey the rules)

5 | customer's request | [C] **a)** a request made by a customer, for example a request for goods to be supplied or for a meal in a restaurant: *May I take your* **order** *now* (=used to ask what a customer in a restaurant wants)*?* | *CBS has* **placed an order** (=made an order) *for four additional episodes of the comedy.* | *Kepler's has 50 copies of the book* **on order** (=ordered but not yet received). | *The carpet we wanted has been* **on back order** (=not currently available from the company that supplies the goods) *for the past three months.* | *There aren't many stores left that* **make suits to order** (=make them especially for a particular customer).* —see also* MADE-TO-ORDER **b)** what a customer has asked for, such as a meal or a type of goods: *We'll call and let you know when your order is ready to collect.* | [+ **of**] *She returned with my order of fries.* —see also SIDE ORDER

6 | command | [C] **a)** also **orders** a command given by someone in authority: *Military people are trained to* **obey orders.** | *I want the report ready by noon – and that's an order.* | *Margaret thinks she can just* **give** *everyone* **orders.** | *General Marshall* **gave the order to** *bomb the city.* | *It's hard to* **take orders from** (=obey) *someone you don't respect.* | *U.S. customs officials* **have orders to** (=have been told to) *seize all imported tobacco.* | *The documents were made public Wednesday,* **by order of** *the court* (=because of someone's order).* | The guards were* **under orders to** (=commanded to) *shoot to kill.* **b)** an official statement from a court of law which says that something must be done; COURT ORDER: *The court has issued an order blocking the sale of this drug.*

7 be out of order a) if a machine or piece of equipment is out of order, it is not working: *Oh no, the copy machine's out of order.* **b)** if things on a list or in a series are out of order, they are not correctly arranged: *Some of the pages were out of order.* **c)** to be breaking the rules in a committee, court, CONGRESS etc.: *Sit down Mr. Phillips! You're out of order.*

8 be in order a) if things on a list or in a series are in order, they are correctly arranged **b)** if an official document is in order, it is legal and correct: *Your work visa seems to be in order.* **c)** FORMAL to be an appropriate thing to do or say on a particular occasion: *I think a brief summary of the situation may be in order.*

9 in (good) working/running order if a vehicle or machine is in good working or running order, it is working well: *All our machines are kept in good working order.*

10 | political/economic situation | [singular] the political, social, or economic situation at a particular time: *It was the rich and powerful families who wanted to maintain* **the existing order.** | **the new order** (=the new situation, following important changes in politics or society) *in Eastern Europe* | **the established order** (=the traditional rules and customs of society)

11 first/main/next etc. order of business the first, most important etc. thing that needs to be done or discussed: *The main order of business is to select the site for the next convention.*

12 of the highest/the first/a high order of the best kind or of a very good kind: *The situation will require diplomatic agility of the highest order.*

13 be the order of the day a) to be a very common or typical feature of a particular time, place etc.: *Downsizing was the order of the day, and thousands of jobs were lost.* **b)** to be appropriate for a particular occasion or situation: *Casual clothes will be the order of the day.*

14 the natural order of things the way that life and the world are organized and intended to be: *For most political commentators, the Cold War was simply part of the natural order of things.*

15 on the order of sth a little more or a little less than a particular amount; APPROXIMATELY: *an increase in profits on the order of $20 million*

16 | religious group | [C] a society of MONKS or NUNS (=people who live a holy life according to religious

rules): *the Benedictine Order* | [+ **of**] *the Order of St. Agnes*

17 take (holy) orders to become a priest

18 | club/society | [C] an organization or society whose members have the same profession, interests etc.: *the Order of the Eastern Star* | *The Fraternal Order of Police*

19 | official honor | [C] **a)** a group of people who have received a special honor from a king, president etc. for their services or achievements: *the National Order of Loyal Knights* **b)** a special piece of metal, silk etc. that members of the order wear at ceremonies

20 | of animals/plants | [C] TECHNICAL a group of animals or plants that are considered together because they are believed to have come from the same plant or animal in EVOLUTION (1) —compare CLASS¹ (9), KINGDOM (3), SPECIES

21 | computer | [C] TECHNICAL a list of jobs that a computer has to do in a particular order —see also **marching orders** (MARCH¹ (5)), MONEY ORDER, PECKING ORDER, **in short order** (SHORT¹ (14)), **standing order** (STANDING¹ (2)), **be a tall order** (TALL (3))

order² v. **1** [I,T] to ask for goods or services to be supplied: *Are you ready to order?* | **order sth** *We all ordered the chef's salad.* | **order sth** *Maybe we should order John a drink too.* | **order sth for sb/sth** *They've ordered a new carpet for the bedroom.* **2** [T] to tell someone to do something, using your authority or power: *"Put your hands up!" the officer ordered.* | [**order sb to do sth**] *Health officials may order the hospital to change its hiring policies.* | *Staff had been ordered not to speak to anyone from the press.* | [**order sth**] *The President's advisers urged him to order an immediate attack.* | [+ **that**] *The court has the power to order that illegal copies of the movie be destroyed.* **3** [T usually passive] to arrange something in an order: *The desks were neatly ordered in rows.* **4** [T] OLD USE to organize things neatly or effectively

order sb around *phr. v.* [T] to continuously give someone orders in an annoying or threatening way: *I wish you'd stop ordering me around!*

order out *phr. v.* **1** [T] to order someone to leave a place: [+ **of**] *Western reporters have been ordered out of the country.* **2** [I] to order food to be delivered to your home or office: *Let's order out tonight.* | [+ **for**] *We ordered out for pizza.* **3** [T] to order soldiers or police to go somewhere to stop violent behavior by a crowd: *The Governor had no choice but to order out the National Guard.*

USAGE NOTE: ORDER

WORD CHOICE: order, command
Use **order** for most situations when someone in a position of authority tells other people to do something: *All foreigners were ordered to leave the city.* Use **command** when it is someone in the military who is telling other people to do something: *General Gaines commanded his men to fire.*

---

or·dered /ˈɔrdɚd/ also **well-ordered** *adj.* well arranged or controlled: *a well-ordered society* | *an ordered universe* —compare DISORDERED

order form /ˈ.. ˌ./ n. [C] special piece of paper for writing orders on: *Have you filled out the order form?*

or·der·ly¹ /ˈɔrdɚli/ *adj.* **1** arranged or organized in a sensible or neat way: *The improvements were put into effect in an orderly manner.* | *an orderly desk* **2** peaceful or well-behaved: *an orderly crowd* —**orderliness** *n.* [U]

orderly² *n.* [C] someone who does unskilled jobs in a hospital

or·di·nal¹ /ˈɔrdn-əl, -nəl/ *adj.* showing a position in a set of numbers

ordinal² *n.* [C] an ordinal number

or·di·nal num·ber /ˌ... ˈ.. ./ *n.* [C] a number such as first, second, third etc. which shows the order of things —compare CARDINAL NUMBER

or·di·nance /ˈɔrdn-əns/ *n.* [C] a law, usually of a city or town, that forbids or restricts an activity: *The ordinance prohibits the sale of fireworks within city limits.*

or·di·nar·i·ly /ˌɔrdnˈɛrəli/ *adv.* [sentence adverb] usually or in most cases: *Counseling ordinarily costs about $100 a session.* | *Ordinarily, it takes six weeks for applications to be processed.* | [+ adj./adv.] *an ordinarily quiet neighborhood*

or·di·nar·y /ˈɔrdnˌɛri/ *adj.* **1** average or usual, not different or special in any way: *Housing prices in New York are out of reach for ordinary people.* | *ordinary household items* | *an ordinary workday* **2 out of the ordinary** very different from what is usual: *Did you notice anything out of the ordinary in Julie's behavior?* **3** not very good, interesting, or impressive: *She was a serious young woman, rather ordinary in appearance.* | *I thought it was a pretty ordinary performance.* —**ordinariness** *n.* [U] —see also EXTRAORDINARY

ordinary shares /ˌ.... ˈ./ *n.* [plural] TECHNICAL the largest part of a company's CAPITAL¹ (2), which is owned by people who have the right to vote at meetings and to receive part of the company's profits

or·di·na·tion /ˌɔrdnˈeɪʃən/ *n.* [C,U] the act or ceremony of making someone a priest: *the ordination of women*

ord·nance /ˈɔrdnəns/ *n.* [U] **1** large guns with wheels; ARTILLERY **2** weapons, explosives, and vehicles used in fighting

or·dure /ˈɔrdʒɚ/ *n.* [U] FORMAL dirt, especially waste matter from a person's or animal's body

ore /ɔr/ *n.* [C,U] rock or earth from which metal can be obtained: *uranium ore* | *ore deposits*

o·reg·a·no /əˈrɛgəˌnoʊ/ *n.* [U] a plant used in cooking, especially in Italian cooking

Or·e·gon /ˈɔrɪgən/ *written abbreviation* **OR** a state in the northwestern U.S.

Oregon Trail, the /ˌ.... ˈ./ one of the main paths across the U.S. to the western part of the country, used by PIONEERS in the mid-19th century. The Trail crossed the Great Plains and the Rocky Mountains before turning toward Idaho, Washington, and Oregon

or·e·o /ˈɔrioʊ/ *n.* [C] OFFENSIVE, SLANG a disapproving word for an African-American person who other people think behaves like a white person

org /ɔrg/ the abbreviation of "organization," used in U.S. Internet addresses

or·gan /ˈɔrgən/ *n.* [C]
1 body part a) a part of the body, such as the heart or lungs, that has a particular purpose: *internal organs* | *an organ transplant* **b)** a word meaning PENIS, used because you want to avoid saying this directly
2 musical instrument a large musical instrument used especially in churches, with one or more KEYBOARDS¹ (1) and large pipes out of which the sound comes: *organ music*
3 organization an organization that is part of a larger organization, especially part of a government: [+ of] *You have to deal with the Foreign Trade Bank, which is an organ of the central government.*
4 newspaper/magazine FORMAL a newspaper or magazine which gives information, news etc. for an organization: [+ of] *Even "L'Unita", the organ of the Italian Communist Party, criticized the strike.*
5 plant a part of a plant, such as a leaf or stem, that has a special purpose

or·gan·die, **organdy** /ˈɔrgəndi/ *n.* [U] very thin stiff cotton, used to make dresses

organ grind·er /ˈ.. ˌ../ *n.* [C] a musician who plays a BARREL ORGAN (=a musical instrument played by turning a handle) in the street

or·gan·ic /ɔrˈgænɪk/ *adj.*
1 living/natural living, or produced by or from living things: *organic material such as leaves, bark, and grass* | *organic dyes* (=made from natural substances, not from chemicals) —opposite INORGANIC
2 food/farming produced by or using farming methods without artificial chemicals: *There was another big increase last year in the demand for organic vegetables.* | *They are demanding more government support for organic farmers.*
3 related parts involving many parts that all work together and all depend on each other: *Clark's proposals see the tax and welfare systems as a single organic whole.* | *There is an organic link in each song between the words and music*
4 development change or development which is organic happens in a natural way, without anyone planning it or forcing it to happen
5 body organs TECHNICAL concerning the organs of the body: *Two studies suggest a possible organic explanation for the disease.* —**organically** /-kli/ *adv.*

organic chem·is·try /.ˌ.. ˈ.../ *n.* [U] the study of CARBON (1) compounds —compare INORGANIC CHEMISTRY

or·gan·i·sa·tion /ˌɔrgənəˈzeɪʃən/ the British spelling of ORGANIZATION

or·gan·ise /ˈɔrgəˌnaɪz/ the British spelling of ORGANIZE

or·gan·ism /ˈɔrgəˌnɪzəm/ *n.* [C] **1** an animal, plant, human, or any other living thing: *The human body is a very complex organism.* | *Food poisoning is caused by a bacterial organism.* —see also MICROORGANISM **2** a system made up of parts that are dependent on each other: *A society is, in essence, an organism.*

or·gan·ist /ˈɔrgənɪst/ *n.* [C] someone who plays the ORGAN (2)

or·ga·ni·za·tion /ˌɔrgənəˈzeɪʃən/ *n.* **1** [C] a group of people, such as a club, a business, or a political party, which has formed for a particular purpose: *a non-profit environmental organization* | *Employees receive health care from a health maintenance organization (HMO).* **2** [U] the act of planning and arranging things effectively: *Callihan's organization and leadership has been invaluable.* | [+ of] *As museum director, she has overseen the organization of about 50 exhibitions.* **3** [U] the way in which the different parts of something are arranged and work together: *There are some good ideas here, but the essay lacks organization and clarity.* | [+ of] *the social organization of primitive cultures* —**organizational** *adj.*: *organizational ability* —**organizationally** *adv.*

organization chart /...ˈ.. ˌ./ also **organizational chart** /ˌ...ˈ... ˌ./ *n.* [C] a chart that shows the names of all the people in a business or other organization, and shows what they are responsible for and how they are related to each other

Organization of A·mer·i·can States, the /...ˌ.. .ˌ... ˈ./ —see OAS, THE

or·ga·nize /ˈɔrgəˌnaɪz/ *v.* **1** [T] to make the necessary arrangements so that an activity can happen: *I agreed to help organize the company picnic.* | *Residents of the city have organized a boycott of the fast-food chain.* **2** [T] to arrange things in a particular way, especially so that they have a clear structure and are easy to use or understand: *A key skill is the ability to organize information effectively.* | *Some day we should sit down and organize the photos from the trip.* | [be organized in/along/around sth] *Our science curriculum is organized around the central theme of the Earth.* | *The Armenian Church is organized along ethnic lines.* **3** [I,T] to form a TRADE UNION (=an organization that protects workers' rights) or persuade people to join one; UNIONIZE

or·ga·nized /ˈɔrgəˌnaɪzd/ *adj.* **1** achieving aims in an effective, ordered, and sensible way: *Barbara's a very organized person.* | *a well-organized company* | *I'll need at least thirty minutes to get organized for the presentation.* | *a highly organized* (=very well organized) *radical student group* —opposite DISORGANIZED **2** an organized activity is arranged for and done by many people: *My son just started playing organized hockey this year.* | *organized religion*

organized crime /ˌ... ˈ./ *n.* [U] illegal activity involving powerful, well-organized groups of criminals

or·gasm /ˈɔrˌgæzəm/ n. [C,U] the greatest point of sexual pleasure

or·gas·mic /ɔrˈgæzmɪk/ adj. **1** TECHNICAL related to orgasm **2** SLANG extremely exciting or enjoyable

org chart /ˈɔrg tʃɑrt/ n. [C] INFORMAL an ORGANIZATION CHART

or·gy /ˈɔrdʒi/ n. plural **orgies** [C] **1** a wild party with a lot of eating, drinking, and especially sexual activity **2 an orgy of sth** an activity that is done in a way that is extreme and not controlled: *a orgy of violence and looting* —**orgiastic** adj.

o·ri·ent¹ /ˈɔriˌɛnt/ v. [T] **1 be oriented to/toward** to have as its main purpose or area of interest: *Our curriculum was heavily oriented toward science and math.* | *an investment plan that is oriented toward steady growth rather than high returns* —see also -ORIENTED **2 orient yourself a)** to learn about and become familiar with a new situation: [+ to] *It often takes a few weeks for new students to orient themselves to college life.* **b)** to find your position with a map or a COMPASS (1): *The climbers stopped to orient themselves.* **3** to position something in a particular direction: *Viewers were told how to orient their satellite dishes to best receive broadcasts.*

orient² n. **the Orient** OLD-FASHIONED OR HUMOROUS the eastern part of the world, especially China and Japan and the countries near them —compare **the East** (EAST (3)), OCCIDENT

o·ri·en·tal¹ /ˌɔriˈɛntl/ adj. from or related to the eastern part of the world, especially China or Japan: *oriental religions* | *a beautiful oriental carpet*

oriental² n. [C] OLD-FASHIONED a word for someone from the eastern part of the world, now considered offensive —compare OCCIDENTAL

o·ri·en·tate /ˈɔriənˌteɪt/ v. [T] another form of the word ORIENT¹

o·ri·en·ta·tion /ˌɔriənˈteɪʃən/ n. **1** [C,U] the aims or interests of a particular activity or organization: *the party's liberal orientation* | [+ toward/to] *The local economy, with its strong orientation toward tourism, was devastated by a series of strikes.* **2 political/religious orientation** [C,U] the political views or religious beliefs that you have **3** [U] training and preparation for a new job or activity: *This is orientation week for the new students.* **4** [C] the angle or position of an object in relation to another object —see also SEXUAL ORIENTATION

-o·ri·ent·ed /ˈɔriɛntɪd/ [in adjectives] **work-oriented/family-oriented etc.** mainly concerned with or paying attention to work, family etc.: *an export-oriented company* | *The resort offers a variety of family-oriented entertainment.*

o·ri·en·teer·ing /ˌɔriənˈtɪrɪŋ/ n. [U] a sport in which people have to find their way quickly across unknown country using a map and a COMPASS (1)

or·i·fice /ˈɔrəfəs, ˈɑr-/ n. [C] FORMAL **1** one of the holes in your body, such as your mouth, nose etc. **2** a hole or opening in something such as a tube or pipe

o·ri·ga·mi /ˌɔrəˈgɑmi/ n. [U] the Japanese art of folding paper to make attractive objects

o·ri·gin /ˈɔrədʒɪn, ˈɑr-/ n. **1** [U] also **origins** [plural] the situation, place, cause etc. from which something begins: [+ of] *The origin of the infection is still unknown.* | *Valentine's Day has its origins in* (=began in) *third-century Rome.* | *This recipe is Spanish in origin* (=it was first made in Spain). | *Federal law requires that every product should show its country of origin* (=should show which country it comes from). **2** [U] also **origins** [plural] the country, race, or class from which a person or their family comes: *Kennedy's Irish-Catholic origins* | *Nine percent of the city's population is of Hispanic origin.* **3** [C] TECHNICAL the point where two axes (AXIS (3)) cross on a GRAPH

o·rig·i·nal¹ /əˈrɪdʒənl/ adj. **1** [only before noun] existing or happening first, before being changed or replaced by something or someone else: *Barnes was one of the three original board members.* | *The orphanage's original budget was just $60,000.* **2** completely new and different from anything that has

---

been thought of before, especially in an interesting way: *Steve comes up with a lot of original ideas.* | *It's not a bad movie, but there's nothing very original about it.* **3** [only before noun] not copied from something else: *an original screenplay*

original² n. **1** [C] a painting, document, etc. that is not a copy, but is the one that was produced first: *It's a new staging of the famous musical, and even better than the original.* | *I'll keep this copy and give you the original.* **2 in the original** in the language that a book, play etc. was first written in, before it was translated: *Tim has read Homer in the original.* **3** [C usually singular] INFORMAL an unusual person who thinks or behaves very differently from other people: *Jack is a true original.*

o·rig·i·nal·i·ty /əˌrɪdʒəˈnæləti/ n. [U] the quality of being completely new and different from anything that anyone has thought of before: *She was a writer of astonishing imagination and originality.*

o·rig·i·nal·ly /əˈrɪdʒənl-i/ adv. in the beginning: *Jeanne's family originally came from Malaysia.* | *They had originally planned to leave the children with a babysitter.* | [sentence adverb] *Originally, we had hoped to be finished by May.*

original sin /ˌ... ˈ./ n. [U] the state of DISOBEDIENCE to God which everyone is in from birth, according to some Christian teaching

o·rig·i·nate /əˈrɪdʒəˌneɪt/ v. **1** [I always + adv./prep., not in progressive] FORMAL to start to develop in a particular place or from a particular situation: *The city has over 300 banks, and this is where much of its wealth originates.* | [+ in/from/with] *This virus is a version of swine fever, which originates in pigs.* **2** [T] to have the idea for something and start it: *a rumor that was probably originated by one of the President's aides* —**origination** /əˌrɪdʒəˈneɪʃən/ n. [U]

o·rig·i·na·tor /əˈrɪdʒəˌneɪtɚ/ n. [C] the person who first has the idea for something and starts it: [+ of] *Caesar Cardini, the originator of the Caesar salad*

O·ri·no·co, the /ˌɔrɪˈnoʊkoʊ/ a river in the northern part of South America, that flows eastward through Venezuela to the Atlantic Ocean

o·ri·ole /ˈɔriˌoʊl, ˈɔriəl/ n. [C] **1** a North American bird that is black with a red and yellow STRIPE on each wing **2** a European bird with black wings and a yellow body

or·mo·lu /ˈɔrməˌlu/ n. [U] a gold-colored mixture of metals, not containing real gold: *an ormolu clock*

or·na·ment¹ /ˈɔrnəmənt/ n. **1** [C] an object that you use for decoration because it is beautiful rather than useful: *Christmas ornaments* **2** [U] decoration that is added to something: *The music building is a structure with simple but gracious ornament.* **3 be an ornament to sth** FORMAL to add honor, importance, or beauty to something: *Sharp is a world-class scientist, and a real ornament to MIT.*

or·na·ment² /ˈɔrnəˌmɛnt/ v. **be ornamented with sth** to be decorated with something: *Her white satin dress was ornamented with silver beads and hearts of pearl.*

or·na·men·tal /ˌɔrnəˈmɛntl/ adj. designed to decorate something: *ornamental vases*

or·na·men·ta·tion /ˌɔrnəmənˈteɪʃən/ n. [U] decoration: *elaborate ornamentation, typical of the Victorian style*

or·nate /ɔrˈneɪt/ adj. with a lot of decoration, especially with many complicated details: *the ornate 18th-century Royal Palace* —**ornately** adv. —**ornateness** n. [U]

or·ne·ry /ˈɔrnəri/ adj. behaving in an unreasonable and angry way, especially by doing the opposite of what people expect you to do: *an ornery 10-year-old*

or·ni·thol·o·gy /ˌɔrnəˈθɑlədʒi/ n. [U] the scientific study of birds —**ornithologist** n. [C] —**ornithological** /ˌɔrnəθəˈlɑdʒɪkəl/ adj.

o·ro·tund /ˈɔrəˌtʌnd, ˈɑr-/ adj. FORMAL **1** an orotund sound or voice is strong and clear **2** orotund speech or writing is trying to sound important and impressive

O·roz·co /ou'rouskou/, **Jo·sé** /hou'zeɪ/ (1883–1949) a Mexican PAINTER famous for his wall paintings of political and social subjects

or·phan[1] /'ɔrfən/ n. [C] a child whose parents are both dead

orphan[2] v. **be orphaned** to become an orphan: *White was orphaned at 14 when his parents died in a car accident.*

or·phan·age /'ɔrfənɪdʒ/ n. [C] a place where orphans live and are taken care of

Orr /ɔr/, **Bob·by** /'babi/ (1948–) a Canadian HOCKEY player, who was the most successful player of the 1970s

or·tho·don·tics /ˌɔrθə'dantɪks/ n. [U] the practice or skill of making teeth move into the right position when they have not been growing correctly —**orthodontic** adj.: *orthodontic braces*

or·tho·don·tist /ˌɔrθə'dantɪst/ n. [C] a DENTIST who makes teeth straight when they have not been growing correctly

or·tho·dox /'ɔrθəˌdaks/ adj. **1** orthodox ideas or methods are generally accepted as being normal or correct: *orthodox methods of treating disease* | *orthodox historical research* —opposite UNORTHODOX **2** believing in or practicing the usual form of a particular set of ideas or methods: *orthodox communism* | *Lacan soon found himself in conflict with more orthodox psychologists.* **3** accepting as true and following all the traditional beliefs and laws of a religion: *an orthodox Jew*

Orthodox Church /ˌ... './ n. **the Orthodox Church** one of the Christian churches in eastern Europe and parts of Asia

or·tho·dox·y /'ɔrθəˌdaksi/ n. plural **orthodoxies 1** [C,U] an idea or set of ideas that is generally accepted as normal or correct: *Early feminists challenged the social and political orthodoxy of their time.* **2** [U] the traditional ideas and beliefs of a group or religion, or the practice of following these strictly: *Ratzinger was seen in the Vatican as the "guardian of Catholic orthodoxy."*

or·thog·ra·phy /ɔr'θagrəfi/ n. [U] TECHNICAL **1** the system for spelling words in a language **2** correct spelling —**orthographic** /ˌɔrθə'græfɪk/ adj.

or·tho·pe·dic, **orthopaedic** /ˌɔrθə'pidɪk◂/ adj. **1** related to or providing medical treatment for problems affecting bones, muscles etc.: *an orthopedic surgeon* **2** an orthopedic **bed/chair/shoe etc.** a bed, chair etc. that is designed to cure or prevent medical problems affecting your bones, muscles etc.

or·tho·pe·dics, **orthopaedics** /ˌɔrθə'pidɪks/ n. [U] the area of medical science or treatment that deals with problems, diseases, or injuries of bones, muscles etc. —**orthopedist** n. [C]

Or·well /'ɔrwɛl/, **George** (1903–1950) a British writer known for his NOVELs about political systems in which people are completely controlled by the government

Or·well·i·an /ɔr'wɛliən/ adj. typical of the political systems described in the novels of George Orwell, in which the state controls everything and ordinary people have no power: *an Orwellian attempt to rewrite history*

-ory /ɔri, əri/ suffix **1** [in nouns] a place or thing used for doing something: *an observatory* (=where people look at the sky and stars) | *a directory* (=book giving lists of information) **2** [in adjectives] doing a particular thing: *an explanatory note* (=that gives an explanation) | *a congratulatory telegram* (=that CONGRATULATEs someone)

or·zo /'ɔrzou/ n. [U] a type of PASTA in the shape of very small round balls

O·sage /'ouseɪdʒ, ou'seɪdʒ/ a Native American tribe from the central area of the U.S.

Os·borne /'azbɔrn/, **John** (1929–1994) a British writer of plays

Os·car /'askə/ n. [C] TRADEMARK the usual name for an ACADEMY AWARD, a prize given each year in the form of a small gold STATUE, to the best movies, actors etc. in the movie industry: *the Oscar for best director*

Os·ce·o·la /ˌasi'oulə/ (?1804–1838) a Seminole chief who tried to stop U.S. soldiers from making his tribe leave Florida

os·cil·late /'asəˌleɪt/ v. [I] **1** FORMAL to keep changing between one level, value etc. and another: *For several days the stock market oscillated wildly.* **2** TECHNICAL to keep moving regularly from side to side, between two limits: *an oscillating fan* **3** TECHNICAL if an electric current oscillates, it changes direction very regularly and very frequently **4** FORMAL to keep changing between one feeling, belief, or attitude and another; VACILLATE —**oscillatory** /'asələˌtɔri/ adj.

os·cil·la·tion /ˌasə'leɪʃən/ n. [C,U] TECHNICAL **1** a regular movement of something from side to side between two limits **2** a regular change in direction of an electrical current **3** a change between one movement, level, value and another: *Economists predict continuing oscillation of the Japanese yen.*

os·cil·la·tor /'asəˌleɪtə/ n. [C] a machine that produces electrical oscillations

-ose /ous/ suffix **1** [in adjectives] full of something, or involving too much of something: *verbose* (=using too many words) **2** [in nouns] used to name sugars, CARBOHYDRATEs, and substances formed from PROTEINs: *sucrose* (=common type of sugar) | *lactose* (=from milk)

-oses /ousiz/ suffix the plural form of -OSIS

OSHA /'ouʃə/ n. the Occupational Safety and Health Administration; a U.S. government organization that makes rules about the safety and health of people at work

O·si·ris /ou'saɪrɪs/ in ancient Egyptian MYTHOLOGY, the god of the dead, who was the husband and brother of ISIS

-osis /ousɪs/ suffix plural **-oses** /ousiz/ [in nouns] **1** TECHNICAL a diseased condition: *tuberculosis* (=a lung disease) | *neuroses* (=mental illnesses) **2** a state or process: *a metamorphosis* (=a change from one state to another) | *hypnosis* (=state that is like sleep) —**-otic** /atɪk/ suffix [in adjectives] *neurotic* —**-otically** /atɪkli/ suffix [in adverbs]

Os·lo /'azlou/ the capital and largest city of Norway

os·mo·sis /az'mousɪs, as-/ n. [U] **1 by/through osmosis** if you learn something or receive ideas by osmosis, you gradually learn them by hearing them often: *Jose seemed to learn English by osmosis.* **2** TECHNICAL the gradual process of liquid passing through a MEMBRANE (2) —**osmotic** adj.

os·prey /'aspri, -preɪ/ n. [C] a type of large HAWK (=type of bird) that eats fish

os·si·fy /'asəˌfaɪ/ v. [I,T] **1** FORMAL to gradually become unwilling or unable to change, or to make something do this: *Gorbachev faced an ossified economic system.* **2** [I,T] TECHNICAL to change into bone or to make something change into bone —**ossification** /ˌasəfə'keɪʃən/ n. [U]

os·ten·si·ble /a'stɛnsəbəl/ adj. [only before noun] the ostensible purpose or reason for something is the one which is openly stated, but which is probably not the true purpose or reason: *The war was fought to remove a cruel dictator – at least that was the ostensible aim* (=this may not have been the real reason).

os·ten·si·bly /a'stɛnsəbli/ adv. pretending to do something for one reason, but having another purpose or reason which is the real one: *A stranger came to the door, ostensibly to ask for directions.*

os·ten·ta·tion /ˌastən'teɪʃən/ n. [U] an unnecessary show of wealth or knowledge intended to make people admire you: *the ostentation and idleness of the rich*

os·ten·ta·tious /ˌastən'teɪʃəs/ adj. DISAPPROVING **1** something that is ostentatious is large, looks expensive, and is designed to make people think that its owner must be very rich: *Stretch limousines were an ostentatious symbol of wealth in the '80s.* | *a big, ostentatious engagement ring* **2** trying to IMPRESS people by showing how rich you are: *an ostentatious lifestyle* —**ostentatiously** adv.

osteo- /ɑstiou, -tiə/ *prefix* TECHNICAL relating to bones: *osteoporosis* (=disease of the joints)

os·te·o·ar·thri·tis /ˌɑstiouɑrˈθraɪtɪs/ *n.* [U] a serious condition which makes your knees and other joints stiff and painful

os·te·o·path /ˈɑstiəˌpæθ/ *n.* [C] someone trained in osteopathy

os·te·op·a·thy /ˌɑstiˈɑpəθi/ *n.* [U] the practice or skill of treating physical problems such as back pain by moving and pressing muscles and bones

os·te·o·po·ro·sis /ˌɑstioupəˈrousɪs/ *n.* [U] a disease in which the bones become very weak and break easily

os·tra·cize /ˈɑstrəˌsaɪz/ *v.* [T] if a group of people ostracize someone, they stop accepting them as a member of the group: *After her arrest, Lang was ostracized by her neighbors.* —**ostracism** /ˈɑstrəˌsɪzəm/ *n.* [U]

os·trich /ˈɑstrɪtʃ, ˈɔs-/ *n.* [C] **1** a very large African bird with long legs, that can run fast but cannot fly **2** INFORMAL someone who refuses to accept that problems exist, instead of trying to deal with them

Os·tro·goth /ˈɑstrəˌgɑθ/ one of a tribe of Goths that ruled Italy in the sixth century A.D.

Os·wald /ˈɑzwəld/**, Lee Har·vey** /li ˈhɑrvi/ (1939–1963) the man who is believed to have shot and killed the U.S. President John F. Kennedy in 1963

OT 1 the written abbreviation of Old Testament **2** the abbreviation of OVERTIME

OTC the abbreviation of OVER-THE-COUNTER (2)

oth·er¹ /ˈʌðɚ/ *determiner, adj.* **1** used before a noun to mean one or more of the rest of a group of people or things, when you have already mentioned at least one person or thing: *I could do it, but none of the other boys in the class could.* | *Fry the onion for five minutes, then add the other ingredients.* | *Here's one sock, but where's **the other one**?* **2** used before a noun to mean someone or something that is different from, or exists in addition to, the person or thing you have already mentioned: *Max was thrown into a cell with three other men.* | *The other good news is that Jan passed her driving test.* | *I'm busy now – could we talk some other time?* **3 the other day/morning etc.** SPOKEN on a recent day, morning etc.: *Mark broke his ankle the other day.* **4 the other side/end etc.** the part of a road, room, place etc. that is opposite where you are or furthest away from where you are: *The children jumped in the river and swam to the other bank.* | *There's a gas station at the other end of the street.* | *My car broke down on the other side of town.* **5 the other way/direction etc.** in a different direction, especially in the opposite direction: *The pickup turned and started back in the other direction.* **6 in other words** said when you are going to express an idea or opinion in a different way, especially one that is easier to understand: *The tax only affects people on incomes over $200,000 – in other words, the very rich.* **7 other than** apart from a particular person or thing; EXCEPT: *He doesn't eat out at all, other than at Burger King.* | *The music was a little loud, but other than that it was a great concert.* **8 the other way around** if the situation, process etc. is the other way around, it is actually the opposite of how you thought it was: *He makes out he's doing me a big favor, but actually it's the other way around.* —see also EACH OTHER, **every other day/week/one** etc. (EVERY (6)), **(on the one hand...) on the other hand** (HAND¹ (3))

other² *pron.* **1 the other/others** one or more people or things that form the rest of a group that you are talking about: *We ate one pizza and froze the other.* | *What time are the others* (=the other people) *going to get here?* | *You pass out these forms and I'll do the others.* —see also **one after the other** (ONE² (4)) **2 none other than** used when saying who someone is, to emphasize that you are surprised or shocked: *The new boss turned out to be none other than my old roommate from college.* **3 be kind to others** used to express the idea that it is important to be kind to other people in general **4 someone/something etc. or other** also **some reason/some person etc. or other** SPOKEN used when you cannot be certain or

definite about what you are saying: *Marcia kept calling for some reason or other.*

oth·er·ness /ˈʌðɚnɪs/ *n.* [U] the quality of being strange, different, or separate: *Many immigrants experience a sense of otherness.*

oth·er·wise /ˈʌðɚˌwaɪz/ *adv.* **1** a word meaning "if not," used especially when there will be a bad result if something does not happen: [sentence adverb] *You should type it; otherwise, they won't be able to read it.* | *An inspection of the building revealed faults that might otherwise have been overlooked* (=if there had not been an inspection). **2** except for what has just been mentioned: [sentence adverb] *The sleeves are a little long, but otherwise it fits fine.* | *The hostages were tired, but otherwise in good health.* | [+ adj./adv.] *Her character is the one bright spot in an otherwise boring play.* **3 say/think/decide etc. otherwise** to say, think etc. something different from what has been mentioned: *He says he has quit politics, but his recent activities suggest otherwise.* **4 or otherwise** or of any other type: *I can't see any advantage in changing my job – financially or otherwise.* **5 otherwise known as** also called: *Global warming is otherwise known as the greenhouse effect.* **6 otherwise engaged/occupied** FORMAL busy doing something else: *The couple was otherwise occupied and did not hear the knock at the door.* **7 it cannot be otherwise** also **how can it be otherwise** FORMAL used to mean that it is impossible for something to be different from the way it is

oth·er·world·ly /ˌʌðɚˈwɚldli/ *adj.* seeming to be more concerned with SPIRITUAL thoughts than daily life, or seeming to come from an unreal place very different from earth: *The humpback whales make otherworldly sounds.*

-otic /ɑtɪk/ *suffix* —see -OSIS

Ot·ta·wa¹ /ˈɑtəwə/ the capital city of Canada

Ottawa² a Native American tribe from the Great Lakes area of North America

ot·ter /ˈɑtɚ/ *n.* [C] a small animal that can swim, has brown fur, and eats fish

ot·to·man /ˈɑtəmən/ *n.* [C] **1** a soft piece of furniture shaped like a box that you rest your feet on when you are sitting down **2** a piece of furniture like a SOFA without arms or a back

Ot·to·man Em·pire, the /ˌɑtəmən ˈɛmpaɪɚ/ a large EMPIRE, based in Turkey and with its capital in Istanbul, which also included large parts of Eastern Europe, Asia, and North Africa. It continued from the 13th century until after World War I, but was most powerful in the 16th century.

Oua·ga·dou·gou /ˌwɑgəˈdugu/ the capital and largest city of Burkina

ouch /aʊtʃ/ *interjection* a sound that you make when you feel sudden pain: *Ouch! That hurt!*

ought·a /ˈɔtə/ *modal verb* NONSTANDARD the spoken short form of "ought to": *He oughta know.*

ought·n't /ˈɔtⁿnt/ *v.* OLD-FASHIONED the short form of "ought not": *She oughtn't to have said that.*

ought to /ˈɔtə; *strong* ˈɔtu/ *modal verb* **1 a)** used to say that someone should do something because it is the best, most sensible, or right thing to do: *Maybe we ought to call the doctor.* | *Don't you think you ought to eat before you go?* | *You ought to email or call her and say you're sorry.* **b)** used to say that you think something will probably happen, probably be true etc.: *The berries ought to be ripe by now.* | *We ought to be able to find someone to do the job pretty quickly.* **2** used to say that someone should do something or that something should happen, because it is right or fair: *Tricking old people like that ought to be illegal.* | *You really ought to apologize to her, you know.* | *That is a type of poverty that ought not to exist at the end of the 20th century.* **3 that ought to do it** SPOKEN used to say that something you have been working on is finished: *Just one more screw – there, that ought to do it.* —see also OUGHTA —compare SHOULD

Oui·ja board /'widʒi ˌbɔrd, -dʒə/ n. [C] TRADEMARK a board with letters and signs on it, used to try to receive messages from the spirits of dead people

s w **ounce** /aʊns/ n. **1** [C] *written abbreviation* **oz.** a unit
3 3 for measuring weight, equal to 1/16 of a pound or 28.35 grams —see also FLUID OUNCE **2 an ounce of sense/truth/decency etc.** a very small amount of a particular quality: *There isn't an ounce of truth in what he says.* **3 every (last) ounce of courage/energy/ strength etc.** all the courage, energy etc. that you have: *I gave every ounce of energy that I had to the job.* **4 not have an ounce of fat on you** an expression meaning "to be thin," used about people who are strong and healthy looking **5 an ounce of prevention is worth a pound of cure** OLD-FASHIONED used to say that it is better to avoid a problem than to try to solve it after it has happened

s w **our** /ɑr; *strong* aʊər/ *possessive adj.* [possessive form of
1 1 "we"] belonging or relating to the person who is speaking and one or more other people: *We drove to Albany and visited our relatives there.* | *It is important that we preserve our natural resources.* —see also OURS

Our Fa·ther /ˌ. '../ n. [singular] the LORD'S PRAYER

Our La·dy /ˌ. '../ n. [singular, not with **the**] a name used by some Christians for Mary, the mother of Jesus Christ

Our Lord /ˌ. '../ n. [singular, not with **the**] a name used by Christians for Jesus Christ

s w **ours** /aʊərz, ɑrz/ *possessive pron.* [possessive form of
2 "we"] the thing or things belonging or relating to the person who is speaking and one or more other people: *They have their tickets, but ours haven't come yet.* | *Ed is a good friend of ours.*

s w **our·selves** /aʊər'sɛlvz, ɑr-/ *pron.* **1** the REFLEXIVE
2 2 form of "we": *Sometimes it's hard for us to think of ourselves as adults.* | *We have to ask ourselves if we could have helped him more.* **2** the strong form of "we," used to emphasize the subject or object of a sentence: *We started this business ourselves.* | *We ourselves were unaware of what was about to happen.* **3 (all) by ourselves a)** alone: *This year we wanted to take a vacation by ourselves.* **b)** without help from anyone else: *We built the wall all by ourselves.* **4 (all) to ourselves** not having to share something with any other people: *When Sarah goes to college we'll finally have the house to ourselves.* —see also YOURSELF

-ous /əs/ *suffix* [in adjectives] having a particular quality: *dangerous* (=full of danger) | *nervous* (=worried or afraid about something) —see also -EOUS, -IOUS

oust /aʊst/ v. [T] to force someone out of a position of power, especially so that you can take their place: [**oust sb from sth**] *Hale was ousted from the company's main board in a big management shake-up.*

oust·er /'aʊstər/ n. [C usually singular] an act of removing someone from a position of power: *Havel's ouster came as a shock to everybody.*

s w **out¹** /aʊt/ *adv., adj.* [adv. only after verb, adj. not
1 1 before noun]
1 from inside sth away from the inside of a place or container: *Gwen reached in the drawer and pulled out a knife.* | *We opened the window to let all the smoke out.* | [+ of] *My keys fell out of my pocket.* | *Sit down, and I'll get a couple of beers out of the cooler.* —see Usage Note at OUTSIDE²
2 leave a place from the inside part of a building, vehicle etc., to the outside: *Watch the step on your way out.* | [+ of] *I saw him come out of the hotel.* | [**out came/jumped/walked etc.**] *The plane door opened, and out stepped the President.*
3 outside not inside a building; outside: *children playing out in the snow* | *In the summer, we sometimes sleep out in the yard.*
4 not there away from the place where you usually are, especially for a short time: *Ms. Nichols is out this morning. Can I take a message?* | *Do you know how long he'll be out?*
5 social activity not at home because you have

gone somewhere to enjoy yourself, for example a restaurant or a movie: *We eat out* (=eat in restaurants) *all the time.* | *He finally asked me out* (=invited me to go somewhere).
6 distant place in or to a place that is far away from city centers, or difficult to get to: *a little hotel out in the desert* | *The Smiths live out on Long Island.*
7 western U.S. toward the West in the U.S.: *We moved out to California when I was little.*
8 completely/carefully completely or carefully: *I got the kids to clean out the garage for me.* | *Poor Steve – the job is just wearing him out* (=making him extremely tired). | *It's a nice idea, but I don't think they've really thought it out* (=considered it carefully and thoroughly).
9 not working power, electricity, a piece of equipment etc. that is out is not working: *I think the electricity went out again last night.* —see also **out of order** (ORDER¹ (1))
10 fire/light a fire or light that is out is not turning or shining anymore: *The lights are out – I don't think anybody's home.* | *I put out my cigarette and went back inside.*
11 not in power a politician or political party that is out does not have power or authority any longer: *The only way to lower taxes is to vote the Democrats out.* | *He may face prosecution once he is out of office.*
12 appear used to say that someone or something has appeared: *It looks like the sun's finally going to come out.* | *The leaves are just starting to come out on the trees.*
13 read/shout etc. sth out (loud) to say something in a voice that is loud enough for others to hear: *"See you later," she called out.* | *What does it say? Read it out loud.*
14 given to many people used to say that something is given to many people: *She got a job handing out pamphlets.* | *I'll send out the invitations tomorrow.*
15 get rid of sth used to say that something does not exist anymore or is getting rid of something: *Can I throw out the corn? Nobody's going to eat it.* | [+ of] *How can I get this wine stain out of my blouse?*
16 not included not included in a team, group etc.: *Darryl has an ankle injury, and could be out for several weeks.* | [+ of] *What did she do to get kicked out of the club?*
17 not possible/allowed INFORMAL not possible or not allowed: *"What do you want to do then?" "Well, skiing's out because I don't have any money."* | *I'm training for the marathon, so things like alcohol and rich foods are out.*
18 origin used to say where someone or something comes from: *The burning complex poured out smoke.* | [+ of] *Kukoc is one of the most talented players to come out of Europe.* | *New product research is financed out of company profits.*
19 out of wood/metal/glass etc. used to say what substance a particular thing is made of: *People were living in shacks made out of metal sheets and bits of wood.*
20 available a product that is out is available to be bought: *Is her new book out yet?* | *I heard there's a cheaper model coming out this fall.*
21 stick out used to say that something is very easy to see, feel etc. because it is not part of the main part of something: *The small peninsula juts out into the sea.* | [+ of] *He walked in the house with a plastic bag sticking out of his pocket.*
22 choose used to say that one person or thing is chosen or taken from a larger group: *You can pick out whatever you want.* | *Why was Kenny singled out for punishment?*
23 be out for sth also **be out to do sth** INFORMAL to have a particular intention: *He's convinced that his colleagues are out to cheat him.* | *Andre's just out for a good time.*
24 be out to get sb to want to punish or do something bad to someone because they have done something bad to you: *He thinks everyone is out to get him.*
25 not awake **a)** asleep: **be/go out like a light** *Billy was out like a light by 8:00 p.m.* **b)** not conscious: *I felt dizzy and almost passed out.* | *He must have hit his head pretty hard. He's out cold.*

26 `sports/games` **a)** a player or team that is out is not allowed to play anymore, or has lost one of their chances to get a point: *If the ball hits you, you're out.* | *Hingis went out in the second round, beaten by an almost unknown Australian.* **b)** a ball that is out in a game such as tennis or basketball is not in the area of play

27 `not fashionable` clothes or styles that are out are not fashionable anymore: *Don't you know tight jeans are out?*

28 `not secret` not secret anymore: *The secret's out.* | *Somehow* **word** *of Beasley's arrest* **got out**.

29 `free` not in prison or kept in a place against your will anymore: *How did the dog get out?* | *[+ of] Dutton has been out of prison since 1976.*

30 `finished/used` be/run/sell etc. out to not have something because you have used it all, sold it all etc.: *Tickets for the show sold out immediately.* | *[+ of] I didn't finish because I ran out of time.* | *We're almost out of gas.*

31 `homosexual` if a HOMOSEXUAL person is out or comes out, they tell everyone that they are homosexual: *The congressman has been out for several years now.*

32 `reason for doing sth` if you do something out of interest, kindness, or some other feeling, you do it because you are interested, kind etc.: *[+ of] Out of respect for the dead woman's family, there were no journalists at the funeral.* | *Why did I go? Just out of curiosity, I guess.*

33 out there **a)** in a place that could be anywhere except here: *My real father is out there and one day I plan to find him.* **b)** where something or someone can be noticed by many people: *Jerry Lewis is out there all the time raising money for disabled kids.* **c)** SPOKEN, INFORMAL used to say that an idea or person seems very strange: *Sheila's ideas can be way out there sometimes.*

34 `ocean` if the TIDE[1] (1) is out, the ocean is at its lowest level

35 be out of control/danger etc. used to say that someone or something is not in a particular condition or situation anymore: *Strong winds sent the boat out of control.* | *The average kid is more out of shape than he used to be.*

36 watch/look out SPOKEN used to tell someone to be careful: *Look out! There's a van coming.*

37 a) be/feel out of it INFORMAL to be unable to think clearly because you are very tired, drunk etc.: *I was so out of it, I didn't really understand what he was saying.* **b)** to not feel completely involved in an activity or situation: *Shelly felt out of it her first week back at work.*

38 out with it! SPOKEN used to tell someone to say something that they are having difficulty saying: *OK, out with it! What really happened?*

39 out (you go)! SPOKEN used to order someone to leave a room

40 be out of work also out of a job to not have a job: *Ramos has been out of work for over 6 months.*

41 get out from under sb/sth to not be controlled by someone anymore, or to not suffer because of a bad situation anymore: *We need to do something to get out from under this debt.*

42 9 out of 10 also 4 out of 5 etc. used to say that there are ten people or things and you are talking about nine of them etc.: *Almost five out of ten marriages end in divorce.*

43 out front **a)** in front of something, especially a building, where everyone can see you: *There's a station wagon waiting out front.* **b)** taking a leading position: *As a civil rights leader, he was always out front.* **c)** INFORMAL very honest and direct: *Molly is very out front in talking about her mistakes.* —see also up front (FRONT[1] (10))

44 out back in a back yard or behind a building: *I think there's an old wheelbarrow out back.* —see also OUTBACK

45 out and about going from one place, house etc. to another, especially for social activities: *Most teenagers would rather be out and about with their friends.*

46 out of earshot/sight so far away from someone that they cannot hear you or see you: *They only use*

those expressions when their parents are out of earshot.

47 before the day/year etc. is out before the day, year etc. has ended: *Derry signed the contract and was performing onstage before the week was out.* —see also out of the blue (BLUE[2] (4)), go out of your mind (MIND[1] (8)), OUT-OF-THE-WAY, out of place (PLACE[1] (14)), be out of the question (QUESTION[1] (6)), out of sight (SIGHT[1] (7)), out of sorts (SORT[1] (4)), be out of this world (WORLD[1] (17))

out[2] *prep.* from inside to the outside of something: *Karen looked out the window at the back yard.* | *[+of] Grass grows out of small holes in the side of the pot.*

out[3] *v.* **1** [T usually passive] to publicly say that someone is HOMOSEXUAL, especially when that person wants it to be a secret: *John knew that he might be outed if he decided to run for office.* **2 truth/murder etc. will out!** used to say that it is difficult to hide the truth, a murder etc.

out[4] *n.* **1** [singular] INFORMAL an excuse for not doing something, or a chance to avoid a difficult situation: *I'm busy Sunday, so that gives me an out.* **2** [C] an act of making a player in baseball lose the chance to get a point **3 on the outs** INFORMAL arguing or not agreeing with someone: *[+ with] Wilson is on the outs with his family because of his relationship with the woman.* —see also the ins and outs (of sth) (INS)

out- /aʊt/ *prefix* **1** used to form nouns and adjectives from verbs that are followed by "out": *an outbreak of flu* (=from "break out") | *outspoken comments* (=from "speak out") **2** [in nouns and adjectives] outside or beyond something: *an outhouse* (=a toilet outside a house) | *the city's outlying areas* (=far from the center of the city) **3** [in verbs] bigger, further, greater etc. than someone or something else: *She outlived her brother* (=he died before her). | *He's outgrown all his clothes* (=become too big for them). **4** [in verbs] better than someone else, so that you defeat them: *I can outrun you any day.*

out·age /ˈaʊtɪdʒ/ *n.* [C] a period when a service such as the electricity supply is not provided: *a power outage*

out-and-out /ˌ. . ˈ./ *adj.* [only before noun] having all the qualities of a particular kind of person or thing, especially someone or something bad: *out-and-out lies* | *The guy is an out-and-out conman.*

out·back /ˈaʊtbæk/ *n.* **the outback** the Australian COUNTRYSIDE far away from cities, where few people live

out·bal·ance /aʊtˈbæləns/ *v.* [T] to be more important or valuable than something else; OUTWEIGH

out·bid /aʊtˈbɪd/ *v. past tense* **outbid** *present participle* **outbidding** [T] to offer a higher price than someone else, especially at an AUCTION[1]: *Shue outbid three competitors for the painting.*

out·board mo·tor /ˌaʊtbɔrd ˈmoʊtɚ/ *n.* [C] a motor fastened to the back end of a small boat

out·bound /ˈaʊtbaʊnd/ *adj.* moving away from you or away from a town, country etc.: *outbound planes*

out box, outbox /ˈ. ./ *n.* [C] **1** a container on an office desk used to hold words and letters which are ready to be sent out or put away **2** a place on a computer where the EMAIL messages that you have sent are kept —compare IN BOX

out·break /ˈaʊtbreɪk/ *n.* [C] the sudden appearance or start of war, fighting, or serious disease: *a cholera outbreak* | *[+ of] the outbreak of World War II* —see also break out (BREAK[1])

out·build·ing /ˈaʊtˌbɪldɪŋ/ *n.* [C] a building such as a BARN or SHED near a main building

out·burst /ˈaʊtbɜrst/ *n.* [C] **1** a sudden powerful expression of strong emotion, especially anger: *I was embarrassed by my husband's outburst.* | *[+ of] outbursts of anger* **2** a sudden temporary increase in activity: *a fresh outburst of violence in the region*

out·cast /ˈaʊtkæst/ *n.* [C] someone who is not accepted by the people they live among, or has been forced out of their home: *After her divorce she was treated as an outcast by her family.* —**outcast** *adj.*

out·class /ˌaʊtˈklæs/ *v.* [T] to be much better than someone at doing something, or to be much better than something else: *De Niro gives a brilliant performance, completely outclassing the other members of the cast.*

out·come /ˈaʊtˌkʌm/ *n.* [C] the final result of a meeting, process, series of events etc., especially when no one knows what it will be until it actually happens: *The negotiations are continuing, and we are hoping for a positive outcome.* | *[+ of] factors that influenced the outcome of the war*

out·crop·ping /ˈaʊtˌkrɑpɪŋ/ also **out·crop** /ˈaʊtˌkrɑp/ *n.* [C] a rock or group of rocks above the surface of the ground

out·cry /ˈaʊtkraɪ/ *n.* [C] an angry protest by a lot of people: *The killings by the military have caused an international outcry.* | *[+ against] a public outcry against the new rule*

out·dat·ed /ˌaʊtˈdeɪtɪd/ *adj.* **1** not useful or modern anymore: *outdated equipment* | *teaching methods that were hopelessly outdated* **2** an outdated document cannot be used because the period of time for which it was effective has passed: *an outdated passport* —see also OUT-OF-DATE

out·did /aʊtˈdɪd/ *v.* the past tense of OUTDO

out·dis·tance /aʊtˈdɪstəns/ *v.* [T] to run, ride etc. faster than other people, especially in a race, so that you are far ahead: *Turner easily outdistanced the other competitors.*

out·do /aʊtˈdu/ *v. past tense* **outdid** *past participle* **outdone** /-ˈdʌn/ [T] **1** to be better or more successful than someone else at doing something: *Kwan outdid Bobek to win the finals.* | *[outdo sb in (doing) sth] The big stores were trying to outdo each other in the lavishness of their window displays.* **2 outdo yourself** to do something extremely well: *The costumes are great. You've really outdone yourself this time.* **3 not to be outdone** in order not to let someone else do better than you: *Not to be outdone by the girls, the boys' team also won its second team title.*

out·door /ˈaʊtdɔr/ *adj.* **1** [only before noun] existing, happening, or used outside, not inside a building: *outdoor sports* | *an outdoor swimming pool* | *outdoor furniture* —opposite INDOOR **2 outdoor type** a person who enjoys camping, and other outdoor activities such as walking, climbing etc.

out·doors¹ /aʊtˈdɔrz/ *adv.* outside, not inside a building; OUT OF DOORS: *He used to work outdoors even in the middle of winter.* —opposite INDOORS —see Usage Note at OUTSIDE²

outdoors² *n.* **the (great) outdoors** the open lands, mountains, rivers etc. far away from buildings and cities: *a love of the great outdoors*

out·door·sy /aʊtˈdɔrzi/ *adj.* INFORMAL enjoying outdoor activities: *Jeff is really outdoorsy.*

out·draw /aʊtˈdrɔ/ *v. past tense* **outdrew** /-ˈdru/ *past participle* **outdrawn** /-ˈdrɔn/ [T] to pull a gun out faster than someone else

out·er /ˈaʊtə/ *adj.* [only before noun] **1** on the outside of something: *Remove the tough outer leaves before cooking.* **2** farther from the center of something: *the outer edge of the solar system* —opposite INNER

out·er·most /ˈaʊtəˌmoʊst/ *adj.* [only before noun] farthest outside or farthest from the middle: *the outermost petals of the flower* —opposite INMOST (2)

outer space /ˌ.. ˈ./ *n.* [U] the space outside the Earth's air, where the PLANETS and stars are

out·er·wear /ˈaʊtəˌwɛr/ *n.* [U] clothes, such as coats, that are worn over ordinary clothes

out·fall /ˈaʊtfɔl/ *n.* [C] a place where water flows out, especially from a DRAIN² (1) or river: *a sewage outfall*

out·field /ˈaʊtfild/ *n.* **the outfield a)** the part of a baseball field furthest from the player who is batting (BAT² (1)) **b)** the players in this part of the field —**outfielder** *n.* [C] —compare INFIELD

out·fit¹ /ˈaʊtˌfɪt/ *n.* [C] **1** a set of clothes worn together: *I love your outfit!* | *a cowboy outfit* **2** a group of people who work together as a team or organization: *an outfit of 120 engineers* | *a five-piece jazz outfit* **3** a set of tools or equipment that you need for a particular purpose or job

outfit² *v.* **outfitted, outfitting** [T] to provide someone with a set of clothes or equipment for a special purpose: *Police had been outfitted with protective riot gear.*

out·fit·ter /ˈaʊtˌfɪtə/ *n.* [C] a store that sells equipment for outdoor activities such as camping

out·flank /aʊtˈflæŋk/ *v.* [T] **1** to go around the side of an enemy during a battle and attack them from behind: *To the west, the army was outflanked by a huge number of British forces.* **2** to gain an advantage over an opponent, especially in politics or business: *Republicans sought to outflank Democrats on the tax bill.*

out·flow /ˈaʊtfloʊ/ *n.* [C,U] **1** a process in which money, goods, people etc. leave a place: *[+ of] A weak stock market led to large outflows of investment funds.* **2** a flow of liquid or air from something: *chemical outflow into the bay* | *outflow pipes* —opposite INFLOW

out·fox /aʊtˈfɑks/ *v.* [T] to gain an advantage over someone by being smarter than they are; OUTWIT: *So far Hutchinson has managed to outfox police.*

out·go·ing /ˈaʊtˌgoʊɪŋ/ *adj.* **1** liking to meet and talk to new people: *Jamie is a friendly, outgoing woman.* | *an outgoing personality* **2 the outgoing President/CEO etc.** someone who will soon be finishing a job as a president etc. **3** [only before noun] going out or leaving a place: *outgoing phone calls*

out·grow /aʊtˈgroʊ/ *v. past tense* **outgrew** /-ˈgru/ *past participle* **outgrown** /-ˈgroʊn/ [T] **1** to grow too big for something: *Kara's already outgrown her shoes.* **2** to not do something or enjoy something anymore, because you have grown older and changed: *Many illicit drug users simply outgrow the habit once they reach their thirties.* **3** to grow or increase faster than someone or something else: *The female population outgrew the male population in most of the experiments.*

out·growth /ˈaʊtgroʊθ/ *n.* [C] **1** something that develops from something else, as a natural result: *[+ of] These new family structures are an outgrowth of rising divorce rates.* **2** something that grows out of something else

out·guess /aʊtˈgɛs/ *v.* [T] to guess what someone or something is going to do before they do it: *Too many investors try to outguess the stock market.*

out·gun /aʊtˈgʌn/ *v. past tense and past participle* **outgunned** *present participle* **outgunning** [T usually passive] **1** to defeat another group or army because you have more or better weapons than they do **2** to defeat someone in a competition, argument etc. because you have more skills, are better prepared etc.: *The prosecution was outgunned by high-priced defense lawyers.*

out·house /ˈaʊthaʊs/ *n.* [C] a small building which is used as a toilet, found in places such as camping areas, and in the past behind houses; a PRIVY

out·ie /ˈaʊti/ *n.* [C] INFORMAL a BELLY BUTTON that sticks out —compare INNIE

out·ing /ˈaʊtɪŋ/ *n.* **1** [C] a short enjoyable trip for a group of people: *a Girl Scout outing in the mountains* **2** [C,U] the practice of publicly naming people as HOMOSEXUALS, when they do not want anyone to know this

out·land·ish /aʊtˈlændɪʃ/ *adj.* very strange and unusual: *outlandish costumes*

out·last /aʊtˈlæst/ *v.* [T] to continue to exist, work etc. for a longer time than someone or something else: *Other restaurants have come and gone in the neighborhood, but Shien's has outlasted them all.* —compare OUTLIVE

out·law¹ /ˈaʊtlɔ, aʊtˈlɔ/ *v.* [T] to make something illegal: *Religious and racial discrimination were outlawed under the 1964 Civil Rights Act.*

outlaw² /ˈaʊtlɔ/ *n.* [C] a word meaning a "criminal," often one who is hiding from the police, used especially in past times

outlaw³ *adj.* [only before noun] not obeying the law or accepted rules: *an outlaw nation*

out·lay /'aʊtˌleɪ/ *n. plural* **outlays** [C,U] the amount of money that you have to spend in order to start a new business, activity etc.: *You can start a fast-food franchise for a relatively modest outlay.* | *[+ on/for] There'll be an initial outlay of $2500 for tools and equipment.*

out·let /'aʊtˌlɛt, -lɪt/ *n.* [C] **1** a place on a wall where you can connect electrical equipment to the supply of electricity —see pictures at PLUG¹ and KITCHEN **2 a)** a store, company, organization etc. through which products are sold: *Toys 'R' Us was the first large U.S. retail outlet to open in Japan.* **b)** a store that sells things for less than the usual price: *an outlet mall* **3** a way of expressing or getting rid of strong feelings: *[+ for] For many unemployed youths, violence is an outlet for their frustrations.* **4** a pipe or a hole through which something such as a liquid or gas can flow out

out·line¹ /'aʊtˌlaɪn/ *n.* [C] **1** the main ideas or facts about something, without all the details: *In a short statement, Akers gave an outline of his plans for the company.* | *an outline agreement* | *The events are familiar, at least in outline, to most of the students.* | **a broad/rough outline** (=a very general outline) **2** a plan for a piece of writing in which each new idea is separately written down: *[+ of/for] The professor wants an outline of our essays by Friday.* **3** a line around the edge of something which shows its shape: *A chalk outline of the victim's body was still visible on the sidewalk.*

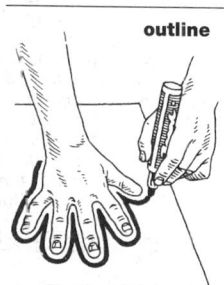

outline

She is drawing an outline of her hand.

outline² *v.* [T] **1** to describe something in a general way, giving the main points but not the details: *The President outlined his peace plan for the Middle East.* **2** to draw or put a line around the edge of something to show its shape: *We could see the huge ferris wheel outlined in colored lights.*

out·live /aʊt'lɪv/ *v.* [T] **1** to live longer than someone else: *Women usually outlive their husbands.* **2** to continue to live or exist after something else has ended or disappeared: *Retired people are beginning to worry that they will outlive their savings.* **3 outlive your usefulness** to become no longer useful: *The organization, started during the war, may have outlived its usefulness.* —see also OUTLAST

out·look /'aʊtˌlʊk/ *n.* **1** [singular] your general attitude to life and the world: *[+ on] Nels has a very positive outlook on life.* | *There are major differences in outlook between the two candidates.* **2** [singular] what is expected to happen in the future: *[+ for] The long-term outlook for the computer industry remains fairly bright.* **3** [singular] a description of what the weather is likely to do: *[+ for] The outlook for Friday is good – sunny and warm.* **4** [C] a place from which something such as an area of land can be seen, or the view from that place

out·ly·ing /'aʊtˌlaɪ-ɪŋ/ *adj.* [only before noun] far from a city, town etc. or its center, or far from a main building: *outlying farm communities*

out·man /aʊt'mæn/ *v. past tense and past participle* **outmanned** *present participle* **outmanning** [T usually passive] to have more people in your group than in your opponent's group; OUTNUMBER: *The Mexicans, though outmanned by three to one, defeated Napoleon's forces at Puebla.*

out·ma·neu·ver /ˌaʊtmə'nuvɚ/ *v.* [T] to gain an advantage over an opponent by using smarter, more skillful methods: *The President found himself consistently outmaneuvered by his rivals in Congress.*

out·mod·ed /aʊt'moʊdɪd/ *adj.* not fashionable or useful anymore: *outmoded economic policies*

out·num·ber /aʊt'nʌmbɚ/ *v.* [T] to be more in

number than another group: *In these mountains the animal population outnumbers the human by three to one.*

out-of-bod·y /ˌ. . '.ɪ/ *adj.* **an out-of-body experience** the feeling, which sometimes happens when someone is close to death, that they are outside of their own body and can look down on it from above

out of bounds /ˌ. . '.ɪ/ *adj.* **1** not inside the official playing area in a sports game: *An official ruled that Burford was out of bounds.* **2** not allowed or acceptable: *[+ for] Certain topics, such as sex, were out of bounds for discussion.* **3** if a place is out of bounds, you are officially forbidden from entering it: *[+ for] Downtown Los Angeles was declared out of bounds for military personnel.* —**out of bounds** *adv.*: *Stark knocked the ball out of bounds.*

out-of-court /ˌ. . '.ɪ/ *adj.* **an out-of-court settlement** an agreement to settle a legal argument, in which one side agrees to pay money to the other so that the problem is not brought to court

out-of-date, out of date /ˌ. . '.ɪ/ *adj.* not useful, correct, or fashionable anymore: *out-of-date theories on education* | *The new manuals are already out of date.* —see also OUTDATED

out of doors /ˌ. . '.ɪ/ *adv.* outside, not in a building; OUTDOORS

out-of-pock·et /ˌ. . '../ *adj.* **out-of-pocket expenses/ costs etc.** costs that you have to pay yourself, rather than costs that someone else, such as your employer pay them

out-of-sight, out of sight /ˌ. . '.ɪ/ *adj.* **1** an amount of money that is out of sight is extremely large: *Our grocery bills are out of sight.* | *out-of-sight housing prices* OLD-FASHIONED, SLANG extremely good: *Wow, man! Out of sight!* —see also **out of sight** (SIGHT¹ (7)), **out of sight, out of mind** (SIGHT¹ (14))

out-of-state /ˌ. . '.ɪ/ *adj.* from, to, or in another state: *out-of-state license plates* —**out of state** *adv.*: *She may go to college out of state.*

out-of-the-way /ˌ. . . '.ɪ/ *adj.* far from other people or towns, or in a place that is difficult to find: *He spent the summer in an out-of-the-way village.* —see also **out of the way** (WAY¹ (14))

out of touch /ˌ. . '.ɪ/ *adj.* **1** not realizing what a situation is really like, how other people live or think etc.: *[+ with] The leadership had grown increasingly out of touch with ordinary people.* **2** someone who is out of touch with someone else has not spoken, written etc. to them for a long time: *Over the years we just sort of fell out of touch.*

out-of-town /ˌ. . '.ɪ/ *adj.* [only before noun] to, from, or in another town: *The museum attracts a lot of out-of-town visitors.*

out-of-work /ˌ. . '.ɪ/ *adj.* unemployed: *out-of-work actors*

out·pace /aʊt'peɪs/ *v.* [T] to go faster, perform better, or develop more quickly than someone or something else: *The problem started when federal spending began to outpace economic growth.*

out·pa·tient /'aʊtˌpeɪʃənt/ *n.* [C] someone who goes to a hospital for treatment but does not stay there —compare INPATIENT

out·per·form /ˌaʊtpɚ'fɔrm/ *v.* [T] to perform better or be more successful than someone or something else: *Spanish students outperformed U.S. students in science.*

out·place·ment /'aʊtˌpleɪsmənt/ *n.* [C,U] a service that a company provides to help its workers find other jobs when it cannot continue to employ them —**outplace** *v.* [T]

out·play /aʊt'pleɪ/ *v.* [T] to beat an opponent in a game by playing with more skill than they do

out·poll /aʊt'poʊl/ *v.* [T] to defeat an opponent by receiving more votes than they do: *Bond outpolled three other Republicans to win the primary.*

out·post /'aʊtˌpoʊst/ *n.* [C] a small town or group of buildings in a place far from city or towns, usually established as a military camp or a place for trade: *The city began its life as a remote border outpost.*

out·pour·ing /ˈaʊtˌpɔrɪŋ/ *n.* [C] **1** an expression of strong feelings by a large number of people: [+ of] *Her death provoked an outpouring of sadness and sympathy.* **2** a lot of something, especially ideas, writings etc., that is produced suddenly: [+ of] *There was an enormous outpouring of "protest literature" in the 60s and 70s.*

out·put /ˈaʊtˌpʊt/ *n.* [C,U] **1** the amount of goods or work produced by a person, machine, factory etc.: *Ford plans to increase its car output next year.* **2** the information produced by a computer, and shown on the screen or printed onto paper —**output** *v.* [T] —compare INPUT[1]

out·rage[1] /ˈaʊtreɪdʒ/ *n.* **1** [U] a feeling of great anger or shock: *The plans brought cries of outrage from residents.* **2** [C] something that causes this feeling: *The prices they charge are an outrage!*

outrage[2] *v.* [T usually passive] to make someone feel very angry and shocked: [+ at/by] *People were outraged at the idea that a convicted killer could be released so soon.*

out·ra·geous /aʊtˈreɪdʒəs/ *adj.* **1** very shocking, because it is unfair or offensive: *outrageous prices | She accused Sloan of telling outrageous lies. | It's outrageous that company executives can vote themselves such massive pay raises.* **2** extremely unusual, amusing or shocking: *an outrageous hairstyle | They showed a scene from Almodovar's outrageous new movie.*

out·ran /aʊtˈræn/ *v.* the past tense of OUTRUN

out·rank /aʊtˈræŋk/ *v.* [T] **1** to have a higher rank or position than someone else in the same group **2** to be more important than something else: *The survey shows that humor and shared activities outrank sex as features of a good relationship.*

ou·tré /uˈtreɪ/ *adj.* FORMAL strange, unusual, and slightly shocking: *a slightly outré theater production*

out·reach /ˈaʊtritʃ/ *n.* [U] the practice of providing help, advice, or other services to people in an area who have particular problems: *an inner city youth outreach program | outreach and education for homeless people*

out·ride /aʊtˈraɪd/ *v.* past tense **outrode** past participle **outridden** /-ˈrɪdn/ [T] to ride faster or farther than someone or something else

out·rid·er /ˈaʊtˌraɪdɚ/ *n.* [C] a guard or police officer who rides on a MOTORCYCLE or horse beside or in front of a vehicle in which an important person is traveling

out·rig·ger /ˈaʊtˌrɪgɚ/ *n.* [C] **1** a piece of wood shaped like a small narrow boat which is fastened to the side of a boat, especially a CANOE[1], to prevent it from turning over in the water **2** a boat that has one of these

out·right[1] /ˈaʊtraɪt/ *adj.* [only before noun] **1** complete and total: *an outright trade ban* **2** clear, direct, and with no attempt to hide what you think: *his outright opposition to the proposal* **3** an outright winner/victor someone who has definitely and easily won

out·right[2] /ˈaʊtraɪt, aʊtˈraɪt/ *adv.* **1** without trying to hide your feelings or intentions: *They laughed outright at my suggestion.* **2** completely or definitely: *Kahn needs 50% plus one vote to win the primary outright.* **3** immediately or without any delay: *Most of the lawmakers rejected the idea outright.* **4** buy/own sth outright to own something such as a house completely because you have paid the full price with your own money

out·rode /aʊtˈroʊd/ *v.* the past tense of OUTRIDE

out·run /aʊtˈrʌn/ *v.* past tense **outran** past participle **outrun** present participle **outrunning** [T] **1** to run faster or farther than someone or something: *The fire was moving so fast you couldn't outrun it.* **2** to develop more quickly than something else: *Consumer demand has outrun our production capabilities.*

out·sell /aʊtˈsɛl/ *v.* past tense and past participle **outsold** [T] **1** to be sold in larger quantities than something else: *They claim their machines are outselling Nintendo's machines.* **2** to sell more goods or products than a competitor: *Chevrolet's desire to outsell Ford*

out·set /ˈaʊtsɛt/ *n.* at/from the outset at or from the beginning of an event or process: *It was clear from the outset that there were going to be problems.*

out·shine /aʊtˈʃaɪn/ *v.* past tense and past participle **outshone** /-ˈʃoʊn/ or **outshined** [T] **1** to be clearly better than someone or something else: *Stone effortlessly outshines the other members of the cast.* **2** to shine more brightly than something else

out·shoot /aʊtˈʃut/ *v.* past tense and past participle **outshot** /-ˈʃɑt/ [T] to get more points than an opponent in HOCKEY, basketball etc.: *Montreal outshot the Blues 39–20.*

out·side[1] /ˌaʊtˈsaɪd, ˈaʊtsaɪd/ *prep.* **1** also **outside of** not inside a building, vehicle etc. but still close to it: *There was a crowd of photographers outside the courtroom.* —opposite INSIDE[1] **2** going out of a building or room: *She walked outside the bank and waited for the police to arrest her.* **3** also **outside of** beyond the limits of a city, country etc.: *They live in a little town outside of Reed City.* **4** also **outside of** beyond the limits or range of a situation, activity, group etc.: *Teachers can't control what students do outside school. | I'm afraid that subject is outside the scope of this discussion.* —compare BEYOND[1] (3)

USAGE NOTE: OUTSIDE

WORD CHOICE: out, outside, outdoors, out of doors
If you are **out**, you are away from a building, especially from the place where you live or work: *Let's go out for dinner. | I'm sorry, Mr. Hartman is out until Thursday.* If you are **outside**, you are not inside a room or a building, but you are usually close to it: *You have to go outside if you want to smoke.* If you are **outdoors** (or **out of doors**), you are away from buildings and in the open air: *Our kids love to play outdoors.*

---

outside[2] *adv.* **1** not inside a building: *It's cold outside. | Lonnie, take the dog outside.* **2** not in a room or building, but close to it: *Could I speak with you outside in the hall for just a minute? | There were a couple of guards standing outside.* **3** **outside of sth** INFORMAL apart from a particular person or thing: *I'm taking one big trip in the summer, but outside of that I'll be around.*

outside[3] *adj.* [only before noun] **1** not inside a building: *The apartment is reached by an outside stairway. | an outside toilet* —opposite INSIDE[4] —compare OUTDOOR, OUTER **2** from or involving people who do not belong to the same group or organization as you: *Both sides say they are opposed to any outside interference in the conflict. | We plan to hire an outside design team to produce our brochures.* **3** the **outside world** the rest of the world which is you do not know much about because you have no communication with it, you are not involved in it etc.: *Since the attack the city has been cut off from the outside world.* **4** **outside interests/experiences etc.** interests, experiences etc. that are separate from those that you have in your job or at your school: *Greene plans to retire and enjoy some of his outside interests.* **5** **an outside chance** a very small possibility that something will happen: *We still have an outside chance of getting into the playoffs.* **6** **outside line/call etc.** a telephone line or telephone call that is to or from someone who is not inside a building or organization **7** **an outside figure/estimate etc.** a number or amount that is the largest something could possibly be

outside[4] *n.* the **outside 1** the outer part or surface of something: [+ of] *They painted the outside of the house green.* —opposite INSIDE[3] **2** the area around something such as a building, vehicle etc.: *The house is a lot bigger than it looks from the outside.* **3** **on the outside a)** used to describe the way someone appears to be or to behave: *Cara was furious, though on the outside she appeared perfectly calm.* **b)** not in prison: *Life on the outside was not as easy as he'd first thought.* **c)** not involved in an activity, or not belonging to a particular group, organization etc.: *It's impossible for anyone on the outside to fully understand the judge's reasoning.* **4 at the outside** used to say that a number or amount is the largest something could possibly be, and it might be less: *It's only a 20-minute walk, half an hour at the outside.* **5** the LANE (1) on a wide road that is away from the inside or center: *In some countries it is only permissible to pass on the outside.* —opposite INSIDE³

out·sid·er /aʊt'saɪdɚ/ *n.* [C] **1** someone who is not accepted as a member of a particular social group: *Italian residents don't like to discuss the matter with outsiders.* | *They've treated us like outsiders ever since we moved in.* **2** someone who does not belong to a particular company or organization, is not involved in a particular activity etc.: *Why do they bring in outsiders to tell us how to run the business?* | *To outsiders, these ideological battles seem completely pointless.* **3** someone who does not seem to have much chance of winning a race or competition

out·size /'aʊtsaɪz/ *adj.* also **out·sized** /-saɪzd/ [only before noun] **1** larger than normal: *an outsize pair of glasses* **2** made for people who are very large: *outsize clothes*

out·skirts /'aʊtskɚts/ *n.* **the outskirts** the parts of a town or city that are farthest from the center: *We stayed on the outskirts of the capital.*

out·smart /aʊt'smɑrt/ *v.* [T] to gain an advantage over someone using tricks or using your intelligence; OUTWIT: *The lizard can outsmart predators by leaving its tail behind to confuse them.*

out·sold /aʊt'soʊld/ *v.* the past tense and past participle of OUTSELL

out·sourc·ing /'aʊt,sɔrsɪŋ/ *n.* [U] the practice of using workers from outside a company, or of buying supplies, parts etc. from another company instead of producing them yourself

out·spend /aʊt'spɛnd/ *v.* past tense and past participle **outspent** /-'spɛnt/ [T] to spend more money than another person or organization: *Gingrich had consistently outspent rival candidates.*

out·spo·ken /,aʊt'spoʊkən⁴/ *adj.* expressing your opinions honestly, even when it is not popular to do so: *She's an outspoken critic of U.S. policy.* | *outspoken views* —**outspokenness** *n.* [U]

out·spread /,aʊt'sprɛd⁴/ *adj.* spread out flat or completely: *He was lying on the beach with arms outspread.*

out·stand·ing /aʊt'stændɪŋ/ *adj.* **1** extremely good: *Ed is an outstanding football player.* | *Her performance was outstanding.* **2** not yet dealt with, solved, or paid: *Two of the lawsuits are still outstanding.* | *an outstanding debt* —**outstandingly** *adv.*

out·stay /aʊt'steɪ/ *v.* [T] to stay somewhere longer than someone else —see also **overstay/outstay your welcome** (WELCOME³ (3))

out·stretched /,aʊt'strɛtʃt⁴/ *adj.* stretched out to full length: *The birds rose with outstretched wings.*

out·strip /aʊt'strɪp/ *v.* **outstripped, outstripping** [T] **1** to be greater in quantity than something else: *Demand for energy is outstripping the supply.* **2** to do something better than someone else: *Even the most primitive computer can outstrip the human brain in certain types of calculation.* **3** to run or move faster than someone or something else

out·ta /'aʊtə/ *prep.* NONSTANDARD used in writing to represent the spoken form of "out of": *I've got to get outta here.*

out·take /'aʊt,teɪk/ *n.* [C] a piece of a movie or television show that is removed before it is broadcast, especially because it contains a mistake

out·vote /aʊt'voʊt/ *v.* [T usually passive] to vote in larger numbers than someone else or to defeat by having a larger number of votes: *They feared that the numerous poor might outvote the few rich.* | *Waddington's proposal was outvoted in the Senate.* —compare OUTPOLL

out·ward¹ /'aʊtwɚd/ *adj.* [only before noun] **1** relating to how a person or situation seems to be, rather than

how it really is: *My parents showed no outward signs of affection.* | **To all outward appearances** (=as much as can be judged by the way things seem) *Jodie seemed like a normal 12-year-old.* **2** directed toward the outside, or away from a place: *an outward movement of the arm* | *The outward flight was very uncomfortable.* —opposite INWARD

out·ward² also **outwards** *adv.* toward the outside or away from the center of something: *Oil began spreading outward from the sinking ship.*

out·ward·ly /'aʊtwɚdli/ *adv.* according to how people, things etc. seem, rather than how they are: *Amy was outwardly calm, but actually very tense.* | [sentence adverb] *Outwardly, nothing seemed to have changed.*

out·weigh /aʊt'weɪ/ *v.* [T] to be more important or valuable than something else: *Benefits of the surgery far outweigh the risk.*

out·wit /aʊt'wɪt/ *v.* **outwitted, outwitting** [T] to gain an advantage over someone using tricks or clever plans; OUTSMART: *Speeders can outwit police radar with a variety of devices.*

out·worn /,aʊt'wɔrn⁴/ *adj.* old-fashioned, and not useful or important anymore: *outworn traditions*

ou·zo /'uzoʊ/ *n.* [U] a Greek alcoholic drink with a strong taste, usually drunk with water

o·va /'oʊvə/ *n.* the plural form of OVUM

o·val /'oʊvəl/ *n.* [C] a shape like a circle, but longer than it is wide —**oval** *adj.*: *an oval swimming pool* —see picture at SHAPE¹

Oval Of·fice /,.. '../ *n.* **the Oval Office** the office of the U.S. President, in the White House in Washington, D.C.

o·var·i·an /oʊ'vɛriən/ *adj.* [only before noun] relating to the ovaries: *ovarian cancer*

o·va·ry /'oʊvəri/ *n. plural* **ovaries** [C] **1** the part of a human female or female animal that produces eggs **2** the part of a female plant that produces seeds

o·va·tion /oʊ'veɪʃən/ *n.* [C] FORMAL if a group of people give someone an ovation, they CLAP their hands to show approval: *The President received a standing ovation* (=everyone stood up to give it) *as he entered the hall.*

ov·en /'ʌvən/ *n.* [C] **1** a piece of equipment that food is cooked inside, shaped like a metal box with a door on it —see picture at KITCHEN **2 like an oven** INFORMAL so hot that you are uncomfortable: *I wish they'd turn off the heat. It's like an oven in here.* —see also **sb has a bun in the oven** (BUN (4))

ov·en·proof /'ʌvən,pruf/ *adj.* ovenproof dishes, plates etc. will not be harmed by the high temperatures in an oven

ov·en·ware /'ʌvən,wɛr/ *n.* [U] cooking pots that can be put in a hot oven without cracking

o·ver¹ /'oʊvɚ/ *prep.* **1** above or higher than something, without touching it: *A thick layer of smoke hung over the city.* | *The sign over the door said "Do Not Enter."* | *Leaning over her desk, she grabbed the phone.* —opposite UNDER¹ (1) —see also ABOVE¹ (1), ACROSS¹ (3) —see picture at ABOVE¹ **2** on something, so that it is covered: *I put another blanket over the baby.* | *A blue vest over that shirt would look great.* | *Sprinkle some sugar over the strawberries.* —opposite UNDER¹ **3** from one side of something to the other side, by going across the top of it: *We followed the trail over the hill.* | *One of the men jumped over the counter and grabbed the money.* **4** more than a particular number, level, age etc.: *The Delaneys spent over $20,000 repairing their house.* | *You could lose over 20 pounds in just six weeks.* | *The game is designed for children over 6 years old.* | **the over-30s/the over-40s etc.** (=people who are more than a particular age) **5** during: *Over a two-year period, Nancy became addicted to painkillers.* | *Did you go anywhere over New Year's?* | *Let's discuss the contract over lunch.* **6 over on** on the opposite side of something from where you already are: *Bill lives over on 32nd Avenue.* **7** down from the edge of something: *Just hang the towel over the back of the chair.* **8** in many parts of a place: *I've traveled over most of Europe but my favorite place was Austria.* | *There was broken glass all over* (=in every part) *the road.* **9 be/get over sth** to feel better after being sick or upset: *Susan's mad at me, but she'll get over it.* | *Are you over your cold now?* **10** in control of someone or having authority to give orders to someone: *He rules over a large kingdom.* | *In this office there is one manager over a staff of 15 workers.* —opposite UNDER[1] (8) **11** using a telephone or other system for communicating information: *I'd prefer not to talk about it over the phone.* | *Almost half their sales are now made over the Internet.* **12** about a particular subject, person or thing: *the long-running dispute over the ownership of the islands* **13 over and above** more than a certain amount: *The city has spent $2 million over and above budgeted funds for the new stadium.* —see also **all over** (ALL[2] (2))

over[2] *adv.* **1** falling down from an upright position: *The wind blew over the table.* | *I got so dizzy that I almost fell over.* **2** to, from, or in a particular place: *I'm over here!* | [+ to/from/in] *We drove over to Grandma's after lunch.* | *You mean you came all the way over from Brazil for the conference?* | *The fax machine is over in the corner.* **3** so that someone or something is not straight or flat anymore and is folded or bent in the middle: *Dan bent over to pick up the keys.* | *Place the cheese filling in the middle of the pastry and fold it over.* **4** so that the side or bottom of someone or something can now be seen: *Turn the box over and open it at that end.* | *Josh rolled over and went back to sleep.* **5** more or higher than a particular amount, number, or age: *The puzzle is for kids aged ten and over.* | *Almost 40 percent of women are size 14 or over.* —opposite UNDER[1] (3) **6** from one person or group to another: *The men agreed to hand over the stolen money to the authorities.* **7 read/ think/talk sth over** to read something, think about something etc. very carefully before deciding what to do: *I'll need to read this contract over before I sign it.* **8 start/do over** to start or do something again: *I got mixed up and had to start over.* **9 over and over (again)** repeatedly: *They just keep playing the same songs over and over.* **10 covered/painted etc. over** covered with a particular substance or material: *Most of the windows have been boarded over.* [+ with] *The door had been painted over with a bright red varnish.* **11 over to sb** used to say that it is now someone else's turn to do something, to speak etc.: *Now over to Bob who's live at the scene of the crime.* **12 over!** SPOKEN used by pilots, soldiers etc. when speaking to each other with a radio, to say that they are finished speaking so that another person can speak **13 over and out** SPOKEN used to say that you are completely finished saying what you have to say, especially when speaking to someone with a radio **14 over against sth** FORMAL compared to someone or something else: *The church is being forced to define itself over against non-religious culture.* —see also **all over** (ALL[2] (2))

over[3] *adj.* [not before noun] **1** if an event or period of time is over, it has finished: *Is the game over yet?* **2 get it/this over with** to do something that you do not want to do, but that is necessary, so that you do not have to worry about it anymore: *Should he tell her everything was OK? Or should he tell the truth and get it over with?* **3 be over (and done) with** if a bad situation or experience is over, it is finished: *I'm so glad that mid-term exams are over and done with.*

over- /ˈoʊvɚ/ *prefix* **1** too much, too many, or to too great a degree: *an overcrowded room* (=with too many people in it) | *overcooked vegetables* **2** above, beyond, or across: *overhanging branches* **3** outside or covering something: *an overcoat* **4** in addition: *I've been working overtime this month* (=longer than the usual time).

o·ver·a·chiev·er, **over-achiever** /ˌoʊvɚəˈtʃivɚ/ *n.* [C] someone who works very hard to be successful, and is very unhappy if they do not achieve everything

they want to —**over-achieve** *v.* [I] —compare UNDER-ACHIEVER

o·ver·act /ˌoʊvɚˈækt/ *v.* [I,T] to act a part in a play with too much emotion or too much movement

o·ver·ac·tive /ˌoʊvɚˈæktɪv◂/ *adj.* too active, in a way that causes problems: *an overactive thyroid gland* | *Jan has an overactive imagination* (=often imagines things that are untrue).

over-age /ˌ. . ˈ.◂/ *adj.* too old for a particular purpose or activity —compare UNDERAGE

o·ver·all[1] /ˌoʊvɚˈɔl◂/ *adj.* [only before noun] including or considering everything: *The overall cost of the trip is $500.* | *You certainly get the overall impression of a very well-run, clearly-focused business.*

overall[2] *adv.* **1** [sentence adverb] generally: *Overall, it's been a good year.* **2** including everything: *The project budget is around $25 million overall.*

o·ver·alls /ˈoʊvɚˌɔlz/ *n.* [plural] heavy cotton pants that have a piece covering your chest and are held up by pieces of cloth that go over your shoulders

o·ver·arch·ing /ˌoʊvɚˈɑrtʃɪŋ/ *adj.* [only before noun] **1** including or influencing every part of something: *Productivity and efficiency are overarching concerns at the factory.* **2** forming a curved shape over something: *the overarching sky*

o·ver·awe /ˌoʊvɚˈɔ/ *v.* [T usually passive] to make someone feel so impressed that they are nervous or unable to say or do anything: *We were overawed to be in the presence of such a great film maker.*

o·ver·bear·ing /ˌoʊvɚˈbɛrɪŋ/ *adj.* always trying to control other people without considering their wishes or feelings; DOMINEERING: *her overbearing husband* —**overbearingly** *adv.*

o·ver·bid /ˌoʊvɚˈbɪd/ *v.* **1** [I + for] to offer too high a price for something, especially at an AUCTION[1] **2** [I,T] to offer more than the value of your cards in a card game such as BRIDGE[1] (4)

o·ver·bite /ˈoʊvɚˌbaɪt/ *n.* [C] a condition in which someone's upper jaw is too far forward beyond their lower jaw

o·ver·blown /ˌoʊvɚˈbloʊn◂/ *adj.* FORMAL made to seem more important or impressive than it really is; EXAGGERATED (1): *Teague believes the incident has been overblown in the press.*

o·ver·board /ˈoʊvɚˌbɔrd/ *adv.* **1 go overboard** INFORMAL to do or say something that is too extreme for a particular situation: *Don't you think you went a little overboard on the decorations?* **2** over the side of a ship or boat into the water: *Eichenburger apparently slipped and fell overboard.* | *Man overboard!* (=said when someone falls off a boat)

o·ver·book /ˌoʊvɚˈbʊk/ [I,T] to sell more tickets for a theater, airplane etc. than there are seats available

o·ver·bur·den /ˌoʊvɚˈbɚdn/ *v.* [T usually passive] to give a person, organization, or system too much work or too many problems to deal with: *Public health systems are already overburdened by patients with no insurance.* —**overburdened** *adj.*: *the overburdened court system*

o·ver·came /ˌoʊvɚˈkeɪm/ *v.* the past tense of OVERCOME

o·ver·ca·pac·i·ty /ˌoʊvɚkəˈpæsəti/ *n.* [singular,U] when a factory or business is able to make more products than people will buy

o·ver·cast /ˈoʊvɚˌkæst/ *adj.* dark with clouds: *The afternoon will be overcast with cooler temperatures.* | *an overcast sky*

o·ver·charge /ˌoʊvɚˈtʃɑrdʒ/ *v.* **1** [I,T] to charge someone too much money for something: *The taxi driver had overcharged us by about $20.* —opposite UNDERCHARGE **2** [T] to put too much power into a BATTERY (1) or electrical system

o·ver·coat /ˈoʊvɚˌkoʊt/ *n.* [C] a long, thick, warm coat worn over other clothes in cold weather

o·ver·come /ˌoʊvɚˈkʌm/ *v. past tense* **overcame** *past participle* **overcome** [T] **1** to successfully deal with a feeling or problem that prevents you from achieving something: *I don't think he'll ever overcome his fear of flying.* | *Sara had overcome the disadvantages of her background to become a successful lawyer.* **2** to fight and win against someone or something:

New York overcame Washington in the final game. **3** [usually passive] if smoke or gas overcomes someone, they become extremely sick or unconscious because they breathe it: *Five employees were overcome by smoke.* **4** if an emotion overcomes someone, they cannot behave normally because they feel the emotion so strongly: *I was overcome with an irresistible urge to hit him.*

o·ver·com·pen·sate /ˌouvəˈkɑmpənˌseɪt/ *v.* [I] to try to correct a weakness or mistake by doing too much of the opposite thing: [+ **for**] *Zoe overcompensates for her shyness by talking a lot.* —**overcompensation** /ˌouvəˌkɑmpənˈseɪʃən/ *n.* [U]

o·ver·cook /ˌouvəˈkuk/ *v.* [T] to cook food for too long, so that it does not taste good —**overcooked** *adj.*: *overcooked vegetables*

o·ver·crowd·ed /ˌouvəˈkraudɪd◂/ *adj.* filled with too many people or things: *overcrowded prisons*

o·ver·crowd·ing /ˌouvəˈkraudɪŋ/ *n.* [U] the condition of living or working too close together, with too many people in a small space

o·ver·de·vel·oped /ˌouvədɪˈvɛləpt◂/ *adj.* **1** too great or large: *Ryan has an overdeveloped sense of his own importance.* **2** if a city or area is overdeveloped, too many houses, buildings, roads etc. have been built there

o·ver·do /ˌouvəˈdu/ *v. past tense* **overdid** /-ˈdɪd/ *past participle* **overdone** /-ˈdʌn/ [T] **1** to do something more than is appropriate or natural: *Don't overdo the praise. She wasn't that good.* **2 overdo it a)** to work too hard or be too active, so that you become tired: *She's been overdoing it lately.* **b)** to do something too much or in an extreme way: *I think Trudy has overdone it with all the lace and frills in her bedroom.*

o·ver·done /ˌouvəˈdʌn/ *adj.* cooked too much: *As usual, the fish was overdone.* —compare UNDERDONE

o·ver·dose¹ /ˈouvəˌdous/ *n.* **1** [C] too much of a drug taken at one time: *The 18-year-old male died of an overdose of sleeping pills.* **2** [singular] INFORMAL a situation in which you do, see, eat etc. too much of one thing: *an overdose of soap operas*

o·ver·dose² *abbreviation* **OD** *v.* [I] **1** to take too much of a drug: [+ **on**] *He overdosed on heroin.* **2** to do or have too much of something so that you do not want to do or have any more: [+ **on**] *OD on chocolate*

o·ver·draft /ˈouvəˌdræft/ *n.* [C] the amount of money you owe to a bank when you have taken out more money than you had in your bank account

o·ver·drawn /ˌouvəˈdrɔn/ *adj.* if your bank account is overdrawn, you have spent more than is in it and you owe the bank money: *If you are overdrawn, there's a $25 fee to pay.* | *The account was overdrawn by $700.*

overdressed

o·ver·dressed /ˌouvəˈdrɛst◂/ *adj.* dressed in clothes that are too formal for the occasion.: *We were completely overdressed for the party.* —**overdress** *v.* [I]

o·ver·drive /ˈouvəˌdraɪv/ *n.* [U] **1** an additional GEAR¹ (1) which allows a car to go fast while its engine produces the least power necessary **2 go into overdrive** to become very excited or active: *Hollywood has gone into overdrive about Spielberg's next movie.*

o·ver·due /ˌouvəˈdu◂/ *adj.* **1** a payment that is overdue should have been paid earlier: *overdue mortgage payments* **2** something that is overdue should have happened or been done a long time ago: [+ **for**] *Our house is overdue for a new paint job.* | *Tougher laws on air pollution are long overdue.* **3** a library book that is overdue was not returned to the library when it should have been **4** [not before noun] a baby that is overdue was not born at the time that it was expected: *Collette's baby is already two weeks overdue.*

over·eas·y /ˌ.. ˈ../ *adj., adv.* eggs that are over-easy are cooked in oil and turned over to cook on the other side for only a moment so that the YOLK is still liquid: *I'd like my eggs done over-easy, please.*

o·ver·eat /ˌouvəˈit/ *v. past tense* **overate** /-ˈeɪt/ *past participle* **overeaten** /-ˈitn/ [I] to eat too much, or eat more than is healthy: *Some people can overeat without putting on much weight.*

o·ver·em·pha·size /ˌouvəˈɛmfəˌsaɪz/ *v.* [T] too emphasize something too much or give it too much importance: *The importance of car safety cannot be overemphasized.* —**overemphasis** /ˌouvəˈɛmfəsɪs/ *n.*: *an overemphasis on money*

o·ver·es·ti·mate¹ /ˌouvəˈɛstəˌmeɪt/ *v.* **1** [I,T] to think that something is larger, more important, more expensive etc. than it really is: *The generals had overestimated the strength of the enemy forces.* | *The significance of these changes cannot be overestimated.* (=they are extremely important) **2** [T] to think that someone is more skillful, intelligent etc. than they really are: *Never overestimate your ability or strength when swimming in the ocean.* —compare UNDERESTIMATE¹

o·ver·es·ti·mate² /ˌouvəˈɛstəmɪt/ *n.* [C] a calculation, judgment, or guess that is too large

o·ver·ex·cit·ed /ˌouvərɪkˈsaɪtɪd◂/ *adj.* too excited to behave sensibly

o·ver·ex·pose /ˌouvərɪkˈspouz/ *v.* [T] **1** to allow too much light to reach the film when taking or developing a photograph **2 be overexposed** someone who is overexposed has appeared too many times on television, in the newspapers etc. and people have become bored by them —opposite UNDEREXPOSE

o·ver·ex·po·sure, over-exposure /ˌouvərɪkˈspouzə/ *n.* [U] **1** the state of having received too much light, sunlight, RADIATION etc., that is harmful to someone's skin, photographic film etc. **2** the fact of being overexposed

o·ver·ex·tend /ˌouvərɪkˈstɛnd/ [T] **overextend yourself a)** to try to do too much, with the result that you become sick, unable to deal with all your jobs or problems etc. **b)** to spend more money than you actually have: *It's common for out-of-work families to overextend themselves.* —**overextended** *adj.*: *The company was badly overextended because of an expensive advertising campaign.*

o·ver·flow¹ /ˌouvəˈflou/ *v.* [I,T] **1** if a river, lake, or container overflows, it is so full that the water or material inside it flows over its edges: *Turn the water off so the sink doesn't overflow.* | *Shoal Creek overflowed its banks today.* | [+ **with**] *The trash can overflowed with beer bottles.* **2** if a place overflows with people or if people overflow a place, there are too many of them to fit into it: *There were more than 30 reporters, overflowing their allotted space in the courtroom* | [+ **with**] *The hospitals are overflowing with victims of the hurricane.* **3 filled to overflowing (with sth)** completely full: *Her little room was filled to overflowing with photos and ornaments.* **4 overflow with love/gratitude etc.** to have a very strong feeling of love etc.: *Hampton overflows with enthusiasm when he talks about jazz.*

overflow

o·ver·flow² /ˈouvəˌflou/ *n.* **1** [C usually singular] the additional people or things that cannot be contained in a place because it is already full: *A temporary*

O

parking lot will be provided to handle the overflow. | [+ **of**] an overflow of students **2** [U] an act of overflowing something **3** [C] a pipe through which water flows out of a container when it becomes too full —**overflow** adj.: The overflow crowd stood in the back of the theater.

o·ver·fly /ˌoʊvɚˈflaɪ/ v. past tense **overflew** /-ˈflu/ past participle **overflown** /-ˈfloʊn/ [T] to fly over an area or country in an aircraft: Air force helicopters overflew the area.

o·ver·grown /ˌoʊvɚˈɡroʊn◂/ adj. **1** covered with plants that have grown in a wild way: an overgrown field | [+ **with**] Both sides of the road were overgrown with weeds. **2 overgrown child/kid/etc.** an adult who behaves like a child: They were fooling around like a bunch of overgrown kids.

o·ver·growth /ˈoʊvɚˌɡroʊθ/ n. [U] plants and branches of trees growing above your head, usually in a forest

o·ver·hand /ˈoʊvɚˌhænd/ adj., adv. an overhand throw in a sport is when you throw the ball with your arm above the level of your shoulder —opposite UNDERHAND

o·ver·hang[1] /ˌoʊvɚˈhæŋ/ v. past tense and past participle **overhung** [I,T] to hang over something or stick out above it: There's a long sweep of farmland that overhangs the Rappahannock River.

o·ver·hang[2] /ˈoʊvɚˌhæŋ/ n. [C usually singular] **1** a rock, roof etc. that hangs over something else: The amphitheater's overhang protects most of the seats from bad weather. **2** the amount by which something hangs over something else

o·ver·haul[1] /ˌoʊvɚˈhɔl, ˈoʊvɚˌhɔl/ v. [T] to repair or improve a machine, system etc., by checking all its parts and fixing anything that does not work well: They promised to reduce taxes and overhaul the whole welfare system. | An engineer is coming in to overhaul the air conditioning.

o·ver·haul[2] /ˈoʊvɚˌhɔl/ n. [C] a process of making necessary changes or repairs to a machine or system: The Chevy needs a complete overhaul. | an overhaul of the election process

o·ver·head[1] /ˌoʊvɚˈhɛd◂/ adv. above your head: Helicopter gunships hovered overhead. —**overhead** adj.: Their bags fit in the overhead compartment.

s w **o·ver·head**[2] /ˈoʊvɚˌhɛd/ n. **1** [U] money spent regularly on rent, insurance, electricity, and other things that are needed to keep a business operating: Working out of my home had significantly lowered my overhead. **2** [C] a piece of transparent material used with an overhead projector to show words, pictures etc. —**overhead** adj.: The company laid off 1500 employees to cut overhead costs.

overhead pro·jec·tor /ˌ... .ˈ../ n. [C] a piece of electrical equipment used by teachers, trainers etc. which makes words and images look larger by showing them on a wall or large screen

o·ver·hear /ˌoʊvɚˈhɪr/ v. past tense and past participle **overheard** /-ˈhɚd/ [I,T] to accidentally hear what other people are saying, when they do not know that you have heard: She claims to have overheard an argument between the President and the First Lady. | an overheard conversation | [**overhear sb do sth/doing sth**] Two U.S. soldiers were overheard discussing the invasion plans. —compare EAVESDROP

o·ver·heat /ˌoʊvɚˈhit/ v. [I,T] **1** to become too hot, or to make something too hot: If the fan doesn't work, the engine could overheat. | Try not to overheat the sauce. **2** if a country's ECONOMY overheats or if something overheats it, it grows too fast and this leads to increases in prices, salaries, interest rates etc.: Critics say the economy overheated because of the recent tax cuts.

o·ver·heat·ed /ˌoʊvɚˈhitɪd◂/ adj. **1** too hot: The smoke was caused by an overheated air conditioner. **2** an overheated economic system is growing too fast, and this leads to increases in prices, salaries, interest rates etc. **3** full of angry feelings: an overheated debate

o·ver·hung /ˌoʊvɚˈhʌŋ/ v. the past tense and past participle of OVERHANG[1]

o·ver·in·dulge /ˌoʊvɚɪnˈdʌldʒ/ v. **1** [I] to eat or drink too much: It's hard not to overindulge during the holidays. **2** [T] to let someone have everything they want, or always let them do what they want: Sam's parents constantly overindulge him. —**overindulgence** n. [U]

o·ver·joyed /ˌoʊvɚˈdʒɔɪd/ adj. [usually after noun] extremely happy about something: I knew my mother would be overjoyed when she heard the news. | **overjoyed to hear/find/see sth** We were overjoyed to see them safely back home.

o·ver·kill /ˈoʊvɚˌkɪl/ n. [U] **1** more of something than is needed or wanted: The coverage of the trial is a clear example of media overkill. **2** more than enough weapons, especially NUCLEAR (3) weapons, to kill everyone in a country

o·ver·land /ˈoʊvɚˌlænd/ adv. across land, not by sea or air: We decided to travel overland to Oaxaca. —**overland** adj.: an overland route

o·ver·lap[1] /ˌoʊvɚˈlæp/ v. **overlapped, overlapping** [I,T] **1** if two or more things overlap, part of one thing covers part of the other: The tiles on the roof overlap. | Overlap the first strip of cloth with the second by about two inches. **2** if two subjects, ideas etc. overlap, they each include some but not all of the same features: The responsibilities of the two departments overlap in certain areas. | Having merged the two companies, his first task is to eliminate overlapping product lines. **3** if two events or activities overlap, the first one finishes after the second one starts: [+ **with**] This year Easter overlaps with Ramadan.

o·ver·lap[2] /ˈoʊvɚˌlæp/ n. [C,U] the degree to which two things, activities etc. overlap: [+ **between**] We're working to reduce overlap between jobs.

o·ver·lay[1] /ˌoʊvɚˈleɪ/ v. past tense and past participle **overlaid** [T] **1** to thinly cover something: The semiprecious stones are partly overlaid with gold. **2** to cover or hide actions or attitudes, often so that real intentions will not show: The legal action overlays an illegal and hidden set of interests. **3** to add new qualities to existing ideas, customs, or works of art: a religious culture in which Buddhism overlays even older folk beliefs | [+ **with**] The rich bass rhythms are overlaid with delicate melodies.

o·ver·lay[2] /ˈoʊvɚˌleɪ/ n. [C] **1** something laid over something else **2** a transparent sheet with a picture or drawing on it which is put on top of another picture to change it **3** an additional quality or feeling: Kupfer added an unnecessary overlay of sexuality to the opera.

o·ver·leaf /ˈoʊvɚˌlif/ adv. on the other side of the page: See the diagram overleaf.

o·ver·lie /ˌoʊvɚˈlaɪ/ v. [T] TECHNICAL **1** to lie over something: A layer of limestone overlies older rocks. **2** if a parent animal overlies its young it kills them by lying on them

o·ver·load /ˌoʊvɚˈloʊd/ v. past participle **overloaded** [T] **1** to fill something with too many things or people: You shouldn't overload the washing machine. **2** to put too much electricity through an electrical system or piece of equipment: Don't overload the outlet by plugging in too many appliances. **3** to give someone too much work: [+ **with**] All the staff are overloaded with work. —**overload** /ˈoʊvɚˌloʊd/ n. [C,U]

o·ver·long /ˌoʊvɚˈlɔŋ◂/ adj. continuing for too long: an overlong romantic melodrama

o·ver·look[1] /ˌoʊvɚˈlʊk/ v. [T] **1** to not notice something: The clerk must have overlooked your name, because he said you weren't here. **2** if a building, room, or window overlooks a place, you can look down on that place from it: Thaden's restored house overlooks an alpine valley. **3** to ignore and forgive someone's mistake, bad behavior etc.: I'll overlook your mistake this time.

o·ver·look[2] /ˈoʊvɚˌlʊk/ n. [C] a high place from which you can see the land below it

o·ver·lord /ˈouvəˌlɔrd/ *n.* [C often plural] someone who has great power over a large number of people, especially in the past

o·ver·ly /ˈouvəli/ *adv.* [often in negatives] too or very: *We weren't overly impressed with the movie.* | *I think you're being overly critical.*

o·ver·manned /ˌouvəˈmænd/ *adj.* OVERSTAFFED

o·ver·much /ˌouvəˈmʌtʃ/ *adv.* LITERARY too much

o·ver·night¹ /ˌouvəˈnaɪt/ *adv.* **1** for or during the night: **stay overnight** *Higgins was not required to stay overnight at the hospital.* **2** quickly or suddenly, in a way that is surprising: *Several members of the board became millionaires overnight.*

o·ver·night² /ˈouvəˌnaɪt/ *adj.* [only before noun] **1** continuing all night: *an overnight flight to Seoul* **2** done in one night: *an overnight delivery service* **3 an overnight success** something that suddenly becomes very popular or successful: *The show was an overnight success on Broadway.*

over·op·ti·mis·tic /ˌ.. ..ˈ.. ./ *adj.* expecting that things will be better than is possible or likely: *Reports that the hostages will be released soon are over-optimistic.*

o·ver·paid /ˌouvəˈpeɪd/ *adj.* [not before noun] given more money for a job than you deserve: *overpaid athletes*

o·ver·pass /ˈouvəˌpæs/ *n.* [C] a structure like a bridge that allows one road to go over another road —see picture at BRIDGE¹

o·ver·pay /ˌouvəˈpeɪ/ *v.* **overpays, overpaid, overpaying 1** [I,T] to pay too much money for something: *We overpaid our taxes this year.* **2** [T] to pay someone more money than they deserve: *Most big companies continue to overpay their top executives.* —**overpayment** *n.* [C,U]

o·ver·play /ˌouvəˈpleɪ/ *v.* **overplays, overplayed, overplaying** [T] **1** to make something seem more important or more exciting than it is: *The press tends to overplay these disagreements among Cabinet members.* —opposite UNDERPLAY (1) **2 overplay your hand** to behave too confidently, and try to gain more advantage than you can reasonably expect: *By opposing even a moderate ban on assault weapons, the gun lobby has overplayed its hand.* **3** to play a piece of music, show something on television, etc. too often

o·ver·pop·u·lat·ed /ˌouvəˈpɑpyəˌleɪtɪd/ *adj.* an overpopulated city, country etc. has too many people: *overpopulated areas* —**overpopulation** /ˌouvəˌpɑpyəˈleɪʃən/ *n.* [U]

o·ver·pow·er /ˌouvəˈpauə/ *v.* [T] **1** to defeat someone, especially by taking hold of them, because you are stronger than they are: *Three inmates overpowered guards at the county jail in Madison.* **2** if a smell or taste or an emotion overpowers someone or something, it has bad effects because it is too strong: *The wine is bland enough not to overpower the fish.*

o·ver·pow·er·ing /ˌouvəˈpauərɪŋ/ *adj.* **1** very strong; INTENSE: *Her loneliness was overpowering.* | *an overpowering smell* **2** someone who is overpowering has such a strong character that they make other people feel uncomfortable or afraid

o·ver·priced /ˌouvəˈpraɪst/ *adj.* something that is overpriced is much more expensive than it should be: *overpriced Italian restaurants* —**overprice** *v.* [I,T]

o·ver·print /ˌouvəˈprɪnt/ *v.* [T + with/on] to print additional words over a document, stamp etc. that already has printing on it

o·ver·pro·duc·tion /ˌouvəprəˈdʌkʃən/ *n.* [U] the act of producing more of something than people need or want: *the overproduction of crude oil* —**overproduce** /ˌouvəprəˈdus/ *v.* [I,T]

o·ver·pro·tec·tive /ˌouvəprəˈtɛktɪv/ *adj.* so anxious to protect someone from harm, danger etc. that you restrict their freedom: *overprotective parents*

o·ver·qual·i·fied /ˌouvəˈkwɑləˌfaɪd/ *adj.* having so much experience or training that people do not want to employ you for particular jobs: *I'm having trouble finding a job – everyone says I'm overqualified.*

o·ver·ran /ˌouvəˈræn/ *v.* the past tense of OVERRUN

o·ver·rat·ed /ˌouvəˈreɪtɪd/ *adj.* not as good or important as some people think or claim: *the most overrated film of the year* —opposite UNDERRATED —**overrate** *v.* [T]

o·ver·reach /ˌouvəˈritʃ/ *v.* [I,T] to try to do more than you have the power, ability, or money to do: *Critics say the commissioner overreached his authority.* | *The company had overreached itself, and ended up with debts that it couldn't pay.*

o·ver·re·act /ˌouvəriˈækt/ *v.* [I] to react to something that happens by showing too much emotion or by doing something that is not really necessary: *Some analysts believe the bank overreacted, and that interest rates did not really need to rise.* | *[+ to] It's normal for parents to overreact to their child getting hurt.* —**overreaction** /ˌouvəriˈækʃən/ *n.* [C,U]

o·ver·ride¹ /ˌouvəˈraɪd/ *v.* past tense **overrode** /-ˈroud/ past participle **overridden** /-ˈrɪdn/ [T] **1** to change someone's official decision by using your power or authority to do so: *City council members voted to override the mayor's veto.* **2** to be regarded as more important than something else: *Should the opinions of experts override the wishes of the people?* **3** to change a process that is normally AUTOMATIC: *Pilots tried to manually override the plane's computer control.*

o·ver·ride² /ˈouvəˌraɪd/ *n.* [C] **1** an act of overriding an official decision **2** a system or piece of equipment that allow you to change a process that is usually AUTOMATIC: *a manual override*

o·ver·rid·ing /ˌouvəˈraɪdɪŋ/ *adj.* [only before noun] more important than anything else: *The overriding theme of the conference is the need to reduce Third World debt.* | *an overriding concern about safety*

o·ver·ripe /ˌouvəˈraɪp/ *adj.* overripe fruit and vegetables are past the point of being fully grown and ready to eat: *overripe bananas*

o·ver·rule /ˌouvəˈrul/ *v.* [T] **1** to change an order or decision that you think is wrong, using your official power: *The Supreme Court overruled the lower court's decision.* **2 (objection) overruled** LAW used by a judge in a court of law to say that someone was not right to object to another person's statement —opposite **(objection) sustained** (SUSTAIN (5)) —compare **objection!** (OBJECTION (3))

o·ver·run¹ /ˌouvəˈrʌn/ *v.* past tense **overran** past participle **overrun** [T] if something unwanted overruns a place or area, it spreads all over it in large quantities: *Vines of morning glory overran the rainforest canopy.* | **be overrun by/with sth** *Some of the housing projects were overrun by gangs and drugs.* **2** [I,T] if a river overruns its banks, it is so full that the water flows over its edges: *Heavy rains caused Stoney Creek to overrun its banks earlier today.* **3** [T] to defeat a place or an area and take control of it: *Soviet troops overran the nation in 1940.* —see also **run over** (RUN¹)

o·ver·run² /ˈouvəˌrʌn/ *n.* [C] an act of spending more money on a program of work, a product etc. than had been planned or agreed: *cost overruns of $7.2 million*

o·ver·seas¹ /ˌouvəˈsiz/ *adv.* to or in a foreign country that is across the ocean: *Lara plans to study overseas.* | *Most of the applications came from overseas.*

o·ver·seas² /ˈouvəˌsiz/ *adj.* [only before noun] coming from, existing, or happening abroad: *overseas travel* | *overseas bank accounts*

o·ver·see /ˌouvəˈsi/ *past tense* **oversaw** /-ˈsɔ/ *past participle* **overseen** /-ˈsin/ *v.* [T] to be in charge of a program of work or a group of workers, and check that everything is done correctly: *Mr. Somers oversaw construction of the water treatment plant.* | *Schultz oversees 61 workers and a $5.9 million budget.*

o·ver·se·er /ˈouvəˌsiə/ *n.* [C] someone in charge of a group of workers, who checks that their work is done correctly, especially in past times

o·ver·sell /ˌouvəˈsɛl/ *past tense and past participle* **oversold** /-ˈsould/ *v.* [T] **1** to praise someone or something too much, or make claims about them that may not be true: *The movie was oversold and ended up disappointing everyone.* **2** to sell more tickets, seats etc. than are actually available

o·ver·sen·si·tive /ˌoʊvɚˈsɛnsətɪv◂/ *adj.* very easily upset or offended

o·ver·sexed /ˌoʊvɚˈsɛkst◂/ *adj.* having too much interest in or desire for sex

o·ver·shad·ow /ˌoʊvɚˈʃædoʊ/ *v.* [T] **1** [usually passive] to make someone or something else seem less important, especially by being more successful than them: *Tim felt constantly overshadowed by his older brother.* **2** to make an occasion, period, event etc. seem less enjoyable by making people feel sad or worried: *Rumors of financial malpractice overshadowed the President's inauguration ceremony.* **3** if a tall building, mountain etc. overshadows a building, place etc., it is very close to it and much taller than it: *An impressive 25-story skyscraper overshadows the temple next door.*

o·ver·shoe /ˈoʊvɚˌʃu/ *n.* [C] a rubber shoe that you wear over an ordinary shoe to keep your feet dry

o·ver·shoot /ˌoʊvɚˈʃut/ *v. past tense and past participle* **overshot** /-ˈʃɑt/ [T] **1** to miss a place where you wanted to stop or turn,, by going too far past it: *A commuter plane overshot the runway Sunday night in Augusta.* **2** to go beyond an intended limit or level, for example by spending more money than you had planned: *The budget deficit will probably overshoot its target of 5.8 percent of GDP.* **3 overshoot the mark** to make the mistake of trying to achieve too much or go farther than you had planned

o·ver·sight /ˈoʊvɚˌsaɪt/ *n.* **1** [C,U] a mistake that you make by not noticing something or by forgetting to do something: *They sent a check along with a letter of apology for the oversight.* **2** [U] the situation of being in charge of a piece of work and checking that it is satisfactory: *a school oversight committee*

o·ver·sim·pli·fy /ˌoʊvɚˈsɪmpləˌfaɪ/ *v.* **oversimplifies, oversimplified, oversimplifying** [I,T] to make a situation or problem seem less complicated than it really is, by ignoring important facts: *Elder's article greatly oversimplifies the causes of the current crisis.* —**oversimplification** /ˌoʊvɚˌsɪmpləfəˈkeɪʃən/ *n.* [C, U]

o·ver·size /ˌoʊvɚˈsaɪz◂/ also **o·ver·sized** /-ˈsaɪzd/ *adj.* bigger than usual or too big: *Oversize, baggy shorts are still popular.*

o·ver·sleep /ˌoʊvɚˈslip/ *v. past tense and past participle* **overslept** /-ˈslɛpt/ [I] to sleep for longer than you intended: *Why are you so late? Did you oversleep again?* —compare **sleep in** (SLEEP¹), **sleep over** (SLEEP¹)

o·ver·spend /ˌoʊvɚˈspɛnd/ *v. past tense and past participle* **overspent** /-ˈspɛnt/ [I,T] to spend more money than you can afford: *Too many people overspend during the holidays.* | *Philadelphia overspent its budget by 10%.*

o·ver·staffed /ˌoʊvɚˈstæft◂/ *adj.* an overstaffed company, organization etc. has more workers than it needs —opposite UNDERSTAFFED

o·ver·state /ˌoʊvɚˈsteɪt/ *v.* [T] to talk about something in a way that makes it seem more important, serious etc. than it really is; EXAGGERATE: *Opponents say Nader is overstating the gravity of the problem.* —**overstatement** *n.* [C,U] —opposite UNDERSTATE

o·ver·stay /ˌoʊvɚˈsteɪ/ *v.* **overstays, overstayed, overstaying** [T] to stay somewhere longer than you intended or longer than you should: *The INS is looking for tourists who have overstayed their visas.* —see also **overstay/outstay your welcome** (WELCOME³ (3))

o·ver·step /ˌoʊvɚˈstɛp/ *v.* **overstepped, overstepping** [T] **overstep the bounds/rules/limits etc.** to do something that goes beyond what is acceptable or what is allowed by the rules: *Lawmakers appear to be overstepping their authority this time.*

o·ver·stock /ˌoʊvɚˈstɑk/ *v.* [I,T] to obtain more of something than is needed for a store, hotel etc.

o·ver·stuffed /ˌoʊvɚˈstʌft◂/ *adj.* **1** an overstuffed chair is filled with thick PADDING: *Alice sank into a big overstuffed armchair.* **2** filled with too much of something or too many things: *overstuffed lockers*

o·ver·sub·scribe /ˌoʊvɚsəbˈskraɪb/ *v.* [T] **be oversubscribed** if an activity, service etc. is oversubscribed, too many people want to do it or use it: *Most publicly funded clinics are oversubscribed.*

o·ver·sup·ply /ˈoʊvɚsəˌplaɪ/ *n. plural* **oversupplies** [C,U] the state of having more of a particular product than you need or can sell: *an oversupply of steel*

o·vert /oʊˈvɚt, ˈoʊvɚt/ *adj.* FORMAL overt actions or feelings are done or shown publicly, without trying to hide anything: *an overt attempt to force landowners to sell* | *overt racism* —**overtly** *adv.* —opposite COVERT¹

o·ver·take /ˌoʊvɚˈteɪk/ *v. past tense* **overtook** *past participle* **overtaken** /-ˈteɪkən/ [T] **1** to become bigger, more advanced, more successful etc. than someone or something that you are competing with: *By 1970 the U.S. had overtaken the Soviet Union in space technology.* **2** to go past a moving vehicle or person because you are going faster than them: *Police overtook and captured the fleeing suspect.* **3** if a bad feeling or bad event overtakes you, it happens to you suddenly and prevents you from doing what you had planned: *He was overtaken by exhaustion.* **4 be overtaken by events** if you are overtaken by events, the situation changes so that your plans or ideas are not useful or appropriate anymore

o·ver·tax /ˌoʊvɚˈtæks/ *v.* [T] **1** to make someone or something do more than they are really able to do: *Since the operation, he's been careful not to overtax himself.* **2** to make people pay too much tax —**overtaxed** *adj.*

over-the-count·er /ˌ... ˈ..◂/ *adj.* [only before noun] **1** over-the-counter drugs can be obtained without a PRESCRIPTION (=a written order) from a doctor **2** *abbreviation* **OTC** over-the-counter business shares are ones that do not appear on an official STOCK EXCHANGE list —**over the counter** *adv.*: *The medicine is available over the counter.*

over-the-top /ˌ... ˈ.◂/ *adj.* INFORMAL an over-the-top remark, performance, type of behavior etc. is so EXAGGERATED that it seems slightly silly or extreme: *She specializes in over-the-top satirical comedy.*

o·ver·throw¹ /ˌoʊvɚˈθroʊ/ *v. past tense* **overthrew** /-ˈθru/ *past participle* **overthrown** /-ˈθroʊn/ [T] **1** to remove a leader or government from a position of power by force: *A small group of military officers overthrew the President in September.* **2** to cause a complete change by getting rid of the existing rules, ideas etc.: *a discovery that could overthrow conventional ideas about computing*

o·ver·throw² /ˈoʊvɚˌθroʊ/ *n.* [U] the defeat and removal from power of a leader or government, especially by force: [+ of] *The organization was dedicated to the overthrow of capitalism.* | *the overthrow of Mussolini*

o·ver·time /ˈoʊvɚˌtaɪm/ *n.* [U] **1** time that you spend working in your job in addition to your normal working hours: *I had to* **work overtime** *three days last week.* **2** the money that you are paid for working more hours than usual: *I don't mind working weekends as long as they* **pay** *me* **overtime.** **3** a period of time added to the end of a sports game to give one of the two teams a chance to win: *Miller scored 9 of his 23 points in overtime.* **4 be working overtime** INFORMAL to be very active: *Price's wit and sarcasm are working overtime in this production.*

o·ver·tone /ˈoʊvɚˌtoʊn/ *n.* [C] **1** [usually plural] signs of an emotion or attitude that is not expressed directly: **racial/political overtones etc.** *The defeat of the city's first black mayor had racial overtones.* **2** TECHNICAL a higher musical note that sounds together with the main note —see also UNDERTONE

o·ver·took /ˌoʊvɚˈtʊk/ *the past tense of* OVERTAKE

o·ver·ture /ˈoʊvɚtʃɚ, -ˌtʃʊr/ *n.* [C] **1** a short piece of music written as an introduction to a longer piece, especially in an OPERA **2** [usually plural] an attempt to begin a friendly relationship with a person, country, or organization etc.: *U.S. business chiefs were beginning to* **make overtures to** *the leadership in*

Beijing. **3** [usually plural] an attempt to begin a romantic or sexual relationship with someone: *sexual overtures* **4 be an overture to sth** to happen before, and seem to lead to, a particular event: *King's ill-treatment by the police was a disturbing overture to the riots that followed.*

o·ver·turn /ˌoʊvəˈtɜrn/ *v.* **1** [T] to change an official decision or result so that it becomes the opposite of what it was before: *Today's ruling overturns part of a lower court's decision on July 25.* **2** [I,T] if you overturn something or if it overturns, it turns upside down or falls over on its side: *Fans roamed the streets, overturning cars with foreign license plates.* | *One of the boats had overturned.* **3** [T] to suddenly remove a government from power, especially by using violence; OVERTHROW[1] (1)

o·ver·use /ˌoʊvəˈyuz/ *v.* [T] to use something too much, or more than is necessary: *Ed tends to overuse management jargon.* —**overuse** /ˌoʊvəˈyus/ *n.* [U]

o·ver·val·ue /ˌoʊvəˈvælyu/ *v.* [T] to believe or say that something is more valuable or more important than it really is: *Analysts grossly overvalued the company's inventories.* —**overvalued** *adj.* —**overvaluation** /ˌoʊvəˌvælyuˈeɪʃən/ *n.* [U]

o·ver·view /ˈoʊvəˌvyu/ *n.* [C usually singular] a short description of a subject or situation that gives the main ideas without all the details: *Janks gave an overview of the Lincoln plan.*

o·ver·ween·ing /ˌoʊvəˈwinɪŋ/ *adj.* [only before noun] FORMAL too proud and confident; ARROGANT: *overweening ambition*

o·ver·weight /ˌoʊvəˈweɪt/ *adj.* **1** too heavy or too fat: *I'm 15 pounds overweight.* | *a special clinic for seriously overweight children* —see Usage Note at FAT[1] **2** something such as a package that is overweight weighs more than it is supposed to weigh: *overweight luggage* —opposite UNDERWEIGHT

o·ver·whelm /ˌoʊvəˈwɛlm/ *v.* [T] **1** if an emotion, event, or problem overwhelms you, you are very affected by it and you do not know what to do, how to react etc.: *Sometimes a sense of deep frustration almost overwhelms her.* | *Auto theft cases seem to be overwhelming local police.* | *I was completely overwhelmed by their generosity.* **2** to defeat an opponent or army completely: *The Lakers overwhelmed the Sonics by the third quarter.* **3** if a color, smell, taste etc. overwhelms another color, taste etc., it is much stronger and more noticeable: *Most preparations overwhelm the flavor of good oysters.* **4** LITERARY if water overwhelms an area of land, it covers it completely and suddenly

o·ver·whelm·ing /ˌoʊvəˈwɛlmɪŋ/ *adj.* **1** large enough in size, number, or amount to be very impressive or have a strong effect: *The evidence against them is overwhelming.* | *An overwhelming majority of the members are women.* **2** an overwhelming situation or feeling affects you so strongly that it is difficult to deal with or fight against: *She had an overwhelming urge to call Mel again in New York.* | *an overwhelming experience* —**overwhelmingly** *adv.*: *Congress voted overwhelmingly in favor of the bill.*

o·ver·work[1] /ˌoʊvəˈwɜrk/ *v.* [I,T] to work too much, or to make someone work too much: *The company has been overworking its employees to try to keep up with demand.*

o·ver·work[2] /ˈoʊvəˌwɜrk, ˌoʊvəˈwɜrk/ *n.* [U] too much hard work: *He literally killed himself with overwork.*

o·ver·worked /ˌoʊvəˈwɜrkt/ *adj.* **1** working too hard and for too long: *overworked teachers* **2** a word or phrase that is overworked is used too much and has become less effective: *overworked metaphors*

o·ver·wrought /ˌoʊvəˈrɔt/ *adj.* **1** very upset, nervous, and worried: *Cecile was emotionally overwrought.* **2** written, acted etc. in a way that is too careful and seems awkward: *an overwrought performance*

o·ver·zeal·ous /ˌoʊvəˈzɛləs/ *adj.* too eager about something you feel strongly about: *overzealous fans* | *an overzealous tax inspector*

Ov·id /ˈɑvɪd/ (43 B.C.–A.D. 17) a Roman poet whose Roman name was Publius Ovidius Naso

o·vi·duct /ˈoʊvɪˌdʌkt/ *n.* [C] TECHNICAL one of the two tubes in a female through which eggs pass to the WOMB

o·vip·a·rous /oʊˈvɪpərəs/ *adj.* TECHNICAL an oviparous animal, fish, bird etc. produces eggs that develop and HATCH outside its body

o·void /ˈoʊvɔɪd/ *adj.* TECHNICAL having a shape like an egg —**ovoid** *n.* [C]

o·vu·late /ˈɑvyəˌleɪt/ *v.* [I] when a woman or female animal ovulates, she produces eggs inside her body —**ovulation** /ˌɑvyəˈleɪʃən/ *n.* [U]

o·vum /ˈoʊvəm/ *n. plural* **ova** /ˈoʊvə/ [C] TECHNICAL an egg, especially one that develops inside a woman or female animal's body

ow /aʊ/ *interjection* said to show that something hurts you: *Ow! My leg!*

owe /oʊ/ *v.* [T] **1** to have to pay someone money because you have borrowed from them, or because they have done something for you or sold you something and you have not paid them for it: *How much do you owe?* | [owe sb sth] *Chris owes me $20.* | [owe sth to sb] *At that time Uganda owed billions of dollars to the World Bank.* | [owe sb for sth] *I still owe him for gas.* **2** to feel that you should do something for someone or give something to someone, because they have done something for you or given something to you: *You're going to owe me if I let you use my car.* | *Joanne will watch the kids – she owes me a favor.* | *I'll write and tell Marie. I owe her a letter anyway.* | *Thanks, Mandy. I really owe you one* (=used to thank someone for helping you). **3 owe sb an apology/explanation** to feel that you should say sorry to someone or explain to them why you did something **4 a)** to have something valuable or important as a result of a particular person, quality etc.: [owe sth to sb/sth] *About 1 million Americans owe their jobs to foreign tourism.* | [owe sb sth] *We owe those firefighters our lives.* **b)** to feel that someone's help has been important to you in achieving something: *I owe my parents a lot for everything they've done for me.* | *Peggy's a good cook now, but she owes it all to her grandmother.* | *The nation owes a debt of gratitude to its brave veterans.* **5 owe it to sb to do sth** to feel you should do something for someone because it is what they deserve: *We owe it to our children to clean up the environment.* | *You owe it to yourself to take some time off.* **6 owe allegiance to sb/sth** to have a duty to obey someone or be loyal to them: *People with dual nationality owe allegiance to more than one country.*

Ow·ens /ˈoʊənz/, **Jes·se** /ˈdʒɛsi/ (1913–1980) a very successful African-American ATHLETE, who won four GOLD MEDALS at the 1936 Olympic Games in Berlin

Jesse Owens

ow·ie /ˈaʊi/ *n.* [C] SPOKEN a word meaning a small injury, used by or to children

ow·ing /ˈoʊɪŋ/ *adj.* **1** FORMAL **owing to sth** because of: *Hundreds of babies are dying, owing to shortages of basic foods.* **2** [not before noun] if money is owing, it has not yet been paid to the person who should receive it: *How much is still owing?*

owl /aʊl/ *n.* [C] a bird with large eyes and a loud call, which hunts at night

owl·ish /ˈaʊlɪʃ/ *adj.* someone who is owlish looks a little like an owl and seems serious and intelligent because they wear glasses: *a friendly fellow with owlish looks*

own[1] /oʊn/ *determiner, pron.* **1** belonging to a particular person and no one else: *Ben wants his own room.* | *This is my newspaper. Go get your own.* | *He left the company to start a business of his own.* | *Now*

*I've got **my very own** credit card.* **2** done or made without the help or influence of someone else: *I'm old enough to make my own decisions.* | *It's his own fault for leaving it there.* | *Why buy it when you can make your own for less?* **3 (all) on your own a)** alone: *Will you be OK here on your own?* **b)** without anyone's help: *Did you build this all on your own?* —see Usage Note at ALONE **4 be your own man/woman** to have strong opinions and intentions which are not influenced by other people —see also **in sb's own back yard** (BACKYARD (2)), **come into your own** at **come into** (COME[1]), **hold your own** (HOLD[1] (25)), **in sb's own way** (WAY[1] (28))

O

USAGE NOTE: OWN

GRAMMAR
Use **own** only after possessive words like *my, Carol's, the company's* etc.: *Becky has her own office.* You can also use **very** to emphasize **own**, especially in informal spoken English: *I love her like my very own child.*

S2 W1 **own**[2] *v.* [T not in progressive] **1** to legally have something because you have bought it, been given it etc.: *I don't even own a car.* | *They own a small electronics company.* | *The horse is owned by a Saudi businessman.* **2 do sth like you own the place** INFORMAL to behave in a way that is too confident and annoys other people: *He walks around here like he owns the place!* **3 own (that)** OLD USE to admit that something is true

own up *phr. v.* [I] to admit something embarrassing or something bad that you have done: *It was five years before the Defense Department owned up and accepted responsibility for the accident.* | [+ **to**] *Chuck wouldn't own up to the fact that he'd been drinking.*

S3 W1 **own·er** /ˈoʊnɚ/ *n.* [C] someone who owns something: *a property owner* | [+ **of**] *the owner of the restaurant* | *Scheer is **the proud owner of** a copy of the Declaration of Independence.* —see also HOMEOWNER

owner-oc·cu·pied /ˌ.. ˈ...◂/ *adj.* owner-occupied houses, apartments etc. are lived in by the people who own them —**owner-occupier** *n.* [C]

own·er·ship /ˈoʊnɚˌʃɪp/ *n.* [U] the fact or state of owning something: *The agency was transferred from public to private ownership.*

own goal /ˌ. ˈ./ *n.* [C] a GOAL that you accidentally SCORE[2] (1) against your own team without intending to in a game of SOCCER, HOCKEY etc.

ox /ɑks/ *n. plural* **oxen** /ˈɑksən/ [C] **1** a BULL whose sex organs have been removed, often used for working on farms **2** a large cow, BULL etc.

ox·bow /ˈɑksboʊ/ *n.* [C] a U-shaped bend in a river

ox cart, oxcart /ˈ. ./ *n.* [C] a vehicle pulled by oxen

ox·eye /ˈɑksaɪ/ *n.* [C] a yellow flower like a DAISY

ox·ford /ˈɑksfɚd/ *n.* **1** [U] also **oxford cloth** a type of thick cotton cloth used for making shirts **2** [C] also **oxford shirt** a shirt made of this cloth **3** [C] a type of leather shoe that fastens with a SHOELACE

ox·i·da·tion /ˌɑksəˈdeɪʃən/ *n.* [U] TECHNICAL the process or result of oxidizing

ox·ide /ˈɑksaɪd/ *n.* [C,U] TECHNICAL a chemical compound in which another substance is combined with oxygen: *iron oxide*

ox·i·dize /ˈɑksəˌdaɪz/ *v.* [I,T] TECHNICAL to combine with oxygen, or make something combine with oxygen, especially in a way that causes RUST: *Through the years, paint oxidizes as it's exposed to air.*

ox·tail /ˈɑks-teɪl/ *n.* [U] the meat from the tails of cattle, used especially in soup

ox·y·a·cet·y·lene /ˌɑksiəˈsɛtl̩ˌin◂, -ˈsɛtl-ən◂/ *n.* [U] TECHNICAL a mixture of oxygen and ACETYLENE that produces a hot white flame that can cut steel

ox·y·gen /ˈɑksɪdʒən/ *n.* [U] *symbol* **O** a gas that is an ELEMENT, has no color, smell, or taste, is present in the air, and is necessary for animals and plants to live

ox·y·gen·ate /ˈɑksɪdʒəˌneɪt/ *v.* [T] TECHNICAL to add oxygen to something —**oxygenated** *adj.* —**oxygenation** /ˌɑksɪdʒəˈneɪʃən/ *n.* [U]

oxygen mask /ˈ... ˌ./ *n.* [C] a piece of equipment that fits over someone's mouth and nose to provide them with oxygen

oxygen tent /ˈ... ˌ./ *n.* [C] a piece of equipment shaped like a tent that is put around someone who is very sick in a hospital, to provide them with oxygen

ox·y·mo·ron /ˌɑksiˈmɔrɑn/ *n.* [C] a combination of two words that seem to mean the opposite of each other, such as "new classics"

o·yez /oʊˈyɛz, -ˈyeɪ, ˈoʊ-/ *interjection* a word used by law officials or by TOWN CRIERS in the past to get people's attention

oys·ter /ˈɔɪstɚ/ *n.* [C,U] a small ocean animal that has a shell and can produce a jewel called a PEARL, or the inside part of this animal, which can be eaten raw or cooked —see also **the world is sb's oyster** (WORLD[1] (26))

oyster bed /ˈ.. ˌ./ *n.* [C] an area at the bottom of the ocean where oysters live

oz. the written abbreviation of OUNCE or ounces

O·zarks, the /ˈoʊzɑrks/ an area of high land covered by forests in the southern central U.S. states of Missouri and Arkansas

o·zone /ˈoʊzoʊn/ *n.* [U] **1** TECHNICAL a poisonous blue gas that is a type of oxygen **2** clean fresh air, especially near the ocean

ozone-friend·ly /ˌ.. ˈ..◂/ *adj.* not containing chemicals that damage the ozone layer: *ozone-friendly hair spray*

ozone lay·er /ˈ.. ˌ../ *n.* [singular] **the ozone layer** the layer of gases that prevents harmful RADIATION (2) from the sun from reaching the Earth

P

P, p /pi/ *n. plural* **P's, p's** [C] the 16th letter of the English alphabet —see also **mind your manners/ p's and q's** (MIND² (11))

p the written abbreviation of "piano," used in written music to show that a part should be played or sung quietly

p. **1** *plural* **pp.** the written abbreviation of "page" **2** the written abbreviation of PARTICIPLE

PA¹ the written abbreviation of Pennsylvania

PA² *n.* [C usually singular] public address system; electronic equipment that makes someone's voice loud enough to be heard by large groups of people

pa /pɑ/ *n.* [C] OLD-FASHIONED a word meaning "father," used by or to children

pab·lum /'pæbləm/ *n.* [U] FORMAL books, speeches, movies etc. that are very simple or boring, and contain no new or original ideas: *The studio had become a purveyor of middle-of-the-road Hollywood pablum.*

PAC /pæk/ *n.* [C] Political Action Committee; an organization that tries to influence politicians so that they support the group's aims, for example, by voting a particular way

pace¹ /peɪs/ *n.*

1 speed of events/changes [singular] the rate or speed at which something happens or is done: [+ **of**] *The pace of technological innovation shows no sign of slowing down.* | *She's been working incredibly hard, but I doubt if she can* **keep up this pace** (=continue working at this rate.) | *Professor Morrey lets us study* **at our own pace.** | **at a slow/rapid/steady** etc. **pace** (=slowly, quickly etc.)

2 speed of walking [singular] the speed at which you walk or run: *The women walked by* **at a brisk pace.**

3 a step [C] a single step when you are running or walking, or the distance moved in one step: *Paul stepped three paces into the room and dropped his bag.* | *About 20 paces from the house is an old oak tree.*

4 **pick/speed/step up the pace** to do something more quickly or to cause something to happen more quickly than before: *Jackson said the slow players need to pick up the pace.* | *The President wants to step up the pace of gun-control reform*

5 **keep pace (with sb/sth)** to move or change as fast as someone or something else: *Funding for the program is unlikely to keep pace with need.* | *If population growth continues at this rate, will food production be able to keep pace?*

6 **a change of pace** a change in the way something is done, the speed at which it is done etc.: *This year's smaller festival is a welcome change of pace from last year's.*

7 **put sb/sth through their/its paces** to make a person, machine etc. show how well they can do something: *The world's most advanced aircraft are put through their paces at this desert test site.*

8 **set the pace** **a)** to establish a rate of development, a level of quality etc. that other people or organizations try to copy: *For most of the nineties, we were setting the pace in mobile phone technology.* **b)** to run at a speed that other runners try to follow

9 **force the pace** to make something happen or develop more quickly than it would normally: *Senator Michaels says he does not intend to force the pace of the legislation.*

10 **the pace of life** the amount of activity in people's lives and how busy they are: *Muriel misses the old days when the pace of life was slower.*

11 horse [C] one of the ways that a horse walks or runs

pace² *v.* **1** [I always + adv./prep.,T] to walk first in one direction and then in another, again and again, when you are waiting for something or worried

about something: *Stewart was pacing the floor while watching the game on TV.* | *When I get nervous I start* **pacing back and forth.** **2** **pace yourself** to do something at a steady speed so that you do not get tired quickly: *It's a long climb, so you have to pace yourself.* **3** [T] to set a speed for someone running or riding in a race: *I need someone to pace me or I fall too far behind.* **4** [T] to be more successful than any other player on a team, for example by getting more points: *Kernan paced the Monarchs with 17 points and 15 rebounds.* **5** also **pace off, pace out** [T] to measure a distance by taking steps of an equal length: *He paced off the distance just to make sure.* —see also PACING

-paced /peɪst/ [in adjectives] **slow-paced/fast-paced/lightning-paced** etc. moving, happening, or developing slowly, quickly etc.: *a fast-paced adventure movie*

pace·mak·er /'peɪs,meɪkɚ/ *n.* [C] **1** a very small machine that is attached to someone's heart to help it beat regularly **2** a PACESETTER

pace·set·ter /'peɪs,sɛtɚ/ *n.* [C] **1** someone or something that establishes a level of quality or achievement which others try to copy: *The French TGV is the pacesetter for high-speed trains.* **2** a team that is ahead of others in a competition **3** someone who runs at the front at the beginning of a race and sets the speed at which others must run

Pa·chel·bel /'pɑkəl,bɛl/, **Jo·hann** /'youhɑn/ (?1653–1706) a German musician who wrote CLASSICAL music

pach·y·derm /'pækɪ,dɚm/ *n.* [C] TECHNICAL a thick-skinned animal such as an ELEPHANT or a RHINOCEROS

Pa·cif·ic /pə'sɪfɪk/ *n.* **1** **the Pacific** the Pacific Ocean **2** [U] SPOKEN a short form of Pacific Time, the TIME ZONE in the western part of the U.S.

pa·cif·ic /pə'sɪfɪk/ *adj.* LITERARY **1** peaceful or loving peace: *a normally pacific community* **2** helping to cause peace

Pacific Day·light Time /.ˌ. '. ˌ./ *abbreviation* **PDT** *n.* [U] the time that is used in the western part of the U.S. for just over half the year, during the summer months, when clocks are one hour ahead of Pacific Standard Time

Pacific North·west /.ˌ.. '.'./ *n.* [U] **the Pacific Northwest** the area of the U.S. that includes the states of Oregon and Washington, and can include the southwestern part of British Columbia, Canada

Pacific O·cean, the /.ˌ.. '../ also **the Pacific** the ocean between the continents of North and South America to the east and Asia and Australia to the west

Pacific Rim /.ˌ.. './ *n.* **the Pacific Rim (countries)** the countries or parts of countries that border the Pacific Ocean, such as Japan, Australia, and the west coast of the U.S., often considered as an economic group

Pacific Stan·dard Time /.ˌ.. ˌ.. '. ˌ.. '.. ˌ./ *abbreviation* **PST** *n.* [U] the time that is used in the western part of the U.S. for almost half the year, during the winter months —compare PACIFIC DAYLIGHT TIME

Pacific Time /.'.. ˌ./ *abbreviation* **PT** *n.* [U] the time that is used in the western part of the U.S.

pac·i·fi·er /'pæsə,faɪɚ/ *n.* [C] **1** a specially shaped rubber object that you give a baby to suck so that it does not cry **2** something that makes people calm

pac·i·fism /'pæsə,fɪzəm/ *n.* [U] the belief that all wars and all forms of violence are wrong

pac·i·fist /'pæsəfɪst/ *n.* [C] someone who believes that all wars are wrong and who refuses to use violence

pac·i·fy /'pæsə,faɪ/ *v.* **pacifies, pacified, pacifying** [T] **1** to make someone calm, quiet, and satisfied after they have been angry or upset: *They had to use drugs to pacify him.* **2** to bring peace to an area or to end war in a place: *On August 20, the army recaptured the city and pacified the surrounding area.* —**pacification** /ˌpæsəfə'keɪʃən/ *n.* [U]

pac·ing /ˈpeɪsɪŋ/ *n.* [U] **1** the rate at which events develop in a book, movie etc.: *As always in King's stories, the pacing is excellent.* **2** the action of walking first in one direction and then in another, again and again, when you are waiting for something or worried about something

s w

pack¹ /pæk/ *v.*

1 boxes, cases etc. [I,T] **a)** to fill a suitcase, box etc. with things: *Why do you always pack at the last minute? | Brent had to pack a suitcase and get to the airport in under an hour.* **b)** to put things in boxes or suitcases: *Don't forget to pack your swimming suit. | Can you pack the kids' lunches?*

2 large crowd [I always + adv./prep., T] to go in large numbers into a space that is not big enough, or to make a lot of people or things do this: *More than 50,000 fans packed into the stadium. | Tourists in North Carolina packed ferries to flee the Outer Banks.*

3 protect sth [T] to cover, fill, or surround something closely with material to protect it: *Pack the knee with ice to reduce swelling.*

4 snow/soil etc. [T] to press soil, snow etc. down firmly: [pack sth into/down etc.] *Kenny packed the snow into a perfect snowball.*

5 food [T] to prepare food, especially meat, and put it into containers for preserving or selling: *The tuna is packed in oil. | a meat packing factory*

6 pack your bags INFORMAL to leave a place and not return, especially because of a disagreement: *She should pack her bags and go back where she came from.*

7 pack a committee/jury/meeting etc. to secretly and dishonestly arrange for a group to be filled with people who support you: *The President tried to pack the court with conservatives.*

8 pack a gun/heat/a piece SLANG to carry a gun

9 pack a punch/wallop INFORMAL **a)** to have a strong effect: *Black Star promises to pack more punch than Budweiser. | The play was written 30 years ago, but it still packs emotional wallop.* **b)** to be able to hit another person hard in a fight —see also **send sb packing** (SEND (11))

pack sth ↔ **away** *phr. v.* [T] to put something back in a box, case etc. where it is usually kept: *I let the engine run while I packed the tools away.*

pack sb/sth **in** *phr. v.* [T] **1 pack them in** INFORMAL to attract a lot of people: *Diana Ross can still pack them in.* **2** [pack sb/sth ↔ **in**] to fit a lot of people, things, activities etc. into a limited space or a limited period of time: *There's not enough space in back to consider packing in three adults.* **3 pack it in** INFORMAL to stop doing something, especially a job, that is not making you feel happy or satisfied: *I'm still frustrated, but I'm not ready to pack it in yet.*

pack sth **into** sth *phr. v.* [T] to fit a lot of something into a limited space, place, or period of time: *We packed a lot of sightseeing into two weeks.*

pack sb **off** *phr. v.* [T] INFORMAL to send someone away quickly because you want to get rid of them: [+ to] *Our folks used to pack us off to camp every summer.*

pack up *phr. v.* **1** [I,T] to put things into boxes, suitcases, bags etc. in order to take or store them somewhere: *When I got home, Sally and the kids were packing up. |* [pack sth ↔ **up**] *Shannon packed up her belongings and left.* **2** [I] INFORMAL to finish work: *I think I'll pack up and go home early.*

s w

pack² *n.* [C]

1 small container a small container made of paper, CARDBOARD etc., with a set of things in it, especially things that are sold together in this way: *Susan took a mint out of the pack. |* [+ of] *a pack of cigarettes* —see picture at CONTAINER

2 group of animals a group of wild animals that live and hunt together, or a group of dogs trained together for hunting: *a wolf pack |* [+ of] *a pack of hounds*

3 group of people a group of people who do something together, especially a group who you do not

approve of: [+ of] *The hostages had to face a pack of reporters and photographers.*

4 things wrapped together several things wrapped or tied together or put in a case, to make them easy to carry, sell, or give to someone: *a video gift pack | a six-pack of beer*

5 bag a BACKPACK¹ —see also FANNY PACK

6 cards also **pack of cards** a complete set of playing cards; DECK

7 be a pack of lies INFORMAL to be completely untrue: *White said the charges against him were "a pack of lies."*

8 Cub/Brownie pack a group of children belonging to a children's organization —see also BROWNIE, CUB SCOUT

9 military a group of aircraft, SUBMARINES etc. that fight the enemy together

10 on a wound a thick mass of soft cloth that you press on a wound to stop the flow of blood —see also ICE PACK, MUDPACK

pack·age¹ /ˈpækɪdʒ/ *n.* [C] **1** the box, bag, or other container that food is put in to be sold: *The cooking instructions are on the package. |* [+ of] *a package of frozen spinach* —see picture at BASKET **2** something packed together firmly or packed in a box and wrapped in paper, especially for mailing: *The mailman left a package for you at our house.* **3** a set of related things or services that are sold or offered together: *a new software package*

s w

package² *v.* [T] **1** to put something in a special package, especially to be sent or sold: *The cocaine was already packaged and ready to be shipped to the U.S.* **2** to try to make a person, idea, or product seem interesting or attractive so that people will like them or want them: *Martin's manager had packaged him to appeal to teenage girls.*

package deal /ˈ.. ˌ./ *n.* [C] an offer or agreement that includes several things that must all be accepted together

package store /ˈ.. ˌ./ *n.* [C] OLD-FASHIONED a store where alcohol is sold

package tour /ˌ.. ˈ./ *n.* [C] a completely planned vacation arranged by a company at a particular price, which includes travel, hotels, meals etc.

pack·ag·ing /ˈpækɪdʒɪŋ/ *n.* [U] **1** bags, boxes, and all the other materials that contain a product that is sold in a store: *More than 30% of the cost of our food goes on packaging.* **2** a way of making a person, idea etc. seem interesting, attractive, or better than they are: *TBS's packaging of its programs has been a key factor in its success.* **3** the process of wrapping food or other products for sale: *The tour of the plant follows the almonds from storage to final packaging.*

pack an·i·mal /ˈ. ˌ../ *n.* [C] an animal such as a horse used for carrying heavy loads

packed /pækt/ *adj.* **1** extremely full of people: *Boy, the zoo is packed today. |* [+ with] *The hotels were packed with tourists.* **2** containing a lot of a particular kind of thing: [+ with] *The new tourist guide is packed with useful information* **3 packed to the rafters/roof/gills** extremely full of people or things: *Auditorium Hall was packed to the rafters with people.* **4** [not before noun] if you are packed, you have put everything you need into bags, suitcases etc. before going somewhere: *Are you packed yet?* **5** put or pressed together: *packed snow | Use half a cup of* **loosely packed** *basil leaves. | a* **tightly packed** *football crowd*

pack·er /ˈpækɚ/ *n.* [C] someone who works in a factory, preparing food and putting it into containers

pack·et /ˈpækɪt/ *n.* [C] **1** a small envelope containing a substance or a group of things: *a packet of carrot seeds* —see picture at CONTAINER **2** a small package: *We received our membership packets in the mail.* **3** TECHNICAL a quantity of information that is sent as a single unit from one computer to another on a network or on the Internet

s w

packet switch·ing /ˈ.. ˌ../ *n.* [C] a method of sending DATA (=information stored on a computer) on telephone lines, that breaks long messages into pieces and puts them together again when they are received

pack ice /'. ./ *n.* [U] a mass of ice that is made of smaller pieces and that floats in a large body of water

pack·ing /'pækɪŋ/ *n.* [U] **1** the act of putting things into cases or boxes so that you can send or take them somewhere: *I usually* **do my packing** *the night before I leave.* **2** paper, plastic, cloth etc. that is put around things you are packing to protect them

packing case /'.. ,./ *n.* [C] a large strong wooden box in which things are packed to be sent somewhere or stored

pack rat /'. ./ *n.* [C] INFORMAL someone who collects and stores things that they do not really need

pack trip /'. ./ *n.* [C] a trip through the countryside on horses, for fun or as a sport

pact /pækt/ *n.* [C] a formal agreement between two groups, nations, or people, especially to help each other or fight together against an enemy: *Four of the countries refused to* **sign the** *economic* **pact.** | *We* **made a pact** *to help each other out.* —see also SUICIDE PACT

SW **pad¹** /pæd/ *n.* [C]
3
1 [soft material] something made of or filled with soft material that is used to protect something, clean something or make something more comfortable: *Cover the wound with a cotton pad.* | *Wipe the pad over the surface until the wood starts to shine.* | *I had to sleep on a foam pad on the floor.* | **knee/elbow/shoulder pad** (=a pad sewn into someone's clothes to protect their knee, elbow etc. or make them look bigger)
2 [paper] many sheets of paper fastened together, used for writing letters, drawing pictures etc.: **a note/message/sketch pad**
3 [for women] a piece of soft material that a woman puts in her underwear during her PERIOD¹ (4) to take up the blood
4 [home] OLD-FASHIONED, INFORMAL a house, room, or apartment where someone lives: *a bachelor pad*
5 [animal's foot] the flesh on the bottom of the foot of a cat, dog, etc.
6 [for ink] a piece of material that has been made wet with ink and is used for covering a STAMP (2) with ink; INK PAD
7 [water plant] the large floating leaf of some water plants such as the WATER LILY: *a lily pad*
8 a LAUNCH PAD
9 a HELICOPTER PAD

pad² *v.* **padded, padding 1** [I always + adv./prep.] to walk softly and quietly: *Rhoda padded across the hall into her sister's room.* **2** [T] to protect something, make it more comfortable, or change its shape by covering or filling it with soft material: *For the movie, he has to pad his body to make himself look 25 pounds heavier.* **3** [T] to dishonestly make bills more expensive than they should be: *They realized their lawyer was padding the court fees.* **4** [T] also **pad sth out** to make a speech or piece of writing longer, by adding unnecessary words or details: *The last chapter is padded out with an extract from an earlier report.* | *Some of the students do "community service," partly in order to* **pad their resumes** (=make them seem more impressive). **5** [T] to add to your points in a game that you are already winning: *The A's padded their lead with two more runs.*

pad·ded /'pædɪd/ *adj.* something that is padded is filled or covered with a soft material to make it thicker or more comfortable: *chairs with padded backs and arms*

padded cell /,.. './ *n.* [C] a special room with thick soft walls in a MENTAL HOSPITAL, used to stop people who are being violent from hurting themselves

pad·ding /'pædɪŋ/ *n.* [U] **1** soft material used to fill or cover something to make it softer or more comfortable **2** unnecessary words or details that are added to make a sentence, speech etc. longer

pad·dle¹ /'pædl/ *n.* [C] **1** a short pole that is wide and flat at one end or both ends, used for moving a small boat along —compare OAR **2** a flat round object with a short handle, used for hitting the ball in PING-PONG **3** a piece of wood with a handle, used for hitting a child to punish them **4** one of the wide blades

on the wheel of a PADDLE STEAMER **5** a tool like a flat spoon, used for mixing food —see also DOG PADDLE

paddle² *v.* **paddled, paddling 1** [I,T] to move a small light boat through water, using one or more paddles: *I watched the market traders paddling their canoes across the lake.* | [**+ along/upstream/toward**] *We got in the boat and paddled upstream.* —compare ROW² **2** [I] to swim by moving your hands and feet up and down —see also DOG PADDLE **3** [T] INFORMAL to hit a child with a piece of wood as a punishment

paddle boat /'.. ,./ *n.* [C] **1** a small boat that one or two people move by turning PEDALS with their feet **2** a paddle steamer

paddle steam·er /'.. ,../ *n.* [C] a STEAMBOAT (=large boat driven by steam) which is pushed forward by two large wheels at the sides

paddle wheel /'.. ,./ *n.* [C] a large wheel on a boat, which has many boards attached to it that push the boat through the water

pad·dock /'pædək/ *n.* [C] **1** a place where horses are brought together before a race so that people can look at them **2** a small field near a house or STABLE in which horses are kept or exercised

pad·dy /'pædi/ also **paddy field** /'.. ,./ *n. plural* **paddies** [C] a field in which rice is grown in water

paddy wag·on /'.. ,../ *n.* [C] INFORMAL a covered truck or VAN used by the police to carry prisoners

pad·lock /'pædlɑk/ *n.* [C] a small metal lock with a rounded bar that you can attach to a door, bicycle etc. —**padlock** *v.* [T]

pa·dre /'pɑdreɪ, -dri/ *n.* [C] INFORMAL a priest, especially one in the army

pae·an /'piən/ *n.* [C] LITERARY a piece of writing, music etc. expressing praise or happiness: [**+ to**] *His new movie is a paean to the "film noirs" of the 1940s.*

pa·el·la /pɑ'elə, -'eɪyə/ *n.* [U] a Spanish dish of rice cooked with pieces of meat, fish, and vegetables

pa·gan¹ /'peɪgən/ *adj.* **1** relating to or believing in a religion that is not one of the main religions of the world, especially one from a time before these religions developed: *ancient pagan beliefs and rituals* | *pagan Germanic tribes* **2** not religious

pagan² *n.* [C] **1** someone who believes in a pagan religion **2** HUMOROUS someone who has few or no religious beliefs —**paganism** *n.* [U]

page¹ /peɪdʒ/ *n.* [C]
SW
11
1 [paper] one side of a sheet of paper in a book, newspaper etc., or the sheet of paper itself: *What page is the picture on?* | *How many pages are we supposed to read?* | *See pages 27–30 for club listings.* | *a ten-page handwritten letter* | *The last page of the book is missing.* | *Did you see what was on* **the front page** *of the paper this morning?* | *Alex was sitting in an armchair,* **turning the pages** *of a magazine.* | **the sports pages/the fashion page** etc. (=part of a newspaper dealing with sports, fashion etc.)
2 [young worker] a young person who works in the U.S. CONGRESS for a short time to gain experience
3 [computer] **a)** a piece of writing or a picture on a computer screen that will fill one side of a piece of paper when it is printed **b)** all the writing that can be seen at one time on a computer screen
4 **a page in history** an important event or period: *The ending of the Civil War* **turns a new page in** *our nation's* **history.**
5 [boy] **a)** a boy who served a KNIGHT during the Middle Ages as part of his training **b)** a PAGEBOY (2) **c)** OLD USE a boy who is a servant to a person of high rank

page² *v.* [T] **1** to call someone's name out in a
SW
2
public place, especially using a LOUDSPEAKER, in order to find them: *I couldn't find Jenny at the airport, so I had her paged.* **2** to call someone by sending a message to their PAGER (=a small machine they carry that receives signals): *Don't page me after 10 o'clock.*

page through sth *phr. v.* [T] to quickly look at a

book, magazine etc., by turning the pages: *Her two-year-old son paged through a toy catalog on the floor.*

pag·eant /'pædʒənt/ *n.* **1** [C] a public competition for young women in which their appearance and other qualities are compared and judged **2** [C] a public show or ceremony where people dress in beautifully decorated clothes and perform historical or traditional scenes: *Parents came to see their children in the annual Christmas pageant.* **3** [singular] LITERARY a continuous series of historical events that are interesting and impressive: *The pageant of African history is so rich and various.*

pag·eant·ry /'pædʒəntri/ *n.* [U] impressive ceremonies or events, involving many people wearing special clothes

page·boy /'peidʒbɔi/ *n.* [C] **1** a style of cutting women's hair in which the hair is cut fairly short and has its ends turned under **2** OLD-FASHIONED a boy or young man employed in a hotel, club, theater etc. to deliver messages, carry bags etc.

pag·er /'peidʒɚ/ *n.* [C] a small electronic machine that you carry or wear, that makes a high noise or VIBRATES to tell you to call someone

pag·i·na·tion /ˌpædʒə'neiʃən/ *n.* [U] FORMAL the process of giving a number to each page of a book, magazine etc. —**paginate** /'pædʒə,neit/ *v.* [T] FORMAL

pa·go·da /pə'goudə/ *n.* [C] a TEMPLE of a type that is common in China, Japan, and other Asian countries, that has several levels with a decorated roof at each level

Pa·go Pa·go /ˌpɑŋou 'pɑŋou/ the capital city of the U.S. TERRITORY of American Samoa

paid /peid/ *v.* the past tense and past participle of PAY

Paige /peidʒ/, **Satch·ell** /'sætʃəl/ (1906–1982) a U.S. baseball player, famous as a PITCHER, who became one of the first African-American players in the Major Leagues in 1948

pail /peil/ *n.* [C] **1** a container with a handle used for holding or carrying liquids, or used by children playing with sand; BUCKET: *a milk pail | a diaper pail* **2** also **pail·ful** /'peilful/ the amount a pail will hold: *a pailful of water*

s w **pain¹** /pein/ *n.* [C,U]
2 2
1 `in your body` the feeling you have when part of your body hurts: *I had a pain in my right shoulder. | A month after surgery she was still in pain* (=feeling pain). *| Bubka said he was tired and felt some pain in his left leg. | Her drugs don't do much to relieve the pain* (=make it hurt less). *| Injuries to the major joints can cause severe pain. | Berg is suing the hospital for $500,000 for pain and suffering. | We had minor aches and pains for days after the game. | Suddenly I felt a sharp pain* (=one that you feel very severely, usually for a short time) *in my neck. | Joe felt a dull pain in his arm after the shot. | Julie woke up about 5 a.m. with labor pains* (=pain felt by women beginning to have a baby). —see also GROWING PAINS
2 `in your mind` a feeling of emotional suffering, caused by something that upsets you or makes you very worried: *the pleasures and pains of trying to earn money as a writer | The scandal has caused me and my family great pain. | She turned to drugs to ease the pain of her family life. | This policy is inflicting needless pain on thousands of American families.*
3 be a pain in the ass/butt VULGAR to be extremely annoying: *That cat's been a real pain in the ass lately.*
4 be a pain (in the neck) SPOKEN to be very annoying: *Everyone thinks he's a pain in the neck. | It's such a pain to have to drive downtown.*
5 on/under pain of death/punishment etc. at the risk of being killed, punished etc.: *Members were sworn to keep the secret, on pain of death.*
6 take pains to do sth also **go to (great) pains to do sth** to try hard to do something, or to be very careful in doing something: *Duke takes pains to avoid racist language.*
7 be at pains to do sth to make a special effort to

do something, because you think it is very important: *The U.S. military has been at pains not to offend its Muslim host.*
8 for sb's pains as a reward for your efforts or hard work, especially an unfair reward: *He works there his whole life, and then he gets fired for his pains!*

pain² *v.* [T] **1 it pains sb to do sth** FORMAL it is very difficult and upsetting for someone to have to do something: *It pained her to see how much older Bill was looking.* **2** OLD USE if a part of your body pains you, it hurts

Paine /pein/, **Thomas** (1737–1809) a U.S. PHILOSOPHER and writer, born in England, who supported the American states in their fight to become independent of Great Britain

pained /peind/ *adj.* worried, upset, or offended: *a pained expression on her face*

pain·ful /'peinfəl/ *adj.* **1** causing physical pain: **s w** *painful surgery | a slow painful death* **2** making you feel very unhappy or upset: *events from her painful and troubled past | Painful memories are never easy to forget. | GM has made the painful decision to lay off 3,000 workers. | [it is painful for sb (to do sth)] It's still painful for him to talk about the divorce.* **3** very bad and embarrassing for other people to watch, hear etc.: *His total humiliation was painful to watch. | painful shyness* **4** if part of your body is painful, you feel pain in it: *painful, swollen knee-joints* —**painfulness** *n.* [U]

pain·ful·ly /'peinfəli/ *adv.* **1** in a way that makes you unhappy or causes you to suffer: *At first, Andrews had found it painfully uncomfortable to play in public. | I am painfully aware of the criticism that has been directed at me.* **2 painfully obvious/clear/evident etc.** a fact or situation that is painfully obvious, clear etc. is easy to see and is disappointing or upsetting: *It was painfully evident that few of the people there knew how to dance.* **3** with pain, or causing pain: *Muriel watched her father die painfully of cancer. | Her rings dug painfully into my fingers.* **4** involving a lot of effort or trouble: *Rebuilding the damaged bridge will be painfully slow. | a painfully learned lesson*

pain·kill·er /'pein,kilɚ/ *n.* [C] a medicine which reduces or removes pain

pain·less /'peinlis/ *adj.* **1** causing no pain: *a painless trip to the dentist* **2** INFORMAL needing no effort or hard work: *a painless way to learn a foreign language* —**painlessly** *adv.*

pains·tak·ing /'peinz,teikiŋ, 'pein,stei-/ *adj.* very careful and thorough: *painstaking research* —**painstakingly** *adv.*

paint¹ /peint/ *n.* **1** [U] a liquid that you put on a sur- **s w** face to make it a particular color: *a can of blue* **2** *paint | This room needs a fresh coat of paint. | There were "wet paint" signs on all the benches.* **2** [singular] the layer of dried paint on a surface: *There was an old iron bed, with rust showing through the white paint.* **3** [U] OLD-FASHIONED: see MAKEUP **4 paints** [plural] a set of small tubes or dry blocks of paint, used for painting pictures: *a set of oil paints*

paint² *v.* **1** [I,T] to put paint on a surface: *We really* **s w** *need to paint the bedroom. | Sarah painted the table* **1 2** *blue. | Don't wear that shirt when you're painting.* **2 a)** [I,T] to make a picture, design etc. using paint: *My neighbor painted that picture. | Anna usually paints in the afternoons. | paint in oils/water-colors/acrylic etc.* (=paint using a particular kind of paint) **b)** [T] to make a picture of someone or something using paint: *an artist who painted my brother* **3 paint sb/sth as sth** to describe someone or something in a particular way: *Her lawyers paint her as an innocent victim.* **4 paint a picture of sb/sth** also **paint a portrait of sb/sth** to describe someone or something in a particular way: *She doesn't paint a very flattering portrait of her first husband. | paint a grim/rosy/gloomy etc. picture of sth Officials paint a bleak picture of the country's economy.* **5** [T] to put a colored substance on part of your face or body to make it more attractive: *All the children had painted their faces. | Her lips and finger-nails were painted bright red.* **6 paint the town (red)**

INFORMAL to go out to bars, clubs etc. to enjoy yourself or celebrate something —see also **paint/tar (sb/sth) with a broad brush** (BROAD¹ (7))

paint sth ↔ **in** phr. v. [T] to fill a space in a picture or add more to it using paint: *The additional figures were painted in at a later date.*

paint sth ↔ **out** phr. v. [T] to remove a design, figure etc. from a picture or surface by covering it with more paint: *She tried to paint out the extra shadows in the picture.*

paint sth ↔ **over** phr. v. [T] to cover a picture or surface with new paint: *Don't just paint over grease and dirt.*

paint·brush /ˈpeɪntˌbrʌʃ/ n. [C] a brush for spreading paint on a surface —see picture at BRUSH¹

Painted Des·ert, the /ˌ. ˈ../ a desert area in Arizona in the southwestern U.S. east of the Little Colorado River

paint·er /ˈpeɪntɚ/ n. [C] **1** someone who paints pictures; ARTIST: *a landscape painter* **2** someone whose job is painting houses, rooms etc.: *a house painter* **3** TECHNICAL a rope for tying a small boat to a ship or to a post on land

paint·er·ly /ˈpeɪntɚli/ adj. LITERARY typical of painters or painting: *painterly images*

paint·ing /ˈpeɪntɪŋ/ n. **1** [C] a painted picture: *an oil painting of Columbus* **2** [U] the skill or process of making a picture using paint: *He's taking a class in drawing and painting.* **3** [U] the act of covering a wall, house etc. with paint: *painting and decorating*

paint job /ˈ. ./ n. [C] the way a car, house, building etc. is painted, or the work done to achieve this: *My dad bought me a '67 Chevy automatic, with a brand new paint job.* | *This place needs a paint job.*

paint strip·per /ˈ. ˌ../ n. [U] a substance used to remove paint from walls, doors etc.

paint thin·ner /ˈ. ˌ../ n. [U] a liquid that you add to paint to make it less thick

paint·work /ˈpeɪntˌwɚk/ n. [U] paint on a car, wall etc.

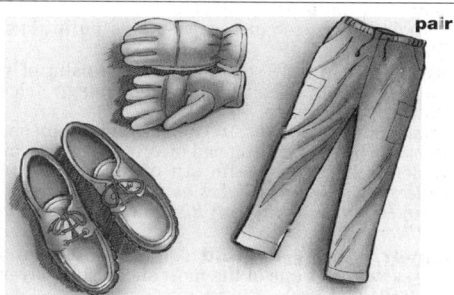

pair

s w **pair¹** /pɛr/ n. plural **pairs** or **pair** [C]
2 3
1 [pants/scissors etc.] a single thing made of two similar parts that are joined together: *If you wear glasses, take an extra pair when you go on vacation.* [+ **of**] *a new pair of jeans*
2 [shoes/gloves etc.] two things of the same kind that are used together: *a pair of socks* | *a pair of clip-on earrings*
3 [two people] two people who are standing or doing something together: *Stein and his business partner are a rather unusual pair.* | [+ **of**] *a pair of dancers* | *At sunset a pair of soldiers walked by.*
4 in pairs in groups of two: *Alexander advises women to travel in pairs or groups.* | *The fighter jets took off in pairs.*
5 [two animals] **a)** two animals, one male and one female, that come together to have sex: [+ **of**] *a pair of blue jays*
6 an extra/another pair of hands SPOKEN additional help from someone when you are busy: *We can use another pair of hands to help us wrap gifts for the holidays.*
7 [cards] two PLAYING CARDS which have the same value: *I've got three pairs.* | [+ **of**] *a pair of queens* —see Usage Note at COUPLE¹

pair² also **pair up** v. [I,T usually passive] to form

groups of two, or be put into groups of two: [**be paired with sb/sth**] *Each Russian student will be paired with an American at the camp.*

pair off phr. v. [I,T] to come together or bring two people together to have a romantic relationship: *Toward the end of the evening everyone at the party started to pair off.*

pair up phr. v. [I] to join together with someone to do something: *Nunn and Lloyd Webber paired up to create "Cats."*

pais·ley /ˈpeɪzli/ adj. made from cloth that is covered with a pattern of shapes that look like curved drops of rain: *a paisley tie* —**paisley** n. [U] *Paisley and plaid are popular this fall.*

Pai·ute /ˈpaɪyut/ a Native American tribe from the southwestern region of the U.S. —**Paiute** adj.

pa·ja·ma /pəˈdʒɑmə, -ˈdʒæ-/ adj. [only before noun] **1 pajama top/bottoms** the shirt or pants of a set of PAJAMAS **2 pajama party** a SLUMBER PARTY

pa·ja·mas /pəˈdʒɑməz, -ˈdʒæ-/ n. [plural] a soft loose pair of pants and a top that you wear in bed

Pak·i·stan /ˈpækɪˌstæn/ a country in Asia, west of India and east of Afghanistan and Iran —**Pakistani** /ˌpækɪˈstæni/ n., adj.

pal¹ /pæl/ n. [C] **1** OLD-FASHIONED, INFORMAL a close friend: *They'd been pals since childhood.* **2** SPOKEN used to address a man in an unfriendly way: *Listen, pal, I know what I'm talking about, okay?* —see also PEN PAL

pal² v. **palled, palling**
pal around phr. v. [I] INFORMAL to go places and do things with someone as a friend: [+ **with**] *The coach seems to pal around with a lot of the players.*

pal·ace /ˈpælɪs/ n. [C] **1** often **Palace** a large house where a king, queen, or ruler officially lives: *If you visit England, you can go see Buckingham Palace.* **2** a large, grand, beautifully decorated house or building: *The nobles of Florence built splendid palaces.* | *After his years of homelessness, Woody's little apartment seemed like a palace.*

palace guard /ˌ.. ˈ./ n. **1** [C,U] someone or the group of people whose job is to protect the king, queen etc. in a palace **2** [U] a small group of people who support and give advice to a powerful person: *He had once been a member of Nixon's palace guard.*

pal·a·din /ˈpælədɪn/ n. [C] **1** FORMAL a respected person who strongly supports a particular action or opinion: *a pro-choice paladin* **2** a KNIGHT (=a soldier of high rank) in the Middle Ages who fought loyally for his prince

pal·at·a·ble /ˈpælətəbəl/ adj. **1** an idea, suggestion etc. that is palatable is acceptable or sounds good: *We made several compromises to make the plan more palatable to voters.* **2** FORMAL having a pleasant or acceptable taste: *a palatable wine* —opposite UNPALATABLE

pal·a·tal /ˈpælətl/ n. [C] TECHNICAL a CONSONANT¹ (1) sound such as /tʃ/ in the word "chin" made by putting your tongue against or near your HARD PALATE —**palatal** adj.

pal·ate /ˈpælɪt/ n. **1** [C,U] the sense of taste: *Fresh tomatoes make the sandwich more pleasing to the palate.* **2** [C] the ROOF (=top inside part) of the mouth —see also **a cleft lip/palate** (CLEFT² (2)), HARD PALATE, SOFT PALATE

pa·la·tial /pəˈleɪʃəl/ adj. very large and beautifully decorated, like a PALACE: *a palatial Beverly Hills estate*

Pa·lau /pəˈlaʊ/ a country consisting of a group of islands in the western Pacific Ocean

pa·lav·er /pəˈlævɚ, -ˈlɑ-/ n. **1** [U] INFORMAL silly and meaningless talk: *There's been a lot of palaver about feminist oversensitivity to language.* **2** [C] OLD USE a long talk about something important

pale¹ /peɪl/ adj. **1** having a much whiter skin color than usual, especially because you are sick, worried, frightened etc.: *You look kind of pale. Are you feeling okay?* | *a pale complexion* **2** lighter than the usual color: *pale blue eyes* —compare DARK¹ (2), DEEP¹ (5), LIGHT² (1) **3** pale light is not bright: *the pale light of early morning* **4 a pale imitation/copy etc.** an unimpressive or bad-quality copy of an earlier performance, movie, event etc.: *Their first hit was a pale remake of a Beatles song.* —**paleness** *n.* [U]

pale² *v.* [I] **1** to seem worse, less important, or less impressive when compared to something else: *This year's "Swan Lake" **pales in comparison** to last year's production.* | *There are still some problems, but they **pale into insignificance** when compared to the difficulties facing Russia.* **2** LITERARY if your face pales, it becomes much whiter than usual because you have had a shock: *Clarence paled visibly. He hated the thought of pain.*

pale³ *n.* **beyond the pale** behavior that is beyond the pale is completely unacceptable: *With his latest, hard-hitting campaign ad, Robertson has really gone beyond the pale.*

pale-face /'peɪlfeɪs/ *n.* [C] an insulting word for a white person used by Native Americans in old movies

paleo- /peɪlioʊ, peɪliə/ *prefix* TECHNICAL extremely ancient, or relating to things that happened before historical times: *paleobotany* (=study of ancient plants)

pa-le-o-lith-ic, Paleolithic /,peɪliə'lɪθɪk/ *adj.* relating to the earliest period of the STONE AGE (=the period many thousands of years ago when people made stone tools and weapons): *the Paleolithic era* —compare NEOLITHIC

pa-le-on-tol-o-gy /,peɪliən'tɑlədʒi, -liən-/ *n.* [U] the study of FOSSILs (=ancient animals and plants that have been preserved in rock) —**paleontologist** *n.* [C]

Pal-es-tine /'pæləstaɪn/ an area of land which is now part of the country of Israel

Pal-es-tin-i-an /,pælə'stɪniən/ *adj.* **1** relating to or coming from the area between the Jordan River and the Mediterranean Sea, which used to be called Palestine **2** relating to the Arab people who come from or live in this area —**Palestinian** *n.* [C]

pal-ette /'pælɪt/ *n.* [C] **1** a board with a curved edge and a hole for the thumb, on which a painter mixes colors **2** [usually singular] the range of colors, tastes, or qualities that are included in things such as pictures, food, and music: [+ of] *Farhi's palette of pale blue, cream, and brown challenges traditional ideas about men's suits.* | *Garlic powder is a terrific addition to the cook's palette of seasonings.*

palette knife /'.. ,./ *n.* [C] a thin knife that bends easily and has a rounded end, used by painters for mixing paint

Pa-li-kir /,pɑlɪ'kɪr/ the capital city of Micronesia

pal-i-mo-ny /'pæləmoʊni/ *n.* [U] money that someone is ordered to pay regularly to a former partner, when they lived together without being married —compare ALIMONY

pal-imp-sest /'pæləmp,sɛst/ *n.* [C] an ancient written document which has had its original writing rubbed out, not always completely, and has been written on again

pal-in-drome /'pælən,droʊm/ *n.* [C] a word or phrase such as "deed" or "level," which is the same when you read it backward

pal-ing /'peɪlɪŋ/ *n.* [C usually plural] a pointed piece of wood used with other pointed pieces in making a fence

pal-i-sade /,pælə'seɪd/ *n.* [C] **1** a fence made of strong pointed poles, used for defense in past times **2** palisades [plural] a line of high straight cliffs, especially along a river or beside the ocean

pall¹ /pɔl/ *n.* **1 cast a pall over/on sth** to spoil an event or occasion that should have been happy and enjoyable: *The earthquake's destruction cast a pall over Christmas celebrations in the region.* **2** [singular] a low dark cloud of smoke, dust etc.: [+ of] *A huge pall of black smoke hangs over the Amazon Basin.* **3** [C] a large piece of cloth spread over a

CASKET (=box in which a dead body is carried) **4** OLD USE [C] a CASKET with a body inside

pall² *v.* [I] to gradually become uninteresting or unenjoyable: *For Sasha, the celebrity lifestyle was beginning to pall.*

pal-la-di-um /pə'leɪdiəm/ *n.* [U] a type of shiny soft whitish metal

pall-bear-er /'pɔl,bɛrɚ/ *n.* [C] someone who walks beside a CASKET (=a box with a dead body inside) or helps to carry it at a funeral

pal-let /'pælɪt/ *n.* [C] **1** a large metal plate or flat wooden frame on which heavy goods can be lifted, stored, or moved **2** OLD-FASHIONED a temporary bed, or a cloth bag filled with STRAW (1) for someone to sleep on

pal-li-ate /'pæli,eɪt/ *v.* [T] FORMAL **1** to reduce the bad effects of illness, pain etc. without curing them **2** to make a bad situation seem better than it really is, for example by explaining it in a positive way —**palliation** /,pæli'eɪʃən/ *n.* [U]

pal-lia-tive /'pælyətɪv, -li,eɪtɪv/ *n.* [C] FORMAL **1** an action taken to make a bad situation seem better, but which does not solve the problem: *Promises of reform are mere palliatives.* **2** a medical treatment that will not cure an illness but will reduce the pain —**palliative** *adj.*: *palliative therapy*

pal-lid /'pælɪd/ *adj.* **1** unusually pale, or pale in an unhealthy way: *Paul looked pallid and sick.* **2** boring, without any excitement: *a pallid performance* —**pallidness** *n.* [U]

pal-lor /'pælɚ/ *n.* [singular,U] unhealthy paleness of the skin or face: *Her skin had a deathly pallor.*

palm¹ /pɑm/ *n.* [C] **1** the inside surface of your hand, between the base of your fingers and your wrist: *A piece of candy stuck to his palm.* | *Julia patted the dog with **the palm of** her hand.* **2** a palm tree **3 hold/have sb in the palm of your hand** to have a strong influence on someone, so that they do what you want them to do: *She's got the whole committee in the palm of her hand.* **4 read sb's palm** to tell someone what is going to happen to them by looking at their hand —see also **grease sb's palm** (GREASE² (2))

palm² *v.* [T] to hide something in the palm of your hand, especially when performing a magic trick or stealing something

palm sth ↔ off *phr. v.* to persuade someone to accept or buy something bad or unwanted, especially by deceiving them: [**palm sth as sth**] *Plenty of dealers try to palm off fakes as works of art.* | [+ on/onto] *He wants to palm off his old car on his younger brother.*

Palm-er /'pɑmɚ/, **Ar-nold** /'ɑrnəld/ (1929–) a U.S. GOLFER who was one of the most successful players of the 1950s and 1960s

pal-met-to /pæl'mɛtoʊ/ *n.* *plural* **palmettos** or **palmettoes** [C] a small PALM TREE that grows in the southeastern U.S.

palm-is-try /'pɑməstri/ *n.* [U] palm reading —**palmist** *n.* [C]

palm oil /'. ./ *n.* [U] the oil obtained from the nut of an African PALM TREE

palm read-er /'. ,../ *n.* [C] someone who claims they can tell what a person is like or what will happen to them in the future, by looking at the PALM of their hand —**palm reading** *n.* [U] —compare FORTUNE TELLER

Palm Sun-day /,. '../ *n.* the Sunday before Easter in Christian religions

palm-top /'pɑmtɑp/ *n.* [C] a very small computer that you can hold in your hand

palm tree /'. ./ also **palm** *n.* [C] a tropical tree which typically grows near beaches or in deserts, with a long straight trunk and large pointed leaves at the top

palm-y /'pɑmi/ *adj.* **1** covered with palm trees: *the palmy beaches of southern California* **2** used to describe a period of time when people have money and life is good: *palmy times for the car industry*

pal-o-mi-no /,pælə'minoʊ/ *n.* *plural* **palominos** [C] a horse of a golden or cream color, with a white MANE and tail

pal·pa·ble /'pælpəbəl/ adj. FORMAL **1** easily and clearly noticed; OBVIOUS: *His frustration was palpable.* **2** able to be touched or physically felt; TANGIBLE: *Tension in the city was as palpable as the dust in the air* —**palpably** adv. —opposite IMPALPABLE

pal·pate /'pælpeɪt/ v. [T] TECHNICAL to touch and press someone's body during a medical examination —**palpation** /pæl'peɪʃən/ n. [C,U]

pal·pi·tate /'pælpə,teɪt/ v. [I] **1** if your heart palpitates, it beats quickly and in an irregular way **2** LITERARY to shake, especially because of fear, excitement etc.: [+ with] *Our hearts were palpitating with excitement.*

pal·pi·ta·tions /,pælpə'teɪʃənz/ n. [plural] irregular or extremely fast beating of your heart, caused by illness or too much effort

pal·sied /'pɔlzid/ adj. NOT TECHNICAL suffering from an illness that makes your arms and legs shake because you cannot control your muscles

pal·sy /'pɔlzi/ n. [U] **1** an illness that makes your arms and legs shake because you cannot control your muscles **2** OLD USE: see PARALYSIS (1) —see also CEREBRAL PALSY

pal·try /'pɔltri/ adj. [usually before noun] **1** a paltry amount of something such as money is too small to be useful or important: *a paltry 1.2% growth rate* **2** worthless and silly: *paltry excuses*

pam·pas /'pæmpəz, -pəs/ n. **the pampas** the large wide flat areas of land covered with grass in some parts of South America

pampas grass /'.. ,./ n. [U] a type of tall grass with silver-white feathery flowers

pam·per /'pæmpə/ v. [T] to take care of someone very kindly, sometimes too kindly: *Mr. Spielvogel pampers all his major clients.* | *She pampered herself at the end of the day with a long hot bath.* —**pampered** adj.

pam·phlet /'pæmflɪt/ n. [C] a very thin book with paper covers, giving information about something

pam·phlet·eer /,pæmflə'tɪr/ n. [C] someone who writes pamphlets giving political opinions

pan-, Pan- /pæn/ prefix including all of something: *the Pan-American highway* | *Pan-Arabism* (=political union of all Arabs)

pans

frying pan   round cake pan   saucepan

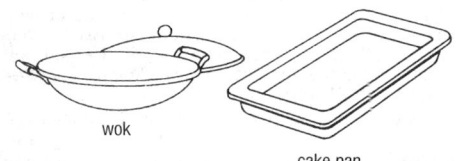

wok

cake pan

pan¹ /pæn/ n. [C] **1** a round metal container used for cooking, usually with one long handle and sometimes a lid: *a frying pan* —see picture at KITCHEN **2** a metal container for baking things in, or the food that this contains: [+ of] *There's a pan of sweet rolls baking in the oven.* **3** a container with low sides, used for holding liquids: *an oil pan* **4** a container used to separate gold from other substances, by washing them in water **5** one of the two dishes on a pair of SCALES (=a small weighing machine) **6** a metal drum that is played in a STEEL BAND —see also BEDPAN, **a flash in the pan** (FLASH² (5)), FRYING PAN, SAUCEPAN, WARMING PAN

pan² v. **panned, panning 1** [T] to strongly criticize a movie, play etc. in a newspaper or on television or radio: *Barnes panned the show in Thursday's "Times."*

---

2 a) [I always + adv./prep.] if a movie or television camera pans in a particular direction, it moves slowly while taking a picture: *The camera panned back to the cat sitting in the corner.* **b)** [I,T] to move a camera in this way **3** [I,T] to wash soil in a pan, especially to separate gold from it: [+ for] *Henkins moved to the Sierras to pan for gold.*

pan out phr. v. [I] SPOKEN to happen or develop in the way you expected or hoped: *None of the job possibilities have panned out.*

pan·a·ce·a /,pænə'siə/ n. [C] **1** something that people think will make everything better and solve all their problems: [+ for] *Debt reduction should not be seen as a panacea for the region's economic problems.* **2** a medicine or form of treatment that is supposed to cure any illness

pa·nache /pə'næʃ, -'nɑʃ/ n. [U] a confident way of doing things with style that makes them seem easy, and makes other people admire you: *Pappano conducted the symphony with great panache.*

Pan·a·ma /'pænə,mɑ/ a country on a narrow piece of land connecting Central and South America, between Costa Rica and Colombia —**Panamanian** /,pænə'meɪniən/ n., adj.

pan·a·ma /'pænə,mɑ/ also **panama hat** /'... ,./ n. [C] a light hat for men, made from STRAW —see picture at HAT

Panama Ca·nal, the /,... .'./ a long narrow CANAL that was built across Panama in 1914 in order to allow ships to sail between the Atlantic and Pacific Oceans

Panama Cit·y /,... '../ the capital city of Panama

Pan A·mer·i·can /,.. .'...‹/ adj. relating to or including all of the countries in North, Central, and South America: *the Pan American Games*

pan·a·tel·la /,pænə'tɛlə/ n. [C] a long thin CIGAR

pan·cake /'pænkeɪk/ n. [C] a thick, round, flat cake made from flour, milk, and eggs that has been cooked in a flat pan and is eaten for breakfast, often with MAPLE SYRUP

pancake land·ing /,.. '../ n. [C] an act of bringing an aircraft down to the ground in such a way that it drops flat from a low height

pancake make·up /,.. '../ n. [U] very thick MAKEUP for the face

pan·cre·as /'pæŋkriəs/ n. [C] a GLAND inside your body, near your stomach, that produces INSULIN and a liquid that helps your body to process the food you eat —**pancreatic** /,pæŋkri'ætɪk/ adj. —see picture at DIGESTIVE SYSTEM

pan·da /'pændə/ n. [C] a large black and white animal similar to a bear that lives in the mountains of China

pan·dem·ic /pæn'dɛmɪk/ n. [C] TECHNICAL an illness or disease that affects the population of a very large area —**pandemic** adj. —compare ENDEMIC

pan·de·mo·ni·um /,pændə'mouniəm/ n. [U] a situation in which there is a lot of noise because people are angry, confused, or frightened: *When the verdict was read, pandemonium broke out in the courtroom.*

pan·der /'pændə/ v.
pander to sb/sth phr. v. [T] to try to please people by doing or saying what they want you to do, even though you know this is wrong: *Liberals charge that the senator is pandering to racist voters.*

pan·der·ing /'pændərɪŋ/ n. [U] the crime of finding customers for PROSTITUTES: *McFadden was arrested for pimping and pandering.* —compare PIMP

P and L state·ment /,.. '. ,../ n. [C] a document that shows the profits and losses (LOSS (2)) of a business

Pan·do·ra's box /pæn,dɔrəz 'bɑks/ n. **open Pandora's box** to cause a lot of problems that did not exist before without meaning to

pane /peɪn/ n. [C] a sheet of glass used in a window or door —see WINDOWPANE

pan·e·gyr·ic /,pænə'dʒɪrɪk/ n. [C] FORMAL a speech or piece of writing that praises someone or something very highly

P

pan·el[1] /'pænl/ n. [C]
1 ‖group of people‖ **a)** a group of people with skills or special knowledge who have been chosen to give advice or opinions on a particular subject: *A panel of scientists met to discuss the issue of nuclear safety.* | *the Senate ethics panel* | *a panel discussion on sexual harassment* **b)** a group of well-known people who answer questions on a television or radio program: *Let me introduce tonight's panel.* —see also PANELIST **c)** a group of people who are chosen to listen to a case in a court of law and to decide the result; JURY
2 ‖part‖ **a)** a flat piece of wood, glass etc. with straight sides, which forms part of a door, wall, fence etc.: *a carved-wood panel* **b)** a piece of metal that forms part of the outer structure of a vehicle **c)** a piece of material that forms part of a piece of clothing
3 **instrument/control panel** a board in a car, airplane, boat etc. where the controls are
4 ‖picture‖ a thin board with a picture painted on it —see also SOLAR PANEL

panel[2] v. **paneled, paneling** [T usually passive] to cover or decorate something with flat pieces of wood, glass etc.: **[be paneled with/in]** *The walls are paneled in walnut.* | **oak-paneled/glass-paneled etc.** *a wood-paneled office*

pan·el·ing /'pænl-ɪŋ/ n. [U] wood, especially in long or square pieces, used to decorate walls etc.: *pine paneling*

pan·el·ist /'pænl-ɪst/ n. [C] one of a group of well-known people who answer questions on a television or radio program

panel truck /'.. ,./ n. [C] a motor vehicle used for delivering goods, which has doors on the sides that slide up and down

pang /pæŋ/ n. [C] a sudden feeling of pain, sadness etc.: *hunger pangs* | **[+ of]** *a pang of guilt*

pan·han·dle[1] /'pæn,hændl/ v. [I] to ask for money in the streets or public places: *Large numbers of the homeless panhandle on the eastern edge of the park.* | *New York's transit authority has banned panhandling in the subway system.* —**panhandler** n. [C]

panhandle[2] n. [C] a thin piece of land that is joined to a larger area like the handle of a pan: *the Texas panhandle*

pan·ic[1] /'pænɪk/ n. **1** [C usually singular,U] a sudden strong feeling of fear or nervousness that makes you unable to think clearly or behave sensibly: *I could see the look of panic on her face.* | *A bomb exploded on the subway, causing panic among rush-hour commuters.* | **[throw/send sb into a panic]** *Rumors of a food shortage could send the population into a panic.* | **(in (a) panic** *Small business owners are in a panic over whether they will survive.* | *I still get horrible **panic attacks** in elevators.* **2** [C usually singular,U] a situation in which people are suddenly made very anxious, and make quick decisions without thinking carefully: *Amid the panic and confusion, police somehow managed to maintain order.* | *Baker had lost a lot of money during the last stock market panic.* **3** [singular] a situation in which there is a lot to do and not much time to do it in: *Every April 15th, there's the usual panic of people trying to file their taxes on time.* **4** **press/push/hit the panic button** to do something quickly without thinking enough about it, because something bad has suddenly happened and made you very anxious: *Even though stock prices have dropped, I wouldn't hit the panic button just yet.*

panic[2] v. **panicked, panicking** [I,T] to suddenly become so frightened that you cannot think clearly or behave sensibly, or to make someone do this: *Lisa panicked when she heard she might be fired.* | *The driver apparently panicked and ran off the road.* | **Don't panic!** (=used to tell people to stay calm) | **panic sb into doing sth** *Any sudden movement could panic the snake into attacking.*

panic buy·ing, panic-buying /'.. ,../ n. [U] a situation in which many people buy all or most of the supply of a product or products at one time because they are afraid there will be none left soon: *With Hurricane Carmen only miles offshore, panic buying has swept the city.*

pan·ick·y /'pænɪki/ adj. INFORMAL very nervous or anxious: *panicky motorists*

panic-strick·en /'.. ,../ adj. so frightened that you cannot think clearly or behave sensibly: *Panic-stricken passengers trampled one another rushing for the exits.*

pan·ni·er /'pæniə/ n. [C] **1** one of a pair of baskets or bags carried one on each side of an animal or a bicycle **2** a basket used to carry a load on someone's back

pan·o·ply /'pænəpli/ n. [U] **1** FORMAL a large number and variety of people or things: *Penicillin was used to treat a whole panoply of conditions.* **2** an impressive show of special clothes, decorations etc., especially at an important ceremony: *the whole panoply of a royal wedding*

pan·o·ram·a /,pænə'ræmə, -'rɑ-/ n. [C usually singular] **1** an impressive view of a wide area of land: *a stunning mountain panorama* | **[+ of]** *a gorgeous panorama of the Gobi Desert* **2** a description or series of pictures that shows all the features of a subject, historical period etc.: **[+ of]** *The paintings are a historical panorama of the First Battle of Bull Run.* —**panoramic** /,pænə'ræmɪk/ adj.: *a panoramic view of the valley* —**panoramically** /-kli/ adv.

pan·pipes /'pænpaɪps/ n. [plural] a simple musical instrument made of several short wooden pipes of different lengths, that are played by blowing across their open ends

pan·sy /'pænzi/ n. plural **pansies** [C] **1** a small garden plant with flat brightly colored flowers **2** OFFENSIVE a man who seems weak and behaves like a woman

pant[1] /pænt/ v. **1** [I] to breathe quickly with short noisy breaths because you have been running, climbing etc. or because it is very hot: *The athletes panted and puffed in the 90-degree heat.* | *After five minutes I was **panting for breath**.* **2** [T] to say something while panting: *"Go on without me," Mike panted.*
pant for sth phr. v. [T] to want something very much: *juicy gossip about the actor, that keeps fans panting for more* —**pant** n. [C]

pant[2] adj. relating to or part of PANTS: *My left pant leg has a tear in it.* | *pant cuffs*

pan·ta·loons /,pæntə'lunz/ n. [plural] long pants with wide legs, which are narrow at the ANKLES

pan·the·ism /'pænθi,ɪzəm/ n. [U] the religious idea that God and the universe are the same thing and that God is present in all natural things —**pantheist** n. [C] —**pantheistic** /,pænθi'ɪstɪk/ adj.

pan·the·on /'pænθiɑn/ n. [C] **1** a group of famous and important people in a particular area of work, sports etc.: *a great album that guarantees her place in the pantheon of jazz singers* **2** all the gods of a particular people or nation: *the Roman pantheon* **3** a TEMPLE built in honor of all gods

pan·ther /'pænθə/ n. [C] **1** a COUGAR **2** a black LEOPARD

pant·ies /'pæntiz/ n. [plural] a piece of women's underwear that covers the area between the waist and the top of the legs: *a pair of silk panties*

pan·to·mime /'pæntə,maɪm/ n. [C,U] a method of performing using only actions and not words, or a play performed using this method; MIME[1]

pan·try /'pæntri/ n. plural **pantries** [C] a very small room in a house where food is kept

pants /pænts/ n. [plural] **1** a piece of clothing that covers you from your waist to your feet and has a separate leg for each leg: *She was wearing red pants and a white shirt.* | *Jason needs a new **pair of pants** for school.* **2** **scare/bore/shock etc. the pants off sb** INFORMAL to make someone feel very frightened, very bored etc.: *That movie scared the pants off Heidi.* **3** **beat the pants off sb/sth** INFORMAL to easily defeat someone in a game, or to be much better than someone or something: *His home-made burgers beat the* *pants off anything you can get in a restaurant.* **4 get in/into sb's pants** IMPOLITE to touch someone in a sexual way, or have sex with someone: *Stay away from Al – he just wants to get in your pants.* **5 sb puts their pants on one leg at a time** SPOKEN used to say that someone who is famous is really just like everyone else —see also **do sth by the seat of your pants** (SEAT¹ (10)), **wear the pants** (WEAR¹ (9))

pant·suit /'pæntsut/ *n.* [C] a woman's suit consisting of a JACKET and matching pants

pan·ty·hose /'pænti,hoʊz/ *n.* [plural] a very thin piece of women's clothing that covers their legs from the toes to the waist and is usually worn with dresses or skirts

pan·ty·lin·er /'pænti,laɪnɚ/ *n.* [C] a very thin SANITARY NAPKIN

panty raid /'.. ,./ *n.* [C] INFORMAL an occasion when young men go into women's rooms to steal their underwear as a joke, especially done at college

pap /pæp/ *n.* [U] **1** DISAPPROVING books, television programs etc. that people read or watch for entertainment but which have no serious value: *Most of the novel is boring, super-sentimental pap.* **2** very soft food eaten by babies or sick people —see also PAP SMEAR

pa·pa /'pɑpə/ *n.* [C] INFORMAL a word meaning "father," especially used by children

pa·pa·cy /'peɪpəsi/ *n.* **1 the papacy** the position and authority of the POPE **2** [U] the time during which a particular POPE is in power

Pa·pa·go /'pɑpə,goʊ/ a Native American tribe from the southern U.S. and northern Mexico

pa·pal /'peɪpəl/ *adj.* [only before noun] relating or belonging to the POPE: *papal authority*

papal bull /,.. './ *n.* [C] an official statement from the POPE

paparazzi

pa·pa·raz·zi /,pɑpə'rɑtsi/ *n.* [plural] newspaper photographers who follow famous people

pa·pa·ya /pə'paɪə/ *n.* [C] a large yellow-green tropical fruit

pa·per¹ /'peɪpɚ/ *n.*
1 for writing on [U] material in the form of thin sheets that is used for writing on, wrapping things etc.: *a piece/sheet of paper Joe handed me a piece of paper with a list of the winners.* | *The glasses were wrapped in white paper.* | **writing/wrapping/drawing paper** *Do you have any writing paper I could borrow?*
2 newspaper [C] a newspaper: *Today's paper is over on the coffee table.* | *Why don't you put an ad in the paper?* | **evening/Sunday/local paper** *Our local paper doesn't have much international news.*
3 with writing on papers [plural] documents, letters, reports, and other pieces of paper with writing on them: *Kim left some important papers in her briefcase.* | *A letter from the President was found among his private papers.*
4 on paper a) if you put ideas or information on paper, you write them down: *As soon as you have an idea, get it down on paper so you don't forget it.* **b)** something that is true on paper seems to be true

---

as an idea, but may not be true in a real situation: *It looks simple enough on paper, but I doubt if it will actually work.* | *On paper, the family is worth over $5 billion.*
5 school work [C] a piece of writing that is done as part of a course at a school or college: *When is your sociology paper due?* | [+ **on**] *I have to write a paper on art during the French Revolution.*
6 speech/piece of writing [C] a piece of writing or a talk by someone who has made a study of a particular subject: *We're **presenting a paper on** (=giving a talk about) on bilingualism at the conference.*
7 official documents papers [plural] official documents such as your PASSPORT, ID etc.: *After checking our papers, the border guards let us through.*
8 for walls [C,U] paper for covering walls; WALLPAPER
9 not worth the paper it is written/printed on if something such as a contract is not worth the paper it is written on, it has no value because whatever is promised in it will not happen —see also **put/set pen to paper** (PEN¹ (3)), TOILET PAPER, WASTE PAPER, WHITE PAPER, WORKING PAPERS

paper² *adj.* [only before noun] **1** made of paper: *a paper cup* **2** existing only as an idea but not having any real value: *paper profits* | *paper promises* **3 paper trail** documents and records that show what someone has done, especially when they prove that someone is guilty of a crime: *Police investigators followed a paper trail that led them straight to Vincenzi.* **4 paper tiger** an enemy or opponent who seems powerful but actually is not

paper³ *v.* [T] **1** to decorate the walls of a room by covering them with special paper **2 paper over the cracks/a problem etc.** to try to hide disagreements or difficulties

pa·per·back /'peɪpɚ,bæk/ *n.* [C] a book with a stiff paper cover: *a shelf full of paperbacks* | **in paperback** *Wiley's latest novel is now available in paperback.* —compare HARDCOVER

pa·per·board /'peɪpɚ,bɔrd/ *n.* [U] —see also CARDBOARD¹

pa·per·boy /'peɪpɚ,bɔɪ/ *n.* [C] a boy who delivers newspapers to people's houses

paper chase /'.. ,./ *n.* [C] INFORMAL an attempt to do something that involves writing and reading a lot of documents, and takes a very long time: *She had gotten involved in the paper chase to obtain U.S. citizenship.*

paper clip /'.. ,./ *n.* [C] a small piece of curved wire used for holding sheets of paper together

paper doll /,.. './ *n.* [C] a piece of stiff paper cut in the shape of a person

paper girl /'.. ,./ *n.* [C] a girl who delivers newspapers to people's houses

pa·per·hang·er /'peɪpɚ,hæŋɚ/ *n.* [C] someone whose job is to decorate rooms with WALLPAPER

pa·per·less /'peɪpɚlɪs/ *adj.* [usually before noun] using computers, EMAIL etc., and without the use of paper: *a paperless office* | *paperless trading on the stock market*

paper mon·ey /'.. ,../ *n.* [U] money consisting of small sheets of paper, not coins

paper-push·er /'.. ,../ *n.* [C] someone whose job is doing unimportant office work

paper route /'.. ,./ *n.* [C] the job of delivering newspapers to a group of homes, or the group of homes you have to deliver newspapers to

paper-thin /,.. './ *adj.* very thin: *paper-thin walls*

paper tow·el /,.. '../ *n.* [C] a sheet of soft thick paper that you use to clean up small amounts of liquid, food etc. or to dry your hands

pa·per·weight /'peɪpɚ,weɪt/ *n.* [C] a small heavy object used to hold pieces of paper in place

pa·per·work /'peɪpɚ,wɜrk/ *n.* [U] **1** work such as writing letters or reports, which must be done but is not very interesting: *I've been buried in paperwork all week.* **2** the documents that you need for a business deal, a trip etc.: *The car dealer will fill out all of the necessary paperwork on the car.*

pa·per·y /ˈpeɪpəri/ *adj.* something such as skin or leaves that is papery is very dry and thin and a little stiff: *the papery outer skin of an onion*

pa·pier-mâ·ché, papermâché /ˌpeɪpə məˈʃeɪ/ *n.* [U] a soft substance made from a mixture of paper, water, and glue, which becomes hard when it dries and is used for making boxes, pots etc.

pa·pist /ˈpeɪpɪst/ *n.* [C] a member of the Catholic Church who believes strongly in the Catholic religion

pa·poose /pæˈpus/ *n.* [C] **1** a type of bag fastened to a frame, used to carry a baby on your back **2** OLD USE a Native American baby or young child

pap·py /ˈpæpi/ *n.* [C] OLD-FASHIONED a word meaning "father"

pa·pri·ka /pəˈprikə, pæ-/ *n.* [U] a red powder made from a type of sweet PEPPER, used to give a strong taste to food

Pap smear /ˈpæp smɪr/ also **Pap test** /ˈ. ./ *n.* [C] a medical test that takes cells from a woman's CERVIX and examines them for signs of CANCER

Pap·u·a New Guin·ea /ˌpæpyuə nu ˈgɪni/ a country in the south western Pacific Ocean, north of Australia, which includes the eastern half of the island of New Guinea and several small islands —**Papuan** *n., adj.*

pa·py·rus /pəˈpaɪrəs/ *n. plural* **papyruses** or **papyri** /-raɪ/ **1** [U] a plant like grass that grows in water **2** [C,U] a type of paper made from this plant and used in ancient Egypt, or a piece of this paper

par /pɑr/ *n.* **1 on a par (with sb/sth)** at the same level or standard: *The new pay deal puts us on a par with other workers in the industry.* | *For Stan, shopping is about on a par with going to the dentist* (=is as bad as going to the dentist). **2 be below/ under par** also **not be up to par a)** to feel a little sick or lacking in energy: *I haven't been up to par since the operation.* **b)** to be less good than usual or below the appropriate standard: *For a second year, economic growth has been substantially below par.* **3** [C,U] the number of STROKEs a player should take to hit the ball into a hole in the game of GOLF: *Oritz needed only a par to win the tournament.* | *Grady shot a 2-under-par 68.* **4 be par for the course** to be the same as you would normally expect, especially to be as bad as you expect: *It rained all week, but I guess that's par for the course in Ireland.* **5** [U] TECHNICAL also **par value** the value of a STOCK or BOND that is printed on it when it is first sold: *The stock's par value decreased from $3.14 to 31 cents.* —see also PAR EXCELLENCE

par. the written abbreviation of PARAGRAPH

para- /ˈpærə/ *prefix* **1** beyond something: *the paranormal* (=strange events that go beyond what normally happens) **2** connected with a profession, and helping more highly trained people: *a paramedic* (=who gives medical help before a doctor does) | *a paralegal* (=someone who helps a lawyer) **3** very similar to something: *a paramilitary group* **4** relating to PARACHUTES: *a paratrooper* | *paragliding*

par·a·ble /ˈpærəbəl/ *n.* [C] a short simple story that teaches a moral or religious lesson, especially one of the stories told by Jesus Christ in the Bible

pa·rab·o·la /pəˈræbələ/ *n.* [C] TECHNICAL a curve in the shape of the imaginary line that a ball makes when it is thrown in the air and comes down a little distance away —**parabolic** /ˌpærəˈbɑlɪk/ *adj.*

par·a·chute¹ /ˈpærəˌʃut/ *n.* [C] a piece of equipment fastened to the back of people who jump out of airplanes which makes them fall slowly and safely to the ground: *a parachute jump*

parachute² *v.* **1** [I always + adv./prep.] to jump from an airplane using a parachute: [+ **into/in/onto** etc.] *Troops parachuted into enemy territory*

overnight. | *Due to bad weather, rescue personnel were unable to parachute in.* **2** [T always + adv./prep.] to drop something from an airplane with a parachute: [**parachute sth to/into**] *A mission to parachute essential supplies to refugees along the border has been proposed.* —**parachuting** *n.* [C]

par·a·chut·ist /ˈpærəˌʃutɪst/ *n.* [C] someone who jumps from an airplane with a parachute

parade

pa·rade¹ /pəˈreɪd/ *n.* [C] **1** a public celebration when musical bands, brightly decorated vehicles etc. move down the street: *Macy's Thanksgiving Day Parade* | *The city has a parade every 4th of July.* **2** a military ceremony in which soldiers stand or march together so that important people can examine them: **be on parade** (=be standing or marching in a parade) **3** a series of many people, events etc. coming one after another: [+ **of**] *For the next six hours, he treated an endless parade of sick children.* —see also HIT PARADE

parade² *v.*
1 |celebrate/protest| [I always + adv./prep.] to walk or march together to celebrate or protest about something: [+ **around/past** etc.] *The players and coaches paraded around the stadium with the trophy.* | *About 50 protesters marched through the hall and paraded right below the stage.*
2 |walk around| [I always + adv./prep.] to walk around, especially in a way that shows that you want people to notice and admire you: [+ **around/past** etc.] *Franklin and his girlfriend paraded arm in arm through the hotel lobby.*
3 |proudly show| [T always + adv./prep.] to proudly show someone or something to other people, because you want to look impressive to them or prove how powerful, rich, good etc. you are: *The captured pilots were paraded through the town.* | *celebrities who parade their perfect marriages before the TV cameras*
4 |soldiers| [I,T] if soldiers parade or if an officer parades them, they march together so that an important person can watch them: *The President stood as a battalion of soldiers paraded past him.*
5 parade as sth/be paraded as sth if something parades as something else that is better, someone is pretending that it is the other better thing: *It's just old-fashioned racism parading as scientific research.*

parade ground /ˈ. ˌ./ *n.* [C] a large flat area where soldiers practice marching or standing together in rows

par·a·digm /ˈpærəˌdaɪm/ *n.* [C] **1** a particular way of doing something or thinking about something, which is generally accepted or copied: *The needs of today's children cannot be met by our old educational paradigms.* | *Community interaction of this kind could be a paradigm for race relations in the future.* **2** FORMAL a very clear or typical example of something: *The Vietnam War has become a powerful anti-war paradigm.* | [+ **of**] *a paradigm of economic failure* **3** TECHNICAL an example or pattern of a word, showing all its forms in grammar, like "child, child's, children, children's" —**paradigmatic** /ˌpærədɪgˈmætɪk/ *adj.* —**paradigmatically** /-kli/ *adv.*

par·a·dise /ˈpærəˌdaɪs, -ˌdaɪz/ *n.* **1** [C] a place or situation that is extremely pleasant, beautiful, or enjoyable: *Tonga is a tropical paradise.* | *For the new immigrants, America seemed like paradise.* **2** [U] a place that is perfect for a particular type of person or activity, because it has everything you need: *With so many inexpensive fashion stores, it's a bargain-*

hunter's paradise. | [+ **for**] *San Felipe is paradise for seafood lovers.* **3 Paradise** [singular] **a)** Heaven, thought of as the place where God lives and where there is no illness, death, or evil **b)** the garden where Adam and Eve lived (=the first humans, according to the Bible) —see also BIRD OF PARADISE, **be living in a fool's paradise** (FOOL¹ (8))

par·a·dox /ˈpærəˌdɑks/ *n.* **1** [C] a situation that seems strange because it involves two ideas or qualities that are opposite or very different: *Isn't it a paradox that the airline with the lowest fares is the one with the most customer satisfaction?* **2** [C] a statement that seems impossible because it contains two opposing ideas that are both true **3** [U] the use of such statements in writing or speech —**paradoxical** /ˌpærəˈdɑksɪkəl/ *adj.*

par·a·dox·i·cal·ly /ˌpærəˈdɑksɪkli/ *adv.* [sentence adverb] in a way that is surprising because it is the opposite of what you would expect: *Perhaps paradoxically, the problem of loneliness is most acute in big cities.*

par·af·fin /ˈpærəfɪn/ *n.* [U] a soft white substance used for making CANDLEs, made from PETROLEUM or coal

par·a·glid·ing /ˈpærəˌglaɪdɪŋ/ *n.* [U] a sport in which you jump off a hill or out of an aircraft and use a PARACHUTE to float back down to the ground

par·a·gon /ˈpærəˌgɑn/ *n.* [C] OFTEN HUMOROUS someone or something that is perfect or is extremely brave, good etc.: [+ **of**] *a paragon of virtue*

sw **par·a·graph** /ˈpærəˌgræf/ *n.* [C] a group of several
2 sentences in a piece of writing, the first sentence of which starts on a new line —**paragraph** *v.* [T]

Par·a·guay /ˈpærəˌgwaɪ/ a country in South America between Brazil and Argentina —**Paraguayan** /ˌpærəˈgwaɪən/ *n., adj.*

par·a·keet /ˈpærəˌkit/ *n.* [C] a small brightly colored bird with a long tail

par·a·le·gal /ˌpærəˈligəl/ *n.* [C] someone whose job is to help a lawyer do his or her work

par·al·lel¹ /ˈpærəˌlɛl/ *n.* **1** [C] a relationship or similarity between two things, especially things that exist or happen in different places or at different times: [+ **between**] *There are many parallels between politics and acting.* | [+ **with**] *When looking at Mozart's life, the parallels with "Hamlet" are astonishing.* | *The article **draws a parallel between** (=shows that two things are similar) the political situation now and that in the 1930s.* **2 in parallel with sb/sth** together with and at the same time as something else: *The CIA is working in parallel with the FBI to solve the case.* **3** [C] an imaginary line drawn on a map of the Earth, that is parallel to the EQUATOR: *The 42nd parallel is the northern border of Pennsylvania.* **4 have no parallel** also **be without parallel** be greater, better etc. than anything else: *Gilmore's voice perhaps has no parallel in country music today.* **5 be in parallel** TECHNICAL if two electrical CIRCUITs (=complete circular paths) are in parallel, they are connected so that any electric current is divided equally between them

parallel² *adj.* **1** two lines, paths etc. that are parallel to each other are the same distance apart along their whole length: *The airport's two parallel runways are only 750 feet apart.* | [+ **to/with**] *Place the boards parallel with each other and six inches apart.* | *The river **runs parallel to** (=is parallel to) the road.* **2** FORMAL similar and happening at the same time: *The film attempts to follow the parallel story lines of the novel.* | *a parallel universe*

parallel³ *v.* [T] FORMAL **1** to be similar to something else: *a period of political change that closely parallels what happened in France in the 18th century* **2** to be in a position that is parallel with something else: *The railroad tracks paralleled the stream for several miles.*

parallel bars /ˈ... ˌ./ *n.* [plural] two wooden bars that are held parallel to each other on a set of posts, used in GYMNASTICS

par·al·lel·ism /ˈpærələˌlɪzəm/ *n.* FORMAL **1** [U] the state of being PARALLEL with something **2** [C] a similarity

par·al·lel·o·gram /ˌpærəˈlɛləˌgræm/ *n.* [C] a flat shape with four sides in which each side is the same length as the side opposite it and parallel to it —see picture at SHAPE¹

parallel park·ing /ˌ... ˈ.../ *n.* [U] **1** a way of parking a car so that it is parallel to the SIDEWALK **2** spaces that are arranged so that you can park a car in this way

parallel pro·cess·ing /ˌ... ˈ.../ *n.* [U] TECHNICAL the use of several computers to work on a single problem at one time, or the process by which a single computer can perform several operations at the same time

pa·ral·y·sis /pəˈræləsɪs/ *n.* [U] **1** the loss of the ability to move all or part of your body or to experience any feeling in it: *Such injuries can cause permanent paralysis.* **2** a state of being unable to take action, make decisions, or operate normally: *The new President promised to end years of government paralysis.* —see also INFANTILE PARALYSIS

par·a·lyt·ic¹ /ˌpærəˈlɪtɪk/ *adj.* [only before noun] suffering from paralysis —**paralytically** /-kli/ *adv.*

paralytic² *n.* [C] someone who is paralyzed

par·a·lyze /ˈpærəˌlaɪz/ *v.* [T] **1** to make a person or animal lose the ability to move part or all of their body, or to feel anything in it: *The spider uses a poison to paralyze its victim.* **2** to make something or someone unable to operate normally: *Labor disputes and strikes have paralyzed the country's transportation network.* | *In October 1973, with Nixon paralyzed by the Watergate crisis, war broke out in the Middle East.*

par·a·lyzed /ˈpærəˌlaɪzd/ *adj.* **1** unable to move part or all of your body or feel things in it: *A diving accident left the lower half of Robert's body paralyzed.* **2** unable to think clearly or operate normally: *They were both paralyzed with fear.* | *Apart from the black market, trade in the country is virtually paralyzed.*

Par·a·mar·i·bo /ˌpærəˈmærəˌboʊ/ the capital city of Suriname

par·a·med·ic /ˌpærəˈmɛdɪk/ *n.* [C] someone who has been trained to help people who are hurt or to do medical work, but who is not a doctor or nurse

par·a·med·i·cal /ˌpærəˈmɛdɪkəl◂/ *adj.* [usually before noun] helping or supporting doctors, nurses, or hospitals: *paramedical staff*

pa·ram·e·ter /pəˈræmətəʳ/ *n.* [C usually plural] a set of agreed limits that control the way that something should be done: *We also need to consider the influence of the media, but that is **outside the parameters of** the present inquiry.* | **establish/set/lay down parameters** *The committee's job is to establish new parameters for allocating public housing.*

par·a·mil·i·tar·y /ˌpærəˈmɪləˌtɛri/ *adj.* [usually before noun] **1** a paramilitary organization is an illegal military force that uses violence to achieve its political aims: *extremist paramilitary groups* **2** relating to or helping a military organization: *paramilitary operations* | *paramilitary gear* —**paramilitary** *n.* [C]

par·a·mount /ˈpærəˌmaʊnt/ *adj.* more important than anything else: *An airline spokesman stated that the safety of passengers was absolutely paramount.* | *The abortion issue is **of paramount importance** to the so-called "religious right."*

par·a·mour /ˈpærəˌmʊr/ *n.* [C] LITERARY someone who has a romantic or sexual relationship with another person who they are not married to; LOVER

par·a·noi·a /ˌpærəˈnɔɪə/ *n.* [U] **1** an unreasonable belief that you cannot trust other people, or that they are trying to harm you: *It seemed possible that Soviet paranoia could spark a war at any time.* **2** TECHNICAL a serious mental illness that makes someone believe that people hate them and treat them badly

par·a·noi·ac /ˌpærəˈnɔɪæk◂, -ˈnɔɪ-ɪk/ *adj.* paranoid —**paranoiac** *n.* [C]

par·a·noid /ˈpærəˌnɔɪd/ *adj.* **1** believing that you cannot trust other people, that other people want to

P

harm you, or that you are always in danger: *I get a little paranoid around big dogs.* | *Jason's so paranoid about getting sick that he washes his hands all the time.* **2** TECHNICAL suffering from a mental illness that makes you believe that other people are trying to harm you

par·a·nor·mal /ˌpærəˈnɔrməl◂/ *adj.* **1** paranormal events cannot be explained by science and seem strange and mysterious: *ESP and other paranormal phenomena* **2 the paranormal** these events in general —compare SUPERNATURAL[1]

Pa·ra·ná River /ˌpærəˈnɑ/ a river in central South America that flows south through Brazil and Paraguay to the Atlantic Ocean on the coast of Argentina

par·a·pet /ˈpærəpət, -pɛt/ *n.* [C] **1** a low wall at the edge of a high roof, bridge etc. **2** a protective wall of earth or stone built in front of a TRENCH[3] in a war

par·a·pher·na·lia /ˌpærəfɚˈneɪlyə, -fəˈneɪl-/ *n.* [U] a lot of small things that belong to someone or are needed for a particular activity: *Their home was decorated with Elvis Presley paraphernalia.* | *drug paraphernalia*

par·a·phrase[1] /ˈpærəˌfreɪz/ *v.* [T] to express in a shorter or clearer way what someone has written or said: *The article only paraphrased Castro's words, and gave no direct quotes.*

paraphrase[2] *n.* [C] a statement that expresses in a shorter or clearer way what someone has said or written

par·a·ple·gi·a /ˌpærəˈplidʒiə, -dʒə/ *n.* [U] the inability to move your legs and the lower part of your body

par·a·ple·gic /ˌpærəˈplidʒɪk/ *n.* [C] someone who is unable to move the lower part of their body including their legs —**paraplegic** *adj.*

par·a·psy·chol·o·gy /ˌpærəsaɪˈkɑlədʒi/ *n.* [U] the scientific study of mysterious abilities that some people claim to have, such as knowing what will happen in the future

par·a·sail·ing /ˈpærəˌseɪlɪŋ/ *n.* [U] a sport in which you wear a PARACHUTE and are pulled behind a motor boat so that you sail through the air —see picture on page 1332

par·a·site /ˈpærəˌsaɪt/ *n.* [C] **1** a plant or animal that lives on or in another plant or animal and gets food from it **2** a lazy person who does not work but depends on other people: *They tend to regard people on welfare as parasites.*

par·a·sit·ic /ˌpærəˈsɪtɪk/ also **par·a·sit·i·cal** /ˌpærəˈsɪtɪkəl/ *adj.* **1** living in or on another plant or animal and getting food from them: *Parasitic beetles often make their homes in the nests of ants.* **2** a parasitic person is lazy, does no work, and depends on other people **3** a parasitic disease is caused by parasites —**parasitically** /-kli/ *adv.*

par·a·sol /ˈpærəˌsɔl, -ˌsɑl/ *n.* [U] a type of UMBRELLA used to provide shade from the sun

par·a·troop·er /ˈpærəˌtrupɚ/ *n.* [C] a soldier who is trained to jump out of an airplane using a PARACHUTE

par·a·troops /ˈpærəˌtrups/ *n.* [plural] a group of paratroopers that fight together as a military unit

par·boil /ˈpɑrbɔɪl/ *v.* [T] to boil something until it is partly cooked

par·cel[1] /ˈpɑrsəl/ *n.* [C] **1** something wrapped so it can be sent by mail: PACKAGE[1] **2** an area of land that is part of a larger area which has been divided up: *a parcel of farmland* —see also **be part and parcel of sth** (PART[1] (21))

parcel[2] *v.* **parceled, parceling**

parcel sth ↔ **out** *phr. v.* [T] to divide or share something among several people: *It's Clare's job to parcel out the work to members of the team.*

parcel sth ↔ **off** *phr. v.* [T] to divide something into small parts so that it can be sold: *Owner Kirk Kerkorian has parceled off many of the company's assets.*

parcel post /ˌ.. ˈ./ *n.* [U] the slowest and cheapest system of sending parcels by mail in the U.S.

parch /pɑrtʃ/ *v.* [T] if sun or wind parches land, plants etc., it makes them very dry

parched /pɑrtʃt/ *adj.* **1** very dry, especially because of hot weather: *Strong winds and high temperatures fueled dozens of fires in parched Oregon.* | *Phil raised a glass of water to his parched lips.* **2 be parched** INFORMAL to be very THIRSTY

Par·chee·si /pɑrˈtʃizi/ *n.* [U] TRADEMARK a children's game in which you move small pieces of plastic around a board after throwing DICE

parch·ment /ˈpɑrtʃmənt/ *n.* **1** [U] a material used in the past for writing on, made from the skin of a sheep or a goat **2** [U] thick yellow-white writing paper, sometimes used for official documents **3** [C] a document written on this paper or material

pard·ner /ˈpɑrdnɚ/ *n.* SPOKEN, HUMOROUS a word used when speaking to someone you know well, thought to be typical of the way COWBOYS speak: *Howdy, pardner!*

par·don[1] /ˈpɑrdn/ *v.* [T] **1** to officially allow someone to be free without being punished, although a court has decided they are guilty of a crime: *Ford immediately pardoned Nixon when he became President.* **2** [not in progressive] to forgive someone for doing something wrong: *I hope you'll pardon the state of the house – I haven't had time to clean it up.*

S W
3

SPOKEN PHRASES

3 pardon me a) used to politely say sorry after you have made an impolite sound such as a BURP or a YAWN **b)** used before you politely correct someone or disagree with them: *Pardon me, but that's not exactly what happened.* **c)** used to politely say sorry when you have accidentally pushed someone, interrupted them etc.: *Pardon me, but I'd better answer that phone.* **d)** used to politely get someone's attention in order to ask them a question: *Pardon me, can you tell me how to get to the library?* —see also PARDON[3] —see Usage Note at EXCUSE[1] **4 pardon me for interrupting/asking/saying** used to politely ask if you can interrupt someone, ask something etc.: *Pardon me for asking, but where did you buy your shoes?* **5 if you'll pardon the expression** used when you are saying sorry for using a slightly impolite phrase: *It's time that guy got off his ass, if you'll pardon the expression.* **6 pardon my French** HUMOROUS used to say sorry after you have said an impolite word **7 pardon my ignorance/rudeness etc.** used when you think that you may seem not to know enough, not to be polite enough etc.: *Pardon my ignorance, but what does OPEC stand for?* **8 pardon me for living/breathing** used when you are annoyed because you think someone has answered you angrily for no good reason

---

pardon[2] *n.* **1** [C] an official order allowing someone to be free without being punished, although a court has decided they are guilty of a crime: *With the promise of a pardon, Wynn was persuaded to give evidence.* | **grant/give sb a pardon** (=pardon them) **2** [U] OLD-FASHIONED the act of forgiving someone | **ask/beg sb's pardon (for)** (=ask someone to forgive you) *Walter begged her pardon for all the pain he had caused her.* —see also **I beg your pardon** (BEG (4)) —see Usage Note at EXCUSE[1]

pardon[3] *interjection* also **pardon me** used when you want someone to repeat something because you did not hear it: *"What time are you leaving?" "Pardon?" "What time do you have to go?"*

S W
2

par·don·a·ble /ˈpɑrdn-əbəl/ *adj.* FORMAL pardonable behavior or mistakes are not very bad and can be forgiven —**pardonably** *adv.*

pare /pɛr/ *v.* [T] **1** to cut off the thin outer part of a fruit or vegetable using a sharp knife: *Pare one small apple and then dice it.* **2** to reduce an amount or number, especially by making a series of small reductions: *The firm has not been able to pare costs fast enough to match competitors.* | **pare sth from sth** *IBM plans to pare 20,000 workers from its payroll.*

pare sth ↔ **down** *phr. v.* [T] to gradually reduce an amount or number: *The Navy has pared its carrier fleet down to 9 ships from 14.* | *Union leaders are* outraged with the company for trying to pare down health benefits. —**pared-down** adj.

par·ent /'pɛrənt, 'pær-/ n. [C] **1** the father or mother of a person or animal: I'd like you to meet my parents sometime. **2** a larger company or organization that owns a particular organization: The airline's parent, AMR Corp., lost $115 million in the first nine months. —see also PARENT COMPANY, SINGLE PARENT

par·ent·age /'pɛrəntɪdʒ/ n. [U] someone's parents and the country or social class they are from: children of French-Canadian parentage

pa·ren·tal /pə'rɛntl/ adj. [usually before noun] related to a child's parent or parents: parental responsibilities

parental leave /.,.. '.,/ n. [U] time that a parent is allowed to spend away from work with his or her baby —compare MATERNITY LEAVE

parent com·pa·ny /'.. ,.../ n. [C] a company that controls a smaller company or organization

pa·ren·the·sis /pə'rɛnθəsɪs/ n. plural **parentheses** /-siz/ [usually plural] one of the marks ( ), used in writing to separate additional information from the main information: Ratings of the movies are shown in parentheses.

par·en·thet·i·cal /,pærən'θɛtɪkəl/ adj. said or written as an additional, usually less important, piece of information: The help given by the police department is briefly acknowledged in a parenthetical comment. —**parenthetically** /-kli/ adv.

par·ent·hood /'pɛrənt,hʊd/ n. [U] the state of being a parent: They felt that they were not yet ready for parenthood.

par·ent·ing /'pɛrəntɪŋ/ n. [U] the skill or activity of taking care of children as a parent

Parent-Teach·er As·so·ci·a·tion /,.. '.. ..,./ n. —see PTA

par ex·cel·lence /,par ɛksə'lɑns/ adj. [only after noun] of the best possible kind: He went on to become the talk-show host par excellence.

par·fait /par'feɪ/ n. [U] a sweet food made of layers of ICE CREAM and fruit

pa·ri·ah /pə'raɪə/ n. [C] **1** a person, organization, country etc. that is hated and avoided by others: a social pariah | Sudan was viewed by the U.S. State Department as a pariah state. **2** OLD USE a member of a very low social class in India

par·i·mu·tu·el /,pærɪ'myutʃuəl/ n. **1** [U] a system in which the money that people have risked on a horse race is shared between the people who have won **2** [C] a machine used to calculate the amount of money people can win by risking it on horse races

paring knife /'.. ,./ n. [C] a small knife used for cutting vegetables and fruit

par·ings /'pɛrɪŋz/ n. [plural] thin pieces of something that have been cut off: nail parings

Par·is /'pærɪs/ the capital and largest city of France —**Parisian** /pə'riʒən/ n., adj.

par·ish /'pærɪʃ/ n. [C] **1** the area that a priest in some Christian churches is responsible for: a parish priest **2** an area in the state of Louisiana that contains several towns that are governed together **3** the parish the people who live in a particular area, especially those who go to church

parish church /,.. './ n. [C] the main Christian church in a particular area

pa·rish·ion·er /pə'rɪʃənɚ/ n. [C] someone who lives in a parish, especially someone who regularly goes to the church there

par·i·ty /'pærəti/ n. [U] **1** the state of being equal, especially having equal pay, rights, or power: The Soviets' aim was to achieve parity in nuclear capability. | The bill would return Senate and House salaries **to parity** (=to an equal level). | [+ with] Employees at NBC want pay parity with their counterparts at TV networks. **2** TECHNICAL equality between the units of money from two different countries: The currency was recently set **at parity** with the U.S. dollar.

park¹ /park/ n. [C] **1** a large open area with grass and trees, especially in a city, where people can walk, play games etc.: Let's go for a walk in the park. | a

park bench **2** a large area of land in the country that has been kept in its natural state to protect the trees, plants, and animals in it, where people can visit, go CAMPING etc. | **national/state/county park** (=one that is controlled by the national, state etc. government) **3** the field where a game of BASEBALL is played —see also AMUSEMENT PARK, BALLPARK, BUSINESS PARK, SCIENCE PARK, THEME PARK, TRAILER PARK

park² v. **1** [I,T] to put a car or other vehicle in a particular place for a period of time: I couldn't find a place to park. | **park sth** Who parked their car in the handicapped zone? | I'm parked over there (=I've parked my car over there). **2 park yourself** INFORMAL to sit or stand in a particular place: My cat always parks herself in front of the heater. **3** [T] SPOKEN to put something in a place, in a way that is inconvenient or annoying: **park sth in/on/here etc.** Hey, don't park those bags down there.

par·ka /'parkə/ n. [C] a thick warm JACKET with a HOOD

park and ride /,. . '. ./ n. [U] a system in which you leave your car in a PARKING LOT on the edge of a city, and then take a special bus to the center of the city

Par·ker, Bon·nie /'parkɚ/, /'bɑni/ (1911–1934) a young criminal who stole money from banks and businesses with Clyde Barrow

Par·ker, Char·lie /'tʃɑrli/ (1920–1955) a JAZZ musician who played the SAXOPHONE and invented the BEBOP style of jazz with Dizzy Gillespie

Parker, Dor·o·thy /'dɔrəθi/ (1893–1967) a U.S. writer and JOURNALIST, famous for her many clever and funny sayings

park·ing /'parkɪŋ/ n. [U] **1** the act of parking a car or other vehicle: The sign said "No Parking." | a **parking fine 2** spaces in which you can leave a car or other vehicle: Parking is available on Lamay Street. | We found **a parking space** near the exit.

parking brake /'.. ,./ n. [C] a piece of equipment in a car that prevents it from moving when it is parked

parking ga·rage /'.. ,./ n. [C] an enclosed building in a public place for cars to be parked in

parking light /'.. ,./ n. [C] one of two small lights next to the main front lights on a car

parking lot

parking lot /'.. ,./ n. [C] an open area for cars to park in

parking me·ter /'.. ,../ n. [C] a machine which you put money into when you park your car next to it

parking tick·et /'.. ,../ n. [C] an official notice fastened to a vehicle, saying that you have to pay money because you have parked your car in the wrong place or for too long

Par·kin·son's dis·ease /'parkənsənz dɪ,ziz/ also **Parkinson's** n. [U] a serious illness in which your muscles become very weak and your arms and legs shake

park·land /'park-lænd/ n. [U] land with grass and trees, which is used as a park

park ran·ger /'. ,../ n. [C] a RANGER (1)

Parks /pɑrks/, **Ro·sa** /ˈroʊzə/ (1913–) an African-American woman who became famous in 1955 because she refused to give her seat on a bus to a white man, which was an important event in the CIVIL RIGHTS movement

Rosa Parks

park·way /ˈpɑrkweɪ/ n. plural **parkways** [C,U] a wide road with an area of grass and trees in the middle or along the sides

par·lance /ˈpɑrləns/ n. **in common/medical/advertising etc. parlance** expressed in words that most people, or a particular group of people, would use: "Two dimes," in street parlance, is $20 worth of crack.

par·lay /ˈpɑrleɪ, -li/ v. **parlays, parlayed, parlaying** [T] to use advantages that you already have, such as your skills, experience, or money, and increase their value by using all your opportunities well: [**parlay sth into sth**] DeLuca parlayed a $1,000 investment into the nation's largest submarine-sandwich chain.

par·ley /ˈpɑrli/ n. [C] OLD-FASHIONED a discussion in which enemies try to achieve peace —**parley** v. [I]

par·lia·ment /ˈpɑrləmənt/ n. [C] **1** the group of people in some countries who are elected to make the country's laws and discuss important national affairs: New budget measures were approved Tuesday by the Russian parliament. **2 Parliament** the main law-making institution in some countries, such as the United Kingdom **3** the period during which this institution meets

par·lia·men·tar·i·an /ˌpɑrləmənˈtɛriən/ n. [C] an experienced member of a parliament

par·lia·men·ta·ry /ˌpɑrləˈmɛntri, -ˈmɛntəri/ adj. [only before noun] relating to or governed by a parliament: parliamentary elections | a parliamentary debate

par·lor /ˈpɑrlɚ/ n. [C] **1 ice cream/massage/funeral etc. parlor** a store or type of business that provides a particular service **2** OLD-FASHIONED a room in a house which has comfortable chairs and is used for meeting guests

parlor game /ˈ.. ˌ./ n. [C] OLD-FASHIONED a game that can be played indoors, such as a guessing game or a word game

par·lous /ˈpɑrləs/ adj. FORMAL in a very bad or dangerous condition: the parlous state of the country's economy

Par·me·san cheese /ˈpɑrməˌzɑn, -ˌʒɑn/ also **Parmesan cheese** /ˈ... ˌ./ n. [U] a hard strong-tasting Italian cheese

pa·ro·chi·al /pəˈroʊkiəl/ adj. **1** only interested in the things that affect you and your local area, and not interested in more important matters: Local newspapers tend to be very parochial. **2** [only before noun] relating to a particular church —**parochialism** n. [U] —**parochially** adv.

parochial school /.ˈ... ˌ./ n. [C] a private school which is run by or connected with a church

par·o·dy¹ /ˈpærədi/ n. plural **parodies 1** [C,U] a song, piece of writing, television show etc. that copies a particular well-known style in an amusing way: [+ **on/of**] The film is a hilarious parody of all those 1970s disaster movies. | Her act contains a strong element of self-parody (=when someone makes fun of their own style). **2** [C] a very bad or unacceptable copy of something: U.N. observers described the election as a parody of democratic process. | an outrageous parody of justice (=a very unfair trial)

parody² v. **parodies, parodied, parodying** [T] to copy someone's style or attitude, especially in an amusing way: The movie parodies such classics as "Gone with the Wind" and "Casablanca." —**parodist** n. [C]

pa·role¹ /pəˈroʊl/ n. [U] permission for someone to leave prison, on the condition that they promise to behave well: Hicks was released **on parole** May 17. | Police arrested Ramos for **violating parole** (=not behaving as he was supposed to while on parole). | She is appearing before the **parole board** (=the official group that can give a prisoner parole) next week.

parole² v. [T usually passive] to allow someone to leave prison on the condition that they promise to behave well

pa·rol·ee /pəˌroʊˈli/ n. [C] someone who is on parole

par·ox·ys·m /ˈpærəkˌsɪzəm, pəˈrɑk-/ n. [C] **1 a paroxysm of rage/laughter/excitement etc.** a sudden expression of strong feeling that you cannot control: The paroxysm of cynicism ignited by the assassination of President Kennedy still lives in the national consciousness. **2** a sudden short attack of pain, coughing, shaking etc.: [+ **of**] paroxysms of coughing

par·quet /pɑrˈkeɪ, ˈpɑrkeɪ/ n. [U] small flat blocks of wood fitted together in a pattern, which cover the floor of a room: a parquet floor

par·ri·cide /ˈpærəˌsaɪd/ n. [U] FORMAL the crime of killing your father, mother, or any other close relative —compare MATRICIDE, PATRICIDE

Par·rish /ˈpærɪʃ/, **Max·field** /ˈmæksfild/ (1870–1966) a U.S. PAINTER and book ILLUSTRATOR

par·rot¹ /ˈpærət/ n. [C] a tropical bird with a curved beak and brightly colored feathers, which can be taught to copy human speech

parrot² v. [T] to repeat someone else's words or ideas without really understanding what you are saying

par·ry /ˈpæri/ v. **parries, parried, parrying** [T] **1** to avoid directly answering a difficult question: Robins repeatedly parried questions from reporters on his personal finances. **2** to defend yourself against someone who is attacking you by pushing their weapon or hand to one side —**parry** n. [C]

parse /pɑrs/ v. [T] TECHNICAL to describe the grammar of a word when it is in a particular sentence, or the grammar of the whole sentence

Par·see, Parsi /ˈpɑrsi, pɑrˈsi/ n. [C] a member of an ancient Persian religious group in India —**Parsee** adj.

par·si·mo·ni·ous /ˌpɑrsəˈmoʊniəs/ adj. FORMAL extremely unwilling to spend money —**parsimoniously** adv. —**parsimony** /ˈpɑrsəˌmoʊni/ n. [U]

pars·ley /ˈpɑrsli/ n. [U] a small plant with curly leaves that have a strong taste, used in cooking or as decoration on food

pars·nip /ˈpɑrsnɪp/ n. [C,U] a plant with a thick white or yellowish root that is eaten as a vegetable

par·son /ˈpɑrsən/ n. [C] OLD-FASHIONED a Christian priest or minister responsible for a small area

par·son·age /ˈpɑrsənɪdʒ/ n. [C] the house where a parson lives

part¹ /pɑrt/ n.
1 piece of sth [C,U] one of the pieces or features of something, for example of an object, place, event, or period of time: [+ **of**] Which part of town do you live in? | It's the lower part of my back that hurts most. | Do you enjoy working as part of a team? | **be (a) part of sth** All this new responsibility is just part of growing up. | **the later/early part of sth** I should have more free time during the later part of the week. | **the best/worst part (of sth)** The best part of the movie was when she slapped him. | **the hard/easy/nice etc. part** I don't mind reading stories to the kids – that's the fun part.
2 machine/equipment [C] one of the separate pieces that something such as a machine or piece of equipment is made of: Where does this part go? | Check inside the box to see if all the parts are there. —see also SPARE PART
3 not all [C,U] some but not all of a particular thing or group of things: [+ **of**] Part of the money will be spent on a new playground. | **in parts** The film is very violent in parts. | Parts of New England got two to three inches of snow Tuesday night. | **(only) part of the problem/explanation/reason etc.** She's

having a tough time at work, and I think that's part of the reason she's so bad-tempered.
4 play a part a) if something or someone plays a part in something, they are involved in it and have a lot of influence on the way it happens or develops: *They've certainly worked very hard, but luck has played a part too.* | **[+ in]** *Tests confirmed that alcohol played a part in the accident.* | **play a big/important part in sth** *In small towns like this, the local church plays an important part in people's lives.* | *Senator Mitchell played such a big part in the Northern Ireland peace talks.*
5 take part to be involved in an activity, sport, event etc. together with other people: **[+ in]** *About 400 students took part in the protest.* | *McCluskey claims he took no part in the fighting.* | **take an active part** *Britain needs to take a more active part in shaping Europe's future.*
6 the better/best part of sth almost all of something: *I spent the better part of the afternoon fixing the printer.*
7 a good/large part of sth a lot or more than half of something: *Married couples make up a large part of the church's congregation.*
8 for the most part also **in large part** mostly or in most places: *LA defeated St. Louis, thanks in large part to Honeycutt's pitching.* | *For the most part, she's a fair person.*
9 in part to some degree, but not completely: *The failure of the project was due in part to his lack of leadership.*
10 hair **[C usually singular]** the line on your head formed by dividing your hair with a comb
11 sb's part in sth what a particular person did in an activity that was shared by several people, especially something bad: *Larkin will definitely go to jail for his part in the robbery.*
12 want no part in/of sth to not want to be involved in something, because you do not agree with or approve of it: *Matthews said he wanted no part of anything illegal.*
13 quantity **[C]** a particular quantity of a substance used when measuring different substances together into a mixture: *Mix one part milk with two parts flour and stir.*
14 acting **[C]** the words and actions of a particular character in a play, movie etc., performed by an actor: *The director has given us until tomorrow to learn our parts.* | *The part of Cyrano was played by Gerard Depardieu (=he performed as this character).*
15 Part One/Two/Three etc. the different parts of something such as a book or television program, sometimes used as a title: *Part Four tells us more about the main character's past.*
16 music **[C]** a tune that a particular type of instrument or voice within a group plays or sings: *I'll sing the bass part if you want.*
17 in/around these parts in the particular area, part of a country etc. that you are in: *I'm not from around these parts.*
18 on sb's part also **on the part of sb** used to say what someone does or feel: *The work all got done, though without much effort on Jim's part (=Jim did not make much effort).* | *There has never been any jealousy on my part.*
19 part of me/him etc. used when you have many different feelings or thoughts about something, so it is difficult to decide what you feel or what you should do: *Part of him wanted to tell her how he felt, but he was too shy.*
20 for sb's part used to say what someone thinks about something, especially when you are comparing this with someone else's opinion: *For my part, I can't see what the problem is.*
21 be part and parcel of sth to be included in something else, as a necessary feature: *Occasional unemployment is part and parcel of being an actor.*
22 take sth in good part OLD-FASHIONED to be able to laugh at a joke which is about you or affects you

part² *v.* **1 [I,T]** to pull the two sides of something apart, or to move apart in this way, making a space in the middle: *The crowd parted as Governor Langley walked to the stage.* | *Very gently, he parted the front of her robe.* | *Ralph's lips parted (=his mouth*

opened) into a delighted smile. **2 [I]** to separate from someone, or end a relationship with them: *Sharon and I parted on friendly terms.* | *With a brief hug, they parted.* **3 part company a)** also **part ways** to separate from someone, or end a relationship with them: **[+ with]** *Stinson parted company with the band in 1985.* | *It's been two years since I parted ways with my former employer.* **b)** to not agree with someone anymore or think the same as they do: *Experts part company on what can be done about the situation.* **4 [T]** if you part your hair, you separate it into two parts with a comb so that it looks neat: *Jen's black hair was parted down the middle.*

part with sth *phr. v.* **[T]** to get rid of something although you do not want to: *We finally had to part with our old station wagon.*

part³ *adv.* **part sth, part sth** if something is part one thing, part another, it consists of both of those things: *The medical exams are part written, part practical.* | *He's one of those evangelists who is part preacher, part TV personality.*

par·take /pɑrˈteɪk/ *v.* past tense **partook** past participle **partaken** /-ˈteɪkən/ **[I]** FORMAL **1** to take part in an activity or event; PARTICIPATE: **[+ in]** *Over 50 international stars were invited to partake in a charity concert.* **2** to eat or drink something: **[+ of]** *Diners here can partake of miso soup, raw fish, and steamed rice.*

partake of sth *phr. v.* **[T]** FORMAL to have a certain amount of a particular quality: *a style of drama that partakes of the unexpected*

par·the·no·gen·e·sis /ˌpɑrθənoʊˈdʒɛnəsɪs/ *n.* **[U]** TECHNICAL the production of a new plant or animal from a female without the sexual involvement of the male

par·tial /ˈpɑrʃəl/ *adj.* **1** not complete: *a partial solution to the problem* | *partial disability* | *Wade received only partial compensation for her injuries.* **2 be partial to sth** FORMAL to like something very much: *I'm quite partial to red wine.* **3** unfairly supporting one person or one side against another: **[+ to/toward]** *Some observers felt that the judge was partial toward the defendant.* —opposite IMPARTIAL

par·ti·al·i·ty /ˌpɑrʃiˈæləti/ *n.* **[U] 1** unfair support of one person or one side against another; BIAS¹: *The chairman must avoid any appearance of partiality.* **2 a partiality for sth** FORMAL a special liking for something: *Chris's partiality for sports cars is what put him into debt.*

par·tial·ly /ˈpɑrʃəli/ *adv.* not completely; partly: *Food shortages were partially responsible for riots.* | *A stroke left her partially paralyzed.*

par·tic·i·pant /pɑrˈtɪsəpənt, pə-/ *n.* **[C]** someone who is taking part in an activity or event: **[+ in]** *Participants in the 10K run will receive a T-shirt.*

par·tic·i·pate /pɑrˈtɪsəˌpeɪt, pə-/ *v.* **[I]** FORMAL to take part in an activity or event: *We asked a company spokesman to join the debate, but he refused to participate.* | **[+ in]** *More than 400 children participated in a clean-up of the park.*

par·tic·i·pa·tion /pɑrˌtɪsəˈpeɪʃən/ *n.* **[U]** the act of taking part in an activity or event: *Voter participation has declined by 5%.* | **[+ in]** *Two bishops were jailed for their participation in the demonstration.*

par·tic·i·pa·to·ry /pɑrˈtɪsəpəˌtɔri/ *adj.* **[usually before noun]** FORMAL a participatory way of organizing something, making decisions etc. is one that involves everyone who is affected by such decisions: *a participatory management style*

par·tic·i·pi·al /ˌpɑrtəˈsɪpiəl/ *adj.* TECHNICAL using a participle, or having the form of a participle: *a participial phrase*

par·ti·ci·ple /ˈpɑrtəˌsɪpəl/ *n.* **[C]** TECHNICAL the form of a verb, usually ending in "-ing" or "-ed," which is used to make compound forms of the verb (such as "She is singing") or used as an adjective (such as "annoying" or "annoyed") —see also PAST PARTICIPLE

an argument: *As he walked out the door, Lee took a parting shot at his wife.*

par·ti·san¹ /ˈpɑrtəzən, -sən/ *adj.* strongly supporting one particular party, plan, leader etc., and not liking all others: *Gore was speaking before a partisan crowd of about 500 Democrats.* —compare BIPARTISAN, NON-PARTISAN

partisan² *n.* [C] someone who supports a particular party, plan, or leader: [+ of] *a well-known partisan of the democratic movement in China* —**partisanship** *n.* [U]

par·ti·tion¹ /pɑrˈtɪʃən, pə-/ *n.* **1** [C] a thin wall that separates one part of a room from another **2** [U] the act of dividing a country into two or more independent countries: [+ of] *the partition of Czechoslovakia*

partition² *v.* [T + adv./prep.] to divide a country, building, or room into two or more parts: *Korea was partitioned at the 38th Parallel after World War II.*

partition sth ↔ **off** *phr. v.* [T] to divide part of a room from the rest by using a partition: *The rest of the room had been partitioned off into smaller offices.*

par·ti·tive /ˈpɑrtətɪv/ *n.* TECHNICAL a word which comes before a noun and shows that part of something is being described, not the whole of it, for example the word "some" in the phrase "some of the money" —**partitive** *adj.*

part·ly /ˈpɑrtli/ *adv.* to some degree, but not completely: *Federal budget cuts are partly to blame for the rise in unemployment.* | *Drunk-driving convictions have increased, partly as a result of more effective policing.* | *Skies were **partly cloudy** across much of Texas today.* s w ☐3

part·ner¹ /ˈpɑrtˈnɚ/ *n.* [C] s w ☐2☐1
1 in business one of the owners of a business, who share the profits and losses: *Previously, Ellsworth was a partner at the accounting firm of Deloitte Touche.* | *The sale of the firm could make each of the senior partners into millionaires.*
2 marriage etc. one of two people who are married or who live together and have a sexual relationship.: *Are we allowed to bring our partners to the staff party?* | *Company health benefits cover not only spouses but **domestic partners** as well.*
3 dancing/games etc. someone you do a particular activity with, for example dancing or playing a game against two other people: *Running with a partner can keep your work-out from being boring.*
4 country/organization a country or organization that has an agreement with another country or organization: *Japan is a major trading partner of the US.*
5 partner in crime OFTEN HUMOROUS one of two people who have planned and done something together, either something illegal or something that annoys other people

partner² *v.* [T usually passive] to be someone's partner in a dance, game, or other activity: *At the American Ballet Theater, Cynthia Gregory was partnered by Fernando Bujones.*

partner up *phr. v.* [I,T] to join with someone as their partner, or make people become partners: [+ with] *I'd like you all to partner up with someone for the square dance.*

part·ner·ship /ˈpɑrtˈnɚˌʃɪp/ *n.* **1** [U] the state of being a partner and working with someone else, for example in a business or other shared activity: *Police and community leaders need to work together in a spirit of partnership.* | **be/work in partnership (with sb)** *At that time, Tannen was in partnership with Jack Baker in the automobile business.* | *Eleven years ago, the sisters **went into partnership with each other**.* **2** [C] a relationship between two people, organizations, or countries that work together regularly: *The YMCA and other youth agencies have set up a partnership to reach the city's poor children.* | *the great movie partnership of De Niro and Scorsese* **3** [C] a business owned by two or more partners who share the profits and losses: *The law firm is run as a partnership.* s w ☐3

part of speech /ˌ. . ˈ./ *n.* [C] one of the types into which words are divided in grammar according to their use, such as noun, verb, or adjective

par·took /pɑrˈtʊk/ the past tense of PARTAKE

P

...**cle** /ˈpɑrtɪkəl/ *n.* [C] **1** a very small piece of ...ething: [+ of] *tiny particles of dust in the air* ... one of the very small pieces of matter that an atom consists of: *subatomic particles such as protons* **3** TECHNICAL a type of word in grammar, such as a CONJUNCTION (3) or PREPOSITION, that is usually short and does not belong to one of the main word classes. Some particles such as "in" and "up" can combine with verbs to form PHRASAL VERBS

particle ac·cel·er·a·tor /ˈ... .ˌ.../ *n.* [C] TECHNICAL a machine used in scientific studies which makes particles (=the pieces that atoms are made of) move at very high speeds

particle phys·ics /ˈ... ˌ../ *n.* [U] TECHNICAL the scientific study of the way particles (=the pieces that atoms are made of) develop and behave

par·tic·u·lar¹ /pəˈtɪkyələ/ *adj.* **1** [only before noun] a particular thing or person is the one that you are talking about, and not any other: *This particular part of Idaho is especially beautiful.* | *I'm looking for a particular book on Asian art.* **2** [only before noun] special or important enough to mention separately: *You should pay particular attention to spelling.* | *Was there any particular reason why he quit?* | *Of particular concern is the rising cost of transportation.* **3** [not before noun] very careful about choosing exactly what you like and not easily satisfied: [+ about] *Mr. Gabbert is very particular about how his business is run.* **4** I'm not particular SPOKEN used to say that you do not care what is decided: [+ what/how/where etc.] *I'm not really particular which movie we go to.* s w ☐2☐1

par·tic·u·lar² *n.* **1** in particular especially: *Automobile prices in particular have fallen in recent months.* | *There was one incident in particular that made us suspicious about him.* | **anything/anyone/anywhere in particular** *Is there anyone in particular you have in mind for the job?* | **nothing/no one/nowhere in particular** *There's nothing in particular I want for my birthday.* **2** particulars [plural] the facts and details about something: [+ of] *Doug worked out the particulars of the contract.* | *At the interview, you'll need to provide all of **your particulars** (=details such as your name, address, profession etc.).* **3** in every particular/in all particulars FORMAL in every detail: *Hann's analysis is right in almost all particulars.* s w ☐3

par·tic·u·lar·i·ty /pəˌtɪkyəˈlærəti/ *n. plural* **particularities** FORMAL **1** [U] the quality of being exact and paying attention to details **2** [C] a detail

par·tic·u·lar·ize /pəˈtɪkyələˌraɪz/ *v.* [I,T] FORMAL to give the details of something; ITEMIZE

par·tic·u·lar·ly /pəˈtɪkyələli, -ˈtɪkyəli/ *adv.* **1** more than usual or more than others; ESPECIALLY: *Yosemite is particularly enjoyable in the winter because there are fewer visitors.* | *Exercise reduces the risk of cancer, particularly colon cancer.* **2 not particularly a)** not very: *Jon isn't particularly worried about money.* **b)** SPOKEN not very much: *"You don't like cats very much, do you?" "No, not particularly."* s w ☐2☐1

par·tic·u·late¹ /pəˈtɪkyəlɪt, pɑr-, -ˌleɪt/ *n.* [C usually plural,U] a substance that consists of very small separate parts, especially a substance in the air that comes from car engines and can damage your health: *toxic particulates*

particulate² *adj.* [only before noun] consisting of very small separate parts: *particulate matter*

part·ing¹ /ˈpɑrtɪŋ/ *n.* **1** [C,U] an occasion when two people leave each other: *an emotional parting at the airport* **2 parting of the ways** a situation in which two people or organizations decide to separate: *They did not say whether Smith was fired, but called it an "amicable parting of the ways."* **3** [U] an act of separating two things or of making two things separate: *the parting of clouds*

parting² *adj.* **1** a parting kiss/gift/glance etc. a kiss, gift etc. that you give someone as you leave **2** a parting shot a cruel or severe remark that you make just as you are leaving, especially at the end of

par·tridge /ˈpɑrtrɪdʒ/ *n.* [C] a fat brown bird with a short tail, which some people shoot as a sport or for food

part-time /ˌ. ˈ.◂/ *adj.* [only before noun] a part-time worker works regularly in a job, but only for part of the usual working time: *She's a part-time bartender.* —compare FULL-TIME —**part-time** *adv.*: *Brenda teaches math part-time.* —**part-timer** *n.* [C] INFORMAL *A part-timer helps us out in the mornings.*

par·tu·ri·tion /ˌpɑrtʃəˈrɪʃən/ *n.* [U] TECHNICAL the act or process of giving birth to a baby

part·way, **part way** /ˌpɑrtˈweɪ◂/ *adv.* **1** after part of a distance has been traveled, or after part of a period of time has passed: [+ **in/through/down** etc.] *A fire alarm went off partway through the meeting.* | *Jose got stuck after climbing partway up the cliff.* **2** in part; not completely: *Cyril opened his eyes partway.*

s w **par·ty¹** /ˈpɑrti/ *n. plural* **parties** [C]
1 for fun an occasion when people meet together, to enjoy themselves by eating, drinking, dancing etc.: *a birthday party* | **give/throw/have a party** *We're having a party for Maria to celebrate her graduation.* | *They had a surprise party for Steve on his 30th birthday.* | **party dress/clothes/hat** (=worn at a party) | *Do you remember that party game* (=played at a party) *called Telephone?* —see also COCKTAIL PARTY, DINNER PARTY
2 in politics an organization of people with the same political beliefs and aims, which you can vote for in elections: *the Republican Party* | **party leader/member** *Party leaders met to discuss their housing policy.* | *Morris continues to have deep support among the party faithful* (=a party's most loyal members). —see also PARTY LINE (1)
3 group of people a group of people that has come together in order to go somewhere or do something in an organized way: *a search party* | *The President was followed around by a small party of journalists.* | *Foster, party of six, your table is ready.*
4 contract/argument FORMAL one of the people or groups involved in an argument, agreement etc., especially a legal one: *Both parties will meet again on Monday to discuss the contract.* | *Really, it is Mrs. Blake who is the injured party here* (=the person who has been unfairly treated). —see also THIRD PARTY
5 the guilty party FORMAL the person who has done something illegal or wrong
6 be (a) party to sth FORMAL to be involved in or have your name connected with an activity, especially something bad or illegal: *I refuse to be a party to anything so dishonest.*
7 party animal INFORMAL someone who enjoys parties very much
8 party school INFORMAL a college or university where the students are not serious about studying and have lots of parties
9 party girl/boy INFORMAL a young attractive woman or man who is not very serious about life and likes to go to parties
10 party foul! SPOKEN, HUMOROUS said when someone does something embarrassing at a party or does something that interrupts the good feelings at a party

par·ty² *v.* **parties, partied, partying** [I] **1** INFORMAL also **party down** to enjoy yourself, especially by drinking alcohol, eating, dancing etc.: *I just got paid and I'm ready to party.* **2** SLANG to use illegal drugs

party fa·vor /ˈ.. ˌ../ *n.* [C usually plural] a small gift such as a paper hat or toy given to children at a party

party line /ˈ.. ˌ./ *n.* **1 the party line** the official opinion of a political party, which its members are expected to agree with and support: *Booth angered conservative Republicans by openly opposing the party line.* **2** [C] a telephone line connected to two or more telephones that belong to different people

party pol·i·tics /ˌ.. ˈ.../ *n.* [U] political activity that is concerned more with getting advantage for a particular party than with doing things to improve the situation in a country

party poop·er /ˈpɑrti ˌpupɚ/ *n.* [C] INFORMAL someone who spoils other people's fun and does not want people to enjoy themselves

party wall /ˈ.. ˌ./ *n.* [C] a dividing wall between two buildings, apartments etc. which belongs to both owners

par·ve·nu /ˈpɑrvəˌnu/ *n.* [C] FORMAL an insulting word for someone from a low social class who suddenly becomes rich or powerful —**parvenu** *adj.*

PASCAL /pæˈskæl/ *n.* [U] a computer language that works well on small computer systems and is used especially in teaching computer science

Pas·cal /pæˈskæl/, **Blaise** /bleɪz/ (1623–1662) a French PHILOSOPHER, MATHEMATICIAN, and PHYSICIST, known for writing about religion, and for his scientific discoveries

pas·chal /ˈpæskəl/ *adj.* **1** relating to the Jewish holiday of Passover **2** relating to the Christian holiday of Easter

pas de deux /ˌpɑ də ˈdu/ *n.* [C] a dance in BALLET performed by a man and a woman

pass

We passed the movie theater.
We drove past the movie theater.

pass¹ /pæs/ *v.*
s w
1 go past [I,T] **a)** to come up to a particular point or object and go past it: *They kept quiet until the soldiers had passed.* | *I pass her house every day on my way to work.* **b)** to move toward another vehicle from behind and then continue going beyond it: *A police car passed us doing 90 miles an hour.*
2 move/go **a)** [I always + adv./prep.] to move, go, or travel from one place to another, following a particular direction: [+ **through/into/from** etc.] *We heard the sound of helicopters passing overhead.* | *Here's the place in the wall where the bullet passed through.* | *The railroad passes around the northern shores of Lake Baikal.* | *I'm just passing through* (=traveling through a place) *on my way to Tulsa.* **b)** [T always + adv./prep.] to move or put something across, through, around etc. something else: [**pass sth around/across/through** etc.] *Lenny frowned and passed a hand through his hair.*
3 time **a)** [I] if time passes, it goes by: *As time passes, the disease progresses through several distinct stages.* | *Twenty-five years have passed since the civil war.* | *She became more frustrated with every passing day* (=as each day passed). | *Hardly a day passed without Carver's face being on the front page of the newspaper* (=it was there almost every day). **b)** [T] if you pass a period of time in a particular way, you spend it in that way: *We would drive up to Canada and pass the summer hiking around.* | *When I'm on the train, I read books to pass the time* (=keep from being bored).
4 give **a)** [T] to take something and put it in someone's hand, especially because they cannot reach it: *Pass the butter, please.* | [**pass sb sth**] *Could you pass me that pen over there?* | [**pass sth to sb**] *Just a minute. I'll pass the phone to Bob.* **b)** to give someone information: *Details of the attack had been passed to enemy agents.*

5 **test** a) [I,T] to succeed on a test: *Do you think you'll pass?* | *Dan's worried he won't pass calculus.* | *Ken passed his physics finals with flying colors* (=got very high grades). b) [T] to officially decide that someone has passed a test: *The driving instructor passed me even though I made a few mistakes.*
6 **sports** [I,T] to kick, throw, or hit a ball etc. to a member of your own team: *Miller passed to Rison for a 24-yard touchdown.* | *Hey, pass me the ball!*
7 **law/proposal** a) [T] to officially accept a law or proposal, especially by voting: **pass a law/motion/resolution etc.** *The city council passed a resolution banning smoking in restaurants.* b) [I,T] if a law or proposal passes an official group, it is officially accepted by that group: *The bill passed by a two-thirds majority in the Senate.*
8 **let sth pass** to deliberately not react when someone says or does something that you do not like: *When she started criticizing my parents, I couldn't let it pass.*
9 **number** to go past a particular number or amount, as a total gradually increases: *The family's hospital bills passed the $200,000 mark last month.*
10 **say/communicate** [I always + adv./prep.] if words, looks, or signs pass between two or more people, they exchange them with one another: [+ **between**] *Not many words passed between us during the trip home.*
11 **pass the time of day (with sb)** to talk to someone for a short time in order to be friendly
12 **end** [I] to gradually come to an end: *Dr. Todd said the pain would pass in a day or two.* | *The storm soon passed.*
13 **not do sth** [I] a) SPOKEN used to say that you do not want to do something: *"Do you want to go fishing Saturday?" "Sorry, I'll have to pass this time."* b) to say that you do not know the answer to a question, especially in a competition: *"What's the capital of Albania?" "Pass."* | [+ **on**] *I had to pass on the last question.*
14 **pass judgment (on sb)** to give your opinion about someone's behavior, especially in order to criticize them
15 **pass (a) sentence (on sb)** to officially decide how a criminal will be punished, and to announce what the punishment will be
16 **change of ownership** [I,T] FORMAL to go from one person's control or possession to someone else's: [+ **from/to**] *The title passes from father to son.* | [**pass sth to sb**] *Last week's election passed control of Congress to the Republicans.*
17 **pass the hat (around)** to collect money from a group of people, especially after a performance or for a particular purpose: *Employees passed the hat and raised $500 to help with the boy's medical costs.*
18 **pass unnoticed** to happen without anyone noticing or saying anything
19 **pass the torch (to sb)** if someone passes the torch to someone else, they give their position or work to them: *In the early '90s, Friedkin passed the torch to Gunaji as director of the foundation.*
20 **change** [I] FORMAL if a substance passes from one condition into another, it changes into another condition: [+ **from/to**] *When water freezes, it passes from a liquid to a solid state.*
21 **pass muster** to be accepted as good enough for a particular job: *Only if a paper passes muster is it accepted for publication.*
22 **pass the buck** to try to blame someone else or make them responsible for something that you should deal with: *a bunch of politicians all trying to pass the buck*
23 **false money** [T] to use false money to pay for something: *The two men were arrested for passing a counterfeit 100-dollar bill at a gas station.*
24 **never/not pass sb's lips** a) used to say that you will not talk about something that is secret: *Don't worry, not a word of this will pass my lips!* b) used to say that you have not eaten or drunk something you do not like, especially alcoholic drinks: *Junk food has never passed his lips.*

25 **die** INFORMAL a word meaning "to die," used when you want to avoid saying this directly
26 **pass gas** a polite way of saying to allow air to come from your BOWELS
27 **pass urine/stools/blood etc.** TECHNICAL to send out something as waste material or in waste material from your BLADDER or BOWELS
28 **pass water** TECHNICAL to send out URINE (=liquid waste) from your body
29 **different race etc.** [I] DISAPPROVING if someone who is not white or who is HOMOSEXUAL passes, they look and behave in a way that makes other people think they are white or HETEROSEXUAL
30 **come to pass** LITERARY OR BIBLICAL to happen

pass sth ↔ **around** *phr. v.* [T] to give something to one person in a group, who then gives it to the person next to them, and so on: *We sat in a circle, passing the bottle around.* | *They passed around the microphone so everyone could have a chance to speak.*

pass as sb/sth *phr. v.* [T] —see **pass for sb/sth** (PASS[1])

pass away *phr. v.* [I] an expression meaning "to die," used because you want to avoid upsetting someone by saying this directly: *It's been over a year since Mrs. Brock passed away.*

pass by *phr. v.* **1** [I,T] to move past or go past a person, place, vehicle etc. on your way to another place: *I was just passing by so I thought I'd stop for a visit.* | [**pass by sb/sth**] *We saw an old woman pass by our window.* —see also PASSERBY **2** [T **pass** sb **by**] if something passes you by, it is there but you do not get any profit or advantage from it: *I never went to college – somehow the opportunity just passed me by.*

pass sth ↔ **down** *phr. v.* [T often passive] to give something or teach something, such as knowledge or traditions, to people who are younger than you or live after you: [**pass sth down (from sb) to sb**] *These remedies have been passed down from generation to generation.*

pass for sb/sth *phr. v.* [T] if someone or something passes for something else, people think that they are that thing, although they are not really: *Even though Shawn's only 17, he's so big and tall he could pass for 21.* | *It's amazing what passes for entertainment on TV* (=what bad quality things people will accept as entertainment).

pass sb/sth **off** *phr. v.* [T] to try to make people think that something or someone is something that it is not or they are not, especially someone important or something valuable: [**pass sb/sth off as sth**] *They tried to pass the crystals off as diamonds.* | *The agents managed to pass themselves off as wealthy businessmen.*

pass on *phr. v.* **1** [T **pass** sth ↔ **on**] to tell someone a piece of information that someone else has told you: [**pass sth on to sb**] *I'll pass your suggestion on to the committee.* **2** [T **pass** sth **on**] to give something to someone else, usually after another person has given it to you: *Take one copy and pass the rest on to the next person.* **3** [T **pass** sth ↔ **on**] a) to infect someone with an illness that you have: *I don't want to pass on my cold to the baby, so I'd better not get too close.* | *The virus can be passed on during unprotected sex.* b) to give something, especially a disease, to your children through your GENES **4** [T **pass** sth **on**] to make someone else pay the cost of something: *Any increase in wage costs is bound to be passed on to the consumer.* **5** [I] an expression meaning "to die," used when you want to avoid saying this directly: *David's father passed on last year.*

pass out *phr. v.* **1** [I] to faint: *It was so hot in there I thought I was going to pass out.* **2** [T **pass** sth ↔ **out**] to give something to each one of a group of people: *Could you help me pass out the worksheets?*

pass sb/sth **over** *phr. v.* [T] **1** [**pass** sb ↔ **over**, usually passive] if you pass over someone for a job, you give the job to someone else who is younger or lower in the organization than they are: **get/be passed over for (a) promotion** (=the job was given to someone else) **2** [**pass over** sth] if you pass over a remark or a subject in a conversation, you do not spend any time discussing it: *I decided to pass over the fact that he had lied on his resume.*

pass sth ↔ **up** *phr. v.* [T] to not make use of an

invitation, opportunity, offer etc.: *I couldn't pass up the peach cobbler, which was great.* | **pass up a chance/opportunity/offer** etc. *You shouldn't pass up the opportunity to visit Florence while in Italy.* | **too good/tempting/cheap** etc. **to pass up** *The money was too good to pass up.*

USAGE NOTE: PASS

WORD CHOICE: pass, passed, past
Remember that **passed** is the past tense and past participle of the verb *pass: I think we just passed Rick's house a second ago.* **Past** is used as a preposition or an adverb: *She walked right past us without even saying hello.* | *Just then, Mike drove past in his new Jeep.* **Past** can also be an adjective: *the past few weeks* or a noun: *In the past, people didn't have as much free time.*

---

^{sw} **pass²** *n.* [C]
1 **official paper** an official paper which shows that you are allowed to enter a building, area etc.: *Students must obtain a pass before leaving campus.* | **movie/zoo/museum** etc. **pass** (=a pass that allows you to enter a movie, zoo etc.) *Receive a free pass to Disneyland when you stay more than two nights at the Hilton.*
2 **bus/train** a special ticket you buy which allows you to ride a bus or train for a specific length of time, such as a week or a month
3 **sports** a single act of kicking, throwing, or hitting a ball etc. to another member of your team: *Davis scored on a 40-yard pass from Elway.*
4 **mountain road** a road or path going through a place that is difficult to cross, especially over a mountain: *a narrow mountain pass* —see picture on page 428
5 **make a pass at sb** INFORMAL to try to kiss or touch another person with the intention of having sex with them
6 **movement past** **a)** a single movement of an aircraft over a place, especially while it is attacking: *They scored a direct hit of the target on their second pass.* **b)** an act of moving past or over something: *Comet Shoemaker-Levy passed through our solar system and crashed into Jupiter July 16, 1994.*
7 **the first/next** etc. **pass** the first, next etc. stage in a process, especially one which involves gradually improving something or removing unwanted things: *This will be our final editing pass before we send the book to be printed.*

pass·a·ble /ˈpæsəbəl/ *adj.* 1 good enough to be satisfactory or acceptable, though not very good: *Linda speaks passable Arabic.* 2 [not before noun] a road or river that is passable is not blocked, so you can travel along or across it: *Despite the snow, all the major highways in upstate New York were still passable.* —**passably** *adv.: passably well*

^{sw} **pas·sage** /ˈpæsɪdʒ/ *n.*
1 **narrow way** also **passageway** [C] a long narrow area with walls on either side, which connects one room or place to another: *an underground passage*
2 **of a law** [U] the process of getting a BILL through Congress so that it can become law: *In March, the district won passage of a $47 million measure to repair city streets.*
3 **way through** [C usually singular] a way through or to something: *The refugees risked crossing the dangerous ocean passage to Florida.*
4 **from a book** etc. [C] a short part of a book, poem, speech, piece of music etc.: *a passage from the Bible*
5 **movement** [U] FORMAL the action of going across, over, along etc. something: *The sun rose as the Delta Queen made steady passage up the Ohio River.*
6 **time** [U] the passing of time: [+ of] *Despite the passage of half a century, tension still exists between the two countries.*
7 **inside a body** [C] a tube in your body that air or liquid can pass through: *nasal passages*
8 **trip** [singular] OLD-FASHIONED travel by ship: [+ to] *My parents couldn't afford the passage to America.* —see also **rite of passage** (RITE (2))

pas·sage·way /ˈpæsɪdʒˌweɪ/ *n. plural* **passageways** [C] a PASSAGE (1)

Pas·sa·ma·quod·dy /ˌpæsəməˈkwɑdi/ a Native American tribe from the northeastern area of the U.S.

pass·book /ˈpæsbʊk/ *n.* [C] a book in which a record is kept of the money you put into and take out of a SAVINGS ACCOUNT

pas·sé /pæˈseɪ/ *adj.* not modern or fashionable anymore. *Neon colors are already passé*

pas·sel /ˈpæsəl/ *n.* [C usually singular] OLD-FASHIONED a group of people or things: [+ of] *a whole passel of kids*

pas·sen·ger /ˈpæsəndʒɚ/ *n.* [C] someone who is traveling in a vehicle, airplane, boat etc., but is not driving it or working on it: *About 70 of the train's 500 passengers were injured in the crash.* | **passenger train/car/ship** (=for people, not for goods) ^{sw}

^P

passenger seat /ˈ... ˌ./ *n.* [C] the seat in the front of a vehicle next to the driver —see picture on page 427

pass·er·by /ˌpæsɚˈbaɪ/ *n. plural* **passersby** [C] someone who is walking past a place by chance: *The robbery was witnessed by several passersby.*

pass·ing¹ /ˈpæsɪŋ/ *adj.* [only before noun] 1 going past: *Noise from the passing traffic could be heard from the backyard.* 2 short, or disappearing after only a short time; BRIEF¹: *a passing glance* | *passing fashions* | *He didn't even give the matter a* **passing thought**. 3 **with each passing day/week** etc. continuously as time passes: *The costs of medical insurance seem to increase with each passing year.* 4 **a passing knowledge/interest/acquaintance** etc. a very slight knowledge of something, interest in something etc.: *Barnes claims he had only a passing knowledge of the two suspects.*

passing² *n.* [U] 1 **in passing** if you say something in passing, you mention it while you are mainly talking about something else: **mention/say/note sth in passing** *The human rights issue was mentioned, but only in passing.* 2 the fact of something ending or disappearing: *the passing of the Cold War* 3 the act or skill of throwing or kicking the ball to another member of your team: *They lost the game partly because of ineffective passing.* 4 **the passing of time/ the years** the process of time going by: *The passing of the years has not weakened his artistic ability.* 5 **sb's passing** an expression meaning someone's death, used when you want to avoid saying this directly: *Celebrities gathered to mourn the passing of Jacobson.*

pas·sion /ˈpæʃən/ *n.* 1 [C,U] a very strong deeply felt emotion, especially of sexual love, anger, or belief in an idea or principle: *a sermon full of passion and inspiration* | [+ for] *Her novel is about a man's passion for a woman who is already married.* 2 [C] a very strong liking for something: *Acting is Turturro's passion.* | [+ for] *the Finns' passion for saunas* 3 **the Passion** FORMAL the suffering and death of Jesus Christ —**passionless** *adj.* —see also **a crime of passion** (CRIME (5)) ^{sw}

pas·sion·ate /ˈpæʃənɪt/ *adj.* 1 having or involving very strong feelings of sexual love: *a passionate kiss* | *a passionate love affair* 2 having or expressing a very strong feeling, especially a strong belief in an idea or principle: *Lau has shown herself to be a passionate defender of the poor.* | *a passionate speech* 3 very eager; INTENSE: [+ about] *Brian is passionate about football.* —**passionately** *adv.: He was passionately committed to the ideal of non-violence.*

pas·sion·fruit, passion fruit /ˈpæʃənˌfrut/ *n.* [C,U] a small fruit that has dry, brown skin and many seeds inside

Passion play /ˈ.. ˌ./ *n.* [C] a play telling the story of the suffering and death of Jesus Christ

pas·sive¹ /ˈpæsɪv/ *adj.* 1 tending to accept situations or things that other people do, without attempting to change them or prevent them; SUBMISSIVE: *The story's main female character is shown as an attractive but rather passive woman.* 2 not actively involved or taking part in: *The student's role in a traditional*

classroom learning environment is a passive one.
3 TECHNICAL a passive verb or sentence has as its subject the person or thing to which an action is done, as in "Two men were injured in the fire." —compare ACTIVE[1] (7) **4 passive vocabulary/knowledge** words or knowledge that you can recognize or understand, but cannot think of or use on your own: Sarah's passive vocabulary in French is quite large. —**passively** adv. —**passiveness, passivity** /pæˈsɪvəti/ n. [U]

passive[2] n. **the passive** TECHNICAL the passive form of a verb, for example "was destroyed" in the sentence "The building was destroyed by an enemy bomb." —compare ACTIVE[2]

passive re·sis·tance /ˌ.. .ˈ../ n. [U] a way of opposing or protesting against something without using violence

passive re·straint /ˌ.. .ˈ. ˌ../ also **passive restraint sys·tem** /ˌ.. .ˈ. ˌ../ n. [C] TECHNICAL a safety system such as an AIR BAG which prevents someone from moving in order to protect them in a car accident

passive smok·ing /ˌ.. ˈ../ n. [U] the act of breathing in smoke from someone else's cigarette, PIPE etc., which can damage your health —compare SECOND-HAND SMOKE

passive voice /ˌ.. ˈ./ n. **the passive voice** the PAS-SIVE[2]

pass·key /ˈpæsˌki/ n. [C] a key that will open many different locks

Pass·o·ver /ˈpæsˌoʊvɚ/ n. [U] an important Jewish religious holiday when the escape of the Jews from Egypt is remembered

pass·port /ˈpæspɔrt/ n. [C] **1** a small official document given by a government to a citizen, which proves who that person is and allows them to leave the country and enter other countries **2 passport to success/romance/happiness etc.** something that makes success, romance etc. possible and likely: Dad believed education was a passport to a better life.

pass·word /ˈpæswɚd/ n. [C] **1** a secret group of letters or numbers that must be put into a computer before you can use a system or program **2** a secret word or phrase that someone has to speak before they are allowed to enter a place such as a military camp

s w **past[1]** /pæst/ adj.
²‾¹
1 before now [only before noun] happening, done, or existing before the present time: We knew from past experience that the job would take at least two weeks. | The problems we face now are a result of past decisions.
2 recent [only before noun] a little earlier than the present, or in the period up until now: **in the past 24 hours/few weeks/year etc.** Weather conditions have worsened in the past 48 hours. | **for the past 24 hours/few weeks/year etc.** For the past 18 years, Arlene has worked as editor of the magazine.
3 former [only before noun] having achieved something in the past, or having held a particular important position in the past: **past President/ champion/heroes etc.** Bruce Jenner, a past Olympic champion
4 finished finished or having come to an end: The time is past for us to continue ignoring our differences. | The divorce is all part of Jenny's **past life**.
5 grammar [only before noun] TECHNICAL being the form of a verb that is used to show a past action or state: the past tense —see Usage Note at PASS[1]

s w **past[2]** prep. **1** further than: My house is four blocks ²‾² past the main intersection. | There's a movie theater **just past** (=a little farther away than) the bank. —see picture at PASS[1] **2** up to and beyond: You drive past the stadium on your way to work, don't you? | **right/straight past** I was so deep in thought I almost walked right past Jerry. **3** later than a particular time: It's ten past nine. | Come on Annie, it's past your bedtime. **4 I wouldn't put it past sb (to do sth)** SPOKEN used to say that you would not be surprised if someone did something bad or unusual because it is typical of them to do that type of thing:

I wouldn't put it past Colin to lie to his wife. **5 be past caring** to not care about something anymore: When we arrived, I was so sick I was way past caring where I slept. **6 be past due** something that is past due has not been paid or done by the time it should have been: Their rent is three months past due.

past[3] n. **1 the past a)** the time that existed before s w the present: Barker had tried in the past to commit ²‾² suicide. | We can study the events of the past. | Good manners seem to have become **a thing of the past** (=something that does not exist anymore). **b)** the PAST TENSE of a verb **2 it's all in the past** SPOKEN used to say that a bad experience has ended and you can now forget about it: Don't worry about what he said. It's all in the past now. **3** [C usually singular] all the things that have happened to someone or something in the time before now: She'd like to forget her past and start over. | There were certain facts about his past that could hurt his chances of being elected. | a woman with **a shady past**

past[4] adv. **1** up to and beyond a particular place: The car sped past at more than 100 miles an hour. **2 go past** if a period of time goes past, it passes: Several days went past without even a phone call.

pas·ta /ˈpɑstə/ n. [U] an Italian food made from flour, s w eggs, and water and cut into various shapes, usually ‾³ eaten with a SAUCE

paste[1] /peɪst/ n. **1** [U] a soft mixture made from crushed solid food that is used in cooking or is spread on bread: tomato paste **2** [U] a type of glue that is used for sticking paper onto things: wallpaper paste **3** [C,U] a soft thick mixture that can easily be shaped or spread: Pound the ingredients together into a smooth paste. **4** [U] TECHNICAL artificial diamonds or other artificial stones

paste[2] v. **1** [T always + adv./prep.] to stick paper to a surface using paste: [**paste sth on/over/across etc.**] Newspaper was pasted over the windows. | Friends had pasted his picture on billboards around the campus. **2** [I,T] to make words appear in a new place on a computer screen **3** [T] INFORMAL to defeat someone easily in a game or other competition: Florida State pasted South Carolina 59–0. —see also PASTING

paste·board /ˈpeɪstbɔrd/ n. [U] flat stiff CARDBOARD made by sticking sheets of paper together

pas·tel[1] /pæˈstɛl/ n. **1 a)** [C,U] a small colored stick used for drawing pictures, made of a substance like CHALK **b)** [C] a picture drawn with pastels: a pastel portrait **2** [C usually plural] a soft pale color, such as pale blue or pink

pastel[2] adj. [only before noun] **1** a pastel color is pale and light: pastel blue **2** drawn using pastels: the child's pastel drawing

Pas·ter·nak /ˈpæstɚˌnæk/, **Bor·is** /ˈbɔrɪs/ (1890–1960) a Russian poet and writer, best known for his NOVEL about the Russian revolution DOCTOR ZHIVAGO

Pas·teur /pæˈstɚ/, **Lou·is** /ˈlui/ (1822–1895) a French SCIENTIST who established the study of MICROBIOLOGY, and proved the disease can be caused by GERMS

pas·teur·ize /ˈpæstʃəˌraɪz, -stə.raɪz/ v. [T] to heat a liquid using a special process that kills any BACTERIA in it —**pasteurization** /ˌpæstʃərəˈzeɪʃən, -stərə-/ n. [U]

pas·tiche /pæˈstiʃ/ n. **1** [C] a work of art that consists of a variety of different styles put together: [+ of] Jong's novel is a pastiche of journals, letters, and interviews. **2** [C + of] a piece of writing, music etc. that is deliberately made in the style of another artist **3** [U] the style or practice of making works of art in either of these ways

pas·time /ˈpæs-taɪm/ n. [C] something that you do in your free time because you find it enjoyable or interesting: A Gallup poll found gardening to be America's leading pastime.

past·ing /ˈpeɪstɪŋ/ n. **1** [singular] INFORMAL an easy defeat of an opponent in a game or other competition: UNC continued their winning streak, with a 93–47 pasting of Eastern Michigan. **2** [U] the act of making words appear in a new place on a computer screen: cutting and pasting

past mas·ter /ˌ. ˈ../ *n.* [C] someone who is very skilled at doing something, and has done it many times before: [+ at] *Duvall is a past master at playing cowboy roles.*

pas·tor /ˈpæstə/ *n.* [C] a Christian priest in some Protestant churches —see Usage Note at PRIEST

pas·tor·al /ˈpæstərəl/ *adj.* **1** [usually before noun] relating to the duties of a priest, minister etc. toward the members of their religious group: *Father Brackley did pastoral work in El Salvador.* **2** LITERARY typical of the simple peaceful life in the country: *The Heber Valley is a pastoral spot ringed by mountains.*

past par·ti·ci·ple /ˌ. ˈ..../ *n.* [C] TECHNICAL a participle that can be used in compound forms of a verb to show the PASSIVE² or the PERFECT³ tenses (for example "broken" in "I have broken my leg"), and sometimes also as an adjective (for example "broken" in "a broken leg")

past per·fect /ˌ. ˈ../ *n.* **the past perfect** TECHNICAL the form of a verb that shows that the action described by the verb was completed before a particular time in the past, formed in English with "had" and a past participle, for example "I had already met her at a previous party" —**past perfect** *adj.*

pas·tra·mi /pəˈstrɑmi/ *n.* [U] smoked BEEF that contains a lot of SPICES

pas·try /ˈpeɪstri/ *n. plural* **pastries** **1** [U] a mixture of flour, fat, and milk or water, used to make the outer part of baked foods such as PIES **2** [C] a small sweet cake, made using this substance: *a Danish pastry*

past tense /ˌ. ˈ./ *n.* **the past tense** TECHNICAL the form of a verb that shows that the action or state described by the verb happened or existed before the present time: *All the verbs in this exercise are in the past tense.*

pas·tur·age /ˈpæstʃərɪdʒ/ *n.* [U] pasture

pas·ture¹ /ˈpæstʃə/ *n.* [C,U] **1** a field or area of land that is covered with grass and is used for cattle, sheep etc. to eat: *a cow pasture* **2 put sth out to pasture** to move cattle, horses etc. into a field to feed on the grass **3 put sb out to pasture** INFORMAL to make someone leave their job because you think they are too old to do it well **4 greener/new pastures** a new job, place, or activity, which you think will be better or more exciting: *Butler decided to head off for greener pastures in Los Angeles.*

pasture² *v.* [T] to put animals outside in a field to feed on the grass

pas·ture·land /ˈpæstʃəˌlænd/ *n.* [U] pasture

past·y¹ /ˈpeɪsti/ *adj.* a pasty face looks very pale and unhealthy

pasty² *n. plural* **pasties** [C usually plural] a small cover for the NIPPLE that NUDE (=without clothes) dancers, models etc. wear

pasty-faced /ˈ.. ˌ./ *adj.* having a very pale face that looks unhealthy

PA sys·tem /ˌ. ˈ. ˌ../ also **public-address system** *n.* [C] an electrical system used to make a person's voice loud enough for large numbers of people to hear it

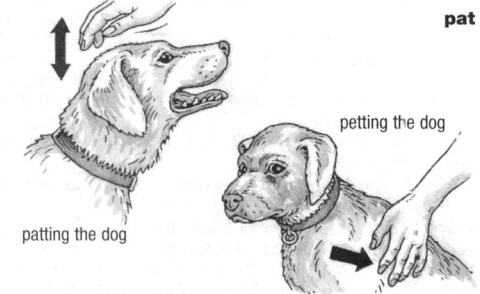

pat

petting the dog

patting the dog

pat¹ /pæt/ *v.* **patted, patting** [T] **1** to touch someone or something lightly with your hand flat: *Nancy patted her pillow, trying to make herself more*

---

comfortable. | [pat sb on the arm/head/back etc.] *I hate it when men pat me on the head.* **2 pat sth dry** to dry something by touching it lightly with a cloth or paper: *Rinse the fish and then pat them dry with paper towels.* **3 pat sb/yourself on the back** to praise someone or feel pleased with yourself for doing something well: *She should pat herself on the back and take a well-earned break.* **4** to touch something with your hand flat in order to shape it: [pat sth into/down] *Pat the dough into a 9-inch square.*

pat sb **down** *phr. v.* [T] to search someone for hidden weapons, drugs etc. by feeling their body with your hands

pat² *n.* [C] **1** a friendly act of touching someone with your hand flat: *Coach Brown gave him a pat on the shoulder.* **2 a pat of butter** a small flat piece of butter **3 a pat on the back** INFORMAL praise for something that you have done well: *She should pat herself on the back and take a well-earned break.* **3 a pat on the back** INFORMAL praise for something that you have done well: *I think you all deserve a pat on the back for your hard work.* **4** the sound made by hitting something lightly with a flat object

pat³ *adj.* a pat answer or explanation seems too quick and too simple, and sounds as if it has been used before: *There are no pat answers or simple solutions to this.*

pat⁴ *adv.* **1 have sth down pat** to know something thoroughly so that you can say it, perform it etc. immediately without thinking about it **2 stand pat** to refuse to change your opinion or decision

Pat·a·go·nia /ˌpætəˈgoʊnyə/ a large area in southern Argentina, which has a small population and many sheep farms

patch¹ /pætʃ/ *n.* [C]

1 part of an area a part of an area that is different or looks different from the parts that surround it: *There were some darker patches on the carpet.* | **patch of dirt/grease/ice** etc. *Patches of weeds had grown up all around the yard.* | **patch of light/sky** *Patches of light from the houses glowed in the darkness.*

patch

2 over a hole a small piece of material used to cover a hole in something: *Both knees of his jeans had patches on them.*

3 fruits/vegetables a small area of ground where fruit or vegetables are grown: *a pumpkin patch*

4 eye a piece of material that you wear over your eye to protect it when it has been hurt

5 time a particular period of time, especially one when you are experiencing a lot of problems: *Morris is going through one of the roughest patches of his presidency.*

6 decoration a small piece of cloth with words or pictures on it that you can sew onto clothes

7 computer a small computer program that is temporarily added to another program to make it work better

8 skin a small piece of material you stick to your skin that sends medicine into your body: *a nicotine patch*

patch² *v.* [T] to put a piece of material over a hole in order to repair it, for example in a piece of clothing

patch sth ↔ **together** *phr. v.* [T] to make something quickly or carelessly from a number of different pieces or ideas: *The three shacks had been patched together from wood scraps.*

patch sth/sb ↔ **up** *phr. v.* [T] **1** to end an argument because you want to stay friendly with someone: *She wanted to patch up her marriage after a decade of separation.* | *You should make an effort to patch things up with John.* **2** to repair something by adding a new piece of material to it: *Road crews are working overtime to patch up potholes.* **3** to give quick and basic medical treatment to someone who is hurt: *Soldiers with minor injuries were patched up and sent back into battle.*

pa·tchou·li /pə'tʃuli/ *n.* [U] a type of PERFUME made from the leaves of an Asian bush.

patch pock·et /ˌ. '../ *n.* [C] a pocket made by sewing a square piece of cloth onto a piece of clothing

patch·work /'pætʃwɚk/ *n.* [U] **1** a type of sewing in which many colored squares of cloth are sewn together to make one large piece: *a patchwork quilt* **2 a patchwork of ideas/techniques etc.** a combination of many different ideas etc.: *a patchwork of architectural styles* **3 a patchwork of fields/hills etc.** a pattern that fields, hills etc. seem to make when you see them from far above

patch·y /'pætʃi/ *adj.* **1** happening or existing in an irregular way in a number of small separate areas: *patchy fog* | *The grass looked pretty patchy.* **2** not complete enough to be useful: *His knowledge of French remained pretty patchy.* | *patchy evidence* —**patchiness** *n.* [U]

pate /peɪt/ *n.* [C] OLD USE the top of your head: *his bald pate*

pâ·té /pɑ'teɪ, pæ-/ *n.* [U] a smooth soft substance made from meat or fish that can be spread on bread

pa·tel·la /pə'tɛlə/ *n.* [C] TECHNICAL your KNEECAP —see picture at SKELETON

pa·tent[1] /'pæt̮nt/ *n.* **1** [C] a special document that says that you have the right to make or sell a new INVENTION or product, and that no one else is allowed to do so: [+ **on/for**] *In 1884, Richards received a patent on a new type of bicycle.* **2** [U] the right given by this document to make or sell something that no one else is allowed to copy: *These drugs are still protected by patent.*

patent[2] *adj.* [only before noun] **patent lie/impossibility/nonsense etc.** FORMAL used to emphasize that something is clearly a lie, clearly impossible etc.; OBVIOUS —see also PATENTLY

patent[3] *v.* [T] to officially obtain a patent for something such as a new invention or product: *Cox made millions by patenting a device used in steel production.*

patent leath·er /ˌ. '../ *n.* [U] shiny, usually black, leather: *a patent leather handbag*

pa·tent·ly /'pæt̮ntli/ *adv.* FORMAL a word meaning "very clearly," used to emphasize that something is clearly bad and no reasonable person could disagree with the fact: *Their marketing strategy has patently failed to work.* | *patently false/unfair/ridiculous etc.* a patently false accusation

patent pend·ing /ˌ. '../ TECHNICAL a phrase written on a product to show that a patent for that product is in the process of being considered

pa·ter·fa·mil·i·as /ˌpɑtɚfə'miliəs, ˌpæ-, ˌpeɪ-/ *n.* [C] FORMAL a father or a man who is the head of a family

pa·ter·nal /pə'tɚnl/ *adj.* **1** paternal feelings or behavior are like those of a father for his children: *Professor Johnson was always there for paternal advice.* **2 paternal grandmother/uncle/grandfather etc.** your father's mother, brother etc. —**paternally** *adv.* —compare MATERNAL

pa·ter·nal·ism /pə'tɚnl̩ˌɪzəm/ *n.* [U] a way of controlling people or organizations, in which people are protected and their needs are satisfied, but they do not have any freedom or responsibility

pa·ter·nal·is·tic /pəˌtɚnl'ɪstɪk/ *adj.* a paternalistic person, government, company etc. takes good care of the people it is responsible for, but also limits their freedom and makes all the important decisions for them: *The company had the reputation of being an old-fashioned, paternalistic employer.*

pa·ter·ni·ty /pə'tɚnəti/ *n.* [U] LAW the fact of being the father of a particular child, or the question of who the child's father is: *A DNA test should establish Wright's paternity of the child.*

paternity leave /.'... ,./ *n.* [U] a period of time away from work that a father of a new baby is allowed —compare MATERNITY LEAVE

paternity suit /.'... ,./ *n.* [C] a legal action in which a mother asks a court of law to say officially that a particular man is the father of her child

path /pæθ/ *n. plural* **paths** /pæðz, pæθs/ [C]
1 **track** a track that people walk along over an area of ground: *a path through the woods* | *Students had worn a path across the courtyard.*
2 **way through** a way through something, made by opening a space to allow you to move forward: *Workers at the plant found their own path was blocked by protesters.* | [+ **through**] *Police cleared a path through the crowd.*
3 **direction** the direction or line along which someone or something moves: *The tornado destroyed everything in its path.* | *the Earth's path around the sun*
4 **plan** a plan or series of actions that helps you to achieve something, especially over a long period of time: *a career path* | [+ **to**] *our country's path to economic recovery*
5 sbs' paths cross if two people's paths cross, they meet by chance: *It was not until 1989 that our paths crossed again.* —see also **beat a path (to sb's door)** (BEAT[1] (27)), FLIGHT PATH, **lead sb down the garden/primrose path** (LEAD[1] (17))

pa·thet·ic /pə'θɛt̮ɪk/ *adj.* **1** something or someone that is pathetic is so useless, unsuccessful, or badly done that they annoy you: *The movie's special effects are absolutely pathetic.* | *You're pathetic! Here, let me do it.* | *a pathetic attempt at seduction* **2** making you feel pity or sympathy: *pathetic images of half-starved children* —**pathetically** /-kli/ *adv.*

path·find·er /'pæθˌfaɪndɚ/ *n.* [C] **1** a person who goes ahead of a group and finds the best way through unknown land **2** a person who discovers new ways of doing things

path·o·gen /'pæθədʒən/ *n.* [C] TECHNICAL something that causes disease in your body —**pathogenic** /ˌpæθə'dʒɛnɪk/ *adj.*

path·o·log·i·cal /ˌpæθə'lɑdʒɪkəl/ *adj.* **1** pathological behavior or feelings are bad or unreasonable, but also impossible to control: *a pathological fear of being alone* | *pathological gambling* | *Kern was a pathological liar.* **2** a mental or physical condition that is pathological is caused by disease **3** relating to pathology —**pathologically** /-kli/ *adv.*: *pathologically shy*

pa·thol·o·gy /pə'θɑlədʒi, pæ-/ *n.* [U] the study of the causes and effects of illnesses —**pathologist** *n.* [C]

pa·thos /'peɪθɑs, -θəs, 'pæ-/ *n.* [U] FORMAL the quality that a person, situation, or artistic work has that makes you feel pity and sadness: *The opera's mixture of comedy, pathos, and desire will break your heart.*

path·way /'pæθweɪ/ *n. plural* **pathways** [C] **1** a path **2** a way in which a process happens in the body of a person or animal: *We know about the pathways through which odors are detected.*

pa·tience /'peɪʃəns/ *n.* [U] **1** the ability to wait calmly, accept delays, or continue doing something difficult for a long time, without becoming angry or anxious: *This type of medical research requires enormous patience.* **2** the ability to accept trouble and other people's annoying behavior without complaining or becoming angry: **have no patience with/for sth** *I wouldn't have the patience to be a driving instructor.* | *Teachers soon* **lost their patience** *(=stopped being patient and got angry) with Sal's childish behavior.* | *Her constant questions were beginning to* **try my patience** *(=make me angry).* **3 the patience of a saint** a very large amount of patience: *My husband, who has the patience of a saint, has helped me a great deal.* —see also **have the patience of Job** (JOB)

pa·tient[1] /'peɪʃənt/ *n.* [C] someone receiving medical treatment from a doctor or in a hospital

patient[2] *adj.* able to wait calmly for a long time or to accept difficulties, people's annoying behavior etc. without becoming angry or anxious: *The long and patient struggle to achieve equal rights will continue.* | [+ **with**] *You have to be very patient with young learners.* —**patiently** *adv.*

pat·i·na /pə'tinə, pæ-/ *n.* [singular,U] **1** a greenish layer that forms naturally on the surface of COPPER or BRONZE **2** a smooth shiny surface that gradually develops on wood, leather, metal etc. **3 a patina of wealth/success/authority etc.** FORMAL the attractive or impressive appearance of wealth, success etc.: *The job involves a lot of foreign travel, which gives it a patina of glamour.*

pat·i·o /'pætiˌoʊ/ *n. plural* **patios** [C] a flat area with a stone floor next to a house, where people sit outside

patio door /'... ˌ./ *n.* [C usually plural] a sliding glass door that opens from a living room onto a patio

pa·tis·se·rie /pə'tisəri/ *n.* [C] a store that sells French cakes and PIES

pat·ois /'pætwɑ/ *n. plural* **patois** /-wɑ, -wɑz/ [C,U] a spoken form of a language used by the people of a small area or within a certain group that is different from the national or standard language: *a patois of the Louisiana backwoods* | *the patois of lawyers* —compare CREOLE (1), DIALECT

pat. pend. TECHNICAL the written abbreviation of PATENT PENDING

patri- /peɪtrə, pætrə/ *prefix* **1** relating to fathers: *patricide* (=killing one's father) **2** relating to men: *a patriarchal society* (=controlled by men) —compare MATRI-

pa·tri·arch /'peɪtriˌɑrk/ *n.* [C] **1** an old man who is respected as the head of a family or tribe —compare MATRIARCH **2** a BISHOP in the early Christian church **3** a chief BISHOP of the Orthodox Christian churches

pa·tri·arch·al /ˌpeɪtri'ɑrkəl/ *adj.* **1** a patriarchal family, social system, way of thinking etc. is one in which men control things and have all the power: *To many feminists, marriage is an inherently patriarchal institution.* | *patriarchal attitudes* **2** connected with a patriarch: *patriarchal authority*

pa·tri·arch·y /'peɪtriˌɑrki/ *n. plural* **patriarchies** [C,U] **1** a social system in which men have all the power **2** a social system in which the oldest man rules his family and passes power and possessions on to his sons —compare MATRIARCHY

pa·tri·cian /pə'trɪʃən/ *adj.* **1** having the appearance, manners, way of speaking etc. that is typical of people from the highest social class; ARISTOCRATIC: *Peterson's patrician image* **2** belonging to the governing classes in ancient Rome —compare PLEBEIAN[2] —**patrician** *n.* [C]

pat·ri·cide /'pætrəˌsaɪd/ *n.* [U] FORMAL the crime of murdering your father —compare MATRICIDE, PARRICIDE

Pat·rick, Saint /'pætrɪk/ (A.D. ?389–?461) the PATRON SAINT of Ireland, who helped to spread the Christian religion there

pat·ri·mo·ny /'pætrəˌmoʊni/ *n.* [U] **1** the art, natural RESOURCES, valuable objects etc. of a country: *the national patrimony of Canada* **2** FORMAL property given to you after the death of your father, which was given to him by your grandfather etc.; INHERITANCE —**patrimonial** /ˌpætrə'moʊniəl/ *adj.*

pa·tri·ot /'peɪtriət/ *n.* [C] APPROVING someone who loves their country and is willing to defend it

pa·tri·ot·ic /ˌpeɪtri'ɑtɪk/ *adj.* APPROVING having or expressing a great love of your country: *patriotic songs* | *Relatives remembered him as a deeply patriotic man.* —**patriotism** /'peɪtriəˌtɪzəm/ *n.* [U] —compare NATIONALISTIC

pa·trol[1] /pə'troʊl/ *v.* **patrolled, patrolling** [I always + adv./prep., T] **1** to go around the different parts of an area or building at regular times to check that there is no trouble or danger: *Riot police patrolled the hotel.* | *Brook had been wounded while patrolling on the border.* **2** to drive or walk again and again around an area in a threatening way: *Striking workers armed with steel pipes patrolled the shipyard.*

patrol[2] *n.* **1** [C,U] the act of going around different parts of an area at regular times to check that there is no trouble or danger: *Police have increased patrols in some neighborhoods.* | *Warships on patrol in the Red Sea spotted two enemy jets.* | **patrol boat/car/ helicopter etc.** (=used by the military or police) **2** [C] a group of police, soldiers, airplanes etc. sent

to patrol a particular area: *the US border patrol* **3** [C] a small group of BOY SCOUTS —see also HIGHWAY PATROL

patrol car /.'. ˌ./ *n.* [C] a police car that drives around the streets of a city

pa·trol·man /pə'troʊlmən/ *n. plural* **patrolmen** /-mən/ [C] a police officer who regularly walks or drives around a particular area to prevent crime from happening

pa·tron /'peɪtrən/ *n.* [C] **1** someone who supports a person, organization, or activity, especially by giving money: *Many artists were dependent on wealthy patrons.* | [+ of] *The Caliph was a great patron of astronomy and science.* **2** FORMAL someone who uses a particular store, restaurant, or hotel —compare CUSTOMER (1)

pa·tron·age /'peɪtrənɪdʒ, 'pæ-/ *n.* [U] **1** FORMAL the fact of being a customer of a particular store, restaurant or hotel: *Thank you for your patronage.* **2** the support, especially financial support, that is given by a patron to a person, activity, or organization: *a patron of the museum* **3** a system by which someone in a powerful position gives people generous help or important jobs in return for their support

pa·tron·ize /'peɪtrəˌnaɪz, 'pæ-/ *v.* [T] **1** to talk to someone or treat someone as if they are unable to understand things or do things: *She's almost 90, but she gets very annoyed with anyone who tries to patronize her.* **2** FORMAL to use or visit a store, restaurant etc.: *It's a charming little restaurant which is mostly patronized by locals.* **3** to support or give money to an organization or activity

pa·tron·iz·ing /'peɪtrəˌnaɪzɪŋ/ *adj.* talking to someone or treating someone as if you think they are stupid, unimportant, or unable to do things: *To its critics, "affirmative action" is seen as patronizing to women and minorities.* | **patronizing attitude/manner/ tone etc.** *the senator's patronizing attitude to the public*

patron saint /ˌ.. './ *n.* [C] a Christian SAINT (=very holy person) who is believed to give special protection to a particular place, activity, or person: [+ of] *St. Christopher, the patron saint of travelers*

pat·sy /'pætsi/ *n. plural* **patsies** [C] INFORMAL someone who is easily tricked or deceived, especially into taking the blame for someone else's crime

pat·ter[1] /'pætɚ/ *v.* [I] to make the quiet sound of something hitting a surface lightly, quickly, and again and again: [+ on] *Rain pattered on the tin roof of the shack.*

patter[2] *n.* **1** [singular] the repeated sound of something hitting a surface lightly and quickly: [+ of] *the patter of raindrops* **2** [U,singular] fast, continuous, and often amusing talk, used for example by someone telling jokes or trying to sell something: *My thoughts wandered as the tour guide began his patter.* | *a salesman's patter* **3 the patter of tiny feet** HUMOROUS used to mean that someone is going to have a baby soon: *Are we going to hear the patter of tiny feet?*

pat·tern[1] /'pætɚn/ *n.* [C]
1 of events the regular way in which something happens, develops, or is done: *San Diego has a very regular weather pattern.* | *behavior patterns* | [+ of] *If you've set a pattern of overspending, try to break it this year.* | **follow/fit a pattern** *Romantic novels tend to follow a fixed pattern.*
2 design **a)** a regularly repeated arrangement of shapes, colors, or lines on a surface, usually intended as decoration: *Eventually, he decided on a suit with a blue-gray check pattern.* | [+ of] *a pattern of light and dark bands* **b)** a regularly repeated arrangement of sounds or words: *A sonnet has a fixed rhyming pattern.*
3 making things a shape used as a guide for making something, especially a thin piece of paper used when cutting material to make clothing: *a skirt pattern*

patterns

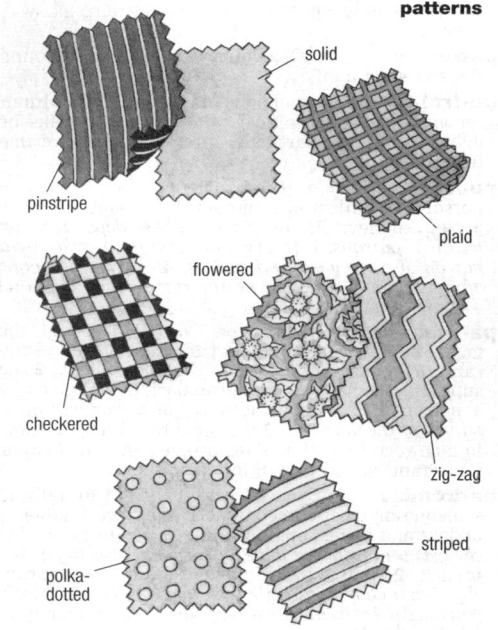

solid

pinstripe

plaid

flowered

checkered

zig-zag

polka-dotted

striped

pattern[2] *v.* [T usually passive] to design or make something in a way that is copied from something else: **pattern sth after/on sb/sth** *The restaurant was patterned after the Oak Lane Diner in Philadelphia.*

pat·terned /ˈpætənd/ *adj.* decorated with a pattern: *patterned pillowcases | floral-patterned tea cups*

pat·tern·ing /ˈpætənɪŋ/ *n.* [U] **1** TECHNICAL the development of definite ways of behaving, thinking, doing things etc. as a result of copying and repeating actions, language etc.: *cultural patterning* **2** patterns of a particular kind: *The giraffes' distinctive patterning makes them difficult to see.*

pat·ty /ˈpæti/ *n. plural* **patties** [C] a round flat piece of meat or other food: *a hamburger patty*

patty melt /ˈ.. ˌ./ *n.* [C] a flat round piece of BEEF that is cooked with cheese on top and served on bread

pau·ci·ty /ˈpɔsəti/ *n.* **a/the paucity of sth** FORMAL less of something than is needed: *Tourism is limited by the paucity of affordable downtown hotel rooms.*

Paul, Saint /pɔl/ (A.D. ?3–?68) a Christian APOSTLE who wrote many of the Epistles in the New Testament of the Bible

Pau·ling /ˈpɔlɪŋ/, **Li·nus** /ˈlaɪnəs/ (1901–1994) a U.S. scientist who studied how atoms join together and form larger structures, and who strongly opposed the use of NUCLEAR WEAPONS

paunch /pɔntʃ, pɑntʃ/ *n.* [C] OFTEN HUMOROUS a man's fat stomach —**paunchy** *adj.*

pau·per /ˈpɔpɚ/ *n.* [C] OLD-FASHIONED someone who is very poor

pause[1] /pɔz/ *v.* [I] to stop speaking or doing something for a short time before starting again: *Jill paused for a moment to look at her notes. | Pausing briefly at the door, Linus straightened his tie.*

pause[2] *n.* [C] **1** a short time during which someone stops speaking or doing something before starting again: *After a brief pause, Sharon said, "You're right." | We worked for four hours without a pause. | [+ in] an awkward pause in the conversation* **2 give sb pause (for thought)** to make someone stop and consider carefully what they are doing: *High real estate prices have given potential buyers pause.* **3** a mark (⌒) over a musical note, showing that the note is to be played or sung longer than usual

pave /peɪv/ *v.* [T usually passive] **1** to cover a path, road, area etc. with a hard level surface such as blocks of stone or CONCRETE: *The road through the valley was only paved last year.* **2 pave the way for sb/sth** to make a later event or development possible by producing the right conditions: *Galileo's achievements paved the way for Newton's scientific discoveries.* —**paved** *adj.*: *a large paved courtyard* —see also **the road to hell is paved with good intentions** (ROAD (7))

pave·ment /ˈpeɪvmənt/ *n.* **1** [U] the hard surface of a road **2** [C,U] paved surface or area of any kind; PAVING: *The saint's remains are buried beneath the pavement of a little chapel.* **3 pound/hit the pavement** to work very hard to get something, especially a job, by going to a lot of different places: *For months, Garcia pounded the pavement for jobs.*

pa·vil·ion /pəˈvɪlyən/ *n.* [C] a large light structure that is built for either temporary or permanent use, especially for public entertainment or EXHIBITIONS: *More than 1,400,000 people visited the Liberty Bell pavilion last year.*

pav·ing /ˈpeɪvɪŋ/ *n.* **1** [U] material used to form a hard level surface on a path, road, area etc. **2** [U] any kind of PAVED surface

paving stone /ˈ.. ˌ./ *n.* [C] one of the flat square pieces of stone that are used to make a hard surface to walk on

Pav·lov /ˈpævləv, ˈpɑvlɔf/, **I·van Pet·ro·vich** /ˈaɪvən ˈpɛtrəvɪtʃ/ (1849–1936) a Russian scientist known especially for his work with dogs, which proved the existence of CONDITIONE*d*[2] REFLEX —**Pavlovian** /pævˈloʊviən/ *adj.*

Pav·lo·va /pɑvˈloʊvə/, **An·na** /ˈɑnə/ (1835–1931) a Russian BALLET dancer who is considered by many to have been the world's greatest ballet dancer

paw[1] /pɔ/ *n.* [C] **1** an animal's foot that has nails or CLAWS: *Our dog cut his paw on a piece of metal.* **2** INFORMAL someone's hand: *Get your paws off my pizza!*

paw[2] *v.* [I,T] **1** if an animal paws a surface, it touches or rubs one place again and again with its paw: [+ at/through/around] *Several coyotes have been seen pawing around in garbage.* **2** INFORMAL to feel or touch someone in a rough or sexual way that is offensive: *First he drank too much, then he started pawing me.*

pawn[1] /pɔn/ *n.* [C] **1** one of the eight smallest and least valuable pieces in the game of CHESS **2** someone who is controlled by a more powerful person or group, and used for the advantage of that person or group: [+ in] *The children became pawns in their parents' divorce battle.*

pawn[2] *v.* [T] to leave something valuable with a pawnbroker in order to borrow money from them

pawn sth ↔ off *phr. v.* **1 pawn sth off on sb** INFORMAL to persuade someone to buy or accept something that you want to get rid of, especially something of low quality: *They were suspected of trying to pawn off the medicines on Third World countries.* **2 pawn sb/sth ↔ off as sth** to present something in a dishonest way: *The tabloids often pawn off stories of gossip and trivia as real news.*

pawn·bro·ker /ˈpɔnˌbroʊkɚ/ *n.* [C] someone whose business is to lend people money in exchange for valuable objects

Paw·nee /ˌpɔˈni/ a Native American tribe from the midwestern region of the U.S. —**Pawnee** *adj.*

pawn·shop /ˈpɔnʃɑp/ *n.* [C] a pawnbroker's shop

pay[1] /peɪ/ *v. past tense and past participle* **paid** **1 give money** [I,T] to give someone money for something you have bought, or for something they have done for you: *They ran off without paying. | [+ for] Let me pay for dinner this time. | [pay sb for sth] Do they pay you for mowing their lawn? | [pay sb sth] We pay our babysitter $5 an hour. | [pay sb to do sth] Maybe it would be best if we paid someone to do the filing. | pay (in) cash You get a discount for paying cash. | pay by check/by credit card If you pay by credit card there's a small extra charge.* **2 debt/bill/tax** [T] to pay money that you owe to a person, organization, or government: *Have you paid* the rent yet? | If you earn below $6000, you pay no income tax.

3 [job] [I,T] to give someone money for the job they do: *How much do they pay you?* | *Bartending can pay pretty well.* | *Some lawyers get paid over $400 an hour.*

4 pay attention (to sb/sth) to give your attention to something, by listening carefully, watching carefully etc.: *I don't think she was paying any attention to what I was saying.*

5 pay a visit to sb or **pay sb a visit** to visit someone: *I think it's time I paid my grandparents a visit.*

6 [good result] [I] if a particular action pays, it brings a good result or advantage for you: *Crime doesn't pay.* | [it pays to do sth] *In my experience, it doesn't pay to argue with her.* | [it would/it might pay to do sth] *It might pay to get your roof fixed before winter comes.* | *Taking care of your customers pays big dividends* (=brings a lot of advantages) *in the long run.*

7 [profit] **a)** [I] if a store or business pays, it makes a profit: *Although both of them worked hard, they couldn't make the business pay.* **b)** [T] to provide a certain amount as profit or in INTEREST[1] (3b): *Our fixed rate savings account currently pays 6.5% interest.*

8 pay sb a compliment to say nice things about someone's appearance, behavior etc.

9 pay tribute to sb/sth to say how much you admire or respect someone or something: *Staff and friends gathered to pay tribute to Professor Collins.*

10 pay your respects (to sb) FORMAL to send polite greetings to someone or to visit them: *Celebrities turned out in large numbers yesterday to pay their last respects* (=go to someone's funeral).

11 pay for itself if something you buy pays for itself, it helps you to save as much money as you paid for it: *Installing solar film on the windows will pay for itself.*

12 pay the penalty/price to experience something bad as a result of a decision or mistake you have made: *She makes plenty of money, but there's a high price to pay in terms of long hours.* | [pay the price/penalty for (doing) sth] *I'm now paying the penalty for not saving enough money for retirement.*

13 sb has paid their debt to society used to say that someone who has done something illegal has been fully punished for it: *After 20 years in jail, Murray feels he has paid his debt to society.*

14 pay your way to pay for everything that you need without having to depend on anyone else for money: *Pfeiffer worked as a shipping clerk to pay his way through college.*

15 pay through the nose (for sth) INFORMAL to pay far too much for something: *Many people end up paying through the nose for their car insurance policies.*

16 pay lip service to sth to say that you support or agree with something without doing anything to prove your support: *City leaders are just paying lip service to affordable housing.*

17 pay your dues if you pay your dues, you work at the lowest levels of a profession or organization in order to earn the right to move up to a better position: *Now a news anchorman, Shaw paid his dues as a reporter.*

18 pay a call on sb or **pay sb a call** OLD-FASHIONED to visit someone

19 pay court to sb OLD-FASHIONED to treat someone, especially a woman, with great respect and admiration

pay sb/sth ↔ **back** *phr. v.* [T] **1** to give someone the money that you owe them; REPAY: *Bob said he would pay me back on Wednesday.* | *You still have to pay back your student loans, don't you?* | [pay sb back (for) sth] *Did you pay Alice back for lunch?* —see picture at LEND **2** to make someone suffer for doing something wrong or bad to you: [pay sb back for sth] *I still haven't paid him back for the way he embarrassed me at the party.*

pay sth ↔ **in/into** *phr. v.* [T] to put money in your bank account, a RETIREMENT account etc.: *If you have a pension fund, consider increasing the amount you pay in each month.* | [pay sth into sth] *The check for $250 was paid into your account on Friday.*

pay off *phr. v.* **1** [T pay sth ↔ off] to pay someone all the money you owe them: *Ed was driving a taxi on the weekends to pay off all his debts.* **2** [I] if a plan or attempt or your hard work pays off, it brings success after a long time: *My persistence finally paid off when they called me in for an interview.* **3** [T pay sb ↔ off] to pay someone to keep quiet about something illegal or dishonest: *According to rumors, several witnesses in the trial were paid off.* —see also PAYOFF

pay out *phr. v.* **1** [I,T pay sth ↔ out] to pay a lot of money for something: *Our company pays out a huge amount in health benefits.* | *As long as your kids are living with you, you just have to keep paying out.* **2** [T pay sth ↔ out] to allow a piece of rope to unwind —see also PAYOUT

pay sth ↔ **over** *phr. v.* [T] to make an official payment of money: [pay sth over to sb] *Clancy's share of the inheritance is to be paid directly over to him.*

pay up *phr. v.* [I,T] to pay money that you owe, especially when you do not want to or you are late: *In most cases, Fadely said, people pay up in response to the first notice the IRS sends them.*

pay² *n.* [U] **1** money that you are given for doing your job; SALARY: *For most fast-food workers, the pay is around $5 an hour.* | **a pay raise/increase/cut** etc. *Workers at the plant say they haven't had a pay raise in two years.* **2 in the pay of sb** someone who is in someone else's pay is working for them, often secretly or illegally: *Several cops were in the pay of Colombian drug lords.*

USAGE NOTE: PAY

WORD CHOICE: pay, salary, wages, fee, income
Money given to someone in return for work is called **pay**: *The pay for entry-level jobs is usually quite low.* | *a big increase in your pay.* A **salary** is paid to someone regularly, for example every two weeks or twice a month, especially to professional people, managers etc.: *a salary of $100,000 a year.* **Wages** are paid by the hour, especially to people who work in restaurants or factories or on farms, and who are not managers: *Assembly-line workers' wages rose to $7.91 an hour.* A **fee** is money that some professions charge for a particular service they have done: *a lawyer's fees.* **Income** means any money you receive regularly, from work or anywhere else: *A large percentage of their income comes from their investments.*

---

pay·a·ble /ˈpeɪəbəl/ *adj.* [not before noun] **1** a bill, debt etc. that is payable must be paid: *A lab fee of $25 is payable during the first week of class.* **2 payable to sb** a check that is payable to someone has that person's name written on it and should be paid to them: *Checks should be made payable to the "Refugee Relief Fund."*

pay·back /ˈpeɪbæk/ *n.* **1** [U] INFORMAL something that harms or punishes someone who has defeated you or done something bad to you; REVENGE: *Now the Knicks want payback for the beating they received from Chicago a month ago.* **2 it's payback time** used to say that it is time to punish someone who has harmed you in the past: *For many voters, this election is payback time for the people who raised their taxes.* **3** [C] a profit or advantage that you get later from something you have spent money on or something you have done: *Now is a good time to invest in mutual funds because the long-term paybacks are potentially large.* **4 payback period/schedule** the amount of time in which you have to pay back money you have borrowed: *a new loan package with a 15-year payback period*

pay·check /ˈpeɪtʃek/ *n.* [C] **1** a check that pays someone's salary: *a bi-weekly paycheck* **2** the amount of money someone earns: *McKinney's paycheck will be nearly $4 million for his next movie.*

pay·day /ˈpeɪdeɪ/ *n.* [U] the day on which you get your salary: *Payday here is always every other Friday.*

pay dirt, paydirt /ˈ. ./ *n.* [U] **hit/strike pay dirt** to

P

make a valuable or useful discovery: *a group of scientists who struck pay dirt*

pay·ee /ˌpeɪˈi/ *n.* [C] TECHNICAL the person to whom money, especially a check, should be paid

pay·er /ˈpeɪɚ/ *n.* [C] TECHNICAL someone who pays for something: *In the case of a disputed payment, the payer would have to show bank account records.*

pay·load /ˈpeɪloʊd/ *n.* [C] **1** the amount of goods or passengers carried by a vehicle or aircraft: *The helicopter is designed to carry a payload of 2640 pounds.* **2** the instruments and equipment carried in a SPACECRAFT: *The shuttle's main payload will be a 37,300-pound satellite.* **3** the amount of explosive that a MISSILE can carry

pay·mas·ter /ˈpeɪˌmæstɚ/ *n.* [C] **1** an official in a factory, the army etc., who gives people their pay **2** someone who pays someone else to do something, especially something illegal: *The assassin's paymasters were never identified.*

pay·ment /ˈpeɪmənt/ *n.* **1** [C] an amount of money that has been paid or must be paid: *Flood victims received a one-time payment of $2000 from the government.* | *As long as we can make our house payments, I'll be happy.* **2** [U] the act of paying: *Most hotels here only accept payment in dollars.* | *penalties for late payment of taxes* | *Doctors expect immediate payment in full* (=paying the entire amount of money) *for health services.* **3** [U] someone's reward for doing something: [+ **for**] *The only payment I got for my effort was insults.* **4 payment in kind** a way of paying for something with goods or services instead of money —see also DOWN PAYMENT

pay·off /ˈpeɪɔf/ *n.* [C] **1** an advantage or profit that you get as a result of doing something: *With electric cars, the development costs are high but there is a big environmental payoff.* **2** a payment that is made to someone, often illegally, in order to stop them from causing you trouble: *It was alleged that union leaders had received huge payoffs from the company's bosses.* **3** a payment made to someone when they are forced to leave their job —see also **pay off** (PAY¹)

pay·o·la /peɪˈoʊlə/ *n.* [U] INFORMAL **1** a secret or indirect payment made to someone who uses their influence to make people buy what your company is selling, especially to make someone play your company's records on the radio —compare BRIBE¹ **2** the practice of giving or taking these payments

pay·out /ˈpeɪaʊt/ *n.* [C] a large payment of money, for example from an insurance claim or from winning a competition, or the act of making this payment —see also **pay out** (PAY¹)

pay-per-view /ˌ. . ˈ. ./ *adj.* [only before noun] a pay-per-view television CHANNEL makes people pay for each program they watch —**pay-per-view** *n.* [U]

pay phone /ˈ. ./ *n.* [C] a public telephone that you can use when you put in coins or a CREDIT CARD

pay raise /ˈ. ./ *n.* [C] an increase in the amount of money you are paid for doing your job: *a 4.2% pay raise*

pay·roll /ˈpeɪroʊl/ *n.* **1** [C] a list of people who are employed by a company and the amount of money each of them is paid: *Burns will be on the payroll* (=a member of the company) *until January 31.* **2** [singular] the total amount that a particular company pays its workers

payroll tax /ˈ.. ˌ./ *n.* [C,U] a tax that an employer must take from workers' salaries to pay to the government

pay stub /ˈ. ./ *n.* [C] a piece of paper that shows how

pay phone

much money an employed person has been paid and how much has been taken away for tax, insurance etc.

pay tel·e·phone /ˌ. ˈ…, ˈ. ˌ…/ *n.* [C] a PAY PHONE

pay toi·let /ˌ. ˈ../ *n.* [C] a toilet that you must pay to use

pay TV /ˌ. . ˈ./ also **pay tel·e·vi·sion** /ˌ. ˈ…./ *n.* [U] television CHANNELS you must pay to watch

Paz /pɑz, pas/, **Oc·ta·vi·o** /ɑkˈtɑvioʊ/ (1914–1998) a Mexican poet

PBS *n.* [U] Public Broadcasting System; a company in the U.S. that broadcasts television programs without advertisements

PC¹ *n.* [C] a personal computer; the most common type of computer, which is used by one person at a time, for business, study, or entertainment

PC² *adj.* the abbreviation of POLITICALLY CORRECT

PCB *n.* [C] one of a group of chemicals that used to be used in industry but are very harmful to the environment

PCP *n.* **1** [U] an ANESTHETIC that is also taken as an illegal drug **2** [U] PNEUMOCYSTIS **3** [C] a PRIMARY-CARE PHYSICIAN

PCS *n.* [U] personal communications service; a communication system that allows CELLULAR PHONES to communicate with each other

pct. a written abbreviation of PERCENT

pd. the written abbreviation of "paid"

pdq /ˌpi di ˈkyu/ *adv.* SPOKEN, INFORMAL pretty damn quick; used to say that something should be done immediately: *I told her to get back here pdq.*

PDT the abbreviation of Pacific Daylight Time

P.E. *n.* [U] physical education; sports and physical activity taught as a school subject

pea /pi/ *n.* [C] **1** a round green seed that is cooked and eaten as a vegetable: *pea soup* | *frozen peas* —see picture at VEGETABLE **2** a plant that produces long green PODS that contain these seeds **3 the size of a pea/pea-sized** small in size: *a pea-sized gland at the base of the brain* **4 pea-brained** INFORMAL a stupid creature or person: *Wilkins called the governor a pea-brained idiot.* **5 like two peas in a pod** INFORMAL exactly the same in appearance, behavior etc. —see also SPLIT PEA, SWEET PEA

Pea·bod·y /ˈpiˌbɑdi, -bədi/, **Elizabeth** (1804–1894) a U.S. educator who started the first KINDERGARTEN in the U.S.

Peabody, George (1795–1869) a U.S. businessman and BANKER who gave a lot of money to help education

peace /pis/ *n.*

1 no war **a)** [U] the situation in which there is no war between countries or within a country: *Some of these children have never known a time of peace.* | *a threat to world peace* | *The U.S. is sending troops overseas again – this time to keep the peace.* | *The country is at peace with its neighbors for the first time in years.* | *peace talks/agreements/treaties* (=discussions, agreements etc. to end or prevent wars) | *The rival armies are now involved in peace negotiations.* | *peace movement/campaign/vigil* etc. (=organized efforts to prevent war) **b)** [singular] a period of time in which there is no war: *a lasting peace* | *An uneasy peace continued until 1939.*

2 no noise [U] a situation that is very calm, quiet, and pleasant: *All I want is some peace and quiet.* | *I'll leave now and let you get dressed in peace* (=without being interrupted).

3 calmness [U] the feeling of being calm, happy, and not worried: *the search for inner peace* | *Having household insurance is supposed to give you peace of mind.*

4 at peace a) someone who is at peace is calm and satisfied, especially after they have had difficult experiences. *It was hard for Owen to quit, but he is at peace with the decision.* | *Lynn never seems to be at peace with herself.* **b)** an expression meaning "dead" when you want to say this in a gentle way

5 no arguing [U] a situation in which there is no arguing or fighting between people who live or work together: *Can't we just have peace in the family?* | *a*

part of the city where Christians and Muslims live together in peace

6 make (your) peace to agree to stop fighting with a person or a group, especially by telling them you are sorry: [+ **with**] *Laurie wanted to make peace with her father before he died.*

7 **document** [singular] a formal agreement that ends a war: *In 1648 the Peace of Westphalia ended the 30 Years War.*

8 keep/hold your peace FORMAL to keep quiet even though there is something you would like to say: *She was tempted to tell them what she thought, but decided to keep her peace.*

9 rest in peace a prayer for someone who has died, said during a funeral service or written on a GRAVESTONE —see also **disturb the peace** (DISTURB (4))

peace·a·ble /ˈpisəbəl/ *adj.* **1** someone who is peaceable dislikes fighting or arguing, and tries not to get involved in fights or arguments: *A peaceable and orderly crowd staged a protest outside city hall.* **2** a peaceable situation or way of doing something is calm, without any violence or fighting: *a peaceable kingdom* —**peaceably** *adv.*

Peace Corps /ˈ. ./ *n.* **the Peace Corps** a U.S. government organization that helps poorer countries by sending VOLUNTEERS (=people who work without payment), especially young people, to teach skills in education, health, farming, etc.: *When John graduates, he'll join the Peace Corps.*

peace div·i·dend /ˈ. ˌ.../ *n.* [singular] the money saved on weapons and available for other purposes, when a government reduces its military strength because the risk of war has been reduced

peace·ful /ˈpisfəl/ *adj.* **1** quiet and calm without any worry or excitement: *It's peaceful out there in the woods.* **2** without war or fighting: *a peaceful transition from military to civilian rule* **3** deliberately avoiding any violence: *a noisy but peaceful group of demonstrators* —**peacefully** *adv.* —**peacefulness** *n.* [U]

peace·keep·ing /ˈpisˌkipɪŋ/ *adj.* **peacekeeping force/troops etc.** a group of soldiers who are sent to a place in order to stop opposing groups from fighting each other: *Traditionally, the United Nations sends peacekeeping forces to a conflict area only after a cease-fire has been agreed to.* —**peacekeeper** *n.* [C]

peace·lov·ing /ˈ. ˌ.../ *adj.* believing strongly in peace rather than war. *peace-loving nations*

peace·mak·er /ˈpisˌmeɪkər/ *n.* [C] someone who tries to persuade other people or nations to stop fighting: *The U.S. sees itself as a peacemaker in the region.*

peace march /ˈ. ./ *n.* [C] a march by people who are protesting against violence or military activities

peace of·fer·ing /ˈ. ˌ.../ *n.* [C] something you give to someone to show them that you are sorry and want to be friendly, after you have annoyed or upset them: *Mike brought in some doughnuts – I think they were a sort of peace offering.*

peace pipe /ˈ. ./ *n.* [C] a pipe which Native Americans use to smoke tobacco, which is shared in a ceremony as a sign of peace

peace·time /ˈpis-taɪm/ *n.* [U] a period of time when a nation is not fighting a war —opposite WARTIME

s w **peach** /pitʃ/ *n.* **1** [C] a round juicy yellow-red fruit
3 that has a PIT (=large rough seed) in the center and soft skin, or the tree that it grows on —see picture at FRUIT¹ **2** [U] a pale pinkish-orange color **3** [C usually singular] OLD-FASHIONED someone or something that you like very much or think is attractive: *Jan's a real peach.* **4 a peaches-and-cream complexion** smooth skin with an attractive pink color

peach fuzz /ˈ. ./ *n.* [U] INFORMAL soft light body hair, especially hair that grows on a boy's face before he becomes a man

peach·y /ˈpitʃi/ *adj.* **1** tasting or looking like a peach **2** SPOKEN, OLD-FASHIONED very good or pleasant: *Everything here's just peachy.*

pea coat /ˈ. ./ *n.* [C] a short DOUBLE-BREASTED coat made with heavy wool that is worn especially by SAILORS

pea·cock /ˈpikɑk/ *n.* [C] a large bird, the male of

which has long shiny blue and green tail feathers that it can spread out

peacock blue /ˌ.. ˈ.◂/ *n.* [U] a deep greenish-blue color —**peacock blue** *adj.*

pea green /ˌ. ˈ.◂/ *n.* [U] a light green color, like that of a PEA —**pea-green** *adj.*

pea jack·et /ˈ. ˌ../ *n.* [C] a PEA COAT

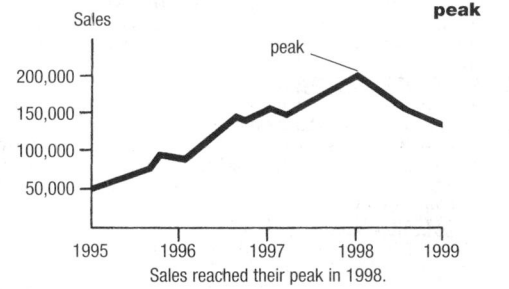

Sales reached their peak in 1998.

peak¹ /pik/ *n.* [C] **1** [usually singular] the time or s w point at which something is biggest, most successful, 3 or best: *The Dow Jones closed at 10,215 points, about 10% down from its peak* | *Pease is at the peak of his career.* | **reach/hit a peak** *LSD use reached a peak in the '60s and early '70s.* **2** the sharply pointed top of a mountain, or the whole mountain: *the Alps' snow-covered peaks* —compare SUMMIT (2) —see picture on page 428 **3** a part that forms a point above a surface or at the top of something: *Whisk the egg whites until they form stiff peaks.* —see also WIDOW'S PEAK

peak² *v.* [I] to reach the highest point or level: *Sales peaked in August, then fell sharply.* | *Commentators feel that the Bears haven't peaked yet this season (=reached their highest level of performance).* | [+ **at**] *Wind speeds peaked at 105 mph yesterday.*

peak³ *adj.* **1 peak level/rate/value etc.** the highest level, rate etc. of something: *Gasoline prices are 14% below the peak level they hit in November.* **2** a peak time or period is when the largest number of people are doing the same thing, using the same service etc.: *Hotel prices rise considerably during peak season.* —compare OFF-PEAK

peaked¹ /ˈpikɪd/ *adj.* pale and looking sick: *You're looking a little peaked this morning.*

peaked² /pikt, ˈpikɪd/ *adj.* **1** having a point at the top: *a peaked roof* **2** a peaked cap has a flat curved part at the front above the eyes

peal¹ /pil/ *n.* [C] **1** a sudden loud repeated sound, such as laughter, THUNDER, or bells ringing: [+ **of**] *We could hear peals of laughter coming from the hall.* | *the peal of church bells* **2** TECHNICAL **a)** a musical pattern made by ringing a number of bells one after the other **b)** a set of bells

peal² *v.* also **peal out** [I] if bells peal, they ring loudly: *The bells of Saint Paul's pealed out on a sleepy Sunday morning.*

Peale /pil/, **Charles** (1741–1827) a U.S. PAINTER famous for his pictures of people

Peale, Nor·man Vin·cent /ˈnɔrmən ˈvɪnsənt/ (1898–1993) a U.S. Protestant minister and SELF-HELP writer

pea·nut /ˈpinʌt/ *n.* [C] a nut which grows in a soft s w shell under the ground and which can be eaten, or 3 the plant this nut grows on: *salted peanuts*

peanut brit·tle /ˌ.. ˈ../ *n.* [U] a type of hard TOFFEE (=type of candy) with peanuts in it

peanut but·ter /ˈ.. ˌ../ *n.* [U] a soft substance made from crushed peanuts, usually eaten on bread: *a peanut butter and jelly sandwich*

peanut gal·ler·y /ˈ.. ˌ.../ *n.* [C] HUMOROUS the cheap rows of seats at the back of a theater, or the people sitting there

pea·nuts /'pinʌts/ *n.* [U] INFORMAL a very small amount of money: *I'm tired of working for peanuts*.

pear /pɛr/ *n.* [C] a sweet juicy fruit that has a round wide bottom and becomes thinner on top near the stem, or the tree that it grows on —see also PRICKLY PEAR —see picture at FRUIT¹

pearl /pɔl/ *n.*
1 jewel [C] **a)** a valuable small white round object with a silvery shine, that is formed inside the shell of an OYSTER, and is used in jewelry: *a string of pearls* | *a pearl-colored dress* **b)** an artificial copy of this jewel
2 hard substance [U] a hard shiny substance of various colors formed inside some SHELLFISH, which is used for decorating objects: *pearl buttons*
3 pearls of wisdom an expression meaning "wise remarks," often used jokingly to mean slightly stupid remarks: *Do you have any other pearls of wisdom for us?*
4 excellent thing/person [C usually singular] OLD-FASHIONED someone or something that is especially good or valuable: *a pearl of a wife*
5 liquid [C] LITERARY a small round drop of liquid: *Pearls of dew sparkled on the grass.* —see also **cast pearls before swine** (CAST¹ (22))

pearl div·er /'. ˌ../ *n.* [C] someone who swims under the water in the ocean, looking for shells that contain pearls

Pearl Har·bor /ˌ. '../ an important U.S. Navy base in Hawaii, which was attacked by Japanese planes in December 1941 without any warning. This made the U.S. start fighting in World War II

pearl on·ion /ˌ. '../ *n.* [C] a type of small white onion

pearl·y /'pɔli/ *adj.* like pearls or having the color of pearls: *a pearly white fish*

pearly gates /ˌ.. '../ *n.* [plural] **the pearly gates** INFORMAL the entrance to heaven

pearly whites /ˌ.. '../ *n.* [plural] INFORMAL, HUMOROUS your teeth

pear-shaped /'. ./ *adj.* someone, especially a woman, who is pear-shaped is larger around the waist and HIPS than around the chest

Pea·ry /'piri/, **Rob·ert** /'rɑbɔt/ (1856–1920) a U.S. EXPLORER who was leader of the first group to reach the North Pole

peas·ant /'pɛzənt/ *n.* [C] **1** a poor farmer who owns or rents a small amount of land, either in past times or in poor countries: *The economic crisis caused famine, epidemics, and peasant revolt.* **2** INFORMAL a stupid uneducated person who does not have good manners

peas·ant·ry /'pɛzəntri/ *n.* [U] **the peasantry** all the peasants of a particular country: *Bazin was believed to have wide support among the peasantry in the countryside.*

pea·shoot·er /'pi,ʃutɔ/ *n.* [C] a small tube used by children to blow small objects, especially dried PEAS, at someone or something

peat /pit/ *n.* [U] a substance formed from decaying plants under the surface of the ground in some areas, which can be burned instead of coal, or mixed with earth to help plants grow well —**peaty** *adj.*

peat moss /'. ./ *n.* [U] **1** a type of MOSS (=soft green plant) that grows in wet areas **2** pieces of this plant used to help other plants grow: *Mix the seeds with moist sand and peat moss.*

peb·ble /'pɛbəl/ *n.* [C] a small smooth stone found on the beach or on the bottom of a river —**pebbly** *adj.*

pe·can /pə'kɑn, -'kæn/ *n.* [C] a long thin sweet nut with a dark shell, or the tree that it grows on, common in the southern states of the U.S.: *pecan pie*

pec·ca·dil·lo /ˌpɛkə'dɪloʊ/ *n. plural* **peccadilloes**, **peccadillos** [C] something bad which someone does, especially involving sex, which is not regarded as very serious or important: *The public is willing to forgive him for his peccadillos.*

pec·ca·ry /'pɛkəri/ *n. plural* **peccaries** [C] a wild

animal like a pig that lives in Central and South America

peck¹ /pɛk/ *v.* **1** [I,T] if a bird pecks something it quickly moves its beak to hit, bite, or pick up something, especially food: [+ at] *Chickens peck at the corn on the ground.* —see picture at BITE¹ **2 peck sb on the cheek/forehead etc.** to kiss someone quickly and lightly —see also HENPECKED, **hunt and peck** (HUNT¹ (4))

peck at sth *phr. v.* [T] to eat only a little bit of a meal without interest.: *My kids only peck at my roasts.*

peck² *n.* [C] **1** a quick light kiss: *He gave me a peck on the cheek.* **2** an action of pecking something with a beak **3** a unit used for measuring dry substances such as fruit or grain, equal to 8 QUARTS or 8.81 liters

peck·er /'pɛkɔ/ *n.* [C] SLANG: see PENIS

pecking or·der /'.. ˌ../ *n.* [C] the social system of a particular group of people or animals, in which each one knows who is more important and less important than themselves: *He seems to have dropped down the Hollywood pecking order.* | *Nobody wants to be at the bottom of the pecking order.*

Pe·cos Bill /ˌpeɪkɑs 'bɪl/ a very strong COWBOY in old American stories

pecs /pɛks/ *n.* [plural] INFORMAL: see PECTORALS

pec·tin /'pɛktɪn/ *n.* [U] a chemical substance like sugar that is found in some fruits and is important in making JAM² (1) and JELL-O —**pectic** *adj.*

pec·to·ral /'pɛktərəl/ *adj.* relating to your chest: *pectoral muscles*

pectoral fin /ˌ... './ *n.* [C] the FIN that is on the side of a fish's head and helps it to control the direction it swims in

pec·to·rals /'pɛktərəlz/ *n.* [plural] your chest muscles: *bulging pectorals*

pe·cu·liar /pɪ'kyulyɔ/ *adj.* **1** strange, unfamiliar, or a little surprising, especially in a way that is not good: *This cheese has a peculiar smell.* | [it is peculiar that] *It seemed peculiar that no-one noticed Tammy leaving.* **2 be peculiar to sb/sth** to be a quality that only one particular person, place, or thing has: *The problem of racism is not peculiar to this country.* **3** behaving in a strange and slightly crazy way: *Martha has been a little peculiar lately.*

pe·cu·li·ar·i·ty /pɪˌkyuli'ærəti/ *n. plural* **peculiarities 1** [C] something that is a feature of only one particular place, person, situation etc.: [+ of] *The pharmacist is familiar with the peculiarities of Dr. Klein's handwriting.* **2** [C] a strange or unusual habit, quality etc.: *Margaret loved her mother, and regarded her peculiarities with a fond tolerance.* **3** [U] the quality of being strange or unfamiliar

pe·cu·liar·ly /pɪ'kyulyɔli/ *adv.* **1** peculiarly American/female/middle-class/ etc. something that is peculiarly American, female etc. is a typical feature only of Americans, only of women etc.: *a peculiarly Japanese institution* **2** in a strange or unusual way: *John and Sylvia looked at me peculiarly.*

pe·cu·ni·ar·y /pɪ'kyuni,ɛri/ *adj.* FORMAL relating to or consisting of money: *pecuniary losses*

ped·a·go·gi·cal /ˌpɛdə'gɑdʒɪkəl/ *adj.* FORMAL relating to methods of teaching or the practice of teaching: *the need to review current pedagogical practices* —**pedagogically** /-kli/ *adv.*

ped·a·go·gy /'pɛdə,goʊdʒi, -,gɑ-/ *n.* [U] FORMAL the practice of teaching, or the study of teaching

ped·al¹ /'pɛdl/ *n.* [C] **1** one of the two parts of a bicycle that you push around with your feet to make the bicycle go forward —see picture at BICYCLE¹ **2** a part in a car or on a machine that you press with your foot to control it: *the gas pedal* **3** a part on a piano or organ that you press with your foot to change the quality of the sound **4 put/press/push the pedal to the metal a)** to drive a car, truck etc. very fast **b)** to work harder or faster, especially so that you can win a game: *By the second half of the game, the Tigers had really started to put the pedal to the metal.* —**pedal-to-the-metal** *adj.*

pedal² *v.* [I,T] to ride a bicycle or other machine by

pushing pedals with your feet: *Tim got on his bike and pedaled around town.* —see also BACKPEDAL, SOFT-PEDAL

ped·al push·ers /'.. ,../ *n.* [plural] a type of pants worn by women, which reach the middle of the lower leg: *His wife was wearing pedal pushers and a sleeveless blouse.*

ped·ant /'pɛdnt/ *n.* [C] someone who pays too much attention to rules or to small unimportant details: *It is the work of a pedant, and shows no originality.* —**pedantry** *n.* [U]

pe·dan·tic /pə'dæntɪk/ *adj.* paying too much attention to rules or to small unimportant details: *Her book is informative and scholarly, but never pedantic.* —**pedantically** /-kli/ *adv.*

ped·dle /'pɛdl/ *v.* [T] **1** to sell goods that are of low quality, dangerous, illegal etc.: *She now peddles cheap jewelry on TV.* | *Melendez's gang made up to $10 million a month peddling heroin.* **2** to try to get people to accept opinions, false information etc.: *Councilman Cobb is peddling his idea for a new freeway.* —see also INFLUENCE-PEDDLING

ped·dler /'pɛdlɚ/ *n.* [C] **1** someone who sells small things either in the street or walking from place to place: *Smithson had been a rose peddler in Portland.* **2** a person who sells things, especially when they are illegal or of low quality: **drug/dope/smut peddler** —compare PUSHER

ped·er·ast /'pɛdə,ræst/ *n.* [C] a man who has sex with a boy —**pederasty** *n.* [U]

ped·es·tal /'pɛdəstl/ *n.* [C] **1** the base on which a PILLAR or STATUE stands **2 put/place sb on a pedestal** to admire someone so much that you treat them or talk about them as though they are perfect: *My last boyfriend put me on a pedestal.* **3 a pedestal table/sink etc.** a table, SINK etc. that is supported by a single COLUMN

pe·des·tri·an¹ /pə'dɛstriən/ *n.* [C] someone who is walking, especially on a city street, instead of driving a car, riding a bicycle etc.

pedestrian² *adj.* **1** [only before noun] relating to pedestrians or used by pedestrians: *pedestrian traffic* **2** ordinary, uninteresting, and without any imagination: *On the main wall was a rather pedestrian portrait of his wife.*

pedestrian cross·ing /.,... '../ *n.* [C] a CROSSWALK

pe·des·tri·an·ize /pə'dɛstriə,naɪz/ *v.* [T] to change a street or shopping area into a place where vehicles are not allowed —**pedestrianization** /pə,dɛstriənə-'zeɪʃən/ *n.* [U]

pedestrian mall /.,... './ *n.* [C] a shopping area in the center of a city where cars, trucks etc. cannot go

pe·di·a·tri·cian /,pidiə'trɪʃən/ *n.* [C] a doctor who treats children

pe·di·at·rics /,pidi'ætrɪks/ *n.* [U] the area of medicine that deals with children and their illnesses —**pediatric** *adj.*: *a pediatric hospital*

ped·i·cure /'pɛdɪ,kyʊr/ *n.* [C,U] a treatment for the feet and TOENAILS, to make them more comfortable or beautiful —**pedicurist** *n.* [C] —compare MANICURE

ped·i·gree /'pɛdə,gri/ *n.* [C,U] **1** the parents and other past family members of an animal or person, or an official written record of this **2** a person's past activities, experiences, and achievements; BACKGROUND: *Given her pedigree in the classical theater, it's not surprising that she wasn't happy working in Hollywood.*

ped·i·greed /'pɛdə,grid/ also **pedigree** *adj.* a pedigreed animal comes from a family that has been recorded for a long time and is considered to be of a very good breed: *pedigreed dogs* —compare PUREBRED, THOROUGHBRED

ped·i·ment /'pɛdəmənt/ *n.* [C] a three-sided piece of stone or other material placed above the entrance to a building, especially in the buildings of ancient Greece

pe·dom·e·ter /pə'dɑmɪtɚ/ *n.* [C] an instrument for measuring distance that has to be pushed by someone walking

ped·o·phile /'pɛdə,faɪl, 'pi-/ *n.* [C] someone who is sexually attracted to young children

pee¹ /pi/ *v.* [I] INFORMAL to pass liquid waste from your body; URINATE: *It smells like the cat peed in there.* | *I have to **go pee**.* S W

pee² *n.* [U] INFORMAL liquid waste passed from your body; URINE

peek¹ /pik/ *v.* [I] to look quickly at something, especially something that you are not supposed to see: *Billy peeked out from under his blanket.* | *No fair! You peeked!* —compare PEEP¹ (1)

peek

peek² *n.* [C] a quick look at something: ***Take a peek** and see if the cake's done.*

peek·a·boo /'pikə,bu/ *interjection n.* [U] a game played to amuse babies and young children, in which you repeatedly hide your face and then show it again, saying "peekaboo!"

peel¹ /pil/ *v.* **1** [T] to remove the skin from fruit or vegetables: *Could you peel an orange for me?* —see picture on page 425 **2** [T always + adv./prep.] to remove the outer layer from something: [+ **away/back**] *Brown peeled back the foil on his hot dog.* | *When the paint is dry, peel away the masking tape.* **3** [I] if skin, paper, or paint peels, it comes off, usually in small pieces: *I got sunburned, and now my face is peeling.* —see also **keep your eyes open/peeled** (EYE¹ (21)) S W

peel off *phr. v.* **1** [I,T **peel** sth ↔ **off**] to become loose and come off in small thin pieces, or to remove a layer of paper, paint etc.: *Jack was peeling the label off the bottle of Heineken.* | *The wallpaper was starting to peel off.* **2** [I,T **peel** sth ↔ **off**] to take your clothes off, especially if they are wet or tight: *She peeled off her jeans and began unbuttoning her shirt.* **3** [I] to leave a moving group of vehicles, aircraft etc. and go in a different direction: *The last two motorcycles peeled off to the left.*

peel out *phr. v.* [I] to suddenly make a car start moving very quickly so that it makes a loud noise: [+ **of**] *He peeled out of the driveway.*

peel² *n.* [C,U] the thick skin of some fruits and vegetables, especially the ones that you usually peel before eating: *a banana peel* —see picture at FRUIT¹

peel·er /'pilɚ/ *n.* [C] a special type of knife for removing the skin from fruit or vegetables

peel·ings /'pilɪŋz/ *n.* [plural] pieces of skin that have been removed from fruit or vegetables: *carrot peelings*

peep¹ /pip/ *v.* [I] **1** to look at something quickly and secretly, especially through a hole or opening: [+ **into/through** etc.] *One morning a reporter even peeped through her bedroom window.* **2** [always + adv./prep.] if something peeps from somewhere, it is just possible to see it: [+ **through/from** etc.] *The wreck of an old car was peeping from the weeds.* —compare PEEK¹, PEER²

peep² *n.* [C] **1 not a peep** INFORMAL not a small sound, a complaint, or a piece of information: *The rumors continue, but there hasn't been a peep out of Basinger.* | *I **didn't hear a peep out of** the kids all afternoon.* **2** a quick or secret look at something: *He got a peep at her face before she slammed the door.* **3** a short weak high sound like the sound a mouse or a young bird makes

peep·ers /'pipɚz/ *n.* [plural] OLD-FASHIONED your eyes

peep·hole /'piphoul/ *n.* [C] a small hole in a door or wall that you can see through

peep·ing Tom /,pipɪŋ 'tɑm/ *n.* [C] INFORMAL someone who secretly watches people, especially when they are undressing, having sex etc.

peep-show /'. ./ *n.* [C] **1** a type of show in which a man pays for a woman to take her clothes off while he watches through a window **2** a box containing moving pictures that you look at through a small hole or LENS

peer[1] /pɪr/ n. [C] **1** someone who is the same age as you, or has the same type of job, rank etc.: *The respect of his peers in the research community is very important to him.* —see also PEER GROUP, PEER PRESSURE **2** a member of the British NOBILITY

peer[2] v. [I always + adv./prep.] to look very carefully or hard, especially because you cannot see something well: [+ at/across/through etc.] *Peering through the fog, we saw a tall figure approaching.*

peer group /'. ./ n. [C] a group of people who are the same age or have the same type of job, rank etc.: *As children reach adolescence, peer groups become a more significant influence.*

peer·less /'pɪrlɪs/ adj. better than anyone or anything else: *B.B. King's peerless blues guitar playing*

peer pres·sure /'. ,../ n. [C] a strong feeling that you must do the same things as other people of your age if you want them to like you: *A lot of kids start drinking because of peer pressure.*

peeve /piv/ n. [C] INFORMAL something that annoys you: *One of my pet peeves is pointless meetings that go on forever.*

peeved /pivd/ adj. INFORMAL annoyed: *Murray is peeved that the club did not offer him a new contract.*

pee·vish /'pivɪʃ/ adj. easily annoyed by small and unimportant things: *The whole team was peevish after losing the game.* —**peevishness** n. [U]

pee·wee /'piwi/ n. [C] INFORMAL a small child, or a very small adult —**peewee** adj.: *a peewee football game* (=for young children)

peg[1] /pɛg/ n. [C] **1** a short piece of wood, metal etc. that fits into a hole or is fastened to a wall, used especially for hanging things on, or instead of nails for fastening things together: *Serena hung her hat on a peg.* **2 take/bring/knock sb down a peg (or two)** to make someone realize that they are not as important or as good at something as they think they are: *an arrogant young man who needed to be brought down a peg or two* **3** a wooden screw used to tighten or loosen the strings of a VIOLIN, GUITAR etc. **4** also **tent peg** a pointed piece of wood or metal that you push into the ground in order to keep a tent in the correct position; STAKE —see also **a square peg in a round hole** (SQUARE[1] (10))

peg[2] v. **pegged, pegging** [T] **1** to set prices, values, salaries etc. at a particular level, or set them in relation to something else: [peg sth to sth] *In the last century, most countries pegged their currencies to gold.* **2** to believe or say that someone has a particular type of character: [peg sb/sth as sth] *Initial reports pegged the crime as drug-related.* | *I didn't have her pegged as a troublemaker.* **3** to fasten something somewhere with a peg

peg·board /'pɛgbɔrd/ n. **1** [C,U] thin board with holes in it, into which you can put pegs or hooks to hang things on, or a piece of this **2** [C] a small piece of board with holes in it, used to record the players' points in some games, especially card games

peg leg /'. ./ n. [C] INFORMAL an artificial leg, or someone who has one, used especially regarding PIRATES

Pei /peɪ/**, I.M.** /aɪ ɛm/ (1917–) a Chinese-American ARCHITECT

Peirce /pɪrs, pərs/**, Charles San·ders** /tʃɑrlz 'sændərz/ (1839–1914) a U.S. PHILOSOPHER

pe·jor·a·tive /pɪ'dʒɔrətɪv, -'dʒɑr-/ adj. FORMAL a pejorative word or expression is used to show disapproval of or to insult someone: *For hard-line Republicans, the word "liberal" had become a pejorative term.* —**pejoratively** adv. —**pejorative** n. [C]

Pe·king /ˌpi'kɪŋ , ˌpeɪ-/ a name for the city of Beijing that was formerly used in English

Pe·king·ese, Pekinese /ˌpikə'niz / n. [C] a very small dog with a short flat nose and long silky hair

pe·lag·ic /pə'lædʒɪk/ adj. TECHNICAL relating to or living in the ocean, far from shore: *a pelagic shark*

Pe·lé /pɛ'leɪ, 'peɪleɪ/ (1940–) a Brazilian SOCCER player, considered the best player ever by many people

pel·i·can /'pɛlɪkən/ n. [C] a large water bird that catches fish for food and stores them in a deep bag of skin under its beak

pel·la·gra /pə'lægrə, -'leɪ, -'lɑ-/ n. [U] a disease caused by a lack of a type of B VITAMIN, that makes you feel tired and causes problems with your skin and CENTRAL NERVOUS SYSTEM

pel·let /'pɛlɪt/ n. [C] **1** a small hard ball made from ice, paper, food etc. **2** a small ball of metal made to be fired from a gun

pell-mell /ˌpɛl 'mɛl / adv. running or moving in a fast uncontrolled way: *Rioters were rushing pell-mell through the streets.* —**pell-mell** adj.

pel·lu·cid /pə'lusɪd/ adj. LITERARY very clear; TRANSPARENT: *a pellucid stream*

pelt[1] /pɛlt/ v. **1** [T] to attack someone or something by throwing a lot of things at them: [pelt sb/sth with sth] *Angry residents pelted Baker's car with tomatoes.* | [pelt sth at sb/sth] *Demonstrators were pelting rocks at police.* **2** [I,T] if rain or snow pelts a place or person, or if it pelts down, it is raining or snowing very heavily: *We were out in the cold rain that pelts northern Arkansas in March.* **3** [I always + adv./prep.] INFORMAL to run somewhere very fast

pelt[2] n. [C] **1** the skin of a dead animal, either with the fur or hair still on it, or with the fur or hair removed so the skin is ready to be prepared as leather: *mink pelts* **2** the fur or hair of a living animal **3 (at) full pelt** moving as fast as possible: *He ran full pelt down the street with a brick in his hand.*

pel·vic /'pɛlvɪk/ adj. within or relating to your pelvis: *a pelvic exam*

pel·vis /'pɛlvɪs/ n. [C] the set of large wide curved bones at the base of your SPINE, to which your legs are joined —see picture at SKELETON

pen[1] /pɛn/ n. [C] **1** an instrument for writing or drawing with ink: *a ballpoint pen* | *a fountain pen* | *a felt-tip pen* | *Write your essays in pen* (=using a pen) *not pencil.* **2** a small piece of land enclosed by a fence, where farm animals are kept —see also PIGPEN, PLAYPEN **3 put/set pen to paper** to begin to write **4 the pen** INFORMAL a PENITENTIARY; a prison

pen[2] v. **penned, penning** [T] **1** FORMAL to write something such as a letter or article, especially with a pen: *The piece was penned by Mozart when he was eight.* **2** also **pen sb/sth ↔ in/up** to shut an animal in a small enclosed area, or prevent someone from leaving an enclosed area: *The flu kept him penned up at home for a week.*

Pen., pen. a written abbreviation of PENINSULA

pe·nal /'pinl/ adj. **1** [only before noun] relating to the legal punishment of criminals: *the penal system* | *a penal colony* (=a place far away from any other city where prisoners are kept) **2 a penal offense** a crime that can be punished by the law

penal code /'.. ,./ n. [C] a set of laws and the punishments for not obeying these laws

pe·nal·ize /'pinl,aɪz, 'pɛn-/ v. [T] **1** to punish someone or treat them unfairly: *Why should I be penalized just because everyone else did a bad job?* | *The proposed energy taxes would unfairly penalize people living in rural areas.* **2** to punish a team or player in sports by giving an advantage to the other team: *Wallace was penalized twice for false starts.* —**penalization** /ˌpinl-ə,zeɪʃən/ n. [U]

pen·al·ty /'pɛnlti/ n. plural **penalties** [C] **1** a punishment for not obeying a law, rule, or legal agreement: [+ of] *Cox's company agreed to pay a penalty of $100,000 for making false claims in its advertising.* | [+ for] *Answer all questions on the test – there's no penalty for guessing.* | *a stiff/heavy penalty* (=a severe penalty) *The U.S. has stiff penalties for drug violations.* —see also DEATH PENALTY **2** a disadvantage in sports given to a player or team for not obeying a rule **3** a chance to kick the ball or hit the PUCK into the GOAL (3) in a game of SOCCER, HOCKEY etc. given because the other team has not obeyed a rule **4** something bad that happens to you because of a bad decision you made in the past or because of the situation you are in: *Unemployed at 30, Brad was now paying the penalty for dropping out of school* as a teenager. | [+ **of**] *One of the penalties of being famous is the loss of privacy*

penalty a·re·a /'... ,.../ *n.* [C] the area in front of the GOAL (3) in SOCCER, in which the team opposing you is given a PENALTY (3) if you do not obey a rule there

penalty box /'... ,./ *n.* [C] **1** an area off the ice where a player in HOCKEY must wait after not obeying a rule **2** a penalty area

penalty clause /'... ,./ *n.* [C] part of a contract which says what someone will have to pay or do if they do not obey the agreement, for example if they fail to complete work on time

penalty kick /'... ,./ *n.* [C] a PENALTY (3) in the game of SOCCER

pen·ance /'penəns/ *n.* [C,U] punishment or suffering that you accept or give to yourself, especially for religious reasons, to show you are sorry for having behaved badly: *Members of the order led a life of prayer, fasting, and penance.*

pen-and-ink /,. . '.◄/ *adj.* [only before noun] a pen-and-ink drawing is drawn with a pen instead of a pencil

pen·chant /'pentʃənt/ *n.* [singular] a liking for something you do as a habit, especially something that is slightly disapproved of by other people: [+ **for**] *a penchant for gambling*

s w **pen·cil¹** /'pensəl/ *n.* [C, U] **1** a narrow pointed
3 wooden instrument, used for writing or drawing, containing a thin stick of a black or colored substance: *Do the math problems in pencil* (=using a pencil), *not pen.* | *a red pencil* **2 a pencil of light** a narrow beam of light beginning from or ending in a small point —see also EYEBROW PENCIL

pencil² *v.* **penciled, penciling** [T] to write something with a pencil or make a mark with a pencil: *I found her name penciled inside the back cover of the book.* —**penciled** *adj.*
　　pencil *sb/sth* ↔ **in** *phr. v.* [T] to make an arrangement for a meeting or other event, knowing that it might have to be changed later: *Let's pencil in a meeting for next Wednesday, and I'll call you later to confirm.*

pencil push·er /'.. ,../ *n.* [C] INFORMAL someone who has a boring unimportant job in an office

pencil sharp·en·er /'.. ,.../ *n.* [C] a small piece of equipment with a blade inside, used for sharpening pencils

pencil-thin /,.. '.◄/ *adj.* very thin: *Allen was a dark-haired man with a pencil-thin mustache* | *pencil-thin models*

pen·dant, pendent /'pendənt/ *n.* [C] a jewel or small decoration that hangs from a chain that you wear around your neck: *a diamond pendant*

pen·dent /'pendənt/ *adj.* LITERARY OR TECHNICAL **1** hanging from something: *a pendent lamp* **2** sticking out beyond a surface: *pendent ledges of rocks*

pend·ing¹ /'pendɪŋ/ *prep.* FORMAL while waiting for something, or until something happens: *The victim's identity is being withheld pending notification of relatives.*

pending² *adj.* FORMAL **1** not yet decided, agreed on, or finished: *Funeral arrangements are pending.* **2** something that is pending is going to happen soon: *More employees are likely to lose jobs in the pending merger.*

pen·du·lous /'pendʒələs/ *adj.* LITERARY hanging down loosely and swinging freely: *pendulous breasts* —**pendulously** *adv.*

pen·du·lum /'pendʒələm/ *n.* **plural pendulums** [C] **1** a long stick or string with a weight at the bottom that swings regularly from side to side, and controls the operation of a large clock **2 the pendulum** used to talk about the tendency of ideas, beliefs etc. to change regularly from one position to an opposite one: *Highly paid banking jobs were seen as very desirable in the 1980s, but the pendulum is swinging the other way now.* | *Today, the fashion pendulum is swinging back to casual clothes.*

Pe·nel·o·pe /pə'nɛləpi/ in ancient Greek stories, the wife of ODYSSEUS, who remained faithful to him while he was away from home for over 20 years

P

pen·e·trate /'penə,treɪt/ *v.*
1 enter/go through [I,T] to enter something or pass through it, especially when this is difficult: *The bomb penetrated the wall and exploded inside the building.* | [+ **into**] *Oil had penetrated into the concrete.*
2 spread through [I,T] to spread through an area: *The fall weather outside penetrated the room.* | *Islam has penetrated vast parts of Africa and Asia.*
3 business [T] to succeed in selling your products in an area or country, especially when this is difficult: *Few U.S. companies have successfully penetrated the Japanese electronics market.*
4 organization [T] to join and be accepted into a group or an organization in order to find out their secrets: *Spies had penetrated the highest ranks of both governments.*
5 see through [T] to see into or through something even though it is difficult: *My eyes couldn't penetrate the gloom.*
6 understand [T] FORMAL to succeed in understanding something very difficult: *Dario was attempting to penetrate Nature's mysteries.*
7 sex [T] FORMAL if a man penetrates someone, he puts his PENIS into a woman's VAGINA or into someone's ANUS when having sex —see also IMPENETRABLE —**penetrable** /'penətrəbəl/ *adj.* —**penetrability** /,penətrə'bɪləṭi/ *n.* [U]

pen·e·trat·ing /'penə,treɪtɪŋ/ *adj.* **1** showing a special ability to understand things very clearly and completely: *The book offers some penetrating insights into how government works.* | *a penetrating question* **2** a penetrating sound is loud, high, and often annoying: *a penetrating whistle* **3** spreading and reaching everywhere: *penetrating cold* | *a penetrating sealer for wood*

pen·e·tra·tion /,penə'treɪʃən/ *n.* **1** [C,U] the act of entering something or passing through it, especially when this is difficult: *Protect the wood against water penetration.* | *Military sources reported several enemy penetrations of U.S. airspace.* **2** [U] the degree to which a product is available or is sold in an area: *Video conferencing is expected to continue its penetration into the corporate marketplace.* **3** [U] the act of joining and being accepted by an organization, business etc. to find out secret information: *foreign penetration of the British secret service* **4** [U] the act of a man putting his PENIS into a woman's VAGINA or into someone's ANUS **5** [U] a special ability to understand things very clearly and completely

pen·e·tra·tive /'penə,treɪtɪv/ *adj.* **1** showing a special ability to understand things very clearly and completely: *a penetrative thinker* **2** [only before noun] penetrative sex involves a man putting his PENIS into a woman's VAGINA or into someone's ANUS

pen·guin /'pengwɪn/ *n.* [C] a large black and white Antarctic sea bird, which cannot fly but uses its wings for swimming

pen·i·cil·lin /,penə'sɪlən/ *n.* [U] a substance used as a medicine to destroy BACTERIA: *The infection can usually be cured by a course of penicillin.*

pe·nile /'pinaɪl/ *adj.* TECHNICAL relating to the penis

pe·nin·su·la /pə'nɪnsələ/ *n.* [C] a piece of land almost completely surrounded by water but joined to a large mass of land: *the Korean peninsula* —**peninsular** *adj.*

pe·nis /'pinɪs/ *n.* [C] the sex organ of men and male animals, used in sexual activity and for getting rid of URINE from the body

penis en·vy /'.. ,../ *n.* [U] the desire of a girl or woman to have a penis, according to the ideas of Sigmund Freud

pen·i·tent¹ /'penətənt/ *adj.* FORMAL feeling sorry because you have done something bad, and showing you do not intend to do it again: *Phil was trying hard to look penitent.* —**penitently** *adv.* —**penitence** *n.* [U]

penitent² *n.* [C] someone who is doing religious PENANCE

P

pen·i·ten·tial /ˌpɛnəˈtɛnʃəl◂/ adj. FORMAL relating to being sorry for having done something wrong: *a penitential journey to a holy shrine*

pen·i·ten·tia·ry /ˌpɛnəˈtɛnʃəri/ n. [C] plural **penitentiaries** another word for a prison, used especially in names: *the North Carolina State Penitentiary*

pen·knife /ˈpɛn-naɪf/ n. plural **penknives** /-naɪvz/ [C] a small knife with blades that fold into the handle, usually carried in your pocket

pen·light /ˈpɛnlaɪt/ n. [C] a small thin FLASHLIGHT that is about the size of a pen

pen·man·ship /ˈpɛnmənˌʃɪp/ n. [U] the art of writing by hand, or skill in this art: *penmanship exercises*

Penn /pɛn/, **William** (1644–1718) an English religious leader who went to North America and established Pennsylvania as a place of religious freedom

pen name /ˈ. ./ n. [C] a name used by a writer instead of their real name

pen·nant /ˈpɛnənt/ n. [C] **1** a long narrow pointed flag used on ships or by schools, sports teams, etc. **2 the pennant** the prize given to the best team in the American and National baseball competitions: *It was the Reds' first pennant since 1976.*

Pen·ney /ˈpɛni/, **James** (1875–1971) a U.S. businessman who started the J.C. Penney chain of stores

pen·ni·less /ˈpɛnɪlɪs/ adj. having no money: *He had gone from being a penniless student to become a multi-millionaire.*

pen·non /ˈpɛnən/ n. [C] a long narrow pointed flag, especially one carried on the end of a long pole by soldiers on horses in the Middle Ages

Penn·syl·va·nia /ˌpɛnsəlˈveɪnyə/ written abbreviation **P.A.** a state in the northeastern U.S. —**Pennsylvanian** n. [C]

pen·ny /ˈpɛni/ n. plural **pennies** [C]
1 U.S. coin a coin that is worth one cent (1/100th of a dollar), used in the U.S. and Canada: *Do you have three pennies?*
2 not a penny no money at all: *It wouldn't cost him a penny to go to college here.*
3 every penny all of an amount of money: *He's worth every penny they paid him.*
4 a penny saved is a penny earned SPOKEN used to say that it is a good idea to save money
5 the/your last penny the only money that is left: *They took everything she had, down to the last penny.*
6 not have a penny to your name to not have any money at all
7 a penny for your thoughts SPOKEN used to ask someone what they are thinking about when they are silent
8 in for a penny, in for a pound used to mean that if something has been started, it should be finished, whatever the cost may be
9 British coin plural also **pence** a British coin that is worth 1/100th of a pound, or the value of this coin —see also **a bad penny** (BAD¹ (29)), **cost a pretty penny** (PRETTY² (8))

penny an·te /ˈ.. ˌ../ adj. INFORMAL involving very small sums of money, and therefore not important: *He'd gotten mixed up in criminal activity, but it was just penny-ante stuff.* | *penny-ante investors*

penny can·dy /ˌ.. ˈ../ n. [C,U] OLD-FASHIONED candy that costs one cent for a piece

penny-pinch·ing /ˈ.. ˌ../ adj. unwilling to spend or give money: *a penny-pinching husband* —**penny pinching** n. [U] —**penny pincher** n. [C]

pen·ny·weight /ˈpɛniˌweɪt/ n. [C] written abbreviation **dwt**, **cwt** a unit for measuring weight, equal to 1/20 of an OUNCE (about 1.555 grams)

penny whis·tle /ˈ.. ˌ../ n. [C] a simple musical instrument shaped like a tube with holes, which you blow down

pen·ny·worth /ˈpɛniˌwəθ/ n. [singular + of] OLD-FASHIONED as much as you can buy with a PENNY

Pe·nob·scot /pəˈnɑbskət, -skɑt/ a Native American tribe from the northeastern area of the U.S.

pe·nol·o·gy /pɪˈnɑlədʒi/ n. [U] the study of the punishment of criminals and the operation of prisons —**penologist** n. [C]

pen pal /ˈ. ./ n. [C] someone you make friends with by writing letters, especially someone in another country whom you have never met

pen·sion /ˈpɛnʃən/ n. [C] **1** the money that a company or organization pays regularly to someone who used to work there, after that person RETIRES (=stops working): *Howe **draws** a yearly **pension** of $12,000.* **2** a house like a small hotel where you can get a room and meals in France and some other European countries

pen·sion·er /ˈpɛnʃənə/ n. [C] someone who is receiving a pension

pension fund /ˈ.. ˌ./ n. [C] a large amount of money that a company or organization etc. INVESTS and uses to pay PENSIONS

pension plan /ˈ.. ˌ./ n. [C] a system organized by a company for paying PENSIONS to its workers when they become to old to work —compare RETIREMENT PLAN

pen·sive /ˈpɛnsɪv/ adj. thinking about something a lot, especially when this makes you seem worried or a little sad: *She appeared pensive and uneasy after the visit.* | *a pensive mood* —**pensively** adv.

penta- /pɛntə/ prefix five: *a pentagon (=shape with five sides)*

Pen·ta·gon /ˈpɛntəˌgɑn/ n. **the Pentagon** the U.S. government building from which the Army, Navy etc. are controlled, or the military officers who work in this building

pen·ta·gon /ˈpɛntəˌgɑn/ n. [C] a flat shape with five, usually equal, sides and five angles —**pentagonal** /pɛnˈtægənl/ adj.

pen·ta·gram /ˈpɛntəˌgræm/ n. [C] a five-pointed star, especially one used as a magic sign

pen·tam·e·ter /pɛnˈtæmətə/ n. [C] a line of poetry with five main beats —see also IAMBIC PENTAMETER

pen·tath·lon /pɛnˈtæθlɑn, -lən/ n. [singular] a sports competition involving five different events; the MODERN PENTATHLON

Pen·te·cost /ˈpɛntɪˌkɑst/ n. [C,U] **1** the seventh Sunday after Easter, when Christians celebrate the time when the Holy Spirit came from Heaven to Jesus Christ's followers **2** a Jewish religious holiday 50 days after Passover, celebrating the time when Moses received the Ten Commandments from God

Pen·te·cos·tal /ˌpɛntɪˈkɑstl/ adj. **1** relating to Christian churches whose members pray in special languages and believe that the Holy Spirit can help them to cure diseases **2** relating to the holiday of Pentecost —**Pentecostal** n. [C]

Pentecostal church·es /ˌ.... ˈ../ a group of Christian churches that are especially interested in the gifts of the HOLY SPIRIT

Pen·te·cos·tal·ist /ˌpɛntɪˈkɑstəlɪst/ n. [C] someone who belongs to a Pentecostal church —**Pentecostalist** adj. —**Pentecostalism** n. [U]

pent·house /ˈpɛnthaʊs/ n. [C] a very expensive and comfortable apartment or set of rooms on the top floor of a building: *a penthouse apartment above Central Park*

pent-up /ˌ. ˈ.◂/ adj. pent-up emotions are prevented from being freely expressed for a long time: *Years of pent-up anger and frustration came out as she cried.* | *The collapse of the Berlin Wall released a pent-up demand for consumer goods*

pe·nul·ti·mate /pɪˈnʌltəmɪt/ adj. [only before noun] FORMAL next to the last: *the penultimate game of the season*

pe·num·bra /pəˈnʌmbrə/ n. [C] TECHNICAL a slightly dark area between full darkness and full light

pe·nu·ri·ous /pəˈnʊriəs/ adj. FORMAL very poor

pen·u·ry /ˈpɛnyəri/ n. [U] FORMAL the state of being very poor; POVERTY: *Over two-thirds of the population lives in penury.*

pe·on /ˈpiɑn/ n. [C] **1** INFORMAL someone who works at a boring or physically hard job for low pay: *We* *don't make those decisions around here – we're just peons.* **2** someone in Mexico or South America who works as a kind of slave to pay his debts

pe·o·ny /'piəni/ *n. plural* **peonies** [C] a garden plant with large round flowers that are dark red, white, or pink

peo·ple¹ /'pipəl/ *n.*

1 persons [plural] used as the plural of **person** to mean men, women, and children: *How many people were at the concert? | an earthquake that left thousands of people homeless | I like the people I work with.*

2 people in general [plural] people in general, or people other than yourself: *People sometimes make fun of my name. | I never understand people who say they don't like vegetables. |* **business/theater etc. people** *Computer people seem to speak a language of their own.*

3 the people [plural] all the ordinary people in a country who do not belong to the government or ruling class: *The mayor should remember that he was elected to serve the people. | Supporters viewed him as* **a man of the people** (=a politician who understands ordinary people).

4 nation [C] the people who belong to a particular country: *The Statue of Liberty was a gift from the people of France.* —see Usage Note at RACE¹

5 the people versus... used as the name of a court case in which the U.S. government officially says that someone is guilty of a crime: *The people versus Thomas Stanton*

6 peoples groups of people who have the same religion, language, or way of life: *The Church provided a bond among the diverse peoples of the world. | Indigenous peoples were very knowledgeable about plants and animals.*

7 of all people SPOKEN used to say that someone is the one person who you would not have expected to do something: *You of all people should have realized the risks. | "Annie" was directed by John Huston, of all people.*

8 sb's people [plural] **a)** INFORMAL the people who work for a person or organization: *As a senior manager, you will be judged by the performance of your people.* **b)** the people that a king or leader rules or leads: *Arafat has urged his people to refrain from violence.* **c)** OLD-FASHIONED your parents, grandparents etc.: *Where do your people come from?*

9 to get attention SPOKEN, INFORMAL used to get the attention of a group of people: *Listen up, people!* —see also **little people** (LITTLE¹ (11)), PERSON

people² *v.* **1 be peopled with/by sth** FORMAL to be filled with people or things of a particular type: *The bookstores and cafes downtown are peopled with college students and teenagers.* **2** [T] to live in a place; INHABIT: *The region has traditionally been peopled by Armenians.*

people-watch·ing /'.. ,../ *n.* [U] the act of watching different kinds of people who you do not know in a public place because you are interested in people and what they do: *Sunday afternoons on this street are great for people-watching.*

Pe·or·i·a /pi'ɔriə/ a Native American tribe from the northeastern central area of the U.S.

pep¹ /pɛp/ *v.* **pepped, pepping**
pep sb/sth ↔ **up** *phr. v.* [T] INFORMAL to make something or someone more active, interesting, or full of energy: *You need a bright scarf to pep up that outfit. | I had a coffee to pep myself up. | Interest rates are being lowered to pep up the economy.*

pep² *n.* [U] INFORMAL physical energy: *His exercise routine keeps him full of pep.* —**peppy** *adj.* —see also PEP BAND, PEP PILL, PEP RALLY, PEP SQUAD, PEP TALK

pep band /'. ./ *n.* [C] a band that plays at sports events at a school or at a PEP RALLY

pep·per¹ /'pɛpə/ *n.* **1** [U] a powder that is usually black or gray which is used to add a slightly strong taste to food: *Pass the salt and pepper, please.* —see also BLACK PEPPER, WHITE PEPPER **2** a red powder like this, especially CAYENNE PEPPER or PAPRIKA **3** [C] a hollow red, green, or yellow fruit with a sweet or SPICY taste that is eaten as a vegetable or added to other foods —see also BELL PEPPER

---

pepper² *v.* [T] **1** to scatter things all over or all through something: [**pepper sth with sth**] *Her speech was peppered with references to family values. | Environmentalists have been peppering the neighborhood with pamphlets.* **2** to hit something with many bullets in a very short time: [**pepper sth with sth**] *Rebel forces had peppered the parliament building with gunfire.* **3 pepper sb with questions** to ask someone many questions, one after the other: *At every stop, reporters peppered her with questions.* **4** to add pepper to food

pepper-and-salt /,.. '.< / *adj.* SALT-AND-PEPPER

pep·per·corn /'pɛpə,kɔrn/ *n.* [C] the small dried fruit from a tropical plant which is crushed to make pepper

pepper mill /'.. ,./ *n.* [C] a small piece of kitchen equipment which is used to crush peppercorns into pepper

pep·per·mint /'pɛpə,mɪnt/ *n.* **1** [U] a MINT plant with strong-tasting leaves, which is often used in candy, tea, and medicine **2** [U] the taste of this plant: *peppermint candy* **3** [C] a candy with this taste

pep·pe·ro·ni /,pɛpə'rouni/ *n.* [C,U] a strong-tasting red Italian SAUSAGE: *pepperoni pizza*

pepper shak·er /'.. ,../ *n.* [C] a small container with little holes in the top used for shaking pepper onto food

pepper spray /'.. ,./ *n.* [C,U] a substance used especially by the police for controlling people, containing red pepper that can be SPRAYed in people's eyes to make them blind for a short time

pep·per·y /'pɛpəri/ *adj.* **1** having the taste of pepper: *a peppery sauce* **2** easily annoyed or made angry

pep pill /'. ./ *n.* [C] INFORMAL a PILL containing a drug that gives you more energy or makes you happier for a short time

pep ral·ly /'. ,../ *n.* [C] a meeting of all the students at a school before a sports event, when CHEERLEADERS lead students in encouraging their team to win

pep·sin /'pɛpsən/ *n.* [U] a liquid in your stomach that changes food into a form that can be used by your body

pep squad /'. ./ *n.* [C] a group of CHEERLEADERS who perform at school sports events or pep rallies

pep talk /'. ./ *n.* [C] INFORMAL a short speech that is intended to encourage you to work harder, win a game etc.: *The Bears' coach* **was giving** *them their pre-game* **pep talk**.

pep·tic ul·cer /,pɛptɪk 'ʌlsə/ *n.* [C] a sore painful place inside the stomach caused by the action of pepsin

Pepys /pips/, **Samuel** (1633–1703) an English writer famous for his DIARY which describes his personal life and the important events of the time

Pe·quot /'pikwɑt/ a Native American tribe from the northeastern area of the U.S.

per /pə/ *prep.* **1** for each: *Oranges are 39 cents per pound. | My car gets about 30 miles per gallon* (=for each gallon of gasoline). | *Entry costs $55* **per head** (=for each person). **2 per hour/day/week etc.** during each hour, day etc.: *City buses carry about 20,000 passengers per day. | The speed limit is 65* **miles per hour**. **3** FORMAL according to what has been agreed or what you have been asked to do: *I purchased a one-way ticket* **as per** *your instructions.* **4 as per usual** SPOKEN used when something, especially something annoying, happens which has often happened before: *Alicia was late, as per usual.* —see also PER ANNUM, PER CAPITA

per·am·bu·late /pə'ræmbyə,leɪt/ *v.* [I,T] OLD-FASHIONED to walk around or along a place without hurrying —**perambulation** /pə,ræmbyə'leɪʃən/ *n.* [C,U]

per an·num /pə 'ænəm/ written abbreviation **p.a.** *adv.* for or in each year: *an inflation rate of about 4% per annum*

per·cale /pə'keɪl, -'kæl/ *n.* [U] a type of cotton cloth, used especially for making bed sheets

per cap·i·ta /pɚˈkæpətə/ adj. adv. TECHNICAL for or by each person in a particular place: *Per capita income rose by 1.2% last year.*

per·ceive /pɚˈsiv/ v. [T not in progressive] **1** to think of something or someone in a particular way: [perceive sb/sth as sb/sth] *The tax system was widely perceived as unfair to ordinary workers* (=many people thought it was unfair). | [perceive sb/sth to be sth] *High-tech industries are perceived to be crucial to the country's economic growth.* | [perceive that] *Many students perceive that on-the-job training is more important than college.* **2** FORMAL to notice something, especially something that is difficult to notice: *The human eye is capable of perceiving thousands of insignificant details.* | *Emma had perceived a certain bitterness in his tone.* —see also PERCEPTION

per·cent¹ /pɚˈsɛnt/ n. plural **percent** [C] an amount equal to a particular number of parts in every 100 parts. The sign for this word is %: *The money was divided up and they each got 25%.* | [+ of] *More than 70 percent of the country's population is younger than 25.*

percent² adj., adv. **1** equal to a particular number of parts in every 100 parts. The sign for this word is %: *Our "Gold" credit card only charges 8.5 percent interest.* | *You're supposed to leave a 15% tip* (=15 cents for every dollar you have spent on a meal). **2 a/one hundred percent** completely; totally: *I agree with you a hundred percent.*

per·cent·age /pɚˈsɛntɪdʒ/ n. **1** [C,U] an amount or number that is part of a total amount, when the total is thought of as having 100 parts: [+ of] *The percentage of students over 35 has increased.* | *Prices have fallen by three **percentage points** this month.* | **a high/low/large/small etc. percentage** *A growing percentage of women are choosing not to get married.* **2** [C usually singular] a share of profits equal to a particular amount of every dollar: *He gets a percentage for every book that is sold.* **3 there is no percentage in (doing) sth** INFORMAL used to say that there is no advantage or profit in doing something

---

USAGE NOTE: PERCENTAGE

GRAMMAR
Percentage is singular, but if the noun that follows **a percentage of** is plural, use a plural verb: *A high percentage of shoppers downtown are tourists.*

---

per·cen·tile /pɚˈsɛnˌtaɪl/ n. [C usually singular] TECHNICAL one of 100 equal-sized groups that a range of information, especially test SCORES, is divided into: *Dumont third-graders scored in the 87th percentile in reading* (=they did better than 87 percent of other students).

per·cep·ti·ble /pɚˈsɛptəbəl/ adj. FORMAL able to be noticed or seen: *a barely perceptible change* —opposite IMPERCEPTIBLE —**perceptibly** adv.

per·cep·tion /pɚˈsɛpʃən/ n. **1** [C] the way you understand or think of something and your beliefs about what it is like: [+ about] *Their aim is to change public perceptions about genetically modified food* (=to change the way people think about it). | [+ of] *She doesn't have a very realistic perception of the situation.* **2** [U] the way that you notice things with your senses: [+ of] *Part of the brain controls our perception of pain.* **3** [U] a natural ability to understand or notice things that are not easy to notice: *I was impressed by her perception and her grasp of the facts.*

per·cep·tive /pɚˈsɛptɪv/ adj. APPROVING good at noticing and understanding what is happening or what other people are thinking or feeling: *a perceptive observer of the political scene* | *perceptive comments* —**perceptively** adv. —**perceptiveness** n. [U]

per·cep·tu·al /pɚˈsɛptʃuəl/ adj. FORMAL relating to the way you see things, hear things, understand things etc.: *children's perceptual abilities*

perch¹ /pɚtʃ/ n. **1** [C] a branch, stick etc. where a bird sits, especially in a CAGE **2** [C] a high place or position, especially one where you sit and watch something: *They get a great view of the game from their perch in the press-box.* **3** [C,U] a type of fish that lives in lakes, rivers, etc., or the meat of this fish

perch² v. **1 be perched on/upon/over etc. sth** to be in a position on top of, or on the edge of something: *The castle is perched on a hill overlooking the town.* **2 perch (yourself) on sth** to sit on top of, or on the edge of, something: *He had perched himself on a tall wooden stool.* **3** [I] if a bird perches on something, it sits on it: [+ in/on] *Birds like to perch in nearby trees.*

per·chance /pɚˈtʃæns/ adv. OLD USE OR LITERARY **1** perhaps **2** by chance

per·cip·i·ent /pɚˈsɪpiənt/ adj. FORMAL quick to notice and understand things; PERCEPTIVE —**percipience** n. [U]

per·co·late /ˈpɚkəˌleɪt/ v. **1** [I,T] if coffee percolates, or if you percolate it, you make coffee by passing hot water through crushed coffee beans in a special pot **2** [I] if an idea, feeling, piece of information etc. percolates, it gradually develops or spreads: *She already has an idea percolating for her next novel.* | *Ideas from these right-wing "think tanks" eventually percolated through into policy decisions.* **3** [I always + adv./prep.] if liquid, air, or light percolates somewhere, it passes slowly through a surface that has very small holes in it: [+ through/down/into] *Rainwater will percolate into the valley's underground water basin.* —**percolation** /ˌpɚkəˈleɪʃən/ n. [C,U]

per·co·la·tor /ˈpɚkəˌleɪtɚ/ n. [C] a pot in which coffee is percolated

per·cus·sion /pɚˈkʌʃən/ n. [U] **1 the percussion** the part of an ORCHESTRA or band that consists of drums and other instruments that are played by being hit with an object such as a stick or hammer **2** these instruments in general, considered as a group: *percussion instruments* **3** the sound or effect of two things hitting each other with great force

per·cus·sion·ist /pɚˈkʌʃənɪst/ n. [C] someone who plays percussion instruments

per di·em¹ /pɚ ˈdiəm/ n. [C] an amount of money that an employer gives a worker each day or allows them to spend each day for additional things while doing their job, especially when they are on a business trip

per diem² adv. FORMAL for or in each day: *Our consultants receive $500 per diem plus expenses.*

per·di·tion /pɚˈdɪʃən/ n. [U] LITERARY complete destruction or failure: *Wilde was now on the brink of perdition.*

per·e·gri·na·tion /ˌpɛrəgrəˈneɪʃən/ n. [C usually plural] LITERARY a long trip, especially in foreign countries: *His peregrinations took him to India and China.*

per·e·grine fal·con /ˌpɛrəgrən ˈfælkən/ also **peregrine** n. [C] a hunting bird with a black and white spotted front

pe·remp·to·ry /pəˈrɛmptəri/ adj. FORMAL **1** peremptory behavior, speech etc. is not polite or friendly and shows that the person speaking does not want to be argued with: *a peremptory tone of voice* **2 a peremptory challenge** LAW an opportunity for a lawyer to have someone removed from a JURY without giving a reason —**peremptorily** adv.

pe·ren·ni·al¹ /pəˈrɛniəl/ adj. happening again and again, or existing for a long time: *Mickey Mouse remains a perennial favorite.* | *perennial problems of the local economy* —**perennially** adv.

perennial² n. [C] a plant that lives for more than two years —see also ANNUAL² (1), BIENNIAL (2)

per·e·stroi·ka /ˌpɛrəˈstrɔɪkə/ n. [U] (POLICY) the policies of social, political, and economic change that happened in the U.S.S.R. in the 1980s just before the end of the COMMUNIST government.

per·fect¹ /ˈpɚfɪkt/ adj. **1** of the best possible type or standard, without any faults or mistakes: *We had perfect weather the whole trip.* | *They seem to have a perfect marriage.* | *Michiko's English is perfect.* | *The* quilt is in nearly perfect condition. **2** exactly right for a particular purpose, situation, or person: *That's a perfect example of what I was talking about.* | [+ **for**] *It's a perfect frame for that picture.* | *I think he'd be perfect for you.* **3** [only before noun] complete or total: *How could you have given that confidential information to a perfect stranger?* | *Cindy's been a perfect angel all morning.* **4 make perfect sense** to be completely reasonable and sensible: *His explanation seemed to make perfect sense.* **5 nobody's perfect** SPOKEN said when you are answering someone who has criticized you or someone else: *OK, so he made some mistakes – nobody's perfect.* **6 have a perfect right to do sth** used to emphasize that someone has the right to do something: *You have a perfect right to say "no" if you don't want to do it.* **7 the perfect gentleman/student/host etc.** someone who behaves exactly as a gentleman, student etc. ought to behave —see also **the perfect crime** (CRIME (6)), PERFECTLY, **practice makes perfect** (PRACTICE¹ (10))

per·fect² /pəˈfɛkt/ v. [T] to make something perfect or as good as you are able to: *Luke perfected his cooking skills after he got married.*

per·fect³ /ˈpəfɪkt/ n. TECHNICAL **the perfect** perfect tenses are formed using a form of the verb "have" with a PAST PARTICIPLE —see also FUTURE PERFECT, PAST PERFECT, PRESENT PERFECT

per·fect·i·ble /pəˈfɛktəbəl/ adj. able to be improved or made perfect

per·fec·tion /pəˈfɛkʃən/ n. [U] **1** the state of being perfect: *Our father expected perfection from all of us.* | *The bacon was cooked to perfection* (=perfectly). **2** the process of making something perfect: *Lehmann had spent years in the development and perfection of his wine-making techniques.* **3** a perfect example of something: *The sushi was beautifully presented and absolutely fresh – pure perfection.*

per·fec·tion·ist /pəˈfɛkʃənɪst/ n. [C] someone who is not satisfied with anything unless it is perfect: *Hoffman is known to be a perfectionist who is often hard on directors.* —**perfectionist** adj. —**perfectionism** n. [U]

per·fect·ly /ˈpəfɪktli/ adv. **1** a word meaning "completely," used to emphasize that there can be no doubt about what you are saying: *The airplane was standing perfectly still.* | *They're not welcome here.* *We made that perfectly clear.* | *They had thrown out a perfectly good stereo.* **2** in a perfect way: *She's always perfectly dressed.*

perfect par·ti·ci·ple /ˌ.. ˈ....ˌ/ n. [C] a PAST PARTICIPLE

perfect pitch /ˌ.. ˈ./ n. [U] the ability to correctly name any musical note that you hear, or to sing any note at the correct PITCH without the help of an instrument

per·fid·i·ous /pəˈfɪdiəs/ adj. LITERARY disloyal and not able to be trusted: *a perfidious scheme* —**perfidy** /ˈpəfədi/ n. [U]

per·fo·rat·ed /ˈpəfəˌreɪtɪd/ adj. **1** paper that is perforated has a line of small holes in it so that part of it can be torn off easily: *a perforated sheet of stamps* **2** something that is perforated, especially a part of the body, has had a hole or holes cut in it or torn in it: *a perforated eardrum* | *Use a perforated spatula to stir the mixture.* —**perforate** v. [T]

per·fo·ra·tion /ˌpəfəˈreɪʃən/ n. **1** [C] a small hole in something, or a line of holes made in a piece of paper so that it can be torn easily **2** [U] the action or process of making a hole or holes in something

perforation

perforation

per·form /pəˈfɔrm/ v. **1** [I, T] to do something to entertain people, for example by acting in a play or playing a piece of music: *The opera was performed in over 100 cities.* | *Perez is currently performing in "The Nutcracker."* **2** [T] to do something such as a job, a ceremony, or a piece

of work, especially something difficult or something useful: *Rubin says he will resign when he is no longer able to perform his duties.* | *Surgery was performed Friday to correct the heart defects.* | *These sharks perform a useful function by cleaning the ocean floor.* | *You can't expect me to perform miracles* (=do things that seem impossible). **3 perform well/badly etc. a)** to work or do something well, badly etc.: *Most students performed very poorly even though they had taken the test before.* | *All systems on the space shuttle appear to be performing well.* **b)** if a product, business etc. performs well or badly, it makes a lot of money, very little money etc.: *The electronics industry continues to perform well.*

per·form·ance /pəˈfɔrməns/ n. **1 a)** [C] an act of performing a play, piece of music etc.: [+ **of**] *The festival opens with a performance of Mozart's Requiem.* | *Lois Smith gives a moving performance as the mother.* **b)** an occasion on which a play, piece of music etc. is performed: *This evening's performance begins at 8:00 pm.* **2** [U] how well or badly you do a particular job or activity: *Some companies link pay to performance.* | *The new program will better evaluate the performance of students and teachers.* **3** [U] how well a car or other machine works: *Its performance on mountain roads was impressive.* | *a high-performance car* (=very powerful car) **4** [U] how much money a product, business etc. makes: *the disappointing performance of the bond market* **5** [U] the act of doing a piece of work, duty etc.: *the performance of his official duties* **6 a performance** SPOKEN, DISAPPROVING an act of behaving in a way that is too loud or attracts too much attention: *She put on quite a performance.*

performance art /.ˈ.. ˌ./ n. [U] a type of art that can combine acting, dance, painting, film etc. to express an idea —**performance artist** n. [C]

per·form·er /pəˈfɔrmə/ n. [C] **1** an actor, musician etc. who performs to entertain people: *jazz performers* **2 a skillful/brilliant/poor etc. performer a)** someone who does a particular job or activity well or badly **b)** a product, business etc. that makes a lot of money or very little money: *RTN was one of last year's top performers on the stock exchange*

per·form·ing arts /.ˌ.. ˈ./ n. **the performing arts** arts such as dance, music, and DRAMA, which are performed to entertain people

per·fume¹ /ˈpəfyum, pəˈfyum/ n. [C,U] **1** a liquid that has a strong pleasant smell, that women put on their skin or clothing to make themselves smell nice: *She always wears too much perfume.* —compare COLOGNE **2** a sweet or pleasant smell: *the rose's heady perfume*

per·fume² /pəˈfyum/ v. [T] **1** LITERARY to fill something with a sweet pleasant smell: *The sweet scent of sagebrush perfumed the air.* **2** to add perfume or something else to make something smell nice —**perfumed** adj.: *a perfumed envelope*

per·fum·er·y /pəˈfyuməri/ n. plural **perfumeries 1** [C] a place where perfumes are made or sold **2** [U] the process of making perfumes

per·func·to·ry /pəˈfʌŋktəri/ adj. FORMAL a perfunctory action is done quickly or without interest, and only because people expect it: *The applause was perfunctory.* | *a perfunctory apology* —**perfunctorily** adv.

per·go·la /ˈpəgələ/ n. [C] a structure made of posts built for plants to grow over in a garden

per·haps /pəˈhæps/ adv. **1** possibly; maybe: *I wonder if perhaps I offended him somehow.* | *Perhaps it'll be warmer tomorrow.* **2** used to give your opinion, when you do not want to be too definite: *Perhaps their biggest problem is that they don't have enough to do.* **3** used to say that a number is only a guess: *It was a big space, perhaps 60 by 80 feet.* **4** SPOKEN used to politely ask or suggest something: *This has been planned for weeks. Perhaps you can change the other meeting.* **5** SPOKEN, FORMAL used to say what you are going to do: *Perhaps I could transfer you to* *our customer service department.* —see Usage Note at MAYBE

per·i·car·di·um /ˌpɛriˈkɑrdiəm/ *n. plural* **pericardia** /-diə/ [C] TECHNICAL the MEMBRANE that is filled with liquid that surrounds the heart

per·il /ˈpɛrəl/ *n.* FORMAL **1** [U] great danger, especially of being harmed or killed: *With food supplies exhausted, two million people are in peril of starving.* | *She defied the soldiers at great peril to herself and her family.* **2 the perils of sth** the dangers or problems relating to a particular activity or situation: *the perils of drinking alcohol during pregnancy* | *Amundsen and his crew had survived the perils of ice, snow, and storms.* **3 do sth at your peril** to do something that is very dangerous and is likely to harm you: *These are grave environmental warnings, which we ignore at our peril* (=it would be dangerous for us to ignore them).

per·il·ous /ˈpɛrələs/ *adj.* LITERARY very dangerous: *a perilous mountain road* —**perilously** *adv.*: *We came to a stop perilously close to the edge.*

pe·rim·e·ter /pəˈrɪmətə/ *n.* [C] **1** the border around an enclosed area of land: *the perimeter of the airfield* | *a perimeter fence* **2** the whole length of the border around an area or shape —compare CIRCUMFERENCE

per·i·na·tal /ˌpɛrəˈneɪtḷ/ *adj.* TECHNICAL at or around the time when a woman gives birth: *perinatal health care*

sw **pe·ri·od**[1] /ˈpɪriəd/ *n.* [C]
1 1
1 length of time a length of time with a beginning and an end: *A five-day waiting period is required to purchase a handgun.* | *The loan has to be repaid over a 15-month period.* | *[+ of] Cleve went through several periods of depression.* | *The new taxes will be introduced over a period of time.* | *After a nine-month trial period* (=period of testing to see how something works), *the state will re-evaluate the program.*
2 history a particular time in history: *the Byzantine period, between the fourth and seventh centuries A.D.*
3 in development a particular time during the development of a person, their artistic style etc.: *"Siesta" is the best example of work from Storni's early period.*
4 women the monthly flow of blood from a woman's WOMB
5 dot the mark (.) used in writing that shows the end of a sentence or of an ABBREVIATION
6 school one of the equal parts that the school day is divided into: *Mike's taking Spanish second period.*
7 sports one of the equal parts that a game is divided into in a sport such as HOCKEY
8 period! SPOKEN used to emphasize that a decision has been made and there is nothing more to discuss: *I'm not giving them any more money, period!*

period[2] *adj.* **period costume/furniture etc.** clothes, furniture etc. in the style of a particular time in history: *actors dressed in period costume* —see also PERIOD PIECE

pe·ri·od·ic /ˌpɪriˈɑdɪk/ *also* **periodical** *adj.* [only before noun] happening many times over a long period, usually at regular times: *periodic crop failures* —**periodically** *adv.*: *Check your dog periodically for ticks. The information on our website is updated periodically.*

pe·ri·od·i·cal /ˌpɪriˈɑdɪkəl/ *n.* [C] a magazine, especially one about a serious or technical subject, that comes out at regular times such as once a month

periodic ta·ble /ˌ.... ˈ../ *n.* **the periodic table** a list of ELEMENTS (=simple chemical substances) arranged according to their ATOMIC structure

per·i·o·don·tal /ˌpɛrioʊˈdɑntḷ/ *adj.* TECHNICAL relating to the part of the mouth at the base of the teeth: *periodontal disease*

period piece /ˈ... ˌ./ *n.* [C] **1** a movie or play whose story takes place during a particular period in history: *an Edwardian period piece* **2** something such

as a piece of furniture or work of art that comes from a particular period in history

per·i·pa·tet·ic /ˌpɛrəpəˈtɛtɪk/ *adj.* FORMAL traveling from place to place, especially in order to do your job: *peripatetic priests who ministered to several villages* | *a peripatetic lifestyle*

pe·riph·e·ral[1] /pəˈrɪfərəl/ *adj.* **1** involved in or connected with an activity or situation, but not as one of the main features or people: *The U.S. State Department had only a peripheral role in the negotiations.* | *Stan plays a peripheral character in the series.* | *[+ to] activities that are peripheral to the organization's educational goals* **2 peripheral vision** what you can see to the side of you when you look straight ahead **3** in the outer area of something, or relating to this area: *the peripheral nervous system* **4** peripheral equipment can be connected to a computer and used with it —**peripherally** *adv.*

peripheral[2] *n.* [C] a piece of equipment that is connected to a computer and used with it, such as a screen or a PRINTER

pe·riph·er·y /pəˈrɪfəri/ *n.* **1** [C usually singular] the outer area or edge that surrounds a place: *[+ of] stores on the periphery of downtown* **2 on the periphery of sth** only slightly involved in a group or activity: *beggars on the periphery of society*

pe·riph·ra·sis /pəˈrɪfrəsɪs/ *n. plural* **periphrases** /-siz/ [C,U] FORMAL the unnecessary use of long words or phrases or unclear expressions —**periphrastic** /ˌpɛrɪˈfræstɪk/ *adj.*

per·i·scope /ˈpɛrəˌskoʊp/ *n.* [C] a long tube with mirrors fitted in it, used to look over the top of something, especially to see out of a SUBMARINE

per·ish /ˈpɛrɪʃ/ *v.* **1** [I] LITERARY to die, especially in a terrible or sudden way: *Sanchez perished in a mudslide in 1985.* **2** [I] LITERARY to stop existing or be destroyed: *We must make sure that democracy does not perish.* **3 Perish the thought!** SPOKEN used as a reply to an unacceptable idea or suggestion, to say that you hope this is impossible or never happens: *You're afraid you might get bored? Perish the thought!* —see also **publish or perish** (PUBLISH (5))

per·ish·a·ble /ˈpɛrɪʃəbəl/ *adj.* perishable food is likely to decay if it is not kept in the correct conditions: *perishable crops like fruits and vegetables* —**perishables** *n.* [plural]

per·i·to·ni·tis /ˌpɛrətˈnaɪtɪs/ *n.* [U] TECHNICAL a poisoned and sore condition of the inside wall of your ABDOMEN (=part around and below your stomach)

per·i·win·kle /ˈpɛriwɪŋkəl/ *n.* **1** [C] a small plant with light blue or white flowers that grows close to the ground **2** [C] a small ocean animal that lives in a shell and can be eaten **3** [U] a light blue color

per·jure /ˈpɝdʒɚ/ *v.* [I] **perjure yourself** to tell a lie after promising to tell the truth in a court of law —**perjurer** *n.* [C]

per·jured /ˈpɝdʒɚd/ *adj.* **perjured statements/testimony** lies that someone tells after promising to tell the truth in a court of law

per·ju·ry /ˈpɝdʒəri/ *n.* [U] the crime of telling a lie after promising to tell the truth in a court of law, or a lie told in this way: *Hall was found guilty of perjury.*

perk[1] /pɝk/ *n.* [C usually plural] money, goods, or other advantages that you get from your job in addition to the money you are paid: *[+ of] One of the perks of my last job was the use of a company car.*

perk[2] *v.* [I,T] INFORMAL to make coffee using a PERCOLATOR

perk up *phr. v.* [I,T] INFORMAL **1** to become more cheerful, active, and interested in what is happening around you, or to make someone feel this way: *The dogs always perk up when we walk in the room.* | *[T perk sb ↔ up] She was taking some herbal energy pills to perk herself up.* **2** to become more active, more interesting, more attractive etc., or to make something do this: *Congress hopes consumer spending will perk up in the fall.* | *[T perk sth ↔ up] You can perk up the sauce by adding a dash of fresh lime juice.*

Per·kins /ˈpɝkənz/, **Fran·ces** /ˈfrænsɪs/ (1882–1965) a

U.S. social REFORMER who was the first woman to hold a CABINET position in the U.S. government

perk·y /'pɔki/ *adj.* perkier, perkiest INFORMAL confidently cheerful and active: *You're awfully perky this morning, Debbie.* —**perkiness** *n.* [U]

perm[1] /pɔm/ *n.* [C] a process of putting curls into straight hair, by chemical treatment: *Did you get a new perm?*

perm[2] *v.* [T] to put curls into straight hair by means of a chemical treatment: *I had my hair permed last week.*

per·ma·frost /'pɔmə,frɔst/ *n.* [U] a layer of soil, in very cold countries, that is always frozen

per·ma·nence /'pɔmənəns/ also **per·ma·nen·cy** /'pɔmənənsi/ *n.* [U] the state of being permanent: *His life, at that time, lacked* **a sense of permanence** (=a feeling that the situation is not constantly changing).

s w **per·ma·nent**[1] /'pɔmənənt/ *adj.* continuing to exist for a long time or for all future time: *Mr. Lo has applied for permanent residence in the U.S.* | *Only five of the firm's employees are permanent.* | *Alex seems to have become* **a permanent fixture** (=someone or something that is always there) *around here.* —opposite TEMPORARY

permanent[2] *n.* [C] a PERM[1]

per·ma·nent·ly /'pɔmənəntli/ *adv.* always, or for a very long time: *Hardy was permanently banned from skating.* | *The accident left him permanently paralyzed.*

permanent press /,... '.‹/ *n.* [U] a process of treating cloth so that it does not WRINKLE easily, or cloth that has been treated in this way

permanent wave /,... './ *n.* [C] OLD-FASHIONED a PERM[1]

per·me·a·ble /'pɔmiəbəl/ *adj.* TECHNICAL material that is permeable allows water, gas etc. to pass through it: *a permeable membrane* —**permeability** /,pɔmiə'bɪləti/ *n.* [U] —opposite IMPERMEABLE

per·me·ate /'pɔmi,eɪt/ *v.* **1** [T] if ideas, beliefs, emotions etc. permeate something, they are present in every part and have an effect on all of it: *There is a culture of racism that permeates the entire organization.* **2** [I always + adv./prep., T] if liquid, gas etc. permeates something, it enters it and spreads through every part of it: *The smell of smoke permeated the house.* | [+ **through/into**] *Toxic vapors can permeate into the plaster and wood.* —**permeation** /,pɔmi'eɪʃən/ *n.* [U]

per·mis·si·ble /pɔ'mɪsəbəl/ *adj* FORMAL allowed by law or by the rules: *The use of racial preferences is not permissible under the new law.*

s w **per·mis·sion** /pɔ'mɪʃən/ *n.* [U] an act of allowing someone to do something, especially in an official or formal way: [**permission to do sth**] *Producers failed to get permission to use the song.* | *You have to* **ask permission** *before you take the car.* | *They* **gave us permission** *to use the pool.*

per·mis·sive /pɔ'mɪsɪv/ *adj.* not strict, and allowing behavior that many other people disapprove of: *permissive divorce laws* | *He had a very permissive upbringing.* —**permissiveness** *n.* [U] *sexual permissiveness*

s w **per·mit**[1] /pɔ'mɪt/ *v.* permitted, permitting [T usually passive] **1** FORMAL to allow something to happen, especially by an official decision, a rule, or a law: *Horseback riding is not permitted in the park.* | [**permit sb to do sth**] *No one was permitted to pick the flowers.* | [**permit sth in/near etc. sb/ sth**] *No one under 17 will be permitted in the theater.* | [**permit sb sth**] *Why was he permitted access to the jail while carrying a weapon?* **2** [I, T] to make it possible for something to happen: *a new system that permits greater flexibility* | [**permit sb/sth to do sth**] *Different package sizes permit consumers to buy only as much as they need.* | *If time permits, you can repeat the process.* | *We're going to the beach this weekend,* **weather permitting** (=if the weather is good enough). **3** also **permit of** [T] FORMAL to make something possible: *The facts permit of no other explanation.*

per·mit[2] /'pɔmɪt/ *n.* [C] an official written statement

giving you the right to do something: *You can't park there without a permit.* | **a travel/work/export etc. permit** (=an official document allowing you to travel, work etc.) —see also WORK PERMIT

per·mu·ta·tion /,pɔmyu'teɪʃən/ *n.* [C] one of the different ways in which a set of things can be arranged or put in order: *The 14 different dinners are mostly permutations of beef, chicken, noodles, and rice.* —**permute** /pɔ'myut/ *v.* [T] —compare COMBINATION

per·ni·cious /pɔ'nɪʃəs/ *adj.* FORMAL very harmful or evil, but often in a way that is difficult to notice: *the pernicious effects of advertising* | *a pernicious lie* —**perniciously** *adv.*

pernicious a·ne·mi·a /,... .'.../ *n.* [U] TECHNICAL a form of severe ANEMIA (=too few red blood cells in the blood) that will kill someone if it is not treated

Pe·rón /pɔ'roun, peɪ-/, **E·va** /'eɪvə/ also **E·vi·ta** /ɛ vitə/ (1919–1952) the first wife of the Argentinian President Juan Perón

Perón, Juan Do·min·go /wɑn dɔ'mɪŋgou/ (1895–1974) the President of Argentina from 1946 to 1955 and again in 1973–1974

per·o·ra·tion /,pɛrɔ'reɪʃən/ *n.* [C] FORMAL **1** the last part of a speech, especially a part in which the main points are repeated **2** a long speech that sounds impressive but does not have much meaning

per·ox·ide /pɔ'rɑk,saɪd/ *n.* [U] a chemical liquid used to make dark hair lighter or to kill BACTERIA

peroxide blonde /,... './ *n.* [C] OLD-FASHIONED, INFORMAL a woman who has changed the color of her hair to very light yellow by using peroxide

per·pen·dic·u·lar[1] /,pɔpən'dɪkyələ/ *adj.* **1** be **perpendicular (to sth)** if one line is perpendicular to another line, they form an angle of 90 degrees **2** not leaning to one side or the other but exactly upright; VERTICAL: *a perpendicular pole* **3** also **Perpendicular** in the style of 14th and 15th century English churches which are decorated with straight upright lines —**perpendicularly** *adv.*

perpendicular[2] *n.* **1 the perpendicular** an exactly upright position or line: *at an angle to the perpendicular* **2** [C] TECHNICAL a line that is perpendicular to another line

per·pe·trate /'pɔpɔ,treɪt/ *v.* [T] FORMAL to do something that is seriously wrong or criminal: *an extremist group that had perpetrated bombings and other acts of terror* | [**perpetrate sth against sb**] *Many abuses have been perpetrated against farm workers.* —**perpetration** /,pɔpɔ'treɪʃən/ *n.* [U]

per·pe·tra·tor /'pɔpɔ,treɪtɔ/ *n.* [C] someone who does something that is seriously wrong or criminal: [+ **of**] *the perpetrator of a sex crime*

per·pet·u·al /pɔ'pɛtʃuəl/ *adj.* **1** continuing all the time without changing: *a perpetual struggle between rich and poor* | *Walker seems to have a perpetual grin on his face.* **2** repeated many times in a way that annoys you: *I'm sick of her perpetual nagging.* **3** LITERARY permanent: *the perpetual snows of the mountaintops* —**perpetually** *adv.*

perpetual mo·tion /,... '../ *n.* [U] **1** the idea that a machine would be able to continue moving forever without getting energy from anywhere else, which is not considered possible **2** INFORMAL the state of being very active for a long time without stopping

per·pet·u·ate /pɔ'pɛtʃu,eɪt/ *v.* [T] to make a situation, attitude etc., especially a bad one, continue to exist: *His view is that the welfare system helps to perpetuate failure and poverty.* —**perpetuation** /pɔ,pɛtʃu'eɪʃən/ *n.* [U]

per·pe·tu·i·ty /,pɔpɔ'tuəti/ *n.* **in perpetuity** LAW for all future time: *The community does not own land* **in perpetuity.**

per·plex /pɔ'plɛks/ *v.* [T] if something perplexes you, it makes you feel worried and confused because it is difficult to understand: *Shea's symptoms perplexed the doctors.* —**perplexing** *adj.*: *perplexing questions*

per·plexed /pɔ'plɛkst/ *adj.* confused and worried by

something that you cannot understand: *What's wrong? You look perplexed.* | [+ **by/about**] *He seemed rather perplexed by these criticisms.*

per·plex·i·ty /pɚˈplɛksəti/ *n. plural* **perplexities** **1** [U] the feeling of being confused or worried by something you cannot understand: *They looked at each other in evident perplexity.* **2** [C usually plural] something that is complicated or difficult to understand: *moral perplexities*

per·qui·site /ˈpɚkwəzɪt/ *n.* [C] FORMAL a PERK[1]

Per·ry /ˈpɛri/, **Gay·lord** /ˈɡeɪlɔrd/ (1938–) a U.S. baseball player

Perry, Matthew (1794–1858) the U.S. navy officer who made the agreement with Japan that started trade between Japan and the U.S.

per se /ˌpɚ ˈseɪ/ *adv.* used to say that something is being considered alone, apart from anything else: *Money per se is not the main reason that people change careers.*

per·se·cute /ˈpɚsɪˌkyut/ *v.* [T] **1** to treat someone cruelly or unfairly, especially because of their religious or political beliefs: *Catholics were often persecuted under communism.* **2** to deliberately cause trouble for someone by annoying them often, asking them too many questions etc.: *Duke said he was being persecuted by a hostile media.* —**persecutor** *n.* [C]

per·se·cu·tion /ˌpɚsɪˈkyuʃən/ *n.* [C,U] the act of persecuting someone: *political and religious persecution*

persecution com·plex /..ˈ.. ˌ../ *n.* [C] a mental illness in which someone believes that other people are always trying to harm them

Per·seph·o·ne /pɚˈsɛfəni/ in Greek MYTHOLOGY, the goddess of the spring, who returns to earth each year after spending the winter months in the UNDERWORLD

per·se·ver·ance /ˌpɚsəˈvɪrəns/ *n.* [U] APPROVING determination to keep trying to achieve something in spite of difficulties: *Captain Benson praised his men's courage and perseverance in dealing with a very dangerous situation.*

per·se·vere /ˌpɚsəˈvɪr/ *v.* [I] APPROVING to continue trying to do something in a very determined way, in spite of difficulties: *Their switchboard is always jammed, but you can get through if you persevere.* | [+ **in/with**] *U.S. leaders have encouraged Adams to persevere in his efforts to bring peace.* —**persevering** *adj.*

Per·shing /ˈpɚʃɪŋ/, **John** (1860–1948) the leader of the U.S. Army Expeditionary Force in Europe during World War I

Per·sian[1] /ˈpɚʒən/ *n.* **1** [U] the language of Iran; FARSI **2** [C] OLD-FASHIONED someone from Iran, especially in the time when it was called Persia

Persian[2] *adj.* relating to or coming from Iran, especially from the time when it was called Persia: *a Persian carpet*

Persian cat /ˌ.. ˈ./ *n.* [C] a type of cat with long silky hair

Persian Gulf, the /ˌ.. ˈ./ a part of the Indian Ocean between Iran and Saudi Arabia

per·sim·mon /pɚˈsɪmən/ *n.* [C] a soft orange-colored fruit that grows in hot countries

per·sist /pɚˈsɪst/ *v.* [I] **1** to continue doing something, even though it is difficult or likely to cause problems: [**persist in (doing) sth**] *Why does Alice persist in believing she doesn't need any help?* | [**persist in/with sth**] *Students must persist in their efforts if they wish to do well.* | *"It does matter," Jill persisted.* **2** to continue to exist or happen: *If the pain persists, call a doctor.*

per·sist·ence /pɚˈsɪstəns/ *n.* [U] **1** determination to do something even though it is difficult or other people oppose it: *His persistence finally paid off this year with an award for best actor.* **2** the state of continuing to exist or happen, especially for longer than is usual or desirable: *the persistence of inequalities*

per·sist·ent /pɚˈsɪstənt/ *adj.* **1** continuing to exist or happen, especially for longer than is usual or desirable: *The U.S. trade deficit has been a persistent problem.* | *persistent headaches* **2** continuing to do something even though it is difficult or other people oppose it: *If she hadn't been so persistent, she might not have gotten the job.* | *persistent efforts to bring the warring factions together* —**persistently** *adv.*

per·snick·e·ty /pɚˈsnɪkəti/ *adj.* INFORMAL worrying too much about small and unimportant things; FUSSY: *persnickety rules*

per·son /ˈpɚsən/ *n.* **1** [C] *plural* **people** /ˈpipəl/ a man, woman, or child, especially considered as someone with their own character: *The person who finishes first gets a special prize.* | *Kevin's not an easy person to get to know.* | *She's a great actor, but what's she like as a person?* | *If you're asking me about Latin, you're asking the wrong person.* | a **computer/cat/city etc. person** (=someone who likes a particular thing or activity) —see also PEOPLE[1] **2 in person** if you do something in person, you do it when you are in a place, not by using a letter, the telephone etc.: *You can apply for a visa by mail, but it's quicker if you go to the embassy in person.* **3 businessperson/ salesperson etc.** someone who works in business, who sells things etc. —see also CHAIRPERSON, SPOKESPERSON **4** [C] *plural* **persons** FORMAL or LAW someone who is not known or not named: *Police are looking for the person or persons responsible for the fire.* | *The club does not allow any person under the age of 21 to enter.* **5 on/about sb's person** FORMAL in someone's pockets or hidden in their clothes: *Hide your passport securely on your person.* **6 in the person of sb** FORMAL used before someone's name to emphasize that this is the person that you are talking about: *A clear leader emerged in the person of Miyazawa.* —see also FIRST PERSON, MISSING PERSON, PERSON-TO-PERSON, SECOND PERSON, THIRD PERSON

USAGE NOTE: PERSON

GRAMMAR

Person means one man, woman, or child: *Will is the smartest person I know.* **Persons** is one possible plural form of **person**, but this is only used in very official language: *Unauthorized persons will be escorted from the premises.* When talking about more than one **person**, use **people** as the plural: *There were at least 30 people at the party.* **People** can also sometimes be a countable noun, meaning a particular race or group that lives in a country or area. With this meaning, its plural is **peoples**: *the peoples of Central Asia.*

---

per·so·na /pɚˈsoʊnə/ *n. plural* **personas** *or* **personae** /-ni/ [C] the way you behave when you are with other people or in a particular situation, which gives people a particular idea about your character: *Green's on-screen persona is cute and innocent.* —see also PERSONA NON GRATA

per·son·a·ble /ˈpɚsənəbəl/ *adj.* having an attractive appearance and a pleasant polite way of talking and behaving: *He seems a very personable young man.*

per·son·age /ˈpɚsənɪdʒ/ *n.* [C] FORMAL **1** a famous or important person: *notable personages* **2** a character in history or in a NOVEL, play etc.

per·son·al /ˈpɚsənəl/ *adj.* **1** relating to you [only before noun] used to emphasize that something is done, known, or experienced by you: *He took personal responsibility for everything that happened.* | *I know from personal experience how difficult this kind of work can be.* **2** private concerning only you, especially the private areas of your life: *Can I ask you a personal question?* | *Beth had a lot of personal problems at that time.* | *I'm not going to tell her anything personal.* | *I'm sorry I can't give you personal information about our customers* (=about where they live, how old they are etc.). **3** belonging to you [only before noun] used to emphasize that something belongs only to you, or someone works only for you: *I've got my own* personal web site. | *a personal fitness trainer* | *After Alan's death, his mother received his personal effects* (=small possessions, clothing, documents etc.). | **personal possessions/property/belongings** (=things belonging only to you)

4 done by humans involving direct communication between people, or done by people rather than by machines or in writing: *You can take English classes through the Internet, but you don't get much personal contact.* | *Small companies can devote more personal attention to each project.*

5 criticism involving rude or upsetting criticism of someone: *Opponents have resorted to personal attacks on Gingrich to stop the legislation.* | *Nothing personal* (=I am not criticizing you), *but I'd like to be alone right now.*

6 **a personal friend** someone that you know well, especially a famous or important person: *David is a close personal friend of Bill and Hillary.*

7 not work not relating to your work, business, or official duties: *We're not allowed to make personal phone calls at work.*

8 your body [only before noun] relating to your body or the way you look: *a manufacturer of personal care products* | *personal hygiene*

9 **a personal touch** something you do to make something special, or that makes someone feel special: *She adds her own personal touch to every recipe.*

10 personal development the improvements in your character that come from your experiences in life

personal ad /,... './ *n.* [C] a short advertisement put in a newspaper or magazine by someone who wants a friend or LOVER —see also PERSONALS

personal as·sis·tant /,... '..' *n.* [C] someone who works for one person and helps them do their job

personal best /,...'./ *n.* [C] a result of a race, competition etc. that is better than anything you have done before: *Plumer's time of 4:05:04 was a personal best.* —**personal-best** *adj.*: *a personal-best time*

personal check /,... './ *n.* [C] a CHECK (=piece of paper you sign and use instead of money) that is written by an ordinary person rather than a company or bank

personal com·put·er /,... '..'/ *n.* [C] a PC; the usual type of computer that is used by one person for business or at home

personal e·lec·tron·ic de·vice /,... '.. .,./ *n.* [C] a piece of electronic equipment, such as a LAPTOP computer or CELL PHONE, that is small and easy to carry

personal ex·emp·tion /,... '..'/ *n.* [C] a specific part of the total amount of money that you earn in a year, on which you do not have to pay INCOME TAX

personal i·den·ti·fi·ca·tion num·ber /,... ...'. ,./ also **PIN** *n.* [C] a number that you use when you get money from an ATM (=machine that provides money from your account) using a plastic card

per·son·al·i·ty /,pɔːsəˈnælətɪ/ *n. plural* **personalities 1** [C,U] someone's character, especially the way they behave toward other people *Dotty was a smart, good-looking 17-year-old with a lively personality.* | *The disease causes memory loss, often leading to changes in behavior and personality.* **2** [C] someone who is very well known and often in the newspapers, on television etc., especially an entertainer or sports person: *a sports personality* **3** [U] qualities of character that make someone interesting or enjoyable to be with: *The Senator is a good, reliable man, but he lacks personality.* **4** [U] the qualities that make a place or thing special and different: *There are three islands off the coast, each with its own personality.* **5 a personality clash/conflict** a situation in which two people cannot live together or work together because their personalities are very different

personality cult /..'... ,./ *n.* [C] also **cult of personality** the officially encouraged practice of giving too much admiration, praise, love etc. to a political leader

per·son·al·ize /ˈpɔːsənəˌlaɪz/ *v.* [T] **1** to put someone's name or INITIALS on something: *You can ask the author to personalize the book with your child's name.* **2** to make or design something so that it is useful or

appropriate for a particular person's needs or wishes: *We try to personalize our presentation for each client.* | *Helena has personalized her office with things she's collected on her travels.* **3** to discuss a subject by talking about and criticizing the people who are involved in it, rather than talking about it in a more general way: *The President has personalized the debate by attacking his opponents by name.* **4** to make someone think about the people involved in a situation or problem, instead of thinking about it in general: *Meeting someone with AIDS can personalize the disease for many people.* —**personalized** *adj.*: *personalized stationery* —**personalization** /,pɔːsənələˈzeɪʃən/ *n.* [U]

personalized li·cense plate /,.... '.. ,./ *n.* [C] a VANITY PLATE

per·son·al·ly /ˈpɔːsənəlɪ/ *adv.* **1** [sentence adverb] ESPECIALLY SPOKEN used to emphasize that you are only giving your own opinion about something: *Personally, I don't care how you do it.* | *Most of our customers like French wine, though I personally prefer Californian.* **2** doing something yourself, or affecting you yourself rather than someone else: *I was personally asked by the governor to run for office.* | *It's best to write about things you have experienced personally.* | *Maureen is personally responsible for all the arrangements.* **3 take sth personally** to let yourself get upset or hurt by the things other people say or do: *Please don't take it personally – he doesn't want to see anyone.* **4** as a friend, or as someone you have met: *I don't know him personally, but I've heard a lot about him.* **5** in a way that unfairly criticizes someone's character or appearance: *Members of the Senate rarely attack each other personally.*

personal organizers

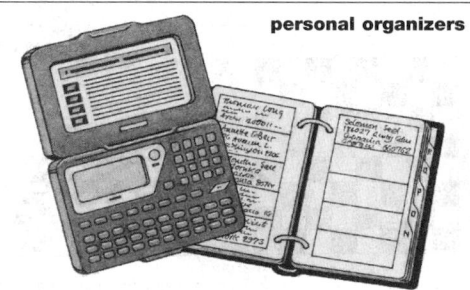

personal or·gan·iz·er /,... '..../ *n.* [C] **1** a small book in which you write addresses, things you must do etc., with loose pages so that you can add more **2** a very small computer used for the same purpose —compare DATEBOOK

personal pro·noun /,... '../ *n.* [C] TECHNICAL a PRONOUN used for the person who is speaking, being spoken to, or being spoken about, such as "I," "you," or "they"

per·so·nals /ˈpɔːsənəlz/ *n.* **the personals** a part of a newspaper in which people can have private or personal messages printed

personal shop·per /,... '../ *n.* [C] someone whose job is to help other people decide what to buy or to go shopping for them

personal space /,... './ *n.* [U] the distance that you like to keep between you and other people in order to feel comfortable, for example when you are talking to someone or traveling on a bus or train

personal ster·e·o /,... '..../ *n.* [C] a small radio, CASSETTE PLAYER, or CD DECK which you carry around with you and listen to through small HEADPHONES; WALKMAN

personal train·er /,... '../ *n.* [C] someone whose job is to help people decide what type of exercise is best for them and show them how to do it

persona non gra·ta /pɔːˌsəʊnə nɑn ˈɡrɑtə/ *n.* [U] **1** FORMAL someone who is not welcome in a particular place or in a particular group: *After the court* *case he found himself persona non grata in the business community.* **2** TECHNICAL a DIPLOMAT (=government representative) who is not acceptable to the government of the country where he or she is sent to work

per·son·i·fi·ca·tion /pɚˌsɑnəfəˈkeɪʃən/ *n.* **1 the personification of sth** someone who is a perfect example of a quality because they have a lot of it: *Sarah is the personification of feminine innocence.* **2** [C,U] the representation of a thing or a quality as a person, in literature or art: *the poem's personification of the moon*

P

per·son·i·fy /pɚˈsɑnəˌfaɪ/ *v.* **personifies, personified, personifying** [T] **1** to perfectly represent a particular quality or idea, by having a lot of that quality or being a typical example of it: *Carter personifies the values of self-reliance and hard work.* | *Bertha will be remembered as kindness personified.* **2** to think of or represent a quality or thing as a person: *The new year is sometimes personified as a baby.*

S W 3 **per·son·nel** /ˌpɚsəˈnɛl/ *n.* **1** [plural] the people who work in a company, organization, or military force: *hospital personnel* | *All personnel must attend the meeting.* **2** [U] the department in an organization that chooses people for jobs and deals with their complaints, problems etc.; HUMAN RESOURCES

person-to-person /ˌ... . ˈ..◂/ *adj.* **1 a person-to-person call** a telephone call that is made to one particular person and does not have to be paid for if they are not there **2** involving communication between people: *Electronic mail provides a way of sending person-to-person messages almost instantaneously.*

perspective

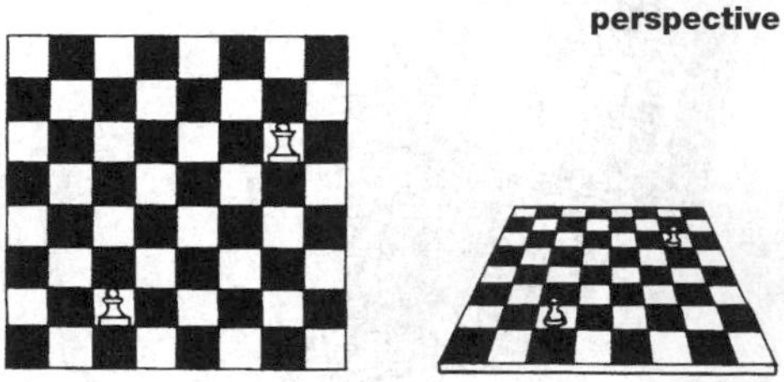

a chessboard drawn in perspective

S W 2 3 **per·spec·tive** /pɚˈspɛktɪv/ *n.* **1** [C] a way of thinking about something, which is influenced by the kind of person you are or by your experiences: [+ **on**] *Students have a unique perspective on matters of school policy.* | *The story is told* ***from the perspective*** *of an ordinary soldier.* | *We need to view the current crisis* ***from a*** *historical* ***perspective***. **2** [C,U] a sensible way of thinking about, judging, and comparing situations, so that you do not imagine that something is more serious than it really is: *Despite all his problems, Tony hasn't* ***lost*** *his* ***sense of perspective***. | *We're trying to* ***keep*** *the team's recent losses* ***in perspective*** (=not get too worried about them). **3** [U] a method of drawing a picture that makes objects look solid and shows distance and depth, or the effect this method produces in a picture: *Giotto's use of perspective* **4** [C] a view, especially one that stretches into the distance

per·spi·ca·cious /ˌpɚspɪˈkeɪʃəs◂/ *adj.* FORMAL good at judging and understanding people and situations, or showing this quality: *a perspicacious critic* —**perspicaciously** *adv.* —**perspicacity** /ˌpɚspɪˈkæsət̬i/ *n.* [U]

per·spi·ra·tion /ˌpɚspəˈreɪʃən/ *n.* [U] **1** liquid that appears on your skin when you are hot or nervous; SWEAT **2** the process of perspiring

per·spire /pɚˈspaɪɚ/ *v.* [I] to become wet on parts of your body, especially because you are hot or have been doing hard work; SWEAT

per·suade /pɚˈsweɪd/ *v.* [T] **1** to make someone decide to do something, especially by giving them reasons why they should do it, or asking them many times to do it: [**persuade sb to do sth**] *I tried to persuade Freddie to see her.* | [**persuade sb**] *Leo wouldn't agree, despite our efforts to persuade him.* **2** to make someone believe something or feel sure about something: *Maguire said he was not persuaded by criticisms in the media.* | [**persuade sb (that)**] *She'll only take me back if I can persuade her that I've changed.* | [**persuade sb of sth**] *McFadden must now persuade the jury of her innocence.* S W 3

per·sua·sion /pɚˈsweɪʒən/ *n.* **1** the act or skill of persuading someone to do something: *Some* ***gentle persuasion*** *by his wife got John to change his mind.* | *We were won over by Kimball's* ***powers of persuasion*** (=skill at persuading people). **2** [C] FORMAL a particular type of belief, especially a political or religious one: *people of all political persuasions* **3 of the female/conservative/vegetarian etc. persuasion** HUMOROUS OR FORMAL belonging to a particular type or group: *a writer of the post-modern persuasion*

per·sua·sive /pɚˈsweɪsɪv/ *adj.* able to influence other people to believe you or to do what you ask them: *persuasive arguments.* | *Diane can be very persuasive.* —**persuasively** *adv.* —**persuasiveness** *n.* [U]

pert /pɚt/ *adj.* **1** having a lot of energy and a lively attractive manner: *Katie is a pert outgoing young woman.* **2** amusing in a way that shows a slight lack of respect: *a pert answer* —**pertly** *adv.* —**pertness** *n.* [U]

per·tain /pɚˈteɪn/ *v.*

pertain to sth *phr. v.* [T] FORMAL to relate directly to something: *Use company e-mail for messages pertaining to business only.*

per·ti·na·cious /ˌpɚtˀnˈeɪʃəs/ *adj.* FORMAL continuing to believe something or to do something in a very determined way —**pertinaciously** *adv.* —**pertinacity** /ˌpɚtˀnˈæsət̬i/ *n.* [U]

per·ti·nent /ˈpɚtˀn-ənt/ *adj.* FORMAL directly relating to something that is being considered; RELEVANT: *pertinent questions* | [+ **to**] *The information is not pertinent to this study.* —**pertinently** *adv.* —**pertinence** *n.* [U] —compare IMPERTINENT

per·turbed /pɚˈtɚbd/ *adj.* worried or annoyed by something: *She seemed a little perturbed by these rumors.* —**perturbation** /ˌpɚt̬ɚˈbeɪʃən/ *n.* [U] —**perturb** /pɚˈtɚb/ *v.* [T]

per·tus·sis /pɚˈtʌsɪs/ *n.* [U] TECHNICAL: see WHOOPING COUGH

Pe·ru /pəˈru/ a country on the west coast of South America, north of Bolivia and south of Ecuador —**Peruvian** /pəˈruviən/ *n., adj.*

pe·ruse /pəˈruz/ *v.* [T] FORMAL OR HUMOROUS to read something in a careful way: *He spent hours perusing the catalog.* —**perusal** *n.* [C,U]

per·vade /pɚˈveɪd/ *v.* [T] if a feeling, idea, or smell pervades a place, it spreads through every part of it: *A culture of violence pervades the local police department.* | *the smell of rain pervading the air*

per·va·sive /pɚˈveɪsɪv/ *adj.* existing or spreading everywhere: *Alcohol is still a pervasive problem with high-school students.* | *the* ***all-pervasive*** (=extremely pervasive) *influence of television* —**pervasiveness** *n.* [U] —**pervasively** *adv.*

per·verse /pɚˈvɚs/ *adj.* **1** behaving in an unreasonable way, especially by doing the opposite of what people want or expect: *People in Minneapolis take a perverse pride in how cold their winters are.* | *a perverse policy* **2** PERVERTED —**perversely** *adv.*

per·ver·sion /pɚˈvɚʒən/ *n.* [C,U] **1** a type of sexual behavior that is considered unnatural and unacceptable **2** the process of changing something that is natural or good into something that is unnatural or wrong, or the result of such a change: *Their views have been condemned as a perversion of Christ's teachings.*

per·ver·si·ty /pɚˈvɚsət̬i/ *n.* [U] **1** the quality of being perverse: *Max refused the money out of sheer perversity.* **2** PERVERSION (1)

per·vert[1] /pə'vɔt/ v. [T] **1** to change something in an unnatural and often harmful way: *Negative advertising is perverting the democratic process.* **2** to influence someone so that they begin to think or behave in an IMMORAL way: *TV sex and violence perverts the minds of young children.*

per·vert[2] /'pɔ·vɔt/ n. [C] someone whose sexual behavior is considered unnatural and unacceptable

per·vert·ed /pə'vɔtɪd/ adj. **1** morally unacceptable, especially in a way that changes something good into its opposite: *the perverted logic of Nazi propaganda* | *Local church leaders described the ceremony as "sick and perverted."* **2** sexually unacceptable or unnatural: *perverted sexual practices*

pe·se·ta /pə'seɪtə/ n. [C] the standard unit of money in Spain

pes·ky /'pɛski/ adj. peskier, peskiest INFORMAL annoying and causing trouble: *pesky reporters*

pe·so /'peɪsoʊ/ n. plural pesos [C] the standard unit of money in various countries, including Mexico, Cuba, Colombia, and the Philippines

pes·si·mis·m /'pɛsə,mɪzəm/ n. [U] a pessimistic feeling, or a tendency to expect bad things to happen: [+ about] *In his speech, he voiced deep pessimism about the economy.* —opposite OPTIMISM

pes·si·mist /'pɛsəmɪst/ n. [C] someone who always expects that bad things will happen: *Don't be such a pessimist – I'm sure things will work out.* —opposite OPTIMIST

pes·si·mis·tic /,pɛsə'mɪstɪk/ adj. expecting that bad things will happen in the future or that a situation will have a bad result: *Some environmentalists take a more pessimistic view.* | [+ about] *Investment analysts are extremely pessimistic about the economic outlook.* —opposite OPTIMISTIC —**pessimistically** /-kli/ adv.

pest /pɛst/ n. [C] **1** a small animal or insect that harms people or destroys things, especially crops or food supplies: *a new strategy for pest control* **2** INFORMAL an annoying person, especially a child: *Stop being such a pest, Timothy.*

pes·ter /'pɛstə/ v. [T] to annoy someone, especially by asking them many times to do something: *I can't get anything done if you keep pestering me.* | [**pester sb for sth**] *She says men are always pestering her for sex.* | [**pester sb to do sth**] *Ryan keeps pestering me to play with him.*

pes·ti·cide /'pɛstə,saɪd/ n. [C] a chemical substance used to kill insects and small animals that destroy crops

pes·ti·lence /'pɛstələns/ n. [C,U] LITERARY a disease that spreads quickly and kills large numbers of people

pes·ti·len·tial /,pɛstə'lɛnʃəl/ also **pes·ti·lent** /'pɛstələnt/ adj. **1** FORMAL causing or relating to pestilence: *pestilential disease* **2** LITERARY OR HUMOROUS extremely bad or annoying: *pestilential kids*

pes·tle /'pɛsəl, 'pɛstl/ n. [C] a short stick with a heavy round end, used for crushing things in a MORTAR (=a special bowl)

pes·to /'pɛstoʊ/ n. [U] a SAUCE made of BASIL, GARLIC, PINE NUTS, OLIVE OIL, and cheese

pet[1] /pɛt/ n. [C] an animal such as a cat or a dog which you keep and care for at home: *Do you have any pets?* —see also TEACHER'S PET

pet[2] v. [T] to touch and move your hand gently over something, especially an animal: *Do you want to pet the kitty?* —see also HEAVY PETTING, PETTING —see picture at PAT[1]

pet[3] adj. **1 a pet project/theory/subject etc.** a plan, idea, or subject that you particularly like or are interested in **2 a pet peeve** something that you strongly dislike because it always annoys you: *Business travelers' pet peeve seems to be the quality of airline food.* **3 a pet rabbit/snake/lion etc.** an animal which is usually wild that you keep as a pet —see also PET NAME

PETA /'pitə/ People for the Ethical Treatment of Animals; a U.S. organization that works to prevent cruelty to animals

pet·al /'pɛtl/ n. [C] the colored part of a flower that is shaped like a leaf: *rose petals* —see picture at ROSE[1]

-petaled /pɛtld/ [in adjectives] **eight-petaled/blue-petaled etc.** having eight petals, blue petals etc.: *many-petaled flowers*

pe·tard /pə'tard/ n. —see **be hoisted with your own petard** (HOIST[1] (3))

Pete /pit/ n. **for Pete's sake** SPOKEN said when you are annoyed, surprised, impatient etc.: *For Pete's sake! Be quiet and listen for a minute.*

Pe·ter /'pitə/ **1 Peter, 2 Peter** two books in the New Testament of the Christian Bible —see also **rob Peter to pay Paul** (ROB (4))

pe·ter[1] /'pitə/ v.

peter out phr. v. [I] to gradually become smaller or happen less often and then come to an end: *Hurricane Fefa petered out in the Pacific before reaching shore.* | *Public interest in the environment may be in danger of petering out.*

peter[2] n. [C] SPOKEN, INFORMAL a PENIS

Peter, Saint, Simon Peter in the Bible, the leader of the 12 APOSTLEs who became the leader of the first Christians

Peter I /,pitə ðə 'fɔst/ also **Peter the Great** (1672–1725) the ruler of Russia from 1682 to 1725

pe·tit bour·geois /,pɛti bʊr'ʒwa, pə,ti-/ also **petty bourgeois** adj. **1** DISAPPROVING paying too much attention to matters such as social position and private possessions, and treating these things as if they are very important: *a petty bourgeois mentality* **2** belonging to the part of the MIDDLE CLASS who are not very wealthy and who own small businesses, stores etc.

petit bour·geoi·sie /,pɛti bʊrʒwa'zi, pə,ti-/ also **petty bourgeoisie** n. DISAPPROVING **the petit bourgecisie** people belonging to the middle class who are not very wealthy

pe·tite /pə'tit/ adj. **1** a petite woman is short and attractively thin **2** small and delicate: *petite hands*

petit four /,pɛti 'fɔr, pə,ti-/ n. [C] a type of very small sweet cake

pe·ti·tion[1] /pə'tɪʃən/ n. [C] **1** a written request signed by a lot of people, asking the government or someone in authority to do something or change something: [+ for/against] *Over 200 residents signed a petition against the traffic signal.* | *Berisha is part of the opposition group that drew up the petition.* **2** an official letter to a court of law, asking for a legal case to be considered: [+ for] *Judge Campbell rejected Thompson's petition for custody of the children.* **3** FORMAL a formal prayer or request to someone in authority or to God or to a ruler

petition[2] v. [I,T] **1** to ask the government or an organization to do something by sending it a petition: [**petition (sb) to do sth**] *Ten American Indian tribes have petitioned the state for the right to run gambling casinos.* **2** to make a formal request to someone in authority, to a court of law, or to God: [+ for] *At the end of March, Moody's wife petitioned for divorce.*

pe·ti·tion·er /pə'tɪʃənə/ n. [C] **1** someone who writes or signs a petition **2** LAW someone who asks for a legal case to be considered in a court of law

petit mal /'pɛti ,mal, ,mæl/ n. [U] TECHNICAL a form of EPILEPSY which is not very serious —compare GRAND MAL

pet name /,. './ n. [C] a special name you call someone you like: *Derwin has pet names for all his employees.*

Pe·trarch /'pɛtrark, 'pi-/ also **Francesco Petrarca** (1304–1374) an Italian poet

pet·rel /'pɛtrəl/ n. [C] a black and white ocean bird

pet·ri·fied /'pɛtrə,faɪd/ adj. **1** extremely frightened, especially when this makes you unable to move or think: [+ of] *Aren't you petrified of earthquakes?* **2 petrified wood/trees/insects etc.** wood, trees etc. that have changed into stone over a long period of

P

time —**petrify** v. [T] —**petrifaction** /ˌpɛtrəˈfækʃən/ n. [U]

pet·ro·chem·i·cal /ˌpɛtrouˈkɛmɪkəl/ n. [C] a chemical substance obtained from PETROLEUM or natural gas: *the petrochemical industry*

pet·ro·dol·lars /ˈpɛtrouˌdɑləʳz/ n. [plural] money earned by the sale of oil

pet·ro·glyph /ˈpɛtrəˌglɪf/ n. [C] a picture or set of marks cut into rock, especially one made thousands of years ago

pet·rol /ˈpɛtrəl/ n. [U] BRITISH: see GASOLINE

pe·tro·le·um /pəˈtrouliəm/ n. [U] oil that is obtained from below the surface of the Earth and is used to make gas, PARAFFIN, and various chemical substances: *petroleum-based plastic*

petroleum jel·ly /ˈ...ˌ.../ n. [U] VASELINE

pe·trol·o·gy /pəˈtrɑlədʒi, pɛ-/ n. [U] the study of rocks —**petrologist** n. [C]

pet·ti·coat /ˈpɛtiˌkout/ n. [C] a long skirt that was worn under a skirt or dress by women in the past

pet·ti·fog·ger·y /ˈpɛtiˌfɑgəri, -ˌfɔ-/ n. [U] unnecessary concern with small unimportant details

pet·ti·ness /ˈpɛtinɪs/ n. [U] behavior and attitudes that are not generous, and too concerned with unimportant matters: *I got sick of the nastiness and pettiness of office politics.*

pet·ting /ˈpɛtɪŋ/ n. [U] **1** the activity of kissing and touching someone as part of a sexual activity —see also HEAVY PETTING **2** the action of touching and moving your hand gently over an animal

petting zoo /ˈ.. ˌ./ n. [C] part of a ZOO which has baby animals in it for children to touch

pet·ty /ˈpɛti/ adj. **pettier, pettiest 1 a petty problem/detail/worry etc.** a problem, detail, etc. that is small and unimportant: *We're spending too much time on petty issues.* | *a petty dispute* **2** not generous, and caring too much about things that are not really important: *a petty personal attack* | *Sometimes he can be so petty about money* (=he thinks too much about exactly how much people owe him). —see also PETTINESS **3 (a) petty crime** a crime that is not serious, for example stealing things that are not expensive **4 a petty thief/criminal etc.** a criminal who steals things that are not expensive or whose crimes are not very important **5 a petty tyrant/dictator/bureaucrat etc.** someone who is not really important but uses their power as if they were important

petty bour·geois /ˌ... ˈ./ adj. PETIT BOURGEOIS

petty bour·geoi·sie /ˌ... ...ˈ./ n. [singular] PETIT BOURGEOISIE

petty cash /ˌ.. ˈ./ n. [U] money that is kept in an office for making small payments

petty lar·ce·ny /ˌ.. ˈ.../ n. [U] LAW the crime of stealing things that are only worth a small amount of money —compare GRAND LARCENY

petty of·fi·cer /ˌ.. ˈ...ˌ/ n. [C] an officer of low rank in the Navy

pet·u·lant /ˈpɛtʃələnt/ adj. behaving in an impatient and angry way for no reason at all, like a child: *Alexis walked out with a petulant look, and slammed the door.* —**petulantly** adv. —**petulance** n. [U]

pe·tu·nia /pəˈtunyə/ n. [C] a garden plant which has pink, purple, or white flowers in the shape of TRUMPETS

pew¹ /pyu/ n. [C] a long wooden seat in a church

pew² interjection said when something smells very bad: *Pew! What stinks?*

pew·ter /ˈpyuṭəʳ/ n. [U] **1** a gray metal made by mixing LEAD and TIN: *a pewter mug* **2** objects made from this metal

pe·yo·te /peɪˈouṭi/ n. **1** [U] a drug made from a Mexican CACTUS, which makes people imagine that strange things are happening to them **2** [C] the plant that produces this drug

Pfc., PFC the abbreviation of PRIVATE FIRST CLASS

pfen·nig /ˈfɛnɪg/ n. [C] a unit of money worth 1/100th of a German MARK² (16)

PG n. [C,U] Parental Guidance; used to show that a movie may include parts that are not appropriate for young children —compare G², PG-13, R³

pg. a written abbreviation of PAGE¹ (1)

PG-13 /ˌpi dʒi θɝˈtin‹ / n. [C,U] Parental Guidance-13; used to show that a movie may include parts that are not appropriate for children under the age of 13 —compare G², PG, R³

pH /piˈeɪtʃ/ also **pH val·ue** /ˈ. ˌ.../ n. [C usually singular] a number on a scale of 0 to 14 which shows how acid or ALKALINE a substance is

phag·o·cyte /ˈfægəˌsaɪt/ n. [C] a blood cell that protects your body by destroying harmful BACTERIA, VIRUSes etc.

pha·lanx /ˈfeɪlæŋks/ n. [C] FORMAL **1** a large group of people, vehicles etc. that are very close together and difficult to move through: *Stepping off the plane, the President faced a phalanx of cameras and reporters.* **2** a group of soldiers who stand or move closely together in battle

phal·lic /ˈfælɪk/ adj. like a phallus or relating to a phallus: *phallic symbols*

phal·lus /ˈfæləs/ n. [C] **1** something that looks like the male sex organ, often used to represent sexual power **2** TECHNICAL the male sex organ; PENIS

phan·tasm /ˈfænˌtæzəm/ n. [C,U] LITERARY something that exists only in your imagination; an ILLUSION —**phantasmal** /fænˈtæzməl/ adj.

phan·tas·ma·go·ri·a /ˌfæntæzməˈgɔriə/ n. [C] LITERARY a confused changing strange scene like something from a dream —**phantasmagorical** adj.

phan·ta·sy /ˈfæntəsi/ n. plural **phantasies** [C,U] an old spelling of FANTASY

phan·tom¹ /ˈfæntəm/ n. [C] LITERARY **1** a frightening and unclear image, especially of a dead person; GHOST **2** something that exists only in your imagination

phantom² adj. [only before noun] **1** seeming or looking like a phantom: *a phantom ship* **2** seeming real or made to appear real, but not really existing: *He planned to fix the election using phantom votes.* | *phantom limb pain in amputees* **3** HUMOROUS used to describe an unknown person that you blame for something annoying: *The phantom pen stealer strikes again!*

phar·aoh, Pharaoh /ˈfɛrou, ˈfæ-/ n. [C] a ruler of ancient Egypt

phar·i·see /ˈfærəˌsi/ n. [C] **1** someone who pretends to be religious or morally good, but who is not sincere; a HYPOCRITE **2 Pharisees** a group of Jews who lived at the time of Jesus Christ and who believed in strictly obeying religious laws —**pharisaic** /ˌfærəˈseɪ-ɪk/ adj.

phar·ma·ceu·ti·cal /ˌfɑrməˈsutɪkəl/ adj. [only before noun] relating to the production of drugs and medicine: *the large pharmaceutical companies*

phar·ma·ceu·ti·cals /ˌfɑrməˈsutɪkəlz/ n. [plural] **1** drugs and medicines **2** the large companies that make drugs and medicines

phar·ma·cist /ˈfɑrməsɪst/ n. [C] someone who is trained to prepare drugs and medicines and who works in a store or in a hospital

phar·ma·col·o·gy /ˌfɑrməˈkɑlədʒi/ n. [U] the scientific study of drugs and medicines —**pharmacologist** n. [C] —**pharmacological** /ˌfɑrməkəˈlɑdʒɪkəl/ adj.

phar·ma·co·poe·ia /ˌfɑrməkəˈpiə/ n. [C] TECHNICAL an official book giving information about medicines

phar·ma·cy /ˈfɑrməsi/ n. plural **pharmacies 1** [C] a store or a part of a store where medicines are prepared and sold **2** [U] the study or practice of preparing drugs and medicines

phar·yn·gi·tis /ˌfærɪnˈdʒaɪtɪs/ n. [U] a medical condition in which you have a sore swollen pharynx

phar·ynx /ˈfærɪŋks/ n. [C] the tube that goes from the back of your mouth to where the separate passages for food and air divide —**pharyngeal** /fəˈrɪndʒəl/ adj.

phase¹ /feɪz/ n. [C] **1** one of the stages of a process of development or change: *The first phase of renovations should be finished by next January.* | *a new drug that is still in the experimental phase* | *It's normal for kids his age to rebel – he's just going through a phase.* —compare STAGE¹ (1) **2** one of the changes in the appearance of the moon or a PLANET when it is seen from the Earth

phase² v. [T]

phase sth → in phr. v. [T] to introduce something such as a new law or rule gradually: *The new rules will be phased in beginning January 1.*

phase sth → out phr. v. [T] to gradually stop using or providing something: *As many as 2,000 jobs could be phased out at the plant by next fall.*

phased /feɪzd/ adj. happening gradually in a planned way: *a phased withdrawal from the territory*

phat /fæt/ adj. SLANG fashionable, attractive, or desirable: *a phat song*

Ph.D. /ˌpi eɪtʃ ˈdi/ n. [C] Doctor of Philosophy; the highest university degree that can be earned, which is given to someone who has done serious RESEARCH, or someone who has this degree —compare DOCTORATE

pheas·ant /ˈfɛzənt/ n. [C,U] a large colorful bird with a long tail that is hunted for food and sport, or the meat of this bird

phe·no·bar·bi·tal /ˌfinoʊˈbɑrbəˌtɔl/ n. [U] a powerful drug that helps you to sleep

phe·nom /fɪˈnɑm/ n. [C] INFORMAL a PHENOMENON (2): *an 18-year-old tennis phenom*

phe·nom·e·nal /fɪˈnɑmənl/ adj. very unusual and impressive: *The restaurant is a phenomenal success.* | *a phenomenal performance* —**phenomenally** adv.: *phenomenally popular*

phe·nom·e·non /fɪˈnɑmənən, -ˌnɑn/ n. plural **phenomena** /-nə/ [C] **1** something that happens or exists in society, science, or nature, often something that people discuss or study because it is difficult to understand: *It's a TV program about strange natural phenomena.* | [+ of] *the phenomenon of international terrorism* | *Homelessness is not a new phenomenon.* **2** [usually singular] something or someone that is very unusual, because of a rare quality or ability that they have: *Still walking five miles a day at the age of 95, the woman was an absolute phenomenon.*

USAGE NOTE: PHENOMENON

GRAMMAR: phenomenon, phenomena
Phenomenon is singular and **phenomena** is plural. However, many people use the word **phenomena** when they are speaking about a single thing.

---

pher·o·mone /ˈfɛrəˌmoʊn/ n. [C] a chemical produced by an animal or insect, which can affect the behavior of other animals of the same type, especially by causing sexual attraction

phew /fyu, hwyu/ interjection said when you feel tired, hot, or RELIEVED: *Phew! I am so glad it's Friday.*

phi·al /ˈfaɪəl/ n. [C] a VIAL

Phi Be·ta Kap·pa /ˌfaɪ ˌbeɪtə ˈkæpə/ n. [singular, not with **the**] a society for college students who have done well in their studies

Phil·a·del·phia /ˌfɪləˈdɛlfyə/ a city in the U.S. state of Pennsylvania, which is the fifth largest city in the U.S.

phi·lan·der·er /fɪˈlændərə/ n. [C] DISAPPROVING a man who has sex with many women, without intending to have any serious relationships —**philandering** adj. —**philandering** n. [U]

phil·an·throp·ic /ˌfɪlənˈθrɑpɪk/ adj. a philanthropic person or institution gives money to people who are poor or who need money in order to do something good or useful —**philanthropically** /-kli/ adv.

phi·lan·thro·pist /fɪˈlænθrəpɪst/ n. [C] a rich person who gives money to help people who are poor or who need money to do useful things: *The city library was built by a 19th-century philanthropist.*

phi·lan·thro·py /fɪˈlænθrəpi/ n. [U] the practice of giving money to help people who are poor or who need money to do useful things

phi·lat·e·ly /fəˈlætl-i/ n. [U] the activity of collecting stamps for pleasure —**philatelic** /ˌfɪləˈtɛlɪk/ adj. —**philatelist** /fəˈlætl-ɪst/ n. [C]

-phile /faɪl/ suffix [in nouns and adjectives] someone who likes something very much: *a bibliophile* (=someone who likes books) | *Francophile* (=liking France or the French)

Phi·le·mon /fɪˈlimən/ a book in the New Testament of the Christian Bible

Phil·har·mon·ic /ˌfɪləˈmɑnɪk◂, ˌfɪlhɑr-/ adj. used in the names of ORCHESTRAS: *the Boston Philharmonic*

-philia /fɪliə/ suffix [in nouns] **1** TECHNICAL a tendency to feel sexually attracted in a way that is not approved of, that may be part of a mental illness: *necrophilia* (=a sexual attraction to dead bodies) **2** TECHNICAL a diseased or unhealthy tendency to do something: *hemophilia* (=a tendency to bleed) **3** a tendency to like something: *Francophilia* (=liking France)

-philiac /fɪliæk/ suffix [in nouns] TECHNICAL **1** someone who feels sexually attracted in a way that is not approved of: *a necrophiliac* **2** someone who has a particular illness: *a hemophiliac*

Phil·ip /ˈfɪlɪp/, **Chief** (died 1676) a Wampanoag chief who fought against COLONISTS from England who settled on his tribe's land

Philip, Saint in the Bible, one of the 12 APOSTLES

Phi·lip·pi·ans /fɪˈlɪpiənz/ a book in the New Testament of the Christian Bible

Phil·ip·pine /ˈfɪləˌpin/ adj. relating to or coming from the Philippines

Phil·ip·pines, the /ˈfɪləˌpinz/ a country that consists of over 7000 islands off the southeast coast of Asia —**Filipino** /ˌfɪləˈpinoʊ/ n., adj. —see also FILIPINO

Phil·is·tine /ˈfɪləˌstin, fɪˈlɪstən/ one of the group of people who lived on the coast of Palestine from the 12th to the 10th century B.C.

phil·is·tine /ˈfɪləˌstin/ n. [C] DISAPPROVING someone who does not like or understand art, literature, music etc. —**philistine** adj. —**philistinism** n. [U]

phil·o·den·dron /ˌfɪləˈdɛndrən/ n. [C] a tropical climbing plant with smooth shiny leaves that many people keep in their houses

phi·lol·o·gy /fɪˈlɑlədʒi/ n. [U] OLD-FASHIONED the study of the way languages develop and the relationships between languages —**philologist** n. [C] —**philological** /ˌfɪləˈlɑdʒɪkəl/ adj. —compare LINGUISTICS

phi·los·o·pher /fɪˈlɑsəfə/ n. [C] **1** someone who studies and develops ideas about the nature and meaning of existence and reality, good and evil etc.: *the ancient Greek philosophers* **2** someone who thinks a lot and asks a lot of questions about the world, the meaning of life etc.

philosopher's stone /.ˈ... ˌ./ n. [singular] an imaginary substance that was thought in the past to have the power to change any other metal into gold

phil·o·soph·i·cal /ˌfɪləˈsɑfɪkəl/ also **phil·o·soph·ic** /ˌfɪləˈsɑfɪk/ adj. **1** relating to philosophy: *Rousseau's philosophic writings* **2** accepting difficult or bad situations calmly: [+ about] *Jerome was disappointed he didn't get the job, but he was philosophical about it.* —**philosophically** /-kli/ adv.

phi·los·o·phize /fɪˈlɑsəˌfaɪz/ v. [I + about] to think about or talk about things in a serious way, for example about the nature and meaning of life

phi·los·o·phy /fɪˈlɑsəfi/ n. plural **philosophies** **1** [U] the study of what it means to exist, what good and evil are, what knowledge is, or how people should live **2** [C] a set of ideas about these subjects: *the philosophy of Nietzsche* | *Eastern religions and philosophies* **3** [C] a set of beliefs or ideas that someone has about how to live their life, do their job etc.: *My philosophy is, I leave work at 5 o'clock and forget all about it till the next day.* —see also NATURAL PHILOSOPHY

phle·bi·tis /flɪˈbaɪtɪs/ n. [U] a medical condition in which your VEINS (=tubes that carry blood through your body) are swollen

phlegm /flɛm/ n. [U] the thick yellowish substance produced in your nose and throat, especially when you have a cold

phleg·mat·ic /flɛgˈmætɪk/ adj. calm and not easily excited or worried: *Though normally phlegmatic, Jan was beginning to get alarmed.*

phlox /flɑks/ n. [C] a low spreading plant with pink, white, or purple flowers

Phnom Penh /pəˌnɑm ˈpɛn/ the capital and largest city of Cambodia

-phobe /foʊb/ suffix [in nouns] someone who has a strong unreasonable dislike or fear of a particular type of person or thing: *a xenophobe* (=someone who hates foreigners) | *technophobes* (=people who are nervous about new TECHNOLOGY, especially computers)

pho·bi·a /ˈfoʊbiə/ n. [C] a strong unreasonable fear of something: [+ about] *I have a real phobia about going to places where I don't know anyone.* —**phobic** adj.

-phobia /foʊbiə/ suffix [in nouns] **1** a strong unreasonable dislike or fear of something, which may be part of a mental illness: *claustrophobia* (=fear of being in a small enclosed space) | *aquaphobia* (=fear of water) **2** a dislike or hatred of a particular type of person or thing: *homophobia* (=dislike of HOMOSEXUALS)

-phobic /foʊbɪk/ suffix **1** [in adjectives] suffering from or relating to a particular phobia: *I'm a little claustrophobic.* **2** [in nouns] someone suffering from a particular phobia: *an agoraphobic* (=who is afraid of large open spaces) —**-phobically** /foʊbɪkli/ suffix [in adverbs]

Phoe·ni·cian /fɪˈnɪʃən/ one of the people that lived in Phoenicia on the eastern coast of the Mediterranean from the 12th century to the fourth century B.C.

Phoe·nix /ˈfiniks/ the capital and largest city of the U.S. state of Arizona

phoe·nix /ˈfiniks/ n. [C] **1** a magic bird which, according to ancient stories, lives for 500 years, burns itself in a fire, and is then born again from the ashes **2 rise like a phoenix from the ashes** to become successful again after seeming to have failed completely

phon- /fən, foʊn/ prefix relating to sound, the voice, or the ability to speak: *phonetics* (=science of speech sounds) | *a phoneme* (=a unit of speech)

s w **phone**[1] /foʊn/ n. [C] **1** a telephone: *Can I use your phone?* | *I could hear a phone ringing in the next apartment.* | *What's your phone number?* | *My sister lives in Canada, but we talk on the phone* (=using the telephone). | **by phone/over the phone** *You can order a new checkbook by phone.* **2** the part of a telephone into which you speak; RECEIVER: *It was another reporter asking questions, so she just slammed down the phone.* —see also CELL PHONE, MOBILE PHONE

phone[2] v. [I,T] to connect your telephone with someone else's in order to speak to them; call: *I phoned her apartment, but she wasn't there.* | *You can register for the program by phoning this number.* —see Usage Note at TELEPHONE[2]

phone in phr. v. [I,T **phone** sth ↔ **in**] to telephone a place to report something, give your opinion, ask a question etc.: *Elliot was arrested in Arizona for phoning in a bomb threat.* —see also PHONE-IN

-phone /foʊn/ suffix **1** [in nouns] an instrument or machine related to sound, hearing, or music: *earphones* (=for listening to a radio etc.) | *a saxophone* **2** [in nouns] TECHNICAL someone who speaks a particular language: *a Francophone* (=who speaks French) **3** [in adjectives] speaking a particular language: *Francophone nations* (=where French is spoken)

phone book /ˈ. ./ n. [C] a book that contains an alphabetical list of the names, addresses, and telephone numbers of all the people who have a telephone in a particular area

phone booth /ˈ. ./ n. [C] a small structure that is partly or completely enclosed, containing a public telephone

phone card /ˈ. ./ n. [C] a plastic card with a special number on it that you can use to pay for calls made on a public telephone

phone-in /ˈ. ./ adj. **phone-in radio/talk/television show** a radio or television program which ordinary people can call on the telephone to ask questions, give opinions etc.

pho·neme /ˈfoʊnim/ n. [C] TECHNICAL the smallest unit of speech that can be used to make one word different from another word, such as the "b" and the "p" in "big" and "pig" —**phonemic** /fəˈnimɪk/ adj.

pho·ne·mics /fəˈnimɪks/ n. [U] TECHNICAL the study and description of the phonemes of languages

phone sex /ˈ. ./ n. [U] the activity of talking with someone on the telephone about sex in order to become sexually excited

phone tag /ˈ. ./ n. [U] INFORMAL a situation in which two people call each other and leave messages on each other's ANSWERING MACHINE but never actually speak to each other: *We've been **playing phone tag** with each other for about two weeks.*

phone-tap·ping /ˈ. ˌ. ./ n. [U] the activity of listening secretly to other people's telephone conversations using special electronic equipment

pho·net·ic /fəˈnɛtɪk/ adj. TECHNICAL **1** relating to the sounds of human speech **2** using special signs, often different from ordinary letters, to represent the sounds of speech: *a phonetic alphabet*

pho·net·ics /fəˈnɛtɪks/ n. [U] the science and study of speech sounds —**phonetician** /ˌfoʊnəˈtɪʃən/ n. [C]

phone tree /ˈ. ./ n. [C] a list of telephone numbers of the members in an organization, the workers in a company etc., and the order of who should call whom if there is important information that everyone should know

pho·ney /ˈfoʊni/ adj. phonier, phoniest another spelling of PHONY

phon·ic /ˈfɑnɪk/ adj. TECHNICAL **1** relating to sound **2** relating to speech sounds

phon·ics /ˈfɑnɪks/ n. [U] a method of teaching people to read in which they are taught to recognize the sounds that letters represent

phono- /foʊnoʊ, -nə/ prefix TECHNICAL relating to sound, the voice, or the ability to speak: *a phonograph* (=a RECORD PLAYER) | *phonology* (=the study of a system of speech sounds)

pho·no·graph /ˈfoʊnəˌgræf/ n. [C] OLD-FASHIONED a RECORD PLAYER

pho·nol·o·gy /fəˈnɑlədʒi/ n. [U] TECHNICAL the study of the system of speech sounds in a language, or the system of sounds itself —**phonologist** n. [C] —**phonological** /ˌfoʊnəˈlɑdʒɪkəl/ adj. —**phonologically** /-kli/ adv.

pho·ny, phoney /ˈfoʊni/ adj. phonier, phoniest INFORMAL **1** false or not real, and intended to deceive someone; FAKE: *a phony Italian accent* | *a phony driver's license* **2** someone who is phony pretends to be friendly, smart, kind etc., but in fact they are insincere —**phony** n. [C] *The photograph is a phony.* —**phoniness** n. [U]

phoo·ey /ˈfui/ interjection OLD-FASHIONED said to express strong disbelief or disappointment

phos·phate /ˈfɑsfeɪt/ n. [C,U] **1** one of the various forms of a salt of PHOSPHORUS, which has various industrial uses **2** [usually plural] a substance containing a phosphate used for making plants grow better

phos·pho·res·cent /ˌfɑsfəˈrɛsənt/ adj. a phosphorescent substance shines slightly in the dark because it contains phosphorus, but it produces little or no heat: *a pale green phosphorescent light* —**phosphorescence** n. [U]

phos·pho·rus /ˈfɑsfərəs/ n. [U] symbol **P** a poisonous yellowish ELEMENT that starts to burn when brought out into the air —**phosphoric** /fɑsˈfɔrɪk/ adj.: *phosphoric acid*

pho·to /ˈfoʊtoʊ/ *n. plural* **photos** [C] INFORMAL a photograph: *a photo album*

photo- /ˈfoʊtoʊ, -tə/ *prefix* TECHNICAL **1** relating to light: *photosensitive paper* (=which changes when light acts on it) **2** relating to photography: *photojournalism* (=use of photographs in reporting news)

photo booth /ˈ.. ˌ./ *n.* [C] a small structure in which you can sit to have photographs taken by a machine

pho·to·cop·i·er /ˈfoʊtəˌkɑpiɚ/ *n.* [C] a machine that quickly copies documents onto paper by photographing them

pho·to·cop·y[1] /ˈfoʊtəˌkɑpi/ *n. plural* **photocopies** [C] a copy of a document made using a photocopier: *Make a photocopy of this page, please.*

photocopy[2] *v.* [T] to make a copy of a document using a photocopier: *Could you photocopy it and give me back the original?*

pho·to·e·lec·tric /ˌfoʊtoʊ-ɪˈlɛktrɪk◂/ *adj.* using an electric effect that is controlled by light: *photoelectric sensors*

photoelectric cell /ˌ..... ˈ./ *n.* [C] **1** an electronic instrument that uses light to start an electrical effect, often used in BURGLAR ALARMS **2** a PHOTOVOLTAIC CELL

photo fin·ish /ˌ.. ˈ../ *n.* [C] **1** the end of a race in which the leading runners finish so close together that a photograph of the end must be examined to decide which is the winner **2** any competition in which the winner wins by only a very small amount: *Latest polls suggest Sunday's election will be a photo finish.*

pho·to·gen·ic /ˌfoʊtəˈdʒɛnɪk/ *adj.* always looking attractive in photographs: *I'm not very photogenic.*

pho·to·graph[1] /ˈfoʊtəˌgræf/ *n.* [C] a picture that is made using a camera and film that is sensitive to light: *black-and-white photographs of the canyon* | *Broder has been **taking** underwater **photographs** since he was 13.*

photograph[2] *v.* **1** [T] to make a picture of someone or something by using a camera and film sensitive to light: *Ruskin refused to be photographed for the article.* **2 photograph well/badly** to look attractive or unattractive in photographs

pho·tog·ra·pher /fəˈtɑgrəfɚ/ *n.* [C] someone who takes photographs, especially as a professional or as an artist: *a fashion photographer*

pho·to·graph·ic /ˌfoʊtəˈgræfɪk◂/ *adj.* **1** relating to photographs, using photographs, or used in producing photographs: *a photographic image* | *a photographic exhibition* | *photographic techniques* **2 a photographic memory** the ability to remember exactly every detail of something you have seen

pho·tog·ra·phy /fəˈtɑgrəfi/ *n.* [U] the art, profession, or method of producing photographs or the scenes in movies: *landscape and wildlife photography*

pho·to·jour·nal·ism /ˌfoʊtoʊˈdʒɚnlˌɪzəm/ *n.* [U] the job or activity of showing news stories in newspapers and magazines using mainly photographs instead of words

pho·tom·e·ter /foʊˈtɑmətɚ/ *n.* [C] an instrument that is used for measuring light

pho·to·mon·tage /ˌfoʊtoʊmɑnˈtɑʒ/ *n.* [C,U] the process of making a picture by putting many smaller photographs together, or a picture made this way

pho·ton /ˈfoʊtɑn/ *n.* [C] TECHNICAL a unit of ENERGY (2) that carries light and has no MASS[1] (1)

photo op·por·tu·ni·ty /ˈ.. ..ˌ.../ also **photo op** /ˈfoʊtoʊ ˌɑp/ *n. plural* **photo opportunities** [C] **1** a chance for someone such as a politician to be photographed for the newspapers or for television in a way that will make them look good **2** a chance to take a picture of someone or something interesting: *You get great photo opportunities from the bridge.*

pho·to·sen·si·tive /ˌfoʊtoʊˈsɛnsət̮ɪv◂/ *adj.* sensitive to the action of light, for example by changing color or form: *photosensitive paper*

photo shoot /ˈ.. ˌ./ *n.* [C] an occasion during which a professional photographer takes pictures of a fashion model, an actor etc. for advertisements

Pho·to·stat, photostat /ˈfoʊtəˌstæt/ *n.* [C] TRADEMARK a type of machine used for making photographic copies, or the copy itself —**photostat, photostatic** /ˌfoʊtəˈstætɪk/ *adj.*

pho·to·syn·the·sis /ˌfoʊtoʊˈsɪnθəsɪs/ *n.* [U] the production by a green plant of special substances like sugar that it uses as food, caused by the action of sunlight on CHLOROPHYLL (=the green substance in leaves)

pho·to·vol·ta·ic /ˌfoʊtoʊvɑlˈteɪ-ɪk◂/ *adj.* able to produce electricity using light: *photovoltaic solar panels*

photovoltaic cell /ˌ..... ˈ./ *n.* [C] an electronic instrument that changes light into electricity

phras·al /ˈfreɪzəl/ *adj.* consisting of or relating to a phrase or phrases

phras·al verb /ˌ.. ˈ./ *n.* [C] TECHNICAL two or more words including a verb and an adverb or PREPOSITION, which are used together as a verb and have a different meaning from the verb alone. In the sentence "The rocket blew up," "blew up" is a phrasal verb. In this dictionary phrasal verbs are marked *phr. v.*

phrase[1] /freɪz/ *n.* [C] **1** a group of words that are often used together and that have a special meaning: *Darwin gave the world the phrase, "survival of the fittest."* | *I'm trying to learn some French phrases for my trip to Paris.* **2** a group of words without a main verb that together make a subject, an object, or a verb tense. In the sentence "Sarah was wearing old gray sneakers," "old gray sneakers" is a noun phrase —compare CLAUSE (2), SENTENCE[1] (1) **3** TECHNICAL a short group of musical notes that is part of a longer piece —see also **to coin a phrase** (COIN[2] (2)), **a turn of phrase** (TURN[2] (10))

phrase[2] *v.* [T] **1** to express something in a particular way: *How was the question phrased?* **2** to perform music so as to produce the full effect of separate musical phrases

phrase·book /ˈfreɪzbʊk/ *n.* [C] a book that explains useful words and phrases of a foreign language, for people to use when they travel to other countries

phra·se·ol·o·gy /ˌfreɪziˈɑlədʒi/ *n.* [U] the way that words and phrases are chosen and used in a particular language or subject: *the standard phraseology of air traffic controllers*

phras·ing /ˈfreɪzɪŋ/ *n.* [U] **1** a way of playing music, reading poetry etc. that separates the notes, words, or lines into phrases: *Sinatra's classic phrasing* **2** the way that something is stated, especially when the words that are used are carefully chosen: *the careful phrasing of the report*

phre·nol·o·gy /frɪˈnɑlədʒi/ *n.* [U] the study of the shape of the human head as a way of showing someone's character and abilities, which was popular especially in the 19th century —**phrenologist** *n.* [C]

phyl·lo dough /ˈfiloʊ ˌdoʊ/ *n.* [U] a type of DOUGH with many very thin layers

phy·lum /ˈfaɪləm/ *n. plural* **phyla** /-lə/ [C] TECHNICAL one of the main groups into which scientists divide plants, animals, and languages, which is a larger group than a CLASS

phys·i·cal[1] /ˈfɪzɪkəl/ *adj.*
1 **body not mind** relating to someone's body rather than their mind or soul: *She was in great physical pain.* | *physical beauty* | *physical fitness*
2 **real/solid** relating to real things that can be seen, tasted, felt etc.: *There is no physical evidence to connect him to the crime scene.* | *The traditional office design creates physical barriers between workers.*
3 **violent** involving violent or forceful body movements: *a physical confrontation* | *I'm aggressive – I like physical sports.*
4 **sex** relating to sexual attraction or activity: *It was a purely physical relationship.*
5 **person** INFORMAL someone who is physical likes touching people a lot
6 **science** [only before noun] a physical science studies energy, natural laws, or things that are not living: *physical chemistry* —see also PHYSICALLY

physical² also **physical ex·am·i·na·tion** /ˌ... ...'../ *n*. [C] a thorough examination of someone's body and general health by a doctor, especially to decide whether they are fit to do a particular job

physical ed·u·ca·tion /ˌ... ...'../ also **phys ed** /ˌfɪz 'ɛd/, or **P.E.** *n*. [U] sports and physical exercise taught as a school subject

physical ge·og·ra·phy /ˌ... .'../ *n*. [U] the study of the Earth's surface and of its rivers, mountains etc. rather than of the countries it is divided into —compare POLITICAL GEOGRAPHY

phys·i·cally /'fɪzɪkli/ *adv*. **1** in relation to the body rather than the mind or soul: *As a child, she had been physically and emotionally abused.* | *People say I'm like my mother, but physically I look more like my father.* | *We try to keep* **physically fit** (=having strong muscles and not much fat). **2** done using violent or forceful body movements: *Police physically removed Ms. Sanders from City Hall.* **3 physically impossible** not possible according to the laws of nature or what is known to be true: *It would be physically impossible to open and check all 2.5 million packages.*

physically chal·lenged /ˌ... '../ *adj*. a word meaning "physically HANDICAPPED," used when you want to avoid offending people

physical sci·ence /ˌ... '../ *n*. [U] also **the physical sciences** [plural] the sciences, such as CHEMISTRY, PHYSICS etc., that are concerned with the study of things that are not living

physical ther·a·pist /ˌ... '../ *n*. [C] someone whose job is to give PHYSICAL THERAPY as a treatment for medical conditions

physical ther·a·py /ˌ... '../ *n*. [U] a treatment that uses special exercises, rubbing, heat etc. to treat illnesses and problems with muscles

phy·si·cian /fɪ'zɪʃən/ *n*. [C] FORMAL a doctor —see Usage Note at DOCTOR¹

physician's as·sis·tant /ˌ.,.. .'../ *n*. [C] someone who is trained to give basic medical treatment, in order to help a doctor

phys·i·cist /'fɪzəsɪst/ *n*. [C] a scientist who has special knowledge and training in physics

phys·ics /'fɪzɪks/ *n*. [U] the science that studies physical objects and substances, and natural forces such as light, heat, and movement

physio- /fɪziou, -ziə/ *prefix* TECHNICAL **1** relating to nature and living things: *physiology* (=study of how the body works) **2** physical: *physiotherapy*

phys·i·og·no·my /ˌfɪzi'ɑnəmi, -'ɑgnə-/ *n*. [C] TECHNICAL the general appearance of a person's face

phys·i·ol·o·gy /ˌfɪzi'ɑlədʒi/ *n*. [U] **1** the science that studies how the bodies of living things work **2** the way the body of a person or an animal works and looks: *a study of the physiology of whales* —compare ANATOMY —**physiologist** *n*. [C] —**physiological** /ˌfɪziə'lɑdʒɪkəl/ *adj*.

phys·i·o·ther·a·py /ˌfɪziou'θɛrəpi/ *n*. [U] PHYSICAL THERAPY —**physiotherapist** *n*. [C]

phy·sique /fɪ'zik/ *n*. [C] the shape and appearance of a human body, especially a man's body: *an athletic physique*

pi /paɪ/ *n*. [U] TECHNICAL a number that is represented by the Greek letter (π) and is equal to the distance around a circle, divided by its width

Pia·get /pyɑ'ʒeɪ/, **Jean** /ʒɑn/ (1896–1980) a Swiss PSYCHOLOGIST who developed important new ideas about the way that children's minds develop

pi·a·nis·si·mo /piə'nɪsɪˌmou/ *adj., adv.* TECHNICAL played or sung very quietly

pi·an·ist /pi'ænɪst, 'piənɪst/ *n*. [C] someone who plays the piano, especially very well

pi·an·o¹ /pi'ænou/ *n. plural* **pianos** [C] a large musical instrument that you play by sitting in front of it and pressing the KEYS (=narrow black and white bars)

piano² *adj., adv.* TECHNICAL played or sung quietly

piano bar /.'.. ,./ *n*. [C] a bar where someone plays the piano for entertainment

pi·a·no·la /ˌpiə'noulə/ *n*. [C] a PLAYER PIANO

piano stool /.'.. ,./ *n*. [C] a small seat with no back that you sit on while you play the piano

piano tun·er /.'.. ,../ *n*. [C] someone who makes pianos play at the right PITCH as their job

pi·az·za /pi'ɑtsə/ *n*. [C] a public square (=large open area in a city) or market place, especially in Italy

pic /pɪk/ *n*. [C] INFORMAL a picture or movie: *Norris made a name for himself by starring in action pics.*

pi·cante sauce /pɪ'kɑnt ,sɔs/ also **picante** *n*. [U] a thick SPICY mixture of crushed TOMATOes, onions, and CHILIS that you put on Mexican food —compare SALSA (1)

pic·a·resque /ˌpɪkə'rɛsk/ *adj*. a picaresque story or NOVEL tells about the adventures and travels of a character whose behavior is not always moral but who is still likable

Pi·cas·so /pɪ'kɑsou/, **Pab·lo** /'pɑblou/ (1881–1973) a Spanish artist regarded as one of the greatest and most original artists of the 20th century, who helped to develop CUBISM and other styles of ABSTRACT art

pic·a·yune /ˌpɪkə'yun/ *adj*. small and unimportant: *a picayune off-Broadway theater*

pic·ca·lil·li /ˌpɪkə'lɪli/ *n*. [U] a SPICY SAUCE made with small pieces of vegetables

pic·co·lo /'pɪkəˌlou/ *n. plural* **piccolos** [C] a musical instrument that looks like a small FLUTE

pick up

Steve picked up the can.

Mom picked up her jacket from the dry cleaners.

The truck driver picked up a hitchhiker.

pick¹ /pɪk/ *v*. [T]

1 choose sth to choose someone or something from a group or range of people or things: *In the end, Katie picked the blue dress.* | [pick sb as sth] *U.S. magazine has picked Turner as one of the 10 sexiest women.* | [pick sb/sth for sth] *Luckily, I didn't get picked for jury duty.* | [pick sb to do sth] *Two students were picked to represent our school at the debate.* —see also **pick out** (PICK¹)

2 flowers/fruit etc. to pull off or break off a flower, fruit, nut etc. from a plant or tree: *Laura's out in the garden picking tomatoes.* | [pick sb sth] *Here, I picked you an apple.* | **pick a bunch/basketful/couple** etc. *We picked two basketfuls of strawberries.* | *These lilacs are* **freshly picked** (=picked very recently). | **go grape/berry etc. picking** (=pick something for your own use)

3 **small things/pieces** to remove small things from something, or pull off small pieces of something: [**pick sth off/from etc.**] *It took hours to pick the nettles off the picnic blanket.* | *Pick the bones out of the fish before you take a bite.* | *Stevie, stop picking your nose* (=putting your finger in your nose to clean it)! | *Sam has an annoying habit of picking his teeth* (=removing pieces of food from between your teeth, with your fingers or something pointed). | *Wolves had picked the sheep's carcass clean* (=ate all of the meat from the bone).

4 **pick and choose** INFORMAL to choose only the things you really like or want from a group and ignore the others: *You can't just pick and choose which laws you're going to follow.*

5 **pick your way through/across/among etc.** to move slowly and carefully, choosing exactly where to put your feet down: *Rescue workers picked their way through the rubble.*

6 **pick a fight (with sb)** to deliberately start an argument or fight with someone: *Jerry's always trying to pick a fight.*

7 **pick sb's brain(s)** to ask someone who knows a lot about something for information and advice about it: *If you have time later, I'd like to pick your brains about some legal matters.*

8 **pick a lock (with sth)** to use something that is not a key to unlock a door, drawer etc.: *Thieves had picked the lock on the back door.*

9 **pick sb's pocket** to quietly steal something from someone's pocket: *On our last day in the city, someone picked my pocket.* —see also PICKPOCKET and see Usage Note at STEAL[1]

10 **pick holes in sth** to criticize a plan, an idea etc.: *I had no trouble picking holes in her theory.*

11 **pick a winner** INFORMAL an expression meaning "to make a very good choice," sometimes used in a joking way when you think someone has made a very bad choice

12 **pick sb/sth to pieces** INFORMAL to criticize someone or something very severely and in a very detailed way

13 **musical instrument** to play a musical instrument by pulling at its strings with your fingers —see also **I have a bone to pick with you** (BONE[1] (5))

pick at sth *phr. v.* [T] **1** to eat something by taking small bites but without much interest, for example because you feel unhappy: *Elaine just sat there picking at her dinner and looking glum.* **2** to touch something repeatedly with your fingers, often pulling it slightly: *Don't pick at your scab, or you'll get it infected.*

pick sb/sth **off** *phr. v.* [T] to shoot people or animals that are some distance away one at a time, by taking careful aim: *One by one, the gunman picked off people below.*

pick on sb/sth *phr. v.* [T] SPOKEN to treat someone in a way that is not kind: *Stop picking on me!* | *Pick on someone your own size!*

pick sb/sth **out** *phr. v.* [T] **1** to choose someone or something carefully: *We had a lot of fun picking out a present for Susan.* **2** to recognize someone or something in a group of people or things: *McNulty was able to pick out her attacker from a police lineup.* **3** to play a tune on a musical instrument, slowly or with difficulty: *Connor sat at the piano picking out a simple melody with one finger.*

pick over sth *phr. v.* [T] to examine a group of small things very carefully in order to choose the ones you want: *All the best fruit had been picked over by the time we got to the store.*

pick through sth *phr. v.* [T] to search through a pile or group of things, and take the one that you want

pick up *phr. v.*
1 **lift sth up** [T **pick** sb/sth ↔ **up**] to lift something up from a surface: *Greg picked his daughter up and put her on his shoulders.* | *The vacuum cleaner won't pick this stuff up.* | [**pick sth up by sth**] *The lioness picked up her cub by its neck.* | *Just as I picked up the phone* (=lifted it to up to talk into it), *it stopped ringing.* | *Ronnie, stop shuffling and pick your feet up* (=walk without sliding your feet on the ground).

2 **pick yourself up** to stand up after falling down: *Carol picked herself up and dusted herself off.*

3 **go get sb/sth** [T **pick** sb/sth ↔ **up**] to go somewhere, usually in a vehicle, in order to get someone or something: *I'll come by tonight to pick up my books.* | *Could you pick me up around eight?* | *For more information, pick up a leaflet at your local post office.*

4 **to buy sth a)** [T **pick** sth ↔ **up**] to buy something, while you are going somewhere or doing something: *Do you want me to pick up something for you at the store?* | **pick up the bill/tab (for sth)** INFORMAL to pay for something: *The company's picking up the bill for my trip to Hawaii.*

5 **clean a place** [T **pick** sth ↔ **up**] to put things away neatly, or to clean a place this way: *Could you pick all those papers up for me?* | *Pick up the living room before you go to bed.* | *I'm always picking up after him* (=putting things away that he has used).

6 **improve** [I] if business, your social life etc. picks up, it improves: *Sales should pick up again in November.*

7 **feel better** [T **pick** sb ↔ **up**] if a medicine, drink etc. picks you up, it makes you feel better —see also PICK-ME-UP

8 **sth picks up speed** also **sth's speed picks up** if something that is moving picks up speed or its speed picks up, it starts to go faster: *The train was gradually picking up speed.* | *Our speed began to pick up as we started downhill.*

9 **pick up speed/steam/momentum etc. a)** if an idea or system picks up speed, it begins to develop, grow, or become more important: *By the end of the year the economy had picked up steam, and voters were hopeful.* **b)** if a person or group picks up steam, they begin to have more energy or confidence: *The Packers seem to be picking up steam after winning in Minnesota last week.*

10 **learn** [T **pick** sth ↔ **up**] to learn a skill, language, or idea without much effort or without being taught in a class: *It's amazing how quickly Lee picked up Russian – he hasn't lived there very long.*

11 **the wind/beat etc. picks up** if the wind, a musical beat etc. picks up, it increases or becomes stronger: *The wind's picking up a little bit.*

12 **pick up the slack** to work harder or take more responsibility for work that needs to be done, when the person who usually does it cannot or is not doing it: *With Nicole gone, all of our staff will be picking up the slack.*

13 **get an illness** [T **pick** sth ↔ **up**] INFORMAL to get an illness from someone, or to become sick: *I think I picked up a cold from someone at work.*

14 **notice sth** [T **pick** sth ↔ **up**] to see, hear, or smell something, especially when it is difficult: *Rescue dogs were able to pick up the scent of the child.*

15 **radio/recording** [**pick** sth ↔ **up**] if a machine picks up a sound, signal, or movement, it is able to change it into pictures, record it etc.: *Our TV doesn't pick up channel 26 very well.* | *Radar has picked up a new storm front.*

16 **start again** [I,T **pick** sth ↔ **up**] if a conversation, meeting etc. picks up or if you pick it up, it starts again from the point where it was interrupted: *Let's pick up again in Chapter 11.* | *Luckily, Maggie was able to pick up where she left off at work, even though she'd been in the hospital for two months.*

17 **a criminal** [T **pick** sb ↔ **up**] if the police or another official group of people pick someone up, they find them and take them somewhere, to answer questions or to be locked up: *Authorities picked Linden up at a border crossing.* | *Rogers was picked up on a drug charge.*

18 **sex** [T **pick** sb ↔ **up**] to talk to someone you do not know because you want to have sex with them: *Kathy said some guy tried to pick her up at a bar.*

19 **pick up the pieces (of sth)** if you pick up the pieces of a business, relationship etc. that has had serious problems, you try to make it work again: *The town is beginning to pick up the pieces after the worst mass shooting in U.S. history.*

P

P

20 pick up the threads (of sth) if you pick up the threads of a relationship, a way of life, or an idea that has been interrupted, you try to start it again: *The good thing is that he's trying to pick up the threads of his life again.*

21 a color [T **pick** sth ↔ **up**] if a color or a piece of furniture picks up the color of something else, it has small amounts of that color in it so that it matches: *I like the way the curtains pick up the red and yellow in the rug.*

pick up on sth *phr. v.* [T] **1** to notice something, especially when this is difficult: *Children easily pick up on tension between their parents.* | *Genny is good at picking up on trends in the stock market.* **2** to continue to talk about something you have noticed or discovered: *Hollywood also has picked up on the tragic story of Brandon Silveria.*

pick² *n.* **1** [U] choice: *The shirt comes in four colors, so take your pick* (=choose one). | *Twenty years ago, you could have your pick of* (=be able to choose any one of many) *engineering jobs.* **2 the pick of sth** the best thing or things of a group: *It's the pick of this month's new movies.* | **the pick of the crop/bunch/litter** (=the best in the group) **3** [C] INFORMAL someone or something that is chosen from among other people or things: *Mutombo, the fourth pick in the NBA draft, is averaging 19 points a game.* **4** [C] a pickax **5** [C] a small flat object used to pull the strings of an instrument such as a GUITAR when you play it **6** a type of COMB used for very curly hair —see also ICE PICK

pick·a·nin·ny /ˈpɪkəˌnɪni/ *n.* [C] OLD-FASHIONED a word for a small African child, now considered offensive

pick·ax /ˈpɪk-æks/ *n.* [C] a large tool that has a curved iron bar with two sharp points at the end of a long handle

pick·er /ˈpɪkɚ/ *n.* [C] **cotton/fruit/apple picker etc.** a person or machine that picks things, especially crops

pick·et¹ /ˈpɪkɪt/ *n.* [C] **1** also **picket line** a group or line of people who stand or march in front of a store, factory, government building etc. to protest about something or to stop people from going to work during a STRIKE: *Protesters staged a noisy picket in front of the hotel where the governor spoke.* | *A few of the nurses crossed picket lines and went back to work.* **2** one person in a picket: *Pro-choice supporters donate money to the clinic for each picket who shows up.* **3** a soldier or group of soldiers who have the special duty of guarding a military camp —see also PICKET FENCE

picket² *v.* **1** [I,T] to stand or march in front of a store, factory, government building etc. to protest about something or to stop people from going to work during a STRIKE: *More than 1,200 teachers picketed that day.* | *Union members have picketed the department store since it opened.* **2** [T] to place soldiers around or near a place as guards

picket fence /ˌ.. ˈ./ *n.* [C] a fence made up of a line of strong pointed sticks fastened in the ground

Pick·ford /ˈpɪkfɚd/, **Mary** (1893–1979) a U.S. movie actress born in Canada

pick·ings /ˈpɪkɪŋz/ *n.* [plural] INFORMAL something or a group of things that you can choose from | **easy/best/richest etc. pickings** *You'll find good decorating ideas in many shops, but the best pickings are usually in expensive department stores.* | **slim/lean/meager etc. pickings** (=when there are not many good things or opportunities to choose from)

pick·le¹ /ˈpɪkəl/ *n.* **1** [C] a CUCUMBER preserved in VINEGAR or salt water, or a piece of this: *a dill pickle* **2** [U] a strong-tasting liquid made with VINEGAR, used to preserve vegetables **3 be in a (pretty) pickle** OLD-FASHIONED to be in a difficult or confusing situation

pickle² *v.* [T] to preserve food in VINEGAR or salt water: *pickled onions*

pick·led /ˈpɪkəld/ *adj.* OLD-FASHIONED INFORMAL drunk

pick-me-up /ˈ. . ˌ./ *n.* [C] INFORMAL something that makes you feel more cheerful and gives you more energy, especially a drink or medicine

pick·pock·et /ˈpɪkˌpɑkɪt/ *n.* [C] someone who steals things from people's pockets, especially in a crowd —see Usage Note at THIEF

pick-up¹ /ˈ. ./ *n.* **1** [C] also **pickup truck** a vehicle with a large open part in the back that is used for carrying goods: *Dad's old pick-up was parked outside.* **2** [U] the rate at which a vehicle can increase its speed; ACCELERATION: *My old car had excellent pick-up.* **3** [C usually singular] an increase or improvement in something: *a pick-up in textbook sales* **4** [C] a time or meeting that has been arranged so that someone can take things or people away from a particular place: *Garbage pick-ups are on Tuesdays and Fridays.* | *a shuttle-bus pick-up* **5** [C] an electronic part on an electric GUITAR that makes the sound louder

pick-up² *adj.* [only before noun] a pick-up game of basketball, football etc. is not planned and happens because people suddenly decide to play, often with other people they do not know: *Occasionally I play a game of pick-up basketball in the park.*

pick-up truck /ˈ. . ˌ./ *n.* [C] a PICK-UP (1)

pick·y /ˈpɪki/ *adj.* **pickier, pickiest** INFORMAL someone who is picky is difficult to please because they only like particular things, or only like things to happen in a particular way: *a picky eater* | [+ about] *Phil's not picky about his appearance.*

pic·nic¹ /ˈpɪknɪk/ *n.* [C] **1** an occasion when people take food and eat it outdoors, especially somewhere such as the beach, a park etc.: *Let's have a picnic Sunday afternoon.* —see also PICNIC BASKET **2 be no picnic** to be difficult or bad: *A two-hour bus ride to work every day is no picnic.* **3 picnic lunch/supper** the food you take for a picnic: *Those attending the conference are invited to bring a picnic lunch.*

picnic² *v.* **picnicked, picnicking** [I] to have a picnic: *Several young couples were picnicking on the beach.* —**picnicker** *n.*

picnic ar·e·a /ˈ.. ˌ.../ *n.* [C] an area near a road where people in cars can stop and rest and have a picnic

picnic bas·ket /ˈ.. ˌ../ *n.* [C] a basket used to carry food for a picnic

Pict /pɪkt/ one of the people who lived in north and central Scotland from the 3rd to the 9th centuries

pic·to·graph /ˈpɪktəˌgræf/ *n.* [C] a SYMBOL or sign that represents a word or idea, especially ones that are used to write a language

pic·to·ri·al /pɪkˈtɔriəl/ *adj.* relating to paintings, drawings, or photographs

pic·ture¹ /ˈpɪktʃɚ/ *n.*
1 image [C] a painting, drawing, or photograph: *Pictures of her family covered the coffee table.* | *Leo's picture* (=a photograph of Leo) *is in the paper today.* | **draw/paint a picture** *The children drew pictures of their houses.* | *Excuse me, could you take a picture of us* (=use a camera to take a photograph)?
2 description [C usually singular] a description of how something is or what it is like: *To get a better picture of how the company is doing, look at sales.* | **paint a clear/grim/optimistic etc. picture of sth** (=describe something in a particular way)
3 the big/overall/larger picture a situation considered as a whole, not just in detail: *Claussen's having trouble getting her fellow council members to see the big picture.*
4 be in/out of the picture if someone is in or out of the picture, they are involved or not involved in a situation: *With his main rival out of the picture, Franklin will surely win the election.*
5 be the picture of health/innocence/despair etc. to look very healthy, innocent etc.: *At 82, Mr. Field is the picture of health.*
6 mental image [C usually singular] an image or memory that you have in your mind: *I still have a vivid picture in my head of my first day in Paris.*
7 get the picture SPOKEN to understand a situation: *Oh, I get the picture. You're in love with Muriel, aren't you?*

8 movie [C] a word meaning a movie, used especially by people in the movie industry: *By the 1930s, Garbo was reportedly earning $250,000 a picture.* | *Beymer has **been in pictures** (=acted in movies) with Paul Newman but has never studied acting.* —see also MOTION PICTURE

9 television [C usually singular] the image that appears on a television or movie SCREEN: *The picture's all fuzzy.* —see also **pretty as a picture** (PRETTY² (4))

picture² sw v. [T] 1 to imagine something, especially by making an image in your mind: *I can still picture her lovely brown eyes.* | [**picture sb doing sth**] *Doris could picture him standing there in his uniform.* | [**picture sb/sth as sth**] *I can't picture Jay as a ballet dancer.* **2 be pictured** to be shown in a photograph, painting, or drawing, especially in a newspaper, magazine, or book: *Here, Thuong is pictured with her son Son Hong Vo.*

picture book /'.. ,./ *n.* [C] a children's book that has a lot of pictures and usually a simple story

picture-per·fect /,.. '..·./ *adj.* exactly right in appearance or quality: *It was a picture-perfect day for going fishing.*

picture post·card /'.. '../ *n.* [C] a POSTCARD with a photograph or picture on the front of it

picture-postcard /'.. ,../ *adj.* [only before noun] very pretty: *a picture-postcard view of the Pacific*

picture show /'.. ,./ *n.* [C] OLD-FASHIONED a movie, or the occasion when a movie is shown

pic·tur·esque /,pɪktʃə'rɛsk/ *adj.* **1** a place that is picturesque is pretty and interesting, especially in an old-fashioned way: *the picturesque town of Monterey* **2** interesting, and unusual or exciting: *Gordon's picturesque account of the battle*

picture win·dow /,.. '../ *n.* [C] a large window made of a single piece of glass

pid·dle /'pɪdl/ *v.* [I] SPOKEN to URINATE
piddle around *phr. v.* [I] SPOKEN to waste time doing things that are not important

pid·dling /'pɪdlɪŋ/ *adj.* small and unimportant: *a piddling amount of money*

pidg·in /'pɪdʒən/ *n.* **1** [C,U] a language that is a mixture of two other languages and is used especially between people who do not speak each other's languages well **2 pidgin English/French etc.** English, French etc. that is either not very good or is mixed with the words or grammar of another language

pie sw /paɪ/ *n.* **1 [C,U] a sweet food usually made with fruit baked inside a PASTRY covering: *cherry pie* | *a piece of pie* **2** [C,U] a food made of meat or vegetables baked in a PASTRY covering: *steak and kidney pie* —see also POT PIE **3 slice/share/piece of the pie** a share of something such as money, profits etc.: *Smaller capitalist countries are maneuvering to gain a bigger share of the pie.* **4 pie in the sky** a good plan, promise, or idea that you do not think will happen: *Building a baseball field downtown is just pie in the sky right now.* —see also **easy as pie** (EASY¹ (11)), **have a finger in every pie** (FINGER¹ (10)), **eat humble pie** (HUMBLE¹ (6)), MUD PIE, PIE CHART

pie·bald /'paɪbɔld/ *adj.* a piebald animal has large areas of skin or fur that are two different colors, usually black and white —**piebald** *n.* [C]

**piece¹ sw /pis/ *n.* [C]
1 separate part a part of something that has been separated, broken, or cut from the rest of it: [+ **of**] *Do you want a piece of pizza?* | *There are pieces of glass all over the road.* | *Our satellite dish has a piece broken off of it.* | *The ship now lies in pieces* (=in small parts) *at the bottom of the ocean.*
2 object a single thing of a particular type, often one that is part of a set of things: *Which piece of luggage is yours?* | *a piece of paper* | *a beautifully made piece of furniture* | *a 100-piece tool set* (=with 100 tools in the set)
3 connected part one of several different parts that must be joined together to make something: *Some of the jigsaw pieces are missing.* | *The cars were shipped in pieces* (=separated into pieces) *and then reassembled.*
4 a piece of advice/information/gossip etc. some

advice, information etc.: *Let me give you a piece of advice – don't mention our conversation to Kim.*
5 a piece of land/property an area of land: *Our condo is located on a fabulous piece of beach-front property.*
6 tear/rip/hack etc. sth to pieces to damage something very severely so that it is in many parts: *Several of the bodies had been hacked to pieces.*
7 cut/rip/tear etc. sb to pieces to criticize someone or their ideas very severely: *The President's plan has been ripped to pieces by the press.*
8 go to pieces to be so upset or nervous that you cannot think or behave normally: *When they lost the family business, Liz went to pieces.*
9 (all) in one piece not damaged or injured: *Somehow we made it to Tibet and back in one piece.*
10 give sb a piece of your mind INFORMAL to tell someone that you are very angry with them: *I was so mad that I called back and gave her a piece of my mind.*
11 be a piece of cake INFORMAL to be very easy to do: *Creating graphs is a piece of cake on the computer.*
12 a piece of the action INFORMAL a share of the profits from a business activity, especially an illegal one
13 money **a)** a coin of a particular value | **fifty-cent/hundred-yen/ten-franc etc. piece** *What can I buy with a fifty-cent piece?* **b)** OLD USE a coin: *30 pieces of silver*
14 art/music etc. something that has been produced by an artist, musician, or writer: *One of the pieces in Greene's sculpture collection is valued at $12,000.*
15 be a piece of crap/junk/poop etc. SPOKEN an impolite way of saying that something is of very low quality: *This printer's a piece of crap!*
16 sb's a (real) piece of work SPOKEN, HUMOROUS used to say that someone behaves in unusual or strange ways, especially when this is annoying or difficult to deal with
17 in a newspaper a short written ARTICLE (1) in a newspaper, magazine, or television program: *The Times did a nice piece on the illegal gambling.*
18 in games also **game piece** a small object or figure used in playing games such as CHESS
19 gun SLANG a small gun
20 piece of ass VULGAR a word for a woman, used by men when they are talking about sex and considered offensive by women
21 a piece OLD-FASHIONED a short distance away: *The store is down the road a piece.* —see also **fall to pieces** (FALL¹ (22)), MUSEUM PIECE, **pick up the pieces (of sth)** at **pick up** (PICK¹), SET PIECE, **the villain (of the piece)** (VILLAIN (2))

piece² v.
piece sth ↔ together *phr. v.* [T] **1** to think about all the details you have about a situation in order to understand the whole thing: *Investigators are still trying to piece together what caused the fire.* **2** to put all the separate parts of an object into the correct order or position: *A team of five pieced together shards of ancient pottery.*

pi·èce de ré·sis·tance /pi,ɛs də reɪzi'stɑns/ *n.* [C] the best or most important thing or event in a series, especially when it comes after all the others: *The concert's pièce de résistance was Mozart's "Requiem."*

piece·meal /'pismil/ *adj.* a process that is piecemeal happens slowly in separate unconnected stages and is not well planned: *Improvements have been largely piecemeal, without adequate government support.* —**piecemeal** *adv.*: *Hargrave might have to sell the company piecemeal.*

piece rate /'. ./ *n.* [C] an amount of money that is paid for each thing a worker produces: *The piece rate was $2.00 per skirt.*

pieces of eight /,.. . './ *n.* [plural] silver coins used in past times in Spain

piece·work /'piswɜk/ *n.* [U] work that is paid according to the number of things you complete or produce rather than the number of hours you work

pie chart /'. ./ *n.* [C] a circle divided into several parts that shows how something such as an amount of money or the population is divided —see picture at CHART[1]

pie crust /'. ./ *n.* [C,U] the PASTRY pastry that is under and sometimes covering the fruit or meat in a PIE

pied /paɪd/ *adj.* [only before noun] having two or more colors in different areas or in the form of spots, especially used to describe animals

pied-à-terre /pi,eɪd ə 'tɛr/ *n.* [C] a small apartment or house that is not your main home but which you own and stay in sometimes

pie-eyed /'. ,./ *adj.* OLD-FASHIONED very drunk

pier /pɪr/ *n.* [C] **1** a structure that is built out into the water, especially so that boats can stop next to it: *The cruise boards at 7 p.m. at Pier 33.* **2** a thick post of stone, wood, or metal used to support something such as a bridge —see picture at BELOW[1]

s w   **pierce** /pɪrs/ *v.* [T] **1** to make a small hole in or through something using an object with a sharp point: *A bullet pierced his spinal cord.* **2** have/get sth pierced to have a small hole made in your ears, nose etc. so that you can wear jewelry in it: *Jennie's getting her ears pierced.* **3** if sound, light, pain etc. pierces something you can suddenly hear it, see it, or feel it: *Orange-red flames pierced the dark sky.*

Pierce /pɪrs/, **Frank·lin** /'fræŋklɪn/ (1804–1869) the 14th President of the U.S.

pierced /pɪrst/ *adj.* a part of your body that is pierced has a small hole or holes in it so that you can wear jewelry there: *Are your ears pierced?* | **pierced ears/nose/tongue etc.** *Anne has a pierced nose.*

pierc·ing[1] /'pɪrsɪŋ/ *adj.* **1** a piercing sound is high, loud, and usually not nice to listen to: *a piercing scream* **2** very cold and seeming to cut through your clothes: *an icy piercing wind* **3** seeming to examine things and notice and understand more than other people would: *his piercing blue eyes* **4** affecting your emotions very much, especially in a sad way: *She had a piercing vision of what life would be like without David.* **5** piercing questions, remarks etc. show that someone understands a situation very well and cannot be tricked: *Letterman's piercing humor* **6** a piercing light is very strong and bright: *piercing beams of light* —**piercingly** *adv.*

piercing[2] *n.* [C,U] a BODY PIERCING

Pierre /pɪr/ the capital city of the U.S. state of South Dakota

pie-shaped /'. ./ *adj.* [usually before noun] having a shape that is pointed at one end and wider with a curved edge at the other end, like a piece that has been cut from a circular PIE

pi·e·ty /'paɪəti/ *n.* [U] respect for God and religion, often shown in the way you behave —opposite IMPIETY —see also PIOUS

s w   **pig[1]** /pɪg/ *n.* [C] **1** a farm animal that is kept for its meat and that is usually pink or black and has short legs, a fat body, and a curled tail —see also GUINEA PIG (2) **2** SPOKEN **a)** someone who eats too much or eats more than their share: *You pig! You ate all of the cookies!* **b)** someone who is very dirty or messy: *How can you live in this mess? You're such a pig!* **c)** someone who is disgusting or offensive: *You're a selfish pig.* —see also **male chauvinist pig** (MALE CHAUVINIST) **3** OFFENSIVE, SLANG a police officer **4 in a pig's eye!** SPOKEN used to show that you do not believe what someone is saying

pig[2]

    pig out *phr. v.* [I] SPOKEN to eat a lot of food: [+ **on**] *We pigged out on pizza in front of the TV.*

pi·geon /'pɪdʒən/ *n.* [C] a gray bird with short legs that is common in cities —see also CARRIER PIGEON, HOMING PIGEON

pigeon-chest·ed /'.. ,../ *adj.* someone who is pigeon-chested has a narrow chest that sticks out

pi·geon·hole[1] /'pɪdʒən,hoʊl/ *n.* [C] **1** one of a set of small boxes built into a desk or into a frame on a wall, into which letters or papers can be put **2 put sb/sth into a pigeonhole** to pigeonhole someone or something

pigeonhole[2] *v.* [T] to decide unfairly that a person, activity etc. belongs to a particular type or group: *Most people don't think of him as a real actor. He is pigeonholed as an action movie star.*

pigeon-toed /'.. ,./ *adj.* someone who is pigeon-toed has feet that point in rather than straight forward

pig·gish /'pɪgɪʃ/ *adj.* someone who is piggish eats too much, is dirty, or is disgusting: *piggish behavior*

pig·gy /'pɪgi/ *n. plural* **piggies** [C] SPOKEN a word meaning a "pig," used especially by or to children

pig·gy·back[1] /'pɪgi,bæk/ *adv.* on someone's back or shoulders, or on top of something: *The space shuttle rode piggyback on a modified jumbo jet.*

piggyback[2] *v.* [I] INFORMAL to use something that someone else has done, developed, or made for your own advantage: [+ **on/onto**] *These new firms are piggybacking onto technology that we developed.*

pig·gy·back ride /'.. ,./ *n.* [C] a ride on someone's back: *Dad, give me a piggyback ride.*

pig·gy bank /'.. ,./ *n.* [C] a small container, often in the shape of a pig, in which children can save coins

pig·head·ed /'pɪg,hɛdɪd/ *adj.* DISAPPROVING determined to do things the way you want and refusing to change your mind, even when there are good reasons to do so; STUBBORN: *The consulate official was being pigheaded about giving us our visas.*

pig i·ron /'. ,../ *n.* [U] a form of iron that is not pure, obtained directly from a BLAST FURNACE

pig·let /'pɪglɪt/ *n.* [C] a young pig

pig·ment /'pɪgmənt/ *n.* [C,U] **1** a natural substance in humans, plants, and animals that gives color to skin, blood, hair etc., or all of these substances considered as a group **2** a dry colored powder that is mixed with oil, water etc. to make paint, or these powders considered as a group

pig·men·ta·tion /,pɪgmən'teɪʃən/ *n.* [U] the coloring of living things: *skin pigmentation*

pig·my /'pɪgmi/ *n. plural* **pygmies** [C] another spelling of PYGMY

pig·pen /'pɪgpɛn/ *n.* [C] **1** a place where pigs are kept, usually with a building and an outdoor area **2** INFORMAL a very dirty or messy place

pig·skin /'pɪgskɪn/ *n.* **1** [singular] INFORMAL the ball used in football: *Let's go toss the pigskin around.* **2** [U] leather made from the skin of a pig

pig·sty /'pɪgstaɪ/ *n. plural* **pigsties** [C] **1** a very dirty or messy place: *This room's a pigsty.* **2** a pigpen

pig·tail /'pɪgteɪl/ *n.* [C] one of two lengths of hair that have been pulled together on either side of the head, and that sometimes are BRAIDed, worn especially by very young girls: *Jenny wore her hair in pigtails.* —see picture at HAIRSTYLE

pike /paɪk/ *n.* [C] **1** a large fish that eats other fish and lives in rivers and lakes **2** SPOKEN a TURNPIKE **3 come down the pike** if an opportunity or something new comes down the pike, it happens or starts to exist: *Job opportunities like this don't come down the pike that often.* **4** a long-handled weapon used in past times by soldiers

pike·man /'paɪkmən/ *n.* [C] a soldier who fought in past times with a pike

pik·er /'paɪkɚ/ *n.* [C] INFORMAL, DISAPPROVING someone who does not like to spend much money: *Harper's glitzy new restaurant made the rest of us in the business look like pikers.*

Pike's Peak /,paɪks 'pik/ one of the Rocky Mountains in the U.S. state of Colorado

pike·staff /'paɪkstæf/ *n.* [C] the long wooden handle of a PIKE

pi·laf, pilaff /'pilɑf/ *n.* [C,U] a dish in which rice and vegetables or meat are cooked together in a pan

pi·las·ter /pɪ'læstɚ, 'pɪlæs-/ *n.* [C] a square COLUMN that sticks out partly beyond the wall of a building and is usually only a decoration

pi·lau /pɪ'laʊ, -'loʊ, 'pɪlaʊ/ *n.* [C,U] PILAF

pile

a pile of books

a heap of sand

s w **pile¹** /paɪl/ n.
2   **1** large amount/mass [C] **a)** a large mass of things collected together or thrown together: *Clare was having too much fun playing in the leaf pile to come inside.* | [+ of] *Piles of cans and bottles littered the ground.* **b)** a neat collection of several things of the same kind placed on top of each other; STACK¹ (1): *The folded laundry was separated into three piles.* | [+ of] *a pile of books* | **the top/bottom of the pile** *The papers you want are at the bottom of the pile.* —compare HEAP¹ (2)
2 a pile of sth also **piles of sth** INFORMAL a lot of something: *We went through piles and piles of songs deciding which were best for my voice.*
3 at the bottom of the pile in a very weak position in society or in an organization: *The mayor has shown little concern for those at the bottom of the pile.*
4 cloth/carpets [C,U] the soft surface of short threads on a CARPET or some types of cloth, especially VELVET: *a thick red pile carpet* —compare NAP¹ (2)
5 make a pile INFORMAL to make a lot of money: *In the '70s, Jones made a pile in real estate.*
6 post [C] a heavy big post made of wood, stone, or metal, pushed into the ground and used to support a building, bridge etc.
7 piles [plural] NOT TECHNICAL: see HEMORRHOIDS

pile² v. [T] **1** also **pile up** to make a pile by collecting things together: *Dirty dishes were left piled in the sink.* **2** to fill something or cover a surface with a lot of something: *Mattie piled her plate with food.* | **be piled (high) with** *Every chair in the room was piled with dirty laundry.*
  pile in/into sth phr. v. [I,T] if people pile into a place or vehicle, many of them go into it quickly or in a disorganized way: *Children pile into the gym two afternoons a week.* | *They all piled in, three on the front seat and five in the back.*
  pile on sth phr. v. [T] INFORMAL **1** also **pile it on** to do or talk about something a lot or too much: *In his book, Garret piles on endless details about his childhood.* | *Once the press begins to criticize someone, they tend to pile it on.* **2** if people pile on something such as a piece of furniture, many of them sit or lie on it together: *We all piled on the sofa to watch the movie.*
  pile out phr. v. [I] if a large number of people pile out of a place, they leave it quickly, especially in a disorganized way: [+ of] *Commuters piled out of the train.*
  pile up phr. v. [I,T] to become much larger in quantity or amount, or to make something do this: *Her medical bills began to pile up.* | *Bryant piled up 20 points in the second half of the game.* —see also PILE-UP

pile driv·er /ˈ. ˌ../ n. [C] a machine for pushing heavy posts into the ground

pile-up /ˈ. ./ n. [C] INFORMAL an accident in which several vehicles crash into each other: *Slick roads caused a six-car pile-up along Highway 30.*

pil·fer /ˈpɪlfɚ/ v. [I,T] to steal small amounts of things, or things that are not worth much, especially from the place where you work: *The kids had been pilfering apples from a farmer's orchard in Binghamton.* —**pilferer** n. [C] —**pilfering** n. [U]

pil·grim /ˈpɪlgrəm/ n. [C] **1** someone who travels a long way to a holy place for a religious reason: *Thousands of Christian pilgrims converged on Bethlehem to celebrate Christmas Eve.* **2 the Pilgrims** the group

of English people who arrived to settle at Plymouth, Massachusetts in North America in 1620

pil·grim·age /ˈpɪlgrəmɪdʒ/ n. [C,U] **1** a trip to a holy place for religious reasons: *a pilgrimage to Mecca* **2** a trip to a place related to someone or something famous: *a pilgrimage to Graceland, Elvis' home* **3** a trip to a place that you like very much and where you go often: *In March, the Lowes made their annual pilgrimage to the Rockies.*

Pilgrim Fa·thers /ˌ.. '../ n. [plural] **the Pilgrim Fathers** the men who were the leaders of the Pilgrims in New England in the 17th century

pil·ing /ˈpaɪlɪŋ/ n. [C] a heavy post made of wood, CEMENT, or metal that is used for supporting a building or bridge

pill /pɪl/ n. **1** [C] a small solid piece of medicine, that s w you swallow whole: *I took a couple of pills for my* 3 *stuffy nose.* | *sleeping pills* —see picture at MEDICATION **2 the pill, the Pill** a pill taken regularly by some women in order to prevent them having babies: **be/go on the pill** *Kayla's mom was shocked to find out that Kayla was on the Pill.* **3** INFORMAL someone who annoys you, often a child: *Hannah's being a real pill today.* —see also **a bitter pill (to swallow)** (BITTER (7)), MORNING-AFTER PILL

pil·lage /ˈpɪlɪdʒ/ v. [I,T] if an army pillages a place, it uses violence to steal from and damage a place that it has taken control of in a war —compare LOOT¹ —**pillage** n. [U] —**pillager** n. [C]

pil·lar /ˈpɪlɚ/ n. [C] **1** a tall upright round post used as a support for a roof —see picture on page 423 **2 pillar of the community/church/society etc.** an active and important member of a group, organization etc. who is respected by many people and is considered to behave in a very moral way: *Sambari is one of the pillars of our community.* **3** a very important part of a system of beliefs, especially religious beliefs: *IBM's three pillars of business wisdom are service, people, and perfection.* **4 from pillar to post** moving or changing frequently from one place or situation to another: *We need to get rid of these corrupt officials, not just move them from pillar to post.* **5 pillar of dust/smoke/flame etc.** LITERARY a tall upright mass of dust, smoke, flame etc.

pill·box /ˈpɪlbɑks/ n. [C] **1** a small round box for holding PILLS **2** a small strong, usually circular, shelter with a gun inside it, built as a defense **3** also **pillbox hat** a small round hat for a woman

pil·lion /ˈpɪlyən/ n. **1** [C] a seat for a second person behind the driver of a motorcycle or a rider on a horse **2 ride pillion** to sit behind someone who is driving a MOTORCYCLE or riding a horse

pil·lo·ry¹ /ˈpɪləri/ v. **pillories, pilloried, pillorying** [T usually passive] if someone is pilloried, they are publicly criticized by a lot of people: *Carter was pilloried for his military policies.*

pillory² n. plural **pillories** [C] a wooden frame with holes for the head and hands to be locked into, used in past times as a way of publicly punishing someone —compare **the stocks** (STOCK¹ (9))

pil·low¹ /ˈpɪloʊ/ n. **1** [C] a cloth bag filled with soft s w material, that you put your head on when you are 3 sleeping —compare CUSHION¹ (1) —see picture at BED¹ **2 a pillow fight** a game in which children hit each other with pillows **3 pillow talk** INFORMAL conversation between lovers in bed

pillow² v. [T] **pillow your head on sth** LITERARY to rest your head somewhere, especially so that you can go to sleep: *Roger slept with his head pillowed on Allison's lap.*

pil·low·case, pillow case /ˈpɪloʊˌkeɪs/ n. [C] a cloth cover for a pillow

pi·lot¹ /ˈpaɪlət/ n. [C] **1** someone who operates the s w controls of an aircraft or SPACECRAFT: *an airline pilot* 2 **2** someone with a special knowledge of a particular area of water, who is employed to guide ships across it: *the ship's pilot* **3** a television program that is made in order to test whether people like it and would watch it again in the future **4 pilot program/ test/project etc.** a test that is done to see if an idea, product etc. will be successful: *a pilot project to produce electric cars* —see also AUTOMATIC PILOT

pilot² *v.* [T] **1** to guide an aircraft, SPACECRAFT, or ship as its pilot: *Who was piloting the Boeing 727 when the planes collided?* **2** to test a new idea, product etc. on people to find out whether it will be successful: *The new housing program will be piloted in Chicago and Kansas City.* **3** [always + adv./prep.] to help someone to go to a place: [**pilot sb toward/ through etc. sth**] *He grabbed Wyatt's elbow and piloted him into the backyard.*

pi·lot·house /ˈpaɪlət,haʊs/ *n.* [C] the covered part of a boat, where it is controlled from

pilot light /ˈ.. ,./ also **pilot burn·er** /ˈ.. ,../ *n.* [C] **1** a small gas flame that burns all the time and is used for lighting larger gas burners **2** a small electric light on a piece of electrical equipment that shows when it is turned on

Pi·ma /ˈpimə/ a Native American tribe from the southwestern region of the U.S. —**Pima** *adj.*

pi·men·to /pəˈmɛntoʊ/ *n.* also **pi·mien·to** /pəˈmyɛntoʊ/ [C,U] a small red PEPPER often put inside green OLIVES

pimp /pɪmp/ *n.* [C] a man who makes money by controlling PROSTITUTES (=women who have sex with men for money) —**pimp** *v.* [I]

pim·per·nel /ˈpɪmpə,nɛl/ *n.* [C] a small wild plant with flowers in various colors, especially red

pim·ple /ˈpɪmpəl/ *n.* [C] a small raised red spot on your skin, especially on your face —see also GOOSE PIMPLES —**pimpled** *adj.* —**pimply** *adj.*

PIN /pɪn/ also **PIN num·ber** /ˈ. ,../ *n.* [C] Personal Identification Number; a number that you use when you get money from an ATM (=machine where you can get money from your bank account) using a plastic card

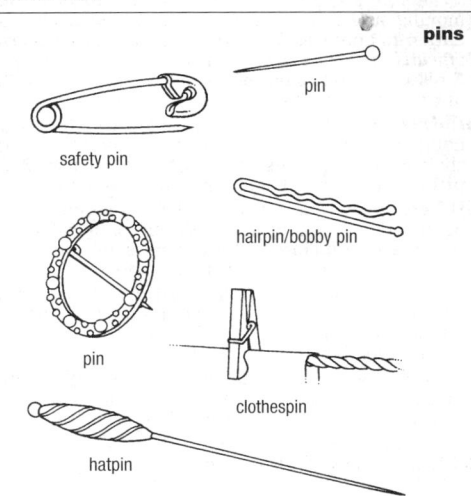

pins

pin

safety pin

hairpin/bobby pin

pin

clothespin

hatpin

s w **pin¹** /pɪn/ *n.* [C]
2 **1** [for cloth] a short thin piece of metal with a sharp point at one end, used especially for fastening together pieces of cloth while making clothes **2** [jewelry] **a)** an attractively shaped piece of metal, sometimes containing jewels, that you fasten to your clothes and wear as a decoration; BROOCH **b)** also **stick pin** a short thin piece of metal with a decoration at one end, used as jewelry **3** [electrical] one of the pieces of metal that stick out of an electric PLUG **4** [for support] a thin piece of metal or wood used as a support for something, or to fasten things together: *After a skiing accident, Dan had a pin inserted in his wrist.*

5 [games] one of the bottle-shaped objects that you try to knock down in a game of BOWLING **6 you could hear a pin drop** SPOKEN used to say that it is very quiet and no one is speaking —see also PINS AND NEEDLES, ROLLING PIN, SAFETY PIN

pin² *v.* **pinned, pinning 1** [T always + adv./prep.] to fasten something somewhere, or to join two things together, using a pin: [**pin sth to/on/onto**] *Some people wore small yellow ribbons pinned to their jackets.* | *Edward had some difficulty pinning the corsage on her dress.* **2 pin your hopes on sb/sth** to hope that something will happen or someone will do something, because all your plans depend on it: *Scientists are pinning their hopes on the new satellite for the information they want.* **3 pin the blame/crime/ killing etc. on sb** to blame someone for something, often unfairly **4** [T always + adv./prep.] to make someone unable to move by putting a lot of pressure or weight on them: [**pin sb to/under/between etc.** sth] *The fourth victim was pinned beneath the car.* **5** [T] to hold someone down on their back or the ground in WRESTLING in order to win

pin sb/sth ↔ down *phr. v.* [T] **1** to make someone give clear details or make a definite decision about something: *Fitzwater refused to be pinned down on details of the investigation.* **2** to understand something clearly or be able to describe it exactly: *It has been difficult to pin down exactly what happened that night.* **3** to not allow someone to move from a particular place by shooting at them: *Jets were used to pin down rebel units.*

pi·ña co·la·da /ˌpinyə koʊˈlɑdə, -kə-/ *n.* [C] an alcoholic drink made from COCONUT juice, PINEAPPLE juice, and RUM

pin·a·fore /ˈpɪnə,fɔr/ *n.* [C] a loose piece of clothing that does not cover your arms, worn by women over their clothes to keep them clean

pi·ña·ta /piˈnyɑtə/ *n.* [C] a decorated paper container filled with candy and sometimes small toys, that children try to hit with sticks and break open as a game

Pi·na·tu·bo, Mount /ˌpinəˈtuboʊ/ a mountain on the island of Luzon in the Philippines that is an active VOLCANO

pin·ball /ˈpɪnbɔl/ *n.* [U] an electric game with lights and bells and a sloping board, in which you push buttons to try to keep a ball from rolling off the board

pinball ma·chine /ˈ.. ,../ *n.* [C] a machine that you play pinball on

pince-nez /ˌpæns ˈneɪ/ *n.* GLASSES worn in past times that were made to fit tightly onto the nose, instead of being held by pieces fitting around the ears

pin·cer /ˈpɪnsə, ˈpɪntʃə/ *n.* **1** [C usually plural] one of the pair of CLAWS¹ (2) that some SHELLFISH and insects have, used for holding and cutting food, and for fighting —see picture at CRUSTACEAN **2 pincers** [plural] a tool made of two crossed pieces of metal, used for holding things tightly —see picture at TOOL¹

pincers move·ment also **pincer movement** /ˈ.. ,../ *n.* [C] a military attack in which two groups of soldiers come from opposite directions in order to catch the enemy between them

pinch¹ /pɪntʃ/ *v.* **1** [T] to press someone's skin very tightly between your finger and thumb, especially so that it hurts: *Stop pinching me!* **2** [I,T] if something you are wearing pinches you, it presses painfully on your skin, because it is too tight: *These shoes pinch my toes.* **3 pinch yourself** SPOKEN to remind yourself that a situation is real and that you are not imagining it: *I keep having to pinch myself, and tell myself that I really did win.* —see also PENNY-PINCHING

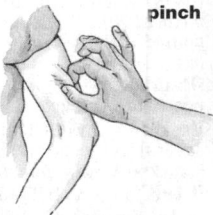

pinch

pinch² *n.* **1 pinch of salt/pepper/cinnamon etc.** a small amount of salt, pepper etc. that you can hold between your finger and thumb: *Stir in a pinch of* nutmeg to the mixture. **2** [C] an act of pressing someone's flesh between your finger and thumb, especially so that it hurts: *Grandma gave us both a pinch on the cheek.* **3 in a pinch** if necessary in a particularly difficult or urgent situation: *The bus service is terrible, but it'll get you to work in a pinch.* **4 take sth with a pinch of salt** to not completely believe what someone says to you: *You have to take most things Dave says with a pinch of salt.* **5 feel the pinch** to have financial difficulties, especially because you are not making as much money as you used to make: *Local stores and businesses are beginning to feel the pinch from the economic crisis.*

pinched /pɪntʃt/ *adj.* **1** not having enough money to do what you want: *Cuts in spending are having a direct effect on the already pinched local schools.* **2** a pinched face looks thin and unhealthy, for example because the person is sick, cold, or tired

pinch-hit /ˌ. './ *v.* [I + for] **1** to HIT¹ (5) for someone else in baseball **2** to do something for someone else because they are suddenly not able to do it: *I've asked Carl to pinch-hit for me at the meeting next week.* —**pinch-hitter** *n.* [C]

pin·cush·ion /ˈpɪnˌkuʃən/ *n.* [C] a soft filled bag for sticking pins in until you need to use them

Pin·dar /ˈpɪndə/ (?518–?438 B.C.) a Greek poet

s w
3
pine¹ /paɪn/ *n.* **1** [C,U] a PINE TREE: *a grove of pines* **2** the soft pale-colored wood of this tree, used to make furniture, floors etc.: *a pine table*

pine² also **pine away (for sb/sth)** *v.* [I] to gradually become weaker, less active, and less healthy because you feel very unhappy: *For months Jennifer stayed at home, pining away for Jack.*
pine for sb/sth *phr. v.* [T] to become unhappy or sick because you cannot be with someone you love or in a place you love: *Les is still pining for home.*

pin·e·al gland /ˈpɪniəl ˌglænd, ˈpaɪ-/ *n.* [C] a part of the brain that scientists think may be sensitive to light

pine·ap·ple /ˈpaɪnˌæpəl/ *n.* [C,U] a large yellow-brown tropical fruit or its sweet juicy yellow flesh: *pineapple juice* —see picture at FRUIT¹

pine·cone /ˈpaɪnkoʊn/ *n.* [C] the brown seed container of the PINE TREE

pine nee·dle /'. ˌ../ *n.* [C] a leaf of the pine tree, that is thin and sharp

pine nut /'. ./ *n.* [C] a small seed that grows on some pine trees, that is eaten in salads and other dishes

pine·tree /ˈpaɪnˌtri/ *n.* [C] a tall tree with long hard sharp leaves that do not fall off in winter; a PINE¹ (1)

pine·wood /ˈpaɪnwʊd/ *n.* **1** [C] a forest of pine trees **2** [U] the wood from a pine tree

pine·y, piny /ˈpaɪni/ *adj.* relating to or containing PINE TREES: *the piney woods of southeast Alabama*

ping¹ /pɪŋ/ *n.* [C] a short high ringing sound

ping² *v.* [I] to make a short high ringing sound

ping-pong, Ping Pong /ˈpɪŋˌpɑŋ, -pɔŋ/ *n.* [U] TRADEMARK an indoor game played on a table top by two people with a small light plastic ball and two PADDLES¹ (2); TABLE TENNIS

pin·head /ˈpɪnhɛd/ *n.* [C] **1** the head of a pin **2** [C] INFORMAL someone who is stupid: *I have to deal with pinheads like him all day at work.*

pin·hole /ˈpɪnhoʊl/ *n.* [C] a very small hole in something, or a small hole made by a pin

pinhole cam·e·ra /ˌ.. '../ *n.* [C] a very simple camera, in which a pinhole is made at one end of a box, and the film is put inside the box on the side across from the hole

pin·ion¹ /ˈpɪnyən/ *v.* **1** [T usually passive] TECHNICAL to cut off the big strong feathers from a bird's wings so that it cannot fly **2** [T always + adv./prep.] LITERARY to hold or tie up someone's arms or legs very tightly, so that they cannot move freely: *Her arms were pinioned tightly behind her.*

pinion² *n.* [C] **1** a small wheel, with tooth-like parts on its outer edge, that fits into a larger wheel and turns it or is turned by it **2** LITERARY a bird's wing **3** TECHNICAL the outer part of a bird's wing, where the strongest flying feathers grow

pink¹ /pɪŋk/ *adj.* red mixed with white: *pink carnations* | *pink and white stripes* —see also **be tickled pink** (TICKLE¹ (3))   **s w**
2

pink² *n.* **1** [C,U] a pale color made by mixing red and white **2** [C] a garden plant with pink, white, or red flowers **3 in the pink** OLD-FASHIONED in very good health

pink-col·lar /ˌ. '..◂/ *adj.* relating to low-paid jobs done mainly by women, for example in offices and restaurants, or relating to the women who do these jobs: *pink-collar jobs* | *pink-collar workers* —compare WHITE-COLLAR, BLUE-COLLAR

Pin·ker·ton /ˈpɪŋkətən/, **Al·lan** /ˈælən/ (1819–1884) a U.S. DETECTIVE who started the Pinkerton National Detective Agency

P

pink·eye /ˈpɪŋk-aɪ/ *n.* [U] NOT TECHNICAL a disease that causes the skin around the eyes to swell and become red, and can easily be given to someone else

pink·ie, pinky /ˈpɪŋki/ also **pinkie fin·ger** /'.. ˌ../ *n.* [C] the smallest finger of the human hand

pink·ing shears /'.. ˌ./ also **pinking scis·sors** /'.. ˌ.◂/ *n.* [plural] a special type of scissors that makes points on the edge of the cloth or paper you are cutting —see picture at SCISSORS

pink·ish /ˈpɪŋkɪʃ/ *adj.* slightly pink: *pinkish-lavender flowers*

pink·o /ˈpɪŋkoʊ/ *n.* [C] OFFENSIVE someone who is a SOCIALIST or COMMUNIST¹ (1) —**pinko** *adj.*

pink slip /'. ./ *n.* [C] **1** INFORMAL an official document that proves you own a particular car **2** INFORMAL a written warning you get when your job is going to end because there is not enough work: *As a result of cutbacks, the plant issued pinkslips to over 300 employees.*

pink·y /ˈpɪŋki/ *n. plural* **pinkies** [C] another spelling of PINKIE

pin mon·ey /'. ˌ../ *n.* [U] OLD-FASHIONED a small amount of money that you can spend on yourself rather than on necessary things

pin·na·cle /ˈpɪnəkəl/ *n.* **1** [singular] the most successful, powerful, exciting etc. part of something: [+ of] *By 1965, Fellini had reached the pinnacle of his commercial success.* **2** [C] a pointed stone decoration, like a small tower, on a building such as a church or castle **3** [C] ESPECIALLY LITERARY a high mountain top

pi·noch·le /ˈpiˌnʌkəl/ *n.* [U] a card game

pin·point¹ /ˈpɪnpɔɪnt/ *v.* [T] **1** to say exactly what the facts about something really are: *Scientists have been unable to pinpoint the exact causes of cancer.* | [pinpoint what/how/why etc.] *Nobody can pinpoint what a company will earn even two years from now.* **2** to find or show the exact position of something: *Satellite pictures helped to pinpoint the locations of 13,000 troops.*

pinpoint² *n.* [C] **1** a very small point or DOT of something: [+ of] *Through a telescope, Jupiter's moons will look like pinpoints of light.* **2 with pinpoint accuracy/precision** very exactly, without even the smallest mistake: *This type of missile can be fired with pinpoint precision.*

pin·prick /ˈpɪnˌprɪk/ *n.* [C] **1** a very small hole in something, similar to one made by a pin **2** [C] a very small area or DOT of something: [+ of] *a pinprick of light* **3** a slight feeling that worries or upsets you: [+ of] *a pinprick of jealousy*

pins and nee·dles /ˌ. . '.◂/ **1 be on pins and needles** to be very nervous and unable to relax, especially because you are waiting for something important: *I was on pins and needles until I found out I'd won.* **2** the small sharp pains that you get in a part of your body when it starts to stop feeling NUMB, for example after you have been in an uncomfortable position for too long

pin·stripe /ˈpɪnstraɪp/ *n.* [C] one of the thin light-colored lines that form a pattern on dark cloth —see picture at PATTERN¹

pin-striped also **pinstripe** /'. ./ *adj.* having a pattern of pinstripes: *a pin-striped suit*

pint /paɪnt/ *n.* [C] a unit for measuring liquid, equal to 16 FLUID OUNCES or 0.4732 liters: *a pint of milk*

Pin·ter /'pɪntə/, **Har·old** /'hærəld/ (1930–) a British writer of plays

pin·to /'pɪntoʊ/ *n.* [C] a horse with irregular markings of two or more colors

pinto bean /'.. ,./ *n.* [C] a small light brown bean

pint-sized also **pint-size** /'. ./ *adj.* [only before noun] small, and often seeming silly or unimportant: *The owners meet regularly to show off their pint-sized pets.*

pin-up /'. ./ *n.* [C] **1** a picture of an attractive person, often a woman without many clothes on, that is put up on a wall to be looked at and admired **2** someone who appears in one of these pictures

pin·wheel /'pɪnwil/ *n.* [C] a toy consisting of a stick with curved pieces of plastic at the end that turn around when they are blown

pin·y /'paɪni/ *adj.* another spelling of PINEY

pi·o·neer[1] /ˌpaɪə'nɪr/ *n.* [C] **1** one of the first people to do something that other people will later develop or continue to do: [+ of/in] *Dr. DeBakey was one of the pioneers of heart-transplant surgery.* | *pioneers in special education* | **pioneer photographer/geologist etc.** (=one of the first people to develop the skill of photography etc.) **2** one of the first people to travel to a new country or area and begin living there, farming etc.: *Many of the early pioneers left after a long cold winter.*

pioneer[2] *v.* [T] to be the first person to do, invent, or use something: *Merrell pioneered the use of Velcro instead of laces on boots.*

pi·o·neer·ing /ˌpaɪə'nɪrɪŋ / *adj.* [only before noun] introducing new and better methods or ideas for the first time: *the pioneering work of Caventou in drug research* | *the pioneering jazz pianist Bud Powell*

pi·ous /'paɪəs/ *adj.* **1** having strong religious beliefs, and showing this in the way you behave **2** DISAPPROVING pious words, promises, attitudes etc. are intended to sound good or moral, although they are not: *pious speeches by politicians* —see also PIETY —**piously** *adv.* —**piousness** *n.* [U]

pip[1] /pɪp/ *n.* [C] **1** a small seed from a fruit such as an apple or orange **2** one of the spots on DICE or PLAYING CARDS

s w **pipe**[1] /paɪp/ *n.* **1** [C] a tube through which a liquid or
3 gas flows, often under the ground: *Let a little water run in your sink so that your pipes don't freeze.* | *Developers in some hill areas are required to lay their own water pipes.* | *sewer pipes* **2** [C] a thing used for smoking tobacco, consisting of a small tube with a container shaped like a bowl at one end: *Dad has smoked a pipe for years.* | *pipe tobacco* **3** [C] **a)** one of the metal tubes through which air passes when an ORGAN (2) is played **b)** a simple musical instrument shaped like a tube and played by blowing **4 pipe dream** a hope, idea, plan etc. that is impossible or will probably never happen: *Making it all the way to the NFL is a pipe dream for most athletes.* **5 put that in your pipe and smoke it!** SPOKEN used to say that someone must accept what you have just said, even though they do not like it

pipe[2] *v.* **1** [T usually passive] to send a liquid or gas through a pipe to another place: [be piped in/into/ to etc.] *Lots of oil is piped in from Alaska.* **2** [I,T] to make a musical sound using a pipe **3** [I,T] LITERARY to speak or sing in a high voice: *I awoke to hundreds of birds piping their morning song.* **4** [T] to decorate food, especially a cake, with thin lines of ICING or cream

pipe down *phr. v.* [I] SPOKEN to stop talking or making a noise, and become calmer and less excited: *Pipe down! I'm trying to study.*

pipe sth in/into *phr. v.* [T] to send radio signals or recorded music into a room or building, so that people can hear it while they do other things: *Soft, soothing music was piped in over the speaker system.*

pipe up *phr. v.* [I] INFORMAL to begin to say something or start speaking, especially when you have been quiet until then: *Suddenly Dennis piped up, "Mom, can I have a Coke?"*

pipe clean·er /'. ,./ *n.* [C] a length of wire covered with soft material, used to clean the inside of a tobacco pipe

piped mu·sic /ˌ. '../ *n.* [U] quiet recorded music played continuously in stores, hotels, restaurants etc.

pipe fit·ter /'. ,./ *n.* [C] someone who puts in and repairs pipes for water, gas etc.

pipe·line /'paɪp-laɪn/ *n.* [C] **1** a line of connecting pipes, often under the ground, used for moving gas, oil etc. over long distances **2 be in the pipeline** if a plan, idea, or event is in the pipeline, it is still being prepared, but it will happen or be completed soon: *Plans for building 1,700 rental units are in the pipeline.*

pipe or·gan /'. ,./ *n.* [C] another word for an ORGAN (2)

pip·er /'paɪpə/ *n.* [C] a musician who plays a PIPE (3b) or the BAGPIPES

pipe rack /'. ./ *n.* [C] a small frame for holding several tobacco pipes

pi·pette /paɪ'pɛt/ *n.* [C] a thin glass tube for sucking up exact amounts of liquid, used especially in chemistry

pip·ing[1] /'paɪpɪŋ/ *n.* [U] **1** thin cloth ropes used as decorations on clothes and furniture **2** several pipes, or a system of pipes, used to send liquid or gas in or out of a building

piping[2] *adj.* INFORMAL **piping hot** very hot: *piping hot soup*

pip·pin /'pɪpɪn/ *n.* [C] a small sweet apple

pip·squeak /'pɪpskwik/ *n.* [C] someone that you think is not worth respecting or paying attention to, especially because they are young or do not have much power: *Fernandez is a pipsqueak compared to other drug dealers.*

pi·quant /pi'kɑnt, 'pikənt/ *adj.* **1** having a pleasantly SPICY taste: *a piquant sauce with garlic and red peppers* **2** interesting and exciting; INTRIGUING: *a tale full of piquant characters and vivid descriptions* —**piquantly** *adv.* —**piquancy** *n.* [U]

pique[1] /pik/ *v.* **1 pique your interest/curiosity** to make you feel interested in something or someone: *The tour of the hospital piqued her interest in studying medicine.* **2** [T usually passive] to make someone feel annoyed or upset, especially because they feel insulted: **be/feel piqued** *Privately, Zarich was piqued that his offer was rejected.*

pique[2] *n.* [U] **1** a feeling of being annoyed or upset, especially because you feel insulted: *In a fit of pique* (=sudden anger), *he tossed his wife's McDonald's meal out of the car window.* **2** also **piqué** a type of material made of cotton, silk, or RAYON

pi·ra·cy /'paɪrəsi/ *n.* [U] **1** the illegal copying and sale of books, TAPES, VIDEOS, electronic technology etc.: *software piracy* **2** the crime of attacking and stealing from ships at sea, especially in past times

Pi·ran·del·lo /ˌpɪrən'dɛloʊ/, **Lu·i·gi** /lu'idʒi/ (1867– 1936) an Italian writer of plays and NOVELS

pi·ra·nha /pə'rɑnə, -'ræn-/ *n.* [C] a South American fish with sharp teeth that lives in rivers and eats flesh

pi·rate[1] /'paɪrɪt/ *n.* [C] **1** someone who dishonestly copies and sells another person's work **2 pirate radio/TV** illegal radio or television broadcasts, or the station sending them out: *a pirate radio station* **3** someone who sailed on the oceans, especially in past times, attacking other boats and stealing things from them —**piratical** *adj.*

pirate[2] *v.* [T] to illegally copy and sell another person's work, such as a book, design, or invention —**pirated** *adj.*: *pirated CDs*

pir·ou·ette /ˌpɪru'ɛt/ *n.* [C] a very fast turn made on one toe or the front part of one foot, especially by a BALLET dancer —**pirouette** *v.* [I]

pis·ca·to·ri·al /ˌpɪskə'tɔriəl / *adj.* FORMAL relating to fishing or fishermen (FISHERMAN)

Pis·ces /ˈpaɪsiz/ *n.* **1** [singular] the twelfth sign of the ZODIAC, represented by two fish, and believed to affect the character and life of people born between February 21 and March 20 **2** [C] someone who was born between February 21 and March 20: *Nick's a Pisces.*

pish /pɪʃ/ *interjection* OLD USE used to express annoyance or impatience

piss¹ /pɪs/ *v.* VULGAR **1** [I] to URINATE **2 not have a pot to piss in** to be extremely poor **3 piss in the wind** to waste time or effort trying to do something that is impossible **4 go piss up a rope!** used to tell someone rudely to go away

piss sth ↔ **away** *phr. v.* [T] VULGAR to waste something very stupidly: *They've pissed away a whole lot of money on expensive vacations.*

piss sb ↔ **off** *phr. v.* [T] IMPOLITE to annoy someone very much: *The way she treats me kind of pisses me off.*

piss² *n.* VULGAR **1** [singular] an act of urinating (URINATE): *I need to* **take a piss.** **2** [U] URINE **3 full of piss and vinegar** full of energy

piss-ant¹, **pissant** /ˈ. ./ *n.* [C] IMPOLITE an annoying person who has a weak character or who thinks they are more important than they are: *Forget Allan, that little pissant. We don't need him anymore.*

piss-ant², **pissant** *adj.* [only before noun] IMPOLITE very low value, quality, or importance: *I get really tired of doing these piss-ant little jobs.*

piss-ass /ˈ. ./ *adj.* [only before noun] VULGAR not important at all, or very silly: *Seth thinks his piss-ass little job makes him special!*

pissed off /ˌ. ˈ./ also **pissed** *adj.* [not before noun] IMPOLITE annoyed, disappointed, or unhappy: *I think my boss is pissed off because I want to leave.* | [+ about/at/with] *What are you so pissed off about?* | [+ with/at] *Judy's pissed at me, I think*

pis·ser /ˈpɪsɚ/ *n.* [C] VULGAR **1** a difficult job or activity, or a bad or annoying situation: *You have to work this weekend? What a pisser!* **2** a toilet

piss-poor /ˌ. ˈ./ *adj.* VULGAR of very low quality or done badly: *The city's been doing a piss-poor job of serving its citizens.*

pis·sy /ˈpɪsi/ *adj.* [not before noun] VULGAR **1 get pissy** to begin to get angry and start treating other people badly: *Stacy likes to tease us, but then she gets pissy when we tease her.* **2** used to describe something annoying: *Our brand new CD player isn't working. Isn't that pissy?*

pis·ta·chi·o /pɪˈstæʃiˌoʊ/ *n. plural* **pistachios** [C] a small green nut

pis·til /ˈpɪstl/ *n.* [C] TECHNICAL the female part of a flower that produces seeds

pis·tol /ˈpɪstl/ *n.* [C] a small gun you can use with one hand

pistol-whip /ˈ.. ˌ./ *v.* [T] to hit someone with a pistol

pis·ton /ˈpɪstən/ *n.* [C] a part of an engine consisting of a short solid piece of metal inside a tube, that moves up and down to make the other parts of the engine move

piston ring /ˈ.. ˌ./ *n.* [C] a circular metal spring used to stop gas or liquid escaping from between a piston and the tube that it moves in

pit¹ /pɪt/ *n.*

1 hole [C] **a)** a hole in the ground, especially one made by digging: *Many of the victims were buried in large pits.* **b)** a large hole in the ground from which stones or minerals have been dug: *a gravel pit*

2 mark [C] **a)** a small hollow mark in the surface of something: *There are tiny scratches and pits on the windshield.* **b)** a small hollow mark that is left on your face by ACNE or some diseases

3 be the pits SPOKEN used to say that something is extremely bad: *Wouldn't it be the pits if your flight got canceled?*

4 in the pit of your stomach if you feel an emotion in the pit of your stomach, you experience it strongly, often as a bad feeling in your stomach: *Before a performance, I would wake up with anxiety in the pit of my stomach.*

5 messy place [C] SPOKEN a house or room that is dirty, messy, or in bad condition: *Eric's house is a total pit.*

6 in fruit [C] the single large hard seed in some fruits: *a peach pit*

7 car racing the pits the place beside the track where cars can come in during a race to be quickly repaired

8 the/a pit of sth a situation in which a particular bad quality is too common, or a bad feeling is extremely strong: *I hate politics – it's just a pit of deceit, and it's the same all over the world.*

9 mine [C] a mine, especially a coal mine

10 in a theater [C] an ORCHESTRA PIT

11 in a garage [C] a hole in the floor of a garage that lets you get under a car to repair it

12 business [C] the area of a STOCK EXCHANGE where people buy and sell STOCKs

13 body part [C] INFORMAL an ARMPIT

14 the pit BIBLICAL: see HELL (1) —see also **money pit** (MONEY (9)), MOSH PIT

pit² *v.* **pitted, pitting 1** [T] to take out the single hard seed inside some fruits: *Peel and pit two avocados.* **2** [T usually passive] to put small marks or holes in the surface of something: *The street was pitted with potholes.* **3** [I] to stop in a car race to get gasoline or to have your car repaired: *Andretti pitted with 16 laps left.* —see also PITTED

pit sb/sth **against** sb/sth *phr. v.* [T] to compete, argue, or fight with someone, or test your strength, ability, power etc. against theirs: *The idea has pitted farmers, developers and environmentalists against each other.* | *Amateur golfers will get to* **pit their skill** *against professionals this weekend at Palm Beach.*

pit out *phr. v.* SLANG [I,T **pit** sth ↔ **out**] to SWEAT so much that your clothes become wet under your arms: *By the end of the meeting, I had pitted out my sport coat.*

pi·ta bread /ˈpitə brɛd/ *n.* [U] a type of flat bread that can be opened so you can put food into it

pit bull /ˈ. ˌ./ also **pit bull ter·ri·er** /ˌ. ˈ.../ *n.* [C] an extremely strong dog with short legs that is sometimes violent

Pit·cairn Is·land /ˌpɪtkɛrn ˈaɪlənd/ an island in the southern Pacific Ocean that is controlled by the U.K.

pitch¹ /pɪtʃ/ *n.*

1 baseball [C] a throw of the ball to the BATTER¹ (2) in baseball: *Ryan's first pitch was high and wide.*

2 persuading [C] INFORMAL the things someone says to persuade people to buy something, do something, or agree with an idea: *The President made his strongest pitch yet for standardized testing in schools.*

3 music a) [C,U] a musical note, or the highness or lowness of a musical note or a sound: *The same syllables were sung repeatedly at a number of different pitches.* | *I've never been able to sing* **on pitch.** **b)** [U] the ability of a musician to play or sing a note at exactly the correct pitch: *Kendrick's pitch was good throughout the first aria.* —see also PERFECT PITCH

4 strong feelings [singular,U] the strength of your feelings or opinions about something: *Racial tensions have risen to* **fever pitch** (=a very excited level) *in recent days.*

5 black substance [U] a black sticky substance that is used on roofs, the bottoms of ships etc. to stop water from coming through —see also PITCH-BLACK, PITCH-DARK

6 as black as pitch very dark or completely black

7 ship/aircraft [C] a movement of a ship or an aircraft in which the front part goes up and the back goes down, and then the front goes down and the back goes up

8 slope [singular,U] the degree to which something slopes or the angle it is at: *the pitch of the roof*

pitch² *v.*

1 baseball a) [I,T] to aim and throw a ball to the BATTER¹ (2) in baseball: *Stanton pitched to two batters in the ninth inning.*

P

s w
pit¹

2 throw [T] to throw something with a lot of force, often aiming carefully: [**pitch sth over/into/through etc.**] *The suspect pitched the gun into the river.*

3 fall [I always + adv./prep.,T always + adv./prep.] to fall suddenly and heavily in a particular direction, or to make someone or something fall in this way: [**pitch sb into/over/forward etc.**] *A sudden stop pitched her into the windshield.* | [**pitch forward/backward/over etc.**] *Greg tripped and pitched forward into the bushes.*

4 business deals [I,T] INFORMAL to try to make a business agreement, or to sell something by saying how good it is: *The investment was pitched to parents as a safe way to deal with rising college costs.* | [**+ for**] *They're a huge airline, and we were pitching hard for their business.*

5 set a level [T always + adv./prep.] if you pitch a speech, explanation etc. at a particular level of difficulty or to a particular group of people, you make sure that it can be understood by people at that level: [**+ at**] *The last two chapters are pitched at a slightly higher level than the rest of the book.* | [**+ to**] *Gardner writes that most successful political speeches are pitched to a five-year-old's level.*

6 ship/aircraft [I] if a ship or an aircraft pitches, it moves up and down in an uncontrolled way with the movement of the water or air —compare ROLL¹ (9), YAW

7 voice/music [T always + adv./prep.] if you pitch your voice or another sound at a particular level, the sound is produced at that level: **pitch sth high/low** *This song is pitched too high for my voice.* —see also HIGH-PITCHED, LOW-PITCHED

8 pitch a tent also **pitch camp** to set up a tent or a camp for a short time: *We'd better pitch the tent before it gets dark.*

9 slope [I always + adv./prep.] to slope down | **pitch gently/steeply etc.** *The roof pitches sharply to the rear of the house.* —see also PITCHED

10 pitch sb a line INFORMAL to tell someone a story or give them an excuse that is difficult to believe: *She pitched me some line about a bomb scare on the metro.*

pitch in *phr. v.* [I] INFORMAL **1** to start to work eagerly as a member of a group: *When the harvest comes, the whole family pitches in.* **2** to add your help, support, or money: *The whole team pitched in to buy Kevin a nice present.*

pitch-black /ˌ. ˈ.◂/ *adj.* completely black or dark: *It was pitch-black outside.*

pitch-dark, pitch dark /ˌ. ˈ.◂/ *adj.* completely dark: *I'm not going in. It's pitch-dark in there!*

pitched /pɪtʃt/ *adj.* a roof that is pitched is sloping rather than flat

pitched bat·tle /ˌ. ˈ../ *n.* [C] **1** an angry and usually long argument: *All three companies are in a pitched battle over who invented the technology.* **2** a battle between armies or groups of people who have already chosen and prepared their positions: *Thirty students were injured in a pitched battle with police.* —compare SKIRMISH¹ (1)

pitch·er /ˈpɪtʃɚ/ *n.* [C] **1** a container for holding and pouring liquids, that has a handle and a SPOUT (=shaped part for pouring): *a pitcher of iced tea* **2** the player in baseball who throws the ball to the BATTER¹ (2) —see picture at BASEBALL

pitch·fork /ˈpɪtʃfɔrk/ *n.* [C] a farm tool with a long handle and two long curved metal points, used especially for lifting HAY (=dried long grass)

pitch·man /ˈpɪtʃmən/ *n.* [C] someone who tells people why they should buy a particular product

pitch·pipe /ˈpɪtʃpaɪp/ *n.* [C] a small pipe that makes a sound when you blow through it, that is used to TUNE² (2) musical instruments

pit·e·ous /ˈpɪtiəs/ *adj.* LITERARY expressing suffering and sadness in a way that makes you feel pity: *the piteous cries of hungry children* —**piteously** *adv.*

pit·fall /ˈpɪtfɔl/ *n.* [C] a problem or difficulty that is likely to happen in a particular job, course of action, or activity: *the pitfalls of fame* | *Wiley wrote the book to help travelers **avoid** the **pitfalls** of cross-cultural encounters.*

pith /pɪθ/ *n.* [U] **1** a white substance just under the outside skin of oranges and similar fruit **2** a soft white substance that fills the stems of some plants —see picture at FRUIT¹ **3 the pith of an argument/issue etc.** the most important and necessary part of an argument etc.

pith hel·met /ˈ. ˌ../ *n.* [C] a large light hard hat worn especially in hot countries, to protect your head from the sun

pith·y /ˈpɪθi/ *adj.* **pithier, pithiest** something you say or write that is pithy is intelligent and strongly stated, without wasting any words: *Zehme wrote the pithy comments that accompany each picture.* —**pithily** *adv.* —**pithiness** *n.* [U]

pit·i·a·ble /ˈpɪtiəbəl/ *adj.* FORMAL making you feel pity: *pitiable victims of war* —**pitiably** *adv.*

pit·i·ful /ˈpɪtɪfəl/ *adj.* **1** someone or something that is pitiful looks so sad and unfortunate that you feel very sorry for them: *Margret looked so pitiful, I had to help her.* **2** very bad in quality: *Stu's bass playing is just pitiful.* —**pitifully** *adv.*: *She looked pitifully thin.*

pit·i·less /ˈpɪtɪlɪs/ *adj.* **1** showing no pity; cruel: *a pitiless dictator* **2** pitiless wind, rain, sun etc. is very severe and shows no sign of changing: *the pitiless desert sun* —**pitilessly** *adv.*

pi·ton /ˈpɪtɑn/ *n.* [C] TECHNICAL a piece of metal used in climbing, that you fasten into the rock to hold the rope

pit stop /ˈ. ./ *n.* [C] **1 make a pit stop** SPOKEN to stop when driving on a long trip to get food, gasoline, or use the toilet **2** a time when you stop in the PIT¹ (7) during a car race to get more gasoline or have repairs done

pit·tance /ˈpɪtns/ *n.* [singular] a very small or unfairly small amount of money: *Smith's salary is a mere pittance compared with others in the NBA.*

pit·ted /ˈpɪtɪd/ *adj.* **1** having small marks or holes in the surface: *The truck went racing down the pitted side streets.* **2** a pitted fruit has had the single hard seed removed from it: *pitted prunes*

pit·ter-pat /ˈpɪtɚ ˌpæt/ *adv.* pitter-patter

pit·ter-pat·ter /ˈpɪtɚ ˌpætɚ/ *adv.* **go pitter-patter** to make a sound or movement consisting of many quick light beats or sounds: *Anna's heart went pitter-patter as she opened the letter.* —**pitter-patter** *n.* [singular] *the pitter-patter of rain on the roof*

Pitts·burgh /ˈpɪtsbɚg/ an industrial city in the U.S. state of Pennsylvania

pi·tu·i·tar·y /pəˈtuəˌtɛri/ also **pituitary gland** /.ˈ....ˌ./ *n.* plural **pituitaries** [C] the small organ at the base of your brain which produces HORMONES that control the growth and development of your body —**pituitary** *adj.*

pit vi·per /ˈ. ˌ../ *n.* [C] a type of poisonous snake, such as RATTLESNAKES or COPPERHEADS, which have small hollow places below their eyes

pit·y¹ /ˈpɪti/ *n.* **1** [singular] SPOKEN used to show that you are disappointed about something and you wish things could happen differently: [**it's a pity (that)**] *It's a pity Joel had to move away.* | [**be a pity to do sth**] *It seems a pity to waste it.* | *Students just don't seem interested in math anymore, which is **a great pity.*** | **That's/What a pity** *"Gene didn't get accepted to Yale." "Oh really? That's a pity."* **2** [U] sympathy for someone who is suffering or unhappy: *I have no pity for people who lie and get caught.* | *Joe hated being an **object of pity** at school.* **3 take/have pity on sb** to feel sorry for someone and do something to help them: *Finally, a truck driver took pity on us and gave us a ride.* **4 more's the pity** OLD-FASHIONED used after describing a situation, to show that you wish it was not true: *The new staff are all women, more's the pity.*

pit·y² *v.* **pities, pitied, pitying** [T not usually in progressive] to feel sorry for someone because they are in a very bad situation: *I pity anyone who has to live with Rick.*

Pi·us IX, Pope /ˌpaɪəs ðə ˈnaɪnθ/ (1792–1878) the POPE who called together the First Vatican Council, a meeting of Catholic Church leaders from all over the world

Pius XII, Pope /ˌpaɪəs ðə ˈtwɛlfθ/ (1876–1958) the POPE at the time of World War II

piv·ot[1] /ˈpɪvət/ n. [C] **1** also **pivot point** the one central idea or event that all parts of a plan, process, or idea are based on or arranged around: *Nuclear weapons and the missiles to deliver them became the pivot around which much of the Cold War revolved.* **2** a central point or pin on which something balances or turns

pivot[2] v. **1** [I,T] to turn or balance on a central point, or to make something do this: *The security cameras can automatically pivot to monitor the entire hallway.* **2** [I] to turn quickly on your feet so that you face in the opposite direction: *Magee pivoted and threw the ball to first base.*
pivot on sth *phr. v.* [T] to depend on or be planned around a particular event, or to have a particular idea as the central one: *The entire project pivots on this meeting with the Board of Directors.*

piv·ot·al /ˈpɪvətl/ adj. a pivotal time, event, or person has a very important effect on the way something develops: *Nixon was pivotal in raising the Republican Party's standing among Jewish people.* | **a pivotal event/moment/role etc.** *Kennedy's assassination was a pivotal event for an entire generation.*

pix /pɪks/ n. [plural] SLANG pictures or photographs

pix·el /ˈpɪksəl/ n. [C] TECHNICAL the smallest unit of an image on a television or computer screen

pix·ie, pixy /ˈpɪksi/ n. [C] an imaginary creature that looks like a very small human being, has magical powers, and likes to play tricks on people

Pi·zar·ro /pɪˈzaroʊ/, **Fran·cis·co** /frənˈsɪskoʊ/ (?1475–1541) a Spanish EXPLORER and soldier who went to South America in 1524, and took control of Peru for Spain

s w
1
piz·za /ˈpitsə/ n. [C,U] a thin flat round bread, baked with TOMATOes, cheese, and sometimes vegetables or meat on top

pizza par·lor /ˈ.. ˌ../ n. [C] a restaurant that serves pizza

piz·zazz /pəˈzæz/ n. [U] INFORMAL an exciting strong quality or style: *I knew I didn't have the pizzazz to be a top news anchor.*

piz·ze·ri·a /ˌpitsəˈriə/ n. [C] a restaurant that serves pizza

piz·zi·ca·to /ˌpɪtsɪˈkɑtoʊ/ n. [U] musical notes played by pulling on the STRINGs of an instrument

pj's, PJ's /ˈpidʒeɪz/ n. [plural] SPOKEN: see PAJAMAS

Pk. the written abbreviation of "park"

pkg. the written abbreviation of "package"

Pkwy. the written abbreviation of PARKWAY

Pl. the written abbreviation of "place"

pl. the written abbreviation of "plural"

plac·ard /ˈplækərd, -kard/ n. [C] a large notice or advertisement put up or carried in a public place: *One placard in the crowd read, "Enough is enough!"*

pla·cate /ˈpleɪkeɪt, ˈplæ-/ v. [T] FORMAL to make someone stop feeling angry: *The noise control law could placate airport neighbors, who oppose growth because of the noise.* —**placatory** /ˈpleɪkəˌtɔri/ adj.: *placatory words*

s w
1 1
place[1] /pleɪs/ n. [C]
1 point/position any area, point, or position: *Always keep your passport in a safe place.* | *This is the place where the accident happened.* | *Nothing had been stolen, and all the CDs and tapes were in their usual places.* | *There's a place near the bottom of the picture where you can see the cracks in the paint.* | *a sore place on my knee* | *In places* (=in some areas), *there was even mold on the walls.* —see Usage Note at POSITION[1]
2 building/town/country etc. a particular place such as a town, country, business etc.: *She was born in a place called Black River Falls.* | *I know a good place to get your car serviced.* | *There's a nice Korean place* (=restaurant) *on the corner.*

3 place for doing sth a place that is used for, or is appropriate for, a particular purpose or activity: [+ for] *Pinnacle State Park is a great place for relaxing.* | **place to live/eat/park etc.** *We're looking for a good place to go dancing.* | *I couldn't find a place to park.*
4 where sb lives INFORMAL the house, apartment, or room where someone lives: *Let's go back to my place for dinner.* | *Stuart bought a nice place over on Oak Street.*
5 take place to happen, especially after being planned or arranged: *The next Olympics will take place in Australia.* | *When did the robbery take place?* —see Usage Note at HAPPEN
6 place of work FORMAL a factory, office etc. where you work
7 place of worship FORMAL a building such as a church, where people have religious ceremonies
8 take the place of sb/sth to exist or be used instead of someone or something else; REPLACE: *Sending e-mail has almost taken the place of writing letters.* | *I don't think anyone could take her place* (=be as important or loved as she is).
9 in place of sb/sth instead of someone or something: *Rolled oats can be used in place of wheat flour in making the bread.*
10 in place **a)** in the correct or usual position: *The decorations are in place for the party.* | **hold/keep sth in place** *Use a piece of twisted wire to hold the material in place.* **b)** if a system, program, or way of doing something is in place, it is being used: *At least 25 percent of communities in this country have teen pregnancy prevention programs in place.*
11 first/second/third etc. place first, second etc. position in a race or competition, with first place being the winner: *Canada finished in third place in the bobsled competition.*
12 in sb's place **a)** if you do something in someone's place, you do it because they were supposed to but could not: *With Leiter injured, Hernandez will pitch in his place.* **b)** SPOKEN used when talking about what you would do if you were in someone else's situation: *What would you do in my place?*
13 space/position a space or position in a line of people who are waiting for something: *If you get there first, can you save me a place in line?*
14 out of place **a)** not appropriate for a particular situation or occasion: *I felt totally out of place at Cindy's wedding.* **b)** not in the correct or usual position: *Look at that! You got all of my notes out of place!*
15 take your place **a)** to go to a particular position that you need to be in for an activity: *Take your places for the next dance.* **b)** to join, and form an important part of, a group of people or things: *Catholics have clearly taken their place on the center stage of American political life.*
16 in the first place **a)** used to introduce a series of points in an argument, discussion etc.: *In the first place, New York is very cold in the winter, and in the second place I don't want to move anyway.* **b)** SPOKEN used when talking about what was done, or should have been done, at the start of a situation: *I should never have gone in the first place!*
17 sth's place the place where something is usually kept: *Please put the screwdriver back in its place when you're finished.*
18 be no place for sb/sth to be a completely inappropriate place someone or something: *A library is no place for a party.*
19 take second place to sb/sth to be thought of or treated as less important than someone or something else: *Brenda's desires and concerns often take second place to Joe's.*
20 all over the place INFORMAL **a)** everywhere: *Dirty clothes were all over the place.* **b)** in a very messy state: *Her hair was all over the place.*
21 activity/class etc. an opportunity to become a member of a group of people who take part in a particular activity, class etc.: *There are three places left on the cheerleading squad.*

P

22 **at a table** a knife, fork, spoon, plate etc. arranged on a table for one person to use: *Don't forget to set a place for Debbie, too.* —see also PLACE SETTING

23 **put sb in their place** to show someone that they are not as intelligent or important as they think they are: *I'd like to put her in her place – she thinks she's so special.*

24 **be the place (to do sth)** used to say that it is an appropriate place, time, or situation to do or say something: *A board meeting is not the place to discuss your salary.* | *If you want to eat good seafood – this is the place.*

25 **not your place (to do sth)** if it is not your place to do something, it is not appropriate for you to do it, or it is not your responsibility to do it: *I know it's not my place to say this, but I think you need to see a doctor.*

26 **lose your place** to not know what point you had reached in a book, speech etc.: *I'm sorry, what page are we on? I've lost my place.*

27 **have no place** FORMAL to be completely unacceptable: [+ **in**] *Some people believe religion has no place in the schools.*

28 **be going places** INFORMAL to start becoming successful in your life: *At only twenty-four, Ailey was going places – he was in a Broadway show.* —see also DECIMAL PLACE, **fall into place** (FALL¹ (7)), **know your place** (KNOW¹ (21))

USAGE NOTE: PLACE

WORD CHOICE: room, space, place, somewhere, anywhere
Use **place** [C] to talk about an area or a particular part of an area: *The best place to sit is right in front of the stage.* Use both **space** [C,U] and **room** [U] to talk about empty areas. **Space** can mean the size of an area, or it can mean the area itself: *There's a lot of space between the two cars.* | *I had trouble finding a parking space.* **Room** means that there is enough space for a particular purpose: *There's room in the back seat for all three of you.* In spoken English, people often use **somewhere** or **anywhere**: *He's looking for somewhere to park his car.* | *I can't find anywhere to park.*

---

s w **place²** *v.*
²|¹

1 **object** [T always + adv./prep.] to put something somewhere, especially with care: [**place sth in/on/under etc.**] *I placed the vase carefully in the center of the table.* | *Seth placed his trophy on the top shelf.*

2 **place emphasis/importance/blame etc. (on sb/sth)** to decide that someone or something should be emphasized, is important, should be blamed etc.: *The growing urban community is placing greater and greater demands on the water supply.* | *Many teachers don't place enough emphasis on good grammar.* | *Companies are placing greater importance on personality in interviews these days.* | *Vargas places the blame for the roads' bad condition on Washington.*

3 **situation** [T always + adv./prep.] to force someone or something into a particular situation: *He felt that Jordan's mistakes had placed the family in great danger.*

4 **position/rank** [T] if something places a person at a particular position or rank within a group, it puts them in that position or rank: *Pallan's latest win places him in the top ten players in Ohio.* | *Guivier's discoveries placed him at the cutting edge of medical research.*

5 **price/age** [T] to decide what price something should be or how old something is: *The value of the jewels has been placed at one million dollars.*

6 **job/home** [T] if an organization or company places someone, it finds an appropriate job or place to live for them: *The temp agency was trying to place me with a law firm.* | *At the age of five, Matthew was placed with a foster family.*

7 **place an order** to ask a store or business to provide a product that you need: *Conoco said it had placed an order for two double-hull oil tankers.*

8 **place a call** FORMAL to make a telephone call: *I'd like to place an overseas call, please.*

9 **place sb** to remember why you recognize someone, what their name is etc.: *I recognize the name, but I can't place him.*

10 **place sb under arrest** if the police place someone under arrest, they take them away because they think the person has done something illegal

11 **place sb under surveillance** if an organization such as the police places someone under surveillance, they watch them because they think they are doing something illegal

12 **place your hopes in sb/sth** to hope for someone to do something or for something to happen, so that there will be a good result for you: *Genda and his superiors placed great hopes in the effectiveness of their new bomber.*

13 **place a/your etc. bet** to risk money by guessing the result of a future event, especially a sports event

14 **place first/second/third etc.** to be first, second etc. in a race

15 **horse race** [I] if a horse places in a race, it comes second

pla·ce·bo /pləˈsiboʊ/ *n. plural* **placebos** also **placeboes** [C] **1** a substance given to a patient instead of medicine, without telling them it is not real, either because they are not really sick or because it is part of a test on a drug **2** **placebo effect** when a patient becomes well after taking a placebo because they think they are taking real medicine

place card /ˈ. ./ *n.* [C] a small card with someone's name on it, put on a table to show where they are going to sit

place kick /ˈ. ./ *n.* [C] a kick at a ball, especially in football, when the ball is placed or held on the ground —**placekicker** *n.* [C]

place mat /ˈ. ./ *n.* [C] a MAT that you put on a table for each person who is eating there, to protect the table

place·ment /ˈpleɪsmənt/ *n.* **1** [U] the process of finding a place for someone to live, work, or go to college: *job placement services* **2** [C,U] the act of placing something in position: *The placement of the buttons and knobs in the car is well thought out.*

place name /ˈ. ./ *n.* [C] the name of a particular place, such as a town, city, mountain etc.: *Many of the place names are Scottish in origin.*

pla·cen·ta /pləˈsɛntə/ *n.* [C] an ORGAN that forms inside a woman's UTERUS to feed an unborn baby —**placental** *adj.*: *placental tissue*

place set·ting /ˈ. ˌ../ *n.* [C] the arrangement on a table of knives, forks, spoons, glasses etc. to be used by one person

plac·id /ˈplæsɪd/ *adj.* calm and peaceful: *The setting sun turned the placid ocean into a sea of gold.* | *his placid round face* —**placidly** *adv.* —**placidity** /pləˈsɪdəti/ *n.* [U]

plack·et /ˈplækɪt/ *n.* [C] an opening at the top front of a dress, shirt etc. that makes it easier to pull over your head, and that often fastens with buttons

pla·gia·rism /ˈpleɪdʒəˌrɪzəm/ *n.* **1** [U] the act of using someone else's words, ideas, or work and pretending they are your own: *Claims of plagiarism are common in the movie business.* **2** [C] an idea, phrase, story etc. that has been copied from someone else's work, without stating that this is where it came from: *His dissertation contained many plagiarisms.* —**plagiarist** *n.* [C]

pla·gia·rize /ˈpleɪdʒəˌraɪz/ *v.* [I,T] to take words, ideas etc. from someone else's work and use them in your work, without stating where they came from and as if they were your own ideas etc.: *Kelty was expelled from the college for plagiarizing a term paper.*

plague¹ /pleɪg/ *n.* **1** [C,U] an attack of a disease that causes death and spreads quickly to a large number of people: *AIDS has been called a sexual plague.* **2** [U] also **the plague** a very infectious disease that produces high fever and swellings on the body, and often leads to death, especially BUBONIC PLAGUE: *an outbreak of plague* —see also BLACK DEATH **3 a** **plague of rats/locusts etc.** an uncontrollable and harmful increase in the numbers of a particular animal or insect **4 a plague on sb/sth** LITERARY used to say that someone or something is very bad and that you are extremely annoyed about them or it: *Domestic violence is a plague on America.* —see also **avoid sb/sth like the plague** (AVOID (2))

plague² v. [T] **1** to cause regular discomfort, suffering, or trouble to someone: *Heavy rains continue to plague the state.* | *Elway has been plagued all season by back problems.* **2** to annoy someone, especially by asking them for something again and again: **plague sb with sth** *The kids have been plaguing me with questions.*

plaid /plæd/ n. [U] a pattern of squares and crossed colored lines, used mainly on cloth —**plaid** adj. [a plaid dress] —compare TARTAN —see picture at PATTERN[1]

s w
3
plain¹ /pleɪn/ adj.
1 clear very clear, and easy to understand or recognize: *It was plain that Cotrell didn't agree with Jim.* | *From the first day I met her, Caroline made it plain that* (=showed clearly) *she didn't like me.* | *Why don't you just say it in plain English* (=without using technical or difficult words)?
2 not decorated without anything added or without decoration; simple: *a plain blue suit* | *plain vanilla ice cream*
3 as plain as day also **as plain as the nose on your face** very clear to see or understand: *Phil loves her – that's as plain as day.*
4 honest showing clearly and honestly what you think about something, without trying to hide anything: *I've never seen her before in my life, and that's the plain truth.*
5 not beautiful someone who is plain is not beautiful in any way, used when you do not want to say this directly —see also PLAIN JANE
6 (just) plain... SPOKEN **a)** used before a noun to emphasize it: *There's no other word for it. It's just plain mismanagement.* **b)** used before someone's name to emphasize that it is simple or ordinary or that they do not have a special title: *No, it's not "Doctor Delaney" – it's just plain Mr. Delaney.* —see also PLAIN[3]
7 in plain sight if something is in plain sight, it is very easy to see or notice, especially in a situation where it should be hidden or someone has not seen it when they should easily have noticed it: *I couldn't believe they'd left the drugs and needles right out in plain sight.*
8 in plain clothes police officers in plain clothes are wearing regular clothes instead of a uniform —see also PLAIN-CLOTHES —**plainness** n. [U] —see also PLAINLY

plain² n. **1** [C] also **plains** a large area of flat dry land: *the central Oahu plain* | *the plains of Nebraska* **2** [U] the ordinary stitch in KNITTING

plain³ adv. **(just) plain...** INFORMAL used before an adjective in order to emphasize it: *Jason's just plain lucky he wasn't hurt.*

plain-chant /'pleɪntʃænt/ n. [U] PLAINSONG

plain-clothes /ˌ '.ˌ/ adj. [only before noun] plain-clothes police are police who wear ordinary clothes so that they can work without being recognized

plain Jane /'. .ˌ/ n. [C] INFORMAL a woman who is not attractive, but is not ugly either: *She's kind of a plain Jane.*

plain-Jane /'. .ˌ/ adj. [only before noun] INFORMAL a plain-Jane person or thing is not attractive or interesting: *cheap plain-Jane houses*

plain·ly /'pleɪnli/ adv. **1** in a way that is easy to hear, see, notice etc.: *The price is marked plainly on the tag.* | *Garver was plainly nervous as she began her speech.* **2** speaking honestly, and without trying to hide the truth: *Woodard would not say plainly what his plans for the future were.* **3** [sentence adverb] if something is plainly true, necessary, correct etc., it is easy to see that it is true etc.; OBVIOUSLY: *Plainly, an investigation into the tragedy would be necessary.* **4** simply or without decoration: *a plainly dressed man*

plain·song /'pleɪnsɒŋ/ n. [U] a type of old Christian

church music in which a group of people sing a simple tune together, without musical instruments

plain·spo·ken /ˌpleɪn'spoʊkən◂/ adj. APPROVING saying exactly what you think, especially in a way that people think is honest rather than impolite

plaint /pleɪnt/ n. [C] LITERARY a complaint or a sad cry

plain·tiff /'pleɪntɪf/ n. [C] LAW the person in a court of law who SUES someone else for doing something wrong or illegal —compare DEFENDANT

plain·tive /'pleɪntɪv/ adj. a plaintive sound is high and sad, like someone crying: *the plaintive cry of wolves* —**plaintively** adv.

plait /plæt, pleɪt/ n. [C] OLD-FASHIONED a BRAID[1] (1) in a person's hair or a horse's MANE —**plait** v. [T]

P

plan¹ /plæn/ n. [C]
s w
1 1
1 intention [usually plural] something you have decided to do at a particular time: *Originally, the plan was to meet at Dave's house, but he's still not home.* | *I'm sorry to make you change your plans, but I don't have the car tonight.* | **a change of plan(s)** *There's been a change of plan – I'm not flying to Seattle today.* | *Do you have plans Friday night?* | *We still haven't made plans for* (=prepared for) *the trip to Tahiti.*
2 method/arrangement a set of actions for achieving something in the future, especially one that has been considered carefully and in detail: *the state's highway improvement plan* | [+ for] *The company has a new plan for reorganizing our department.* | [a/the plan to do sth] *Next week, world leaders will meet to discuss plans to eliminate all chemical weapons.* | *They've devised a plan to ease the flow of traffic downtown.* | *The plans for merging the two companies have fallen through* (=it became impossible because something unexpected happened). | *Last fall, the city council devised a plan of action to help the homeless.* —see also INSTALLMENT PLAN
3 go according to plan to happen in the way that was arranged: *If everything goes according to plan, we'll be done in October.*
4 plan A INFORMAL your first plan, which you will use if things happen as you expect: *So, plan A is for Christen to come down on the bus.*
5 plan B INFORMAL your second plan, which you can use if things do not happen as you expect: *If the bus doesn't run on Sunday, then plan B is to drive up and pick her up.*
6 drawing **a)** TECHNICAL a drawing of a building, room, or machine as it would be seen from above, showing the shape, measurements, position of the walls etc. —see also FLOOR PLAN, GROUND PLAN **b)** a drawing that shows exactly how something will be arranged: *I have to organize a seating plan for the dinner.*
7 map a drawing similar to a map, showing roads, towns, and buildings: *a street-plan of Hartford*

plan² v. **planned, planning 1** [I,T] to think carefully about something you want to achieve, and decide exactly how you will do it: *She started planning her career change after taking an evening class in nutrition.* | [plan to do sth] *I was planning to leave as early as possible to beat the traffic.* | *Call to find specific prices for the days you travel and plan ahead* (=make plans for a long time in the future). | *The graduation ceremony went exactly as planned.* **2** [I,T] to intend to do something: [plan to do sth] *I was planning to call you tonight.* —see also **plan on sth 3** [T] to think about something you are going to make and decide what it will be like; DESIGN[1] (3): *The team is still planning the layout of the magazine cover.*

s w
1 1

plan sth ↔ out phr. v. [T] to plan something carefully, considering all the possible problems: *The restructuring of the company was planned out months in advance.*

plan on sth phr. v. [T] **1** to expect something to happen in a particular way: *Don't plan on Todd being on time.* **2** to intend to do something: *How long are you planning on staying?*

Planck /plæŋk/, **Max** /mæks/ (1858–1947) a German scientist who developed the ideas on which QUANTUM THEORY is based

plane[1] /pleɪn/ *n.* [C] **1** a vehicle that flies in the air and has wings and at least one engine; airplane: *It's quicker to go by plane.* | *We were **on the plane** (=riding inside of a plane) for more than ten hours.* **2** a level or standard of thought, conversation etc.: *Let's try to keep the discussion on a friendly plane.* **3** TECHNICAL a completely flat surface in GEOMETRY **4** a tool that has a flat bottom with a sharp blade in it, used for making wooden surfaces smooth —see picture at TOOL[1]

plane[2] *v.* [T] to use a PLANE on a piece of wood to make it smooth

plane[3] *adj.* [only before noun] TECHNICAL completely flat and smooth: *a plane surface*

plane ge·om·e·try /ˌ. .ˈ.../ *n.* [U] the study of lines, shapes etc. that are TWO-DIMENSIONAL (=with measurements in only two directions, not three)

plane·load /ˈpleɪnloʊd/ *n.* [C] the number of people or amount of something that an airplane will hold: *A planeload of ambassadors arrived for the economic summit.*

plan·er /ˈpleɪnɚ/ *n.* [C] a machine or electrical tool for making wooden surfaces smooth —see picture at TOOL[1]

plan·et /ˈplænɪt/ *n.* **1** [C] a very large round object in space that moves around the sun or another star; Earth is a planet: *Saturn is the planet with rings around it.* | *Is there life on other planets?* **2 the planet** an expression meaning Earth or the world, used when talking about the environment: *the future of the planet* **3 what planet is sb on/from?** also **sb is (living) on another planet** SPOKEN, HUMOROUS used to say that you think someone is behaving in a strange way: *He's giving all his money to that woman? What planet is he on?* —**planetary** *adj.*

plan·e·tar·i·um /ˌplænəˈtɛriəm/ *n.* [C] a building where lights on a curved ceiling show the movements of planets and stars

plan·gent /ˈplændʒənt/ *adj.* LITERARY a plangent sound is loud and deep and sounds sad

plank /plæŋk/ *n.* [C] **1** a long narrow, usually heavy, piece of wooden board, used especially for making structures to walk on: *a small bridge made of planks* —see also **walk the plank** (WALK[1] (15)) **2** one of the main principles that makes up a political PARTY's statement of its aims: *Cracking down on illegal immigration was one of the state Republicans' major campaign planks.* —compare PLATFORM (3)

plank·ing /ˈplæŋkɪŋ/ *n.* [U] many planks that are put together to make a floor

plank·ton /ˈplæŋktən/ *n.* [U] the very small forms of plant and animal life that live in water, especially the ocean, and are eaten by fish

planned ob·so·les·cence /ˌ. ..ˈ../ *n.* [U] the practice of making products that will not be useful or popular for very long, so that people will always have to buy newer, more useful, or popular products to replace them

Planned Pa·rent·hood /ˌ. ˈ.../ a U.S. organization, with offices all over the country, that provides advice on FAMILY PLANNING

plan·ner /ˈplænɚ/ *n.* [C] someone who plans something, especially someone whose job is to plan the way towns grow and develop: *I worked as a city planner in New York for 15 years.*

plant[1] /plænt/ *n.* **1** [C] a living thing that has leaves and roots and grows in earth, especially one that is smaller than a tree: *Don't forget to water the plants.* | *a tomato plant* —see also HOUSEPLANT **2** [C] a factory or building where an industrial process happens: *an aluminum plant* —see also POWER PLANT **3** [C usually singular] something illegal or stolen that is hidden in someone's clothes or possessions to make them seem guilty: *Carlson swore to the police that the drugs were a plant.* **4** [C] someone who is put somewhere or sent

somewhere secretly to find out information: *a KGB plant in the Washington establishment*

plant[2] *v.*
1 plant/seeds [T] to put plants or seeds in the ground to grow: *About a dozen school children helped plant trees in the park.*
2 plant a field/garden/area etc. (with sth) to plant seeds, plants, or trees in a field, garden etc.: *The field over there is planted with soy beans.*
3 put sth somewhere [I,T always + adv./prep.] INFORMAL to put something firmly in or on something else, or to move somewhere and stay there: [+ in/on etc.] *Larry's always planted on the sofa in front of the TV when I get home.* | [plant sth in/on etc.] *Grandma planted a big wet kiss on my cheek.*
4 hide illegal goods [T] INFORMAL to hide stolen or illegal goods in someone's clothes, bags, room etc. in order to make them seem guilty: [plant sth on sb] *Someone must have planted the drugs on her.*
5 plant a bomb INFORMAL to put a bomb somewhere: *Police discovered that a bomb had been planted in the bus station.*
6 person [T] to put or send someone somewhere, especially secretly, so that they can find out information: [plant sb in/at etc.] *The FBI had planted two agents in the paramilitary organization.*
7 plant an idea/doubt/suspicion (in sb's mind) to make someone begin to believe an idea, begin to doubt something etc., especially so that they do not realize it was you who gave them the idea: *Their conversation had planted doubts in Dennis' mind about the partnership.*
plant sth ↔ **out** *phr. v.* [T] to put a young plant into the soil outdoors, so that it has enough room to grow

Plan·tag·e·net /plænˈtædʒənɪt/ the name of the Royal Family of England from 1154 to 1399

plan·tain /ˈplænt[ə]n/ *n.* [C,U] a type of BANANA that is cooked before it is eaten, or the plant on which it grows

plan·tar /ˈplæntɚ, -ˌtɑr/ *adj.* relating to the SOLE (=bottom) of your feet: *plantar warts*

plan·ta·tion /plænˈteɪʃən/ *n.* [C] **1** a large area of land in a hot country, where crops such as tea, cotton, and sugar etc. are grown: *a coffee plantation* **2** a large group of trees grown to produce wood

plant·er /ˈplæntɚ/ *n.* [C] **1** an attractive, often decorated, container for growing plants in **2** someone who owns or is in charge of a plantation: *a rice planter* **3** a machine used for planting

plant·ing /ˈplæntɪŋ/ *n.* [C usually plural] **1** the action of planting a plant or crop: *Conway's city council has banned further park plantings until next spring.* **2** a plant or crop that has been planted: *The car had plunged into the freeway plantings near exit 29.*

plaque /plæk/ *n.* **1** [C] a piece of flat metal or stone with writing on it, used as a prize in a competition or to remind people of an event or person: *Near the door was a bronze plaque which told of the building's historic past.* **2** [U] a substance that forms on your teeth, in which BACTERIA that can damage your teeth can live

plas·ma /ˈplæzmə/ *n.* [U] **1** the yellowish liquid part of the blood that contains blood cells **2** the living substance inside a cell **3** a gas at a very high temperature inside stars, in flashes of electricity etc.

plas·ter[1] /ˈplæstɚ/ *n.* [U] **1** a substance used to cover walls and ceilings and give a smooth surface, consisting of LIME, water, and sand **2** PLASTER OF PARIS

plaster[2] *v.* [T usually passive] **1** to spread or stick something all over a surface so that it is thickly covered: [plaster sth with sth] *The wall was plastered with old movie posters.* **2** to cover the pages of a newspaper with a particular story or report: *The news of the wedding was plastered all over the morning papers.* **3** to put wet plaster on a wall or ceiling **4** to make your hair lie flat or stick to your head: [+ down/to etc.] *His hair was plastered to his forehead with sweat.*
plaster sth ↔ **over** *phr. v.* [T] to cover a hole or an old surface by spreading plaster over it

plas·ter·board /ˈplæstɚˌbɔrd/ *n.* [U] DRYWALL

plaster cast /ˌ. ˈ./ *n.* [C] **1** a hard cover that is used to keep a broken bone in place while it grows together; CAST[2] **2** a copy of a STATUE made using plaster of Paris

plas·tered /'plæstəd/ adj. [not before noun] INFORMAL very drunk: *Chris was plastered that night.*

plas·ter·er /'plæstərə/ n. [C] someone whose job is to cover walls and ceilings with PLASTER

plaster of Par·is /,.. '../ n. [U] a mixture of white powder and water that dries quickly, used especially for making STATUEs

s w
2
3 **plas·tic**[1] /'plæstɪk/ adj. **1** [only before noun] made of plastic: *a plastic spoon | plastic bags* **2** INFORMAL something that is plastic looks or tastes artificial or not natural: *I hate that plastic smile of hers.* **3** TECHNICAL a plastic substance can be formed into many different shapes, and it keeps a shape until it is changed

s w
3 **plas·tic**[2] n. **1** [C,U] a light strong material that is chemically produced, that can be made into different shapes when it is soft and is used to make many things: *The doors are made of plastic so they don't dent. | The company experimented with various plastics but found that aluminum was still the best option.* **2** [singular,U] INFORMAL a CREDIT CARD, or credit cards considered as a group: *I didn't have the cash for a trip home, so I paid with plastic.*

plastic art /,.. './ n. [C,U] TECHNICAL art that shows things in ways in which they can be clearly seen, especially painting or SCULPTURE

plastic bul·let /,.. '../ n. [C] a large bullet made of hard plastic that is intended to injure but not kill, and is used for controlling violent crowds

plastic ex·plo·sive /,.. .'../ n. [C,U] an explosive substance that can be shaped by hand, or a small bomb made from this

plas·tic·i·ty /plæ'stɪsəti/ n. [U] TECHNICAL the quality of being easily made into any shape

plastic sur·geon /,.. '../ n. [C] a doctor who does plastic surgery

plastic sur·ger·y /,.. '.../ n. [U] the medical practice of changing the appearance of people's faces or bodies, either to improve their appearance or to repair injuries

plastic wrap /'.. ,./ n. [U] thin transparent plastic used to cover food in order to keep it fresh

Pla·ta /'plɑtə/, **Río de la** /'riou də lɑ/ a BAY on the eastern coast of South America, between Argentina and Uruguay, where the Paran and Uruguay rivers join the Atlantic Ocean

plat du jour /,plɑ də 'ʒʊr, ,plæ-/ n. [C] a dish that a restaurant prepares specially on a particular day in addition to its usual food

s w
1
2 **plate**[1] /pleɪt/ n.
1 food [C] **a)** a flat and usually round dish that you eat from or serve food from: *a salad plate |* **clean/empty your plate** (=eat everything on your plate) **b)** also **plateful** the amount of food that is on a plate: [+ of] *The waiter brought us two heaping plates of spaghetti.*
2 a sheet of metal [C] a sheet of metal used to protect something: *Doctors had to insert a steel plate to repair the damage done to his head.*
3 **have a lot on your plate** INFORMAL to have a lot of problems to deal with or a lot of things to worry about: *With all that you have on your plate, you shouldn't start something new.*
4 sign [C] a flat piece of metal with words or numbers on it, for example on a door or a car: *The engine model number is on a plate just above the spark plug.* —see also NAMEPLATE
5 plates [plural] INFORMAL: see LICENSE PLATEs: *The truck had New Jersey plates.*
6 Earth's surface [C] TECHNICAL one of the very large areas of rock that form the surface of the Earth —see also PLATE TECTONICS
7 the plate **a)** the place in baseball where the person hitting the ball stands; HOME PLATE —see also **step up to the plate** at step up STEP[2] **b)** a small plate or container, used to collect money in a Christian church
8 gold/silver etc. **a)** gold/silver etc. plate ordinary

metal with a thin covering of gold, silver etc. **b)** [U] articles such as plates, cups, forks, or knives covered with gold or silver
9 pictures/photos [C] **a)** a sheet of metal that has been cut or treated so that words or pictures can be printed from its surface **b)** a picture in a book, usually in color, that is printed on good-quality paper **c)** TECHNICAL a thin sheet of glass used especially in past times in photography, with chemicals on it that are sensitive to light
10 protective covering [C] TECHNICAL one of the thin sheets of bone, horn etc. that covers and protects the outside of an animal: *The reptile's body is covered with horny protective plates.*
11 teeth [C] **a)** a thin piece of plastic that fits inside a person's mouth, which false teeth are attached to **b)** a thin piece of plastic with wires attached to it, that people wear to make their teeth straight; BRACEs —see also -PLATED

plate[2] v. [T] **be plated with sth a)** to have a thin covering of gold, silver etc.: *Even their faucets had been plated with gold.* **b)** to be covered in thin pieces of a hard material such as metal or bone: *The President's limousine is plated with armor.*

pla·teau[1] /plæ'tou/ n. plural **plateaus** or **plateaux** /-'touz/ [C] **1** a large area of flat land that is higher than the land around it **2** a period during which the level of cost, achievement etc. does not change much, especially after a period when it was increasing: **reach/hit a plateau** *Attendance at health clubs has reached a plateau.*

plateau[2] v. [I] if costs, achievement etc. plateau, they do not change much, especially after increasing for a period of time: *The athletic footwear market has not yet plateaued.*

-plated /pleɪtɪd/ [in adjectives] **gold-plated/silver-plated/brass-plated etc.** covered with a thin covering of gold, silver etc.: *a gold-plated necklace*

plate·ful /'pleɪtfʊl/ n. [C] all the food that is on a plate: *The pasta was so good, I just had to have a second plateful.*

plate glass /,. '.< / n. [U] big pieces of glass made in large thick pieces, used especially for store windows

plate·let /'pleɪtlət/ n. [C] one of the very small plate-shaped cells in your blood that help it become solid when you bleed, so that you stop bleeding

plate tec·ton·ics /,. .'../ n. [U] the study of the forming and movement of the large areas of rock that form the surface of the Earth

plat·form /'plætfɔrm/ n. [C] s w
3
1 for speeches a raised floor or stage for people to stand on when they are making a speech, performing etc.: *Professor Allen stepped up onto the platform. | Please address your comments to the platform* (=the people on the platform).
2 structure a tall structure built so that people can stand or work above the surrounding area: *a gas drilling platform*
3 politics **a)** [usually singular] the main ideas and aims of a political party, especially the ones that they state just before an election: *The party's new platform emphasizes rural development.* —compare PLANK (2) **b)** a chance for someone to express their opinions, especially their political opinions: *Actors have a good platform to promote their causes.*
4 support something that gives you the support, help, power etc. that you need to do something: *"The deal provides us with a platform for expansion into new markets," Weldon said.*
5 computers used to describe the type of computer system or SOFTWARE someone uses: *Which platform does your department use, Windows or Macintosh?*
6 train the raised place beside a railroad track where you get on and off a train in a station: *The train to Boston leaves from Platform 9.*
7 platforms [plural] also **platform shoes** shoes with a thick layer of wood, leather etc. beneath the front part and the heel

P

Plath /plæθ/,   **Syl·vi·a**
/'sɪlviə/ (1932–1963) a U.S.
poet

plat·ing /'pleɪtɪŋ/ n. [U] a
thin layer of metal that
covers another metal sur-
face: *gold plating*

plat·i·num /'plætˀnəm,
'plætˀn-əm/ n. [U] *symbol*
Pt a silver-gray metal that
is an ELEMENT, that does
not change color or lose its
brightness, and used in
making expensive jewelry
and in industry: *a plat-
inum ring*

Sylvia Plath

platinum blonde /ˌ.. '. / n.
[C] a young woman whose hair is a silver-white
color, especially one whose hair has been colored
with chemicals —**platinum blonde** *adj.*

plat·i·tude /'plætə͜tud/ n. [C] a statement that has
been made many times before and is not interesting
or smart: *empty political platitudes* —**platitudinous**
/ˌplætə'tudn-əs/ *adj.*

Pla·to /'pleɪtoʊ/ (?427–347 B.C.) an ancient Greek
PHILOSOPHER, who had a very great influence on
European philosophy

pla·ton·ic /plə'tɑnɪk/ *adj.* **1** a relationship that is
platonic is just friendly, and is not a sexual relationship **2 Platonic** relating to or influenced by the
ideas of Plato: *Platonic thinkers* —**platonically** /-kli/
adv.

pla·toon /plə'tun/ n. [C] a small group of soldiers that
is part of a COMPANY and is usually led by a LIEU-
TENANT

plat·ter /'plætɚ/ n. [C] **1** a large plate from which
food is served **2 chicken/seafood/combo etc. platter** chicken or other foods arranged on a plate and
served in a restaurant **3** OLD-FASHIONED a RECORD[1] (5)

plat·y·pus /'plætəpəs/ n. [C] a small furry Australian
animal that has a beak and feet like a duck, lays
eggs, and gives milk to its young

plau·dits /'plɔdɪts/ n. [plural] FORMAL praise and
admiration: *Albright won plaudits for her tough
stance on terrorism.*

plau·si·ble /'plɔzəbəl/ *adj.* a statement that is plausible is reasonable and seems likely to be true: *Langham's story sounded plausible at the time.* —opposite
IMPLAUSIBLE —**plausibly** *adv.* —**plausibility** /ˌplɔzə-
'bɪləti/ n. [U]

s w **play**[1] /pleɪ/ v. **plays, played, playing**
11

1 sports/games **a)** [I,T] to take part or compete
in a game or sport: *The guys are outside playing
basketball.* | *I've only played chess a few times.* |
[play (against) sb] *The Rockets are playing the Bulls
this weekend.* | [+ for] *Iverson plays for the Philadel-
phia 76ers.* **b)** [T] to use a particular piece, card,
person etc. in a game or sport: *I played the ace of
clubs and won the game.*

2 children [I,T] when children play, they do things
that they enjoy, often with other people or with toys:
Kendra's in her room playing. | [play sth] *Andy loves
to play hide-and-go-seek.* | [+ with] *He enjoys playing
with his grandchildren.* | *Tony has a lot of toys to
play with.*

3 music/instrument [I,T] **a)** to perform a piece of
music on a musical instrument: *I have a recording of
Kreisler playing Bach's E major concerto.* | *There's a
good band playing at the Club 39 Saturday night.*
b) to have the ability to play a musical instrument:
Matt plays the drums.

4 radio/tape/cd etc. if a radio, STEREO etc. plays or
you make it play, it produces sound, especially music:
The bedside radio played softly. | **play a tape/CD/
record** *I usually play my jazz CDs to relax.*

5 play a part/role in sth to have an effect on or an
influence on something: *Politics played no part in my
decision.*

6 theater/movie **a)** [T] to perform the actions and
say the words of a particular character in a theater
performance, movie etc.: *Polly is playing "Celia" in
"As You Like It."* | **play a role/part** *Gibson convinc-
ingly played the part of the villain.* **b)** [I] if a play or
movie is playing at a particular theater, it is being
performed or shown there: *"Cats" is still playing on
Broadway.* | *What's playing at the discount theater
tonight?* **c)** [T] if actors play a theater, they perform
there in a play

7 behave [T always + adv./prep.] to behave in a
particular way in a situation in order to achieve the
result or effect that you want: *We have to talk about
how we're going to play this situation – these are
important clients.* | *Janet wants to **play it safe**
(=avoid taking any risks) and not put all of our
money in stocks.* | **play it carefully/cool etc.** *If you
like a guy, you've got to play it cool and not let know
how much you like him.*

8 play it by ear to decide what to do according to
the way a situation develops, without making plans
before that time: *So just leave me a message when you
know what you're doing – we'll play it by ear.*

9 pretend [linking verb] to pretend to be a particular kind of person or to have a particular feeling or
quality, when this is not typical or true: *If he asks
where I was,* **play dumb** (=pretend you do not know
the answer). | *The snake fools predators by **playing
dead**.* | *Don't **play the fool** (=pretend to be stupid,
or behave in a silly way) with me, young man.* | **play
the idiot/teacher etc.** *Susan felt she had to play the
good wife.*

10 play ball a) to throw, kick, hit, or catch a ball as
a game or activity: *You kids should go outside if you
want to play ball.* **b)** INFORMAL to do what someone
asks you to do; COOPERATE (2): *Their loan officer
refuses to play ball, so we have to get a loan from a
different bank.*

11 play the ball [always + adv./prep.] to hit a ball
in a particular way or to a particular place in a game
or sport: *She played the ball low, just over the net.*

12 play a joke/trick on sb to do something to someone as a joke or trick: *They do all the things children
do – play tricks on each other, tease.*

13 play tricks to confuse someone so that they do
not know what is really happening: **your mind/
memory plays tricks on you** *My mind must be playing tricks on me – I'm sure I left my bag on the chair.*

14 play games to hide your real feelings or wishes
in order to achieve something in a smart or secret
way: *We're all tired of politicians playing games with
the budget.*

15 play your cards right to behave in a smart or
skillful way in a situation, so that you gain as much
as possible from it: *If you play your cards right, you
might get them to reduce the price.*

16 play second fiddle (to sb) to be slightly lower in
rank or less important than someone or something
else: *He was never more than a B-movie actor, playing
second fiddle to actors like Errol Flynn.*

17 play with fire to do something that is likely to
have a very dangerous or harmful result: *Dating the
boss's daughter is playing with fire.*

18 play hard to get to pretend that you are not
romantically interested in someone so that they will
become more interested in you: *You should call her
again – I think she's just playing hard to get.*

19 play for time to try to delay something so that
you have more time to prepare for it or prevent it
from happening: *The U.S. strategy over the past weeks
has been to play for time.*

20 play the system to use the rules of a system in
a smart way, to gain advantage for yourself: *Accountants know how to play the tax system.*

21 play the market to risk money on the STOCK
MARKET as a way of trying to earn more money

22 play the field to have romantic relationships
with a lot of different people

23 play the game to do things in the way you are
expected to do them or in a way that is usual in a
particular situation: *Diillon won't get promoted if
he's not willing to play the game.*

24 play fast and loose with sb/sth to treat someone
in a SELFISH careless way, or to not obey rules or the

law carefully: The *Mayor liked to play fast and loose with the rules.*

25 play hooky to stay away from school without permission

26 light [I always + adv./prep.] if light plays on something, it shines on it and moves around on it: *She watched the sunlight playing on the water.*

27 play sb for a sucker to show by the way that you behave toward someone that you think they are stupid

28 smile [I always + adv./prep.] LITERARY if a smile plays over someone's lips, they smile quickly and only a little

play along *phr. v.* [I] to pretend that you agree with someone's ideas, because you want to gain an advantage for yourself or to avoid an argument: *I don't like the idea of Valentine's Day, but I play along every year and buy chocolates for my girlfriend.*

play around with sb *phr. v.* [T] to have a sexual relationship with someone that is not serious or not intended to last very long: *He wondered if his father had ever played around with other women.* —see also **play with**

play at sth *phr. v.* [T] **1** if you play at doing something, you do not do it seriously or correctly: *They are a group of college students who play at being rock stars.* **2** if children play at doing something or being someone, they pretend to do it or be that person: *At two years old, Henry would hold a book and play at reading.*

play sth ↔ **back** *phr. v.* [T] to play something that has been recorded on a machine so that you can listen to it or watch it: *Which button do I push to play back the last phone message?*

play sth ↔ **down** *phr. v.* [T] to try to make something seem less important than it really is: *The White House is trying to play down the latest scandal.*

play sb **off against** sb *phr. v.* [T] if you play one person off against another, you encourage them to argue with each other so that you can gain something: *The secret service is reportedly playing the rebel groups off against each other.*

play on sth *phr. v.* [T] to use someone's fears, worries, or problems in order to gain an advantage for yourself: *His campaign message plays on people's fear of losing their jobs.*

play out *phr. v.* [I,T usually passive] if an exciting or complicated situation or event is played out or plays itself out, it continues: *Reporters and legal commentators around the nation will watch carefully as the trial plays itself out.*

play sth ↔ **up** *phr. v.* [T] if you play something up, you make it seem more important than it really is: *The press has been playing up the racial aspects of the case.*

play up to sb *phr. v.* [T] to behave in a very polite or kind way to someone because you want something from them: *Connie always plays up to her parents when she wants money.*

play with sth *phr. v.* [T] **1** [also **play around with** sth] to keep touching something or moving it around: *Stop playing with the remote control!* **2 play (around) with the idea of doing sth** to consider the possibility of doing something, often not very seriously: *I've been playing with the idea of traveling around the world.* **3** [also **play around with** sth] to try doing something in different ways to decide what works best: *I've been playing around with the design of the newsletter all morning.* **4 play with words** to use words in a smart or amusing way: *Danny enjoys playing with words.* **5 have time/money to play with** to have time or money that is available to be used: *We don't have much time to play with since the deadline is Friday.* **6 play with yourself** to touch your own sex organs for pleasure

s w **play²** *n. plural* **plays**

![11 grid icon]

1 theater [C] a story that is written to be performed by actors, especially in a theater: *The play is about two men on trial for murder.* | *"Pygmalion" was one of Shaw's most famous plays.* | *The drama club puts on a play* (=performs a play) *every spring.*

2 children [U] things that people, especially children, do for amusement rather than as work: *Parents need to understand the importance of play in a child's*

development. | *By observing children at play* (=playing), *teachers can understand more about how they see the world.*

3 game/sport [C,U] the actions of the people who are playing a game or a sport, or one particular action or set of actions during the game: *There's a huge difference in the level of play from college to the NFL.* | *On the next play, Ervin caught a forty-yard pass to score a touchdown.*

4 in play/out of play if a ball is in play or out of play, it is inside or outside the area allowed by the rules of the game: *Courier put only 50 percent of his first serves in play.*

5 come into play to be used or have an effect on something: *During the negotiations, cultural differences will certainly come into play.*

6 bring/put sth into play to use something or make it have an effect: *I try to imagine the arguments another lawyer might bring into play.*

7 at play having an effect on something: *There are some important medical considerations at play in this tropical locale.*

8 a play on words a use of a word that is interesting or amusing because it can be understood as having two very different meanings; PUN

9 make a play for sb/sth to try to begin a romantic relationship with someone or to try to gain something: *It was obvious that she was making a play for Donnel.*

10 looseness [U] if there is some play in something, it is loose and can be moved: *There needs to be a little more play in the fan belt for it to work right.*

11 the play of light the patterns made by light as it moves gently over a surface: *the play of light on the water*

play·a·ble /ˈpleɪəbəl/ *adj.* **1** able to be played on a particular machine: [+ **on**] *The disks are playable on home computers.* **2 a)** a field or court that is playable is in good enough condition for a sports game to be played on it **b)** a ball that is playable in a sports game is within the playing field, so that a player can try to catch, throw, or hit it **3** able to be played by people of a particular age or ability: *The string quartet is looking for music that will be playable for all members of the group.*

play·act·ing /ˈ. ˌ../ *n.* [U] behavior in which someone pretends to be serious or sincere, but is not —**playact** *v.* [I]

play·ac·tion /ˈ. ˌ../ *n.* **a play-action pass/play** the act of throwing a football after pretending to give it to another player

play·back /ˈpleɪbæk/ *n.* [C,U] a recording of something, especially one that you play soon after it is made: *You can skip the commercials during playback.*

play·bill /ˈpleɪbɪl/ *n.* [C] a printed paper advertising a play

play·book /ˈpleɪbʊk/ *n.* [C] a book that contains all the PLAYS (=actions in a sports game) that a team uses

play·boy /ˈpleɪbɔɪ/ *n.* [C] a rich man who does not work and who spends his time enjoying himself with beautiful women and fast cars

play-by-play /ˌ. . ˈ.ˌ/ *n.* [U] **1** also **play-by-play commentary/description** a description of the action in a sports game or other event as it happens, usually given on television or on the radio: *Hahn does play-by-play for the Kings.* **2 a play-by-play man/announcer/broadcaster** someone who tells what is happening in a sports game as it is happening

play clothes /ˈ. ./ *n.* [U] clothing that children wear to play in

play date /ˈ. ./ *n.* [C] a planned time for children to get together to play

Play-Doh /ˈpleɪ doʊ/ *n.* [U] TRADEMARK a soft substance like clay made in many different colors, used by children for making shapes

played-out /ˌ. ˈ.ˌ/ *adj.* **1** someone or something who is played-out is not as strong, powerful, attractive

P

etc. as they used to be: *a played-out pony* **2** old-fashioned and not useful anymore: *played-out ideas* —see also **play out** (PLAY¹)

play·er /ˈpleɪɚ/ *n.* [C] **1** someone who takes part in a game or sport: *a tennis player* **2** one of the people, companies, or organizations that is involved in and influences a situation: *Poland is a major player in the transformation of Eastern Europe.* **3** a CD/record/tape etc. player a piece of equipment that is used to play CDs, records etc. **4** someone who plays a musical instrument: *a bass player* **5** OLD-FASHIONED an actor

player pi·an·o /ˌ.. .ˌ../ *n.* [C] a piano that is played by machinery, with the music controlled by a continuous roll of paper with holes cut into it for the notes

play·ful /ˈpleɪfəl/ *adj.* **1** intended to be fun rather than serious, or showing that you are having fun: *a playful song* | *The Milk Board has produced a playful series of ads for milk.* | *a playful smile* **2** very active and happy: *a playful kitten* —**playfully** *adv.* —**playfulness** *n.* [U]

play·go·er /ˈpleɪˌɡoʊɚ/ *n.* [C] someone who often goes to see plays

play·ground /ˈpleɪɡraʊnd/ *n.* [C] **1** a piece of ground for children to play on, especially at a school or in a park **2** a place where a particular group of people go to enjoy themselves: *The Catskill resorts were once the playground of the rich and famous.*

play group /ˈ. ./ *n.* [C,U] a group of children, usually between two and four years old, whose parents meet each week so that the children can play together

play·house /ˈpleɪhaʊs/ *n.* [C] **1** a word meaning a "theater," often used as part of a theater's name: *We saw "The Crucible" last night at the Berkshire Playhouse.* **2** a small structure like a little house for children to play in

playing card /ˈ.. ,./ *n.* [C] FORMAL a CARD¹ (5)

playing field /ˈ.. ,./ *n.* [C] a large piece of ground with particular areas marked out for playing football, SOCCER etc. —see also **a level playing field** (LEVEL¹ (7))

play·list, **play list** /ˈpleɪlɪst/ *n.* [C] the list of songs that a radio station plays

play·mak·er /ˈpleɪˌmeɪkɚ/ *n.* [C] someone who is skillful at making points or giving their team an advantage in sports such as football and basketball

play·mate /ˈpleɪmeɪt/ *n.* [C] a friend that a child plays with

play mon·ey /ˌ. ˈ.. / *n.* [U] money used in games that is not real

play-off /ˈ. ./ *n.* [C] a game or series of games played by the best teams or players in a sports competition in order to decide the final winner

play·pen /ˈpleɪpɛn/ *n.* [C] an enclosed space in which a small child can play safely, consisting of a type of box with sides made of bars or a net

play·room /ˈpleɪrum/ *n.* [C] a room for children to play in

play·thing /ˈpleɪˌθɪŋ/ *n.* [C] **1** a toy **2** someone who you use for your own amusement, without caring about their feelings or needs: *The ads portray women as stupid but sexy playthings.*

play·time /ˈpleɪtaɪm/ *n.* [U] a period of time at a school when children can play

play·wright /ˈpleɪraɪt/ *n.* [C] someone who writes plays —**playwriting** *n.*

pla·za /ˈplɑzə, ˈplæzə/ *n.* [C] **1** a group of stores and other small business buildings in a town, with outdoor areas between them: *Oak Hill Plaza* —compare MALL **2** a public area or market place surrounded by buildings, especially in towns in Spanish-speaking countries **3** an area near a HIGHWAY (=large road) where you can stop to buy food or gasoline, use the toilet etc.: *a service plaza* —see also TOLL PLAZA

plea /pli/ *n.* **1** [C] a request that is urgent or full of emotion: *Taylor made an emotional plea for donations.* | *a mother's plea for help* **2** [C usually singular] LAW a statement by someone in a court of law saying whether they are guilty or not: **make/enter a plea** *Clark entered a plea of not guilty.* **3** [singular] an excuse for something: *He refused to come on the plea that he had work to do at home.*

plea bar·gain /ˈ. ,../ *n.* [C] an agreement in which you say you are guilty of a crime in order to avoid punishment for a more serious one —**plea bargain** *v.* [I,T] —**plea bargaining** *n.* [U]

plead /plid/ *v. past tense and past participle* **pleaded** or **pled 1** [I,T] to ask for something that you want very much, in a sincere and emotional way: *"You've got to help me," Magruder pleaded.* | **[+ for]** *Regional officials have come to Washington, pleading for assistance.* | **[plead with sb (to do sth)]** *Leslie pleaded with him to let her out.* **2** [I] LAW to state in a court of law whether or not you are guilty of a crime: *"How do you plead?" "Not guilty, your honor."* | **plead guilty/innocent/no contest** etc. *Hoskins pled guilty to four charges of theft.* **3 plead ignorance/poverty/insanity** etc. to give a particular excuse for your actions: *Goldman has pleaded ignorance, saying he knew nothing about the violations.* **4** [T] to give reasons why you think something is true or why something should be done: *Residents have a chance to plead their case at tonight's council meeting.* | **[plead that]** *Taylor pleaded that the proposal would cost the city too much money.*

plead·ing·ly /ˈplidɪŋli/ *adv.* if you say something pleadingly, or look at someone pleadingly, you speak to them or look at them in an emotional way, as though you are asking them to do something

pleas·ant /ˈplɛzənt/ *adj.* **1** enjoyable, nice, and making you feel happy: *It's been a very pleasant evening.* | *What a pleasant surprise!* **2** friendly, polite, and easy to talk to: *Marcia's always pleasant to everybody.* | *a pleasant-looking man* **3** weather that is pleasant is dry and not too hot or cold —opposite UNPLEASANT —**pleasantly** *adv.*

pleas·ant·ry /ˈplɛzəntri/ *n. plural* **pleasantries** [C usually plural] things that are not very important that you say to someone in order to be polite: *She and McDermott exchanged pleasantries.*

please¹ /pliz/ *interjection* **1** used to be polite when asking someone to do something: *Please be quiet.* | *Paige, sit down, please.* | *Would you please hurry up – we're going to be late.* | *Please feel free to ask questions at any time.* **2** used to be polite when asking for something: *Two pancakes for me, please.* | *Could I please borrow the car?* **3** said in order to politely accept something that someone offers you: *"Would you like some more wine?" "Yes, please."* **4 Please!** INFORMAL **a)** said when you think what someone has just said or asked is not possible or reasonable: *"Maybe we'll win." "Oh, please! We don't have any chance at all."* **b)** used to ask someone to stop behaving badly: *Allison! Please!*

please² *v.* [not in progressive] **1** [I,T] to make someone happy or satisfied: *Most young children are eager to please their teachers.* | *I think he tries a little too hard to please.* | *Choose room colors to please yourself, not your friends.* | **be easy/hard** etc. **to please** *Some people are easier to please than others.* | *Corey is impossible to please* (=it is impossible to please him). **2 whatever/however** etc. **sb pleases** whatever, however etc. someone wants: *She lets her kids do whatever they please.* **3 as sb pleases** doing whatever someone wants to do: *She's free to come and go as she pleases.* **4 please yourself** SPOKEN said when telling someone to do whatever they like, even though really you think that they are making the wrong choice: *"I don't think I'll go." "Oh, well, please yourself. I'm going anyway."* **5 if you please** SPOKEN, FORMAL used to make a polite request: *Spell it for me, if you please.* **6 please God** used to express a very strong hope or wish: *Everything's going to be fine, please God.* **7 (as) big/nice/bold** etc. **as you please** SPOKEN very big, nice etc., often in a surprising way: *She walked down the street in her swimming suit, as bold as you please.*

pleased /plizd/ adj. **1** happy or satisfied: *I was so pleased when they said they'd be able to stay another week.* | [+ **with**] *Republican leaders were pleased with the news.* | [**pleased (that)**] *We're all pleased you could come.* | **be pleased to see/hear/learn/announce etc. sth** *I'm pleased to see that after 10 years in the courts, this case is finally heading toward a conclusion.* —opposite DISPLEASED **2** (**I'm) pleased to meet you** SPOKEN used as a polite greeting when you meet someone for the first time **3 pleased with yourself** feeling proud or satisfied because you think you have done something smart, in a way that annoys other people: *Selina looks awfully pleased with herself.*

pleas·er /'plizɚ/ n. **crowd-pleaser/people-pleaser etc.** someone or something that makes other people happy: *A chocolate dessert is a guaranteed crowd-pleaser.*

pleas·ing /'plizɪŋ/ adj. FORMAL giving pleasure, enjoyment, or satisfaction: *a pleasing nutty flavor* | [+ **to**] *Though pleasing to the eye, the building is drafty and cold.* —**pleasingly** adv.

pleas·ur·a·ble /'plɛʒərəbəl/ adj. FORMAL enjoyable: *We want this to be a pleasurable experience for everyone.*

pleas·ure[1] /'plɛʒɚ/ n. **1** [U] the feeling of happiness, satisfaction, or enjoyment that you get from an experience: *I don't get to read much for pleasure anymore.* | *It gives me great pleasure to introduce the champions.* | *He seems to take pleasure in proving other people wrong.* **2** [C] an activity or experience that you enjoy very much: *the simple pleasures of life* | *It's a pleasure to finally meet you, Colonel.* | *Sleeping on the soft, warm sand was a pleasure.* **3 have the pleasure of (doing)** FORMAL to enjoy the experience of something: *We had the pleasure of meeting with the President privately.*

SPOKEN PHRASES

4 (**it's) my pleasure** used when someone has thanked you for doing something and you want to say that you were glad to do it: *"Thanks for coming." "My pleasure."* **5 what's your pleasure?** OLD-FASHIONED used to ask someone what they want: *What is your pleasure, Sire?* **6 with pleasure** FORMAL used to say politely that you are happy to do something that someone has just asked you to do: *"Give the kids a hug for me." "With pleasure."*

pleasure[2] v. [T] INFORMAL to give someone feelings of sexual pleasure by touching them

pleasure boat also **pleasure craft** /'.. ,./ n. [C] a boat that someone uses for fun rather than for business

pleat /plit/ n. [C] a flat narrow fold in a skirt, a pair of pants, a dress etc. —**pleat** v. [T]

pleat·ed /'plitɪd/ adj. a pleated skirt, pair of pants, dress etc. has a lot of flat narrow folds —see picture at PLEAT

pleat

a pleated skirt

plebe /plib/ n. [C] INFORMAL a first year student at the U.S. Military Academy or the U.S. Naval Academy

ple·be·ian[1] /plɪ'biən/ adj. **1** DISAPPROVING not impressive, expensive, fashionable etc.: *The food selection – hot dogs and beer – was rather plebeian.* **2** relating to ordinary people rather than people with a high social class

plebeian[2] n. [C] an ordinary person who had no special rank in ancient Rome —compare PATRICIAN (2)

pleb·i·scite /'plɛbə,saɪt/ n. [C,U] a system by which everyone in a country, area etc. votes on an important decision that affects the whole area: *Puerto Rico held a plebiscite in 1991 on whether to become a state.* —compare REFERENDUM

plec·trum /'plɛktrəm/ n. [C] a small thin piece of plastic, metal, or wood that you use for playing some STRINGED INSTRUMENTS such as a GUITAR; PICK[2]

pled /plɛd/ a past tense and past participle of PLEAD

pledge[1] /plɛdʒ/ n. [C] **1** a serious promise or agreement to do something or to give money to an organization, country etc., especially one made publicly or officially: [**a pledge to do sth**] *All six nations have signed a pledge to fight terrorism.* | *Donors have made pledges totaling nearly $4 million.* | *Humphrey fulfilled his pledge by resigning after two terms in Congress.* **2 a pledge of love/friendship etc.** a serious promise of love etc. made by two people **3** someone who has promised to become a member of a college FRATERNITY or SORORITY but is not yet a member **4** something valuable that you leave with someone else as proof that you will do what you have agreed to do, pay back what you owe etc.

pledge[2] v. [T] **1** to make a formal, usually public, promise to do something or to give money to an organization, country etc.: *Moore has pledged $100,000 to the symphony.* | [**pledge to do sth**] *The President has pledged to make welfare reform a success.* | [**pledge that**] *Cohen pledge that the troops would be home by Christmas.* | **pledge support/loyalty/solidarity etc.** (=promise to give your support, be loyal etc.) **2** to make someone formally promise something: *We were all pledged to secrecy.* **3** to promise to become a member of a college FRATERNITY or SORORITY **4** to leave something with someone as a PLEDGE[1] (4)

Pledge of Al·le·giance /,. . .'../ n. **the Pledge of Allegiance** an official statement said by Americans in which they promise to be loyal to the United States, usually said every morning by children in school

Pleis·to·cene /'plaɪstə,sin/ adj. relating to the period in the Earth's history that started about two million years ago and ended about 10,000 years ago, when much of the Earth was covered with ice

ple·na·ry /'plinəri, 'plɛ-/ adj. [only before noun] FORMAL **1** involving all the members of a committee, organization etc.: *The party held a plenary session in April.* | *a plenary speech* (=to all the members) **2** plenary power or authority is complete and has no limit: *The envoy was given plenary powers to negotiate with the rebels.* —**plenary** n. [C]

plen·i·po·ten·ti·ar·y /,plɛnəpə'tɛnʃi,ɛri, -ʃəri/ n. [C] FORMAL someone who has full power to take action or make decisions, especially as a representative of their government in a foreign country —**plenipotentiary** adj.

plen·i·tude /'plɛnə,tud/ n. LITERARY **1 a plenitude of sth** a large amount of something: *a plenitude of hope* **2** [U] completeness or fullness

plen·te·ous /'plɛntiəs/ adj. LITERARY plentiful

plen·ti·ful /'plɛntɪfəl/ adj. more than enough in quantity: *a plentiful harvest* | *Opportunities for teaching abroad are plentiful.* —**plentifully** adv.

plen·ty[1] /'plɛnti/ pron. a large quantity that is enough or more than enough: *There's plenty to do and see in this beautiful vacation area.* | *"More dessert?" "No thanks, I've had plenty."* | [+ **of**] *Come at 8. That'll give me plenty of time to get ready.* | *Make sure you drink plenty of water.*

plenty[2] adv. SPOKEN, INFORMAL a lot, or more than enough: *Those pants are plenty big on you.* | *There's plenty more chicken if you want it.*

plenty[3] n. [U] FORMAL **1** a situation in which there is a large supply of something, especially something that is needed for life: *It is a disgrace that we still have hunger in this land of plenty.* **2 in plenty** many, or more than enough: *You'll find errors in plenty if you look hard enough.* —see also HORN OF PLENTY

pleth·o·ra /'plɛθərə/ n. **a plethora of sth** FORMAL a very large amount of something: *The city faces a plethora of problems.*

pleu·ri·sy /'plʊrəsi/ n. [U] a serious illness that affects your lungs, causing severe pain in your chest

Plex·i·glas, plexiglass /'plɛksi,glæs/ n. [U] TRADEMARK a strong clear type of plastic that can be used instead of glass

plex·us /'plɛksəs/ *n.* —see SOLAR PLEXUS

pli·a·ble /'plaɪəbəl/ *adj.* **1** able to bend without breaking or cracking: *The clay should be moistened regularly to keep it soft and pliable.* **2** easily influenced by other people to do what they want: *The system helps make workers more pliable to the demands made by management.* —**pliability** /,plaɪə-'bɪləti/ *n.* [U]

pli·ant /'plaɪənt/ *adj.* pliable —**pliancy** *n.* [U]

pli·ers /'plaɪɚz/ *n.* [plural] a small tool made of two crossed pieces of metal, used to hold small things, pull things, or to bend and cut wire: *Hand me that pair of pliers, please.* —see picture at TOOL¹

plight /plaɪt/ *n.* [usually singular] a bad, serious, or sad condition or situation: *the plight of homeless children*

plinth /plɪnθ/ *n.* [C] a square block, usually made of stone, that is used as the base for a PILLAR or STATUE

Plin·y the El·der /,plɪni ði 'ɛldɚ/ (A.D. 23–79) an ancient Roman writer known for his NATURAL HISTORY, a very long book full of information about the ideas of his time

Pliny the Young·er /,plɪni ðə 'yʌŋgɚ/ (A.D. ?61–113) an ancient Roman politician and writer known for his letters

Pli·o·cene /'plaɪə,sin/ *adj.* relating to the period in the Earth's history that started about five million years ago and continued until about two million years ago

plod /plɑd/ *v.* **plodded, plodding 1** [I] also **plod along/on** to happen or do something very slowly in a boring or bored way: *The movie plods along with predictable twists and turns.* **2** [I always + adv./prep.] to walk along slowly because you are tired or bored: [+ **through/along** etc.] *Nathan plodded up the stairs to his room.* —**plodding** *adj.*: *the plodding pace of negotiations*

plonk /plɑŋk/ *v.* [T] INFORMAL another form of PLUNK

plop¹ /plɑp/ *v.* **plopped, plopping 1** [I always + adv./prep., T] to fall somewhere, making a sound like something dropping into water, or to make something do this: *The frog plopped back into the river.* **2** [T always + adv./prep.] to drop something or put it down in a careless way: [+ **on/into**] *The children plopped their coats on the floor of the classroom.* **3** **plop (yourself) down** to sit down or lie down heavily: *Stanley plopped down on the sofa beside me.*

plop² *n.* [C] the sound made by something when it falls or is dropped into liquid

plo·sive /'plousɪv/ *n.* [C] TECHNICAL a CONSONANT sound that is made by completely stopping the flow of air out of your mouth and then suddenly letting it out, as when saying, for example, /b/ or /t/ —**plosive** *adj.*

plot¹ /plɑt/ *n.* [C] **1** the events that form the main story of a book, movie, or play: *The plot was boring, but the special effects were good.* **2** a secret plan made by several people to do something harmful or illegal: [a **plot to do sth**] *The diplomat was involved in a plot to bomb UN headquarters.* | [+ **against**] *a plot against the government* | *Peters hatched the plot* (=started making plans) *to kidnap the baby even before it was born.* **3 the plot thickens** SPOKEN, HUMOROUS used to say that events seem to be becoming more complicated and difficult to understand **4** a small piece of land for building or growing things on **5** a piece of land in a CEMETERY, in which one person or a group of people are buried when they die: *a family plot* **6** a drawn plan of a building at ground level; GROUND PLAN

plot² *v.* **plotted, plotting 1** [I,T] to make a secret plan to harm a particular person or organization, especially a political leader or government: *She spent months plotting revenge.* | [**plot to do sth**] *Jurors ruled that Nichols plotted to blow up the building.* | [+ **against**] *The king believed his advisors were plotting against him.* **2** [T] also **plot out** to make lines

and marks on a CHART that represent facts, numbers etc.: *The results are plotted in figure 6.1.* **3** [T] also **plot out** to mark, calculate, or follow the position of a moving aircraft, a ship, stars etc.: *Ahab plotted a course which he hoped would take him to the whale.* —**plotter** *n.* [C]

plough /plaʊ/ the British and Canadian spelling of PLOW

plov·er /'plʌvɚ, 'plou-/ *n.* [C] a small bird with a round body that lives near the ocean

plow¹ /plaʊ/ *n.* [C] a large piece of equipment used on farms, that cuts up the surface of the ground so that seeds can be planted and is usually pulled by a TRACTOR or animal —see also SNOWPLOW

plow² *v.* **1** [I,T] to use a plow to cut the earth: *Medina plows his sugar-cane fields using an ox.* **2** to push snow off streets using a SNOWPLOW **3** [I always + adv./prep.] to move with a lot of effort or force: [+ **along/across** etc.] *Lindy's truck plowed through the mud.*

plow sth ↔ **back** *phr. v.* [T] to put money that you have earned back into a business in order to make the business bigger and more successful: *Companies can plow back their profits into new equipment.*

plow into sb/sth *phr. v.* [T] to crash into something or someone, causing damage or harm: *A train derailed and plowed into two houses.*

plow on *phr. v.* [I] to continue trying to achieve something even though you feel annoyed or impatient: *It was not the reaction Margaret had been hoping for, but she plowed on regardless.*

plow through sth *phr. v.* [T] **1** to make progress slowly and with difficulty: *The justices are plowing through 500,000 pages of testimony this week.* **2** to do something completely but without wasting time: *Lovett's band plowed though a wide range of country and western hits.* | *We plowed through the photos of his trip to Italy.* **3** to move powerfully through something without regard for what is in your path: *The tornado plowed through Huntsville on Friday.* | *The car plowed through a fence.*

plow·man /'plaʊmən/ *n.* [C] OLD USE a man whose job was to guide a plow that was being pulled by a horse

plow·share /'plaʊʃɛr/ *n.* [C] the broad curved metal blade of a plow, which turns over the soil —see also **beat/turn swords into plowshares** (SWORD (2))

ploy /plɔɪ/ *n. plural* **ploys** [C] a way of tricking someone in order to gain an advantage: *The ploy didn't work.* | [**a ploy to do sth**] *Criminals will try all kinds of ploys to divert your attention.*

pluck¹ /plʌk/ *v.*
1 <u>pull sth</u> [T] to pull something quickly in order to remove it or separate it from something else: [**pluck sth from/off** etc. **sth**] *He reached to the side and plucked an apple off the tree.* | *Aunt Viva always plucked her eyebrows* (=pulled out hairs from the edges of them).
2 <u>take sb/sth away</u> [T always + adv./prep.] to take someone away from a place or situation in a quick and unexpected way: [**pluck sb from/off/away** etc.] *A large seagull swooped down and plucked a fish out of the water.*
3 <u>chicken/bird etc.</u> [T] to pull the feathers off a dead chicken or other bird before cooking it
4 <u>music</u> [I,T] to quickly pull hard at the strings of a musical instrument: [+ **at**] *Someone was plucking at the strings of an old guitar.*
5 **pluck up (the) courage** to force yourself to be brave and do something you are afraid of doing: *It took me weeks to pluck up the courage to try out for the play.*
6 **pluck sth out of the/thin air** to say or suggest a number, name etc. that you have just thought of without thinking about it carefully: *We haven't plucked these ten principles out of thin air.*

pluck at sth *phr. v.* [T] to pull something quickly and repeatedly with your fingers: *Kitty's restless hands plucked at her black cotton skirt.*

pluck² *n.* [U] OLD-FASHIONED courage and determination: *It takes a lot of pluck to do what he's done.*

pluck·y /'plʌki/ *adj.* INFORMAL brave and determined: *a plucky heroine* s w **plug**[1] /plʌg/ n. [C]

1 ▮electricity▮ **a)** the small object at the end of a wire that is used for connecting a piece of electrical equipment to an OUTLET (=supply of electricity): *the plug on the electric blanket* **b)** INFORMAL a place, usually on a wall, where electrical equipment is connected to the electricity supply; OUTLET: *Where's the plug in here?*

2 ▮bathtub▮ a round flat piece of rubber or plastic used for blocking the hole in a bathtub or SINK[2]

3 ▮object▮ an object used to fill or block a hole, tube etc.: *He sleeps with plugs in his ears.* —see also EARPLUG

4 ▮advertisement▮ INFORMAL a way of advertising a book, movie, idea etc., by talking about it publicly, especially on a television or radio program: *Jennings put in a plug for his new building project Thursday.*

5 ▮in an engine▮ INFORMAL the part of an engine that makes the SPARK to start the gas burning; SPARK PLUG: *Change the plugs every 10,000 miles.*

6 pull the plug INFORMAL **a)** to stop a business, or activity from continuing, especially by deciding not to give it any more money: [+ **on**] *NBC has pulled the plug on the new comedy series.* **b)** to turn off the machines that are keeping someone who is in a COMA alive: *If I ever get that way, just pull the plug.* **c)** to take out the plug that is connecting a piece of electrical equipment such as a television or computer to the supply of electricity

7 ▮piece▮ a piece of a substance that has been pressed tightly together: *a plug of tobacco*

plug

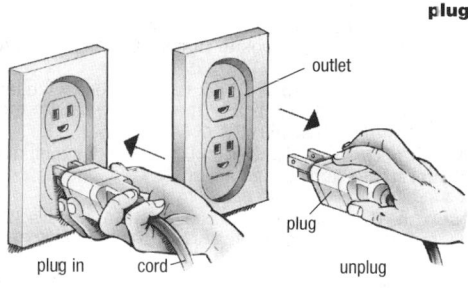

plug in — cord — unplug

s w **plug**[2] v. plugged, plugging [T] **1** also **plug up** to fill or block a hole: *Don't pour oil in the sink – it'll plug up the drain.* **2** to advertise a book, movie, idea etc. by talking about it on a television or radio program: *Whitaker was there to plug his new movie.* **3 plug the gap** to provide more of something that is needed: *The mayor wants to raise property taxes to plug the gap in the budget.* **4** OLD-FASHIONED to shoot someone: *They plugged him full of lead.*

plug away phr. v. [I] to keep working hard at something: [+ **at**] *We need to find out where we can improve, and keep plugging away at it.*

plug sth ↔ **in** phr. v. [T] **1** to connect a piece of electrical equipment to the main supply of electricity, or to another piece of electrical equipment: *Plug the VCR in and see if it still works.* **2** to add or include numbers or data: *We still have to plug in more data.*

plug into sth phr. v. [T] **1** to connect one piece of electrical equipment to another or to be connected: [plug sth into sth] *Can you plug the speakers into the stereo for me?* **2** to realize that something is available to be used and use it: *The campaign aims to give people the knowledge necessary to plug into the city's social service resources.*

plug-in /'. ./ adj. able to be connected to a supply of electricity or to another piece of electrical equipment: *a plug-in microphone*

plum[1] /plʌm/ n. **1** [C] a small round juicy fruit that is purple, red, or yellow and has a single large seed, or the tree that produces this fruit —see picture at FRUIT[1] **2** a good part in a play or movie, a good job etc. that other people wish they had: *The contract is a plum for Browning and Co.* **3** [U] a dark reddish purple color —see also PLUMMY

plum[2] adj. **1 a plum role/job etc.** INFORMAL a good

part in a play or movie, a good job etc. that other people wish they had: *Regina is one of the plum roles for women in American theater.* **2** having a dark reddish purple color

plum·age /'plumɪdʒ/ n. [U] the feathers covering a bird's body: *the duck's colorful plumage*

plumb[1] /plʌm/ v. [T] **1** to make an effort to learn, understand, or explain something completely: *Dubus, in his essays, tries to plumb the feelings of women.* **2 plumb the depths of despair/misery/bad taste etc.** to reach the lowest or worst point of something bad: *When his wife left him, Matt plumbed the depths of despair.* **3** to measure the depth of water or to check to see if something is exactly upright using a PLUMB LINE

plumb[2] adv. INFORMAL **1** HUMOROUS completely: *I'm sorry. I plumb forgot.* **2** [always + adv./prep.] INFORMAL exactly: *The bullet hit him plumb between the eyes.*

plumb[3] adj. TECHNICAL **1** exactly upright or level **2 out of plumb** not exactly upright or level

plumb bob /'. ./ n. [C] a small heavy object at the end of a PLUMB LINE

plumb·er /'plʌmɚ/ n. [C] someone whose job is to repair water pipes, SINKs, toilets etc.

plumber's help·er /,. '../ n. [C] OLD-FASHIONED a PLUNGER (1)

plumb·ing /'plʌmɪŋ/ n. [U] **1** the pipes that water flows through in a building: *I think there's something wrong with the plumbing.* **2** the work of fitting and repairing water pipes, toilets etc.

plumb line /'. ./ n. [C] a piece of string with a small heavy object tied to one end, used for measuring the depth of water or for marking a position that is exactly upright, for example when building a wall

plume /plum/ n. [C] **1** a small cloud of smoke, dust etc. that rises up into the air: [+ **of**] *Plumes of hot gas shoot up from Jupiter's surface.* **2** a large feather or group of feathers, especially one that is used as a decoration on a hat —see also NOM DE PLUME

plumed /plumd/ adj. [only before noun] having or decorated with feathers: *the knights' plumed helmets*

plum·met /'plʌmɪt/ v. [I] **1** to suddenly and quickly decrease in value or amount: *Enrollment at the school has plummeted to 25 students.* **2** to fall very suddenly and quickly from a very high place: *The helicopters slammed together before plummeting to the ground.* —compare PLUNGE[1] (1)

plum·my /'plʌmi/ adj. tasting like a PLUM or containing a lot of PLUMs: *a plummy wine*

plump[1] /plʌmp/ adj. **1** a word meaning "slightly fat," often used in order to be polite: *a plump woman in her fifties* **2** attractively round and slightly fat: *plump juicy strawberries* —**plumpness** n. [U] —see Usage Note at FAT[1]

plump[2] v. [T] **1** also **plump up** to make CUSHIONs, PILLOWs etc. softer and rounder by shaking or hitting them **2** [I,T] also **plump up** to make someone or something fatter by giving them food or filling them with something: *Boil the dried fruit until it plumps up in the cooking liquid.* **3 plump (yourself) down** to sit down suddenly and heavily: *Peggy plumped down in the chair beside Otto.* **4** [T always + adv./prep.] to put something down suddenly and carelessly: *You can plump the bags down anywhere you like.*

plum to·ma·to /,. .'../ n. [C] a type of TOMATO that is egg-shaped and that is often used in cooking

plun·der[1] /'plʌndɚ/ v. [I,T] to steal money or property from a place, especially while fighting in a war: *Many works of art were plundered by Nazi troops.* | *Critics claim the President has plundered the national treasury.* —**plunderer** n. [C]

plunder[2] n. [U] **1** things that have been stolen during a violent attack, especially during a war: *He fled the country with $600 million in plunder.* **2** the act of plundering: *the plunder of Africa by the European nations*

P

plunge¹ /plʌndʒ/ v.
1 ‖fall downward‖ [I always + adv./prep.] to move, fall, or be thrown suddenly forward or down: [+ off/into/through etc.] *Her car swerved and plunged through the guardrail.* | *A waterfall plunges off the cliff to the river below.* | *The skydiver **plunged to** her **death** from 8000 feet.*
2 ‖decrease‖ [I] to suddenly decrease by a large amount: *The President's popularity has plunged dramatically in recent weeks.*
3 ‖bad situation‖ [T] to suddenly put someone or something into a bad situation: [plunge sb/sth into sth] *Economic changes have plunged many of the elderly into poverty.* | *The hall was suddenly plunged into darkness.* | **plunge sb into gloom/despair** etc. (=to suddenly make someone feel very unhappy)
4 ‖into water‖ [I always + adv./prep.] to jump or DIVE into water: [+ in/into] *Burt plunged into the river fully clothed to save the boy.*
5 ‖push down‖ [T] to push something firmly and deeply into something else: [plunge sth into sth] *She plunged the knife into his neck.* | *Plunge the potatoes into cold water to stop the cooking.*
6 ‖start doing sth‖ [I,T] to begin to do something or become involved in something suddenly, especially without thinking about the possible results: *She plunged herself into her writing.* | *The two women sat down in a corner and plunged into an animated conversation.*
7 ‖go suddenly‖ [I always + adv./prep.] to suddenly go into a place or area: *Three men left the truck and plunged into the woods.*
8 ‖ship‖ [I] if a ship plunges, it moves violently up and down, usually because of high waves

plunge² n. **1 take the plunge** to decide to do something risky, especially after delaying it or worrying about it for a long time: *We've decided to take the plunge and get married.* **2** [C usually singular] a sudden quick fall down or forward: *Myers was severely injured in the plunge from the top of the hotel.* **3** [C] a sudden large decrease in the price, value, or amount of something: *There has been a 10% plunge in stock prices.* **4** [C usually singular] a jump into water, or a quick swim: *a plunge in the lake*

plung·er /ˈplʌndʒɚ/ n. [C] **1** a tool used for unblocking a pipe in a toilet or SINK², consisting of a straight handle with a large rubber cup on its end **2** TECHNICAL a part of a machine that moves up and down

plunging neck·line /ˌ.. ˈ../ n. [C] a very low curve or V shape at the neck of a woman's dress

plunk¹ /plʌŋk/ v. [T] INFORMAL **1** also **plunk down** to spend a lot of money for something: *I was too cheap to plunk down $25 for a one-hour lesson.* **2** to put something down somewhere, especially in a careless noisy way: [plunk sth in/on etc.] *Workers just plunk the bags of frozen meat into boiling water.* **3 plunk (yourself) down** to sit down heavily and then relax: *Americans love to plunk themselves down in front of the TV.*

plunk² n. [C,U] the sound something makes when it is dropped

plu·per·fect /ˌpluˈpɚfɪkt/ n. **the pluperfect** TECHNICAL the PAST PERFECT tense of a verb

plu·ral¹ /ˈplʊrəl/ n. **1 the plural** the form of a word that represents more than one person or thing. For example, "hands" is the plural of "hand." **2** [C] a plural noun

plural² adj. **1** a plural word or form shows you are talking about more than one thing, person etc.: *a plural pronoun* | *"Have" is the plural form of "has."* **2** FORMAL involving more than one person or thing or different types of people or things: *the plural makeup of the United States*

plu·ral·ism /ˈplʊrəˌlɪzəm/ n. [U] FORMAL the principle that people of different races, religions, and political beliefs can live together peacefully in the same society, or the situation in which this happens —**pluralist** n. [C] —**pluralistic** /ˌplʊrəˈlɪstɪk/, **pluralist** adj.: *a pluralistic society*

plu·ral·i·ty /plʊˈræləti/ n. plural **pluralities 1** [C,U] the number of votes received by the winning person in an election where there are three or more people trying to be elected: *The mayor won with a plurality of 12,000 votes, while the other two candidates had 9000 and 7000 votes, respectively* —compare MAJORITY **2** [C] FORMAL a large number of different things: [+ of] *In the U.S., there is a plurality of religious beliefs.* **3** [U] TECHNICAL the state of being plural

plur·i·bus /ˈplʊrɪbəs/ —see E PLURIBUS UNUM

plus¹ /plʌs/ prep. used when one number or amount is added to another: *Three plus six equals nine. (3 + 6 = 9)* | *The jacket costs $49.95 plus tax.* —opposite MINUS¹

plus² conjunction INFORMAL and also: *He's really cute, plus he's got a good job.* | *You need a birth certificate, plus a photo I.D.*

plus³ adj. **1 A plus/B plus/C plus** etc. a grade used in a system of marking students' work, usually written A+, B+ etc.; a C plus (C+) is higher than a C, but lower than a B MINUS (B–) —opposite MINUS³ (2) **2** more than a particular amount, number, or level, or greater than zero: *He works 10 hours a day plus.* | *a temperature of plus 12°* **3 on the plus side** used before giving the advantages of something when there might also be disadvantages: *On the plus side, this online service is a lot cheaper than some of the larger ones.* **4 a plus factor/point** an advantage or favorable feature that something has

plus⁴ n. [C] **1** INFORMAL something that is an advantage, or a quality you think is good: *"The office is really close to my house." "That's a plus."* | *There are* **pluses and minuses** (=both good and bad things) *to living in the city.* —opposite MINUS² **2** [usually singular] a PLUS SIGN

plus-fours /ˌ. ˈ./ n. [plural] pants with loose wide legs that are fastened just below the knee, worn by men in past times when playing GOLF

plush¹ /plʌʃ/ also **plush·y** /ˈplʌʃi/ adj. **1** expensive, comfortable, and of good quality: *a plush hotel* **2** made of plush: *plush green carpet*

plush² n. [U] silk or cotton cloth with a surface like short fur: *Clara wants the seats to be upholstered in plush.*

plus sign /ˈ. ./ n. [C] the sign (+), showing that you should add two or more numbers together, or that a number is more than zero

Plu·tarch /ˈplutɑrk/ (A.D. ?46–?120) an ancient Greek HISTORIAN who wrote about famous Greek and Roman politicians and military leaders

Plu·to /ˈplutoʊ/ **1** in Greek MYTHOLOGY, another name for Hades, the god of the Underworld where the spirits of dead people live **2** the smallest PLANET, ninth in order from the Sun

plu·toc·ra·cy /pluˈtɑkrəsi/ n. plural **plutocracies** [C] DISAPPROVING **1** a country ruled by rich people, or a government that is controlled by them **2** a group of rich people who rule a country

plu·to·crat /ˈplutəˌkræt/ n. [C] DISAPPROVING someone who has power because they are rich —**plutocratic** /ˌplutəˈkrætɪk/ adj.

plu·to·ni·um /pluˈtoʊniəm/ n. [U] symbol **Pu** a metal that is an ELEMENT and is used in the production of NUCLEAR power

ply¹ /plaɪ/ v. **plied, plying 1 ply your trade** FORMAL to work at your business or special skill: *A number of drug dealers ply their trade in the park.* **2** [I always + adv./prep., T] LITERARY if a boat or vehicle plies between two places, it travels to those two places regularly: [+ between/across etc.] *Small fishing boats are plying back and forth across the harbor.* | [ply sth] *Graceful sailboats ply the Nile.* **3** [T] OLD USE OR LITERARY to use a tool skillfully

ply sb with sth phr. v. **1** to keep giving someone one large quantities of food and drink: *Agents plied him with liquor to get him talking.* **2 ply sb with questions** to keep asking someone questions

ply² n. [U] **two-ply/three-ply** etc. a unit for measuring the thickness of plywood, toilet paper, thread, rope etc. based on the number of layers or threads that it has: *double-ply toilet paper*

Plym·outh /'plɪməθ/ **1** the place in the U.S. state of Massachusetts where the Pilgrim Fathers first settled in America **2** a port in southwestern England from which the Pilgrim Fathers sailed to America

ply·wood /'plaɪwʊd/ *n.* [U] a material made of several thin sheets of wood stuck together to form a strong board

PM *n.* [C] an abbreviation for PRIME MINISTER

p.m. /ˌpiː 'ɛm/ used after numbers to show times from NOON to just before MIDNIGHT: *The party starts at 7 p.m.* (=in the evening) —compare A.M.

PMS *n.* [U] Premenstrual Syndrome; the feelings of anger or sadness and the physical pain many women feel just before their PERIOD (=monthly flow of blood)

pneu·mat·ic /nʊ'mætɪk/ *adj.* **1** able to work using air pressure: *a pneumatic pump* **2** TECHNICAL filled with air: *pneumatic tires*

pneumatic drill /.ˌ.. './ *n.* [C] a JACKHAMMER

pneumatic tube /.ˌ.. './ *n.* [C] a tube that you can send things through very quickly using air pressure

pneu·mo·coc·cus /ˌnuːmə'kɒkəs/ *n. plural* **pneumo·cocci** /-'kɒsaɪ, -'kɒkaɪ/ [C] a type of BACTERIA (=very small living things) that causes disease —**pneumococcal** *adj.*

pneu·mo·cys·tis /ˌnuːmə'sɪstɪs/ *n.* [U] a serious type of pneumonia that people with AIDS often get

pneu·mo·nia /nʊ'moʊnyə/ *n.* [U] a serious illness of the lungs that makes it difficult for you to breathe

P.O. 1 the written abbreviation of POST OFFICE **2** the written abbreviation of PETTY OFFICER

Po, the /poʊ/ a river in northern Italy that flows into the Adriatic Sea

poach /poʊtʃ/ *v.* **1** [T] **a)** to cook eggs without their shells in water that is almost boiling **b)** to cook fish or meat in water or another liquid that is almost boiling: *The chicken was poached with basil and pepper.* **2** [I,T] to persuade someone to leave a team or company and join yours: *Volkswagen poached Lopez from GM in 1993.* **3** [I,T] to illegally catch or shoot animals, birds, or fish, especially on private land without permission **4** [T] to unfairly or illegally use someone else's ideas

poached /poʊtʃt/ *adj.* poached food has been cooked in water that is almost boiling: *poached fruit*

poach·er /'poʊtʃɚ/ *n.* [C] someone who illegally catches or shoots animals, birds, or fish, especially on private land without permission

poach·ing /'poʊtʃɪŋ/ *n.* [U] the activity of illegally catching or shooting animals, birds, or fish, especially on private land without permission: *Kenya wants to prevent the poaching of elephants for their tusks.*

P.O. Box /ˌpiː 'oʊ ˌbɑks/ *n.* [C] a box in a post office that has a special number, to which you can have your mail sent instead of to your home: *For more information write: P.O. Box 680E, Dorset, Minnesota.*

Po·ca·hon·tas /ˌpoʊkə'hɑntəs/ (1595–1617) a Native American woman who helped to develop friendly relations between the English and the Native Americans

pocked /pɑkt/ *adj.* covered with small holes or marks: *the meteor-pocked surface of the moon* —**pock** *v.* [T]

pock·et¹ /'pɑkɪt/ *n.* [C]

1 `in clothes` a small bag sewn onto or into coats, shirts, pants, or skirts, where you can put things such as money or keys: *Maggie put her hands in her pockets to keep them warm.* | *Fred searched his pockets for the ticket.* | **coat/pants/jacket etc. pocket** *He stuffed the phone number in his shirt pocket.*

2 `money` the amount of money available for you to spend: *The ruling means less money in the pockets of investors.* | *Gaylor had to pay the fine out of his own pocket* (=with his own money). | *They're looking for someone with deep pockets* (=a lot of money to spend) *to pay for the research.* | **an out-of-pocket expense/ charge/cost** (=something you must pay for yourself, rather than your company, your insurance company etc. paying for it) —see also DEEP-POCKETED

3 `in a bag/door etc.` a small bag, net, or piece of material that is attached to something, so you can

put things in it: *You will find the air safety card in the seat pocket in front of you.*

4 `small area/amount` a small area or amount of something that has a particular quality which is very different from what surrounds it: [+ of] *There will be pockets of colder temperatures over the valley today.* | *Government troops crushed the last pockets of resistance in the city.*

5 **in sb's pocket** if a politician or person in authority is in someone's pocket, they are completely controlled by them and willing to do what they want: *He argues that foreign agents have the administration in their pocket.*

6 `games` a hole or a small bag on a POOL¹ (2) table that you have to hit the ball into

7 `food` the hollow area in some kinds of food, which can be filled with other foods: *Stuff the meat into the pocket of the pita bread.*

8 **have sth in your pocket** to be very sure that you are going to win something such as a competition or election: *It looks like the team has a chance at the Aloha Bowl firmly in their pocket.* —see also AIR POCKET, **burn a hole in your pocket** (BURN¹ (15)), **line your own pockets** (LINE² (3)), **pick sb's pocket** (PICK¹ (9))

pocket² *v.* [T] **1 a)** to steal money, especially money that you are responsible for: *Robbins admitted pocketing $5300 of the campaign money.* **b)** to get money in a slightly dishonest way: *It's simple – we buy them for $5, sell them for $8, and pocket the difference.* **2** to put something into your pocket: *Tom slipped off his rings and pocketed them.* **3** to hit a ball into a pocket in games such as POOL

pocket³ *adj.* [only before noun] also **pocket-sized** small enough to be carried in your pocket: *a pocket dictionary*

pock·et·book /'pɑkɪt,bʊk/ *n.* [C] **1** the amount of money you have, or your ability to pay for things: *Higher prices will hit consumers in the pocketbook* (=cost them a lot of money). **2** OLD-FASHIONED a woman's PURSE (=small bag), especially one without a STRAP¹ **3** a small book with a soft cover that can be carried in a pocket **4** OLD-FASHIONED a WALLET —see also **vote with your pocketbook** (VOTE¹ (7))

pocket change /'.. ˌ./ *n.* [U] **1** coins that you carry in your pocket **2** a small or unimportant amount of money

pock·et·ful /'pɑkɪt,fʊl/ *n.* [C] the amount that a pocket will hold: [+ of] *a pocketful of quarters*

pocket knife /'.. ˌ./ *n.* [C] a small knife with one or more blades that fold into the handle

pocket mon·ey /'.. ˌ../ *n.* [U] INFORMAL a small amount of money that you can use to buy things you want, especially given to children by their parents: *He earned pocket money by repairing furniture for neighbors.*

pocket pro·tec·tor /'.. .ˌ../ *n.* [C] **1** a piece of plastic worn in a shirt pocket to carry pens and prevent ink from ruining your shirt **2 pocket-protector types/guys etc.** someone who likes technical subjects too much, is unfashionable, and is slightly strange

pocket ve·to /'.. ˌ../ *n.* [C] a method used by the U.S. President to stop a BILL (=suggestion for a new law), in which the President keeps the bill without signing it until Congress is on vacation, so that it cannot become a law

pock·mark /'pɑkmɑrk/ *n.* [C] **1** a small round hollow mark on someone's skin left by a disease such as ACNE, CHICKENPOX etc. **2** a small hollow mark on the surface of something

pock·marked /'pɑkmɑrkt/ *adj.* covered with small holes or marks: *a pockmarked face* | *The government buildings were pockmarked with bullet holes.* —**pockmark** *v.* [T]

Po·co·nos, the /'poʊkəˌnoʊz/ also **the Pocono Mountains** a group of mountains in the state of Pennsylvania in the northeastern U.S. that are part of the Appalachians

p.o.'d /ˌpi ˈoʊd‹ / adj. SPOKEN, INFORMAL very annoyed: *She was really p.o.'d when she didn't get the job.*

pod /pɑd/ n. [C] **1** the part of plants such as PEAS and beans that the seeds grow in: *Slice the vanilla pod along one side.* **2** a part of a vehicle or building that is separate from the main part: *Fiers sits in the cockpit pod between the two engines.* **3** a long narrow container for gasoline or other substances, especially one carried under an aircraft wing **4** a group of sea animals such as WHALES and DOLPHINS that swim together **5** a type of natural bag that holds the eggs of some types of insects and fish

po·di·a·trist /pəˈdaɪətrɪst/ n. [C] a doctor who takes care of people's feet and treats foot diseases —**podiatry** n. [U]

po·di·um /ˈpoʊdiəm/ n. [C] **1** a small raised area for a performer, speaker, or musical CONDUCTOR to stand on **2** a tall thin desk that you stand behind when giving a speech to a lot of people: *Hillie rose and went to the podium where he addressed the audience.*

Po·dunk, podunk /ˈpoʊdʌŋk/ adj. SPOKEN used to describe a place you think is small, unimportant, and boring: *His car broke down in some podunk little town.*

Poe /poʊ/, **Ed·gar Al·lan** /ˈɛdɡər ˈælən/ (1809–1849) a U.S. poet and writer of short stories

po·em /ˈpoʊəm/ n. [C] a piece of writing that expresses emotions, experiences, and ideas, especially in short lines using words that RHYME (=have a particular pattern of sounds)

po·e·sy /ˈpoʊəzi, -əsi/ n. [U] OLD USE poetry

po·et /ˈpoʊɪt/ n. [C] someone who writes poems

po·et·ess /ˈpoʊətɪs/ n. [C] OLD-FASHIONED a female poet

po·et·ic /poʊˈɛtɪk/ also **po·et·i·cal** /poʊˈɛtɪkəl/ adj. **1** relating to poetry or typical of poetry: *poetic language* | *poetic imagery* **2** graceful, beautiful, and having deep feelings: *Cliburn's playing was poetic and sensitive.* —**poetically** /-kli/ adv.

poetic jus·tice /ˌ… ˈ../ n. [U] a situation in which someone is made to suffer for something bad they have done, in a way that you think they deserve: *After the way she treated Sean, it's poetic justice that Darrin left her.*

poetic li·cense /ˌ… ˈ../ n. [U] the freedom you have to change facts and not to obey grammar rules etc. because you are making art or writing poetry

poet lau·re·ate /ˌ… ˈ../ n. [C] a poet who is chosen by a king, queen, president etc. to write poems on important occasions

po·et·ry /ˈpoʊətri/ n. [U] **1** poems: *He read me some of his poetry.* **2** the art of writing poems: *a poetry class* **3** APPROVING a quality of beauty, gracefulness, and deep feeling: *The way she moves is pure poetry.*

po·gey /ˈpoʊgi/ n. [U] CANADIAN, SPOKEN: see WELFARE (1)

po·go stick /ˈpoʊgoʊ ˌstɪk/ n. [C] a toy used for jumping, that consists of a pole with a spring near the bottom, a bar across the pole that you stand on, and a handle on top

po·grom /ˈpoʊgrəm/ n. [C] a planned killing of large numbers of people, especially Jews, usually done for reasons of race or religion

poign·ant /ˈpɔɪnyənt/ adj. making you have strong feelings of sadness or pity: *a poignant love story* —**poignancy** n. [U] —**poignantly** adv.: *She writes poignantly of her childhood.*

poin·set·ti·a /pɔɪnˈsɛtiə/ n. [C] a tropical plant with groups of large red or white leaves that look like flowers

point¹ /pɔɪnt/ n.

1 **idea** [C] a single fact, idea, or opinion in an argument or discussion: *They only agreed on one point – to have another meeting.* | *Visser makes some interesting points* (=gives facts, ideas, or opinions) *about our relationship to food.* | *Grinde referred to the book to prove his point* (=show that his idea or opinion is right). | *He lectures foreign students on the finer points of* (=details about) *democracy.*

2 **the point/sb's point** the main meaning or idea in something that is said or done: *The point is you've got to get some kind of job.* | *So what's your point?* | *Those issues are beside the point* (=they do not relate to the subject). | *Would you just get to the point* (=say the important part of what you want to say)? | *Whitney missed the point* (=did not understand the main meaning) *of the whole discussion.*

3 **in time/development** [C] a specific moment, time, or stage in something's development: *We're not planning to hire anyone else at this point.* | *The family moved to Oregon at some point in the last century.* | *Both sides accepted the proposal as a starting point* (=stage from which something can start) *for negotiations.* | *He was tired to the point of crying.* | *We've reached a point where we don't have enough money to continue all our services.*

4 **the point of no return** a stage in a process or activity when it becomes impossible to stop it or do something different: *The dam project has reached the point of no return.*

5 **on the point of (doing) something** going to do something very soon: *Experts are convinced Vietnam's economy is on the point of improving greatly.*

6 **purpose** [U] the purpose or aim of doing something: *The whole point of setting goals is to encourage progress.* | *There's no point in paying rent on the apartment if you're not going to live there.*

7 **quality/feature** [C] a particular quality or feature that someone or something has: *His plan has both good and bad points.* | *The main selling point of the drug is that it has fewer side effects.* | *Getting along with other people is not Nick's strong point* (=he is not very good at it).

8 **measure on a scale** [C] a mark or measure on a scale: *Stock prices moved up 27 points today.*

9 **the high/low point (of sth)** the best or worst part of something, or the best or worst moment of something: *Meeting the Pope was the high point of our trip.* | *Faith in government is at a low point.*

10 **the boiling/freezing/melting etc. point (of sth)** the temperature at which something boils, freezes, melts etc.

11 **games/sports** [C] a unit used to show the SCORE in a game or sport: *Reeves scored 23 points for Arizona.* | *If you forget to draw a card, you lose a point.*

12 **in numbers** [C] the sign (.) used to separate a whole number from the DECIMALS that follow it: *one point nine percent* (=1.9%)

13 **sharp end** [C] a sharp end of something: *a pencil point*

SPOKEN PHRASES

14 **sb has (got) a point** said when you think someone's idea or opinion is right: *She has a point – some of the so-called family movies are the worst things you could take your kid to.*

15 **(that's a) good point** said when someone mentions an important fact or detail that you had not thought of: *"But the bank is closed tomorrow." "Good point. I guess I'll have to go today."*

16 **that's not the point** said when you think that someone's facts or explanations are not acceptable because they do not relate to the most important facts or ideas: *"I gave it back." "That's not the point – you shouldn't have taken it in the first place."*

17 **what's the point** said when you do not think something is worth doing: *I could tell him, but what's the point? He never listens to anyone.*

18 **I see your/her etc. point** used to say that you can understand why someone has a particular idea or opinion: *At first I was against her, but now I see her point.*

19 **that's the (whole) point** used when emphasizing what the main fact, idea, or purpose of something is: *Advertisers want to make you buy things you don't need. That's the whole point.*

20 **not see any point in (doing) sth** used to say that you do not think something has any real purpose: *I don't see any point in waiting around.*

21 **point taken** said when you are accepting that what someone has said is true: *OK, point taken. I won't interfere anymore.*

22 not to put too fine a point on it used when you are saying something in a very direct way that might upset someone: *Everyone there – not to put too fine a point on it – was crazy.*

23 up to a point partly, but not completely: *That's true, up to a point.*

24 make a point of doing sth to do something deliberately: *Bridget made a point of thanking each of us for the gift.*

25 to the point only talking about the most important facts or ideas: *The letter was short and to the point.*

26 in point of fact used when giving correct information when someone has previously given the wrong information: *Many people believe surgery is the only answer. In point of fact, a change in diet is often enough.*

27 more to the point used to say that a particular fact or reason is more important than the one that was just mentioned: *Willis doesn't have children, and more to the point, he doesn't like children.*

28 place [C] an exact place or position: *Line A crosses line B at point C.* | *a border crossing point*

29 piece of land [C] a long thin piece of land that stretches out into the ocean

30 print [C,U] a unit for measuring the size of TYPE (=individual letters, numbers etc.) in printing: *I need a 12-point font.*

31 small spot [C] a very small spot: *tiny points of light*

32 direction [C] one of the marks on a COMPASS that shows direction: *the points of the compass* —see also **get/earn brownie points** (BROWNIE (3))

s w point² *v.*

1 show sth with your finger [I] to hold out your finger or a thin object toward something in order to make someone notice it: *Babies learn to point before they learn to talk.* | [+ at] *She pointed at my plate and asked why I wasn't eating.* | [+ to] *"There's a spider," he said, pointing to the ceiling.*

2 aim [I always + adv./prep., T] to aim something in a particular direction, or to be aimed in that direction: [+ at/to/toward etc.] *There were TV cameras pointing at us every time we turned around.* | [point sth at sb/sth] *The man pointed the gun at her head.*

point

She pointed at the broken window.

3 machine/clock etc. [I always + adv./prep.] to show a particular amount, number, time, direction etc. on a machine, clock, COMPASS etc.: *The arrow always points north.* | *It will be time to go when the big hand points to 12 and the little hand points to 6.*

4 show sb where to go [I always + adv./prep., T always + adv./prep.] to show someone which direction to go: *Could you point me in the right direction?* | *A simple sign for the party pointed down a dirt road.*

5 point the finger at sb INFORMAL to blame someone or say that they have done something wrong: *There's no reason to point the finger at him; there's no proof.*

6 point the way a) to show how something could change or develop successfully: *Several themes at the conference point the way for new nursing research.* **b)** to show which direction you need to go to find something: *No signs point the way to Carson's grave.*

7 point your toes to stretch the ends of your feet down, for example when you are dancing

point out *phr. v.* [T] **1** [point sth ↔ out] to tell someone something that they do not already know or have not thought about: *He got very angry when Emily pointed out his mistake.* | *I hadn't noticed the ad until Bill pointed it out.* | [point out that] *Critics point out that there is little evidence to support Abramson's theory.* | [point sth out to sb] *Robinson pointed out to them that the changes would actually improve the property.* **2** [point sb/sth ↔ out] to show

someone or something to someone by pointing at them: *Point out your office when we go by.* | *Helpful passengers pointed him out to the police.*

point to sth *phr. v.* [T] **1** also **point toward** if something points to a fact, it makes it seem very likely that it is true: *His symptoms all point to a stomach ulcer.* **2** to mention something because you think it is important: *Rollings points to improved test scores to justify the spending on schools.*

point sth ↔ **up** *phr. v.* [T] to make something seem more important or more noticeable: *The crash points up the need for new safety regulations.*

point-blank /ˌ. ˈ./ *adv.* **1** if you say something point-blank, you do it directly and without trying to explain your reasons: *I told Fred point-blank that he had made a mistake.* **2** a gun fired point-blank is fired very close to the person or thing it is aimed at: *Rutledge shot him point-blank in the chest.* —**point-blank** *adj.*: *Edwards was shot at point-blank range.*

point-ed /ˈpɔɪntɪd/ *adj.* [usually before noun] **1** having a point at the end: *the dog's pointed brown ears* **2 a pointed comment/question/look etc.** a direct question, look etc. that deliberately shows that you are annoyed, bored, or that you disapprove of something: *Jones could not avoid the reporter's pointed questions.* —**pointedly** *adv.*

point-er /ˈpɔɪntɚ/ *n.* [C] **1** a useful piece of advice or information that helps you do or understand something; TIP¹: [+ on] *Larry gave me a few pointers on giving a presentation.* **2** a long stick used to point at things on a map, board etc.: *General Peckam swung his pointer across the map of Italy.* **3** the thing, usually a thin piece of metal, that points to a number or direction on a piece of equipment, for example a scale or COMPASS: *Players win the amount of money shown by the pointer when the wheel stops moving.* **4** the small picture, usually an ARROW, that you move using a computer's MOUSE to point to the place on the screen where you want to work or start a program: *Move the pointer to the program's icon and double click.* **5** a hunting dog that stands very still and points with its nose to where birds or animals are hiding —see also THREE-POINTER

poin-til-lism /ˈpwɑntlˌɪzəm, ˈpɔɪn-/ *n.* [U] a style of painting popular in the late 19th century, that uses small spots of color all over the painting, rather than BRUSH STROKES —**pointillist** *adj.* —**pointillist** *n.* [C]

point-less /ˈpɔɪntlɪs/ *adj.* **1** without any purpose or meaning: *People stood in groups, making pointless small talk.* | *a pointless, brutal murder* **2** not likely to have any useful result: *Officials say the investigation is pointless.* | [it is pointless to do sth] *It is pointless to look at the budget again.* | [it is pointless doing sth] *It's pointless talking to Ken – he won't listen.* —**pointlessly** *adv.* —**pointlessness** *n.* [U]

point man /ˈ. ./ *n.* [C] **1** someone with a very important job or a lot of responsibility for a particular subject in a company or organization: *Brown was the point man for Clinton's technology policies.* **2** a soldier who goes ahead of a group to see if there is any danger

point of or-der /ˌ. . ˈ../ *n.* [C] FORMAL a rule used to organize an official meeting: *The Russian delegation was allowed to speak on a point of order* (=according to a rule).

point of ref-er-ence /ˌ. . ˈ../ *n.* [C] a REFERENCE POINT

point of sale /ˌ. . ˈ./ *n.* [C usually singular] the place or store where a product is sold: *Cash registers at the point of sale keep track of the store's stock.*

point of view /ˌ. . ˈ./ *n.* [C] **1** a particular way of thinking about or judging a situation: *The story is written from a child's point of view.* **2** someone's own personal opinion or attitude about something: *A trip to the island can be either very relaxing or very boring, depending on your point of view.*

poin-ty /ˈpɔɪnti/ *adj.* **pointier, pointiest** INFORMAL: see POINTED (1)

pointy-head-ed /ˈ.. ˌ../ *adj.* INFORMAL, DISAPPROVING intelligent in a way that is not practical, and showing you think you know more than anyone else —**pointy head** *n.* [C]

poise /pɔɪz/ *n.* [U] **1** a calm confident way of behaving, and the ability to control your feelings or reactions in difficult situations: *The Bears were 13 points behind, but Coach Stenstrom maintained his poise and confidence.* **2** a graceful way of moving or standing, so that your body seems balanced and not awkward: *Anne is tall and thin, but lacks poise.*

poised /pɔɪzd/ *adj.* **1** [not before noun] completely ready to do something or for something to happen, when it is likely to happen soon: [**poised to do sth**] *Hargrove is poised to become the city's first black mayor.* | [**+ for**] *The company seems poised for success.* **2** [not before noun] not moving, but completely ready to move or do something immediately: [**+ for/on/over etc.**] *The runners stood poised at the start of the race.* | [**poised to do sth**] *A tabby cat was poised to pounce at any second.* **3** behaving in a calm confident way, and able to control your feelings and reactions: *Heather looked poised and relaxed as she made her way to the stage.* **4** [not before noun] not moving, and leaning over something or seeming to hang in the air: [**+ over/above**] *Harriet was poised over her son's bed, wondering what he was dreaming.* **5 be poised between sth** [not before noun] to be in a position or situation in which two things have an equally strong influence: *The government stands poised between economic collapse and a loss of power.*

s w poi·son¹ /'pɔɪzən/ *n.* [C,U] **1** a substance that kills you or makes you very sick if you eat it, breathe it etc.: *The child was rushed to the hospital after eating rat poison.* | *These fruits contain a **deadly poison**.* **2** a person, feeling, idea etc. that makes you behave badly or become very unhappy: *Nationalism is a poison that has caused much suffering.* **3 what's your poison?** SPOKEN a humorous way of asking someone which alcoholic drink they would like

poison² *v.* [T] **1** to give someone poison, especially by adding it to food or drink, in order to harm or kill them: *Hill poisoned her husband and daughter for the insurance money.* | *Steven thought that someone had poisoned his food.* | [**poison sb with sth**] *Two of the victims had been poisoned with arsenic.* **2** if a substance poisons someone, it makes them very sick or kills them: *A small amount of lead paint can severely poison a child.* | *Seabirds are being poisoned by toxins in the water.* **3** to make land, rivers, air etc. dangerous by adding harmful chemicals to them: *Chemical waste has poisoned the city's water supply.* **4** to influence someone's thoughts or emotions in a bad way, or to make them feel very unhappy: *Kendall believes that sex on TV is poisoning our children's minds.* **5** to infect a part of the body: *For over a year, Jane fought against the cancer that had poisoned her blood.* **6 poison sb's mind against sb** to make someone dislike another person by saying bad and untrue things. —**poisoner** *n.* [C]

poison gas /ˌ.. './ *n.* [U] gas that causes death or serious injury, used especially against an enemy in a war

poi·son·ing /'pɔɪzənɪŋ/ *n.* [C,U] **1** illness that is caused by swallowing, touching, or breathing a poisonous substance | **alcohol/lead/radiation poisoning** (=caused by a particular substance) **2** the act of giving poison to someone: *There was no evidence of poisoning in the death of John Wallace.* —see also BLOOD POISONING, FOOD POISONING

poison i·vy /ˌ.. './. *n.* [U] a plant that has leaves with three parts and white berries, which has an oily substance on its leaves that makes your skin hurt and ITCH if you touch it

poison oak /ˌ.. './ *n.* [U] a plant with leaves similar to an OAK tree's, that makes your skin hurt and ITCH if you touch it

poi·son·ous /'pɔɪzənəs/ *adj.* **1** containing poison or producing poison: *The plant's white berries are extremely poisonous.* | *poisonous snakes* **2** causing

harm and anger: *Citizens demanded that the mayor apologize for his poisonous racist comments.* —**poisonously** *adv.*

poison-pen let·ter /ˌ.. '. ˌ../ *n.* [C] a letter that is usually not signed and that says things that are not nice about the person it has been sent to

poison su·mac /ˌpɔɪzən 'sumæk/ *n.* [U] a plant that has leaves with two parts and green-white berries, that makes your skin hurt and ITCH if you touch it

poke¹ /poʊk/ *v.*

1 with a finger/stick etc.
[T] to quickly push into something or someone using something pointed, such as your finger or a stick: *Someone poked me in the eye during basketball practice.*

poke

2 through a space/hole
a) [T always + adv./prep.] to move or push something through a space or out of an opening, so that you can see part of it: *Sherman poked his camera through the curtains.* | **poke your head around the door/through the window etc.** *Hannah poked her head around the corner to say "Hi."* **b) be seen** [I always + adv./prep.] if something is poking through or out of something else, you can see part of it but not all of it: *Curly strands of red hair poked out from under her hat.* | *Weeds poked through the cracks in the sidewalk.*

3 poke a hole a) to make a hole or hollow area in something by pushing something pointed into or through it: [**+ in/through**] *Fire crews poked holes in the roof to lower temperatures inside.* **b)** to find mistakes or problems in a plan or in what someone has said: [**+ in**] *Defense attorneys tried to poke holes in Jimmy's story.*

4 poke fun at sb/sth to joke about someone or something in a way that is not nice: *Reid was poking fun at his fellow Texans.*

5 poke your nose in/into sth INFORMAL to try to find out information about or get involved in someone else's private affairs: *My mother-in-law is always poking her nose in our business.*

6 poke the fire to move coal or wood in a fire with a stick to make it burn better

7 sex [T] VULGAR to have sex with a woman

poke along *phr. v.* [I] INFORMAL to move very slowly: *I wish this car in front of me would stop poking along.*

poke around *phr. v.* [I,T] INFORMAL **1** to look for something by moving a lot of things around: *Fossil collectors come to poke around the mud banks of Brays Bayou.* | [**+ in**] *Dan loves poking around in hobby shops, looking for new airplanes.* **2** to try to find out information about other people's private lives, in a way that annoys them: [**+ in**] *I'm tired of the press poking around in my private life.*

poke at sth *phr. v.* [T] to push something repeatedly with your finger or a sharp object: *The three girls poked at each other and giggled.* | *Jennie just poked at her food all evening* (=she moved food on her plate but did not want very much)

poke² *n.* **1 give sb/sth a poke** to quickly push your fingers, a stick etc. into something or someone: *Vanessa gave me a poke in the ribs.* **2 take a poke at sb** SPOKEN to hit or try to hit someone: *He insulted my wife, so I took a poke at him.* **3** INFORMAL a criticism of someone or something: [**+ at**] *Keillor is known for his fond pokes at small-town America.* | *Bennet took a poke at the President's recent refusal to sign the bill.*

pok·er /'poʊkɚ/ *n.* **1** [U] a card game that people usually play for money **2** [C] a metal stick used to move wood in a fire to make it burn better

poker-faced /'.. ˌ./ *adj., adv.* showing no expression on your face: *The jury sat poker-faced through six weeks of graphic testimony.* —**poker face** *n.* [singular]

pok·ey¹, **poky** /'poʊki/ *adj.* INFORMAL doing things very slowly, especially in a way that is annoying: *My old pokey car can only go sixty miles an hour.*

pokey² *n.* [C] OLD-FASHIONED, INFORMAL a JAIL

pol /pɑl/ *n.* [C] INFORMAL a politician

Po·lack /'poʊlæk/ *n.* [C] TABOO from Poland. Do not use this word.

Po·land /'poʊlənd/ a country in central Europe, east of Germany and west of Belarus

po·lar /'poʊlə/ *adj.* **1** close to or relating to the North Pole or the South Pole: *The crew flew a polar route to Detroit from Eastern Russia.* **2 polar opposite/opposites** something exactly or completely opposite in character or nature: *O'Brien's dark, troubled pictures are the polar opposites of Wheelan's cheerful abstractions.* **3** TECHNICAL related to one of the POLES (=ends) of a MAGNET

polar bear /'.. ,./ *n.* [C] a large white bear that lives near the North Pole

polar cap /'.. ,./ also **polar ice cap** /,.. '. ,./ *n.* [C] one of two masses of ice on the North and South Poles

po·lar·i·ty /poʊ'lærəti, pə-/ *n.* [C,U] **1** FORMAL a state in which people, opinions, or ideas are completely different or opposite to each other: [+ **between**] *There is a growing polarity between the workers and the management.* **2** TECHNICAL the state of having either a positive or negative electric charge

po·lar·ize /'poʊlə,raɪz/ *v.* [I,T] FORMAL to divide into clearly separate groups with opposite beliefs, ideas, or opinions, or to make people do this: *The community has been polarized by the police brutality case.* —**polarization** /,poʊlərə'zeɪʃən/ *n.* [U]

Po·lar·oid /'poʊlə,rɔɪd/ *n.* TRADEMARK **1** [C] a camera that uses a special film to produce a photograph very quickly **2** [C] a photograph taken with a Polaroid camera **3** [U] a special substance that is put on the glass in SUNGLASSES, car windows etc. to make the sun seem less bright

s w
3
Pole /poʊl/ *n.* [C] someone who comes from Poland

pole¹ /poʊl/ *n.* [C]

1 stick/post a long stick or post usually made of wood or metal, often set upright in the ground to support something: *a telephone pole* | *a flag pole* | *a fishing pole*

2 north/south pole the most northern or most southern point on a PLANET, especially the Earth: *Amundsen's expedition was the first to reach the pole.*

3 be poles apart two people or things that are poles apart are as different from each other as it is possible to be: *Tokyo and Washington remain poles apart on the issue of free trade.*

4 opposites one of two situations, ideas, or opinions that are the complete opposite of each other: *At one pole in the debate is keeping our personal freedoms, and at the other is reducing crime.*

5 electrical **a)** one of two points at the ends of a MAGNET where its power is the strongest **b)** one of the two points at which wires can be attached to a BATTERY (1) in order to use its electricity

6 the pole POLE POSITION

pole² *v.* [I,T] to push a boat along in the water using a pole

pole·cat /'poʊlkæt/ *n.* [C] **1** INFORMAL a SKUNK **2** a small dark brown wild animal that lives in northern Europe and defends itself by producing a bad smell

po·lem·ic /pə'lɛmɪk/ *n.* FORMAL OR TECHNICAL **1** [C] a written or spoken statement that strongly criticizes or defends a particular idea, opinion, or person: *Essentially, the play is a polemic on the judicial system.* **2** [U] also **polemics** the practice or skill of making such statements: *We discussed, planned, and engaged in passionate polemics.*

po·lem·i·cal /pə'lɛmɪkəl/ also **polemic** *adj.* FORMAL OR TECHNICAL using strong arguments to criticize or defend a particular idea, opinion, or person: *polemical literature* —**polemically** /-kli/ *adv.*

pole po·si·tion /'. .,../ *n.* [C,U] the best front position at the beginning of a car or bicycle race

Pole Star /'. ./ *n.* **the Pole Star** a star that is almost directly over the North Pole and that can be seen from the northern part of the world

pole vault /'. ./ *n.* **the pole vault** the sport of jumping over a high bar using a long pole —**pole vaulter** *n.* [C] —**pole vaulting** *n.* [U]

pole vault

po·lice¹ /pə'lis/ *n.* **1 the police** an official organization whose job is to make sure that people obey the law, to catch criminals, and to protect people and property: *Friends convinced Marla to report the robbery to the police.* | *If you don't leave, I'll call the police.* **2** [plural] the people who work for this organization: *On Monday, both men finally surrendered to police.* —see also MILITARY POLICE, SECRET POLICE

police² *v.* [T] **1** to control an activity or industry by making sure that people obey the rules: *The agency was set up to police the nuclear power industry.* | *The proposal says that if schools don't start to* **police** *themselves, others will come in to do the job.* **2** to use police officers or the army etc. in order to keep control over a particular area and protect people and property: *The five security zones are policed by U.N. forces.* **3** to walk around an outside area in order to clean it up: *All campers are required to police their campsite before they leave.* —**policing** *n.* [U] *The community is demanding a less aggressive style of policing.*

police bru·tal·i·ty /.,. .'.../ *n.* [U] violence or threats made by the police against someone who they believe is guilty of a crime

police de·part·ment /.'. .,../ *n.* [C] the official police organization in a particular area or city

police dog /.'. ,./ *n.* [C] a dog trained by the police to find hidden drugs or catch criminals

police force /.'. ,./ *n.* [C] all the people who work for a police organization: *Ferdinand resigned from the police force last May.*

po·lice·man /pə'lismən/ *n. plural* **policemen** /-mən/ [C] a male police officer

police of·fi·cer /.'. ,.../ *n.* [C] a member of the police

police state /.'. ,./ *n.* [C] a country in which the government strictly controls people's freedom to meet, write, or speak about politics, travel where they want to etc.

police sta·tion /.'. .,../ *n.* [C] the local office of the police in a town, part of a city etc.

po·lice·wom·an /pə'lis,wʊmən/ *n. plural* **policewomen** /-,wɪmɪn/ [C] a female police officer

pol·i·cy /'pɑləsi/ *n. plural* **policies 1** [C,U] a way of doing something that has been officially agreed on and chosen by a political party, business, or other organization: *Few journalists liked Reagan's policies.* | [+ **on**] *The company's policy on maternity leave is very generous.* | **defense/housing/foreign etc. policy** *the President's economic policy* **2** [C] a contract with an insurance company, or an official written statement giving all the details of such a contract: *Your homeowner's policy probably doesn't cover damage to your house from mudslides.* **3** [C,U] a particular principle that you believe in and that influences the way you behave: *I make it my policy not to gossip.*

pol·i·cy·hold·er /'pɑləsi,hoʊldə/ *n.* [C] someone who has bought insurance for something

pol·i·cy·mak·er, policy maker /'pɑləsi,meɪkə/ *n.* [C] someone who helps to decide what an organization's way of doing things will be

po·li·o /'poʊli,oʊ/ also **po·li·o·my·e·li·tis** /,poʊlioʊ-maɪə'laɪtɪs/ TECHNICAL *n.* [U] a serious infectious disease of the nerves in the SPINE, which often causes a permanent loss of the ability to move part or all of your body

P

pol·i sci /ˌpɑli 'saɪ/ *n.* [U] SPOKEN: see POLITICAL SCIENCE

Po·lish¹ /'poʊlɪʃ/ *adj.* from or relating to Poland, its people, or their language

Polish² *n.* [U] the language of Poland

pol·ish¹ /'pɑlɪʃ/ *v.* [T] **1** to make something smooth, bright, and shiny by rubbing it: *Jerome spent all afternoon polishing the car.* **2** to improve a piece of writing, a speech etc. by making slight changes before it is completely finished: *Edward's essay is good, but he needs to polish it a little bit.* —**polisher** *n.* [C] —**polishing** *n.* [U]

    polish sth ↔ **off** *phr. v.* [T] INFORMAL to finish food, work etc., quickly or easily: *Justin polished off a whole pie last night.*

    polish sb ↔ **off** *phr. v.* [T] INFORMAL to kill or defeat someone: *Miami has polished off eleven teams in a row this season.*

    polish sth ↔ **up** *phr. v.* [T] **1** also **polish up on sth** to improve a skill or an ability by practicing it: *I need to polish up on my writing skills.* **2** to make something seem better or more attractive to other people: *The boxing federation is trying to polish up their image.* **3** to polish or make something clean and new looking: *Every summer they polish up the opera house.*

polish² *n.* **1** [C,U] a liquid, powder, or other substance that you rub into a surface to make it smooth and shiny: *furniture polish* | *shoe polish* **2** [U] great skill and style in the way someone performs, writes, or behaves: *What this dance troupe lacks in polish, they make up for in enthusiasm.* **3** [singular] an act of polishing a surface to make it smooth and shiny: *A good polish now and then will keep the table looking new.* **4** [singular] a smooth shiny surface produced by polishing —see also **spit and polish** (SPIT² (4))

pol·ished /'pɑlɪʃt/ *adj.* **1** shiny because of being rubbed, usually with polish: *All their furniture was made of dark red polished wood.* | *a polished granite counter* **2** a polished performance, piece of writing, musician, actor etc. is skillful and stylish: *Guillem is a polished ballerina.* **3** polite, confident, and graceful: *a polished and handsome lawyer* | *polished manners*

pol·it·bu·ro /'pɑlɪt,byʊroʊ/ *n.* [C usually singular] the chief decision-making committee of a Communist party or Communist government, especially of the former Soviet Union

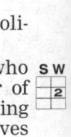

po·lite /pə'laɪt/ *adj.* **1** behaving or speaking in a way that is correct for the social situation you are in, and showing that you are careful to consider other people's needs and feelings: *The clerks were very polite and helpful.* | [**it is polite to do sth**] *It's not polite to talk with your mouth full.* —opposite RUDE (1), IMPOLITE **2 just/only being polite** SPOKEN saying something you may not really believe or think, in order to avoid offending someone: *Did she really like the flowers, or was she just being polite?* **3** polite conversation, remarks etc. are made because it is considered socially correct to do this: *We exchanged polite goodbyes before getting on the train.* | *a polite smile* **4 in polite society/circles/company** OFTEN HUMOROUS among people who are considered to have a good education and correct social behavior: *You can't use words like that in polite company.* —**politely** *adv.* —**politeness** *n.* [U]

pol·i·tesse /ˌpɑli'tɛs/ *n.* [U] FORMAL the ability to behave or speak in a polite way

pol·i·tic /'pɑlə,tɪk/ *adj.* FORMAL sensible and likely to bring advantage; PRUDENT: *Had Stiles been more politic, he would have used the information in court.* —see also BODY POLITIC, POLITICS

po·lit·i·cal /pə'lɪtɪkəl/ *adj.* **1** [no comparative] relating to the government, politics, and public affairs of a country: *The U.N. is seeking a political solution rather than a military one.* | *The U.S. has two main political parties.* | *political activists* **2** [no comparative] relating to the ideas or activities of a particular person, party, or group in politics: *Nixon had many political enemies.* | *political jokes and satire* **3** [no comparative] relating to the way that people, groups, companies etc. try to get advantages for themselves: *Harris has his own political agenda in the company.* **4** interested in or active in politics: *Mike's never been a political person.* **5 political football** a difficult problem which opposing politicians argue about or which each side deals with in a way that will bring them advantage: *Airline safety has become a political football.* —see also POLITICALLY

political ac·tion com·mit·tee /.ˌ... '.. .ˌ../ *abbreviation* **PAC** *n.* [C] an organization formed by a business, UNION, or INTEREST GROUP to help raise money so that people who support their ideas can try to be elected for Congress

political a·sy·lum /.ˌ... .'../ *n.* [U] the right to remain in another country if you cannot live safely in your own because of the political situation there: *The family was finally granted political asylum in the United States.*

political e·con·o·my /.ˌ... .'.../ *n.* [U] the study of the way nations organize the production and use of wealth

political ge·og·ra·phy /.ˌ... .'.../ *n.* [U] the study of the way the Earth's surface is divided up into different countries, rather than the way it is marked by rivers, mountains etc. —compare PHYSICAL GEOGRAPHY

po·lit·i·cally /pə'lɪtɪkli/ *adv.* in a political way: *Women were becoming more politically active.* | *Larkin's decision is widely believed to be politically motivated.* | [sentence adverb] *Politically, the region is very unstable.*

politically cor·rect /.ˌ... .'./ *adj.* language, behavior, and attitudes that are carefully chosen so that they do not offend or insult anyone —**political correctness** *n.* [U] —see also PC²

political ma·chine /.ˌ... .'../ *n.* [singular] the system used by people with the same political interests to make sure that political decisions bring an advantage to themselves or to their group

political pris·on·er /.ˌ... '.../ *n.* [C] someone who is put in prison because they oppose and criticize the government of their own country

political sci·ence /.ˌ... '../ *n.* [U] the study of politics and government —**political scientist** *n.* [C]

pol·i·ti·cian /ˌpɑlə'tɪʃən/ *n.* [C] **1** someone who works in politics, especially an elected member of the government **2** someone who is skilled at dealing with people or at getting advantages for themselves within an organization: *As a salesman, I have to be part politician and part psychologist.*

po·lit·i·cize /pə'lɪtə,saɪz/ *v.* [T] to make something more political or more involved in politics: *Sheppard cautioned against politicizing the study's findings.*

po·lit·i·cized /pə'lɪtə,saɪzd/ *adj.* having been made more political or having become involved in politics: *Abortion is already a highly politicized issue.* —**politicization** /pəˌlɪtəsə'zeɪʃən/ *n.* [U]

pol·i·tick·ing /'pɑlə,tɪkɪŋ/ *n.* [U] political activity, usually done for your own advantage: *The House's session will be shortened due to election-year politicking.*

po·lit·i·co /pə'lɪtə,koʊ/ *n. plural* **politicos** [C] a politician or someone who is active in politics, often used in a disapproving way: *Many local politicos were surprised at McKasson's resignation.*

politico- /pəlɪtəkoʊ/ *prefix* political and something else: *politico-military strategy*

pol·i·tics /'pɑlə,tɪks/ *n.* **1** [U] ideas and activities that are concerned with gaining and using power in a country,: *Brock's been involved in city politics since college.* | *Politics doesn't interest me much.* **2** [U] the profession of being a politician: *Helping people is why I went into politics* (=became a politician) *in the first place.* | *Flynn retired from politics in 1986.* **3** [plural] the activities of people who are concerned with gaining personal advantage within a group, organization etc.: *I'm tired of dealing with all of the office politics.* **4** [plural] someone's political beliefs and opinions: *I don't agree with Michael's politics,* *but he's sure a nice guy.* **5** [U] the study of political power and systems of government; POLITICAL SCIENCE

pol·i·ty /'pɑləti/ n. [C,U] FORMAL a particular form of political or government organization, or a condition of society in which political organization exists

Polk /pouk/, **James** (1795–1849) the 11th President of the U.S.

pol·ka /'poulkə, 'poukə/ n. [C] a very quick simple dance for people dancing in pairs, or a piece of music for this dance —**polka** v. [I]

polka dot /'.. ,./ n. [C] one of a number of round spots that form a pattern, especially on cloth made into clothing: *Kate's shirt was green with purple polka dots.* —**polka-dot** —**polka-dotted** adj.: *a polka-dot dress* —see picture at PATTERN[1]

s w **poll**[1] /poul/ n. [C] **1** the process of finding out what people think about something by asking many people the same question: *In our poll, we asked teachers how they felt about teacher testing.* | **take/conduct/do a poll** *The newspaper did a poll and found that people are in favor of campaign-finance reform.* **2** a record of the result of this: *Recent polls indicate strong support for cutting taxes.* **3 the polls** [plural] **a)** an election to choose a government or political representative: *City officials do not expect many people at the polls.* | *We're trying to encourage young people to* **go to the polls** (=vote in an election). **b)** the place where you can go to vote in an election: *The polls open at 7 a.m.* —see also EXIT POLL, STRAW POLL

poll[2] v. [T] to try to find out what people think about a subject by asking many people the same question: *Only 16 percent of the freshmen polled said they intended to major in business.*

pol·len /'pɑlən/ n. [U] a fine powder produced by flowers, which is carried by the wind or by insects to other flowers of the same type, making them produce seeds

pollen count /'.. ,./ n. [C] a measure of the amount of pollen in the air, usually given to help people who are made sick by it: *The pollen count is usually much lower in the winter.*

pol·li·nate /'pɑləneɪt/ v. [T] to make a flower or plant produce seeds by giving it pollen: *Bees help pollinate more than 100 crop plants in the United States.* —**pollination** /,pɑlə'neɪʃən/ n. [U]

poll·ing /'poulɪŋ/ n. [U] **1** the activity of voting in a political election: *Polling will take place from 7 a.m. to 10 p.m.* **2** the activity of asking people their opinions

polling sta·tion /'.. ,../ also **polling place** /'.. ,./ n. [C] the place where people go to vote in an election

pol·li·wog, **pollywog** /'pɑli,wɑg/ n. [C] a TADPOLE

Pol·lock /'pɑlək/, **Jackson** (1912–1956) a U.S. artist known for his very large ABSTRACT paintings which are full of color

poll·ster /'poulstɚ/ n. [C] someone who prepares and asks questions to find out what people think about a particular subject

poll tax /'. ./ n. [C] a tax of a particular amount that is collected from every citizen of a country, especially in order to be allowed to vote

pol·lut·ant /pə'lutnt/ n. [C,U] a substance that makes air, water, soil etc. dangerously dirty, and is caused by cars, factories etc.: *Although low-sulfur coal produces fewer pollutants, it's more expensive than mine.*

pol·lute /pə'lut/ v. [T] **1** to make air, water, soil etc. dangerously dirty and not good enough for people to use: *The group wants to ban logging activities that could pollute the water.* | *Many of these factories pollute the air with hydrogen sulfide.* **2** to make something bad that used to be good: *Money has polluted*

the democratic spirit of American politics. **3** to give someone immoral thoughts and make their character bad: *Violent movies and video games are polluting our children's minds.* —**polluted** adj.: *polluted rivers* —**polluter** n. [C]

pol·lu·tion /pə'luʃən/ n. [U] **1** the process of making air, water, soil etc. dangerously dirty and not good enough for people to use: *Pollution and overfishing have reduced the population of coastal fish.* | *The use of electric cars could be a key factor in fighting pollution.* **2** substances that make air, water, soil etc. dangerously dirty: *Pollution levels are often dangerously high in large cities.* | *The city is looking into ways to reduce air pollution.*

Pol·ly·an·na /,pɑli'ænə/ n. [C usually singular] someone who is always cheerful and always thinks something good is going to happen

po·lo /'poulou/ n. [U] a game played between two teams of players riding horses, who use wooden hammers with long handles to hit a small ball —see also WATER POLO

Po·lo /'poulou/, **Mar·co** /'markou/ (1254–1324) an Italian traveler whose writings gave Europeans their first knowledge of life in the Far East

pol·o·naise /,pɑlə'neɪz/ n. [C] a slow Polish dance popular in the 18th century, or the music for this dance

polo shirt /'.. ,./ n. [C] a sport shirt, usually made of cotton, that has a collar, a few buttons near the neck, and that is pulled on over the head

Pol Pot /,poul 'pɑt, ,pɑl/ (1926–1998) the leader of the Communist Khmer Rouge group, and Prime Minister of Cambodia from 1975 to 1979, during which time about 3 million people were killed

pol·ter·geist /'poultɚ,gaɪst/ n. [C] a GHOST that makes objects move around and makes strange noises

poly- /pɑli/ prefix many: *polysyllabic* (=with three or more SYLLABLES) | *polyglot* (=speaking more than one language)

pol·y·an·dry /'pɑli,ændri/ n. [U] TECHNICAL the custom or practice of having more than one husband at the same time —compare BIGAMY, POLYGAMY —**polyandrous** /,pɑli'ændrəs/ adj.

pol·y·es·ter /'pɑli,ɛstɚ, ,pɑli'ɛstɚ/ n. [C,U] **1** a type of strong SYNTHETIC cloth: *a blue polyester shirt* **2** TECHNICAL a chemical compound used to make cloth and plastics

pol·y·eth·yl·ene /,pɑli'ɛθə,lin/ n. [U] a strong light plastic used to make bags, material for covering food, small containers etc.

po·lyg·a·my /pə'ligəmi/ n. [U] TECHNICAL the custom or practice of having more than one husband or wife at the same time —compare BIGAMY, MONOGAMY —**polygamous** adj.

pol·y·glot /'pɑli,glɑt/ adj. FORMAL speaking or using many languages; MULTILINGUAL —**polyglot** n. [C]

pol·y·gon /'pɑli,gɑn/ n. [C] TECHNICAL a flat shape with three or more sides —**polygonal** /pə'ligənl/ adj.

pol·y·graph /'pɑli,græf/ n. [C] TECHNICAL a piece of equipment that is used by the police to find out whether someone is telling the truth; LIE DETECTOR

pol·y·he·dron /,pɑli'hidrən/ n. [C] a solid shape with many sides

pol·y·math /'pɑli,mæθ/ n. [C] FORMAL someone who has a lot of knowledge about many different subjects

pol·y·mer /'pɑləmɚ/ n. [C] a chemical compound that has a simple structure of large MOLECULEs

pol·y·mor·phous /,pɑli'mɔrfəs◂/ also **pol·y·mor·phic** /,pɑli'mɔrfɪk◂/ adj. TECHNICAL having many forms, styles etc. during different stages of growth or development

pol·y·no·mi·al /,pɑli'noumiəl/ n. [C] TECHNICAL a mathematical expression in ALGEBRA (=type of math) that contains two or more TERMS[1] (24) —**polynomial** adj.: *a polynomial equation*

pol·yp /'pɑləp/ *n.* [C] **1** a small LUMP that grows inside someone's body and is caused by an illness **2** a very simple sea animal that has a body like a tube

po·lyph·o·ny /pə'lɪfəni/ *n.* [U] a type of music in which several different tunes or notes are sung or played together at the same time —**polyphonic** /ˌpɑli'fɑnɪk/ *adj.*

pol·y·pro·pyl·ene /ˌpɑli'proʊpəˌlin/ *n.* [U] a hard light plastic material

pol·y·se·mous /ˌpɑli'siməs, pə'lisəməs/ *adj.* TECHNICAL a polysemous word has two or more different meanings —**polysemy** /'pɑliˌsimi, pə'lisəmi/ *n.* [U]

pol·y·sty·rene /ˌpɑli'staɪrin‹/ *n.* [U] a soft light plastic material that prevents heat or cold from passing through it, used especially for making containers; STYROFOAM: *polystyrene cups*

pol·y·syl·lab·ic /ˌpɑlisɪ'læbɪk/ *adj.* TECHNICAL a word that is polysyllabic contains more than three SYLLABLES —**polysyllable** /'pɑliˌsɪləbəl/ *n.*

pol·y·tech·nic /ˌpɑli'tɛknɪk/ *n.* [C] a college where you can study technical or scientific subjects: *Sam is a junior at Baltimore Polytechnic Institute.*

pol·y·the·ism /'pɑliθiˌɪzəm/ *n.* [U] the belief that there is more than one god —compare MONOTHEISM —**polytheistic** /ˌpɑliθi'ɪstɪk/ *adj.*

pol·y·un·sat·u·rate /ˌpɑliʌn'sætʃərɪt/ *n.* [C] a FATTY ACID (=chemical that helps your body produce energy) that is POLYUNSATURATED

pol·y·un·sat·u·rat·ed /ˌpɑliʌn'sætʃəˌreɪtɪd/ *adj.* polyunsaturated fats or oils come from vegetables and plants, and are considered to be better for your health than animal fats —compare SATURATED FAT

pol·y·ur·e·thane /ˌpɑli'yʊrəˌθeɪn/ *n.* [U] a plastic used to make paints and VARNISH

pol·y·vi·nyl chlor·ide /ˌpɑlivaɪnl 'klɔraɪd/ *n.* [U] PVC

po·made /poʊ'meɪd/ *n.* [U] a sweet-smelling oily substance rubbed on men's hair to make it smooth, which was used especially in past times

po·man·der /'poʊˌmændə/ *n.* [C] a box or ball that contains dried flowers and HERBS and is used to make clothes or a room smell nice

pom·e·gran·ate /'pɑməˌgrænɪt/ *n.* [C] a juicy round fruit with a thick red skin and many small seeds inside

pom·mel /'pʌməl, 'pɑ-/ *n.* [C] the high rounded part at the front of a horse's SADDLE[1] (1)

pommel horse /'.. ˌ./ *n.* [C] a piece of equipment used in GYMNASTICS that has two handles on top, which you hold onto and jump over

pomp /pɑmp/ *n.* [U] FORMAL all the impressive clothes, decorations, music etc. that are traditional for an important official or public ceremony: *The queen was welcomed with great pomp and circumstance* (=impressive clothes and ceremonies).

pom·pa·dour /'pɑmpəˌdɔr/ *n.* [C] a hair style in which the hair in front in worn brushed up and back over the FOREHEAD (=top part of the face)

Pom·pey /'pɑmpi/ (106–48 B.C.) a Roman general and politician who opposed Julius Caesar but was defeated by him in 48 B.C.

pom·pom /'pɑmpɑm/ also **pom·pon** /'pɑmpɑn/ *n.* [C] **1** a small wool ball used as a decoration on clothing, especially hats **2** a large round ball of loose plastic strings connected to a handle, used by CHEERLEADERS —see picture at CHEERLEADER

pomp·ous /'pɑmpəs/ *adj.* trying to make people think you are important, especially by using very formal and important sounding words —**pompously** *adv.* —**pompousness, pomposity** /pɑm'pɑsəṭi/ *n.* [U]

Pon·ce de Le·ón /ˌpɑnsə deɪ leɪ'oʊn/, **Juan** /wɑn/ (1460–1521) a Spanish EXPLORER who took control of Puerto Rico for Spain in 1508 and discovered Florida in 1513

pon·cho /'pɑntʃoʊ/ *n. plural* **ponchos** [C] **1** a coat that keeps rain off you and is made of one large piece of material with a cover for your head **2** a coat consisting of one large piece of thick wool cloth like a BLANKET, with a hole in the middle for your head

pond /pɑnd/ *n.* [C] **1** a small area of fresh water that is smaller than a lake: *a goldfish pond* **2 across the pond** also **on the other side of the pond** INFORMAL on the other side of the Atlantic Ocean in the U.K.

pon·der /'pɑndə/ *v.* [I,T] FORMAL to spend time thinking carefully and seriously about a problem, a difficult question, or something that has happened: *Webber has been pondering retirement since June.* | [+ on/over/about] *Scientists still ponder over the origin of man.* | [ponder how/what/ whether etc.] *Policy-makers are pondering how to improve California's highway system.*

pon·der·ous /'pɑndərəs/ *adj.* **1** moving slowly or awkwardly, especially because of being very big and heavy: *Holyfield had a considerable advantage over his opponent.* **2** boring and too serious: *the professor's ponderous voice* **3** very big and heavy: *an elephant's ponderous head* —**ponderously** *adv.* —**ponderousness** *n.* [U]

pond scum /'. ./ *n.* [U] SLANG **1** someone that you do not like, respect, or trust: *Bernie's nothing but pond scum. You don't need him.* **2** ALGAE

Pon·ti·ac /'pɑnṭiæk/ (?1720–1769) an Ottawa chief who fought against the British in 1763–1766

pon·tiff /'pɑntɪf/ *n.* [C] the POPE

pon·tif·i·cal /pɑn'tɪfɪkəl/ *adj.* FORMAL **1** relating to the POPE **2** speaking as if you think your judgment or opinion is always right —**pontifically** /-kli/ *adv.*

pon·tif·i·cate[1] /pɑn'tɪfəˌkeɪt/ *v.* [I] to give your opinion about something in a way that shows you think you are always right: [+ about/on] *Politicians will happily pontificate on any issue, but not all of them really know anything about it.*

pon·tif·i·cate[2] /pɑn'tɪfɪkɪt, -ˌkeɪt/ *n.* [C] TECHNICAL the position or period of being POPE

pon·toon /pɑn'tun/ *n.* [C] **1** one of several metal containers or boats that are fastened together to support a floating bridge **2** one of two hollow metal containers that are attached to the bottom of an airplane so that it can come down onto water and float

pontoon bridge /.'. ˌ./ *n.* [C] a floating bridge that is supported by several pontoons

po·ny[1] /'poʊni/ *n. plural* **ponies** [C] a small horse —see also SHETLAND PONY

pony[2] *v.*

pony up *phr. v.* [I,T **pony up** sth] INFORMAL to pay for something: *Opera fans will have to pony up $50 for even the cheapest seats.*

Pony Ex·press /ˌ.. .'./ *n.* [singular] a mail service in the 1860s that used horses and riders to carry the mail

po·ny·tail /'poʊniˌteɪl/ *n.* [C] hair tied together at the back of your head —see picture at HAIRSTYLE

Pon·zi scheme /'pɑnzi ˌskɪm/ *n.* [C] another name for a PYRAMID SCHEME

poo /pu/ *n.* INFORMAL **1** [U] a word meaning solid waste from your BOWELS, used especially by children **2** [singular] a word meaning the act of passing waste or gas from your BOWELS, used especially by children —**poo** *v.* [I,T] INFORMAL —compare POOP[1]

pooch /putʃ/ *n.* INFORMAL [C] a dog

poo·dle /'pudl/ *n.* [C] a dog with thick curly hair

poof /puf, pʊf/ *interjection* used when talking about something that happened suddenly: *Then poof! She was gone.*

poof·y /'pufi/ *adj.* INFORMAL poofy hair or clothes look big and soft or filled with air: *She wore a poofy blond wig.*

pooh /pu/ *interjection* INFORMAL **1** used when you think an idea, suggestion, effort etc. is stupid or not very good: *Pooh! You can't finish that paper by tomorrow.* **2** used when you are slightly upset about something, especially to avoid saying a swear word: *Oh pooh! I forgot my keys.*

pooh-bah /'pu bɑ/ *n.* [C] INFORMAL a word meaning someone who is important or powerful, used to show that you do not respect them very much: *the pooh-bahs down at city hall*

pooh-pooh /'pupu, pu'pu/ v. [T] INFORMAL to say that you think an idea, suggestion, effort etc. is stupid or not very good: *Energy companies have pooh-poohed the seriousness of global warming.*

pool¹ /pul/ n.

1 [for swimming] [C] a hole that has been specially built and filled with water so that people can swim or WADE in it: *The Kohlers' have a pool in their backyard.* | *I spent the entire afternoon relaxing by the pool.* —see picture on page 423

2 [game] [U] a game in which you use a stick to knock numbered balls into holes around a cloth-covered table, which is often played in bars: **play/shoot pool** *Then we went to the bar and played pool.*

3 **a pool of water/blood/light etc.** a small area of liquid or light on a surface: *There was a pool of oil under the car.*

4 [area of water] [C] a small area of still water in a hollow place: *Kids were looking at the starfish and anemones in the tide pools.*

5 [sports] [C] a game in which people try to win money by guessing the results of football, basketball etc. games, or the money that is collected from these people for this: *the office basketball pool*

6 [group of people] [C] a group of people who are available to work or to do an activity when they are needed: *a pool of volunteers for community projects* | *a secretarial pool*

7 [group of things] [C] a number of things or an amount of money that is shared by a group of people: *He won $50,000 from the pool.*

8 dirty pool something that is not fair or that deceives someone —see also CARPOOL¹, GENE POOL

pool² v. [T] to combine your money, ideas, skills etc. with those of other people so that you can all use them: *The family pooled all of their financial resources to start the business.*

pool hall /'. ./ n. [C] a building where people go to play pool

pool·room /'pulrum/ n. [C] a room used for playing pool, especially in a bar

pool·side /'pulsaɪd/ adj. [only before noun] near or on the side of a swimming pool: *a poolside barbecue* —**poolside** n. [U]

pool ta·ble /'. ,../ n. [C] a cloth-covered table with pockets in the corners and sides that is used for playing pool

poon·tang /'puntæŋ/ n. [U] TABOO a woman's VAGINA (=sex organ), often used offensively to mean "a woman"

poop¹ /pup/ n. **1** [U] INFORMAL solid waste from your BOWELS **2** [singular] INFORMAL an act of passing waste from your BOWELS **3 the poop** SPOKEN the most recent news about something that has happened, which someone tells you in an unofficial way: *So, what's the poop on the new guy?* **4** [C] TECHNICAL the raised part at the back end of an old sailing ship

poop² v. INFORMAL [I,T] to pass solid waste from your BOWELS —see also PARTY POOPER

poop out phr. v. INFORMAL **1** [I,T **poop** sb **out**] to stop trying to do something because you are tired, bored etc., or to make someone feel this way: *I pooped out after just ten minutes of basketball.* | *The late nights at the office are pooping me out.* **2** [I] if something poops out, it stops working: *The laptop's battery pooped out after only two hours.* **3** [I] to decide not to do something you have already said you would do, because you are tired or not interested: [**poop out on sb**] *Don't poop out on us – I know you'll have a good time.*

poop deck /'. ./ n. [C] the floor on the raised part at the back of an old sailing ship

pooped /pupt/ also **pooped out** /,. './ adj. [not before noun] INFORMAL very tired; EXHAUSTED

pooper scoop·er /'.. ,../ n. [C] INFORMAL a small SHOVEL and a container, used by dog owners for removing their dogs' solid waste from the streets

poo-poo /'. ./ n. [U] POOP¹ (1)

poop sheet /'. ./ n. [C] INFORMAL written instructions or information

poop·y /'pupi/ adj. SPOKEN full of POOP or covered with poop: *a poopy diaper*

poor /pʊr, pɔr/ adj.

1 [no money] having very little money and not many possessions: *Elaine comes from a poor family.* | *The Scotts are so poor they can barely afford milk and bread.* | *a poor neighborhood*

2 the poor people who are poor: *Several local churches are involved in giving out food to the poor.*

3 [not good] not as good as it could be or should be: *Her chances of recovery are poor.* | *Attendance at the meeting was poor.* | *The jacket was of very poor quality* (=not made well or of good materials). | *His memory is poor, so you may need to repeat things.* —opposite GOOD¹

4 poor boy/girl/Joe etc. SPOKEN used to show pity for someone because they are so unlucky, unhappy etc.: *Poor Dad, he's had an exhausting week.* | *I feel sorry for the poor animals at the zoo.* | *The poor thing looks like she hasn't eaten in days.* | **Poor old** *Phil hasn't been on a date in years.*

5 [not good at sth] not good at doing something: *a poor math student* | [+ at] *He's poor at reading.* —opposite GOOD¹ (3)

6 do a poor job (of) doing sth to do something badly: *Public schools have done a poor job educating ethnic minorities.*

7 [health] someone whose health is poor is sick or weak for a long period of time: *My parents are both in rather poor health.*

8 poor in sth lacking things that people need: *The country is poor in natural resources.*

9 poor loser someone who behaves badly if they lose a game

10 finish a poor second/third etc. to finish a race, competition etc. a long way behind the person ahead of you: *Smits finished a poor second to Zamperini in the 5000 meters.*

11 a poor man's sb HUMOROUS used to say that someone is like a very famous performer, writer etc. but is not as good as they are: *Gallen considers himself a poor man's Ted Turner.*

12 a poor man's sth used to say that something can be used for the same purpose as something else, and is much cheaper: *Biological weapons have been called the poor man's atomic bomb.* —**poorness** n. [U] —see also **be (in) good/bad/poor taste** (TASTE¹ (6)), POORLY

poor boy also **po' boy** /'. ./ n. [C] a word used especially in the southern U.S. for a long bread roll that is cut open and filled with meat, cheese etc.; SUBMARINE SANDWICH

poor·house /'pʊrhaʊs/ n. [C] **1** a building in past times where people could live and be fed, which was paid for with public money **2** the state of not having any money: *If Jimmy keeps spending like this, he's going to end up in the poorhouse.*

poor·ly /'pʊrli/ adv. badly: *The article is really poorly written.* | *a poorly lit room*

poor-spir·it·ed /,. '...◂/ adj. LITERARY having no confidence or courage —**poor-spiritedly** adv.

pop¹ /pɑp/ v. **popped, popping**

1 [short sound] [I,T] to suddenly make a short sound like a small explosion, or to make something do this: *The wood sizzled and popped in the fire.* | *Jody, please don't pop my balloon.*

2 [come out of sth] [I always + adv./prep.] to come suddenly or surprisingly out of or away from something: [+ out/off/up etc.] *A button popped off my jacket.* | *Godreau's shoulder popped out of its socket.*

3 [put sth somewhere] [T always + adv./prep.] INFORMAL to quickly put something somewhere for a short time: [**pop sth in/around/over etc.**] *I'll just pop these cookies into the oven.*

4 [go quickly] [I always + adv./prep.] SPOKEN to go somewhere quickly, suddenly, or in a way that you did not expect: [+ in/out/around/to etc.] *I need to pop into the drug store for a second.* | [+ on] *I might just pop in on Sarah on the way home.*

P

5 corn [I,T] to cook POPCORN (=dried corn) until it swells and bursts open, or to be cooked in this way: *I'll pop some popcorn before the movie starts.*
6 ears [I] if your ears pop, you feel the pressure in them suddenly change, for example when you go quickly up or down in an airplane
7 pop the question INFORMAL to ask someone to marry you: *When are you going to pop the question?*
8 pop pills INFORMAL to take PILLS too often
9 hit [T] SPOKEN to hit someone: *If you say that again, I'll pop you one.*
10 sb's eyes popped (out of their head) used to say that someone looked extremely surprised or excited
11 pop into your head to think of something suddenly: *The idea just popped into my head.*
12 pop the clutch to take your foot off the CLUTCH in a car when the car is moving slowly, in order to start the engine

pop off *phr. v.* [I] INFORMAL **1** to die suddenly **2** to speak quickly without thinking first

pop out *phr. v.* [I] INFORMAL to say something suddenly without thinking about it first: *I didn't mean to say it like that – it just popped out.*

pop up *phr. v.* [I] **1** to appear suddenly in a way, or at a time that you did not expect: *There seem to be new restaurants popping up everywhere.* | *A screen popped up saying there was a system error.* **2** to hit a ball into the air in a game of baseball so that it only travels a short distance: *The game ended when Javier popped up in the infield.* —see also POP-UP

s w **pop²** *n.* **1 a)** [C,U] INFORMAL a sweet drink that contains BUBBLES and has no alcohol in it, or a glass or can of this drink; SODA: *There's a pop in the fridge for you.* | *a can of pop* **2** [U] POP MUSIC: **pop singer/concert/festival etc.** *a pop album* **3** [C] a sudden short sound like a small explosion: *The pop we heard turned out to be just an air gun.* | *The balloon went pop* (=made a sudden short sound). **4 $7/$50/25¢ etc. a pop** SPOKEN used when each of something costs a particular amount of money: *Those freeze-dried meals for backpacking cost seven dollars a pop.* **5** [singular, not with **the**] also **Pops** OLD-FASHIONED a word meaning your "father," used especially when you are talking to him: *Hi, Pop, what are you doing?* **6 pops** [U] CLASSICAL music that is familiar to many people, especially people who do not usually like CLASSICAL MUSIC: **pops concert/orchestra** *the Boston Pops Orchestra*

pop³ *adj.* [only before noun, no comparative] produced or written for people who do not have special knowledge of a particular field: *pop science*

pop. the written abbreviation of "population"

pop art /ˌ. ˈ./ *n.* [U] a type of art that was popular in the 1960s, which shows ordinary objects, such as advertisements, or things you see in people's homes

s w **pop·corn** /ˈpɑpkɔrn/ *n.* [U] a type of corn that swells and bursts open when heated, and is usually eaten warm with salt and butter

pop cul·ture /ˌ. ˈ../ *n.* [U] music, movies, products etc. in a particular society that are familiar to and popular with most ordinary people in that society

Pope /poup/ *n.* [C] **1** the leader of the Catholic Church: *Several thousand people came to hear the Pope speak.* | *Pope John Paul II* —see also PAPAL **2 Is the Pope Catholic/Polish?** HUMOROUS used to say that something is clearly true or certain: *"Do you think he's guilty?" "Is the Pope Catholic?"*

pop-eyed /ˈ. ./ *adj.* INFORMAL **1** having your eyes wide open, because you are surprised, excited, or angry **2** having eyes that stick out slightly; BUGEYED

pop fly /ˈ. ./ *n.* [C] a type of hit in BASEBALL in which the ball is hit straight up into the air and only travels a short distance —see picture at BASEBALL

pop gun /ˈ. ./ *n.* [C] a toy gun that fires small objects, such as CORKS¹, with a loud noise

pop·lar /ˈpɑplə/ *n.* [C] a very tall thin tree that grows very fast

pop·lin /ˈpɑplɪn/ *n.* [U] a strong shiny cotton cloth

pop mu·sic /ˈ. ˌ../ *n.* [U] modern music that is popular with young people and usually consists of simple tunes with a strong beat

pop·o·ver /ˈpɑpˌouvə/ *n.* [C] a light hollow MUFFIN (=small cake) made with eggs, milk, and flour

pop·pa /ˈpɑpə/ *n.* [singular] INFORMAL another spelling of PAPA

pop·pers /ˈpɑpəz/ *n.* [plural] INFORMAL a type of illegal drug that makes you feel more active and full of energy

pop psy·chol·o·gy /ˌ. .ˈ.../ *n.* [U] ways of dealing with personal problems that are made popular on television or in books, but that are not considered scientific

pop·py /ˈpɑpi/ *n. plural* **poppies 1** [C] a plant that has brightly colored, usually red, flowers and small black seeds **2** [U] a red color

pop·py·cock /ˈpɑpiˌkɑk/ *n.* [U] OLD-FASHIONED nonsense: *Much of what he said was pure poppycock.*

pop·py·seed /ˈpɑpiˌsid/ *n.* [U] the small black seeds of the poppy plant, used in cakes, bread etc.

pop quiz /ˌ. ˈ./ *n.* [C] a short test that a teacher gives without any warning in order to check whether students have been studying

Pop·si·cle /ˈpɑpsɪkəl/ *n.* [C] TRADEMARK a food made of juice that is frozen onto sticks: *a cherry Popsicle*

pop star /ˈ. ./ *n.* [C] a famous and successful entertainer who plays or sings POP MUSIC

pop·u·lace /ˈpɑpyələs/ *n.* [singular] FORMAL the ordinary people who live in a country: *A large group of the American populace attends church regularly.*

s w **pop·u·lar** /ˈpɑpyələ/ *adj.* **1** liked by a lot of people: *The Sears Tower is a popular tourist destination.* | *Hilary was the most popular girl at school.* | *Jazz has been popular in Japan since the 1960s.* | [+ **with**] *Baggy jeans are now popular with teenagers.* —opposite UNPOPULAR **2 popular belief/opinion/misconception** a belief, opinion etc. that a lot of people have: **Contrary to popular belief**, *dogs are not colorblind* (=although many people believe that dogs are colorblind, they really are not). **3** [only before noun] relating to ordinary people, or intended for ordinary people: *"Cracker Jacks" are a snack with a long history in American popular culture.* | *popular entertainment such as TV* —see also POP MUSIC **4** [only before noun] done by a lot of people in a society, group etc.: *Opposition leaders are calling for a popular uprising* (=violent action by a lot of people) *against the government.* **5 that'll make you popular with sb** SPOKEN used when telling someone that other people will be annoyed with them: *You're giving a test on Monday? That'll make you popular with your students.*

pop·u·lar·i·ty /ˌpɑpyəˈlærəti/ *n.* [U] the quality of being liked or supported by a large number of people: *The popularity of cellular phones has grown in the last five years.* | *Lee's popularity started to fade somewhat.*

pop·u·lar·ize /ˈpɑpyələˌraɪz/ *v.* [T] **1** to make something well known and liked: *Self-service shopping was popularized by Clarence Saunders.* **2** to make a difficult subject or idea easily understandable for ordinary people who have no special knowledge about it: *Skinner was the psychologist who popularized behavior modification.* —**popularization** /ˌpɑpyələrəˈzeɪʃən/ *n.* [U]

pop·u·lar·ly /ˈpɑpyələli/ *adv.* **1** by most or many people: *Yeltsin was Russia's first popularly elected president.* | **popularly known/thought/believed etc.** *Musculoligamentous Neck Sprain is popularly known as "whiplash injury."* **2 popularly priced** if something is popularly priced, it does not cost very much, which makes many people want to buy it: *popularly priced wines*

pop·u·late /ˈpɑpyəˌleɪt/ *v.* [T usually passive] if an area is populated by a particular group of people, they live there: [**be populated by sb**] *The Filipino island of Mindanao is heavily populated by Muslims.* | **densely/sparsely populated** *Biella is the most densely populated province in the region.*

s w **pop·u·la·tion** /ˌpɑpyəˈleɪʃən/ *n.* **1** [C] the number of people living in a particular area, country etc.: *Austria has a population of 7.5 million.* | *What is the population of Montana?* **2** [C usually singular] all of the people who live in a particular area: *Most of the population of Canada lives relatively near the U.S. border.* | *A large portion of the population lives in poverty.* | **the white/urban/American etc. population** (=part of the group of people who live in a particular area who are white, live in cities etc.) **3 population explosion** a rapid increase in the population of an area or the whole world **4 population center** also **center of population** a city, town etc.: *Crime is more prevalent in the major population centers.*

pop·u·list /'papyəlɪst/ *adj.* claiming to represent ordinary people: *Edwards is seen as a populist Democrat.* —**populist** *n.* [C] —**populism** *n.* [U]

pop·u·lous /'papyələs/ *adj.* FORMAL a populous area has a large population in relation to its size: *China is the most populous country in the world.* —**populousness** *n.* [U]

pop-up /'. ./ *adj.* **pop-up book/card/toaster etc.** a book, card, TOASTER etc. that is designed to make something suddenly spring up out of it

por·ce·lain /'pɔrsəlɪn/ *n.* [U] **1** a hard shiny white substance that is used for making expensive plates, cups etc. **2** plates, cups etc. made of this

porch /pɔrtʃ/ *n.* [C] a structure built onto the front or back entrance of a house, with a floor and a roof but no walls: *They were sitting on the front porch drinking beer.* —see picture on page 423

por·cine /'pɔrsaɪn/ *adj.* FORMAL looking like or relating to pigs

por·cu·pine /'pɔrkyə,paɪn/ *n.* [C] an animal with long, sharp, needle-like parts growing all over its back and sides

pore¹ /pɔr/ *n.* [C] one of the small holes in your skin that liquid, especially SWEAT, can pass through, or a similar hole in the surface of a plant

pore² *v.*
  pore over sth *phr. v.* [T] to read or look at something very carefully for a long time: *We spent all night poring over the contract.*

pork /pɔrk/ *n.* [U] **1** the meat from pigs: *pork chops* **2** INFORMAL government money spent in a particular area in order to get political advantages: *More taxes and more government pork won't help the economy.*

pork bar·rel /'. ,../ *n.* [singular,U] INFORMAL a government plan to increase the amount of money spent in a particular area in order to gain political advantage: *Money for water projects is a common type of Washington pork barrel.* —**pork-barrel** *adj.*: *pork-barrel spending*

pork·er /'pɔrkə/ *n.* [C] **1** a young pig that is made fat before being killed for food **2** INFORMAL, HUMOROUS a fat person

pork-pie hat /,. . './ also **pork-pie** *n.* [C] a hat made of FELT with a small soft BRIM (=edge)

pork rinds /'. ./ *n.* [plural] small pieces of pig fat that have been cooked in hot oil and are eaten as a SNACK

por·ky /'pɔrki/ *adj.* INFORMAL, HUMOROUS fat

porn /pɔrn/ *n.* [U] INFORMAL pornography: *The theater shows mainly kung fu movies and porn.* | *a porn star* —see also **hardcore pornography** (HARDCORE (2)), SOFT PORN

por·no /'pɔrnoʊ/ *n.* INFORMAL pornography —**porno** *adj.*: *a porno magazine*

por·nog·ra·phy /pɔr'nagrəfi/ *n.* [U] **1** magazines, movies etc. that show sexual acts and images in a way that is intended to make people feel sexually excited **2** the activity of making these magazines or movies —**pornographer** *n.* [C] —**pornographic** /,pɔrnə'græfɪk‹/ *adj.*: *pornographic magazines* —**pornographically** /-kli/ *adv.*

po·rous /'pɔrəs/ *adj.* allowing liquid, air etc. to pass through slowly: *porous rock* —**porousness** *n.* [U]

por·phy·ry /'pɔrfəri/ *n.* [U] a type of hard dark red or purple rock that contains CRYSTALS

por·poise /'pɔrpəs/ *n.* [C] a large sea animal that looks similar to a DOLPHIN and breathes air

por·ridge /'pɔrɪdʒ, 'par-/ *n.* [U] soft CEREAL that is cooked with milk or water

port /pɔrt/ *n.* **1** [C,U] a place where ships can be loaded and unloaded: *The submarine was back in port after three months at sea.* | **come into port/ leave port** *U.S.S. Kentucky is scheduled to come into port at noon.* **2** [C] a town or city with a HARBOR or DOCKS where ships can be loaded and unloaded: *the shipping port of New Bedford* | *Port Angeles, Washington* **3** [U] strong sweet Portuguese wine that is usually drunk after a meal: *a glass of port* **4** [U] the left side of a ship or aircraft when you are looking toward the front: *on the port side* | **To port**, *we could see the tiny island of Yurishima.* —opposite STARBOARD **5** [C] TECHNICAL a part of a computer where you can connect another piece of equipment such as a PRINTER **6 any port in a storm** SPOKEN an expression meaning that you should take whatever help you can when you are in trouble, even if it has some disadvantages —see also FREE PORT, PORT OF CALL, PORT OF ENTRY

port·a·ble¹ /'pɔrtəbəl/ *adj.* **1** able to be carried or moved easily: *a portable phone* | *portable toilets* **2** a portable computer program can be used on different computer systems **3 portable benefits** health insurance, PENSION PLANS, etc. that workers can take with them when they move from one job to another —**portability** /,pɔrtə'bɪləti/ *n.* [U]

portable² *n.* [C] a piece of electronic equipment that can be easily carried or moved: *You don't need a big TV, why don't you just get a portable?*

port·age /'pɔrtɪdʒ/ *n.* [U] the act of carrying boats over land from one river to another —**portage** *v.* [T]

por·tal /'pɔrtl/ *n.* [C] **1** a WEBSITE on the Internet that helps you find other websites **2** [usually plural] LITERARY a tall and impressive gate or entrance to a building: *the Gothic portal of the cathedral*

Por·ta Pot·ti, porta-potty /'pɔrtə 'pati/ *n.* [C] TRADEMARK a toilet that is in a small plastic building that can be moved

Port-au-Prince /,pɔrt oʊ 'prɪns/ the capital and largest city of Haiti

por·tend /pɔr'tɛnd/ *v.* [T] LITERARY to be a sign that something is going to happen, especially something bad: *Rising infection rates portend a health-care disaster.*

por·tent /'pɔrtɛnt/ *n.* [C] LITERARY a sign or warning that something is going to happen: [+ of] *The strikes are viewed as a portent of revolution.* —compare OMEN

por·ten·tous /pɔr'tɛntəs/ *adj.* **1** LITERARY portentous events are very important, especially because they show that something bad is going to happen: *Recent developments are as portentous as the collapse of the Berlin Wall.* **2** trying to appear important and serious: *a portentous film*

por·ter /'pɔrtə/ *n.* **1** [C] someone whose job is to carry travelers' bags at airports, hotels etc. **2** [C] someone whose job is to take care of the part of a train where people sleep **3** [C] someone whose job is to take care of a building by cleaning it, repairing things etc.

Por·ter, Cole /koʊl/ (1891–1964) a U.S. musician who wrote many popular songs and MUSICALS

Porter, Kath·er·ine Anne /'kæθrɪn æn/ (1890–1980) a U.S. writer of NOVELS and short stories

Porter, William the real name of the U.S. writer O. Henry

por·ter·house /'pɔrtə,haʊs/ *n.* [C,U] also **porterhouse steak** /,... './ a thick flat piece of high quality BEEF¹ (1)

port·fo·li·o /pɔrt'foʊliˌoʊ/ *n. plural* **portfolios** [C] **1** a large flat case used especially for carrying drawings, documents etc. **2** a collection of drawings, paintings, or other pieces of work by an artist, photographer etc. **3** a collection of STOCKS owned by a particular person or company: *an investment portfolio* **4** FORMAL the area of responsibility that a particular government official has: *the foreign affairs portfolio*

port·hole /'pɔrthoʊl/ n. [C] a small round window on the side of a ship or airplane

por·ti·co /'pɔrtɪˌkoʊ/ n. [C] a covered entrance to a building, consisting of a roof supported by PILLARS: *the south portico of the White House*

s w **por·tion¹** /'pɔrʃən/ n. [C] **1** a part of something larger, especially a part that is different from the other parts: [+ **of**] *There were no windows in the lower portion of the hall.* | *A large portion of the book is made up of photographs.* **2** an amount of food for one person, especially when served in a restaurant: *Do you have any children's portions?* | [+ **of**] *a portion of ice cream* **3** [usually singular] a share of something, such as responsibility, blame, or a duty, that is divided among a small number of people: [+ **of**] *Both drivers must bear a portion of the blame.* **4** sb's portion FORMAL OR LITERARY something that happens in your life that you cannot avoid; FATE: *Sorrow has always been her portion.*

portion² v.

portion sth ↔ **out** *phr. v.* [T] to divide something into parts, especially to give them to several people: *Could you portion out the cake?*

Port·land /'pɔrtlənd/ **1** the largest city in the U.S. state of Oregon **2** the largest city in the U.S. state of Maine

Port Lou·is /ˌpɔrt 'luɪs, 'luɪ/ the capital and largest city of Mauritius

port·ly /'pɔrtli/ adj. someone who is portly, especially an older man, is fat and round: *a portly old gentleman* —**portliness** n. [U]

port·man·teau¹ /pɔrt'mæntoʊ/ n. [C] OLD-FASHIONED a very large SUITCASE that opens into two parts

portmanteau² adj. [only before noun] FORMAL a portmanteau word is made by combining the sound and meaning of two other words, for example "infomercial" combines "information" and "commercial"

Port Mores·by /pɔrt 'mɔrzbi/ the capital and largest city of Papua New Guinea

port of call /ˌ. . '. / n. [C usually singular] **1** a port where a ship stops on a trip from one place to another: *Hong Kong has been an important port of call for the U.S. Navy.* **2** INFORMAL one of a series of places that you visit: *My next port of call was the City Records Department.*

port of en·try /ˌ. . '../ n. [C] a place, such as a port or airport, where people or goods enter a country

Port of Spain /ˌpɔrt əv 'speɪn/ the capital and largest city of Trinidad and Tobago

Por·to No·vo /ˌpɔrtə 'noʊvoʊ/ the capital city of Benin

por·trait /'pɔrtrɪt/ n. **1** [C] a painting, drawing, or photograph of a person: *a family portrait* | [+ **of**] *a portrait of George Washington* —see picture at CARICATURE¹ **2** [C] a description or representation of something: [+ **of**] *His stories are all harsh portraits of life on the street.* —see also SELF-PORTRAIT

por·trait·ist /'pɔrtrətɪst/ n. [C] someone who paints portraits

por·trai·ture /'pɔrtrɪtʃəʳ/ n. [U] the art of painting or drawing pictures of people

por·tray /pɔr'treɪ, pə-/ v. **portrays, portrayed, portraying** [T] **1** to describe or represent something or someone: *Fink is not the only writer portrayed in the film.* | *Their music portrays a lifestyle that no longer exists.* **2 portray sb/sth as sth** to describe or show someone or something in a particular way, according to your opinion of them: *Many fairy tales portray women as victims.* | *Liberals are portrayed by the group as sensitive and caring.* **3** to act the part of a character in a play: *In the movie, Burg portrays a real-life Holocaust survivor.*

por·tray·al /pɔr'treɪəl/ n. [C,U] the action of portraying someone or something, or the book, movie, play etc. that results from this: *Spacek won an Oscar for her portrayal of Loretta Lynn.*

Por·tu·gal /'pɔrtʃəgəl/ a country in southwest Europe, west of Spain

Por·tu·guese /ˌpɔrtʃə'giz / n. [U] **1** the language of Portugal, Brazil, and some other countries **2 the Portuguese** the people of Portugal —**Portuguese** adj.

Portuguese man-of-war /ˌ... . . '. / n. [C] a large sea creature, like a JELLYFISH, which has long poisonous parts hanging down from its body

Port Vi·la /ˌpɔrt 'vilə/ the capital and largest city of Vanuatu

pose

The family posed for their wedding photo.

pose¹ /poʊz/ v. **1 pose a problem/threat/challenge etc.** to exist in a way that may cause a problem, s w danger, difficulty etc.: *Some of the more extreme militia members may pose a terrorist threat.* | *The fish oil apparently poses no danger to humans.* **2** [I,T] to sit or stand in a particular position in order to be photographed or painted, or to make someone do this: [+ **for**] *A group of fans wanted Romano to pose for pictures.* | [**pose sb**] *He had to pose us just the way he wanted us.* **3 pose a question** to ask a question, especially one that needs to be carefully thought about: *The magazine posed a list of questions to each of the candidates.* **4 pose as sb** to pretend to be someone else, in order to deceive people: *Cox posed as a doctor to gain entrance to the day care center.* **5** [I] to dress or behave as if you have a quality or social position that you do not really have, in order to seem more impressive to other people

pose² n. [C] **1** the position in which someone stands or sits, especially in a painting, photograph etc.: *Each child is photographed in a glamorous pose.* | *Lyn struck a pose* (=stood or sat in a particular position) *with her head to one side.* **2** behavior in which someone pretends to have a quality or social position they do not really have, usually in order to seem impressive to other people: *He shed the pose of the sophisticated lawyer and became his real self at last.*

Po·sei·don /pə'saɪdn/ in Greek MYTHOLOGY, the god of the sea

pos·er /'poʊzəʳ/ n. [C] a POSEUR

po·seur /poʊ'zɚ/ n. [C] someone who pretends to have a quality or social position they do not really have, usually in order to seem impressive to other people: *They're just a group of rock poseurs, but the Clash is the real thing.*

posh /pɑʃ/ adj. a posh restaurant, hotel, car etc. is expensive and looks as if it is used or owned by rich people: *a posh five-star hotel*

pos·it /'pɑzɪt/ v. [T] FORMAL to suggest that a particular idea should be accepted as a fact: *Ptolemy posited that each planet moved in a perfect circle.*

po·si·tion¹ /pə'zɪʃən/ n. s w
1 **standing/sitting etc.** [C] the way someone stands, sits, or lies, or the direction in which an object is pointing: *Make sure you are in a comfortable position before you start to drive.* | **a sitting/kneeling/standing position** *Horton pulled himself slowly to a standing position.*
2 **situation** [C usually singular] the situation that someone is in, or the situation relating to a particular subject: *I'm not sure what I'd do if I were in your position.* | *After our third touchdown, the team was in a pretty good position.* | **put sb in a difficult/awkward/uncomfortable position** *His request puts us in a difficult position.*

3 `place where sb/sth is` [C,U] the place where someone or something is, especially in relation to other objects and places: *It's difficult to determine the exact position of the plane.* | *the position of the sun in the sky* | **be in/out of position** (=be in the correct or not in the correct place)

4 `opinion` [C] an opinion or judgment on a particular subject, especially the official opinion of a government, party, or someone in authority: **[+ on]** *I disagree with Lundgren's position on abortion.* | *The airline **takes the position** that its security is adequate.* | *Flores says she will **reconsider her position** on the new law.*

5 `direction` [C] the direction in which an object is pointing | **an upright/vertical/horizontal position** *Put your tray tables in the upright and locked position.*

6 `job` [C] a job: *I have an interview for a position at the university.* | *Massy has **held the position** (=had the job) of marketing manager for 14 years.* | *I'm sorry, **the position has been filled** (=the company has found someone to do the job).* —see Usage Note at JOB

7 `sports` [C] the area where someone plays in a sport, or the type of actions they are responsible for doing in the game: *"What position do you play?" "Second base."*

8 `level/rank` [C] someone's or something's level or rank in a society or organization: **[+ of]** *the traditional position of women in society* | *May was in **a position of trust** (=one in which people trust you) as a church leader.* | *It is clear that he **abused** his **position** as head of the organization (=used his authority wrongly).* | **a position of authority/influence/responsibility** *Eleanor was soon placed in a position of responsibility in the convent.*

9 be in a position to do sth to be able to do something because you have the ability, money, or power to do it: *Maybe next year we'll be in a better position to buy a house.* —opposite **be in no position to do sth**

10 `race/competition` [C,U] the place of someone or something in a race, competition, list etc.: *Mears has moved from fifth to fourth position.*

11 take up (a) position to move to a particular place so that you are ready to shoot a gun, fight in a war etc.: *Police marksmen took up positions on nearby rooftops.*

12 sb is in no position to talk SPOKEN used to say that someone should not criticize another person, because they have made the same mistakes

13 jockey/maneuver/jostle etc. for position a) to try to get an advantage over other people who are all trying to succeed in doing the same thing: *Republicans are jockeying for position prior to the presidential campaign.* **b)** to try to move into a particular place, especially a place that gives you an advantage, when a lot of other people are trying to move into the same place: *A dozen cameramen jockeyed for position as Keegan left the building.*

14 a position of strength a situation in which you should be able to succeed or win: *The President will be able to negotiate from a position of strength.* —opposite **a position of weakness**

15 `army` [C] a place where an army has put soldiers, guns etc.: *Government forces destroyed military positions and captured enemy soldiers.*

16 `sex` [C] one of the ways in which two people can sit or lie to have sex: *the missionary position*

USAGE NOTE: POSITION

WORD CHOICE: place, position, location, spot, where
Place is the usual word you use to talk about where something is or happens: *I can't find a place to park.* | *We visited the place where Hoover was born.* **Position** is used to talk about the place where something that can move is in relation to other things or places: *the position of the cursor on the screen* | *More and more people are asking if our lives are affected by the position of the stars.* **Location** is a more formal word for a place where someone works or lives, or where something is built: *Come visit our store in its new location.* | *My book lists the location of all the embassies.* **Spot** is a more informal word used especially for a pleasant

place: *This looks like a nice spot for a picnic.* In spoken English you usually use **where, anywhere, somewhere, someplace** etc. instead of these words: *I'll show you where I work.* | *I've looked everywhere, but I can't find my other shoe.* | *Can we put the TV someplace else?*

position² *v.* [T] to put someone or something in a particular position: *Nate positioned himself so he could keep an eye on the door.*

position pa·per /'.. ,../ *n.* [C] a written statement that shows how a department, organization etc. intends to deal with something

pos·i·tive¹ /'pazətɪv/ *adj.*
1 `sure` [not before noun] very sure, with no doubt at all, that something is right or true: *"Are you sure you don't want another drink?" "Positive."* | **[position (that)]** *I'm positive I told him we were leaving at 4.* | **[+ of/about]** *I'm not positive of the address, but it's around here somewhere.*

2 `confident` considering the good qualities of a situation, person etc., and expecting success: **[+ about]** *Vernon tried to be positive about the team's 2–6 record.* | **positive attitude/approach/outlook etc.** *You need a positive attitude to find the right job.* —opposite NEGATIVE¹ (2) —see also **think positively/positive** (THINK (14))

3 `likely to be successful` showing that something is likely to succeed or improve: *The fact that he's breathing on his own again is a positive sign.*

4 `agreement/support` showing that someone agrees with you, supports what you are doing, and wants you to succeed: *Public response to the ads has been overwhelmingly positive.* | **positive criticism/feedback** (=criticism that includes praise for things done well, and encourages you to do better) —opposite NEGATIVE¹

5 positive proof/evidence/identification etc. proof, EVIDENCE etc. that shows that there is no doubt that something is definitely true: *The body was flown to Honolulu for positive identification.*

6 `medical/scientific test` showing signs of what is being looked for: *Officials say he will be banned from the sport if he **tests positive** for cocaine.* | **come out/up positive** *Phoebe's pregnancy test came out positive.* —opposite NEGATIVE¹ (4)

7 `good/useful` having a good or useful effect, especially on someone's character: *We're glad that something positive has come out of the situation.* | *a very positive experience* —opposite NEGATIVE¹ (1)

8 `morally good` [usually before noun] showing or encouraging someone, especially a child, to behave in a way that is morally good: *a positive message for the youth of today* | *positive role models*

9 positive reinforcement the action of rewarding someone when they do something well, rather than punishing them when they do something wrong

10 `mathematics` TECHNICAL a positive number or quantity is more than zero; (+) is the positive sign —opposite NEGATIVE¹ (5)

11 `electricity` [no comparative] TECHNICAL having the type of electrical charge that is carried by a PROTON, shown by a (+) sign on a BATTERY —opposite NEGATIVE¹ (6)

12 `blood` TECHNICAL having RHESUS FACTOR in your blood: *type AB positive* —opposite NEGATIVE¹ (7)

13 `grammar` relating to the basic form of an adjective or adverb, such as "small" or "quietly" as opposed to the COMPARATIVE or SUPERLATIVE forms

14 `force` relating to the end of a MAGNET that turns naturally toward north —**positiveness** *n.* [U]

positive² *n.* [C] **1** a quality or feature of something that is good or useful: *You can find positives in any situation.* —opposite NEGATIVE² **2** a number that is higher than zero **3 the positive** TECHNICAL the basic form of an adjective or adverb, such as "small" or "quietly," as opposed to the COMPARATIVE or the SUPERLATIVE —see also **a false positive/negative** (FALSE (8))

pos·i·tive·ly /'pazətɪvli, ,pazə'tɪvli‹/ *adv.* **1** used to emphasize a strong opinion or surprising statement:

Ed's positively the funniest guy I know. | *positively beautiful* **2** SPOKEN used to emphasize that you mean what you are saying: *I absolutely, positively must remember to send that check.* **3** in a good or useful way: *We were affected very positively by the experience.* **4** in a way that shows you agree with something, want it to succeed, or think it is good: *Wall Street reacted positively to the announcement.* **5** in a way that leaves no possibility of doubt: *They all said positively that they had seen it.* **6 positively charged** TECHNICAL having the type of electrical charge that is carried by PROTONs —see also **think positively/positive** (THINK (14))

pos·i·tiv·ism /ˈpɑzətɪˌvɪzəm/ *n.* [U] a type of PHILOSOPHY based only on real facts that can be scientifically proven, rather than on ideas —**positivist** *n.* [C]

pos·it·ron /ˈpɑzəˌtrɑn/ *n.* [C] a very small piece of matter that has the same mass as an ELECTRON but has a positive electrical CHARGE

pos·se /ˈpɑsi/ *n.* [C] **1** a group of men gathered together by a SHERIFF (=local law officer) in past times to help catch a criminal **2 a posse of sth** a large group of the same kind of people: *Will plays with a posse of Los Angeles musicians.* **3** SLANG someone's group of friends

pos·sess /pəˈzɛs/ *v.* [T not in progressive] **1** FORMAL to own or have something, especially something valuable, important, or illegal: *Too many nations already possess chemical weapons.* | *The Church possesses a bone from the saint's leg.* **2** FORMAL to have an ability, quality etc.: *Zorna is said to possess miraculous healing powers.* **3 what possessed sb (to do sth)?** SPOKEN said when you cannot understand why someone did something: *I don't know what possessed me to buy such an ugly dress.* **4** LITERARY if a feeling possesses you, you suddenly feel it very strongly and it affects your behavior: *A sense of fear possessed him as he walked into the old house.* **5** if an evil spirit possesses someone, it takes control of their mind: *Jo believed that demons possessed her.*

pos·sessed /pəˈzɛst/ *adj.* [not before noun] **1** controlled by an evil spirit: *Her family thought that she was possessed, and called in a priest.* **2 like a man/woman possessed** with a lot of energy or violence: *Young played the game like a man possessed.* **3 be possessed of sth** LITERARY to have a particular quality, ability, belief etc.: *He felt possessed of great strength and fearlessness.* —see also SELF-POSSESSED

pos·ses·sion /pəˈzɛʃən/ *n.*
1 sth you own [C usually plural] something that someone owns and keeps or uses themselves: *They lost their home and all their possessions in the storm.* | *One of Ron's **most prized possessions** (=most important possessions) is a home run ball hit by Babe Ruth.*
2 state of having sth [U] FORMAL the state of having or owning something, especially something valuable or important: *The tape is **in the possession of** prosecutors.* | *Is it legal to **have** marijuana **in your possession**?* | *The country is **not in possession of** nuclear weapons.* | *Anderson says he **has possession of** the records.*
3 take possession of sth to get or start using a house, car, or valuable object after you have bought it: *We don't take possession of the house till next month.*
4 drugs/gun [U] LAW the crime of having illegal drugs or a gun with you or in your home: *Kortz was charged with theft and possession of stolen property.*
5 country [C] a country controlled or governed by another country: *Britain's former overseas possessions*
6 ball [U] the state of having control of the ball in some sports | **gain/lose/get etc. possession** *Pittsburgh got possession and scored.*
7 evil spirits [U] a situation in which someone's mind is being controlled by an evil spirit
8 in (full) possession of your faculties/senses able to think in a clear and intelligent way, because you are not crazy or affected by old age: *He's difficult to get along with but still in full possession of his faculties.*

9 possession is nine-tenths of the law used to mean that someone who has something is likely to keep it even if it does not really belong to them

pos·ses·sive¹ /pəˈzɛsɪv/ *adj.* **1** wanting someone to have feelings of love or friendship only for you: *I broke up with Lyle because he was as possessive as a two-year-old.* **2** unwilling to let other people use something you own: [+ of/about] *He's pretty possessive about his car.* **3** TECHNICAL relating to a word or form of a word such as "my," "theirs," or "Charlene's" that shows that one thing or person belongs to or relates to another thing or person —**possessiveness** *n.* [U]

possessive² *n.* TECHNICAL **1 the possessive** the form of words such as "your," "its," or "Joshua's" that shows that one thing or person belongs to or is related to another thing or person **2** [C] an adjective, PRONOUN, or noun in the possessive form

possessive ad·jec·tive /.,.. '.../ *n.* [C] TECHNICAL an adjective such as "my," "your," or "our" that shows that one thing or person belongs to or is related to another thing or person

possessive pro·noun /.,.. '../ *n.* [C] TECHNICAL a word that can take the place of a noun such as "mine," "yours," or "ours" which shows that one thing or person belongs to another thing or person or is related to that thing or person

pos·ses·sor /pəˈzɛsɚ/ *n.* [C] FORMAL someone who has or owns something, especially something valuable or illegal: [+ of] *the world's largest possessor of chemical weapons*

pos·si·bil·i·ty /ˌpɑsəˈbɪləti/ *n. plural* **possibilities**
1 [C,U] how likely it is that something will happen or is true: [+ of] *Is there any possibility of that happening?* | **[a possibility (that)]** *There's a possibility we won't be here that weekend.* | **a good/definite/distinct etc. possibility** *I don't know if he's leaving, but it's a strong possibility.* **2** [C] an opportunity to do something, or something that can be done or tried: [+ for] *Fuel cells are another possibility for powering electric cars.* | *Right now I'm focusing on possibilities for the future.* | *Archer is **exploring the possibilities** (=thinking about or trying different opportunities) of opening a club in the city.* | *The U.S. has not yet **exhausted all** diplomatic **possibilities** (=tried every possible way).* **3 have possibilities** if something has possibilities, it could be made into something much better: *This place has a lot of possibilities, but it will need some work.* —see also **within the realm(s) of possibility** (REALM (2))

pos·si·ble¹ /ˈpɑsəbəl/ *adj.* **1 as long/much/soon etc. as possible** as long, soon, quickly etc. as you can: *Keep your explanation as simple as possible.* | *I want to collect as many of the stickers as possible.* **2** able to be done or likely to happen, exist, or be true: *Sudden snowstorms are always possible this time of year.* | *Here's a list of possible topics for your next essay.* | **[it is possible (for sb) to do sth]** *Is it possible to use the program on a Macintosh?* | **[it is possible (that)]** *So you're saying it's possible that Mark did it.* | *Computer technology **makes it possible** for many people to work at home now.* | *I'd like an appointment on Friday afternoon **if possible**.* **3 would it be possible (for sb) to do sth?** SPOKEN said when asking politely if you can do or have something: *Would it be possible to get together at 6:30 instead of 5?* **4 the best/biggest/fastest etc. possible sth** the best, biggest etc. thing that can exist or be achieved: *Of course, buyers want to get the property at the lowest possible price.* **5 whenever/wherever possible** every time you have an opportunity to do something: *I try to avoid speaking to her whenever possible.*

possible² *n.* [C] someone or something that might be appropriate or acceptable for a particular purpose: *Dern is another possible for the award.*

pos·si·bly /ˈpɑsəbli/ *adv.* **1** used when saying that something may be true or likely; PERHAPS: *He's going to stay at least three weeks, possibly longer.* | *Boyd is **quite possibly** the laziest man ever to hold down a job.* **2** used with MODAL VERBS, especially "can" and "could," to emphasize that something is or is not possible: *You can't possibly go to all those stores in one day.* | *I have everything I could possibly need.* **3 could/can you possibly...?** SPOKEN said when politely asking someone to do something: *Could you possibly wait until later to practice?* **4** SPOKEN used with MODAL VERBS, especially "can" and "could," to emphasize that you are very surprised or shocked by something, or that you cannot understand it: *How could anyone possibly do that to her?*

pos·sum /'pɑsəm/ *n.* [C] **1** an OPOSSUM **2 play possum** INFORMAL to pretend to be asleep or dead so that someone will not annoy or hurt you

post¹ /poʊst/ *n.*

1 piece of wood/metal [C] a strong upright piece of wood, metal etc. that is set into the ground, especially to support something: *a fence post*

2 job [C] FORMAL an important job, especially one in the government or military: *the post of deputy environmental secretary* | *General Swart took up his new post* (=started his job) *in the capital on Tuesday.* | *Montes has said that he will not resign his post.*

3 soldier/guard etc. [C] the place where someone is expected to be in order to do their job: *Soldiers are not allowed to leave their posts.*

4 military [C] a military BASE (=place where soldiers live, work etc.)

5 sports [C] one of the two upright pieces of wood that players try to kick or hit the ball between in football, HOCKEY etc.; GOALPOST

6 jewelry [C] the small metal bar that goes through your ear as part of an EARRING

7 furniture [C] one of the upright parts on the corners of a piece of furniture such as a bed: *Her nightgown hung on a bed post.*

8 race **the post** also **the finishing post** the place where a race finishes, especially a horse race

9 BRITISH: see MAIL —see also STAGING POST, TRADING POST

post² *v.* [T]

1 public notice to put up a public notice about something on a wall, BULLETIN BOARD, computer system etc.: *Rangers have posted warnings at the entrance to the trails.*

2 keep sb posted SPOKEN to regularly tell someone the most recent news about something: *We don't have any plans yet, but I'll keep you posted.*

3 job [usually passive] to send someone to a different country or place in order to work for a company, or in order to work for a period of time in the army, navy, or government: [post sb to sth] *In 1942 he was posted to India as a fighter pilot.* | *Burton has been posted overseas for two years.* —see Usage Note at JOB

4 profit/loss etc. if a company posts its profits, sales, losses etc., it records the money gained or lost in its accounts: *In the third quarter the company posted profits of $14.6 million.*

5 post bail LAW to pay a specific amount of money in order to be allowed to leave JAIL before your TRIAL: *Mott was released after posting $10,000 bail.*

6 guard [usually passive] to send someone somewhere in order to guard a building, check who enters or leaves a place, watch something etc.: [post sb at sth] *Extra guards were posted at the cemetery during the funeral.*

post- /poʊst/ *prefix* later than or after something: *the postwar years* (=after a particular war) | *We'll have to postpone the meeting* (=have it later). —compare PRE-

post·age /'poʊstɪdʒ/ *n.* [U] the money charged for sending a letter, package etc. by mail: *Please add $3.95 for postage and handling* (=charge for packing and sending something you have ordered).

postage me·ter /'.. ,../ *n.* [C] a machine used by businesses that puts a mark on letters and packages to show that postage has been paid

postage stamp /'.. ,./ *n.* [C] FORMAL a stamp

post·al /'poʊstl/ *adj.* [only before noun] **1** relating to the official system that takes letters from one place to another: *postal workers* **2 go postal** SLANG to become very angry and behave in a violent way

postal serv·ice /'.. ,../ *n.* **the postal service** the organization that provides the service of carrying letters, packages etc. from one part of a country to another

post·card /'poʊstkard/ *n.* [C] a card, often with a picture on it, that can be sent in the mail without an envelope: *a postcard of the Statue of Liberty*

post·date /ˌpoʊst'deɪt/ *v.* [T] **1** to write a check with a date that is later than the actual date, so that it cannot be used or become effective until that time **2** to happen, live, or be made later in history than something else: *The mosaic postdates this period, although the style is quite similar.* —compare ANTEDATE, BACKDATE, PREDATE

post doc /'. ./ *n.* [C] INFORMAL someone who is studying after they have finished their PH.D.

post·doc·tor·al /ˌpoʊst'daktərəl/ *adj.* [only before noun] relating to study done after a PH.D.

post·er /'poʊstɚ/ *n.* [C] a large printed notice, picture etc. used to advertise something or as a decoration: *Two of her photos became posters for the Monterey Jazz festival.* —see picture on page 426

poster child /'.. ,./ *n.* [C usually singular] **1** also **poster boy**, **poster girl** a child with a particular illness or DISABILITY (=physical problem) whose picture appears on a poster advertising the work of an organization that helps children with that problem **2** OFTEN HUMOROUS someone whose behavior represents a particular quality: *Washburn is the poster child for wasted talent.*

pos·te·ri·or¹ /pɑ'stɪriɚ, poʊ-/ *n.* [C] HUMOROUS the part of the body you sit on; BUTTOCKS

posterior² *adj.* [only before noun] TECHNICAL near or at the back of something, especially someone's body —opposite ANTERIOR (1)

pos·ter·i·ty /pɑ'stɛrəti/ *n.* [U] people who will live after you are dead: *The shows have been taped for posterity.*

post·game /ˌpoʊst 'geɪm◂/ *adj.* happening after a sports game: *postgame celebrations*

post·grad /ˌ. '.◂/ *adj.* INFORMAL postgraduate —**postgrad** *n.* [C]

post·grad·u·ate¹ /ˌpoʊst'grædʒuɪt/ *adj.* [only before noun] **1** relating to studies done after finishing college: *postgraduate degrees* **2** relating to studies done after completing a PH.D.: *postgraduate work at the Sorbonne*

postgraduate² *n.* [C] someone who is studying to obtain a higher degree after college

post·haste /ˌpoʊst'heɪst/ *adv.* LITERARY very quickly: *We need to enact the law posthaste.*

post hoc /ˌpoʊst 'hak◂/ *adj.* FORMAL a post hoc explanation, argument etc. makes a connection between two events that have happened, even though there is no real connection

post·hu·mous /'pastʃəməs/ *adj.* happening after someone's death, or given to someone or printed after their death —**posthumously** *adv.*: *Versace will be honored posthumously at the dinner.*

post·hyp·not·ic sug·ges·tion /ˌpoʊsthɪpˌnɑtɪk səg'dʒɛstʃən/ *n.* [C] something that someone tells you while you are HYPNOTIZEd that is intended to affect you or your behavior when you are not hypnotized anymore

post·in·dus·tri·al, **post-industrial** /ˌpoʊstɪn'dʌstriəl◂/ *adj.* relating to the period in the late 20th century when older types of industries, such as making things in factories, became less important, and computers became more important: *the postindustrial, information-based society*

post·ing /'poʊstɪŋ/ *n.* [C] **1** a public notice, especially one advertising a job: *job postings* **2** the act of sending someone to a place to do their job, especially a soldier: *He had a military background with postings overseas.* | [+ to] *a posting to Beirut*

Post-it /'poʊst ɪt/ *n.* [C] TRADEMARK a small piece of paper that sticks to things, used for leaving notes for people

post·lude /'poʊstlud/ n. [C] a piece of music played at the end of a long musical piece or church ceremony —compare PRELUDE (2)

post·man /'poʊstmən/ n. plural **postmen** /-mən/ [C] a MAILMAN

post·mark /'poʊstmɑrk/ n. [C] an official mark made on a letter, package etc. that shows the place and time it was sent —**postmark** v. [T] All entries must be postmarked by May 1.

post·mas·ter /'poʊst,mæstɚ/ n. [C] the person who is in charge of a post office

postmaster gen·e·ral /,... '.../ n. [C] the person in charge of a national POSTAL SERVICE

post·men·o·paus·al /,poʊstmɛnə'pɔzəl/ adj. TECHNICAL a postmenopausal woman has gone through MENOPAUSE (=stopped having her monthly flow of blood)

post·mod·ern·ism, **post-modernism** /,poʊst'mɑdɚnɪzəm/ n. [U] a style of building, painting, writing etc. in the late 20th century that uses an unusual mixture of old and new styles as a reaction against MODERNISM —**postmodern** adj.: postmodern architecture —**postmodernist** adj.: postmodernist fiction —**postmodernist** n. [C]

post·mor·tem, **postmortem** /,poʊst'mɔrtəm/ n. [C] **1** also **post-mortem examination** FORMAL an examination of a dead body to discover why the person died; AUTOPSY: No evidence of drugs was found in the post-mortem examination. **2** an examination of a plan or event that failed, in order to discover why it failed: [+ of/on] a post-mortem of Brock's campaign

post·na·sal /,poʊst'neɪzəl◂/ adj. TECHNICAL happening or existing behind your nose inside your head

post·na·tal /,poʊst'neɪtl◂/ adj. TECHNICAL relating to the time after a baby is born: postnatal care —compare PRENATAL

postnatal de·pres·sion /,... .'../ n. [U] POSTPARTUM DEPRESSION

post of·fice /'. ,../ n. [C] a place where you can buy stamps and send letters, packages etc.

post of·fice box /'. .. ,./ n. [C] FORMAL a P.O. BOX

post-op /'. ./ adj. INFORMAL postoperative —compare PRE-OP

post·op·er·a·tive /,poʊst'ɑpərətɪv/ adj. TECHNICAL relating to the time after someone has had a medical operation: postoperative pain —compare PREOPERATIVE

post·paid /,poʊst'peɪd◂/ adj. with the POSTAGE (=charge for sending something) already paid: Calendars are available for $10.95 postpaid. —**postpaid** adv.

post·par·tum /,poʊst'pɑrtəm◂/ adj. TECHNICAL relating to the time just after a woman has a baby: postpartum exhaustion

postpartum de·pres·sion /,... .'../ n. [U] an illness in which a woman feels DEPRESSED (=very unhappy and tired) after her baby has been born

post·pone /poʊst'poʊn/ v. [T] to change an event, action etc. to a later time or date: [postpone sth until/for sth] The meeting's been postponed until tomorrow. | Another delay could postpone the space mission for a year. —**postponement** n. [C,U]

post·script /'poʊst,skrɪpt/ n. [C] **1** written abbreviation **P.S.** a message written at the end of a letter below the place where you sign your name: The hand-written postscript read, "Thank you Jim!" **2** something that you add at the end of a story or account that you have been telling someone: There's an interesting postscript to this tale.

post·sea·son /,poʊst'sizən◂/ adj. [only before noun] relating to the time after the usual sports SEASON (=time when the sport is regularly played) is over: a postseason game —**postseason** n. [singular] —compare PRESEASON

post·sec·ond·a·ry /,poʊst'sɛkənderi/ adj. relating to schools or education after you have finished high school: postsecondary education

post·test /'poʊsttɛst/ n. [C] a test that you take to see how much you have learned after you have studied something or after you have done an activity —compare PRETEST

post-trau·mat·ic stress dis·or·der /,... ... '. .../ n. [U] TECHNICAL a mental illness that can develop after a very bad experience such as an airplane crash

pos·tu·late[1] /'pɑstʃə,leɪt/ v. [T] FORMAL to suggest that something might have happened or be true: Darwin postulated the modern theory of evolution. | [+ that] From his experience Keller postulates that such abuse is quite common. —**postulation** /,pɑstʃə'leɪʃən/ n. [C,U]

pos·tu·late[2] /'pɑstʃəlɪt, -,leɪt/ n. [C] FORMAL something that is believed to be true, but is not proven, on which an argument or scientific discussion is based: a proof of Kepler's mathematical postulate

pos·ture /'pɑstʃɚ/ n. **1** [C,U] the position you hold your body in when you sit or stand: Kerry has really good posture. **2** [C usually singular] the way you behave or think in a particular situation: The North has maintained a hostile military posture for 40 years.

pos·tur·ing /'pɑstʃərɪŋ/ n. **1** to pretend to have a particular opinion or attitude: He dismissed the Senator's comments as "political posturing." **2** the action of standing or behaving in a way that you hope will make other people notice and admire you: Ken's muscular posturing in front of the mirror is making me sick. —**posture** v. [I]

post·war, **post-war** /,poʊst'wɔr◂/ adj. [only before noun] happening or existing after a war, especially World War II: postwar economic growth —**postwar** adv. —compare PREWAR

po·sy /'poʊzi/ n. plural **posies** [C] OLD-FASHIONED a flower, or a small group of cut flowers

pot[1] /pɑt/ n.

1 cooking [C] a container used for cooking which is round, deep, and usually made of metal: pots and pans | a soup pot

2 tea/coffee [C] a container with a handle and a small tube for pouring, used to make tea or coffee: a coffee pot

3 for a plant [C] a container for a plant, usually made of plastic or baked clay: Do you think I should put it in a bigger pot?

4 go to pot INFORMAL if something such as a place or an organization goes to pot, it becomes much worse because no one is interested in taking care of it or making it work: My God, they've really let the house go to pot.

5 drug [U] INFORMAL, MARIJUANA

6 bowl [C] a dish, bowl, plate, or other container that is made by shaping clay and then baking it: broken shards of Roman pots

7 the pot all the money that people have risked in a game of cards, especially POKER

8 storing food [C] a glass or clay container used for storing food: a pot of honey

9 (a case of) the pot calling the kettle black INFORMAL used to say that you should not be criticizing someone for a fault that you also have —see also CHAMBER POT, MELTING POT

pot[2] v. **potted, potting** [T] to put a plant in a pot filled with soil —see also POTTED

po·ta·ble /'poʊtəbəl/ adj. FORMAL potable water is safe to drink

pot·ash /'pɑtæʃ/ n. [U] a type of potassium used especially in farming to make the soil better

po·tas·si·um /pə'tæsiəm/ n. [U] symbol **K** a silver-white soft metal that is an ELEMENT and usually exists in compounds formed with other substances

po·ta·to /pə'teɪtoʊ, -tə/ n. plural **potatoes 1** [C,U] a round white root with a brown, red, or pale yellow skin, cooked and eaten as a vegetable: mashed potatoes | a baked potato —see picture at VEGETABLE **2** [C] a plant that has potatoes growing at its roots —see also HOT POTATO, SWEET POTATO

potato chip /.'. ,./ n. [C] one of many thin pieces of potato that have been cooked in oil to make them hard, and that are sold in packages —see picture at CHIP[1]

potato peel·er /.'.. ,../ n. [C] a small tool like a knife, used for removing the skin of a potato

Pot·a·wat·o·mi /,pɑtə'wɑtəmi/ a Native American tribe from the northeastern central area of the U.S.

pot·bel·lied /'pɑt ̩bɛlid/ adj. having a large stomach that sticks out: *a potbellied office worker*

potbellied pig /,... './ n. [C] a type of small pig that people keep as a pet

potbellied stove /,... './ n. [C] a small round metal STOVE that you burn wood or coal in for heating or cooking, used especially in past times

pot·bel·ly /'pɑt ̩bɛli/ n. [C] a large round stomach that sticks out

pot·boil·er /'pɑt ̩bɔɪlə/ n. [C] a book or movie that is produced quickly to make money, especially one that is exciting and romantic

po·ten·cy /'poʊt ̩nsi/ n. [U] **1** the strength of the effect of a drug, medicine, food etc. on your mind or body: *high-potency marijuana* | *the potency of the chili* **2** the ability of a man to have sex **3** the power that an idea, argument, action etc. has to influence people: *the political potency of the crime issue*

po·tent /'poʊt ̩nt/ adj. **1** having a powerful effect or influence on your body or mind: *His speech had a potent emotional impact.* | *unusually potent drugs* **2** powerful and effective: *potent weapons* **3** a man who is potent is able to have sex or able to make a woman PREGNANT —**potently** adv. —compare IMPO-TENT

po·ten·tate /'poʊt ̩n ̩teɪt/ n. [C] LITERARY a ruler with direct power over his people: *Eastern potentates*

s w **po·ten·tial[1]** /pə'tɛnʃəl/ adj. [only before noun] a potential customer, problem, effect etc. is not a cus-tomer, problem etc. yet, but may become one in the future; POSSIBLE: *The 60 potential jurors filled the front of the courtroom.* | *The potential side effects of the drug are unknown.*

s w **potential[2]** n. [U] **1** the possibility that something will develop in a certain way, or have a particular effect: [+ for] *Consult a doctor to minimize the poten-tial for health risks.* **2** a natural ability or quality that could develop to make a person or thing very good: *This room has potential.* | *In his third year Stokes is finally showing his great potential.* | **achieve/reach/realize your (full) potential** (=succeed in doing as well as you possibly can) **3** TECHNICAL the difference in VOLTAGE between two points on an electrical CIRCUIT

po·ten·ti·al·i·ty /pə ̩tɛnʃi'æləti/ n. [C,U] FORMAL the possibility that something may develop in a particu-lar way

po·ten·tial·ly /pə'tɛnʃəli/ adv. [+ adj./adv.] some-thing that is potentially dangerous, useful, embar-rassing etc. does not have that quality now, but it may develop it later: *Sculpture workshops are poten-tially dangerous work sites.* | *a potentially fatal dis-ease* (=one that could kill you)

pot·ful /'pɑt ̩fʊl/ n. [C] the amount that a pot can contain

pot·head /'pɑthɛd/ n. [C] SLANG someone who smokes a lot of MARIJUANA

pot·hold·er /'pɑt ̩hoʊldə/ n. [C] a piece of thick mate-rial used for holding hot cooking pans

pot·hole /'pɑthoʊl/ n. [C] a large hole in the surface of a road caused by traffic and bad weather that makes driving difficult or dangerous —**potholed** adj.: *a potholed highway*

po·tion /'poʊʃən/ n. [C] **1** LITERARY a drink intended to have a special or magic effect on the person who drinks it: *a love potion* **2** HUMOROUS a medicine, espe-cially one that seems strange, old-fashioned, or unnecessary: *pills and potions*

pot·luck[1] /,pɑt'lʌk◂/ n. **1** [C] a potluck meal **2 take potluck a)** to choose something without knowing very much about it and hope that it will be what you want: *We hadn't booked a hotel so we had to take potluck.* **b)** to have a meal at someone's home in which you eat whatever they have available

potluck[2] adj. **a potluck meal/dinner/lunch etc.** a

meal in which everyone who is invited brings some-thing to eat

Po·to·mac, the /pə'toʊmək/ a river in the eastern U.S. that separates the state of Maryland and the city of Washington, D.C. from the states of Virginia and West Virginia

pot pie /,. './ n. [C] meat and vegetables covered with PASTRY and baked in a deep dish

pot·pour·ri /,poʊpʊ'ri/ n. **1** [U] a mixture of pieces of dried flowers and leaves kept in a bowl to make a room smell nice **2** [C usually singular] a combina-tion or mixture of things, especially things that are not usually put together: *a potpourri of religious ideas*

pot roast /'. ./ n. [C] a dish that consists of a piece of meat, usually BEEF, cooked slowly in a pan with pota-toes or other vegetables

pot shot /'. ./ n. **take a pot shot at sb/sth a)** to shoot at someone or something without aiming very care-fully **b)** to criticize someone unfairly without think-ing carefully about it: *There is a small but vocal minority that likes to take pot shots at the United Nations.*

pot·ted /'pɑtɪd/ adj. [only before noun] a potted plant grows indoors in a pot: *a potted palm*

pot·ter /'pɑtə/ n. [C] someone who makes pots, dishes etc. out of clay

potter's wheel /'.. ,./ n. [C] a special round flat object that spins around very fast, onto which wet clay is placed so that it can be shaped into a pot

pot·ter·y /'pɑtəri/ n. **1** [U] objects made out of baked clay: *American Indian pottery* | *a pottery bowl* **2** [U] the activity of making pots, dishes etc. out of clay: *experts in pottery* | *a pottery class* **3** [C] a factory where pottery objects are made

potting soil /'.. ,./ n. [U] special dirt that is used in pots to grow plants in

pot·ty /'pɑti/ n. [C] **1** a word meaning a potty chair, used by or to children **2 go potty** SPOKEN an expres-sion meaning "to use the toilet," said by or to young children: *Do you have to go potty?* **3 a potty mouth** SPOKEN, INFORMAL a person who has or is a potty mouth uses offensive language **4 potty break** SPOKEN, HUMOROUS a chance to stop what you are doing and use the toilet

potty chair /'.. ,./ n. [C] a small chair with a hole in the seat and a bowl under it that is used as a toilet for young children

potty-train /'.. ,./ v. [T] to teach a child to use a potty chair or toilet —**potty training** n. [U] —**potty-trained** adj.

pouch /paʊtʃ/ n. [C] **1** a small leather, cloth, or plas-tic bag that you can keep things such as tobacco or money in: *a concealed pouch for your passport* **2** a large bag for holding mail or papers: *a mail pouch* **3** a pocket of skin on the stomach that MARSUPIALS such as KANGAROOS keep their babies in —see picture at MARSUPIAL **4** a fold of skin like a bag that animals such as SQUIRRELS have inside each cheek to carry and store food **5** an area of loose skin under some-one's eyes

Pou·lenc /pu'læŋk/, **Fran·cis** /'frænsɪs/ (1899–1963) a French musician who wrote CLASSICAL music

poul·tice /'poʊltɪs/ n. [C] something that is put on someone's skin to make it less swollen or painful, often made of a wet cloth with milk, HERBS, or CLAY on it

poul·try /'poʊltri/ n. [plural,U] birds such as chickens and ducks that are kept on farms for supplying eggs and meat, or the meat from these birds: *a poultry farmer*

pounce /paʊns/ v. [I] to suddenly jump on an animal, person, or thing after waiting to attack them: *Josh was waiting like a cat, ready to pounce.* | [+ on] *The other woman pounced on her and began fighting.* —**pounce** n. [C]

pounce on sb/sth *phr. v.* [T] **1** to notice a mistake, someone's opinion etc. and immediately criticize or disagree with it: *Daub pounced on Baker's reluctance to support the military.* **2** to accept an offer or invitation eagerly: *That was an opportunity you should have pounced on.*

pound¹ /paʊnd/ *n.* **1** *written abbreviation* **lb.** [C] a unit for measuring weight, equal to 16 OUNCES or about 0.454 kilograms: *an 8-pound 3-ounce baby girl | I've gained 10 pounds since Thanksgiving. | Navel oranges are only 39 cents a pound.* **2** [C] **the pound a)** a place where dogs and cats that are found on the street are kept until someone comes to get them **b)** a place where cars that have been parked illegally are kept until the owners pay to get them back **3** [C] **a)** *written abbreviation* **£** the standard unit of money in the U.K. **b)** the standard unit of money in various other countries, such as Egypt and Sudan **4** [U] also **the pound sign/key** the SYMBOL (#), or the button on a telephone with this symbol: *Enter your five-digit code, and then press pound.* **5 get/take etc. a pound of flesh** to make someone suffer or pay more money than they can afford, especially because they owe you money

pound² *v.* **1** [I,T] to hit something several times to make a lot of noise, damage it, make it lie flat etc.: [+ **against/on**] *Bill jumped up, pounding on his desk in anger.* | [**pound** sth] *One of the attackers pounded the victim's head on the concrete several times.* | *Pound the cutlets with a mallet until they are tender.* **2** [I] if your heart pounds, it beats very hard and quickly: *Jessica felt her heart pounding but forced herself to remain calm.* **3** [I always + adv./prep.] to walk or run quickly with heavy loud steps: [+ **along/through/down**] *He was already pounding up the narrow trail.* **4** [T] to attack a place continuously for a long time with bombs or SHELLS¹ (3): *Army cannons continued to pound the city from the hillsides.* —see also **pound/hit the pavement** (PAVEMENT (3))

pound away *phr. v.* [I] **1** to continue to do something difficult without stopping: [+ **at**] *Top scientists around the country are pounding away at different parts of the puzzle.* **2** to continue to hit or attack something: [+ **at**] *Allied warplanes continue to pound away at their targets.*

pound sth ↔ **out** *phr. v.* **1** to play music loudly by hitting your piano, drum etc. very hard: *At one point Crowes even pounded out a version of the Beatle's "Get Back."* **2** to TYPE (=write with a machine) something quickly, especially by hitting the KEYS very hard: *How can he expect me to pound out this report for him by 5:00?*

Pound /paʊnd/, **Ez·ra** /ˈɛzrə/ (1885–1972) a U.S. poet who lived mostly in Europe, and supported FASCISM and Mussolini during World War II

pound·age /ˈpaʊndɪdʒ/ *n.* [U] **1** TECHNICAL an amount charged for every pound in weight **2** INFORMAL weight: *Men's extra poundage is usually in the stomach area.*

pound cake /ˈ. ./ *n.* [C] a heavy cake made from flour, sugar, and butter

pound·er /ˈpaʊndə/ *n.* **1 a 3-pounder/24-pounder/185-pounder etc. a)** an animal, fish, or person that weighs 3 pounds, 24 pounds etc.: *A 36-pounder is the biggest halibut caught from the pier so far.* **b)** a gun that fires a SHELL¹ (3) that weighs 3 pounds, 24 pounds etc. **2 a quarter/half pounder** a HAMBURGER with a quarter or half pound of meat in it

pound·ing /ˈpaʊndɪŋ/ *n.* **1** [singular,U] the action or the sound of something repeatedly hitting a surface very hard, or of your heart beating: *The pounding of hooves was getting nearer.* **2 take a pounding a)** to be completely defeated: *Our football team took a real pounding.* **b)** to be hit many times by a lot of bombs or SHELLS

pound ster·ling /ˌ. ˈ../ *n.* [singular] TECHNICAL the POUND¹ (3a)

pour /pɔr/ *v.*

1 liquid [T] to make a liquid or a substance such as salt or sand flow out of or into something: *You hold the cup and I'll pour the juice.* | [**pour** sth **into/on/down** etc.] *Don't pour that out – I'm going to drink it.* | [**pour** sb sth] *Do you want me to pour you a glass of water?* —see picture on page 425

2 it pours/it pours (down) rain [I] if it pours, a lot of rain comes out of the sky: *It poured all night.* | *When I got ready to leave it was pouring down rain.*

pour

3 liquid/smoke [I always + adv./prep.] to flow quickly and in large amounts: [+ **from/down/out**] *Smoke poured out of the upstairs windows.*

4 arrive/leave [I always + adv./prep.] if people or things pour into or out of a place, a lot of them arrive or leave at the same time: [+ **into/from/through**] *The city awoke as fans poured into the streets to celebrate the victory.* | *Offers of help poured in from all over the country.*

5 pour money/aid/dollars into sth to provide a lot of money over a period of time: *Despite the problems, banks continued to pour money into real estate lending.*

6 pour cold water over/on sth to spoil someone's plan, idea, or desire to do something by criticizing them: *Mieno is pouring cold water on the report before she's even seen it.*

7 pour scorn on sb/sth to say that something or someone is stupid and not worth considering: *Iraqi Radio poured scorn on the concept of "a new world order."*

pour on sth *phr. v.* [T] **1** to show a quality in a way that is easy to notice: *Clinton poured on the charm during his visit to the heartland.* **2 pour it on** INFORMAL to work very hard and use a lot of energy: *The Warriors continued to pour it on in the third quarter, taking a 20 point lead.*

pour sth ↔ **out** *phr. v.* [T] if you pour out your thoughts, feelings etc., you tell someone everything about them, especially because you feel very unhappy: [**pour out** sth **to** sb] *It's sometimes easier to pour out your troubles to a complete stranger.* | **pour out your heart/soul** (=tell someone all your feelings, including your most secret ones)

pour·ing /ˈpɔrɪŋ/ *adj.* pouring rain is very heavy rain

Pous·sin /puˈsæn/, **Nic·o·las** /ˈnɪkələs/ (1594–1665) a French PAINTER famous for his LANDSCAPES

pout /paʊt/ *v.* [I,T] to push out your lower lip because you are annoyed or unhappy, or in order to look sexually attractive: *Stop pouting and eat your dinner.* —**pout** *n.* [C] —**pouty** *adj.*

pou·tine /puˈtin/ *n.* [U] FRENCH FRIES covered in cheese CURDS and GRAVY, eaten in Canada

pov·er·ty /ˈpɑvəti/ *n.* **1** [U] the situation or experience of being poor: *Too many of our children are being raised in poverty.* | **extreme/dire/abject etc. poverty** *Filho came from the northeast to escape that region's grinding poverty.* **2 the poverty line/level** the income below which a person or a family is officially considered to be very poor and in need of help: *Nearly a quarter of the city's residents live below the poverty line.* **3** [singular,U] FORMAL a lack of a particular quality: [+ **of**] *The novel shows a surprising poverty of imagination.* —opposite WEALTH

poverty-strick·en /ˈ... ,../ *adj.* extremely poor and having problems because of this: *poverty-stricken neighborhoods*

POW *n.* [C] a PRISONER OF WAR: *All POWs have been released.*

pow /paʊ/ *interjection* used to represent the sound of a gun firing, an explosion, or someone hitting another person hard, especially in children's COMIC BOOKS

pow·der[1] /'paʊdɚ/ n. **1** [C,U] a dry substance in the form of very small grains: *talcum powder* | *curry powder* —see picture at MAKEUP **2** [U] also **powder snow** dry light snow consisting of extremely small pieces: *There's a foot of powder on the slopes.* **3 take a powder** to stop doing something or to leave a place quickly, especially to avoid a difficult situation

powder[2] v. **1** [T] to put powder on something, especially your skin: *The makeup man rushed forward to powder Zack's face.* **2 powder your nose** an expression meaning "to go to the toilet," used by women to avoid saying this directly

powder blue /ˌ.. '.◂/ n. [U] a pale blue color —**powder blue** adj.

pow·dered /'paʊdɚd/ adj. **1** produced or sold in the form of a powder: *powdered milk* **2** covered with powder or with something like powder: *a powdered wig* | [+ **with**] *Their faces were powdered with white dust.*

powder keg /'.. ./ n. [C] **1** a dangerous situation or place where violence or trouble could suddenly start: *The city's ethnic mix is a powder keg waiting to explode.* **2** a small container like a BARREL used for holding GUNPOWDER or other substances that explode

powder puff /'.. ./ n. [C] a small piece of soft material used by women to spread POWDER on their face or body

powder room /'.. ./ n. [C] **1** a polite phrase meaning a "woman's public toilet" **2** a small room with a toilet and SINK in someone's home

pow·der·y /'paʊdɚi/ adj. **1** like powder or easily broken into powder: *The snow was dry and powdery.* **2** covered with powder

pow·er[1] /'paʊɚ/ n.

1 control [U] the ability or right to control people or events: *It sounds like you've got a lot of power at work.* | *She liked the feeling of power that gang membership gave her.* | [+ **over**] *Many people see poverty as something we have little power over.* —see Usage Note at FORCE[1]

2 political [U] the position of having political control of a country or government: *He's been in power now for eight years.* | *Everything changed when the Communists came to power.* | *Many feared a return to power of the Khmer Rouge.* | **take/seize power** *Taking power in 1985, Gorbachev tried to reform the Soviet Union.*

3 energy [U] energy such as electricity that can be used to make a machine, car etc. work: *a power source* | *Anawalt's plane lost power almost immediately after taking off Thursday.* | *Did the power go out* (=did the electricity supply stop?) *last night?* | *The ship is sailing for Scotland under its own power* (=without help from another machine, ship etc.). | **nuclear/wind/solar etc. power** *You can't rely strictly on solar power to move a car very far.* —see also POWER OUTAGE

4 right/authority [C,U] the legal right or authority to do something: *China has threatened to use its veto power in the Security Council.* | *The bill would give the President new powers to declare war.* | [**the power to do sth**] *As general manager Wolf has the power to fire or retain the coach.* | [+ **over**] *Local governments have little power over cable television companies.*

5 strong country [C] a country that is strong and important, or has a lot of military strength: *Iran is a major power in the Persian Gulf region.* | *The U.S. must improve its education system if it hopes to remain a world power.* —compare SUPERPOWER

6 influence [U] the ability to influence people or give them strong feelings: [+ **of**] *Horton was fascinated by the power of dance.* | *the power of sex*

7 strength [U] the physical strength of something such as an explosion, animal, or natural force, or of a person: [+ **of**] *The house was rocked by the power of the explosion.* | *Seifert stood and walked out of the room under his own power.*

8 natural ability [C,U] a natural or special ability to do something: [+ **of**] *After several strokes, her father lost the power of speech.* | *She claims to have psychic powers.* | [**the power to do sth**] *Locals believe the plant has the power to cure all kinds of ailments.*

9 a power struggle a situation in which groups or leaders try to defeat each other and get complete control: *The search for a new premier has led to a power struggle in the government.*

10 do everything in your power to do everything that you are able or allowed to do: *Doctors are doing everything in their power to save him.*

11 earning/purchasing/bargaining power the ability to earn money, buy things etc.: *The shrinking buying power of the dollar is beginning to affect Wall Street.*

12 the powers that be INFORMAL the people who have important positions of authority and power, and whose decisions affect your life: *The powers that be do not seem interested in solving the city's transportation problems.*

13 have it in your power to do sth also **be in your power to do sth** to have the authority or ability to do something: *He has it in his power to end the war immediately.*

14 be in sb's power to be in a situation in which someone has complete control over you: *He is worried his son will be entirely in his ex-wife's power.*

15 to the power of 3/4/5 etc. if a number is increased to the power of three, four, five etc., it is multiplied by itself three, four, five etc. times

16 making things look bigger [U] a measure of how much bigger the LENSes of BINOCULARS, TELESCOPES etc. make things look

17 air/sea power ships or aircraft that help an army on the ocean or in the air: *The outcome will be decided by air power.*

18 student/black/kid etc. power the political or social influence that a particular group of people has

19 more power to sb SPOKEN used to say that you approve of what someone is trying to do, especially when you would not want to: *If Patty's willing to work on the weekend, more power to her.*

20 be beyond/outside sb's power to do sth to not have the authority or ability to do something: *The potential cost in human lives is beyond our power to measure.*

21 be on a power trip INFORMAL to enjoy the power or authority that you have been given, in a way that other people do not like

22 the powers of good/evil spirits or magical forces that are believed to influence events in a good or evil way

23 the power behind the throne someone who is able to secretly control and influence decisions made by the leader or government of a country, but who does not have an official government position themselves

24 a power in the land OLD-FASHIONED someone or something that has a lot of power and influence in a country —see also BALANCE OF POWER, HIGH-POWERED, LOW-POWER, STAYING POWER

power[2] v. **1** [T usually passive] to supply power to a vehicle or machine: *Most chain saws are powered by two-cycle gasoline engines.* **2 battery-powered/solar-powered/nuclear-powered etc.** working or moving by means of power from a BATTERY, the sun etc.: *a jet-powered airplane* **3** [I + adv./prep.] to move quickly and with a lot of strength: [+ **through/up/down**] *Jones powered his way through the San Diego line of defense.* —see also HIGH-POWERED, LOW-POWER

power sth ↔ up phr. v. [T] to make a machine start working: *Never move a computer while it is powered up.*

power[3] adj. **1** controlled by a motor: *Does this car have power windows?* | *power steering* **2** INFORMAL **power breakfast/lunch etc.** a meal at which people meet to discuss business **3 a power tie/suit etc.** a piece of clothing that makes you look important or confident **4 power dressing** a way of dressing in which you choose the color and style of your clothes to make others think you are important and confident

power base /'.. ./ n. [C] the group of people in a particular area whose support gives a politician or leader their power: *McClardy's power base is among working-class Catholics.*

pow·er·boat /ˈpaʊəˌboʊt/ *n.* [C] a powerful MOTOR-BOAT that is used for racing

power bro·ker /ˈ.. ˌ../ *n.* [C] someone who controls or influences which people get political power in a particular area

power drill /ˈ.. ˌ., ˌ... ˈ./ *n.* [C] a tool for making holes that works by electricity

power fail·ure /ˈ.. ˌ../ *n.* [C] a POWER OUTAGE

pow·er·ful /ˈpaʊəfəl/ *adj.*
1 important a powerful person, organization, group etc. is able to control and influence events and other people's actions: *Ten of the world's most powerful men met to discuss trade barriers.* | *a powerful civil rights group*
2 country having a lot of influence, and a lot of economic or military strength: *Nigeria is the most powerful and populous nation in black Africa.*
3 machine/weapon etc. a powerful machine, engine, weapon etc. works very effectively and quickly or with great force: *This Civic is more powerful than the last model.* | *a powerful bomb*
4 affecting sb's feelings/ideas having a strong effect on someone's feelings or on the way they think: *I was impressed with Dinsmore's powerful command of language.* | *a powerful story of love and forgiveness.* | **powerful reasons/arguments** (=reasons that make you think that something must be true)
5 team/army etc. a powerful team, army etc. is very strong and can easily defeat other teams or armies: *The Steelers' powerful offense has scored over 25 points a game.*
6 medicine a powerful medicine or drug has a very strong effect on your body: *The drug is a thousand times more powerful than LSD.*
7 physically strong physically strong: *John held her in his powerful arms.*
8 light/sound/taste etc. very strong, bright, loud etc.: *There was a powerful smell coming from the laundry basket.*
9 explosion/kick/punch etc. a powerful blow, explosion etc. hits someone with a lot of force or has a lot of force: *Tyson landed a powerful left hook on Douglas' chin.* —**powerfully** *adv.* —see also ALL-POWERFUL

pow·er·house /ˈpaʊəˌhaʊs/ *n.* [C] INFORMAL **1** an organization or place that produces a lot of ideas and has a lot of influence: *This small company has become a powerhouse in the software market.* **2** someone who is very strong and has a lot of energy: *Vocal powerhouse Dorothy Reid will perform at Thursday's gospel concert.* **3** someone or something that is very successful, especially in sports: *Atlanta was the powerhouse team of the '90s.*

pow·er·less /ˈpaʊəlɪs/ *adj.* unable to stop or control something because you do not have the power, strength, or legal right to do so: [**powerless to do sth**] *The security guards were powerless to hold back the enraged crowd.* | [+ **against**] *Smith was powerless against office gossip.* —**powerlessly** *adv.* —**powerlessness** *n.* [U]

power line /ˈ.. ˌ./ *n.* [C] a large wire carrying electricity above or under the ground

power of at·tor·ney /ˌ... . ˈ../ *n.* [C,U] LAW the legal right to do things for another person in their personal or business life, or a document giving this right

power out·age /ˈ.. ˌ../ *n.* [C] a period of time when there is no electricity supply

power pack /ˈ.. ˌ./ *n.* [C] INFORMAL a BATTERY that is used to make electrical objects run

Pow·erPC /ˌpaʊə pi ˈsi/ *n.* [C] TRADEMARK a fast CPU that is used in many modern computers

power plant /ˈ.. ˌ./ *n.* [C] **1** a building where electricity is produced to supply a large area **2** TECHNICAL the machine or engine that supplies power to a factory, airplane, car etc.

power pol·i·tics /ˌ.. ˈ.../ *n.* [U] the attempt to get power and influence by using or threatening to use force, especially against another country: *Cambodia has long been a victim of power politics.*

power-shar·ing /ˈ.. ˌ../ *n.* [U] a situation in which two or more people or groups of people run a government together —**power-sharing** *adj.* [only before noun] *a power-sharing arrangement*

power sta·tion /ˈ.. ˌ../ *n.* [C] a POWER PLANT (1)

power steer·ing /ˌ.. ˈ../ *n.* [U] a system for STEERing a vehicle that uses power from the vehicle's engine and so needs less effort from the driver

power struc·ture /ˈ.. ˌ../ *n.* [C] the group of people who have power in a society or country

power tool /ˈ.. ˌ./ *n.* [C] a tool that works by electricity

Pow·ha·tan[1] /ˌpaʊəˈtæn/ a group of Native American tribes from the eastern U.S.

Powhatan[2] (1550–1618) an Algonquin chief, father of Pocahontas, who made a peace agreement in 1614 with the English settlers of Jamestown

pow·wow /ˈpaʊ waʊ/ *n.* [C] **1** HUMOROUS a meeting or discussion **2** a meeting or council of Native Americans

pox /pɑks/ *n.* **1** [U] OLD USE the disease SMALLPOX **2 a pox on sb** OLD-FASHIONED used to show that you are angry or annoyed with someone **3 the pox** OLD USE the disease SYPHILIS —see also CHICKENPOX

p.p. written before the name of another person when you are signing a letter for them

pp. the written abbreviation of "pages": *See pp. 15–17.*

ppm *n.* [singular] TECHNICAL parts per million; a measurement of very small pieces of something, especially something in the air or water: *ozone levels between 0.07 and 0.12 ppm*

PPO *n.* [C] Preferred Provider Organization; a type of health insurance plan in which members can go to any hospital or doctor, but the insurance company pays more for hospitals and doctors in their system than those outside their system —compare HMO

PPP *n.* [C] TECHNICAL point-to-point protocol; the information that your computer gives to an ONLINE SERVICE PROVIDER over telephone lines, so that you can connect your computer with them and use the Internet, send EMAIL etc.

P.P.S. *n.* [C] a note added after a P.S. in a letter or message

PR *n.* [U] **1** PUBLIC RELATIONS; the work of persuading people to think that a company or organization is a good one: *Last year, we hired a PR firm to help change our corporate image.* | **good/bad PR** *The company got some good PR from giving money to the orphanage.* **2** the written abbreviation of Puerto Rico

prac·ti·ca·ble /ˈpræktɪkəbəl/ *adj.* FORMAL able to be used or done successfully in a particular situation: *The company merger will take place as soon as practicable.* —**practicably** *adv.* —**practicability** /ˌpræktɪkəˈbɪləti/ *n.* [U]

prac·ti·cal /ˈpræktɪkəl/ *adj.*
1 real situations relating to real situations and events rather than ideas: *Instructors have a master's degree in business plus a lot of **practical experience**.* | *Voters make their choices based on practical considerations.* —compare THEORETICAL
2 sensible sensible and basing your decisions on what is possible and likely to succeed, or showing this quality: *We have to be practical and not spend so much money.* | *Campbell considers himself a practical man.* —opposite IMPRACTICAL
3 likely to work practical plans, methods, advice etc. are likely to succeed or be effective in a situation: *Automakers are trying to develop a practical electric car design.* | *Liederman offers practical advice about coping with losing your job.* —opposite IMPRACTICAL
4 useful designed to be useful rather than attractive or interesting: *Babysitting coupons are a practical gift any parent will love.*
5 suitable appropriate for a particular purpose or for normal life: *Small economy cars are more practical if you live in the city.* —opposite IMPRACTICAL

6 for all practical purposes used when saying what the real effect of a situation is: *For all practical purposes, the country is bankrupt.*

7 good at fixing things good at repairing or making things: *He's really smart and really practical – he can fix anything.*

prac·ti·cal·i·ty /ˌpræktɪˈkæləti/ *n.* **1 practicalities** [plural] the real facts of a situation rather than ideas about how it might be: *The committee is looking into the practicalities of renovating the train station.* **2** [U] how appropriate an idea, method, or plan is for a situation, and whether or not it is likely to succeed: *Some Congressmen doubt the practicality of the new legislation.* **3** [U] the quality of being sensible and basing your plans on what you know is likely to succeed

practical joke /ˌ... ˈ./ *n.* [C] a trick that is intended to give someone a surprise or shock and make other people laugh —**practical joker** *n.* [C]

s w prac·ti·cal·ly /ˈpræktɪkli/ *adv.* **1** INFORMAL almost: *Linda practically jumped out of her chair when the phone rang.* | *Practically everyone from work was at the party.* **2** in a sensible way that considers problems: *Joey just doesn't think practically.*

practical nurse /ˌ... ˈ./ *n.* [C] ≈ LICENSED PRACTICAL NURSE

s w prac·tice¹ /ˈpræktɪs/ *n.*

1 a skill a) [U] regular activity that you do in order to improve a skill or ability: *Cooking is something that improves with practice.* | *Learning to write isn't easy, it takes practice.* **b)** [C,U] a period of time you spend training to improve your skill in doing something: *soccer practice* | *During the summer, the team has two practices a day.*

2 tradition [C] something that you do often because of your religion or your society's tradition: *the religious beliefs and practices of Hindus* | [**the practice of doing sth**] *It took me a while to adjust to the practice of eating with my bare hands.*

3 in practice used when saying what really happens rather than what should happen or what people think happens: *In practice, the city's transportation system is very inefficient.* —compare **in theory** (THEORY (4))

4 sth done often [C,U] something that people do often, especially a particular way of doing something: *Doctors want to educate teenagers about unsafe sexual practices.* | **standard/common/general etc. practice** *Lowering prices after the holidays is common practice in the U.S.* —see Usage Note at HABIT

5 doctor/lawyer [C,U] the work of a doctor or lawyer, or the place where they work: *Both dentists have been in practice* (=worked as dentists) *for twenty years.* | **medical/legal practice** *Mitchelson has a successful medical practice in L.A.* —see also GENERAL PRACTICE, PRIVATE PRACTICE

6 good/bad practice an example of a good or very bad way of doing something, especially in a particular job: *Changing your computer passwords regularly is considered good practice.*

7 be out of practice to have not done something for a long time so that you are unable to do it well: *I'd love to play tennis with you, but I'm really out of practice.*

8 put sth into practice if you put an idea, plan, some knowledge etc. into practice, you start to use it and see if it is effective: *New safety guidelines for factory workers will be put into practice next month.*

9 be in practice if you are in practice, you have practiced something regularly and are able to do it well

10 practice makes perfect used to say that if you do an activity regularly, you will become very good at it

s w practice² *v.* **1** [I,T] to do an activity regularly in order to improve your skill or to prepare for a test: *Teresa practices karate twice a day.* | [**practice doing sth**] *Gene needs to practice writing essays.* | [**practice for sth**] *The stunt pilots are practicing for an upcoming air show.* | [**practice sth on sb**] *For weeks, Rob has been practicing his comedy routine on me.* | *Coach says I need to **practice hard** (=practice a lot) if I want to become a starter.* **2** [I,T] to work as

a doctor or lawyer | **practice law/medicine/psychiatry etc.** *Harris has practiced law for over thirty years.* | [**+ as**] *In 1975, Blanks began practicing as a radiologist.* **3** [T] to use a particular method or custom: *The custom of arranging marriages is practiced in some parts of Asia.* **4** [T] if you practice a religion, system of ideas etc., you live your life according to its rules: *Tricia practices Zen Buddhism.* **5 practice what you preach** to do the things that you advise other people to do: *The environmental magazine practices what it preaches, using recycled paper and soy ink.*

prac·ticed /ˈpræktɪst/ *adj.* **1** someone who is practiced in a particular job or skill is good at it because they have done it many times before: *Gerhardt is a practiced outdoorsman.* **2** [only before noun] a practiced action has been done so often that it now seems very easy: *With a practiced, easy motion, Brickman grabbed the snake.*

prac·tic·ing /ˈpræktɪsɪŋ/ *adj.* **1 a practicing Catholic/Muslim/Jew etc.** someone who follows the rules and traditions of a particular religion: *Meyers has been a practicing Buddhist since the early 1970s.* **2 a practicing doctor/lawyer/architect etc.** someone who is working as a doctor, lawyer etc. **3 a practicing homosexual/lesbian/gay etc.** someone who is HOMOSEXUAL and who has sex

prac·ti·cum /ˈpræktɪkəm/ *n.* [C] a school or college course in which students use the knowledge that they have learned in a practical way

prac·tise /ˈpræktɪs/ *v.* the British and Canadian spelling of PRACTICE²

prac·ti·tion·er /prækˈtɪʃənɚ/ *n.* [C] **1 a medical/legal/tax etc. practitioner** someone who does a particular job such as a doctor or a lawyer **2** someone who regularly does a particular activity or follows the rules of a particular religion or PHILOSOPHY: *a Christian Science practitioner* | [**+ of**] *a practitioner of Taoist philosophy* —see also FAMILY PRACTITIONER, GENERAL PRACTITIONER, NURSE PRACTITIONER

prae·sid·i·um /prɪˈsɪdiəm, -ˈzɪ-/ *n.* [C] another spelling of PRESIDIUM

prae·to·ri·an guard /priˌtɔriən ˈɡɑrd/ *n.* [singular] LITERARY a group of people who are very loyal to someone important or powerful

prag·mat·ic /præɡˈmætɪk/ *adj.* dealing with problems in a sensible practical way, instead of strictly following a set of ideas: *Our nation needs to take a pragmatic approach to lowering trade barriers.* —**pragmatically** /-kli/ *adv.*

prag·mat·ics /præɡˈmætɪks/ *n.* [U] TECHNICAL the study of how words and phrases are used with special meanings in particular situations

prag·ma·tism /ˈpræɡməˌtɪzəm/ *n.* [U] a way of dealing with problems in a sensible practical way, instead of following a set of ideas: *Strauss' pragmatism has kept the company profitable.* —**pragmatist** *n.* [C]

Prague /prɑɡ/ the capital and largest city of the Czech Republic

Prai·a /ˈpraɪə/ the capital and largest city of Cape Verde

prai·rie /ˈprɛri/ *n.* [C] a wide open area of mostly flat land that is covered with grass, especially in North America

prairie dog /ˈ... ˌ./ *n.* [C] a small animal with a short tail, which lives in holes on the prairies

s w praise¹ /preɪz/ *v.* [T] **1** to say that you admire and approve of someone or something, especially publicly: *The new freeway plan has been praised by local business leaders.* | [**praise sb/sth for sth**] *Nadine praised Dorothy for her hard work.* | *The university's work in cancer research has been **highly praised**.* **2** to give thanks to God and show your respect to him, especially by singing or praying in a church **3 God/Heaven be praised** also **Praise the Lord** used to say that you are pleased something has happened and thank God for it **4 praise sb/sth to**

the skies OLD-FASHIONED to praise someone or something a lot

praise[2] *n.* [U] **1** words that you say or write in order to praise someone or something: *Residents were full of praise for the fire department's quick actions* (=they praised it a lot). | *Ueberroth got high praise* (=a lot of praise) *for his management of the 1984 Olympics.* | *The film has won praise from* (=received praise) *audiences and critics alike.* **2** an expression of respect and thanks to God: *Let us give praise unto the Lord.* **3 praise be!** OLD-FASHIONED used when you are very pleased about something that has happened —see also **sing sb's praises** (SING (4))

praise·wor·thy /ˈpreɪzˌwɚði/ *adj.* deserving praise: *Honesty is the most praiseworthy quality one can possess.* —**praiseworthiness** *n.* [U]

pra·line /ˈprɑlin, ˈpreɪ-/ *n.* [C,U] a sweet food made of nuts cooked in boiling sugar

prance /præns/ *v.* [I] **1** to walk moving your body in a confident way in order to make people notice and admire you: [+ **around/in/up**] *Models pranced along the catwalk in long wrap skirts.* **2** if a horse prances, it moves with high steps

prank /præŋk/ *n.* [C] a trick, especially one that is intended to make someone look silly: **pull/play a prank** *Every April Fool's Day, Sun employees pull a prank on their managers.*

prank·ster /ˈpræŋkstɚ/ *n.* [C] someone who plays tricks on people to make them look silly

prate /preɪt/ *v.* [I + **on/about**] OLD-FASHIONED to talk in a meaningless boring way about something

prat·fall /ˈprætfɔl/ *n.* [C] an embarrassing accident or mistake, especially one in which you fall down

prat·tle /ˈprætl/ *v.* [I] to talk continuously about silly and unimportant things: *What's Sarah prattling on about?* —**prattle** *n.* [U] —**prattler** *n.* [C]

prawn /prɔn/ *n.* [C] a sea animal like a large SHRIMP, that is used for food

pray[1] /preɪ/ *v.* **prays, prayed, praying 1** [I,T] to speak to God or gods in order to ask for help or give thanks: *You don't have to go to church to pray.* | [+ **for**] *I would like everyone to pray for my grandmother to get well.* | [+ **to**] *Billy prayed to God for help.* **2** [I,T] to wish or hope very strongly that something will happen: [**pray that**] *Mel prayed that the lawyers could help him.* | [+ **for**] *We're praying for good weather tomorrow.*

pray[2] *adv.* [sentence adverb] OLD-FASHIONED used when politely asking a question or telling someone to do something: *And who, pray tell, is this?*

prayer /prɛr/ *n.* **1** [C] words that you say when praying to God or gods: *Our thoughts and prayers are with the Hinson family.* | [+ **for**] *a prayer for the poor* **2** [U] the act of praying, or the regular habit of praying: *the power of prayer* | *a prayer meeting* | *The congregation knelt in prayer* (=praying). **3** [C] a wish or hope that something will happen: *His constant prayer was for an end to the war.* **4 not have a prayer (of doing sth)** INFORMAL to have no chance of succeeding: *The Seahawks don't have a prayer of winning the Superbowl.* **5 sb's prayers are answered** INFORMAL used to say that someone has gotten something that they wanted very much: *I thought all my prayers were answered when I got that job.* **6 prayers** [plural] a regular religious meeting in a church, school etc., at which people pray together: *Prayers are at o'clock.* —see also LORD'S PRAYER

prayer beads /ˈ. ./ *n.* [plural] a string of BEADs used for counting prayers —see also ROSARY

prayer book /ˈ. ./ *n.* [C] a book containing prayers used in some Christian church services

prayer mat also **prayer rug** /ˈ. ./ *n.* [C] a small MAT which Muslims kneel on when praying

prayer wheel /ˈ. ./ *n.* [C] a piece of wood or metal that is shaped like a drum and turns around on a pole, on which prayers are written, used by Tibet Buddhists

praying man·tis /ˌpreɪ-ɪŋ ˈmæntɪs/ *n.* [C] a long thin green insect that eats other insects

pre- /pri/ *prefix* [in adjectives] **1** before a particular event or period of time: *pre-holiday shopping* | *a prewar movie* —compare POST- **2** done before something, or in order to prepare for something: *a prenatal test* | *You have to pre-register by January 24.* | *prerecorded music* **3** before a particular person lived or had power: *pre-Franco Spain* (=Spain before Franco ruled it)

preach /pritʃ/ *v.* **1** [I,T] to give a talk in public about a religious subject, especially about the correct moral way for people to behave: [+ **to/on/about**] *Christ began preaching to large crowds.* | [**preach sth**] *Pastor Young preached a sermon on forgiveness.* **2** [T] to talk about how good or important something is and try to persuade other people about this: *You're always preaching honesty, and then you lie to me.* **3** [I] to give someone advice in a way that they think is boring or annoying: *Mom, stop preaching – I'm old enough to take care of myself.* **4 preach to the choir/converted** to talk about what you think is right or important to people who already have the same opinions as you —see also **practice what you preach** (PRACTICE[2] (5))

preach·er /ˈpritʃɚ/ *n.* [C] someone who gives talks at religious meetings, especially at a church —see Usage Note at PRIEST

preach·y /ˈpritʃi/ *adj.* INFORMAL trying too much to persuade people to accept a particular opinion: *The last part of your report gets a little preachy.*

pre·am·ble /ˈpriˌæmbəl/ *n.* [C] FORMAL a statement at the beginning of a book, document, or talk, explaining what it is about: *the preamble to the Constitution*

pre·ar·ranged /ˌpriəˈreɪndʒd◂/ *adj.* if something is prearranged, it is planned before it happens: *The driver met us at the prearranged time.* —**prearrange** *v.* [T] —**prearrangement** *n.* [U]

pre·car·i·ous /prɪˈkɛriəs, -ˈkær-/ *adj.* **1** a precarious situation or state is likely to become very dangerous: *Levin is in a precarious state of health.* | *c precarious peace* **2** likely to fall, or likely to cause someone to fall: *We had to cross a precarious rope bridge.* —**precariously** *adv.* —**precariousness** *n.* [U]

pre·cast /ˌpriˈkæst◂/ *adj.* precast CONCRETE is already formed into blocks ready for use to make buildings

pre·cau·tion /prɪˈkɔʃən/ *n.* [C usually plural] something you do in order to prevent something dangerous or bad from happening: *All safety precautions must be followed.* | [+ **against**] *Take precautions against bicycle theft by always using a U-lock.* | *Residents of the building were evacuated by firefighters as a precaution.* | *I took the precaution of insuring my camera.*

pre·cau·tion·a·ry /prɪˈkɔʃəˌnɛri/ *adj.* done in order to prevent something dangerous or bad from happening | **a precautionary measure/step** *Vega was taken to El Camino Hospital as a precautionary measure.*

pre·cede /prɪˈsid/ *v.* [T] FORMAL **1** to happen or exist before someone or something or to come before something else in a series: *The fire was preceded by a loud explosion.* | *A planning session at 11:30 will precede the noon lunch discussion.* **2** to go somewhere before someone else: *The bride and groom preceded the family out of the church.* **3** to say or write something as an introduction to a speech, book etc.: *The first chapter was preceded by a brief biography of the author.*

prec·e·dence /ˈprɛsədəns/ *n.* [U] **take/have precedence** to be more important or urgent than someone or something else, and so need to be done first: *Helping the kids with their homework takes precedence over housework.*

prec·e·dent /ˈprɛsədənt/ *n.* **1** [C] an action or official decision that can be used to give legal support to later actions or decisions: **set/create a precedent** *The case set a precedent for civil rights legislation.* **2** [C,U] something of the same type that has happened or existed before: [+ **for**] *There is no precedent for an empire as vast as that of Russia.* | *The protest was without precedent* (=had never happened before) *in a land where strikes are taboo.* **3** [U] the way that things have always been done: *The principal* **broke with precedent** (=did something different than was normal) *in letting the students wear shorts.*

pre·ced·ing /prɪˈsidɪŋ, ˈprisɪdɪŋ/ *adj.* [only before noun] FORMAL happening or coming before the time, place, or part mentioned: *This seems to contradict the argument in the preceding paragraph.* —opposite FOLLOWING[1]

pre·cept /ˈprisɛpt/ *n.* [C] FORMAL a rule on which a way of thinking or behaving is based: *basic moral precepts*

pre·cinct /ˈprisɪŋkt/ *n.* **1** [C] an area within a town or city that has its own police force, local government representatives etc.: *the 12th Precinct* | *With 99 percent of precincts reporting, Fordice had 359,884 votes.* **2** [C] the main police station in a particular area of a town or city: *The suspect was taken to the 40th precinct in South Bronx.* **3 precincts** [plural] the area that surrounds an important building: *the precincts of the cathedral*

pre·ci·os·i·ty /ˌprɛʃiˈɑsəti/ *n.* [U] LITERARY the attitude of being too concerned about style or detail in your writing or speech, so that it sounds unnatural

pre·cious[1] /ˈprɛʃəs/ *adj.* **1** something that is precious is valuable and important and should not be wasted or used without care: *Antelope herds in the Rocky Mountains have lost precious winter pasture.* | [+ to] *These schools are too precious to the community to close them.* **2** precious memories or possessions are important to you because they remind you of people you like or events in your life: *That bear is Ellie's most precious possession.* **3** rare and worth a lot of money: **precious jewels/metal/stones** (=valuable jewels, metal etc.) **4** too concerned about style or detail in your writing or speech, so that it seems unnatural: *The novel may be too precious for some, but it's good summer reading.*

SPOKEN PHRASES

5 used in order to describe someone or something that is small and pretty: *What a precious little baby girl!* **6** [only before noun] said to show that you are annoyed that someone seems to care too much about something: *Apparently I'd ruined her precious towel.* **7** used to speak to someone you love, especially a baby or small child: *Hello, precious, are you having fun?*

—**preciously** *adv.* —**preciousness** *n.* [U]

precious[2] *adv.* INFORMAL **precious little/few** very little or very few: *There are precious few seats inside the court room.*

precious met·al /ˌ.. ˈ../ *n.* [C,U] a rare and valuable metal such as gold or silver

precious stone also **precious gem** /ˌ.. ˈ./ *n.* [C] a rare and valuable jewel such as a DIAMOND or an EMERALD —compare SEMI-PRECIOUS

prec·i·pice /ˈprɛsəpɪs/ *n.* [C] a very steep side of a high rock, mountain, or cliff

pre·cip·i·tant /prɪˈsɪpətənt/ *n.* [C] TECHNICAL something that causes PRECIPITATION

pre·cip·i·tate[1] /prɪˈsɪpəˌteɪt/ *v.* **1** [T] FORMAL to make something serious happen suddenly or more quickly than was expected: *An attack on the country could precipitate a world war.* **2** [I,T + out] TECHNICAL to separate a solid substance from a liquid by chemical action, or to be separated in this way **3 precipitate sb somewhere** FORMAL to make someone fall down or forward with great force

pre·cip·i·tate[2] /prɪˈsɪpətɪt, -ˌteɪt/ *n.* [C,U] TECHNICAL a solid substance that has been chemically separated from a liquid

pre·cip·i·tate[3] /prɪˈsɪpətɪt/ *adj.* FORMAL done too quickly, especially without thinking carefully enough —**precipitately** *adv.*

pre·cip·i·ta·tion /prɪˌsɪpəˈteɪʃən/ *n.* **1** [C,U] TECHNICAL rain, snow etc. that falls on the ground, or the amount of rain, snow etc. that falls: *In the last four days, we've had three inches of precipitation.* **2** [C,U] TECHNICAL a chemical process in which a solid substance is separated from a liquid **3** [U] FORMAL the act of

doing something too quickly in a way that is not sensible

pre·cip·i·tous /prɪˈsɪpətəs/ *adj.* **1** a precipitous change is sudden and bad: *a precipitous drop in property values* **2** a precipitous action or event happens too quickly and is not well planned: *a precipitous decision* **3** dangerously high or steep: *A precipitous path led down the cliff.* —**precipitously** *adv.* —**precipitousness** *n.* [U]

pré·cis /ˈpreɪsi/ *n. plural* **précis** /-siz/ [C] a statement that gives the main idea of a piece of writing, speech etc. —**précis** *v.* [T]

pre·cise /prɪˈsaɪs/ *adj.* **1** precise details, costs, measurements etc. are exact: *There is no precise method of measuring intelligence.* | *Divers have been unable to find the precise location of the sunken ship.* **2** [only before noun] used to emphasize that something happens exactly in a particular way or that you are describing something correctly in every detail: *At that precise moment, the telephone rang.* **3 to be precise** used to show that you are giving more exact details relating to something you have just said: *He was born in April – on the 4th to be precise.* **4** someone who is precise is very careful about small details or about the way they behave —**preciseness** *n.* [U]

pre·cise·ly /prɪˈsaɪsli/ *adv.* **1** exactly: *We arrived at the hotel at precisely 10:30.* | **precisely what/how/where etc.** *Nick can't remember precisely what he said to her.* **2** used to emphasize that a particular thing is completely true or correct: *She's precisely the kind of person we're looking for.* **3** SPOKEN used to say that you agree completely with someone: *"So it was Clark's mistake." "Precisely."*

pre·ci·sion[1] /prɪˈsɪʒən/ *n.* [U] the quality of being very exact: *The work is done with consistency and precision.*

precision[2] *adj.* [only before noun] **1** made or done in a very exact way: *Golf is a precision sport.* **2 a precision tool/instrument** a precision tool or instrument is used for making or measuring something in a very exact way

pre·clude /prɪˈklud/ *v.* [T] FORMAL to prevent something or make something impossible: [**preclude sb from doing sth**] *The contract precludes the singer from performing at any other Atlantic City casino.* —**preclusion** /prɪˈkluʒən/ *n.* [U]

pre·co·cious /prɪˈkoʊʃəs/ *adj.* a precocious child behaves like an adult in some ways, for example by asking difficult and intelligent questions: *The book's narrator is a precocious 12-year-old boy.* —**precociously** *adv.* —**precociousness** *n.* [U]

pre·cog·ni·tion /ˌprikɑgˈnɪʃən/ *n.* [U] FORMAL the knowledge that something will happen before it does

pre·co·lo·ni·al /ˌ.. .ˈ.../ *adj.* relating to or happening before a place was COLONIZED

pre·Co·lum·bi·an /ˌ.. .ˈ.../ *adj.* relating to or happening before 1492, when Christopher Columbus came to the Americas: *pre-Columbian Indian cultures*

pre·con·ceived /ˌprikənˈsivd/ *adj.* [only before noun] preconceived ideas, opinions etc. are formed before you really have enough knowledge or experience: *Karl had a lot of preconceived notions about Americans.*

pre·con·cep·tion /ˌprikənˈsɛpʃən/ *n.* [C] a belief or opinion that you have already formed before you know the actual facts: *Everyone has certain preconceptions of what a drug addict is.*

pre·con·di·tion /ˌprikənˈdɪʃən/ *n.* [C] something that must happen or exist before something else can happen [+ of/for] *Statewide tests could become a precondition for high school graduation.*

pre·cooked /ˌpriˈkʊkt/ *adj.* precooked food has been partly or completely cooked at an earlier time so that it can be quickly heated up later —**precook** *v.* [T]

pre·cur·sor /ˈprikɜsə, priˈkɜsə/ *n.* [C] FORMAL something that happened or existed before something else and influenced its development: [+ of/to] *The Office of Strategic Services was the precursor of the CIA.*

P

pre·date /pri'deɪt/ v. [T] to have happened or existed earlier in history than something else: *Stone knives predate bows and arrows.* —compare ANTEDATE, BACKDATE, POSTDATE

pred·a·tor /'predətɚ/ n. [C] **1** an animal that kills and eats other animals **2** someone who tries to use another person's weakness to get advantages

pred·a·to·ry /'predə,tɔri/ adj. **1** a predatory animal kills and eats other animals for food **2** trying to use someone's weakness to get advantages for yourself: *predatory sales practices*

pre·dawn /,pri'dɔn⁴/ adj. relating to or happening before the sun rises: *a predawn police raid*

pre·de·cease /,pridi'sis/ v. [T] FORMAL to die before someone else

pred·e·ces·sor /'predə,sesɚ/ n. [C] **1** someone who had your job before you started doing it: *Vandenberg has been a more aggressive CEO than his predecessor.* **2** a machine, system etc. that existed before another one in a process of development: *The new Corvette is only 1.2 inches longer than its predecessor.* —opposite SUCCESSOR

pre·des·ti·na·tion /,pridɛstə'neɪʃən/ n. [U] the belief that God or FATE has decided everything that will happen and that people cannot change this

pre·des·tined /pri'dɛstɪnd/ adj. something that is predestined is certain to happen because it has been decided by God or FATE: **[predestined to do sth]** *He's a man who seems predestined to die lonely.* —predestine v. [I,T]

pre·de·ter·mined /,pridi'tɚmɪnd/ adj. FORMAL decided or arranged before something happens, so that it does not happen by chance: *The lights go on at a predetermined time.* —predetermination /,pridi,tɚmə'neɪʃən/ n. [U]

pre·de·ter·min·er /,pridi'tɚmɚ/ n. [C] TECHNICAL in grammar, a special kind of DETERMINER that is used before other determiners such as "the," "that," or "his." In the phrases, "all the boys" and "both his parents," the words "all" and "both" are predeterminers

pre·dic·a·ment /prɪ'dɪkəmənt/ n. [C] a difficult or bad situation in which you do not know what to do, or in which you have to make a difficult choice: *Almost everyone who owns a house is in the same predicament.*

pred·i·cate¹ /'predɪkɪt/ n. [C] TECHNICAL in grammar, the part of a sentence that has the main verb, and that tells what the subject is doing or describes the subject. In the sentence, "He ran out of the house," "ran out of the house" is the predicate —compare SUBJECT¹ (5)

pred·i·cate² /'predɪ,keɪt/ v. [T] FORMAL **be predicated on/upon sth** to be based on something as the reason for doing something else: *The company's $1.6 million budget was predicated on selling 10,000 subscriptions.*

pred·i·ca·tive /'predɪkətɪv, -,keɪtɪv/ adj. TECHNICAL a predicative adjective or phrase comes after a verb, for example "happy" in the sentence "She is happy" —predicatively adv.

pre·dict /prɪ'dɪkt/ v. [T] to say that something will happen before it happens: *The newspapers are predicting a close election.* | **[predict (that)]** *The Census Bureau predicts that there will be 53 million people over 65 by 2020.* | **[predict whether/what/how etc.]** *It's almost impossible to predict when or where a tornado will occur.*

pre·dict·a·ble /prɪ'dɪktəbəl/ adj. **1** if the result of something is predictable, you know what it will be before it happens: *The snow had a predicable effect on traffic.* **2** behaving or happening in the way that you expect, especially when this seems boring or annoying: *Horror movies can be so predictable.* —predictably adv. [sentence adverb] —predictability /prɪ,dɪktə'bɪləti/ n. [U]

pre·dic·tion /prɪ'dɪkʃən/ n. [C,U] something that you say is going to happen, or the act of saying what you think is going to happen: *One prediction is that 50%* of households will have two microwaves.* | *I'd rather not make a prediction about how popular the book will be.* —predictive /prɪ'dɪktɪv/ adj.

pre·di·gest·ed /,pridi'dʒɛstɪd⁴/ adj. predigested information etc. has been put in a simple form and explained so that it is easy to understand

pred·i·lec·tion /,predl'ɛkʃən, ,prid-/ n. [C] FORMAL if you have a predilection for something, especially something unusual, you like it very much

pre·dis·posed /,pridi'spouzd/ adj. **predisposed to/toward** tending to behave in a particular way, or to have a particular health problem: *Some women may be predisposed toward breast cancer.*

pre·dis·po·si·tion /,pridispə'zɪʃən/ n. [C] a tendency to behave in a particular way or suffer from a particular illness: **[+ to/toward]** *a predisposition to alcoholism*

pre·dom·i·nance /prɪ'dɑmənəns/ n. **1** [singular] if there is a predominance of one type of person or thing in a group, there are more of that type than of any other type: **[+ of]** *the predominance of Latinos in the community* **2** [U] someone or something that has predominance has the most power or importance in a particular group or area: *Japan's predominance in the world of finance*

pre·dom·i·nant /prɪ'dɑmənənt/ adj. more powerful, more common, or more easily noticed than others: *Immigration is the predominant social issue of the day.*

pre·dom·i·nant·ly /prɪ'dɑmənəntli/ adv. mostly or mainly: *a predominantly middle-class neighborhood*

pre·dom·i·nate /prɪ'dɑmə,neɪt/ v. [I] **1** to have the most importance or influence, or to be most easily noticed: *This is a district where Democrats predominate.* **2** if one type of person or thing predominates in a group or area, there are more of this type than any other: *Before 1860, buffalo predominated in the Great Plains.*

pree·mie /'primi/ n. [C] INFORMAL a PREMATURE (=born too early) baby

pre·em·i·nent, pre-eminent /pri'ɛmənənt/ adj. much more important, more powerful, or much better than any others: *For decades, the Gershwin brothers were America's pre-eminent songwriting team.* —preeminently adv. —preeminence n. [U]

pre·empt, pre-empt /pri'ɛmpt/ v. [T] to make what someone has planned to do or say unnecessary or ineffective by doing or saying something else first: *The deal would preempt a strike by city employees.* —preemption /pri'ɛmpʃən/ n. [U]

pre·emp·tive, pre-emptive /pri'ɛmptɪv/ adj. a preemptive action is done to harm someone else before they can harm you, or to prevent something bad from happening: **a preemptive strike/attack/move etc.** *Planes bombed the area in a preemptive strike.* —preemptively adv.

preen /prin/ v. **1** [I,T] if a bird preens or preens itself, it cleans itself and makes its feathers smooth using its beak **2** [I] to look proud because of something you have done **3 preen yourself a)** to spend a lot of time in front of a mirror making yourself look neater and more attractive **b)** to be very pleased with yourself

pre·ex·ist·ing /,.·.'..⁴/ adj. FORMAL existing before something else: *Insurers will not always pay for a pre-existing medical condition.* —preexist v. [I,T]

pre·fab /'prifæb/ n. [C] INFORMAL a small prefabricated building —prefab adj.

pre·fab·ri·cat·ed /pri'fæbrə,keɪtɪd/ adj. built from parts made in standard sizes in a factory, so that they can be put together somewhere else: *prefabricated houses* —prefabricate v. [T] —prefabrication /,prifæbrə'keɪʃən/ n. [U]

pref·ace¹ /'prefɪs/ n. [C] an introduction at the beginning of a book or speech

preface² v. [T] FORMAL to say or do something before the main part of what you are going to say: *Al-Hosni prefaced his speech with a phrase from the Koran.*

pref·a·to·ry /'prefə,tɔri/ adj. FORMAL forming a preface or introduction: *The chairman stood up and made a few prefatory remarks.*

pre·fect /'prifɛkt/ n. [C] a public official in France, Italy etc. who is responsible for a particular area

pre·fec·ture /'prifɛktʃə/ n. [C] a large area which has its own local government in France, Italy, Japan etc.: *Saitama prefecture*

s w **pre·fer** /prɪ'fə/ v. **preferred, preferring** [T not in
2 2 progressive] **1** to like someone or something more than someone or something else, so that you would choose it if you could: *Which color do you prefer – blue or red?* | [prefer sb/sth to sb/sth] *I prefer turkey to chicken.* | [prefer to do sth] *Mom prefers to rent movies and watch them at home.* | [prefer doing sth] *John prefers having morning meetings.* | *Marsha would prefer giving birth at home, rather than at the hospital.* **2 I would prefer it** SPOKEN **a)** used when telling someone politely not to do something: *I'd prefer it if you would not insult my friends.* **b)** used to say that you wish a situation was different: *I would prefer it if we had a bigger house, but we can't afford it.*

pref·er·a·ble /'prɛfərəbəl/ adj. better or more appropriate: [preferable to (doing) sth] *Full-time work is definitely preferable to part-time work.*

pref·er·a·bly /'prɛfərəbli/ adv. used in order to show which person, thing, place, or idea you think would be the best choice: *You should see a doctor, preferably a specialist.*

pref·er·ence /'prɛfrəns, -fərəns/ n. **1** [C,U] if you have a preference for something, you like it more than another thing: *Do you have any preference as to what kind of pizza we should order?* | *Shawn has a preference for athletic women.* | *Ellis expressed a preference* (=said that she wants one thing more than others) *for inviting workers to give suggestions.* | *have no strong/particular preference* (=not prefer one thing more than anything else) **2 give/show preference to sb** to treat someone more favorably than you treat other people: *Some employers give preference to non-smokers.* **3 in preference to sth** if you choose one thing in preference to another, you choose it because you think it is better: *I like paying with credit cards in preference to cash.*

pref·er·en·tial /,prɛfə'rɛnʃəl/ adj. [only before noun] preferential treatment, rates etc. are deliberately different in order to give an advantage to particular people: *Bank officials denied giving the senator any preferential treatment.* —**preferentially** adv.

pre·fer·ment /prɪ'fəmənt/ n. [U] FORMAL the act of getting a more important job

pre·fig·ure /,pri'fɪgyə/ v. [T] FORMAL to be a sign that shows that something will happen later —**prefiguration** /pri,fɪgyə'reɪʃən/ n. [C,U]

pre·fix¹ /'pri,fɪks/ n. [C] **1** a group of letters that is added to the beginning of a word to change its meaning and make a new word, such as "un" in "untie" or "mis" in "misunderstand" —compare AFFIX², SUFFIX **2** the first group of numbers in a telephone number **3** a title such as "Ms." or "Dr." used before someone's name

prefix² v. [T] **1** to add a prefix to a word, name, or set of numbers **2** FORMAL to say something before the main part of what you have to say

pre·game /'prigeɪm/ adj. happening before a game of football, basketball, baseball etc.: *the pregame show* —**pregame** n. [C]

preg·nan·cy /'prɛgnənsi/ n. plural **pregnancies** [C,U] the condition of being pregnant, or the period of time when a woman is pregnant: *It's harmful to drink alcohol during pregnancy.* | *This will be her third pregnancy.*

s w **preg·nant** /'prɛgnənt/ adj. **1** if a woman or female
2 3 animal is pregnant, she has an unborn baby growing inside her: *When did you find out you were pregnant?* | [+ with] *At the time, my wife was pregnant with our third child.* | *six weeks/four months etc. pregnant I think she's only three months pregnant.* | *After five years, Susan finally got pregnant* (=became pregnant). | *Tony got his girlfriend pregnant* (=made her pregnant by having sex with her). **2 a pregnant pause/silence** a pause or silence that is full of meaning or emotion, even though no one

says anything: *A pregnant silence filled the air before the winner was announced.* **3 pregnant with sth** FORMAL containing a lot of a quality or feeling: *His voice was pregnant with contempt.*

pre·heat /pri'hit/ v. [T] to heat an OVEN to a particular temperature before it is used to cook something: *Preheat the oven to 375°.*

pre·hen·sile /pri'hɛnsəl/ adj. TECHNICAL a prehensile tail, foot etc. can curl around things and hold on to them

pre·his·tor·ic /,prihɪ'stɔrɪk/ adj. relating to the time in history before anything was written down: *prehistoric cave drawings* —**prehistorically** /-kli/ adv.

pre·his·to·ry /,pri'hɪstəri/ n. [U] the time in history before anything was written down

pre·judge /,pri'dʒʌdʒ/ v. [T] to form an opinion about someone or something before you know or have considered all the facts: *I'm not going to prejudge those decisions.* —**prejudgment** n. [C,U]

prej·u·dice¹ /'prɛdʒədɪs/ n. **1** [C,U] an unreasonable dislike and distrust of people who are different from you in some way, especially because of their race, sex, religion etc.: *Being a black man, I have to deal with prejudice every day.* | [+ against] *There still is a lot of public prejudice against single mothers.* | *racial/sexual/religious prejudice* (=prejudice against people who belong to a different race, sex, or religion) **2 without prejudice** FORMAL without treating someone or something else in an unfair way because of opinion you already have: *As a principal, I have to resolve conflict between students without prejudice.* **3 to the prejudice of sb/sth** FORMAL having a harmful effect or influence on someone or something else

prejudice² v. [T] **1** to influence someone so that they have an unfair or unreasonable opinion about someone or something: [prejudice sb against sb/sth] *Seidel tried to prejudice the jury against Davis.* **2** to have a bad effect on your opportunities, chances etc. of succeeding in doing something: *A criminal record will prejudice your chances of getting a job.*

prej·u·diced /'prɛdʒədɪst/ adj. **1** having an unfair feeling of dislike for someone who is different from you in some way, especially because they belong to a different race, sex, or religion etc.: *She's the most prejudiced person I've ever known.* | [+ against] *Many of them admitted being prejudiced against white people.* **2** having an unreasonable dislike of something: [+ against] *Some of the older employees are prejudiced against using e-mail.*

prej·u·di·cial /,prɛdʒə'dɪʃəl/ adj. FORMAL having a bad effect on something

prel·ate /'prɛlət/ n. [C] TECHNICAL a BISHOP, CARDINAL, or other important priest in some Christian churches

pre·lim /'prilɪm/ n. [C usually plural] INFORMAL a PRELIMINARY² (2)

pre·lim·i·nar·y¹ /prɪ'lɪmə,nɛri/ adj. happening before something that is more important, often in order to prepare for it: *Preliminary tests showed that pollution was very high in the river.* | [+ to] *Renaissance artists considered drawing preliminary to painting.*

preliminary² n. plural **preliminaries** [C usually plural] **1** something that is done first, to introduce or prepare for something else: *The official opening is in September, but preliminaries include a showing of sculptures in August.* **2** the first part of a competition, when it is decided who will go on to the main competition

pre·lit·er·ate /,pri'lɪtərət/ adj. TECHNICAL a society that is preliterate has not developed a written language —compare ILLITERATE

prel·ude /'preɪlud, 'prɛlyud/ n. [C] **1 be a prelude to sth** if an event is a prelude to a more important event, it happens just before it and makes people expect it: *Some analysts see the violence as a prelude to civil war.* **2** a short piece of music at the beginning of a large musical piece, or before a church ceremony —compare POSTLUDE **3** TECHNICAL a short piece of music for piano or ORGAN: *Chopin's preludes*

pre·mar·i·tal /ˌpriˈmærətḷ/ *adj.* happening or existing before marriage: *Students were counseled about the dangers of premarital sex.* —**premaritally** *adv.*

pre·ma·ture /ˌpriməˈtʃʊr‹, -ˈtʊr‹/ *adj.* **1** happening before the natural or appropriate time: *Payton's premature death was caused by lung cancer.* **2** a premature baby is born before the usual time of birth: *a premature birth* | *The baby was six weeks premature.* **3** done too early or too soon: *It would be premature to conclude that Wilson will lose the election.* —**prematurely** *adv.*

pre·med, pre-med /ˌpriˈmɛd/ *adj.* INFORMAL relating to classes that prepare a student for medical school, or to the students who are taking these classes: *a premed student* —**premed** *n.* [U]

pre·med·i·cal /ˌpriˈmɛdɪkəl/ *adj.* premed

pre·med·i·tat·ed /ˌpriˈmɛdəˌteɪtɪd/ *adj.* a premeditated action, especially a crime, is planned before it happens and done deliberately: *a premeditated murder*

pre·med·i·ta·tion /ˌpriˌmɛdəˈteɪʃən/ *n.* [U] the act of thinking about something and planning it before you actually do it

pre·men·stru·al /ˌpriˈmɛnstrəl/ *adj.* TECHNICAL happening just before a woman's PERIOD (=monthly flow of blood)

premenstrual syn·drome /.ˌ.. '../ *n.* [U] FORMAL PMS

pre·mier[1] /prɪˈmɪr, -ˈmyɪr, ˈprimɪr/ *n.* [C] a PRIME MINISTER: *the Chinese Premier Li Peng*

premier[2] *adj.* FORMAL [only before noun] best or most important: *The Super Bowl is America's premier sporting event.*

pre·miere, première /prɪˈmɪr, prəˈmyɛr/ *n.* [C] the first public performance of a movie, play etc.: *The premiere of the miniseries "Roots" took place on Jan. 23, 1977.* | *The opera had its world premiere (=the first performance in the world) in March.* —**premiere** *v.* [I,T] —see also SEASON PREMIERE

pre·mier·ship /prɪˈmɪrʃɪp/ *n.* [C,U] the period when someone is PRIME MINISTER

prem·ise /ˈprɛmɪs/ *n.* [C] **1** a statement or idea that you accept as true and use as a base for developing other ideas: [**premise that**] *The program is based on the premise that drug addiction can be cured.* **2** premises [plural] the buildings and land that a store, restaurant, company etc. uses: *A religious group rents the premises on weekends.* | *Smoking is not allowed on the premises.* | *The man was escorted off the premises.*

pre·mi·um[1] /ˈprimiəm/ *n.* **1** [C] an amount of money that you pay for something such as insurance: *We pay over $1200 in annual car insurance premiums.* **2** [U] HIGH-OCTANE (=very good quality) gasoline: *Premium costs around $1.35 a gallon.* **3 at a premium a)** if something is at a premium, there is little of it available or it is difficult to get: *Hotel rooms are at a premium during the summer.* **b)** if something is sold at a premium, it is sold at a higher price than usual because a lot of people want it: *Top quality cigars are being sold at a premium.* **4 put/place a premium on sth** to consider one thing or quality as being much more important than others: *Modern economies place a premium on educated workers.* **5** [C] an additional amount of money, above a standard rate or amount: *Farmers are being offered a premium for organically grown vegetables.*

premium[2] *adj.* **1** of very high quality: *premium-quality wine* | *The cable company offers both standard and premium services.* **2 premium prices** prices that are higher than usual, especially because there is not much of something available

pre·mo·ni·tion /ˌpriməˈnɪʃən, ˌprɛ-/ *n.* [C] a strange feeling that cannot be explained that something, especially something bad, is going to happen: *She had a premonition that she would die in a plane crash.*

pre·mon·i·to·ry /prɪˈmɑnəˌtɔri/ *adj.* FORMAL giving a warning that something bad is going to happen: *a disease with few premonitory symptoms*

pre·na·tal /ˌpriˈneɪtḷ‹/ *adj.* [only before noun] TECHNICAL relating to unborn babies and the care of PREGNANT women: *Poor women seldom receive good prenatal care.* —compare POSTNATAL

pre·nup·ti·al a·gree·ment /priˌnʌptʃəl əˈgrimənt/ *n.* [C] a legal document that is written before a man and a woman get married, in which they agree to things such as how much money each will get if they DIVORCE

pre·oc·cu·pa·tion /priˌɑkyəˈpeɪʃən/ *n.* **1** [singular, U] the condition of being preoccupied: [**+ with**] *Rockburne's new paintings show her preoccupation with color and measurement.* **2** [C] something that you give all your attention to: *Brad's main preoccupations were eating and sleeping.*

pre·oc·cu·pied /priˈɑkyəˌpaɪd/ *adj.* thinking or worrying about something a lot, with the result that you do not pay attention to other things: *What's wrong with Cindy? She seems a little preoccupied.* | [**+ with**] *The governor has been preoccupied with budget battles.*

pre·oc·cu·py /priˈɑkyəˌpaɪ/ *v.* **preoccupies, preoccupied, preoccupying** [T] if something preoccupies someone, they think or worry about it a lot

pre-op /ˌpriˈɑp‹/ *adj.* INFORMAL preoperative

pre·op·er·a·tive /priˈɑpərətɪv/ *adj.* TECHNICAL relating to the time before a medical operation —compare POSTOPERATIVE

pre·or·dained /ˌpriɔrˈdeɪnd/ *adj.* [not before noun] FORMAL if something is preordained, it is certain to happen in the future because God or FATE has decided it

pre-owned /ˌpriˈoʊnd‹/ *adj.* a word meaning having been previously owned by someone else, used especially as a nice way of saying that something is USED[2] (1): *They have a nice selection of pre-owned cars.*

prep[1] /prɛp/ *v.* **prepped, prepping** INFORMAL **1** [T] to prepare someone for an operation, examination etc. **2** [I] to prepare for something you will do: *I have to prep for my afternoon class.* **3** [T] to prepare food for cooking in a restaurant

prep[2] *n.* [C] the written abbreviation of PREPOSITION

pre·pack·aged /ˌpriˈpækɪdʒd‹/ also **pre·packed** /ˌpriˈpækt‹/ *adj.* prepackaged or prepacked food or other goods are already wrapped and are sold ready to use: *prepackaged salads*

pre·paid /ˌpriˈpeɪd‹/ *adj.* if something is prepaid, it is paid for before it is needed or used: *The shipping charges are prepaid.* | *a prepaid envelope* (=one with a stamp already on it)

prep·a·ra·tion /ˌprɛpəˈreɪʃən/ *n.* **1** [U] the act or process of preparing something: *Most of the dessert's preparation can be done ahead of time.* | [**+ for**] *I think this game was good preparation for the playoffs.* | [**+ of**] *Graham stressed the need for thorough preparation of the sales staff.* | *Boitano is practicing every day in preparation for* (=in order to prepare for) *his upcoming ice-skating show.* | *Plans for the new school are now in preparation* (=being prepared). **2 preparations** [plural] arrangements for something that is going to happen: [**+ for**] *Preparations for the upcoming Olympic Games are nearing completion.* | *Preparations are being made for the President's visit.* **3** [C] a type of medicine, COSMETIC etc.: *Grant uses a homemade preparation for his sore muscles.* **4** [C] a way of cooking food, or a particular dish: *Karahi chicken is a spicy Indian preparation that is also done with lamb.*

pre·par·a·to·ry /prɪˈpærəˌtɔri, -ˈpɛr-, ˈprɛprə-/ *adj.* **1** [only before noun] done in order to get ready for something: *Months of preparatory work needs to be done before construction can begin.* **2 preparatory to sth** FORMAL before something else and in order to prepare for it: *The partners held several meetings preparatory to signing the agreement.*

preparatory school /.ˌ.... ,., '.... ,./ *n.* [C] a PREP SCHOOL

pre·pare /prɪˈpɛr/ *v.* **1** [T] to make something such as a place, a meal, a piece of writing etc. ready to be used, eaten etc.: *Brenda spent all day preparing the meal.* | [**prepare sth for sb/sth**] *I haven't prepared my report for the meeting yet.* —see Usage Note at COOK[1] **2** [I,T] to make plans or arrangements for something that will happen in the future: [+ **for**] *The Bears are busy preparing for their game against the Redskins next week.* | [**prepare sth**] *Organizers recently met in Chicago to prepare the agenda for the conference.* | [**prepare to do sth**] *Kenny has spent months preparing to take the entrance exam.* **3** [T] to provide someone with the training, skills, experience etc. that they need to do something or to deal with a bad situation: [**prepare sb for sth**] *Romano said the Marines prepared him for the challenges of a professional career.* | [**prepare sb to do sth**] *Since he was born, his parents have been preparing him to become a doctor.* **4** [I,T] to make yourself mentally or physically ready for something that you expect to happen soon: [**prepare yourself (for sth)**] *I took a few moments to prepare myself before going out on stage.* **5 prepare the way/ground for sth** to make it possible for something to be achieved, or for someone to succeed in doing something: *The Secretary of State's visits are designed to prepare the way for peace negotiations.*

pre·pared /prɪˈpɛrd/ *adj.* **1 be prepared to do sth** to be willing to do something, especially something difficult or something that you do not usually do: *The Pentagon is prepared to build an emergency camp for refugees.* **2** [not before noun] ready to do something or to deal with a situation: [+ **for**] *Professor Robbins never seems prepared for class.* | *There was no news and we were **prepared for the worst** (=expected that something very bad may have happened).* | **well/badly/poorly etc. prepared** *It was clear that we were poorly prepared to handle such a huge increase in business.* **3** [not before noun] arranged and ready to be used: *The dining room is all prepared for our guests.* | *I have to **get** these packages **prepared** (=make them ready) to send out by tomorrow.* **4** planned, made, or written at an earlier time: *In a prepared statement, Riggs denied being responsible for the murder.* **5 I'm not prepared to do sth** SPOKEN used when saying strongly that you refuse to do something: *I'm not prepared to let them take my business without a fight.*

pre·par·ed·ness /prɪˈpɛrdnɪs/ *n.* [U] the state of being ready for something: *Military preparedness is important to prevent war.*

pre·pay /priˈpeɪ/ *v.* [I,T] to pay for something before it is needed or used: *The cost of the buffet breakfast is $7 for club members who prepay.*

pre·pon·der·ance /prɪˈpɑndərəns/ *n.* FORMAL **1 a preponderance of sb/sth** if there is a preponderance of people or things of a particular type in a group, there are more of that type than of any others: *All three volumes contain a preponderance of love poems.* **2 a preponderance of evidence** LAW a phrase meaning most of the EVIDENCE (=facts and statements) used in a law case shows that one fact is true, but not all of it

pre·pon·der·ant /prɪˈpɑndərənt/ *adj.* FORMAL main or most important —**preponderantly** *adv.*

prep·o·si·tion /ˌprɛpəˈzɪʃən/ *n.* [C] TECHNICAL in grammar, a word that is used before a noun, PRONOUN, or GERUND to show place, time, direction etc. In the phrase "a tree in the park," "in" is a preposition —**prepositional** *adj.* —**prepositionally** *adv.*

prepositional phrase /...,... '../ *n.* [C] TECHNICAL a phrase consisting of a preposition and the noun, PRONOUN, or GERUND following it, such as "in bed" or "about traveling"

pre·pos·sess·ing /ˌpripəˈzɛsɪŋ/ *adj.* FORMAL looking attractive or pleasant: *a prepossessing smile*

pre·pos·ter·ous /prɪˈpɑstərəs/ *adj.* FORMAL completely unreasonable or silly; ABSURD: *Ticket prices for football games are absolutely preposterous!* | *a preposterous excuse* —**preposterously** *adv.* —**preposterousness** *n.* [U]

prep·py /ˈprɛpi/ *adj.* INFORMAL preppy clothes or

styles are very neat, in a way that is typical of students who go to expensive private schools in the U.S.

prep school /'. ./ *n.* [C] INFORMAL a private school that prepares students for college

pre·pu·bes·cent /ˌpripyuˈbɛsənt/ *adj.* FORMAL relating to the time just before a child reaches PUBERTY

pre·quel /ˈprikwəl/ *n.* [C] a book, movie, television program etc. that tells you what happened before the story that has already been told in a popular book or movie: *"The Phantom Menace" is a prequel to "Star Wars."*

Pre-Raph·a·el·ite /priˈræfeɪəˌlaɪt/ *n.* [C] a member of a group of late 19th century English painters and artists —**Pre-Raphaelite** *adj.*

pre·re·cord /ˌpririˈkɔrd/ *v.* [T] to record a message, music, a radio program etc. on a machine so that it can be used later —**prerecorded** *adj.*: *a prerecorded message* —**prerecording** *n.* [C,U]

pre·reg·is·ter /priˈrɛdʒɪstə/ *v.* [I] to put your name on a list for a particular class, school etc. before the official time to do so —**preregistered** *adj.* —**preregistration** /ˌprirɛdʒɪˈstreɪʃən/ *n.* [U]

pre·req·ui·site /priˈrɛkwəzɪt/ *n.* [C] FORMAL something that is necessary before something else can happen or be done: [+ **for/to/of**] *Hunter proved that experience is not a prerequisite for winning a marathon.*

pre·rog·a·tive /prɪˈrɑgətɪv/ *n.* [C usually singular] a right that someone has, especially because of their importance or position: *If you want to leave early, that's your prerogative.* | *Congress has the prerogative to raise taxes.*

pres. 1 the written abbreviation of "present" **2 Pres.** the written abbreviation of "president"

pres·age /ˈprɛsɪdʒ, prɪˈseɪdʒ/ *v.* [T] FORMAL to be a warning or a sign that something is going to happen, especially something bad: *Recent small earthquakes may presage a much larger one.* —**presage** /ˈprɛsɪdʒ/ *n.* [C]

Pres·by·te·ri·an /ˌprɛzbəˈtɪriən, ˌprɛs-/ *n.* [C] a member of the Presbyterian Church —**Presbyterian** *adj.* —**Presbyterianism** *n.* [C]

Pres·by·te·ri·ans /ˌprɛzbəˈtɪriənz, ˌprɛs-/ a Protestant Christian group that is one of the largest churches in the U.S. and the national church of Scotland

pres·by·ter·y /ˈprɛzbəˌtɛri/ *n.* [C] **1** a local court or council of the Presbyterian church, or the area controlled by that church **2** a house in which a Catholic priest lives **3** the eastern part of a church, behind the area where the CHOIR (=trained singers) sits

pre·school[1] /ˈpriskul/ *n.* [C] a school for young children between two and five years of age, where they learn such things as numbers, colors, and letters; NURSERY SCHOOL

preschool[2], pre-school *adj.* relating to the time in a child's life before they are old enough to go to school: *preschool children*

pre·school·er, pre-schooler /ˈpriˌskulə/ *n.* [C] a child who does not yet go to school, or one who goes to PRESCHOOL

pre·sci·ent /ˈprɛʃiənt, -ʃənt/ *adj.* FORMAL able to imagine or know what will happen in the future —**prescience** *n.* [U]

pre·scribe /prɪˈskraɪb/ *v.* [T] **1** to officially say what medicine or treatment a sick person should have: [**prescribe sth for sb/sth**] *Doctors commonly prescribe steroids for children with asthma.* **2** to state officially what someone can and cannot do, or what should be done in a particular situation: *Four years is the minimum jail sentence that federal law prescribes.*

pre·scribed /prɪˈskraɪbd/ *adj.* decided by a rule: *All schools must follow the district's prescribed curriculum.*

pre·script /ˈpriˌskrɪpt/ *n.* [C] FORMAL an official order or rule

pre·scrip·tion /prɪˈskrɪpʃən/ *n.* **1** [C] a piece of paper on which a doctor writes what medicine a sick person should have, so that they can get it from a PHARMACIST: *I need to go to the drug store to get this prescription filled* (=get the medicine that is described in the prescription). **2** [C] a particular medicine or treatment ordered by a doctor for a sick person: *With my insurance, prescriptions cost a maximum of $5.* **3 by prescription** a drug that you get by prescription can only be obtained with a written order from the doctor —compare **over the counter** (COUNTER¹ (3)) **4** [C usually singular] an idea or suggestion about how to make a situation, activity etc. successful: [+ for] *Sandra tried to give me her prescription for a happy marriage.* **5** [U] the act of prescribing a medicine or drug

prescription drug /.,.. ˈ./ *n.* [C] a type of medicine that you can only get by having a prescription from your doctor

pre·scrip·tive /prɪˈskrɪptɪv/ *adj.* **1** FORMAL stating or ordering how something should be done or what someone should do: *prescriptive teaching methods* **2** TECHNICAL stating how a language should be used, rather than describing how it is used: *prescriptive grammar* —**prescriptively** *adv.*

pre·sea·son /ˌpriˈsizən‹ / *adj.* relating to the time before the beginning of the time of year when a sport is regularly played: *preseason injuries* —**preseason** *n.* [singular] —compare POSTSEASON

pres·ence /ˈprɛzəns/ *n.*
1 **in a place** [U] the state of being present in a place: *The ambassador's presence at the reception was a surprise.* | [+ of] *Because of the presence of chemicals, many fish are inedible.* —opposite ABSENCE
2 **in sb's presence** also **in the presence of sb** with someone or in the same place as them: *Some staff routinely ignored the rule, though never in my presence.*
3 **appearance/manner** [singular,U] the ability to appear impressive to people because of your appearance or the way you behave: *The African dancers have a powerful stage presence.*
4 **official group** [singular] an official group of people from another country, an army, or the police, who are in a place to watch and influence what is happening: *There was a strong police presence at the march.*
5 **business** [singular,U] the ability to gain sales because your business is strong or noticeable: *The sale gives USAir a greater presence in the Northeast.*
6 **make your presence felt** to have a strong and noticeable effect on the people around you or the situation you are in: *Bruce wasted little time making his presence felt by scoring in the first ten minutes of the game.*
7 **spirit** [C usually singular] a spirit or influence that cannot be seen, but is felt to be near: *It was as if an evil presence lived in the room.*

presence of mind /,... ˈ./ *n.* [U] the ability to deal with a dangerous situation calmly and quickly: *Bill had the presence of mind to call 911 when the fire got out of control.*

pres·ent¹ /ˈprɛzənt/ *adj.* **1** [not before noun] existing in a particular place: *Traces of the chemical are present in drinking water.* | *A feeling of sadness was present in the room.* | *Copies were given to all the members present.* —opposite ABSENT¹ **2** [only before noun] happening or existing now: *The new library will be double the size of the present one.* | *In the present economic climate, investors should be cautious.* | *Cancer cannot be cured at the present time.* **3 the present day** FORMAL in modern times; NOW: *Traditional Indian pottery designs are still used in the present day.* **4 all present and accounted for** used to say that everyone who is supposed to be in a place, at a meeting etc. is now here **5 present company excepted** SPOKEN used when you are saying something bad or impolite about a group of people, in order to tell the people you are with that you do not mean to include them in the statement: *All men are selfish pigs – present company excepted.* —see also PRESENTLY, PRESENT TENSE

pres·ent² /prɪˈzɛnt/ *v.*
1 **give** [T] to give something to someone, especially at a formal or official occasion: *The Golden Globe Awards will be presented January 18.* | [present sb with sth] *Captain Dave Schilling presented Patrick with a commendation from the fire department.*
2 **a speech** [T] to give a speech in which you offer an idea, plan etc. to be considered or accepted: *The researchers will present their findings at the annual meeting of the Radiological Society.* | [present sth to sb] *The report will be presented to the district board this week.*
3 **information** [T] to offer or show information about something in a particular way: *All of the following data is presented in metric tons.*
4 **theater/television** [T] to give a performance in a theater etc., or broadcast it on television or radio: *The Roxy is presenting a production of "Waiting for Godot" this weekend.*
5 **cause sth to happen** [T] to cause something to happen or exist: **present a problem/difficulty/opportunity** etc. *Heavy rains have presented new difficulties for relief workers.*
6 **appearance** [T] to give something or someone a particular appearance or quality: *Restaurants take care to present their food with style.*
7 **seem true** [T] to make something seem true, especially when it is not: [present sb/sth as sth] *Almost every media story presented these ideas as fact.* | *John presented himself as a conservative Republican.*
8 **document/ticket** [T] FORMAL to show something such as an official document or ticket to someone in an official position: *Arguello presented his passport to the border guards.*
9 sth presents itself if a situation, opportunity etc. presents itself, it suddenly happens or exists: *After independence, the opportunity to stop slavery presented itself, but was not acted upon.*
10 **introduce sb** [T] FORMAL to introduce someone formally, especially to someone important: *May I present my parents, Mr. and Mrs. Benning?*
11 **arrive** **present yourself** FORMAL if you present yourself at a place, you arrive there and tell someone that you have come: *Mendez presented himself at the Marine base in Virginia.*
12 present arms a command to soldiers to hold their weapons upright in front of their bodies as a greeting to someone important
13 present your apologies/compliments etc. FORMAL used to greet someone, tell them you are sorry etc. very politely: *Mrs. Gottlieb presents her apologies and regrets she will not be able to attend.*
14 **illness** [I,T] TECHNICAL to show an illness by having a particular SYMPTOM (=sign of an illness): [+ with] *The disease may present with a headache.*

pres·ent³ /ˈprɛzənt/ *n.* **1** [C] something you give someone on a special occasion: *The knife was a present from his father.* | **a birthday/Christmas/anniversary present** (=something that you give someone on their birthday, at Christmas etc.) **2 the present a)** the time that is happening now: *The book details the history of France from the Renaissance to the present.* **b)** TECHNICAL the form of a verb that shows what exists or is happening now **3 at (the) present** FORMAL at this time; NOW: *We have no plans at the present for closing the factory.* **4 there's no time like the present** used to say that if you are going to do something, you should do it now: *There's no time like the present to change your eating habits.*

pre·sent·a·ble /prɪˈzɛntəbəl/ *adj.* neat and attractive enough to be seen or shown to someone: *It will take about $7,500 to make the house presentable to buyers.* | *At least try and look presentable when we go out.* —**presentably** *adv.*

pres·en·ta·tion /ˌprɛzənˈteɪʃən, ˌprɛ-/ *n.*
1 **give prize** [C] the act of giving someone a prize or present at a formal ceremony: [+ of] *Most Scouts were there for the presentation of the awards.*
2 **speech** [C] a formal talk about a particular subject: *Our presentation was followed by about two hours of discussion.* | *Walters gave a presentation on ancient Korean art.*

3 way of saying/showing [C,U] the way in which something is said, offered, shown, explained etc. to others: *We blamed the lawyers for a weak presentation of the case.* | *Bear's Cafe needs to pay more attention to presentation and taste*
4 proof [C,U] the act of showing someone something, so that it can be checked or considered: [+ of] *The tourist card is issued upon presentation of proof of U.S. citizenship.*
5 performance [C] the act of performing something in front of a group of people or on television, radio etc.: *Thompson has the lead role in the Children's Theater presentation of "Annie."*
6 baby [C,U] TECHNICAL the position in which a baby is lying in its mother's body just before it is born: *a breech presentation* —**presentational** *adj.*

pres·en·ta·tion cop·y /ˌ..ˈ.. ˌ../ *n.* [C] a book that is given to someone by the writer or PUBLISHER

pres·ent-day /ˌ.. ˈ.◂/ *adj.* [only before noun] modern or existing now: *The colonists settled near present-day Charleston.*

pre·sen·tenc·ing /ˌpriˈsɛntˈnsɪŋ/ *adj.* [only before noun] happening before someone receives their SENTENCE (=punishment) in a court of law: *a presentencing report*

pre·sent·er /prɪˈzɛntɚ/ *n.* [C] someone who gives a speech or who officially gives a prize or present to someone

pre·sen·ti·ment /prɪˈzɛntəmənt/ *n.* [C] FORMAL a strange and uncomfortable feeling that something is going to happen: [+ of] *a presentiment of danger*

pres·ent·ly /ˈprɛzəntli/ *adv.* FORMAL **1** at this time; now: *The university presently operates two cancer research centers.* | [**sentence adverb**] *Presently, I am unemployed.* **2** OLD-FASHIONED in a short time; SOON: *Tea will be served presently.*

present par·ti·ci·ple /ˌ.. ˈ..../ *n.* [C] TECHNICAL a PARTICIPLE that is formed in English by adding "ing" to the verb, as in "sleeping." It can be used in COMPOUND[1] (4) forms of the verb to show PROGRESSIVE or CONTINUOUS tenses, as in "She's sleeping," as an adjective, as in "the sleeping child," or as a GERUND, as in "I like cooking."

present per·fect /ˌ.. ˈ../ *n.* **the present perfect (tense)** TECHNICAL the form of a verb that shows what happened during the period of time up to and including the present, which is formed in English with the present tense of the verb "have" and a PAST PARTICIPLE. In the sentence "Tina has seen the movie twice," "has seen" is in the present perfect.

present tense /ˌ.. ˈ./ *n.* **the present tense** TECHNICAL the form of a verb that shows what is true, what exists, or what happens at the present time. In the sentence "James works for a computer company," "works" is in the present tense.

pres·er·va·tion /ˌprɛzɚˈveɪʃən/ *n.* [U] **1** the act of keeping something unharmed or unchanged: *wildlife preservation* | [+ of] *The tribe is concerned with the preservation of its culture and traditions.* | *Cripple Creek residents voted in favor of gambling to support historic preservation.* **2** the degree to which something has remained unchanged or unharmed by weather, age etc.: *Ironically, the older buildings were in a much better state of preservation.* —see also SELF-PRESERVATION

pres·er·va·tion·ist /ˌprɛzɚˈveɪʃənɪst/ *n.* [C] someone who works to prevent historical places, buildings etc. from being destroyed

pre·serv·a·tive /prɪˈzɚvətɪv/ *n.* [C U] a chemical substance that prevents food or wood from decaying

pre·serve[1] /prɪˈzɚv/ *v.* [T] **1** to save something or someone from being harmed or destroyed: *We want to preserve as much open land as possible.* | *The house is part of local history and should be preserved.* | [**preserve sb/sth from sth**] *Dalton's aides were determined to preserve him from embarrassment.* **2** to make something continue without changing: *The new law preserves the national guarantee of health care for poor children.* **3** to treat food in a special way so that it can be stored for a long time without decaying: *Here's a recipe for preserving fruit in brandy.* —see also WELL-PRESERVED —**preservable** *adj.*

preserve[2] *n.* **1** [C] an area of land or water in which animals, fish, or trees are protected: *the nation's first wilderness preserve* **2** [singular] an activity that only one particular group of people can do, or a place that only those people can use: *a profession that was for years an all-white, all-male preserve* | [+ of] *Sending satellites into space was once the preserve of governments.* **3** also **preserves** [U,plural] a sweet substance such as JAM made from boiling large pieces of fruit with sugar

pre·set /ˌpriˈsɛt◂/ *adj.* [usually before noun] decided or set at an earlier time: *The TV turns itself off at a preset time.* —**preset** *v.* [T]

pre·shrunk /ˌpriˈʃrʌŋk◂/ *adj.* preshrunk clothes are sold after they have been made smaller by being washed: *preshrunk jeans*

pre·side /prɪˈzaɪd/ *v.* [I] to be in charge of an important event, organization, ceremony etc.: *Judge Richter is presiding in the Poindexter case.* | [+ at] *Queen Elizabeth II presided at the state dinner held Tuesday.*
   preside over sth *phr. v.* [T] to be in a position of authority at a time when important things happen: *It was Prime Minister Yoshida who presided over Japan's post-war economic boom.*

pres·i·den·cy /ˈprɛzədənsi/ *n. plural* **presidencies** [C] **1** the job or office of president: *Buckman needs 57 votes to retain the Presidency of the company.* **2** the period of time for which a person is president: *Truman's popularity had fallen to the lowest point of his presidency.*

pres·i·dent /ˈprɛzədənt/ *n.* [C] **1** the official leader of government, in some countries: *Mandela was already in his seventies when he became president.* | *President Lincoln* | [+ of] *the President of Mexico* **2** someone who is in charge of a business, bank, club, college etc.: [+ of] *the President of Drew University* —see also VICE PRESIDENT

president-e·lect /ˌ... .ˈ./ *n.* [singular] someone who has been elected as a new president, but who has not yet started the job

pres·i·den·tial /ˌprɛzəˈdɛnʃəl/ *adj.* [usually before noun] relating to a president, or done by a president: *presidential candidates* | *a presidential proclamation*

Presidents' Day /ˈ... ˌ./ *n.* a U.S. holiday on the third Monday in February to remember the BIRTHDAYS of George Washington and Abraham Lincoln

Elvis Presley

pre·sid·i·um, praesidium /prɪˈsɪdiəm, -ˈzɪ-/ *n.* [C] a committee chosen to represent a large political organization, especially in a COMMUNIST country

Pres·ley /ˈprɛzli/, **El·vis** /ˈɛlvɪs/ (1935–1977) a U.S. singer and GUITAR player, who first became popular as a ROCK 'N' ROLL singer in the mid-1950s, and became one of the most successful and popular singers ever

press[1] /prɛs/ *v.*
1 with finger [T] to push something, especially with your finger, in order to make a machine start, a bell ring etc.: *Without thinking, he pressed a button on the desktop.* | *Which key do I press to save?*

press

2 push against [T always + adv./prep.] to push something firmly against a surface: *His hands pressed down on both her shoulders.* | *Andy pressed the cool glass to his* *forehead.* | *Their tiny faces were pressed against the window.*

3 iron [T] to make clothes smooth using heat: *I'm not going to press those shirts for you.*

4 try to persuade [I,T] to try hard to persuade someone to do something or tell you something: [+ for] *Employees are pressing for better pay and benefits.* | [press sb on sth] *When pressed on the point, the mayor offered no explanation.* | [press sb for sth] *She really couldn't say much when we pressed her for more details.* | [press sb to do sth] *Both leaders are being pressed to agree quickly on the new treaty.*

5 press charges to say officially that someone has done something illegal and must go to court: [+ against] *Davis refused to press charges against her husband.*

6 heavy weight [T] to put pressure or weight on something to make it flat, crush it etc.: *The hand-operated machine presses the grapes to produce a dark liquid.*

7 move [I always + adv./prep.] to move in a particular direction by pushing: *Kate pressed forward through the crowd to take her place.*

8 keep saying/asking [T] to continue to say something or ask for something, because you want to make people accept what you are saying: **press a demand/claim/case/point** *She was convinced of Hanson's innocence, and repeatedly pressed his case in Congress.*

9 press sb's hand/arm to hold someone's hand or arm tightly for a short time, to show friendship, sympathy etc.

10 exercise [T] to push a weight up from your chest without moving your legs or feet: *How much can you press?*

11 press sb/sth into service/duty to persuade someone to help you, or to use something to help you do something, because of an unexpected problem or need: *The National Guard was pressed into service to help fight forest fires.*

12 press home sth to repeat or emphasize something, so that people remember it: *Poland will join the talks to press home its concerns.*

13 press the flesh HUMOROUS to shake hands with a lot of people: *Smiling happily, the President reached into the crowd to press the flesh.*

14 record [T] to make a CD or PHONOGRAPH record

press ahead/on *phr. v.* [I] to continue doing something in a determined way: *We've decided to ignore the setbacks and press on.* | [+ with] *The government seems determined to press ahead with its nuclear arms program.*

s w **press**[2] *n.*

1 news **a)** [used with singular or plural verb] all the organizations, especially newspapers, that provide news and information for the public, or the people who report the stories: **The auto press** *have already seen and written about most of the cars on display.* | *As usual the conservatives are saying that* **the press** *has a liberal bias.* | *Taylor refuses to speak to* **the press**. | *a press photographer* (=who takes photographs for newspapers etc.) | *Details of their love affair have shown up* **in the press**. | *I don't think the* **press coverage** (=the way something is reported by the press) *has been very objective.* | *The editors, citing* **freedom of the press**, *refused to pay fines.*

2 printing [C] **a)** a business that prints and sometimes also sells books: *Wesleyan University Press* **b)** also **printing press** a machine that prints books, newspapers, or magazines

3 get good/bad press to be praised or criticized in reports in the newspapers or on television or the radio: *They expected to get some good press for donating the land.*

4 go to press if a newspaper, magazine, or book goes to press, it begins to be printed: *The May issue was ready to go to press when the magazine closed down.*

5 machine [C] a piece of equipment used to put weight on something in order to make it flat or to

force liquid out of it: *a wine press* | *Put the garlic through a press.*

6 push [singular] a light steady push against something small: *The box opens with the press of a button.*

7 crowd [singular] a crowd of people pushing against each other: *Making her way through the press of fans and well-wishers, Halliwell got into a taxi.*

8 responsibility [singular] FORMAL the fact of having a lot of difficult things to do in a short time: [+ of] *the press of government business*

9 exercise [C] an exercise in which you push a weight up from your chest without moving your legs or feet, or a piece of equipment you use to do this: *a bench press* —see also FULL-COURT PRESS, stop the presses (STOP[1] (10))

press a·gen·cy /'. ,.../ *n.* [C] a NEWS AGENCY

press a·gent /'. ,../ *n.* [C] someone whose job is to supply information or photographs about a particular actor, musician etc. to newspapers, television, or radio

press box /'. ./ *n.* [C] an enclosed area at a sports ground used by people from newspapers, television, or radio

press clip·ping /'. ,../ *n.* [C usually plural] a short piece of writing or a picture, cut out from a newspaper or magazine

press con·fer·ence /'. ,.../ *n.* [C] a NEWS CONFERENCE

press corps /'. ./ *n.* [C] a group of news reporters working at the same place where something important is happening: *the White House press corps*

pressed /prɛst/ *adj.* **be pressed for time/money etc.** to not have enough time, money etc.: *Frozen dinners can be a lifesaver when you are pressed for time.* —see also HARD-PRESSED

press gal·le·ry /'. ,.../ *n.* [C] an area where news reporters sit, above or at the back of a court of law, Congress, or similar place

press·ing[1] /'prɛsɪŋ/ *adj.* very important and needing to be dealt with immediately; URGENT: *Survival is the most pressing concern of any new company.* | *a pressing need for medical supplies*

pressing[2] *n.* [C] a number of CDs or PHONOGRAPH records made at one time

press·man /'prɛsmən/ *n. plural* **pressmen** /-mən/ *n.* INFORMAL someone who writes news reports

press of·fice /'. ,../ *n.* [C] the office of an organization or government department which gives information to the newspapers, television, or radio —**press officer** *n.* [C]

press re·lease /'. ,./ *n.* [C] an official statement giving information to the newspapers, television, or radio: *Woodward's attorney said she would* **issue a press release** *within a week.*

press sec·re·tar·y /'. ,.../ *n.* [C] someone who works for an important organization or person and gives information about them to the newspapers, television, or radio

pres·sure[1] /'prɛʃɚ/ *n.* **1** [U] an attempt to persuade s w someone by using influence, arguments, or threats: [+ for] *The government faces heavy union pressure for higher wages.* | [pressure to do sth] *So far, she has resisted pressure to tell her story to the newspapers.* | *Teachers are* **under** *a lot of* **pressure from** *school authorities to improve test scores.* | *His parents have been* **putting pressure on** *him to find a job.* | *Privately, French diplomats had* **exerted pressure on** *the kidnappers* (=persuaded them, threatened them etc.) *to release their hostages.* **2** [C,U] a way of working or living that causes you a lot of anxiety, especially because you feel you have too many things to do: *I just can't take the pressure at work anymore.* | [+ on] *Economic and social pressures on the family finally forced them to move.* | [+ of] *the pressures of daily deadlines at the newspaper office* | *He performs best* **under pressure**. **3** [C,U] events or conditions that cause changes and affect the way a situation develops, especially in economics or politics: *Inflationary pressures will lead to higher prices.* | *The yen fell in value again after* **coming under pressure** *on the foreign exchanges.* **4** [U] the force or weight that is being put on something: *To stop the bleeding,* **put pressure** *directly on the wound* (=push on the wound with your hands or a substance). | *There was no water pressure in the bathroom this morning.* **5** [C,U] a condition of the air in the Earth's ATMOSPHERE, which affects the weather: **high/low/rising/falling pressure** *Tomorrow's chart shows falling pressure, so we can expect a lot of wind and rain.* —see also BLOOD PRESSURE, HIGH-PRESSURE

pressure[2] *v.* [T] to try to make someone do something by making them feel it is their duty to do it: [pressure sb to do sth] *Sherry's boyfriend is pressuring her to have sex with him.* | [pressure sb into doing sth] *Don't let yourself be pressured into signing something you haven't read.*

pressure cook·er /'.. ,../ *n.* [C] **1** a tightly covered cooking pot in which food is cooked very quickly by the pressure of hot steam **2** a situation or place which causes anxiety or difficulties: *By the spring of 1989, more and more bills put Perry in a financial pressure cooker.*

pres·sured /'preʃəd/ *adj.* feeling worried because of the number of things you have to do: *I've been feeling pretty pressured at work recently.*

pressure group /'.. ,../ *n.* [C] a group or organization that tries to influence the opinions of ordinary people and persuade the government to do something: *environmental pressure groups* —compare INTEREST GROUP

pressure point /'.. ,./ *n.* [C] **1** a point on the body where an ARTERY (=a tube that carries blood) that runs near a bone can be pressed and closed off, to stop blood loss **2** a place on the body that is MASSAGEd or used in treatments such as REFLEXOLOGY or ACUPUNCTURE **3** a place or situation that may involve trouble or problems: *a pressure point for racial tension*

pres·sur·ize /'preʃə,raɪz/ *v.* [T usually passive] to keep air or another gas or liquid at a controlled pressure: *a pressurized spray can* | *The submarine is pressurized just like an airplane.* —**pressurized** *adj.* —**pressurization** /,preʃərə'zeɪʃən/ *n.*

pres·tige /pre'stiʒ, -'stidʒ/ *n.* [U] the respect and importance that a person, organization, or profession has, because of their high position in society or the quality of their work: *Many are worried the current scandal could damage the mayor's prestige.*

pres·tig·ious /pre'stɪdʒəs, -'sti-/ *adj.* admired as one of the best and most important: *One of the most prestigious universities in the country is looking for a new president.*

pres·to[1] /'prestoʊ/ *interjection* said when something happens so suddenly that it seems hard to believe or seems magical: *You fold it like this and presto! It turns into a hat.*

presto[2] *adj., adv.* played or sung very quickly

pre·sum·a·bly /prɪ'zuməbli/ *adv.* [sentence adverb] used to say that you think something is likely to be true: *Presumably he's going to come back and get this stuff.* | *In the center of the photo is a tall, well-dressed woman – presumably the firm's boss.*

pre·sume /prɪ'zum/ *v.* [T] **1** to think that something is likely to be true, although you are not certain: *The price includes all your transportation and hotels, I presume?* | [presume (that)] *I presume you haven't told anyone else about this.* | [be presumed to do sth] *The killers are presumed to have fled to Mexico.* **2** to accept something as true until it is proven to be untrue, especially in law: **be presumed (to be) innocent/dead** *She is missing and presumed to be dead.* **3** FORMAL to behave without respect or politeness by doing something that you have no right to do: [presume to do sth] *I would never presume to tell you what you should do.* **4** [usually in present tense] FORMAL to depend on something that is expected to be true: [presume that] *The curriculum presumes that students already have a working knowledge of German.*

pre·sump·tion /prɪ'zʌmpʃən/ *n.* **1** [C] something thought to be true because it is very likely: [+ of] *Profit forecasts are based on the presumption of a steady rise in sales.* | [presumption that] *We sent in*

troops with the presumption that they would only stay a year. **2** [C,U] LAW the act of accepting something as true, until it is proven to be untrue: *the presumption of innocence* **3** [U] FORMAL behavior that is not respectful or polite, and that shows you are too confident

pre·sump·tive /prɪ'zʌmptɪv/ *adj.* FORMAL OR TECHNICAL based on a reasonable belief about what is likely to happen or be true: *a presumptive diagnosis* —**presumptively** *adv.*

pre·sump·tu·ous /prɪ'zʌmptʃuəs/ *adj.* doing something you have no right to do, because of a lack of respect or politeness: *It would be presumptuous of me to speak on behalf of my colleagues.* —**presumptuousness** *n.* [U]

pre·sup·pose /,prisə'poʊz/ *v.* [T usually in present tense] FORMAL to depend on something that is thought to exist or be true: *Their whole system of belief presupposes a benevolent God.* | [presuppose (that)] *The manual presupposes that the reader is already fairly computer-literate.* —**presupposition** /pri,sʌpə'zɪʃən/ *n.* [C,U]

pre·tax /,pri'tæks◂/ *adj.* considered before taxes have been calculated or paid: *a pretax profit of $1.4 million* —**pretax** *adv.*

pre·teen /,pri'tin◂/ *adj.* [only before noun] relating to, or made for children who are 11 or 12 years old: *preteen girls* | *preteen fashions* —**preteen** /'pritin/ *n.* [C]

pre·tend[1] /prɪ'tɛnd/ *v.* **1** [I,T] to behave as if something is true when you know that it is not: *I don't think he's asleep – I think he's just pretending.* | [pretend (that)] *We can't just go on pretending that everything is OK.* | [pretend to be] *Rose didn't even pretend to be interested.* | [pretend to do sth] *Jake pointed the gun at them and pretended to shoot.* | [pretend sth] *"My goodness!" she said, pretending shock.* **2** [T usually in negatives] to claim that something is true: [pretend to do sth] *I can't pretend to understand all this* (=I admit I do not understand it). | [pretend (that)] *We somehow managed to finish it, but I won't pretend it was easy.* **3** [I,T] to imagine something is true or real, as a game: [pretend (that)] *Let's pretend we live in a cave!*

pretend[2] *adj.* a word meaning "imaginary," used especially by or with children: *We're building a pretend rocket to the moon.*

pre·tend·ed /prɪ'tɛndɪd/ *adj.* false or unreal, although seeming to be true or real: *a pretended suicide attempt*

pre·tend·er /prɪ'tɛndə/ *n.* [C] **1** someone who claims a right to be king, leader etc., that many people do not accept [+ to] *a pretender to the English throne* **2** someone who pretends to be or do something

pre·tense /'pritɛns, prɪ'tɛns/ *n.* [singular,U] **1** an attempt to pretend that something is true: [pretense that] *Whiting has abandoned the pretense that* (=has stopped pretending that) *she wrote the book alone.* | *He made no pretense of intending to repay the money.* | *How long are you going to keep up the pretense of being sick?* | *Eric moved in with his girlfriend under the pretense of wanting to save money.* **2** under false pretenses if you do something under false pretenses, you do it by pretending that something is true when it is not: *He would get the women to come into his house under false pretenses, then attack them.* **3** have no pretense to doing sth FORMAL to not claim that you have a particular quality, skill etc.: *These movies are just about making money – they have no pretense to being art.*

pre·ten·sion /prɪ'tɛnʃən/ *n.* [C,U] an attempt to seem more important, more intelligent, of a higher social class etc. than you really are: *Part of his charm lies in his complete lack of pretension.* | *a neighborhood with middle-class pretensions* | [+ to] *The musical comedy has few pretensions to high art.*

pre·ten·tious /prɪ'tɛnʃəs/ *adj.* trying to seem more important, more intelligent etc. than you really are: *The restaurant is stuffy, pretentious, and ridiculously* *expensive.* | *a pretentious movie* —opposite UNPRETEN-TIOUS —**pretentiously** *adv.* —**pretentiousness** *n.* [U]

pret·er·ite, **preterit** /'prɛtərət/ *n.* **the preterite** TECHNICAL the PAST TENSE —**preterite** *adj.*

pre·term /ˌpri'tɜm◂/ *adj. adv.* happening before the time that a baby is expected to be born: *a preterm delivery*

pre·ter·nat·u·ral /ˌpritə'nætʃərəl/ *adj.* FORMAL **1** beyond what is usual or normal; EXTRAORDINARY: *The story emphasizes the heroine's preternatural beauty.* **2** strange, mysterious, and unnatural: *a preternatural spirit* —**preternaturally** *adv.*: *Kissin may be preternaturally talented, but he works harder than any other pianist today.*

pre·test /'pritɛst/ *n.* [C] a test that you take before you have studied something or done an activity to see how much you already know —compare POSTTEST

pre·text /'pritɛkst/ *n.* [C] a reason given for an action, used in order to hide your real intentions: [+ **for**] *Mr. Baines was glad to have a pretext for leaving the party early.* | [**a pretext to do sth**] *They used "poor performance" as a pretext to fire him.* | **on/under the pretext of doing sth** *The gang enters people's houses under the pretext of making repairs, and then steals everything of value.* | **on/under the pretext that** *His rental car was stopped by police on the pretext that it had a broken tail light.* —see Usage Note at EXCUSE²

Pre·to·ri·a /pri'tɔriə/ a city in South Africa which is one of South Africa's two capital cities. The other is Cape Town

pre·tri·al /ˌpri'traɪəl◂/ *adj.* [only before noun] happening before the official TRIAL in a court of law: *a pretrial hearing*

pret·ti·fy /'prɪtəˌfaɪ/ *v.* [T] to change something with the intention of making it nicer or more attractive, but often with the effect of spoiling it

pret·ty¹ /'prɪti/ *adv.* [+ adj./adv.] INFORMAL **1** fairly, but not completely: *I thought the test was pretty easy.* | *"How are you doing?" "Pretty good."* **2** very: *Six o'clock? That's pretty early.* **3** **pretty much** SPOKEN almost completely: *These meetings are pretty much a waste of time.* | *"Are you sure you know how to work this?" "Pretty much."* **4** **pretty near** SPOKEN almost: *I pretty near froze to death out there.* **5** **pretty please** SPOKEN, HUMOROUS said to emphasize that you really want something when you are asking someone for it: *Can I go? Pretty please?* —see also **be sitting pretty** (SIT (8)) —see Usage Note at RATHER

pretty sth/sb ↔ **up** *phr. v.* [T] to try to make something look more attractive or acceptable to people: *This formerly run-down street was prettied up with flowers and fresh paint.*

pret·ty² *adj.* **prettier, prettiest 1** a woman or girl who is pretty has a nice attractive face: *Nancy is younger than I am and much prettier.* | *a pretty little girl* **2** something that is pretty is pleasant to look at or listen to, without being very beautiful or impressive: *a pretty dress* | *pretty flowers* | *You have a really pretty voice.* **3** **not a pretty picture/sight** very bad, upsetting, or worrying: *The plane was completely destroyed – it's not a pretty sight.* **4** **pretty as a picture** very pretty **5** **not just another/a pretty face** HUMOROUS someone who not only looks attractive, but also has other good qualities or abilities: *Critics tended to dismiss her as dumb, but she's not just another pretty face.* **6** a boy who is pretty looks attractive, but in a way that is more typical of a girl **7** **a pretty boy** a man or boy who is very attractive in a way that is typical of a girl, and who is considered to have succeeded because of his appearance, rather than because of his ability or hard work **8** **cost a pretty penny** OLD-FASHIONED to cost a lot of money —**prettily** *adv.* —**prettiness** *n.* [U] —see Usage Note at BEAUTIFUL

pret·zel /'prɛtsəl/ *n.* [C] a hard salty type of bread baked in the shape of a stick or a loose knot

pre·vail /pri'veɪl/ *v.* [I] FORMAL [not in progressive] **1** if a person, idea, or principle prevails in a

fight or argument, they achieve success in the end: *If they prevail in court, they could receive up to $100,000.* | [+ **over**] *Not surprisingly, good prevails over evil in this film.* | *The use of force cannot be allowed to prevail over international law.* **2** if a belief, custom, situation etc. prevails, it exists among a group of people or in a certain place: [+ **in/among etc.**] *After the riots, a mood of uncertainty still prevails in the neighborhood.* | *Dry mild weather prevailed over much of the nation today.*

prevail on/upon sb *phr. v.* [T] FORMAL to persuade someone: [**prevail on/upon sb to do sth**] *Human rights groups have prevailed upon the governor to intervene.*

pre·vail·ing /pri'veɪlɪŋ/ *adj.* [only before noun] **1** existing or accepted in a particular place or at a particular time: *the prevailing minimum wage* | *prevailing local customs* **2** **a prevailing wind** a wind that blows over a particular area most of the time

prev·a·lent /'prɛvələnt/ *adj.* common at a particular time or in a particular place: *Drug abuse is the most prevalent problem among patients in the hospital.* | *Everyone knows that crime is more prevalent in big cities.* —**prevalence** *n.* [U] *The prevalence of alcoholism among females is estimated to be less than 1 percent.*

pre·var·i·cate /pri'værəˌkeɪt/ *v.* [I] FORMAL to try to hide the truth by not answering questions directly: *Judge Greene said Tate was prevaricating to avoid having to testify against his ex-boss.* —**prevarication** /priˌværə'keɪʃən/ *n.* [C,U]

pre·vent /pri'vɛnt/ *v.* [T] to do something so that something harmful or bad does not happen: *To prevent injuries you should always stretch before exercising.* | [**prevent sb/sth from doing sth**] *Guards stood at the doors to prevent anyone from leaving.* —**preventable** *adj.*: *Smoking is the leading preventable cause of death.*

pre·ven·ta·tive /pri'vɛntətɪv/ *adj.* another form of the word PREVENTIVE

pre·ven·tion /pri'vɛnʃən/ *n.* [U] the act of preventing something, or the actions that you take in order to prevent something: *AIDS prevention efforts* | [+ **of**] *the prevention of cruelty to animals*

pre·ven·tive /pri'vɛntɪv/ also **preventative** *adj.* [only before noun] intended to prevent something that you do not want to happen, such as illness or crime: *preventive health care* (=designed to prevent people from becoming sick) | *Troops were sent to the region as a preventive measure.*

preventive med·i·cine /.ˌ. '.../ *n.* [U] medical treatment, advice, and health education that is designed to prevent disease from happening rather than to cure it

pre·view¹ /'privyu/ *n.* [C] **1** an advertisement for a movie or television program that consists of short parts from it to show what it will be like **2** an occasion when you can see a movie, play etc. before it is shown to the public **3** an opportunity to see or experience what something will be like: *Last night's speech provides a preview of the campaign ahead.* —see also SNEAK PREVIEW

preview² *v.* [T] **1** to see or watch something before someone else or before the public: *The movie was partly re-edited after being previewed by critics.* **2** to show or perform something before it is shown to or performed for the public: *Cliff previewed five of the new songs from his upcoming album in Boston.*

pre·vi·ous /'privias/ *adj.* **1** [only before noun] happening or existing before the event, time, or thing that is being mentioned: *The previous owner did not take very good care of the place.* | *Andi has two children from a previous marriage.* | *Do you have any previous experience with computers?* | *previous offenses/convictions* (=things that a criminal has done, or been judged guilty of, before) | *Some of his previous offenses have involved violence.* **2** **previous to sth** FORMAL before a particular time or event; PRIOR to: *Previous to 1981 there were no women on the Supreme Court.*

pre·vi·ous·ly /'priviasli/ *adv.* before now, or before a particular time: *It's a book of some of his previously* *unpublished stories.* | *Industrial robots perform tasks that were previously done by human operators* | *The car was now worth twice what we'd paid for it six months previously.*

pre·war, pre-war /ˌpriˈwɔr/ *adj., adv.* happening or existing before a war, especially World War II: *The Soviet Union claimed 46% of prewar Poland.* —compare POSTWAR

prey[1] /preɪ/ *n.* [U] **1** an animal that is hunted and eaten by another animal or by a person: *Snakes track their prey by its scent.* **2 a bird/beast of prey** a bird or animal which lives by killing and eating other animals **3 fall prey to sth** to be affected by something bad or harmful: *Increasingly, their industries have fallen prey to foreign competition.* **4** someone who can easily be deceived or influenced: *The elderly are easy prey for such con men.*

prey[2] *v.*
prey on sb/sth *phr. v.* [T] **1** to try to influence, deceive, or harm weaker people: *There is national concern over sex offenders who prey on children.* **2** if an animal or bird preys on another animal or bird it hunts and eats it: *Spiders prey on insects and sometimes small rodents.* **3 prey on your mind** to make you worry continuously: *The accident has been preying on my mind all week.*

prez /prez/ *n.* [C] INFORMAL, HUMOROUS a PRESIDENT

price[1] /praɪs/ *n.*
1 money [C,U] the amount of money for which something is sold, bought, or offered: *House prices are beginning to fall again.* | *[– of] the price of gold* | *They're selling two bras for the price of one at Macy's.* | *The major oil companies raised their prices again last week.* | *We're trying to find the right car at the right price.* | *We could rent a car or take the plane – there's almost no difference in price.* | *high/low price I can't believe how high their prices are!* | **half/full price** *We got all the furniture for half price.* —see Usage Note at COST
2 something bad [U] something bad that you must accept or experience in order to have or do something that you want: *[+ of] He's very busy, but I guess that's the price of success.* | *Travel insurance can be a small price to pay for a vacation without worries.* | *She's gotten the job she wanted, but at what price?*
3 at/for a price used to say that you can buy something, but only if you pay a lot of money: *All this modern equipment comes at a price, you know.*
4 put a price (tag) on sth to say how much something costs or is worth: *How can you put a price on a 150-year-old tree?*
5 at any price if you want to do something at any price you are determined to do it, even if it is very difficult or involves results you do not like: *We all want peace at any price.*
6 not at any price used to say that you would never sell something or do something, even for a lot of money: *Sorry, the car's not for sale at any price.*
7 everyone has their price used to say that you can persuade people to do anything if you give them what they want
8 a price on sb's head a reward for catching or killing someone: *The former drug lord has a $3 million price on his head.*
9 what price fame/glory etc.? SPOKEN, FORMAL used to suggest that perhaps it was not worth achieving something good, because too many bad things have happened as a result: *As we look at the growing trash heaps we may ask ourselves, what price materialism?*
10 at a horse race [C] the chance that a horse will win a race, expressed in numbers; ODDS —see also ASKING PRICE, LIST PRICE, MARKET PRICE, **name your price** (NAME[2] (7)), **pay the penalty/price** (PAY[1] (12))

price[2] *v.* [T] **1** [usually in passive] to set the price of something that is for sale: *These shoes are pretty reasonably priced.* | **[be priced at]** *The wine is priced at $15 to $23 per bottle.* **2** to put the price on goods to show how much they cost **3** to compare the prices of things: *I've been pricing VCRs* **4 price yourself out of the market** to demand too much money for the services or goods that you are selling

price con·trol /ˈ. ˌ./ *n.* [C,U] a system in which the government sets the prices of things: *There was a period of hyper-inflation after price controls were eased in 1992.*

price fix·ing /ˈ. ˌ./ *n.* [U] **1** an illegal agreement between producers and sellers of a product to set its price and make it stay at a high level **2** a system in which the government sets the prices of things

price in·dex /ˈ. ˌ./ *n.* [C] a system of numbers by which the prices of goods can be compared with what they were in the past

price·less /ˈpraɪsləs/ *adj.* **1** so valuable that you cannot calculate a financial value: *priceless works of art* **2** extremely important or useful: *The tablet gives us priceless knowledge about civilization 3,500 years ago.* **3** INFORMAL extremely funny or silly: *There were moments in the movie that were just priceless.*

price list /ˈ. ./ *n.* [C] a list of prices for things being sold

price sup·port /ˈ. ˌ./ *n.* [U] a system in which the government keeps the price of a product at a set level by giving the producer money or buying the product itself

price tag /ˈ. ./ *n.* [C] **1** a small ticket showing the price of something **2** the amount that something costs or is worth: *They stole my favorite jewelry, and you can't really put a price tag on things like that.*

price war /ˈ. ./ *n.* [C] a period when two or more companies reduce the prices of their products, because they are all trying to get the most customers

pric·ey /ˈpraɪsi/ *adj.* **pricier, priciest** INFORMAL expensive: *The food's great, but it's a little pricey.*

prick[1] /prɪk/ *v.* [T] **1** to make a small hole in the surface of something, using a sharp point: *With a fork, prick holes in the cake layers.* | *She accidentally pricked herself with a contaminated needle.* **2** to cause a painful stinging feeling on your skin: *Tears pricked my eyes and stung in my throat.* —compare PRICKLE[2] **3 prick sb's conscience** to make someone feel guilty or ashamed: *Gordimer's novels pricked the conscience of white South Africans.*
prick up *phr. v.* **1** [I,T **prick** sth ↔ **up**] if someone pricks up their ears, or their ears prick up, they start listening carefully because they have heard something interesting: *Jay pricked up his ears when I mentioned vacation.* **2** [I,T **prick** sth ↔ **up**] if an animal pricks up its ears, or its ears prick up, it raises them and points them toward a sound

prick[2] *n.* [C] **1** a slight pain you get when something sharp goes into your skin: *He felt a sudden sting like the prick of a needle in his back.* **2** an act of pricking something: *The lamb rolls fall apart with the first prick of the fork.* —see also PINPRICK **3** a small hole made by a sharp point, especially in your skin: *Blood was dripping from several pricks on his arm.* **4** SPOKEN, OFFENSIVE a stupid nasty man **5** VULGAR a PENIS

prick·le[1] /ˈprɪkəl/ *n.* [C] **1** a long thin sharp point on the skin of some plants and animals **2** a stinging feeling on your skin: *prickles of perspiration*

prickle[2] *v.* [I,T] to have an uncomfortable stinging feeling on your skin, or to make someone feel this: *She could feel the hair prickling the back of her neck.*

prick·ly /ˈprɪkli/ *adj.* **1** covered with prickles: *prickly bushes* **2** something prickly has small points and feels rough and slightly sharp: *His cheeks were prickly with a two-day growth of beard.* **3** causing problems or disagreements: *Myer carefully avoided the prickly issue of offshore drilling rights.* **4** INFORMAL someone who is prickly gets annoyed or offended easily: *Problems at the office were making Todd very prickly.* —**prickliness** *n.* [U]

prickly pear /ˌ.. ˈ./ *n.* [C,U] a type of CACTUS with yellow flowers, or the fruit of this plant

pric·y /ˈpraɪsi/ *adj.* another spelling of PRICEY

pride[1] /praɪd/ *n.*
1 satisfaction/pleasure [U] a feeling of satisfaction and pleasure in what you have achieved, or in

what someone connected with you has achieved: *Lance takes obvious pride in his restaurant and in serving his customers.* | *She always speaks of her daughter's achievements with great pride.* | *The team's success is a source of pride for the whole school.*
2 respect [U] a feeling that you like and respect yourself and that you deserve to be respected by other people; SELF-ESTEEM: *gay pride* | *It's easy for people in these situations to lose their pride.* | *I think you may have hurt his pride.*
3 too much pride [U] a feeling that you are more important, skillful etc. than you really are: *In the end, the main character is destroyed by his own pride and ambition.*
4 sb's pride and joy someone or something that someone is very proud of, and that is important to them: *We don't have any children, so Snowball is our pride and joy.*
5 the pride of sb/sth a) the thing or person that the people in a particular place are most proud of: *Olympic champion Mosley is the pride of Tiburon.* **b)** the best thing in a group: *The ship was the pride of the U.S. fleet.*
6 lions [C] a group of lions
7 pride of place the most important position: *A statue of Buddha from Thailand holds pride of place in the living room.* —see also **swallow your pride** (SWALLOW[1] (4))

pride² v. **pride yourself on sth** to be especially proud of something that you do well, or of a quality that you have: *Arthur prided himself on his knowledge of Italian art.*

s w
3 3
priest /prist/ n. [C] **1** someone who is specially trained to perform religious duties and ceremonies in some Christian churches **2** a man with religious duties and responsibilities in some non-Christian religions

---

USAGE NOTE: PRIEST

WORD CHOICE: priest, minister, pastor, preacher, clergyman, clergy, chaplain
A **priest** is someone, usually but not always a man, in charge of the prayers, ceremonies etc. in the Catholic, Episcopal, or Orthodox churches and in some other non-Christian religions. Someone who does the same job in a Protestant church is called a **minister** or **pastor**. A **preacher** is someone who gives sermons (=a religious talk as part of a church service) in certain Protestant churches: *a Southern Baptist preacher.* More general words are **the clergy** (=religious leaders as a group) or a **clergyman** (=any type of religious leader): *Members of the clergy are relatively well respected in this country.* A priest who takes care of the religious needs of an organization such as a college, hospital, or prison is a **chaplain**. A priest who takes care of the religious needs of members of the military is also a **chaplain**.

---

priest·ess /'pristɪs/ n. [C] a woman with religious duties and responsibilities in some non-Christian religions
priest·hood /'pristhʊd/ n. **1 the priesthood** the job or position of a priest: *He began his religious training for the priesthood.* **2** [C,U] all the priests of a particular religion or country: *the Babylonian priesthood*
Priest·ley /'pristli/**, Joseph** (1733–1804) a British scientist who did important work on the chemistry of gases
priest·ly /'pristli/ adj. relating to a priest: *priestly robes*
prig /prɪg/ n. [C] DISAPPROVING someone who obeys moral rules very carefully, and behaves as if they think they are better than other people —**priggish** adj. —**priggishness** n. [U]
prim /prɪm/ adj. **1** DISAPPROVING very formal and careful in the way you behave, and easily shocked by anything offensive, sexual etc.: *She's a very prim and proper lady.* **2** OLD-FASHIONED small and neat: *a prim bouquet of white flowers* —**primly** adv. —**primness** n. [U]

pri·ma bal·le·ri·na /ˌprimə bælə'rinə/ n. [C] the main woman dancer in a BALLET company
pri·ma·cy /'praɪməsi/ n. [U] FORMAL the state of being the most powerful or important thing or person: *The two companies are struggling for primacy in the software market.* | [**the primacy of sb/sth (over sb/sth)**] *the primacy of the FBI over local organizations*
pri·ma don·na /ˌprimə 'dɑnə, ˌprimə-/ n. [C] **1** someone who thinks that they are very good at what they do, and demands a lot of attention, admiration etc. from other people: *I wouldn't want either player on my team – they're both prima donnas.* **2** the most important woman singer in an OPERA company —compare DIVA
pri·ma fa·cie /ˌpraɪmə 'feɪʃə/ adj. LAW [only before noun] seeming to be true, or based on what seems to be true, even though it may be disproved later: *a prima facie case against him* | *prima facie evidence* —**prima facie** adv.
pri·mal /'praɪməl/ adj. [only before noun] FORMAL **1** primal feelings or behavior seem to belong to a part of people's character that is ancient and animal-like: *What primal urge makes these men want to ride the bull?* **2** basic: *the primal truths of human existence*
pri·mar·i·ly /praɪ'mɛrəli/ adv. mainly: *At my last job I worked primarily with immigrants.* | *Language is primarily a system of signs.* s w
pri·mar·y¹ /'praɪ,mɛri, -məri/ adj. [usually before noun] **1** most important or most basic: *Low attendance was the primary reason for canceling the shows.* | *What is the primary role of parents in bringing up children?* **2** [only before noun] relating to the education of children between five and eleven years old; ELEMENTARY: *primary students* | *primary grades* **3** existing or developing before other things: *a primary infection* —compare SECONDARY s w
primary² n. plural **primaries** [C] **1** an election in the U.S. in which members of a political party in one area vote to decide who will be their party's CANDIDATE for a political position **2** a primary color s w
primary care /ˌ... '.../ also **primary health care** /ˌ... '. ./ n. [U] basic medical treatment that you receive from a doctor that includes advice as to whether you should see a SPECIALIST (=a doctor who deals only with specific types of medical problems): *a primary care physician* (=a doctor who provides primary care)
primary col·or /ˌ... '../ n. [C] in art, one of the three colors – red, yellow, and blue – that can be mixed together to make any other color. Green is sometimes also thought of as a primary color.
primary e·lec·tion /ˌ... .'../ n. [C] a PRIMARY (1)
primary school /'... ,./ n. [C] an ELEMENTARY SCHOOL
primary source /ˌ... '../ n. [C] TECHNICAL something such as a piece of literature or a historical document that people examine in ESSAYs, books etc. —compare SECONDARY SOURCE
primary stress /ˌ... '. / n. [C,U] TECHNICAL the strongest force given, when you are speaking, to a part of a long word, like the force given to "pri" when you say "primary." It is shown in this dictionary by the mark (').
pri·mate /'praɪmeɪt/ n. [C] **1** a member of the group of MAMMALs that includes humans and monkeys **2** also **Primate** the most important BISHOP (=priest with high rank) in a country or an area, especially in the Catholic Church
prime¹ /praɪm/ adj. [only before noun] **1** most important: *Our prime concern is for the child's safety.* | *Bigley was named the prime suspect in the murder.* **2** of the very best quality or kind: *The mall is in a prime location, visible from the freeway.* | *prime cuts of beef* **3 a prime example** a very typical example of something: *Ken is a prime example of someone who always gets what he wants.* **4 be a prime candidate/target etc. (for sth)** to be the person or thing that is most appropriate or most likely to be chosen for a particular purpose: *Their high disposable income makes this group a prime target for advertisers.*
prime² n. **1** [singular] the time in your life when

you are strongest and most active: *He's as handsome as Tyrone Power was in his prime.* | *Ali was by then a little past his prime* (=not as strong or good as he used to be). **2** [U] PRIME RATE **3** [C] A PRIME NUMBER

prime³ v. [T] **1** [usually passive] to prepare someone for a situation, so that they know what to do: [**prime sb to do sth**] *Second baseman Gonzalez is being primed to take over as shortstop.* | [**be primed for sth**] *The riot police were primed for action.* **2** to put a special layer of paint on a surface, to prepare it for the main layer **3** to prepare a gun or MINE² (1) so that it can fire or explode **4 prime the pump** to encourage a business, industry, or activity to develop by putting money or effort into it

prime fac·tor /ˌ. ˈ../ n. [C] TECHNICAL a number that can be divided only by itself and the number one, and is a FACTOR of another number. For example, 7 is a prime factor of 21

prime me·rid·i·an /ˌ. .ˈ.../ n. **the prime meridian** the imaginary line that goes from north to south through Greenwich, England, from which east and west are measured

prime min·is·ter /ˌ. ˈ.../ n. [C] the chief minister and leader of the government in some countries that have a PARLIAMENTARY system of government

prime mov·er /ˌ. ˈ../ n. [C] **1** someone who has great influence in the development of something important: *Kohl always wanted to be seen as a prime mover for European unity.* **2** TECHNICAL a natural force, such as wind or water, that can be used to produce power

prime num·ber /ˌ. ˈ../ n. [C] a number that can be divided only by itself and the number one, for example 3

prim·er¹ /ˈpraɪmɚ/ n. **1** [C,U] paint that is spread over the surface of wood, metal etc. before the main covering of paint is put on **2** [C] a tube containing explosive, used to fire a gun, explode a bomb etc.

prim·er² /ˈprɪmɚ/ n. [C] **1** a set of basic instructions, explanations etc.: *a primer of good management techniques* **2** OLD-FASHIONED a beginner's book in a school subject

prime rate /ˈ. ./ n. [C] the lowest rate of interest at which money can be borrowed, which banks offer to certain customers

prime rib /ˌ. ˈ./ n. [singular,U] a piece of good quality BEEF that is cut from the chest of the animal

prime time /ˌ. ˈ.◂/ n. [U] the time in the evening when the greatest number of people are watching television, between about 7:00 and 10:00 or 11:00 —**prime-time** adj. [only before noun] *prime-time TV*

pri·me·val /praɪˈmivəl/ adj. **1** belonging to the earliest period in the existence of the universe or the Earth: *The sun and planets formed from a primeval cloud of gas about 5 billion years ago.* **2** very ancient: *primeval tropical rainforests* **3** primeval emotions or attitudes are very strong, and seem to come from a part of people's character that is ancient and animal-like

prim·i·tive¹ /ˈprɪmətɪv/ adj. **1** belonging to a society that has a very simple way of life, without modern industries and machines: *Mead's research focused on three primitive New Guinea tribes.* | *primitive art* **2** belonging to an early stage in the development of humans or of plants or animals: *primitive man* | *fossils of primitive algae* **3** very simple or uncomfortable, without modern features: *primitive machinery* | *The cabin is primitive and lacks running water.* —**primitively** adv. —**primitiveness** n. [U]

primitive² n. [C] **1** used in past times to mean someone from a simple society who is not used to modern machines or ways of life, now considered offensive **2** a painter who paints simple pictures like those of a child **3** a painter or SCULPTOR of the time before the Renaissance

pri·mo·gen·i·ture /ˌpraɪmouˈdʒɛnətʃɚ/ n. [U] TECHNICAL the system by which property owned by a man goes to his oldest son after his death, used especially in past times

pri·mor·di·al /praɪˈmɔrdiəl/ adj. FORMAL **1** existing at the beginning of time and the beginning of the Earth:

the primordial origins of life **2** in the simplest most basic form: *primordial instincts*

primp /prɪmp/ v. [I,T] to make yourself look attractive by arranging your hair, putting on MAKEUP etc.: *Are you through primping? I need to use the bathroom.*

prim·rose /ˈprɪmrouz/ n. **1** [C] a small wild plant with colored flowers, or a flower from this plant **2** [U] primrose yellow

primrose yel·low /ˌ.. ˈ..◂/ n. [U] a light yellow color —**primrose yellow** adj.

prince /prɪns/ n. [C] **1** the son of a king or queen, or one of their close male relatives: *Prince William* **2** a male ruler of a small country or state: *Prince Rainier of Monaco* **3** LITERARY OR HUMOROUS a man who is regarded as very special or as the best of a group of men: *Robbins was a prince among story-tellers.* | *the prince of the junk bond salesmen*

Prince Charm·ing /ˌ. ˈ../ n. [C] INFORMAL OR HUMOROUS a perfect man that a young girl might dream about meeting

Prince Ed·ward Is·land /prɪns ˌɛdwɚd ˈaɪlənd/ a PROVINCE in southeast Canada that is an island in the Gulf of St. Lawrence

prince·ly /ˈprɪnsli/ adj. [only before noun] **1 princely sum/fee/price etc.** an expression meaning a large amount of money, often used in a joking way to mean a very small amount of money: *Harris earned the princely sum of $24 for all her work.* **2** belonging to or relating to a prince: *the princely states* **3** FORMAL very good or generous: *a princely gift*

prin·cess /ˈprɪnsɪs, -sɛs/ n. [C] **1** the daughter of a king or queen, or one of their close female relatives: *Princess Anne* **2** the wife of a prince

prin·ci·pal¹ /ˈprɪnsəpəl/ adj. [only before noun] most important; MAIN: *Oil is the country's principal source of income.* | *Your taxes depend on where your principal residence is located.* —see also PRINCIPALLY

principal² n. **1** [C] someone who is in charge of a school **2** [singular] an amount of money lent to someone, put into a business etc., on which INTEREST is paid **3** [C often plural] the main person in a business or organization who can make business decisions **4** [C] the main performer in a play, group of musicians etc.

prin·ci·pal·i·ty /ˌprɪnsəˈpæləti/ n. plural **principalities** [C] a country ruled by a PRINCE

prin·ci·pal·ly /ˈprɪnsəpli/ adv. mainly: *The road is used principally for military purposes.*

principal parts /ˌ... ˈ./ n. [plural] TECHNICAL the parts of a verb from which other parts are formed. In English they are the INFINITIVE, past tense, present participle, and past participle

prin·ci·ple /ˈprɪnsəpəl/ n. **1** [C,U] a moral rule or set of ideas about right and wrong, which influences you to behave in a particular way: *He'll do anything to make money. The man has no principles.* | *They refused to print the photographs as a matter of principle.* | *Julie doesn't eat meat on principle* (=because she thinks it is morally wrong, not because she dislikes it). | *No, it wasn't a lot of money, but it's the principle of the thing. You have to ask before you borrow.* | *I wouldn't work for a tobacco company – it's against my principles.* **2** [C] a belief or idea on which a set of ideas, a set of laws, a system for doing something etc. is based: [**+ of**] *the principle of separation of church and state* | *the basic principles of Marxism* | [**principle that**] *The method is based on the principle that children learn best through stories.* | *It is a principle of international law that every state has the right to defend itself.* | *Many of the ideals that the U.S. was built on have become democratic first principles* (=most important and basic beliefs). **3** [C] a basic rule that explains the way something works, such as a machine or a natural force in the universe: *The principles governing the world of physics are unchanging.* | *Archimedes' principle* **4 in principle a)** if you agree in principle, you agree about a general plan or idea but have not thought about the details yet: *The government has agreed in principle to hold elections next year.* **b)** if you believe in something in principle, you believe in the idea of it but are sometimes willing to take actions that do not support this belief: *Many people who support the First Amendment in principle want to restrict free speech in certain situations.* **5 a man/woman of principle** someone who has strong ideas about what is morally right or wrong

prin·ci·pled /'prɪnsəpəld/ *adj.* [usually before noun] **1** having strong clear beliefs about what is morally right and wrong: *principled leadership* **2** based on clear beliefs or ideas: *principled opposition to the idea of lower taxation*

P

SW
1
3

print[1] /prɪnt/ *v.*
1 words by machine **a)** [I,T] to produce words, numbers, or pictures on paper or other material, using a machine which puts ink onto the surface: *Why won't this printer print?* | *I'd like to print it in color if I can.* | [print sth with sth] *Stan had the cards printed with his name and address.* | [print sth on/across sth] *I called the 800 number that was printed on the form.* | [print sth in sth] *This part should be printed in italics.* | *The words to the song are printed in Japanese.* **b)** [I] to be printed by a computer: *How long will it take for this file to print?*
2 produce books etc. [T] to produce many copies of a book, newspaper etc.: *His second novel was originally printed in Paris.*
3 in a newspaper [T] to include a letter, speech, picture etc. in a newspaper, book, or magazine; PUBLISH: *Brown's suing the magazine for printing nude photos of him.* | *They printed my letter in the Sunday paper.*
4 write [I,T] to write words by hand without joining the letters: *Please print your name in the blank.*
5 photograph [T] to produce a photograph on special paper: *How do you want the pictures printed?*
6 print money if a government prints money, it produces paper money, especially in order to pay for something: *The government was printing money to finance a reckless war.* —see also **a license to print money** (LICENSE[1] (7))
7 the printed word language in printed form, especially when compared with spoken language
8 the printed page writing that has been PUBLISHed
9 mark [T usually passive] to make a mark on a surface by pressing something onto it: *The mark of a child's shoe was clearly printed in the mud.*
print sth ↔ **out/off** *phr. v.* [T] to produce a printed copy of something you have written using a computer: *I'm going to go print my essay out at the computer lab.*

SW
2
3

print[2] *n.*
1 books/newspapers [U] writing that has been printed in books, newspapers etc.: *The information is available in several formats including print, CD-ROM, and from our website.* | *It's always exciting to see your own work in print* (=printed in a book, newspaper etc.). | *By the time the news appeared in print, most people had already heard about it.* | *They pay $50 for each story that makes it into print* (=gets printed).
2 be out of print if a book is out of print, it is not being printed anymore, and you cannot buy new copies
3 be in print if a book is in print, new copies of it are still being printed: *More than 40 of her books are still in print.*
4 the fine/small print the details of a legal document, often in very small writing: *Don't sign anything until you've read the fine print.*
5 letters [U] the letters in which something is printed: *Most of her novels are also available in large-print editions.*
6 picture [C] **a)** a picture or design that has been printed from a small sheet of metal, block of wood etc. **b)** a copy of a painting produced by photography
7 photograph [C] a photograph in the form of a

picture that has been produced from a film: *I'll order two sets of prints, and you can have one of them.*
8 mark [C] **a)** a mark made on a surface or in a soft substance by something that has been pressed onto it: *Some cat left its paw prints on my car* | *I don't want your dirty hand prints all over the walls.* —see also FOOTPRINT **b)** a word for a mark made by the pattern of lines on the ends of your finger, used especially by police; FINGERPRINT: *We found a set of prints on the door.*
9 movie [C] a copy of a movie: *A new print of "Citizen Kane" has just been released.*
10 cloth [C,U] cloth, especially cotton, on which a colored pattern has been printed, or the pattern itself: *She was wearing a print dress and white shoes.* | *a floral print*

print·a·ble /'prɪntəbəl/ *adj.* [usually in negatives] appropriate, polite enough etc. to be printed and read by everyone: *Some of the comments we received were not even printable* (=contained offensive or sexual language). —compare UNPRINTABLE

printed cir·cuit /,.. '../ *n.* [C] a set of connections between points in a piece of electrical equipment which uses a thin line of metal, not wire, to CONDUCT (=carry) the electricity

printed mat·ter /'.. ,..., ,.. '../ *n.* [U] printed material, such as advertisements or books, that can be sent by mail at a cheap rate

print·er /'prɪntə/ *n.* [C] **1** a machine connected to a computer that puts documents from the computer onto paper —compare PRINTING PRESS —see picture on page 426 **2** someone employed in the business of printing

SW
2

print·ing /'prɪntɪŋ/ *n.* **1** [U] the action, process, or business of making books, magazines, etc. by pressing or copying letters or photographs onto paper: *printing technology* **2** [C] an action of printing copies of a book for sale: *The book is in its fourth printing.*

printing ink /'.. ,./ *n.* [U] a type of ink that dries very quickly and is used in printing books, newspapers etc.

printing press /'.. ,./ also **printing ma·chine** /'.. .,./ *n.* [C] a machine that prints newspapers, books etc., used especially before computers were common

print·mak·ing /'prɪnt͵meɪkɪŋ/ *n.* [U] the art of printing pictures using a small sheet of metal, a block of wood etc.

print·out /'prɪntaʊt/ *n.* [C,U] a sheet or length of paper with printed information on it, produced from a computer

print run /'. ./ *n.* [C] all the copies of a book, newspaper etc. that are printed at one time: *an initial print run of 1 million copies*

print shop /'. ./ *n.* [C] a small store that prints and copies documents, cards etc. for customers

pri·on /'prɪɒn/ *n.* [C] a very small piece of PROTEIN that is thought to cause some infectious brain diseases

pri·or[1] /'praɪə/ *adj.* **1** prior to sth FORMAL before: *Prior to 1492, no human in the Old World had ever eaten corn.* | *They're planning to talk to Joe prior to the meeting.* **2** [only before noun] arranged or happening before the present situation or before something else happens: *Most applicants had no prior experience of working with children.* | *Pets are permitted only by prior arrangement with the management.* | *I'm sorry, I have a prior engagement* (=something you have planned to do) and *won't be able to attend.* **3** prior notice/warning a warning or announcement made before something else happens, especially something bad: *He was thrown out of the apartment without prior notice.* **4** a prior arrest/conviction LAW a previous occasion when someone has been ARRESTed for a crime or found guilty of it in a court of law: *Jackson has no history of violence, and no prior convictions.*

prior[2] *n.* [C] **1** INFORMAL a previous occasion when someone has been found guilty of a crime: *two priors for homicide* **2** the man in charge of a PRIORY, or the priest next in rank to the person in charge of an ABBEY

pri·or·ess /ˈpraɪərɪs/ *n.* [C] the woman in charge of a PRIORY

pri·or·i·tize /praɪˈɔrəˌtaɪz/ *v.* **1** [I,T] to put several jobs, problems etc. in order of importance, so that you can deal with the most important ones first: *Identify all the tasks you have to do, then prioritize.* **2** [T] to deal with one job or problem before everything else, because it is the most important: *The public wants to see the fight against crime prioritized.* —**prioritization** /praɪˌɔrətəˈzeɪʃən/ *n.* [U]

s w **pri·or·i·ty** /praɪˈɔrəti/ *n. plural* **priorities 1** [C] the thing that you think is most important and that needs attention before anything else: *Our priority right now is to get food and medical supplies to the region.* | *the need to establish priorities* (=to decide what is most important and urgent). | *Hawkins is frustrated by the low priority the government has put on education.* | *a top/high/first priority Balancing the budget is one of his top priorities.* **2 have/ take/get priority** also **be given priority** to be considered most important and dealt with before anything or anyone else: *Restaurant seating is limited and hotel guests are given priority.* | [+ over] *It's normal among teenagers for socializing to take priority over schoolwork.* **3 get your priorities straight/ right** etc. to form a clear idea of what is most important or urgent: *I need to take a little time off just to get my priorities in order.* —**priority** *adj.* [only before noun] *We can only deal with priority cases.*

priority mail /ˈ... ˌ./ *n.* [U] a type of mail service that is faster and more expensive than regular mail

pri·o·ry /ˈpraɪəri/ *n.* a place for a group of MONKS or NUNS (=Christian men or women living a religious life separately from other people) which is smaller and less important than an ABBEY.

prism /ˈprɪzəm/ *n.* [C] **1** a transparent block of glass that breaks up white light into different colors **2** TECHNICAL a solid object with matching ends and several sides which are the same width all the way up

pris·mat·ic /prɪzˈmætɪk/ *adj.* TECHNICAL **1** using or containing a PRISM: *prismatic crystal* **2** a prismatic color is very clear and bright

s w **pris·on** /ˈprɪzən/ *n.* **1** [C,U] a large building where people are kept as a punishment for a crime, or while waiting to go to court for their TRIAL: *a maximum security prison* | *Schenk spent 26 years in prison for killing his girlfriend.* | *He is serving a 15-year prison sentence* (=the length of time someone must stay in prison). | *Nine of the 15 men were sent to prison for their role in the conspiracy.* **2** [U] the system of sending people to be kept in a prison: *Prison is an expensive and inefficient way to deal with social problems.* —see also IMPRISON

prison camp /ˈ.. ˌ./ *n.* [C] a special prison in which PRISONERS OF WAR are kept

prison cell /ˈ.. ˌ./ *n.* [C] a locked room where prisoners are kept

s w **pris·on·er** /ˈprɪzənə/ *n.* [C] **1** someone who is kept in a prison as a punishment for a crime: *The county has 90 prisoners in a jail designed for 29.* **2** someone who is taken by force and kept somewhere, for example during a war: *enemy prisoners* | *Rebels were still holding two Americans prisoner at the end of the week.* | *George fought in World War II and was taken prisoner by the Germans* (=caught and kept as a prisoner).

prisoner of con·science /ˌ... ˈ. ˌ./ *n.* [C] someone who is put in prison because of their political beliefs

prisoner of war /ˌ... ˈ./ *n.* [C] a soldier, member of the navy etc. who is caught by the enemy during a war and kept as a prisoner: *Only about 150 of the prisoners of war were freed.*

pris·sy /ˈprɪsi/ *adj.* very worried about behaving correctly, and easily shocked by anything offensive or sexual: *She always irritated me – she was so prissy.* | *a look of prissy disapproval* —**prissily** *adv.* —**prissiness** *n.* [U]

pris·tine /ˈprɪˌstin, prɪˈstin/ *adj.* completely unspoiled by use, or completely clean: *the pristine whiteness of newly fallen snow* | *It was an old Ford Thunderbird in pristine condition.*

prith·ee /ˈprɪði/ *interjection* OLD USE please

pri·va·cy /ˈpraɪvəsi/ *n.* [U] **1** the condition of being able to be alone, and not seen or heard by other people: *If you want privacy you can close the door.* **2** the condition of being able to keep your own affairs secret: *the constitutional right to privacy*

pri·vate¹ /ˈpraɪvɪt/ *adj.*
1 **not for everyone** only for use by one particular person or group, not for everyone: *private property* | *Each guest has a private bathroom.*
2 **secret a)** private feelings, information, or opinions are personal or secret and not for other people to know about: *After his death the author's family released many of his private papers.* | *Don't read that – it's private.* **b)** a private meeting, conversation etc. involves only a small number of people, and is not for other people to know about: *The two leaders held private talks in June to try to resolve the dispute.*
3 **not government** [only before noun] not relating to owned by, or paid for by the government: *a private college*
4 **not work** separate from and not relating to your work or your official position: *Earlier the Dalai Lama had spent six days in England on a private visit.* | *Susan is trying to balance her private life and her work.*
5 **quiet place** quiet and without lots of people: *We found a private little spot to set up our tent.*
6 **person** [only before noun] a private person is one who likes being alone, and does not talk much about their thoughts or feelings: *He doesn't talk much about his family – he's a very private person.*
7 **a private joke** a joke made between friends, family members etc. that other people do not understand —see also PRIVATELY

private² *n.* **1 in private** without other people being present: *I'd rather talk about it with you in private, if you don't mind.* —opposite **in public** (PUBLIC² (2)) **2** [C] also **Private** a soldier of the lowest rank **3 privates** [plural] PRIVATE PARTS

private de·tec·tive /ˌ.. .ˈ../ *n.* [C] someone who can be employed to look for information or missing people, or to follow people and report on what they do

private ed·u·ca·tion /ˌ.. ..ˈ../ *n.* [U] education that you must pay for, rather than public education which is provided by the government

private en·ter·prise /ˌ.. ˈ...ˌ./ *n.* **1** [U] the economic system in which private businesses are allowed to compete freely with each other, and the government does not control industry —see also PRIVATE SECTOR **2** [C] a business established by a single person or group

pri·va·teer /ˌpraɪvəˈtɪr/ *n.* [C] **1** an armed ship in past times that was not in the navy but attacked and robbed enemy ships carrying goods **2** someone who commanded or sailed on a ship of this type

private eye /ˌ.. ˈ./ *n.* [C] INFORMAL a PRIVATE DETECTIVE

private first class /ˌ.. . ˈ./ *n.* [C] a soldier in the U.S. Army or Marines with a rank above PRIVATE² (2)

private in·ves·ti·ga·tor /ˌ.. .ˈ....ˌ./ *n.* [C] a PRIVATE DETECTIVE

pri·vate·ly /ˈpraɪvɪtli/ *adv.* **1** without other people around: *Could I speak to you privately?* **2** not publicly or as part of your official duties: [sentence adverb] *Privately, officials admit that mistakes were made.* **3** if you feel or think something privately, you do not tell anyone about it: *Many villagers privately feared the worst.* | [sentence adverb] *Privately, I knew the treatment wasn't working.* **4** without the involvement of the government or without money from the government: *privately owned land*

private parts /ˌ.. ˈ./ *n.* [plural] OFTEN HUMOROUS an expression meaning "sex organs," used when you want to avoid naming them directly

private prac·tice /ˌ.. ˈ..ˌ./ *n.* [U] the business of a professional person, especially a doctor or lawyer, who works alone rather than with others

private school /ˌ.. ˌ./ n. [C] a school not supported by government money, where education must be paid for by the parents of the children

pri·vate sec·re·tar·y /ˌ.. ˈ..../ n. [C] a secretary who is employed to help one person, especially with secret business

private sec·tor /ˈ.. ˌ../ n. **the private sector** the industries and services in a country that are owned and run by private companies, and not by the state or government: *Increasingly, researchers are seeking funds from the private sector.* —**private-sector** adj. [only before noun] *private-sector jobs* —compare PUBLIC SECTOR

private view·ing /ˌ... ˈ../ n. [C] an occasion when a few people are invited to see a show of paintings, a movie etc. before the public sees it

pri·va·tion /praɪˈveɪʃən/ n. [C,U] FORMAL a lack or loss of the things that everyone needs, such as food, warmth, and shelter: *He had endured times of privation as a boy, but he never dwelled on it.*

pri·va·ti·za·tion /ˌpraɪvətəˈzeɪʃən/ n. [C, U] the action or process of privatizing something

pri·vat·ize /ˈpraɪvəˌtaɪz/ v. [T] to sell an organization, industry, or service that was previously controlled and owned by a government to a private company: *The company was privatized by the government in 1987.* —compare NATIONALIZE

priv·et /ˈprɪvət/ n. [U] a bush with leaves that stay green all year, often grown to form a HEDGE

priv·i·lege /ˈprɪvlɪdʒ, -vəlɪdʒ/ n. **1** [C] a special advantage or right that is given only to one person or group: *If convicted, he could lose his diplomatic privileges.* | [the privilege of (doing) sth] *Commuters pay high prices for the privilege of parking close to their offices.* **2** [singular] something that you are lucky to have the chance to do, and that you enjoy very much: [the privilege of (doing) sth] *I had the privilege of working with him once back in 1972.* | [a privilege to do sth] *It's a privilege to finally meet you.* **3** [U] a situation in which people who are rich or of a high social class have many more advantages than other people: *Compton grew up in an atmosphere of privilege in the best part of St. Louis.*

priv·i·leged /ˈprɪvlɪdʒd/ adj. **1** having advantages because of your wealth, high social position etc.: *a member of the privileged class* | *Some see the Republicans as the party of the privileged few.* **2** having a special advantage or a chance to do something that most people cannot do: *Taylor enjoyed privileged access to the presidential files.* | [privileged to do sth] *I feel privileged to serve on the committee.* **3** LAW privileged information does not have to be given even if a court of law asks for it

priv·y¹ /ˈprɪvi/ adj. **1 privy to sth** FORMAL sharing in the knowledge of facts that are secret: *Only a handful of executives were privy to the business plan.* **2** OLD USE secret and private —**privily** adv.

privy² n. [C] an outside toilet, used in past times

prix fixe /ˌpri ˈfiks◂, ˈfɪks/ adj. **a prix fixe meal/dinner/menu** a complete meal in a restaurant that is offered for a single price: *a $40 prix fixe four-course dinner*

prize¹ /praɪz/ n. [C] **1** something that is given to someone who is successful in a competition, race, game of chance etc.: *First prize is a trip to Orlando.* | [+ for] *She should win the prize for the most original costume.* | *Enter now for the chance to win any of these fabulous prizes.* | *Suu Kyi was awarded the peace prize in 1991.* —see also CONSOLATION PRIZE **2** something that is very valuable to you or very important to try to get: *New York State, with 33 votes in the electoral college, is seen as a major prize.* | *She's going to marry Simon, but I don't think he's much of a prize.*

prize² adj. [only before noun] **1 prize money** that is given to the person who wins a competition, race etc. **2** good enough to win a prize or to have

won a prize: *a herd of prize cattle* —see also PRIZE-WINNING **3** [no comparative] best, most important, or most useful: *one of the team's prize players* —compare PRIZED

prize³ v. [T] to regard something as very important or valuable: *This culture prizes conformity, and frowns on any form of rebellion.*

prized /praɪzd/ adj. extremely important or valuable to someone: *Matsutake mushrooms are highly prized for their fragrance.* | *The transistor radio was the old man's most prized possession.*

prize·fight /ˈpraɪzfaɪt/ n. [C] a BOXING match in which the competitors are paid —**prizefighter** n. [C] —**prizefighting** n. [U]

prize win·ner /ˈ. ˌ../ n. [C] someone who wins a prize: *a Pulitzer Prize winner*

prize-win·ning /ˈ. ˌ../ adj. [only before noun] a prize-winning movie, book, person, animal etc. has won a prize: *a prize-winning composer*

pro¹ /proʊ/ n. plural **pros** [C] **1** INFORMAL someone who earns money by doing a particular sport or using a particular skill; PROFESSIONAL: *a golf pro* **2** INFORMAL someone who has had a lot of experience with a particular type of situation: *He answered reporters' questions like an old pro.* | *Megan's become a real pro at manipulating people.* **3 the pros and cons (of sth)** the advantages and disadvantages of something: *The brochure explains the pros and cons of each health-care plan.* —see also PRO FORMA, PRO RATA

pro² adj. INFORMAL **1** doing a job, sport, or activity for money; PROFESSIONAL: *a pro basketball player* | **turn/go pro** (=become a pro) *Both skaters turned pro last year.* **2** done by or relating to people who are paid for what they do; PROFESSIONAL: *pro wrestling*

pro³ prep. if you are pro an idea, plan, suggestion etc., you support it or hope that it will succeed: *The party claims to be very pro family.*

pro- /proʊ/ prefix favorable toward or supporting something: *a pro-environment governor* | *a pro-democracy demonstration*

pro·ac·tive /ˌ. ˈ../ adj. making changes to improve something before problems happen, rather than reacting to problems and then changing things: *School officials need to be proactive in minimizing dangers on campus.*

pro-am /ˌproʊ ˈæm◂/ n. [C] a competition, especially in GOLF, for both PROFESSIONALs (=people who play for money) and AMATEURs (=people who play just for fun)

prob·a·bil·i·ty /ˌprɑbəˈbɪləti/ n. plural **probabilities 1** [singular,U] how likely it is that something will happen, exist, or be true: [+ of] *For a woman over the age of 40, the probability of remarrying is small.* | **there is a strong/high/distinct etc. probability that** *Deaf couples face a very high probability that any child they have will be deaf, too.* | **The probability is that** (=it is likely that) *education will be the main issue in the election.* **2 in all probability** used to say that you think something is very likely to happen: *In all probability, Kelsey will resign by the end of the year.* **3** [C] something that is likely to happen or exist: *War is a real probability.* **4** [C,U] the mathematically calculated chance that something will happen: *Genetic tests show a 99.4 percent probability that Hill is the child's father.*

prob·a·ble¹ /ˈprɑbəbəl/ adj. likely to exist, happen, or be true: *Light rain is probable tomorrow evening.* | *Measles is the probable cause of illness in the three athletes.* | **It is probable that** *the jury will find the defendant guilty.* —opposite IMPROBABLE (1)

probable² n. [C] someone who is likely to be chosen for a team, to win a race etc.

prob·a·ble cause /ˌ... ˈ./ n. [U] LAW good reasons to believe that someone has done something illegal: *The police had probable cause to search the two men for drugs.*

prob·a·bly /ˈprɑbəbli/ adv. used to say that something is likely to happen, exist, or be true: *I'll probably be late for dinner tonight.* | *"Where is Joan?" "She's probably still at work."* | [sentence adverb] *"Are* you going to take the job if they offer it to you?" "Yeah I will, probably."

pro·bate[1] /ˈproʊbeɪt/ n. [U] LAW the legal process of deciding that someone's WILL[2] (2) has been correctly made, or the court where this takes place

probate[2] v. [T] LAW to prove that a WILL[2] (2) is legal

pro·ba·tion /proʊˈbeɪʃən/ n. [U] **1** a system that allows some criminals to avoid going to prison, if they behave well and see a PROBATION OFFICER regularly for a specific period of time: *A judge gave Brown six months probation.* | **put/place sb on probation** *Preston was put on probation for three years.* —compare PAROLE[1] **2** a specific period of time in which you must improve your work so that you will not have to leave your job: **put/place sb on probation** *Lubbell will be put on probation and fired if the situation does not improve.* **3** a specific period of time during which someone who has just started a job is tested to see whether they are appropriate for that job: *All new employees are on probation for nine months.* —**probationary** adj.

pro·ba·tion·er /proʊˈbeɪʃənɚ/ n. [C] **1** someone who has broken the law and has been put on probation **2** someone who has recently started a job and who is being tested to see whether they are appropriate for it

probation of·fi·cer /.ˈ.. ,.../ n. [C] someone whose job is to watch, advise, and help people who have broken the law and are on probation

probe[1] /proʊb/ v. [I,T] **1** to ask questions in order to find things out, especially things that other people do not want you to know: [+ into] *A federal grand jury will probe into the financial dealings between the two men.* | [probe sth] *Investigators are probing the causes of the train wreck.* **2** to put a long thin instrument into something, in order to examine it or to try to find something: *I'm tired of the doctors poking and probing me with needles and tubes.* —**probing** adj.: *probing questions* —**probingly** adv.

probe[2] n. [C] **1** a long thin metal instrument that doctors and scientists use to examine parts of the body inside you **2** a SPACE PROBE **3** a word meaning a very thorough process of asking questions about something, used especially in newspapers: *Ammiano called for a probe into reports of voter fraud.*

pro·bi·ty /ˈproʊbəti/ n. [U] FORMAL complete honesty: *Politicians are not known for their probity or punctuality.*

prob·lem /ˈprɑbləm/ n. [C] **1** a situation that causes difficulties: [+ of] *the problem of homelessness* | *Unemployment is a **serious problem** in our community.* | *These chemicals could **cause** health **problems** in babies.* | *Give me a call if you **have** any more **problems** with your back.* | **a drug/crime/alcohol etc. problem** *Mike might have an alcohol problem.* | *Blaming the doctors will not **solve** your **problem**.* —see Usage Note at TROUBLE[1] **2** a question that must be answered, especially one relating to numbers or facts on a test: *The first section of the test will contain twenty algebra problems.* **3** **a problem child/family/drinker etc.** a child, family, drinker etc. who behaves in a way that is difficult for other people to deal with

reason. **9 Do you have a problem with that?** also NONSTANDARD **You got a problem with that?** used to ask someone why they oppose you or disagree with you, in a way that shows you think they are wrong: *"You're going to wear that dress?" "Do you have a problem with that?"*

prob·lem·at·ic /ˌprɑbləˈmætɪk/ also **prob·lem·at·i·cal** /ˌprɑbləˈmætɪkəl/ adj. full of problems and difficult to deal with: *Enforcing this law has been problematic.* —**problematically** /-kli/ adv.

problem-solv·ing /ˈ.. ,../ n. [U] finding ways of doing things, or finding answers to problems: *Most of the test questions involve problem-solving.* —**problem-solving** adj. [only before noun]

pro bo·no /ˌproʊ ˈboʊnoʊ/ adj. LAW used to describe work that someone, especially a lawyer, does without getting paid for it: *Turner has agreed to handle the case on a pro bono basis.*

pro·bos·cis /prəˈbɑsɪs, -ˈbɑskɪs/ n. plural **pro·boscises** TECHNICAL [C] **1** a long thin tube that forms part of the mouth of some insects and worms **2** the long thin nose of certain animals, such as the ELEPHANT

pro·ce·dure /prəˈsidʒɚ/ n. **1** [C,U] the correct or normal method of doing something: [+ for] *Could you explain the procedure for shutting down the computer?* | **correct/proper/standard etc. procedure** *The police did not **follow standard procedure** in investigating the murder.* **2** [C] a medical treatment or operation that is done in a particular way: *Parcells underwent a procedure last week to repair his knee.* —**procedural** adj.   S W

pro·ceed /prəˈsid, proʊ-/ v. [I] **1** to continue to do something that has already been started: *Contract negotiations are proceeding smoothly.* | [+ with] *Russia decided to proceed with economic reforms.* | [+ to] *Let's proceed to the next item on the agenda.* **2 proceed to do sth** an expression meaning to do something next, used especially about something annoying or surprising: *Royston then proceeded to deny all the accusations.* **3** [always + adv./prep.] FORMAL to move in a particular direction: [+ in/to etc.] *Passengers for the Miami flight should proceed to gate 25.* —see also PROCEEDS   S W

proceed against sb phr. v. [T] LAW to begin a legal case against someone: *The agency decided not to proceed against Cowley.*

pro·ceed·ing /prəˈsidɪŋ/ n. [C usually plural] **1** an event or series of actions: *Brady directs the proceedings at the board meetings.* **2** actions taken in a law court or in a legal case: *divorce proceedings* **3** the official records of meetings

pro·ceeds /ˈproʊsidz/ n. [plural] the money that has been gained from doing or selling something: *All the proceeds from the concert will go to charity.*

pro·cess[1] /ˈprɑsɛs, ˈproʊ-/ n. [C]   S W
1 developments a series of natural developments or events that produce gradual change: *the human reproductive process* | *the aging process*
2 actions a series of actions that someone takes in order to achieve a particular result: *The process of applying to a college is often very time-consuming.*
3 be in the process of doing sth to have started doing something and not yet be finished: *Our office is in the process of upgrading all the computers.*
4 process of elimination a way of discovering the cause of something by carefully examining each possibility until only the correct one is left: *By process of elimination, scientists were able to find a cure.*
5 in the process while you are doing something or while something is happening: *The Warriors won, but almost gave their coach a heart attack in the process.*
6 industry a system or a treatment of materials that is used to produce goods: *an advanced industrial process*
7 law TECHNICAL a legal case, considered as a series of actions —see also DUE PROCESS

s w
3 3

process² *v.* [T] **1** to treat food or some other substance by adding other substances to it or heating it in order to give it color, keep it fresh etc.: *The milk must be maintained at this temperature until it is processed.* **2** to deal with information in an official way: *It will take four to six weeks to process your loan application.* **3** to print a picture from a photographic film **4** to put information into a computer to be examined —see also DATA PROCESSING

pro·cess³ /prəˈsɛs/ *v.* [I always + adv./prep.] FORMAL to move in a procession, or to move very slowly and seriously

pro·cessed /ˈprɑsɛst/ *adj.* processed foods are specially treated to give them color, keep them fresh etc.: *Highly processed foods are not as nutritious as fresh foods.* | **processed cheese/meat/food etc.** *processed American cheese slices*

pro·ces·sion /prəˈsɛʃən/ *n.* **1** [C,U] a line of people or vehicles moving slowly as part of a ceremony: *a funeral procession* | *They marched **in procession** to the Capitol Building.* **2** [C] several people or things of the same kind, appearing or happening one after the other: [+ of] *The family has endured an endless procession of tragic events.*

pro·ces·sion·al¹ /prəˈsɛʃənl/ *n.* [C] **1** a procession **2** a piece of music that is played during a procession

processional² *adj.* [only before noun] relating to or used during a procession: *Flags lined the processional route.*

pro·ces·sor /ˈprɑsɛsɚ/ *n.* [C] the central part of a computer that does the calculations needed to deal with the information it is given; CENTRAL PROCESSING UNIT —see also FOOD PROCESSOR, WORD PROCESSOR

pro-choice /ˌ. ˈ./ *adj.* someone who is pro-choice believes that women have a right to ABORTION, and uses this word to describe their own beliefs: *pro-choice activists* —compare PRO-LIFE

pro·claim /proʊˈkleɪm, prə-/ *v.* [T] FORMAL **1** to say publicly or officially that something important is true or exists: *Phillips has repeatedly proclaimed his innocence.* | [proclaim sb/sth sth] *The cave was proclaimed a national monument in 1909.* **2** to show something clearly or be a sign of something: *Nearly everyone there wore a pin proclaiming their support of the union.*

proc·la·ma·tion /ˌprɑkləˈmeɪʃən/ *n.* **1** [C] an official public statement about something that is important: *The President issued a proclamation declaring the county a national disaster area.* **2** [U] the act of stating something officially and publicly: *the country's proclamation of independence*

pro·cliv·i·ty /proʊˈklɪvəti/ *n. plural* **proclivities** [C] FORMAL a strong liking for something or a natural tendency to do something, especially something bad: [+ for] *Children have a proclivity for acting without thinking of the danger.*

pro·con·sul /proʊˈkɑnsəl/ *n.* [C] someone who governed a part of the ancient Roman Empire —**proconsular** *adj.*

pro·con·su·late /proʊˈkɑnsəlɪt/ also **pro·con·sul·ship** /proʊˈkɑnsəlˌʃɪp/ *n.* [C] the rank of a proconsul, or the time during which someone was a proconsul

pro·cras·ti·nate /prəˈkræstəˌneɪt/ *v.* [I] to delay doing something that you ought to do, usually because you do not want to do it: *It's time to stop procrastinating and get the job done.* —**procrastination** /prəˌkræstəˈneɪʃən/ *n.* [U] —**procrastinator** /prəˈkræstəˌneɪtɚ/ *n.* [C]

pro·cre·ate /ˈproʊkriˌeɪt/ *v.* [I,T] FORMAL to produce children or baby animals —**procreation** /ˌproʊkriˈeɪʃən/ *n.* [U]

proc·tor¹ /ˈprɑktɚ/ *n.* [C] someone who watches students during a test to make sure that they do not cheat

proctor² *v.* [T] to watch students during a test to make sure that they do not cheat

proc·u·ra·tor /ˈprɑkyəˌreɪtɚ/ *n.* [C] **1** someone who manages the government of an area, especially someone who did this during the Roman Empire **2** someone such as a lawyer who manages someone's affairs

pro·cure /proʊˈkyʊr, prə-/ *v.* [T] FORMAL to obtain something, especially something that is difficult to get: [procure sth for sb] *The money will be used to procure medicine and food for local orphanages.* —**procurable** *adj.* —**procurement** *n.* [U] —**procurer** *n.* [C]

prod¹ /prɑd/ *v.* **prodded, prodding** [I,T] **1** to strongly encourage someone to do something: *His wife prodded him for years before he began writing his first novel.* | [prod sb into (doing) sth] *Politicians have failed to prod local industries into reducing pollution levels.* **2** to push or press something with your finger or a pointed object

prod² *n.* [C usually singular] **1** an instrument used for prodding an animal in order to make them move in a particular direction: *a cattle prod* **2** something that is said or done to encourage or remind someone to do something: *The new law will serve as a prod to make the airline industry increase their safety measures.* **3** a sudden pressing or pushing movement, using your finger or a pointed object: *Jerry gave me a sharp prod in the back.*

prod·i·gal¹ /ˈprɑdɪgəl/ *adj.* tending to waste what you have, especially money: *a prodigal lifestyle*

prodigal² *n.* [C] HUMOROUS someone who spends money carelessly and wastes their time

pro·di·gious /prəˈdɪdʒəs/ *adj.* extremely or surprisingly large or powerful: *Building the bridge was a prodigious feat of engineering and finance.* —**prodigiously** *adv.*

prod·i·gy /ˈprɑdədʒi/ *n. plural* **prodigies** [C] **1** a young person who is extremely smart or good at doing something: *a tennis prodigy* | *David Helfgott, the pianist, was considered a **child prodigy**.* **2** something strange and surprising: *Everest climbers display prodigies of endurance.*

pro·duce¹ /prəˈdus/ *v.*

s w
2

1 grow/make [T] to grow something or make it naturally: *The region produces most of the state's corn.* | *Cancer is destroying his body's ability to produce white blood cells.*

2 result [T] to make something happen or develop, or have a particular result or effect: *The drug is known to produce severe side effects in some people.* | *Poisonous gases are produced by improperly burned fuel.*

3 show [T] to show, bring out, or offer something so it can be seen or considered: *During the argument, one of the men produced a knife.* | *The defendants were able to produce documents showing they were the legal heirs.*

4 make with skill [T] to make something using skill and imagination: *Very few artists are producing the kind of original work Larson is.* | *Kuleto's Bakery produces some of the finest pastries in town.*

5 goods [I,T] to make things to be sold, using an industrial process: *Nuclear power plants produce twenty percent of the country's energy.* | *The company produces over 200 sewing machines a month.* —see also MASS-PRODUCED

6 play/film [T] to control the preparation of a play, movie etc. and then show it to the public: *Aaron Spelling has produced numerous hit TV shows.* —see also PRODUCER (2)

7 baby [T] FORMAL to have a baby: *Anthea felt pressure from the family to produce a son.* —see also PRODUCTION —see Usage Note at PRODUCT

prod·uce² /ˈprɑdus, ˈproʊ-/ *n.* [U] food that has been grown, especially fruits and vegetables: *fresh produce* | *a produce market*

pro·duc·er /prəˈdusɚ/ *n.* [C] **1** a person, company, or country that makes or grows goods, foods, or materials: [+ of] *Allergan is a leading producer of contact lenses.* | **a coffee/wine/car etc. producer** *an international group of steel producers* —compare CONSUMER **2** someone who has general control of the preparation of a play, movie, broadcast etc., but who does not direct the actors: *record producer Michael*

s w
2

Fine —compare DIRECTOR (1) —see Usage Note at PRODUCT

prod·uct /ˈprɑdʌkt/ *n.* [C] **1** something useful that is made in a factory, grown, or taken from nature: *None of our products are tested on animals.* | *The bill will restrict the advertising of tobacco products.* | *I'm allergic to dairy products.* **2 be a/the product of sth a)** if someone is the product of a particular experience or situation, that experience has strongly influenced the way they behave, their opinions etc.: *Sex offenders are often the products of child abuse.* **b)** if something is the product of particular conditions or actions, it is a result of those conditions or actions: *Health problems may be a product of poor housing.* **3** TECHNICAL the number you get by multiplying two or more numbers in MATHEMATICS: [+ of] *The product of 3 times 5 is 15.* **4** TECHNICAL a new chemical compound produced by chemical action

---

USAGE NOTE: PRODUCT

WORD CHOICE: product, produce, production, producer

Production [U] is the process in which things are made, usually with the help of people, or in a factory: *We need to increase production* (NOT *the production*). | *mass production of computers.* A **production** [C] is a play, movie, or program made for the theater, television, or radio: *a new production of Thornton Wilder's play.* A **product** [C] is something that is made to be sold, often in a factory, or a natural substance like wood, coal etc. that is taken from the ground or land to sell: *Dow produces a lot of chemical products.* | *household products such as cleaning liquids and detergents* | *The country's main products are natural gas, coal, and sugar.* In business, sales, and advertising language, a wider range of things may be called products. For example, a life insurance company might call the services it sells its products. **Produce** [U] (which is pronounced differently from the verb) is a general word for fresh fruit and vegetables: *There are more salad dressings available in the produce section.* If a person, company, or country produces something, they are a **producer** [C]: *Brazil is the world's most important producer of coffee.*

---

pro·duc·tion /prəˈdʌkʃən/ *n.* **1** [U] the process of making or growing things to be sold as products, or the amount that is produced: *Steel production has decreased by thirty-four percent.* | *Prices have increased to cover production costs.* | *The booklet, now in production* (=being made), *will be available in early January.* | *This type of engine never went into production* (=began to be produced in large numbers). **2** [C] something produced by skill or imagination, especially a play, movie, broadcast etc.: *the Northside Theater Company's production of "A Christmas Carol"* **3** [U] the act or process of making something new, or of bringing something into existence: *the body's production of white blood cells* **4 make a (major) production out of sth** INFORMAL to do something in a way that takes more effort or shows more emotion than is necessary, so that people notice: *Just wash the dishes! You don't have to made a production out of it.* **5** [U] the act of showing something —see Usage Note at PRODUCT

production line /ˈ.. ˌ./ *n.* [C] an arrangement of machines and workers in a factory, in which each worker or machine does one job in the making of a product, and the product is then passed on to the next worker or machine

production num·ber /ˈ.. ˌ./ *n.* [C] a scene in a MUSICAL involving many people singing and dancing

production plat·form /ˈ.. ˌ./ *n.* [C] a large piece of equipment standing on very long legs, used for getting oil out of the ground under the ocean

pro·duc·tive /prəˈdʌktɪv/ *adj.* **1** producing or achieving a lot: *Most of us are more productive in the morning.* | *It was a very productive meeting* (=it had useful results). | *Despite his health problems, Gilbert lives a productive life* (=he achieves a lot). —opposite UNPRODUCTIVE **2** producing goods, crops, or wealth: *Companies receive tax credits for buying productive equipment.* | *Fertilizers make the land more*

productive. **3 productive of sth** FORMAL causing or producing something: *Few ideas have been more productive of controversy than Communism.* —**productively** *adv.* —**productiveness** *n.* [U]

pro·duc·tiv·i·ty /ˌproudəkˈtɪvəṭi, ˌprɑ-/ *n.* [U] the rate at which goods are produced, and the amount produced, compared with the work, time, and money needed to produce them: *Managers are always looking for ways to increase worker productivity.*

product mix /ˈ.. ˌ./ *n.* [C] TECHNICAL the number and type of different products made by a particular company

product place·ment /ˈ.. ˌ./ *n.* [U] the practice of using particular products in movies or television shows as a form of advertising

prof /prɑf/ *n.* [C] **1** INFORMAL a PROFESSOR **2 Prof.** the written abbreviation of PROFESSOR

pro·fane¹ /prouˈfeɪn, prə-/ *adj.* **1** showing disrespect for God or for holy things, by using offensive words or religious words wrongly: *College officials expressed concern over profane language used in the play.* | *Taylor was a loud, profane man.* **2** FORMAL not religious or holy but dealing with human life: *sacred and profane art* —opposite SACRED —**profanely** *adv.*

pro·fane² *v.* [T] FORMAL to treat something holy in a way that is not respectful —**profanation** /ˌprɑfəˈneɪʃən, ˌprou-/ *n.* [C,U]

pro·fan·i·ty /prouˈfænəṭi, prə-/ *n. plural* **profanities** [C,U] **1** offensive words, or religious words used wrongly **2** an act of showing disrespect for God or for holy things

pro·fess /prəˈfɛs, prou-/ *v.* [T] FORMAL **1** to make a claim about something, especially a false one: *Lewis professed his innocence.* | [profess to be sth] *Although he professes to be a vegetarian, he admits to eating chicken.* | [profess to do sth] *Duke professes to have abandoned his racist views.* **2** to state a personal feeling or belief openly and freely: *For months, Derek had wanted to profess his love for Beth.* | *Speaking softly, Prucell professed her dislike of giving interviews.* **3** to have a religion or belief: *In Mexico, ninety percent of the people profess Catholicism.*

pro·fessed /prəˈfɛst/ *adj.* [only before noun] FORMAL **1** clearly stating what you believe: *a professed socialist* **2** pretended, rather than real or sincere: *Celia's professed admiration for her sister worried their parents.* —**professedly** *adv.*

pro·fes·sion /prəˈfɛʃən/ *n.* **1** [C,U] a job that needs special education and training: *I'm a writer – that's my profession.* | *He's a lawyer by profession.* —see Usage Note at JOB **2** [singular] all the people in a particular profession: *In 1950, Jones entered the teaching profession.* **3** [C] a statement of your belief, opinion, or feeling: *She was surprised by Clark's profession of love for her.* **4 the world's oldest profession** HUMOROUS the job of being a PROSTITUTE

pro·fes·sion·al¹ /prəˈfɛʃənl/ *adj.* **1** [no comparative] doing a job, sport, or activity for money: *a professional singer* | *a professional football player* | *turn/go professional* (=start to do something as a job) —compare AMATEUR¹ (1) **2** [no comparative] done by or relating to people who are paid: *the glamorous world of professional skating* | *professional basketball games* —compare AMATEUR¹ (1) **3** [only before noun, no comparative] relating to a job that needs special education and training: *None of the applicants have any professional job experience.* | *You should speak to a lawyer for a professional opinion.* **4** showing that someone has been well trained and is good at their work, or done by such a person: *These glossy brochures look very professional.* | *I was impressed with William's professional manner on the phone.* **5 professional person/man/woman etc.** someone who works in a profession, or who has an important position in a company or business: *Most professional women find it difficult to balance working with having children.* **6 a professional liar/complainer etc.** HUMOROUS someone who lies or complains too much

s w **professional**[2] n. [C] **1** someone who earns money by doing a job, sport, or activity: *Professionals were first allowed to compete in the Olympics in 1992.* —compare AMATEUR[2] (1) **2** someone who works in a job that needs special education and training: *Electrical repairs should be left to a professional.* **3** someone who has a lot of experience and does something very skillfully: *Mr. Soloff was a true professional in the field of insurance.* **4 tennis/golf/swimming etc. professional** someone who is very good at a sport and is employed by a private club to teach its members

pro·fes·sion·al·ism /prəˈfɛʃnəlˌɪzəm, -ʃənl-/ n. [U] the skill and high standards of behavior expected of a professional person: *Keeley's competence and professionalism will be missed.*

pro·fes·sion·al·ly /prəˈfɛʃənl-i/ adv. **1** as a paid job rather than just for enjoyment, or as part of your work: *Schneider has cooked professionally in France and the United States.* **2** in a way that shows high standards and good training: *a professionally edited video*

professional wres·tling /.ˌ... ˈ../ n. [U] a form of entertainment in which actors, often wearing funny clothing, pretend to fight by holding, pulling, and pushing each other —**professional wrestler** n. [C]

s w **pro·fes·sor,** Professor /prəˈfɛsɚ/ n. [C] a teacher at a college or university, especially one who has a high rank: *Professor Paterson will give the keynote address.* | *Who is your economics professor?* | *a professor of physics* —see also ASSISTANT PROFESSOR, ASSOCIATE PROFESSOR, FULL PROFESSOR

USAGE NOTE: PROFESSOR

WORD CHOICE: professor, assistant professor, associate professor, full professor, instructor
In the U.S. most university teachers are called **professor**, which is used for any full-time member of the teaching staff of a university or college. There are three specific ranks: **assistant professor, associate professor,** and **full professor. Assistant professor** is the least important position and **full professor** is the most important. An **instructor** is usually a part-time member of a university or college teaching staff. School teachers are never called professors in the U.S.

---

pro·fes·so·ri·al /ˌprɑfəˈsɔriəl/ adj. relating to the job of a professor, or considered typical of a professor: *Malachowski looks very professorial in wire-rimmed glasses and tweed jacket.* —**professorially** adv.

pro·fes·sor·ship /prəˈfɛsɚˌʃɪp/ n. [C] the job or position of a college or university professor: *a professorship in psychology*

prof·fer /ˈprɑfɚ/ v. [T] FORMAL **1** to give someone advice, an explanation etc.: *Spencer refused to proffer an apology.* **2** to offer something to someone, especially by holding it out in your hands: *A tray of exquisite desserts was proffered at the end of the meal.* —**proffer** n. [C]

pro·fi·cien·cy /prəˈfɪʃənsi/ n. plural **proficiencies** [C,U] a high standard of ability and skill: [+ in/with/at] *The students' proficiency in speaking English is also tested.* | *Nick's proficiency with computers is well known.*

pro·fi·cient /prəˈfɪʃənt/ adj. able to do something well or skillfully: [+ in/at] *Gwen is proficient in three languages.* | *a proficient typist* —**proficiently** adv.

s w **pro·file**[1] /ˈproufaɪl/ n. [C] **1** a side view of someone's head: *He has an attractive profile.* | *On the wall was a drawing of her in profile.* **2** a short description that gives important details about a person, a group of people, or a place: [+ of] *The agency also gave a brief biographical profile of Buckley to the press.* | *Barcelona was the subject of a recent travel section profile.* **3 keep a low profile** to behave quietly and avoid doing things that will make people notice you: *Western visitors to the region are asked to keep a low profile.* **4** an edge or shape of something seen against a background: *Amid the smoke, one could see*

the unmistakable profile of the Claremont Hotel. —see also HIGH-PROFILE

profile[2] v. [T] to write or give a short description of someone or something: *Dorsey is one of the Harvard medical students profiled in the magazine.*

pro·fil·ing /ˈproufaɪlɪŋ/ n. [U] **1** DNA PROFILING **2** the way in which some police organizations stop people from particular races or other groups in society etc., in order to ask them questions, search them etc., because the police think that people in those groups are more likely to be involved in crimes or do bad things

prof·it[1] /ˈprɑfɪt/ n. **1** [C,U] money that you gain by selling things or doing business: *All the profits from the auction will go to cancer research.* | [+ of] *Genentech Inc. reported a profit of $13.5 million for the third quarter.* | **make/turn a profit** *We could sell the CDs for $3 apiece and still make a profit.* | *Finley's plan was to fix up the property and sell it at a profit.* | **net profit** (=the profit after taxes etc. are paid) | **gross profit** (=the profit before taxes etc. are paid) **2** [U] an advantage that you gain from doing something: *There's no profit to be found in lying.* —see also NONPROFIT

s w

profit[2] v. **1** [I,T] FORMAL to be useful or helpful to someone: [**profit sb to do sth**] *It might profit you to learn about the company before your interview.* | [+ from/by] *Many companies profit from hiring minorities.* **2** [I] to gain money from doing something: *In the end, the stocks soared and everyone profited.* | [+ from/by] *Convicted criminals are not permitted to profit from their crimes.*

prof·it·a·bil·i·ty /ˌprɑfɪtəˈbɪləti/ n. [U] the state of producing a profit, or the degree to which a business or activity is profitable: *They plan to increase profitability by making the factory more efficient.*

prof·it·a·ble /ˈprɑfɪtəbəl/ adj. **1** producing a profit: *Many small hospitals are struggling to stay profitable.* | *a profitable business* **2** producing a useful result: *I had a very profitable conversation with Jack today.* —**profitably** adv. —opposite UNPROFITABLE

profit and loss state·ment /ˌ... ˈ. ˌ../ n. [C] a financial statement showing a company's income, spending, and profit over a particular period

prof·it·eer /ˌprɑfəˈtɪr/ n. [C] someone who makes unfairly large profits, especially by selling things at very high prices when they are difficult to get: *black market profiteers* —**profiteer** v. [I] —**profiteering** n. [U]

prof·it·less /ˈprɑfətlɪs/ adj. not making a profit, or not worth doing —**profitlessly** adv.

profit-mak·ing /ˈ.. ˌ../ adj. making a profit: *Government will never be a profit-making enterprise.*

profit mar·gin /ˈ.. ˌ../ n. [C] the difference between the cost of producing something and the price you sell it at

profit shar·ing /ˈ.. ˌ../ n. [U] a system by which all the people who work for a company share in its profits

prof·li·gate[1] /ˈprɑfləgɪt/ adj. FORMAL **1** wasting money in a stupid and careless way: *profligate spending of the taxpayer's money* **2** behaving in an immoral way and not caring about it at all —**profligacy** n. [U]

profligate[2] n. [C] FORMAL someone who is profligate

pro for·ma /proʊ ˈfɔrmə/ adj. adv. FORMAL if something is approved, accepted etc. pro forma, this is part of the usual way of doing things and does not involve any actual choice or decision: *pro forma approval*

pro·found /prəˈfaʊnd/ adj. **1** important and having a strong influence or effect: *The impact of these changes will be profound.* | *a book with profound social implications* **2** showing strong serious feelings: *Her death left me with a profound sense of sadness.* **3** showing great knowledge and understanding: *a profound remark* | *Much of what he had to say was very profound.* **4** complete; TOTAL: *profound deafness* | *There was a profound silence after his remark.* **5** LITERARY deep or far below the surface of something —**profoundly** adv.: *profoundly disturbing news*

pro·fun·di·ty /prəˈfʌndəti/ *n. plural* **profundities** FORMAL **1** [U] the quality of knowing and understanding a lot, or having strong serious feelings: *Fairy tales have a surprising profundity.* **2** [C usually plural] something that someone says that shows this quality: *The profundities of his speech were lost on the young audience.* —**profusely** *adv.*

pro·fuse /prəˈfyus, prou-/ *adj.* **1** given, flowing, or growing freely and in large quantities: *Profuse sweating is one of the symptoms of heat exhaustion.* **2** very eager or generous with your praise, thanks etc.: [+ in] *Noriko was profuse in her thanks.* —**profuseness** *n.* [U]

pro·fu·sion /prəˈfyuʒən/ *n.* [singular,U] a supply or amount that is almost too large: [+ of] *A profusion of fresh flowers surrounded the tables.* | *Condominiums and shopping malls have sprung up* **in profusion**.

pro·gen·i·tor /prouˈdʒenətə/ *n.* [C] TECHNICAL **1** a person or animal that lived a long time ago, to whom someone or something living now is related; ANCESTOR **2** FORMAL someone who first thought of an idea a long time ago: [+ of] *Graham was a great progenitor of modern dance.*

prog·e·ny /ˈprɑdʒəni/ *n.* [U] **1** TECHNICAL the DESCENDANTS of a person, animal, or plant form, or the things that can develop from something else: *We are dooming our progeny by ruining the environment.* **2** FORMAL someone's children: *The salmons' progeny will be large enough to catch by next summer.*

pro·ges·ter·one /prouˈdʒestəˌroun/ *n.* [U] a female sex HORMONE that is produced by a woman when she is going to have a baby and is also used in CONTRACEPTIVE drugs

prog·na·thous /ˈprɑgnəθəs, prɑgˈneɪθəs/ *adj.* TECHNICAL with a jaw that sticks out more than the rest of your face

prog·no·sis /prɑgˈnousɪs/ *n. plural* **prognoses** /-siz/ [C] **1** TECHNICAL a doctor's opinion of how an illness or disease will develop: *Doctors say his prognosis is good, and they expect a full recovery.* —compare DIAGNOSIS **2** FORMAL a judgment about the future that is based on information or experience: *The report's prognosis for unemployment was very pessimistic*

prog·nos·ti·cate /prɑgˈnɑstəˌkeɪt/ *v.* [T] to say what will happen, or to be a sign of what will happen —**prognostication** /prɑgˌnɑstəˈkeɪʃən/ *n.* [C,U]

s w
1 1
pro·gram[1] /ˈprougræm, -grəm/ *n.* [C]
1 plan an important plan, especially one organized by a government or large organization: *the U.S. space program* | *a government program to feed the poor*
2 television/radio a show or performance on television or radio, especially one that is played regularly: *"ER" is the most popular program on TV.* | [+ about] *Last night, I watched a program about the history of Brazil.*
3 computer a set of instructions given to a computer to make it do a particular job: *a word processing program*
4 education a set of planned activities in education or training, which have a specific purpose: *Brian was able to get into a good nursing program.* | *the company's management training program*
5 play/performance a printed description of what will happen at a play, concert etc. and of the people who will be performing: *a circus program*
6 activities the planned order of activities or events at a performance or meeting; SCHEDULE[1]: *Square dancing is on tonight's program at the rec center.*
7 **get with the program** SPOKEN used to tell someone to pay attention to what needs to be done, and to do it

s w
2 2
program[2] *v.* **programmed, programming** **1** [T] to set a machine to operate in a particular way: [program sth to do sth] *I've programmed the VCR to record the 9 o'clock movie.* **2** [I,T] to write a set of instructions for a computer or give a computer instructions that it can use to perform a particular operation: *The computers have been programmed to automatically save whatever you're working on.* | *Hal spends most of his time programming.* **3** [T usually passive] to make someone behave or think in a

---

particular way, especially by the influence of a society, group, or situation: [program sb to be sth] *Some psychologists believe women are programmed to not be aggressive.* **4** to arrange something as part of series of planned events: *The orchestra programs very little music by living composers.* —see also PROGRAMMER

program di·rec·tor /ˈ.. .,../ *n.* [C] **1** someone who manages an organization or a PROGRAM (=set of planned activities) **2** someone who decides what PROGRAMS to show on a television or radio station

pro·gram·ma·ble /prouˈgræməbəl, ˈprougræm-/ *adj.* able to be controlled by a computer or electronic program: *a programmable heating system*

pro·gram·mat·ic /ˌprougrəˈmætɪk/ *adj.* FORMAL relating to a program or to how something is organized: *The agency needs to make programmatic reforms.*

pro·gramme /ˈprougræm/ the British spelling of PROGRAM, also used in Canada

programmed in·struc·tion /ˌ... .ˈ../ *n.* [U] a method of teaching in which the subject to be learned is divided into small parts, and you have to get one part right before you can go on to the next

pro·gram·mer /ˈprouˌgræmə, -grəmə/ *n.* [C] someone whose job is to write computer PROGRAMS

pro·gram·ming /ˈprougræmɪŋ/ *n.* [U] **1** television or radio PROGRAMS, or the activity of producing them: *Much of the evening programming is too violent for children.* **2** the activity of writing PROGRAMS for computers **3** something written by a computer programmer: *Computer viruses are bits of destructive programming.*

program mu·sic /ˈ.. ,../ *n.* [U] descriptive music which uses sound to suggest a story, picture etc.

prog·ress[1] /ˈprɑgrəs, -grɛs/ *n.* [U] **1** the process of getting better at doing something, or getting closer to finishing or achieving something: *Congress has* **made** *little* **progress** *in reaching an agreement.* | [+ of/on/toward] *The country's progress toward democratic elections has been frustrating.* **2** all the improvements, developments, and achievements that happen in science, society, work etc.: *The older generation is simply afraid of progress.* | *Technological progress has allowed people to build immensely tall skyscrapers.* **3 in progress** happening now, and not yet finished: *When we arrived at the studio, filming was already in progress.* **4** movement toward a place: *The ship* **made** *slow* **progress** *through the rough sea.*

s w
3 2

pro·gress[2] /ˈprɑgrɛs/ *v.* [I] **1** to develop, improve, or become more complete over a period of time: *Repair work has progressed more quickly than expected.* | [+ to] *If events progress to civil war, the UN may be forced to intervene.* **2** to move forward slowly: *Both of the men progressed slowly up the stairs.* **3** to move on from doing one thing to doing another: [+ to] *We started with a bottle of wine, and then progressed to whiskey.* —compare REGRESS

pro·gres·sion /prəˈgrɛʃən/ *n.* **1** [U] a process of change or development: [+ of] *A blood test will help doctors measure the progression of the disease.* | [progression (from sth) to sth] *Yamaguchi made a rapid progression from young skater to world favorite.* **2** [U] movement toward a GOAL or particular place: *the river's progression toward the Gulf of Mexico* **3** [C] a number of things coming one after the other —see also ARITHMETIC PROGRESSION, GEOMETRIC PROGRESSION

pro·gres·sive[1] /prəˈgrɛsɪv/ *adj.* **1** supporting new or modern ideas and methods, especially in politics and education: *Lotus had always prided itself on its progressive employee policies.* | *the progressive wing of the Republican Party* **2** happening or developing gradually over a period of time: *Patients are taught progressive muscle relaxation techniques.* | *a progressive brain disorder* **3** TECHNICAL the progressive form of a verb is used to show that an action or activity is continuing to happen, and is shown in English by the verb "be" followed by a PRESENT

P

PARTICIPLE, as in "I was waiting for the bus" —**progressively** adv. —**progressiveness** n. [U]

progressive[2] n. [C] someone with modern ideas who wants to change things

progressive tax /.,.. '. / n. [singular] TECHNICAL a tax that takes a larger PERCENTAGE of money from people with higher incomes than from people with lower incomes —compare REGRESSIVE TAX

progress re·port /'.. .,./ n. [C] a statement about how something, especially work, is developing

pro·hib·it /proʊˈhɪbɪt, prə-/ v. [T] **1** to officially stop an activity by making it illegal or against the rules: *Selling alcohol to people under 21 is prohibited.* | [prohibit sb from doing sth] *At that time, there were laws that prohibited blacks from owning property.* **2** to make something impossible or prevent it from happening: *His poor eyesight prohibited him from becoming a pilot.* —see Usage Note at FORBID

pro·hi·bi·tion /ˌproʊəˈbɪʃən/ n. **1** [C,U] the act of officially stopping something by law, or the order that does this: [+ on/against/of] *The group is pushing for a prohibition on cigarette advertising.* | *the prohibition of chemical weapons* **2** Prohibition the period from 1919 to 1933 in the U.S. when the production and sale of alcoholic drinks were forbidden by law

pro·hi·bi·tion·ist /ˌproʊəˈbɪʃənɪst/ n. [C] someone who supported Prohibition —**prohibitionism** n. [U]

pro·hib·i·tive /proʊˈhɪbətɪv, prə-/ adj. **1** prohibitive prices are so high that they prevent people from buying something: *The cost of renovating the old buildings would be prohibitive.* **2** a prohibitive tax or rule prevents people from doing things: *a prohibitive tax on imports* **3** prohibitive favorite the person, team, or group that is most likely to win a game, election etc.: *The Huskies are prohibitive favorites against Toledo.* —**prohibitively** adv.

pro·hib·i·to·ry /proʊˈhɪbəˌtɔri/ adj. intended to stop something

proj·ect[1] /ˈprɑdʒɛkt, -dʒɪkt/ n. [C] **1** an important and carefully planned piece of work, especially one that is intended to build or produce something new, or that is intended to deal with a problem: *Work on the new freeway project began yesterday.* | *The project still must be approved by the Board of Supervisors.* **2** a part of a school course that involves careful study of a particular subject over a period of time: [+ on] *Our class is doing a project on Virginia state history.* **3** the projects INFORMAL the buildings that are part of a HOUSING PROJECT —see also HOUSING PROJECT

pro·ject[2] /prəˈdʒɛkt/ v.
1 calculate [T] to calculate the size, amount, or rate of something as it probably will be in the future, using the information you have now: *School officials are projecting a rise in student numbers next semester.* | [project sth to do sth] *Profits of 400 major firms are projected to drop 11.2% in the current fiscal year.*
2 movie/photograph [T] to make the picture of a movie, photograph etc. appear in a larger form on a screen or flat surface: *A computer image of an eyeball was projected onto a screen on stage.*
3 plan be projected to be planned to happen in the future: *The ambassador's visit is projected to take place in June.*
4 how sb seems [T] to make other people have a particular idea about you: *Kirk doesn't realize how arrogant an image he projects.* | *Lang is trying to project himself as a progressive politician.*
5 stick out [I] to stick out beyond an edge or surface: [+ out/from/through etc.] *The garage roof projects two feet over the driveway.*
6 feelings [T] to imagine that other people have the same feelings as you, especially when you do not realize you are doing this: [project sth on/onto sb] *Jay's finally realizing that he projects his own insecurities onto his friends.*
7 project your voice to speak clearly and loudly so that you can be heard by everyone in a big hall or room

8 throw [T] TECHNICAL to throw something up or forward with great force
9 picture [T] TECHNICAL **a)** to make a picture of a solid object on a flat surface **b)** to make a map using this method

pro·jec·tile /prəˈdʒɛktl, -ˌtaɪl/ n. [C] an object that is thrown or is fired from a weapon, such as a bullet, stone, or SHELL[1] (3) —**projectile** adj.

pro·jec·tion /prəˈdʒɛkʃən/ n. **1** [C] a statement or calculation about what will probably happen, based on information available now: *The city's sales-tax revenues are running $800,000 below projections.* | *next year's sales projections* **2** [C] FORMAL something that sticks out from a surface: *The tires have short metal projections to improve traction on snow and ice.* **3** [U] the act of projecting a movie or picture: *projection equipment* **4** [U] the act of imagining that other people are feeling the same emotions as you **5** [C] TECHNICAL an image of something that has been projected, especially an image of the world's surface on a map

pro·jec·tion·ist /prəˈdʒɛkʃənɪst/ n. [C] someone whose job is to operate the projector in a movie theater

pro·jec·tor /prəˈdʒɛktɚ/ n. [C] a piece of equipment that makes a movie appear on a screen or on a flat surface —see also OVERHEAD PROJECTOR

Pro·kof·iev /prəˈkɔfiɛf, -fyəf/, **Ser·gei** /ˈsɔɹgeɪ/ (1891–1953) a Russian musician who wrote CLASSICAL music

pro·lapse /ˈproʊlæps, proʊˈlæps/ n. [C] TECHNICAL the falling down or slipping of an inner part of your body, such as the UTERUS, from its usual position

pro·le·tar·i·an /ˌproʊləˈtɛriən◂/ adj. relating to or involving the proletariat

pro·le·tar·i·at /ˌproʊləˈtɛriət/ n. the proletariat the class of workers who own no property and work for WAGES, especially in factories, building things etc.

pro-life /ˌ. './ adj. someone who is pro-life is opposed to ABORTION and uses this word to describe their views —compare PRO-CHOICE —see also RIGHT-TO-LIFE

pro·lif·er /ˌ. '../ n. [C] a member of a pro-life group

pro·lif·er·ate /prəˈlɪfəˌreɪt/ v. [I] if something proliferates, it increases rapidly and spreads to many different places: *Fast-food restaurants have proliferated in the area.*

pro·lif·er·a·tion /prəˌlɪfəˈreɪʃən/ n. **1** [singular,U] a rapid increase in the amount or number of something: [+ of] *the proliferation of nuclear weapons* **2** [U] TECHNICAL the very fast growth of new parts of a living thing, such as cells or BUDS

pro·lif·ic /prəˈlɪfɪk/ adj. **1** someone who is prolific produces a lot of something, especially works of art, books etc.: *Since then, Hull has become hockey's most prolific scorer.* **2** an animal or plant that is prolific produces many babies or many other plants **3** LITERARY existing in large numbers: *Strawberries are prolific in the area.* —**prolifically** /-kli/ adv.

pro·lix /proʊˈlɪks, ˈproʊlɪks/ adj. FORMAL a prolix piece of writing has too many words and is boring

PROLOG /ˈproʊlɑg/ n. [U] TRADEMARK a computer language that is similar to human language

pro·logue /ˈproʊlɑg, -lɔg/ n. [C usually singular] **1** the introduction to a play, a long poem etc. **2** LITERARY an act or event that leads to a much more important event: *The past is the prologue to the future.* —compare EPILOGUE

pro·long /prəˈlɔŋ/ v. [T] to deliberately make something such as a feeling or activity last longer: *Doctors say these drugs can reduce pain and prolong lives.*

pro·lon·ga·tion /ˌproʊlɔŋˈgeɪʃən/ n. **1** [U] the act of making something last longer **2** [C + of] something added to another thing, which makes it longer

pro·longed /prəˈlɔŋd/ adj. continuing for a long time: *a prolonged illness*

prom /prɑm/ n. [C] a formal dance party for HIGH SCHOOL students, often held at the end of a school year: *the senior prom*

prom·e·nade /ˌprɑməˈneɪd, -ˈnɑd/ n. [C] **1** a wide road next to the beach where people can walk for pleasure **2** OLD-FASHIONED a walk for pleasure in a public place

promenade deck /ˌ..'. ,.ˈ...ˌ./ n. [C] the upper level of a ship where people can walk for pleasure

Pro·me·the·us /prəˈmiθiəs/ in Greek MYTHOLOGY, a TITAN who stole fire from heaven to give to humans

prom·i·nence /ˈprɒmənəns/ n. **1** [U] the fact of being important and well known: *The case gained prominence* (=became well known) *because of the brutal nature of the murders.* | *come/rise to prominence Brubeck rose to prominence as a jazz pianist in the 1950s.* **2** [C] FORMAL a part or place that is higher or larger than what is around it

prom·i·nent /ˈprɒmənənt/ adj. **1** [C] well known and important: *a prominent business leader* | *The federal government should play a prominent role* (=be very involved) *in fighting crime.* **2** something that is prominent is large and sticks out: *a prominent nose* **3 a prominent place/position** somewhere that is easily seen and is usually used for things that are important: *His college diploma occupied the most prominent place in the living room.*

pro·mis·cu·ous /prəˈmɪskyuəs/ adj. **1** having sex with a lot of people: *Rumors spread through the school that Jill was promiscuous.* **2** OLD USE made of many different parts **3** OLD USE not choosing carefully —**promiscuously** adv. —**promiscuity** /ˌprɒmɪˈskyuəti/ n. [U]

prom·ise[1] /ˈprɒmɪs/ v. **1** [I,T] to tell someone that you will definitely do something or that something will happen: [**promise (that)**] *Todd promises that he will write often.* | [**promise sb (that)**] *You promised me you would be on time.* | [**promise to do sth**] *I had promised to bring her back a gift from Thailand.* | [**promise sb sth**] *Mom promised us ice-cream if we were good at the store.* | *I/we promise "Promise me you won't do anything stupid." "I promise."* | *"I'll help you write your term paper." "Promise?"* (=used to ask if someone promises) | *On Monday, the hostages were released as promised* (=at the time or place that was promised). **2** [T] to make you expect that something will happen: *The game promises to be exciting.* **3 I can't promise anything** SPOKEN used to tell someone that you will try to do what they want, but may not be able to: *I'll try to get us tickets, but I can't promise anything.* **4 I promise you...** SPOKEN used to emphasize that what you are saying is true: *I promise you, I didn't tell anyone that you're pregnant.* **5 promise (sb) the moon/world** to promise to give someone a lot of things, which may be impossible for you to do: *Politicians promise the world and deliver nothing.*

promise[2] n. **1** [C] a statement that you will definitely do something or that something will definitely happen: *You made a promise, so you have to keep it.* | [**a promise to do sth**] *Jim made a promise to quit smoking.* | [**+ of**] *a promise of cooperation* | **keep/break a promise** (=to do or fail to do something you promised) **2** [U] signs that something or someone will be good or successful: *John shows a lot of promise* (=is likely to be good) *as a writer.* | [**+ of**] *More research is needed to fulfil the promise of this powerful technology.*

Promised Land /ˈ.. ,./ n. **a) the Promised Land** a situation or condition that you have wanted for a long time because it will bring you happiness and make you feel safe: *Jordan has repeatedly led his team to the Promised Land of the NBA Finals.* **b)** the land of Canaan, which was promised by God to Abraham and his people in the Bible

prom·is·ing /ˈprɒmɪsɪŋ/ adj. showing signs of being successful in the future: *a promising career in law* | *a promising young actor* —**promisingly** adv.

prom·is·so·ry note /ˈprɒməsɔri ˌnoʊt/ n. [C] a document promising to pay money before a particular date

pro·mo /ˈproʊmoʊ/ n. plural **promos** [C] **1** INFORMAL a short movie that advertises an event or product **2** a free product, given away in order to advertise something

prom·on·to·ry /ˈprɒmənˌtɔri/ n. plural **promontories** [C] a high, long, and narrow piece of land that goes out into the ocean

pro·mote /prəˈmoʊt/ v. [T] **1** to help something to develop and be successful: *Chambers says the council could do more to promote recycling.* | *Include workout activities that promote flexibility and strength.* **2** [usually passive] to give someone a better more responsible job in a company: [**promote sb to sth**] *Verdoorn was promoted to senior vice president.* —opposite DEMOTE **3** to make sure people know about a new product, movie etc., especially by offering it at a reduced price or advertising it on television: *Kits promoting "Sesame Street" have been sent to day-care centers.* **4** to try to persuade people to believe or support an idea or way of doing things: *Allen goes from school to school to promote his anti-drug message.* **5** to be responsible for arranging a large public event such as a concert or a sports game

pro·mot·er /prəˈmoʊtə/ n. [C] **1** someone who arranges and advertises concerts or sports events **2** someone who tries to make people believe or support an idea or way of doing things: *a promoter of healthy living*

pro·mo·tion /prəˈmoʊʃən/ n. **1** [C,U] a move to a more important job or rank in a company or organization: *With the promotion came a $3,890 raise.* | [**+ to**] *Cooper announced the promotion of Moore to vice chairman.* **2** [C,U] an activity intended to help sell a product, or the product that is being promoted: *Renee won a year's supply of chocolate as part of a promotion for the candy maker.* **3** [U] the activity of persuading people to support an idea or way of doing things: *the promotion of women's rights* **4** [U] the activity of helping something develop and succeed: *the promotion of solar energy*

pro·mo·tion·al /prəˈmoʊʃənl/ adj. promotional movies, events etc. are made or organized to advertise something: *a promotional brochure*

prompt[1] /prɒmpt/ v. **1** [T] to make someone decide to do something, especially something that they had been thinking of doing: *News of the scandal prompted a Senate investigation.* | [**prompt sb to do sth**] *The decision prompted steel workers to strike.* **2** to make people say or do something as a reaction: *What prompted that remark?* **3** [I,T] to remind an actor or actress of the next words in a speech

prompt[2] adj. **1** done quickly, immediately, or at the right time: *Complaints receive a prompt response.* **2** [not before noun] someone who is prompt arrives at the right time or does something on time: *Lunch is at two. Try to be prompt.* —**promptly** adv.: *We'll start the meeting promptly at 10 a.m.* —**promptness** n. [U]

prompt[3] n. [C] **1** a sign on a computer screen that shows that the computer has finished one operation and is ready to begin the next: *When you see the "C" prompt, type "WP."* **2** a word or words said to an actor in a play, to help them remember what to say

prompt·er /ˈprɒmptə/ n. [C] someone who tells actors in a play what words to say when they forget

prompt·ing /ˈprɒmptɪŋ/ n. **1** [C,U] the act of reminding or encouraging someone to do something: *It took some prompting, but I finally got Jared to clean his room.* **2** [U] telling an actor what to say when they forget

prom·ul·gate /ˈprɒmlˌgeɪt/ v. [T] FORMAL **1** to spread an idea or belief to as many people as possible **2** to make a new law come into effect by announcing it officially —**promulgation** n. [C] —**promulgation** /ˌprɒmlˈgeɪʃən/ n. [U]

pron. n. the written abbreviation of PRONOUN

prone /proʊn/ adj. **1** likely to do something or suffer from something, especially something bad or harmful: [**+ to**] *Tight muscles are prone to injury.* | [**prone to do sth**] *Dr. MacLaughlin is prone to say exactly what she thinks.* | **injury-prone/fire-prone/ accident-prone** etc. *leak-prone fiberglass boats* **2** FORMAL lying down with the front of your body facing down: *Many of the injured were lying prone on the floor.* —compare PROSTRATE[1] (1) —**proneness** n. [U]

P

prong /prɔŋ, prɑŋ/ *n.* [C] **1** a thin sharp point of something that has several points, such as a fork **2** SLANG a PENIS (=male sexual organ)

-pronged /prɔŋd, prɑŋd/ [in adjectives] **two-pronged/three-pronged etc. a)** having two, three etc. prongs **b)** a two-pronged or three-pronged attack, approach plan etc. comes from two or three directions or uses two or three methods at the same time: *The project uses a three-pronged approach in fighting drug use.*

pro·nom·i·nal /proʊˈnɑmənl/ *adj.* TECHNICAL relating to or used like a PRONOUN —**pronominally** *adv.*

pro·noun /ˈproʊnaʊn/ *n.* [C] a word that is used instead of a noun or noun phrase, such as "he" instead of "Peter" or instead of "our boss," or "it" instead of "the car" —see also DEMONSTRATIVE PRONOUN, PERSONAL PRONOUN

SW **pro·nounce** /prəˈnaʊns/ *v.* **1** [T] to make the sound
3 of a letter, word etc., especially in the correct way: *How do you pronounce your last name?* **2** [T] to officially state that something is true: [pronounce sb/sth (to be) sth] *Martins was pronounced dead at 11:07 p.m.* | *I now pronounce you husband and wife.* **3 pronounce sentence** LAW if a judge pronounces sentence, he or she tells the court what kind of punishment a criminal will have **4** [I,T] FORMAL to give a judgment or opinion in an official or legal situation: [+ on] *Leffert used the award ceremony to pronounce on the evils of drugs.*

pro·nounced /prəˈnaʊnst/ *adj.* very easy to notice: *Mrs. Jones walks with a pronounced limp.* | *Her Polish accent is very pronounced.* —**pronouncedly** /prəˈnaʊnsɪdli/ *adv.*

pro·nounce·ment /prəˈnaʊnsmənt/ *n.* [C] FORMAL an official public statement: [+ on] *the Pope's latest pronouncement on birth control*

pron·to /ˈprɑntoʊ/ *adv.* SPOKEN quickly or immediately: *The boss wants this report pronto.*

pro·nun·ci·a·tion /prəˌnʌnsiˈeɪʃən/ *n.* **1** [C,U] the way in which a language or a particular word is pronounced: *Speak as much French as you can, and don't worry about your pronunciation.* **2** [singular, U] a particular person's way of pronouncing a word or words

proof¹ /pruf/ *n.* **1** [C,U] facts, information, documents etc. that prove something is true: [+ of] *To receive the discount, you must show proof of student status.* | [proof that] *His fingerprints on the gun are proof that he's guilty.* | **proof positive** (=definite proof) **2** [C usually plural] TECHNICAL a printed copy of a piece of writing, used to find and remove mistakes before the final printing is done **3** [C] a photograph that is used as a test copy before an official copy is made **4** [C] **a)** a test in MATHEMATICS of the correctness of a calculation **b)** a list of reasons that shows a THEOREM (=statement) in GEOMETRY or science to be true **5 the proof is in the pudding** also **the proof of the pudding (is in the eating)** used to say that you can only know whether something is good or bad after you have tried it —see also **the burden of proof** (BURDEN¹ (2)), **living proof** (LIVING¹ (2))

proof² *adj.* **1 30/40 etc. proof** strong alcoholic drinks such as VODKA or BOURBON that have a particular proof contain a specific amount of alcohol **2 be proof against sth** FORMAL if something is proof against something else, it is not affected by it: *The varnish makes the wood proof against water.*

-proof /pruf/ *suffix* **1** [in adjectives] designed or made so as not to be harmed by something, or to protect people against something: *an ovenproof dish* (=that cannot be harmed by heat) | *a bulletproof vest* (=to protect you from bullets) | *tamper-proof packages* (=packages that are made in a way that prevents someone from opening them before they are sold) —compare -RESISTANT **2** [in verbs] to design or make something so that it cannot be affected by something else, or prevent it from being affected: *We're going to child-proof the living room before my*

3-year-old niece comes to visit (=arrange the room so that anything that is dangerous to a baby is out of reach).

proof of pur·chase /ˌ. . ˈ../ *n. plural* **proofs of purchase** [C] a special marking on a package of something that proves that you bought it: *Send in three proofs of purchase and receive a free roll of film.*

proof·read /ˈprufrid/ *v. past tense and past participle* **proofread** /-rɛd/ [I,T] to read through something that is written or printed in order to correct any mistakes in it —**proofreader** *n.* [C]

prop¹ /prɑp/ *v.* **propped, propping** [T always + adv./prep.] to support something or keep it in a particular position, by leaning it against something or by putting something else under, next to, or behind it: [prop sth against/on sth] *The painter began by propping a ladder against the house.* | [prop sth open] *Give me something to prop the door open.*

prop up

She used some bricks to prop up some books on the shelf.

prop sth ↔ up *phr. v.* [T] **1** to prevent something from falling by putting something against it or under it: *Steel beams were used to prop up the sagging roof.* **2** to help an ECONOMY, industry, or government so that it can continue to exist, especially by giving money: *For years, the U.S. government propped up the savings and loan industry.* **3 prop yourself up (on/against/with etc. sth)** to stand or sit straight by leaning against something: *I propped myself up against the wall.*

prop² *n.* [C] **1** a small object such as a book, weapon etc. used by actors in a play or movie: *stage props* **2** INFORMAL a short form of the word PROPELLER **3** something that helps an ECONOMY, industry, or government so that it can continue to exist or be successful, for example money or special laws: *Low interest rates are the stock market's most important prop.* **4** an object placed under or against something to hold it in a position

Prop. *n.* the abbreviation of PROPOSITION¹ (3): *I voted against Prop. 209.*

prop·a·gan·da /ˌprɑpəˈgændə/ *n.* [U] false or partly false information used by a government or political party to make people agree with them: *Neo-Nazi propaganda* | *a propaganda film* | **propaganda campaign** (=an organized plan to spread propaganda) —**propagandize** *v.* [I,T] —**propagandist** *n.* [C]

prop·a·gate /ˈprɑpəˌgeɪt/ *v.* FORMAL **1** [T] to spread an idea, belief etc. to many people: *The belief that the king was a living god was propagated early in the 18th century.* **2** [I,T] to grow and produce new plants or to make a plant do this: *Rasberries can be propagated in two different ways.* **3** [T] if an animal, insect, or CELL etc. propagates itself or is propagated, it increases in number by reproducing (REPRODUCE (1)) —**propagation** /ˌprɑpəˈgeɪʃən/ *n.* [U]

prop·a·ga·tor /ˈprɑpəˌgeɪtə/ *n.* [C] **1** someone who spreads ideas, beliefs etc. **2** a covered box of soil in which seeds are planted to grow quickly

pro·pane /ˈproʊpeɪn/ *n.* [U] a colorless gas used for both cooking and heating

pro·pel /prəˈpɛl/ *v.* **propelled, propelling** [T] **1** to move, drive, or push something forward: *Four jet engines propel the 8,300-ton ship.* | *The pelican's strong legs and webbed feet propel it in water.* **2** to make someone achieve something, or to make something happen or develop: *Rachel's stunning good looks helped propel her to stardom.* —see also PROPULSION

pro·pel·lant, propellent /prəˈpɛlənt/ *n.* [C,U] **1** an explosive for firing a bullet or ROCKET[1] **2** gas pressed into a small space in a container of liquid, which pushes out the liquid when the pressure is taken away —**propellant** *adj.*

pro·pel·ler /prəˈpɛlə/ *n.* [C] a piece of equipment consisting of two or more blades that spin around, making an aircraft or ship move

pro·pen·si·ty /prəˈpɛnsəti/ *n. plural* **propensities** [C] FORMAL a natural tendency to behave in a particular way or cause something: [a propensity for (doing) sth] *the group's propensity for violence* | [a propensity to do sth] *Some drugs have a propensity to cause birth defects.*

s w
2
3
prop·er /ˈprɑpə/ *adj.* **1** [only before noun, no comparative] right, appropriate, or correct: *Higher math skills are not given proper attention in schools.* | *We need to put the books back in their proper place.* **2** socially correct and acceptable: *It just wouldn't have been proper to not invite Jeff.* **3** very polite, and careful to do what is socially correct: *Bill is a very proper young man.* **4** [only after noun] relating to the main or most important part of something such as a place or a subject: *It's the main road which links Santa Cruz proper and the mountains.* **5 proper to sth** FORMAL natural or normal in a particular place or situation: *Please dress in a way proper to the occasion.* —see also PROPERLY

proper frac·tion /ˌ.. ˈ../ *n.* [C] a FRACTION such as 3/4, in which the number above the line is smaller than the one below it —compare IMPROPER FRACTION

prop·er·ly /ˈprɑpəli/ *adv.* **1** correctly, or in a way that is considered right: *Finding running shoes that fit properly can be tricky.* | *The company had failed to properly train their workers.* **2** completely and thoroughly: *Make sure the door is properly closed.*

proper noun also **proper name** /ˌ.. ˈ./ *n.* [C] a noun such as "James," "New York," or "China" that is the name of a particular person, place, or thing and is spelled with a CAPITAL[1] (4) letter —compare COMMON NOUN —see also NOUN

prop·er·tied /ˈprɑpətid/ *adj.* [only before noun] FORMAL owning a lot of property or land: *the propertied classes*

s w
2
2
prop·er·ty /ˈprɑpəti/ *n. plural* **properties 1** [C,U] a building, a piece of land, or both together: *What's the full market value of the property?* | *Vandals wrecked school property.* | *property taxes* | *There was no criminal violation because the party occurred on **private property**.* **2** [U] the thing or things that someone owns: *At that time, a slave was considered property.* | *Police recovered some of the **stolen property**.* | *The 17-karat diamond ring had once been the **personal property** of Ann-Margret.* **3** [C] a quality or power that belongs naturally to something: *People are becoming more aware of garlic's medicinal properties.* | *All sound has three properties: pitch, volume, and duration.* —see also REAL PROPERTY

property de·vel·op·er /ˈ... ˌ.../ *n.* [C] someone who makes money by buying land and building on it

property tax /ˈ... ˌ./ *n.* [C,U] a tax based on the value of someone's house

proph·e·cy /ˈprɑfəsi/ *n. plural* **prophecies 1** [C] a statement that something will happen in the future, especially one made by someone with religious or magic powers: *the biblical prophecy of a world war* **2** [U] the making of statements about what will happen in the future, or the ability to do this —see also SELF-FULFILLING PROPHECY

proph·e·sy /ˈprɑfəˌsaɪ/ *v.* **prophesies, prophesied, prophesying** [I,T] **1** to use religious or magical knowledge to say what will happen in the future; FORETELL: *History reports that she prophesied her own death.* **2** to use special knowledge or experience to say that something will happen in the future; PREDICT: *Many brokers on Wall Street prophesied the downfall of the company.*

proph·et /ˈprɑfɪt/ *n.* [C] **1** a man whom people in the Christian, Jewish, or Muslim religion believe has been sent by God to lead them and teach them their religion: *the prophet Isaiah* **2 the Prophets** the Jewish holy men whose writings form part of the

OLD TESTAMENT, or the writings themselves **3 prophet of doom/disaster** someone who believes that bad things will happen in the future **4** someone who introduces and teaches a new idea: [+ of] *Gandhi, the prophet of non-violent protests*

proph·et·ess /ˈprɑfɪtɪs/ *n.* [C] a woman whom people believe has been sent by God to lead them

pro·phet·ic /prəˈfɛtɪk/ *adj.* correctly saying what will happen in the future: *Lundgren's warnings proved **prophetic**.* —**prophetically** /-kli/ *adv.*

pro·phet·i·cal /prəˈfɛtɪkəl/ *adj.* like a prophet, or related to the things a prophet says or does

pro·phy·lac·tic[1] /ˌproufəˈlæktɪk/ *adj.* TECHNICAL intended to prevent disease

prophylactic[2] *n.* [C] TECHNICAL **1** a CONDOM **2** something used to prevent disease

pro·phy·lax·is /ˌproufəˈlæksɪs/ *n.* [C,U] TECHNICAL a treatment for preventing disease

pro·pin·qui·ty /prəˈpɪŋkwəti/ *n.* [U + of/to] FORMAL the fact of being near someone or something, or of being related to someone

pro·pi·ti·ate /prouˈpɪʃiˌeɪt/ *v.* [T] FORMAL to make someone who has been unfriendly or angry with you feel more friendly by doing something to please them —**propitiation** /prouˌpɪʃiˈeɪʃən/ *n.* [U]

pro·pi·ti·a·to·ry /prouˈpɪʃiəˌtɔri/ *adj.* FORMAL intended to please someone and make them feel less angry toward you and more friendly: *a propitiatory gift of flowers*

pro·pi·tious /prəˈpɪʃəs/ *adj.* FORMAL good and likely to bring good results: *The most propitious time for an attack was lost.* —**propitiously** *adv.*

pro·po·nent /prəˈpounənt/ *n.* [C] someone who supports something or persuades people to do something: [+ of] *Gephardt is a leading proponent of tax relief for middle-income families.* —compare OPPONENT

proportion

The car is out of proportion to the person.

pro·por·tion[1] /prəˈpɔrʃən/ *n.* **s w**
3
1 number/amount [C] a part or share of a larger amount or number of something: [+ of] *Americans spend a large proportion of their income on housing.* | *The proportion of residents receiving welfare has dropped.*
2 appearance [U] the correct relationship between the size, shape, and position of the different parts of something: *Architects must learn about scale and proportion.* | *Reduce the drawing so that all the elements stay **in proportion**.* | *Her head was rather large **in proportion to** her thin figure.* | *The porch is **out of proportion with** (=is too big or too small compared to) the rest of the house.*
3 size/importance **proportions** how large, important, serious etc. something is: *It may reduce the task to more manageable proportions.* | *The region faces a financial crisis **of huge proportions**.* | *reach crisis/epidemic proportions* (=become so common or frequent that it is a serious problem)
4 relationship [C,U] the relationship between the amounts, numbers, or sizes of different things that go together to form a whole: [proportion of sth to sth] *Girls in the class outnumber the boys by a proportion of three to two.* | *Seventy-five percent of California's immigrants are foreign-born, and that proportion is likely to increase.*

5 in proportion (to sth) according to a particular relationship in size, amount etc.: *Gasoline prices have risen in proportion to the price of crude oil.*
6 out of proportion (to sth) a reaction, result, emotion etc. that is out of proportion is too strong or great, compared to the situation in which it happens: *The two men received prison terms that are completely out of proportion to their crime.*
7 blow sth (way/totally/all etc.) out of proportion to react to a situation as if it is much worse or more serious than it really is: *I think this whole incident has been blown way out of proportion.*
8 a sense of proportion the ability to judge what is most important in a situation: **have/keep/lose a sense of proportion** *McCartney seems to have a good sense of proportion about his fame.*
9 mathematics [U] TECHNICAL equality in the mathematical relationship between two sets of numbers, as in the statement "8 is to 6 as 32 is to 24" —compare RATIO

pro·por·tion² v. [T usually passive] FORMAL **1 well/beautifully etc. proportioned** if something is well, beautifully etc. proportioned, its different parts are in a correct relationship to each other, so that it is pleasant to look at: *Arnold's well-proportioned, muscular body* | *a beautifully proportioned dining room* —opposite BADLY/ILL PROPORTIONED **2** to make something stay in a particular relationship with something else according to size, amount, position etc.: **[proportion sth to sth]** *Farmers pay a small amount for use of the pasture, proportioned to the number of animals grazed there.*

pro·por·tion·al /prəˈpɔrʃnəl, -ˈpɔrʃənl/ adj. something that is proportional to something else stays in a correct or appropriate relationship to the other thing in size, amount, importance etc.: **[+ to]** *The number of representatives each state has is proportional to its population.* —**proportionally** adv.

proportional rep·re·sen·ta·tion /ˌ.…, …ˈ.../ abbreviation **PR** n. [U] a system of voting in elections by which all political parties are represented in the government according to the number of votes they receive in the whole country

pro·por·tion·ate /prəˈpɔrʃənɪt/ adj. something that is proportionate to something else stays in a correct or appropriate relationship to the other thing in size, amount, importance etc.: *The cruise tries to keep the bookings balanced, with a proportionate ratio of men and women.* —**proportionately** adv. —opposite DISPROPORTIONATE

s w **pro·pos·al** /prəˈpoʊzəl/ n. **1** [C,U] a plan or suggestion that is given formally to an official person or group, or the act of giving it: *the President's budget proposals* | **[proposal to do sth]** *The governor has made a proposal to raise the tax on gasoline by two cents.* | **[proposal that]** *Unions were opposed to a proposal that would shift health insurance costs to employees.* **2** [C] the act of asking someone to marry you: *Did she accept his proposal?* —see Usage Note at PROPOSE

s w **pro·pose** /prəˈpoʊz/ v. **1** [T] to formally suggest a plan, time, or way of doing something: *We proposed several dates for the next meeting, but they were all rejected.* | **[propose sth to sb]** *We'll have to wait and see what kind of solutions they propose to us.* | **[propose that]** *What do you propose that Michael do?* | **[propose doing sth]** *The new administration has proposed scrapping more than 400 obsolete government programs.* | **[propose to do sth]** *One council member proposed to close three of the schools to save money.* | **[propose sb]** *I didn't feel comfortable proposing him for the award* (=suggesting he receive the award). **2** [T] FORMAL to intend to do something: **[propose to do sth]** *What do you propose to do about it?* **3 a)** [I] to ask someone to marry you, especially in a formal way: **[+ to]** *Did he propose to her, or did she propose to him?* **b) propose marriage** FORMAL to ask someone to marry you **4** [T] FORMAL to suggest an idea, method etc. as an answer to a scientific question: **[propose that]** *It has been proposed that*

Japanese and Korean are descendants of a common language. **5 propose a toast (to sb)** to formally ask a group of people at a social event to join you in wishing someone success, happiness etc., while raising a glass and then drinking from it —**proposer** n. [C]

USAGE NOTE: PROPOSE

WORD CHOICE: propose, proposal, suggest, suggestion, let's, why don't we?
Use **propose** or **proposal** in formal situations to say what you think someone should do, especially after you have thought a lot about it: *I propose that the extra tax money be returned to the taxpayers.* | *Lawmakers are considering a proposal to change the regulations.* Use **suggest** or **suggestion** in less formal situations for ideas you have about what someone should do, even if you have not thought carefully about it: *I suggest you go over your notes to prepare for the test.* | *Can I make a suggestion?* In spoken English, people do not usually say **I suggest that...** but rather **Let's...** or **Why don't we/you...?**: *Let's go to a movie.* | *Why don't we take the other car?*

---

pro·posed /prəˈpoʊzd/ adj. [only before noun] formally suggested to an official person or group: *The proposed regulations would take effect next year.*

prop·o·si·tion¹ /ˌprɑpəˈzɪʃən/ n. [C] **1** a statement in which you express an opinion or belief: *Most of Aristotle's propositions have proven wrong over time.* | **[proposition that]** *Erling has based his legal defense on the proposition that the photos of him are fake.* **2** an offer, plan, idea, or suggestion, especially in business or politics: *We're still studying the proposition.* | **[proposition to do sth]** *I have a proposition to make – why don't we do it together?* | **an attractive/interesting/practical etc. proposition** (=an idea that is attractive etc.) **3** also **Proposition** a suggested change or addition to the law of a state of the U.S., which citizens vote on: *Proposition 209 outlawed affirmative action in California.* **4** TECHNICAL something that must be proved, or a question to which the answer must be found in GEOMETRY (=type of math dealing with shapes and angles) **5** a statement to someone that you would like to have sex with them —**propositional** adj.

proposition² v. [T] to suggest to someone that they have sex with you: *She complained that her boss propositioned her on several occasions.*

pro·pound /prəˈpaʊnd/ v. [T] FORMAL to suggest an idea, explanation etc. for other people to consider: *The theory they propound isn't really very complicated.*

pro·pri·e·tar·y /prəˈpraɪəˌtɛri/ adj. [no comparative, usually before noun] FORMAL **1** a proprietary product is one that can only be sold by a particular company: *proprietary software* **2 proprietary information** information about a company's products, methods etc. that is known only to people who work for the company **3** proprietary behavior or feelings show that someone or something belongs to you: *He would never have married her, but he had a proprietary feeling toward her anyway.*

proprietary school /.ˈ…. ,./ n. [C] a school or college that is owned by a person and that teaches a special skill, such as how to repair a car

pro·pri·e·tor /prəˈpraɪətə/ n. [C] FORMAL an owner of a business —**proprietorial** /prəˌpraɪəˈtɔriəl/ adj.

pro·pri·e·tress /prəˈpraɪətrɪs/ n. [C] OLD-FASHIONED a woman who owns a business

pro·pri·e·ty /prəˈpraɪəti/ n. FORMAL **1** [U] correct social or moral behavior: *Kids today have no sense of propriety.* | **[+ of]** *Critics have questioned the propriety of some of the Senator's loans.* —opposite IMPROPRIETY **2 the proprieties** the accepted rules of correct social behavior

pro·pul·sion /prəˈpʌlʃən/ n. [U] TECHNICAL the force that moves a vehicle forward, or the system used to make this happen: *jet propulsion* —**propulsive** /prəˈpʌlsɪv/ adj.: *propulsive force*

pro ra·ta /ˌproʊ ˈreɪtə, -ˈrɑtə/ adj. TECHNICAL a pro rata

pro·rate /'prooreit, proo'reit/ v. [T] to calculate a charge, price etc. according to the actual amount of service received rather than by a standard sum: *The fee will be prorated for the days you do not attend.*

pro·sa·ic /proo'zei-ik/ adj. boring, ordinary, or lacking in imagination: *a prosaic writing style* | *The furniture is prosaic and modern.* —**prosaically** /-kli/ adv.

pro·sce·ni·um /proo'siniəm, prə-/ n. [C] the part of a theater stage that comes forward beyond the curtain

pro·sciut·to /proo'ʃutoo/ n. [U] uncooked dried Italian HAM (=salted meat) that is cut in very thin pieces

pro·scribe /proo'skraib/ v. [T] **1** FORMAL to officially stop the existence or use of something: *Many Shiite clergymen maintain that birth control is proscribed by Islam.* **2** OLD USE to state publicly that a citizen is not protected by the law anymore —**proscription** /proo'skripʃən/ n. [C,U]

prose /prooz/ n. [U] written language in its usual form, as opposed to poetry: *Brown's prose is simple and direct.*

pros·e·cute /'prasə,kyut/ v. **1** [I,T] to officially say that you think someone is guilty of a crime and have them judged by a court of law: *Shoplifters will be prosecuted.* | [**prosecute sb for sth**] *Police are under pressure to find someone to prosecute for the murder.* **2** [I,T] if a lawyer prosecutes someone or a case it is their job to try to prove that the person is guilty of a crime: *Who is going to prosecute the case?* —compare DEFEND (4) **3** [T] FORMAL to continue doing something, usually until it is finished: *We will continue to prosecute the war to the end.*

prosecuting at·tor·ney /,.... '../ n. [C] a prosecutor who works for a state, COUNTY, or city government in the U.S.

pros·e·cu·tion /,prasə'kyuʃən/ n. **1 the prosecution** the people in a court of law who are trying to prove that someone is guilty of a crime: *The prosecution does not have a case against my client.* —compare DEFENSE (4) **2** [C,U] the process or act of bringing a legal charge against someone for a crime, or of being judged for a crime in a court of law: *Maxwell could face prosecution for his role in the robbery.* | *Since January, three hate-crime prosecutions have gone to trial.* **3** [U] FORMAL the action of doing something until it is finished: *the prosecution of her duties*

s w **pros·e·cu·tor** /'prasə,kyutə/ n. [C] a lawyer who is **2** trying to prove in a court of law that someone is guilty of a crime

pros·e·lyte /'prasə,lait/ n. [C] FORMAL someone who has recently been persuaded to join a religious group, political party etc.; CONVERT

pros·e·ly·tiz·ing /'prasələ,taiziŋ/ n. [C] FORMAL the activity of trying to persuade someone to join a religious group, political party etc., especially in a way that people find offensive: *Under Stalin, proselytizing was officially forbidden.* —**proselytize** v. [I,T] —**proselytizer** n. [C]

prose po·em /'. ,../ n. [C] something that is written in PROSE but that has some of the qualities of poetry —**prose poetry** n. [U]

Pro·ser·pi·na /prə'sɜpinə/ the Roman name for the goddess Persephone

pros·o·dy /'prasədi, -zə-/ n. [U] the rules for arranging the patterns of sounds and beats in poetry, or the study of these rules —**prosodic** /prə'sadik/ adj.

s w **pros·pect**[1] /'praspekt/ n. **1** [C,U] something that is **2** possible or likely to happen in the future, or the possibility itself: *Job prospects for college graduates this spring don't look good.* | [**+ of**] *Laura was dreading the prospect of spending her first Christmas alone.* | [**+ for**] *Both sides are still hopeful about the prospects for peace.* **2** [C] a person, job, plan etc. that has a good chance of success in the future: *Wilder is considered a good prospect for the next election.* **3** [C usually plural] chances of future success: *You can't marry a man with no job and no prospects!* **4** [C usually singular] FORMAL a view of a wide area of land,

especially from a high place: *a fine prospect of the valley below* **5 in prospect** FORMAL likely to happen in the near future: *A new round of trade talks are in prospect.*

prospect[2] v. [I + **for**,T] to examine an area of land or water, in order to find gold, silver, oil etc.

pro·spec·tive /prə'spɛktɪv/ adj. [only before noun] **1** likely to do a particular thing or achieve a particular position: *Prospective jurors waited in the hallway.* **2** likely to happen or exist: *the prospective costs of the deal*

pros·pec·tor /'praspɛktə/ n. [C] someone who looks for gold, minerals, oil etc.

pro·spec·tus /prə'spɛktəs/ n. [C] **1** a small book that advertises a college, university, new business etc. **2** a formal statement giving details about a business opportunity such as an INVESTMENT

pros·per /'praspə/ v. **1** [I] to be successful and earn a lot of money: *Businesses across the state are prospering.* **2** [I] to grow and develop in a healthy way; THRIVE: *The children seemed to prosper under their grandparent's care.* **3** [T] OLD USE to make something succeed

pros·per·i·ty /pra'spɛrəti/ n. [U] a condition in which people have money and everything that is needed for a good life: *a time of economic prosperity*

pros·per·ous /'praspərəs/ adj. successful and having a lot of money: *Deng was the son of a prosperous landowner.*

pros·tate /'prasteit/ also **prostate gland** /,.. './ n. [C] the organ in the male body that produces a liquid in which SPERM are carried

pros·the·sis /pras'θisis/ n. plural **prostheses** /-siz/ [C] TECHNICAL an artificial leg, tooth, or other part of the body that takes the place of a missing part —**prosthetic** /pras'θɛtik/ adj.

pros·ti·tute[1] /'prastə,tut/ n. [C] someone, especially a woman, who earns money by having sex with people

prostitute[2] v. [T] **1** FORMAL if someone prostitutes a skill, ability, important principle etc., they use it in a way that does not show its true value, usually to earn money: *Friends from the theater criticized him for prostituting his talent in movies.* | *After the trial, defense lawyers said that justice had been "prostituted."* **2** to force someone to work as a prostitute to get money **3 prostitute yourself a)** to have sex in return for money **b)** to do something bad or do low quality work because you need money, even though you have the ability to do better

pros·ti·tu·tion /,prastə'tuʃən/ n. [U] **1** the work of prostitutes **2** FORMAL the use of a skill, ability, principle etc., in a way that does not show its true value

pros·trate[1] /'prastreit/ adj. **1** lying on your front with your face toward the ground: *They found him lying prostrate on the floor.* —compare PRONE (2) **2** too shocked, upset, damaged etc. to do anything or be effective: *the nation's prostrate economy* | [**+ with**] *Judy was prostrate with grief after her father's death.*

prostrate[2] v. [T] **1 prostrate yourself** to lie on your front with your face toward the ground, as an act of praise or a sign of your willingness to obey someone **2 be prostrated** FORMAL to have lost all your strength, courage, or energy —**prostration** /pra'streiʃən/ n. [C,U]

prot- /proot/ prefix another spelling of PROTO-, used before some vowels

pro·tag·o·nist /proo'tægənist/ n. [C] **1** the most important character in a play, movie, or story **2** FORMAL someone who is in a competition, battle, or struggle: *The U.N. Security Council has influence with some of the protagonists in the conflict.* **3** one of the main supporters of a social or political idea or way of thinking: [**+ of/for**] *McKinley was elected in 1896 as the protagonist of the views of the conservative classes.* —compare ANTAGONIST

pro·te·an /'prootiən, proo'tiən/ adj. LITERARY having the ability to change your appearance or behavior again and again: *an actor's protean talents*

P

s w **pro·tect** /prə'tɛkt/ v. [I,T] **1** to keep someone or something safe from harm, damage, or illness: *Are we doing enough to protect the environment?* | [protect sb/sth from sth] *The laws are designed to protect consumers from unsafe products.* | *The cover protects the machine from dust.* | [protect sb/sth] *You don't have to lie to protect me anymore, Bill.* | *To protect his investment, he put another $140,000 into the company.* | [protect sb/sth against sth] *The "Open Skies" plan was designed to protect nations against military buildup and surprise attack.* | [+ against] *Waxing your car will help protect against rust.* **2** [T usually passive] if an insurance company protects your home, car, life etc., it agrees to pay you money if things are stolen or damaged or you are hurt or killed: *Unemployment insurance means that you are partially protected when you lose your job.* **3** [T] to help the industry and trade of your own country by taxing foreign goods —see also PROTECTIONISM, PROTECTIVE

pro·tect·ed /prə'tɛktɪd/ an animal or plant that is protected is kept safe from harm or destruction by special laws: *Spotted owls are a protected species.*

s w **pro·tec·tion** /prə'tɛkʃən/ n. **1** [U] the act of protecting, or the condition of being protected: *24-hour police protection* | [+ against] *Always wear safety goggles for protection against flying pieces of wood and metal.* | **give/offer/provide protection** *Hard-shell bike helmets offer better protection than soft-shell helmets.* **2** [C] something that protects: *a bill providing environmental protections* | [+ against] *American troops were asked to remain as a protection against further fighting.* **3** [U] the promise of payment from an insurance company if something bad happens; COVERAGE **4** [U] protection money

pro·tec·tion·ism /prə'tɛkʃə,nɪzəm/ n. [U] the system of helping your country's trade, especially by taxing foreign goods —**protectionist** adj. —**protectionist** n. [C]

protection mon·ey /.'.. ,../ n. [U] money paid to criminals to stop them from damaging your property

protection rack·et /.'.. ,../ n. [C] INFORMAL a system in which criminals demand money from you to stop them from damaging your property

pro·tec·tive /prə'tɛktɪv/ adj. **1** [only before noun] used or intended for protection: *protective gloves* | *Some countries have taken more drastic protective measures to save the rhinos.* **2** wanting to protect someone from harm or danger: [+ of] *He's very protective of his younger brother.* **3** intended to give an advantage to your own country's industry: *a protective tariff on foreign textiles* —**protectively** adv. —**protectiveness** n. [U]

protective cus·to·dy /.,.. '.../ n. [U] a situation in which the police make you stay somewhere in order to protect you from people who could harm you: *The three children were taken into protective custody.*

protective serv·ic·es /.,.. '.../ n. [U] **child/adult protective services** a government organization that is responsible for making sure that children or old people are being taken care of well by their families

pro·tec·tor /prə'tɛktɚ/ n. [C] someone or something that protects someone or something else: *He sees himself as her protector.* | *a plastic pocket protector*

pro·tec·tor·ate /prə'tɛktərɪt/ n. [C] a country that is protected and controlled by a more powerful country, especially in the areas of defense and foreign affairs —compare COLONY (1)

pro·té·gé /'proʊtə,ʒeɪ, ,proʊtə'ʒeɪ/ n. [C] someone, especially a young person, who is taught and helped by someone who has influence, power, or more experience

pro·té·gée /'proʊtə,ʒeɪ, ,proʊtə'ʒeɪ/ n. [C] a girl or woman who is guided and helped by someone who has influence, power, or more experience

pro·tein /'proʊtin/ n. [C,U] one of the substances that exist in food such as meat, eggs, and beans, which

help your body to grow and keep it strong and healthy

pro tem, **Pro Tem** /proʊ 'tɛm/ also **pro tem·po·re** /proʊ 'tɛmpəri/ FORMAL adj. [only after noun] happening or existing now but only for a short time: *President/Mayor/Judge etc. pro tem the President pro tem of the Senate*

pro·test¹ /'proʊtɛst/ n. **1** [C,U] a strong complaint s w that shows you disagree with or are angry about something that you think is wrong or unfair: *Despite angry protests from environmentalists, building will go ahead as planned.* | [+ against] *Many observers see the demonstrations as a protest against the government.* | *Six teachers quit in protest of the board's decision.* | *the radical protest movements* (=group of people who are protesting) *of the 1960s* | **a storm/wave/firestorm of protest** (=a lot of angry protest) **2** [C] an occasion when people come together in public to express disapproval or opposition to something: *Three people died Thursday in violent street protests.* **3** **do sth under protest** to do something in a way that shows you do not want to do it because you think it is wrong or unfair: *They finally paid the full bill under protest.* **4** **without protest** calmly and without complaining: *How can she accept that kind of treatment without protest?*

pro·test² /prə'tɛst, 'proʊtɛst/ v. **1** [I,T] to say or do something publicly to show that you disagree with or are angry about something that you think is wrong or unfair: [+ against/at/about] *Thousands blocked the streets, protesting against the ruling.* | [protest sth] *Students protested the change.* | *"I don't think that's fair!" she protested.* **2** [T] to state very firmly that something is true, especially when other people do not believe you: [protest that] *Everyone laughed as Ashley protested that she wasn't Tom's girlfriend.* | *He was led away to his jail cell, still protesting his innocence.*

Prot·es·tant /'prɑtəstənt/ adj. relating to a part of the Christian church that separated from the Catholic Church in the 16th century —**Protestant** n. [C] —**Protestantism** n. [U]

prot·es·ta·tion /,prɑtə'steɪʃən ,proʊ-/ n. [C] FORMAL a strong statement saying that something is true or not true: [+ of] *protestations of love*

pro·test·er /'proʊtɛstɚ, proʊ'tɛstɚ/ n. [C] someone who takes part in a public activity to show their opposition to something

proto- /proʊtoʊ, -tə/ prefix TECHNICAL existing or coming before other things of the same type; ORIGINAL: *a proto-fascist group* | *a prototype* (=first form of a new car, machine etc.)

pro·to·col /'proʊtə,kɔl, -,kɑl/ n. **1** [U] the system of rules on the correct and acceptable way to behave in an official situation: *What is the correct protocol when you meet the Queen?* **2** [C] TECHNICAL a set of rules for what form electronic information should be in, so that it can be sent successfully from one computer to another —see also FTP **3** [C] an official statement of the rules that a group of countries have agreed to follow in dealing with a particular problem: *the Montreal Protocol on greenhouse warming* **4** [C] the rules that are followed when treating or dealing with a particular illness or medical problem: *Under the new protocol, women will stay in the clinic for four hours to be watched for the appearance of new symptoms.*

pro·ton /'proʊtɑn/ n. [C] a very small piece of matter with a positive electrical CHARGE that is in the central part of an atom —compare ELECTRON, NEUTRON

pro·to·plasm /'proʊtə,plæzəm/ n. [U] TECHNICAL the colorless substance that forms the cells of plants and animals

pro·to·type /'proʊtə,taɪp/ n. [C] **1** the first form that a new design of a car, machine etc. has, or a model of it used to test the design before it is produced: [+ of/for] *a working prototype of the new model* **2** someone or something that is one of the first and most typical examples of a group or situation: *Baltimore is now cited as the prototype of successful civic entrepreneurship.*

pro·to·typ·i·cal /ˌprouṭə'tɪpɪkəl/ adj. [no comparative] very typical of a group or a type: *"All I Want for Christmas" is the prototypical comedy for 8- to 12-year-olds.*

pro·to·zo·an /ˌprouṭə'zouən/ also **pro·to·zo·on** /ˌprouṭə'zouɑn/ /-'zouɑ/ n. plural **protozoa** /-'zouə/ [C usually plural] a very small living thing that has only one cell —**protozoan** adj.

pro·tract·ed /prou'træktɪd, prə-/ adj. [only before noun] continuing for a long time, especially longer than usual or necessary: *There was a protracted silence before Lydia spoke again.*

pro·trac·tor /prou'træktɚ, prə-/ n. [C] an instrument, usually in the shape of a half-circle, used for measuring and drawing angles

pro·trude /prou'trud/ v. [I] to stick out from somewhere: [+ from] *A tuft of gray hair protruded from beneath her knit hat.* —**protruding** adj.: *a protruding stomach*

pro·tru·sion /prou'truʒən/ n. 1 [C] something that sticks out 2 [U] the condition of sticking out

pro·tu·ber·ance /prou'tubərəns/ n. [C] FORMAL something that sticks out from the surface of something else —**protuberant** adj.

s w
3 3
proud /praud/ adj. 1 feeling pleased with your achievements, family, country etc. because you think they are very good: *You did it all by yourself? You should be very proud.* | [+ of] *Your dad and I are so proud of you.* | [proud to do/be sth] *I'm proud to be an American.* | [proud (that)] *Yes, I did oppose the changes, and I'm proud that I did.* | *Scheer is the proud owner of a copy of the Declaration of Independence.* | *Three new fathers stood holding their babies, looking proud as peacocks* (=extremely pleased). | *Pearman's proudest moment was becoming an Eagle Scout at age 15.* —opposite HUMBLE[1] 2 thinking that you are more important, skillful etc. than you really are: *He was a proud man who refused to admit his mistakes.* 3 do sb proud INFORMAL to make people feel proud of you by doing something well: *The soldiers have done their country proud.* 4 having respect for yourself, so that you are too embarrassed to accept help from other people when you are in a difficult situation: *Many farmers then were too proud to ask for government help.* 5 LITERARY tall and impressive: *the proud cathedral spire* —see also PRIDE[1] —**proudly** adv.

Proust /prust/, **Mar·cel** /mar'sɛl/ (1871–1922) a French writer of NOVELS who is considered one of the greatest writers of modern times

s w
2 1
prove /pruv/ v. past tense **proved** past participle **proved** or **proven** 1 [T] to show that something is definitely true, especially by providing facts, information etc.: *He claims the police destroyed records that could prove the officer's guilt.* | *To prove her point, Garth cites a book by John Quincy Adams.* | [prove (that)] *Can you prove that you had nothing to do with it?* | **prove sb wrong/innocent etc.** *They say I'm too old, but I'm going to prove them all wrong.* —compare DISPROVE 2 [linking verb] if someone or something proves to be difficult, helpful, a problem etc., you find out that they are difficult, helpful, a problem etc. | **prove (to be) useful/difficult etc.** *Some of the experiments proved disastrous for the biology department's reputation.* | *The recent revelations may prove to be embarrassing to the President.* | **prove (to be) a disaster/problem/benefit etc.** *The magazine proved to be a financial disaster and was eventually sold off.* 3 **prove yourself** also **prove something** to show how good you are at doing something: *When I started the job, I felt I had to prove myself.* | *I don't have to prove anything to anyone – I just do what I want.* 4 **What is sb trying to prove?** SPOKEN said when you are annoyed by someone's behavior, because you think that they are trying too hard to show that they are right or that they know something: *What is he trying to prove? It's like he wants to show us he's a real man, or something.* 5 **prove a point** if someone does something to prove a point, they do it to show that they are right or that they can do something without having any other good reason: *I'm not going to run the marathon just*

to prove a point. I know I could do it if I wanted to. 6 [T] LAW to show that a WILL has been made in the correct way —**provable** adj. —**provably** adv.

prov·en[1] /'pruvən/ adj. [usually before noun] tested and shown to be true or good, or shown to exist: *Saudi Arabia controls a quarter of the world's proven oil supply.*

proven[2] v. a past participle of PROVE

prov·e·nance /'prɑvənəns/ n. [U] FORMAL the place where something originally came from: *a rug of Iranian provenance*

prov·en·der /'prɑvəndɚ/ n. [U] OLD-FASHIONED dry food for horses and cattle

prov·erb /'prɑvɚb/ n. [C] a short well-known statement that contains advice about life in general. For example, "A penny saved is a penny earned" is a proverb.

prov·er·bi·al /prə'vɚbiəl/ adj. 1 **the proverbial sth** used when you describe something using a well-known expression: *The store had everything including the proverbial kitchen sink.* 2 relating to a proverb: *a proverbial expression* 3 well known by a lot of people: *His modesty is proverbial.* —**proverbially** adv.

Pro·verbs /'prɑvɚbz/ a book in the OLD TESTAMENT in the Bible

s w
2 1
pro·vide /prə'vaɪd/ v. [T] 1 to give something to someone or make it available to them, because they need it or want it: [provide sth for sb] *The clinic will provide basic health care for people in the community.* | [provide sb with sth] *Someone had provided the reporters with photographs.* | [provide sth] *A useful summary of the information is provided in Table 8b.* 2 to produce a useful result, opportunity etc.: *Liz's painful story provides a clear example of the dangers of drug abuse.* | [provide sb with sth] *Even a cigarette butt could provide investigators with clues about what happened.* | [provide sth to/for sb] *Her letter provided hope to women in similar situations.* 3 **provide that** FORMAL if a law or rule provides that something must happen, it states that it must happen

provide against sth phr. v. [T] FORMAL to make plans in order to deal with a bad situation that might happen

provide for sb/sth phr. v. [T] 1 to give someone the things they need, such as money, food etc.: *It's important to me to be able to provide for my family.* 2 FORMAL if a law, rule, or plan provides for something, it states that something will be done and makes it possible for it to be done: *The new constitution provides for a 650-seat legislature.* 3 FORMAL to make plans in order to deal with something that might happen in the future: *Commanders failed to provide for the enemy's attack by sea.*

pro·vid·ed /prə'vaɪdɪd/ also **provided that** conjunction used to say that something will only be possible if something else happens or is done first: *There's no annual fee provided that you use the credit card at least six times a year.*

Prov·i·dence /'prɑvədəns/ the capital and largest city of the U.S. state of Rhode Island

prov·i·dence, Providence /'prɑvədəns/ n. [U] LITERARY a force that some people believe organizes what happens in our lives, especially what God wants to happen: *divine providence* —compare FATE (2)

prov·i·dent /'prɑvədənt/ adj. FORMAL careful and sensible, especially in saving money for the future —opposite IMPROVIDENT

prov·i·den·tial /ˌprɑvə'dɛnʃəl/ adj. FORMAL happening just when you need it or in just the way you need it to happen: *Blackwell's arrival at that moment was providential.* —**providentially** adv.

pro·vid·er /prə'vaɪdɚ/ n. [C] 1 a company or person that provides a service: *day-care providers* 2 someone who supports a family

pro·vid·ing /prə'vaɪdɪŋ/ also **providing that** conjunction used to say that something will only be possible if something else happens or is done first; PROVIDED: *They'll have it built by November, providing we don't get an early snow.*

prov·ince /'prɑvɪns/ *n.* **1** also **Province** [C] one of the large areas into which some countries are divided, which usually has a government for that area: *a Chinese province* **2** FORMAL a subject that someone knows a lot about or something that only they are responsible for; DOMAIN: [+ **of**] *Computers were once the province of scientists and mathematicians.* **3 the provinces** [plural] the parts of a country that are not near to the capital or other large city: *Life in the provinces was difficult.* **4** an area that an ARCHBISHOP (=a Christian priest of the highest rank) is responsible for —compare DIOCESE

pro·vin·cial¹ /prə'vɪnʃəl/ *adj.* **1** [only before noun] relating to or coming from a province or from the parts of a country that are not near the capital or other large city: *the provincial government of Quebec* **2** DISAPPROVING not interested in anything new or different or in anything that does not relate to your own life and experiences: *provincial attitudes*

provincial² *n.* [C] DISAPPROVING someone who comes from a part of a country that is not near the capital or other large city, especially someone who is not interesting in anything new or different

pro·vin·cial·ism /prə'vɪnʃə,lɪzəm/ *n.* [U] DISAPPROVING the attitude of not being interested in anything new or different or in anything that does not relate to your own life or experience

prov·ing ground /'.. ,./ *n.* [C] **1** a place or situation in which something new is tried for the first time or tested: *Chicago was becoming an influential proving ground for bands like Smashing Pumpkins.* **2** an area for scientific testing, especially of vehicles

s w **pro·vi·sion¹** /prə'vɪʒən/ *n.* **1** [C,U] the act of providing something that someone needs now or will need in the future: [+ **of**] *the provision of drinking water to rural communities* | *He made provisions for his wife and children in his will.* **2** [C] a condition in an agreement or law: *The agreement includes a provision for each side to check the other side's weapons.* **3 provisions** [plural] food supplies, especially for a long trip: *We had enough provisions for two weeks.*

provision² *v.* [T] to provide someone or something with a lot of food and supplies, especially for a trip

pro·vi·sion·al /prə'vɪʒənl/ *adj.* **1** intended to exist for only a short time and likely to be changed in the future: *a provisional government* —compare TEMPORARY **2** provisional offers, arrangements etc. are not yet definite but should become definite in the future: *We accept provisional bookings by phone.* —**provisionally** *adv.*

pro·vi·so /prə'vaɪzoʊ/ *n. plural* **provisos** [C] FORMAL a condition that you ask for before you will agree to something: *The money was given to the museum with the proviso that it be spent on operating costs.*

pro·voc·a·teur /proʊ,vɑkə'tɚ/ *n.* [C] someone who is employed to encourage people who are working against a government to do something illegal so that the government can catch them

prov·o·ca·tion /,prɑvə'keɪʃən/ *n.* [C,U] an action or event that makes someone angry or that is intended to do this: *Carter claims that she attacked him without provocation.*

pro·voc·a·tive /prə'vɑkətɪv/ *adj.* **1** provocative behavior, remarks etc. are intended to make people angry or to cause a lot of discussion: *The book's provocative statements have led to it being banned in some schools.* **2** provocative clothes, movements, pictures etc. are intended to make someone sexually excited: *a provocative bikini* —**provocatively** *adv.*

pro·voke /prə'voʊk/ *v.* [T] **1** to make someone very angry, especially by annoying them: *The dog would not have attacked if it hadn't been provoked.* [**provoke sb into (doing) sth**] *Paul tried unsuccessfully to provoke Fletch into a fight.* **2** to cause a reaction or feeling, especially a sudden one: *Dole's comments*

provoked laughter from the press. | [**provoke sb to do sth**] *His criticisms only provoked her to work harder.* | [**provoke sb into (doing) sth**] *She hopes her editorial will provoke readers into thinking seriously about the issue.* —see also THOUGHT-PROVOKING

pro·vost, Provost /'proʊvoʊst/ *n.* [C] an important official at a college or university

prow /praʊ/ *n.* [C] ESPECIALLY LITERARY the front part of a ship or boat

prow·ess /'praʊɪs/ *n.* [U] FORMAL great skill at doing something: *athletic prowess*

prowl¹ /praʊl/ *v.* [I,T] **1** if an animal prowls, it moves around an area quietly, especially because it is hunting another animal **2** if someone prowls, they move around an area slowly and quietly, especially because they are looking for something: *Officer Watson prowls the streets at night, looking for drug dealers.*

prowl² *n.* **1 be on the prowl** to be moving around looking for something or someone in different places: *Lucille is always on the prowl for bargains.* **2** [singular] an act of prowling

prowl car /'. ./ *n.* [C] OLD-FASHIONED a car used by the police to drive around an area

prowl·er /'praʊlɚ/ *n.* [C] someone who moves around secretly or hides in or near someone's house, especially at night, in order to harm them or steal something

prox·i·mate /'prɑksəmɪt/ *adj.* FORMAL **1** a proximate cause or result is a direct one, when there are other possible causes as well: *The proximate cause of death was colon cancer.* **2** nearest in time, order, or family relationship —**proximately** *adv.*

prox·im·i·ty /prɑk'sɪməti/ *n.* [U] FORMAL nearness in distance or time: [+ **to**] *We chose the house for its proximity to the school.* | *In Rio the rich and poor continue to live in close proximity.*

prox·y /'prɑksi/ *n.* [C] **1** someone that you choose to represent you, especially to vote for you **2 (do sth) by proxy** to do something by arranging for someone else to do it for you

proxy vote /'.. ,./ *n.* [C] a vote you make by officially sending someone else to vote for you

Pro·zac /'proʊzæk/ *n.* [U] TRADEMARK a type of drug that is used to treat DEPRESSION (=a mental illness that makes people very unhappy)

prude /prud/ *n.* [C] DISAPPROVING someone who is very easily shocked by anything relating to sex —see also PRUDISH

pru·dence /'prudns/ *n.* [U] a sensible and careful attitude that makes you avoid unnecessary risks

pru·dent /'prudnt/ *adj.* sensible and careful, especially by trying to avoid unnecessary risks: *prudent house buyers* | *It is prudent to give children only pasteurized milk and juices, to avoid food poisoning.* —opposite IMPRUDENT —**prudently** *adv.*

pru·den·tial /pru'dɛnʃəl/ *adj.* OLD-FASHIONED PRUDENT

prud·er·y /'prudəri/ *n.* [U] DISAPPROVING prudish behavior

Prud·hoe Bay /'prudoʊ ,beɪ/ a BAY of the Arctic Ocean on the northern coast of Alaska, where large amounts of oil were discovered in 1968

prud·ish /'prudɪʃ/ *adj.* DISAPPROVING very easily shocked by things relating to sex: *American culture is in many ways still fairly prudish.* —**prudishly** *adv.* —**prudishness** *n.* [U] —see also PRUDE

prune¹ /prun/ *v.* [T] **1** also **prune sth ↔ back** to cut some of the branches of a tree or bush to make it grow better: *Red dogwoods should be pruned regularly.* **2** to get rid of the unnecessary parts of something: *The state has pruned $275 million from this year's budget.* —**pruning** *n.* [U]

prune² *n.* [C] a dried PLUM (=type of fruit): *stewed prunes*

pruning hook /'.. ,./ *n.* [C] a knife that is shaped like a hook and is usually on a long pole, used for cutting branches off trees

pru·ri·ent /'prʊriənt/ *adj.* FORMAL too strongly interested in sex: *The material would appeal only to prurient interests.* —**prurience** *n.* [U]

prus·sic ac·id /ˌprʌsɪk ˈæsɪd/ n. [U] a very poisonous acid

pry /praɪ/ v. **pried, prying** 1 [T always + adv./prep.] to force something open, or force it away from something else | **pry** sth ↔ **loose/off/apart** etc. A raccoon was trying to pry open the lid of the garbage can. 2 [I] to try to find out details about someone else's private life in an impolite way: Anna is a private person, and I did not want to pry. 3 **prying eyes** people who want to see or know what you are doing: She is finally able to relax with friends, away from prying eyes.

pry sth **out of** sb/sth phr. v. [T] to get money or information from someone with a lot of difficulty: If you want to know his name, you're going to have to pry it out of her.

P.S. n. [C] 1 also **p.s.** postscript; a note added at the end of a letter, giving more information: Love, Lucinda P.S. Tell Abby "hello." 2 the abbreviation of PUBLIC SCHOOL: P.S. 121 3 the abbreviation of Police Sergeant

psalm /sɑm/ n. [C] a song or poem praising God

psalm·ist /ˈsɑmɪst/ n. [C] someone who has written a psalm

Psalms /sɑmz/ a book in the Old Testament of the Christian Bible

psal·ter /ˈsɑltər/ n. [C] a book containing the psalms from the Bible, often with music, for use in a church

psal·ter·y /ˈsɑltəri/ n. [C] an ancient musical instrument with strings stretched over a board

pseudo- /sudoʊ/ prefix not real; false: pseudo-intellectuals (=people who pretend to be intelligent) | Popular opinion is that astrology is just a pseudoscience (=not a real science).

pseu·do·nym /ˈsudnˌɪm, ˈsudəˌnɪm/ n. [C] an invented name used by someone, especially a writer, instead of their real name: Charlotte Brontë wrote under the pseudonym of Currer Bell.

pseu·don·y·mous /suˈdɑnəməs/ adj. written or writing under a pseudonym: Martin writes the pseudonymous advice column "Miss Manners." —**pseudonymously** adv.

pshaw /pʃɔ/ interjection OLD-FASHIONED said to show annoyance, disapproval, or disagreement

psi, p.s.i. n. [U] pounds per square inch; a measure of pressure against a surface

pso·ri·a·sis /səˈraɪəsɪs/ n. [U] a disease that makes your skin dry, red, and FLAKY (=coming off in small pieces)

psst /pst/ interjection a sound you make very quietly, used to attract someone's attention without other people noticing: Psst! Come over here – I want to show you something.

PST the abbreviation of Pacific Standard Time

psych¹ /saɪk/ v.

psych sb/sth ↔ **out** phr. v. [T] INFORMAL to do or say things that will make your opponent in a game or competition feel nervous or confused, so that it is easier for you to win: Lawyers try to psych out their opponents.

psych sb/yourself **up** phr. v. [T] INFORMAL to prepare someone mentally before doing something, so that they feel confident: [+ for] He was pacing the room, trying to psych himself up for the meeting.

psych² n. [U] SPOKEN, INFORMAL a short form of PSYCHOLOGY: a psych major

psych³ adj. [only before noun] SPOKEN, INFORMAL a short form of PSYCHIATRIC: the hospital's psych ward

psych- /saɪk/ prefix TECHNICAL relating to the mind, as opposed to the body: a psychiatrist | psychosis (=serious mental illness) —see also PSYCHO-

psy·che /ˈsaɪki/ n. [C usually singular] TECHNICAL OR FORMAL someone's mind, or their basic nature, which controls their attitudes and behavior: The war in Vietnam still lingers in the American psyche.

psyched /saɪkt/ adj. [not before noun] also **psyched up** to be mentally prepared for an event and excited about it: [+ about/for] I'm really psyched about this semester!

psy·che·del·ic /ˌsaɪkəˈdɛlɪk/ adj. 1 psychedelic

drugs such as LSD make you HALLUCINATE (=see things that do not really exist) 2 psychedelic art, clothing etc. has complicated patterns of strong bright colors, shapes etc.

psy·chi·at·ric /ˌsaɪkiˈætrɪk/ adj. [only before noun] relating to the study and treatment of mental illness: psychiatric evaluation

psychiatric hos·pi·tal /..ˈ.. ˌ.../ n. [C] a hospital where people with mental illnesses are treated

psy·chi·a·trist /saɪˈkaɪətrɪst, sə-/ n. [C] a doctor trained in the treatment of mental illnesses —compare PSYCHOLOGIST

psy·chi·a·try /saɪˈkaɪətri/ n. [U] the study and treatment of mental illnesses

psy·chic¹ /ˈsaɪkɪk/ adj. [no comparative] 1 also **psychical** relating to mysterious events involving the power of the human mind: psychic phenomena | psychic healers 2 having the ability to know what other people are thinking or what will happen in the future, or showing this quality: How did you know I wanted one? You must be psychic! | a psychic prediction —compare CLAIRVOYANT 3 also **psychical** affecting the mind rather than the body: psychic disorders —**psychically** /-kli/ adv.

psychic² n. [C] someone who has mysterious powers, such as the ability to receive messages from dead people or to know what will happen in the future

psy·cho /ˈsaɪkoʊ/ n. plural **psychos** [C] INFORMAL someone who is likely to suddenly behave in a violent or crazy way —**psycho** adj.

psycho- /saɪkoʊ, -kə/ prefix TECHNICAL relating to the mind, as opposed to the body: a psychoanalyst (=person who helps people with mental illnesses) —see also PSYCH-

psy·cho·ac·tive /ˌsaɪkoʊˈæktɪv/ adj. TECHNICAL psychoactive drugs, chemicals etc. have an effect on the mind

psy·cho·a·nal·y·sis /ˌsaɪkoʊəˈnæləsɪs/ n. [U] a way of treating someone who is mentally ill by talking to them about their life in the past, their feelings etc., in order to find out the hidden causes of their problems —**psychoanalytic** /ˌsaɪkoʊˌænlˈɪtɪk/ also **psychoanalytical** adj. —**psychoanalytically** /-kli/ adv.

psy·cho·an·a·lyst /ˌsaɪkoʊˈænlɪst/ n. [C] someone who is trained in psychoanalysis

psy·cho·an·a·lyze /ˌsaɪkoʊˈænlˌaɪz/ v. [I,T] to treat someone or think about a problem using psychoanalysis

psy·cho·bab·ble /ˈsaɪkoʊˌbæbəl/ n. [U] INFORMAL, DISAPPROVING language that sounds scientific but is not really, that some people use when talking about their emotional problems

psy·cho·bi·ol·o·gy /ˌsaɪkoʊbaɪˈɑlədʒi/ n. [U] the study of the body in relation to the mind

psy·cho·dra·ma /ˈsaɪkoʊˌdrɑmə/ n. [C] 1 a serious movie, play etc. that examines the complicated psychological relationships of the characters 2 a way of treating mental illness in which people are asked to act in a situation together to help them understand their emotions

psy·cho·ki·ne·sis /ˌsaɪkoʊkəˈnisɪs/ n. [U] the action of moving solid objects using only the power of the mind, which some people believe is possible —**psychokinetic** /ˌsaɪkoʊkəˈnɛtɪk/ adj.

psy·cho·log·i·cal /ˌsaɪkəˈlɑdʒɪkəl/ adj. [no comparative] 1 relating to the way that people's minds work and the way that this affects their behavior: psychological problems | Sometimes psychological abuse is worse than physical abuse. 2 relating to what is in someone's mind rather than what is real: Doctors dismissed her complaints of pain as psychological. 3 psychological warfare behavior that is intended to make your opponents less confident —**psychologically** /-kli/ adv.

psy·chol·o·gist /saɪˈkɑlədʒɪst/ n. [C] someone who is trained in psychology: a child psychologist —compare PSYCHIATRIST

psy·chol·o·gy /saɪˈkɑlədʒi/ n. **1** [U] the study of the mind and how it works: *clinical psychology* | *a psychology class* **2** the mental processes involved in doing a certain activity: [+ **of**] *Eckman's research has focused on the psychology of lying.* | *the psychology of video games* **3** [C,U] the usual way in which a particular person or group thinks and reacts: *a terrorist's psychology* **4** [U] INFORMAL knowledge of the way that people think, that makes you able to control what they do: *You have to use psychology to get people to stop smoking.*

psy·cho·met·ric /ˌsaɪkouˈmɛtrɪk◂/ adj. relating to the measurement of mental abilities and qualities: *psychometric tests*

psy·cho·path /ˈsaɪkə,pæθ/ n. [C] someone who has a serious and permanent mental illness that makes them behave in a violent or criminal way —compare SOCIOPATH —**psychopathic** /ˌsaɪkə,pæθɪk/ adj.: *a psychopathic killer*

psy·cho·sis /saɪˈkoʊsɪs/ n. plural **psychoses** /-siz/ [C,U] TECHNICAL a serious mental illness that can change your character and make you unable to behave in a normal way —see also PSYCHOTIC

psy·cho·so·cial /ˌsaɪkouˈsouʃəl/ adj. TECHNICAL relating to both someone's mind and how they behave with other people: *the pychosocial concerns of cancer patients*

psy·cho·so·mat·ic /ˌsaɪkousəˈmæt̮ɪk/ adj. **1** a psychosomatic illness is caused by fear or anxiety rather than by any physical problem **2** relating to the relationship between the mind and physical illness —**psychosomatically** /-kli/ adv.

psy·cho·ther·a·py /ˌsaɪkouˈθɛrəpi/ n. [U] the treatment of mental illness, for example DEPRESSION, by talking to someone and discussing problems, rather than by using drugs or medicine —**psychotherapist** n. [C]

psy·chot·ic /saɪˈkɑt̮ɪk/ adj. suffering from PSYCHOSIS, or caused by psychosis: *psychotic delusions* —**psychotic** n. [C] —**psychotically** /-kli/ adv.

psy·cho·tro·pic /ˌsaɪkəˈtroupɪk◂/ adj. TECHNICAL psychotropic drugs have an effect on your mind or behavior

PT the written abbreviation of Pacific Time

pt. 1 the written abbreviation of "part": *Pt. III* **2** the written abbreviation of PINT **3** the written abbreviation of "payment" **4** also **Pt.** the written abbreviation of "point" **5** also **Pt.** the written abbreviation of PORT (1): *Pt. Moresby*

PTA n. [C] Parent-Teacher Association; an organization of parents and teachers that tries to help and improve a particular school

pter·o·dac·tyl /ˌtɛrəˈdæktl/ n. [C] a type of large flying animal that lived many millions of years ago

PTO n. [C] **1** Parent Teacher Organization; an organization similar to the PTA **2** please turn over; written at the bottom of a page of writing to show that there is more written on the back

Ptol·e·ma·ic sys·tem /ˌtɑləˈmeɪ-ɪk ˌsɪstəm/ n. [singular] the old system of belief that the Earth was at the center of the universe, with the sun, stars, and PLANETS moving around it

Ptol·e·my¹ /ˈtɑləmi/ (A.D. ?100–?170) a Greek ASTRONOMER and MATHEMATICIAN who lived and worked in Egypt, and developed the PTOLEMAIC SYSTEM

Ptolemy² the name used by the family of kings who ruled Egypt from the 4th century B.C. to the 1st century B.C.

pto·maine /ˈtoumeɪn, touˈmeɪn/ n. [C,U] a poisonous substance formed by BACTERIA in decaying food

pub /pʌb/ n. [C] a comfortable BAR that often serves food, especially one in the U.K. or Ireland

pu·ber·ty /ˈpyubət̮i/ n. [U] the stage of physical development during which you change from a child to an adult, for example when a girl begins to MENSTRUATE: **reach/enter puberty** *Girls often reach puberty*

earlier than boys.* | *Cameron admits it was hard, going through puberty on TV.*

pu·bes /pyubz/ n. [plural] SLANG pubic hair

pu·bes·cent /pyuˈbɛsənt/ adj. a pubescent boy or girl is going through puberty

pu·bic /ˈpyubɪk/ adj. [only before noun] relating to or near the sexual organs: *pubic hair*

pub·lic¹ /ˈpʌblɪk/ adj.
1 ordinary people [no comparative] relating to or coming from all the ordinary people in a country or city: *Reiner insisted that public pressure did not influence his decision.* | *Allowing the two banks to merge would not be in the public interest* (=helpful or useful to ordinary people). | *Public outcry has led to the lowering of gasoline prices.*
2 for anyone [no comparative] available for anyone to use: *a public restroom* | *a public beach* | *Smoking is no longer allowed in indoor public places.*
3 government [no comparative] relating to the government and with the services it provides for people: *An estimated $20,000 dollars in public money was spent on the celebration.* | *Jones had never run for public office* (=a job that is part of a government) *before being elected Senator.* | *The government is not allowed to aid religion in U.S. public life* (=the actions and services that are for all people).
4 known about [no comparative] known about by most people: *The name of the victim has not been made public.* | *Yeltsin's heart problems did not become public knowledge until after his re-election.* | *This is not the first time Collins has been in the public eye* (=on television, radio etc. a lot because you are famous). | *Hudson was one of the first public figures* (=famous people) *to die of AIDS.*
5 not hidden intended for anyone to know, see, or hear: *We feel he owes us a public apology.* | *public display of emotion/grief/affection etc.* (=showing your emotions so that everyone can see)
6 go public a)** to tell everyone about something that was secret: *The chairman didn't want to go public with the information.* **b)** to begin to sell STOCK in your company to become a PUBLIC COMPANY: *Several biotech companies went public this year.*
7 public life work that you do, especially for the government, that makes you well known to many people: *Monnerville retired from public life in 1983.* | *Ms. Levin has been in public life for 23 years.*
8 public image the character or attitudes that a famous person, organization etc. is thought by most people to have: *Armstrong is working hard to rebuild his public image.*
9 a public appearance a visit by a famous person in order to make a speech, advertise something etc.: *White will make no more public appearances for the rest of the year.*
10 public enemy number one, public enemy No. 1 the criminal, problem etc. that is considered the most serious threat to people's safety: *Rats have been branded public enemy No. 1 in Bangladesh.* —compare PRIVATE¹

public² n. **1 the public** all the ordinary people in a country or city: *The class is free and open to the public.* | *We want the committee to include at least five members of the general public.* **2 in public** in a place where anyone can know, see, or hear: *You're not going to wear that in public, are you?* —opposite **in private** (PRIVATE² (1)) —see also **wash your dirty laundry/linen in public** (DIRTY¹ (8)) **3** [singular,U] the people who like listening to a particular singer, reading the books of a particular writer etc.: *He goes out of his way to make sure his public is satisfied.*

public ac·cess /ˌ.. ˈ../ n. [U] the right of ordinary people to go onto particular areas of land or read particular documents: [+ **to**] *Public access to these beaches is guaranteed.*

public access chan·nel /ˌ.. ˈ.. ˌ../ n. [C] a television CHANNEL provided by CABLE television, on which anyone can broadcast a program

public-ad·dress sys·tem /ˌ.. ˈ. ˌ../ n. [C] a PA²

public af·fairs /ˌ.. ˈ./ n. [plural] events and questions, especially political ones, that have an effect on people in general: *the university's vice president for public affairs*

public as·sist·ance /ˌ.. .ˈ../ n. [U] the government programs that help poor people get food, homes, and medical care: *Almost half the community lives on public assistance.*

pub·li·ca·tion /ˌpʌblɪˈkeɪʃən/ n. **1** [U] the process of printing a book, magazine etc. and offering it for sale: *The Weekly began publication December 1, 1982.* **2** [C] a book, magazine etc.: *a monthly publication* **3** [U] the act of making something known to people in general: *The publication of his results has inspired a new wave of research.*

public com·pa·ny /ˌ.. ˈ.../ n. [C] a company that offers its STOCK for sale to people who are not part of the company

public cor·po·ra·tion /ˌ.. .ˈ../ n. [C] **1** a PUBLIC COMPANY **2** a business that is run by the government

public de·fend·er /ˌ.. .ˈ./ n. [C] a lawyer who is paid by the government to defend people in court, because they cannot pay for a lawyer themselves —compare DISTRICT ATTORNEY

public do·main /ˌ.. .ˈ./ n. LAW **in the public domain** a play, idea etc. that is in the public domain is available for anyone to perform or use

public fund·ing /ˌ.. ˈ../ n. [U] money that the government gives to support organizations or events: *public funding for the arts*

public health /ˌ.. ˈ./ n. [U] the health of all the people in an area: *The food additives do not appear to pose a public health risk.*

public hol·i·day /ˌ.. ˈ../ n. [C] a special day when people do not go to work and many stores do not open

public hous·ing /ˌ.. ˈ../ n. [U] houses or apartments built by the government for poor people

public in·quir·y /ˌ.. ˈ..., ˌ.. .ˈ../ n. [C] **1** an official attempt to find out the cause of something, especially an accident: *The administration has promised a public inquiry into the bombing.* **2** a request for information from an official organization, by people who are not part of that organization

pub·li·cist /ˈpʌbləsɪst/ n. [C] someone whose job is to make sure that people find out about a new product, movie, book etc., or about what a famous person is doing

pub·lic·i·ty /pəˈblɪsəti/ n. [U] **1** the attention that someone or something gets from newspapers, television etc.: *Wilder **received** national **publicity** after the rescue.* | *How can we get some **free publicity** for our company?* | **bad/negative publicity** (=publicity that makes you look bad) | **good/favorable publicity** (=publicity that makes you look good) **2** the business of making sure that people know about a new product, movie etc., or about what a particular famous person is doing: *Who did you get to do the publicity for the show?* | *Jackson has launched **a** massive **publicity campaign** to promote her book (=a series of activities intended to get attention for her book).* **3** a **publicity stunt** something that is done only to get publicity

publicity a·gent /.ˈ... ˌ../ n. [C] a PRESS AGENT

pub·li·cize /ˈpʌbləˌsaɪz/ v. [T] to give information about something to people in general, so that they know about it: *Rumors should be investigated, not publicized.* | **well/much/widely/highly publicized** *He was found not guilty of the highly publicized murders.*

public li·brar·y /ˌ.. ˈ../ n. [C] a building where people can go to read or borrow books without having to pay

pub·lic·ly /ˈpʌblɪkli/ adv. **1** in a way that is intended for anyone to know, see, or hear: *No one is complaining publicly, but few are happy with the new policy.* | *This will be the first time he has talked publicly about the accident.* **2** by the government as part of its services: *The jobs program is publicly funded.* **3** a company that is publicly owned has sold STOCK in it to people who are not part of the company **4** among the ordinary people in a country or city: *We believe the current proposals will prove publicly acceptable.*

public nui·sance /ˌ.. ˈ../ n. [C] **1** LAW an action that

is harmful to many people: *Six protesters were charged with **creating a public nuisance** for blocking the highway.* **2** a person who does things that annoy a lot of people

public o·pin·ion /ˌ.. .ˈ../ n. [U] the opinions or beliefs that ordinary people have about a particular subject: *a recent public opinion poll about the election*

public own·er·ship /ˌ.. ˈ.../ n. [U] businesses, property etc. that are under public ownership are owned by the government

public prop·er·ty /ˌ.. ˈ.../ n. [U] **1** something, especially an area of land, that is provided for anyone to use, and is usually owned by the government: *Disaster aid helps pay for repairs to bridges, roads, and other damaged public property.* **2** INFORMAL something that everyone has a right to know about: *What happens in an open courtroom is public property.*

public re·la·tions /ˌ.. .ˈ../ abbreviation **PR** n. **1** [plural] the relationship between an organization and the public: *Messer admits that clear-cutting forests is bad for public relations.* **2** [U] the work of explaining to the public what an organization does, so that they will understand it and approve of it: *a public relations firm*

public relations ex·er·cise /ˌ.. .ˈ.. ˌ.../ n. [C] something that an organization does just to make itself popular, rather than because it is the right thing to do: *Management's offer is little more than a public relations exercise.*

public school /ˈ.. ˌ./ n. [C] a free local school that any child can go to, which is controlled and paid for by the government —compare PRIVATE SCHOOL

public sec·tor /ˌ.. ˈ../ n. **the public sector** the industries and services in a country that are owned and run by the government: *a job **in the public sector*** —**public-sector** adj. [only before noun] —compare PRIVATE SECTOR

public serv·ant /ˌ.. ˈ../ n. [C] someone who works for the government, especially someone who is elected

public serv·ice /ˌ.. ˈ../ n. **1** [C usually plural] a service or product that a government provides, such as electricity, TRANSPORTATION etc.: *Essential public services are supported by property taxes.* **2** [C] a service provided to people because it will help them, and not for profit: *Local TV stations ran the ads as a public service.* **3** [U] jobs in the government or its departments: *a long career of public service*

public-service an·nounce·ment /ˌ.. ˈ.. .ˌ../ n. [C] a special message on television or radio, giving information about an important subject

public speak·ing /ˌ.. ˈ../ n. [U] the activity of making speeches in public: *a course in public speaking.*

public spend·ing /ˌ.. ˈ../ n. [U] the money that the government spends on public services: *Public spending for education must be increased.*

public-spir·it·ed /ˌ.. ˈ...◂/ adj. willing to do what is helpful for everyone in society: *public-spirited citizens*

public tel·e·vi·sion /ˌ.. ˈ.../ n. [U] a television program or service that is paid for by the government, large companies, and the public —see also PBS

public trans·por·ta·tion /ˌ.. .ˈ../ n. [U] bus services, train services etc., that are provided for everyone to use

public u·til·i·ty /ˌ.. .ˈ.../ n. [C] a private company that is allowed by the government to provide an important service or product, such as electricity or water, to the people in a particular area

public works /ˌ.. ˈ./ n. [plural] buildings, roads, PORTS etc. that are provided and built by the government

pub·lish /ˈpʌblɪʃ/ v. **1** [I,T] to arrange for a book, magazine etc. to be written, printed, and sold: *"Moby Dick" was first published in London in 1851.* | *We publish mainly textbooks and other educational* *materials.* **2** [T] if a newspaper, magazine etc. publishes something such as a letter, it prints it for people to read: *The newspaper published a list of the elected school district officials.* **3** [T usually passive] to make official information such as a report available for everyone to read: *So far none of the members' names have been published.* **4** [I,T] if a writer or musician publishes their work, they arrange for it to be printed and sold **5 publish or perish** used to say that people with particular jobs, especially college or university PROFESSORS, must have things that they write published if they want to succeed

pub·lish·er /'pʌblɪʃə/ *n.* [C] a person or company whose business is to arrange the writing, production, and sale of books, newspapers etc.

pub·lish·ing /'pʌblɪʃɪŋ/ *n.* [U] the business of producing books, magazines etc.: *Marcia has worked in publishing for at least 10 years.* —see also DESKTOP PUBLISHING, ELECTRONIC PUBLISHING

publishing house /'... ,./ *n.* [C] a company whose business is to arrange the writing, production, and sale of books

Puc·ci·ni /pu'tʃini/, **Gia·co·mo** /'dʒɑkəmoʊ/ (1858–1924) an Italian musician who wrote OPERAS

puce /pyus/ *adj.* dark brownish purple —**puce** *n.*

puck /pʌk/ *n.* [C] a hard flat circular piece of rubber that you hit with the stick in the game of HOCKEY

puck·er /'pʌkə/ also **pucker up** *v.* [I,T] **1** INFORMAL if your mouth puckers or if you pucker it, you pull your lips tightly together: *Even the thought of eating raw rhubarb makes my mouth pucker.* **2** [I] if cloth puckers, it gets lines or folds in it and is not flat anymore —**pucker** *n.* [C] —**puckered** *adj.*

puck·ish /'pʌkɪʃ/ *adj.* LITERARY showing that you are amused by other people, and like to make jokes about them: *a puckish grin* —**puckishly** *adv.*

pud·ding /'pʊdɪŋ/ *n.* [C,U] **1** a thick sweet creamy food, made with milk, eggs, sugar, and a little flour, and usually served cold: *chocolate pudding* **2** a hot sweet dish, made from cake, rice, bread etc. and milk and eggs, and sometimes with fruit or other sweet things added: *bread pudding* —see also **the proof is in the pudding** (PROOF[1] (5))

pud·dle[1] /'pʌdl/ *n.* [C] a small pool of water, especially rain water, on a path, street etc.: *a mud puddle*

puddle[2] *v.* [I] if a liquid puddles, it forms a puddle

puddle jum·per /'.. ,../ *n.* [C] INFORMAL a small airplane that is used to fly short distances

pu·den·dum /pyu'dɛndəm/ *n. plural* **pudenda** /-də/ [C] TECHNICAL the sexual organs on the outside of the body, especially a woman's

pudg·y /'pʌdʒi/ *adj.* **pudgier, pudgiest** fatter than usual: *He's short, pudgy, and bald.* —**pudginess** *n.* [U]

Pueb·lo /'pwɛbloʊ/ a group of Native American tribes from the southwestern region of the U.S., including the Hopi. They are known for their ADOBE buildings —**Pueblo** *adj.*

pueb·lo /'pwɛbloʊ/ *n.* [C] a small town, especially in the southwest U.S.

pu·er·ile /'pyʊrəl, -raɪl/ *adj.* FORMAL silly and stupid; CHILDISH: *puerile jokes*

Puer·to Ri·co /,pɔrtə 'rikoʊ, ,pwɛrtoʊ-/ an island in the Caribbean Sea, southeast of the U.S. state of Florida. People who live in Puerto Rico are U.S. citizens, but Puerto Rico is not a U.S. state and it governs itself. —**Puerto Rican** *n., adj.*

puff[1] /pʌf/ *v.* **1** [I,T] to breathe in and out while smoking a cigarette, pipe etc.: [+ **on/at**] *He sat at the bar puffing on a cigar.* **2** [I] to breathe quickly and with difficulty after running, carrying something heavy etc.: [+ **up/along** etc.] *A couple of pudgy joggers were puffing along the path.* —see also **huff and puff** (HUFF[2] (1)) **3 a)** [T always + adv./prep.] to blow smoke or steam out of something: *factory chimneys puffing smoke* **b)** [I] if smoke or steam puffs from somewhere, it comes out in little clouds **4** [I always

+ adv./prep.] if a steam train puffs along, it moves while sending out little clouds of steam

puff sth ↔ **out** *phr. v.* [T] **puff out your cheeks/ chest** to make your cheeks or chest bigger by filling them with air: *Gillespie's cheeks puffed out as he blew into his bent-bell trumpet.*

puff up *phr. v.* **1** [I,T **puff** sth ↔ **up**] to become bigger by increasing the amount of air inside, or to make something bigger in this way: *Birds puff up their feathers to keep warm.* | *As the noodles puff up, flip them over in the pan.* **2** [I] if your eye, face etc. puffs up, it swells painfully because of an injury or infection: *The skin where he had brushed against the plant was puffing up.* **3** [T **puff** sb **up**] to make someone feel very pleased or proud

puff[2] *n.* [C] **1** the action of taking the smoke from a cigarette, pipe etc. into your lungs: [+ **on**] *a nervous puff on a cigarette* | *I took a puff* (=smoked a cigarette or MARIJUANA) *once or twice in college.* **2** a sudden small movement of wind, air, or smoke: [+ **of**] *a puff of smoke* | *It only took a puff of wind to tip the boat over.* **3** a **cream/cheese/lemon** etc. **puff** a piece of light PASTRY with a soft mixture of cream or cheese etc. inside

puff·ball /'pʌfbɔl/ *n.* [C] a type of round FUNGUS that bursts to let its seeds go

puffed sleeve /,. './ *n.* [C] a short SLEEVE that is wider in the middle than at each end

puffed up /,. '. ◄/ *adj.* **1** behaving in a way that shows you are too proud: *John was all puffed up about being chosen for the conference.* **2** PUFFY

puffed wheat /,. './ *n.* [U] grains of wheat that have been cooked to make them very light, usually eaten with milk for breakfast

puf·fin /'pʌfɪn/ *n.* [C] a North Atlantic sea bird with a black and white body and a large brightly colored beak

puff pas·try /,. '../ *n.* [U] a type of very light PASTRY that PUFFS up when you bake it and has many thin layers

puff piece /'. ./ *n.* [C] an article in a newspaper, a report on television etc. that is not very serious and makes the person that it is about look very good

puff·y /'pʌfi/ *adj.* **puffier, puffiest 1** puffy eyes, faces, or cheeks are swollen: *She answered the door, her eyes still puffy from crying.* **2** soft and filled with a lot of air: *puffy white clouds* —**puffiness** *n.* [U]

pug /pʌg/ *n.* [C] a small fat short-haired dog with a wide flat face and a short flat nose

Pu·get Sound /'pyudʒɪt/ a long narrow BAY of the Pacific Ocean on the northwestern coast of the U.S. in the state of Washington

pu·gi·lism /'pyudʒə,lɪzəm/ *n.* [U] FORMAL the sport of BOXING (=fighting with your hands) —**pugilistic** /,pyudʒə'lɪstɪk/ *adj.*

pu·gi·list /'pyudʒəlɪst/ *n.* [C] FORMAL a BOXER

pug·na·cious /pʌg'neɪʃəs/ *adj.* FORMAL very eager to argue or fight with people: *When drinking, he becomes pugnacious and rude.* —**pugnaciously** *adv.* —**pugnacity** /pʌg'næsəti/ *n.* [U]

pug nose /'. ./ *n.* [C] a short flat nose that turns up at the end

puke[1] /pyuk/ also **puke up** *v.* [I,T] **1** INFORMAL to bring food back up from your stomach through your mouth; VOMIT: *I feel like I'm going to puke again.* **2 it makes me (want to) puke!** SPOKEN used to say that something makes you very angry or annoyed: *It makes me puke when I hear rich people complaining about taxes.*

puke[2] *n.* [U] INFORMAL food brought back up from your stomach through your mouth; VOMIT[2]

pukey, puky /'pyuki/ *adj.* SLANG very disgusting or unattractive

pul·chri·tude /'pʌlkrə,tud/ *n.* [U] FORMAL beauty, especially of a woman

Pu·lit·zer /'pʊlɪtsə/, **Joseph** (1847–1911) a U.S. JOURNALIST and newspaper owner, who established the Pulitzer Prizes

Pulitzer Prize /,... './ *n.* one of the eight prizes given every year in the U.S. to people who have produced especially good work in JOURNALISM, literature, or music

push

pull

pull

pull¹ /pʊl/ v.

1 ▮move sth toward you▮ [I,T] to use your hands to make something move toward you: *Don't start pulling yet – wait till I say go.* | [**pull sth**] *Mom, Ellie's pulling my hair!* | [**pull sth into/onto/away** etc.] *Help me pull the trunk into the corner.* **pull sth open/shut** *Tim got in the car and pulled the door shut.*

2 ▮remove▮ [T] to use force to take something out of the place where it is attached or held: *She's going to have her wisdom teeth pulled* | [**pull sth out/up/ off** etc.] *When I got back to the kitchen, the baby had pulled everything out of the cupboards.*

3 ▮make sth follow you▮ to use a rope, chain, your hands etc. to make something move behind you in the direction that you are moving: *a train pulling 64 boxcars* | [**pull sth into/away/over** etc.] *He goes by here every day pulling that little wagon behind him.*

4 ▮move your body▮ [T always + adv./prep.] **a)** to move your body or a part of your body away from someone or something: [**pull sth away/off/out** etc.] *Janice pulled her hand out of the cookie jar guiltily.* **b)** to hold onto something and use your strength to move your body somewhere: [**pull yourself up/ through** etc.] *Bobby had to pull himself up out of the hole.*

5 ▮muscle▮ [T] to injure one of your muscles by stretching it too much during physical activity; STRAIN: *Sampras dropped out of the tournament after pulling a calf muscle.*

6 **pull strings** to secretly use your influence with important people in order to get what you want or to help someone else: *Samuels pulled strings to get her daughter a job in Mitchell's office.*

7 **pull the/sb's strings** to control something or someone, especially when you are not the person who is supposed to be controlling it: *Who is really pulling the strings at the White House?*

8 **pull your weight** to do your share of the work *If you don't start pulling your weight around here, you're fired.*

9 ▮clothing▮ [T always + adv./prep.] to put on or take off clothing, usually quickly: [**pull sth on/off/ up/down**] *He ran out the door, pulling on his shirt as he went.* | *I pulled my hat down over my eyes.*

10 ▮gun/knife▮ [T] to take out a gun or knife ready to use it: [**pull sth on sb**] *Richards allegedly pulled a gun on Dalton.*

11 ▮trick/joke/lie▮ **a) pull sb's leg** INFORMAL to tell someone something that is not true, as a joke: *I think he was just pulling your leg.* **b) pull a stunt/trick/ joke/prank** etc. INFORMAL to do something that annoys or harms other people: *boys pulling practical jokes* **c)** [T] SPOKEN to deceive or trick someone: *What are you trying to pull?* | *Are you trying to pull a fast one on me?*

12 ▮car▮ [I] if a car pulls to the left or right as you are driving, it moves in that direction because of a problem with its machinery: *The car seems to be pulling to the left.*

13 ▮use a control▮ [T] to move a control such as a SWITCH or TRIGGER toward you to make a piece of equipment work: *She raised the gun and pulled the trigger.*

14 ▮make sb/sth not take part▮ [T] to remove someone from an organization, activity etc., so that they do not take part anymore: *The team was pulled at the last minute.* | *She was angry enough to pull her kids from the school.*

15 **pull the curtains/blinds** to open or close curtains or BLINDS: *Could you pull the blinds, please?*

16 **sth is like pulling teeth** used to say that it is very difficult or unpleasant to persuade someone to do something: *Getting the kids to do their homework was like pulling teeth.*

17 ▮crowd/votes etc.▮ [T] if an event, performer etc. pulls crowds or a politician pulls a lot of votes, a lot of people come to see them or vote for them: *Bagert is expected to pull just enough votes to win.*

18 **pull a punch** to deliberately hit someone with less force than you could use, so that it hurts less —see also **not pull any punches** (PUNCH² (6))

19 **pull sb's license** INFORMAL to take away someone's LICENSE (=special permission) to do something, especially to drive a car, because they have done something wrong —compare REVOKE

20 ▮baseball/golf▮ [I,T] to hit the ball in baseball, GOLF etc. so that it does not go straight but moves to one side

21 ▮row a boat▮ [I,T] to make a boat move by using OARS —compare PUSH¹ —see also **pull rank (on sb)** (RANK¹ (5)), **pull the plug** (PLUG¹ (6)), **pull the rug (out) from under sb** (RUG (2)), **pull the wool over sb's eyes** (WOOL (4)), **pull yourself up by your bootstraps** (BOOTSTRAPS), **tear/pull your hair out** (HAIR (5))

pull ahead *phr. v.* [I] if one vehicle pulls ahead of another, it gets in front of it by moving faster

pull apart *phr. v.* **1** [T **pull** sth ↔ **apart**] to separate something into two or more pieces or groups: *Pull apart the dough into four equal pieces.* | *Nationalist tensions have pulled the country apart.* **2** [T **pull sb apart**] to upset someone or make the relationship between people difficult: *My father's drinking problem pulled the family apart.* **3** [T **pull** sth ↔ **apart**] to carefully examine or criticize something: *The selection committee pulled each proposal apart.* **4** [T **pull** sb ↔ **apart**] to separate people or animals when they are fighting **5** [I] if something pulls apart, it breaks into pieces when you pull on it: *Barbecued ribs should pull apart easily with your fingers.*

pull at/on sth *phr. v.* [T] **1** to take a hold of something and pull it several times: *It's nice to relax with a cup of coffee without the kids pulling at my leg.* **2** to take smoke from a pipe or cigarette into your lungs **3** OLD-FASHIONED to take a long drink from a bottle or glass

pull away *phr. v.* [I] **1** to start to drive away from a place where you have stopped: [+ from] *Children should not chase a bus after it has pulled away from a bus stop.* **2** to move ahead of a competitor by going faster or being more successful: *In the final quarter the Bulls pulled away, winning 105–80.* **3** to move away from someone quickly when they are trying to touch you or hold you: *I tried to kiss her but she pulled away.*

pull down *phr. v.* [T] **1** [**pull** sth ↔ **down**] to destroy something or make it stop existing: *Houses were pulled down to make way for a new highway.* | *The Population Registration Act was the final pillar of apartheid to be pulled down.* **2** [**pull down** sth] INFORMAL to earn a particular amount of money at your job: *He pulls down at least $65,000 a year.* **3** [**pull** sb/sth ↔ **down**] to make someone or something less successful: *There are worries that the new sales figures could pull the economy down.* **4 pull down a menu** to make a computer PROGRAM show you a list of the things it can do —see also PULL-DOWN (1)

pull for sb/sth *phr. v.* [T] INFORMAL to encourage a person or team to succeed: *Which team are you pulling for?*

P

pull in *phr. v.* **1** [T **pull** sth ↔ **in**] INFORMAL if you pull in a lot of money, you earn it: *Smith will pull in about $1.2 million a year.* **2** [I,T **pull in** sth] to move a car into a particular space and stop it: *Ken pulled in behind me and parked.* **3** [T **pull in** sth] to get money, business etc. by doing something to attract people's attention: *Hall pulled in 58% of the vote.* **4** [T **pull** sb/sth **in**] if an event, a show etc. pulls in a lot of people, they go to it or see it: *"Titanic" was still pulling in crowds after 18 weeks.* **5** [I] if a train pulls in, it arrives at a station **6** [T **pull** sb ↔ **in**] if a police officer pulls someone in, they take them to a police station because they think they may have done something wrong

pull off *phr. v.* **1** [T **pull** sth ↔ **off**] INFORMAL to succeed in doing something difficult: *The Huskies pulled off a win in Saturday's game.* **2** [I,T **pull off** sth] to drive a car off a road to stop or to turn onto another road: *We pulled off for a bite to eat.*

pull on sth *phr. v.* [T] —see **pull at/on** (PULL¹)

pull out *phr. v.* **1** [I] to drive onto a road from another road, or from where you have stopped: [+ **of**] *Be careful when you pull out of the driveway.* **2** [I,T **pull** sb/sth **out**] to get out of a dangerous place or to stop taking part in something, or make someone else do this: *Most of the troops have been pulled out.* | [+ **of**] *After the injury, he had to pull out of the race.* **3 pull out all the stops** to do everything you can in order to make something succeed: *Fred's pulling out all the stops for his daughter's wedding.* **4** [I] if a train pulls out, it leaves a station

pull over *phr. v.* [I,T **pull** sb/sth **over**] to drive to the side of a road and stop your car, to make someone do this: *I got pulled over for speeding.*

pull through *phr. v.* [I,T **pull** sb **through**] **1** to stay alive after you have been very sick or badly injured, or help someone do this: *We're all praying that he'll pull through.* —compare **bring** sb **through** (sth) (BRING) **2** to succeed or to continue to exist after being in a difficult or upsetting situation, or to help someone do this: *The city managed to pull through its financial crisis.*

pull together *phr. v.* **1** [I] if a group of people pull together, they all work hard to achieve something: *After the hurricane, neighbors pulled together to help each other.* **2 pull yourself together** to force yourself to stop behaving in a nervous, frightened, or disorganized way: *Pull yourself together – you don't want him to see you crying like that.* **3** [T **pull** sth ↔ **together**] to organize something that is not organized and make it work more effectively: *It must have been a lot of work pulling a show like that together.*

pull up *phr. v.* **1** [I] to stop the vehicle that you are driving: *Who is that pulling up out front?* **2 pull up a chair/stool etc.** to get a chair and sit down next to someone who is already sitting **3** [T **pull** sth ↔ **up**] to use force to take plants out of the ground

pull² *n.*
1 act of pulling [C] an act of using force to move something toward you or in the same direction that you are moving: *Give the rope a good pull.* —compare TUG¹

2 force [C usually singular] a strong force such as GRAVITY, that makes things move in a particular direction: *The moon's pull on the Earth's oceans creates the tides.*

3 influence [singular,U] INFORMAL special influence that gives you an unfair advantage: *The former Senator has a lot of pull with the Republicans in Congress.*
4 attraction [U] the ability to attract people: *The pull of the Bavarian countryside is strong.*
5 muscle an injury to one of your muscles caused by stretching it too much during exercise: *a groin pull*
6 handle [C] a rope or handle that you use to pull something: *I couldn't remember where the pull was to open the parachute.*
7 drink [C] an act of taking a long drink of something: *I took one last pull from the water jug.*

8 baseball/golf [C] a way of hitting the ball in baseball or GOLF so that it does not go straight, but moves to one side
9 smoke [C] an act of taking the smoke from a cigarette, pipe etc. into your lungs

pull·back /'pʊlbæk/ *n.* [C] **1** an action of moving an army back to a position where it was before: *a pullback of troops from the occupied territories* **2** an situation in which STOCK prices return to a lower level **3** a situation in which a company, organization, or people in general stop doing something or do it less: *The recession has led to a pullback in consumer spending.*

pull·down /'. ./ *adj.* **1 a pull-down menu** a list of things a computer program can do that you can make appear on a computer SCREEN **2** [only before noun] able to be pulled into a lower position: *a pull-down window shade*

pul·let /'pʊlət/ *n.* [C] a young chicken during its first year of laying eggs

pul·ley /'pʊli/ *n. plural* **pulleys** [C] a piece of equipment consisting of a wheel over which a rope or chain is pulled to lift heavy things

Pull·man /'pʊlmən/ *n.* [C] **1** also **Pullman car** a very comfortable train car, especially one that you can sleep in, or a train made up of these cars **2** also **Pullman case** OLD-FASHIONED a very large suitcase

pull·on /'. ./ *adj.* [only before noun] a pull-on shirt, dress etc. does not have any buttons, so you pull it on over your head

pull·out¹ /'pʊlaʊt/ *n.* [C] **1** the act of an army, business etc. leaving a particular place or area of activity: *There is still no date for the pullout of troops from the region.* **2** part of a magazine, newspaper etc. that can be removed: *a 16-page pull-out of office furnishings*

pullout², **pull-out** *adj.* [only before noun] able to be removed from something: *a special pullout calendar* | *pull-out shelves*

pull·o·ver /'pʊl,oʊvɚ/ *n.* [C] a SWEATER without buttons

pull·up /'. ./ *n.* [C] an exercise in which you use your arms to pull yourself up toward a bar above your head, until your chin is over the bar

pul·mo·nar·y /'pʊlmə,nɛri, 'pʌl-/ *adj.* TECHNICAL relating to the lungs or having an effect on the lungs

pulp¹ /pʌlp/ *n.* [singular,U] **1** the soft inside part of a fruit or vegetable: *He won't drink the orange juice if there's a lot of pulp in it.* **2** a very soft substance that is almost liquid, especially a substance made from wood or other plants and used for making paper, or a substance made by crushing and mixing fruit or vegetables with water: *paper pulp* | *Stir vigorously to break the cranberries into a pulp.* **3 beat** sb **to a pulp** INFORMAL to hit someone until they are seriously injured **4** part of the inside of a tooth **5** books, magazines, movies etc. that are of poor quality or are badly written, and that are often about sex or violence —**pulpy** *adj.*

pulp² *adj.* [only before noun] pulp magazines, stories etc. are of poor quality or are badly written, and are often about sex and violence: *pulp fiction*

pulp³ *v.* [T] **1** to beat or crush something until it becomes so soft that it is almost liquid **2** to cut up and add water to books, newspapers etc. in order to make paper: *Forms will be shredded, pulped, and recycled.*

pul·pit /'pʊlpɪt, 'pʌl-/ *n.* [C] a structure like a tall box at the front of a church, that a priest or minister stands behind when they speak

pulp·wood /'pʌlpwʊd/ *n.* [U] crushed wood that is used to make paper

pul·sar /'pʌlsɑr/ *n.* [C] an object like a star that is far away in space and produces a regular radio signal

pul·sate /'pʌlseɪt/ *v.* [I] **1** to make sounds or movements that are strong and regular, like a heart beating: *Marley's mellow reggae music pulsates from the speakers.* **2** LITERARY to be strongly affected by a powerful emotion or feeling: [+ **with**] *The whole city seemed to be pulsating with excitement.* —**pulsating** *adj.*

1 [C] a beat of the heart or any regular beat that can be measured **2** [U] movement that pulsates

pulse¹ /pʌls/ *n.*

1 heart beat [C] **a)** the regular beat that can be felt, for example at your wrist, as your heart pumps blood around your body: *The man on the ground had no pulse.* **b)** [usually singular] also **pulse rate** the number of these beats per minute: *Roll up your sleeve so I can take your pulse* (=to count how many times someone's heart beats in a minute, usually by feeling their wrist).
2 sound/light/electricity [C] an amount of sound, light, or electricity that continues for a very short time: *An electrical pulse sends the atom to the tip of the microscope needle.*
3 music/drum [C,U] a strong regular beat as in music, or on a drum: *the pulse of steel drums in the parks*
4 important ideas/feelings [U] the ideas, feelings, opinions etc. that are most important or have the most influence in a particular group of people at a particular time: *Stock brokers with a feel for Hong Kong's financial pulse were worried.*
5 your pulse quickens/races if your pulse quickens etc., it becomes faster because you are excited or nervous: *Feel your pulse quicken as the ocean rolls beneath your surfboard.*
6 pulses [plural] seeds such as beans, PEAS, and LENTILS that can be eaten —see also **have/keep your finger on the pulse** (FINGER¹ (8))

pulse² *v.* [I] **1** to move or flow with a steady rapid beat or sound: *Often you can feel the brake pedal pulsing when the ABS system is operating.* **2** if a feeling or emotion pulses through someone, they feel it very strongly **3** to push a button on a FOOD PROCESSOR to make the machine go on and off regularly, rather than work continuously: *Pulse several times until the mixture looks like oatmeal.*

pul·ver·ize /ˈpʌlvəˌraɪz/ *v.* [T usually passive] **1** to crush something into a powder **2** INFORMAL to completely defeat someone —**pulverization** /ˌpʌlvərəˈzeɪʃən/ *n.* [U]

pu·ma /ˈpumə, ˈpyumə/ *n.* [C] a COUGAR

pum·ice /ˈpʌmɪs/ also **pumice stone** /ˈ.. ./ *n.* **1** [U] very light silver-gray rock that has come from a VOLCANO, and is crushed and used as a powder for cleaning **2** [C] a piece of this stone used for rubbing your skin to clean it or make it soft

pum·mel /ˈpʌməl/ *v.* [T] **1** to hit someone or something many times quickly with your FISTS (=closed hands): *Ali leaned against the ropes and allowed Foreman to pummel him.* **2** INFORMAL to completely defeat someone at a sport: *On Saturday, Penn State pummeled Arizona 54–0.*

pump¹ /pʌmp/ *n.* **1** [C] a machine for forcing liquid or gas into or out of something: **water/air/oil** etc. **pump** (=for moving water, air etc.) | **hand/foot pump** (=operated by your hand or foot) —see also STOMACH PUMP and see picture at BICYCLE¹ **2** also **gas pump** INFORMAL [C] a machine at a GAS STATION that is used to put gasoline into cars **3** [C usually plural] a woman's plain shoe that has a short HEEL and does not fasten: *a pair of blue leather pumps* —see picture at SHOE¹ **4** [C] an act of pumping —see also HEAT PUMP, **prime the pump** (PRIME³ (4))

pump² *v.*
1 move in a direction [T always + adv./prep.] to make liquid or gas move in a particular direction with a pump: **pump sth into/through/from** etc. *A pipe accidentally pumped tons of sewage into Boston Harbor.*
2 from under ground [T] to bring a supply of water, oil etc. to the surface from under the ground: *We were able to pump clean groundwater from several of the wells.* | **pump gas** (=put gasoline into your car at a gas station)
3 come out quickly [I always + adv./prep.] when a liquid pumps from somewhere, it comes out in sudden large amounts: [+ from/out of etc.] *Oil continued to pump out of the ship's damaged hull.*
4 questions [T] INFORMAL to ask someone a lot of questions, in order to find out something: [**pump sb**

for sth] *Viktor wanted to pump Jody for more information about her program.*
5 move in and out also **pump away** [I] to move very quickly in and out or up and down: *My heart was pumping fast.*
6 use a pump [I] also **pump away** to operate a pump: *He pumped away furiously.*
7 pump sb full of sth to put a lot of drugs into someone's body: *The doctor had him pumped full of pain killers.*
8 pump iron INFORMAL to do exercises by lifting heavy weights
9 have your stomach pumped to have the things inside your stomach removed by a pump, after swallowing something harmful

pump sth into sb/sth *phr. v.* [T] **1** to spend money on something such as a business, industry, or ECONOMY: *So far, the program has pumped $750,000 into communities for playground equipment.* **2 pump bullets into sb/sth** INFORMAL to shoot someone several times

pump out *phr. v.* **1** [I,T **pump** sth ↔ **out**] if something such as music, information, or a supply of products is pumped out or pumps out, a lot of it is produced: *The factory pumps out 400 million electronic devices a year.* **2** [T **pump** sth ↔ **out**] to remove liquid from something using a pump: *It took all afternoon to pump out our flooded basement.*

pump sth ↔ **up** *phr. v.* [T] **1** to fill a tire, ball etc. with air until it is correctly filled; INFLATE **2** to increase the value, amount etc. of something: *The success of the computer industry has pumped up the local economy.* **3 pump up the music/volume etc.** SLANG to play music louder

pump sb **up** *phr. v.* [T] INFORMAL to encourage someone or make them excited about something: *By putting articles about gangs in the paper, you just pump them up.*

pump-ac·tion /ˈ. ˌ../ *adj.* **a pump action shotgun/bottle/hairspray etc.** a SHOTGUN, bottle etc. that is operated by pulling or pressing part of it in or out

pumped /pʌmpt/ also **pumped up** *adj.* INFORMAL very excited about something: *She often makes big plays that gets the whole team pumped up.*

pum·per·nick·el /ˈpʌmpəˌnɪkəl/ *n.* [U] a heavy dark brown bread

pump·kin /ˈpʌmpkɪn, ˈpʌŋkɪn/ *n.* **1** [C,U] a very large orange fruit that grows on the ground, or the inside of this fruit eaten as food: *pumpkin pie* —see picture at VEGETABLE **2** [singular, not with **the**] a way of talking to someone you love, especially a child: *What's wrong, pumpkin?*

pump room /ˈ. ./ *n.* [C] a room at a SPA where you can go to drink the water

pun¹ /pʌn/ *n.* [C] an amusing use of a word or phrase that has two meanings, or of words with the same sound but different meanings: **pardon/excuse/forgive the pun** (=used to tell someone that you will make a pun) *Reuschel carries considerable weight in the Assembly,* **no pun intended** (=used to tell someone that you did not mean to make a pun).

pun² *v.* **punned, punning** [I + on] to make a pun

punch¹ /pʌntʃ/ *v.* [T]
1 hit to hit someone or something hard with your FIST (=closed hand): [**punch sb in/on sth**] *Then the guy walked up and punched Jack in the face.* | [**punch sb/sth**] *My older brother's always punching me.*
2 make hole to make a hole in something using a metal tool or other sharp object: **punch a ticket/card** etc. *The bus driver will punch your ticket.* | **punch a hole in/through sth** *I got so mad that I punched a hole in the door.*
3 push buttons to push a button or key on a machine: *All you have to do is punch a few buttons and the computer will do the rest for you.*
4 punch holes in an argument/idea/plan etc. to disagree with someone's idea or plan and show what is wrong with it

P

a lot of energy: *punchy melodies* **3** **punch-drunk** —**punchiness** *n.* [U]

punc·til·i·ous /pʌŋkˈtɪliəs/ *adj.* FORMAL being very careful to behave correctly and keep exactly to rules —**punctiliously** *adv.* —**punctiliousness** *n.* [U]

punc·tu·al /ˈpʌŋktʃuəl/ *adj.* arriving, happening etc. at exactly the time that has been arranged: *Michael's a very punctual, reliable worker.* | *We've always been punctual in paying our rent.* —**punctually** *adv.* —**punctuality** /ˌpʌŋktʃuˈæləti/ *n.* [U]

punc·tu·ate /ˈpʌŋktʃu,eɪt/ *v.* **1** [T] to divide written work into sentences, phrases etc. using COMMAS, PERIODS etc. **2 be punctuated by/with sth** to be interrupted by something, especially in a repeated way: *Brant often punctuates her conversations with quotes from musicians.* **3** [T] to complete or end something in a way that people notice, especially a period of time: *Danoff's resignation punctuated a decade of tremendous change at the museum.*

punc·tu·a·tion /ˌpʌŋktʃuˈeɪʃən/ *n.* [U] the marks used in dividing a piece of writing into sentences, phrases etc.

punctuation mark /..ˈ.. ,./ *n.* [C] a sign, such as a COMMA or QUESTION MARK, that is used in dividing a piece of writing into sentences, phrases etc.

punc·ture¹ /ˈpʌŋktʃɚ/ *n.* [C] a small hole made by a sharp point

puncture² *v.* **1** [T] to make a small hole through the surface of something, so that air or liquid can get out: *Workers accidentally punctured a natural gas main.* **2** [T] to suddenly destroy a feeling or belief, making someone feel unhappy, silly, or confused: *Gonick's books puncture the myths about American history.*

pun·dit /ˈpʌndɪt/ *n.* [C] someone who knows a lot about a particular subject, and is often asked for their opinions on it: *political pundits*

pun·gent /ˈpʌndʒənt/ *adj.* **1** a pungent taste or smell is strong and sharp: *the pungent smell of onions* **2** pungent remarks or writing criticize something in a very direct and intelligent way: *Borsky made several pungent comments about the government.* —**pungently** *adv.* —**pungency** *n.* [U]

pun·ish /ˈpʌnɪʃ/ *v.* [T] **1** to make someone suffer because they have done something wrong or broken the law: *Sanders should be punished to the fullest extent of the law.* | [**punish sb for (doing) sth**] *Janson says she's being punished for publicly criticizing the department.* **2** if you punish a crime, you punish anyone who is guilty of it: *Deserting the army during war can be punished by death.* **3 punish yourself (for sth)** to blame yourself for something: *The accident wasn't your fault; stop punishing yourself.*

pun·ish·a·ble /ˈpʌnɪʃəbəl/ *adj.* a punishable action may be punished by law, especially in a particular way: *a punishable offense* | [+ **by**] *Misuse of state funds is punishable by two to four years in prison.*

pun·ish·ing /ˈpʌnɪʃɪŋ/ *adj.* long, difficult, or extreme, and making you feel tired and weak: *Wang has a punishing schedule.* | *the desert's punishing climate* —**punishingly** *adv.*

pun·ish·ment /ˈpʌnɪʃmənt/ *n.* **1** [C] a way in which someone or something is punished: [+ **for**] *The maximum punishment for robbery is 40 years in prison.* | **a harsh/severe punishment** (=one that makes someone suffer a lot) **2** [U] the act of punishing someone or the process of being punished: [+ **for**] *Baylor was suspended for one game as punishment for violating team rules.* **3** [U] INFORMAL rough treatment; DAMAGE: *With five children in the house, the furniture has to take a lot of punishment.* —see also CAPITAL PUNISHMENT, CORPORAL PUNISHMENT

pu·ni·tive /ˈpyunətɪv/ *adj.* **1** punitive actions/measures/damages etc. actions etc. that are intended to punish someone: *The airline had to pay over $50 million in punitive damages.* **2** so severe that people find it very difficult to pay: *punitive taxes* —**punitively** *adv.*

punk /pʌŋk/ *n.* **1** [U] also **punk rock** a type of loud violent music popular in the late 1970s and the

---

5 punch the air to make a movement like a punch toward the sky, to show that you are very pleased about something

6 punch the clock INFORMAL to record the time that you start or finish work by putting a card into a special machine: *Bob is glad to have a job where he doesn't have to punch the clock.*

7 punch sb's lights out INFORMAL to hit someone hard in the face so that they become unconscious

8 punch it! SPOKEN used to tell someone to start driving faster immediately

9 **cattle** [T] to move cattle from one place to another

punch in *phr. v.* **1** [I] to record the time that you arrive at work, by putting a card into a special machine: *Mitch made sure he punched in exactly at 8 a.m.* **2** [T **punch sth ↔ in**] to put information into a computer by pressing buttons or keys: *What command do I punch in to open the program?*

punch out *phr. v.* **1** to record the time that you leave work, by putting a card into a special machine: *You should punch out now and take the rest of the day off.* **2** [T **punch sb out**] to hit someone so hard that they fall over or become unconscious: *If Jeff ever sees the guy again, he's going to punch him out.*

punch² *n.*

1 **hit** [C] a quick strong hit made with your FIST (=closed hand): [+ **in/on**] *Mike gave me a punch on the arm.* | **throw a punch** (=try to hit someone)

2 **drink** [C,U] a drink made from fruit juice, sugar, water, and sometimes alcohol: *a bowl of rum punch*

3 **effective quality** [U] a strong, effective, and interesting quality in the way something does something: *Thomas's novel loses its punch toward the end.* | *The new Ford Mustang has a lot of punch.*

4 **tool** [C] also **hole punch** a metal tool for cutting holes or for pushing something into a small hole

5 beat sb/sth to the punch INFORMAL to do or get something before someone else: *Hitachi has beaten their competition to the punch with a new line of mainframe computers.*

6 not pull any punches INFORMAL to express your disapproval or criticism very clearly, without trying to hide what you feel: *The report doesn't pull any punches in describing human rights abuses around the world.*

7 a one-two punch two events that happen close together and that cause problems: *The city faced the one-two punch of an earthquake followed by a recession.*

8 as pleased as punch INFORMAL very happy: *He's as pleased as punch about the baby.* —see also **pack a punch/wallop** (PACK¹ (9))

punch bowl /ˈ. ./ *n.* [C] a large bowl in which punch is served

punch card /ˈ. ./ *n.* [C] **1** also **punched card** a card with a pattern of holes in it that was used in past times for putting information into a computer **2** a card that some businesses give you that allows you to get something free or for a reduced price after you have used the business a certain number of times and have had a small hole put in the card each time

punch-drunk /ˌ. ˈ./ *adj.* **1** INFORMAL very confused, especially because you have had continuous bad luck or have been treated badly **2** a BOXER who is punch-drunk is suffering brain damage from being hit too much

punch·ing bag /ˈ.. ,./ *n.* [C] **1** a heavy leather bag hung from a rope, that is PUNCHed for exercise **2 use sb as a punching bag** INFORMAL to hit or PUNCH someone

punch line /ˈ. ./ *n.* [C] the last few words of a joke or story that make it funny or surprising

punch·y /ˈpʌntʃi/ *adj.* **punchier, punchiest** **1** a punchy piece of writing or speech is very effective because it expresses ideas clearly in only a few words: *punchy political jokes* **2** a punchy performance or punchy music is done or played well with

1980s **2** [C] SLANG a young man or a boy who fights and breaks the law: *I'd like to find the punk who broke off my car antenna.* **3** [C] also **punk rocker** someone who dresses like people who like or play punk rock, with brightly colored hair, chains and pins, and torn clothing: *punk hairstyles* **4** [U] a substance that burns without a flame and is used to light FIREWORKS etc.

pun·kin /ˈpʌŋkən/ *n.* [C] a non-standard spelling of PUMPKIN

pun·ster /ˈpʌnstɚ/ *n.* [C] someone who makes PUNS

punt¹ /pʌnt/ *n.* **1** [C] a long kick that you make after dropping the ball from your hands, in football **2** [C] a long narrow river-boat with a flat bottom and square ends, that is moved by pushing a long pole against the bottom of the river **3** [singular] the act of going out in a punt

punt² *v.* **1** [I,T] to drop the ball from your hands and kick it before it touches the ground, especially in football: *Prokop punted five times for a 39-yard average.* **2** [I,T] to go or take someone on a river by punt

punt·er /ˈpʌntɚ/ *n.* [C] the player who punts the ball in football

pu·ny /ˈpyuni/ *adj.* **punier, puniest 1** small, thin, and weak: *a puny kid* **2** unimpressive and ineffective: *puny profits* —**puniness** *n.* [U]

pup¹ /pʌp/ *n.* [C] **1** a PUPPY **2** a young SEAL¹ (1) or OTTER: *seal pups* **3** OLD-FASHIONED an insulting word for a young man who is impolite or too confident, and who does not have much experience

pup² *v.* [I] TECHNICAL to give birth to pups

pu·pa /ˈpyupə/ *n. plural* **pupas** or **pupae** /-pi/ [C] an insect in the middle stages of its development, when it is protected inside a special cover —**pupal** *adj.* —see picture at METAMORPHOSIS

pu·pate /ˈpyupeɪt/ *v.* [I] TECHNICAL to become a pupa

pu·pil /ˈpyupəl/ *n.* [C] **1** FORMAL someone who is being taught, especially a child **2** the small black round area in the middle of your eye

pup·pet /ˈpʌpɪt/ *n.* [C] **1** a model of a person or animal that you can move by pulling wires or strings, or by putting your hand inside it: *a puppet show* **2** a person or organization that is not independent but is controlled by someone else: *He was considered a puppet of the ruling party.* | **puppet government/regime/state etc.** (=a government controlled by a more powerful country or organization)

pup·pet·eer /ˌpʌpɪˈtɪr/ *n.* [C] someone who performs with puppets

pup·pet·ry /ˈpʌpɪtri/ *n.* [U] the art of performing with puppets, or the study of this

pup·py /ˈpʌpi/ *n. plural* **puppies** [C] **1** a young dog **2 this/that puppy** SPOKEN, INFORMAL used instead of the name of a thing, especially when you do not know the name: *How do you shut this puppy off?*

puppy love /ˈ.. ˌ./ *n.* [U] a young boy's or girl's love for someone, which people do not regard as serious: *a boy with a bad case of puppy love*

pup tent /ˈ. ./ *n.* [C] a small TENT for two people

pur·blind /ˈpɚblaɪnd/ *adj.* FORMAL OR LITERARY stupid or dull

Pur·cell /ˈpɚsəl/**, Henry** (1659–1695) an English musician who wrote CLASSICAL music

pur·chase¹ /ˈpɚtʃəs/ *v.* [T] FORMAL to buy something, especially something big or expensive: *Ogburn purchased the property in 1989.*

purchase² *n.* **1** [C,U] FORMAL the act of buying something: *The money will be used for the purchase of $40,000 worth of computer equipment.* | *Many stores will let you* **make a purchase** (=buy something) *by telephone.* | *Tickets may be returned to the* **place of purchase** (=where you bought them) *for a full refund.* **2** [C] FORMAL something that has been bought: *This coupon will give you ten dollars off any fifty dollar purchase at the store.* **3** [singular,U] FORMAL a firm hold with your hands or feet: *Holman attempted to gain a purchase on the narrow ledge.*

purchase price /ˈ.. ˌ./ *n.* [singular] FORMAL the price that you have to pay to buy something or that you

paid for something: *The purchase price of the house was $177,500.*

pur·chas·er /ˈpɚtʃəsɚ/ *n.* [C] FORMAL the person who buys something

purchasing pow·er /ˈ... ˌ../ *n.* [U] **1** the amount of money that a person or group has available to spend, compared to other people: *The average Mexican employee's purchasing power is still relatively low compared with U.S. workers.* **2** the value of a unit of money considered in relation to how much you can buy with it: *The purchasing power of the dollar has declined.*

pur·dah /ˈpɚdə/ *n.* [U] **1** the custom, especially among Muslim people, in which women stay in their home or cover their faces so that they cannot be seen by men **2 in purdah a)** women who are in purdah live according to this custom **b)** staying away from other people

pure /pyʊr/ *adj.*

s w
3 3

1 not mixed not mixed with anything else: *Pure olive oil is usually light gold in color.* | *The cocaine was 95% pure.* —opposite IMPURE (1)

2 complete complete or total: *It was by pure luck that we found the place.* | *In terms of pure natural ability, Rick's the best athlete on the team.*

3 clean clean, without anything harmful or unhealthy: *pure drinking water*

4 color clear and not mixed with other colors: *These flowers also come in pure white.*

5 sound very clear and beautiful to hear: *a pure tenor voice*

6 without evil having the quality of being completely good or moral, especially not having sexual thoughts or experience; INNOCENT: *a pure young girl* | *I'm sure he had the purest of motives.*

7 pure science/math etc. work done in science, math etc. in order to increase our knowledge of it rather than to make practical use of it: *pure research* —compare APPLIED

8 pure and simple INFORMAL used to say that there is only one reason for something: *The motive for the robbery was greed, pure and simple.*

9 art a pure form of art is done exactly according to an accepted standard or pattern

10 as pure as the driven snow an expression meaning "morally perfect," often used in a joking way to describe someone who is not like this at all —**pureness** *n.* [U] —see also IMPURE, PURELY, PURIFY, PURITY

pure·blood·ed /ˈpyʊrˌblʌdɪd/ *adj.* with parents, grandparents etc. from only one group or race of people, with no mixture of other groups

pure·bred /ˈpyʊrbrɛd/ *adj.* coming from only one breed of animal, with no mixture of other breeds: *a purebred greyhound* —**purebred** *n.* [C] —compare PEDIGREED, THOROUGHBRED

pu·ree, purée /pyʊˈreɪ/ *n.* [C,U] food that is boiled or crushed until it is a soft mass that is almost liquid: *apple puree* | *tomato puree* —**puree, purée** *v.* [T]

pure·ly /ˈpyʊrli/ *adv.* completely and only, without anything else being involved: *Goldman said attendance on the program is purely voluntary.* | *I don't enjoy it, but I jog purely for the sake of good health.*

pur·ga·tive /ˈpɚgətɪv/ *n.* [C] a medicine or food that makes your BOWELS empty themselves —**purgative** *adj.*

pur·ga·to·ry /ˈpɚgəˌtɔri/ *n.* [U] **1** a place, situation, or time when you suffer a lot or wait a lot: *The island was turned into a purgatory for slaves before they were sold.* **2 Purgatory** a place where, according to Catholic beliefs, the souls of dead people must suffer for the bad things they did, until they are pure enough to enter heaven —**purgatorial** /ˌpɚgəˈtɔriəl/ *adj.*

purge¹ /pɚdʒ/ *v.* [T] **1** to force your opponents or people who disagree with you to leave an organization or place, often by using violence: [**purge sth of sb/sth**] *On many occasions, Stalin purged the armed forces of senior commanders.* | [**purge sb/sth (from sth)**] *Noriega routinely purged potential enemies.*

P

2 FORMAL to remove something or throw something away: *Employees leaving the government were encouraged to purge their computer files.* **3** LITERARY to get rid of your bad feelings, such as hatred: [**purge sb/sth of sth**] *It took her months to purge herself of her feelings of guilt.* **4** TECHNICAL to take a medicine to clear all the waste from your BOWELS

purge² *n.* [C] **1** an action to remove your opponents or people who disagree with you from an organization or place, often using violence: *There was a purge of the military commanders who had supported the coup.* **2** OLD-FASHIONED a medicine that clears all the waste from your BOWELS

pu·ri·fi·ca·tion /ˌpyʊrəfəˈkeɪʃən/ *n.* [U] **1** a process that removes the dirty or unwanted parts from something: *a water purification plant* **2** acts or ceremonies to remove evil from someone: *The tribe is building a new sweat lodge for purification ceremonies.*

pu·ri·fi·er /ˈpyʊrəˌfaɪəʳ/ *n.* [C] a machine that makes water or air clean: *a water purifier*

pu·ri·fy /ˈpyʊrəˌfaɪ/ *v.* **purifies, purified, purifying** [T] **1** to remove the dirty or unwanted parts from something: *The system purifies water by filtering it through sand.* **2** to get rid of evil from your soul

Pu·rim /ˈpʊrɪm, pʊˈrim/ *n.* [U] a religious holiday on which Jews celebrate their escape from being killed by a king in ancient Persia

pur·ist /ˈpyʊrɪst/ *n.* [C] someone who has very strict ideas about what is right or correct in a particular subject, for example in grammar, art, music etc.: *Baseball purists would be against reducing the number of games.* —**purism** *n.* [U]

Pu·ri·tan /ˈpyʊrət̮n/ *n.* a member of a Protestant religious group in England in the 16th and 17th centuries, who wanted to make religion simpler and get rid of complicated ceremonies. Many of them went to America to find religious freedom, and their beliefs had a strong influence on the American way of life. —**Puritan** *adj.*

pu·ri·tan /ˈpyʊrət̮n/ *n.* [C] someone who has very strict moral standards and thinks that pleasure is unnecessary or wrong —**puritan** also **Puritan** *adj.*: *a Puritan background* | *puritan beliefs*

pu·ri·tan·i·cal /ˌpyʊrəˈtænɪkəl/ *adj.* having extreme attitudes about religion and moral behavior: *Americans tend to be more puritanical than Europeans.* —**puritanically** /-kli/ *adv.*

pu·ri·tan·ism /ˈpyʊrət̮nˌɪzəm/ *n.* [U] **1** a way of living according to very strict rules, especially concerning religion and moral behavior **2** **Puritanism** the beliefs and practices of the Puritans

pu·ri·ty /ˈpyʊrət̮i/ *n.* [U] the quality or state of being pure: *Use of the chemicals could harm the purity of dairy products.* | *In literature, the swan has been a symbol of purity and virtue.* —opposite IMPURITY

purl¹ /pɚl/ *v.* [I,T] to use the purl stitch when you KNIT (=make clothes from wool)

purl² *n.* [U] one of the types of stitches that you use when you KNIT (=make clothes from wool)

pur·lieus /ˈpɚlyuz, -luz/ *n.* [plural] LITERARY the area in and around a place

pur·loin /pɚˈlɔɪn, ˈpɚlɔɪn/ *v.* [T] FORMAL OR HUMOROUS to steal something, or borrow something without permission: *Thieves purloined about $4 million in jewels from the mansion.*

pur·ple /ˈpɚpəl/ *n.* [U] **1** a dark color that is a mixture of red and blue **2 purple with rage/purple in the face etc.** very red in the face as a result of being angry or embarrassed **3 purple passage/prose/patch** a piece of writing that uses longer or more LITERARY words than are really necessary, in order to appear impressive to people —**purple** *adj.*

Purple Heart /ˌ.. ˈ./ *n.* [C] a special MEDAL given to U.S. soldiers who have been wounded in battle

pur·plish /ˈpɚplɪʃ/ *adj.* slightly purple: *a purplish-blue sweater*

pur·port¹ /pɚˈpɔrt/ *v.* [I,T] FORMAL to claim to be someone or something, or to make people believe that something is true, even if it is not: [**purport to do/be sth**] *The photograph purports to show American pilots missing in Vietnam.* —**purported** *adj.*: *the purported leader of the group* —**purportedly** *adv.*

pur·port² /ˈpɚpɔrt/ *n.* [U] FORMAL the general meaning of what someone says

pur·pose¹ /ˈpɚpəs/ *n.*
1 aim [C] the thing that an event, process, or activity is supposed to achieve, or the job that something is supposed to do: [+ of] *The purpose of this exercise is to increase your strength.* | [**the purpose of doing sth**] *The purpose of storing photos in a dark, dry place is to prevent fading.* | *The water can be treated for drinking purposes.* | *The new tax will serve the purpose* (=have the particular purpose) *of raising money for our schools.* —see Usage Note at REASON¹
2 on purpose deliberately: *Fire investigators believe the fire was set on purpose.*
3 plan [C] an intention or a plan: *The group's purpose is to help disabled teenagers have fun and meet new friends.* | [**for the purpose of doing sth**] *Compton bought the land for the purpose of developing it.* | [**purpose in/of doing sth**] *The primary purpose in traveling to Washington was to meet with the Vice President.*
4 reason to live [U] the feeling of determination that you have when you want to succeed in something: *Starting his own business gave him a new sense of purpose in his life.*
5 for all practical purposes also **for all intents and purposes** used to say that something may not exactly be true, but it is true in general: *For all practical purposes, the cleanup of the oil spill is complete.*
6 for the purpose(s) of sb/sth used to say that someone or something will be considered in a particular way in a discussion, document etc.: *For the purposes of this survey, "white" did not include Hispanics.*
7 serve its purpose if something serves its purpose, it does what you intended it to do: *The midnight-to-5 a.m. curfew has served its purpose of restoring order to the city.*
8 to no purpose FORMAL with no results: *The negotiations lasted for days, apparently to no purpose.* —opposite **to good purpose**
9 to the purpose OLD-FASHIONED useful or helpful —see also **accidentally on purpose** (ACCIDENTALLY (2)), PURPOSELY

purpose² *v.* [T] OLD USE to intend to do something

pur·pose·ful /ˈpɚpəsfəl/ *adj.* having a clear aim or purpose: *For young children, workbooks are often not purposeful enough.* —**purposefully** *adv.* —**purposefulness** *n.* [U]

pur·pose·less /ˈpɚpəslɪs/ *adj.* not having a clear aim or purpose: *The violence is purposeless and impulsive.* —**purposelessly** *adv.* —**purposelessness** *n.* [U]

pur·pose·ly /ˈpɚpəsli/ *adv.* deliberately: *Tom was purposely not invited to the party.*

purr /pɚ/ *v.* **1** [I] if a cat purrs, it makes a soft, low sound in its throat to show that it is pleased **2** [I] if the engine of a vehicle or machine purrs, it works perfectly and makes a quiet smooth sound: *Our limo purred smoothly down the tree-lined road.* **3** [I,T] if someone purrs, they speak in a soft, low, and SEXY voice: *"What a good idea," she purred.* —**purr** *n.* [C]

purse¹ /pɚs/ *n.* **1** [C] a bag, often made of leather, in which a woman carries her money and personal things: *I can never find anything in my purse.* —see picture at BAG¹ **2** [singular] FORMAL the amount of money that a person, organization, or country has available to spend: *Income from the new sales tax will go into the purse and will pay for the sports complex.* | *Haze says his plan would help small businesses without draining the public purse* (=money controlled by a government). **3** [C] the amount of money given to someone who wins a sports event, such as a BOXING match or car race: *The purse for Friday's title fight is more than $50 million.* **4 hold/control the purse strings** to control the money in a family, company etc.: *Maureen definitely holds the purse strings.* **5** [C] a small container for keeping coins in, made of leather, cloth, plastic etc., used especially by women

purse² *v.* **purse your lips** to bring your lips together tightly into a small circle, especially to show disapproval or doubt: *Hardin pursed his lips and said, "Lee, you'll never learn."*

purs·er /'pɜːsə/ *n.* [C] an officer who is responsible for the money on a ship and is also in charge of the passengers' rooms, comfort etc.

pur·su·ance /pə'suːəns/ *n.* **in pursuance of sth** FORMAL with the aim of doing or achieving something, or during the process of doing this

pur·su·ant /pə'suːənt/ *adj.* FORMAL **pursuant to sth** if you do something pursuant to a law, rule, contract etc., you do it according to what the law, rule, contract etc. says: *This money was spent legally and pursuant to city regulations.*

pur·sue /pə'suː/ *v.* [T] **1** to continue doing an activity or trying to achieve something over a long period of time: *After college, Jeffrey said he hopes to pursue a career in medicine.* **2** to chase or follow someone or something, in order to catch them, attack them etc.: *Police pursued the suspect for 20 minutes along Highway 5.* **3 pursue the matter/argument/question** to continue trying to ask about, find out about, or persuade someone about a particular subject: *Vardell pursued matter in court, and won.* **4** to keep trying to persuade someone to have a relationship with you: *Carol's been pursuing him for months.*

pur·su·er /pə'suːə/ *n.* [C] someone or something that is chasing you: *Sherman got away from his pursuers by running into a nearby train yard.*

pur·suit /pə'suːt/ *n.* **1** [U] the act of trying to achieve something in a determined way: [+ of] *the pursuit of truth and justice* | *I was too involved in the pursuit of wealth to spend time with my kids.* **2** [U] the act of chasing or following someone: *The suspect crossed the bridge, with four police cars in pursuit (=following behind).* | *Liz ran out the front door, with Tony in hot pursuit (=following close behind).* **3** [C usually plural] FORMAL an activity such as a sport or HOBBY, which you spend a lot of time doing: *Moriarty spent the summer focusing on his musical pursuits.*

pur·ty /'pɜːti/ *adj.* SPOKEN, NONSTANDARD pretty

pu·ru·lent /'pjʊərələnt/ *adj.* TECHNICAL containing or producing PUS —**purulence** *n.* [U]

pur·vey /pə'veɪ/ *v.* [T + to] FORMAL to supply goods, services, or information to people

pur·vey·or /pə'veɪə/ *n.* [C] FORMAL someone who supplies information, goods, or services to people, especially as a business: *Petrossian Inc. is the world's largest purveyor of caviar.*

pur·view /'pɜːvjuː/ *n.* **within/outside the purview of sth** FORMAL within or outside the limits of someone's job, activity, or knowledge: *Such social issues are not within the purview of the commission.*

pus /pʌs/ *n.* [U] a thick yellowish liquid produced in an infected part of your body: *If the blister becomes red and drains pus, see your doctor.*

push¹ /pʊʃ/ *v.*

1 ■ **move** ■ [I,T] to make someone or something move by pressing with your hands, arms, shoulders etc.: *It's still stuck – you'll have to push harder.* | *When I give the signal, I want you all to push.* | [push sb/sth] *Stop pushing me!* | [push sb/sth up/across/away etc.] *Help me push the car into the garage.* | **push the door open/shut** *I slowly pushed the door open.* —see picture at PULL¹

2 ■ **button/switch** ■ [I,T] to press a button, SWITCH etc., especially in order to make a piece of equipment start or stop working: *Push the green button to turn on the machine.*

3 ■ **try to get past sb** ■ [I,T always + adv./prep.] to use your hands, arms, shoulders etc. to make someone move, especially so that you can get past them: *There's no need to push. There are enough tickets for everyone.* | [push past/through] *Security guards pushed their way through the crowd to help the injured man.* | **push your way toward/across/to** etc. *Sandra and I had to push our way to the front of the bus.*

4 ■ **encourage/persuade** ■ [I,T] to encourage or persuade someone to accept or do something, especially something that they do not want to do: *Animal-rights groups are pushing to ban the capture of dolphins.* | [push sb to do sth] *My boss keeps pushing me to work more overtime.* | [push (sb) for sth] *Kehoe will push for spending more on after-school activities.* | [push sb into doing sth] *I think she pushed Derek into marrying her.*

5 ■ **work hard** ■ [T] to make someone work very hard: *Coach Koepple pushes his players pretty hard.* | *You have to push yourself if you want to be a professional dancer.*

6 ■ **increase/decrease** ■ to increase or decrease an amount, number, or value: [+ down/up] *Economists hope recent events will not push down the value of the yen.* | *Inflation has pushed up prices by 35%.* | **push sth higher/lower** *New technology has pushed the cost of health care even higher.*

7 ■ **drugs** ■ [T] INFORMAL to sell illegal drugs —see also PUSHER

8 ■ **advertise** ■ [T] INFORMAL to try to sell more of a product by advertising it a lot: *"Who was at the door?" "It was some guy pushing magazine subscriptions."*

9 ■ **ideas/opinions** ■ [T] to try to make people accept your ideas or opinions, especially by talking about them a lot: *I got tired of Robin pushing her environmental agenda at the office.*

10 push sb's buttons to make someone angry by doing or saying something that annoys them: *He really knows how to push Dad's buttons.*

11 push your luck also **push it** INFORMAL to do something or ask for something, when this is likely to annoy someone or be risky: *If we don't leave until 5 p.m., we'll be pushing it to get to the airport on time.*

12 push sth to the back of your mind to try to forget about a bad feeling or situation: *I pushed those memories to the back of my mind and went on with my life.*

13 be pushing up (the) daisies HUMOROUS to be dead

14 push the point OLD-FASHIONED to keep trying to make someone accept your opinion in a way that they find annoying —see also PULL¹, PUSHING

push ahead *phr. v.* [I] to continue with a plan or activity, especially in a determined way: [+ with] *The Navy plans to push ahead with putting women on combat ships.*

push along *phr. v.* [T] to make something continue to happen and be successful: *The new policies should help push along the nation's economic reform.* —see also **push forward** (PUSH¹)

push sb around *phr. v.* [T] **1** to tell someone what to do in an impolite or threatening way: *You shouldn't let people push you around like that.* **2** to push someone in a threatening way, often while talking to them in an impolite way: *Some of the bigger boys are pushing the little kids around.*

push sth ↔ aside *phr. v.* [T] to try not to think about something, especially something bad, so that you can give your attention to something else: *Somehow he manages to push personal feelings aside and work with convicted murderers.*

push forward *phr. v.* **1** [I,T push sth ↔ forward] to make something continue to happen and be successful: *New ideas are needed to push the peace process forward.* **2** [I] to continue moving toward a place, in spite of difficulties: *As the army pushed forward, the death toll mounted.*

push off *phr. v.* [I] **1** if a boat pushes off from the shore, it moves away from it **2** OLD-FASHIONED to leave a place

push on *phr. v.* **1** [I] to continue doing an activity [+ with] *Even with disagreement growing, they decided to push on with the negotiations.* **2** [T push sth on sb] to try to make someone accept your ideas or beliefs or buy something that you are selling, especially in a very determined way: *We don't try to push our religion on anybody.* **3** [I] to continue traveling somewhere, especially after you have had a rest: *Hungry and exhausted, the backpackers pushed on.*

P

push sb/sth ↔ **over** phr. v. [T] to make someone or something fall to the ground by pushing them: *They also pushed over a stand that held the VCR.*

push sth ↔ **through** phr. v. [T] to get a new law officially accepted: *Ohio representatives tried to push through a bill that would declare the site a historic landmark.*

push² n. **1** [C] the act of pushing or pressing something: *If the door's stuck, just give it a push.* **2** [C] to attempt to get or achieve something: *The President has renewed a push to get the hostages freed.* | *In a push to capture more of the market, Conoco will start selling propane.* **3 if/when push comes to shove** SPOKEN used to say what you can do if a situation becomes very difficult: *If push comes to shove, you can always rent out the house.* **4** [C] a planned military attack into the area where the enemy is: *Rebel forces are believed to be preparing a final push into the city.* **5 at/with the push of a button** used to emphasize how easy a machine is to use because it is controlled by pushing a button: *The instrument can gauge a distance with the push of a button.*

push-but·ton /'. ,../ adj. [only before noun] **1** operated by pressing a button with your finger: *a push-button phone* **2** using computers or electronic equipment rather than traditional methods: *push-button warfare* | *the push-button piloting of a ship*

push·cart /'puʃkɑrt/ n. [C] a large flat container like a box with wheels, used especially by people who sell goods in the street

push·er /'puʃɚ/ n. [C] INFORMAL someone who sells illegal drugs —see also PENCIL PUSHER

push·ing /'puʃɪŋ/ prep. **be pushing 18/30/60 etc.** SPOKEN to be nearly 18, 30, 60 etc. years old: *Sheila must be pushing 40 by now.*

Push·kin /'puʃkɪn/, **Al·ek·san·dr** /ˌælɪgˈzændɚ/ (1799–1837) one of Russia's greatest writers who wrote NOVELS, plays, and poetry, and greatly influenced the development of Russian literature

push·o·ver /'pʌʃ,ouvɚ/ n. INFORMAL **be a pushover** to be easy to persuade, influence, or defeat: *Mr. Corry quickly showed the students that he was no pushover.* | [+ for] *Alan's a pushover for beautiful women.*

push-start /'. ./ v. [T] to push a vehicle while someone stops pressing on the CLUTCH in order to make the engine start —**push-start** n. [C]

push-up /'. ./ n. [C] an exercise in which you lie on the floor on your chest and push yourself up with your arms

push·y /'puʃi/ adj. **pushier, pushiest** DISAPPROVING so determined to succeed and to get what you want that you behave in an impolite way: *a pushy salesman* —**pushily** adv. —**pushiness** n. [U]

pu·sil·lan·i·mous /ˌpyusə'lænəməs/ adj. FORMAL weak and frightened of taking even small risks —**pusillanimously** adv. —**pusillanimity** /ˌpyusələ'nɪməti/ n. [U]

puss /pus/ n. [usually singular] **1** OLD-FASHIONED a name for a cat, or a way of calling a cat **2** INFORMAL face —see also SOURPUSS

pus·sy /'pusi/ n. plural **pussies 1** [C,U] TABOO a word for a woman's sex organs, often used to talk about a woman in a way that is very offensive **2** [C] VULGAR, OFFENSIVE a man who is weak or not brave **3** [C] INFORMAL a cat

puss·y·cat /'pusi,kæt/ n. [C] INFORMAL **1** a cat **2** [usually singular] someone who is very nice and gentle, especially when they may not seem this way: *Jake's a real pussycat once you get to know him.*

puss·y·foot /'pusi,fut/ also **pussyfoot a·round** /ˌ... .'./ v. [I] INFORMAL to be too careful or frightened to make decisions or tell someone exactly what you think: *When Cranston wants something, he doesn't pussyfoot around.*

pussy-whip·ped /'.. ,./ adj. VULGAR, SLANG, DISAPPROVING a man who is pussy-whipped does whatever his GIRLFRIEND or wife wants him to do; HENPECKED —compare WHIPPED

pussy wil·low /ˌ.. '.. ./ n. [C,U] a tree with white flowers that are soft like fur

pus·tule /'pʌstʃul/ n. [C] TECHNICAL a small raised spot on your skin containing PUS (=a thick yellow liquid)

put /put/ v. past tense and past participle **put** present participle **putting**

1 ⟨move to place/position⟩ [T always + adv./prep.] to move something to a particular place or position, especially using your hands: *Where did you put the newspaper?* | [put sth in/on/over etc. sth] *I think I put the keys in my coat pocket.* | *We had to put netting over the plants to protect them from birds.* | *Just put the package **over there** on the table.*

2 ⟨change sb's situation/feelings⟩ [T always + adv./prep.] to change someone's situation or the way they feel: *Winning their last six games has put Utah into first place.* | *This is music to put you in a relaxed mood.* | *Listening to Larry's stories just about put me to sleep (=made me feel sleepy).* | *The boys put themselves in danger (=created a situation in which they could have been hurt) by ignoring the safety regulations.* | *Higher transportation costs put many companies out of business (=make the companies close down).*

3 ⟨write/print sth⟩ [T] to write or print something: [put sth in/on/under sth] *Put your name at the top of each answer sheet.* | *Last week we put an ad in the newspaper for a new secretary.*

4 put a stop/an end to sth to stop an activity that is harmful or unacceptable: *It's time the community worked together to put an end to the violence.*

5 put pressure/emphasis/blame etc. on sb/sth to do something that affects someone or something: *Congress is putting pressure on the military to investigate the accident.*

6 put sth behind you to try to forget about a bad experience or mistake so that it does not affect you now: *Counseling helped her put the trial behind her.*

7 put sb in charge/control/command (of sth) to give someone authority or control over a group, activity, organization etc.: *Hargrave will be put in charge of all overseas marketing.*

8 ⟨express⟩ [T always + adv./prep.] to say something in a particular way, especially in a way that helps people understand how you feel or what you want: *put sth well/cleverly/succinctly etc. At press conferences, Wickford's answers are always succinctly put.* | *Nancy often has trouble putting her thoughts into words (=expressing her ideas or feelings).* | *You don't have to put it like that (=say it in that particular way).*

SPOKEN PHRASES

9 as sb puts it used to repeat what someone else has said: *As Jerry's wife, Lois, puts it, "He wasn't a very strong player."*

10 to put it mildly used to say that a situation is actually worse than the way you are describing it: *The movie contains some scenes that are, to put it mildly, rather difficult to watch.*

11 to put it bluntly used to tell someone that you are going to say exactly what you think: *To put it bluntly, you are not pretty enough to be a movie star.*

12 how shall/can I put it? used when what you are going to say might sound strange or impolite, or when it is difficult to say exactly what you mean: *The dessert was – how shall I put it? – like a chocolate sunset.*

13 put it there OLD-FASHIONED used to tell someone to shake hands with you, either as a greeting or after making an agreement with them: *$500? OK, it's a deal. Put it there!*

14 put sb/sth to work a) to make someone or a machine work: *During the war, Giacchi was put to work on a Navy newspaper.* **b)** to use something such as an idea or money to do something: *In the meantime, the money could be put to work for repairing streets.*

15 put sb out of work/out of a job to make someone lose their job: *The closing of the steel mill put over 300 employees out of work.*

16 put money in/into sth to make money available to be used in a business, or add it to something such as a bank account: *GM is putting lots of money into development of new safety features.* | *Each month I put at least $300 into my savings account.*

17 put faith/trust/confidence in sb/sth to trust someone or something or believe that they can do something: *Young says he doesn't put much trust in the polls.*

18 to put it another way used when trying to explain something in a different way and make it clearer: *The liquid dumped in the river was extremely acidic. To put it another way, it's not good for the fish.*

19 put sth into action/effect/practice to start using a plan, idea, knowledge etc.: *Forest managers have been slow to put the plan into practice.*

20 put energy/work/enthusiasm etc. into sth to use a lot of energy etc. when you are doing an activity: *The kids have put a lot of energy into planning the trip.*

21 have importance/quality [T always + adv./prep.] to consider something to have a particular level of importance or quality: [**put sb as/among/in etc.**] *I'd put Harris among the top three sprinters in the country.* | [**put sth before sth**] *He puts his work before everything else.* | **put sth first/second etc.** *It's obvious that Jan puts her family first and herself second.*

22 send sb somewhere [T always + adv./prep.] to arrange for or order someone to go to a place for a particular purpose: [**put sb in/on etc.**] *Pneumonia put him in the hospital for more than a week.* | *The new law will put twenty new policemen on the street.* | *It's time to put the boys to bed* (=make them go into their beds).

23 put sb in a bad/good/terrible etc. mood to make someone angry or happy: *Exercising usually helps put me in a better mood.*

24 put a question to sb to ask a question, especially when you want to get someone's opinion about something: *The Toronto Sun recently put this question to fans: Who is the top fighter in the NHL?*

25 put a proposition/proposal/case to sb to suggest something to a person or group and usually ask them to agree to it or make a decision about it: *We then put our proposal to the city's board of supervisors.*

26 put one/sth over on sb INFORMAL to deceive someone into believing something that is not true or that is useless: *They think they've found a way to put one over on the welfare office.*

27 put sb on a plane/train to take someone to an airplane, train etc. to start a trip: *We went to the airport this morning to put my Mom on a plane home.*

28 add sth [T] to add a quality to something: *Put a little romance into your life.*

29 put sth right to make a situation better, especially after someone has made a mistake or behaved badly: *Larson has promised to put the city's finances right by the end of the year.*

30 throw [I,T] to throw a SHOT (=a heavy metal ball) in a sports competition —see also **put your back into it** (BACK² (16)), **put your finger on sth** (FINGER¹ (4)), **put your foot down** (FOOT¹ (10)), **put pressure on** (PRESSURE¹ (1)), **put sth to (good) use** (USE² (4))

put about *phr. v.* [I,T **put** sth **about**] TECHNICAL if a ship puts about or if you put it about, it changes direction

put sth **↔ across** *phr. v.* [T] **1** to explain your ideas, beliefs etc. in a way that people can understand: *To put his point across, my dad locked me out when I was late.* **2** to sing or play music in a clear, effective way: *Laurel puts across a song with lots of style.*

put sth **↔ aside** *phr. v.* [T] **1** to try to stop thinking about a problem, argument, or disagreement, because you want to achieve something: *Try to put aside your feelings and look at the facts.* **2** to save money regularly, usually for a particular purpose: *Fortunately, they had put aside money for such an emergency.* **3** to stop reading or working with something, in order to start doing something else: *Let's put this question aside for now and continue with the discussion.* **4** to keep a period of time free in order

---

to be able to do something: *Try to put aside an hour each day for exercise.*

put sth **at** sth *phr. v.* [T] to calculate and state an amount, someone's age etc., without trying to be very exact: *Official estimates put the damage at over $10 million.*

put sb/sth **↔ away** *phr. v.* [T] **1** [**put** sth **↔ away**] to put something in the place where it is usually kept: *Could you put the dishes away before you go to bed?* **2** [**put** sb **↔ away**] INFORMAL to put someone in a prison or in a mental hospital: *A maniac like him needs to be put away for a long time.* **3** [**put** sth **↔ away**] INFORMAL to eat or drink a lot: *Jack can really put away the food.* **4** [**put** sth **↔ away**] to save money: *Mom had put away almost $100,000 for retirement.*

put back *phr. v.* [T] **1** [**put** sth **↔ back**] to arrange for an event to start at a later time or date; POSTPONE: *The meeting has been put back to next Thursday.* **2** [**put** sth **↔ back**] to delay a process or activity by a number of weeks, months etc.: *This fire could put back the opening date by several weeks.* **3** [**put** sb/sth **↔ back**] to put things or people in the place or situation they were in before: *Put the milk back in the fridge.* | *The program should put 250 people back to work.*

put down *phr. v.*
1 criticize [T **put** sb **↔ down**] to criticize someone and make them feel silly or stupid: *It seems like Meg's mother-in-law is always putting her down.* | *Stop putting yourself down* (=criticizing yourself)!
2 write [T **put** sth **↔ down**] to write something, especially a name or number, on a piece of paper or on a list: *Put down your name and address and we'll send you a free copy of the magazine.*
3 put down a revolution/revolt/rebellion etc. to use force to stop people who are fighting against the government: *Military police were called in to put down the riot.*
4 pay [T **put** sth **↔ down**] to pay part of the total cost of something, so that you can pay the rest later: *We had enough to put 20% down on our car.*
5 baby [T **put** sb **down**] to put a baby in its bed: *I put Jessica down for her afternoon nap a few minutes ago.*
6 put the phone down to put the part of the telephone that you talk into back onto the telephone when you have finished speaking to someone
7 kill [T **put** sth **↔ down**] to kill an animal without causing it pain, usually because it is old or sick: *We had to have the dog put down.*
8 I couldn't put it down SPOKEN used to say that you found a book, toy etc. extremely interesting: *It's such a good book that I couldn't put it down.*
9 aircraft [I,T **put** sth **↔ down**] FORMAL if an aircraft puts down or if a pilot puts it down, it lands, especially because of an EMERGENCY: *The pilot managed to put down in a field away from the buildings.*
10 put down a motion/an amendment to suggest a subject, plan, change in the law etc. for Congress or a committee to consider

put sb **down as** sth *phr. v.* [T] to guess what someone is like or what they do, without having much information about them: *Some people have put me down as a skeptic.*

put sb **down for** sth *phr. v.* **1** [T **put** sb **down for** sth] to put someone's name on a list so that they can take part in an activity, join an organization etc.: *I'll put you down for an appointment on Thursday at 3 p.m.* **2 put sb down for $5/$10 etc.** to write someone's name on a list with an amount of money that they have promised to give: *You can put me down for a $25 donation.*

put sth **down to** sth *phr. v.* [T] to explain the reason for something, especially when you are guessing: *The burger was a little tasteless, which I put down to the quality of the meat.*

put sth **↔ forth** *phr. v.* [T] FORMAL **1** to suggest a plan, proposal etc. or support it in discussions: *Arguments have been put forth in favor of the construction project.* **2 put forth leaves/shoots/roots**

etc. LITERARY if a tree or bush puts forth leaves etc. it begins to grow them

put sb/sth ↔ **forward** *phr. v.* [T] **1** [put sth ↔ forward] to suggest a plan, proposal etc., especially in order to start discussions about something that needs to be decided: *The Dutch delegation put forward a new trade deal.* **2** [put sb ↔ forward] to suggest someone who would be good for a particular job, position etc.: *No other candidate has been put forward to succeed Fontaine, who is retiring in December.*

put in *phr. v.* **1** [T put sth ↔ in] to put a piece of equipment somewhere and connect it so that it is ready to be used: *After we bought the car, we had a better stereo put in.* **2** [T put sth ↔ in] to spend time or use energy working or practicing something: *Our team put in some long hours getting the presentation ready.* **3 put your two cents in** INFORMAL to say what you really think about something: *At least I got to put in my two cents before the meeting ended.* **4** [T put sth ↔ in] to ask for something in an official way: *Susan put in her application for graduate school last week.* **5** [I] if a ship puts in, it enters a port

put in for sth *phr. v.* [T] to make an official request for something: *Jones put in for a transfer to our Dallas office.*

put off *phr. v.* [T] **1** [put sth ↔ off] to arrange to do something at a later time or date, especially because there is a problem, difficulty etc.: *Cheney has put off any action until after the panel studies the issue.* | [put off doing sth] *Commissioners decided to put off voting on the proposal until next month.* **2** [put sth ↔ off] to delay doing something until later because you do not want to do it now: *You shouldn't put off going to the dentist.* **3** [put sb ↔ off] to make you dislike something or not want to do something: *Don't let the restaurant's cheap-looking decor put you off – the food's really good.* **4** [put sb ↔ off] to make someone wait because you do not want to meet them, pay them etc. until later: *I just don't have the money right now – I'll have to put him off for another week.*

put on *phr. v.* [T]

1 clothes [put sth ↔ on] to put a piece of clothing on your body: *Hurry up and put your shoes on.* —see picture and Usage Note at DRESS[1]

2 affect/influence sth [put sth on sth] to do something that affects or influences something else: *The government has put a limit on foreign imports of textiles.*

3 start equipment [put sth ↔ on] to make a piece of equipment begin working: *It's cold in here. Why don't you put on the heat?*

4 on skin [put sth ↔ on] to put MAKEUP, cream etc. on your skin: *I hardly ever put on lipstick.*

5 music [put sth ↔ on] to put a record, TAPE, VIDEO, or CD into a machine and start playing it

6 pretend [put sth ↔ on] to pretend to have a certain feeling, opinion, way of speaking etc. especially in order to get attention: *It annoys me when she puts on her phony British accent.*

7 put on weight/ 5 pounds etc. to become fatter and heavier: *It looks like Dennis has put on a few pounds since he got married.*

8 event/concert/play etc. [put sth ↔ on] to arrange an event, concert, play etc. or perform in it: *The West Valley Symphony is putting on a free concert in the park.*

9 cook [put sth ↔ on] to start cooking something: *Let me just put the potatoes on first.*

10 you're putting me on! SPOKEN used to tell someone that you think they are joking: *Seth is moving to Alaska? You're putting me on!*

11 risk money [put sth on sth] to risk an amount of money on the result of a game, race etc.: *I put $30 on Miami to win the Super Bowl.*

12 put on the brakes to make a vehicle stop or slow down by pressing a PEDAL or handle

13 add [put sth on sth] to add an amount of money or tax onto the cost of something: *The new tax could put another ten cents on the price of gas.*

put out *phr. v.*

1 fire/cigarette etc. [T put sth ↔ out] to make a fire, cigarette etc. stop burning: *It took firefighters several hours to put the blaze out.* —see Usage Note at FIRE[1]

2 [T put sth ↔ out] to place things where people can find and use them: *Could you help me put out the sandwiches for lunch?*

3 make extra work [T put sb ↔ out] to make additional work or cause problems for someone: *Will it put you out if I bring another guest?*

4 put yourself out to make an effort to do something that will help someone: *I wouldn't want to put yourself out just for me.*

5 move/take outside [T put sth ↔ out] to put something outside the house: *Remember to put the cat out before you go to bed.* | **put the trash/garbage out** (=put dirty or unwanted things outside your house to be taken away) | **put the wash/laundry out** (=put clothes outside to dry)

6 put your hand/foot/arm etc. out also **put out your hand/foot etc.** to move your hand, foot etc. forward and away from your body: *He put his hand out to keep from falling over.*

7 make unconscious [T put sb out] to make someone unconscious before a medical operation

8 produce sth [T put sth ↔ out] to produce radio signals, print books, broadcast programs etc.: *In the last five years, Williams has put out three new CDs.*

9 put out information/statements/statistics etc. to give information, statements etc. for people to read or listen to: *The company has put out a statement saying that they will replace all the defective products.*

10 put out a light to make a light stop working by pressing or turning a button

11 put out feelers/antenna to try to discover information or opinions by listening to people or watching what is happening: *Several prospective buyers for the airline have already put out feelers.*

12 ship [I] if a ship puts out, it starts to sail

13 have sex [I] VULGAR, SLANG if a woman puts out, she has sex with a man

14 baseball [T put sb out] to prevent a baseball player from winning a point, for example, by catching the ball that they have hit

put through *phr. v.* [T] **1** [put sb ↔ through] to connect someone to someone else on the telephone: *"I'd like to speak with Mr. Croft." "I'll put you right through."* **2 put sb through school/college/university** to pay for someone to study at school or college: *I'm grateful to my wife for putting me through law school.* **3** [put sb through sth] to make someone do something that is very bad or difficult: *Nelson put the team through a rugged practice Friday.* | *My father's drinking problem put my mother through hell.* **4** [put sth ↔ through] to do what is necessary in order to get a plan or suggestion accepted or approved: *Conservatives in the legislature also put through amendments protecting defense funding.*

put sth **to** sb *phr. v.* [T] **1** [put sth to sb] to suggest something such as a proposal or plan to a group of people: *The new marketing plan was put to the board this morning.* | **put sth to a/the vote** (=get people to vote on it) **2** [put sth to sb] to ask someone a question or make a suggestion to them: *I'll put the question to the group for discussion.* **3 put sb to trouble/inconvenience etc.** to make someone do something that will cause them trouble or inconvenience: *I hope I'm not putting you to any trouble by asking for your help.* **4 put your name/signature to** sth to sign a letter, document etc. saying that you agree with what is written in it

put sth ↔ **together** *phr. v.* **1** [T put sth ↔ together] to prepare or produce something by collecting pieces of information, ideas etc.: *Callahan has put together a proposal for new after school activities.* **2** [T put sth ↔ together] to make a machine, model etc. by joining all the different parts: *It took days to put the engine together again.* **3 more... than the rest put together** used when comparing two sets of people or things to say that one set contains more than the total of all the other sets: *David earns more than the rest of us put together.*

put sb **under** *phr. v.* [T] if a doctor puts you under, they give you drugs to make you UNCONSCIOUS before SURGERY: *The doctor explained the operation one more time before putting me under.*

put up *phr. v.* [T]
1 build [put sth ↔ up] to build something such as a wall, fence, building etc.: *A new traffic light will be put up at the intersection of 4th and Pine.*
2 for people to see [put sth ↔ up] to attach a picture, etc. to a wall or to decorate things so that people can see them: *Let's put a few of these posters up in the hallway.* | *Stores are already putting up Christmas decorations.*
3 let sb stay [put sb ↔ up] to let someone stay in your house and give them meals: *I could put you up for the night if you can't find a hotel.*
4 **put** sth **up for sale** to make something available for someone to buy, especially a house or a business: *Thirteen of the bank's branches will be put up for sale.*
5 **put** sth **up for discussion/review** etc. to suggest that an idea, plan, report etc. be discussed or examined
6 **put** sb **up for adoption** to make a child available for another family to ADOPT: *Within days after being born, Dana was put up for adoption.*
7 **put up a fight/a struggle/resistance** to argue against or oppose something in a determined way, or to fight against someone who is attacking you: *Ferris threatened to put up a fight in court if the sign was not taken down.*
8 **put up money/$500/$5 million** to give an amount of money for a particular purpose: *Part of that money is being put up by local businessmen.*
9 elections [put sb ↔ up] FORMAL to suggest someone as an appropriate person to be elected to a position: *The new party plans to put up candidates in every state.*

put sb **up to** sth *phr. v.* [T] to encourage someone to do something stupid or dangerous: *Someone must have put Chris up to stealing the bike.*

put up with sb/sth *phr. v.* [T] to accept a bad situation or person without complaining: *For many years, residents have put up with inadequate roads.* | *You see what I have to put up with!*

pu·ta·tive /ˈpyutətɪv/ *adj.* [only before noun] FORMAL believed or accepted by most people: *Hess is the ballet's putative lead dancer.*

put-down /ˈ. ./ *n.* [C] something you say that is intended to make someone feel stupid or unimportant: *I took his criticism of my work as a real put-down.* —see also **put down** (PUT)

put-on /ˈ. ./ *n.* [C] INFORMAL something you say or do to try to make someone believe something that is not true

put out /ˌ. ˈ./ *adj.* INFORMAL **be/feel put out** to feel upset or offended: *Anne was put out about not being invited to the dance.*

pu·tre·fac·tion /ˌpyutrəˈfækʃən/ *n.* [U] FORMAL the process of decay in a dead animal or plant, during which it smells very bad

pu·tre·fy /ˈpyutrəˌfaɪ/ *v.* **putrefies, putrefied, putrefying** [I,T] FORMAL if a dead animal or plant putrefies, it decays and smells very bad

pu·tres·cent /pyuˈtrɛsənt/ *adj.* FORMAL beginning to decay and smell very bad —**putrescence** *n.* [U]

pu·trid /ˈpyutrɪd/ *adj.* **1** dead animals, plants, or parts of the body that are putrid are decaying and smell very bad **2** INFORMAL very bad or disgusting: *a putrid smell*

putsch /pʊtʃ/ *n.* [C] a secretly planned attempt to remove a government by force: *Both generals were convicted for their role in the failed putsch.*

putt /pʌt/ *v.* [I,T] to hit a GOLF BALL lightly a short distance along the ground toward the hole —**putt** *n.* [C]

put·tee /pʌˈti/ *n.* [C usually plural] a long piece of cloth that is wrapped around the leg from the knee down, worn as part of an army uniform in the past

put·ter¹ /ˈpʌtɚ/ *n.* a type of GOLF CLUB (=stick) to hit the ball a short distance toward or into the hole

putter² *v.* [I always + adv./prep.] **1** to spend time doing things that are not very important, in a

relaxed way: [+ **around/in**] *Grandpa spends most of his time puttering around the garden.* **2** to walk or move slowly and without hurrying: [+ **along/down** etc.] *drivers puttering along in the slow lane*

put·ting /ˈpʌtɪŋ/ *n.* [U] the action of lightly hitting a GOLF BALL a short distance so that it goes into a hole, or the ability to this: *I need to work on my putting.*

putting green /ˈ.. ˌ./ *n.* [C] one of the smaller smooth areas of grass on a GOLF COURSE where you hit the ball into the hole

put·ty /ˈpʌti/ *n.* [U] **1** a soft substance that dries hard and is used to fasten glass into window frames **2** **be putty in sb's hands** to be easily controlled or influenced by someone

put-up job /ˈ. . ˌ./ *n.* [C] INFORMAL a secret arrangement for something to happen, especially something illegal or something done to trick someone

put-up·on /ˈ. ˌ./ *adj.* [not before noun] **be/feel put upon** to think that other people are treating you unfairly by expecting you to do too much: *Don had a way of getting people to work without feeling put upon.*

putz¹ /pʌts, pʊts/ *n.* [C] INFORMAL **1** someone, especially a man, who is stupid, annoying, and impolite **2** VULGAR a PENIS

putz² *v.*

putz around *phr. v.* [I] to spend time without doing very much, or without doing anything important: *It's time the City Council stopped putzing around.*

puz·zle¹ /ˈpʌzəl/ *n.* [C] **1** a game or toy that has a lot of pieces that you have to fit together: *a child's wooden puzzle* —see also JIGSAW PUZZLE **2** a game in which you have to think hard to solve a difficult question or problem: *a crossword puzzle* **3** [usually singular] something that is difficult to understand or explain: *Women have always been a puzzle to Brad.* **4** **a piece of the puzzle** a piece of information that helps you to understand part of a difficult question, mystery etc.

puzzle² *v.* **1** [T usually passive] to confuse someone or make them feel slightly anxious because they do not understand something: *Astronomers continue to be puzzled by the existence of black holes.* **2** [I,T] to think for a long time about something, especially because you cannot understand or solve it: [+ **over/about**] *At the counter, a couple puzzled over which lottery numbers to choose.*

puz·zled /ˈpʌzəld/ *adj.* confused and unable to understand something: *Her reaction left me puzzled.* | **puzzled look/expression/stare** *I noticed her looking at me with a puzzled stare.*

puz·zle·ment /ˈpʌzəlmənt/ *n.* [U] FORMAL a feeling of being confused and unable to understand something

puz·zler /ˈpʌzlɚ/ *n.* [C] INFORMAL something that is difficult to understand or explain

puz·zling /ˈpʌzlɪŋ/ *adj.* confusing and difficult to understand or explain: *Most puzzling was the fact that Mason waited a week to report the crime.*

PVC *n.* [U] a type of plastic, usually used to make pipes, coverings for floors, or other things used in building houses

pvt. the written abbreviation of PRIVATE, the lowest military rank in the army

pwr. the written abbreviation of "power"

PX *n.* [C] a special store for food and other supplies on a U.S. military base

pyg·my /ˈpɪgmi/ *n. plural* **pygmies** [C] **1** also **Pygmy** a person belonging to a race of very small people, especially one of the tribes of central Africa **2** **pygmy rabbit/hippo/elephant** etc. a very small type of rabbit, HIPPO etc.

py·ja·mas /pəˈdʒɑməz, -dʒæ-/ *n.* [plural] the British spelling of PAJAMAS

py·lon /ˈpaɪlɑn/ *n.* [C] **1** one of a set of plastic CONES placed on a road to control traffic and protect people who are working there **2** one of the tall metal structures that supports wires carrying electricity **3** a tall structure or post used to support something heavy, especially something that is used to guide aircraft to land

Pyn·chon /'pɪntʃən/, **Thomas** (1937–) a U.S. writer of NOVELS

Pyong·yang /ˌpyʌŋ'yaŋ, ˌpyɔŋ-/ the capital and largest city of North Korea

py·or·rhe·a /ˌpaɪə'riə/ n. [U] a DISEASE of your GUMS that makes your teeth become loose

pyr·a·mid /'pɪrəmɪd/ n. [C] **1** a large stone building with four TRIANGULAR (=three-sided) walls that slope in to a point at the top, found especially in Egypt and Central America **2** [usually singular] a system or organization in which a small number of people have power or influence over a much larger number of people: *At the bottom of the pyramid are the uneducated poor.* **3** a pile of objects that have been put into the shape of a pyramid: [+ **of**] *a pyramid of cans* **4** a pyramid-shaped object —see picture at SHAPE¹ —**pyramidal** /'pɪrəmɪd/ *adj.*

pyramid scheme /'... ˌ./ n. [C] an illegal system of INVESTing money, in which the money of people who invest later is used to pay people in the system who invested earlier

pyre /paɪə/ n. [C] a high pile of wood on which a dead body is placed to be burned in a funeral ceremony

Pyr·e·nees, the /'pɪrəˌniz/ a range of mountains in southern Europe, that runs between France and Spain, from the Bay of Biscay to the Mediterranean Sea

Py·rex /'paɪrɛks/ n. [U] TRADEMARK a special type of strong glass that does not break at high temperatures and is used for making cooking dishes

py·rite /'paɪraɪt/ n. [U] a yellow-colored compound of iron and SULFUR; FOOL'S GOLD

py·ri·tes /pə'raɪtiz, 'paɪraɪts/ n. [C] any of various compounds of SULFUR with a type of metal, usually iron, or iron and COPPER: *iron pyrites*

py·ro·ma·ni·a /ˌpaɪrou'meɪniə/ n. [U] a mental illness that gives you a strong desire to start fires

py·ro·ma·ni·ac /ˌpaɪrou'meɪniæk/ n. [C] **1** someone who suffers from the mental illness of pyromania **2** INFORMAL, HUMOROUS someone who enjoys making and watching fires

py·ro·tech·nics /ˌpaɪrə'tɛknɪks/ n. **1** [plural] FORMAL OR TECHNICAL a public show of FIREWORKS **2** [U] TECHNICAL the skill or business of making FIREWORKS **3** [plural] an impressive show of someone's skill as a public speaker, musician etc. —**pyrotechnic** *adj.*

Pyr·rhic vic·to·ry /ˌpɪrɪk 'vɪktəri/ n. [C] a victory in which the person who wins suffers so much that the victory was hardly worth winning

Py·thag·o·ras /pɪ'θægərəs/ (?582–?507 B.C.) a Greek PHILOSOPHER and MATHEMATICIAN, known for the Pythagorean Theorem, about the relationship between the sides of a TRIANGLE which has one angle of 90°

py·thon /'paɪθɑn, -θən/ n. [C] a large tropical snake that kills animals for food by winding itself around them and crushing them

pyx /pɪks/ n. [C] a small container in which the holy bread used for the Christian ceremony of COMMUNION (1) is kept

Q, q /kyu/ *n. plural* **Q's, q's** [C] the 17th letter of the English alphabet

Q., q. the written abbreviation of "question"

QA *n.* [U] QUALITY ASSURANCE

Qad·da·fi /gəˈdɑfi, kə-/, **Colonel Mu·am·mar al-** /ˈmuəmɑr æl/ (1942–) the leader of Libya since 1969

Qa·tar /ˈkɑtɑr, kəˈtɑr/ a country in the Middle East, east of Saudi Arabia —**Qatari** /kəˈtɑri/ *n., adj*

QB the written abbreviation of QUARTERBACK

QED the abbreviation of the Latin phrase "quod erat demonstrandum," used to say that a fact, event etc. proves that what you say is true

Q-rat·ing /ˈkyu ˌreɪtɪŋ/ *n.* [C] a way of describing how well-known by the public someone is

qt. the written abbreviation of QUART

Q-tip /ˈkyu tɪp/ *n.* [C] TRADEMARK a small thin stick with cotton at each end, used for cleaning places that are difficult to reach, such as your ears

Qtr., qtr. the written abbreviation of "quarter"

Quaa·lude /ˈkweɪlud/ also **lude** *n.* [C] TRADEMARK an illegal drug that makes you feel very relaxed or sleepy

quack¹ /kwæk/ *v.* [I] to make the sound that a duck makes

quack² *n.* [C] INFORMAL **1** someone who pretends to be a doctor **2** the sound a duck makes

quack³ *adj.* relating to the activities or medicines of someone who pretends to be a doctor: *a quack remedy for colds*

quack·er·y /ˈkwækəri/ *n.* [U] the activities of someone who pretends to have medical knowledge or skills

quad /kwɑd/ *n.* [C] **1** a square open area with buildings all around it, especially in a school or college **2** a short form of QUADRUPLET **3 quads** [plural] INFORMAL: see QUADRICEPS

quadr- /kwɑdr/ *prefix* four: *a quadrangle* (=flat shape with four sides) | *a quadrilateral* (=shape with four straight sides) | *a quadruped* (=animal with four legs)

quad·ran·gle /ˈkwɑdræŋɡəl/ *n.* [C] **1** a formal word for a QUAD (1) **2** TECHNICAL a flat shape that has four straight sides

quad·rant /ˈkwɑdrənt/ *n.* [C] **1** a quarter of a circle —see picture at SHAPE¹ **2** an area that is one of four equal parts that a larger area is divided into: *the town's southwest quadrant* **3** an instrument for measuring angles, used when sailing or when looking at the stars

quad·ra·phon·ic, quadrophonic /ˌkwɑdrəˈfɑnɪk◂/ *adj.* using a system of sound recording, broadcasting etc. in which the sound comes from four different SPEAKERS at the same time —compare MONO², STEREO²

quad·rat·ic e·qua·tion /kwɑˌdrætɪk ɪˈkweɪʒən/ *n.* [C] TECHNICAL an EQUATION such as $ax^2+bx+c=y$, which includes numbers or quantities multiplied by themselves

quad·ri·ceps /ˈkwɑdrəˌsɛps/ *n.* [plural] the large muscle at the front of your THIGH

quad·ri·lat·er·al /ˌkwɑdrəˈlætərəl/ *n.* [C] a flat shape with four straight sides —**quadrilateral** *adj.*

qua·drille /kwɑˈdrɪl/ *n.* [C] a dance, popular especially in the 19th century, in which the dancers form a square

quad·ril·lion /kwɑˈdrɪlyən/ *number* 1,000,000,000,000,000

quad·ri·ple·gic /ˌkwɑdrəˈplidʒɪk/ *n.* [C] someone who cannot move any part of their body below their neck: *A drunken driving accident left him a quadriplegic* —**quadriplegia** *n.* [U] —**quadriplegic** *adj.*

quad·ro·phon·ic /ˌkwɑdrəˈfɑnɪk◂/ *adj.* another spelling of QUADRAPHONIC

quad·ru·ped /ˈkwɑdrəˌpɛd/ *n.* [C] TECHNICAL an animal that has four legs —compare BIPED

quad·ru·ple¹ /kwɑˈdrupəl/ *v.* [I,T] to increase and become four times as big or as high, or to make something do this: *Food prices quadrupled during the war.* | *The company has quadrupled its profits in just three years.*

quadruple² *adv.* **1** four times as big or as many: *The subjects were given quadruple the normal dosage of the drug.* **2** having four parts —**quadruple** *adj.*

quad·ru·plet /kwɑˈdruplɪt/ *n.* [C] one of four babies born at the same time to the same mother

quaff /kwɑf, kwæf/ *v.* [T] LITERARY to drink a lot of something quickly

quag·mire /ˈkwæɡmaɪə, ˈkwɑɡ-/ *n.* [C usually singular] **1** an area of soft wet muddy ground: *In the rainy season the roads become a quagmire.* **2** a difficult or complicated situation: *For the U.S., the war in Vietnam was a moral and military quagmire.*

quail¹ /kweɪl/ *n.* [C,U] a small fat bird with a short tail that is hunted and shot for food and sport, or the meat from this bird

quail² *v.* [I + at] LITERARY to be afraid and show it by shaking a little bit

quaint /kweɪnt/ *adj.* unusual and attractive, especially in an old-fashioned way: *the town's quaint charm*

quake¹ /kweɪk/ *v.* [I] **1** to shake slightly in an uncontrolled way, usually because you are afraid: [+ **with**] *Her voice was quaking with fear.* **2** if the earth, a building etc. quakes, it shakes violently: *The explosion made the whole house quake.* **3 quake in your boots** INFORMAL to feel very afraid or nervous

quake² *n.* [C] INFORMAL an EARTHQUAKE

quake-proof /ˈ. ./ *v.* [T] to build or repair a building so that it is not easily damaged by EARTHQUAKES —**quake-proof** *adj.* —**quake-proofing** *n.* [U]

Quak·ers, the /ˈkweɪkəz/ a Christian religious group, also called the Society of Friends, that opposes all violence, has no priests or ceremonies, and holds its religious meetings in silence —**Quaker** *adj.*

qual·i·fi·ca·tion /ˌkwɑləfəˈkeɪʃən/ *n.* **1** [C usually plural] a skill, personal quality, or type of experience that makes you right for a particular job or position: *Zabriskie is a political newcomer with impressive qualifications.* | [**qualification to do sth**] *Does this man really have the qualifications to run the CIA?* | [+ **for**] *Several senators questioned his qualifications for the Supreme Court.* **2** [C,U] the official standard that must be achieved in order to do a job, enter a sports competition etc., or the achievement of this standard: [+ **for**] *Banks require different qualifications for borrowing money.* | *The team ensured its qualification for the finals with a win over Kennedy High.* **3** [C,U] something that you add to a statement to limit its effect or meaning: *Bryant always says what he means, without qualification or evasion.*

qual·i·fied /ˈkwɑləˌfaɪd/ *adj.* **1** having the right or officially approved knowledge, experience, skills etc., especially for a particular job: *Have the house inspected by a qualified building contractor.* | *three qualified applicants* | [**qualified to do sth**] *The purchaser must be legally qualified to own a gun.* | [+ **for**] *Gibbons is highly qualified for the job.* **2** qualified agreement, approval etc. is limited in some way, because you do not completely agree or approve: *The FDA gave its qualified approval to the drug, but suggested that more studies be done.*

qual·i·fi·er /ˈkwɑləˌfaɪə/ *n.* [C] **1** someone who has reached the necessary standard for entering a competition: *Ramoz is a qualifier for the National Rodeo Finals* **2** a game that you have to win in order to be able to take part in a competition: *The U.S. beat Panama in the Olympic soccer qualifier.* **3** TECHNICAL in grammar, a word or phrase that acts as an adjective or adverb, that limits or adds to the meaning of another word or phrase. In the sentence "She rode off happily on her new red bike," the words "happily," "new," and "red" are qualifiers.

s w **qual·i·fy** /'kwɑlə,faɪ/ v. **qualifies, qualified, qualifying**
3 3
1 ‖have a right‖ [I,T] to have a right to have or do something, or give someone the right to have or do something: *Free school lunches are provided to those children who qualify.* | [+ for] *Only members of the credit union can qualify for loans.* | [qualify sb/sth for sth] *Does this qualify me for citizenship?*
2 ‖reach a standard‖ [I] to pass an examination or reach the standard of knowledge or skill that you need in order to do something: *After qualifying, stock brokers must work for the company for five years.* | [+ as] *Fifty hours of flight training is enough to qualify as a pilot.*
3 ‖make sb suitable‖ [T] if your knowledge, ability etc. qualifies you to do something, it makes you a good person to do it: [qualify sb/sth for sth] *Tomita's fluency in English and Japanese helped qualify her for the job.*
4 ‖have the right qualities‖ [I] to have all the necessary qualities to be considered as a particular thing: [+ as] *Does photography qualify as an art form?* | *The fees qualify as a Medicaid expense.*
5 ‖competition‖ [I] to reach the necessary standard to enter or continue in a competition or sports event: [+ for] *Officials will soon decide how many skaters will qualify for the Olympic team.*
6 ‖add something‖ [T] to add to something that has already been said, in order to limit its effect or meaning: *He qualified his statement, saying that "the peace process will take some time."*

qual·i·ta·tive /'kwɑlə,teɪtɪv/ adj. relating to the quality or standard of something, rather than to the amount or number: *The research involves qualitative analysis of students' performance.* —compare QUANTITATIVE

s w **qual·i·ty**[1] /'kwɑləti/ n. plural **qualities** **1** [C usually
2 1 plural] a good or bad part of someone's character: *Lucas has outstanding leadership qualities.* | *Her jealousy is one of her worst qualities.* | *the qualities of honesty and independence* **2** [U] the degree to which something is good or bad: *The recent hot, humid weather is affecting air quality.* | *They serve* **high quality** (=very good) *food in a clean, well-lighted room.* | *The paints are* **of poor quality** (=not very good).* **3** [C] something that is typical of a substance or object and that makes it different from other things: *There is a wild quality in his books that keeps you reading.* | *Khat is a leaf with narcotic qualities.* **4** [U] a high standard: *The company guarantees the quality of its service.* | *Tiled bathroom walls are usually a sign* **of quality** *in new houses.* **5** **quality of life** how good or bad your life is, shown for example by whether or not you are happy, healthy, able to do the things you want to do etc.: *The city's low population and openness contribute to the high quality of life in Phoenix.* | *Quality of life could be improved for many of the terminally ill patients.*

quality[2] adj. [only before noun, no comparative] having a high standard: *The students will receive a quality education.*

quality as·sur·ance /'... .,../ n. [U] the management of the way goods or services are produced in order to keep the quality good

quality con·trol /'... .,./ n. [U] the practice of checking goods as they are produced, to be sure that their quality is good enough —**quality controller** n. [C]

quality time /'... ,./ n. [U] the time that you spend giving someone your full attention, especially time spent with your children: *Parents might spend only 15 minutes of quality time a day with their kids.*

qualm /kwɑm, kwɔm/ n. [C usually plural] a feeling of slight worry because you are not sure that what you are doing is right: *Doctors expressed qualms about the ethics of the treatment.* | *I had no qualms about enrolling my child at the company's day-care center.*

quan·da·ry /'kwɑndri, -dəri/ n. plural **quandaries** [C] a difficult problem or situation about which you are

uncertain what to do: *A new book thoughtfully analyzes the quandary.* | *Several committee members are* **in a quandary over** *how to vote.*

quan·ti·fi·er /'kwɑntə,faɪə/ n. [C] TECHNICAL in grammar, a word or phrase that is used with a noun to show quantity. In the sentence "There were a few people at the party," "few" is a quantifier.

quan·ti·fy /'kwɑntə,faɪ/ v. **quantifies, quantified, quantifying** [T] to measure something and express it as a number, especially something that is difficult to measure: *It is impossible to quantify what an active cultural life does for a city.* —**quantifiable** /,kwɑntə-'faɪəbəl/ adj. —**quantification** /,kwɑntəfə'keɪʃən/ n. [U]

quan·ti·ta·tive /'kwɑntə,teɪtɪv/ adj. relating to amounts rather than to the quality or standard of something: *a quantitative analysis of stock market trends* —**quantitatively** adv. —compare QUALITATIVE

quan·ti·ty /'kwɑntəti/ n. plural **quantities** [C,U] an amount of something that can be counted or measured: *The price varies depending on the quantity purchased.* | [+ of] *There large quantities of bacteria in the water.* | *The cards are cheaper if you buy them* **in quantity** (=a large amount). —see also **be an unknown quantity** (UNKNOWN[1] (4))

quan·tum /'kwɑntəm/ n. plural **quanta** /-tə/ [C] TECHNICAL an amount of energy in NUCLEAR PHYSICS, which can change from the next possible smaller or larger amount by a specific degree

quantum leap, quantum jump /,.. './ n. [C] a very large and important improvement: *The orchestra's performance took a quantum leap forward.*

quantum me·chan·ics /,.. .'../ n. [U] the study of the way that atoms and smaller pieces of MATTER[1] (2) behave

quantum the·o·ry /'.. ,.../ n. [singular] the idea that energy, especially light, travels in separate pieces and not in a continuous form

quar·an·tine[1] /'kwɔrən,tin, 'kwɑr-/ n. [U] a period of time when a person or animal is kept apart from others in case they have a disease: *The quarantine makes it illegal to transport honey bees out of the area.* | *Koko the gorilla will be* **in quarantine** *until next week.* | *Doctors have placed the town* **under quarantine**.

quarantine[2] v. [T often passive] to put a person or animal in quarantine

quark /kwɑrk/ n. [C] TECHNICAL one of the smallest known amounts of MATTER[1] (2) that forms part of an atom

quar·rel[1] /'kwɔrəl, 'kwɑrəl/ n. [C] **1** an angry argument: *a bitter family quarrel* | [+ with] *She got into a quarrel with her son's coach.* | [+ about/over] *a neighbors' quarrel over a property line* **2** a reason or subject for disagreement: *Thomas said he* **had no quarrel with** (=had no reason to dislike or disagree with something) *being judged on those standards.*

quarrel[2] v. [I] to have an angry argument: *I could hear them quarreling next door.* | [+ with] *Rivera had quarreled with his tenants once before.* | [+ about/over] *Cattle and sheep farmers quarreled over grazing rights.*

quarrel with sth phr. v. [T] to disagree with something or complain about something: *The complaints are justified, but I quarrel with the solution.*

quar·rel·some /'kwɔrəlsəm/ adj. LITERARY often arguing, or seeming to enjoy arguing —**quarrelsomeness** n. [U]

quar·ry[1] /'kwɔri, 'kwɑri/ n. plural **quarries** [C] **1** a place where large amounts of stone, sand etc. are dug out of the ground: *a slate quarry* —compare MINE[2] (2) **2** [singular] an animal or person that someone is hunting or chasing: *The hunter closed in on his quarry.*

quarry[2] v. [T] to dig out stone, sand etc. from a quarry

quart /kwɔrt/ n. written abbreviation **qt.** [C] a unit for measuring liquid, equal to 2 PINTS or 0.9463 liters

quar·ter[1] /'kwɔrtə/ n. [C]
s w **1** ‖amount‖ one of four equal or almost equal parts
1 1 into which something can be divided: *Cut the*

sandwiches into quarters. | *The article is about two and a quarter pages long.* | [+ **of**] *A quarter of Canada's population is French speaking.* —see picture at QUICHE

2 part of an hour one of the four periods of 15 minutes into which each hour can be divided: *I'll meet you in three-quarters of an hour* (=in 45 minutes). | *It's a quarter to/of five* (=15 minutes before five o'clock; 4:45). | *The movie starts at a quarter after seven* (=15 minutes after seven o'clock; 7:15).

3 money a coin that is worth 25 cents (=¹/₄ of a dollar), used in the U.S. and Canada

4 sports one of the four equal periods of time into which games of some sports are divided: *Houston was ahead by 15 points at the end of the first quarter.*

5 business a period of three months, used when discussing business and money: *The company's profits rose in the first quarter of the year.* —see also QUARTERLY[1]

6 college one of the four periods into which a year at school or college is divided, usually continuing for 10 to 12 weeks: *What classes are you taking this quarter?* —compare SEMESTER

7 house/room quarters [plural] the house or rooms where someone lives, especially someone in the army: *Sleeping quarters are in the barracks.* | **cramped/close/tight quarters** (=a living place where there are too many people and not enough room)

8 part of a city an area in some cities where a particular type of people typically live or work: *We rented a house in the Creole quarter of New Orleans.*

9 in/from... quarters in or from different groups of people: *"I expect criticism from some quarters,"* said Wilson.

10 moon the period of time twice a month when you can see a quarter of the moon's surface

11 all quarters of the Earth/globe LITERARY everywhere in the world

12 give no quarter OLD USE to show no pity for someone, especially an enemy whom you have defeated —see also **in/at close quarters** (CLOSE[2] (16))

quarter[2] *v.* [T] **1** to cut or divide something into four parts: *Quarter two large apples.* **2** to provide someone with a place to sleep and eat, especially a soldier

quarter[3] *quantifier* being a fourth (=¹/₄) of an amount, size, distance, number etc.: *a quarter-century* | *a quarter-mile* | *It has an area a quarter the size of California's.*

quar·ter·back[1] /ˈkwɔrtəˌbæk/ *n.* [C] the player in football who directs the OFFENSE and throws the ball —see also MONDAY MORNING QUARTERBACK

quarterback[2] *v.* **1** [I,T] to play in the position of quarterback in football **2** [T] INFORMAL to organize or direct an activity, event etc.: *She quarterbacked the new sales campaign.*

quar·ter·deck /ˈkwɔrtərˌdɛk/ *n.* [C] the back part of the upper DECK (=floor level) of a ship, used mainly by officers

quar·ter·fi·nal /ˌkwɔrtərˈfaɪnl/ *n.* [C] one of the set of four games near the end of a competition, whose winners play in the two SEMIFINALS

quarter horse /ˈ.. ˌ./ *n.* [C] a strong horse that is bred to run short races, usually of a quarter of a mile

quar·ter·ly[1] /ˈkwɔrtərli/ *adj., adv* produced four times a year: *a quarterly newsletter*

quarterly[2] *n. plural* **quarterlies** [C] a magazine that is produced four times a year

quar·ter·mas·ter /ˈkwɔrtərˌmæstər/ *n.* [C] **1** a military officer in charge of providing food, uniforms etc. **2** a ship's officer in charge of signals and guiding the ship on the right course

quarter note /ˈ.. ˌ./ *n.* [C] a musical note that continues for a quarter of the length of a WHOLE NOTE —see picture at MUSIC

quar·ter·staff /ˈkwɔrtərˌstæf/ *n.* [C] a long wooden pole used as a weapon, especially in past times

quar·tet /kwɔrˈtɛt/ *n.* [C] **1** four singers or musicians who perform together: *a jazz quartet* | **wood-wind/string/brass quartet** *They hired a string quartet for the wedding.* **2** a piece of music written

for four performers **3** four people or things of the same type: [+ **of**] *50 amateur actors led by a quartet of professionals* —compare QUINTET, TRIO

quar·to /ˈkwɔrtoʊ/ *n.* [C] TECHNICAL **1** the size of a piece of paper made by folding a large sheet of paper twice, to produce four sheets, or the paper itself **2** a book with pages of quarto size

quartz /kwɔrts/ *n.* [U] a hard mineral substance, used in making electronic watches and clocks: *a quartz gold watch*

qua·sar /ˈkweɪzɑr/ *n.* [C] TECHNICAL a very bright, very distant object similar to a star

quash /kwɑʃ/ *v.* [T] FORMAL **1** to stop someone from doing or wanting something: *The company tried to quash the unwanted publicity.* **2** to use force to end protests or to stop people who are not obeying the law: *The police were brought in to quash the strike.* **3** to officially state that a judgment or decision is not legal or correct: *The court quashed the convictions after a nine-day hearing.*

quasi- /ˈkwɑzi, ˈkweɪzaɪ/ *prefix* like something in some ways; PARTLY: *the chairman's quasi-judicial role* (=acting in some ways like a judge) | *a quasi-scientific theory* (=not entirely scientific)

qua·ter·cen·ten·a·ry /ˌkwɑtərsɛnˈtɛnəri/ *n.* [C] the day or year exactly 400 years after a particular event: *the quatercentenary of Shakespeare's birth*

quat·rain /ˈkwɑtreɪn/ *n.* [C] a group of four lines in a poem

qua·ver /ˈkweɪvər/ *v.* [I,T] if your voice quavers, it shakes as you speak, especially because you are nervous: *Her voice quavered as she recounted details of the attack.* —**quaver** *n.* [C] —**quavery** *adj.*

quay /keɪ, ki/ *n. plural* **quays** [C] a place where boats can be tied up or can stop to load and UNLOAD: *a quay lined with fishing boats*

quay·side /ˈkeɪsaɪd/ *n.* [C] the area next to a quay: *a quayside restaurant*

quea·sy /ˈkwizi/ *adj.* **1** feeling that you are going to VOMIT; NAUSEATED: *The sway of the boat made passengers queasy.* **2** feeling uncomfortable because an action seems wrong, especially morally wrong: **be/feel queasy about sth** *Many Democrats feel queasy about the issue.* —**queasiness** *n.* [U]

Que·bec /kwɪˈbɛk/ **1** a PROVINCE in eastern Canada, in which most people speak French as their first language **2** the capital city of Quebec province

queen[1] /kwin/ *n.* [C]
1 ruler also **Queen a)** the female ruler of a country: *Elizabeth II became Queen of England in 1952* **b)** the wife of a king
2 card a playing card with a picture of a queen on it: *the queen of hearts*
3 competition the woman who wins a beauty competition, or who is chosen to represent a school, area etc.: *Michelle is going to be the homecoming queen.* | *the queen of the Kalispell County Fair*
4 homosexual OFFENSIVE a male HOMOSEXUAL, especially one who behaves like a woman
5 insect a large female BEE, ANT etc., which lays the eggs for a whole group
6 chess the most powerful piece in the game of CHESS
7 a woman who is regarded as the best at a particular activity or in a particular field: *Cooper is a former B-movie queen.* | *Tammy Wynette, the queen of country music*
8 queen bee a woman who behaves as if she is the most important person in a place —see also BEAUTY QUEEN, DRAG QUEEN, **homecoming king/queen** (HOMECOMING (3))

queen[2] *v.* [T] TECHNICAL to change a PAWN into a queen in the game of CHESS

queen·ly /ˈkwinli/ *adj.* appropriate for or like a queen

Queen Moth·er /ˌ. ˈ../ *n.* [singular] the mother of the ruling king or queen

Queens /kwinz/ one of the five BOROUGHS of New York City, which is at the western end of Long Island

queen-size /ˈ../ adj. **1** a queen-size bed, sheet etc. is larger than the standard size for a bed for two people **2** queen-size clothing is for women who are larger than average size —compare DOUBLE BED, KING-SIZE, TWIN BED

queer¹ /kwɪr/ adj. **1** OLD-FASHIONED strange or difficult to explain: *a queer sound* **2** OFFENSIVE: see HOMOSEXUAL **3** an offensive word for HOMOSEXUAL, BISEXUAL, or TRANSGENDER people, used especially by people in these groups **4 queer in the head** OLD-FASHIONED talking or behaving strangely; crazy —**queerly** adv. —**queerness** n. [U]

queer² n. [C] OFFENSIVE a HOMOSEXUAL person

quell /kwɛl/ v. [T] FORMAL **1** to end a violent situation, especially when people are protesting: *Police fired tear gas to quell the rioting.* **2** to reduce or stop feelings of doubt, worry, and anxiety: *They hope to quell public anxiety about offshore oil drilling.*

quench /kwɛntʃ/ v. [T] **1 quench your thirst** to drink enough to stop you from feeling THIRSTY: *Iced tea really quenches your thirst.* **2 quench a fire/ blaze etc.** to make a fire stop burning

quer·u·lous /ˈkwɛrələs, -yələs/ adj. FORMAL complaining all the time in an annoying way: *a querulous voice* —**querulously** adv. —**querulousness** n. [U]

que·ry¹ /ˈkwɪri/ n. plural **queries** [C] FORMAL a question you ask to get information, or to check that something is true or correct: *Menlo angrily replied to a query from a reporter.*

query² v. **queries, queried, querying** [T] FORMAL **1** to ask a question: *Not one of the customers queried liked the service.* **2** to express doubt that something is true or correct: *The manager queried the figures.*

que·sa·dil·la /ˌkeɪsəˈdiə/ n. [C] a Mexican dish made of TORTILLAS filled with cheese and sometimes meat

quest /kwɛst/ n. [C] ESPECIALLY LITERARY a long search for something: *a spiritual quest* | [+ **for**] *Industries are still engaged in a quest for increased productivity.* —**quest** v. [I]

ques·tion¹ /ˈkwɛstʃən, ˈkwɛʃtʃən/ n. [C]
1 asking for information a sentence or phrase used to ask for information: [+ **about**] *Are there any questions about the homework?* | *Reporters had a few questions for the mayor.* | *Hi Lori, can I ask you a quick question?* | *Answer three out of the five questions on the test.*
2 subject/problem a subject that needs to be discussed or a problem that needs to be solved: ISSUE¹ (1): *Several questions had still not been resolved.* | [+ **of**] *Congress has been discussing the question of term limits.* | *The question is, are you going to meet the deadline?*
3 doubt a feeling of doubt about something: *There is no question that the market for computer products will continue to grow.* | *The recent fighting has called into question* (=made people feel doubt about) *the government's ability to keep the peace.* | *Scientists have raised questions about* (=expressed doubt about) *the drug's long-term safety.* | *Whether the promises will be kept is open to question* (=making people feel doubt).
4 without question a) without any doubt; DEFINITELY: *Their weapons technology is without question a threat to us.* b) without complaining or asking why: *Insurance companies once paid medical bills almost without question, but no longer.*
5 in question the things, people etc. in question are the ones that are being discussed or talked about: *Housing in the area in question would not violate zoning laws.*
6 be out of the question used to emphasize that what someone wants to do is not possible or not allowed: *Some of these families are so poor that Christmas presents are out of the question.*
7 (that's a) good question! SPOKEN said when you are admitting that you do not know the answer to a question: *"Does the program allow you to do that?" "That's a good question – I don't know."*
8 be a question of sth used when you are giving the most important fact, part, or feature or something: *More train stations will be approved, it's just a question of when and where.*
9 there's no question of doing sth used to say that there is no possibility of something happening: *There is no question of tearing the building down.*
10 there is no question of/that sth used when something is definitely true: *There is no question that the painting is genuine.*
11 it's just a question of sth SPOKEN used to say that something is easy or not complicated: *It's just a question of putting in a couple of screws.*
12 pop the question INFORMAL, HUMOROUS to ask someone to marry you —see also **a leading question** (LEADING¹ (4)), **beg the question** (BEG (7)), **rhetorical question** (RHETORICAL (1))

question² v. [T] **1** to ask someone questions to find out what they know about something, especially about a crime: *Roughly 1000 people were questioned in the November poll.* | [**question sb about sth**] *Byner was questioned by police about the photograph.* —see Usage Note at ASK **2** to have doubts about something or tell someone about these doubts: *His leadership and integrity are being questioned.*

ques·tion·a·ble /ˈkwɛstʃənəbəl/ adj. **1** likely to be dishonest or morally wrong: *Barton has been involved in some questionable financial deals.* **2** uncertain or possibly not true or correct: *The research is questionable because the sample used was very small.* | *The picture's value is questionable.* **3** if a sports player is questionable for a game, they may not be able to play

ques·tion·er /ˈkwɛstʃənɚ/ n. [C] someone who is asking a question, for example in a public discussion

ques·tion·ing /ˈkwɛstʃənɪŋ/ adj. a questioning look or expression shows that you have doubts about something or need some information: *the questioning eyes of a child* —**questioningly** adv.

question mark /ˈ.. ˌ./ n. [C] **1** the mark (?) that is used in writing at the end of a question **2 a question mark over sth** if there is a question mark over something, there is a possibility that it will not be successful or will not continue to exist: *A big question mark hangs over the company's future.*

ques·tion·naire /ˌkwɛstʃəˈnɛr/ n. [C] a written set of questions about a particular subject given to a large number of people, in order to collect information: *Readers were asked to fill out a questionnaire on health issues.*

queue /kyu/ n. [C] **1** TECHNICAL a list of jobs that a computer has to do in a particular order; ORDER¹ (1): *the print queue* **2** a number of telephone calls that are waiting to be answered in an electronic telephone system: *Your call is being held in a queue. Please hold for the next available operator.* **3** BRITISH a line of people, vehicles etc.

quib·ble¹ /ˈkwɪbəl/ v. [I] to argue about something that is not very important: [+ **about/over**] *I didn't feel like quibbling over the price.*

quibble² n. [C] a complaint or criticism about something that is not very important: *I have a few minor quibbles about the car's performance.*

quiche

quarter

quiche /kiʃ/ n. [C,U] a type of food that consists of PASTRY filled with a mixture of eggs, cheese, vegetables etc.

s w | **quick¹** /kwɪk/ *adj.*

1 **fast** done, happening, or existing for only a short time: *I'll just take a quick shower first.* | *That was quick! I thought you'd be gone for hours.* | *Chicken can be quick to prepare.* | *Don't make any quick movements, or you'll scare the birds.*

2 **smart** able to learn and understand things fast: *Carrie's very quick. I never had to explain anything twice.* | *He rarely missed work and was considered* **a quick study** (=someone who learns things quickly). | *He's a good interviewer, tough and* **quick on the uptake** (=quick to understand what someone is saying).

3 **a quick fix** INFORMAL a repair to something or an answer to a problem that happens quickly, but may work for only for a short time: *There's no quick fix for stopping pollution.* | *Congress is trying to resist quick-fix solutions.*

4 **no delay** happening without any waiting or delay: *Even lowering the price won't guarantee a quick sale.*

5 **be quick to do sth** to react quickly to what someone says or does: *I don't think he'll be so quick to forgive you.* | *Coach Killick was quick to point out that the team is playing very well.*

6 **be quick on your feet** to be able to move quickly and gracefully: *Tom's a big guy, but he's quick on his feet.*

7 **be quick (about it)** used to tell someone to hurry: *"Can I just finish this first?" "OK, but be quick about it."*

8 **a quick one** INFORMAL an alcoholic drink that you have in a hurry: *Let's just have a quick one before they close the bar.*

9 **quick-and-dirty** done fast and using as little money and effort as possible: *The management was looking for a quick-and-dirty solution to their tax problems.*

10 **be quick on the draw a)** to be able to pull a gun out quickly in order to shoot **b)** INFORMAL to be good at reacting quickly and intelligently to difficult questions or in difficult situations: *Amy was very quick on the draw in her interview.*

11 **a quick draw** someone who is able to pull a gun out quickly in order to shoot

12 **have a quick temper** to get angry very easily

13 **quick as a wink** very quickly —see also QUICKLY —**quickness** *n.* [U]

quick² *interjection* used to tell someone to hurry or come quickly: *Quick! We'll miss the bus!*

s w | **quick³** *adv.* SPOKEN, NONSTANDARD quickly: *Come quick! Larry's on TV!* | *It all happened pretty quick.*

quick⁴ *n.* [U] **1** **the quick** the sensitive flesh under your FINGERNAILS and TOENAILS: *Her nails were bitten to the quick.* **2** **cut sb to the quick** if a remark or criticism cuts you to the quick, it makes you very upset **3** **the quick** OLD USE all people who are alive

quick bread /'. ./ *n.* [C,U] a bread that you can bake immediately, because it uses BAKING POWDER or BAKING SODA rather than YEAST: *muffins and other quick breads*

quick-change ar·tist /ˌ. '. ˌ../ *n* [C] an entertainer who can change their clothes or appearance very quickly

quick·en /'kwɪkən/ *v.* [I,T] **1** to become quicker or make something do this: *New laws will* **quicken the pace** *at which cars must have certain safety features.* | *Everyone's* **pulse quickens** (=your heart beats faster, especially because you are afraid or nervous) *at the sound of a fire alarm.* **2** FORMAL if a feeling quickens, or if something quickens it, it becomes stronger or more active: *Interest in the idea has quickened recently.* **3** OLD USE OR LITERARY to come alive or make something come alive

quick·en·ing /'kwɪkənɪŋ/ *n.* [U] the first movements of a baby that has not been born yet

quick·ie /'kwɪki/ *n.* [C] INFORMAL **1** something done or made quickly and easily: *a quickie wedding ceremony in Las Vegas* **2** HUMOROUS a sexual act done in a hurry —**quickie** *adj.*: *a quickie divorce*

quick·lime /'kwɪk-laɪm/ *n.* [U] a white substance obtained by burning LIMESTONE

quick·ly /'kwɪkli/ *adv.* **1** fast, or done in a very short amount of time: *Don't eat too quickly.* | *Kids grow up so quickly.* **2** for a short amount of time: *Let me just talk to Eve quickly before we go.* **3** after only a very short time: *I realized fairly quickly that this wasn't going to be easy.* **s w**

quick·sand /'kwɪksænd/ *n.* [C,U] wet sand that is dangerous because it pulls you down into it if you walk on it

quick·sil·ver /'kwɪkˌsɪlvə/ *n.* [U] OLD USE **1** APPROVING changing or moving quickly and in a way that you do not expect: *the quicksilver beauty of Khan's singing* | *Hunt, the team's quicksilver guard, slipped in and made the basket.* **2** MERCURY

quick·step /'kwɪkstɛp/ *n.* [C] a dance with fast movements of the feet, or the music for this dance

quick-tem·pered /ˌ. '..ˌ/ *adj.* easily becoming angry: *My father was quick-tempered and often drunk.*

quick-wit·ted /ˌ. '..ˌ/ *adj.* able to understand things quickly and to say things that are funny and smart: *Brady is quick-witted and articulate.* —**quickwittedness** *n.* [U]

Q

quid pro quo /ˌkwɪd proʊ 'kwoʊ/ *n.* [C] something that you give or do in exchange for something else, especially when this arrangement is not official: *It is clearly illegal to require sex as a quid pro quo for promotion.*

qui·es·cent /kwaɪ'ɛsənt, kwi-/ *adj.* FORMAL not developing or doing anything, especially when this is only a temporary state —**quiescently** *adv.* —**quiescence** *n.* [U]

qui·et¹ /'kwaɪət/ *adj.* **s w**

1 **no noise** not making a lot of noise: *The baby's sleeping, so we need to be quiet.* | *The engine is 20% quieter than in previous models.* | *People sat drinking coffee and having quiet conversations.*

2 **(be) quiet!** SPOKEN used to tell someone to stop talking or making noise: *Morgan, be quiet, please.*

3 **not much activity** a quiet place or time is one where there is not much activity: *We live in a quiet neighborhood.* | *I'm just going to have a quiet evening at home.* | *The city was quiet after overnight shelling that wounded 15 people.*

4 **not many people** not having many people near you: *She said it was beautiful, very quiet, with deserted beaches and clear water.* | *a quiet place in the mountains*

5 **not speaking a)** someone who is quiet does not usually talk very much: *He's nice, but kind of quiet.* **b)** not saying much or not saying anything: *Missy's very quiet – is she sick?*

6 **business** if business is quiet, there are not many customers: *Retailers are worried, as business has been quiet for much of December.*

7 **keep (sth) quiet** also **keep quiet about sth** to keep information secret: *The company kept quiet about its work until it had obtained a patent.*

8 **keep sb quiet** to stop someone from talking, complaining, or causing trouble: *Give the kids some crayons, that will keep them quiet for a while.* —**quietness** *n.* [U] —see also QUIETLY

quiet² *v.* **1** [I,T] also **quiet down** to become calmer and less noisy or active, or to make someone or something do this: *The kids finally quieted down and read their books.* | *White has quieted the skeptics who said he couldn't do the job.* **2** [T] to make someone feel less frightened or worried: *Her mother quieted her after the nightmare.*

quiet³ *n.* [U] **1** the state of being quiet, calm, and peaceful: *the quiet of the forest* | *I sat and enjoyed a few minutes of* **peace and quiet**. **2** silence: *Can I have quiet, please!*

qui·et·ly /'kwaɪətli/ *adv.* **1** without making much noise: *Rosa shut the door quietly.* | *"I'm sorry," she said quietly.* **2** in a way that does not attract attention: *The meeting was quietly arranged to avoid reporters.* **s w**

qui·e·tude /ˈkwaɪəˌtud/ *n.* [U] FORMAL calmness, peace, and quiet

qui·e·tus /kwaɪˈitəs, -ˈeɪtəs/ *n.* [singular] FORMAL **1** death **2** the end of something

quill /kwɪl/ *n.* [C] **1** a bird's feather, especially a large one, including the stiff, hard part at the base where the feather joins to the bird's body **2** also **quill pen** a pen made from a large bird's feather, used in past times **3** one of the sharp needles that grow on the backs of some animals, such as the PORCUPINE

quilt

quilt /kwɪlt/ *n.* [C] a warm thick cover for a bed, made by sewing two layers of cloth together with cloth or feathers in between them: *a patchwork quilt*

quilt·ed /ˈkwɪltɪd/ *adj.* quilted cloth has a thick layer of material sewn to it in a pattern of stitches: *a quilted bathrobe*

quilt·ing /ˈkwɪltɪŋ/ *n.* [U] the work of making a quilt, or the material and stitches that you use

quince /kwɪns/ *n.* [C,U] a hard, yellowish fruit like a large apple, used for making JELLY, or the tree that grows this fruit

qui·nine /ˈkwaɪnaɪn/ *n.* [U] a drug used for treating fevers, especially MALARIA

quinine wa·ter /ˈ.. ˌ../ *n.* [U] a bitter-tasting drink often mixed in alcoholic drinks such as GIN

quint /kwɪnt/ *n.* [C] INFORMAL a QUINTUPLET

quin·tes·sence /kwɪnˈtɛsəns/ *n.* **the quintessence of sth** FORMAL a perfect type or example of something: *He is the quintessence of Middle America.*

quint·es·sen·tial /ˌkwɪntəˈsɛnʃəl/ *adj.* being a perfect example of a particular type of person or thing: *New York is the quintessential big city.* —**quintessentially** *adv.*

quin·tet /kwɪnˈtɛt/ *n.* [C] **1** five singers or musicians who perform together **2** a piece of music written for five performers —compare QUARTET, SEXTET, TRIO

quin·tup·let /kwɪnˈtʌplɪt, -ˈtu-/ *n.* [C] one of five babies born to the same mother at the same time —compare QUADRUPLET, SEXTUPLET

quip /kwɪp/ *v.* [I] to say something short and amusing: *"It's the 40th anniversary of my 29th birthday,"* *quipped Reagan.* —**quip** *n.* [C]

quire /kwaɪɚ/ *n.* [C] TECHNICAL 24 sheets of paper

quirk /kwɚk/ *n.* [C] **1** a strange habit or feature that someone or something has: *Greg is a nice guy, but he has a few weird personality quirks.* | *It's a quirk of the language that pronunciation has changed, but not spelling.* **2** something strange that happens by chance: [+ of] *By a quirk of nature, half the frogs in the pond had more than four legs.*

quirk·y /ˈkwɚki/ *adj.* **quirkier, quirkiest** slightly strange or unusual, in an unexpected way: *a quirky, hour-long TV drama* —**quirkily** *adv.* —**quirkiness** *n.* [U]

quis·ling /ˈkwɪzlɪŋ/ *n.* [C] someone who helps an army or enemy country that has taken control of his own country

quit /kwɪt/ *v.* past tense and past participle **quit** present participle **quitting 1** [I,T] to leave a job, school etc., especially because you are annoyed or unhappy: *Four or five people have either quit or been fired.* | *He* had to **quit his job** to take care of her. **2** [T] INFORMAL to stop doing something bad or annoying: *Quit it, Robby, or I'll tell Mom!* | **[quit doing sth]** *I quit smoking two years ago.* | *Quit treating me like I'm a baby.* **3** [I,T] INFORMAL to stop doing something: *That kid just never quits moving.* | *I've always regretted quitting piano lessons.* **4** [T] OLD USE to leave a place —see also QUITS

quite /kwaɪt/ *adv.* **1** [+ adj./adv.] very, but not extremely: *His hair is quite thin on top now.* | *The food's good, but it's quite expensive.* | *Keegan's quite tall.* **2 not quite** not completely or not exactly: *I'm not quite sure how the system works.* | *"Are you ready?" "Not quite."* | *He didn't say it quite that way, but that's what he meant.* | *Traffic wasn't quite as bad as I expected.* **3** used when an amount or number is large, but not extremely large: *There were quite a few people there.* | *We've had quite a bit of snow this year so far.* | *I haven't seen Ed in quite a while.* **4** used in order to emphasize the fact that something is unusually good, bad etc.: *We got quite a deal on the car.* | *Darby made quite an impression on the kids.* —see Usage Note at RATHER

Qui·to /ˈkitoʊ/ the capital city of Ecuador

quits /kwɪts/ *adj.* **call it quits** INFORMAL to stop doing something: *At midnight the band still showed no sign of calling it quits.* | *After 8 years of marriage, they're calling it quits.*

quit·tance /ˈkwɪtⁿs/ *n.* [C] LAW a statement saying that someone does not have to do something anymore, such as paying back money that they owe

quit·ter /ˈkwɪtɚ/ *n.* [C] INFORMAL, DISAPPROVING someone who stops doing a job, activity, or duty because it becomes difficult: *I'm not a quitter, but this job is starting to affect my health.*

quiv·er¹ /ˈkwɪvɚ/ *v.* [I] **1** to shake slightly, especially because you feel angry, excited, or upset: *Her lip quivered, and tears rolled down her cheeks.* | **[+ with]** *Elaine's voice quivered with emotion.* **2** to shake slightly: *The ground quivered under my feet.*

quiver² *n.* [C] **1** a slight shake: *I felt a quiver of excitement run through me.* **2** a long case for carrying ARROWS

quix·ot·ic /kwɪkˈsɑtɪk/ *adj.* having ideas and plans that are based on hopes, and that are not reasonable or practical: *He began a quixotic search for the mother who abandoned him.*

quiz¹ /kwɪz/ *n.* plural **quizzes** [C] **1** a short test that a teacher gives to a class: *a biology quiz* **2** a competition in which you have to answer questions: *a quiz show on TV* —see also POP QUIZ

quiz² *v.* **quizzes, quizzed, quizzing** [T] **1** to ask someone a lot of questions: *Journalists quizzed the governor during the half-hour program.* **2** to give a student a short test: *Students are quizzed on their reading.* —see also POP QUIZ

quiz show /ˈ. ./ *n.* [C] a television show in which people answer questions to test their knowledge in order to try to win prizes or money —compare GAME SHOW

quiz·zi·cal /ˈkwɪzɪkəl/ *adj.* seeming to ask a question, often in an amused way: *The child gave him a quizzical look.* —**quizzically** /-kli/ *adv.*

quo /kwoʊ/ —see QUID PRO QUO, STATUS QUO

quoit /kɔɪt, kwɔɪt/ *n.* [C] a ring used in the game of quoits

quoits /kɔɪts, kwɔɪts/ *n.* [U] a game in which you throw rings over a small upright post

quon·dam /ˈkwɑndəm/ *adj.* FORMAL relating to an earlier time

Quon·set hut /ˈkwɑnsət ˌhʌt/ *n.* [C] TRADEMARK a metal building shaped like half a circle, where soldiers live or where things are stored

quo·rum /ˈkwɔrəm/ *n.* [C usually singular] the smallest number of people who must be present at a meeting for official decisions to be made: *Do we have a quorum?*

quo·ta /ˈkwoʊtə/ *n.* [C] **1** an amount or number of something that you are expected to produce, sell, achieve etc., especially in your job: **fill/meet a quota** *Salespeople who fill their quotas earn bonuses.*

2 a limit, especially an official limit, on the number or amount of something you are allowed to have: *Most countries have an immigration quota.* | *a strict quota on imports* | *I think I've had my quota of coffee for the day.*

quot·a·ble /'kwoʊtəbəl/ *adj.* a quotable remark or statement is interesting and noticeable, especially because it is intelligent or amusing

quo·ta·tion /kwoʊ'teɪʃən/ *n.* **1** [C] words from a book, poem etc. that you repeat in your own speech or piece of writing: *a quotation from the Bible* **2** [U] the act of quoting something that someone else has written or said **3** [C] a written statement of exactly how much money a service will cost: *We got two completely different quotations for fixing the roof.* —compare ESTIMATE² (2)

quotation mark /.'.. ,./ *n.* [C usually plural] a mark (" or ") used in writing before and after any words that are being quoted or before and after the exact words someone says

s w **quote¹** /kwoʊt/ *v.* **1** [I,T] to repeat exactly what
2 2 someone else has said or written: [quote (sth) from sth] *He quoted a line from a play by Brecht.* | [quote sb/sth] *Ross quoted a study on the use of sexist language.* | *"It is a threat to world peace," the general was quoted as saying.* | *I think he's a racist, and you can quote me on that.* | *There's no question it was illegal, but don't quote me* (=said when what you are saying is not official). **2** [T] to give proof for what you are saying by mentioning a particular example of something: *Dr. Morse quoted three*

successful cases in which the drug was used. **3** [T] to tell a customer the price you will charge them for a service or product: *If you call the hotel directly, you may get a rate lower than those quoted by travel agents.* —compare ESTIMATE¹ **4 quote ... unquote** SPOKEN used when you are repeating the exact words that someone has said: *...and Mr. Wigan said, quote, "Go to hell," unquote.*

quote² *n.* [C] INFORMAL **1** a QUOTATION **2 in quotes** s w words that are in quotes are between a pair of 2
QUOTATION MARKS   3

quoth /kwoʊθ/ *v.* [T] OLD USE **quoth I/he/she etc.** a way of saying "I said," "he said" etc.

quo·tid·i·an /kwoʊ'tɪdiən/ *adj.* FORMAL daily or ordinary

quo·tient /'kwoʊʃənt/ *n.* [C] **1** TECHNICAL the number which is obtained when one number is divided by another **2** the amount or degree of a quality, feeling etc. in a person or situation: *Is all this healthy food supposed to increase my happiness quotient?*

Qur.'an /kə'ræn, -'rɑn/ *n.* **the Qur'an** another spelling of the KORAN

q.v. quod vide; used to tell readers to look in another place in the same book for a piece of information

qwert·y /'kwɜ·ti/ *adj.* a qwerty KEYBOARD on a computer or TYPEWRITER has the keys arranged in the usual way, with Q,W,E,R,T, and Y on the top row

Q

R

R¹, r /ɑr/ *n. plural* **R's, r's** [C] the 18th letter of the English alphabet —see also THREE R'S

R² 1 the written abbreviation of "Republican," used to show that someone belongs to that political party: *Senator Charles Grassley, R–Iowa* **2** also **R.** the written abbreviation of "river," used especially on maps

R³ *n.* [C,U] Restricted; a letter used to show that no one under the age of 17 can go to a particular movie unless a parent goes with them —compare NC-17, PG-13

Ra /rɑ/ in Egyptian MYTHOLOGY, the god of the sun

Ra·bat /rəˈbɑt/ the capital city of Morocco

rab·bi /ˈræbaɪ/ *n.* [C] a Jewish priest

rab·bin·ate /ˈræbənɪt, -neɪt/ *n.* **the rabbinate** rabbis considered together as a group

rab·bin·i·cal /rəˈbɪnɪkəl/ *adj.* relating to the writings or teaching of rabbis

rab·bit /ˈræbɪt/ *n.* **1** [C] a common small animal with long ears and soft fur, that lives in a hole in the ground **2** [U] the fur or meat of a rabbit

rabbit hutch /ˈ.. ˌ./ *n.* [C] a wooden CAGE for pet rabbits

rabbit punch /ˈ.. ˌ./ *n.* [C] a quick hit on the back of the neck, made with the side of the hand

rabbit war·ren /ˈ.. ˌ./ *n.* [C] **1** an area under the ground where wild rabbits live in their holes **2** a building or place with a lot of narrow passages or streets where you can easily get lost

rab·ble /ˈræbəl/ *n.* [singular] **1** a noisy crowd of people who are likely to cause trouble: *If any of the rabble attempts to enter the palace, shoot them.* **2** DISAPPROVING an insulting word for a group of people that you do not respect: *the Hollywood movie rabble*

rabble-rous·er /ˈ.. ˌ./ *n.* [C] someone who tries to make a crowd of people angry and violent, especially in order to achieve political aims —**rabble-rousing** *adj.*: *a rabble-rousing speech* —**rabble-rousing** *n.* [U]

Ra·be·lais /ˌræbəˈleɪ/**, Fran·çois** /frɑnˈswɑ/ (?1494–1553) a French writer who is known for his SATIRE and jokes about sex

rab·id /ˈræbɪd/ *adj.* **1** having very extreme and unreasonable opinions, especially about politics; FANATICAL: *rabid liberals* **2** suffering from rabies: *a rabid dog*

ra·bies /ˈreɪbiz/ *n.* [U] a disease that kills animals and people, that you can get if you are bitten by an infected animal

Ra·bin /rɑˈbin/**, Itz·hak** /ˈɪtʃɑk/ (1922–1995) an Israeli politician who was Prime Minister 1974–1977 and 1992–1995

rac·coon, racoon /ræˈkun/ *n.* **1** [C] a small North American animal with black fur around its eyes and black and white rings on its tail **2** [U] the thick fur of a raccoon

race

race¹ /reɪs/ *n.*

1 [sports] [C] a competition in which each competitor tries to run, drive etc. fastest and finish first: *Lewis won his final race.* | *the Transpacific yacht race*

2 [people] **a)** [C] one of the main groups that humans can be divided into according to the color of their skin and other physical features: *human beings of all races* **b)** [U] the fact of belonging to one of these groups: *Mary was discriminated against because of her age and race.* | *a person of mixed race* **c)** [C] a group of people with the same customs, history, language etc.: *the Nordic races* —see also HUMAN RACE

3 [politics] [C usually singular] a competition for power or a political position: *He lost to Pfeiffer in the race for district attorney.*

4 [get/do sth first] [C usually singular] a situation in which one group of people tries to obtain or achieve something before another group does: [+ **for**] *Athens' main competition in the race for the 2004 Olympic Games is Rome.* | [**the race to do sth**] *The company has joined the race to develop the television of the future.* | **The race was on** *for domination of the continent.*

5 a race against time also **a race against the clock** an attempt to quickly finish doing something very important

6 [animal/plant] [C] TECHNICAL a type of animal or plant

7 the races an event at which horses are raced against each other, especially for money: *a day at the races* —see also ARMS RACE, RAT RACE

USAGE NOTE: RACE

WORD CHOICE: race, nation, state, people, tribe
These words are all used to talk about groups of people. The largest group is a **race**, which means people who have the same skin color and physical features: *Race and sex are not factors in our admission policy.* A **nation** is a country and its social and political structure, but it also means a group of people with the same history and language: *the Japanese nation* | *the Sioux Indian nation.* A race or nation may also be called a **people** (plural **peoples**): *the Jewish people* | *the peoples of eastern and central Europe.* **State** is used when talking about politics or the government of a country: *a state-owned bank.* A state usually contains people of different races or nations. A **tribe** is a social group, smaller than a nation, that shares the same customs and usually the same language, and often follows an ancient or traditional way of life: *the Aguaruna tribe of Peru* | *Chippewa tribes.*

---

race² *v.*

1 [sports] **a)** [I,T] to compete against someone or something in a race: *Schumacher will be racing in the Monaco Grand Prix.* | [**race sb to/back/across** etc.] *I'll race you to the other side of the pool.* **b)** [T] to use an animal, vehicle, or toy to compete in a race: *Some kids were racing rubber ducks in the stream.*

2 [move quickly] [I always + adv./prep.,T always + adv./prep.] to move very quickly, or make someone or something do this: *Turner grabbed the ball and raced 65 yards for a touchdown.* | [+ **out/into/ by** etc.] *I watched the children race across the playground.* | [**race sb/sth to sth**] *Samples were raced to the lab for testing.*

3 [heart/mind etc.] [I] if your heart, PULSE, or mind races, it works harder and faster than usual, especially because you are sick or anxious: *Trent woke at three a.m., his heart racing.*

4 [engine] [I] if an engine races, it works faster than it should

race car /ˈ. ./ also **racing car** /ˈ.. ./ *n.* [C] a car that is specially designed for car races

race·course /ˈreɪs-kɔrs/ *n.* [C] a track around which runners, cars etc. race

race·horse /ˈreɪshɔrs/ *n.* [C] a horse specially bred and trained for racing

rac·er /ˈreɪsɚ/ *n.* [C] someone who races a car, bicycle, boat etc.: *a motorcycle racer*

race re·la·tions /'. .,../ *n.* [plural] the relationship that exists between people from different races who are living in the same place: *Hawaii has a tradition of good race relations.*

race ri·ot /'. ,../ *n.* [C] violent behavior, such as fighting and attacks on property, caused by hatred between people of different races

race·track /'reɪs-træk/ *n.* [C] a track around which runners, horses, cars etc. race

Rach·ma·ni·noff /rɑk'mɑn,nɔf/, **Ser·gei** /'sɝgeɪ/ (1873–1943) a Russian musician who wrote CLASSICAL music

SW 2 ra·cial /'reɪʃəl/ *adj.* [only before noun] **1** relating to the relationships between different races of people: *racial equality* | *The event is designed to promote racial harmony.* | *He spoke of the racial discrimination* (=unfair treatment because of race) *he had experienced.* **2** relating to the various races that humans can be divided into: *Los Angeles County has over 150 racial and ethnic groups in it.* | *We welcome all of you, whatever your racial background.* —**racially** *adv.*: *a racially mixed school*

Ra·cine /ræ'sin/, **Jean** /ʒɑn/ (1639–1699) a French writer of plays

rac·ing¹ /'reɪsɪŋ/ *n.* [U] the sport of running in races or racing horses, cars etc.: **horse/car/dog** etc. **racing** *He began his career in horse racing at the age of 15.*

racing² *adj.* [only before noun] relating to, designed, or bred for racing: *a racing bicycle* | *racing dogs*

racing car /'.. ,./ *n.* [C] a RACE CAR

racing form /'.. ,./ *n.* [C] a printed sheet that gives information about horse races

rac·ism /'reɪsɪzəm/ *n.* [U] **1** unfair treatment of people, or violence against them, because they belong to a different race from your own: *We will not tolerate racism.* **2** the belief that different races of people have different characters and abilities, and that the qualities of your own race are the best

rac·ist /'reɪsɪst/ *adj.* believing that people of your own race are better than others, and treating people of other races unfairly: *The propaganda was blatantly racist.* | *racist comments* —**racist** *n.* [C]

racks

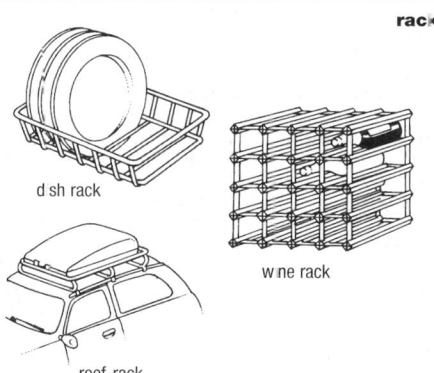

dish rack

wine rack

roof-rack

SW 3 rack¹ /ræk/ *n.* [C] **1** a frame or shelf, usually with bars or hooks, for holding things on: *a spice rack* | *Let the cake cool on a rack for ten minutes.* | *a bicycle rack* | **book/magazine/newspaper rack** *Celia lingered in front of the magazine rack.* —see also LUGGAGE RACK, OFF-THE-RACK, ROOF-RACK **2 a rack of lamb/ribs** a fairly large piece of meat from the side of an animal **3 the rack** a piece of equipment used in the past to make people suffer severe pain by stretching their bodies **4** a three-sided frame used for arranging the balls at the start of a game of POOL **5 go to rack and ruin** to gradually get into a very bad condition as a result of not being taken care of: *The old farmhouse had gone to rack and ruin.*

rack² *v.* **1 rack your brain(s)** to think very hard or for a long time: *He racked his brain for something sensible to say.* **2** another spelling of WRACK —see also NERVE-RACKING **3** [T] also **rack up** to put the

---

balls in the rack at the beginning of a game of POOL

rack sth ↔ up *phr. v.* INFORMAL to increase the number or amount of points, experiences, debt etc. that you have over a period of time: *Mullin racked up 41 points in last night's game.* | *At age 37, Tad has racked up an impressive list of achievements.*

rack-and-pin·ion steer·ing /,. . ,.. '../ *n.* [U] TECHNICAL a type of system for STEERing a car, truck etc. that uses special bars and COGs

rack·et /'rækɪt/ *n.* **1** [singular] INFORMAL a lot of loud noises: *Would you stop that racket, please?* **2** also **racquet** [C] a piece of equipment used for hitting the ball in games such as tennis, consisting of a stick with a net in a round frame: *a tennis racket* **3** [C] a dishonest way of obtaining money, such as by threatening people or selling them illegal goods: *Police have uncovered an insurance racket in Cleveland.* —see also PROTECTION RACKET **4** [C] INFORMAL a job, especially one in which you make a lot of money easily: *the advertising racket*

rack·et·eer /,rækə'tɪr/ *n.* [C] someone who is involved in a dishonest method of obtaining money

rack·et·eer·ing /,rækə'tɪrɪŋ/ *n.* [U] the crime of obtaining money dishonestly by means of a carefully planned system: *Kelly is awaiting trial on fraud and racketeering charges.*

rac·on·teur /,rækɑn'tɔ/ *n.* [C] someone who is good at telling stories in an interesting and amusing way

ra·coon /ræ'kun/ *n.* [C] another spelling of RACCOON

rac·quet /'rækɪt/ *n.* the British and Canadian spelling of RACKET (2)

rac·quet·ball /'rækɪt,bɔl/ *n.* [U] an indoor game in which two players use RACKETs to hit a small rubber ball against the four walls of the court

rac·y /'reɪsi/ *adj.* **racier, raciest** racy speech, writing, clothing etc. is exciting and entertaining, usually because it involves sex: *a racy underwear ad* —**racily** *adv.* —**raciness** *n.* [U]

ra·dar /'reɪdɑr/ *n.* [C,U] a method of finding the position of things such as airplanes or MISSILEs by sending out radio waves: *Enemy radar must have detected our approach.*

radar de·tect·or /'.. .,../ *n.* [C] a piece of electronic equipment that can be used in a car to tell you whether police are using RADAR to check how fast you are driving

radar screen /'.. ,./ *n.* **1** [C] a screen that shows where other things such as planes and ships are by using radar **2 the radar screen** a situation in which something is noticed or considered important: *Six years ago the company wasn't even on the radar screen.*

radar trap /'.. ,./ *n.* [C] a situation in which police use radar to catch drivers who are going faster than the legal speed

ra·di·al¹ /'reɪdiəl/ *adj.* arranged in a circular shape with bars, lines etc. coming from the center: *First, the spider lays down a strong radial framework for the web.*

radial² *n.* [C] INFORMAL a radial tire

ra·di·al tire /,... '../ *n.* [C] a car tire with wires inside the rubber that go completely around the wheel to make it stronger and safer

ra·di·ance /'reɪdiəns/ *n.* [U] **1** great happiness, or energy that shows in the way someone looks: *When she returned, she had a kind of radiance about her.* **2** a soft light that shines from or onto something: *the moon's radiance*

ra·di·ant /'reɪdiənt/ *adj.* **1** full of happiness and love, in a way that shows in your face, eyes etc.: *a radiant bride* | *She looked at him with radiant eyes.* **2** [only before noun] very bright: *radiant rubies and diamonds* **3** TECHNICAL [only before noun] radiant heat, energy etc. is sent out by radiation —**radiantly** *adv.*: *radiantly beautiful*

ra·di·ate /'reɪdi,eɪt/ *v.* **1** [I,T] if someone radiates a feeling or quality, or if it radiates from them, they

R

show it or feel it in a way that is easy to notice: *Syd radiates warmth as he greets his guests.* | [+ **from**] *There is an energy that seems to radiate from her* **2** [I always + adv./prep.,T] if something radiates light or heat, or if light or heat radiates from something, it is sent out in all directions: *The log fire radiated a cozy glow.* | [+ **from/out etc.**] *CFCs trap energy that radiates from Earth.* **3** [I] to spread out from a central point: [+ **from**] *A web of boulevards radiates from the traffic circle.*

ra·di·a·tion /ˌreɪdi'eɪʃən/ *n.* **1** [U] a form of energy that comes from changes in the NUCLEAR structure of substances such as URANIUM or RADIUM, which is very harmful to living things if present in large amounts: *Sensors detected a dangerous level of radiation.* | *The tumors are treated with radiation.* **2** [U] energy in the form of heat or light sent out as beams that you cannot see: *solar radiation* **3** [C,U] the action or process of spreading out from a central position: *Clouds prevent the radiation of Earth's warmth into space.*

radiation sick·ness /..ˈ.. ˌ../ *n.* [U] an illness caused by your body receiving too much radiation

ra·di·a·tor /'reɪdiˌeɪtɚ/ *n.* [C] **1** a thing used for heating a room, consisting of a hollow metal container attached to a wall, through which hot water passes **2** the part of a car or aircraft which stops the engine from getting too hot —see picture at ENGINE

rad·i·cal¹ /'rædɪkəl/ *adj.* **1** radical changes or decisions are thorough and complete and have important effects: *He recommended a radical change in her diet.* | *It was an incredibly radical decision.* **2** radical opinions, ideas, leaders etc. support thorough and complete social or political change: *a radical leftist group* **3** relating to the central or most important qualities of something: *Radical differences within the group began to appear.* **4** SLANG very good or enjoyable: *That was one radical party!* —**radically** /-kli/ *adv.*

radical² *n.* [C] someone who wants thorough and complete social and political change —**radicalism** *n.* [U]

rad·i·cal·ize /'rædɪkəˌlaɪz/ *v.* [T] to make a system or idea more extreme, or to make someone want complete social or political change: *Young people have been radicalized by the struggle with the government.*

ra·dic·chi·o /ræ'dikioʊ/ *n.* [U] a type of plant used in SALADS, that is red and has a bitter taste

rad·i·i /'reɪdiaɪ/ *n.* the plural of RADIUS

ra·di·o¹ /'reɪdiˌoʊ/ *n. plural* **radios** **1 a)** [C] a piece of electronic equipment which you use to listen to programs that are broadcast, such as music and news: *Can you turn your radio down a little bit?* | *I'm going to buy a new radio for the car.* **b)** [U] the process of sending or receiving programs by radio: *We encourage more use of radio in the public interest.* **2 the radio** programs that are broadcast on the radio, considered in general: *Sometimes you just want to* **listen to the radio.** | *I heard* **on the radio** *that they blocked off Fulton Street.* **3** [U] the business or activity of making and broadcasting programs which can be heard on a radio: *a radio personality* | *Manley plans to pursue a career* **in radio.** | **local/ national radio** (=programs or companies broadcasting for a local area, or for the whole country) **4 a)** [C] a piece of electronic equipment, especially on an airplane or a ship, which can send and receive spoken messages **b)** [U] the action of sending or receiving these messages: *We've lost radio contact.*

radio² *v.* **radios, radioed, radioing** [I,T] to send a message using a radio: *I urgently radioed the information back to headquarters.*

radio- /reɪdioʊ/ *prefix* TECHNICAL **1** relating to energy that is sent out as beams: *a radiometer* (=used to measure the amount of energy sent out by something) | *radiography* (=the taking of X-RAYS) **2** relating to something that uses RADIO WAVES: *a radiogram* (=a message sent by radio) **3** relating to energy that comes from NUCLEAR REACTIONS: *radioactive elements*

ra·di·o·ac·tive /ˌreɪdioʊˈæktɪv◂/ *adj.* containing or producing RADIATION (=a form of energy that can harm living things): *a highly radioactive material* | *radioactive decay*

radioactive dat·ing /ˌ..... '../ *n.* [U] a scientific method of calculating the age of a very old object by measuring the amount of a certain substance in it; CARBON DATING

radioactive waste /ˌ..... '../ *n.* [U] harmful radioactive substances that remain after energy has been produced in a NUCLEAR REACTOR

ra·di·o·ac·tiv·i·ty /ˌreɪdioʊæk'tɪvəti/ *n.* [U] **1** a quality that certain substances have which makes them send out RADIATION (=a form of energy that can harm living things) **2** the energy which is produced in this way: *Workers were exposed to high levels of radioactivity.*

radio bea·con /'... ˌ../ *n.* [C] a station that sends out radio signals to help aircraft stay on the correct course

ra·di·o·car·bon dat·ing /ˌreɪdioʊkarbən 'deɪtɪŋ/ *n.* [U] FORMAL: see CARBON DATING

radio-cas·sette play·er /ˌ... '. ˌ../ *n.* [C] a piece of electronic equipment that contains both a radio and a CASSETTE DECK

radio-con·trolled /ˌ.... '.◂/ *adj.* **a radio-controlled airplane/car/vehicle** an airplane, car etc., or a toy copy of this, that is controlled from far away using radio signals

ra·di·o·gram /'reɪdioʊˌgræm/ *n.* [C] a message sent by radio

ra·di·og·ra·pher /ˌreɪdi'ɑgrəfɚ/ *n.* [C] someone whose job is to take X-RAY photographs of the inside of someone's body, or who treats people for illnesses using an X-ray machine

ra·di·og·ra·phy /ˌreɪdi'ɑgrəfi/ *n.* [U] the taking of X-RAY photographs of the inside of someone's body for medical purposes

ra·di·ol·o·gist /ˌreɪdi'ɑlədʒɪst/ *n.* [C] a doctor who is trained in the use of RADIATION to treat people

ra·di·ol·o·gy /ˌreɪdi'ɑlədʒi/ *n.* [U] the study and medical use of RADIATION

radio tel·e·phone, radiotelephone /ˌ... '...ˌ/ *n.* [C] a telephone, used especially in cars, that works by sending and receiving radio signals

radio tel·e·scope /ˌ... '.../ *n.* [C] a very large piece of equipment that receives and records the RADIO WAVES that come from stars and other objects in space

ra·di·o·ther·a·py /ˌreɪdioʊ'θɛrəpi/ *n.* [U] the treatment of illnesses using RADIATION —**radiotherapist** *n.* [C]

radio wave /'... ˌ./ *n.* [C usually plural] a form of electric energy that can move through air or space

rad·ish /'rædɪʃ/ *n.* [C] a small vegetable whose red or white root is eaten raw and has a strong SPICY taste

ra·di·um /'reɪdiəm/ *n.* [U] *symbol* **Ra** a rare metal that is an ELEMENT, is RADIOACTIVE, and is used in the treatment of diseases such as CANCER

ra·di·us /'reɪdiəs/ *n. plural* **radii** /-diaɪ/ [C] **1** the distance from the center to the edge of a circle: *The moon has a radius of approximately 1737 kilometers.* **2 within a 10 mile/200 yard etc. radius** within a distance of 10 miles, 200 yards etc. in all directions from a particular place: *The bomb caused damage and injuries within a half-mile radius.* **3** TECHNICAL a line drawn straight out from the center of a circle to its edge **4** TECHNICAL the outer bone of the lower part of your arm

ra·don /'reɪdɑn/ *n.* [U] *symbol* **Rn** a RADIOACTIVE gas that is an ELEMENT and that can be dangerous in large amounts

raf·fi·a /'ræfiə/ *n.* [U] a soft substance like string that comes from the leaves of a PALM tree and is used for making baskets, hats, MATS etc.

raff·ish /'ræfɪʃ/ *adj.* LITERARY behaving or dressing in a confident and cheerful way that shows no concern for what other people think but is still attractive: *He became friendly with a slightly raffish group of actors.* —**raffishness** *n.* [U]

raf·fle¹ /'ræfəl/ *n.* [C] a type of competition or game in which people buy numbered tickets and can win prizes

raffle² also **raffle off** *v.* [T] to offer something as a prize in a raffle: *They're raffling off a new Cadillac at the carnival.*

raft¹ /ræft/ *n.* [C] **1** a flat floating structure, usually made of pieces of wood tied together, used as a boat **2** a small flat rubber boat filled with air **3 a (whole) raft of sth** INFORMAL a large number of things or large amount of something: *The book offers a whole raft of important information about China-town.* **4** a flat floating structure that you can sit on, jump from etc. when you are swimming

raft

raft² *v.* [I,T] to travel by raft or carry things by raft

raf·ter /'ræftə/ *n.* [C]
1 [usually plural] one of the large sloping pieces of wood that form the structure of a roof **2** someone who travels on a raft

raft·ing /'ræftɪŋ/ *n.* [U] the sport of traveling down a fast-flowing river in a rubber raft

rag¹ /ræg/ *n.*
1 cloth [C] a small piece of old cloth, for example one used for cleaning things: *Just get a rag and wipe it up.*
2 in rags wearing old torn clothes: *an old man in rags*
3 go from rags to riches to become very rich after starting your life very poor
4 newspaper [C] INFORMAL a newspaper that you think is of low quality: *That paper's nothing but a fascist rag.*
5 sb is on the rag VULGAR used to say that a woman is angry because she is having her PERIOD¹ (4)
6 music [C] a piece of RAGTIME music: *Maple Leaf Rag* —see also GLAD RAGS

rag² *v.* **ragged, ragging**
rag on sb *phr. v.* [T] INFORMAL **1** to make jokes and laugh at someone in order to embarrass them: *Everybody ragged on Steve about his new haircut.* **2** to criticize someone in an angry way: *Can't you do anything except rag on the team for losing?*

ra·ga /'rɑgə/ *n.* [C] **1** a piece of Indian music based on an ancient pattern of notes **2** one of the ancient patterns of notes that are used in Indian music

rag·a·muf·fin /'rægə,mʌfɪn/ *n.* [C] LITERARY a dirty young child wearing torn clothes

rag·bag /'rægbæg/ *n.* **a ragbag of sth** a confused mixture of things that do not seem to go together or make sense: *There is a ragbag of over 100 federal programs to help the poor.*

rag doll /'. ./ *n.* [C] a soft DOLL made of cloth

rage¹ /reɪdʒ/ *n.* [C,U] **1** a strong feeling of uncontrollable anger: *She threw open the door in a rage and confronted Ellis.* | *Major Sanderson instantly flew into a rage* (=suddenly became very angry). | **shaking/trembling/quivering with rage** *I was literally shaking with rage when I heard the news.* **2 be (all) the rage** INFORMAL to be very popular and fashionable: *Short skirts are all the rage this spring.* **3 the rage for sth** the popularity of or desire for something: *Princess Diana helped create the current rage for pearls.*

rage² *v.* [I] **1** if something rages, such as a battle, disagreement, or storm, it continues with great violence or strong emotions: *A debate still rages on bilingual education in public schools.* | *Outside, a thunderstorm was raging and the lights flickered.* **2** LITERARY to feel very angry about something and show this in the way you behave or speak: [+ at/about/against] *For twenty years, Evans raged against minority injustices.*

rag·ged /'rægɪd/ *adj.* **1** torn and in bad condition: *Alex was wearing ragged jeans with holes in the knees.* | *He touched his ragged hat as she passed.* **2** wearing clothes that are old and torn: *She looked quite ragged and unkempt.* **3** not straight or neat, but with rough uneven edges: *a ragged shoreline* **4** tired after using a lot of effort: *Bev's voice was ragged with fatigue.* | *I was run ragged for hours at the press conference.* **5** a ragged performance, game, ESSAY etc. is not done, played, written etc. well: *Much of Cassidy's concert seemed ragged and under-rehearsed.* —**raggedly** *adv.* —**raggedness** *n.* [U]

rag·ged·y /'rægədi/ *adj.* OLD-FASHIONED **1** torn and in bad condition: *raggedy gloves* **2** not straight or neat, but with rough uneven edges: *raggedy hair*

rag·ing /'reɪdʒɪŋ/ *adj.* **1** [only before noun] raging feelings and emotions are extremely strong: *Spencer immediately got into a raging argument with her teammates.* | *a raging thirst* **2 raging stream/torrent/waters** water that flows fast and with a lot of force **3 a raging headache/toothache etc.** a very bad pain in your head, tooth etc.

rag·lan /'ræglən/ *adj.* **1 a raglan coat/sweater etc.** a coat, SWEATER etc. which has arms that are joined in a sideways line from the arm to the neck **2 a raglan sleeve** an arm of a coat, SWEATER etc. joined in this way

ra·gout /ræ'gu/ *n.* [C,U] a mixture of vegetables and meat boiled together; STEW

rag·tag /'rægtæg/ *adj.* **1** disorganized and not working well together: *a ragtag army of rebel soldiers* **2** looking messy, poor, and dirty: *a ragtag refugee camp*

rag·time /'rægtaɪm/ *n.* [U] a type of music and dancing with a quick RHYTHM that was popular in the early part of the 20th century

rag·weed /'rægwid/ *n.* [U] a North American plant that produces a substance which causes HAY FEVER

rah-rah¹ /'rɑrɑ/ *adj.* INFORMAL, DISAPPROVING **1** supporting something without thinking about it enough: *I find the rah-rah patriotism of most American war movies annoying.* **2** used to describe someone who tries to encourage people by saying only positive things: *Until recently, he had been known as the rah-rah college coach.*

rah-rah² *interjection* an expression used in some CHEERS (=shouts of encouragement) at a sports game, or the written expression of what a crowd at a sports game sounds like

raid¹ /reɪd/ *n.* [C] **1** a quick attack on a place by soldiers, airplanes, or ships, intended to cause damage but not take control: *a bombing raid* | [+ on] *They planned a surprise, early-morning raid on the naval base.* | **launch/make etc. a raid** *Allied forces carried out a successful raid on the port.* **2** a sudden visit by the police searching for something illegal: *Zavala led a series of raids on marijuana plantations.* | *Over 200 assault rifles were confiscated in the police raid.* **3** DISAPPROVING to take and use money that should be used for something else, especially money that belongs to a company or government: *The law will limit corporate raids on company pension funds.* **4** TECHNICAL an attempt by a company to buy enough STOCK in another company to take control of it: [+ on] *Fisher earned $50 million in a successful raid on Emhart Corporation.* —see also AIR RAID, PANTRY RAID

raid² *v.* [T] **1** if police raid a place, they go there suddenly to search for something illegal: *Police raided a pirate video factory in Glendale.* **2** to make a sudden attack on a place: *In 1943, allied bombers repeatedly raided Hamburg.* **3** to take or steal a lot of things from a place: *Thieves raided an Italian villa that housed a number of valuable paintings.* | **raid the refrigerator/closet/pantry etc.** *It looks like someone raided the liquor cabinet as well as the refrigerator last night.*

R

rail¹ /reɪl/ n. **1** [C] a bar that is attached along the side or on top of something such as stairs or a BALCONY: *Hold on to the rail as you walk up the stairs.* —see also RAILING **2** [C] one of the two long metal tracks attached to the ground that trains move along **3** [U] traveling by train: *Visitors can enter the city by rail or by boat.* | *rail travel* **4 go/run off the rails** if a system, plan, process etc. goes off the rails, it stops working the way it is supposed to: *The peace process is in danger of going off the rails.* **5** [C] a bar that you use to hang things on that is attached to a wall or door: *a towel rail*

rail² v. [I] LITERARY to complain angrily about something, especially something that you think is very bad or unfair: [+ **against/at**] *During his sermon, the priest railed against greed.*

rail·ing /ˈreɪlɪŋ/ n. [C] a fence consisting of a piece of wood or metal supported by upright posts, especially used on the sides stairs or the edge of a BALCONY —see also RAIL¹ (1)

rail·ler·y /ˈreɪləri/ n. [U] FORMAL friendly joking about someone

rail·road¹ /ˈreɪlroʊd/ n. **1** [C] a method of traveling or moving things around by train: *the Southern Pacific railroad* | *a railroad track* **2 the railroad** all the work, equipment etc. relating to a train system: *Smithers worked on the railroad for more than 50 years.*

railroad² v. [T] to force or persuade someone do something without giving them enough time to think about it: *This complex proposal should not be railroaded through Congress.* | [**railroad sb into doing sth**] *Claudia was railroaded into selling her late husband's land.*

railroad cross·ing /ˌ.. ˈ../ n. [C] a place where a road and railroad tracks cross each other at the same level

railroad line /ˈ.. ˌ./ n. [C] a part of the railroad system that connects two places: *the transcontinental railroad line*

railroad sta·tion /ˈ.. ˌ../ n. [C] a TRAIN STATION

rail trail /ˈ. ./ n. [C] a path that used to be a railroad track but that has been covered with a hard surface for people to walk, run, or ride bicycles on

rail·way /ˈreɪlweɪ/ n. plural **railways** [C] ESPECIALLY CANADIAN, BRITISH a RAILROAD

rai·ment /ˈreɪmənt/ n. [U] LITERARY clothes

rain¹ /reɪn/ n. **1** [C,U] water that falls in small drops from clouds in the sky: *There's an 80% chance of rain.* | *Someone left the ladder and the toolbox out in the rain.* | *It looks like rain* (=it is probably going to rain) – *we'd better go inside.* | **(a) heavy/light rain** (=a large or small amount of rain) **2 (come) rain or shine** whatever happens or whatever the weather is like: *Burrow runs two miles, rain or shine, everyday.* **3 a rain of arrows/comets/blows etc.** many ARROWS, COMETS etc. falling or coming down from above at the same time —see also ACID RAIN, **(as) right as rain** (RIGHT¹ (13)) —**rainless** adj.: *a rainless summer*

rain² v. **1** [I] if it rains, drops of water fall from clouds in the sky: *Think it'll rain this weekend?* | *It was raining hard.* **2 be/get rained out** if an event or activity is rained out, it has to stop because there is too much rain: *Yesterday's St. Louis–New York game was rained out.* **3 when it rains, it pours** SPOKEN used to say that as soon as one thing goes wrong, a lot of other things go wrong as well **4 it's raining cats and dogs** SPOKEN it is raining very hard **5 rain on sb's parade** if you rain on someone's parade, you say or do something that prevents them from enjoying something good that is happening to them

rain down phr. v. [I,T] if something rains down, or is rained down, it falls in large quantities: *Tears rained down her cheeks.* | *Bombs rained down on the town.*

rain·bow /ˈreɪnboʊ/ n. [C] a large curve of different colors that can appear in the sky when there is both sun and rain

rain check /ˈ. ./ n. **1 take a rain check (on sth)** SPOKEN used to say that you would like to accept an invitation or offer later, but you cannot right now: *I'm sorry but I'm busy on Saturday – can I take a rain check?* **2** a piece of paper which allows you to buy a particular product at a special price, given by a store when it does not have any more of the product **3** [C] a ticket for an outdoor event, such as a sports game, that you can use later if rain stopped an event you were at

rain·coat /ˈreɪnkoʊt/ n. [C] a coat that you wear to protect yourself from the rain

rain drop /ˈ. ./ n. [C] a single drop of rain

rain·fall /ˈreɪnfɔl/ n. [C,U] the amount of rain that falls on an area in a particular period of time: *Below-normal rainfall has led to a major water shortage.*

rain for·est /ˈ. ˌ../ n. [C] a tropical forest with tall trees that are very close together, growing in an area where it rains a lot: *the Brazilian rain forest*

rain gauge /ˈ. ./ n. [C] an instrument that is used for measuring the amount of rain that falls

Rai·ni·er, Mount /rəˈnɪr/ a mountain in the U.S. state of Washington which is the highest mountain in the Cascade Range

rain·mak·er /ˈreɪnˌmeɪkə/ n. [C] **1** someone who makes a lot of money for a company, usually by attracting rich CLIENTS (=customers) **2** someone who claims to be able to make it rain

rains /reɪnz/ n. **the rains** a period in the year when there is a lot of rain in tropical countries; MONSOON: *The rains have started early this year.*

rain·storm /ˈreɪnstɔrm/ n. [C] a sudden heavy fall of rain

rain·water /ˈreɪnˌwɔtə/ n. [U] water that has fallen as rain

rain·wear /ˈreɪnwɛr/ n. [U] WATERPROOF clothes that you wear when it rains

rain·y /ˈreɪni/ adj. **rainier, rainiest** **1 rainy day/afternoon/weather etc.** a day, afternoon etc. when it rains a lot **2 save sth for a rainy day** also **put sth away/aside for a rainy day** to save something, especially money, for a time when you will need it

raise¹ /reɪz/ v. [T]

1 [to a higher position] to move or lift something to a higher position, place, or level: *She raised her glass to make a toast.* | *Roy's car raised a cloud of dust as he drove off.* | *I raised my hand to get her attention.*
2 [increase] to increase an amount, number, or level: *He's raising the rent because he's fixed up the apartment.* | *Efforts are being made to raise employee morale.*
3 [children] to take care of your children and help them grow; BRING UP: *You can't raise a child in an environment like that.* | **raise sb Catholic/Muslim** etc. *I was raised Catholic.* | **raise sb (as) a Catholic/Muslim** etc. *John was raised as a New England Quaker.* | *Were you born and raised in Alabama?*
4 [improve] to improve the quality or standard of something: *They're hoping to raise living conditions in the area.*
5 [farming] to grow plants or keep cows, pigs etc. so that they can be sold or used as food: *His sister raises horses in Colorado.* | *These pheasants are raised on a corn diet.*
6 raise hopes/consciousness/awareness etc. to make people more hopeful etc.: *We hope Stephen's story will raise awareness of mental illness.*
7 raise a question/point etc. to begin to talk or write about a question etc. that you want to be considered: *Johnson's case also raises the issue of free speech.* | *Each time Woodward raised a question about it, she said, "I don't know."*
8 [collect money] to collect money, support etc. so that you can use it to help people: *Our objective is to raise $200 for the school band.*
9 raise your voice to speak loudly or shout because you are angry: *Stop raising your voice, Amanda.*
10 [your eyes or face] to move your eyes or face so

that you are looking up: *I raised my head and looked suspiciously around me.*

11 ‖upper part of your body‖ also **raise up** to lift the upper part of your body from a lying position: *She raised herself up on her elbows and looked around sleepily.*

12 ‖to an upright position‖ to move or lift something to an upright position: *If you raise that metal bar, it turns off the ice maker.*

13 ‖emotion/reaction‖ **a)** to cause a particular emotion or reaction: *The news raised concern among many in the district.* **b)** to try to show a particular feeling or emotion although you do not really feel it: *She felt so sad, she couldn't even raise a smile.*

14 raise your eyebrows (at sth) to show surprise, doubt, disapproval etc. by moving your EYEBROWS up: *His candid remarks raised more than a few eyebrows.*

15 raise hell/Cain to behave in a wild noisy way that upsets other people: *He spent his teenage years raising hell and stealing cars.*

16 raise your glass (to sth) to celebrate something by holding up your glass and drinking from it: *Members of the club raised their glasses in a salute to Anderson.*

17 ‖card game‖ to make a higher BID than an opponent in a card game: *I'll see your $5 and raise you $10.*

18 raise the alarm LITERARY to warn people about danger: *Fearing the bag might contain a bomb, a passenger raised the alarm.*

19 raise a siege/embargo FORMAL to allow goods to go in and out of a place again after they have been stopped by force or by a law

20 ‖build‖ FORMAL to build something such as a MONUMENT

21 ‖wake sb‖ LITERARY to wake someone who is difficult to wake: *Try as he might, he could not raise her.*

22 ‖dead person‖ BIBLICAL to make someone who has died live again: *Jesus raised Lazarus from the grave.*

23 raise the roof INFORMAL to make a very loud noise when singing, celebrating etc.: *The crowd's cheers raised the roof.*

24 ‖army‖ OLD-FASHIONED to collect together a group of people, especially soldiers

25 raise 2/4/10 etc. to the power of 2/3/4 etc. TECHNICAL to multiply a number by itself a particular number of times: *2 raised to the power of 3 (=2^3) is 8.*

USAGE NOTE: RAISE

WORD CHOICE: raise, lift, increase, rise, bring up, rear, grow, improve

People or other forces **raise** things to a higher position, though in informal language **lift** is usually used: *The crane raised/lifted the whole house.* In a court of law you may hear *Please raise your right hand and repeat after me.* People, governments etc. **raise** or **increase** the price, cost, or amount of something *Do you think they'll raise the price of gasoline again?* | *High taxes could increase the number of unemployed people.* When things or prices move upward on their own, they **rise**: *The balloon rose slowly from the ground.* | *the problem of rising inflation* | *Industrial production is likely to rise over the next year.* You can also **raise** or **bring up** children (or, in more formal contexts, you can **rear** children), meaning you take care of them as they grow up. You can **raise** or **bring up** a point, question etc. in a discussion. You may **raise** cattle or other animals on a farm. You can also **grow** wheat, flowers, or vegetables. When you are talking about making something better, people often use either **raise** or **improve**: *I'm working hard to raise/improve my TOEFL score.* | *Women still need to raise/improve their position in society* (NOT *raise up*). When something gets better on its own, you can use **rise** or **improve**: *Standards are rising/improving.* The noun **raise** means a pay increase. Otherwise the noun is always **rise**: *a rise in house prices/standards* | *the rise of the Roman Empire.*

---

raise² *n.* [C] an increase in the money you earn: *Library employees have not received a raise for six years.*

rai·sin /ˈreɪzən/ *n.* [C] a dried GRAPE (=the fruit that wine is made from)

rai·son d'ê·tre /ˌreɪzoʊn ˈdetrə, -zɑn-/ *n.* [C] the reason something exists, why someone does something etc.: *Winning is the raison d'être of a professional coach.*

ra·jah, raja /ˈrɑdʒə, -dʒɑ/ *n.* [C] the king or ruler of an Indian state

rake¹ /reɪk/ *n.* **1** [C] a tool with a row of metal teeth at the end of a long handle, used for making soil level, gathering up dead leaves etc. **2** [C] OLD-FASHIONED a man who behaves in an unacceptable way, having many sexual relationships, drinking too much alcohol etc. **3** [C] a stick used by a CROUPIER for gathering in the CHIPS at a table where games are played for money **4** [singular] the angle of a slope: *the rake of the stage*

rake

rake² *v.* **1** also **rake up** [I,T] to move a rake across a surface in order to make the soil level, gather dead leaves etc.: *They paid me $20 to rake the leaves in their front yard.* **2** [I always + adv./prep.] to search a place very carefully for something: [+ **through/ around/about**] *Stacy and her children raked through the rubble of their house.* **3** [T] FORMAL to point something such as a gun, camera, strong light etc., so that it covers a wide area, by slowly moving it from one side to another: *Guerrillas raked the room with gunfire.* | *The women raked us with their cold stares.* **4 rake sb over the coals** to criticize someone severely for something they have done: *Senator Hartley has been raked over the coals for his sexist remarks.* **5 rake your fingers/nails** to pull your fingers or nails through something or across a surface: *Ken raked his fingers through his hair.* **6 rake (the) ashes/coals** to push a stick backward and forward in a fire in order to make the fire go out

rake sth ↔ **in** *phr. v.* [T] INFORMAL to earn a lot of money without trying very hard: *For a few years, his business was raking in $5,000 a week.* | *"Titanic" is still raking it in at the box office.*

rake sth ↔ **up** *phr. v.* [T] INFORMAL to talk about something from the past that people would rather not remember

rak·ish /ˈreɪkɪʃ/ *adj.* **1** making you look relaxed, confident, and stylish, or looking this way: *a rakish suit* **2 at a rakish angle** if you wear a hat at a rakish angle, you do not wear it straight, and this makes you look relaxed and confident **3** OLD-FASHIONED a rakish man behaves in an unacceptable way, having many sexual relationships, wasting money, drinking too much alcohol etc. —**rakishly** *adv.*

Ra·leigh /ˈrɑli, ˈrɔ-/ the capital city of the U.S. state of North Carolina

Raleigh, Sir Wal·ter /ˈwɔltər/ (?1552–1618) an English EXPLORER who made several trips to North and South America and later wrote books about them

ral·ly¹ /ˈræli/ *v.* **rallies, rallied, rallying 1** [I,T] to come together or bring people together to support an idea, a political party etc.: *Albright tried to rally support for the plan from Congress.* | [+ **to**] *The children rallied to save the 111-year-old lighthouse.* **2** [I] to become stronger again after a period of weakness or defeat: *On the stock market, share prices rallied after a four-day decline.* | *Miami rallied to defeat New Orleans 28–24.*

rally around *phr. v.* [I,T] if a group of people rally around, they all try to help you in a difficult situation: *In times of crisis, the public tends to rally around the president and the military.*

rally² *n. plural* **rallies** [C] **1** a large public meeting, especially one that is held outdoors to support a political idea, protest etc.: *a pro-democracy rally* —see also PEP RALLY **2** a car race on public roads:

the Monte Carlo Rally **3** an occasion when something becomes stronger again after a period of weakness or defeat: *A 30-point rally in the fourth quarter gave the New York the win.* | *There was a late rally on the stock exchange.* **4** a series of hits of the ball between players in games like tennis

rallying cry /'... ,./ *n. plural* **rallying cries** [C] a word or phrase used to unite people in support of an idea: *"Land and Liberty" was the rallying cry of revolutionary Mexico.*

rallying point /'... ,./ *n.* [C] an idea, event, person etc. that makes people come together to support something they believe in: *The Pittston coal strike served as a rallying point for organized labor.*

RAM /ræm/ *n.* [U] TECHNICAL Random Access Memory; the part of a computer that keeps information temporarily so that it can be used immediately —compare ROM

ram[1] /ræm/ *v.* **rammed, ramming** **1** [I always + adv./ prep.,T] to run or drive into something very hard: *The driver lost control and rammed into a car waiting at a stoplight.* | *Hancock tried to ram the police car.* **2** [T always + adv./prep.] to push something into a position using great force: *He rammed a clip of bullets into the gun.* **3 ram sth down sb's throat** to try to make someone accept an idea or opinion by repeating it again and again, especially when they are not interested **4 ram sth home** to make sure someone fully understands something by emphasizing it and by providing a lot of examples, proof etc.

ram[2] *n.* [C] **1** an adult male sheep —compare EWE **2** a BATTERING RAM **3** TECHNICAL a machine that hits something again and again to force it into a position

Ram·a·dan /'rɑmə,dɑn/ *n.* [U] the ninth month of the Muslim year, during which Muslims are not allowed to eat or drink during the hours of daylight

ram·ble[1] /'ræmbəl/ *v.* [I] **1** to talk for a long time in a way that does not seem to be clearly organized, with the result that other people find it hard to understand you: *Dean Wilford tends to ramble when he speaks.* **2** [always + adv./prep.] to go on a walk for pleasure: *We spent three wonderful days rambling around Palermo.* **3** a plant that rambles grows in all directions

ramble on *phr. v.* [I] to talk or write for a long time in a way that other people find boring: *She rambled on but Anastasia was not listening.* | *He had been rambling on about himself for over an hour.*

ramble[2] *n.* [C] **1** a long walk for pleasure: *My favorite ramble is the nine-mile hike to West Potrero Road.* **2** a speech or piece of writing that is very long and does not seem to be clearly organized: *In a ten-page ramble, Barre explains why he wrote the book.*

ram·bler /'ræmblɚ/ *n.* [C] a rose bush that grows in many different directions

ram·bling /'ræmblɪŋ/ *adj.* **1** a building that is rambling has an irregular shape and covers a large area: *a rambling New England farmhouse* **2** speech or writing that is rambling is very long and does not seem to have any clear organization or purpose: *Perot's rambling speech swung from economics to education.*

ram·bunc·tious /ræm'bʌŋkʃəs/ *adj.* noisy, full of energy, and behaving in a way that cannot be controlled: *two rambunctious boys* —**rambunctiously** *adv.* —**rambunctiousness** *n.* [U]

ram·e·kin /'ræmɪkən, 'ræmkən/ *n.* [C] a small dish in which food for one person can be baked and served

Ram·e·ses II /,ræməsiz ðə 'sɛkənd/ also **Rameses the Great** the king of Egypt from about 1292 to 1225 B.C.

ram·ie /'reɪmi, 'ræ-/ *n.* [C,U] a plant from which cloth is made, or the cloth itself

ram·i·fi·ca·tion /,ræməfə'keɪʃən/ *n.* [C usually plural] FORMAL a result or effect of something you do, which may not have expected when you first decided to do it: *At the time, I was not aware of the ramifications of my actions.*

ram·i·fy /'ræmə,faɪ/ *v.* **ramifies, ramified, ramifying** [I] FORMAL to spread out and form a system or network

ramp[1] /ræmp/ *n.* [C] **1** a road for driving onto or off a large main road: *I hit a patch of ice as I entered the ramp to the expressway.* | **an off/on-ramp** *Take the Lake Herman Road on-ramp to Interstate 80.* **2** a slope that has been built to connect two places that are at different levels: *Ramps are needed at exits and entrances for wheelchair users.*

ramp[2] *v.*

ramp down *sth phr. v.* [T] to decrease the amount or quantity of something

ramp up *phr. v.* [I,T **ramp** sth ↔ **up**] to start happening more quickly, or to make something do this: *Two new steel mills are ramping up production.*

ram·page[1] /'ræmpeɪdʒ/ *n.* [C] an occasion when a person or a group rushes around in a wild and violent way, causing damage: *University students went on a rampage after another tuition increase was announced.* | **a shooting/crime/murder rampage** *Farley will stand trial for killing seven people in a shooting rampage.*

ram·page[2] /ræm'peɪdʒ, 'ræmpeɪdʒ/ *v.* [I] to rush about in groups wildly or violently, causing damage: [+ **through**] *Anti-government demonstrators rampaged through the capital today.*

ramp·ant /'ræmpənt/ *adj.* **1** if something such as crime or disease is rampant, it is bad, happens often in many different places, and is difficult to control: *Pickpocketing is rampant in the downtown area.* | *The drug problem continues to run rampant.* **2** a plant that is rampant grows and spreads in an uncontrolled way: *rampant garden weeds* —**rampantly** *adv.*

ram·part /'ræmpɑrt/ *n.* [C usually plural] a wide pile of earth or a stone wall built to protect a castle or city in past times

ram·rod[1] /'ræmrɑd/ *n.* [C] **1** a stick for pushing GUN-POWDER into an old-fashioned gun, or for cleaning a small gun **2** someone who tries very hard to make someone or a group of people do something or agree with something: *Connerly became the ramrod on anti-affirmative action legislation.*

ramrod[2] *adv.* **ramrod straight/stiff** sitting or standing with your back straight and your body stiff —**ramrod** *adj.: ramrod posture*

ram·shack·le /'ræm,ʃækəl/ *adj.* a ramshackle building or vehicle is in bad condition and in need of repair: *a row of ramshackle homes*

ran /ræn/ *v.* the past tense of RUN

ranch /ræntʃ/ *n.* [C] **1** a very large farm in the western U.S. and Canada where sheep, cattle, or horses are raised: *a cattle ranch* **2** a RANCH HOUSE: *a four-bedroom ranch* —see also **bet the ranch/farm** (BET[1] (8))

ranch dress·ing /,. '../ *n.* [U] a type of SAUCE that is put on SALADS, made with YOGURT, HERBS and SPICES

ranch·er /'ræntʃɚ/ *n.* [C] someone who owns or is in charge of a ranch: *a cattle rancher*

ranch house /'. ./ *n.* [C] **1** a long, narrow house built on one level, usually with a roof that does not slope much **2** a house on a ranch, in which the rancher lives

ranch·ing /'ræntʃɪŋ/ *n.* [U] the activity or business of operating a RANCH

ran·cid /'rænsɪd/ *adj.* oily or fatty food that is rancid smells or tastes bad because it is not fresh anymore: *rancid butter* —**rancidity** /ræn'sɪdəṭi/ *n.* [U]

ran·cor /'ræŋkɚ/ *n.* [U] FORMAL a feeling of hatred, especially when you cannot forgive someone: *John and Nancy's divorce was carried out with a minimum of rancor.* —**rancorous** *adj.* —**rancorously** *adv.*

rand /rænd/ *n. plural* **rand** [C] the standard unit of money in South Africa

Rand /rænd/**, Ayn** /aɪn/ (1905–1982) a U.S. writer of NOVELS

R & B /,ɑr ən 'bi/ *n.* [U] rhythm and blues; a style of popular music that is a mixture of BLUES and JAZZ

R & D /,ɑr ən 'di/ *n.* [U] research and development; the part of a business concerned with studying new ideas and planning new products

R & R /ˌɑr ən 'ɑr/ n. [U] rest and relaxation; a vacation given to people in the army, navy, etc. after a long period of hard work or during a war

ran·dom /'rændəm/ adj. **1** happening or chosen without any definite plan, aim, or pattern: *random drug tests* | *Random dashes of color highlight the painting.* **2 at random** if something is done or happens at random, it does so without any definite plan, aim, or pattern: *We selected the agencies at random from the phone book.* —**randomly** adv. —**randomness** n. [U]

random ac·cess mem·o·ry /ˌ.. ˌ.. '.../ n. [C,U] RAM

rang /ræŋ/ v. the past tense of RING

sw **range¹** /reɪndʒ/ n.
2 **1** group [C, usually singular] a number of things which are all different, but of the same general type: [+ of] *Herbs provide a range of aromas and flavors for cooking.* | *We teach the full range of ballroom dances.* | **a wide/broad range of sth** *The party is trying to appeal to a broader range of voters.*
2 number limits [C] the limits within which amounts, quantities, ages etc. can vary: **age/price etc. range** *Sandwiches come in three sizes and price ranges.* | [in the range of sth] *Starting salaries are in the range of $28,000 to $33,000.* | **beyond/out of sb's range** (=more than someone's limit on price, age etc.)
3 limits to power/activity [C] the amount of power or area of responsibility that a person or organization has, or the types of activities they are allowed to do: [+ of] *Companies with under 20 employees were outside the range of our survey.*
4 distance **a)** [singular,U] the distance within which something can be seen or heard: [+ of] *Voice radio has a range of about 100 miles.* | *We just want to get within range to use our binoculars.* | *Make sure towels and shower curtains are out of range* (=too far away to reach, hear etc.) *of the spray.* | *The walls appear smooth except at close range* (=very near). **b)** [singular,U] the distance over which a particular weapon can hit things: *What's the gun's range?* | [+ of] *missiles with a range of 500 miles* | *Once within range* (=near enough to hit) *of the target, the plane will drop the bomb.* | *Until the attack began, allied forces stayed out of range* (=too far away to hit) *of enemy artillery.* | **at close/point-blank/short range** (=from very close) | **long-/short-range missile** *a Pershing short range missile* **c)** [C] the distance which a vehicle such as an airplane can travel before it needs more fuel etc.: [+ of] *The Type-2 boat has a range of 4000 miles.*
5 products [C] a set of similar products made by a particular company or available in a particular store: *Sansui planned to broaden its product range to include video equipment.*
6 music [C usually singular] all the musical notes that a particular singer or musical instrument can make: *Williams is blessed with a 2¹⁄₄-octave range.*
7 ability [C,U] someone's area of ability, especially as an actor or actress: *an actor of extraordinary range and intensity*
8 mountains [C] a group of mountains or hills, usually in a line: *the Hajar mountain range*
9 practice with weapons [C] an area of land where you can practice using weapons: *a rifle range* —see also DRIVING RANGE
10 land [C,U] a large area of land covered with grass, which cattle can eat —see also FREE-RANGE
11 cooking [C] a STOVE: *a gas range*

sw **range²** v.
3 **1** include **a)** [I always + adv./prep.] if prices, levels, temperatures etc. range from one amount to another, they include both those amounts and anything in between: [range from sth to sth] *The five men are serving prison sentences ranging from 35 to 105 years.* | [range between sth and sth] *Ticket prices range between $12 and $14.* | **range in age/size etc.** (=include many different ages, sizes etc.) **b)** to include a variety of different feelings, actions etc.: [range from sth to sth] *His expression ranges from a painful grimace to a slight smile.*
2 area of land [I always + adv./prep.] to move around in or cover an area of land: [+ over/

through] *Experts say a single mountain lion can range over as much as 64,000 acres.*
3 include many subjects [I] to deal with a wide range of subjects or ideas in a book, speech, conversation etc.: [range over sth] *The show ranges over many settings, from 18th-century sailing ships to concert halls.* —see also WIDE-RANGING
4 be ranged FORMAL to be in a particular order or position: *A group of sullen men were ranged along the bar.*
5 be ranged against sth FORMAL to publicly state your opposition to a particular group's beliefs and ideas: *Ranged against the fundamentalists are dozens of political parties.*

range·find·er /'reɪndʒˌfaɪndər/ n. [C] an instrument for finding the distance of an object when firing a weapon or taking photographs

rang·er /'reɪndʒər/ n. [C] **1** someone who is in charge of protecting a forest or area of COUNTRYSIDE: *a park ranger* **2** a police officer in past times, who rode on a horse through country areas **3** a soldier who has been specially trained to make quick attacks

Ran·goon /ræŋ'gun/ the capital and largest city of Myanmar (Burma)

rank¹ /ræŋk/ n.
1 position in army/organization [C,U] the position or level that someone holds in an organization, especially in the police or armed forces: *State your name, rank, and serial number.* | **high/senior/low/junior rank** *It was the first time that a leader of such high rank had visited the islands.*
2 the ranks a) the people who belong to an organization or group: *The layoffs cut deep into the ranks of the city's health workers.* | *A further 450 workers are due to join the ranks of the jobless.* **b)** all the members of the armed forces who are not officers: *After the war, Gilroy rose quickly in the ranks.*
3 close ranks if the people in a group close ranks, they join together to support each other against other people: *He called for the Lebanese to close ranks behind his government.*
4 break ranks a) to stop supporting a group that you are a member of: *31 Republicans in the Assembly broke ranks to vote with Democrats.* **b)** if soldiers break ranks, they do not stay in line
5 pull rank (on sb) to use your authority over someone to make them do what you want, especially unfairly: *She never acted like an authority figure or pulled rank on me.*
6 line [C] a line of people or things: *They were all standing in ranks next to each other.*
7 swell the ranks to increase the number of people or things in a group: *Ecological and economic disasters are swelling the ranks of refugees worldwide.*
8 of the first rank of the highest quality: *Washington has emerged as an actor of the first rank.*
9 social class [C,U] someone's position in society: *She always wore rich fabrics and jewels, as befitted one of her rank.* —see also RANK AND FILE

rank² v. **1 a)** [I always + adv./prep.] to have a particular position in a list of people or things that are put in order of quality or importance: *The Rams have ranked near the bottom of the NFL for two seasons.* | [+ among/as/with] *Sandoz ranks as one of the ten largest drug companies in the world.* | **high-/low-ranking** *Several high-ranking officers were called to testify in the case.* **b)** [T] to decide the position of someone or something on a list, based on quality or importance: **be ranked fourth/number one etc.** *Mexico's soccer team is ranked 11th in the world.* | [rank sb/sth in order] *Rank the candidates in order of preference.* **2** [T] to have a higher rank than someone else; OUTRANK: *A general ranks a captain.*

rank³ adj. **1** [only before noun] complete; total: *Her students range from rank beginners to professionals.* | *rank hypocrisy* **2** having a very strong and bad smell or taste: *rank cheese* —**rankly** adv. —**rankness** n. [U]

R
sw
3

rank and file /ˌ. . './ *n.* **the rank and file** the ordinary members of an organization rather than the leaders: *The policy will now have to be approved by the rank and file.* —**rank-and-file** *adj.* [only before noun] *rank-and-file members of the union*

Ran·kin /'ræŋkɪn/, **Jean·nette** /dʒɪ'nɛt/ (1880–1973) a U.S. woman who helped women get the right to vote and was the first woman member of the U.S. House of Representatives

rank·ing[1] /'ræŋkɪŋ/ *n.* [C] a position on a scale that shows how good someone or something is when compared with others: *Sampras clinched the number one ranking again this year.*

ranking[2] *adj.* [only before noun] a ranking person has the highest position in an organization: *Helms is the ranking Republican on the Senate Foreign Relations Committee.*

ran·kle /'ræŋkəl/ *v.* [I,T] if something rankles or rankles you, it makes you very annoyed or angry: *His casual style of dress rankled his superiors.*

ran·sack /'rænsæk/ *v.* [T] **1** to go through a place stealing things and causing damage: *Roth found his home had been ransacked by burglars.* **2** to search a place very thoroughly, often making it messy: *She ransacked the dresser drawer, looking for the ring.*

ran·som[1] /'rænsəm/ *n.* [C] **1** an amount of money paid to free someone who is held as a prisoner: *They're demanding $10,000 in ransom to return Drake unharmed.* **2 hold sb for ransom** to keep someone as a prisoner until money is paid

ransom[2] *v.* [T] to set someone free by paying a ransom

rant /rænt/ *v.* [I] to talk or complain in a loud, excited, and rather confused way because you feel strongly about something: *Thompson was ranting about American youth again.* | *You don't have to rant and rave to get your point across.*

rap[1] /ræp/ *n.*
1 music [C,U] a type of popular music in which the words of a song are not sung, but spoken in time to music with a steady beat
2 knock [C] a quick light hit or knock: *We heard a sharp rap on the door.*
3 crime INFORMAL a statement by the police that someone is responsible for a serious crime; CHARGE[1]: *murder/robbery etc. rap The kid's been cited twice on drunk driving raps.* —see also RAP SHEET
4 take the rap (for sth) to be blamed or punished for a mistake or crime, especially unfairly: *Bo was left to take the rap for Victor's murder.*
5 beat the rap to avoid being punished for a crime: *He's been indicted three times, but beat the rap each time.*
6 get a bum/bad rap to be unfairly criticized, or to be treated badly: *Cleveland always gets a bum rap in the press.*
7 a rap on the knuckles a punishment or criticism that is not very severe: *In the past, securities firms had gotten away with a rap on the knuckles.*

rap[2] *v.* **rapped, rapping**
1 hit [I,T] to hit or knock something quickly: *She rapped the table with her pen and called for silence.* | [+ at/on] *Nina rapped on my door and called out my name.*
2 music [I] to say the words of a RAP[1] (1): *L.L. Cool J raps on a new album of Disney songs.*
3 criticize [T] to criticize someone angrily: *Nelson is being rapped for his team's loss.*
4 conversation [I] OLD-FASHIONED to talk in an informal way to friends: *Sammy was rapping about some guy in L.A.*
5 rap sb on the knuckles to punish or criticize someone for something, but not very severely: *We should rap them on the knuckles and make them agree to work together.*
6 say [T] to say something loudly, suddenly, and in a way that sounds angry: *Yoshinaka rapped an order at his men.*

ra·pa·cious /rə'peɪʃəs/ *adj.* FORMAL taking everything that you can, especially by using violence: *rapacious real estate developers* —**rapaciously** *adv.* —**rapaciousness** *n.* [U] —**rapacity** /rə'pæsəti/ *n.* [U]

rap art·ist /'. ../ *n.* [C] someone who speaks the words of a RAP[1] (1)

rape[1] /reɪp/ *v.* [T] to force someone to have sex, especially by using violence: *Lula was raped on her way home from work.*

rape[2] *n.* **1** [C,U] the crime of forcing someone to have sex, especially by using violence: *Wilson has been charged with attempted rape.* | *a rape victim* —see also DATE RAPE, RAPIST **2** [singular] sudden unnecessary destruction, especially of the environment: *the rape of the American West* **3** [U] a plant with yellow flowers, grown as animal food and for its oil; CANOLA

Raph·a·el[1] /'ræfiəl/ in the Christian religion, an ARCHANGEL

Raphael[2] (1483–1520) an Italian painter and ARCHITECT who was one of the most important artists of the RENAISSANCE. His full name in Italian is Raffaello Sanzio.

rap·id /'ræpɪd/ *adj.* done or happening very quickly and in a very short time: *Adolescence is a period of great and rapid change.* | *Will cast a rapid glance at the clock.* —**rapidly** *adv.* —**rapidity** /rə'pɪdəti/ *n.* [U]

rap·id-fire /ˌ.. '. ./ *adj.* [only before noun] **1** rapid-fire questions, jokes etc. are said quickly one after another **2** a rapid-fire gun can fire shots quickly one after another

rap·ids /'ræpɪdz/ *n.* [plural] part of a river where the water looks white because it is moving very fast over rocks

rapid tran·sit sys·tem /ˌ.. '.. ˌ../ also **rapid transit** *n.* [C] a system for moving people quickly around a city using SUBWAYS or trains above the ground

ra·pi·er /'reɪpiə/ *n.* [C] **1** a long thin sword with two sharp edges **2 rapier wit** the ability to say things that are very funny, and that often criticize other people

rap·ine /'ræpən, -paɪn/ *n.* [U] LITERARY the taking away of property by force

rap·ist /'reɪpɪst/ *n.* [C] someone who has forced someone else to have sex, especially by using violence

rap·pel /ræ'pɛl, rə-/ *v.* **rappelled, rappelling** [I] to go down a cliff or a rock by sliding down a rope and touching the cliff or rock with your feet —**rappel** *n.* [C]

rap·per /'ræpə/ *n.* [C] someone who speaks the words of a RAP[1] (1) (=type of popular music)

rap·port /ræ'pɔr, rə-/ *n.* [singular,U] friendly agreement and understanding between people: [+ with/ between] *He established a good rapport with his students.*

rap·proche·ment /ˌræprouʃ'mɑn/ *n.* [singular,U] the establishment of a good relationship between two countries or groups of people, after a period of unfriendly relations: *Nixon's visit set in motion the rapprochement between Beijing and Washington.*

rap·scal·lion /ræp'skælyən/ *n.* [C] OLD USE someone who behaves badly, but whom you still like

rap sheet /'. ./ *n.* [C] INFORMAL a list kept by the police of someone's criminal activities: *He's got a rap sheet longer than a giraffe's neck!*

rapt /ræpt/ *adj.* so interested in something that you do not notice anything else: *The congregation listened in rapt attention.*

rap·ture /'ræptʃə/ *n.* [U] great excitement and happiness: *He stared in rapture at his baby son.*

rap·tur·ous /'ræptʃərəs/ *adj.* FORMAL expressing great happiness or admiration: *The exhibition has drawn huge crowds and rapturous reviews.* —**rapturously** *adv.*

rare /rɛr/ *adj.* **1** not seen or found very often, or not happening very often: *Tim collects rare stamps.* | *Shannon suffers from a rare form of cancer.* | [it is rare for sb to do sth] *It is rare for him to ask my help.* | [it is rare to do sth] *It's fairly rare to find a teacher who can teach writing well.* **2** meat that is rare has only been cooked for a short time and is still red: *I like my steak rare.* —compare MEDIUM[1] (2), WELL-DONE **3** TECHNICAL air that is rare has less oxygen than usual because it is in a high place —see also RARELY, RARITY —**rareness** *n.* [U]

USAGE NOTE: RARE

WORD CHOICE: rare, scarce
Rare is used to talk about something that is valuable and that there is not much of, or about things that do not happen very often: *a rare first edition of the poems of John Keats* | *A rare tornado struck in Washington state.* **Scarce** is used to talk about something that is difficult to get at a particular time or in a particular place, although it may be available at other times: *Consumer goods are scarce and of poor quality.* | *Jobs for college graduates were scarce.*

---

rare earth /ˌ. ˈ./ also **rare earth el·e·ment** /ˌ. ˈ. ˌ.../ *n.* [C] TECHNICAL one of a group of chemical ELEMENTS which are considered metals

rar·e·fied /ˈrɛrəˌfaɪd/ *adj.* **1** DISAPPROVING rarefied ideas, opinions etc. can only be understood by, or only involve, one small group of people: *the rarefied New York literary world* **2** rarefied air is the air in high places, which has less oxygen than usual

rare·ly /ˈrɛrli/ *adv.* not often: *Very rarely does she eat any kind of meat.* | *Alan rarely talked about his own work.* | *Brian rarely, if ever* (=almost never) *gets to bed before 3 am.*

rar·ing /ˈrɛrɪŋ/ *adj.* **raring to go** very eager to start an activity: *Carlos was raring to go soon after leaving the hospital.*

rar·i·ty /ˈrɛrəti/ *n. plural* **rarities 1 be a rarity** to not happen or exist very often: *I decided to skip dessert, which is a rarity for me.* **2** [C] something that is valuable or interesting because it is rare: *The Go-Gos' latest album is packed with live versions, B-sides, and other rarities.* **3** [U] the quality of being rare: *Such stamps are expensive because of their rarity.*

ras·cal /ˈræskəl/ *n.* [C] **1** OLD-FASHIONED a dishonest man **2** HUMOROUS a child who behaves badly but whom you still like —**rascally** *adj.: a rascally trick*

rash¹ /ræʃ/ *n.* [C] **1** a lot of red spots on someone's skin, caused by an illness or an ALLERGY: *Symptoms include high fever and a rash.* | *My mother breaks out in a rash if she eats seafood.* | **heat/diaper rash** (=a rash caused by heat or wearing DIAPERS) **2 a rash of sth** INFORMAL a large number of bad events, changes etc. within a short time: *A rash of chemical accidents took place at the refinery.*

rash² *adj.* doing something too quickly, without thinking carefully about whether it is sensible or not: *a rash decision* | *It would be rash to put too much into stocks right now.* —**rashly** *adv.* —**rashness** *n.* [U]

rasp¹ /ræsp/ *v.* **1** [I,T] to make a rough sound that is not nice to listen to: *I heard John's voice rasping in the other room.* **2** [T] to rub a surface with something rough

rasp² *n.* **1** [singular] a rough noise that is not nice to listen to: *Roger lowered his voice to a rasp.* | *the rasp of a rake on dead leaves* **2** [C] a metal tool with a rough surface, like a FILE, used for shaping wood or metal

rasp·ber·ry /ˈræzˌbɛri/ *n. plural* **raspberries** [C] **1** a soft sweet red berry that has many small parts, or the bush that this berry grows on: *raspberry jam* **2** INFORMAL an impolite sound made by putting your tongue out and blowing; BRONX CHEER

Ras·pu·tin /ræˈspyutˈn/, **Gri·go·ri** /grɪˈgɔri/ (1871–1916) a Russian who claimed to be a holy man, and who had a lot of power in the Russian government because of his influence over Alexandra, the wife of Czar Nicholas II

rasp·y /ˈræspi/ *adj.* **raspier, raspiest** a raspy voice or sound is rough and not nice to listen to

Ras·ta /ˈræstə, ˈrɑs-/ *n.* [C] INFORMAL a Rastafarian —**Rasta** *adj.*

Ras·ta·far·i·an /ˌræstəˈfɛriən, ˌrɑs-/ *n.* [C] someone who believes in a religion that is originally from

---

Jamaica, which has Haile Selassie as its religious leader, and has the belief that people from the Caribbean islands will return to Africa —**Rastafarian** *adj.* —**Rastafarianism** *n.* [U]

Ras·ta·man /ˈræstəˌmæn/ *n.* [C] INFORMAL a male Rastafarian, especially one with long hair that has been twisted into DREADLOCKS

rat¹ /ræt/ *n.* [C] **1** an animal that looks like a large mouse with a long tail **2** SPOKEN someone who has been disloyal to you or deceived you: *This is a good way to get back at that rat Yossarian.* **3 look like a drowned rat** to look very wet and uncomfortable: *Out in the field, we looked like a bunch of drowned rats.* **4 not give a rat's ass (about sb/sth)** VULGAR to not care at all about someone or something —see also PACK RAT, RAT RACE, RATS, RAT TRAP, **smell a rat** (SMELL² (6))

rat² *v.* **ratted, ratting** [I] INFORMAL to be disloyal to someone, especially by telling someone in authority about something wrong that person has done: [+ on] *I wouldn't rat on Albert.*

rat-a-tat /ˈ. . ./ also **rat-a-tat-tat** /ˈ. . . ./, **rat-tat-tat** *n.* [singular] a series of short repeated sounds, for example from a MACHINE GUN

ra·ta·tou·ille /ˌrætəˈtui, ˌrɑ-/ *n.* [U] a dish originally from France, made of cooked vegetables such as EGG-PLANT, ZUCCHINI, TOMATOES, and onions

ratch·et¹ /ˈrætʃɪt/ *n.* [U] a machine part consisting of a wheel or bar with teeth on it, which allows movement in only one direction

ratchet² *v.* [I,T always + adv./prep.] to increase or decrease by small amounts over a period of time: [+ up/down] *Raising the minimum wage would ratchet up real incomes in general.*

rate¹ /reɪt/ *n.* [C]
1 how often the number of times something happens, or the number of examples of something within a certain period: *Prisoners escaped from the center at the rate of one every five days.* | **birth/ unemployment/divorce etc. rate** *Death rates for some forms of cancer continue to rise.* | **a high/low rate of sth** *There is a high rate of street crime against tourists.* | **success/failure rate** (=the number of times that something succeeds or fails)
2 money a charge or payment that is set according to a standard scale: *Hotel rates advertised are per person, not per room.* | *The State Bank charges lower rates on personal loans.* | **hourly/weekly rate** *In most cases, lawyers charge on an hourly rate.* | *We found the going rate* (=the usual amount paid for something) *to be about $12 per day.*
3 speed the speed at which something happens over a period of time: *Our money was running out at an alarming rate.* | [+ of] *We were both traveling at the same rate of speed.*
4 at any rate SPOKEN **a)** used when you are stating one definite fact in a situation that is uncertain or unsatisfactory: *That's what they said, at any rate.* **b)** used to introduce a statement that is more important than what was said before, especially if it was confusing or unclear: *Well, at any rate, the next meeting will be on Wednesday.*
5 at this rate SPOKEN used to say what will happen if things continue to happen in the same way as now: *At this rate, I'll lose $30 million by the end of the season.* —see also CUT-RATE, EXCHANGE RATE, INTEREST RATE, PRIME RATE, -RATE

rate² *v.* **1 a)** [T usually passive] to think that someone or something has a particular quality, value, or standard: [be rated (as) sth] *Rhodes was rated as the top high-school player in the country.* | *Californian wines are very highly rated.* **b)** [I] to be considered as having a particular quality, value, or standard: [+ as] *That rates as one of the best meals I've ever had.* **2 be rated G/PG/R/X etc.** if a movie is rated G, PG etc. it is officially approved for people of a particular age to see —see also X-RATED **3** [T] to deserve something: *Our restaurant didn't even rate a mention in Beck's guide.*

-rate /reɪt/ [in adjectives] **first-rate/second-rate/ third-rate** of good, bad, or very bad quality: *Morgan surrounds himself with first-rate musicians on his latest album.*

rate of ex·change /ˌ. . . ˈ./ *n.* [C] the EXCHANGE RATE

rate of re·turn /ˌ. . . ˈ./ *n.* [singular] a company's profit for a year, expressed as a PERCENTAGE of the money that the company has spent during the year

rat fink /ˈ. ./ *n.* [C] OLD-FASHIONED someone who you trusted who has told the police, a teacher, or someone else in authority about something you have done wrong

rath·er /ˈræðɚ/ *adv.* **1 rather than** a phrase meaning "instead of," used when you are comparing two things or situations: *Rather than fly directly to LA, why not stop in San Francisco first?* | *Bryson decided to quit rather than accept the new rules.* | *I prefer cooking with olive oil rather than butter.* **2 would rather** used when you would prefer to do or have one thing more than another: *We could eat later, if you would rather do that.* | *I'd rather not talk about it, okay?* | [**would rather do sth than do sth**] *Tina would rather die than apologize to Doug.* | [**would rather sb did sth**] *I'd rather you stayed over at Barb's than drive home so late.* **3** [+ adj./adv.] FORMAL fairly or to some degree: *He was rather irritated that they didn't say anything.* | *Some of the photographs are rather blurry.* **4 or rather** used to correct something that you have said, or give more specific information: *There is a problem with parking, or rather with the lack of it.* **5 not... but rather...** used to say that someone does not do something but does something else instead: *The problem is not their lack of funding, but rather their lack of planning.*

USAGE NOTE: RATHER

WORD CHOICE: fairly, quite, pretty, rather, kind of
You use **fairly** to emphasize an adjective or adverb a little: *The weather was fairly cold* (=more than a little cold, but not extremely cold). You use **quite** to emphasize something: *It's quite expensive* (=more than a little expensive). **Rather** is more formal than "fairly": *It was a rather disappointing season for the Giants.* **Pretty** is the most usual way of saying "fairly" or "very," and is especially common in spoken English: *Charlie's Restaurant is pretty good, especially if you want somewhere cheap.* | *You'd better wear a coat – it's pretty cold out.*
GRAMMAR
Note that you say: *a rather/fairly/pretty long road* but *quite a long road*. **Rather** is not used before *than* when you are comparing people or things: *Books are more interesting than TV* (NOT *Books are interesting rather than TV*). But it is used when you are using adjectives to compare: *TV is relaxing rather than interesting.* **Rather** can only be used to mean **prefer** in the phrase *sb would rather* followed by the base form of a verb or a clause: *They'd rather walk* (NOT *they rather to walk/ walking/a walk*). | *I'd rather not answer that question.*

---

rat·i·fy /ˈrætəˌfaɪ/ *v.* **ratifies, ratified, ratifying** [T] to make a written agreement official by signing it: *Congress failed to ratify the treaty until two years later.* —**ratification** /ˌrætəfəˈkeɪʃən/ *n.* [U]

rat·ing /ˈreɪtɪŋ/ *n.* [C] **1** a level on a scale that shows how good, important, popular etc. someone or something is: *The President's approval rating rose to 78%.* | *NBC's new comedy had the highest television rating this season.* **2** [usually singular] a letter used to show how much violence, sex, and offensive language a movie contains: *Almodovar's film was given an X rating in the U.S.* **3** the military class or rank into which an army, navy etc. member is placed, according to their special skills and abilities —see also CREDIT RATING

ra·tings /ˈreɪtɪŋz/ *n.* **the ratings** a list that shows which television programs, movies etc. are the most popular: *CBS will end the series if it continues to drop in the ratings.*

ra·ti·o /ˈreɪʃiˌoʊ, ˈreɪʃoʊ/ *n. plural* **ratios** [C] a relationship between two amounts, represented by a pair of numbers showing how much bigger one amount is than the other: *The ratio of women to men on campus is 3:1.* —compare PROPORTION[1]

ra·tion[1] /ˈræʃən, ˈreɪ-/ *n.* **1** [C] a specific amount of something such as food or gasoline that you are allowed to have, when there is not much available: *In the army we received a daily ration of meat.* **2 rations** [plural] the food that is given to a soldier or member of a group each day: *U.S. planes dropped army rations to refugees along the border.*

ration[2] *v.* [T] to control the supply of something such as food or gasoline by allowing people to have only a limited amount of it, usually because there is not enough: *Sugar, cooking oil and rice will also be rationed.* —**rationing** *n.* [U]

ra·tion·al /ˈræʃənəl/ *adj.* **1** based on clear, practical, or scientific reasons: *There is no rational explanation for Melanie Hawkin's disappearance.* **2** sensible and able to make decisions based on intelligent thinking rather than on emotion: *No rational person would have agreed to those terms.* | *rational behavior* —**rationally** *adv.* —**rationality** /ˌræʃəˈnæləti/ *n.* [U] —opposite IRRATIONAL

ra·tion·ale /ˌræʃəˈnæl/ *n.* [C,U] the reasons and principles on which a decision, plan, belief etc. is based: [+ **for**] *The rationale for recruiting so many new players is to create a strong, fresh team.*

ra·tion·al·ist /ˈræʃənl-ɪst/ *n.* [C] someone who bases their opinions and actions on intelligent thinking, rather than on emotion or religious belief —**rationalism** *n.* [U] —**rationalist, rationalistic** /ˌræʃənəˈlɪstɪk/ *adj.*

ra·tion·al·ize /ˈræʃnəˌlaɪz, -nlˌaɪz/ *v.* **1** [I,T] to find or invent a reasonable explanation for your behavior or attitudes: *Glen tries to rationalize his drinking by saying he deserves a beer after a hard day.* **2** to think about something or improve it in a practical, sensible way: *The Social Security system needs to be rationalized.* —**rationalization** /ˌræʃnələˈzeɪʃən/ *n.* [C,U]

rat race /ˈ. ./ *n.* [U] **the rat race** the bad situation in business, politics etc. in which people are always competing against each other for success: *We retired early to get out of the rat race.*

rats /ræts/ *interjection* SPOKEN used to express annoyance: *Rats. I forgot to pick up my dry cleaning.*

rat·tan /ræˈtæn, rə-/ *n.* [U] the plant from which WICKER furniture is made

rat-tat-tat /ˌræt tæt ˈtæt/ *n.* [singular] RAT-A-TAT

rat·tle[1] /ˈrætl/ *v.* **1** [I,T] to shake, or make something shake, with quick repeated knocking sounds: *Monday's earthquake rattled windows and woke residents.* | *Keys rattled in his pocket as he walked.* **2** [I] to move quickly, making a RATTLING sound: [+ along/ past/over etc.] *Jenny rattled down the block on her old bike.* **3** [T] INFORMAL to make someone lose confidence or become nervous: *Nothing rattles him.* | *News of the shoot-out rattled nerves in the community* (=made people nervous). **4 rattle sb's cage** SPOKEN, HUMOROUS to make someone feel angry or annoyed: *Who rattled your cage?* —see also SABER-RATTLING

rattle around *phr. v.* [I] to move around in an empty space, often making a noise: *The ball is filled with small pebbles that rattle around inside.*

rattle sth ↔ **off** *phr. v.* [T] to say something quickly and easily, from memory: *Mark rattled off the list of movies he'd seen.*

rattle on *phr. v.* [I] INFORMAL to talk quickly for a long time, about things that are not interesting: [+ **about**] *Deanna just loves to rattle on about her boyfriend.*

rattle[2] *n.* **1** [singular] the sound that you hear when the parts of something knock against each other: [+ **of**] *the rattle of chains* **2** [C] a baby's toy that makes a noise when it is shaken **3** [C] a wooden or plastic instrument that makes a loud knocking noise, used by people on New Year's Eve and at parties —see also DEATH RATTLE

rat·tled /ˈrætld/ *adj.* [not before noun] nervous and not confident because of something that has happened: *He's a good player because he doesn't **get rattled** easily.*

rat·tler /'rætlɚ, 'rætl-ɚ/ *n.* [C] INFORMAL a rattlesnake

rattlesnake

rat·tle·snake /'rætl,sneɪk/ *n.* [C] a poisonous American snake that makes a noise like a rattle with its tail

rat·tle·trap /'rætl,træp/ *adj.* a rattletrap vehicle is in very bad condition

rat·tling /'rætlɪŋ/ *adj. adv.* OLD-FASHIONED **a rattling good story/tale etc.** a very good or interesting story

rat trap /'. ./ *n.* [C] a dirty old building that is in very bad condition

rat·ty /'ræti/ *adj.* **rattier, rattiest 1** in bad condition; SHABBY: *a ratty bathrobe* **2** like a rat

rau·cous /'rɔkəs/ *adj.* **1** impolite disorganized, noisy, and violent: *Raucous crowds yelled and cheered.* **2** very loud and rough-sounding: *raucous laughter* —**raucously** *adv.* —**raucousness** *n.* [U]

raun·chy /'rɔntʃi, 'rɑn-/ *adj.* **raunchier, raunchiest** INFORMAL **1** sexually exciting or intended to make you think about sex: *raunchy jokes* **2** a raunchy smell is extremely disgusting —**raunchily** *adv.* —**raunchiness** *n.* [U]

Rausch·en·berg /'raʊʃən,bɚg/, **Rob·ert** /'rɑbɚt/ (1925–) a U.S. artist famous for his work in the style of POP ART that sometimes includes photographs or real objects

rav·age /'rævɪdʒ/ *v.* [T often passive] to destroy, ruin, or damage something very badly [**be ravaged by sth**] *The population was ravaged by cholera.*

rav·ag·es /'rævɪdʒɪz/ *n.* **the ravages of war/time/disease etc.** the damage or destruction caused by something such as war, disease, storms etc.: *The church has miraculously escaped most of the ravages of civil war.*

rave[1] /reɪv/ *v.* [I] **1** to talk in a very excited way about something, saying how much you admire or enjoy it: [+ **about/over**] *Everyone's raving about the new sushi restaurant on 4th Ave.* **2** to talk in an angry, uncontrolled way: *Rosen ranted and raved about the team's poor performance.* **3** to talk in a crazy way that is impossible to understand, especially because you are very sick: *Newman was raving and banging his head on the wall of his cell.* —see also RAVING

rave[2] *adj.* **rave reviews/notices** strong praise for a new movie, book, restaurant, product, etc.: *Pryce won rave reviews for his performance in "Miss Saigon."*

rave[3] *n.* [C] **1** an event at which a very large group of young people dance all night to loud music with a strong beat: **rave band/party/culture etc.** *The band became successful in the rave scene of the early 1990s.* **2** a piece of writing in a newspaper, magazine etc. that praises a movie, play, or performance very much

rav·el /'rævəl/ *v.* [I] **1** if something made from wool or cloth ravels, the threads in it become separated from one another **2** if threads ravel, they become knotted and twisted —compare UNRAVEL

Ra·vel /ræ'vɛl/, **Mau·rice** /mɔ'ris/ (1875–1937) a French musician who wrote CLASSICAL music

ra·ven[1] /'reɪvən/ *n.* [C] a large shiny black bird with a large black beak

raven[2] *adj.* [only before noun] raven hair is black and shiny

raven-haired /'.. ,./ *adj.* LITERARY having shiny black hair

rav·en·ing /'rævənɪŋ/ *adj.* LITERARY ravening animals are extremely hungry: *a ravening beast*

rav·en·ous /'rævənəs/ *adj.* extremely hungry: *a ravenous appetite* | *The boys ran in, ravenous after their game.* —**ravenously** *adv.*

ra·vine /rə'vin/ *n.* [C] a deep narrow valley with steep sides: *A bus plunged 250 feet into a ravine, killing thirty people.*

rav·ing /'reɪvɪŋ/ *adj.* INFORMAL **1** talking or behaving in a crazy way: *a raving lunatic* **2 raving success** something that is very successful —see also **stark raving mad** (STARK[2] (2))

rav·ings /'reɪvɪŋz/ *n.* [plural] things someone says that are crazy and have no meaning: [+ **of**] *Salieri's confession was dismissed as the ravings of a madman.*

ra·vi·o·li /,rævi'ouli/ *n.* [U] small squares of PASTA filled with meat or cheese

rav·ish /'rævɪʃ/ *v.* [T] LITERARY **1** to RAPE a woman **2** to make someone feel great pleasure and happiness: *music to ravish the soul*

rav·ish·ing /'rævɪʃɪŋ/ *adj.* FORMAL very beautiful: *a ravishing young woman* —**ravishingly** *adv.*

raw[1] /rɔ/ *adj.*
1 food not cooked: *raw fish* | *The dill sauce also works well as a dip with raw vegetables.* | *Mayonnaise is traditionally made with raw eggs.*
2 information information or ideas that have not yet been arranged, checked, or prepared for use: *Scientists are analyzing raw data from the shuttle's telescope.* | *Dickinson's quiet life provides the raw material* (=ideas) *for her poetry.* | **raw footage** (=film of an event that is not changed before it is shown)
3 materials raw cotton, sugar, wool etc. are in their natural state and have not been prepared for people to use or deal with: **raw sewage** (=waste material that has not yet been treated with chemicals) —see also RAW MATERIALS
4 not developed not experienced, not fully trained, or not developed: *Good coaches develop raw talent into seasoned players.* | *We were impressed by the singer's raw, husky voice.* | **raw recruits** (=people who have just joined the army, navy etc.)
5 get a raw deal to be treated unfairly
6 skin a part of your body that is raw is red and sore: *His face was raw and blistered.*
7 language INFORMAL containing a lot of sexual details
8 emotions/qualities raw emotions or qualities are strong and natural, but not completely developed or controlled: *Audiences admire his raw courage and daring.*
9 descriptions giving facts which may not be favorable or nice, without trying to make them seem more acceptable: *a raw account of poverty in the cities*
10 weather very cold and wet: *raw, gusty winds* —**rawness** *n.* [U] —see also **strike/touch/hit a (raw) nerve** (NERVE[1] (5))

raw[2] *n.* **in the raw a)** in a natural state and not changed or developed: *Her films portray nature in the raw.* **b)** INFORMAL not wearing any clothes

raw·boned /'rɔboʊnd/ *adj.* someone who is rawboned, especially a man, is thin and has large bones with the skin stretched over them

raw·hide /'rɔhaɪd/ *n.* [U] natural leather that has not been specially treated

raw ma·te·ri·als /,. .'.../ *n.* [plural] materials such as coal, oil etc. in their natural state, before being treated in order to make things

ray /reɪ/ *n. plural* **rays** [C] **1** a narrow beam of light from the sun or from something such as a lamp: *the sun's rays* | [+ **of**] *Rays of light filtered through the pine trees.* **2** TECHNICAL a beam of heat, electricity, or other form of ENERGY (2): *a gun that fires invisible rays* —see also COSMIC RAY, GAMMA RAY, X-RAY[1] **3 ray of hope/light/comfort etc.** something that provides a small amount of hope or happiness in a difficult situation: *If only I could see some ray of hope for the future.* **4 ray of sunshine** INFORMAL an expression meaning someone or something that makes a situation seem better: *Little Annie was an unexpected ray of sunshine in her life.* **5** a large flat ocean fish with a long pointed tail

Ray /reɪ/, **Man** /mæn/ (1890–1976) a U.S. artist and photographer, who was one of the leaders of the DADA and SURREALIST movements

ray gun /'. ./ *n.* [C] an imaginary gun in SCIENCE FICTION stories that fires rays that kill people

ray·on /'reɪɑn/ *n.* [U] a smooth material like silk used for making clothes

raze /reɪz/ *v.* [T] to completely destroy a town or building: *The old theater will be razed and replaced with housing.*

ra·zor /'reɪzɚ/ *n.* [C] **1** a sharp instrument used for removing hair, especially from a man's face: *an electric razor* **2 be on a razor edge** to be in a dangerous position where a mistake could be very dangerous: *Politically we are on a razor edge. Whatever judgment we make could have dire consequences.*

razor blade /'.. ,./ *n.* [C] a small flat blade with a very sharp cutting edge, used in some types of razors

razor-sharp /,.. '. ◂/ *adj.* **1** very sharp: *a razor-sharp hunting knife* **2** able to think and understand things very quickly

razor wire /'.. ,./ *n.* [U] sharp metal wire in long strings, usually twisted into large circles, that is used to protect buildings or as a fence

razz /ræz/ *v.* [T] INFORMAL to make a joke about someone that is insulting or makes them feel embarrassed; TEASE[1]: *Eddie was razzed by his teammates after the game.*

raz·zle-daz·zle /,ræzəl 'dæzəl/ *n.* [U] INFORMAL **1** a lot of activity that is intended to be impressive and excite people: *Behind all the razzle-dazzle is a good play.* **2** a complicated series of actions intended to confuse your opponent

razz·ma·tazz, **razzamatazz** /,ræzəmə'tæz/ *n.* [U] INFORMAL busy or noisy activity that is intended to attract people's attention: *Audiences love the old Broadway razzmatazz.*

RC the written abbreviation of Roman Catholic

RCMP *n.* the abbreviation of the Royal Canadian Mounted Police —see also MOUNTIE

R.D. *n.* [U] Rural Delivery; the system of addresses the post office uses to deliver mail in country areas

Rd. the written abbreviation of Road, used in addresses

-rd /rd/ *suffix* used with the number 3 to form ORDINAL numbers: *the 3rd (=third) of June | his 53rd birthday*

RDA *n.* [singular] recommended daily allowance; the amount of substances such as VITAMINS or MINERALS that you should have each day

re[1] /ri/ *prep.* used especially in business letters to introduce the subject that you are going to write about: *re your e-mail dated November 27th* —see also IN RE

re[2] /reɪ/ *n.* [singular] the second note in a musical SCALE[1] (9) according to the SOL-FA system

re- /ri/ *prefix* **1** again: *They're rebroadcasting the speech.* **2** again in a new and better way: *You'd better rewrite that letter.* **3** back to a former state: *After years of separation they were finally reunited.*

're /r, ɚ/ *v.* the short form of "are": *We're going to go see them when they're back in town.*

S W
reach[1] /ritʃ/ *v.*
1 1
1 **arrive** [T] to arrive at a particular place, especially when it has taken a long time or a lot of effort to get there: *Snow prevented workers from reaching the broken pipeline. | It took seven hours before we reached the border.*
2 **with your hand** a) [I always + adv./prep.,T always + adv./prep.] to move your hand or arm in order to touch, hold, or pick up something: [+ for/

in/over etc.] *Paul reached into his pocket and pulled out a pen. | Someone reached out and grabbed her arm.* **b)** [I,T not in progressive] to be able to touch something by stretching out your hand or arm, especially something that is above your head: *I can't reach the top shelf. | Babies will put everything they can reach in their mouths.* **c)** [T] to take or pick up something by stretching your arm, especially over your head: *Can you reach the salt for me?* —see picture at ENOUGH[2]
3 **level/standard** [T] to increase, improve, or develop to a particular level or standard over a period of time: *Temperatures are expected to reach the 80s and 90s. | After you reach a certain age, nobody wants to hire you. | I've **reached the point** (=my situation has developed) where I just don't care anymore.*
4 **achieve an aim** [T] to succeed in doing what you were trying to do: **reach a decision/agreement/result etc.** *Attorneys were able to reach an out-of-court settlement.*
5 **length/height** [I always + adv./prep.,T not in progressive] to be big enough, long enough, or high enough to get to a particular point or level: *The flood waters reached the lower floor of the houses. | [**reach down to sth**] Her skirt reaches down to her ankles.*
6 **speak to sb** [T] to speak to someone or leave a message for them, especially by telephone; CONTACT[2]: *Have you tried reaching her at home? | You can reach us at (915) 532-7864.*
7 **be seen/heard by sb** [T] if a message, television program etc. reaches a lot of people, they hear it or see it: *The sales campaign reached a target audience of 12,000 women. | Community workers were praised for **reaching out to** poorer families (=talking and listening to them).*
8 reach for the stars to aim for something that is very difficult to achieve

---

USAGE NOTE: REACH

WORD CHOICE: reach, arrive, get to, achieve, catch
To **arrive** somewhere is to get there after traveling: *Leslie and Pat arrived at the hotel at almost the same time. | The flight is scheduled to arrive at 7:20.* **Reach** suggests more time or effort is involved: *At last we reached the base camp.* In spoken English, people usually use **get to**: *By the time we got to the airport, our flight had already left.* Note that you **get/arrive/reach etc. home** (NOT **to home**). You may **reach** a standard or level, especially through your own efforts, but **achieve** is often a better word: *I want to achieve a good level of English. | He achieved his aim in life - to write a book* (NOT *reached*). If you get to a bus, train etc. in time, you **catch** it: *You'd better hurry if you want to catch that bus.*
GRAMMAR
You **reach** a place (NOT **reach at** or **reach to** it): *He reached Tokyo at 5 a.m.* You **arrive at** a particular place or building: *When are they arriving at the airport?* You **arrive in** a country or a big city: *to arrive in LA/Tokyo/France.* Sometimes you do not need a preposition at all: *When will they get there/here/home?*

---

reach[2] *n.* **1** [singular,U] the distance that you can stretch out your arm to touch something: *a boxer with a long reach | **out of reach/beyond reach** Keep all medicines out of children's reach. | Adjust the car seat so that all the controls are **within reach**.* **2 within reach (of sth) a)** within a distance that you can easily travel: *All the main tourist attractions are **within easy reach** of the hotel.* **b)** also **in reach** easy to achieve or get with the skills, power, money etc. that you have: *The goal of saving the wetland is now **within reach**.* **3 beyond the reach/out of reach** difficult to achieve or get because you do not have enough skill, power, or money: *Houses are still priced **beyond the reach** of most middle-class families.* **4** [C] a straight part of a river between two bends

re·act /ri'ækt/ *v.* [I] **1** to behave in a particular way S W because of something that has happened or something that has been said to you: *How did Dad 3 3 react when he found out Vicky was pregnant? | [+ to]*

Residents reacted angrily to the city council's decision. | [**react by doing sth**] *Parents reacted by setting up their own neighborhood watch.* —see also OVERREACT **2** to become sick when you take a particular drug, eat a particular kind of food etc.: [+ **to**] *The patient reacted badly to penicillin.* **3** TECHNICAL if a chemical substance reacts, it changes when it is mixed with another chemical substance: [+ **with/on**] *An acid reacts with a base to form a salt.* —compare RESPOND

react against sth *phr. v.* [T] to show that you dislike someone else's rules or way of doing something by deliberately doing the opposite: *Feminists reacted against the limitations of women's traditional roles.*

re·ac·tion /riˈækʃən/ *n.*

1 to a situation/event [C,U] something that you feel or do because of what has happened to you or been said to you: *What was Jeff's reaction when you told him about the job?* | [+ **to**] *Her parents' reaction to the news was surprisingly calm.* | *The pay offer brought a **mixed reaction** from union members* (=both good and bad reactions). | *My **gut reaction** (=immediate reaction before you have time to think) to her story was disbelief!*

2 to food/drugs [singular] a bad effect, such as illness, caused by food that you have eaten or a drug that you have taken: *an allergic reaction* | [+ **to**] *Some people **have a mild reaction to** the drug.*

3 change [singular] a change in people's attitudes, behavior, fashions etc. that happens because they disapprove of what was done in the past: [+ **against**] *The attitudes of this generation are a reaction against the selfish values of the 1980s.*

4 reactions [plural] your ability to move quickly when something happens suddenly, especially something dangerous: **quick/slow reactions** *Fighter pilots need to have very quick reactions.*

5 science [C,U] **a)** a chemical change that happens when two or more chemical substances are mixed together; CHEMICAL REACTION **b)** a physical force that is the result of an equally strong physical force in the opposite direction —see also NUCLEAR REACTION

6 tired/sad [singular] a sudden feeling of weakness, tiredness, or sadness that you sometimes get after a lot of activity

7 against change [U] FORMAL strong and unreasonable opposition to all social and political changes: *The revolution was defeated by the forces of reaction.* —see also CHAIN REACTION

re·ac·tion·ar·y /riˈækʃəˌnɛri/ *adj.* DISAPPROVING strongly opposed to social or political change in a way that is unreasonable: *Reactionary politicians voted against the proposal.* —**reactionary** *n.* [C]

re·ac·ti·vate /riˈæktəˌveɪt/ *v.* [T] to make something start working again, or to start a process again

re·ac·tive /riˈæktɪv/ *adj.* **1** reacting to events or situations rather than starting something new: *Many businesses follow a reactive strategy rather than initiating new products.* **2** TECHNICAL a reactive chemical substance changes when it is mixed with another chemical substance

re·ac·tor /riˈæktɚ/ *n.* [C] a NUCLEAR REACTOR

read out

The professor read out a poem to the class.

read[1] /rid/ *v. past tense and past participle* **read** /rɛd/
1 words/books [I,T] to look at written words and understand what they mean: *My parents taught me how to read.* | *Jean can't read a word without her*

glasses on. | *Have you read Stephen King's new book yet?* | *Always read the label before you wash your clothes.* | *I can read Spanish but I can't speak it very well.*

2 information [I,T not in progressive] to find out information from books, newspapers etc.: *Don't believe everything you read in the papers.* | [+ **about/of**] *Did you read about the big snow storm in Canada?* | *I read of his death in the local newspaper.* | [+ **that**] *Somewhere I read that garlic is good for your heart.*

3 read and speak [I,T] to say the written words in a book, newspaper etc. so that people can hear them: [**read sb sth**] *Daddy, will you read me a story?* | [**read to sb**] *Mom always read to us at bedtime.* | **read (sth) aloud/out loud** *He looked at the letter and began to read it aloud.*

4 music/maps/signs etc. [T] to look at signs, pictures etc. and understand what they mean: *I learned to read music when I was taking piano lessons.* | *map reading*

5 computer [T] TECHNICAL if the DISK DRIVE of a computer reads information from a DISK, it takes the information and puts it into the computer's memory

6 understand sth in a particular way [T] to choose to understand a situation, remark, etc. in one of several possible ways: [**read sth as sth**] *People read his silence as an admission of guilt.* | *Low test scores should not be read as a sign of failure.*

7 have a particular sign/meaning [I not in progressive] if words read in a particular way, they have a particular form, or produce a particular effect when you read them: *The headline read: "Firefighters Save Girl From Flames."* | *Johnson's travel guide **reads well** (=is easy to read) and is very informative.*

8 measuring [T] **a)** to look at the number or amount shown on a measuring instrument such as a gas or electricity meter: *Soon utility companies may be able to read your meter by computer.* **b)** if a measuring instrument reads a particular number, it shows that number: *The thermometer read 46 degrees.*

9 read between the lines to guess someone's real feelings from something they say or write: *While Anderson did not say directly that changes needed to be made, it was easy to read between the lines.*

10 read sb's mind/thoughts to guess what someone else is thinking: *Don't expect your spouse to be able to read your mind.*

11 read sb like a book to know someone so well that you immediately know what they are thinking or feeling

12 well-read having read a lot of books and gained a lot of knowledge: *a well-read young man*

13 widely read/little read etc. read by a lot of people, few people etc.: *the nation's most widely read newspaper*

14 read sth as sth also for sth read sth used to tell someone to replace a wrong number or word with the correct one: *Please read "5.2% interest" as "5.5% interest".* | *For "November" (=instead of November) on line 6, read "September."*

15 do you read me? SPOKEN used to ask someone whether they fully understand what you are saying: *I do not want this to happen again! Do you read me?*

16 read sb's lips to understand what someone is saying by watching the way their lips move —see also LIP-READ

17 read sb's palm to look carefully at someone's hand, in order to find out about their future

18 take it as read to accept a report, statement etc. as correct and complete without reading or hearing it: *We'll have to take the secretary's report as read.* —see also READING, **read (sb) the riot act** (RIOT[1] (5))

read for sth *phr. v.* [T] to perform the part of a particular character from a play, as a test of your ability to act in the play; AUDITION[2]

read sth **into** sth *phr. v.* [T] to think that a situation, action etc. has a meaning or importance that it does not really have: *It was only a casual remark. I think you're reading too much into it.*

read sth ↔ **out** *phr. v.* [T] to say the words that are written in a message, list etc. so that people can hear: *He opened the envelope and read out the name of the winner.*

read sth ↔ **through/over** *phr. v.* [T] to read something carefully from beginning to end in order to check details or find mistakes: *Read the contract over carefully before you sign it.*

read up on sth *phr. v.* [T] INFORMAL to read a lot about something because you will need to know about it: *I'll have to read up on the tax laws before the meeting tomorrow.*

read² *n.* [singular] **a good read** something that you enjoy reading: *It's not great literature, but it's a good read.*

read·a·ble /'ridəbəl/ *adj.* **1** interesting or enjoyable to read, and easy to understand: *Toobin's book is a dense yet readable account of the O.J. Simpson trial.* **2** writing or print that is readable is clear and easy to read —**readability** /ˌridə'bɪləti/ *n.* [U] —opposite UNREADABLE —see also MACHINE READABLE

read·er /'ridə/ *n.* [C] **1** someone who reads a particular book, newspaper etc.: *At this point in the novel, the reader still does not know the hero's true identity.* **2** someone who reads a lot, or reads in a particular way: **a fast/slow/good/careful etc. reader** *I'm a really slow reader.* **3** an easy book to help children learn to read, to help people learn a foreign language etc. —see also MIND READER

read·er·ship /'ridə,ʃɪp/ *n.* [C,U] the people who read a particular newspaper or magazine: *The magazine has a readership of 60,000.*

read·i·ly /'rɛdl-i/ *adv.* **1** quickly and easily: *Fresh cilantro is readily available in most supermarkets.* **2** quickly, willingly, and without complaining: *McGrath readily agreed to go.*

read·i·ness /'rɛdinɪs/ *n.* **1** [singular,U] willingness to do something: **[readiness to do sth]** *Both sides expressed their readiness to begin peace talks.* **2** [U] a state of being prepared and ready for what is going to happen: *Troops were kept **in readiness for** a possible military attack.*

read·ing /'ridɪŋ/ *n.*
1 activity/skill [U] the activity of looking at and understanding written words: *His hobbies include reading and hiking.* | *The children are separated into groups for reading.* | **reading material** (=books, articles etc. that you read)
2 books [U] the books, articles etc. that you read: *Handouts and additional reading will be provided in class.* | **light reading** (=books that are enjoyable and easy to read)
3 understanding [C] your opinion of what a particular statement, situation, piece of music etc. means; INTERPRETATION: *What's George's reading of the situation at work?* | *an energetic reading of Beethoven's "Pastoral Symphony"*
4 to a group [C] **a)** an occasion when a piece of literature is read to a group of people: *a poetry reading* **b)** a piece of literature or part of the Bible that is read to a group of people: *The first reading is from Corinthians I, Chapter 3.*
5 measurement [C] a number or amount shown on a measuring instrument: *Temperature readings were as cold as –2°.*
6 act of reading sth [singular] the act of reading something: *Even a casual reading of the text gives you an idea of the theme.*
7 in congress [C] one of the three occasions in the U.S. Congress when a BILL (=suggested new law) is read and discussed: *the second reading of the Industrial Relations Bill*
8 make good/interesting/boring etc. reading to be enjoyable, interesting etc. to read: *Your report made fascinating reading.*

re·ad·just /ˌriə'dʒʌst/ *v.* **1** [I] to change the way you do things because of a new situation, job, or way of life: **[+ to]** *NASA is studying ways to help astronauts readjust to life on Earth.* **2** [T] to make a small change to something or to its position: *Remember to readjust the mirrors in the car.* —**readjustment** *n.* [C,U]

read-on·ly mem·o·ry /ˌ. ˌ.. '.../ *n.* [C,U] ROM

read-out /'. ./ *n.* [C] a record of information that has been produced by a computer, shown on a SCREEN or in print: *This program gives you a read-out of all the areas where sales have increased.* —compare PRINTOUT

read·y¹ /'rɛdi/ *adj.*
1 prepared [not before noun] prepared for what you are going to do: *Wait a minute. I'm not ready yet.* | **[ready to do sth]** *Are you guys ready to go?* | **[+ for]** *I'm not ready for a serious relationship.* | *She's still **getting ready** for work.* | *The ship was **made ready** to sail.* | *"You have to be **ready for anything** if you want to win," coach Bryant explained.* | *"Got it?" "Yeah, **ready when you are**." "Okay, let's go!"* | *The building is completed and the service should be **ready to roll** (=ready to start working) in January.*
2 for immediate use [not before noun] something that is ready has been prepared and can be used, eaten etc. immediately: *Is dinner ready yet?* | *Your dry cleaning will be ready on Thursday.* | **[+ for]** *Is everything ready for the exhibition?* | *Can you **get** breakfast **ready** for the kids?* | *I've got to have this report **ready** by Monday morning.*
3 be ready for a vacation/drink/change etc. SPOKEN to need or want a vacation etc. as soon as possible: *You must be ready for a drink after all that hard work.*
4 be ready to cry/drop etc. INFORMAL to be so upset or tired that you feel you will cry, fall down etc.: *She looked like she was ready to throw up.*
5 willing willing and quick to do or give something: **[+ with]** *Jim's father is always ready with advice.* | **[ready to do sth]** *Management was all too ready to declare the project a failure.* | *There are hundreds of people who are **ready, willing, and able** to work, but there aren't any jobs here.*
6 quick [only before noun] quick or without delay: *a ready answer* | *On the Internet, you have ready access to huge amounts of information.*
7 ready money/cash money that can be spent at once in coins or paper money: *He was only willing to sell it for ready cash.*
8 (get) ready, (get) set, go! SPOKEN used to tell people to start a race —see also READILY, READINESS, **rough and ready** (ROUGH¹ (13))

read·y² *n.* FORMAL **at the ready** available to be used immediately: *The crowd stood around, cameras at the ready.*

read·y³ *v.* **readies, readied, readying** [T] FORMAL to make something ready

read·y-made /ˌ.. '.◂/ *adj.* [only before noun]
1 already prepared, and ready to be used immediately: *ready-made curtains* **2** ready-made opinions or ideas have been copied from someone else **3** READY-TO-WEAR

read·y-to-wear /ˌ... '.◂/ *adj.* OLD-FASHIONED ready-to-wear clothes are made in standard sizes, not made specially to fit one person

re·af·firm /ˌriə'fəm/ *v.* [T] to formally state an intention, belief etc. again, especially as an answer to a question or doubt: **[+ that]** *The statement reaffirmed that the government would never make concessions to terrorists.* —**reaffirmation** /ˌriæfə'meɪʃən/ *n.* [C,U]

Rea·gan, Ron·ald /'reɪgən/, /'rɑnəld/ (1911–) the 40th President of the U.S.

re·a·gent /ri'eɪdʒənt/ *n.* [C] TECHNICAL a substance that shows that another substance in a compound exists, by causing a chemical REACTION (6)

real¹ /ril/ *adj.*
1 not imaginary actually existing and not just imagined: *All of the characters are based on real people.* | **very real danger/possibility/risk etc.** *There is a very real possibility that the medication won't work.* | *She's much prettier in real life than she is in this picture.* | *In the **real world**, (=in actual situations where people have to deal with practical problems) few of these students will make it to college.*
2 not artificial something that is real is actually what it seems to be and not false, artificial, or pretended: *Marilyn Monroe's real name was Norma Jean*

Baker. | real leather | Jack isn't their real father. | I scored much better on the practice test than I did on **the real thing**. | This is genuine malt whiskey – **the real McCoy** (=used to emphasize that something really is what it seems).

3 used to emphasize what you are saying: *The house is a real mess.* | *He sounds like a real jerk.* | *The noise is becoming a real problem.*

4 **true** actual and true, not what people think or say: *So what's the real reason you were late?*

5 **right qualities** [only before noun] having all the right qualities that you expect a particular kind of thing or person to have: *He's never had a real job.*

6 **no real chance/hope/reason etc.** if there is no real chance etc., there is almost no chance: *There's no real reason why the plane should have crashed.*

7 **most important** the real questions, problems etc. are the most important ones: *The real issue is how can we help prevent heart disease?*

8 **real income/costs/value etc.** income etc. that is calculated after including in the calculation the general decrease in the value of money: *a 2% annual growth in real income* | **In real terms** (=calculated in this way), *the value of their wages has fallen*

SPOKEN PHRASES

9 **real live...** an expression used in order to emphasize that something surprising has been seen or exists, used especially by or to children: *Take the kids to a children's farm, with real live farm animals.*

10 **for real** seriously, not pretending: *He quit smoking? For real?*

11 said when something is the way you think it should be: *Now that's real coffee!*

12 **get real!** used to tell someone that they are being very silly or unreasonable: *'Get real! He'll never make the team."*

13 **keep it real** used to tell someone to behave in an honest way and not pretend to be different from how they really are

14 **are you for real?** used when you are very surprised by or disapprove of what someone has done or said

---

real² *adv.* SPOKEN very: *Carla's little boy is real cute.* | *It was real nice to see you again.*

real³ *n.* [C] the standard unit of money used in Brazil

real es·tate /'. .,./ *n.* [U] **1** property in the form of land or houses **2** the business of selling houses or land

real estate a·gent /'. .. ,../ *n.* [C] someone whose job is to sell houses or land for other people

re·a·lign /ˌriəˈlaɪn/ *v.* **1** [T] to arrange something differently in relation to something else: *You'll have to realign your text columns if you change the typeface.* **2** to change the aims and relationships that a political party or other organization has: *Teams are now realigned according to players' ages.*

re·a·lign·ment /ˌriəˈlaɪnmənt/ *n.* [C,U] **1** a change in the way two or more things are organized, so that they have a different relationship to each other: [+ of] *The senator called for a realignment of the political parties.* **2** the process of arranging parts of something so that they return to their correct positions in relation to each other: *the realignment of broken bones*

re·al·ism /ˈriəˌlɪzəm/ *n.* [U] **1** the ability to accept and deal with situations in a practical way, without being influenced by feelings or false ideas **2** also **Realism** the style of art and literature in which everything is shown or described as it really is in life —compare CLASSICISM, IDEALISM, ROMANTICISM —**realist** *n.* [C]

re·al·is·tic /ˌriəˈlɪstɪk/ *adj.* **1** judging and dealing with situations in a practical way, according to what is actually possible: *We want to play in the championships, but right now that's not very realistic.* | *realistic goals* | [+ about] *Parents need to be realistic about their child's attention span* | **Be realistic**, *Dennis. You know we can't afford it.* —opposite UNREALISTIC **2** pictures, models, plays etc. that are realistic show things as they are in real life: *The game's 3-D graphics are amazingly realistic.* | *a realistic television drama*

re·al·is·ti·cally /ˌriəˈlɪstɪkli/ *adv.* **1** in a practical way and according to what is actually possible: *You can realistically expect to pay between $25 and $50 a ticket.* | [sentence adverb] *Realistically, there was not much we could do to help.* **2** in a way that shows or describes things as they are in real life: *Proulx's novel realistically portrays life in early 20th century America.*

re·al·i·ty /riˈæləti/ *n.* **1** [U] things that actually happen or are true, not things that are imagined or thought about: *Small children often can't tell the difference between fantasy and reality.* | *Delane turned to drugs as an escape from reality.* **2 in reality** used to say something is different from what people think: *Henry always seems so self-confident, but in reality he's extremely shy.* **3 become a reality** also **make sth a reality** to actually happen: *Frank's dream of opening a restaurant became a reality in 1987.* **4** the **reality/realities of sth** what actually happens in a situation, rather than what you think might happen: *They were unprepared for the reality of city life.* | the **harsh realities of prison** **5** **the reality is that** used to say that the truth about a situation is very different from what people say: *They keep saying we'll get the money, but the reality is that there's none left.* **6 reality check** INFORMAL an occasion when you consider the facts of a situation, as opposed to what you would like or what you have imagined: *It's time for a reality check. The Bears aren't as good a team as you think.*

re·al·iz·a·ble /ˌriəˈlaɪzəbəl/ *adj.* **1** possible to achieve: *realizable goals* **2** in a form that can be changed into money: *realizable value*

re·al·i·za·tion /ˌriələˈzeɪʃən/ *n.* [singular,U] **1** the act of understanding something that you had not noticed before: [+ that] *There is a realization that more work needs to be done.* | *The city council has* **come to the realization that** *transportation problems are costing the city money.* **2** the act of achieving what you had planned, hoped, or aimed for: [+ of] *Getting this role in a major film was a realization of her childhood dreams.* **3** FORMAL [+ of] the act of changing something into money by selling it

re·al·ize /ˈriəˌlaɪz/ *v.* [T not usually in progressive] **1** **know sth's importance** to know and understand the importance of something: [realize (that)] *You realize that I don't have a choice.* | [realize who/what/how etc.] *I wonder if the kids who stole that stuff realize its value.* | [realize sth] *Teenagers don't realize the danger of unprotected sex.* **2** **know sth new** to start to know something that you had not noticed before: [realize (that)] *Margaret suddenly realized he was crying.* | *We didn't realize that it would take so long to get here.* | [realize who/what/how etc.] *I didn't realize how chilly it is.* | [realize sth] *He'd hurt his arm, but didn't realize it until later.* **3** **realize an ambition/hope/goal etc.** FORMAL to achieve something that you were hoping to achieve: *Gates thought he would probably never realize his career ambition.* **4** **sb's worst fears were realized** used to say that the thing that you were afraid of actually happened: *My worst fears were realized when I saw the test questions.* **5** **money** FORMAL **a)** to obtain an amount of money, especially by selling something: *The initial campaign has realized $5000 in cash and pledges.* | *We realized a profit on the house.* **b)** to change something that you own into money, especially by selling it: *We were obliged to realize most of our assets.*

real·ly /ˈrili/ *adv.* **1** a word meaning "very" or "very much," used to emphasize something: *Tom's a really nice guy.* | *His letter really irritated her.* | *My kids would really like this.* | *It doesn't really matter, does it?* | *I really, really miss living near the woods.* **2** used when you are saying what is actually the truth of a situation, rather than what people might wrongly think: *What really happened?* | *He really* *doesn't trust me, does he? | That doll might really be valuable.*

SPOKEN PHRASES

3 used to emphasize something you are saying: *I really don't mind. | No, really, I'm fine. Don't worry.* **4 really? a)** used to show that you are surprised by what someone has said: *"He'll be ninety-two this year." "Really?"* **b)** used in conversation to show that you are listening to or interested in what the other person is saying: *"She came to the baby shower we gave for Beth." "Oh, really?"* **5 not really** used to say "no," especially when something is not completely true: *"Are you hungry yet?" "Not really."* **6 (yeah) really** used to express agreement: *"Jeez, Glen can be such a jerk sometimes." "Yeah, really."* **7** used to express disapproval: *Really, Matt, did you have to make such a mess?* **8 really, truly** also **really and truly** used to emphasize a statement or opinion: *He was really, truly a devoted family man.*

USAGE NOTE: REALLY

Really is often used with an adjective or adverb to mean "very": *I'm really fed up with this job. | Mike did really well on his physics test.* **Real** is also used to mean "very," but only in informal speech, and is considered by some people to be grammatically incorrect: *That's a real nice car.*
GRAMMAR
Really meaning "very" must go immediately before the adjective it strengthens: *He's a really nice man (=a very nice man). | Kim's really excited about going to Paris.* **Really** in other positions usually emphasizes that what you are saying is true, even though it might not seem to be true: *Really, I'm fine (=I feel good, even though you might not think so). | Deep down, Shane really is a nice guy.* **Really** is usually used before a verb but not immediately after it (except after the verb **to be**): *It's really cold in here. | Dad never really did like traveling.*
SPELLING
Remember there are two l's in **really**.

---

realm /rɛlm/ *n.* [C] **1** a general area of knowledge, interest, or thought: *the spiritual realm | [+ of] new discoveries in the realm of science* **2 within the realm(s) of possibility** possible: *Such a thing is not within the realms of possibility.* **3** LITERARY a country ruled over by a king or queen

re·al·po·li·tik /reɪˈælpɑlɪˌtik/ *n.* [U] politics based on practical situations and needs rather than on principles or ideas

real prop·er·ty /ˌ. '.../ *n.* [U] LAW: see REAL ESTATE (1)

real-time /'. ./ *adj.* [only before noun] TECHNICAL a real-time computer system deals with information as fast as it receives it —**real time** *n.* [U] *Airline booking systems need to work in real time.*

Real·tor, realtor /'riltɚ/ *n.* [C] TRADEMARK a REAL ESTATE AGENT who belongs to the National Association of Realtors

real·ty /'rilti/ *n.* [U] TECHNICAL: see REAL ESTATE

ream¹ /rim/ *n.* **1 reams** [plural] INFORMAL a large amount of writing on paper: *[+ of] Lawyers examined reams of documents.* **2** [C] TECHNICAL a standard amount of paper, consisting of 500 pieces of paper

ream² *v.* [T] **1** to treat someone badly, especially by cheating **2** TECHNICAL to make a hole larger

re·an·i·mate /ri'ænəˌmeɪt/ *v.* [T] FORMAL to give someone or something new strength or the energy to start again

reap /rip/ *v.* [I,T] **1** to get something as a result of what you have done: *Don't let others reap the benefits of your research. | In five years' time you can reap the profits of your investment.* **2** to cut and gather a crop of grain **3 you reap what you sow** SPOKEN used to say that if you do bad things, bad things will happen to you, and if you do good things, good things will happen to you —compare HARVEST²

---

reap·er /'ripɚ/ *n.* [C] a machine or person that cuts and gathers a crop of grain —see also GRIM REAPER

re·ap·pear /ˌriə'pɪr/ *v.* [I] to appear again after not being seen for some time: *In March, his cancer reappeared.* —**reappearance** *n.* [C,U]

re·ap·por·tion·ment /ˌriə'pɔrʃənmənt/ *n.* [U] TECHNICAL the process of changing the numbers of members of the House of Representatives that each state has, based on changes in the states' populations —**reapportion** *v.* [T]

re·ap·praise /ˌriə'preɪz/ *v.* [T] to examine something again in order to consider whether you should change your opinion of it: *Many analysts have reappraised their economic forecasts.* —**reappraisal** *n.* [C,U]

rear¹ /rɪr/ *n.* **1 the rear** the back part of an object, vehicle, or building, or a position at the back of an object or area: *The engine is in the rear. | [+ of] There are more seats at the rear of the theater.* —compare FRONT¹ (1) **2** [C] also **rear end** INFORMAL the part of your body that you sit on; BUTTOCKS: *Get up off your rear end!* **3 be bringing up the rear** to be at the back of a line of people or in a race: *Bringing up the rear is the smallest yacht in the race.* **4 get your rear in gear** SPOKEN, HUMOROUS used to tell someone to start doing something, or to do something faster

rear² *adj.* [only before noun] at or near the back of something: *the rear door of the car | Go around back and knock at the rear entrance.*

rear³ *v.* **1** [T] to take care of a person or animal until they are fully grown: *She's reared a large family. | cattle rearing* —see Usage Note at RAISE¹ **2** [I] also **rear up** if an animal rears, it rises upright on its back legs: *The horse reared and threw me off.* —compare BUCK² (1) **3 be reared on sth** to be given a particular kind of food, books, entertainment etc. regularly while you are a child: *We were reared on junk food and B-movies.* **4 sth rears its ugly head** INFORMAL if a problem or difficult situation rears its ugly head, it appears and is impossible to ignore: *Scandal in the White House rears its ugly head again.*

rear ad·mi·ral, Rear Admiral /ˌ. '...ˌ/ *n.* [C] a high rank in the navy, or someone who has this rank

rear·guard /'rɪrgɑrd/ *n.* **fight a rearguard action a)** to make a determined effort to prevent a change that you think is bad, although it seems too late to stop it: *A rearguard action is being fought against the sale of the land for business development.* **b)** if an army fights a rearguard action, it defends itself at the back against an enemy that is chasing it

re·arm, re-arm /ri'ɑrm/ *v.* [I,T] to obtain weapons again or provide someone else with new weapons: *Both sides' armies were rearming heavily for combat.* —**rearmament** *n.* [U]

rear·most /'rɪrmoust/ *adj.* [only before noun] furthest back; last: *Exits are also located in the rearmost section of the plane.*

re·ar·range /ˌriə'reɪndʒ/ *v.* [T] **1** to change the position or order of things: *We'll have to rearrange all the furniture once they deliver the new sofa.* **2** to change the time of a meeting or planned event: *Can we rearrange your appointment for next Thursday?* —**rearrangement** *n.* [C,U]

rear·view mir·ror /ˌrɪrvyu 'mɪrɚ/ *n.* [C] a mirror in a vehicle that lets the driver see the area behind them —see picture on page 427

rear·ward /'rɪrwɚd/ *adj.* in or toward the back of something —**rearward** also **rearwards** *adv.*

rea·son¹ /'rizən/ *n.*
1 cause [C] the cause or fact that explains why something has happened or why someone has done something: *The real reason we weren't getting along wasn't so simple. | [+ for] Time pressure is a major reason for job-related stress. | [reason (that)] The reason that the administration is unwilling to act is because Turkey is an ally. | [reason why] One reason why students should study a variety of subjects is to become knowledgeable citizens. | McNamara left without giving any reason. | for personal/health etc. reasons She resigned for health reasons. | The main tower has been closed for reasons of safety. | Geiger*

was found not guilty *by reason of* insanity. | *They've decided to change all our job titles, **for some reason*** (=for a reason you do not know or cannot understand). | *"Why did you tell him?" "Oh, I **had my reasons**."* (=had a secret reason for doing it) | ***For reasons best known to** herself,* (=for reasons other people do not understand) *she's sold the house and left the country.* —see Usage Note at EXCUSE²

2 good or fair reason [U] a fact that makes it right or fair for someone to do something: [**reason to do sth**] *Porter **has reason to** be cautious.* | *There is **no reason to** panic.* | *Under the circumstances we **had every reason to** be suspicious* (=had very good reasons). | *There is **no reason to** believe he will not recover.* | *Natalie was alarmed by the news, and **with good reason**.*

3 all the more reason to do sth SPOKEN used to say that what has just been mentioned is an additional reason for doing what you have suggested: *The division has a lot of good teams, so that's all the more reason to be proud of winning.*

4 good judgment [U] sensible judgment and understanding: *In times of war, reason can give way to racism.* | *Sonnenberg shrugged, as if to say that his client wouldn't **listen to reason*** (=would not be persuaded by sensible advice). | *They tried to make her **see reason*** (=accept advice and make a sensible decision).

5 within reason within sensible limits: *Do what you can, within reason, to prevent accidents.*

6 go/be beyond (all) reason to be more than is acceptable or reasonable: *Their demands go beyond all reason.*

7 ability to think [U] the ability to think, understand, and form judgments that are based on facts: *Political negotiation always involves a balance between reason and force.* | *Maya feared that she was losing her reason* (=becoming mentally ill).

8 no reason SPOKEN used when someone asks you why you are doing something and you do not want to tell them: *"Why do you want to go that way?" "Oh, no reason."* —see also **rhyme or reason** (RHYME¹ (4)), **it stands to reason** (STAND¹ (37))

USAGE NOTE: REASON

WORD CHOICE: cause, reason, purpose
A **cause** is anything that produces a result, often not a person: *the causes of inflation* | *What was the cause of the accident?* A **reason** explains something, often after it has happened or been done: *There was no reason for the attack.* | *There are several reasons why the plan won't work.* | *Give me one good reason.* A **purpose** is what you hope to achieve by something you do, and is intentional: *Their purpose is to attract attention to environmental issues.*

GRAMMAR
Reason is often followed by **for, that,** or **why**: *What's the reason for all this noise?* (NOT "the reason **of**" or "**to**") | *the reason that/why he left* (NOT "the reason because/how he left..."). It is also possible to leave out **that**: *the reason he left.* The nature of a **reason** is usually described in a *that* clause: *The reason for the party was that it was Sue's birthday.* In spoken English you may also hear *because* used, although this is considered incorrect by many speakers: *The reason for the party is because it's Sue's birthday.* **Purpose** is often followed by **of** or **in**: *The purpose of the trip/of my coming is to see the President* (NOT "The purpose why I'm coming..."). | *My purpose in coming is to see the President* (NOT "of/for coming..."). People usually say *For this reason/purpose...* (NOT "from/because of this reason...", "in/on this purpose" or "for this cause").

---

s w
2 2

reason² v. **1** [T] to form a particular judgment about a situation after carefully considering the facts: [**reason (that)**] *They reasoned that forcing schools to compete for kids would force them to improve their classes.* **2** [I] to think and make judgments: *the ability to reason*

reason sth **out** *phr. v.* [T] to find an explanation or solution to a problem, by thinking of all the possibilities

reason with sb *phr. v.* [T] to talk to someone in

order to try to persuade them to be more sensible: *They tried to reason with him and persuade him to come home.*

rea·son·a·ble /ˈriznəbəl, -zən-/ *adj.* **1** fair and sensible: *Cole accepted that Moe's views were reasonable and valid.* | *A reasonable request* | *Mason is a reasonable man.* | *It is reasonable to suppose that prices will come down soon.* —opposite UNREASONABLE **2** fairly good, but not especially good: *The Dolphins have a reasonable chance of winning the Super Bowl.* **3** a reasonable amount is not too much or too many: *Teachers need a reasonable amount of time to prepare course work.* **4** prices that are reasonable seem fair because they are not too high: *good quality furniture at reasonable prices* **5 beyond a reasonable doubt** LAW if something is proved beyond a reasonable doubt, it is shown to be almost certainly true —**reasonableness** *n.* [U]

s w
3 3

rea·son·a·bly /ˈriznəbli/ *adv.* **1** [+ adj./adv.] to a satisfactory degree, although not completely: *Dad's in reasonably good shape for a 68-year-old.* | *a reasonably priced* (=not too expensive) *restaurant* **2** in a way that is right or fair: *How long before we can reasonably expect to see any improvement?* **3** in a sensible and reasonable way: *It was the high-school students who reasonably and responsibly found a solution to the problem.*

rea·soned /ˈriznd/ *adj.* [only before noun] based on careful thought, and therefore sensible: *a well-reasoned response*

rea·son·ing /ˈriznɪŋ/ *n.* [U] the process of thinking carefully about something in order to make a judgment: *logical reasoning* | *What is **the reasoning behind** this proposal?*

re·as·sur·ance /ˌriəˈʃʊrəns/ *n.* **1** [U] help or advice that makes you feel less worried or frightened about a problem: *Parents turned to **give reassurance to** their children.* **2** [C] a remark or statement that makes someone feel less worried about something: [+ **that**] *Carter received reassurances that he would not lose his job.*

re·as·sure /ˌriəˈʃʊr/ *v.* [T] to make someone feel calmer and less worried or frightened about a problem or situation: *Officials reassured callers who were worried about the fires.* | [**reassure sb (that)**] *They apologized and reassured us that the matter would be dealt with immediately.* —see Usage Note at INSURE

re·as·sur·ing /ˌriəˈʃʊrɪŋ/ *adj.* making you feel less worried or frightened: *Routines are reassuring to a child.* —**reassuringly** *adv.*

re·bate /ˈribeɪt/ *n.* [C] an amount of money that is paid back to you when you have paid too much tax, rent etc.: *In the end I managed to claim a tax rebate.*

reb·el¹ /ˈrɛbəl/ *n.* [C] **1** someone who opposes or fights against people in authority: *Anti-government rebels have seized the radio station.* | *rebel soldiers* **2** someone who refuses to do things in the normal way, or in the way that other people want them to: *a teenage rebel*

re·bel² /rɪˈbɛl/ *v.* **rebelled, rebelling** [I] to oppose or fight against someone in a position of authority: [+ **against**] *The novel tells the story of a teenager who rebels against his father.* | *In Croatia, Serbs rebelled against the republic's authorities.*

re·bel·lion /rɪˈbɛlyən/ *n.* [C,U] **1** an organized attempt to change the government, or other authority, using violence: *Threats of an armed rebellion caused tightened security measures across the country.* | [+ **against**] *a rebellion against the military regime* | *put down/crush a rebellion* (=use violence to stop it) **2** opposition to someone in authority or to normal or usual ways of doing things: *Government officials feared a rebellion by right-wing members of the party.* | [+ **against**] *a clear rebellion against parental control* | *Evans' pictures reflect his rebellion against the styles of other popular photographers.* —compare REVOLUTION

re·bel·lious /rɪˈbɛlyəs/ *adj.* **1** deliberately disobeying someone in authority: *the rebellious daughter of* a *military man* | *rebellious behavior* **2** fighting against the government of your country: *Aristide, the elected president, was ousted by rebellious soldiers.* —**rebelliously** *adv.* —**rebelliousness** *n.* [U]

re·birth /riˈbɜθ, ˈribɜθ/ *n.* [singular] FORMAL a change by which an important idea, feeling, or organization becomes active again: *The 1980s saw a rebirth of conservative thinking.* | *spiritual rebirth*

re·boot /riˈbut/ *v.* [I,T] if you reboot a computer, or if it reboots, it starts up again after it has stopped working: *Try rebooting the machine and see what happens.*

re·born /riˈbɔrn/ *adj.* [not before noun] LITERARY **1** having become active again after being inactive: *Our hopes of success were reborn when we received thousands of letters of support.* **2 be reborn** to be born again, especially according to some religions, ancient stories etc.

re·bound¹ /ˈribaʊnd, rɪˈbaʊnd/ *v.* **1** [I] if a ball or other moving object rebounds, it moves quickly back through the air, after hitting something: [+ **off**] *The ball rebounded off the wall and I caught it.* **2** [I] if prices, values etc. rebound, they increase again after decreasing: *Share prices rebounded today after last week's losses.* **3** [I,T] to catch a basketball after a player has tried but failed to get a point

rebound on/upon sb *phr. v.* [T not in passive] if a harmful action rebounds on someone, it has a bad effect on the person who did it

re·bound² /ˈribaʊnd/ *n.* **1 a) on the rebound** someone who is on the rebound is upset or confused because a romantic relationship they had has ended: *We met when I was on the rebound from a very messy affair.* **b)** in basketball, a ball that is on the rebound has been caught after someone else has failed to get a point: *Anderson scored the sixth goal on the rebound.* **c)** a ball that is on the rebound is moving back through the air after hitting something **d)** something that is on the rebound is starting to increase or improve again: *John Travolta's acting career was on the rebound with "Look Who's Talking."* **2** [C] TECHNICAL an act of catching a BASKETBALL after a player has tried but failed to get a point

re·buff /rɪˈbʌf/ *n.* [C] FORMAL an unkind or unfriendly answer to a friendly suggestion or offer of help: *Despite several rebuffs, Farley refused to leave Laura alone.* —**rebuff** *v.* [T]

re·build /riˈbɪld/ *v. past tense and past participle* **rebuilt** /-ˈbɪlt/ [T] **1** to build something again, after it has been damaged or destroyed: *Much of the city had to be rebuilt after the 1906 earthquake.* **2** to make something strong and successful again: *The first priority is to rebuild the area's manufacturing industry.*

re·buke /rɪˈbyuk/ *v.* [T] FORMAL to speak to someone severely about something they have done wrong: [**rebuke sb for doing sth**] *Members of the jury were sharply rebuked for speaking with the press.* —**rebuke** *n.* [C,U]

re·bus /ˈribəs/ *n.* [C usually singular] a set of pictures in which the names of the objects in the pictures are similar to a word or phrase when they are said out loud. For example, a picture of an eye would represent the word "I."

re·but /rɪˈbʌt/ *v.* **rebutted, rebutting** [T] FORMAL to prove that a statement or a charge made against you is false; REFUTE —**rebuttal** *n.* [C]

re·cal·ci·trant /rɪˈkælsətrənt/ *adj.* FORMAL refusing to do what you are told to do, even after you have been punished: *recalcitrant children* —**recalcitrantly** *adv.* —**recalcitrance** *n.* [U]

sᴡ **re·call¹** /rɪˈkɔl/ *v.* [T]
₂
₃ **1** remember sth [not in progressive] to deliberately remember a particular fact, event, or situation from the past, especially in order to tell someone about it: [**recall that**] *You may recall that only three U.S. athletes won gold medals.* | [**recall doing sth**] *I don't recall ever meeting her.* | [**recall what/how/where etc.**] *Mrs. Adkins cannot recall what happened*

the night she was attacked. | **As I recall** (=used when you are telling someone what you remember about something), *it was particularly hot that summer.*
2 product if a company recalls one of its products, it asks you to return it because there may be something wrong with it: *Over 10,000 of the faulty irons had to be recalled from store shelves.*
3 person to officially tell someone to come back from a place where they have been sent: [+ **from**] *The Ambassador was recalled from Washington.*
4 on a computer to bring information back onto the screen of a computer
5 be similar to FORMAL if something recalls something else, it makes you think of it because it is very similar: *a style of film-making that recalls Alfred Hitchcock*
6 politics to vote in order to decide whether a politician should be removed from their political position —**recallable** *adj.*

re·call² /ˈrikɔl, rɪˈkɔl/ *n.* **1** [U] the ability to remember something that you have learned or experienced: *Twenty years later, Brady had total recall* (=the ability to remember everything) *of the night his father was killed.* **2** [singular,U] a vote to decide whether to remove an officer from their political position, or the act of being removed from a political position: [+ **of**] *the recall of four city council officials* **3** a command in which a company tells people to return a product they bought because there is something wrong with it **4** a command telling someone to return from a place where they have been officially sent: *Families were overjoyed to hear about the recall of Allied seamen to their own countries.* **5 beyond recall** someone or something that is beyond recall is unable to be changed back to the way they or it used to be: *In Russia, efforts at political change are linked beyond recall with the problem of supplying food.*

re·cant /rɪˈkænt/ *v.* [I,T] FORMAL to say publicly that you no longer have a political or religious belief that you had before: *Galileo was forced to recant his belief in the Copernican theory.* —**recantation** /ˌrikænˈteɪʃən/ *n.* [C,U]

re·cap /ˈrikæp, riˈkæp/ *v.* **recapped, recapping** [I,T] to repeat the main points of something that has just been said; short for RECAPITULATE: *Let me just recap what's been said so far.* —**recap** /ˈrikæp/ *n.* [C]

re·cap·i·tal·ize /riˈkæpɪt̮l̩ˌaɪz/ *v.* [T] to INVEST more money into a company or bank, so that it can operate correctly: *The government fund will be used to recapitalize two financially troubled banks.* —**recapitalization** /riˌkæpɪt̮l̩əˈzeɪʃən/ *n.* [U]

re·ca·pit·u·late /ˌrikəˈpɪtʃəˌleɪt/ *v.* [I,T] FORMAL to repeat the main points of something that has just been said —**recapitulation** /ˌrikəpɪtʃəˈleɪʃən/ *n.* [C,U]

re·cap·ture /riˈkæptʃɚ/ *v.* [T] **1** to make someone experience or feel something again: *His book recaptures the excitement of life in the Old West.* **2** to catch a prisoner or animal that has escaped: *Nine of the fugitives were later recaptured.* **3** to take control of a piece of land again by fighting for it —**recapture** *n.* [U]

re·cast /riˈkæst/ *v. past tense and past participle* **recast** [T] **1** to give something a new shape or a new form of organization: *Brennan has worked diligently to recast the company's image.* **2** to give parts in a play or movie to different actors —**recasting** *n.* [C,U]

recd. the written abbreviation of "received"

re·cede /rɪˈsid/ *v.* [I] **1** if something you can see or hear recedes, it gets further and further away until it disappears: *She walked away, her footsteps receding down the hall.* | [+ **into/from**] *The two figures receded into the mist.* **2** if a memory, feeling, or possibility recedes, it gradually goes away: *As the threat of attack receded, village life returned to normal.* | [+ **into/from**] *The postwar division of Europe is receding into the past.* **3** if water recedes, it moves back from an area that it was covering: *Flood waters finally began to recede in November.* **4** if your hair recedes, you gradually lose the hair at the front of your head: *He has a fuzzy beard and a receding hairline.* **5 receding chin** a chin that slopes backward

re·ceipt /rɪˈsit/ n. **1** [C] a piece of paper that shows you have received money, goods, or services: *Keep your credit card receipts until your statement arrives.* | *Purchases may be returned if you show your receipt.* **2** [U] FORMAL the act or fact of receiving something: [+ of] *Please respond within 10 days of receipt of this letter.* | *Payment is due upon receipt of merchandise* (=when the goods are received). **3 receipts** [plural] the money that a business, bank, or government receives: *Tax receipts were $123 million lower than expected.*

re·ceiv·a·ble /rɪˈsivəbəl/ adj. needing or waiting to be paid: *Lenora is responsible for the company's accounts receivable* (=sales that have been made but not yet paid for).

re·ceiv·a·bles /rɪˈsivəbəlz/ n. [plural] money that a company owns but that has not yet been paid to it: *The bank purchased $110 million in credit card receivables.*

re·ceive /rɪˈsiv/ v. [T]

1 be given sth to be officially given something: *Officials have received numerous complaints about airport noise.* | *Are you still receiving financial aid?* | [receive sth from sb] *In 1962 she received an honorary doctorate from Harvard.*

2 be sent sth FORMAL to get a letter, message, telephone call etc.: *Police received calls from residents who heard the gunshots.* | *Richardson received invitations to speak at all three universities.*

3 treatment FORMAL if you receive a particular type of treatment, an injury etc., it is done to you or it happens to you: *Three firefighters received minor injuries while fighting the blaze.* | *Rovner is still in the hospital receiving treatment for a heart problem.*

4 ideas/information [usually passive] to react in a particular way to a suggestion, idea, or piece of information: *Hawke's first novel was well received by many book critics.* | *When she received news of her father's death, she returned home.*

5 by radio **a)** if a radio or television receives radio waves or other signals, it makes them become sounds or pictures **b)** to be able to hear a radio message that someone is sending: *"Are you receiving me?" "Receiving you loud and clear."*

6 people FORMAL to accept or welcome someone officially as a guest or member of a group: *Hotel guests may not receive visitors after 10 p.m.* | [receive sb into sth] *He was later received into the priesthood.*

7 be on the receiving end (of sth) to be the person who is most affected by someone else's actions, usually in a bad way: *I know what it's like to be on the receiving end of criticism.* —see Usage Note at OBTAIN

re·ceived /rɪˈsivd/ adj. [only before noun] FORMAL accepted or considered to be correct by most people: *Sontag's articles challenged received notions about photography.*

re·ceiv·er /rɪˈsivər/ n. [C] **1** the part of a telephone that you hold next to your mouth and ear: *Cory slammed down the receiver.* **2** someone who is officially in charge of a business or company that is BANKRUPT (=has no money): *Carlson is the court-appointed receiver for the firm.* **3** a player in football who is in a position to catch the ball **4** FORMAL a piece of electronic equipment in a STEREO, television, or radio that changes electrical signals into sounds, then makes them loud enough to hear, or the television, stereo, or radio itself **5** someone who buys and sells stolen property **6** someone who is given something: *The gift should be something the receiver will like.*

re·ceiv·er·ship /rɪˈsivərˌʃɪp/ n. [U] the state of being controlled by an official receiver: *The resort has closed and gone into receivership.*

re·cent /ˈrisənt/ adj. [usually before noun] **1** having happened or begun to exist only a short time ago: *a recent poll of voters* | *Anything that happened after World War II is too recent to be considered "history."* | *This is the most recent memo from KD.* | *Air traffic has grown rapidly in recent years.* **2 in recent memory** during the time that most people are able to remember: *It was one of the worst storms in recent memory.* —**recentness** n. [U] —see Usage Note at NEW

re·cent·ly /ˈrisəntli/ adv. not long ago, or during the recent days or weeks: *The hospital recently installed a new heating system.* —see Usage Note at LATELY

re·cep·ta·cle /rɪˈsɛptəkəl/ n. FORMAL a container for putting things in: *a trash receptacle*

re·cep·tion /rɪˈsɛpʃən/ n. **1** [C] a large formal party to celebrate an event or to welcome someone: *a wedding reception* | *There will be a reception for the visiting professors.* **2** [C usually singular] a way of reacting to a person or idea that shows what you think of them or it: *Winfrey received a warm reception* (=people welcomed her in a friendly way). | *Congress gave the idea a cool reception* (=they did not like the idea). **3** [U] the quality of television or radio signals that you receive: **get good/bad reception** *We get better reception with the satellite dish.* **4 reception desk/area** the desk or area where visitors arriving in a hotel or large organization go first: *Please leave your key at the reception desk.* **5** [C] the act of catching the ball in football: *a 24-yard touchdown reception*

re·cep·tion·ist /rɪˈsɛpʃənɪst/ n. [C] someone whose job is to welcome and help people arriving in a hotel or office building, visiting a doctor etc.

re·cep·tive /rɪˈsɛptɪv/ adj. willing to consider new ideas or listen to someone else's opinions: *a receptive audience* | [+ to] *Viewers were receptive to the movie's anti-war message.* —**receptively** adv. —**receptiveness** also **receptivity** /ˌrisɛpˈtɪvəti/ n. [U]

re·cess[1] /ˈrisɛs, rɪˈsɛs/ n. **1** [C,U] a time of rest during the working day or year at a law court, government etc.: *Congress will return in January from its holiday recess.* | *One of the lawyers asked the judge for a recess.* **2** [U] a time when children are allowed to go outside to play during the school day: *As a punishment, she had to stay inside at recess.* **3** [C] a space in the wall of a room for shelves, cupboards etc. **4 the recesses of sth** the hidden parts inside something such as a room: *the dark recesses of the basement*

re·cess[2] v. [I,T] to take an official time of rest in government or court activities: *The judge recessed the trial for two hours.*

re·cessed /ˈrisɛst, rɪˈsɛst/ adj. something that is recessed is built into the material of a wall or ceiling, so that it does not stick out: *recessed lighting*

re·ces·sion /rɪˈsɛʃən/ n. [C] a period of time during which there is less trade, business activity etc. than usual: *the recession of the 1980s*

re·ces·sive /rɪˈsɛsɪv/ adj. TECHNICAL a recessive GENE is only seen as a physical feature if both parents have the gene and pass it to their child —compare DOMINANT[1] (3)

re·charge /ˈritʃɑrdʒ, riˈtʃɑrdʒ/ v. [T] **1** to put a new supply of electricity into a BATTERY **2** INFORMAL to get your strength and energy back again: *A workout leaves me feeling recharged.* —**rechargeable** adj. —**recharge** /ˈritʃɑrdʒ/ n. [C]

re·charg·er /riˈtʃɑrdʒər/ n. [C] a machine that recharges batteries (BATTERY (1))

re·cid·i·vist /rɪˈsɪdəvɪst/ n. [C] TECHNICAL a criminal who starts doing illegal things again, even after they have been punished —**recidivism** n. [U]

rec·i·pe /ˈrɛsəpi/ n. [C] **1** a set of instructions for cooking a particular type of food: [+ for] *a recipe for tomato soup* **2 be a recipe for sth** to be likely to cause a particular result, often a bad one: *I think the new regulations are a recipe for economic disaster.*

re·cip·i·ent /rɪˈsɪpiənt/ n. FORMAL someone who receives something: *welfare recipients* | [+ of] *the recipient of the Nobel Peace Prize*

re·cip·ro·cal /rɪˈsɪprəkəl/ adj. FORMAL a reciprocal arrangement or relationship is one in which two people or groups do or give similar things to each other: *Iran's leaders expected a reciprocal gesture of goodwill.* —compare MUTUAL (1) —**reciprocally** /-kli/ adv.

R

re·cip·ro·cate /rɪˈsɪprəˌkeɪt/ v. [I,T] **1** to do or give something, because something similar has been done or given to you: *In 1979, Egypt made a genuine offer of peace, and Israel reciprocated with an offer of territory.* **2** to feel the same about someone as they feel about you: *Her love was not reciprocated.* —**reciprocation** /rɪˌsɪprəˈkeɪʃən/ n. [U]

rec·i·proc·i·ty /ˌrɛsəˈprɑsəti/ n. [U] FORMAL a situation in which two people, groups, or countries give each other similar kinds of help or special rights

re·cit·al /rɪˈsaɪtl/ n. [C] **1** a performance of music or poetry, usually by one performer: *a piano recital* | [+ **of**] *a recital of operatic arias* **2** FORMAL a spoken description of a series of events

rec·i·ta·tion /ˌrɛsəˈteɪʃən/ n. [C,U] an act of saying a poem, piece of literature etc. that you have learned, for people to listen to: *The service ended with a recitation of the Lord's Prayer.*

rec·i·ta·tive /ˌrɛsətəˈtiv/ n. [C,U] TECHNICAL a speech set to music which is sung by one person and continues the story of an OPERA (=musical play) between the songs

re·cite /rɪˈsaɪt/ v. **1** [I,T] to say a poem, piece of literature etc. that you have learned, for people to listen to: *Each student had to recite a poem.* **2** [T] to tell someone a series or list of things: *Detective Clark recited the facts of the case.* —**reciter** n. [C]

reck·less /ˈrɛklɪs/ adj. not caring or worrying about danger or about the bad results of your behavior: *reckless spending* | *The driver was arrested for reckless driving.* —**recklessly** adv. —**recklessness** n. [U]

reck·on /ˈrɛkən/ v. [T not in progressive] **1** to guess a number or amount, without calculating it exactly: *The TV audience in China is reckoned at 800 million.* | [**reckon (that)**] *Scientists reckon a third of global-warming gases are produced by cars and trucks.* **2** to think that someone or something is a particular type of person or thing: [**reckon sb/sth as sth**] *An earthquake of magnitude 7 is reckoned as a major quake.* **3** SPOKEN to think or suppose something: *How long do you reckon it will take?* **4** FORMAL to calculate an amount
   reckon on sth *phr. v.* [T] to expect something to happen when you are making plans: *I didn't reckon on how angry he'd be at the idea.*
   reckon sth ↔ **up** *phr. v.* [T] to add up an amount, cost etc., in order to get a total: *The human costs of the war are only beginning to be reckoned up.*
   reckon with sb/sth *phr. v.* [T] **1 a ... to be reckoned with** something or someone that is powerful or has influence, and must be regarded seriously as a possible opponent, competitor, danger etc.: *The Huskies are a team to be reckoned with this season.* | *The rebels are still **a force to be reckoned with**.* **2** to consider a possible problem when you think about the future: *Capital gains taxes must be reckoned with.*

reck·on·ing /ˈrɛkənɪŋ/ n. **1** [U] a calculation that is based on a careful guess rather than on exact knowledge: *By Silva's reckoning, property owners in the city could save $91,000 in bills.* **2 day of reckoning** the time when the results of your actions or behavior become clear and start to affect you, especially in a bad way —see also DEAD RECKONING

re·claim /rɪˈkleɪm/ v. [T] **1** to get back something that once belonged to you: *You may be entitled to reclaim some tax.* **2** to obtain useful products from waste material: *The golf course will use reclaimed wastewater to water the grass.* **3** to make land that has never been used, or that is not good enough to be used, able to be used for farming, housing etc.: *The organization is trying to reclaim desert land for farming.* —**reclamation** /ˌrɛkləˈmeɪʃən/ n. [U]

re·cline /rɪˈklaɪn/ v. **1** [I] FORMAL to lie or lean back in a relaxed way: [+ **in/on**] *Davis was reclining in an easy chair.* **2** [I,T] if you recline a seat or if it reclines, the back of the seat is lowered, so that you can lean back in it

reclining chair /.ˌ... ˈ./ also **re·clin·er** /rɪˈklaɪnɚ/ n. [C] a large comfortable chair that you can lean back in, with your feet supported by the chair

rec·luse /ˈrɛklus/ n. [C] someone who chooses to live alone, and avoids seeing or talking to other people: *Hudson became a recluse after her husband's death.* —**reclusive** /rɪˈklusɪv/ adj.

rec·og·ni·tion /ˌrɛkəgˈnɪʃən/ n. **1** [U] the act of recognizing someone or something: *She stared at him without recognition for a few seconds.* | *Many of the bodies were burned **beyond recognition**.* (=they had become impossible to recognize) **2** [singular,U] the act of realizing and accepting that something is true or important: [+ **of**] *There is a growing recognition of the need for more preventive treatment.* | [+ **that**] *These Supreme Court cases forced the recognition that religious freedom also means freedom to be non-religious.* **3** [singular,U] public admiration and thanks for someone's work or achievements: *Women painters got little recognition in those days.* | *Ruiz was presented with a gold watch **in recognition of** his 25 years of service.* **4** [U] the act of officially accepting that an organization, government, document etc. has legal or official authority: *In 1991, Bush granted diplomatic recognition to Russia.* | [+ **of**] *the recognition of treaties and borders* **5 speech/voice/image etc. recognition** the ability of a computer to recognize voices, shapes etc.

re·cog·ni·zance /rɪˈkɑgnəzəns/ n. [U] LAW **1 be released on your own recognizance** if a person who has been CHARGEd in a court of law is released on their own recognizance, they are allowed to stay out of prison if they promise to come back to court at a specific time **2** money that someone pays a court etc. in order to promise that they will come back on a particular day or time: *Howe posted a $250 recognizance bond.*

rec·og·nize /ˈrɛkəgˌnaɪz/ v. **1** [T not in progressive] to know who someone is or what something is, because you have seen, heard, experienced, or learned about them in the past: *We hadn't seen each other in thirty years, but I recognized her right away.* | *Aaron was humming a tune I didn't recognize.* | *The campaign is aimed at helping doctors recognize abuse victims.* **2** [T] to officially accept that an organization, government, document etc. has legal or official authority: *The U.S. has not recognized the Cuban government since 1961.* **3** [T usually passive] to realize that something is important or very good: *Franklin is a recognized leader in her field.* | [**recognize sb/sth as sth**] *They will one day be recognized as the best repertory theater company in the country.* **4** [T] to admit or accept that something is true: [**recognize (that)**] *Hudson recognized that she had to make a change in her lifestyle.* | [**recognize what/how/who etc.**] *Our record shows that we recognize how important safety is.* **5** [T] to officially and publicly thank someone for something they have done, by giving them a special honor: *Carnegie heroes are recognized for trying to save lives while risking their own.* —**recognizable** /ˌrɛkəgˈnaɪzəbəl, ˈrɛkəgˌnaɪ-/ adj. —**recognizably** adv.

re·coil¹ /ˈrikɔɪl, rɪˈkɔɪl/ v. [I] **1** to feel such a strong dislike of a particular situation that you want to avoid it: [+ **from/at**] *The MPAA ratings board recoiled at the sex scenes and gave the movie an X rating.* | *People recoiled in horror from the destruction of the war.* **2** to move back suddenly and quickly from something you do not like or are afraid of: [+ **from/at**] *She recoiled from his touch.* **3** if a gun recoils, it moves backward very quickly when it is fired

recoil² n. [singular,U] the backward movement of a gun when it is fired

rec·ol·lect /ˌrɛkəˈlɛkt/ v. [T] to be able to remember something, especially by deliberately trying to remember: *The events were so dreadful that even now it is painful to recollect them.* | [**recollect how/when/what etc.**] *Davenport tried to recollect who he had spoken to at the company.*

rec·ol·lec·tion /ˌrɛkəˈlɛkʃən/ n. FORMAL **1** [U] an act of remembering something, especially something you try hard to remember: *The driver said she had no recollection of what had happened.* | **To the best of my recollection**, (=used when you remember something, but cannot be sure that it is correct) *they* have never asked us for any money. **2** [C] something from the past that you remember: *She knew her father only through photographs and her mother's recollections.*

S W **rec·om·mend** /ˌrekəˈmend/ *v.* [T] **1** to advise someone to do something, especially because you have special knowledge of a situation or subject: *The prosecutor recommended a 15-year sentence.* | *The recommended dosage for children is 20 milligrams.* | [recommend that] *Doctors recommend that all children should be immunized.* | [recommend doing sth] *The manufacturers recommend changing the oil every 6,000 miles.* | *We strongly recommend buying a bicycle helmet.* **2** to say that something or someone is good, and suggest them for a particular purpose or job: *Can you recommend a good restaurant?* | [recommend sth to sb] *It's a children's book, but I recommend it to everyone.* | [recommend sth for sth] *He recommended some computer equipment for his employers.* | [recommend sb for sth] *Bennett recommended him for the rank of distinguished professor.* | *Capra's film is a classic that I highly recommend.* **3** sth has much/little/nothing to recommend it used to say that something has many, few, or no good qualities: *The hotel has little except price to recommend it.*

USAGE NOTE: RECOMMEND

WORD CHOICE: recommend, suggest, advise
Use **suggest** when you are giving someone your ideas about what they should do or where they should go: *He suggested that I talk to a counselor.* Use **advise** when you tell someone what you think they should do, because it is the most sensible thing to do: *Drivers are advised to avoid Highway 203.* Use **recommend** to suggest that someone do something, after you have thought about it carefully: *The report recommends a number of changes to the current law.*
GRAMMAR
When you use **recommend, suggest, advise, ask, insist, request,** and **demand** with "that," use only the infinitive form of the verb without "to," even if the subject is singular: *I recommend that this plan be accepted.* | *We ask that the committee review the facts.*

S W **rec·om·men·da·tion** /ˌrekəmənˈdeɪʃən/ *n.* **1** [C] official advice given to someone, especially about what to do: [+ for] *The Council has made recommendations for changes in the space program.* | [recommendation that] *Congress accepted a recommendation that the military base be closed.* | [recommendation to do sth] *They made a recommendation to limit household water use.* | *The committee will make a recommendation in the next month.* **2** [U] the action of suggesting to someone that they should choose a particular thing or person that you think is very good: *The council decided, at the recommendation of the city staff, to extend the deadline.* | *Page was hired on Flournoy's recommendation.* **3** [C] also **letter of recommendation** a formal letter or statement saying that someone would be an good choice to do a job, study at a particular college etc.: *Schatz's former employer wrote him a recommendation.*

rec·om·pense¹ /ˈrekəmˌpens/ *v.* [T] FORMAL to give someone a payment for trouble or losses that you have caused them, or a reward for their efforts to help you: [recompense sb for sth] *The reason for the lawsuit is to recompense the victims for their injuries.* —compare COMPENSATE (2)

recompense² *n.* [singular,U] FORMAL something that you give to someone for trouble or losses that you have caused them, or as a reward for their help: [+ for] *The guidelines say what is fair recompense for church musicians.* —compare COMPENSATION (1)

rec·on·cile /ˈrekənˌsaɪl/ *v.* **1** [T] to show that two ideas, situations, or facts can exist together and are not opposed to each other: *Senate and House members are trying to reconcile different versions of the transportation bill.* | *How do people reconcile a belief in God with the suffering of innocent people?* **2** be reconciled (with sb) to have a good relationship again with someone after

---

arguing with them: *Ransom hoped to be reconciled with his wife and children.*

reconcile sb **to** sth *phr. v.* [T] to make someone able to accept a bad situation: *The food was so good I was almost able to reconcile myself to the price.*

rec·on·cil·i·a·tion /ˌrekənˌsɪliˈeɪʃən/ *n.* [singular,U] a situation in which two people, countries etc. become friendly with each other again after arguing or fighting: *Her ex-husband asked for a reconciliation.* | [+ between/with] *Janikowski called for reconciliation between the people of the two countries.*

rec·on·dite /ˈrekənˌdaɪt, rɪˈkɑn-/ *adj.* [only before noun] FORMAL recondite information, knowledge etc. is not known about or understood by many people

re·con·di·tion /ˌrikənˈdɪʃən/ *v.* [T] to repair something, especially an old machine, so that it works like a new one —**reconditioned** *adj.*: *a reconditioned engine*

re·con·nais·sance /rɪˈkɑnəsəns, -zəns/ *n.* [C,U] the military activity of sending soldiers and aircraft to find out information about the enemy: *a reconnaissance mission*

re·con·noi·ter /ˌrikəˈnɔɪtər/ [I,T] to try to find out the position and size of your enemy's army, for example by flying airplanes over land where their soldiers are

re·con·sid·er /ˌrikənˈsɪdər/ *v.* [I,T] to think again about something in order to decide if you should change your opinion: *Please reconsider. We'd love it if you came with us.* | *The governor can ask the board to reconsider parole decisions.* —**reconsideration** /ˌrikənsɪdəˈreɪʃən/ *n.* [U]

re·con·sti·tute /rɪˈkɑnstəˌtut/ *v.* **1** [T] to make a group, organization etc. exist again in a different form: *The parliament has been reconstituted, but is essentially powerless.* **2** to change dried food back to its original form by added water to it: *reconstituted orange juice* —**reconstitution** /ˌrikɑnstəˈtuʃən/ *n.* [U]

re·con·struct /ˌrikənˈstrʌkt/ *v.* [T] **1** to produce a complete description of something that happened by collecting pieces of information: *Police are trying to reconstruct the events of last Friday.* **2** to build something again after it has been destroyed or damaged: *Kramer had several operations to reconstruct the bones in her leg.*

re·con·struc·tion /ˌrikənˈstrʌkʃən/ *n.* **1** [U] the work that is done to repair the damage to a city, industry etc., especially after a war: *Gorbachev began the reconstruction and reform of the Soviet system.* **2** [C] a medical operation to replace a bone or a part of the body that has been damaged: *a hip reconstruction* **3** [C usually singular] a description or copy of something that you produce by collecting information about it: [+ of] *a reconstruction of a Native American village* | *a reconstruction of the crime* **4 Reconstruction** the period after the U.S. Civil War, when the South was trying to repair damage to farms, houses, industries etc.

rec·ord¹ /ˈrekərd/ *n.* **S W**
1 information [C] information about something that is written down so that it can be looked at in the future: *Medical records are now kept on computers.* | [+ of] *Records of births, marriages, and deaths are filed at City Hall.* | *The past decade has been the warmest since people began keeping records* (=writing down information). | *The drop in stock prices is the fifth worst decline on record.*
2 highest/best ever [C] the fastest speed, longest distance, highest or lowest level etc. that has ever been reached: *Dyer scored 36 points, a tournament record.* | *Melissa broke a school record* (=she did something better than the previous record) *by making all of her free throws.* | *Lewis holds the record in the dash.* | *Walsh set a pentathlon record* (=achieved a new record) *in 1953.* | *Six million jobs were created in 1978 and 1979 – an all-time record* (=the best ever achieved).
3 past activities [singular] the facts about how successful, good, honest etc. someone or something

has been in the past: *Coach Rogers has boosted the team's record to 12 wins and only 4 losses.* | [+ **on**] *The Attorney General defended his record on civil rights.* | *Mobile homes have a **good record** for surviving earthquakes.* —see also TRACK RECORD

4 police document [singular] also **criminal record** a document that the police keep that shows a person's criminal activities, time spent in prison etc.: *Hoyle **has a record** as long as your arm.*

5 music [C] a round flat piece of plastic with a hole in the middle on which music and sound are stored: *an old Beatles record*

6 off the record if something you tell someone is off the record, you do not want them to officially report that you said it: *Officials, speaking off the record, said they were still worried about the situation.*

7 on (the) record said publicly or officially: *I'm willing to **go on record** to support the new housing development.* | *Rowe is **on record as saying** she would consider an advisory position.*

8 for the record used to tell someone that what you are saying should be remembered or written down: *For the record, the official score was France 3, the U.S. 1.*

9 set/put/keep the record straight to tell people the truth about something, because you want to be sure that they understand what the truth really is: *Feinstein said she wanted to set the record straight about her positive drug test last month.*

re·cord² /rɪˈkɔrd/ v. **1** [T] to write information down so that it can be looked at in the future: *The expedition recorded many new species of plants.* | *Washington, D.C. police recorded 483 murders in 1990.* **2** [I,T] to store music, sound, television programs etc. on TAPE etc. so that people can listen to them or watch them again: *Are we recording? Push that red button to start it.* | *Would you set the VCR to record ER for me tonight?* | *The whole incident was recorded on an amateur video tape.* **3** [T] if an instrument records the size, speed, temperature etc. of something, it measures it and keeps that information: *Wind speeds of up to 100 mph have been recorded.*

re·cord³ /ˈrɛkɔrd/ adj. [only before noun] a record event, number, or level is the best, worst, highest, lowest etc. of its type that has ever happened or existed: *Record flooding (=the worst flooding ever) was reported on the Colorado River.* | *The game was played in front of a record crowd (=the biggest crowd ever).* | *record high/low Temperatures reached a record high yesterday in Tuscon.*

record-break·ing /ˈ.. ˌ../ adj. [only before noun] a record-breaking number, level, performance, or person is the highest, lowest, biggest, best etc. of its type that has ever happened or existed: *a record-breaking run* | *record-breaking heat* | *a record-breaking swimmer*

re·cord·er /rɪˈkɔrdɚ/ n. [C] **1** a piece of electrical equipment that records information, music, movies etc.: *a tape recorder* | *the flight data recorder* **2** a simple wood or plastic musical instrument shaped like a tube, that you play by blowing into it **3** someone whose job is to officially record things: *The deed must be filed with the county recorder.*

record-hold·er /ˈ.. ˌ../ n. [C] the person who has achieved the fastest speed, the longest distance etc. in a sport

re·cord·ing /rɪˈkɔrdɪŋ/ n. **1** [C] a piece of music, speech etc. that has been recorded: *I called her office but just got a recording.* | [+ **of**] *a recording of Vivaldi's "Gloria"* **2** [U] the act of storing music, movies etc. on a TAPE etc.: *This VCR is easy to program for automatic recording.* | **recording equipment/studio etc.** (=equipment etc. used for recording)

record play·er /ˈ.. ˌ../ n. [C] a piece of equipment for playing records —compare STEREO¹ (1)

re·count¹ /rɪˈkaʊnt/ v. [T] FORMAL to tell a story or describe a series of events: *"The plane dropped slowly," passenger Ken Argos recounted.*

re·count² /ˈrikaʊnt/ n. [C] a process of counting votes again: *Opponents demanded a recount.* —**recount** /rɪˈkaʊnt/ v. [T]

re·coup /rɪˈkup/ v. [T] to get back an amount of money you have lost or spent: *The movie will have to be a huge hit to recoup its cost.*

re·course /ˈrikɔrs, rɪˈkɔrs/ n. FORMAL something you can do to help yourself in a difficult situation, or the act of doing this: *You **have** legal **recourse** if the guarantee is in writing.* | *The family was forced to survive **without recourse to** (=without being able to use) government aid.*

re·cov·er /rɪˈkʌvɚ/ v. **1** [I] to become better after an illness, accident, shock etc.: *Doctors say she will recover quickly.* | [+ **from**] *It will take several months for Boyle to recover from the knee injury.* **2** [I] to return to a normal condition after a period of trouble or difficulty: *The Eagles had a 37–20 lead at halftime, and the Broncos couldn't recover.* | [+ **from**] *The economy has not yet recovered from the recession.* **3** [T] to have something returned that was taken from you, lost, or almost destroyed: *A number of bodies were recovered from the wreckage.* **4** [T] to get back the same amount of money that you have spent or that you have lost on an INVESTMENT: *The company hopes to recover the cost of developing their new product.* **5** [T] to have the ability to control your feelings or your body again after not having it: *He never recovered the use of his legs.* | *Joyce quickly **recovered herself** (=controlled her emotions) and blew her nose.* —**recoverable** adj.

re·cov·er /riˈkʌvɚ/ v. [T] to put a new cover on a piece of furniture: *The sofa had been re-covered in yellow.*

re·cov·er·y /rɪˈkʌvəri/ n. **1** [singular,U] a process of getting better after an illness, injury etc.: [+ **from**] *The group supports members during their recovery from alcoholism.* | *Wendy has an 85% chance of a **full recovery**. (=complete recovery)* **2** [singular,U] the process of returning to a normal condition after a period of trouble or difficulty: *Economic recovery is forecast.* | [+ **from**] *The team finally **made a recovery from** their season-long problems.* **3** [U] the act of getting something that has been taken or lost back: [+ **of**] *the recovery of the stolen jewels*

recovery pro·gram /.ˈ... ˌ../ n. [C] a period of treatment for people who are ADDICTed to drugs or alcohol

recovery room /.ˈ... ˌ./ n. [C] a room in a hospital where people first wake up after an operation

re·cre·ate /ˌrikriˈeɪt/ v. [T] to make something from the past exist again in a new form or be experienced again: *Arjelo's novel vividly recreates 15th-century Spain.* —**recreation** /ˌrikriˈeɪʃən/ n. [C,U]

rec·re·a·tion /ˌrɛkriˈeɪʃən/ n. [C,U] an activity that you do for pleasure or fun: *Families use the space for recreation.* —**recreational** adj.

recreational ve·hi·cle /.ˌ..., ˈ.../ n. [C] an RV

re·crim·i·na·tion /rɪˌkrɪməˈneɪʃən/ n. [C usually plural,U] a situation in which people blame each other, or the things they say when they are blaming each other: *We promised each other there would be no recriminations if it didn't work out.*

rec room /ˈrɛk rum/ also **recreation room** /..ˈ.. ˌ../ n. [C] **1** a public room, for example in a hospital, used for social activities or games **2** a room in a private house, where you can relax, play games etc.

re·cru·des·cence /ˌrikruˈdɛsəns/ n. [usually singular] FORMAL a time when something, especially something bad, returns or happens again

re·cruit¹ /rɪˈkrut/ v. **1** [I,T] to find new people to work in a company, join an organization, do a job etc.: *Efforts to recruit more men to the priesthood have not been successful.* **2 a)** [I,T] to get people to join the army or navy **b)** [T] to form a new army in this way **3** [T] INFORMAL to persuade someone to do something for you: [**recruit sb to do sth**] *We recruited a few of our friends to help us move.* —**recruitment** n. [U] —compare CONSCRIPT¹

recruit² n. [C] **1** someone who has just joined the Army, Navy, or Air Force: *Forty **raw recruits** (=new recruits) have just started boot camp.* —compare

CONSCRIPT² **2** someone who has recently joined an organization, team, group of people etc.: *At most banks, young recruits spend a few months working as tellers.*

rec·tal /'rɛktəl/ *adj.* TECHNICAL relating to the RECTUM

rec·tan·gle /'rɛk,tæŋgəl/ *n.* [C] a shape that has four straight sides, two of which are usually longer than the other two, and four 90° angles at the corners —compare SQUARE² (1) —see picture at SHAPE¹

rec·tan·gu·lar /rɛk'tæŋgyələ/ *adj.* having the shape of a rectangle

rec·ti·fy /'rɛktə,faɪ/ *v.* **rectifies, rectified, rectifying** [T] FORMAL to correct something that is wrong: *A number of steps have been taken to rectify the error.* —**rectifiable** *adj.* —**rectification** /,rɛktəfə'keɪʃən/ *n.* [C,U]

rec·ti·lin·e·ar /,rɛktə'lɪniə/ *adj.* TECHNICAL formed or moving in a straight line, or consisting of straight lines

rec·ti·tude /'rɛktə,tud/ *n.* [U] FORMAL honesty and moral correctness

rec·to /'rɛktoʊ/ *n.* [C] TECHNICAL a page on the RIGHT-HAND side of a book —compare VERSO

rec·tor /'rɛktə/ *n.* [C] **1** a priest in some Christian churches who is responsible for a particular area, group etc. **2** the person in charge of certain colleges and schools

rec·to·ry /'rɛktəri/ *n.* [C] a house where the priest of the local church lives

rec·tum /'rɛktəm/ *n.* [C] TECHNICAL the lowest part of your BOWEL —see picture at DIGESTIVE SYSTEM

re·cum·bent /rɪ'kʌmbənt/ *adj.* FORMAL lying down on your back or side

re·cu·per·ate /rɪ'kupə,reɪt/ *v.* [I] **1** to get better again after an illness or injury: *Tina spent nine months recuperating.* | [+ **from**] *Arkwright is recovering from a knee injury.* **2** to return to a more normal condition after a difficult time: *Winston proposed several ways for the industry to recuperate.* —**recuperation** /rɪ,kupə'reɪʃən/ *n.* [U]

re·cu·per·a·tive /rɪ'kupə,reɪtɪv, -pərətɪv/ *adj.* relating to the ability something has to help someone or something to get better again: *the recuperative powers of nature*

re·cur /rɪ'kə/ *v.* **recurred, recurring** [I] **1** if something, especially something bad, recurs, it happens again or happens several times: *There is a danger that the disease may recur.* | *He has a small recurring role as Earl the barber.* **2** TECHNICAL if a number or numbers after a DECIMAL POINT recur, they are repeated forever in the same order

re·cur·rence /rɪ'kʌrəns, -'kə-/ *n.* [C,U] FORMAL an occasion when something that has happened before happens again: [+ **of**] *Job stress may cause a recurrence of the condition.*

re·cur·rent /rɪ'kʌrənt/ *adj.* happening or appearing repeatedly: *a recurrent infection* —**recurrently** *adv.*

re·cuse /rɪ'kyuz/ *v.* [T] FORMAL **recuse yourself** to say that you cannot give advice or take part in a something, because you might be too closely involved to be fair —**recusal** *adj.*

re·cy·cla·ble /ri'saɪkləbəl/ *adj.* used materials or substances that are recyclable can be recycled: *recyclable bottles* —**recyclable** *n.* [C usually plural]

re·cy·cle /ri'saɪkəl/ *v.* [I,T] to put used objects or materials through a special process, so that they can be used again: *Plastic bottles can be recycled into clothing.* —**recycled** *adj.*: *recycled paper*

re·cy·cling /ri'saɪklɪŋ/ *n.* [U] the process of treating things such as paper or steel so that they can be used again: *the city's recycling program*

red¹ /rɛd/ *adj.* **redder, reddest 1** having the color of blood: *a red dress* | *He drove straight through a red light.* **2** hair that is red is an orange-brown color **3** skin that is red is a bright pink color: *Her cheeks were red with excitement.* **4** red wine has a red or purple color **5 red flag** something that shows or warns you that something might be wrong, illegal etc.: *The transfer of $750,000 from Bowman's account*

raised the red flag for investigators. **6 be/turn as red as a beet** to have a very red face, usually because you are embarrassed **7 not one red cent** INFORMAL used to emphasize that you mean no money at all: *Carter said she wouldn't pay one red cent of her rent until the landlord fixed her roof.* **8** INFORMAL an insulting word meaning COMMUNIST², used especially in past times —**redness** *n.* [U] —see also **paint the town (red)** (PAINT² (6)), **be like waving a red flag in front of a bull** (WAVE¹ (7))

red² *n.* **1** [C,U] the color of blood: *The corrections were marked in red* (=in red ink). | *the reds and yellows of the fall trees* **2** [C,U] red wine: *a nice bottle of red* **3 be in the red** INFORMAL to owe more money than you have: *The state is already $3 billion in the red this year.* —opposite **be in the black** (BLACK² (3)) **4 see red** to become very angry: *I immediately saw red and wanted to prove him wrong.* **5** [C] INFORMAL an insulting word for someone who has COMMUNIST ideas or opinions, used especially in past times

red a·lert /,. .'./ *n.* [C usually singular] a warning of that there is very great danger: *Government troops were put on red alert after the assassination attempt.*

red blood cell /,. '. ./ also **red cor·pus·cle** /,. '.../ *n.* [C] one of the cells in your blood that carry oxygen to every part of your body —compare WHITE BLOOD CELL

red-blood·ed /,. '../ *adj.* **red-blooded male/American/patriot etc.** HUMOROUS used in order to emphasize that someone has all of the qualities that a typical man, American etc. is supposed to have

red car·pet /,. '../ *n.* [C usually singular] **1** a long piece of red CARPET that is put on floors for important people to walk on **2** special treatment that you give to someone important who is visiting you: *Williams' hometown rolled out the red carpet to welcome her.*

red chip /,. './ *n.* [C] a STOCK in a Chinese company that is shown on the Hong Kong STOCK MARKET —compare BLUE CHIP

Red Cloud /'rɛd klaʊd/ (1822–1909) a Sioux chief who tried to stop U.S. soldiers from helping people to settle on Sioux land in the northwest U.S.

red·coat /'rɛdkoʊt/ *n.* [C] a British soldier during the 18th and 19th centuries

Red Cross /,. './ **the Red Cross** an international organization that helps people who are suffering as a result of war, floods, disease etc.

red·den /'rɛdn/ *v.* [I,T] to become red, or make something red: *Her face reddened in embarrassment.*

red·dish /'rɛdɪʃ/ *adj.* slightly red: *reddish-brown lipstick*

re·dec·o·rate /ri'dɛkə,reɪt/ *v.* [I,T] to change the way a room looks by painting, changing the furniture etc. —**redecoration** /,ridɛkə'reɪʃən/ *n.* [U]

re·deem /rɪ'dim/ *v.* [T] FORMAL **1** to make something less bad: *The system had failed so badly there was no way to redeem it.* | **redeeming feature/quality/trait etc.** (=the one good thing about someone or something that is generally bad) **2** to exchange a piece of paper representing an amount of money for that amount of money or for goods equal in cost to that amount of money: *Travelers can redeem the coupons for one-way flights.* **3 redeem yourself** to do something that will improve what other people think of you, after you have behaved badly or failed: *The Bears will have a chance to redeem themselves in Saturday's game.* **4** a word meaning to free someone from the power or evil, used especially in the Christian religion: *Christ came to Earth to redeem us from our sins.* —see also REDEEMER **5 redeem a promise/pledge/obligation etc.** FORMAL to do what you promised to do **6** to buy something back that you left with someone in order to borrow money from them: *I finally redeemed my watch from the pawnbrokers.* —**redeemable** *adj.*

Re·deem·er /rɪ'dimə/ *n.* LITERARY **the Redeemer** Jesus Christ

re·demp·tion /rɪ'dɛmpʃən/ *n.* [U] **1** the act of

exchanging a piece of paper worth a particular amount of money for money, goods, or services: *State redemption centers pay 5 cents for every two recyclable containers.* **2** the state of doing something to improve what people think of you, after you have failed or done something bad: *After his last movie bombed, this script is Brown's shot at redemption.* **3** the state of being freed from the power of evil, believed by Christians to be made possible by Jesus Christ **4 past/beyond redemption** too bad to be saved, repaired, or improved: *His lawyer believes Manson is beyond redemption.* **5** TECHNICAL the exchange of STOCKs, BONDs etc. for money —**redemptive** /rɪ'dɛmptɪv/ *adj.*

re·de·ploy /ˌridɪ'plɔɪ/ *v.* [T] to move someone or something to a different place or job, especially in the military: *Army tanks were redeployed elsewhere in the region.* —**redeployment** *n.* [U]

re·de·vel·op /ˌridə'vɛləp/ *v.* [T] to make an area more modern by putting in new buildings or changing or repairing the old ones: *Tourism in Baltimore has increase since the city redeveloped the Inner Harbor.*

re·de·vel·op·ment /ˌridə'vɛləpmənt/ *n.* [C,U] the act of redeveloping an area, especially in a city: *The city has spent millions on downtown redevelopment.*

red-eye /'. ./ *n.* [U] INFORMAL **1** an airplane with PASSENGERS on it that flies at night: *I took the red-eye from Chicago to LA.* **2** if someone in a photograph has red-eye, their eyes look red because the photograph was taken using a FLASH (=very bright light on the camera) **3** cheap WHISKEY

red-faced /ˌ. '.◂/ *adj.* embarrassed or ashamed: *A red-faced Meyer apologized for his choice of words.*

red flag /ˌ. './ *n.* [C] INFORMAL something that warns you that something is wrong or that there may be problems in the future: *When he mentioned his ex-wife, a little red flag went up.*

red gi·ant /ˌ. '../ *n.* [C] a star that is near the middle of its life, and is larger and less solid than the sun

red-handed

The security guard caught him red-handed.

red-hand·ed /ˌ. '..◂/ *adj.* **catch sb red-handed** to catch someone at the moment when they are doing something wrong: *The FBI caught the mayor red-handed using drugs.*

red·head /'rɛdhɛd/ *n.* [C] someone who has red hair

red her·ring /ˌ. '../ *n.* [C] a fact or idea that is not important but that is introduced to take your attention away from the facts that are important

red-hot /ˌ. '.◂/ *adj.* **1** INFORMAL extremely active, exciting, or interesting: *a red-hot news story* | *The Braves have been red-hot in the last few games.* **2** very sexually exciting: *Their friendship turned into a red-hot love affair.* **3** metal or rock that is red-hot is so hot that it shines red: *Red-hot lava flowed down the sides of the volcano.* **4** INFORMAL very hot: *Be careful with those plates – they're red-hot.*

re·dial /'ri,daɪəl, ri'daɪəl/ *v.* [I,T] to DIAL a telephone number again

red ink /ˌ. './ *n.* [U] money that a business loses because it spends more than it can earn: *This marks the sixth straight quarter of red ink for the $1.3 billion firm.*

re·di·rect /ˌridɪ'rɛkt, -daɪ-/ *v.* [T] to send something in

a different direction, or use something for a different purpose: *The plane was redirected to Cleveland.*

re·dis·trib·ute /ˌridɪ'strɪbyut/ *v.* [T] to give something to each member of a group so that it is divided up in a different way than it was before: *Taxes are a way of redistributing income for the welfare of the whole society.* —**redistribution** /ˌridɪstrə'byuʃən/ *n.* [U]

red-let·ter day /ˌ. '.. ˌ./ *n.* [C] INFORMAL a day when something special happens that makes you very happy

red-light dis·trict /ˌ. '. ˌ../ *n.* [C] the area of a town or city where there are many PROSTITUTES (=people who have sex for money)

red-lin·ing /'. ˌ../ *n.* [U] the act of refusing to give insurance, CREDIT, LOANs etc. to people who live in poor areas of a city, or the act of charging more money for insurance, loans etc. to people in these areas

red meat /ˌ. './ *n.* [U] dark colored meat such as BEEF or LAMB

red·neck /'rɛdnɛk/ *n.* [C] INFORMAL, DISAPPROVING a man who lives in a country area, is not educated, and has strong unreasonable opinions —**redneck** *adj.*

re·do /ri'du/ *v. past tense* **redid** /-'dɪd/ *past participle* **redone** /-'dʌn/ [T] **1** to do something again: *Blair stood at the mirror, redoing her makeup.* **2** to change the way a room is decorated: *We're redoing the bathroom.*

red·o·lent /'rɛdl-ənt/ *adj.* FORMAL **1 redolent of sth** making you think of something: *The movie's scenery is redolent of mystery.* **2** smelling strongly like something: [+ **of/with**] *a sauce redolent of garlic* —**redolence** *n.* [U]

re·dou·ble /ri'dʌbəl/ *v.* [T] **redouble your efforts** to greatly increase your effort as you try to do something: *Society should redouble its efforts to give everyone equal opportunities.*

re·doubt·a·ble /rɪ'daʊtəbəl/ *adj.* LITERARY someone who is redoubtable is a person you respect or fear

re·dound /rɪ'daʊnd/ *v.* **redound to sb's fame/credit/honor etc.** FORMAL to make someone more famous, more respected etc.

red pep·per /ˌ. '../ *n.* **1** [C] a red vegetable that you can eat raw or use in cooking **2** [U] a SPICY red powder used in cooking; CAYENNE PEPPER

re·dress¹ /rɪ'drɛs/ *v.* [T] FORMAL to correct something that is wrong or unfair: *Congress has done little to redress these injustices.* | *Affirmative action was meant to redress the balance* (=make the situation fair) *for minorities.*

re·dress² /'ridrɛs, rɪ'drɛs/ *n.* [U] FORMAL money that someone pays you because they have caused you harm, or damaged your property; COMPENSATION: *The courts provide the means of redress for victims of crime.*

Red Sea, the /ˌ. './ a sea which separates Egypt, Sudan, and Ethiopia from Saudi Arabia and Yemen

red·shirt /'rɛdʃərt/ *v.* [I,T] to keep a college sports player from playing during one year, so that he or she will still be allowed to play during later years of college: *Drew was redshirted in his freshman year.* —**redshirt** *n.* [C]

red·skin /'rɛdskɪn/ *n.* [C] OLD-FASHIONED a word meaning a Native American, now considered offensive

red tape /ˌ. './ *n.* [U] official rules that seem unnecessary and prevent things from being done quickly and easily: *U.S. companies fear the red tape will scare off customers.* | *The new rules should help cut the red tape for farmers.*

re·duce /rɪ'dus/ *v.* **1** [T] to make something smaller or less in size, amount, or price: *The helmet law should reduce injuries in motorcycle accidents.* | [**reduce sth by sth**] *To meet the budget, the city must reduce its spending by 15%.* | [**reduce sth (from sth) to sth**] *Reduce the oven temperature to 350 degrees.* —see also REDUCTION **2** [T] to boil a liquid so that there is less of it **3** [I] to become thinner by losing weight **4 in reduced circumstances** OLD-FASHIONED poorer than you were before

reduce sb/sth **to** sth *phr. v.* [T] **1 reduce sb to tears/silence etc.** to make someone cry, be silent etc.: *The music can reduce a listener to tears.* **2 reduce sth to rubble/ashes/ruins etc.** to destroy something, especially a building, completely **3 reduce sb to doing sth** to make someone do something they would rather not do, especially when it involves behaving or living in a way that is not as good as before: *They were reduced to begging on the streets.*

re·duc·tion /rɪ'dʌkʃən/ *n.* **1** [C,U] a decrease in size, price, amount etc.: *The U.S. has agreed to an arms reduction proposal.* | [+ **in**] *Consumers will benefit from the reduction in gasoline prices.* | *The central bank will make no further reductions in interest rates.* **2** [C] a smaller copy of a photograph, map, or picture —opposite ENLARGEMENT (1)

re·dun·dant /rɪ'dʌndənt/ *adj.* **1** not necessary because something else means or does the same thing **2** TECHNICAL having additional parts that will make a system work if other parts fail —**redundancy** *n.* [U] —**redundantly** *adv.*

re·dux /ˌriː'dʌks◂/ *adj.* [only after noun] done again, or having come again: *For some, the recession of the 1990s seemed like the 1930s redux.*

red·wood /'rɛdwʊd/ *n.* [C,U] a very tall tree that grows in Oregon and California, or the wood from this tree

reed /riːd/ *n.* [C] **1** a type of tall plant like grass that grows in wet places: *Reeds grew all along the river bank.* —see picture on page 428 **2** a thin piece of wood that is attached to a musical instrument such as an OBOE or CLARINET, and that produces a sound when you blow over it

Reed /riːd/, **Wal·ter** /'wɔltɚ/ (1851–1902) a U.S. doctor who discovered that YELLOW FEVER is caused by MOSQUITO bites

re·ed·u·cate /ri'ɛdʒə,keɪt/ *v.* [T] to teach someone to think or behave in a different way: *Young criminals must be re-educated.*

reed·y /'riːdi/ *adj.* **1** a voice that is reedy is high and not nice to listen to **2** a place that is reedy has a lot of reeds growing there

reef[1] /riːf/ *n.* [C] a line of sharp rocks, often made of CORAL, or a raised area of sand near the surface of the ocean: *the Great Barrier Reef*

reef[2] also **reef in** *v.* [T] TECHNICAL to tie up part of a sail in order to make it smaller

ree·fer /'riːfɚ/ *n.* [C] OLD-FASHIONED a cigarette containing the drug MARIJUANA

reek /riːk/ *v.* [I] **1** to have a strong bad smell: *This room absolutely reeks.* | [+ **of**] *Beggars slept on street corners that reeked of urine.* **2** to strongly express a particular quality, especially a bad quality: [+ **of**] *A wooden sculpture titled "Abraham" reeked of anti-Semitism.* —**reek** *n.* [singular]

reel[1] /riːl/ *v.* **1** [I always + adv./prep.] to walk in an unsteady way and almost fall over, as if you are drunk: *The drunk reeled across the road, talking loudly to nobody.* **2** [I] to be confused or have no control over a situation, because something bad or shocking has just happened: *The economy was still reeling from the previous year's recession.* **3** [I always + adv./prep.,T always + adv./prep.] to make something move on or off a reel by winding it: *Sam reeled in a 7 pound fish.* **4** [I] also **reel back** to step backward suddenly and almost fall over, especially after being hit or getting a shock: *A punch in his stomach sent him reeling.* **5** [I] to seem to go around and around: *The room reeled before my eyes, and I fainted.*

reel sth ↔ **off** *phr. v.* [T] INFORMAL **1** to repeat a lot of information quickly and easily: *Jack reeled off a list of names.* **2** to do something repeatedly and quickly: *The UNLV team reeled off 14 straight points to take the lead.*

reel[2] *n.* [C] **1** a round object onto which things such as film or a special string for fishing can be wound: *a fishing rod and reel* **2** the amount that one of these objects will hold: *a reel of film* **3** one of the parts of a movie that is contained on a reel: *a scene from the final reel of "High Noon"* **4** a quick FOLK

dance, especially one from Scotland or Ireland, or the music for this

re·e·lect, reelect /ˌri ɪ'lɛkt/ *v.* [T] to elect someone again: *Soloman was re-elected director of the corporation.* —**re-election** /-'lɛkʃən/ *n.* [C,U]

re·en·act /ˌri ɪ'nækt/ *v.* [T] to perform the actions of a story, crime etc. that happened in past times: *At the church, children re-enacted the Christmas story.* —**re-enactment** *n.* [C] *a re-enactment of the crime*

re·en·try /ri'ɛntri/ *n.* [C,U] an act of entering a place again: *The shuttle made a successful re-entry into the Earth's atmosphere.*

reeve /riːv/ *n.* [C] the official who is in charge of the town governments in some Canadian PROVINCES

ref /rɛf/ *n.* [C] INFORMAL a REFEREE

ref. the written abbreviation of REFERENCE

re·fec·to·ry /rɪ'fɛktəri/ *n.* [C] a large room in a MONASTERY, college etc. where meals are served and eaten

re·fer /rɪ'fɚ/ *v.* referred, referring

refer to *phr. v.* [T] **1** [**refer to** sb/sth] to mention or speak about someone or something: *One woman used a racist term to refer to African-Americans.* | [**refer to** sth/sb **as** sth] *Holland teaches what her students refer to as "the sex course," or sex education.* **2** [**refer to** sth] to look at a book, map, piece of paper etc. for information: *If you don't know what book to get, refer to the list on page 3.* **3** [**refer to** sth/sb] if a statement, number, report etc. refers to someone or something, it is about that person or thing: *The blue line on the graph refers to sales.* **4** [**refer** sb/sth **to** sb/sth] to send someone or something to another place or person for information, advice, or a decision: *The clinic refers patients needing specialized care to the University Hospital.* —see also CROSS-REFER

ref·er·a·ble /rɪ'fʌrəbəl, -'fɚ-/ *adj.* [+ **to**] FORMAL something that is referable to something else can be related to it

ref·er·ee[1] /ˌrɛfə'ri/ *n.* [C] **1** someone who makes sure that the rules are followed in sports such as football, basketball, or BOXING —compare UMPIRE[1] **2** LAW someone whose job is to be a judge in certain types of law cases: *a juvenile court referee* **3** someone who judges an article or RESEARCH idea before it is PUBLISHed or given money: *Articles submitted to the journal are read by several referees.* **4** someone who is asked to settle a disagreement: *A referee can be called in for some disputes between neighbors.*

USAGE NOTE: REFEREE

WORD CHOICE: referee, umpire
Both of these words mean the person who makes sure that the rules are followed in a sports game. Use **referee** with basketball, boxing, hockey, soccer, wrestling, and volleyball. Use **umpire** with baseball. Tennis and football have both umpires and referees.

---

referee[2] *v.* refereed, refereeing [I,T] to be the referee for a game

ref·er·ence /'rɛfrəns/ *n.* **1** [C,U] something you say or write that mentions another person or thing: [+ **to**] *There is no direct reference to her own childhood in the novel.* | *Oddly, the ad makes no reference to the product being sold.* **2 reference point** also **point of reference a)** an idea, fact, event, etc. that helps you understand or make a judgment about a situation: *Fitzgerald's case will be the reference point for lawyers in tomorrow's trial.* | *The time he spent in prison serves as a point of reference for Bowden – the lessons are worth remembering.* **b)** something that you can see that helps you to know where you are when you are traveling in an area **3** [C,U] the act of looking at something for information, or the book, magazine etc. you get the information from: *One shelf was filled with reference works (=reference books).* | *Microfilm copies will be kept for future reference (=so that they can be looked at in the future).* **4 in/with reference to sth**

FORMAL used to say what you are writing or talking about: *With reference to our agents, we have complete confidence in their honesty.* **5** [C] **a)** also **letter of reference** a letter containing information about you that is written by someone who knows you well, usually to a new employer: *For the adoption, the Millers provided references and numerous other documents.* **b)** the person who writes this letter: *Ask a teacher to act as one of your references.* **6** [C] **a)** a note that tells you where the information that is used in a book, article etc. comes from: *a list of references at the end of the article* **b)** a number that tells you where you can find the information you want in a book, on a map etc.: *map reference SG49* —see also CROSS-REFERENCE, **terms of reference** (TERM[1] (21))

reference book /'.. ,./ n. [C] a book such as a dictionary or ENCYCLOPEDIA that you look at to find information

reference li·brar·y /'.. ,.../ also **reference room** /'.. ,./ n. [C] a public library or a room in a library, that contains books that you can use but not take away —compare LENDING LIBRARY

ref·er·en·dum /ˌrɛfəˈrɛndəm/ n. plural **referenda** /-də/ or **referendums** [C,U] an occasion when you vote in order to make a decision about a particular subject, rather than voting for a person: *Denmark planed to* **hold a referendum** *on the issue.*

re·fer·ral /rɪˈfʌrəl, -ˈfɝ-/ n. [C,U] FORMAL an act of sending someone or something to another place for help, information, a decision etc.: *The agency provides referrals for elderly people who need help finding health care.*

re·fill[1] /riˈfɪl/ v. [T] to fill something again: *The waiter refilled our glasses.* —**refillable** adj.: *a refillable lighter*

re·fill[2] /ˈrifɪl/ n. [C] **1** a container filled with a particular substance that you use to fill or replace an empty container, or the substance itself: *refills for an ink pen* | *a prescription refill* **2** SPOKEN another drink to refill your glass: *A large soda is $1.50. Refills are free.*

re·fine /rɪˈfaɪn/ v. [T] **1** to improve a method, plan, system etc. by gradually making slight changes to it: *Engineers are working on developing and refining the car engines.* **2** to make a substance more pure using an industrial process: *There are huge profits in growing and refining cocaine.*

re·fined /rɪˈfaɪnd/ adj. **1** [no comparative] a substance that is refined has been made pure by an industrial process: *refined oil* | *refined beet sugar* **2** having qualities that are related to being well-educated, polite, and interested in high quality books, music, food etc.: *a refined audience of music-lovers* **3** well made and of high quality: *The food could be described as healthy, rather than refined.* **4** improved and made more effective: *a refined method of measurement* —opposite UNREFINED

re·fine·ment /rɪˈfaɪnmənt/ n. **1** [C] an addition or improvement to an existing product, system etc.: *Several rule refinements come into force this season.* **2** [U] the quality of being polite and well-educated, and interested in high quality books, music, food etc.: *His manners showed refinement and good breeding.* **3** [U] the quality of being very good and well-made: *a wine of great delicacy and refinement* **4** [U] the process of improving something: [+ of] *The contract calls for refinement and completion of the aircraft.* **5** [U + of] the process of making a substance more pure

re·fin·er·y /rɪˈfaɪnəri/ n. plural **refineries** [C] a factory where something such as metal, sugar, or oil is refined: *an oil refinery*

re·fin·ish /riˈfɪnɪʃ/ v. [T] to make the surface of something wooden look new again: *Hardwood floors can be sanded and refinished.* —**refinishing** n. [U]

re·fit /riˈfɪt/ v. **refitted, refitting** [I,T] to make a ship, airplane, building etc. ready to be used again, by doing repairs and putting in new machinery: *a refitted shrimp boat* —**refit** /ˈrifɪt/ n. [C,U]

re·flect /rɪˈflɛkt/ v. **1** [T] if a surface reflects light, heat, sound it throws back the light etc. that hits it: *The moon reflects the sun's rays.* | [+ off] *Sunlight reflected off the whitewashed houses.* **2 be reflected in sth** if an object, person, view etc. is reflected in a mirror or in water, you can see the person or thing in it: *The mountains were reflected in the still water of the lake.* **3** [T not in progressive] to show or be a sign of a particular situation, idea, or feeling: *The poll results reflect widespread anxiety about the economy.* | [be reflected in sth] *People's unhappiness with Congress has been reflected in the recent elections.* | [reflect who/what/how etc.] *The department's name was changed to reflect what it does more accurately.* **4** [I,T] to think carefully and often for a long time about something, or to express this type of thought: [+ on] *She sat reflecting on how much had changed since she'd bought the farm.* | [reflect that] *Parker reflected that most people have no idea how hard teachers work.*

reflect on/upon phr. v. [T] to make people have a particular type of opinion about something: *The economic record reflects badly on the president's policies.*

re·flec·tion /rɪˈflɛkʃən/ n. **1** [C] an image reflected in a mirror or similar surface: *I could see my reflection in his glasses.* **2** [C,U] careful thought, or an idea or opinion based on this: *Many working women have little time for reflection.* | [+ on] *In his latest poems, Paz gives us a series of reflections on death.* | **Upon reflection,** (=after thinking about something) *I came to appreciate my father's wisdom.* **3** [C] something that shows, or is a sign of, a particular situation, fact, or feeling: [+ of] *The amount you tip should be a reflection of the kind of service you got.* **4 be a reflection on sb/sth** to show someone's character, abilities, work etc. in an unfavorable way: *Your children's bad behavior is seen as a reflection on you.* | *No matter how hard you clean, the dirt will return. It* **is no reflection on** *your housekeeping.* **5** [U] the light, heat, sound, or image that is being reflected

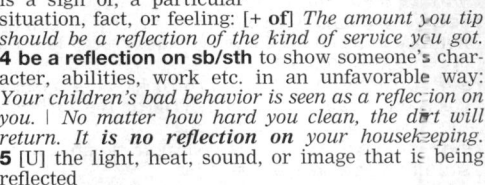

reflect on

mirror

re·flec·tive /rɪˈflɛktɪv/ adj. **1** someone who is reflective thinks carefully and deeply about things: *a reflective and soft-spoken man* **2** a reflective surface reflects light: *Bicyclists should wear reflective vests at night.* **3 be reflective of sth** to show something that is typical or true about a situation: *The data is reflective of the eating habits of American children.*

re·flec·tor /rɪˈflɛktɚ/ n. [C] **1** a small piece of plastic that reflects light and can be fastened to something such as a bicycle, so that it can be seen more easily at night —see picture at BICYCLE[1] **2** a surface that reflects light

re·flex /ˈriflɛks/ n. **1** [C] a sudden movement that your muscles make as a natural reaction to a physical effect: *Though in a coma, the patient shows signs of brain activity, such as reflexes.* **2 reflexes** [plural] the natural ability to react quickly and well to something sudden: *Computer games require quick reflexes.* **3** [C,U] also **reflex action** something that you do when you react to a situation without thinking: *Hawthorne said she fired the gun as a reflex when her husband shouted.*

re·flex·ive /rɪˈflɛksɪv/ adj. TECHNICAL a reflexive verb or PRONOUN shows that the action in a sentence affects the person or thing that does the action. In the sentences "I enjoyed myself" and "I cut myself," "myself" is reflexive. —**reflexive** n. [C]

re·flex·ol·o·gy /ˌriflɛkˈsalədʒi/ n. [U] a type of ALTERNATIVE MEDICINE in which areas of the feet are touched or rubbed in order to cure or help a medical problem

re·for·es·ta·tion /ˌrifɔrəˈsteɪʃən/ n. [U] the practice of planting trees in an area where they were previously cut down, in order to grow them for industrial use or to improve the environment —**reforest** /ri'fɔrəst/ v. [I,T]

re·form¹ /rɪ'fɔrm/ v. **1** [T] to improve a system, law, organization etc. by making a lot of changes to it, so that it operates in a fairer or more effective way: *Plans to reform the health care system have failed more than once.* **2** [I,T] to improve your behavior by making a lot of changes to it, or to make someone do this: *Dogs that bite can be reformed with good training.* | *reformed criminal/sinner/alcoholic etc.* (=someone who is no longer a criminal, sinner etc.)

s w **reform²** n. [C,U] a change or changes made to a
2 system or organization, in order to improve it: *Tax reforms did not benefit the middle class.* | [+ of] *The governor has called for reform of the forestry laws.*

re-form /ˌri'fɔrm/ v. [I,T] **1** to start to exist again or to make something start to exist again: *The band isn't re-forming.* **2** to form into lines again, or to make soldiers do this: *The soldiers re-formed their line five deep at the entrance.*

ref·or·ma·tion /ˌrɛfəˈmeɪʃən/ n. **1** [C,U] an improvement made by changing something a lot: *the reformation of the welfare system* **2 the Reformation** the religious changes in Europe in the 16th century that resulted in the Protestant churches being established

re·for·ma·to·ry /rɪ'fɔrmə,tɔri/ n. plural **reformatories** [C] a REFORM SCHOOL

re·form·er /rɪ'fɔrmə/ n. [C] someone who tries to improve a system, law, or society: *a great social reformer*

re·form·ist /rɪ'fɔrmɪst/ adj. wanting to improve systems or situations, especially in politics —**reformist** n. [C]

reform school /.'. ,./ n. [C] a special school where young people who have broken the law are sent to live

re·fract /rɪ'frækt/ v. [T] TECHNICAL if glass or water refracts light, the light changes direction when it passes through the glass or water —**refraction** /rɪ'frækʃən/ n. [U]

re·frac·to·ry /rɪ'fræktəri/ adj. FORMAL deliberately not obeying someone in authority and being difficult to deal with or control

re·frain¹ /rɪ'freɪn/ v. FORMAL to not do something that you want to do: [+ from] *Please refrain from smoking.*

refrain² n. [C] **1** a part of a song that is repeated, especially at the end of each VERSE **2** FORMAL a remark or idea that is repeated often: *"Never again" is the refrain associated with the Holocaust.*

re·fresh /rɪ'frɛʃ/ v. **1** [T] to make someone feel less tired or less hot: *A brief nap was enough to refresh him after the flight.* **2 refresh sb's memory/recollection** to make someone remember something: *Leopold looked at the files to refresh his memory.* **3 refresh sb's drink** SPOKEN to add more of an alcoholic drink to someone's glass **4** [I,T] TECHNICAL to make a computer screen show any new information that has arrived while you have been looking at it —**refreshed** adj.

re·fresh·er course /.'.. ,./ n. [C] a course that teaches you about new developments in a particular subject or skill, especially one that you need for your job: *a nursing refresher course*

re·fresh·ing /rɪ'frɛʃɪŋ/ adj. **1** making you feel less tired or less hot: *The ocean breeze was refreshing.* | *Lemon sorbet makes a refreshing treat on a hot night.* **2** pleasantly different from what is familiar and boring: *The show's sophisticated writing makes it **a refreshing change** from TV's usual programs.* —**refreshingly** adv.

re·fresh·ment /rɪ'frɛʃmənt/ n. **1** [C usually plural] food and drinks that are provided at a meeting, party, sports event etc.: *Admission to the dance is $5, and refreshments are provided.* | *a refreshment stand* **2** [U] food and drinks in general: *Hosts ought to offer their guests some refreshment.* **3** [U] the experience of being made to feel less tired or hot

ref·ried beans /ˌrifraɪd 'binz/ n. [plural] a Mexican

dish in which beans that have already been cooked are fried FRY¹ (1) again with SPICES

re·frig·er·ant /rɪ'frɪdʒərənt/ n. [C] TECHNICAL a substance used in refrigerators, AIR-CONDITIONING systems etc.

re·frig·er·ate /rɪ'frɪdʒə,reɪt/ v. [T] to make something such as food or liquid cold in order to preserve it: *Refrigerate the mixture overnight.* —**refrigeration** /rɪ,frɪdʒə'reɪʃən/ n. [U]

re·frig·er·a·tor /rɪ'frɪdʒə,reɪtə/ n. [C] a large piece of **s w** electrical kitchen equipment, shaped like a cupboard, used for keeping food and drinks cold —compare FREEZER —see picture at KITCHEN

re·fuel /ri'fyul/ v. **1** [I,T] to fill a vehicle or airplane with FUEL before continuing a trip: *Some military planes can refuel in mid-air.* **2** [T] to make feelings, emotions, or ideas stronger: *The attack refueled fears the war would begin again.*

ref·uge /'rɛfyudʒ/ n. [C] a place that provides protection from bad weather or danger: *a wildlife refuge* | [+ from] *Small huts along the trail provide a refuge from the rain.* | [+ for] *a refuge for abused women and children* | *We **took refuge** from the heat under the whirling ceiling fans.* | *Several reporters **sought refuge** in the U.S. embassy.*

ref·u·gee /ˌrɛfyʊ'dʒi/ n. [C] someone who has been forced to leave their country, especially during a war: *Refugees were streaming across the border.* | *a refugee camp*

re·ful·gent /rɪ'fʊldʒənt/ adj. LITERARY very bright —**refulgence** n. [U]

re·fund¹ /'rifʌnd/ n. [C] an amount of money that is given back to you if you are not satisfied with the goods or services that you have paid for: *You can return it within 30 days for a full refund.* | *Two cups were broken, so the store **gave me a refund**.*

re·fund² /rɪ'fʌnd, 'rifʌnd/ v. [T] to give someone their money back, especially when they are not satisfied with the goods or services they have paid for: *Saturday's concert is canceled, and tickets will be refunded.* —compare REIMBURSE

re·fur·bish /ri'fɜbɪʃ/ v. [T] to thoroughly repair and improve a building by painting it, cleaning it etc.: *A developer wants to refurbish the Green Street Hotel.* —**refurbishment** n. [C,U]

re·fus·al /rɪ'fyuzəl/ n. [C,U] **1** an act of saying or showing that you will not do something that someone has asked you to do: [refusal to do sth] *Samuelson's refusal to take a drug test cost him his job.* **2** an act of not accepting something that is being offered to you: [+ of] *Layoff decisions were blamed on the refusal of the unions to accept pay cuts.*

re·fuse¹ /rɪ'fyuz/ v. **1** [I] to say or show that you will **s w** not do something that someone has asked you to do: **2** *He tried to persuade her to come with him, but she refused.* | [refuse to do sth] *Steen refused to answer any questions.* **2** [I,T] to say that you do not want something that someone tries to give you: *Sutton refused food in protest against conditions in the prison.* | *Their offer is too good to refuse.* —opposite ACCEPT **3** [T] to not give or allow someone to have something that they want: [refuse sb sth] *Immigration authorities refused him a visa.* —compare DECLINE¹ (2)

R

USAGE NOTE: REFUSE

WORD CHOICE: refuse, reject, decline, turn down
Use all of these words to show that you do not accept something or will not do something that someone has asked you to do. You can **refuse** an invitation, application, offer, or permission: *Connors refused all offers of help.* You can also **refuse to** say or do something: *She refused to come with us.* If you **reject** something or someone, you say firmly that you will not accept an offer, suggestion, plan etc.: *They have until December 19 to accept or reject the proposal.* | *Her first novel was rejected by over 30 publishers.* If you **decline** an invitation or offer, you say politely that you cannot or will

not accept it: *We had to decline the invitation.* | *Maxwell declined the job offer.* **Turn down** is a less formal way of saying **reject**: *He has turned down several offers to play in Europe.*

ref·use² /ˈrɛfyus/ *n.* [U] FORMAL waste material; TRASH¹

re·fute /rɪˈfyut/ *v.* [T] FORMAL to prove that a statement or idea is not correct or not fair: *Several scientists have attempted to refute Moore's theories.* —**refutable** *adj.* —**refutation** /ˌrɛfyʊˈteɪʃən/ *n.* [C,U]

reg. a written abbreviation of REGISTRATION

re·gain /rɪˈgeɪn/ *v.* [T] **1** to get something back, especially an ability or quality, that you have lost: *Iowa State regained the lead in the second half.* | *It is unsure whether Kahn will regain full use of his right hand.* **2** LITERARY to reach a place again

re·gal /ˈrigəl/ *adj.* FORMAL typical of a king or queen, appropriate for a king or queen, or similar to a king or queen in behavior, looks etc.: *Jones watched, arms folded, with regal detachment.* —**regally** *adv.*

re·gale /rɪˈgeɪl/ *v.*
regale sb **with** sth *phr. v.* to entertain someone by telling them about something: *Burns regaled his interviewer with tale after tale of his political life.*

re·ga·lia /rɪˈgeɪlyə/ *n.* [U] traditional clothes and decorations, used at official ceremonies: *Campbell, a Cheyenne tribe member, wore full Indian regalia.*

re·gard¹ /rɪˈgɑrd/ *n.*
1 respect [U] feelings of respect for a person or idea: [+ for] *His statements show little regard for women.* | *Most people in the community* **have high regard for** (=have a lot of respect for) *the local elementary school.* | *Seventy percent of the voters* **hold him in low regard** (=have little respect for him).
2 attention [U] careful attention that is given to something: *Leland seems to have* **have little regard for** *detail in his work.* | *The best people are hired,* **without regard to** (=without thinking about) *race.*
3 **with/in regard to** sth used to introduce the subject you are talking or writing about: *Important changes are being made in regard to security.*
4 **in this/that regard** used to relate something you say to the statement or idea that came before it: *Last quarter we stated the need for developing a new appraisal system. The department's efforts in this regard have been impressive.*
5 **as regards** used to introduce the subject you are talking or writing about: *It is too early to judge the success of these plans, especially as regards the environment.*
6 **regards** [plural] good wishes: *Send my regards to Mark if you're writing him, okay?* | *I asked Jim to* **give my regards** *to his mother.*
7 look [singular] LITERARY a long look without moving your eyes

regard² *v.* [T] **1** [not in progressive] to think about someone or something in a particular way: [**regard** sb/sth **as** sth] *Though 20 years old, the book is still regarded as the authority on the subject.* | [**regard** sb/sth **with** **admiration/fear/concern** etc.] *Robert's classmates regarded him with curiosity.* | *The product* **is highly regarded** (=people have a very good opinion of it) *worldwide.* **2** FORMAL to look at someone or something, especially in a particular way: *She regarded him thoughtfully.* **3** FORMAL to pay attention to something

re·gard·ing /rɪˈgɑrdɪŋ/ *prep.* used in letters or speeches to introduce the subject you are writing or talking about: *Regarding your recent inquiry, I've enclosed a copy of our new brochure.*

re·gard·less /rɪˈgɑrdlɪs/ *adv.* **1** without being affected by different situations, problems etc.: *I love you, regardless.* | [+ of] *The law requires equal treatment for all, regardless of race, religion, or sex.* **2** if you continue doing something regardless, you do it in spite of difficulties or opposition: *Some actors want to play the role their way, regardless.* | [+ of] *He does what he wants, regardless of what I say.*

re·gat·ta /rɪˈgɑtə, -ˈgæ-/ *n.* [C] a sports event in which boats race

re·gen·cy /ˈridʒənsi/ *n.* [C,U] a period of government by a regent

re·gen·er·ate /rɪˈdʒɛnəˌreɪt/ *v.* [T] FORMAL to make something develop and grow strong again: *Given time, the forest will regenerate itself.* | *The Marshall Plan sought to regenerate the shattered Europe of 1947.* —**regenerative** /-nəˌreɪtɪv, -nərətɪv/ *adj.* —**regeneration** /rɪˌdʒɛnəˈreɪʃən, ˌri-/ *n.* [U]

re·gent /ˈridʒənt/ *n.* [C] someone who governs instead of a king or queen, because the king or queen is sick, absent, or still a child —**regent** *adj.* [only after noun] *the Prince Regent*

reg·gae /ˈrɛgeɪ/ *n.* [U] a type of popular music from the West Indies with a strong regular beat

reg·i·cide /ˈrɛdʒəˌsaɪd/ *n.* FORMAL **1** [U] the crime of killing a king or queen **2** [C] someone who does this

re·gime /reɪˈʒim, rɪ-/ *n.* [C] **1** a government that has not been elected in fair elections: *the region's military regime* **2** a particular system of government or management, especially one you disapprove of: *Baker was part of the Reagan regime.* (=the government when Reagan was president) **3** a regimen

reg·i·men /ˈrɛdʒəmən/ *n.* [C] FORMAL a special plan of food, exercise etc. that is intended to improve your health: *a fitness regimen*

reg·i·ment /ˈrɛdʒəmənt/ *n.* [C] **1** a large group of soldiers, usually consisting of several BATTALIONs: *the 11th Armored Cavalry Regiment* **2** a large number of people, animals, or things: *He cooked Thanksgiving dinner for a regiment of friends and family.*

reg·i·men·tal /ˌrɛdʒəˈmɛntl/ *adj.* relating to a regiment: *the regimental commander*

reg·i·ment·ed /ˈrɛdʒəˌmɛntɪd/ *adj.* organized and controlled strictly, often too strictly: *Prison inmates follow a regimented schedule.* —**regimentation** /ˌrɛdʒəˌmənˈteɪʃən, -mɛn-/ *n.* [U]

re·gion /ˈridʒən/ *n.* [C] **1** a fairly large area of a state, country etc., usually without exact limits: *Snow is expected in mountain regions.* | *The soil varies widely in this region of the country.* —see Usage Note at AREA **2** a particular part of someone's body: *Alzheimer's disease affects the regions of the brain that control memory.* **3** **(somewhere) in the region of** sth used to describe an amount of time, money, etc. without being exact; APPROXIMATELY: *The cost of the plan would be in the region of $40 to $60 billion.*

re·gion·al /ˈridʒənl/ *adj.* relating to a particular region: *Nuclear programs are a threat to regional and world peace.*

re·gion·al·ism /ˈridʒənlˌɪzəm/ *n.* [U] loyalty to a particular region of a country and the desire for it to be more politically independent

reg·is·ter¹ /ˈrɛdʒəstə/ *n.* **1** [C] an official list containing the names of all the people, organizations, or things of one particular type: *The railroad station is listed in the National Register of Historic Places.* **2** [C] a book that people write their names or other information in, to show that they have done something or been somewhere: *Hyatt signed the hotel guest register.* | *a check register* **3** [C] a CASH REGISTER **4** [C] a small movable metal plate that controls how much cool or warm air comes into a room: *Keep plants away from the hot air registers.* **5** [C] TECHNICAL the range of musical notes that someone's voice or a musical instrument can reach **6** [C,U] TECHNICAL the words, style, and grammar used by speakers and writers in a particular situation or in a particular type of writing: *Business letters should be written in a formal register.*

register² *v.* **1** [I,T] to record a name, details about something etc. on an official list: *Owners had until the end of 1990 to register their weapons.* | *Dyson is the boat's registered owner.* | [+ as] *Four candidates in the primary are registered as Democrats.* **2** [I,T] to officially arrange to attend a particular school, college, or class; ENROLL: [+ for] *When do you have to register for classes?* **3** [T] to show or express a feeling: *The faces of the jury registered no emotion.* **4** [I usually in negatives, T] if a fact or something you see registers, or if you register it, you realize or notice it and then remember it: *She told me her name, but it just didn't register at the time.* **5** [T] FORMAL to officially state your opinion about something so that everyone knows what you think: *Call or write to the consumer affairs board to register your complaint.* **6** [I,T] if an instrument registers an amount or if an amount registers on it, the instrument shows or records that amount: *Rare roast beef should register 115 degrees in the center when tested.*

registered nurse /ˌ... ˈ./ *n.* [C] *abbreviation* **RN** someone who has been trained and is officially allowed to work as a nurse

reg·is·trar /ˈrɛdʒəˌstrɑr/ *n.* [C] someone who is in charge of official records, especially at a college

reg·is·tra·tion /ˌrɛdʒəˈstreɪʃən/ *n.* **1** [U] the process of officially arranging to attend a particular school, college, or class: *The registration fee is $75.* **2** [U] the act of recording names and details on an official list: *voter registration* | [+ **of**] *the registration of births and deaths* **3** [C] an official piece of paper containing details about a vehicle and the name of its owner: *May I see your license and registration, Ma'am?*

reg·is·try /ˈrɛdʒəstri/ *n. plural* **registries 1** [C] a place where official records are kept: *the Registry of Motor Vehicles* **2** [U] the act of recording information on an official list, or the state of being recorded on such a list: *ships of U.S. registry* **3** [C] a list of gifts that people would like to receive when they get married, usually kept at a store: *the bridal registry at Robinson's Department Store*

re·gress /rɪˈgrɛs/ *v.* [I] to return to an earlier and worse condition, or to a less developed way of behaving: [+ **to**] *The patient had regressed to an infantile state.* —**regressive** *adj.*

re·gres·sion /rɪˈgrɛʃən/ *n.* [C,U + **to**] **1** the act of returning to an earlier condition that is worse or less developed **2** TECHNICAL the act of thinking or behaving as you did at an earlier time in your life, such as when you were a child

regressive tax /.,.. ˈ./ *n.* [C] TECHNICAL a tax that has less effect on the rich than on the poor —compare PROGRESSIVE TAX

re·gret[1] /rɪˈgrɛt/ *v.* [T] **1** to feel sorry about something you have done and wish you had not done it: *Do you ever regret taking this job?* | [**regret doing sth**] *I regretted not having worn a thicker coat.* | [**regret (that)**] *Most of the men regretted that they hadn't stayed in school.* | **bitterly/deeply regret sth** (=regret something very much) | *If we don't deal with the problem now, we'll **live to regret** it* (=we'll regret it in the future). | *You'll regret it if you leave your job now.* **2** [not in progressive] FORMAL to be sorry and sad about a situation: *We truly regret any inconvenience this mistake caused you.* | *I regret that I have to impose such a short deadline for this project.* **3 I regret to say/inform/tell you that** FORMAL used when you are going to give someone bad news: *I regret to inform you that your contract will not be renewed.*

USAGE NOTE: REGRET

GRAMMAR
Regret is often followed by an *-ing* form of a verb. It can be followed by the *to* form, but this is used mainly in very formal writing. So if you say: *I regret to inform you that your application was not successful,* you mean *I'm sorry, but your application was not successful.* Compare this with: *I regret telling her about my affair.* This means *I'm sorry I told her about my affair.* You **regret** something (NOT "regret about/for sth").

---

regret[2] *n.* [C,U] **1** sadness that you feel about something, because you wish it had not happened or that you had not done it: *Jason detected a note of regret in her voice.* | *She **has no regrets about** (=does not regret) not pursuing a TV career.* | [+ **at**] *Dunne expressed regret at having joined the club.* | **with (great/deep) regret** *It is with deep regret that I accept your resignation.* **2 much to my regret** FORMAL used to say that you are sorry about something: *Much to*

---

his regret, Brant never met Ives. **3 give/send your regrets** FORMAL to say that you are unable to go to a meeting, accept an invitation etc.: *Henry sends his regrets – he has the flu.*

re·gret·ful·ly /rɪˈgrɛtfəli/ *adv.* **1** feeling sad because you do not want to do what you are doing: *"We'd better go back," she said regretfully.* **2** [sentence adverb] used to talk about a situation that you wish was different or that you are sorry about: *Regretfully, Elliot was forced to close the business.* —**regretful** *adj.*

re·gret·ta·ble /rɪˈgrɛtəbəl/ *adj.* something that is regrettable makes you feel sorry or sad because it has bad results: *Any job losses are regrettable.* | *It's regrettable that we can't go in June when the weather is best.*

re·gret·ta·bly /rɪˈgrɛtəbli/ *adv.* used when you consider a particular situation to be unsatisfactory: [sentence adverb] *Regrettably, a lot of the work in the show is of poor quality.* | [+ adj./adv.] *Mr. Hart's comments were regrettably inappropriate.*

re·group /ˌriˈgrup/ *v.* **1** [I] to organize what you are doing in a new or different way, in order to be calmer or more effective: *After a tantrum, a child needs time to regroup.* **2** [I,T] to form new groups or form a group again in order to be more effective, or to make people do this: *Several of the remaining members may regroup for a new project.*

reg·u·lar[1] /ˈrɛgyələ/ *adj.*

1 repeated a regular series of things has the same amount of time or space between each thing and the next: *His breathing was slow and regular.* | *These women were given blood tests **at regular intervals** for a year.*
2 ordinary ordinary, without any special features or qualities: *Dr. Garrison is a regular doctor, not a specialist.* | *Do you want decaffeinated or regular coffee?*
3 normal size [only before noun] of a MEDIUM size, neither large nor small: *I'd like a cheeseburger and a regular Coke.*
4 every day [usually before noun] happening many times or doing something many times, especially at the same times every day, month, year etc.: *a regular churchgoer* | *Nancy entertains at home **on a regular basis**.*
5 often [only before noun] happening or doing something very often: *Infants require regular health screening.* | *Hemingway was a **regular customer** here.*
6 usual [only before noun] normal or usual: *What's the regular procedure for filing a complaint?*
7 shape evenly shaped with parts or sides of equal size: *a regular hexagon* | *Nat got his fine, regular features from his mother.*
8 regular guy/Joe a man who is ordinary, honest, and friendly: *Steven sounds like a regular guy.*
9 be/keep regular INFORMAL **a)** to get rid of waste from your BOWELS often enough to be healthy **b)** a woman who is regular has her PERIOD at the same time each month
10 grammar TECHNICAL a regular verb or noun changes its forms in the same way as most verbs or nouns. The verb "dance" is regular, but "be" is not.
11 regular army a regular army has permanent soldiers, whether there is a war or not —**regularity** *n.* [U]

regular[2] *n.* **1** [C] INFORMAL a customer who goes to the same store, bar, restaurant etc., very often: *Early morning regulars were surprised to find the coffee shop closed.* **2** [U] gasoline that contains LEAD —compare UNLEADED **3** [C] a soldier whose permanent job is in the army

reg·u·lar·ize /ˈrɛgyələˌraɪz/ *v.* [T] to make a situation that has existed for some time legal or official —**regularization** /ˌrɛgyələrəˈzeɪʃən/ *n.* [U]

reg·u·lar·ly /ˈrɛgyələli, ˈrɛgyəli/ *adv.* **1** at regular times, for example every day, week, or month: *Children are required to attend school regularly.* **2** often:

The teenage Presley regularly visited Memphis blues clubs. **3** evenly arranged or shaped: *regularly shaped crystals*

s w **reg·u·late** /ˈrɛɡyəˌleɪt/ v. [T] **1** to control an activity or process, especially by rules: *Meat and poultry are regulated by the Agriculture Department.* **2** to make a machine, your body etc. work at a particular speed, temperature etc.: *The drug helps to regulate Ryan's heartbeat.*

s w **reg·u·la·tion¹** /ˌrɛɡyəˈleɪʃən/ n. **1** [C] an official rule or order: **building/safety/fire etc. regulations** *The government is working on new food-labeling regulations.* | *There are **rules and regulations** that we all have to abide by.* **2** [U] control over something, especially by rules: *Some reforms have been made in the regulation of childcare.*

regulation² adj. [only before noun] having or doing all the things asked for in an official rule: *a regulation nine-hole golf course*

reg·u·la·tor /ˈrɛɡyəˌleɪtə/ n. [C] **1** someone who makes sure that a system operates in the right way, or makes it possible for a system to operate correctly or fairly: *federal bank regulators* **2** an instrument for controlling the temperature, speed etc. of something

reg·u·la·to·ry /ˈrɛɡyələˌtɔri/ adj. FORMAL having the purpose of controlling an activity or process, especially by rules: *the Nuclear Regulatory Commission*

re·gur·gi·tate /rɪˈɡədʒəˌteɪt/ v. FORMAL **1** [I,T] to bring food that you have already swallowed back out of your mouth; VOMIT: *Birds regurgitate food to feed their young.* **2** DISAPPROVING [T] to repeat facts, ideas etc. that you have read or heard without thinking about them yourself: *Horton regurgitated the popular, but wrong, idea that poverty creates crime.* —**regurgitation** /rɪˌɡədʒəˈteɪʃən/ n. [U]

re·hab /ˈrihæb/ n. [U] INFORMAL the process of curing someone who has an alcohol or drug problem: *a rehab center* | *I spent seven months in rehab.*

re·ha·bil·i·tate /ˌriəˈbɪləˌteɪt, ˌrihə-/ v. **1** [I,T] to help someone to live a healthy, useful, or active life again after they have been injured, very sick, or in prison: *This fund was set up to help rehabilitate victims of landmines.* | *Programs have been established to help young adults rehabilitate or achieve their potential.* **2** [T] to improve a building or area so that it returns to the good condition it was in before: *The city will be using some of its tax dollars to rehabilitate its downtown area.* **3** [T] to make people think that someone is good again after a period when they thought that person was bad: *Deaver devised the campaign to rehabilitate the First Lady's image.* —**rehabilitation** /ˌriəˌbɪləˈteɪʃən/ n. [U]

re·hash /riˈhæʃ/ v. [T] **1** to use the same ideas again in a new form that is not really different or better: *I get the feeling that Smith rehashed parts of his life for the movie.* **2** to repeat something that was discussed earlier, especially in an annoying way: *The committee members just rehashed arguments made weeks before.* —**rehash** /ˈrihæʃ/ n. [C]

s w **re·hears·al** /rɪˈhəsəl/ n. [C,U] a period of time or a particular occasion when all the people in a play, concert etc. practice it before a public performance: *Some of the play was rewritten while it was in rehearsal.* —see also DRESS REHEARSAL

re·hearse /rɪˈhəs/ v. **1** [I,T] to practice or make people practice something such as a play or concert in order to prepare for a public performance: *They rehearsed the scene in her dressing room.* **2** [T] to practice something that you plan to say to someone: *Norm spent the night before rehearsing what he'd say to the senator.* **3** [T] FORMAL to repeat an opinion that has often been expressed before

re·heat /ˌriˈhit/ v. [T] to make a meal or drink hot again: *Reheat the sauce before serving.*

Rehn·quist /ˈrɛnkwɪst/, **William H.** (1924–) the Chief Justice of the U.S. Supreme Court since 1986

Reich /raɪk/ n. **the Third Reich** the German state between 1933 and 1945

reign¹ /reɪn/ n. [C] **1** the period of time during which someone is king or queen: *the reign of Henry VIII* **2** a period or time during which an important or noticeable feature exists in a particular state or situation: *Jones ended Woodson's six-year reign as driving champion last night.* **3** **reign of terror** a period during which a government kills many of its political opponents or puts them in prison: *The invasion ended the four-year-long reign of terror.*

reign² v. [I] **1** to be the king or queen: *King George VI reigned from 1936 to 1952.* **2** to exist for a time as the most important or noticeable feature of a place, business, industry etc.: *Hyperinflation reigned in Argentina during the 1980s.* **3** **the reigning champion** the most recent winner of a competition: *the reigning Super Bowl champions*

re·im·burse /ˌriɪmˈbəs/ v. [T] FORMAL to pay money back to someone: [**reimburse sb for sth**] *Workers will not be reimbursed for any travel expenses.* —compare REFUND² —**reimbursement** n. [C,U]

rein¹ /reɪn/ n. [C] **1** [usually plural] a long narrow band of leather that is fastened around a horse's head in order to control it **2** **give sb (a) free rein** to give someone complete freedom to do something in whatever way they choose **3** **keep a (tight) rein on sb/sth** to control something strictly: *Candidates traditionally promise to keep a rein on taxes.* **4** **the reins** control over an organization or country: *Chef Thuilier will hand over the reins of the restaurant to his grandson.* **5** **free rein** freedom to express emotions or to do what you want to do: *The right boss will give you free rein as long as you are clearly loyal.*

rein² v.

rein sth ↔ in phr. v. [T] **1** to start to control a situation more strictly: *3000 jobs were cut in an attempt to rein in costs.* **2** to make a horse go more slowly by pulling on the reins

re·in·car·nate /ˌriɪnˈkɑrˌneɪt/ v. **be reincarnated** to be born again in another body after you have died

re·in·car·na·tion /ˌriɪnkɑrˈneɪʃən/ n. **1** [U] the act of being born again in another body after you have died **2** [C] the person or animal that a reincarnated person has become: [+ **of**] *Many Nepalis view him as the reincarnation of the Hindu god, Vishnu.*

rein·deer /ˈreɪndɪr/ n. plural **reindeer** [C] a large DEER with long wide horns that lives in very cold places

re·in·force /ˌriɪnˈfɔrs/ v. [T] **1** to give support to an opinion, idea, or feeling, and make it stronger: *This reinforces the stereotype that blondes have no brains.* **2** to make part of a building, structure, piece of clothing etc. stronger: *The dam was reinforced with 20,000 sandbags.* **3** to make a group of people, especially an army, stronger by adding people, equipment etc.

reinforced con·crete /ˌ... ˈ../ n. [U] CONCRETE with metal RODS in it, used to make buildings stronger

re·in·force·ment /ˌriɪnˈfɔrsmənt/ n. **1** [U] the act of making something stronger: *More than 17 bridges in the area need reinforcement.* **2** **reinforcements** [plural] additional soldiers who are sent to an army to make it stronger: *Hundreds of troop reinforcements arrived and pushed back the crowd.*

re·in·state /ˌriɪnˈsteɪt/ v. [T] **1** to put someone back into a job or position of authority that they had before: *Hannigan was reinstated after students protested his dismissal.* **2** to begin to use a law, system etc. again after not using it for a period of time: *The state reinstated capital punishment in 1976.* —**reinstatement** n. [C,U]

re·in·sure /ˌriɪnˈʃʊr/ v. [T] TECHNICAL to share the insurance of something between two or more companies, so that there is less risk for each —**reinsurance** n. [U]

re·in·ter·pret /ˌriɪnˈtəprɪt/ v. [T] to think about or perform something again or in a different way, especially to understand it in a new way —**reinterpretation** /ˌriɪntəprəˈteɪʃən/ n. [C,U] *a feminist reinterpretation of history*

re·in·vent /ˌriɪnˈvɛnt/ v. [T] **1** to produce an idea, method etc. that is based on something that existed in the past, but is slightly different: *The American educational system needs to be reinvented.* **2 reinvent yourself** to do something differently than you did before, especially in order to improve or change the way people think of you: *Mcdonna kept winning new fans as she reinvented herself.* **3 reinvent the wheel** INFORMAL to waste time trying to find a way of doing something when someone else has already discovered the best way to do it

re·is·sue /ri'ɪʃu/ v. [T] to produce a record book etc. again, after it has not been available for some time: *Collins' recordings are being reissued on CD.* —**reissue** n. [C]

re·it·er·ate /ri'ɪtəˌreɪt/ v. [T] FORMAL to repeat a statement or opinion in order to make your meaning as clear as possible: *Rosamond reiterated her wish to leave Middlemarch.* —**reiteration** /riˌɪtə'reɪʃən/ n. [C,U]

re·ject /rɪ'dʒɛkt/ v. [T]
1 offer/suggestion to refuse to accept an offer, suggestion, or request: *Ceara rejected calls for his resignation.* | *The Lottery Commission has rejected the advice of accountants.* —see Usage Note at REFUSE[1]
2 idea/belief to decide that you do not believe in or agree with something: *Some scholars reject parts of the Gospel as untrue.* | *People are free to accept or reject Stone's interpretation of the facts.*
3 not employ to refuse to accept someone for a job, school etc.: *Mitchell was rejected by several law schools.*
4 product to throw away something that has just been made, because its quality is not good enough: *Green or rotten apples are rejected.*
5 not love to refuse to give someone any love or attention: *Catherine rejected many suitable men before settling on Tom.* | *The child feels that if he fails, he will be rejected.*
6 organ if your body rejects an organ, such as a heart, after a TRANSPLANT operation, it produces substances that attack that organ —**rejection** /-'dʒɛkʃən/ n. [C,U] —opposite ACCEPT

re·ject[2] /'ridʒɛkt/ n. [C] **1** a product that has been rejected because it is damaged or imperfect **2** SLANG a person who is unsuccessful at everything they do; LOSER (3)

re·jec·tion /rɪ'dʒɛkʃən/ n. **1** [C,U] the act of not accepting, believing in, or agreeing with something: [+ of] *I think a rejection of their bid at this stage is unlikely.* **2** [C] the act of not accepting someone for a job, school, etc.: *He faced rejection after rejection before finding a job.* **3** [U] a situation in which someone stops giving you love or attention: *Eugenie's rejection of Vincent had a profound impact on his work.*

re·jig·ger /rɪ'dʒɪgə/ v. [T] INFORMAL to arrange or organize something in a different way, especially in order to make it better, more appropriate, more useful etc.: *Maybe they could rejigger the lanes so the bus could stop here.*

re·joice /rɪ'dʒɔɪs/ v. [I] LITERARY to feel or show that you are very happy: [+ at/over] *Local farmers rejoiced at the steady rain that fell.* —**rejoicing** n. [U] *The palace became the center for national rejoicing.*
rejoice in sth phr. v. [T] to be very happy about something: *Mia rejoiced in the diversity and possibilities of her new country.*

re·join[1] /ˌri'dʒɔɪn/ v. [T] **1** to go back to a group of people that you were with before: *I promised to rejoin Jane in an hour.* **2** to join an organization again: *Schroeder will rejoin the company as President and CEO.* **3** to join two things together again: *The cables need to be rejoined.*

re·join[2] /rɪ'dʒɔɪn/ v. [T] FORMAL to say something in reply, especially rudely or angrily: *"I won't be here long," he rejoined.*

re·join·der /rɪ'dʒɔɪndə/ n. [C] FORMAL a clever reply, especially one that criticizes someone or something: *Sharpton has a funny rejoinder for every occasion.*

re·ju·ve·nate /rɪ'dʒuvəˌneɪt/ v. [T] **1** [usually passive] to make someone look or feel young and strong again: *After a workout, I feel rejuvenated.* **2** to make a system or place better again: *Mr. Maynard has an*

excellent chance to rejuvenate the Tribune. —**rejuvenation** /rɪˌdʒuvə'neɪʃən/ n. [singular,U]

re·kin·dle /ri'kɪndl/ v. [T] **1** to make someone have a particular feeling, thought etc. again: *His recent move to Utah rekindled Jack's interest in skiing.* **2** to light a fire or flame again

re·lapse /'rilæps/ n. [C] **1** a situation in which someone feels sick again after feeling better: *A sudden relapse forced Peggy to stay in the hospital until Monday.* **2** a situation in which someone or something gets worse after being better for a while: *Relapses are common among some recovering alcoholics.* —**relapse** /rɪ'læps/ v. [I]

re·late /rɪ'leɪt/ v. **1** [I,T] to show or prove a connection between two or more things: *I don't understand how the two ideas relate.* | [**relate sth to sth**] *Most writing systems relate letters to sounds fairly closely.* **2** [T] FORMAL to tell someone about events that have happened to you or to someone else: *Paige related the story of her legal battles in great detail.* **3** [I] SPOKEN to feel that you understand someone's problem, situation etc.: *"I can't do a thing with my hair." "I can totally relate."*
relate to sb/sth phr. v. [T] **1** to be concerned with or directly connected to a particular subject: *How does this job relate to your career goals?* **2** to be able to have a good relationship with people because you understand their feelings and behavior: *Laurie has a hard time relating to children.* **3** SPOKEN to feel that you understand or sympathize with a particular idea or situation: *I can really relate to that article you sent me.*

re·lat·ed /rɪ'leɪtɪd/ adj. **1** connected in some way: *Applicants must hold a degree in accounting or a related field.* | [+ **to**] *Fox writes about how culture is related to art.* | **drug-related/stress-related etc.** *career-related education* **2** [not before noun] connected by a family relationship: [+ **to**] *Is Connie related to him?* **3** animals, plants, languages etc. that are related belong to the same group —**relatedness** n. [U]

relating to /.'.. ./ prep. about: *Type any comments relating to the document.*

re·la·tion /rɪ'leɪʃən/ n. **1 in relation to sth** used when comparing two things or showing the relationship between them: *Where is Fort Collins in relation to Denver?* **2** [C,U] a connection between two or more things: [+ **between**] *There's no relation between income and how much health care a person will use.* | *Most jobs* **bear no relation to** (=are not connected to) *people's schooling.* **3** [C] a member of your family; RELATIVE: **be a relation to sb** *Dad, what relation are you to Max?* | *His name's Johnson too, but there's* **no relation** (=he is not a relative). —see also BLOOD RELATIVE **4 relations** [plural] official connections between companies, countries etc.: *Japan established* **diplomatic relations** *with South Korea in 1965.* **5 relations** [plural] the way in which people or groups of people behave toward each other: [+ **between/among**] *Relations among the two groups have not always been cordial.* **6 have (sexual) relations with sb** OLD-FASHIONED to have sex with someone —see also PUBLIC RELATIONS —see Usage Note at RELATIONSHIP

re·la·tion·al /rɪ'leɪʃənəl/ adj. TECHNICAL a relational word is used as part of a sentence but does not have a meaning of its own, for example the word "have" in "I have gone" —compare NOTIONAL

re·la·tion·ship /rɪ'leɪʃənˌʃɪp/ n. **1** [C] the way in which two people or two groups behave toward each other: *Professional relationships should not be affected by personal feelings.* | [+ **between**] *Munro explores the relationship between daughters and stepmothers.* | [+ **with**] *We've developed a good relationship with our customers.* **2** [C,U] the way in which two or more things are connected and affect each other: [+ **between**] *The relationship between religion and sexual behavior is unclear.* **3** [C] a situation in which two people spend time together or live together, and have romantic or sexual feelings for each other: *His relationship with Amy wasn't going to last forever.* | *No, I'm not married, but I'm **in a relationship** right now.* **4** [U] the way in which you are related to someone in your family: [+ **to**] *"What's your relationship to Sue?" "She's my cousin."*

USAGE NOTE: RELATIONSHIP

WORD CHOICE: relationship, relations, relation, connection

A **relationship with** someone or something is usually close, and may involve strong feelings: *Jane's stormy relationship with her husband* | *What kind of relationship does she have with her mother?* **Relations** between people, groups, countries etc. are often about working together or communicating: *Relations between the union and management have improved recently.* **Relations** is a more official word: *friendly relations in the workplace.* A **relation** or **relationship to** someone or something, like a **connection,** is usually about a simple fact: *"What's Jane's relationship to Jeff?" "He's her uncle."* | *What relation does temperature have to humidity?* A **relationship between** people and other people or things may be either close and full of emotion, or simply a matter of fact: *The relationship between Cynthia and her mother has not always been a loving one.* | *What's the relationship between inflation and interest rates?*

R

rel·a·tive¹ /ˈrɛlətɪv/ *n.* [C] a member of your family: *Are your relatives from Denmark coming to the wedding?*

relative² *adj.* **1** having a particular quality when compared with something else: *Kim lived a life of relative ease and privilege.* | *Farr escaped to the relative quiet of his room.* **2 relative to sth** relating to or compared with a particular subject: *The value of the dollar relative to the yen has dropped slightly.*

relative clause /ˌ... ˈ./ *n.* [C] TECHNICAL a part of a sentence that has a verb in it, and is joined to the rest of the sentence by "who," "which," "where" etc. For example, in the sentence "The man who lives next door is a doctor," the phrase "who lives next door" is a relative clause.

relative hu·mid·i·ty /ˌ... .ˈ.../ *n.* [U] the amount of water, in the form of VAPOR, that is in the air, usually expressed as a PERCENTAGE: *The lab is kept at 72° and 50% relative humidity.*

rel·a·tive·ly /ˈrɛlətɪvli/ *adv.* **1** to a particular degree, especially when compared with something similar: *It's a relatively inexpensive restaurant.* | *The phone has been relatively quiet today.* **2 relatively speaking** used when comparing something with all similar things: *Relatively speaking, land prices in Ventura are still pretty cheap.*

relative pro·noun /ˌ... ˈ../ *n.* [C] TECHNICAL a PRONOUN such as "who," "which," or "that" by which a relative clause is connected to the rest of the sentence

rel·a·tiv·ism /ˈrɛlətɪvɪzəm/ *n.* [U] the belief that truth and right and wrong are not always the same but change according to the situation or society —**relativist** *adj.* —**relativist** *n.* [C]

rel·a·tiv·i·ty /ˌrɛləˈtɪvəṭi/ *n.* [U] the relationship in PHYSICS between time, space, and MOTION (=movement), according to Einstein's THEORY

re·launch /ˈriˈlɔntʃ, riˈlɔntʃ, -ˈlɑntʃ/ *v.* [T] to make a new effort to sell a product that is already on sale: *The magazine will be relaunched next month.* —**relaunch** /ˈriˈlɔntʃ/ *n.* [C]

re·lax /rɪˈlæks/ *v.* **1 calm** [I,T] to feel calm and comfortable and stop worrying, or to make someone do this: *Hey, relax, you're going to be all right.* | *Just sit back and relax, and enjoy the music.* | *What Robin needed was a good drink to relax her.* **2 muscle** [I,T] if you relax a part of your body or it relaxes, it becomes less stiff or less tight: *Gentle exercise can relax stiff shoulder muscles.*

3 relax rules/controls/regulations etc. to make rules etc. less strict: *Sutter hasn't in any way relaxed his standard for the team.* **4 relax your hold/grip a)** to hold something less tightly than before: [+ **on**] *Molassi relaxed his grip on my arm.* **b)** to become less strict in the way you control something: [+ **on**] *The party has no intention of relaxing its hold on the country.* **5 hair** [T] to use strong chemicals such as LYE to straighten curly hair, especially of an African-American person **6 relax your vigilance/concentration etc.** to reduce the amount of attention you give to something

re·lax·ant /rɪˈlæksənt/ *n.* [C] something, especially a drug, that makes you relax: *a muscle relaxant*

re·lax·a·tion /ˌrilækˈseɪʃən/ *n.* **1** [C,U] a way of feeling calm and comfortable and enjoying yourself: *I like to cook for relaxation.* | *relaxation therapy* **2** [U] the process of making rules on the control of something less strict: [+ **of**] *a relaxation of export controls*

re·laxed /rɪˈlækst/ *adj.* **1** feeling calm and comfortable and not worried: *Everyone looked happy and relaxed, even Bill.* **2** a situation that is relaxed is comfortable and informal: *Old couches and armchairs set a relaxed mood at Java.*

re·lax·ing /rɪˈlæksɪŋ/ *adj.* making you feel relaxed: *a relaxing bath*

re·lay¹ /ˈrileɪ/ *n.* **1** [C] a relay race: *the 4 x 100 meter relay* **2** [C,U] a piece of electrical equipment that receives radio or television signals and sends them to a wider area

re·lay² /ˈrileɪ, rɪˈleɪ/ *v.* **relays, relayed, relaying** [T] **1** to pass a message from one person or place to another: [**relay sth to sb**] *Terry relayed the offer to his boss.* **2** to send out radio or television signals by relay: *Once the information is recorded, it will be relayed to mission control.*

re·lay³ /ˌriˈleɪ/ *v.* **relays, relaid, relaying** [T] to lay something such as a CARPET again

relay race /ˈ.. ./ *n.* [C] a race in which each member of a team runs or swims part of the total distance

re·lease¹ /rɪˈlis/ *v.* [T]

release

1 set sb free to let someone go, after having kept them somewhere: *The turtles will be released back into the sea.* | [**release sb from sth**] *They're going to release me from the hospital tomorrow.* **2 stop holding** to stop holding something that you have been holding tightly or carefully: *Paul released her hand as she sat down.* | *release your hold/grip/grasp on sth Iris released her hold on Carl and stepped aside.* **3 make public** to let news or official information be known and printed: *Police have not released the names of any of the people involved.* **4 feelings** to express or get rid of feelings such as anger or worry: *Physical exercise is a good way of releasing tension.* **5 movie/record** to make a record, CD, movie etc. available for people to buy or see **6 chemical** to let a substance flow out: *Carbon stored in trees is released as carbon dioxide.* **7 from a duty** to allow someone not to do their duty or work: [**release sb from sth**] *Williams asked to be released from her teaching contract.* **8 weapon** to make a weapon fly or fall **9 machinery** to allow part of a piece of machinery or equipment to move from the position in which it is fastened: *Release the clamp gently.*

release² *n.*

1 from prison [singular,U] the act of allowing someone to go free or being allowed to go free: *The judge denied Larsen early release.* | [+ **from**] *Since his release from prison, Logan's become very religious.*

2 **record/movie** [C,U] a new record, CD, movie etc., or the act of making a movie, CD, record etc. available to buy or see: *The movie is slated for release in January.* | *New releases include previously unheard recordings by Marvin Gaye and Miles Davis.*

3 **feelings** [U] **a)** a feeling that you are free from the worry or pain that you have been suffering: [+ from] *A new treatment could mean a release from pain for arthritis sufferers.* **b)** freedom to show or express your feelings: *Music has always provided me with an emotional release.*

4 **official statement** [C,U] an official statement, report etc. that is made available to be printed or broadcast, or the act of making this available: *The release of the Roswell report proved very controversial.* —see also PRESS RELEASE

5 **chemicals** [U] the act of letting a chemical, gas etc. flow out of its usual container: *There was an accidental release of toxic waste.*

6 **on a machine** [C] a handle, button etc. that can be pressed to allow part of a machine to move

rel·e·gate /'rɛlə,geɪt/ v. [T] TECHNICAL to give someone or something a less important position than before: [relegate sb to sth] *I was relegated to the kids' table for Thanksgiving.* —**relegation** /,rɛlə-'geɪʃən/ n. [U]

re·lent /rɪˈlɛnt/ v. [I] to change your attitude and become less severe or cruel toward someone or something: *Dobbs finally relented and gave an interview to "People" magazine.*

re·lent·less /rɪˈlɛntlɪs/ adj. **1** someone who is relentless never stops being strict, cruel, or determined: *Ridge's success is due to a relentless pursuit of perfection.* [+ in] *Sanders is relentless in his attacks on the government.* **2** something bad that is relentless continues without ever stopping or getting less severe: *relentless population growth* | *Hugh felt the relentless sun on his back.* —**relentlessly** adv.

rel·e·vant /'rɛləvənt/ adj. directly relating to the subject or problem being discussed or considered: *Do you have any relevant experience in advertising?* | [+ to] *Kids have to understand how school is relevant to their lives.* —**relevance** also **relevancy** n. [U] —**relevantly** adv. —opposite IRRELEVANT

re·li·a·ble /rɪˈlaɪəbəl/ adj. someone or something that is reliable can be trusted or depended on: *Don't worry, my car is reliable.* | *reliable statistics* —**reliably** adv. —**reliability** /rɪ,laɪə'bɪləti/ n. [U] —opposite UNRELIABLE

re·li·ance /rɪˈlaɪəns/ n. [singular,U] the state of being dependent on something: [+ on] *Our cities need to reduce their reliance on the car.*

re·li·ant /rɪˈlaɪənt/ adj. **be reliant on sb/sth** to depend on someone or something: *Many of these people are reliant on international aid to keep from starving.* —see also SELF-RELIANT

rel·ic /'rɛlɪk/ n. **1** [C] an old object or custom that reminds people of the past: *Civil War relics* | [+ of] *Obelisks are among the least-understood relics of ancient Egypt.* **2** [C] a part of the body or clothing of a holy person which is kept after their death, because it is thought to be holy: *the sacred relics of John the Baptist*

re·lief /rɪˈlif/ n.

1 **comfort** [singular,U] a feeling of comfort or happiness when something frightening, worrying, or painful has ended or has not happened: *Tears of joy and relief ran down Nina's cheeks.* | *In a way, however, his dismissal was a relief.* | *To our relief, the deal went though without any problems.* | *What a relief to finally get away from the office.* | *She heaved a sigh of relief when he finally answered the phone.* | *Alice turned with relief from the messy kitchen.*

2 **reduction of pain** [U] the reduction of pain or unhappy feelings: *Ice decreases inflammation and provides pain relief.* | [+ from] *A spa can provide relief from everyday stresses.* | [+ of] *the relief of human suffering*

3 **help** [U] money, food, clothes etc. given to people who need them: *relief supplies* | **disaster/earthquake/flood relief** *We're seeking donations for earthquake relief in Assisi.*

4 **money** [U] **a)** money given by the government to help people who are poor, old, unemployed etc.: *Once people get on relief it is hard to get off.* **b)** a reduction in money owed to someone, such as the government: *tax relief*

5 **replace sb** [C] a person or group of people that replaces another one, in order to do their duties: *Ensign Korn turned over the watch to his relief.* | *a relief driver*

6 **decoration** [C] a shape or decoration that is raised above the surface it is on —see also BAS-RELIEF

7 **in relief a)** a shape or decoration that is in relief sticks out above the rest of the surface it is on: **in high/low relief** (=sticking out a lot or a little) **b)** if you show a part of the Earth's surface on a map in relief, you show the differences in height between different parts of it

8 **bring/throw sth into relief** also **stand out in relief** to make something very noticeable, or to be very noticeable: **into stark/sharp relief** *The shooting of 22 people in Texas throws the issue of gun control into stark relief.*

9 **comic relief** a funny moment during a serious movie, book, or situation: *The dog provides most of the comic relief in this tedious sitcom.*

10 **freeing a town** FORMAL the act of freeing a town when it has been surrounded by an enemy: *the relief of Khe Sanh*

relief map /.'. ,./ n. [C] a map with the mountains and high parts shown differently from the low parts, especially by being printed in a different color or by being raised

re·lieve /rɪˈliv/ v. [T]

1 **pain/problem** to make a pain, problem, or bad feeling less severe: *Just take some Tylenol to relieve the pain.* | *Regular exercise can relieve depression and anxiety.*

2 **replace sb** to replace someone when they have completed their duty or when they need a rest: *After about 20 hours, they were relieved by another crew.*

3 **relieve yourself** a polite expression meaning to URINATE

4 **relieve the boredom/monotony** to make something less boring: *Cross-country skiing relieves the monotony of winter.*

5 **town** FORMAL to free a town that an enemy has surrounded

relieve sb of sth phr. v. [T] **1** FORMAL to take away someone's job because they have done something wrong: **relieve sb of their command/duties/post** *Col. Hayes was relieved of his command for violating attack guidelines.* **2** FORMAL to help someone by taking something from them, especially something difficult they are doing or something heavy that they are carrying: *Efforts will be made to relieve the country of its massive debt.* **3** HUMOROUS to steal something from someone: *Hoskins was relieved of his wallet while sleeping on the beach.*

re·lieved /rɪˈlivd/ adj. [not before noun] feeling happy because you are no longer worried about something: *By the time Lew left, Meier felt greatly relieved.* | [be **relieved to see/hear/know etc. sth**] *Vicki was relieved to hear that Clint wasn't badly wounded.* | [+ that] *Cara was relieved that the pregnancy test was negative.*

re·li·gion /rɪˈlɪdʒən/ n. **1** [U] a belief in the life of the spirit and usually in one or more gods: *My beliefs about abortion are not influenced by religion.* | *The Constitution guarantees freedom of speech and religion.* **2** [C] a particular system of this belief and all the ceremonies and duties that are related to it: *the Muslim religion* | *people of all religions* | *Birth control is against her religion* (=not allowed by her church). | *Frost has the right to practice his religion.* **3** **find/get religion** INFORMAL to suddenly become interested in religion in a way that seems strange to other people: *Nichols found religion during his fifteen years in prison.* **4** [singular] an activity or area of interest that is extremely or unreasonably important in your life: *Exercise is almost like a religion to Mina.*

re·li·gious /rɪ'lɪdʒəs/ *adj.* **1** relating to religion in general or to a particular religion: *religious studies* | *They didn't attend because of religious reasons.* **2** believing strongly in your religion and obeying its rules carefully: *My mother is so religious that she won't even watch TV on Sundays.*

re·li·gious·ly /rɪ'lɪdʒəsli/ *adv.* **1** if you do something religiously, you are always very careful to do it: *I've been watching that show religiously for four years.* **2** in a way that is related to religion: *religiously oriented education*

re·lin·quish /rɪ'lɪŋkwɪʃ/ *v.* [T] FORMAL to let someone else have your position, power, or rights, especially not willingly: *Captain Weiss will relinquish command after this mission.* | [relinquish sth to sb] *Single mother Lisa had relinquished her baby to her parents.*

rel·i·quar·y /'rɛlə,kwɛri/ *n.* [C] a container for RELICS (=religious objects)

rel·ish[1] /'rɛlɪʃ/ *v.* [T] to enjoy an experience or the thought of something that is going to happen: *Ella relished her short freedom during the summer.* | *Ida clearly relishes proving other people wrong.*

relish[2] *n.* **1** [C,U] a cold SAUCE made with foods that are cut up very small, eaten especially with meat to add taste to it: *sweet pickle relish* **2** [U] great enjoyment of something: *General Peckham chuckled with relish.*

re·live /,ri'lɪv/ *v.* [T] to remember or imagine something that happened in the past so clearly that you experience the same emotions again: *Over lunch, we relived our adventures in Tanzania.*

re·load /,ri'loʊd/ *v.* [I,T] to put another bullet into a gun, film into a camera, or PROGRAM into a computer: *Reload the pistol, quick!*

re·lo·cate /ri'loʊ,keɪt/ *v.* [I,T] if a group of people or a business relocates or is relocated, they move to a different place: [+ to] *I really don't see myself relocating to England.* | [relocate sb/sth to sth] *Relocating the airport to Miramar would give an economic boost to the region.* —**relocation** /,riloʊ'keɪʃən/ *n.* [U]

re·luc·tant /rɪ'lʌktənt/ *adj.* slow and unwilling: *She gave a reluctant smile.* | [reluctant to do sth] *At first, the bank was reluctant to lend me the money.* —**reluctance** *n.* [singular,U] —**reluctantly** *adv.*

re·ly /rɪ'laɪ/ *v.*

rely on/upon sb/sth *phr. v.* [T] **1** to trust someone or something to do what you need or expect them to do: *Many basketball teams rely on one star player.* [rely on sb/sth to do sth] *Students rely on the pictures to help them understand.* | [rely on sb/sth for sth] *Most people rely on TV for information about the world.* **2** to depend on something in order to continue to live or exist: [rely on sth/sb for sth] *50% of Americans with AIDS rely on Medicaid for their health care.*

re·main /rɪ'meɪn/ *v.* [I] **1** [always + adv./prep., linking verb] to continue to be in the same state or condition: *Sean remained close to his kids after the divorce.* | *Two men remain in captivity.* | *You have the right to remain silent.* **2** FORMAL to stay in the same place without moving away: [+ at/in/with etc.] *Rosie remained at the bar, smoking a cigarette.* **3** to continue to exist, after others are gone or have been destroyed: *What little remained of the original structure has been converted into a farmhouse.* | *Byrd is likely to lose what remains of his fortune.* **4 it remains to be seen** FORMAL used to say that it is still uncertain whether something will happen or is true: *Whether the team can sustain its winning streak remains to be seen.* **5 sth remains to be done** something still needs to be done, after other things have been dealt with: *Many questions remain to be answered.* | *The appointment remains to be approved by the board.* **6 the fact remains** used to say that a particular fact cannot be ignored: *I know Benson has a Ph.D., but the fact remains that he has no practical experience.*

re·main·der /rɪ'meɪndə/ *n.* **the remainder** the part of something that is left after everything else is gone or has been dealt with: *The state will provide $4.6 million, with the county supplying the remainder.* | [+ of] *Mattie gulped down the remainder of the Coca Cola.*

re·main·ing /rɪ'meɪnɪŋ/ *adj.* [only before noun] the remaining people or things are those that are left when the others are gone, have been used, or have been dealt with: *Add all the remaining ingredients and bring to the boil.* | *One remaining couple carried on dancing.*

re·mains /rɪ'meɪnz/ *n.* [plural] **1** the parts of something that are left after the rest has been destroyed or has disappeared: [the remains of sth] *The McDonald family picked through the remains of their house.* **2** FORMAL the body of someone who has died: *A special chapel was built to house Spencer's remains.*

re·make[1] /'rimeɪk/ *n.* [C] a record or movie that has the same music or story as one that was made before: *Mitchum has a cameo in the remake of "Cape Fear."*

re·make[2] /,ri'meɪk/ *v.* past tense and past participle **remade** /-'meɪd/ [T] **1** to film a story or record a song again: *"Mutiny on the Bounty" has been remade at least three times.* **2** to build or make something again

re·mand[1] /rɪ'mænd/ *v.* [T usually passive] TECHNICAL **1** to send a case to be dealt with in another court: *The case should be remanded to state court.* **2** if a court remands someone, it sends them to prison to wait for their TRIAL: *Individuals may be remanded to the custody of the Marshals Service.*

remand[2] *n.* [U] **on remand** if a case is on remand, it has been sent by one court to another to be dealt with

re·mark[1] /rɪ'mɑrk/ *n.* [C] something that you say when you express an opinion or say what you have noticed: *The audience roared with laughter at Carson's remarks.* | *Dan made a sarcastic remark about my being on the phone all the time.*

remark[2] *v.* [T] to say something, especially about something you have just noticed: *"I hate that machine," Anderson remarked.* | [+ that] *Several people remarked that Bill seemed like a nice man.*

remark on/upon sth *phr. v.* [T] to notice that something has happened and say something about it: *Balter remarked on the orchestra's improvement when he returned.*

re·mark·a·ble /rɪ'mɑrkəbəl/ *adj.* unusual or surprising and therefore deserving attention or praise: *Josephine was a truly remarkable woman.* *Clark did a remarkable job setting things up for the meeting.* | [+ about] *Was there anything remarkable about his injuries?* | [+ for] *Yank Shing's buffet is remarkable for the quality of the food.*

re·mark·a·bly /rɪ'mɑrkəbli/ *adv.* in an amount or to a degree that is unusual or surprising: [+ adj./adv.] *Prague is a remarkably beautiful place.* | [sentence adverb] *Remarkably, both the kids and the grown-ups enjoyed themselves.*

Re·marque /rə'mɑrk/, **Er·ich Ma·ri·a** /'ɛrɪk mə'riə/ (1898–1970) a German writer of NOVELS

re·mar·ry /ri'mæri/ *v.* **remarries, remarried, remarrying** [I,T] to marry again after your husband or wife dies, or after the end of a previous marriage: *Widowed in 1949, Mrs. Hayes never remarried.* —**remarriage** /ri'mærɪdʒ/ *n.* [C]

re·mas·ter /ri'mæstə/ *v.* [T] TECHNICAL to make a musical recording sound better or a movie look better by using a computer to improve the original: *The album includes ten digitally remastered songs.*

re·match /'rimætʃ, ri'mætʃ/ *n.* [C] a second game that is played between two teams or people because there was no winner in the first game or there was a disagreement about the result

Rem·brandt /'rɛmbrænt/ (1606–1669) a Dutch artist, Rembrandt van Rijn, who is regarded as one of the greatest European painters

re·me·di·al /rɪ'midiəl/ *adj.* [usually before noun] **1 remedial class/course/program etc.** a special class, course etc. that helps students who are having

difficulty learning something: *remedial math classes*
2 intended to improve something that is wrong or to cure a problem with someone's health: *The company is taking **remedial action**.*

rem·e·dy¹ /'rɛmədi/ *n. plural* **remedies** [C] **1** a way of dealing with a problem or making an unsatisfactory situation better: *The best remedy would be to install a separate meter.* | [+ **for**] *There is no adequate remedy for discrimination.* **2** something such as a medicine that is used to cure an illness or pain that is not very serious: *Inhaling steam is a good home remedy for a sore throat.* | *a Chinese folk remedy* (=something that people use as a medicine, but that is not a drug used by doctors) *for upset stomachs*

remedy² *v.* **remedies, remedied, remedying** [T] to deal with a problem or improve a bad situation: *Her superiors took steps to remedy the situation.*

re·mem·ber /rɪ'mɛmbər/ *v.*
1 the past [I,T] to have a picture or idea in your mind of people, events, places etc. from the past: *Do you remember that kid Anthony from art class?* | [**remember (that)**] *I remember he had a broken leg that summer.* | [**remember sb doing sth**] *She remembered him saying a friend of his was in trouble.* | [**remember doing sth**] *I can remember playing canasta over at Fran's house.* | *If I remember correctly, there was a big bay window at the back.* | **clearly/distinctly/vividly remember** sth *I clearly remember my grandfather pushing me around in his red wheelbarrow.*
2 information/facts [I,T] to bring information or facts that you know back into your mind: *Sometimes I have trouble remembering her name.* | *Bud, do you remember the exact date of their wedding?* | [**remember (that)**] *I suddenly remembered that I'd left the stove on.* | [**remember what/how/why etc.**] *Mr. Kovacs couldn't remember when the last tenant moved out.*
3 to do/get sth [I,T] to not forget something that you must do, get, or bring: *Did you remember the bread?* | *You were supposed to pick her up on your way home, remember?* | [**remember to do sth**] *It's often hard to remember to take vitamin pills.*
4 keep sth in mind [T] to keep a particular fact about a situation in your mind [**remember (that)**] *Remember that dark colors will make a room look smaller.*
5 honor the dead [T] to think about someone who has died with special respect, often in a ceremony: *On Memorial Day, Americans remember their war dead.*
6 be remembered for/as sth to be famous for something that happened or something important that you once did: *James Dickey is best remembered for his 1972 novel "Deliverance."* | *Graf will be remembered as one of the best women's tennis players.*
7 give sb a present [T] to give someone a present on a particular occasion: *Aunt Sara always remembers me at Christmas.*
8 **remember me to sb** OLD-FASHIONED, SPOKEN used to ask someone to give a greeting from you to someone else

USAGE NOTE: REMEMBER

WORD CHOICE: remember and remind
Remember is used to say that you are the person who is remembering something: *Do you remember Tom and Missy?* | *I can't remember how this thing works.* Use **remind** to say that a person or a thing is making you remember something: *It really reminds me of my hometown.* | *She reminds me of Carla.*

re·mem·brance /rɪ'mɛmbrəns/ *n.* **1** [U] the act of remembering and giving honor to someone who has died: *Ware will speak **in remembrance** of Martin Luther King.* **2** [C,U] FORMAL a memory that you have of a person or event: *They shared their remembrances of Christmases past.*

re·mind /rɪ'maɪnd/ *v.* [T] **1** to make someone remember something that they must do: *I'd better write this down to remind myself.* | [**remind sb to do sth**] *Remind me to give you Tracy's number before you*

go. | [**remind sb about sth**] *Let's go down and remind Mr. Lee about the meeting.* | [**remind sb (that)**] *Mrs. Welland reminded her son they still had several people to see.* | [**remind sb what/how/when etc.**] *Can you remind me what poison oak looks like?*
2 to make someone remember someone that they know or something that happened in the past: [**remind sb of sb/sth**] *That reminds me of a joke I heard last week.* | [**remind sb what/how etc.**] *The view across the bay reminded me why so many people want to live here.*

SPOKEN PHRASES

3 that reminds me used when something has just made you remember something you were going to say or do: *Oh, that reminds me, I have to deposit a check at the bank.* **4 Don't remind me** used in a joking way when someone has mentioned something that embarrasses or annoys you: *"We have a test tomorrow." "Don't remind me!"* **5 let me remind you** also **may I remind you** FORMAL used to add force to a warning or criticism: *Let me remind you of your original statement.*

—see Usage Note at REMEMBER

remind sb **of** sb/sth *phr. v.* [T not in progressive] to seem similar to someone or something else: *Doesn't she remind you of Nicole?* | *These cookies remind me of my mother's.*

re·mind·er /rɪ'maɪndər/ *n.* [C] **1** something that reminds you of something that happened or existed in the past: [+ **of**] *Several vacant lots are reminders of the earthquake.* | *Lorna kept the photos as reminders of happier times.* **2** something that makes you notice something or understand it better: [+ **of**] *All night there were small explosions, reminders of the war.* | [**a reminder that**] *It's a painful reminder that discrimination occurs in every community.* | *The President's bodyguards serve as a reminder that he's no ordinary guy out for a walk.* **3** something, for example a letter, that reminds you to do something which you might have forgotten: *We sent a reminder, but have not yet received a reply.*

Rem·ing·ton /'rɛmɪŋtən/**, Fred·er·ic** /'frɛdrɪk/ (1861–1909) a U.S. PAINTER and SCULPTOR famous for his work showing Native Americans and life in the American West

rem·i·nisce /ˌrɛmə'nɪs/ *v.* [I] to talk or think about pleasant events in your past: [+ **about**] *Peter and June talked for hours, reminiscing about the Summer of Love.*

rem·i·nis·cence /ˌrɛmə'nɪsəns/ *n.* [C often plural,U] a spoken or written story about events that you remember: [+ **of**] *reminiscences of the '60s* —compare MEMOIR

rem·i·nis·cent /ˌrɛmə'nɪsənt/ *adj.* **1 reminiscent of sth** reminding you of something: *We ate in a cozy dining room slightly reminiscent of a ski lodge.* **2** [only before noun] thinking about the past: *"Those were the days," agreed Barrow with a reminiscent sigh.*

re·miss /rɪ'mɪs/ *adj.* FORMAL [not before noun] careless about doing something that you ought to do: *The editor would be remiss in her duties if the information were not reported.* | [**it would be remiss of sb to do sth**] *It would be remiss of the team not to make use of Cone's pitching talent.* —**remissness** *n.* [U]

re·mis·sion /rɪ'mɪʃən/ *n.* [C,U] a period when a serious illness improves for a time: *Juan has cancer, although it is in remission for now.*

re·mit /rɪ'mɪt/ *v.* **remitted, remitting** FORMAL **1** [I,T] to send a payment by mail: *He filed a tax return but failed to remit what he owed.* **2** [T] to free someone from a debt or punishment

remit sth **to** sb/sth *phr. v.* [T] FORMAL to send a proposal, plan, or problem back to someone for them to make a decision about: *On Thursday the bill was remitted to a committee for review.* —compare UNREMITTING

re·mit·tance /rɪˈmɪtⁿns/ *n.* **1** [C] FORMAL an amount of money that you send by mail to pay for something **2** [U] the act of sending money by mail

re·mit·tent /rɪˈmɪtⁿnt/ *adj.* FORMAL a remittent fever or illness is severe for short periods but improves between those times

rem·nant /ˈremnənt/ *n.* [C] **1** [usually plural] a small part of something that remains after the rest of it has been used, destroyed, or eaten: [+ of] *Burning cinders showered down from the remnants of the roof.* **2** a small piece of cloth left from a larger piece and sold for a cheaper price

re·mod·el /ˌriˈmɑdl/ *v.* [I,T] to change the shape or appearance of something such as a house, room, building etc.: *We're remodeling the basement this winter.*

re·mold /ˌriˈmould/ *v.* [T] FORMAL to change an idea, system, way of thinking etc.: *Technology has remolded the way the stock market operates.*

re·mon·strance /rɪˈmɑnstrəns/ *n.* [C,U] FORMAL a complaint or protest

rem·on·strate /ˈremənˌstreɪt, rɪˈmɑnˌstreɪt/ *v.* [I] FORMAL to tell someone that you strongly disapprove of something they have said or done: [+ with/against] *Dean frequently remonstrated with writers and directors about how to play a role.*

re·morse /rɪˈmɔrs/ *n.* [U] a strong feeling of being sorry that you have done something very bad: *Watson expressed deep remorse for his crimes and is no longer considered a threat to others.* —**remorseful** *adj.* —**remorsefully** *adv.*

re·morse·less /rɪˈmɔrslɪs/ *adj.* **1** something bad or threatening that is remorseless continues to happen and seems impossible to stop: *A remorseless gray drizzle fell all day long.* **2** cruel, and not caring how much other people are hurt: *Farley was shown to be a remorseless killer and a chronic liar.* —**remorselessly** *adv.* —**remorselessness** *n.* [U]

re·mort·gage /ˌriˈmɔrgɪdʒ/ *v.* [T] to borrow money by having a second MORTGAGE on your house, or increasing the one you have: *Remortgaging your house is a big risk if you're retired.* —see also REVERSE MORTGAGE, SECOND MORTGAGE

re·mote¹ /rɪˈmout/ *adj.* **1** far away in space or time: *Space probes operate in dark, cold, remote parts of the solar system.* | *Analysts say a political solution is more remote than ever.* **2** far from towns: *The plane went down in a remote forest area.* **3 remote possibility/chance** a very slight or small possibility or chance: *There is a very remote chance that the hurricane will veer toward the east coast.* **4** very different from something else, or not closely related to it: [+ from] *This discussion of artistic meaning seems very remote from a convict's experience.* **5** unfriendly, and not interested in people: *Peter's father was always remote and silent around his family.* **6** [only before noun] controlled by a piece of equipment that is not directly connected: *The procedure was monitored with remote cameras.* —**remoteness** *n.* [C]

remote² *n.* [C] SPOKEN a remote control: *Hand me the remote.*

remote ac·cess /.ˌ. ˈ../ *n.* [U] a system that allows you to use information on a computer that is far away from your computer

remote con·trol /.ˌ. .ˈ./ *n.* **1** [C] a thing you use for controlling a piece of electrical or electronic equipment without having to touch it, for example for turning a television on or off —see picture on page 426 **2** [U] the process of controlling equipment from a distance, using radio or electronic signals: *The bomb is guided by remote control.* **3** [U] a type of computer SOFTWARE that lets you use a particular computer by connecting it to another one that is far away —**remote-controlled** *adj.*

re·mote·ly /rɪˈmoutli/ *adv.* **1** slightly: *Most of the low-alcohol brews taste only remotely like beer.* | *This is not even remotely funny.* **2** from far away: *remotely operated vehicles*

remote sens·ing /.ˌ. ˈ../ *n.* [U] the use of SATELLITES to obtain pictures and information about the Earth

re·mov·a·ble /rɪˈmuvəbəl/ *adj.* easy to remove: *The trench coat features a removable fur collar.*

re·mov·al /rɪˈmuvəl/ *n.* [C,U] the act of taking something away: *hair removal* | *the removal of investment controls*

re·move /rɪˈmuv/ *v.* [T] **1** **take away** to take something away from, out of, or off the place where it is: *Remove the spice bag before serving the soup.* | *The old paint will have to be removed first.* | [remove sth from sth] *Phil removed a notebook and pencil from his coat pocket.* **2** **get rid of** to get rid of something so it does not exist anymore: *What's the best way to remove red wine stains?* | *The plan will remove unneeded layers of bureaucracy.* **3** **from a job** to force someone out of an important position or dismiss them from a job: [+ from] *If the recall succeeds, the mayor will be removed from office.* **4** **clothes** FORMAL to take off a piece of clothing: *Irvin paused to remove his sunglasses.* **5** **be far removed from sth** to be very different from something: *The world of TV sitcoms is far removed from reality.* **6 cousin once/twice etc. removed** the child, GRANDCHILD etc. of your COUSIN, or your cousin's father, grandfather etc. **7 removed from sth** OLD USE hidden from someone or something

re·mov·er /rɪˈmuvɚ/ *n.* [C,U] **paint/stain etc. remover** a substance that takes away paint marks etc.

REM sleep /ˈrem slip/ *n.* [U] a period during sleep when there is rapid movement of the eyes, when you are dreaming

re·mu·ner·ate /rɪˈmyunəˌreɪt/ *v.* [T] FORMAL to pay someone for something they have done for you —**remuneration** /rɪˌmyunəˈreɪʃən/ *n.* [C,U]

re·mu·ner·a·tive /rɪˈmyunərətɪv, -ˌreɪtɪv/ *adj.* FORMAL making a lot of money —**remuneratively** *adv.*

Ren·ais·sance /ˈrenəˌzɑns, -ˌsɑns, ˌrenəˈsɑns/ *n.* **1 the Renaissance** the period of time in Europe between the 14th and 17th centuries, when art, literature, PHILOSOPHY, and scientific ideas became very important and a lot of new art etc. was produced **2 Renaissance art/architecture etc.** art, architecture etc. belonging to the Renaissance period

renaissance *n.* [singular] a new interest in something, especially a particular form of art, music etc., that had not been popular for a long period of time: *American classical music is enjoying a renaissance.*

Renaissance man /.ˈ... ˌ./ *n.* [C] a man who can do many things well, such as writing, painting etc., and who knows a lot about many different subjects

Renaissance wom·an /.ˈ... ˌ./ *n.* [C] a woman who can do many things well, such as writing, painting etc., and who knows a lot about many different subjects

re·nal /ˈrinl/ *adj.* [only before noun] TECHNICAL relating to the KIDNEYS: *acute renal failure*

re·name /riˈneɪm/ *v.* [T usually passive] to give something a new name: *In 1930, the bank was renamed Bank of America.*

rend /rend/ *v.* past tense and past participle **rent** [T] LITERARY to tear or break something violently into pieces

ren·der /ˈrendɚ/ *v.* [T] FORMAL **1** to cause someone or something to be in a particular condition: *Digital technology could render today's televisions useless.* | [render obsolete/helpless/meaningless etc.] *The new Nintendo game deck renders obsolete all the old game cartridges.* **2** to give something to someone or do something, because it is your duty or because they expect you to: *The bill would allow unions to charge for services rendered to non-members.* | **render a decision/judgment/opinion etc.** *It is the court's task to render a fair and impartial verdict.* **3** FORMAL to express or present something in a particular way: *Maestas' sculptures were rendered in bronze.* | *In beautifully rendered prose, she relates her daily struggles.* | **render sth into English/Russian/**

Chinese etc. (=to translate something into English, Russian etc.) **4** to draw something, especially something that you plan to build, to show what it will look like when it is finished: *Galan rendered his drawing of a new commercial center in less than a week.* **5** to melt the fat of an animal as you cook it: *Steam the goose to render some of the fat.*

render sth ↔ **up** *phr. v.* [T] OLD USE to give something to someone, especially to a ruler or enemy

ren·der·ing /ˈrɛndərɪŋ/ *n.* [C] **1** the particular way a painting, story etc. is expressed: *a poetic rendering* **2** a drawing or plan of something such as a building, that shows what it will look like when it is built: *an architectural rendering*

ren·dez·vous¹ /ˈrɑndeɪˌvu, -dɪ-/ *n. plural* **ren·dez·vous** /-ˌvuz/ [C] **1** an arrangement to meet at a particular time and place: [+ with] *She flew to Paris for a secret rendezvous with Jean-Jacques.* **2** [usually singular] a place where two or more people have arranged to meet: *Old Town Square is one of Prague's best known tourist rendezvous.* **3** an occasion when two SPACECRAFT or military airplanes or vehicles meet, for example to move supplies from one to the other

rendezvous² *v.* [I] **1** to meet someone as you have arranged: [+ with] *The yacht was scheduled to rendezvous with a Coast Guard patrol on Monday.* **2** if two SPACECRAFT or military vehicles or airplanes rendezvous, they meet, for example to move supplies from one to the other

ren·di·tion /rɛnˈdɪʃən/ *n.* **1** [U] the way a play or piece of music is performed: *Vaughn's rendition of "Body and Soul" won the competition.* **2** [C] a TRANSLATION of a piece of writing: *an English rendition of a Greek poem*

ren·e·gade /ˈrɛnəˌgeɪd/ *n.* [C] someone who joins the opposing side in a war, political, or religious organization etc., or who does or believes things that are not approved of by the organization they belong to —**renegade** *adj.* [only before noun] *renegade cops*

re·nege /rɪˈnɛg, -ˈnɪg/ *v.* [I] FORMAL to not do something you have promised or agreed to do: **renege on a promise/agreement** *The gunmen reneged on their promise to release the hostages.*

re·ne·go·ti·ate /ˌrɪnɪˈgoʊʃiˌeɪt/ *v.* [I,T] to change a previous agreement between two or more people or groups, especially because one of the groups believes the conditions are unfair: *The company was forced to renegotiate contracts with several of its remaining customers.* —**renegotiable** *adj.*

re·new /rɪˈnu/ *v.* [T] **1** to arrange for a contract, membership of a club etc. to continue: *To renew your license, contact the Department of Motor Vehicles.* | *There was nothing to prevent the President from renewing the bombing in the North.* **2 renew a book** to arrange to continue borrowing a library book for an additional period of time: *Library books can be renewed by telephone.* **3** to begin to do something again: *His firm is renewing efforts to provide in-house computer training.* | **renew a friendship/acquaintance etc.** (=start a relationship again) **4** to replace something that is old or broken with something new: *The state desperately needs to renew its road system.* —see also RENEWED

re·new·a·ble /rɪˈnuəbəl/ *adj.* **1** something that is renewable can be replaced by natural processes or good management, so that it is never used up: **renewable energy/resources** *Water is a natural renewable resource.* **2** a renewable contract, ticket etc. can be made to continue after the date on which it ends: *a six-month renewable visa* —opposite NONRENEWABLE

re·new·al /rɪˈnuəl/ *n.* [singular,U] an act of renewing something: [+ of] *Martinez will not seek renewal of his company's contract.* —see also URBAN RENEWAL

re·newed /rɪˈnud/ *adj.* **1** increasing or starting again after not being very strong *The departure of UN troops could lead to renewed fighting.* | **renewed confidence/faith/interest etc.** *There has been a renewed interest in art deco buildings.* **2** [not before noun] feeling healthy and relaxed again, after feeling sick or tired

ren·net /ˈrɛnət/ *n.* [U] a substance used for making milk thicker in order to make cheese

Re·no /ˈrinoʊ/ a city in the U.S. state of Nevada which is a popular place of people to go to in order to GAMBLE

Reno, Jan·et /ˈdʒænɪt/ (1938–) a U.S. lawyer who, in 1993, became the first woman to have the job of ATTORNEY GENERAL

Janet Reno

Ren·oir /rənˈwɑr/, **Pierre Au·guste** /pyɛr ɔˈgust/ (1841–1919) a French PAINTER who was one of the first IMPRESSIONISTS

re·nounce /rɪˈnaʊns/ *v.* [T] **1** to publicly say that you will no longer try to keep something, or will not stay in an important position: *Rudolph voluntarily renounced his U.S. citizenship.* | *Von Bulow renounced all claims to his wife's fortune.* **2** to publicly say that you no longer believe in or support something: *We absolutely renounce all forms of terrorism.* —see also RENUNCIATION

ren·o·vate /ˈrɛnəˌveɪt/ *v.* [T] to repair and paint an old building so that it is in good condition again: *It will take over a year to renovate the historic hotel.* —**renovation** /ˌrɛnəˈveɪʃən/ *n.* [U]

re·nown /rɪˈnaʊn/ *n.* [U] FAME and admiration, that you get because of some special skill or something that you have achieved: [+ as] *Rostropovich gained international renown as a cello soloist.* | *an artist of great renown*

re·nowned /rɪˈnaʊnd/ *adj.* known and admired by a lot of people, especially for some special skill, achievement, or quality: *a renowned university* | *Rangoon was renowned for its dazzling buildings and pagodas.* | **renowned statesman/architect etc.** *We later learned that Stark was a renowned scientist in his field.* —see Usage Note at FAMOUS¹

rent¹ /rɛnt/ *v.* **1** [I,T] to regularly pay money to live in a house or room that belongs to someone else or use something that belongs to someone else: *He finally decided to rent a condo on the lake.* | *Beck and his wife are renting while they look for a house to buy.* —see Usage Note at BORROW **2** [T] to pay money for the use of something for a short period of time: *We rented a couple of movies this weekend.* **3** [I,T] to let someone live in a house, room etc. that you own, in return for money: [+ to] *Some landlords refuse to rent to unmarried couples.*

rent at/for sth *phr. v.* [I] if a house rents at or rents for a particular amount of money, that is how much someone pays in order to use it: *What are studio apartments renting for in this area?*

rent sth ↔ **out** *phr. v.* [T] to make a house, room etc. that you own available to someone in return for money: *We're thinking of renting out the basement.*

rent² *n.* **1** [C,U] the amount of money you pay for the use of a house, room, car, etc. that belongs to someone else: *The rent is $850 a month.* | *Danny always pays the rent on time.* **2 for rent** available to be rented **3** [C] LITERARY a long narrow cut or hole in something such as cloth

rent·al¹ /ˈrɛntl/ *n.* **1** [C usually singular] the money that you pay to use a car, television, tools etc. over a period of time: *Ski rental is $14.* **2** [C,U] an arrangement by which you rent something, or the act of renting something: *rental costs* | *Card holders get special deals on car rentals and hotels.* **3** [C] something that is rented, especially a car or house: *the pros and cons of buying a rental*

rental² *adj.* [only before noun] available to be rented, or being rented: *a rental car*

rent con·trol /ˈ. .ˌ./ *n.* [U] a situation in which a city or state uses laws to control the cost of renting apartments

rent-free /ˌ. ˈ. ◂/ *adj., adv.* without payment of rent:

Laurie is still living rent-free in our house. | *rent-free housing*

rent strike /'. ./ *n.* [C] a time when all the people living in a group of houses or apartments refuse to pay their rent, as a protest against something

re·nun·ci·a·tion /rɪˌnʌnsi'eɪʃən/ *n.* [C,U] FORMAL a decision not to keep a particular set of beliefs, way of life, power, or object: [+ **of**] *The agreement depends on their renunciation of violence.*

re·o·pen /ri'oupən/ *v.* **1** [I,T] if a theater, restaurant etc. reopens or is reopened, it opens again after being closed **2** [I,T] if you reopen a discussion or law case, or if it reopens, you begin it again after it has stopped: *Garrett reopened the murder investigation in May.* **3** [T] if a government reopens the border of their country, they allow people to pass through it again after it has been closed

re·or·der /ri'ɔrdə/ *v.* [I,T] **1** to order a product again: *Levi's computers automatically reorder supplies when needed.* **2** to change things or put them in a more appropriate order: *New parents quickly find themselves reordering their priorities.*

re·or·ga·nize /ri'ɔrgəˌnaɪz/ *v.* [I,T] to arrange or organize something in a new way: *I've been meaning to reorganize the kitchen cabinets for ages.* —**reorganization** /riˌɔrgənə'zeɪʃən/ *n.* [U]

rep /rɛp/ *n.* **1** [C] INFORMAL someone who speaks officially for a company or organization; REPRESENTATIVE: *MTV reps confirmed that the station will not show the video.* **2** [C] INFORMAL a SALES REPRESENTATIVE **3** [C] INFORMAL a REPERTORY theater or company **4** [C] SPOKEN a REPUTATION: *Williams has a bad rep, both on and off the field.* **5** one exercise that you do in a series of exercises; REPETITION: *Do 15 reps of each exercise.*

Rep. *n.* [C] **1** the written abbreviation of REPRESENTATIVE: *Rep. Lamar Smith* **2** the written abbreviation of REPUBLICAN

re·pack·age /ˌri'pækɪdʒ/ *v.* [T] **1** to change the way someone or something is shown to the public, so that people will think of them in a new and different way: *The attempt to repackage the gas tax was a complete failure.* **2** to change the way that a product is PACKAGED (PACKAGE²), usually in a more attractive way **3** to put something into a different package or container

re·paid /ri'peɪd/ *v.* the past tense and past participle of REPAY

repairing the fence

re·pair¹ /rɪ'pɛr/ *v.* [T] **1** to fix something that is damaged, broken, or not working correctly: *They had to move out while the condo was being repaired.* | *Jones had cosmetic surgery to repair the damage to his face.* **2** FORMAL to do something to remove the harm that your mistake or wrong action has caused: *The first step in repairing a relationship is a willingness to communicate.* —see also IRREPARABLE

repair to sth *phr. v.* [T] OLD-FASHIONED to go to a place: *Shall we repair to the drawing room?*

repair² *n.* **1** [C,U] an act of repairing something: *Many ships dock at Kure Naval Base for repairs.* | *The building across the street was burned beyond repair* (=so badly that it cannot be repaired). | *Your house is in serious need of repair.* | *Two sections of*

Highway 101 are under repair (=being repaired). **2 in good/bad/poor repair** in good or bad condition: *You can prevent falls by keeping stairways in good repair.* **3** [C] a place on something that has been repaired: *Sanding is unnecessary if the repair is reasonably smooth.* —**repairer** *n.* [C]

re·pair·a·ble /rɪ'pɛrəbəl/ *adj.* able to be repaired

rep·a·ra·ble /'rɛpərəbəl/ *adj.* FORMAL able to be repaired —opposite IRREPARABLE

rep·a·ra·tion /ˌrɛpə'reɪʃən/ *n.* **1 reparations** [plural] money paid by a defeated country after a war, for all the deaths, injuries, and damage it has caused: *Germany paid $50 billion in reparations for Nazi crimes.* **2** [C,U] FORMAL payment made to or something done for someone for damage, loss, or injury that you have caused them in the past: *What should be the reparation for a mother whose child was murdered?*

rep·ar·tee /ˌrɛpə'ti, -pɑr'ti/ *n.* [U] FORMAL conversation that is very fast and full of intelligent and amusing remarks: *witty repartee*

re·past /rɪ'pæst/ *n.* [C] FORMAL a meal

re·pa·tri·ate /ri'peɪtriˌeɪt/ *v.* [T] **1** to send someone back to their own country: *So far, 51 boat people have been forcibly repatriated.* **2** to send profits or money you have earned back to your own country —**repatriation** /riˌpeɪtri'eɪʃən/ *n.*

re·pay /rɪ'peɪ/ *v.* **repays, repaid, repaying** [T] **1** to pay back money that you have borrowed: *Failure to repay a student loan can ruin a person's credit rating.* **2** to reward someone for helping you: [**repay sb for sth**] *We'll never be able to repay you for all you've done.*

re·pay·a·ble /rɪ'peɪəbəl/ *adj.* money that is repayable at a specific time has to be repaid by that time

re·pay·ment /rɪ'peɪmənt/ *n.* **1** [U] the act of paying back money: *They're demanding repayment for the cost of the uniforms.* **2** [C] an amount of money that you pay back: *Canceled checks show when repayments were made.*

re·peal /rɪ'pil/ *v.* [T] if a government repeals a law, it officially ends that law: *Congress repealed the ban on women flying Naval combat missions.* —**repeal** *n.* [U]

re·peat¹ /rɪ'pit/ *v.*
1 ▸state again◂ [T] to say something again: *Could you repeat question number six, please?* | [**repeat that**] *Martin kept repeating that he was hungry.* | *An interpreter asked Karpov to repeat himself* (=say the same thing again). | *Do not, I repeat* (=used to emphasize what you are saying), *do not leave the area.* **SW 2 2**
2 ▸do again◂ [T] to do something again: *Holmes repeated his experiments to verify the existence of atoms.* | *Willy has to repeat kindergarten.*
3 ▸tell sth you hear◂ [T] to say something that you have heard someone else saying: *Sam came out of the room and repeated what the doctor had said.*
4 ▸learn◂ [T] to say something you have learned: *Repeat after me*: "The customer is always right."
5 ▸history◂ [T] if history or an event repeats itself, it is like something that happened before: *If history repeats itself, Taylor could be up for her second Grammy award.*
6 ▸broadcast◂ [T often passive] to broadcast a television or radio program again: *The awards show will be repeated on TNN Saturday night at six.*
7 ▸pattern◂ [I,T] if a pattern repeats or is repeated, it appears the same way several times or in several places: *A pattern of red and green flowers is repeated on the bedspread and drapes.*
8 repeat yourself to say something that you have already said, usually without realizing that you have done it: *It's sad, that Grandpa just repeats himself a million times, and asks you the same questions over again.*
9 be worth/bear repeating used to say that something is interesting or important enough to say again: *I've dealt with this problem before, but it's well worth repeating.*

re·peat² *n.* [C] **1** an event very like something that happened before: [+ **of**] *We simply can't afford a repeat of the Alaska oil spill here.* | *I will not tolerate a repeat performance* (=I do not want something bad to happen again). **2 repeat customer/buyer** someone who buys goods or services from the same business they bought from before: *Close to 70 percent of their business is from repeat customers.* **3** a television or radio program that is broadcast again; RERUN: *There's a repeat of "ER" on tonight.* **4** TECHNICAL the sign at the end of a line of written music that tells the performer to play the music again, or the act of playing the music again

re·peat·ed /rɪˈpiːtɪd/ *adj.* [only before noun] done or happening again and again: *Motorists used the roads despite repeated warnings of snow.* | *Repeated attempts to fix the satellite have failed.*

re·peat·ed·ly /rɪˈpiːtɪdli/ *adv.* many times: *Davis repeatedly denied that he had ever taken drugs.*

re·peat·er /rɪˈpiːtə/ *n.* [C] **1** TECHNICAL a repeating gun **2** someone who does an activity again, such as a sport, competition, or class: *Demter is the only repeater from the 1996 team.*

re·peat·ing /rɪˈpiːtɪŋ/ *n.* [C] **1** a repeating gun can be fired several times without being loaded again **2** a repeating watch or clock can be made to repeat the last STRIKE (=sound made at an hour or quarter of an hour)

re·pel /rɪˈpɛl/ *v.* repelled, repelling **1** [T] if something repels you, you want to avoid it because you do not like it: *Her heavy make-up and cheap perfume repelled him.* **2** [T] to fight a group or military force and make them stop attacking you: *Guerrilla fighters were soon able to repel the army's attack.* **3** [T] to keep something or someone away from you: *Use cedar or citronella candles to repel biting insects.* **4** [I,T] TECHNICAL if two things repel each other they push each other away with an electrical force

re·pel·lent¹ /rɪˈpɛlənt/ *n.* [C,U] a substance that keeps insects away: *mosquito repellent* —see also WATER-REPELLENT

repellent² *adj.* disgusting: *Women found him physically repellent.*

re·pent /rɪˈpɛnt/ *v.* [I,T] **1** to say you are sorry and to feel shame about something, used especially by religious people: *Repent your sins and you will be forgiven.* **2** to feel sorry for something and wish you had not done it: *At a press conference, Cheng repented her crimes.* | [+ for] *Wilson publicly repented for the pain he had caused the family.*

re·pen·tance /rɪˈpɛntns/ *n.* [U] the state of being sorry for something you have done

re·pen·tant /rɪˈpɛntnt/ *adj.* sorry for something wrong that you have done —opposite UNREPENTANT —**repentantly** *adv.*

re·per·cus·sions /ˌriːpəˈkʌʃənz/ *n.* [plural] **1** the effects of an event or action, especially bad effects that happen much later: *The government is making a major effort to deal with poverty and its repercussions.* | [+ of/for/on etc.] *California Democrats are concerned about the repercussions of last week's election.* **2 repercussion** [C] TECHNICAL a sound or force coming back after it hits something

rep·er·toire /ˈrɛpəˌtwɑr/ *n.* [C usually singular] **1** all of the plays, pieces of music etc that a performer or group has learned and can perform **2** the total number of things that someone or something is able to do: *Kate shouldn't have any problem finding a job with her repertoire of skills.*

rep·er·to·ry /ˈrɛpəˌtɔri, -pə-/ *n. plural* **repertories** **1** [U] a type of theater work in which a group of actors perform different plays on different days, instead of only doing the same play for a long time *a repertory company* **2** [C] a repertoire: *Aiko and Koko performed material from their existing repertories.*

rep·e·ti·tion /ˌrɛpəˈtɪʃən/ *n.* **1** [U] doing the same thing many times: *Students are taught math by constant repetition.* **2** [C] something that is done again: [+ of] *We don't want a repetition of last year's disaster.*

rep·e·ti·tious /ˌrɛpəˈtɪʃəs/ *adj.* saying or doing the same thing several times, especially in such a way that people become bored: *repetitious drills*

re·pet·i·tive /rɪˈpɛtətɪv/ *adj.* done many times in the same way, and often boring: *A lot of the work we*

have to do is repetitive. —**repetitively** *adv.*

repetitive strain in·ju·ry /ˌ.,... ˈ. ,.../ *n.* [U] TECHNICAL: see RSI

re·phrase /riˈfreɪz/ *v.* [T] to express something in different words so that its meaning is clearer or more acceptable: *OK. Let me rephrase the question.*

re·place /rɪˈpleɪs/ *v.* [T] **1** to start doing something instead of another person, or start being used instead of another thing: *Have they hired anybody to replace Ken?* | *Typewriters have basically been replaced by computers.* **2** to remove someone from their job or something from its place, and put a different person or thing there: *Anderson was replaced in the fifth inning after a wrist injury.* | [**replace sth with sth**] *The apartments will be torn down and replaced with a shopping plaza.* **3** to get something new to put in the place of something that is broken, stolen, too old etc.: *I've replaced the batteries in your Walkman.* **4** to put something back in its correct place: *Please replace your tray and return your seat to an upright position for landing.* —**replaceable** *adj.*

re·place·ment /rɪˈpleɪsmənt/ *n.* **1** [C] someone or something that replaces another person or thing: [+ for] *John's planning to retire as soon as they find a replacement for him.* **2** [U] the act of replacing something, often with something newer, better etc.: [+ of] *Replacement of the bridge is expected to cost $38 million.* | *hip/knee/joint replacement She's had two hip replacements.* —**replacement** *adj.*: *a replacement passport*

re·play¹ /ˈriːpleɪ/ *n. plural* **replays** [C] **1** an action in a sport seen on television, that is immediately shown again: *Instant replays showed that Griffith caught the ball.* **2** something that is done exactly as it was before: [+ of] *Republicans are hoping for a replay of the 1988 elections.*

re·play² /riˈpleɪ/ *v.* replays, replayed, replaying [T] **1** to play again something that has been recorded, such as a VIDEO, television show, or telephone message: *Channel 5 will replay the game's highlights at midnight.* **2** to play a game or sport again: *This is a key series that both teams would like to replay in October.* **3** to do something or think about something exactly as it was done before: *Another of Ray's comments replayed in my head.*

re·plen·ish /rɪˈplɛnɪʃ/ *v.* [T] FORMAL to fill something again or put new supplies into something: *As more workers retire, new employees are needed to replenish the workforce.* —**replenishment** *n.* [U]

re·plete /rɪˈpliːt/ *adj.* [not before noun] **1** FORMAL fully supplied with something: [+ with] *a military ceremony replete with honors* **2** OLD-FASHIONED so full of food or drink that you want no more —**repletion** /rɪˈpliːʃən/ *n.* [U]

rep·li·ca /ˈrɛplɪkə/ *n.* [C] a very good copy, especially of a painting or other work of art: [+ of] *a replica of a wooden Viking boat*

rep·li·cate /ˈrɛpləˌkeɪt/ *v.* [T] FORMAL to do or make something again, so that you get the same result or make an exact copy: *Other scientists were unable to replicate the experiment.* —**replication** /ˌrɛpləˈkeɪʃən/ *n.* [C,U]

re·ply¹ /rɪˈplaɪ/ *v.* replies, replied, replying **1** [I,T] to answer someone by saying or writing something: *Sorry it took me so long to reply.* | *"Of course," Nathalie replied.* | [+ to] *Has anyone replied to your ad in the paper?* | [+ that] *Mills replied that the car belonged to his brother.* —see Usage Note at ANSWER¹ **2** [I] to react to an action by doing something else: [**reply (to sth) with sth**] *Rebel troops replied with increased violence.*

reply² *n. plural* **replies** [C] **1** something that is said, written, or done as a way of replying: *I tried calling, but there was no reply.* | [+ to] *We have still not received any replies to our letters.* | *Aitkins frowned but made no reply* (=did not say anything). **2 in reply (to sth)** FORMAL as a way of replying to something: *I am writing in reply to your letter dated May 12.* | *The renewed violence was in reply to continued*

R

government pressure on the rebels. **3** an EMAIL message that is an answer to a message that was sent earlier

re·po man /'ripou ˌmæn/ n. [C] INFORMAL someone whose job is to REPOSSESS (=take away) cars whose owners have stopped paying for them

re·port¹ /rɪ'pɔrt/ n. [C] **1** a piece of writing in a newspaper about something that is happening, or part of a television or radio news program: *According to recent **news reports**, two of the victims are Americans.* | *the weather report* **2** a written or spoken description of a situation or event, giving people the information they need: [+ **about/of/on**] *a police officer's report of the accident* | *Martens **gave a report on** his sales trip to Korea.* **3** a piece of writing that carefully considers a particular subject, and is often written by a group of people: [+ **on**] *The Agriculture Department recently issued a report on world population.* —see also BOOK REPORT **4** a description of a situation or event, that may or may not be true: [+ **of**] *Police received reports of a bomb threat at the airport at 11:28 p.m.* **5** FORMAL the noise of an explosion or shot: *a loud report*

report² v.
1 news [I,T] to give people information about recent events, especially in newspapers and on television and radio: *We aim to report the news as fairly as possible.* | *Kathy Wilhelm has reported for The Associated Press since 1987.* | [+ **on**] *Here's Mike Bryer, reporting on the day's stock exchange.* | [+ **that**] *Journalists in Cairo reported that seven people had been shot.* | [**report doing sth**] *Witnesses reported seeing three people flee the scene.* | [**be reported to be**] *The stolen necklace is reported to be worth $57,000.*
2 job/work [I,T] to tell someone about what has been happening, or what you are doing as part of your job: *To report a change of address, please call our toll-free number.* | [**report (to sb) on sth**] *Come back next week to report on your progress.*
3 public statement [T] to officially give information to the public: *Doctors reported a 13% increase in the number of people with heart disease.*
4 crime/accident [T] to tell the police or someone in authority that an accident or crime has happened: *I'd like to report a theft.* | [**report sth to sb**] *We immediately reported the incident to the police.* | **report sb missing/injured/killed etc.** *Francis was reported missing when he failed to arrive home Saturday night.*
5 complain [T] to complain about someone to people in authority: [**report sb to sb**] *His drinking problem led co-workers to report him to supervisors.*
6 arrival [I] to go somewhere and officially state that you have arrived: [+ **to**] *Bradley will report to a federal prison in Petersburg, VA.* | *All soldiers were required to **report for duty** (=go somewhere and officially say you are ready to work) on Friday.*
report back phr. v. [I,T] to bring or send back information that you have been asked to find: [+ **to**] *The committee has 60 days to report back to Congress.* | [+ **on**] *Students were asked to report back on their results.*
report to sb phr. v. [T] to be responsible to someone at work and be managed by them: *In his new post, he will report to Greg Carr, Boston Technology's chief executive.*

re·port·age /rɪ'pɔrtɪdʒ, ˌrɛpɔr'tɑʒ/ n. [U] **1** the particular style of reporting used in newspapers, radio, or television **2** the act of reporting news

report card /'. ./ n. a written statement by teachers about a child's work at school, sent to their parents

re·port·ed·ly /rɪ'pɔrtɪdli/ adv. [sentence adverb] according to what people say: *Her husband's assets are reportedly worth over $15 million.*

re·port·ed speech /.ˌ.. './ n. [U] TECHNICAL in grammar, the style of speech or writing used to report what someone says without repeating their actual words. The sentence "She said she didn't feel well." is an example of reported speech.

re·port·er /rɪ'pɔrtə/ n. [C] someone whose job is to write about events for a newspaper or to tell people about events on television or the radio —compare JOURNALIST —see also COURT REPORTER

re·pose¹ /rɪ'pouz/ n. [U] FORMAL a state of calm or comfortable rest: *A human body **in repose** has a graceful shape.* —**reposeful** adj.

repose² v. FORMAL **1** [I] if something reposes in a place, it is put there **2** [I] if someone reposes somewhere they rest there **3 repose your trust/hope etc. in sb** to trust someone to help you

re·pos·i·to·ry /rɪ'pɑzəˌtɔri/ n. plural **repositories** [C] **1** a place where things are stored in large quantities: *a furniture repository* | [+ **of/for**] *a repository for nuclear waste* **2** FORMAL a person or book that gives a lot of information: [+ **of/for**] *Parry became a repository for the tribe's oral history.*

re·pos·sess /ˌripə'zɛs/ v. [T] to take back cars, furniture, or property from people who stop paying for them as they had arranged: *His car was eventually repossessed by the auto loan agency.* —**repossession** /-'zɛʃən/ n. [C,U]

rep·re·hend /ˌrɛprɪ'hɛnd/ v. [T] FORMAL to express disapproval of a person or an action

rep·re·hen·si·ble /ˌrɛprɪ'hɛnsəbəl/ adj. FORMAL bad and deserving criticism: *I find their behavior morally reprehensible.*

rep·re·sent /ˌrɛprɪ'zɛnt/ v. [T]
1 speak for sb **a)** to speak officially for someone in a court of law and to prepare arguments to support them in court: *Who is representing the defendant?* | *She decided to **represent herself** (=speak for herself, without a lawyer) during the trial.* **b)** to speak officially for another person or group of people, giving their opinions and taking action for them: *As a top agent, Ovitz represented some of Hollywood's biggest stars.*
2 be an example to be a clear example which shows that something happens or exists: **represent a change/advance/increase etc.** *This treatment represents a significant advance in the field of cancer research.* | *Some pesticides represent a major threat to public health.*
3 amount to make up a particular amount or part of something: *European orders represented 30 percent of our sales last year.*
4 government to have been elected to an official government position by the people in a particular area and to do things and make decisions in order to help them: *the Congressman who represents the taxpayers of District 1*
5 sports if you represent your country, school, town etc. in a sport, you play for the team from that country etc.: *Her greatest ambition was to represent her country at the Olympics (=to compete on her country's team).*
6 be well represented if a group, organization, area etc. is well represented at an event, a lot of people from it are at the event: *Local parents were well represented at the school board meeting.*
7 represent sb/sth as sth to describe someone or something in a particular way, so that people have a particular opinion of them or it: *The article represents the millionaire as a simple family man* | *The poll represented college students as mainly uninterested in politics.*
8 represent yourself as sth to say that you are something that you are not: *He had represented himself as an employee in order to gain access to the files.*
9 sign to be a sign or mark that shows the position of a particular thing, especially on a map or plan; SYMBOLIZE: *Brown areas represent deserts on the map.*
10 art if a painting, STATUE, piece of music etc. represents something or someone, it shows that thing in a particular way: *Paintings representing religious themes were common in medieval times.* | *The dummies represent average-sized adult males.*

rep·re·sen·ta·tion /ˌrɛprɪzɛn'teɪʃən, -zən-/ n. **1** [U] the state of having someone to speak, vote, or make decisions for you: *There has been a decline in union representation in the auto industry.* | *Each state receives equal representation in the U.S. Senate.* —see also PROPORTIONAL REPRESENTATION **2** [C] a painting, sign etc. that shows or describes something else: *The clock in the painting is a symbolic representation of the passage of time.* **3** [U] the act of representing someone or something: *She received praise for her effective representation of Garcia during the trial.* **4 make false/fraudulent representations** FORMAL to describe or explain something in a way that you know is not true

rep·re·sen·ta·tion·al /ˌreprɪzenˈteɪʃənəl/ *adj.* **1** a representational painting or style of art shows things as they actually appear in real life —compare ABSTRACT[1] (1) **2** relating to a situation in which someone officially speaks or does something for someone else: *The union provides the same level of representational assistance to all divisions.*

rep·re·sen·ta·tive[1] /ˌreprɪˈzentətɪv/ *adj.* [C] **1** like other members of the same group; typical: [+ of] *The latest incident is representative of a larger trend.* | *The pollsters asked a representative sample of New York residents for their opinions.* **2** a representative system of government allows people to vote for other people to represent them in the government: *a representative democracy*

representative[2] *n.* [C] **1 Representative** a member of the House of Representatives, the Lower House of Congress in the United States **2** a person who has been chosen to speak, vote, or make decisions for someone else: [+ of] *an elected representative of the people* —see also SALES REPRESENTATIVE

re·press /rɪˈpres/ *v.* [T] **1** to stop yourself from doing something, especially something you want to do: *Brenda repressed the urge to shout at him.* | *I repressed a smile.* **2** if someone represses feelings, memories etc., their mind has hidden them because they are too upsetting to think about: *He had long ago repressed the painful memories of his childhood.* **3** to control a group of people by force: *Other nations condemned the ruler for repressing dissent.* —compare SUPPRESS

re·pressed /rɪˈprest/ *adj.* having feelings or desires that you do not allow yourself to express or think about, especially sexual feelings: *The actress plays a repressed young woman trapped in a loveless marriage.* | *repressed anger*

re·pres·sion /rɪˈpreʃən/ *n.* [C,U] **1** very strong control of feelings or desires that you are ashamed of, until you feel as if you do not have them anymore: *Religious ideas about sin made sexual repression commonplace.* **2** cruel and severe control of a large group of people: *During Stalin's repressions, countless people were sent to labor camps and starved to death.*

re·pres·sive /rɪˈpresɪv/ *adj.* **1** a repressive government or law is severe and cruel: *The country has repressive laws and jails full of political prisoners.* **2** relating to feelings or desires that you do not allow yourself to express, especially sexual ones: *The customs were exceedingly repressive toward women.*

re·prieve[1] /rɪˈpriv/ *n.* [C] **1** a delay before something bad continues: *Shoppers will get a temporary reprieve from the new sales tax.* **2** an official order stopping the killing of a prisoner as a punishment: *The U.S. Supreme Court voted against granting Smith a reprieve.*

reprieve[2] *v.* [T usually passive] to officially stop a prisoner from being killed as a punishment

rep·ri·mand /ˈreprəˌmænd/ *v.* to tell someone officially that something they have done is very wrong: *Breslin was sharply reprimanded for insulting an Asian-American reporter.* —**reprimand** *n.* [C]

re·print[1] /ˌriˈprɪnt/ *v.* [T] to print a book, story, newspaper article etc. again

re·print[2] /ˈriprɪnt/ *n.* [C] **1** a book, story, newspaper article etc. that is printed again **2** an act of printing a book again because all the copies of it have been sold

re·pris·al /rɪˈpraɪzəl/ *n.* [C,U] an act of violence or other strong reaction, to punish your enemies or opponents for something they have done: [+ against] *There were reprisals against unarmed civilians.* | *They didn't tell the police for fear of reprisal.* | *Alfred was shot in reprisal for killing a rival gang member.*

re·prise /rɪˈpriz/ *n.* [C] the repeating of all or part of a piece of music, movie etc.

re·proach[1] /rɪˈproutʃ/ *n.* FORMAL **1** [C,U] criticism or disapproval, or a remark that expresses this: *"You don't need me," she said quietly, without reproach.* | *Fernandez argued the reproaches were harsh and unfair.* **2 above/beyond reproach** impossible to criticize; perfect: *Vernon's work in the community has been beyond reproach.* **3 a reproach to sth** something that makes a person, society etc. feel bad or ashamed: *These derelict houses are a reproach to the city.*

reproach[2] *v.* [T] **1** FORMAL to blame or criticize someone in a way that shows you are disappointed, but not angry: [reproach sb for sth] *King Victor publicly reproached his son for his behavior.* | [reproach sb for doing sth] *Moviemakers have been reproached for showing violence.* **2 reproach yourself** to feel guilty about something that you think you are responsible for

re·proach·ful /rɪˈproutʃfəl/ *adj.* a reproachful look, remark etc. shows that you are criticizing someone or blaming them: *She shot me a reproachful glance.* —**reproachfully** *adv.*

rep·ro·bate /ˈreprəˌbeɪt/ *n.* [C] FORMAL OR HUMOROUS someone who behaves in an immoral way: *a nasty old reprobate*

re·proc·ess /riˈprɑses/ *v.* [T] to treat a waste substance so that it can be used again: *The plant's main function has been to reprocess uranium.*

re·pro·duce /ˌriprəˈdus/ *v.* **1** [I,T] if a plant or animal reproduces, or reproduces itself, it produces young plants or animals: *The turtles return to the Mexican coast to reproduce.* **2** [T] to make a photograph or printed copy of something: *Klimt's artwork is reproduced in this exquisite collector's book.* **3** [T] to make something that is just like something else, or make something happen again in the same way as it happened the first time: *Scientists were unable to reproduce the results claimed on the television program.* | *With a good set of speakers, you can reproduce the orchestra's sound in your own home.* —**reproducible** *adj.*

re·pro·duc·tion /ˌriprəˈdʌkʃən/ *n.* **1** [U] the act or process of producing young animals or plants: *Scientists studied the reproduction, diet and health of the dolphins.* **2** [U] the act of producing a copy of a book, picture, piece of music etc.: *Unauthorized reproduction of this publication is strictly forbidden.* | *high quality sound reproduction* **3** [C] a copy of a work of art, piece of furniture etc.: [+ of] *a reproduction of Vincent van Gogh's "Sunflowers"* | **reproduction furniture/chairs** etc. *a reproduction Victorian bed*

re·pro·duc·tive /ˌriprəˈdʌktɪv/ *adj.* [only before noun] relating to the process of producing young animals or plants: *the human reproductive system*

re·proof /rɪˈpruf/ *n.* FORMAL **1** [U] blame or disapproval: *She greeted me with a look of cold reproof.* **2** [C] a remark that blames or criticizes someone: *a sharp reproof*

re·prove /rɪˈpruv/ *v.* [T] FORMAL to criticize someone for something that they have done: [reprove sb for doing sth] *Employees were reproved for smoking in the building's restrooms.*

re·prov·ing /rɪˈpruvɪŋ/ *adj.* FORMAL expressing criticism of something that someone has done: *a reproving stare* —**reprovingly** *adv.*

rep·tile /ˈreptaɪl, ˈreptl/ *n.* [C] a type of animal such as a snake or LIZARD whose blood changes according to the temperature around it, and that usually lays eggs

rep·til·i·an[1] /repˈtɪliən/ *adj.* like a reptile or relating to reptiles

reptilian[2] *n.* [C] TECHNICAL a reptile

re·pub·lic /rɪˈpʌblɪk/ *n.* [C] a country governed by elected representatives of the people, and led by a President, not a king or queen —compare MONARCHY

re·pub·li·can[1] /rɪˈpʌblɪkən/ n. [C] **1 Republican** a member or supporter of the Republican Party in the U.S. —compare DEMOCRAT (1) **2** someone who believes in government by elected representatives only, with no king or queen

republican[2] adj. **1 Republican** relating to or supporting the Republican Party in the U.S.: *the Republican candidate for president* **2** relating to or supporting a system of government that is not led by a king or queen and is elected by the people —**republicanism** n. [U]

Republican Par·ty /.,... ˈ../ n. **the Republican Party** one of the two main political parties of the U.S. —compare DEMOCRATIC PARTY

re·pu·di·ate /rɪˈpyudiˌeɪt/ v. [T] FORMAL **1** to disagree strongly with someone or something and refuse to have any association with them or it; REJECT[1]: *Government officials were urged to repudiate the treaty.* **2** to state or show formally that something is not true or correct: *The book repudiates all the racist stereotypes about black women.* **3** OLD-FASHIONED to say formally that you do not have any connection with someone anymore, especially a relative; DISOWN **4** to refuse to pay a debt —**repudiation** /rɪˌpyudiˈeɪʃən/ n. [U]

re·pug·nance /rɪˈpʌgnəns/ n. [U] FORMAL a strong feeling of dislike for something: [+ for/of etc.] *a repugnance for pornography*

re·pug·nant /rɪˈpʌgnənt/ adj. FORMAL very bad and offensive: *Congressmen found Cray's behavior deeply repugnant.*

re·pulse[1] /rɪˈpʌls/ v. [T] FORMAL **1** if something or someone repulses you, you feel they are very bad or disgusting: *The very thought of his cold clammy hands repulsed me.* —see also REPULSIVE (1) **2** to defeat a military attack: *Government troops repulsed an attack by rebel forces.* **3** to refuse an offer of friendship or help in a way that is impolite

repulse[2] n. [singular] **1** FORMAL the act of refusing in an impolite way when someone offers to help you or be your friend **2** TECHNICAL the defeat of a military attack

re·pul·sion /rɪˈpʌlʃən/ n. **1** [singular,U] a feeling that you want to avoid something or move away from it, because it is disgusting: *Looking at Ed's tattoos, I felt a mixture of amazement and repulsion.* **2** [U] TECHNICAL the electric or MAGNETIC force by which one object pushes another one away from it —opposite ATTRACTION

re·pul·sive /rɪˈpʌlsɪv/ adj. **1** disgusting, in a way that almost makes you feel sick: *Baine's tale is both intriguing and repulsive.* **2** TECHNICAL repulsive forces push objects away from each other —**repulsively** adv. —**repulsiveness** n. [U]

re·pur·pose /riˈpɜpəs/ v. [T] if something such as equipment, a building, or a document is repurposed, it is used in a new way that is different from its original use, without having to be changed very much

rep·u·ta·ble /ˈrɛpyətəbəl/ adj. respected for being honest or for doing good work: *the nation's most reputable newspaper* —**reputably** adv.

rep·u·ta·tion /ˌrɛpyəˈteɪʃən/ n. [C] **1** the opinion that people have about a particular person or thing because of what has happened in the past: [+ for] *The college's reputation for a sound education is strong.* | [+ as] *In her last job she got a reputation as a trouble maker.* | *Judge Kelso* **has a reputation for** *being strict but fair.* | **a good/bad reputation** *Stanford University has maintained its good reputation.* | **earn/gain/win** etc. **a reputation as sth** *He gained a national reputation as a campaigner against drugs.* **2 live up to your reputation** to behave in the way that people expect: *"Touchdown Tom" lived up to his reputation, scoring six times.* **3 live up to its reputation** to be at least as bad or good as people had thought: *The service at Heron Lodge failed to live up to its reputation.*

re·pute /rɪˈpyut/ n. [U] FORMAL reputation: **of good/**

low/international etc. **repute** *a man of great repute* | *a hotel* **of some repute** (=having a good reputation)

re·put·ed /rɪˈpyutɪd/ adj. [only before noun] according to what most people say or think, but not definitely: *the reputed leader of the Crips gang* | **be reputed to be/do sth**] *She is reputed to be extremely wealthy.*

re·put·ed·ly /rɪˈpyutɪdli/ adv. [sentence adverb] according to what most people say or think: *The committee had reputedly spent over $3000 on "business entertainment."*

re·quest[1] /rɪˈkwɛst/ n. [C] **1** an act of asking for something politely or formally: [+ for] *They have* **made an urgent request** *for international aid.* | [+ that] *Anderson repeated his request that we postpone the meeting.* | *The study was done* **at the request** *of the Chairman* (=because the Chairman asked for it). | *Further details will be sent* **on request** (=when you ask for it). | *There were no flowers at the funeral,* **by request** (=because they asked specially not to have flowers).* | **any requests?** (=used to ask people if they want anything) **2** a piece of music that is played on the radio because someone has asked for it

request[2] v. [T] **1** FORMAL to ask for something politely or formally: *To request more information, please call our toll free number.* | [**request that**] *Students requested that the school provide more computer classes.* | [**request sb to do sth**] *Guests are requested to wear formal attire.* **2** to ask for a particular piece of music to be played on the radio

USAGE NOTE: REQUEST

WORD CHOICE: ask (for), request, demand
Ask is the usual word for speaking or writing to someone in order to get something done: *I asked one of my friends to help me.* You use **ask for** when you are trying to get something: *I asked for help.* **Request** is more formal and official. If you **request** something, you often have the right to get what you are asking for: *I'd like to request a copy of my transcript.* | *The mayor has requested a meeting with community leaders.* **Demand** is even stronger. If you **demand** something, you feel strongly that you have the right to it: *I demand to see the manager!*
GRAMMAR
You **request** something (NOT "request for" sth). But you do use **for** with the noun: *requests for money* (NOT *"requests of money"*).

req·ui·em /ˈrɛkwiəm/ also **requiem mass** /,... ˈ./ n. [C] **1** a Christian religious ceremony of prayers for someone who has died **2** a piece of music written for this ceremony

re·quire /rɪˈkwaɪɚ/ v. [T not in progressive] **1** if a problem or situation requires something, it makes it necessary: *Higgins' broken leg will probably require surgery.* | *The job requires a college degree and a knowledge of computers.* **2** to need something: *Most house plants require good light and regular watering.* **3** [usually passive] to officially demand that people do something, because of a law or rule: *You are required by law to wear seat belts.* | [+ that] *State law requires that dogs be kept on leashes in public areas.* | **the required standard/level/period** etc. *The bill failed to get the required number of votes.* **4** SPOKEN, FORMAL used to ask someone what they need: *Is there anything further you require, sir?*

re·quire·ment /rɪˈkwaɪɚmənt/ n. [C] **1** something that is needed or asked for, especially a quality or skill that is needed in a particular situation: [+ for] *Current laws specify parking requirements for new buildings.* | *Pilots and their aircraft must* **meet** *strict safety* **requirements** (=have what is needed for safety). **2** something that a college, employer etc. says you must have or do: [+ for] *To find out about entry requirements for students, write to the college admissions board.*

req·ui·site /ˈrɛkwəzɪt/ adj. FORMAL needed for a particular purpose: *He lacks the requisite qualifications.*

req·ui·sites /ˈrɛkwəzɪts/ n. [plural] FORMAL things,

skills, or qualities that are needed for a particular purpose: [+ **of/for**] *He lacked the mental and moral requisites for marriage.*

req·ui·si·tion[1] /ˌrɛkwəˈzɪʃən/ *v.* [T] to officially demand to have something, especially so that it can be used by an army: *All food in the city had been requisitioned by the army.*

requisition[2] *n.* [C,U] an official demand to have something, usually made by an army or military authority

re·quit·al /rɪˈkwaɪt̬l/ *n.* [U] FORMAL **1** payment for something done or given **2** something that you do to harm someone who has harmed you

re·quite /rɪˈkwaɪt/ *v.* [T] FORMAL to give or do something in return for something done or given to you in the past

re·re·lease /ˌri rɪˈlis/ *v.* [T] if a record or movie is re-released, it is produced and sold for a second time, usually with small changes: *Star Wars was re-released in 1997.* —**re-release** /ˈri rɪˌlis/ *n.* [C]

re·route /riˈrut, -ˈraʊt/ *v.* [T] to send vehicles, airplanes, telephone calls etc. to a different place than the one where they were originally going

re·run[1] /ˈriˌrʌn/ *n.* [C] a movie or old television program that is being shown again: *We watched a rerun of "The Brady Bunch."*

re·run[2] /riˈrʌn/ *v.* [T] to show a movie or old television program again

re·sched·ule /riˈskɛdʒəl/ *v.* [T] **1** to arrange for something to happen at a different time, because the time you had planned is not convenient anymore: [+ **for**] *The press conference had to be rescheduled for March 19.* **2** TECHNICAL to arrange for a debt to be paid back later than was originally agreed

re·scind /rɪˈsɪnd/ *v.* [T] to officially end a law, decision, or agreement that has been made in the past

re·scis·sion /rɪˈsɪʒən/ *n.* [C,U] FORMAL an official decision or statement that a planned sale, law, agreement etc. will not happen; CANCELLATION

rescue

res·cue[1] /ˈrɛskyu/ *v.* [T] to save someone or something from a situation of danger or harm: *Survivors of the crash were rescued by helicopter.* | [**rescue sb/sth from sth**] *She died trying to rescue her children from the blaze.* | *Investors hope the merger will rescue the company from bankruptcy.* —**rescuer** *n.* [C]

rescue[2] *n.* [C] **1** an occasion when someone or something is rescued from danger: [+ **of**] *Storms delayed the rescue of the crash victims.* | **rescue team/boat/equipment etc.** *Rescue workers arrived at the scene two hours later.* | **rescue attempt/ effort/operation etc.** *a military rescue mission.* **2 come to the rescue a)** to save someone who is in a dangerous situation **b)** to help someone who is having problems or difficulties: *Carol's brother and sister once again came to the rescue and sent her $1000.*

SW **re·search**[1] /ˈrisət̬ʃ, rɪˈsət̬ʃ/ *n.* [U] also **researches** [plural] **1** serious study of a subject, that is intended to discover new facts or test new ideas: [+ **into/on**] *research into the causes of cancer* | *The* book draws on Gardner's own research. | **research project/team/grant etc.** *Scolaro joined work on several AIDS research projects.* | *I'm still* **doing research** *for my thesis.* **2** the activity of finding information about something that you are interested in or need to know about: *It's a good idea to* **do** *some* **research** *before you buy a house.* —see also MARKET RESEARCH, R & D

re·search[2] /rɪˈsət̬ʃ, ˈrisət̬ʃ/ *v.* [T] **1** to study a subject in detail, especially in order to discover new facts or test new ideas: *He spent four years researching material for the play.* **2** to supply all the necessary facts and information for something: *Joslin's legal documents were praised for being well researched.* —**researcher** *n.* [C]

research and de·vel·op·ment /ˌ. . .ˈ..., .ˌ. .ˈ.../ *n.* [U] R & D

re·sell /ˌriˈsɛl/ *v.* past tense and past participle **resold** /-ˈsoʊld/ [T] to sell something that you have bought: *Brokers buy the tickets and then resell them at higher prices.* —**resale** /ˈriseɪl/ *n., adj.:* **resale shops**

re·sem·blance /rɪˈzɛmbləns/ *n.* [C,U] a SIMILARITY between two things, especially in the way they look: [– **between**] *You can see a family resemblance between me and Uncle Mike.* | *Tina* **bears a** *striking* **resemblance to** (=looks like) *Madonna.*

re·sem·ble /rɪˈzɛmbəl/ *v.* [T not in progressive or passive] to look like, or be similar to, someone or something: *It's amazing how* **closely** *Brian and Steve* **resemble** *each other.*

re·sent /rɪˈzɛnt/ *v.* [T] to feel angry or upset about a situation or about something that someone has done, especially because you think that it is not fair: [**resent (sb) doing sth**] *I resented having to work such long hours.* | *Alex deeply* **resented the fact that** *Carol didn't trust him.*

re·sent·ful /rɪˈzɛntfəl/ *adj.* feeling angry and upset about something that you think is unfair: [+ **of/ about etc.**] *Father was bitterly resentful of the praise given to Mr. Foerster.* —**resentfully** *adv.* —**resentfulness** *n.* [U]

re·sent·ment /rɪˈzɛntˈmənt/ *n.* [U] a feeling of anger because something has happened that you think is unfair: *Patrick stared at her with resentment.* | [+ **at/ against/of etc.**] *She couldn't let go of her resentment over the divorce.*

res·er·va·tion /ˌrɛzəˈveɪʃən/ *n.* **1** [C] an arrangement made so that a place is kept for you in a hotel, restaurant, airplane etc.: *Customers are advised to* **make** *seat* **reservations** *well in advance.* **2** [C,U] a feeling of doubt because you do not agree completely with a plan, idea, or suggestion: **have/express reservations (about sth)** *Fred has serious reservations about signing the McKinley deal.* | *We welcomed her back* **without reservation** (=completely). **3** [C] an area of land in the U.S. kept separate for Native Americans to live on: *a Navajo reservation* **4** [C] an area of land where wild animals can live without being hunted; RESERVE: *a 50,000 acre private wildlife reservation*

re·serve[1] /rɪˈzɚv/ *v.* [T] **1** to arrange for a place in a hotel, restaurant, airplane etc. to be kept for you: *Do you have to reserve tickets in advance?* | *I'd like to reserve a table for two.* **2** to keep something separate so that it can be used by a particular person or for a particular purpose: [**reserve sth for sb/sth**] *A separate, smaller room is reserved for smokers.* | *Reserve half of the chicken stock for the sauce.* **3** to use or show something only in one particular situation: [**reserve sth for sb/sth**] *She spoke in a tone of voice she usually reserved for dealing with officials.* **4 reserve the right to do sth** FORMAL an expression meaning that you will do something if you think it is necessary, used especially in notices or official documents: *The management reserves the right to refuse admission.* —see also **suspend/reserve judgment** (JUDGMENT (3))

reserve[2] *n.* **1** [C] an amount of something kept for future use, especially for difficult or dangerous situations: *$10 million in cash reserves* | [+ **of**] *reserves of food* | *Somehow Debbie maintained an inner reserve of strength.* **2 in reserve** ready to be used if needed in an unexpected situation: *We always keep some money in reserve, just in case.* **3** [U] a quality in someone's character that makes them not like expressing their emotions or talking about their problems: *Later, Darcy drops his reserve and confesses that he loves her.* **4** a RESERVATION (4) **5** [C] a price limit below which something will not be sold, especially in an AUCTION **6 reserves** [plural] a military force that a country has in addition to its usual army: *the army reserves* **7** CANADIAN a RESERVATION (4)

re·served /rɪ'zɜːvd/ *adj.* **1** unwilling to express your emotions or talk about your problems: *He was particularly reserved around women.* **2** kept specially to be used by one particular person: *reserved parking spaces* | [+ **for**] *The front row is reserved for the family of the bride.* —**reservedly** /rɪ'zɜːvɪdli/ *adv.* —**reservedness** *n.* [U] —see also **all rights reserved** (RIGHT³ (8)), UNRESERVED

Reserve Of·fi·cer Train·ing Corps /.ˌ. '... ˌ.. ˌ./ —see ROTC

reserve price /.'. ˌ./ RESERVE² (5)

re·serv·ist /rɪ'zɜːvɪst/ *n.* [C] a soldier in the reserves, who is trained to fight and may join the professional army during a war: *a Marine Corps reservist*

res·er·voir /'rɛzə,vwɑr, -zə-, -,vwɔr/ *n.* [C] **1** a lake, especially an artificial one, where water is stored before it is supplied to people's houses **2** a large amount of something that has not yet been used: [+ **of**] *She found she had reservoirs of unexpected strength.* **3** TECHNICAL a place where something, such as liquid, is kept before it is used

re·set¹ /ˌri'sɛt/ *v.* past tense and past participle **reset** present participle **resetting** [T] **1** to change a clock, control etc. so that it shows a different time or number: *Have you reset the alarm clock?* **2** to put a broken bone back into its correct place so that it grows back together correctly **3** to load an OPERATING SYSTEM for a small computer from a DISK into the computer's memory **4** to put a jewel into a new piece of jewelry **5** TECHNICAL to make new pages from which to print a book —**reset** /'riset/ *n.* [C,U]

re·set² /'riset/ *adj.* a reset button is used to make a machine or instrument ready to work again

re·set·tle /ˌri'sɛtl/ *v.* **1** [I,T] to go to live in a new country or area, or help people to do this: *During the 1980s, about 284,000 refugees resettled in California.* | *Families still living on the polluted farmland will be resettled.* **2** [T] to start using an area again as a place to live: *The area was resettled in the latter half of the century.* —**resettlement** *n.* [U]

re·shuf·fle¹ /ri'ʃʌfəl/ *v.* [T] to change the jobs of the people who work in an organization, especially in government: *Perez hired replacements and reshuffled job responsibilities.*

re·shuf·fle² /ri'ʃʌfəl, 'riʃʌfəl/ *n.* [C] the act of changing the jobs of people who work in an organization, especially in a government: *Major policy changes are expected from the corporate reshuffle.*

re·side /rɪ'zaɪd/ *v.* [I always + adv./prep.] FORMAL to live in a particular place
reside in sth/sb *phr. v.* [T not in passive] FORMAL **1** to be present in something: *Momaday's talent resides in his storytelling abilities.* **2** also **reside within** sth/sb if a power, right etc. resides in something or someone, it belongs to them: *Political power often resides within prominent families.*

res·i·dence /'rɛzədəns/ *n.* **1** [U] legal permission to live in a country for a certain amount of time: *Joel needed a passport and a residence permit before he could move to the Bahamas.* | **permanent/temporary residence** *Jeff has permanent residence in Canada, but as a U.S. citizen, he still has to file taxes with the IRS.* —see also GREEN CARD **2** [C] FORMAL a house, especially a large one: *One of the greatest residences that Wright designed is Hollyhock House.*

3 [U] the state of living in a place **4 artist/poet/scholar etc. in residence** an artist etc. who has been officially chosen by a college or other institution to work there **5 take up residence** FORMAL to start living in a place: *In 1951 he took up residence in Chicago.* **6 in residence** living in a place or present there —see also RESIDENCE HALL

residence hall /'... ˌ./ *n.* [C] a DORMITORY at a college

res·i·den·cy /'rɛzədənsi/ *n.* [U] **1** a period of time when a doctor receives special training in a particular type of medicine, especially at a hospital **2** permission to live somewhere permanently; RESIDENCE

res·i·dent¹ /'rɛzədənt/ *n.* [C] **1** someone who lives or stays in a place such as a house, town or country: *Residents of Westville complained about the town's bus system.* **2** a doctor working at a hospital where he is being trained

resident² *adj.* **1** [only before noun] living or working in a particular place or institution: *the resident conductor at the Oregon Symphony* **2** FORMAL living in a place: [+ **in**] *While resident in Vienna he continued his musical studies.* **3** [only before noun] HUMOROUS belonging to a particular group: *He's our resident expert on computer games.*

resident a·li·en /ˌ... '.../ *n.* TECHNICAL someone from a foreign country who has the legal right to live in the U.S.: *It is illegal for foreign nationals to contribute to U.S. campaigns unless they hold resident alien status.*

res·i·den·tial /ˌrɛzə'dɛnʃəl◂/ *adj.* **1** a residential part of town consists of private houses, with no offices or factories: *a quiet residential neighborhood* **2** relating to homes, rather than offices or businesses: *telephone services for residential and commercial customers*

residential care /ˌ.... '. ./ *n.* [U] a system in which people who are too old or sick to take care of themselves at home live in a special house with other sick people and are taken care of by professionals: *a residential care facility*

residential treat·ment /ˌ.... '.. ./ *n.* [U] treatment that a person receives while they live in a special home similar to a hospital, especially if they are mentally ill, ADDICTED to drugs or alcohol, or too old or weak to take care of themselves

resident phy·si·cian /ˌ... .'.. ./ *n.* [C] another name for a RESIDENT¹ (2)

residents' as·so·ci·a·tion /'... ...ˌ.. ./ *n.* [C] an association of people who meet to discuss the problems and needs of the area where they live

re·sid·u·al /rɪ'zɪdʒuəl/ *adj.* [only before noun] remaining after a process, event etc. is finished: *the residual effects of the drug treatment*

res·i·due /'rɛzə,du/ *n.* [C] **1** the part of something that is left after the rest has gone or been taken away: *Soap can leave a slight residue on your skin.* | [+ **of**] *a residue of anger and hatred* **2** TECHNICAL a substance that is left after a chemical process

re·sign /rɪ'zaɪn/ *v.* [I,T] **1** to officially and permanently leave your job or position because you want to: [+ **from**] *Shea resigned from the union last year.* | **resign your post/position etc.** *Paul Bartini eventually resigned his position as chief executive.* **2 resign yourself to (doing) sth** to make yourself accept something that you do not like but that cannot be changed: *He seems to have resigned himself to living without her.* —see also RESIGNED

res·ig·na·tion /ˌrɛzɪg'neɪʃən/ *n.* **1** [C,U] the act of resigning, or a written statement to say you are doing this: *Wong's sudden resignation was announced at the meeting.* | *a letter of resignation* | **hand in your resignation/tender your resignation** (=officially say that you are leaving your job) **2** [U] the act of calmly accepting a bad situation that cannot be changed: *"All we can do now is wait," Lee said with resignation.*

re·signed /rɪ'zaɪnd/ *adj.* **1** accepting a situation that you do not like, but cannot change: [**resigned to (doing) sth**] *Resigned to waiting another hour, Maria found a chair and sat down.* | *We became resigned to the fact that our team would lose.* **2** a resigned look, sound, action etc. shows that you are making yourself accept something that you do not like: *"Oh well,"* she *said with a resigned look in her eyes.* —**resignedly** /rɪ'zaɪnɪdli/ *adv.*

re·sil·ience /rɪ'zɪlyəns/ also **re·sil·i·en·cy** /rɪ'zɪlyənsi/ *n.* [U] **1** the ability to quickly become strong, healthy, or happy after a difficult situation, illness etc.: *Their courage and resilience inspired us all.* | *the resilience of the state's economy* **2** the ability of a substance such as rubber to return to its former shape when pressure is removed; FLEXIBILITY

re·sil·ient /rɪ'zɪlyənt/ *adj.* **1** able to quickly become strong, healthy, or happy again after an illness, difficult situation, change etc.: *The enemy proved far more resilient than expected.* **2** a resilient substance returns to its former shape when pressure is removed —**resiliently** *adv.*

res·in /'rɛzən/ *n.* **1** [U] a thick sticky liquid that comes out of some trees **2** [C] an artificial plastic substance that is produced chemically and used in industry —**resinous** *adj.*

re·sist /rɪ'zɪst/ *v.* **1** [I,T usually in negatives] to stop yourself having something that you like very much or doing something that you want to do: **[resist (doing sth)]** *Aren't these shoes cute? I couldn't resist getting them.* | *They made me an offer I can't resist.* | **hard/impossible to resist** *It's pretty hard to resist Jacob's smile.* | **resist the temptation/impulse etc.** *I put the phone back down, resisting the urge to call her.* **2** [I,T] to oppose or fight someone or something: *When security guards came to stop him, he did not resist.* | *Congress continues to resist the anti-weapons bill.* | *He was charged with resisting arrest* (=fighting against the police who were trying to take him to the police station). **3** [T] to try to prevent change or prevent yourself being forced to do something: *The university resisted pressure to close its art department.* **4** [T] to not be changed or harmed by something: *Test-tube studies show that the virus is able to resist most antibiotics.* —**resistable** *adj.*

re·sist·ance /rɪ'zɪstəns/ *n.*
1 against change [singular,U] a refusal to accept new ideas or changes: *Attempts to move the prison have met with strong resistance from the community.* | **[+ to]** *It's surprising how little resistance there's been to the new budget plan.*
2 fighting [singular,U] fighting against someone or something that is attacking you: **put up resistance/offer resistance** *Protesters put up some resistance when the police arrived.*
3 against infection/illness [singular,U] the natural ability of an animal or plant to stop diseases from harming it: *Vitamins can build up your resistance to colds and flu.*
4 wind resistance the degree to which a moving object, such as a car or airplane, is made to move more slowly by the air it moves through
5 electricity [U] the degree to which a substance can stop an electric current passing through
6 the resistance an organization that secretly fights against an enemy that controls their country: *During World War II, he joined the resistance against the Nazis.*
7 the path/line of least resistance the easiest thing to do in a difficult situation
8 equipment [C] a RESISTOR —see also PASSIVE RESISTANCE

re·sis·tant /rɪ'zɪstənt/ *adj.* **1** not damaged or affected by something: **[+ to]** *After two years the AIDS virus becomes resistant to the drug AZT.* **2** opposed to something and wanting to prevent it happening: **[+ to]** *Manhattan's community planners are notoriously resistant to change.*

-resistant /rɪzɪstənt/ *suffix* [in adjectives] not easily affected or damaged by something: *child-resistant packaging* (=boxes or bottles that are difficult for children to open) | *stain-resistant carpets* (=carpets that are not easily damaged when things are spilled on them) —compare -PROOF (1) —see also HEAT-RESISTANT, TAMPER-RESISTANT, WATER-RESISTANT

re·sis·tor /rɪ'zɪstə/ *n.* [C] a piece of wire or other material used for increasing electrical resistance

res·o·lute /'rɛzə,lut/ *adj.* doing something in a very determined way because you have very strong

beliefs, aims etc. —opposite IRRESOLUTE —**resolutely** *adv.* —**resoluteness** *n.*

res·o·lu·tion /,rɛzə'luʃən/ *n.* **1** [C] a formal decision or statement agreed on by a group of people, especially after a vote: *The UN passed a Human Rights resolution by a vote of 130–2.* **2** [singular,U] the final solution to a problem or difficulty: **[+ of]** *a peaceful resolution of the conflict* | **[+ to]** *Drivers may go on strike Monday if there is no resolution to the pay dispute.* **3** [U] APPROVING the quality of having strong beliefs and determination **4** [C] a promise to yourself to do something: *My New Year's resolution* (=a resolution made on January 1st) *is to lose weight.* | *Hass made a resolution never to return to the South.* —compare RESOLVE[1] (2) **5** [C,U] the power of a television, camera, MICROSCOPE etc. to give a clear picture of things, or a measure of this: *a high resolution microscope*

re·solve[1] /rɪ'zɑlv/ *v.* **1** [T] to find a satisfactory way of dealing with a problem or difficulty; settle: *We're hoping they'll resolve their differences* (=stop arguing and become friendly again) *soon.* | *Congressmen called for a third meeting to resolve the conflict.* **2** [I,T] to make a definite decision to do something: **[resolve to do sth]** *After the divorce she resolved never to marry again.* | **[+ that]** *Alma resolved that one day she would return to her homeland.* **3** [I,T] to make a formal decision, especially by voting: **[+ that]** *The city council resolved that all street repairs be postponed until June.*

resolve into *phr. v.* [T] **1 [resolve sth into** sth] FORMAL to separate or become separated into parts: *As a civilization grows larger, it will resolve itself into smaller districts.* **2 [resolve into** sth/sb] to gradually change into something else; become: *The dark shape resolved into the figure of Mr. Markham.*

resolve[2] *n.* [U] strong determination to succeed in doing something: *News of the attack strengthened our resolve to keep fighting.*

res·o·nance /'rɛzənəns/ *n.* **1** [U] the deep, loud, continuing quality of a sound: *the powerful resonance of Jessie's voice* **2** [C,U] FORMAL the special meaning that something has for you because it relates to your own experiences: *The movie had a special emotional resonance for me.* **3** [C,U] TECHNICAL sound that is produced or increased in an object by sound waves from another object

res·o·nant /'rɛzənənt/ *adj.* **1** having a deep, loud, clear sound that continues for a long time: *the baritone's resonant voice* **2** filled with a special meaning, effect, or feeling that continues for a long time: **[+ with]** *Lawrence's story was resonant with the joys of summer.* **3** TECHNICAL resonant materials increase any sound produced inside them —**resonantly** *adv.*

res·o·nate /'rɛzə,neɪt/ *v.* [I] **1** if something such as an event or message resonates, it continues to have a special meaning or effect: *Martin Luther King Jr.'s name resonates in the heart of every American.* **2** to make a deep, loud, clear sound that continues for a long time: *The rumble of the taiko drum resonated through the air.* **3** to make a sound that is produced as a reaction to another sound

resonate with sth *phr. v.* [T] **1** to be full of a sound: *a hall resonating with laughter* **2** FORMAL to be full of a particular meaning or feeling: *Stein's speech resonated with bursting hope.*

res·o·na·tor /'rɛzə,neɪtə/ *n.* [C] a piece of equipment for making the sound louder in a musical instrument

re·sort[1] /rɪ'zɔrt/ *n.* **1** [C] a place where many people often go for vacation, with hotels, swimming pools etc.: **seaside/beach/mountain etc. resort** *an exclusive island resort in Hawaii* | **resort hotel/beach/town** (=a hotel etc. that is a resort) | **ski/health/golf etc. resort** (=a resort where you can ski, improve your health etc.) **2 last resort** what you will do if everything else fails: *I might have to get a second job as a last resort.* | *Everybody else is too busy to help – you're the last resort.* | *a weapon of* *last resort* (=only used if every other type of weapon fails)

re·sort² v.

resort to sth *phr. v.* [T] to use something or do something that is bad in order to succeed or deal with a problem: *When polite requests failed, Paul resorted to threats.* | [**resort to doing sth**] *Many homeless teenagers resort to stealing when their money runs out.*

re·sound /rɪˈzaʊnd/ v. [I] **1** if a place resounds with a sound, it is filled with it; ECHO¹: [+ **with/to**] *The auditorium resounded with thunderous applause.* **2** if a sound such as a musical note resounds, it continues loudly and clearly for a long time: [+ **through/around** etc.] *Laughter and cheers resounded throughout the building.*

re·sound·ing /rɪˈzaʊndɪŋ/ adj. **1 resounding success/victory/defeat etc.** a very great or complete success, victory etc., that many people know about: *The Wolves suffered a resounding defeat at home Thursday night.* **2 a resounding yes/no** a very strong answer of "yes" or "no": *The answer appears to be a resounding yes.* **3** [only before noun] a resounding noise is so loud that it seems to continue for a few seconds: *Her remarks were met with resounding cheers.* —**resoundingly** adv.

re·source /ˈrisɔrs, rɪˈsɔrs/ n. [C] **1** something such as land, minerals, or natural energy that exists in a country and can be used to increase its wealth: *Canada's vast mineral resources* | *a country rich in natural resources* **2** something that is available to be used when needed: *The police used every available resource to track down the killer.* **3** something such as a book, movie, or picture that provides information: *important educational resources* | *a valuable new computer resource* | **resource room/center etc.** (=a room, building etc. where resources are kept) **4 resources** [plural] **a)** all the money, property, skills etc. that you have available: *We need to devote more time and resources to the important projects.* | *Some students are without adequate financial resources to attend college.* | **pool your resources** (=put together all the resources that each of you can provide) **b)** personal qualities, such as courage and a determination, that you need to deal with a difficult situation: *Jan relied on her **inner resources** to get her through that tough time.* —see also HUMAN RESOURCES

-resourced /ˈrisɔrst, rɪ-/ also **resourced** [in adjectives] **be well-resourced/under-resourced/badly-resourced** having plenty of money and supplies, or not enough money and supplies, to do a particular job, PROJECT etc.: *This is the best equipped, best resourced army in the world.*

re·source·ful /rɪˈsɔrsfəl/ adj. APPROVING good at finding ways of dealing with practical problems: *She's a shrewd, resourceful woman and will certainly be able to cope.* —**resourcefully** adv. —**resourcefulness** n. [U]

re·spect¹ /rɪˈspɛkt/ n.

1 admiration [U] admiration for someone, especially because of their personal qualities, knowledge, or skill: [+ **for**] *I have a lot of respect for Mike's ability as a skier.* | **win/earn/gain the respect of sb** *Her hard work won her the respect of her male coworkers.* | *He **commands the respect of** (=has and deserves the respect of) many Latino voters in the district.* —compare DISRESPECT¹

2 consideration [U] an attitude of regarding something or someone as important, so that you are careful not to harm them, be impolite to them etc.: [+ **for**] *I don't think these companies have any respect for the environment.* | *They stayed away out of respect for the wishes of the victim's family.* | *Sales staff should treat all customers **with courtesy and respect.***
3 in one respect/in some respects/in every respect etc. used to say that something is true in one way, in some ways, or in every way: *In many respects, Barb's background is very similar to Jon's.* | *When I was a kid, this town was pretty boring. Not much has changed in that respect.*

4 for danger [U] a careful attitude toward something or someone that is dangerous: [+ **for**] *Brady has a healthy respect for guns.*
5 with respect to sth FORMAL **a)** concerning or in relation to: *Analysts produced a detailed report, particularly with respect to the system's cost.* **b)** used to introduce a new subject, or to return to one that has already been mentioned: *With respect to your second question, it's still too early to tell.*
6 in respect of sth FORMAL concerning or in relation to: *In respect of civil rights, all citizens are equal under the law.*
7 with (all due) respect SPOKEN, FORMAL used before disagreeing with someone who is in a position of authority, in order to make what you say seem less rude: *With all due respect, sir, that is not going to help anything.*
8 pay your (last/final) respects to go to someone's funeral: [+ **to**] *We were there to pay our last respects to Uncle Frank.* —see also SELF-RESPECT

re·spect² v. [T] **1** [not in progressive] to admire someone because they have high standards and good personal qualities such as fairness and honesty: *Most of the students liked and respected Mrs. Moline.* | *I totally disagree with him, but I still respect his opinion.* | *Dawn never gives up, and **I respect her for that.*** **2** to be careful not to do anything against someone's wishes, rights etc.: *The doctors respected the dying man's wishes.* | *When traveling abroad, it is important to respect local customs and laws.*

re·spect·a·bil·i·ty /rɪˌspɛktəˈbɪləti/ n. [U] the quality of being considered morally correct and socially acceptable: *South Africa has regained international respectability.*

re·spect·a·ble /rɪˈspɛktəbəl/ adj. **1** having standards of behavior, appearance etc. that are socially acceptable and approved of: *a respectable neighborhood* | *Put on a tie – it'll make you look a little more respectable.* **2** good or satisfactory: *A "B" is a perfectly respectable grade.* —**respectably** adv.

re·spect·ed /rɪˈspɛktɪd/ adj. admired by many people because of your work, achievements etc.: *a highly respected surgeon*

re·spect·ful /rɪˈspɛktfəl/ adj. feeling or showing respect: *They stood a respectful distance away from the casket.* | [+ **of**] *We always try to be respectful of each other's preferences.* —**respectfully** adv.

re·spec·tive /rɪˈspɛktɪv/ adj. [only before noun] relating or belonging separately to each person who has been mentioned: *The leaders met to discuss the problems facing their respective countries.*

re·spec·tive·ly /rɪˈspɛktɪvli/ adv. FORMAL each separately in the order mentioned: *In terms of population, California and New York rank first and second respectively.*

res·pi·ra·tion /ˌrɛspəˈreɪʃən/ n. [U] TECHNICAL the process of breathing —see also ARTIFICIAL RESPIRATION

res·pi·ra·tor /ˈrɛspəˌreɪtə/ n. [C] **1** a piece of equipment that pumps air into and out of someone's lungs when they cannot breathe without help: *She's on a respirator in the intensive care unit.* **2** something you wear that covers your nose or mouth so you do not breathe dangerous substances

res·pi·ra·to·ry /ˈrɛsprəˌtɔri/ adj. TECHNICAL relating to breathing: *respiratory diseases* | *the respiratory system*

res·pite /ˈrɛspɪt/ n. [singular,U] a short time when something bad stops happening, so that the situation is temporarily better: [+ **from**] *a brief respite from the recent hot weather*

re·splen·dent /rɪˈsplɛndənt/ adj. FORMAL very beautiful in appearance, in a way that looks expensive: *The bride entered the church, **resplendent in** a white silk gown.* —**resplendently** adv.

re·spond /rɪˈspɑnd/ v. **1** [I] to react to something that has been said or done: [+ **to**] *The fire department responded to the call within minutes.* | [**respond (to sth) by doing sth**] *Rebels responded by firing missiles into the town's crowded market square.* —see Usage Note at ANSWER¹ **2** [I,T] to say or write something as a reply: [**respond that**] *Government officials responded that the policy was likely to be changed.* |

[+ **to**] *How did they respond to your criticism?* **3** [I] to improve as a result of a particular kind of treatment: [+ **to**] *Her cancer responded well to the new medication.*

re·spon·dent /rɪˈspɒndənt/ *n.* [C] FORMAL someone who answers questions

S W
2 1
2
re·sponse /rɪˈspɒns/ *n.* **1** [C,U] something that is done as a reaction to something that has happened or been said: *The decision provoked an angry response from local residents.* | [+ **to**] *The public response to the new model has been very positive.* | *She said she was writing in response to* (=as a response to) *an ad in the paper.* **2** [C] something that is said or written as a reply: *I wrote to them a month ago but haven't gotten a response yet.* **3** [C] a part of a religious service that is spoken or sung by the people as an answer to a part that is spoken or sung by the priest

S W
2 1
2
re·spon·si·bil·i·ty /rɪˌspɒnsəˈbɪləti/ *n. plural* **responsibilities**

1 in charge [U] a duty to be in charge of or take care of something or someone, so that you make decisions and can be blamed if something bad happens: *Kelly's promotion meant more money and more responsibility.* | *The children are your responsibility.* | *Mike agreed to take responsibility for organizing the party.* | *The ship's owner has assumed responsibility for* (=agreed to be in charge of) *cleaning up the wreckage.*

2 sth you should do [C] something you should or must do: *Nick has a lot of responsibilities at home.* | *We all have a responsibility to protect the environment.*

3 blame [U] blame for something bad that has happened: **accept/take responsibility** *Vince refused to accept responsibility for the accident.*

4 sense of responsibility an ability to behave sensibly so that you can be trusted to do the right thing: *Activities like these help kids develop a sense of responsibility.*

5 claim responsibility (for sth) to officially say that you are the person or organization that did something, especially an act of TERRORISM: *No one has yet claimed responsibility for yesterday's bombing.*

6 a responsibility to sb a duty to help or serve someone because of your work, position in society etc.: *Parents' primary responsibility* (=most important responsibility) *is to their children.*

S W
2 2
re·spon·si·ble /rɪˈspɒnsəbəl/ *adj.*

1 guilty [not before noun] if someone is responsible for an accident, mistake, crime etc., it is their fault or they can be blamed: *I would feel responsible if anything happened to the kids.* | [+ **for**] *Police have not yet found the people responsible for the theft.* | *If anything goes wrong, I will hold you personally responsible.*

2 cause [not before noun] something that is something for a change, problem, event etc. causes it: [+ **for**] *A diet high in fat may be responsible for several types of cancer.*

3 in charge of [not before noun] having a duty to be in charge of or to take care of someone or something: [+ **for**] *Mills is responsible for a budget of over $5 million.* | *Kari will be responsible for the kids while we're away.*

4 be responsible to sb if you are responsible to someone, that person is in charge of your work and you must explain your actions to them: *Our department manager is directly responsible to the vice-president of sales.*

5 sensible sensible and able to make good judgments so that you can be trusted: *Supporters say the program helps teens become sexually responsible.* —opposite IRRESPONSIBLE

re·spon·si·bly /rɪˈspɒnsəbli/ *adv.* in a sensible way that makes people trust you: *You can trust Jamie to act responsibly.*

re·spon·sive /rɪˈspɒnsɪv/ *adj.* **1** ready to react in a useful or helpful way: [+ **to**] *Management needs to be more responsive to the needs of employees.* **2** easily controlled, and reacting quickly in the way that you want: *Her condition is usually responsive to drug therapy.* **3** willing to give answers or show your

feelings about something: *She's a very responsive baby.* —opposite UNRESPONSIVE —**responsively** *adv.* —**responsiveness** *n.* [U]

taking a rest

rest¹ /rest/ *n.*
S W
1 1
1
1 the rest what is left after everything else has been used, dealt with etc.: *I ate half the pizza and put the rest in the fridge.* | *A few students got A's on the exam, but the rest didn't do so well.* | [+ **of**] *She will have to take medication for the rest of her life.*

2 relaxing [singular,U] a period of time when you can relax or sleep: *You need to get some rest.* | *Try and give your ankle a rest so it will heal better.* | *They decided to stop driving and take a short rest.*

3 come to rest a) to stop moving: *The plane skidded along the runway and came to rest in a cornfield.* **b)** if your eyes come to rest on something, you stop looking around and look at that one thing: *Lynn's eyes came to rest on a framed picture on the bookshelf.*

4 put sb's mind to/at rest to make someone feel less anxious or worried: *She tried to put Alan's mind to rest about the money.*

5 give sth a rest SPOKEN used to say that someone should stop doing or saying something, especially because it is boring or annoying: *You've been complaining all day. Why don't you just give it a rest?*

6 at rest TECHNICAL not moving: *The mass was measured while the object was at rest.*

7 lay/put sth to rest to get rid of a false idea or belief by showing that it is not true: *Many of the public's doubts have now been laid to rest.*

8 no rest for the wicked/weary SPOKEN, HUMOROUS said by someone who is tired but who has a lot of things that they must do

9 lay sb to rest an expression meaning "to bury someone," used when you want to avoid saying this directly: *She was laid to rest next to her husband, who died in 1993.*

10 music [C] **a)** a period of silence of a particular length in a piece of music **b)** a written sign that shows how long the period of silence should be —see picture at MUSIC

rest² *v.*
S W
3 3
1 relax [I] to stop working or doing an activity for a time and sit down or lie down: *We stopped and rested for a while at the top of the hill.*

2 rest your feet/legs/eyes etc. to stop using a part of your body because it is feeling sore or tired

3 give support [T always + adv./prep.] to support an object or part of your body by putting it on or against something: [**rest sth against/on etc.**] *He rested his head on my shoulder.*

4 lie/lean on [I always + adv./prep.] to lie or lean on something for support: [+ **against/on etc.**] *Their bikes were resting against the fence.* | *He slept peacefully, his head resting on one arm.*

5 rest assured (that) used to tell someone not to worry, because what you say about a situation is true: *Lasorda can rest assured that his place in baseball history is secure.*

6 sb will not rest until used to say that someone will not be satisfied until something happens: *We will not rest until our demands for justice are met.*

7 court of law if one side rests in a court of law, they stop giving information because they believe

Native Americans are demanding the restoration of their lands.

they have said enough to prove what they want to prove: *The defense plans to* **rest its case** *Tuesday morning after calling one more witness.*

8 I rest my case SPOKEN, HUMOROUS used when something happens or is said which proves that you were right

9 `dead person` [I always + adv./prep.] if a dead person rests somewhere, they are buried there: *My mother rests beside my father in the family graveyard.* | **final/last resting place** (=the place where someone is buried) —see also RIP

10 rest on your laurels DISAPPROVING to not make any further effort because you are so satisfied with what you have done: *In such a competitive market, the leading company can't afford to rest on its laurels.*

rest on/upon sth *phr. v.* [T not in progressive] **1** FORMAL to depend on or be based on something: *Her whole argument rests on the assumption that the two systems are identical.* **2** if your eyes rest on something, you look at it

rest with sb *phr. v.* [T not in progressive] if a decision or responsibility rests with someone, they are in charge of it: *Responsibility for training rests with the human resources manager.*

rest a·r·ea /ˈ. ˌ.../ *n.* [C] a place near a road where you can stop and rest, use the toilet etc.; REST STOP

re·start /riˈstɑrt/ *v.* [T] to start something such as a machine, a process etc. again after it has stopped: *attempts to restart the peace talks* —**restart** /ˈristɑrt/ *n.* [C usually singular]

re·state /riˈsteɪt/ *v.* [T] to say something again or in a different way, so that it is clearer or more strongly expressed: *The President restated his intention to veto the bill.* —**restatement** *n.* [C,U]

res·tau·rant /ˈrɛsˌtrɑnt, ˈrɛstəˌrɑnt, ˈrɛstərənt/ *n.* [C] a place where you can buy and eat a meal: *a Chinese restaurant*

res·tau·ra·teur /ˌrɛstərəˈtɚ/ also **res·tau·ran·teur** /ˌrɛstərɑnˈtɚ/ *n.* [C] someone who owns and manages a restaurant

rest·ed /ˈrɛstɪd/ *adj.* [not before noun] feeling healthier, stronger, or calmer because you have had time to relax: *We came back from the trip feeling rested and full of energy.*

rest·ful /ˈrɛstfəl/ *adj.* peaceful and quiet, and making you feel relaxed: *restful music* —**restfully** *adv.*

rest home /ˈ. ./ *n.* [C] a place where old or sick people can live and be taken care of —see also NURSING HOME

res·ti·tu·tion /ˌrɛstəˈtuʃən/ *n.* [U] FORMAL the act of giving back something that was lost or stolen to its owner, or of paying for damage: *The defendant was ordered to pay $350,000 restitution to the victims.*

res·tive /ˈrɛstɪv/ *adj.* FORMAL impatient because of strict rules or laws, and difficult to control: *The southern region was growing increasingly restive.* —**restively** *adv.* —**restiveness** *n.* [U]

rest·less /ˈrɛstlɪs/ *adj.* **1** unable or unwilling to keep still, especially because you are nervous or bored: *The kids quickly grew restless and impatient.* **2** unwilling to stay in one place, and always wanting new experiences: *His restless imagination led him to develop a revolutionary software product.* **3 a restless night** a night during which you cannot sleep or rest —**restlessly** *adj.* —**restlessness** *n.* [U]

re·stock /ˌriˈstɑk, ˈristɑk/ *v.* [I,T] to bring in more supplies to replace those that have been used: [+ **with**] *Stores restocked their shelves with fans following last week's heat wave.*

res·to·ra·tion /ˌrɛstəˈreɪʃən/ *n.* [C,U] **1** the act of thoroughly repairing something such as an old building or a piece of furniture so that it looks the same as it did when it was first made: *The state has completed a major restoration of the governor's mansion.* **2** the act of bringing back a law, tax, or system of government: [+ **of**] *Their priority is the restoration of law and order in the region.* **3** the act of officially giving something back to its former owner: *Some*

re·stor·a·tive /rɪˈstɔrətɪv/ *adj.* FORMAL making you feel healthier or stronger: *He's a great believer in the restorative power of short naps.*

re·store /rɪˈstɔr/ *v.* [T]

1 `former situation` to make something return to its former level or condition: *The utility company is still working to restore power supplies in rural areas.* | [**restore** sth **to** sth] *It will take time to restore the company to profitability.*

2 restore hope/confidence/calm etc. to make a person or group feel hopeful, confident, calm etc. again: *The legislature wants to restore the public's confidence in the economy.*

3 `repair` to repair an old building, piece of furniture, painting etc. so that it is in its original condition: *She's restoring her grandmother's antique dresser.*

4 restore (law and) order to make people stop fighting and breaking the law: *The National Guard was called in to restore order.*

5 `bring back a law` to bring back a law, tax, right etc.: *a campaign to restore the death penalty*

6 restore sb's sight/hearing etc. to make someone able to see, hear etc. again: *He underwent an operation to restore his hearing.*

7 `give sth back` FORMAL to give back to someone something that was lost or taken from them: [**restore** sth **to** sb] *Many works of art looted by the Nazis have been restored to their original owners.*

8 restore sb to power/the throne FORMAL to give back power to a king, queen, or president

re·stor·er /rɪˈstɔrɚ/ *n.* [C] someone who repairs an old building, piece of furniture, painting etc. so that it is in its original condition: *antique furniture restorers*

re·strain /rɪˈstreɪn/ *v.* [T] **1 restrain yourself (from doing sth)** to control your emotions, especially anger: *She couldn't restrain herself any longer and started screaming abuse at him.* **2** to physically prevent someone from doing something, especially because they are being violent: *It took four officers to restrain Wilson before he could be handcuffed.* **3** to control or limit something that tends to increase: *The economy's growth will slow down enough to restrain inflation.*

re·strained /rɪˈstreɪnd/ *adj.* **1** behavior that is restrained is calm and controlled and does not show the stronger emotions you feel: *She replied in a low, restrained voice.* **2** not too brightly colored or decorated: *The room was painted in light, restrained colors.*

restraining or·der /.ˈ.. ˌ../ *n.* [C] an official legal document that prevents someone from doing something, for example one that makes it illegal for a person who is threatening another person to go near or talk to that person: *Susan got a restraining order against her ex-husband.*

re·straint /rɪˈstreɪnt/ *n.* **1** [U] the ability not to do something that you very much want to do, because you know it is more sensible not to do it: *The situation called for great care and restraint.* | **show/exercise/practice restraint** *Bush asked oil companies to show restraint in gasoline pricing.* **2** [C usually plural,U] a rule or principle that limits people's activity or behavior: [+ **on**] *The treaty will remove all restraints on exports between the countries.* | **impose/lift restraints** (=make or remove rules that control something) **3** [C] something that prevents someone from moving freely, such as a rope or a SEAT BELT: *Psychiatric hospitals have rules on the use of restraints on patients.* **4** [U] FORMAL physical force used to stop someone from moving freely, especially because they are likely to be violent: *Death was due to a lack of oxygen, caused by physical restraint.*

re·strict /rɪˈstrɪkt/ *v.* [T] **1** to control something or keep it within limits: *Many cities have restricted smoking in public places.* | *Can the school board restrict teachers' rights to express their views?* **2 restrict yourself to sth** to allow yourself to have only a particular amount of something, or do only a particular type of activity: *In this seminar, we will restrict ourselves to Plath's later poems.*

re·strict·ed /rɪ'strɪktɪd/ *adj.* **1** limited or controlled, especially by laws or rules: *Since Dave's heart attack, he's been on a restricted diet.* | *restricted parking* | *Visiting hours are restricted to evenings and weekends only.* **2 be restricted to sth** to only affect a limited area, group etc.: *The damage was restricted to the west side of town.* **3** limited in what you can do, or in your movements: *ramps for people with restricted mobility* **4** a restricted area, document or information can only be seen or used by a particular group of people because it is secret or dangerous: *documents containing restricted data*

re·stric·tion /rɪ'strɪkʃən/ *n.* **1** [C usually plural] a rule or system that limits or controls what you can do or what is allowed to happen: [+ on] *The U.S. is seeking tighter restrictions on weapon sales to the region.* | *Some border states have* **imposed restrictions** (=made restrictions) *on liquor imports from Mexico.* | *Congress might* **lift restrictions** (=remove restrictions) *on foreign aid for birth control.* **2** [U] the act of restricting the size, amount, or range of something

re·stric·tive /rɪ'strɪktɪv/ *adj.* tending to restrict particular types of activity too much: *The labor laws are too restrictive.* | *Some restrictive diets can be dangerous to your health.*

restrictive clause /.ˌ.. '.ˌ/ *also* **restrictive rel·a·tive clause** /.ˌ.. '... ˌ./ *n.* [C] TECHNICAL a part of a sentence that says which person or thing is meant. For example in "the man who came to dinner," the phrase "who came to dinner" is a restrictive clause.

restrictive prac·tic·es /.ˌ.. '...ˌ/ *n.* [plural] **1** unreasonable limits that one TRADE UNION puts on the kind of work that members of other trade unions are allowed to do **2** an unfair trade agreement between companies that limits the amount of competition there is

rest room, restroom /'. ./ *n.* [C] a room with a toilet, in a public place such as a restaurant, office, or theater

re·struc·ture /ˌri'strʌktʃə/ *v.* [T] to change the way in which something such as a government, business, or system is organized: *If the company is to survive, it must be seriously restructured.*

rest stop /'. ./ *n.* [C] a place near a road where you can stop and rest, use the toilet etc.

re·sult¹ /rɪ'zʌlt/ *n.* **1** [C,U] something that happens or exists because of something that happened before: [+ of] *Violotti stressed that hunger is not the result of overpopulation.* | *Elizabeth suffers memory loss* **as a result of** *Alzheimer's disease.* | *Consumer incomes have risen,* **with the result that** *more jewelry has been purchased.* | **end/final/net result** *The end result of the new regulations will be cleaner air.* —see Usage Note at THUS **2** [C] the final number of points, votes etc. at the end of a competition, game, or election, so that you know who won or lost: *Election results are not expected to be announced until Friday.* **3** [C] the answers that are produced by a scientific study or test: *The results of the study were published in the New England Journal of Medicine.* | *My doctor wants to talk to me about my test results.* **4 results** [plural] **a)** things that happen successfully because of your efforts: *In order to* **get results** (=succeed in doing something) *teachers need support and training.* | *For* **best results**, *use only fresh ingredients.* **b)** a company's results are the accounts that show how successful it has been over a period of time, usually a year

re·sult² /rɪ'zʌlt/ *v.* [I] to happen or exist because of something that happened before: [+ from] *Karlin's novels resulted from his experience in the Vietnam War.*

result in sth *phr. v.* [T not in passive] to make something happen; CAUSE: *Improved farming technology has resulted in larger harvests.*

re·sult·ant /rɪ'zʌltənt, -t'nt/ *adj.* [only before noun] FORMAL happening or existing as a result of something: *The blast and resultant fire destroyed the building.*

re·sume /rɪ'zum/ *v.* **1** [I,T] FORMAL to start doing something again after stopping or being interrupted: *"As I was saying," resumed Dahlberg.* | *Sherman resumed his walk toward First Avenue.* **2** [I] if an

activity or process resumes, it starts again after a pause: *The trial will resume on Wednesday morning.* **3 resume your seat/place/position** FORMAL to go back to the seat, place, or position where you were before: *Will the delegates please resume their seats?*

ré·su·mé /'rɛzəˌmeɪ, ˌrɛzə'meɪ/ *n.* [C] **1** a short written description of your education and your previous jobs, that you send to an employer when you are looking for a new job **2** [+ of] a short description of something such as an article or speech, that gives the main points but no details

re·sump·tion /rɪ'zʌmpʃən/ *n.* [singular,U] FORMAL the act of starting an activity again after a pause: [+ of] *The application deadline is two weeks before the resumption of classes.*

re·sur·face /ˌri'sɜfɪs/ *v.* **1** [I] to be seen, heard, or noticed again after having disappeared: *Rumors resurfaced that the sale of the company might fall through.* **2** [T] to put a new surface on a road **3** [I] to come back up to the surface of the water

re·sur·gence /rɪ'sɜdʒəns/ *n.* [singular,U] the growth of a belief or activity that was common in the past, especially one that is harmful: *Cigar smoking is experiencing a resurgence.* | [+ of] *There was a resurgence of tuberculosis at the start of the decade.* —**resurgent** *adj.*

res·ur·rect /ˌrɛzə'rɛkt/ *v.* [T] to start an old custom, belief etc. again, after it has not existed for a long time: *"Silverado" was an entertaining but unsuccessful attempt to resurrect the Western.*

res·ur·rec·tion /ˌrɛzə'rɛkʃən/ *n.* **1 the resurrection** *also* **the Resurrection** the return of Jesus Christ to life after his death on the CROSS, which is one of the main beliefs of the Christian religion **2** [U] *also* **(the) Resurrection (of the Dead)** the return of all dead people to life at the end of the world **3** [U] a situation in which something returns to its previous state or condition: *the city's economic resurrection*

re·sus·ci·tate /rɪ'sʌsəˌteɪt/ *v.* [T] to make someone breathe again or become conscious after they have almost died —**resuscitation** /rɪˌsʌsə'teɪʃən/ *n.* [U]

re·tail¹ /'riteɪl/ *n.* [U] the sale of goods in stores to customers, for their own use and not for selling to anyone else: *I've worked in retail for two years.* | **retail trade/business** etc. *He owns a chain of retail stores.* —compare WHOLESALE¹

retail² *v.* **1 retail for/at sth** to be sold at a particular price in stores: *A Big Mac retails for $1.90 nationally.* **2** [T] FORMAL to tell people about something, especially about other people's private affairs

retail³ *adv.* from a store at the regular price most stores sell something for: *We bought it retail.*

re·tail·er /'riteɪlə/ *n.* [C] someone who owns a store that sells goods, or a store that does this

re·tail·ing /'riteɪlɪŋ/ *n.* [U] the business of selling goods in stores: *Direct marketing is the fastest growing segment of retailing.* | *the retailing industry*

re·tain /rɪ'teɪn/ *v.* [T] FORMAL **1** to keep something or continue to have something: *The town has retained much of its country charm.* | *Florian's relatives will retain rights to the property.* —see also RETENTION (2) **2** to keep facts in your memory: *Children would retain more if the summer vacation were shorter.* **3** to make sure that you will have someone's help or services, by paying for them before they actually help you: *The Commission retains the services of consultants in specialized fields.*

re·tain·er /rɪ'teɪnə/ *n.* [C] **1** an amount of money paid to someone, especially a lawyer, for work that they are going to do: *Insurance companies keep the finest legal talent on retainer.* **2** a plastic and wire object that you wear in your mouth to make your teeth stay straight **3** OLD USE a servant, especially one who has always worked for a particular person or family

retaining wall /.'.. ˌ./ *n.* [C] a wall that is built to prevent land or water from moving beyond a particular place

re·take¹ /ˌriˈteɪk/ v. [T] **1** to get control of an area again in a war: *Government forces have retaken control of the city.* **2** to film or photograph something again **3** to take a test again because you have previously failed it

re·take² /ˈriteɪk/ n. [C] an act of filming or photographing something again: *Sitcom work requires a lot of retakes.*

re·tal·i·ate /rɪˈtæliˌeɪt/ v. [I] to do something bad to someone because they have done something bad to you: *Walker retaliated only after Thomas hit him several times.*

re·tal·i·a·tion /rɪˌtæliˈeɪʃən/ n. [U] action against someone who has done something bad to you: *O'Connor was shot in retaliation for an attack on a rival gang member.* | *military retaliation*

re·tal·i·a·to·ry /rɪˈtæliəˌtɔri/ adj. [usually before noun] FORMAL done against someone because they have harmed you: *Will the government take retaliatory action?*

re·tard¹ /rɪˈtard/ v. [T] FORMAL to delay the development of something, or to make something happen more slowly than expected: *Even in small amounts, lead can retard development in children.* —**retardation** /ˌritarˈdeɪʃən/ n. [U]

re·tard² /ˈritard/ n. [C] SPOKEN, OFFENSIVE a stupid person

re·tard·ed /rɪˈtardɪd/ adj. OLD-FASHIONED a word for someone who is less intelligent or mentally developed than other people, now sometimes considered offensive: *As a child, he was considered **mentally retarded**.* —compare MENTALLY HANDICAPPED

retch /rɛtʃ/ v. [I] to try to VOMIT, or feel as if you are going to VOMIT when you do not: *The smell from the creek was enough to make you retch.*

re·tell /ˈriˈtɛl/ v. past tense and past participle **retold** /-ˈtoʊld/ [T] to tell a story again, often in a different way or in a different language

re·ten·tion /rɪˈtɛnʃən/ n. [U] **1** TECHNICAL the ability or tendency of something to hold liquid, heat etc. within itself: *One of the side effects of the drug is water retention.* **2** FORMAL the act of keeping something: [+ of] *The retention of valued employees is worth more than a little inconvenience.* **3** the ability to keep something in your memory: *powers of retention*

re·ten·tive /rɪˈtɛntɪv/ adj. a retentive memory or mind is able to hold facts and remember them —**retentively** adv. —**retentiveness** n. [U]

re·think /ˌriˈθɪŋk/ v. past tense and past participle **rethought** /-ˈθɔt/ [I,T] to think about a plan or idea again, in order to decide if any changes should be made: *Perhaps it's time to rethink our priorities.*

ret·i·cent /ˈrɛtəsənt/ adj. unwilling to talk about what you feel or what you know: *John always was more reticent than his sister.* | [+ about] *Shaw is clearly reticent about discussing his private life.* —**reticence** n. [U] —**reticently** adv.

re·tic·u·lat·ed /rɪˈtɪkyəˌleɪtɪd/ adj. TECHNICAL forming or covered with a pattern of squares and lines that looks like a net —**reticulation** /rɪˌtɪkyəˈleɪʃən/ n. [C,U]

ret·i·na /ˈrɛtˈnə/ n. [C] the area at the back of your eye that receives light and sends an image of what you see to your brain

ret·i·nue /ˈrɛtˈnˌu/ n. [C] a group of helpers or supporters who are traveling with an important person: *Gerstein strode past with a retinue of aides.*

re·tire /rɪˈtaɪə/ v.
1 stop working [I,T] to stop working, usually because of old age, or to make someone do this: *At 75, Stevens has no plans to retire.* | [+ from] *DiMaggio retired from baseball after the '51 season.*
2 quiet place [I] FORMAL to go away to a quiet place: *The jury has retired to consider its verdict.*
3 bed [I] FORMAL to go to bed
4 sports number [T] if a team retires a player's uniform or number, they do not use it anymore, in order to show respect to that player: *The 49ers are planning to retire Montana's No. 16 jersey.*
5 baseball [T] in baseball, if a PITCHER retires the BATTER, he makes him STRIKE out
6 army [I] FORMAL to move back from a battle after being defeated —compare RETREAT¹ (2)

re·tired /rɪˈtaɪəd/ adj. having stopped working, usually because of your age: *I'm a retired school teacher.* | *Aunt Pat and Uncle Joe are both retired.*

re·tir·ee /rɪˌtaɪəˈri/ n. [C] someone who has stopped working, usually because of their age

re·tire·ment /rɪˈtaɪəmənt/ n. **1** [C,U] the act of retiring from your job, or the time when you do this: *I have less than a year to go before retirement.* | *Dr. Franklin took early retirement and moved to Hawaii.* | *Stitch announced her retirement this year.* **2** [singular,U] the period after you have retired: *How much do I need to save for a comfortable retirement?*

retirement com·mu·ni·ty /.ˈ.. .ˌ.../ n. [C] an area where old people can live independently in separate houses, but close to each other, and where there are various services and activities available to them

retirement home /.ˈ.. ˌ./ n. [C] a building for old people to live in, where various services are provided for them such as food, social activities and medical care —compare NURSING HOME

retirement plan /.ˈ.. ˌ./ n. [C] a system for saving money for your retirement, done either through your employer or arranged by yourself —compare PENSION PLAN

re·tir·ing /rɪˈtaɪərɪŋ/ adj. **1** not wanting to be with other people, especially people you do not know; SHY: *Librarians are normally thought of as being retiring.* **2** the retiring president/manager/director etc. a president, manager etc. who is soon going to leave their job

re·tool /riˈtul/ v. **1** [T] INFORMAL to organize something in a new way: *They've successfully retooled their corporate image.* **2** [I,T] to change or replace the machines or tools in a factory

re·tort¹ /rɪˈtɔrt/ v. [T] to reply quickly, in an angry or humorous way: *"Nonsense," retorted Simpson.*

retort² n. [C] **1** a short and angry or humorous reply: *She's always ready with a quick retort.* **2** a bottle with a long narrow bent neck, used for heating chemicals

re·touch /riˈtʌtʃ/ v. [T] to improve a picture or photograph by painting over marks or making other small changes: *All the pictures were heavily retouched so he would look younger.*

re·trace /riˈtreɪs/ v. [T] **1** to go back exactly the way you have come: *I retraced my steps for two blocks looking for my keys.* **2** to repeat exactly the same trip that someone else has made: *Riders can retrace the trail taken by Chief Big Foot to the battle site.* **3** to do something that someone else has done, in order to find out about a series of past actions or events: *Researchers are retracing their steps to see if they missed something.*

re·tract /rɪˈtrækt/ v. **1** [T] to make an official statement saying that something which you said previously is not true; WITHDRAW: *Bingham retracted his remarks and apologized to those concerned.* **2** [I,T] if part of a machine or an animal's body retracts or is retracted, it moves back into the main part: *The cat scratched him and then retracted its claws.*

re·tract·a·ble /rɪˈtræktəbəl/ adj. **1** a retractable part of something can be pulled back into the main part: *The new stadium will have a retractable roof.* **2** having a retractable part: *a retractable razor*

re·trac·tion /rɪˈtrækʃən/ n. **1** [C] an official statement saying that something which someone said previously is not true: *If I don't get a retraction, I am going to take legal action.* **2** [U] the act of an animal or machine pulling something back in to its main part

re·train /riˈtreɪn/ v. [I,T] to learn or to teach someone the skills that are needed to do a different job: *A federal program was set up to retrain workers who have lost their jobs.* —**retraining** n. [U]

re·tread[1] /'ritrɛd/ n. [C] **1** a retreaded tire **2** INFORMAL something that is made or done again, with a few changes added: *"Modern Romance" is a retread of some of his earlier work.* **3** INFORMAL someone who has been trained to do work which is different from what they did before

re·tread[2] /ri'trɛd/ v. [T] to put a new rubber surface on an old tire

re·treat[1] /rɪ'trit/ v. [I]

1 change your decision to change your decision about a promise you have publicly made or about a principle you have stated, because the situation has become too difficult: [+ from] *The administration is retreating from its goal of buying 75 Stealth bombers.*
2 of an army to move away from the enemy after being defeated in battle: *After the battle, Santa Anna retreated with his forces.*
3 to a quiet place to go away to a place that is quiet or safe: [+ from/into/to] *Ralph retreated upstairs to his room.*
4 move back to walk away from someone or something because you are afraid or embarrassed: [+ to/ from etc.] *I retreated from the window before he saw me.* | *A stunned Phelps retreated to his seat.*
5 become smaller LITERARY if an area of water, snow, or land retreats, it gradually gets smaller: *The flood waters are slowly retreating.*
6 business TECHNICAL if the price of STOCKS, INVESTMENTS etc. retreat, they go down: *Gold prices retreated after reaching a record price yesterday.*
7 retreat into yourself/your thoughts etc. to ignore what is happening around you and give all your attention to your private thoughts

retreat[2] n.

1 change of intention [C,U] an act of changing your decision about a promise you publicly made or a principle you stated, because the situation has become too difficult: *Today's statement represents a retreat from their previous position.*
2 thought and prayer [C] a period of time that you spend praying, studying, or thinking about things in a quiet place: *a retreat for writers and artists* | *We're going on a retreat this weekend.*
3 place [C] a place you can go to that is quiet or safe: *The room was an intimate retreat from the rest of the house.* | *the presidential retreat at Camp David*
4 of an army [C,U] a movement away from the enemy after a defeat in battle: *The soldiers made a strategic retreat.* —opposite ADVANCE[2] (3)
5 movement back [C,U] a movement back and away from someone or something, because you are afraid, embarrassed etc.: *He made a hasty retreat as soon as he saw me.* | *Officials beat a hasty retreat* (=made one) *as reporters shouted questions.*
6 business [C] TECHNICAL an occasion when the price of STOCKS, INVESTMENTS etc. goes down: *Stock prices turned downward today in a retreat led by IBM.*

re·trench /rɪ'trɛntʃ/ v. [I] if a government, group, or organization retrenches, it spends less money —**retrenchment** n. [C,U]

re·tri·al /,ri'traɪəl, 'ritraɪəl/ n. [C] a process of judging a law case in court again, usually because a mistake was made before or because no judgment was reached: *District Attorney McKittrick has asked the judge for a retrial.*

ret·ri·bu·tion /,rɛtrə'byuʃən/ n. [singular,U] severe punishment that is deserved: [+ for] *We can accomplish nothing by seeking retribution for his death.* | *The boy's parents believe his illness is divine retribution* (=punishment from God) *for their sins.* —**retributive** /rɪ'trɪbyətɪv/ adj.

re·triev·al /rɪ'trivəl/ n. [U] **1** TECHNICAL the process of getting back information from a computer system: *information retrieval* | *a retrieval system* **2** [U] FORMAL the act of getting back something you have lost or left somewhere

re·trieve /rɪ'triv/ v. **1** [T] FORMAL to find something and bring it back: *Right now we're concentrating on retrieving the spacecraft.* | [**retrieve sth from sth**] *Divers retrieved a body from the icy river on Wednesday.* **2** [T] TECHNICAL to get back information that has been stored in the memory of a computer **3** [I,T]

if a dog retrieves, it finds and brings back birds and small animals its owner has shot —**retrievable** adj.

re·triev·er /rɪ'trivər/ n. [C] a type of dog that can be trained to retrieve birds that its owner has shot —see also GOLDEN RETRIEVER, LABRADOR

ret·ro[1] /'rɛtroʊ/ adj. deliberately using styles of fashion or design from the recent past: *Although the sound is retro, the band performs only original tunes.*

retro[2] n. [C] INFORMAL a RETROSPECTIVE

retro- /rɛtroʊ, -trə/ prefix back toward the past or an earlier state: *retroactive legislation* (=which has an effect on things already done) | *in retrospect* (=looking back at what has happened) | *a retrograde step* (=returning to an earlier and worse state)

ret·ro·ac·tive /,rɛtroʊ'æktɪv/ adj. FORMAL a law or decision that is retroactive is made now but is effective from a particular date in the past: [+ to] *The 3% raise will be retroactive to July 1.* —**retroactively** adv.

ret·ro·fit /'rɛtroʊfɪt/ v. [T] to improve a machine, piece of equipment etc. by putting new and better parts in it after it is made: [**retrofit sth with sth**] *It is not possible to retrofit an existing car with air bags.* —**retrofit** n. [C] —**retrofitting** n. [U]

ret·ro·flex /'rɛtrəflɛks/ adj. TECHNICAL a retroflex speech sound is made with the end of your tongue pointing backward and up

ret·ro·grade /'rɛtrəgreɪd/ adj. FORMAL **1** moving backward: *Venus's rotation is retrograde.* **2** involving a return to an earlier and worse situation: *retrograde racial politics*

ret·ro·gress /,rɛtrə'grɛs/ v. [I + to] FORMAL to go back to an earlier and worse state —compare REGRESS

ret·ro·gres·sion /,rɛtrə'grɛʃən/ n. [singular,U] FORMAL the action or process of going back to an earlier and worse state: *There has been a major retrogression in relations between the two nations.*

ret·ro·gres·sive /,rɛtrə'grɛsɪv/ adj. FORMAL returning to an earlier and worse situation: *a retrogressive plan* —**retrogressively** adv.

ret·ro·spect /'rɛtrəspɛkt/ n. **in retrospect** thinking back to a time in the past, especially with the advantage of knowing more now than you did then: *In retrospect, I would have handled it differently.* | *My discussion with Charles seemed significant only in retrospect.*

ret·ro·spec·tion /,rɛtrə'spɛkʃən/ n. [U] FORMAL thought about the past

re·tro·spec·tive[1] /,rɛtrə'spɛktɪv/ adj. [only before noun] relating to or thinking about the past: *a retrospective look at the 1974 election*

retrospective[2] n. [C] something that collects some of the best work an ARTIST, singer, FILMMAKER etc. has done, for example in a single show in a MUSEUM: *The retrospective includes 10 of the 12 films written and directed by Sturges.*

re·try /ri'traɪ/ v. **retried, retrying** [I] to judge a law case again in court

ret·si·na /rɛt'sinə/ n. [U] a Greek wine that tastes like the RESIN (=juice) of certain trees

re·turn[1] /rɪ'tɚn/ v.   S W
    1
    2

1 go back [I] to go back to a place where you were before, or come back from a place where you have just been: *It was a bright, hot day when she returned.* | [+ to] *He returned to Georgia after receiving his law degree.* | [+ from] *Amador had just returned from an appointment.* | *I travel a lot, often returning home late at night.* | *Many of the villagers will leave, never to return.*
2 give back [T] **a)** to give something back to its owner or put something back in its place: *I've got to go by Blockbuster and return these tapes.* | [**return sth to sb/sth**] *Part of the job was returning borrowed books to the shelves.* **b)** to take something back to the store where you bought it, because you do not like it, it does not fit etc.: *I'm going to return these shoes – they're a little tight.*

3 happen again [I] to start to exist again or to have an effect again: *If the pain returns, take two of the tablets every four hours.* | [+ to] *Republicans warned against returning to isolationism.*

4 start again [I] to go back to an activity, job etc. that you were doing before you stopped or were interrupted: [+ to] *Santa Anna eventually returned to power in 1853.* | *Yeltsin was anxious to **return to work** after his bout with pneumonia.*

5 previous state [I] to be in a previous state or condition again: *Slowly, my breathing **returned to normal**.*

6 react [T] to do something or give something to someone because they have given the same thing to you: *Hitchcock **returned the favor** by playing on the band's new album.* | *We will **return your call** as soon as we can.* | *Police took cover in combat positions but did not **return fire** (=shoot back at someone shooting at them).*

7 discuss again [I] to start discussing or dealing with a subject that you have already mentioned, especially in a piece of writing: [+ to] *I'll return to your question in a few minutes.*

8 ball [T] to send the ball back to your opponent in a game such as tennis

9 return a verdict if a JURY returns a VERDICT, they say whether someone is guilty or not

10 profit [T] if an INVESTMENT returns a particular amount of money, that is how much profit it produces: *Their investment list returned a profit of 34% last year.*

SW **return²** n.

1 going back [singular] the act of returning from somewhere, or your arrival back in the place where you started from: *We were anxiously awaiting Pedro's return.* | **on/upon sb's return** *On his return from the Holy Land, he stopped at Cotignola.*

2 of a feeling/problem [U] the fact of something such as a problem, feeling, or activity starting to happen or exist again: [+ of] *Perhaps her rapid shifts in mood signaled the return of madness.*

3 giving back [U] the act of giving, putting, or sending something back: *She begged for the return of her kidnapped baby.* | *Both sides are demanding the return of territory lost in the war.*

4 to an activity [singular] the action of going back to an activity, job, or way of life: [+ to] *Cohen says he is not ruling out a return to public life.*

5 in return (for sth) in exchange for something, or as payment for something: *Navy officials reduced the punishment in return for his cooperation.* | *She gave us food and clothing and asked for nothing in return.*

6 profit [U] also **returns** [plural] the amount of profit that you get from something: *Most people get fairly low returns from their personal investments.* | **return on investment/capital/sales** *U.S. citizens found that they could get a higher return on their capital by investing abroad.*

7 taxes [C] a TAX RETURN

8 computer [U] the key that you press on a computer or TYPEWRITER after you have finished the line you are writing: *Type in your file name and press return.*

9 many happy returns said to someone on their BIRTHDAY, in order to wish them a long life and happiness —see also **the point of no return** (POINT¹ (4))

return³ *adj.* **by return mail** if you reply to a letter by return mail, you send your reply almost immediately

re·turn·a·ble /rɪ'tɜnəbəl/ *adj.* **1** returnable bottles, containers etc. can be given back to the store, so they can be used again or RECYCLED **2** FORMAL something such as money or an official paper that is returnable must be given or sent back: *a returnable deposit*

return ad·dress /.,. '../ *n.* [C] the address of the person sending a letter or package, usually shown on the upper left hand corner of an envelope

return tick·et /.,. '../ *n.* [C] a ticket for your trip back to your home: *Immigrations agents will ask to see your passport and return ticket.*

Reu·ben /'rubən/ in the Bible, the head of one of the 12 tribes of Israel

Reuben sand·wich /,.. '../ *n.* [C] also **Reuben** a hot SANDWICH made with CORNED BEEF, Swiss cheese, and SAUERKRAUT on RYE bread

re·u·ni·fy /ri'yunə,faɪ/ *v.* **reunified, reunifying** [T] to join the parts of something together again, especially a country that was divided —compare REUNITE —**reunification** /ri,yunəfə'keɪʃən/ *n.* [U] *the reunification of Germany*

re·un·ion /ri'yunyən/ *n.* **1** [C] a social meeting of people who have not met for a long time, especially families or people who were at school or college together: *My twenty-year high school reunion is in August.* | *a family reunion* **2** [U] the state of being brought together again after a period of being separated: *David is hoping for an eventual reunion with his wife.*

Ré·un·ion /ri'yunyən/ a country consisting of a group of islands in the Indian Ocean, which is controlled by France

re·u·nite /,riyu'naɪt/ *v.* [I,T usually passive] to come together again or bring people together again: [be reunited with sb] *She was recently reunited with the son she gave up for adoption.*

re·use /,ri'yuz/ *v.* [T] to use something again: *Sterilized needles for taking blood are never reused.* —**reusable** *adj.* —**reuse** /ri'yus/ *n.* [U]

rev¹ /rɛv/ *n.* [C] INFORMAL a complete turn of a wheel or engine part, used as a unit for measuring the speed of an engine; REVOLUTION

rev² *v.* **revved, revving** [I,T] also **rev up** if you rev an engine, or if an engine revs, you make it work faster: *Joe donned his black helmet and revved up his Harley.*

rev up *phr. v.* [I,T **rev** sth ↔ **up**] INFORMAL if you rev up a system or organization, or it revs up, it becomes more active: *Investors keep putting money in U.S. companies, revving up the economy even more.* —see also REVVED UP

Rev. the written abbreviation of REVEREND: *the Rev. Jesse Jackson*

re·val·ue /ri'vælyu/ *v.* [T] **1** to examine something again in order to calculate its present value: *Once it's sold, the property is revalued at the sale price.* **2** to increase the value of a country's money in relation to that of other countries: *In 1985, the yen was revalued by more than 40%.* —compare DEVALUE —**revaluation** /ri,vælyu'eɪʃən/ *n.* [C,U]

re·vamp /ri'væmp/ *v.* [T] INFORMAL to change something in order to improve it: *ABC plans to revamp the show before next season.* —**revamping** *n.* [C,U] —**revamp** *n.* [singular]

re·veal /rɪ'vil/ *v.* [T] **1** to show something that was previously hidden: *The wooden doll opened to reveal a smaller doll within.* **2** to make known something that was previously secret or unknown: *His letters reveal a different side of his personality.* | [reveal (that)] *Medical tests in late August revealed that a virus was slowly destroying his heart.*

re·veal·ing /rɪ'vilɪŋ/ *adj.* **1** a remark or event that is revealing shows you something interesting or surprising about a situation or someone else's character: *His second book on Mitterrand is filled with revealing anecdotes and interviews.* **2** revealing clothes allow parts of your body that are usually kept covered to be seen: *revealing swimsuits*

rev·eil·le /'rɛvəli/ *n.* [singular,U] a special tune played as a signal to wake soldiers in the morning, or the time at which it is played: *The cadets wake to reveille at 6:55 a.m.*

rev·el /'rɛvəl/ *v.* [I] OLD USE to spend time dancing, eating, drinking etc., especially at a party —**revel** *n.* [C usually plural] *drunken revels*

revel in sth *phr. v.* [T] to enjoy something very much: *Leo reveled in his children's success.*

rev·e·la·tion /,rɛvə'leɪʃən/ *n.* **1** [C] a surprising fact about someone or something that was previously secret but that is now being made known: *Each new revelation received extensive news coverage.* **2 be a revelation** to be good, enjoyable, or useful in a surprising way: *Among the cast, Bob Sorensen is* something of a revelation in this show. **3** [U] the act of suddenly making known a surprising fact that had previously been secret **4** [C,U] an event, experience etc. that is considered to be a message from God

Rev·e·la·tions /ˌrɛvəˈleɪʃənz/ the last book of the New Testament of the Bible, in which the story of the end of the world is told

rev·el·er /ˈrɛvələ/ n. [C usually plural] someone who is having fun singing, dancing etc. in a noisy way, usually because they are celebrating something or are at a party: *A crowd of happy revelers danced behind the brass band.*

rev·el·ry /ˈrɛvəlri/ n. [U] also **revelries** [plural] wild noisy dancing, eating, drinking etc., usually as a celebration of something: *People came from miles around to join in the revelry.*

re·venge¹ /rɪˈvɛndʒ/ n. [U] **1** something you do in order to punish someone who has harmed or offended you: [+ for] *Together, the brothers sought revenge for the murder of their parents.* | *The caller said the bombing was carried out in revenge for Sunday's massacre.* | **get/take revenge (on sb)** *He vowed that someday he would get revenge.* **2 get your revenge** INFORMAL to defeat someone who has previously defeated you, especially in a sport —**revengeful** adj.

revenge² v. [T] FORMAL **revenge yourself on sb** also **be revenged on sb** to punish someone who has harmed you: *He vowed to be revenged on those who had killed his father.*

s w **rev·e·nue** /ˈrɛvəˌnu/ n. [U] also **revenues** [plural]
2 **1** money that a business or organization receives over a period of time, especially from selling goods or services: *Nintendo's estimated revenue totals $9 billion worldwide.* **2** money that the government receives from tax —see also INTERNAL REVENUE SERVICE

re·ver·ber·ate /rɪˈvɜbəˌreɪt/ v. [I] **1** if a loud sound reverberates, it is heard many times as it is sent back from different surfaces, so that the room or building where it is seems to shake: [+ through/across/in etc.] *The sound of a 20-gun salute reverberated throughout the city.* —compare ECHO¹ (1) **2** if an event, action, or idea reverberates, it has a strong effect over a wide area: *News of his resignation continues to reverberate in the media.*

re·ver·ber·a·tion /rɪˌvɜbəˈreɪʃən/ n. **1** [C usually plural] a strong effect that is caused by a particular event: *The June 5 union election will have reverberations throughout the auto industry.* **2** [C,U] a loud sound that is heard again and again as it is sent back from different surfaces

re·vere /rɪˈvɪr/ v. [T] FORMAL to respect and admire someone or something very much: *Most of us revere the Bible, but few of us read it regularly.*

Re·vere /rɪˈvɪr/, **Paul** (1735–1818) an American who rode at night on April 18, 1775, to the town of Concord, Massachusetts, in order to warn the people there that the British soldiers were coming

rev·er·ence¹ /ˈrɛvrəns/ n. **1** [U] FORMAL great respect and admiration for someone or something: [+ for] *Human conduct must be guided by compassion and reverence for all forms of life.* **2 your/his reverence** OLD USE used when speaking to or about a priest

reverence² v. [T] OLD USE to revere someone or something

Rev·er·end /ˈrɛvrənd/ n. a title of respect used before the name of a minister of a Christian church: *Do you remember Reverend Ward?*

rev·er·end¹ /ˈrɛvrənd/ n. [C] a minister of a Christian church: *The reverend was on his way to Rome.*

reverend² adj. [only before noun] OLD USE deserving respect

Reverend Moth·er /ˌ... ˈ../ n. [C] OLD USE a title of respect for the woman in charge of a CONVENT; MOTHER SUPERIOR

rev·er·ent /ˈrɛvrənt/ adj. FORMAL showing a lot of respect and admiration: *Jacobs' tone becomes reverent when he speaks of Salzer.* —**reverently** adv.

rev·er·en·tial /ˌrɛvəˈrɛnʃəl/ adj. FORMAL having the qualities of great respect and admiration: *Stewart*

was honored with reverential speeches and affectionate anecdotes. —**reverentially** adv.

rev·er·ie /ˈrɛvəri/ n. [C,U] a state of imagining or thinking about pleasant things, that is like dreaming: *Auntie interrupted my reveries.*

re·ver·sal /rɪˈvɜsəl/ n. [C,U] **1** a change to an opposite arrangement, process, or course of action: *The decision marks a sharp reversal in federal policy.* **2** [C] a failure or other problem that prevents you from being able to do what you want: *Wilson's campaign suffered a number of embarrassing reversals in recent months.*

re·verse¹ /rɪˈvɜs/ v. **1** [T] to change something, such as a decision, judgment, or process so that it is the opposite of what it was before or so that it goes back to what it originally was: *It may take a century or two to reverse the damage done by pollution.* | *It's clear that our priorities need to be reversed.* | **reverse a decision/ruling/verdict etc.** *The judgment was reversed by a higher court.* **2** [T] to change the usual order of the parts of something: *Half the new police squad cars have the colors reversed.* **3** [T] to turn something over, so as to show the back of it or so that it faces the opposite way: *The image on the screen was reversed and upside down.* **4** [I,T] if a car or its driver reverses, they go backward: *Drive down to where I am, then start reversing.* —**reversible** adj.: *a reversible jacket* —**reversibility** /rɪˌvɜsəˈbɪləti/ n. [U]

reverse² n. **1 the reverse** the exact opposite of what has just been mentioned: *Lewis is known as a difficult interview subject, but my own experience with him was quite the reverse.* **2 go into reverse** if a TREND or process goes into reverse, it starts to happen in the opposite way: *Economic expansion has slowed to a crawl and may soon go into reverse.* **3** [U] the control in a vehicle that makes it go backward: **into/in reverse** *Maria put the car into reverse and drove away.* **4** [C] FORMAL a defeat or a problem that delays your plans: *Financial reverses forced Thomas to sell his business.* **5** [singular] the side of a coin that does not show a person's head: *The reverse side has two eagles with a dead hare.* —opposite OBVERSE

reverse³ adj. [only before noun] **1** opposite to what is usual or to what has just been stated: *Dyslexia sufferers often write the letters of a word in reverse order.* **2 the reverse side** the back of something: *Please fill in the information requested on the reverse side of the form.*

reverse dis·crim·i·na·tion /ˌ... ...ˈ../ n. [U] the practice of giving unfair treatment to a group of people who usually have advantages, in order to be fair to the group of people who have been unfairly treated in the past —compare AFFIRMATIVE ACTION

reverse gear /ˌ. ˈ./ n. [U] the control in a vehicle that makes it go backward

reverse mort·gage /ˌ. ˈ../ n. [C] TECHNICAL a legal arrangement by which you borrow money from a bank equal to the value of your house, and the LOAN is paid off when the house is sold after your death

re·vers·i·ble /rɪˈvɜsəbəl/ adj. **1** able to be changed so that something is the opposite of what it was before, or so that it goes back to what it originally was: *Smokers gradually lose their sense of smell, but this is reversible when they quit.* **2** a piece of clothing that is reversible can be worn with the part that is normally on the inside showing on the outside: *a reversible jacket*

reversing light /.ˈ.. ˌ./ n. [C] a light on the back of a car that comes on when the car is going backward —see picture on page 427

re·ver·sion /rɪˈvɜʒən/ n. [singular, U] **1** FORMAL a return to a former, usually bad, condition or habit: [+ to] *Our task is to guarantee that there will be no reversion to the past totalitarian regime.* **2** LAW the return of property to a former owner: *the reversion of Hong Kong to China*

re·vert /rɪˈvɜt/ v.
   revert to sth phr. v. [T] **1** to go back to a former

condition or habit, especially one that was bad: *Adults tend to revert to childhood patterns when they visit their parents' homes.* | *Brian reverted to his normal happy self as soon as his father returned.* **2** LAW if land or a building reverts to someone, it becomes the property of its former owner again **3** to return to an earlier subject of conversation

re·vet·ment /rɪˈvetˈmənt/ n. [C] TECHNICAL a surface of stone or other building material that is added to give strength to a wall that holds back loose earth, water etc.

re·view¹ /rɪˈvyu/ n. **1** [C,U] an act of carefully examining and considering a situation or process: *After a review by the city council, his license was revoked.* | *A post-census review found that many homes had been missed.* | *A new housing plan for the city is now **under review** (=being considered).* | *The ban on whaling **came up for review** (=the time arrived when it needed to be given a review) in 1990.* **2** [C] an article in a newspaper or magazine that gives an opinion about a new book, play, movie etc.: *a restaurant review* | *The movie opened to good reviews.* **3** [C] an official show of the Army, Navy etc. in the presence of a president or officer of high rank: *a naval review* **4** [C] a REVUE

review² v. **1** [T] to examine, consider, and judge a situation or process carefully: *The finance committee is reviewing the budget proposal.* **2** [I,T] to write an article judging a new book, play, movie etc.: *Hayes used to review books for the local paper.* **3** [I,T] to prepare for a test by studying books, notes, reports etc.: *I'll just review my notes and go to bed.* | *We'll spend this week reviewing for the final.* **4** [T] to officially examine a group of soldiers, ships etc. at a military show

re·view·er /rɪˈvyuɚ/ n. [C] someone who writes about new books, plays etc. in a newspaper or magazine

re·vile /rɪˈvaɪl/ v. [T] to express hatred of someone or something: *Faulkner's neighbors both loved and reviled him in the same breath.* —**reviler** n. [C]

re·vise /rɪˈvaɪz/ v. **1** [T] to change your opinions, plans etc. because of new information or ideas: *Cheney is urging that the policy be revised.* | *The plan was revised and the fee lowered to $600.* **2** [T] to change a piece of writing by adding new information, making improvements, or correcting mistakes: *I'd like you read my story once I've revised it.* | *In 1881, Duhousset published a **revised edition** of his earlier book.* —**reviser** n. [C]

re·vi·sion /rɪˈvɪʒən/ n. **1** [C,U] the process of improving something, especially a piece of writing, by correcting it or including new information or ideas, or the new information or changes themselves: *The city's general development plan is undergoing revision.* | *Make sure your revisions are improvements, not just changes.* **2** [C] a piece of writing that has been improved and corrected

re·vi·sion·ist /rɪˈvɪʒənɪst/ adj. a word meaning not accepting or showing the usual beliefs or opinions about a subject, especially in history, often used in a disapproving way: *a revisionist history of the Korean War* —**revisionist** n. [C] —**revisionism** n. [U]

re·vis·it /riˈvɪzɪt/ v. [T] **1** to return to a place you once knew well: *Mary Stout, a combat nurse, revisited Vietnam two years ago.* **2** to come back to something in order to discuss it, think about it etc. again: *Mayer has encouraged the actors to revisit the familiar text.* **3** sth revisited an event, fashion etc. revisited reminds you very much of something like it: *1965 revisited, proclaimed a sign above a rack of shirts.*

re·vi·tal·ize /riˈvaɪtˌlaɪz/ v. [T] to put new strength or power into something: *Large cities across the nation are revitalizing their business districts.* —**revitalization** /riˌvaɪtˌl-əˈzeɪʃən/ n. [U]

re·viv·al /rɪˈvaɪvəl/ n. **1** [C,U] a process of something becoming active or strong again: *Hopefully, the new marketplace will spark a neighborhood economic revival.* | *[+ of] His comments caused a revival of*

takeover rumors. **2** [C,U] the fact of something becoming popular again: *Opera is enjoying a revival.* | *[+ of] a revival of '60s styles* **3** [C] a public religious meeting that is intended to make people interested in Christianity **4** [C] a new production of a play that has not been performed recently: *a Broadway revival of "A Streetcar Named Desire"*

re·viv·al·ism /rɪˈvaɪvəˌlɪzəm/ n. [U] an organized attempt to make a religion more popular —**revivalist** adj.

revival meet·ing /.ˈ.. ,../ n. [C] a REVIVAL (3)

re·vive /rɪˈvaɪv/ v. **1** [I,T] to become or make someone become conscious, healthy, or strong again: *Paramedics rushed him to the hospital, but could not revive him.* **2** [T] to come back or bring something back into existence or popularity: *Seeing Dan revived all my old feelings of inadequacy.* | *The movie revives Ali's reputation as a boxer.*

re·viv·i·fy /rɪˈvɪvəˌfaɪ/ v. plural **revivifies, revivified, revivifying** [T] FORMAL to give new life and health to someone or something: *Monadnock succeeds in revivifying Thomson's opera.*

rev·o·ca·tion /ˌrɛvəˈkeɪʃən/ n. [C,U] the act of revoking a law, decision etc.

re·voke /rɪˈvoʊk/ v. [T] to officially state that a law, decision, contract etc. is not effective or being used anymore; CANCEL: *His license was revoked for selling alcohol to minors.*

re·volt¹ /rɪˈvoʊlt/ n. **1** [C,U] strong and often violent action by a lot of people against their ruler or government: *[+ against] Poland's trade union Solidarity became the spearhead for revolt against Communist rule.* | *Marcos and his wife left the Philippines after a popular revolt in 1986.* **2** [C,U] a refusal to accept someone's authority or to obey rules, laws etc.: *[+ against] The French Revolution began with a popular revolt against a new "salt tax."* | *The whole city is in revolt about the new curfew.*

revolt² v. **1** [I] if a group of people revolt, they take strong and often violent action against the government, usually with the aim of taking power away from them; REBEL: *[+ against] Two hundred years ago our forefathers revolted against oppression and formed a new nation.* **2** [I] to refuse to accept someone's authority or obey rules, laws etc.: *The community revolted at the proposal to move the bank downtown.* **3** [T] if something revolts you, it is so bad or upsetting that it makes you feel sick and shocked: *I don't wear fur, I was so revolted by what I saw at a fox farm once.* —see also REVULSION

re·volt·ing /rɪˈvoʊltɪŋ/ adj. very bad or upsetting, often in a way makes you feel sick; DISGUSTING: *a revolting idea for a situation comedy* | *The smell from the river was revolting.* —**revoltingly** adv.

rev·o·lu·tion /ˌrɛvəˈluʃən/ n. **1** [C] a complete change in ways of thinking, methods of working etc.: *Penicillin began a revolution in the treatment of infectious disease.* | *the technological revolution* —see also INDUSTRIAL REVOLUTION **2** [C,U] a time of great, usually sudden, social and political change, especially the changing of a ruler or political system by force: *the Bolshevik Revolution of 1917* —compare REBELLION —see also COUNTERREVOLUTION **3** [C,U] one complete circular movement, or continued circular movement, around a certain point: *The Earth makes one revolution around the sun each year.* **4** [C] one complete circular spinning movement, made by something such as a wheel fastened on a central point: *a speed of 100 revolutions per minute* —see also REVOLVE

rev·o·lu·tion·ar·y¹ /ˌrɛvəˈluʃəˌnɛri/ adj. **1** completely new and different, especially in a way that leads to great improvements: *Women have made revolutionary changes in their roles in the past 25 years.* **2** [only before noun] relating to a political or social revolution: *I was very involved in revolutionary activity then.*

revolutionary² n. plural **revolutionaries** [C] someone who joins in or supports a political or social revolution: *They think they're revolutionaries, but they're nothing but common criminals.*

Revolutionary War, the /.ˌ.... '../ the war in which

people in Britain's colonies (COLONY) in North America became independent and established the United States of America. The war began in 1775 and ended in 1781, and a peace agreement was signed in 1783.

rev·o·lu·tion·ize /ˌrɛvə'luʃəˌnaɪz/ v. [T] to completely change the way people think or do things, especially because of a new idea or invention: *Satellites have revolutionized the science of weather prediction.*

re·volve /rɪ'vɑlv/ v. [I,T] to spin around or make something spin around on a central point; ROTATE: *A green and blue mobile revolved slowly above our heads.*

revolve around sth *phr. v.* [T not in passive] **1** [not in progressive] to have something as a main subject or purpose: *Most of the discussion revolved around money.* | *Her life revolves around her children.* **2 think the world revolves around you** INFORMAL to think that you are more important than anyone or anything else: *You're so selfish – you think the world revolves around you, don't you?* **3** to move in circles around something: *It was once thought that the sun revolves around the Earth.*

re·volv·er /rɪ'vɑlvə/ n. [C] a small gun that has a container for bullets that spins around, so that several shots can be fired without having to put more bullets in

re·volv·ing /rɪ'vɑlvɪŋ/ adj. a revolving object is designed so that it turns with a circular movement: *The lead dancer appeared on a revolving pedestal.*

revolving cred·it /.'..,../ n. [U] an arrangement with a store, bank etc. that allows you to borrow money up to a particular amount, and when you pay back some of that money, you can later borrow up to the limit again

revolving door /.,.. '../ n. [C] **1** a type of door in the entrance of a large building, that goes around and around a central point as people go through it **2** used to say that the people involved in a situation, organization etc. change often: *The park director position has been a revolving door for seven appointees.* **3** used to say that people return to a situation, position etc. often, but usually for a different reason: *Term limits could mean that we end up with a revolving door Congress, in which former members return as lobbyists.*

revolving door

re·vue /rɪ'vyu/ n. [C] a show in a theater, that includes songs, dances, and jokes about recent events

re·vul·sion /rɪ'vʌlʃən/ n. [U] a strong feeling of shock and very strong dislike: *Foley expressed revulsion at the killings.*

revved up, revved-up /ˌrɛvd 'ʌp/ adj. INFORMAL **1** very excited about doing something: *These kids never did well in high school, but are revved up about going to college.* **2** more active, exciting, or interesting than before: *a revved-up version of an old American folk song* —see also **rev up** (REV²)

re·ward¹ /rɪ'wɔrd/ n. **1** [C,U] something that you receive because you have done something good or helpful: [+ for] *The best reward for an author is sales.* | *He was given Archima's hand in marriage as a reward for his bravery.* **2** [C] an amount of money that is offered to someone who finds something that was lost or gives the police information: *They're offering a reward for information on the killer.* **3 be its own reward** if something that you do is its own reward, it makes you feel happy and satisfied: *For Harper, playing the music has been its own reward.*

reward² v. [T] to give something to someone because they have done something good or helpful: *How can I reward your kindness?* | [reward sb with sth] *The performers were rewarded with flowers and candy from the audience.* | [reward sb for sth] *It's a great feeling finally getting rewarded for all our hard work.*

re·ward·ing /rɪ'wɔrdɪŋ/ adj. making you feel happy and satisfied because you feel you are doing something useful, important, or interesting, even if you do not earn much money: *International travel can be a rich and rewarding adventure.*

re·wind /ri'waɪnd/ to make a CASSETTE tape or VIDEOTAPE go backward so you can see or hear it again from the beginning

re·wire /ri'waɪə/ v. [T] to put new electric wires in a building, machine, light etc.

re·word /ri'wɔd/ v. [T] to say or write something again in different words, in order to make it easier to understand or more appropriate: *Let me reword my question.*

re·work /ri'wɔk/ v. [T] to make changes in music or a piece of writing, in order to use it again or to improve it

re·write /ri'raɪt/ v. past tense **rewrote** /-'rout/ past participle **rewritten** /-'rɪt'n/ [T] to change something that has been written, especially in order to improve it, or because new information is available: *Usually Woodward would do a first draft, then Bernstein would rewrite it.* —**rewrite** /'riraɪt/ n. [C]

Rey·kja·vik /'reɪkyəvɪk/ the capital and largest city of Iceland

RFD n. [U] the written abbreviation of Rural Free Delivery; used in the addresses of people who live in the country far from cities and towns

rhap·so·dize /'ræpsəˌdaɪz/ v. [I] to talk about something in an eager, excited, and approving way: [+ about/over] *Gottfried rhapsodized about our musical heritage.*

rhap·so·dy /'ræpsədi/ n. [C] **1** a piece of music that is written to express emotion, and does not have a regular form **2** an expression of eager and excited approval: *I typed out a rhapsody about the delectable meal I had eaten.*

Rhe·a /'riə/ in Greek MYTHOLOGY, the wife of the god Cronus and the mother of Zeus

rhe·o·stat /'riəˌstæt/ n. [C] a piece of equipment that controls the loudness of a radio or the brightness of an electric light, by limiting the flow of electric current

Rhe·sus fac·tor /'risəs ˌfæktə/ n. [singular] TECHNICAL a substance that some people have in their red blood cells, which may have a dangerous effect if, for example, a baby that does not have the substance is born to a woman with the substance

rhesus mon·key /'risəs ˌmʌŋki/ n. [C] a small monkey from northern India that is often used in medical tests

rhet·o·ric /'rɛtərɪk/ n. [U] **1** speech or writing that sounds impressive, but is not actually sincere or very useful: *Don't try to fool us with all those facts and bureaucratic rhetoric.* **2** language used to persuade or influence people, especially by politicians: *the rhetoric of campaigning politicians* **3** the art of speaking or writing to persuade or influence people

rhe·tor·i·cal /rɪ'tɔrɪkəl, -'tɑ-/ adj. **1 rhetorical question** a question that you ask as a way of making a statement, without expecting an answer, such as "Who knows what might happen?" **2** using speech or writing in special ways in order to persuade people or to produce an impressive effect: *She delivered her speech with her usual rhetorical fire.* —**rhetorically** /-kli/ adv.

rhet·o·ri·cian /ˌrɛtə'rɪʃən/ n. [C] FORMAL someone who is trained or skillful in the art of persuading or influencing people through speech or writing

rheum /rum/ n. [U] a thin liquid that comes out of your nose and eyes, especially when you have a COLD —**rheumy** adj.

rheu·mat·ic /rʊ'mætɪk/ adj. **1** relating to rheumatism: *a treatment center for children with rheumatic diseases* **2** suffering from rheumatism

rheumatic fe·ver /.,.. '../ n. [U] a serious infectious disease that causes fever, swelling in your joints, and sometimes damage to your heart

rheu·ma·tism /'rumə,tɪzəm/ *n.* [U] a disease that makes your joints or muscles painful and stiff

rheu·ma·toid ar·thri·tis /,rumətɔɪd ɑr'θraɪtɪs/ *n.* [U] a disease that continues for many years, and makes your joints painful and stiff, and often makes them lose their correct shape

RH fac·tor /,ɑr 'eɪtʃ ,fæktɚ/ *n.* [C] the RHESUS FACTOR

Rhine, the /raɪn/ an important river in western Europe that flows northward from Switzerland to the Netherlands and into the North Sea

rhine·stone /'raɪnstoʊn/ *n.* [C,U] a jewel made from glass or a transparent rock that is intended to look like a DIAMOND

rhi·no /'raɪnoʊ/ *n. plural* **rhinos** [C] INFORMAL a rhinoceros

rhi·noc·er·os /raɪ'nɑsərəs/ *n.* [C] a large heavy African or Asian animal with thick skin and either one or two horns on its nose

rhi·no·plas·ty /'raɪnoʊ,plæsti/ *n.* [U] PLASTIC SURGERY on your nose —**rhinoplastic** /,raɪnoʊ'plæstɪk/ *adj.*

rhi·zome /'raɪzoʊm/ *n.* [C] TECHNICAL the thick stem of some plants such as the IRIS, which lies flat along the ground with roots and leaves growing from it

Rhode Is·land /roʊd 'aɪlənd/ *written abbreviation* **RI** a state in the northeast of the U.S. which is the smallest U.S. state

Rhodes /roʊdz/ a large Greek island near the coast of Turkey

Rhodes, Cec·il /'sɛsəl/ (1853–1902) a South African politician who was born in the U.K.

Rho·de·sia /roʊ'diʒə/ a former name for Zimbabwe that was used during the period of British rule —**Rhodesian** *n., adj.*

rho·do·den·dron /,roʊdə'dɛndrən/ *n.* [C] a bush with bright flowers that keeps its leaves in winter

rhom·boid¹ /'rɑmbɔɪd/ *n.* [C] TECHNICAL a shape with four sides whose opposite sides are equal; PARALLELO-GRAM —see picture at SHAPE¹

rhomboid² also **rhom·boid·al** /rɑm'bɔɪdl/ *adj.* TECHNICAL shaped like a rhombus

rhom·bus /'rɑmbəs/ *n.* [C] TECHNICAL a shape with four equal straight sides, especially a shape that is not a square

Rhone, the /roʊn/ a river in southern Europe that flows from southern Switzerland to France and into the Mediterranean Sea

rhu·barb /'rubɑrb/ *n.* [U] a plant with broad leaves and a thick red stem that can be eaten

rhyme¹ /raɪm/ *n.* **1** [C] a short poem or song, especially for children, using words that rhyme —see also NURSERY RHYME **2** [U] the use of words that rhyme in poetry, especially at the ends of lines **3** [C] a word that rhymes with another word, for example "hop" and "pop": [+ **for**] *I can't find a rhyme for "orange."* **4** **rhyme or reason** a phrase that means a way of doing something that can be reasonably explained or easily understood, used in negative sentences: *There was no rhyme nor reason to his decisions.* | *The book is full of trivial facts presented one after another without rhyme or reason.*

rhyme² *v.* [not in progressive] **1** [I] if two words or lines of poetry rhyme, they end with the same sound, for example "hop" and "pop": [+ **with**] *Why doesn't Arkansas rhyme with Kansas?* **2** [T] to put two or more words together to make them rhyme: [**rhyme sth with sth**] *Crystal sang a hilarious song that rhymed "Corleone" with "Home Alone."* **3** **rhymed/rhyming couplets** two lines of poetry that end in words that rhyme

rhythm /'rɪðəm/ *n.* [C,U] **1** a regular repeated pattern of sounds or movements: *the rhythm of the music* | *The air conditioner beat a steady rhythm.* **2** a regular pattern of changes or events: *I was finally fitting in with the rhythm of their household.*

rhythm and blues /,... '../ *n.* [U] R & B (=a type of music)

rhyth·mic /'rɪðmɪk/ also **rhyth·mic·al** /'rɪðmɪkəl/ *adj.* having rhythm: *the rhythmic beat of the horses hooves* —**rhythmically** /-kli/ *adv.*

rhythm meth·od /'.. ,../ *n.* **the rhythm method** a method of BIRTH CONTROL that depends on having sex only at a time when the woman is not likely to become PREGNANT

rhythm sec·tion /'.. ,../ *n.* [C] the part of a band that provides a strong RHYTHM using drums and other similar instruments

RI the written abbreviation of Rhode Island

ri·al /ri'æl, -'ɑl/ *n.* [C] a RIYAL

rib¹ /rɪb/ *n.* [C] **1** one of the 12 pairs of curved bones that surround your chest: *A bruised rib sent Shaw out of the game.* —see picture at SKELETON **2** a piece of meat that includes an animal's rib: *barbecued ribs* **3** a curved piece of wood, metal etc. that is used as part of the structure of something such as a boat or building —see also PRIME RIB, SPARERIBS

rib² *v.* **ribbed, ribbing** [T] to make jokes and laugh at someone so that you embarrass them, but in a friendly way: *Jose's teammates ribbed him about the flowers he got.*

rib·ald /'raɪbəld, 'rɪbəld/ *adj.* ribald songs, remarks, riddles, or jokes are humorous and usually about sex

rib·ald·ry /'rɪbəldri, 'raɪ-/ *n.* [U] ribald songs, remarks, or jokes

ribbed /rɪbd/ *adj.* having a pattern of raised lines: *a ribbed turtleneck sweater*

rib·bing /'rɪbɪŋ/ *n.* [U] **1** friendly jokes and laughter about someone that embarrasses them: *What's the matter? Can't you take a little ribbing?* **2** a pattern of raised lines in KNITTING

rib·bon /'rɪbən/ *n.* **1** [C,U] a long narrow piece of cloth used to tie things or as a decoration: *Christmas ornaments hung from red ribbons on the tree.* **2** [singular] something that is long and narrow: *Fire Island is a 30-mile-long ribbon of beachland.* **3** [C] a small arrangement of colored ribbons in the form of a flat flower, that is given as a prize in a competition: *Holly's tomatoes won the blue ribbon* (=first prize). **4** [C] a piece of ribbon with a special pattern or colors on it, worn to show that you have received a military honor **5** **be cut/torn to ribbons** to be very badly damaged by being cut or torn in many places: *Her feet were cut to ribbons on the rocks.* **6** [C] a long narrow piece of cloth or plastic with ink on it that is used in a TYPEWRITER

rib cage /'. ./ *n.* [C] the structure of RIBS around your lungs, heart, and other organs

ri·bo·fla·vin /,raɪbə'fleɪvən, 'raɪbə,fleɪvən/ *n.* [U] TECHNICAL, VITAMIN B2, a substance that exists in meat, milk, and some vegetables, and that is important for your health

rice /raɪs/ *n.* [U] **1** a food that consists of small white or brown grains that you boil in water until they become soft enough to eat: *long-grain rice* **2** the plant that produces this grain

rice pad·dy /'. ,../ *n.* [C] a field in which rice is grown

rice pa·per /'. ,../ *n.* [U] **1** a type of thin paper made especially in China, used for painting or writing **2** a type of thin paper that can be eaten, which is used in cooking

rice pud·ding /,. '../ *n.* [U] a sweet food made of rice, milk, and sugar cooked together

rich /rɪtʃ/ *adj.*
1 wealthy **a)** having a lot of money or valuable possessions: *Esmeralda was the rich and beautiful daughter of Count Calafato.* | *Gates is one of the world's richest men.* | *For most actors, showbiz is no way to get rich* (=become rich). **b)** **the rich** people who have a lot of money and possessions: *The rich send their kids to exclusive private schools.*
2 large amount having or containing a lot of something: [+ **in**] *Nearly all nuts are rich in protein.* | *oxygen-rich/oil-rich/calcium-rich etc.* (=containing a lot of oxygen etc.)
3 full of interest full of interesting or important events, ideas etc.: *We provide a rich learning environment for our students.* | [+ **in**] *Old San Juan is rich in history and culture.*

4 food containing foods such as butter, cream, and eggs, which make you feel full very quickly: *a rich chocolate cake*
5 smell having a strong pleasant smell: *The hot sun drew a rich scent from the honeysuckle vines.*
6 color having a beautiful strong color: *Rich golds and elegant silvers are the colors for this season.*
7 music/sounds having a pleasant low sound: *His guitar produces a warm, rich sound.*
8 soil/land good for growing plants in; FERTILE: *Carnations require sun, rich soil, and even watering.*
9 cloth/jewelry etc. expensive and beautiful: *She stroked the rich velvet of the dress enviously.*

Rich·ard I, King /ˌrɪtʃəd ðə ˈfɜrst/ (1157–1199) a king of England who spent a lot of time fighting in the CRUSADES and in France. He is often called Richard the Lion-Heart.

Richard III, King /ˌrɪtʃəd ðə ˈθɜrd/ (1452–1485) a king of England who took the position of king from his brother's son

Ri·che·lieu, Cardinal /ˈrɪʃəˌlu/ (1585–1642) a French CARDINAL who was the chief minister of France under King Louis XIII

rich·es /ˈrɪtʃɪz/ *n.* [plural] ESPECIALLY LITERARY expensive or beautiful possessions and large amounts of money: *He had soon squandered his family's riches.*

rich·ly /ˈrɪtʃli/ *adv.* **1** heavily or strongly: *The bread was dark and richly flavored.* **2** in a beautiful or expensive way: *richly furnished rooms* **3 richly colored** having beautiful strong colors: *She wore long, richly colored skirts.* **4 richly deserve** to completely deserve something such as success or punishment: *Stewart received a richly deserved ovation from the crowd.* **5** in large amounts: *He accepted a richly paid position with the company.*

Rich·mond /ˈrɪtʃmənd/ the capital city of the U.S. state of Virginia

Richter scale /ˈrɪktɚ ˌskeɪl/ *n.* [singular] a scale that shows how strong an EARTHQUAKE is, with 1 being very weak and 10 being the strongest

Richt·ho·fen /ˈrɪktoʊfən/**, Baron von** (1892–1918) a German pilot known as the Red Baron, who commanded a group of fighter planes in World War I

rick /rɪk/ *n.* [C] **1** a large pile of STRAW or grass that is kept in a field until it is needed **2** a pile of wood: *a rick of neatly stacked logs*

rick·ets /ˈrɪkɪts/ *n.* [U] a disease that children get in which their bones become soft and bent, caused by a lack of VITAMIN D

rick·et·y /ˈrɪkəti/ *adj.* a rickety piece of furniture or part of a building is in such bad condition that it looks as if it will break if you use it: *We climbed up two flights of rickety wooden stairs.*

Rick·o·ver /ˈrɪkoʊvɚ/**, Hy·man** /ˈhaɪmən/ (1900–1986) a U.S. Navy ADMIRAL and engineer who directed the development of the first SUBMARINE driven by NUCLEAR ENERGY

rick-rack /ˈ. ./ *n.* [U] a type of RIBBON with a shape like small waves, that is used for decoration on clothes

rick·shaw /ˈrɪkʃɔ/ *n.* [C] a small vehicle that is pulled by someone walking or riding a bicycle, used in South East Asia for carrying one or two passengers

ric·o·chet¹ /ˈrɪkəˌʃeɪ/ *v.* [I] if a moving object, such as a bullet or stone, ricochets, it changes direction when it hits a surface at an angle: [+ **off**] *Bullets were ricocheting off the blacktop road no more than 40 feet away.*

ricochet² *n.* [C] **1** something such as a bullet or a stone that has ricocheted: *He was hit by a ricochet.* **2** an act of ricocheting

ri·cot·ta /rɪˈkɑtə/ *n.* [U] a type of soft white Italian cheese

rid¹ /rɪd/ *adj.* **1 get rid of sb/sth a)** to throw away, sell etc. something you do not want or use anymore: *It's about time you got rid of that old gas-guzzling car.* **b)** to take action so that you do not have something bad or unwanted anymore: *They burned the ship to get rid of the evidence.* | *I can never get rid of the lumps in my gravy.* **c)** to make someone leave because you do not like them or because they are

causing problems: *My mother made me get rid of my dog.* **2 be rid of sb/sth** to do something so that someone or something is not there to worry or annoy you anymore: *I'd give anything to be rid of this headache.*

rid² *v.* past tense and past participle **rid** present participle **ridding**
rid sb/sth of sth *v.* [T] **1** to remove something or someone that is bad or harmful from a place, organization etc.: *Ridding the border region of guns will not be easy.* **2 rid yourself of sth** to do something so that you do not have a feeling, thought, or problem that was causing you trouble anymore: *She's taking classes to rid herself of her Southern accent.*

rid·dance /ˈrɪdns/ *n.* [U] **good riddance** SPOKEN used when you are glad that someone or something has gone away

-ridden /rɪdn/ *suffix* [in adjectives] too full of something, especially something bad: *guilt-ridden* (=feeling very guilty) | *mosquito-ridden swamps* | *a violence-ridden demonstration*

rid·dle¹ /ˈrɪdl/ *n.* [C] **1** a question that is deliberately confusing and usually has a humorous or clever answer: *Oedipus came to Thebes and solved the riddle of the Sphinx.* **2** a mysterious action, event, or situation that you do not understand and cannot explain: *How do we solve the riddle of the disappearing marriage?*

riddle² *v.* [T] to make a lot of small holes in something: *Gunmen riddled the bus with bullets.*

rid·dled /ˈrɪdld/ *adj.* **1** full of something bad: *She lives in a drug-riddled neighborhood.* | [+ **with**] *a report riddled with errors* **2** damaged or full of holes, especially from bullets: *12 bullet-riddled bodies were discovered at the ranch.* | [+ **with**] *The highway was riddled with potholes.*

ride¹ /raɪd/ *v.* past tense **rode** past participle **ridden** /ˈrɪdn/
1 animal [I,T] to sit on an animal, especially a horse, and make it move along: *Louise taught her kids to ride and rope on the ranch.* | [ride sth] *Shoemaker rode a horse named Patchy Groundfog.* | [+ **away/across/back etc.**] *He thanked him and then watched him ride away.* | [ride on sth] *The bride rode to her wedding on a white horse.*
2 bicycle/motorcycle [I always + adv./prep.,T] to sit on a bicycle or MOTORCYCLE and make it move along: *Bicyclists should ride on the right side of the street.* | [+ **away/down/back etc.**] *Nick rode in on his Harley-Davidson.* | [ride sth] *We used to ride our bikes a lot in the summer.*
3 vehicle [I always + adv./prep.,T] to travel in a bus, car, or other vehicle: [ride sth] *Have you ever ridden the Sandia Peak tram?* | [ride in/on sth] *Children 12 and under should always ride in the back seat.* | [ride to/into/back etc.] *I had to ride back to New York on the bus.*
4 be riding high to feel very happy and confident: *Before today's defeat, the Broncos had been riding high.*
5 in water **a)** [I always + adv./prep.,T] to move or float on the water: *The kayak rode the waves gently.* | *Ships awaiting dock space rode at anchor in the middle of the bay.* **b) ride a wave** to SURF: *Trevor has been riding the waves for more than half his life.*
6 let sth ride INFORMAL **a)** if you let a bad situation ride, you let it continue for a time without doing anything about it, before deciding whether to take any action: *We can't just let this ride – this kid's future is at stake.* **b)** also **let sth slide** if you let a remark that has annoyed you ride, you do not say anything about it
7 annoy sb [T] to annoy someone by repeatedly criticizing them or asking them to do things: *His teammates are still riding him about striking out.*
8 ride roughshod over sth to ignore someone else's feelings or ideas because you have the power or authority to do this: *Marshall accused the court of riding roughshod over individual rights.*
9 ride on sb's shoulders/back if a child rides on someone's shoulders or back, they are carried in that way

R

10 ride a punch/blow to move back slightly when someone hits you, so that you are not hit with so much force

ride on sth *phr. v.* [T] if someone's success or the respect that they get is riding on something, it depends on it: *A medical resident's career rides on their supervisor's evaluation.*

ride sth ↔ **out** *phr. v.* [T] **1** if a ship rides out a storm, it manages to keep floating until the storm has ended **2** if you ride out a difficult situation, you are not badly harmed by it: *Graduate school is a good place to ride out an economic crisis.*

ride up *phr. v.* [I] if a skirt rides up, it moves up so that it is not covering your body in the way it should

ride² *n.* [C]

1 car/train etc. a trip in a vehicle: *It's a two-hour ride to the Canadian border.* | [+ in/on] *He took us for a ride in his snazzy new car.* | *Can we give you a ride home?* | *We could all go for a ride out to Irene's.* | *She usually gets a ride from her sister in the mornings.* | *Maybe I'll be able to hitch a ride* (=get a ride) *with Steph.* | *a car/train/subway etc.* ride *John took me on my first plane ride.*

2 horse/bike an occasion when you ride a horse or bicycle somewhere: *The two girls went for a ride in the early morning.* | *"Fun" for her is a long bike ride on weekends.*

3 take sb for a ride INFORMAL to trick someone, especially in order to get money from them: *Well, at least he's not going to take her for a ride, like her first husband.*

4 come/go along for the ride INFORMAL to join what other people are doing just for pleasure, not because you are seriously interested in it: *I had nothing better to do, so I thought I'd go along for the ride.*

5 have a bumpy/rough ride INFORMAL a situation that is difficult or causes problems: *Volatile sector funds can give investors a very bumpy ride.*

6 machine a large machine that people ride on for fun at a FAIR or AMUSEMENT PARK: *a rollercoaster ride*

Ride /raɪd/**, Sal·ly** /ˈsæli/ (1951–) a U.S. scientist and ASTRONAUT who was the first American woman in space

rid·er /ˈraɪdɚ/ *n.* [C] **1** someone who rides a horse, bicycle etc. **2** a statement that is added, especially to an official decision or judgment: *The rider states that paragraph 27 applies only to foreign imports.*

ridge¹ /rɪdʒ/ *n.* [C] **1** a long area of high land, especially at the top of a mountain: *The sun disappeared behind the ridge.* —see picture on page 428 **2 a)** a line of something that rises above a surface: *They came out onto a sand ridge that curved away toward the rocks.* | *Cycles of freezing and thawing caused an ice ridge to build up.* **b)** a long narrow raised part of a surface: *My fingers traced the ridges and folds of his hand.* **3 a ridge of high pressure** TECHNICAL a long area of high ATMOSPHERIC pressure

ridge² *v.* [T] to make a ridge or ridges in something

ridged /rɪdʒd/ *adj.* something that is ridged has ridges on its surface: *Cook the chicken in a ridged cast-iron skillet.*

rid·i·cule¹ /ˈrɪdəˌkyul/ *n.* [U] **1** laughter or remarks that are not nice and are intended to make someone or something seem stupid: *If a child lives with ridicule, he learns to be shy.* **2 an object of ridicule** a person or thing that everyone laughs at and regards as stupid: *Sophisticated critics regarded him as an object of ridicule.*

ridicule² *v.* [T] to laugh at a person, idea, institution etc. because you think it is stupid: *Petrocelli ridiculed the police conspiracy theory.*

ri·dic·u·lous /rɪˈdɪkyələs/ *adj.* silly or unreasonable: *She gave some sort of ridiculous cowgirl getup.* | *Oh, for goodness sake, don't be ridiculous.* | *It's/that's ridiculous A 50-pound bag of corn is $11. That's ridiculous.* —**ridiculously** *adv.* —**ridiculousness** *n.* [U]

rid·ing /ˈraɪdɪŋ/ *n.* **1** [U] the sport or activity of riding horses **2** [C] an official area in Canada represented by a member of the Canadian PARLIAMENT

RIF *n.* [C] Reduction In Force; an expression used by companies to mean an occasion when many people are forced to leave their jobs so the company can save money —compare LAYOFF

rife /raɪf/ *adj.* **1 rife with sth** full of something bad: *From the start, their romance was rife with complications.* **2** [not before noun] if something bad is rife, it is very common: *Drug abuse is rife despite a nation-wide crackdown.*

riff /rɪf/ *n.* [C] a repeated series of notes in popular or JAZZ music: *Berry's guitar riffs inspired several generations of bands.*

rif·fle /ˈrɪfəl/ *v.* [T] to quickly turn over the pages of a book, magazine etc.: *Harry riffled through the comics.*

riff·raff /ˈrɪf ræf/ *n.* [U] DISAPPROVING people who are noisy, badly-behaved, or not socially acceptable, who you do not want to have around: *A high metal fence protected the house from riffraff.*

ri·fle¹ /ˈraɪfəl/ *n.* [C] a gun with a long BARREL (=tube-shaped part) that you hold up to your shoulder

rifle² *v.* [T] **1** also **rifle through** to search quickly through a cupboard, drawer etc.: *He rifled through a filing cabinet in search of the memo.* **2** to steal things from a place: *The robbers rifled the cash register and fled with $188 in cash.* **3** SLANG to throw or hit a ball with a lot of force: *Fisher rifled a pass to Dreher for an easy layup.*

rifle range /ˈ. ˌ./ *n.* [C] a place where people practice shooting with rifles

rift /rɪft/ *n.* [C] **1** a situation in which two people or groups have begun to dislike or distrust each other, usually because of a serious disagreement: *Joe's marriage caused a huge rift in the family.* **2** a crack or narrow opening in a large mass of rock, cloud etc.

rift val·ley /ˈ. ˌ./ *n.* [C] a valley with very steep sides, formed by the cracking and moving of the Earth's surface

rig¹ /rɪg/ *v.* **rigged, rigging** [T] **1** to arrange or influence an election, competition etc. in a dishonest way, so that you get the result that you want: *Many of the game shows of the 1950s turned out to be rigged.* **2** [usually passive] to provide a ship with ropes, sails etc.: *a fully-rigged vessel* **3** also **rig up** to make equipment, furniture etc., especially from objects that you find around you: *Lou had a buzzer rigged up beside his bed so he could call his wife.*

rig² *n.* [C] **1** a large structure used for getting oil from the ground under the ocean: *an offshore oil rig* **2** a large TRUCK: *Highway 53 is closed due to an accident involving a big rig.* **3** the way in which a ship's sails and MASTS are arranged

Ri·ga /ˈrigə/ the capital city of Latvia

rig·a·ma·role /ˈrɪgəməˌroʊl/ *n.* [C] another spelling of RIGMAROLE

rig·ging /ˈrɪgɪŋ/ *n.* [U] all the ropes, chains etc. that hold up a ship's sails

right¹ /raɪt/ *adj.*

1 true/correct based on true facts; correct: *The right answer is "spinal cord."* | *You're right, there's another train in five minutes.* | [be right about sth] *Summers was right about one thing – this album is going to sell in the millions.* | *Their prediction turned out to be half right.*

2 correct/normal in the position, order, or state that is correct or where something works best: *The doctor made sure that the patient was getting the right medicine.* | *Something didn't look right about the two couples that walked into the supermarket.*

3 not left side [only before noun] **a)** relating to or belonging to the side of your body that has the hand that most people write with: *You start this step with your right foot.* | *Chris tore a ligament in his right elbow.* —opposite LEFT² (1) **b)** on the same side of something as your right side: *Rich made a right turn into the parking lot.* | *A color picture of her takes up the right side of the card.* —opposite LEFT² (2)

4 appropriate most appropriate for a particular occasion or purpose: *She gave a lecture on how to choose the right wine for dinner.* | *Ben struggled to find the right words.* | [be right for sth] *I have a friend who would be just right for the job.* | [be right for sb] *Melissa knew that she and Peter were right for each other.*

5 that's right said when something that is said or done is correct, or when you remember something or are reminded of it: *That's right, Jim's been a friend of mine for years.* | *Yeah, that's right – it was based on a Raymond Chandler novel.*

6 as question used as a question to ask if what you have said is correct: *He's the drummer for that band, right?*

7 yeah, right said when you do not believe what has just been said: *He says, "I'll call you," and I'm like, "yeah, right."*

8 to agree used to agree with what someone says, to show that you are listening, or to show that what they have said is correct: *"We'll have to leave soon." "Right."*

9 make sure sb understands used to check that someone understands what you are saying: *So I was scheduled for surgery, right, but then my doctor goes on vacation.*

10 morally correct an action that is right is morally correct: *They're just deciding things on the color of your skin, and that's not right.* | **[be right to do sth]** *Scientists are still debating whether it's right to clone human beings.* —opposite WRONG¹ (4)

11 right side up with the top part at the top, in the correct position: *Dip the pretzels in salt, then place them right side up on a baking sheet.* —opposite UPSIDE DOWN¹

12 be in the right place at the right time to be in a place or position that allows you to gain an advantage for yourself, or to do something useful: *An off-duty cop happened to be in the right place at the right time to stop a robbery.*

13 (as) right as rain OLD-FASHIONED completely healthy, especially after an illness: *Just get lots of rest, and you'll be as right as rain in no time.*

14 socially the right people, places, schools etc. are considered to be the best or most important: *I wanted to make sure I was getting involved with the right people.*

S W
1 1
right² *adv.*
1 exactly in a particular position or place: *The TV lights were shining right in his face.* | *The plane touched down right at the water's edge.* | *Your keys are right there where you left them.*

2 immediately immediately and without any delay | **right now/away/after** *We decided to get married right away.* | *It's on right after the 6:30 news.* | *I could see right off the bat that there were going to be problems.*

3 correctly correctly: *Hey, they actually spelled my name right!*

4 direction/side toward the direction or side that is on the right: *Just as you enter town, turn right onto Main Street.* —opposite LEFT³

5 right through/into/down etc. all the way through, into etc.: *I drank the delicious shake right down to the bottom of the glass.* | *A bird flew right into the window.*

6 sb will be right with you also **sb will be right there** SPOKEN used to ask someone to wait because you are coming very soon: *Wait in the lounge for me, Gerard, I'll be right there.*

7 be/rank right up there (with sth) INFORMAL to be as good or as important as the very best: *The American dream of owning a little inn is right up there with owning a little book store.*

8 right and left everywhere or in every way: *Buildings were burning down right and left.*

S W
1 1
right³ *n.*
1 allowed [C usually singular] if you have the right to do something, you are morally, legally, or officially allowed to do it: **[the right to do sth]** *Fernandez has the right to fire anyone without explanation.* | *People have a right to feel safe in their streets.*

2 freedom/advantages rights [plural] the freedom and advantages that everyone should be allowed to have: *We must stand up and fight for our rights.* | **women's/workers' rights etc.** *Smokers' rights*

---

groups tried to block the new ban on smoking in public places. | *We must commit ourselves to promoting equal rights for all Americans.* —see also CIVIL RIGHT, HUMAN RIGHTS

3 have no right to do sth used to say that someone's actions are completely unreasonable or unfair: *You have no right to tell me what I can and can't do!*

4 the right a) the side of your body that has the hand that most people write with, or this side of anything else: *Owens sat on the right, facing Smith.* | *My bedroom is off to the right.* | *Take two steps to the right.* **b)** also **the Right** political parties or groups such as the REPUBLICANS in the U.S., which strongly support the CAPITALIST economic system

5 correct behavior [U] behavior that is generally agreed to be morally correct: *I urged her time and again to do what's right.* | *It's the job of families to teach their children about right and wrong.*

6 the rights and wrongs of sth all the different reasons for and against something: *My sisters and I got a long lecture on the rights and wrongs of wearing makeup.*

7 legal permission rights [plural] legal permission to print or use a story, movie etc. in another form: **[+ to]** *Thorn EMI owns the rights to music from many top Broadway shows.*

8 all rights reserved used at the end of printed or recorded material to show that it is illegal to copy it without special permission

9 be within sb's rights if it is within someone's rights to do something, they are legally allowed to do it: *Your landlady is within her rights to give you notice.*

10 in your own right without depending on anyone or anything else: *Kahlo was the wife of painter Diego Rivera and an artist in her own right.*

11 by rights used to describe what should happen if things are done fairly or correctly: *He's worked the land all his life, so by rights it's his.*

12 do right by sb OLD-FASHIONED to do what is morally correct for someone: *We have not yet done right by Native Americans.*

13 hit [C] a hit using your right hand: *Leonard counters with a right to the jaw.* —**rightness** *n.* [U]

two wrongs don't make a right (WRONG³ (6))

S W
3
right⁴ *v.* [T] **1 right a wrong** to do something to prevent an unfair situation from continuing **2** to put something back into the state or situation that it should be in: *Keating promised to right the country's troubled economy.* **3** to put something, especially a boat, back into its correct upright position: *A tow truck was called to attempt to right the trailer.*

right an·gle /ˌ. ˈ../ *n.* [C] **1** an angle of 90°, like the angles at the corners of a square **2 at right angles (to sth)** if two things are at right angles, they make a 90° angle where they touch: *The aisles intersect at right angles to form the shape of a cross.* —**right angled** *adj.*: *a right-angled triangle*

right-click /ˈ. ./ *v.* [I,T] to press the right button on a computer MOUSE to make the computer do something

right·eous /ˈraɪtʃəs/ *adj.* **1 righteous indignation/anger etc.** strong feelings of anger when you think a situation is not morally right or fair: *Wilson's proposed budget cuts brought righteous anger from Democrats.* **2** FORMAL morally good and fair: *No matter how good and righteous you think your cause is, you cannot break the law.* **3** SLANG extremely good: *a righteous dude* —**righteously** *adv.* —**righteousness** *n.* [U] —see also SELF-RIGHTEOUS

right field /ˌ. ˈ./ *n.* **1** [singular] the area in baseball in the right side of the OUTFIELD **2** [U] the position of the person who plays in this area —compare LEFT FIELD

right·ful /ˈraɪtfəl/ *adj.* [only before noun] according to what is legally and morally correct: *The city wants to return the houses to their rightful owners.* | *Historians are debating Columbus' rightful place in history* (=trying to agree on how important he was). —**rightfully** *adv.* —**rightfulness** *n.* [U]

R

R

right-hand, right hand /'. ./ *adj.* [only before noun] on the right side of something: *Look on page fifty-one up in the right hand corner.* | *Washington Avenue will be on your right-hand side.* —opposite LEFT-HAND

right-hand·ed /ₗ. '..◂/ *adj.* **1** a right-handed person uses their right hand for writing, throwing etc. **2** a right-handed tool is designed for right-handed people: *right-handed scissors* —**right-handed** *adv.* —opposite LEFT-HANDED

right-hand·er /ₗ. '../ *n.* [C] **1** someone who uses their right hand for writing, throwing etc. **2** a hit with your right FIST (=closed hand) —opposite LEFT-HANDER

right-hand man /ₗ. . './ *n.* [singular] the person who supports and helps you the most, especially in your job

right·ist /'raɪtɪst/ *adj.* supporting RIGHT-WING ideas or groups: *a rightist government* —**rightist** *n.* [C] —**rightism** *n.* [U] —opposite LEFTIST

right·ly /'raɪtli/ *adv.* **1** correctly, or for a good reason: *Doctorow's "Billy Bathgate" novel has been rightly hailed as an American classic.* | *Voters are rightly concerned about paying higher taxes.* **2 rightly or wrongly** used to say that whether you think someone's actions are right or wrong, this is what they did: *Rightly or wrongly, most employees regard annual raises as just cost-of-living increases.* **3 and rightly so** used to say that a decision or action you have just described is fair and morally right: *We were blamed, and rightly so, for this mess.* **4 I don't rightly know** also **I can't rightly say** SPOKEN used to say that you are not sure whether something is correct or not

right-mind·ed /ₗ. '..◂/ *adj.* a right-minded person has opinions, principles, or standards of behavior that you approve of; RIGHT-THINKING —**right-minded-ness** *n.* [U]

right of ap·peal /ₗ. . '.../ *n. plural* **rights of appeal** [C] LAW the legal right to ask for a court's decision to be changed

right-of-cen·ter /ₗ. . . '..◂/ *adj.* supporting ideas and aims that are between the center and the right in politics —opposite LEFT-OF-CENTER

right of way, right-of-way /ₗ. . './ *n.* **1** [U] the right to drive into or across a road before other vehicles: *I had the right of way at the intersection, but I let him go by first.* **2** *plural* **rights-of-way** [C,U] the right to go across private land, or the place where you can do this: *Private property – no right of way.*

right on /ₗ. '.◂/ *adj.* INFORMAL **1** someone is right on when they say something that is correct or that you completely agree with: *Parker's column on teenage sexuality is right on.* **2 right on** SPOKEN used to emphasize that you agree with what someone says or does

rights is·sue /'. ₗ../ *n.* [C] TECHNICAL an offer of STOCK in a company at a cheaper price than usual, to people who own some already

right·size /'raɪtsaɪz/ *v.* [I,T] if a company or organization rightsizes, or if it rightsizes its operations, it reduces the number of people it employs in order to reduce costs —**rightsizing** *n.* [U] —compare DOWNSIZE

right-think·ing /ₗ. '..◂/ *adj.* a right-thinking person has opinions, principles, or standards of behavior that you approve of; RIGHT-MINDED: *Any right-thinking individual has got to be really concerned about the situation.*

right-to-die /ₗ. . './ *adj.* [only before noun] supporting the rights of people who are extremely sick, injured, or unconscious to refuse to use machines or methods that would keep them alive —see also LIVING WILL

right-to-life /ₗ. . './ *adj.* [only before noun] members of a right-to-life organization are opposed to ABORTION, and they use this word to describe their views: *the right-to-life movement* —see also PRO-LIFE, PRO-CHOICE

right tri·an·gle /ₗ. '...◂/ *n.* [C] TECHNICAL a TRIANGLE in which the angle opposite the longest side measures 90°

right·ward /'raɪtwəd/ *adj. adv.* **1** on or toward the right **2** on or toward the political RIGHT: *a rightward shift in American politics* —opposite LEFTWARD

right wing /ₗ. '.◂/ *n.* **1 the right wing** political groups that believe in a CONSERVATIVE and traditional system of government and way of living **2** [C] the right side of a playing area in sports such as SOCCER or HOCKEY, or a player who plays on this side —**right-winger** *n.* [C] —opposite LEFT WING

right-wing /ₗ. '.◂/ *adj.* [only before noun] belonging to or relating to the right wing: *a right-wing fund raising group* —opposite LEFT-WING

rig·id /'rɪdʒɪd/ *adj.* **1** rigid methods, systems etc. are very strict and difficult to change: *The French maintain a rigid separation of personal and professional life.* | *rigid academic standards* **2** someone who is rigid is very unwilling to change their ideas: *The key to success is flexibility. If you're too rigid, you could be in trouble.* **3** stiff and not moving or bending —**rigidly** *adv.* —**rigidity** /rɪ'dʒɪdəti/ *n.* [U]

rig·ma·role /'rɪgmə,roʊl/ also **rigamarole** *n.* [singular,U] a long confusing series of actions that seems silly: *We had to take a day off work to go through the rigmarole of getting state ID cards.*

rig·or /'rɪgə/ *n.* **1** [U] great care and thoroughness in making sure that something is correct: *His study was flawed by a lack of scientific rigor.* **2 the rigors of sth** the problems and difficulties of a situation: *Teachers try to prepare their students for the rigors of their senior year.* **3** [U] the state of being strict or severe

rig·or mor·tis /ₗrɪgə 'mɔrtɪs/ *n.* [U] the condition in which someone's body becomes stiff after they die

rig·or·ous /'rɪgərəs/ *adj.* **1** careful, thorough, and exact: *The car is put through rigorous road performance tests.* **2** very severe or strict: *rigorous academic standards* —**rigorously** *adv.*

rile /raɪl/ *v.* [T] also **rile** sb **up** to make someone extremely angry: *The policy has people riled up and ready to take action.*

Ril·ke /'rɪlkə/, **Rai·ner Ma·ri·a** /'raɪnə mə'riə/ (1875–1926) an Austrian poet born in Prague

rim[1] /rɪm/ *n.* [C] the outside edge of something circular: *The ball hit the rim of the basket and bounced off.* | *Her lipstick left a red mark on the rim of the cup.* —see also HORN-RIMMED, -RIMMED, WIRE-RIMMED

rim[2] *v.* **rimmed, rimming** [T] to be around the edge of something: *Her eyes were rimmed with black.*

Rim·baud /ræm'boʊ/, **Ar·thur** /'ɑrtʊr/ (1854–1891) a French poet

rime /raɪm/ *n.* [U] LITERARY: see FROST (=powdery ice)

-rimmed /rɪmd/ [in adjectives] **gold-rimmed/silver-rimmed etc.** having a particular color or type of rim: *a chipped gold-rimmed saucer*

Rim·sky-Kor·sa·kov /ₗrɪmski 'kɔrsəkɔf/, **Nik·o·lai** /'nɪkəlaɪ/ (1844–1908) a Russian musician who wrote CLASSICAL music

rind /raɪnd/ *n.* [C,U] **1** the thick outer skin of some types of fruit, such as oranges: *grated lemon rind* —compare PEEL[2] **2** the thick outer skin of some foods, such as BACON or cheese

ring[1] /rɪŋ/ *n.*
1 jewelry [C] a piece of jewelry that you wear on your finger: *On her right hand was a huge diamond ring.* —see also CLASS RING, ENGAGEMENT RING, WEDDING RING

2 circle [C] **a)** an object in the shape of a circle: *napkin rings* | *They make great onion rings there.* | *There were two car keys on a ring that said FIAT.* **b)** a circular line or mark: *My glass left a wet ring on the table.* **c)** a group of people or things arranged in a circle: *A ring of mountains encircles the Val d'Aosta.*

3 bells [C] the sound made by a bell, or the act of making this sound: *There was a ring at the door.*

4 criminals [C] a group of people who illegally control a business or criminal activity | **drug/crime/spy etc. ring** *Evidence shows he was at the center of a drug and prostitution ring.*

5 have a familiar ring (to it) if something has a familiar ring, you feel that you have heard it before: *His name had a familiar ring to it.*
6 have a ring of truth (to it) to seem likely to be true: *The judge admitted that their testimony had a ring of truth to it.*
7 sports/entertainment a) a small square area surrounded by ropes, where people BOX or WRESTLE **b)** a large circular area surrounded by seats at a CIRCUS **c) the ring** the sport of BOXING: *He retired from the ring at 34.*

ring² *v. past tense* **rang** *past participle* **rung**
1 bell a) [I,T] to make a bell make a sound, especially to call someone's attention to you: *We heard them ringing the temple bell.* | [+ for] *Roberts walked across the lobby and rang for the elevator.* **b)** [I] if a bell rings, it makes a noise: *All the students were out of their seats as soon as the bell rang.*
2 telephone [I] if a telephone rings, it makes a sound to show that someone is calling you: *She was about to go out when the phone rang.*
3 sounds [I] **a)** if your ears ring, they make a continuous sound that only you can hear, after you have been somewhere very noisy or heard a loud sound: *My ears were still ringing hours after the concert.* **b)** LITERARY if a place rings with a sound, it is full of that sound: *The cathedral rang with the amazing voices of the choir.*
4 ring a bell INFORMAL if something rings a bell, you think you have heard it before: *Does the name Bill Buckner ring a bell?*
5 not ring true if something does not ring true, you do not believe it, even though you are not sure why: *None of her explanations rang true.*
6 ring in your ears if a sound or remark rings in your ears, you remember it clearly and think about it often: *My father's discouraging words still ring in my ears.*
7 ring hollow if words ring hollow, you do not feel that they are true or sincere: *His assurances that things will change rang hollow.*
ring in *phr. v.* [T] **ring in the New Year** to celebrate the beginning of the New Year
ring out *phr. v.* **1** [I] a voice, bell etc. that rings out is making a sound that is loud and clear: *Roars of laughter rang out from the bar.* **2 ring out the old (year)** to celebrate the end of the previous year and the beginning of the new year
ring sth ↔ **up** *phr. v.* [T] **1** to press buttons on a CASH REGISTER to record how much money is being put inside when you are selling something: *Can I ring that up for you, sir?* **2** to spend a particular amount of money: *Gillman rang up about $1,000 at the gift shop.*

ring³ *v. past tense and past participle* **ringed** [T] **1** to surround something, especially by forming a circle: *Thousands of protesters ringed the embassy.* | [ring sth with sth] *The area was ringed with barbed wire.* **2** to draw a circular mark around something: *Her eyes were ringed with heavy black liner.* **3** to put a metal ring around a bird's leg

ring·er /'rɪŋə/ *n.* [C] **1** a piece of equipment that makes a ringing noise: *Turn down the ringer on your phone.* **2** someone who rings church bells or hand bells **3** someone who pretends not to have a skill that they really have, in order to play on a team, enter a competition etc.: *A couple of professional ballplayers were brought in as ringers for the softball game.* —see also **a dead ringer** (DEAD¹ (22))

ring fin·ger /'. ,../ *n.* [C] the finger, which is next to the smallest finger on your left hand, that you traditionally wear your WEDDING RING on

ring·git /'rɪŋgɪt/ *n.* [C] the standard unit of money used in Malaysia

ring·ing /'rɪŋɪŋ/ *adj.* a ringing sound or voice is loud and clear

ring·lead·er /'rɪŋ,lidə/ *n.* [C] someone who leads a group that is doing something illegal or wrong: *The ringleaders are facing life in prison.*

ring·let /'rɪŋlɪt/ *n.* [C] a long curl of hair that hangs down

ring·mas·ter /'rɪŋ,mæstə/ *n.* [C] someone who is in charge of the performances in a CIRCUS

ring·side /'rɪŋsaɪd/ *n.* [singular] **1** the area nearest to the performance in a CIRCUS, BOXING match etc. **2 ringside seat** a seat very near to the performers in a CIRCUS, BOXING match etc.

ring·worm /'rɪŋwəm/ *n.* [U] a skin infection that causes red rings, especially on your head

rink /rɪŋk/ *n.* [C] **1** a specially prepared area of ice for skating (SKATE) **2** a special area with a smooth surface where you can go around on ROLLER SKATES

rink·y-dink /'rɪŋki ,dɪŋk/ *adj.* INFORMAL cheap and of bad quality

rinse¹ /rɪns/ *v.* [T] to use clean water, especially flowing water, to remove dirt, soap etc. from something: *Drain and rinse the noodles under cold water.* | *Keith stood by the sink, rinsing the dishes.* | [rinse sth out/away/off etc.] *Irene rinsed the dirt off her hands.*
rinse sth ↔ **out** *phr. v.* [T] to wash something in clean water without soap: *Don't forget to rinse out your swimsuit.*

rinse² *n.* **1** [C] an act of rinsing something: *Add fabric softener during the final rinse.* **2** [C,U] a product you use to change the color of your hair or to make it more shiny: *It's just a rinse, so I can wash the color right out.*

Ri·o de Ja·nei·ro /,riou deɪ ʒə'nɛrou/ also **Rio** a large city and port in east Brazil

Ri·o Grande, the /,riou 'grænd/ a river in the south of the U.S. that forms part of the border between the U.S. and Mexico. The Mexican name for it is Rio Bravo.

ri·ot¹ /'raɪət/ *n.* **1** [C] a situation in which a large crowd of people are behaving in a violent and uncontrolled way, especially when they are protesting about something: *A peaceful rally turned into a riot after police fired into the crowd.* | *The boy's death touched off race riots* (=riots caused by a racial problem) *and divided the town.* **2 run riot a)** if a plant runs riot, it grows very quickly: *Roses ran riot up the wall.* **b)** if your imagination, thoughts etc., run riot, you cannot or do not control them: *Ann let her imagination run riot as she wrote.* **c)** if people run riot, they behave in a violent, noisy, and uncontrolled way **3** [singular] SPOKEN someone or something that is very funny or enjoyable: *This guy is a riot.* | *Isn't that a riot?* **4 a riot of color** LITERARY something with many different bright colors: *The garden was a riot of color.* **5 read (sb) the riot act** INFORMAL to give someone a strong warning that they must stop causing trouble: *Stephanie read Ted the riot act for seeing his old girlfriend.*

riot² *v.* [I] if a crowd of people riot, they behave in a violent and uncontrolled way, for example by fighting the police and damaging cars or buildings: *Hundreds of prisoners rioted on April 1 in the overcrowded prison.* —**rioting** *n.* [U] —**rioter** *n.* [C]

ri·ot·ous /'raɪətəs/ *adj.* **1** wild, exciting, and uncontrolled: *The riotous celebration continued late into the night.* **2** uncontrolled, noisy, and perhaps dangerous: *riotous behavior* —**riotously** *adv.* —**riotousness** *n.* [U]

riot po·lice /'.. .,./ *n.* [plural] police whose job is to stop riots

RIP the written abbreviation of Rest in Peace (=words written on a stone over a grave)

rip¹ /rɪp/ *v.* **ripped, ripping 1** [I,T] to tear something or be torn quickly and violently: *We both fell and I heard his shirt rip.* | *A bomb blast ripped the plane apart at 31,000 feet.* | *My fingers trembled as I ripped open the envelope.* **2** [T always + adv./prep.] to remove something quickly and violently, using your hands: [rip sth out/off/down/away] *The kids quickly ripped off the wrapping paper on the Christmas presents.* **3 rip sth/sb to shreds a)** to destroy something or damage it badly by tearing it in many places: *Unexpected hailstorms have ripped crops to shreds.* **b)** to strongly criticize someone, or criticize their opinions, remarks, behavior etc.: *Carson ripped* him to shreds in his monologue. **4 let rip** INFORMAL to speak or behave violently or emotionally: *Harriet finally let rip with 20 years of stored resentment.* **5 let her/it rip** INFORMAL to make a car, boat etc. go as fast as it can: *I just cranked it up and let it rip.* **6 rip sb's heart out** to end a relationship with someone who loves you, and treat them in a way that is not nice **7 rip the heart out of sth** to remove the most important part of a plan, law, organization etc.: *Weakening the penalties would rip the heart out of the bill.*

rip into sb *phr. v.* [T] to attack or criticize someone very strongly, especially unfairly: *The lead defense attorney ripped into Baker on cross examination.*

rip off *phr. v.* [T] INFORMAL **1** [rip sb ↔ off] to charge someone too much money for something: *Insurance companies have been ripping people off for years.* **2** [rip sth ↔ off] to steal something: *A burglar ripped off $3,000 worth of stereo and TV equipment.* **3** [rip sb/sth ↔ off] to take words, ideas etc. from someone else's work and use them in your work as if they were your own ideas; PLAGIARIZE —see also RIP-OFF

rip on sb/sth *phr. v.* [T] SLANG to complain a lot about someone or something: *Ginny's always ripping on her boss.*

rip through sth *phr. v.* [T] to move through a place quickly and with violent force: *A tornado ripped through the town.*

rip sth ↔ **up** *phr. v.* [T] to tear something into several pieces: *Linen tablecloths were ripped up and used for bandages.*

rip² *n.* [C] a long tear or cut: *Anne's jacket has a rip in it.*

rip·cord /'rɪpkɔrd/ *n.* [C] **1** the string that you pull to open a PARACHUTE **2** the string that you pull to let gas out of a HOT-AIR BALLOON

ripe /raɪp/ *adj.* **riper, ripest 1** ripe fruit or crops are fully grown and ready to eat: *You'll need a pound of ripe tomatoes.* —opposite UNRIPE **2 be ripe for sth** to be ready for something to happen, especially for some kind of change to happen: *If ever a songwriting team were ripe for revival, it's Bacharach and David.* **3 the time is ripe (for sth)** used to say it is a good time for something to happen: *The time was ripe for change in the company.* **4 ripe old age a)** if you live to a ripe old age, you are very old when you die: *Da Ponte lived to the ripe old age of 89.* **b)** HUMOROUS used to show that you find it surprising or impressive that someone is doing something or has achieved something at a very young age: *Angie was the orchestra's soloist at the ripe old age of 22.* **5** ripe cheese has developed a strong taste and is ready to eat **6** HUMOROUS a ripe smell is strong and disgusting: *We were pretty ripe after a week of hiking.* —**ripeness** *n.* [U]

rip·en /'raɪpən/ *v.* [I,T] to become ripe or to make something ripe: *Strawberries do not ripen after picking.*

rip-off /'. ./ *n.* [C] SPOKEN **1** something that is expensive in a way that is unreasonable: *We shouldn't have gone there – it was such a rip-off.* **2** music, art, movies etc. that are rip-offs copy something else without admitting this: *This band is nothing but a Pearl Jam rip-off, with no original sound of its own.* —see also **rip off** (RIP¹)

ri·poste¹ /rɪ'poust/ *n.* [C] **1** FORMAL a quick, intelligent, and amusing reply: *Capote took such pleasure in his witty ripostes.* **2** TECHNICAL a quick return STROKE with a sword in FENCING (=the sport of fighting with swords)

riposte² *v.* **1** [I] FORMAL to reply quickly and in an amusing way **2** [I] TECHNICAL to make a riposte in FENCING

ripped /rɪpt/ *adj.* SLANG having muscles with shapes that are clear and easy to see

rip·ple¹ /'rɪpəl/ *v.* **1** [I,T] to move in small waves, or to make something move in this way: *The occasional dip of an oar rippled the lake's glassy surface.* | *A flag*

rippled in the breeze. **2** [I] to make a noise like water that is flowing gently: *He saw ahead of him the rippling waters of the river.* **3** [I always + adv./prep.] to pass from one person to another like a wave: [+ across/through etc.] *A smattering of applause rippled across the audience.*

ripple

ripple² *n.* [C] **1** a small low wave on the surface of a liquid: *A soft breeze made ripples on the lake.* **2** a sound that gets gradually louder and softer: **a ripple of applause/laughter** etc. *His remark brought a ripple of laughter among the crowd.* **3** a feeling that spreads through a person or a group because of something that has happened: **a ripple of shock/ nervousness** etc. *The measures have aroused a ripple of protest abroad.* **4 ripple effect** a situation in which one action causes another, which then causes a third etc. **5** a shape or pattern that looks like a wave: *potato chips with ripples* **6 raspberry/ chocolate etc. ripple** a type of ICE CREAM that has different colored bands of fruit, chocolate etc. in it

rip-roar·ing /ˌ. '..ˌ/ *adj.* INFORMAL noisy, exciting, and uncontrolled: *The football season got off to a rip-roaring start.*

rise¹ /raɪz/ *v.* past tense **rose** past participle **risen** /'rɪzən/ [I]
1 increase to increase in number, amount, or value: *Student test scores have been rising gradually since the 1970s.* | [rise by 10%/$5 etc.] *The Earth's average temperature will rise by about 4 degrees Fahrenheit by 2020.* | **rise sharply/rapidly/dramatically** *The costs of bringing up a child have risen rapidly.* | *The divorce rate has risen steadily since the 1950s.* | *As with any investment, earnings rise and fall.* | *Traffic on Saratoga Avenue is high and rising.*
2 go upward also **rise up** to go up: *Beat the mixture until large bubbles rise to the surface.* | *She touched the cup and felt steam rise up from it.* | *Flood waters are still rising in parts of Missouri.*
3 become successful to become important, powerful, successful, or rich: [+ from] *Thomas rose from a childhood of poverty to a federal judgeship.* | [+ to] *She quickly rose to the position of supervisor.* | *Khrushchev rose to power after Stalin's death in 1953.* | *Lydon rose to fame as Johnny Rotten of the Sex Pistols.* | *Though marketing is not a difficult field to break into, rising to the top is.*
4 rise through the ranks to start working for an organization in a low-paid job, and to gradually improve your position, until you get a very important, well-paid job
5 voice/sound **a)** to be heard: [+ from] *A roar rose from the crowd.* | [+ above] *He could hear the rhythm of chanting voices rising above the sound of the traffic.* | [+ up] *Their young voices rose up in prayer.* **b)** to become louder or higher: *Her voice rose with an anger that had built up over months.*
6 emotion if a feeling or emotion rises, you feel it more and more strongly: *Public anxiety about the economy was rising.* | *Our spirits rose* (=we became much happier) *when we heard of the ship's safe return.*
7 mountain/building/tree etc. to be very tall: *Our*

newest ride rises 320 feet into the air. | [+ **up**] *Coffee Pot Mountain rises up off the Sonoran Desert floor.*
8 rise from sth if something tall rises from a place, its base is in that place: *Nearby, Midas Peak rises from the evergreen forests.*
9 stand FORMAL to stand up: *Everyone rose and followed him into the dining room.* | **rise from the table/your chair etc.** *"I'm going home," Alice said, rising from the table.* | *The audience rose to its feet, cheering the dancers.*
10 all rise SPOKEN, FORMAL used to tell people to stand up at the beginning of a meeting of a court of law
11 bed OLD-FASHIONED to get out of bed in the morning: *early to bed, early to rise*
12 rise and shine SPOKEN, HUMOROUS used to tell someone to wake up and get out of bed
13 protest/opposition [I always + adv./prep.] also **rise up** if a large group of people rise or rise up, they oppose or fight against people in authority who are controlling them: *The Russian people rose in rebellion in 1917.* | [+ **against**] *Indiana steel workers rose up against their bosses, demanding safer work conditions and better pay.*
14 rise to the occasion/challenge to deal successfully with a difficult situation or problem: *Barragan rose to the occasion and defeated his opponent.*
15 wind if the wind rises, it becomes stronger: *A strong wind rose off the coast of Florida.*
16 sun/moon/star to appear in the sky: *A slim crescent of moon rose in the sky.*
17 bread/cakes etc. if bread, cakes etc. rise, they become bigger before they bake or as they bake
18 rise from the ashes to become successful again after being almost completely destroyed: *Japan has risen from the ashes of World War II to become an industrial power.*
19 rise from the dead/grave to come alive after having died: *He truly believed his wife would rise from the dead.*
20 rise to sth if you rise to a remark, you reply to it rather than ignoring it, especially because it has made you angry: *She refused to rise to his sexist remarks.*
21 rise out of sth to be caused by something or begin with something: *The quarrel had risen out of a misunderstanding.*
22 rise from the ranks to become an officer in the army after having been an ordinary soldier
23 river if a river rises somewhere, it begins there: *The River Rhine rises in Switzerland.*

rise above *phr. v.* [T] **1** to go above or beyond the limits of something: *He had managed to rise above the deprivations of his childhood.* | *I am confident the company will rise above its financial problems.* **2** to be morally good or wise enough to be able to avoid something that you should not do or to understand things that other people do not: *Let us all rise above our hatreds and band together in national unity.* | *The law should rise above popular opinion.* **3** to be of a higher standard than other things that are similar: *The restaurant needs something to help it rise above the competition.*

rise against *phr. v.* [T] LITERARY to be very angry and upset by something: *His whole heart rose against this.*

USAGE NOTE: ROSE

The past tense of **rise** is **rose**, and the perfect tense is **have risen** (NOT raised).

S W ② **rise²** *n.* **1** [C] an increase in number, amount, or value: [+ **in**] *They reported a 20% rise in sales last year.* | **rise in costs/prices/taxes etc.** *Officials fear that sudden rises in food prices could cause riots.* | *Many Representatives opposed the tax rise.* | *Violent crime is on the rise in some European nations.* —see Usage Note at RAISE² **2** [singular] the achievement of importance, success, or power: [+ **of**] *"Citizen Kane" details the rise of a ruthless tycoon.* | *Few in the 1960s would have predicted the Latino rise to power.* | *Smith credits the popularity of professional beach volleyball for his sudden rise to fame.* **3 the rise and**

fall a) if you see, hear, or feel the rise and fall of something, you see, hear or feel it go up and then down again: *Jerry couldn't catch what they were saying, but he could hear the rise and fall of their voices.* **b)** an increase in power, popularity, influence etc. followed by a decrease: *the rise and fall of the Roman Empire* **4 give rise to sth** a phrase meaning to be the reason why something happens or begins to exist, used especially in writing: *The success of "Pamela" gave rise to a number of imitations.* | *Daily shaving can give rise to a number of skin problems.* **5 get a rise out of sb** to make someone become annoyed or embarrassed by making a joke about them: *Bill likes to get a rise out of people, to say things just for effect.* **6** [C] a piece of ground that slopes up: *We topped the rise and saw the spread of land below us.* —see also HIGH-RISE

ris·er /ˈraɪzɚ/ *n.* [C] **1 early/late riser** someone who usually gets out of bed very early or very late **2** the upright part of a step on a set of stairs **3 risers** [plural] a movable set of wooden or metal steps for a group of people to stand on

ris·i·ble /ˈrɪzəbəl/ *adj.* FORMAL something that is risible is so stupid that it deserves to be laughed at —**risibility** /ˌrɪzəˈbɪləti/ *n.* [U]

ris·ing /ˈraɪzɪŋ/ *adj.* **1** increasing in amount or level: *the rising cost of living* **2** [only before noun] becoming more important or famous: *a rising young actor*

R

risk¹ /rɪsk/ *n.*

S W ① **1 chance of bad result** [C,U] the possibility that something bad or dangerous may happen: *Nothing worthwhile is accomplished without risk or danger.* | [+ **of**] *the risk of infection* | [+ **that**] *There is a real risk that the wheat crop may be lost.* | **reduce/increase the risk of sth** *There are measures you can take to reduce the risk of accidents.* | *There's an element of risk* (=some risk, but not too much) *in any kind of investment.*
2 take a risk to decide to do something even though you know there is a chance something bad will happen: *I encourage people to take risks by trying new things.*
3 at risk be in a situation where you may be harmed: *Millions of lives are at risk because of food shortages.* | [**be at risk of sth**] *Evidence shows that the spotted owl is at risk of extinction.* | [**be at risk from sth**] *Hundreds of people are at risk from radiation poisoning.* | *We would never make a decision that put public health at risk.*
4 cause of danger [C] something or someone that is likely to hurt you or be dangerous: [+ **to**] *I'm worried that my age may be a risk to my unborn child.* | *Pollution is a health risk to the elderly.* | *Untended camp fires pose a tremendous fire risk.* | *the risk factors* (=things that influence whether something bad will happen) *for heart disease*
5 run a risk to be in a situation where something bad may happen to you: *If your body temperature rises above 106 degrees, you run a great risk of getting heat stroke.*
6 at your own risk if you do something at your own risk, you do it even though you understand the possible dangers and have been warned about them: *Danger – enter at your own risk.*
7 at the risk of doing sth used when you think that what you are going to say or do may have a bad result, may offend or annoy people etc.: *At the risk of being boring, I have to say again how much I enjoyed myself.*
8 insurance/business [C] a person or business to whom it is a good or bad idea to give insurance or lend money: **a good/bad/poor risk** *Students are not a very good credit risk.* —see also **a calculated risk** (CALCULATED (1)), SECURITY RISK

risk² *v.* [T] **1** to put something in a situation in **S W ③** which it could be lost, destroyed, or harmed: *He had risked his own health to help the sick during the epidemic.* | [**risk sth on sth**] *The senators are willing to risk their careers on a matter of principle.* | *Jim risked his life to help save his partner.* | *I'm getting* too old to **risk life and limb** (=risk being killed or hurt) *for a cheap thrill.* **2** to get into a situation where something bad may happen to you: *They had risked death in order to get their families to America.* | [**risk being defeated/killed/fired etc.**] *Any young athlete caught taking gifts or money risks being kicked off the team.* **3** to do something that you know may have dangerous or bad results: [**risk doing sth**] *No one wanted to risk dining on Ollie's cooking.* | *If that's my only chance of getting my husband back, I'll risk it.*

risk man·age·ment /ˈ. ˌ.../ *n.* [U] a system to prevent or reduce dangerous accidents or mistakes

risk-tak·ing /ˈ. ˌ.../ *n.* [U] the practice of doing things that involve risks in order to achieve something —**risk-taker** *n.* [C]

risk·y /ˈrɪski/ *adj.* **riskier, riskiest** involving a risk that something bad will happen: *Travel in the region is still considered risky.* | *Banks don't want to finance us because this is a risky business.* —**riskily** *adv.* —**riskiness** *n.* [U]

ri·sot·to /rɪˈzɑtou, -ˈsɑtou, -ˈzou-/ *n.* [U] a hot food made by adding hot liquid to rice a little at a time, often with cheese and pieces of meat, fish, or vegetables

ris·qué /rɪsˈkeɪ/ *adj.* a joke, remark etc. that is risqué is slightly shocking, especially because it is about sex: *risqué humor*

rite /raɪt/ *n.* [C] **1** a ceremony that is always performed in the same way, usually for religious purposes: *Buddhist rites* | *A cleansing rite was performed before building started.* **2 rite of passage** a special ceremony or action that is a sign of a new stage in someone's life, especially when a boy starts to become a man **3 last rites** final prayers or religious ceremonies for someone who is dying: *A priest came to give him the last rites.*

S W **rit·u·al¹** /ˈrɪtʃuəl/ *n.* [C,U] **1** a ceremony that is
3 always performed in the same way, in order to mark an important religious or social occasion: *traditional dances and rituals* | *The Chinese surround silk with myth and ritual.* **2** something that you do regularly and in the same way each time: *Set up a regular time for homework; make it a ritual.*

rit·u·al² *adj.* [only before noun] **1** done as part of a rite or ritual: *ritual prayers* **2** done in a specific and expected way, but without real meaning or sincerity: *ritual campaign promises* —**ritually** *adv.*

rit·u·al·is·tic /ˌrɪtʃuəˈlɪstɪk◂/ *adj.* ritualistic words, types of behavior etc. always follow the same pattern, especially because they form part of a ritual: *ritualistic ceremonies* | *ritualistic violence* —**ritualistically** /-kli/ *adv.*

ritz·y /ˈrɪtsi/ *adj.* **ritzier, ritziest** INFORMAL fashionable and expensive: *We had dinner at the ritzy Drake Hotel.*

S W **ri·val¹** /ˈraɪvəl/ *n.* [C] **1** a person, group, or organi-
3 zation that you compete with in sports, business, a fight etc.: [**+ for**] *Cunningham and Da Silva are rivals in tonight's boxing match.* | **rival company/ nation/team etc.** *two rival Arab tribes* | *The David Letterman show's* **arch-rival** (=most important rival) *is "The Tonight Show."* **2** something that is equally as good or important as something else: *The cult of Mithras was Christianity's main rival at the time of Constantine.* | **have no/few rivals** *Nunn has few rivals for the title of top golfer in the Senate.*

ri·val² *v.* [T] to be as good or important as someone or something else: *Chef Shawn's apple pie rivals the best I've tasted.* —see also UNRIVALED

ri·val·ry /ˈraɪvəlri/ *n.* plural **rivalries** [C,U] continuous competition: *Most of the killings result from gang rivalry.* | *ethnic rivalries* —see also **sibling rivalry** (SIBLING (2))

riv·en /ˈrɪvən/ *adj.* FORMAL split violently apart: *Somalia's south remains riven by tribal feuds.*

S W **riv·er** /ˈrɪvɚ/ *n.* [C] **1** a natural and continuous flow
2 of water in a long line across a country into an

ocean, lake etc.: *the Mississippi River* | **up/down river** (=in the same direction as the river flows, or in the opposite direction) *We went down river in a canoe.* —see picture on page 428 **2** a large amount of moving liquid: [**+ of**] *The cut caused a small river of blood to flow down his arm.* —see also **sell sb down the river** (SELL¹ (11))

Ri·ve·ra /rɪˈvɛrə/, **Di·e·go** /diˈeɪgou/ (1886–1957) a Mexican PAINTER famous for his wall paintings showing the life and history of the Mexican people

river ba·sin /ˈ.. ˌ../ *n.* [C] an area from which all the water flows into the same river

river bed /ˈ.. ˌ./ *n.* [C] the ground over which a river flows

riv·er·side /ˈrɪvɚˌsaɪd/ *n.* [singular] the land on the banks of a river: **riverside city/home etc.** *a beautiful riverside park*

riv·et¹ /ˈrɪvɪt/ *v.* [T] **1** to attract and hold someone's attention: *A rash of high-profile crimes riveted the city's attention this summer.* | [**be riveted on/to sth**] *All eyes were riveted to the tiny television set.* **2** to fasten something with rivets

rivet² *n.* [C] a metal pin used to fasten pieces of metal together

riv·et·ing /ˈrɪvɪtɪŋ/ *adj.* something that is riveting is so interesting or exciting that you cannot stop watching it or listening to it: *Kevin Bacon gives a riveting performance as O'Keefe.*

riv·i·er·a /ˌrɪviˈɛrə/ *n.* **the Riviera** a warm coast that is popular with people who are on vacation, especially the Mediterranean coast of France

riv·u·let /ˈrɪvyəlɪt/ *n.* [C] a very small stream of liquid, especially water: *The snow began to melt and run in small rivulets.*

Riy·adh /ˈriyɑd/ the capital and largest city of Saudi Arabia

ri·yal, rial /riˈyɑl, -ˈyæl/ *n.* [C] the standard unit of money in Saudi Arabia and other Arab countries

RN *n.* [C] the abbreviation of REGISTERED NURSE

RNA *n.* [U] ribonucleic acid; an important chemical that exists in all living cells and controls CHEMICAL activities in cells

roach /routʃ/ *n.* **1** a COCKROACH **2** SLANG the part of a MARIJUANA cigarette that you suck smoke through **3** a European fish similar to a CARP

road /roud/ *n.* **1** [C,U] a specially prepared hard sur- **S W** face for cars, buses, bicycles etc. to travel on: *Susie* **1 1** *used to live on this road.* | *a small Texas road* | **up/ down/along the road** (=further along the road) *The child-care center is just down the road.* | *Alaska's ferry system connects cities that can't be reached by road.* | *I think the next* **main road** *is where we need to turn left.* | *They turned off the highway onto a* **side road** *to elude the police.* | *A twisting* **dirt road** (=without a hard surface) *led to her house.* | **road accident/repairs/user etc.** *He was killed in a road accident.* —see Usage Note at STREET **2 on the road a)** traveling in a car, especially for long distances: *We were back on the road before dawn.* **b)** if a group of actors or musicians is on the road, they are traveling from place to place giving performances **c)** if your car is on the road, you have paid for the repairs, tax etc. necessary for you to legally drive it: *It costs a lot of money to keep these old cars on the road.* **3 on the road to peace/recovery/democracy etc.** developing in a way that will result in peace etc.: *We are already on the road to economic recovery.* **4 down the road** INFORMAL in the future: *We might get married, but that's down the road.* **5 go down a road** INFORMAL to follow a particular course of action: *The country is making efforts to go down the thermonuclear road.* **6 one for the road** SPOKEN a last alcoholic drink before you leave a party, bar etc. **7 the road to hell is paved with good intentions** used to say that it is not enough to intend to do something good, because people are judged by the results of what they do, not by their intentions —see also the **end of the road** (END¹ (11)), **hit the road** (HIT¹ (19))

road·block /ˈroudblɑk/ *n.* [C] **1** a place where the police are stopping traffic: *Within an hour of the shootings, police set up ten roadblocks around Las*

Cruces. **2** something that stops the progress of a plan: *Inappropriate clothing can be a roadblock to promotion.*

road hog /'. ./ *n.* [C] INFORMAL someone who drives with their car taking up most of a road and does not let others drive by

road·house /'roodhaus/ *n.* [C] a restaurant or bar on a main road outside a city

road·ie /'roodi/ *n.* [C] INFORMAL someone whose job is moving equipment for musicians

road·kill /'roodkɪl/ *n.* [U] INFORMAL animals that are killed by cars on a road or HIGHWAY

road man·ag·er /'. ,.../ *n.* [C] someone who makes arrangements for entertainers when they are traveling

road rage /'. ./ *n.* [U] violence and angry behavior by car drivers toward other car drivers: *a road rage attack*

road·run·ner /'rood,rʌnɚ/ *n.* [C] a small American bird that runs very fast and that usually lives in deserts

road·show /'roodʃoʊ/ *n.* [C] a performance for entertainment or business purposes, done by a person or group that travels around the country: *Caldor's managers will soon begin a roadshow to promote the company to investors.*

road·side /'roodsaɪd/ *n.* [singular] the land at the edges of a road: **a roadside cafe/restaurant etc.** *a roadside hamburger place*

road sign /'. ./ *n.* [C] a sign next to a road, that gives information to drivers

road test /'. ./ *n.* [C] a test to check that a vehicle is in good condition and safe to drive —**roadtest** *v.* [T]

road trip /'. ./ *n.* [C] a long trip you take in a car, usually with friends

road·way /'roodweɪ/ *n.* **plural roadways** [C,U] the part of the road used by vehicles

road·work /'roodwɚk/ *n.* [U] repairs that are being done to a road: *Roadwork has slowed traffic to a crawl.*

road·wor·thy /'rood,wɚði/ *adj.* a vehicle that is roadworthy is in good condition and safe enough to drive —**roadworthiness** *n.* [U]

roam /room/ *v.* **1** [I,T] to walk or travel, usually for a long time, with no clear purpose or direction: *At one point, buffalo freely roamed North America.* | *The kids roamed the neighborhood on their bikes.* | [+ **around/through/over etc.**] *He's been roaming around Italy for the last two or three months.* **2** [I] if your eyes roam over something, you look slowly at all parts of it: [+ **over**] *Harry's eyes roamed over her body.*

roam·ing /'roomɪŋ/ *n.* [U] **1** the use of your CELLULAR PHONE outside its normal area **2** the act of walking or traveling, usually for a long time, with no clear purpose or direction: *After 18 years of roaming, Shirley finally settled down in Missouri.*

roan /roon/ *n.* [C] a horse that is a light reddish brown color —**roan** *adj.*

roar¹ /rɔr/ *v.* **1** [I] to make a deep, very loud noise, like the noise a LION makes: *The lions roared in their cages.* **2** [T] to say or shout something in a deep, powerful voice: *"I don't need to listen to this," roared Maxie.* **3** [I always + adv./prep.] a word meaning "to move very quickly and noisily," used especially about vehicles or other things that are not alive: [+ **past/down etc.**] *Cars full of young kids roared by with streamers flying.* | *The fire roared across 1000 acres of hillside.* **4** [I] to laugh loudly and continuously: *When she told him about the call, he roared with laughter.*

roar back *phr. v.* [I] to start performing much better in a sport, competition, election etc., when you were losing before: *Logan High roared back to win by 11 points.*

roar² *n.* [C] **1** a deep, loud noise made by an animal such as a LION, or by someone's voice: *Nadia let out a roar of laughter.* **2** a continuous loud noise, especially made by a machine or a strong wind: *the roar of the surf*

roar·ing /'rɔrɪŋ/ *adj.* **1** [only before noun] making a deep, very loud, continuous noise: *Our train passed over a roaring waterfall.* **2 roaring fire** a roaring fire burns with a lot of flames and heat **3 roaring drunk** very drunk and noisy

roast¹ /roost/ *v.* **1** [I,T] to cook something, such as meat, in an OVEN or over a fire **2** [I,T] to heat nuts, coffee, beans etc. quickly in order to dry them and give them a particular taste: *dry-roasted peanuts* **3** [T] INFORMAL to strongly criticize or make insulting remarks about someone or something: *Even the judge joined in roasting the media for their coverage of the case.*

roast² *n.* [C] **1** a large piece of roasted meat —see also POT ROAST **2** an occasion at which people celebrate a special event in someone's life by telling funny stories or giving speeches about them: *We're going to have a roast for Jack when he retires.* **3** an outdoor party at which food is cooked on an open fire: *a hamburger roast at the beach*

roast³ *adj.* [only before noun] roasted: *roast beef*

roast·ing /'roostɪŋ/ also **roasting hot** /,.. '. ./ *adj.* INFORMAL very hot, especially so that you feel uncomfortable: *a roasting hot day*

rob /rɑb/ *v.* **robbed, robbing** [T] **1** to steal money or property from a person, bank etc.: *Police are looking for a man who robbed a gas station on Van Ness Avenue.* | *We got robbed last summer.* | [**rob sb of sth**] *Her first husband had robbed her of her fortune.* —see Usage Note at STEAL¹ **2** to take away an important quality, ability etc. from someone or something: [**rob sb/sth of sth**] *A hamstring injury had robbed him of his speed.* **3 rob the cradle** INFORMAL to have a sexual relationship with someone who is a lot younger than you **4 rob Peter to pay Paul** INFORMAL to use money that you needed for something to pay for something else

rob·ber /'rɑbɚ/ *n.* [C] someone who steals money or property: *a bank robber* —see Usage Note at THIEF

robber bar·on /'.. ,../ *n.* [C] a powerful person who uses money and influence to get more money, businesses, land etc., in a way that is slightly dishonest

rob·ber·y /'rɑbɚi/ *n.* **plural robberies** [C,U] the crime of stealing things from a bank, store etc., especially using violence: *Many travelers have been the victims of robberies on this road.* | *He got a 20-year sentence for* **armed robbery** (=robbery using a gun).

robe¹ /roob/ *n.* [C] **1** also **robes** a long loose piece of clothing, especially one worn for official ceremonies: *Kovitsky was up on the bench, in his black robes.* **2** a long loose piece of clothing that you wear over your night clothes or after a bath; BATHROBE

robe² *v.* FORMAL **be robed in sth** to be dressed in a particular way: *The hostess looked very glamorous, robed in emerald velvet.*

Robes·pierre /,roobz'pyɛr/, **Max·i·mil·i·en** /,mæksɪ'mɪliən/ (1758–1794) one of the leaders of the French Revolution

rob·in /'rɑbɪn/ *n.* [C] **1** a common North American bird with a red breast and brown back **2** a European bird like an American robin, but smaller

Robin Hood /'rɑbɪn ,hʊd/ in old English stories, a man who is remembered especially for robbing the rich and giving to the poor

Rob·in·son /'rɑbənsən/, **Jack·ie** /'dʒæki/ (1919–1972) a baseball player who was the first African-American person to be allowed to play in the MAJOR LEAGUES

Robinson, Sug·ar Ray /'ʃʊgɚ reɪ/ (1920–1989) a BOXER who was the world CHAMPION in the 1940s and 1950s

ro·bot /'roobɑt, -bʌt/ *n.* [C] **1** a machine that can move and do some of the work of a person, and is usually controlled by a computer: *assembly line robots* **2** someone who works or behaves like a machine, without having thoughts or feelings —**robotic** /roo'bɑtɪk/ *adj.*

ro·bot·ics /rou'bɑtɪks/ n. [U] the study of how robots are made and used

ro·bust /rou'bʌst, 'roubʌst/ adj. **1** a robust person is strong and healthy: *Mrs. Lutu is a robust, energetic mother of four.* **2** a robust system, organization etc. is strong and not likely to have problems: *Retail sales have been robust this year.* **3** a robust object is strong and not likely to break: *The chair was more robust than it looked.* **4** robust food or FLAVORS have a good, strong taste: *a robust cheese* **5** behaving or speaking in a strong and determined way: *"I plead not guilty," Zhivkov stated in a robust voice.* —**robustly** adv. —**robustness** n. [U]

s w **rock**[1] /rɑk/ n.
₂₂ **1** |stone| **a)** [U] stone, or a type of stone that forms part of the Earth's surface: *Geologists study the exposed sections of rock.* | *igneous rock* (=rock formed by volcanoes) | *The road was flanked by boulders and tall rock formations* (=shapes made naturally from rock). **b)** [C] a piece of stone, especially a large one: *Eugene stood on a rock and called for help.* | *A ship had been driven onto the rocks* (=a line of rocks under or next to the ocean) *during the storm.*
2 |music| [U] also **rock music** a type of popular modern music with a strong loud beat, played using GUITARS and drums: *a rock concert* | *KXCI plays rock, blues, jazz, world beat, and folk music.*
3 be on the rocks INFORMAL a relationship or business that is on the rocks is having a lot of problems and is likely to fail soon: *His third marriage was on the rocks.*
4 scotch/vodka etc. on the rocks INFORMAL an alcoholic drink that is served with ice but no water
5 be (stuck) between a rock and a hard place INFORMAL to have a choice between two things, both of which are bad or dangerous
6 |jewel| [C usually plural] INFORMAL a DIAMOND or other jewel
7 as solid/steady as a rock a) very strongly built or well supported and not likely to break or fall **b)** someone who is as solid or steady as a rock is very strong and calm in difficult situations and you can depend on them —see also ROCK-SOLID
8 get your rocks off VULGAR, SLANG if a man gets his rocks off, he has sex

s w **rock**[2] v. **1** [I,T] to move gently, leaning backward
₃ and forward or from one side to the other, or to make something do this: *The chair squeaked as I rocked back and forth* | *Waves from a passing freighter rocked the boat.* **2** [T] to make the people in a place or organization feel very shocked or surprised, especially because they have to deal with problems or changes: *The company was rocked by massive changes in the computer business.* **3 rock the boat** INFORMAL to cause problems for other members of a group by criticizing something or trying to change the way something is done: *As long as you don't rock the boat, nobody cares what you do.* **4 sb/ sth rocks** SLANG said to show that you strongly approve of someone or something: *You rock.* **5** [T] if an explosion or EARTHQUAKE (=violent movement of the earth) rocks an area, it makes it shake

rock·a·bil·ly /'rɑkə,bɪli/ n. [U] a type of music that combines rock music and traditional country music

rock and roll /ˌ. . '. / n. [U] ROCK 'N' ROLL

rock bot·tom /ˌ. '../ n. **hit/reach rock bottom** INFORMAL to become as unhappy or unsuccessful as it is possible to be: *Joan Rivers reveals how she hit rock bottom and recovered in her autobiography.*

rock-bottom /ˌ. '..‹/ adj. a rock-bottom price is as low as it can possibly be: *rock-bottom real estate prices*

rock climb·ing /'. ,../ n. [U] the sport of climbing up very steep rock surfaces such as the sides of mountains —**rock climber** n. [C] —see picture on page 1332

rock-crys·tal /'. ,../ n. [U] pure natural QUARTZ (=a very hard mineral) that is transparent

Rock·e·fel·ler /'rɑkə,fɛlɚ/, **John D.** (1839–1937) a

U.S. businessman and PHILANTHROPIST who started the Standard Oil Company in 1870

Rockefeller, John D., II (1874–1960) the son of John D. Rockefeller who gave the U.N. the land for its HEADQUARTERS, and built the Rockefeller Center in New York City

Rockefeller Foun·da·tion, the /ˈ.... .,../ an organization that supports scientific RESEARCH, especially to improve the environment and social conditions

rock·er /'rɑkɚ/ n. [C] **1** a ROCKING CHAIR **2** one of the curved pieces of wood fastened to the bottom of a ROCKING CHAIR, that allows it to move backward and forward if you push it **3** a musician who plays ROCK 'N' ROLL music, or someone who likes this kind of music: *rocker Carl Perkins* **4 be off your rocker** SPOKEN to be crazy

rock·et[1] /'rɑkɪt/ n. [C] **1** a vehicle used for traveling s w
or carrying things into space, which is shaped like a ₃
big tube **2** a similar object used as a weapon, especially one that carries a bomb: *Heavy artillery and rocket attacks rained down on the camp.* **3** a small tube fastened to a stick, that contains explosive powder and is used as a FIREWORK **4 sth isn't rocket science** HUMOROUS used to say that something is very easy to do, and only stupid people would be unable to do it —see also ROCKET SCIENTIST

rocket[2] v. [I] **1** also **rocket up** if a price or amount rockets, it increases quickly and suddenly: *Interest rates have rocketed as credit has become scarce.* **2** [always + adv./prep.] to move somewhere very fast: [+ **through/along** etc.] *They rocketed by in their sleek limousines.* **3** [always + adv./prep.] to achieve a successful position very quickly: [+ **to**] *Krickstein first rocketed to prominence at the 1983 U.S. Open.*

rocket launch·er /'.. ,../ n. [C] a weapon like a tube used for firing military rockets into the air

rocket sci·en·tist /'.. '../ n. **1** a scientist whose work is related to rockets **2 it doesn't take a rocket scientist (to do sth)** also **you don't have to be a rocket scientist (to do sth)** HUMOROUS used to say that something is very easy to do, and only stupid people would be unable to do it: *It doesn't exactly take a rocket scientist to realize that the chain of events was no coincidence.* **3 sb is no rocket scientist** HUMOROUS used to say that someone is very stupid

rock·fall /'rɑk,fɔl/ n. [C] a pile of rocks that are falling or have fallen

rock gar·den /'. ,../ n. [C] a type of garden where there are rocks with small plants growing between them

rock-hard /ˌ. '.‹/ adj. extremely hard

rock·ing chair /'.. ,./ n. [C] a chair that has two curved pieces of wood under its legs, so that it moves backward and forward smoothly —see picture at CHAIR[1]

rocking horse /'.. ,./ n. [C] a wooden horse for children that moves backward and forward when you sit on it

rock mu·sic /'. ,../ n. [U] a type of popular modern music with a strong loud beat, played using GUITARS and drums

Rock·ne /'rɑkni/, **Knute** /nut/ (1888–1931) a U.S. football COACH famous for developing new methods of playing that made his team extremely successful

rock 'n' roll /ˌrɑk ən 'roul/ n. [U] a type of music with a strong loud beat and played on GUITARS and drums, which first became popular in the 1950s: *It was rock 'n' roll that originally inspired me to become a musician.*

rock salt /'. ./ n. [U] a type of salt that is obtained from under the ground

rock-sol·id /ˌ. '..‹/ adj. **1** very strong, so that you can depend on it: *rock-solid commitment* **2** very hard and not likely to break

rock-stead·y /ˌ. '..‹/ adj. very strong or very calm: *rock-steady nerves*

Rock·well /'rɑkwɛl/, **Nor·man** /'nɔrmən/ (1894–1978) a U.S. artist famous for his pictures of the lives of ordinary people

rock·y /'rɑki/ *adj.* **rockier, rockiest 1** covered with rocks or made of rock: *The village sits on a rocky hill overlooking the Mediterranean.* **2** INFORMAL a relationship or situation that is rocky is difficult and may not continue or be successful: *Negotiations got off to a rocky start today.* —**rockiness** *n.* [U]

Rocky Moun·tains, the /ˌ... '../ also **the Rockies** a long range of high mountains in North America that runs from Alsaka down to New Mexico, and separates the Midwest of the U.S. from the West Coast

ro·co·co /rə'koukou/ *adj.* rococo buildings and furniture have a lot of curly decoration and were fashionable in Europe in the 18th century

rod /rɑd/ *n.* [C] **1** a long thin pole or bar: *a curtain rod* **2** a long thin pole used with a line and hook for catching fish: *a fishing rod* **3** a long thin CELL (1) in your eye, that helps you see areas of light and darkness —compare CONE (5) —see also HOT ROD, LIGHTNING ROD

rode /roud/ *v.* the past tense of RIDE¹

ro·dent /'roudnt/ *n.* [C] one of a group of small animals with long sharp front teeth, such as rats or rabbits

ro·de·o /'roudiˌou, rou'deiou/ *n. plural* **rodeos** [C] a type of entertainment in which COWBOYs ride wild horses, catch cattle with ropes, and ride in races

Rod·gers /'rɑdʒɚz/, **Richard** (1902–1979) a U.S. COMPOSER famous for writing MUSICALs with Lorenz Hart and Oscar Hammerstein

Ro·din /rou'dæn/, **Au·guste** /ɔu'gust/ (1840–1917) a French SCULPTOR who is considered the greatest sculptor of his time

roe /rou/ *n.* [C,U] fish eggs eaten as a food

roent·gen, röntgen /'rɛntˈgɚ, 'rʌnt-/ *n.* [C] TECHNICAL the international measure for X-RAYS

Roent·gen, Röntgen /'rɛntgən, 'rʌnt-/, **Wil·helm,** /'vɪlhɛlm/ (1845–1923) a German scientist who discovered X-rays

Roeth·ke /'rɛtki/, **The·o·dore** /'θiədɔr/ (1908–1963) a U.S. poet

rog·er /'rɑdʒɚ/ *interjection* used in radio conversations to say that a message has been understood

Rog·ers /'rɑdʒɚz/, **Will** /wɪl/ (1879–1935) a U.S. humorous writer and performer, famous for his jokes that criticized politicians

Ro·get /rou'ʒei/, **Peter Mark** (1779–1869) a British doctor who wrote the first English THESAURUS

rogue¹ /roug/ *adj.* [only before noun] **1** a rogue person or organization does not follow the usual rules or methods and often causes trouble: *Rogue trader Nick Leeson lost millions of dollars for his company.* **2** a rogue wild animal lives apart from the main group and is often dangerous

rogue² *n.* [C] a man who behaves in a slightly bad or dishonest way, but whom people still like —**roguery** *n.* [U]

rogu·ish /'rougɪʃ/ *adj.* someone with a roguish expression or smile looks amused, especially because they have done something slightly dishonest or wrong —**roguishly** *adv.* —**roguishness** *n.* [U]

roil /rɔɪl/ *v.* [T] **1** to make water, clouds etc. move violently: *Joy-riding boaters roiled the water.* **2** to make someone or a group feel nervous or annoyed: *Wild swings in prices roiled the stock market.*

role, rôle /roul/ *n.* [C] **1** the way in which someone or something is involved in an activity or situation, and how much influence they have on it: *School staff take an active role in providing career guidance.* | **play a leading/major/key role** *The Red Cross played a major role in the country's rehabilitation.* **2** the character played by an actor in a play or movie: *Birney played the role of a doctor on TV's "St. Elsewhere."* | **the lead/leading role** *Alexander had sung leading roles in more than 50 operas.* | *Costner only plays a minor role in the movie.* **3** the position that someone has in society, in an organization etc., or the way they are expected to behave in a relationship with someone else: *The traditional male role in marriage is to provide for women and children.* **4 role reversal** a situation in which two people,

especially a man and a woman, take each other's traditional roles

role mod·el /'. ../ *n.* [C] someone whose behavior, attitudes etc. people try to copy because they admire them: *She is a leader and role model for many women in business.*

role-play /'. ./ *n.* [C,U] an exercise in which you behave in the way that someone else would behave in a particular situation, especially to help you learn something: *ideas for classroom role-play* —**role-play** *v.* [I,T]

roll¹ /roul/ *v.*

roll

1 **round object** [I always + adv./prep.,T] if something that is round rolls or if you roll it, it moves along a surface by turning over and over: *One of the eggs rolled off the edge of the counter.* | [**roll sth**] *Roll the scallops in the Cajun spice mix.*

2 **person/animal** [I always + adv./prep.] to turn your body over one or more times while lying down: *I'm trying to teach my dog to roll over.* | *Ralph rolled onto his stomach.*

3 **sth with wheels** [I always + adv./prep.,T always + adv./prep.] to move on wheels, or make something that has wheels move: [+ **into/forward/past etc.**] *Cars rolled slowly forward toward the toll booth.* | [**roll sth to/around/by etc.**] *The waitress rolled the dessert cart over to our table.*

4 **paper/string etc.** [T] also **roll up** to bend or wind something such as paper, string etc. into the shape of a tube or ball: *Roll the tortilla around the chicken and serve with salsa.* | *She rolled up the poster and put it in a cardboard tube.*

5 **drop of liquid** [I always + adv./prep.] to move over a surface smoothly without stopping: [+ **down/onto etc.**] *Perspiration rolled off his forehead.*

6 **waves/clouds** [I always + adv./prep.] to move in a particular direction: [+ **into/toward etc.**] *In 1987, a tidal wave rolled over the island nation.*

7 **roll your eyes** to move your eyes around and up, especially in order to show that you are annoyed: *Every time he leaves the room, everybody rolls their eyes.*

8 **game** [I,T] if you roll DICE, you throw them as part of a game

9 **ship/plane** [I] if a ship or airplane rolls, it leans one way and then another with the movement of the water or air

10 **make sth flat** [T] to make something flat by moving something heavy over it: *Use a rolling pin to roll the dough into a 12-inch square.* —see picture on page 425

11 **sound** [I] if drums or THUNDER roll, they make a long low series of sounds

12 **machine/camera** [I] if a machine such as a movie camera or a PRINTING PRESS rolls, it operates: *Quiet! The cameras are rolling!*

13 **(all) rolled into one** if something is several different things rolled into one, it includes qualities of all those things: *The band's sound was metal and punk and rap all rolled into one.*

14 **get rolling** if a plan, business etc. gets rolling, it starts operating: *Although started in 1965, Wedtech didn't really get rolling until 1975.*

15 **be rolling in money/dough/cash/it** to have or earn a lot of money: *Mel Levine is rolling in dough.*

16 **roll out of bed** INFORMAL to get out of bed: *As a student, he rarely rolled out of bed before noon.*

17 **be rolling in the aisles** if people in a theater, AUDIENCE etc. are rolling in the aisles, they are laughing a lot

18 **be ready to roll** INFORMAL used to say you are ready to do something or go somewhere: *After months of planning, we were finally ready to roll.*

19 **roll with the punches** to deal with problems or difficulties by doing whatever you need to do, rather

than by trying only one method: *Many industries were able to roll with the punches in a tough economy.*
20 attack [T] INFORMAL to rob someone, especially when they are drunk and asleep: *Punks on the streets would roll drunks for small change.*
21 roll your r's to pronounce the sound /r/ using your tongue in a way that makes the sound very long
22 a rolling stone gathers no moss used to say that someone who often changes jobs, moves to different places etc. is not able to have any real relationships or responsibilities
23 roll a cigarette to make your own cigarette, using loose tobacco and special paper —see also **set/start the ball rolling** (BALL¹ (5)), **heads will roll** (HEAD¹ (29)),

roll around *phr. v.* [I] if something that happens regularly rolls around, it happens again: *By the time bedtime rolls around, the boys are pretty worn out.*

roll sth ↔ **back** *phr. v.* [T] **1** to reduce the price of something: *Ticket prices will be rolled back to 1968 levels.* **2** to reduce the influence or power of a system, government etc., especially because it has too much power: *Dulles saw communism as something evil to be rolled back, not just contained.* **3** to force your opponents in a war to move back from their position

roll sth ↔ **down** *phr. v.* [T] **roll a window down** to open a car window

roll in *phr. v.* [I] **1** to happen or arrive in large numbers or quantities: *After restructuring under new management, the company's profits began rolling in.* **2** to arrive later than usual or expected without seeming to be worried about it: *Rebecca sometimes rolls in around noon.* **3** if clouds, mist etc. roll in, they begin to cover an area of the sky or land: *It looks like the fog is already rolling in.*

roll sth ↔ **out** *phr. v.* [T] **1** to make something flat and thin by pushing a special wooden roller over it: *On a floured surface, roll out the dough as thin as possible.* **2** to make something flat and straight after it has been curled into a tube shape or a ball: *We rolled out our sleeping bags under the stars.* **3** to make a new product available for people to buy or use: *L'Oreal rolled out a line of skin-care products called Plenitude.* **4 roll out the red carpet** to make special preparations for an important visitor

roll over *phr. v.* **1** [I] to turn your body around once so that you are lying in a different position: *I rolled over and went back to sleep.* **2** [T **roll** sb/sth **over**] to turn someone's body over on the ground: *We have to roll him over onto his back.*

roll up *phr. v.* **1** to curl something such as cloth or paper into a tube shape —see picture at FOLD¹ **2 roll your sleeves/pants up** to turn the ends of your sleeves, pants etc. over several times so that they are shorter **3 roll your sleeves up** to start doing a job, even though it is difficult or you do not want to do it: *We've got a crisis on our hands, and we need to roll up our sleeves and do something about it.* **4 roll a window up** to close the window of a car **5** [I] to arrive somewhere, especially late or when you are not expected: *A man and his family rolled up in their car.*

sw **roll²** *n.*
2
3 **1** paper/film/money etc. [C] a piece of paper, film, money etc. that has been rolled into the shape of a tube: [+ of] *I sent two rolls of film in yesterday to be developed.* | *Some rolls of wallpaper were stacked in the corner.*
2 bread [C] a small round LOAF of bread for one person: *Hot, fresh rolls were served throughout the meal.* | *a cinnamon roll*
3 list of names an official list of names, especially of people at a meeting, in a class etc.: *The roll is called to see which members are present.*
4 rolls [plural] a list with the names of people that are officially allowed to vote: *More than 23,000 people on the rolls haven't voted in the past eight city elections.*
5 roll of drums/guns/thunder a long, low, fairly loud sound made by drums etc.

6 be on a roll INFORMAL to be having a lot of success with what you are trying to do
7 game [C] the action of throwing DICE as part of a game: *You have another roll, don't you?*
8 ship/plane [C] the movement of a ship or airplane when it leans from side to side with the movement of the water or air
9 skin/fat [C + of] a thick layer of skin or fat, usually just below your waist
10 a roll in the hay INFORMAL, HUMOROUS an act of having sex with someone

roll bar /'. ./ *n.* [C] a strong metal bar over the top of a car, intended to protect the people inside if the car turns over

roll call /'. ./ *n.* [C,U] the act of reading out an official list of names to check who is there

rolled oats /ˌ. './ *n.* [plural] a type of OATS, used for making OATMEAL

roll·er /'roʊlɚ/ *n.* [C] **1** a tube-shaped piece of wood, metal etc. that can be rolled over and over, used for painting, crushing, making things smoother etc.: *a paint roller* **2** CURLER **3** a long, powerful wave: *Booming rollers crashed on the beach.* **4** a tube-shaped piece of metal or wood, used for moving heavy things that have no wheels —see also HIGH ROLLER

Roll·er·blade /'roʊlɚˌbleɪd/ *n.* [C] TRADEMARK: see IN-LINE SKATE —**rollerblade** *v.* [I] —**rollerblading** *n.* [U] —compare ROLLER SKATE

roller coast·er /'.. ˌ../ *n.* [C] **1** a track with sudden steep slopes and curves, which people ride on in special cars at FAIRS and AMUSEMENT PARKS **2** a situation that is impossible to control, because it keeps changing very quickly: *I would like to get off the emotional roller coaster I've been on.*

roller skate /'.. ˌ./ *n.* [C] a special boot with four wheels attached under it —**roller-skate** *v.* [I] —**roller skating** *n.* [U] —compare IN-LINE SKATE

roller tow·el /'.. ˌ../ *n.* [C] a cloth you use for drying your hands in a public place, which is joined together at the ends and wound around a bar of wood or metal

rol·lick·ing /'rɑlɪkɪŋ/ *adj.* [only before noun] OLD-FASHIONED noisy and cheerful: *a rollicking song*

roll·ing /'roʊlɪŋ/ *adj.* **1** [only before noun] rolling hills have many long gentle slopes **2** if you have a rolling walk, you move from side to side as you walk

roll·ing mill /'.. ˌ./ *n.* [C] a factory or machine in which metal is rolled into large, flat, thin pieces

rolling pin /'.. ˌ./ *n.* [C] a long tube-shaped piece of wood used for making PASTRY flat and thin before you cook it

rolling stock /'.. ˌ./ *n.* [U] all the trains, BOXCARS, passenger cars etc. that are used on a railroad

roll-on /'. ./ *n.* [C] also **roll-on de·o·dor·ant** /ˌ. . '.../ a bottle which contains liquid that you rub under your arms in order to stop your SWEAT from smelling bad

roll·o·ver /'roʊlˌoʊvɚ/ *n.* **1 a)** [C] if an INVESTMENT or bank account is a rollover, the money in it is moved from one account to another without having to pay any tax or other FEES: *Many CD rollovers happen in October.* **b)** [C,U] the action of making a bank account, INVESTMENT etc. do this: *The law allows a rollover of retirement money from a company pension to an IRA.* **2** [C] an accident in which a car turns over onto its roof

roll-top desk /ˌ. . '. ./ *n.* [C] a desk that has a cover that you roll back when you open it

Ro·lo·dex /'roʊloʊˌdɛks/ *n.* [C] TRADEMARK a small container that sits on a desk and holds cards with people's names, addresses, and telephone numbers on them

ro·ly-po·ly /ˌroʊli 'poʊli‹/ *adj.* a roly-poly person is round and fat

ROM /rɑm/ *n.* [U] Read-Only Memory; the part of a computer where permanent information and instructions are stored —compare RAM

ro·maine /roʊ'meɪn, 'roʊmeɪn/ *n.* [U] a type of bitter-tasting LETTUCE with long leaves

Ro·man /'roʊmən/ *adj.* **1** relating to ancient Rome or the Roman Empire **2** relating to the city of Rome —**Roman** *n.* [C]

roman *n.* [U] TECHNICAL the ordinary style of printing that uses small upright letters, like the style used for printing these words —compare ITALICS

ro·man à clef /roʊˌmɑn ɑ ˈkleɪ/ *n.* [C] a NOVEL in which real events and people are given different names or changed slightly, so that they seem to be invented and not real

Roman al·pha·bet /ˌ.. ˈ.../ *n.* **the Roman Alphabet** the alphabet used in English and many other European languages, which begins with the letters A, B, C

Roman can·dle /ˌ.. ˈ./ *n.* [C] a type of FIREWORK in the shape of a large CANDLE that burns quickly and brightly and shoots SPARKS into the air

Roman Cath·o·lic /ˌ.. ˈ../ *adj.* belonging or related to the part of the Christian religion whose leader is the Pope —**Roman Catholic** *n.* [C] —**Roman Catholicism** /ˌ.. ˈ..../ *n.* [U]

Roman Cath·o·lic Church, the /ˌ.. ˌ.. ˈ./ the largest church of the Christian religion, that has the Pope as its leader

SW **ro·mance¹** /ˈroʊmæns, roʊˈmæns/ *n.* **1** [C] an exciting and often short relationship between two people who love each other: *Some viewers objected to the interracial romance the show portrays.* | *It was just a summer romance* (=one that happens during a vacation). | *Paris is where her whirlwind romance* (=one that happens very suddenly and quickly) *started.* **2** [U] love, or a feeling of being in love: *The romance had gone out of their relationship.* **3** [U] the feeling of excitement and adventure that is related to a particular place, activity etc.: *the romance of life in the Wild West* **4** [C] a story about the love between two people: *romance novels* **5** [C] a story that has brave characters and exciting events: *a Medieval romance*

ro·mance² /roʊˈmæns/ *v.* [T] OLD-FASHIONED to try to persuade someone to love you

Romance lan·guage /ˈ.. ˌ../ *n.* [C] a language that comes from Latin, for example French or Spanish

Ro·man·esque /ˌroʊməˈnɛsk◂/ *adj.* in the style of building that was popular in Western Europe in the 11th and 12th centuries, which had many round ARCHes and thick PILLARS

Ro·ma·ni·a /roʊˈmeɪniə, ru-/ a country in southeast Europe, east of Hungary and west of the Black Sea —**Romanian** *n.*, *adj.*

Roman law /ˌ.. ˈ./ *n.* [U] LAW: see CIVIL LAW

Roman nose /ˌ.. ˈ./ *n.* [C] a nose that curves out near the top

roman nu·mer·al /ˌ.. ˈ.../ *n.* [C] a number in a system first used in ancient Rome, that uses the combinations of the letters I, V, X, L, C, D, and M to represent numbers —compare ARABIC NUMERAL

Romano- /roʊmɑnoʊ, rə-/ *prefix* ancient Roman and something else: *Romano-British art*

Ro·ma·nov /ˈroʊmənɑf/ the name of a family of Russian CZARS who ruled from 1613 to 1917

Ro·mans /ˈroʊmənz/ a book in the New Testament of the Christian Bible

SW **ro·man·tic¹** /roʊˈmæntɪk/ *adj.* **1** showing strong feelings of love: *Why don't you send him a little romantic card and see how he reacts?* **2** relating to feelings of love or a loving relationship: *I'm in the most stable romantic relationship I've ever had.* **3** beautiful in a way that affects your emotions and makes you think of love or adventure: *We shared a gourmet meal in a romantic, candle-lit restaurant.* **4** not practical, and basing your actions too much on an imagined idea of the world: *You have a very romantic and foolish idea of science.* **5** a romantic story or movie is about love: *a romantic comedy* **6 Romantic art/literature etc.** art or literature that is based on the ideas of romanticism —**romantically** /roʊˈmæntɪkli/ *adv.*

romantic² *n.* [C] **1** someone who shows strong feelings of love and likes doing things that are related to love, such as buying flowers, presents etc.: *I'm a*

romantic who likes picnics and candlelight dinners. **2** someone who is not practical, and bases their ideas too much on an imagined idea of the world **3** also **Romantic** a writer, painter etc., whose work is based on romanticism

ro·man·ti·cism, Romanticism /roʊˈmæntəˌsɪzəm, rə-/ *n.* [U] a way of writing or painting that was popular in the late 18th and early 19th century, in which feelings and wild natural beauty were considered more important than anything else —compare CLASSICISM, REALISM

ro·man·ti·cize /roʊˈmæntəˌsaɪz/ *v.* [T] to talk or think about things in a way that makes them seem more romantic or attractive than they really are: *Much of the film takes a highly romanticized view of life on the streets.*

Ro·ma·ny /ˈroʊməni/ *n.* **1 the Romany** the GYPSY people **2** [U] the language of the GYPSY people

Rome /roʊm/ the capital and largest city of Italy

Ro·me·o /ˈroʊmioʊ/ *n.* [C] OFTEN HUMOROUS a man who tries to attract all the women he meets in a ROMANTIC or sexual way: *"I'm going out with Ellen tonight." "Way to go, Romeo!"* | *the office Romeo*

romp¹ /rɑmp/ *v.* [I] **1** [always + adv./prep.] to play in a noisy way, especially by running, jumping etc.: [+ around/through etc.] *Children romped around happily in the mud.* **2** to defeat another team or player in a sports competition very easily: *Payne Stewart romped to a nine-stroke win at the Dutch Open.*

romp² *n.* [C] **1** an occasion when people play noisily and roughly **2** an occasion when one sports team defeats another one very easily: *Nebraska's 59–28 romp over Utah State* **3** INFORMAL a piece of amusing entertainment that has a lot of exciting scenes: *"Tom Jones" is a bawdy romp through 18th century England.*

romp·ers /ˈrɑmpərz/ *n.* [plural] a piece of clothing for babies, made like a top and pants joined together

ron·do /ˈrɑndoʊ/ *n. plural* **rondos** [C] a piece of music in which the main tune is repeated several times

rönt·gen /ˈrɛntˌgən, ˈrʌnt-/ *n.* [C] another spelling of ROENTGEN

roof¹ /ruf, rʊf/ *n.* [C] **SW**
1 of a building the outside surface or structure on top of a building, vehicle, tent etc.: *We'll need a ladder to get up on the roof.* | *I left my coffee cup on the roof of the car.* —see picture on page 423
2 a roof over your head somewhere to live: *We always had food on the table and a roof over our heads.*
3 go through the roof INFORMAL **a)** if a price, cost etc. goes through the roof, it increases to a very high level **b)** also **hit the roof** to suddenly become very angry: *Put that back before Dad sees you and hits the roof!*
4 of your mouth the hard upper part of the inside of your mouth
5 under the same roof also **under one roof** in the same building or home: *Superstores offer groceries, a bakery, a deli, and other services all under one roof.*
6 under my roof SPOKEN in your home: *Karla discovered her husband was fooling around with his secretary under her own roof.*
7 the roof falls in/caves in a) INFORMAL if the roof falls in or caves in, something bad suddenly happens to you when you do not expect it: *The Warriors were leading, with only a few minutes of the game to go, when the roof fell in.* **b)** if the roof of a building, cave etc. falls in, it falls down on top of the rooms or area beneath it —see also **raise the roof** (RAISE¹ (23)), SUNROOF

roof² *v.* [T usually passive] **1** to put a roof on a building **2 metal-roofed/tile-roofed etc.** having a roof that is covered with a particular material

roof·ies /ˈrufiz/ *n.* [plural] SLANG an illegal drug that is sometimes used to make someone unconscious so they can be RAPEd

roof·ing /'rufɪŋ/ n. [U] material such as SHINGLES or TILES etc., used for making or covering roofs

roof-rack /'. ./ n. [C] a LUGGAGE RACK —see picture at RACK¹

roof·top /'ruftɑp/ n. [C] the upper surface of a roof: *A cat was up on the rooftop.* —see also **shout sth from the rooftops** (SHOUT¹ (2))

rook¹ /rʊk/ n. [C] **1** one of the pieces in a game of CHESS; CASTLE **2** a large black European bird like a CROW

rook² v. [T] OLD-FASHIONED to cheat someone, especially to get their money

rook·er·y /'rʊkəri/ n. [C] a group of NESTS made by rooks or other birds that live together, such as PENGUINS

rook·ie /'rʊki/ n. [C] **1** someone who is in their first year of playing a professional sport: *Lisa Hackney is the LPGA's Rookie of the Year.* **2** someone who has just started doing a job and has little experience: *a rookie radio reporter*

s w **room¹** /rum, rʊm/ n.

1 █in a building█ [C] an area of the inside of a building that has its own walls, floor, and ceiling: *Amanda, can you clean up your room, please? | We're on the eighth floor, room 804.* | **bathroom/dining room/meeting room etc.** *I think I'll put the lamp in the guest room.* | **one-room/two-room** *Carl lives in a one-room apartment downtown.* | **single/double room** (=a room in a hotel for one person or for two)
2 █space█ [U] enough space for a particular purpose: *There isn't any more room in the closet.* | **[room for sb/sth]** *Move over and make some room for me.* | **[room to do sth]** *The kids don't have much room to play in the yard.* | **[have room (for sth)]** *We have plenty of room here for a party.* | *I'll make room for the turkey in the refrigerator.* | *Leave room in the trunk for another suitcase.* | *That old TV takes up too much room.* | **leg-room/head-room** (=space for your legs or head in a vehicle) —see also **elbow room** (ELBOW¹ (5)) —see Usage Note at PLACE¹
3 █possibility█ [U] the possibility that something may exist or will happen: **[+ for]** *Does the position offer room for advancement?* | *There was no room for error on Powell's final long-jump attempt.* | **room for debate/discussion/doubt** *There is room for disagreement over what the test results really tell us.*
4 there's room for improvement used to say that someone's work or performance is not perfect and needs to be improved: *You did well on the last project, but there's room for improvement.*
5 █opportunity█ [U] the chance to do the things that you want to do or need to do: **[+ for]** *You should make room in your diet for more nutritious foods.* | **[room to do sth]** *Dad always gave us room to make mistakes and learn from them.*
6 there's not enough room to swing a cat INFORMAL used to say that an area or room is not very big —see also LIVING ROOM, SITTING ROOM

s w **room²** v. [I] **1 room with sb** to share a room or a house with someone, especially when you are in college: *Dan roomed with Steve at Harvard.* **2** to rent and live in a room somewhere: **[+ in]** *Didn't you used to room in their house?*

room and board /,. . './ n. [U] a room to sleep in and food: *Room and board at school costs $450 a month.*

room·er /'rumə/ n. [C] someone who pays rent to live in a house with its owner

room·ful /'rumfʊl/ n. [C] a large number of things or people that are all together in one room: **[+ of]** *a roomful of reporters*

room·ie /'rumi/ n. [C] SPOKEN a ROOMMATE

room·ing house /'. ,./ n. [C] a house where you can rent a room to live in

s w **room·mate** /'rum-meɪt/ n. [C] **1** someone who you share a room with, especially when you are in college: *I ran into my old college roommate today.* **2** someone you share a room, apartment, or house with: *We were roommates back in Chicago.*

room serv·ice /'. ,../ n. [U] a service provided by a hotel, by which food, drink etc. can be sent to a guest's room

room tem·per·a·ture /,. '..../ n. [U] the normal temperature inside a house: *Red wine tastes best at room temperature.*

room·y /'rumi, 'rʊmi/ adj. **roomier, roomiest** a house, car etc. that is roomy is large and has a lot of space inside it — **roominess** n. [U]

Roo·se·velt /'rouzə,vɛlt/, **El·ea·nor** /'ɛlɪnə/ (1884–1962) the wife of President Franklin D. Roosevelt, known for her work on human rights

Roosevelt, Frank·lin D. /'fræŋklɪn di/ (1882–1945) the 32nd President of the U.S., who helped to end the Depression of the 1930s by starting a program of social and economic changes called the New Deal —see picture on page 1331

Roosevelt, The·o·dore /'θiədɔr/ (1858–1919) the 26th President of the U.S.

roost¹ /rust/ n. [C] a place where birds rest and sleep —see also **rule the roost** (RULE² (5))

roost² v. [I] **1** if a bird roosts, it rests or sleeps somewhere **2 sb's chickens come home to roost** also **sth comes home to roost** used to say that someone's past mistakes are causing problems for them now: *Their extravagant overspending has come home to roost.*

roost·er /'rustə/ n. [C] a male chicken

s w **root¹** /rut, rʊt/ n. [C]
1 █plant█ the part of a plant or tree that grows under the ground and gets water from the soil: *Cover the roots with plenty of soil.* | *Truffles are parasites that grow on the roots of trees.* —see picture at OAK
2 █cause of a problem█ the main cause of a problem: *The love of money is the root of all evil.* | **be/lie at the root of** *There is not just a single gene at the root of alcoholism.* | *A competent mechanic should be able to get to the root of the problem.* | *What do you see as the root cause* (=main reason) *of the Civil War?*
3 roots [plural] **a)** the origins of a custom or TRADITION that has continued for a long time: *Jazz has its roots in the folk songs of the southern U.S.* **b)** your relation with a place because you were born there, or your family used to live there: *He decided to return to his East Coast roots after his marriage failed.*
4 put down roots if you put down roots somewhere, you start to feel that this place is your home and to have relationships with the people there: *Just as I was putting down roots, our family had to move up north.*
5 █of an idea/belief█ the main part of an idea or belief which all the other parts come from: **be/lie at the root of sth** *Biblical writings lie at the root of Western culture.*
6 █tooth/hair etc.█ the part of a tooth, hair etc. that connects to the rest of your body
7 take root a) if an idea, method, activity etc. takes root, people begin to accept or believe it: *Women's professional basketball has yet to take root in this country.* **b)** if a plant takes root, it starts to grow where you have planted it
8 █language█ TECHNICAL the basic part of a word that shows its main meaning, to which other parts can be added. For example, the word "coldness" is formed from the root "cold" and the suffix "ness." —compare STEM¹ (4)
9 █mathematics█ TECHNICAL a number that when multiplied by itself a certain number of times, equals the number that you have: *2 is the fourth root of 16.* —see also CUBE ROOT, SQUARE ROOT, GRASS ROOTS

root² v. **1 a)** [I] to grow roots: *New shrubs will root easily in summer.* **b)** [T usually passive] to hold a plant in the ground firmly by its roots: *The bush was too firmly rooted in the hard earth to dig up easily.*
2 be rooted in sth to have developed from something and be strongly influenced by it: *A lot of his problems are rooted in his relationship with his mother.* **3** [I always + adv./prep.] INFORMAL to search for something by moving things around: **[–through/ in/around]** *I rooted through my purse for a pen and*

a notebook. **4 be rooted to the spot/chair/floor etc.** to be so shocked, surprised, or frightened that you cannot move

root for sb *phr. v.* [T] INFORMAL **1** to give support and encouragement to someone in a competition, test, or difficult situation, because you want them to succeed: *We're all rooting for you, Bill.* **2** to support a sports team or player by shouting and cheering: *Most of the crowd was rooting for Foreman.*

root sth ↔ **out** *phr. v.* [T] **1** to find out where a particular kind of problem exists and get rid of it: *Drastic measures have been taken to root out corruption.* **2** to find something by searching for it: *Their mission was to root out and capture the remaining enemy soldiers.*

root sth ↔ **up** *phr. v.* [T] to dig or pull a plant up with its roots

root beer /'. ./ *n.* [C,U] a sweet brown non-alcoholic drink made from the roots of some plants

root ca·nal /'. ,./ *n.* [C] a treatment in which a DENTIST removes a diseased area in the root of a tooth

root cel·lar /'. ,./ *n.* [C] a room under the ground in which vegetables such as potatoes are kept, used especially in past times

root crop /'. ./ *n.* [C] a vegetable or plant that is grown so that its root parts can be used

root·less /'rutlıs/ *adj.* having nowhere that you feel is really your home: *His life in California felt rootless.* —**rootlessness** *n.* [U]

root vege·ta·ble /'. ,.../ *n.* [C] a vegetable such as a potato or CARROT that grows under the ground

rope[1] /roup/ *n.* **1** [C,U] very strong, thick string, made by twisting together many threads of HEMP, NYLON, or other material: *They used a piece of rope to tie the clerk up.* | *She lowered the basket on a rope.* **2 the ropes a)** all the things someone needs to know to do a job or deal with a system: *Nathan knows the ropes – he's been in the company for 15 years.* | *She's working in a burger joint to **learn the ropes** of the fast-food business.* | *New employees are assigned a buddy to **show them the ropes**.* **b)** the rope fence that surrounds an area used for BOXING or WRESTLING **3 be at the end of your rope** INFORMAL to have no more PATIENCE or strength left to deal with a problem or a difficult situation: *I'm about at the end of my rope with my son. What should I do?* **4 give sb enough rope to hang themselves** INFORMAL to give someone freedom to do what they want to do, because you think they will cause problems for themselves **5 be on the ropes** INFORMAL to be in a very bad situation, in which you are likely to be defeated: *Primary election results show the governor is on the ropes.* —see also JUMP ROPE

rope[2] *v.* **1** [T always + adv./prep.] to tie things together using rope: [**rope sth to sth**] *We roped the Christmas tree to the top of the car and drove home.* | [**rope sb/sth together**] *Team members roped themselves together to climb up the mountain.* **2** [T] to catch an animal using a circle of rope: *I had always wanted to learn how to rope a calf.*

rope sb ↔ **into** *phr. v.* [T] INFORMAL to persuade someone to help you in a job, or to join in an activity, especially when they do not want to: [**rope sb into doing sth**] *My wife and I have been roped into going to this fund-raising dinner.*

rope sth ↔ **off** *phr. v.* [T] to surround an area with ropes, especially in order to separate it from another area: *Sidestreets had been roped off for the parade.*

rope lad·der /'. ,../ *n.* [C] a LADDER made of two long ropes connected by wooden pieces that you stand on

Roque·fort /'roukfət/ *n.* [U] a type of cheese that is white with STRIPES of blue MOLD

Ror·schach test /'rɔrʃak ,tɛst/ *n.* [C] a method of testing someone's character, by making them say what spots of ink with various shapes look like

ro·sa·ry /'rouzəri/ *n. plural* **rosaries** **1** [C] a string of BEADS used by Catholics for counting prayers **2 the Rosary** the set of prayers that are said by Catholics while counting rosary BEADS

rose[1] /rouz/ *n.* **1** [C] a flower that has a pleasant smell, and is usually red, pink, white, or yellow, or the bush that this grows on: *a dozen red roses* **2** [U] a pink color **3 sth is not a bed of roses** INFORMAL if a job or situation is not a bed of roses, it is not always pleasant and there are often difficult things to deal with: *Our marriage hasn't been a bed of roses.* **4 be coming up roses** INFORMAL be happening or developing in the best possible way **5 come out (of sth) smelling like a rose** also **come out smelling like roses** INFORMAL to get an advantage from a situation, when you ought to have been blamed, criticized, or harmed by it: *Zeller is the only one who came out of the scandal smelling like a rose.*

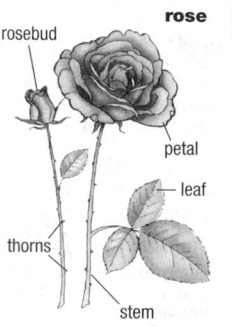

rose
rosebud
petal
leaf
thorns
stem

rose[2] *adj.* having a pink color

rose[3] *v.* the past tense of RISE

ro·sé /rou'zeɪ/ *n.* [C,U] pink wine

ro·se·ate /'rouziɪt/ *adj.* POETIC pink

Ro·seau /rou'zou/ the capital and largest city of Dominica

rose·bud /'rouzbʌd/ *n.* [C] the flower of a rose before it opens

rose bush /'. ./ *n.* [C] the plant that roses grow on

rose-col·ored /'. ,../ *adj.* **1** having a pink color **2 see/view etc. sth through rose-colored glasses** to think that something is better than it really is, because you do not notice anything bad: *A lot of city people look at life in the country through rose-colored glasses.*

rose hip /'. ./ *n.* [C] the small red fruit from some kinds of rose bushes, used in medicines and juices

rose·mar·y /'rouz,mɛri/ *n.* [U] leaves that have a strong, pleasant smell and are used in cooking, or the bush that these come from

Ro·sen·berg /'rouzən,bɔrg/, **Ju·li·us** /'dʒuliəs/ (1918–1953) a U.S. citizen who was a SPY for the Soviet Union with his wife Ethel Rosenberg (1915–1953)

rose-tint·ed /'. ,../ *adj.* ROSE-COLORED

Ro·set·ta Stone, the /rou'zɛtə ,stoun/ a large, ancient stone that was found in Egypt in 1799, which had the same piece of writing on it in three different writing systems: Greek letters, Egyptian letters, and ancient Egyptian HIEROGLYPHICS. This important discovery made it possible for people to translate hieroglyphics for the first time.

ro·sette /rou'zɛt/ *n.* [C] a shape like a round flat flower that has been made from stone, wood, cloth etc. and is used for decoration

rose-wa·ter /'rouz,wɔtɚ/ *n.* [U] a liquid made from roses which has a pleasant smell

rose·wood /'rouzwod/ *n.* [U] a hard dark red wood, used for making expensive furniture

Rosh Ha·sha·nah, Rosh Hashana /,rɑʃ hə'ʃɑnə/ *n.* [C,U] the Jewish New Year, in late September or early October

ros·in /'rɑzən/ *n.* [U] a solid, slightly sticky, substance that you rub on the BOW of a VIOLIN etc., to help it move smoothly on the strings —**rosin** *v.* [T]

Ross /rɑs/, **Bet·sy** /'bɛtsi/ (1752–1836) the woman who is believed to have made the first U.S. flag

Ros·tand /rou'stɑnd/, **Ed·mond** /'ɛdmənd/ (1868–1918) a French writer of plays

ros·ter /'rɑstɚ/ *n.* [C] **1** a list of the names of people on a sports team, in an organization etc.: *Williams took Carney's place on the Miami Dolphin roster.* | *The nightclub's roster has always featured young punk bands.* **2** a list of people's names that shows the jobs they must do and the times when they must do them: *Here is the duty roster for all the members of the scout troop.*

ros·trum /ˈrɑstrəm/ *n.* [C] a small PLATFORM (=raised area) that you stand on when you are making a speech or CONDUCTing musicians

ros·y /ˈroʊzi/ *adj.* **rosier, rosiest 1** pink: *rosy cheeks* **2** seeming to offer hope of success or happiness: *a rosy financial report* | *Things were looking less rosy all of a sudden.* —**rosiness** *n.* [U]

rot¹ /rɑt/ *v.* **1** [I,T] to decay by a gradual natural process, or to make something do this: *Moisture can rot your house's foundation.* | *Many of the tomatoes had rotted on their stems.* **2 rot in jail/prison etc.** to get into a bad mental or physical condition because you have been forced to stay in a place such as a prison: *He's a liar and he should rot in hell.*

rot away *phr. v.* [I,T **rot** sth ↔ **away**] to decay completely and disappear or break into small pieces, or to make something do this: *The top of the coffin had rotted away.*

rot² *n.* **1** [U] the natural process of decaying, or the part of something that has decayed: *The wood was soft with rot.* **2** LITERARY a state in which something becomes bad or does not work as well as it should: *Economic specialists hope to guide the country out of its economic rot.* **3** [U] OLD-FASHIONED nonsense: *They went through all that boring rot about the war again.* —see also DRY ROT

ro·ta·ry /ˈroʊtəri/ *adj.* [usually before noun] **1** turning in a circle around a central point, like a wheel: *the rotary movement of the helicopter's blades* **2** having a main part that does this: *a rotary dial phone*

Ro·ta·ry Club /ˈroʊtəri ˌklʌb/ *n.* an organization of business people in a town who work together to raise money for people who are poor or sick

ro·tate /ˈroʊteɪt/ *v.* **1** [I,T] to turn with a circular movement around a central point, or to make something do this: *Night and day are created by the Earth rotating on its axis.* | *Rotate the handle a half turn to the left.* **2** [I,T] to change the places of things or people, or to change places, especially in a circular direction: *Rotating the tires every few months helps them last longer.* | *The players rotate before each serve.* **3** [I,T] if a job rotates, or if people rotate jobs, they each do a job for a particular period of time and then change to another: *Cleaning duties are rotated among the various groups.* **4** [T] TECHNICAL to regularly change the crops grown on a piece of land, in order to preserve the quality of the soil

ro·ta·tion /roʊˈteɪʃən/ *n.* **1** [U] the action of turning with a circular movement around a central point: *the rotation of the Earth* **2** [C] one complete turn around a central point: *It takes 243 Earth days for Venus to complete one rotation.* **3** [U] the practice of changing regularly from one thing to another, or regularly changing the person who does a particular job: *We need to do more cross-training and job rotation.* **4** [C] a period of time spent doing a particular job, when you will soon change to a different job for the same employer: *Robinson's first rotation at the hospital was in the emergency room.* **5** [U] also **crop rotation** TECHNICAL the practice of regularly changing the crops that are grown on a piece of land, in order to preserve the quality of the soil **6 in rotation** done or used one after the other in a regular order: *Employees shall be assigned to cases in rotation.* | *Three Shakespearean comedies will be performed in rotation during the festival.* —**rotational** *adj.*

ROTC /ˈrɑtsi, ˌɑr oʊ ti ˈsi/ *n.* Reserve Officers Training Corps; an organization that trains students to be U.S. Army or Navy officers

rote /roʊt/ *n.* [U] FORMAL **1** a rote action, process etc. involves repeating something many times, without thinking about it carefully or without understanding: *rote memorization* | *Simon's concert was rote and uninspired.* **2 by rote** if you do something by rote, you do it the same way every time, without thinking about it: *Each morning, we recited the Pledge of Allegiance by rote.*

ROTFL, rotfl a written abbreviation of "rolling on the floor laughing," used by people communicating in CHAT ROOMs on the Internet to say that they are laughing very hard at something that someone else has written

rot·gut /ˈrɑtgʌt/ *n.* [U] SLANG strong cheap low-quality alcohol: *rotgut whiskey*

Roth·ko /ˈrɑθkoʊ/, **Mark** (1903–1970) a U.S. artist, born in Russia, famous for his large paintings of squares and RECTANGLES in different colors

ro·tis·ser·ie /roʊˈtɪsəri/ *n.* [C] a piece of equipment for cooking meat by turning it around and around on a metal ROD over heat

ro·to·gra·vure /ˌroʊtəgrəˈvyʊr/ *n.* **1** [U] a method of printing words and pictures from a COPPER CYLINDER **2** [C] part of a newspaper that has been printed in this way

ro·tor /ˈroʊtɚ/ *n.* [C] TECHNICAL **1** a part of a machine that turns around on a central point **2** also **rotor blade** the long flat part on top of a HELICOPTER that turns around and around

ro·to·till·er, Rototiller /ˈroʊtəˌtɪlɚ/ *n.* [C] a machine with a motor and sharp blades that is used to cut up land to prepare it for growing plants —**rototill** *v.* [I,T]

rot·ten¹ /ˈrɑt̬n/ *adj.* **1** badly decayed: *rotten eggs* | *The floor in the bathroom is all rotten.* **2** INFORMAL very bad or disgusting: *We want to get rid of the whole rotten tax system.* | *I've had a rotten day.* **3** INFORMAL a word meaning very bad at doing something, or very badly done, used especially when you feel annoyed about this: *Tom complained loudly about the rotten service.* | *You're rotten at lying.* **4 feel rotten a)** to feel sick: *I've felt rotten all day.* **b)** to feel unhappy and guilty about something: [+ **about**] *I feel rotten about having to fire him.* **5 a rotten apple** one bad person who has a bad effect on all the others in a group —**rottenly** *adv.* —**rottenness** *n.* [U]

rotten² *adv.* INFORMAL **spoil sb rotten** to treat someone too well or too kindly, especially a child: *Brittany's grandparents spoil her rotten.*

Rott·wei·ler, rottweiler /ˈrɑtˌwaɪlɚ/ *n.* [C] a type of strong and sometimes dangerous dog, often used as a guard dog

ro·tund /roʊˈtʌnd/ *adj.* HUMOROUS having a fat round body —**rotundity** *n.* [U]

ro·tun·da /roʊˈtʌndə/ *n.* [C] a round building or hall, especially one with a DOME (=a round bowl-shaped roof)

rou·ble /ˈrubəl/ *n.* [C] another spelling of RUBLE

rou·é /ruˈeɪ/ *n.* [C] LITERARY, DISAPPROVING a man who believes that pleasure is the most important thing in life

rouge /ruʒ/ *n.* [U] pink or red powder or cream that women put on their cheeks —**rouge** *v.* [T]

rough¹ /rʌf/ *adj.*

1 not smooth having an uneven surface: *Photographs show the rough surface of the moon.* | *His hands were big and rough.* —opposite SMOOTH¹

2 not exact not exact, not containing many details, or not in a final form; APPROXIMATE: *Prices shown are only a rough guideline.* | *McNeil has just finished the rough draft (=first writing) of his first novel.* | *Can you give me a rough idea of what courses I have to take?* | *A rough estimate is that 50 to 70 civilians were killed in the attack.*

3 not gentle using force or violence: *Football's a rough sport.* | *Some of the refugees complained of rough treatment from guards.*

4 having a lot of problems/difficulties [usually before noun] a rough period of time is one in which you have a lot of problems or difficulties *I've had a rough day.* | *This year has been a rough ride (=difficult time) for Pacific Bank.* | *Melody admitted that there have been rough patches (=difficult times) in her marriage.* | *The project may run into some rough sledding (=a difficult period of time).*

5 city/area etc. a rough area is a place where there is a lot of violence or crime: *Max grew up in a particularly rough part of Brooklyn.*

6 **unfair** difficult, or not fair or kind: *The last few years have been rough on wine producers.* | *"He was orphaned the day he was born." "That's rough, poor kid."*

7 **have rough edges** also **be rough around the edges** to have small parts that are not completely correct, finished etc. but are not a serious problem: *The play still has a few rough edges, but by next week it should be all right.*

8 **weather/sea** with strong wind or storms: *The seas were so high and rough the Coast Guard wouldn't let us go out.*

9 **not comfortable** uncomfortable, with difficult conditions: *Traveling thousands of miles in a compact car was pretty rough*

10 **voice/sound** not sounding soft or gentle, and often sounding fairly angry: *The foreman had a deep, rough voice.*

11 **rough stuff** SPOKEN violent behavior

12 **simple/not well made** simple and often not very well made: *a rough wooden table*

13 **rough and ready** not perfect for a particular situation or purpose, but good enough

14 **rough justice** punishment that is not decided in a court in the usual legal way, and that is often severe or unfair: *the rough justice of the Old West* —**roughness** *n.* [U] —see also ROUGH DIAMOND, ROUGHLY

rough² *n.* **1 the rough** uneven ground with long grass on a GOLF course **2 take the rough with the smooth** to accept the bad things in life as well as the good ones **3** [C] a picture drawn very quickly, that does not show all the details —see also **a diamond in the rough** (DIAMOND (5))

rough³ *v.* **rough it** INFORMAL to live for a short time in conditions that are not very comfortable, especially when CAMPing: *It's backpacking, but with horses carrying the load and first-class meals, it's not roughing it.*

rough sb **up** *phr. v.* [T] INFORMAL to attack someone and hurt them by hitting them: *He's accused of roughing up a nightclub doorman.*

rough⁴ *adv.* **play rough** to play in a violent way in which someone could get hurt

rough·age /ˈrʌfɪdʒ/ *n.* [U] a substance contained in some vegetables and fruits that is not easily DIGESTed, and so helps your BOWELS to work; FIBER

rough-and-tum·ble /ˌ. '.ˌ./ *adj.* full of people competing, often in a cruel way: *the rough-and-tumble world of Wall Street*

rough di·a·mond /ˌ. '.../ *n.* [C] a DIAMOND that has not yet been cut and polished to use as jewelry —see also **a diamond in the rough** (DIAMOND (5))

rough·en /ˈrʌfən/ *v.* [I,T] to become rough, or to make something rough: *Sand the surface to roughen it before repainting.*

rough-hewn /ˌ. '.ˌ./ *adj.* rough-hewn wood or stone has been roughly cut and its surface is not yet smooth

rough·house /ˈrʌfhaʊs/ *v.* [I] to play roughly or fight: *No more roughhousing, you two!*

s w **rough·ly** /ˈrʌfli/ *adv.* **1** not exactly; APPROXIMATELY: *Martin makes roughly $150,000 a year.* | *Jill spends roughly four hours a day working on her book.* **2** not gently or carefully: *She roughly pushed me toward the door.*

rough·neck /ˈrʌfnɛk/ *n.* [C] **1** a member of a team of people who make or operate an OIL WELL **2** INFORMAL someone who usually behaves in a rough, rude, or angry way

rough·shod /ˈrʌfʃɑd/ *adj.* **run/ride roughshod over sth** to behave in a way that ignores other people's feelings or opinions: *The court cannot be allowed to ride roughshod over the rights of the accused.*

rou·lette /ruˈlɛt/ *n.* [U] a game in which a small ball is spun around on a moving wheel, and people try to win money by guessing which hole it will fall into —see also RUSSIAN ROULETTE

s w **round¹** /raʊnd/ *adj.* **1** shaped like a circle: *a round table* | *He wore round glasses with wire rims.* **2** shaped like a ball: *small round berries* **3** fat and curved: *a short round man* **4** a round number is a whole number, often ending in 0, that is usually not

exact: *It probably costs more, but $200 is a nice round number.* | **In round numbers**, *you'll need to make about $1000 to break even.* —**roundness** *n.* [U] —see also ROUNDLY, **a square peg in a round hole** (SQUARE¹ (10))

round² *n.* [C]

1 **series** a number or set of events that are related: [– of] *A final round of talks is scheduled in Tokyo next year.*

2 **competition** one of the parts of a competition that you have to finish or win before you can go to the next part: *Purdue lost to Kansas State in the third round.*

3 **alcohol** if you buy a round of drinks in a bar, you buy drinks for all the people in your group: *I'll buy the next round of beers.*

4 **a round of applause** a period when people CLAP¹ (1) to show that they enjoyed a performance

5 **rounds** [plural] the usual visits that someone, especially a doctor, regularly makes as part of their job: *The theft was discovered by a security guard making his rounds.*

6 **gun shot** a single shot from a gun, or a bullet for one shot: *More than 30 rounds were fired at the guards.*

7 **make the rounds of sth** to go around from one place to another, often looking for work: *Ryan is making the rounds of talk shows to promote her new movie.*

8 **make/do the rounds** INFORMAL if an illness or piece of news does the rounds, it is passed on from one person to another: *I just got this new chain letter that's making the rounds.*

9 **golf** a complete game of GOLF

10 **boxing** one of the periods of fighting in a BOXING or WRESTLING match that are separated by short rests: *Hamed won the fight in the seventh round.*

11 **circle** something that has a circular shape: *Cut the carrots into half-inch rounds.*

12 **song** a song for three or four singers, in which each one sings the same tune, starting at different times

13 **the daily round (of sth)** the things that you have to do every day: *He dreaded the daily round of phone calls from unhappy customers.*

14 **in the round** a play that is performed in the round is performed on a central stage surrounded by the people watching it

round³ *v.* [T] **1** to go around something such as a bend or the corner of a building: *As I rounded the corner, I could see that the house was on fire.* **2** to make something into a round shape: *The edges of the counter have been rounded to make them safer.*

round sth ↔ **down** *phr. v.* [T] to reduce an exact figure to the nearest whole number —compare **round up**

round off *phr. v.* **1** [I,T **round** sth ↔ **off**] to change an exact figure to the nearest whole number: *Prices are rounded off to the nearest dollar.* **2** [I,T **round** sth ↔ **off**] to do something as a way of ending an event, performance etc. in an appropriate or satisfactory way: *We rounded off our dinner with homemade apple pie.* **3** [T **round** sth ↔ **off**] to take the sharp edges off something: *Round off the corners with a pair of scissors.*

round sth ↔ **out** *phr. v.* [T] to make an experience more thorough or complete: *Next week's performance of Strauss' "Elektra" rounds out the opera season.*

round sb/sth ↔ **up** *phr. v.* [T] **1** [**round** sb/sth ↔ **up**] to find and gather together a group of people or things: *Neighbors helped round up the escaped pigs.* —see also ROUND-UP (1) **2** [**round** sb ↔ **up**] to find a particular group of people and force them to go to prison: *Officers succeeded in rounding up most of the gang's members.* **3** [**round** sth ↔ **up**] to increase an exact figure to the next highest whole number —compare **round down**

round⁴ *adv.* [only after verb] **1** AROUND² **2 round about** SPOKEN about a particular time or amount: *She's round about 26 or 27.*

round[5] *prep.* AROUND: *Doris was running round the playground with the kids.* —see also ROUND-THE-CLOCK

round·a·bout /ˈraʊndəˌbaʊt/ *adj.* not done in the shortest, most direct way possible: *The taxi driver took a roundabout route to the hotel.* | *In a roundabout way, she admitted she was wrong.*

round·ed /ˈraʊndɪd/ *adj.* having a round shape; CURVED —see also WELL-ROUNDED

round·house /ˈraʊndhaʊs/ *n.* [C, usually singular] a hit or kick in which you swing your FIST (=closed hand) or foot with a wide circular movement at someone: *Reid ducked away from a roundhouse.* —**roundhouse** *adj.*

round·ly /ˈraʊndli/ *adv.* **roundly condemn/criticize etc.** to condemn or criticize etc. someone strongly and severely: *All the major parties roundly condemned the attack.*

round rob·in /ˌ. ˈ../ *n.* [C] a competition in which every player or team plays against each of the other players or teams

round-shoul·dered /ˈ. ˌ../ *adj.* having shoulders that are bent forward or that slope down

round steak /ˈ. ./ *n.* [U] a piece of meat from the top part of the leg of a cow

round-ta·ble /ˈ. ˌ../ *adj.* [only before noun] a round-table discussion or meeting is one in which everyone can talk about things in an equal way

round-the-clock /ˌ. . ˈ.◂/ *adj.* [only before noun] all the time, both day and night: *round-the-clock weather reports* —see also **around the clock** (CLOCK[1] (3))

round trip /ˌ. ˈ./ *n.* [C] a trip to a place and back again: *It takes four round trips to qualify for a free ticket.*

round-trip /ˌ. ˈ.◂/ *adj.* [only before noun] a round-trip ticket is for a trip to a place and back again —compare ONE-WAY

round-up /ˈ. ./ *n.* [C] **1** an occasion when people or animals of a particular type are all brought together, often using force: *a cattle round-up* **2** a short description of the main parts of the news, on the radio or on television —see also **round up** (ROUND[3])

rouse /raʊz/ *v.* **1** [I,T] to wake up, or to wake someone up: *Around 2 a.m., I was roused by the sound of screaming.* **2** [T] to make someone start doing something, especially when they have been too tired or unwilling to do it: *Kemp's speech roused the crowd to cheers.* **3** [T] to make someone feel a particular emotion, such as hope or fear: *The project is a NASA scheme to rouse interest in science and space.* —compare AROUSE

rous·ing /ˈraʊzɪŋ/ *adj.* a rousing song, speech etc. makes people feel excited and eager to do something

Rous·seau /ruˈsoʊ/, **Hen·ri** /ɑnˈri/ (1844–1910) a French PAINTER famous for his paintings in bright colors and a simple flat-looking style

Rousseau, Jean-Jacques /ʒɑn ˈʒɑk/ (1712–1778) a French writer and PHILOSOPHER whose work had a great influence on the French Revolution

roust /raʊst/ *v.* [T] to make someone move from a place, especially using force or for a reason that is not nice: *Thousands of people were rousted from their homes by the fire.*

roust·a·bout /ˈraʊstəˌbaʊt/ *n.* [C] a man who does work for which he needs to be strong but not skilled, especially in a port, an OILFIELD, or a CIRCUS

rout[1] /raʊt/ *v.* [T] to defeat someone completely in a battle, competition, or election: *The Seattle Super-Sonics routed Atlanta 111–88.*

rout[2] *n.* [singular] a complete defeat in a battle, competition, or election: *A 3–0 rout of Canada qualified the U.S. for the World Cup.*

route[1] /rut, raʊt/ *n.* [C] **1** the way from one place to another, especially a way that is regularly used and can be shown on a map: *Why don't you take the scenic route?* | [+ to/from] *Columbus set off to find a new route to the Orient.* | **take/follow a route** *We weren't sure about which route we should take.* **2** a road, railroad, or imaginary line along which vehicles often travel: *TWA sold some of its European routes to American Airlines.* | *a bus route* **3** a way of doing something or achieving a particular result: *Kennedy arrived at the same conclusion by a different route.* | *War has never been a painless route to peace.* **4** **Route 66/54 etc.** used to show the number of a main road in the U.S.: *I took Route 20 east from Chicago.* —see also EN ROUTE, SNOW ROUTE, TRADE ROUTE

route[2] *v.* [T] to send something or someone using a particular route: [+ through/by] *All calls were routed through a switchboard to my office.* —see also REROUTE

rou·tine[1] /ruˈtin/ *n.* **1** [C,U] the usual or normal way in which you do things, or the usual series of things that you do: *The daily routine starts early, around 6:00 a.m.* | *I was looking for a way out of the monotonous routine at the factory.* **2** [C] a set of steps learned and practiced by a dancer for a public performance **3** [C] TECHNICAL a set of instructions given to a computer so that it will do a particular operation —**routinize** /ruˈtinaɪz, ˈrutˌnaɪz/ *v.* [T]

rou·tine[2] /ˌruˈtin◂/ *adj.* **1** regular and usual: *The infection was detected during a routine blood test.* | *Systems need to be updated on a routine basis.* **2** ordinary and boring: *My job at the newspaper had become routine.*

rou·tine·ly /ruˈtinli/ *adv.* if something is routinely done, it is usually done as part of the normal process of working, doing a job etc.: *The staff routinely ignored my requests.*

roux /ru/ *n. plural* **roux** /ruz/ [C,U] a mixture of flour and butter that is used for making SAUCEs

rove /roʊv/ *v.* [I] **1** to travel from one place to another: *Bands of armed men rove the countryside.* **2** **a roving reporter/photographer** someone who works for a newspaper or television company and travels from place to place to do their job **3** if someone's eyes rove, they look continuously from one part of something to another: *Benedict's eyes roved over her sleeping body.* **4** **a roving eye** OLD-FASHIONED someone who has a roving eye is always looking for a chance to have sexual relationships

rov·er /ˈroʊvɚ/ *n.* [C] LITERARY someone who travels or moves around from place to place

row[1] /roʊ/ *n.* [C] **1** a line of things or people next to each other: [+ of] *A row of palm trees lined the street.* | *Tommy arranged his toy soldiers in a row* (=next to each other). | *The hills are planted with row upon row of grape vines.* **2** a line of seats in a theater, large room etc.: *Gabrielle found a seat in the front row.* **3** **three/four etc. times in a row** happening a number of times one after the other, in exactly the same way or with the same result: *That's the second year in a row we forgot her birthday.* **4** **a hard/tough row to hoe** INFORMAL used to say that a particular situation is difficult: *Improving schools with little funding is a tough row to hoe.*

row[2] *v.* **1** [I,T] to make a boat move across water using OARs (=long poles that are flat at one end): *In the afternoon, we rowed out to the island.* **2** [I] to be able to make a boat move in this way, or to do this as a sport: *Jenny used to row in college.*

row·boat /ˈroʊboʊt/ *n.* [C] a small boat that you move through the water with OARs (=long poles that are flat at the end)

row·dy[1] /ˈraʊdi/ *adj.* **rowdier, rowdiest** behaving in a noisy, rough, uncontrolled way that is likely to cause arguments and fighting: *a rowdy fraternity party* | *Our fans may be a little rowdy, but they don't throw things.* —**rowdily** *adv.* —**rowdiness** *n.* [U]

rowdy[2] *n.* [C usually plural] OLD-FASHIONED someone who behaves in a rough noisy way

row house /ˈ. ./ *n.* [C] a house that is part of a line of houses that are joined to each other —see picture on page 423

row·ing /ˈroʊɪŋ/ *n.* [U] the sport or activity of making a boat move through water with OARs

rowing ma·chine /ˈ.. ˌ./ *n.* [C] a piece of exercise equipment on which you perform the action of rowing a boat

s w **roy·al¹** /ˈrɔɪəl/ *adj.* [only before noun] **1** relating to or
3 belonging to a king or queen: *the royal palace* | *the
royal house of Austria* —compare REGAL **2** very
impressive, as if done for a king or queen: *Williams
got the royal treatment on her visit to Washington.*
3 INFORMAL used to emphasize how bad or annoying
someone or something is: *They've made a royal mess
of things.* | *My friends think my sister is a royal pain
in the butt.* —**royally** *adv.*

royal² *n.* [C] INFORMAL a member of a royal family

royal blue /ˌ.. ˈ./ *n.* [U] a strong, bright blue color
—**royal blue** *adj.*

royal flush /ˌ.. ˈ./ *n.* [C usually singular] a set of
cards that someone has in a card game, which are
the five most important cards in a SUIT (=one of the
four different types of card)

Royal High·ness /ˌ.. ˈ../ *n.* [C] **your/his/her Royal
Highness** used when speaking about or to a royal
person, especially a prince or PRINCESS

roy·al·ist /ˈrɔɪəlɪst/ *n.* [C] someone who supports a
king or queen, or believes that a country should be
ruled by kings or queens —**royalist** *adj.*

roy·al·ty /ˈrɔɪəlti/ *n. plural* **royalties 1** [C usually
plural] a payment made to the writer of a book or
piece of music depending on how many books etc.
are sold, or to someone whose idea, invention etc. is
used by someone else to make money: *He receives a
royalty of 2% on each card sold* | *Simon's royalties
for the book will go to charity.* **2** [U] members of a
royal family

rpm /ˌɑr pi ˈɛm/ revolutions per minute; a measurement of the speed at which an engine or RECORD
PLAYER turns

RR, R.R. 1 rural route; used in addresses in country
areas of the U.S., to show which mail delivery area
a letter should go to **2** a written abbreviation of
"railroad"

RSI *n.* [U] repetitive strain injury; pain in your hands,
arms etc. caused by doing the same movements very
many times, especially when typing (TYPE² (2))

RSVP¹ 1 an abbreviation that is used on invitations
to ask someone to tell you if they can come or
not **2** the reply you give to an invitation: *I forgot to
mail my RSVP.*

RSVP² *v. present tense* **RSVP's** *past tense and past
participle* **RSVP'd 1** [I,T] to tell someone who gave
you an invitation whether you can go or not: *Eighteen people hadn't RSVP'd for the wedding.* **2** [I] to
arrange for a place to be kept for you at an event:
The cost is $25 per couple. To RSVP, call 555-9120.

rte. a written abbreviation of ROUTE

s w **rub¹** /rʌb/ *v.* **rubbed, rubbing**
2 **1** move over a surface [I,T] to move your hand, a
cloth etc. over a surface while pressing against it:
Ann woke up and rubbed her eyes. | *Rodriguez
rubbed his leg to ease the pain.* | *I had to rub hard to
get the marks off.*
2 rub sth against/on sth [T] to make something
press against something else and move it around:
[rub sth against/on] *He rubbed the toe of his shoe
against his calf.* | [rub sth together] *We tried to
make a fire by rubbing two sticks together.*
3 put substance on sth [T always + adv./prep.] to
put a substance into or onto the surface of something
by pressing it and moving it around with your hand,
a cloth etc.: [+ on/into/over etc.] *He rubbed lini-
ment on the horse's front legs.*
4 cause pain/damage [I,T] to move around while
pressing against another surface, often causing pain,
damage etc.: [+ against/on] *These shoes rub against
my heels.*
5 rub it in INFORMAL to remind someone about something they want to forget, especially because they
are embarrassed about it: *You don't need to rub it in,
I know you got a better grade on the test.*
6 rub shoulders with sb INFORMAL to spend time
with rich or famous people: *As a reporter he gets to
rub shoulders with all the big names in politics and
the media.*
7 rub sb the wrong way INFORMAL to annoy someone by the way you behave toward them: *Brock
admits he sometimes rubs people the wrong way.*

8 rub salt into a wound INFORMAL to make a bad
situation even worse for someone

9 rub sb's nose in it also **rub sb's nose in the dirt**
INFORMAL to keep reminding someone about something they did wrong or failed to do, especially in
order to punish them

10 be rubbing your hands INFORMAL to be pleased
because something has happened which gives you an
advantage, especially because something bad has
happened to someone else

rub down *phr. v.* [T] **1** [rub sth ↔ down] to make
a surface dry or smooth by rubbing it with a cloth or
SANDPAPER **2** [rub sb down] **a)** to MASSAGE someone
(=rub their muscles), especially after hard exercise
b) [rub sb/sth down] to dry a person or animal by
rubbing them with a cloth, TOWEL etc. —see also RUB-
DOWN

rub off *phr. v.* [I,T **rub** sth ↔ **off**] to remove something from a surface by rubbing it, or to come off a
surface because of being rubbed: *Newspaper ink had
rubbed off on my hand.*

rub off on sb *phr. v.* [I] if a feeling, quality, or habit
rubs off on someone, they start to have it because
they are with another person who has it: [+ on]
Maybe grandpa's good luck will rub off on me.

rub sb **out** *phr. v.* [T] OLD-FASHIONED to murder
someone

rub² *n.* **1** the action of rubbing something or massaging (MASSAGE) someone for a short time: *Can I
have a back rub?* | *Give the table a good rub with
a damp cloth.* **2 the rub** LITERARY a particular problem or difficult situation: *The rub is that disposable
diapers will last 500 years in a landfill.* **3** a mixture
of SPICES, oil etc. that you put on meat before cooking
it to give it more FLAVOR: *lemon and ginger rub*

rub·ber /ˈrʌbɚ/ *n.* **1** [U] a substance used to make **s w**
tires, gloves, boots etc., which is made from the juice **3**
of a tropical tree or artificially: *a rubber ball* **2** [C]
INFORMAL a CONDOM **3** [C] the piece of white rubber
where the PITCHER (=person who throws the ball)
stands in a baseball game **4 rubbers** [plural] OLD-
FASHIONED a rubber shoe or boot that you wear over
an ordinary shoe when it rains or snows; GALOSHES
5 [C] a series of games of BRIDGE (=a card game)

rubber band /ˌ.. ˈ., ˈ.. ˌ./ *n.* [C] a thin circular piece
of rubber used for holding things together

rubber boot /ˌ.. ˈ./ *n.* [C] a tall boot made of rubber
that keeps your foot and the lower part of your leg
dry

rubber bul·let /ˌ.. ˈ../ *n.* [C] a bullet made of rubber
that is not intended to seriously hurt or kill people,
but is used to control violent crowds

rubber ce·ment /ˌ.. .ˈ./ *n.* [U] a type of glue that
dries slowly, allowing you to change the position of
something

rubber check /ˌ.. ˈ./ *n.* [C] INFORMAL a check that
the bank refuses to accept because the person who
wrote it does not have enough money in the bank to
pay it

rub·ber·neck /ˈrʌbɚˌnɛk/ *v.* [I] INFORMAL, DISAPPROV-
ING to look around at something, especially something such as an accident, while you are driving
past: *People rubbernecking in the southbound lane
caused a second accident.* —**rubbernecker** *n.* [C]

rubber plant /ˈ.. ˌ./ *n.* [C] a plant with large shiny
dark green leaves that is often grown indoors

rubber stamp /ˌ.. ˈ./ *n.* [C] a small piece of rubber
with a handle, used for printing dates or names on
paper

rubber-stamp /ˌ.. ˈ./ *v.* [T] to give official approval to
something without really thinking about it: *The
board rubber-stamped the plan at its meeting Friday.*

rub·ber·y /ˈrʌbəri/ *adj.* **1** looking or feeling like
rubber: *The steak was a little rubbery.* **2** if your legs
or knees are rubbery, they feel weak or unsteady

rub·bing /ˈrʌbɪŋ/ *n.* [C] a copy of a shape or pattern
made by rubbing a pencil, WAX, CHALK etc. onto a
piece of paper laid over it: *a brass rubbing*

R

R

rubbing al·co·hol /'.. ,.../ *n.* [U] a type of alcohol used for cleaning wounds or skin

rub·bish /'rʌbɪʃ/ *n.* [U] **1** INFORMAL an idea, statement etc. that is rubbish is silly or wrong and does not deserve serious attention; NONSENSE: *If you believe all this rubbish, you'll believe anything.* **2** GARBAGE

rub·ble /'rʌbəl/ *n.* [U] broken stones or bricks from a building or wall that has been destroyed

rub·down /'rʌbdaʊn/ *n.* [C] **1** if you give someone a rubdown, you rub their body to make them relaxed, especially after exercise; MASSAGE **2** if you give a surface a rubdown, you rub it to make it smooth or clean —see also **rub down** (RUB¹)

rube /rub/ *n.* [C] INFORMAL someone, usually from the country, who has no experience of other places and thinks in a simple way

Rube Gold·berg /,rub 'goʊldbɚg/ *adj.* a Rube Goldberg machine etc. is very complicated and not practical, in an amusing way

ru·bel·la /ru'bɛlə/ *n.* [U] TECHNICAL an infectious disease that causes red spots on your body, and can damage an unborn child; GERMAN MEASLES

Ru·bens /'rubənz/, **Peter Paul** (1577–1640) a Flemish PAINTER, famous for his paintings in which the women have fairly large fat bodies

Ru·bi·con /'rubɪ,kɑn/ *n.* **cross the Rubicon** to do something that you cannot later change, that will have extremely important effects in the future

ru·bi·cund /'rubɪkənd/ *adj.* LITERARY someone who is rubicund is fat and has a red face

ru·ble /'rubəl/ *n.* [C] the standard unit of money in the former U.S.S.R.

ru·bric /'rubrɪk/ *n.* [C] FORMAL **1** a title for a group of things that all have the same particular qualities: *I think the general rubric for the conference will be business-climate issues.* **2** the title written at the top of a piece of writing: *The names were listed under the rubric "Contributors."*

ru·by /'rubi/ *n. plural* **rubies** **1** [C] a red jewel **2** [U] the color of this jewel

ruched /ruʃt/ *adj.* a ruched curtain or piece of clothing has parts of it gathered together so that it has soft folds in it

ruck·sack /'rʌksæk/ *n.* [C] a BACKPACK

ruck·us /'rʌkəs/ *n.* [singular] INFORMAL a noisy argument or confused situation: *He woke up when he heard the ruckus outside his front door.*

rud·der /'rʌdɚ/ *n.* [C] a flat part at the back of a ship or aircraft that can be turned in order to control the direction in which the ship or aircraft moves

rud·der·less /'rʌdɚləs/ *adj.* without a leader who can make decisions: *Some historians think that when Mao died, China was left rudderless.*

rud·dy /'rʌdi/ *adj.* **ruddier, ruddiest** **1** a ruddy face looks pink and healthy: *ruddy cheeks* **2** LITERARY red: *The fire cast a ruddy glow over the room.* —**ruddiness** *n.* [U] —**ruddy** *adv.*

rude /rud/ *adj.* **1** speaking or behaving in a way that is not polite and is likely to offend or annoy people: *I don't mean to be rude, but I have to get going.* | *She is always frank and direct, but she is never rude.* | [**be rude to sb**] *He got detention for being rude to the substitute teacher.* | [**be rude of sb**] *It was rude of him to not say hello.* | [**It's rude to do sth**] *Stop that! It's rude to stare.* —opposite POLITE (1) **2 a rude awakening/shock** a situation in which you suddenly realize something upsetting or bad: *They were in for a rude awakening when they started inquiring about magazine production costs.* **3** LITERARY made in a simple, basic way: *The inhabitants lived in rude mud huts.* —**rudely** *adv.* —**rudeness** *n.* [U]

ru·di·men·ta·ry /,rudə'mɛntri, -'mɛntəri/ *adj.* **1** a rudimentary knowledge or understanding of a subject is very simple and basic: *I have a rudimentary understanding of computer programming.* **2** rudimentary equipment, methods, systems etc. are very basic and not advanced: *The boys had built a*

rudimentary two-way radio. **3 a rudimentary tail/ wing/eye** a part of an animal that has only developed into a very simple form

ru·di·ments /'rudəmənts/ *n.* [plural] FORMAL the most basic parts of a subject, which you learn first: [+ of] *Coach Phillips taught me the rudiments of the game.*

rue /ru/ *v.* [T] LITERARY to wish that you had not done something; REGRET¹: *She rued the day she first spoke to Remi.*

rue·ful /'rufəl/ *adj.* feeling or showing that you wish you had not done something: *Jane looked at her with a rueful smile.* —**ruefully** *adv.*

ruff /rʌf/ *n.* [C] **1** a stiff circular white collar, worn in the 16th century **2** a circle of feathers or fur around the neck of an animal or bird

ruf·fi·an /'rʌfiən/ *n.* [C] OLD-FASHIONED a violent man who is involved in crime: *a gang of ruffians*

ruf·fle¹ /'rʌfəl/ *v.* [T] **1** to make a smooth surface uneven: *The wind ruffled Jill's hair.* **2** to offend or upset someone slightly: *Yancy's aggressive style has ruffled some feathers* (=annoyed some people). | *They did their best to soothe the ruffled customers who were waiting for car repairs.*

ruffle² *n.* [C] a band of thin cloth sewn in folds, used as a decoration around the edge of something such as a dress

rug /rʌg/ *n.* [C] **1** a piece of thick cloth or wool that covers part of a floor, used for warmth or as a decoration: *a large circular rug* —compare CARPET¹ (1) **2 pull the rug (out) from under sb** also **pull the rug (out) from under sb's feet** INFORMAL to suddenly take away something that someone was depending on to achieve what they wanted: *He promised support, then pulled the rug out from under us.* **3** HUMOROUS a TOUPEE —see also **sweep sth under the rug/ carpet** (SWEEP¹ (14))

rug·by /'rʌgbi/ *n.* [U] an outdoor game played by two teams with an OVAL (=egg-shaped) ball that you kick or carry

rug·ged /'rʌgɪd/ *adj.* **1** land that is rugged is rough and uneven: *The coastline is rugged and harsh.* | *He loved the rugged landscape of the West.* **2** a rugged car or piece of equipment etc. is strongly built and not likely to break easily; STURDY: *a rugged mountain bike* **3** a man who is rugged is good-looking and has strong features which are often not perfect: *Ann admired Joe's rugged good looks.* **4** rugged behavior is confident and determined but not always polite: *a rugged individual* —**ruggedly** *adv.* —**ruggedness** *n.* [U]

rug·rat /'rʌgræt/ *n.* [C] SPOKEN, HUMOROUS a small child

ru·in¹ /'ruɪn/ *v.* [T] **1** to spoil or destroy something completely: *The Zimmerman's house was ruined by the flood.* | *Alcohol and drugs almost ruined his career.* **2** to make someone lose all their money: *A long strike would ruin the company.* —**ruined** *adj.* [only before noun] *ruined houses* —see Usage Note at DESTROY

ruin² *n.* **1** [U] a situation in which you have lost all your money, your social position, or the good opinion that people had about you: *financial ruin* | *A dictatorship would lead the country to ruin.* | *An unwise investment could be the road to ruin.* **2** [C] the part of a building that is left after the rest has been destroyed: *We visited the ruins of the old abbey.* | *an 800-year-old Mayan ruin* **3 be/lie in ruins a)** if a building is in ruins, it has fallen down or been badly damaged: *Whole blocks of the city were in ruins after the war.* **b)** if someone's life, hopes, plans, or an organization is in ruins, they are having great problems and cannot continue: *Our economy lies in ruins.* **4 the ruins of sth** the parts of something such as an organization, system, or set of ideas that remain after the rest has been destroyed: *They created a stable and prosperous society on the ruins of the old totalitarian regime.* **5 fall into ruin** also **go to ruin** if something falls into ruin, it becomes damaged or destroyed because no one is taking care of it: *The 18th century mansion has fallen into ruin.* **6 the ruin of sb** OLD-FASHIONED to make someone lose all their money, their good health, the good opinion that other people have about them etc.: *Manning's love for alcohol was the ruin of him.* —see also **go to rack and ruin** (RACK[1] (5))

ru·in·a·tion /ˌruəˈneɪʃən/ *n.* [U] FORMAL a situation in which someone or something is ruined, or the cause of this

ru·in·ous /ˈruɪnəs/ *adj.* **1** causing a lot of damage: *Alcohol is as ruinous as illegal drugs.* **2** costing much more than you can afford: *ruinous taxes* —**ruinously** *adv.*: *ruinously expensive*

s w **rule[1]** /rul/ *n.*
1 1

1 **instruction** [C] an official instruction that says how things must be done or what is allowed, especially in a game, organization, or job: *What are the rules of the game?* | *Ben always follows the rules.* | *You can't come in if you're not a member – it's against the rules.* | *Elizabeth was expelled for breaking the school's rules.* | **bend/stretch the rules** (=allow someone to not obey a particular rule on a particular occasion) | *Each mobile home park has its own rules and regulations.* | *There are really no hard and fast rules* (=definite rules) *for decorating.* | *We have unwritten rules* (=unofficial rules) *about what kind of behavior is considered normal.* | *I'm sorry, but rules are rules* (=used when you are saying that a rule cannot be broken) *and you can't go in there.*

2 **government** [U] the government of a country by a particular group of people or using a particular system: *Late in 1991, Communist rule ended in Russia.* | *Under colonial rule, India was treated as a single territory.* | *South Africa has made a somewhat peaceful transition to majority rule* (=the situation in which the largest group of people control the government). | *An efficient state is based on the rule of law* (=a situation in which the people in a country obey the laws).

3 **as a (general) rule** used to say that something usually happens or is usually true: *I like older women as a rule.*

4 **be the rule** used to say that something is the usual situation: *Early marriage used to be the rule in the Arab world.*

5 **behavior** [C] the way of behaving that is accepted as right by most people: *the rules of etiquette*

6 **rule of thumb** a rough method of calculation, based on practical experience: *You should tip bellmen $1–$2 per bag, as a rule of thumb.*

7 **make it a rule (to do sth)** to try to make sure that you always do something: *I make it a rule not to take friends on as clients.*

8 **of grammar/of a system** [C] a statement about what is usually allowed in the grammar of a language, or according to a particular system: *The rules of grammar in French are very complex.*

9 **the rule is** SPOKEN used when advising someone what to do in a particular situation: *The rule in the museum is "Look, but don't touch."*

10 **for measuring** [C] OLD-FASHIONED a RULER (1) —see also **the exception not the rule** (EXCEPTION (1)), **sb/sth is the exception that proves the rule** (EXCEPTION (4)), GOLDEN RULE, GROUND RULES, HOME RULE, SLIDE RULE

s w **rule[2]** *v.*
1
3

1 **government** [I,T] to have the official power to control a country and the people who live there: *African tribal societies were traditionally ruled by a council of elders.* | **[rule (over) sth/sb]** *Marcos ruled the Philippines for 20 years.*

2 **court/law** [I always + adv./prep.,T] to make an official decision about something, especially a legal problem: *The Medical Examiner's office ruled the death a murder.* | **[+ that]** *The government ruled that he was not eligible for Social Security payments.* | **[+ on]** *The Supreme Court has yet to rule on the case.* | **[+ against]** *A state appeals court ruled against her last month.* | *On May 19, Judge Karlton ruled in favor of the plaintiffs* —see also RULING[1]

3 **control/influence** [T] if a feeling or desire rules someone, it has a powerful and controlling influence on their actions: *Ashley's life was ruled by her addiction to drugs.*

4 **rule sb/sth with an iron fist/hand** to control a

group of people in a very severe way: *Ceauşescu ruled Romania with an iron fist until 1989.*

5 **rule the roost** INFORMAL to be the most powerful person in a group: *Amanda pretty much rules the roost in that house.*

6 **let your heart rule your head** to make decisions based on what you feel, not what you think

7 **sb/sth rules** SPOKEN used to say that the team, school, place etc. mentioned is better than anyone else: *In football, Jefferson High rules!*

8 **draw a line** [T usually passive] to draw a line using a ruler or other straight edge: *Paper ruled into one-inch squares is used to practice writing Chinese characters.* —see also OVERRULE

rule out *phr. v.* [T] **1** **[rule sb/sth ↔ out]** to decide that something is not possible or appropriate, or that someone is not appropriate: *You should not rule out a school because it costs too much.* | *Doctors have ruled out the possibility of surgery.* **2** **[rule sth ↔ out]** to make it impossible for something to happen: *His injuries rule out a return to the field before the end of the season.*

rule·book /ˈrulbʊk/ *n.* [C] a book of rules, especially one that is given to workers in a job or that contains the rules of a sport

ruled /ruld/ *adj.* ruled paper has parallel lines printed across it

rul·er /ˈrulər/ *n.* [C] **1** a flat narrow piece of plastic, metal etc. with straight edges, that you use for measuring things or drawing straight lines: *a 12-inch ruler* **2** someone such as a king or queen who has official power over a country or area

rul·ing[1] /ˈrulɪŋ/ *n.* [C] an official decision, especially one made by a court: **[+ on]** *Conservatives didn't like his rulings on civil rights cases.*

ruling[2] *adj.* [only before noun] the ruling group in a country or organization is the group that controls it: *the ruling party*

rum /rʌm/ *n.* [C,U] a strong alcoholic drink made from sugar, or a glass of this drink

rum·ba /ˈrʌmbə/ *n.* [C,U] a popular dance from Cuba, or the music for this dance

rum·ble[1] /ˈrʌmbəl/ *v.* **1** [I] to make a series of long low sounds: *Loud applause rumbled through the hall.* **2** [I always + adv./prep.] if a car, truck, airplane rumbles somewhere, it moves slowly while making this sound: **[+ along/past etc.]** *A truck rumbled past, leaving a trail of diesel fumes.* **3** if your stomach rumbles, it makes a noise, especially because you are hungry **4** [I,T] OLD-FASHIONED to fight with someone

rumble[2] *n.* **1** [singular] a series of long low sounds: *The rumble of the train going by woke me up.* **2** [C] OLD-FASHIONED a fight

rum·bling /ˈrʌmblɪŋ/ *n.* **1** [C usually plural] remarks that show that people are becoming annoyed, or that a difficult situation is developing: *There were rumblings of discontent among the students.* **2** [C usually singular] a rumbling noise: *the rumbling of thunder*

ru·mi·nant /ˈrumənənt/ *n.* [C] TECHNICAL an animal such as a cow that has several stomachs and eats grass

ru·mi·nate /ˈruməˌneɪt/ *v.* [I] **1** FORMAL to think for a long time about something: **[+ about/on etc.]** *Hamlet ruminates on the nature of life and death in the gravedigger's scene.* **2** TECHNICAL if animals such as cows ruminate, they bring food back into their mouths from their stomachs and CHEW it again —**rumination** /ˌruməˈneɪʃən/ *n.* [C,U]

rum·mage[1] /ˈrʌmɪdʒ/ *v.* [I always + adv./prep.] also **rummage around** to search for something by moving things around in a careless way: **[+ in/through etc.]** *Andrea rummaged through her purse for a tissue.*

rummage[2] *n.* [U] old clothes, toys etc. that you do not want anymore

rummage sale /ˈ.. ˌ./ *n.* [C] an event at which old clothes, toys etc. are sold as a way of getting money, for example to help a school or church

R

rum·my /'rʌmi/ *n.* [U] a simple card game

ru·mor /'rumɚ/ *n.* [U] **1** information that is passed from one person to another and which may or may not be true, especially information about someone's personal life or about an official decision: [+ **about/of**] *Rumors of war were everywhere.* | [+ **that**] *Knox denied rumors that he might be running for office.* | *Rumor has it that the romance is over between Ryder and Depp.* **2 the rumor mill** the people, considered as a group, that discuss something and pass rumors to each other: *Skinner's name has come up in the rumor mill as a possible director for the project.*

ru·mored /'rumɚd/ *adj.* if something is rumored to be true, people are saying secretly or in an unofficial way that it may be true: *It's rumored that they're going to sell the old Anderson farm.* | [**be rumored to be sth**] *Allen is rumored to be moving to Montana.*

ru·mor·mon·ger /'rumɚ,mʌŋgɚ, -,mɑŋ-/ *n.* [C] someone who tells other people rumors

rump /rʌmp/ *n.* **1** [C] the part of an animal's back that is just above its back legs **2** [C] HUMOROUS the part of your body that you sit on **3** [singular] the part of a country, organization etc. that remains after most of the other parts have left or been taken away: [+ **of**] *the rump of Yugoslavia*

rum·ple /'rʌmpəl/ *v.* [T] to make hair, clothes etc. less neat —**rumpled** *adj.*: *rumpled sheets*

rump steak /'. ./ *n.* [C,U] meat that comes from the part of a cow that is just above its back legs

rum·pus /'rʌmpəs/ *n.* [singular] INFORMAL a lot of noise, especially made by people arguing or playing: *The kids were making quite a rumpus in the living room.*

rumpus room /'.. ,./ *n.* [C] OLD-FASHIONED a room in a house that is used by the family for games, parties etc.

run[1] /rʌn/ *v. past tense* **ran** *past participle* **run** *present participle* **running**

1 move [I] to move very quickly, by moving your legs more quickly than when you walk: *If we run we can still catch the bus.* | [+ **down/over/through** etc.] *He ran over to the flower bed and picked some flowers for her.* | *She ran along the whole length of the field.* | *I ran screaming out of the house.* | *He ran for his life* (=to avoid being killed) *as bullets flew around him.*

2 be in charge of [T] to control or be in charge of a company, an organization, or system: *Christina runs a restaurant in Houston.* | *well/badly run I try hard to keep a neat and well-run home.* | *Eliseo works in a large state-run factory.*

3 in a race [I,T] to take part in a running race: *I've never run a marathon before.* | [+ **in**] *Owens is running in the 200 meters.*

4 machines **a)** [I] if a machine runs, it operates: *How has your car been running lately?* | *The ad says the computer can be up and running* (=working) *in less than an hour.* | *run on/off sth Deb's car runs on diesel.* | *The hot water heater in our mountain cabin runs off solar energy.* **b)** [T] to make a machine operate: *Let me just run the vacuum over the carpet quickly.* | *They don't run the furnace in the summertime.*

5 money/numbers [I,T] to be at a particular level, amount, price etc.: *New headlights are going to run you about forty bucks.* | [**be running at sth**] *Unemployment in Europe is currently running at 10.6 percent.* | *Weekly rates run to $3,750 during June, July, and August.*

6 computers [I,T] to operate a computer program: *You'd better run the spell checker before you print it.*

7 go somewhere [I] SPOKEN to go somewhere quickly, either walking or in a car: [+ **to**] *I need to run to the store for some milk.* | [+ **over/out/back** etc.] *Let me just run out to the car and get it.*

8 election [I] to try to be elected in an election: [**run for sth**] *Laszlo ran for Congress in 1994.* | [**run against sb**] *Kovic has not said if he will run against Dornan.*

9 test/process [T] to do something such as a medical test or an EXPERIMENT, in which you do things in a particular order: *The doctors need to run a few tests first.*

10 run late/early/on time to arrive, go somewhere, or do something late, early, or at the right time: *Don called – he's running late, so we'll start without him.*

11 news/stories/advertisements [I,T] to print or broadcast a story etc. in a newspaper or magazine or on television: *Dorothy was reunited with her family after the newspaper ran her story.*

12 water/liquids [I] to flow, especially in or from a particular direction or place: [+ **down/along** etc.] *Allen could feel the sweat running down his back.* | *A stream ran through the garden.*

13 fast/out of control [I always + adv./prep.] to move too fast or in an uncontrolled way: [+ **into/down/through** etc.] *The truck ran downhill at a frightening speed.*

14 play/movie etc. [I] to continue being performed or shown regularly in one place: *The exhibit runs through May at the Museum of Art.*

15 happen [I] to happen or take place, especially in the way that was intended: *Riboli and his wife keep the winery running smoothly* (=with no unexpected problems). | *The general reassured us that the military campaign was running according to plan.*

16 buses/trains etc. **a)** [I] if a bus, train etc. service runs, it takes people from one place to another at specific times of the day: *Metro North trains are running on a weekend schedule.* **b)** [T] if someone runs a bus, train etc. service, they make it operate: *Caltrain runs commuter trains to San Jose.*

17 official papers [I] to officially be able to be used for a particular period of time: *Barkley's contract only runs through next season.*

18 sb's nose [I] if someone's nose is running, liquid is flowing out of it

19 roads/pipes/fences/lines [I always + adv./prep.,T always + adv./prep.] to exist in a particular place or continue in a particular direction: [+ **along/through** etc.] *A strip of embossed gold ran along the top of the invitation.* | *A small path runs between the dunes.* | [**run sth along/through** etc.] *They want to run a pipeline through protected parts of Alaska.*

20 be running short (of sth) to have very little of something left: *Food and medical supplies are running short in the area.*

21 time is running short used to say that there is little time left: *With time running short we were worried that he wouldn't show up.*

22 be running low (on sth) to have very little left of something that you normally keep a supply of: *The plane was running low on fuel and had to make an emergency landing.*

23 touch [T always + adv./prep.] to move or rub something lightly along a surface: [**run sth down/through/along**] *She ran her hand along the silky scarf.*

24 feelings/thoughts [I always + adv./prep.] if thoughts or feelings run through you, you think about them or feel them in a very strong way: [+ **through**] *All these thoughts are running through my head that I can't put into words.* | *I felt a mixture of emotion running through me during the performance.*

25 pain [I always + adv./prep.] if pain runs through you, it feels sharp and sudden: [+ **through/down** etc.] *Alvin felt a sharp pain run down his left arm.*

26 run drugs/guns to bring drugs or guns into a country illegally in order to sell them —see also DRUG RUNNER, GUN-RUNNING

27 run in the family if something such as a quality, disease, or skill runs in the family, many people in that family have it: *Twins run in the family, so it didn't surprise us when we heard the news.*

28 run a temperature/fever to have a body temperature that is higher than normal because you are sick: *The baby was fussing and running a fever, so I called the doctor.*

29 run a light to drive quickly through TRAFFIC LIGHTS instead of stopping: *The ambulance ran a red light.*

30 run an errand to go to a store, office etc. to buy or get something that you need: *I have to stop off near here to run an errand.*
31 colors [I] if color runs, it spreads from one area of cloth to another, when the cloth is wet: *I hope these jeans don't run when I wash them.*
32 paint [I] if paint runs, it moves onto an area where you did not intend it to go
33 run for cover a) to run toward a place where you will be safe from being attacked, especially by bullets: *At the sound of gunfire, people ran for cover.* **b)** to try to protect yourself from criticism, a bad situation etc.: *Signs of trouble on Wall Street sent investors running for cover.*
34 run for it to run as quickly as possible in order to escape: *Ridley decided to make a run for it and try to escape.*
35 up and running working fully and correctly: *Hopefully, the telescope will be up and running as early as next year.*
36 run (sth) aground/ashore if a ship runs aground, or someone runs it aground, it hits rocks or the ground and cannot move because the water is not deep enough: *At least 20 small boats were run aground by the storm.*
37 run its course to continue in the expected way until finished: *Once the disease has run its course, it's not likely to return.*
38 run a bath to fill a bathtub with water: *Christine got out of bed and ran a hot bath.*
39 be running high if feelings are running high, people are becoming angry or upset about something: *Emotions were running high during the Woodward trial.*
40 run dry a) if a river or WELL (=hole in the ground for getting water) runs dry, there is no water left **b)** if something like ideas, money etc. run dry, you do not have any more of them: *The show's creativity had run dry after the second season.*
41 run a check/test on sb to arrange for something or someone to be checked or tested: *The police are running a background check on him.* | *Health officials ran tests to check the purity of the water.*
42 hole in clothes [I] if a hole in PANTYHOSE runs, it gets longer in a straight line
43 come running a) INFORMAL to react in a very eager way when someone asks or tells you to do something: *When Bob Dylan calls, musicians come running.* **b)** SPOKEN to ask someone for help, advice, or sympathy when you have a problem: [+ to] *Well I warned you, so don't come running to me when everything goes wrong!*
44 run sb's life INFORMAL to keep telling someone what they should do all the time, in a way that they find annoying: *Don't try to run my life!*
45 be running scared to have become worried about the power of an enemy or opponent: *Their new software has the competition running scared.*
46 run and do sth SPOKEN used to ask a child to get or do something quickly for you: *Run and get me a towel, Susie.*
47 run rings/circles around sb INFORMAL to be able to do something much better than someone else can: *People could run rings around him in scientific arguments.*
48 run wild to behave in an uncontrolled way: *Football fans ran wild through the city.*
49 run like hell INFORMAL to run very quickly, especially in order to escape from something: *If this thing catches on fire, then run like hell.*
50 run sth into the ground to use something a lot without taking care of it or repairing it, so that you destroy it: *Some slum landlords run their properties into the ground.* —see also **run amok** (AMOK), **make your blood run cold** (BLOOD (11)), **run counter to** (COUNTER³), **cut and run** (CUT¹ (30)), **run/go deep** (DEEP² (4)), **run the gauntlet** (GAUNTLET (3)), **run riot** (RIOT¹ (2)), RUNNING

run across sb/sth *phr. v.* [T] to meet or find someone or something by chance: *As he came out into the lobby, Archer ran across his friend Ned.*
run after sb/sth *phr. v.* [T] to chase someone or something: *Nately jumped out of the car and ran after Santiago.*

run along *phr. v.* SPOKEN used to tell someone, especially children, that they must leave, or that you must leave: *Sorry, but I should be running along now.* | *Now you kids run along to bed.*
run around *phr. v.* [I] **1** to run in an area, without a definite direction or purpose: *Put your puppy on the floor and let him run around.* **2** INFORMAL to be very busy doing many small jobs: *She's been running around all day getting things ready for the wedding.* **3 run around with sb** to spend a lot of time with someone, especially in a way that other people disapprove of: *I was always out, running around with the guys.* —see also RUNAROUND
run away *phr. v.* [I] **1** to leave a place, especially secretly, in order to escape from someone or something: *He wanted to run away and join the circus when he was a kid.* | [+ from] *Sandy had run away from home several times in her teens.* —see also RUNAWAY² **2** to try to avoid a problem or situation because it is difficult or embarrassing: *Baker is not one to run away from a fight.*
run away with *phr. v.* [T] **1** [run away with sb] to leave a place secretly or illegally with someone else: *Mallie moved to California after her husband ran away with another woman.* **2 run away with you** if your feelings, ideas etc. run away with you, they start to control how you behave because you cannot think in a sensible way anymore: *I can't let my emotions run away with me.* **3** [run away with sth] INFORMAL to win a competition or sports game very easily: *Murphy ran away with the 1992 mayoral race.* **4** [run away with sth] to steal something: *They found that the treasurer had run away with the funds.*
run sth **by** sb *phr. v.* [T] **1** to ask someone about something in order to get their opinion or permission: *You'd better run that contract by a lawyer.* **2 run that by me again** SPOKEN used to ask someone to explain by something again, because you did not completely understand
run down *phr. v.* **1** [T run sb/sth ↔ down] to drive into a person or animal and kill or injure them: *He was run down by a drunken woman.* **2** [I,T run sth ↔ down] if a clock, machine, BATTERY etc. runs down, it has no more power and stops working: *I left the tape playing and it's run down the battery.* **3** [T run sb/sth ↔ down] INFORMAL to say things that are impolite, bad, or unfair about someone or something: *Never run down your previous employer to a new one.* **4** [T run down] sth to read a list of people or things: *Let me run down the proposed guestlist.* **5** [T run sth ↔ down] to let a company, organization etc. gradually become smaller or stop working: *Things were allowed to run down by the restaurant's previous owners.* —see also RUNDOWN, RUN-DOWN
run into *phr. v.* [T] **1** [run into sb] INFORMAL to meet someone by chance: *We ran into Ruth Ann this morning.* **2** [run into sb/sth] to hit someone or something with a car or other vehicle: *I nearly ran into a tree.* **3** [run into sth] to accidentally hit a part of your body on something: *His legs are all bruised because he's always running into things.* **4 run into difficulties/problems/debt etc.** to start to experience difficulties: *Make sure your bills are paid a month in advance so you don't run into cash flow problems.*
run off *phr. v.* **1** [I] to leave a place or person in a way that people disapprove of: [+ to] *When she ran off to Germany, Luke was left to take care of her son.* **2** [T run sth ↔ off] to quickly print several copies of something: *We need to run off a hundred and fifty copies of this.* **3** [T run sb off] to force someone to leave a particular place, especially a road: *Gates had run them off his property with a rifle.* | *Someone tried to run me off the road.* **4 run off at the mouth** INFORMAL to talk too much: *Boyd seems to enjoy running off at the mouth to the press.*
run off with sb/sth *phr. v.* [I] INFORMAL **1** to leave a place with someone, because you are having a sexual relationship that people do not approve of: *Maria left her husband and ran off with Henry.* **2** to take something without permission: *The attackers ran off with Robert's scuba gear.*

R

run on *phr. v.* [I] to continue happening for longer than expected or planned: *Our meetings usually run on for hours.*

run out *phr. v.* **1** [I] if something runs out, or you run out of something, you use all of it and do not have any left: *My patience was running out.* | [+ **of**] *I hope we don't run out of paint.* | *We're starting to run out of ideas.* | *We've run out of milk. Could you stop at the store on your way home?* **2** [I] if an agreement, contract, official document etc. runs out, it reaches the end of the period when it is officially allowed to continue; EXPIRE: *The company's patent on Prozac runs out in 2002.* **3 run out on sb** to leave someone, especially your family, when you should not because you are responsible for them: *My dad ran out on me and my mom when I was ten.* **4 run out of steam/gas etc.** INFORMAL to have no energy or eagerness left for something that you are trying to do: *I'm running out of steam – why don't we quit for the day?* **5 run sb out of town** OLD-FASHIONED to force someone to leave a place, because they have done something wrong

run out

The ink ran out before I'd finished writing the address.

run over *phr. v.* **1** [T **run** sb/sth ↔ **over**] to hit someone or something with a car or other vehicle, and drive over them: *Birds that nest on the ground are sometimes run over by lawn mowers.* **2** [I] if a container runs over, there is so much liquid inside that some flows out; OVERFLOW **3** [T **run over** sth] to look at or read something again so that you understand it better, or so that you are prepared for something: *Larry was still running over the script as we prepared to go on the air.* **4** [I] also **run over time** to continue past the arranged time: *We've run over time, so, sorry, there's no time for questions.*

run through *phr. v.* [T] **1** [**run through** sth] to repeat something so that you remember it or get better at it: *They ran through their lines twice while the scenery was set up.* **2** [**run through** sth] to read, look at, or explain something quickly: *Joette ran through a list of the jobs to be done.* **3** [**run through** sth] to be present in many parts of something or continue through it, for example in an artist's work or in a society: *A thread of violence runs through the lives of everyone in the community.* **4** [**run** sb **through**] LITERARY to push a sword completely through someone —see also RUN-THROUGH

run sth ↔ **up** *phr. v.* [T] **1 run up a bill/expenses/debts** to use a lot of something or borrow a lot of money, so that you will have to pay a lot of money: *Stop running up the phone bill!* **2** to raise a flag on a pole

run up against sth/sb *phr. v.* [T] to have to deal with unexpected problems or a difficult opponent: *The Rockets finally ran up against a team they couldn't beat.*

run² *n.*
1 on foot [C] a period of time spent running, or a distance that you run: *a 5-mile run* | *I'm about to go for a run.* | *I broke into a run* (=started running) *when I spotted her playing across the field.* | *The kids set off at a run* (=running) *for the swing sets.*
2 baseball [C] a point won in baseball
3 play/movie [C] a continuous series of performances of a play, movie etc. in the same place: *Dunaway is starring in a six-week run of "Master Class" in Los Angeles.*
4 do sth on the run while you are on your way somewhere, or doing something else: *I always seem to eat on the run these days.*
5 a run on sth a situation in which a lot of people suddenly buy a particular product: *Since the break-ins, stores have reported a run on deadbolt locks.*

6 bank [C] an occasion when a lot of people all take their money out of a bank at the same time
7 run on the dollar/pound/yen etc. a situation in which a lot of people sell dollars etc. and the value goes down
8 a run of failures/wins/strikes etc. a series of failures, wins etc.: *Saturday's game may well be the end of De La Salle's historic run of victories.*
9 election [C, usually singular] an attempt to be elected: *Turner is making his first run for public office.*
10 be on the run a) to be trying to escape or hide, especially from the police: *Mel had been on the run since he escaped from jail.* **b)** if an army or an opponent is on the run, they may soon be defeated
11 trip [C, usually singular] a trip by train, ship, truck etc., made regularly between two places: *They left Anchorage at nine for the forty-mile run to Matanuska.*
12 skiing [C] a sloping area of land that you can SKI down: *Both resorts offer beginner to expert runs.*
13 in clothes [C] a long hole in a pair of PANTYHOSE
14 make a run for (sth) to suddenly start running, in order to escape: *It was still raining hard, but we made a run for it to the car.*
15 a run of good/bad luck several lucky or unlucky things happening quickly after each other: *After a run of bad luck, Carla decided to make a new start in California.*
16 give sb a (good) run for their money to do well in an election, competition etc. so that your opponent has to use all their skill and effort to defeat you: *Slosser gave Boyd a run for his money in the 1996 GOP primary.*
17 have the run of sth to be allowed to use a place when and how you want: *Leroy and I had the run of the weight room.*
18 the runs [plural] INFORMAL DIARRHEA (=an illness that makes you need to go to the toilet often)
19 music [C] a set of notes played or sung quickly up or down a SCALE in a piece of music
20 card games [C] a set of cards with numbers in a series, held by one player
21 sled [C] a special area or track for people to slide down on a SLED or BOBSLED
22 for animals [C] an enclosed area where animals such as chickens or rabbits are kept —see also DRY RUN, FUN RUN, **in the long run** (LONG¹ (8)), **in the short term/run** (SHORT¹ (10)), TRIAL RUN

run·a·bout /ˈrʌnəˌbaʊt/ *n.* [C] OLD-FASHIONED a small car used for short trips, especially within a city

run·a·round /ˈrʌnəˌraʊnd/ *n.* **give sb the runaround** INFORMAL to deliberately avoid giving someone a definite answer, especially when they are asking you to do something: *I called the insurance company about this claim, but they kept giving me the runaround.* —see also **run around** (RUN¹)

run·a·way¹ /ˈrʌnəˌweɪ/ *adj.* [only before noun] **1** a runaway vehicle or animal is moving fast while not being controlled by anyone any longer: *a runaway freight train* **2** runaway success/inflation etc. success, INFLATION etc. that happens quickly or in an uncontrolled way: *"Scarlett" became a runaway best-seller.* **3** a runaway person has left the place where they are supposed to be: *Weiss runs a drop-in center for runaway teens.*

runaway² *n. plural* **runaways** [C] someone, especially a child, who has left home without telling anyone and does not intend to go back —see also **run away** (RUN¹)

run·down /ˈrʌndaʊn/ *n.* [C usually singular] a quick report or explanation of an idea, situation, event etc.: *Here's a rundown of the wines you're most likely to find in local wine stores.*

run-down /ˌ. ˈ.◂/ *adj.* **1** a building or area that is run-down is in very bad condition: *He made a fortune buying run-down houses and fixing them up to sell.* **2** [not before noun] someone who is run-down is tired or not healthy: *I was feeling too run-down to go for my morning jog.*

rune /run/ *n.* [C] **1** one of the letters of an ancient alphabet once used by people in Northern Europe **2** a magic song or written sign —**runic** *adj.*

rung[1] /rʌŋ/ v. the past participle of RING[2]

rung[2] n. [C] **1** one of the bars that form the steps of a LADDER **2** INFORMAL a particular level or position in an organization or system: *Community colleges are the bottom rung of the state's higher education ladder.* **3** a bar between two legs of a chair

run-in /'. ./ n. [C] **1** an argument or disagreement, especially with someone in an official position: *Ken had a terrible run-in with his boss yesterday.* **2 a run-in with the police/authorities/law** if you have a run-in with the police, the authorities etc., you have trouble with them because you have broken a law: *Mike's addiction to heroin has led to several run-ins with the law.*

run·ner /'rʌnə/ n. [C] **1** someone who runs as a sport: *a long-distance runner* **2** someone who walks or runs from place to place carrying messages, especially in past times **3** one of the two thin pieces of metal under a SLED, or the single piece of metal under a SKATE, that allows it to go over snow and ice smoothly **4** a long narrow piece of cloth or CARPET: *a red table runner for Christmas* **5** the bar of wood or metal that a drawer or curtain slides along **6** TECHNICAL a stem with which a plant such as a STRAWBERRY spreads itself along the ground —see also DRUG RUNNER, FRONTRUNNER

runner-up /,.. './ n. plural **runners-up** [C] the person or team that comes second in a race or competition

run·neth /'rʌnəθ/ v. —see **my cup runneth over** (CUP[1] (11))

run·ning[1] /'rʌnɪŋ/ n. **1** [U] the act or sport of running: *Do you want to go running with me?* | *running shoes/shorts etc. I put on a T-shirt and a pair of running shorts.* **2 the running of sth** the way in which a business, home, organization etc. is managed or organized: *Maria helped her mother with the running of the household.* **3 be in the running to** have some hope of winning a race or competition: *Jacques Villeneuve will find out this week if he is still in the running for the Formula One title.* —opposite **be out of the running**

running[2] adj. [only before noun] **1 running water a)** a building that has running water has pipes which provide water to a BATHROOM, kitchen etc.: *They lived in a one-room trailer with no running water.* **b)** water that is flowing or moving: *The sound of running water could be heard like faint background music.* | *Scrub the potatoes thoroughly under running water.* **2 running commentary** a spoken description of an event, especially a race or game, made while the event is happening: *A woman behind us kept up a running commentary on what was happening in the movie.* **3 running battle/argument** an argument that continues or is repeated over a long period of time: *Thomas and his neighbor had a running battle about the fence.* **4 running total** a total that is continuously increased as new costs, amounts etc. are added: *Keep a running total of your expenses.* **5 running sore** a sore area on your skin, that has liquid coming out of it **6 in running order** a machine that is in running order is working correctly **7 the running order** the order in which the different parts of an event have been arranged to take place: *There are a few changes in the running order for the teachers' conference.*

running[3] adv. **two years/five times etc. running** for three years etc. without a change or interruption: *We've been enjoying increased sales for three years running.*

running back /'.. ,./ n. [C,U] a player whose main job is to run with the ball in football

running costs /'.. ,./ n. [plural] the amount of money that is needed to operate an organization, system etc.

running jump /,.. './ n. [C] a jump made by running up to the point at which you leave the ground

running mate /'.. ,./ n. [C usually singular] the person chosen by someone who is trying to become president, GOVERNOR etc. who will then be their VICE PRESIDENT, LIEUTENANT GOVERNOR etc. if they are elected: *Kennedy chose Johnson as his running mate in the 1960 presidential election.*

run·ny /'rʌni/ adj. INFORMAL **1** a runny nose, runny eyes etc. have liquid coming out of them, usually because you have a cold **2** something, especially a food, that is runny is not solid or thick enough: *The scrambled eggs were a little bit runny.*

run-off /'. ./ n. **1** [C] a second competition or election that is arranged when there is no clear winner of the first one: *a run-off election* —compare PLAY-OFF —see also **run off** (RUN[1] **2** [U] rain or other liquid that flows off the land into rivers, oceans etc.: *The Piedmontese plain is well watered by the run-off from the Alps.*

run-of-the-mill /,. . . '.◂/ adj. not special or interesting in any way; ORDINARY: *Detective Harris could see this was not going to be a run-of-the-mill case.*

run-on sen·tence /,. . '../ n. [C] a sentence that has two main CLAUSES without connecting words or correct PUNCTUATION

runt /rʌnt/ n. [C] **1** the smallest and least developed baby animal of a group born at the same time: *the runt of the litter* **2** INFORMAL a small, unimportant person who you do not like

run-through /'. ./ n. [C] a short practice before a performance, test etc.: *There will be a brief run-through the afternoon before the concert.*

run-up /'. ./ n. **1 the run-up to sth** the period of time just before an important event: *These performances are part of the run-up to the Center's anniversary celebrations.* **2** [C] the act of running, or the distance that you run, before you kick a ball, jump over a pole etc.

run·way /'rʌnweɪ/ n. plural **runways** [C] **1** a long specially prepared hard surface like a road that aircraft leave from or come down on **2** a long narrow part of a stage that goes out into the area where the AUDIENCE sits —see picture at MODEL[1]

Run·yon /'rʌnyən/, **Da·mon** /'deɪmən/ (1884–1946) a U.S. writer of humorous stories

ru·pee /'rupi, ru'pi/ n. [C] the standard unit of money in some countries such as India and Pakistan

ru·pi·ah /ru'piə/ n. [C] the standard unit of money in Indonesia

rup·ture[1] /'rʌptʃə/ n. **1** [C,U] an occasion when something suddenly breaks apart or bursts: *A pipeline rupture halted supplies of natural gas.* **2** [C] a situation in which two countries or groups of people suddenly disagree and often end their relationship with each other: *Terrorist attacks led to the rupture of relations between the two countries.* **3** [C,U] a medical condition in which an organ of the body sticks out through the wall of muscle that normally surrounds it; HERNIA

rup·ture[2] v. [I,T] to break or burst, or make something break or burst: *A stroke is often caused by a blood vessel in the brain ruptures.*

ru·ral /'rurəl/ adj. **1** happening in or relating to the country, not the city: *a magazine about rural life* | *Crime is a concern in both rural and urban areas.* **2** like the country or reminding you of the country: *Compared to Los Angeles, Santa Barbara is rural.* —opposite URBAN

rural de·liv·er·y /,.. .'.../ n. R.D.

rural route /'.. ,./ n. RR

ruse /ruz/ n. [C] something you do in order to deceive someone; trick: *He wore a fake mustache in a ruse to conceal his identity.*

rush[1] /rʌʃ/ v.

1 move quickly [I always + adv./prep.] to move very quickly, especially because you need to be somewhere very soon: [+ out/past/through/along etc.] *I rushed into the hall to get a ticket for the next train to Singapore.*

2 do sth quickly [I,T] to do something very quickly, especially so that you do not have time to do it carefully or well: *There's plenty of time — we don't need to rush.* | **rush it/things** *He's recovering from surgery well, but shouldn't rush things.*

3 rush to do sth to do something eagerly and without delay: *Investors rushed to buy the newly issued stocks.*

4 take/send urgently [T always + adv./prep.] to take or send something somewhere very quickly, especially because of an unexpected problem: [**rush sb to somewhere**] *Miss Tish was rushed to the hospital with severe chest pain.* | *The army rushed reinforcements to the front.*

5 make sb hurry [T] to try to make someone do something more quickly than they want to: *I don't mean to rush you but I really need to get going.* | [**rush sb into doing sth**] *Don't let them rush you into signing the contract.*

6 blood [I] if blood rushes to your face, your face becomes red because you feel embarrassed or shy about something: [+ **to**] *Val felt the blood rush to her face when she realized the whole class was staring at her.*

7 liquid [I always + adv./prep.] if water or another liquid rushes somewhere, it moves quickly through or into a place: *Water rushed through the gutters during the heavy thunderstorm.*

8 football [I,T] to carry the ball forward: *Lawrence rushed for 68 yards and one touchdown.*

9 attack [T] to attack someone suddenly and in a group: *Police in riot gear rushed the demonstrators.*

10 universities **a)** [T] to consider letting new students join a FRATERNITY or SORORITY (=type of club) by giving parties, having meetings with them etc. to see if you want to accept them **b)** [I,T] to go through the process of trying to be accepted into these clubs: *She decided to rush the Tri-Delta sorority.*

rush around *phr. v.* [I] to try to do a lot of things in a short period of time: *Dean rushed around trying to get the necessary papers.*

rush into sth *phr. v.* [T] to get involved in something without taking enough time to think carefully about it: *She's made it clear she won't be rushed into any decision.* | *He's asked me to marry him, but I don't want to rush into anything.*

rush sth ↔ **out** *phr. v.* [T] to make a new product, book etc. available for sale very quickly

rush sth ↔ **through** *phr. v.* [T] to deal with official or government business more quickly than usual: *The environmental bill was rushed through the House of Representatives in one month.*

rush² *n.*
1 hurry [singular,U] a situation in which you need to hurry: *Slow down! What's the big rush?* | [**be in a rush to do sth**] *Eric was in no rush to make a decision.* | *"I'll bring it right back." "Take your time. There's no rush."* | *If you are in a rush and can't stop to eat, grab a carton of yogurt or some fruit.*

2 busy period [singular] the time in the day, month, year etc. when a place or group of people are particularly busy: *The accident happened during the evening rush.* | *the Christmas rush* —see also RUSH HOUR

3 people wanting sth [singular] a situation in which a lot of people suddenly try to do or get something: [+ **on**] *A scheduled increase in passport fees has caused a rush on the passport office.* | [**the rush to do sth**] *Libraries are being sacrificed in the rush to put computers in schools.* —see also GOLD RUSH

4 fast movement [singular] a sudden fast movement of things or people: *From the darkness behind her there came a rush of wings.*

5 plant [C] a type of tall grass that grows in water, often used for making baskets, MATS etc.

6 feeling **a)** [C] INFORMAL a strong, usually pleasant feeling that you get from taking a drug or from doing something exciting: *Skateboarding is a real rush once you know how to do it.* **b) rush of excitement/panic etc.** a sudden very strong feeling of excitement etc.: *I felt a rush of passion I had never known before.*

7 students [C usually singular] the time when university students who want to join a FRATERNITY or SORORITY (=type of club) go to a lot of parties in order to see which one they would like to join: *rush week* | *a rush party*

8 rushes [plural] the first prints of a movie before it has been EDITed; dailies (DAILY³ (2))

rushed /rʌʃt/ *adj.* done very quickly or too quickly, because there was not enough time: *The restaurant's service was rushed and impersonal.*

rush hour /'. ./ *n.* [C,U] the time of day when the roads, buses, trains etc. are most crowded, because people are traveling to or from work: *heavy rush hour traffic*

Mount Rushmore

Rush·more, Mount /'rʌʃmɔr/ **Mount Rushmore National Memorial** a mountain in the U.S. state of South Dakota, where the rock has been cut into the shape of the faces of four U.S. presidents: Washington, Jefferson, Lincoln, and Theodore Roosevelt

Rus·sell /'rʌsəl/, **Ber·trand** /'bɜtrənd/ (1872–1970) a British PHILOSOPHER and mathematician

Russell, Bill /bɪl/ (1934–) a U.S. basketball player

Russell, Charles (1852–1916) a U.S. religious leader who started the JEHOVAH'S WITNESSES

rus·set /'rʌsɪt/ *n.* [U] LITERARY a reddish-brown color —**russet** *adj.*

Rus·sia /'rʌʃə/ a very large country in Eastern Europe and northern Asia, officially called the Russian Federation, that reaches from the Arctic Ocean in the north and Ukraine in the west to the Pacific Ocean in the east —**Russian** *n., adj.*

Russian Or·tho·dox Church, the /,.. ,.. './ the main Christian church in Russia, that was formed in the 11th century by separating from the Catholic Church, and is closely related to the Greek Orthodox Church

Russian rou·lette /,.. './ *n.* [U] a game in which you risk killing yourself by shooting at your head with a gun that has a bullet in only one of six CHAMBERs

rust¹ /rʌst/ *n.* [U] **1** the reddish-brown substance that forms on iron and steel when they get wet: *Clean and oil gardening tools to prevent rust.* **2** a plant disease that causes reddish-brown spots —see also RUSTPROOF, RUSTY

rust² *v.* [I,T] to become covered with rust or make something become covered in rust: *The old typewriter had been rusting in my basement for years.*

rust away *phr. v.* [I] to be gradually destroyed by rust

Rust Belt, the /'. ./ an area in the northern U.S., including parts of the states of Illinois, Michigan, Indiana, Ohio, and Wisconsin, where many large industries, especially the steel and car industries, used to employ many people but have become less successful

rus·tic¹ /'rʌstɪk/ *adj.* **1** simple, old-fashioned, and not spoiled by modern developments, in a way that is typical of the country: *We stayed in a rustic old lodge.* **2** [only before noun] roughly made from wood: *a rustic bench* —**rusticity** /rʌ'stɪsəti/ *n.* [U]

rustic² *n.* [C] LITERARY someone from the country, especially a farm worker

rus·tle¹ /'rʌsəl/ *v.* **1** [I,T] if leaves, papers, clothes etc. rustle, or if you rustle them, they make a soft noise as they rub against each other: *A light breeze rustled the treetops.* | *Her taffeta dress rustles as she moves past.* **2** [T] to steal farm animals such as cattle, horses, or sheep

rustle sth ↔ **up** *phr. v.* [T] INFORMAL to find or make something quickly, especially food or a meal: *Ma, can you rustle up some breakfast for me before I go?*

rustle² *n.* [singular] the noise made when something rustles: *a rustle of leaves*

rus·tler /'rʌslɚ/ *n.* [C] someone who steals farm animals such as cattle, horses, or sheep

rust·proof /'rʌstpruf/ *adj.* metal that is rustproof will not RUST

rust·y /'rʌsti/ *adj.* **1** metal that is rusty is covered in RUST: *an old rusty bicycle* **2** if someone's skill in a particular activity or subject is rusty, it is not as good as it used to be, because they have not practiced it for a long time: *We haven't played in a long time, we might be a little rusty.* —**rustiness** *n.* [U]

rut¹ /rʌt/ *n.* **1** [C] a deep narrow track left in soft ground by a wheel **2 in a rut** living or working in a situation that never changes, so that you feel bored: *I sometimes feel my that my relationship with Jeff is stuck in a rut.* **3 the rut** TECHNICAL the period of the year when some male animals, especially DEER, are sexually active

rut² *v.* [I] TECHNICAL if animals, especially DEER, are rutting, they are having sex or are ready to have sex because of the time of year

ru·ta·ba·ga /'rutə,beɪgə/ *n.* [C] a large round yellow vegetable that grows under the ground

Ruth /ruθ/ a book in the Old Testament of the Christian Bible

Ruth, Babe /beɪb/ (1895–1948) a baseball player who is famous for getting more HOME RUNS than anyone before him

Ruth·er·ford /'rʌðɚfɚd/, **Er·nest** /'ɚnɪst/ (1871–1937) a British scientist, born in New Zealand, who

discovered the structure of the atom and was the first person to split the NUCLEUS of an atom

ruth·less /'ruθlɪs/ *adj.* **1** so determined to get what you want that you do not care if you have to hurt other people in order to get it: *You could see the cold, ruthless look in her eyes.* | *a ruthless criminal* **2** determined and firm when making difficult decisions: *He ran the company with ruthless efficiency.* —**ruthlessly** *adv.* —**ruthlessness** *n.* [U]

Rut·ledge /'rʌtlɪdʒ/, **John** (1739–1800) a CHIEF JUSTICE on the U.S. Supreme Court

rut·ted /'rʌtɪd/ *adj.* a surface that is rutted has deep narrow tracks in it left by the wheels of vehicles: *After the snow melted, the roads were rutted and muddy.*

RV *n.* [C] recreational vehicle; a large vehicle, usually with cooking equipment and beds in it, that a family can use for traveling or camping

Rw·an·da /ru'andə/ a country in east central Africa between Tanzania and the Democratic Republic of Congo —**Rwandan** *n., adj.*

Rx. *n.* the written abbreviation of PRESCRIPTION

rye /raɪ/ *n.* [U] **1** a type of grain that is used for making bread and WHISKEY: *rye bread* | *a pastrami sandwich on rye* **2** also **rye whis·key** /'. .../ a type of WHISKEY made from rye: *a bottle of rye*

rye·grass /'raɪgræs/ *n.* [U] a type of grass that is grown as food for animals

R

S

S, s /ɛs/ *n. plural* **S's, s's** [C] **1** the 19th letter of the English alphabet **2** the written abbreviation of "south" or "southern" **3** used to show that a television show has scenes involving sex

-'s /z, s/ INFORMAL **1** the short form of "is": *Alan's on vacation.* | *What's in here?* | *Pam's leaving today.* **2** the short form of "has": *Paul's already left.* **3** a short form of "us," used only in "let's": *Let's go.* **4** INFORMAL a short form of "does," used in questions after "who," "what" etc.: *How's that look?*

sab·ba·tar·i·an /ˌsæbəˈtɛriən/ *n.* [C] FORMAL someone who strongly believes that the Sabbath should be a holy day on which people do not work —**sabbatarian** *adj.*

Sab·bath /ˈsæbəθ/ *n.* **1 the Sabbath a)** Sunday, considered as a day of rest and prayer by most Christian churches **b)** Saturday, considered as a day of rest and prayer in the Jewish religion and some Christian churches **2 keep/break the Sabbath** to obey or not obey the religious rules of this day

sab·bat·i·cal /səˈbætɪkəl/ *n.* [C,U] a period when someone, especially someone in a college or university job, stops doing their usual work in order to study or travel: *He's going* **on sabbatical** *next fall.* —**sabbatical** *adj.*

sa·ber /ˈseɪbɚ/ *n.* [C] **1** a light pointed sword with one sharp edge, used in FENCING **2** a heavy sword with a curved blade, used in past times

saber-rat·tling /ˈ.. ˌ../ *n.* [U] threats to use military force that someone makes, especially when you do not think they are very frightening or serious

Sa·bin /ˈseɪbɪn/**, Al·bert** /ˈælbɚt/ (1906–1993) a U.S. doctor who developed a new VACCINE against POLIO

sa·ble¹ /ˈseɪbəl/ *n.* [C,U] an expensive fur used to make coats, or the small animal that this fur comes from

sable² *adj.* POETIC black or very dark

sab·o·tage¹ /ˈsæbəˌtɑʒ/ *v.* [T] **1** to secretly damage or destroy equipment, vehicles etc. that belong to an enemy or opponent, so that they cannot be used: *The plane's landing gear had been sabotaged.* **2** to deliberately spoil someone's plans because you do not want them to succeed: *Mitchell accused the party of trying to sabotage his campaign.*

sabotage² *n.* [U] the act of deliberately damaging or destroying equipment, vehicles etc. in order to prevent an enemy or opponent from using them: *The rebels stopped their sabotage of the power distribution network.*

sab·o·teur /ˌsæbəˈtɚ/ *n.* [C] someone who deliberately damages, destroys, or spoils someone else's property or activities, in order to prevent them from doing something

sac /sæk/ *n.* [C] TECHNICAL a part inside a plant or animal that is shaped like a bag and contains liquid or air

Sac·a·ja·we·a /ˌsækədʒəˈwiə/ (1786–1812) a Native American woman who acted as a guide to Meriwether LEWIS and William CLARK on their travels from St. Louis to the Pacific Ocean

sac·cha·rin /ˈsækərɪn/ *n.* [U] a chemical substance that tastes sweet and can be used instead of sugar in drinks and foods

sac·cha·rine /ˈsækərɪn/ *adj.* too romantic in a way that seems silly and insincere: *The movie's saccharine ending is a disappointment.*

sac·er·do·tal /ˌsæsɚˈdoʊtl̩, ˌsækɚ-/ *adj.* LITERARY relating or belonging to a priest

sa·chet /sæˈʃeɪ/ *n.* [C] a small bag that contains something that has a nice smell or gives a special taste to food: *a lavender sachet*

sack¹ /sæk/ *n.* [C] **1** a large bag, usually made of paper, that you use for carrying food or other things that you have bought: *a sack of groceries* | *a brown paper sack* **2** a large bag made of strong rough cloth, that you use for storing or carrying flour, coal, vegetables etc.: *a sack of potatoes* **3 hit the sack** SPOKEN to go to bed: *I'm ready to hit the sack.* **4 in the sack** INFORMAL in bed: *Carla caught the two of them in the sack together.* **5** an occasion in a football game when someone makes the QUARTERBACK fall down

sack² *v.* [T] **1** to make the QUARTERBACK fall down in a football game **2** if an army sacks a place, they go through it destroying or stealing things, and attacking people: *The invaders sacked Delphi and founded Galatia.*

   sack out *phr. v.* [I] SPOKEN to go to sleep: *Jill sacked out pretty early last night.*

sack·cloth /ˈsæk-klɔθ/ also **sack·ing** /ˈsækɪŋ/ *n.* [U] **1** rough cloth used for making sacks **2 wear sackcloth and ashes** to behave in a way that shows everyone you are sorry about something you have done wrong

sack race /ˈ. ./ *n.* [C] a race in which the competitors have to jump forward with both legs inside a large cloth bag

sac·ra·ment /ˈsækrəmənt/ *n.* [C] **1 the Sacrament** the bread and wine that are eaten at COMMUNION (1) (=an important Christian ceremony) **2** one of the important Christian ceremonies, such as marriage or communion —**sacramental** /ˌsækrəˈmɛntl̩/ *adj.*

Sac·ra·men·to /ˌsækrəˈmɛntoʊ/ the capital city of the U.S. state of California

sa·cred /ˈseɪkrɪd/ *adj.* **1** relating to a god or religion: *sacred writings* | *sacred rites* —opposite PROFANE¹ **2** greatly respected, or believed to be holy: *These burial grounds are sacred to the Native Americans.* **3** extremely important to you: *Our time at home with our kids is sacred.* **4 is nothing sacred?** SPOKEN used to express shock when something that you think is very important is being changed or harmed: *Look at how those girls are dressed! Is nothing sacred anymore?* —**sacredly** *adv.* —**sacredness** *n.* [U]

sacred cow /ˌ. './ *n.* [C] DISAPPROVING a belief that is so important to some people that they will not let anyone criticize it

sac·ri·fice¹ /ˈsækrəˌfaɪs/ *n.* **1** [C,U] something valuable that you decide not to have, in order to get something that is more important: *Parenthood often calls for sacrifice.* | *David's mother* **made** *many* **sacrifices** *to send him to college.* **2** [C,U] the act of offering something to a god, especially in past times, by killing an animal or a person in a religious ceremony: *They* **made sacrifices to** *their gods to keep them happy.* **3** [C] an object or animal that is offered to a god in a ceremony of sacrifice: *The ceremony included a* **human sacrifice** (=a person killed as a sacrifice). **4** LITERARY **the ultimate/supreme sacrifice** the act of dying while you are fighting for something that you strongly believe in: *These soldiers were prepared to make the ultimate sacrifice in defense of freedom.* **5** a hit in baseball that you make so that a runner can go ahead to the next BASE, even though you are OUT¹ (26) (=not allowed to play anymore at that time): *Puckett's sacrifice let Gladden score.*

sacrifice² *v.* [T] **1** to willingly stop having something you want or stop doing something you like, in order to get something more important: [**sacrifice sth for sth**] *Rugiero was willing to sacrifice his life for his country.* | [**sacrifice sth to do sth**] *Jim sacrificed a television career to stay home with his kids.* **2** to lose or give up something that is important to you: *Her letters reveal the extent to which she had sacrificed her identity.* **3** to offer something or someone to a god as a sacrifice

sac·ri·fi·cial /ˌsækrəˈfɪʃəl◂/ *adj.* **1** relating to or offered as a sacrifice: *a sacrificial ceremony* **2 a sacrificial lamb** someone or something that suffers, loses their job, is destroyed etc., especially unfairly, in order to protect another person, group, or organization: *Domestic textile workers are being used as sacrificial lambs in the nation's efforts to save its trade relations.* —**sacrificially** *adv.*

sac·ri·lege /'sækrəlɪdʒ/ *n.* [C U] **1** the act of treating something holy in a way that does not show respect **2** the act of treating something badly when someone else thinks it is very important: *Sending a guest away with no food is sacrilege to my mother.* —**sacrilegious** /ˌsækrə'lɪdʒəs/ *adj.* —**sacrilegiously** *adv.*

sac·ris·tan /'sækrəstən/ *n.* [C] TECHNICAL someone whose job is to take care of the holy objects in a church

sac·ris·ty /'sækrɪsti/ *n.* [C] TECHNICAL a small room in a church where holy cups and plates are kept, and where priests put on their ceremonial clothes; VESTRY

sac·ro·sanct /'sækrouˌsæŋkt/ *adj.* something that is sacrosanct is considered to be so important that no one is allowed to criticize or change it: *Marriage is no longer sacrosanct – in fact, it isn't even seen as necessary.*

SAD *n.* [U] SEASONAL AFFECTIVE DISORDER

sad /sæd/ *adj.* **sadder**, **saddest 1** unhappy, especially because something bad has happened to you or someone else: *I felt so sad when I heard about Ronald's death.* | [**be sad to do sth**] *We're sad to see him go – he's been a good friend.* | [+ **about**] *Tim was excited about this new opportunity, but sad about leaving.* | **a sad smile/face/expression etc.** *What she remembered most was the sad expression in his eyes.* —opposite HAPPY (1) **2** making you feel unhappy: *My brother told us the sad news.* | **a sad book/song/movie etc.** *She sang a sad, nostalgic song about love.* | **it is sad to see/hear etc.** *It was sad to see all that food going to waste.* | **a sad time/day/moment etc.** *This is a sad day for me and everyone at the company.* **3** very bad or unacceptable: *It's pretty sad that in an Italian restaurant they can't cook pasta well.* | *America's public schools are in a* **sad state.** | **Sad to say**, *many children fail to appreciate their parents until it's too late.* **4 sad sack** INFORMAL someone who is very boring or not skillful at doing things **5 sadder but wiser** having learned something from a bad experience: *He came out of the relationship sadder but wiser.* **6** SPOKEN a sad person is someone who you think is boring, stupid, or very bad at doing something: *You stayed home waiting for him to call? You are so sad.* —**sadness** *n.* [singular, U] —see also SADLY

Sa·dat /sə'dɑt/, **An·war al-** /'ɑnwɑr æl/ (1918–1981) the President of Egypt from 1970 to 1981, who tried to bring peace between the Arabs and Israelis

Sad·dam Hus·sein /sə,dɑm hu'seɪn, ˌsɑdəm/ (1937–) the President of Iraq since 1979

sad·den /'sædn/ *v.* [T] FORMAL to make someone feel sad or disappointed: *It saddens me that the children have been dragged into this mess.*

sad·dle¹ /'sædl/ *n.* **1** [C] a seat made of leather that is put on a horse's back so that someone can ride it **2** [C] a seat on a bicycle or MOTORCYCLE **3 be in the saddle** INFORMAL **a)** to be in a position in which you have power or authority: *Madison is back in the saddle at company headquarters.* **b)** to be riding a horse: *They were weary after many hours in the saddle.*

sad·dle² *v.* [T] to put a saddle on a horse
saddle up *phr. v.* [I,T] to put a saddle on a horse: *We'd better saddle up and get ready to go.*
saddle sb with sth *phr. v.* [T] to give someone a job, problem etc. that is difficult or boring and that they do not want: *My parents had gone out and left me saddled with my little brother for the night.*

sad·dle·bag /'sædl,bæg/ *n.* [C] a bag used for carrying things, that is attached to the saddle on a horse or bicycle

sad·dler /'sædlɚ/ *n.* [C] someone who makes saddles and other leather products

sad·dler·y /'sædləri, 'sædl,ri/ *n.* **1** [C,U] leather goods, such as saddles, made by a saddler, or the store where these are sold **2** [U] the art of making saddles and other leather goods

saddle shoe /'.. ,./ *n.* [C] a shoe that has a toe and heel of one color, with a different color in the middle

saddle soap /'.. ,./ *n.* [U] a type of soap used for cleaning and preserving leather

saddle sore¹ /'.. ,./ *n.* [C usually plural] a sore spot on someone's BUTTOCKs or legs that they get after riding a horse for a long period of time

saddle sore² *adj.* [not before noun] feeling stiff and sore after riding a horse or bicycle

sa·dism /'seɪdɪzəm/ *n.* [U] **1** a way of behaving in which someone gets pleasure from being cruel to someone else: *He looked grim as he recalled the sadism of the prison guards.* **2** a way of behaving in which someone gets sexual pleasure from hurting someone else

sa·dist /'seɪdɪst/ *n.* [C] someone who enjoys being cruel to other people

sa·dis·tic /sə'dɪstɪk/ *adj.* cruel and enjoying making other people suffer: *Carter turned to her with a sadistic glint in his eye.* —**sadistically** /-kli/ *adv.*

sad·ly /'sædli/ *adv.* **1** in a way that shows that you are sad: *Sam looked sadly out the window.* **2** [sentence adverb] UNFORTUNATELY: *Sadly, Anne suffered from emotional problems most of her life.* **3** in a way that makes you sad: *Low wages are sadly typical in service industries.* **4 sadly lacking/neglected etc.** in a way that seems bad or wrong: *Dan's language abilities were sadly lacking.* **5 be sadly mistaken** to be completely wrong about something: *They're sadly mistaken if they think they're going to win.*

sa·do·mas·o·chism /ˌseɪdou'mæsəˌkɪzəm/ *n.* [U] FORMAL the practice of getting sexual pleasure from hurting someone or being hurt —**sadomasochist** *n.* [C] —**sadomasochistic** /ˌseɪdou,mæsə'kɪstɪk/ *adj.*

sa·fa·ri /sə'fɑri/ *n.* [C] **1** a trip through the country areas of eastern or southern Africa, during which you watch wild animals: **go/be on safari** *Amy and John went on safari for their honeymoon.* **2 safari suit/jacket** a suit or JACKET that is made of light-colored material, and usually has a belt and two pockets on the chest

safe¹ /seɪf/ *adj.*
1 not causing harm not likely to cause any physical injury or harm: *Flying is one of the safest forms of travel.* | [**be safe to do sth**] *Is it safe to drink the water?* | [+ **for**] *Make your home safer for your children.* —opposite DANGEROUS
2 not in danger [not before noun] not in danger of being lost, harmed, or stolen: *I feel pretty safe in this building.* | [+ **from**] *Umpires need to be safer from attacks by angry players.* | *Keeping art safe from thieves is a worry for museums everywhere.* | *I pray that I'll be home* **safe and sound** (=unharmed) *with all of you soon.*
3 place a safe place is one where something is not likely to be stolen or lost: *Keep your passport* **in a safe place.**
4 no risk not involving any risk and very likely to succeed: *a safe investment* | *Tom's plan seemed simple and safe.*
5 safe trip/arrival/return etc. a trip etc. that ends safely: *They prayed for their father's safe return.*
6 subject a safe subject of conversation is not likely to upset anyone or make people argue: *She tends to choose safe, politically acceptable topics for her films.*
7 better (to be) safe than sorry SPOKEN used to say that it is better to be careful now, even if this takes time, effort etc., so that nothing bad will happen later: *I think I'll take my umbrella along – better safe than sorry.*
8 be on the safe side to do something especially carefully in order to avoid an bad situation: *Just to be on the safe side, drink bottled water.*
9 be in safe hands to be with someone who will take good care of you: *Parents want to make sure they're leaving their children in safe hands.* —**safely** *adv.*: *Drive safely!* —see also **play it safe** (PLAY¹ (7)), **it's a safe/sure bet (that)** (BET² (5))

safe[2] *n.* [C] a strong metal box or cupboard with special locks where you keep money and valuable things

safe con·duct /,. '../ *n.* [singular,U] official protection for someone when they are passing through a dangerous area: *Rafael was granted safe conduct out of the country.*

safe·crack·er /'seif,krækɚ/ *n.* [C] someone who opens SAFES illegally, in order to steal things from them

safe-de·pos·it box /'. .,.. ,./ *n.* [C] a small box used for storing valuable objects, usually kept in a special room in a bank

safe·guard[1] /'seifgard/ *v.* [I,T] to protect something from harm or damage: *Be sure to safeguard your passport at all times.* | [safeguard (sth) against sth] *Appropriate precautions are needed to safeguard against chemical spills.*

safeguard[2] *n.* [C] something such as a rule, action etc. that is intended to protect someone or something from possible dangers or problems: [+ against] *Save your files regularly as a safeguard against loss of data.*

safe ha·ven /,. '../ *n.* [C,U] a place where someone can go to in order to escape from possible danger or attack

safe house /'. ./ *n.* [C] a house where someone can hide when their enemies are looking for them

safe·keep·ing /,seif'kipiŋ/ *n.* [U] **1 for safekeeping** if you put something somewhere for safekeeping, you put it in a place where it will not get damaged, lost, or stolen: *The artworks are stored in a bank vault for safekeeping.* **2** the state of being in a position or situation where there is no danger of being damaged, lost, or stolen, or the action of putting something in this position: *One of Durie's duties was the safekeeping of legal documents.*

safe sex /,. './ *n.* [U] ways of having sex that reduce the risk of the spread of AIDS and other sexual diseases, especially the use of a CONDOM

S W
2 2 **safe·ty** /'seifti/ *n.*

1 not in danger [U] the state of being safe from danger or harm: *Our job is to maintain safety on the streets.* | *We need to know that we can send our children to school in safety.* | *For safety's sake, keep kids away when deep frying food.*

2 not dangerous [U] the state of not being dangerous or likely to cause harm or injury: *There is concern over the safety of silicone breast implants.* | **safety measures/precautions/checks** (=things that are done in order to make sure that something is safe)

3 sb's safety how safe someone is in a particular situation: *Captain Billings just wants to ensure his passengers' safety.* | *For your safety, have your vehicle serviced regularly.*

4 safe place [U] a place where you are safe from danger: *She finally reached the safety of the shelter.* | **lead/take etc. sb to safety** *We had just enough time to rush the kids to safety.* | *He swam at least 3 miles before he reached safety*

5 there's safety in numbers SPOKEN used to say that a dangerous or bad situation is better if there are a lot of people with you

6 sports [C] TECHNICAL a way of getting two points in football by making the other team put the ball down in its own GOAL (3)

7 gun a small SWITCH on a gun that stops it from being fired by accident

safety belt /'.. ,./ *n.* [C] a SEAT BELT

safety cur·tain /'.. ,../ *n.* [C] a thick curtain that can be lowered at the front of a theater stage to prevent fire from spreading

safety de·pos·it box /'.. .,.. ,./ *n.* [C] a SAFE-DEPOSIT BOX

safety glass /'.. ,./ *n.* [U] **1** strong glass that has been specially heated and cooled so that it breaks into very small pieces that are not sharp, used for example in car windows **2** glass that is made by putting a thin plastic sheet between two pieces of glass, so that if the glass is broken the pieces stay on the plastic

safety lamp /'.. ,./ *n.* [C] a special lamp used by MINERS, that has a flame which will not make gases below the surface of the earth explode

safety match /'.. ,./ *n.* [C] a match that can only be lit by rubbing it along a special surface on the side of its box

safety net /'.. ,./ *n.* [C] **1** a large net that is used to catch someone who is performing high above the ground if they fall **2** a system or arrangement that exists to help you if you have serious problems or get into a difficult situation: *Welfare provides a safety net for people who are unable to work.*

safety pin /'.. ,./ *n.* [C] a curved wire pin with a cover at one end that its point fits into, so that it cannot hurt you accidentally —see picture at PIN[1]

safety ra·zor /'.. ,./ *n.* [C] a RAZOR that has a cover over part of the blade to protect your skin

safety valve /'.. ,./ *n.* [C] **1** a part of a machine that allows gas, steam etc. to be let out when the pressure becomes too great **2** something you do that allows you to express strong feelings such as anger without doing any harm: *Humor can be a safety valve in high pressure situations.*

saf·flow·er /'sæflauɚ/ *n.* [C,U] a plant with orange flowers, grown for its oil which is used in cooking

saf·fron /'sæfrən/ *n.* [U] **1** bright orange thread-like pieces from certain flowers, used in cooking to give food a special taste and orange-yellow color **2** a bright orange-yellow color

sag[1] /sæg/ *v.* **sagged, sagging** [I] **1** to sink or bend down and away from the usual position: *The shelves sagged under the weight of hundreds of records and CDs.* | *His whole body seemed to sag with relief.* **2** to become weaker or less valuable: *Stock prices sagged again today.* | *Edberg seemed to sag after losing the second set.*

sag[2] *n.* [singular,U] a sinking movement or position: *There was a slight sag in the ceiling.*

sa·ga /'sɑgə/ *n.* [C] **1** a long story, especially one that continues over a period of many years: *Chang's novel is the real-life saga of a Chinese family.* **2** INFORMAL a long and complicated series of events, or a description of this: *Getting here from Milwaukee was a real saga.* **3** one of the stories written about the Vikings of Norway and Iceland

sa·ga·cious /sə'geifəs/ *adj.* FORMAL able to understand and judge things very well; WISE[1] (2) —**sagaciously** *adv.*

sa·ga·ci·ty /sə'gæsəti/ *n.* [U] FORMAL good judgment and understanding; WISDOM

Sa·gan /'seigən/, **Carl** /karl/ (1934–1996) a U.S. ASTRONOMER famous for his books and television programs

sage[1] /seidʒ/ *n.* **1** [U] a plant with gray-green leaves that are used in cooking **2** [C] LITERARY someone, especially an old man, who is very wise

sage[2] *adj.* LITERARY very wise, especially as a result of a lot of experience: *sage advice* —**sagely** *adv.*

sage·brush /'seidʒbrʌʃ/ *n.* [U] a small plant that is very common in dry areas in the western U.S.

sag·gy /'sægi/ *adj.* **saggier, saggiest** INFORMAL having a shape that sinks or drops down: *saggy blue socks*

Sag·it·tar·i·us /,sædʒə'tɛriəs/ *n.* **1** [U] the ninth sign of the ZODIAC, represented by an animal that is half-horse and half-human, and believed to affect the character and life of people born between November 22 and December 21 **2** [C] someone who was born between November 22 and December 21

sa·gua·ro /sə'gwarou/ *n. plural* **saguaros** [C] a type of large CACTUS (=plant with many sharp points, that grows in dry areas) with branches that curve up, that grows in the southwestern U.S.

Sa·har·a, the /sə'hærə/ also **the Sahara Des·ert** /,... '../ the world's largest desert which covers a very large area of North Africa

said[1] /sɛd/ *v.* the past tense and past participle of SAY[1]

said[2] *adj.* [only before noun] LAW mentioned before: *It seems likely that said person has committed similar offenses in the past.*

sail[1] /seɪl/ *v.* **1** [I always + adv./prep.,T] to travel across an area of water in a boat or ship: *The Pequod sailed toward the island.* | *We'll sail from Miami to Nassau.* | *I just want to quit my job and sail the South Pacific.* **2** [I,T] to direct or control the movement of a boat or ship: *There was a picture of Dick sailing his boat in the Caribbean.* | *My father taught me to sail when I was 14.* **3** [I] to start a trip by boat or ship: *The ship sailed at dusk.* | [+ for] *What year did Columbus sail for the New World?* **4** [I always + adv./prep.] to move quickly and smoothly through the air: *Jeff ducked as the ball sailed past his head.* **5** [I always + adv./prep.] to move forward gracefully and confidently: *She sailed by without looking at him.*

sail through *phr. v.* [I,T] to succeed very easily on a test or in a competition, a difficult process etc. *The Paperwork Reduction Act sailed through Congress without much opposition.*

sail[2] *n.* [C] **1** a large piece of strong cloth attached to the MAST (=tall pole) of a boat, so that the wind will push the boat along: **raise/lower the sails** (=put the sails up or down) **2 set sail (for sth)** to begin a trip by boat or ship: *We set sail for Savannah in the morning.* **3 under sail** LITERARY moving along on a ship or boat that has sails

sail·board /'seɪlbɔrd/ *n.* [C] a flat board with a sail, that you stand on in the sport of WINDSURFING

sail·board·ing /'seɪlbɔrdɪŋ/ *n.* [U] WINDSURFING —**sailboarder** *n.* [C]

sail·boat /'seɪlboʊt/ *n.* [C] a boat with one or more sails, that is moved by the wind

sail·ing /'seɪlɪŋ/ *n.* **1** [U] the sport or activity of traveling in or controlling a small boat with sails: *Visitors to the resort can go sailing in the clear waters off the island.* **2 sth is smooth/clear sailing** used to say that a situation is not causing problems and is easy to deal with: *The bill should have smooth sailing in the Senate.* **3** [C] a time when a passenger ship leaves a port: *Luckily, there was another sailing at 2 o'clock that afternoon.*

sailing ship /'.. ,./ also **sailing ves·sel** /'.. ,../ *n.* [C] a large ship with sails

sail·or /'seɪlɚ/ *n.* [C] **1** someone who works on a ship, especially a member of a navy **2 a good/bad sailor** someone who does or does not feel sick when they are in a boat

sailor suit /'.. ,./ *n.* [C] a blue and white suit that looks like an old-fashioned sailor's uniform, worn by small boys

saint /seɪnt/ *n.* [C] **1** *abbreviation* St. someone who is given a special honor by the Christian church after they have died, because they were very good or holy: *Saint Patrick* **2** INFORMAL someone who is extremely good, kind, or patient: *Thanks so much for doing that. You're a saint.* **3 sb is no saint** used to say that someone has done some bad things and is not an honest person: *He may have been successful, but Taylor was definitely no saint.* —see also **the patience of a saint** (PATIENCE (3))

saint·ed /'seɪntɪd/ *adj.* **1** [only before noun] LITERARY having been made a saint by the Christian church **2** HUMOROUS someone who is sainted is extremely good, kind, or patient, often in a way that people find annoying

saint·hood /'seɪnthʊd/ *n.* [U] the state of being a saint

saint·ly /'seɪntli/ *adj.* **saintlier, saintliest** seeming to be completely good and honest, with no faults: *She was a simple, loving and saintly woman.* —**saintliness** *n.* [U]

Saint Pat·rick's Day /seɪnt 'pætrɪks ,deɪ/ *n.* [C,U] a holiday on March 17 when people, especially people whose families originally came from Ireland, wear green clothes and honor Saint Patrick

Saint-Saëns /sæn'sɑns/, **Ca·mille** /kæ'mil/ (1835–1921) a French musician who wrote CLASSICAL music

saint's day /'. ./ *n.* [C] the day of the year when the Christian church remembers a particular SAINT

saith /'seɪəθ, sɛθ/ OLD USE says

sake[1] /seɪk/ *n.* [U] **1 for the sake of sb/sth** also **for sb's/sth's sake** in order to help, improve, or please someone or something: *They tried to keep their marriage together for the sake of the children.* | *She reluctantly agreed to go for James' sake.* **2 for God's/Christ's/goodness'/Heaven's etc. sake** SPOKEN said when you are annoyed, surprised, impatient etc.: *I was coming to that – for God's sake, be patient!* **3 for its own sake** because of the thing itself, not for any other reason: *Weber says he is interested in writing for its own sake – an uncommon attitude in Hollywood these days.* **4 for the sake of it** if you do something for the sake of it, you do it because you want to and not for any particular reason: *He was just talking for the sake of it.* **5 for the sake of argument** SPOKEN if you say something for the sake of argument, what you say may not be true, but it will help you to have a discussion: *Let's just say, for the sake of argument, that you've got $5,000 to invest.*

sake[2] /'sɑkeɪ/ *n.* [U] a Japanese alcoholic drink made from rice, usually served warm in small cups

Sa·kha·rov /'sɑkərɔf/, **An·drei** /'ɑndreɪ/ (1921–1989) a Russian scientist who helped to develop the Soviet HYDROGEN BOMB and was also known for his criticism of the Soviet government

sal·a·ble, saleable /'seɪləbəl/ *adj.* something that is salable can be sold, or is easy to sell: *It will be two years before the trees produce a salable crop.* —**salability** /,seɪlə'bɪləti/ *n.* [U]

sa·la·cious /sə'leɪʃəs/ *adj.* showing too much interest in sex: *The tabloid newspapers love salacious gossip.* —**salaciously** *adv.* —**salaciousness** *n.* [U]

sal·ad /'sæləd/ *n.* [C,U] **1** a mixture of raw vegetables, especially one that has LETTUCE in it: *a salad bowl* | *Serve hot, accompanied by a tomato and cucumber salad.* | *Can you toss the salad* (=mix it all together) *and take it to the table?* **2** raw or cooked food that is cut into small pieces and served cold: *potato salad*

salad bar /'.. ,./ *n.* [C] a place in a restaurant where you can make your own salad

salad days /'.. ,./ *n.* [plural] OLD-FASHIONED the time of your life when you are young and not very experienced

salad dress·ing /'.. ,../ *n.* [C,U] a SAUCE that you put on SALADS to give them a special taste

sal·a·man·der /'sælə,mændɚ/ *n.* [C] a small animal similar to a LIZARD, which lives in water and on land

sa·la·mi /sə'lɑmi/ *n.* [C,U] a large SAUSAGE with a strong taste, that is eaten cold in thin SLICES

sal·a·ried /'sælərid/ *adj.* **1** salaried workers receive a salary, rather than being paid for the number of hours they have worked **2** a salaried job or position is one for which a worker is paid a salary

sal·a·ry /'sæləri/ *n. plural* **salaries** [C,U] money that you receive as payment from the organization or business you work for, paid to you at regular times, for example every two weeks: *How can they afford that car on Todd's salary?* | *He reportedly earns an annual salary of $20 million.* —compare WAGE[1] (1) —see Usage Note at PAY[2]

sal·a·ry·man /'sælərimæn/ *n. plural* **salarymen** /-mɛn/ [C] a man who works in an office in Japan, often for many hours every day

sale /seɪl/ *n.*
1 act of selling [C,U] the act of giving property or other goods to someone in exchange for money: *Deb's biggest sale today was a guitar for $500.* | [+ of] *The 18th Amendment banned the manufacture and sale of alcohol.* | *Every time Harvey makes a sale, he gets $50 commission.*
2 for sale available to be bought: *Sorry, the decorations aren't for sale.* | *The airline was recently put up for sale* (=made available to be bought).
3 lower prices [C] a period of time when stores sell their goods at lower prices than usual: *All the Christmas sales start right after Thanksgiving.*

4 on sale a) available to be bought at a lower price than usual: *I got my shoes on sale for half price.* **b)** available to be bought: **be/go on sale** *Tickets for the concert will go on sale in June.*

5 sales a) [plural] the total number of products that a company sells during a particular period of time: *We're expecting sales to top $5 million this year.* | *sales figures* **b)** [U] the part of a company that deals with selling products: *She works as sales manager at a magazine.* | *Are you interested in a career in sales?*

6 available to buy [C] an occasion when people bring particular things to a place in order to sell them: *a craft sale*

7 garage/yard sale an occasion when people sell things they do not want or use anymore, that takes place in the area outside their house

8 offering prices [C] an event at which things are sold to the person who offers the highest price; AUCTION[1]: *an exhibit and sale of Chinese art*

9 sales drive/campaign an effort made by a company to try to increase the number of products it sells

10 sales pitch/talk the things that someone says when they are trying to persuade you to buy something —see also BILL OF SALE, POINT OF SALE

sale·a·ble /ˈseɪləbəl/ *adj.* another spelling of SALABLE

Sa·lem /ˈseɪləm/ **1** the capital city of the U.S. state of Oregon **2** a town in the U.S. state of Massachusetts, famous for the Salem Witch Trials in 1692, when many women were taken to a court of law and then officially killed for using magic

sales·clerk /ˈseɪlzklɚk/ *n.* [C] someone who sells things in a store

sales·girl /ˈseɪlzgɚl/ *n.* [C] OLD-FASHIONED a young woman who sells things in a store

sales·man /ˈseɪlzmən/ *n. plural* **salesmen** /-mən/ [C] a man whose job is selling things, especially by persuading people to buy his company's products

sales·man·ship /ˈseɪlzmənˌʃɪp/ *n.* [U] the skill of selling something or making someone interested in buying something: *Many stores spend too much on technology and too little on salesmanship and service.*

sales·per·son /ˈseɪlzˌpɚsən/ *n.* [C] someone whose job is selling things, especially by persuading people to buy their company's products

sales rep·re·sent·a·tive /ˈ. ..,.../ *also* **sales rep** /ˈ. ./ *n.* [C] someone who travels around, usually within a particular area, selling their company's products

sales slip /ˈ. ./ *n.* [C] a small piece of paper that has the amount something cost printed on it, that you are given in a store when you buy something; RECEIPT (1)

sales tax /ˈ. ./ *n.* [C,U] a tax that you have to pay in addition to the cost of something you are buying

sales·wom·an /ˈseɪlzˌwʊmən/ *n. plural* **saleswomen** /-ˌwɪmɪn/ [C] a woman whose job is selling things, especially by persuading people to buy her company's products

sa·li·ent /ˈseɪliənt/ *adj.* FORMAL the salient points or features of something are the most important or most noticeable parts of it: *Four salient points emerged from our study* —**salience** *n.* [U]

sa·line¹ /ˈseɪlin, -laɪn/ *adj* containing or consisting of salt: *saline solution* —**salinity** /səˈlɪnəti/ *n.* [U]

saline² *n.* [U] a special mixture of water and salt, used in medical treatment

Sal·in·ger /ˈsælɪndʒɚ/, **J.D.** /dʒeɪ di/ (1919–) a U.S. writer best known for his book "The Catcher in the Rye"

Salis·bur·y steak /ˌsɔlzbəri ˈsteɪk, ˌsælz-, -bəri/ *n.* [C] a food made of GROUND BEEF that is formed into a large flat shape, mixed with SPICEs, and cooked

Sa·lish /ˈseɪlɪʃ/ a group of Native American tribes from the northwestern U.S. and western Canada that speak the same language

sa·li·va /səˈlaɪvə/ *n.* [U] the liquid that is produced naturally in your mouth

sal·i·var·y gland /ˈsæləˌvɛri ˌglænd/ *n.* [C] a part of your mouth that produces saliva

sal·i·vate /ˈsæləˌveɪt/ *v.* [I] **1** to produce more saliva in your mouth than usual, especially because you see or smell food **2** HUMOROUS to be very interested or eager to do something or try something: *Investors are salivating at the thought of a vast new market.* —**salivation** /ˌsæləˈveɪʃən/ *n.* [U]

Salk /sɔk, sɔlk/, **Jo·nas** /ˈdʒoʊnəs/ (1914–1995) a U.S. scientist famous for producing the first successful VACCINE against POLIO

sal·low /ˈsæloʊ/ *adj.* sallow skin looks slightly yellow and unhealthy —**sallowness** *n.* [U]

sal·ly¹ /ˈsæli/ *n.* [C] **1** an amusing intelligent remark **2** a sudden quick attack and return to a position of defense

sally² *v.* **sallied, sallying**
sally forth *phr. v.* [I] to leave somewhere that is safe in order to do something that you expect to be difficult or dangerous: *Several members of Congress sallied forth with a tough message for the leaders of the tobacco industry.*

salm·on /ˈsæmən/ *n.* [C,U] **1** *plural* **salmon** a large fish with silver skin and pink flesh that lives in the ocean but swims up rivers to lay its eggs, or the meat of this fish **2** [U] a pink-orange color

sal·mo·nel·la /ˌsælməˈnɛlə/ *n.* [U] a type of BACTERIA in food, especially chicken or eggs, that makes you sick

sa·lon /səˈlɑn/ *n.* [C] **1** a place where you can get your hair cut, have beauty treatments etc.: *a beauty salon* **2** a store where fashionable and expensive clothes are sold: *a bridal salon* **3** OLD-FASHIONED a room in a very large house where people can meet and talk **4** a regular meeting of famous people at which they talk about art, literature, or music

sa·loon /səˈlun/ *n.* [C] **1** a public place where alcoholic drinks were sold and drunk in the western U.S. in the 19th century **2** a large comfortable room on a ship, especially in past times, where passengers could sit and relax

sal·sa /ˈsælsə, ˈsɔl-/ *n.* **1** [U] a SAUCE usually made from onions, TOMATOes and CHILIes, that you put on Mexican food —compare PICANTE SAUCE **2** [C,U] a type of Latin American music, or the dance done to this music

salt¹ /sɔlt/ *n.* **1** [U] a natural white mineral, usually in the form of very small grains, that is added to food to make it taste better or to preserve it: *Season the sauce with salt and pepper.* | *a pinch of salt* —see also ROCK SALT, SEA SALT, TABLE SALT **2 the salt of the earth** someone who is ordinary, but good and honest **3** [C] TECHNICAL a type of chemical substance that is formed when an acid is combined with a BASE[2] (12) **4 old salt** a SAILOR who has had a lot of experience sailing on the ocean —see also BATH SALTS, EPSOM SALTS, **take sth with a grain of salt** (GRAIN (6)), **rub salt into a wound** (RUB[1] (8)), SMELLING SALTS, **worth his/her salt** (WORTH[1] (10))

salt² *v.* [T] **1** to add salt to food to make it taste better **2** to add salt to food to preserve it **3** to put salt on the roads to prevent them from becoming icy
salt sth ↔ away *phr. v.* [T] to save money for the future: *They had salted away over $45 million in overseas bank accounts.*

salt³ *adj.* [only before noun] **1** preserved by salt: *salt pork* **2** consisting of SALTWATER: *a salt lake*

salt-and-pep·per /ˌ. . ˈ../ *adj.* colored with small areas of black and white mixed together: *a salt-and-pepper beard*

salt·box /ˈsɔltˌbɑks/ *n.* [C] a house that has two levels in front and one level in back

salt cel·lar /ˈ. ˌ../ *n.* [C] a small bowl used for holding salt on a table

sal·tine /sɔlˈtin/ *n.* [C] a type of CRACKER (=thin hard dry bread) with salt on top of it

J. D. Salinger

Salt Lake Cit·y /ˌ. .ˈ../ the capital and largest city of the U.S. state of Utah

salt·pe·ter /ˌsɔltˈpitɚ/ n. [U] a substance used in making GUNPOWDER (=powder that causes explosions) and matches

salt shak·er /ˈ. ˌ../ n. [C] a small container for salt, with holes in the top

salt truck /ˈ. ./ n. [C] a large vehicle that puts salt or sand on the roads in the winter to make them less icy

salt·wa·ter¹, salt water /ˈsɔltˌwɔtɚ/ n. [U] water that contains salt, especially naturally in the ocean

saltwater² adj. [only before noun] living in salty water or in the ocean: saltwater fish —compare FRESHWATER

salt·y /ˈsɔlti/ adj. **saltier, saltiest 1** tasting like or containing salt: The soup is a little too salty. **2** OLD-FASHIONED using language that is slightly impolite or about sex, but which you think is amusing: She's a surprisingly salty lady.

sa·lu·bri·ous /səˈlubriəs/ adj. FORMAL pleasant and good for your health: the salubrious climate of northern Italy

sal·u·ta·ry /ˈsælyəˌtɛri/ adj. FORMAL a salutary experience has a positive result or teaches you something, although it is often unpleasant: The war could have a salutary effect on other countries in the region.

sal·u·ta·tion /ˌsælyəˈteɪʃən/ n. **1** [C] a word or phrase used at the beginning of a letter or speech, such as "Dear Mr. Smith" **2** [C,U] FORMAL something you say or do when greeting someone

sa·lu·ta·to·ri·an /səˌlutəˈtɔriən/ n. [C] a student who has received the second-best grades in their class all through high school or college, and who usually gives a speech at the GRADUATION ceremony —compare VALEDICTORIAN

sa·lute¹ /səˈlut/ v. **1** [I,T] to move your right hand to your head in order to show respect to an officer in the Army, Navy etc.: He turned around and saluted the captain. | It's against their religion to salute the U.S. flag. **2** [T] to praise someone for the things they have achieved, especially publicly: [salute sb as sth] Bush saluted Madison as "the father of our Constitution." | [salute sb for sth] Today we salute these citizens for their commitment to our community.

salute² n. [C] **1** an act of raising your right hand to your head as a sign of respect, usually done by a soldier to an officer **2** something that expresses praise to someone for something they have achieved, or that expresses honor or respect to something: [a salute to sb/sth] Our program is a musical salute to Hollywood movies of the 1940's. **3** an occasion when guns are fired into the air in order to show respect for someone important: a 21-gun salute

sal·vage¹ /ˈsælvɪdʒ/ v. [T] **1** to save something from a situation in which other things have already been damaged, destroyed, or lost: [salvage sth from sth] They stood clutching the possessions they had salvaged from their homes. **2** to do something to make sure that you do not completely fail or lose something: Some observers doubt whether the peace process can be salvaged. | He fought to salvage his reputation (=do something so that he would not lose people's respect).

salvage² n. [U] **1** the act of saving things from a situation in which other things have already been damaged, destroyed, or lost: The developers have planned for the salvage and reuse of the building's decorations. **2** things that have been saved in this way: We found the statue in a local salvage yard.

sal·va·tion /sælˈveɪʃən/ n. [U] **1** the state of being saved from evil or death in the Christian religion **2** something that prevents danger, loss, or failure: Construction of the factory proved to be the salvation of the local economy.

Salvation Ar·my /ˌ..ˈ../ n. **the Salvation Army** a Christian organization that tries to help poor people

salve¹ /sæv/ n. [C,U] **1** a substance that you put on sore skin to make it less painful **2** something you do to reduce bad feelings in a situation: Our goal is to provide a salve for consumers' fears.

salve² v. [T] **salve your conscience/feelings/ego** to do something to make yourself or someone else feel less guilty or less emotionally hurt: Baker was convinced that Nelson needed a new challenge to help salve his grief.

sal·ver /ˈsælvɚ/ n. [C] a large metal plate used for serving food or drinks at a formal meal: a silver salver

sal·vo /ˈsælvoʊ/ n. plural **salvos** or **salvoes** [C] **1** the firing of several guns during a battle or as part of a ceremony: [+ of] Just then, snipers let off a salvo of automatic gunfire. **2** one of a series of questions, statements etc. that you use to try to win an argument or competition: He directed a series of verbal salvos at his opponent during the debate. | This could be the **opening salvo** of a campaign to get the arena built elsewhere.

Sa·mar·i·tan /səˈmærətn/ also **good Samaritan** n. [C] someone who helps you when you have problems or are in a difficult situation

sam·ba /ˈsɑmbə, ˈsæm-/ n. [C,U] a fast dance from Brazil, or the type of music played for this dance

same¹ /seɪm/ adj. [only before noun] **1 the same person/place/thing etc. a)** one particular person, thing etc. and not a different one: Harry and I went to the same school. | [+ as] Don't worry if large items aren't picked up on the same day as your garbage. | **the same... (that)** Put the book back in the same place you took it from. **b)** used to say two or more people, things etc. are exactly like each other: I know how you feel – I have the same problem. | They both have the same hairstyle. | [+ as] He gets the same grades as I do, but he never studies. | **the same... (that)** Brenda came in wearing the same dress that Jean had on. **2 at the same time a)** if two things happen at the same time, they both happen together: We both started talking at the same time. **b)** used to introduce a fact which must also be considered: The media's criticism can be hard to take. But at the same time, we've got to keep doing our jobs. **3 the same old person/place/thing** INFORMAL used to say that a particular person or thing does not change: It's just the same old boring routine at work every day. | He's still the same old Jerry. **4 the very/exact same** SPOKEN, INFORMAL used when you are surprised that someone or something is the same person or thing and not a different one: The exact same thing happened to Linda yesterday. **5 same difference** SPOKEN used to say that different actions, behavior etc. have the same result or effect: "We'll have to use lemons instead of limes." "Same difference." **6 by the same token** in the same way, or for the same reasons: I want to win, but by the same token, I don't want to hurt Sam's confidence. **7 be on the same page** SPOKEN used to say that two or more people understand each other and are thinking about something in the same way: I just want to make sure we're all on the same page before we start. **8 same old, same old** SPOKEN used to say that a situation has not changed at all: "How are you doing, Dave?" "Same old, same old." **9 be in the same boat** be in the same difficult situation that someone else is in —see also **amount to the same thing** (AMOUNT² (4))

USAGE NOTE: SAME

GRAMMAR
Remember that the adjective **same** always has "the" or "this," "that" etc. before it: We all ordered the same thing. | He's driving back to Fairview that same night.

same² pron. **1 the same a)** someone or something that is exactly like another: Oranges are an excellent source of vitamin C. The same is true for strawberries and spinach. | Temperatures were in the mid-80s today; expect **more of the same** for the weekend. **b)** someone or something that does not change: Things just won't be the same without you around. **2 just/all the same** in spite of a particular situation, opinion etc.: The potatoes were a little overcooked, but

delicious all the same. **3 (and the) same to you!**
SPOKEN used as a friendly reply to a greeting, or as
an angry reply to an impolite remark: *"Have a happy
New Year!" "Thanks – same to you."* | *"You jerk! I
hope you get run over!" "Same to you!"*—see also **it's
all the same to sb** (ALL² (13)), **one and the same**
(ONE² (20))

same³ *adv.* **1 the same (as sth)** in the same way:
*"Pain" and "pane" are both pronounced exactly the
same.* | *I used your recipe, but my cookies don't taste
the same as yours.* **2 same as sb** SPOKEN just like
someone else: *He works hard, same as you.* **3 same
here** SPOKEN used to say that you feel the same way as
someone else: *"I'm really thirsty." "Yeah, same here."*

same·ness /ˈseɪmnɪs/ *n.* [U] a boring lack of variety,
or the quality of being very similar to something else

same-sex /ˌ. ˈ.◂/ *adj.* **same-sex marriage/relation-
ship etc.** a marriage, relationship etc. between two
men or two women

Sa·mo·a /səˈmoʊə/—see AMERICAN SAMOA, WESTERN
SAMOA —**Samoan** *n., adj.*

sam·o·var /ˈsæməvɑr/ *n.* [C] a large metal container
used in Russia to boil water for making tea

sam·pan /ˈsæmpæn/ *n.* [C] a small boat used in China
and Southeast Asia

s w **sam·ple¹** /ˈsæmpəl/ *n.* [C] **1** a small part or amount
3 3 of something that is examined in order to find out
something about the whole thing: [+ **of**] *I'll need to
look at a sample of his handwriting.* | **blood/urine/
water etc. sample** *Montzka's study is based on air
samples taken in seven locations.* **2** a small amount
of a product that people can try in order to find out
what it is like: [+ **of**] *They were giving out free samples of ice cream at the store.* **3** a group of people who
have been chosen to give information or answers to
questions: *The sample consisted of 344 elementary
school teachers.* | *The survey was based on telephone
interviews with a **random sample** (=one in which
you choose people without knowing anything about
them) of Americans.* | *We selected a **representative
sample** (=one that is planned to include several different types of people) of 650 students and asked them
to rate teaching techniques.* **4** a small part of a song
from a CD or record that is used in a new song

sample² *v.* [T] **1** to try a small amount of food, go to
a place, try an activity etc. in order to see what it is
like: *I decided to sample the chocolate cheesecake.* |
*You should sample the local nightlife while you're
here.* —see Usage Note at TASTE² **2** [often passive] to
choose some people from a larger group in order to
ask them questions or get information: *The results are
based on a poll of 1000 randomly sam-
pled adults.* **3** to use a small part of a song from a
CD or record in a new song

sam·pler /ˈsæmplə/ *n.* [C] **1** a piece of cloth with different stitches on it, made to show how good someone is at sewing **2** a set of small amounts of each
different type of something: *The chef made up a
dessert sampler platter for us.*

Samp·ras /ˈsæmprəs/, **Pete** /pit/ (1971–) a U.S.
tennis player

Sam·u·el /ˈsæmyuəl/ **1 Samuel, 2 Samuel** two books
in the Old Testament of the Christian Bible

sam·u·rai /ˈsæmʊˌraɪ/ *n. plural* **samurai** [C] a
member of a powerful military class in Japan in past
times —**samurai** *adj.: a samurai sword*

Sa·n'a /sæˈnɑ/ the capital city of Yemen

san·a·to·ri·um /ˌsænəˈtɔriəm/ *n.* [C] a type of hospital for sick people who are getting better but still
need rest and a lot of care, especially in past times
when many people suffered from TUBERCULOSIS (=a
serious disease of the lungs)

sanc·ti·fy /ˈsæŋktəˌfaɪ/ *v.* **sanctified, sanctifying** [T]
1 to make something holy **2** to make something
socially or religiously acceptable, or to give something official approval: *These arbitrary customs have
been sanctified over a long time.* —**sanctification**
/ˌsæŋktəfəˈkeɪʃən/ *n.* [U]

sanc·ti·mo·ni·ous /ˌsæŋktəˈmoʊniəs/ *adj.* behaving
as if you are morally better than other people, in a
way that is annoying: *Many sanctimonious speeches
were made about the need for honesty in government.*
—**sanctimoniously** *adv.* —**sanctimoniousness** *n.* [U]

sanc·tion¹ /ˈsæŋkʃən/ *n.* **1 sanctions** [plural] official
orders or laws stopping trade, communication etc.
with another country, as a way of forcing its leaders
to make political changes: [+ **against**] *International
sanctions against Iraq are still in force.* | *Several
countries **imposed sanctions on** (=started using
sanctions against) Yugoslavia in an attempt to stop
the fighting.* | *The government is not yet ready to **lift
these sanctions** (=stop using them).* **2** [U] official
permission, approval, or acceptance: *He acted without religious or government sanction.* **3** [C] a form of
punishment that can be used if someone disobeys a
rule or law: *The court **imposed** the harshest possible
sanction.*

sanction² *v.* [T] FORMAL **1** to officially accept or
allow something: *Gambling will be not be sanctioned
in any form.* **2 be sanctioned by sth** to be made
acceptable by something: *The social hierarchy was
determined by birth and sanctioned by religion.*

sanc·ti·ty /ˈsæŋktəti/ *n.* [U] **1 the sanctity of life/
marriage etc.** the quality that makes life, marriage
etc. so important that it must be respected and preserved: *We wish to respect traditional values and the
sanctity of human life.* **2** FORMAL the holy or religious character of a person or place: *Numerous miracles were proof of his sanctity.*

sanc·tu·ar·y /ˈsæŋktʃuˌɛri/ *n. plural* **sanctuaries**
1 [U] safety and protection from danger, or protection from police, soldiers etc.: *He is suspected of
giving sanctuary to terrorists.* | **find/seek sanctu-
ary** *Hundreds of civilians have sought sanctuary at
churches and embassies.* **2** [C] a place that is safe
and provides protection, especially for people who
are in danger: *The center is a sanctuary for battered
women.* **3** [C] an area for birds or animals where
they are protected and cannot be hunted: **bird/
wildlife etc. sanctuary** *Radioactive waste is threatening the marine sanctuary.* **4** [C] the part of a
church where Christian religious services take place
5 [C] the part of a religious building that is considered to be the most holy

sanc·tum /ˈsæŋktəm/ *n.* [C] **1 inner sanctum** HUMOR-
OUS a place or room that only a few important people
are allowed to enter: *He was soon accepted into the
inner sanctums of city government.* **2** also **sanctum
sanc·to·rum** /-sæŋkˈtɔrəm/ a holy place inside a
TEMPLE

sand¹ /sænd/ *n.* [U] **1** a substance consisting of very **s w**
small grains of rocks and minerals, that forms **2**
beaches and deserts and is part of soil and CONCRETE:
*The neighbors' children played happily in the
sand.* **2 the sands of time** LITERARY moments of time
that pass quickly **3** a light yellowish or grayish
brown color

sand² *v.* **1** [I,T] also **sand down** to make a surface **s w**
smooth by rubbing it with SANDPAPER or using a spe- **3**
cial piece of equipment **2** [T] to put sand onto an icy
road to make it safer

san·dal /ˈsændl/ *n.* [C] a light open shoe that is fastened onto your foot by bands of leather, cloth etc.,
and that is worn in warm weather —see picture at
SHOE¹

san·dal·wood /ˈsændlˌwʊd/ *n.* [U] wood from a
southern Asian tree that has a strong smell, or the
oil from this wood, which is often used in PERFUMES

sand·bag¹ /ˈsændbæg/ *n.* [C] a bag filled with sand,
which is used for protection against floods, explosions etc.

sandbag² *v.* **sandbagged, sandbagging** **1** [I,T] to
build walls with sandbags in order to protect a
place from a flood, explosion etc. **2** [T] to treat someone unfairly in order to prevent them from doing
something or being successful: *Morley accused
Franklin of sandbagging him by not telling him the
full story.*

sand·bank /ˈsændbæŋk/ *n.* [C] a raised area of sand
in or by a river, ocean etc.

sand·bar /'sændbɑr/ n. [C] a long pile of sand in a river or the ocean formed by the movement of the water

sand·blast /'sændblæst/ v. [T] to clean or polish metal, stone, glass etc. with a machine that sends out a powerful stream of sand

sand·box /'sændbɑks/ n. [C] a special box or area with clean sand for children to play in

Sand·burg /'sændbɚg/, **Carl** /'kɑrl/ (1878–1967) a U.S. writer and poet

sand·cas·tle /'sænd,kæsəl/ n. [C] a small model of a castle made out of wet sand, usually built by children playing on a beach

sand dune /'. ./ n. [C] a hill of sand formed by the wind in a desert or near the ocean —see picture on page 428

sand·er /'sændɚ/ also **sanding ma·chine** /'.. .,./ n. [C] an electric tool with a rough surface that moves very quickly, used for making surfaces smooth

sand fly /'. ./ n. [C] a small fly that bites people and lives on beaches

S & L /,ɛs ən 'ɛl/ n. [C] INFORMAL a SAVINGS AND LOAN ASSOCIATION

sand·lot /'sændlɑt/ n. [C] an area of empty land in a town or city, where children often play sports or games: **sandlot baseball/volleyball etc.** (=an informal sports game played on a sandlot) —compare PARK¹ (1)

sand·man /'sændmæn/ n. **the sandman** an imaginary man who is supposed to make children go to sleep by putting sand in their eyes

sand·pa·per¹ /'sænd,peipɚ/ n. [U] strong paper covered on one side with sand or a similar substance, that you rub on wood in order to make the surface smooth

sandpaper² v. [T] to rub something with sandpaper

sand·pip·er /'sænd,paipɚ/ n. [C] a small bird with long legs and a long beak that lives around muddy or sandy shores

sand·stone /'sændstoun/ n. [U] a type of soft yellow or red rock, often used in buildings

sand·storm /'sændstorm/ n. [C] a storm in the desert in which sand is blown around by strong winds

sand trap, sandtrap /'. ./ n. [C] a hollow place on a GOLF COURSE, filled with sand, from which it is difficult to hit the ball

sand·wich¹ /'sændwɪtʃ/ n. [C] two pieces of bread with cheese, meat etc. between them: *a ham and egg sandwich* —see also CLUB SANDWICH, **give sb a knuckle sandwich** (KNUCKLE¹ (3)), OPEN-FACED SANDWICH

sandwich² v. **be sandwiched between sth** to be in a very small space between two other things: *I sat there, sandwiched between two huge women.*

sandwich board /'.. ,./ n. [C] two boards with advertisements or messages on them that hang in front and behind someone as they walk around in public

sand·y /'sændi/ adj. **sandier, sandiest 1** covered with sand: *a sandy beach* **2** hair that is sandy is a yellowish-brown color —**sandiness** n. [U]

sane /sein/ adj. **1** mentally healthy and able to think in a normal and reasonable way —opposite INSANE **2** reasonable and using or showing sensible thinking: *Mass transit is the only sane way to get around New York.* | *No sane person would accept a high-level job there.* —**sanely** adv. —see also SANITY

San Fran·cis·co /,sæn frən'sɪskou/ a city in the U.S. state of California which is built on hills next to the Pacific Ocean

San Francisco Bay /,. ... './ an INLET of the Pacific Ocean on the western coast of the U.S. in the state of California

sang /sæŋ/ v. the past tense of SING

Sang·er /'sæŋɚ/, **Mar·garet** /'mɑrgrɪt/ (1883–1966) a U.S. woman who started the attempt to make BIRTH CONTROL available to everyone in the U.S.

sang-froid /,sæŋ'fwɑ/ n. [U] FORMAL courage and the ability to keep calm in dangerous or difficult situations

San·gre de Cris·to Mountains, the /,sɑŋgrei də 'krɪstou/ a RANGE of mountains in the southwestern

U.S. that is part of the Rocky Mountains and runs from Colorado to New Mexico

san·gri·a /sæŋ'griə, sæn-/ n. [U] a drink made from red wine, fruit, and fruit juice

san·gui·na·ry /'sæŋgwə,nɛri/ adj. LITERARY involving violence and killing: *a bitter and sanguinary war*

san·guine /'sæŋgwɪn/ adj. FORMAL **1** cheerful and hopeful about the future; CONFIDENT: *Traders are taking a sanguine view of interest-rate prospects.* **2** red and healthy looking: *a sanguine complexion* —**sanguinely** adv.

san·i·tar·i·um /,sænə'tɛriəm/ n. [C] another spelling of SANATORIUM

san·i·tar·y /'sænə,tɛri/ adj. **1** clean and not involving any danger to your health: *All food should be prepared under sanitary conditions.* **2** [only before noun] relating to health, especially the removal of dirt, infection, or human waste: *We didn't even have sanitary facilities* (=toilets) *in the fields.*

sanitary land·fill /,.... './ n. [C] a place where waste is buried under the ground; DUMP

sanitary nap·kin /,.... './ also **sanitary pad** /,.... './ n. [C] a piece of soft material that a woman wears in her underwear for the blood when she has her PERIOD¹ (4)

san·i·ta·tion /,sænə'teiʃən/ n. [U] the protection of public health by removing and treating waste, dirty water etc.

sanitation work·er /,..'.. ,./ n. [C] FORMAL someone who removes the waste material that people put outside their houses; GARBAGE MAN

san·i·tize /'sænə,taɪz/ v. [T] **1** DISAPPROVING to remove all the offensive parts from news, literature etc., with the result that it is not complete or interesting: *Forman has sanitized the film to fit its R-rating.* **2** to clean something thoroughly, removing dirt and BACTERIA

san·i·ty /'sænəṭi/ n. [U] **1** the ability to think in a normal and sensible way: *Let's hope sanity prevails on Capitol Hill and they vote against this bill.* **2** the condition of being mentally healthy: *The pressures of his arrest and trial may have caused Garcia to lose his sanity.* —opposite INSANITY

San Jo·sé /,sæn hou'zei/ the capital and largest city of Costa Rica

San Juan /sæn 'wɑn/ the capital city of the U.S. TERRITORY of Puerto Rico

sank /sæŋk/ v. a past tense of SINK

San Ma·ri·no /,sæn mə'rinou/ a very small country in northeast Italy

sans /sænz, sɑn/ prep. HUMOROUS without: *He was wearing running shoes, sans socks.*

San Sal·va·dor /sæn 'sælvə,dɔr/ the capital and largest city of El Salvador

San·skrit /'sænskrɪt/ n. [U] an ancient language of India

sans ser·if /,sæn 'sɛrəf, ,sænz-/ n. [U] TECHNICAL a style of printing in which letters have no SERIFS (=wider parts at the ends of lines)

San·ta Claus /'sæntə ,klɔz/ also **Santa** n. an imaginary old man with red clothes and a long white BEARD who, children believe, brings them presents during the night before Christmas

San·ta Fe /,sæntə 'fei/ the capital city of the U.S. state of New Mexico

Santa Fe Trail, the /,... './ an important road in the western area of the U.S. starting in Missouri and ending in Santa Fe, which was used in the 19th century by American SETTLERS

San·tee /sæn'ti/ also **Santee Sioux** /,.. './ the eastern part of the Sioux tribe of Native Americans

San·te·ri·a /,sæntə'riə/ a religion based on traditional African beliefs and Catholic Christian beliefs

San·ti·a·go /,sænti'ɑgou/ the capital and largest city of Chile

San·to Do·min·go /ˌsæntoʊ dəˈmɪŋgoʊ/ the capital and largest city of the Dominican Republic

São Pau·lo /saʊm ˈpaʊloʊ/ the largest city in southeast Brazil

São To·mé /ˌsaʊn təˈmeɪ/ the capital city of São Tomé and Príncipe

São Tomé and Prín·ci·pe /ˌsaʊn təˈmeɪ ən ˈprɪnsɪpə/ a small country that consists of a group of islands off West Africa in the Gulf of Guinea

sap¹ /sæp/ n. **1** [U] the watery substance that carries food through a plant **2** [C] INFORMAL a stupid person who is easy to deceive or treat badly

sap² v. **sapped, sapping** [T] to gradually take away something such as strength or energy: **sap sb's courage/energy/strength** The illness had sapped Diane's strength.

sa·pi·ent /ˈseɪpiənt/ adj. LITERARY very wise —**sapiently** adv. —**sapience** n. [U]

sap·ling /ˈsæplɪŋ/ n. [C] a young tree

sap·phic /ˈsæfɪk/ adj. LITERARY: see LESBIAN

sap·phire /ˈsæfaɪɚ/ n. **1** [C,U] a transparent bright blue jewel **2** [U] a bright blue color

sap·py /ˈsæpi/ adj. **sappier, sappiest 1** expressing love and emotions in a way that seems silly: a sappy love song **2** full of SAP (=liquid in a plant)

sap·wood /ˈsæpwʊd/ n. [U] the younger outer wood in a tree, that is paler and softer than the wood in the middle

sar·a·band, sarabande /ˈsærəbænd/ n. [C] a slow piece of music based on a type of 17th century dance

Sar·a·cen /ˈsærəsən/ n. [C] OLD USE a word for a Muslim, used in the Middle Ages

Sar·a·je·vo /ˌsærəˈyeɪvoʊ/ the capital and largest city of Bosnia-Herzegovina

Sa·ran Wrap /səˈræn ˌræp/ n. [U] TRADEMARK thin transparent plastic that you use to wrap or cover food, in order to keep it fresh

sar·casm /ˈsɑrˌkæzəm/ n. [U] a way of speaking or writing that involves saying the opposite of what you really mean in order to make a joke that is not nice, or to show that you are annoyed: There was a tinge of sarcasm in his voice.

sar·cas·tic /sɑrˈkæstɪk/ adj. saying things that are the opposite of what you mean in order to make a joke that is not nice, or to show that you are annoyed: His story prompted a sarcastic question from Fitch, the prosecuting attorney. —**sarcastically** /-kli/ adv.

sar·coph·a·gus /sɑrˈkɑfəgəs/ n. [C] a decorated stone box for a dead body, used in ancient times and sometimes displayed as a monument

sar·dine /sɑrˈdin/ n. **1** [C] a small fish that can be eaten, that is often packed in flat metal boxes **2 be packed like sardines** to be crowded tightly together in a small space: We were packed like sardines on the train.

sar·don·ic /sɑrˈdɑnɪk/ adj. speaking or smiling in a way that is not nice and shows you do not have a good opinion of someone or something: He gave a brief, sardonic laugh. —**sardonically** /-kli/ adv.

sarge /sɑrdʒ/ n. [singular] SPOKEN, INFORMAL: see SERGEANT

Sar·gent /ˈsɑrdʒənt/, **John Sing·er** /dʒɑn ˈsɪŋɚ/ (1856–1925) a U.S. painter who worked mainly in London, known for his paintings of rich and important people

sa·ri /ˈsɑri/ n. [C] a long piece of cloth that you wrap around your body like a dress, worn especially by women from India

sa·rong /səˈrɑŋ, -ˈrɔŋ/ n. [C] a loose skirt consisting of a long piece of cloth wrapped around your waist, worn especially by men and women in Malaysia and some islands in the Pacific Ocean

sarsa·pa·ril·la /ˌsæspəˈrɪlə, ˌsɑrs-/ n. [U] a sweet drink made from the root of the SASSAFRAS plant

sar·to·ri·al /sɑrˈtɔriəl/ adj. [only before noun] FORMAL relating to good-quality clothes or how they are made: McEnery is known for her sartorial elegance. —**sartorially** adv.

Sar·tre /ˈsɑrtrə/, **Jean-Paul** /ʒɑn pɔl/ (1905–1980) a French PHILOSOPHER and writer, famous for his influence on the development of EXISTENTIALISM

SASE n. [C] self-addressed stamped envelope; an envelope that you put your name, address, and a stamp on, so that someone else can send you something

sash /sæʃ/ n. [C] **1** a long piece of cloth that you wear around your waist like a belt **2** a long piece of cloth that you wear over one shoulder and across your chest as a sign of a special honor **3** a wooden frame that has a sheet of glass fastened it to form part of a window

sa·shay /sæˈʃeɪ/ v. **sashayed, sashaying** [I always + adv./prep.] to walk in a confident way while moving your body from side to side, especially so that people look at you: [+ around/along/down etc.] All eyes were on Kelli as she sashayed around the stage.

sa·shi·mi /sɑˈʃimi/ n. [U] a type of Japanese food consisting of small pieces of fresh fish that have not been cooked

Sas·katch·e·wan /səˈskætʃəwən, -ˌwɑn/ a PROVINCE in central Canada

Sas·quatch /ˈsæskwɑtʃ/ n. another name for BIGFOOT

sass¹ /sæs/ v. [T] INFORMAL to talk in an impolite way to someone you should respect: And don't sass the teacher, Billy.

sass² n. [U] INFORMAL **1** impolite remarks made to someone who should be respected: Watch your sass, missy! **2** a confident attitude that shows you do not care what other people think: John was full of sass and could talk anyone into doing anything.

sas·sa·fras /ˈsæsəˌfræs/ n. [C,U] a small Asian or North American tree, or the pleasant-smelling roots of this tree used in food and drinks

sas·sy /ˈsæsi/ adj. **sassier, sassiest 1** a child who is sassy is not polite to someone they should respect **2** confident and showing that you do not care what other people think

SAT n. [C] TRADEMARK Scholastic Aptitude Test; an examination that high school students take before they go to college: What was your SAT score?

sat /sæt/ v. the past tense and past participle of SIT

Sat. a written abbreviation of Saturday

Sa·tan /ˈseɪtn/ n. the Devil, considered to be the main evil power and God's opponent

sa·tan·ic /səˈtænɪk, seɪ-/ adj. **1** relating to practices that treat the Devil like a god: a satanic cult **2** extremely cruel or evil: He has a satanic influence over her. —**satanically** /-kli/ adv.

sa·tan·ism /ˈseɪtnˌɪzəm/ n. [U] the practice of respecting or WORSHIPping the Devil as if he were a god —**satanist** n. [C] —**satanist** adj.

sa·tay /ˈsɑteɪ/ n. [U] a dish originally from southeast Asia, made of pieces of meat which are cooked on small sticks and eaten with a PEANUT SAUCE

satch·el /ˈsætʃəl/ n. [C] a leather bag that you carry over your shoulder, used especially in past times by children for carrying books to school

sate /seɪt/ v. [T] LITERARY **be sated (with sth)** to have had enough, or more than enough, of something to satisfy you

sat·el·lite /ˈsætlˌaɪt/ n. [C] **1** a machine that has been sent into space and goes around the Earth, moon etc., used for radio, television, and other electronic communication: The central convention site will be linked by satellite to other sites around the country. **2** a moon that moves around a PLANET **3** a country, organization, store etc. that is controlled by or is dependent on another larger one: Soviet satellite countries | Susan Bruce plans to open a satellite store in St. Paul.

satellite dish /ˈ... ˌ./ n. [C] a large circular piece of metal that receives special television signals so that you can watch satellite television

satellite tel·e·vi·sion /ˌ... ˈ..../ also **satellite TV**

/ˌ… .'./ *n.* [U] television programs that are broadcast using satellites in space, and that can only be received by people who have a satellite dish

sa·ti·ate /ˈseɪʃiˌeɪt/ *v.* [T usually passive] LITERARY to completely satisfy a desire or need for something such as food or sex, sometimes so that you feel you have had too much —**satiated** *adj.* —**satiety** /səˈtaɪəti/ *n.* [U]

sat·in /ˈsætˀn/ *n.* [U] a type of cloth that is very smooth and shiny —**satin** *adj.*

sat·in·wood /ˈsætˀnˌwʊd/ *n.* [C,U] a tree that grows in India and Sri Lanka, or the hard smooth wood that comes from this tree

sat·in·y /ˈsætˀn-i/ *adj.* smooth, shiny, and soft

sat·ire /ˈsætaɪə/ *n.* **1** [U] a way of talking or writing about something, for example politics and politicians, in which you deliberately make them seem funny so that people will see their faults: *Gelbart is a writer of comedy and social satire.* **2** [C] a play, book, story etc. written in this way: *a political satire* —**satirical** /səˈtɪrɪkəl/ *adj.* —**satiric** *adj.* —**satirically** /-kli/ *adv.*

sat·i·rist /ˈsætərɪst/ *n.* [C] someone who writes satire

sat·i·rize /ˈsætəˌraɪz/ *v.* [T] to use satire to make people see someone or something's faults: *Glick's book satirizes small-town politics.*

sat·is·fac·tion /ˌsætɪsˈfækʃən/ *n.* [U] **1** a feeling of happiness or pleasure because you have achieved something or gotten what you wanted: *Our goal is 100% customer satisfaction.* | *She got profound satisfaction from her career.* | *I'm looking for greater job satisfaction* (=enjoyment of your job) *and independence.* —opposite DISSATISFACTION **2** FULFILLMENT of a need, demand, claim, desire etc.: *Infants are concerned only with the satisfaction of their physical needs.* | *sexual satisfaction* **3 have/get the satisfaction of doing sth** to get a small amount of pleasure from a situation that is unsatisfactory in other ways: *It's unfair, but at least you have the satisfaction of knowing you were right.* **4 to sb's/sth's satisfaction** if something is done to someone's satisfaction, it is done as well or as completely as they want, so they are pleased: *It took me twenty minutes to iron the shirt to my satisfaction.* | *The question could not be resolved, at least not to Brenner's satisfaction.*

sat·is·fac·to·ry /ˌsætɪsˈfæktəri, -tri/ *adj.* acceptable, or good enough for a particular situation or purpose: *Nobody could give Donna a satisfactory answer to her question.* | [+ to] *We need to work out arrangements that are satisfactory to both sides.* —see Usage Note at ADEQUATE —**satisfactorily** *adv.*

sat·is·fied /ˈsætɪsˌfaɪd/ *adj.* **1** pleased because something has happened in the way that you want, or because you have achieved something: *"I like being forty," she said with a satisfied grin.* | [+ with] *We ask all our customers if they are satisfied with the service they received.* —opposite DISSATISFIED **2** feeling sure that something is right or true: [+ that] *She was not satisfied that her brother was serious about becoming a pilot.* **3 (are you) satisfied?** SPOKEN used to show that someone has annoyed you by asking too many questions or making too many demands: *I'm here now – are you satisfied?* —see also SELF-SATISFIED

sat·is·fy /ˈsætɪsˌfaɪ/ *v.* **satisfied, satisfying** [T] **1** to make someone happy by providing what they want or need: *The changes I made seemed to satisfy Cooley.* | *Magazines like this satisfy people's curiosity about celebrities' lives.* | **satisfy a request/desire/need etc.** *The new stadium will help satisfy the public demand for sports facilities.* **2** FORMAL to make someone feel sure that something is right or true; CONVINCE: *Once Phil had satisfied himself that no one else was listening, he began to tell me what had happened.* **3** FORMAL to be good enough for a particular purpose, standard etc.: *The cheapest products satisfy only minimum safety requirements.* **4** FORMAL to pay a debt that you owe: **satisfy a debt/obligation** *Wilco said it will satisfy all its obligations to its banks and creditors.* **5** TECHNICAL to be a correct answer to an EQUATION in mathematics etc.: *What numbers will satisfy the equation $2x + 3 > 13$?*

sat·is·fy·ing /ˈsætɪsˌfaɪ-ɪŋ/ *adj.* **1** making you feel

pleased and happy, especially because you have gotten what you wanted: *June was looking for a new and satisfying career.* | **It's satisfying to** *know that people enjoyed our performance.* **2** food that is satisfying is good and makes you feel that you have eaten enough: *a satisfying meal* —**satisfyingly** *adv.*

sat·u·rate /ˈsætʃəˌreɪt/ *v.* [T] **1** FORMAL to make something very wet; SOAK[1] (2): *The bathtub overflowed, and water saturated the carpeting.* **2** to fill something completely with a large number of things, or with a large amount of something: *Issa is saturating local radio time with his campaign ads.* **3 saturate the market** to offer so much of a product for sale that there is more of it than people want to buy **4** TECHNICAL to DISSOLVE (=mix until something becomes part of a liquid) as much of a solid into a chemical mixture as possible

sat·u·rat·ed /ˈsætʃəˌreɪtɪd/ *adj.* [no comparative] **1** extremely wet: [+ with] *The pillow was saturated with blood.* **2** completely filled with something or a large number of things: [+ with] *The welfare program is completely saturated with fraud and corruption.* **3** TECHNICAL if a chemical mixture is saturated, it has had as much of a solid DISSOLVEd (=mixed until it has become part of the liquid) into it as possible: *a saturated salt solution*

saturated fat /ˌ… './ *n.* [C,U] a type of fat from meat and milk products that is less healthy than other kinds of fat from vegetables or fish

sat·u·ra·tion /ˌsætʃəˈreɪʃən/ *n.* [U] **1** the act or result of making something completely wet **2** a situation in which something is very full of a particular type of thing, so that no more can be added: *Falling sales suggest that the VCR market may have reached saturation.* **3 saturation bombing** a military attack in which the whole of a particular area has a lot of bombs dropped on it **4 saturation coverage/advertising** a situation in which there is so much information, advertising etc. about something that everyone has heard about it **5** TECHNICAL the state of a chemical mixture that has reached its SATURATION POINT

saturation point /..'.. ,./ *n.* [C usually singular] **1** a situation in which no more people or things can be added because there are already too many: *The coffee bar market has almost reached its saturation point.* **2** TECHNICAL the state that a chemical mixture reaches when it has had as much of a solid substance DISSOLVEd (=mixed until it becomes part of the liquid) into it as possible

Sat·ur·day /ˈsætədi, -ˌdeɪ/ *n.* [C,U] the seventh day of the week, between Friday and Sunday: *Carrie's plane leaves Saturday.* | *Jim's going to Tucson on Saturday.* | *We were in Hawaii last Saturday.* | *Would next Saturday be a good time for me to visit?* | *Let's get together this Saturday* (=the next Saturday that is coming). | *Jack always washes his car on Saturdays* (=each Saturday). | *Steve's birthday is on a Saturday this year.* | **Saturday morning/afternoon/night etc.** *Don't forget that we have a soccer game Saturday morning.* —see Usage Note at SUNDAY

Saturday night spe·cial /ˌ… '../ *n.* [C] a small cheap gun that is easy to buy and easy to hide in your clothing

Sat·urn /ˈsætən/ *n.* **1** the PLANET that is sixth in order from the sun and is surrounded by large rings **2** in Roman MYTHOLOGY, the father of Jupiter and god of farming

sat·ur·na·li·a /ˌsætəˈneɪliə/ *n.* [C] LITERARY an occasion when people enjoy themselves in a very wild and uncontrolled way

sat·ur·nine /ˈsætəˌnaɪn/ *adj.* [no comparative] LITERARY looking sad and serious, especially in a threatening way: *a dark, saturnine expression*

sa·tyr /ˈseɪtə/ *n.* [C] **1** a creature in ancient Greek literature who was half human and half goat and represented pleasure and enjoyment **2** FORMAL OR HUMOROUS a man who is always thinking about sex or trying to get sexual pleasure

S

sauce /sɔs/ n. **1** [C,U] a thick liquid that is served with food to add a particular taste: *chicken in a rich, creamy sauce* | **tomato/chocolate etc. sauce** *scallops with garlic sauce* | **barbecue/teriyaki/white sauce** (=a particular type of sauce) **2 the sauce** OLD-FASHIONED alcoholic drinks: *Alice seems to be **hitting the sauce** (=drinking a lot) a lot lately.*

sauce·pan /ˈsɔs-pæn/ n. [C] a deep round metal container with a handle that is used for cooking on top the STOVE —see pictures at PAN¹ and KITCHEN

sau·cer /ˈsɔsɚ/ n. [C] a small round plate that curves up at the edges, that you put a cup on —see also FLYING SAUCER

sau·cy /ˈsɔsi/ adj. **saucier, sauciest 1** slightly shocking, but amusing or sexually attractive: *saucy headlines* | *saucy swimwear* **2** OLD-FASHIONED impolite and not showing enough respect, but often in a way that is amusing: *a saucy, spirited girl* —**saucily** adv. —**sauciness** n. [U]

Saudi A·ra·bi·a /ˌsɔdi əˈreɪbiə, ˌsaʊ-/ a country in the Middle East, east of the Red Sea —**Saudi Arabian** also **Saudi** n., adj.

sau·er·kraut /ˈsaʊɚˌkraʊt/ n. [U] a German food made from CABBAGE that has been left in salt so that it tastes sour

Sauk, Sac /sɔk/ a Native American tribe from the northeastern central area of the U.S.

Sault Sainte Ma·rie Ca·nals /ˌsu seɪnt məˌri kəˈnælz/ a system of three CANALS connecting two of the Great Lakes in North America, Lake Superior and Lake Huron

sau·na /ˈsɔnə/ n. [C] **1** a room that is heated to a very high temperature by hot air, where people sit because it is considered healthy **2** a period of time when you sit or lie in a room like this: *Gordon took a sauna after his swim.*

saun·ter /ˈsɔntɚ, ˈsɑn-/ v. [I always + adv./prep.] to walk in a slow way, that makes you look confident or proud: [+ **along/around/in etc.**] *Glass in hand, Jonnie sauntered back into the ballroom.* —**saunter** n. [singular]

sau·sage /ˈsɔsɪdʒ/ n. [C,U] a mixture of meat, especially PORK (=meat from a pig), that has been cut up very small and SPICES, usually made into a tube shape: *Do you want bacon or sausage with your eggs?*

Saus·sure, Fer·di·nand de /ˈfɚdɪnan də/ (1857–1913) a Swiss LINGUIST whose ideas are considered the beginning of modern LINGUISTICS

sau·té /sɔˈteɪ/ v. [T] to cook something quickly in a little hot oil: *Sauté the onions until soft.*

sav·age¹ /ˈsævɪdʒ/ adj. **1** very cruel and violent: *a savage warrior* | *Daniels was found dead in his apartment, the victim of a savage beating.* **2** criticizing someone or something very severely: **savage attack/criticism etc.** *They launched a savage assault on Ms. Armstrong's credibility.* **3** very severe and harmful: *savage tax increases* **4** [only before noun] OLD-FASHIONED a word to describe a person or group from a country where the way of living seems very simple and undeveloped, now considered offensive; PRIMITIVE¹ (1) —**savagely** adv. —**savageness** n. [U]

savage² n. [C] OLD-FASHIONED a word for someone from a country where the way of living seems very simple and undeveloped, now considered offensive: *The movie reinforces the stereotype of Indians as heathens and savages.* —see also **noble savage** (NOBLE¹ (4))

savage³ v. [T] **1** to criticize someone or something very severely: *Stevens was savaged in the sports press after his defeat.* **2** to attack someone violently, causing serious injuries: *Troops savaged the weakened enemy army.*

sav·age·ry /ˈsævɪdʒri/ n. [C,U] extremely cruel and violent behavior: *Karlin witnessed inhumane savagery during the war.*

sa·van·na, savannah /səˈvænə/ n. [C,U] a large flat area of grassy land in a warm part of the world

Sa·van·nah /səˈvænə/ the oldest city in the U.S. state of Georgia

sa·vant /sæˈvɑnt, sə-/ n. [C] LITERARY someone who knows a lot about a particular subject

save¹ /seɪv/ v.
1 from harm/danger [T] to make someone or something safe from danger, harm, or destruction: [**save sb/sth from sth**] *Neighbors were able to save both children from the fire.* | *The children campaigned to save the playground from being closed.* | *Jane was able to put out the fire and **save his life** (=prevent him from dying).*

2 money in a bank [I,T] also **save up** to keep money, and often to gradually add more money over a period of time, so that you can use it later: *We're trying to save money to buy a house.* | [+ **for**] *I'm saving up for a trip to Europe.* —see also SAVER

3 not waste [T] to use less money, time, energy etc. so that you do not waste any: *We can save fifteen minutes by taking the expressway.* | *money-saving coupons* | [**save sb sth**] *These changes could save the company up to $500,000 a year.*

4 to use later [T] to keep something so that you can use or enjoy it in the future: *Why don't we save these chips for the party?* | *Save the chicken bones to make stock later.*

5 collect [T] also **save up** to keep all the objects of a particular kind that you can find, so that they can be used for a special purpose: *My grandmother saved up all her old magazines.*

6 help to avoid [T] to help someone by making it unnecessary for them to do something that is inconvenient or that they do not want to do: [**save sb doing sth**] *A template document saves you having to type the same letter over and over.* | [**save sb sth**] *Could you fax me the letter? It would save me a trip across town.* | *Just use canned soup and **save yourself the trouble**.*

7 keep for sb [T] to stop people from using something, so that it is available for someone else: [**save sth for sb**] *Kate asked us to save some dinner for her.* | *We'll **save you a seat** at the theater.*

8 computer [I,T] to make a computer keep the work that you have done on it: *Don't forget to save before you close the file.*

9 save sb's skin/butt/bacon INFORMAL to make it possible for someone to escape from an extremely difficult or dangerous situation: *The money arrived just in time to save my lazy butt.*

10 you saved my life SPOKEN used to thank someone who has gotten you out of a difficult situation or solved a problem for you: *Thanks for the ride – you really saved my life.*

11 can't do sth to save your life SPOKEN to be completely unable to do something: *I can't read a map to save my life.*

12 saving grace the one good thing that makes someone or something acceptable: *The movie's only saving grace was its dazzling special effects.*

13 save the day to make a situation end successfully when it seemed likely to end badly: *Will saved the day by lending me his suit for the interview.*

14 sports [T] to stop the other team from getting a GOAL in a sport such as SOCCER or HOCKEY

15 save sb from themselves to prevent someone from doing something that is likely to harm them in the end

16 religion [I,T] in the Christian church, to free someone from the power of evil and SIN —see also **save your breath** (BREATH (4)), **save face** (FACE¹ (7))

save on sth phr. v. [T] to avoid wasting something by using as little as possible of it: *To save on expenses, Tracy moved in with her mother.*

save² n. [C] an action by the GOALKEEPER in SOCCER or HOCKEY that prevents the other team from getting a GOAL

save³ prep. FORMAL except for: *The fee covers everything, save one dinner.*

sav·er /ˈseɪvɚ/ n. [C] **1 time-saver/money-saver/energy-saver etc.** something that prevents loss or waste: *Shopping by mail is a great time-saver.* **2** someone who saves money in a bank: *Mutual funds have been attractive to **small savers** (=people* who save small amounts of money). —see also FACE SAVER, SCREEN SAVER

sa·vi·ng /ˈseɪvɪŋ/ n. **1 savings** [plural] all the money that you have saved, especially in a bank: *She lost their life savings in a Vegas casino.* **2** [C] an amount of something that you have not used or do not have to spend: *The sale price of $599 represents a saving of $100 off the regular price.* **3** [U] the act of keeping money and adding to it so that you can use it later

savings ac·count /ˈ.. .,./ n. [C] a bank account that pays INTEREST[1] (3) on the money you have in it —compare CHECKING ACCOUNT

savings and loan /,... ˈ./ n. [C] a business that lends money, usually so that you can buy a house, and into which you can pay money to be saved

savings bank /ˈ.. ,./ n. [C] a bank whose business is mainly from savings accounts and from LOANS on houses

savings bond /ˈ.. ,./ n. [C] TECHNICAL a BOND sold by the U.S. government that cannot be sold from one person to another

sav·ior /ˈseɪvyɚ/ n. **1** [C usually singular] someone or something that saves you from a difficult or dangerous situation: *A wealthy investor turned out to be the troubled computer company's savior.* **2 the Savior** in the Christian religion, a name for Jesus Christ, because he is believed to save people from SIN and death

sa·voir-faire /ˌsævwɑr ˈfɛr/ n. [U] the ability to do or say the right things, especially in social situations: *people with money and savoir-faire*

sa·vor[1] /ˈseɪvɚ/ v. [T] **1** to enjoy the taste or smell or something very much: *Marty took time to savor each bite of his steak.* **2** to make an activity or experience last as long as you can, because you are enjoying every moment of it: *We savored the early morning quiet.*

savor[2] n. [singular,U] FORMAL **1** a taste or smell, especially one that is pleasant: *a delicate savor* **2** interest and enjoyment: *Life seems to have lost its savor.*

sa·vor·y[1] /ˈseɪvəri/ adj. **1** having a pleasant and attractive smell or taste: *savory grilled vegetables* **2** having a taste that is not sweet, especially a salty or SPICY taste: *Americans eat about six billion pounds of savory snacks a year.* **3** [used with negative] something that is not savory seems morally unacceptable, or not nice: *There were some less savory businesses at the south end of Sewell Street.*

savory[2] n. [U] a plant whose leaves are used in cooking to add taste to meat, vegetables etc.

sav·vy[1] /ˈsævi/ adj. **savvier, savviest** having the practical knowledge and ability to deal with a situation successfully: *Lisa had become a savvy young woman.* | *computer-savvy/media-savvy* etc. (=having knowledge about a particular subject)

savvy[2] n. [U] practical knowledge and ability: *political savvy*

saw[1] /sɔ/ v. the past tense of SEE

saw

saw[2] n. [C] **1** a tool that has a flat metal blade with an edge that has been cut into a series of "V" shapes, used for cutting wood —see picture at TOOL[1] **2** a well-known wise statement; PROVERB: *That reminds me of that old saw about being careful what you wish for.*

saw[3] v. past tense **sawed** past participle **sawed** or

sawn [I,T] to cut something using a saw: [+**through**] *The prisoners escaped by sawing through the bars in their cell.*

saw at sth phr. v. [T] to try to cut something with a repeated backward and forward movement: *Dad sawed at the steak.*

saw sth ↔ **off** phr. v. [T] to remove something by cutting it off with a saw: *The metal railing had to be sawed off by the firefighters.*

saw·bones /ˈsɔboʊnz/ n. [C] HUMOROUS a medical doctor, especially a SURGEON

saw·buck /ˈsɔbʌk/ n. [C] OLD-FASHIONED a $10 BILL

saw·dust /ˈsɔdʌst/ n. [U] very small pieces of wood that fall when you cut wood with a SAW

sawed-off /ˈ. ./ adj. **sawed-off shotgun/rifle** a SHOTGUN that has had its BARREL (=long thin part) cut short, so that it is easier to hide

saw·horse /ˈsɔhɔrs/ n. [C] a small wooden structure shaped like an "A," usually used in pairs, on which you put a piece of wood that you are sawing

saw·mill /ˈsɔmɪl/ n. [C] a factory where trees are cut into boards using machines

sawn /sɔn/ v. a past participle of SAW

saw·yer /ˈsɔyɚ/ n. [C] OLD USE someone whose job is sawing wood

sax /sæks/ n. [C] INFORMAL a saxophone

Sax·on /ˈsæksən/ n. [C] a member of the German race that went to live in England in the 5th century —**Saxon** adj.

sax·o·phone /ˈsæksəˌfoʊn/ also **sax** INFORMAL n. [C] a metal musical instrument with a single REED, used mostly in JAZZ and dance music

sax·o·pho·nist /ˈsæksəˌfoʊnɪst/ n. [C] someone who plays the saxophone

say[1] /seɪ/ v. past tense and past participle **said** 3rd person singular **says**

1 word/sound [T] to pronounce a word, sentence, or sound: *What did you say?* | *"I'm in love," said Dennis.* | *How do you say your last name?*

2 thought/opinion [I only in questions and negatives,T] to express a thought, opinion, explanation etc. in words: *"Is Joyce coming over later?" "She didn't say."* | [**say (that)**] *Stevie said you did an excellent job.* | **say how/why/who etc.** *Did she say how long she's going to be gone?* | **anything/something/ nothing to say** *It was an awful interview – I had nothing to say.* | **a nice/stupid/weird etc. thing to say** *That's a terrible thing to say, Wayne.* | **say yes/ no (to sth)** *Every time I volunteer to cook for Mom, she says no.* | **say hello/goodbye/please/ thank you etc.** (=greet someone, speak to them when you are leaving, ask for something politely etc.) | *I think he's a little scared, even if he won't say so.* | *He said something about being glad he was home.* | *Look, I've said I'm sorry* (=apologized) – *what more do you want?* | *I'd just like to say a few words* (=make a short speech) *about the schedule.*

3 give information [T not in passive] to give information in written words, numbers, or pictures: *The clock in the hall said it was almost midnight.* | [**say (that)**] *It said back there you have to make a left turn.* | [**say to do sth**] *Didn't it say to slice the sausage first?* | **say who/what/how etc.** *The card doesn't even say who sent the flowers.*

4 tell sb to do sth [T not in progressive] to tell someone to do something: [**say to do sth**] *Lois said to stay at the Waterside Inn when we're in Maine.*

5 rules [T] to state what people are allowed to do: [**say (that)**] *Did Mom say you could come?*

6 say to yourself to think something: *"Face it, Jack, you're getting old," he said to himself.*

7 say your prayers/say grace etc. to speak the particular set of words that form a prayer etc.: *We will start by saying the Pledge of Allegiance.*

8 say sth to sb's face to make a remark that is negative or not nice directly to the person that the remark is about: *Never write anything in an e-mail that you wouldn't say to the person's face.*

9 `not directly` [T] used when someone has expressed what they mean in an indirect way, and you want to make sure you understand it more directly: *What are you trying to say?* | [say (that)] *Are you saying I'm fat?*

10 `common opinion` [T] to express an opinion that a lot of people have: *Well, you know what folks say – everything in moderation.* | **They say** (=many people say) *you only ever use a small portion of your brain.*

11 be said to do/be sth to be considered by many to do something or to have certain qualities: *Queen Elizabeth is said to be the richest woman in the world.*

12 `show character/qualities` [T] to show what someone or something's real character or qualities are: [say a lot about sb/sth] *What you wear says a lot about who you are.* | [not say much for sb/sth] *His track record doesn't say much for the sincerity of his intentions.*

13 `have meaning` [T] to have or show a meaning that someone can understand: *Most modern art doesn't say much to me.* | *Julie's clothes and her whole attitude just said "New York"* (=they were typical of what you would find there).

14 this/that is not to say used to make it clear that something is not true, when you think someone might think that it is: *I had a bad experience in therapy, but this is not to say that all therapists are incompetent.*

15 to say nothing of sth used to say that you have described only some of the bad points about something: *A bounced check will cost you $25 or more, to say nothing of your credit rating.*

SPOKEN PHRASES

16 be saying used to emphasize that you are trying to explain what you mean in a way that someone will understand better, especially in a situation in which you are arguing with someone and do not want them to be angry: *I'm not saying it's a bad idea, just that we need to think about it.* | *I'm just saying it would be easier if we made a copy.* | *Teachers have to try and understand their students more,* **you know what I'm saying?** | **All I'm saying is** *that it would be better to do this first.*

17 [T usually in imperative] to suggest or suppose that something might happen or might be true: *Say a student came to you with a problem. You'd try to help them, right?* | **let's say (that)** *Let's just say they don't approve our plan. What do we do then?*

18 say $45/100 years/Tuesday etc. used to suggest a possible example, amount etc. when discussing something: *Can you come to dinner? Say, 7:00?*

19 Say what? SLANG used when you have not heard something that someone said, or when you cannot believe that something is true

20 who says? used to say that you do not agree with a statement, opinion etc.: *Who says Tommy and I are still going out?*

21 anything/whatever you say used to tell someone that you agree to do what they want, accept their opinion etc., especially because you do not want an argument: *"I want fifty copies of this by 3:00." "Anything you say, Mrs. DeVere."*

22 you can say that again used to say that you completely agree with someone: *"We're too old for that sort of stuff." "You can say that again."*

23 having said that used before saying something that makes the opinion you have just given seem less strong: *Of course he deserves prison. Having said that, I don't think any good will come of locking him up forever.*

24 I can't say (that sth) used to say that you definitely do not think or feel something: *"Do you know what I mean?" "No, Willie, I can't say that I do."*

25 who can say? used to say that no one knows the answer to a question: *It's unlikely that we'll find anything of value there. Still, who can say?*

26 who's to say? used to say that your judgment of a situation might not be correct, because you can never be sure what will happen in the future: *If they do it once, who's to say they won't do it again?*

27 what do you say? used to ask someone if they agree with a suggestion: *How about going to Europe this summer? What do you say?* | **What do you say** *we split the two sandwiches?*

28 say when said when you want someone to tell you when to stop doing something or when you have given them the correct amount of something, especially a drink

29 enough said used to say that something is clear, and does not need to be explained any further: *"Then I saw Jill coming out of Alex's apartment." "Enough said."*

30 you don't say! HUMOROUS used to show that you are not surprised at all by what someone has just told you: *"I think Bob and Susan are having an affair." "You don't say! That's been common knowledge for months."*

31 say the word used to tell someone they have only to ask and you will do what they want: *Just say the word and I'll get rid of her.*

32 I'll say this (much) for sb used when you want to mention something good about someone, especially when you have been criticizing them: *I'll say this much for Barkley – the guy never lacks confidence.*

33 that's not saying much used to emphasize even though one thing is better or different from another, the difference is not very large: *I'm better with computers than my sister, but that's not saying much.*

34 when all is said and done used to remind someone about an important point that they should remember: *Tricia has had a few problems, but when all is said and done, she's still part of our family.*

35 to say the least used to say that you could have described something, criticized someone etc. a lot more severely than you have: *These maps are difficult to understand, to say the least.*

36 sth goes without saying used to say that something is so clear that it does not really need to be stated: *It goes without saying that a well-rested person is a better worker.*

37 something/a lot/not much etc. to be said for sth used to say that there are a lot of, not many etc. good reasons for doing something: *Despite the fog and dampness, there are a few things to be said for living next to the ocean.*

38 that/which is to say used before describing what you mean in more detail: *Laura uses a special, which is to say expensive, shampoo and conditioner.*

39 you said it! a) used to say that you agree with someone: *"The second part of the race was super easy." "You said it."* **b)** also **you said it, not me** used when someone says something that you agree with, although you would not have actually said it yourself because it is not nice or not polite: *"Does that mean Sherri lied about where she went?" "You said it."*

40 what do you have to say for yourself? used to ask someone for an explanation when they have done something wrong: *What did Floyd have to say for himself when you asked about the broken window?*

41 say no more used to show that you understand what someone means, although it has not been said directly: *"Angela is so... you know." "Say no more."*

42 I'd rather not say used when you do not want to tell someone something: *"What were you doing at the time of the accident?" "I'd rather not say."*

43 have something to say about sth to be angry about something: *You'd better tell your dad about the dent in the car – I'm sure he'll have something to say about it.*

44 I wouldn't say no (to sth) used to say that you would like something, and would accept it you were offered it: *I wouldn't say no to a cup of coffee.*

45 what sb says, goes used to emphasize who is in control in a situation: *Around here, what the boss says, goes.*

—see also **say cheese** (CHEESE (2)), **easier said than done** (EASY² (5)), **say a mouthful** (MOUTHFUL (4)), **no sooner said than done** (SOON (11))

USAGE NOTE: SAY

WORD CHOICE: say, tell, talk, and **speak**

Use **say** when you want to show the exact words that someone else spoke: *"I'd like to see you again," she said.* | *"Consider it done," said Ralph.* You can also talk about what someone said without using the same words. In this type of statement, **say** is often followed by "that": *Shawna said that she'd call you later.* | *Mom said I look like a tennis player in this dress.* Use **tell** when you want to mention the person that spoke and the person that was listening to them: *Susan told me that Pam is getting a divorce.* | *Did I tell you I bumped into Bob today? You* **tell** *a story a joke etc.: Daddy, tell me that story again.* You also use **tell** to mention someone who gave an order or instruction to someone else: *Tell Mark to bring the pictures over.* | *I told her to come back at 10:30.* If you want to mention the subject that someone was discussing, use **talk** rather than **say**. In these statements, **talk** is followed by "about": *Who are you talking about?* | *We talked about Brandon's wedding.* **Speak** is often used for more formal situations: *Prof. Bridges spoke about the effects of interest rates on the housing market.* | *Hello, could I please speak to Mrs. O'Neil?*

say² *n.* [singular,U] **1** the right to take part in deciding something: [+ **in**] *Citizens should have a say in how their tax money is spent.* **2** **have/get your say** to have the opportunity to give your opinion about something: *Taiwan's voters finally had their say on Saturday.*

say³ *interjection* used to express surprise, or to get someone's attention so that you can tell them something: *Say, my lights don't work.* | *Say, Mike, how about a beer after work?*

say·ing /ˈseɪ-ɪŋ/ *n.* [C] **1** a well-known short statement that expresses an idea most people believe is true and wise —compare PROVERB **2** **as the saying goes** used to introduce a particular phrase that people often say: *Blondes, as the saying goes, have more fun.*

say-so /ˈ. ./ *n.* [singular] INFORMAL **1** sb's **say-so** someone's permission: *Nobody here leaves without my say-so.* **2** **on sb's say-so** based on someone's personal statement without any proof: *I'd feel terrible if anyone went to see the play on my say-so and hated it.*

SC the written abbreviation of South Carolina

scab /skæb/ *n.* [C] **1** a hard layer of dried blood that forms over a cut or wound while it is getting better **2** an insulting word for someone who works while the other people in the same factory, office etc. are on STRIKE —**scab** *v.* [I]

scab·bard /ˈskæbəd/ *n.* [C] LITERARY a metal or leather cover for the blade of a knife or sword

scab·by /ˈskæbi/ *adj.* **scabbier, scabbiest** scabby skin is covered with scabs: *scabby knees*

sca·bies /ˈskeɪbiz/ *n.* [U] a skin disease caused by very small insects

scab·rous /ˈskæbrəs/ *adj.* LITERARY impolite or shocking, especially in a sexual way: *scabrous rumors*

scads /skædz/ *n.* [plural] INFORMAL **scads of sth** large numbers or quantities of something: *They got scads of calls from reporters.*

scaf·fold /ˈskæfəld, -foʊld/ *n.* [C] **1** a structure built next to a building or high wall, for workers to stand on while they build, repair, or paint the building **2** a structure that can be moved up and down to help people work on high buildings **3** a structure with a raised PLATFORM on which criminals are killed, especially in past times, by hanging or cutting off their heads

scaf·fold·ing /ˈskæfəldɪŋ/ *n.* [U] poles and boards that are built into a structure for workers to stand on when they are working on the outside of a building or next to a high wall

scag /skæg/ *n.* [U] SLANG: see HEROIN

scal·a·wag /ˈskæləwæg/ *n.* [C] OLD-FASHIONED a dishonest person who causes trouble

scald¹ /skɔld/ *v.* [T] **1** to burn your skin with hot liquid or steam: *He was badly scalded when a cup of hot coffee spilled on him.* **2** to heat a liquid to a temperature just below the BOILING POINT: *Scald the milk and add it to the bowl.*

scald² *n.* [C] a burn caused by hot liquid or steam

scald·ing /ˈskɔldɪŋ/ *adj.* **1** extremely hot: *a cup of scalding coffee* **2** scalding criticism is very severe

scale¹ /skeɪl/ *n.*

1 size/level [singular,U] the size, level, or amount of something, especially in relation to something else or to what is normal: [+ **of**] *The scale of the disaster soon became evident.* | **on a large/small/broad etc. scale** *Civil unrest in the region requires the use of force on a massive scale.* | **large-scale/small-scale** *a small-scale research project*

2 measuring system [C] a system for measuring the force, speed, amount etc. of something, or for comparing it with something else: *Hurricanes are graded on a scale from one to five, with five the strongest.* | *The salary scale goes from $60,000 to $175,000.*

3 on a scale of 1 to 10 SPOKEN used when you are telling someone how good you think something is: *On a scale of 1 to 10, this book rates a nine and a half* (=it is very good).

4 weight **a)** a machine that you use to weigh people or objects: *Greg stood on the bathroom scale and looked in the mirror.* **b)** also **scales** a piece of equipment with two dishes, used especially in the past for weighing things by comparing them to a known weight —see also **tip the balance/scales** (TIP² (4)), **tip the scales at 150/180/200 etc. pounds** (TIP² (7))

5 range [C usually singular] the whole range of different types of people, things, ideas etc., from the lowest level to the highest: *At the upper end of the scale is the Parker School, with tuition of over $9,000 a year.*

6 measuring marks [C] a set of marks with regular spaces between them that are on a tool or instrument used for measuring: *a ruler with a metric scale* | *the scale on a thermometer*

7 map/model [C,U] the relationship between the size of a map, drawing, or model and the actual size of the place or thing that it represents: *The map was drawn to a scale of one inch to the mile.*

8 fish [C usually plural] one of the small flat pieces of skin that cover the bodies of fish, snakes etc. —see picture at BARRACUDA

9 music [C] a series of musical notes moving up or down in PITCH¹ (3) with particular distances between each note: *the F major scale*

10 pay [U] an amount of money that must be paid to someone who belongs to a UNION: *Many of the actors worked for scale as a favor to the director.*

11 water pipes [U] a white substance that forms around the inside of hot water pipes or containers in which water is boiled

12 the scales fell from my eyes LITERARY used to say that you suddenly realized what had been clear to other people —see also FULL-SCALE

scale² *v.* [T] **1** FORMAL to climb to the top of something that is high and difficult to climb: *Corbett has scaled El Capitan in Yosemite a record 46 times.* **2** to make something the right size for use by a particular person or group: *a human-scaled business district* | [+ **to**] *The dollar-sized pancakes are great for kids who love food scaled to their size.* **3** to remove the SCALES (=skin) from a fish

scale sth ↔ back/down *phr. v.* [T] to reduce the size of an organization, plan etc. so that it operates at a lower level: *Due to slow sales, the company is scaling back its expansion plans.*

sca·lene /ˈskeɪlin/ *adj.* TECHNICAL a scalene TRIANGLE is a three-sided shape in which the sides are all different lengths —compare EQUILATERAL, ISOSCELES

scal·lion /ˈskælyən/ *n.* [C] a young onion with a small round end and a long green stem; GREEN ONION

scal·lop /ˈskæləp, ˈskɑləp/ *n.* [C] **1** a small sea creature that has a hard flat shell made of two parts that fit together, or the flesh from this animal eaten as food **2** one of a row of small curves decorating the edge of clothes, curtains etc.

scal·loped /ˈskæləpt, ˈskɑ-/ *adj.* **1** having a series of small curves around the edges for decoration: *a dress with a scalloped neckline* **2 scalloped potatoes/ corn etc.** potatoes, corn etc. that have been baked in a cream or cheese SAUCE

scalp¹ /skælp/ *n.* [C] **1** the skin on the top of your head **2 want sb's scalp** to want to defeat or punish someone severely: *It is clear that some Republican senators are after the President's scalp.*

scalp² *v.* [T] **1** INFORMAL to buy tickets for an event and sell them again at a much higher price **2** to cut off a dead enemy's scalp as a sign of victory

scal·pel /ˈskælpəl/ *n.* [C] a small very sharp knife used by doctors in operations

scal·per /ˈskælpɚ/ *n.* [C] a person who makes money by buying tickets for an event and selling them again at a very high price

scal·y /ˈskeɪli/ *adj.* **scalier, scaliest 1** an animal, such as a fish, that is scaly is covered with small flat pieces of hard skin **2** scaly skin is dry and rough —**scaliness** *n.* [U]

scam¹ /skæm/ *n.* [C] INFORMAL a smart but dishonest plan, usually to get money: *What are some ways to recognize phony charity scams?*

scam² *v.* **scammed, scamming** [T] INFORMAL to trick someone into giving you money

scam ar·tist /ˈ. ˌ../ *n.* [C] INFORMAL someone who tries to get money by tricking people

scamp /skæmp/ *n.* [C] OLD-FASHIONED a child who has fun by tricking people, especially in an amusing way

scam·per /ˈskæmpɚ/ *v.* [I always + adv./prep.] to run with quick short steps, like a child or small animal: [+ **across/out/off etc.**] *A mouse scampered away through the grass.*

scam·pi /ˈskæmpi/ also **shrimp scampi** /ˌ. ˈ../ *n.* [U] a dish of large SHRIMP cooked with butter and GARLIC

scan¹ /skæn/ *v.* **scanned, scanning 1** also **scan through** [I,T] to read something quickly in order to understand its main meaning or to find some particular information: *Stern started every day by scanning the want ads.* **2** [T] if a machine scans an object or a part of your body, it passes a BEAM¹ (1) of ELECTRONs over it to produce a picture of its surface or of what is inside: *Dr. Schlaug scanned the brains of several musicians as part of his research.* | [**scan sth in/ into**] *You could scan the picture into your computer and paste it into your paper.* —see also SCANNER (2) **3** [T] to examine an area carefully but quickly, because you are looking for a particular person or thing: *Surveillance cameras constantly scan the sidewalks.* | [**scan sth for sth**] *I scanned the beach for familiar faces.* **4** [T] if a machine or instrument scans an area, it searches it with RADAR or SONAR **5** TECHNICAL **a)** [I] poetry that scans has a correct regular pattern of beats **b)** [T] to find or show a regular pattern of beats in a poem or line of poetry —see also SCANSION

scan² *n.* [C] **1** a test done by a SCANNER (=special machine that produces a picture of the inside of something): *A bone scan showed a small fracture in Conway's right ankle.* **2** the act of scanning something: *After a quick scan of the headlines, Joan put the newspaper down.*

scan·dal /ˈskændl/ *n.* [C,U] behavior or events, often involving famous people, that are considered to be shocking or not moral: *a financial scandal* | *The administration has been plagued by scandal and controversy.* | *Jameson lost his job and split up with his wife after the **scandal broke** (=became known to everyone).*

scan·dal·ize /ˈskændlˌaɪz/ *v.* [T usually passive] to do something that shocks people very much: *In the 1800s, writer George Sand, really a woman, scandalized society by dressing like a man.*

scan·dal·mon·ger /ˈskændlˌmʌŋgɚ, -ˌmɑŋgɚ/ *n.* [C] someone who tells people shocking things about someone else, often things that are not true —**scandalmongering** *n.* [U]

scan·dal·ous /ˈskændl-əs/ *adj.* completely immoral and shocking: *scandalous behavior* —**scandalously** *adv.*

Scan·di·na·vi·a /ˌskændɪˈneɪviə/ an area of northern Europe consisting of Norway, Sweden, Denmark, Finland, and Iceland

Scan·di·na·vi·an /ˌskændəˈneɪviən◂/ *n.* [C] someone from the area of northern Europe that is considered to include Norway, Sweden, Denmark, Finland, and Iceland —**Scandinavian** *adj.*: *Scandinavian languages*

scan·ner /ˈskænɚ/ *n.* [C] **1** a piece of computer equipment that copies an image from paper onto the screen —see picture on page 426 **2** a machine that moves a BEAM¹ (1) of ELECTRONs over something in order to produce a picture of what is inside: *scanners for medical use*

scan·sion /ˈskænʃən/ *n.* [U] TECHNICAL the pattern of regular beats in poetry, or the marks you write to represent this

scant /skænt/ *adj.* [only before noun] **1** not enough: *We had scant time to rehearse.* | *Many people in the U.S. give scant attention to European affairs.* **2 a scant cup/teaspoon etc.** a little less than a full amount of a particular measurement: *Add a scant tablespoon of dry yeast.*

scant·y /ˈskænti/ *adj.* **scantier, scantiest** not big enough for a particular purpose: *Beautiful women paraded by in scanty clothing.* —**scantily** *adv.*: *scantily clad models*

-scape /skeɪp/ *suffix* [in nouns] a wide view of a particular area, especially in a picture: *the impressive cityscape of New York* | *some old Dutch seascapes* (=pictures of the ocean)

scape·goat /ˈskeɪpgoʊt/ *n.* [C] someone who is blamed for something bad that happens, even if it is not their fault: *They'll be looking for a scapegoat if things don't go their way.* —**scapegoat** *v.* [T]

scap·u·la /ˈskæpyələ/ *n.* [C] TECHNICAL one of the two flat bones on each side of your upper back; SHOULDER BLADE —see picture at SKELETON

scar¹ /skɑr/ *n.* [C] **1** a permanent mark that is left after you have had a cut or wound **2** a permanent emotional or mental effect caused by a bad experience: *Divorce can **leave** permanent **scars** on a child.* **3** an ugly permanent mark on something *Some parts of Northridge still **bear the scars of** the 1994 earthquake.*

scar² *v.* **1** [T] to have or be given a permanent mark on your skin because of a cut or wound: *Her arm was scarred with cigarette burns.* | *David survived the crash but will **be scarred for life**.* **2** [T] if a bad, difficult, or upsetting experience scars you, it has a permanent effect on your character or feelings: *battle-scarred young men* | *The scandals have scarred Garcia's life.* **3** [I] also **scar over** if a wound scars, it becomes healthy but leaves a permanent mark on your skin

scar·ab /ˈskærəb/ also **scarab bee·tle** /ˈ.. ˌ../ *n.* [C] a large black BEETLE (=insect with a hard shell), or a representation of this

scarce¹ /skɛrs/ *adj.* **1** if food, clothing, water etc. is scarce, there is not enough of it available: *Water is always scarce in these parts.* | *Mayors have to juggle scarce resources to keep their cities working.* —see Usage Note at RARE **2 make yourself scarce** INFORMAL to leave a place, especially in order to avoid a bad situation: *For the next few days I made myself scarce, hoping his bad mood would pass.*

scarce² *adv.* LITERARY scarcely

scarce·ly /ˈskɛrsli/ *adv.* **1** almost not, or almost none at all: *We've seen scarcely a drop of rain for over six months.* | **scarcely any/ever** *There was scarcely any decoration in the room.* | **can/could scarcely do sth** *She could scarcely believe her eyes.* **2** just barely: [**have scarcely done sth when**] *He had scarcely gone to sleep when the phone rang.* **3** definitely not, or almost certainly not: *There can scarcely be any doubt that Sullivan is guilty.* —see Usage Note at ALMOST

scar·ci·ty /'skɛrsəti/ *n.* [singular,U] a situation in which there is not enough of something: *The scarcity of medical supplies was becoming critical.*

s w **scare**[1] /skɛr/ *v.* **1** [T] to make someone feel frightened: *All the stuff he said about spiders kind of scared me.* | **scare the hell/shit/daylights etc. out of sb** *A siren went off somewhere, scaring the hell out of him.* **2** [I] to become frightened: *I don't scare easily, you know.*

scare sb ↔ **into** sth *phr. v.* [T] to make someone do something by frightening them or threatening them: [**scare sb into doing sth**] *Pictures of diseased lungs scared me into quitting smoking.*

scare sb/sth ↔ **off/away** *phr. v.* [T] **1** to make someone or something go away by frightening them: *Install an alarm system to scare burglars away.* **2** to make someone uncertain or worried, so that they do not do something they were going to do: *News of the Gulf War scared many travelers off visiting the Mediterranean.*

scare sth ↔ **up** *phr. v.* [T] INFORMAL **1** to get or find something, even though this is difficult: *I might be able to scare up two tickets to the Tampa Bay game.* **2** to make something, although you have very few things to make it from: *Susie scared up some lunch while we unpacked.*

scare[2] *n.* **1** [singular] a sudden feeling of fear: *Lisa gave her parents a scare when she didn't come home after school.* **2** [C] a situation in which a lot of people become frightened about something: *The game was delayed due to a bomb scare.* | *a health scare*

scare·crow /'skɛrkroʊ/ *n.* [C] an object made to look like a person, that a farmer puts in a field to frighten birds away

s w **scared** /skɛrd/ *adj.* frightened of something, or nervous about something: [+ of] *He's really scared of snakes.* | *A lot of people are scared of computers.* | [+ (that)] *She was scared that she might slip and fall on the ice.* | [**scared to do sth**] *Janice lay on the floor trembling, too scared to move.* | **scared stiff/scared to death** (=extremely frightened)

scare·dy-cat /'skɛrdi,kæt/ *n.* [C] INFORMAL an insulting word for someone who is easily frightened, used especially by children

scare sto·ry /'. ,../ *n.* [C] a report, especially in a newspaper, that makes a situation seem more serious or worrying than it really is

scare tac·tics /'. ,../ *n.* [plural] methods of persuading people to do something by frightening them: *The company used scare tactics to sell medical alert systems to the elderly.*

scarf[1] /skarf/ *n. plural* **scarfs** or **scarves** /skarvz/ [C] **1** a long narrow piece of material that you wear around your neck to keep it warm **2** a square piece of material that a woman wears over her head or around her neck, usually as a decoration

scarf[2] *v.* [T] INFORMAL also **scarf down/up** to eat something very quickly: *I scarfed down a candy bar between classes.*

scar·i·fy /'skɛrəfaɪ, 'skær-/ *v.* **scarified, scarifying** [T] **1** to break and make the surface of a road or field loose, using a pointed tool **2** TECHNICAL to make small cuts on an area of skin using a sharp knife **3** LITERARY to criticize someone very severely

scar·let /'skarlɪt/ *n.* [U] a bright red color —**scarlet** *adj.*

scarlet fe·ver /,.. '../ *n.* [U] a serious infectious illness that mainly affects children, causing a sore throat and red spots on your skin

scarlet wom·an /,.. '../ *n.* [C] OLD-FASHIONED a woman who has sexual relationships with many different people

scarp /skarp/ *n.* [C] TECHNICAL a line of natural cliffs

scarves /skarvz/ *n.* a plural of SCARF

s w **scar·y** /'skɛri/ *adj.* **scarier, scariest** INFORMAL frightening: *a scary movie*

scat[1] /skæt/ *n.* [U] **1** a style of JAZZ singing, in which

a singer sings sounds rather than words **2** solid waste from the body of a wild animal; DROPPINGS: *bear scat*

scat[2] *interjection* OLD-FASHIONED used to tell an animal, especially a cat, or a small child to go away: *Go on, scat! And don't come back!*

scath·ing /'skeɪðɪŋ/ *adj.* scathing remarks, COMMENTS etc. criticize someone or something very severely: *Bloom paints a scathing portrait of Meinke in his memoirs.* | *Their criticism was scathing.* —**scathingly** *adv.*

scat·o·log·ic·al /,skæt̮l'ɑdʒɪkəl/ *adj.* FORMAL too interested in or relating to human waste, in a way that people find offensive: *scatological humor* —**scatology** /skæ'tɑlədʒi/ *n.* [U]

scat·ter /'skæt̮ɚ/ *v.* [I,T] **1** if a lot of things scatter, or if someone scatters them, they are thrown or dropped over a wide area in an irregular way: [+ over/on etc.] *The marbles scattered and rolled across the room.* | *Scatter a few flower petals over the table for a decorative effect.* | [**scatter sth with sth**] *The work table was scattered with pencils and crayons.* **2** if a group of people scatter, or if something scatters them, everyone suddenly moves in different directions, especially to escape danger: *Soldiers used tear gas to scatter the crowd.* **3 be scattered to the four winds** LITERARY to be broken apart or separated and lost —see also SCATTERED, SCATTERING

scat·ter·brained /'skæt̮ɚ,breɪnd/ *adj.* not thinking in a practical way, so that you forget or lose things —**scatterbrain** *n.* [C]

scat·tered /'skæt̮ɚd/ *adj.* **1** spread over a wide area or over a long period of time: *There was scattered gunfire and looting in the area.* **2 scattered showers/thunderstorms/rain** used in weather reports to say there will be some short periods of rain

scat·ter·ing /'skæt̮ɚɪŋ/ *n.* [C usually singular] a small number of things or people spread out over a large area: [+ of] *Only a scattering of people applauded as he finished his speech.*

scav·enge /'skævɪndʒ/ *v.* [I,T] **1** if someone scavenges, they search through things that other people do not want for food or useful objects: [+ for] *In the garbage dumps, women and children scavenge for glass and plastic bottles.* **2** if an animal scavenges, it eats anything that it can find —**scavenger** *n.* [C]

scavenger hunt /'... ,./ *n.* [C] a game in which people are given a list of unusual things that they must find and bring back

sce·nar·i·o /sɪ'nɛri,oʊ, -'nær-/ *n. plural* **scenarios** [C] **1** a situation that could possibly happen but has not happened yet: *A common scenario is that a woman marries and sacrifices her career for her husband.* | **worst-case/nightmare scenario** (=the worst possible situation) **2** a written description of the characters, place, and things that will happen in a movie, play etc.

scene /sin/ *n.* [C]

s w **1** **play/movie** **a)** part of a play during which there is no change in time or place: *Act V, Scene 2 of Hamlet* **b)** a single piece of action that happens in one place in a movie, book etc.: *In the final scene, Harry tells Sabrina he loves her.* | *the death scene*

2 **view/picture** a view of a place as you see it, or as it appears in a picture: *She stared out the window at the lively street scene.* | *On the wall were several framed floral scenes.*

3 **accident/crime** [usually singular] the place where an accident, crime etc. happened: *One witness placed Smith at the scene of the crime.* | **on/at the scene** *Genoa was on the scene to report the murders for "The Examiner."*

4 **the music/fashion/political etc. scene** a particular set of activities and the people who are involved in them: *Haskell has been immersed in the jazz scene since he was 12.* | *the literary scene*

5 behind the scenes secretly, while other things are happening publicly: *Although he had retired, Brown remained active behind the scenes for years.*

6 situation all the things that are happening in a place, and the effect or situation that they cause: [+ of] *Harriet's house was a scene of utter confusion.*
7 set the scene a) to provide the conditions in which an event can happen: *Government tanks rolled into town, setting the scene for a bloody battle.* **b)** to describe the situation before you begin to tell a story
8 not your scene SPOKEN not the type of thing you like: *Vegas isn't really my scene.*
9 argument a loud angry argument, especially in a public place: *Rather than make a scene, I kept quiet and climbed in the back.*
10 be/come on the scene to be or become involved in a situation, activity etc.: *By then, there was a boyfriend on the scene.*
11 bad scene INFORMAL a difficult or bad situation: *It was a very bad scene at work today.*

scen·er·y /ˈsinəri/ *n.* [U] **1** the natural features of a particular part of a country, such as mountains, forests, deserts etc.: *The train passes by some breathtaking scenery in the Canadian Rockies.* **2** the painted background, furniture etc. used on a theater stage —see also **a change of scenery** (CHANGE² (3))

sce·nic /ˈsinɪk/ *adj.* surrounded by views of beautiful COUNTRYSIDE: *Highway 55 takes you up a very scenic route along the river.* —**scenically** /-kli/ *adv.*

scent¹ /sɛnt/ *n.* [C,U] **1** a pleasant smell that something has: *The sweet scent of incense filled the air.* —see Usage Note at SMELL¹ **2** the smell of a particular animal or person that some other animals, for example dogs, can follow: *Two police bloodhounds followed the boy's scent to the old house.* **3 throw sb off the scent** to give someone false information to prevent them from catching you or discovering something: *Companies developing new products try to throw their competitors off the scent.* **4** OLD-FASHIONED a liquid that you put on your skin to make it smell nice; PERFUME

scent² *v.* [T] **1** to give a particular smell to something: *The fragrance of lilacs scented the evening air.* **2 scent fear/danger/victory etc.** LITERARY to feel sure that something is going to happen: *Something inside him scented danger.* **3** if an animal scents another animal or a person, it knows that they are near because it can smell them

scent·ed /ˈsɛntɪd/ *adj.* having a particular smell, especially a nice one: *scented paper*

scent·less /ˈsɛntləs/ *adj.* without a smell

scep·ter /ˈsɛptə/ *n.* [C] a short decorated stick carried by kings or queens at ceremonies

scep·ti·cal /ˈskɛptɪkəl/ the British and Canadian spelling of SKEPTICAL

scep·ti·cism /ˈskɛptəˌsɪzəm/ the British and Canadian spelling of SKEPTICISM

scha·den·freu·de /ˈʃɑdnˌfrɔɪdə/ *n.* [U] FORMAL a feeling of pleasure that you get when something bad happens to someone else

sched·ule¹ /ˈskɛdʒəl, -dʒul/ *n.* [C] **1** a plan of what someone is going to do and when they are going to do it: *What's your schedule like on Wednesdays?* **busy/full schedule** *Because of his busy schedule, Art doesn't get to spend much time with his sons.* | **ahead of/on/behind schedule** (=before, at, or after the planned time) **2** a list that shows the times that buses, trains etc. leave or arrive at a particular place **3** a formal list of something, for example prices: *Medicare pays for each test according to its schedule of fees.*

schedule² *v.* [T usually passive] **1** to plan that something will happen at a particular time: [+ for] *We have a rehearsal scheduled for four o'clock.* | [be scheduled to do sth] *I'm scheduled to see Dr. Good next week.* **2 scheduled flight** an airplane service that flies at the same time every day or every week

Schel·ling /ˈʃɛlɪŋ/, **Frie·drich von** /ˈfridrɪk vɑn/ (1775–1854) a German PHILOSOPHER

sche·ma /ˈskimə/ *n. plural* **schemas** or **schemata** /skiˈmɑtə/ [C] TECHNICAL a plan showing only the important parts of something; DIAGRAM

sche·mat·ic¹ /skiˈmætɪk/ *adj.* in the form of a basic plan or arrangement: *His business card had a small schematic map on the back.* | *a schematic drawing* —**schematic** *n.* [C] —**schematically** /-kli/ *adv.*

schematic² *n.* [C] a DIAGRAM (=a correct drawing) of a structure, especially of an electrical or MECHANICAL system: *The software can help you produce blueprints, schematics, and maps.*

sche·ma·tize /ˈskiməˌtaɪz/ *v.* [T] FORMAL to arrange something in a system

scheme¹ /skim/ *n.* [C] **1** an intelligent plan, especially to do something bad or illegal: *Young came up with the scheme to pass phony checks.* | *a get-rich-quick scheme* **2** a system that you use to organize information, ideas etc.: *a classification scheme* | *It's a modern salon with a color scheme* (=the colors chosen for something) *of blue and beige.* **3 in the scheme of things** in the way things generally happen, or are organized: *What I'm doing is unimportant in the big scheme of things, but people find it interesting.*

scheme² *v.* [I] to secretly make intelligent and dishonest plans to get or achieve something: [scheme to do sth] *He was charged with scheming to defraud the government.* | [scheme against sb] *Newman and Marvin play ranch hands who are scheming against their crooked employer.* —**schemer** *n.* [C] —**scheming** *adj.*: *a scheming woman*

scher·zo /ˈskɛrtsoʊ/ *n. plural* **scherzos** [C] a cheerful piece of music played quickly —**scherzo** *adj. adv.*

Schil·ler /ˈʃɪlə/, **Frie·drich von** /ˈfridrɪk vɑn/ (1759–1805) a German writer of plays, poetry, and history

schism /ˈsɪzəm, ˈskɪzəm/ *n.* [C,U] the separation of a group into two groups, caused by a disagreement about its aims and beliefs, especially a separation in the Christian church —**schismatic** /sɪzˈmætɪk, skɪz-/ *adj.*

schist /ʃɪst/ *n.* [U] TECHNICAL a type of rock that naturally breaks apart into thin flat pieces

schiz·o /ˈskɪtsoʊ/ *n.* [C] SLANG a SCHIZOPHRENIC

schiz·oid /ˈskɪtsɔɪd/ *adj.* **1** TECHNICAL typical of schizophrenia: *a schizoid personality disorder* **2** INFORMAL quickly changing between opposite opinions or attitudes: *Martin's latest play is as schizoid and erratic as its characters.*

schiz·o·phre·ni·a /ˌskɪtsəˈfriniə/ *n.* [U] a serious mental illness in which someone's thoughts and feelings are not based on what is really happening around them

schiz·o·phren·ic¹ /ˌskɪtsəˈfrɛnɪk/ *adj.* **1** TECHNICAL relating to schizophrenia, or typical of schizophrenia **2** INFORMAL quickly changing from one opinion, attitude etc. to another: *The survey shows the schizophrenic nature of Americans' views on crime.*

schizophrenic² *n.* [C] someone who has schizophrenia

schle·miel /ʃləˈmil/ *n.* [C] a stupid person, especially one who is easily tricked

schlep /ʃlɛp/ *v.* **schlepped, schlepping** [T] INFORMAL to carry or pull something heavy: [+ down/out/along etc.] *There were no carts available, so we had to schlep our luggage up the hill.*
schlep around *phr. v.* [I] to spend your time doing nothing useful: *I usually just schlep around the house on Saturdays.*

Schlie·mann /ˈʃlimən/, **Hein·rich** /ˈheɪnrɪk/ (1822–1890) a German ARCHEOLOGIST who discovered the ancient city of Troy

schlock /ʃlɑk/ *n.* [U] INFORMAL things that are cheap, bad, or useless: *The gift store sells both tasteful gifts and cheap schlock.* —**schlocky** *adj.*

schlong, schlang /ʃlɑŋ/ *n.* [C] VULGAR, SLANG a PENIS

schmaltz·y /ˈʃmɔltsi, ˈʃmɑl-/ *adj.* **schmaltzier, schmaltziest** INFORMAL a schmaltzy piece of music, book etc. deals with strong emotions such as love and sadness in a way that seems silly and not serious enough: *a schmaltzy love song* —**schmaltz** *n.* [U]

schmo /ʃmoʊ/ *n. plural* **schmoes** [C] INFORMAL a

stupid person —see also **Joe Blow/Schmo** (JOE (1))

schmooze /ʃmuz/ v. [I] INFORMAL to talk about unimportant things at a social event in a friendly way that is not always sincere: *Leno spent time schmoozing with local TV executives.* —**schmoozer** n. [C]

schmuck /ʃmʌk/ n. [C] SPOKEN a stupid person

schnapps /ʃnæps/ n. [U] a strong alcoholic drink

schnau·zer /'ʃnauzɚ, 'ʃnautsɚ/ n. [C] a type of small gray or black dog with fairly short wavy hair

schnit·zel /'ʃnitsəl/ n. [C,U] a flat piece of meat, especially VEAL, covered with small pieces of bread and cooked in oil

schnook /ʃnʊk/ n. [C] SPOKEN a stupid or unimportant person

schnoz, schnozz /ʃnaz/ n. [C] HUMOROUS a nose

Schoen·berg /'ʃɔnbɚg/, **Ar·nold** /'arnəld/ (1874–1951) an Austrian musician who wrote modern CLASSICAL music

schol·ar /'skalɚ/ n. [C] **1** someone who knows a lot about a particular subject, especially one that is not a science subject: *Biblical scholars* **2** someone who has been given a SCHOLARSHIP (=money) to study at a college or university: *a Rhodes scholar*

schol·ar·ly /'skalɚli/ adj. **1** relating to the serious study of a particular subject: *scholarly research* **2** someone who is scholarly spends a lot of time studying, and knows a lot about a particular subject

schol·ar·ship /'skalɚʃɪp/ n. **1** [C] an amount of money that is given to someone by an organization to help pay for their education, especially because they are very smart or for another particular reason —compare FINANCIAL AID GRANT[1] **2** [U] the knowledge, work, or methods involved in serious studying: *Burns's book is a work of great scholarship.*

scho·las·tic /skə'læstɪk/ adj. [only before noun] FORMAL **1** relating to schools, learning, or teaching: *Mel received an award for outstanding scholastic achievement.* **2** relating to scholasticism

scho·las·ti·cism /skə'læstə,sɪzəm/ n. [U] a way of studying thought, especially religious thought, based on things written in ancient times

school[1] /skul/ n.

1 where children learn [C] a place where children are taught: *What school does your son go to?* | *Lisa always buys her lunch at school.* | **school** *bus/* **building** etc. *school books* —see also CHARTER SCHOOL, PAROCHIAL SCHOOL, PRIVATE SCHOOL, PUBLIC SCHOOL

2 time at school [U] a day's work at school: *Did you have a good day at school?* | **before/after school** *I have football practice after school.* **b)** the time during your life when you go to a school: *Joanne's one of my old friends from school.*

3 in school **a)** attending a school or university, as opposed to having a job: *Aaron's girlfriend is still in school.* **b)** in the school building: *The kids are in school between nine and three.*

4 university **a)** [C,U] a college or university, or the time when you study there: *Both their kids are away at school now.* | *You should apply to Swarthmore – it's a good school.* **b)** [C] a department or group of departments that teaches a particular subject at a university: [+ of] *the Harvard School of Business* | **law/medical/graduate** etc. **school** *I worked my way through grad school.*

5 teachers/students [singular,U] the students and teachers at a school: *The whole school was sorry when she left.*

6 one subject [C] a place where a particular subject or skill is taught: *a language school* | [+ of] *the Eastman School of Music*

7 art/literature [C] a number of artists, writers etc. who are considered as a group because of their styles of work are very similar: *the Impressionist school*

8 school of thought an opinion or way of thinking about something that is shared by a group of people: *There are many schools of thought on how yoga should be taught.*

9 fish [C] a large group of fish, WHALES, DOLPHINS etc. that swim together: [+ of] *a school of whales*

10 of/from the old school having old-fashioned traditional values or qualities, and not willing to

change them: *As a soldier of the old school, Eisenhower felt his responsibility was to protect the nation's security.*

11 the school of hard knocks OLD-FASHIONED the difficult or bad experiences you have in life: *Pete learned everything he knows about business from the school of hard knocks.*

school[2] v. [T usually passive] to train or teach someone: [be schooled in sth] *Although never schooled in fashion, Ramirez is a talented designer.*

school·bag /'skulbæg/ n. [C] a bag that a child carries his or her books and other things for school in

school board /'. ./ n. [C] a group of people who are elected to govern a school or group of schools in the U.S.

school·book /'skulbʊk/ n. [C] a book that is used in school classes; TEXTBOOK

school·boy /'skulbɔɪ/ n. [C] OLD-FASHIONED a boy attending school

school·child /'skul-tʃaɪld/ n. plural **schoolchildren** [C] OLD-FASHIONED a child attending school

school·day /'skuldeɪ/ n. [C] **1** a day of the week when children are usually at school **2 schooldays** [plural] the time of your life when you go to school: *I've known Wally since our schooldays.*

school dis·trict /'. ,../ n. [C] an area in a U.S. state that includes a number of schools which are governed together

school·girl /'skulgɚl/ n. [C] OLD-FASHIONED a girl attending school

school·house /'skulhaʊs/ n. [C] a building for a small school, especially in a small town or the country in past times: *a one-room schoolhouse*

school·ing /'skulɪŋ/ n. [U] school education: *Walter only had seven years of schooling.*

school·kid /'skul-kɪd/ n. [C] INFORMAL a child attending school

school·marm /'skulmarm/ n. [C] a woman teacher who is considered to be old-fashioned, strict, and easily shocked by immoral things —**schoolmarmish** adj.

school·mas·ter /'skul,mæstɚ/ n. [C] OLD-FASHIONED a male teacher

school mis·tress /'. ,../ n. [C] OLD-FASHIONED a female teacher

school night /'. ./ n. [C] a night before you have to go to school the next morning: *You guys should be in bed – it's a school night.*

school·room /'skulrum/ n. [C] a room where classes are taught

school·teach·er /'skul,titʃɚ/ n. [C] a teacher

school·work /'skulwɚk/ n. [U] work done for or during school classes

schoo·ner /'skunɚ/ n. [C] **1** a fast sailing ship with two sails **2** a large tall glass for beer

Scho·pen·hau·er /'ʃoupən,haʊɚ/, **Ar·tur** /'artʊr/ (1788–1860) a German PHILOSOPHER

Schrö·ding·er /'ʃroudɪnɚ/, **Er·win** /'ɚvɪn/ (1887–1961) an Austrian scientist whose ideas were an important part of the development of QUANTUM MECHANICS

Schu·bert /'ʃubɚt/, **Franz** /franz/ (1797–1828) an Austrian musician who wrote CLASSICAL music

Schu·mann /'ʃumən/, **Rob·ert** /'rabɚt/ (1810–1856) a German musician who wrote CLASSICAL music

schuss /ʃʊs/ v. [I] to SKI quickly down a mountain in a straight line

schwa /ʃwa/ n. [C] **1** a vowel typically heard in parts of a word that are spoken without STRESS[1] (4), such as the "a" in "about" **2** the sign (ə), used to represent this sound

Schweit·zer /'ʃwaɪtsɚ/, **Al·bert** /'ælbɚt/ (1875–1965) a German doctor, famous for starting a hospital in Gabon and treating people who were suffering from LEPROSY

sci·at·ic /saɪˈætɪk/ *adj.* TECHNICAL relating to the HIPS: *the sciatic nerve*

sci·at·i·ca /saɪˈætɪkə/ *n.* [U] pain in the lower back, HIPS, and legs

sci·ence /ˈsaɪəns/ *n.* **1** [U] knowledge about the physical world, especially based on examining, testing, and proving facts: *Through these lessons, students learn the basics of science.* | *science and technology* **2** [U] the study of science: *Mr. Paulson is a science teacher.* **3** [C] a particular part of science, for example BIOLOGY, CHEMISTRY, or PHYSICS: *the physical sciences* **4 sth is not an exact science** used to say that something involves a lot of guessing, and that there is not just one right way to do it: *Opinion polling is hardly an exact science.* **5 have sth down to a science** to have so much experience doing something that you can do it very well without making any mistakes, wasting anything etc.: *After cooking for six years on the Orient Express, chef Bodiguel has it down to a science.* —see also NATURAL SCIENCE, **sth isn't rocket science** (ROCKET[1] (4)), SOCIAL SCIENCE

science fic·tion /ˌ.. '../ *n.* [U] a type of writing that describes imaginary future developments in science and their effect on life, for example traveling in time or to other PLANETS with life on them

science park /'.. ˌ./ *n.* [C] an area in a city where there are a lot of companies or organizations that do scientific work

sci·en·tif·ic /ˌsaɪənˈtɪfɪk/ *adj.* **1** [no comparative] relating to science, or using its methods: *scientific research* | *There is no scientific basis for such policies.* **2** done very carefully, using an organized system: *There isn't a very scientific filing system in the office.* **3 the scientific method** the usual process of finding out information in science, which involves testing your ideas by performing EXPERIMENTS and making decisions based on the results —**scientifically** /-kli/ *adv.*

sci·en·tist /ˈsaɪəntɪst/ *n.* [C] someone who works or is trained in science —see also ROCKET SCIENTIST

Sci·en·tol·o·gy /ˌsaɪənˈtɑlədʒi/ *n.* [U] a religion that was started in the 1950s by the U.S. SCIENCE FICTION writer L. Ron Hubbard, officially called the Church of Scientology —**Scientologist** *n.*

sci-fi /ˌsaɪ ˈfaɪ/ *n.* [U] INFORMAL: see SCIENCE FICTION

scim·i·tar /ˈsɪmɪt̬ə, -ˌtɑr/ *n.* [C] a sword with a curved blade

scin·til·la /sɪnˈtɪlə/ *n.* [singular] FORMAL a very small amount of something: *There was **not a scintilla of** evidence to prove that Grover committed the murders.*

scin·til·late /ˈsɪntˌl̩eɪt/ *v.* [I] LITERARY to shine with small quick flashes of light; SPARKLE —**scintillation** /ˌsɪntˌl̩ˈeɪʃən/ *n.* [U]

scin·til·lat·ing /ˈsɪntˌl̩eɪt̬ɪŋ/ *adj.* FORMAL interesting, intelligent, and amusing: *scintillating conversation*

sci·on /ˈsaɪən/ *n.* [C] **1** LITERARY a young member of a famous or important family: [+ of] *Baker is the scion of one of Houston's most distinguished families.* **2** TECHNICAL a living part of a plant that is cut off, especially to be fastened to another plant

scis·sors /ˈsɪzəz/ *n.* [plural] a tool for cutting paper, fabric, card etc., made of two sharp blades that are fastened in the middle and have two holes for your fingers at one end: *a pair of scissors*

scle·ro·sis /skləˈroʊsɪs/ *n.* [C,U] TECHNICAL a disease that causes an organ or soft part of your body to become hard —**sclerotic** /skləˈrɑtɪk/ *adj.* —see also MULTIPLE SCLEROSIS

scoff /skɔf, skɑf/ *v.* [I] FORMAL to laugh at a person or idea, and talk about them in a way that shows you think they are stupid: [+ at] *Parker scoffed at the movie's critics.*

scof·flaw /ˈskɔflɔ, ˈskɑf-/ *n.* [C] someone who often breaks the law, but in a way that is not very serious: *The mayor announced plans to track down scofflaws who refuse to pay their parking fines.*

scold[1] /skoʊld/ *v.* [T] to angrily criticize someone, especially a child, about something they have done: [**scold sb for doing sth**] *June scolded the boys for taking the candy without asking first.* —**scolding** *n.* [C,U]

scold[2] *n.* [C] OLD-FASHIONED someone who often complains or criticizes

sco·li·o·sis /ˌskoʊliˈoʊsɪs/ *n.* [U] TECHNICAL a medical condition in which someone's SPINE is curved in a way that is not normal

sconce /skɑns/ *n.* [C] an object that is attached to a wall and holds CANDLES or electric lights

scone /skoʊn, skɑn/ *n.* [C] a small round type of bread, sometimes containing dried fruit

scoop[1] /skup/ *n.* [C] **1** a round deep spoon used for holding or serving food such as flour, sugar, or ICE CREAM: *an ice cream scoop* **2** also **scoopful** an amount of food served with this kind of spoon: [+ of] *a big scoop of mashed potatoes* **3** an important or exciting news story that is printed in one newspaper or shown on one television station before any of the others know about it: *CNN recognized its opportunity for a scoop.* **4 what's the scoop?** SPOKEN used to ask someone for information or news about something

scoop[2] *v.* [T] **1** to pick something up with a scoop, a spoon, or with your curved hand: [**scoop sth up/out/off etc.**] *Cut the squash in half and scoop out the seeds.* **2** to be the first newspaper to print an important news report: *Charlie loved to scoop the competition.*

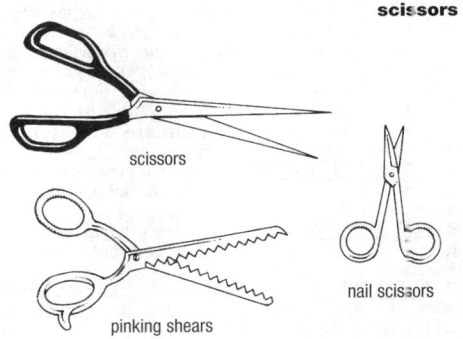

scoop out

scoop sth ↔ up *phr. v.* [T] if a lot of people scoop something up, they buy it quickly so that soon there is none left: *Fans scooped up the trading cards in the first few hours of the sale.*

scoop neck /'. ./ *n.* [C] a round, fairly low neck on a woman's TOP or dress

scoot[1] /skut/ *v.* INFORMAL **1** [I] to move to one side, especially to make room for someone or something else: [+ over] *Can you scoot over?* **2** [I] to move quickly and suddenly: *Matt scooted over the bridge on his skateboard.* **3** [T] to make someone or something move a short distance by pushing or pulling: *I scooted my chair over to their table.*

scoot[2] *interjection* used to tell someone to move or to leave a place quickly: *Time for bed, Andy – scoot!*

scoot·er /ˈskut̬ə/ *n.* [C] **1** also **motor scooter** a type of small, less powerful MOTORCYCLE —see picture at MOTORCYCLE **2** a child's vehicle with two small wheels, an upright handle, and a narrow board that you stand on with one foot, while the other foot pushes against the ground

scissors

scissors

pinking shears

nail scissors

scope[1] /skoʊp/ *n.* [U] **1** the range of things that a subject, activity, book etc. deals with: *Student science projects should vary in length and scope.* | **beyond/ within the scope of sth** *A discussion of all the possible treatments is beyond the scope of this book.* | **broaden/expand the scope of sth** *The network is* *trying to expand the scope of children's TV.* **2** the opportunity to do or develop something: [+ **for**] *Is there much scope for initiative in this job?*

scope² *v.* [T]

scope sb/sth out *phr. v.* [T] INFORMAL to look at something or someone to see what they are like: *A couple of guys were scoping out the girls.*

scorch¹ /skɔrtʃ/ *v.* **1** [I,T] if you scorch something, or if it scorches, its surface burns slightly and changes color: *Stir the onions frequently to prevent scorching.* | *The iron was too hot, and I scorched my shirt.* **2** [T] if strong heat scorches you, it burns you: *The hot sand scorched our feet.* **3** [T] if strong heat scorches plants, it dries them and kills them

scorch

Rob scorched his shirt.

scorch² *n.* **1** [C] a mark made on something where its surface has been burned **2** [U] brown coloring on plants caused by some plant diseases

scorched-earth pol·i·cy /ˌ. '. ˌ.../ *n.* [C] the destruction by an army of everything useful in an area, especially crops and buildings, so that the land cannot be used by an enemy

scorch·er /'skɔrtʃɚ/ *n.* [C usually singular] INFORMAL an extremely hot day: *Today's going to be a scorcher.*

scorch·ing /'skɔrtʃɪŋ/ *adj.* extremely hot: *Here in Houston, it was a scorching 93° today.*

s w **score¹** /skɔr/ *n.* [C]

1 in a game the number of points that each team or player has won in a game or competition: *What's the score?* | *With only nine seconds left to go, the score is tied at 82.* | *Barbara, can you keep score* (=keep a record of the points won)?

2 on a test the number of points a student has earned for correct answers on a test: *Average test scores have fallen in recent years.*

3 music a written or printed copy of a piece of music, especially for a large group of performers, or the music itself: *a jazz score* | *Williams has written the score for many of Spielberg's movies.*

4 on that score SPOKEN concerning the particular thing you have just mentioned: *You won't get any complaints from me on that score.*

5 scores of sth a lot of: *Scores of reporters gathered outside the courthouse.*

6 settle a score to do something to harm or hurt someone who has harmed or hurt you in the past: *Stanford settled an old score Friday by defeating Siena 94–72.*

7 mark a mark that has been cut onto a surface with a sharp tool: *deep scores in the wood*

8 number OLD USE twenty —see also **know the score** (KNOW¹ (17))

s w **score²** *v.*

1 win points [I,T] to win a point in a game, competition, or on a test: *Students who listened to Mozart scored higher on IQ tests than students who took the test in silence.* | *Anyone who scores under 70 percent will have to retake the exam.* **score a point/run/touchdown etc.** *Mays scored the winning goal.*

2 give points to give a particular number of points in a game, competition, or test: *Participants will be scored on their performance in each event.*

3 score points (with sb) INFORMAL to do or say something to please someone or to make them feel respect for you: *Score points with your girlfriend by sending her a big bunch of flowers.*

4 succeed [I,T] INFORMAL to be very successful in something you do: *Van Zandt has scored again with this enjoyable film about young urban types.* | *Dr. John scored a huge hit with his cover of "Makin' Whoopee."*

5 music **a)** to write the music for a movie, BALLET etc. **b)** to arrange a piece of music for a group of instruments or voices

6 sex [I] SLANG to have sex with someone: *Did you score last night?*

7 get drugs [I,T] SLANG to succeed in buying or getting illegal drugs

8 paper [T] to mark a line on a piece of paper, using a sharp instrument: *Scoring the paper first makes it easier to fold.*

score·board /'skɔrbɔrd/ *n.* [C] a board on which the points won in a game are shown

score·card /'skɔrkɑrd/ *n.* [C] a printed card used by someone watching a game or race to record what happens

score·keep·er /'skɔrˌkipɚ/ *n.* [C] someone who keeps an official record of the points won in a game

scor·er /'skɔrɚ/ *n.* [C] **1** a player who wins a point or GOAL (2) **2** a scorekeeper

scorn¹ /skɔrn/ *n.* [U] strong criticism of someone or something that you think is stupid or not as good as other people or things and does not deserve respect: [+ **for**] *He could barely disguise his scorn for her.* | **heap/pour scorn on** *Republican leaders are heaping scorn on the plan.*

scorn² *v.* [T] to show in an unkind way that you think that a person, idea, or suggestion is stupid or not worth accepting: *Skinner's ideas were scorned by many American psychologists.*

scorn·ful /'skɔrnfəl/ *adj.* feeling or showing scorn: *a scornful look* | [+ **of**] *He remained scornful of religion and its influence over people.* —**scornfully** *adv.*

Scor·pi·o /'skɔrpiˌoʊ/ *n.* **1** [singular] the eighth sign of the ZODIAC, represented by a scorpion, and believed to affect the character and life of people born between October 23 and November 21 **2** [C] someone who was born between October 23 and November 21

scor·pi·on /'skɔrpiən/ *n.* [C] a tropical creature like an insect with a curving tail and a poisonous sting

Scot /skɑt/ *n.* [C] someone from Scotland

Scotch¹ /skɑtʃ/ *n.* [C,U] a type of WHISKEY (=strong alcoholic drink) made in Scotland, or a glass of this: *Scotch and soda*

Scotch² *adj.* SCOTTISH

scotch /skɑtʃ/ *v.* [T] to stop something happening by firmly doing something to prevent it: *The mayor held a press conference to* **scotch rumors of** *his plans to run for the Senate.*

Scotch tape /ˌ. './ *n.* [U] TRADEMARK thin clear plastic in a narrow band that is sticky on one side, used for sticking light things such as pieces of paper together

scotch-tape /ˌ. './ *v.* [T] to stick things together with Scotch tape

scot-free /ˌskɑt 'fri/ *adv.* **get off scot-free** INFORMAL to avoid being punished, although you deserve to be

Scot·land /'skɑtlənd/ a country in the United Kingdom, north of England

Scots·man /'skɑtsmən/ *n.* [C] a man who comes from Scotland

Scots·wom·an /'skɑtsˌwʊmən/ *n.* [C] a woman who comes from Scotland

Scott /skɑt/**, Dred** /drɛd/ (?1795–1858) an African-American who was born a slave, famous for a legal case in which he claimed that he should be a free man

Scott, Sir Wal·ter /'wɔltɚ/ (1771–1832) a Scottish writer and poet

Scot·tish /'skɑtɪʃ/ *adj.* from or relating to Scotland

scoun·drel /'skaʊndrəl/ *n.* [C] OLD-FASHIONED a bad or dishonest man

scour /skaʊɚ/ *v.* [T] **1** to search very carefully and thoroughly through an area, a document etc.: *Rescue teams scoured the ruins for signs of more victims.* **2** also **scour out** to clean something very thoroughly by rubbing it with a rough material: *Scour the bowl with a mixture of vinegar and baking soda.* **3** also **scour out** to form a hole by continuous movement over a long period: *Over the years, the stream had scoured out a round pool in the rock.* —**scour** *n.* [singular]

scourge¹ /skɚdʒ, skɔrdʒ/ *n.* [C] **1** something that

causes a lot of harm or suffering: [+ of] *Gun violence is the scourge of my daughter's generation.* **2** a WHIP used to punish people in past times

scourge² *v.* [T] LITERARY **1** to cause a lot of harm or suffering to a place or group of people **2** to hit someone with a whip as punishment in past times

scouring pad /ˈ.. ˌ./ *n.* [C] a small ball of wire or rough plastic for cleaning cooking pots and pans

scout¹ /skaʊt/ *n.* [C] **1** a soldier who is sent to search an area in front of an army and get information about the enemy **2** someone whose job is to look for good sports players, musicians etc. in order to employ them: *Davis caught the attention of NBA scouts a few years ago.* —see also TALENT SCOUT **3** a member of the BOY SCOUTS or the GIRL SCOUTS

scout² *v.* **1** [I] also **scout around** to look for something in a particular area: [+ for] *Lou was scouting for a site on which to build her house.* **2** [T] also **scout out** to examine a place or area in order to get information about it, especially in a military situation: *In the morning, he set out to scout the surrounding countryside.* **3** [T] also **scout for** to find out about the abilities of sports players, musicians etc.

scout·ing /ˈskaʊtɪŋ/ *n.* [U] the activities that BOY SCOUTS and GIRL SCOUTS take part in

scout·mas·ter /ˈskaʊtˌmæstɚ/ *n.* [C] a man who is the leader of a group of BOY SCOUTS

scow /skaʊ/ *n.* [C] a large boat with a flat bottom, used mainly for carrying heavy goods

scowl¹ /skaʊl/ *v.* [I] to look at someone in an angry way: [+ at] *Nancy scowled at me from across the room.*

scowl² *n.* [C] an angry or disapproving expression on someone's face

Scrab·ble /ˈskræbəl/ *n.* [U] TRADEMARK a game in which players try to make words from the separate letters they have

scrab·ble /ˈskræbəl/ *v.* [I always + adv./prep.] to try to find something by feeling with your fingers, especially quickly among a lot of other things: [**scrabble for sth**] *She scrabbled under the bed for her slippers.*

scrag·gly /ˈskrægli/ *adj.* INFORMAL growing in a way that looks uneven and not well taken care of: *a scraggly beard*

scram /skræm/ *v.* [I usually in imperative] SPOKEN to leave a place very quickly, especially so that you do not get caught: *Scram, kid!*

scram·ble¹ /ˈskræmbəl/ *v.*
1 climb [I always + adv./prep.] to climb up or over something quickly and with difficulty, especially using your hands to help you: [+ up/down/over etc.] *The suspect scrambled over a fence.* | *Fans scrambled onto the stage.*
2 move quickly [I always + adv./prep.] to move somewhere quickly, especially in an awkward way: [+ to/out/from etc.] *Campers scrambled to safety when a flash flood came down the canyon.* | *I scrambled out of bed, late as usual.*
3 do sth quickly [T] to try to do something difficult very quickly: [**scramble to do sth**] *Everyone had to scramble to finish the project on time.* | *Officials scrambled for ways to meet the demand.*
4 compete [I] to struggle or compete with other people to get or reach something: [+ for] *People were scrambling for the seats in the front row.*
5 information/message [T] to use special equipment to mix messages, radio signals etc. into a different form, so that they cannot be understood by other people without the correct equipment: *Most cable TV companies began scrambling their signals in the mid–1980s.*
6 scramble an egg to cook an egg by mixing the white and yellow parts together and heating it
7 football if a football player, especially the QUARTERBACK, scrambles, he runs around with the football in order to avoid being TACKLEd (=stopped by the defense)

8 to mix words, ideas, sentences etc., so that they are not in the right order and do not make sense: *In this game, the letters of the words are scrambled.*
9 scramble to your feet to stand up quickly and awkwardly: *He scrambled to his feet as the ambassador entered the room.*
10 scramble sb's brains INFORMAL to make someone unable to think clearly or reasonably: *This amount of LSD is enough to scramble anyone's brains.*
11 aircraft [I,T] TECHNICAL if a group of military airplanes scrambles or if someone scrambles them, they are sent up into the air very quickly in order to escape or to attack an enemy

scramble² *n.* [singular] **1** a situation in which people compete with and push each other in order to get what they want: [+ for] *There was a scramble for the best seats in the auditorium.* | [**a scramble to do sth**] *Everyone was in a scramble to reach the exits.* **2** a situation in which something has to be done very quickly, with a lot of rushing around: *It was a mad scramble trying to get things ready in time.*

scrambled eggs /ˌ.. ˈ./ *n.* [plural] eggs that have been cooked after mixing the white and yellow parts together

scram·bler /ˈskræmblɚ/ *n.* [C] a machine that mixes up a radio or telephone message so that it cannot be understood without special equipment —see also DESCRAMBLER

scrap¹ /skræp/ *n.* **1** [C] a small piece of paper, cloth etc.: [+ of] *She wrote the message on a scrap of paper and handed it to Bill.* | *Save those fabric scraps to make a quilt.* **2** [U] materials or objects that are not used anymore for the purpose they were made for, but can be used again in another way: *The Kempers sold their old car to a scrap dealer.* | **scrap metal** (=metal from old cars, machines etc. that is melted and used again) **3** [C] a small piece of information, truth etc.: [+ of] *Detectives gathered up every scrap of evidence that might support their case.* **4 scraps** [plural] pieces of food that are left after you have finished eating: **table/kitchen scraps** | *They fed the dog on table scraps.* **5** [C] INFORMAL a short fight or argument: *Wilson came in, slightly bruised from his scrap with a photographer.*

scrap² *v.* **scrapped, scrapping** **1** [T] to decide not to use a plan or system: *The state poured millions of dollars into this program before it was finally scrapped.* **2** [T] to get rid of an old machine, vehicle etc., and use its parts in some other way: *Thousands of older planes will be scrapped as a result of budget cuts.* **3** [I] INFORMAL to have a short fight or argument

scrap·book /ˈskræpbʊk/ *n.* [C] a book with empty pages where you can stick pictures, newspaper articles, or other things you want to keep

scrape¹ /skreɪp/ *v.* **1** [T] to remove something from a surface or clean a surface, using the edge of a knife, stick etc.: *You'll need to scrape the windshield – it's covered in ice.* | **scrape sth away/off** etc. *Barbara used a stick to scrape the mud off her boots.* | **scrape sth clean** *Scrape your plate clean and put it in the sink.* **2** [I always + adv./prep.,T] to rub against a rough surface in a way that causes slight damage or injury, or to make something do this: [+ on/against etc.] *I heard the side of the car scrape against the wall.* | [**scrape sth on/against etc. sth**] *Tim fell down and scraped his knee on the sidewalk.* **3** [I,T] to make a noise by rubbing roughly against a surface: *Metal scraped loudly as the snowplow drove past.* | [**scrape (sth) along/down/against etc.**] *The branches were scraping against the house in the wind.* **4 scrape the bottom of the barrel** INFORMAL to have to use something even though it is not very good, because there is nothing better available: *We'll really be scraping the bottom of the barrel if we hire him.*

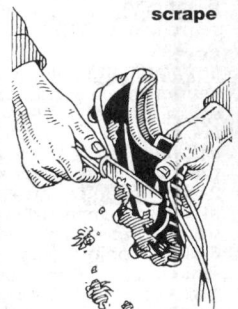
scrape

scrape by *phr. v.* [I] **1** to have just enough money to live: [+ **on**] *We had to scrape by on welfare checks and food stamps for two years.* **2** to just manage to succeed in passing a test or dealing with a difficult situation

scrape in/into *phr. v.* [I,T **scrape into** sth] to just manage to succeed in getting a job, getting into college, etc.: *Dave just scraped into the local college.*

scrape through *phr. v.* [I,T **scrape through** sth] to just manage to succeed in passing a test or dealing with a difficult situation: *Dani just scraped through her driving test.*

scrape sth ↔ **together/up** *phr. v.* [T] to get enough money for a particular purpose, when this is difficult: *We had to scrape together $15,000 for Kenny's surgery.*

scrape² *n.* **1** [C] a mark or slight injury caused by rubbing against a rough surface: *Fortunately, Tonya only suffered a few cuts and scrapes in the accident.* **2** [C] a situation in which you get into trouble or have difficulties: [+ **with**] *He got into several scrapes with the school authorities.* **3** [C usually singular] the noise made when one surface rubs roughly against another: *We heard the scrape of a chair downstairs, followed by footsteps.*

scrap·er /'skreɪpə/ *n.* [C] a tool whose edge is used to remove something from a surface: *a paint scraper*

scrap heap /'. ./ *n.* **1 the scrap heap** INFORMAL the situation of not being wanted or used any longer, especially in a way that seems unfair: *Are these older employees just going to end up on the scrap heap after the layoffs?* **2** [C] a pile of unwanted things, especially pieces of metal

scra·pie /'skreɪpi/ *n.* [U] a serious disease that sheep get

scrap·ings /'skreɪpɪŋz/ *n.* [plural] small pieces that have been SCRAPED from a surface

scrap·py /'skræpi/ *adj.* **scrappier, scrappiest** INFORMAL, APPROVING having a strong determined character and being willing to fight or argue with people: *This scrappy little software company has decided to take on the market leader.*

scrap yard, scrapyard /'. ./ *n.* [C] a business that buys old materials and goods and sells the parts that can be used again

scratch

scratching our heads. | *Budget directors are scratching their heads about how to deal with the shortfall.*
7 remove sth [T always + adv./prep.] to remove something from a surface by rubbing it with something sharp: [**scratch** sth **off/away** etc.] *I scratched some of the varnish off the table with a knife.*
8 stop planning [T] if you scratch an idea, a plan etc., you stop planning to do it because it is not possible or practical anymore: *Well, I guess we can scratch that idea.*
9 you scratch my back, I'll scratch yours SPOKEN used to say that you will help someone if they agree to help you
10 scratch sb/sth off a list to remove someone's name or something else from a list
11 remove from race [T usually passive] to remove someone from a race or competition before it begins
12 scratch (out) a living to get just enough to eat or live: *The area's farming communities scratch out a living from the rocky terrain.*

scratch sth ↔ **out** *phr. v.* [T] to draw a line through a word, in order to remove it: *Phil's name had been scratched out with a black pen.*

scratch² *n.* **1** [C] a thin mark or cut on the surface of something or on someone's skin: *a scratch on the car door* **2 from scratch** if you do or start something from scratch, you begin it without using anything that existed or was prepared before: *The company was started from scratch in 1995, but its annual sales are already over $20 million.* | *Doug baked the cake from scratch* (=not using a cake mix from a box). **3 without a scratch** if you escape from a dangerous situation without a scratch, you are not injured at all: *Miraculously, Liz survived the fall without a scratch.*

scratch³ *adj.* [no comparative] a scratch player in a sport, especially GOLF, does not have a HANDICAP¹ (3)

scratch-and-sniff /,. . '. ./ *adj.* [only before noun] a scratch-and-sniff book, magazine advertisement etc. has a special dry substance on its surface that produces a smell when you scratch it

scratch pad /'. ./ *n.* [C] several sheets of cheap paper fastened together at the top or side, used for writing notes or lists

scratch pa·per /'. ,../ *n.* [U] cheap paper, or paper that has already been used on one side, that you use for making notes, lists etc.

scratch·y /'skrætʃi/ *adj.* **scratchier, scratchiest** **1** scratchy clothes or materials feel rough and uncomfortable **2** a scratchy voice sounds deep and rough **3** a scratchy throat feels sore **4** a scratchy record makes a lot of noise because it is old or damaged —**scratchiness** *n.* [U]

scrawl¹ /skrɔl/ *v.* [T] to write in a careless and messy way, so that your words are not easy to read: *Jim scrawled his signature across the bottom of the page.*

scrawl² *n.* [C singular] something written in a messy careless way, or a messy careless way of writing: *The note was written in Gwen's childish scrawl.*

scraw·ny /'skrɔni/ *adj.* **scrawnier, scrawniest** thin, unattractive, and looking weak: *a scrawny kid*

scream¹ /skrim/ *v.* **1** [I] to make a loud high noise with your voice because you are hurt, frightened, excited etc.: *There was a loud bang, and people started screaming.* | *a screaming baby* | [+ **with/in**] *She lay in the street, screaming with pain.* **2** [I,T] also **scream out** to shout something in a very loud high voice because you are angry or frightened: *"Get out!" she screamed.* | [**scream** sth] *They were screaming insults at each other.* | [+ **for**] *I screamed for help.* | [+ **at**] *Carla's been screaming at her kids all morning.* **3** [I] to make a very loud high noise: *The police car sped around the corner with its siren screaming.* —see also **scream/yell bloody murder** (BLOODY¹ (3))

scream² *n.* [C] **1** a loud high sound made with your voice because you are very frightened, angry, hurt, or excited: *We heard a piercing scream followed by*

---

scratch¹ /skrætʃ/ *v.*
1 rub your skin [I,T] to rub your skin with your nails, especially because it ITCHes: *The medicine relieves the itching, so the child doesn't scratch so much.*
2 make a mark [T] to rub something sharp or rough against a hard surface so that it makes a thin mark: *Don't use that cleaner – it'll scratch the sink.*
3 cut your skin [I,T] to make a small cut by pulling something sharp against someone's skin: *I scratched my hand on a rusty nail.* | *The cat will scratch if you make her mad.*
4 make a noise [I always + adv./prep.] to make a noise by rubbing something with a sharp or pointed object: *The dog kept scratching at the door to be let in.*
5 scratch the surface to deal with only a very small part of a subject: *So far, we have only scratched the surface of the information available on this topic.*
6 scratch your head INFORMAL to not know the answer or solution to something, and to have to think hard about it.: *The last question really left us*

two gunshots. | **scream of joy/pain etc.** *The class greeted the news with screams of excitement.* | *He* ***let out a scream*** *of terror.* **2 be a scream** INFORMAL used to describe someone or something that is very funny: *Did you see that show last night? What a scream!*

scree /skri/ *n.* [U] an area of small loose broken rocks on the side of a mountain

screech /skritʃ/ *v.* **1** [I] if a vehicle or its wheels screech, they make a loud high noise: *The plane's tires screeched as it touched down on the runway.* | *screeching brakes* **2** [I,T] to make a loud high noise with your voice, especially because you are angry: *I heard Heather screech, "Hit him, Jim!"* **3 screech to a halt/stop/standstill** if a vehicle screeches to a halt, stop, etc., it stops very suddenly, so that the wheels make a loud noise —**screech** *n.* [singular] *a screech of tires*

S W 2 2 **screen¹** /skrin/ *n.* **1** [C] the flat glass part of a television or computer, on which you see words, pictures etc.: *It's easier to correct your work* ***on screen*** *than on paper.* —see picture on page 426 **2 a)** [C] the large white surface that pictures are shown on in a movie theater **b)** [singular,U] movies in general: *Her play was adapted for* ***the big screen.*** | *She was well-known as a star of stage and screen.* **3** [C] a wire net fastened inside a frame in front of a window or door that allows air into the house but keeps insects out **4** [C] a type of wall that can be moved around, used to divide one part of a room from another **5** [C] a player or group of players in a BASKETBALL game who protect the player who has the ball —see also SMOKESCREEN, SUNSCREEN

S

S W 3 **screen²** *v.* [T] **1** to do tests on people to find out whether they have a particular illness: [**screen sb for sth**] *Doctors recommend that women over 50 be screened for breast cancer.* **2** to hide or protect something by putting something in front of it: [**screen sth (off) from sth**] *The hedge screens the back yard from the street.* **3** to examine or test people to make sure that they will be loyal to your company, organization etc.: *Management has announced new procedures for screening applicants.* **4** to show a movie or television program: *Spielberg's 1995 blockbuster is being screened on network TV for the first time tonight.* **5 screen (your) calls** to find out who is calling you on the telephone, especially by using an ANSWERING MACHINE, so that you do not have to speak to someone you do not want to speak to

screen sth ↔ **out** *phr. v.* [T] **1** to decide that someone or something is not appropriate for a job, position etc.: *We use a personality test to screen out unsuitable job applicants.* **2** to prevent something from entering or passing through: *The low clouds screened out all but a hint of sunshine.*

screen door /ˌ. ˈ./ *n.* [C] a door that will let air in but keep insects out, that consists of a wire net inside a frame and is put outside the main door

screen dump /ˈ. ./ *n.* [C] a picture of the information on a computer screen that you can print or save in your computer

screened porch also **screen porch** /ˌ. ˈ./ *n.* [C] a room or area built onto the outside of the ground floor of a house, with SCREENS¹ (3) on it to let air in but keep insects out

screen·ing /ˈskrinɪŋ/ *n.* **1** [C,U] tests done to make sure that someone does not have a disease or is generally healthy: *Does your HMO offer cancer screening for women?* **2** [C,U] the showing of a movie or television program: *The director answered questions following the 7:30 screening.* **3** [U] tests or checks done to make sure that someone or something is appropriate for a particular purpose: *The screening of potential jurors will continue next week.*

screen·play /ˈskrinpleɪ/ *n. plural* **screenplays** [C] a play written to be made into a movie or television program: *a screenplay based on a novel by John O'Brien*

screen print·ing /ˈ. ˌ../ *n.* [U] SILK-SCREENING

screen sav·er /ˈ. ˌ../ *n.* [C] a computer program that makes a moving image appear on a computer screen when no work has been done on the computer for a particular period of time, so that the screen does not become damaged

screen test /ˈ. ./ *n.* [C] an occasion when someone is filmed while performing, in order to see if they are good enough to act in a movie

screen·writ·er /ˈskrinˌraɪtɚ/ *n.* [C] someone who writes plays for movies or television programs —**screenwriting** *n.* [U]

screw¹ /skru/ *n.* **1** [C] a thin pointed piece of metal that you push and turn in order to fasten pieces of metal or wood together: *You just need to tighten these two screws here.* —see picture at NAIL¹ **2 have a screw loose** also **have a few screws loose** INFORMAL, HUMOROUS to be slightly crazy **3 tighten/put the screws (on sb)** INFORMAL to force someone to do something by threatening them: *The government plans to tighten the screws on industries that pollute the environment.* S W 3

screw² *v.* S W 2

1 **attach** [I,T always + adv./prep.] to attach one object to another using a screw: [**screw (sth) into/onto/to sth**] *The kitchen cabinets were screwed to the brick walls.* | *The table legs just screw into the top like this.*

2 **close by turning** [T always + adv./prep.] to fasten or close something by turning it until it cannot be turned anymore: [**screw sth on/together etc.**] *Be sure to screw the cap back onto the soda bottle.*

3 screw you/him/that etc. SPOKEN, TABOO used to show that you are very angry with someone: *Oh, yeah? Well, screw you!* | *Screw it – I'm not waiting around for them anymore.*

4 screw sb also **screw sb over** SLANG to cheat someone or treat them in a dishonest or unfair way: *The dealer really screwed us over when we bought this car.*

5 be screwed SLANG to be in a lot of trouble or in a very difficult situation: *If Dad finds out about this, we're screwed!*

6 **face** [T always + adv./prep.] to move the muscles around your eyes, mouth etc. in a way that makes them seem narrow: *Lynn screwed her eyes shut and blew as hard as she could.*

7 **sex** [I,T] VULGAR to have sex with someone —see also **have your head screwed on (right/straight)** (HEAD¹ (25))

screw around *phr. v.* **1** [I] INFORMAL to spend time doing silly things: *Usually, the kids just screw around downtown until about 11 o'clock.* **2** [I] INFORMAL to cause trouble or problems for someone, especially by changing something that they think should not be changed: [**+ with**] *Someone's been screwing around with my computer.* **3** [I] TABOO to have sex with a lot of different people

screw sb **out of** sth *phr. v.* [T] SLANG to cheat someone or treat them in a dishonest or unfair way, so that they do not get something that they should get: *Sue's sister screwed her out of her share of the money.*

screw up *phr. v.* **1** [I] INFORMAL to make a bad mistake or do something very stupid: *If you screw up again, you're fired!* **2** [T **screw** sth ↔ **up**] INFORMAL to spoil something, especially by making it so that it is not arranged in the right order, by doing something stupid: *Dave screwed up my files, so now I can't find anything.* **3** [T **screw** sb ↔ **up**] INFORMAL to make someone feel very unhappy, confused, or anxious, especially for a long time: *Living with my parents is enough to screw anybody up.* —see also SCREWED UP **4 screw your eyes/mouth/face up** to move the muscles around your eyes, mouth etc. in a way that makes them seem narrow: *Vicki took one sip and screwed up her face in disgust.* **5 screw up your courage** to try to be brave enough to do something you are very nervous about: *Mike screwed up his courage and started dialing her number.*

screw·ball /ˈskrubɔl/ *n.* [C] INFORMAL **1** someone or something that seems very strange or crazy **2 screwball comedy** a movie or television program that is funny because crazy things happen

screw·driv·er /ˈskruˌdraɪvɚ/ n. [C] **1** a tool with a narrow blade at one end that you use for turning screws —see picture at TOOL[1] **2** an alcoholic drink made from VODKA and orange juice

screwed up /ˌ.ˈ./ adj. INFORMAL **1** unhappy or anxious because you have had bad experiences in the past: *He plays a screwed-up rich kid who gets expelled from school.* **2** not arranged in the correct order, or not in the correct place: *Kirtley supported the plan to straighten out the state's screwed-up finances.*

screw top /ˈ. ./ n. [C] a cover that you twist onto the top of a bottle or other container

screw·y /ˈskrui/ adj. **screwier, screwiest** INFORMAL an idea, plan, etc. that is screwy seems strange or crazy: *It sounded like a pretty screwy idea to me.*

scrib·ble[1] /ˈskrɪbəl/ v. **1** [T] to write something quickly and in a messy way: *She scribbled her name on a slip of paper.* **2** [I] to draw marks that have no meaning: *Ashley scribbled all over her bedroom walls in crayon.*

scribble[2] n. **1 scribbles** [plural] meaningless marks or pictures, especially done by children **2** [singular, U] messy writing that is difficult to read

scrib·bler /ˈskrɪblɚ/ n. [C] INFORMAL a writer, especially an unimportant one

scribe /skraɪb/ n. [C] someone employed to copy things in writing, especially before printing was invented

scrim·mage /ˈskrɪmɪdʒ/ n. [C] a practice game of football, basketball etc. —see also **line of scrimmage** (LINE[1] (39)) —**scrimmage** v. [I]

scrimp /skrɪmp/ v. [I] to try to save as much money as you can, even though you have very little, especially by buying cheaper things: *My parents scrimped and saved to pay for my education.*
scrimp on sth phr. v. [T] to pay too little money for something or buy something that is cheap and of bad quality: *There is a temptation to scrimp on software when buying your first computer.*

scrip /skrɪp/ n. **1** [U] an official piece of paper especially a STOCK that is given instead of money or a DIVIDEND **2** [C] SPOKEN a PRESCRIPTION (1): *a scrip for Prozac*

script[1] /skrɪpt/ n. **1** [C] the written form of a speech, play, movie etc.: *He read the announcement from a prepared script.* **2** [C,U] the set of letters used in writing a language; ALPHABET: *Arabic script* **3** [singular,U] FORMAL writing done by hand, especially with the letters of the words joined: *The letter was written in beautiful 18th-century script.*

script[2] v. [T] **1** to write a speech, play, movie etc.: *The film was scripted by author Armistead Maupin.* **2** to plan all the details of an event, with the result that it does not seem natural: *The convention has been carefully scripted to appeal to TV viewers.*

script·ed /ˈskrɪptɪd/ adj. **1** a speech or broadcast that is scripted has been written down before it is read **2** an event that is scripted has been very carefully planned, in a way that does not seem natural: *The leaders met during a carefully scripted visit to the White House.*

scrip·tur·al /ˈskrɪptʃərəl/ adj. relating to or based on holy books

scrip·ture /ˈskrɪptʃɚ/ n. **1** [U also **the (Holy) Scriptures** [plural] the Christian Bible **2** [C,U] the holy books of a particular religion: *Buddhist scriptures*

script·writ·er /ˈskrɪptˌraɪtɚ/ n. [C] someone who writes SCRIPTs for movies, television etc.

scrod /skrɑd/ n. [U] the white meat of a young fish, especially COD or HADDOCK

scroll[1] /skroʊl/ n. [C] **1** a long piece of paper that can be rolled up, and is used as an official document, especially in past times **2** a decoration shaped like a roll of paper

scroll[2] v. [I,T] to move information on a computer screen up or down so that you can read it: [+ **up/down**] *Use the mouse button to scroll the text down.*

scroll·work /ˈskroʊlwɚk/ n. [U] TECHNICAL decoration in the shape of scrolls

Scrooge, scrooge /skrudʒ/ n. [C] INFORMAL someone who hates spending money, and who often spoils other people's fun because of this: *My scrooge of a wife won't let me buy new golf clubs.*

scro·tum /ˈskroʊtəm/ n. plural **scrota** /-tə/ or **scrotums** [C] the bag of skin that contains the TESTICLES of men and male animals

scrounge /skraʊndʒ/ v. [I,T] to get money or something you want by asking other people for it, rather than by paying for it yourself: [**scrounge** sth **from** sb] *She scrounged materials for her artworks from local lumberyards.* | [**scrounge** sth **up**] *I just used whatever I could scrounge up.* —**scrounger** n. [C]
scrounge (around) for sth phr. v. [T] to search through other things, looking for something such as food or supplies: *We saw children scrounging around in garbage cans for something to eat.*

scrub[1] /skrʌb/ v. **1** [I,T] to rub something hard, especially with something rough, in order to clean it: *The kitchen floor needs to be scrubbed and waxed.* | *The children's freshly-scrubbed faces beamed up at us.* **2** [T usually passive] INFORMAL to decide not to do something that you had planned, especially because there is a problem: *Yesterday's shuttle launch was scrubbed just ten minutes before liftoff.*
scrub up phr. v. [I] to wash your hands and arms before doing a medical operation

scrub[2] n. **1** [U] low bushes and trees that grow in very dry soil **2 scrubs** [plural] INFORMAL a loose green shirt and pants worn by doctors during medical operations

scrub·ber /ˈskrʌbɚ/ n. [C] a plastic or metal object or a brush that you use to clean pans or floors

scrub brush /ˈskrʌb brʌʃ/ n. [C] a stiff brush that you use for cleaning things —see picture at BRUSH[1]

scrub·by /ˈskrʌbi/ adj. covered by low bushes: *scrubby terrain*

scrub·land /ˈskrʌblænd/ n. [U] land that is covered with low bushes

scruff /skrʌf/ n. **by the scruff of the neck** if you hold a person or animal by the scruff of their neck, you hold the flesh, fur, or clothes at the back of the neck

scruff·y /ˈskrʌfi/ adj. **scruffier, scruffiest** dirty and messy and not taken care of very well: *a scruffy sweatshirt*

scrum /skrʌm/ n. [C] an arrangement of players in the game of RUGBY, in which they are pushing very close together

scrump·tious /ˈskrʌmpʃəs/ adj. INFORMAL food that is scrumptious tastes very good: *scrumptious cheesecake*

scrunch /skrʌntʃ/ v. [T always + adv./prep.] INFORMAL to crush and twist something into a small round shape: [**scrunch** sth **up/into** etc.] *She tore out the pages and scrunched them up into a ball.*

scrunch·ie /ˈskrʌntʃi/ n. [C] a circular rubber band that is covered with cloth, used for holding hair in place

scru·ple[1] /ˈskrupəl/ n. [C usually plural] a belief about right and wrong that prevents you from doing something bad: *He has absolutely no scruples about claiming other people's work as his own.*

scruple[2] v. **not scruple to do** sth FORMAL to be willing to do something, even though it may have harmful or bad effects: *They did not scruple to bomb innocent civilians.*

scru·pu·lous /ˈskrupyələs/ adj. **1** careful to be honest and fair, and making sure that every detail is correct: *The finance department is always scrupulous about their bookkeeping.* —opposite UNSCRUPULOUS **2** done very carefully so that every detail is correct: *This job requires scrupulous attention to detail.* —**scrupulously** adv.: *Employees' hands must be kept scrupulously clean.* —**scrupulousness** n. [U]

scru·ti·nize /ˈskrutnˌaɪz/ v. [T] to examine someone or something very thoroughly and carefully: *Detectives scrutinized the area, looking for clues.*

scru·ti·ny /'skrut⌐n-i/ n. [U] careful and thorough examination of someone or something: **careful/ close/intense scrutiny** *Upon closer scrutiny, some of the regulations were found to discriminate against minority groups.* | *The senator's office later* **came under scrutiny** *from the Justice Department.*

SCSI n. [U] Small Computer Systems Interface; something that helps a small computer work with another piece of electronic equipment, such as a PRINTER, especially when they are connected by wires

scu·ba div·ing /'skubə ˌdaɪvɪŋ/ n. [U] the sport of swimming under water while breathing from a container of air on your back —**scuba diver** n. [C]

scud /skʌd/ v. [I + **across/along/past** etc.] LITERARY if clouds scud past, they move quickly across the sky

scuff /skʌf/ v. [T often passive] to make a mark on a smooth surface by rubbing it against something rough: *scuffed brown shoes* —**scuff** n. [C]

scuf·fle /'skʌfəl/ n. [C] a short fight that involves only a few people and that is not very violent or serious: *A brief scuffle broke out between fans after the game.* —**scuffle** v. [I]

scuf·fling /'skʌflɪŋ/ n. [U] noises made by someone or something that you cannot see, that is moving around: *There were some scuffling noises behind the wall.*

scuff mark /'. ./ n. [C] a mark made on something by scuffing: *scuff marks on the kitchen floor*

scull[1] /skʌl/ n. [C] **1** a small light boat for only one person **2** one of the OARS that you use when you are sculling a boat

scull[2] v. [I,T] to ROW a small light boat, especially a boat that is only for one person

scul·le·ry /'skʌləri/ n. [C] a room next to the kitchen, especially in a large old house, where cleaning jobs were done in past times

sculpt /skʌlpt/ v. [T often passive] **1** to shape stone, wood, clay etc. in order to make a solid object that represents someone or something.: *The statue is sculpted in solid marble.* **2** to make something into a particular shape as a result of a natural process, for example the movement of a river

sculpt·ed /'skʌlptɪd/ adj. [only before noun] having a clear, smooth shape that looks as though an artist had made it: *high, sculpted cheekbones*

sculp·tor /'skʌlptə/ n. [C] someone who makes sculptures

sculp·tur·al /'skʌlptʃərəl/ adj. [only before noun] having a clear shape that looks as though an artist had made it: *Four sleek, sculptural figures guard the top of the building.*

sculp·ture /'skʌlptʃə/ n. **1** [U] the art of making solid objects representing people or animals out of stone, wood, clay etc.: *the history of European painting and sculpture* **2** [C] an object produced in this form of art: *a life-size bronze sculpture*

sculp·tured /'skʌlptʃəd/ adj. **1** [only before noun] decorated with sculptures, or formed into a particular shape by an artist: *sculptured plaques and statues* **2 sculptured features/muscles etc.** features etc. that have an attractive clear shape, as if they had been made by an artist

scum /skʌm/ n. **1** [singular,U] a disgusting substance that forms on the surface of a liquid: *soap scum on the bathtub* **2** *plural* **scum** [C] SPOKEN a bad disgusting person: *I don't want that scum coming back into my restaurant!* | **scum of the earth** (=the worst people you can imagine) —see also POND SCUM —**scummy** adj.

scum·bag /'skʌmbæg/ n. [C] SPOKEN a bad disgusting person

scup·per /'skʌpə/ n. [C] TECHNICAL a hole in the side of a ship that allows water to flow back into the ocean

scur·ri·lous /'skə·ələs, 'skʌr-/ adj. FORMAL scurrilous remarks, articles etc. contain damaging and untrue statements about someone

scur·ry /'skə·i, 'skʌri/ v. **scurries, scurried, scurry-ing** [I always + adv./prep.] to move quickly with short steps: [+ **along/past/across**] *A mouse scurried across the floor.*

S-curve /'ɛs kə·v/ n. [C] a curve in a road in the shape of an "S," that can be dangerous to drivers

scur·vy /'skə·vi/ n. [U] a disease caused by not eating foods such as fruit and vegetables that contain VITA-MIN C

scut·tle[1] /'skʌtl/ v. **1** [T] to ruin or end someone's plans or chance of being successful: *The senator did his best to scuttle the tax increase.* **2** [I always + adv./prep.] to move quickly with short steps: [+ **along/past/down**] *Crabs scuttled out of their holes.* **3** [T] to sink a ship by making holes in the bottom, especially in order to prevent it from being used by an enemy

scut·tle[2] n. [C] a container for carrying coal

scut·tle·butt /'skʌtlˌbʌt/ n. [U] INFORMAL stories about other people's personal lives, especially containing things that are unkind and untrue about them; GOSSIP

scuz·zy /'skʌzi/ adj. **scuzzier, scuzziest** INFORMAL disgusting and dirty: *a scuzzy part of the city*

scythe /saɪð/ n. [C] a farming tool that has a long curved blade attached to a long wooden handle, and is used to cut grain or long grass

SD the written abbreviation of South Dakota

S.E., **SE** the written abbreviation of SOUTHEAST

sea /si/ n. **1** [C] a large area of salty water that is mostly enclosed by land: *the Mediterranean Sea* **2** [singular,U] a word meaning the "ocean," used especially when talking about traveling in a ship or boat: *land and sea* | *Waste is dumped* **in the sea** | *ships* **at sea** (=on the ocean). | *Five sailors were* **lost at sea** (=drowned). | *The bottle gradually drifted* **out to sea** (=away from land). **3 a sea of sth** a large number or quantity of something: *She looked out over a vast sea of cars.* **4 the seas** LITERARY the ocean, used especially when you are not talking about a particular ocean **5** [C] one of the broad plains on the moon and Mars —see also **on the high seas** (HIGH[1] (23)), **the seven seas** (SEVEN (4))

sea a·nem·o·ne /'. .ˌ.../ n. [C] a brightly-colored animal that sticks onto rocks under the surface of the ocean and looks like a flower

sea bed /'. ./ n. [singular] the land at the bottom of the ocean

sea·bird /'sibəd/ n. [C] a bird that lives near the ocean and finds food in it

sea·board /'sibɔrd/ n. [C] **the eastern/Atlantic seaboard** the part of the eastern U.S. that is near the Atlantic Ocean

sea·borne /'sibɔrn/ adj. carried on or arriving in ships: *a seaborne attack*

sea breeze /'. ./ n. [C] a cool light wind that blows from the ocean onto the land

sea cap·tain /'. ˌ../ n. [C] the CAPTAIN of a ship

sea change /'. ./ n. [singular] a very big change in something: *a sea change in society's values*

sea dog /'. ./ n. [C] LITERARY OR HUMOROUS someone with a lot of experience of ships and sailing

sea·far·ing /'siˌfɛrɪŋ/ adj. [only before noun] **1** relating to the life and activities of a sailor: *an author of seafaring tales* **2** having a strong relationship with ships and the ocean, especially because of international trade: **seafaring nation/people** *The Portuguese are an ancient seafaring nation.* —**seafaring** n. [U] —**seafarer** n. [C]

sea·floor /'siflɔr/ n. [singular] the land at the bottom of a sea or ocean

sea·food /'sifud/ n. [U] animals from the ocean that you can eat, especially SHELLFISH

sea·front /'sifrʌnt/ adj. [only before noun] relating to the land along the edge of the ocean: *a seafront hotel*

sea·go·ing /'siˌgoʊɪŋ/ adj. [only before noun] built to travel on the ocean; OCEANGOING: *a seagoing vessel*

sea·gull /'sigʌl/ also **gull** n. [C] a common gray and white bird that lives near the ocean

sea·horse /'sihɔrs/ *n.* [C] a small sea fish with a head and neck that look like those of a horse

seal[1] /sil/ *n.* [C] **1** a large sea animal that has smooth fur, eats fish, and lives by the ocean, especially in cold areas **2 a)** a piece of rubber or plastic used on a pipe, machine, container etc. to prevent air, water, dirt etc. from going into or out of it: *an airtight seal* **b)** a piece of WAX[1] (1), paper etc. that you have to break in order to open a new container: *Check that the seal on the medicine has not been broken.* **3 seal of approval** if you give something your seal of approval, you say that you approve of it, especially officially: *The project has received the city council's seal of approval.* **4** a mark that has a special design and shows the legal or official authority of a person or organization: *stationery decorated with the Texas state seal* **5** a special type of stamp with a picture on it, that you cannot use to mail a letter but that is bought to help a CHARITY **6 under seal** information or documents that are under seal are kept secret, especially by a court of law: *Court papers regarding pretrial information are under seal.*

seal[2] *v.* [T] **1** also **seal up** to close an entrance or a container with something that stops air, water etc. from coming into or out of it: *The doorway had been sealed up with bricks.* **2** to close an envelope, package etc. by using something sticky to hold its edges in place: *She sealed the box with clear tape.* **3 seal a deal/agreement/promise etc.** to do something that makes a deal, agreement etc. more formal or definite **4 seal sb's fate** to make something, especially something bad, seem certain to happen: *Rogerson's fate was sealed when he got behind the wheel of his car, completely drunk.* **5** if a court of law or a business seals information, documents, offers etc., they keep them secret —compare UNSEAL —see also **my lips are sealed** (LIP (5))

seal sth ↔ **in** *phr. v.* [T] to stop what something contains from getting out: *Cook the meat over a high heat to seal in the juices.*

seal sth ↔ **off** *phr. v.* [T] to stop people from entering an area or building, because it is dangerous: *Following the gas leak, authorities sealed off an area of fifteen square blocks.*

sea lane /'. ./ *n.* [C] a SHIPPING LANE

seal·ant /'silənt/ *n.* [C,U] a substance that is put on the surface of something or in the space between two surfaces to prevent air, water etc. from passing through

sealed /sild/ *adj.* **1** closed in a way that prevents something from getting in or out: *The list of winners' names was delivered in a sealed envelope.* **2** sealed information, documents, offers etc. are kept secret by a court of law or business —compare UNSEALED

sea legs /'. ./ *n.* [plural] **get your sea legs** to begin to be able to walk normally, not feel sick etc. when you are traveling on a ship

seal·er /'silə/ *n.* **1** [C,U] a layer of paint, polish etc. put on the surface of something to protect it from air, water etc. **2** [C] a person or ship that hunts SEALS

sea lev·el /'. ,./ *n.* [U] the average height of the ocean, used as a standard for measuring other heights and depths, such as the height of a mountain: **above/below sea level** *The city is 2500 feet above sea level.*

sea·lift /'silıft/ *n.* [C] an act of moving people or things by boat, when it is difficult or dangerous to use roads or aircraft

seal·ing /'silıŋ/ *n.* [U] the hunting or catching of SEALS

sealing wax /'.. ,./ *n.* [U] a red substance that melts and becomes hard again quickly, used for SEALing letters, documents etc., especially in past times

sea li·on /'. ,./ *n.* [C] a large type of SEAL[1] (1)

seal·skin /'silskın/ *n.* [C,U] the skin or fur of some types of SEALS, used for making leather or clothes

seam /sim/ *n.* [C] **1** a line where two pieces of cloth, leather etc. have been stitched together: *Neil's shirt was torn at the shoulder seam.* **2** a layer of a mineral, especially coal, under the ground **3 be coming/falling apart at the seams a)** if a plan, organization etc. is coming or falling apart at the seams, so many things are going wrong with it that it will probably fail: *The country's whole economy is coming apart at the seams.* **b)** if a piece of clothing etc. is coming or falling apart at the seams, the stitches on it are coming unfastened **4 be bursting/bulging at the seams** if a room, building etc. is bursting or bulging at the seams, it's so full of people that hardly anyone else can fit into it: *The auditorium was bulging at the seams during the governor's talk.* **5** a line where two pieces of metal, wood etc. have been fastened together

sea·man /'simən/ *n. plural* **seamen** /-mən/ [C] **1** a sailor on a ship or in the navy who is not an officer **2** someone who has a lot of experience of ships and the ocean

sea·man·ship /'simən,ʃıp/ *n.* [U] the skills and knowledge that an experienced sailor has

sea mile /'. ./ *n.* [C] a NAUTICAL MILE

seam·less /'simlıs/ *adj.* **1** done or happening so smoothly that you cannot tell where one thing stops and another begins: *a seamless transition between musical pieces* **2** not having any SEAMS: *seamless stockings*

seam·less·ly /'simlısli/ *adv.* happening or done so smoothly that you cannot tell where one thing stops and another begins: *The novel shifts seamlessly from the present to the past.*

seam·stress /'simstrıs/ *n.* [C] OLD-FASHIONED a woman whose job is SEWING and making clothes

seam·y /'simi/ *adj.* **seamier, seamiest** involving bad things such as crime, violence, POVERTY, or immoral behavior: *the seamy side of Hollywood*

sé·ance /'seıɑns/ *n.* [C] a meeting where people try to talk to or receive messages from the spirits of dead people

sea·plane /'siplein/ *n.* [C] an airplane that can take off from and land on the surface of water

sea·port /'sipɔrt/ *n.* [C] a town or city on or near a coast with a HARBOR that large ships can use

sea pow·er /'. ,../ *n.* **1** [U] the size and strength of a country's navy **2** [C] a country with a powerful navy

sear /sır/ *v.* **1** [I always + adv./prep.,T] to burn something with a sudden powerful heat: *Brush fires seared the hillsides.* **2** [T] to cook the outside of a piece of meat quickly at a high temperature, in order to keep its juices in **3** [I,T always + adv./prep.] to have a very strong sudden and bad effect on you: [+ **into/in**] *The image of the crash was seared into her memory.*

search[1] /sɜtʃ/ *n.* **1** [C usually singular] an attempt to find someone or something that is difficult to find: [+ **for**] *the search for the wreck of the Titanic* | *Police have* **called off the search for** (=officially stopped looking for) *the missing children.* | *The company* **launched a** nationwide **search** *for Mr. Weiss' replacement as President.* **2** [C] if a computer does a search or if someone does a search on a computer, they command the computer to find certain information: **perform/run/do a search** *Police ran a database search of the license numbers of stolen cars.* **3 in search of sb/sth** looking for someone or something: *They traveled widely in search of work.* **4** [singular,U] an attempt to find a solution to a problem or an explanation for something: [+ **for**] *the search for the meaning of life* **5 search and rescue** the process of searching for someone who is lost and who may need medical help, for example in the mountains or in the ocean —see also STRIP SEARCH

search[2] *v.* **1** look for [I,T] to look carefully for someone or something that is difficult to find: *We searched the whole house for Diane's ring.* | [+ **for**] *Lynn searched for a parking place.* | [+ **through**] *I searched through the papers on my desk, looking for the receipt.* | [**search sth for sth**] *Investigators searched the records for evidence of illegal business activities.*

S

2 computer to tell a computer to find certain information: [**search sth for sth**] *You could try searching the Internet for information on hotels in Paris.*

3 person [T] to look in someone's pockets, clothes etc. in order to find something, especially drugs or weapons: *All visitors will be searched before entering the prison.*

4 solution/explanation etc. [I] to try to find a solution to a problem, an explanation for something etc.: [+ **for**] *The accident has left residents searching for answers and explanations.*

5 Search me! SPOKEN used to tell someone that you do not know the answer to a question: *"How much longer is it going to take?" "Search me!"*

6 examine [T] to examine something very carefully in order to find something out, decide something etc.: *Our leaders will have to search their consciences before agreeing to this deal.*

7 search-and-destroy mission/operation an attempt to find and destroy something such as an enemy's property during a military battle

search sth ↔ **out** *phr. v.* [T] to find or discover something by looking carefully for it: *The gallery's owners search out works by the most talented young artists.*

search en·gine /'. ˌ../ *n.* [C] a computer program that helps you find information on the Internet

search·ing /'sɜtʃɪŋ/ *adj.* [only before noun] **1 searching examination/critique/inquiry** an examination, report etc. that looks thoroughly at all the facts **2 searching look** a look from someone who is trying to find out as much as possible about someone else's thoughts and feelings: *She gave Mike a long, searching look.* —**searchingly** *adv.*

search·light /'sɜtʃlaɪt/ *n.* [C] a powerful light that can be turned in any direction, used for finding people, vehicles etc. in the dark

search par·ty /'. ˌ../ *n. plural* **search parties** [C] a group of people organized to look for someone who is missing or lost: *Anxious parents sent out a search party to look for the two boys.*

search war·rant /'. ˌ../ *n.* [C] a legal document that gives the police official permission to search a building, for example in order to look for stolen goods

sear·ing /'sɪrɪŋ/ *adj.* [only before noun] **1** extremely hot: *the searing heat of the desert* **2** searing pain is severe and feels like a burn **3** searing writing or remarks criticize someone or something in a severe way: *Her novel is a searing portrait of 1950s society.*

Sears /sɪrz/**, Richard** (1863–1914) a U.S. businessman who started the MAIL ORDER company Sears Roebuck

sea salt /'. ./ *n.* [U] a type of salt used in cooking, that is made by allowing ocean water to dry and form large CRYSTALS

sea·scape /'. ./ *n.* [C] a picture or painting of the ocean

sea ser·pent /'. ˌ../ *n.* [C] an imaginary large snake-like animal that people used to think lived in the ocean

sea·shell /'siʃɛl/ *n.* [C] a word meaning the shell that covers some types of ocean animals, used especially when the animal is not inside it anymore: *seashells on the beach*

sea·shore /'siʃɔr/ *n.* **the seashore** the land along the edge of the ocean, usually consisting of sand and rocks —compare BEACH[1] —see Usage Note at SHORE[1]

sea·sick /'si,sɪk/ *adj.* feeling very sick because of the movement of a boat or ship —**seasickness** *n.* [U]

sea·side /'sisaɪd/ *adj.* [only before noun] relating to the land next to a sea or ocean: *a seaside resort*

sea·son[1] /'sizən/ *n.* [C]
1 in a year one of the four main periods in a year, which are spring, summer, fall, or winter
2 usual time for sth a period of time in a year when something happens most often or when something is usually done: *The Lakers need to work on their defense this season.* | *The network has several new dramas lined up for the fall season* (=the time in

the fall when new television programs are shown . | *This region has a fairly short growing season* (=when flowers and plants grow). | **the rainy/dry/wet etc. season** (=when there is a lot of rain, dry weather etc.) | **football/basketball/hockey etc. season** (=when football, basketball etc. is officially played)

3 the holiday season the period of time between Thanksgiving and New Year's Day

4 high/peak season the time of year when a place is most busy, especially a place where many people go on vacation

5 in season a) if vegetables or fruit are in season, it is the time of year when they are ready to eat **b)** during the period of time in a year when something is usually done: *A double room will cost around $125 in season.*

6 out of season a) if vegetables or fruit are out of season, it is not the time of year when they are normally ready to eat **b)** if you catch a fish or hunt an animal out of season, you do it during the time of year when it is illegal

7 legal time for sth a period of time in a year when it is legal to do something, especially to catch fish or hunt wild animals: **hunting/fishing season** *When does fishing season open this year?* | **deer/duck etc. season** (=when it is legal to hunt deer, ducks etc.)

8 season's greetings used especially on cards to say that you hope someone has a nice Christmas, Hanukkah etc. —see also OPEN SEASON

season[2] *v.* [T] **1** to add salt, pepper, SPICES etc. to something you are cooking to make it taste better: [**season sth with sth**] *a creamy sauce lightly seasoned with herbs* **2** to make wood hard and ready to use by gradually drying it

sea·son·a·ble /'sizənbəl/ *adj.* FORMAL seasonable weather conditions are typical for the time of year: *Sunny skies and seasonable temperatures are forecast for this weekend.* —**seasonably** *adv.* —see also UNSEASONABLY

sea·son·al /'sizənəl/ *adj.* [usually before noun] **1** happening or needed only at a particular time of year, or changing from one time to another: *seasonal variation in rainfall levels* | **seasonal workers/labor/employment etc.** *seasonal farm workers* **2** usually happening or available during a particular season: *waffles served with fresh seasonal fruits*

seasonal af·fec·tive dis·or·der /,... .,.. .'../ also **SAD** *n.* [U] a feeling of sadness and lack of energy that some people get in the winter because there is not enough light from the sun

sea·son·al·ly /'sisənəli/ *adv.* according to what is usual for a particular season: **seasonally adjusted figures/rates/data etc.** (=numbers about sales, unemployment etc. that are changed according to what usually happens at a particular time of year)

sea·soned /'sizənd/ *adj.* **1 seasoned traveler/campaigner/veteran etc.** someone who has a lot of experience in a particular activity etc. **2** seasoned food has salt, pepper, SPICES etc. added

seasoned salt /'.. ./ *n.* [U] a mixture of salt and other SPICES, especially PAPRIKA, used in cooking and to give food a special taste

sea·son·ing /'sizənɪŋ/ *n.* [C,U] salt, pepper, SPICES etc. that add a more interesting taste to food

season pre·miere /,... .'../ *n.* [C] the first show of the year for a continuing television series, usually shown in the fall

season tick·et /,.. '../ *n.* [C] a ticket that allows you to go to all the sports games played by a particular team in a year, all the concerts in a series etc. and that costs less than buying a separate ticket for each game, concert etc.: *a season ticket to the Pasadena Playhouse*

seat[1] /sit/ *n.*
1 place to sit [C] a place where you can sit, for example, a chair, especially in a restaurant, airplane, theater etc.: *There are two seats left in the back row.* | *a 65,000-seat stadium* | *Please take a seat* (=sit down). | *Mr. Benson came in and took his seat* (=sat

down in his seat). | *Would you like a window or aisle seat* (=in an airplane)? | *Anne, in the passenger seat* (=the seat next to the driver in a car), *was not hurt.* | **the back/front seat** (=the seats in the back or front of a car) | *Reserved seats* (=specific seats that you say you want when you buy a ticket) *for the game are $15.* —see Usage Note at SIT

2 official position [C] a position as a member of a government or a group that makes official decisions: *a seat on the board of directors* | *Republicans hold 235 of the 435 seats in the House.*

3 part of a chair [C usually singular] the flat part of a chair etc. that you sit on: *a chair with a broken seat* | *Who left the toilet seat up?*

4 bicycle etc. the part of a bicycle, MOTORCYCLE etc. that you sit on; SADDLE —see picture at BICYCLE

5 seat of government FORMAL a place, usually a city, where a government is based

6 take a back seat (to sb/sth) to let someone else make the important decisions, or to be considered less important than someone or something: *Quality will have to take a back seat to price when we buy the new furniture.*

7 on the edge of your seat waiting with great excitement to see what will happen next: *The movie's last scenes kept us on the edge of our seats.*

8 be in/on the hot seat INFORMAL to be in a position in which you have to make important decisions or answer a lot of difficult questions: *The Eagles' coach found himself in the hot seat after Sunday's huge loss.*

9 be in the driver's seat to control everything that happens in an organization, relationship, or situation

10 do sth by the seat of your pants to do something by using only your own skill and experience, without any help from anyone or anything else

11 the seat of your pants the part of your pants that you sit on —see also **a back seat driver** (BACK SEAT (2)), COUNTY SEAT, LOVESEAT, WINDOW SEAT

seat² *v.* [T] **1 be seated a)** to be sitting down: *Jan was seated near the door.* **b)** SPOKEN, FORMAL used to ask people politely to sit down: *Please be seated so we can start the meeting.* —see Usage Note at SIT **2 remain/stay seated** FORMAL to stay in your seat: *Ellen remained seated on the couch, completely motionless.* **3 seat yourself beside/in/on etc.** FORMAL to sit down somewhere: *Archer seated himself in the velvet armchair.* **4** [always + adv./prep.] to arrange for someone to sit somewhere: **seat sb beside/on/near etc.** *The hostess seated us next to the kitchen door.* **5** [not in progressive] if a room, vehicle, table etc. seats a certain number of people, it has enough seats for that number: *The arena seats 30,000.*

seat belt /'. ./ *also* **safety belt** *n.* [C] a strong belt attached to the seat of a car or airplane, that you fasten around yourself for protection in an accident —see picture on page 427

seat·er /'sitər/ *n.* [C] **two-seater/four-seater etc.** a vehicle or aircraft with two seats, four seats etc.

seat·ing /'sitɪŋ/ *n.* [U] **1** all the seats in a theater, STADIUM etc.: *The restaurant has a **seating capacity** of only 30.* **2** a way of arranging seats, or a plan of who will sit in them: **seating plan/arrangements** etc. *the seating plan for the banquet*

seat·mate /'sitˌmeɪt/ *n.* [C] someone who sits next to you on an airplane

seat-of-the-pants /ˌ. . . '. / *adj.* **a seat-of-the-pants approach/operation etc.** INFORMAL a way of doing something in which you do not plan ahead, but instead do things using your skill and knowledge of the current situation: *a quirky, seat-of-the-pants approach to business*

Se·at·tle /si'ætl/ a city and port in the U.S. state of Washington in the northwest of the U.S.

sea ur·chin /'. ,../ *n.* [C] a small round animal that lives in the ocean and has a hard shell, sometimes with sharp points

sea·wall /'siwɔl/ *n.* [C] a wall built along the edge of the ocean to stop the water from flowing over an area of land

sea·ward /'siwərd/ *adj.* facing or directed toward the sea or the ocean: *the seaward slope of the ridge* —**seaward** *also* **seawards** *adv.*

sea·wat·er /'siˌwɔtər/ *n.* [U] salty water from a sea or ocean

sea·way /'siweɪ/ *n. plural* **seaways** [C] **1** a river or CANAL used by ships to go from the ocean to places that are not on the coast **2** a line of travel regularly used by ships on the ocean

sea·weed /'siwid/ *n.* [U] one of several different types of common plants that grow in the ocean

sea·wor·thy /'siˌwərði/ *adj.* a ship that is seaworthy is safe and in good condition —**seaworthiness** *n.* [U]

se·ba·ceous /sɪ'beɪʃəs/ *adj.* TECHNICAL related to a part of the body that produces special oils

se·bum /'sibəm/ *n.* [U] a special oil that is produced by the skin

SEC —see SECURITIES AND EXCHANGE COMMISSION, THE

sec /sɛk/ *n.* **a sec** SPOKEN a very short time: *"Are you coming?" "Just a sec"* (=wait a short time) *– I'm almost ready."* | *I'll be there in a sec.*

se·cant /'sikænt, -kənt/ *n.* [singular] TECHNICAL **1** a line that crosses a curve at two or more places **2** the RATIO of the HYPOTENUSE of a RIGHT TRIANGLE to the side next to a particular angle

se·cede /sɪ'sid/ *v.* [I] FORMAL to formally stop being part of a country or organization: [+ **from**] *Quebec voted on seceding from Canada.* —**secession** /sɪ'sɛʃən/ *n.* [U] —**secessionist** *n.* [C]

se·clude /sɪ'klud/ *v.* [T] FORMAL to keep yourself or someone else away from other people

se·clud·ed /sɪ'kludɪd/ *adj.* **1** a secluded place is private and quiet because it is a long way from other places and people: *a secluded beach* **2 a secluded life/existence** a way of living that is quiet and private because you do not see many people

se·clu·sion /sɪ'kluʒən/ *n.* [U] the state of being private and away from other people: *The victim's family has remained in seclusion since the shooting.*

sec·ond¹ /'sɛkənd/ *adj.* **1** 2nd; the person, thing, event etc. after the first one: *Amy's in her second year of grad school.* | *His character dies during the second act of the play.* | *King's second novel became a bestseller.* **2 the second-largest/second-fastest/second-best etc.** the one next in rank after the largest, the fastest etc.: *the second-largest city in the state* **3 a second chance/opinion/look etc.** another chance, opinion etc. in addition to the usual one: *The program for teen mothers gives them a second chance to finish high school.* | *Most insurance companies ask you to get a second opinion before having major medical treatment.* **4 be second only to sth** to be the most important, most common, best etc. thing, except for one other particular thing: *Breast cancer is second only to lung cancer in U.S. cancer-related deaths.* **5 have second thoughts (about sth)** to have doubts about a decision you have made: *Stan was having second thoughts about marrying Julie.* **6 on second thought** SPOKEN used to say that you have changed your opinion or decision about something: *On second thought, I don't think I'll wear this jacket.* **7 not give sth a second thought** to not think or worry about something at all: *Most people just drive around and don't give the environment a second thought.* **8 without a second thought** if you do something without a second thought, you do it without worrying about it at all: *Those people would have killed him without a second thought.* **9 be second to none** to be the best: *His musical technique is second to none.* **10 second home/car etc.** another home, car etc. besides the one you use most of the time **11 second best** something that is not as good as the best: *We shouldn't have to settle for second best* (=accept something that is not as good as the best). **12 second wind** if you get your second wind, you begin to feel less tired than before, especially when playing a sport, doing physical work etc. **13 every second year/day/thing etc.** the second, then the fourth, then the sixth etc. year, day, or thing: *The committee meets every second Monday.*

second² *n.* **1** [C] a unit for measuring time that is equal to 1/60 of a minute: *Heat the sauce in the microwave* **for** *45* **seconds**. | *It should only* **take** *four or five* **seconds** *to transfer the data.* —see Usage Note at MOMENT **2** [C] a very short period of time: *I'll be ready in* **a few seconds**. | *Hold still, this will only* **take a second**. | *He should be here* **any second** (=in a very short time). | *The whole thing was over* **in seconds** (=after a few seconds). | *At least 30 shots were fired* **in a matter of seconds** (=in a very short time). —see also SPLIT SECOND **3 just a second** SPOKEN used to tell someone to wait a short time: *"Are you coming?" "Just a second – I have to put my shoes on."* **4 seconds** [plural] **a)** another serving of the same food after you have eaten your first serving: *Are you going back for* **seconds**? **b)** clothes or other goods that are sold cheaply in stores because they are not perfect **5** [U] INFORMAL: see SECOND BASE

second³ [adverb] **1** next after the first one: *finish second/come in second* *Alice finished second in the 100-meter dash.* **2** [sentence adverb] used to add another piece of information to what you have already said or written; SECONDLY: *Well, first of all, it's too expensive and second, we don't have anywhere to put it.*

second⁴ *pron.* **1 the second a)** the next thing on a list etc. after the first one: *A third reason for rejecting the plan, closely related to the second, is the effect on the environment.* | *Maria's birthday is on the second* (=the 2nd day of the month). **2 the Second** *abbreviation* II used after the name of a king, queen, pope etc. who has the same name as someone who held that position in the past: *Pope John Paul the Second* (=written as "Pope John Paul II")

second⁵ *v.* [T] **1** to formally support a suggestion or plan made by another person in a meeting: **second a motion/proposal etc.** *The motion to purchase a new copier was seconded by Ms. Green.* **2 I'll second that** SPOKEN used to say that you completely agree with what someone has just said: *"I could use a cold drink right now." "I'll second that!"*

sec·ond·ar·y /ˈsɛkənˌdɛri/ *adj.* **1** not as important or urgent as something else: *Price is the most important factor for us – location is a secondary issue.* | [be secondary to sth] *In their movies, character development is secondary to flashy special effects.* | **be of secondary importance/be a secondary consideration** *Teenagers want their clothes to look good – comfort is of secondary importance to them.* **2 secondary education/schooling etc.** the education, teaching etc. of children between the ages of 11 and 18 —**secondarily** *adv.*

secondary in·fec·tion /ˌ.... .ˈ../ *n.* [C] an infection that develops from another illness that someone has

secondary school /ˈ.... ˌ./ *n.* [C] a school for children between the ages of 11 and 18 —compare ELEMENTARY SCHOOL, MIDDLE SCHOOL

secondary source /ˌ.... ˈ./ *n.* [C] TECHNICAL a book, article etc. that ANALYZES something such as a piece of literature or a historical event and that can be used to support your ideas in an ESSAY —compare PRIMARY SOURCE

secondary stress /ˌ.... ˈ./ *n.* [C,U] TECHNICAL the second strongest STRESS¹ (4) given in speech to part of a word or sentence, and shown in this dictionary by the mark (ˌ)

second ba·nan·a /ˌ.. .ˈ../ *n.* [C usually singular] HUMOROUS someone who plays a less important part than another person on a television show or in another form of entertainment, or someone who helps someone else

second base /ˌ.. ˈ./ *n.* [singular] the second of the four places you have to run to in games such as baseball before gaining a point

second child·hood /ˌ.. ˈ../ *n.* [singular] **1** a time when someone, especially a man who is between 40 and 60 years old, decides that they want to behave like a young person again and have an exciting life **2** a polite expression meaning a time when an old person starts to behave and think like a small child,

because their mental abilities are not as good as they used to be

second class /ˌ.. ˈ./ *n.* [U] **1** the system in the U.S. for delivering newspapers, magazines, advertisements etc. through the mail —compare FIRST CLASS, THIRD CLASS **2** the part of a train or ship in some countries outside the U.S., that is cheaper but not as comfortable as FIRST CLASS

second-class /ˌ.. ˈ.◂/ *adj.* **1** [only before noun] considered to be less important or good than other people or things: *We will not accept a second-class education for our children.* **2 second-class citizen** someone who is not as important as other people in a society, and who is treated badly **3 second-class ticket/fare/compartment/cabin etc.** relating to cheaper and less comfortable travel on a train or ship in some countries outside the U.S. —compare FIRST-CLASS

second com·ing /ˌ.. ˈ../ *n.* **the Second Coming** the time when Christians believe that Jesus Christ will return to Earth

second cous·in /ˌ.. ˈ../ *n.* [C] a child of a COUSIN (1) of one of your parents

second-de·gree /ˌ.. .ˈ.◂/ *adj.* **1 second-degree murder/manslaughter/burglary etc.** a crime that is less serious than the most serious type, especially because it was not planned **2 second-degree burns** TECHNICAL the second most serious form of burns

second-guess /ˌ.. ˈ./ *v.* [T] **1** to criticize something after it has already happened: *It's no use second-guessing his decision to sell the company.* **2** to try to say what will happen or what someone will do before they do it: *She was trying to second-guess which card Jeff would play next.*

second hand /ˌ.. ˈ./ *n.* [C] the HAND (29) that shows seconds on a clock or watch

second·hand /ˌsɛkəndˈhænd/ *adj.* **1** not new, and used by someone else before you: *secondhand clothing* **2 secondhand store/bookstore/shop etc.** a store that sells things that have been used by other people, at cheap prices **3** secondhand information, reports, opinions etc. are told to you by someone different from the person who originally said it —**secondhand** *adv.*

secondhand smoke /ˌ.... ˈ./ *n.* [U] smoke from someone else's cigarette, pipe etc. that you breathe in

second-in-com·mand /ˌ.. . .ˈ./ *n.* [C] the person who has the next highest rank to the most important person, especially in a military organization

second lan·guage /ˌ.. ˈ../ *n.* [C usually singular] a language that you speak in addition to the language you learned as a child

second lieu·ten·ant /ˌ.. .ˈ.../ *n.* [C] a middle rank in several of the U.S. military forces, or someone who has this rank

sec·ond·ly /ˈsɛkəndli/ *adv.* [sentence adverb] used to introduce the second fact, reason, subject etc. that you want to talk about: *With annoyance calls,* **first of all***, don't carry on a conversation.* **And secondly***, hang up quickly and quietly.*

second mort·gage /ˌ.. ˈ../ *n.* [C] a legal arrangement in which you borrow additional money from a bank when you already have one MORTGAGE that you are still paying back

second na·ture /ˌ.. ˈ../ *n.* [U] **be/become second nature (to sb)** something that is second nature to you is something you have done so often that you do it almost without thinking: *Typing becomes second nature after a while.*

second per·son /ˌ.. ˈ../ *n.* TECHNICAL **the second person** a form of a verb or PRONOUN that is used to show the person you are speaking to. For example, "you" is a pronoun in the second person, and "you are" is the second person singular and plural of the verb "to be" —**second-person** *adj.* [only before noun] —compare FIRST PERSON, THIRD PERSON

second-rate /ˌ.. ˈ.◂/ *adj.* [usually before noun] not very good: *a second-rate author*

second sight /ˌ.. ˈ./ *n.* [U] the ability to know what will happen in the future, or to know about things that are happening somewhere else

second-string /ˌ.. '.ˌ/ *adj.* [only before noun] not regularly part of a team, group etc., but sometimes taking someone else's place in it: *the Vikings' second-string quarterback* —compare FIRST-STRING

Second World War /ˌ.. . '.ˌ/ *n.* **the Second World War** WORLD WAR II

se·cre·cy /'sikrəsi/ *n.* [U] **1** the process of keeping something secret, or the state of being kept a secret: *The entire project has been shrouded in secrecy* (=kept completely secret). | **absolute/complete secrecy** *They stressed the need for complete secrecy.* **2 swear sb to secrecy** to make someone promise that they will not repeat what you have told them: *Mia swore me to secrecy after she told me about the affair.*

se·cret¹ /'sikrɪt/ *adj.* **1** known about by only a few people and kept hidden from others: *secret information* | *He made a secret trip to the White House in order to secure an agreement.* | *They kept their relationship secret from Jenny's parents* (=they did not tell her parents). | **secret compartment/passage/hiding place etc.** *Federal agents found the drugs in a secret compartment in Campbell's suitcase.* | **secret ingredient/recipe/formula** *The cookies are made to a secret recipe.* —see also TOP-SECRET **2 secret weapon** something that will help you gain a big advantage over your competitors, that they do not know about **3** [only before a noun] secret feelings, worries, or actions are ones that you do not want other people to know about: *Her secret fear was that Jim would find out where she was living.* **4 secret admirer** someone who is in love with another person, without that person's knowledge

se·cret² *n.* [C] **1** something that is kept hidden or that is known about by only a few people: *I can't tell you that – it's a secret.* | *Can you keep a secret* (=not tell a secret to anyone)? | *I'll tell you a secret, if you promise not to tell anybody else.* | **It is certainly no secret that** (=many people know that) *the store is losing a lot of money.* | *Journalists have uncovered the company's dirty little secret: business deals with the Mafia.* | *Promise you won't tell anybody – it'll just be our little secret.* | **The secret is out** (=it is not a secret anymore)– *their new product is to be launched on May 1.* | *Pam's lasagna recipe is a closely-guarded secret* (=one that is carefully kept). **2 in secret** in a private way or place that other people do not know about: *The negotiations were conducted in secret.* **3** a particular way of achieving a good result, that is the best or only way: **[the secret to doing sth/the secret to sth]** *The secret to making good pie crust is to use very cold water.* | *Your hair always looks so great – what's your secret* (=how do you do it)? | *What do you think is the secret of her success?* **4 make no secret of sth** to make your opinions about something clear: *Marge made no secret of her dislike for Terry.* **5 the secrets of nature/the universe etc.** the things no one yet knows about nature, the universe etc. —see also TRADE SECRET

secret a·gent /ˌ.. '.ˌ/ *n.* [C] someone whose job is to find out and report on the military and political secrets of other countries

sec·re·tar·i·al /ˌsɛkrə'tɛriəl/ *adj.* relating to the work of a secretary: *She's held several secretarial jobs.*

Sec·re·tar·i·at /ˌsɛkrə'tɛriət/ a horse famous for winning many horse races in the U.S.

sec·re·tar·i·at /ˌsɛkrə'tɛriət/ *n.* [C] a government office or the office of an international organization with a secretary or secretary-general who is in charge: *the United Nations Secretariat in New York*

sec·re·tar·y /'sɛkrəˌteri/ *n. plural* **secretaries** [C] **1** someone who works in an office typing (TYPE² (1)) letters, keeping records, answering telephone calls, arranging meetings etc.: *My secretary will fax you all the details.* —see also PRESS SECRETARY **2** an official who is chosen by the President of the U.S. to be a member of the CABINET in charge of a large government department: *the Secretary of Defense* —see also SECRETARY OF STATE **3** a member of an organization who is chosen to write down notes from meetings, write letters etc.: *the secretary of the chess club*

secretary-gen·er·al /ˌ.... '...ˌ/ *n.* [C] the most important official in charge of a large organization, especially an international organization: *the U.N. Secretary-General*

Secretary of State /ˌ.... . '.ˌ/ *n.* [C] the official who is chosen by the President of the U.S. to be a member of the CABINET and who is in charge of America's relations with other countries

secret bal·lot /ˌ.. '.ˌ/ *n.* [C,U] a way of voting in which people write their choices on a piece of paper in secret, or an act of voting in this way: *The chairman was elected by secret ballot.*

se·crete /sɪ'krit/ *v.* [T] **1** TECHNICAL if a part of an animal or plant secretes a substance, it produces that substance: *The toad's skin secretes a deadly poison.* —see also EXCRETE **2** FORMAL to hide something: *They had secreted $120 million in a Swiss bank account.*

se·cre·tion /sɪ'kriʃən/ *n.* TECHNICAL **a)** [C] a substance, usually liquid, produced by part of a plant or animal **b)** [U] the production of this substance: *The disorder is caused by excessive secretion of certain hormones.*

se·cre·tive /'sikrətɪv/ *adj.* a secretive person or organization likes to keep their thoughts, intentions, or actions hidden from others: *North Korea is a secretive nation.* | **[be secretive about sth]** *Saturn officials have been secretive about sales projections.* —**secretively** *adv.* —**secretiveness** *n.* [U]

se·cret·ly /'sikrɪtli/ *adv.* in a way that is kept hidden from other people: *Harris secretly recorded his conversation with the senator.*

secret po·lice /ˌ.. '.ˌ/ *n.* **the secret police** a police force controlled by a government, that secretly tries to defeat the political enemies of that government

secret serv·ice /ˌ.. '.ˌ/ *n.* **the Secret Service** a U.S. government department that deals with special kinds of police work, especially protecting the President

secret so·ci·e·ty /ˌ.. .'..ˌ/ *n. plural* **secret societies** [C] a social, political etc. organization that meets in secret and whose members must keep its activities and rules secret from other people

sect /sɛkt/ *n.* [C] a group of people with their own particular set of beliefs and practices, especially one that has separated from a larger religious group

sec·tar·i·an /sɛk'tɛriən/ *adj.* **1 sectarian violence/conflict/fighting etc.** violence, CONFLICT etc. that is related to the strong feelings between people of different religious groups **2** supporting a particular religious group and its beliefs: *a sectarian school* —**sectarianism** *n.* [U]

sec·tion¹ /'sɛkʃən/ *n.* **1** place/object [C] one of the parts that something, such as an object or place, is divided into: *The plane's tail section was found in a cornfield.* | *Swimsuits are next to the lingerie section.* | *Garnish the salad with fresh grapefruit sections.* | [+ of] *This is one of the older sections of town.* | *the reference section of the library* | *Are there any seats left in the smoking section* (=where smoking is allowed)? | *The bookcase can be taken apart and stored in sections.* **2** group of people [C] a separate group within a larger group of people: [+ of] *a large section of the American public* **3 brass/rhythm/woodwind/string etc. section** the part of a band or ORCHESTRA that plays the BRASS, RHYTHM etc. instruments **4** book/newspaper/report [C] a separate part of something that is written, such as a newspaper or part of a book: *Who has the sports section?* | *the final section of this chapter* **5** law one of the parts of a law or legal document: *Article I, Section 8 of the U.S. Constitution* **6** medical/scientific TECHNICAL **a)** [C,U] a medical operation that involves cutting —see also **cesarean section** (CESAREAN) **b)** [C] a very thin flat piece that is cut from skin, a plant etc. to be looked at under a MICROSCOPE

S

7 side/top view [C,U] a picture that shows what a building, part of the body etc. would look like if it were cut from top to bottom or side to side —see also CROSS SECTION

8 area of land [C] a square area of land in the central and western U.S. that is one mile long on each side

9 mathematics [C] TECHNICAL the shape that is made when a solid figure is cut by a flat surface in mathematics: *conic sections*

section[2] *v.* [T] TECHNICAL **1** to separate something into sections: *Peel and section the oranges.* **2** to cut a section from skin, a plant etc. **3** to use a flat surface to cut a solid figure in mathematics **4** TECHNICAL to cut a part of the body in a medical operation

section sth ↔ **off** *phr. v.* [T] to divide an area into parts, by making a dividing line between them: *Part of the yard had been sectioned off for growing fruit trees.*

sec·tion·al /'sɛkʃənl/ *adj.* **1** relating to a particular area: *the sectional tennis tournament* **2** limited to one particular group or area within a larger group: *Members of the church's administration were divided among sectional lines.* **3** sectional sofa a SOFA made up of sections that can be put together or taken apart

sec·tor /'sɛktə/ *n.* [C] **1** a part of an area of activity, especially of business, trade etc.: [+ **of**] *growth in the manufacturing sector of the state's economy* | **the public/private sector** (=business controlled by the government or by private companies) **2** one of the parts into which an area is divided, especially for military reasons: *recent disturbances in the city's Christian sector* **3** TECHNICAL an area in a circle enclosed by two straight lines drawn from the center to the edge

sec·u·lar /'sɛkyələ/ *adj.* **1** not relating to or controlled by a church or other religious authority: *The government is secular.* | *secular music* —compare SACRED (1) **2** TECHNICAL a secular priest lives among ordinary people, rather than with other priests in a MONASTERY

sec·u·lar·ism /'sɛkyələ,rɪzəm/ *n.* [U] **1** a system of social organization that does not allow religion to influence the government, or the belief that religion should not influence a government: *Turkey's secularism* **2** the quality of behaving in a way that shows religion does not influence you: *the secularism of American popular culture* —**secularist** *n.* [C]

sec·u·lar·ize /'sɛkyələ,raɪz/ *v.* [T] to remove a society or an institution from the control or influence of religious groups —**secularization** /,sɛkyələrə'zeɪʃən/ *n.* [U]

se·cure[1] /sɪ'kyʊr/ *adj.* **1** a situation that is secure is one that you can depend on because it is not likely to change: *Wilson had no secure job.* | *Gorbachev's place in history is secure.* **2 a)** locked or guarded so that people cannot get in or out, or steal anything: *Keep your passport in a secure place.* | *a secure area near the governor's office* **b)** safe from and protected against damage or attack: *Companies can offer secure credit card transactions over the Internet.* | [+ **from**] *They spent the night in a little cave, secure from the storm.* **3** feeling safe and protected from danger: *People should feel secure when they walk the streets of this city.* **4 a)** feeling confident and certain about a situation and not worried that it might change: *Bill was successful and **financially secure** (=having enough money to live on), but still unsatisfied.* | *Babysitters are available so that you can dance till dawn, **secure in the knowledge that** your kids are safe and sound.* **b)** feeling confident about yourself and your abilities: *I don't think Marie is as secure as she would have liked us to believe.* —opposite INSECURE (1) **5** firmly attached, tied, or fastened: *Are you sure that shelf is secure?*

secure[2] *v.* [T] **1** to get or achieve something that will be permanent, especially after a lot of effort: *Oregon secured a place in the NCAA basketball tournament.* | *Ms. Ferrer and Santos are working*

together to secure the hostages' release. **2** to make something safe from being attacked, harmed, or lost: *Troops were brought in to secure the area.* **3** to attach or tie something firmly in a particular position: [**secure sth to sth**] *Dana secured the boat to the dock with a strong rope.* **4** to legally promise that if you cannot pay back money you have borrowed from someone, you will give them goods or property of the same value instead: *Fox had used company money to secure a personal loan.*

se·cure·ly /sɪ'kyʊrli/ *adv.* **1** tied, attached etc. tightly, especially in order to make something safe: **securely locked/fastened/tied etc.** *Nancy found that the front door was securely locked.* **2** in a way that keeps something safe from being stolen or lost: *The system will let consumers buy products securely and quickly over the Internet.*

Securities and Ex·change Com·mis·sion, the /.'...... .'. .,../ a U.S. government organization which makes sure that people and companies obey laws about the sale of company STOCKs and BONDs

se·cu·ri·ty /sɪ'kyʊrəti/ *n.*

1 keep sb/sth safe [U] things that are done in order to keep a place, person, or thing safe: **security measures/checks/procedures etc.** *These security checks must be made before the President's arrival.* | **national/state security** (=protection of a country from attack or harm) | *He was transferred to a **high security** federal prison.* | *They maintain very **tight security** (=careful protection using a lot of soldiers, police etc.) along the border.*

2 safe from bad situations [U] protection or a feeling of protection from the bad things that could happen to you: *Parenting is about giving a child security and love.* | *Unions are working for greater **job security** (=not being in danger of losing your job) for low-paid workers.* | *This insurance plan offers your family **financial security** (=enough money to live on) in the event of your death.*

3 **securities** [plural] official documents such as STOCKs or BONDs that people buy in order to earn money from INTEREST[1] (3)

4 not lose/steal [U] protection from being lost, stolen, or damaged: *Your paycheck is deposited directly into your account for greater security.*

5 guards [U] people who deal with the protection of buildings and equipment, especially people who do this for a company or store: *A salesclerk called security.* | *Airport **security personnel** can perform checks on carry-on luggage.* —see also SECURITY GUARD

6 borrowing money [U] something such as property that you promise to give someone if you cannot pay back money you have borrowed from them: [+ **for**] *Reiss used his Brooklyn home as security for the loan.*

security blan·ket /.'... ,../ *n.* [C] **1** a BLANKET that children like to hold and touch to comfort themselves **2** something that makes someone feel less nervous or anxious in bad or worrying situations: *Computer customers no longer need the security blanket of a brand name.*

security clear·ance /.'... ,../ *n.* [C,U] official permission for someone to see secret documents etc., or to enter a building, after a strict checking process

security de·pos·it /.'... .,../ *n.* [C] an amount of money that you give to a LANDLORD before you rent a house or apartment, and that is returned to you after you leave if you have not damaged the property

security force /.'... ,./ *n.* [C usually plural] a group of people whose job is to protect a country, an official building etc.

security guard /.'... ,./ *n.* [C] someone whose job is to guard a building, a vehicle carrying money etc.

security light /.'... ,./ *n.* [C] a light that turns on when someone tries to enter a dark building or area

security risk /.'... ,./ *n.* [C] someone or something that you cannot trust, and that could cause serious problems for the safety of a government or organization: *Videotaping inside the prison could create a security risk for guards and officials.*

security serv·ice /.'... ,../ *n.* [C] a government organization that protects a country's secrets against enemy countries or protects the government against attempts to take away its power

secy. a written abbreviation of "secretary"

se·dan /sɪˈdæn/ *n.* [C] a large car that has four doors, seats for at least four people, and a TRUNK

sedan chair /.'. ˌ./ *n.* [C] a seat on two poles with a cover around it, on which an important person was carried in past times

se·date¹ /sɪˈdeɪt/ *adj.* calm, serious, and formal: *Overall, the wedding was a sedate affair.* —**sedately** *adv.* —**sedateness** *n.* [U]

sedate² *v.* [T usually passive] to give someone drugs to make them sleepy or calm, especially so that they do not feel pain: *She was **heavily sedated** for the pain.*

se·da·tion /sɪˈdeɪʃən/ *n.* [U] the use of drugs to make someone sleepy or calm, often so that they do not feel pain: *The patient was still **under sedation**.*

sed·a·tive /ˈsɛdətɪv/ *n.* [C] a drug used to make someone sleepy or calm

sed·en·tar·y /ˈsɛdnˌtɛri/ *adj.* FORMAL **1** a sedentary job etc. is one in which you sit down a lot and do not move or exercise very much: *People with sedentary lifestyles have a greater risk of heart attacks.* **2** a sedentary person is someone who sits a lot and does not exercise: *America's young people are too sedentary.* **3** a sedentary group of people tend always to live in the same place: *a sedentary population*

Se·der /ˈseɪdə/ *n.* [C] a special dinner which takes place on the first two nights of Passover and is held to remember the occasion when the Jewish people left Egypt

sedge /sɛdʒ/ *n.* [U] a plant similar to grass that grows in groups on low wet ground

sed·i·ment /ˈsɛdəmənt/ *n.* [C,U] solid substances that settle at the bottom of a liquid: *sediment in the wine*

sed·i·men·ta·ry /ˌsɛdəˈmɛntri, -ˈmɛntəri/ *adj.* made of the solid substances that settle at the bottom of oceans, rivers, lakes etc.: *sedimentary rock*

sed·i·men·ta·tion /ˌsɛdəmənˈteɪʃən/ *n.* [U] TECHNICAL the natural process by which small pieces of rock, earth etc. settle at the bottom of the ocean etc. and form a solid layer

se·di·tion /sɪˈdɪʃən/ *n.* [U] FORMAL speech, writing, or actions intended to encourage people to disobey a government, in places where this is considered a crime

se·di·tious /sɪˈdɪʃəs/ *adj.* FORMAL intended to encourage people to disobey the government, in places where this is considered a crime: *seditious statements* —**seditiously** *adv.*

se·duce /sɪˈdus/ *v.* [T] **1** to persuade someone to have sex with you, especially in a way that is attractive and not too direct: *Are you trying to seduce me?* **2** [usually passive] to make someone want to do something by making it seem very attractive or interesting to them: *A majority of law school graduates are seduced by the huge salaries offered by large firms.* —**seducer** *n.* [C]

se·duc·tion /sɪˈdʌkʃən/ *n.* **1** [C,U] an act of persuading someone to have sex with you for the first time: *The story describes the seduction of a young girl by a middle-aged professor.* **2** [C usually plural] something that strongly attracts people, but often has a bad effect on their lives: *The distractions and seductions of modern life are everywhere in our busy world.*

se·duc·tive /sɪˈdʌktɪv/ *adj.* **1** sexually attractive: *a charming and seductive man* **2** something that is seductive is very interesting or attractive to you, in a way that persuades you to do something you would not usually do: *L.A. is a dangerous yet seductive city.* —**seductively** *adv.* —**seductiveness** *n.* [U]

se·duc·tress /sɪˈdʌktrɪs/ *n.* [C] a woman who uses her sexual attractiveness to persuade someone to have sex with her

sed·u·lous /ˈsɛdʒələs/ *adj.* LITERARY hard working and determined: *a sedulous worker* —**sedulously** *adv.*

see¹ /si/ *v. past tense* **saw** *past participle* **seen**
1 ability to see [I,T not in progressive] to be able to use your eyes to look at things and know what they

are: *Dad doesn't see as well as he used to.* | **can/can't see** *Newborn babies can see only blurred shapes.*

see

Karen was blindfolded so she couldn't see anything.

They looked at the paintings.

Dad's watching TV.

2 notice/examine [T not in progressive] to notice, examine, or recognize someone or something by looking: *Let me see your pen.* | *Can't you see I'm eating?* | **can/can't see** *Hey, you can see the Empire State Building from here.* | [+ where/what/who etc.] *Did you see who it was?* | [+ (that)] *Oh, I see you've got cable TV.* | [see sb/sth doing sth] *She could see Tom eyeing the crowd for some sign of his wife.* | [see sb/sth do sth] *He had seen five women arrive at the hotel that morning.* | [+ if/whether] *Can you see if Robert's there?*

3 understand sth [I,T not in progressive] to understand or realize something: [+ that] *Now I see that you were both correct.* | [+ why/what/who etc.] *I wish Jeff could see how important this interview is to me.* | *I see what you mean – her voice is really irritating.* | *I **could never see the point of** (=could not understand the reason for or importance of something) making us write in pencil.*

4 find out [T] to find out information or a fact: [+ what/when/who/how etc.] *Did you see how many inches of snow we had?* | *Let's go see what Mom is doing.* | [+ if/whether] *I'll call Tina and see if she's going.*

5 in the future [I,T] to find out about something in the future: [+ if/whether] *I'll see if I can sneak out for a drink later.* | [+ how/what/when etc.] *It'll be a while before we see what results the new system will bring.* | *We just have to **wait and see** what happens.* | **see how it goes/see how things go** (=used when you are going to do something and will deal with problems as they appear)

6 where information is [T only in imperative] used to tell you where you can find information: *See p.58.* | *See local listings for movie times.* | **see above/below** *The results are shown in Table 7a (see below).*

SPOKEN PHRASES

7 **see you!** used to say goodbye when you know you will see someone again: **see you tomorrow/at 3:00/Sunday etc.** *I'll see you all in two weeks.* | **see you in a while/in an hour etc.** *We'll see you folks in a little while.* | *See you later, Colleen.* | *Okay then, I'll be seeing you (=see you soon)!*

8 I see used to show that you are listening to what someone is telling you and that you understand it: *"You have to put the TV on channel three first." "Oh, I see."*

9 we'll see said when you do not want to make a decision about something immediately, especially when you are talking to a child: *"Can I come with you, Mommy?" "We'll see, sweetheart."*

10 let's see also **let me see** used to show that you are trying to remember or find something: *Okay, let's see, what were we talking about?*

11 you see used when you are explaining something to someone: *You see, he spends most of his time over at Bart's house.*

12 ...see used to check that someone is listening and understands what you are explaining to them: *You mix the flour and the eggs like this, see.*

13 I'll see what I can do used to say that you will try to help someone: *"I really need it by tomorrow." "I can't make any promises, but I'll see what I can do."*

14 see what sb/sth can do a) to find out if you can deal with a situation or problem: [+ **about**] *Skeeter and I are going into town to see what we can do about this stupid bike.* **b)** to find out how good someone or something is at what they are supposed to be able to do: *Let's take this car out to the track and see what it can do.*

15 I don't see why not used to say yes in answer to a question or request: *"Are you sure they'll let us walk on their land?" "I don't see why not."*

16 be seeing things to imagine that you see something which is not really there

17 seen one, seen them all also **once you've seen one, you've seen them all** used to say that things of a particular type become boring because they are very similar to each other: *Once you've seen one children's Christmas play, you've seen them all.*

18 see your way (clear) to do sth FORMAL to be able and willing to help someone: *If you could see your way to help us, it would be greatly appreciated.*

19 check sth [T not in progressive] to make sure or check that something is done correctly: [+ **that**] *See that the housekeeper does her job.*

20 warning [T only in imperative] used as a warning that something is important and must be done: [**see (that)** sth] *Just see that you behave while you're there.*

21 consider sth in a particular way [T always + adv./prep.] to regard or consider something in a particular way: *Jack could see nothing wrong with their approach to the situation.* | *As Janice sees it, the only way to finish the project is to work late every night.*

22 visit/meet sb [T] **a)** to visit or meet someone: *Hi, I'm here to see Mary Jorgensen.* | *I'll see you* (=meet you) *at two-thirty at the mall.* **b)** to be visited by someone: *Danielle's still too sick to see anyone today.*

23 meet by chance [T not in progressive] to meet someone by chance: *We saw Kathy and her mom at the airport.*

24 spend time with sb [T] to spend time with someone: *I've been seeing Joanne a lot lately.* | *see more/less etc. of sb Do you see much of Rick these days?*

25 have a meeting [T] to have an arranged meeting with someone: *Ally has been seeing an analyst for years.* | [**see sb about sth**] *Why don't you see Bryan about the job?*

26 television/movie [T not in progressive] to watch a television program, movie, play etc.: *We saw a great show on Channel 5 last night.*

27 see sb/sth as sth to consider something to be a particular thing or to have a particular quality: *Climbers see the Himalayas as the final frontier.* | [**be seen as sth**] *Marsalis is seen as a role model for young black musicians.*

28 be seeing sb to be having a romantic relationship with someone: *Is Marge still seeing Tom?*

29 see for yourself to look at something so that you can find out if it is true, rather than believing what someone else tells you: *Ed came outside to see for himself what was going on.*

30 see sth coming to realize that there is going to be a problem before it actually happens: *Everyone had seen the layoffs coming, but nobody could do anything to stop them.*

31 imagine [T not in progressive] to form a picture or idea of something or someone in your mind; IMAGINE: *He could see a great future for her in music.* | [**can't see sb as sth**] *I just can't see Marla as a teacher.*

32 experience before [T not in progressive] to have experience of something: *Dr. McNeil had never seen an injury like this before.*

33 see fit (to do sth) FORMAL to consider an action to be appropriate and sensible: *Management has not seen fit to replace the system yet.* | *The committee is free to use the funds as it sees fit.*

34 time/place [T] if a time or place has seen a particular event or situation, it happened or existed in that time or place: *The U.S. saw a huge wave of immigration in the early 1900s.*

35 have seen better days INFORMAL to be in a bad condition: *Virginia's car had definitely seen better days.*

36 see sth for what it is also **see sb for what they are** to realize that someone or something is not as good or nice as they seem

37 not see the forest for the trees to be unable to understand something because you are looking too much at small details rather than the whole thing

38 see the last of sb/sth to not see someone or something again because they have gone or are finished: *I hope we've seen the last of Tina Hughes' stupid boyfriend!*

39 be seen to be noticed by people who are important in society: *Spago is still the place to be seen in L.A.*

40 see the world to travel to many different countries so that you can get a lot of different experiences

41 see the light a) to realize that something is true or must be done: *We can only hope the mayor will see the light and close down all these sex shops.* **b)** to have a special experience that makes you believe in a religion

42 see the light of day to begin to exist or appear: *Most observers predict the bill won't see the light of day until at least January.*

43 see reason/sense to realize that you are being stupid or unreasonable: *Thank God the judge saw sense and set her free.*

44 see sb to the door to go to the door with someone when they leave your house, to say goodbye to them

45 not see beyond the end of your nose to be so concerned with yourself and what you are doing that you do not realize what is happening to other people around you

46 game of cards [T not in progressive] to risk the same amount of money as your opponent in a card game: *I'll see your $5, and raise you another $5.*

see about sth *phr. v.* [T] **1** to find out about something in order to make arrangements or deal with it: *I bought a newspaper to see about houses for rent.* | [**see about doing sth**] *Kenji will have to see about getting a visa.* **2 we'll see about that** SPOKEN **a)** also **we'll have to see about that** used to say that you do not know if something will be possible: *"I want to go to Joshua's tonight." "Well, we'll have to see about that."* **b)** used to say that you intend to stop someone from doing something they are planning to do: *Kim wants to go to this party, huh? Well, we'll see about that!*

see sth **against** sth *phr. v.* [T usually passive] to consider something together with something else: *This growth must be seen against the backdrop of the city's overall economic expansion.*

see sb **around** *phr. v.* [T] INFORMAL **1 see you around** SPOKEN used to say goodbye to someone when you have not made a definite arrangement to meet again: *"Have a good trip." "OK, see you around."* **2** to notice someone regularly in places where you go, without speaking to them: *"How's Judd doing?"* *"I don't know. I've just seen him around a few times."*

see in *phr. v.* [T] **1** [see sth in sb/sth] to notice a particular quality in someone or something that makes you like them: *Janna gave me a look that conveyed the same sense of fun that I saw in her father.* **2 not know what sb sees in sb** also **what does sb see in sb?** used to say that you do not understand why someone likes someone else: *What does Ron see in her?* **3 see in the new year** to celebrate the beginning of a new year

His family came to the airport to see him off.

see sb/sth **off** *phr. v.* [T] **1** to go to an airport, train station etc. to say goodbye to someone: *Carlo and I went to see Maria off.* **2** to defend yourself successfully in a fight or battle, or beat an opponent in a game: *Coca-Cola and Pepsi have largely seen off the threat from cheap unbranded colas.*

see sb **out** *phr. v.* [T] to go to the door with someone to say goodbye to them when they leave: *Don't get up – I'll see myself out* (=used to tell someone they do not have to come to the door with you).

see through *phr. v.* [T] **1** [see through sth] to recognize the truth about something that is intended to deceive you: *Sloper saw right through Morris' intentions toward his daughter.* **2** [see through sb] to know what someone is really like, especially what their bad qualities are: *I'm no good at bluffing – she'll see right through me.* **3** [see sth through] to continue doing something, especially something difficult or not nice, until it is finished: *Martin made it clear that he intends to see the project through.* **4** [see sb through sth] to give help and support to someone during a difficult time: *She had enough money saved to see her through about six months of unemployment.*

see to sb/sth *phr. v.* [T] to deal with something or do something for someone: *Lynn hired Cowie to see to all the details for the reception.* | *Would you see to it that Michelle gets that report?* —see also **the color of sb's money** (COLOR¹ (11)), **see red** (RED² (4)), **it remains to be seen** (REMAIN (4)), SEEING

USAGE NOTE: SEE

WORD CHOICE: see, look, watch
See is a general word that means "to use your eyes to notice things": *Yuck! I saw a roach in the bathroom.* Use **look** when someone deliberately turns their eyes toward someone or something and pays attention to them or it: *Hey, look at that!* | *He looked at me and smiled.* Use **watch** for something that you pay attention to for a period of time: *Do you want to watch TV tonight?*

---

see² *n.* [C] TECHNICAL an area governed by a BISHOP

seed¹ /sid/ *n.* **1 a)** [C] a small, hard object produced by plants, from which a new plant of the same kind grows: *sunflower seeds* | **plant/sow seeds** *Sow the seeds one inch deep in the soil.* **b)** [U] a quantity of seeds: *grass seed* —see picture at FRUIT¹ **2 seeds of sth** something that makes a new situation start to grow and develop: *The report planted seeds of doubt in Sally's mind about the future of the research project.* **3 number one/three etc. seed** a player or

---

team which is given a particular position according to how likely they are to win a competition: *Tulane plays the No. 1 seed South Florida today.* **4 go to seed a)** if a plant or vegetable goes to seed, it starts producing flowers and seeds as well as leaves **b)** if someone or something goes to seed, they become ugly, fat, or unhealthy, especially because they are getting old or are not taken care of well: *The old central bus station is now seldom used and is going to seed.* **5** BIBLICAL OR HUMOROUS: see SEMEN or SPERM **6** [U] BIBLICAL the group of people who have a particular person as their father, grandfather etc., especially when they form a particular race

seed² *v.* **1** [T usually passive] to remove seeds from fruit or vegetables: *Add 2 green peppers, seeded and sliced.* **2** [T usually passive] to give a player or team in a competition a particular position, according to how likely they are to win: *Top-seeded Hingis beat the defending champion.* **3** [T usually passive] to plant seeds in the ground: *a newly-seeded lawn* **4** [T] to put a chemical substance into clouds from an airplane, in order to produce rain **5** [I] to produce seeds

seed·bed /'sidbed/ *n.* [C] **1** a place or condition that encourages something to develop: [+ of] *The city's slums were a seedbed of rebellion.* **2** an area of ground where young plants are grown from seeds before they are planted somewhere else —see also HOTBED

seed cap·i·tal /'. ,.../ *n.* [U] seed money

seed·ling /'sidlɪŋ/ *n.* [C] a young plant grown from seed

seed mon·ey /'. ,../ *n.* [U] the money you have available to start a new business

seed pearl /'. ./ *n.* [C] a very small and often imperfect PEARL

seed·y /'sidi/ *adj.* seedier, seediest INFORMAL a seedy person or place looks dirty or poor, and is often involved in or connected with illegal, immoral, or dishonest activities: *a seedy nightclub* —**seediness** *n.* [U]

see·ing /'siɪŋ/ *conjunction* SPOKEN because a particular fact or situation is true: [+ as/that] *It might be tough to get one of those gadgets, **seeing as how** they're illegal.*

Seeing Eye dog /,.. '. ,./ *n.* [C] TRADEMARK a dog trained to guide blind people

seek /sik/ *v.* past tense and past participle **sought** [T] **1** FORMAL to try to achieve or get something: *Do you think the President will seek re-election?* | [seek to do sth] *Local schools are seeking to reduce the dropout rate.* | **attention-seeking/publicity-seeking** (=trying to get people's attention) **2 seek (sb's) advice/help/assistance etc.** FORMAL to ask someone for advice or help: *Brenda was encouraged to seek counseling for her drinking problem.* **3** FORMAL to look for something you need: *The number of needy Americans seeking emergency food and shelter increased by 7% last year.* **4 seek your fortune** LITERARY to go to another place hoping to gain success and wealth: *Coles came to the Yukon in the 1970s to seek his fortune.* **5** to move naturally toward something or into a particular position: *Water seeks its own level.* —see also HEAT-SEEKING, SELF-SEEKING, SOUGHT-AFTER

seek sb/sth **out** *phr. v.* [T] to look very hard for someone or something: *The Demo Derby was set up to seek out local music talent.*

seek·er /'sikɚ/ *n.* [C] someone who is trying to find or get something: **job/asylum/treasure etc. seeker** *Autograph seekers should arrive early at the game.*

seem /sim/ *v.* [linking verb, not in progressive] **1** to appear to be a particular thing or to have a particular quality, feeling, or attitude: *You seem kind of nervous.* | [seem sth to sb] *Doesn't that seem a little bit weird to you?* | *Teri seemed like a nice girl.* | *She waited for what seemed a long time.* **2** to appear to exist or be true: [seem to do sth] *Mr. Naylor seems to take very good care of his car.* | *It seems like you're* catching a cold, Taylor. | *It seems to me that* what he's doing is a mistake. | **it seems as if/ though** *It almost seemed as if we could hear the corn growing in the night.* | **it seems (that)/it would seem (that)** *It seems that one of your students cheated on the test.* | *"So Bill is leaving her?" " So it seems* (=it appears to be true)*."* **3** to appear to be happening or to be doing something: [**seem to be doing sth**] *Jill's voice seemed to be coming from very far away.* | *It seemed like everything was happening in slow motion.* **4 can't/couldn't seem to do sth** used to say that you have tried to do something, but cannot do it: *I just can't seem to come up with lyrics for this song.*

seem·ing /'simɪŋ/ *adj.* [only before noun] FORMAL appearing to be something, especially when this is not actually true; APPARENT: *Don't be fooled by her seeming fragility.*

seem·ing·ly /'simɪŋli/ *adv.* **1** [+ adj.] appearing to have a particular quality when this is not actually true; APPARENTLY: *We now have a seemingly endless choice of TV channels.* **2** [sentence adverb] FORMAL according to the facts as you know them: *There is seemingly nothing we can do to stop the plans from going ahead.*

seem·ly /'simli/ *adj.* **seemlier, seemliest** LITERARY appropriate for a particular situation or social occasion, according to accepted standards of behavior: *It would not have been very seemly for the ladies to hear all the shouting.* —opposite UNSEEMLY

seen /sin/ *v.* the past participle of SEE

seep /sip/ *v.* [I always + adv./prep.] **1** to flow slowly through small holes or spaces: [+ **in/into/through** etc.] *Toxic chemicals have seeped from the factory into groundwater.* **2** to gradually affect all of something: *Work has seemingly seeped into everything, including dinner parties.*

seep·age /'sipɪdʒ/ *n.* [singular,U] a gradual flow of liquid through small spaces or holes: *There was some oil seepage from the valves in the car's engine.*

seer /'siə/ *n.* [C] ESPECIALLY LITERARY someone who can see into the future and say what will happen

seer·suck·er /'sɪr,sʌkə/ *n.* [U] a light cotton cloth with an uneven surface and a pattern of lines on it

see·saw[1] /'sisɔ/ *n.* [C] a piece of equipment that children play on, made of a board that is balanced in the middle, so that when the child sitting on one end goes up the other goes down; TEETER-TOTTER

seesaw[2] *v.* [I] to move repeatedly from one condition to another and back again: *Stock prices seesawed* (=moved up and down) *throughout the morning.*

seethe /sið/ *v.* [I] **1** to feel a bad emotion, especially anger, so strongly that you are almost shaking: *He went to bed seething.* | [+ **with**] *Daniel was seething with jealousy.* **2** if a place is seething with people, insects etc., there are a lot of them all moving quickly in different directions: [+ **with**] *The harbor of the naval base seethed with activity.*

see-through /'. ./ *adj.* a see-through material or surface allows you to see through it: *a see-through blouse* —compare TRANSPARENT (1)

seg·ment /'sɛgmənt/ *n.* [C] **1** a part of something that is in some way different from or affected differently than the whole: *The program included a short segment about pet owners.* | [+ **of**] *A large segment of the population regularly takes vitamins.* | *We offer products for a variety of* **market segments**. **2** a part of a fruit, flower, or insect that naturally divides into parts: *orange segments* —see picture at FRUIT[1] **3** TECHNICAL the part of a line between two points **4** TECHNICAL a part of a circle that is separated from the rest of the circle by a straight line across it —**segment** /'sɛgmɛnt, sɛg'mɛnt/ *v.* [T]

seg·men·ta·tion /,sɛgmən'teɪʃən/ *n.* [U] the act of dividing something into smaller parts, or the state of being divided in this way

seg·ment·ed /'sɛgmɛntɪd/ *adj.* made up of separate parts that are connected to each other: *an insect's segmented body*

seg·re·gate /'sɛgrə,geɪt/ *v.* [T often passive] to separate one group of people from others, or to separate people into several groups: *The practice of segregating children by ability in schools seems to be spreading.* | [**segregate sb from sb**] *Juvenile offenders should be segregated from adults.* —opposite DESEGREGATE —compare INTEGRATE (1)

seg·re·gat·ed /'sɛgrə,geɪtɪd/ *adj.* a segregated school or other institution can only be used by members of one race, religion, sex etc.: *racially segregated public restrooms* —compare INTEGRATED

seg·re·ga·tion /,sɛgrə'geɪʃən/ *n.* [U] the practice of keeping people of different races or religions apart and making them live, work, or study separately: *Racial segregation was outlawed by the Supreme Court in 1954.* —compare INTEGRATION (2)

se·gue /'sɛgweɪ/ *v.* **segued, segueing** [I] to move or change smoothly from one song, idea, activity, condition etc. to another: [+ **into**] *The band started with "96 Tears" and then segued into "I Feel Good."* —**segue** *n.* [C]

Seine, the /seɪn, sɛn/ a river in northern France that flows through Paris and Rouen and northward into the English Channel

seis·mic /'saɪzmɪk/ *adj.* [only before noun] TECHNICAL **1** relating to or caused by EARTHQUAKES or powerful explosions: *an increase in seismic activity* **2** very great, serious, or important: *seismic changes in international relations*

seis·mo·graph /'saɪzmə,græf/ *n.* [C] an instrument that measures and records the movement of the earth during an EARTHQUAKE —**seismographic** /,saɪzmə'græfɪk/ *adj.*

seis·mol·o·gy /,saɪz'mɑlədʒi/ *n.* [U] the scientific study of EARTHQUAKES —**seismologist** *n.* [C]

seize /siz/ *v.* [T] **1** to take firm hold of someone or something suddenly and violently; GRAB: *"Come with me," said Nat, seizing him by the arm.* **2** to take someone prisoner very suddenly and violently: *Three women were seized at gunpoint.* **3** to take control of a place suddenly and quickly, using military force: *seize power/control Pinochet seized power in a 1973 coup.* **4** if the police or government officers seize something, they take away illegal goods such as drugs or guns: *Authorities have seized over 200 pounds of marijuana since Feb. 1.* **5** [usually passive] to suddenly be affected by an extremely strong feeling: *Sudden alarm seized Frith.* | [**be seized with sth**] *Diane was suddenly seized with hysterical laughter.* **6 seize a chance/opportunity etc.** to quickly and eagerly do something when you have the chance to do it: *As usual, I seized the opportunity to voice my own opinion.* **7 seize the day/moment** used to say that you should do something now, when you have the chance to do it, rather than waiting until a later time

seize on/upon sth *phr. v.* [T] to suddenly become very interested in an idea, excuse, what someone says etc.: *White House staffers seized upon the senator's comments.*

seize up *phr. v.* [I] **a)** if an engine or part of a machine seizes up, its moving parts stop working and cannot move anymore, for example because of lack of oil **b)** if a part of your body such as your back seizes up, you suddenly cannot move it and it is very painful

sei·zure /'siʒə/ *n.* **1** [C,U] the act of suddenly taking control or possession of something: *The raid led to the seizure of 25 kilograms of pure heroin.* **2** [C] a sudden condition in which someone becomes unconscious and cannot control the movements of their body, which continues for a short time: *have/suffer a seizure One of the restaurant customers suffered an epileptic seizure.*

sel·dom /'sɛldəm/ *adv.* very rarely; almost never: *Anna seldom eats at home.* | *Council meetings are seldom longer than an hour.* | *Seldom have I read a book with such a powerful message.*

se·lect[1] /sɪ'lɛkt/ *v.* [T] to choose something or someone by carefully thinking about which is the best, most appropriate etc.: *I selected four postcards.* | [**select sb to do sth**] *Chu has been selected to attend the National Young Leaders Conference.*

select² *adj.* FORMAL **1** [only before noun] a select group of people or things is a small special group that has been carefully chosen: *DiTucci tested the formula on a select number of patients.* | *Nowadays careers in medicine and law are open to everyone, not just a select few.* **2** only lived in, visited, or used by a small number of rich people; EXCLUSIVE: *select golfing vacations*

select com·mit·tee /ˌ. .ˈ../ *n.* [C] a small group of politicians and advisers from various parties that has been chosen to examine a particular subject: *the Senate Select Committee on Ethics*

se·lect·ed /sɪˈlɛktɪd/ *adj.* [only before noun] carefully chosen from among a group of similar people or things: *Prices have been reduced on selected sofas and loveseats.*

SW
33
se·lec·tion /sɪˈlɛkʃən/ *n.* **1** [U] the careful choice of a particular person or thing from among a group of similar people or things: *The selection of a politician as ambassador was highly controversial.* | *The judges will **make** their final **selection** this afternoon.* **2** [C usually singular] a collection of things of a particular type, especially of things that are for sale: [+ **of**] *There was a **wide selection of** fresh fish and shellfish.* **3** [C] something that has been chosen from among a group of things: [+ **from**] *Whitney read a selection from Dickens' "A Christmas Carol."* —see also NATURAL SELECTION

se·lec·tive /sɪˈlɛktɪv/ *adj.* **1** careful about what you choose to do, buy, allow etc.: [+ **about**] *Companies are becoming more selective about the TV shows they sponsor.* **2** affecting or relating to the best or most appropriate people or things from a larger group: *the selective breeding of horses* —**selectively** *adv.* —**selectivity** /sɪˌlɛkˈtɪvəti/ *n.* [U]

Selective Serv·ice /.ˌ.. ˈ../ *n.* [U] the U.S government system in which young men must put their names on an official list and choose which part of the armed forces they would join if there were a war

se·lec·tor /sɪˈlɛktər/ *n.* [C] TECHNICAL a piece of equipment that helps you find the right position for something, for example the correct station on a radio

se·le·ni·um /sɪˈliniəm/ *n.* [U] *symbol* Se a poisonous ELEMENT that is not a metal and is used in some electrical instruments to make them sensitive to light

SW
2
self /sɛlf/ *n. plural* **selves** /sɛlvz/ **1** [usually singular] the type of person you are, including your character, your typical behavior, your abilities etc.: *sb's usual/normal self Marcus wasn't his normal self today.* | *be/look/feel (like) your old self After a disappointing first half, Johnson was his old self in the second.* | *Many people deny their true selves* (=what they are really like). **2** [U] TECHNICAL someone's consciousness of being a separate person, different from other people: *Most Jewish people said that their faith is an important part of their sense of self.* **3** *be a shadow/ghost of your former self* to not be at all like the cheerful, healthy strong etc. person that you used to be **4** [U] a word written in business letters, official documents etc. meaning the same person that has just been mentioned: *He may be in danger of injuring self or others.*

self- /sɛlf/ *prefix* **1** by yourself or by itself: *He's self-taught.* (=he taught himself) | *self-adhesive labels* (=that stick by themselves) **2** done by or to yourself or itself: *a self-portrait* (=a picture of yourself, that you have drawn or painted yourself) | *self-restraint* (=the ability to stop yourself from doing something that is not sensible)

self-ab·ne·ga·tion /ˌ. .ˈ../ *n.* [U] FORMAL a lack of interest in your own needs and desires; ABNEGATION

self-ab·sorbed /ˌ. .ˈ.◂/ *adj.* concerned only with yourself and the things that affect you: *I was too self-absorbed to notice how unhappy she was.* —**self-absorption** *n.* [U]

self-ac·tu·al·i·za·tion /ˌ. ....ˈ../ *n.* [U] FORMAL the process of developing and improving your own abilities so that you become happier and more satisfied with your life: *Many people seek self-actualization and fulfillment through parenthood.*

self-ad·dressed /ˌ. ..◂/ *adj.* a self-addressed envelope has your name and address on it, so that

someone can use it to send you something in the mail —see also SASE

self-ad·he·sive /ˌ. .ˈ../ *adj.* a self-adhesive stamp, BANDAGE etc. has a sticky surface and does not need liquid or glue to make it stay attached to something else

self-ag·gran·dize·ment /ˌ. .ˈ.../ *n.* [U] the act of making yourself seem bigger, more important, or more powerful than you are —**self-aggrandizing** *adj.*

self-ap·point·ed /ˌ. .ˈ..◂/ *adj.* [only before noun] thinking that you are the best person to lead other people or represent their wishes and opinions, especially when you are not: *We won't be intimidated by self-appointed guardians of educational standards.*

self-as·sem·bly /ˌ. .ˈ.◂/ *adj.* something that is self-assembly, for example furniture, is sold as separate parts that you put together yourself at home

self-as·sur·ance /ˌ. .ˈ../ *n.* confidence and the belief that you are able to deal with people and problems easily

self-as·sured /ˌ. .ˈ.◂/ *adj.* calm and confident about what you are doing: *A woman's voice came on the line, firm and self-assured.*

self-a·ware·ness /ˌ. .ˈ../ *n.* [U] knowledge and understanding of yourself: *Steiner promotes greater self-awareness in her books.* —**self-aware** *adj.*

self-cen·tered /ˌ. ˈ..◂/ *adj.* interested only in yourself and not really caring what is happening to other people; SELFISH —**self-centeredness** *n.*

self-con·fessed /ˌ. .ˈ.◂/ *adj.* [only before noun] admitting that you have a particular quality, especially one that is bad: *a self-confessed television addict*

self-con·fi·dent /ˌ. ˈ.../ *adj.* sure that you can do things well, that people have a good opinion of you, that you are attractive etc., and not shy or nervous in social situations —**self-confidently** *adv.* —**self-confidence** *n.* [U]

self-con·grat·u·la·to·ry /ˌ. .ˈ...../ *adj.* behaving in an annoying way that shows you think you have done very well at something: *a self-congratulatory smile* —**self-congratulation** /ˌ. ...ˈ../ *n.* [U]

self-con·scious /ˌ. ˈ../ *adj.* **1** worried and embarrassed about what you look like or what other people think of you: *"I've never drunk wine before," I said, suddenly self-conscious.* | [+ **about**] *Leo's still self-conscious about his accent.* **2** TECHNICAL self-conscious art, writing etc. shows that the artist or writer is paying too much attention to how the public will react to their work: *Her diary was written in a strangely self-conscious style.* —**self-consciously** *adv.* —**self-consciousness** *n.* [U]

self-con·tained /ˌ. .ˈ.◂/ *adj.* **1** something that is self-contained is complete in itself, and does not need other things or help from somewhere else to make it work: *a self-contained heating unit* **2** someone who is self-contained tends not to be friendly or show their feelings

self-con·tra·dic·to·ry /ˌ. ..ˈ.../ *adj.* containing two opposite statements or ideas that cannot both be true —**self-contradiction** *n.* [C,U]

self-con·trol /ˌ. .ˈ./ *n.* [U] the ability to behave calmly and sensibly even when you feel very excited, angry etc.: *In school, his problems with self-control led to academic difficulties.* —**self-controlled** *adj.*

self-de·cep·tion /ˌ. .ˈ../ *n.* [U] the act of making yourself believe something is true, when it is not really true: *Perhaps he was engaging in self-deception to block out the troubling facts.* —**self-deceptive** *adj.*

self-de·feat·ing /ˌ. .ˈ..◂/ *adj.* causing more problems and difficulties in a situation, instead of preventing or dealing with the ones that already exist: *It's time to end the self-defeating cycle of overeating and dieting.*

self-de·fense /ˌ. .ˈ./ *n.* [U] **1** something that you do to protect yourself or your property: *Keller insists he shot the guy in self-defense* (=to protect himself).

S

2 skills that you learn to protect yourself if you are physically attacked: *a self-defense class*

self-de·ni·al /ˌ. .'./ *n.* [U] the practice of not doing or having the things you enjoy, either because you cannot afford it, or for moral or religious reasons —self-denying *adj.*

self-dep·re·cat·ing /ˌ. '..../ *adj.* trying to make your own abilities or achievements seem unimportant: *self-deprecating humor*

self-de·scribed /ˌ. .'.◂/ *adj.* [only before noun] using a particular word or words to describe yourself, even if other people would not describe you in this way: *Arya is a self-described gambling man.*

self-de·struct /ˌ. .'./ *v.* [I] if something such as a bomb self-destructs, it destroys itself, usually by exploding: *The package was set to self-destruct if it was opened by anyone else.*

self-de·struc·tion /ˌ. .'.◂/ *n.* [U] the practice of deliberately doing things that are likely to seriously harm or kill you: *Her poems reveal that she was bent on self-destruction* (=determined to harm or kill herself).

self-de·struc·tive /ˌ. .'../ *adj.* self-destructive actions are likely to harm or kill the person who is doing them: *In spite of Cobain's self-destructive lifestyle, he managed to create some classic songs.*

self-de·ter·mi·na·tion /ˌ. ...'../ *n.* [U] the right of the people of a particular country to govern themselves and to choose the type of government they will have

self-dis·ci·pline /ˌ. '.../ *n.* [U] the ability to make yourself do the things you know you ought to do, without someone making you do them: *Taking part in plays teaches kids focus and self-discipline.* —self-disciplined *adj.*

self-doubt /ˌ. './ *n.* [U] the feeling that you and your abilities are not good enough

self-ed·u·cat·ed /ˌ. '..../ *adj.* having taught yourself by reading books etc., rather than learning things in school

self-ef·fac·ing /ˌ. .'../ *adj.* FORMAL not wanting to attract attention to yourself or your achievements, especially because you are not socially confident; MODEST: *Jack faced this minor crisis with typical self-effacing humor.* —self-effacement *n.* [U]

self-em·ployed /ˌ. .'.◂/ *adj.* working for yourself, and not directly employed by a company: *Kerry is a self-employed graphic designer.* —self-employment *n.* [U] —compare FREELANCE

self-es·teem /ˌ. .'./ *n.* [U] the feeling that you are someone who deserves to be liked, respected, and admired: *Losing the job was a real blow to his self-esteem.* | *low/poor self-esteem* (=not much self-esteem)

self-ev·i·dent /ˌ. '...◂/ *adj.* FORMAL clearly true and needing no more proof; OBVIOUS: *self-evident truths*

self-ex·am·i·na·tion /ˌ. ...'../ *n.* **1** [C,U] the practice of checking parts of your body for early signs of some diseases: *Regular self-examination of your breasts is important.* **2** [U] careful thought about whether your actions and your reasons for them are right or wrong

self-ex·plan·a·to·ry /ˌ. .'..../ *adj.* clear and easy to understand without needing further explanation: *The Maxim toaster wins points for its elegant design and self-explanatory controls.*

self-ex·pres·sion /ˌ. .'../ *n.* [U] the expression of your feelings, thoughts, ideas etc., especially through activities such as painting, writing, or acting etc.: *Corporate dress codes don't give workers much room for self-expression.* —self-expressive *adj.*

self-ful·fil·ling proph·e·cy /ˌ. ..,... '.../ *n.* [C usually singular] a statement about what is likely to happen in the future that becomes true, because you expected it to happen and therefore changed your behavior so that it did happen

self-gov·ern·ing /ˌ. '...◂/ *adj.* a country or organization that is self-governing is controlled by its own members rather than by someone from another country or organization: *a self-governing territory*

self-gov·ern·ment /ˌ. '.../ *n.* [U] the government of a country by its own citizens, without people from other countries having any control or influence

self-help /ˌ. './ *n.* [U] the use of your own efforts to deal with your problems instead of depending on other people: *self-help books* | *a self-help group* (=a group of people with a particular illness or problem who help each other)

self-hood /'selfhʊd/ *n.* [U] TECHNICAL the knowledge of yourself as an independent person separate from others

self-i·mage /ˌ. '../ *n.* [C] the idea you have of your own abilities, physical appearance, and character: *A positive self-image can help you achieve anything you decide to do.*

self-im·por·tant /ˌ. .'..◂/ *adj.* behaving in a way that shows you think you are more important than other people: *a self-important, pompous little man* —self-importantly *adv.*

self-im·posed /ˌ. .'.◂/ *adj.* a self-imposed rule, condition, responsibility etc. is one that you have made yourself accept, and which no one has asked you to accept: *Until his death, he lived in self-imposed exile in France.*

self-im·prove·ment /ˌ. .'../ *n.* [U] the activity of trying to learn more skills or to deal with problems better

self-in·dul·gent /ˌ. .'..◂/ *adj.* allowing yourself to have or do things you enjoy but do not need, especially if you do this too much: *Bobbi's just a spoiled and self-indulgent rich kid.* —self-indulgence *n.* [U] —self-indulgently *adv.*

self-in·flict·ed /ˌ. .'..◂/ *adj.* self-inflicted pain, problems, illnesses etc. are those you have caused yourself: *Redman died of a self-inflicted gunshot wound to the chest.*

self-in·terest /ˌ. '../ *n.* [U] consideration only of what is best for you rather than other people: *His offer was motivated solely by self-interest.* —self-interested *adj.*

self·ish /'selfɪʃ/ *adj.* caring only about yourself and not about other people: *He's completely selfish.* | *She agreed to go along for purely selfish reasons.* —selfishly *adv.* —selfishness *n.* [U]

self-knowl·edge /ˌ. '../ *n.* [U] FORMAL an understanding of your own character, your reasons for doing things etc.

self·less /'selflɪs/ *adj.* caring about other people more than about yourself: *He dedicated his entire life to selfless service to his country.* —selflessly *adv.* —selflessness *n.* [U]

self-made /ˌ. '.◂/ *adj.* a self-made man or woman has become successful and rich by their own efforts, and did not have advantages such as money or a high social position when they started: *a self-made millionaire*

self-o·pin·ion·at·ed /ˌ. .'..../ *adj.* believing that your own opinions and ideas are always right and that everyone else should always agree with you

self-pit·y /ˌ. '../ *n.* [U] the feeling of being sorry for yourself because you have been unlucky or you think people have treated you badly: *Haslet never gave in to self-pity, despite her illness.* —self-pitying *adj.*

self-por·trait /ˌ. '../ *n.* [C] a drawing, painting, or description that you do of yourself

self-pos·sessed /ˌ. .'.◂/ *adj.* calm, confident, and in control of your feelings, even in difficult or unexpected situations —self-possession *n.* [U]

self-pres·er·va·tion /ˌ. ...'../ *n.* [U] protection of yourself in a threatening or dangerous situation: *What seems to motivate Congress is self-preservation – a desire to get re-elected.*

self-pro·claimed /ˌ. .'.◂/ *adj.* [only before noun] having given yourself a position or title without the approval of other people: *So many people are self-proclaimed environmentalists that it doesn't mean much anymore.*

self-reg·u·la·to·ry /ˌ. '...../ also **self-reg·u·lat·ing** /ˌ. '..../ adj. a self-regulatory system, industry, or organization is one that controls itself, rather than having an independent organization or laws to make sure that rules are obeyed —**self-regulation** /ˌ. ..'../ n. [U]

self-re·li·ant /ˌ. '..'../ adj. able to decide what to do by yourself, without depending on the help or advice of other people: *David learned to be self-reliant at a young age.* —**self-reliance** n. [C]

self-re·spect /ˌ. .'../ n. [U] a feeling of being happy about what you are, what you do, and what you believe in: *Tom's job teaching young kids gives him pride and self-respect.*

self-re·spect·ing /ˌ. .'../ adj. [only before noun] having respect for yourself and your abilities and beliefs: *No self-respecting wine drinker would enjoy wine that came from a box.*

self-re·straint /ˌ. .'../ n. [U] the ability not to do or say something you really want to, because you know it is more sensible not to do or say it: *If you practice self-restraint and moderation, you should be able to stay on your diet.*

self-right·eous /ˌ. '../ adj. proudly sure that your beliefs and attitudes are good and right, in a way that annoys other people: *Bike riders seems to have this self-righteous attitude toward people in cars.* —**self-righteously** adv. —**self-righteousness** n. [U]

self-ris·ing flour /ˌ. .. '../ n. [U] a type of flour that contains BAKING POWDER

self-rule /ˌ. '../ n. [U] the government of a country or part of a country by its own citizens; SELF-GOVERNMENT

self-sac·ri·fice /ˌ. '.../ n. [U] the act of doing without things you want, need, or care about in order to help someone else —**self-sacrificing** adj.

self·same /'sɛlfseɪm/ adj. [only before noun] LITERARY exactly the same: *They met and were married on the selfsame day.*

self-sat·is·fied /ˌ. '.../ adj. too pleased with yourself and what you have done: *Sonnenberg strolled in, his chin held up at a self-satisfied angle.* —**self-satisfaction** /ˌ. ..'../ n. [U]

self-seek·ing /ˌ. '..../ adj. DISAPPROVING doing things only because they will give you an advantage that other people do not have: *self-seeking politicians*

self-serv·ice /ˌ. '..../ also **self serve** /ˌ. '..'/ adj. a self-service restaurant, store etc. is one in which you get things for yourself and then pay for them: *a self-service gas station* —**self-service** n. [U]

self-serv·ing /ˌ. '..../ adj. DISAPPROVING showing that you will only do something if it will gain you an advantage: *a self-serving political maneuver*

self-start·er /ˌ. '..'/ n. [C] someone who is able to work successfully on their own without needing other people's help or a lot of instructions

self-styled /ˌ. '.'/ adj. [only before noun] having given yourself a title or position without having a right to it: *a self-styled religious leader*

self-suf·fi·cient /ˌ. .'..'/ adj. providing all the things you need without help from outside: *a self-sufficient farm* —**self-sufficiency** n. [U]

self-sup·port·ing /ˌ. .'..'/ adj. able to earn enough money to support yourself: *University athletic departments have to be self-supporting for the most part.*

self-taught /ˌ. '.'/ adj. having learned a skill or subject by yourself, rather than in a school: *Flo is a self-taught cook.*

self-ti·tled /'. ../ adj. [only before noun] a self-titled CD, record etc. has as its title the name of the group or singer who performs on it: *Caravan is still performing 26 years after the release of its self-titled debut album.*

self-willed /ˌ. '.'/ adj. very determined to do what you want, even when this is unreasonable —**self-will** n. [U]

self-wind·ing /ˌ. '..'/ adj. a self-winding watch is one that you do not have to WIND² (2) to make it work

self-worth /ˌ. '.'/ n. [U] the feeling that you deserve to be liked and respected: *Basic trust is necessary to develop inner security and a feeling of self-worth.*

sell¹ /sɛl/ v. past tense and past participle **sold** S W / 1 1

1 **give sth for money** [I,T] to give something to someone in exchange for money: *My parents sold the stereo at a garage sale.* | [**sell sth to sb**] *The school board sold the land to a real estate developer.* | **sell sth for $100/$50 etc.** *I sold my car for five hundred bucks.* | **sell sth at a profit/loss** (=to gain or lose money when you sell something) —opposite BUY¹

2 **for sale** [T] to offer something for people to buy: *Do they sell brake fluid here?*

3 **be bought** [I] to be bought by someone in exchange for money: *We're hoping the house will sell quickly.* | *Their first album sold millions.* | **sell well/badly** *Lower-priced homes continue to sell well.* | **sell for $100/$50/$3 etc.** *Nierman's paintings sell for thousands of dollars.*

4 **make sb want sth** [T] to make people want to buy something: [**sell sth to sb**] *The motorcycle's eco-friendly design should help sell it to consumers.*

5 **idea/plan** [I,T] to try to make someone accept a new idea or plan, or to become accepted: *Jackson faces a difficult struggle in selling his proposal to the city council.* | *It's all right for Washington, but will it sell in small-town America?*

6 **be sold on (doing) sth** to think that an idea or plan is very good: *Local merchants aren't sold on banning car traffic from Market Street.*

7 **sell yourself a)** to be able to make yourself seem impressive to other people: *If you want a promotion, you've got to sell yourself better.* **b)** also **sell your body** to have sex with someone for money; to be a PROSTITUTE

8 **sell like hotcakes** to sell quickly and in large amounts

9 **sell sb/sth short** to not give someone or something the praise, attention, or reward that they deserve: *Don't sell this guy short – there's more to him than just good looks.*

10 **sell your soul (to the devil)** to do something bad in exchange for money, power etc.

11 **sell sb down the river** INFORMAL to do something that harms a group of people who trusted you to help them, in order to gain money or power for yourself

12 **sell your vote** to take money from someone who wants you to vote for a particular person or plan: *Nine legislators were charged with selling their votes for cash.*

sell sth ↔ **off** phr. v. [T] **1** to sell something because you need the money, or because you do not need it anymore: *After Dad died, Mom had to sell off the house.* **2** to try to get rid of things that no one seems to want to buy by selling them cheaply: *Many video stores sell off old movies to make space for new titles.*

sell out phr. v. **1** [I] if a product, tickets, places at a concert etc. sell out, they are all sold and there are none left: *Tickets for Berky's New Year's Eve party sell out every year.* | *All the dates on Streisand's concert tour are sold out.* **2** [I] if a store sells out of something, it has no more of that particular thing left to sell: [**be/have sold out (of sth)**] *Sorry, we're sold out.* | *Toys 'R' Us had sold out of the game before Christmas.* **3** [I,T] to not keep to your beliefs or principles because you want more money, a comfortable life, or a political advantage: *Can you make it in advertising without selling out?* | *Pratt promised that he would never sell his audience out.* **4** [I] to sell your business or your share in a business: *He was forced to sell out to pay off his debts.*

sell² n. **a hard/tough sell** something that is difficult to persuade people to buy or accept: *This tax hike is going to be a hard sell to voters.* —see also SOFT SELL

sell·er /'sɛlə/ n. [C] **1** someone who sells something —opposite BUYER **2** **good/bad etc. seller** a product that sells well, badly etc. —see also BESTSELLER

seller's mar·ket /ˌ. . '../ n. [singular] a situation in which there is not much of a particular thing, such as houses or property, available for sale, so prices tend to be high —opposite BUYER'S MARKET

S

sell·ing point /'.. ˌ./ *n.* [C] something about a product that will make people want to buy it: *One of the car's strongest selling points is its V-12 engine.*

selling price /'.. ˌ./ *n.* [C] the price at which something is actually sold —compare ASKING PRICE

sell·out, sell-out /'sɛlaʊt/ *n.* [C usually singular] **1** a performance, sports game etc., for which all the tickets have been sold: *The Nebraska game is expected to be a sellout.* | *The Cornhuskers played before a sellout crowd of 65,000.* **2** INFORMAL someone who other people think has not done what they promised to do or who is not loyal to their old friends or supporters anymore, especially because they are trying to become more popular, richer etc.: *If I took the job, I thought I would feel like a sell-out.* **3** INFORMAL a situation in which someone has not done what they promised to do or were expected to do by the people who trusted them: *Waters' new film may be considered a sell-out by his older fans.*

selt·zer /'sɛltsɚ/ also **seltzer wa·ter** /'.. ˌ./ *n.* [U] water that contains BUBBLES of gas

sel·vage /'sɛlvɪdʒ/ *n.* [C] the edge of a piece of cloth, made strong in such a way that the threads will not come apart

selves /sɛlvz/ *n.* the plural of SELF

Selz·nick /'sɛlznɪk/**, Da·vid O.** /'deɪvɪd oʊ/ (1902–1965) a U.S. movie PRODUCER

se·man·tic /sə'mæntɪk/ *adj.* relating to the meanings of words: *The semantic distinction between "criticism" and "feedback" can be important.* —**semantically** /-kli/ *adv.*

se·man·tics /sə'mæntɪks/ *n.* [U] **1** the study of the meaning of words and other parts of language **2** [U, plural] the meaning of words or writing, especially as they are used by people in a particular area of work: *Money managers are in a better position to understand the semantics of the business.*

sem·a·phore /'sɛməˌfɔr/ *n.* **1** [U] a system of sending messages using two flags, that you hold in different positions to represent letters and numbers **2** [C] a light that is used to send signals, for example on a railroad

sem·blance /'sɛmbləns/ *n.* **a/some semblance of sth** a condition or quality that is similar to another one: *Life went back to a semblance of normalcy.* | *These countries now have at least some semblance of* (=a little bit of) *a free press.*

se·men /'simən/ *n.* [U] the liquid containing SPERM that is produced by the male sex organs in humans and animals

se·mes·ter /sə'mɛstɚ/ *n.* [C] one of the two periods of time, usually about 15 to 18 weeks long, into which a year in high schools, colleges, and universities is divided —compare QUARTER[1] (6)

sem·i /'sɛmaɪ/ *n. plural* **semis** [C] **1** a very large heavy truck consisting of two connected parts, that carries goods over long distances —see also SEMITRAILER **2** [usually plural] INFORMAL a SEMIFINAL: *Phebus beat Stanford's Ania Blezynski in the semis.*

semi- /sɛmi, sɛmaɪ/ *prefix* **1** exactly half: *a semicircle* **2** partly but not completely: *a semi-invalid* (=someone who is not well enough to go out very much) | *semi-literate people* (=who can only read a little) **3** happening, appearing etc. twice in a particular period: *a semi-weekly visit* —compare BI-

sem·i·an·nu·al /ˌsɛmi'ænyuəl, -maɪ-/ *adj.* happening, appearing etc. twice a year: *a semiannual report* —**semiannually** *adv.*

semi-ar·id, semiarid /ˌ.. '../ *adj.* having only a little rain and producing only some small plants: *a semi-arid climate*

semi-au·to·bi·o·graph·i·cal /ˌ.. ....'.../ *adj.* a semi-autobiographical book contains some true information about the writer's own life and some descriptions of events that did not really happen: *a semi-autobiographical novel*

sem·i·au·to·mat·ic /ˌsɛmiˌɔtə'mætɪk, -maɪ-/ *adj.* a semi-automatic weapon moves each new bullet into position ready for you to fire, so that you can fire the next shot very quickly —**semiautomatic** *n.* [C] —compare AUTOMATIC[2] (2)

sem·i·cir·cle /'sɛmiˌsɚkəl/ *n.* [C] **1** half a circle —see picture at SHAPE[1] **2** a group arranged in a curved line, as if on the edge of half a circle: *A semicircle of chairs faced his desk.* —**semicircular** /ˌsɛmi'sɚkyələ/ *adj.*

sem·i·co·lon /'sɛmiˌkoʊlən/ *n.* [C] a PUNCTUATION MARK (;) used to separate independent parts of a sentence or list

sem·i·con·duc·tor /'sɛmikənˌdʌktɚ, -maɪ-/ *n.* [C] a substance, such as SILICON, that allows some electric currents to pass through it and that is used in electronic equipment for this purpose —**semiconducting** *adj.* [only before noun] —compare CONDUCTOR (3), INSULATOR

sem·i·con·scious /ˌsɛmi'kɑnʃəs, -maɪ-/ *adj.* only partly conscious and not able to understand everything that is happening around you

sem·i·dark·ness /ˌsɛmi'dɑrknɪs, -maɪ-/ *n.* [U] a place or situation in which there is not much light: *They saw shadowy figures in the semidarkness and started firing.*

sem·i·fi·nal /ˌsɛmi'faɪnl, 'sɛmaɪ-, ˌsɛmi'faɪnl/ *n.* [C] one of two sports games, whose winners then compete against each other to decide who wins the whole competition: *Today's winners will move into the semifinal on Saturday.*

sem·i·fi·nal·ist /ˌsɛmi'faɪnl-ɪst, ˌsɛmaɪ-/ *n.* [C] a person or team that competes in a semifinal

sem·i·gloss /'sɛmiglɔs, -maɪ-/ *n.* [U] semigloss paint has a smooth and slightly shiny surface when it is dry

sem·i·nal /'sɛmənl/ *adj.* **1** FORMAL a seminal book, piece of music etc. is new and important, and influences the way in which literature, music etc. develops in the future: *Chuck Berry is one of the seminal figures of rock 'n' roll.* **2** [only before noun] TECHNICAL producing or containing SEMEN

sem·i·nar /'sɛməˌnɑr/ *n.* [C] a class or series of classes for a small group of students, in which they study or talk about a particular subject: *a sales seminar*

sem·i·nar·i·an /ˌsɛmə'nɛriən/ *n.* [C] a student at a seminary

sem·i·nary /'sɛməˌnɛri/ *n. plural* **seminaries** [C] a college for training priests or ministers

Sem·i·nole /'sɛmɪˌnoʊl/ *n.* a group of Native Americans of the Creek tribe, from the southwestern area of the U.S.

se·mi·ot·ics /ˌsɛmi'ɑtɪks/ also **sem·i·ol·o·gy** /ˌsɛmi'ɑlədʒi/ *n.* [U] TECHNICAL the way in which people communicate through signs and images, or the study of this —**semiotician** /ˌsɛmiə'tɪʃən/ *n.* [C] —**semiologist** /ˌsɛmi'ɑlədʒɪst/ *n.* [C] —**semiotic** /ˌsɛmi'ɑtɪk/ *adj.*

sem·i·per·me·a·ble /ˌsɛmi'pɚmiəbəl, -maɪ-/ *adj.* TECHNICAL a semipermeable surface allows some substances to pass through it, but not others: *a semipermeable membrane*

sem·i·pre·cious, semiprecious /ˌ.. '..ʌ/ *adj.* a semiprecious jewel or stone is valuable, but not as valuable as a DIAMOND, RUBY etc.

sem·i·pri·vate /ˌsɛmi'praɪvɪt, -maɪ-/ *adj.* a semiprivate hospital room is one that you share with one or two other people

semi-pro·fes·sion·al /ˌ.. .'...ʌ/ also **sem·i·pro** /ˌsɛmi'proʊ, -maɪ-/ INFORMAL *adj.* [usually before noun] relating to being paid for doing a sport, playing music etc., but not doing it as a main job: *a semipro boxer* | *the semiprofessional baseball leagues* —**semiprofessional** also **semipro** *n.* [C]

sem·i·re·tired /ˌsɛmiri'taɪɚd, -maɪ-/ *adj.* a semi-retired person only works part of the time they used to work, especially because they are getting older and want time to do other things

semi-skilled /ˌ.. '.ʌ/ *adj.* **a)** a semi-skilled worker is not highly skilled or professional, but needs some skills for the job they are doing **b)** a semi-skilled job is one that you need some skills to do, but you do not have to be highly skilled

sem·i·sweet /ˌsɛmi'swit◂, -maɪ-/ *adj.* semisweet chocolate is only slightly sweet and has a darker color than MILK CHOCOLATE

Sem·ite /'sɛmaɪt/ *n.* [C] someone who belongs to the race of people that includes Jews, Arabs and, in ancient times, Babylonians, Assyrians etc. —see also ANTI-SEMITISM

Se·mit·ic /sə'mɪtɪk/ *adj.* **1 a)** belonging to the race of people that includes Arabs, some Jews, and, in ancient times, Babylonians, Assyrians etc. **b)** belonging or relating to any of the languages of these people **2** OLD USE another word for JEWISH

sem·i·trail·er /'sɛmaɪˌtreɪlɚ/ *n.* [C] a part of a large truck like a long box, that is pulled by the main part of the truck and has its front end supported by the main part —see also SEMI

sem·i·trop·i·cal /ˌsɛmi'trɑpɪkəl◂/ *adj.* SUBTROPICAL

semi-vow·el /'.. ,../ *n.* [C] TECHNICAL a sound made in speech that sounds like a vowel, but is in fact a CONSONANT, such as /w/

sem·i·week·ly /ˌsɛmi'wikli -maɪ-/ *adj., adv.* appearing or happening twice a week: *Broder writes a semiweekly column for the paper.*

sem·o·li·na /ˌsɛmə'linə/ *n.* [U] small grains of crushed wheat, used especially in making PASTA

Sen. *n.* [C] the written abbreviation of SENATOR: *Sen. Biden*

sen·ate /'sɛnɪt/ *n.* **1 a)** the Senate the smaller and higher-ranking of the two parts of the government with the power to make laws, in countries such as the U.S., Canada, and Australia: *Bradley was elected to the Senate in 1978.* **b)** [C] a similar part of the government in many U.S. states: *Mr. Bradley served for 28 years in the Kansas state Senate.* —compare HOUSE OF REPRESENTATIVES **2** [C] the governing council at some universities **3** [singular] the highest level of government in ancient Rome

s w **2** **sen·a·tor, Senator** /'sɛnətɚ/ *n.* [C] a member of a senate: *Senator Kennedy* —**senatorial** /ˌsɛnə'tɔriəl/ *adj.*: *senatorial duties*

s w **1 1** **send** /sɛnd/ *v. past tense and past participle* **sent**
1 **take sth by mail etc.** [T] to arrange for something to go or be taken to another place, especially by mail: *Kristen sent some pictures from the party.* | [**send sb sth**] *You should send Pat some flowers to say thank you.* | [**send sth up/over/to etc.**] *He ordered coffee and rolls sent up to his room.* | **send sb a letter/message/card etc.** *Did you send Grandma a birthday card?* | **send sth by mail/ship/air etc.** *I'll send you the documents by courier.*
2 **electronic/computer etc.** [T] to make a message, electronic signal etc. go somewhere using radio equipment, computers etc.: *I'll **send you an email** when I know more.* | *The ship sent a distress call.*
3 **tell sb to do sth** [T] to tell someone to go somewhere, usually so that they can do something for you there: *Who sent you?* | [**send sb to do sth**] *I was sent to bring Mr. Helmsley his breakfast.* | *Russia sent two ships to help in the cleanup of the oil spill.* | **send sb over/home/to etc.** *Chris sent me over to pick up his dry cleaning.*
4 **make sb stay somewhere** [T always + adv./ prep.] to make someone go somewhere and spend some time there: [**send sb to sth**] *They send people to jail for doing stuff like that.* | *Last summer my mom sent me to tennis camp.*
5 **send sth out/up/forth etc.** to produce small pieces or parts, or to make them come out: *In the fireplace, a log broke in two and sent up a shower of sparks.*
6 **send your love/regards/best wishes etc.** SPOKEN to ask someone to give your greetings, good wishes etc. to someone else: *Send my love to Troy, and tell him congratulations.*
7 **send sb/sth flying/sprawling/reeling etc.** to make someone or something move quickly through the air: *The force of the blow sent me reeling to the floor.*
8 **send shivers/chills up (and down) your spine** to

make you feel very frightened or excited: *Stephen King's novels have sent shivers up readers' spines for more than 20 years.*
9 **send word** to tell someone something by sending them a letter or message: *Ruth **sent word that** she would be in town for a few days.* | [**send word through sb**] *He had sent word through his secretary that he wanted to see me.*
10 **affect someone** [T always + adv./prep.] to affect someone's feelings or condition: [**send sb into sth**] *Her presence in the kitchen sent me into waves of agitation.*
11 **send sb packing** to tell someone who is not wanted that they must leave immediately: *Dozens of workers were sent packing because of harsh new environmental rules.*

send away *phr. v.* **1** [T send sb ↔ away] to send someone to another place, especially to live there: *Greg was sent away to school at the age of seven.* **2** **send away for sth** to order something to be sent to you in the mail: *I sent away for one of their catalogs.*

send sth ↔ **back** *phr. v.* [T] to return something to where it came from: [+ to] *Would you fill that form out and send it back to us?*

send for sb/sth *phr. v.* [T] **1** FORMAL to ask or order someone to come to you by sending them a message: *Once Oleg found a job, he'd send for Nina and the baby.* | **send for help/send for a doctor etc.** *Louie had a bad cough, so we sent for the doctor.* **2** to ask or order that something be brought or sent to you: *Now's the time to send for gardening catalogs.*

send sth ↔ **in** *phr. v.* [T] **1** to take something, usually by mail, to a place where it can be dealt with: *If you send in more than one recipe, put each on a separate sheet of paper.* **2** to make soldiers, police etc. go somewhere to deal with a very difficult or dangerous situation: *It's time to send in the ground troops.*

send off *phr. v.* [T] **1** [send sth ↔ off] to take something somewhere by mail: *Don't wait till the deadline to send off your application.* **2** [send sb ↔ off] to make someone go to another place: *When she was 16, Eleanor was sent off to boarding school in Europe.*

send sth ↔ **on** *phr. v.* [T] to send something that has been received to another place so that it can be dealt with: *The nomination will be sent on to the Senate for consideration.*

send out *phr. v.* [T] **1** [send sb/sth ↔ out] to send someone or something from a central point to various other places: *Procter & Gamble send out millions of new product samples.* | *Sean just called – we're being sent out on another job.* **2** [send sth ↔ out] to broadcast or produce a signal, light, sound etc.: *The satellites send out radio signals that pinpoint the ships' positions.* **3** **send out for sth** to ask a restaurant or store to deliver food to you at home or at work: *What do you say we send out for Chinese?*

send up *phr. v.* [T] **1** [send sth ↔ up] to make something increase in value: *The shortage is bound to send prices up.* **2** [send sb/sth] to make something look silly or stupid by copying it in a very funny way: *Cundieff's new film sends up rap culture.*

send·er /'sɛndɚ/ *n.* [C] **1** the person who sent a particular letter, package, message etc. **2** **Return to Sender** a message printed on a letter or package when it could not reach the person it was sent to

send·off /'sɛndɔf/ *n.* [C] a party or other occasion when people gather together to say goodbye to someone who is leaving: [**give sb a good/big/warm etc. sendoff**] *Craig's teammates gave him a rousing send-off.*

send-up /'. ./ *n.* [C] the act of copying someone or something in a way that makes them look funny or stupid: [+ of] *Ives performed a very funny send-up of the mayor's speech.*

Sen·e·ca[1] /'sɛnɪkə/ (?4 B.C.–A.D. ?65) a Roman PHILOSOPHER, politician, and writer of plays

Seneca[2] [plural] a Native American tribe from the northeast region of the U.S.

Sen·e·gal /'sɛnɪ,gɔl/ a country in west Africa on the Atlantic coast —**Sengalese** /,sɛnɪgɔ'liz/ *n., adj.*

se·nes·cent /sɪ'nɛsənt/ *adj.* FORMAL becoming old and showing the effects of getting older: *a senescent industry* —**senescence** *n.* [U]

se·nile /'sinaɪl/ *adj.* NOT TECHNICAL mentally confused or behaving strangely, because of old age: *His lawyers claim he is senile and incompetent to stand trial.* —**senility** /sɪ'nɪləti/ *n.* [U]

senile de·men·tia /,sinaɪl dɪ'mɛnʃə/ *n.* [U] a medical condition that can affect the minds of old people, making them confused and not able to think well —compare ALZHEIMER'S DISEASE

Se·nior /'sinyɔr/ *written abbreviation* **Sr.** *adj.* [only after noun] used after the name of a father who has the same name as his son: *Ken Griffey, Sr.*

ꜱ ᴡ **senior¹** *adj.* having a higher position or rank: *Mr. Swenson is the senior partner in his law firm.* | [+ **to**] *Most men had no problems taking orders from women senior to them in command.* —opposite JUNIOR¹

ꜱ ᴡ **senior²** *n.* [C] **1** a student in the last year of HIGH SCHOOL or college: *I took French when I was a senior.* —compare FRESHMAN, JUNIOR² (1), SOPHOMORE **2** a senior citizen: *Rossmoor was designed as a housing development for active seniors.* **3 be two/five/ten etc. years sb's senior** to be two, five, ten etc. years older than someone: *Kim married a man 15 years her senior.* —opposite JUNIOR² (2)

senior cit·i·zen /,.. '../ *n.* [C] someone who is over 60 or who is RETIRED —see Usage Note at OLD

senior high school /,.. '. ,./ also **senior high** /,.. '. / *n.* [C] a school for students between 14 and 18 —compare JUNIOR HIGH SCHOOL

se·nior·i·ty /,sin'yɔrəti, -'yɑr-/ *n.* [U] **1** the situation of being older or higher in rank than someone else: *There is no substitute for seniority and experience.* **2** official advantage that you have because of the length of time you have worked in a company or organization: *People should be promoted and rewarded on merit, not seniority.*

senior prom /,.. './ *n.* [C] a formal dance party for students in their last year of HIGH SCHOOL

sen·na /'sɛnə/ *n.* [U] a tropical plant with a fruit that is often used to make a medicine to help your BOWELS work

sen·sa·tion /sɛn'seɪʃən/ *n.* **1** [C,U] a feeling that you get from one of your five senses (SENSE¹ (4)), especially the sense of touch: *A cold sensation suddenly ran down my spine.* | [+ **of**] *She felt the ticklish sensation of wanting to sneeze.* **2** [U] the ability to feel, especially through your sense of touch: *The drug helps to improve muscle function and sensation after an accident.* **3** [C] a feeling that is hard to describe, caused by a particular event, experience, or memory: *On the roller coaster, you* **have the sensation that** *you have fallen off the track.* **4** [C usually singular] extreme excitement or interest, or someone or something that causes this: **cause/create a sensation** *The opera caused a sensation in Moscow.* | **pop/fashion/football etc. sensation** *Piano sensation Eugeny Kissin will perform next month.*

sen·sa·tion·al /sɛn'seɪʃənl/ *adj.* **1** very interesting and exciting: *sensational findings* | *Stanford made a sensational comeback in the second half.* **2** DISAPPROVING intended to interest, excite, or shock people rather than inform them: *The media played up the more sensational aspects of the case.* **3** INFORMAL very good or impressive: *She still looks sensational at 56.* —**sensationally** *adv.*

sen·sa·tion·al·ism /sɛn'seɪʃənl,ɪzəm/ *n.* [U] DISAPPROVING a way of reporting events or stories that makes them seem as strange, exciting, or shocking as possible —**sensationalist** *adj.*

sen·sa·tion·al·ize /sɛn'seɪʃənl,aɪz/ *v.* [T] DISAPPROVING to deliberately make something seem as strange, exciting, or shocking as possible: *The story has been sensationalized for the sole purpose of selling newspapers.*

sense¹ /sɛns/ *n.*
1 judgment [U] good understanding and judgment, especially about practical things: *We lost sight of each other on the trail, but we* **had the sense to** *keep in radio contact.* —see also COMMON SENSE
2 make sense a) to have a clear meaning and be easy to understand: *Read this and tell me if it makes sense.* **b)** to have a good reason or explanation: *It just doesn't make sense to keep all these people on the payroll.* | *Stern made the deal because it made good business sense.* **c)** to be a sensible thing to do: *It doesn't make sense to drive if you can walk.*
3 feeling [C] a feeling about something: [+ **of**] *The neighborhood has a real sense of community.* | *Employees get a real sense of satisfaction from helping customers.* | **get/have the sense that** *I got the sense that things weren't exactly right.*
4 see/smell/touch etc. [C] one of the five natural powers of sight, hearing, feeling, taste, and smell, that give us information about the things around us: *Roaming across the island is a feast for all* **the senses.** | **sense of smell/taste/touch etc.** *Dogs have an incredibly keen sense of smell.* —see also SIXTH SENSE
5 come to your senses to realize that what you are doing is not sensible: *Hopefully the government will come to its senses and work this out without violence.*
6 bring sb to their senses to make someone think or behave in a reasonable and sensible way: *It's too bad it took a lawsuit to bring them to their senses.*
7 make sense of sth to understand something, especially something difficult or complicated: *From birth, children strive to make sense of their experiences.*
8 talk/knock some sense into sb to try to persuade someone to stop behaving in a way that you think is silly: *I hope you can talk some sense into Denise's head before she gets into real trouble.*
9 there is no sense in (doing) sth SPOKEN used to say that it is not sensible to do something: *There's no sense in my painting the door if we're going to replace it later.*
10 ability [singular] a natural ability to judge something: **a sense of rhythm/timing/form etc.** *Steiner's drawings show a strong sense of color.* —see also FASHION SENSE
11 sense of direction a) the ability to know which way you should be going in a place you do not know well **b)** an idea about what your aims in life are: *Rehabilitation programs have created a sense of direction for the inmates.*
12 a sense of humor the ability to understand or enjoy things that are funny, or to make people laugh: *Jessica managed to keep her sense of humor throughout the ordeal.*
13 the meaning of sth [C] the meaning of a word, phrase, sentence etc.: *The word "record" has several different senses.* | *He's a gentleman* **in every sense of the word** (=using all possible meanings of this word).
14 in a/one sense in one particular way, but without considering all the other facts or possibilities: *The whole point of a screen saver program is, in a sense, to do nothing at all.*
15 in no sense used to emphasize that something is definitely not true: *Social Security is in no sense an insurance program.*
16 in a (very) real sense used to emphasize the fact that something is definitely true: *As the person who knew most about weather patterns, Kimball was, in a real sense, in charge of the expedition.*
17 a sense of occasion a feeling or understanding that an event or occasion is very serious or important
18 take leave of your senses to start to behave in an unreasonable or stupid way: *You challenged him to a fight? Have you taken leave of your senses?*
19 regain your senses OLD-FASHIONED to stop feeling FAINT¹ (5) or slightly sick: *Out in the fresh air, she quickly regained her senses.* —see also **see reason/sense** (SEE¹ (43))

sense² *v.* [T] **1** if you sense something, you feel that it exists or is true, without being told or having proof: *She sensed his impatience and tried to hurry.* |

[sense (that)] *Fanny sensed that the Mansfield family needed her help.* | **sense what/how/who etc.** *I could sense how hurt he was by that rejection letter.* **2** if a machine senses something, it discovers and records it: *This new dishwasher senses how many dishes are loaded and sets itself accordingly.*

sense·less /'sɛnslɪs/ *adj.* **1** happening or done for no good reason or with no purpose: *We don't want our men and women to die in a senseless war.* | *a senseless act of terror* **2** unconscious: *They beat him senseless, and left him for dead.* —**senselessly** *adv.* —**senselessness** *n.* [U]

sense or·gan /'. ˌ../ *n.* [C] a part of your body through which you see, hear, taste, or feel something

sen·si·bil·i·ty /ˌsɛnsə'bɪləti/ *n. plural* **sensibilities** **1** [C,U] the way that someone reacts to particular subjects or types of behavior: *Never put anything on your screen that might offend the sensibilities of your fellow workers.* **2** [U] the ability to understand feelings, especially those expressed in literature or art: *Very few people have the refined sensibility needed to appreciate these paintings.*

sen·si·ble /'sɛnsəbəl/ *adj.* **1** showing good judgment; REASONABLE: *On the whole, Sam was a sensible, intelligent person.* | *He was sensible enough to see that Jake was the best candidate for the job.* | *We aim to help clients make financially sensible choices.* **2** appropriate for a particular purpose; PRACTICAL: *An old lady in a pink sweater and sensible shoes walked by.* **3 be sensible of sth** LITERARY to know or recognize something: *Now all of us are sensible of the inconvenience this is causing, so we'll try to hurry.* **4** FORMAL noticeable: *a sensible increase in temperature* —**sensibly** *adv.*

S W
2 3
sen·si·tive /'sɛnsətɪv/ *adj.*

1 understanding people able to understand other people's feelings and problems: *Underneath all that macho stuff, he's really a sensitive guy.* | [+ **to**] *Nurses have to be sensitive to patients' needs.* —opposite INSENSITIVE

2 easily offended easily hurt, upset, or offended by things that people say: *Joel is such a sensitive boy.* | [+ **about**] *As a young man he was very sensitive about his gawky looks.* —see also HYPERSENSITIVE (2)

3 cold/pain etc. able to feel physical sensations, especially pain, more than usual: *Tell me if any of these spots are sensitive.* | [+ **to**] *My teeth are really sensitive to hot and cold.*

4 heat/light etc. able to measure or react to very small changes in heat, light etc.: *This is a very sensitive recorder – it picks up every word you say.* | **light-sensitive/heat-sensitive etc.** *light-sensitive photographic paper*

5 situations/subjects a situation or subject that is sensitive needs to be dealt with very carefully because it is secret or it may offend people or make them angry: *In the Navy, Whitworth had access to highly sensitive information.*

6 art/music etc. able to understand or express yourself through art, music, literature etc.: *a sensitive musician* —**sensitively** *adv.* —**sensitiveness** *n.* [U]

sen·si·tiv·i·ty /ˌsɛnsə'tɪvəti/ *n.* **1** [U] the ability to understand other people's feelings and problems: *Female employees praise Moore's sensitivity to women's issues.* **2** [C,U] the quality of being able to express emotions through art, music, literature etc.: *There's a sensitivity in his music that is remarkable for someone so young.* **3** [U] the fact of being easily hurt, offended, or upset by the things that people say: *He misjudged the sensitivity of many Hispanics on the issue.* **4 sensitivities** [plural] someone's feelings and the fact that they could be upset or offended: *The sensitivities of the black community were largely ignored.* **5** [C,U] the fact of reacting to chemicals, animal fur, or other substances in a way that makes you sick: *Rashes and difficulty in breathing can be a result of a chemical sensitivity.* **6** [U] the ability to measure and react to very small changes in heat, light etc.: *the sensitivity of the telescope's instruments* **7** [C,U] the fact of quickly reacting to new situations: *the market's price sensitivity*

sensitivity train·ing /ˌ..'... ˌ../ *n.* [U] a type of training that teaches people to have more respect for people of different races, people who are DISABLED, etc.

sen·si·tize /'sɛnsəˌtaɪz/ *v.* **1** [T usually passive] to give someone some experience of a particular problem or situation so that they can notice it and understand it easily: [**sensitize sb to sth**] *The public is being sensitized to the level of handgun violence.* **2** [T] TECHNICAL to treat a material or a piece of equipment so that it will react to physical or chemical changes: *sensitized photographic paper* —**sensitization** /ˌsɛnsətə'zeɪʃən/ *n.* [U]

sens·or /'sɛnsɚ, -sɔr/ *n.* [C] TECHNICAL a piece of equipment used for discovering the presence of light, heat, sound etc., especially in small amounts

sen·so·ry /'sɛnsəri/ *adj.* relating to or using your senses of sight, hearing, smell, taste or touch: *sensory stimuli* | *sensory deprivation* —see also ESP (1)

sen·su·al /'sɛnʃuəl/ *adj.* **1** interested in or making you think of physical pleasure, especially sexual pleasure: *A majority of Americans think that women are more sensual than men.* | *sensual lips* **2** relating to the feelings of your body rather than your mind: *She loved the sensual pleasures of taking care of a baby.* —**sensuality** /ˌsɛnʃu'æləti/ *n.* [U] —**sensually** /'sɛnʃuəli/ *adv.*

sen·su·al·ist /'sɛnʃuəlɪst/ *n.* [C] someone who is only interested in physical pleasure

sen·su·ous /'sɛnʃuəs/ *adj.* **1** pleasing to your senses: *a rich sensuous smell* **2** full of powerful images or sounds that suggest physical pleasure: *We saw a performance of Wagner's sensuous opera, "Tristan und Isolde."* —**sensuously** *adv.* —**sensuousness** *n.* [U]

S

sent /sɛnt/ the past tense and past participle of SEND

sen·tence[1] /'sɛntns, -təns/ *n.* [C] **1** a group of words that usually contains a subject and a verb, expresses a complete idea or asks a question, and that, when written in English, begins with a capital letter and ends with a PERIOD **2** a punishment that a judge gives to someone who has been found guilty of a crime: *a six-year prison sentence* | *He faces a possible life sentence* (=staying in prison until he dies). | *The murder charge could result in a death sentence* (=punishment by death) | *He had served a short sentence* (=spent time in prison) *for robbery.* | *a heavy/light sentence* (=long or short time in prison) **3 pass/pronounce sentence** to officially state what a punishment will be

S W
2 2

sentence[2] *v.* [T often passive] if a judge sentences someone found guilty of a crime, they officially and legally give them a punishment: [**sentence sb to sth**] *She was sentenced to three years in prison.*

sentence ad·verb /'.. ˌ../ *n.* [C] an adverb that expresses an opinion about the whole sentence that contains it

sen·ten·tious /sɛn'tɛnʃəs/ *adj.* FORMAL saying intelligent things about morality or the way people should behave: *sententious remarks* —**sententiously** *adv.*

sen·tient /'sɛnʃənt/ *adj.* FORMAL OR TECHNICAL having feelings and knowing that you exist: *Man is a sentient being.*

sen·ti·ment /'sɛntəmənt/ *n.* **1** [C,U] FORMAL an opinion or feeling you have about something: *Those are fine sentiments, boy, but they're only going to cause you trouble.* | *"I hate all this junk mail we get." "My sentiments exactly* (=I agree).*"* | **public/popular sentiment** *Popular sentiment against the war was growing.* | **anti-war/anti-Washington etc. sentiment** *The two women turned their anti-abortion sentiment into a crusade.* **2** [U] feelings of pity, love, sadness etc. that are often considered to be too strong or not appropriate for a particular situation: *He was overwhelmed by sentiment as he thought of his wife.*

sen·ti·men·tal /ˌsɛntə'mɛntl/ *adj.* **1** relating to or easily affected by emotions such as love, sympathy, sadness etc., often in a way that is not appropriate for a particular situation: *I suppose we get more sentimental as we grow older.* | *Vladimir shook my hand and said a sentimental farewell.* **2** based on or relating to your feelings rather than on practical reasons: *Robinson found the car and bought it for sentimental reasons.* **3** a story, movie, book etc. that is sentimental deals with emotions such as love and sadness in a way that seems silly and insincere: *Westerberg writes unabashedly sentimental, romantic lyrics.* **4 sentimental value** if something has sentimental value, it is not worth much money, but it is important to you because it reminds you of someone you love or a happy time in the past: *The piano has great sentimental value to her – it belonged to her grandmother.* —**sentimentally** *adv.*

sen·ti·men·tal·ist /ˌsɛntəˈmɛntl-ɪst/ *n.* [C] someone who behaves or writes in a sentimental way —**sentimentalism** *n.* [U]

sen·ti·men·tal·i·ty /ˌsɛntəmɛnˈtæləti, -mən-/ *n.* [U] the quality of being sentimental

sen·ti·men·tal·ize /ˌsɛntəˈmɛntl.aɪz/ *v.* [I,T] to speak, write or think about something in a way that mentions only the good or happy things about something, but not the bad things: *These historical novels tended to sentimentalize the past.*

sen·ti·nel /ˈsɛnt˺nl, -tɪnəl/ *n.* [C] OLD-FASHIONED a sentry

sen·try /ˈsɛntri/ *n. plural* **sentries** [C] a soldier standing outside a building as a guard

sentry box /ˈ.. ˌ./ *n.* [C] a tall narrow shelter with an open front where a soldier can stand while guarding a building

Seoul /soʊl/ the capital and largest city of South Korea

se·pal /ˈsipəl, ˈsɛ-/ *n.* [C] TECHNICAL one of the small leaves directly under a flower

sep·a·ra·ble /ˈsɛpərəbəl/ *adj.* two things that are separable can be separated or considered separately: *The culture of a people is not separable from its physical surroundings.* —opposite INSEPARABLE —**separably** *adv.* —**separability** /ˌsɛpərəˈbɪləti/ *n.* [U]

s w **sep·a·rate¹** /ˈsɛprɪt/ *adj.* [no comparative] **1** things,
2 2 places, buildings etc. that are separate are not joined to each other or touching each other: *separate bedrooms* | [+ **from**] *Smoking sections in restaurants should be kept separate from non-smoking sections.* **2** ideas, information, activities etc. that are separate are not related or do not affect each other in any way: *A separate study found that 77% of students are spending less time on homework.* | [+ **from**] *Dale and Terry have little trouble keeping their work life separate from their married life.* **3** different: *In a separate saucepan, heat the milk and the cream.* | *He asked her out on two separate occasions.* **4 go your separate ways a)** to finish a relationship with someone, especially a romantic relationship **b)** to start traveling in a different direction from someone you have been traveling with —**separately** *adv.*

s w **sep·a·rate²** /ˈsɛpəˌreɪt/ *v.*
2 2 **1** be between [T often passive] if something separates two places or two things, it is between them so that they are not touching each other or connected with each other: *She looked over the picket fence that separates her lawn from the neighbor's.* | *Steaks and meat patties should be separated by wax paper before freezing.*
2 divide [I,T] to divide or split into different parts, or layers, or to make something do this: *The milk had soured and separated.* | [+ **from**] *Atlantis is scheduled to separate from Mir space station on Thursday night.* | [**separate sth into sth**] *My loose-leaf binder was neatly separated into subjects.* | *You have to separate the eggs* (=divide the white part from the yellow part) *and beat the yolks with the sugar.*
3 stop living together [I] to start to live apart from your husband, wife or sexual partner: *After years of abuse, Ginny finally separated from her husband.*

4 recognize difference [T] to recognize that one idea is different from another, and to deal with each idea alone: [**separate sth from sth**] *Human behavior cannot be separated from its biological base.*
5 move apart [I T] to move apart, or make people move apart: *We had to separate Philip and Jason because they were talking all the time.* | [+ **from**] *They got lost on the mountain when they separated from the rest of their climbing party.*
6 make sb/sth different [T] to be the thing that makes someone or something different from other similar people or things: [**separate sb/sth from sb/sth**] *What is it that you think separates her from the other applicants?*
7 separate the men from the boys INFORMAL to make it clear which people are brave or strong and which are not
8 separate the sheep from the goats also **separate the wheat from the chaff** to choose the good and useful things or people and get rid of the others
separate sth ↔ **out** *phr. v.* [I,T] if part of something separates out or is separated out, it becomes separate from the other parts

sep·a·rat·ed /ˈsɛpəˌreɪtɪd/ *adj.* not living with your husband, wife or sexual partner anymore: *David and I have been separated for six months but we're not divorced yet.*

sep·a·rates /ˈsɛprɪts/ *n.* [plural] women's clothing, such as skirts, shirts, and pants, that can be worn in different combinations

sep·a·ra·tion /ˌsɛpəˈreɪʃən/ *n.* **1** [U] the act of separating or the state of being separate: *the separation of church and state* **2** [C,U] a period of time that two or more people spend apart from each other: *The worst part of the divorce was the separation from his three children.* **3** [C] a situation in which a husband and wife agree to live apart even though they are still married —compare DIVORCE¹ (1)

separation anx·i·e·ty /..ˈ.. .ˌ.../ *n.* [U] TECHNICAL a feeling of being very nervous and upset when someone important to you leaves you, especially that a child has when its parents go away

sep·a·ra·tist /ˈsɛprətɪst/ *n.* [C] a member of a group in a country that wants to establish a new separate country with its own government —**separatism** *n.* [U]

sep·a·ra·tor /ˈsɛpəˌreɪtɚ/ *n.* [C] a machine for separating liquids from solids, or cream from milk

se·pi·a /ˈsipiə/ *n.* [U] **1** a dark reddish brown color **2 a sepia photograph/print** a photograph, picture etc., especially an old one, that is this color **3** an ink used for drawing which has this color

sep·sis /ˈsɛpsəs/ *n.* [U] TECHNICAL an infection in part of the body, in which PUS is produced

Sep·tem·ber /sɛpˈtɛmbɚ/ *n.* [C,U] the ninth month of the year, between August and October: *Students go back to school in September.* | *Classes start on September 5th.* | *Noah started first grade last September.* | *Next September I'll be a senior in high school.* | *Quinn will arrive September 24.* —see Usage Note at JANUARY

sep·tet /sɛpˈtɛt/ *n.* [C] **1** a group of seven singers or musicians who perform together **2** a piece of music written for seven performers

sep·tic /ˈsɛptɪk/ *adj.* TECHNICAL, INFECTED: *a septic wound*

sep·ti·ce·mi·a /ˌsɛptəˈsimiə/ *n.* [U] TECHNICAL a serious condition in which infection spreads from a small area of your body through your blood; BLOOD POISONING

septic tank /ˈ.. ˌ./ *n.* [C] a large container kept under ground used for putting human body waste into

sep·tu·a·ge·nar·i·an /ˌsɛptuədʒəˈnɛriən/ *n.* [C] someone who is between 70 and 79 years old

sep·tum /ˈsɛptəm/ *n.* [C] TECHNICAL a thin MEMBRANE that separates two hollow areas in a body organ, especially in the nose

sep·ul·cher /ˈsɛpəlkɚ/ *n.* [C] a small room or building in which the bodies of dead people were put in the past

se·pul·chral /səˈpʌlkrəl/ *adj.* **1** LITERARY sad, serious and slightly frightening: *a sepulchral voice* **2** TECHNICAL relating to burying dead people

se·quel /ˈsikwəl/ *n.* **1** [C] a book, movie, play etc. that continues the story of an earlier one, usually written or made by the same person **2** [C usually singular] an event that happens as a result of something that happened before

se·quence /ˈsikwəns/ *n.* [C,U] **1** a series of related events, actions etc. which have a particular order and usually lead to a particular result: *Owen closed his eyes and thought about the sequence of events that led up to this.* **2** [C,U] the order that events or actions happen in, or are supposed to happen in: *The system follows a logical sequence.* | **in sequence/out of sequence** *Each edition is numbered separately in sequence.* **3** [C] one part of a story, movie etc. that deals with a single subject or action: *The action sequences are the best part of the film.*

se·quenc·ing /ˈsikwənsɪŋ/ *n.* [U] FORMAL the arrangement of things into an order, especially events or actions

se·quen·tial /sɪˈkwɛnʃəl/ *adj.* FORMAL relating to or happening in a sequence: *a sequential arrangement* —**sequentially** *adv.*

se·ques·ter /sɪˈkwɛstə/ *v.* [T] to force a group of people, such as a JURY, to stay away from other people

se·ques·tered /sɪˈkwɛstəd/ *adj.* LITERARY a sequestered place is quiet and far away from people

se·quin /ˈsikwɪn/ *n.* [C] a small shiny round flat piece of plastic that you SEW onto clothing for decoration —**sequined, sequinned** *adj.*

se·quoi·a /sɪˈkwɔɪə/ *n.* [C] a tree from the western U.S. that can grow to be very tall —see picture on page 428

Se·quoy·ah /sɪˈkwɔɪə/ (?1760–1843) a Native American of the Cherokee tribe, famous for inventing a way of writing the Cherokee language

se·ra·glio /səˈrælyou, -ˈral-/ *n.* [C] LITERARY a HAREM

ser·aph /ˈsɛrəf/ *n. plural* **seraphs** or **seraphim** /-rəfɪm/ [C] one of the ANGELS that protect the seat of God, according to the Bible

se·raph·ic /səˈræfɪk/ *adj.* LITERARY extremely beautiful or pure, like an ANGEL

Ser·bi·a /ˈsəbiə/ a country of eastern Europe which became part of Yugoslavia and has now joined Montenegro to form the Federal Republic of Yugoslavia

sere /sɪr/ *adj.* LITERARY very dry

ser·e·nade¹ /ˌsɛrəˈneɪd/ *n.* [C] **1** a song that a man performs for the woman he loves, especially standing below her window at night **2** a piece of gentle music

serenade² *v.* [T] if you serenade someone, you sing or play music to them to show them that you love them

ser·en·dip·i·ty /ˌsɛrənˈdɪpəti/ *n.* [U] LITERARY the natural ability to make interesting or valuable discoveries by accident

se·rene /səˈrin/ *adj.* **1** someone who is serene is very calm and relaxed: *She had a small serene face, like on a cameo.* **2** a place or situation that is serene is very peaceful: *Jan looked out over a serene landscape of gentle hills.* —**serenely** *adv.* —**serenity** /səˈrɛnəti/ *n.* [U]

serf /səf/ *n.* [C] someone who lived and worked on land that they did not own and who had to obey the owner of this land during the Middle Ages in Europe —compare SLAVE¹ (1)

serf·dom /ˈsəfdəm/ *n.* [U] the state of being a serf

serge /sədʒ/ *n.* [U] strong cloth, usually made of wool

ser·geant /ˈsɑrdʒənt/ *n.* [C] a low rank in the army, air force, police etc., or someone who has this rank

sergeant-at-arms /ˌ... . ˈ./ *n.* [C] an officer in an organization such as Congress whose job is to make sure that members obey the rules and that meetings stay organized

sergeant ma·jor /ˌ... ˈ.../ *n.* [C] a military rank in the U.S. Army or Marine Corps, or someone who has this rank

se·ri·al¹ /ˈsɪriəl/ *n.* [C] a story that is broadcast or

printed in several separate parts on television, in a newspaper etc.: *I love the old Saturday morning serials from the 1940s.*

serial² *adj.* [only before noun] **1** doing something in the same way time after time: **serial murders/killings** *The news of serial killings led to near mass hysteria.* **2** arranged or happening one after the other in the correct order: *Nearly all present-day digital computers are of the serial type, executing one program at a time.* —**serially** *adv.*

se·ri·al·ize /ˈsɪriəˌlaɪz/ *v.* [T usually passive] to print or broadcast a story in several separate parts: *His book was first serialized in "The New Yorker."* —**serialization** /ˌsɪriələˈzeɪʃən/ *n.* [U]

serial kill·er /ˌ... ˈ../ *n.* [C] someone who has killed several people, one after the other, often in the same way

serial mo·nog·a·my /ˌ... .ˈ.../ *n.* [U] HUMOROUS the practice of having a series of MONOGAMOUS relationships that continue for only a short time —**serial monogamist** *n.* [C]

serial num·ber /ˈ... ˌ../ *n.* [C] a number put on things that are produced in large quantities so that each one is slightly different: *The stolen weapon was identified by its serial number.*

se·ries /ˈsɪriz/ *n. plural* **series** [C]
1 similar actions [usually singular] several events or actions of the same kind that happen one after the other: [+ of] *There has been a series of attacks on tourists in the city this summer.*
2 events with a result a group of events that are related and have a particular result: [+ of] *An ongoing series of problems made the sale of the company necessary.*
3 tv/radio [usually singular] a set of television or radio programs in which each one tells the next part of a story or deals with the same kind of subject: *The new movie is based on the classic TV series from the '60s.*
4 books/magazines etc. a set of books, magazines etc. that deal with the same subject, tell stories about the same characters etc.: *Jance has written a series of books that take place in Seattle.*
5 similar things a group of similar things: *a series of numbers at the bottom of the computer screen* | *As she smiled, her mouth pushed her cheeks into a series of tiny wrinkles.*
6 planned events a group of events or actions of the same kind that are planned to happen one after another in order to achieve something: *a lecture series* | *Beethoven's Ninth Symphony will be the first in a series of concerts at the new concert hall.* —see also WORLD SERIES
7 in series TECHNICAL being connected so that electricity passes though the parts of something electrical in the correct order

ser·if /ˈsɛrəf/ *n.* [C] a short flat line at the top or bottom of some printed letters —see also SANS SERIF

se·ri·ous /ˈsɪriəs/ *adj.*
1 situation/problem a serious situation, problem, accident etc. is extremely bad or dangerous: *Violent crime is a serious and growing problem throughout the country.* | *Ben's been involved in a serious car accident.*
2 be serious to not joke or pretend, and say what you really mean: [+ about] *Look, I know you're not really serious about visiting, so quit pretending.* | *Stop pushing me! I'm serious* (=used to emphasize that something is important)! | *My God, you're dead serious* (=extremely serious), *aren't you?*
3 careful careful and thorough: *Paying serious attention to public opinion is a recent phenomenon.* | *We'll give your point serious consideration.*
4 romantic relationship a serious romantic relationship is intended to continue for a long time: *JJ and Chuck seemed pretty serious.* | [+ about] *Stella, you aren't serious about this boy?* | **a serious boyfriend/girlfriend** *Dee's got a serious boyfriend – she lives with him in New York.*

5 person someone who is serious is always very sensible and quiet: *He's always serious, but he still makes me laugh.*
6 important: *Work was a serious business to Tom.*
7 sports/activities etc. very interested in something, and spending a lot of time involved with it: [+ about] *People in France are very serious about their food.* | *My brother is a serious golfer.*
8 you can't be serious! SPOKEN used to tell someone that what they have just said is silly or impossible: *"Winston's leaving his wife." "You can't be serious!"*
9 serious money/exercise/time etc. INFORMAL a large amount of money, exercise etc.: *If you plan to replace it, you're talking serious money.*
10 worried/unhappy seeming slightly worried or unhappy: *We both chuckled for a second, then got serious again.*
11 very good INFORMAL [only before noun] very good and often expensive: *That's a pretty serious Swiss Army knife.* —**seriousness** *n.* [U]

se·ri·ous·ly /'sɪriəsli/ *adv.* S W 2 2
1 not joking **a)** in a way that shows you are not joking and you mean what you say: *Allow me to speak seriously for a moment.* **b)** [sentence adverb] SPOKEN used to show that what you say next is not a joke: *Seriously, though, are you going to see her again?*
2 very much/badly very badly or to a great degree: *There was something seriously wrong.*
3 take sb/sth seriously to believe that someone or something is worth paying attention to or should be respected: *You really take this stuff seriously, don't you?* | *Sandy used to take herself so seriously all the time.*
4 carefully very carefully and thoroughly: *My plan is to train seriously from January to July.*
5 romantic relationship in a way that shows that you intend to continue a romantic relationship for a long time: *They started dating seriously about 8 months ago.*
6 seriously? SPOKEN used to ask someone if they really mean what they have just said: *"What do you think? I painted it myself." "Seriously?"*

ser·mon /'sɔmən/ *n.* [C] **1** a religious talk given as part of a Christian church service, usually based on a part of the Bible: *Reverend Read **preached** the most beautiful sermon I ever heard.* **2** INFORMAL a talk in which someone tries to give you unwanted moral advice; LECTURE

ser·mon·ize /'sɔmə,naɪz/ *v.* [I] to give a lot of unwanted moral advice in a serious way

ser·o·to·nin /,sɛrə'toʊnɪn/ *n.* [U] a chemical in the body that helps carry messages from the brain

ser·pent /'sɔpənt/ *n.* [C] **1** LITERARY a snake, especially a large one **2 the Serpent** the evil snake in the Garden of Eden according to the Bible

ser·pen·tine /'sɔpən,tin, -,taɪn/ *adj.* **1** twisting or winding like a snake: *a serpentine river* **2** complicated and difficult to understand: *a serpentine plot*

ser·rat·ed /sə'reɪtɪd, 'sɛ,reɪtɪd/ *adj.* having a sharp edge made of a row of connected V shapes like teeth: *Use **a serrated knife** to slice the bread.* —**serration** /sə'reɪʃən/ *n.* [C,U]

ser·ried /'sɛrid/ *adj.* LITERARY pressed closely together; CROWDED

se·rum /'sɪrəm/ *n.* [C,U] **1** a liquid containing substances that fight infection, that is put into a sick person's blood —compare VACCINE **2** TECHNICAL the watery part of blood or the liquid from a plant —**serous** *adj.*

serv·ant /'sɔvənt/ *n.* [C] **1** someone who is paid to clean someone's house, cook for them, answer the door etc. **2 servant of sb/sth** someone who is controlled by someone or something: *I am and remain a faithful servant of the state.* —see also CIVIL SERVANT

serve¹ /sɔv/ *v.* S W 1 1
1 food/drink [I,T] to give someone food or drink, especially as part of a meal: *Light refreshments will be served.* | [serve sb] *A team of waiters served the*

guests. | [serve sth with sth] *I'm planning to serve the chicken with a light cream sauce.* | **serve sth hot/cold etc.** *Serve the pie warm or at room temperature.* | **serve breakfast/lunch/dinner** *Dinner will be served at five p.m. sharp.*
2 serve two/three/four etc. (people) if food serves two, three etc. people, there is enough for that number of people: *One three-pound terrine serves 10 to 12 people.*
3 be useful/helpful [I,T] to be useful or helpful for a particular purpose or reason: [serve as sth] *Your birth certificate will serve as evidence of your age.* | *The designs **serve** no functional **purpose** other than to dazzle the beholder.* | *McKenna's background in publishing **serves her well** in her new position.* | *We don't get enough aid to **serve our needs.***
4 do a helpful job [I,T] to spend a period of time doing a job, especially one that helps the organization: *School board members serve a two-year term.* | [+ in] *She served in the Peace Corps in the 1960s.* | [+ on] *LaSuer has served on the city transit board for six years.* | [+ as] *Powell served as deputy national security adviser for Reagan.* | [serve sb/sth] *Christine was proud to serve her country.*
5 store/restaurant [T] to help the customers in a store, restaurant etc., especially by bringing them the things that they want: *Please fill out this questionnaire so that we may better serve you.*
6 have an effect [I,T] to have a particular effect or result: [serve to do sth] *The budget debate has served to polarize the country.* | [serve (sb) as sth] *The school's report can serve as a starting point for the discussion.*
7 prison [T] to spend a particular period of time in prison: *He's **serving a life sentence** for murder.* | *McAllen is still **serving time** (=spending time in prison) for manslaughter.*
8 (it) serves sb right SPOKEN used to say that you think someone deserves it if something bad happens to them, because they have been stupid or not nice: *Serves him right – he shouldn't have cheated in the first place.*
9 provide sth [T] to provide a group of people with something that is necessary or useful: *The airline now serves 37 cities.*
10 sports [I,T] to start playing in a game such as tennis or VOLLEYBALL by throwing the ball up in the air and hitting it to your opponent
11 serve a summons/writ etc. to officially send or give someone a written order to appear in a court of law
12 serve an apprenticeship to learn a job or skill by working for a particular period of time for someone who has a lot of experience
13 church [I] to help a priest during the EUCHARIST —see also **if memory serves** (MEMORY (9)), **justice has been done/served** (JUSTICE (5))

serve sth **↔ out** *phr. v.* [T] to continue doing something until the end of a particular period of time: *The Senator's failing health means he may not be able to serve out his term.*

serve sth **↔ up** *phr. v.* [T] to put food onto plates so that people can eat it

serve² *n.* [C] the action in a game such as tennis or VOLLEYBALL in which you throw the ball in the air and hit it to your opponent

serv·er /'sɔvɚ/ *n.* [C] **1** someone who brings you your food in a restaurant: *Our server told us about the day's specials.* **2** a special spoon or tool for putting a particular kind of food onto a plate: *a silver cake server* **3 a)** the main computer on a NETWORK¹ (3), that controls all the others **b)** one of the computers on a network that provides a special service: **a file/print/mail server** *All important data is stored on a central file server.* **4** a player who hits a ball to begin a game in tennis, VOLLEYBALL etc. **5** someone who helps a priest during the EUCHARIST

serv·ice¹ /'sɔvɪs/ *n.* S W 1 1
1 store/hotel etc. [U] the help that people who work in a store, restaurant, bar etc. give you: *We got incredibly good service at that French restaurant.* | *Retailers have to improve **customer service** and make stores convenient and attractive.*
2 help [singular,U] help that you give to someone:

Don't thank me – I'm glad to **be of service** (=be able to help someone). | *Suzuki has done a great service to older Americans.* | *Unions may charge for services rendered* (=help that has been given) *to non-members.*

3 |employment| [plural,U] the work you do for a person or organization: [+ to] *Horne was given an award in recognition of services to the city.* | *Jordan had a long and distinguished career in **public service*** (=work done for the public or the government). | *20/30 years etc. of service After six years of service he is entitled to a six-month paid sabbatical.*

4 |business| [C] a business that provides help or does jobs for people rather than producing things: *I just subscribed to a new e-mail service.* | *a babysitting/cleaning/delivery etc. service We offer a gift-buying service for busy businesspeople.* —see also SERVICE INDUSTRY

5 |religion| [C] a formal religious ceremony, for example in church: *A special church service was held in the city for victims of the fire.* | *a marriage/funeral etc. service A larger memorial service will be held for Burns later this month.*

6 |organization| [C] an organization that provides advice and help, for example with legal or personal problems: *I'm looking for information on family planning services.*

7 jury/military/community etc. service something that ordinary people can be asked to do for the public as a public duty or as a punishment: *He was ordered to perform 2,400 hours of community service for shipping obscene materials.*

8 police/medical/fire etc. service help that is provided by the police, hospitals etc.: *Emergency ambulance service will be provided by the Fire Department.* —see also PUBLIC SERVICE

9 be at sb's service FORMAL if someone or something is at your service, they are available to help you in some way if you need them: *Alfred Descoyne at your service, sir!*

10 |government| [C usually singular] an organization that works directly for a government: *the foreign service* | *the U.S. customs service*

11 the service a country's military forces, especially considered as a job: *My first duty station in the service was in North Carolina.*

12 |sports| [C] an act of hitting a ball through the air in order to start a game, for example in tennis

13 |car/machine| [U] an examination and repair of a machine or car to keep it working correctly

14 dinner/tea service a set of matching plates, bowls, cups etc. —see also **on active duty/service** (ACTIVE[1] (5)), **pay lip service to sth** (PAY[1] (6)), **press sb/sth into service/duty** (PRESS[1] (11))

service[2] *v.* [T] **1** to examine a machine or vehicle and repair it if necessary: *I'm having the car serviced next week.* **2** to provide people with something they need or want: *Dunn's firm services 72 arts organizations across the nation.* **3** TECHNICAL to pay the INTEREST on a debt **4** SLANG to give someone sexual pleasure, especially by touching a man's sex organ with the lips and tongue **5** SLANG to have sex with someone or give them sexual pleasure without being concerned about your own pleasure —**servicing** *n.* [U]

service[3] *adj.* **service door/elevator etc.** a door, ELEVATOR etc. that is only for the use of people working in a place, rather than the public

serv·ice·a·ble /'səvɪsəbəl/ *adj.* **1** ready or appropriate to be used for a particular purpose: *He insisted that the boat was perfectly serviceable.* **2** fairly good, but not excellent: *The food was serviceable, if not stunning.* —**serviceability** /ˌsəvɪsə'bɪləti/ *n.* [U]

service charge /'.. ./ *n.* [C] an amount of money that is added to the price of something in order to pay for services that you use when buying it: *The service charge for advance tickets is $1 per ticket.*

service club /'.. ./ *n.* [C] a usually national organization made of smaller local groups in which members do things to help their COMMUNITY

service in·dus·try /'.. ,../ *n.* [C,U] an industry that provides a service such as insurance, bank accounts or advertising rather than a product

serv·ice·man /'səvɪsˌmæn, -mən/ *n. plural* **servicemen** /-ˌmɛn, -mən/ [C] a man who is a member of the military

service road /'.. ./ *n.* [C] a FRONTAGE ROAD

service sta·tion /'.. ,../ *n.* [C] a place that sells gas, food, etc.

serv·ice·wom·an /'səvɪsˌwʊmən/ *n. plural* **servicewomen** /-ˌwɪmɪn/ [C] a woman who is a member of the military

ser·vi·ette /ˌsəvi'ɛt/ *n.* [C] CANADIAN, BRITISH a paper NAPKIN

ser·vile /'səvəl, -vaɪl/ *adj.* **1** too eager to obey someone without questioning them: *The cruel king and his servile courtiers entered the room.* **2** relating to SLAVES or to being a slave —**servilely** *adv.* —**servility** /sə'vɪləti/ *n.* [U]

serv·ing[1] /'səvɪŋ/ *n.* [C] an amount of food that is enough for one person; HELPING: *Eat two or three servings from the dairy group per day.*

serving[2] *adj.* **a serving spoon/dish/platter etc.** a spoon, dish etc. that is used to serve food

ser·vi·tor /'səvətə/ *n.* [C] OLD USE a male servant

ser·vi·tude /'səvəˌtud/ *n.* [U] the condition of being a SLAVE or being forced to obey someone else: *The 13th Amendment forbade slavery and involuntary servitude.*

ses·a·me /'sɛsəmi/ *n.* [U] a tropical plant grown for its seeds and oil and used in cooking —see also OPEN SESAME

ses·sion /'sɛʃən/ *n.* [C] **1** a meeting or period of time used for a particular purpose, especially by a group of people: *He wrote the new song during a recording session.* | *a practice session* **2** a formal meeting or group of meetings, especially of a law court or government organization: *Court will remain **in session**.* **3** a part of the year when classes are given at a college or university: *This course will only be offered during the fall session.*

set[1] /sɛt/ *v. past tense and past participle* **set** *present participle* **setting**

1 |put| [T always + adv./prep.] to carefully put something down somewhere, especially something that is difficult to carry: [+ **down/on/aside etc.**] *She smiled and set down her cup of coffee.*

2 set a pattern/tone/trend to happen or do something in a particular way that is then repeated many times or which continues for a long time: *Abrams spoke first and set a somber tone for the session.*

3 set fire to sth also **set sth on fire/ablaze/alight** to make something start burning: *Protesters set fire to a truck and two buses.*

4 set a time/date/price etc. to decide that something should happen at a particular time, cost a particular amount of money etc.: *Have you set a date for the wedding?*

5 set guidelines/standards/conditions/limits etc. to officially establish rules, standards etc. for doing something: *The government has set strict guidelines for building and sewage disposal.*

6 set a precedent if an event or action sets a precedent, it shows people a way of doing something which they can use or copy: *Jackson's new contract could set a new salary precedent for top recording artists.*

7 set sth in motion to make something start happening, especially by means of an official order: *Tressler plans to continue many of the ambitious projects McEnery set in motion.*

8 set the table to arrange plates, knives, cups etc. on a table so that it is ready for a meal

9 |movie/play/story| [T usually passive] if a movie, play, story etc. is set in a place or period, it happens there or at that time: *The play is set in Madrid in the year 1840.*

10 set a record to run a race in a faster time than anyone else, jump further than anyone else, win a competition more times than anyone else etc.: *The Bulls set a team record with its 15th successive victory.*

11 set (yourself) a goal to decide that you should try to achieve something, especially something that needs a lot of effort: *It's better to set realistic goals, and actually achieve them.* | *In college, Spencer set himself the goal of being sports editor of the campus paper.*

12 set your mind/sights/heart on sth to be determined to achieve something or decide that you definitely want to have it: *Heath had set her sights on the U.S. Senate seat for Colorado.*

13 set a trap a) to make a trap ready to catch an animal **b)** to invent a plan to show that someone is doing something wrong: *The cheaters were caught when one teacher set a trap by casually leaving a copy of the test on her desk.*

14 move part of a machine/clock etc. [T] to move part of a machine, clock etc. so that it is in a particular position and is ready to be used: *We set our alarm for five a.m. so we could get an early start.* | *I still haven't figured out how to set the VCR to tape while I'm away.*

15 set to work to start doing something in a determined way, especially something that is difficult and needs a lot of effort: *Yolanda set to work changing the tire.* | [+ **on**] *Thomas went to his desk and set to work on the illustrations to go with the advertising copy.*

16 set sail to start sailing somewhere: *We set sail at sunrise.*

17 set sb to work to make someone start doing a particular kind of work for you: *They set her to work in the hot fields.*

18 sun [I] if the sun sets, it seems to move close to the horizon and then goes below it

19 liquid/glue/cement etc. [I] to become hard and solid: *Let the dessert set in the fridge for two hours.*

20 set an example to behave in a way that shows other people how to behave: *Parents should set a good example for their children by being active and keeping fit.*

21 set sb straight/right to tell someone the right way to do something or the true facts about something: *Someone had to set Dave straight on company policies and procedures.* —see also **set/put/keep the record straight** (RECORD¹ (9))

22 set the world on fire INFORMAL an expression meaning "to have a big effect" or "be very successful," often used when you think someone or something has failed to do this: *She went to New York expecting to set the world on fire.*

23 set sth to music to write music for a story or a poem, so that it can be sung

24 set sb free/loose to allow someone or an animal to be free: *After six years in prison, Louis was set free.*

25 set store by sth to consider something to be very important: *Mama always set such store by honesty and truthfulness.*

26 printing to arrange the words and letters of a book, newspaper etc. so it is ready to be printed: *In those days books had to be set by hand.*

27 set sth right also **set sth to rights** to deal with any problems, mistakes etc. and make a situation the way it should be: *This company needs a dramatic shake-up to set things right.*

28 bone a) [T] if you set a broken bone, you move the broken ends so that they are in the right place to grow together again **b)** [I] if a broken bone sets, it joins together again

29 hair [T] to arrange someone's hair while it is wet so that it has a particular style when it dries

30 be set with gems/jewels etc. to be decorated with jewels: *He gave her a golden ring set with four precious stones.*

31 be set into sth to be attached to the surface of something: *We cooked the meat on a grill set into the table.*

set about sb/sth *phr. v.* [T] **1** to start doing something, especially something that needs a lot of time and effort: *He set about his task in a workmanlike way.* | [**set about doing sth**] *Lou set about decorating their new house in blues and yellows.* **2** ESPECIALLY LITERARY to attack someone by hitting and kicking them: *They set about him with their fists.*

set sb/sth **against** sb/sth *phr. v.* [T] **1** to make someone start to fight or argue with another person, especially a person who they had friendly relations with before: *From our earliest youth he set us against one another, the better to control us.* **2** [usually passive] if a movie, play, story etc. is set against a place or period it happens there or at that time: *It's a novel of passion and love set against the glitter of the international jet set.*

set sb/sth **apart** *phr. v.* to make someone or something different and often better than other people or things: *Its sheer size sets Sports Nation apart from other health clubs.*

set sth ↔ **aside** *phr. v.* [T] **1** to keep something, especially money or time, for a special purpose and only use it for that purpose: [+ **for**] *I set aside a good dowry for my daughter.* | *The shelter said 32 spaces for homeless kids.* **2** to decide that you will not be influenced by a particular feeling, belief, or principle, because something else is more important: *Jurors must set aside their opinions and give the accused a fair trial.* **3** to decide that a previous legal decision or agreement does not have any effect anymore: *The judge set aside the verdict of the lower court.*

set back *phr. v.* [T] **1** [**set** sb/sth ↔ **back**] to delay the progress or development of something, or delay someone from finishing something: *It is too early to say how much the fire has set back construction of the house.* **2** [**set** sb **back**] INFORMAL to cost someone a particular amount of money: *Most of these wines will set you back $15 – $20.*

set sth ↔ **down** *phr. v.* [T] **1** to establish how something should be done in an official set of rules or an official document: *Pension plans have to meet certain conditions set down by the tax law.* **2** to write about something so that you have a record of it: *Harriet would spy on her parents and neighbors, then set it all down in her notebook.*

set forth *phr. v.* **1** [T **set** sth ↔ **forth**] FORMAL to write or talk about an idea, argument, or a set of figures: *The review committee has set forth its conclusions in a report.* **2** [I] LITERARY to begin a journey: *Parsifal left his mother's home and set forth for King Arthur's court.*

set in *phr. v.* [I] if something sets in, especially something bad, it begins and seems likely to continue for a long time: *Panic set in as the tornado approached.* | *Other complications soon set in, including internal bleeding and pneumonia.*

set off *phr. v.* **1** [T **set** sth ↔ **off**] to make something start happening or make people suddenly start doing something, especially when you do not intend to do so: *Her 1962 book, "Silent Spring," set off a movement to ban DDT and other pesticides.* **2** [I] to start to go somewhere: *Jeri and I set off on foot for the beach.* **3** [T **set** sth ↔ **off**] to make something such as an ALARM system start operating, especially when you do not intend to do so: *Karen set off the alarm when she came in early that morning.* **4** [T **set** sth ↔ **off**] to make a bomb explode, or cause an explosion: *A short circuit set off an explosion in the hospital basement.* **5** [T **set** sth ↔ **off**] if a piece of clothing, color, decoration etc. sets something off, it makes it look noticeable and attractive: *The blue in your shirt really sets off your eyes* **6** [T **set** sb **off**] to make someone start laughing, crying, talking etc. about something: *That picture of him really set me off – I nearly started crying again.*

set out *phr. v.* **1** [I] to start a trip, especially a long one: [+ **on**] *Next morning at five o'clock they set out on the 12-hour drive to Lake Tahoe.* | [+ **for**] *She took off her apron and set out for her evening walk.* **2 set out to do sth** to start doing something or making plans to do something in order to achieve a particular result: *When she was 18, Amy set out to find her biological parents.* **3** [T **set** sth ↔ **out**] to write or talk about something such as a group of facts, ideas, or reasons, especially in a clearly organized way: *The Maastricht Treaty sets out guidelines for European monetary union.* **4** [T **set** sth ↔ **out**] to put a group of things down and arrange them in order: *Lois had already set out the sugar bowl and the napkins on the coffee table.* **5 set out on a career/**

course of action to start a particular kind of job or start doing something in a particular way: *My nephew is just setting out on a career in journalism.*

set up *phr. v.*

1 company/organization etc. [I,T set sth ↔ up] to start a company, organization, committee etc.; ESTABLISH: *They want to set up their own import-export business.*

2 arrange/organize [T set sth ↔ up] to make the necessary arrangements so that something can happen, such as a meeting, an event, or a system for doing something: *I can set up an appointment for you to have a massage.* | *Kurri scored a goal and set up the Kings' second goal.*

3 equipment [I,T] to prepare the equipment that will be needed for an activity so that it is ready to be used: *The next band was already setting up on the other stage.* | [set sth ↔ up] *Art's coming by to set up the modem on my computer.*

4 build/put up [T set sth ↔ up] to place or build something such as a sign or STATUE somewhere: *A press headquarters was set up outside the stadium.*

5 set up shop to start a business: *Jack got his law degree, then set up shop as a real estate lawyer.*

6 set up housekeeping/house to start living in your own home, especially with someone else, instead of living with your parents: *I have to save enough money to set up house on my own.*

7 set up camp **a)** to put up a tent or group of tents in a place so that you can stay there: *We should finish setting up camp before we start dinner.* **b)** INFORMAL to move all your things to a place so that you can start to live or work there: *She's set up camp in my office.*

8 make sb seem guilty [T set sb ↔ up] to deliberately make other people think that someone has done something wrong or illegal: *He said following his arrest that the FBI had set him up.*

9 relationship [T set sb ↔ up] to arrange for someone to meet someone, especially in order to start a romantic relationship: *No, I wasn't trying to set her up, I just thought she'd like to ride with Carl.*

set² *n.*

1 group of things [C] a group of things that form a whole: *a train set* | [+ of] *I'm thinking of buying a set of golf clubs.* | *It was a peculiar set of events that brought me here.*

2 television/radio [C] a television, or a piece of equipment for receiving radio signals: *a color television set* —see also CRYSTAL SET

3 movie [C] a place where a movie or television program is acted and filmed: *She was on the set early to read over her new lines.*

4 stage [C] the painted background, furniture etc. that is put on a stage to represent where the action of the play is taking place: *Wagner won a Tony for the set of "On the Twentieth Century."*

5 sports [C] one part of a game such as tennis or VOLLEYBALL: *In the second set, Sampras led 5 – 4.*

6 music [C] a series of songs performed by one band or singer as part of a concert

7 people [C usually singular] a group of people with similar interests: *He soon hooked up with the set of young people he knew who had already moved to the city.* —see also JET SET

8 hair [singular] an act of arranging your hair in a particular style when it is wet

9 firmness [singular] the state of becoming firm or solid: *You'll get a better set if you use gelatin.*

10 part of body [singular] the way in which you are sitting, standing etc., especially when you look stiff: [+ of] *His determination to win was evident in the set of his jaw.*

11 math [C] TECHNICAL a collection of numbers, shapes etc. in MATHEMATICS: *The set (x,y) has two members.*

12 onion [C] a small brown root planted in order to grow onions: *onion sets*

set³ *adj.* [no comparative]

1 amount/time a set time, amount etc. has been decided by someone and cannot be changed: *Workers earn a set amount for each piece they sew.* | *The*

company will match your donations to charity, up to a set limit.

2 ready [not before noun] INFORMAL prepared for something: [+ for] *Get set for a full evening of hot and spicy entertainment.* | [be set to do sth] *He was set to go, but Mel held up a hand.* | *Okay, I'm all set, let's get going.* | *"On your marks – get set* (=get ready) *– go!"*

3 be (dead) set on/upon/against sth to be very determined about something: *Mark is absolutely set on owning his own business.* | *Dana wanted to drop out of college, but her parents were dead set against the idea.*

4 have your heart/sights set on sth to be determined to do something: *Teng is thought to have her sights set on the Board of Supervisors' presidency.*

5 set smile/teeth/jaw a set smile etc. shows that you are not happy about something or are determined to do something: *Gloria greeted her guests with a set smile.*

6 set opinions/beliefs etc. set opinions or beliefs are ones you are not likely to change

7 be set in your ways to be used to doing things in a particular way and not willing to change: *Nancy's mother seemed set in her ways and not very open to new influences.*

8 be set to do sth likely to happen or do something: *Sculptor Javier Marín is set to become an international name in the coming year.* | *The submarine's repairs are set to last about two months.*

set·back /'setbæk/ *n.* [C] something that delays or prevents progress, or makes things worse than they were: *Judge Cook's ruling will be a major setback for civil rights activists.* —see also **set back** (SET¹)

Se·ton /'sitn/, **Saint Elizabeth** (1774–1821) the first woman in the U.S. to be made a SAINT by the Catholic Church

set piece /ˌ. './ *n.* [C] part of a play, piece of music, painting etc. that follows a well-known formal pattern or style, and is often very impressive: *The State of the Union address is one of the great set pieces of American public life.*

set·tee /sɛˈti/ *n.* [C] a long seat with a back and usually with arms, for more than one person to sit on

set·ter /'sɛtɚ/ *n.* [C] **1** a long-haired dog often trained to find where animals or birds are so they can be shot **2** a policy-setter/record-setter/price-setter etc. someone who decides something as part of their job, who does things that other people try to copy, etc.: *Turner became a high-profile example-setter by donating $1 billion to the U.N.* —see also PACESETTER, TRENDSETTER

set·ting /'sɛtɪŋ/ *n.* **1** [C usually singular] all the things that surround someone or something at a particular time, including the events that happen, their environment, or the people they are with: *Imagine working in a beautiful setting overlooking the bay.* | *Most patients were initially treated in a hospital setting.* **2** [C usually singular] the place or time that the action of a book, movie etc. happens: *Dashwood Manor sounds like the setting for a Victoria Holt novel, doesn't it?* **3** [C] the position in which you put the controls on a machine or instrument: *The heater has three temperature settings.* **4** [C] the metal that holds a stone in a piece of jewelry, or the way the stone is fastened: *a diamond ring with a gold setting* **5** [C] music that is written to go with a poem, prayer etc. **6** the setting of the sun LITERARY the time when the sun goes down —see also PLACE SETTING

set·tle¹ /'sɛtl/ *v.*

1 court of law/argument [I,T] to end an argument by agreeing on something: [+ with] *He finally settled with his former employers for an undisclosed sum.* | *Maybe they'll be willing to settle out of court* (=come to an agreement before going to a court of law). | *We hope the factions will be able to settle their differences* (=agree to stop arguing or fighting) *by peaceful means.* | settle a lawsuit/dispute/case etc. British Petroleum agreed to pay $185 million to settle a 14-year-old lawsuit.* | *Mom, we need your opinion to settle a bet.*

2 live in a place **a)** [I,T] to go to a place where no people have lived permanently before and start to live there: *Historians are unsure when the territory was first settled.* **b)** [I always + adv./prep.] to go to live in a new place, and stay there for a long time: *Many Jewish immigrants settled in the Lower East Side.*
3 comfortable [I,T always + adv./prep.] to put yourself or someone else in a comfortable position: [+ back/into/down etc.] *When they had all left, Stan settled back to read his paper.* | *She settled herself by an oak tree on a hill overlooking the town.*
4 move down [I] **a)** if dust, snow etc. settles, it comes down and stays in one place: [+ on/in] *Kahn could see a layer of fine white dust settling on the wet pavement.* | *The coffee grounds had settled in the bottom of the pot.* —see also **the dust settles** (DUST¹ (3)) **b)** if something such as a building or the ground settles, it sinks slowly to a lower level: *The existing chimney's foundation has settled and needs to be replaced.*
5 **settle a bill/account/claim** to pay money that is owed: *Officials can seize a home and sell it to settle a tax bill.* | *Many Japanese companies settle their annual accounts at the end of March.*
6 organize business/money [T] to put all the details of a business or someone's money and property in order and deal with them, for example before you travel or because you may die soon: *When it is finally settled, the Menendez estate may be worth no more than $100,000.* | *After her husband's death, Jackie went to the city to settle her husband's affairs.*
7 decide [T] to decide on something, especially so that you can make definite arrangements: *Nothing is settled yet.* | *There's not much time to **settle the details** of our trip.*
8 feeling/quality [I always + adv./prep.] if a quality or feeling settles over a place or on someone, it has a strong effect: [+ over/on] *A sense of peace settled on the town's inhabitants.*
9 weather/night if something such as darkness or FOG settles over an area, it comes into the sky: [+ on/over] *Dusk began to settle over the island.*
10 bird/insect if a bird, insect etc. settles, it flies down and rests on something: [+ on] *We watched as a butterfly settled on a branch near our window.*
11 quiet/calm [I,T] to become quiet or calm, or to make someone or something quiet or calm: **settle your nerves/stomach** (=stop your nerves or stomach from being upset)
12 **settle a score** also **settle an account** to do something to hurt or cause trouble for someone because they have harmed or offended you: *She's got a few old scores to settle with her former friend.*
13 face [I] if a particular expression settles on your face, it stays there: *A look of fury settled on his face.*

settle down *phr. v.* **1** [I,T] to stop talking or behaving in an excited way, or to make someone do this: *Would you kids just settle down for a minute?* | [settle sb ↔ down] *Sometimes we take the baby for a ride in the car to settle him down.* **2** [I] to start living in a place with the intention of staying there and behaving in a responsible way, getting married, having a good job etc.: *Tony's parents looked forward to the day when he would settle down and start a family of his own.* **3** [I] to start giving all of your attention to a job, activity etc.: [+ to] *She settled down to work on the manuscript after lunch.*

settle for sth *phr. v.* [T not in passive] to accept or agree to something, especially something that is worse than what you want: *There wasn't any real coffee, so we had to settle for the instant kind.* | *There's no need to settle for less than you deserve.*

settle in/into *phr. v.* **1** [I,T] to become used to a new home, job, surroundings etc. or to help someone do this: *Are you settling in OK?* | [settle in/into sth] *They'll need time to get settled into their new house.* | [settle sb in/into sth] *Church members helped settle the young family in the community.* **2** [I] to make yourself comfortable and prepare to stay somewhere

for a period of time: [+ for] *At least 3,000 people settled in for an afternoon of music in the park.*

settle on/upon sth/sb *phr. v.* [T] **1** to decide or agree on something: *Doug finally settled on the broiled salmon for $14.95.* | *Three ballots were needed before the committee settled on a new leader.* **2** if your eyes settle on someone or something, you look at them carefully for a period of time: *Just then, my eyes settled on a door I hadn't seen before.*

settle up *phr. v.* [I] to pay what you owe on an account or bill: *It's time to settle up.*

settle² *n.* [C] a long wooden seat with a high back that usually has a hollow place for storing things under the seat

set·tled /ˈsɛtld/ *adj.* **1** unlikely to change; FIXED: *We can accept that as settled, then.* | *a well-to-do, settled community* **2** **feel/be settled** to feel comfortable about living or working in a particular place: *Well, they seem to be very settled, from what you've said.* —compare UNSETTLED

set·tle·ment /ˈsɛtlmənt/ *n.* **1** official agreement [C,U] an official agreement or decision that ends an argument between two sides: **reach/achieve a settlement** *A settlement of the conflicts in Georgia must be reached soon.* | *An amicable **out-of-court settlement** is always the best and least expensive way to settle a dispute.* | **divorce/peace/financial etc. settlement** (=the agreement about what the two sides will do after a divorce, after fighting stops etc.) | **negotiated/political/peaceful etc. settlement** (=agreement after discussions are held, political decisions are made etc.) **2** group of houses [C] a group of houses and buildings where people live, in an area where no group lived before: *a Mormon settlement* | *There were only a few scattered settlements of squatters by the river.* **3** new area/places [U] the movement of a new population into a place to live there: [+ of] *the settlement of the American West* **4** payment [C,U] the payment of money that you owe someone: *The defendant paid over $200,000 **in settlement** of the matter.* **5** sinking [U] the slow sinking of a building, the ground under it etc.

set·tler /ˈsɛtlɚ, ˈsɛtl-ɚ/ *n.* [C] someone who goes to live in a new place where there are few people: *Eddie's grandfather was one of the town's first settlers.*

set·up /ˈsɛtʌp/ *n.* **1** [C usually singular] the way something is organized or arranged: *Instead of the usual classroom setup, our desks were in a circle.* **2** [C,U] the act of organizing something new, such as a business or a computer system: *Trained technicians can help with installation and setup.* **3** [C] several pieces of equipment that work together in a system: *If you're serious about photography, you'll need your own darkroom setup.* **4** [C usually singular] INFORMAL a dishonest plan that is intended to trick you: *How do I know this isn't a setup?* **5** [C usually singular] the first part of a story, movie, or joke that describes the general situation and introduces the characters in it —see also **set up** (SET¹)

Seu·rat /səˈrɑ/, **Georges** /ʒɔrʒ/ (1859–1891) a French painter famous for developing the method of painting known as POINTILLISM

Seuss /sus/, **Dr.** (1904–1991) a U.S. children's writer whose funny stories, poems, and pictures are very popular with young children

sev·en /ˈsɛvən/ *number* **1** 7 **2** seven o'clock: *Come over at around seven.* **3** **the seven-year itch** HUMOROUS the idea that after seven years of being married, people feel less satisfied with their relationship and may want to have sex with other people **4** **the seven seas** LITERARY all the oceans of the world: *They traveled the seven seas, hoping to find new lands.* —see also SEVENTH¹, **be at sixes and sevens** (SIX (5))

sev·en·teen /ˌsɛvənˈtin◂/ *number* 17 —**seventeenth** *adj., pron., n.*

sev·enth¹ /ˈsɛvənθ/ *adj.* **1** 7th; next after the sixth: *The store is on Seventh Avenue.* **2** **be in seventh**

heaven INFORMAL to be extremely happy: *We got Darren a puppy for Christmas, and he was in seventh heaven.*

seventh[2] *pron.* **the seventh** the 7th thing in a series: *I'll call you when I get back on the seventh* (=the 7th day of the month).

seventh[3] *n.* [C] 1/7; one of seven equal parts

Seventh-Day Ad·vent·ist /ˌsɛvənθ deɪ ˈædvəntɪst/ *n.* [C] a member of a Christian group that goes to church on Saturdays and that believes that Jesus Christ will soon come again to Earth

seventh-inn·ing stretch /ˌ.. ˌ. '. / *n.* [singular] a period of time in the middle of the seventh INNING of a baseball game, when the teams stop playing and the people watching the game can stand up and walk around

sev·en·ti·eth[1] /ˈsɛvəntiɪθ/ *adj.* 70th; next after the sixty-ninth: *It's my father's seventieth birthday tomorrow.*

seventieth[2] *pron.* **the seventieth** the 70th thing in a series

sev·en·ty /ˈsɛvənti/ *number* **1** 70 **2 the seventies** also **the '70s** the years from 1970 through 1979 **3 sb's seventies** the time when someone is 70 to 79 years old: **in your early/mid/late seventies** *I'd guess she's in her late seventies.* **4 in the seventies** if the temperature is in the seventies, it is between 70° and 79° FAHRENHEIT: **in the high/low seventies** *The weather was nice. It was in the high seventies and sunny.*

seventy-eight /ˌ... '. / *n.* [C] an old-fashioned record that turns 78 times a minute while it is being played

sev·er /ˈsɛvə/ *v.* [T] FORMAL **1** to cut off a part of someone's body, especially in an accident: *Doctors worked to reattach his severed finger.* **2** to cut through something, separating it into two parts: *High winds severed power lines in many areas last night.* **3** to end a relationship with someone, or a connection with something: *She wanted to **sever** all **ties with** (=have no more contact with) her family.*

sev·er·al[1] /ˈsɛvrəl/ *quantifier, pron.* a number of people or things that is more than a few, but not a lot: *I've been to Florida several times.* | *Several people volunteered to help.* | [+ **of**] *Several of the students received awards for their work.*

several[2] *adj.* [only before noun, no comparative] FORMAL OR LAW different and separate: *Business partners have a joint and several liability where taxes are concerned.* —**severally** *adv.*

sev·er·ance /ˈsɛvrəns/ *n.* [U] **1** a situation in which someone has to leave a company because their employer does not have a job for them anymore: *The company has a voluntary severance and early retirement program.* **2** severance pay: *Kramer reportedly got severance worth tens of millions.* **3** the act of ending a relationship with someone or a connection with something: *the severance of all economic ties between the two nations*

severance pay /ˈ.. ˌ. / *n.* [U] money that you get when you leave a company because your employer does not have a job for you anymore

se·vere /səˈvɪr/ *adj.* **1** very bad, or serious enough for you to worry about: *severe pain* | *The victims suffered severe head injuries in the accident.* | *severe economic problems* **2** severe weather conditions are extremely hot, cold, dry etc. and are bad or dangerous: *The weather station issued a warning for severe thunderstorms.* **3** severe punishment or criticism is extreme, and intended to prevent more crimes or wrong behavior: *Severe penalties will be imposed for late payment.* **4** someone who is severe is very strict and demands that rules of behavior be obeyed or standards be followed **5** simple and formal in style with little or no decoration: *She wore a severe black dress and no make-up.* —**severity** /səˈvɛrəti/ *n.* [C,U] *We didn't realize the severity of her illness.*

se·vere·ly /səˈvɪrli/ *adv.* **1** very badly or to a great degree: *a severely damaged building* | *severely disabled children* | *Medical facilities are severely limited in the area.* **2** in a way that shows you disapprove greatly: *Martinson spoke severely about his opponent's*

voting record in the Senate. **3** in a way that is strict and intended to prevent more crimes or wrong behavior: *She grew up in a house where the children were often severely punished.* **4** in a plain simple style with little or no decoration: *Her hair was pulled back severely from her face.*

sew /soʊ/ *v. past tense* **sewed** *past participle* **sewn** also **sewed** [I,T] to use a needle and thread to fasten pieces of cloth together, or to attach something such as a button to clothes: *Where did you learn to sew so well?* | **sew sth on/onto sth** *The AIDS quilts have messages sewn onto them.*

sew sb/sth ↔ **up** *phr. v.* [T] **1 have sth sewn up** to gain control over a situation so that you are sure to win or gain something: *IBM had the market for electric typewriters sewn up.* **2** INFORMAL to close a wound on someone's body using stitches: *Jared had to be held down while the doctor sewed up his arm.* **3** to close or repair something by sewing it: *You should sew up that rip in your pants.*

sew·age /ˈsuɪdʒ/ *n.* [U] the mixture of waste from the human body and used water that is carried away from houses by sewers: *a sewage treatment plant*

Sew·ard /ˈsuəd/, **William Henry** (1801–1872) a U.S. politician who helped to arrange the deal in which the U.S. bought Alaska from Russia in 1867

sew·er /ˈsuə/ *n.* [C] a pipe or passage under the ground that carries away waste material and used water from houses, factories etc.

sew·er·age /ˈsuərɪdʒ/ *n.* [U] the system by which waste material and water are carried away in sewers and then treated to stop them from being harmful

sew·ing /ˈsoʊɪŋ/ *n.* [U] **1** the activity or skill of making or repairing clothes or other things made of cloth, or decorating cloth with a needle and thread **2** something you have sewn or are going to sew: *The quilt was a truly beautiful piece of sewing.*

sewing ma·chine /ˈ.. ˌ./ *n.* [C] a machine used for stitching cloth or clothes together

sewn /soʊn/ *v.* a past participle of SEW

sex[1] /sɛks/ *n.* **1** [U] the activity in which two people join their sexual organs in order to produce babies, or for pleasure: *I don't want my kids seeing all that sex and violence on TV.* | *Should students be taught about sex in elementary school?* | *They believe it's wrong to **have sex** (=do this activity) outside marriage.* | *He had **had sex with** several partners.* **2** [C,U] the male or female nature of a person, animal, or plant: *The test can be used to determine a baby's sex before it is born.* | *He's very nervous around members of **the opposite sex** (=people that are not his own sex).* —see also SAME-SEX, SINGLE-SEX

sex[2] *v.* [T] TECHNICAL to find out whether an animal is male or female

sex act /ˈ. ./ *n.* [C] a particular way in which people have sex

sex ap·peal /ˈ. ˌ./ *n.* [U] the quality of being sexually attractive: *a star with real glamour and sex appeal*

sex change /ˈ. ./ *n.* [C usually singular] a medical operation or treatment that changes someone's body so that they look like someone of the other sex

sex dis·crim·i·na·tion /ˈ. ...ˌ./ also **sexual discrimination** /ˈ... ...ˌ./ *n.* [U] unfair treatment because of which sex you are

sex drive /ˈ. ./ *n.* [U] someone's ability or physical need to have sex

sex ed·u·ca·tion /ˈ. ...ˌ./ also **sex ed** /ˌsɛks ˈɛd/ INFORMAL *n.* [U] education in schools about the physical processes and emotions involved in sex

sex god·dess /ˈ. ˌ./ *n.* [C] INFORMAL a woman, especially an actress, who many people think is sexually attractive

sex in·dus·try /ˈ. ...ˌ./ *n.* [singular] the businesses and activities related to PROSTITUTION and PORNOGRAPHY (=movies, magazines, etc. that show sex)

sex·ism /ˈsɛkˌsɪzəm/ *n.* [U] unfair attitudes and behavior based on the belief that women are weaker, less intelligent, and less important than men: *The armed forces have worked to eliminate racism and sexism in their organizations.*

sex·ist /ˈsɛksɪst/ *adj.* **1** relating to the belief that women are weaker, less intelligent, and less important than men: *sexist comments* **2** believing in sexism: *He's such a sexist pig.* —**sexist** *n.* [C]

sex kit·ten /ˈ. ˌ../ *n.* [C] OLD-FASHIONED a woman who is considered to be very sexually attractive and who behaves like a young girl

sex·less /ˈsɛkslɪs/ *adj.* **1** not sexually attractive; not SEXY **2** not involving sexual activity, in a way that does not seem normal or usual: *a sexless relationship*

sex life /ˈ. ./ *n.* [C] someone's sexual activities: *Jim's too busy to have much of a sex life.*

sex ma·ni·ac /ˈ. ˌ.../ *n.* [C] INFORMAL someone who always wants to have sex, thinks about it all the time, and is unable to control these feelings

sex ob·ject /ˈ. ˌ../ *n.* [C] someone you consider only as a means of satisfying your sexual desire, rather than as a person with feelings and desires of their own

sex of·fend·er /ˈ. .ˌ../ *n.* [C] someone who is guilty of a crime related to sex —**sex offense** *n.* [C]

sex·pot /ˈsɛkspɑt/ *n.* [C] INFORMAL a word meaning a "sexually attractive woman," that many women think is offensive

sex sym·bol /ˈ. ˌ../ *n.* [C] someone famous who represents society's idea of what is sexually attractive

sex·tant /ˈsɛkstənt/ *n.* [C] a tool for measuring angles between stars in order to calculate the position of your ship or aircraft

sex·tet /sɛksˈtɛt/ *n.* [C] **1** a group of six singers or musicians performing together **2** a piece of music for six performers

sex ther·a·py /ˈ. ˌ.../ *n.* [U] the treatment of someone's sexual problems by talking to them for a long time about their feelings —**sex therapist** *n.* [C]

sex·ton /ˈsɛkstən/ *n.* [C] someone whose job is to take care of a church building, and sometimes ring the church bells and dig graves

Sex·ton /ˈsɛkstən/, **Ann** /æn/ (1928–1974) a U.S. poet

sex tour·ism /ˈ. ˌ.../ *n.* [U] the activity of traveling to other countries in order to have sex, especially in order to do sexual activities that are illegal in your own country —**sex tourist** *n.* [C]

sex·tup·let /sɛkˈstʌplɪt/ *n.* [C] one of six people who are born at the same time and have the same mother

s w **sex·u·al** /ˈsɛkʃuəl/ *adj.* [no comparative] **1** relating to sex: *Herpes is a disease passed on by sexual contact.* | *sexual relationships* **2** relating to the social relationships between men and women: *sexual stereotypes* **3** relating to the way people or animals have babies: *sexual reproduction* —**sexually** *adv.*: *a sexually experienced young man*

sexual as·sault /ˌ... .ˈ./ *n.* [C,U] LAW the crime of forcing someone to have sex or touching someone sexually while threatening them

sexual con·gress /ˌ... ˈ../ *n.* [U] LITERARY sexual intercourse

sexual ha·rass·ment /ˌ... .ˈ.., ˌ... ˈ../ *n.* [U] sexual remarks, looks, or touching done to someone who does not want it, especially from someone that they work with

sexual in·ter·course /ˌ... ˈ.../ *n.* [U] FORMAL the act of two people having sex with each other

sex·u·al·i·ty /ˌsɛkʃuˈæləti/ *n.* [U] **1** the things people do and feel that are related to their desire or ability to have sex: *a study of human sexuality* **2** SEXUAL ORIENTATION

sexually trans·mit·ted dis·ease /ˌ..... .ˌ... .ˈ./ *n.* [C,U] STD; a disease that is passed on through having sex, such as AIDS, HERPES etc.

sex or·gan /ˈ. ˌ../ *n.* [C] a part of the body that is involved with the production of children, such as the PENIS or VAGINA

sexual o·ri·en·ta·tion, /ˌ... ...ˈ./ also **sexual pref·er·ence** /ˌ... ˈ.../ *n.* [U] the fact that someone is sexually attracted to men or women, especially whether they are HETEROSEXUAL or HOMOSEXUAL

sexual re·la·tions /ˌ... .ˈ./ *n.* [plural] FORMAL sexual activity between two people

sex work·er /ˈ. ˌ../ *n.* [C] a polite expression for a PROSTITUTE

sex·y /ˈsɛksi/ *adj.* **sexier, sexiest 1** sexually exciting or attractive: *a sexy woman* | *a sexy black dress* —see Usage Note at BEAUTIFUL **2** INFORMAL sexy ideas or products are ones that many people think are very interesting and exciting: *a political campaign that lacked sexy issues* —**sexily** *adv.* —**sexiness** *n.* [U]

Sey·chelles, the /seɪˈʃɛlz/ a country that consists of about 85 small islands in the Indian Ocean, to the east of Kenya —**Seychellois** /ˌseɪʃɛlˈwɑ/ *adj.*

SF *adj. n.* the abbreviation of SCIENCE FICTION

SGML *n.* [U] TECHNICAL Standard Generalized Markup Language; a special computer language used to send computer information from one piece of computer SOFTWARE to another

Sgt. the written abbreviation of SERGEANT

Shab·bat /ʃəˈbɑt, ˈʃɑbəs/ *n.* [C,U] Saturday, considered as a day of rest and prayer in the Jewish religion

shab·by /ˈʃæbi/ *adj.* **shabbier, shabbiest 1** old and in bad condition from being used for a long time: *a shabby suit* | *shabby hotel rooms* **2** shabby treatment behavior toward someone that is unfair and not nice: *I don't know what we did to deserve such shabby treatment.* **3** sth is not (too) shabby INFORMAL used to show that you think something is very good: *Our profits were up by 35% last year. That's not too shabby.* **4** wearing clothes that are old and in bad condition: *a shabby old man* —**shabbily** *adv.* —**shabbiness** *n.* [U]

shack¹ /ʃæk/ *n.* [C] a small building made of cheap materials: *They lived in a one-room shack.*

shack² *v.*

shack up *phr. v.* [I] INFORMAL to live with someone who you have sex with but are not married to: [+ with] *When they let him out of prison, he shacked up with some woman in Newark.*

shack·le /ˈʃækəl/ *v.* [T usually passive] **1** to restrict what someone can do: *The company is shackled by a lack of capital.* **2** to put shackles on someone

shack·les /ˈʃækəlz/ *n.* [plural] **1** the shackles of slavery/communism etc. LITERARY the limits put on your freedom and happiness by SLAVERY, COMMUNISM etc.: *They were determined to free themselves from the shackles of colonialism.* **2** a pair of metal rings joined by a chain that are used for fastening together a prisoner's hands or feet: *He was led into the courthouse in shackles.*

shad /ʃæd/ *n.* [C,U] a north Atlantic fish used for food

shade¹ /ʃeɪd/ *n.*

1 area of darkness [U] an area that is cooler and darker because the light of the sun cannot reach it: *Let's find a table in the shade.* | *They were sitting in the shade of an old oak tree.* —compare SHADOW¹ (2)

2 slight darkness slight darkness, caused by the sun's light being partly blocked by something: *a plant that likes shade*

3 color [C] a particular degree of a color: *The room was decorated in pastel shades.* | [+ of] *a delicate shade of pink*

4 cover [C] something that reduces or blocks light especially a piece of cloth or other material that can be rolled up and down to cover a window inside a building: *I don't think they're home – all the shades are drawn* (=pulled down to cover the windows). | *a cardboard sun shade for the car window*

5 in a picture [U] the dark places in a picture: *Note the artist's skillful use of light and shade to create the impression of depth.*

6 a shade very slightly, or a little bit: **a shade too big/hot/fast** etc. *Matt's clothes were just a shade too small for Rick.* | **a shade better/quicker/more** etc. *The results were a shade better than expected.* | **a shade over/under/above/behind** etc. **sth** *She was a shade under five feet tall.*

7 shade of meaning/opinion/feeling etc. a meaning etc. that is slightly different from other ones; NUANCE: *One phrase can have many shades of meaning, depending on the context.*

8 shades [plural] INFORMAL: see SUNGLASSES

9 shades of sb/sth used to say that something reminds you of someone or something else: *He's an educated, ambitious young politician from the South – shades of Bill Clinton.*

10 shades of gray slightly different opinions or ways of looking at a situation that are not completely right or wrong, or completely good or bad: *Tom's view of the world doesn't allow for many shades of gray.*

11 lamp [C] a part of a lamp that makes the light from the lamp less bright

12 put sth in the shade to be so good or impressive that other similar things or people seem much less important or interesting: *They're planning a festival that will put all the others in the shade.*

13 have it made in the shade HUMOROUS to have everything you need in order to be happy

shade² *v.* [T] **1** to protect something from direct light: *a narrow road shaded by rows of trees* | **shade your eyes/face etc.** *She shaded her eyes and watched as the plane flew by overhead.* **2** also **shade in** to make part of a picture or drawing darker: *The shaded areas on the map represent national parks.*

shade into sth *phr. v.* [T] FORMAL if one thing shades into another, it gradually changes into the other thing: *Bedford felt his impatience shading into anger.*

shade tree /'. ./ *n.* [C] a tree that is planted in order to give SHADE¹ (1)

shad·ing /'ʃeɪdɪŋ/ *n.* **1** [U] the areas of a drawing or painting that have been made to look darker **2 shadings** [plural] also **shading** [U] slight differences between things, situations, or ideas: *He didn't understand the subtle shadings of legal language.*

shad·ow¹ /'ʃædoʊ/ *n.*

1 dark shape [C] **a)** a dark shape that someone or something makes on a surface when they are between that surface and the light: *As we walked along, our shadows lengthened with the setting sun.* | *The apple tree cast a shadow across the front lawn.* **b)** a dark shape, especially of a person, that you cannot see well because it is in a dark place; SILHOUETTE: *Just then, a dark shadow emerged from the mist.*

2 darkness [U] also **shadows** PLURAL darkness caused by something that prevents light from entering a place: *The room was half in shadow* | *a thief lurking in the shadows*

3 in the shadow of sth very near something large and important, and often affected or influenced by it: *Families living in the shadow of the nation's largest nuclear power plant are concerned.*

4 cast a shadow over/on sth to make something seem less attractive or impressive: *The scandal cast a shadow over his reputation for the rest of his career.*

5 beyond a shadow of a doubt leaving no doubt at all: *His guilt has been proved beyond a shadow of a doubt.*

6 be a shadow of your former self to be much weaker or less powerful than before: *Following years of heavy losses, the company is only a shadow of its former self.*

7 in the shadow of sb also **in sb's shadow** less happy and successful than you could be, because someone else gets noticed much more: *All his life, he struggled in the shadow of a celebrity father and a successful, powerful mother.*

8 shadows under sb's eyes small dark areas under someone's eyes that show they are tired

9 sb's shadow someone who follows someone else everywhere they go —see also **afraid of your own shadow** (AFRAID (7)), EYE SHADOW, FIVE O'CLOCK SHADOW

shadow² *v.* [T] **1** to follow someone closely in order to watch what they are doing: *Detectives shadowed them for weeks, collecting evidence.* **2** to spend time with someone at work in order to learn about their job: *Several students spent a week in the office, shadowing attorneys and office staff.* **3** [usually passive]

to cover something with a shadow, or make it dark: *The module will pass over several of the moon's permanently shadowed craters.*

shadow box·ing /'.. ,../ *n.* [U] fighting with an imaginary opponent, especially as training for BOXING —**shadow-box** *v.* [I]

shadow pup·pet /'.. ,../ *n.* [C] a flat PUPPET that makes special shapes on a wall when you shine a light behind it

shad·ow·y /'ʃædoʊi/ *adj.* **1** mysterious and difficult to know anything about: *a shadowy network of terrorist groups* **2** full of shadows, or difficult to see because of shadows: *a shadowy room* | *a shadowy figure at the back of the crowd*

shad·y /'ʃeɪdi/ *adj.* **shadier, shadiest 1** protected from the sun or producing shade: *These plants will grow best in shady conditions.* | *shady trees* **2** probably dishonest or illegal: *She's been involved in some shady deals.*

shaft¹ /ʃæft/ *n.* **1** [C] a passage that goes up through a building or down into the ground, so that someone or something can get in or out: **mine/elevator/ventilation shaft** *They survived a six-story fall down an elevator shaft.* **2 shaft of light/sunlight** a narrow beam of light **3** [C] a long handle on a tool, SPEAR etc. **4 get the shaft** SLANG to be treated unfairly, for example by being dismissed from your job without a good reason **5** [C] a thin long piece of metal in an engine or machine that turns and passes on power or movement to another part of the machine —see also DRIVE SHAFT **6** [C] LITERARY an ARROW (1)

shaft² *v.* [T usually passive] SLANG to treat someone unfairly, especially by dishonestly getting money from them: *Once again, ordinary consumers are going to get shafted when the price increase goes into effect.*

shag¹ /ʃæg/ *n.* **1** [U] a covering for a floor, with a rough surface made from long pieces of YARN: **shag carpeting/rug** (=with a surface like this) **2** [C] a type of hair style in which the hair is cut to different lengths all over the head, so that it is not smooth **3** [U] strong-tasting TOBACCO with thick leaves cut into small thin pieces

shag² *v.* [I,T] to practice catching a baseball that has been hit rather than thrown: *The fielders were shagging balls hit by the coach.*

shag·gy /'ʃægi/ *adj.* **shaggier, shaggiest 1** shaggy hair or fur is long and messy: *a shaggy black beard* **2** having shaggy hair or fur: *a shaggy dog* —**shagginess** *n.* [U]

shaggy-dog sto·ry /,.. '. ,../ *n.* [C] a long joke that often ends in a silly or disappointing way

Shah /ʃɑ/ *n.* [C] the title of the kings of Iran, used in past times

shake¹ /ʃeɪk/ *v. past tense* **shook** /ʃʊk/ *past participle* **shaken** /'ʃeɪkən/

1 movement [I,T] to move up and down or from side to side with quick repeated movements, or to make someone or something do this: *His hand shook as he signed the paper.* | *Shake the bottle well to mix all the ingredients together.* | *What's the matter? You're shaking like a leaf* (=shaking a lot because you are very nervous or frightened). | **shake with anger/fear/laughter etc.** (=be so angry, frightened etc. that you cannot stop shaking)

shaking hands

2 remove by shaking [I,T always + adv./prep.] to remove something or move it into a different position by shaking it or something it is attached to, or to be removed in this way: *Coat the chicken pieces in flour and shake off any excess.* | **[shake sth out/off/from etc.]** *Patti had to stop and shake the sand out of her shoes.* | *The earthquake shook several ceiling lights loose in our office.*

3 shake your head to turn your head from side to side as a way of saying no or of showing that you are disappointed

4 shake hands (with sb) also **shake sb's hand** to hold someone's hand in your hand and move it hand up and down, as a greeting or as a sign you have agreed on something: *The governor shook hands with everyone in the room.*

5 shock [T] to shock and upset someone or a group of people very much: *News of the accident shook the tiny farming community.* | *She was **badly shaken** by the experience.*

6 push sb [T] to hold someone by their shoulders and push and pull them backward and forward roughly, because you are angry with them or in order to wake them up: *Never shake a baby.* | *She went into Ben's room and gently **shook** him **awake**.*

7 shake sb's confidence/faith/belief to make someone feel less confident, less sure about their beliefs etc.: *The outcome of the trial had shaken his belief in the legal system.*

8 shake your fist (at sb) to show that you are angry by holding up and shaking your tightly closed hand

9 voice [I] if your voice shakes, it sounds nervous or uncertain: [+ with] *Tim's voice shook with emotion.*

10 escape [T] also **shake off** to escape from someone who is chasing you: *They raced around corners and down dark alleys, trying to shake the police.*

11 get rid of [T] also **shake off** to get rid of an illness, a problem, something annoying etc.: *I can't seem to shake off this cold.* | *Parker hopes to shake his image as a dull, unimaginative politician.*

12 be shaking in your boots INFORMAL to be very nervous or worried: *Employees were shaking in their boots at the thought of more layoffs.*

13 more sth than you can shake a stick at HUMOROUS a lot or very many: *There are more fast-food places in this town than you can shake a stick at.*

14 shake a leg SPOKEN to hurry and start doing something now: *If we want to get there by 11:00, we'd better shake a leg.*

15 shake your booty HUMOROUS to dance to popular music —see also **shake/rock sth to its foundations** (FOUNDATION (8))

shake sb ↔ **down** *phr. v.* **1** INFORMAL to get money from someone by using threats or by searching them or their property: *Corrupt officials were shaking down local business owners.* **2** to search a person or place thoroughly —see also SHAKEDOWN

shake on sth *phr. v.* [T] SPOKEN to agree on a decision or business agreement by shaking hands: *Let's shake on it.*

shake out *phr. v.* **1** [T **shake** sb **out of** sth] to make someone change an attitude, emotion, or opinion, especially one that you do not approve of: *She tried to **shake herself out of it**, but soon began crying again.* **2** [I] to change naturally over a period of time until the final result is clear: *The project was put on hold for a year to see how things were going to shake out.*

shake up *phr. v.* [T] **1** [shake sth ↔ up] to make changes to an organization in order to make it more effective: *The new manager says she's going to **shake things up** around here.* —see also SHAKEUP **2** [shake sb ↔ up] to give someone a very bad shock, so that they feel very upset and frightened: *Hearing their screams was what really shook me up.* —see also SHAKEN, SHOOK UP

shake² *n.* [C] **1** an act of shaking: *Give the bottle a good shake before you pour.* **2** a cold drink made of milk, ICE CREAM, and fruit or chocolate; MILKSHAKE: *a strawberry shake* **3 the shakes** NOT TECHNICAL nervous shaking of your body caused by illness, fear, too much alcohol etc.: *She would always **get** a bad case of **the shakes** before going on stage.* **4 no great shakes** INFORMAL if you say that someone or something is no great shakes, you think they are not very good: *He's no great shakes as a singer.* —see also **give/get a fair shake** (FAIR¹ (10))

shake·down /ˈʃeɪkdaʊn/ *n.* **1** [C] INFORMAL an act of getting money from someone by using threats **2** [C] a thorough search of a place or a person: *No firearms were found during the shakedowns at the prison, but guards did recover several knives.* **3 shakedown flight/cruise/process** a final test of something such as a boat or airplane before it is put into general use, to find any remaining problems

shak·en /ˈʃeɪkən/ also **shaken up** *adj.* [usually not before noun] upset, shocked, or frightened: *The Bronskis appeared visibly shaken as they viewed the damage to their home.*

shake·out /ˈʃeɪkaʊt/ *n.* [C] **1** [usually singular] a situation in which several companies fail because they cannot compete with stronger companies in difficult economic conditions **2** a SHAKEUP

Shak·er /ˈʃeɪkə/ *adj.* Shaker furniture is made in a plain, simple, and attractive style: *a Shaker chair*

shak·er /ˈʃeɪkə/ *n.* [C] **1** a container with holes in the lid, used to shake salt, sugar etc. onto food: *a salt shaker* **2** also **cocktail shaker** a container in which drinks are mixed —see also **mover and shaker** (MOVER (2))

Shak·ers /ˈʃeɪkəz/ a Christian religious group that started in England in 1747 and was established in the U.S. in 1774. Members live and work together in their own small towns, and do not have sex. No new members were accepted after the 1970s.

Shakes·peare /ˈʃeɪkspɪr/, **William** (1564–1616) an English writer of plays and poems, who is generally regarded as the greatest of all English writers

Shake·spear·e·an /ʃeɪkˈspɪriən/ *adj.* [only before noun] **1** relating to the work of Shakespeare: *Shakespearean scholars* **2** in the style of Shakespeare: *a drama of Shakespearean length and complexity*

shake·up /ˈʃeɪk-ʌp/ *n.* [C] a process in which an organization makes a lot of big changes in a short time to improve its effectiveness: *a sweeping shakeup in the company's middle management*

shak·y /ˈʃeɪki/ *adj.* **shakier, shakiest 1** weak and unsteady because of old age, illness, or shock: *a shaky voice* **2** not thorough, complete, or certain: *a shaky relationship* | *The evidence is shaky, at best.* **3** not firm or steady: *a shaky ladder* **4 on shaky ground** not certain, or using reasons to support your opinions or actions that are not completely correct: *She refused to admit she was wrong, even though she was on very shaky ground.* —**shakily** *adv.* —**shakiness** *n.* [U]

shale /ʃeɪl/ *n.* [U] a smooth soft rock that breaks easily into thin flat pieces

shall /ʃəl; *strong* ʃæl/ *modal verb* **1** FORMAL used in official documents to show a law, command, promise etc.: *No such authorization shall be given without the manager's written consent.* **2 shall I/we?** SPOKEN used to make a suggestion, or ask a question that you want the other person to decide about: *Shall I turn on the light?* | *Shall we meet around 6 o'clock?* **3** FORMAL OR OLD-FASHIONED used to describe what will happen to someone, especially when you are saying that it is very definite: *The truth shall make you free.* | *As we shall see in the next chapter, many of these practices are still in use.* **4 we shall see** FORMAL used when you do not know what will happen in the future, or when you do not want to give someone a definite answer

shal·lot /ˈʃælət, ʃəˈlɑt/ *n.* [C] a vegetable like a small onion

shal·low /ˈʃæloʊ/ *adj.* **1** not deep, and measuring only a short distance from the top to the bottom: *a shallow drawer* | *Don't dive in. The water's too shallow here.* —see picture at DEEP¹ **2** not interested in or not showing any understanding of important or serious matters: *a shallow argument* | *If he's only interested in your looks, that just shows how shallow he is.* **3 shallow breathing** breathing that only takes in small amounts of air —**shallowly** *adv.* —**shallowness** *n.* [U]

shal·lows /ˈʃæloʊz/ *n.* **the shallows** an area of shallow water: *A number of small fish live in the shallows.*

sha·lom /ʃɑˈloʊm, ʃə-/ *interjection* a Hebrew word used to say hello or goodbye

shalt /ʃəlt; *strong* ʃælt/ *v.* **thou shalt** BIBLICAL you shall

sham /ʃæm/ *n.* [C] **1** [usually singular] something that deceives people by seeming good or true when it is not: *The competition has been exposed as a complete sham.* | *These immigrants entered into sham marriages just to stay in the country.* **2** someone who pretends to be something they are not, especially to gain an advantage or sympathy: *He was a sham and a liar.* **3** a cover for a PILLOW, that has decorated edges

sha·man /ˈʃɑmən, ˈʃeɪ-/ *n.* [C] someone with religious authority in some tribes, who is believed to be able to talk to spirits, cure illnesses etc. —**shamanism** *n.* [U] —**shamanistic** /ˌʃɑməˈnɪstɪk/ *adj.*

sham·ble /ˈʃæmbəl/ *v.* [I always + adv./prep.] to walk slowly and awkwardly, without lifting your feet off the ground very much: [+ **along/in/over** etc.] *He talked to the other guests for a while, then shambled over toward me.*

sham·bles /ˈʃæmbəlz/ *n.* **1** [singular,U] an event or situation that is a complete failure because it has not been well organized or planned: *The whole meeting was a shambles from start to finish.* | *By 1985, the economy was **in a** complete **shambles**.* | *At that time, his life was **in shambles**.* **2** [singular] a place where there is a lot of damage, destruction, and confusion: *This kitchen is a shambles!*

shame¹ /ʃeɪm/ *n.*

1 **it's a shame (that)** also **what a shame** SPOKEN used to say that a situation is disappointing, and you wish things had happened differently: *It's a shame you have to leave so soon.* | *What a shame we missed the beginning of the concert!* | *"Jeff says he can't come tonight." "Oh, that's such a shame!"*

2 guilty feeling [U] the uncomfortable feeling of being guilty and embarrassed that you have when you have done something wrong: *He felt a deep sense of shame.* | **hang/bow your head in shame** (=look downward and avoid looking at other people because you feel ashamed)

3 **Shame on you!** SPOKEN used to tell someone that they should feel shame because of something they have done

4 **put sb/sth to shame** INFORMAL to be so much better than someone or something else that it makes the other thing seem very bad or ordinary: *Matt's gourmet dinner really put my cooking to shame.*

5 **it's a crying/damn shame (that)** SPOKEN used to say that you are angry and disappointed about something: *It's a crying shame that our schools don't have enough money for textbooks.*

6 **have no shame** to not feel any shame, even when someone else thinks you should: *How could you do that in public? Have you no shame?*

7 no respect [U] loss of honor and respect: *There's no shame in finishing second* (=it should not make you feel ashamed). | *You've **brought shame on** this family.* —compare ASHAMED

USAGE NOTE: SHAME

WORD CHOICE: shame, embarrassment
Shame is an uncomfortable feeling you have when you have done something wrong, and you feel that people will not respect you anymore. If you make a mistake, this may cause **embarrassment,** but not usually **shame** because **shame** is a stronger feeling that lasts a lot longer.

---

shame² *v.* **1** **shame sb into doing sth** to force someone to do something by making them feel ashamed: *His wife shamed him into handing the money back.* **2** [T] to make someone feel ashamed: *It shamed him to have to ask Jan for help.*

shame·faced /ˈʃeɪmfeɪst/ *adj.* looking ashamed or embarrassed about having behaved badly: *A shamefaced spokesperson admitted that mistakes had been made.* —**shamefacedly** /ˈʃeɪmˌfeɪsɪdli/ *adv.*

shame·ful /ˈʃeɪmfəl/ *adj* shameful behavior is so bad that people think you should be ashamed of it: *This is a shameful waste of our natural resources.* —**shamefully** *adv.*

shame·less /ˈʃeɪmlɪs/ *adj.* not seeming to be ashamed of your bad behavior, although other people think you should be ashamed: *He's a shameless flirt.* —**shamelessly** *adv.* —**shamelessness** *n.* [U]

sham·poo¹ /ʃæmˈpu/ *n. plural* **shampoos** **1** [C,U] a liquid soap for washing your hair **2** [C,U] a liquid soap used for cleaning CARPETS **3** [C] an act of shampooing or having your hair shampooed: *She made an appointment for a shampoo, cut, and blow-dry.*

shampoo² *v.* [T] to wash something with shampoo

sham·rock /ˈʃæmrɑk/ *n.* [C] a small plant with three green leaves on each stem that is the national sign of Ireland

Shang·hai /ʃæŋˈhaɪ/ the largest city in China

shang·hai /ʃæŋˈhaɪ/ *v.* [T usually passive] to trick or force someone into doing something they do not want to do: *The boys feared being shanghaied into the army.*

Shan·gri-La /ˌʃæŋɡrɪˈlɑ/ *n.* [singular, not with **the**] a perfect place that is very beautiful and where everyone is happy; PARADISE: *Every summer, the family would return to their private Shangri-La on the lake.*

shank /ʃæŋk/ *n.* **1** [C,U] a piece of meat cut from the leg of an animal: *lamb shanks* **2** [C] a straight narrow part of a tool or other object: *the shank of a button* **3** [C usually plural] OLD USE the part of a person's or animal's leg between the knee and ANKLE

shan't /ʃænt/ *modal verb* OLD USE the short form of "shall not"

shan·ty /ˈʃænti/ *n. plural* **shanties** [C] **1** a small, roughly built house made from thin sheets of wood, TIN¹ (1), plastic etc. that very poor people live in **2** also **shantey** another spelling of CHANTEY

shan·ty·town /ˈʃæntiˌtaʊn/ *n.* [C] an area in or near a city where people live in shanties

shape¹ /ʃeɪp/ *n.*

1 outer form a) [C,U] the outer form of something, that you see or feel: *You can recognize a tree by the shape of its leaves.* | *What shape is your kitchen table?* | *They baked him a cake in the shape of* (=having the same shape as) *a football.* | **round/square etc. in shape** *The lamp was triangular in shape.* b) [C] a particular shape, or a thing that is that shape: *They cut out shapes from the piece of cardboard.* | *a toddler's book about shapes and colors*

2 **in good/bad/poor etc. shape** in good, bad etc. condition, or in good, bad etc. health: *My old bike is still in pretty good shape.* | *The economy is in better shape now than it was last year.*

3 **in shape, out of shape** to be in a good or bad state of physical FITNESS (1): *I really need to **get in shape** before summer.* | **keep/stay in shape** *He plays basketball to **keep in shape**.*

4 **take shape** to develop into a clear and definite form: *An idea was **beginning to take shape** in his mind.*

5 character of sth [singular] a particular combination of qualities and features that something has: *Computers have completely **changed the shape of** our industry.* | *We will **not** tolerate racism **in any way, shape or form** (=not of any type).* | *They claim that this new technique is **the shape of things to come*** (=an example of the way things will develop in the future).

6 **be in no shape to do sth** to be sick, weak, drunk etc., and so not able to do something well: *Mel was in no shape to drive home after the party.*

7 **in/of all shapes and sizes** of many different types: *The store was filled with gadgets of all shapes and sizes.* | *Clothing manufacturers don't always realize that women **come in all shapes and sizes**.*

8 thing not seen clearly [C] a thing or person that you cannot see clearly enough to recognize: *We could just see a couple of shapes in the distance.* —see also **bent out of shape** (BENT² (3)), **whip sb/sth into shape** (WHIP¹ (6))

shape² *v.* [T] **1** to influence something such as a belief, opinion etc. and make it develop in a particular way: *Teenagers' tastes and preferences are shaped by what they see in the media.* **2** to make something have a particular shape, especially by pressing it: *Shape the dough into small balls.*

shape up *phr. v.* [I] INFORMAL **1** to improve your behavior or work: *If you don't shape up, I'll have to contact your parents.* **2** to make progress and develop in a particular way: *Ken's plans for the business are shaping up nicely.* | [**shape up as sth**] *Immigration is shaping up as a major issue in the campaign.* | [**shape up to be sth**] *February is shaping up to be one of the wettest months on record.* **3 shape up or ship out** SPOKEN used to tell someone that if they do not improve, they will be made to leave a place or their job

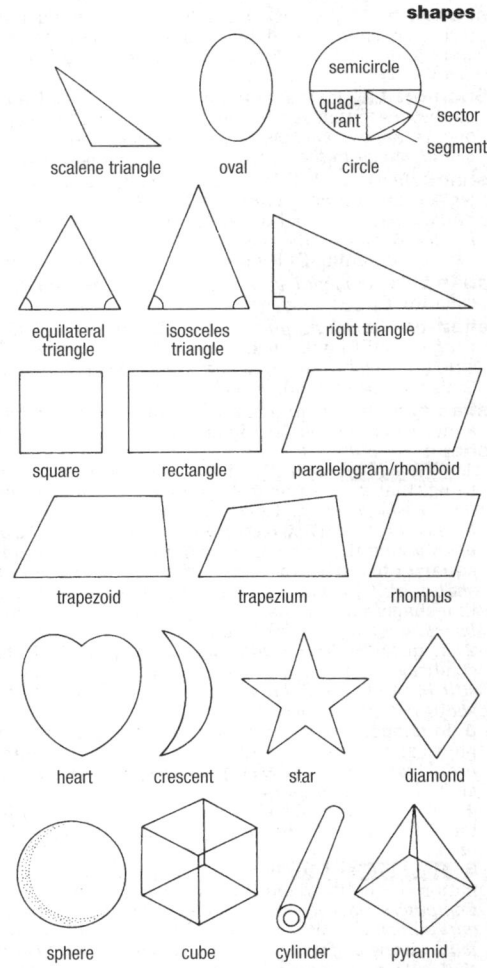

shapes

scalene triangle — oval — circle
semicircle — quadrant — sector — segment

equilateral triangle — isosceles triangle — right triangle

square — rectangle — parallelogram/rhomboid

trapezoid — trapezium — rhombus

heart — crescent — star — diamond

sphere — cube — cylinder — pyramid

shaped /ʃeɪpt/ *adj.* having a particular shape: *The building was shaped like a giant pyramid.* | **egg-shaped/V-shaped** etc. *an L-shaped living room*

shape·less /'ʃeɪplɪs/ *adj.* not having a clear or definite shape, especially in a way that looks unattractive: *The prisoners wear shapeless orange uniforms.*

shape·ly /'ʃeɪpli/ *adj.* having an attractive shape: *her long, shapely legs* —**shapeliness** *n.* [U]

shard /ʃɑrd/ *n.* [C] a sharp piece of broken glass, metal etc.: [+ of] *Archeologists discovered shards of ancient pottery at the site.*

share¹ /ʃɛr/ *v.*
1 [use equally] [I,T] to have or use something that other people also have or use at the same time: *We*

don't have enough books for everyone, so you'll have to share.* | [**share sth with sb**] *Do you mind sharing a room with Jenny?*

2 [let sb use sth] [I,T] to let someone have or use something that belongs to you: *Learning to share is a difficult process for toddlers.* | [**share sth with sb**] *You'll have to share your toys with your little brother.*

3 [same interest/opinion etc.] [T] to have the same opinion, experience, feeling etc. as someone else: *I share your concern about this.* | [**share sth with sb**] *His writing shares certain characteristics with the poems of Robert Frost.* | *Mike finally found a girl who shares his interest in football.*

4 [divide] [I,T] to divide something between two or more people: *We can share the cost of gas for the ride.* | *Everybody brings a dish to share with everyone else.*

5 [responsibility] [T] to be equally responsible for doing something, paying for something etc.: *We all share some of the blame for the accident.*

6 [tell sb sth] [I,T] to tell other people about an idea, secret, problem etc.: *If you think it would help to share, we're here to listen.* | [**share sth with sb**] *Sonia shared a very touching story with the group.*

7 share and share alike SPOKEN used to say that you should share things fairly and equally with everyone

share in sth *phr. v.* [T] to take part in something, or to have a part of something that other people also have: *Thousands of fans flooded the streets to share in the celebration of their team's victory.* | *Owning stock will allow you to share in a corporation's profits.*

share² *n.* **1** [C, usually singular] **a)** the part of something that belongs to you, or that should be paid for or done by you: [+ of] *I wrote a check for my share of the phone bill.* | [+ in] *Richardson recently sold his share in the restaurant for $500,000.* **b)** [singular] your part in an activity, event etc.: [+ in] *The political reforms offered ordinary people more of a share in the running of the country.* **2 your (fair) share a)** as much as or more of something than you could reasonably expect to have: *She's had more than her fair share of problems recently.* | *You've sure had your share of bad luck, haven't you?* **b)** as much as everyone else: *We'll make sure everyone gets their fair share.* | *I've made my share of mistakes.* **3** [C] a part of an amount: [+ of] *A large share of their income goes toward rent.* **4** [C] one of the equal parts into which the ownership of a company is divided, used especially when you are talking about the number of parts or the price of each one: *The price has gone up to $4.50 a share.* | [+ in/of] *Sandy owns 200 shares of Microsoft stock.* —compare STOCK¹ (2) **5** [C] OLD-FASHIONED a PLOWSHARE —see also **the lion's share (of sth)** (LION (2)), TIMESHARE —**sharing** *n.* [U]

share·crop·per /'ʃɛrˌkrɑpɚ/ *n.* [C] a poor farmer who uses someone else's land, and gives the owner part of the crop in return

share·hold·er /'ʃɛrˌhoʊldɚ/ also **share·own·er** /'ʃɛrˌoʊnɚ/ *n.* [C] someone who owns STOCK¹ (2) in a business; STOCKHOLDER

share·ware /'ʃɛrwɛr/ *n.* [U] free or cheap computer SOFTWARE, usually produced by small companies, that you can use for a short time before you decide whether to buy it —compare FREEWARE

sha·ri·a /ʃɑˈriə/ *n.* [U] a system of religious laws followed by Muslims

shark /ʃɑrk/ *n.* [C] **1** *plural* **shark** or **sharks** a large fish with several rows of very sharp teeth, that is sometimes considered to be dangerous to humans **2** INFORMAL someone who cheats other people out of money: **card/pool shark** (=someone who cheats when playing cards or POOL¹ (2) in order to win money) —see also LOAN SHARK

shark·skin /'ʃɑrkskɪn/ *n.* [U] a type of material with a smooth shiny surface

sharp¹ /ʃɑrp/ *adj.*
1 [thin edge/point] having a very thin edge or point that can cut things easily: *Peel the apples using a sharp knife.* | *Make sure your pencils are sharp before we begin the test.* | *The blade has a razor-sharp* (=very sharp) *edge.* —compare BLUNT¹ (1), DULL¹ (6)

2 [change] a sharp increase, fall etc. is very sudden and very big: *a sharp rise in prices*

3 *direction* a sudden extreme change of direction: *We came to a **sharp turn** in the road.*
4 *intelligent* able to think and understand things very quickly: *a sharp young attorney* | *My great-aunt Nellie is 87, but she's still **as sharp as a tack** (=able to think very quickly and clearly).*
5 *criticism* severe, angry, and criticizing: *We were surprised by the sharp tone of her comments.* | *The proposed tax increase drew **sharp criticism** from Republican senators.*
6 *difference* clear and definite, so that there is no doubt: *There is not always a sharp distinction between murder and manslaughter.* | *In sharp contrast to last year, businesses are now reporting sales increases of up to 6%.*
7 *pain* sudden and severe, but not continuing for a long time: *I felt a sharp pain in my back.*
8 *sounds* loud, short, and sudden: *a sharp cry of pain*
9 *eyes* able to see and notice details very well: *The job requires someone with **a sharp eye for detail** (=the ability to notice and deal with details).*
10 **keep a sharp eye out for sth** to watch carefully so that you do not miss something: *We ought to keep a sharp eye out for animal tracks.*
11 **keep a sharp eye on sb** to watch someone very carefully, especially because you do not trust them: *Security guards kept a sharp eye on Mattson as he walked through the store.*
12 *clothes* attractive and stylish: *lawyers in sharp suits*
13 *shape* not rounded or curved; ANGULAR: *Mia has a sharp nose and very dark eyes.*
14 **have a sharp tongue** to often talk to people in an angry, cruel, or criticizing way
15 *taste* having a strong, slightly bitter taste: *sharp Cheddar cheese*
16 *picture* having a shape that is clear and detailed: *This TV set gives you a very sharp picture.*
17 *movement* quick and sudden: *The wind blew across the lake in sharp gusts.* | *a sharp intake of breath*
18 *music* **a)** F/D/C etc. *sharp* a musical note that is sharp has been raised by one HALF STEP from the note F, D, C etc. and is shown by the sign (#) **b)** if music or singing is sharp, it is played or sung at a slightly higher PITCH¹ (3) than it should be —see picture at MUSIC —**sharpness** *n.* [U] —see also SHARPLY

sharp

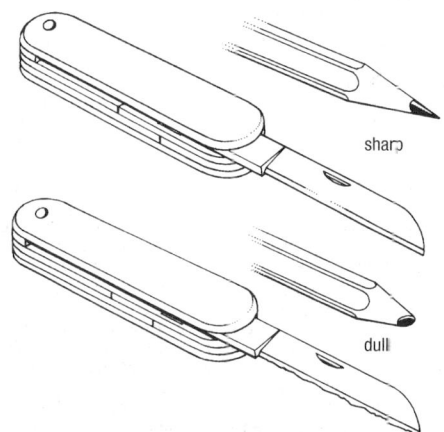

sharp

dull

sharp² *adv.* **1** **at ten-thirty/2 o'clock etc. sharp** at exactly 10:30, 2:00 etc.: *We're meeting at 10 o'clock sharp.* **2** if you sing or play music sharp, you sing or play slightly higher than the correct note so that it sounds bad —compare FLAT² (2)

sharp³ *n.* [C] **1** a musical note that has been raised one HALF STEP above the note written —compare FLAT³ (2), NATURAL² (2) **2** the sign (#) in a line of written music used to show this

sharp·en /ˈʃɑrpən/ *v.* **1** [I,T] to become sharp or make something sharp: *Sharpen all your pencils before the test.* | *The images sharpened on screen as the camera focused.* **2** [T] to develop a skill, ability etc. so that you are able to do things more quickly: *This course will give students a chance to sharpen their problem-solving skills.* **3** [T] to make a feeling stronger and more urgent: *Recent developments have given our leaders a sharpened sense of responsibility.*

sharp·en·er /ˈʃɑrpənə/ *n.* [C] a tool or machine for sharpening pencils, knives etc.

sharp-eyed /ˈ. ./ *adj.* able to see very well and notice small details: *Two sharp-eyed readers spotted the mistake.*

sharp·ly /ˈʃɑrpli/ *adv.* **1** if something rises, falls, increases etc. sharply, it rises, falls, increases etc. quickly and suddenly: *Our sales declined sharply in the last quarter.* | *sharply rising prices* **2** in a severe and disapproving way: *The White House reacted sharply to the accusations of improper deals.* | *The committee's report is **sharply critical** of the safety procedures at the plant.* **3** clearly and definitely: *Opinion is sharply divided in the local community.* | *The administration's latest policy **contrasts sharply with** (=is very different from) its earlier statements.* **4** quickly and suddenly: *Bill **turned sharply** and punched Paul in the eye.*

sharp·shoot·er /ˈʃɑrpˌʃutə/ *n.* [C] someone who is very skillful at hitting what they aim at when shooting a gun

sharp-tongued /ˌ. ˈ.ᵈ/ *adj.* [usually before noun] often saying things in an cruel or criticizing way

sharp-wit·ted /ˌ. ˈ.ᵈ/ *adj.* able to think and react very quickly

Shas·ta /ˈʃæstə/, **Mount** a mountain in the Cascade Range that is in the U.S. state of California and is an inactive VOLCANO

shat /ʃæt/ *v.* a past tense and past participle of SHIT²

shat·ter /ˈʃætə/ *v.* **1** [I,T] to break suddenly into very small pieces, or to make something break in this way: *The force of the crash shattered the windshield.* | *Trees fell down and windows shattered during the storm.* **2** [T] to completely destroy someone's hopes or beliefs: *Our lives were completely shattered by the accident.*

shat·ter·ing /ˈʃætərɪŋ/ *adj.* very shocking and upsetting: *He related his shattering war experiences in his autobiography.* —see also EARTH-SHATTERING

shat·ter·proof /ˈʃætəˌpruf/ *adj.* glass that is shatterproof is specially made so that it will not form sharp dangerous pieces if it is broken

shave¹ /ʃeɪv/ *v.* **1** [I,T] to cut off hair very close to the skin, especially from the face: *He was filthy and hadn't shaved in over a week.* | **shave your head/ legs/armpits etc.** *Many European women do not shave their legs.* **2** [T] to remove very thin pieces from the surface of something, especially a piece of food, using a sharp tool: *Shave some fresh Parmesan cheese over the salad before serving.*

shave

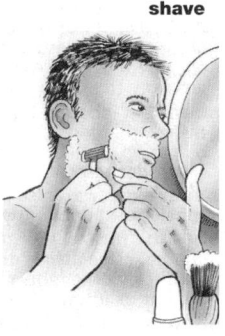

S W
3

shave sth → off *phr. v.* [T] **1** to remove hair by shaving: *Dave really looked different after he shaved off his mustache.* **2** to reduce an amount or number very slightly: *She shaved two seconds off her previous time in the Boston Marathon.* **3** to remove very thin pieces from the surface of something, using a knife or other cutting tool: *Fill the crack with putty and shave off any excess after it dries.*

shave² *n.* [C usually singular] **1** an act of shaving your face: *He badly needed a shower and a shave.* **2 a**

S

close shave a) a situation in which you just avoid an accident or something bad: *Mike's had three car accidents, plus a few other pretty close shaves.* **b)** a shave that cuts a man's hair very close to his face

shav·en /'ʃeɪvən/ *adj.* with all the hair shaved off: *He was chased by white youngsters, some with shaven heads.* —see also CLEAN-SHAVEN, UNSHAVEN

shav·er /'ʃeɪvə/ *n.* [C] **1** a tool used for shaving, especially a small electric machine —compare RAZOR (1) **2** INFORMAL, OLD-FASHIONED a small boy

shav·ing brush /'.. ,./ *n.* [C] a brush used for spreading soap or shaving cream over a man's face when he shaves

shaving cream /'.. ,./ *n.* [U] a mixture made of soap that a man puts on his face when he SHAVES

shav·ings /'ʃeɪvɪŋz/ *n.* [plural] very thin pieces, especially of wood, cut from a surface with a sharp blade: *a pile of wood shavings on the floor*

Shaw /ʃɔ/, **George Ber·nard** /dʒɔrdʒ bə'nɑrd/ (1856–1950) an Irish writer famous especially for his funny plays which criticized society and the moral values of the time

shawl /ʃɔl/ *n.* [C] a piece of soft cloth, usually in a square or TRIANGULAR shape, that is worn around the shoulders or head, especially by women

Shaw·nee /ʃɔ'ni/ *n.* a Native American tribe from the central northern region of the U.S. —**Shawnee** *adj.*

s/he /ˌʃi ə 'hi/ *pron.* used in writing when the subject of the sentence can be either male or female: *If any student witnesses a crime, s/he should contact campus police immediately.*

she¹ /ʃi/ *pron.* [used as the subject of a verb] **1 a)** a woman or girl who has been mentioned already, or who the person you are talking to already knows about: *What did she tell you to do? | You'd better ask Amy – she knows how to use the copier. | I saw you talking to that girl. Who is she?* **b)** a female animal who has been mentioned already **2** used to talk about a car, ship or other vehicle that has been mentioned already: *She's a good, reliable little car.*

she² *n.* [singular] INFORMAL a female: *What a cute puppy! Is it a he or a she?*

she- /ʃi/ *prefix* a female, especially a female animal: *a she-goat*

sheaf /ʃif/ *n. plural* **sheaves** /ʃivz/ [C] **1** several pieces of paper held or tied together: [+ of] *She stood up and took a sheaf of papers out of her bag.* **2** a bunch of wheat, corn etc. tied together after it has been cut

shear¹ /ʃɪr/ *v. past tense* **sheared** *past participle* **sheared** *or* **shorn** [T] **1** to cut the wool off a sheep **2 be shorn of sth** to have something valuable or important taken away from you: *Many of the party leaders were shorn of their power in the revolution.* **3** [T] *also* **shear off** to cut something off, using a lot of force or a heavy cutting tool: *The tornado sheared off part of the Swensons' roof.* **4** [T usually passive] LITERARY to cut off someone's hair

shear² *n.* **shears** [plural] a heavy tool for cutting things, that looks like a big pair of scissors: *Sam was trimming the hedge with a pair of garden shears.* —see also PINKING SHEARS, WIND SHEAR

shear·er /'ʃɪrə/ *also* **sheep shearer** /'. ,./ *n.* [C] someone who cuts the wool off sheep

sheath /ʃiθ/ *n. plural* **sheaths** /ʃiðz, ʃiθs/ [C] **1** a simple, close-fitting dress **2** a cover for the blade of a knife or other sharp object **3** a close-fitting part of a plant or animal that acts as a protective covering

sheathe /ʃið/ *v.* **1 be sheathed in sth** to be enclosed in a protective outer cover: *Their sofa was sheathed in clear plastic.* **2** [T] LITERARY to put a knife or sword into a sheath

sheath·ing /'ʃiðɪŋ/ *n.* [C usually singular] a protective outer cover, for example for a building or a ship

sheaves /ʃivz/ *v.* the plural of SHEAF

she·bang /ʃɪ'bæŋ/ *n.* **the whole shebang** INFORMAL the whole thing; everything: *We'll have to take the table, chairs, dishes, silverware – the whole shebang.*

she'd /ʃid/ **1** the short form of "she had": *She'd taken everything with her.* **2** the short form of "she would": *She'd like to come with us.*

shed¹ /ʃɛd/ *n.* [C] **1** a small building, often made of wood or metal, used especially for storing things: *We keep the ladder in the tool shed. | a storage shed* **2** a large industrial building where work is done, large vehicles are kept, or machinery is stored

shed² *v. past tense and past participle* **shed** *present participle* **shedding**

1 get rid of [T] to get rid of something that you do not need or want anymore: *The senator hopes to shed his old-fashioned image to appeal to younger voters. | I'd like to shed a few pounds* (=lose weight and become thinner).

2 drop/take off [T] to drop something, allow it to fall, or to take it off quickly: *Inside, the two leaders shed their coats and sat down facing each other.*

3 shed tears to cry: *I imagine a few tears will be shed at Monica's farewell party.*

4 shed blood to kill or injure people, especially during a war or a fight: *Too much blood has already been shed in this conflict.* —see also BLOODSHED

5 animal/plant [I,T] to have hair, skin, or leaves fall off as part of a natural process: *Short-haired dogs don't shed as much as long-haired ones. | As it grows, a snake will regularly shed its skin.*

6 water [T] if something sheds water, the water flows off its surface, instead of sinking into it

7 lamp etc. [T] if a lamp or other SOURCE of light sheds a particular type of light, it lights the area around it: *The candle shed a dim glow over her face.* —see also **throw/shed/cast light on sth** (LIGHT¹ (11))

she-dev·il /'. ,../ *n.* [C usually singular] HUMOROUS a very cruel woman

sheen /ʃin/ *n.* [singular,U] a soft smooth shiny appearance: *A sheen of perspiration soon covered Ron's forehead.*

shee·ny /'ʃini/ *n. plural* **sheenies** [C] TABOO a Jewish person. Do not use this word.

sheep /ʃip/ *n. plural* **sheep** [C] a grass-eating farm animal that is kept for its wool and its meat: *a sheep ranch | a flock/herd of sheep* (=a group of sheep) —compare LAMB¹ (1), MUTTON —see also BLACK SHEEP, **count sheep** (COUNT¹ (9)), **a wolf in sheep's clothing** (WOLF¹ (2))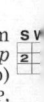

sheep dip /'. ./ *n.* [C,U] a chemical used to kill insects that live in sheep's wool, or a special bath in which this chemical is used

sheep dog, sheepdog /'. ./ *n.* [C] a dog that is trained to control sheep —see also OLD ENGLISH SHEEP-DOG

sheep·ish /'ʃipɪʃ/ *adj.* uncomfortable or embarrassed because you know that you have done something silly or wrong: *She looked relieved at first, then a little sheepish.* —**sheepishly** *adv.* —**sheepishness** *n.* [U]

sheep·skin /'ʃip,skɪn/ *n.* **1** [C,U] the skin of a sheep with the wool still on it: *a sheepskin coat* **2** [C] INFORMAL a DIPLOMA (=official document that shows you have completed your studies at a college or university): *Get your sheepskin if you want a good job.*

sheer /ʃɪr/ *adj.* [no comparative] **1 the sheer amount/weight/size etc.** used to emphasize how much of something there is or how heavy, big etc. something is: *The building's sheer size makes it extremely expensive to heat. |* [+ of] *We were overwhelmed by the sheer number of applications.* **2 sheer luck/happiness/stupidity etc.** luck, happiness etc. with no other feeling or quality mixed with it: *The sheer joy of the occasion made her burst into tears. | It was sheer luck that the last shot went into the basket.* **3** a sheer drop, cliff, slope etc. is very steep and almost VERTICAL¹ (1) **4** NYLON, silk etc. that is sheer is very thin and fine, so that it is almost transparent: *sheer curtains*

sheet /ʃit/ *n.* [C] **1** a large piece of thin cloth that you put on a bed to lie on or lie under: *Hotel housekeepers change the sheets* (=put clean sheets on a bed) *every day.* **2** a thin flat piece of something such as paper, glass, or metal, that usually has four sides:

Write each answer on a separate sheet. | [+ **of**] *Cover the dish with a sheet of plastic wrap.* —see also SHEET METAL **3** a large flat area of something such as ice or water that is spread over a surface: [+ **of**] *The temperature dropped quickly, turning puddles into sheets of ice.* **4** a sheet of rain or fire is a very large moving mass of it: *During monsoon season, the rain comes down in sheets.* | [+ **of**] *The gas leak triggered a huge blast and a sheet of flames.* **5 between the sheets** INFORMAL, HUMOROUS in bed, especially in relation to having sex: *What do you suppose he's like between the sheets?* —see also BAKING SHEET, BALANCE SHEET, COOKIE SHEET, RAP SHEET, TIME SHEET, **as white as a sheet** (WHITE¹ (3))

sheet·ing /ˈʃiːtɪŋ/ *n.* [U] cloth or other material that is made into sheets, or used in the form of a sheet: *The roof was covered in plastic sheeting.*

sheet met·al /ˈ. ˌ../ *n.* [U] metal in the form of thin sheets

sheet mu·sic /ˈ. ˌ../ *n.* [U] music that is printed on single sheets and not fastened together inside a cover

Sheet·rock /ˈʃiːtˌrɑk/ *n.* [U] TRADEMARK a type of board made of two large sheets of CARDBOARD with PLASTER between them, used to cover walls and ceilings

sheik, sheikh /ʃik, ʃeɪk/ *n.* [C] **1** an Arab chief or prince **2** a Muslim religious leader or teacher

sheik·dom, sheikhdom /ˈʃikdəm/ *n.* [C] a place that is governed by an Arab chief or prince

shek·el /ˈʃɛkəl/ *n.* [C] **1** the standard unit of money in Israel **2** HUMOROUS money: *Cahn made a few shekels on the deal.*

S W 2

shelf /ʃɛlf/ *n. plural* **shelves** /ʃɛlvz/ **1** [C] a long flat narrow board fastened to a wall or in a frame or cupboard, that you can put things on or store things on: *Put it back on the top shelf.* | *shelves of books* | *supermarket shelves* | *Breakfast cereals take up more **shelf space** than most other products in the grocery store.* **2 off the shelf** available to be bought immediately, without having to be specially designed or ordered: *off-the-shelf computer software packages* **3 on the shelf** if a plan, idea etc. is on the shelf, it is not used or considered: *The proposal will have to be put on the shelf until we can get more funding.* **4** [C] a narrow surface of rock or ice shaped like a shelf **5 fly off the shelves** to be sold in large numbers: *We can't keep the toy in stock – it's just been flying off the shelves.* —see also SHELVE

shelf life /ˈ. ./ *n.* [C, usually singular] the length of time that food, chemicals etc. can be stored before they become too old to eat or use: *Chocolate has a shelf life of 9 months.*

she'll /ʃɪl, ʃil/ the short form of "she will": *She'll be back in a minute.*

S W 3

shell¹ /ʃɛl/ *n.* [C] **1** a hard outer part that covers or protects a nut, egg, or seed and some types of animals: *Throw away any eggs with cracked shells.* | *The turtle poked its head out of its shell.* | *clam shells* **2** a metal tube containing a bullet and an explosive substance, used in a gun: *shotgun shells* **3** a metal container, like a large bullet, which is full of an explosive substance and is fired from a large gun: *Rebels fired mortar shells directly into the town square.* **4** a covering made of PASTRY that surrounds a food: *Pour the mixture into a prepared pie shell and bake at 375° for 45 minutes.* | *taco shells* **5** the outside part or covering of something: *Most buildings in the area are just burned-out shells.* | *a parka with a waterproof nylon shell* **6 come out of your shell** also **bring sb out of their shell** to become less shy and more confident and willing to talk to people, or to make someone do this: *She's really come out of her shell since she went to college.*

shell² *v.* [T] **1** to fire shells at something: *They targeted the area's most vital structures, shelling power plants and hospitals.* **2** to remove something such as beans, nuts, or SHELLFISH from a shell or a POD² (1): *Add one pound of cooked, shelled shrimp.*

shell out *phr. v.* INFORMAL [I,T **shell out** sth] to pay a lot of money for something, especially when it is more than you want to spend: *Dave ended up shelling*

out over $2000 to get his car fixed.* | *As the night wore on, I kept shelling out for drinks and cab rides.*

shel·lac¹ /ʃəˈlæk/ *n.* [U] a type of transparent paint used to protect surfaces or to make them hard

shellac² *v. past tense and past participle* **shellacked** *present participle* **shellacking** [T] **1** to paint something with shellac **2** to completely defeat someone

shel·lack·ing /ʃəˈlækɪŋ/ *n.* [U] a complete defeat: *He played a key role in Washington's 56–3 shellacking of Kansas State.*

Shel·ley /ˈʃɛli/, **Ma·ry Woll·stone·craft** /ˈmɛri ˈwʊlstənˌkræft/ (1797–1851) an English writer, whose best-known NOVEL is "Frankenstein"

Shelley, Per·cy Bysshe /ˈpɜːsi bɪʃ/ (1792–1822) an English poet

shell·fire /ˈʃɛlˌfaɪə/ *n.* [U] SHELLING

shell·fish /ˈʃɛlˌfɪʃ/ *n. plural* **shellfish** [C,U] an animal that lives in water, that has a shell but no BACKBONE, and that may be eaten as food

shell game /ˈ. ./ *n.* [C] **1** a dishonest method of doing something, in which you appear to be doing one thing when you are really doing another: *The new program to help science students is just a shell game, as an older program that helps more students is being cut.* **2** a game in which a player guesses which cup a small object is hidden under, after the cups have been moved around several times

shell·ing /ˈʃɛlɪŋ/ also **shellfire** *n.* [U] the firing of large guns at a place: *The shelling of the town continued well into the night.*

shell shock /ˈ. ./ *n.* [U] OLD-FASHIONED a type of mental illness caused by the terrible experiences of fighting in a war or battle

shell-shocked /ˈ. ./ *adj.* **1** INFORMAL feeling tired, confused, or anxious because of a recent difficult experience: *Cindy looked a little shell-shocked after her driving test.* **2** OLD-FASHIONED mentally ill because of the terrible experiences of war

shel·ter¹ /ˈʃɛltə/ *n.* **1** [U] a place to live, considered as one of the basic needs of life: *They are in desperate need of food, clothing and shelter.* **2** [U] protection from danger or from wind, rain, hot sun etc.: *We eventually reached the shelter of the caves.* | *Several people took shelter indoors when the rain started.* | *They had to run for shelter when gunshots rang out.* **3** [C] a safe place where people who are in danger can go to live and receive help: *a shelter for battered women* | *a homeless shelter* (=for people who do not have a place to live) **4** [C] a building or an area with a roof over it that protects you from the weather or other dangerous conditions outside: *a bus shelter* (=a small structure with a roof, where you wait for a bus) | *an air-raid shelter* (=a place that protects people from bombs dropped by airplanes) —see also BOMB SHELTER, TAX SHELTER

shelter

taking shelter

shelter² *v.* **1** [T] to provide a place where someone or something is protected, especially from the weather or from danger: *Federal agents knew the family had been sheltering criminals in their home.* | [**shelter sth from sth**] *A row of tall trees will shelter the house from the afternoon sun.* **2** [I] to stay in or under a place where you are protected from the weather or from danger: [+ **from**] *Groups of people were standing in doorways, sheltering from the wind and rain.*

shel·tered /ˈʃɛltəd/ *adj.* **1 a sheltered life/childhood/existence etc.** a life etc. in which someone has been too protected from difficult or bad experiences: *Paula grew up in a small town and had a very sheltered upbringing.* **2** a place that is sheltered is protected from weather conditions: *Let's find a nice sheltered spot for a picnic.*

shelve /ʃɛlv/ *v.* [T] **1** to decide not to continue with a plan, idea etc., although you might continue with it at a later time: *Plans for the new stadium have been shelved due to a lack of funding.* **2** to put something on a shelf, especially books

shelves /ʃɛlvz/ *n.* the plural of SHELF

shelv·ing /ˈʃɛlvɪŋ/ *n.* [U] **1** a set of shelves attached to a wall **2** wood, metal etc. used for shelves

Shen·an·do·ah /ˌʃɛnənˈdoʊə/ a river in northwest Virginia in the eastern U.S.

Shen·an·do·ah Valley, the /ˌ....ˈ../ a valley in northwest Virginia in the eastern U.S., between the Blue Ridge Mountains and the Allegheny Mountains

she·nan·i·gans /ʃəˈnænɪgənz/ *n.* [plural] INFORMAL **1** bad behavior that is not very serious; MISCHIEF **2** slightly dishonest activities

Shep·ard /ˈʃɛpəd/, **Al·an** /ˈælən/ (1923–1998) a U.S. ASTRONAUT who was the first American in space

Shepard, Sam /sæm/ (1943–) a U.S. actor and writer of plays

shep·herd[1] /ˈʃɛpəd/ *n.* [C] someone whose job is to take care of sheep

shepherd[2] *v.* [T always + adv./prep.] to lead or guide a group of people somewhere, making sure that they go where you want them to go: **shepherd sb into/out/toward etc.** *The tour guides shepherded the rest of the group onto the bus.*

shep·herd·ess /ˈʃɛpədɪs/ *n.* [C] OLD-FASHIONED a woman or girl whose job is to take care of sheep

sher·bert /ˈʃəbət/ *n.* [U] NONSTANDARD: see SHERBET

sher·bet /ˈʃəbɪt/ *n.* [U] a sweet frozen food, similar to ICE CREAM, made with water, fruit, sugar, and milk

Sher·i·dan /ˈʃɛrədən/, **Rich·ard Brins·ley** /ˈrɪtʃəd ˈbrɪnzli/ (1751–1816) an Irish writer of plays

sher·iff /ˈʃɛrɪf/ *n.* [C] the highest-ranking law officer of a COUNTY in the U.S., who is elected

Sher·lock /ˈʃəlɑk/ *n.* SPOKEN used when you think someone is being stupid, because they should have understood something more easily or sooner: *"It's Saturday tomorrow, right?" "Yeah, Sherlock."*

Sher·man /ˈʃəmən/, **William** (1820–1891) a Union general in the U.S. Civil War

Sher·pa /ˈʃəpə/ *n.* [C] a Himalayan person who is often employed to guide people through mountains

sher·ry /ˈʃɛri/ *n.* [C,U] a pale or dark brown strong wine, originally from Spain

Sher·wood /ˈʃəwʊd/, **Rob·ert** /ˈrɑbət/ (1896–1955) a U.S. writer of plays

she's /ʃiz/ **1** the short form of "she is": *She's coming now.* **2** the short form of "she has": *She's changed the guidelines.*

Shet·land po·ny /ˌʃɛtlənd ˈpoʊni/ *n.* [C] a small strong horse with long rough hair

shh /ʃʃ/ *interjection* used to tell people to be quiet: *Shh! I can't hear what he's saying.*

Shi·a /ˈʃiə/ *adj.* relating to the Shiite branch of the Muslim religion —**Shia** *n.* [C]

shi·at·su /ʃiˈɑtsu/ *n.* [U] a Japanese form of MASSAGE (=pressing and rubbing someone's body), used to prevent or treat physical or emotional problems

shib·bo·leth /ˈʃɪbələθ, -lɛθ/ *n.* [C] FORMAL **1** an old idea, custom, or principle that you think is not important or appropriate for modern times **2** a word, phrase, or pronunciation that is used mainly by a particular group of people, for example very educated people or uneducated people, and which makes people who say it easily recognized as belonging to that group

shield[1] /ʃild/ *n.* [C] **1 a)** a thing that soldiers used to protect themselves in past times, consisting of a broad piece of metal or leather **b)** also **riot shield** a piece of equipment made of strong plastic, used by police or soldiers to protect themselves against angry crowds —see also **a human shield** (HUMAN[1]

(4)) **2** something that protects a person or thing from harm or damage: [+ against] *The immune system is our body's shield against infection.*

shield[2] *v.* [T] to protect someone or something from being harmed or damaged: *Beneath him, shielded by his body, lay a baby.* | [**shield sb/sth from sb/sth**] *Tara's manager had shielded her from a lot of the bad publicity and hostile reviews.*

shift[1] /ʃɪft/ *v.*

1 move [I,T] to move from one place or position to another, or make something do this: *Jonas stood and listened, shifting uncomfortably from one foot to another.* | *She shifted her gaze from me to Bobby with a look of suspicion.*

2 new subject [T always + adv./prep.] to change a situation, discussion etc. by giving special attention to one idea or subject instead of to a previous one: **shift attention/emphasis/focus etc.** *The White House hopes this success will shift the media's attention away from foreign policy issues.* | **attention/emphasis/focus etc. shifts** *The focus shifted to whether the team would make the playoffs.*

3 opinions [I] if someone's opinions, beliefs etc. shift, they change: *Public opinion was beginning to shift to the right.* | *shifting attitudes toward homosexuality*

4 costs/spending [T always + adv./prep.] to change the way that money is paid or spent: *Investors were shifting funds from U.S. to Asian stocks.* | *There is a strong need to shift more resources toward health care.*

5 shift the blame/responsibility to make someone else responsible for something, especially for something bad that has happened: *It was a blatant attempt to shift the responsibility for the crime on to the victim.*

6 in a car [I,T] to change the GEARs when you are driving: *I shifted into second gear.*

shift[2] *n.* [C] **1** a change in the way people think about something, in the way something is done etc.: [+ from/to] *a major shift from manufacturing to service industries* | [+ in] *a fundamental shift in the state's education policy* **2 a)** one of the periods during each day and night when a particular group of workers in a factory, hospital etc. are at work: *Dave had to work a twelve-hour shift yesterday.* | *They had been asked to work double shifts* (=two shifts, one immediately after the other) *over the weekend.* | *Thirty employees worked around the clock in shifts to get the job done.* | **the day/night shift** *Earl's on the night shift this week.* **b)** the workers who work during one of these periods **3** a simple straight loose-fitting woman's dress **4** the KEY[1] (3) on a computer KEYBOARD or TYPEWRITER that you press to print a capital letter: *To run the spellchecker, press SHIFT and F7.*

shift key /ˈ. ./ *n.* [C] the KEY[1] (3) on a computer KEYBOARD or TYPEWRITER that you press to print a capital letter

shift·less /ˈʃɪftlɪs/ *adj.* OLD-FASHIONED lazy and seeming to have no interest in working hard or trying to succeed: *my shiftless nephew*

shift·y /ˈʃɪfti/ *adj.* someone who is shifty or has shifty eyes looks as though they cannot be trusted: *a shifty, fast-talking lawyer* —**shiftiness** *n.* [U]

shi·i·ta·ke /ʃiˈtɑki/ *n.* plural **shiitake** [C] a type of MUSHROOM that is often used in Chinese and Japanese cooking

Shi·ite /ˈʃiaɪt/ *n.* [C] a member of one of the two main branches of the Muslim religion —compare SUNNI —**Shiite** *adj.*

shik·sa /ˈʃɪksə/ *n.* [C] a word used by Jewish people to talk about a woman who is not Jewish

shill /ʃɪl/ *n.* [C] DISAPPROVING **1** someone who is paid to say that they like and use a product in an advertisement, in order to encourage other people to buy that product: *weight-loss products advertised by celebrity shills* **2** someone who pretends to be a customer in order to make other people interested in doing something such as GAMBLING —**shill** *v.* [I + for]

shil·ling /ˈʃɪlɪŋ/ *n.* [C] **1** a unit of money used in past times in Great Britain. There were 20 shillings in a pound. **2** a unit of money used in Kenya, Uganda, Tanzania, and Somalia

shil·ly-shal·ly /'ʃɪli ˌʃæli/ v. **shilly-shallies, shilly-shallied, shilly-shallying** [I] INFORMAL to waste time or take too long to make a decision

Shi·loh /'ʃaɪloʊ/ a place in the U.S. state of Tennessee where many soldiers on both sides were killed in a battle in 1862 during the Civil War

shim /ʃɪm/ n. [C] a piece of wood, metal etc. that is wider at one end than the other, used to fill a space between two things that do not fit together well

shim·mer /'ʃɪmə/ v. [I] to shine with a soft light that seems to shake slightly: *The lake shimmered in the moonlight.* —**shimmer** n. [singular,U]

shim·my /'ʃɪmi/ v. **shimmies, shimmied, shimmying** [I] to move forward or back while also quickly moving slightly from side to side

shin /ʃɪn/ n. [C] the front part of your leg between your knee and your foot —see also SHIN SPLINTS —see picture at BODY

shin·bone /'ʃɪnboʊn/ n. [C] the front bone in your leg below your knee —see picture at SKELETON

shin·dig /'ʃɪndɪg/ n. [C] OLD-FASHIONED a noisy party

shine¹ /ʃaɪn/ v. past tense and past participle **shone**
1 [I] to produce light: *It wasn't very warm, but at least the sun was shining.* | *The moon shone brightly in the sky.* | [+ in/on] *That lamp's shining in my eyes.* **2** [I] to look bright and shiny: *She polished the table until it shone.* **3** past tense and past participle **shined** to make something bright by rubbing it; polish: *You'd better shine your shoes before you go out.* **4** [T] to hold or point a lamp, light etc so that the light from it goes in a particular direction: [**shine sth into/across/onto etc.**] *She shone the flashlight around the room.* **5** [I] if your eyes shine, or your face shines, you have an expression of happiness: *The kids' eyes shone with excitement as the snow started to fall.* **6** [I not in progressive] to be very good at something and be noticed doing it: *You've put in a lot of work, and the concert will be your chance to shine.*

shine through phr. v. [I] if a quality that someone or something has shines through, you can easily see that it is there: *The simple musical arrangement lets the brilliance of Harburg's lyrics shine through.*

shine² n. **1** [singular,U] the brightness that something has when light shines on it: *This shampoo says it will add body and shine to your hair.* **2 take a shine to sb/sth** INFORMAL to like someone or something very much when you have just met them or seen them for the first time: *Ron took a shine to Amy the minute she walked in.* **3** [singular] an act of making something bright by polishing it: *Your shoes need a shine.* —see also **(come) rain or shine** (RAIN¹ (2))

shin·er /'ʃaɪnə/ n. [C] INFORMAL a black or purple area of skin around your eye, because you have been hit there

shin·gle¹ /'ʃɪŋgəl/ n. **1** [C] one of many thin flat pieces of building material, fastened in rows to cover a roof or wall **2 hang out your shingle** to start your own business, especially as a doctor or lawyer **3 shingles** [U] a disease caused by an infection of the nerve endings, which produces painful red spots, usually on one side of the body only **4** [U] small round pieces of stone on a beach

shin·gle² v. [T] to put shingles on a roof

shin·ing /'ʃaɪnɪŋ/ adj. [only before noun] **1** excellent in a way that is easy to see: **a shining achievement/moment** *For one brief, shining moment, the nation's attention was focused on our little town.* **2 a shining example of sth** someone or something that should be admired because it clearly shows a particular quality: *The house is a shining example of Art Deco architecture.*

shin·ny /'ʃɪni/ v. **shinnies, shinnied, shinnying** [I] **shinny up/down** to climb up or down a tree, pole etc. by using your hands and legs

shin splints /'. ./ n. [plural] a condition in which you have pain and swelling in your shins, usually caused by running on hard surfaces

Shin·to /'ʃɪntoʊ/ also **Shin·to·ism** /'ʃɪntoʊˌɪzəm/ n. [U] the ancient religion of Japan that has gods who represent various parts of nature, and gives great importance to people who died in the past

shin·y /'ʃaɪni/ adj. **shinier, shiniest** smooth and bright: *a shiny black limousine* | *Her hair was thick and shiny.* —**shininess** n. [U]

ship¹ /ʃɪp/ n. [C] **1** a large boat used for carrying people or things on the ocean: *a cruise ship* | *a cargo ship* | *Most of the island's supplies are brought in by ship.* **2** a large vehicle used for traveling in space —see also **jump ship** (JUMP¹ (23)), **run a tight ship** (TIGHT¹ (9))

ship² v. **shipped, shipping 1** [I,T] to deliver goods to someone, or to deliver them to a store so that they are available for people to buy: *We can ship a replacement to you within 24 hours.* | *The updated version is scheduled to ship on July 1.* **2** [T] to send or carry something by ship: [**ship sth out/to etc.**] *In the 18th century, fine French furniture was shipped to England in pieces and assembled later.* **3** [T usually passive] to order someone to go somewhere: [**ship sb off/out etc.**] *He was shipped off to a juvenile detention center at the age of 14.* —see also **shape up or ship out** at **shape up** (SHAPE²)

-ship /ʃɪp/ suffix [in nouns] **1** a particular position, condition, or state: *A year's membership costs $35.* | *a long friendship* **2** a particular art or skill: *her fine musicianship* | *a work of great scholarship* —see also -MANSHIP **3** all the people in a particular group: *a magazine with a readership of 9000* (=with 9000 readers) **4** used to form particular titles for people: *your Ladyship*

ship·board¹ /'ʃɪpbɔrd/ n. [U] **on shipboard** on a ship

shipboard² adj. [only before noun] on a ship: *shipboard navigation systems*

ship·build·ing /'ʃɪpˌbɪldɪŋ/ n. [U] the industry of making ships —**shipbuilder** n. [C]

ship·load /'ʃɪploʊd/ n. [C] the amount of goods or the number of people a ship can carry: [+ of] *Several shiploads of grain arrived in the harbor that day.*

ship·mate /'ʃɪpmeɪt/ n. [C] a SAILOR's shipmate is another sailor who is working on the same ship

ship·ment /'ʃɪpmənt/ n. [C,U] a load of goods being delivered, or the act of sending them: *Your order will be ready for shipment tomorrow.* | [+ of] *a large shipment of auto parts*

ship·per /'ʃɪpə/ n. [C] a company that sends goods to places

ship·ping /'ʃɪpɪŋ/ n. [U] **1 shipping and handling** the price charged for delivering goods: *Please enclose a check for $17.95 plus $2.00 shipping and handling.* **2** ships considered as a group, or the business done by ship: *The port is closed to all shipping.*

shipping clerk /'.. ˌ./ n. [C] someone whose job is to send and receive goods at a company

shipping lane /'.. ˌ./ also **sea lane** n. [C] an officially approved path of travel that ships must follow

ship·shape /ˌʃɪpˈʃeɪp/ adj. [not before noun] neat and clean: *Hotels are warned when rooms aren't shipshape.*

ship-to-shore /ˌ.. '.ˌ/ adj. [only before noun] providing communication between a ship and people on land: *ship-to-shore radio*

ship·wreck¹ /'ʃɪp-rɛk/ n. [C] **1** the destruction of a ship in an accident: *Morgan was the lone survivor of a shipwreck off the California coast.* **2** a ship that has been destroyed in an accident: *Divers discovered a 450-year-old shipwreck near here.*

shipwreck² v. **be shipwrecked** if someone or a boat or ship is shipwrecked, they are in an accident in which a ship is destroyed: *The characters in the series were shipwrecked on a desert island.*

ship·wright /'ʃɪp-raɪt/ n. [C] someone who builds or repairs ships

ship·yard /'ʃɪp-yard/ n. [C] a place where ships are built or repaired

shirk /ʃɚk/ v. [T] FORMAL to deliberately avoid doing something you should do, because you are lazy: **shirk your responsibilities/duties/obligations** *We must not shirk our responsibilities to the citizens of our great state.* —**shirker** n. [C] —**shirking** n. [U]
   shirk from sth *phr. v.* [T] FORMAL to deliberately avoid something or refuse to do something, especially because you are afraid: *The President made it clear he would not shirk from a fight over the tax credit.*

shirred /ʃɚd/ adj. shirred material is decorated with several lines of stitches sewn in a way that makes many small folds between the stitches

shirt /ʃɚt/ n. [C] **1** a piece of clothing that covers the upper part of your body and your arms, and usually has a collar and buttons down the front: *I have to wear a shirt and tie to work.* —compare BLOUSE, T-SHIRT **2 sb would give you the shirt off their back** INFORMAL used to say that someone is very generous: *Dan's the kind of guy who would give you the shirt off his back.* **3 keep your shirt on** SPOKEN used to tell someone who is becoming angry that they should stay calm **4 no shirt, no shoes, no service** used on signs in restaurants and stores to say that if you are not wearing a shirt or shoes, you cannot come in —see also STUFFED SHIRT

shirt·dress /'ʃɚtdrɛs/ n. [C] a woman's dress in the style of a long shirt; SHIRTWAIST

shirt·front /'ʃɚtfrʌnt/ n. [C] the part of a shirt that covers your chest

shirt·sleeve /'ʃɚtsliv/ n. **1 in (your) shirtsleeves** wearing a shirt but no JACKET: *Most of the men were working in their shirtsleeves.* **2** [C] the part of a shirt that covers your arm

shirt·tail /'ʃɚtteɪl/ n. [C] the part of a shirt that is below your waist and is usually inside your pants, especially in the back: *Tuck your shirttail in before you go outside.*

shirt·waist /'ʃɚtweɪst/ also **shirtwaist dress** /'.. ˌ./ n. [C] a SHIRTDRESS

shish ke·bab /'ʃɪʃ kəˌbɑb/ n. [C] small pieces of meat and vegetables that are put on a long thin metal stick and cooked

shit¹ /ʃɪt/ n. VULGAR
   1 shit! also **oh shit!** said when you are angry or annoyed about something: *Oh, shit! I forgot my passport!*
   2 body waste [U] solid waste that comes out of your body from your BOWELS: *There's a pile of dog shit on the sidewalk.*
   3 take a shit to push out solid waste from your BOWELS
   4 have/get the shits to have or get DIARRHEA (=an illness in which solid waste comes out of your body in a more liquid form than usual)
   5 sth unpleasant/bad quality [U] something that you think is bad or of very bad quality, or a bad situation: *I'm not eating that shit!* | *This radio is a total piece of shit.* | *She put up with a lot of shit from her ex-husband.*
   6 shit happens used to say that sometimes bad things happen, and people cannot always prevent them from happening: *Yeah, well, shit happens.*
   7 sb's possessions [U] someone's possessions, especially the things they have with them; STUFF: *Just put your shit on the chair over there.*
   8 stupid/not true [U] something that you think is stupid or untrue: *You expect me to believe that shit?* | *You're full of shit* (=what you are saying is stupid), *Rudy.*
   9 not give a shit to not care at all about something: *I don't give a shit what you think!*
   10 take shit (from sb) to let someone insult or criticize you: *Donna won't take any shit from her students.*
   11 give sb shit to insult someone or argue with them in a way that annoys them: *Go out and mow the lawn, and don't give me any shit about it, either.*
   12 ...and shit used to say that there are more

details that you could mention, but it should be clear to someone else what you mean: *We were gonna go out for a pizza and shit.*
   13 no shit a) used to express surprise or to check whether what someone has just said is true: *"I can get you one for $50." "No shit?"* **b)** used to emphasize that what you are saying is true, or to agree that what someone else says is true: *They had, like, no shit, forty different kinds of beer on tap.* | *"This case is a waste of time." "No shit."* **c)** used to say that someone is being stupid, especially because they should have understood or realized something earlier or more easily: *"Oh, the ticket guy gave me the wrong ticket." "No shit. You should have checked it."*
   14 no shit, Sherlock! used to tell someone rudely that what they have just said was very easy to notice or understand and was not surprising at all: *"We're going to need a key to open that trunk." "No shit, Sherlock!"*
   15 feel/look like shit to feel very sick or not look as neat, clean etc. as you should: *I woke up with a hangover and felt like shit for the rest of the day.*
   16 beat/kick the shit out of sb to beat or kick someone very violently
   17 person [C] someone who is very cruel or impolite, or who you do not respect: *What are you looking at, you little shit?*
   18 be in deep shit to be in a lot of trouble
   19 the shit hits the fan used to say that there is a lot of trouble when someone finds out about something: *The shit really hit the fan when Andy saw the phone bill.*
   20 be up shit creek (without a paddle) to be in a very difficult or dangerous situation
   21 sb thinks their shit don't/doesn't stink used to say that someone thinks that everything they do is good and that they do not make mistakes
   22 a shit-eating grin a smile that show someone is very pleased because they have done something smart —see also **hot shit** (HOT (17)), **scare the hell/shit/daylights etc. out of sb** (SCARE¹ (1)), **tough shit** (TOUGH¹ (6))

shit² v. past tense and past participle **shit** or **shat** VULGAR **1** [I] to pass solid waste out of your body from your BOWELS **2 shit (in) your pants** to feel very worried or frightened: *I was so scared, I could've shit my pants.* **3 shit a brick/shit bricks** HUMOROUS to be extremely frightened or worried: *I bet they're shitting bricks right now.* **4 shit sb** to tell someone something that is untrue: *Are you shitting me?* **5 shit or get off the pot** used to tell someone to do something, when they have been talking about doing it for too long without actually taking any action

shit·faced /'ʃɪtˌfeɪst/ adj. [not before noun] VULGAR very drunk: *The guys got totally shitfaced on Friday.*

shit-for-brains /ˌ. . './ n. [C] VULGAR someone who you think is very stupid

shit·head /'ʃɪthɛd/ n. [C] VULGAR someone who you think is very stupid or who you are very angry with

shit·hole /'ʃɪthoʊl/ n. [C] VULGAR a place that is very dirty and disgusting: *They live in a total shithole.*

shit·less /'ʃɪtlɪs/ adj. VULGAR **scare sb shitless** to make someone feel very frightened

shit list /'. ./ n. VULGAR **be on sb's shit list** to have annoyed someone very much: *Uh oh – I'm really gonna be on Jody's shit list if I forget to bring her stuff back.*

shit·load /'ʃɪtloʊd/ n. [C] SPOKEN, TABOO a lot of something: [+ of] *I've got a shitload of homework tonight.*

shit·ty /'ʃɪti/ adj. **shittier, shittiest** VULGAR very bad or disgusting: *Paul's been in a shitty mood all morning.*

shiv·er¹ /'ʃɪvɚ/ v. [I] to shake slightly because you

shiver

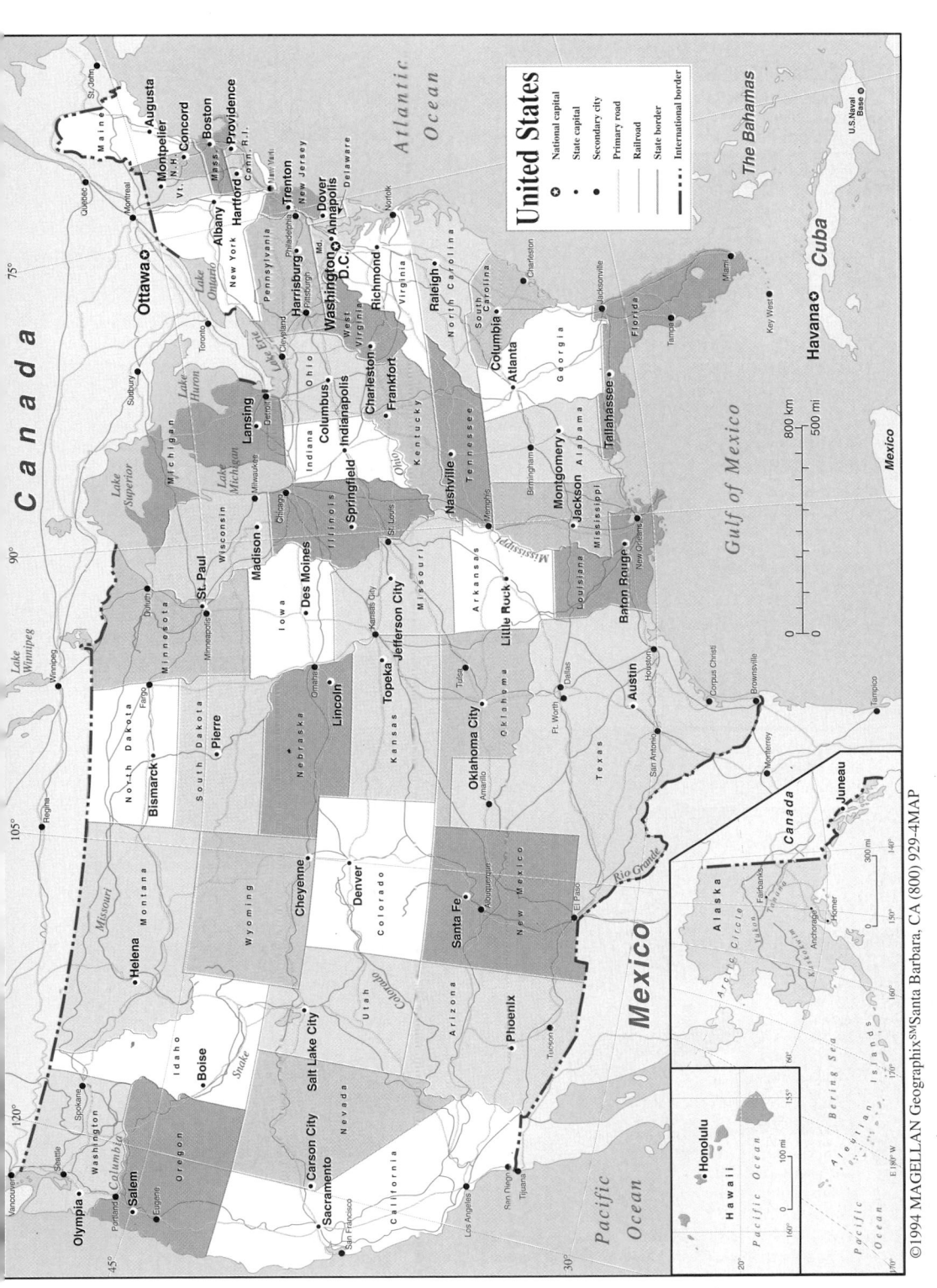

The movie industry was born in Hollywood in the 1920s.

The first great steel plants were constructed in Pennsylvania in the mid-nineteenth century.

Oil was first discovered in what is now Texas in 1543.

Michigan has been the center of the U.S. auto industry since 1899.

Florida has been at the heart of the American space industry since the 1950s.

Washington, D.C., has been at the center of American political life since 1800.

Las Vegas became the entertainment and gambling capital in 1931.

North Dakota has been a defense center since the establishment of several air bases in the 1960s.

Silicon Valley in California has been at the center of the computer industry since the late 1960s.

New York's first stock exchange was set up on Wall Street in 1792.

The Wright Brothers made the first successful flight in an airplane in 1903.

Industrialist Henry Ford founded the Ford Motor Company in 1903.

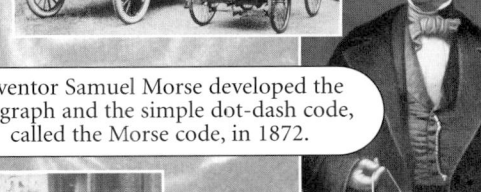

Inventor Samuel Morse developed the telegraph and the simple dot-dash code, called the Morse code, in 1872.

German-born physicist Albert Einstein published the general theory of relativity in 1915.

Inventor Thomas Edison patented the incandescent light bulb in 1872.

Inventor Eli Whitney developed the cotton gin, a machine for removing the seeds from cotton, in 1793.

Astronaut John Glenn was the first American to orbit the Earth in 1962. In 1998 he became the oldest person to travel in space.

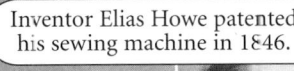

Inventor Elias Howe patented his sewing machine in 1846.

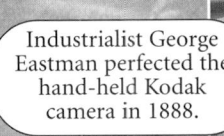

Industrialist George Eastman perfected the hand-held Kodak camera in 1888.

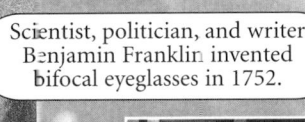

Scientist, politician, and writer Benjamin Franklin invented bifocal eyeglasses in 1752.

Scientist George Washington Carver announced the results of his experiments to make products from peanuts and sweet potatoes in 1914.

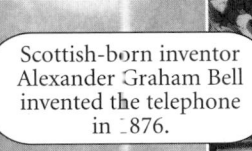

Scottish-born inventor Alexander Graham Bell invented the telephone in 1876.

In 1927, the pilot Charles Lindbergh became the first person to fly alone across the Atlantic without stopping, in his plane, The Spirit of St. Louis.

In 1906, violent earthquakes and fire devastated San Francisco, California.

In 1929, the New York Stock Exchange slumped dramatically in the Wall Street Crash, causing financial chaos and worldwide economic depression.

In 1949, the North Atlantic Treaty Organization (NATO) was established to provide mutual protection for the U.S., Canada and Western Europe.

In 1963, President John F. Kennedy was assassinated in Dallas, Texas.

In 1968, the black religious and civil rights leader Martin Luther King was assassinated in Memphis, Tennessee.

In 1969, a huge popular music festival was held near the town of Woodstock, New York.

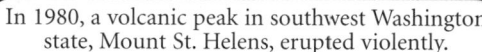

In 1980, a volcanic peak in southwest Washington state, Mount St. Helens, erupted violently.

In 1969, the spacecraft Apollo 11 landed on the moon and astronaut Neil Armstrong became the first man to walk on its surface.

In 1982, the Space Shuttle Columbia made its first operational flight into space.

Arizona: the sunniest state
(4,000 hours of sun per year in Yuma)

The Sears Tower in
Chicago, Illinois: the tallest
habitable building
(1,454 feet or 443 meters)

New York, New York: the city
with the largest population
(7,311,966 people)

Franklin D. Roosevelt: the
longest-serving U.S. President
(12 years and 39 days)

The Golden Gate Bridge in
San Francisco, California: the longest
suspension bridge on the West Coast
(4,200 feet or 1,280.2 meters).

O'Hare Airport in Chicago, Illinois:
the busiest airport
(65,091,000 passengers per year)

The New York Public Library:
the biggest public library
(10,505,079 books)

Mount McKinley (or Denali)
in Alaska: the highest mountain
(20,320 feet or 6,194 meters)

Crater Lake in Oregon: the deepest freshwater
lake (1,932 feet or 589 meters)

The MBTA in Boston,
Massachusetts: the oldest
subway system
(constructed in 1897)

Chief Crazy Horse on Thunderhead
Mountain in South Dakota: the tallest
free-standing statue (563 feet or 172 meters)

whitewater rafting

snowboarding

skydiving

rock climbing

bungee jumping

mountain biking

hang gliding

parasailing

ICE STORMS CAUSE POWER OUTAGES IN NORTHEAST

VIOLENT HURRICANE BATTERS GULF COAST

MUDSLIDE ENGULFS HOUSES IN MALIBU

AVALANCHE BURIES HOMES IN CALIFORNIA

SEVERE BLIZZARD STRIKES NEW YORK STATE

EXTENSIVE FLOODING DEVASTATES EASTERN IOWA

SAVAGE TORNADOES HIT CENTRAL OKLAHOMA

HIGH WINDS FUEL FOREST FIRES IN OREGON

SEVERE THUNDERSTORMS DOWN POWER LINES IN MIDWEST

THICK FOG BLANKETS NEW ENGLAND

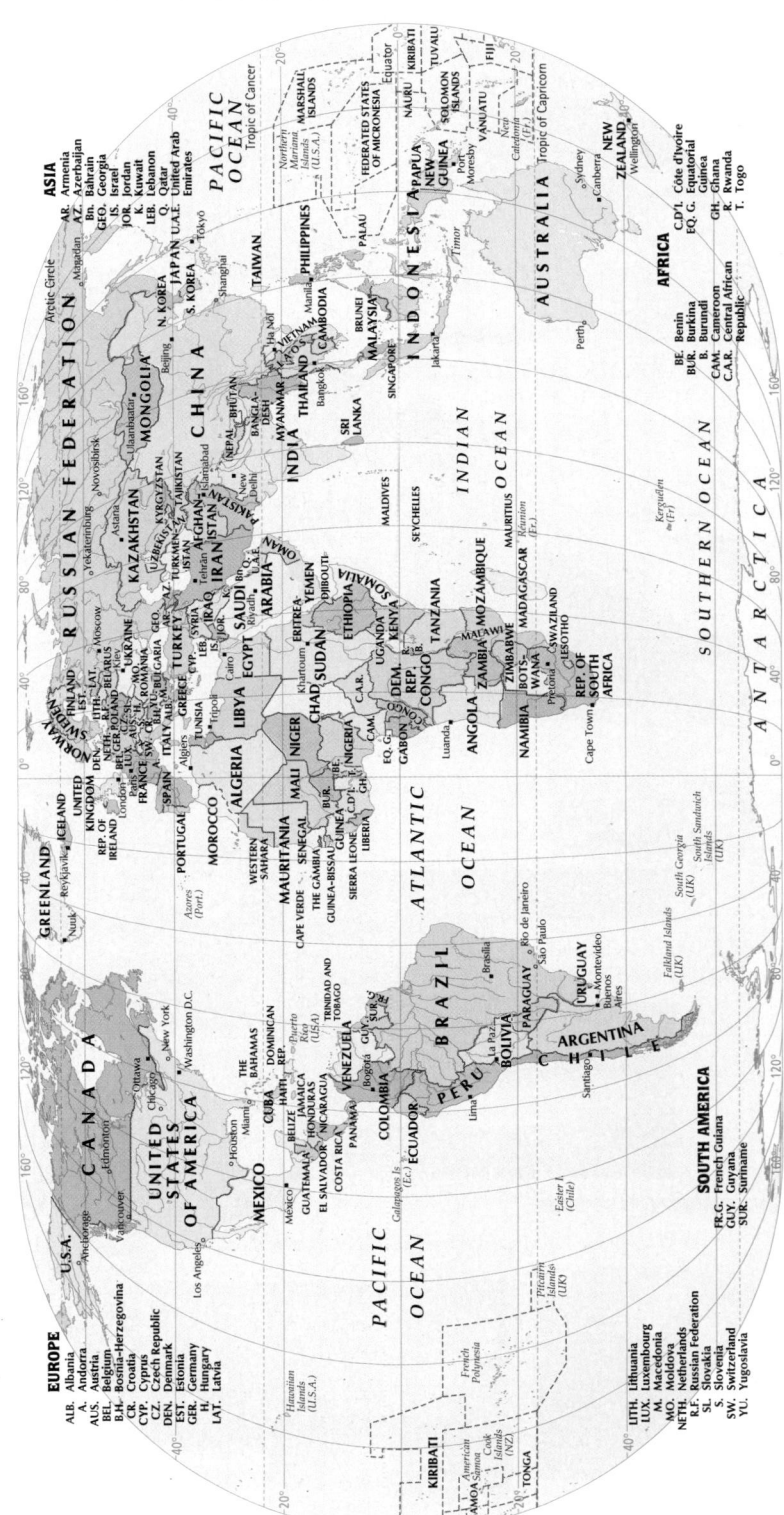

are cold or frightened: *The water was cold, and Robbie shivered.* | [+ **with**] *Juanita was shivering with fear.*

shiver² *n.* [C] **1** a slight shaking movement of your body caused by cold or fear: *The thought of sleeping in such an old house sent a shiver through her.* **2 give you the shivers** INFORMAL to make you feel afraid: *Just thinking about flying in an airplane gives me the shivers.* —see also **send shivers/chills up (and down) your spine** (SEND (8))

shiv·er·y /ˈʃɪvəri/ *adj.* shaking slightly because of cold, fear, or illness

shoal /ʃoʊl/ *n.* [C] **1** a large group of fish swimming together **2** a small hill of sand just below the surface of water that makes it dangerous for boats

s w **shock¹** /ʃɑk/ *n.*
3
1 event/situation [C usually singular] an unexpected and bad event, situation, or piece of news that surprises and upsets you: *It was a big shock when Connie said she was leaving her husband.* | *Chuck's death came as a complete shock to all of us.*
2 bad feeling [singular,U] the feeling of surprise you have when something very bad happens that you do not expect: *Several campaign workers wandered around, still in shock at their candidate's huge defeat.* | *Dad'll get a huge shock when he sees the dent in his car.*
3 electricity [C] also **electric shock, electrical shock** a sharp, painful feeling caused by a dangerous flow of electricity passing through your body: *Ouch! The light switch just gave me a shock.*
4 medical [U] TECHNICAL a medical condition in which someone looks pale and their heart and lungs are not working correctly, usually after a sudden very bad experience: *Several passengers were taken to the hospital to be treated for shock.*
5 shaking [C,U] violent shaking caused for example by an explosion or a sudden movement of the earth's surface: *The shock of the explosion could be felt miles away.* —see also SHOCK WAVE
6 a SHOCK ABSORBER
7 a shock of hair a very thick mass of hair —see also CULTURE SHOCK, SHELL SHOCK, SHOCKED, TOXIC SHOCK, SYNDROME

USAGE NOTE: SHOCK

WORD CHOICE: shock, surprise, shocking, surprising
Shock and **shocking** are both fairly strong words, and you may have to think whether they are the words you really need to express your meaning. If something **is, comes as,** or **gives you a shock,** it is unexpected and often very bad: *It came as a real shock to hear she was in the hospital.* | *It will take a long time to get over the shock of his wife's death.* You can use **surprise** and **surprising** to talk about something that is unexpected, but is not necessarily bad: *It was a nice surprise when Brenda dropped in.* | *There are a number of surprising differences between life in America and in my country.* Something that is **shocking** is extremely bad, often in an offensive or immoral way: *shocking cruelty* | *The shocking news of her murder came late Friday night.* So you would not use **shocking** to describe, for example, your first day at school, or something that was simply an unpleasant surprise.

---

shock² *v.* [T] **1** to make someone feel very surprised and upset, and unable to believe what has happened: *Obviously, her suicide shocked the whole school.* **2** to make someone feel very offended, by talking or behaving in an immoral or socially unacceptable way: *Many readers were shocked by the number of obscenities in the article.* **3** to give an electric shock to someone

shock ab·sorb·er /ˈ. .ˌ../ *n.* [C] a piece of equipment connected to each wheel of a vehicle to make traveling more comfortable and less BUMPY

s w **shocked** /ʃɑkt/ *adj.* feeling surprised and very upset by something unexpected and bad: [+ **at**] *We were shocked at their terrible working conditions.* | **shocked to see/hear/learn etc.** *I was very shocked to hear of Brian's death.*

shock·er /ˈʃɑkɚ/ *n.* [C] a movie, news story etc. that shocks you

shock·ing /ˈʃɑkɪŋ/ *adj.* very offensive or upsetting: *shocking photographs of mass graves* —**shockingly** *adv.* —see Usage Note at SHOCK²

shocking pink /ˌ.. '.ˌ/ *n.* [U] a very bright pink color —**shocking pink** *adj.*

shock jock /ˈ. ./ *n.* [C] someone on a radio show who plays music and talks about subjects that offend many people

shock·proof /ˈʃɑkpruf/ *adj.* something that is shockproof is made or designed so that it is not easily damaged if it is dropped or hit

shock tac·tics /ˈ. ˌ../ *n.* [plural] methods of achieving what you want by deliberately shocking someone

shock ther·a·py /ˈ. ˌ.../ *n.* [U] **1** also **shock treatment** treatment of mental illness using powerful electric shocks **2** also **shock treatment** the use of extreme methods to change a system or solve a problem as quickly as possible: *Several Eastern European nations adopted programs of economic shock therapy to convert to capitalism.*

shock troops /ˈ. ./ *n.* [plural] soldiers who are specially trained to make attacks on the enemy

shock wave /ˈ. ./ *n.* **1 shock waves** [plural] strong feelings of shock that people feel when something bad happens suddenly: *The plane crash sent shock waves through the aviation industry.* **2** [C,U] a very strong wave of air pressure or heat from an explosion, an EARTHQUAKE etc.

shod¹ /ʃɑd/ *v.* the past tense and past participle of SHOE²

shod² *adj.* FORMAL wearing a particular type of shoes: [**be shod in sth**] *His feet were shod in thick-soled sandals.*

shod·dy /ˈʃɑdi/ *adj.* **shoddier, shoddiest 1** made or done cheaply or carelessly: *shoddy workmanship* **2** unfair and dishonest: *shoddy journalism* —**shoddily** *adv.*: *shoddily built housing* —**shoddiness** *n.* [U]

shoe¹ /ʃu/ *n.* [C] **1** something that you wear to cover your feet, made of leather or some other strong material: *Billy needs a new pair of shoes for school.* | *I can't walk in high-heeled shoes.* —compare BOOT¹ (1), SANDAL, SLIPPER —see also TENNIS SHOE **2 be in sb's shoes** to be in someone else's situation, especially a bad one: *I wouldn't want to be in Frank's shoes right now. How's he going to get the money?* **3 step into sb's shoes** also **fill sb's shoes** to do a job that someone else used to do, and do it as well as they did: *Will anyone ever be able to fill Pam's shoes in the post office?* **4 if the shoe fits (, wear it)** SPOKEN used to say that if a remark that has been made about you is true, then you should accept it: *"Are you saying I'm a liar?" "Well, if the shoe fits..."* **5** a U-shaped piece of iron that is nailed onto a horse's foot; HORSESHOE **6** the part of a BRAKE that presses on a wheel to make a vehicle stop —see picture on page 1300

shoe² *v.* past tense, past participle **shod** present participle **shoeing** [T] to put a shoe on a horse

shoe·box /ˈʃubɑks/ *n.* [C] a CARDBOARD box that shoes are sold in, and that people often keep other things in

shoe·horn¹ /ˈʃuhɔrn/ *n.* [C] a curved piece of metal or plastic that you can put inside the back of a shoe when you put it on, to help your heel go in easily

shoehorn² *v.* [T] to put someone or something into a space that is too small: [+ **into**] *Twelve players are shoehorned into a tiny dressing room.*

shoe·lace /ˈʃuleɪs/ *n.* [C] a thin piece of material, like string, that goes through holes in the front of your shoes and is used to tie them

shoe·mak·er /ˈʃumeɪkɚ/ *n.* [C] someone who makes shoes and boots

Shoe·mak·er /ˈʃumeɪkɚ/, **Wil·lie** /ˈwɪli/ (1931–) a U.S. JOCKEY who won thousands of horse races and is considered one of the best jockeys ever

shoe·shine /ˈʃuʃaɪn/ *n.* [C usually singular] an act of polishing your shoes or having them polished by someone else

shoe·string /'ʃuˌstrɪŋ/ *n.* **1 on a shoestring** INFORMAL if you do something on a shoestring, you do it without spending much money: *The program was run on a shoestring for years until they found a sponsor.* **2 a shoestring business/operation/budget etc.** a business, organization etc. that does not have much money available to spend: *Willis ran a shoestring campaign for governor and came within 50,000 votes of the winner.* **3** a shoelace

shoes

lining
tongue
lace
eyelet
seam
upper
heel
sole
toe

wingtip
moccasin
loafer
clog
tennis shoe/sneaker
slipper
pump
sandal
slingback
thong

shoestring po·ta·toes /ˌ.. '../ *n.* [plural] potatoes that have been cut into very thin pieces, thinner than FRENCH FRIES, and then cooked in hot oil

shoe·tree /'ʃuˌtri/ *n.* [C] an object shaped like a shoe that you put inside a shoe so that it keeps its shape

sho·gun /'ʃoʊgən/ *n.* [C] a military leader in Japan until the middle of the 19th century

shone /ʃoʊn/ *v.* the past tense and past participle of SHINE

shoo¹ /ʃu/ *interjection* used to tell a child or an animal to go away

shoo² *v.* [T always + adv./prep.] to make a child, animal, or insect go away by waving your arms around, especially because they are annoying you: [**shoo sb out/away etc.**] *He shooed the kids out of the kitchen.*

shoo-in /'. ./ *n.* [C usually singular] someone who is expected to win a race, election etc. easily: *He looked like **a shoo-in to win** the Democratic nomination.*

shook /ʃʊk/ *v.* the past tense of SHAKE
shook up /ˌ. '. ./ *adj.* [not before noun] INFORMAL very frightened, shocked, or upset because of something that has happened: *She was too shook up to talk about the accident.*
shoot¹ /ʃut/ *v.* past tense and past participle **shot**
1 kill/injure [T] to injure or kill someone or an animal using a gun: *Police shot one suspect when he pulled a gun on them.* | *She shot herself with one of her husband's hunting rifles.* | **shoot sb in the leg/head etc.** *He was shot in the leg while trying to escape.* | **shoot sb to death/shoot sb dead** *One woman was shot to death in an attempted robbery.* | *The guards have orders to **shoot intruders on sight** (=shoot as soon as you see someone).*
2 fire a gun [I,T] to fire a weapon at someone or at an animal, or make a weapon fire: *Stop or I'll shoot!* | [+ **at**] *Two guys walked in and just started shooting at people.* | *The soldiers had orders to **shoot to kill** (=shoot at someone with the intention of killing them).* | **shoot bullets/arrows etc.** *It's just a toy – it doesn't shoot real bullets.* | **shoot a gun/rifle etc.** *Todd's grandfather taught him how to shoot a rifle.*
3 move quickly [I,T always + adv./prep.] to move quickly in a particular direction, or to make something move in this way: [+ **past/along etc.**] *Two kids shot past us on in-line skates.* | *Flames were shooting skyward.* | [**shoot sth up/in/along etc.**] *The fountain shoots water 20 feet into the air.*
4 go up in level/rank [I] to rise in level or rank very quickly: *Her second novel shot straight to the top of the bestseller lists.*
5 pain [I always + adv./prep.] if pain shoots through your body, you feel it going quickly through it: [+ **through/along/down**] *A sharp pain suddenly shot down her right arm.*
6 shooting pain/pains sudden short pain that passes through a part of your body: *People often had backaches with shooting pains.*
7 sports [I,T] to throw or hit a ball or PUCK in a sport such as basketball or HOCKEY toward the place where you can gain points: *O'Neal turned and shot from behind the 3–point line.*
8 shoot hoops/baskets INFORMAL to practice throwing a basketball through the basket: *Let's go out and shoot a few hoops.*
9 shoot pool INFORMAL to play a game of POOL¹ (2)
10 photo/movie [I,T] to take photographs or make a movie of something: *The opening scenes of the program were shot in northern Oregon.*
11 start speaking [used in the imperative] SPOKEN, INFORMAL used to tell someone to start speaking: *"I have a couple of questions for you." "Okay, shoot."*
12 shoot yourself in the foot to say or do something stupid that will cause you a lot of trouble: *If we just let him keep talking, pretty soon he's going to shoot himself in the foot.*
13 shoot the bull/breeze INFORMAL to have an informal conversation about unimportant things: *Cal and I were sitting on the porch, shooting the breeze.*
14 shoot a look/glance (at sb) to look at someone quickly, especially so that other people do not see, to show them how you feel: *Linda shot an angry glance in Doug's direction.*
15 shoot your mouth off INFORMAL to talk about something that you should not talk about or that you know nothing about
16 shoot from the hip to speak or act without thinking first
17 shoot questions at sb to ask someone a lot of questions very quickly: *The prosecutor shot a series of rapid questions at Hendrickson.*
18 shoot your wad INFORMAL to have used all of your money, power, energy etc. —see also **blame/shoot the messenger** (MESSENGER (2))
shoot sb/sth ↔ down *phr. v.* [T] **1** to destroy an airplane while it is flying: *Schmidt was shot down behind enemy lines.* **2** to kill someone with a gun, especially someone who cannot defend themselves: *They shot him down in the middle of an empty parking lot.* **3** shoot sb/sth down (in flames) INFORMAL to tell someone that what they are saying or suggesting is wrong or stupid: *The boss is just going to shoot down all my suggestions at the meeting.*

shoot for/at sth *phr. v.* [T] INFORMAL to try to achieve a particular aim, especially one that is very difficult: *Mandy's shooting for an "A" in history this quarter.*

shoot up *phr. v.* **1** [I] to increase quickly in number or amount: *Insurance premiums shot up following the earthquake.* **2** [I] to grow taller or higher very quickly: *Suddenly, a huge orange flame shot up.* | *Peter really shot up over the summer.* **3** [T shoot sb/sth ↔ up] to injure or damage someone or something by shooting them with bullets: *Then two men came in and shot up the entire lobby.* **4** [I,T] SLANG to take illegal drugs by using a needle

shoot² *n.* [C] **1** the part of a plant that that comes up above the ground when it is just beginning to grow **2** an occasion when someone takes photographs or makes a movie: *Stevens had just finished a photo shoot for a clothing company* **3** an occasion when people shoot birds or animals as a sport: *Some of the guys are going on a duck shoot this weekend.* —see also **sth is a crap shoot** (CRAP¹ (6)), TURKEY SHOOT

shoot³ *interjection* INFORMAL used to show that you are annoyed or disappointed about something: *Oh, shoot! I forgot to go to the bank.*

shoot·er /ˈʃutɚ/ *n.* [C] **1** a basketball player who is good at throwing the ball through the basket in order to gain points **2** someone who shoots a gun **3** INFORMAL a gun —see also SIX-SHOOTER, TROUBLE-SHOOTER

shoot·ing /ˈʃutɪŋ/ *n.* [C] a situation in which someone is injured or killed by a gun: *Ambulances rushed to the scene of the shooting.*

shooting gal·le·ry /ˈ.. ˌ.../ *n.* [C] **1** a place where people shoot guns at objects to win prizes **2** SLANG an empty building in a city, where people buy illegal drugs and put them into their bodies with needles

shooting star /ˌ.. './ *n.* [C] a small piece of rock or metal from space, that burns brightly as it falls toward the Earth; METEOR

shoot·out /ˈʃutaʊt/ *n.* [C] **1** a fight using guns: *Brown was killed in a shootout with police.* **2** a sports competition, especially in basketball or GOLF, in which people take turns throwing or hitting a ball to see who can gain the most points

s w **shop¹** /ʃɑp/ *n.*
¹₂ **1** ▢small store▢ [C] a small store that sells one particular type of goods: *a card shop* —see also COFFEE SHOP
2 ▢making/repairing things▢ [C] a place where things are made or repaired: *After assembly, the cars go to the paint shop to be painted.* | *Our car's still in the shop* (=being repaired). —see also BODY SHOP, SHOP STEWARD
3 ▢school subject▢ [U] also **shop class** a subject taught in schools that shows students how to use tools and machinery to make or repair things: *Doug made this table in shop.* | **wood/metal/print etc. shop** *One auto shop class is run just for girls.*
4 set up shop INFORMAL to start a business: *Dr. Rosen closed his downtown practice and set up shop in a suburban neighborhood.*
5 close up shop INFORMAL to close a business, usually permanently: *Finnegan's Bar is closing up shop after 35 years.* —see also **talk shop** (TALK³ (3))

s w **shop²** *v.* **shopped, shopping** [I] to go to one or more
₂ stores to buy things: [+ for] *I was shopping for a new dress but couldn't find anything I liked.* | [+ at] *I usually shop at Lucky's.* —see also SHOPPING, WINDOW SHOPPING

shop around *phr. v.* [I] to compare the price and quality of different things before you decide which to buy: [+ for] *We shopped around for the best deal on a new car.*

shop·a·hol·ic /ˌʃɑpəˈhɔlɪk, -ˈhɑlɪk/ *n.* [C] HUMOROUS someone who goes shopping very often and buys more things than they should

shop floor /ˈ. ./ *n.* **the shop floor** the area in a factory where the ordinary workers do their work

shop·keep·er /ˈʃɑpˌkipɚ/ *n.* [C] someone who owns or is in charge of a small store; STOREKEEPER

shop·lift /ˈʃɑpˌlɪft/ *v.* [I] to take something from a store without paying for it —**shoplifter** *n.* [C]

Shoplifters will be prosecuted. —see Usage Notes at STEAL¹ and THIEF

shop·lift·ing /ˈʃɑpˌlɪftɪŋ/ *n.* [U] the crime of stealing things from stores, for example by hiding them in your bag or under your clothes

shoppe /ʃɑp/ *n.* [C usually singular] a way of spelling "shop," used especially in the names of stores to make them seem old-fashioned and attractive: *Ye Olde Candy Shoppe*

shop·per /ˈʃɑpɚ/ *n.* [C] **1** someone who buys things in stores, or who is looking for something to buy: *The streets were crowded with holiday shoppers.* —see Usage Note at CUSTOMER **2** a type of newspaper, filled mainly with advertisements, that is delivered free to every house in a particular area

shop·ping /ˈʃɑpɪŋ/ *n.* [U] **1 go shopping** to go to one s w or more stores to buy things, often for enjoyment: ₂ [+ for] *Kari and I went shopping for swimsuits.* | **go grocery/clothes/shoe etc. shopping** (=to go to one or more stores in order to buy food, clothes etc.) **2** the activity of going to stores to buy things: *Ben listed his hobbies as watching TV, shopping, and going to the movies.* | *She was tired after doing all the shopping, washing, and ironing.* | **Christmas/holiday shopping** (=buying presents for Christmas, Hanukkah etc.)

shopping bag /ˈ.. ˌ./ *n.* [C] a large bag made of heavy paper with a flat bottom and two handles, that you get when you buy something in a store

shopping cart /ˈ.. ˌ./ *n.* [C] a large metal basket on wheels that you push around in a store when you are shopping

shopping cen·ter /ˈ.. ˌ../ *n.* [C] a group of stores built together in one area, often in one large building

shopping list /ˈ.. ˌ./ *n.* [C] a list of things, especially food, that you need to buy

shopping mall /ˈ.. ˌ./ *n.* [C] a large, specially built covered area where there are a lot of stores; MALL —see picture on page 430

shopping pla·za /ˈ.. ˌ../ *n.* [C] a row of stores built together with an area for parking cars in the front; STRIP MALL

shopping spree /ˈ.. ˌ./ *n.* [C] an occasion when you buy a lot of things from a lot of stores and spend a lot of money: *She went on a shopping spree and spent over $1500 on clothes in one afternoon.*

shop stew·ard /ˌ. './ *n.* [C] a worker who is elected by members of a UNION in a factory or other business to represent them in dealing with managers

shop talk /ˈ. ./ *n.* [U] INFORMAL conversation about your work, which other people may find boring

shop·worn /ˈʃɑpwɔrn/ *adj.* **1** something that is shopworn is slightly damaged or dirty because it has been in a store for a long time **2** an idea that is shopworn is not interesting anymore because it has been discussed many times before

shore¹ /ʃɔr/ *n.* **1** [C,U] the land along the edge of a s w large area of water, such as an ocean or lake: *We* ₃ *could see a boat about a mile from shore.* | *a resort on the shores of Lake Michigan* | *We only had a couple of hours on shore* (=away from a ship). —see picture on page 428 **2 these/American/our etc. shores** ESPECIALLY LITERARY a particular country that has a border on the ocean: *It was the first college founded on these shores.* —see also ASHORE, OFFSHORE, ONSHORE

USAGE NOTE: SHORE

WORD CHOICE: shore, bank, coast, seashore, beach
The usual word for the land at the edge of an ocean or lake is **shore**: *At night he would stand on the shore and gaze out to sea.* | *There was a little cabin on the opposite shore.* The edges of a river are its **banks**. When you are talking about a country, or a large area of a country, you call the land next to the ocean the **coast**: *Spain's Atlantic coast* | *I could tell from his clothes that he was from the West Coast.* **Seashore** is similar in meaning to

S

coast, and is used especially in the names of places: *Point Reyes National Seashore.* A **beach** is part of the **shore**, usually covered with sand or small smooth stones, where you go for pleasure: *In summer, my mother used to take me to the beach.* | *They walked hand in hand along the beach.*

shore² *v.*

shore sth ↔ **up** *phr. v.* [T] **1** to help or support something that is likely to fail or is not working well: *Russian leaders have made attempts to shore up the struggling economy.* **2** to support a wall with large pieces of wood, metal etc. to stop it from falling down: *Brick buildings must be shored up within four years to prevent serious earthquake damage.*

shore leave /'. ./ *n.* [U] a period of time that a SAILOR is allowed to spend on land, away from their work: *The crew members were on shore leave in New York.*

shore·line /'ʃɔrlaɪn/ *n.* [C,U] the land at the edge of a lake, river, ocean etc.: *The reeds grow along a 50-mile stretch of shoreline.*

shorn /ʃɔrn/ *v.* the past participle of SHEAR

short¹ /ʃɔrt/ *adj.*
1 length/height/distance measuring a small amount in distance, length, or height: *It's a short drive from the airport.* | *a short skirt* | *The yard is surrounded by a short hedge.* | *Anita had her hair cut short.* —opposite LONG¹ (1)
2 time **a)** happening or continuing for only a little time: *a short pause in the conversation* | *A short while later, the doorbell rang.* | *I've just been living here a short time.* | *Ken gave a short speech at the award ceremony.* | *Both her parents died within a short space of time.* **b)** happening or seeming to happen for less time than usual: *Today's meeting should be fairly short.* | *Winter is coming, and the days are getting shorter.* —opposite LONG¹ (2)
3 person of less than average height: *Brad is fairly short and stocky.*
4 book/name/list etc. a short piece of writing or name etc. does not have many words or details in it: *a short novel* —see also SHORT STORY —opposite LONG¹ (6)
5 be short (of sth) to not have enough of something that you need, especially when you need a particular amount more: *Can you lend me a couple of dollars? I'm still a little short.* | *The Democrats are three votes short of a majority in the Senate.* | *Jill dropped out of college two credits short of graduation.*
6 just short of sth also a little short of sth a little less than something: *The total cost will be just short of $17 million.*
7 be short on sth to have less of something than you should have: *Sometimes I think he's a little short on common sense.* | *The mayor's speech was short on specific policies and long on colorful phrases.*
8 time is short used to say that there is probably not enough time to do what you need to do: *Let's get to work – time's getting short.*
9 on short notice with very little warning that something is going to happen: *Yolanda had to fly to New York on very short notice.*
10 in the short term/run during the period of time that is not very far into the future: *These measures may save some money in the short term, but we'll just end up spending more later.* —see also SHORT-TERM
11 be in short supply if something is in short supply, there is not enough of it available: *Fresh fruit was in very short supply.*
12 short and sweet not taking a long time, and better or less boring than you expect: *They won't listen to a long lecture, so just keep it short and sweet.*
13 short of breath unable to breathe easily, especially because of being unhealthy
14 in short order in a short time and without delay: *The bombers destroyed the enemy's camp in short order.*
15 make short work of sth to finish something quickly and easily, especially a meal or a job: *Computers can make short work of complex calculations.*

16 be short for sth to be a shorter way of saying a name: *Her name is Alex, short for Alexandra.*
17 nothing/little short of sth used to emphasize that something is very good, very surprising etc.: *Dana's recovery seemed nothing short of a miracle.* | *His performance was little short of amazing.*
18 give sb/sth short shrift to not give much attention or sympathy to someone: *Her suggestions were given short shrift by the chairman.*
19 have a short temper/fuse to get angry very easily
20 draw/get the short straw also get the short end of the stick to be given something difficult or bad to do, especially when other people have been given something better
21 life's too short (to do sth) SPOKEN used to say that something is too unimportant to worry about or spend time on: *Don't worry about it. Life's too short to dwell on little mistakes.*
22 vowel TECHNICAL short vowels in English are the sounds of a in "bat," e in "bet," i in "bit," o in "box," and u in "but"
23 be short with sb to speak to someone using very few words, in a way that seems impolite or unfriendly: *Sorry I was short with you on the phone this morning.* —**shortness** *n.* [U]

short² *adv.* **1** short of (doing) sth SENTENCE ADVERB without actually doing something: *Short of selling the house, I don't know how we're going to get that amount of money.* **2** 3 feet/5 miles etc. short of sth without reaching a place you are trying to get to, because you are still a particular distance from it: *The plane touched down 200 yards short of the runway.* **3** short (of sth) without enough of something that you need, especially when you need a particular amount more: *The documentary ends in 1975, over a decade short of the end of the Cold War.* **4** be running short (of/on sth) if you are running short of something, or if something is running short, it is being used up and there will soon not be enough left: *Many stores are running short on bottled water.* | *Our supply of firewood was running short.* | *Let's go – time's running short.* **5** fall short of sth to be less than the result, level, or standard that you expect, or to fail to achieve something you are hoping for: *The results fell far short of our expectations.* **6** stop short of doing sth to almost do something but decide against actually doing it: *Paula stopped just short of calling me a thief.* **7** cut sth short to suddenly bring something to an end before it is completely finished: *His death at the age of 38 cut short a brilliant career.* **8** come up short to be in a situation in which you do not have enough of something that you need, or in which you are not successful: *We've been to the state tournament four times, but we've come up short every time.* **9** cut sb short to stop someone before they have finished speaking, by interrupting them: *I was halfway through my explanation when Walter cut me short.* **10** stop short to suddenly stop speaking or stop what you are doing, for example because something has surprised you or you have just thought of something: *At the crest of the hill, she stopped short as she read a warning sign next to the trail.*

short³ *n.* **1** shorts [plural] **a)** short pants ending at or above the knees: *a pair of tennis shorts* **b)** men's underwear; BOXER SHORTS: *He came to the door in his shorts.* **2** in short used when you want to say, in just a few words, what is the most important point about a situation: *In short, the project is just too expensive.* **3** for short as a shorter way of saying a name: *His name's Maximilian, but we just call him Max for short.* **4** [C] INFORMAL a short movie shown before the main movie in a theater, especially in past times **5** [C] INFORMAL a SHORT CIRCUIT: *There must be a short in the system.* —see also the long and the short of it (LONG¹ (19))

short⁴ *v.* INFORMAL **1** [I,T] also short out to SHORT-CIRCUIT, or make something do this: *The fire was caused by a toaster that shorted out.* **2** [T] to give someone less of something than they should receive: *Customers were being shorted about two ounces per glass of beer.*

short·age /ˈʃɔrtɪdʒ/ *n.* [C,U] a situation in which there is not enough of something that people need: [+ of] *a severe shortage of skilled labor* | **water/oil/food etc. shortage** *water shortages in the summer*

short·bread /ˈʃɔrtˌbrɛd/ *n.* [U] a hard, sweet cookie made with a lot of butter

short·cake /ˈʃɔrtˌkeɪk/ *n.* [U] cake over which a sweet fruit mixture is poured: *strawberry shortcake*

short-change /ˌ. ˈ./ *v.* [T often passive] **1** to treat someone unfairly by not giving them what they deserve: *Fans felt they had been short-changed when the band only played for half an hour.* **2** to give back too little money to someone who has paid for something with more money than was needed

short cir·cuit /ˌ. ˈ../ *n.* [C] the failure of an electrical system caused by bad wires or a fault in a connection in the wires

short-cir·cuit /ˌ. ˈ../ *v.* **1** [I, T] to have a short circuit or cause a short circuit in something **2** [T] to get something done without going through the usual long methods: *You can short-circuit all the complicated messages by pressing 0.*

short·com·ing /ˈʃɔrtˌkʌmɪŋ/ *n.* [C usually plural] a fault in someone's character or abilities, or in a product, system etc., that makes something less successful or effective than it should be: *He bravely acknowledged his own personal shortcomings.* | [+ in/of] *The inspection revealed some serious shortcomings in our safety procedures.*

short·cut, short cut /ˈʃɔrtˌkʌt/ *n.* [C] **1** a quicker more direct way of going somewhere than the usual one: *Carlos decided to take a shortcut home across the field.* **2** a quicker way of doing something: [+ to] *There aren't really any shortcuts to learning English.*

short·en /ˈʃɔrtn/ *v.* [I,T] to make something shorter, or to become shorter: *The new procedure could shorten hospital stays by two to three days.* | *The plane's wings can shorten for a jet-boosted takeoff.* —opposite LENGTHEN

short·en·ing /ˈʃɔrtn-ɪŋ, -nɪŋ/ *n.* [U] butter, LARD or solid fat made from vegetable oil that you mix with flour when making cookies, PASTRY etc.

short·fall /ˈʃɔrtfɔl/ *n.* [C] the difference between the amount you have and the amount you need or expect: *Government aides predicted a $4 billion budget shortfall for this year.* | [+ in/of] *a shortfall in world food supplies*

short·hand /ˈʃɔrthænd/ *n.* [U] **1** a fast method of writing that uses special signs or shorter forms to represent letters, words, and phrases: *The notes from the meeting were written in shorthand.* —compare LONGHAND **2** a shorter but sometimes less clear way of saying something: [be shorthand for sth] *"SRS" is auto-industry shorthand for "supplemental restraint system," or what we know as an airbag* | *Over the years, the phrase became a shorthand way of saying that someone wasn't qualified for the job.*

short·hand·ed /ˌʃɔrtˈhændɪd/ *adj.* having fewer helpers or workers than you need: *Dave's been working long hours because they're shorthanded at the plant.*

short-haul /ˈ. ./ *adj.* a short-haul aircraft or flight travels a fairly short distance —compare LONG-HAUL

short·ie /ˈʃɔrti/ *n.* INFORMAL **1** a shortie coat, JACKET, skirt etc. is one that is shorter than the usual length **2** also **shortie pajamas** [plural] a set of clothes consisting of a shirt and a pair of short pants, for a woman to wear in bed —see also SHORTY

short list /ˈ. ./ *n.* [C] a list of the most appropriate people for a job, chosen from all the people who were considered: *Weber's name was on the short list of candidates for the superintendent's job.*

short-lived /ˌʃɔrtˈlɪvd/ *adj.* continuing for only a short time: *Our happiness was short-lived.*

short·ly /ˈʃɔrtli/ *adv.* **1** soon: *Ms. Jones will be back shortly.* | *shortly before/after The accident happened shortly before noon.* **2** speaking in an impatient, unfriendly way: *"I've already told them that," Jim said shortly.*

short-or·der cook /ˌ. ˌ.. ˈ./ *n.* [C] someone in a restaurant kitchen who makes the food that can be prepared easily or quickly

short-range /ˌ. ˈ.◂/ *adj.* [only before noun] **1** designed to travel or operate only within a short distance: *a short-range nuclear missile* **2** short-range plan/goal/forecast etc. relating only to the period that is not very far into the future: *We are working to improve the accuracy of our short-range predictions.*

short ribs /ˈ. ./ *n.* [plural] a piece of meat from a cow that includes part of the bones that go around its chest

short sell·ing /ˈ. ˌ../ *n.* [U] the practice of selling STOCKS, currencies (CURRENCY) etc. immediately after buying them, and then buying them back again later, when the price has become lower, in order to make a profit

short-sheet /ˌ. ˈ., ˈ. ./ *v.* [T] to fold the top sheet on a bed so that no one can get into it, as a trick

short·sight·ed, short-sighted /ˌʃɔrtˈsaɪtɪd◂/ *adj.* **1** not considering the possible effects in the future of something that seems to save time, money, or effort now: *The company has a shortsighted policy of letting managers retire early.* **2** NEARSIGHTED —**shortsightedly** *adv.* —**shortsightedness** *n.* [U]

short-staffed /ˌ. ˈ.◂/ *adj.* [not before noun] having fewer than the usual or necessary number of workers: *The nursing home is so short-staffed that most nurses are working 12 hours a day.*

short·stop /ˈʃɔrtstɑp/ *n.* [C] the player on a baseball team who tries to stop any balls that are hit between second and third BASE² (9)

short sto·ry /ˌ. ˈ../ *n.* [C] a short written story about imaginary situations, usually containing only a few characters

short-tem·pered /ˌ. ˈ..◂/ *adj.* easily becoming angry or impatient: *He tends to be very short-tempered when he's hungry.*

short-term /ˌ. ˈ.◂/ *adj.* [usually before noun] continuing for only a short time, or relating only to the period that is not very far into the future: *Some of the apartments are available for short-term rentals.* | *short-term economic forecasts* —opposite LONG-TERM

short·wave, short wave /ˈʃɔrtweɪv/ *n.* [U] radio broadcasting on waves of less than 60 meters in length, which can be sent around the world —see also LONG WAVE, MEDIUM WAVE

short·y /ˈʃɔrti/ *n.* [C usually singular] SPOKEN, OFFENSIVE someone who is not very tall

Sho·sho·ne /ʃoʊˈʃoʊni/ *n.* a group of Native American tribes from the southeastern region of the U.S. —**Shoshone** *adj.*

Shos·ta·ko·vich /ˌʃɑstəˈkoʊvɪtʃ/, **Dmi·tri** /dɪˈmitri/ (1906–1975) a Russian musician who wrote CLASSICAL music

shot¹ /ʃɑt/ *n.*

1 **gun** an act of firing a gun: *The first shot missed Randy's head by just a few inches.* | *He quickly fired three shots.* | *Someone took a shot at her as she was getting out of her car.*

2 **sound** [C] the sound of a gun being fired: *Where were you when you heard the shot?*

3 **sports** [C] an attempt to throw, kick, or hit the ball toward the place where you can gain points, especially in basketball, tennis, HOCKEY, or SOCCER: *Shaw made the shot and turned to run down the court.*

4 **photograph** [C] a photograph of a particular thing, view, person etc.: [+ of] *Al got some good shots of the parade as it went past.*

5 **movie/tv** [C] a continuous view of something in a movie or television program, that is produced by having the camera in a particular position: *In the opening shot, we see Travolta's feet walking down the sidewalk.*

6 **attempt** [C] an attempt to do something or achieve something: [+ at] *This will be his second shot at the championship.* | *take/have a shot (at sth) Rhonda was willing to take a shot at singing on stage.*

7 **medicine** [C] an amount of a medicine that is put into your body with a needle, or the act of doing this:

*You should **have a** tetanus **shot** every ten years or so.*
8 `drink` [C] a small amount of a strong alcoholic drink: [+ of] *He poured himself another shot of whiskey.* —see picture at GLASS
9 `bullets` [U] **a)** small metal balls that are shot, many at a time, from a SHOTGUN **b)** OLD USE large metal balls that are shot from a CANNON¹
10 a good/bad etc. shot someone who can shoot a gun well, badly etc.: *Sgt. Cooper is an excellent shot.*
11 `heavy ball` [C] a heavy metal ball that competitors try to throw as far as possible in the sport of the SHOT PUT
12 a shot in the dark an attempt to guess something without having any facts or definite ideas: *My answer to the last question was a complete shot in the dark.*
13 `remark` [C] an angry remark: *As Eve was leaving, she couldn't resist a **parting shot** at Brian: "I never loved you anyway!"* | *His jokes were generally well-chosen, except for one **cheap shot** (=a rude remark that is not necessary) about short people.*
14 big shot INFORMAL an important or powerful person, especially in business: *a meeting of insurance-industry big shots*
15 a shot in the arm something that makes you more confident or more successful: *The new factory will give the local economy a real shot in the arm.*
16 like a shot if you do something like a shot, you do it very quickly and eagerly: *She slammed the phone down and was out of the room like a shot.*
17 a 10-to-1/50-to-1 etc. shot a horse, dog etc. in a race, whose chances of winning are expressed as numbers that show the ODDS —see also **call the shots** (CALL¹ (12)), **not by a long shot** (LONG¹ (13)), MUG SHOT

shot² *adj.* [not before noun] **1 be shot** SPOKEN to be in bad condition after being used too much or treated badly: *My back tires are shot.* | *I used to be able to sing pretty well, but now my voice is all **shot to hell**.* **2 be shot through with sth** FORMAL **a)** if a piece of cloth is shot through with a color, it has very small threads of that color woven into it: *fine silk shot through with gold threads* **b)** to have a lot of a particular quality or feeling: *All the stories were shot through with Hurley's dry, gentle humor.*

shot³ *v.* the past tense and participle of shoot

shot·gun /ˈʃɑt¬gʌn/ *n.* [C] **1** a long gun that fires a lot of small round bullets and that is held to your shoulder to fire, used especially for killing birds or animals **2 ride/call shotgun** SLANG to ride in the front seat of a car next to the driver, or to say you want to do this: *My kids always argue over who gets to ride shotgun.*

shotgun wed·ding also **shotgun mar·riage** /ˌ.. ˈ../ *n.* [C] a wedding that has to take place immediately because the woman is going to have a baby

shot put /ˈ. ./ *n.* **the shot put** a sports competition in which you throw a heavy metal ball as far as you can —**shot putter** *n.* [C] *an Olympic shot putter*

should /ʃəd; *strong* ʃʊd/ *modal verb negative short form* **shouldn't 1** used when giving or asking for advice or an opinion: *The city should clean the streets more often.* | *You should have called me right away.* | *Children shouldn't take candy from strangers.* | *What should I do?* **2** used to say that you expect something to happen or be true: *It should be a nice day tomorrow.* | *They should be here by 8:00.* **3 should it rain/should there be a problem etc.** FORMAL if it rains, if there is a problem etc.: *Should you encounter any difficulties, do not hesitate to call us.* **4 I should think/hope** SPOKEN used to show a strong reaction to something, based on what you think is correct or morally right: *"I wasn't going to give her any extra help." " I should think not, after the way she treated you last time." | "My new car is really nice." "Well, I should hope so, considering how much you paid for it!"* **5 I should think (that)...** FORMAL, SPOKEN used to say what you believe or expect to be true or correct: *I should think he'd be grateful for some time off.* **6 what should happen but/who should appear but**

etc. OLD-FASHIONED OR HUMOROUS used to show that you were surprised when something happened, a particular person appeared etc.: *Just then, who should appear but old St. Nicholas himself!*

should·a /ˈʃʊdə/ *v.* SPOKEN, NONSTANDARD a way of saying "should have"

shoul·der¹ /ˈʃoʊldɚ/ *n.*
1 `body part` [C] one of the two parts of the body at each side of the neck where the arm is connected: *Ben put his arm around Kari's shoulders.* | *When we asked Mike about it, he just **shrugged his shoulders** (=raised his shoulders to show that he did not know or care).* —see picture at BODY
2 watch/look/read over sb's shoulder to stand behind someone and look at, read etc. something in front of them, sometimes so that you can criticize it: *I can't work at the computer when somebody is watching over my shoulder.*
3 `clothes` [C] the part of a piece of clothing that covers your shoulder: *a jacket with padded shoulders*
4 `road` [C usually singular] an area of ground beside a road where drivers can stop their cars if they are having trouble: *Several cars with their hoods up were on the shoulder.*
5 a shoulder to cry on if you need a shoulder to cry on, you want someone to listen to your problems and give you sympathy: *If you ever need a shoulder to cry on, just call me.*
6 `meat` [C,U] the upper part of the front leg of an animal that is used for meat: *a pork shoulder roast*
7 stand/walk etc. shoulder to shoulder to stand, walk etc. very close together in a row
8 shoulder to shoulder (with sb) together, in order to achieve the same thing: *They were working shoulder to shoulder with local residents.*
9 on sb's shoulders if a difficult or unpleasant responsibility is on someone's shoulders, they are the person that has that responsibility: *The blame rests squarely on Jim's shoulders.* —see also **have a chip on your shoulder** (CHIP¹ (5)), **give sb/ sth the cold shoulder** (COLD¹ (9)), **head and shoulders above the rest/others** (HEAD¹ (47)), **rub shoulders with sb** (RUB¹ (6)), -SHOULDERED

shoulder² *v.* **1** [T] **shoulder a responsibility/duty/ cost etc.** to accept a difficult or unpleasant responsibility, duty etc.: *Most of the cost was shouldered by a private corporation.* **2** [T] to lift something onto your shoulder to carry it: *He shouldered his ax and began walking into the woods.* **3 shoulder your way through/into etc.** to move through a large crowd of people by pushing with your shoulder: *She shouldered her way through the onlookers.*

shoulder bag /ˈ.. ˌ./ *n.* [C] a bag or PURSE that you use for carrying things, that hangs from a long STRAP over your shoulder

shoulder blade /ˈ.. ˌ./ *n.* [C] one of the two flat bones on each side of your back —see picture at SKELETON

-shouldered /ˈʃoʊldɚd/ [in adjectives] **broad-shouldered/square-shouldered/round-shouldered etc.** having shoulders that have a particular size or shape

shoulder-high /ˌ.. ˈ.◂/ *adj.* as high as your shoulder: *a shoulder-high hedge*

shoulder-length /ˈ.. ˌ./ *adj.* **shoulder-length** hair hangs down to your shoulders

shoulder pad /ˈ.. ˌ./ *n.* [C usually plural] a thick flat piece of material that is attached under the shoulder of a piece of clothing to make your shoulders look bigger

shoulder strap /ˈ.. ˌ./ *n.* [C] a long narrow piece of material that goes over the shoulder on a piece of women's clothing or on a bag etc.

should·n't /ˈʃʊdnt/ *v.* the short form of "should not": *You shouldn't have told her.*

shouldst /ʃʊdst/ *v.* OLD USE OR BIBLICAL the second person singular form of the verb "should"

should've /ˈʃʊdəv/ *v.* the short form of "should have": *Dana should've come with us.*

shout¹ /ʃaʊt/ *v.* **1** [I,T] to say something very loudly: *You don't need to shout. I'm standing right here.* | *"Get out of the way!" she shouted.* | [+ for] *We could hear them shouting for help.* | [+ at] *The men shouted* at them to stay away. | [**shout sth at sb**] *He was shouting obscenities at the kids next door.* **2 shout sth from the rooftops** to tell everyone about something, because you want them to know about it: *He felt as though he wanted to shout the good news from the rooftops.*

shout sb ↔ **down** *phr. v.* T] to shout in order to prevent someone from being heard: *Some of the speakers were shouted down by the crowd.*

shout sth ↔ **out** *phr. v.* [T] to say something suddenly in a loud voice: *Several students shouted out the answer.*

shout² *n.* **1** [C] a loud call expressing anger, pain, excitement etc.: *Lisa's voice rose to a shout.* | *Mindy gave a little* **shout** *when her name was called.* | **a shout of joy/delight/pain** etc. *The news was greeted with shouts of excitement.* **2 give sb a shout** SPOKEN to go and find someone and tell them something: *Give me a shout when you're ready to go.* **3 send a shout out to sb** SLANG to say hello to someone you know when you are on the radio or TV

shove¹ /ʃʌv/ *v.* **1** [I,T] to push someone or something, in a rough or careless way, using your hands or shoulders: *The officer removed Schultz' handcuffs and shoved him into a cell.* | *People were* **pushing and shoving** *at the barriers to get a better view.* **2** [T always + adv./prep.] to put something somewhere carelessly or without thinking about it much: [**shove sth into/under** etc.] *Amy just shoved everything under the bed.* | *He shoved a handful of popcorn into his mouth.* **3 shove it/sth** used to tell someone in a very rude way that you do not want something and that you are very angry: *Tell him he can shove his stupid $5.00-an-hour job.* | *For all I care, Brad can take that engagement ring and shove it.*

shove sb **around** *phr. v.* [T] INFORMAL to treat someone in a rude way, especially by giving them orders: *Pretty soon, they won't be able to shove me around anymore.*

shove off *phr. v.* [I] **1** INFORMAL to go away: *If those guys are still there, tell them to shove off.* **2** to push a boat away from the land, usually with a pole

shove² *n.* [C] a strong push: *Give the door a good shove – it might open.* —see also **if/when push comes to shove** (PUSH² (3))

shov·el¹ /ˈʃʌvəl/ *n.* [C] **1** a tool used for digging or moving soil, snow etc., that has a rounded blade and a long handle —compare SPADE (1) **2** a part of a large vehicle or machine used for moving or digging soil

shovel² *v.* **shoveled, shoveling** also **shovelled, shovelling 1 a)** [I,T] to lift and move soil, snow etc. with a shovel: *They shoveled dirt back into the grave.* **b)** [T] to make a surface clean by using a shovel: **shovel the driveway/sidewalk** etc. *Chris, I asked you two days ago to shovel the front walk.* **2 shovel sth into/onto** etc. **sth** to put something into a place quickly: *He was shoveling spaghetti into his mouth.*

shov·el·ful /ˈʃʌvəlˌfʊl/ *n.* [C] the amount of soil, snow etc. that you can carry on a shovel

_{S W
1 1} **show¹** /ʃoʊ/ *v.* past tense **showed** past participle **shown**

1 make sth clear [T] to provide facts or information that make it clear that something is true or that something exists: *The latest figures show a rise in unemployment.* | [**show (that)**] *Studies have shown that consumers are buying more organic produce.* | [**show how/what** etc.] *Applicants must show how their qualifications make them suitable for the job.* | [**be shown to do sth**] *Red wine has been shown to reduce the risk of heart disease.* —see Usage Note at LEARN

2 information/numbers [T] **a)** if a picture, map etc. shows something, you can see it in the picture, on the map etc.: *Fig. 3 shows the average monthly rainfall in Miami.* **b)** if a clock or other measuring instrument shows a time, a number etc., you can see that time etc. on it: *When Gretzky scored, the clock showed 1:22.*

3 feelings/qualities [T] to let your feelings, attitudes, or personal qualities be clearly seen in the way you behave, the way you look etc.: *I wish she would show some consideration for other people.* | *Mark isn't afraid to show his feelings.* | *Martha's*

short response clearly showed her displeasure. | [**show how/what** etc.] *All right. Show us how tough you are.*

4 let sb see [T] to let someone see something, for example by holding it out so that they can look at it: [**show sb sth**] *Billy showed us the scar from his operation.* | [**show sth to sb**] *You have to show your ticket to the woman at the gate.*

5 explain sth [T] to tell someone how to do something, by explaining it to them, often by doing it yourself so that they can see you: [**show sb sth**] *Show her the right way to do it.* | *My grandma showed me* **how** *to make cornbread.*

6 show signs of sth used to say that something is starting to become noticeable: *At 65, Nelson* **shows no signs** *of slowing down.* | *Data from the second quarter* **showed some signs** *of improvement.*

7 guide sb [T] to go with someone and guide them to a place: *I'll show you the master bedroom upstairs.* | [**show sb to/in/out/up**] *Carlos showed us up to a corner suite.*

8 tell sb where [T] to tell someone where a place or thing is, for example by pointing to it: *I'll show you where I work.*

9 can be seen a) [I] if something shows, it is easy to see: *Margaret's love of Italy showed in her photographs.* | *Is my slip showing?* **b)** [T] if material shows dirt or a mark, it is easy to see the dirt or mark on it: *Light-colored carpeting really shows the dirt.*

10 have something/nothing etc. **to show for sth** if you have something to show for your efforts, hard work etc., you have achieved something as a result of them: *They ended up with very little to show for their investment.*

11 movie/pictures/art a) [I] if a movie is showing in a theater or if paintings or works of art are showing in a GALLERY, you can see them there **b)** [T] if a theater shows a movie or if a GALLERY shows paintings or works of art, it makes them available for people to see —see also SHOWING (1)

12 it just shows also **it just goes to show** SPOKEN said when an event or experience you have been talking about proves something: *Then he used salt instead of sugar. It just goes to show how much men know about cooking.*

13 show a profit/loss if a company shows a profit or loss, it makes a financial profit or loss

14 show sb the door to make it clear that someone is not welcome and should leave a building: *Then one of his bodyguards showed me the door.*

15 show sb a good time HUMOROUS to take someone to a lot of social events and other types of entertainment so that they enjoy themselves: *They both said they knew how to show a girl a good time.*

16 show your true colors to behave in a way that shows what your real character is, especially if you are dishonest or not nice

17 animal [T] to put an animal into a competition with other animals

18 show your face to go somewhere, especially when there is a good reason for you not to be there or you are embarrassed about being there: *It was a dangerous place for a non-Italian to show his face.*

19 arrive [I] INFORMAL to arrive at the place where someone is waiting for you; show up: *I came to meet Hank, but he never showed.*

20 ...and it shows used to say that something, especially something bad, is very clear to see: *This is the director's first feature film, and it shows* (=it is obviously not very good).

21 show your hand to make your true power or intentions clear, especially after you have been keeping them secret: *He said that he wouldn't be bullied into showing his hand first.*

22 I'll show him/them etc. SPOKEN used to say that you will prove to someone that you are better, more effective etc. than they think you are: *Is that so? Well, I'll show them!*

23 show sb who's boss INFORMAL to prove to someone who is threatening your authority that you are more powerful than they are: *Don't let her treat you like that, Cyril. Show her who's boss.*

24 show the way if you show the way for other people, you do something new that others then try to copy: *Short hair is in again, and Johnny Depp shows the way with a cool new cut.*

25 |horse race| [I] if a horse shows in a race, it finishes third

show sb ↔ **around** (sth) *phr. v.* [T] to go around a place with someone when they first arrive there, to show them what is interesting, useful etc.: *Tim showed us around while we were waiting for Mike.*

show off *phr. v.* **1** [I] to try to make people admire your abilities, achievements, or possessions: *They always show off in front of the neighbors.* **2** [T **show** sth ↔ **off**] to show something to a lot of people because you are very proud of it: *Gary was looking for an opportunity to show off his boxing skills.* **3** [T **show** sth ↔ **off**] if one thing shows off something else, it makes the other thing look especially attractive: *She wore a cream-colored dress that showed off her tan.*

show up *phr. v.* **1** [I] to arrive, especially at the place where someone is waiting for you: *I was almost asleep when Chris finally showed up.* **2** [I] to be easy to see or notice: *The white marks really show up against the dark fabric.* | *Her tumor didn't show up on the scan.* **3** [T **show** sb ↔ **up**] to make someone feel stupid or embarrassed in public, especially by doing something better than they can do it: *Robin's not talking to me because I showed her up at racquetball.*

show² *n.*

1 |tv/radio| [C] a program on television or on the radio: *She appeared on several hit TV shows in the '70s.* —see also GAME SHOW, TALK SHOW

2 |theater/music etc.| [C] an entertaining performance, especially one that includes music, dancing, or jokes: *a Broadway show* | *Brad got tickets to the Grateful Dead show on the 12th.* | *The kids* **put on a** *puppet* **show** *in the back yard.* —see also FLOOR SHOW

3 |collection of things| [C] an occasion when a lot of similar things are brought together in one place so that people can come and look at them: **a flower/dog/cat etc. show** *Dad took us to the boat show at the civic center.* | **hold/stage a show** *The school is holding a show of students' artwork in the commons area.* —see also FASHION SHOW

4 a show of sth something that someone does in order to make a particular feeling or quality clear to someone else: *The dolphins may rub up against you as* **a show of affection.** | *In* **a show of force,** *several fighter planes flew low over the enemy's camp.* | *Demonstrators flooded the streets as* **a show of support** *for the king.*

5 make a show of sth to do something in a very clear way because you want other people do notice that you are doing it: *The government made a show of moving troops and tanks near the border.*

6 for show if something is for show, or is done for show, its main purpose is to look attractive to people: *We don't eat off those plates. They're just for show.*

7 a show of hands a vote taken by counting the raised hands of the people at a meeting, in a class etc.: *Let's see a show of hands. Who wants to go outside?*

8 run the/this show INFORMAL to be in charge of a situation: *I totally ran that show.*

9 let's get this show on the road SPOKEN used to tell people it is time to start working or start a trip

10 on show if something is on show, it is in a place where it can be seen by the public: *We have placed one of the pieces on show in the lobby.* | **be/go on show** *Her sculptures will go on show at the Electra Gallery on May 10.* —see also steal the show/scene/limelight (STEAL¹ (4))

show and tell /ˌ. . './ *n.* [U] an activity for children in which they bring an object to school and tell the other children about it: *You can take your doll to show and tell.*

show·biz /'ʃoubɪz/ *n.* [U] INFORMAL: see SHOW BUSINESS

show·boat¹ /'ʃoubout/ *v.* [I] INFORMAL to do things to try to make people notice and admire you

showboat² *n.* [C] a large river boat, usually with an engine that is run by steam, with a theater on it

show busi·ness /'. ˌ../ *n.* [U] the entertainment industry, for example television, movies, theater etc.: *He's celebrating 50 years in show business.*

show·case¹ /'ʃoukeɪs/ *n.* [C] **1** an event or situation that is designed to show the good qualities of a person, organization, product etc.: [+ **for**] *The convention is a major showcase for new software products.* **2** a glass box containing objects for people to look at in a store, at an art show etc.

showcase² *v.* [T] to show someone or something to the public in a favorable way: *Four stages will showcase the talents of Bay Area performers.*

show·down /'ʃoudaʊn/ *n.* [C usually singular] a meeting, argument, fight etc. that will settle a disagreement or competition that has continued for a long time: [+ **between/with**] *a showdown between the top two teams in the league* | *The Senate moved toward another showdown with the President over the budget.*

show·er¹ /'ʃaʊɚ/ *n.* [C]

1 |place for washing| a place where you can stand to wash your whole body with water that comes from above you: *If anybody calls, tell them I'm* **in the shower.**

2 |act of washing| an act of washing your body while standing under a shower: *You'll feel better after a nice hot shower.* | *Steve didn't even have time to* **take a shower** *this morning.*

3 |rain/snow| a short period of rain or snow: *Tomorrow's forecast calls for a few scattered showers.* | *a snow shower*

4 |things in the air| a lot of small, light things falling or appearing together: [+ **of**] *The aircraft skidded off the runway in a shower of sparks.*

5 |party| a party at which presents are given to a woman who is going to get married or have a baby: *a baby shower* | *Donna's having a* **bridal shower** *for Julie next week.*

shower² *v.* **1** [I] to wash your whole body while standing in a shower **2** [I always + adv./prep., T] to scatter a lot of small light things onto a person or place, or to be scattered in this way: *The Earth is constantly showered by rocky debris from space.* | [+ **down/over/upon**] *Confetti showered down as the crowd cheered wildly.* | [**shower** sb/sth **with** sth] *After the ceremony, the bride and groom were showered with handfuls of rice.* **3** to generously give someone a lot of things, or a large amount of something: *Medals were showered on the soldiers returning from battle.* | **shower** sb **with praise/admiration/honors etc.** *Visitors to the resort are showered with attention.*

shower cap /'.. ˌ./ *n.* [C] a plastic hat that keeps your hair dry in a shower

shower gel /'.. ˌ./ *n.* [U] a type of liquid soap that you use to wash yourself in a shower

shower head /'.. ˌ./ *n.* [C] the part of a SHOWER that has many small holes in it for water to come out

show·er·y /'ʃaʊəri/ *adj.* raining frequently for short periods

show·girl /'ʃougɚl/ *n.* [C] one of a group of women who sing or dance in a musical show, usually wearing clothing decorated in bright colors, feathers, etc.

show house /'. ./ *n.* [C] a house that has been built and filled with furniture to show buyers what similar new houses look like

show·ing /'ʃouɪŋ/ *n.* **1** [C] an occasion when a movie, collection of art works etc. is shown to the public: *We went to the 7:30 showing at the theater on Third Avenue.* | [+ **of**] *This is the first major showing of Khaldei's photographs in America.* **2** [C usually singular] the level of success or failure someone is achieving in a competition, process etc.: **a good/strong/poor etc. showing** *Despite his disastrous showing in the New Hampshire primary, he is now the party's leading candidate.*

show jump·ing /'. ,../ n. [U] a sport in which horses with riders have to jump a series of fences as quickly and skillfully as possible

show·man /'ʃoʊmən/ n. plural **showmen** /-mən/ [C] someone who is good at entertaining people and getting a lot of public attention: He is a versatile performer and a born showman.

show·man·ship /'ʃoʊmən,ʃɪp/ n. [U] skill at entertaining people and getting public attention

shown /ʃoʊn/ the past participle of SHOW

show·off /'ʃoʊɔf/ n. [C] INFORMAL someone who always tries to show how smart or skillful they are so that other people will admire them

show·piece /'ʃoʊpis/ n. [C usually singular] something that is intended to show the public how good, successful etc. someone or something is: The school's showpiece is its respected teacher-training program. | He built the casino as the showpiece of his business empire.

show·place /'ʃoʊpleɪs/ n. [C] a place that someone wants people to see, because of its beauty, historical interest, etc.: They turned their home into a seven-bedroom showplace.

show·room /'ʃoʊrum/ n. [C] a large room where you can look at things that are for sale such as cars or electrical goods: a car showroom

show-stop·ping /'. ,../ adj. a show-stopping performance or song is extremely good or impressive: In some of the show-stopping solos, the dancers even danced on their hands. —**showstopper** n. [C]

show·time /'ʃoʊtaɪm/ n. 1 [C,U] the time when a movie or other type of entertainment is supposed to begin 2 [U] INFORMAL the time when an activity is supposed to begin: Okay, everybody. It's showtime!

show tri·al /'. ,../ n. [C] an unfair legal TRIAL that is organized by a government, especially a Communist one, for political reasons, not in order to find out whether someone is guilty

show tune /'. ./ n. [C] a song that is used in a MUSICAL (=play in a theater with music)

show·y /'ʃoʊi/ adj. **showier**, **showiest** very colorful, big, expensive etc., especially in a way that is meant to attract people's attention: She wore a lot of cheap, showy jewelry. | The species is distinguished by its showy white flowers. —**showily** adv. —**showiness** n. [U]

shrank /ʃræŋk/ the past tense of SHRINK

shrap·nel /'ʃræpnəl/ n. [U] small pieces of metal from a bomb, bullet etc. that are scattered when it explodes: Many civilians suffered burns and shrapnel wounds.

shred¹ /ʃrɛd/ n. 1 [C] a small thin piece that is torn or cut roughly from something: [+ of] a shred of paper | **tear/rip/cut sth to shreds** The force of the hurricane tore the boat's sails to shreds. 2 **a shred of sth** a very small amount of something: He took away her last shred of dignity. | **not a shred of proof/evidence/doubt** etc. | The police didn't have a shred of evidence (=none at all) against her. 3 **in shreds a)** torn in many places: Earl's shirt hung in shreds and one of his eyes was swollen shut. **b)** completely ruined: A series of violent attacks has left the peace talks in shreds.

shred

shred² v. **shredded, shredding** [T] 1 to cut or tear something into small thin pieces: Shred the mozzarella cheese and sprinkle it on the pizza. 2 to put a document into a shredder: He had told his secretary to shred the memo.

shred·der /'ʃrɛdɚ/ n. [C] a machine that cuts documents into long, narrow pieces so that no one can read them

shrew /ʃru/ n. [C] 1 a very small animal like a mouse with a long pointed nose 2 a woman who is

not nice and always argues and disagrees with people

shrewd /ʃrud/ adj. 1 good at judging what people or situations are really like, especially in a way that makes you successful in business, politics etc.: Kyle is a shrewd, aggressive manager. 2 well judged and likely to be right or successful: Thanks to some shrewd investments, they've got plenty of money left. —**shrewdly** adv.: They have shrewdly taken advantage of the latest trends in the market. —**shrewdness** n. [U]

shrew·ish /'ʃruɪʃ/ adj. a shrewish woman is one who always argues and disagrees with people

shriek¹ /ʃrik/ v. [I,T] to make a very high, loud sound, especially because you are excited, afraid, or angry: Anne began to shriek and jerked her arm away. | [shriek sth] Suddenly she shrieked, "You lied to me!" | **shriek with joy/pain/fright** etc. Several people in the audience shrieked with laughter.

shriek² n. [C] 1 a loud high sound that you make with your voice because you are frightened, excited, angry etc.: Then he let out a piercing shriek. | [+ of] a shriek of terror 2 a loud high sound made by an animal or a machine: The vehicles pulled over when they heard the shriek of the police siren.

shrift /ʃrɪft/ —see **give sb/sth short shrift** (SHORT¹ (18))

shrill¹ /ʃrɪl/ adj. 1 a shrill sound is very high and not nice to listen to; PIERCING: Mike could hear his aunt's shrill voice downstairs. | She gave a brief, shrill laugh. 2 shrill words express repeated, often unreasonable complaints or criticism: The media's shrill criticism of Newton has reached a new level. —**shrillness** n. [U] —**shrilly** adv.

shrill² v. ESPECIALLY LITERARY 1 [I,T] to say something in a very high voice: "Stop it!" she shrilled. 2 [I] to produce a very high sound that is not nice to listen to: The metal detector shrilled as Whitney attempted to walk through.

shrimp /ʃrɪmp/ n. [C] 1 plural **shrimp** or **shrimps** a small curved sea creature that you can eat, which has ten legs and a soft shell and turns pink when it is cooked —see picture at CRUSTACEAN 2 INFORMAL an insulting word for someone who is very small

shrimp cock·tail /ˌ. '../ n. [C,U] shrimp served with a red SAUCE, eaten before the main part of a meal

shrimp·ing /'ʃrɪmpɪŋ/ n. [U] the activity of fishing for shrimp —**shrimper** n. [C]

shrine /ʃraɪn/ n. [C] 1 a place that is connected with a religion, a holy event, or holy person, and that people visit to pray: a Shinto shrine 2 a place that people visit and respect because it is connected with a famous person or event: the Lenin shrine in Moscow 3 **a shrine to sb/sth** a place that is connected with someone or something and often has been specially decorated to honor them: Linda transformed a corner of her bedroom into a shrine to Elvis.

Shrin·er /'ʃraɪnɚ/ n. [C] someone who belongs to a secret society, in which members help each other become successful, do good things for others etc.

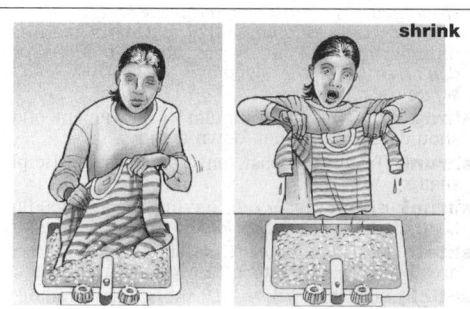
shrink

shrink¹ /ʃrɪŋk/ v. past tense **shrank** or **shrunk** past participle **shrunk** 1 [I,T] to become smaller or to make something smaller through the effects of heat or water: *My sweater shrank in the dryer.* —see also PRESHRUNK, SHRUNKEN **2** [I,T] to become smaller in amount, size, or value: *Profits have been shrinking over the last year.* | *We hope these reforms will shrink the nation's budget deficit.* **3** [I always + adv./prep.] to move back and away from something, especially because you are frightened: [+ **back/away/from**] *Paul's wife shrank away from him and told him he was disgusting.*

shrink from sth *phr. v.* [T] to avoid doing something that is difficult or that you do not want to do: *We do not intend to shrink from our fundamental responsibility.* | *Many people tend to shrink from discussing such personal issues.*

shrink² *n.* [C] INFORMAL, HUMOROUS a PSYCHIATRIST

shrink·age /'ʃrɪŋkɪdʒ/ *n.* [C] the act of shrinking, or the amount that something shrinks: *This move is intended to stop the shrinkage in the banking industry.*

shrinking vi·o·let /ˌ... '.../ *n.* [C] HUMOROUS someone who is very shy: *Maggie is definitely **no shrinking violet**.*

shrink-wrap /'. ./ *n.* [U] a type of clear plastic that is used for wrapping goods for sale —**shrink-wrapped** *adj.*

shriv·el /'ʃrɪvəl/ also **shrivel up** *v.* [I,T] **1** if something shrivels or is shriveled, it becomes smaller and its surface is covered in lines because it is very dry or old: *Why do Kate's onions grow so well, while mine shrivel and rot in the ground?* **2** to gradually become less and less or smaller and smaller, or to make something do this: *Profits have shriveled since the start of the economic crisis.* —**shriveled** *adj.*: *Avoid buying plants with yellowing leaves or shriveled stems.*

'shroom /ʃrum/ *n.* [usually plural] SLANG a MUSHROOM¹ (2)

shroud¹ /ʃraʊd/ *n.* [C] **1** a cloth that is wrapped around a dead person's body before it is buried **2** something that hides or covers something: *Smoke cast a gray shroud over the city yesterday afternoon.* | [+ **of**] *What could explain the shroud of secrecy surrounding the project?*

shroud² *v.* [T usually passive] to cover or hide something: *A thickening fog shrouded the top of the mountain.* | **be shrouded in mist/smoke** etc. *The ship was shrouded in clouds of steam and gray smoke.* **2 be shrouded in mystery/secrecy** etc. to be mysterious, secret etc.: *The rapper's murder is still shrouded in mystery.*

Shrove Tues·day /ˌʃroʊv 'tuzdi/ *n.* [C,U] the day before the beginning of the Christian period of Lent —compare ASH WEDNESDAY, MARDI GRAS

shrub /ʃrʌb/ *n.* [C] a small bush with several woody stems

shrub·ber·y /'ʃrʌbəri/ *n. plural* **shubberies** [C,U] a group of shrubs planted close together

shrug¹ /ʃrʌg/ *v.* [I,T] to raise and then lower your shoulders in order to show that you do not know something or do not care about something: *He shrugged his shoulders and went back to his work.*

shrug sth ↔ **off** *phr. v.* [T] to treat something as unimportant and not worry about it: *Many people don't recognize the symptoms of a stroke and just shrug them off.*

shrug² *n.* [C usually singular] a movement of your shoulders up and then down again

shrunk /ʃrʌŋk/ the past tense and past participle of SHRINK

shrunk·en /'ʃrʌŋkən/ *adj.* having become smaller or been made smaller: *She looked frail and shrunken.*

shtetl /'ʃtɛtl, 'ʃteɪtl/ *n.* [C] a small Jewish town or area of a city in Eastern Europe in past times

shtick, schtick /ʃtɪk/ *n.* [U] the style of humor that a particular actor or COMEDIAN typically uses

shuck /ʃʌk/ *v.* [T] **1** to remove the outer cover of a vegetable such as corn, or the shell of OYSTERS **2** also

shuck off to take off a piece of clothing: *He shucked off his wet coat and hat in the hallway.* **3** also **shuck off** to get rid of something that you do not want anymore: *Hong Kong wanted to shuck its image as a producer of cheap merchandise.*

shucks /ʃʌks/ *interjection* INFORMAL used to show you are a little disappointed or annoyed about something: *Well, shucks, why pay for one when you can just borrow mine?* —see also AW SHUCKS²

shud·der¹ /'ʃʌdə/ *v.* [I] **1** to shake for a short time because you are afraid or cold, or because you think something is disgusting: *Fred shuddered as he brought the cup to his mouth.* | [+ **at**] *Kari shuddered at the sight of the dead squirrel.* **2** if a vehicle or machine shudders, it shakes violently: *The car shuddered briefly as its engine died.* **3 I shudder to think** used to say that you do not want to think about something because it is too bad or disgusting: *I shudder to think what will happen to him now.*

shudder at sth *phr. v.* [T] to think that something is very bad or disgusting: *Citizens shuddered at the cost of the cleanup following the oil spill.*

shudder² *n.* [C usually singular] **1** a shaking movement: *"Do you think he'll come back?" she asked with a shudder.* **2 send a shudder through sb/sth** to cause someone or an organization to be afraid: *A financial crisis is sending a shudder through all levels of the church.*

shuf·fle¹ /'ʃʌfəl/ *v.* **1** [I always + adv./prep.] to walk without lifting your feet off the ground, often in a slow and awkward way: [+ **along/toward/down** etc.] *She shuffled across the floor to answer the telephone.* **2** [I,T] to move something such as papers into a different order or into different positions: *She shuffled her pile of papers, then began to speak.* | [+ **through**] *Mr. Murphy shuffled through some files in the drawer.* **3** [T] to move people around into different positions or jobs, usually within the same organization or department: [**shuffle sb around**] *Bryant has shuffled the team's starting players around several times this season.* **4** [I,T] to mix PLAYING CARDS around into a different order before playing a game with them: *Is it my turn to shuffle?* **5 shuffle your feet** to move your feet slightly, especially because you are bored or embarrassed: *Monica shuffled her feet nervously and stared at the floor.* —**shuffler** *n.* [C] —see also RESHUFFLE¹

shuffle² *n.* **1** [singular] a slow walk in which you do not lift your feet off the ground **2** [C usually singular] an act of moving things or people around to different positions: *The latest management shuffle involved the heads of sales, finance, and personnel.* **3** [C] the act of mixing cards into a different order before playing a game

shuf·fle·board /'ʃʌfəlˌbɔrd/ *n.* [U] a game played especially by passengers on ships, in which you use a long stick to push a flat round object toward an area with numbers on it

shui /ʃweɪ/ —see FENG SHUI

shun /ʃʌn/ *v.* [T] to avoid someone or something deliberately: *Wilson is a quiet man who shuns publicity.* | *When the rumors started, the children found themselves shunned by their classmates.*

shunt¹ /ʃʌnt/ *v.* [T] **1** to move someone or something to another place, especially in a way that seems unfair: [**shunt sb aside/off/around** etc.] *Students with limited English ability tend to be shunted aside into the slower classes.* **2** TECHNICAL to make something such as blood flow between two parts of the body, especially by making a special passage in a medical operation: *Blood is shunted to the liver, where it can be filtered.* **3** TECHNICAL to make electricity flow through a different path

shunt² *n.* [C] TECHNICAL **1** a small passage that a doctor puts between two parts of someone's body to let something such as blood flow between them; BYPASS **2** TECHNICAL a connection that allows electricity to flow through a different path

shush¹ /ʃʌʃ, ʃʊʃ/ *v.* [T] to tell someone to be very quiet, especially by putting your fingers against your lips or by saying "shush": *He stood up and shushed the class.*

shush² *interjection* used to tell someone, especially a child, to be quiet: *"Shush," she said, "you'll scare the birds."*

S W
1 2
shut¹ /ʃʌt/ *v. past tense and past participle* **shut** *present participle* **shutting 1** [I,T] to close something, or to become closed: *You'd better shut the window. | Did you hear the back door shut? | She lay down on the bed and shut her eyes.* —see Usage Note at OPEN² **2 shut your mouth/trap/face!** SPOKEN used to tell someone in a rude and angry way to stop talking **3 shut your eyes/ears to sth** FORMAL to deliberately refuse to notice or pay attention to something: *We must not shut our ears to the voices of suffering people.* **4 shut your ears (to sth)** to deliberately not listen to something: *Then they started talking about laxatives, and I just shut my ears.*

shut sb/sth ↔ **away** *phr. v.* [T] **a)** to put someone or something in a place away from other people where they cannot be seen **b)** **shut yourself away** to stay home or go somewhere quiet, so that you can be alone: *She shut herself away in her room to work on her novel.*

shut down *phr. v.* **1** [I,T] if a company, factory, large machine etc. shuts down or is shut down, it stops operating: *A faulty switch was causing the printing press to shut down frequently. |* [**shut** sth ↔ **down**] *Activists are fighting to shut down the nuclear processing plant.* **2** [T **shut** sb ↔ **down**] to prevent an opposing sports team or player from playing well or getting points: *The Redskins shut down three quarterbacks Sunday.*

shut off *phr. v.* **1** [I,T] if a machine, tool etc. shuts off or if you shut it off, it stops operating: *The iron shuts off automatically if it gets too hot. |* [**shut** sth ↔ **off**] *Shut your ignition off for a minute.* **2** [T **shut** sth ↔ **off**] to prevent goods or supplies from being available or being delivered: *Crews had to shut off gas service to make repairs to one of the mains.* **3 shut yourself off** to avoid meeting and talking to other people: [+ **from**] *After his wife's death, Pete shut himself off from the rest of his family.* **4 be shut off from sth** to be separated from other people or things, especially so that you are not influenced by them: *These people are completely shut off from the rest of society.* —see Usage Note at OPEN²

shut sb/sth ↔ **out** *phr. v.* [T] **1** to deliberately not let someone join in an activity or share your thoughts and feelings: *Don't just shut me out. I want to help. | Many of the working poor are being shut out of the healthcare system.* **2** to prevent someone or something from entering a place: *Heavy curtains shut out the sunlight.* **3** to stop yourself from thinking about or noticing something, so that you are not affected by it: *She could not shut out the noise of the lawnmower.* **4** to defeat an opposing sports team and prevent them from getting any points: *Colorado shut out Kansas City 3–0.*

shut up *phr. v.* **1 shut up!** SPOKEN used to tell someone rudely to stop talking: *Just shut up, you two!* **2** [I,T] INFORMAL to stop talking or be quiet, or to make someone do this [+ **about**] *I wish Ted would shut up about that stupid bike. |* [**shut** sb **up**] *Maybe this will shut her up.* **3** [T **shut** sb ↔ **up**] to keep someone in a place away from other people, and prevent them from leaving: *All the stores were closed and citizens were shut up in their houses.*

shut² *adj.* [not before noun; no comparative] not open; closed: *Make sure you keep the doors and windows shut. | He sat with his eyes tightly shut. |* **slam/bang/swing etc. shut** *She heard the cell door clang shut. |* **pull/kick/slide etc. sth shut** *Dave got in the car and pulled the door shut.* —see also **keep your mouth shut** (MOUTH¹ (2))

shut·down /'ʃʌtˌdaʊn/ *n.* [C] the act of stopping a factory, business, or piece of machinery from operating: *The strike prompted a temporary shutdown of the airline.*

shut-eye /'. ./ *n.* [U] INFORMAL sleep: **get/catch some shut-eye** *Let's try and get some shut-eye tonight.*

shut-in /'. ./ *n.* [C] someone who is sick or DISABLED and cannot leave their house very easily: *The office provides services for shut-ins and elderly people in Cook County.*

shut·off /'ʃʌtɔf/ *n.* [C,U] the act of stopping the supply of something such as gas or water, or something that can stop the supply: *A chemical leak forced the shutoff of water to two towns. | This model has an automatic shutoff for safety.*

shut·out /'ʃʌtaʊt/ *n.* [C] a sports game in which one team prevents the other from getting any points

shut·ter¹ /'ʃʌtɚ/ *n.* [C] **1** [usually plural] one of a pair of wooden or metal covers fastened to the sides of a window on the outside of a house, used either to protect the window or for decoration —see picture on page 423 **2** a part of a camera that opens for a very short time to let light onto the film —see picture at CAMERA

shutter² *v.* [T usually passive] to close a business, office etc. for a short time or permanently: *The snowstorm forced the company to shutter 100 of its stores.*

shut·ter·bug /'ʃʌtɚˌbʌg/ *n.* [C] someone who likes to take a lot of photographs

shut·tered /'ʃʌtɚd/ *adj.* with closed shutters: *Every window was shuttered along the street.*

shut·tle¹ /'ʃʌtl/ *n.* [C] **1** a SPACE SHUTTLE —see picture on page 1330 **2** an airplane, bus, or train that makes regular short trips between two places: *If I take the 6:30 shuttle, I'll be there in time for the meeting.* **3** a pointed tool used in weaving, to pass a thread over and under the threads that form the cloth

shuttle² *v.* **1** [I always + adv./prep.] to travel frequently between two places: [+ **between**] *Susan shuttles between New York and Washington for her job.* **2** [T] to move people from one place to another place that is fairly near: *Passengers were herded onto buses and shuttled to hotels downtown.*

shut·tle·cock /'ʃʌtlˌkak/ *n.* [C] a BIRDIE¹ (3)

shuttle di·plo·ma·cy /ˌ.. '.../ *n.* [U] international talks in which someone travels between countries and talks to members of the governments, for example to make a peace agreement

shy¹ /ʃaɪ/ [I] *adj.* **shier, shiest** or **shyer, shyest 1** nervous and embarrassed about talking to other people, especially people you do not know: *Carl is a very quiet, shy boy. | a shy smile | He was painfully shy* (=extremely shy) *as a teenager.* **2 sb is not shy about sth** used to say that someone is very willing to do something or get involved in something: *John has strong opinions, and he's not shy about sharing them.* **3 be shy (of sth)** to have less than a particular amount of something: *The Democrats are three votes shy of a majority. | She was one week shy of her twentieth birthday when she got married.* —**shyly** *adv.: She smiled shyly and started to blush.* —**shyness** *n.* [U] —see also CAMERA-SHY, GUN-SHY, **once bitten twice shy** (BITE¹ (18))

shy² *v.* **shies, shied, shying**

shy at sth *phr. v.* [T] if a horse shies at something, it makes a sudden movement away from it because it is frightened

shy (away) from sb/sth *phr. v.* [T] also **shy away** [I] **1** to avoid doing or dealing with something because you are not confident enough or you are worried or nervous about it: *The board members tend to shy away from controversial topics.* **2** to move away from someone avoid them because you are nervous or frightened

shy·ster /'ʃaɪstɚ/ *n.* [C] INFORMAL a dishonest person, especially a lawyer or BUSINESSMAN

Si·a·mese cat /ˌsaɪəmiz 'kæt/ *n.* [C] a type of cat that has blue eyes, short gray or brown fur, and a dark face and feet

Siamese twin /ˌsaɪəmiz 'twɪn/ *n.* [C usually plural] one of two people who are born joined to each other

Si·be·ri·a /saɪ'bɪriə/ a very large area in Russia, between the Ural Mountains and the Pacific Ocean

sib·i·lant¹ /'sɪbələnt/ *adj.* FORMAL making or being a sound such as "s" or "sh": *sibilant whispers*

sibilant² *n.* [C] TECHNICAL a sibilant sound such as "s" or "sh" in English

S

sib·ling /'sɪblɪŋ/ n. [C] **1** FORMAL a brother or sister **2 sibling rivalry** competition between brothers and sisters for their parents' attention or love

sib·yl /'sɪbəl/ n. [C] one of a group of women in ancient Greece and Rome who were thought to know the future

sic[1] /sɪk/ adv. FORMAL used in PARENTHESES or BRACKETS after a word in writing that you have copied from another document in order to show that you know the word was not spelled or used correctly: *Jenna's letter began, "Dear Santa Clouse [sic], ..."*

sic[2] v. **sicced, siccing** [T] **1 sic sb on sb** to tell a dog or person to attack someone: *He sicced his dog on me.* **2 sic 'em!** SPOKEN used to tell a dog to attack someone

Si·ci·ly /'sɪsəli/ an island in the Mediterranean Sea, which is part of Italy and is close to Italy's most southern point —**Sicilian** /sɪ'sɪliən/ n., adj.

S W
1 2
sick[1] /sɪk/ adj. **1** not healthy suffering from a disease or illness: *Maria can't come in today because she's sick.* | *Dan got* (=became) *really sick when we were on vacation.* | *Three employees were out sick* (=not at work because they were sick) *yesterday.* | *Ron was sick as a dog* (=very sick) *all week.* | *Leslie called in sick* (=telephoned to say she would not come to work because she was sick) *today.* —compare ILL[1] **2 be sick** to bring food up from your stomach through your mouth; VOMIT: *I think I'm going to be sick.* —compare **throw up** (THROW[1]) **3 feel sick** also **be/feel sick to your stomach** to feel as if you are going to VOMIT: *I felt sick after I ate all that candy.* **4 be sick (and tired) of** sth also **be sick to death of** sth to be angry and bored with something that has been happening for a long time: *I am sick and tired of her excuses.* | *They must be sick of living in that crummy little apartment.* **5 make me/you sick** SPOKEN **a)** to make you feel very angry: *It's enough to make you sick, the way they treat old people.* **b)** SPOKEN, HUMOROUS used to say that someone has more beauty, wealth etc. than anyone deserves to have: *He's so cute it makes me sick.* **6 be worried sick** also **be sick with worry** to be extremely worried: *Why didn't you call us? We were worried sick about you!* **7** strange/cruel **a)** someone who is sick does things that are strange and cruel, and seems mentally ill: *One of the suspect's neighbors described him as "a very sick man."* | *This letter must be the product of a sick mind.* **b)** sick stories, jokes etc. deal with death and suffering in a cruel or disgusting way: *Is this somebody's idea of a sick joke?* **8 sick at heart** very unhappy, upset, or disappointed about something: *All the cruelty and injustice made her sick at heart.* —see also CARSICK, HOMESICK, SEASICK, **take ill/sick** (TAKE[1] (39))

sick[2] n. **the sick** [plural] people who are sick: *She devoted herself to the care of the sick and poor.*

sick·bay /'sɪkbeɪ/ n. [C] a room on a ship, at a military BASE etc. where there are beds for people who are sick

sick·bed /'sɪkbɛd/ n. [C usually singular] the bed where a sick person is lying: *He responded in a message from his sickbed.*

sick build·ing syn·drome /ˌ. ˌ.. '.., ˌ. '.. ˌ../ n. [U] a condition in which chemicals and GERMs stay in the air in an office building and make the people who work there sick

sick day /'. ./ n. [C] a day that you are allowed to spend away from work because you are sick: *I haven't taken any sick days this year.*

sick·en /'sɪkən/ v. **1** [T] to make you feel shocked and angry, because you strongly disapprove of something: *The thought of such cruelty sickened her.* **2** [I,T] to become very sick, or to make someone sick: *A gas attack in the main train station sickened hundreds of people.* | *The buffalo sickened and died in captivity.*

sicken of sth phr. v. [T] FORMAL to lose your desire for something or your interest in it: *She soon sickened of City Hall politics and moved on.*

sick·en·ing /'sɪkənɪŋ/ adj. **1** very shocking, annoying, or upsetting; DISGUSTING: *The police described it as a sickening racial attack.* **2** disgusting, and making you feel as if you want to VOMIT: *the sickening smell of rotting meat* **3 a sickening thud/crash etc.** a sound that is not nice to listen to, and that makes you think someone has been injured or something has been broken: *I heard the sickening whack of clubs on their skulls.* —**sickeningly** adv.

sick·ie /'sɪki/ n. [C] INFORMAL, HUMOROUS a SICKO

sick·le /'sɪkəl/ n. [C] a tool with a blade in the shape of a hook, used for cutting wheat or long grass

sick leave /'. ./ n. [U] time that you are allowed to spend away from work because you are sick

sickle cell a·ne·mi·a /ˌ... .'..ˌ../ n. [U] a serious illness that mainly affects people whose families originally came from Africa, in which the blood cells change shape, causing weakness and fever

sick·ly /'sɪkli/ adj. **1** weak, unhealthy, and often sick: *Daryl was a pale, sickly child.* **2** a sickly smell, taste etc. is disgusting and makes you feel sick —**sickly** adv.: *the sickly sweet smell of cheap perfume*

sick·ness /'sɪknɪs/ n. **1** [U] the state of being sick: *Several crew members had to leave due to sickness and exhaustion.* —see Usage Note at DISEASE **2 motion/car/air sickness** a feeling that some people get while traveling, that they are about to VOMIT —see also ALTITUDE SICKNESS, MORNING SICKNESS, SLEEPING SICKNESS **3** [C] a particular illness: *Many veterans claim the army has not compensated them for war-related sicknesses.* **4** [C,U] the serious problems and weaknesses of a social, political, or economic system: *They said that the murders were a sign of a new, terrible sickness in our society.*

sick·o /'sɪkoʊ/ n. [C] INFORMAL someone who gets pleasure from things that most people find disgusting or upsetting: *What kind of sicko would write something like that?*

sick·out /'sɪkaʊt/ n. [C] an organized protest by workers at a company who say they are sick and stay home on the same day

sick pay /'. ./ n. [U] money paid by an employer to a worker who cannot work because of illness

sick·room /'sɪk-rum/ n. [C] a room where someone who is very sick lies in bed

Sid·dhar·tha /sɪ'dɑrθə, -tə/ the original name of the Buddha

side[1] /saɪd/ n. [C]
S W
1 1
1 part of an area one of the two areas that are on either the left or the right of an imaginary line, or on either the left or the right of a border, wall, river etc.: *The south side of town is pretty run down.* | *Mike always puts his feet on my side of the bed.* | *Cars pulled over to one side to let the ambulance past.* | **the far/other side** (=the area farthest from you or across from you) | **the right-hand/left-hand side** *Assets are listed on the left-hand side of the chart.* **2** next to [usually singular] the place or area directly next to someone or something, on the right or the left: *Dick selected an armchair to the left side of the desk.* | *She faced the reporters with her husband at her side* (=standing next to her). | *Two large screens stood on either side* (=one on the left side and one on the right side) *of the stage.* —see also **not leave sb's side** (LEAVE[1] (33)) **3 side by side a)** next to each other: *They lay side by side on the couch until Sonia fell asleep.* **b)** if people live, work etc. side by side, they do it together, have a good relationship and help each other: *Doctors and scientists are working side by side to find a cure for AIDS.* **c)** if two things exist side by side, they exist at the same time, even though this may seem difficult or impossible: *In Egypt, fundamentalism and feminism have long existed side by side.* **4** outer surface **a)** an outer surface of something that is not its front, back, top, or bottom: *You can use the door at the side of the building.* | *Toni ran her finger up and down the side of her glass.* | *The name*

of the restaurant was painted on both sides of the van.
b) one of the usually flat surfaces of something: *A cube has six sides.*

5 `edge` the part of an object or area that is farthest from the middle, at or near the edge: *After a while, she grew tired and sat down by the side of the road.* | *Shawna bumped her head on the side of the table.*

6 `inner surface` one of the usually flat surfaces on the inside of a hollow object or area: *Scrape the batter from the sides of the bowl.* | *They began a two-hour hike up the opposite side of the valley.*

7 `of a thin object` one of the two surfaces of a thin flat object: *You can write on both sides of the paper.* | *The record has a scratch on one side.*

8 from side to side moving continuously, first in one direction then in the other: *The boat swayed from side to side as waves hit it.*

9 `subject/situation` one part or feature of a subject, problem, or situation, especially when compared with another part: *Tell me your side of the story.* | *Look on the bright side* (=think about the positive parts), *Tim. Things could be a lot worse.* | **technical/financial/social etc. side** *Who's in charge of the creative side of the project?* | **serious/ funny etc. side** *Jack's reports usually look at the lighter side of the news.* | **on the plus/minus side** *Verrett's singing was sometimes hard to hear. On the plus side, though, she conveyed a rich, warm tone.*

10 `argument/war etc.` one of the people, groups, or countries opposing each other in an argument, war etc.: *At least we're on the winning side.* | *You're on my side, aren't you, Pat?* | *"All right, Steelers!" "Hey, whose side are you on, anyway* (=why are you supporting the other side)?*'

11 take sides to choose to support a particular person or opinion: *We're not here to take sides in this case.*

12 from all sides a) from every direction: *Immediately, the troops opened fire from all sides.* **b)** from a lot of people with different opinions: *Panel members expect criticism from all sides.*

13 on all sides also **on every side a)** in every direction: *The golden fields of wheat were surrounded on all sides by mountains.* **b)** among a lot of people with different opinions: *Current trade agreements are being questioned on all sides.*

14 `part of sb's character` [usually singular] one part of someone's character, especially when compared with another part: *It was a side of Shari I hadn't seen before.* | **sb's emotional/romantic/ funny etc. side** *Todd seldom lets people see his softer side.*

15 `part of your body` the left or right part of your body from under your arm to the top of your leg: *We need to roll her onto her left side.*

16 `family` the parents, grandparents etc. of your mother or your father: *Ken is Scottish on his mother's side.*

17 on the high/heavy/small etc. side a little too high, too heavy etc.: *Alice is a little on the quiet side, but she's a good worker.*

18 on the side a) in addition to your regular job: *They run a catering business on the side.* —see also SIDELINE[1] (1) **b)** food that is served on the side in a restaurant is served next to the main food on a plate: *The blueberry pie came with a mound of whipped cream on the side.*

19 have sth on your side also **sth is on your side** to have an advantage that increases your chances of success: *Time is on our side – sooner or later, they'll do something stupid.*

20 get on sb's good/bad side SPOKEN to make someone very pleased with you or very angry with you: *I don't know what I did to get on her bad side.*

21 a side of beef/pork one half of an animal's body, cut along the BACKBONE, to be used for food

22 put/set sth to one side to save something to be dealt with or used later: *Victims with head wounds had to be put to one side.*

23 on the right/wrong side of 30, 40 etc. SPOKEN, HUMOROUS younger or older than 30, 40 etc.

24 on the wrong/right side of the law INFORMAL breaking or not breaking the law: *De Niro plays a lawyer, on the right side of the law.*

25 this side of sth/sb when you consider everyone or everything except the person or thing mentioned: *They serve the best baked beans this side of Boston.*

26 criticize/nag/hassle etc. sb up one side and down the other to criticize someone, treat them in an unkind way etc. a lot, without worrying about how they feel

27 the other side of the coin a different or opposite way of thinking about something: *The food wasn't exceptional, but the other side of the coin is that lunches are reasonably priced.*

28 two sides of the same coin two problems or situations that are so closely connected that they are really just two parts of the same thing: *Kohl later said that German unity and European integration were "two sides of the same coin."* —see also **get up on the wrong side of the bed** (BED[1] (9)), ERR (1), FLIP SIDE, **right side up** (RIGHT[1] (11)), **to be on the safe side** (SAFE[1] (8)), -SIDED, **split your sides** (SPLIT[1] (9))

side[2] *adj.* [only before noun] **1** in or on the side of something | **a side door/panel etc.** *Josie slipped out through a side exit.* **2 a side view** a view of something as it looks from the side: *The next slide shows a side view of the building.* **3 a side street/road** a street, road etc. that is smaller than a main street but is often connected to it: *He parked the car on a side street so it wouldn't be spotted.*

side[3] *v.*

side against sb *phr. v.* [T] to argue against a person or group in an argument, fight etc.

side with sb *phr. v.* [T] to support a person or group in an argument, fight etc.: *Liz tends to side with her Dad in difficult family decisions.*

side·arm[1] /'saɪdɑrm/ *n.* [C often plural] a weapon carried or worn at someone's side, for example a gun or sword

sidearm[2] *adj. adv.* a sidearm throw in a sport is one in which you throw the ball with a sideways movement of your arm

side·bar /'saɪdbɑr/ *n.* [C] **1** an area next to a newspaper article, often with lines around it, that gives additional information relating to the article **2** LAW an occasion when the lawyers and the judge in a legal CASE discuss something without letting the JURY hear

side ben·e·fit /'. ˌ.../ *n.* [C] an additional advantage or good result that comes from something, besides its main purpose: *A side benefit to filming close-up shots is that your microphone will pick up clearer sound.*

side·board /'saɪdbɔrd/ *n.* [C] a long low piece of furniture usually in a DINING ROOM, used for storing plates, glasses etc.

side·burns /'saɪdbɜrnz/ *n.* [plural] hair that grows down the sides of a man's face in front of his ears

side·car /'saɪdkɑr/ *n.* [C] a small vehicle with a seat but no motor, that can be attached to the side of a MOTORCYCLE for an additional passenger

-sided /saɪdɪd/ [in adjectives] **six-sided/hard-sided etc.** having the number or type of sides mentioned: *a naïve, one-sided view of the issue* | *soft-sided luggage*

side dish /'. ./ *n.* [C] a small amount of food such as a vegetable that you eat with a main meal

side ef·fect /'. ˌ.,./ *n.* [C] **1** an effect that a drug has on your body, in addition to curing pain or illness: *Possible side effects of the treatment include nausea and diarrhea.* **2** an unexpected result of a situation or event: *A side effect of tuna fishing was the death of over 100,000 dolphins annually.*

side is·sue /'. ˌ.../ *n.* [C] a subject or problem that is not as important as the main one, and may take people's attention away from the main subject: *The brothers would usually find smaller side issues to debate.*

side·kick /'saɪd,kɪk/ *n.* [C] someone, especially on a television show or in a movie, who spends time with or helps another more important person

side·line[1] /'saɪdlaɪn/ n. **1** [C] an activity that you do in addition to your main job or business in order to earn more money: *Over his 25-year career, recording has been a sideline to performing.* **2** [C] a line at the side of a sports field, which shows where the players are allowed to play **3 the sidelines** [plural] **a)** the area just outside the lines that form the edge of a sports field: *Tom stood **on the sidelines**, cheering his teammates.* **b)** the state of not taking part in an activity even though you want to or should do it: **on/to the sidelines** *Trading was light yesterday as small investors remained on the sidelines.*

side·line[2] v. [T usually passive] to make someone unable to play in a sports game because they are injured, or unable to take part in an activity because they are not as good as someone else: *Horn will be sidelined for three weeks by a sprained ankle.*

side·long /'saɪdlɔŋ/ adj. **a sidelong glance/look** a way of looking at someone by moving your eyes to the side, especially so that it seems secret, dishonest, or disapproving: *Fred kept sneaking sidelong glances at Lynn during dinner.* —**sidelong** adv.

side or·der /'. ˌ../ n. [C] a small amount of food ordered in a restaurant to be eaten with a main meal, but served on a separate dish: *a side order of onion rings*

si·de·re·al /saɪ'dɪriəl/ adj. TECHNICAL relating to or calculated using the stars: *the sidereal day*

side·sad·dle /'saɪdˌsædl/ adv. **ride/sit sidesaddle** to ride or sit on a horse with both of your legs on the same side of the horse

side·show /'saɪdʃoʊ/ n. [C] **1** a separate small part of a CARNIVAL or CIRCUS, where you pay to see something, such as people with strange physical appearances **2** an event that is much less important or serious than another one, but that people may find more interesting: *In a way, the presidential race is a sideshow to the real struggle for power in Washington.*

side·split·ting /'saɪdˌsplɪtɪŋ/ adj. extremely funny: *His stage show includes a side-splitting imitation of the Vice President.*

side·step /'saɪdstɛp/ v. **sidestep a problem/question/rule etc.** to avoid doing or talking about something that is difficult or inconvenient: *The board decided to sidestep the issue of discrimination.* —**sidestep** n. [C]

side·swipe /'saɪdswaɪp/ v. [T] to hit the side of a car while passing in another car so that the two sides touch quickly: *The bus sideswiped several parked cars.*

side·track /'saɪdtræk/ v. [T] **1** to make someone stop doing what they should be doing, or stop talking about what they started talking about, by making them interested in something else: *We were talking about the book, but then we **got sidetracked**.* **2** to delay or stop the progress of something: *An effort to improve security has been sidetracked by budget problems.*

side-view mir·ror /'. . ˌ../ n. [C] a mirror attached to the side of a car

side·walk /'saɪdwɔk/ n. [C] a raised hard surface along the side of a street for people to walk on —see picture on page 423

sidewalk ca·fé /ˌ.. .'./ n. [C] a type of restaurant with tables and chairs outdoors on the sidewalk

sidewalk su·per·in·ten·dent /'.. ...ˌ../ n. [C] HUMOROUS someone who stands on a sidewalk in their free time, watching workers build a new building

side·wall /'saɪdwɔl/ n. [C] **1** the surface on the side of a car tire, that does not touch the road **2** a wall that forms the side of a room or building

side·ways /'saɪdweɪz/ adv. **1** to or toward one side: *He leaned sideways slightly to let Jane past.* **2** with the side, rather than the front or back, facing forward: *She sat sideways across her boyfriend's lap.* —**sideways** adj.: *Mike gave her a sideways glance.*

side-wheel·er /'saɪdˌwilɚ/ n. [C] an old-fashioned type of ship which is pushed forward by a pair of large wheels at the sides

side-wind·er /'saɪdˌwaɪndɚ/ n. [C] a type of snake that lives in dry areas of Mexico and the southwestern U.S., and that moves along the ground in a sideways movement

sid·ing /'saɪdɪŋ/ n. **1** [U] long, narrow pieces of wood, metal, or plastic, used for covering the outside walls of houses **2** [C] a short railroad track connected to a main track, where trains are kept when they are not being used

si·dle /'saɪdl/ v. [I always + adv./prep.] to walk toward something or someone slowly and quietly, as if you do not want to be noticed: [+ up/toward/along] *Rosa sidled up to him and murmured, "Can I ask you something?"*

SIDS /sɪdz/ n. [U] SUDDEN INFANT DEATH SYNDROME

siè·cle /si'ɛklə/ —see FIN DE SIÈCLE

siege /sidʒ/ n. [C,U] **1** a situation during which an army or the police surround a place and try to gain control of it by stopping supplies of food, weapons etc. from reaching it: [+ of] *the 900-day-long Nazi siege of Leningrad* | *Security forces have **laid siege to** (=started a siege in) two areas of the city.* **2** a situation in which someone or a group of people enters a place and holds the people inside as prisoners **3 be under siege a)** to be surrounded by an army or the police in a siege **b)** to be criticized or attacked by a lot of questions, problems, threats etc. over a period of time: *The President was under siege from war protesters on the sidewalk.* **4 siege mentality** the feeling among a group of people that they are surrounded by enemies and must do everything they can to protect themselves

si·en·na /si'ɛnə/ n. [U] a yellowish-brown color

si·er·ra /si'ɛrə/ n. [C,U] mountains that have a rough uneven top edge

Sierra Club /.'. ˌ./ a U.S. organization that tries to protect the environment, especially natural area such as forests, mountains, and rivers

Sierra Le·one /siˌɛrə li'oʊn/ a country in west Africa between Liberia and Guinea —**Sierra Leonean** n., adj.

Sierra Ma·dre, the /siˌɛrə 'mɑdreɪ/ a system of mountain ranges in central Mexico

Sierra Ne·va·da, the /siˌɛrə nə'vædə, -'vɑ-/ also **the Sierras** a mountain range in the U.S. state of California, which separates the coast of California from the rest of the U.S.

si·es·ta /si'ɛstə/ n. [C] a short sleep in the afternoon, especially in warm countries: *We finished lunch and went inside to **take a siesta**.*

sieve[1] /sɪv/ n. [C] **1** a round wire kitchen tool with a lot of small holes, used for separating solid food from liquid or small pieces of food from large pieces —see picture on page 425 **2** a round wire tool for separating small objects from large objects

sidewalk café

sieve[2] v. [T] to put something through a sieve

sift /sɪft/ v. [T] **1** to put flour, sugar etc. through a sifter or similar container in order to remove large pieces —see picture on page 425 **2** also **sift through** to examine information, documents etc. carefully in order to find something out or decide what is important and what is not: *It will take a while to sift through all these magazines.*

sift sth ↔ **out** *phr. v.* [T] to separate something from other things: [+ from] *It's hard to sift out the truth from the lies in this case.*

sift·er /'sɪftə/ *n.* [C] a container with a handle and a lot of small holes in the bottom, used for removing large pieces from flour or for mixing flour and other dry things together in cooking

sigh¹ /saɪ/ *v.* **1** [I,T] to breathe out making a long sound, especially because you are bored, disappointed, tired etc.: *"I know," she sighed.* | *Russ sighed deeply and looked at the ceiling.* | *When it was over, Penny sighed with relief.* **2** [I] LITERARY if the wind sighs, it makes a long sound like someone sighing: *The wind sighed in the trees.* **3 sigh for sth** LITERARY to be sad because you are thinking about a pleasant time in the past: *Emilia sighed for her lost youth.*

sigh² *n.* [C] an act or sound of sighing: [+ of] *With a sigh of exhaustion, she let them leave.* | **breathe/give/heave etc. a sigh of relief** *"I'm glad that's over," she said, breathing a sigh of relief.*

SW
2
3
sight¹ /saɪt/ *n.*
1 sth that proves sth [U] the physical ability to see: *She recently underwent an operation to restore her sight.* | *Mrs. Rosen is losing her sight.*
2 act of seeing [singular,U] the act of seeing something: [+ of] *Martha couldn't bear the sight of children begging in the streets.* | *Ray always faints at the sight of blood.* | *We caught sight of* (=suddenly saw) *the mayor on her way into City Hall.*
3 thing you see [C] something you can see, especially something unusual, beautiful etc.: *Stretch limousines are a common sight in Los Angeles.* | *We saw all the important sights on our first day in Chicago.* | *Are you sure you want to come in? It's not a pretty sight* (=very ugly or frightening). —see also SIGHTSEEING
4 in/within sight a) inside the area that you can see: *Al wanted to smoke, but there were no ashtrays in sight.* | *Lynn leaned out of the window, snapping pictures of everything in sight.* **b)** likely to happen soon: *Today is the fifteenth day of the heat wave, with no end in sight.*
5 within/in sight of sth a) in the area where you can see something: *The refugees' boat was stopped by the Coast Guard within sight of land.* **b)** in a position where you will soon be able to get something or achieve something: *Just when he was within sight of his goal, the funding for Dr. Wilson's research was cut.*
6 on sight as soon as you see someone: *A lot of people assume on sight that Lisa's not American.* | *Troops were given orders to shoot on sight.*
7 out of sight outside the area that you can see: *Keep your car windows rolled up and valuables out of sight.* —see also OUT-OF-SIGHT
8 disappear/vanish from sight to disappear: *Then the plane vanished from sight on the radar screen.*
9 come into sight to appear or come inside the area that you can see: *We stood at the window until their car came into sight.*
10 not let sb out of your sight to make sure that someone stays near you: *Stay here, and don't let the baby out of your sight.*
11 sight unseen if you buy or choose something sight unseen, you do it without looking at the thing first: *If I didn't take the car, the other guy was willing to buy it sight unseen.*
12 can't stand the sight of sb/sth also **hate the sight of sb/sth** to dislike someone or something very much: *Alan and Sam can't stand the sight of each other.*
13 a sight for sore eyes SPOKEN someone or something that you feel very happy to see
14 out of sight, out of mind used to say that if you cannot see someone or something, you stop thinking about it/them and forget about them: *I tucked it in the back of a drawer, figuring out of sight, out of mind.*

15 gun [C usually plural] the part of a gun or other weapon that guides your eye when you are aiming at something
16 be/look a sight to look very funny, stupid, or messy: *She must have been quite a sight with her hair in curlers.* —see also **a damn sight more/better etc.** (DAMN² (4)), **at first sight/glance** (FIRST¹ (4)), **know sb by sight** (KNOW¹ (5)), **lose sight of sb/sth** (LOSE (17)), **set your mind/sights/heart on sth** (SET¹ (12))

sight² *v.* [T] to see something from a long distance away or for a short time: *When the haze cleared, the sailors sighted land straight ahead.* | *A mountain lion was sighted in the local area last night.*

sight·ed /'saɪtɪd/ *adj.* someone who is sighted can see, and is not blind —see also CLEAR-SIGHTED, FARSIGHTED, NEARSIGHTED

sight gag /'. ./ *n.* [C] something that an actor or COMEDIAN does that makes people laugh because it looks funny

sight·ing /'saɪtɪŋ/ *n.* [C] an occasion on which something is seen, especially something rare or something that people are hoping to see: *There were two unconfirmed sightings of UFOs in the area.*

sight·less /'saɪtlɪs/ *adj.* LITERARY blind

sight-read /'saɪt rid/ *v. past tense and past participle* **sight-read** /-red/ [I,T] to play or sing written music when you look at it for the first time, without practicing it first —**sight-reader** *n.* [C] —**sight-reading** *n.* [U]

sight·see·ing /'saɪt siɪŋ/ *n.* [U] the activity of visiting famous or interesting places, especially as a tourist: *We can go sightseeing downtown tomorrow.*

sight·se·er /'saɪt siə/ *n.* [C] someone, especially a tourist, who is visiting a famous or interesting place

S

sign¹ /saɪn/ *n.*
SW
1 1
1 sth that proves sth [C] an event, fact etc. that shows that something is happening or that something is true or exists; INDICATION: [+ of] *Do you see any signs of improvement in her condition?* | [sign (that)] *The drop in unemployment is one sign that the economy is improving.* | *After ten miles, some runners were starting to show signs of fatigue.* | *Police who investigated the burglary found no sign of forced entry.* | *I waited for two hours, but there was still no sign of her.* | *Holiday decorations in the stores are a sure sign that summer is over.*
2 movement or sound [C] a movement, sound etc. that you make in order to tell someone to do something or give them information; GESTURE: [sign that] *I made a sign that I understood Anna.* | **give/make a sign** *The President gave reporters the thumbs-up sign.*
3 information on a wall/pole etc. [C] a piece of paper, metal etc. in a public place, with words or drawings on it that give people information, warn them not to do something etc.: *a stop sign* | *What did that sign say?*
4 picture/symbol [C] a picture, shape etc. that has a particular meaning; SYMBOL: *Write your answer after the equals sign.*
5 a sign of life a) a movement that shows that someone is alive, or something that shows that there are people in a particular place: *Apart from a few lights, there was no sign of life on the block.* **b)** something that shows that a situation is becoming more active: *The nation's economy is starting to show a few faint signs of life.*
6 a sign of the times something that shows how the world or society has changed recently: *The sheer amount of government research available to farmers on the Internet is a real sign of the times.*
7 the sign of the cross the hand movement that some Christians make in the shape of a cross, to show respect for God or to protect themselves from evil
8 stars [C] also **star sign** a group of stars, representing one of 12 parts of the year, that some people believe influences your behavior and your life: *What's your sign?*

S W
1 1

sign² *v.* **1** [I,T] to write your SIGNATURE on a letter or document to show that you wrote it, agree with it etc.: *Just sign here by the X.* | *Would you like to sign our guest book?* | *She signed her name at the bottom of the page.* **2** [T] to make a document, agreement etc. official and legal by writing your SIGNATURE on it: *Each tenant will have to sign the lease.* | *The President signed the telecommunications reform bill into law yesterday.* **3** [T] if an organization such as a football team or music company signs someone, that person signs a contract agreeing to work for it: *Simmons was signed as a free agent in 1994.* **4 sign on the dotted line** INFORMAL to officially agree to something, especially by signing a contract **5** [I,T] to use SIGN LANGUAGE: *The governor's speech will be signed by an interpreter for the hearing-impaired.* **6 signed, sealed, and delivered** also **signed and sealed** with everything finished and taken care of as needed: *Please use caution until everything is signed, sealed, and delivered.* —**signer** *n.* [C]

sign sth **↔ away** *phr. v.* [T] to sign a document that takes away your legal right to do something, or that gives your property or legal right to someone else: *Several people had been tricked into signing away their right to sue.* | *The contract was so complicated, I felt like I was signing my life away.*

sign for sth *phr. v.* [T] to sign a document to prove that you have received something: *Who signed for the package?*

sign in *phr. v.* **1** [I] to write your name on a form, in a book etc. when you enter a place such as a hotel, office or club: *All visitors must sign in at the front desk.* **2** [T **sign** sb **in**] to write someone else's name in a book so that they are allowed to enter a club that you are a member of

sign off *phr. v.* [I] to say goodbye at the end of a television or radio broadcast, or at the end of a letter

sign off on sth *phr. v.* [T] to officially say or show that you approve of a document, plan, or idea: *Congress has not yet signed off on the deal.*

sign on *phr. v.* [I,T] to sign a document agreeing to help or work for someone, or to persuade someone to do this: *All the show's stars have signed on for another season.* | [**sign** sb **↔ on**] *The RTC is signing on about 1000 contractors a week.*

sign out *phr. v.* **1** [I] to write your name in a book when you leave a place such as a hotel, office or club **2** [T **sign** sth **↔ out**] to write your name on a form or in a book to show that you have taken or borrowed something: *Somebody had already signed out the last VCR.*

sign sth **↔ over** *phr. v.* [T] to sign an official document that gives your property or rights to someone else: [+ to] *Richard signed over his shares in the biotech company to his son.*

sign up *phr. v.* **1** [I] to put your name on a list because you want to take part in an activity, such as a class: [+ for] *Over 25 people have signed up for the self-defense class.* | [**sign up to do** sth] *All four of their sons signed up to join the army.* **2** [T **sign** sb **↔ up**] to officially allow someone to work for a company or join an organization: *Unions have been having trouble signing up enough new members.*

sign with sth *phr. v.* [T] to sign a contract agreeing to work for a particular organization, such as a sports team, a television or record company etc.: *Morris signed with Toronto for over $5 million per year.*

sign·age /ˈsaɪnɪdʒ/ *n.* [U] all the signs used in a building, along a road, etc.

S W
3 3

sig·nal¹ /ˈsɪgnəl/ *n.* [C] **1** a sound or action that you make in order to give information to someone or tell them to do something: *During mating season, female butterflies respond to subtle signals from the males.* | *That afternoon, the general gave the signal for his troops to advance.* —see also BUSY SIGNAL, SMOKE SIGNAL **2** something that happens, or something that someone does, which shows how they feel or what is likely to happen: [**signal (that)**] *The unemployment figures are a signal that the economy is improving.* |

The trade agreement is a clear signal of our commitment to a market economy. | *People give off signals that let others know how they feel.* | **send/give a signal** *Grogan's speech may send the wrong signal to potential investors.* **3** a series of light waves, sound waves etc. that carry an image, sound, or message, such as in radio or television: *The telephone changes sound waves into electrical signals.* | *The Coast Guard picked up a distress signal from a freighter near the shore.* **4** a piece of equipment with colored lights, used on a road or railroad to tell drivers when they can continue or when they must stop: *We just sat there, waiting for the signal to turn green.*

signal² *v.* **1** [I,T] to give a signal in order to give information or tell someone to do something: *The display will flash "L," signaling the user to change the batteries.* | [+ for] *Kolodney stepped onto the stage and signaled for silence.* **2** [T] to make something clear by what you say or do: *He'd been signaling his desire to leave for over a year.* | [**signal that**] *The beach community tightened law enforcement, signaling that college students weren't welcome during spring break.* **3** [T] to be a sign or proof of something: *The melting of the ice on the lake signals the start of spring.* **4** [I] to show the direction you intend to turn in a vehicle, by using lights: *The driver in front of us was signaling left, but he didn't turn off.*

signal³ *adj.* FORMAL **a signal achievement/success/ failure etc.** a very important achievement, success etc.: *The episode turned into one of the signal moments in our cultural history.*

sig·nal·ize /ˈsɪgnəˌlaɪz/ *v.* [T] FORMAL to be a clear sign of something: *The agreement was regarded as signalizing the end of the South African struggle.*

sig·nal·ly /ˈsɪgnəli/ *adv.* FORMAL in a way that is very noticeable: *Conventional ideas have signally failed to deal with new developments in technology.*

sig·nal·man /ˈsɪgnəlmən/ *n.* [C] **1** a member of the army or navy who is trained in SIGNALing (SIGNAL² (4)) **2** someone whose job is to control railroad signals

sig·na·to·ry /ˈsɪgnəˌtɔri/ *n. plural* **signatories** [C] one of the people or countries that sign an official agreement, especially an international one: [+ to/of] *a meeting of the 35 signatories of the Helsinki Pact*

sig·na·ture¹ /ˈsɪgnətʃɚ/ *n.* [C] **1** your name written in the way you usually write it, for example at the end of a letter or contract or on a check: *I couldn't read his signature.* | *a petition with four thousand signatures* **2** something that is closely connected in people's minds with a particular event, person, company etc. because they use it a lot: [+ of] *Negative TV ads soon became the signature of the '96 Presidential campaign.* —compare AUTOGRAPH¹ —see also KEY SIGNATURE, TIME SIGNATURE

S W
2

signature² *adj.* [only before noun] closely connected in people's minds with a particular person, company etc. because it is used a lot by that person or company: *The First Lady's signature red knit suits were designed by Adolfo.*

sign·board /ˈsaɪnbɔrd/ *n.* [C] a flat piece of wood, CARDBOARD etc. in a public place, with writing on it that gives people information

sig·net /ˈsɪgnɪt/ *n.* [C] a metal object used for printing a small pattern in WAX as an official SEAL¹ (4)

signet ring /ˈ.. ˌ./ *n.* [C] a ring that has a signet on it

sig·nif·i·cance /sɪgˈnɪfəkəns/ *n.* [U] **1** the importance of an event, action etc., especially because of the effects or influence it will have in the future: [+ of] *City leaders are just starting to realize the significance of the drug problem.* | [+ for] *Recent research findings will have enormous significance for arthritis sufferers.* | [+ to] *We have identified political issues of significance to the union's members.* | **be of great/little significance** *The few policies he has introduced were of very little significance.* **2** the meaning of a word, sign, action etc., especially when this is not immediately clear: [+ of] *a discussion about the significance of the poem*

sig·nif·i·cant /sɪgˈnɪfəkənt/ *adj.* **1** having an important effect or influence, especially on what will

S W
3 2

happen in the future: *There has been a significant change in the tone of the media's coverage.* | *Volunteer tutoring programs can have a significant impact on student achievement.* **2** large enough to be noticeable or have noticeable effects: *A significant number of drivers still refuse to wear seat belts.* | *There was no statistically significant difference between the two test groups.* **3** [only before noun] a significant look, smile etc. has a special meaning that is not known to everyone: *They exchanged significant glances.*

sig·nif·i·cant·ly /sɪɡˈnɪfɪkəntli/ *adv.* **1** in an important way or to a large degree: *It is not possible to reduce costs without significantly altering the quality of the product.* | **significantly better/greater/ worse etc.** *People living near the reactor have significantly higher rates of cancer.* **2** [sentence adverb] used to say that something is very important: *But perhaps more significantly, the only person to mention America's role in the scandal was a non-American.* **3** in a way that seems to have a special meaning: *Barb paused and glanced significantly in my direction.*

significant oth·er /.,... '../ *n.* [C] someone you have been having a close personal relationship with for a long time, especially your GIRLFRIEND, BOYFRIEND, wife, or husband

sig·ni·fi·ca·tion /ˌsɪɡnəfəˈkeɪʃən/ *n.* [C] FORMAL the intended meaning of a word

sig·ni·fy /ˈsɪɡnəˌfaɪ/ *v.* **signifies, signified, signifying** [T not in progressive] **1** to represent, mean, or be a sign of something: *The red star signified his membership in the Communist Party.* | [**signify (that)**] *"N/A" signifies that the information was not available.* **2** FORMAL to make a wish, feeling, or opinion known by doing something: *Many people wore red ribbons to signify their support for AIDS awareness.*

sign·ing /ˈsaɪnɪŋ/ *n.* **1** [U] the act of putting your SIGNATURE on something such as an agreement or contract: *Both leaders were present for the signing of the peace treaty.* **2** [C] a ceremony or event at which someone puts their SIGNATURE on something: *Northcott attended several book signings around the state to promote her autobiography.*

sign lan·guage /'. ,../ *n.* [C,U] a language that uses hand movements instead of spoken words, used by people who cannot hear

sign·post¹ /ˈsaɪnpoʊst/ *n.* [C] **1** a pole that supports a sign near a road, or a sign that is supported by a pole: *Malcolm's car hit a signpost before crashing into a tree.* **2** something that helps you to understand how something is organized, or to notice something: *Clear signposts at the beginning of each section will help the audience follow your ideas.*

signpost² *v.* [T] to show something clearly so that everyone will notice and understand it: *They have signposted their conclusions in the report.*

Sikh /sik/ *n.* [C] a member of an Indian religious group that developed from Hinduism in the 16th century —**Sikhism** *n.* [U] —**Sikh** *adj.*

Si·kor·sky /sɪˈkɔrksi/, **I·gor** /ˈigor/ (1889–1972) a U.S. engineer, born in the Ukraine, who designed the first HELICOPTER

si·lage /ˈsaɪlɪdʒ/ *n.* [U] grass or other plants cut and stored so that they can be used as winter food for farm animals

si·lence¹ /ˈsaɪləns/ *n.*

1 no noise [U] complete absence of sound or noise: *A voice echoed in the silence.* | [+ **of**] *Nothing disturbed the silence of the night.* | *Silence fell* (=it began to be quiet) *over the desert.* | **break/shatter the silence** *The silence was suddenly broken by a loud scream.* | **absolute/complete/dead silence** *the complete silence of the forest at night*

2 no talking/discussion [C,U] **a)** complete quiet because no one is talking, or a period of complete quiet: *There was a long silence before anyone answered.* | *The school observed a minute of silence in honor of the students who had died.* | *We walked along in silence for a few blocks.* | **embarrassed/awkward/stunned etc. silence** *Peter's comments were met with an awkward silence.* **b)** failure or

refusal to discuss something or answer questions about something: [+ **on**] *The government's silence on such an important issue seems very strange.* | *Most of the demonstrators maintained a stony silence* (=angry or offended silence). | *Activists criticized the state's deafening silence* (=very noticeable refusal to discuss) *on the issue of immigration.*

3 no communication [C,U] failure to write a letter to someone, call them on the telephone etc.: *After years of silence, we were talking on the phone every few weeks.*

silence² *v.* [T] **1** to make someone stop expressing opposition or criticism: *Police used violence and threats to silence the party's political opponents.* | *At last, Switzer had a chance to silence his critics.* **2** to make someone stop talking, or stop something from making a noise: *Angry residents are suing the church to silence the bell at night.*

si·lenc·er /ˈsaɪlənsə/ *n.* [C] a thing that is put on the end of a gun so that it makes less noise when it is fired

si·lent /ˈsaɪlənt/ *adj.* **1** not saying anything: *Phil was silent for a moment as he thought about his reply.* | *The audience fell silent* (=became completely quiet) *as Jackson began to speak.* —see also **sb is the strong, silent type** (STRONG (24)) **2** failing or refusing to talk about something or express an opinion: [+ **on/about**] *The company is suspiciously silent about its plans for cutting costs.* | *You have the right to remain silent.* **3** without any sound, or not making any sound: *The hours before the attack were strangely silent.* | *Police responded to a silent alarm at the bank's Hope Street branch.* **4** **give sb the silent treatment** to not speak to someone because you are angry or upset about something they did **5** a silent letter in a word is not pronounced: *The "b" at the end of "thumb" is silent.* —**silently** *adv.*

silent ma·jor·i·ty /,.. .'.../ *n.* **the silent majority** all the people in a country who are not politically active, whose opinions are believed to represent the ideas that most ordinary people have

silent mov·ie /,.. '../ also **silent film** /,.. './ *n.* [C] an old-fashioned movie with no sound, mainly made before about 1928

silent part·ner /,.. '../ *n.* [C] someone who owns part of a business, but is not actively involved in the way it operates

sil·hou·ette¹ /ˌsɪluˈɛt, ˈsɪluˌɛt/ *n.* **1** [C] a dark image, shadow, or shape, seen against a light background: *We could see her silhouette through the curtains.* **2** [C,U] a drawing of someone or something that shows their outer shape, filled in with black against a light background: *The 32¢ stamp depicted a woman in silhouette.* **3** [C] a particular shape that clothes have: *Lauren's fall collection includes wool suits with a new, narrower silhouette.*

silhouette² *v.* **be silhouetted (against sth)** to appear as a dark shape in front of a light background: *Vogel gazed at the mountains silhouetted against the sky.*

sil·i·ca /ˈsɪlɪkə/ *n.* [U] a chemical compound that exists naturally as sand, QUARTZ, and FLINT, used in making glass

sil·i·cate /ˈsɪləˌkeɪt, -kət/ *n.* [C,U] TECHNICAL one of a group of common solid mineral substances that exist naturally in the Earth's surface

sil·i·con /ˈsɪlɪkən, -ˌkɑn/ *n.* [U] *symbol* **Si** an ELEMENT that is often used for making glass, bricks, and parts for computers

silicon chip /,... './ *n.* [C] a computer CHIP

sil·i·cone /ˈsɪləˌkoʊn/ *n.* [U] one of a group of chemicals that are not changed by heat or cold, do not let water pass through them, and are used in making artificial rubber, body parts, and many other products: *silicone breast implants*

Silicon Val·ley /,... '../ a part of California in the area between San Francisco and San José, which is known as a center of the computer industry —see picture on page 1328

sil·i·co·sis /ˌsɪləˈkoʊsɪs/ n. [U] an illness of the lungs caused by breathing SILICA, common among people who work in mines

silk /sɪlk/ n. **1** [U] a thin, smooth, soft cloth made from very thin thread which is produced by a silkworm: *a silk blouse* **2 silks** [plural] TECHNICAL the colored shirts worn by JOCKEYS (=people who ride horses in races) **3 you can't make a silk purse out of a sow's ear** SPOKEN used to say that there is no possibility of improving a situation or person because they are so bad, stupid etc.

silk·en /ˈsɪlkən/ adj. LITERARY **1** soft, smooth, and shiny like silk: *silken hair* **2** made of silk: *The prince was dressed in red silken robes.*

silk-screen·ing /ˈ. ˌ../ also **screen print·ing** n. [U] a way of printing by forcing paint or ink onto a surface through a stretched piece of cloth —**silk-screen** v. [T]

silk·worm /ˈsɪlk-wɜːm/ n. [C] a type of MOTH whose young produces silk thread

silk·y /ˈsɪlki/ adj. **silkier, silkiest 1** soft, smooth and shiny, like silk: *The treatment will leave your hair feeling soft and silky.* **2** a silky voice is gentle and pleasant to listen to —**silkiness** n. [U]

sill /sɪl/ n. [C] the narrow shelf at the base of a window frame

S W
2
sil·ly[1] /ˈsɪli/ adj. **sillier, silliest 1** stupid in a childish or embarrassing way: *I feel so silly in this outfit.* | *a silly hat* | *Don't pay any attention to her – she's just being silly.* **2** not sensible, or showing bad judgment; FOOLISH: *Do you mind if I ask a silly question?* | *It's silly to build another room onto the house now.* **3** SPOKEN not serious or practical: *We saw all these city people with their silly little sandals on.* **4 bore/scare/beat etc. sb silly** to make someone extremely bored, SCARED etc. **5 drink yourself silly** to get very drunk —**silliness** n. [U]

silly[2] n. [singular, not with **the**] SPOKEN a name used to tell someone that you think they are being stupid: *No, silly, put it over there!*

si·lo /ˈsaɪloʊ/ n. plural **silos** [C] **1** a tall structure like a tower that is used for storing grain, winter food for farm animals etc. **2** a large structure under the ground from which a large MISSILE can be fired

silt[1] /sɪlt/ n. [U] moving sand, mud, soil etc. that is carried in water and then settles at a curve in a river or where a river flows into the ocean

silt[2] v.

silt up phr. v. [I,T] to fill or become filled with silt: *The reservoirs had silted up as a result of the climate change.*

sil·ver[1] /ˈsɪlvɚ/ n. **1** [U] symbol **Ag** a shiny whitish valuable metal that is an ELEMENT and is used to make jewelry, knives, coins etc. **2** [U] spoons, forks, dishes etc. that are made of silver or a similar metal: *Use a soft cloth to polish the silver.* **3** [U] the color of silver **4** [C] a SILVER MEDAL

S W
3 3
silver[2] adj. **1** made of silver: *a silver pitcher* **2** having the color of silver: *a silver Mercedes* **3 give/hand sth to sb on a silver platter** to make it very easy for someone to get something or succeed at something: *It was no real contest – we handed them the victory on a silver platter.* **4 silver bullet** a quick, painless cure for an illness, or something that solves a difficult problem in an easy way: *More investment isn't a silver bullet for poor neighborhoods.* —see also **be born with a silver spoon in your mouth** (BORN (7)), **every cloud has a silver lining** (CLOUD[1] (6))

silver[3] v. [T] to cover something with a thin shiny silver-colored surface, for example in order to make a mirror —compare GILD (1)

silver an·ni·ver·sa·ry /ˌ.. ..ˈ.../ n. [C] the date that is exactly 25 years after the beginning of something, especially a marriage —compare DIAMOND ANNIVERSARY, GOLDEN ANNIVERSARY

silver dol·lar /ˌ.. ˈ../ n. [C] a one-dollar coin used in the U.S. in past times

sil·ver·fish /ˈsɪlvɚfɪʃ/ n. plural **silverfish** or **silverfishes** [C] a small silver-colored insect that is found in houses and sometimes damages paper or cloth

silver med·al /ˌ.. ˈ../ n. [C] a MEDAL made of silver that is given to the person who finishes second in a race or competition —see also GOLD MEDAL, SILVER MEDAL

silver med·al·ist /ˌ.. ˈ.../ n. [C] someone who has won a silver medal

silver plate /ˌ.. ˈ./ n. [U] metal with a thin covering of silver —**silver-plated** adj.: *a silver-plated candlestick*

silver screen /ˌ.. ˈ./ n. **the silver screen** the movie industry in Hollywood, in past times: *stars of the silver screen*

sil·ver·smith /ˈsɪlvɚˌsmɪθ/ n. [C] someone who makes things out of silver

silver-tongued /ˈ.. ˌ./ adj. good at talking to people and persuading them

sil·ver·ware /ˈsɪlvɚˌwɛr/ n. [U] knives, spoons and forks made of silver or some other metal —see picture at KITCHEN

sil·ver·y /ˈsɪlvəri/ adj. **1** shiny and silver in color: *Salmon have pink flesh and silvery skin.* **2** ESPECIALLY LITERARY having a pleasant, light, musical sound: *a silvery laugh*

Sim·e·on /ˈsɪmiən/ in the Bible, the head of one of the 12 tribes of Israel

sim·i·an /ˈsɪmiən/ adj. TECHNICAL relating to monkeys or similar to a monkey or APE —**simian** n. [C]

S W
2 1
sim·i·lar /ˈsɪmələ/ adj. **1** almost the same, but not exactly the same: *We have similar tastes in music.* | *The law has served as a model for similar policies in other states.* | [+ to] *Tom's voice is very similar to his brother's.* | [+ in] *a cheese that is similar in texture to Cheddar* **2** [no comparative] TECHNICAL if GEOMETRIC figures are similar, they have the same shape and equal angles, but are not the same size

sim·i·lar·i·ty /ˌsɪməˈlærəti/ n. plural **similarities 1** [singular,U] the fact of being similar to something else, or the degree to which two or more things are similar to each other; RESEMBLANCE: [+ between] *a striking similarity between the two designs* | [+ to] *The drug's effectiveness is due to its similarity to natural hormones.* | *The hostage crisis bore a remarkable similarity to another attack last year.* **2** [C] a way in which things or people are similar: *Kraut's study looked at the similarities and differences among managerial jobs.* | [+ in] *Related languages often have similarities in their sound structures.*

S W
3
sim·i·lar·ly /ˈsɪmələli/ adv. **1** [sentence adverb] used to say that a situation is similar to something you have just mentioned: *Sales of existing homes went up 2% last month. Similarly, construction of new homes rose as well.* **2** in a similar way: *The most commonly used rocks are granite, quartz, or other similarly stable materials.*

sim·i·le /ˈsɪməli/ n. **1** [C] an expression that describes something by comparing it with something else, using the words "as" or "like," for example "as white as snow" **2** [U] the use of expressions like this

SIMM /sɪm/ n. [C] TECHNICAL Single In-line Memory Module; a piece of electronic equipment that gives a computer more RAM

sim·mer[1] /ˈsɪmɚ/ v. **1** [I,T] to cook something slowly in a liquid that is gently boiling: *Bring the stew to a boil, then let it simmer for 20 minutes.* **2** [I] if something such as an argument is simmering, it develops slowly over a long period of time before people express their feelings strongly: *The debate about school closures has been simmering among locals for years.* | *long-simmering ethnic conflicts* **3 simmer down!** SPOKEN used to tell someone to be less excited, angry etc.: *Simmer down, you two! Supper's almost ready.*

simmer[2] n. [singular] the condition of simmering: *Bring the vegetables to a simmer.*

Si·mon /ˈsaɪmən/**, Neil** /nil/ (1927–) a U.S. writer of humorous plays and movies

Simon Ze·lo·tes /ˌsaɪmən ziˈloʊtiz/ **Simon the Canaanite** in the Bible, one of the 12 APOSTLES

sim·pa·ti·co /sɪmˈpɑtɪkoʊ, -ˈpæ-/ *adj.* INFORMAL **1** someone who is simpatico is easy to like **2** in agreement: *Not all couples are simpatico during long car trips.*

sim·per /ˈsɪmpɚ/ *v.* [I] to smile in a silly, annoying way —**simper** *n.* [C]

S W
2 1
sim·ple /ˈsɪmpəl/ *adj.*
1 **easy** not difficult or complicated: *I'm sure there's a perfectly simple explanation.* | *He couldn't even answer very simple questions.* | *Just call her up – it's* **as simple as that.**
2 **plain** without a lot of decoration or unnecessary things added: *a simple black dress* | *The chicken was served with a simple cream sauce.* | *She liked the building's simple, clean lines.*
3 **only** [only before noun] not complicated or involving anything else: *Even the simple act of eating dinner together can make an evening special.* | *Milk is cheap now for one simple reason: there's too much of it available.* | **the simple truth/fact is...** *The simple truth is that we don't have enough money.*
4 **not having many parts** consisting of only a few necessary parts: *simple organisms such as bacteria* | *You will need a few simple tools for this job.*
5 **not special** honest and ordinary, and without much experience of the world: *Joe was just a simple farmer.*
6 **the simple life** life without all the problems of the modern world, especially life in the COUNTRYSIDE, without too many possessions or modern machines
7 **stupid** OLD-FASHIONED not intelligent: *Billy was a very simple boy.* —see also **pure and simple** (PURE (8))

simple frac·ture /ˌ.. '../ *n.* [C] TECHNICAL a broken or cracked bone that does not cut through the flesh that surrounds it —compare COMPOUND FRACTURE

simple in·terest /ˌ.. '../ *n.* [U] INTEREST¹ (3) that is calculated on the sum of money that you first INVESTed and does not include the interest it has already earned —compare COMPOUND INTEREST

simple-mind·ed /ˌ.. '.. ◂/ *adj.* unable to understand complicated things, and not showing much understanding of the world

sim·ple·ton /ˈsɪmpəltən/ *n.* [C] OLD-FASHIONED someone who has a very low level of intelligence

sim·plic·i·ty /sɪmˈplɪsəti/ *n.* [U] APPROVING the quality of being simple, especially when this is attractive or useful: *The design was beautiful in its simplicity.* | *For the sake of simplicity, we will ignore seasonal changes in population.* | *His plan for gaining control of the company was simplicity itself* (=was very simple).

sim·pli·fy /ˈsɪmpləˌfaɪ/ *v.* **simplifies, simplified, simplifying** [T] to make something easier or less complicated: *The laws have been simplified to shorten the process of divorce.* —see also OVERSIMPLIFY —**simplified** *adj.*: *a simplified version of Chinese script* —**simplification** /ˌsɪmpləfəˈkeɪʃən/ *n.* [C,U]

sim·plis·tic /sɪmˈplɪstɪk/ *adj.* DISAPPROVING treating difficult subjects in a way that is too simple: *a naïve and simplistic view of the world* —**simplistically** /-kli/ *adv.*

S W
2 1
sim·ply /ˈsɪmpli/ *adv.* **1** only; just: *Simply fill out the coupon and take it to your local store* | *It's not simply a matter of hiring more people – they also need to be trained.* | *They fired Elaine simply because she was a woman.* **2** used to emphasize what you are saying: *The strain on the rope was simply too much, and it broke in two.* | *We simply don't have the resources to compete with large corporations.* **3** in a way that is easy to understand: *She writes very simply and clearly.* | **Simply put** (=expressing it in a simple clear way), *I am very disappointed.* **4** in a plain and ordinary way, without spending much money: *They live very simply in the country.*

sim·u·la·crum /ˌsɪmyəˈlækrəm, -ˈleɪ-/ *n. plural* **simulacra** /-krə/ [C + of] FORMAL an image or copy of something

sim·u·late /ˈsɪmyəˌleɪt/ *v.* [T] **1** to make or produce something that is not real but has the appearance of something real: *This machine can simulate conditions*

---

in space. | *The navy's maneuvers were designed to simulate an enemy invasion of the island.* **2** LITERARY to pretend to have a feeling; FEIGN: *James felt obliged to simulate reluctance.*

sim·u·lat·ed /ˈsɪmyəˌleɪtɪd/ *adj.* not real, but made to look, feel etc. like a real thing, situation, or feeling: *simulated leather* | *The movie's simulated tropical storm used up huge quantities of water.*

sim·u·la·tion /ˌsɪmyəˈleɪʃən/ *n.* **1** [C,U] an activity or situation that produces conditions which are not real, but have the appearance of being real, used especially for testing something: *Pilots receive additional training by means of computer simulations.* | [+ of] *Rescue crews are participating in a simulation of a major traffic accident.* **2** [U] the act or process of simulating something

sim·u·la·tor /ˈsɪmyəˌleɪtɚ/ *n.* [C] a piece of equipment used for training people by letting them feel what real conditions are like, for example in an aircraft: *a flight simulator*

sim·ul·cast /ˈsaɪməlˌkæst/ *v. past tense and past participle* **simulcast** [T usually passive] to broadcast a program on television and radio, or on more than one television or radio station, at the same time —**simulcast** *n.* [C]

si·mul·ta·ne·ous /ˌsaɪməlˈteɪniəs/ *adj.* happening or done at exactly the same time: *In simultaneous raids on five homes, police seized over $5 million worth of cocaine.* —**simultaneously** *adv.*: *Two pictures are taken simultaneously from different camera angles.* —**simultaneity** /ˌsaɪməltəˈneɪəti/ *n.* [U]

sin¹ /sɪn/ *n.* **1** [C,U] something you do that is against religious laws or offensive to God, or the act of doing something like this: *The Bible says adultery is a sin.* | *the sin of greed* | *No one is completely without sin.* **2** [C usually singular] something that you strongly disapprove of: **It's a sin to** *waste all this food.* | **It's no sin to** (=it is acceptable to) *look at other men once in a while.* **3 as miserable/ugly/guilty etc. as sin** SPOKEN very unhappy, ugly etc. —**sinless** *adj.* —see also **live in sin** (LIVE¹ (16)), **cover/hide a multitude of sins** (MULTITUDE (3)), ORIGINAL SIN, SINFUL

sin² *v.* **sinned, sinning** [I] **1** to break God's laws: [+ against] *He has sinned against God.* **2 be more sinned against than sinning** OLD-FASHIONED used to say that someone should not be blamed for what they have done wrong, because they have been badly treated by other people

sin³ TECHNICAL the written abbreviation of SINE

Si·nai /ˈsaɪnaɪ/ the northeastern part of Egypt, which is a piece of land between the two narrow upper parts of the Red Sea, the Gulf of Suez and the Gulf of Aqaba

S W
1 1
since¹ /sɪns/ *conjunction* **1** at a time after a particular time or event in the past: *A lot has happened since we graduated from college.* | *Steele has not visited Arizona since he sold his house last October.* **2** continuously during the period of time after a particular time or event in the past: *Darla's been really happy since she started work.* | *We've been friends ever since we met in school.* **3** used to give the reason for something: *I'll be forty next month, since you ask.* | *Since nobody's replied yet, we'll assume they're not interested.*

S W
2 1
since² *prep.* **1** at or from a time after a particular time or event in the past: *Unemployment is now at its lowest point since World War II.* | *Sarah's been sick since Friday.* | **Ever since** *the accident, I haven't been able to use my right hand.* —compare FOR¹ (8) **2 since when?** SPOKEN used in questions to show surprise, anger etc.: *Oh, yeah? Since when are you in charge around here?* —see Usage Note at FROM

USAGE NOTE: SINCE

WORD CHOICE: since, for, ago
Since is mainly used when you want to talk about a situation or activity that started at some time in the past

and has continued to the time when you are speaking. It is used with verbs in the present perfect tense: *We've been here since Tuesday morning.* | *Doug hasn't been the same since his father died six months ago* (NOT *"He hasn't been the same since six months/six months before."*). **For** is used where you want to give the length of a period of time, but do not need to say exactly when it started or finished. It goes with all tenses of verbs: *We lived there for a long time.* | *Tony will be staying with us for three days.* When you use **for** with the present perfect tense, it gives a period of time that ends at the time of speaking: *I've been waiting for two hours* (NOT *"since two hours"*). **Ago** is used mainly with the simple past tense to show the point in time when something happened: *Marlene called ten minutes ago* (NOT *"since ten minutes"*).

S **W**
2 2 **since**[3] *adv.* [used with the present perfect and the past perfect tenses] **1** at a time in the past after a particular time or event: *Her husband died over ten years ago, but she has since remarried.* | *Many of our friends have since moved away.* | *Greg left work Tuesday afternoon and hasn't been seen since.* **2** for the whole of a long period of time after a particular time or event in the past: *We bought this house in 1986 and have lived here ever since.* —see also **long since** (LONG[2] (9))

sin·cere /sɪnˈsɪr/ *adj.* **1** a sincere feeling, belief, statement etc. is honest and true, and based on what you really feel and believe; GENUINE: *Over the years, he has made a sincere effort to improve race relations.* | *I would like to express my sincere appreciation for your hard work.* **2** someone who is sincere is honest and says that they really feel or believe: *She's a hardworking, sincere person.* | [+ **in**] *They were completely sincere in their beliefs.* —opposite INSINCERE

sin·cere·ly /sɪnˈsɪrli/ *adv.* **1** in a sincere, honest way: *Steve sincerely believed he was doing the right thing.* | *We sincerely regret any trouble this has caused.* **2** **Sincerely (yours), ...** or **Yours sincerely, ...** an expression that you write at the end of a formal letter before you sign your name

sin·cer·i·ty /sɪnˈsɛrəti/ *n.* [U] **1** the quality of honestly believing something or really meaning what you say: *Several people expressed doubts about the sincerity of her offer.* **2** **in all sincerity** very sincerely and honestly: *I think in all sincerity it would be better to give up now.*

Sin·clair /sɪnˈklɛr/**, Up·ton** /ˈʌptən/ (1878–1968) a U.S. writer best known for his NOVEL about the MEAT-PACKING industry in Chicago

sine /saɪn/ *n.* [C] TECHNICAL a number relating to an angle in a RIGHT TRIANGLE that is calculated by dividing the length of the side across from the angle by the length of the HYPOTENUSE (=longest side) —compare COSINE, TANGENT (3)

si·ne·cure /ˈsaɪnɪˌkyʊr, ˈsɪn-/ *n.* [C] a job which you get paid for, even though you do not have to do very much work

si·ne qua non /ˌsaɪni kwɑ ˈnɑn/ *n.* [singular] FORMAL something that you must have, or which must exist, for something else to be possible: [+ **for/of**] *Strength of character is the sine qua non of leadership.*

sin·ew /ˈsɪnyu/ *n.* **1** [C,U] NOT TECHNICAL a long strong piece of TISSUE in your body that connects a muscle to a bone; TENDON **2** [C usually plural] LITERARY a means of strength or support: *The plan was designed to provide the sinews of enhanced military power.*

sin·ew·y /ˈsɪnyui/ *adj.* **1** having strong sinews that you can see through the skin: *a big man with long, sinewy arms* **2** sinewy meat has a lot of sinews in it, and is not easy to cut or eat

sin·ful /ˈsɪnfəl/ *adj.* **1** morally wrong, or guilty of doing something morally wrong: *sinful behavior* | *They believe that humans are sinful by nature.* **2** very wrong or bad: *a sinful waste of taxpayers' money* —**sinfully** *adv.*

sing /sɪŋ/ *v. past tense* **sang** *past participle* **sung** **S W** **1 2** **1** [I,T] to produce musical sounds, songs etc. with your voice: *Daryl sang in his high school choir.* | [+ **to**] *She sang softly to herself as she worked.* | [**sing sb sth**] *Sing me a little of it, and I'll see if I know it.* | *They drove along,* **singing** *old Beatles* **songs.** **2** [I] if birds sing, they produce high musical sounds **3 sing sb to sleep** to sing to a baby or child until they go to sleep **4 sing sb's praises** to praise someone very much: *Diane really admires you – she's always singing your praises.* **5** [I always + adv./prep.] LITERARY to make a high, continuous, ringing sound: *Beth ran toward the stream that sang on the other side of the woods.* **6** [I] OLD-FASHIONED to tell someone or the police everything you know about a crime, especially a crime you were involved in yourself: *Pretty soon, Vinnie was singing like a canary.* **7** [I + **of**,T] LITERARY to praise someone in poetry

sing along *phr. v.* [I] to sing with someone else who is already singing: [+ **to**] *Jackie was singing along to the radio and didn't hear the doorbell.* | [+ **with**] *Kern invited the audience to sing along with him on some of his greatest hits.*

sing out *phr. v.* [I,T] to sing or shout out clearly and loudly: *"Good morning, Mrs. James!" Eddie sang out.*

sing. the written abbreviation of "singular"

sing·a·long /ˈsɪŋəˌlɔŋ/ *n.* [C] an informal occasion when people sing songs together

Sing·a·pore /ˈsɪŋgəˌpɔr/ **1** a small country on an island in southeast Asia, between Malaysia and Indonesia **2** the capital city of Singapore —**Singaporean** /ˌsɪŋgəˈpɔriən/ *n., adj.*

singe /sɪndʒ/ *v.* **singeing, singed** [I,T] to burn something slightly on its surface or edge, or to be burned in this way: *The heat was so intense that it singed our hair.*

sing·er /ˈsɪŋɚ/ *n.* [C] someone who sings, especially as a profession: *an opera singer* | *a jazz singer* **S W** **3**

Sing·er /ˈsɪŋɚ/**, I·saac** /ˈaɪzək/ (1811–1875) a U.S. inventor who was the first person to make and sell SEWING MACHINES

Singer, Isaac Ba·shev·is /bəˈʃɛvɪs/ (1904–1991) a Jewish-American writer, born in Poland, who is best known for his short stories written in Yiddish

singer-song·writ·er /ˌ...ˈ.../ *n.* [C] someone who writes songs and sings them

sin·gle[1] /ˈsɪŋgəl/ *adj.* **S W** **1 1**
1 **one** [only before noun] only one: *The Cubs won the game by a single point.* | *These trees can grow over a foot in a single summer.* | *We hope to establish a single safety standard for all airlines.* | *There was* **not a single** (=not even one) *person in sight.*
2 every single thing/person/one etc. used to emphasize that something is true for every thing, person etc. in a group: *Mike's mom calls him every single day.* | *Every single time I go on a plane, I get sick.*
3 the single biggest/greatest/worst etc. used to emphasize that something or someone is the biggest, greatest etc. of their kind: *Education is the single most important issue facing the city today.* | *Housing is our single biggest monthly expense.*
4 **person** **a)** not married: *Jeff is 38 years old and still single.* **b)** not involved in a romantic relationship: *How does it feel to be single again?* —see also SINGLE PARENT
5 single bed/room etc. something that is meant for or used by only one person: *You have to pay extra for a single room.* —compare DOUBLE[1] (3)
6 **one part** having only one part, quality etc., rather than having two or more: *Carla wore a single strand of pearls around her neck.* | *a single-lane bridge*

single[2] *n.* [C] **1** a musical recording of only one song, that can be bought separately: *the Top 40 singles chart* **2** a hit that allows the person who is hitting the ball to reach first BASE in baseball **3 singles** [U] a game, especially in tennis, played by one person against another: *the women's singles championship* —compare **doubles** (DOUBLE[2] (5)) **4** a piece of paper money worth one dollar: *Does anybody have*

five singles? **5 singles** [plural] people who are not married or involved in a romantic relationship: *The show is especially popular among young singles.* | *a singles bar* (=where single people can go to drink and meet new people)

single³ v. **[I]** to hit the ball far enough to be able to run as far as first BASE in baseball: *Rodriguez singled to left field.*

single sb/sth ↔ **out** *phr. v.* **[T]** to choose someone or something from among a group of similar people or things, especially in order to praise them or criticize them: *I don't know why I was singled out.* | **single sb out for praise/blame** etc. *It is absurd to single out one group for special treatment.*

single-breast·ed /ˌ.. '..↓/ *adj.* a single-breasted JACKET or suit has only one set of buttons at the front —compare DOUBLE-BREASTED

single dig·its /ˌ.. '../ *n.* **in (the) single digits** a number, rate etc. that is in single digits is less than 10: *Temperatures dipped into the single digits overnight.* —**single-digit** *adj.* [only before noun] *single-digit inflation*

single-fam·ily /ˌ.. '..↓/ *adj.* [only before noun] **a single-family house/home etc.** a house that is built for one family to live in

single file /ˌ.. '../ *n.* **in single file** moving in a line, with one behind another: *The class walked in single file down the hall.* —**single file** *adv.:* *They passed single file through the gap in the hedge.*

single-hand·ed·ly /ˌ.. '..../ also **single-handed** /ˌ.. '../ *adv.* done by one person without help from anyone else: *Nader almost single-handedly changed the public's opinion of the big car companies.* —**single-handed** *adj.* [only before noun] *a single-handed yacht race*

single-mind·ed /ˌ.. '..↓/ *adj.* having one clear aim and working very hard to achieve it: *a single-minded pursuit of success* —**single-mindedly** *adv.* —**single-mindedness** *n.* [U]

sin·gle·ness /'sɪŋgəlnɪs/ *n.* FORMAL **1 singleness of purpose** great determination when you are working to achieve something **2** [U] the state of being unmarried

single par·ent /ˌ.. '..↓/ *n.* [C] a mother or father who takes care of their children on their own, without a partner

single-sex /ˌ.. '.↓/ *adj.* **single-sex school/college/ education etc.** a school, college etc. for either males or females, but not for both together —opposite COED¹

single-spaced /ˌ.. '.↓/ *adj.* [usually before noun] single-spaced lines of words on a printed page are close together, rather than having a space between them: *Donna received a three-page, single-spaced letter from her lawyer.* —**single-space** *v.* [T] —**single-spacing** *n.* [U] —compare DOUBLE-SPACED

sin·gle·ton /'sɪŋgəltən/ *n.* [C] someone who does something or goes somewhere alone

sin·gly /'sɪŋgli/ *adv.* one at a time; separately: *Are the rolls sold singly or by the dozen?*

sing·song /'sɪŋsɔŋ/ *n.* [singular] a way of speaking in which your voice repeatedly rises and falls —**singsong** *adj.: a singsong voice*

sin·gu·lar¹ /'sɪŋgələ/ *adj.* **1** a singular noun, verb, form etc. is used when writing or speaking about one person or thing: *If the subject is singular, use a singular verb.* **2** [only before noun] FORMAL very great or very noticeable: *Enya's music possesses a singular sense of vision and originality.* **3** [only before noun] used to emphasize the fact that there is only one of something; single: *The singular objective of this partnership is to improve the company's safety performance.* **4** [only before noun] LITERARY very unusual or strange: *We saw another singular item on the list of objects for sale: Napoleon's reading glasses.*

singular² *n.* **the singular** the form of a word used when writing or speaking about one person or thing

sin·gu·lar·i·ty /ˌsɪŋgjə'lærəti/ *n.* **1** [C] TECHNICAL an extremely small point in space that contains an extremely large amount of material, which does not obey the usual laws of nature, especially inside a BLACK HOLE or at the beginning of the universe **2** [U]

OLD-FASHIONED strangeness **3** [U] FORMAL the fact of being the only one of its kind: *He is just trying to assert his singularity as a writer.*

sin·gu·lar·ly /'sɪŋgjələli/ *adv.* **1** in a way that is very noticeable: *a singularly beautiful woman* **2** OLD-FASHIONED in an unusual way; strangely

Sin·ha·lese /ˌsɪnhə'liz/ *n.* [C] **1** someone from one of the groups of people who live in Sri Lanka **2** one of the languages of Sri Lanka —**Sinhalese** *adj.*

sin·is·ter /'sɪnɪstə/ *adj.* making you feel that something evil, wrong, or illegal is happening or will happen: *a sinister laugh* | *A sinister figure lurked in the shadows.* | *There may be more sinister forces at work behind the scenes.*

sink¹ /sɪŋk/ *v. past tense* **sank** *or* **sunk** *past participle* **sunk**

1 ‹in water› **a)** [I] to go down below the surface of water, mud etc.: *The kids watched as the coin sank to the bottom of the pool.* | *Fortunately, the sinking barge did not leak any fuel into the harbor.* **b)** [T] to damage a ship so badly that it goes down below the surface of water: *Three ships were sunk that night by enemy torpedoes.* —see picture at FLOAT¹

2 ‹move lower› [I] **a)** to move down to a lower level: *The building's foundations have sunk several inches in recent years.* | *Gradually, the sun sank below the horizon.* **b)** to fall down or sit down heavily, especially because you are very tired and weak: [+ **into/on/down** etc.] *Tom sank down on the sofa, completely exhausted.*

3 ‹get worse› [I always + adv./prep.] to gradually get into a worse condition: *She couldn't stand the poverty, seeing people sinking lower and lower, with no ambition.* | **sink into crisis/despair/decay etc.** *The country was sinking into political crisis.* | *Two days after the accident, Joyce sank into a coma.*

4 ‹lower amount/value› [I] to go down in amount or value: *The stock index had sunk 197.92 points by midday.* | *The price of crude oil could sink even further.*

5 ‹sports› [T] to put a ball into a hole or basket in games such as GOLF or basketball: *Pierce sank a 3-point basket two minutes into the game.*

6 ‹dig into ground› [T] if you sink something such as a well or part of a building, you dig a hole to put it into the ground: *The first exploratory oil well was sunk in late 1987.*

7 sb's heart sinks also **sb's spirits sink** used to say that someone loses hope or confidence: *My heart just sank when I read Patty's letter.*

8 be sunk SPOKEN to be in a situation when you are certain to fail or have a lot of problems: *If that check doesn't come today, we're really sunk.*

9 sink like a stone/rock also **sink without a trace a)** if something in water sinks like a stone, it sinks to the bottom very quickly **b)** if someone or something sinks like a stone, it is not popular and people forget about it very quickly: *Shore's 1995 movie sank like a stone.*

10 ‹sound› [I] if a sound sinks, it becomes very quiet: [+ **into**] *Sarah's voice sank into a whisper.*

11 a/that sinking feeling the bad feeling that you get when you suddenly realize that something bad is going to happen: *I had a sinking feeling in the pit of my stomach.*

12 sink so low also **sink to doing sth** to be dishonest enough or SELFISH enough to do something very bad or unfair: *How could he have sunk so low?*

13 sink or swim to succeed or fail without help from anyone else: *Some people advocate leaving the jobless to sink or swim.*

sink in *phr. v.* [I] if information, facts etc. sink in, you gradually understand them or realize their full meaning: *I don't know what we're going to do now that Jamie's gone - it hasn't really sunk in yet.*

sink sth **into** sth *phr. v.* **1** [T] to spend a lot of money on something; INVEST: *They had sunk their entire savings into their house.* **2** [T] to put something sharp into someone's flesh, into food, etc.: *Walters sank his harpoon into the whale.* **3 sink your teeth into sth a)** to bite into something or start to eat it: *We couldn't wait to sink our teeth into one of Dave's juicy burgers.* **b)** to become actively involved in something that you think is very interesting: *Bruce says he's waiting for a movie role he can really sink his teeth into.*

s w **sink²** *n.* [C] an open container in a kitchen or BATHROOM that you can fill with water and use for washing your hands or face, or for washing dishes etc. —see also **everything but the kitchen sink** (KITCHEN) —see picture at KITCHEN

sink·er /'sɪŋkɚ/ *n.* [C] **1** a small heavy object that is attached to a string or net to keep it in the water when you are fishing —see also **hook, line, and sinker** (HOOK¹ (12)) **2** a type of throw in baseball in which the ball drops very low as it crosses HOME PLATE

sink·hole /'sɪŋkhoʊl/ *n.* [C] **1** a large hole that forms in the ground **2** something that costs a lot of money over a long period of time, or uses a lot of time and other things: *Sen. Leahy argued that the fighter plane program was a budget sinkhole.*

sink·ing fund /'.. ,./ *n.* [C] TECHNICAL money saved regularly by a business to pay for something in the future

sin·ner /'sɪnɚ/ *n.* [C] someone who has SINned by not obeying God's laws

Sino- /saɪnoʊ/ *prefix* relating to China: *Sino-Japanese trade*

sin tax /'. ./ *n.* [C] an additional tax that is put on the price of certain things that are thought to be unhealthy, such as cigarettes and alcohol

sin·u·ous /'sɪnyuəs/ *adj.* curving and twisting smoothly, like the movements of a snake: *a tree with sinuous branches* | *I watched the sinuous movements of her head and arms.*

si·nus /'saɪnəs/ *n.* [C] one of the hollow spaces in the bones of your face that are filled with air and are connected to your nose

si·nus·i·tis /,saɪnə'saɪtɪs/ *n.* [U] a condition in which your sinuses swell up and become painful

Sioux /su/ a Native American tribe from the central northern region of the U.S. —**Sioux** *adj.*

sip¹ /sɪp/ *v.* [I,T] to drink something slowly, taking very small mouthfuls: *Tom sipped his martini thoughtfully.* | *[+ on]* *We sipped on some cocktails before ordering our meals.*

sip² *n.* [C] a very small amount of a drink: *Fraker nodded and took a sip of wine.*

si·phon¹ /'saɪfən/ *n.* [C] **1** a bent tube used for getting liquid out of a container, by holding the other end of the tube at a lower level than the container **2** a type of bottle for holding SODA WATER that is forced out of the bottle using gas pressure

siphon² *v.* [T] **1** to remove liquid from a container by using a siphon: **siphon sth off/out/into etc.** *Crews began siphoning oil from the leaking barge.* **2** to take money from a business, account etc. dishonestly, in order to use it for a purpose for which it was not intended: **siphon sth off/from etc.** *Over $30 billion had been siphoned off into foreign bank accounts.*

Si·quei·ros /sɪ'keɪroʊs/**, Da·vid** /'deɪvɪd/ (?1896–1974) a Mexican PAINTER famous for his wall paintings of political subjects

s w **sir** /sɚ/ *n.* **1** FORMAL used to address a man in order to be polite or to show respect: *Excuse me, sir. Is this your jacket?* | *"Are you on duty tonight, Corporal?" "Yes, sir."* | *Dear Sir or Madam...* (=used at the beginning of a formal letter to someone you do not know) —compare MA'AM **2** Sir a title used before the first name of a man who was made a KNIGHT by the king or queen of Great Britain, or who was born with the rank of BARONET: *Sir James Wilson* **3** no/ yes sir! SPOKEN, INFORMAL used to emphasize a statement or an answer to a question: *I'm not doing any more work for them. No sir!*

sire¹ /saɪɚ/ *n.* **1** Sire OLD USE a way of addressing a king: *Please excuse me, Sire.* **2** [C usually singular]

TECHNICAL the father of a four-legged animal, especially a horse —compare DAM¹ (2)

sire² *v.* [T] **1** to be the father of an animal, especially a horse: *The stallion has sired several race winners.* **2** OLD-FASHIONED to be the father of a person

sir·ee, sirree /sə'ri/ *n.* **no/yes siree (Bob)!** SPOKEN, INFORMAL used to emphasize a statement or an answer to a question: *"Did you hear that, everybody?" "Yes siree!"*

si·ren /'saɪrən/ *n.* [C] **1** a piece of equipment that makes very loud warning sounds, used on police cars, FIRE TRUCKS etc. **2 a siren call/song** encouragement to do something that sounds very attractive, especially when this could have bad results: *Still more investors have been lured by the siren call of Internet stocks.* **3** a word used especially in newspapers meaning a woman who is very attractive, but also dangerous to men **4 the Sirens** a group of women in ancient Greek stories, whose beautiful singing made SAILORs sail toward them into dangerous water

sir·loin /'sɚlɔɪn/ also **sirloin steak** /'.. ,./ *n.* [C,U] expensive meat, cut from a cow's lower back

si·roc·co /sɪ'rɑkoʊ/ *n.* [C] a hot wind blowing from the desert of North Africa across to southern Europe

sir·ree /sə'ri/ *n.* another spelling of SIREE

sis /sɪs/ *n.* SPOKEN a name used when speaking to your sister

si·sal /'saɪsəl/ *n.* [C,U] a Central American plant whose leaves produce strong FIBERs which are used in making rope

sis·sy /'sɪsi/ *n. plural* **sissies** [C] INFORMAL, OFFENSIVE a boy that other boys dislike because he prefers doing things that girls enjoy —**sissy** *adj.* [only before noun] *I'm not playing that sissy game!*

sis·ter /'sɪstɚ/ *n.* [C] **1** a girl or woman who has the **s w** same parents as you: *My little sister* (=younger sister) *was watching TV in the next room.* | *Kari's big sister* (=older sister) *drove us home.* | *older/ younger sister* | *Tim's older sister is in college.* **2** also **Sister** a NUN: *Sister Mary Margaret* **3 a sister company/organization/ship etc.** a company etc. that belongs to the same group or organization: *Some customers were contacted by employees of the bank's sister company, Western Financial Securities.* **4** SPOKEN a way of talking to or about an African American woman, used by African Americans: *I thought she would be sympathetic because she's a sister.* **5** SPOKEN a word used by women to talk about other women and to show that they have feelings of friendship and support toward them: *We have to support our sisters in southern Africa.*

sister cit·y /'.. ,./ *n.* [C] a city or town that has formed a relationship with a similar city in another country in order to encourage visits between them

sis·ter·hood /'sɪstɚ,hʊd/ *n.* **1** [U] a strong loyalty among women who share the same ideas and aims, especially relating to the improvement of women's rights and opportunities **2** [C] an organization of women, especially a religious one

sister-in-law /'.. . ,./ *n. plural* **sisters-in-law** [C] **1** the sister of your husband or wife **2** your brother's wife **3** the wife of the brother of your husband or wife

sis·ter·ly /'sɪstɚli/ *adj.* typical of a loving sister: *sisterly affection*

sit /sɪt/ *v. past tense and past participle* **sat** *present* **s w** *participle* **sitting**
1 in a chair etc. a) [I] to be on a chair, in a seat or on the ground, with the top half of your body upright and your weight resting on your BUTTOCKS: *[+ on/ in/by etc.]* *We sat on the floor, sorting through the pictures.* | *She was sitting in her rocking chair by the window.* | *Who usually sits next to you in class?* | *[sit doing sth]* *Todd just sat staring into space for a while.* | *sit at a desk/table etc.* *I walked in and saw Steve sitting at the kitchen table.* **b)** [I always + adv./ prep.] to get into a sitting position after you have been standing up: *Jim walked over and sat beside her.* **c)** [T always + adv./prep.] to make someone sit somewhere or help them to sit somewhere: *sit sb on/in etc.* *Just sit him over here and give him something to drink.*

sitting on a chair   sitting at a desk   sitting in an armchair

2 objects/buildings etc. [I] to be in a particular position or condition: [+ on/in etc.] *Your book is sitting on the shelf, right where you left it.* | **sit empty/unused/vacant etc.** *Most of the stores had sat vacant for years.*

3 do nothing [I always + adv./prep.] to stay in one place for a long time, especially sitting down, doing nothing useful or helpful: *Are you just going to **sit there** all afternoon?* | *I'm not going to **sit here** and listen to you two argue.*

4 animal/bird **a)** [I always + adv./prep.] to be in, or get into, a resting position, with the tail end of the body resting on a surface: *Jeff's dog sat next to his chair as we talked.* **b) Sit!** used to tell a dog to sit with the tail end of its body on the ground or floor **c)** [I always + adv./prep.] if a bird sits on its eggs, it covers them with its body to make the eggs HATCH (=open)

5 sit tight a) SPOKEN to stay where you are and not move: *Just sit tight – I'll be there in ten minutes.* **b)** to stay in the same situation, and not change your mind or do anything new: *You might want to sit tight a few months and see what happens to the stock market.*

6 not sit well with sb if a situation, plan etc. does not sit well with someone, they do not like it: *Buchanan's opposition to trade treaties did not sit well with voters.*

7 committee/court etc. [I] **a)** to be a member of a committee, court, or other official group: [+ on] *Critics have claimed that he is not qualified to sit on the court.* **b)** to have a meeting in order to carry out official business: *The Court of Appeals sits in San Francisco.*

8 be sitting pretty to be in a very good or favorable position: *At that stage in the campaign, she was sitting pretty in the polls.*

9 sit on the fence to avoid saying which side of an argument you support or what your opinion is about a particular subject: *You can't sit on the fence any longer – what's it going to be?* —see also FENCE-SITTER

10 sit on your hands to delay taking action when you should do something: *Most delegates sat on their hands while a few radicals took control of the discussion.*

11 sit in judgment (on/over sb) to give your opinion about whether someone has done something wrong, especially when you have no right to do this

12 picture/photo [I + for] to sit somewhere so that you can be painted or photographed

13 baby/child [I + for] SPOKEN to take care of a baby or child while its parents are out; BABYSIT

sit around *phr. v.* [I] to spend a lot of time sitting and doing nothing useful: *Mostly we sat around and told each other stories about ourselves.*

sit back *phr. v.* [I] **1** to get into a comfortable position and relax: *You sit back and relax – I'll fix dinner.* **2** to make no effort to get involved in something or influence what happens: *All we have to do now is sit back and watch the checks roll in.*

sit by *phr. v.* [I] to take no action that would stop something bad from happening: *We're not going to sit by and let the same thing happen next year.*

sit down *phr. v.* **1** [I] to get into a sitting position or be in a sitting position: *Come on in and sit down.* | *I've been sitting down all day – I don't mind standing for a while.* **2** [T **sit sb down**] to make someone sit down somewhere, especially if you are angry with them or want to tell them something important: *I think you need to sit Bobby down and explain why we can't afford to go.* **3 sit down and do sth** to try to solve a problem or deal with something that needs to be done, by giving it all your attention: *First we should sit down and work out the financing.*

sit in *phr. v.* [I] **1** to be present at a meeting, but not take an active part in it: [+ on] *We sat in on a couple of French classes.* **2** to do a job, go to a meeting etc. instead of the person who usually does it: [– for] *Diane Sawyer sat in for Jennings on the evening news for a week.*

sit on sth *phr. v.* [T] INFORMAL to delay dealing with something: *If you have a genuine complaint, don't just sit on it.*

sit sth ↔ **out** *phr. v.* [T] **1** to not take part in something such as a game or dance, especially after you have been taking part for a while: *I'm a little tired, so I think I'll sit the next dance out.* **2** to stay where you are until something finishes, especially something boring or bad; WAIT OUT: *When the war started, her family decided to stay in the country and sit it out.*

sit through sth *phr. v.* [T] to attend a meeting, performance etc., and stay until the end, even if it is very long and boring: *New council members had to sit through three hours of speeches.*

sit up *phr. v.* **1** [I] to get into a sitting position or get into a sitting position after you have been lying down: *By Monday, Tina was well enough to sit up in bed.* **2** [T **sit sb up**] to help someone to sit after they have been lying down **3** [I] to sit in a chair with your back up straight: *Sit up straight and finish your dinner.* **4** [I] to stay up very late: *Rick sat up all night studying for his physics final.* **5 sit up and take notice** to suddenly start paying attention to someone or something: *The success of cable news stations has made other broadcasters sit up and take notice.*

S

USAGE NOTE: SIT

WORD CHOICE: sit, sit at/in front of/on/in, sit down, seat, be seated

You **sit at** a table, piano, or desk (unless you choose to **sit on** them!), and also **at** a computer or the controls of a car or airplane. However, you sit **in front of** the television or the fire (though you can also sit *by* or *around* a fire). You **sit on** something that has a flat level surface such as the floor, the grass, a simple hard chair, a bench, a sofa, or a bed. You **sit in** a tree, long grass, a car, a room, an armchair, or the driver's seat of a car. When you are talking about the action of moving from standing to sitting, it is more common to use **sit down** rather than **sit** on its own: *Afterward, everyone sat down again* (NOT *"sat again"*). | *Please sit down.* You usually only say *Sit!* to a dog. Note that **seat** as a verb is only transitive. It is fairly formal, and is used in these ways: *The theater seats 500 people* (=has seats for 500 people). | *The hostess will seat you* (=show you where you can sit). **Be seated** is a formal expression for **sit down.** At a formal dinner or in church, for example, you might hear: *Please be seated* (=please sit down).

sit·ar /'sitar/ *n.* [C] a musical instrument from India that has two sets of strings, a long wooden neck, and a round body

sit·com /'sitkam/ *n.* [C,U] a funny television program in which the same characters appear in different situations each week

sit-down /ˌ. '.ˌ/ *adj.* **1** a sit-down meal or restaurant is one in which you sit at a table and eat a formal meal **2 a sit-down strike/protest** an occasion when a large group of people protests something by not moving from a particular area until their problem is solved

site[1] /saɪt/ *n.* [C] **1** a place where something important or interesting happened: *a historical site* | [+ of] *the site of a Civil War battle* **2** an area of ground where something is being built or will be built: *a construction site* | [+ of/for] *The school board has approved the site for the high school.* **3 on site** at the place where something happens: *An engineer will be on site to supervise the construction.* **4** a WEB SITE

site[2] *v.* **be sited** be placed or built in a particular place: [+ in/near etc.] *The zoo is sited in the middle of the city.*

site-spe·cif·ic /ˌ. .'..◂/ *adj.* designed and made to be used in a particular place, or relating to a particular place: *site-specific artworks*

sit-in /'. ./ *n.* [C] a type of protest in which people refuse to leave the place where they work or study until their demands are dealt with: **hold/stage a sit-in** *Students staged a sit-in to protest the firing of a popular professor.*

sit·ter /'sɪtɚ/ *n.* [C] **1** SPOKEN a BABYSITTER **2** someone who sits or stands somewhere so that someone else can paint them or take photographs of them

sit·ting /'sɪtɪŋ/ *n.* [C] **1 at/in one sitting** during one continuous period when you are sitting in a chair: *Jeff ate a whole bag of potato chips in one sitting.* **2** one of the times when a meal is served in a place where there is not enough space for everyone to eat at the same time: *Dinner is served in three sittings.* **3** an occasion when you have yourself painted or photographed

Sitting Bull /ˌ.. './ (?1834–1890) a Sioux chief famous for fighting against General George CUSTER

sitting duck /ˌ.. './ *n.* [C] someone who is easy to attack or easy to cheat: *We were like sitting ducks for pickpockets in the city.*

sitting room /'.. ˌ./ *n.* [C] OLD-FASHIONED the room in a house where you sit, relax, watch television etc.; LIVING ROOM

sit·u /'sɪtu, 'saɪtu/ —see IN SITU

sit·u·ate /'sɪtʃuˌeɪt/ *v.* **1 be situated** to be in a particular place or position: *The house is situated on a small hill.* | **beautifully/conveniently/ideally etc. situated** *Troops later occupied Langson, a town strategically situated near the Chinese border.* **2** [T] to describe or consider something as being part of something else or relating to something else: **situate sth in sth** *Students will be expected to situate the novel in its historical context.* **3** [T always + adv./prep.] to put something in a particular place or position: *Tax preparation services generally situate themselves in storefront offices.*

sit·u·a·tion /ˌsɪtʃu'eɪʃən/ *n.* [C] a combination of all the things that are happening and all the conditions that exist at a particular time in a particular place: *Everyone knew how serious the situation was.* | *What's the best way to deal with an embarrassing situation at work?* | *What would you do if you were in my situation?* | **economic/political/financial situation** *In view of the company's financial situation, there will be no salary increases this year.* —see also NO-WIN SITUATION, WIN-WIN SITUATION

situation com·e·dy /ˌ.... '.../ *n.* [C,U] FORMAL a SITCOM

sit-up /'. ./ *n.* [C] an exercise in which you sit up from a lying position, while keeping your feet on the floor

six /sɪks/ *number* **1** 6 **2** 6 o'clock: *I'll be home at six.* **3 it's six of one and half a dozen of the other** SPOKEN used to say there is not much difference between two possible choices, situations etc. **4 six figures** a number that is between 100,000 and one million dollars: *LaRose is currently earning a salary in the low six figures.* **5 be at sixes and sevens** if someone or a group of people is at sixes and sevens, they are confused and cannot agree: *Likewise, the President is at sixes and sevens over foreign affairs.*

six·fold /ˌsɪks'foʊld◂/ *adv.* by six times as much or as many: *The plant has increased its production sixfold.*

—sixfold *adj.* [only before noun] *a sixfold increase in teenage pregnancies*

six-foot·er /ˌ. './ *n.* [C] INFORMAL someone who is at least six feet (1.83 meters) tall

six-pack /'. ./ *n.* [C] **1** six cans of a drink, especially beer, sold together as a set: [+ of] *Doug brought a six-pack of beer to the party.* **2** HUMOROUS well-developed muscles that you can see on a man's stomach —see also **Joe Six-Pack** (JOE (3))

six-shoot·er /'. ˌ./ *n.* [C] INFORMAL a type of short gun that can hold six bullets, especially one that was used in the western U.S. in past times

six·teen /ˌsɪk'stin◂/ *number* 16

six·teenth[1] /ˌsɪk'stinθ◂/ *adj.* 16th; next after the fifteenth: *the sixteenth century*

sixteenth[2] *pron.* **the sixteenth** the 16th thing in a series: *Let's have dinner on the sixteenth* (=the 16th day of the month).

sixteenth[3] *n.* [C] $1/16$; one of sixteen equal parts

sixteenth note /.'. ./ *n.* [C] a musical note which continues for a sixteenth of the length of a WHOLE NOTE —see picture at MUSIC

sixth[1] /sɪksθ/ *adj.* 6th; next after the fifth: *June is the sixth month.*

sixth[2] *pron.* **the sixth** the 6th thing in a series: *I'll call you on the sixth* (=the 6th day of the month).

sixth[3] *n.* [C] $1/6$; one of six equal parts: *The money represents about a sixth of my income.* | **one-sixth/five-sixths** *Only one-sixth of the electorate voted.*

sixth sense /ˌ. './ *n.* [singular] a special feeling or ability to know things, without using any of your five ordinary senses such as your hearing or sight: *Rob has a sixth sense for making the right investment.*

six·ti·eth[1] /'sɪkstiɪθ/ *adj.* 60th; next after the fifty-ninth: *It's my father's sixtieth birthday tomorrow.*

sixtieth[2] *pron.* **the sixtieth** the 60th thing in a series

six·ty /'sɪksti/ *number* **1** 60 **2 the sixties** also **the '60s** the years from 1960 through 1969 **3 sb's sixties** the time when someone is 60 to 69 years old: **in your early/mid/late sixties** *I'd guess she's in her late sixties.* **4 in the sixties** if the temperature is in the sixties, it is between 60° and 69° FAHRENHEIT: **in the high/low sixties** *The weather was nice. It was in the high sixties and sunny.*

sixty-nine, 69 /ˌ.. './ *v.* [I] VULGAR, SLANG to touch another person's sexual organs with your mouth or lips for pleasure while they do the same to your sexual organs —**sixty-nine** *n.* [U]

siz·a·ble, sizeable /'saɪzəbəl/ *adj.* fairly large: *a sizable crowd*

size[1] /saɪz/ *n.*
1 ▶**how big**◀ [C,U] how big or small something is: *There are restrictions on the size and weight of packages we can ship.* | *Jensens' house is about the same size as ours.* | *They served us hamburgers the size of* (=the same size as) *dinner plates.* | *You need a frame that's strong enough to support the vine at its full size.* | *Leave the dough in a warm place until it has doubled in size.* | **in all/different/various shapes and sizes** *Good athletes come in all shapes and sizes.*
2 ▶**very big**◀ [U] the fact of being very big: *Look at the size of that house!* | *The most impressive thing about the diamond is its sheer size.*
3 **that/this size** also **of that/this size** as big as the thing mentioned: *Nobody thought a town this size could support an orchestra.* | *We can't give loans of that size to just anyone.*
4 ▶**clothes/products**◀ [C] one of a set of standard measures according to which clothes and other goods are produced and sold: *These shoes are one size too big.* | *Do you have these pants in a size 12?* | *What size shoes does Kelly wear?*
5 **to size** if you cut, make, or prepare something to size, you make it the right size for a particular use: *The beams were smoothed and trimmed to size with axes.*
6 **size matters** HUMOROUS used to say that larger things are better than smaller things, especially when talking about the size of men's sexual organs
7 **that's about the size of it** SPOKEN used to agree that what someone has said about a situation is a good or correct way of describing it

8 **glue** [U] SIZING (1) —see also **cut sb down to size** at **cut down** (CUT¹), -SIZE, **try sth on for size** at **try sth on** (TRY¹)

size² *v.* [T] **1** [usually passive] to sort things according to their size: *Shrimp are sized for canning into large, medium and small.* **2** [usually passive] to make something into a particular size or sizes: *Most costume patterns are sized for children.* **3** to cover or treat something with SIZING

size sb/sth ↔ **up** *phr. v.* [T] to look at or consider a person or situation and make a judgment about them: *They stood at opposite sides of the room, sizing each other up.*

-size /saɪz/ [in adjectives] **pocket-size/head-size etc.** about the same shape and size as the thing mentioned: *a pocket-size mirror | dust-size particles | poster-size color photos* —see also BITE-SIZE, KING-SIZE, QUEEN-SIZE

size·a·ble /ˈsaɪzəbəl/ *adj.* another spelling of SIZABLE

-sized /saɪzd/ *adj.* of a particular size, or about the same size and shape as something: *a medium-sized dog | pea-sized hailstones | good-sized/fair-sized/decent-sized* (=big enough for a particular purpose)

siz·ing /ˈsaɪzɪŋ/ *n.* [U] **1** a thick sticky liquid used for giving stiffness and a shiny surface to cloth, paper etc. **2** the way things are grouped according to size: *How does the sizing system work for children's clothes?*

siz·zle /ˈsɪzəl/ *v.* [I] **1** to make a sound like water falling on hot metal: *Bacon was sizzling in the pan downstairs.* **2** to be very exciting: *The movie sizzles with Morris and Elisa's sexy dialogue.* —**sizzle** *n.* [singular,U]

siz·zler /ˈsɪzlɚ/ *n.* [C] something that is very exciting: *The San Jose production of Cavalli's opera turned into the season's sizzler.*

siz·zling /ˈsɪzlɪŋ/ *adj.* **1** very hot: *a sizzling summer day* **2** very exciting, especially in a sexual way: *sizzling sex scenes*

SJ a written abbreviation used after a priest's name, to show that he is a JESUIT

ska /skɑ/ *n.* [U] a kind of popular music originally from Jamaica with a fast regular beat, similar to REGGAE

skank /skæŋk/ *n.* [C] OFFENSIVE, SLANG a woman who you have a bad opinion of, because she has sex with a lot of men —**skanky** *adj.*

skate¹ /skeɪt/ *n.* **1** [C] one of a pair of boots with metal blades on the bottom, for moving quickly on ice; ICE SKATE **2** [C] one of a pair of boots or frames with small wheels on the bottom, for moving quickly on flat smooth surfaces; ROLLER SKATE **3** [C,U] *plural* **skate** or **skates** a large flat ocean fish that can be eaten

skate

in-line skating   ice skating

s w **skate²** *v.* [I] **1** to move on skates: *The children skated on the frozen pond.* **2 be skating on thin ice** INFORMAL to be doing something that may get you into trouble —**skater** *n.* [C]

skate over/around sth *phr. v.* [T] to avoid mentioning a problem or subject, or not give it enough attention: *The mayor either skates over developing crises or ignores them completely.*

skate·board /ˈskeɪtbɔrd/ *n.* [C] a short board with two small wheels at each end, which you can stand on and ride for fun or as a sport —**skateboarder** *n.* [C]

skate·board·ing /ˈskeɪtbɔrdɪŋ/ *n.* [U] the activity of riding a skateboard for fun or as a sport

skat·ing /ˈskeɪtɪŋ/ *n.* [U] the activity of moving around on SKATES for fun or as a sport

skating rink /ˈ.. ˌ./ *n.* [C] a place or building where you can SKATE²

ske·dad·dle /skɪˈdædl/ *v.* [I] HUMOROUS to leave a place quickly, especially because you do not want to be caught

skee·ter /ˈskitɚ/ *n.* [C] SPOKEN, INFORMAL a word meaning MOSQUITO, used mainly in the southern U.S.: *That looks like a big skeeter bite.*

skeet shoot·ing /ˈskit ˌʃutɪŋ/ *n.* [U] the sport of shooting at clay objects that have been thrown into the air —**skeet shooter** *n.* [C]

skein /skeɪn/ *n.* [C] **1** a long loosely wound piece of YARN **2** a complicated series of things that are related to each other: [+ **of**] *a complex skein of stories*

skel·e·tal /ˈskɛlətl/ *adj.* like a skeleton, or relating to a skeleton: *Daly's skeletal remains were found almost a month later.*

skeleton

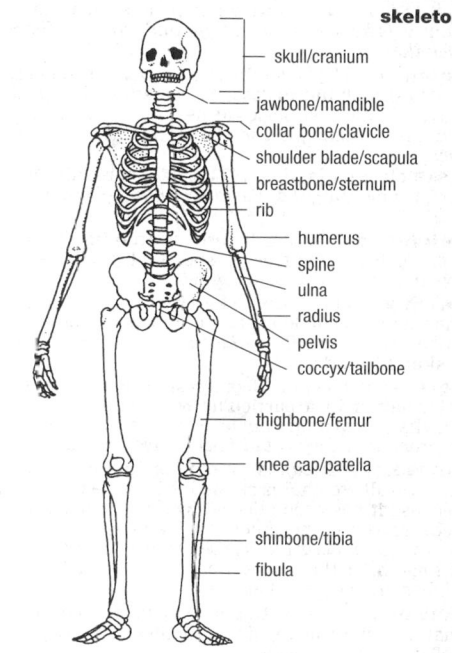

skull/cranium
jawbone/mandible
collar bone/clavicle
shoulder blade/scapula
breastbone/sternum
rib
humerus
spine
ulna
radius
pelvis
coccyx/tailbone
thighbone/femur
knee cap/patella
shinbone/tibia
fibula

S

skel·e·ton /ˈskɛlətn/ *n.* [C]
1 **bones** a) the structure consisting of all the bones in a human or animal body: *the human skeleton* b) a set of these bones or a model of them, fastened in their usual positions, used for example by medical students
2 **structure** the supporting structure of a building, bridge, etc.: *The office building's steel skeleton rose above the skyline.*
3 **thin** an extremely thin person or animal: *We watched her go from a healthy girl to a skeleton in just a few months.*
4 **basic part** the most important parts of something, to which more detail can be added later: *We have agreed on a skeleton outline of the research proposal.*
5 a skeleton in the closet an embarrassing or bad secret about something that happened to you in the past: *Everyone has a few skeletons in the closet.*
6 a skeleton staff/crew/service etc. only enough workers or services to keep an operation or organization running: *On the weekend, we only have a skeleton crew.*

skeleton key /'... ˌ./ *n.* [C] a key made to open a number of different locks

skep·tic /'skɛptɪk/ *n.* [C] someone who has doubts about whether something is true, right, or good: *religious skeptics | Some skeptics question whether the Pell program would cause colleges to raise fees even more.*

skep·ti·cal /'skɛptɪkəl/ *adj.* **1** having doubts about whether something is true, right, or good: [+ **about**] *Initially, he was skeptical about whether the stories were true.* | [+ **of**] *In Washington, many officials were skeptical of the plan.* **2** tending to doubt or not believe what other people tell you: *It will take a lot to convince the increasingly skeptical American public.* —**skeptically** /-kli/ *adv.*

skep·ti·cism /'skɛptəˌsɪzəm/ *n.* [U] an attitude of doubt about whether something is true, right, or good

sketch¹ /skɛtʃ/ *n.* [C] **1** a simple, quickly made drawing that does not show much detail: [+ **of**] *Cantor drew a rough sketch of a cell on his napkin.* **2** a short humorous scene on television, in the theater etc., that is part of a larger show: *a comedy sketch show* **3** a short written or spoken description: *a brief sketch of the life and times of Herman Melville*

sketch² *v.* [I,T] **1** to draw a sketch of something **2** also **sketch out** to describe something in a general way, giving the basic ideas: *Yeltsin sketched an aggressive battle plan for winning back his countrymen.*

   sketch sth ↔ **in** *phr. v.* [T] to add more information about something: *I'd like to sketch in a few details for you.*

sketch·pad /'skɛtʃpæd/ also **sketch·book** /'skɛtʃbʊk/ *n.* [C] a number of sheets of paper fastened together and used for drawing

sketch·y /'skɛtʃi/ *adj.* **sketchier, sketchiest** not thorough or complete, and not having enough details to be useful: *Details of the accident are still sketchy.* —**sketchily** *adv.*

skew /skyu/ *v.* [T] to affect a test or an attempt to get information in a particular way, which makes the results incorrect: *Some samples were handled improperly, which could have skewed the results.*

skewed /skyud/ *adj.* **1** an opinion, piece of information, result etc. that is skewed is incorrect, especially because it has been affected by a particular thing or because you do not know all the facts: *Many people heard only inaccurate, skewed reports about the trial.* **2** something that is skewed is not straight and is higher on one side than the other

skew·er¹ /'skyuɚ/ *n.* [C] a long metal or wooden stick that is put through pieces of meat and vegetables before they are cooked

skewer² *v.* [T] **1** to make a hole through a piece of food, an object etc. with a skewer or with some other pointed object: *They nibbled chunks of Cheddar cheese skewered with toothpicks.* —see picture on page 425 **2** to criticize someone very strongly, often in a way that other people find humorous: *Simon skewers the Rolling Stones in their old age in her song, "The Reason."*

ski¹ /ski/ *n. plural* **skis** [C] **1** one of a pair of long thin narrow pieces of wood or plastic that you fasten to your boots and use for moving on snow **2** a long thin narrow piece of strong material, fastened under a small vehicle so that it can travel on snow

ski² *v. past tense and past participle* **skied** *present participle* **skiing** [I] to move on skis as a sport, or in order to travel on snow: *I'm learning to ski.* —see also SKIER

ski boot /'. ./ *n.* [C] a specially made stiff boot that fastens onto a ski

skid¹ /skɪd/ *v.* **skidded, skidding** [I] if a vehicle or wheel skids, it suddenly slides sideways and you cannot control it: *The plane touched down and skidded off the runway.*

Alice skidded to avoid the old lady.

skid² *n.*
1 ▐sliding movement▐ [C] a sudden sliding movement of a vehicle, that you cannot control: *Long **skid marks** on the pavement showed that the driver had tried to brake.* | *Tony slammed on the brakes and the car **went into a skid** (=started to skid).*
2 on the skids INFORMAL in a situation that is bad and getting worse: *Car and truck sales have been on the skids.*
3 hit the skids to suddenly become much worse or lower in value: *The main character is a defense lawyer whose career has hit the skids.*
4 grease the skids to prepare a situation so that something can happen more easily: *Hundt is already greasing the skids for the deal to be finalized.*
5 put the skids on sth INFORMAL to make it likely or certain that something will fail: *When the payment didn't come through, it put the skids on all our plans.*
6 ▐helicopter▐ [C usually plural] a flat narrow part that is under some aircraft such as HELICOPTERS, used in addition to wheels for landing
7 ▐used to lift/move▐ [C usually plural] a piece of wood that is put under a heavy object to lift or move it

skid row, Skid Row /ˌ. './ *n.* **1 be on skid row** if someone is on skid row, they drink too much alcohol and have no job, nowhere to live etc. **2** [U] a part of a city with a lot of old buildings in bad condition, where poor people who drink too much alcohol spend their time

ski·er /'skiɚ/ *n.* [C] someone who SKIS

skies /skaɪz/ *n.* the plural of SKY

skiff /skɪf/ *n.* [C] a small light boat for one person

ski·ing /'ski-ɪŋ/ *n.* [U] the sport of moving down hills or across land in the snow, wearing SKIS: *We're going skiing in Colorado this winter.*   S W ▢▢ 3

ski jump /'. ./ *n.* [C] a long steep sloping PLATFORM, which people go down on SKIS and jump off in sports competitions

ski jump·ing /'. ˌ../ *n.* [U] a sport in which people wearing SKIS slide down a ski jump and jump off the end as far as possible

skil·ful /'skɪlfəl/ *adj.* the British spelling of SKILLFUL

ski lift /'. ./ *n.* [C] a piece of equipment that carries SKIERS up to the top of a slope

skill /skɪl/ *n.* [C,U] an ability to do something well, especially because you have learned and practiced it: *You have to be able to learn new skills quickly.* | *Marcia's computer skills were not good enough for the job.* | [+ **at/in**] *Gibson's skill at hitting the ball is simply outstanding.* | *The whole team played **with great skill** and determination.* —see Usage Note at ABILITY   S W ▢▢ 1 2

skilled /skɪld/ *adj.* **1** someone who is skilled has the training and experience that is needed to do something well: *There is a shortage of skilled workers in the area.* | [+ **at/in**] *The whole family was skilled in handling horses.* | *She is a **highly skilled** (=very skilled) dancer.* **2** skilled work needs people with special abilities or training to do it: *More women are entering skilled trades such as carpentry and cooking.* —opposite UNSKILLED

skil·let /'skɪlɪt/ *n.* [C] a flat heavy cooking pan with a long handle; FRYING PAN

skill·ful /'skɪlfəl/ *adj.* **1** good at doing something, especially something that needs special ability or training: *a skillful team player* **2** made or done very well, showing a lot of ability: *Thanks to Jackson's skillful management, profits are up this year.* | *the skillful use of sound effects* —**skillfully** *adv.*

skim /skɪm/ *v.* **skimmed, skimming 1** [T] to remove something from the surface of a liquid, especially floating oil or solids: [+ **off/from**] *Skim any fat off the surface of the soup.* **2** [I,T] to read something quickly to find the main facts or ideas in it: *Jack opened the paper and skimmed the headlines.* | [+ **through**] *Save time by reading the questions first, then skimming through the text for answers.* **3** [T] to move along quickly, nearly touching a surface: *seagulls skimming the waves*

skim sth ↔ **off** *phr. v.* [T] **1** to take money illegally or dishonestly: *The communist elite skimmed off wealth to pay for its own luxuries.* **2** to take part of something that other people want, especially the best part of it: *Magnet schools skim off the best facilities, teachers and students from the system.*

ski mask /'. ./ *n.* [C] a warm KNIT hat that covers most of your head and face

skim·mer /'skɪmɚ/ *n.* [C] **1** a ship that is used for cleaning up oil from the surface of the ocean **2** a bird that flies low over the ocean

skim milk /ˌ. './ *n.* [U] milk that has had all the fat and cream removed from it —compare ONE PERCENT MILK, TWO PERCENT MILK, WHOLE MILK

skimp /skɪmp/ *v.* [I] to not spend enough money or time on something, or not use enough of something, so that what you do is unsuccessful or of bad quality: [+ **on**] *Don't skimp on the cream.*

skimp·y /'skɪmpi/ *adj.* **skimpier, skimpiest 1** a skimpy dress, skirt etc. is very short and does not cover very much of a woman's body **2** not providing enough of something: *a skimpy meal* —**skimpily** *adv.* —**skimpiness** *n.* [U]

s w
2 2

skin¹ /skɪn/ *n.*

1 **body** a) [C,U] the natural outer layer of a human or animal body: *He brushed against her beautifully soft skin.* | *a skin disease* | *The toad's skin produces a poisonous substance.* **b)** [U] the skin on your face: *a cleanser for oily skin* | *Todd has really **bad skin** (=unhealthy looking skin).*

2 **from an animal** [C,U] the skin of an animal, sometimes including its fur, used to make leather, clothes etc.: *leopard skins* | *a sheepskin jacket*

3 **food** [C,U] a) the natural thin outer cover of some fruits and vegetables: *potato skins* | *onion skin* —see picture at FRUIT¹ **b)** the outer cover of a SAUSAGE

4 **on a liquid** a thin solid layer that forms on the top of some liquids when they get cold or are left without a cover: *a skin on the top of the pudding*

5 **by the skin of your teeth** if you do something by the skin of your teeth, you just barely succeed in doing it: *Jeff just got into college by the skin of his teeth.*

6 **have thin/thick skin** to be easily upset or not easily upset by criticism: *You need to have thick skin to be a salesperson.* —see also THICK-SKINNED, THIN-SKINNED

7 **be skin and bones** INFORMAL to be extremely thin in a way that is unattractive and unhealthy: *She was all skin and bones, weighing barely 80 pounds.*

8 **get under sb's skin** if someone gets under your skin, they annoy you, especially by the way they behave: *Kids will say some mean things to try and get under your skin.*

9 **make sb's skin crawl** to make someone feel uncomfortable, nervous, or slightly afraid: *The thought of him touching me just makes my skin crawl.*

10 **it's no skin off sb's nose** SPOKEN used to say that someone does not care what another person thinks or does, because it does not affect them: *It's no skin off our nose if they don't want to come along.* —see also **jump out of your skin** (JUMP¹ (5)), **save sb's skin/butt/bacon** (SAVE¹ (9)), -SKINNED

skin² *v.* **skinned, skinning 1** [T] to remove the skin from an animal, fruit, or vegetable: *Add four boned and skinned duck breasts.* **2** [T] to hurt a part of your body by rubbing off some skin: *She skinned her knee when she fell off her bike.* **3 skin** sb **alive** HUMOROUS to punish someone very severely: *Richard*

would skin me alive if he ever found out. **4 there is more than one way to skin a cat** used to say that there is more than one way to achieve something **5** [T] INFORMAL to completely defeat someone: *The football team really skinned Watertown last year.*

skin·care /'skɪnkɛr/ *adj.* skincare products are intended to improve the condition of your skin, especially the skin on your face —**skin care** *n.* [U]

skin deep /ˌ. './ *adj.* [not before noun] something that is skin deep seems to be important or effective, but in fact it is not, because it only affects the way things appear: *Beauty is only skin deep.*

skin div·ing /'. ˌ../ *n.* [U] the sport of swimming under water with light breathing equipment, but without a protective suit —**skin diver** *n.* [C]

skin flick /'. ./ *n.* [C] SLANG a movie that shows a lot of sexual activity; a PORNOGRAPHIC movie

skin·flint /'skɪnˌflɪnt/ *n.* [C] DISAPPROVING someone who hates spending money or giving it away; MISER

skin·graft /'skɪngræft/ *n.* [C] a medical operation in which healthy skin is removed from one part of your body and used on another to replace burned or damaged skin

skin·head /'skɪnhɛd/ *n.* [C] a young white person who has hair that is cut very short, especially one who behaves violently toward people of other races

skin·less /'skɪnlɪs/ *adj.* [only before noun] skinless meat, especially chicken, has had the skin removed from it

-skinned /skɪnd/ [in adjectives] **dark-skinned/ smooth-skinned/brown-skinned etc.** having a particular type or color of skin: *a pale-skinned Englishman*

S

Skin·ner /'skɪnɚ/, **B.F.** /bi ɛf/ (1904–1990) a U.S. PSYCHOLOGIST famous for developing the ideas of BEHAVIORISM

skin·ny¹ /'skɪni/ *adj.* **skinnier, skinniest** very thin, especially in a way that is unattractive: *skinny little kids* —see Usage Note at THIN¹

s w
3

skinny² *n.* **the skinny** SPOKEN information, especially secret information, about someone or something: *What's the skinny on the new guy?*

skinny-dip·ping /'.. ˌ../ *n.* [U] swimming with no clothes on: *Some of us **went skinny-dipping** in the lake.*

skin-tight /ˌ. './ *adj.* [only before noun] skin-tight clothes fit tightly against your body: *skin-tight jeans*

skip¹ /skɪp/ *v.*

1 **not do sth** [T] to not do something that you usually do, or that you should do: *Skipping meals is not a good way to lose weight.* | **skip class/school** *Jeff got caught skipping math class again.*

2 **not deal with sth** [I,T] to not read, mention, or deal with something that would normally come or happen next: *I decided to skip the first two chapters.* | [+ **to**] *Well, let's skip to question 8 for now.* | [+ **over**] *Dana just skipped over the difficult words in the story.*

3 **change subjects** [I always + adv./prep.] to go from one subject or activity to another in no particular order: [+ **around/from**] *Don't keep skipping around from one topic to another in your paper.*

4 **movement** [I] to move forward with quick steps and jumps: *Shelly skipped down the sidewalk.*

5 **skip town/the country** to leave a place suddenly and secretly, especially to avoid being punished or paying debts: *Once he was out of jail, he planned to skip the country.*

6 **skip a year/grade** to start a new school year in a class that is one year ahead of the class you would normally enter

7 **skip rocks/stones** to throw smooth, flat stones into a lake, river etc. in a way that makes them jump across the surface

8 **ball** [I always + adv./prep.] if a ball or something similar skips off a surface, it quickly moves away from that surface after hitting it: [+ **off/along/ across** etc.] *The ball skipped off Bonds' glove and bounced toward the fence.*

s w
3

9 skip rope to jump over a rope as you swing it over your head and under your feet, as a game or for exercise; JUMP ROPE

skip out on sth also **skip out of** sth *phr. v.* [T] to leave suddenly and secretly, especially in order to avoid being punished or paying money: *Tenants who skip out on water and other utility bills are the focus of a new law.*

skip² *n.* [C] a quick light stepping and jumping movement

ski pants /'. ./ *n.* [plural] **1** thick pants with long thin pieces of cloth that fasten over your shoulders, worn while SKIing **2** tight pants with a band of cloth that goes under your foot, worn by women

ski plane /'. ./ *n.* [C] an airplane that has long thin narrow parts on the bottom instead of wheels, for landing on snow

ski pole /'. ./ *n.* [C] one of two pointed short poles used for balancing and for pushing against the snow when SKIing

skip·per¹ /'skɪpɚ/ *n.* [C] **1** the person in charge of a ship **2** INFORMAL the person in charge of a sports team; COACH

skipper² *v.* [T] to be in charge of a ship, sports team, business etc.

skirl /skɔl/ *v.* [I] to make a high sharp sound, like the sound of BAGPIPES —**skirl** *n.* [singular]

skir·mish¹ /'skɔmɪʃ/ *n.* [C] **1** a fight between small groups of soldiers, ships etc., especially one that happens away from the main part of a battle **2** a short argument, especially between political opponents: *SAIC's previous skirmishes with investigators had attracted little attention.*

skirmish² *v.* [I + with] to be involved in a short fight or argument

skirt¹ /skɔt/ *n.* [C] **1** a piece of outer clothing worn by women and girls, which hangs down from the waist like the bottom part of a dress: *She wore a white blouse and a plain black skirt.* —compare DRESS² (1) **2** the part of a dress or coat that hangs down from the waist

skirt² also **skirt around** *v.* [T] **1** to go around the outside edge of a place or area: *Hurricane Ben skirted the Florida coast before moving back out to sea.* **2** to avoid talking about an important subject, especially because it is difficult or embarrassing: *The report skirted the issue of the government's responsibility for the crisis.*

ski run /'. ./ *n.* [C] a marked track on a slope for SKIing

ski slope /'. ./ *n.* [C] a snow-covered part of a mountain which has been prepared for people to SKI down

skit /skɪt/ *n.* [C] a short humorous performance or piece of writing

skit·ter /'skɪtɚ/ *v.* [I] to run very quickly and lightly, like a small animal

skit·tish /'skɪtɪʃ/ *adj.* **1** a horse or other animal that is skittish gets excited or frightened very easily **2** a person who is skittish is nervous and afraid to do anything because of something bad that could happen: *Some skittish Wall Street investors are staying away from the market.* —**skittishly** *adv.* —**skittishness** *n.* [U]

skiv·vies /'skɪviz/ *n.* [plural] HUMOROUS a man's underwear

Skop·je /'skoupyeɪ, 'skɔ-/ the capital and largest city in Macedonia

skul·dug·ger·y /ˌskʌl'dʌgəri/ *n.* [U] OFTEN HUMOROUS secretly dishonest or illegal activity: *He is serving a prison sentence for financial skulduggery.*

skulk /skʌlk/ *v.* [I always + adv./prep.] to hide or move around secretly, trying not to be noticed, especially when you are intending to do something bad: [+ around/in/behind etc.] *People tend to think of spies as people in gray coats, skulking around on street corners.*

skull /skʌl/ *n.* [C] the bones of a person's or animal's head —see picture at SKELETON

skull and cross·bones /ˌ. . '../ *n.* [singular] **1** a picture of a human skull with two bones crossed below it, used in former times on the flags of PIRATE¹ (3) ships —compare JOLLY ROGER **2** a picture of a human skull with two bones crossed below it, used on containers to show that what is inside is poison or very dangerous

skull·cap /'skʌlkæp/ *n.* [C] a small round close-fitting hat for the top of the head, worn sometimes by Christian priests or Jewish men —compare YARMULKE

skunk¹ /skʌŋk/ *n.* **1** [C] a small black and white North American animal that produces a very strong bad smell if it is attacked or afraid **2** [U] SLANG a strong type of MARIJUANA

skunk² *v.* [T] INFORMAL to defeat a player or team very easily

skunk cab·bage /'. ˌ../ *n.* [C,U] a large North American plant that grows in wet areas and has a bad smell

skunk works /'. ./ *n.* [plural] INFORMAL the part of a business concerned with having and developing new ideas

sky /skaɪ/ *n. plural* **skies 1** [singular,U] the space above the earth, where clouds and the sun and stars appear: *The rocket shot up into the sky.* | *The sky turned dark just before the storm.* | **a blue/cloudy etc. sky** *The sun shone down from a clear blue sky.* **2 skies** a word meaning "sky," used especially when describing the weather or what they sky looks like in a place: *a land of blue skies and warm sunshine* | *The skies above Los Angeles were a dull brown.* **3 the sky's the limit** used to say that there is no limit to what someone can achieve, spend, win etc. —see also **pie in the sky** (PIE (4)), **praise sb/sth to the skies** (PRAISE¹ (4))

sky blue /ˌ. '.◂/ *n.* [U] the bright blue color of a clear sky —**sky-blue** *adj.*

sky·cap /'skaɪkæp/ *n.* [C] someone whose job is to carry passengers' bags and SUITCASEs at an airport

sky·div·ing /'skaɪˌdaɪvɪŋ/ *n.* [U] the sport of jumping from an airplane and falling through the sky before opening a PARACHUTE —**skydive** *v.* [I] —**skydiver** *n.* [U] —see picture on page 1332

sky-high /ˌ. '.◂/ *adj. adv.* **1** extremely high: *sky-high real estate prices* **2 blow sth sky-high** to destroy something completely with an explosion

sky·jack /'skaɪdʒæk/ *v.* [T] to use violence or threats to take control of an airplane —**skyjacker** *n.* [C] —**skyjacking** *n.* [C]

sky·lark /'skaɪlɑrk/ *n.* [C] a small bird that sings while flying high in the sky

sky·light /'skaɪlaɪt/ *n.* [C] a window in the roof of a building

sky·line /'skaɪlaɪn/ *n.* [C] the shape made by tall buildings or hills against the sky

sky·rock·et /'skaɪˌrɑkɪt/ *v.* [I] to increase suddenly and greatly: *skyrocketing inflation*

sky·scrap·er /'skaɪˌskreɪpɚ/ *n.* [C] a very tall modern city building

sky·ward /'skaɪwɚd/ also **skywards** *adv.* up into the sky, or toward the sky: *The bird soared skyward.* —**skyward** *adj.*

sky·writ·ing /'skaɪˌraɪtɪŋ/ *n.* [U] words that are written high in the air by an airplane that leaves lines of white smoke behind it

slab /slæb/ *n.* [C] **1** a thick flat four-sided piece of a hard material such as stone: *New concrete slabs have been laid in the back yard.* **2 a slab of cake/beef/butter etc.** a large flat piece of cake, meat etc.

slack¹ /slæk/ *adj.* **1** with less business activity than usual: *Corporate profits have been hurt by slack demand.* **2** hanging loosely, or not pulled tight: *The fan belt is a little slack.* | *Keep the rope slack till I say "pull."* **3** not taking enough care or making enough effort to do things right: *The report criticized airport security as "disgracefully slack."* —**slackly** *adv.* —**slackness** *n.* [U]

slack² *n.* **1 pick/take up the slack** to do something that needs to be done because someone else is not doing it anymore: *As fewer employers provide health insurance, people rely on state programs to pick up the slack.* **2** [U] looseness in the way that something such as a rope hangs or is fastened: *Leave a little slack in the line.* **3** [U] money, space, or people that an organization has, but does not need: *The workforce has been reduced, so there's very little slack in the system.* **4 slacks** [plural] pants, especially ones made out of good material but that are not part of a suit: *He wore black slacks and a sweater.* **5** [U] INFORMAL a period of time when you are not very busy and you can relax: *People in San Francisco seem to have no slack in their lives anymore.* **6 cut/give sb some slack** SPOKEN to allow someone to do something without criticizing them or making it more difficult: *Hey, cut me some slack, man, I'm only a few bucks short.*

slack³ *v.* [I] also **slack off** to make less of an effort than usual, or to be lazy in your work: *This is no time to be slacking off!*

slack·en /ˈslækən/ *v.* [I,T] **1** to gradually become slower, weaker, less active etc., or to make something do this: *Workers can be trained to do other tasks when sales slacken.* | **slacken your pace/ speed** (=go or walk more slowly) **2** to make something looser, or to become looser: *The skin of her face had slackened.*

slack·er /ˈslækə/ *n.* [C] HUMOROUS someone who is lazy and does not do all the work they should

slack-jawed /ˈslæk dʒɔd/ *adj.* having your mouth slightly open: *The audience sat slack-jawed with disbelief.*

slag /slæg/ *n.* [U] a waste material similar to glass, which is left when metal is obtained from rock

slag heap /ˈ. ./ *n.* [C] a pile of waste material at a mine or factory

slain /sleɪn/ *v.* the past participle of SLAY

slake /sleɪk/ *v.* [T] LITERARY **1 slake your thirst** to drink so that you are not THIRSTY anymore **2 slake a desire/craving etc.** to satisfy a desire, etc.

sla·lom /ˈslɑləm/ *n.* [U] a race for people on SKIS or in KAYAKS (=a type of boat) down a curving course marked by flags

slam¹ /slæm/ *v.* **slamming, slammed**

1 door etc. [I,T] if a door, window etc. slams, or if someone slams it, it closes with a loud noise: *We heard a car door slam outside.* | *Greg came in and slammed the door shut behind him.*

2 put sth somewhere [T always + adv./prep.] to put something on or against a surface with a fast violent movement: [**slam sth on/down etc.**] *"I have no comment," said Hunt, before slamming the phone down.*

3 criticize sb/sth [T] to criticize someone or something strongly: *Bankers slammed Congress' plans to cap interest rates on credit cards.*

4 hit with force [I always + adv./prep.,T] to hit or attack someone or something with a lot of force: *Conditions over the Pacific could cause huge storms to slam California this winter.* | [+ into/against etc.] *A commuter plane slammed into a field about 18 miles from Detroit Metropolitan Airport.*

5 slam on the brakes to make a car stop very suddenly by pressing on the BRAKES very hard

6 slam the door in sb's face a) to close a door hard when someone is trying to come in **b)** to rudely refuse to meet someone or talk to them

slam² *n.* [C usually singular] the noise or action of a door, window etc. slamming —see also GRAND SLAM

slam danc·ing /ˈ. ,../ *n.* [U] a way of dancing to PUNK music in which people jump around violently and hit each other with their bodies —**slam-dance** *v.* [I]

slam dunk /ˈ. ./ *n.* [C] **1** an act of putting the ball through the net in basketball, by throwing it down very hard from above the net **2** a very forceful impressive act: *The biggest legal slam dunk came when a judge sentenced four men to 505 years in prison.*

slam-dunk /ˈ. ./ *v.* [I, T] to put a ball through the net in basketball, by jumping very high and throwing the ball down through the net using a lot of force

slam·mer /ˈslæmə/ *n.* **the slammer** HUMOROUS prison

slan·der¹ /ˈslændə/ *n.* [U] **1** false spoken statements about someone that are intended to damage the good opinion that people have of that person **2** the crime of making false spoken statements of this kind: *Later, he learned that he was being sued for slander.* —compare LIBEL¹ —**slanderer** *n.* [C]

slander² *v.* [T] to say untrue things about someone in order to damage other people's good opinion of them —compare LIBEL²

slan·der·ous /ˈslændərəs/ *adj.* a slanderous statement about someone is not true, and is intended to damage other people's good opinion of them: *slanderous remarks*

slang /slæŋ/ *n.* [U] very informal language that includes new and sometimes offensive words, and that is used especially only by people who belong to a particular group, such as young people or criminals: **a slang word/expression/term** *Dino learned a number of slang expressions from the movies.* —**slangy** *adj.*

slant¹ /slænt/ *v.* [I] to slope, or move in a sloping line: *The sun's rays slanted through the trees.*

slant² *n.* [singular] **1** a way of writing or thinking about a subject that shows strong support for a particular opinion or set of ideas: *Several readers objected to the article's strong Republican slant.* | *Recent events have **put a new slant on** the President's earlier comments.* **2** a sloping position or angle: **at/ on a slant** *The house seems to be built on a steep slant.*

slant·ed /ˈslæntɪd/ *adj.* **1** providing facts or information in a way that unfairly supports one opinion, one side of an argument etc.; BIASED: [+ **toward**] *The report was heavily slanted toward the city council's version of events.* **2** sloping to one side

slant-eyed /ˈ. ./ *adj.* TABOO used to describe the appearance of someone whose family came from an Asian country, such as China, Japan, or Korea. Do not use this word.

slap¹ /slæp/ *v.* **slapped, slapping 1** [T] to hit someone quickly with the flat part of your hand: *Sarah slapped Zack across the face.* | *Mrs. Williams slapped the children's hands away from the candy.* **2** [T always + adv./prep.] to put something down on a surface with force, especially when you are angry: [**slap sth on/down**] *Ed slapped his hand down on the table.* **3 slap sb on the back** to hit someone on the back in a friendly way, often as a way of praising them **4** [I always + adv./prep.] to hit a surface with a lot of force, making a loud sharp sound: [+ **against**] *Gray sheets of rain slapped against the windowpanes.*

slap sb down *phr. v.* [T] to criticize someone in an unfair and cruel way, so that they lose confidence: *As a child, he was slapped down in school for speaking Spanish.*

slap sth → on *phr. v.* [T] **1** to put or spread something quickly or carelessly onto a surface: *Campaign workers were slapping posters on every available surface.* **2** to suddenly announce a new charge, tax etc., especially unfairly or without warning: *Buchanan's answer is to slap more tariffs on imports.*

slap² *n.* [C] **1** a quick hit with the flat part of your hand: *Sheila woke Ted up with a slap across the face.* **2 a slap in the face** an action that seems to be deliberately intended to offend or upset someone, especially someone who has tried very hard to do something: *Gwynn considered the salary they were offering a slap in the face.* **3 a slap on the wrist** a punishment that you think is not severe enough **4 a slap on the back** an action of hitting someone on the back in a friendly way, especially as a way of praising them: *a congratulatory slap on the back*

slap·dash /ˈslæpdæʃ/ *adj.* careless and done too quickly: *The program is just a slapdash mix of old, tired ideas.*

slap·hap·py /ˈslæpˌhæpi/ *adj.* silly, careless, and likely to make mistakes

slap shot /ˈ. ./ *n.* [C] a way or act of hitting the PUCK in HOCKEY by moving your stick a long way back and then hitting the puck with a lot of force

slap·stick /ˈslæpˌstɪk/ *n.* [U] humorous acting in which the performers fall down, throw things at each other etc.: *slapstick comedy*

s w **slash¹** /slæʃ/ *v.* **1** [I always + adv./prep.,T] to cut or try to cut something violently with a knife, sword etc.: *Someone had slashed the car's tires.* | [+ at/through] *The leopard's claws slashed through soft flesh.* **2** [T] to reduce an amount, price etc. by a large amount: *Congress has slashed the budget for programs to help poor families.* **3 slash your wrists** to cut the VEINS in your wrists with the intention of killing yourself

slash² *n.* [C] **1** a quick movement made with a knife, sword etc. in order to cut someone or something **2** also **slash mark** a line (/) used in writing to separate words, numbers, or letters **3** a long narrow wound on someone's body, or a long narrow cut in something: *Cut several slashes across the top of the loaf before baking.*

slash-and-burn /ˌ. . ˈ.◂/ *adj.* [only before noun] **1** slash-and-burn farming is a way of clearing land in tropical areas by cutting down and burning plants so that crops can be grown there for a few years **2** used to describe an action that is too extreme and has a harmful effect: *Viewers are disgusted by politicians' slash-and-burn attacks on each other.*

slat /slæt/ *n.* [C] a thin flat piece of wood, plastic etc., used especially in furniture —**slatted** *adj.*: *a slatted bench*

slate¹ /sleɪt/ *n.* **1** [U] a dark gray rock that can easily be split into flat thin pieces **2 slate blue/gray** a dark blue or gray color **3** [C] a list of people that voters can choose in an election, or who are being considered for an important job **4** [C] a small black board or a flat piece of SLATE (1) in a wooden frame, that can be written on with CHALK or a special stick made of rock, used in schools in past times —see also **a clean slate** (CLEAN¹ (9)), **wipe the slate clean** (WIPE¹ (3))

slate² *v.* [T usually passive] to expect or plan something: [be slated to do/be sth] *The National Guard is slated to lose 30,000 troops in the Pentagon's plan.* | [be slated for sth] *Every house on this block is slated for demolition.*

slath·er /ˈslæðɚ/ *v.* [T] to cover something with a thick layer of a soft substance: *toast slathered with butter*

slat·tern /ˈslætɚn/ *n.* [C] OLD-FASHIONED a dirty, messy woman

slaugh·ter¹ /ˈslɔtɚ/ *v.* [T] **1** to kill an animal for food **2** to kill a lot of people in a cruel or violent way: *Hundreds of civilians had been slaughtered by government troops.* —see Usage Note at KILL¹ **3** to defeat an opponent in a sports game by a large number of points: *The Knicks got slaughtered in the semifinal.*

slaughter² *n.* [U] **1** the act of killing large numbers of people in a cruel or violent way **2** the act of killing animals for food —see also **like a lamb to the slaughter** (LAMB¹ (5))

slaugh·ter·house /ˈslɔtɚˌhaʊs/ *n.* [C] a building where animals are killed

s w **slave¹** /sleɪv/ *n.* [C] **1** someone who is owned by another person and works for them for no money —compare MASTER¹ (2) **2 be a slave to/of sth** to be completely influenced by something, so that you cannot make your own decisions: *You don't need to be a slave to fashion.*

slave² *v.* [I always + adv./prep.] to work very hard with little time to rest: [+ away/over/for] *Carla's parents had slaved in the lettuce fields of California.* | *I slaved all day over a hot stove to cook this meal.*

slave driv·er /ˈ. ˌ../ *n.* [C] **1** someone who forces SLAVES to work **2** HUMOROUS an employer who makes people work extremely hard

slave la·bor /ˌ. ˈ../ *n.* [U] **1** work done by SLAVES, or the people who do this work: *The death camps were*

built by slave labor. **2** work for which you are paid an unfairly small amount of money —**slave laborer** *n.* [C]

slav·er¹ /ˈslævɚ, ˈsleɪ-, ˈslɑ-/ *v.* [I] LITERARY to let SALIVA (=liquid produced inside your mouth) come out of your mouth, especially because you are hungry: *The dogs started racing toward us, howling and slavering.*

slaver over sth *phr. v.* [T] to be very excited about something, especially in an impolite or stupid way: *The governor's aides were slavering over news of her opponent's difficulties.*

slav·er² /ˈsleɪvɚ/ *n.* [C] **1** someone who sells slaves **2** OLD USE a ship for slaves

slav·er·y /ˈsleɪvəri/ *n.* [U] **1** the system of having slaves: *Slavery was abolished after the Civil War.* **2** the condition of being a slave: *Her grandfather had been captured and sold into slavery.*

slave state /ˈ. ./ *n.* [C] one of the southern U.S. states in which it was legal to own slaves before the Civil War

slave trade /ˈ. ./ *n.* **the slave trade** the buying and selling of slaves, especially Africans who were taken to America in the 18th and 19th centuries

Slav·ic /ˈslɑvɪk/ *adj.* from or relating to Russia or countries of Eastern Europe, such as Poland or Bulgaria: *Slavic languages*

slav·ish /ˈsleɪvɪʃ/ *adj.* **slavish devotion/imitation etc.** behavior or actions that show that you cannot make your own decisions about what you should do: *the slavish adherence to old ideas* —**slavishly** *adv.* —**slavishness** *n.* [U]

slaw /slɔ/ *n.* [U] COLE SLAW

slay /sleɪ/ *v.* past tense **slew** past participle **slain** [T] **1** a word meaning "to kill someone," used especially in newspapers; murder: *Coretta King is the widow of slain civil rights leader Martin Luther King Jr.* **2** SPOKEN to amuse someone a lot: *That guy really slays me!* —**slayer** *n.* [C]

slay·ing /ˈsleɪɪŋ/ *n.* [C] a word meaning an act of killing someone, used especially in newspapers; murder: *Half a dozen gang-related slayings have been reported this year.*

sleaze /sliz/ *n.* **1** [U] immoral behavior, especially involving sex or lies: *Many citizens are tired of all the sleaze on TV.* **2** [C] also **sleazebag, sleazebucket** INFORMAL someone who behaves in an immoral or dishonest way

slea·zy /ˈslizi/ *adj.* **sleazier, sleaziest** **1** low in quality, and relating to immoral behavior: *sleazy porn movies* | *The bar was cheap and sleazy.* **2** someone who is sleazy is immoral or dishonest and makes you feel uncomfortable: *sleazy drug smugglers* —**sleaziness** *n.* [U]

sled¹ /slɛd/ *n.* [C] a small vehicle used for riding or traveling over snow, made from a board with two long narrow pieces of metal fastened under it, often used by children on in some sports —see also BOBSLED, DOGSLED —compare SLEIGH —see picture at HUSKY²

sled² *v.* [I] to travel or ride on a sled

sled dog /ˈ. ./ *n.* [C] a dog that is used in a team to pull a sled over snow

sledge·ham·mer /ˈslɛdʒˌhæmɚ/ *n.* [C] a large heavy hammer

sleek¹ /slik/ *adj.* **1** a vehicle or other object that is sleek has a smooth attractive shape: *the car's sleek, aerodynamic profile* **2** sleek hair or fur is straight, shiny, and healthy-looking: *The cat purred as Ben stroked its sleek fur.* —**sleekly** *adv.* —**sleekness** *n.* [U]

sleek² *v.* [T] LITERARY to make hair or fur smooth and shiny by putting water or oil on it

sleep¹ /slip/ *v.* past tense and past participle **slept** s w **1** rest [I] to rest your mind and body, usually at night when you are lying in bed with your eyes closed: *I normally sleep on my back.* | *Don't set the alarm – I want to sleep late (=sleep until late in the morning) tomorrow.* | **sleep well/soundly** *Did you sleep well?* **2 sleep like a log** to sleep very well, without waking up for a long time **3 not sleep a wink** to not sleep at all

4 sleep tight SPOKEN used especially to children before they go to bed, to say that you hope they sleep well: *Good night, kids. Sleep tight!*

5 sleep on it SPOKEN to not make a decision about something important until the next day

6 number of people [T] to have enough beds for a particular number of people: **sleep two/four/six** etc. *Expect to pay $115 in peak season for a cabin that sleeps four.*

7 let sleeping dogs lie to deliberately avoid mentioning a problem or argument that you had in the past, so that you do not cause any problems: *The best plan is just to let sleeping dogs lie.*

sleep around phr. v. [I] DISAPPROVING to have sex with a lot of different people

sleep in phr. v. [I] to deliberately sleep later than usual in the morning: *I'm going to sleep in tomorrow.* —compare OVERSLEEP

sleep sth ↔ **off** phr. v. [T] to sleep until you do not feel sick anymore, especially after drinking too much alcohol: *It's better to let him sleep it off.*

sleep over phr. v. [I] a word meaning "to sleep at someone else's house for a night," used especially by children: *Is it okay if I sleep over at Kristi's tonight?*

sleep through sth phr. v. [T] **1** to sleep while something is happening and not be woken by it: *I can't believe I slept through my alarm!* **2 sleep through the night** to sleep continuously during the whole night: *At least the baby's sleeping through the night now.*

sleep together phr. v. [I] to have sex: *I'm sure those two are sleeping together.*

sleep with sb phr. v. [T] to have sex with someone, especially someone you are not married to: *Everybody in the office knows he's been sleeping with Kathy.*

sleep² **1 being asleep** [U] the natural state of resting your mind and body, usually at night: *I didn't get much sleep last night.* | *Sometimes Mike has a hard time getting to sleep* (=starting to sleep). | *Ed often talks in his sleep* (=while he is sleeping).

2 go to sleep a) to start sleeping **b)** if a part of your body goes to sleep, you cannot feel it for a short time because it has not been getting enough blood

3 period of sleeping [singular] ESPECIALLY LITERARY a period of sleeping: *The princess fell into a deep sleep after eating the poisoned apple.*

4 a good night's sleep a night when you sleep well, and which makes you feel healthy and active

5 lose sleep over sth to worry about something: *It's just a practice game – I wouldn't lose any sleep over it.*

6 put sb/sth to sleep a) to give drugs to a sick animal so that it dies without too much pain **b)** to make someone unconscious before a medical operation by giving them drugs

7 sb can do sth in their sleep used to say that someone is able to do something very easily, especially because they have done it many times before

8 sing/rock/lull etc. sb to sleep to sing to someone, move them gently etc. until they start sleeping: *The movement of the waves soon lulled us to sleep.*

9 in your eyes [U] NOT TECHNICAL a substance that forms in the corners of your eyes while you are sleeping

sleep·er /'slipə/ n. [C] **1** someone who is asleep: **a light/heavy sleeper** (=someone who wakes easily, or does not wake easily) **2** a movie, book etc. which is successful, even though people did not expect it to be **3 a)** also **sleeper car** a part of a train with beds for passengers to sleep in **b)** a bed on a train for a passenger to sleep in **4** a piece of clothing for a baby, that covers its whole body including its feet, and that is usually worn to sleep in

sleeping bag /'.. ,./ n. [C] a large warm bag that you sleep in, especially when camping

sleeping car /'.. ,./ n. [C] a part of a train with beds for passengers

sleeping pill /'.. ,./ n. [C] a PILL which helps you to sleep

sleeping sick·ness /'.. ,../ n. [U] a serious disease that is carried by the TSETSE FLY (=a type of African insect) and that causes extreme tiredness and fever, and makes you lose weight

sleep·less /'sliplɪs/ adj. **1 a sleepless night** a night when you are unable to sleep **2** unable to sleep: *the sleepless parents of newborn babies* —**sleeplessly** adv. —**sleeplessness** n. [U]

sleep·o·ver /'slip,ouvə/ n. [C] a party for children in which they spend the night at someone's house

sleep·walk·er /'slip,wɔkə/ n. [C] someone who walks while they are sleeping —**sleepwalk** v. [I] —**sleepwalking** n. [U]

sleep·wear /'slipwɛr/ n. [U] clothes such as PAJAMAS, that you wear in bed

sleep·y /'slipi/ adj. **sleepier, sleepiest 1** tired and ready to sleep **2** a sleepy town or area is very quiet, and not much happens there —**sleepily** adv. —**sleepiness** n. [U]

sleep·y·head /'slipi,hɛd/ n. [C] SPOKEN someone, especially a child, who looks as if they want to go to sleep: *It's time for bed, sleepyhead.*

sleet /slit/ n. [U] snow and rain that fall when it is very cold —**sleet** v. [I]

sleeve /sliv/ n. [C] **1** the part of a piece of clothing that covers your arm, or that covers part of your arm: *a dress with long sleeves* **2 have something up your sleeve** to have a secret plan or idea that you are going to use later: *Don't worry. He still has a few tricks up his sleeve.* —see also **have an ace up your sleeve** (ACE¹ (5)) **3** a stiff paper cover that a record is stored in; JACKET (4) **4** a tube that surrounds a machine part —see also **laugh up your sleeve** (LAUGH¹ (10)), **roll your sleeves up** at **roll up** (ROLL¹)

-sleeved /slivd/ also **-sleeve** [in adjectives] **long-sleeved/short-sleeved** also **long-sleeve/short-sleeve** having sleeves that are long or short: *a short-sleeved shirt*

sleeve·less /'slivlɪs/ adj. a sleeveless JACKET, dress etc. has no sleeves

sleigh /sleɪ/ n. [C] a large vehicle pulled by animals, in which you sit to travel over snow —compare SLED¹

sleight of hand /,slaɪt əv 'hænd/ n. [U] **1** quick skillful movements with your hands, especially when performing magic tricks **2** the use of skillful tricks and lies to achieve something: *Miller's financial sleight of hand resulted in the loss of $2 million in tax revenue.*

slen·der /'slɛndə/ adj. **1** thin, graceful, and attractive: *She is slender and stylish.* | *The path led through the slender birch trees.* —see Usage Note at THIN¹ **2** not enough to be useful, helpful, or effective: *The third quarter's slender profit was still an improvement on previous results.* | *The Democrats had only a slender majority in Congress.* —**slenderness** n. [U]

slept /slɛpt/ v. the past tense and past participle of SLEEP

sleuth /sluθ/ n. [C] OLD-FASHIONED someone who tries to find out information about a crime; DETECTIVE

sleuth·ing /'sluθɪŋ/ n. [U] the activity of finding information about someone or something, especially information about a crime: *DNA testing is a form of genetic sleuthing.*

slew¹ /slu/ n. [+ singular/plural verb] **a slew of sth** a large number of things: *A whole slew of cheap motels are springing up west of town.*

slew² v. the past tense of SLAY

slew³ v. [I,T + **around/out**] to turn or swing suddenly and violently, or to make something do this

slice¹ /slaɪs/ n. **1** [C] a flat piece of bread, meat etc. cut from a larger piece: *Cut the roast into thin slices.* | [+ **of**] *a slice of bread* —see picture on page 425 **2** [C] a part or share of something good: [+ **of**] *Telephone banking services are aiming to take a slice of retail banks' profits.* **3** [C] a way of hitting the ball in sports such as tennis and GOLF that makes the ball go to one side with a spinning movement, rather than straight ahead **4 a slice of life** a description or scene in a movie, play, or book that shows life as it really is

slice[2] *v.* **1** [T] also **slice up** to cut meat, bread etc. into thin flat pieces: *Slice the tomatoes about ¼ inch thick.* **2** [I always + adv./prep.,T] to cut something easily with one long movement of a sharp knife or edge: [+ **into/through**] *The mayor sliced through the ribbon across the doorway and officially opened the new school.* | **slice sth in two/half** (=slice something into two equal pieces) **3** [I always + adv./prep.,T] to move quickly and easily through something such as water or air, or to make something do this: [+ **through/into**] *Jets sliced through the air high above the Gulf.* **4 sth is the best/greatest thing since sliced bread** HUMOROUS used to say that something is new and very helpful, useful, etc. **5** [T] to hit the ball in sports such as tennis or GOLF so that it spins sideways instead of moving straight forward **6 any way you slice it** SPOKEN in any way you choose to consider the situation: *It's the truth, any way you slice it.*

slice sth ↔ **off** *phr. v.* [T] to separate something by cutting it with one long movement of a sharp knife or edge: *Part of Jim's ear had been sliced off in an accident.*

slick[1] /slɪk/ *adj.* **1** a slick movie, program etc. is attractive and looks expensive, but contains no important or interesting ideas: *a slick Hollywood production* **2** good at persuading people, often in a way that does not seem honest: *a slick used-car salesman* **3** smooth and slippery: *slick paper* | [+ **with**] *Cars were sliding off roads that were slick with snow.* **4** working or moving very smoothly, skillfully, and effectively: *Thanks to O'Neil's slick fielding, the Giants won 3–1.* **5** OLD-FASHIONED very good or attractive —**slickly** *adv.* —**slickness** *n.* [U]

slick[2] *n.* [C] **1** an area of oil on the surface of water or on a road; OIL SLICK **2** a magazine printed on good quality paper with a shiny surface, usually with a lot of color pictures **3** a smooth car tire used for racing

slick[3] *v.*

slick sth ↔ **down/back** *phr. v.* [T] to make hair smooth and shiny by using oil, water etc.: *Miller slicked back his hair and put on a black leather vest.*

slick·er /'slɪkɚ/ *n.* [C] a coat made of smooth shiny material to keep out the rain —see also CITY SLICKER

slide

S W
3 3 **slide**[1] /slaɪd/ *v. past tense and past participle* **slid** /slɪd/ **1** [I,T] to move smoothly over a surface while continuing to touch it, or to make something move in this way: [+ **along/across/down etc.**] *Francesca slid across the ice.* | [**slide sth across/along etc.**] *He opened the oven door and slid the pan of cookies in.* **2** [I,T always + adv./prep.] to move somewhere quietly without being noticed, or to move something in this way: [+ **into/out etc.**] *While Frank was still asleep, I slid out of bed and into the kitchen.* | [**slide sth into/out etc.**] *She slid a gun into her pocket.* **3** [I] if prices, amounts, rates etc. slide, they become lower: *Stocks slid a further 3% on the major markets today.* **4** [I] to gradually become worse, or to begin to have a problem: *Students' test scores started to slide in the mid-1980s.* | [+ **into**] *Murphy gradually slid into a pattern of drug abuse.* **5 let sth slide a)** SPOKEN to ignore a mistake, problem, remark etc. without trying to improve or stop it: *Well, I guess we*

can **let it slide** *this time.* **b)** to let a situation get gradually worse, without trying to stop it: *Management has let safety standards slide at the plant.*

slide[2] *n.* [C]
1 for children a large structure with steps leading to the top of a long sloping surface for children to slide down: *Don't go down the slide head first.*
2 picture a small piece of film in a frame that shows a picture on a screen or wall, when you shine light through it: *a slide show*
3 price/amount [usually singular] a fall in prices, amounts etc.: [+ **in**] *a slide in the President's approval rating*
4 getting worse [usually singular] a situation in which something gradually gets worse, or someone develops a problem: *School administrators were unable to explain the slide in student performance.*
5 science a small piece of thin glass used for holding something when you look at it under a MICROSCOPE
6 music/machine a movable part of a machine or musical instrument, such as the U-shaped tube of a TROMBONE
7 earth/snow a sudden fall of earth, stones, snow etc. down a slope
8 movement [usually singular] a sliding movement across a surface —see also LANDSLIDE

slide pro·ject·or /'. .,../ *n.* [C] a piece of equipment that shines a light through SLIDES (SLIDE[2] (2)) so that pictures appear on a screen or wall

slid·er /'slaɪdɚ/ *n.* [C] a fast throw of a baseball in which the ball suddenly changes direction when it gets close to the BATTER

slide rule /'. ./ *n.* [C] an old-fashioned instrument that looks like a ruler with a middle part that slides, used for calculating

sliding door /,.. '../ *n.* [C] a door that slides open from side to side, rather than swinging from one side on HINGES

sliding scale /,.. '../ *n.* [C usually singular] a system for calculating how much you pay for taxes, medical treatment etc., in which the amount that you pay changes when there are different conditions: *Therapists' fees are figured on a sliding scale.*

slight[1] /slaɪt/ *adj.* **1** [usually before noun] not severe, or not important: *a slight headache* | *a slight improvement* | *Officials reported a slight increase in inflation.* **2 not the slightest chance/doubt/difference etc.** no chance, doubt etc. at all: *It won't make the slightest bit of difference what we say.* | *I didn't have the slightest idea who that man was.* **3** thin and delicate: *He was slight and frail, even as a young man.*

slight[2] *v.* [T] FORMAL to offend someone by treating them rudely or without respect: *It was never our intention to slight minority communities.*

slight[3] *n.* [C] a remark or action that offends someone: [+ **to/against**] *The writer of the article intended no slight to the skill of Shaw.*

slight·ly /'slaɪtli/ *adv.* **1** a little: *a slightly different color* | *Let the cookies cool slightly before removing them from the baking sheet.* | *She moved the picture ever so slightly* (=by a very small amount) *to the right.* **2 slightly built** having a thin and delicate body

slim[1] /slɪm/ *adj.* **slimmer, slimmest 1** someone who is slim is attractively thin: *a slim waist* —see Usage Note at THIN[1] **2 slim chance/hope etc.** very little chance etc. of getting what you want: *The Raiders only have a very slim chance of winning now.* **3** very small in amount or number: *The Republicans held a slim majority in the Senate.* | *a slim margin of profit* **4** not wide or thick: *Rob took a slim volume from the shelf.* | *a slim crescent moon* **5 slim pickings** used to say that there is not enough of something available: *It was pretty slim pickings at the Christmas tree farm on Christmas Eve.*

slim[2] *v.* **slimmed, slimming**
slim down *phr. v.* **slim** [I,T **slim** sth ↔ **down**] to reduce the size or number of something: *So far, the federal workforce has been slimmed down by over 160,000 workers.*

slime /slaɪm/ *n.* [U] **1** a thick slippery substance that looks or smells bad **2** a slippery substance that comes from the bodies of SNAILS and SLUGS

slime·ball /'slaɪmbɔl/ *n.* [C] SLANG someone who is immoral, disgusting, and cannot be trusted

slim·ming /'slɪmɪŋ/ *adj.* making you look thinner: *Solid colors are more slimming than patterns.*

slim·y /'slaɪmi/ *adj.* **slimier, slimiest 1** covered with slime, or wet and slippery like slime: *slimy mud* **2** INFORMAL friendly in a disgusting way that makes you feel uncomfortable and seeming dishonest: *a slimy politician* —**sliminess** *n.* [U]

sling[1] /slɪŋ/ *v.* past tense and past participle **slung** [T always + adv./prep.] **1** to throw or put something somewhere with a wide careless movement: [**sling sth around/over etc.**] *Pat picked up his bag and slung it over his shoulder.* **2** [usually passive] to hang something loosely: *Dave wore a tool belt slung around his waist.* **3 sling hash** OLD-FASHIONED SLANG to work as a WAITRESS or WAITER in a cheap restaurant —see also GUNSLINGER, LOW-SLUNG, MUDSLINGING

sling[2] *n.* [C] **1** a piece of cloth tied around your neck to support your injured arm or hand: *She had her arm* **in a sling** *for months.* **2** a set of ropes or strong pieces of cloth that hold heavy objects to be lifted or carried **3 slings and arrows** criticism and remarks that are intended to hurt someone's feelings: *Many of us have had to* **suffer the slings and arrows** *of our political enemies.* **4** a special type of bag that fastens over your shoulders, in which you can carry a baby next to your body **5** a narrow piece of leather or cloth on a gun, used for carrying it over your shoulder **6** a long, thin piece of rope with a piece of leather in the middle, used in past times as a weapon for throwing stones

sling·back /'slɪŋbæk/ *n.* [C] a type of woman's shoe that is open at the back and has a narrow band going around the heel —see picture at SHOE[1]

sling·shot /'slɪŋʃɑt/ *n.* [C] a small stick in the shape of a Y with a thin band of rubber at the top, used by children to shoot stones

slink /slɪŋk/ *v.* past tense and past participle **slunk** [I always + adv./prep.] to move somewhere quietly and secretly, especially because you are afraid or ashamed: [+ **away/off/around** etc.] *He lowered his eyes and slunk back into his office.*

slink·y /'slɪŋki/ *adj.* **slinkier, slinkiest** a slinky dress, skirt etc. is smooth and tight and shows the shape of a woman's body

slip

slippery

slip[1] /slɪp/ *v.* **slipped, slipping**
1 slide/fall [I] to slide a short distance quickly by accident, or to fall by sliding in this way: *Brenda slipped on the icy sidewalk.* | *Her bag slipped off her shoulder.* | *The knife slipped and cut my finger.*
2 move secretly [I always + adv./prep.] to move quickly, smoothly, or secretly: *slip out/through/by etc. After an hour, she slipped through the door without saying goodbye.* | *The F22 plane was designed to slip past Soviet radar defenses.*
3 put sth somewhere [T] to put something somewhere or give someone something quietly, secretly, or smoothly: *Dave slipped me $20 when Jerry wasn't looking.* | [**slip sth around/into/through etc.**] *Someone slipped a note under my door.*
4 get worse [I] to become worse or lower than before: *Sales slipped to $4.5 million from $5 million*

---

the previous quarter. | *Standards have really slipped there recently.*
5 gradual change [I always + adv./prep.] to gradually change or pass by, in a way that is not very noticeable: [+ **away/by/into**] *The older you get, the quicker time seems to slip by.* | *Analysts predict that Germany may slip into a recession.*
6 slip through the cracks if someone or something slips through the cracks, they are not caught or helped by the system that is supposed to catch or help them: *Some kids slip through the cracks of the educational system.*
7 slip your mind if something slips your mind, you forget it or forget to do something, especially because you are too busy: *I was supposed to go to a meeting this morning, but it completely slipped my mind.*
8 slip through your fingers if something such as an opportunity, offer etc. slips through your fingers, you just fail to get or keep it: *Kevin often thought of Michelle, the love that had slipped through his fingers.*
9 time [I] if a SCHEDULE (=plan of times when things are supposed to happen) slips, things begin to happen or be done later than they are supposed to: *The results will not be announced before Tuesday, and the timetable may slip even further because of the strike.*
10 let (it) slip (that) to accidentally mention a piece of information that you had wanted to keep a secret: *During a chat with reporters, Baker let slip that he would receive the Manager of the Year award.*
11 slip a disk to suffer an injury when one of the connecting parts between the bones in your back moves out of place —see also SLIPPED DISK
12 slip one over on sb to deceive someone or play a trick on them: *How often have they bribed city workers to slip one over on an ignorant city council?*

slip into sth *phr. v.* [T] **1** to put clothes on quickly: *I'll just slip into something more comfortable.* **2 slip into sleep/unconsciousness etc.** to gradually fall asleep, become unconscious etc.: *Grandma slipped into a coma and died peacefully that night.*
slip sth ↔ **off** *phr. v.* [T] to take clothes off quickly: *Greg sat down and slipped his shoes off.*
slip sth ↔ **on** *phr. v.* [T] to put clothes on quickly: *Amanda slipped on her robe.*
slip out *phr. v.* [I] if something slips out, you say it without really intending to: *Occasionally, a sarcastic comment slipped out.*
slip out of sth *phr. v.* [T] to take clothes off quickly: *Keith slipped out of his jacket.*
slip up *phr. v.* [I] to make a mistake: *Johnson does occasionally slip up and forget to take his medication.* —see also SLIP-UP

slip[2] *n.*
1 paper [C] a small or narrow piece of paper: *There was a credit-card slip stapled to the receipt.* | [+ **of**] *She wrote the address on a slip of paper.* —see also PINK SLIP
2 mistake [C] a small mistake: *If you make one slip, it could cost you a lot.*
3 a slip of the tongue/pen something that you say or write by accident, when you meant to say or write something else: *Thompson introduced Henry Graham as Graham Henry, without realizing his slip of the tongue.* —see also FREUDIAN SLIP
4 give sb the slip to successfully escape from someone who is chasing you: *Eddie gave her the slip in the hotel lobby.*
5 getting worse [C usually singular] an occasion when something becomes worse or lower than before: [+ **in**] *a slip in stock prices*
6 slide/fall [C] an act of sliding a short distance, or of falling by sliding
7 underwear [C] a piece of underwear similar to a thin dress or skirt, that a woman wears under a dress or skirt
8 a slip of a girl/boy etc. OLD-FASHIONED, HUMOROUS a small thin young person: *It happened when she was just a slip of a thing.*

S W
3

9 boat [C] a space in the water in which you can keep a boat when it is not being used

10 clay [U] a thin mixture of clay and water, used in making pots

11 plant a small part of a plant that has been cut off and put into soil or water to grow into a new plant, or that has been attached to another plant

slip·case /'slɪpkeɪs/ n. [C] a hard cover like a box that a book is kept in

slip cov·er /'. ˌ../ n. [C] a loose plastic or cloth cover for furniture

slip·knot /'slɪpnɑt/ n. [C] a knot that you can make tighter or looser by pulling one of its ends

slip-on /'. ./ n. [C] a type of shoe without a fastening, that you can slide onto your foot —**slip-on** adj.: slip-on shoes

slip·page /'slɪpɪdʒ/ n. [C,U] **1** the act of sliding slightly, especially accidentally: Any slippage in the heel of the shoe means it is too big. **2** the act of becoming worse or lower than before, or of gradually changing, especially to a worse state: a slippage in profits

slipped disk /ˌ. './ n. [C usually singular] a painful injury caused when one of the connecting parts between the bones in your back moves out of place

slip·per /'slɪpɚ/ n. [C] a light soft shoe that you wear indoors, especially to keep your feet warm —see picture at SHOE[1]

slip·per·y /'slɪpəri/ adj. **slipperier, slipperiest** **1** something that is slippery is difficult to hold, walk on etc. because it is wet or GREASY: Dean lost control of his car on a slippery road. —see picture at SLIP[1] **2** a/the slippery slope the beginning of a process or habit that is hard to stop and that will develop into something extremely bad: Any changes to the Bill of Rights would set the government on a slippery slope toward censorship. **3** a problem, job etc. that is slippery is difficult to deal with: a slippery economic problem **4** someone who is slippery cannot be trusted and usually manages to avoid being punished: a slippery salesperson —**slipperiness** n. [U]

slip·shod /'slɪpʃɑd/ adj. done too quickly and carelessly: The research project was shelved due to slipshod management.

slip·stream /'slɪpstrim/ n. [C usually singular] the area of low air pressure just behind a fast-moving vehicle

slip-up /'. ./ n. [C] a careless mistake that spoils a process or plan: Despite a few unfortunate slip-ups, we finished on time.

slip·way /'slɪpweɪ/ n. [C] a sloping track that is used for moving boats into or out of the water

slit[1] /slɪt/ v. past tense and past participle **slit** present participle **slitting** [T] **1** to make a straight narrow cut in cloth, paper, skin etc.: Deb **slit** the letter **open** with a knife. **2** slit sb's throat to kill someone by cutting their throat with a knife **3** slit your wrists to cut the VEINS in your wrists with the intention of killing yourself

slit[2] n. [C] a long straight narrow cut or hole: a skirt with a slit up the side

slith·er /'slɪðɚ/ v. [I always + adv./prep.] to slide smoothly across a surface, twisting or moving from side to side: [+ through/across etc.] A snake slithered through the weeds. | Vines slithered out of the dry bushes.

slith·er·y /'slɪðəri/ adj. slippery in a disgusting way

sliv·er /'slɪvɚ/ n. [C] **1** a very small thin sharp piece of something that has broken off a larger piece: slivers of broken glass **2** a narrow piece or part of something: a sliver of cake —compare SPLINTER[1]

sliv·o·vitz /'slɪvəvɪts, 'sli-/ n. [U] a strong alcoholic drink made in southeastern Europe from PLUMs

slob /slɑb/ n. [C] INFORMAL someone who is lazy, dirty, messy, and impolite: Why are you going out with that fat slob?

slob·ber /'slɑbɚ/ v. [I] INFORMAL to let SALIVA (=the liquid produced by your mouth) come out of your mouth and run down: Weber's dog slobbered all over my hand.

slobber over sb/sth phr. v. [T] to keep saying how much you love someone or something in a way that embarrasses or annoys other people: Maggie squirmed while he held her and slobbered over her.

sloe /sloʊ/ n. [C] a small bitter fruit like a PLUM

sloe gin /ˌ. './ n. [U] an alcoholic drink made with SLOEs, GIN, and sugar

slog[1] /slɑg/ v. [I always + adv./prep.] **1** to walk with difficulty through mud, over wet ground etc.: [+ down/up/through etc.] Cheney slogged through mud and fog to the hilltop. **2** to work hard at something without stopping, especially when the work is boring and difficult: [+ through/on] Students were slogging through volumes of medical reference books.

slog[2] n. [singular] something you do that takes a lot of effort and time: The campaign promises to be a long, hard slog.

slo·gan /'sloʊgən/ n. [C] a short easily remembered phrase used in advertising, politics etc.: an advertising slogan | a campaign slogan

sloop /slup/ n. [C] a type of boat with one central MAST (=pole for sails)

slop[1] /slɑp/ v. **slopped, slopping** **1** [I always + adv./prep.] if liquid in a container slops, it moves quickly around or over the edge: [+ around/about/over] The water slopped around in the bucket. **2** [T always + adv./prep.] to make liquid in a container move quickly around or over the edge: [slop sth over/into etc.] Don't slop your soup on the tablecloth. **3** [T] to feed slop to pigs

slop[2] n. **1** [U] also **slops** PLURAL food waste that is used to feed animals **2** food that is too soft and tastes bad: I'm not eating that slop.

slope[1] /sloʊp/ n. [C] **1** a piece of ground or a surface that is higher at one end than the other: The car rolled down the slope into the lake. **2** [usually singular] the angle at which something slopes in relation to a HORIZONTAL (=flat) surface: a 30° slope **3** [usually plural] an area in the mountains where people go SKIing: the beginner slopes | David and Adam can't wait to get **on the slopes** (=to begin skiing). —see also **a/the slippery slope** (SLIPPERY), SKI SLOPE

slope[2] v. [I] if the ground or a surface slopes, it is higher at one end than the other: a sloping tile roof | [+ up/down/away etc.] The front yard slopes down to the street.

slop·py /'slɑpi/ adj. **sloppier, sloppiest** **1** not done carefully or thoroughly: Ben has very sloppy handwriting. | a sloppy investigation **2** sloppy clothes are loose-fitting and do not look neat: a sloppy old sweater **3** wet and disgusting: He gave me a sloppy kiss on the cheek. —**sloppily** adv. —**sloppiness** n. [U]

sloppy joe, sloppy Joe /ˌslɑpi 'dʒoʊ/ n. [C] a type of SANDWICH made with GROUND BEEF that has been cooked in TOMATO SAUCE

slosh /slɑʃ/ v. **1** [I always + adv./prep.] if a liquid sloshes in a container, it moves quickly against the sides of its container and makes a noise: [+ around] Water sloshed around in the bottom of the boat. **2** [T always + adv./prep.] to make a liquid move quickly against the sides of a container and make a noise: [slosh sth around] Phil sloshed the rum around in the bottom of the bottle. **3** [I always + adv./prep.] to walk through water or mud in an active, loud way: We sloshed over to the other side of the street.

sloshed /slɑʃt/ adj. [not before noun] INFORMAL drunk: Tom was sloshed by seven p.m.

slot[1] /slɑt/ n. [C] **1** a long narrow hole in a surface, especially one that you can put things through: The disk goes into this slot here. **2** a time, position, or opportunity for something: Ron's show has been moved from its 9 p.m. slot on WKDH. | a parking slot

slot[2] v. **slotted, slotting** [I,T always + adv./prep.] to go into a slot, or to make something do this: [+ in/into] The shelf units can be slotted into wall brackets.

sloth /slɔθ, sloʊθ/ n. **1** [C] an animal of Central and South America that moves very slowly, has gray fur, and lives in trees **2** [U] LITERARY laziness: *Workers could be punished for incompetence or sloth.*

sloth·ful /'sloθfəl/ *adj.* LITERARY lazy or not active —**slothfully** *adv.* —**slothfulness** *n.* [U]

slot ma·chine /'. .,./ *n.* [C] a machine which you put a coin into, and which gives you more money back if three of the same pictures appear on a screen

slotted spoon /,.. '.'./ *n.* [C] a large spoon with holes in it

slouch[1] /slautʃ/ *v.* [I] to stand, sit, or walk with your shoulders bent forward in a way that makes you look tired or lazy: *Ralph sat slouching at the dining room table.*

slouch[2] *n.* **1 be no slouch** to be very good or skillful at something: *Franken is no slouch when it comes to innovative projects.* **2** [singular] a way of standing, sitting, or walking with your shoulders bent forward that makes you look tired or lazy

slough[1] /slau, slu/ *v.*
　slough off *phr. v.* **1** [I,T] to get rid of a dead outer layer of skin, or to come off in this way **2** [T slough sth ↔ off] to get rid of a feeling, belief etc.: *Gregson hoped to slough off his reputation as a drug addict.*

slough[2] *n.* **1** [C] an area of land covered in deep dirty water or mud **2 a slough of despair/neglect etc.** LITERARY a bad situation or condition that you cannot get out of easily: *Kerner gradually sank into a slough of despondency.*

Slo·vak Republic, the /'slouvæk/ also **Slo·va·ki·a** /slou'vækiə/ a country in eastern Europe between the Ukraine and the Czech Republic, that was formed in 1993 when Czechoslovakia was divided —**Slovakian, Slovak** *n., adj.*

Slo·ve·nia /slou'viniə/ a country in southeast Europe, between Austria and Croatia, that was formerly part of Yugoslavia —**Slovenian** *n., adj*

slov·en·ly /'slʌvənli, 'slɑ-/ *adj.* dirty, messy, and careless: *She was fat, slovenly, and out of shape.* —**slovenliness** *n.* [U]

s w **slow**[1] /slou/ *adj.*
2 2 **1** move etc. not moving, being done, or happening quickly: *They are notoriously slow workers.* | *We danced to all the slow songs.* | *"Where are y'all from?" he asked in a slow Southern drawl.*
2 long time taking a long time, or a longer time than usual: *slow economic growth* | *Climate change is a very slow process.* | **slow to recognize/see/follow etc.** *Some companies have been very slow to react to foreign competition.*
3 business if business or trade is slow, there are not many customers, or not much is sold: *It's been a pretty slow day.*
4 clock [not before noun] if a clock is slow, it is showing a time earlier than the correct time: **ten minutes/five minutes etc. slow** *My watch is about five minutes slow.*
5 the slow lane a) the slow lane on a large road is the one farthest to the right, where the slowest vehicles are supposed to drive **b)** if someone is in the slow lane, they are not making progress as quickly as other people, organizations etc.: *Vanguard Health-care prefers to stay in the slow lane.*
6 stupid not good or quick at understanding things: *Danny is a little bit slow.* | *a slow learner*
7 slow on the uptake not good at understanding things quickly
8 slow off the mark not reacting to a situation quickly
9 do a slow burn also **go into a slow burn** to slowly become angry: *Coach Bower stood on the sidelines, doing a slow burn.*
10 a slow news day a day on which nothing important happens and there is nothing interesting in the newspapers or on the television news
11 a slow oven an OVEN that is set at a fairly low temperature: *Toast the slices in a slow oven until they are crisp.* —see also SLOWLY

s w **slow**[2] *v.* [I,T] also **slow up** to become slower or make
2 something slower: *All this paperwork has really
3 slowed up our application process.* | *Traffic slowed to a crawl as we approached the accident site.*
　slow down *phr. v.* **1** to become slower or

make something slower: *Slow down, or you're going to hit somebody!* | *Small rockets slow the space shuttle down as it re-enters the atmosphere.* **2** to become less active or busy than you usually are, or to make someone less active or busy: *Marge's arthritis is starting to slow her down.*

slow[3] *adv.* SPOKEN slowly: *You'd better go pretty slow around this corner.*

slow·down /'sloudaun/ *n.* **1** [C usually singular] a reduction in activity or speed: *a slowdown in consumer spending* **2** [C] a period when people deliberately work slowly in order to protest about something

slow·ly /'slouli/ *adv.* **1** at a slow speed or rate: *Ann s w drove away slowly.* | *Her condition is slowly improv- 2 ing.* **2 slowly but surely** if you do something slowly 3 but surely, you do it more slowly than expected, but it is clear that you are making progress: *He's slowly but surely making his way through college.*

slow mo·tion /,. '../ *n.* [U] movement on television or in a movie that is shown at a slower speed than it really happened: *Let's see that spectacular touchdown again in slow motion.*

slow-pitch /'. ./ *n.* [U] a game like SOFTBALL, played by mixed teams of men and women

slow·poke /'sloupouk/ *n.* [C] SPOKEN someone who moves or does things too slowly: *Hurry up, slowpoke!*

slow-wit·ted /,. '..◂/ *adj.* not good at understanding things; stupid

sludge /slʌdʒ/ *n.* [U] **1** the thick, nearly solid substance that is left when SEWAGE (=the liquid waste from houses, factories etc.) has been cleaned **2** a soft thick substance like mud, especially at the bottom of a liquid —**sludgy** *adj.*

slug[1] /slʌg/ *n.* [C] **1** a small slow-moving creature with a soft body like a SNAIL, but without a shell **2** [C] a bullet: *King ended up with two 9 mm slugs in his chest.* **3** INFORMAL a small amount of a strong alcoholic drink: *a slug of whiskey* **4** [C] a piece of metal shaped like a coin, used to get a drink, ticket etc. from a machine illegally

slug[2] *v.* **slugging, slugged** [T] **1** to hit someone hard with your closed hand: *Jimmy slugged Paul in the stomach and pushed him to the ground.* **2** to hit a baseball hard **3 slug it out** if two people slug it out, they fight in a fierce way: *Coca-Cola and Pepsi have been slugging it out in the cola wars for years.*

slug·fest /'slʌgfɛst/ *n.* [C] INFORMAL **1** a situation in which people are arguing or fighting with each other in a very angry and rude way: *The race for senator has become a political slugfest.* **2** a very rude and loud competition between two or more people, sports teams or musical groups

slug·ger /'slʌgɚ/ *n.* [C] a baseball player who hits the ball very hard

slug·gish /'slʌgɪʃ/ *adj.* moving, happening, or reacting more slowly than normal: *If you don't eat breakfast, you'll feel tired and sluggish.* | *Sales were sluggish in the first half of the year.* —**sluggishly** *adv.* —**sluggishness** *n.* [U]

sluice[1] /slus/ *n.* [C] a passage for water to flow through, with a special gate that can be opened or closed to control the flow

sluice[2] *v.* [T] to wash something with a lot of water: *City sweepers sluice down Telegraph Street every morning.*

slum[1] /slʌm/ *n.* [C] an area of a city that is in very bad condition, where very poor people live: *She grew up in the slums of Detroit.*

slum[2] *v.* [I] also **be slumming it** OFTEN HUMOROUS to spend time in conditions that are much worse than you are used to: *She made it clear that she was just slumming for a while in this business.*

slum·ber[1] /'slʌmbɚ/ *v.* [I] LITERARY to sleep

slumber[2] *n.* [singular,U] also **slumbers** LITERARY sleep: *They were awoken from their slumber by a knock at the door.*

slumber par·ty /ˈ.. ˌ../ *n.* [C] a children's party at which a group of children spend the night at one child's house

slum·lord /ˈslʌmlɔrd/ *n.* [C] DISAPPROVING someone who owns houses in a poor area and charges high rents for buildings that are in bad condition

slum·my /ˈslʌmi/ *adj.* INFORMAL a slummy area is one where very poor people live and the buildings are in bad condition

slump¹ /slʌmp/ *v.* **1** [I] to suddenly go down in price, value, or number: *Sales slumped by 20% last year.* **2** [I always + adv./prep.] to suddenly fall down or sit down because you feel weak or become unconscious: [+ **back/over/on** etc.] *Diane slumped back against the pillows.* | *Pat gasped as he slumped further forward.* **3 be slumped** to be sitting with your body leaning completely backward or forward, because you are tired or unconscious: [+ **in/against**] *Alex spotted an old woman slumped in a chair by the window.*

slump² *n.* [C] **1** a sudden decrease in prices, sales, business activity etc.: [+ **in**] *a slump in exports* **2** a period of time when a company, sports team etc. is not successful: *Smith is in the deepest batting slump of his eight-year career.*

slung /slʌŋ/ *v.* the past tense and past participle of SLING

slunk /slʌŋk/ *v.* the past tense and past participle of SLINK

slur¹ /slɚ/ *v.* **slurred, slurring 1** [I,T] to speak in an unclear way, without separating your words or sounds correctly: **slur your speech/words** *After a few drinks, Bev was starting to slur her speech.* **2** [T] to criticize someone or something unfairly **3** [T] to play a group of musical notes smoothly together —**slurred** *adj.*: *slurred speech*

slur² *n.* **1** [C] an unfair criticism, or an offensive remark: [+ **on**] *a slur on my reputation* | **racial/ethnic/anti-Semitic** etc. **slur** (=an offensive remark, based on someone's race, religion etc.) **2** [singular] an unclear way of speaking, in which the words are not separated **3** [C] a curved line written over or under musical notes to show they must be played together smoothly

slurp /slɚp/ *v.* [I,T] to make a noisy sucking sound while drinking a liquid: *Kids slurped strawberry shakes and ate hamburgers.* —**slurp** *n.* [C]

Slur·pee /ˈslɚpi/ *n.* [C,U] TRADEMARK a SLUSH (2)

slur·ry /ˈslɚi, ˈslʌri/ *n.* [U] a thin mixture of water and another substance such as mud, CEMENT, or animal waste

slush /slʌʃ/ *n.* **1** [U] partly melted snow: *Everything had melted into brown slush within a few hours.* **2** [C,U] a drink made with crushed ice and a sweet liquid: *a cherry slush* —**slushy** *adj.*

slush fund /ˈ. ./ *n.* [C] a sum of money kept for dishonest purposes, especially by a politician

slut /slʌt/ *n.* [C] OFFENSIVE a woman who has had many sexual partners —**slutty** also **sluttish** *adj.*

sly /slaɪ/ *adj.* **slier, sliest** also **slyer, slyest 1** very skillful in the way that you use tricks and lies to get what you want: *The sly old Congressman knows what it takes to get elected.* **2 a sly smile/glance/wink** etc. a smile, look etc. that shows that you are hiding something you know from other people: *Max had a sly grin and a twinkle in his eye.* **3 on the sly** secretly, especially when you are doing something that you should not do: *Dick had started drinking again on the sly.* —**slyly** *adv.* —**slyness** *n.* [U]

smack¹ /smæk/ *v.* [T] **1** to hit something against something else so that it makes a short loud noise: [**smack sth against/into** etc.] *Canseco smacked the last pitch into the left-field seats.* **2 smack your lips** to make a short loud noise with your lips because you are hungry **3** to hit someone hard with your hand: *The cop beside him smacked him on the arm.*

smack of sth *phr. v.* [T] FORMAL to seem to have a particular quality: *Their failure to publish the controversial article smacks of censorship.*

smack² *n.* **1** [C] a hard hit with your hand: *She gave Danny's hand a smack.* **2** [C] a short loud noise, caused especially when something hits something else **3 give sb a smack on the lips/cheek** INFORMAL to kiss someone loudly **4** [U] SLANG: see HEROIN (=a dangerous illegal drug)

smack³ *adv.* INFORMAL **1 smack (dab) in the middle** exactly or directly in the middle of something: *We found ourselves right smack in the middle of a huge fight.* **2** if something moves smack into or against something, it hits it with a lot of force, making a loud noise: *I drove smack into the side of the garage.*

smack·er /ˈsmækɚ/ also **smack·er·oo** /ˌsmækəˈru/ *n.* [C] INFORMAL **1** a dollar: *It cost me fifty smackers.* **2** a loud kiss: *He planted a big, wet smacker on Jill's cheek.*

small¹ /smɔl/ *adj.*

1 size not large in size or amount: *a small increase in food prices* | *Smaller cars use less gas.* | *Rhode Island is the smallest state in the nation.* —see also LITTLE¹ —see Usage Note at LITTLE¹

2 group/number consisting of only a few people or things: *A small number of protesters stood near the entrance to the plant.* | *Private schools can offer smaller classes and more individual attention.*

3 unimportant a small problem, job, mistake etc. is not important or severe: *There were just a couple of small mistakes on your test.* | *We have made a few small changes to the original design.*

4 child a small child is young: *Be aware that women and small children, as well as men, can be pickpockets.*

5 small business a business that does not have many EMPLOYEES, and usually deals with a limited number of products or activities

6 small farmer/investor someone whose activities do not involve large amounts of land or money

7 a small fortune a lot of money: *It's going to cost us a small fortune to fix the roof.*

8 in a/some small way if something helps, affects, influences etc. something else in a small way, it has an effect, but not an important one: *Recent events may, in some small way, change our perception of world politics.*

9 small wonder used to say that something is not surprising: *Salonen has worked in cities all over the world. Small wonder, then, that he has mastered five languages.*

10 alphabet small letters are the smaller of the two forms that we use, for example "b" rather than "B"; LOWER CASE

11 feel small to feel stupid, unimportant, or ashamed: *At times, I felt very small and vulnerable.*

12 in no small measure to a great degree; mainly: *The success of the movie is due in no small measure to its spectacular special effects.*

13 voice a small voice is quiet and soft: *"It still hurts," he said in a small voice.*

14 small potatoes also **small beer** something that is not very important, especially when compared with something else: *In today's corporate world, our little company's profits look like pretty small potatoes.*

15 (it's a) small world SPOKEN said when you are surprised to learn that someone knows a person who you know, goes to a place where you go etc.: *"I graduated from St. John's." "Really? So did my brother. Small world."*

16 small fry INFORMAL **a)** children: *Check out our new $2.99 menu for the small fry.* **b)** unimportant people or things: *Making money is getting even harder for us small fry.*

17 a socialist with a small "s"/a libertarian with a small "l" etc. someone who believes in the principles you have mentioned, but is not a member of a political party or group with that name —**small** *adv.*: *He writes so small I can't read it.* —**smallness** *n.* [U]

small² *n.* **the small of your back** the lower part of your back where it curves, just above your BUTTOCKS

small arms /ˌ. ˈ./ *n.* [plural] guns that are held in one or both hands for firing

small-boned /ˌ. ˈ. ◂/ *adj.* a small-boned person is short and thin

small-cal·i·ber /ˌ. '...ˌ/ *adj.* [only before noun] a small-caliber gun fires small bullets

small change /ˌ. './ *n.* [U] **1** money in coins of low value: *They put some small change in the collection box.* **2** an amount of money that seems small, when it is compared with another amount: *The fund receives under $20 million a year, which is small change in Washington.*

small claims court /ˌ. '. ˌ./ *n.* [C] a court where people can try to get small amounts of money from other people or from companies, when they have been treated unfairly

small hours /'. ./ *n.* [plural] **the small hours** the early morning hours, between about one and four o'clock: *We danced until the small hours.*

small in·tes·tine /ˌ. .'./ *n.* [singular] the long tube that food goes through after it has gone through your stomach —compare LARGE INTESTINE —see picture at DIGESTIVE SYSTEM

small·ish /'smɔlɪʃ/ *adj.* fairly small: *The M3 coupe is a smallish car that's comfortable enough for four people.*

small-mind·ed /ˌ. '...ˌ/ *adj.* DISAPPROVING only interested in things that affect you, and too willing to judge people according to your own opinions: *The tone of the book is small-minded and intolerant.* —**small-mindedness** *n.* [U] —compare NARROW-MINDED

small·pox /'smɔlpɑks/ *n.* [U] a serious infectious disease that causes spots which leave marks on your skin —compare CHICKENPOX

small print /ˌ. './ *n.* [U] **the small print** FINE PRINT

small-scale /ˌ. '.ˌ/ *adj.* [only before noun] **1** not involving a lot of people, money etc.: *small-scale research projects* **2** a small-scale map, model etc. is drawn or made smaller than usual and does not show many details —compare LARGE-SCALE

small screen /'. ./ *n.* **the small screen** television: *The story of Hearst's life made it to the small screen last spring.*

small talk /'. ./ *n.* [U] polite friendly conversation about unimportant subjects: *Guests stood with their drinks, making small talk about the weather.*

small-time /ˌ. '.ˌ/ *adj.* [only before noun] not important or successful: *a small-time drug dealer | Most of Jenkins' articles were about small-time police corruption.* —**small-timer** *n.* [C] —compare BIG-TIME

small-town /'. ./ *adj.* [only before noun] **1** relating to a small town: *a small-town newspaper* **2** relating to the qualities, ideas, and opinions that people who live in small towns are supposed to have, such as honesty and politeness, but sometimes also a lack of interest in anything new or different: *small-town values*

smarm·y /'smɑrmi/ *adj.* **smarmier, smarmiest** polite in an insincere way that you do not like or trust: *He fooled us with his soft smarmy ways.*

s w **smart¹** /smɑrt/ *adj.*

1 intelligent intelligent: *Quinn's a smart guy, but he talks too much. | Kelly wasn't sure if she was smart enough to go to law school.* —compare DUMB¹ (1)

2 good decision **a)** making good judgments or decisions: *Here are a few tips every smart traveler should know.* **b)** a smart decision, plan etc. shows good judgment or thinking: *The report shows investors that the takeover was a smart move* (=a good decision).

3 smart money opinions and judgments made by intelligent people who know a lot about a particular situation, especially relating to INVESTMENTS: *The smart money says that digital TV is the next big thing.*

4 impolite saying funny things in a way that does not show respect: *That's enough of your smart remarks for now.*

5 fashionable OLD-FASHIONED fashionable, or used by fashionable people: *a smart suit | an atmosphere of smart elegance*

6 well-dressed OLD-FASHIONED wearing neat attractive clothes and having a generally neat and clean appearance

7 quick a smart movement is done quickly and with force: *Marvin gave me a smart kick under the table.* —**smartness** *n.* [U] —see also SMARTS

smart² *adv.* INFORMAL in a way that shows intelligence and good judgment: *We've got to work smarter, not harder.*

smart³ *v.* [I] **1** to be upset because someone has hurt your feelings or offended you: [+ **from**] *The Eagles were still smarting from their loss to Arizona.* **2** if a part of your body smarts, it hurts with a stinging pain: *The smoke made my eyes smart.*

smart off *phr. v.* [I] INFORMAL to make funny impolite remarks: [+ **to**] *You'd better not smart off to the teacher.*

smart al·eck /'smɑrt ˌælɪk/ *n.* [C] INFORMAL someone who always says funny impolite things, or who always has the right answer in a way that is annoying

smart ass /'. ./ *n.* [C] VULGAR a smart aleck —**smart-ass** *adj.* [only before noun] *smart-ass remarks*

smart bomb /'. ./ *n.* [C] a bomb that is fired from an aircraft and guided by a computer

smart card /'. ./ *n.* [C] a small plastic card with an electronic part that records information

smart·ly /'smɑrtli/ *adv.* **1** in a neat, fashionable way: *a smartly dressed man* **2** quickly: *Stocks rose smartly in active trading.* **3** using force: *He hit the ball smartly toward left field.*

smart-mouthed /ˌ. '.ˌ/ *adj.* INFORMAL making a lot of funny impolite remarks: *Moesha's smart-mouthed little brother*

smarts /smɑrts/ *n.* [plural] INFORMAL the ability to think quickly and make good judgments; intelligence: *Cusack plays the mayor with passion and political smarts.* —see also STREET SMARTS

smart·y /'smɑrti/ *n. plural* **smarties** [C] a SMART ALECK

smart·y·pants /'smɑrti,pænts/ *n.* [C] HUMOROUS someone who always says funny impolite things or always has the right answer, in an annoying way

smash¹ /smæʃ/ *v.* **1** [I,T] to break into many small pieces violently or loudly, or to make something do this by dropping, throwing, or hitting it: *The burglars entered the house by smashing a window. | The vase fell and smashed into a million tiny pieces.* **2** [I,T always + adv./prep.] to hit an object or surface violently, or to make something do this: [+ **against/down/into** etc.] *Carlson was killed when her car smashed into a tree.* **3** [T] to do much better than someone or something has done before in a race, competition etc.: *The stock market rose so quickly it smashed all previous records.* **4** [T] to destroy something such as a political system or criminal organization: *Police authorities say they have smashed a sophisticated insurance fraud ring.* **5** [T] to hit a high ball with a strong DOWNWARD action, in tennis or similar sports

smash sth ↔ **in** *phr. v.* [T] to hit something so violently that you break it and make a hole in it: *One child nearly had her head smashed in when the ceiling collapsed.*

smash sth ↔ **up** *phr. v.* [T] to damage or destroy something: *Forty inmates smashed up their prison cells.* —see also SMASH-UP

smash² *n.* **1** [C] a very successful new play, book, movie etc.; SMASH HIT: *the latest Broadway smash* **2** [singular] the loud sound of something breaking: *Suddenly, there was a smash in the kitchen.* **3** [C] a hard DOWNWARD hit of the ball in tennis or similar sports

smashed /smæʃt/ *adj.* **be/get smashed** INFORMAL to be or become very drunk or affected by a drug: *She's smashed out of her mind.*

smash hit /ˌ. './ *n.* [C] a very successful new play, book, movie etc.: *"Falcon Crest" was only a modest success in the U.S., but a smash hit in Europe.*

smash·ing /'smæʃɪŋ/ *adj.* OLD-FASHIONED very good

smash-up /'. ./ n. [C] a serious car or train accident

smat·ter·ing /'smæṭərɪŋ/ n. **a smattering of sth** a small number or amount of something: *The boys learned English and also picked up a smattering of French.*

smear[1] /smɪr/ v. **1** [I,T] to spread a liquid or soft substance over a surface, especially in a careless or messy way, or to be spread in this way: *I knew Deanna had been crying because her makeup had smeared.* | [**smear sth on/over etc.**] *Researchers will take a drop of blood and smear it on a slide.* **2** [T] to make dirty or oily marks on something: *The rain had dribbled on his glasses and smeared them.* | [**smear sth with sth**] *Halle's face was smeared with butter.* **3** [I,T] to become unclear, or make something unclear by rubbing it; SMUDGE: *The printing wasn't dark enough, and many letters were smeared around the edges.* **4** [T] to spread an untrue story about someone in order to harm them: *Carter refused to take part in an attempt to smear his campaign opponent.*

smear[2] n. [C] **1** a dirty or oily mark on something: *There were paint smears visible on the doorknob.* **2** an attempt to harm someone by spreading untrue stories about them —**smeary** adj. —see also PAP SMEAR

smear cam·paign /'. .,./ n. [C] a deliberate plan to tell untrue stories about someone, especially a politician, in order to harm them

smell[1] /smɛl/ n. **1** [C] the quality that people and animals recognize by using their nose: *Each wine has its own unique flavor and smell.* | *Perfectly pure water has no smell.* | [**+ of**] *The smell of baking bread filled the whole house.* —compare AROMA, FRAGRANCE, SCENT[1] **2** [C] a bad smell: *Where's that smell coming from?* —compare ODOR, STINK[2] (1) **3** [U] the ability to notice or recognize smells: *A mole finds its food by smell alone.* | *Humans' **sense of smell** is not very well developed.*

USAGE NOTE: SMELL

WORD CHOICE: smell, odor, scent, fragrance, aroma
You can use **smell** in a general way to talk about something that you notice or recognize using your nose: *There was a strong smell of fish in the house.* | *The smell of bread baking always reminds me of my grandma.* An **odor** is a bad smell: *the odor of sour milk.* A **scent** is what something smells like, especially something that smells good: *a fresh floral scent.* A **fragrance** is a very good **scent**: *the fragrance of roses and lilacs.* An **aroma** is a pleasant smell from food or drinks: *The aroma of fresh coffee filled the kitchen.*

---

smell[2] v.
1 **have a smell** [I always + adv./prep.,linking verb + adj.] to have a particular smell: **smell nice/good/spicy etc.** *Whatever you're cooking, it smells great!* | *a sweet-smelling flower* | [**+ like**] *Your perfume smells like roses.*
2 **bad** [I not in progressive] to have a bad smell; STINK: *Take the garbage out before it starts to smell.*
3 **recognize a smell** [T not in progressive] to notice or recognize a particular smell: *Do you smell smoke?*
4 **use your nose** [T] to put your nose near something to discover what type of smell it has; SNIFF[1]: *Diane smelled his breath to see if he'd been drinking.*
5 **smell trouble/danger etc.** to feel that something bad is going to happen: *Actually, I should have smelled trouble earlier.*
6 **smell a rat** to guess that something wrong or dishonest is happening: *The investor doesn't start to smell a rat until the payments aren't coming in.*
7 **smell fishy** also **smell something fishy** if a story, excuse etc. smells fishy or if you smell something fishy, you think it is likely to not be true: *Some of the centers did not let the inspectors in because they smelled something fishy.*
8 **sth doesn't smell right (to sb)** used to say that a situation does not seem right

9 **able to smell** [I] to have the ability to notice and recognize smells

smell sb/sth ↔ out phr. v. [T] **1** to find something because you have a natural ability to do this: *Good agents smell out new performers who are full of promise and energy.* **2** to find something by smelling: *Dogs are able to smell out their prey.*

smelling salts /'.. ,./ n. [plural] a strong-smelling chemical that you hold under someone's nose to make them conscious again

smell·y /'smɛli/ adj. **smellier, smelliest** having a strong bad smell: *smelly socks* —**smelliness** n. [U]

smelt[1] /smɛlt/ v. [T] to melt a rock that contains metal in order to remove the metal

smelt[2] v. an old-fashioned form of the past tense and past participle of SMELL

smelt[3] n. [C] a small fish that lives in cold lakes and oceans

smidg·en /'smɪdʒən/ n. **a smidgen** a very small amount of something: *They don't have a smidgen of evidence.*

smile[1] /smaɪl/ v. **1** [I] to have or make a happy expression on your face in which your mouth curves up: *a roomful of smiling children* | [**+ at**] *This guy kept smiling at me from across the room.* —compare GRIN[1] (1) **2** **smile to yourself** to be amused by something, often without showing it: *Warner smiled to himself as he jotted down a few notes.* **3** [T] to say or express something with a smile: *"I knew you'd come," she smiled.* **4** **God/luck/fortune smiles on sb** if God, luck etc. smiles on you, you have very good luck —**smilingly** adv.: *Melissa smilingly reached for a cigarette.*

smile[2] n. [C] **1** an expression on your face in which your mouth curves up to show that you are happy, amused, friendly, etc.: *Juan had a wide smile on his face.* | *"How's it going?" Maya asked with a smile.* | *Give the camera a big smile as you walk past.* **2** **be all smiles** to look very happy, especially because of something good that has happened

smil·ey /'smaɪli/ n. [C] a sign that looks like a face when you look at it sideways, for example :-) used in EMAIL messages to show that you are happy or pleased about something

smiley face /'.. ,./ n. [C] a simple picture of a smiling face, drawn as a circle with two eyes and a mouth inside it

smirk /smɚk/ v. [I] to smile in a way that is not nice, and that shows that you are pleased by someone else's bad luck: [**+ at**] *I sat in the airport lounge, smirking at travelers struggling with heavy luggage.* —**smirk** n. [C]

smite /smaɪt/ v. *past tense* **smote** *past participle* **smitten** [T] **1** OLD USE to hit something or someone hard **2** BIBLICAL to destroy, attack, or punish someone —see also SMITTEN[1]

smith /smɪθ/ n. [C] someone who makes and repairs things made of iron; BLACKSMITH

-smith /smɪθ/ suffix [in nouns] someone who makes something: *a gunsmith* (=someone who makes guns) | *a silversmith* (=someone who makes things out of silver) | *a wordsmith* (=someone who writes, for example a JOURNALIST)

Smith /smɪθ/, **Ad·am** /'ædəm/ (1723–1790) a Scottish ECONOMIST famous for his belief in FREE ENTERPRISE, which has had an important influence on modern economic and political ideas

Smith, John (1580–1631) an English EXPLORER who started Jamestown, Virginia, the first permanent COLONY in America

Smith, Joseph (1805–1844) a U.S. religious leader who started the MORMON religion

Smith, Mar·garet Chase /'mɑrgrɪt tʃeɪs/ (1897–1995) a U.S. politician who was the first woman to be elected to both the Senate and the House of Representatives

smith·er·eens /ˌsmɪðə'rinz/ n. **smash/blow/blast etc. sth to smithereens** to destroy something completely by breaking it violently into very small pieces: *The boat had been smashed to smithereens in the storm.*

Smith·son /'smɪθsən/, **James** (1765–1829) a British scientist who left the money to start the Smithsonian Institution after his death

Smith·so·ni·an In·sti·tu·tion, the /smɪθ‚souniən ɪnstɪ'tuʃən/ also **the Smithsonian** a large group of MUSEUMS and scientific institutions in Washington, D.C., which was established in 1846 using money left by James Smithson

smith·y /'smɪθi/ n. *plural* **smithies** [C] a place where iron objects such as HORSESHOES were made and repaired in past times

smit·ten[1] /'smɪt‑n/ adj. feeling that you love someone or like something very much, especially suddenly: *Eric's completely smitten with Jenny.*

smitten[2] v. the past participle of SMITE

smock /smak/ n. [C] a loose piece of clothing like a long shirt, worn over your clothes to prevent them from getting dirty: *an artist's smock*

smock·ing /'smakɪŋ/ n. [U] a type of decoration made on cloth by pulling the cloth into small regular folds which are held tightly with stitches —**smock** v. [T] —**smocked** adj.

smog /smag, smɔg/ n. [U] unhealthy air, often brown in color, caused by gases from cars and smoke from factories etc. —**smoggy** adj.

S W
3 3
smoke[1] /smouk/ n. **1** [U] white, gray, or black gas that is produced by something burning: *We could see a cloud of smoke rising above the trees.* | *The smell of cigarette smoke hung in the air.* **2** [C] INFORMAL a cigarette: *Maybe you could get a smoke off somebody at the bar.* **3** [C usually singular] INFORMAL an act of smoking a cigarette etc.: *I haven't had a smoke in nine days.* **4 smoke and mirrors** actions that are intended to deceive people, or to make them believe something that is not true: *Our proposal is not smoke and mirrors. It will really get the debt down.* **5 go up in smoke a)** to be destroyed by fire **b)** if your plans go up in smoke, you cannot do what you intended to do **6 there's no smoke without fire** used to say that if something bad is being said about someone or something, it is probably partly true —**smokeless** adj.

S W
1 2
smoke[2] v. **1 a)** [I] if someone smokes, they regularly use cigarettes, a pipe etc.: *Do you smoke?* | *Dana started smoking again when her husband left her.* **b)** [I,T] to suck or breathe in smoke from a cigarette, pipe etc.: *Greg sat alone, smoking a cigarette.* **2** [I] if something smokes, it has smoke coming out of it: *a smoking chimney* **3** [T] to give fish and meat a special taste by hanging it in smoke to preserve it —**smoking** n. [U]

    smoke sb/sth ↔ **out** phr. v. [T] **1** to fill a place with smoke in order to force someone or something to come out **2** to discover who is causing a particular problem and force them to make themselves known: *New guidelines are intended to smoke out unauthorized users of office equipment.*

smoke a·larm /'. ‚./ n. [C] a piece of electronic equipment that warns you when there is smoke or fire in a building

smoke bomb /'. ./ n. [C] something that you throw that produces clouds of smoke, used to prevent people from seeing clearly

smoked /smoukt/ adj. **smoked salmon/bacon/sausage etc.** fish, meat etc. that has been left in smoke to preserve it and give it a special taste

smoke de·tec·tor /'. .‚./ n. [C] ≈ SMOKE ALARM

smoked glass /‚. '.‚/ n. [U] glass that is a dark gray color

smoke-filled room /‚. . '.‚/ n. [C] a place where a group of powerful people meet in secret to make decisions, especially about politics

smoke-free /‚. '.‚/ adj. **smoke-free area/zone etc.** a place where you are not allowed to smoke

smoke·house /'smoukhaus/ n. [C] a building where meat, fish etc. is hung in smoke to preserve them and give it a special taste

smokeless to·bac·co /‚. . '.‚/ n. [U] a type of tobacco that is held in the mouth for a long time and sometimes CHEWed, but not swallowed or smoked

smok·er /'smoukə/ n. [C] **1** someone who smokes cigarettes, CIGARS etc.: *Mike is a very heavy smoker* (=he smokes a lot). —opposite NONSMOKER **2** a piece of equipment that produces smoke, used to give meat, fish etc. a special taste

smoke·screen /'smoukskrin/ n. [C] **1** something that you do or say to hide your real plans or actions: *The rumors were a smokescreen for their own illegal activities.* **2** a cloud of smoke produced so that it hides soldiers, ships etc. during a battle

smoke sig·nal /'. ‚../ n. [C] a signal that is sent out to people who are far away, using the smoke from a fire

smoke·stack /'smoukstæk/ n. [C] a tall CHIMNEY at a factory or on a ship

smokestack in·dus·try /'.. ‚.../ n. [C usually plural] a big traditional industry, such as making cars

smok·ing /'smoukɪŋ/ adj. [only before noun, no comparative] **smoking area/section/room etc.** a place where people are allowed to smoke

smok·ing gun /‚.. './ n. [C usually singular] definite proof of who is responsible for something or how something really happened: *Investigators have failed to find a smoking gun to connect the mayor to the missing money.*

smoking jack·et /‚.. ‚../ n. [C] a type of man's formal JACKET (1) made of expensive material, usually worn at home in the evening

smok·y /'smouki/ adj. **smokier, smokiest 1** filled with smoke: *a smoky room* **2** producing too much smoke: *a smoky old diesel engine* **3** having the taste, smell, or appearance of smoke: *smoky bacon* —**smokiness** n. [U]

smol·der /'smouldə/ v. [I] **1** if something smolders, it burns slowly without a flame: *Forest Service crews routinely discover smoldering campfires along trails.* **2** if someone smolders or if their feelings smolder, they are very sexually attractive or have strong sexual feelings: *Greene found himself seated across from smoldering sex object Fabio.*

smooch /smutʃ/ v. [I,T] INFORMAL if two people smooch, they kiss each other in a romantic way —**smooch** n. [C] *He gave her a smooch and a big hug.*

smooth[1] /smuð/ adj.
1 surface a smooth surface is completely even, without any BUMPS: *a smooth pebble* | *a smooth, freshly-paved driveway* | *a board with smooth edges* —opposite ROUGH[1] (1)
2 soft skin or fur that is smooth is soft and pleasant to touch, and your hand moves easily over it: *Moisturizers promise to leave your skin softer and smoother.*
3 liquid a liquid mixture that is smooth has no big pieces in it: *Add the remaining ingredients and beat until smooth.* —opposite LUMPY
4 without problems a system, operation, or process that is smooth operates well and without problems: *We hope that most students will make a smooth transition into high school.* —see also **go smoothly** (SMOOTHLY (2))
5 smooth sailing if something is smooth sailing, it is easy and happens without any problems: *Case knows the months ahead are not going to be smooth sailing for the company.*
6 movement a smooth movement, style, way of doing something etc. is graceful and has no sudden awkward changes: *a series of smooth, graceful ripples on the lake* —opposite JERKY[1]
7 trip a trip that is smooth is comfortable because the vehicle you are in does not shake much while you are traveling: *a smooth flight* —opposite BUMPY
8 person someone who is smooth is polite, confident, and relaxed, but also makes you feel that you cannot trust them: *a smooth lawyer* —see also SMOOTH-TALKING
9 good taste a drink such as WHISKEY or coffee that is smooth is not bitter, but tastes good and is easy to swallow —**smoothness** n. [U] —see also SMOOTHLY

S

smooth[2] v. [T] **1** to take away the roughness from the surface of something: *The logs were smoothed and trimmed to size with axes.* | [+ **down/off/out** etc.] *Press the filler into the crack, smoothing it off with a wide knife.* **2** to make something flat by moving your hands across it: [+ **out/open** etc.] *Omar unfolded a piece of paper, which he smoothed out on the table.* | [+ **down/back** etc.] *She smoothed back her hair.* **3** [always + adv./prep.] to rub a liquid, cream etc. gently over a surface or into a surface: [**smooth sth into/over sth**] *She smoothed suntan lotion over her legs.* **4 smooth the way (for sth)** to make it easier for something to happen, by dealing with any problems first: *Negotiators have smoothed the way for passage of the controversial handgun law.*

smooth sth ↔ **out** *phr. v.* [T] to get rid of problems or difficulties: *The Access Fund has struggled to smooth out the conflicts between mountain climbers and private owners.*

smooth sth ↔ **over** *phr. v.* [T] to make problems or difficulties seem less important: *Keeley hopes to smooth over personal differences between state and county officials.*

smooth·ie /'smuði/ *n.* [C] **1** a thick drink made of fruit and fruit juices that have been mixed together until they are smooth **2** INFORMAL someone who is good at persuading people, but does not seem to be sincere: *You could see why she was attracted to him, the old smoothie.*

smooth·ly /'smuðli/ *adv.* **1** in a smooth way: *Practice the scales until you can play them smoothly.* | *With one-way streets, cars will move more smoothly and rapidly through the neighborhood.* **2 go/work/run etc. smoothly** if a planned event, piece of work etc. goes smoothly, there are no problems to spoil it: *All departments should function smoothly together.*

smooth talk·ing /'. ,../ *adj.* a smooth-talking person is good at persuading people and saying nice things, but you do not trust them: *a smooth-talking salesman* —**smooth talker** *n.* [C]

smor·gas·bord /'smɔrgəs,bɔrd/ *n.* [C] **1** a large variety of foods which are put on a long table so that people can serve themselves **2 a smorgasbord of sth** a large variety of different things: *Self-guided tours will take you through a smorgasbord of galleries, from ancient sculpture to '60s pop art.*

smote /smoʊt/ *v.* the past tense of SMITE

smoth·er /'smʌðɚ/ *v.* [T] **1** to cover the whole surface of something with something else: [**smother sth with/in sth**] *My steak arrived, smothered in onions and gravy.* **2** to kill someone by putting something over their nose and mouth to stop them from breathing: *When she was 18, she smothered her 11-month-old daughter.* **3** to express your feelings for someone too strongly, so that your relationship with them cannot develop normally: *I had to end it with Tim – I felt like I was being smothered.* **4** to hide your feelings: *Nancy smothered a smile.* **5** to make a fire stop burning by preventing air from reaching it **6** to completely defeat someone who opposes you: *The Phillies' Curt Schilling smothered the Blue Jays, 5–9.*

smudge

smudge[1] /smʌdʒ/ *n.* [C] a dirty mark: *There was a lipstick smudge on the rim of my cup.* —**smudgy** *adj.*

smudge[2] *v.* **1** [I,T] to make writing, painting etc. become unclear by touching or rubbing it, or to become unclear in this way: *Renille wiped at her eyes, smudging her makeup.* **2** [T] to make a dirty mark on a surface: *Carlos had a smudged repair manual propped open on the car's windshield.*

smug /smʌg/ *adj.* showing too much satisfaction with your own skill or success: *Frank patted his pocket and smiled, looking awfully smug.* | *a smug grin* —**smugly** *adv.* —**smugness** *n.* [U]

smug·gle /'smʌgəl/ *v.* [T] **1** to take something or someone illegally from one country to another: [**smuggle sth into/to/from/out of sth**] *Cars are usually used to smuggle drugs into the U.S. from Mexico.* | *The documents apparently were smuggled across the border to Jordan.* **2** to take something or someone secretly to a place where they are not allowed to be: *I'll smuggle you in through the back door.*

smug·gler /'smʌglɚ/ *n.* [C] someone who takes something illegally from one country to another: *a drug smuggler*

smug·gling /'smʌglɪŋ/ *n.* [U] the crime of taking things illegally from one country to another: *Mexico has made efforts to reduce smuggling.*

smut /smʌt/ *n.* [U] **1** DISAPPROVING books, stories, pictures etc. that offend some people because they are about sex **2** a type of plant disease that attacks crops and causes a black substance to form on the plants: *corn smut*

smut·ty /'smʌti/ *adj.* **smuttier, smuttiest** DISAPPROVING books, stories, pictures etc. that are smutty offend some people because they are about sex: *smutty jokes* —**smuttiness** *n.* [U]

snack[1] /snæk/ *n.* [C] **1** a small amount of food that is eaten between main meals or instead of a meal: *I only had time to grab a quick snack.* **2** also **snack food** a food, such as POTATO CHIPS or PEANUTS, that is sold to be eaten as a snack

snack[2] *v.* [I] to eat small amounts of food between main meals or instead of a meal: [+ **on**] *Stop snacking on junk food if you want to lose weight.*

snack bar /'. ./ *n.* [C] a place where you can buy snacks, such as SANDWICHes and CANDY BARS

sna·fu /'snæfu, snæ'fu/ *n.* [C] a situation in which a plan does not happen in the way it should: *AOL had suffered several technical snafus over those three days.*

snag[1] /snæg/ *n.* [C] **1** a disadvantage or problem, especially one that is not very serious: *The process hit a snag Tuesday when a vital meeting had to be canceled.* **2** a thread that has been pulled out of a piece of cloth by accident because it has gotten stuck on something sharp or pointed **3** a part of a dead tree that sticks out, especially one that is under water and can be dangerous

snag[2] *v.* **snagged, snagging** **1** [T] INFORMAL to get someone to notice you, or to succeed in getting something: *The parking lot was almost full, but I snagged a space in the last row.* **2** [I,T] to damage something by getting it stuck on something, or to become damaged in this way: *Danny's kite snagged in the upper branches of a tree.*

snail /sneɪl/ *n.* [C] **1** a small soft creature that moves very slowly and has a hard shell on its back **2 at a snail's pace** if something happens or is done at a snail's pace, it happens extremely slowly

snail mail /'. ./ *n.* [U] HUMOROUS an expression meaning letters that are sent through the mail and not by EMAIL

snake[1] /sneɪk/ *n.* [C] **1** an animal with a long thin body and no legs, that often has a poisonous bite **2** also **snake in the grass** someone who cannot be trusted

snake[2] *v.* [I always + adv./prep.] if a river, road, train, or line snakes somewhere, it moves in long, twisting curves: [+ **along/past/down** etc.] *The line for tickets snaked around the block.* | *Trickles of water were **snaking their way** down the hillside.*

snake·bite /'sneɪkbaɪt/ *n.* **1** [C,U] the bite of a poisonous snake **2** [C] an alcoholic drink that contains TEQUILA, which is drunk quickly from a small glass before you suck a piece of LEMON with salt on it in your hand

snake charm·er /'. ,../ n. [C] someone who entertains people by controlling snakes as they play music to them

snake eyes /'. ./ n. [plural] a situation in a game in which a pair of DICE both show the number 1

snake oil /'. ./ n. **1** [U] something that is claimed to be a solution to a problem, but is not effective **2 snake oil salesman/peddler** someone who deceives people by persuading them to accept false information, solutions that are not effective etc.

snake pit /'. ./ n. [C] **1** a place or situation that is not organized and where people are quick to criticize one another **2** INFORMAL a hospital for people who have mental problems

snake·skin /'sneɪkˌskɪn/ n. [U] the skin of a snake used to make shoes, bags etc.

snak·y /'sneɪki/ adj. moving or lying in twisting curves: *a snaky road*

snap[1] /snæp/ v.

1 break [I,T] if something snaps or if you snap it, it breaks with a sudden sharp noise: *Cheaper versions are made of metal that could rust and snap.* | [**snap sth ↔ off**] *The storm snapped off several branches from the oak tree out front.* | **snap sth in two/half etc.** (=to break something into two pieces)
2 move into position [I,T always + adv./prep.] to move into a particular position suddenly, making a short sharp noise, or to make something move like this: *The cops snapped the handcuffs back onto the prisoner.* | *The pieces just snap together like this.* | **snap open/shut** *She snapped her briefcase shut.*
3 say sth angrily [I,T] to say something quickly in an angry or annoyed way: *"Can't you see I'm eating?" Mattie snapped.* | [+ **at**] *Pitino snapped at one reporter who approached him after the game.*
4 snap your fingers to make a short, sharp noise by moving one of your fingers quickly against your thumb, for example in order to get someone's attention
5 become angry/anxious etc. [I] **a)** to suddenly stop being able to control your anger, anxiety, or other feelings in a difficult situation: *When he hit me across the face, I just snapped.* **b)** if someone or someone's mind snaps, they suddenly become mentally ill
6 stop [T] to end a series of events: *The Rockets finally snapped a seven-game losing streak by defeating Portland.*
7 animal [I] if an animal such as a dog snaps, it tries to bite you: [+ **at**] *Ginger was snapping at their heels.*
8 photograph [T] to take a photograph: *Mel snapped a picture with his pocket camera.*
9 snap to it SPOKEN used to tell someone to hurry and do something immediately: *Come on, snap to it, get that room cleaned up!*
10 snap to attention if soldiers snap to attention, they suddenly stand very straight —see also SNAP-ON

snap out of sth *phr. v.* [T not in passive] **1 snap out of it** to stop being sad or upset and make yourself feel better **2** to suddenly start paying attention or behaving normally again: *When I snapped out of my daydream, it was already 10:00.*

snap on/off *phr. v.* [I,T] if a light or a piece of electrical equipment snaps on or off, or if you snap it on or off, it starts or stops working with a short sharp noise: [**snap sth ↔ on/off**] *I snapped on the television and went through the channels.*

snap sb/sth **↔ up** *phr. v.* [T] **1** to buy something immediately, especially because it is very cheap: *People from out of state are coming in and snapping up real estate.* **2** to eagerly take an opportunity to have someone as part of your company, team etc.: *They needed a good quarterback and would have snapped him up if they'd had a chance.*

snap[2] n. **1 be a snap** INFORMAL to be very easy to do: *Pasta dough is a snap to make.* **2** [singular] a sudden loud sound, especially made by something breaking or closing: *Nick closed the lid with a snap.* **3** [C] the act of throwing the ball from one football player to another, especially over a short distance **4** [C] a small metal fastener on clothes that works

---

when you press its two parts together **5 a snap of your fingers** a sudden sound made by quickly moving one of your fingers against your thumb —see also COLD SNAP

snap[3] adj. **snap judgment/decision** a judgment or decision made quickly and without enough thought or preparation

snap bean /'. ./ n. [C] a long thin green bean that is very CRISP

snap·drag·on /'snæpˌdrægən/ n. [C] a garden plant with white, red, or yellow flowers

snap-on /'. ./ adj. [only before noun] a snap-on part of a toy or tool can be attached and removed easily

snap·per /'snæpə/ n. [C,U] a type of fish that lives in warm parts of the ocean, or the meat from this fish

snapping tur·tle /'.. ,../ n. [C] a type of TURTLE with a powerful mouth that makes a short, sharp noise when it closes quickly

snap·pish /'snæpɪʃ/ adj. easily annoyed and often speaking in an angry way

snap·py /'snæpi/ adj. **snappier, snappiest 1** spoken or written in a short, clear, and often funny way: *We need to come up with a snappier slogan.* | *Keep your answer short and snappy.* **2 make it snappy** SPOKEN used to tell someone to hurry: *Get me a drink, and make it snappy.* **3** snappy clothes, objects etc. are attractive and fashionable: *Fashion editors love her snappy, colorful designs.* —**snappily** adv. —**snappiness** n. [U]

snap·shot /'snæpʃɑt/ n. [C] **1** an informal photograph: *I sent some snapshots of the kids.* **2** a piece of information or a description that quickly gives you an idea of what the situation is like at a particular time: [+ **of**] *The survey results give us a snapshot of employees' opinions of the new training program.*

snare[1] /snɛr/ n. [C] **1** something that is intended to trick someone and get them into a difficult situation **2** a snare drum **3** a trap for catching an animal, especially one that uses a wire or rope to catch the animal by its foot

snare[2] v. [T] **1** to catch an animal by using a snare **2** to catch someone, especially by tricking them: *Boggs is one of three people snared in an ongoing federal investigation.*

snare drum /'. ./ n. [C] a small flat drum that makes a hard sharp sound when you hit it

snarf /snɑrf/ v. [T] INFORMAL to eat something quickly, often in a messy or noisy way: *Office workers were snarfing deli sandwiches.*

snarl /snɑrl/ v. **1** [I + **at**] if an animal snarls, it makes a low angry sound and shows its teeth **2** [I,T] to speak or say something in a nasty angry way: *"What do they want?" snarled Weinstein.* **3** [I,T usually passive] also **snarl up** if traffic snarls or is snarled, it cannot move **4** [I,T usually passive] also **snarl up** if hair, thread, wires etc. snarl, they become twisted and messy and are difficult to separate **5** [I,T usually passive] also **snarl up** if a situation, process etc. snarls, it becomes confused and it is difficult to make any progress: *They're going to give us the information, but it keeps getting snarled up in paperwork.* —**snarl** n. [C] *traffic snarls*

snarl-up /'. ./ n. [C] a confused situation that prevents work from continuing

snatch[1] /snætʃ/ v. [T] **1** to take something away from someone with a quick or violent movement; GRAB[1]: [**snatch sth away/up/back etc.**] *"Wait a second," said Berman, snatching the tape recorder away.* **2** to take someone or something away from a place by force: *Masked gunmen snatched two members of the group from their hotel.* **3** to steal something quickly, when you have an opportunity, especially by taking it in your hands suddenly: *Unfortunately, street crimes such as purse snatching are common.* **4** to quickly take the opportunity to do something when you do not have much time: *Coles tried to snatch a few hours' sleep.*

snatch at sth *phr. v.* [T] to quickly put out your

hand to try to take or hold something: *The dog turned as I snatched at the leash and caught it.*

snatch sth ↔ **up** *phr. v.* [T] to eagerly buy or take something because it is cheap or because you want it very much: *When the deal with Shell fell apart, Ethyl Corp. snatched up the assets.*

snatch² *n.* [C] **1 a snatch of conversation/music/ song etc.** a short and incomplete part of a conversation, song etc. that you hear **2 in snatches** for short periods: *He'd only slept in snatches, an hour at most.* **3** VULGAR a woman's VAGINA

snaz·zy /'snæzi/ *adj.* **snazzier, snazziest** INFORMAL bright, fashionable, and attractive: *a snazzy new car* —**snazzily** *adv.*

Snead /snid/, **Sam** /sæm/ (1912–) a U.S. GOLF player

s w
3

sneak¹ /snik/ *v. past tense and past participle* **snuck** or **sneaked** FORMAL **1** [I always + adv./prep.] to go somewhere secretly and quietly in order to avoid being seen or heard: [+ **in/past/around** etc.] *Local kids used to sneak into the theater through a side door.* **2** [T always + adv./prep.] to take someone or something somewhere secretly: [**sneak** sth **across/ through/by/past** etc.] *The Abrego gang had no trouble sneaking drugs across the border.* **3 sneak a look/ glance/peek** to look at something quickly and secretly, especially something that you are not supposed to see: *Jeff snuck a quick look at the actor eating lunch across the restaurant.* **4** [T] INFORMAL to quickly and secretly steal something that is not important or that does not have much value: *I snuck a drink of Dad's beer when he wasn't looking.*

sneak up *phr. v.* [I] to come close to someone very quietly, so that they do not see you until you reach them: [+ **on/behind** etc.] *Don't sneak up on me like that!* —see also SNEAK PREVIEW

sneak² *n.* [C] INFORMAL someone who is not liked because they do things secretly and cannot be trusted

sneak·er /'snikɚ/ *n.* [C usually plural] a type of light soft shoe, used for sports; TENNIS SHOE —see picture at SHOE¹

sneak·ing /'snikɪŋ/ *adj.* **1 a sneaking suspicion/ feeling (that)** a slight feeling that something is wrong, without being sure: *I had a sneaking suspicion that there was someone else in the room with Rob.* **2 a sneaking admiration for sb/sth** a secret feeling of admiration for someone or something

sneak pre·view /ˌ. ˈ../ *n.* [C] an occasion when you can see a movie, play etc. before it is shown to people in general

sneak·y /'sniki/ *adj.* **sneakier, sneakiest** doing things in a secret and dishonest or unfair way: *It's a sneaky move designed to reduce the company's tax bill.* —**sneakily** *adv.*

sneer¹ /snɪr/ *v.* [I,T] to smile or speak in a way that is not nice and shows you have no respect for someone or something: *"I wouldn't be seen in public wearing that," Janina sneered.* | [+ **at**] *How can you sneer at vegetarians when you're wearing a leather jacket?* —**sneering** *adj.*: *a sneering letter* —**sneeringly** *adv.*

sneer² *n.* [C] a smile or remark that is not nice and shows you have no respect for something or someone

sneeze¹ /sniz/ *v.* [I] **1** to have a sudden uncontrolled burst of air come out of your nose and mouth, for example when you have a cold **2 sth is nothing to sneeze at** used to say that something is good or impressive enough to be considered carefully: *A good old Maryland thunderstorm is nothing to sneeze at.*

sneeze² *n.* [C] an act or sound of sneezing

sneeze guard /ˈ. ./ *n.* [C] a piece of plastic that is hung over food at a restaurant where people serve themselves, to keep them from sneezing on the food

snick·er /'snɪkɚ/ *v.* [I] to laugh quietly in a way that is not nice at something which is not supposed to be funny: [+ **at**] *Some listeners might be tempted to snicker at the childishly simple song titles.* —**snicker** *n.* [C]

snide /snaɪd/ *adj.* funny, but not nice: *snide remark/ comment Joyce then made a few snide comments about her ex-husband.* —**snidely** *adv.*

sniff¹ /snɪf/ *v.* **1** [I,T] to breathe air in through your nose in order to smell something: *He opened the milk and sniffed it.* | *Customs officers used drug-sniffing dogs to find 26 pounds of marijuana hidden in suitcases.* | [+ **at**] *Rex, the dog, was sniffing at the carpet.* **2** [I] to breathe air into your nose in short breaths, loudly enough so that it can be heard: *She sniffed a few times and stopped crying.* **3** [T] to say something in a proud way that shows you do not approve of something: *"It looks overcooked," she sniffed.* **4** [T] to take an illegal drug such as COCAINE through your nose —see also GLUE SNIFFING

s w
3

sniff at sth *phr. v.* **1** to refuse something in a proud way, or to think that something is not good enough for you: *Veteran audio fans may sniff at such ready-made stereo packages.* **2 sth is nothing to sniff at** used to say that something is good or impressive enough to be considered carefully: *Sloan's predictions are nothing to sniff at, according to analyst Frank Dunn.*

sniff sb/sth ↔ **out** *phr. v.* [T] **1** to discover or find something by its smell: *Officers used dogs to sniff out bodies in the rubble.* **2** to find out or discover something: *Olsen's real genius was for sniffing out talent in others.*

sniff² *n.* [C] an act or sound of sniffing

snif·fle¹ /'snɪfəl/ *v.* [I] to sniff repeatedly to stop liquid from running out of your nose, especially when you are crying or when you are sick

sniffle² *n.* **1** an act or sound of sniffling **2 have the sniffles** to have a slight cold

snif·ter /'snɪftɚ/ *n.* [C] a special large round glass for drinking BRANDY

snig·ger /'snɪgɚ/ *v.* [I] SNICKER

snip¹ /snɪp/ *v.* [I,T] to cut something with scissors using quick small cuts: *Lois snipped the wires before loosening the screws.* | [**snip** sth ↔ **off/open** etc.] *Using kitchen shears, snip away the backbone.*

snip² *n.* [C] a quick small cut with scissors

snipe¹ /snaɪp/ *v.* [I] **1** to criticize someone in an angry way: [+ **at**] *Ranchers and activists have been sniping at each other about grazing on public lands.* **2** to shoot from a hidden position at unprotected people: [+ **at**] *At that time, guerrillas were beginning to snipe at travelers.* —**sniping** *n.* [U]

snipe² *n.* [C] a bird with a very long thin beak that lives in wet areas, and is often shot as a sport

snip·er /'snaɪpɚ/ *n.* [C] someone who shoots at unprotected people from a hidden position

snip·pet /'snɪpɪt/ *n.* [C] a small piece of information, music etc.: *The book includes historical snippets and essays from longtime Tucson residents.* | [+ **of**] *a few snippets of conversation*

snip·py /'snɪpi/ *adj.* INFORMAL criticizing in a slightly angry way: *a snippy response*

snit /snɪt/ *n.* **be in a snit** to be annoyed about something, in a way that seems unreasonable: *Dominic was still in a snit the next morning.*

snitch¹ /snɪtʃ/ *v.* INFORMAL **1** [I + **on**] to tell someone in authority about something that another person has done wrong, because you want to cause trouble for that person **2** [T] to quickly steal something that is not important or that does not have much value: *Grover snitched a couple of sugar packets from behind the counter.*

snitch² *n.* [C] someone who is not liked because he or she tells someone in authority when other people do thing that are wrong or against the rules

sniv·el /'snɪvəl/ *v.* [I] to behave or speak in a weak complaining way, especially when you are crying

snob /snɑb/ *n.* [C] **1** someone who thinks they are better than people from a lower social class **2 movie/ wine/fashion etc. snob** someone who knows a lot about movies, wine etc. and thinks their opinions are better than other people's **3 snob appeal** something, especially an expensive product, that has snob appeal is liked by people who think they are better than other people

snob·ber·y /ˈsnɑbəri/ n. [U] the attitudes and behavior of snobs

snob·bish /ˈsnɑbɪʃ/ also **snob·by** /ˈsnɑbi/ adj. having attitudes, behavior etc. that are typical of a snob —**snobbishly** adv. —**snobbishness** n. [U]

snoop /snup/ v. [I] to try to find out private information about someone or something by secretly looking at their things: [+ **around/through** etc.] *I caught him snooping around in my office.* —**snoop** n. [C] —**snooper** n. [C]

snoop·y /ˈsnupi/ adj. **snoopier, snoopiest** INFORMAL always trying to find out private information about someone or something; NOSY

snoot /snut/ n. [C] INFORMAL your nose

snoot·y /ˈsnuti/ adj. **snootier, snootiest** INFORMAL, DISAPPROVING impolite and unfriendly, because you think you are better than other people

snooze¹ /snuz/ v. [I] to sleep for a short time: *Dad was snoozing on the beach.*

snooze² n. **1** [C usually singular] a short period of sleep **2** [C] HUMOROUS something that is boring: *The general opinion is that the show is a huge snooze.*

snore /snɔr/ v. [I] to breathe in a loud way through your mouth and nose while you are sleeping —**snore** n. [C]

snor·kel¹ /ˈsnɔrkəl/ n. [C] **1** a tube that allows a swimmer to breathe air under water **2** a piece of equipment that allows a SUBMARINE to take in air when it is under water

snorkel² v. [I] to swim under water using a snorkel —**snorkeling** n. [U] *We went snorkeling in the Caribbean last winter.*

snort¹ /snɔrt/ v. **1** [I] to make a loud noise by forcing air out through your nose, in order to express anger or annoyance, or while laughing: [+ **at**] *Foster snorted at the idea.* **2** [T] to say something in a way that shows you are angry or annoyed, or that you think something is stupid: *"You must be nuts," Carla snorted.* **3** [T] to take illegal drugs such as COCAINE by breathing them in through your nose

snort² n. [C] **1** a loud sound made by breathing through your nose, especially to show anger, annoyance, or amusement: *Susskind gave a loud snort.* **2** a small amount of a drug that is breathed in through the nose: *a snort of cocaine* **3** INFORMAL a small amount of a strong alcoholic drink: [+ **of**] *a snort of whiskey*

snot /snɑt/ n. INFORMAL, IMPOLITE **1** [U] the thick MUCUS (=liquid) produced in your nose **2** [C] someone who is SNOTTY (1)

snot-nosed /ˈ. ./ adj. **snot-nosed kid/brat etc.** INFORMAL, IMPOLITE an expression used to describe a child by someone who does not like the child

snot·ty /ˈsnɑti/ adj. **snottier, snottiest** INFORMAL **1** thinking that you are better than other people, and criticizing people in an unkind way because of this: *Don't get all snotty with me.* **2** wet and dirty with MUCUS from your nose: *a snotty handkerchief*

snout /snaʊt/ n. [C] the long nose of some kinds of animals, such as pigs

s w **snow¹** /snoʊ/ n. **1** [U] water frozen into soft white pieces that fall from the sky in cold weather and cover the ground: *Over six inches of snow fell last night.* | *The trees were covered with snow.* **2** [C] a period of time in which snow falls: *The recent storm was one of the heaviest snows this winter.* **3 snows** a large amount of snow that has fallen at different times during a season: *The mountain streams had been swollen by melting snows.* **4** [U] NOT TECHNICAL small white spots on a television picture that are caused by bad weather conditions, weak television signals etc. **5** [U] SLANG: see COCAINE

s w **snow²** v. **1 it snows/it is snowing etc.** if it snows, snow falls from the sky: *It snowed all night.* | *We got back home before it started snowing.* **2** [T] to persuade someone to believe or support something, especially by lying to them: *McDonald is manipulating his supporters, snowing them with his good looks.* **3 be snowed in** to be unable to travel from a place because so much snow has fallen there: *We were snowed in for three days last winter.* **4 be snowed**

under a) if an area is snowed under, a lot of snow has fallen there so that people are unable to travel **b)** to have more work than you can deal with

snow·ball¹ /ˈsnoʊbɔl/ n. [C] **1** a ball made of snow that someone has pressed together: *The kids were having a snowball fight outside.* **2 not have a snowball's chance in hell** INFORMAL to have no chance at all **3 a snowball effect** if something has a snowball effect on other things, it starts a series of events or changes that grow bigger and bigger, faster and faster etc.

snowball² v. [I] if a plan, problem, business etc. snowballs, it grows bigger at a faster and faster rate: *By Tuesday, the rumors had snowballed into a huge loss on the stock market.*

snow belt /ˈ. ./ n. **the Snow Belt** the north-central and northeastern parts of the U.S., where the weather is very cold and there is a lot of snow in the winter

snow·bird, Snowbird /ˈsnoʊbərd/ n. [C] someone, especially a RETIRED person, who leaves their home in a cold part of the U.S. or Canada to live in a warm part of the U.S. for the winter

snow blind·ness /ˈ. ˌ../ n. [U] eye pain and difficulty in seeing things, caused by looking at snow in bright light

snow·blow·er /ˈ. ˌ../ n. [C] a machine that clears snow from SIDEWALKS, roads etc. by picking it up and blowing it away with a lot of force

snow·board /ˈsnoʊbɔrd/ n. [C] a long wide board made of plastic, which people stand on and ride down snow-covered hills for fun

snow·board·ing /ˈsnoʊˌbɔrdɪŋ/ n. [U] the sport or activity of going down snow-covered hills while standing on a snowboard —**snowboarder** n. [C] —see picture on page 1332

snow·bound /ˈsnoʊbaʊnd/ adj. blocked or prevented from leaving a place by large amounts of snow: *Snowbound travelers were stuck at the Denver airport for almost 24 hours this week.*

snow bun·ny /ˈ. ˌ../ n. [C] INFORMAL a word meaning a very attractive young woman at a SKI RESORT, considered offensive by most women

snow-capped /ˈ. ./ adj. LITERARY snow-capped mountains are covered in snow at the top

snow cone /ˈ. ./ n. [C] a type of food made from crushed ice with a colored fruit-FLAVORed liquid poured over it, served in a CONE -shaped paper cup

snow day /ˈ. ./ n. [C] a day when schools, businesses etc. are closed because there is too much snow for people to travel

snow·drift /ˈsnoʊˌdrɪft/ n. [C] a deep mass of snow piled up by the wind

snow·drop /ˈsnoʊdrɑp/ n. [C] a European plant with a small white flower which appears in early spring

snow·fall /ˈsnoʊfɔl/ n. [C,U] an occasion when snow falls from the sky, or the amount that falls in a particular period of time: *There was very little snowfall last year.* | *the first snowfall of the season*

snow·field /ˈsnoʊfild/ n. [C] a wide area of land that is always covered in snow

snow·flake /ˈsnoʊfleɪk/ n. [C] a small soft flat piece of frozen water that falls as snow

snow job /ˈ. ./ n. [C usually singular] INFORMAL an act of making someone believe something that is not true

snow line /ˈ. ./ n. **the snow line** the level above which snow on a mountain never melts

snow·man /ˈsnoʊmæn/ n. [C] a figure of a person made of big balls of snow, made especially by children

snow melt /ˈ. ./ also **melt** n. [singular,U] the water that flows out of an area as snow melts, or the time when this happens

snow·mo·bile /ˈsnoʊmoʊˌbil/ n. [C] a small vehicle with a motor, that moves over snow or ice easily

snow pea /'. ./ *n.* [C] a type of PEA whose outer part is eaten as well as its seeds

snow·plow /'snouplau/ *n.* [C] a vehicle or piece of equipment on the front of a vehicle that is used to push snow off roads or railroad tracks

snow route /'. ./ *n.* [C] an important road in a city that cars must be removed from when it snows, so that the snow can be cleared away from it

snow·shoe /'snouʃu/ *n.* [C] one of a pair of wide flat frames with many thin pieces of leather or plastic across, which you attach to your shoes so that you can walk on snow without sinking

snow·storm /'snoustɔrm/ *n.* [C] a storm with strong winds and a lot of snow

snow·suit /'snousut/ *n.* [C] a warm piece of clothing that covers a child's whole body

snow tire /'. ./ *n.* [C] a special car tire with a pattern of deep lines, used when driving on snow or ice

snow-white /ˌ. '.◂/ *adj.* pure white

snow·y /'snoui/ *adj.* **snowier, snowiest 1** full of snow or snowing: *snowy weather* **2** LITERARY pure white: *snowy hair* —**snowiness** *n.* [U]

snub[1] /snʌb/ *v.* **snubbed, snubbing** [T] **1** to treat someone rudely, especially by ignoring them when you meet: *Executives who had once snubbed Miller were now calling him to chat.* **2 snub your nose (at sb)** to show that you do not respect someone, or do not care what they think of you

snub[2] *n.* [C] an act of snubbing someone: *The mayor's comments were not meant as a deliberate snub to the French visitors.*

snub[3] *adj.* **snub nose** a nose that is short and flat and points slightly up

snub-nosed also **snub-nose** /'. ./ *adj.* [only before noun] **1 snub-nosed pistol/revolver etc.** a small gun with a very short BARREL (=tube where the bullets come out) **2** having a short nose that points slightly up

snuck /snʌk/ *v.* a past tense and past participle of SNEAK

snuff[1] /snʌf/ *v.* **1** [T] also **snuff out** to stop a CANDLE from burning by pressing the burning part with your fingers or by covering it with a snuffer **2** [T] also **snuff out** to stop or end something in a sudden, forceful way: *Any hopes of a comeback by the Raiders were snuffed at the start of the second half.* **3** [T] also **snuff out** to kill someone: *How could anyone be so evil that they could snuff out the life of a young girl?* **4** [I,T] to breathe air into your nose in a noisy way; SNIFF[1]

snuff[2] *n.* [U] **1 a)** a type of tobacco in powder form, which people breathe in through their noses **b)** a type of tobacco in small pieces, which people put in their mouth and chew, but do not swallow **2 not be up to snuff** to not be good enough for a particular purpose: *Kemp said the economy still isn't up to snuff.*

snuff·er /'snʌfɚ/ *n.* [C] a tool with a small cup-shaped end on a handle, used for stopping CANDLES from burning

snuff film /'. ./ also **snuff mov·ie** /'. ˌ../ *n.* [C] a movie that shows violent sexual activity that ends in the death of one of the actors

snuf·fle /'snʌfəl/ *v.* [I] to breathe through your nose in a noisy way, making low sounds: *He started making snuffling noises.* —**snuffle** *n.* [C]

snug /snʌg/ *adj.* **1** someone who is snug feels comfortable, happy, and warm: *The children were safe and snug in their beds.* **2** a room or space that is snug is small, warm, and comfortable and makes you feel protected: *Nichols writes novels in his snug home in Taos, New Mexico.* **3** clothes that are snug fit closely —**snugly** *adv.* —**snugness** *n.* [U]

snug·gle /'snʌgəl/ *v.* [I always + adv./prep.] **1** to settle into a warm comfortable position: [+ **up/down/into** etc.] *I blew out the candle and snuggled down under the covers.* **2** to fit into a small space, in

a way that seems comfortable: *Charleston is snuggled along the Kanawha River.*

so[1] /sou/ *adv.* **1** [+ adj./adv.] used to describe or emphasize a quality: *What's so bad about getting a B in math? | I felt so sick yesterday. | Thank you so much! | I never knew Rob could sing so well. | It's too bad that so many kids come from broken homes these days.* **2 so tall/fat/tired etc. (that)** used to say that because someone or something is very tall, fat etc., something happens or someone does something: *The newest model is so simple that even a child could use it. | I was so scared I couldn't think straight.* **3** a word meaning "also," used before a MODAL VERB, an AUXILIARY VERB, or a form of "be" to add a positive statement to another positive statement that has just been mentioned: *If you're going to order dessert, then* **so will I.** *| Average incomes have risen recently, but* **so have** *prices. | "I have a lot to do today." "* **So do I.**" *| Ashley's a great swimmer, and* **so is** *her brother.* **4** used to talk about an idea, suggestion, situation etc. that has been mentioned before: *If you have not sent in your payment yet, please do so immediately. | Dave felt comfortable at Mandy's, even more so than in his own home.* **| think/hope so** *"Is it supposed to rain tomorrow?" "No, I don't think so."* **5 and so forth** also **and so on** used after a list to show that there are other similar things that could also be mentioned, without actually naming them: *The study included women of different ages, races and so forth. | "Non-food" items include cosmetics, plants, magazines, and so on. | Well, Diane was talking about how smart Taylor is and what a good student she is* **and so on and so forth.** **6 ...or so** used when you cannot be exact about a number, amount, or period of time: *I'll be there at around three or so. | There must have been thirty people or so in the class.* **7 so to speak** SPOKEN used when you are saying something in words that do not have their usual meaning: *We have to pull down the barriers, so to speak, of poverty.* **8 sb/sth is not so much...as...** used to say that one description of someone or something is less appropriate or correct than another: *Sarah had made the trip before and was not so much nervous as impatient to be home. | The animals kept dying, not so much from disease as from neglect.* **9 not/without so much as sth** used when you are surprised or annoyed that someone did not do something: *The car survived the accident without so much as a dent. | I never received so much as a reply* **10 so...as to be sth** FORMAL used with two adjectives or adverbs with similar meanings, to emphasize how extreme a particular quality is: *The risk of infection is so small as to be impossible to measure. | Progress has been so slow as to be almost painful.* **11 so tall a man/so high a mountain etc.** FORMAL used to emphasize an adjective, especially when what is being mentioned is surprising or unusual: *It was amazing how much they accomplished in so short a time. | For so large a group of people, they were surprisingly quiet.* **12 so much the better** used to say that if something happens, it will make the situation even better than it already is: *You can use dried parsley, but if you have fresh, so much the better.* **13 so as (not) to do sth** FORMAL in order to do something, or not to do something: *Groups have been chosen so as to ensure maximum fairness. | Work carefully so as not to tear the delicate material.*

SPOKEN PHRASES

14 used to get someone's attention, especially in order to ask them a question: *So, Lisa, how's the new job going?* **15** used with a movement of your hand to show how big, high etc. something or someone is: *Oh, he must be about so tall.* **16** used to check that you understand something: *So this one's the original, and this one's the copy, right?* **17** used when asking a question about what has just been said: *"I'm not exactly sure what this thing does." "So who does it belong to?"* **18 like so** used when you are showing someone how to do something: *Then turn the paper over and fold it, like so.* **19 so much for sb/sth** used to say that something you tried to do did not work as it was supposed to, or that something that was promised did not happen: *I can't get it off the pan –*

so much for it being nonstick. | So much for getting up early every morning. **20 so long!** INFORMAL used to say goodbye **21 so be it** used to show that you do not like or agree with something, but you will accept it anyway: *If we have to break the rules, then so be it.* **22 I do so/it is so etc.** used especially by children to say that something is true, can be done etc. when someone else says that it is not, cannot etc.: *"You don't know how to ride a bike." "I do so!"* **23** NONSTANDARD used before noun phrases to emphasize what you are saying: *Orange is just so not the right color for Kari.* **24 sth is so Bob/Mary etc.** NONSTANDARD used to say that some behavior, attitude etc. is typical of someone: *Jenna's hairstyle is just so Lisa Bonet.* **25 so help me** also **so help me God** used to emphasize how determined you are: *It's immoral, and so help me God, I'm not going to let it happen in my house again.*

—see also **even so** (EVEN[1] (5)) **so far** (FAR[1] (6)), **just so** (JUST[1] (33)), **as/so long as** (LONG[2] (4)) —see Usage Note at SUCH[1]

so² conjunction **1** used to give the reason why something happens, why someone does something etc.: *I got hungry, so I made a sandwich.* **2 So?** also **So what?** SPOKEN, IMPOLITE used to say that you do not think that something is important: *"There are dirty clothes all over your room." "So?" | So what if we're a little late?* **3** SPOKEN used to introduce the next part of a story you are telling someone: *So anyway, we decided to go to the mall.* **4 so (that) a)** in order to make something happen, make something possible etc.: *We've planned a variety of activities, so there'll be something for everyone. | Prune the tree at a young age so that it will have a strong central trunk.* **b)** used to say that something happens as a result of something else: *The ropes got twisted, so I couldn't climb down again.* —see Usage Note at THUS

so³ adj. [not before noun] **1 sth is so** to be true or correct: *You stated earlier that you saw the defendant on May 31. Is that so? | Please, say it isn't so!* **2 more so/less so/too much so etc.** phrases in which "so" is used instead of repeating an adjective that you have mentioned before: *Just as important as jobs, if not more so, is the need for affordable housing. | "You're serious, aren't you?" "Very much so."* **3 be just/exactly so** to be arranged neatly, with everything in the right place: *Everything has to be just so at Maxine's dinner parties.* —see also SO-SO

so⁴ n. [singular] the fifth note in a musical SCALE[1] (9) according to the SOL-FA system

soak¹ /souk/ v. **1** [I,T] if you soak something or let it soak, you keep it covered with a liquid for a period of time, especially in order to make it softer or easier to clean: *Soak the beans overnight. | Let the pan soak a while before you scrub it.* **2** [I always + adv./prep., T] to make something completely wet, or to become completely wet: *If you don't take your umbrella, you're going to get soaked. | [+ through/into etc.] The gravy had soaked into my bread roll. | [be soaked in/with sth] Vardell's shirt was soaked in sweat.* **3** [T always + adv./prep.] to remove something by leaving it covered with a liquid for a period of time: [soak sth off/out] *Soak the label off the jar.* **4** [I] to spend a long time taking a bath **5** [T] to make someone pay too much money in prices or taxes: *a tax designed to soak the rich*

soak sth ↔ **up** phr. v. **1** if something soaks up a liquid, it takes the liquid into itself: *Serve the chicken on a bed of rice to soak up the juices.* **2** to enjoy something by watching it closely or becoming involved in it: *The best way to soak up the atmosphere of Times Square is to walk around it.* **3** to learn something quickly and easily: *Small children soak up language at a fantastic rate.*

soak² n. [C] **1** a long and enjoyable time spent taking a bath **2 an old soak** HUMOROUS someone who is often drunk

soak·ing¹ /'soukɪŋ/ also **soaking wet** /,.. '. ./ adj. very wet: *Tom's shoes were soaking wet.*

soaking² n. [C usually singular] an act of making something completely wet: *We all got a good soaking on the water slides.*

so-and-so /'. . ./ n. plural **so-and-so's 1** [U] an expression meaning some person or thing, used when you do not give a specific name: *He'd say, "Lula, let's do so-and-so," and expect me to do it. | The paper is full of stories about how so-and-so violated this or that law.* —compare SUCH AND SUCH **2** [C] a word meaning a very nasty or unreasonable person, used to avoid saying a stronger word: *Johnson was a mean old so-and-so.*

soap¹ /soup/ n. **1** [U] the substance that you use to wash your body or other things: *Wash thoroughly with soap and water. | a bar of soap* —compare DETERGENT **2** [C] INFORMAL a SOAP OPERA

soap² v. [T] to rub soap on or over someone or something

soap·box /'soupbaks/ n. **be/get/climb on your soapbox** to tell people your own strong opinions about something in a loud forceful way: *I don't get on my soapbox and preach to the kids. I can only show them by example.*

soap ope·ra /'. ,../ n. [C] a television or radio story about the daily lives of the same group of people, which is broadcast regularly

soap·stone /'soupstoun/ n. [U] a soft stone that feels like soap

soap·suds /'soupsʌdz/ n. [plural] the mass of small BUBBLES that form on top of soapy water

soap·y /'soupi/ adj. **soapier, soapiest** containing soap, or like soap: *warm soapy water* —**soapiness** n. [U]

soar /sɔr/ v. [I] **1** to increase quickly to a high level: *The temperature soared to 90°. | soaring real estate prices* **2 a)** to fly, especially very high up in the sky, floating on air currents: *An eagle soared above us.* **b)** to go quickly upward to a great height: *The space shuttle soared into orbit.* **3** if your spirits or hopes soar, you begin to feel very happy or hopeful: *Adam's smile sent her spirits soaring.* **4** [not in progressive] if buildings, trees, towers etc. soar, they look very tall and impressive: *In Montreal, gleaming office towers soar above 18th-century cathedrals.*

SOB, S.O.B. n. [C] OFFENSIVE a short way of saying "SON OF A BITCH"

sob /sab/ v. **sobbed, sobbing** [I] to cry loudly while breathing in short, sudden bursts: *My mother was sobbing uncontrollably.* —**sob** n. [C] —see Usage Note at CRY[1]

so·ber¹ /'soubər/ adj. **1** not drunk: *Was Garcia sober when he drove off?* **2** having a serious attitude to life: *He's a sober, thoughtful, intelligent guy.* **3** plain and not brightly colored: *a sober gray suit* —**soberly** adv.

sober² v. [I,T]

sober up phr. v. [I,T] to gradually become less drunk, or make someone become less drunk: [sober sb ↔ up] *They tried to sober her up by giving her some coffee and food.*

so·ber·ing /'soubərɪŋ/ adj. making you feel very serious: *a sobering thought | The news had a sobering effect on all of us.*

so·bri·e·ty /sə'braɪəti/ n. [U] **1** the condition of not being drunk or not drinking alcohol: *Terry had many periods of sobriety, including eight years in the 1980s.* **2** FORMAL behavior that shows a serious attitude toward life

so·bri·quet /'soubrɪˌkeɪ/ n. [C] LITERARY an unofficial title or name; NICKNAME

sob sto·ry /'. ,../ n. [C] INFORMAL a story, especially one that is not true, that someone tells you in order to make you feel sorry for them

so-called /, . '. ./ adj. [only before noun] **1** used to describe someone or something that has been given a name which you think is wrong: *Maggie's so-called apartment consisted of one small room with a closet-sized bathroom.* **2** used to show that something or someone is usually called a particular name: *He was one of the defendants in the so-called Conspiracy Eight trial.*

soc·cer /'sɑkə/ *n.* [U] a sport played by two teams of 11 players, who try to kick a round ball into their opponents' GOAL (3) —compare FOOTBALL

soccer mom /'.. ,./ *n.* [C] a mother who spends a lot of time driving her children to sports practice, music lessons etc., considered as a typical example of women from the middle to upper classes in U.S. society

so·cia·ble /'souʃəbəl/ *adj.* friendly and liking to be with other people: *She had her back to me and didn't seem very sociable.* —opposite UNSOCIABLE —**sociably** *adv.* —**sociability** /,souʃə'bɪləti/ *n.* [U]

so·cial¹ /'souʃəl/ *adj.* **1** relating to human society and its organization, or the quality of people's lives: *the struggle for social justice* | *demands for social change* **2** relating to the position in society that you have, according to your job, family, wealth etc.: *Governments have made efforts to improve women's social and economic status.* | *Students come from a wide variety of social classes* (=groups of people who have the same social position). **3** relating to the way you meet people and form relationships: *Josh seems to have a complete lack of social skills* (=the ability to meet people easily and deal well with them). **4** relating to the time you spend with your friends for enjoyment: *The church organizes a number of social events during the summer.* | *Brenda had a very active social life* (=activities done with friends for fun) *in college.* | *Even social drinking* (=drinking alcohol with friends, at parties etc.) *is dangerous for an alcoholic.* **5** forming groups or living together in their natural state: *Elephants are social animals.* —see also ANTISOCIAL, SOCIABLE —**socially** *adv.*: *socially acceptable behavior* | *Jan only drinks socially.*

social² *n.* [C] OLD-FASHIONED a party for the members of a group, club, or church

social climb·er /'.. ,../ *n.* [C] DISAPPROVING someone who tries to get accepted into a higher social class by becoming friendly with people who belong to that class

social Dar·win·ism /,.. '../ *n.* [U] the belief that some people in society are naturally more intelligent and skillful than others, and that these people will rise to the top of society

social de·moc·ra·cy /,.. '.../ *n.* **1** [U] a political and economic system, especially in many European countries, based on some ideas of socialism combined with DEMOCRATIC principles, such as personal freedom and government by elected representatives **2** [C] a country, especially in Europe, with a government based on this system —**social democrat** /,.. '.../ *n.* [C]

social di·sease /'.. .,./ *n.* [C] OLD-FASHIONED an expression meaning VENEREAL DISEASE, used to avoid saying this directly

social en·gi·neer·ing /,.. '..'../ *n.* [U] the practice of making changes in laws in order to change society according to a political idea

so·cial·is·m /'souʃə,lɪzəm/ *n.* [U] an economic and political system in which large industries are owned by the government, and taxes are used to take some wealth away from richer citizens and give it to poorer citizens —compare CAPITALISM, COMMUNISM

so·cial·ist¹ /'souʃəlɪst/ *adj.* **1** based on socialism, or relating to a political party that supports socialism: *socialist principles* **2** a socialist country or government has a political and economic system based on socialism

socialist² *n.* [C] someone who believes in socialism, or who is a member of a political party that supports socialism —compare CAPITALIST¹, COMMUNIST¹

socialist re·al·ism /,.. '..../ *n.* [U] a set of beliefs about art, literature, and music which says that their main purpose is to educate people about Marxism and socialism

so·cial·ite /'souʃə,laɪt/ *n.* [C] someone who is well known for going to many fashionable parties

so·cial·i·za·tion /,souʃələ'zeɪʃən/ *n.* [U] **1** the process by which people are made to behave in a way that is acceptable in their society: *Schools are a tool in the socialization of American citizens.* **2** the process of making something work according to SOCIALIST ideas: *the socialization of medicine*

so·cial·ize /'souʃə,laɪz/ *v.* **1** [I] to spend time with other people in a friendly way: [+ **with**] *They don't socialize with their neighbors much.* **2** [T] to train someone to behave in a way that is acceptable in the society they are living in: *Many young women believe they have better things to do than socialize single men.*

socialized med·i·cine /,... '.../ *n.* [U] a phrase meaning social medical care provided by a government and paid for through taxes, used especially by people who believe the government should not pay for medical care

social sci·ence /,.. '../ *n.* **1** [U] the study of people in society, which includes history, politics, ECONOMICS, SOCIOLOGY, and ANTHROPOLOGY **2** [C] one of these subjects —compare NATURAL SCIENCE —**social scientist** *n.* [C]

Social Se·cu·ri·ty /,.. .'.../ *n.* [U] a U.S. government program into which workers must make regular payments, and which pays money regularly to old people and people who are unable to work: *people living on Social Security* —compare PENSION

Social Security num·ber /,.. '.. ,../ *n.* [C] a number that is given to each person in the U.S. by the government and is used to IDENTIFY people on official forms, in computer records etc.

social serv·ice /,.. '../ *n.* [C usually plural] a service that is provided by the government to help people who are poor or have problems such as mental illness, difficulty finding a job, family problems etc.

social stud·ies /'.. ,../ *n.* [U] a subject of study in school that includes history, government, GEOGRAPHY etc.

social work /'.. ,./ *n.* [U] work done by government or private organizations to improve bad social conditions and help people who are poor or who have family problems etc.

social work·er /'.. ,../ *n.* [C] someone who is trained to help people with particular social problems, such as family problems, being unable to work etc.

so·ci·e·tal /sə'saɪətl/ *adj.* [only before noun] relating to a particular society, or the way society is organized: *societal changes*

so·ci·e·ty /sə'saɪəti/ *n. plural* **societies**
1 people in general [U] people in general, considered in relation to the structure of laws, organizations etc. that makes it possible for them to live together: *Children are the most vulnerable members of society.* | *Prisons are meant to protect society from criminals.*
2 a particular group [C,U] a particular large group of people who share laws, organizations, customs etc.: *We live in a society that values hard work.* | *recent changes in American society*
3 organization [C] used in the names of some organizations that have members who share similar interests, aims etc.: *the National Society of Public Accountants*
4 upper class [U] the fashionable group of people who are rich and go to many social events: *a society wedding* | *members of New York's high society*
5 with other people [U] FORMAL the act of being together with other people, or the people you are together with: *We will soon be unable to enjoy the society of our dearest friends.* | *You don't talk about things like that in polite society.*

Society of Friends, the /.. ,.... '../ —see QUAKERS, THE
Society of Je·sus, the /.,.... '../ —see JESUITS

socio- /sousiou, souʃiou/ *prefix* TECHNICAL **1** relating to society; SOCIAL: *sociology* (=study of society) **2** social and something else: *socioeconomic factors*

so·ci·o·cul·tur·al /,sousiou'kʌltʃərəl/ *adj.* based on a combination of social and CULTURAL conditions: *individuals with similar sociocultural values* —**socioculturally** *adv.*

so·ci·o·ec·o·nom·ic /,sousiou,ɛkə'nɑmɪk, -,ikə-/ *adj.* [only before noun] based on a combination of social and economic conditions —**socioeconomically** /-kli/ *adv.*

so·ci·ol·o·gy /ˌsousiˈaləʤi/ n. [U] the scientific study of societies and the behavior of people in groups —**sociologist** n. [C] —**sociological** /ˌsousiəˈlɑʤɪkəl/ adj.: a sociological study of the working class —**sociologically** /-kli/ adv. —compare ANTHROPOLOGY, ETHNOLOGY, SOCIAL SCIENCE

so·ci·o·path /ˈsousiə,pæθ, -ʃiə-/ n. [C] TECHNICAL someone whose behavior toward other people is considered unacceptable, strange, and possibly dangerous —**sociopathic** /ˌsousiəˈpæθɪk/ adj.

so·ci·o·po·lit·i·cal /ˌsousioupəˈlɪtɪkəl, ˌsouʃi-/ adj. [only before noun] based on a combination of social and political conditions: How has technology contributed to changes in the sociopolitical system? —**sociopolitically** /-kli/ adv.

sock¹ /sɑk/ n. **1** [C] a piece of clothing made of soft material that you wear on your foot inside your shoe: I just need to put my socks and shoes on. **2** [C usually singular] INFORMAL to hit someone or something very hard, especially with your hand closed: Larry gave him a sock in the arm. **3 put a sock in it** SPOKEN used to tell someone in a joking way to stop talking —see also **knock sb's socks off** (KNOCK¹ (7))

sock² v. [T] **1** to hit someone very hard: Bill socked her so hard that the bruise lasted a week. **2** [usually passive] if someone is socked with something bad, they are suddenly affected by it: Airline passengers are being socked with fuel surcharges. **3 sock it to sb** [usually in imperative] to do something or tell someone something in a direct and forceful way **4 be socked in** if an airport or area is socked in, it is very difficult to see far and no one can travel because of bad FOG, snow, or rain

sock sth **away** phr. v. [T] to keep money in a safe place, to use later: Gregg has quite a bit of cash socked away for his retirement.

sock·et /ˈsɑkɪt/ n. [C] **1** a hollow part of something that another part fits into: the eye sockets **2** a place in a wall where you can connect electrical equipment to the supply of electricity; OUTLET

sock·eye /ˈsɑk-aɪ/ n. plural **sockeye** [C,U] a type of SALMON (=fish) that is commonly used for food

Soc·ra·tes /ˈsɑkrə,tiz/ (?469–399 B.C.) a Greek PHILOSOPHER from Athens, who was the teacher of Plato and is known for developing a method of examining ideas according to a system of questions and answers —**Socratic** /səˈkrætɪk/ adj.

sod /sɑd/ n. [U] a piece of dirt with grass growing on top of it

so·da /ˈsoudə/ n. **1** [C,U] also **soda pop** a sweet drink that contains BUBBLES and has no alcohol in it: SOFT DRINK: a can of soda **2** [U] also **soda water** water containing BUBBLES of gas, often added to alcoholic drinks **3** [C] an ICE-CREAM SODA **4** [U] one of several types of chemical compound containing SODIUM in powder form, that is used for cleaning or in making other products in industry —compare CAUSTIC SODA, LYE —see also BAKING SODA

soda crack·er /ˈ.. ,../ n. [C] a type of thin hard dry bread with salt on it; SALTINE

soda foun·tain /ˈ.. ,../ n. [C] a place, often inside a DRUGSTORE, with a long COUNTER (=type of high table) at which SOFT DRINKS, drinks made with ICE CREAM etc. were served, especially in the 1940s and 1950s

soda jerk /ˈ.. ,./ n. [C] someone who worked at a soda fountain, making drinks

soda pop /ˈ.. ,./ n. [U] SODA (1)

soda wa·ter /ˈ.. ,../ n. [U] SODA (2)

sod·den /ˈsɑdn/ adj. very wet and heavy: the sodden ground | Mike's potato was sodden with sour cream and butter.

so·di·um /ˈsoudiəm/ n. [U] symbol **Na** a silver-white metal that is an ELEMENT and usually exists in combination with other substances

sodium bi·car·bon·ate /ˌ... ˈ.../ n. [U] TECHNICAL: see BAKING SODA

sodium chlo·ride /ˌ... ˈ../ n. [U] TECHNICAL the type of salt that is used in cooking and on foods

sod·om·ite /ˈsɑdə,maɪt/ n. [C] OLD USE someone who is involved in sodomy

sod·om·y /ˈsɑdəmi/ n. [U] LAW OR OLD USE a sexual act in which a man puts his sexual organ into someone's ANUS, especially that of another man

so·fa /ˈsoufə/ n. [C] a comfortable piece of furniture with raised arms and a back, that is wide enough for three or more people to sit on —compare COUCH¹ (1), LOVESEAT

sofa bed /ˈ.. ,./ n. [C] a sofa that has a bed inside that can be folded out

So·fi·a /ˈsoufiə/ the capital and largest city of Bulgaria

soft /sɔft/ adj.
1 not hard a) not hard, firm, or stiff, but easy to press: a soft pillow | The ground was still soft after the rain. **b)** less hard than average: a soft lead pencil | a soft cheese —opposite HARD¹ (1)

2 not rough having a surface that is smooth and pleasant to touch: A good moisturizer will leave your skin softer and smoother. | Polish the chrome with a soft cloth.

3 not loud a soft sound, voice, or music is quiet and often pleasant to listen to: He spoke in a whisper so soft that I could hardly hear it. | There was some soft music playing in the background.

4 color/light [only before noun] soft colors or lights are pleasant and relaxing because they are not too bright: Soft lighting creates a romantic atmosphere. | We're going to decorate the bedroom in soft blues and grays.

5 no hard edges not having any hard edges or pointed shapes: The 2001 model has a softer, more curved shape.

6 gentle gentle and not strong or forceful: a soft breeze | The senator's advisers want to create a softer, more open image for him.

7 not strict not strict or cruel toward other people: This time, opponents of the peace process decided to take a softer line on the issue. | [+ on] The governor does not want to seem soft on crime. —opposite TOUGH¹ (3)

8 weak character not having a strong character; weak: Just because a guy is bright and plays the guitar doesn't mean he's soft.

9 sales/markets decreasing in price, value, or in the amount sold: Analysts expressed fears of a softer U.S. market for large cars. | Soft land prices have helped boost new home sales.

10 water not containing many minerals, so that it forms BUBBLES from soap easily

11 have a soft spot for sb/sth to like someone or something, even though other people might not: Garner has always had a soft spot for stray animals.

12 too easy a soft job, life etc. is too easy and does not involve much work or much hard physical work: We're all used to a soft life, with hot showers, phones and such.

13 a soft touch a) someone from whom you can easily get money, because they are nice or easy to deceive: Brad knew I was a soft touch. **b)** a gentle way of dealing with something: Negotiators will need a soft touch and strong nerves.

14 weak body having a body that is not in a strong physical condition, because you do not do enough exercise: Compared with today's ideal, 19th-century ladies appear much softer.

15 soft in the head HUMOROUS crazy: I think the old woman's going soft in the head.

16 be soft on sb OLD-FASHIONED to be sexually attracted to someone —**softly** adv.: She stroked his head softly. | Music played softly in the background. —**softness** n. [U]

soft·ball /ˈsɔftbɔl/ n. **1** [U] a game similar to baseball that is played on a smaller field with a special ball **2** [C] a ball that is slightly larger and less hard than a baseball, used to play this game

soft-boiled /ˌ. ˈ.◂/ adj. a soft-boiled egg has been boiled in its shell long enough for the white part to become solid, but the yellow part in the center is still soft —compare HARD-BOILED

S

soft-core /ˌ.ˈ.◂/ adj. [usually before noun] showing or describing sexual behavior and situations in a way that is intended to be sexually exciting, but without fully showing sexual acts or organs: **soft-core pornography/movies/magazines** etc. *cable TV channels featuring soft-core porn* —compare HARD-CORE (2) —see also SOFT PORN

soft·cov·er /ˈ. ˌ../ n. [C] a book with a cover made of thick paper that can bend; PAPERBACK —compare HARDCOVER

soft drink /ˈ. ./ n. [C] a cold drink that does not contain alcohol, especially one that is sweet and has BUBBLES —compare SODA (1)

soft·en /ˈsɔfən/ v. **1** [I,T] also **soften up** to become softer or make something softer: *Choose a good moisturizer to soften and protect your skin.* | *Leave the butter at room temperature to soften.* **2** to make the effect of something less severe: *Republicans agreed to soften their projected cuts in welfare spending.* | **soften the blow/impact** etc. *If you have bad news to tell someone, try to find a way to soften the blow.* **3** [I,T] if your attitude, image etc. softens, or if something softens it, it becomes nicer and less severe: *Lawmakers have softened their stance on immigration in recent months.* **4** [I,T] if your expression or voice softens, or if something softens it, you look or sound nicer and more gentle: *His voice softened when he spoke to her.* —opposite HARDEN

soften sb/sth ↔ **up** phr. v. [T] **1** to be nice to someone before you ask them to do something, so that they will agree to help you: *Perhaps the way to soften up your sweetheart is at the weekly meeting of the French Film Club.* **2** to make an enemy's defenses weaker so that they will be easier to attack, especially by bombing them

soft·en·er /ˈsɔfənə/ n. [C] a substance that you add to water to make clothes feel soft after washing: *a fabric softener* —see also WATER SOFTENER

soft fo·cus /ˌ. ˈ..◂/ n. [U] a way of photographing or filming things so that the edges of the objects in the photograph do not appear clear or sharp

soft·heart·ed /ˌsɔftˈhɑrtɪd◂/ adj. easily affected by feelings of pity or sympathy for other people

soft·ie, softy /ˈsɔfti/ n. [C] someone who is too easily affected by feelings of pity or sympathy, or who is too easily persuaded: *Call me a softy, but I couldn't cook a live crab.*

soft land·ing /ˌ. ˈ../ n. [C] a situation in which a SPACECRAFT comes down onto the ground gently and without any damage

soft mon·ey /ˈ. ˌ../ n. [U] **1** money that a person, company, or activity gives an organization, that is not earned and that is not paid regularly: *Special fund-raising events bring in soft money.* **2** money that is given to a political group rather than to a specific politician, so that the amount that can be given is not limited by law: *The winery donated $15,000 in soft money to the Democratic Party committee.*

soft pal·ate /ˌ. ˈ../ n. [C] the soft part of the back of the top of your mouth

soft-ped·al /ˈ. ˌ../ v. [T] to make something seem less important or less urgent than it really is: *The studios soft-pedal the rivalry between their animation departments.*

soft porn /ˌ. ˈ.◂/ n. [U] magazines, pictures etc. that show people wearing no clothes in a way that is intended to be sexually exciting, but that does not fully and clearly show sexual acts —compare **hardcore pornography** (HARDCORE (2)) —see also SOFT-CORE

soft rock /ˌ. ˈ./ n. [U] a type of ROCK MUSIC that does not have a strong beat and that includes many songs about love —compare HARD ROCK

soft sell /ˌ. ˈ./ n. [singular] a way of advertising or selling things that involves gently persuading people to buy something in a friendly and indirect way —compare HARD SELL

soft-shoe /ˈ. ./ n. [U] a way of dancing in which you make soft noises with your shoes on the floor

soft shoul·der /ˌ. ˈ../ n. [C] the edge of a road, when this edge is made of dirt rather than a hard material

soft-spok·en /ˌ. ˈ..◂/ adj. having a pleasant gentle voice, and not talking very much: *a tall, soft-spoken woman in her 30s*

soft·ware /ˈsɔft-wɛr/ n. [U] the sets of programs that tell a computer what to do: *word-processing software* | *a software developer* —compare HARDWARE (1)

soft·wood /ˈsɔft-wʊd/ n. [C,U] wood from trees such as PINE and FIR that is cheap and easy to cut, or a tree with this type of wood —compare HARDWOOD

soft·y /ˈsɔfti/ n. [C] another spelling of SOFTIE

sog·gy /ˈsɑgi/ adj. **soggier, soggiest** too wet and soft: *Rick couldn't face another picnic lunch on a soggy paper plate.* | *These cornflakes get soggy really fast in milk.* —**soggily** adv. —**sogginess** n. [U]

soi·gné, soignée /swɑnˈyeɪ/ adj. FORMAL dressed or arranged in an attractive fashionable way

soil[1] /sɔɪl/ n. **1 a)** [U] the top layer of the earth in which plants grow; dirt: *soil and water pollution* | *Most herbs grow well in dry soil.* **b)** [C] a particular type of dirt: *The island was a jungle of palm trees in a sandy soil.* —see Usage Note at LAND[1] **2** [U] a place or situation where something can develop: *Right-wing activists found fertile soil for their anti-immigrant ideas in southeastern regions.* **3 on U.S./French/foreign** etc. **soil** in the U.S., in France, in a foreign country etc.: *We were glad to be back on American soil.* **4 sb's native soil** your own country **5 the soil** LITERARY farming as a job or way of life: *Medieval peasants were bound to the soil.*

soil[2] v. [T] **1** FORMAL to make something dirty, especially with waste from your body: *soiled diapers* **2 not soil your hands** to not do something because you consider it too dirty, disgusting, or dishonest: *Keep your drug money – I wouldn't want to soil my hands with it.*

soi·ree, soirée /swɑˈreɪ/ n. [C] LITERARY OR HUMOROUS a fashionable evening party

so·journ /ˈsoʊdʒɚn/ n. [C] LITERARY a short period of time that you stay in a place that is not your home: *a brief sojourn in Europe* —**sojourn** v. [I]

SOL adj. VULGAR **sb is SOL** a short way of saying that someone is "shit out of luck," used to say that someone has lost the opportunity to do something: *If he's not here by 10:30, he's SOL.*

sol /sɑl, soʊl/ n. [U] so[4]

sol·ace /ˈsɑlɪs/ n. [U] a feeling of emotional comfort at a time of great sadness or disappointment | **seek/find solace in sth** *After his wife's death, Rob sought solace in religion.*

so·lar /ˈsoʊlə/ adj. [only before noun] **1** relating to the sun: *a solar observatory* **2** using the power of the sun's light and heat: *solar energy*

solar cell /ˈ.. ˌ./ n. [C] a piece of equipment that can produce electric power from SUNLIGHT

solar e·clipse /ˌ.. .ˈ./ n. [C] an occasion when the moon moves between the sun and the Earth, so that the sun cannot be seen for a short time from the Earth

so·lar·i·um /səˈlɛriəm, soʊ-/ n. [C] a room, usually enclosed by glass, where you can sit in bright SUNLIGHT

solar pan·el /ˌ.. ˈ../ n. [C] a piece of equipment, usually on the roof of a building, that uses the sun's energy to heat water or to make electricity

solar plex·us /ˌsoʊlə ˈplɛksəs/ n. [singular] NOT TECHNICAL the front part of your body below your chest, which hurts very much if you are hit there

solar sys·tem /ˈ.. ˌ../ n. **1 the solar system** the sun and the PLANETS that go around it **2** [C] this type of system around another star

solar year /ˌ.. ˈ./ n. the period of time in which the Earth travels once around the sun, equal to 365¼ days

sold /soʊld/ v. the past tense and past participle of SELL

sol·der[1] /ˈsɑdɚ, ˈsɔ-/ n. [U] a soft metal, usually a mixture of LEAD and TIN, which can be melted and used to fasten together two metal surfaces, wires etc.

solder² *v.* [T] to fasten or repair metal surfaces with solder

soldering i·ron /'... ,../ *n.* [C] a tool which is heated, usually by electricity, and used for melting solder and putting it on surfaces

sol·dier¹ /'souldʒɚ/ *n.* [C] a member of a country's army, especially someone who is not an officer

soldier² *v.*

soldier on *phr. v.* [I] to continue working in spite of difficulties: *The band soldiered on with a variety of different members until 1995.*

sol·dier·ing /'souldʒɚɪŋ/ *n.* [U] the life or job of a soldier: *They have little to learn about bravery, but a lot about basic soldiering.*

sol·dier·ly /'souldʒɚli/ *adj.* FORMAL typical of a good soldier

soldier of for·tune /,... '...' *n.* plural **soldiers of fortune** [C] someone who works as a soldier for anyone who will pay him; MERCENARY

sol·dier·y /'souldʒɚi/ *n.* [singular,U] LITERARY a group of soldiers

sold out /,. '..' / *adj.* a concert, performance etc. that is sold out has no more tickets left —see also **sell out** (SELL¹)

sole¹ /soul/ *adj.* [only before noun] **1** the sole person, thing etc. is the only one: *The sole purpose of his trip was to attend a concert at Carnegie Hall.* | *the sole survivor of the crash* **2** a sole duty, right, responsibility etc. is one that is not shared with anyone else: *Arthur will retain sole ownership of the company.*

sole² *n.* **1** [C] the bottom surface of your foot, especially the part you walk or stand on: *Don't go barefoot, or you'll burn the soles of your feet.* **2** [C] the flat outer part on the bottom of a shoe, not including the heel —see picture at SHOE¹ **3** [C,U] plural **sole** or **soles** a flat ocean fish, or the meat from this fish —see also -SOLED

sole³ *v.* [T usually passive] to put a new sole on a shoe

sol·e·cism /'salə,sɪzəm, 'sou-/ *n.* [C] FORMAL **1** a mistake in grammar **2** a mistake that breaks the rules of polite behavior

-soled /sould/ [in adjectives] **thick-soled/leather-soled etc.** having soles that are thick, made of leather etc.

sole·ly /'souli/ *adv.* not involving anything or anyone else; only: *Scholarships are awarded solely on the basis of financial need.* | *If the business is sued, the owner will be held solely responsible for any damages.*

sol·emn /'saləm/ *adj.* **1** very serious in behavior or style: *a solemn expression* | *solemn music* **2 solemn promise/pledge/word etc.** a promise that is made very seriously and with no intention of breaking it: *The jurors have sworn a solemn oath to obey the judge's instructions.* **3** a solemn ceremony is performed in a very serious way —**solemnity** /sə'lɛmnəti/ *n.* [U] —**solemnly** /'saləmli/ *adv.*

sol·em·nize /'saləm,naɪz/ *v.* **1 solemnize a marriage** FORMAL to perform a wedding ceremony in a church **2** [T] to make a ceremony more formal and serious, especially by having a prayer or other religious part in it

sole pro·pri·e·tor·ship /,. .'...../ *n.* [C] a situation in which only one person owns a business or company

sol-fa /sal 'fa/ *n.* [U] the system in which the notes of the musical SCALE are represented by seven short words (DO, RE, MI, FA, SO, LA, TI), used especially in singing

so·lic·it /sə'lɪsɪt/ *v.* [I,T] **1** to ask someone for money, help, or information: *Certain federal employees are forbidden to solicit campaign funds.* | [**solicit sth from sb**] *School officials have been soliciting ideas from parents.* **2** to sell something by taking orders for a product or service, usually by going to people's houses or businesses: *Two households signed the contract when the cable company solicited them.* **3** LAW to offer to have sex with someone in exchange for money: *She was arrested for soliciting.* —**solicitation** /sə,lɪsə'teɪʃən/ *n.* [C,U]

so·lic·i·tor /sə'lɪsətɚ/ *n.* [C] **1** FORMAL someone who

---

tries to sell things to people, usually by going to people's houses or calling them on the telephone **2** the main lawyer for a city, town, or government department **3** a type of lawyer in the U.K. who gives advice, does the necessary work when property is bought and sold, and defends people, especially in the lower courts of law —compare BARRISTER

solicitor gen·e·ral /.,... '...'/ *n.* [C] a government lawyer next in rank below the ATTORNEY GENERAL

so·lic·it·ous /sə'lɪsətəs/ *adj.* FORMAL caring very much about someone's safety, health, or comfort: *Larry spoke to Davis in sympathetic and solicitous tones during the interview.* | [+ **of**] *He was always very solicitous of other people's opinions.* —**solicitously** *adv.* —**solicitousness** *n.* [U]

so·lic·i·tude /sə'lɪsɪ,tud/ *n.* [U + **for**] FORMAL eager care about someone's health, safety etc.

sol·id¹ /'salɪd/ *adj.*
1 **firm/hard** having a firm shape, and usually hard; not in liquid or gas form: *I was so seasick that it was a relief to be back on solid ground.* | *Is the baby eating solid foods yet?* | *The lake was frozen solid.*
2 **strongly made** strong and well made: *good, solid furniture*
3 **good work/preparation** having a lot of practical value because of good preparation, strong principles etc.: *Wegman's writing combines solid reporting with a sense of humor.* | *Kids need a good, solid education in high school.* | *We have a solid foundation for a global PC business.*
4 **can depend on** someone or something that is solid can be trusted and depended on: *a company with a solid reputation* | *Romer gave every impression of being a solid citizen.* | **solid evidence/facts** *They could not support their claims with solid evidence.*
5 **solid gold/silver/oak etc.** consisting completely of gold, silver, oak etc.: *solid gold bracelets*
6 **not hollow** having no holes or spaces inside: *a solid chocolate bunny* | *The figure was carved out of a solid block of wood.*
7 **color** consisting of one color only, with no pattern: *a solid green background* | *Solid colors would be more flattering than stripes.* —see picture at PATTERN¹
8 **time** without any pauses: **five solid hours/two solid weeks etc.** *Josh stayed in bed for three solid days.*
9 **on solid ground** confident because you are dealing with a subject you are sure about, or because you are in a safe situation: *Our main objective is to get the city's finances onto solid ground.*
10 **line** a solid line is one continuous line
11 **full** without any empty space remaining: *The marchers were met by a solid wall of police officers.*
12 **geometry** TECHNICAL having length, width, and height; THREE-DIMENSIONAL: *A sphere is a solid figure.* —**solidly** *adv.*: *solidly built* —**solidness** *n.* [U] —see also SOLIDITY

solid² *adv.* **1 be booked/jammed/packed solid** to have no more seats, places etc. available at all: *Most state park campgrounds are already booked solid for the summer.* **2 five hours solid/two weeks solid etc.** used to emphasize that something happened or someone did something for a continuous period of time: *We drove for four hours solid to get here on time.*

solid³ *n.* **1** [C] a firm object or substance that has a shape that does not change; not a gas or a liquid: *Water changes from a liquid to a solid when it freezes.* **2 solids** [plural] **a)** foods that are not in liquid form: *She hasn't been able to eat solids for a week.* **b)** TECHNICAL the part of a liquid that has the qualities of a solid when it is separated from the SOLVENT²: *By law, whole milk must contain at least 8.25% milk solids.* **3** [C usually plural] a solid color: *Whether you prefer solids or stripes, polo shirts are big for school this fall.* **4** TECHNICAL a shape that has length, width, and height

sol·i·dar·i·ty /,salə'dærəti/ *n.* [U] loyalty and general agreement between all the people in a group, or between different groups, because they all have the

S

same aim: *A lot of people joined with us as an act of solidarity.* | [+ **with**] *He said the attack was carried out to show his solidarity with the Chechen people.*

so·lid·i·fy /səˈlɪdəˌfaɪ/ *v.* **solidifies, solidified, solidifying** [I,T] **1** to become solid, or make something solid: *Remove any solidified fat from the top of the soup.* **2** to make an agreement, plan, attitude etc. firmer and less likely to change, or to become firmer and less likely to change: *This is the play that solidified William's reputation as a leading playwright.* —**solidification** /səˌlɪdəfəˈkeɪʃən/ *n.* [U]

so·lid·i·ty /səˈlɪdəṭi/ *n.* [U] **1** the strength or hardness of something: *the massive solidity of his muscles* **2** the quality of something that is permanent and can be depended on: *These data confirm the underlying solidity of the labor market.*

solid-state /ˌ.. ˈ.◂/ *adj.* **1** solid-state electrical equipment contains electronic parts, such as SILICON CHIPs, rather than MECHANICAL parts **2** solid-state PHYSICS is concerned with the qualities of solid substances, especially the way in which they CONDUCT[1] (4) electricity

so·lil·o·quy /səˈlɪləkwi/ *n. plural* **soliloquies** [C,U] a speech in a play in which a character talks to himself or herself, so that the AUDIENCE knows the character's thoughts —compare COLLOQUY, MONOLOGUE (1) —**soliloquize** *v.* [I + **about**]

sol·ip·sism /ˈsɑləpˌsɪzəm, ˈsɒ-/ *n.* [U] TECHNICAL the idea in PHILOSOPHY that only the SELF exists or can be known

sol·ip·sis·tic /ˌsɑləpˈsɪstɪk/ *adj.* **1** concerned only with yourself and the things that affect you: *Di Rosa's view that art can change the world is perhaps solipsistic.* **2** TECHNICAL relating to the view in PHILOSOPHY that only the SELF exists or can be known

sol·i·taire /ˈsɑləˌtɛr/ *n.* **1** [C] a single jewel, or a piece of jewelry with a single jewel in it, especially a large DIAMOND: *a diamond solitaire* **2** [U] a game of cards for one person

sol·i·tar·y[1] /ˈsɑləˌtɛri/ *adj.* **1** [only before noun] a solitary person or thing is the only one you can see in a place: *A solitary figure stood at the end of the bar.* —see Usage Note at ALONE **2** [only before noun] done or experienced without anyone else around: *Helena took long solitary walks to the lake.* **3** spending a lot of time alone, usually because you like being alone: *Hamilton was described as a solitary man.* **4 not a solitary word/thing etc.** used to emphasize that there is not even one word, thing etc.: *We don't have a solitary bed available.* —**solitariness** *n.* [U]

solitary[2] *n.* [U] INFORMAL solitary confinement

solitary con·fine·ment /ˌ.... .ˈ../ *n.* [U] an additional punishment for a prisoner in which they are kept alone and are not allowed to see anyone else

sol·i·tude /ˈsɑləˌtud/ *n.* [U] the state of being alone, especially when this is what you enjoy: *The President read his briefing material in solitude.*

so·lo[1] /ˈsoʊloʊ/ *n. plural* **solos** [C] **1 a)** a piece of music written for one performer —compare DUET **b)** a part of a musical work in which one performer plays the most important part, with or without the other performers playing along: *Krupa plays a drum solo on the band's nine-minute version of "Sing, Sing, Sing."* **2** a job or performance that is done alone, especially an aircraft flight

solo[2] *adj., adv.* **1** done alone, without anyone else helping you: *LeRoy took his first solo flight that weekend.* | *Computer bridge programs will let you play solo.* **2** related to or played as a musical solo: *a solo passage for viola* | *Winans released her solo album at age 31.*

solo[3] *v.* [I] **1** to perform a solo in a piece of music **2** to fly an aircraft alone

so·lo·ist /ˈsoʊloʊɪst/ *n.* [C] a musician who performs a solo

Sol·o·mon /ˈsɑləmən/ (10th century B.C.) a king of Israel, the son of King David who built the TEMPLE in Jerusalem, and is known for being extremely wise

Solomon Is·lands, the /ˌ... ˈ../ a country that consists of several islands in the southwest Pacific, to the east of Papua New Guinea

sol·stice /ˈsɑlstɪs, ˈsɒl-/ *n.* [C] the time when the sun is farthest north or south of the EQUATOR: **the summer/winter solstice** (=the longest or shortest day of the year) —compare EQUINOX

sol·u·ble /ˈsɑlyəbəl/ *adj.* **1** a soluble substance can be DISSOLVEd in a liquid —see also WATER-SOLUBLE **2** FORMAL a soluble problem can be solved —opposite INSOLUBLE —**solubility** /ˌsɑlyəˈbɪləṭi/ *n.* [U]

so·lu·tion /səˈluʃən/ *n.* **1** [C] a way of solving a problem or dealing with a difficult situation: *Making the parts smaller is the cheapest solution, but is it the best one?* | [+ **to/for**] *City council members are still seeking solutions to the problem of unemployment.* | *We're trying to find a solution that both sides can support.* **2** [C] the correct answer to a question or problem, for example on a test or in a piece of school work: [+ **to**] *The solution to last week's puzzle is on page 12.* **3** [C,U] a mixture of two or more substances, especially a solid and a liquid, with no chemical change: *a weak sugar solution*

solve /sɑlv/ *v.* [T] **1** to find or provide a way of dealing with a problem: *Simply making drugs legal will not solve our nation's drug problem.* **2** to find the correct answer to a question or problem, or the explanation for something that is difficult to understand: *Casey is very good at solving crossword puzzles.* | **solve a crime/mystery/case** *Rice's murder has never been solved.* —**solvable** *adj.*

sol·vent[1] /ˈsɑlvənt/ *n.* [C,U] a liquid that is able to turn a solid substance into a liquid, or that can remove a substance from a surface

solvent[2] *adj.* having enough money to pay your debts: *Now the question is how to keep the business solvent.* —**solvency** *n.* [U] —opposite INSOLVENT

Sol·zhe·ni·tsyn /ˌsoʊlʒəˈnɪtsən/, **Alexander** (1918–) a Russian writer of NOVELS

So·ma·li·a /səˈmɑliə/ a country in east Africa that is east of Ethiopia and Kenya, and next to the Indian Ocean —**Somali** *n., adj.*

som·ber /ˈsɑmbɚ/ *adj.* **1** sad and serious; GRAVE[2]: *a somber expression* | *The minister spoke in somber tones.* **2** dark and without any bright colors: *long windows covered by somber curtains* —**somberly** *adv.* —**somberness** *n.* [U]

som·bre·ro /səmˈbrɛroʊ, sɑm-/ *n. plural* **sombreros** [C] a Mexican hat for men that is tall with a wide, round edge

some[1] /səm; *strong* sʌm/ *quantifier* **1** a number of people or things or an amount of something, when the exact number or amount is not stated: *There's some butter in the fridge.* | *It's a good idea to take some cash with you.* | *Of course you'll make some new friends in college.* | *They've already gotten some offers to buy their house.* —compare ANY[1] (1) **2** a number of people or things or an amount of something, but not all: *Some people believe in life after death.* | *In some cases, the damage could not even be repaired.* **3** FORMAL a fairly large amount of something: *The talks have been continuing for some time.*

USAGE NOTE: SOME

GRAMMAR
Some of cannot be followed directly by a noun. Use "the," "this," "those" etc., or a possessive: *Some of the students went home early* (NOT *"Some of students..."*). | *I talked to some of my friends after the concert* (NOT *"some of friends..."*). However, **some of** can be followed directly by a pronoun: *Some of us thought the food was overcooked.* **Some** is followed directly by a noun when you are talking about part of something in general: *Some people have trouble staying within a budget.* | *Some foods need to be refrigerated.* Use **some of** when you are talking about part of a particular thing, group etc.: *Some of us left before the end of the movie.* | *Some of the strawberries we bought were bad.*

S W
1 1

some² /sʌm/ *pron.* **1** a number of people or things or an amount of something, but not all: *Many local businesses are having difficulties, and some have even gone bankrupt.* | *It's true that some have suggested that the mayor resign.* | [+ **of**] *Some of us had to leave the meeting early.* | *Can I have some of your cake?* **2** a number of people or things or an amount of something, when the exact number or amount is not stated: *We're out of milk. Could you bring some home from the store?* | *"Do you have any tape?" "Yeah, there's some in my desk drawer."* | *We've ordered more blue shirts, though we still have some in stock.* —compare ANY¹ (1) **3 and then some** INFORMAL and more: *This book will tell you everything you wanted to know about wine – and then some.*

S W
1 1

some³ /sʌm/ *determiner* **1** used to talk about a person or thing, when you do not know or say exactly which: *Can you give me some idea of the cost?* | **some kind/type/form/sort of sth** *Tina must be suffering from some kind of depression.* **2** INFORMAL used when you are talking about a person or thing that you do not know, remember, or understand, or when you think it does not matter: *Some guy called for you today.* **3 some...or other/another** used when you do not want to mention a specific person or thing, or when you think it does not matter: *Everyone will need to see a doctor at some time or another.* | *Mike was always talking to some girl or other.* **4 some friend/help! etc.** SPOKEN used especially when you are annoyed, to mean someone or something has disappointed you by not behaving in the way you think they should: *"Jeff's wife ran off with his best friend." "Some friend!"* **5** used to say that something was very good or very impressive: *That was some party last night!*

some⁴ /səm/ *adv.* **1 some more** an additional number or amount of something: *Would you like some more pie?* | *I think we still need to practice some more.* **2 some 10 people/50%/$100 etc.** an expression meaning about 10 people, 50%, $100 etc.: *Dr. Brown began his career some 30 years ago.* **3** SPOKEN a little: *We could work some and then rest a while.*

-some /səm/ *suffix* **1** [in adjectives] tending to behave in a particular way, or having a particular quality: *a troublesome boy* (=who causes trouble) | *a bothersome back injury* (=that BOTHERS you very much) **2** [in nouns] a group of a particular number: *a golf foursome* (=four people playing GOLF together) | *a loving twosome* (=two people in a relationship)

S W
1 2

some·bod·y¹ /ˈsʌmˌbɑdi, -ˌbɑdi/ *pron.* used to mean a person, when you do not know, or do not say, who the person is; someone: *There's somebody waiting to see you.* | *Somebody's car alarm kept me awake all night.* | **somebody new/different etc.** *I think they are getting somebody famous to sing at the festival.* | *If you can't make it, we can always invite somebody else* (=a different person). | *I bet she told Jill or Terry or somebody* (=or a similar person) *about it.*

some·body² *n.* **be somebody** to be or feel important: *She's hoping that she might be somebody one day.*

some·day /ˈsʌmdeɪ/ *adv.* at an unknown time in the future, especially a long time in the future: *Maybe someday our grandchildren will want to read these magazines.*

S W
2 2

some·how /ˈsʌmhaʊ/ *adv.* **1** in some way, or by some means, although you do not know how: *Somehow they managed to climb in through the bathroom window.* | *I knew he was connected somehow or other with the CIA.* **2** for some reason that is not clear: *Somehow I had a feeling you were going to say that.*

S W
1 1

some·one¹ /ˈsʌmwʌn/ *pron.* used to mean a person, when you do not know, or do not say, who the person is; SOMEBODY: *Someone was pounding on the door.* | *Could someone please turn on the lights?* | **someone new/different etc.** *That limo must be for someone important.* | *We'll have to find someone else* (=a different person) *to finish the job.* | *Maybe you could ask a teacher or someone* (=or a similar person) *about it.*

some·one² *n.* **be someone** to be or feel important: *I'd always wanted to be someone.*

S W
2

some·place /ˈsʌmpleɪs/ *adv.* [not usually in questions or negatives] in or to a place, but you do not say or know exactly where: *I know my glasses must be around here someplace.* | **someplace to live/sleep etc.** *Greg still needs someplace to store his stuff this summer.* | **someplace safe/different etc.** *Let's find someplace quiet to study.* | *If the cafeteria is full, we can just go someplace else* (=to a different place). | *We could drive to Rockport or Ipswich or someplace* (=or a similar place).

som·er·sault /ˈsʌmərˌsɔlt/ *n.* [C] a movement in which someone rolls or jumps forward or backward, so that their feet go over their head before they stand up again: **do/turn a somersault** *Janice did a backward somersault on the mat.* —**somersault** *v.* [I]

S W
1 1

some·thing /ˈsʌmθɪŋ/ *pron.* [not usually in questions or negatives] **1** used to mean a particular thing when you do not know its name, do not know exactly what it is etc.: *There's something in my eye.* | *Sarah said something about coming over later.* | *Come here – I want to show you something.* | **something new/old/big/better etc.** *We knew they were working on something important.* | *I like this car, but I need something bigger.* | *I wish they'd do something about the noise.* | *Maybe you'll be able to find something else* (=a different thing) *at the mall.* | *There's something wrong with* (=a problem with) *the printer.* **2 something to eat/drink/read/do etc.** some food, a drink, a book, an activity etc.: *We stopped to get something to eat in Springfield.* | *See if you can find the kids something to play with.* | *Linda needs to find something to wear to Amy's wedding.* **3 have something to do with sth** to be connected with or related to a particular person or thing, but in a way that you are not sure about: *I know Steve's job has something to do with investments.* **4 something like 100/2000 etc.** APPROXIMATELY 100, 2000 etc.: *There must have been something like fifty people waiting in line.* **5 thirty-something/forty-something etc.** used to say that someone's age is between 30 and 39, between 40 and 49 etc., when you do not know exactly **6 something about sb/sth** a quality or feature of someone or something that you recognize, but cannot say exactly what it is: *Something about Frank's attitude just makes you want to hit him.* | *There's something strange about the woman's eyes in the painting.* **7 make something of yourself** to become successful or famous **8 something of a surprise/shock/tradition etc.** FORMAL used to say that something is a surprise, shock, tradition etc., but not completely or not in a strong or severe way: *The news came as something of a surprise.* | *Kenny had always been something of a disappointment to his parents.* **9 there is something to sth** used to admit that something must be good, helpful etc., when you did not believe this earlier: *Well, if therapy worked for Jean, there must be something to it.*

S

SPOKEN PHRASES

10 ...or something used when you cannot remember, or do not want to give, another example of something you are mentioning: *Here's some money. Get yourself a sandwich or something.* | *Her name was Judy or Julie or something like that.* **11 be something** to be impressive and deserve admiration: *The way the dancers leaped around sure was something.* **12 be something else** to be unusual and sometimes funny to other people: *You're really something else, Jeff.* **13 a little something** a small or inexpensive gift: *Here's a little something from the girls in the office.* **14 sixty something/John something etc.** used when you cannot remember the rest of a number or name: *The last bus leaves at eleven something* (=sometime between 11:00 and 12:00). **15 something fierce** INFORMAL very much, or in a very severe way: *It rained something fierce during our trip.*

S W
2

some·time¹ /ˈsʌmtaɪm/ *adv.* at a time in the future or in the past, although you do not know exactly when: *The burglary must have happened sometime* after 8:00. | *It's a long story. I'll tell you about it some-time.* | *I hope we can get together again* ***sometime soon***.

sometime² *adj.* [only before noun] **1** used to say that someone does or is something part of the time, but not always: *Downey's uncle is a* ***sometime*** *actor and screenwriter.* **2** FORMAL former: *Duval spoke at the funeral of his friend and sometime rival.*

some·times /'sʌmtaɪmz/ *adv.* on some occasions, but not all: *Sometimes I stay late in the library after class.*

some·what /'sʌmwʌt/ *adv.* more than a little, but not very: *The price is somewhat higher than I expected.*

some·where /'sʌmwɛr/ *adv.* [not usually in questions or negatives] **1** in or to a place, but you do not say or know exactly where: *I know their house is* ***somewhere*** *near here.* | ***somewhere to live/sleep*** etc. *Tonya needs somewhere to keep her skis.* | ***some-where warm/different*** etc. *Is there somewhere safe where I can leave my bike?* | *You might be able to find a cheaper one* ***somewhere else*** (=in a different place). | *We could go to the park* ***or somewhere*** (=or a similar place). —see Usage Note at SOMEWHERE **2** ***somewhere around/between*** etc. a little more or a little less than a particular number or amount, a number or amount that is not known but is between two other numbers etc.; APPROXIMATELY: *It would cost somewhere between $12 million and $20 million to build a ship like that today.* **3** ***be getting some-where*** to be making progress: *Now we're really getting somewhere!*

some·wheres /'sʌmwɛrz/ *adv.* SPOKEN, NONSTANDARD somewhere

som·me·lier /ˌsʌməl'yeɪ/ *n.* [C] someone who works in a restaurant and whose job is to advise people on the right wines to drink

som·nam·bu·list /sʌm'næmbyəlɪst/ *n.* [C] FORMAL someone who walks while they are asleep; SLEEP-WALKER —**somnambulism** *n.* [U] —**somnambulistic** /sʌmˌnæmbyə'lɪstɪk/ *adj.*

som·no·lent /'sʌmnələnt/ *adj.* LITERARY **1** making you want to sleep: *a slow, somnolent folk song* **2** almost starting to sleep —**somnolence** *n.* [U]

Som·nus /'sʌmnəs/ the Roman name for the god Hypnos

son /sʌn/ *n.* **1** [C] someone's male child: *Our son Jamie is five years old.* | *They have three sons and a daughter.* —see also **like father like son** (FATHER¹ (5)) **2** [singular, not with **the**] used by an older person as a friendly way to address a boy or young man: *What's your name, son?* **3** ***the Son*** Jesus Christ; the second member of the group in the Christian religion that includes God the Father and the HOLY SPIRIT **4** ***my son*** used by a priest to address a man or boy **5** [C usually plural] a man from a particular place or country, often used in the names of organizations: *members of the Sons of Italy* —see also **favorite son** (FAVORITE¹ (2))

so·nar /'soʊnɑr/ *n.* [U] equipment on a ship or SUB-MARINE that uses sound waves to find out the position of objects under the water

so·na·ta /sə'nɑtə/ *n.* [C] a piece of music with three or four parts that is written for a piano, or for a piano and another instrument: *a violin sonata*

Sond·heim /'sɑndhaɪm/**, Ste·phen** /'stivən/ (1930–) a U.S. SONGWRITER and COMPOSER famous for writing many successful MUSICALs

song /sɔŋ/ *n.* **1 a)** [C] a short piece of music with words that you sing: *The students played guitars and sang folk songs.* **b)** [U] songs or singing in general: *The story of America's independence has been cele-brated in song.* **2 burst/break into song** to suddenly start singing **3** [C,U] the musical sounds made by birds or some other animals, such as WHALES: *a recording of the swallow's song* **4 for a song** very cheaply: *One woman bought a whole armful of clothes for a song.* **5 a song and dance** INFORMAL an expla-nation or excuse that is too long and complicated: *Then he gave us some boring song and dance about*

being a citizen of the world. **6 sb's song** a song that reminds two people in a romantic relationship of when they first met: *Listen, they're* ***playing our*** *song.*

song·bird /'sɔŋbɚd/ *n.* [C] a bird that can make musi-cal sounds

song·book /'sɔŋbʊk/ *n.* [C] a book with the words and music of many songs

Song of Sol·o·mon /ˌ. . '.../ also **Song of Songs** /ˌ. . './ a book in the Old Testament of the Christian Bible

song·ster /'sɔŋstɚ/ *n.* [C] LITERARY **1** a songbird **2** someone who sings and sometimes writes songs

song·stress /'sɔŋstrɪs/ *n.* [C] a woman who sings and sometimes writes popular songs

song·writ·er /'sɔŋˌraɪtɚ/ *n.* [C] someone who writes the words and usually the music of a song —**song-writing** *n.* [U]

son·ic /'sɑnɪk/ *adj.* [only before noun] relating to sound, SOUND WAVES, or the speed of sound

sonic boom /ˌ.. './ *n.* [C] a loud sound like an explo-sion, that an airplane makes when it starts to travel faster than the speed of sound

son-in-law /'. . ˌ./ *n. plural* **sons-in-law** [C] the hus-band of your daughter —compare DAUGHTER-IN-LAW

son·net /'sɑnɪt/ *n.* [C] a poem with 14 lines that RHYME with each other in a special pattern

son·ny /'sʌni/ *n.* [singular, not with **the**] OLD-FASHIONED, SPOKEN used when speaking to a boy or young man who is much younger than you: *Now, you just listen to me, sonny.*

son of a bitch /'. . . . ˌ./ *n. plural* **sons of bitches** SPOKEN **1** [C] OFFENSIVE a man or object that you are very angry or annoyed with: *I'll personally sue that son of a bitch if he does that.* **2 son of a bitch!** IMPO-LITE said when you are annoyed: *Son of a bitch! The car won't start!* **3 be a son of a bitch** IMPOLITE to be very difficult: *Getting the new tire on was a real son of a bitch.*

son of a gun /'. . . ˌ./ *n. plural* **sons of guns** [C] SPOKEN **1** HUMOROUS a man you like or admire: *Billy's a tough old son of a gun.* **2** a man that you are annoyed with: *Somebody go and tell that son of a gun that we're all waiting to go here.* **3** something that is difficult to deal with: *This son of a gun had better work this time.* **4 son of a gun!** used to express surprise

Son of God /ˌ. . './ *n.* **the Son of God** also **the Son of Man** used by Christians to mean Jesus Christ

son·o·gram /'sɑnəˌgræm/ *n.* [C] TECHNICAL an image, for example of an unborn baby inside its mother's body or of a body organ, that is produced by a machine that passes ELECTRONs through the body; ULTRASOUND

son·o·rous /'sɑnərəs/ *adj.* having a pleasantly deep loud sound: *a sonorous voice*

soon /sun/ *adv.* **1** in a short time from now, or a short time after something else happens: *It will be getting dark soon.* | *They came back much sooner than we had anticipated.* | *We soon realized how dif-ficult the job was going to be.* | *They should be back* ***pretty soon***. | ***Soon after*** *his return, Ailey received a letter from Mrs. St. Denis.* | ***How soon*** (=How quickly) *can you finish the report?* **2 as soon as** immediately after something has happened: *I came as soon as I heard the news.* | *I'll come over to your place* ***as soon as I can***. **3 as soon as possible** abbreviation **ASAP** as quickly as possible: *Please send us your reply as soon as possible.* **4 sooner or later** used to say that something is certain to happen at some time in the future, though you cannot be sure exactly when: *She's bound to find out sooner or later.* **5 the sooner (...) the better** used to say that it is important for something to happen very soon: *The sooner we get these bills paid off, the better.* | *They knew they had to leave town, and the sooner the better.* **6 the sooner... the sooner...** used to say that if something happens soon, something else that you want will happen soon after that: *The sooner I get this work done, the sooner I can go home.* **7 too soon** too early: *It's still too soon to say whether the* operation was successful. | Baumer, an enthusiastic young soldier, learned *all too soon* (=much earlier than you would like) *about the horrors of war.* **8 sb would (just) as soon do sth** used to say that you would prefer to do something, or would prefer that something happen: *I'd just as soon forget what happened back there.* **9 soon enough** very soon, or earlier than you expect: *Soon enough, it started to rain.* **10 no sooner had/has/is/does... than...** used to say that something happened almost immediately after something else: *No sooner had he sat down than the phone rang.* **11 no sooner said than done** used to say that you will do something immediately **12 not a moment too soon** also **none too soon** almost too late, and when you thought that something was not going to happen in time: *"Dinner's ready." "And not a moment too soon!"* **13 would sooner do sth (than sth)** if you would sooner do something, you would really prefer to do it, especially instead of something that seems bad: *Mr. Watt would sooner kill himself than sell his store.*

soot /sut/ n. [U] black powder that is produced when something is burned —**sooty** adj.

soothe /suð/ v. [T] **1** to make someone feel calmer and less anxious, upset, or angry: *Lucia soothed the baby with soft words and smiles.* **2** to make a pain or a bad feeling less severe: *Alcohol was the only thing she knew to soothe the pain of her divorce.* | *A massage would soothe his aching muscles.* —**soothing** adj.: *gentle, soothing music* —**soothingly** adv.

sooth·say·er /ˈsuθ,seɪə/ n. [C] OLD USE someone who people believe has the ability to say what will happen in the future

sop¹ /sap/ v. **sopped, sopping**
  sop sth ↔ up phr. v. [T] to remove liquid from a surface by using a piece of cloth, a PAPER TOWEL etc. that ABSORBS (=takes the liquid into itself) the liquid: *Jesse sopped up the spilled drink with a towel.* —see also SOPPING

sop² n. [C usually singular] something not very important or valuable that you offer to someone in order to prevent them from complaining or getting angry about something: [+ to] *The real truth is: that bill is a sop to the rich.*

so·phis·ti·cate /səˈfɪstəkɪt, -ˌkeɪt/ n. [C] someone who is sophisticated

so·phis·ti·cat·ed /səˈfɪstəˌkeɪtɪd/ adj. **1** confident and having a lot of experience of life and good judgment about socially important things such as art, fashion etc.: *a sophisticated, witty woman* | *Sondheim's lyrics have a sophisticated brilliance.* **2** a sophisticated machine, system, method etc. is very well designed, very advanced, and often works in a complicated way: *a highly (=very) sophisticated alarm system* **3** having a lot of knowledge and experience of difficult or complicated subjects, and therefore able to understand them well: *Even experienced and sophisticated readers have been known to have trouble with Thoreau's books.* —**sophistication** /səˌfɪstəˈkeɪʃən/ n. [U] *These organizations vary greatly in size, structure, and degree of sophistication.*

soph·ist·ry /ˈsafɪstri/ n. plural **sophistries** FORMAL **1** [U] the skillful use of reasons or explanations that seem correct but are really false, in order to deceive people **2** [C] a reason or explanation used like this

Soph·o·cles /ˈsafəˌkliz/ (?496–405 B.C.) a Greek writer of plays, who developed Greek TRAGEDY as a style of theater

soph·o·more /ˈsafmɔr/ n. [C] a student in the second year of high school or college —compare FRESHMAN, JUNIOR² (1), SENIOR² (1)

soph·o·mor·ic /safˈmɔrɪk/ adj. childish and not very sensible: *a sophomoric sense of humor*

sop·o·rif·ic¹ /ˌsapəˈrɪfɪk/ adj. FORMAL making you feel ready to sleep: *His voice had an almost soporific effect.*

soporific² n. [C] FORMAL something that makes you feel ready to sleep: *They used television as a soporific for their children.*

sop·ping /ˈsapɪŋ/ also **sopping wet** /ˌ.. ˈ. ◂/ adj. [usually before noun] very wet: *My shoes were sopping.*

so·pra·no /səˈprænoʊ/ n. plural **sopranos** [C] a woman, girl, or young boy whose singing voice is very high —**soprano** adj. [only before noun] *a soprano saxophone* (=that plays very high notes)

sor·bet /sɔrˈbeɪ, ˈsɔrbət/ n. [C,U] a frozen sweet food made of fruit juice, sugar, and water

sor·cer·er /ˈsɔrsərə/ n. [C] a man in stories who uses magic and receives help from evil spirits

sor·cer·ess /ˈsɔrsərɪs/ n. [C] a woman in stories who uses magic and receives help from evil spirits

sor·cer·y /ˈsɔrsəri/ n. [U] magic that uses the power of evil spirits

sor·did /ˈsɔrdɪd/ adj. **1** involving immoral or dishonest behavior: *a sordid crime* | *The details of their affair were sordid and ugly.* **2** very dirty and disgusting: *the sordid slums of modern cities*

sore¹ /sɔr/ adj. **1** a part of your body that is sore is painful and often red because of a wound or infection, or because you have used a muscle too much: *My legs are still sore today.* | *Val woke up with a sore throat and a temperature of 102°.* **2 a sore point/ spot** something that is likely to make someone upset or angry when you talk about it: *Money is still a sore point with many employees.* **3 a sore loser** someone who always gets very angry and upset when they lose a game, competition etc. **4** [not before noun] OLD-FASHIONED upset, angry, and annoyed, especially because you have not been treated fairly: *She was sore because she wasn't asked to the wedding.* | [+ at/about] *Is he still sore at us?* —see also **a sight for sore eyes** (SIGHT¹ (13)), **stick out (like a sore thumb)** at STICK OUT (STICK¹)

sore² n. [C] a painful, often red, place on your body caused by a wound or infection: *They were starving and covered with sores.* —see also BEDSORE, COLD SORE

sore·head /ˈsɔrhɛd/ n. [C] INFORMAL someone who is angry in an unreasonable way

sore·ly /ˈsɔrli/ adv. very much or very seriously: **be sorely needed/lacking/missed etc.** *In the process, Kissinger's patience was sorely tested.* | *Several people may have been sorely tempted to accept Wilson's offer.*

sor·ghum /ˈsɔrgəm/ n. [U] a type of grain that is grown in tropical areas

so·ror·i·ty /səˈrɔrəti, -ˈrɑr-/ n. plural **sororities** [C] a club for women students at some colleges and universities —compare FRATERNITY (1)

sor·rel /ˈsɔrəl, ˈsɑ-/ n. **1** [U] a plant with sour-tasting leaves that are used in cooking **2** [C] a light brown or reddish-brown horse

sor·row¹ /ˈsɑroʊ, ˈsɔ-/ n. **1** [U] a feeling of great sadness, usually because someone has died or because something terrible has happened to you: *Her life was filled with heartache and sorrow.* **2** [C] an event or situation that makes you feel great sadness: *We shared all of our family's joys and sorrows.* —see also **drown your sorrows** (DROWN (4))

sorrow² v. [I] LITERARY to feel or express sorrow

sor·row·ful /ˈsɑroʊfəl, -rəfəl/ adj. FORMAL very sad: *a sorrowful poem* —**sorrowfully** adv.

sor·ry /ˈsɑri, ˈsɔri/ adj. **sorrier, sorriest**
1 ashamed [not before noun, no comparative] feeling ashamed or unhappy about something bad you have done: [+ about] *We're sorry about all the mess, Mom.* | [+ (that)] *Casey was sorry he'd gotten so angry at the kids over nothing.* | [+ for] *Willie said he was sorry for the pain he had caused them.* | *I wish he would just call and say he's sorry.*
2 a) be/feel sorry for sb to feel pity or sympathy for someone because something bad has happened to them or because they are in a bad situation: *For a minute, she felt sorry for the girl.* | *I just feel sorry for the ones who didn't make the team.* **b) feel sorry for yourself** to feel unhappy because you are in a bad situation, especially when other people think you should not be unhappy
3 disappointed [not before noun, no comparative] feeling sad about a situation, and wishing it were

different: [+ (that)] *Brigid was always sorry she hadn't kept up her piano lessons.* | *I'm sorry you didn't enjoy the meal.* | [**be sorry to do sth**] *We'll all be sorry to see Julie go.* | *I won't be sorry to leave this place.* | *I was sorry to hear of your father's death.*

4 very bad [only before noun] very bad, especially in a way that makes you feel pity or disapproval: *This whole sorry episode shows just how bad things have become.* | *Education is in a very **sorry state** in this district.*

5 a sorry excuse for sth something that is of very poor quality, someone who is bad at their job etc.: *I actually paid $7 to see that sorry excuse for a movie.*

SPOKEN PHRASES

6 sorry/I'm sorry a) used to tell someone that you feel ashamed and unhappy because of something bad you have done to them: *I'm really sorry.* | *I didn't mean to hurt your feelings.* | *"Kevin! Don't do that!" "Sorry."* | [+ **about**] *Sorry about that. I'll buy you a new one.* | [+ (that)] *I'm so sorry I forgot your anniversary.* **b)** used as a polite way of excusing yourself in a social situation: *Oh, sorry, am I sitting in your chair?* | [+ (that)] *Sorry we're a little late – we got lost.* | [**sorry to do sth**] *I'm sorry to call you at home, but this is important.* **c)** used as a polite way of introducing disappointing information or a piece of bad news: *Sorry, but that part is out of stock.* **d)** used when you have said something that is not correct, and want to say what is correct: *Turn in your pink form – sorry, your green form – by tomorrow.* **e)** used to politely disagree with someone: *Well, I'm sorry, but to me, drugs are just not funny.* **f)** used to refuse an offer or to say "no": *"I'll give you $500 for it." "Sorry, no deal."*

7 sorry? used to ask someone to repeat something that you have not heard correctly: *Sorry? What was the last point?* | *"Hi, my name's Bob Skluzacek." "Sorry?" "Bob Skluzacek."*

8 you'll be sorry used to tell someone they will wish they had not done something: *You'll be sorry when your dad hears about this.*

9 I'm sorry to say used to say that you are disappointed that something has happened: *No, I'm sorry to say I missed Alice's birthday again.*

—see also **better (to be) safe than sorry** (SAFE[1] (7)) —see Usage Note at EXCUSE[1]

s w sort¹ /sɔrt/ *n.*

1 type/kind [C] a group or class of people, things etc. that have similar qualities or features; type: [+ **of**] *What sort of shampoo do you use?* | *They had **all sorts of** (=many different kinds of) seafood on the menu.* | *Violence **of one sort or another** (=of various different types) is a fact of life in modern cities.* | **of this/that sort** *Events of this sort are reported locally, but seldom get picked up by national media.* —see Usage Note at KIND[1]

2 some sort of sth also **sth of some sort** used when something is of a particular type, but you do not know the exact details about it: *He was some sort of market-research expert.* | *There was a game of some sort going on inside.*

3 of sorts also **of a sort** used when something is of a particular type, but is not a very good example of it, or is similar to something in some way: *The cooler air acts as a barrier of sorts, trapping elements below it.*

4 out of sorts feeling a little upset, annoyed, or sick: *Mandy explained that she'd been feeling out of sorts and had overreacted.*

5 person [C usually singular] someone with a particular type of character: *Uncle Ralph was always a good-natured sort.*

6 computer [C] if a computer does a sort, it puts things in a particular order —compare KIND[1]

SPOKEN PHRASES

7 sort of a) used to say that something is partly true, but does not describe the exact situation: *I sort of organize things and help out in the office.* | *It's sort*

of a condensed one-day version of the course.* | *"Are you finished with your homework?" "Well, sort of."* **b)** used when you are not sure you are using the best word to describe something: *They were covered in this sort of slime, you know, that comes from the chemicals.* | *The car was sort of a greenish-gray color.* **c)** used to make what you are saying sound less strong or direct: *Well, I sort of thought we could maybe go out sometime.* | *It was sort of a shock when I found out.*

8 sort of like used when you are trying to describe something, but cannot think of the exact words: *You shouldn't take too many of those pills, because they're sort of like hard on your liver.*

sort² *v.* [T] to put things in a particular order, or **s w** arrange them in groups according to size, rank, type [1] etc.: *The eggs are sorted according to size.* | [**sort sth into sth**] *Applications will be sorted into three categories.*

sort sb/sth **out** *phr. v.* [T] **1** to organize something that is mixed up or messy: *It took us all day to sort out all the paperwork.* **2** to separate something from a group: *Go through your closet and sort out any stuff that's too small.* **3** to deal with problems: *Mike's still trying to sort out his personal life.*

sort through sth *phr. v.* [T] to look for something among a lot of similar things, especially while you are arranging these things into an order: *Maria sorted through the mail until she found a letter addressed to her.*

sort·a /ˈsɔrtə/ SPOKEN, INFORMAL a short form of "sort of": *I was sorta worried about them.*

sor·tie¹ /ˈsɔrti, sɔrˈti/ *n.* [C] **1** a short flight made by an airplane over enemy land, in order to bomb a city, military defenses etc.: *The enemy generally flew very few sorties at night.* **2** a short trip: *George makes frequent sorties on his private jet.*

sortie² *v.* [I] TECHNICAL to make a short flight over enemy land or an attack on an enemy's position

SOS *n.* [singular] a signal or urgent message that a ship, airplane, or person is in trouble and needs help: *Their frantic SOS message was picked up by a Coast Guard vessel.*

so-so /ˈ. ./ *adj., adv.* neither very good nor very bad; average: *"How are you feeling?" "Oh, so-so."* | *a so-so movie*

sot /sɑt/ *n.* [C] OLD-FASHIONED someone who is drunk all the time

sot·to vo·ce /ˌsɑtoʊ ˈvoʊtʃi/ *adv.* FORMAL in a very quiet voice, so that other people cannot easily hear

souf·flé /suˈfleɪ/ *n.* [C,U] a baked food that contains a lot of air and is made with eggs, flour, milk and often cheese

sough /saʊ, sʌf/ *v.* [I] LITERARY if the wind soughs, it makes a soft sound when passing through trees —**sough** *n.* [U]

sought /sɔt/ *v.* the past tense and past participle of SEEK

sought-af·ter /ˈ. ˌ../ *adj.* [usually before noun] wanted by a lot of people, but rare or difficult to get: **most/highly sought-after** *Quentin became one of the most sought-after speakers in the state.*

souk /suk/ *n.* [C] a market in an Arab city

soul /soʊl/ *n.* **s w**

1 spirit [C] the part of a person that is not physical [2] and contains their thoughts, feelings, character etc., that many people believe continues to exist after they die: *Mabel felt sure that her soul would be saved* (=would go to heaven). —compare SPIRIT[1] (2)

2 inner character [U] the part of a person that contains their true character, where their deepest thoughts and feelings come from: *He knew in his soul that Linda was never going to change.* | *Meditation is good for the soul* (=makes you feel better inside).

3 person [C] a person: *Only a few brave souls ventured outdoors in Monday's storm.* | *Tina swore she would **not tell a soul** (=no one).*

4 strong emotions [U] a special quality of a painting, piece of music, performance etc. that makes people feel strong emotions: *Her performance was technically perfect, but it lacked soul.*

5 music [U] SOUL MUSIC

6 special quality [U] the special quality or part that gives something its true character: *A lot of local residents say the downtown area is losing its soul.*

7 be the soul of discretion HUMOROUS to always be extremely careful to keep secrets

8 bless my soul OLD-FASHIONED, SPOKEN used to express surprise —see also **bare your soul** (BARE[2] (2)), **keep body and soul together** (BODY (10)), **the heart and soul of sth** (HEART (25)), **sell your soul (to the devil)** (SELL[1] (10)), SOUL MUSIC

soul broth·er /ˈ. ˌ../ *n.* [C] INFORMAL an expression meaning an "African-American man," used especially by young African-Americans in the 1960s and 1970s

soul-des·troy·ing /ˈ. .ˌ./ *adj.* something soul-destroying is extremely boring or makes you feel extremely unhappy: *Most people are unaware of the back-breaking, soul-destroying labor required in past centuries.*

soul food /ˈ. ./ *n.* [U] traditional foods that are cooked and eaten by African-Americans in the southern U.S.

soul·ful /ˈsoulfəl/ *adj.* expressing deep, usually sad emotions: *a soulful voice* —**soulfully** *adv.* —**soulfulness** *n.* [U]

soul·less /ˈsoul-lıs/ *adj.* lacking emotions or sympathy: *To the soulless insurance companies, this was just another entry in their profits and losses.* —**soullessly** *adv.* —**soullessness** *n.* [U]

soul mate /ˈ. ./ *n.* [C] someone you have a close relationship with because you share the same emotions and interests

soul mu·sic /ˈ. ˌ../ *n.* [U] a type of popular music that often expresses deep emotions, usually performed by African-American singers and musicians

soul patch /ˈ. ./ *n.* [C] a small square area of hair that a man grows just below his bottom lip

soul-search·ing /ˈ. ˌ../ *n.* [U] careful examination of your thoughts and feelings, because you are very worried about whether or not it is right to do something: *Officials are likely to do some serious soul-searching on whether it was right to continue the mission.*

soul sis·ter /ˈ. ˌ../ *n.* [C] INFORMAL an expression meaning an "African-American woman," used especially by young African-Americans in the 1960s and 1970s

sound[1] /saund/ *n.* **1** [C,U] something that you hear, or what can be heard: *There were strange sounds coming from the next room.* | *Some of these planes can travel faster than the speed of sound.* | *a vowel sound* | [+ **of**] *Just then, we heard the sound of voices outside.* | *We tried not to make a sound* (=to be completely quiet) *as we went upstairs.* —see Usage Note at NOISE **2** [U] what you hear coming from a television, a radio, in a movie theater etc.: *There's no sound coming from the TV.* **3** [C usually singular] the particular quality that a singer's or group's music has: *We're trying to develop a harder, funkier sound.* **4 not like the sound of sth** to feel worried by something that you have heard or read: *"There's been a slight change in our plans." "I don't like the sound of that."* **5 from the sound of it/sth** judging from what you have heard or read: *From the sound of it, Phil had already drunk quite a bit that night.*

sound[2] *v.*

1 seem [linking verb + adj.] if something or someone sounds good, bad, strange etc. that is how they seem to you when you hear or read about them: *The trip sounds really exciting.* | *$50 sounds about right.* | *That sounds pretty good to me.*

2 sound like also **sound as if/though** used to say that someone or something seems a particular way to you: *Nick sounds like a nice guy. Will we get to meet him soon?* | *He sounded like he had a cold or something.* | *It sounds as though Nancy will need another operation.*

3 voice [linking verb + adj.] to seem to show a particular quality with your voice: *Jen sounded kind of tired on the phone.*

4 warning [T] to publicly give a warning or tell people to be careful: *Several earlier studies had*

sounded similar warnings. | **sound a note of caution/optimism/despair** etc. *Louvois was now sounding a note of concern.* | *Several health officials began sounding the alarm* (=warning about danger) *about the hazards of the sun's rays.*

5 make a noise [I,T] if something sounds or if you sound it, it makes a noise: *If gas levels get too high, a warning bell will sound.*

6 measure depth [T] TECHNICAL to measure the depth of the ocean, a lake etc. —see also SOUNDINGS (2)

sound off *phr. v.* [I] **1** to express strong opinions about something, especially when you are complaining angrily: [+ **on/about**] *Madden regularly sounds off on a variety of topics.* **2** if soldiers sound off, they shout out numbers or their names to show that they are there

sound sb/sth ↔ **out** *phr. v.* [T] **1** to talk to someone in order to find out what they think about a plan or idea: *Baker is sounding out our allies on their willingness to go to war.* **2** to pronounce a new or difficult word by slowly saying the sounds of each letter in it: *In first grade, children learn to print and sound out words.*

sound[3] *adj.* **1** sensible, correct, and likely to produce the right results: **sound advice/judgment/policy** etc. *We're looking for someone who can make sound decisions.* | *environmentally sound farming practices* | *sound investments* —opposite UNSOUND **2 be of sound mind** LAW to not be mentally ill: *The hearing will try to determine whether Mr. Kane was of sound mind when he wrote the documents.* **3** in good condition, not damaged: *On the surface, the house appeared to be structurally sound.* **4** sound sleep is deep and peaceful —**soundness** *n.* [U]

sound[4] *adv.* **sound asleep** deeply asleep

sound bar·ri·er /ˈ. ˌ../ *n.* **1 the sound barrier** the sudden increase in the pressure of air against a vehicle, especially an aircraft, when it reaches the speed of sound: *The world's fastest car broke the sound barrier* (=went faster than the speed of sound) *during a test in Nevada yesterday.* **2** [C] a high wall that is built along the side of a road to block the noise of the traffic on the road

sound bite /ˈ. ./ *n.* [C] a very short part of a speech or statement, especially one made by a politician, that is broadcast on television or the radio: *a 20-second sound bite*

sound card /ˈ. ./ *n.* [C] a piece of electronic equipment that allows a computer to produce sounds

sound check /ˈ. ./ *n.* [C] the process of checking that all the equipment needed for broadcasting or recording is working correctly

sound ef·fects /ˈ. .ˌ./ *n.* [plural] sounds produced artificially for a television or radio program, a movie etc.

sounding board /ˈ.. ˌ./ *n.* [C] **1** someone you discuss your ideas with in order to find out if they are good: [+ **for/to**] *Often he serves as a sounding board for other detectives.* **2** a board that is placed behind someone who is speaking to a large group of people so that the speaker can be heard more easily

sound·ings /ˈsaundıŋz/ *n.* [plural] **1** careful or secret questions that you ask someone in order to find out what they think about something: *During the break, lawmakers spend time taking soundings from voters on various issues.* **2** measurements you make to find out how deep water is

sound·less /ˈsaundlıs/ *adj.* without any sound: *The rain had changed into a soundless light sprinkle.* —**soundlessly** *adv.*: *Hawks flew soundlessly above us.*

sound·ly /ˈsaundli/ *adv.* **1** if you sleep soundly, you sleep deeply and peacefully: *I slept soundly for the first time since I left Denver.* **2** completely or severely: *Our proposal was soundly rejected by the board.*

sound·proof[1] /ˈsaundpruf/ *adj.* a soundproof wall, room etc. is one that sound cannot pass through or into

soundproof² v. [T] to make something soundproof

sound sys·tem /'. ,../ n. [C] a very large STEREO system, especially one that includes the equipment a band needs to control its sound at a performance

sound·track /'saʊndtræk/ n. [C] **1** the recorded music from a movie **2** the part of a piece of film where the sound is recorded

sound wave /'. ./ n. [C] the form that sound takes when it travels

soup¹ /sup/ n. **1** liquid cooked food often containing small pieces of meat, fish, or vegetables: *tomato soup* **2 be in the soup** INFORMAL to be in trouble: *For now, his political career is in the soup.*

soup² v.

soup sth ↔ **up** phr. v. [T] INFORMAL to improve something by making it bigger, more attractive, or more exciting: *We spent half a year souping up my old Volkswagen Beetle.* —see also SOUPED-UP

soup·çon /sup'soʊn/ n. [singular] a small amount of something: *Caroline Goodall lends a soupçon of class to the role of Moira.*

souped-up /,. '.◄/ adj. a souped-up car or other machine has been made more powerful, especially by adding special parts to it: *a souped-up gray Chevy*

soup kitch·en /'. ,../ n. [C] a place where people with no money and no homes can get free food

soup spoon /'. ./ n. [C] a wide spoon that is used for eating soup

soup·y /'supi/ adj. INFORMAL having a thick liquid quality like soup: *The fine, powdery soil turned to soupy mud with the first heavy rains.*

sour¹ /saʊɚ/ adj. **1** having a sharp acid taste that stings your tongue, like the taste of a LEMON: *These cherries are really sour.* —compare BITTER (4), SWEET¹ (1) **2** milk or other food that is sour is not fresh and has a bad taste: *The milk smells a little sour.* | **turn/ go sour** (=become sour) **3** looking unfriendly or unhappy: *She always had the same sour expression.* —see also SOUR-FACED **4 sour grapes** DISAPPROVING the attitude of dislike or disrespect that someone has for something, when they want it but cannot have it: *Whatever I say about my ex-wife will probably sound like sour grapes.* **5 turn/go sour** INFORMAL if a relationship or plan turns or goes sour, it becomes less enjoyable, pleasant, or satisfactory: *We dated for two years and then things went sour.* —**sourly** adv. —**sourness** n. [U]

sour² v. [I,T] **1** if a relationship or someone's attitude sours, or if something sours it, it becomes unfriendly or unfavorable: *The incident soured relations between the two countries.* | [+ on] *Investors seem to have soured on the company.* **2** if milk sours or something sours it, it begins to have a bad taste because it is not fresh anymore

source¹ /sɔrs/ n. [C] **1** a thing, place, activity etc. that you get something from: *The sun is perhaps the least expensive energy source we have.* | [+ of] *Milk is a very good source of calcium.* | *Her waitress job is the family's only source of income.* **2** the cause of something, especially a problem, or the place where it starts: [+ of] *Richard's learning disability was a source of embarrassment for him.* | *Money is often a major source of tension for married couples.* **3** a person, book, or document that supplies you with information: *All of your sources have to be listed at the end of the paper.* | *A reliable source in the Justice Department confirmed the story.* **4** the place where a stream or river starts

source² v. [T] to find out where something can be obtained from

source code /'. ./ n. [U] TECHNICAL the original form a computer program is written in before it is changed into a form that a particular type of computer can read —compare MACHINE CODE

source lan·guage /'. ,../ n. [C usually singular] TECHNICAL the original language of something such as a document, from which it is to be translated —compare TARGET LANGUAGE

sour cream /,. './ n. [U] cream which has been made sour by adding a type of BACTERIA

sour·dough /'saʊɚdoʊ/ n. [U] uncooked DOUGH (=bread mixture) that is left to FERMENT¹ before being used to make bread: *sourdough bread*

sour-faced /,. '.◄/ adj. someone who is sour-faced looks unfriendly or unhappy: *sour-faced immigration officials*

sour·puss /'saʊɚpʊs/ n. [C] HUMOROUS someone who is always in a bad mood, complains a lot, and is never satisfied

sou·sa·phone /'suzəˌfoʊn/ n. [C] a very large musical instrument made of metal, which you blow into, used especially in marching bands

souse /saʊs/ v. [T] to put something in water or pour water over something, making it completely wet

soused /saʊst/ adj. INFORMAL drunk: *She was completely soused last night.*

south¹ /saʊθ/ n. [singular,U] **1** *written abbreviation* **S.** the direction toward the bottom of the world, that is on the right of someone facing the rising sun: *Which way is south?* | *Joel came up from the south for the holidays.* | *To the south of the art museum is the International Trade Center.* **2 the south** the southern part of a country, state etc.: *Her uncle runs a hotel in the south of Italy.* **3 the South** the southeastern part of the U.S.: *Don spent most of his childhood in the South.* **4 down South** in or to the south of a particular country, state etc., especially the southeastern part of the U.S.: *The recent fires down South have been causing crises in the major southern cities.* —compare **up North** (NORTH¹ (4)) —see Usage Note at NORTH¹

south² adj. **1** *written abbreviation* **S.** in, to, or facing the south: *Our office is located on the south side of the street.* | [+ of] *Hua Hin is about 120 miles south of Bangkok.* **2** a south wind comes from the south

south³ adv. **1** toward the south: *Go south on Highway 1 until you get to Monterey.* | *The window faces south.* **2 go south** INFORMAL if a situation, organization, or standard of quality goes south, it becomes very bad although it was once very good: *After four years, their relationship began to go south.*

South, the the southeastern states of the U.S. which were part of the Confederacy during the Civil War

South Af·ri·ca /,. '.../ a country at the southern end of Africa —**South African** n., adj.

South A·mer·i·ca /,. .'.../ n. one of the CONTINENTS which includes land south of the Caribbean Sea and north of Antarctica —**South American** n., adj.

south·bound /'saʊθbaʊnd/ adj., adv. traveling or leading toward the south: *southbound traffic* | *The car was driving southbound on Route 43.*

South Car·o·li·na /,saʊθ kærə'laɪnə/ *written abbreviation* **S.C.** a state in the southeast U.S.

South Da·ko·ta /,saʊθ də'koʊţə/ *written abbreviation* **S.D.** a state in the northern central U.S.

south·east¹ /,saʊθ'ist◄/ n. [U] **1** *written abbreviation* **S.E.** the direction that is exactly between south and east **2 the Southeast a)** the part of a country, state etc. that is in the southeast **b)** the area of the U.S. that can include the states of Alabama, Florida, Georgia, and South Carolina

southeast² adj. [only before noun] **1** *written abbreviation* **S.E.** in or from the southeast: *the southeast corner of the state* **2** a southeast wind comes from the southeast

southeast³ adv. [only before noun] toward the southeast: *a car driving southeast*

south·east·er /,saʊθ'istɚ/ n. [C] a strong wind or storm coming from the southeast

south·east·er·ly /,saʊθ'istɚli/ adj. **1** toward or in the southeast: *The rain front is moving in a southeasterly direction.* **2** a southeasterly wind comes from the southeast

south·east·ern /,saʊθ'istɚn/ adj. in or from the southeast part of a country

south·east·ward /,saʊθ'istwɚd/ adj. going toward the southeast: *His ranch is located a few miles southeastward from Pine Ridge.* —**southeastward** adv.

south·er·ly /ˈsʌðəli/ *adj.* **1** in or toward the south **2** a southerly wind comes from the south

south·ern /ˈsʌðən/ *adj.* in or from the south part of a country, state, etc.: *southern Mexico*

south·ern·er, southerner /ˈsʌðənə/ *n.* [C] someone who lives in or comes from the southern part of a country

southern hem·i·sphere /ˌ. ˈ.../ *n.* **the southern hemisphere** the half of the world that is south of the EQUATOR

Southern Lights /ˌ.. ˈ./ *n.* **the Southern Lights** bands of colored light in the night sky, seen in the most southern parts of the world such as Australia —compare NORTHERN LIGHTS

south·ern·most /ˈsʌðənmoʊst/ *adj.* furthest south: *Tierra del Fuego is the southernmost tip of South America.*

South Ko·re·a /ˌ. ˈ.../ a country in East Asia, west of Japan and east of China. It is officially called the Republic of Korea. —**South Korean** *n., adj.*

South Pa·cif·ic /ˌ. ˈ.../ *n.* **the South Pacific** the southern part of the Pacific Ocean where there are groups of islands, such as New Zealand and Polynesia

south·paw /ˈsaʊθpɔ/ *n.* [C] someone who uses their left hand more than their right hand, especially said about baseball PITCHERS and BOXERS

South Pole /ˌ. ˈ./ *n.* **the South Pole** the most southern point on the Earth's surface, and the land around it —see also MAGNETIC POLE, NORTH POLE

south·ward /ˈsaʊθwəd/ also **southwards** *adv.* toward the south: *The fleet turned and sailed southward.* —**southward** *adj.*: *the annual southward movement of icebergs*

south·west[1] /ˌsaʊθˈwest◂/ *n.* [U] **1** written abbreviation **S.W.** the direction that is exactly between south and west **2 the Southwest a)** the part of a country, state etc. that is in the southwest **b)** the area of the U.S. that can include the states of New Mexico, Arizona, Texas, California, Nevada, and sometimes Colorado and Utah

southwest[2] *adj.* **1** written abbreviation **S.W.** in or from the southwest: *the southwest part of the county* **2** a southwest wind comes from the southwest

southwest[3] *adv.* toward the southwest: *We were going southwest on the main highway.*

south·west·er /saʊθˈwestə/ *n.* [C] a strong wind or storm coming from the southwest

south·west·er·ly /saʊθˈwestəli/ *adj.* **1** in or toward the southwest **2** a southwesterly wind comes from the southwest

south·west·ern /ˌsaʊθˈwestən/ *adj.* in or from the southwest part of a country, state etc.: *southwestern Indiana*

south·west·ward /ˌsaʊθˈwestwəd/ also **southwestwards** *adv.* going or leading toward the southwest —**southwestward** *adj.*

sou·ve·nir /ˌsuvəˈnɪr, ˈsuvəˌnɪr/ *n.* [C] an object that you keep to remind yourself of a special occasion or a place you have visited: *a souvenir shop* | *souvenir T-shirts* | [+ **of**] *This towel is the only souvenir of Cancun that I bought.*

sou'west·er /saʊˈwestə/ *n.* [C] **1** a hat made of shiny material that keeps the rain off, with a wide piece at the back that covers your neck **2** INFORMAL a SOUTHWESTER

sov·er·eign[1] /ˈsavərɪn/ *n.* [C] **1** FORMAL a king or queen **2** a gold coin used in past times

sovereign[2] *adj.* **1** a sovereign country or state is independent and governs itself: *The U.S. said it could not negotiate on behalf of other sovereign states.* **2** having the highest power in a country: *the sovereign authority of the Supreme Court*

sove·reign·ty /ˈsavrənti/ *n.* [U] **1** complete freedom and power to govern: *the sovereignty of God* **2** the power that an independent country has to govern itself

So·vi·et /ˈsoʊviɪt, -viˌet/ *adj.* from or relating to the former U.S.S.R. (Soviet Union) or its people

Soviet Un·ion, the /ˌ... ˈ../ a country in Europe and Asia that existed from 1917 to 1991 and was the largest country in the world. It was officially called the Union of Soviet Socialist Republics, or U.S.S.R.

sow[1] /soʊ/ *v. past tense* **sowed** *past participle* **sown** or **sowed** [I,T] **1** to plant or scatter seeds on a piece of ground: *Seeds of these plants are sown in moist sand.* | [**sow sth with sth**] *One year they decided to sow the field with barley instead.* **2 sow the seeds of sth** to do something that will cause a bad situation in the future: *Through their greed and arrogance, they sowed the seeds of their own destruction.* **3 sow your wild oats** if a man sows his wild oats, he has sex with many different women, especially when he is young —**sower** *n.* [C] —see also **you reap what you sow** (REAP (3))

sow[2] /saʊ/ *n.* [C] a fully grown female pig —opposite BOAR —see also **you can't make a silk purse out of a sow's ear** (SILK (3))

sown /soʊn/ the past participle of sow

sox /saks/ *n.* [plural] NONSTANDARD another spelling of socks, used especially in advertising

soy /sɔɪ/ also **soy·a** /ˈsɔɪə/ *n.* [U] soy beans

soy bean /ˈ. ./ also **soya bean** /ˈ.. ./ *n.* [C] the bean of an Asian plant from which oil and food containing a lot of PROTEIN is produced

soy sauce /ˈ. ./ *n.* [U] a dark brown liquid that is used especially in Japanese and Chinese cooking

spa /spa/ *n.* [C] **1** also **health spa** a place where people go in order to improve their health, especially a place where the water has special minerals in it **2** a bath or pool that sends currents of hot water around you; JACUZZI

space[1] /speɪs/ *n.*
1 amount of space [U] the amount of an area, room, container etc. that is empty or available to be used: *We have enough space in the garage to put a washer.* | *Let's make space on the shelf for my books.* | *Leave enough space for the suitcases.* | *The large windows give the dining room a sense of space* (=a feeling that a room has lots of space).
2 area [C,U] an area, especially one used for a particular purpose: *a parking space* | **closet/cupboard/office** etc. **space** *They have around 6,500 square feet of office space.*
3 beyond Earth [U] the area beyond the Earth where the stars and PLANETs are: *space exploration* | *the icy blackness of outer space* (=the farthest areas of space)
4 between things [C] an empty area between two things, or between two parts of something; GAP: *The cat was in the space between the refrigerator and the wall.*
5 around all things [U] all of the area in which everything exists, and in which everything has a position or direction: *Now calculate the exact position in space where the two lines meet.* | *In Judaism, God is not restricted by time and space.*
6 in/during the space of sth within a particular period of time: *In the space of two years, about 30 people on his staff quit or were fired.*
7 a short space of time a short period of time: *5000 cars cannot be built in such a short space of time.*
8 empty land [C,U] land, or an area of land that has not been built on: *Much of the land will be preserved as open space.* | *the wide-open spaces of Australia*
9 freedom [U] the freedom to do what you want or to be alone when you need to: *Do you want me to go home and give you some space?*
10 in writing [C] **a)** an empty space between written or printed words, lines etc.: *Be sure to put two spaces between sentences.* **b)** the width of a TYPEd letter of the alphabet: *The word "the" takes up three spaces.* **c)** a place provided for you to write your name or other information on a document, piece of paper etc.: *Please write any comments in the space provided.*
11 in a newspaper [U] the amount of space in a

newspaper, magazine or book that is used for a particular subject: *The story got very little space in the
major newspapers.*
12 stare/look into space to look straight in front of
you without looking at anything in particular, usually because you are thinking: *I asked him a question, but he just sat there staring into space.* —see
also BREATHING SPACE —see Usage Note at PLACE[1]

s w **space²** *v.* **1** [T always + adv./prep.] to arrange
objects or events so that they have a particular
amount of space or time between them: *The three
injections are spaced several months apart.* | *evenly
spaced bulbs on the tunnel's inside walls* | **[space sth
out/along etc.]** *Neat rows of tall pines were spaced
along both sides of the street.* —see also DOUBLE-
SPACED, SINGLE-SPACED, SPACING **2** [I] also **space out**
INFORMAL to stop paying attention and just look in
front of you without thinking, especially because
you are bored or because you have taken drugs: *I
completely spaced out during the lecture.* —see also
SPACED-OUT

space-age /'. ./ *adj.* very modern: *space-age design*

space bar /'. ./ *n.* [C] the part at the bottom of a TYPE-
WRITER or KEYBOARD that you press to make a space

space ca·det /'. .,./ *n.* [C] INFORMAL someone who
forgets things, does not pay attention, and often
behaves strangely: *Jimmy's a total space cadet.*

space cap·sule /'. .,../ *n.* [C] the part of a spacecraft
that is designed to carry and protect people in space

space·craft /'speɪs-kræft/ *n.* [C] a vehicle that is able
to travel in space

spaced-out /,. '.◄/ also **spaced** *adj.* INFORMAL not
fully conscious of what is happening around you,
especially because you are extremely tired or
because you have taken drugs: *I was so spaced-out I
didn't even realize I'd left my wallet.* —see also **space
out** (SPACE² (2))

space heat·er /'. ,../ *n.* [C] a small machine for heating a room

space·man /'speɪsmæn, -mən/ *n. plural* **spacemen**
/-mɛn, -mən/ [C] **1** INFORMAL a man who travels into
space; ASTRONAUT **2** a creature from another world,
especially in children's stories

space probe /'. ./ *n.* [C] a SPACECRAFT without people
in it, that is sent into space to collect information
about the conditions there and send it back to Earth

space·ship /'speɪsˌʃɪp/ *n.* [C] a vehicle for carrying
people through space, especially in stories

space shut·tle /'. ,../ *n.* [C] a space vehicle that can
land like an airplane, so that it can be used more
than once

space sta·tion /'. ,../ *n.* [C] a place or vehicle in
space that is used as a base for people traveling in
space or for scientific tests

space·suit /'speɪs-sut/ *n.* [C] a special suit for wearing in space, that covers and protects your whole
body and provides an air supply

space-time con·tin·u·um /,. ,. .'.../ *n.* [U] TECH-
NICAL the universe considered as having four measurements: length, width, depth, and time

space·walk /'speɪswɔk/ *n.* [C] the act of moving
around outside a SPACECRAFT while in space, or the
time spent outside it

space·y /'speɪsi/ *adj.* INFORMAL behaving as though
you are not fully conscious of what is happening
around you: *Angela's kind of spacey, isn't she?*

spac·ing /'speɪsɪŋ/ *n.* [U] **1** the amount of space
between each printed letter, word, or line on a page:
single spacing/double spacing etc. (=the arrangement of lines of words on a page with no spaces, one
space etc. between them) —see also SPACE¹ (10) **2** the
amount of space or time between objects or events:
*The proper spacing of plants is critical for their
growth.* —see also SPACE¹ (4)

spa·cious /'speɪʃəs/ *adj.* a spacious house, room etc.
is large and has lots of space to move around in
—**spaciousness** *n.* [U]

spack·le /'spækəl/ *n.* [U] a substance used to fill
holes in walls, that becomes very hard when it dries
—**spackle** *v.* [I,T]

spade /speɪd/ *n.* [C] **1** a SHOVEL **2** a PLAYING CARD
belonging to the set of cards that have one or more
black shapes that look like pointed leaves printed on
them: *the queen of spades* **3 call a spade a spade** to
say exactly what you think is true, without trying to
be polite **4 in spades** INFORMAL to a great degree, or
in large amounts: *Beauty, love-of-life, wealth – Mary
had it all, in spades.* **5** TABOO, OLD-FASHIONED a person
with dark or black skin. Do not use this word.

spade·work /'speɪdwə˞k/ *n.* [U] hard work that has to
be done in preparation before something can
happen: *Most of the spadework in the research was
done by grad students.*

spa·ghet·ti /spə'gɛti/ *n.* [U] a type of PASTA in very s w
long thin pieces, that is cooked in boiling water
—compare MACARONI, TAGLIATELLE, VERMICELLI

spaghetti west·ern /.,.. '../ *n.* [C] a movie about
American COWBOYS, especially one made in Europe
by an Italian director during the 1960s and 1970s

Spain /speɪn/ a country in southwest Europe, between
France and Portugal —**Spanish** /'spænɪʃ/ *adj.*

spake /speɪk/ BIBLICAL OR POETIC a past tense of SPEAK

Spam /spæm/ *n.* [U] TRADEMARK a type of inexpensive
CANNED meat made mainly of PORK

spam /spæm/ *v.* **spammed, spamming** [I,T] DISAP-
PROVING to send the same computer message to many
different people, usually as a way of advertising
something —**spam** *n.* [U] —**spamming** *n.* [U]

span¹ /spæn/ *n.* [C] **1** a period of time between two
dates or events: *During a fifty-year span, Baldwin
produced close to ninety novels.* **2** the length of time
over which someone's attention, life etc. continues:
Shrimp have a life span of about one year. —see also
ATTENTION SPAN **3** the part of a bridge, ARCH¹ etc. that
goes across from one support to another, or the
bridge itself **4** the distance from one side of something to the other

span² *v.* **spanned, spanning** [T] **1** to include all of a
period of time: *Cecil Pickett's teaching career spanned
33 years.* **2** to include all of a particular space or
area: *The Mongol Empire spanned much of Central
Asia.* **3** if a bridge spans an area of water, it goes
from one side to the other

span³ a past tense of SPIN

Span·dex, spandex /'spændɛks/ *n.* [U] TRADEMARK a
type of stretchy material that fits tightly on your
body, especially used to make sports clothes

span·gle /'spæŋgəl/ *n.* [C] a small piece of shiny
metal or plastic sewn on to clothes to give them a
shining effect; SEQUIN

span·gled /'spæŋgəld/ *adj.* **1** covered with lights or
bright shapes: **[be spangled with sth]** *As night fell,
the city became spangled with lights.* | **star-spangled/
gold-spangled/sun-spangled etc.** (=covered in
bright stars, gold, sunlight etc.) **2** covered in span-
gles: *her spangled evening gown*

Spang·lish /'spæŋglɪʃ/ *n.* [U] INFORMAL a mixture of
the Spanish and English languages

Span·iard /'spænyə˞d/ *n.* [C] a Spanish person

span·iel /'spænyəl/ *n.* [C] a type of dog with long ears
that hang down —see also COCKER SPANIEL

Span·ish¹ /'spænɪʃ/ *adj.* from or relating to Spain

Spanish² *n.* [U] **1** the language of Spain and parts of
North, Central, and South America **2 the Spanish**
the people who live in Spain or are from Spain

Spanish fly /,.. '. ./ *n.* [U] a substance made from dried
insects, that is supposed to be an APHRODISIAC (=drug
causing sexual excitement)

spank /spæŋk/ *v.* [T] **1** to hit a child on his or her
BUTTOCKS as a punishment: *I often got spanked by
my parents.* **2** INFORMAL to defeat someone in a sport:
Arizona spanked Nevada 100–85. **3 spank the
monkey** SLANG if a man spanks the monkey, he MAS-
TURBATES

spank·ing¹ /'spæŋkɪŋ/ *n.* [C] the act of hitting a child
on his or her BUTTOCKS as a punishment: *If you do
that again, you're going to get a spanking!*

spanking[2] *adv.* INFORMAL **spanking new/clean etc.** very new, clean etc.: *a spanking new community center*

spar /spar/ *v.* **sparred, sparring** [I] **1** to practice BOXING with someone: *Foreman was cut over his right eye while sparring.* **2** to argue with someone especially in a pleasant, friendly way: *The two have sparred for months over the health bill.* —see also SPARRING MATCH, SPARRING PARTNER

spare[1] /sper/ *adj.*
1 additional **a spare key/battery/bulb etc.** a key, BATTERY etc. that you have in addition to the ones you normally use, so that it is available if another is needed
2 available not being used by anyone and available to be used: *We've got a spare sleeping bag that you can borrow.*
3 **spare time/moments** time when you are not working: *In his spare time, he volunteers at a homeless shelter.*
4 **spare change** coins that you do not need and can give to other people: *I need some spare change for the phone.*
5 plain a spare style of writing, painting etc. is plain or basic and uses nothing unnecessary: *the artist's spare use of color | a spare bass guitar line | a precise, spare style of writing*
6 thin tall and thin —see also SPARE ROOM, SPARE TIRE

spare[2] *v.*
1 give [T] if you can spare something, you let someone have or use it because you do not need it or are not using it: *I'm afraid we can't spare the staff. Everybody's busy right now. | [spare sb sth] Could you spare me a dollar or two?*
2 **money/time to spare** if you have time, money etc. to spare, there is some left in addition to what you have used or need: *Monica had arrived with time to spare, so she decided to have lunch.*
3 **spare sb the trouble/difficulty/pain etc. of (doing) sth** to prevent someone from having to do something difficult or upsetting: *I wanted to spare them the trouble of buying me a present.*
4 not damage or harm [T usually passive] to not damage or harm someone or something even though other people or things are being damaged, killed or destroyed: *Luckily, the hostages' lives were spared.*
5 **spare sb (the details)** to not tell someone all the details about something, because it is boring, it makes them angry etc.: *"They own three houses: one in the country, one in..." "Spare me."*
6 **spare no expense** to spend as much money as necessary to make something really good, even if it is a lot: *They spared no expense in building the library.*
7 **spare sb's feelings** to avoid doing something that would upset someone: *He destroyed parts of Diane's diary to spare the feelings of their children.*
8 **spare a thought for sb** to think about another person who is in a worse situation than you are: *We should spare a thought for those less fortunate.*
9 **spare the rod, spoil the child** OLD-FASHIONED used to say that if you do not SPANK (1) your child when he or she is bad, he or she will not learn how to behave well

spare[3] *n.* [C] **1** an additional thing of a particular kind that you keep so that it is available: *I brought two batteries just in case I needed a spare.* **2** a SPARE TIRE **3** a situation in BOWLING in which you knock down all the PINS (=bottle shaped objects) with a ball in two attempts —compare STRIKE[2] (5)

spare part /ˌ. ˈ./ *n.* [C] a new part for a vehicle or machine, that is used to replace a part that is damaged or broken

spare·ribs /ˈsperˌrɪbz/ *n.* [plural] the meat from the RIBS (=chest bones) of a pig, served on the bones as a meal

spare room /ˌ. ˈ./ *n.* [C] a BEDROOM in your house, that is kept for guests to use when they come to stay

spare tire /ˌ. ˈ./ *n.* [C] **1** an additional wheel with a tire on it, that you keep in a car for use if another tire gets damaged —see picture on page 427 **2** HUMOROUS a large area of fat around someone's waist

spar·ing·ly /ˈsperɪŋli/ *adv.* using or doing only a little of something: *Salt should be used sparingly in cooking. | Davis played sparingly during his freshman season.* —**sparing** *adj.*

spark[1] /spark/ *n.*
1 fire [C] a very small piece of brightly burning material produced by a fire or by hitting or rubbing two hard objects together: *A single spark could set the whole hillside on fire.*
2 electricity [C] a flash of light caused by electricity passing across a space: *A spark created by loose wires was the cause of the explosion.*
3 cause [C] a small action or event that quickly causes trouble or violence: *Tax cuts could be the spark for the troubled economy.*
4 intelligence/energy [U] a quality of intelligence or energy that makes someone successful or fun to be with: *Turner provided the team the spark they needed in the second half.*
5 **spark of interest/excitement/anger etc.** a small amount of a feeling or quality, or the beginning of a feeling or quality that could grow: *There was a spark of interest in Buck's eyes when I mentioned her name.*
6 sexual attraction [singular] a feeling of sexual attraction: *Jim is a really nice guy, but there's just no spark.*
7 **sparks fly** if sparks fly between two people, they argue angrily: *Sparks flew when Julia accused David of cheating.*

spark[2] *v.* **1** also **spark off** [T] to be the cause of trouble or violence: *The shootings have sparked a national debate over gun control.* **2** **spark (sb's) interest/hope/curiosity etc.** to make someone become interested in something, make someone feel hopeful, curious etc.: *Field trips could spark students' interest in science careers.* **3** to encourage someone to try harder to do something well, by doing it well yourself; INSPIRE: *USC was sparked by the aggressive play of Rich Jackson.* **4** [I] to produce sparks of fire or electricity: *Faulty wiring could have sparked the explosion.*

spar·kle[1] /ˈsparkəl/ *v.* [I] **1** to shine in small bright flashes: *The place sparkled with cleanliness.* **2** if someone's eyes sparkle, they shine brightly, especially because the person is happy or excited: [+ with] *Charlie's eyes sparkled with happiness.* —see also SPARKLING

spar·kle[2] *n.* [C,U] **1** a bright shiny appearance, with small points of flashing light **2** a quality that makes something seem interesting and full of life: *The movie has plenty of sparkle.*

spark·ler /ˈsparklɚ/ *n.* [C] a FIREWORK in the shape of a thin stick, that gives off SPARKs of fire as you hold it in your hand

spark·ling /ˈsparklɪŋ/ *adj.* **1** shining brightly with points of flashing light: *a sparkling lake* **2** a sparkling drink has BUBBLEs of gas in it: *sparkling apple juice* **3** full of life and intelligence: *a sparkling personality*

sparkling wine /ˌ.. ˈ./ *n.* [C,U] a white wine with a lot of BUBBLEs, such as CHAMPAGNE

spark plug /ˈ. ./ *n.* [C] a part in a car engine that produces an electric SPARK[1] (2) to make the mixture of gas and air start burning

sparring match /ˈ.. ˌ./ *n.* [C] a friendly argument that is not serious

sparring part·ner /ˈ.. ˌ../ *n.* [C] **1** someone you practice BOXING with **2** someone you regularly have friendly arguments with

spar·row /ˈspæroʊ/ *n.* [C] a small brown bird, very common in many parts of the world

sparse /spars/ *adj.* existing only in small amounts: *He combed back his sparse hair. | Information on the disease is sparse.* —**sparsely** *adv.*: *a sparsely populated area* —**sparseness** *n.* [U]

spar·tan /ˈspartn/ *adj.* spartan conditions or ways of living are simple and without any comfort: *a spartan apartment*

spasm /'spæzəm/ n. [C] **1** a sudden uncontrolled TIGHTENING of your muscles: *Grant missed Monday night's game due to back spasms.* **2 a spasm of grief/laughter/coughing etc.** a sudden strong feeling or reaction that continues for a short period

spas·mod·ic /spæz'mɑdɪk/ adj. **1** of or relating to a muscle spasm **2** happening for short irregular periods, not continuously: *Spasmodic displays of genius are evident in her music.* —**spasmodically** /-klɪ/ adv.

spas·tic /'spæstɪk/ adj. **1** an insulting word used to describe someone who drops things, falls easily etc. or becomes too excited or upset, used especially by children and considered offensive by some people **2** OLD-FASHIONED having CEREBRAL PALSY, a disease that prevents control of the muscles —**spastic** n. [C]

spat[1] /spæt/ the past tense and past participle of SPIT

spat[2] n. [C] **1** INFORMAL a short unimportant argument: *Walter said what happened between him and Marian was just a lovers' spat.* **2** [usually plural] one of a set of special pieces of cloth worn in past times over men's shoes and fastened with buttons

spate /speɪt/ n. **a spate of sth** a large number of similar things that happen in a short period of time, especially bad things: *Reports indicate a recent spate of gun attacks on troops.*

spa·tial /'speɪʃəl/ adj. relating to the position, size, shape etc. of things —**spatially** adv.

spat·ter /'spætɚ/ v. [I always + prep.,T] if liquid spatters on something or something spatters it, drops of it fall on or are thrown on the surface: *Blood spattered across the floor.* | [spatter sth on/over etc.] *Grease was spattered all over the counter.* | [spatter sb/sth with sth] *A passing truck spattered us with mud.* —**spatter** n. [C]

spat·u·la /'spætʃələ/ n. [C] **1** a kitchen tool with a wide flat part at the end of a long handle for lifting food out of a cooking pan **2** a tool with a wide flat part used for spreading and mixing things

spawn[1] /spɔn/ v. **1** [I,T] if a fish or FROG spawns it produces eggs in large quantities at the same time **2** [T] to make a series of things happen or start to exist: *The Arab-Israeli War of 1973 spawned the 1973 oil crisis.*

spawn[2] n. [U] the eggs of a fish, FROG etc. laid together in a soft mass

spay /speɪ/ v. **spays, spayed, spaying** [T] to remove part of the sex organs of a female animal so that it is not able to have babies —compare NEUTER[1]

spaz[1] /spæz/ n. [C] SLANG an insulting word for someone who drops things, falls easily etc. or becomes too excited or upset, used especially by children and considered offensive by some people

spaz[2] also **spaz out** v. **spazzes, spazzed, spazzing** [I] SLANG to become so upset or excited that it is difficult to become calm again, considered offensive by some people

S W
1 1 **speak** /spik/ v. past tense **spoke** past participle **spoken**
1 in conversation [I always + adv./prep.] to talk to someone about something or have a conversation: [+ to] *I haven't spoken to him since last Monday.* | [+ with] *The director would like to speak with you this afternoon.* | [+ of] *None of us ever heard her speak of the war again.* | [speak to/with sb about sth] *Have you spoken to Harriet about going out for lunch?* —see Usage Note at SAY[1]
2 say words [I] to use your voice to produce words: *She was too nervous to speak.* | [+ to] *John! Speak to me! Are you OK?*
3 a language [T not in progressive] to be able to speak a particular language: *Elaine speaks Spanish and Russian.* | *He doesn't speak a word of French* (=he doesn't speak French at all). | **French-speaking/Italian-speaking etc.** *a German-speaking secretary*
4 generally/personally/technically speaking used when you are expressing a general, personal etc. opinion: *Personally speaking, I don't like the way she dresses.*

5 formal speech [I] to make a formal speech: *Ambassador Simons has been asked to speak at the dinner.* | *Kendrick spoke in favor of* (=said things that showed he supports) *cutting taxes.* | *On several occasions, Mother Teresa spoke against* (=said things that showed she opposes) *abortion.* —see also SPEAKER
6 speak your mind to say exactly what you think about something, even when this might offend people: *Sam has never been shy about speaking his mind.*
7 sth speaks volumes used to say that something expresses a feeling or idea very clearly, without using words: *The look on his face spoke volumes about the amount of stress he was feeling.*
8 express ideas/opinions [I always + adv./prep.] to say something that expresses your ideas or opinions: *Dan speaks highly of* (=says good things about) *you.* | **speaking as a parent/teacher/democrat etc.** *Speaking as a citizen of the world, what happens in one country affects all countries.* | **speak well/badly/ill of sb** (=say good or bad things about someone)
9 not be on speaking terms also **not be speaking** if two people are not on speaking terms, they do not talk to each other, especially because they have argued: *The two brothers haven't been on speaking terms for years.*
10 speak out of turn to say something when you do not have the right or authority to say it: *Wagner spoke out of turn when he said the election would be delayed.*
11 speak with one voice if a group of people speak with one voice, they all express the same opinion
12 speak of the devil SPOKEN said when the person you have just been talking about arrives at the place where you are
13 no...to speak of also **nothing to speak of** used to say that something is not large or important enough to be mentioned or easily noticed: *Grace had no personality to speak of.* | *"Have you had any rain?" "Nothing to speak of."* —see also **so to speak** (SO[1] (7))

speak for phr. v. **1** [T **speak for** sb/sth] to express the feelings, thoughts, or beliefs of a person or group of people: *I speak for the families of this city in saying that we want better schools.* **2 speak for yourself** SPOKEN used to tell someone that you do not have the same opinion as they do: *"We're not interested in going to the game." "Hey, speak for yourself."* **3 speak for itself/themselves** to show something so clearly that no explanation is necessary: *He's a good coach – his success speaks for itself.* —see also **actions speak louder than words** (ACTION (15)), **in a manner of speaking** (MANNER (4)), **be spoken for** (SPOKEN[2] (2))

speak of sth phr. v. [T] LITERARY to show clearly that something happened or that it exists: *The lines on her face spoke of her frustration.*

speak out phr. v. [I] to publicly speak in protest about something, especially when protesting could be dangerous: [+ about/against] *Smith was not afraid to speak out against the Vietnam War.*

speak to sb/sth phr. v. [T] to talk to someone who has done something wrong, to tell them not to do it again: *Someone needs to speak to him about slamming the door.*

speak up phr. v. [I] **1** used to ask someone to speak louder: *Speak up, please, I can't hear you.* **2** to express your opinion freely and clearly: *If anyone is against the plan, now is the time to speak up.* **3 speak up for sb** to speak in support of someone: *You'll have to learn to speak up for yourself.*

-speak /spik/ suffix [in nouns] the special language or difficult words that are used in a particular business or activity: *computerspeak*

speak·eas·y /'spik,izi/ n. [C] a place in the U.S. in the 1920s and 1930s where you could buy alcohol illegally

speak·er /'spikɚ/ n. [C] **1** someone who makes a S W
speech, usually at a meeting: *Former President* 1 2
Carter will be the main speaker at the graduation. **2 a French speaker/English speaker etc.** someone who speaks French, English etc. **3** the part of a radio, record player, or sound system where the sound

comes out **4 the Speaker of the House** the politician who controls discussions in the House of Representatives in the U.S. Congress

spear[1] /spɪr/ n. [C] **1** a pole with a sharp pointed blade at one end, used as a weapon **2** a thin pointed stem of a plant, shaped like a spear: *asparagus spears*

spear[2] v. [T] **1** to push a pointed object, usually a fork, into something, so that you can pick it up **2** to push or throw a spear into someone or something, especially in order to kill them

spear·head[1] /'spɪrhed/ v. [T] to lead an attack or organized action: *Evita spearheaded legislation for compulsory public education.*

spearhead[2] n. [C usually singular] a person or group of people who lead an attack or organized action: *Moran was the spearhead of the valley's conservation movement.*

spear·mint /'spɪrmɪnt/ n. [U] **1** a fresh MINT[1] (2) taste, often used in sweets: *spearmint chewing gum* **2** the MINT plant that this taste comes from

spec /spek/ n. INFORMAL **1** [C usually plural] one of the details in the plan for how fast, large etc. something such as a building, car, or piece of electrical equipment should be: *Our CD-ROM drive is three times faster than the software specs require.* | **build/make sth to (sb's) spec(s)** (=build something exactly according to the details of the plan) **2 specs** [plural] GLASSES (4) to help you see **3 on spec** if you do something on spec, you do it without being sure that you will get what you are hoping for: *Families moved west, essentially, on spec.*

spe·cial[1] /'speʃəl/ adj. **1** not ordinary or usual, but different in some way and often better or more important: *A special committee was formed to study various bridge designs.* | *No special equipment is needed to install the heater.* | *We light the fireplace only on* **special occasions** (=important social events). | *This is* **a special edition** (=a special type of something produced only for a short time) *of Faulkner's first novel.* **2** particularly important to someone and deserving special attention, love etc.: *Jane's bringing a very special friend of hers to the party.* **3 a special offer** a low price charged for a product for a short time: *There's a special offer on potatoes this week.* **4** unusually good: *Ann's making her special spaghetti sauce.* **5** more than usual: *Special care was taken in selecting the best learning material for the students.* —see also **nothing special** (NOTHING[1] (9))

special[2] n. [C usually singular] **1** something that is not usual or ordinary, and is made or done for a special purpose: *We watched an interesting TV special on coyotes in Yellowstone Park.* **2** a lower price than usual for a particular product for a short period of time: *Today's lunch special is smoked salmon with rice.* | *Breyer's ice cream is* **on special** *this week.*

special a·gent /ˌ.. '../ n. [C] someone who works for the FBI

special de·liv·er·y /ˌ.. .'../ n. [C, U] a service that delivers a letter or package very quickly

special ed·u·ca·tion /ˌ.. ...'../ n. [U] the education of children who have particular physical problems or learning problems

special ef·fect /ˌ.. .'./ n. [C usually plural] an unusual image or sound in a movie or television program that has been produced artificially: *The only reason to see the movie is for the special effects.*

special forc·es /ˌ.. '../ n. [plural] soldiers who have been specially trained to fight against GUERRILLA or TERRORIST groups

special in·terest group /ˌ.. '.. ˌ./ n. [C] a group of people who all share the same aims

special in·terests /ˌ.. '../ n. [plural] special interest groups in general

spe·cial·ist /'speʃəlɪst/ n. [C] **1** someone who knows a lot about a particular subject, or is very skilled at it: [+ in] *a specialist in African politics* **2** a doctor who knows more about one particular type of illness or treatment than other doctors: *a cancer specialist*

spe·cial·ize /'speʃəˌlaɪz/ v. [I] to limit all or most of your study, business etc. to a particular subject or activity: [+ in] *The store specializes in interior design books.* —**specialization** /ˌspeʃələ'zeɪʃən/ n. [C,U]

spe·cial·ized /'speʃəˌlaɪzd/ adj. trained or made for a particular purpose or type of work: *Many of the employees receive specialized training in programing.* | *The agency helps businesses fill* **highly specialized** (=very specialized) *positions.* —opposite GENERAL[1]

spe·cial·ly /'speʃəli/ adv. **1** for one particular purpose, and only for that purpose: *The kayaks are specially designed for use in the ocean.* **2** SPOKEN: see ESPECIALLY: *We ordered pizza specially for you.*

special needs /ˌ.. './ n. [plural] needs that someone has because they have mental or physical problems: *Teachers are trained to help students with special needs.*

Special O·lym·pics In·ter·na·tion·al /ˌ.. .ˌ.. ..'.ˌ./ an organization that gives sports training to children and adults who have disabilities (DISABILITY) and organizes sports competitions for them

special school /'.. ˌ./ n. [C] a school for children with physical problems or problems with learning

spe·cial·ty /'speʃəlti/ n. plural **specialties** [C] **1** a type of food that is always very good in a particular area or restaurant: *Their specialty is prime rib.* | *They are the largest retailer of specialty coffee in North America.* **2** a subject or job that you know a lot about or have a lot of experience of: *Sports medicine is her specialty.*

spe·cies /'spiʃiz, -siz/ n. plural **species** [C] a group of animals or plants which are all similar and can breed together to produce young animals or plants of the same kind as them: *Many species of aquatic plants can exist in very little light.* —see also ENDANGERED SPECIES

spe·cif·ic[1] /spɪ'sɪfɪk/ adj. **1** [only before noun] a specific thing, person, or group is one particular thing, person, or group: *Rooney wouldn't comment on specific candidates for the job.* | *The Senate voted to ban nine specific models of assault weapons.* **2** detailed and exact: *Power plant employees must follow very specific safety guidelines.* | *Tauscher refused to be specific about his future plans.* **3 specific to sth** FORMAL limited to, or affecting, only one particular thing: *The conference is held to discuss issues specific to senior citizens.*

specific[2] n. **1 specifics** [plural] particular details that must be decided exactly: [+ of] *Dawson would not comment on the specifics of the lawsuit.* | *I don't want to* **go into specifics.** | **give/offer/discuss etc. specifics** *Representatives refused to give specifics of the company's strategy.* **2** [C] TECHNICAL a drug that has an effect only on one particular DISEASE

spe·cif·i·cally /spɪ'sɪfɪkli/ adv. **1** concerning or intended for one particular type of person or thing only: *Intel built the computer specifically for the movie.* **2** in a detailed or exact way: *Kerr said he specifically told employees to keep the door locked.* **3** [sentence adverb] used when you are adding more exact information: *We're talking about money – specifically, the money we need to repair our schools.*

spec·i·fi·ca·tion /ˌspesəfə'keɪʃən/ n. [C usually plural] a detailed instruction about how something should be designed or made: **build/manufacture/make sth to specifications** *Even their socks are manufactured to unique military specifications.*

specific grav·i·ty /ˌ.ˌ.. '../ n. [U] TECHNICAL the weight of a substance divided by the weight of the amount of water that would fill the same space

spe·ci·fy /'spesəˌfaɪ/ v. **specifies, specified, specifying** [T] to state something in an exact and explicit way: *The President did not specify a date for his visit to Peru.* | **[specify who/what/how etc.]** *He did not specify what surgery was required.* | **[specify that]** *A learner's permit specifies that the driver be accompanied by a licensed motorist.* —**specified** adj.: *Applications forms must be submitted before the specified deadline.*

spec·i·men /'spɛsəmən/ n. [C] **1** a small amount or piece of something that is taken from a plant or animal, so that it can be tested or examined: *a blood specimen* **2** a single example of something: *a very fine specimen of 12th century glass* **3** someone who has a very attractive or strong body, especially an ATHLETE: *Johnston is a 6-foot-2, 242-pound specimen from Syracuse University.*

spe·cious /'spiʃəs/ adj. FORMAL seeming to be true or correct, but actually false: *specious logic* —**speciously** adv. —**speciousness** n. [U]

speck /spɛk/ n. [C] a very small mark, spot, or piece of something: *There were a few specks of paint on the floor.*

speck·le /'spɛkəl/ n. [C] small marks or spots covering a background of a different color: *The eggs are covered with gray-brown speckles.*

speck·led /'spɛkəld/ adj. covered with many small marks or spots: *orange-speckled fish*

spec·ta·cle /'spɛktəkəl/ n. [C] **1 make a spectacle of yourself** to behave in an embarrassing way that is likely to make other people notice you and laugh at you: *Jody made a complete spectacle of herself by getting drunk at the wedding.* **2** a very impressive show or scene: *From our tent, we could see the grand spectacle of Mount Blue.* **3** [usually singular] an unusual thing or situation to be seen or noticed: *Seeing Hank in a dress was quite a spectacle.* **4 spectacles** [plural] OLD-FASHIONED GLASSES (4)

spec·tac·u·lar¹ /spɛk'tækyələ/ adj. **1** very impressive and exciting: *The view from the top floor is absolutely spectacular.* **2** unusually great or large: *Houston experienced spectacular growth after the Civil War.* —**spectacularly** adv.

spectacular² n. [C] an event or performance that is very large and impressive: *a television spectacular*

spec·tate /'spɛkteɪt/ v. [I] to watch a sports event

spec·ta·tor /'spɛkteɪtə/ n. [C] someone who is watching an event or game: *Spectators cheered and clapped as the ship came into the harbor.*

spectator sport /'... ,./ n. [C] a sport that people go and watch

spec·ter /'spɛktə/ n. [C] **1 the spectre of sth** something that people are afraid of because it may affect them soon: *The country now faces the specter of civil war.* **2** [C] LITERARY a GHOST

spec·tra /'spɛktrə/ the plural of SPECTRUM

spec·tral /'spɛktrəl/ adj. **1** TECHNICAL relating to or made by a SPECTRUM **2** LITERARY relating to or like a specter

spec·tro·scope /'spɛktrə,skoup/ n. [C] an instrument used for forming and looking at spectra (SPECTRUM (2)) —**spectroscopy** /spɛk'trɑskəpi/ n. [U] —**spectroscopic** /,spɛktrə'skɑpɪk/ adj.

spec·trum /'spɛktrəm/ n. plural **spectra** /-trə/ [C] **1** a complete range of opinions, ideas, situations etc., going from one extreme to its opposite: *People from across the religious spectrum are now working together.* | [+ of] *a wide spectrum of opinions* **2** the set of bands of colored light into which a beam of light can be separated by passing it through a PRISM **3** a complete range of radio, sound etc. waves: *the electromagnetic spectrum*

spec·u·late /'spɛkyə,leɪt/ v. **1** [I,T] to think or talk about the possible causes or effects of something without knowing all the facts or details: [+ on/about] *He didn't want speculate on who might have killed Maguire.* | [speculate that] *Scientists speculate that a giant asteroid hit Earth millions of years ago.* **2** [I] to buy goods, property, STOCK in a company etc. hoping that you will make a large profit when you sell them: [+ in] *Both men made their fortunes by speculating in real estate.* —**speculator** n. [C]

spec·u·la·tion /,spɛkyə'leɪʃən/ n. [C,U] **1** the act of guessing without knowing all the facts about something, or the guesses that you make: [+ about] *She*

would not comment on speculations about her running for Congress. | [speculation that] *There is speculation that he may have left the country.* | **pure/wild/idle speculation** (=speculation that is unlikely to be true) **2** the act of trying to make a profit by speculating (SPECULATE (2)): *In the last quarter, there has been a rise in bond speculation.*

spec·u·la·tive /'spɛkyələtɪv, -,leɪtɪv/ adj. **1** based on guessing, not on information or facts: *Descriptions of how this ancient tribe lived are speculative at best.* **2** bought or done in the hope of making a profit later: *speculative stocks* —**speculatively** adv.

sped /spɛd/ the past tense and past participle of SPEED

speech /spitʃ/ n. **1** [C] a talk, especially a formal one about a particular subject, given to a group of people: *a wedding speech* | **give/make/deliver a speech** *Cassidy gave a speech titled "The Future of Water Development."* **2** [U] the ability to speak: *Only humans are capable of speech.* | *Jerry's worked hard to overcome his* **speech impediment** (=a physical or nervous problem that affects your speech). **3** [U] spoken language rather than written language: *In speech we use a smaller vocabulary than in writing.* **4** [U] the particular way in which someone speaks: *Her speech was slow and distinct.* **5** [C] a set of lines that an actor must say in a play —see also DIRECT SPEECH, FIGURE OF SPEECH, **freedom of speech/religion etc.** (FREEDOM), INDIRECT SPEECH, PART OF SPEECH, REPORTED SPEECH

speech·i·fy /'spitʃə,faɪ/ v. [I] INFORMAL to make speeches in order to seem important: *The festival usually begins with local politicians taking turns speechifying.*

speech·less /'spitʃlɪs/ adj. unable to speak because you are so angry, upset, surprised etc.: [+ with] *Allen was pale and nearly speechless with hysterical fear.* | *The attorney's question* **left** the young witness **speechless** (=made the witness speechless). —**speechlessly** adv. —**speechlessness** n. [U]

speech syn·the·siz·er /'. ,.../ n. [C] a computer system that produces sounds like human speech

speech ther·a·py /'. ,.../ n. [U] treatment that helps people who have difficulty speaking correctly —**speech therapist** n. [C]

speech·writ·er /'spitʃ,raɪtə/ n. [C] someone who writes speeches for other people as their job

speed¹ /spid/ n.

1 of movement [C,U] how fast something moves or travels: *Watch your speed when the roads are wet.* | *The train can travel at* **a speed of** *110 mph.* | *The ferry* **has a top speed of** (=the fastest it can possibly go is) *25 mph.* | *No one can catch him when he's running* **at full speed** (=as fast as a person or thing to can move). | *We raced down the mountain at* **breakneck speed** (=dangerously fast). | *The rocks began to* **gather speed** (=gradually start to travel faster) *as they tumbled down the hillside.*

2 of action [U] the rate at which something happens or is done: *The speed of change in the region has stunned everyone.*

3 photography [C] **a)** the degree to which photographic film is sensitive to light **b)** the time it takes for a camera SHUTTER (2) to open and close: *a shutter speed of 1/250 second*

4 drug [U] SLANG an illegal drug that makes you very active; AMPHETAMINE

5 bring/get sb up to speed to give someone the information they need to understand what has been happening in a particular situation: *We need to bring everyone up to speed on the negotiations.*

6 speed demon HUMOROUS someone who drives a car, MOTORCYCLE etc. very fast —see also -SPEED

speed² v. past tense **sped** also **speeded 1** [I always + adv./prep.] to go quickly: [+ along/down/past etc.] *We stood back as the train sped through the station.* **2** [T always + adv./prep.] to take someone or something somewhere very quickly: [speed sb to/away/back etc.] *Security guards sped her to a waiting helicopter.* **3 be speeding** to be driving faster than the legal limit: *Rob swore he hadn't been speeding when the police stopped him.* —see also SPEEDING

speed by *phr. v.* [I] if time speeds by, it seems to pass very quickly: *The first week sped by, and suddenly we realized how little time we had left.*

speed up *phr. v.* [I,T] **speed** sth ↔ **up**] to move or happen faster or make something move or happen faster: *Speed up – we're going to be late.* | *Cruz hopes to speed up production by 5 percent.*

-speed /spid/ [in adjectives] **five-speed/ten-speed etc.** having five, ten etc. GEARS: *a five-speed transmission* —see also TEN-SPEED

speed-boat /'spidbout/ *n.* [C] a small boat with a powerful engine, designed to go fast

speed bump /'. ./ *n.* [C] a narrow raised part across a road that forces traffic to go slowly

speed di-al /'. ,../ also **speed di-al-ing** /'. ,.../ *n* [U] a special feature on a telephone that lets you DIAL someone's telephone number very quickly by pressing one button —**speed-dial** *v.* [I,T]

speed-ing /'spidɪŋ/ *n.* [U] the offense of driving faster than the law allows: *He's already gotten two tickets for speeding this year.*

speed lim-it /'. ,../ *n.* [C] the fastest speed allowed by law on a particular piece of road, water, railroad etc.: *The speed limit is 55 mph.*

speed-om-e-ter /spɪ'dɑmətɚ/ *n.* [C] an instrument in a vehicle that shows how fast it is going —see picture on page 427

speed read-ing /'. ,../ *n.* [U] the skill of reading very quickly

speed skat-ing /'. ,../ *n.* [U] the sport of racing on ice wearing ICE SKATES

speed-ster /'spidstɚ/ *n.* [C] **1** someone who drives or runs very fast **2** a car that is designed to go very fast: *Porsche's new speedster*

speed trap /'. ./ *n.* [C] a place on a road where police wait to catch drivers who are going too fast

speed-up /'spidʌp/ *n.* [C usually singular] an increase in the speed of something or the rate at which a process happens: [+ **in**] *a speedup in the economy*

speed-way /'spidweɪ/ *n.* [C] a special track that is used for racing MOTORCYCLES or cars as a sport

speed-y /'spidi/ *adj.* **speedier, speediest 1** happening or done quickly or without delay: *Everyone would like to see a speedy resolution to the conflict.* | *We hope you make a speedy recovery.* **2** a speedy car, boat etc. goes fast —**speedily** *adv.* —**speediness** *n.* [U]

spell[1] /spɛl/ *v.* **1** [I,T] to form a word by writing or naming the letters in order: *"How do you spell your name?" "S-M-I-T-H."* | *Excuse me, but my name is spelled wrong* (=not spelled correctly) *on the list.* **2** [T not in passive] if letters spell a word, they form it: *"B-O-O-K" spells "book."* **3 spell trouble/disaster/danger etc.** if a situation or action spells trouble, disaster, danger etc., it makes you expect trouble etc.: *A rise in the value of the dollar could spell trouble for overseas investments.*

spell sth ↔ **out** *phr. v.* [T] **1** to explain something clearly and in detail | **spell out how/what etc.** *At the press conference, Morgan spelled out how he would make the company profitable again.* **2** to show how a word is spelled by writing or saying the letters separately and in order: *"Could you spell your last name out for me?" "T-U-R-N-E-R."* **3** to write a word in its complete form instead of using an ABBREVIATION

spell[2] *n.* [C] **1** a piece of magic that someone does or the special words or ceremonies used in doing it: *The witch cast a spell on* (=did a piece of magic to change something about) *the young prince.* | *Only a kiss could break the spell* (=stop the spell from working). **2** a period of a particular type of activity, weather etc., usually a short period: *After a brief spell in the army, I returned to teaching.* | [+ **of**] *a spell of bad luck* | a **cold/wet/dry spell** *We had another cold spell last week.* **3** a power that attracts and influences you so strongly that it completely controls your feelings | **be/fall under sb's spell** *After college, Corinne fell under the spell of the cult's leader.* **4** a very short period of feeling sick: *I've had a few dizzy spells lately.*

spell-bind-ing /'spɛl,baɪndɪŋ/ *adj.* extremely interesting and holding your attention completely: *You'll especially enjoy the movie's spellbinding ending.* —**spellbinder** *n.* [C]

spell-bound /'spɛlbaʊnd/ *adj.* extremely interested in something you are listening to: *Stories of his trips to Asia held us spellbound for hours.*

spell-check-er /'. ,../ *n.* [C] a computer PROGRAM that checks what you have written and makes your spelling correct —**spell-check** *v.* [I,T]

spell-er /'spɛlɚ/ *n.* [C] **1 a good/bad/poor speller** someone who is good or bad at spelling words correctly **2** a book for teaching spelling

spell-ing /'spɛlɪŋ/ *n.* **1** [U] the act of spelling words correctly or the ability to do this: *Ben has always been good at spelling.* **2** [C] the way in which a word is spelled: *"Tyre" is the British spelling of "tire."*

spelling bee /'. ,../ *n.* [C] a competition for students in a school in which the winner is the one who spells the most words correctly

spe-lunk-ing /spɪ'lʌŋkɪŋ, 'spilʌŋk-/ *n.* [U] the sport of walking and climbing in CAVES —**spelunker** *n.* [C]

spend /spɛnd/ *v. past tense and past participle* **spent** **1** money [I,T] to use your money to buy goods or services: *I sat down and tried to figure out where I'd been spending all my money.* | [**spend sth on sth**] *More money should be spent on health and education.* | [**spend sth on sb**] *I spent eighty bucks on her* (=bought $80 worth of things for her), *and she didn't even say thank you!* | **spend $5/$10/$20 etc.** *I only want to spend about $20.* | *The $100 I used for my new shoes was money well spent* (=a sensible way of spending money). **2** time [T] to use time doing a particular thing or pass time in a particular place: *Mom spent most of the weekend cleaning up the house.* | *We spent the week in a dingy motel off Route 9.* | *It's good to see him spending more time with his wife.* **3 spend the night (at)** if a child spends the night at someone's house, they sleep at a friend's house for a night: *Mom, can Kyle spend the night tonight?* **4 spend the night with sb** to stay for the night and have sex with someone **5** effort [T] to use effort or energy to do something: *We spent a lot of energy looking for a nice apartment.*

spen-der /'spɛndɚ/ *n.* [C] someone who spends money: *The beach front hotels are perfect if you're a big spender* (=someone who likes to spend large amounts of money).

spend-ing /'spɛndɪŋ/ *n.* [U] the amount of money spent, especially by a government or organization, or the activity of spending money: **government/public/defense spending** *The city has increased public spending for repairing roads.*

spending mon-ey /'.. ,../ *n.* [U] money that you have available to spend on your own personal pleasure: *My parents give me $10 a week for spending money.*

spend-thrift /'spɛnd,θrɪft/ *n.* [C] someone who spends money carelessly, even when they do not have a lot of it

spent[1] /spɛnt/ the past tense and past participle of SPEND

spent[2] *adj.* **1** already used, and now empty or useless: *Spent bullet shells littered the ground.* **2 be a spent force** if a political idea or organization is a spent force, it does not have any power or influence anymore: *The Independent Party is commonly thought to be a spent force.* **3** LITERARY extremely tired

sperm /spɚm/ *n.* **1** [C] plural **sperm** or **sperms** a cell produced by the sex organs of a male animal, which is able to join with the female egg to produce a new life **2** [U] the liquid from the male sex organs that these cells swim in; SEMEN **3 sperm count** a medical measurement of the number of sperm a man has, which shows if he is able to make a woman PREGNANT

sper-ma-ce-ti /,spɚmə'siti, -'sɛ-/ *n.* [U] a solid oily substance found in the head of the SPERM WHALE and used in making skin creams, CANDLES etc.

sper·mat·o·zo·on /spəˌmætəˈzoʊɑn, -ˈzoʊən/ *n.* *plural* **spermatozoa** /-ˈzoʊə/ [C] TECHNICAL a sperm

sperm bank /ˈ. ./ *n.* [C] a place where SEMEN is kept to be used in medical operations that help women to become PREGNANT

sper·mi·cide /ˈspəməˌsaɪd/ *n.* [C,U] a cream or liquid that kills SPERM, used while having sex to prevent the woman from becoming PREGNANT —**spermicidal** /ˌspəməˈsaɪdl/ *adj.*: *spermicidal jelly*

sperm whale /ˈ. ./ *n.* [C] a large WHALE, hunted for its oil, fat, and SPERMACETI

spew /spyu/ *v.* **1** also **spew out/forth** [I always + adv./prep.,T] to flow out of something in quantities that are too large, or to make something, especially something unwanted, flow out in this way: [+ from/into/over etc.] *Black smoke spewed from the car's exhaust pipe.* | [**spew sth (out)**] *Burning coal spews huge amounts of carbon dioxide into the air.* **2** also **spew out/forth** [I always + adv./prep., T] to say a lot of bad or negative things very quickly: *Groups like these use the Internet to spew racial and religious hatred.* | *People are sick of candidates spewing out one-line political solutions.* **3** [I,T] SPOKEN to VOMIT

SPF Sun Protection Factor; a number on a bottle of SUNTAN cream that tells you how much protection it gives you from the sun: *SPF 25*

sphere /sfɪr/ *n.* [C] **1** something in the shape of a ball: *The Earth is not a **perfect sphere** (=it is not perfectly round).* —see picture at SHAPE[1] **2** a particular area of activity, work, knowledge etc.: *She has a good reputation in scientific spheres.* **3 sphere of influence** a person's, country's, organization's etc. sphere of influence is the area where they have power to change things: *By the end of 1946, spheres of influence in Europe were clearly drawn.*

-sphere /sfɪr/ *suffix* [in nouns] TECHNICAL relating to the air or gases surrounding the Earth: *the atmosphere*

spher·i·cal /ˈsfɪrɪkəl, ˈsfɛr-/ *adj.* having the shape of a sphere

sphe·roid /ˈsfɪrɔɪd/ *n.* [C] TECHNICAL a shape that is similar to a ball, but not perfectly round

sphinc·ter /ˈsfɪŋktə/ *n.* [C] TECHNICAL a muscle that surrounds an opening or passage in your body, and can become tight in order to close it: *the anal sphincter*

sphinx /sfɪŋks/ *n.* [C] an ancient Egyptian image of a lion with a human head, lying down

spic, spik /spɪk/ *n.* [C] TABOO a Spanish-speaking person. Do not use this word.

spic-and-span /ˌ. . ˈ./ *adj.* another spelling of SPICK-AND-SPAN

spice[1] /spaɪs/ *n.* **1** [C,U] one of the various types of powders or seeds that you put into food you are cooking to give it a special taste: *Add oregano and other Italian spices to the mixture.* **2** [singular,U] interest or excitement that is added to something: *Adding real-life drama can add spice to a high school history lesson.* —see also **variety is the spice of life** (VARIETY (5))

spice[2] also **spice up** *v.* [T] **1** to add spice to food: [+ with] *The sauce can be spiced up with a little chili powder.* **2** to add interest or excitement to something: *CBS spiced up its Monday night line-up with a new sexy drama.*

spick-and-span /ˌspɪk ən ˈspæn/ *adj.* a room, house etc. that is spick-and-span is completely clean and neat: *By the time I got home, Paul had the kitchen looking spick-and-span.*

spic·y /ˈspaɪsi/ *adj.* **spicier, spiciest** **1** food that is spicy has a pleasantly strong taste, and gives you a pleasant burning feeling in your mouth: *spicy Italian sausage* **2** a story or picture that is spicy is slightly shocking because it tells about or shows something

relating to sex: *The magazine published several spicy pictures of the actress at the beach.* —**spiciness** *n.* [U]

spi·der /ˈspaɪdə/ *n.* [C] a small creature with eight legs, which catches insects using a spiderweb

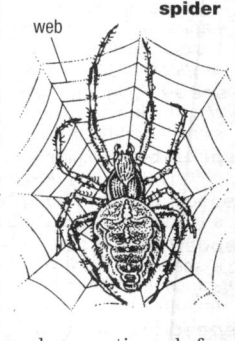

spider
web

spi·der·web /ˈspaɪdəˌwɛb/ also **web** *n.* [C] a very fine network of sticky threads made by a spider to catch insects —compare COBWEB

spi·der·y /ˈspaɪdəri/ *adj.* covered with or made of lots of long thin uneven lines: *spidery handwriting*

spiel /ʃpil, spil/ *n.* [C] IN-FORMAL fast talking that is intended to persuade people to buy something and that the speaker has used many times before: *She gave us a spiel about how the batteries couldn't leak and would last forever.*

Steven Spielberg

Spiel·berg /ˈspilbɔg/, **Ste·ven** /ˈstivən/ (1947–) a U.S. movie DIRECTOR

spif·fy /ˈspɪfi/ *adj.* INFORMAL looking new, neat, and attractive: *a spiffy blue pinstripe suit*

spig·ot /ˈspɪgət, ˈspɪkət/ *n.* [C] **1** an outdoor TAP[1] (1) **2** a TAP on a large container that controls the flow of liquid from it

spik /spɪk/ *n.* [C] another spelling of SPIC

spike[1] /spaɪk/ *n.* [C] **1** something long and thin with a sharp point, especially a pointed piece of metal: *A row of spikes lined the top of the wall.* **2 spikes** [plural] special sports shoes with metal points on the bottom that are worn by people who run races, play GOLF, or play baseball **3** a sudden large increase in the number or rate of something: *In the last six months, there has been a spike in unemployment.* **4** TECHNICAL a sharp point on a GRAPH which shows that the number or rate of something has increased quickly

spike[2] *v.* **1** [I] if the number or rate of something spikes, it increases quickly and by a large amount: *New telephone line orders have spiked in the last two years.* **2** [T] to add alcohol or a drug to what someone is drinking: [+ with] *Lab results confirmed that the lemonade had been spiked with rat poison.* **3** [T] to push a sharp tool or object into something: *Anti-logging activists often spike trees to prevent them from being cut down.* **4 spike the ball a)** to powerfully throw a football down on the ground to celebrate a TOUCHDOWN **b)** to powerfully hit a VOLLEYBALL down over the net

spik·y /ˈspaɪki/ *adj.* **1** hair that is spiky is stiff and stands up on top of your head **2** having long sharp points: *a spiky cactus*

spill[1] /spɪl/ *v.* past tense and past participle **spilled, spilt** **1** **liquid** [I,T] if you spill a liquid or if it spills, it accidentally flows over the edge of a container: *I almost spilled my coffee.* | [spill sth down/on/over] *Someone spilled beer on my shoe.* | [+ on/over etc.] *Oil had spilled onto the concrete.* **2** **people** [I always + adv./prep.] if people spill out of somewhere, they move out in large groups:

[**+ out/into/onto** etc.] *On summer nights, crowds of baseball fans spill into downtown.*

3 spill the beans SPOKEN to tell something that someone else wanted you to keep a secret: *Someone spilled the beans about Rick's surprise party.*

4 spill your guts SPOKEN to tell someone everything about your private life or about a personal secret: *Rob let Al talk until he finally spilled his guts about his affair with Louise.*

5 spill blood LITERARY to kill or wound people —see also **cry over spilled milk** (CRY[1] (6))

spill into/onto sth *phr. v.* [T] if light spills onto or into something, it shines through a window, door, hole etc. onto something else: *A shaft of light spilled onto the porch from the open doorway.*

spill over *phr. v.* [I] if a problem or bad situation spills over, it spreads and begins to affect other places, people etc.: [**+ into**] *The conflict in Rwanda eventually spilled over into Zaire.*

spill² *n.* [C] **1** an act of spilling something or an amount of something that is spilled: *It was the biggest oil spill in the country's history.* **2** a fall from a horse, bicycle etc.: *Tyler broke his arm when he took a spill on his motorcycle.* **3** a piece of wood or twisted paper for lighting lamps, fires etc.

spill·age /ˈspɪlɪdʒ/ *n.* [C,U] a SPILL² (1)

spill·o·ver /ˈspɪlˌoʊvɚ/ *n.* [C,U] the effect that one situation or problem has on another situation: *Not all of the violence in Miami was spillover from the trial.* | **a spillover effect/benefit/cost** *The crisis will have a spillover effect on other small banks.*

spill·way /ˈspɪlweɪ/ *n.* [C] a passage that lets water flow over or around a DAM (=wall for holding back water)

spilt /spɪlt/ a past tense and past participle of SPILL

spin¹ /spɪn/ *v. past tense and past participle* **spun**

1 turn around [I,T] to turn around and around very quickly, or to make something do this: *I sat back and watched the ceiling fan spin above me.* | *On the sidewalk, children took turns spinning a top.* | [**spin (sb/sth) around**] *Dobbs spun around with clenched fists, ready to fight.*

2 sb's head spins also **the room spins** if your head spins, you feel as if you might FAINT because you are shocked, excited, or drunk: *When I stood up, my head began to spin, but I managed to get to the phone.*

3 spin a yarn/story/tale to tell a story, especially using a lot of imagination: *On Saturdays, he's often in the coffee shop spinning yarns with other old-timers.*

4 insect [T] if a SPIDER or insect spins a WEB or COCOON, it produces thread to make it

5 wool/cotton [I,T] to make cotton, wool etc. into thread by twisting it: *The village has a reputation for spinning fine wool yarn.*

6 spin your wheels to try to do something without having any success: *I felt like I was just spinning my wheels trying to make him understand.*

7 drive [I always + adv./prep.] to drive or travel quickly: [**+ past/along** etc.] *The rock band's limousine spun past fans and reporters toward the hotel.*

spin sth ↔ **off** *phr. v.* [T] **1** to form a separate and partly independent company from parts of an existing company: *AT&T spun off Lucent Technology in the mid 1990s.* **2** to produce a new television program using characters from another program: *Producers have spun off only one successful show from "Cheers."* —see also SPIN-OFF

spin out *phr. v.* [I] if a car spins out, the driver loses control of it and the car spins around

spin² *n.*

1 turning [C] an act of turning around quickly: *Bicycle riders performed dangerous spins and flips off ramps and curved walls.*

2 car [C] INFORMAL a short trip in a car for pleasure: *Let's take your new car for a spin.*

3 ball [U] if you put spin on a ball in a game such as tennis or SOCCER, you deliberately make the ball turn very quickly so that it is difficult for your opponent to hit: *Seles puts a tremendous amount of spin on the ball when she serves.*

4 fall/go into a (flat) spin a) to become very confused and anxious: *The sudden fall on the*

stock-market sent brokers into a spin. **b)** if an aircraft goes into a spin it falls suddenly, turning around and around

5 politics/business [singular,U] the things someone, especially a politician or business person, tells people about a situation in order to influence the way people think: *Company representatives tried to put a positive spin on the lay-offs.* —see also SPIN CONTROL, SPIN DOCTOR

6 sb's attitude [singular,U] the way someone thinks about a particular subject or the attitude they have toward it; ANGLE: *Dickenson has her own spin on bringing up children, which is why she wrote the book.*

7 science [singular] a quality of an ELEMENTARY PARTICLE that influences its behavior with other particles

spi·na bif·i·da /ˌspaɪnə ˈbɪfədə/ *n.* [U] a serious condition in which a person's SPINE does not develop correctly before they are born, so that their SPINAL CORD is not protected

spin·ach /ˈspɪnɪtʃ/ *n.* [U] a vegetable with large dark green leaves

spi·nal /ˈspaɪnl/ *adj.* belonging to or affecting your SPINE (1): *spinal injuries*

spinal col·umn /ˈ.. ˌ../ *n.* [C] TECHNICAL your SPINE (1)

spinal cord /ˈ. ˌ./ *n.* [C] the thick string of nerves enclosed in your SPINE (1) by which messages are sent to and from your brain

spin con·trol /ˈ. ˌ./ *n.* [U] the act of describing a situation in politics or business so that the public has a particular opinion of it: *Carville was in charge of the election campaign's spin control.*

spin·dle /ˈspɪndl/ *n.* [C] **1** a part of a machine shaped like a stick, around which something turns **2** a round pointed stick used for twisting the thread when you are spinning wool

spin·dly /ˈspɪndli/ *adj.* long and thin in a way that looks weak: *spindly legs*

spin doc·tor /ˈ. ˌ../ *n.* [C] INFORMAL someone whose job is to give information to the public in a way that gives the best possible advantage to a politician or organization: *The senator's spin doctors are working overtime to explain away his recent lawsuit.*

spine /spaɪn/ *n.* [C] **1** the row of bones down the center of your back that supports your body and protects your SPINAL CORD —see picture at SKELETON **2** the part of a book that the pages are fastened onto **3** a stiff sharp point on an animal or plant: *Hedgehogs' backs are covered with stiff, sharp spines.*

spine-chill·ing /ˈ. ˌ../ *adj.* a spine-chilling story or film is very frightening in a way that people enjoy —**spine-chiller** *n.* [C]

spine·less /ˈspaɪnləs/ *adj.* **1** lacking courage and determination: *He's nothing but a spineless coward.* **2** without a spine: *spineless creatures such as jellyfish* —**spinelessly** *adv.* —**spinelessness** *n.* [U]

spin·et /ˈspɪnət/ *n.* [C] **1** a small UPRIGHT PIANO **2** a musical instrument of the 16th and 17th centuries, which is played like a piano

spine-tin·gling /ˈ. ˌ../ *adj.* making you feel very excited or frightened: *a spine-tingling movie*

spin·na·ker /ˈspɪnəkɚ/ *n.* [C] a sail with three points that is at the front of a boat, used when the wind is directly behind

spin·ner /ˈspɪnɚ/ *n.* [C] **1** someone whose job is to make thread by twisting cotton, wool etc. **2** a thing used for catching fish that moves around and around when pulled through the water

spin·ning /ˈspɪnɪŋ/ *n.* [U] a type of exercise in which a group of people ride EXERCISE BIKES together while they listen to music or a teacher

spinning jen·ny /ˈspɪnɪŋ ˌdʒɛni/ *n. plural* **spinning jennies** [C] an industrial machine used in past times for making cotton, wool etc. into thread

spinning wheel /ˈ.. ˌ./ *n.* [C] a simple machine consisting of a wheel on a frame that people used in their homes in past times for making cotton, wool etc. into thread

spin-off /'. ../ n. [C] **1** a television program involving characters that were previously in another program or movie: *"Frasier" was a spin-off from "Cheers."* **2** a separate and partly independent company that is formed from parts of an existing company, or the action of forming a company in this way —see also **spin** sth **off** (SPIN¹)

Spi·no·za /spɪ'nouzə/, **Ba·ruch** /bə'ruk/ (1632–1677) a Dutch PHILOSOPHER

spin·ster /'spɪnstɚ/ n. [C] OLD-FASHIONED an unmarried woman, usually one who is not young anymore and who seems unlikely to marry —**spinsterhood** n. [U]

spin the bot·tle /ˌ. . '../ n. [U] a game in which people sitting in a circle spin a bottle in the middle and when the bottle stops spinning and points to someone, that person must do something, such as kiss another person

spin·y /'spaɪni/ adj. **spinier, spiniest** having a lot of SPINES (3): *a spiny lobster*

spi·ral¹ /'spaɪrəl/ n. [C] **1** a line in the form of a curve that winds around a central point, moving farther away from the center all the time **2** a process, usually a harmful one, in which something gradually but continuously rises, falls, gets worse etc.: [+ **of**] *Clinton criticized the spiral of violence in the region.* | *The dollar's downward spiral seems to have stopped for now.* **3 inflationary spiral** a situation in which salaries and prices rise continuously because the level of INFLATION is high —**spiral** adj.

spiral² v. **spiraled, spiraling** also **spiralled, spiralling** [I] **1** [always + adv./prep.] to move in a continuous curve that gets nearer to or farther from its central point as it goes around: [+ **to/around etc.**] *The plane spiraled down till it hit the ocean.* **2** if a situation spirals, it gets worse, more violent etc. in a way that cannot be controlled: *The controversy has spiraled out of control.* **3** if debt or the cost of something spirals, it increases quickly in a way that cannot be controlled —**spiraling** adj.: *the spiraling cost of health care*

spiral note·book /ˌ.. '../ n. [C] a book made of plain pieces of paper that are attached to a metal spiral, which you can write notes in

spiral stair·case /ˌ.. '../ n. [C] a set of stairs arranged in a circular pattern so that they go around a central point as they get higher

spire /spaɪɚ/ n. [C] a roof that rises steeply to a point on top of a tower, especially on a church

spir·it¹ /'spɪrɪt/ n. [s w / 2 2]

1 character [singular,U] the qualities that make someone live the way they do, and make them different from other people: *I'm 85, but I still feel young in spirit.* | **a free/proud/wild etc. spirit** (=a particular type of character, or someone with this character)

2 soul [C] the part of someone that you cannot see, that consists of the qualities that make up their character, which many people believe continues to live after the person has died: *Burning the bodies is supposed to convince the spirits of the dead to go to the next world.* —compare SOUL (1)

3 no body [C] a creature without a physical body that some people believe exists, such as an ANGEL or a dead person who has returned to this world and has strange or magical powers: *Firecrackers are lit to scare off evil spirits.*

4 determination [U] APPROVING courage, energy, and determination: *I admire the team's fighting spirit.* | *Everything they did to us in the camps was designed to break our spirit* (=make us lose our courage and determination).

5 spirits [plural] the way someone feels at a particular time, for example if they are cheerful or sad: *Devon was sipping coffee and in good spirits.* | *At first it lifted our spirits to think someone would finally help us* (=made us feel happier and more

hopeful). | *She listens to the Ramones to keep her spirits up* (=avoid becoming less cheerful). | **be in high/low spirits** (=be excited and happy, or sad) | **sb's spirits lift/sink** (=someone becomes more or less cheerful)

6 attitude/feeling [singular] the attitude that you have toward something or while you are doing something: [+ **of**] *We need a new spirit of cooperation to solve the problems in this neighborhood.* | *There is a true spirit of hope among the people.*

7 time/place/group [C, usually singular] the set of ideas, beliefs, feelings etc. that are typical of a particular period in history, a place, or a group of people: [+ **of**] *The cookbook invokes the spirit of Sicily and southern Italy.* | **the spirit of the age/times** *Good art should represent the spirit of the times.*

8 team/community/public etc. spirit a strong feeling of belonging to a particular group and wanting to help them

9 drink [C usually plural] OLD-FASHIONED a strong alcoholic drink such as WHISKEY or BRANDY

10 get/enter into the spirit (of sth) to start to feel as happy, excited etc. as the people around you: *The children are making decorations to get into the spirit of the season.*

11 law/rule [U] the way a law or rule was intended to be used when it was written: *Gere's actions may not actually be illegal, but they have violated the spirit of the law.* —compare **the letter of the law** (LETTER¹ (4))

12 the Spirit the HOLY SPIRIT

13 in spirit you say you will be somewhere in spirit or with someone in spirit, when you cannot be with them but are thinking about them: *If I can't make it to the wedding, I'll be there in spirit.*

14 that's the spirit SPOKEN used to express approval of someone's behavior or attitude

15 the spirit is willing but the flesh is weak HUMOROUS used to say that you would like to do something, but are not strong enough, either physically or mentally, to do it

16 when/as the spirit moves you when you feel that you want to do something

spirit² v. [T] **spirit sb/sth away** also **spirit sb/sth off** to remove someone or something in a secret or mysterious way: *Rogers was spirited away from reporters by his aides.*

spir·it·ed /'spɪrɪtɪd/ adj. APPROVING having energy and determination, or showing this quality: *Anne is a spirited girl who wants to become a writer.* | **a spirited defense/debate etc.** *Grieg joined Maher last week in a spirited discussion of rodeos.*

-spirited /spɪrɪtɪd/ [in adjectives] **sweet-spirited/ tough-spirited/rebellious-spirited etc.** having a particular type of character —see also HIGH-SPIRITED, LOW-SPIRITED, MEAN-SPIRITED, PUBLIC-SPIRITED

spir·it·less /'spɪrɪtlɪs/ adj. **1** having no energy or determination **2** not cheerful: *spiritless celebrations* —**spiritlessness** n. [U]

spir·i·tu·al¹ /'spɪrɪtʃuəl, -tʃəl/ adj. [only before noun] [s w / 3] **1** relating to your spirit rather than to your body or mind: *In the 13th century Jalaludin Rumi wrote poetry about his spiritual life.* | *spiritual values* **2** relating to religion: *The decision was made by the spiritual leaders of the tribe.* **3 a spiritual home** a place where you feel you belong because you share the ideas and attitudes of that society —**spiritually** adv.

spiritual² n. [C] a religious song of the type sung originally by African-Americans

spir·i·tu·al·ism /'spɪrɪtʃu,lɪzəm/ n. [U] the belief that dead people may send messages to living people, usually through a MEDIUM (=someone with special powers) —**spiritualist** n. [C] —**spiritualistic** /ˌspɪrɪtʃə'lɪstɪk/ adj.

spir·i·tu·al·i·ty /ˌspɪrɪtʃu'æləti/ n. [U] the quality of being interested in religion or religious matters

spir·i·tu·ous /'spɪrɪtʃuəs/ adj. [only before noun] TECHNICAL containing alcohol

spit¹ /spɪt/ v. past tense and past participle **spit** or **spat** present participle **spitting**

1 liquid from your mouth [I] to force a small

amount of SALIVA (=the liquid in your mouth) out of your mouth: [+ at/on/into] *Somebody spit at me.* | *Eli, stop spitting on the floor.*
2 food/drink etc. [T] to force something out of your mouth: [**spit sth out**] *I tried a bite, but it was so bad, I spit it out.*
3 say sth [T] also **spit out** to say something quickly in a very angry way: *"You're worthless!" Greg spat out.*
4 small pieces [I,T] to send out small pieces of something, for example fire or hot oil, into the air: *The volcano began rumbling and spitting ash on July 3.*
5 cat [I] if a cat spits, it makes short, angry sounds

spit sth **up** *phr. v.* [I,T] **1** to bring food or drink up from your stomach out through your mouth; VOMIT: *The baby is always crying and spitting up.* **2 spit up blood** to cough so that blood comes out through your mouth, especially because you are injured or sick

spit² *n.* **1** [U] the watery liquid that is produced in your mouth; SALIVA **2** [C] a long thin stick that you put through meat so that you can turn it when cooking it over a fire **3** [C] a long narrow piece of land that sticks out into the ocean, a river etc. **4 spit and polish** INFORMAL the condition of having been thoroughly cleaned and polished

spit·ball /'spɪt'bɔl/ *n.* [C] a small piece of paper that children put in their mouths and then spit or throw at each other

spite¹ /spaɪt/ *n.* **1 in spite of sth** without being affected or prevented by something; DESPITE: *In spite of her success, Spencer continues to get depressed.* | *Kelly loved her husband in spite of the fact that he drank too much.* —see Usage Note at DESPITE **2** [U] a feeling of wanting to hurt or upset people for example because you are JEALOUS or think you have been unfairly treated: *Officials think he may be infecting others with the disease out of spite* (=because of spite). | **pure/ sheer spite** (=spite and nothing else) **3 in spite of yourself** if you do something in spite of yourself, you do it although you did not expect or intend to do it: *The picture made her laugh in spite of herself.*

spite² *v.* [T only in infinitive] to deliberately annoy or upset someone: *Now he's asking to keep the dog just to spite his ex-wife.* —see also **cut off your nose to spite your face** at **cut off** (CUT¹)

spite·ful /'spaɪtfəl/ *adj.* deliberately nasty to someone in order to hurt or upset them: *a spiteful liar* —**spitefully** *adv.* —**spitefulness** *n.* [U]

spit·fire /'spɪtfaɪr/ *n.* [C] someone, especially a woman, who becomes angry very easily

spitting im·age /,.. '../ *n.* **be the spitting image of sb** to look exactly like someone else

spit·tle /'spɪtl/ *n.* [U] SALIVA (=liquid from your mouth) that is outside your mouth

spit·toon /spɪ'tun/ *n.* [C] a container used to SPIT into

Spitz /spɪts/**, Mark** (1950–) a U.S. swimmer famous for winning seven GOLD MEDALS at the Olympic Games in Munich in 1972

splash¹ /splæʃ/ *v.* **1** [I] if a liquid splashes, it hits or falls on something and makes a noise: [+ against/ on/over] *Fat tears rolled down her cheeks and splashed on the paper.* **2** [T always + adv./prep.] to make someone or something wet with a lot of small drops of water or other liquid: [**splash sth on/over/ with etc. sth**] *Glen splashed cold water on his face before walking back into the restaurant.* **3** also **splash around** [I] to make water fly up in the air with a loud noise by hitting it or by moving around in it: *Maggie watched the children splash around in the pool.* **4** [T] INFORMAL if a newspaper splashes a story or picture over its pages, it prints it very large so that it is easy to notice

splash down *phr. v.* [I] if a SPACECRAFT splashes down, it deliberately lands in the ocean —see also SPLASHDOWN

splash

splash² *n.* [C] **1** the sound of a liquid hitting something or being moved around quickly: *I heard the splash of oars in the water.* **2** a mark made by a liquid splashing onto something else: *There were splashes of paint all over my clothes.* **3 make a splash** INFORMAL to do something that gets a lot of public attention: *Cameron Diaz made a big splash in "The Mask."* **4 a splash of color** a small area of a bright color **5** [usually singular] a small amount of liquid added to a drink or food: *Then add just a splash of lemon.*

splash·down /'splæʃdaʊn/ *n.* [C,U] a landing by a SPACECRAFT in the ocean

splash·y /'splæʃi/ *adj.* **splashier, splashiest** big, bright, or very easy to notice; FLASHY: *a splashy orange shirt*

splat¹ /splæt/ *n.* [singular] INFORMAL a noise like something wet hitting a surface hard

splat² *v.* **splatted, splatting** [I,T] to make a noise like something wet hitting a surface, or to make something make this noise: *Big fat raindrops started splatting on the windows.*

splat·ter /'splætɚ/ *v.* [I,T] to cover something with small drops of liquid: *Frank's shirt was splattered with blood.*

splay /spleɪ/ also **splay out** *v.* [I, T] if fingers or legs splay or are splayed, they spread farther apart, often in a way that looks strange: *Cows with the disease foam at the mouth and their legs splay out.*

splay-foot·ed /'. ,../ *adj.* having very flat wide feet

spleen /splin/ *n.* **1** [C] an organ near your stomach that controls the quality of your blood —see picture at DIGESTIVE SYSTEM **2** [U] FORMAL anger: *After reading the letter, he vented his spleen on* (=got angry with) *the nearest person available.*

splen·did /'splɛndɪd/ *adj.* FORMAL **1** excellent or very fine: *The troops are doing a splendid job of keeping the peace.* **2** beautiful and impressive: *a splendid view of the pyramids* —**splendidly** *adv.*: *The plan worked splendidly.*

splen·dif·er·ous /splɛn'dɪfərəs/ *adj.* INFORMAL, HUMOROUS splendid

splen·dor /'splɛndɚ/ *n.* [plural, U] impressive beauty and richness, or features that show this quality, especially in a large building or large place: *He showed us some of the splendors of Zimbabwe's landscape.* | *the splendor of imperial Rome*

sple·net·ic /splɪ'nɛtɪk/ *adj.* LITERARY often in a bad mood and angry

splice¹ /splaɪs/ *v.* [T] to join the ends of two pieces of rope, film etc. so that they form one continuous piece

splice² *n.* [C] the act of joining the ends of two things together, or the place where this connection has been made —see also COMMA SPLICE

splic·er /'splaɪsɚ/ *n.* [C] a machine for joining pieces of film or recording TAPE neatly together

splint /splɪnt/ *n.* [C] a flat piece of wood, metal etc., used for keeping a broken bone in position while it HEALS

splin·ter[1] /ˈsplɪntɚ/ n. [C] a small sharp piece of wood, glass, or metal, that has broken off a larger piece: *I've got a splinter in my finger.* | [+ of] *splinters of glass* —**splintery** adj. —compare SLIVER (1)

splinter[2] v. [I,T] **1** if something such as wood splinters, or you splinter it, it breaks into thin sharp pieces: *Ice storms splintered whole forests of trees in British Columbia.* **2** to separate into smaller groups or parts, or to make a large group or organization do this, especially because of a disagreement: *In the late 1980s the Communist party splintered into two factions.*

splinter group /ˈ.. ˌ./ also **splinter or·ga·ni·za·tion** /ˈ.. ..ˌ../ n. [C] a group of people that has separated from a political or religious organization because they have different ideas: *They are a hard-line conservative splinter group of the Republican Party.*

split[1] /splɪt/ v. past tense and past participle **split** present participle **splitting**

split

1 disagree [I,T] if a group of people splits or is split, it divides into two or more groups, because one group strongly disagrees with the other: *The debate over the use of military force has split legal scholars.* | [+ over/on] *Lawmakers split along party lines over the budget.* | [be split on/over sth] *The administration is split on the issue of nuclear disarmament.*

2 into parts [I,T] to divide or separate into different parts or groups, or to make something do this: [+ into] *Finally the corporation split into three smaller companies.* | [split sth into sth] *Ross split the department into ten teams to work on the project.*

3 break or tear [I,T] if something splits or if you split it, it tears or breaks along a straight line: [split (sth) down/across/along etc. sth] *Split the birds along the backbone before cooking.* | *After about 24 hours the seed coating splits open.* | split (sth) in two/half *The board had split in two.*

4 share [T] to divide something into separate parts, so that two or more people each get a part: [split sth with/between/among sb] *Do you want some of this sandwich? I'll split it with you.* | *Walton split his money among five family members.* | split the bill/cost *Automakers and the Energy department will split the cost of the program.* | split sth three/four etc. ways (=into three, four, or more equal parts)

5 injure [T] also **split open** to cut someone's head or lip, by hitting them: *His head was split open in the accident.*

6 leave [I] SLANG to leave quickly: *Those guys split about an hour ago.*

7 split the difference to agree on an amount that is exactly between two amounts that have been mentioned: *Their offer is only about $500 dollars less than we're asking, so we'll probably just split the difference.*

8 split hairs to argue that there is a difference between two things, when the difference is really too small to be important: *Let's stop splitting hairs and get back to the main issue.*

9 split your sides to laugh very hard

split off phr. v. **1** [I] to completely separate from a group: [+ from] *Lithuanian Communists voted to split off from the national party.* **2** [I,T] to break something away from something so that it is completely separate, or to break off in this way: *A large piece of the cliff split off and fell to the floor of the valley.*

split up phr. v. **1** [I] to end a marriage or relationship: *Marcia's parents split up when she was 13.* |

[+ with] *Taylor's splitting up with his wife.* **2** [I,T split sb/sth ↔ up] to divide into groups, or make someone or something do this: *Let's split up and meet back here in a half an hour.* | *The teacher split up the class into three groups.* **3** [T split sth ↔ up] to divide or separate something into different parts: *The article would be easier to read if you split it up into sections.*

split[2] n. [C] **1** a serious disagreement that divides an organization or group of people into smaller groups: *The new policy has led to a split in the armed forces.* **2** a long straight hole caused when something breaks or tears: *a split in the seam of his pants* **3** the part of something you receive when something, especially money, is shared: **a three-way/four-way etc. split** (=a share of something that is divided equally between three, four etc. people) **4** a difference between two things, ideas etc.: *There is a startling split between men's and women's views of sexual harassment.* **5** do the splits to spread your legs wide apart so that your legs touch the floor along their whole length —see also BANANA SPLIT, STOCK SPLIT

split ends /ˈ. ˈ./ n. [plural] a condition of someone's hair in which the ends have split into several parts

split in·fin·i·tive /ˌ. .ˈ.../ n. [C] a phrase in which you put an adverb or other word between "to" and an INFINITIVE, as in "to easily win." Some people think this is incorrect English.

split-lev·el /ˌ. ˈ../ adj. a split-level house, room, or building has floors at different heights in different parts

split pea /ˌ. ˈ.◂/ n. [C] a dried PEA split into its two halves

split per·son·al·i·ty /ˌ. ..ˈ.../ n. [C] NOT TECHNICAL a condition in which someone has two very different ways of behaving

split screen /ˌ. ˈ.◂/ n. [C] a method of showing two different scenes or pieces of information at the same time on a movie, television, or computer screen

split sec·ond /ˌ. ˈ../ n. **a split second** an extremely short period of time: *For a split second I thought we were going to crash.* —**split-second** adj.: *a split-second decision*

split shift /ˌ. ˈ./ n. [C] a period of work that is divided into two or more parts on the same day

split tick·et /ˌ. ˈ../ n. [C] a vote in U.S. elections in which the voter has voted for some CANDIDATES of one party and some of the other party —**split-ticket** adj.

split·ting /ˈsplɪtɪŋ/ adj. a splitting HEADACHE is very bad

splotch /splɑtʃ/ n. [C] INFORMAL a large mark with an irregular shape, for example of mud, paint etc.: *The french fries leave big greasy splotches on the paper bags they're served in.* —**splotchy** adj.

splurge /splɚdʒ/ v. [I] INFORMAL to spend more money than you can usually afford: *We splurged on an expensive hotel in Chicago.* —**splurge** n. [C]

splut·ter /ˈsplʌtɚ/ v. [I] to SPUTTER

Spock /spɑk/, **Dr. Benjamin** (1903–1998) a U.S. doctor whose books giving advice on how parents should take care of their children had a great influence on parents

spoil /spɔɪl/ v.

1 ruin sth [T] to have a bad effect on something, so that it is not attractive, enjoyable, useful etc. anymore: *It's too bad her good looks are spoiled by her nose.* | *One thoughtless comment spoiled the whole evening.* | *Mom got home early, which spoiled everything* (=completely ruined someone's plan).

2 food [I] to start to decay: *Most of the food in the refrigerator had spoiled.*

3 child [T] to give a child whatever they want or let them do what they want, with the result that they behave badly: *His grandparents spoil him rotten.*

4 treat kindly [T] to take care of or treat someone in a way that is too kind or generous: *Roses? You're spoiling me, Bill.* | **Spoil yourself** *and select the deluxe vacation package.*

5 always expect quality to provide someone with something very good, with the result that they always expect everything else to be as good *We've been spoiled by all the good restaurants around here.* **6** voting [T] to mark a BALLOT wrongly so that your vote is not included

7 be spoiling for a fight/argument to be very eager to fight or argue with someone —see also SPOILER, SPOILS —see Usage Note at DESTROY

spoil·age /'spɔɪlɪdʒ/ *n.* [U] TECHNICAL the process of food spoiling, or the condition of being spoiled

spoiled /spɔɪld/ *adj.* someone, especially a child, who is spoiled is impolite and behaves badly because they are always given what they want or allowed to do what they want: *Mary, you're just **a spoiled brat*** (=a spoiled annoying child). | *A lot of older people think the younger generation is **spoiled rotten*** (=very spoiled).

spoil·er /'spɔɪlɚ/ *n.* [C] **1** a raised part on a car that stops the car from lifting off the road at high speeds **2** a piece of an aircraft wing that can be lifted up to slow the airplane down **3** a person or team that spoils another's winning record **4** a book, article etc. that is produced to take attention away from another similar book and spoil its success

spoils /spɔɪlz/ *n.* [plural] **the spoils** FORMAL OR LITERARY **a)** things taken by an army from a defeated enemy, or things taken by thieves: *the spoils of war* **b)** profits or advantages gained through political power or through competition —see also **to the victor go/belong the spoils** (VICTOR (2))

spoil·sport /'spɔɪlspɔrt/ *n.* [C] INFORMAL someone who spoils other people's fun: *Don't be a spoilsport, Richard. Come play with us.*

spoils sys·tem /'. ,../ *n.* [C] a situation in which someone who has been elected to a government position gives jobs or advantages to their supporters

spoke¹ /spoʊk/ *v.* the past tense of SPEAK

spoke² *n.* [C] one of the thin metal bars that connect the outer ring of a wheel to the center, especially on a bicycle —see picture at BICYCLE¹

spok·en¹ /'spoʊkən/ *v.* the past participle of SPEAK

spoken² *adj.* **1 spoken language/word/English/Chinese etc.** the form of language that you speak rather than write **2 be spoken for a)** if someone is spoken for, they are married or already have a serious relationship with someone **b)** if something is spoken for, it is being kept for someone, so you cannot buy it or use it —see also SOFT-SPOKEN, WELL-SPOKEN

-spoken /spoʊkən/ *suffix* [in adjectives] speaking in a particular way: *a soft-spoken man* (=who speaks quietly)

spoken-word /,.. './ *adj.* relating to language that is spoken rather than written or sung: *Radner won a spoken-word award for her comedy album.*

spokes·man /'spoʊksmən/ *n.* plural **spokesmen** /-mən/ [C] someone, especially a man, who has been chosen to speak officially for a group, organization, or government: [+ **for**] *a spokesman for NASA*

spokes·per·son /'spoʊks,pɚsən/ *n.* plural **spokespeople** /-,pipəl/ [C] a spokesman or spokeswoman

spokes·wom·an /'spoʊks,wʊmən/ *n.* plural **spokeswomen** /-,wɪmɪn/ [C] a woman who has been chosen to speak officially for a group, organization, or government: *a hospital spokeswoman*

spo·li·a·tion /,spoʊli'eɪʃən/ *n.* [U] FORMAL the violent or deliberate destruction or spoiling of something: *the spoliation of the environment*

sponge¹ /spʌndʒ/ *n.* **1** [C,U] a piece of a soft natural or artificial substance that is full of small holes and is used for washing or cleaning something **2** [C] a simple sea creature from which natural sponge is produced **3** [C] a SPONGER

sponge² *v.* **1** [T] to wash something with a wet cloth or sponge: *When I opened my eyes, Polly was sponging my face and neck.* **2** [T always + adv./prep.] to put paint, a liquid etc. on a surface using a sponge: [**sponge sth on/over etc. sth**] *A second coat of paint is then sponged onto a wall that already has been painted.* **3** [T always + adv./prep.] to remove liquid or a mark with a wet cloth or sponge: [**sponge sth off/out/up**] *Spilled wine should be sponged up promptly with cold water.* **4** [I] to get money, free

meals etc. from other people, without doing anything for them: [+ **off**] *Pauly's been sponging off his friends for years.*

sponge bath /'. ./ *n.* [C] an act of washing your whole body with a wet cloth, usually when you cannot use a BATHTUB or SHOWER

sponge cake /'. ./ *n.* [C,U] a light cake made from eggs, sugar, and flour but usually no butter or oil

spong·er /'spʌndʒɚ/ *n.* [C] someone who gets money, free meals etc. from other people and does nothing for them in return

spong·y /'spʌndʒi/ *adj.* **spongier, spongiest** soft and full of holes that contain air or liquid like a SPONGE: *The earth was soft and spongy underfoot.* —**sponginess** *n.* [U]

spon·sor¹ /'spɑnsɚ/ *n.* [C] **1** a person or company that pays for a show, broadcast, sports event etc. in exchange for the right to advertise at that event: *If the show is too controversial, we'll lose our sponsors.* **2** someone who officially introduces or supports a proposal for a new law **3** someone who officially agrees to help someone else, or to be responsible for what they do: *You cannot get a work visa without an American sponsor.* **4** someone who agrees to give someone else money for a CHARITY if they walk, run, swim etc. a particular distance **5** a GODPARENT

sponsor² *v.* [T] **1** to give money to or pay for a sports event, show, broadcast etc., especially so that you can advertise your products at the event: *The race is being sponsored by the Traveler's Club.* **2** to officially support a proposal for a new law: *Baucus and Chafee sponsored the bill together.* **3** to agree to help someone or be responsible for what they do **4** to agree to give someone money for CHARITY if they walk, run, etc. a particular distance

spon·sor·ship /'spɑnsɚˌʃɪp/ *n.* [U] **1** support, usually financial support for an activity or event, often so that you can advertise at that event: *The tobacco industry's sponsorship of sporting events is controversial.* **2** an agreement to help someone or be responsible for what they do: *The government has tightened regulations for sponsorship of new immigrants.* **3** the condition of having officially introduced or supported a proposal for a new law

spon·ta·ne·i·ty /,spɑntə'neɪəti, ,spɑnt'n'eɪ-/ *n.* [U] the quality of being spontaneous: *Performing the show live gives it a spontaneity other programs lack.*

spon·ta·ne·ous /spɑn'teɪniəs/ *adj.* APPROVING **1** happening or done without being planned or organized: *The group was greeted by spontaneous applause.* **2** doing things when you want to, without planning or organizing them: *I'm trying to be more spontaneous.* —**spontaneously** *adv.* —**spontaneousness** *n.* [U]

spontaneous com·bus·tion /,..... '../ *n.* [U] burning caused by chemical changes inside something rather than by heat from outside

spoof /spuf/ *n.* [C] a funny book, play, movie etc. that copies a serious or important one and makes it seem silly: [+ **of/on**] *"Austin Powers" is a spoof on spy films of the '60s.* —**spoof** *v.* [T]

spook¹ /spuk/ *v.* [T] INFORMAL to frighten someone: *Something must have spooked the horses.*

spook² *n.* [C] INFORMAL **1** a GHOST **2** SLANG a SPY **3** TABOO someone with dark or black skin. Do not use this word.

spook·y /'spuki/ *adj.* **spookier, spookiest** INFORMAL strange or frightening, especially in a way that makes you think of GHOSTS: *a spooky old house* | *We think so much alike it's almost spooky.*

spool /spul/ *n.* [C] a small CYLINDER or object shaped like a small wheel that you wind thread, wire, TAPE, camera film etc. around

spoon¹ /spun/ *n.* [C] **1** a tool used for eating, cooking, or serving food, consisting of a small bowl-shaped part and a long handle —see picture on page 1368 **2** a SPOONFUL —see also **be born with a silver spoon in your mouth** (BORN (7)), GREASY SPOON, SOUP SPOON, WOODEN SPOON

spoons

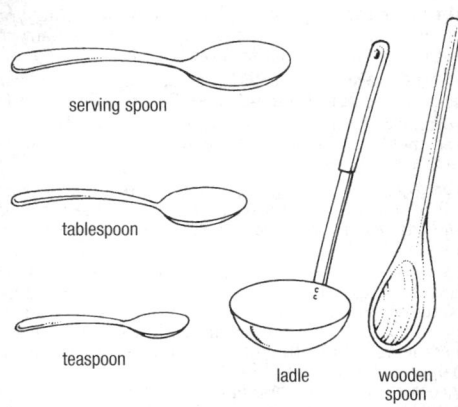

serving spoon

tablespoon

teaspoon

ladle

wooden spoon

spoon² *v.* [T] to pick up or move food with a spoon: [+ **into/on** etc.] *Spoon the rhubarb sauce over the chicken.* —see also SPOONING

spoon·bill /'spunbɪl/ *n.* [C] a type of large water bird with long legs and a long flat BILL

spoo·ner·ism /'spunə,rɪzəm/ *n.* [C] a phrase in which the speaker makes the mistake of exchanging the first sounds of two words, with a funny result, for example "sew you to a sheet" for "show you to a seat"

spoon-feed /'. ./ *v. past tense and past participle* **spoon-fed** [T] **1** to give too much information and help to someone: *Teachers should avoid spoon-feeding facts to students.* **2** to feed someone, especially a baby, with a spoon

spoon·ful /'spunfʊl/ *n.* [C] the amount that a SPOON will hold: [+ **of**] *a spoonful of sugar*

spoon·ing /'spunɪŋ/ *n.* [U] OLD-FASHIONED romantic behavior, especially kissing

spoor /spʊr, spɔr/ *n.* [C] the track of foot marks or FECES (=solid waste) left by a wild animal

spo·rad·ic /spə'rædɪk/ *adj.* happening often but not regularly or continuously; INTERMITTENT: *Sporadic gunfire continued through the night.* —**sporadically** /-kli/ *adv.*

spore /spɔr/ *n.* [C] a cell like a seed, produced by some simple living things such as MUSHROOMS or BACTERIA, which is able to develop into a new mushroom, bacterium etc.

spork /spɔrk/ *n.* [C] a plastic object shaped like a spoon but with points on the end like a fork, usually given to customers in FAST FOOD restaurants

sport¹ /spɔrt/ *n.*
1 games [C] a physical activity in which people compete against each other: *Soccer is Mark's favorite sport.* | *I've been **playing sports** all my life.* —see also SPECTATOR SPORT
2 outdoor activity [C] an outdoor activity such as hunting, fishing, HIKING etc. —see also BLOOD SPORT
3 cheerful person also **good sport** a helpful cheerful person who lets you enjoy yourself and never complains when there is trouble: *Minnie's been a real sport about all the houseguests.*
4 a good sport someone who can deal with defeat or being joked about without becoming angry or upset: *I don't like playing with him – he's not a very good sport.*
5 fun [U] FORMAL fun or amusement: *Lions are usually hunted **for sport**, not for food.* | *The press is having **great sport** with the latest scandal.*
6 boy SPOKEN, OLD-FASHIONED a friendly way of addressing a boy
7 make sport of sb FORMAL to joke about someone in a way that makes them seem stupid

8 the sport of kings horse racing —see also WATER SPORTS, WINTER SPORTS

sport² *v.* **1** to wear or show something publicly, especially in a proud way: *Will came back from his trip sporting a mustache and a beard.* **2** [I] LITERARY to play together happily: *Whales were spouting and sporting with each other.*

sport coat /'. ./ *n.* [C] a SPORTS JACKET

sport·fish·ing /'spɔrt,fɪʃɪŋ/ *n.* [U] the activity of fishing as a HOBBY, rather than a job

sport·ing /'spɔrtɪŋ/ *adj.* **1 a)** [only before noun] relating to sports: *The store sells clothes and **sporting goods** (=sports equipment).* | *a sporting event* **b)** relating to or joining in outdoor sports such as hunting or horse racing: *the sporting life* **2 a sporting chance** a fairly good chance of succeeding or winning: *Neil has a sporting chance of getting on the football team.*

spor·tive /'spɔrtɪv/ *adj.* LITERARY **1** enjoying fun and making jokes in a friendly way; PLAYFUL **2** interested in sports

sport jack·et /'. ,./ *n.* [C] a SPORTS JACKET

sports /spɔrts/ *adj.* [only before noun] **1** relating to sports or used for sports: *a sports tournament* | *sports equipment* **2** on the subject of sports: *Are you finished with **the sports section** (=part of a newspaper)?*

sports car /'. ./ *n.* [C] a low fast car, often with a roof that can be folded back

sports·cast /'spɔrts-kæst/ *n.* [C] a television broadcast of a sports game —**sportscaster** *n.* [C]

sports cen·ter /'. ,./ *n.* [C] a building where many different types of indoor sport are played

sports coat /'. ./ *n.* [C] a SPORTS JACKET

sports day /'. ./ *n.* [C] a FIELD DAY (2)

sport shirt /'. ./ *n.* [C] a SPORTS SHIRT

sports jack·et /'. ,./ *n.* [C] a man's comfortable JACKET, worn on informal occasions

sports·man /'spɔrtsmən/ *n. plural* **sportsmen** /-mən/ [C] a man who plays several different sports, especially outdoor sports —compare SPORTSWOMAN

sports·man·like /'spɔrtsmən,laɪk/ *adj.* behaving in a fair, honest, and polite way when competing in sports, or showing this quality: *a sportsmanlike game of basketball*

sports·man·ship /'spɔrtsmən,ʃɪp/ *n.* [U] behavior that is fair, honest and polite in a game or sports competition: **good/bad sportsmanship** *We try to teach the kids good sportsmanship.*

sports schol·ar·ship /'. ,../ *n.* [C] money given to some college students to pay for all or part of their education, because they are good enough to play for one of the college's sports teams

sports shirt /'. ./ *n.* [C] a shirt for men that is worn on informal occasions

sports·wear /'spɔrtswɛr/ *n.* [U] **1** clothes that are appropriate for informal occasions **2** clothes that are worn to play sports or when you are relaxing

sports·wom·an /'spɔrts,wʊmən/ *n. plural* **sportswomen** /-,wɪmɪn/ [C] a woman who plays many different sports, especially outdoor sports

sports·writ·er /'spɔrts,raɪtɚ/ *n.* [C] someone whose job is to write about sports for a newspaper or magazine

sport top /'. ./ *n.* [C] a special top that can be moved up and down to open or close a bottle, used especially on plastic bottles of drinking water

sport-u·til·i·ty ve·hi·cle /,. .'... ,../ *n.* [C] a type of vehicle that is bigger than a car and is made for traveling over rough ground

sport·y /'spɔrti/ *adj.* **sportier, sportiest** INFORMAL designed to look attractive in a bright informal way: *That's a sporty little car.* —**sportiness** *n.* [U]

spot¹ /spɑt/ *n.* [C]
1 place a particular place or area, especially a pleasant place where you spend time: *This looks like a good spot to stop and rest.* | *It took me about twenty minutes to find a parking spot.* | **the exact/very/same spot** *The church was built on the same spot*

where Juan had seen the Virgin. | **a camping/ swimming/vacation spot** (=a place that is suitable for a particular activity) —see Usage Note at POSITION[1]

2 [area] a usually round area on a surface, that is a different color or is rougher, smoother etc. than the rest: *Our cat is covered with big brown spots.* | *He has a bald spot on the top of his head.*

3 [mark] a small mark on something, especially one that is made by a liquid: *grease spots* | [+ of] *There were spots of blood on the rag.*

4 on the spot a) immediately, without careful planning: *They offered me a job on the spot.* **b)** at the place where something is happening: *The Americans did not have troops on the spot and could not control events.*

5 [position] a position in a competition or event: *Gabel's wins earned him a spot on the Olympic team.*

6 [advertisement] a short radio or television advertisement, especially one for a politician: *a 30-second spot on the local radio station*

7 [appearance] a short appearance on television, radio etc.: *Thomas's promotional tour included a guest spot on "The Tonight Show."*

8 [mark on skin] a small round red area on someone's skin that shows that they are sick: *a chickenpox spot*

9 [part] a particular part of a performance, a piece of writing etc.: *The essay is good, but a few spots still need some work.*

10 a bright spot something that is good in a bad situation: **the one/only bright spot** *The improved trade balance is the only bright spot in the economic report.*

11 put sb on the spot to try to make someone do something or answer a question when they do not want to, by making them feel embarrassed not to do it: *You shouldn't put friends on the spot by asking them to hire your family members.*

12 [situation] INFORMAL a difficult situation: *They put us in a very difficult spot by canceling at the last minute.* | **a tough/rough/difficult etc. spot** *There have already been a few rough spots for the new recycling company.*

13 [light] a SPOTLIGHT[1] (1)

14 a five-spot/ten-spot etc. SPOKEN, OLD-FASHIONED a piece of paper money worth five dollars, ten dollars etc. —see also BLIND SPOT, **a bright spot** (HIGH[1] (12)), **hit the spot** (HIT[1] (16)), **hot spot** (HOT (29)), **be rooted to the spot/chair/floor etc.** (ROOT[2] (4)), **have a soft spot for sb/sth** (SOFT (11)), TROUBLE SPOT, **a weak point/spot** (WEAK (11))

s w **spot[2]** v. [T] **1** to notice someone or something, especially when you are looking for them or when they are difficult to see: *They've spotted us – let's get out of here.* | [spot sb/sth doing sth] *I had just sat down to work when I spotted something moving in the trees.* | **be easy/hard/difficult to spot** *When Maria finally appeared in a blue cape, she wasn't hard to spot.* **2** to recognize the good or bad qualities in someone or something: *She quickly spotted the danger of relying on Hal for everything.* **3** to give the other player in a game an advantage: [spot sb sth] *He spotted me six points and he still won.* **4** to make sure that someone does not get hurt while they do an activity such as GYMNASTICS or WEIGHTLIFTING, by being there to help them move in the correct way if needed **5** to put small round marks on a surface, usually without intending to: *Drops of milk spotted the table.* —see also SPOTTED

spot[3] adj. TECHNICAL for buying or paying immediately, not at some future time: **spot price/sale etc.** *The spot price for crude oil went up 29 cents.*

spot check /ˈ. ./ n. [C] a quick examination of a few things or people from a group, to check whether everything is correct or satisfactory: *Customs officers make random spot checks.* —**spot-check** v. [I,T + for]

spot·less /ˈspɑtlɪs/ adj. **1** completely clean: *Mother always kept the house spotless.* **2 a spotless reputation/record/character** a completely honest and good character, or honest and good past behavior: *a spotless military record* —**spotlessly** adv. —**spotlessness** n. [U]

spot·light[1] /ˈspɑtlaɪt/ n. **1 a)** [C] a very powerful light whose beam can be directed at someone or something **b)** [C, usually singular] the round area of light made by this beam on the ground, stage etc.: *Johnson stepped into the spotlight to make his speech.* **2 the spotlight** attention that someone receives in the newspapers, on television etc.: *The glare of the media spotlight has made it very difficult for Dr. Ho to do his work.* | *Jones has found himself in the spotlight* (=receiving a lot of attention) *when he didn't want to be.* **3 shine/put/turn a spotlight on sth** to direct attention to something: *Watkins is shining a spotlight on his opponent's past mistakes.*

spotlight[2] v. past tense and past participle **spotlighted** or **spotlit** [T] **1** to direct attention to someone or something: *The article spotlights the growth of Islam in the U.S.* **2** to shine a strong beam of light on something

spot·ted /ˈspɑtɪd/ adj. [usually before noun] having small round marks on the surface: *a spotted dog* | [+ with] *The patio was spotted with bird droppings.*

spot·ter /ˈspɑtɚ/ n. [C] **1** someone whose job is to look for a particular thing or person: **weather/traffic/celebrity etc. spotter** *The National Weather Service relies on weather spotters for much of their information.* **2** someone who prevents someone else from getting hurt while they do an activity like GYMNASTICS or WEIGHTLIFTING, by being there to help them move correctly if needed —see also TREND-SPOTTER

spot·ty /ˈspɑti/ adj. **spottier, spottiest 1** good only in some parts, but not in others; PATCHY: *a spotty performance* **2** happening or done sometimes, but not as regularly as you expect: *spotty bus service* **3** covered with spots

spouse /spaʊs/ n. [C] FORMAL a husband or wife —**spousal** /ˈspaʊzəl/ adj.

spout[1] /spaʊt/ n. [C] **1** a small tube or pipe on a container that you pour liquid out through: *the spout of a teapot* **2** a sudden strong stream of liquid that comes out of somewhere very fast: [+ of] *The whale blew a spout of water into the air.* —see also WATERSPOUT

spout[2] v. **1 a)** [I always + adv./prep.] if liquid or fire spouts from somewhere, it comes out very quickly in a powerful stream: [+ from] *Oil continues to spout from the damaged well.* **b)** [T] to send out liquid or flames very quickly in a powerful stream: *The car's radiator was spouting out steam.* **2** [I,T] also **spout off** INFORMAL to talk a lot about something in a boring way, especially without thinking about what you are saying: [+ about] *I got a letter from some idiot spouting off about the work ethic.* | [spout sth (off)] *The singer sat on stage spouting his philosophy of life.* **3** [I] if a WHALE spouts, it sends out a stream of water from a hole in its head

sprain /spreɪn/ v. [T] to damage a joint in your body by suddenly twisting it: *Amy fell down and sprained her ankle.* —**sprain** n. [C]

sprang /spræŋ/ v. the past tense of SPRING

sprat /spræt/ n. [C] a small European HERRING

sprawl[1] /sprɔl/ v. [I always + adv./prep.] **1** also **sprawl out** to lie or sit with your arms or legs stretched out in a lazy or careless way: [+ in/on etc.] *J.D. was sprawled on the floor looking through her records.* **2 send sb sprawling** to hit or push someone so that they fall over in an uncontrolled way: *His slap sent her sprawling over the table.* **3** if buildings or a town sprawl, they spread out over a wide area in a messy and unattractive way: *The middle-class neighborhoods sprawl outward from the city center.*

sprawl[2] n. [U] **1** a large area of buildings that are spread out in a messy and unattractive way: *More freeways will just mean more urban sprawl.* **2** [singular] a position in which you have your arms or legs stretched out in a lazy or careless way

sprawl·ing /ˈsprɔlɪŋ/ adj. spreading over a wide area in a messy or unattractive way: *Mexico City is a sprawling city of more than 20 million inhabitants.*

spray

spray
can

S W
3

spray[1] /spreɪ/ v. **sprays, sprayed, spraying 1** [T] to make a liquid come out of a container, HOSE etc. in a stream of very small drops: [**spray sb/sth with sth**] *She was cleaning the porch by spraying it with water.* | [**spray sth on sb/sth**] *We took turns spraying insect repellent on the backs of each other's legs.* | **spray crops/plants etc.** (=cover them with liquid chemicals to protect them from insects or disease) **2** [I always + adv./prep.] if liquids or small pieces spray somewhere, they are quickly scattered through the air: [+ **over/around/from** etc.] *Grass cuttings sprayed from the mower.* **3 spray (sb/sth with) bullets/gunfire** to shoot many bullets from a gun quickly: *Someone went into the restaurant and started spraying people with bullets.*

S W
3

spray[2] n. plural **sprays 1** [C,U] liquid that is forced out of a special container in a stream of very small drops: *Get some **bug spray** (=spray used for killing insects) while you're at the store.* —see also HAIR SPRAY **2** [C] a can or other container with a special tube that forces liquid out in a stream of small drops: *Use pump sprays instead of aerosol sprays.* **3** [U] water in very small drops blown from the ocean or a wet surface: *During the storm, spray from the waves reached houses half a mile inland.* **4** [C] an attractive arrangement of flowers, jewels, or small branches used for decoration: [+ **of**] *a spray of irises* **5 a spray of bullets/dust etc.** a lot of very small objects or pieces moving quickly through the air **6** [C] liquid that an animal such as a SKUNK forces out of its body in very small drops, that usually has a strong smell —see also PEPPER SPRAY

spray bot·tle /'. ,../ n. [C] a bottle with a pump inside it and a special top that you press in order to make water or a liquid chemical come out of it

spray can /'. ./ n. [C] a can that keeps what is inside it under pressure so it can be sprayed out, used for substances such as paint, HAIR SPRAY, and cooking oil

spray·er /'spreɪɚ/ n. [C] a piece of equipment used for SPRAYing liquid, especially to protect crops from insects or disease

spray gun /'. ./ n. [C] a piece of equipment held like a gun, which SPRAYs liquid in very small drops

spray paint /'. ./ n. [U] paint that is SPRAYed from a can —**spray-paint** v. [I,T]

S W
2 2

spread[1] /spred/ v. past tense and past participle **spread**
1 open or arrange [T] also **spread out** to open something so that it covers a bigger area, or arrange a group of things so that they cover a flat surface: **spread sth on/over/ across etc. sth** *She spread the pages of the letter on the table.* | *After spreading her napkin over her lap, Alice began to eat.*
2 affect more people/places [I,T] to get bigger or worse and affect more people, places, or a larger area, or to make something do this: *The fire is spreading out of control.* | [+ **throughout/to/across** etc.] *It appears the cancer has spread to her bones.* | [**spread sth**] *He was a happy man who spread joy wherever he went.*
3 information/ideas a) [I] to become known about or used by people more and more: [+ **to/through/over** etc.] *Islam spread throughout northern Africa and parts of Asia.* | *Word spread that Mr. Casey's health was not good.* | *News of Polk's arrival spread like wildfire* (=became known very quickly). b) [T] to tell a lot of people about something: *Johnson is working to spread the word about how to prevent AIDS.* | **spread lies/rumors/gossip** *After they broke up, he spread nasty rumors about her.*
4 soft substance a) [T] to put a soft substance onto a surface in order to cover it: [**spread sth on/over sth**] *She spread the frosting evenly over the*
cake. | [**spread sth with sth**] *Spread the bread lightly with butter.* b) [I] to be soft enough to be put onto a surface in order to cover it: *If you warm up the butter it'll spread more easily.* —see picture on page 425
5 cover a large area a) [I always + adv./prep.] also **spread out** to cover or stretch over a large area: [+ **across/over** etc.] *The tables and chairs of the café spread across the plaza.* b) **be spread (out) across/over** etc. to exist or be present over a large area: *The ski resort is spread out over six mountains.*
6 people/plants/animals [I always + adv./prep.] to begin to live or grow in other areas or countries: [+ **throughout/over/to** etc.] *The hemp plant spread to India sometime before 800 B.C.*
7 **spread (out/apart) your legs/arms/fingers etc.** to push your legs, arms etc. as far apart as possible: *Cindy spread out her arms and turned slowly around.*
8 do sth gradually [T] also **spread out** to do something or make something happen gradually over a period of time: [**spread sth over sth**] *The various musical performances will be spread over three days.*
9 work/responsibility/money [T] to share work, responsibility, or money among several people: *Spreading the work around will help us meet the project deadline.* | *The city plans to spread the burden of new taxes as evenly as possible.*
10 **spread yourself too thin** to accept too many duties so you are always too busy: *I think Marge has been spreading herself a little too thin lately.*
11 expression [I always + adv./prep.] to gradually become noticeable on someone's face or mouth: [+ **across/over**] *A sly little smile spread across his lips.*
12 **spread 'em** SPOKEN used by police to tell someone to stand with their arms and legs wide apart so their bodies can be searched
13 **spread seeds/manure/fertilizer** to scatter seeds, MANURE etc. on the ground
14 **spread its wings** if a bird or insect spreads its wings, it opens them wide
15 **spread your wings** to start to have an independent life: *Recently she's begun spreading her wings, taking courses in real estate.*

spread out phr. v. **1** [I] if a group of people spread out, they move apart from each other so that they cover a wider area: *Before we start the exercises I want you all to spread out.* **2** [T **spread sth ↔ out**] to open something or arrange a group of things on a flat surface: [+ **on/over/across** etc.] *Edwin was studying the law books he had spread out on the dining room table.* | *Old women spread out their goods along the dusty road.* **3** [T **spread sth ↔ out**] to do something gradually over a period of time: *You can spread out the payments over a year.* **4** [I] to cover or stretch over a large area: *The rays of the sinking sun spread out across the horizon.*

spread[2] n.
1 the spread of sth the increase in the area or number of people affected by something, or in the number of people who do something: *We must work to prevent the spread of diseases such as malaria and cholera.* | *the spread of capitalism*
2 soft food [C,U] a soft food that you spread on bread: **cheese/chocolate etc. spread** (=cheese, chocolate etc. in a soft form)
3 large meal [C] INFORMAL a large meal for several guests on a special occasion: *There was a nice spread at the reception after the wedding.*
4 article/advertisement [C] a special article or advertisement in a newspaper or magazine: *There's a big three-page spread about them in Sunday's paper.*
5 cloth [C] a BEDSPREAD
6 farm [C] a large farm or RANCH
7 game [singular] the number of points between the SCORES of two opposing teams: *a four-point spread*
8 money TECHNICAL [singular] the difference between the buying price and the selling price of a SHARE on the STOCK EXCHANGE
9 hand/wings [U] the area covered when the fingers of a hand, or a bird's wings, are fully stretched
10 range [C, usually singular] a range of people, things, or numbers

11 a spread of land/water an area of land or water —see also **middle-aged spread** (MIDDLE-AGED (2))

spread-ea-gled /ˌsprɛd ˈiɡəld◂/ also **spread-eagle** adj. lying with arms and legs stretched out: *A fat young man lay spread-eagled on the floor.*

spread-sheet /ˈsprɛdʃit/ n. [C] **1** a type of computer PROGRAM that can show and calculate information about sales, taxes, profits etc. **2** an arrangement of this information in COLUMNS and rows, which can be printed out by the computer

spree /spri/ n. [C] a short period of time in which you do a lot of something that you enjoy, especially spending money or drinking alcohol: *Mom went on a shopping spree and bought three new outfits.* | **a buying/drinking/shooting etc. spree** *Tyson began his crime spree in 1978 by robbing a liquor store.*

sprig /sprɪɡ/ n. [C] a small stem or part of a branch with leaves or flowers on it: [+ of] *a sprig of parsley*

spright-ly /ˈspraɪtli/ adj. sprightlier, sprightliest **1** a sprightly person, especially an old person, is active and full of energy **2** done with a lot of energy: *a sprightly collection of songs* —**sprightliness** n [U]

s w
2 2
spring¹ /sprɪŋ/ n.
1 season [C,U] the season between winter and summer, when leaves and flowers appear: *spring flowers* | *The festival is usually held in the spring.* | *Ned and Mindy were married in the spring of 1997.* | *The store just opened this spring.* | **last/next spring** (=the spring before or after this spring)
2 water [C] a place where water comes up naturally from the ground: *The hot springs in the mountain smell of sulfur.*
3 piece of metal [C] something, usually a twisted piece of metal, that will return to its previous shape after it has been pressed down or pulled —see also BOX SPRING
4 bed/chair etc. [U] the ability of a chair, bed etc. to return to its normal shape after being pressed down: *There's not much spring left in this mattress.*
5 with a spring in sb's step if someone walks with a spring in their step, they move quickly and cheerfully
6 sudden jump [singular] a sudden quick movement or jump in a particular direction

spring² v. past tense **sprang** also **sprung** past participle **sprung**
1 move suddenly [I always + adv./prep.] to move suddenly and quickly in a particular direction, especially by jumping: [+out of / from / towards etc.] *Dobbs sprang off his bed with a look of terror.* | *Springing into the air, the puppy grabbed the leaf with its mouth.* | *Ward sprang to his feet* (=stood up suddenly) *when she entered the room.*

spring out
The cat sprang out of the bush.

2 move back [I always + adv./prep.] to move quickly back again after being pushed down or to the side: [+ back/up] *When it is cold, the rubber doesn't spring back after you press it.*
3 spring to mind if someone or something springs to mind, you immediately think of them: *"What do you think we should buy him?" "Nothing really springs to mind."*
4 spring into action also **spring to life** to suddenly become active: *Church members have sprung into action to save the school.*
5 spring open/shut to open or close suddenly and quickly: *As she turned the key, the door sprang open.*
6 expression/tears [I always + adv./prep.] to appear suddenly on someone's face or in their eyes: [+ into/to] *Tears sprang to his eyes.*
7 spring a leak if a boat or a container springs a leak, it begins to let liquid in or out through a crack or hole
8 spring into existence to suddenly begin to exist: *New businesses do not spring into existence just because taxes are reduced.*
9 spring to sb's defense to quickly defend someone

who is being criticized: *Pete sprang to Carla's defense.*
10 spring a trap a) if an animal springs a trap, it makes the trap move and catch it **b)** to make someone say or do something by tricking them
11 spring a surprise to make something unexpected or unusual happen
12 spring to attention if soldiers spring to attention, they stand suddenly upright
13 prison [T] INFORMAL to help someone leave prison or escape from there —see also **hope springs eternal** (HOPE² (6))
spring for sth phr. v. [T] INFORMAL to pay for something: *I'll spring for the beer tonight.*
spring from sth phr. v. [T] to be caused by something: *Everything I have achieved in my life springs from my faith in God.*
spring sth **on** sb phr. v. [T] to tell someone some news that surprises or shocks them: *I wish you wouldn't spring these things on me when I'm trying to get ready for work.*
spring up phr. v. [I] to suddenly appear or start to exist: *Several bars have sprung up on South Railroad Street.*

spring-board /ˈsprɪŋbɔrd/ n. [C] **1** something that helps you to start doing something, especially by giving you ideas about how to do it: [+ for] *He used his years in the Senate as a springboard for his presidential campaign.* **2** a strong board for jumping on or off, used when DIVING (2) or doing GYMNASTICS

spring-bok /ˈsprɪŋbɑk/ n. [C] a small DEER that can run fast and lives in South Africa

spring break /ˌ. ˈ./ n. [C] a vacation from school in the spring that is usually one or two weeks long

spring chick-en /ˌ. ˈ../ n. [C] **sb is no spring chicken** HUMOROUS used to say that someone is not young anymore

spring-clean-ing /ˌ. ˈ../ n. [U] the process of cleaning a house thoroughly, usually once a year: *It's great to do a little early spring-cleaning after the holidays.* —**spring-clean** v. [I,T]

spring-er span-iel /ˌsprɪŋɚ ˈspænyəl/ n. [C] a type of SPANIEL (=type of dog)

spring fe-ver /ˌ. ˈ../ n. [U] a sudden feeling of energy and a desire to do something new and exciting that you have in the spring

Spring-field /ˈsprɪŋfild/ the capital city of the U.S. state of Illinois

spring on-ion /ˌ. ˈ../ n. [C] a GREEN ONION

spring roll /ˈ. ./ n. [C] an EGG ROLL

spring tide /ˌ. ˈ./ n. [C] a large rise and fall in the level of the ocean at the time of the NEW MOON and the FULL MOON

spring-time /ˈsprɪŋtaɪm/ n. [U] the time of the year when it is spring

spring train-ing /ˌ. ˈ../ n. [U] the period during which a baseball team gets ready for competition

spring-y /ˈsprɪŋi/ adj. springier, springiest **1** something that is springy comes back to its former shape after being pressed or walked on: *The grass was springy and fresh-smelling.* | *springy curls* **2 a springy step/walk** a way of walking which is quick and full of energy

sprin-kle¹ /ˈsprɪŋkəl/ v. **1** [T] to scatter small drops of liquid or small pieces of something: [sprinkle sth on/over sth] *He had sprinkled rose petals on the bed.* | [sprinkle sb/sth with sth] *Sprinkle the mixture with water to keep it from drying out.* —see picture on page 425 **2** [T often passive] to put some jokes, phrases, objects etc. in every part of something, especially something such as a speech or piece of writing: *Reagan sprinkled his conversations with phrases from famous Americans.* | [be sprinkled with sth] *The Colca valley is sprinkled with ruins from the Huari culture.* **3 it is sprinkling** if it is sprinkling, it is raining lightly

sprinkle² n. [C] **1** small pieces of food, or a light

layer of these: *chocolate sprinkles* | *Add a sprinkle of coconut.* **2** a light rain

sprin·kler /'sprɪŋklɚ/ *n.* [C] **1** a piece of equipment with holes that is on the ground, used for scattering water on grass or soil **2** a piece of equipment with holes that is on a ceiling and scatters water if there is a fire

sprin·kling /'sprɪŋklɪŋ/ *n.* **a sprinkling of sth** a small quantity or amount of something: *There was a sprinkling of freckles across her cheeks.*

sprint¹ /sprɪnt/ *v.* [I] to run very fast for a short distance: [+ **along/across/up** etc.] *Lewis sprinted across the finish line.*

sprint² *n.* **1** [singular] a short period of running very fast **2** [C] a short race in which runners run very fast, swimmers swim very fast etc. over a short distance: *a 200-meter sprint*

sprint·er /'sprɪntɚ/ *n.* [C] someone who runs in fast races over short distances

sprite /spraɪt/ *n.* [C] a FAIRY, especially one who is graceful or who likes playing tricks on people

spritz /sprɪts/ *v.* [T] to SPRAY a liquid in short bursts: *She spritzes her throat backstage to help her voice.* —**spritz** *n.* [C] *a spritz of perfume*

spritz·er /'sprɪtsɚ/ *n.* [C,U] a drink made with SODA WATER and white wine

sprock·et /'sprɑkɪt/ *n.* [C] **1** also **sprocket wheel** a wheel with a row of teeth (TOOTH (2)) that fit into and turn something such as a bicycle chain or a photographic film with holes **2** one of the teeth on a wheel of this kind

sprout¹ /spraʊt/ *v.* **1** [I] if leaves or BUDS sprout, they appear and begin to grow **2** [I,T] if vegetables, seeds, or plants sprout, they start to grow, producing SHOOTS, or BUDS: *Weeds are starting to sprout through cracks in the sidewalk.* | [**sprout sth**] *Plants grown underwater never sprout leaves above the surface of the water.* **3** [I + adv./prep.] also **sprout up** to appear suddenly in large numbers: [+ **in/through-out**] *After World War II, suburbs sprouted up all over America.* **4** [I,T] to grow suddenly, or grow something suddenly, especially hair, horns, or wings: *Jim seemed to have sprouted a beard overnight.*

sprout² *n.* [C] **1** [usually plural] an ALFALFA seed that has grown a short stem and is eaten **2** a BEAN SPROUT **3** a new growth on a plant; SHOOT **4** a BRUS-SELS SPROUT

spruce¹ /sprus/ *n.* [C,U] a tree that grows in northern countries and has short leaves shaped like needles

spruce² *v.*

spruce up *phr. v.* [I,T **spruce sb/sth ↔ up**] INFORMAL to make yourself or something look neater and cleaner: *I'll just go upstairs and spruce up a bit before dinner.* | *The article gives some suggestions on how to spruce up your house.*

sprung /sprʌŋ/ *v.* a past tense and the past participle of SPRING

spry /spraɪ/ *adj.* **sprier, spriest** or **spryer, spryest** a spry old person is active and cheerful: *a spry silver-haired grandmother* —**spryly** *adv.*

spud /spʌd/ *n.* [C] INFORMAL a POTATO

spume /spyum/ *n.* [U] LITERARY a type of FOAM that forms on the top of waves when the ocean is rough

spun /spʌn/ *v.* the past tense and past participle of SPIN

spunk /spʌŋk/ *n.* [U] INFORMAL the quality of being brave and determined and having a lot of energy: *Erma's got a lot of spunk.* —**spunky** *adj.*

spur¹ /spɚ/ *n.* [C]
1 on a boot a sharp pointed object on the heel of a rider's boot which is used to encourage a horse to go faster
2 on the spur of the moment without planning ahead of time: *On the spur of the moment, she decided to enter the race that she had come to watch.* —see also SPUR-OF-THE-MOMENT
3 influence a fact or event that makes you try

harder to do something: *The desire to make a profit has always been a spur to expanded trade.*
4 railroad a railroad track or road that goes away from a main line or road
5 bone a short piece of bone that grows out inside a part of your foot or body where it should not: *a small bone spur in the right shoulder*
6 land a piece of high ground that sticks out from the side of a hill or mountain
7 chicken the stiff sharp part that sticks out from the back of a male chicken's leg

spur² *v.* **spurred, spurring** **1** [T] to make an improvement or change happen faster: *Lower taxes would spur investment and help economic growth.* **2** [T] also **spur on** to encourage someone to try harder in order to succeed: [**spur sb (on) to (do) sth**] *Their criticism actually spurred the young watchmaker to work harder.* | *The thought of losing our house was enough to spur me into action* (=make me start doing something). **3** [I,T] to encourage a horse to go faster, especially by kicking it with the spurs on your boots

spu·ri·ous /'spyʊriəs/ *adj.* **1** a spurious statement, argument etc. is not based on facts or good reasoning and is likely to be incorrect: *A jury has rejected the spurious claim that the police created evidence.* **2** insincere: *a spurious smile* —**spuriously** *adv.* —**spuriousness** *n.* [U]

spurn /spɚn/ *v.* [T] LITERARY to refuse to accept something or to have a relationship with someone, especially because you think you are better than they are: *When she spurned his advances, he started to stalk her.*

spur-of-the-mo·ment /ˌ. . . '...ɪ/ *adj.* [only before noun] a spur-of-the-moment decision or action is made or done suddenly without planning it

spurt¹ /spɚt/ *v.* **1** [I] if liquid, flames etc. spurt from something, they pour out of it quickly and suddenly and with force: [+ **from/out of**] *Blood spurted from the wound.* **2** [T] to send out liquid, flames etc. up: *The volcano spurted sulfur miles into the atmosphere.* **3** [I always + adv./prep.] to move forward or up very quickly

spurt² *n.* [C] **1** a stream of liquid, flames etc. that comes out of something suddenly and with force: [+ **of**] *The whale headed for the other side of the pool with a spurt of his blow hole.* **2** a short sudden increase of activity, effort, or speed: *a growth spurt* | [+ **of**] *a spurt of rapid inflation* **3 in spurts** if something happens or is done in spurts, it happens suddenly and for short periods of time: *The rain was light and came in spurts.*

sput·ter /'spʌtɚ/ *v.* **1** [I] to make several quick soft sounds, with no sound in between: *The engine sputtered and died.* **2** [I,T] to talk quickly in short confused phrases, especially because you are angry or shocked: *Solano sputtered that there must be some mistake.* **3** [I] also **sputter along** if a system, team, machine etc. sputters, it does not work very effectively: *The country's transition to democracy continues to sputter along.*

spu·tum /'spyutəm/ *n.* [U] TECHNICAL liquid in your mouth which you have coughed up from your lungs

spy¹ /spaɪ/ *n. plural* **spies** [C] someone whose job it is to find out secret information about another country, organization, or group: *an enemy spy*

spy² *v.* **spies, spied, spying** **1** [I] to secretly collect information about an enemy country or an organization you are competing against: [+ **for**] *The three men were accused of having spied for the Soviet Union.* **2 spy on sb** to watch someone secretly: *You mean all this time you've been spying on me?* **3** [T] LITERARY to suddenly see someone or something, especially after searching for them: *I spied him standing on the other side of the room.* —**spying** *n.* [U]

spy sth ↔ **out** *phr. v.* [T] **1** to secretly find out information about something **2 spy out the land** to secretly find out more information about a situation before deciding what to do

spy·glass /'spaɪglæs/ *n.* [C] a small TELESCOPE used by SAILORS in past times

spy mas·ter, spymaster / . ,../ *n.* [C] a spy who is responsible for a group of spies

sq. the written abbreviation of "square"

squab /skwɑb/ *n.* [C,U] a young PIGEON, or the meat of this bird

squab·ble /ˈskwɑbəl/ *v.* [I] to argue continuously about something unimportant: [+ **about/over**] *My wife and I are always squabbling about money.* —**squabble** *n.* [C]

squad /skwɑd/ *n.* [C] **1** the group of police officers responsible for dealing with a particular type of crime: **the drug/riot/vice etc. squad** *The bomb squad was called in to deactivate the bomb.* **2** an organized group of players that make up a sports team: *a football squad* **3** a small group of soldiers working together for a single purpose: *a drill squad* **4** a group of CHEERLEADERS —see also DEATH SQUAD, FIRING SQUAD, PEP SQUAD

squad car /'. ./ *n.* [C] a car used by police when they are on duty; PATROL CAR

squad·ron /ˈskwɑdrən/ *n.* [C] a military force consisting of a group of aircraft or ships: *a squadron of bombers*

squal·id /ˈskwɑlɪd/ *adj.* **1** dirty and disgusting, because of a lack of care or money: *The living conditions these immigrants endure are squalid, at best.* | *squalid slums* **2** involving DISHONESTY or low moral standards: *a squalid and corrupt political system* —see also SQUALOR

squall[1] /skwɔl/ *n.* [C] a sudden strong wind, especially one that brings rain or snow: *A violent squall sank both ships.*

squall[2] *v.* [I] if a baby or child squalls, it cries loudly

squal·or /ˈskwɑlɚ/ *n.* [U] the condition of being SQUALID: *The refugees are forced to* **live in squalor.**

squan·der /ˈskwɑndɚ/ *v.* [T] to spend money or use your time carelessly on things that are not useful: [**squander sth on sth**] *She has squandered nearly $41 million of the family fortune on bad investments.* —**squanderer** *n.* [C]

Squan·to /ˈskwɑntoʊ/ (?1585–1622) a Native American who helped the first English people to come to live in America, by showing them where to hunt and fish and how to plant corn

S W **square**[1] /skwɛr/ *adj.*
3
1 [shape] having four straight equal sides and 90° angles at the corners: *a square backyard* —see picture at SHAPE[1]
2 **a square mile/meter etc.** an area of measurement equal to a square with sides that are a mile long, a meter long etc.: *The three-story building has about 60,000 square feet of office space.*
3 [angle] forming a 90° angle, or seeming to do this: *a square corner* | *a square jaw*
4 **5 feet/2 meters etc. square** having the shape of a square with sides that are 5 feet, 2 meters etc. long: *The tablecloth is about 54 inches square.*
5 **a square meal** a good satisfying meal
6 [honest] OLD-FASHIONED honest and fair, especially in business: *It's important to be square with clients.* | *We just want* **a square deal.**
7 **be (all) square** INFORMAL if two people are square, they do not owe each other any money: *Here's your $20 – now we're square.*
8 [unfashionable] INFORMAL someone who is square is boring and unfashionable
9 [straight/level] parallel to a straight line: [+ **with**] *The walls should be square with each other.*
10 **a square peg in a round hole** INFORMAL someone who is in a job or situation that is not appropriate for them —**squareness** *n.* [U]

S W **square**[2] *n.* [C]
3
1 [shape] **a)** a shape with four straight equal sides with 90° angles at the corners **b)** a piece of something in this shape: [+ **of**] *a square of green cloth*
2 [in a town] a broad open area in the middle of a town, that is usually in the shape of a square, or the buildings surrounding it: *Have you been to the bank on the square?*
3 **be back to square one** to be back in exactly the same situation that you started from, so that you

have made no progress: *The development deal fell through and now we're back to square one.*
4 [number] TECHNICAL the result of multiplying a number by itself. For example, the square of 4 is 16. —see also SQUARE ROOT
5 [in a game] a space on a board used for playing a game such as CHESS
6 [person] OLD-FASHIONED, SLANG someone who is boring because they are not interested in the newest styles of music, clothes etc.
7 [tool] a flat tool with a straight edge, often shaped like an L, used for drawing or measuring 90° angles

square[3] *v.*
1 [multiply] [T] to multiply a number by itself
2 **square your shoulders** to push back your shoulders with your back straight, usually to show your determination
3 **square an account** also **square the books** to give someone money or do something for them so that you do not owe them anything anymore
4 [make sth straight] [T] to make something straight or parallel
5 [sports] [T] to win the same number of points or games as your opponent: *The Braves beat the Twins and squared the World Series at two games each.*
6 **square the circle** to attempt something impossible
square sth ↔ **away** *phr. v.* [T usually passive] INFORMAL to finish something, especially by putting the last details in order: *I need to get some stuff squared away before I leave Friday.*
square off *phr. v.* **1** [I] to get ready to fight or argue with someone: [+ **with**] *Local ranchers are squaring off with the federal government over the regulations.* **2** [T **square** sth ↔ **off**] to make something square with straight edges
square up *phr. v.* [I] to pay money that you owe
square with *phr. v.* [I,T not in progressive] if you square two ideas, statements etc. with each other or if they square with each other, they can be accepted together even though they seem different: *I don't think her memory really squares with reality.* | [**square** sth **with sth**] *How do you square playing this role with your feminism?*

square[4] *adv.* [only after verb] **1** directly and firmly; SQUARELY: *Look him* **square in the eye** *and tell him you won't do it.* **2** [+ **to**] at 90° to a line; SQUARELY —see also **fair and square** (FAIR[3] (1))

squared /skwɛrd/ *adj.* **1** **3/9/10 etc. squared** the number 3, 9, 10 etc. multiplied by itself: *3 squared equals 9.* **2** having a square shape: *I like the squared corners better than the rounded ones.*

square dance /'. ./ *n.* [C] a type of dance in which four pairs of dancers face each other in a square, and someone calls out the movements they should do

square knot /ˌ. './ *n.* [C] a knot that will not come undone easily

square·ly /ˈskwɛrli/ *adv.* [only after verb] **1** exactly or directly: *He turned and faced her squarely.* **2** completely and with no doubt: *The report puts the blame squarely on the government.* **3** straight on something and centrally: *Dr. Soames jammed his hat squarely on his head.* **4** at 90° to a line

square-rigged /ˌ. '. / *adj.* a ship that is square-rigged has its sails set across it and not along its length

square root /ˌ. './ *n.* [C] the square root of a number is the number which, when multiplied by itself, equals that number: *The square root of 9 is 3.*

squar·ish /ˈskwɛrɪʃ/ *adj.* shaped almost like a square

squash[1] /skwɑʃ, skwɔʃ/ *v.* **1** [T] to press something into a flat shape, often breaking or damaging it: *I'm afraid the chocolates will get squashed in my suitcase.* | *Hey! You're squashing me!* —see picture on page 424 **2** [I always + adv./prep.,T always + adv./prep.] to push yourself or something else into a space that is too small: [**squash (sth) into/under sth**] *He squashed his jacket under the seat.* **3** [T] INFORMAL to use your power or authority to stop something, especially something that is causing trouble; QUASH

S

squash² *n.* **1** [C,U] one of a group of large heavy hard fruits, such as PUMPKINS and ZUCCHINI, that are eaten as vegetables —see picture at VEGETABLE **2** [U] a game played by two people who use RACKETS to hit a small rubber ball against the four walls of a square court

squashed /skwɑʃt/ *adj.* broken or made flat by being pressed hard: *a squashed soda can*

squat¹ /skwɑt/ *v.* **squatted, squatting** [I] **1** also **squat down** to sit with your knees bent under you, your bottom off the ground, and balancing on your feet: [+ **on/behind/in** etc.] *Howard squatted down to check the tire.* **2** to live in a building or on a piece of land without permission and without paying rent: *Thousands of families are still squatting in war-damaged buildings.* **3** SLANG to pass solid waste from your BOWELS

squat² *adj.* short and thick or low and wide in an unattractive way: *a squat old man* | *The brown buildings were old and squat.*

squat³ *n.* **1** [C] a squatting position **2 not pay/do/know** etc. **squat** SLANG not pay, do, know etc. anything: *I didn't learn squat in that class.* —compare DIDDLY

squat·ter /'skwɑt̬ɚ/ *n.* [C] someone who lives in an empty building or on a piece of land without permission and without paying rent

squaw /skwɔ/ *n.* [C] OLD-FASHIONED a word for a Native American woman, now usually considered offensive

squawk /skwɔk/ *v.* [I] **1** if a bird squawks, it makes a loud sharp angry sound: *The parakeet began to squawk when I walked in.* **2** INFORMAL to complain loudly and angrily —**squawk** *n.* [C]

squeak¹ /skwik/ *v.* [I] **1** to make a very short high noise or cry that is not loud: *Kramer's running shoes squeaked on the marble floor.* | *Is that your chair squeaking?* **2 squeak by/through/past (sth)** INFORMAL to succeed, win, or pass a test, class, or competition by a very small amount, so that you just barely avoid failure: *I just squeaked by in algebra.* **3 squeak out a victory/pass** etc. to just barely win, pass etc. a test or competition: *Blue Ridge High School squeaked out a 22–20 victory.*

squeak² *n.* [C] a very short high noise or cry: *The only sound is the soft squeak of the marker on the board.*

squeak·y /'skwiki/ *adj.* **squeakier, squeakiest** **1** making very high noises that are not loud: *a squeaky door* | *Her voice is kind of high and squeaky.* **2 squeaky clean** INFORMAL **a)** never having done anything morally wrong: *John has a squeaky clean reputation.* **b)** completely clean: *a squeaky clean kitchen* —**squeakily** *adv.* —**squeakiness** *n.* [U]

squeal¹ /skwil/ *v.* [I] **1** to make a long loud high sound or cry: *The truck squealed to a stop.* | [+ **with/in**] *The children squealed with delight as he gave them each a gift.* **2 squeal (on sb)** INFORMAL to tell the police or someone in authority about someone you know who has done something wrong

squeal² *n.* [C] a long loud high sound or cry: [+ **of**] *Squeals of laughter were coming from under the bed.* | *a squeal of tires*

squeam·ish /'skwimɪʃ/ *adj.* easily shocked or upset, or easily made to feel sick by disgusting sights: [+ **about**] *Some people are squeamish about worms.* —**squeamishly** *adv.* —**squeamishness** *n.* [U]

squee·gee /'skwidʒi/ *n.* a tool with a thin rubber blade and a short handle, used for removing or spreading a liquid on a surface

s w **squeeze¹** /skwiz/ *v.*
3   **1** press with hand [T] to press something firmly in, especially with your hand: *Cathy gently squeezed my hand.*
   2 get liquid out [T] to press or twist something in order to get liquid out of it: [**squeeze sth out**] *Squeeze excess juices out of the spinach and stir it into the cheese mixture.* —see picture on page 425

[**squeeze sth on/onto sth**] *Emily squeezed lemon into her tea.*
3 fit into small space [I always + adv./prep.,T always + adv./prep.] to try to make something fit into a space that is too small, or to try to get into such a space: [+ **into/through/past/between**] *We squeezed through the crowd to the exit doors.* | [**squeeze sb/sth into sth**] *Somehow I squeezed the car into the tiny parking space.*
4 manage to do sth [T] to manage to do something although you are very busy: [**squeeze sth in/into sth**] *Even on business trips, he manages to squeeze in a few rounds of golf.* | *I can squeeze you in* (=see you) *at four o'clock.*
5 squeeze sb out (of sth) also **squeeze out sb** to make it difficult for someone to continue in business or to be able to buy something: *Higher ticket prices are squeezing out the average fan.*
6 squeeze out/into/through to succeed, win, or pass a test, class, or competition by a very small amount, so that you just barely avoid failure: *Atlanta managed to squeeze out a one-point victory.*
7 squeeze sth out of sb to force someone to tell you something: *See if you can squeeze more information out of them.*
8 limit money [T] to strictly limit the amount of money that is available to a company or organization, so that it is difficult for them to do things: *Cuts in federal funding are squeezing public housing agencies.*

squeeze² *n.* **1 a (tight) squeeze** a situation in which there is just barely enough room for things or people to fit somewhere: *It'll be a tight squeeze, but you can ride in the back seat.* **2** [C] an act of pressing something firmly, usually with your hands: *Henry put an arm around her, giving her a squeeze.* **3** [singular] a situation in which salaries, prices, borrowing money etc. are strictly controlled, so that it becomes difficult for someone to do something: *Small businesses are beginning to feel the financial squeeze.* **4 a squeeze of lemon/lime** etc. a small amount of juice obtained by squeezing a piece of fruit **5 put the squeeze on sb** INFORMAL to try to persuade someone to do something, especially by using threats **6** a SQUEEZE PLAY **7 your/her/his (main) squeeze** INFORMAL someone's BOYFRIEND or GIRLFRIEND

squeeze·box /'skwizbɑks/ *n.* [C] INFORMAL an ACCORDION

squeeze play /'. ./ *n.* [C] **1** a play in baseball in which a BATTER tries to BUNT the ball in order to give a RUNNER on third base a chance to gain a point **2** pressure put on someone in order to get what you want: *The U.N. squeeze play was intended to bring both countries to the bargaining table.*

squeez·er /'skwizɚ/ *n.* [C] a small tool for squeezing (SQUEEZE¹) juice from fruit such as LEMONS

squelch /skwɛltʃ/ *v.* [I] **1** [T] to stop something such as an idea or action from developing or spreading: *Barrett squelched rumors that the bank will change its name.* **2** to make a sucking sound by walking in soft wet mud: [+ **through/along/up**] *We squelched up the muddy path.* —**squelch** *n.* [C]

squelch·y /'skwɛltʃi/ *adj.* squelchy mud or ground is soft and wet and makes a sucking noise when you walk on it

squib /skwɪb/ *n.* [C] **1** LITERARY a short amusing piece of writing **2** a small exploding FIREWORK

squid /skwɪd/ *n. plural* **squid** or **squids** [C] a sea creature with a long body and ten arms around its mouth

squig·gle /'skwɪgəl/ *n.* [C] a short line that curls and twists, especially in writing or drawing: *a pattern of brightly colored squiggles* —**squiggly** *adj.*: *squiggly lines*

squint¹ /skwɪnt/ *v.* [I] to look at something with your eyes partly closed in order to see better, especially because the light is very bright: *She smiled and squinted against the sun.* | [+ **at**] *Mrs. Fanning squinted at the writing on the door.*

squint² *n.* [U] **1** an act of partly closing your eyes in order to see better, especially because the light is very bright **2** a condition of your eye muscles that makes it difficult for both eyes to look in the same direction

squire /skwaɪəʳ/ *n.* [C] a young man in the Middle Ages who learned how to be a KNIGHT by serving one

squirm /skwɜːm/ *v.* [I] **1** to twist your body from side to side, especially because you are uncomfortable or nervous: *The baby squirmed in her arms.* **2** to feel very embarrassed or ashamed: *Pornography is a subject that makes most Americans squirm.* —**squirm** *n.* [singular] —**squirmy** *adj.*

squirm out of sth *phr. v.* [T] INFORMAL to avoid doing something you do not want to do, or to avoid a bad situation: *Langham always seems to squirm out of trouble and win games.*

squir·rel¹ /'skwɜːl/ *n.* [C] a small animal that climbs trees and eats nuts and that has a long furry tail

squirrel

squirrel² *v.*
squirrel sth ↔ **away** *phr. v.* [T] to keep something in a safe place to use later: *She had $12,000 squirreled away in an Arkansas bank account.*

squir·rel·ly, **squirrely** /'skwɜːli/ *adj.* INFORMAL, DISAPPROVING unable to sit still or be quiet

squirt¹ /skwɜːt/ *v.* **1** [I,T] if you squirt liquid or it squirts, it is forced out of a narrow hole in a thin fast stream: [+ **from**] *Blood squirted from the wound.* | [**squirt** sth (**on** sb/sth)] *David squirted ketchup on his fries.* **2** [T] to hit or cover someone or something with a thin fast stream of liquid: [**squirt** sb/sth **with** sth] *Police squirted the man with pepper spray.*

squirt² *n.* [C] **1** a fast thin stream of liquid **2** (**little**) **squirt** SPOKEN a word used when speaking to a small child: *Hey squirt – it's time to wake up.*

squirt bot·tle /'. ,../ *n.* [C] a plastic bottle that you SQUEEZE to make a substance come out of it, used especially for food such as KETCHUP and MUSTARD

squirt gun /'. ./ *n.* [C] a WATER PISTOL

squish /skwɪʃ/ *v.* **1** [I always + adv./prep.] to make a soft sucking sound by moving in or through something soft and wet like mud **2** [I,T] INFORMAL to SQUASH¹ something, or to become squashed

squish·y /'skwɪʃi/ *adj.* **squishier**, **squishiest** **1** soft and able to be SQUEEZEd: *a squishy red ball* **2** soft and wet or full of liquid: *a squishy jellyfish* —**squishiness** *n.* [U]

Sr. 1 [only after noun] the written abbreviation of SENIOR: *Douglas Fairbanks, Sr.* **2** the written abbreviation of Sister, used in front of the name of a NUN: *Sr. Bernadette*

Sri Lan·ka /sri 'læŋkə, ʃri-/ a country in south Asia which is an island in the Indian Ocean, southeast of India —**Sri Lankan** *n., adj.*

SRO, S.R.O. 1 standing room only; used when all the seats in a theater, sports STADIUM etc. are full and there is only room left for people to stand **2** single-room occupancy; a small cheap apartment consisting of one room, a toilet, and a small kitchen area

S.S. 1 the abbreviation of Social Security **2** the abbreviation of STEAMSHIP

SSA Social Security Administration; the U.S. government department that manages SOCIAL SECURITY programs

ssh /ʃʃ/ *interjection* used to ask for silence or less noise: *Ssh! Be quiet.*

St. 1 [only after noun or adjective] the written abbreviation of "street": *Wall St.* **2** the written abbreviation of SAINT: *St. Andrew*

-st /st/ *suffix* used with the number 1 to form ORDINAL numbers: *the 1st* (=first) *prize* | *my 21st birthday*

stab¹ /stæb/ *v.* **stabbed, stabbing 1** [T] to push a knife into someone or something: *Two men were stabbed to death during the riot.* | **stab** sb **in the**

heart/arm etc. *Someone came up behind Bastidas and stabbed him in the back.* **2** [I,T] to make quick pushing movements with your finger or something pointed **3 stab** sb **in the back** to do something that harms someone who likes and trusts you; BETRAY —see also STABBING¹, STABBING²

stab² *n.* [C] **1** an act of stabbing or trying to stab someone: *Sims had multiple stab wounds to his chest and neck.* **2** [C] INFORMAL an attempt at doing something: **take/make a stab at (doing)** sth *Ten years ago, Griggs took a stab at running his own art gallery.* **3 a stab of fear/disappointment/pain** etc. a sudden sharp feeling of fear etc.: *I felt a sudden stab of envy when he showed me his car.* **4** [C] a quick movement, especially with a stick or your hand: *Wood avoided goalie Kelly Hrudey's stab at the puck before scoring.* **5 a stab in the back** something bad that someone does to you, especially someone whom you like and trust: *Molly stealing the money from us was a real stab in the back.*

stab·bing¹ /'stæbɪŋ/ *n.* [C] a crime in which someone is stabbed

stabbing² *adj.* a stabbing pain is sharp and sudden, as if it had been made by a knife

sta·bil·i·ty /stə'bɪləti/ *n.* [U] **1** the condition of being strong, steady, and not changing: *Our relationship provided the stability and comfort we both needed.* | [+ **of**] *the financial stability of the community* **2** TECHNICAL the ability of a substance to stay in the same state —opposite INSTABILITY

sta·bi·lize /'steɪbə,laɪz/ *v.* [I,T] to become firm or steady or to make something do this: *The patient's condition has now stabilized.* —**stabilization** /,steɪbələ'zeɪʃən/ *n.* [U]

sta·bi·liz·er /'steɪbə,laɪzəʳ/ *n.* [C] **1** a chemical that helps something such as a food to stay in the same state **2** a piece of equipment that helps make something such as an aircraft or ship steady

sta·ble¹ /'steɪbəl/ *adj.* **1** steady and not likely to move or change: *That chair doesn't look very stable.* | *a stable family environment* | *a stable government* **2** calm, reasonable, and not easy to upset: *Most people described her as a stable, intelligent woman.* **3** TECHNICAL a stable substance tends to stay in the same chemical or ATOMIC state —opposite UNSTABLE —see also STABILITY —**stably** *adv.*

stable² *n.* [C] **1** a building where horses, cattle etc. are kept **2 stables** [plural] a stable or a group of stables **3 a)** a group of racing horses that has one owner or trainer **b)** a group of people working for the same company or playing on the same team: *Ohio's football team has a talented stable of freshmen.*

stable³ *v.* [T] to put or keep a horse in a stable

sta·ble·man /'steɪbəlmæn/ *n.* [C] a man who works in a stable and takes care of horses

sta·ble·mate /'steɪbəl,meɪt/ *n.* [C] something that is made by the same company or someone who works for the same company: *The Pontiac Grand Am and Oldsmobile Achieva are the Skylark's stablemates.*

sta·bling /'steɪblɪŋ/ *n.* [U] space for horses to be stabled

stac·ca·to /stə'kɑːtoʊ/ *adv.* when music is played staccato, the notes are cut short and do not flow smoothly —compare LEGATO —**staccato** *adj.*

stack¹ /stæk/ *n.* [C] **1** a neat pile of things, one on top of the other: [+ **of**] *a stack of books* | *Stacks of unopened boxes filled the room.* **2 the stacks** [plural] the part of a library where most of the books are kept **3 a stack of** sth also **stacks of** sth INFORMAL a large amount: *We get stacks of junk mail every day.* **4** a temporary store of information on a computer **5** a tall CHIMNEY **6** a large pile of grain, grass etc. that is stored outside —see also HAYSTACK —see also **blow your top/stack** (BLOW¹ (8))

stack² *v.* **1** [I,T] also **stack up** to form a neat pile or make things into a neat pile: *These chairs are designed to stack easily.* | [**stack** sth] *You can stack the plates up here.* **2** [T usually passive] to put piles of things on a place or in a place: [+ **with**] *The coffee table was stacked with magazines.* **3 stack the deck/ cards a)** INFORMAL to make a situation difficult so that someone cannot succeed: [+ **against**] *In the world of business, the deck is often stacked against women.* **b)** INFORMAL to arrange cards dishonestly in a game **4** [I,T] also **stack up** if aircraft stack or are stacked around an airport, they are made to fly around it until they can land —see also **the odds are (stacked) against sb/sth** (ODDS (4))

stack up *phr. v.* [I] INFORMAL to judge how good something is when compared to something else: [+ **against**] *Parents want to know how their kids' schools stack up against others.*

stacked /stækt/ *adj.* SPOKEN a word used to describe a woman who has large breasts, considered offensive by many women

sta·di·um /ˈsteɪdiəm/ *n. plural* **stadiums** or **stadia** /-diə/ [C] a building for sports, consisting of a field surrounded by rows of seats: *a baseball stadium*

staff¹ /stæf/ *n.* **1** [C,U] *plural* **staffs** the people who work for an organization, especially a school or business: *The entire staff has done an outstanding job this year.* | *Our department has a staff of 7.* | *Both the Dodgers and the Reds have strong pitching staffs.* | *Staff members were encouraged to make suggestions.* | *Joan is the only lawyer we have on staff.* **2** [C] *plural* **staffs** a pole for flying a flag on; FLAGPOLE **3** [C] *plural* **staves a)** a long thick stick to help you walk **b)** a long thick stick that an official holds in some ceremonies **4** [C] *plural* **staves** or **staffs** the set of five lines that music is written on **5 the staff of life** LITERARY a basic food, especially bread —see also GENERAL STAFF, GROUND STAFF

staff² *v.* [T usually passive] to provide the workers for an organization: *The clinic is staffed by retired doctors.* —see also OVERSTAFFED, UNDERSTAFFED —**staffing** *n.* [U] *staffing levels*

staff·er /ˈstæfɚ/ *n.* [C] someone who is paid to work for an organization: *He had been a staffer in George Bush's administration.*

staff of·fi·cer /ˈ. ˌ.../ *n.* [C] an officer who helps a military commander of a higher rank

staff ser·geant /ˈ. ˌ../ *n.* [C,U] a lower rank in the U.S. Army, Air Force. or Marines, or someone who has this rank

stag /stæg/ *n.* [C] **1** a fully grown male DEER **2 go stag** INFORMAL if a man goes stag, he goes to a party without a woman —see also STAG PARTY

stage¹ /steɪdʒ/ *n.*

1 time/state [C] a particular time or state that something reaches as it grows or develops: *Construction of the bridge is in its final stage.* | *The initial stages of the disease are difficult to recognize.* | *At this stage, it would be wrong to back out of the deal.* —compare PHASE¹ (1), STEP¹ (4)

2 theater **a)** [C] the raised floor in a theater on which plays are performed: *I get nervous every time I go **on stage.*** | **stage left/right** (=from the left or right side of the stage) **b) the stage** plays as a form of entertainment: *The show was directed for the stage by James Lapine.*

3 acting **the stage** acting as a profession, especially in plays: *After the success of the movie, Brando never **went on stage** (=acted in plays) again.*

4 take center stage to have everyone's attention, or to be very important: *Immigration has taken center stage in the election.*

5 place [singular] a place where something important happens: *Geneva has been the stage for many such conferences.*

6 set the stage for sb/sth to prepare for something or make something possible: *Last year's economic summit set the stage for major changes.*

7 he's/she's going through a stage also **it's just a stage** INFORMAL used to say that someone young will soon stop behaving badly or strangely

stage² *v.* [T] **1** to organize an event, especially one that you hope many people will notice: **stage a**

strike/demonstration/concert etc. *Yesterday activists staged a protest in front of City Hall.* | *Colombian police have staged several raids on drug dealers.* **2** to organize how a play will be done: *Leverich also staged "The Glass Menagerie" here.* **3 stage a comeback** to start doing something again after you have stopped for a while: *After almost two seasons away from the game, Jordan staged a successful comeback.*

stage·coach /ˈsteɪdʒkoʊtʃ/ *n.* [C] a closed vehicle pulled by horses, that in past times carried passengers who paid to go to a particular place

stage·craft /ˈsteɪdʒkræft/ *n.* [U] the skill of making a performance of a play or show interesting: *"Figaro" combines great singing with fine stagecraft.*

stage di·rec·tion /ˈ. ˌ../ *n.* [C] a written instruction to an actor to do something in a play

stage door /ˌ. ˈ◂/ *n.* [C] the side or back door in a theater, used by actors and theater workers

stage fright /ˈ. ./ *n.* [U] nervousness felt by someone who is going to perform in front of a lot of people

stage·hand /ˈsteɪdʒhænd/ *n.* [C] someone who works on a theater stage, getting it ready for a play or for the next part of a play

stage-man·age /ˈ. ˌ../ *v.* [T] INFORMAL to organize a public event, such as a meeting, in a way that will give you the result that you want: *The First Lady has been known to stage-manage press conferences.*

stage man·ag·er /ˈ. ˌ.../ *n.* [C] someone in charge of a theater stage during a performance

stage moth·er /ˈ. ˌ../ *n.* [C] DISAPPROVING a mother who tries too hard to make her child succeed in SHOW BUSINESS (=the business of entertainment)

stage name /ˈ. ./ *n.* [C] a name used by an actor instead of his or her real name

stage·struck /ˈsteɪdʒstrʌk/ *adj.* loving to see plays, or wanting very much to become an actor

stage whis·per /ˈ. ˌ../ *n.* [C] **1** an actor's loud WHISPER that other actors on the stage pretend not to hear **2** a loud WHISPER that is intended to be heard by everyone

stag·ey /ˈsteɪdʒi/ *adj.* another spelling of STAGY

stag·fla·tion /stægˈfleɪʃən/ *n.* [U] an economic condition in which there is INFLATION (=a continuing rise in prices) but many people do not have jobs and businesses are not doing well

stag·ger¹ /ˈstægɚ/ *v.* **1** [I always + adv./prep.] to walk or move in an unsteady way, almost falling over: [+ **away/into/down** etc.] *I got out of bed and staggered to the window.* | *The explosion caused him to stagger backward.* **2** [T usually passive] to make someone feel very surprised or shocked: *We were all staggered by the news of her death.* **3** [T] to arrange people's working hours, vacations etc. so that they do not all begin and end at the same time **4** [T] to start a race with each runner at a different place on a curved track

stagger² *n.* [C usually singular] an unsteady movement of someone who is having difficulty walking

stag·ger·ing /ˈstægərɪŋ/ *adj.* very surprising, shocking, and hard to believe: *A staggering $3 trillion was spent in building the U.S. nuclear arsenal.* —**staggeringly** *adv.*

stag·ing /ˈsteɪdʒɪŋ/ *n.* **1** [C,U] the activity or art of performing a play, including the acting, clothes etc.: *Critics have praised Schneider's dramatic staging.* **2** [U] movable boards and frames for standing on

staging a·re·a /ˈ.. ˌ.../ *n.* [C] **1** a place where soldiers meet and where military equipment is gathered before an attack **2** a place where an event is organized from: *Firefighters met at the staging area at a local high school.*

staging post /ˈ.. ˌ./ *n.* [C] **1** a place where a stop is regularly made on a long trip, especially to rest or get supplies: *The city of Mondovi was a main staging post on the road to Genoa.* —compare STOPOVER **2** a staging area

stag·nant /ˈstægnənt/ *adj.* [no comparative] **1** stagnant water or air does not move or flow and often smells bad: *The moss grows in stagnant pools of* *water.* **2** not changing, developing, or making progress; INACTIVE: *Ticket sales have been stagnant.* —**stagnancy** *n.* [U] —**stagnantly** *adv.*

stag·nate /'stægneɪt/ *v.* [I] to stop developing or making progress: *a stagnating economy* | *In the last ten years, the country's agricultural output has stagnated.* —**stagnation** /stæg'neɪʃən/ *n.* [U] *economic stagnation*

stag par·ty /'. ,../ *n.* [C] a party for men only, especially on the night before a man's wedding —compare BACHELOR PARTY

stag·y, stagey /'steɪdʒi/ *adj.* **stagier, stagiest** behavior that is stagy is not natural, so that people move in a way that is slightly too deliberate, speak slightly too loudly or softly etc.: *I thought the program "I, Claudius" was a stagy bore.* —**stagily** *adv.*

staid /steɪd/ *adj.* serious, old-fashioned, and boring in the way you live, dress, or work: *staid scientific journals* | *The group managed to seem staid in comparison to Rollins' music.* —**staidly** *adv.* —**staidness** *n.* [U]

SW
3
stain¹ /steɪn/ *v.* **1** [I,T] to accidentally make a mark on something, especially one that cannot be removed, or to be marked in this way: *Sweat stained his dusty cowboy hat.* | [+ with] *The collar of his jacket was stained with something yellow.* **2** [T] to change the color of something, especially something made of wood, by using a special chemical or DYE **3 stain sb's name/honor/reputation etc.** LITERARY to damage the good opinion that people have about someone

stain² *n.* **1** [C] a mark that is difficult to remove, especially one made by a liquid such as blood, coffee, or ink: *The pillow had a large stain on it the color of tobacco.* | **a blood/ink/wine etc. stain** *There appeared to be blood stains on the floor.* **2** [C,U] a special liquid used to make something such as wood dark **3 a stain on sb's character/reputation etc.** LITERARY something that someone has done that is wrong or illegal, that other people know about

stained glass /, '. ./ *n.* [U] glass of different colors used for making pictures and patterns in windows, especially in a church

stain·less /'steɪnlɪs/ *adj.* made of stainless steel: *stainless flatware*

stainless steel /,.. '. / *n.* [U] a type of steel that does not RUST: *stainless steel tables*

SW
22
stair /stɛr/ *n.* **1 stairs** [plural] a set of steps built for going from one level of a building to another: *We carried the sofa up four **flights of stairs** (=sets of stairs).* | *There was a letter at **the foot of the stairs** (=the bottom of the stairs).* | **up/down the stairs** *Jerry ran up the stairs.* | **the top/head of the stairs** *I left my briefcase at the top of the stairs.* —compare STEP¹ (3) —see also DOWNSTAIRS, UPSTAIRS¹ —see picture on page 423 **2** [C] one of the steps in a set of stairs: *The second stair creaks when you step on it.* **3** [C] LITERARY a set of stairs: *I heard footsteps coming up the stair.*

stair·case /'stɛrkeɪs/ *n.* [C] a set of stairs inside a building, including its supports and the side parts that you hold on to

stair·way /'stɛrweɪ/ *n. plural* **stairways** [C] a staircase, especially a large or impressive one

stair·well /'stɛrwɛl/ *n.* [C] the space going up through all the floors of a building, where the stairs go up

SW
3
stake¹ /steɪk/ *n.*

1 be at stake if something that you value very much is at stake, you will lose it if a plan or action is not successful: *Thousands of lives are at stake if a war is not avoided.* | *At stake is the company's survival.*

2 (have) a stake in sth to have an important part or share in a business, plan etc., so that you will gain a profit if it succeeds: *Hudson had an 80% stake in the airline.* | *A bonus payment system gives workers a stake in the company.*

3 the stake a post to which a person was tied in past times to be killed by being burned: *In 1536, Tyndale was **burned at the stake** for printing a new translation of the Bible.*

4 ‖money risked‖ [C usually plural] money that

people risk on the result of a game, race etc., all of which is taken by the winner: *a game of high-stakes poker*

5 play for high stakes a) to risk a lot of money in a game **b)** to be in a situation where you may gain or lose a lot

6 ‖sharp post‖ [C] a pointed piece of wood, metal etc. that is pushed into the ground to hold a rope, mark a particular place etc.: *tent stakes*

7 pull up stakes INFORMAL to move from one place to another: *Our family pulled up stakes every few years when Dad was in the Army.*

stake² *v.* [T] **1** to risk losing something that is valuable or important to you, if a plan or action is not successful: [stake sth on sb/sth] *She didn't want to stake her son's future on one doctor's opinion.* | *Bush staked much on the ability of Gorbachev to continue his reforms.* **2 stake (out) a claim a)** to say publicly that you think you have a right to have or own something: *Both countries have staked a claim to the islands.* **b)** to prove that you are the best at something or deserve to have something: *Griffey has already staked a claim to this year's Most Valuable Player award.* **3** to risk money on a race or competition: *One time he even staked his house on a roll of the dice.* **4** also **stake off** to mark or enclose an area of ground with stakes: *Part of the park was staked off to allow the grass to grow back.* **5** also **stake up** to fasten or strengthen something with stakes: *I spent the afternoon staking up our tomato plants.*

stake sth ↔ **out** *phr. v.* [T] INFORMAL **1** to watch a place secretly and continuously: *Patrol officers staked out the apartment all evening.* **2** to mark or control a particular area so that you can have it or use it: *Flower sellers arrive early to stake out a good spot at the fair.* **3** to be successful in a particular area of business: *In three years, they have staked out over 30% of the shoe market.* —see also STAKEOUT

stake·hold·er /'steɪk,hoʊldər/ *n.* [C] **1** someone who will be affected by something, especially someone who puts money into a business: *Stakeholders resent production being cut after they have invested.* **2** LAW someone, usually a lawyer, who is given the responsibility of a property or amount of money during a legal disagreement or during a sale **3** someone chosen to hold the money that is risked by people on a race, competition etc. and to give all of it to the winner

stake·out /'steɪkaʊt/ *n.* [C] the activity of watching a place secretly and continuously, especially done by the police in order to catch people doing something illegal

sta·lac·tite /stə'læktaɪt/ *n.* [C] a sharp pointed object hanging down from the roof of a CAVE, which is formed gradually by water that contains minerals as it drops slowly from the roof

sta·lag·mite /stə'lægmaɪt/ *n.* [C] a sharp pointed object coming up from the floor of a CAVE, formed by drops from a stalactite

stale¹ /steɪl/ *adj.* **1** bread or cake that is stale is not fresh or good to eat because it is slightly old: *stale cookies* | *Their French bread is really good but it goes stale very quickly.* **2** news, ideas, relationships etc. that are stale are not interesting or exciting anymore: *All we hear around here is stale, old gossip.* | *After two years, their marriage began to **go stale**.* **3** air or breath that is stale is not fresh or pleasant —**staleness** *n.* [U]

stale² *v.* [I] FORMAL to become less interesting or exciting

stale·mate /'steɪlmeɪt/ *n.* [C,U] **1** a situation in which it seems impossible to settle an argument or disagreement, and neither side can get an advantage; DEADLOCK: *Congress remains in a stalemate over the federal budget.* **2** a position in CHESS in which neither player can win —**stalemate** *v.* [T]

Sta·lin /'stɑlɪn/**, Joseph** (1879–1953) a Russian politician, born in Georgia, who was leader of the former Soviet Union from the death of Lenin (1924) until his own death

stalk¹ /stɔk/ *n.* [C] a long narrow stem of a plant, that supports the leaves, fruits, or flowers: *Two flowers usually develop on each stalk.* —see picture at FRUIT¹

stalk² *v.* **1** [T] to follow an animal quietly in order to catch or kill it: *Crocodiles have been known to actively stalk and kill humans.* | *Police are making more effort to catch criminals who stalk women.* **2** [T] to follow someone over a long period of time, sometimes sending them letters or gifts, especially in order to force them to have sex or to kill them **3** [I always + adv./prep.] to walk in a proud or angry way, with long steps: [+ **out/off/away**] *Yvonne turned and stalked out of the room in disgust.*

stalk·er /ˈstɔkə/ *n.* [C] someone who follows a person over a long period of time, sometimes sending them letters or gifts, especially in order to force them to have sex or to kill them

stalk·ing /ˈstɔkɪŋ/ *n.* [U] the crime of following someone over a long period of time, especially in order to force them to have sex or to kill them

stalking horse /ˈ.. ,./ *n.* [C] someone or something that draws attention away from the real person who is doing the action or the real purpose of an action: *London has been seen as Washington's stalking horse.*

stall¹ /stɔl/ *n.* **1** [C] a table or a small store with an open front, especially outdoors, where goods are sold: *a stall at a flea market* **2** [C] also **shower/toilet/bathroom stall** a small enclosed private area for washing or using the toilet **3** [C] an enclosed area in a building for an animal **4** [C usually singular] an occasion when an engine stops working: *The plane went into a stall* (=the engine stopped working). **5** [C] an occasion when something stops improving, or developing: *The economy has gone into a stall.* **6** [C usually plural] a seat in a row of long seats for priests and singers in some larger churches: *choir stalls*

stall² *v.* **1** [I,T] if an engine stalls or you stall it, it stops because there is not enough power or speed to keep it going: *Bond was trying to gain altitude when his plane stalled.* | [**stall sth**] *It's easy to stall the engine on cold mornings.* **2** [I] if an activity stalls, it stops happening: *Trade negotiations have stalled.* **3** [I] to deliberately delay because you are not ready to do something, answer questions etc.: *Management seems to be stalling for time on the new contracts.* **4** [T] INFORMAL to make someone wait or stop something from happening until you are ready: *Many consumers are stalling the purchase of new cars.* | *Dad's coming! Stall him for a minute while I hide this.*

stal·lion /ˈstælyən/ *n.* [C] a male horse kept for breeding —compare MARE

stal·wart¹ /ˈstɔlwət/ *n.* [C] someone who works hard and is loyal to a particular organization or set of ideas: *a stalwart of the Democratic Party*

stalwart² *adj.* **1** stalwart supporter/ally etc. a very loyal and strong supporter **2** FORMAL strong in appearance —**stalwartly** *adv.*

sta·men /ˈsteɪmən/ *n.* [C] TECHNICAL the male part of a flower that produces POLLEN

stam·i·na /ˈstæmənə/ *n.* [U] physical or mental strength that lets you continue doing something for a long time without getting tired: *Brooks just doesn't have the stamina to play the whole game.*

stam·mer¹ /ˈstæmə/ *v.* [I,T] to speak or say something with a lot of pauses and repeated sounds, either because you have a speech problem, or because you are nervous, excited etc.: *Patterson often stammered during speeches.* —**stammerer** *n.* [C] —**stammeringly** *adv.* —compare STUTTER¹ (1)

stammer² *n.* [C usually singular] a speech problem which makes someone speak with a lot of pauses and repeated sounds: *"G-g-get up," she said with a slight stammer.*

stamp¹ /stæmp/ *n.* [C]
1 [mail] also **postage stamp** FORMAL a small piece of paper that you buy and stick onto an envelope or

package, that shows you have paid to mail it: *a 32-cent stamp* | **a sheet/book of stamps** (=set of stamps that you buy)
2 [tool] a tool for pressing or printing a mark or pattern onto a surface, or the mark made by this tool: *a date stamp* | *a stamp in your passport*
3 sb's stamp of approval someone's statement that they accept something or give permission for something: *The Federal Reserve gave its stamp of approval to the $10.7 billion bank merger.*
4 put your stamp on sth to affect something so that it changes in a particular way, especially in a way that makes people notice you: *With innovative ideas, Davis has put his stamp on the electronics industry.*
5 [foot] an act of stamping, especially with your foot: *"Louis, get over here!" Margaret demanded with a stamp of her foot.*
6 the stamp of sth if something has the stamp of a particular quality, it clearly has that quality: **have/bear the stamp of sth** *Ms. Harlin's speech bore the stamp of authority.*
7 a TRADING STAMP: *Do you save stamps?* —see also FOOD STAMP, RUBBER STAMP

stamp² *v.*
1 [make a mark] [T] to put a pattern, sign, or letters on something using a special tool: [**stamp sth on sth**] *The medicine had a September 1 expiration date stamped on it.* | [**stamp sth with sth**] *Your passport must be stamped with your entry date.*
2 stamp your foot to lift your foot off the ground and bring it down again very hard because you are angry: *"Be quiet!" she said, stamping her foot.*
3 stamp your feet to keep lifting each foot and bringing it down again very hard, to make a noise or because you are cold: *She stood at the bus stop stamping her feet to keep warm.*
4 [foot] [I] to lift your foot off the ground and put it down hard on something: [+ **on**] *He threw down the glasses and stamped on them.*
5 stamp sb as sth to show that someone has a particular type of character: *Some Republicans are trying to stamp him as unpatriotic.*
6 [affect sb/sth] [T] to have an important or permanent effect on someone or something: [**stamp sb with sth**] *Television news has forever stamped our generation with images of the war.*
7 [mail] [T] to stick a stamp onto a letter, package etc.: *The letters are stamped and are ready to be mailed.*

stamp sth ↔ out *phr. v.* [T] **1** to prevent something bad from continuing: *The new law is an attempt to stamp out political corruption.* **2** to put out a small fire by stepping hard on the flames **3** to make a shape or object by pressing hard on something using a machine or tool

stam·pede¹ /stæmˈpid/ *n.* [C] **1** a sudden rush of frightened animals all running in the same direction **2** a sudden rush by a lot of people, all wanting to do the same thing or go to the same place: *Competitors are hoping for a stampede of unhappy customers from the troubled bank.*

stampede² *v.* [I,T] **1** if animals stampede, they suddenly start running together in the same direction, because they are frightened: *The cattle began stampeding toward the town.* **2** be/get stampeded to be forced to do something you do not really want to do, because a lot of other people are doing it and putting pressure on you: [**be stampeded into doing sth**] *Kennedy refused to be stampeded into starting new nuclear tests.*

stamp·ing ground /ˈ.. ./ *n.* [C] STOMPING GROUND

stance /stæns/ *n.* [C usually singular] **1** an opinion that is stated publicly: [+ **on/against**] *Senator Reilly's stance on tax cuts has not changed.* | **take/adopt a stance** *The city has taken a tough stance on drugs and crime.* **2** a position in which you stand, especially when doing a particular activity: *The club's golf pro gave me some pointers on my stance and swing.* —compare POSTURE (1)

stanch /stæntʃ/ *v.* [T] to STAUNCH²

stan·chion /ˈstæntʃən/ *n.* [C] a strong upright bar used to support something

stand¹ /stænd/ *v. past tense and past participle* **stood**

1 **stand** [I] to support yourself on your feet in an upright position: *She was so weak that she could barely stand.* | *I was standing only a few feet away from where lightning struck.* | *Don't just stand there – help me!* | *Could you stand still* (=not move) *for just a minute and listen to me?* | **stand on your toes/stand on tiptoe** (=support yourself on your toes) —see also STANDSTILL

2 **rise** [I,T] also **stand up** to rise to an upright position on your feet, or to make someone do this: *At the end of his speech, we all stood and clapped.* | *Stand up and tell them what really happened.* | [**stand sb (up) on sth**] *Dad would stand me up on an orange crate to sing solos.*

3 **stand somewhere to do sth** [I always + adv./prep.] to take a particular position or do something in particular while standing: *Now I want the blue team to stand over to my right.* | [**stand somewhere doing sth**] *She stood behind the counter looking at me.* | [+ at/beside/by etc.] *I'll stand outside and wait for you.* | [+ on] *Don't stand on the box or it'll break.* | **stand back/aside** (=step backwards or sideways) | *Stand clear of* (=move away from) *the doors, please.*

4 **on a base** [I,T always + adv./prep.] to stay upright on a base or on an object, or to put something there: *Few houses were left standing after the tornado.* | *There's a parking lot where the theater once stood.* | [**stand sth on/in/over etc.**] *You can stand the bookcase against the wall over there.*

5 **in a state/situation** [I always + adv./prep., linking verb] to be in, stay in, or get into a particular state or situation: *Warships are standing on alert in case there is an attack.* | **the way things stand/as things stand** *As things stand, we'll be lucky to finish the job by Monday.* | **where/how do things stand?** *Where do things stand in terms of the budget?* | **stand united/divided** (=agree or disagree completely) | **stand prepared/ready to do sth** (=be prepared to do something whenever it is necessary) | *We teachers need to* **stand together** (=stay united) *if we want better pay.* —see also **be/stand in awe of sb** (AWE[1] (2))

6 **accept a situation** [I,T] to be able to accept or deal with a difficult situation; TOLERATE: [+ for] *Maggie won't stand for any alcohol in her house.* | **can/could stand** *I could barely stand the pain.* | **stand letting/allowing etc. sb doing sth** *How can you stand letting her talk to you like that?*

7 **be good enough** [T] to be done or made well enough to be successful, strong, or useful for a long time: *The paint is designed to stand all kinds of weather.* —see also **stand up** (STAND[1])

8 **stand to do sth** to be likely to do or have something: *He stands to make a good deal of money* | **stand to win/lose** *Kirkland stands to lose his business if he misses a payment.*

9 **in a position/state** [I, linking verb] to stay in a particular position, place, or state without being moved or used: *The car's been standing in the garage for weeks.* | **stand empty/idle** *Due to the strike, many of GM's factories stood idle.*

10 **at a level/amount** [I always + adv./prep.] to be at a particular level or amount: [+ at] *Unemployment stands at 6%.*

11 **a rank/position** [I always + adv./prep.] to have a particular rank or position when compared to similar things or people: *I know your son stands high on the list of suitable candidates.* | **stand in relation to sb/sth** *How does our country's level of debt stand in relation to other countries?*

12 **height** [I always + adv./prep.,/linking verb] FORMAL to be a particular height: *The radio antenna stands 867 feet high.* | *John stands six feet tall.*

SPOKEN PHRASES

13 **not like** **can't stand** to not like someone or something at all, or think that something is extremely bad or disgusting: *Her father can't stand liver and onions.* | [**can't stand sb/sth doing sth**] *Bert can't stand anyone touching him.* | **can't stand the sight/smell/taste etc. of sth** *Alison can't stand the sight of blood.* | **can't stand to see/hear/do etc.** *I can't stand to see good food going to waste.* | **can't stand seeing/hearing/doing etc.** *I can't stand*

listening to her complain. —see also **sb can't bear sth/ sb** (BEAR[1] (6)), **stand for sth** (STAND[1])

14 **suggest sth to sb** **could stand** used to say very directly that it would be a good idea for someone to do something or for something to happen: *It looks like the kitchen could stand a good cleaning.* | [**could stand to do sth**] *You could stand to lose a few pounds.*

15 **if you can't stand the heat, get out of the kitchen** used to say that you should leave a job or situation if you cannot deal with its difficulties

16 **do sth standing on your head** to do something easily: *I could design that kind of house standing on my head.*

17 **I stand corrected** FORMAL used to admit that your opinion or something that you just said was wrong

18 **stand trial** to be brought to a court of law to have your case examined and judged: [+ on/for] *Jenkins will stand trial on corruption charges.*

19 **stand alone a)** to continue to do something alone, without help from anyone else: *The vote on the ban was 14–1, with Britain standing alone.* **b)** to be much better than anyone or anything else: *For talent, popularity, and style, Muhammad Ali stands alone.* **c)** to stand somewhere with no one else near you: *I stood alone on the shore of the lake.*

20 **stand fast/firm** also **stand your ground a)** to refuse to change your opinions, intentions, or decisions: *The city council stood firm, rejecting the plan to build a new art museum.* | [+ on/against] *Priests were urged to stand firm against divorce.* **b)** to not allow someone to force you to move backward: *The Eagles' defense stood firm, not letting Washington score.*

21 **stand in line** to stand in a line of people, in order to wait for your turn to do something: *At 6 a.m. people were already standing in line to buy bread.*

22 **still exist** [I not in progressive] to continue to exist, be correct, or be VALID: *My offer to take you to dinner still stands.* | *The court of appeal has ruled that the conviction should stand.*

23 **stand still** to not change or progress at all, although time has passed: *Space technology has not stood still.* | *As if time had stood still, he looked the same as he did 10 years ago.*

24 **stand a chance/hope (of doing sth)** to be likely to be able to do something or to succeed: *You'll stand a better chance of getting a job with a degree.* | *The Eagles don't stand a chance against New York in the Super Bowl.*

25 **liquid** [I] a liquid that stands does not flow or is not made to move: *Mosquitos usually lay their eggs in standing water.*

26 **stand tall** to be proud and feel ready to deal with anything: *Fenton stood tall and stared down the gunmen.*

27 **know how/where you stand (with sb)** to know how someone feels about you: *Larry is so quiet that I never know where I stand with him.*

28 **stand the test of time** to be good enough, strong enough etc. to last for a long time: *Our friendship has stood the test of time.*

29 **stand pat** INFORMAL to refuse to change a decision, plan etc.: *The team can't stand pat – we needed to change our starting line-up.* | [+ on] *For now, the German central bank is standing pat on interest rates.*

30 **stand at attention** if soldiers stand at attention, they stand very straight and stiff to show respect: *The Marine guards stood at attention as the general walked past.*

31 **stand on your head/hands** to support yourself on your head or hands, with your feet in the air

32 **where sb stands** someone's opinion about something, or the official rule about something: [+ on] *I'm not sure where I stand on the issue of gun control.*

33 **from where I stand, from where I'm standing** according to what you know or feel: *Well from where I stand, it looks like you've found a good job.*

34 stand guard (over sb/sth) to have the responsibility of watching someone or something so that they do not do anything wrong or so that nothing happens to them: *If you stand guard over our stuff, I'll run get the tickets.*

35 stand accused to be the person in a court of law who is being judged for a crime: *Irvin stands accused of sexual harassment.*

36 stand on your own two feet INFORMAL to be able to do what you need to do, earn your own money etc., without help from others: *She needs to learn to stand on her own two feet.*

37 it stands to reason used to say that something should be completely clear to anyone who is sensible: *If the thefts are all in the same area, it stands to reason it's the same kids doing it.*

38 stand in sb's way also **stand in the way** to prevent someone from doing something: *I wouldn't want to stand in the way of progress.*

39 stand sb in good stead FORMAL to be very useful to someone when needed: *Saving the company millions should stand me in good stead for a promotion.*

40 stand sth on its head to show that a belief, idea etc. is completely untrue: *Galileo's discovery stood medieval thought on its head.*

41 stand or fall by/on to depend on something for success: *The whole nation stands or falls on the Constitution.*

42 not stand on ceremony FORMAL to not worry about the formal rules of polite behavior —see also **make sb's hair stand on end** (HAIR (11)), **not have a leg to stand on** (LEG (10))

stand against sb/sth *phr. v.* [T] to oppose a person, organization, plan, decision etc.: *As a nation, we stand against terrorism.*

stand around *phr. v.* [I] to stand somewhere and not do anything: *I saw two strange men standing around the entrance.*

stand by *phr. v.* **1** [T **stand by** sth] to decide what to do, say, or believe, and not change this: *I stand by what I said earlier.* **2** [T **stand by** sb] to stay loyal to someone and support them, especially in a difficult situation: *He's really stood by her during her illness.* **3** [I] to be ready to do something if necessary: *We have a helicopter standing by when you're ready to go.* | [+ **for**] *Stand by for the countdown.* **4** [I] to not do anything to help someone or prevent something from happening: *They will not stand by and let you take away their homes.* —see also BYSTANDER, STANDBY

stand down *phr. v.* **1 a)** [T **stand** sb ↔ **down**] to order a soldier to stop what he is doing and obey you **b)** [I] if a soldier stands down, he stops what he is doing and obeys you **2** [I] FORMAL to agree to leave your position or to stop trying to be elected, so that someone else can have a chance: *Mitterrand stood down as President after 14 years in power.* —see also **step down** (STEP¹)

stand for sth *phr. v.* [T] **1** if a letter, number, picture, or sign stands for something, it represents a word, name, or idea, especially in a short form: *V.A. stands for Veterans Administration.* **2** to support a particular set of ideas, values, or principles: *Samuels hasn't made it clear to voters exactly what he stands for.*

stand out *phr. v.* [I] **1** to be very easy to see or notice by looking or sounding different from other things or people: *We want the picture on the cover of the newspaper to stand out.* | *At six foot seven, Rich really stands out in a crowd.* **2** to be clearly better or the best: [**stand out as sth**] *Owen stands out as the best young player in the game.* | [+ **from/among/above**] *As a student, Molly stands out from the rest of her classmates.* **3 stand out like a sore thumb** also **stand out a mile** to be very clear or noticeable: *His bright green jacket stands out a mile.* —see also STANDOUT

stand out against sth *phr. v.* [T] to be strongly opposed to an idea, plan etc.: *We must stand out against child abuse.*

stand over sb *phr. v.* [T] to stand very close behind

someone and watch as they work to make sure they do nothing wrong: *Reporters chose their words carefully, as the censors were standing over them.*

stand to *phr. v.* [I] to order a soldier to move into a position so that they are ready for action, or to move into this position

stand up *phr. v.* **1** [I usually in progressive] to be in a standing position: *After standing up all day, I just want a comfortable place to sit down.* **2 stand up straight** to stand in a very upright way, so that your shoulders are not forward: *Stand up straight and pay attention.* | *A desert storm can be so fierce that it's hard to stand up straight.* **3** [I always + adv./prep.] to stay healthy in a difficult environment or in good condition after a lot of hard use: [+ **to**] *My old truck can stand up to just about anything.* **4** [I] to be proved to be true, correct, useful etc. when tested: **stand up under/to sth** *The data may not stand up to further testing.* | *Without a witness, these charges will never stand up in court* (=be successfully proved in a court of law). **5** [T **stand** sb **up**] INFORMAL to not meet someone after you have promised to do something with them: *I can't believe she stood me up.* **6 stand up and be counted** to make it very clear what you think about something, when this is dangerous or might cause trouble for you —see also STAND-UP¹

stand up for sb/sth *phr. v.* [T] to support or defend a person or idea when they are being attacked: *Thanks for standing up for me.* | *Don't be afraid to stand up for what you believe in.*

stand up to sb/sth *phr. v.* [T] to refuse to accept unfair treatment from a person or organization: *He's a hero to Arabs because he stood up to the United States.*

stand² *n.*

1 for support [C] a piece of furniture or equipment used to support something: *a music stand* | *an umbrella stand*

2 for selling [C] a table or small structure, usually outside or in a large building, used for selling or showing things: *They have the largest stand at the conference.* | *an ice cream stand* —see also NEWSSTAND

3 the stands a) the place where people sit to watch a sports game: *There were over 40,000 people in the stands.* **b)** the places where magazines and newspapers can be bought: *The new edition of "Time" will hit the stands* (=become available to be bought) *Tuesday.*

4 opinion/attitude [C usually singular] a position or opinion that you state firmly and publicly: **take a stand (on/against sth)** *The organization has not taken a stand on abortion.*

5 the stand the place in a court of law where someone sits when lawyers ask them questions: *On Monday, Lieutenant Richards will take the stand* (=begin answering questions). | *Wilcox looked nervous on the stand* (=when he was answering questions).

6 oppose/defend [C] a strong effort to defend yourself or to oppose someone or something: **take/make/mount a stand (against sth)** *Neighborhood residents are taking a stand against drug dealers.* —see also GRANDSTAND, ONE-NIGHT STAND

stand·a·lone /ˈstændəˌloʊn/ *adj.* TECHNICAL a standalone computer works on its own without being part of a NETWORK¹ (3)

stan·dard¹ /ˈstændəd/ *n.*

1 level of quality [C,U] a level of quality, skill, ability, or achievement by which someone or something is judged, that is considered to be necessary or acceptable in a particular situation: *Air quality standards vary from state to state.* | [+ **of**] *The agency establishes and enforces standards of food production.* | *School officials will meet to set new standards for hiring teachers.* | *Lofgren insists on the hotel maintaining its high standards* (=keeping things the way they are) *of service.* | *Unless your scuba diving equipment is up to standard* (=good enough), *do not use it.* | *a high/low standard Research indicates that high standards encourage students to achieve more.* | *meet/reach/attain a standard They have to reach a certain standard or they won't pass.* | *raise/lower a standard Asher launched a* campaign to raise standards of health care. | **above/ below standard** (=better than usual, or not good enough)

2 used when comparing [C usually plural] the ideas of what is good or normal that someone uses to compare one thing with another: **high/low stan- dards** *Mrs. Miller had high standards of dress and manners.* | *It was a luxurious house by Indian stan- dards.* | *Ella was 41 years old, hardly a girl by any standard* (=according to anyone's opinion or values).

3 measurement [C] a particular official rule for measuring weight, PURITY, value etc.: *The industry standard of temperature for shipping produce is 41 degrees Fahrenheit.*

4 a standard a car that uses a STICK SHIFT system to control its GEARS: *Eric can't drive a standard.* —com- pare AUTOMATIC[2] (1)

5 song [C] a popular song that has been sung by many different singers, especially over many years: *Haggard relied on old standards from the '60s and '70s.*

6 flag [C] a flag used in ceremonies: *the royal standard*

7 military pole [C] a pole with a picture or shape at the top carried in past times at the front of an army —see also DOUBLE STANDARD, LIVING STANDARD

s w **standard**[2] adj. **1** accepted as normal or usual: *A work week of forty hours is standard in the U.S.* | *Supermarkets typically have six standard food depart- ments.* | *Modems have long been standard equip- ment on PCs sold for home use.* | **standard practice/ procedure** (=the usual way of doing things) **2** regu- lar and usual in shape, size, quality etc.: *standard size paper* **3 standard English/spelling/pronuncia- tion etc.** the form of English, spelling, pronunciation etc. that most people use and consider correct —see also NONSTANDARD, SUBSTANDARD

standard-bear·er /'.. ,../ n. [C] **1** an important leader in a moral argument or political group **2** the soldier who carried the STANDARD (=flag) at the front of an army

standard de·duc·tion /,.. .'../ n. [C usually singu- lar] a specific amount of the money you earn that you do not have to pay tax on

standard de·vi·a·tion /,.. ...'../ n. [C] TECHNICAL a number in STATISTICS that shows how widely mem- bers of a mathematical set vary from the average set

standard-is·sue /,.. '..‹/ adj. included in ordinary military equipment

stan·dard·ize /'stændə,daɪz/ v. [T] to make all the things of one particular type the same as each other: *The committee hopes to standardize school curriculum and teaching techniques.* —**standardization** /,stæn- dədə'zeɪʃən/ n. [U]

standardized test /,... './ n. [C] a test that is taken by a large number of people and is designed to mea- sure their knowledge or ability: *standardized tests of reading ability*

standard of liv·ing /,.. '../ n. [C usually singular] the amount of wealth, comfort, and goods that a par- ticular person, group, country etc. has: *Many cross the border seeking work and a better standard of living.*

standard time /,.. './ n. [singular] **1** the time to which all clocks in a particular area of the world are set **2** the time of the year from late October to early April when clocks are set one hour back from DAY- LIGHT SAVING TIME

stand·by, stand-by /'stændbaɪ/ n. **1** [C] something that is kept ready so that it can be used when needed: *Oatmeal was Mom's standby for breakfast.* | *The station was built to provide standby power in emergencies.* **2** [U] a situation in which you are ready to travel on an airplane if there are any seats left when it is ready to leave: *a cheap standby ticket* | *Other airlines said they would accept the passengers on standby* (=in this situation). **3 on standby** ready to help immediately if you are needed: *City fire- fighters have been on standby for the past three days.* **4** [C] someone or something that you can always depend on or that will always be appropriate: *Duck*

à l'orange is an old standby on traditional French menus. —**standby** adv.: *I was able to fly standby to Miami.* —see also **stand by** (STAND[1])

stand-in /'. ./ n. [C] **1** someone who takes the place of an actor for some of the action in a movie: *Russell used a stand-in for most of the action scenes.* **2** some- one who does the job or takes the place of someone else for a short time: *Perot is just a stand-in for whomever the Reform Party nominates for president.* —see also **stand in** (STAND[1])

stand·ing[1] /'stændɪŋ/ adj. [only before noun] **1** per- manently agreed or arranged | **a standing invita- tion/offer** *We have a standing offer to use their boat.* **2 standing order a)** a permanent rule that a group of people such as a committee, council etc. follow: *U.N. troops have standing orders to launch an attack if they are fired upon.* **b)** an agreement to buy some- thing regularly: *Two of the firm's key customers canceled their standing orders for medical supplies.* **3** done from or in a standing position: *He pulled him- self up very slowly to a standing position.* | *Seifert received a standing ovation* (=when people stand up to CLAP[1] (1) after a good performance or speech) *at the end of his speech.* **4 a standing joke** something that happens often and that people make jokes about: *My spelling mistakes became a standing joke in the office.*

standing[2] n. **1** [U] someone's rank or position in a system, organization, society etc., based on what other people think of them or compared to others of the same type: *TBS has maintained its standing among the top four cable stations.* | *Japan wants a U.N. Security Council seat, to match the country's international standing.* **2 standings** [plural] the list that shows what rank a team, person etc. has in a competition: *The Rockets are second in the NBA standings.* **3 of five/many etc. years' standing** used to show the time during which something such as an agreement has existed: *It was a social policy of 60 years' standing.*

standing ar·my /,.. '../ n. [C] a professional, perma- nent army, rather than one that has been formed for a war

standing com·mit·tee /,.. .'../ n. [C] a group of members of Congress chosen to consider possible new laws

standing room /'.. ,./ n. [U] space for standing in a theater, STADIUM etc.: *There was standing room only* (=no seats were left) *in the court room.*

Stan·dish /'stændɪʃ/, **Miles** /maɪlz/ (?1584–1656) an English soldier who came to America with the Pilgrim Fathers on the Mayflower ship

stand-off /'stændɔf/ n. [C] a situation in which nei- ther side in a fight or battle can gain an advantage

stand-off·ish /stæn'dɔfɪʃ/ adj. INFORMAL fairly unfriendly and formal: *She was cold and stand-offish.* —**stand-offishly** adv. —**stand-offishness** n. [U]

stand-out /'stændaʊt/ n. [C] someone who is better at doing something or more attractive than other people in a group: *Marple was a standout on his high school track team.* —**standout** adj.: *a standout performance*

stand·pipe /'stændpaɪp/ n. [C] a pipe that provides water in a public place in the street

stand·point /'stændpɔɪnt/ n. [C usually singular] a way of thinking about people, situations, ideas etc.; POINT OF VIEW: *From an economic standpoint, the war was a good idea.*

stand·still /'stænd,stɪl/ n. **a standstill** a situation in which there is no movement or activity at all: *The sudden snow storm brought the entire city to a standstill.* | **come/grind to a standstill** *The World Cup has caused business to come to a virtual stand- still.* | *Traffic was at a standstill on the freeway.*

stand-up[1], standup /. ./ adj. [only before noun] **1** stand-up COMEDY involves one person telling jokes as a performance: *a stand-up comedian* **2** able to stay upright: *a stand-up mirror* **3 a stand-up guy**

S

APPROVING a man who other people like because he is honest and admits when he is wrong: *Fred's a stand-up guy.* **4** done or intended to be used by people who are standing up: *People paid $100 each to hear Quayle speak at a stand-up reception.* —see also **stand up** (STAND¹)

stand-up², **stand up** *n.* [U] stand-up COMEDY: **do stand-up** *Mark used to do stand-up at Roxy's bar.*

Stan·i·slav·sky /ˌstænɪˈslɑfski/, **Con·stan·tin** /ˈkɑnstəntɪn/ (1863–1938) a Russian actor and theater DIRECTOR who developed a new way of acting, called method acting, which involves actors using their own emotions and experiences

stank /stæŋk/ *v.* the past tense of STINK

Stan·ley /ˈstænli/, **Hen·ry Mor·ton** /ˈhɛnri ˈmɔrtn/ (1841–1904) a British EXPLORER who was sent by a U.S. newspaper to find David Livingstone in Africa in 1871

Stan·ton /ˈstæntn/, **E·liz·a·beth Ca·dy** /ɪˈlɪzəbəθ ˈkeɪdi/ (1815–1902) a U.S. woman who helped women get the right to vote

stan·za /ˈstænzə/ *n.* [C] a group of lines in a repeated pattern that form part of a poem

staph /stæf/ *n.* [C] a type of BACTERIA that causes serious infections: *a staph infection*

sta·ple¹ /ˈsteɪpəl/ *n.* [C] **1** a small piece of thin wire that is used to hold pieces of paper together, by using a special tool to push the ends through the paper and bend them over **2** a small U-shaped piece of metal with pointed ends, used to hold something in place **3** a food that is needed and used all the time: *Tortillas are a staple of Mexican cooking.* **4** someone or something that is often seen or often happens in a particular place: *Ice skating has long been a staple of ABC's sports programming.*

staple² *v.* [T] to fasten two or more things together with a staple

staple³ *adj.* [only before noun] **1** forming the greatest or most important part of something: *Oil is Nigeria's staple export.* | *In Brazil, the black bean is a staple crop.* **2 staple diet/food** the food that you normally eat: *Potatoes are part of the staple diet in Russia.*

staple gun /ˈ.. ˌ./ *n.* [C] a tool used for putting strong staples into walls or pieces of wood

sta·pler /ˈsteɪplər/ *n.* [C] a tool used for putting STAPLES into paper

star¹ /stɑr/ *n.* [C]

1 in the sky a large amount of burning gases in space that can be seen at night as a point of light in the sky: *The stars are beautiful tonight.* —see also FALLING STAR, SHOOTING STAR

2 performer/player a famous and successful performer in entertainment or a famous player in sports: *His first movie made him a star.* | *Former tennis star Björn Borg also attended the reception.* | *By the age of 20, she was already a big star* (=very famous performer). —see also MOVIE STAR, POP STAR, STAR²

3 shape **a)** a shape with four or more points that is supposed to look like a star in the sky: *The flag's fifty stars represent the fifty states.* **b)** a mark in this shape, used to draw attention to something written; ASTERISK: *I put stars next to the items we still need to buy.* **c)** a piece of cloth or metal in this shape, worn to show someone's rank or position —see picture at SHAPE¹

4 hotels/restaurants a mark used in a system for judging the quality of hotels and restaurants: **three-star/four-star/five-star** *a five-star restaurant*

5 successful person INFORMAL someone who is particularly successful at a job, course of study etc.: *After college, Weiss became a star in sports journalism.* | **a star player/performer/salesman etc.** *Goodrich was a star bank executive.* | *Hashimoto is known as a rising star* (=someone who is becoming successful and famous) *in Japanese politics.*

6 the star of the show the person who gives the best performance in a play, movie etc.: *In Italy, Mehta was the star of the show.*

7 see stars to see flashes of light, especially because you have been hit on the head: *I had bumped my head so hard that I began to see stars.*

8 the star attraction the most interesting person or thing, that most people want to see: *Keiko, a killer whale, had been the star attraction at the amusement park.*

9 star turn a great performance in a play, movie etc.: *Rivera's first star turn was in "West Side Story."*

10 have stars in your eyes to imagine that something you want to do, especially something that might make you famous, is much more exciting or attractive than it really is —see also STARRY-EYED

11 sth is written in the stars INFORMAL used to say that what happens is controlled by FATE (=a power that some people believe controls the future) —see also **be born under a lucky/unlucky star** (BORN (8)), EVENING STAR, FIVE-STAR GENERAL, FOUR STAR GENERAL, MORNING STAR, **reach for the stars** (REACH¹ (8)), **thank your lucky stars** (THANK (4))

star² *v.* **starred, starring 1** [I] to act the part of the main character in a movie or play: *Silverman also starred in "Brighton Beach Memoirs."* **2** [T] if a movie or play stars someone, that person acts the part of the main character: *Attenborough's 1987 "Cry Freedom" starred Denzel Washington.* **3 a/the starring role** the most important acting part in a movie, play etc. **4** [T] to put an ASTERISK (=a star-shaped mark) next to something written: *The most important points have been starred.*

star·board /ˈstɑrbərd/ *n.* [U] the side of a ship or aircraft that is on your right when you are facing forward —**starboard** *adj.* —opposite PORT (4)

starch¹ /stɑrtʃ/ *n.* **1** [U] a white substance that has no taste and forms an important part of foods such as grain, rice, and potatoes **2** [C,U] a food that contains this substance: *Starches such as potatoes are a necessary part of most good diets.* **3** [U] a substance that is mixed with water and is used to make cloth stiff

starch² *v.* [T] to make cloth stiff, using starch: *These shirts need to be starched and ironed.* —**starched** *adj.: a starched white uniform*

star cham·ber /ˌ. ˈ../ *n.* [C] a group of people that meets secretly and makes decisions that are important or judgments that are severe

starch·y /ˈstɑrtʃi/ *adj.* **starchier, starchiest 1** containing a lot of starch: *starchy foods* **2** DISAPPROVING very formal and correct in your behavior: *Her comments drew a starchy response from the State Department.* —**starchily** *adv.* —**starchiness** *n.* [U]

star-crossed /ˈ. ./ *adj.* LITERARY being in a situation that prevents something from happening: *star-crossed lovers* (=who are in a situation that prevents them from being together)

star·dom /ˈstɑrdəm/ *n.* [U] the situation of being famous, especially as a performer or sports player: *Known for his crisp country tenor voice, Denver rose to stardom* (=became famous) *in the 1970s.*

star·dust /ˈstɑrdʌst/ *n.* [U] LITERARY an imaginary magic substance like shiny powder

stare¹ /stɛr/ *v.* [I] **1** to look at something or someone for a long time without moving your eyes: [+ at] *Zach stared at him in disbelief.* | **stare into space** (=looking for a long time at nothing). | *I stood and stared out the window* (=looked for a long time at something through a window). —see Usage Note at GAZE¹ **2 be staring sb in the face a)** INFORMAL to be very clear and easy to see; be OBVIOUS: *The solution is staring you in the face.* **b)** to seem impossible to avoid: *Defeat was staring us in the face.*

stare sb **down** *phr. v.* [T] to look at someone for so long that they start to feel uncomfortable and look away —**staredown** *n.* [C]

stare² *n.* [C] a long steady look or a way of staring: *Their argument attracted the stares of passing shoppers.*

star·fish /ˈstɑrˌfɪʃ/ *n.* [C] a flat sea animal that has five arms forming the shape of a star

star·fruit /ˈstɑrfrut/ n. [C] a pale green fruit that has a shape similar to a star

star·gaz·er /ˈstɑrˌgeɪzɚ/ n. [C] **1** someone who likes to look at stars **2** INFORMAL someone who studies ASTRONOMY or ASTROLOGY **3** someone with ideas or plans that are impossible or not practical

star·gaz·ing /ˈstɑrˌgeɪzɪŋ/ n. [U] the activity of looking at stars —**stargaze** v. [I]

stark[1] /stɑrk/ adj. **1** very simple and severe in appearance: *Gone are the gray industrial carpeting and the stark white walls.* | *the stark beauty of the desert* **2** something that is stark, especially something bad, is clear and impossible to avoid; HARSH: *Ethnic divisions in the region remain stark.* | *The film shows the stark realities of life in the slums.* **3** [only before noun] complete or total: *This year's dryness is in stark contrast to* (=completely opposite) *the record rains of last spring.* —**starkly** adv. —**starkness** n. [U]

stark[2] adv. **1 stark naked** INFORMAL not wearing any clothes at all **2 stark raving mad** completely crazy

star·less /ˈstɑrlɪs/ adj. with no stars showing in the sky

star·let /ˈstɑrlɪt/ n. [C] a young actress who plays small parts in movies and is hoping to become famous

star·light /ˈstɑrlaɪt/ n. [U] the light that comes from the stars, often considered to be romantic

star·ling /ˈstɑrlɪŋ/ n. [C] a greenish-black bird that is very common in Europe and North America

star·lit /ˈstɑrˌlɪt/ adj. LITERARY made brighter by stars: *a starlit night*

Star of Da·vid /ˌstɑr əv ˈdeɪvɪd/ n. [C usually singular] a star with six points that is strongly connected with Judaism or the state of Israel

star·ry /ˈstɑri/ adj. having many stars: *a starry winter sky*

starry-eyed /ˌ.. ./ adj. INFORMAL happy and hopeful about things in a way that is silly or UNREALISTIC: *starry-eyed young actresses*

Stars and Stripes /ˌ. . ˈ./ n. **the Stars and Stripes** the flag of the U.S.

star·ship /ˈstɑrʃɪp/ n. [C] a word for a SPACECRAFT that can take people between stars and PLANETS, used in SCIENCE FICTION stories

star sign /ˈ. ./ n. [C] a ZODIAC SIGN

star-six·ty-nine /ˌ... ˈ./ also **star-six-nine** /ˌ. . ˈ./ v. [T] SPOKEN to call back the last person who called you by pressing the buttons *, 6, and 9 on the telephone

Star-Span·gled Ban·ner /ˌ. .. ../ n. **the Star-Spangled Banner 1** the NATIONAL ANTHEM (=national song) of the U.S. **2** LITERARY the flag of the U.S.

star-stud·ded /ˈ. ˌ../ adj. including many famous performers: *a star-studded charity event*

S W
1 1
start[1] /stɑrt/ v.
1 begin doing sth [I,T] to do something you were not doing before and continue doing it, often without finishing it; BEGIN: *There's so much to do, I don't know where to start.* | [**start doing sth**] *I'm going to start washing the dishes.* | [**start to do sth**] *She started to say something, but Bob stopped her.* | *When we walked outside, it had just started to rain.* | [**start sth**] *They're supposed to start construction of the airport next spring.* | *"My skirt's all wet," she said and started crying again* (=began crying after she had stopped). | *We'd better get started* (=start doing something, especially when you have not been able to do anything yet) *if we want to finish this job today.*
2 begin happening [I,T] to begin happening, or to make something begin happening: *What time does the movie start?* | [**start sth**] *Police are still looking for the two men who started the fire.* | [**start sb doing sth**] *Some dust in the closet started him sneezing.* | *The party was just getting started when we arrived.* | *starting now/today/tomorrow etc. The series will be shown on CBS starting next fall.*
3 a particular beginning [I,T] also **start off** if you start an activity, situation, or period of time in a particular way, or it starts in this way, the first part of it happens in this way or has this quality: [**+ with/**

in/on etc.] *The festivities started with a huge fireworks display.* | [**+ as**] *The whole thing started as a joke, but soon everyone believed it.* | [**start (sth) by doing sth**] *Chao starts by explaining some basic legal concepts.* | [**start sth**] *Taking a walk around the lake was a lovely way to start the day.* | [**start sth with/on etc. sth**] *I like to start my workout with some sit-ups and pushups.* | *start well/badly/slowly etc. The season has started badly for the Giants.*
4 job/school [I,T] to begin a new job, or to begin going to school, college etc.: *It sounds like an exciting job. When do you start?* | *start school/college/work When she started school, Mari couldn't speak English at all.*
5 car/engine etc. also **start up** [I,T] if you start a car or engine or if it starts, it begins to work: *The car wouldn't start this morning.* | *get the car/engine etc. started Can you help me get the lawn mower started?*
6 life/profession [I always + adv./prep.,T] also **start out** to begin your life or profession in a particular way or place: [**+ as**] *At age 13 she started as a cook in a Chinese restaurant.* | [**start sth doing sth**] *Collins started his adult life driving a taxi.* | *Can you give me any tips on how to get started in business?*
7 trip [I] also **start off/out** to begin traveling or moving in a particular direction: *We'll have to start early if we want to get to Grandma's by lunchtime.* | [**+ from/across/up etc.**] *I started up the mountain at noon and reached the top by four.*
8 business/organization etc. [T] also **start up** to make something begin to exist: *A group of women in the neighborhood have started an investment club.* | *start a business/company/firm Brad left his father's company to start a business of his own.*
9 start from scratch/zero to begin doing a job or activity completely from the beginning: *Peter the Great had to start from scratch when he built St. Petersburg.*
10 road/river [I always + adv./prep.] if a river, road etc. starts somewhere it begins in that place: [**+ in/at**] *The creek starts in the mountains and runs down onto private land.*
11 prices [I always + adv./prep.] if prices start at or from a particular figure, that is the lowest figure at which you can get or buy something: [**+ at/from**] *Summer rates at the hotel start at $199.*
12 sports [I,T] if a player starts in a game, or if someone starts them, they begin playing when the game begins, especially because they are one of the best players on a team: [**+ for**] *Astacio started for the Dodgers on Tuesday night.*
13 move suddenly [I] to move your body suddenly, especially because you are surprised or afraid: *A loud knock at the door made her start.* | [**+ from**] *Emma started from her chair and rushed to the window.*
14 start afresh/anew to stop doing what you are doing and begin doing it again better or differently: *She moved to Texas to start anew after the divorce.*
15 start a family to have your first baby: *His mom hopes he'll settle down and start a family.*
16 start a fight/argument etc. to deliberately cause a fight, argument etc.: *I never start fights, but I'll fight if someone else starts one.*
17 start a rumor to tell other people something, usually something bad or untrue: *Someone started a rumor that I was pregnant.*
18 start young to begin doing something when you are young: *You have to start young if you want to be a great musician.*

SPOKEN PHRASES

19 to start with SPOKEN **a)** said to emphasize the first of a list of facts or opinions you are stating: *I'm not going to Vegas. To start with, I don't like gambling, and I also can't get time off work.* **b)** said when talking about the beginning of a situation, especially when it changes later: *I was nervous to start with, but after a while I was fine.*
20 sb started it! used to say that someone else has

caused an argument or problem: *"Tim, stop fighting with your sister." "She started it."*
21 start something/anything to begin causing trouble: *If you start something in there, don't expect me to back you up.*
22 Don't (you) start with me! used to tell someone not to complain, argue, or annoy you

start in *phr. v.* [I] to begin criticizing someone or complaining to them about something: *Mother, don't you start in again, or I'll leave.* | [+ **on**] *Before I knew it, she'd started in on my wife.*
start in on sth *phr. v.* [T] INFORMAL to begin eating something: *By the time we got to the table, he'd already started in on his second burger.*
start off *phr. v.* **1** [I,T] to begin an activity, or to help someone do this: *Let's start off by introducing ourselves.* | [**start** sb/sth ↔ **off**] *Our coach started us off slowly with some simple exercises.* **2** [I always + adv./prep.] to begin happening in a particular way: *The week started off slowly, but by Wednesday I was busy again.* **3** [I] to move in a particular direction, or begin a trip: *I started off in the opposite direction and quickly found the main road.*
start on *phr. v.* **1** [T **start on** sth] to begin doing something or using or eating something: *Don't you think you should start on your homework?* | *Mona started on a second piece of chicken, eating just the skin.* **2** [T **start** sb **on** sth] to make someone start doing something regularly, especially because it will be good for them: *Churchill is the one who started him on painting.* **3 get (sb) started on sth** if you get started on something or someone gets you started on it, you start talking about it for a long time without stopping: *Don't get him started on one of his old war stories, or we'll never be able to leave.*
start out *phr. v.* **1** [I] to begin happening or existing in a particular way, especially when this changes later: *"The Star" started out as a small weekly newspaper in 1933.* **2** [I,T] to begin your life, profession, or an important period of time: *When we were just starting out, no one came to our concerts.* | [+ **as**] *Blake started out as a salesman, but afterward got into advertising.* | [**start** sth ↔ **out**] *Kate started her career out working as a model in New York.* **3** [I] to begin a trip, or begin moving in a particular direction: *They had just started out when Peggy's horse began to gallop.*
start over *phr. v.* [I] to start doing something again from the beginning, especially because you want to do it better: *When I'm drawing, if I make one mistake, I have to start over.*
start up *phr. v.* **1** [I,T **start** sth ↔ **up**] if you start up a business, company etc., or it starts up, it begins to exist: *I've heard that new software companies are starting up in the area.* —see also START-UP² **2** [I,T **start** sth ↔ **up**] if an engine, car etc. starts up, or you start it up, it begins to work: *The whistle blew and the train started up.* **3** [I] to become louder, more active etc., especially after being quiet or calm for a while: *After a few minutes the music started up again.* —see Usage Note at COMMENCE

USAGE NOTE: START

WORD CHOICE: start, begin
These words usually mean the same thing. However, **start** has some special meanings for which **begin** cannot be used. Use **start** to talk about making a machine work: *I couldn't start the car this morning.* We also use **start** to talk about making something begin to exist: *Matt's thinking about starting his own business.*

---

s w **start²** *n.*
2 2 **1** of an activity/event [C usually singular] the first part of an activity, event, period of time etc., or the point at which it begins to develop: [+ **of**] *Since the start of 1992, the company has doubled in size.* | *The sudden roar of planes overhead marked the start of the war.* | *From the start, their marriage seemed headed for disaster.* | *"Cats" is first-rate entertainment from*

start to finish. | *We won't be able to finish, but we can at least make a start.* | **get off to a good/bad start** *The day had gotten off to a bad start.*
2 it's a start SPOKEN used to say that something you have achieved may not be impressive, but it will help with a bigger achievement: *So far we only have 15 signatures on the petition, but it's a start.*
3 for a start INFORMAL used to emphasize the first of a list of facts or opinions you are stating: *I don't think she'll get the job. She's too young, for a start.* —compare **for starters** (STARTER (2))
4 sudden movement [singular] a sudden movement of the body, usually caused by fear or surprise: *I awoke* **with a start** *and reached for the phone.* | *The sound of scratching on the window* **gave** me a **start** (=frightened or surprised me).
5 child [singular] also **start in life** the condition of a child's early life: *We want to give our kids the best possible start in life.*
6 advantage [C usually singular] a situation in which you have an advantage over other people: [+ **on**] *Germany's military buildup in the 1930s gave it a huge start on Britain and France.*
7 in a race/competition [C usually singular] the amount of time or space by which one person is ahead of another, especially in a race or competition; HEAD START
8 the start the place where a race begins: *The horses were all lined up at the start.* —see also FALSE START, **in/by fits and starts** (FIT² (6))

start·er /ˈstɑrtɚ/ *n.* **1** [C] a member of a sports team who plays when the game begins, especially because they are one of the best players: *John was one of the starters before he broke his leg.* **2 for starters** INFORMAL used to emphasize the first of a list of facts, opinions, questions etc.: *"What do you want to know about him?" "What's his name, for starters?"* **3** [C,U] a substance containing BACTERIA that is used to start the process of making cheese, YOGURT etc. **4** a piece of equipment for starting a machine, especially an electric motor for starting an engine **5** [C] a person, horse, car etc. that is in a race when it starts **6** [C] someone who gives the signal for a race to begin **7** [C] an APPETIZER —see also NONSTARTER, SELF-STARTER

starter home /ˈ.. ˌ./ *n.* [C] a small house or apartment bought by people who are buying their first home
starter kit /ˈ.. ˌ./ *n.* [C] the basic equipment and instructions that you need to start doing something, especially working on a computer
starter mo·tor /ˈ.. ˌ../ *n.* [C] a STARTER (4)
starting block /ˈ.. ˌ./ *n.* [C] one of a pair of blocks attached to the ground, that a runner pushes their feet against at the start of a race
starting gate /ˈ.. ˌ./ *n.* [C] a gate or pair of gates that open to allow a horse or dog through at the start of a race
starting line /ˈ.. ˌ./ *n.* **the starting line** the line at which a race begins —compare FINISH LINE
starting line-up /ˌ.. ˈ. ˌ./ *n.* [C] the best players on a sports team, who play when the game begins
starting point /ˈ.. ˌ./ *n.* [C] **1** an idea or situation from which a discussion, process, or PROJECT can develop: *Frye emphasized that his suggestions were just a starting point for discussion.* **2** a place from which you start a trip, race etc.
starting price /ˈ.. ˌ./ *n.* [C] the lowest possible price for a certain type of thing such as a car or house without any special features, or the lowest price you are willing to accept for something you are selling
star·tle /ˈstɑrtl/ *v.* [T] to make someone suddenly surprised or slightly shocked: *You startled me! I didn't hear you come in.* | [**be startled to see/hear/learn etc.**] *We were both equally startled to see each other.*
star·tling /ˈstɑrtlɪŋ/ *adj.* very unusual or surprising: *DuPont's 1988 survey showed a startling change in the attitude of male employees.* —**startlingly** *adv.*: *startlingly beautiful*
start-up¹ /ˈ. ./ *adj.* relating to beginning and developing a new business: *a start-up budget of $90,000* | *start-up companies*

start-up[2] *n.* [C] a new small company or business: *Internet start-ups*

star·va·tion /stɑr'veɪʃən/ *n.* **1** [U] suffering or death caused by lack of food: *The four-year drought threatens two million people with starvation.* **2 a starvation diet** INFORMAL a situation in which you eat very little food, especially to become thinner **3 starvation wages** extremely low WAGES

starve /stɑrv/ *v.* [I,T] **1** to suffer or die because you do not have enough to eat, or to make someone else do this: *The world cannot stand by and watch while these people starve.* | [**starve sth**] *The dog looked like it had been starved.* | *The young elephants must eat several times daily, or they will starve to death.* **2** to not give or not be given something very important such as love or money, with harmful results: [**starve (sb) for sth**] *The children seemed to be starved for any kind of affection.* | [**be starved of sth**] *Trapped on the island, we were starved of information from the outside world.* **3 be starving** also **be starved** SPOKEN to be very hungry: *I'm starving! When do we eat?* **4 starve sb into (doing) sth** to force someone to do something by preventing them from getting food or money: *The Navy thought they could starve the enemy into submission through a blockade.*

starve sb **out** *phr. v.* [T] to force someone to leave a place by preventing them from getting food: *The sheriff spent three weeks at the cave entrance trying to starve out the bandits.*

stash[1] /stæʃ/ *v.* [T always + adv./prep.] INFORMAL to store something in a safe, often secret, place: [**stash sth away**] *She found the bottle of liquor that Bill had stashed away.* | [**stash sth in/under sth**] *They say he has stashed millions in foreign banks.*

stash[2] *n.* [C] INFORMAL an amount of something that is kept in a secret place: [+ **of**] *a stash of weapons*

sta·sis /'steɪsɪs, 'stæ-/ *n.* [U] FORMAL a situation in which everything stays the same and does not change or develop —see also STATIC[1]

stat /stæt/ *n.* [C] INFORMAL a STATISTIC

state[1] /steɪt/ *n.*
1 condition [C] the mental, emotional, or physical condition that someone or something is in at a particular time: *When the gas cools, it condenses back to its liquid state.* | [+ **of**] *We were in a state of shock when they told us how much it would cost.* | *Exercise can improve your state of mind* (=the way you think and feel) *as well as your physical health.* | *Our nation's schools are in a sorry state of disrepair* (=need to be repaired). | *a state of war/siege The two countries are still officially in a state of war.* —see also STATE OF EMERGENCY
2 part of a country [C] one of the areas with separate but limited law-making powers that some countries, such as the U.S., are divided into: *the state of Iowa* | **state employees/property/regulations** etc. *Most state employees will have the day off on Presidents' Day.* | **state-owned/state-funded/state-subsidized** etc. *Politicians are pushing for reform of the state-run pension plan.*
3 a country [C] FORMAL a country considered as a political organization: *Not all member states of the EU will join the currency union.* | **a democratic/totalitarian etc. state** (=with that type of government) —see also POLICE STATE and Usage Note at RACE
4 government [singular,U] also **the State** the government or political organization of a country: *It is the duty of the state to pass laws for the common good.* | **matters/affairs of state** (=the business of the government) —see also HEAD OF STATE, WELFARE STATE
5 ceremony [U] the official ceremonies and events relating to governments and rulers: *The Queen will visit Texas as part of her official state visit.* —see also lie in state (LIE[1] (10))
6 a state of affairs a situation: *It's a sad state of affairs when you can kill someone and only spend a year in jail.*
7 in a state SPOKEN very nervous, anxious, or excited: *I knew I was working myself into a state, but I couldn't stop worrying about them.*
8 the state of play the position reached in an activity or process that has not finished yet: *I can't comment on the state of play in the negotiations.*

state[2] *v.* [T] **1** to formally give a piece of information or your opinion, especially by saying it clearly: *Please state your full name for the record.* | [**state (that)**] *The president has stated that the new law requires several improvements.* | *To say the city has serious problems is stating the obvious* (=saying something that is already clear). **2** if a document, newspaper, ticket etc. states information, it contains the information written clearly: *The receipt clearly states that refunds are not allowed.*

state at·tor·ney /ˌ. .ˈ../ *n.* [C] a lawyer who represents the state in court cases

state col·lege /ˌ. ˈ../ *n.* [C] a college that receives money from the U.S. state it is in to help pay its costs

state court /ˌ. ˈ./ *n.* [C] a court in the U.S. which deals with legal cases that are concerned with state laws or a state's CONSTITUTION

state·craft /'steɪtkræft/ *n.* [U] the skill or activity of working in government or DIPLOMACY

State De·part·ment /ˈ. .ˌ../ —see DEPARTMENT OF STATE, THE

state·hood /'steɪthʊd/ *n.* [U] **1** the condition of being an independent nation **2** the condition of being one of the states making up a nation, such as the U.S.

State·house, statehouse /'steɪthaʊs/ *n.* **the Statehouse** the building where the people who make laws in a U.S. state do their work

state·less /'steɪtlɪs/ *adj.* not officially being a citizen of any country: *Millions of refugees remain stateless.* —**statelessness** *n.* [U]

state line /ˌ. ˈ./ *n.* [C] the line between two states in the U.S.: *Jenkins was arrested for illegally transporting explosives across state lines.*

state·ly /'steɪtli/ *adj.* **1** done slowly and with a lot of ceremony: *She turned and walked back in the same stately manner as before.* **2** impressive in style and size: *a stately old house*

state·ment /'steɪtˌmənt/ *n.* [C] **1** something you say or write publicly or officially to let people know your intentions or opinions, or to record facts: [+ **that**] *The statement that boys are good at math and girls are not is plain wrong.* | [+ **about**] *The report contained misleading statements about Frank.* | *Robinson refuses to make a statement of any kind concerning his involvement.* | *Vernon issued a statement* (=wrote something that could be read in public or given to newspapers) *today, confirming his resignation.* | *In a sworn statement* (=one that you officially say is true), *Thomas denied any improper behavior.* | **get/take a statement** (=officially write down what someone says) **2** a list showing amounts of money paid, received, owing etc. and their total: *a bank statement* | *According to its financial statement, the company made a profit of $15 million last year.* **3** something you do, make, wear etc. to make people understand something clearly or feel a particular way: *The type of car you drive can make a statement about the type of person you are.* —see also FASHION STATEMENT

Stat·en Is·land /ˌstætⁿn 'aɪlənd/ an island which is the smallest of the five BOROUGHS of New York City

state of e·mer·gen·cy /ˌ. . .ˈ.../ *n.* [C] a situation that a government officially says is very dangerous, and in which it uses special laws so that it can react very quickly: *Governor Ridge declared a state of emergency during the blizzard.*

state-of-the-art /ˌ. . . .ˈ.◂/ *adj.* using the most modern and recently developed methods, materials, or knowledge: *state-of-the-art electronics*

state park /ˌ. ˈ./ *n.* [C] a large park owned and managed by a U.S. state, often in an area of natural beauty

state·room /'steɪtrum/ *n.* [C] a private room or place for sleeping on a ship, train etc.

States /steɪts/ *n.* INFORMAL **the States** a word meaning the U.S., used especially by someone when they are outside the U.S.

state's at·tor·ney /ˌ. '..ˌ/ n. a STATE ATTORNEY

state school /'. ˌ./ n. INFORMAL a STATE COLLEGE or STATE UNIVERSITY

state's ev·i·dence /ˌ. '...ˌ/ n. **turn state's evidence** if a criminal turns state's evidence, they give information in a court of law about other criminals

state·side, Stateside /'steɪtsaɪd/ adj., adv. INFORMAL a word meaning "in the U.S." or "relating to the U.S.," used by people especially when they are not in the U.S.: *Jazz has always been more appreciated in Europe than it is stateside.*

states·man /'steɪtsmən/ n. [C] a political or government leader, especially one who is respected as being wise, honorable, and fair —**statesmanlike** adj. —**statesmanship** n. [U]

states' rights /ˌ. '.ˌ/ n. [plural] the right of U.S. states to make their own decisions rather than being told what to do by the national government: *Jefferson was a strong advocate of states' rights.*

states·wo·man /'steɪts,wʊmən/ n. [C] a political or government leader, especially one who is respected as being wise, honorable, and fair

state troop·er /ˌ. '.ˌ/ n. [C] a member of a police force that is controlled by one of the U.S. state governments who works anywhere in that state

state u·ni·ver·si·ty /ˌ. ..'...ˌ/ n. plural **state universities** [C] a university which receives money from the U.S. state it is in to help pay its costs

state·wide /'steɪtˀwaɪd/ adj. affecting or involving all people or parts of a U.S. state: *The next statewide elections will be held in June.*

stat·ic¹ /'stætɪk/ adj. not moving, changing, or developing, especially when movement or change would be good: *Unfortunately, the high divorce rate remains static.* —see also STASIS —compare DYNAMIC¹

static² n. [U] **1** noise caused by electricity in the air that blocks or spoils the sound from radio or TV **2** static electricity **3** INFORMAL complaints or opposition to a plan, situation, or action: *That's my final decision, so don't give me any static.*

static cling /ˌ. ˌ./ n. [U] a force caused by static electricity, that causes things such as clothes to stick together

static e·lec·tric·i·ty /ˌ... ..'...ˌ/ n. [U] electricity that is not flowing in a current, but collects on the surface of an object and gives you a small ELECTRIC SHOCK

stat·ics /'stætɪks/ n. [U] the science dealing with the forces that produce balance in objects that are not moving —compare DYNAMIC² (1)

sta·tion¹ /'steɪʃən/

1 travel [C] a place where public vehicles regularly stop so that passengers can get on and off, goods can be loaded etc., or the building or buildings at such a place: *a bus station* | *I'll meet you at the train station.*

2 activity or service [C] a building or place that is a center for a particular type of service or activity: *a police station* | *I need to stop at the gas station on the way home.* | *a radar station*

3 broadcasting [C] **a)** one of the many different signals you can receive on your television or radio, that a company broadcasts on: *See if you can find a country music station.* | *I can only get a couple of stations on this radio.* **b)** an organization which makes television or radio broadcasts, or the building where this is done: *She works for a television station in Utah.* —compare CHANNEL¹ (1)

4 position [C] a place where someone stands or sits in order to be ready to do something quickly if needed: *You're not to leave your station unless told.*

5 social rank [C] OLD-FASHIONED your position in society

6 military [C] a small military establishment

7 ships [U] TECHNICAL a ship's position in relation to others in a group, especially a military ship

station² v. [T usually passive] to put someone in a particular place in order to do a particular job or military duty: *My father was stationed in Europe during World War II.* | *There were police officers stationed at every exit.*

sta·tion·a·ry /'steɪʃə,nɛri/ adj. standing still instead of moving: *The stars appear stationary because they are so far away.*

stationary bike /ˌ.... '.ˌ/ also **stationary bi·cy·cle** /ˌ.... '...ˌ/ n. [C] an EXERCISE BIKE

station break /'. ˌ./ n. [C] a pause during a radio or television program, so that local stations can give their names or broadcast advertisements

sta·tion·er /'steɪʃənɚ/ n. [C] FORMAL someone in charge of a shop that sells stationery

sta·tion·er·y /'steɪʃə,nɛri/ n. [U] **1** special paper for writing letters on, usually with matching envelopes **2** materials that you use for writing, such as paper, pens, pencils etc.

station house /'. ˌ./ n. [C] the local office of the police or fire department in a town, part of a city etc.

station mas·ter /'.. ˌ.ˌ/ n. [C] someone who is in charge of a train station

station wag·on /'.. ˌ.ˌ/ n. [C] a large car with a door and a lot of space at the back for boxes, suitcases etc.

sta·tis·tic /stə'tɪstɪk/ n. **1 statistics a)** [plural] a collection of numbers which represents facts or measurements: *Government crime statistics indicate that the murder rate is falling.* **b)** [U] the science of dealing with and explaining such numbers: *Did you take statistics in graduate school?* —see also VITAL STATISTICS **2** [singular] a single number which represents a fact or measurement: [**a statistic that**] *I read a statistic that there'll be over 15 coffee chains in the city within two years.* **3 become/be a statistic** INFORMAL to die of a disease, in an accident etc. and be considered only as an example of the way you died, not as a person —**statistical** adj.: *statistical analysis* —**statistically** /-kli/ adv.: *The variation is not statistically significant.*

stat·is·ti·cian /ˌstætəs'tɪʃən/ n. [C] someone who works with statistics

sta·tive /'steɪtɪv/ adj. TECHNICAL a stative verb describes a state rather than an action or event, and is not usually used in PROGRESSIVE forms. For example, in the sentence "This book belongs to me," "belong" is stative.

stats /stæts/ n. [plural,U] INFORMAL statistics

stat·u·ar·y /'stætʃu,ɛri/ n. [U] FORMAL statues: *a fine collection of Greek statuary*

stat·ue /'stætʃu/ n. [C] an image of a person or animal that is made in solid material such as stone or metal and is usually large: *The committee will try to raise $20,000 to erect a commemorative statue on City Hall's front lawn.* | [+ **of**] *Statues of Lenin were torn down across Eastern Europe.* —compare SCULPTURE

stat·u·esque /ˌstætʃu'ɛsk/ adj. large and beautiful in a formal way, like a statue: *a tall statuesque woman*

stat·u·ette /ˌstætʃu'ɛt/ n. [C] a very small statue for putting on a table or shelf —compare BUST² (4)

stat·ure /'stætʃɚ/ n. [C,U] FORMAL **1** the degree to which someone is admired or regarded as important: *Supporters say there is no one of equal stature to replace him in the party.* **2** someone's height or size: *Cecilia is short in stature.*

sta·tus /'steɪtəs, 'stæ-/ n. **1** [C,U] the legal position or condition of a person, group, country etc.: *By accepting the prize money, Wilkerson will probably lose his amateur status.* | *Both sides are arguing over the future status of the disputed city.* | *It is illegal to discriminate based on marital status* (=whether someone is married or not). **2** [U] your social or professional rank or position, considered in relation to other people: *In many cultures, children remain the major source of status for women.* | **high-status/low-status** *He worked for years in high-stress, low-status jobs.* **3** [U] respect and importance that a person or organization has because of their high social position or the quality of their work; PRESTIGE: *Rutan has achieved legendary status for his airplane designs.* **4 the status of sth** what is happening at a particular time in a situation: *Bundy would not comment on the status of negotiations.*

status quo /ˌsteɪtəs ˈkwoʊ. ˌstæ-/ *n.* **the status quo** the condition of a situation as it is: **maintain/preserve the status quo** *The U.S. was willing to use force to maintain the status quo in Europe.*

status sym·bol /'.. ˌ../ *n.* [C] something that you have or own that you think shows high social status: *These shoes have become an important status symbol among teenagers.*

stat·ute /'stætʃut/ *n.* [C] **1** a law that has been passed by a LEGISLATURE and formally written down: *The Board is required by statute to report to Congress each year.* **2** a formal rule of an institution or organization: *university statutes*

statute book /'.. ˌ./ *n.* [C] NOT TECHNICAL **on the statute book** used to say that something is a written law: *Some of those old laws are still on the statute book.*

statute law /'.. ˌ./ *n.* [U] the whole group of written laws established by a LEGISLATURE —compare COMMON LAW

statute of lim·i·ta·tions /ˌ... ....'../ *n.* [C] a law which gives the period of time within which action may be taken on a legal question or crime: *Police did not investigate because the three-year statute of limitations had run out.*

stat·u·to·ry /'stætʃəˌtori/ *adj.* FORMAL decided or controlled by law: *statutory requirements for clinical laboratories* —**statutorily** *adv.*

statutory of·fense /ˌ..... .'../ *n.* [C] TECHNICAL a crime described by a law and punished by a court

statutory rape /ˌ..... '.../ *n.* [C] LAW the act of having sex with someone who is below a particular age

staunch[1] /stɔntʃ, stɑntʃ/ *adj.* giving strong, loyal support to another person, organization, belief etc.: *a staunch conservative* | *staunch allies* —**staunchly** *adv.* —**staunchness** *n.* [U]

staunch[2] also **stanch** *v.* [T] to stop the flow of liquid, especially of blood from a wound: *He used the cloth to try to staunch the flow of blood.*

stave[1] /steɪv/ *v.*
stave sth ↔ off *phr. v.* [T] to keep someone or something from reaching you or affecting you for a period of time: *Villagers are storing up grain to stave off food shortages this winter.*

stave[2] *n.* [C] **1** one of the thin curved pieces of wood forming the sides of a BARREL **2** a STAFF[1] (4)

staves /steɪvz/ *n.* a plural of STAFF

stay[1] /steɪ/ *v.* **stays, stayed, staying**
1 `in a place` [I] to remain in a place rather than go or leave: *Are you sure you can't stay a little longer?* | *They stayed later than I thought they would.* | *Violet had to stay behind to take care of a sick grandmother* (=had to remain after others had gone). | *We asked him to stay for dinner, but he had to leave.* | *If you stay around* (=do not leave) *long enough, sometimes you meet one of the stars.* | **stay here/there** *I'm going to look for a telephone. You stay here.*
2 `in a condition` [I always + adv./prep.,/linking verb] to continue to be in a particular state, condition, or state, without changing: *Let's just stay calm and try to figure out what to do.* | *After what she said, I don't think we can stay friends.* | [+ **in/on/out** etc.] *See if you can stay out of trouble for once.* | *Why do some people stay in abusive relationships?* | [+ **away/out/back** etc.] *I told you to stay away from my sister, Adrian.* | *Get out of this house and stay out!* | *Hotel rates will stay the same next year.*
3 `live somewhere` [I] to live in a place for a short time as a visitor or guest: *Where are you staying while you're here?* | [+ **at/with**] *He always likea staying at the Carlton.* | *You're welcome to stay with us till you find a place of your own.*
4 **stay the night** also **stay over/overnight** remain somewhere, especially someone else's house, from one evening to the next day: *You can stay the night if you want, Paul.*
5 **stay put** SPOKEN to remain in one place and not move: *I'm just going to stay put unless you need me to help you.*
6 **stay out of sth** SPOKEN to not get involved in an argument or fight: *Stay out of this, Ben – it's none of your business.*

7 **stay after (school)** to remain at school after the day's classes are finished, often as a punishment
8 **stay the course** to finish something in spite of difficulties: *Republicans are vowing to stay the course.*
9 **stay an order/ruling/execution** etc. LAW if a judge stays an order, ruling, execution etc., they stop a particular decision from being used or a particular action from happening
10 **stay!** SPOKEN used to tell a dog not to move
11 **stay sb's hand** LITERARY to stop someone from doing something: *There is little we can do to stay his hand without damaging East–West relations.* —see also **here to stay** (HERE[1] (6))
stay in *phr. v.* [I] to spend the evening at home rather than go out: *I'm kind of tired. I think I'll stay in and watch TV.*
stay on *phr. v.* [I] to continue to do a job or to study after the usual or expected time for leaving: *Stein said he would retire in May, but he stayed on as a favor to the mayor.*
stay out *phr. v.* [I] to remain away from home during the evening or night: *My parents won't let me stay out late on weeknights.*
stay up *phr. v.* [I] to not go to bed when you would normally go to bed: *We stayed up all night talking about old times.*

stay[2] *n.* **1** [C usually singular] a limited time of living in a place: *a short stay in the hospital* **2** [C,U] LAW the stopping or delay of an action because a judge has ordered it: **a stay of execution/deportation** etc. (=a delay of the punishment) **3** [C] a strong wire or rope used for supporting a ship's MAST **4** [C] a short piece of plastic, bone, or wire used to keep a shirt COLLAR or a CORSET stiff

stay-at-home /'. . ˌ./ *adj.* [only before noun] **1** INFORMAL always staying at home and never doing exciting things **2** staying at home, rather than working somewhere else, usually to take care of children: *a stay-at-home mom* —**stay-at-home** *n.* [C]

staying pow·er /'.. ˌ../ *n.* [U] the ability or energy to keep doing something difficult until it is finished: *No one should doubt our staying power or determination in this mission.*

St. Ber·nard /ˌseɪnt bɚˈnɑrd/ *n.* [C] a large strong Swiss dog that was trained in the past to help find people who were lost in the snow

St. Chris·to·pher and Ne·vis /ˌseɪnt ˌkrɪstəfɚ ən ˈnivɪs/ —see ST. KITTS AND NEVIS

STD *n.* [U] Sexually Transmitted Disease; a disease that is passed on through having sex, such as AIDS, HERPES etc.

std. a written abbreviation of "standard"

stead /stɛd/ *n.* **1** **do sth in sb's stead** FORMAL to do something that someone else usually does or was going to do: *Garcia is unable to attend, but will send the foreign minister in his stead.* **2** **stand/put/hold sb in good stead** to be very useful to someone when needed: *Throughout her career, Morris' speaking abilities have stood her in good stead.*

stead·fast /'stɛdfæst/ *adj.* LITERARY **1** giving strong, loyal support to another person, organization, belief etc.: *steadfast devotion* **2** being certain that you are right about something and refusing to change your position or opinion in any way: [+ **in**] *Lindros has been steadfast in his refusal to sell the property.* —**steadfastly** *adv.* —**steadfastness** *n.* [U]

stead·y[1] /'stɛdi/ *adj.* **steadier, steadiest**
1 `not moving` firmly held in a particular position and not moving or shaking: *Hold the ladder steady.* | *Gluing china takes a steady hand and a lot of patience.*
2 `continuous` moving, happening, or developing in a continuous or gradual way: *steady rain* | *the steady destruction of the forests* | *Marisol has made steady progress this year.* | **a steady stream of visitors/cars** etc. *Each day a steady stream of refugees made their way across the border.*
3 **steady work/income/employment** etc. work or pay that will definitely continue over a long period of time: *a steady job*

4 [not changing] a steady level, speed etc. stays about the same: *Chen maintained a steady pace throughout the race.*

5 [person] someone who is steady is sensible and you can depend on them: *a steady worker*

6 a steady boyfriend/girlfriend someone that you have been having a regular romantic relationship with

7 steady relationship a serious and strong relationship that continues for a long time —**steadily** *adv.* —**steadiness** *n.* [U]

steady[2] *v.* **steadies, steadied, steadying 1** [I,T] to hold someone or something so they become more balanced or controlled, or to become more balanced or controlled: *When the plane had steadied, Nancy went back to her seat.* | [**steady sb/sth**] *He grabbed the desk to steady himself.* **2** [I,T] to become calmer, or to make someone do this: *They finally found him in the bar where he had gone to* **steady** *his* **nerves.** **3** [I] to stop increasing or decreasing and remain about the same: [+ **above/at/below**] *The price of gold steadied above $405 an ounce.*

steady[3] *adv.* **go steady (with sb)** to have a long regular romantic relationship with someone

steady[4] *n.* [C] OLD-FASHIONED, INFORMAL a BOYFRIEND or GIRLFRIEND that someone has been having a romantic relationship with

steady[5] *interjection* used when you want to tell someone to be careful or not to cause an accident: *Steady! Watch what you're doing.*

steady-state the·o·ry /ˌ.. '. ˌ.../ *n.* TECHNICAL the idea that the degree to which space is filled with things has always been the same and that these things move away from each other as new atoms begin to exist —compare BIG BANG THEORY

steak /steɪk/ *n.* **1** [C,U] good quality BEEF (=meat from a cow), or a large thick piece of any good quality red meat **2 a cod/salmon/tuna etc. steak** [C] a large thick piece of fish

steak·house /'steɪkhaʊs/ *n.* [C] a restaurant that serves steak

steak tar·tare /ˌ. .'./ *n.* [U] steak that is cut into very small pieces and eaten raw, usually with a raw egg

steal[1] /stil/ *v.* past tense **stole** past participle **stolen**

1 [take sth] [I,T] to take something that belongs to someone else: [+ **from**] *You have to be careful – Sadie steals from everybody.* | [**steal sth**] *Someone stole my sunglasses out of the car.* | [**steal sth from sb**] *Robins is accused of stealing thousands of dollars from his employer.*

2 [use ideas] to use someone else's ideas without getting permission or admitting they are their ideas: *Kenner accused the director of stealing ideas from her novel in making his movie.*

3 [move somewhere] LITERARY [I always + adv./prep.] to move quietly without anyone noticing you: [+ **into/across etc.**] *Garrick stole into her room and opened the dresser drawer.*

4 steal the show/scene/limelight to do something, especially when you are acting in a play, that makes people pay more attention to you than to other people: *As soon as she appears as the "older woman," Cusack steals the show.*

5 steal a look/glance etc. to look at someone or something quickly and secretly

6 [baseball] [I,T] to run to the next BASE in the game of baseball before someone hits the ball

7 steal a kiss to kiss someone quickly when they are not expecting it

8 steal sb's thunder to get the success and praise someone else should have gotten, by doing what they had intended to do

9 steal sb's heart LITERARY to make someone fall in love with you

10 steal a march on sb to secretly or suddenly start something that someone else had planned to do, so that you gain an advantage over them

WORD CHOICE: steal, take, shoplift, rob, mug, burglarize, pick sb's pocket
People **steal** things (from people, cars, houses, stores, banks etc.): *Somebody stole my bike!* (NOT *"stole me"* or *"robbed my bike"*). **Take** is also often used in this sense: *They took the TV and VCR too.* If someone takes something from a store without paying, they **shoplift**: *Michelle was caught shoplifting.* People **rob** other people, especially in public places: *I've been robbed!* If they use physical violence on the street, they **mug** them: *On her way home, she was mugged by a man wearing a ski mask.* People also **rob** banks, or gas stations, but usually **burglarize** a house or office: *The Ramos' one-bedroom home was burglarized Thursday.* If someone **picks your pocket**, they steal things from your pocket or purse, usually when you are in a crowd of people.

steal[2] *n.* [C] INFORMAL **1 be a steal** to be very cheap: *This crisp dry wine is a steal at $9.* **2** the act of running to the next BASE in the game of baseball before someone hits the ball

stealth /stɛlθ/ *n.* [U] **1** the action of doing something very quietly, slowly, or secretly so that no one notices you: *Cats rely on stealth to catch their prey.* **2** also **Stealth** a system of making military aircraft that cannot be discovered by RADAR instruments: *stealth technology* | **a stealth bomber/fighter/aircraft etc.** (=an airplane made using this system)

stealth·y /'stɛlθi/ *adj.* moving or doing something quietly and secretly: *the stealthy movements of a hunter* —**stealthily** *adv.*

steam[1] /stim/ *n.* [U]

1 [gas] the hot mist that water produces when boiled

2 [mist on surface] the mist that forms on windows, mirrors etc. when warm wet air suddenly becomes cold

3 [power] power that is produced by boiling water to make steam, in order to make things work or move | **a steam engine/locomotive etc.** (=an engine, train etc. that works by the power produced by steam)

4 let/blow off steam to get rid of your anger or excitement in a way that does not harm anyone, by doing something active: *Recess is a good chance for kids to blow off steam.*

5 pick/build/get up steam also **gather steam a)** if an engine picks up steam, it gradually starts to go faster **b)** if plans, beliefs, actions etc. pick up steam, they gradually become more important and more people become interested in them: *The plan to rebuild the neighborhood is picking up steam.*

6 under your own steam if you go somewhere under your own steam, you get there without help from anyone else —see also **full speed/steam ahead** (FULL[1] (13)), **run out of steam/gas etc.** at **run out** (RUN[1])

steam[2] *v.* **1** [I] if something steams, steam rises from it, especially because it is hot: *I could smell the burning oil steaming up from the motor.* **2** [T] to cook something in steam: *Do you want me to steam the broccoli?* **3** [I always + adv./prep.] to travel somewhere in a boat or train that uses steam to produce power: [+ **into/from etc.**] *During the next two weeks, we steamed from port to port.* **4 be steaming (mad)** also **be steamed (up)** SPOKEN to be very angry: *Pierce was steaming mad after he got the second penalty.*

steam sth ↔ **open/off** *phr. v.* [T] to use steam to open an envelope or to remove a stamp from an envelope: *Letters and packages were analyzed by metal detectors or steamed open.*

steam up *phr. v.* [I,T] to cover something with steam, or become covered with steam: *When I walked inside, my glasses steamed up.* | [**steam** sth ↔ **up**] *His heavy sigh steamed up the window.*

steam·boat /'stimboʊt/ *n.* [C] a boat that uses steam for power and is sailed along rivers and coasts

steam clean /'. ./ *v.* [T] to clean something by using a machine that produces steam

steam·er /'stimɚ/ *n.* [C] **1** a STEAMSHIP **2** a container used to cook food in steam

steamer trunk /'. ˌ./ *n.* [C] a large box, used especially in past times for carrying clothes and other objects when you travel

steam·ing /ˈstimɪŋ/ *adv.* **steaming hot** very hot: *a bowl of steaming hot soup* —see also **be steaming (mad)** (STEAM² (4))

steam i·ron /ˈ. ˌ../ *n.* [C] an electric IRON that produces steam in order to make clothes easier to IRON

steam·roll /ˈstimroul/ *v.* [I,T] INFORMAL to defeat someone badly, or to make sure something happens by using all your power and influence: *Santos' supporters are attempting to steamroll his appointment through Congress.*

steam·roll·er¹ /ˈstimˌroulə/ *n.* [C] **1** a heavy vehicle with very wide wheels that you drive over road surfaces to make them flat **2** someone or something that defeats or destroys its opponents completely

steamroller² *v.* [I,T] INFORMAL to steamroll

steam·ship /ˈstimˌʃɪp/ *n.* [C] a large ship that uses steam to produce power

steam shov·el /ˈ. ˌ../ *n.* [C] a large machine that digs and moves earth

steam·y /ˈstimi/ *adj.* **steamier, steamiest 1** full of steam or covered in steam: *a steamy locker room* **2** sexually exciting and slightly shocking: *steamy love scenes*

steed /stid/ *n.* [C] POETIC a strong fast horse

steel¹ /stil/ *n.* **1** [U] strong metal that can be shaped easily, consisting of iron and CARBON: *The concrete is reinforced with steel.* **2** [U] the industry that makes steel **3** [C] a thin bar of steel used to make knives sharp —see also **nerves of steel** (NERVE¹ (6)), STAINLESS STEEL

steel² *adj.* [only before noun] **1** made of steel: *a steel gate* **2** relating to steel or the industry that makes steel: *the steel towns of Pennsylvania* **3** very strong: *a steel grip*

steel³ *v.* [T] **steel yourself for sth** to prepare yourself for something that will be uncomfortable or upsetting: *"What happened?" she asked, steeling herself for the bad news.*

steel band /ˌ. ˈ./ *n.* [C] a group of people who play music on steel drums together

steel drum /ˌ. ˈ./ *n.* [C] a type of drum from the West Indies made from oil BARRELS, which you hit in different areas to produce different musical sounds

steel-gray /ˌ. ˈ./ *adj.* having a dark gray color: *steel-gray hair* —**steel gray** *n.* [U]

steel gui·tar /ˌ. .ˈ./ *n.* [C] a musical instrument with ten strings that is played using a steel bar and a PEDAL (=a bar you press with your foot)

steel·mak·er /ˈstilˌmeɪkə/ *n.* [C] a company that makes steel —**steelmaking** *n.* [U]

steel mill /ˈ. ./ *n.* [C] a factory where steel is made

steel wool /ˌ. ˈ./ *n.* [U] a rough material made of fine steel threads, that is used to make surfaces smooth, remove paint etc.

steel·work·er /ˈstilˌwəkə/ *n.* [C] someone who works in a factory that makes steel

steel·works /ˈstilwəks/ *n.* a steel mill

steel·y /ˈstili/ *adj.* **1 2 steely determination/pride/ stare** etc. an extremely strong and determined attitude, expression etc. **3** having a gray color like steel: *A steely haze hung over the factory.*

steely-eyed /ˈ.. ˌ./ *adj.* having an expression in your eyes that shows you are strong and determined: *a steely-eyed tough guy*

steep¹ /stip/ *adj.* **1** a road, hill etc. that is steep slopes at a high angle: *The road's too steep to ride up on a bike.* **2** steep prices, charges etc. are unusually expensive: *The show is Sunday, July 27, and though tickets are somewhat steep at $27, it should be well worth seeing.* **3** a steep increase or rise in something is a very big increase: *They've proposed a steep increase in the cigarette tax.* —**steeply** *adv.* —**steepness** *n.* [U]

steep² *v.* [I,T] **1 be steeped in history/tradition/politics** etc. to have a lot of a particular quality: *Fairfield is a conservative school steeped in tradition.* **2** to put food in a liquid and leave it there so that it becomes soft or has the same taste as the liquid, or gives the liquid its taste: [**steep sth in sth**] *Steep the herbs in hot water.*

steep·en /ˈstipən/ *v.* [I,T] if a slope, road etc. steepens or something steepens in it, it becomes steeper

stee·ple /ˈstipəl/ *n.* [C] a tall pointed tower on the roof of a church

stee·ple·chase /ˈstipəlˌtʃeɪs/ *n.* [C] **1** a long race in which horses jump over gates, water etc. **2** a long race in which people run and jump over fences, water etc.

stee·ple·jack /ˈstipəlˌdʒæk/ *n.* [C] someone whose work is repairing towers, tall CHIMNEYS etc.

steer¹ /stɪr/ *v.*

1 change sb/sth [T] to guide someone's behavior or the way a situation develops: [**steer sb/sth away from sth**] *The program aims to steer teenagers away from crime and drugs.* | [**steer sb/sth toward sth**] *Kyle kept steering the conversation back toward politics.*

2 car/boat etc. [I,T] to control the direction a vehicle is going, for example by turning a wheel: *Floyd was going to be too drunk to steer the boat.*

3 steer clear (of sb/sth) INFORMAL to try to avoid someone or something bad or difficult: *British politicians tend to steer clear of religious topics.*

4 guide sb to a place to guide someone to a place, especially while touching them: [**steer sb toward/to etc. sth**] *Len took my arm and steered me toward the group of men.*

5 be in charge of [T always + adv./prep.] to be in charge of an organization, team etc. and make decisions that help it be successful, especially during a difficult time: [**steer sth through/to etc. sth**] *Corbin steered the company through the hard years of recession.*

6 steer a middle course to choose a course of action that is not extreme

steer² *n.* [C] a young male cow that has had its sex organs removed —compare BULLOCK, HEIFER

steer·age /ˈstɪrɪdʒ/ *n.* [U] the part of a passenger ship where people who had the cheapest tickets used to travel in the past

steer·ing /ˈstɪrɪŋ/ *n.* [U] the parts of a car, truck, boat etc. that allow you to control its direction: *power steering*

steering col·umn /ˈ.. ˌ../ *n.* [C] a long piece of metal in a car or other vehicle that connects the steering wheel to the equipment that moves the wheels

steering com·mit·tee /ˈ.. .ˌ../ *n.* a committee that guides or directs a particular activity

steering wheel /ˈ.. ˌ./ *n.* [C] a wheel that you turn to control the direction of a car, boat etc. —see picture on page 427

steers·man /ˈstɪrzmən/ *n.* [C] someone who STEERS a ship

Stei·chen /ˈstaɪkən/, **Ed·ward** /ˈɛdwəd/ (1879–1973) a U.S. PHOTOGRAPHER

stein /staɪn/ *n.* [C] a tall cup for drinking beer, often decorated and with a lid

Stein /staɪn/, **Ger·trude** /ˈgətrud/ (1874–1946) a U.S. writer famous for the new and unusual style of her NOVELS, poems, and other work

Stein·beck /ˈstaɪnbɛk/, **John** (1902–1968) a U.S. writer of NOVELS

Stein·em /ˈstaɪnəm/, **Glo·ri·a** /ˈglɔriə/ (1934–) a U.S. writer and FEMINIST who was a leading member of the WOMEN'S MOVEMENT in the 1960s

Stel·la /ˈstɛlə/, **Frank** (1936–) a U.S. PAINTER famous for his ABSTRACT paintings using GEOMETRIC shapes

stel·lar /ˈstɛlə/ *adj.* [usually before noun] **1** extremely good: *Pacino and*

John Steinbeck

*Keaton give **stellar** **performances**.* **2** TECHNICAL relating to the stars —see also INTERSTELLAR

stem¹ /stɛm/ *n.* [C] **1** a long thin part of a plant, from which leaves, flowers, or fruit grow —see picture at ROSE¹ **2** the long thin part of a wine glass, VASE etc., between the base and the wide top **3** the narrow tube of a pipe used to smoke tobacco **4** the part of a word that stays the same when different endings are added to it, for example "driv-" in "driving" and "driven" **5 from stem to stern** all the way from the front to the back, especially of a ship —see also BRAIN STEM

stem² *v.* **stemmed, stemming** [T] **1 stem the tide/ flow/growth etc. of sth** to stop something from spreading or developing: *The police are trying to stem the flow of drugs into the country.* **2** FORMAL to stop the flow of a liquid: *He used a rag to stem the bleeding.* **3 long-stemmed/short-stemmed etc.** having a long stem, a short stem etc.: *long-stemmed roses*

stem from sth *phr. v.* [T] to develop as a result of something else: *A lot of her emotional problems stem from her childhood.*

stench /stɛntʃ/ *n.* [C usually singular] **1** a very strong bad smell: *the stench of urine* **2 the stench of privilege/injustice/corruption etc.** something that makes you believe that something very bad and dishonest is happening

sten·cil¹ /ˈstɛnsəl/ *n.* [C] a piece of plastic etc. in which patterns or letters have been cut, or the pattern or words made by putting paint or ink over this

stencil² *v.* [T] to make a pattern, letters etc. using a stencil

Sten·dhal /stænˈdɑl, stɑn-/ (1783–1842) a French writer of NOVELS

Sten·gel /ˈstɛŋgəl/, **Ca·sey** /ˈkeɪsi/ (1891–1975) a U.S. baseball player and manager, famous for making the New York Yankees very successful

sten·o /ˈstɛnoʊ/ *n.* INFORMAL **1** [C] a stenographer **2** [U] stenography

ste·nog·ra·pher /stəˈnɑgrəfər/ *n.* [C] someone whose job is to write down what someone else is saying, using stenography, and then type a copy of it

ste·nog·ra·phy /stəˈnɑgrəfi/ *n.* [U] a system of writing quickly by using signs or shorter forms for letters, words, and phrases; SHORTHAND

sten·to·ri·an /stɛnˈtɔriən/ *adj.* LITERARY a stentorian voice is very loud and powerful

[SW 1 1] **step¹** /stɛp/ *n.*
1 movement [C] the movement you make when you put one foot in front of the other when walking: *Sal quickened his steps toward the hotel.* | *Seeing him, she **took a step** back and began to cry.* | *I **retraced** my steps (=went back the way I had come) for two blocks looking for the money.*
2 action [C] one of a series of things that you do in order to deal with a problem or produce a particular result: *Baker said his next step will be to demand a new trial.* | [+ **toward**] *The treaty is **a first step** toward arms control.* | *In 1974 Congress **took steps** (=took action) to limit the powers of the CIA.* | *The new techniques are **a major step forward** for law enforcement.* | *Hiring more people won't fix everything, but it's **a step in the right direction**.* | *The government decision is viewed by many as **a step backward** (=an action that makes a situation worse) for human rights.* —see also STEP-BY-STEP
3 stair [C] a flat narrow piece of wood or stone, especially one in a series, that you put your foot on when you are going up or down, especially outside a building: *Ellen ran up the steps and banged on the door.* —see also DOORSTEP (1)
4 in a process [C] a stage in a process, or a position on a scale: *Completing your degree would move you up a step on the salary scale.* | *Pam has been very careful about expenses **every step of the way** (=during every stage of the process).* | **a step up/ down** *I think Mike's a step up from Rosa's last boyfriend.* —compare STAGE¹ (1)

5 dancing [C] a movement of your feet in dancing: *I can't remember all the steps.*
6 in step a) having ideas that agree with what other people think or with what is usual, acceptable etc.: [+ **with**] *It's important for a president to keep in step with public opinion.* **b)** moving your feet in the same way as people you are walking or marching with
7 out of step a) having ideas that are different from what other people think or from what is usual, acceptable etc.: [+ **with**] *Uriah's out of step with modern life.* **b)** moving your feet in a different way from people you are walking or marching with
8 sound [C] the sound you make when you set your foot down while walking: *Marge could hear a man's steps in the hall.* —compare FOOTSTEP
9 distance [C] the distance you move when you take a step while walking: *Nelson was no more than four or five steps away.*
10 stay one step ahead of police/investigators etc. to manage not to be caught by someone who is trying to find or catch you: *Morton moved frequently, staying one step ahead of the law.*
11 be one step ahead (of sb) to be better prepared for something or know more about something than someone else: *Waters has always been one step ahead of her colleagues.*
12 exercise [C,U] a type of exercise you do by walking onto and off a flat piece of equipment several inches high, or that piece of equipment itself: *a beginners' step class*
13 music [C] the difference in PITCH¹ (3) between two musical notes that are separated by one KEY¹ (3) on the piano —see also **fall into step with sb/sth** (FALL¹ (33)), **with a spring in sb's step** (SPRING¹ (5)), **watch your step** (WATCH¹ (11))

[SW 2 2] **step²** *v.* **stepped, stepping** [I always + adv./prep.]
1 movement to raise one foot and put it down in front of the other one to move along: [+ **forward/ back/down etc.**] *Step aside and let the doctor through.* | [+ **inside/outside etc.**] *Could you step into the hall for a minute?* | *Please **step this way** (=come the way I am showing you).*
2 stand on sth to bring your foot down on something: [+ **in/on etc.**] *Yuck! What did you step in?*
3 step forward to come and offer help, information etc.: *No witnesses to the robbery have yet stepped forward.*
4 step on sb's toes to offend or upset someone, especially by trying to do their work: *I'm new here, so I don't want to step on anyone's toes.*
5 step out of line to behave badly by breaking rules or disobeying orders
6 step on it also **step on the gas** to drive faster: *If you don't step on it we'll miss the plane.*

step down/aside *phr. v.* [I] to leave your job or official position because you want to or think you should: [**step down as sth**] *Arnez will step down as the chairwoman of the review board in May.*

step in *phr. v.* [I] to become involved in a discussion or disagreement, especially in order to stop the trouble; INTERVENE: *If the dispute continues, the government will have to step in.*

step into sth *phr. v.* [T] to become involved in a situation, or start doing something: *Because of her previous experience, she easily stepped into the role of producer.* —see also **step into the breach** (BREACH¹ (5))

step out *phr. v.* [I] to leave your home or office for a short time: *Rhonda just stepped out – may I take a message?*

step up *phr. v.* **1** [T **step** sth ↔ **up**] to increase the amount of an activity or the speed of a process in order to improve a situation: *Local groups are stepping up their anti-drug campaign.* —see also STEPPED-UP **2** [I] also **step up to the plate** to agree to become directly involved in solving a problem or improving a situation: *Local business leaders should step up to the plate to help resolve inner-city problems.*

step- /stɛp/ *prefix* related, not by birth, but because a parent has remarried: *my stepfather (=the man who has married my mother)* | *her stepchildren (=her husband's children from an earlier relationship)*

step·broth·er /ˈstɛpˌbrʌðɚ/ n. [C] a boy or man whose father or mother has married your father or mother

step-by-step /ˌ.. ˈ.ˈ.◂/ adj. [only before noun] a step-by-step plan, method etc. does things carefully and in a particular order —**step by step** adv.: Rich went through the instructions step by step.

step·child /ˈstɛp-tʃaɪld/ n. [C] a stepdaughter or STEPSON

step·daugh·ter /ˈstɛpˌdɔtɚ/ n. [C] a daughter that your husband or wife has from a relationship before your marriage

step·fa·ther /ˈstɛpˌfɑðɚ/ n. [C] the man who is married to your mother but who is not your father

Ste·phen, Saint /ˈstivən/ in the Bible, a follower of Jesus who was the first Christian MARTYR

step·lad·der /ˈstɛpˌlædɚ/ n. [C] a LADDER with two sloping parts that are joined at the top so that it can stand without support, and which can be folded flat

step·moth·er /ˈstɛpˌmʌðɚ/ n. [C] a woman who is married to your father but who is not your mother

step·par·ent /ˈstɛpˌpɛrənt/ n. [C] a STEPFATHER or stepmother

steppe /stɛp/ n. [C,U] also **the steppes** a large area of land without trees, especially an area in Russia, parts of Asia, and southeast Europe

stepped-up /ˌ. ˈ.◂/ adj. done more quickly or with more effort than before: stepped-up factory production —see also **step up** (STEP²)

stepping stone, stepping-stone /ˈ.. ˌ./ n. [C] **1** something that helps you to progress toward achieving something, especially in your work: Brown used the government position as a stepping stone to other political goals. **2** one of a row of large flat stones that you walk on to get across a stream

step·sis·ter /ˈstɛpˌsɪstɚ/ n. [C] a girl or woman whose father or mother has married your mother or father

step·son /ˈstɛpsʌn/ n. [C] a son that your husband or wife has from a relationship before your marriage

-ster /stɚ/ suffix [in nouns] **1** someone who is connected with, deals with, or uses a particular thing: a gangster (=member of a group of criminals) | a trickster (=someone who deceives people with tricks) | a pollster (=someone who asks people for their opinions) **2** someone who has a particular quality: a youngster (=a young person)

ster·e·o¹ /ˈstɛriˌou, ˈstɪr-/ n. plural **stereos 1** [C] a machine for playing CDs, records etc. that produces sound from two or more SPEAKERS —see picture on page 426 **2 in stereo** if music, a radio program etc. is in stereo, it is being played or broadcast using a system in which sound is directed through two speakers

stereo² also **ster·e·o·phon·ic** /ˌstɛriəˈfɑnɪk, ˌstɪr-/ adj. using a system of sound recording or broadcasting in which the sound is directed through two SPEAKERS to make it seem more real: stereo equipment —compare MONO², QUADRAPHONIC

ster·e·o·scop·ic /ˌstɛriəˈskɑpɪk, ˌstɪr-/ adj. a stereoscopic photograph, picture etc. is made so that when you look at it through a special machine it looks solid

stereo sys·tem /ˈ... ˌ../ n. [C] a set of equipment for playing music on, usually including a CD PLAYER, CASSETTE DECK, and radio

ster·e·o·type¹ /ˈstɛriəˌtaɪp, ˈstɪr-/ n. [C] an idea of what a particular group of people is like that many people have, especially one that is wrong or unfair: racial stereotypes | Lee does not fit the stereotype of a district attorney. —**stereotypical** /ˌstɛriəˈtɪpɪkəl/ adj.

stereotype² v. [T usually passive] to decide, usually unfairly, that some people have particular qualities or abilities because they belong to a particular race, sex, or social class: [+ as] Too many children's books stereotype girls as helpless and weak. —**stereotyped** adj. —**stereotyping** n. [U]

ster·ile /ˈstɛrəl/ adj. **1** completely clean and not containing any BACTERIA: a sterile laboratory **2** not able to produce babies: Some women who used the birth

control device became sterile. —opposite FERTILE **3** lacking new ideas or imagination: a sterile, meaningless relationship **4** a sterile building, room, place etc. is not interesting, exciting, or attractive and does not make you feel comfortable: a group of sterile skyscrapers **5** sterile land cannot be used for growing crops —**sterility** /stəˈrɪləti/ n. [U]

ster·il·ize /ˈstɛrəˌlaɪz/ v. [T] **1** to make something completely clean and kill any BACTERIA in it: Sterilize the needle in boiling water. **2** to perform an operation that makes a person or animal unable to have babies —**sterilization** /ˌstɛrələˈzeɪʃən/ n. [C,U] —**sterilizer** /ˈstɛrəˌlaɪzɚ/ n. [C]

ster·ling¹ /ˈstɚlɪŋ/ adj. sterling **qualities/character/record** etc. excellent qualities, character etc.: a man of sterling character

sterling² n. [U] **1** sterling silver **2** the standard unit of money in the United Kingdom, based on the POUND¹ (3)

sterling sil·ver /ˌ.. ˈ../ n. [U] metal that is over 92% pure silver

stern¹ /stɚn/ adj. **1** very serious and strict, often in a way that does not seem nice: a stern judge **2** a **stern look/expression/rebuke** something that someone does or says that expresses disapproval —**sternly** adv. —**sternness** n. [U]

stern² n. [C usually singular] the back part of a ship —compare BOW³ (3)

ster·num /ˈstɚnəm/ n. plural **sternums** or **sterna** /-nə/ [C] TECHNICAL your BREASTBONE —see picture at SKELETON

ste·roid /ˈstɛrɔɪd, ˈstɪrɔɪd/ n. [C] a chemical compound produced in the body, but also given as a drug by doctors for injuries and used illegally by people doing sports to improve their performance

steth·o·scope /ˈstɛθəˌskoup/ n. [C] an instrument used by doctors to listen to someone's heart or breathing

Stet·son, stetson /ˈstɛtsən/ n. [C] TRADEMARK a tall hat with a wide BRIM (=edge), worn especially in the American West

ste·ve·dore /ˈstivəˌdɔr/ n. [C] someone who loads and unloads ships as their job

Ste·vens /ˈstivənz/, **Wal·lace** /ˈwɑləs/ (1879–1955) a U.S. poet

Ste·ven·son /ˈstivənsən/, **Ad·lai** /ˈædleɪ/ (1900–1965) a U.S. politician who competed twice in the election for President, and helped to establish the U.N. in 1946

Stevenson, Rob·ert Lou·is /ˈrɑbɚt ˈlui/ (1850–1894) a Scottish writer of NOVELS

stew¹ /stu/ n. **1** [C] a cooked dish, made of meat and vegetables that are cooked slowly together in liquid: beef stew **2 in a stew** INFORMAL confused or anxious, especially because you are in a difficult situation

stew² v. **1** [T] to cook something slowly in liquid **2 stew (in your own juices)** INFORMAL to worry or become angry because of something bad that has happened or a mistake you have made: I just sat there stewing in the front seat, trying to control my temper.

stew·ard /ˈstuɚd/ n. [C] **1** ship someone who is responsible for the comfort of the passengers on a ship **2** protector someone who takes care of something and protects it, such as nature or public property or money: Not all ranchers are good stewards of the land. **3** airplane OLD-FASHIONED a male FLIGHT ATTENDANT **4** union a SHOP STEWARD **5** house and land someone whose job is to take care of a house and its land, such as a large farm **6** food a man who arranges the supply and serving of food in a club, college etc. **7** race someone who is in charge of a horse race, meeting, or other public event

stew·ard·ess /ˈstuɚdɪs/ n. [C] OLD-FASHIONED a female FLIGHT ATTENDANT

stew·ard·ship /ˈstuɚdˌʃɪp/ *n.* [U] the way in which someone controls and takes care of an event, an organization, or someone else's property

stewed /stud/ *adj.* **1** cooked slowly in liquid: *stewed tomatoes* **2** [not before noun] INFORMAL drunk

St. George's /seɪnt ˈdʒɔrdʒɪz/ the capital city of Dominica

sw **stick¹** /stɪk/ *v.* past tense and past participle **stuck**
1 attach [I,T] to attach something to something else with a substance such as glue, or to become attached to a surface: *Put some butter on the pan so the cookies don't stick.* | [+ **to**] *It was so hot his shirt was sticking to his back.* | [**stick sth to/in/on etc. sth**] *I should have written a note and stuck it on the refrigerator.*
2 put [T always + adv./prep.] INFORMAL to put something somewhere, especially quickly and without thinking carefully: [**stick sth in/on etc.**] *You can stick those books on the table.* | *Don't let the baby stick it in her mouth.*
3 push [I always + adv./prep., T always + adv./prep.] if a pointed object sticks into something or you stick it into something, it is pushed into it: [**stick in/through etc.**] *Walking into the room, she noticed a letter stuck into the mirror's frame.* | [**stick sth in/into/through etc. sth**] *He looked away as the nurse stuck the needle in his arm.*
4 difficult to move [I] if something sticks, it becomes firmly attached in one position so that it is difficult to move: *This cupboard door keeps sticking.*
5 **stick in sb's mind** if something sticks in your mind, you remember it very well, especially because it is unusual or interesting: *My uncle told me the story when I was little, and it's always stuck in my mind.*
6 **make sth stick** INFORMAL **a)** to make a change become permanent or effective: *Mulroney agreed that a blockade may be necessary to make the sanctions stick.* **b)** to prove that someone is guilty of something: *The case never got to trial, because the police didn't think they could make the charges stick.*
7 **stick in sb's throat** if words stick in someone's throat, they are unable to say what they want, especially because they are upset: *When the time came to say "I do," the words stuck in my throat.*
8 **stick in sb's craw** if a situation or someone's behavior sticks in someone's craw, it is so annoying that they cannot accept it: *What sticks in my craw is that she never even asked if I would mind.*
9 name [I] if a name that someone has invented sticks, people continue to use it: *Clark called him "Mule," because he looked like a pack mule, and the name stuck.*
10 **stick to sb's ribs** food that sticks to your ribs makes you feel satisfied and become heavier
11 **sb can stick sth (up their ass)** VULGAR used to say rudely and angrily that you do not want what someone is offering you
12 **stick fast** to become firmly attached in one position and unable to move: *He pushed so hard on the pole that it stuck fast in the mud at the bottom of the river.*
13 **stick a fork in sb – they're done** SPOKEN, HUMOROUS used to say that someone is finished with something, especially because they have been doing it a long time, they are tired etc.
14 card game [I] to decide not to take any more cards in some card games: *I'm sticking.* —see also **stick/poke your nose into sth** (NOSE¹ (4)), STUCK¹

stick around *phr. v.* [I] INFORMAL to stay in the same place for a little longer, especially in order to wait for something that you expect to happen: *Stick around – there'll be dancing later.*

stick by sb/sth *phr. v.* [T] **1** to continue to give your support to a friend who has problems: *My wife has **stuck by** me **through thick and thin.*** **2** to do what you said you would do or what you think you should do: **stick by a decision/promise etc.** *Richards is sticking by her decision not to approve the spending bill.*

stick out *phr. v.*
1 come up or forward [I] if a part of something sticks out, it comes out further than the rest of a surface or comes out through a hole: *It's kind of cute the way his ears stick out.* | [+ **of/from/through**] *A neatly folded handkerchief stuck out of his jacket pocket.*
2 put sth out [T **stick** sth ↔ **out**] to deliberately make part of your body come forward or out from the rest of your body: *"Nice to meet you," Pat said, sticking out her hand.*
3 **stick your tongue out (at sb)** to quickly put your tongue outside your mouth and back in again, to be rude
4 **stick out (in sb's mind)** to seem more important to someone than other people or things: *One concern that sticks out in everyone's mind is the cost of the new stadium.*
5 **stick out (like a sore thumb)** INFORMAL to look very different from everyone or everything around: *I'm not going to the party dressed like this – I'd stick out like a sore thumb.*
6 **stick it out** to continue to the end of an activity that is difficult, painful, or boring: *I'm going to stick it out just to prove to him that I can do it.*
7 **stick your neck out** INFORMAL to take the risk of saying or doing something that may be wrong or that other people may disagree with

stick to sth *phr. v.* [T]
1 **stick to your decision/principles etc.** to do or keep doing what you said you would do or what you believe in: *I told you I'd be there, and I stuck to my word.*
2 **stick to your knitting** HUMOROUS to continue to pay attention to your own work, and not get involved in or ask questions about things that other people are doing
3 continue with same thing to keep using or doing one particular thing and not change to anything else: *He should stick to writing fiction.* | *Most fashion designers are sticking to browns, blacks, and grays this fall.*
4 **stick to it** to continue to work or study in a very determined way in order to achieve something: *When I set a goal, I stick to it.* —see also STICK-TO-IT-IVENESS
5 **stick to the point/subject/facts** to talk only about what you are supposed to be talking about or what is certain: *"Please stick to the facts," said the judge.*
6 **stick to the rules** INFORMAL to do something exactly according to the rules
7 **stick to your guns** INFORMAL to refuse to change your mind about something even though other people are trying to persuade you that you are wrong
8 **stick it to sb** to make someone suffer, pay a high price etc.: *When it comes to taxes, politicians like to stick it to the tourists.*
9 **that's my story and I'm sticking to it** SPOKEN used to say that you are refusing to change any part of what you have already said, and often seen as an admission that what you are saying is not the whole truth

stick together *phr. v.* **1** [I] INFORMAL if people stick together, they continue to support one another even when they have problems: *We've got to stick together through this thing.* **2** [I,T **stick** sth ↔ **together**] to be attached to something else, or to make two or more things do this: *Wrap the candy in waxed paper to keep it from sticking together.*

stick up *phr. v.* **1** [I] if a part of something sticks up, it is raised up or points up above a surface: *My hair is sticking up, isn't it?* | [+ **from/through etc.**] *Dawn saw one of the rabbit's ears sticking up through the hole.* **2** **stick 'em up** SLANG used to tell someone to raise their hands when threatening them with a gun

stick up for sb *phr. v.* [T] INFORMAL to defend someone who is being criticized, especially when no one else will defend them: *You're her husband – you should stick up for her.* | *Shawna's always known how to stick up for herself.*

stick with *phr. v.* INFORMAL **1** [T **stick with** sb) to stay close to someone: *The streets aren't safe at night,* so stick with each other when walking back to your car. **2** [T **stick with** sth] to continue doing or using something the way you did or planned to do before: *Let's stick with the original arrangements.* **3** [T **stick with** sth] to continue doing something, especially something difficult: *We're going to **stick with it** till we get the job done.*

    stick with sb *phr. v.* **1** to stay loyal to someone and support them, especially in a difficult situation: *Some of the older fans stuck with their team for 40 years before it became good.* **2** [T usually passive **stick** sb **with** sb/sth] to make someone accept something, do something, spend time with someone etc. when they do not want to: *Business owners are worried they will get stuck with the bill for the redevelopment.* —see also **be stuck with sth** (STUCK² (4)) **3** [T **stick with** sb] INFORMAL to remain in someone's memory: *The day I met Ricky will stick with me forever.*

stick² *n.*

1 from a tree [C] a long thin piece of wood that has fallen or been cut from a tree
2 a stick of celery/gum/dynamite etc. also a carrot/bread/cinnamon etc. stick a long thin piece of something —see also FISH STICK
3 sports [C] a long specially shaped piece of wood that you use for hitting the ball or PUCK in sports such as HOCKEY
4 car [C] INFORMAL a STICK SHIFT
5 for a particular purpose [C] a long thin piece of wood used for a particular purpose: *a walking stick* | *a measuring stick* —see also CANE¹ (1), NIGHTSTICK
6 get on the stick SPOKEN to start doing something you should be doing: *We really need to get on the stick and get those trees planted.*
7 the sticks INFORMAL a place that is very far from a town or city: *They live somewhere out in the sticks.*
8 have a stick up your butt/ass/behind etc. DISAPPROVING, SLANG to be too formal, stiff, or awkward in your behavior or movements
9 sticks and stones can/may break my bones (but words can never hurt/harm me) OLD-FASHIONED, SPOKEN used to say that it does not worry you if someone says things to you that are not nice —see also **a carrot-and-stick approach** (CARROT (3)), **more sth than you can shake a stick at** (SHAKE¹ (13))

stick·ball /ˈstɪkbɔl/ *n.* [U] a game like BASEBALL that is played in the street by children in the U.S., using a small ball and a stick

stick·er /ˈstɪkɚ/ *n.* [C] a small piece of paper or plastic with a picture or writing on it that you can stick on to something —compare LABEL¹ (1)

sticker price /ˈ.. ˌ./ *n.* [C usually singular] the price of something, especially a car, that is written on it or given in advertisements, but that may be reduced by the person selling it

sticker shock /ˈ.. ˌ./ *n.* [U] HUMOROUS the surprise you feel when you find out how expensive something is, especially a car

stick fig·ure /ˌ. ˈ../ *n.* [C] a very simple drawing of a person that uses straight lines for the arms, body, and legs

sticking point /ˈ.. ˌ./ *n.* [C] the thing that prevents an agreement being made in a discussion: *Reforming health care is one of the key sticking points in the budget negotiations.*

stick-in-the-mud /ˈ. . . ˌ./ *n.* [C] someone with old-fashioned attitudes who is not willing to try anything new

stick·ler /ˈstɪklɚ/ *n.* **be a stickler for rules/detail/punctuality etc.** to think that rules etc. are very important and that other people should also think they are very important: *Montgomery is a stickler for detail* (=he makes sure all the details are right).

stick man /ˈ. ./ *n.* [C] a STICK FIGURE

stick-on /ˈ. ./ *adj.* [only before noun] stick-on material has a sticky substance on its back so that you can stick it on to something: *stick-on name tags*

stick·pin /ˈstɪkˌpɪn/ *n.* [C] a decorated pin worn as jewelry

stick shift /ˈ. ./ *n.* [C] **1** a movable metal bar in a car

that you use to control its GEARS **2** a car that uses a stick shift system to control its gears —compare AUTOMATIC² (1) STANDARD¹ (4)

stick-to-it-ive·ness /ˌstɪk ˈtu ɪt əvnɪs/ *n.* [U] INFORMAL the ability to continue doing something that is difficult or tiring to do

stick-up /ˈ. ./ *n.* [C] INFORMAL a situation in which someone steals money from people in a bank, store etc. by threatening them with a gun

stick·y /ˈstɪki/ *adj.* **stickier, stickiest 1** made of or covered with a substance that sticks to surfaces: *There's something sticky on the floor.* **2** weather that is sticky makes you feel uncomfortable and very hot, wet, and dirty: *a hot sticky day in August* **3** a sticky situation, question, or problem is difficult or dangerous to deal with: *The issue of equal school funding remains a sticky political issue.* **4 have sticky fingers** INFORMAL to be likely to steal something —**stickiness** *n.* [U]

sticky note /ˈ.. ˌ./ also **sticky** *n.* [C] a small piece of paper that sticks to things, used for leaving notes for people; POST-IT NOTE

stiff¹ /stɪf/ *adj.*

1 body if a part of your body is stiff or you are stiff, your muscles hurt and it is difficult to move: *My legs are stiff from going running last night.* | *As you get older, your muscles become stiffer.* | *a stiff neck/back/joint etc. Sleeping on the plane gave me a stiff back.* | *I felt really stiff after playing basketball last week.*
2 paper/material etc. hard and difficult to bend: *The leaves of the anubias plant are very stiff.*
3 mixture thick and almost solid, so that it is not easy to mix: *Beat the egg whites until stiff.*
4 unfriendly unfriendly or very formal, so that other people feel uncomfortable: *Their good-byes were stiff and formal.*
5 strict/severe more difficult, strict, or severe than usual: *stiff sentence/penalty/fine Mexico imposes stiff prison terms for importing illegal firearms.* | *stiff competition/opposition Land developers ran into stiff opposition from environmental groups.*
6 a stiff wind/breeze a fairly strong wind
7 a stiff drink/whiskey etc. a very strong alcoholic drink
8 stiff as a board SPOKEN if something is stiff as a board, it is very hard and difficult to bend
9 keep a stiff upper lip to try to keep calm and not show your feelings in a situation when most people would become upset —**stiffly** *adv.* —**stiffness** *n.* [U]

stiff² *adv.* **bored/scared stiff** INFORMAL extremely bored or SCARED: *I thought I was having a heart attack. I was scared stiff.*

stiff³ *n.* [C] SLANG the body of a dead person —see also WORKING STIFF

stiff⁴ *v.* [T] INFORMAL to not pay someone money that you owe them or that they expect to be given, especially by not leaving a TIP¹ (2) in a restaurant: *I can't believe that couple stiffed me.*

stiff-arm /ˈ. ./ *v.* [T] to prevent someone from getting close to you by pushing them with your arm stretched out: *Sanders stiff-armed Greene at the 30-yard line to score a touchdown.* —**stiff-arm** *n.* [C]

stiff·en /ˈstɪfən/ *v.* **1** [I] to suddenly become unfriendly, angry, or anxious: *Nora stiffened when she heard her ex-boyfriend's name mentioned.* **2** [I,T] to become stronger, more severe, or more determined: *The council wants to stiffen the penalty for drunk driving.* | *stiffen sb's resolve/resistance etc. Senator Smith's arrogance stiffened resistance to him.* **3** [I] also **stiffen up** to become painful and difficult to move: *My back had stiffened up overnight.* **4** [T] to make material, hair etc. stiff so that it will not bend easily: *Moisture will only stiffen the leather of your shoes.*

stiff-necked /ˌ. ˈ./ *adj.* DISAPPROVING proud and refusing to change or obey; STUBBORN

sti·fle /ˈstaɪfəl/ v. **1** [T] to stop something from happening or developing: *Martial law continues to stifle political debate in the country.* **2** [T] to stop a feeling from being expressed: *She stifled the urge to scream.* | **stifle a yawn/smile etc.** *I was unable to stifle my laughter.* **3** [I,T] to stop someone from breathing or be unable to breathe comfortably, especially because the air is too hot or not fresh: *He was almost stifled by the fumes.*

sti·fling /ˈstaɪflɪŋ/ adj. **1** a room or weather that is stifling is very hot and difficult to breathe in: *It was difficult to work in the stifling heat of the warehouse.* **2** a situation that is stifling stops you from developing your own ideas and character: *the city's stifling bureaucracy*

stig·ma /ˈstɪgmə/ n. **1** [singular,U] a strong feeling in society that a type of behavior or a particular condition is shameful: *For children, being fat carries a stigma that starts early.* | *There is a stigma attached to single parenthood.* | **the stigma of** *alcoholism/abortion/poverty etc. People don't get treatment for panic attacks to avoid the stigma of mental illness.* **2** [C] TECHNICAL the top of the center part of a flower that receives the POLLEN that allows it to form new seeds

stig·ma·ta /stɪgˈmɑtə, ˈstɪgmətə/ n. [plural] the marks on Christ's body caused by nails, or similar marks on the bodies of some holy people

stig·ma·tize /ˈstɪgmə.taɪz/ v. [T] **be stigmatized** to be treated by society as if you should be ashamed of your situation or actions: *Single mothers often feel that they are stigmatized by society.* —**stigmatization** /ˌstɪgmətəˈzeɪʃən/ n. [U]

stile /staɪl/ n. [C] a set of steps placed on either side of a fence so that people can climb over it

sti·let·to /stɪˈlɛtoʊ/ n. plural **stilettos** or **stilettoes** [C] **1** also **stiletto heel** a high thin heel of a woman's shoe **2** a shoe that has this kind of heel **3** a small knife with a thin BLADE

still¹ /stɪl/ adv. **1** up to a particular point in time and continuing at that moment: *Do you still have her phone number?* | *I think John is still in medical school.* **2** in spite of what has just been said or done: *Traffic was bad, but we still made it to the movie on time.* | [sentence adverb] *My car looks old and ugly. Still, it's better than having no car at all.* **3** **still more/another/other etc.** even more in amount: *Kevin grew still more depressed.* | *There's still another two months of winter left.* **4** **better/harder/worse etc. still** still better/harder/worse etc. than something else: *Dan found biology difficult, and physics harder still.* **5** **be still going strong** to continue to be active or successful, even after a long time: *They've been married for 42 years, and they're still going strong.*

USAGE NOTE: STILL

WORD CHOICE: still, already, yet

Still can mean that you are surprised that something has continued for longer than you might expect: *You mean Jenny still hasn't found a job?* **Already** is usually used in positive sentences can mean that you are surprised that something has happened earlier than you thought it would: *Are they here already?* **Yet** is used in negatives and questions to talk about things that you expect to happen, but have not happened or might not have happened: *I haven't had breakfast yet.* | *Has Bill arrived yet?* When you compare **yet** with **already** in a question, *Have you eaten lunch yet?* asks for information, while *Have you eaten lunch already?* may express surprise that lunch has already been eaten. Using **yet** instead of **still** in a positive sentence is rare and a little formal: *We have yet to hear the truth.* | *The city council may yet surprise us.* In conversation, however, you are more likely to say something like: *We don't know the truth yet.*

GRAMMAR

Still usually comes immediately before any negative word: *She still isn't ready.* | *You still don't understand.* |

A solution has still not been found (or ...still hasn't, NOT "has not still"). **Still** usually comes immediately after a positive modal verb: *I can still remember* (NOT "still can remember"). | *He may still be there* (NOT "be still there"). Otherwise **still** comes after the verb **to be** and immediately before any main verb: *She's still eating* (NOT "still is eating"). | *It's still wet outside.* | *We still have time* (NOT "have still time"). | *I still love her.* **Yet** often comes either immediately after a negative word or at the end of a clause, but there is a difference of style. In formal written English, you might read: *We do not yet know the answer.* In informal conversation you might say: *I don't know the answer yet* (NOT "I don't know yet the answer"). **Yet** may be placed immediately after the verb where a clause follows: *I don't know yet whether she'll come or not.*

still² adj. [no comparative] **1** not moving: *a still pond* | **keep/stand/lie etc. still** *We stood still and watched as the deer came closer.* **2** quiet and calm: *For once, the house was completely still.* **3** not windy: *a hot, still, airless day* **4** **still waters run deep** used to say that someone who is quiet may have very strong feelings or a lot of knowledge —**stillness** n. [U]

still³ n. [C] **1** a photograph of a scene from a movie **2** a piece of equipment for making alcoholic drinks out of grain or potatoes **3** **the still of the night/evening etc.** LITERARY the calm and quiet of the night, evening etc.

still⁴ v. [T] LITERARY **1** to make someone or something become quiet or calm: *The ground beneath them trembled, then stilled.* **2** if a doubt or fear is stilled, it becomes weaker or goes away

still·birth /ˈstɪlbɚθ, ˌstɪlˈbɚθ/ n. [C,U] a birth in which the baby is born dead —compare ABORTION, MISCARRIAGE

still·born /ˌstɪlˈbɔrn◂/ adj. **1** born dead: *a stillborn baby* **2** ending before having had a chance to start: *a stillborn romance*

still life /ˈ. ./ n. plural **still lifes** [C,U] a painting or photograph of an arrangement of objects, especially flowers and fruit

stilt /stɪlt/ n. [C usually plural] **1** one of two poles on which you can stand and walk high above the ground: *As a child, I loved walking around **on stilts**.* **2** one of a set of poles that support a building, so that it is raised above ground or water level

stilt·ed /ˈstɪltɪd/ adj. a stilted style of writing or speaking is formal and unnatural: *The dialogue was stilted and robotlike.* —**stiltedly** adv.

Stil·ton /ˈstɪltn̩/ n. [U] a type of English cheese that has a strong taste

stim·u·lant /ˈstɪmyələnt/ n. [C] **1** a drug or substance that makes you feel more active and full of energy: *Nicotine, the drug found in tobacco, is a stimulant.* **2** something that encourages more of a particular activity; STIMULUS: [+ to] *Increases in new construction would be a stimulant to the economy.*

stim·u·late /ˈstɪmyə.leɪt/ v. [T] **1** to encourage or help an activity to begin or develop further: *City leaders hope the amusement park will stimulate tourism.* **2** to encourage someone by making them excited about and interested in something: *The activities are designed to stimulate classroom discussions.* **3** to make a plant or part of the body become active or stronger: *The herb echinacea seems to stimulate the body's immune system.* —**stimulative** adj. —**stimulation** /ˌstɪmyəˈleɪʃən/ n. [U]

stim·u·lat·ing /ˈstɪmyəleɪtɪŋ/ adj. **1** exciting or full of new ideas: *a stimulating discussion of world politics* **2** making you feel more active: *the stimulating effects of coffee and tea*

stim·u·lus /ˈstɪmyələs/ n. plural **stimuli** /-laɪ/ **1** [C usually singular, U] something that helps a process to develop more quickly or more strongly: *Tax cuts provided the stimulus the slow economy needed.* **2** [C] something that makes someone or something move or react: *At this age, the infant begins to react more to visual stimuli.*

sting¹ /stɪŋ/ *v. past tense and past participle* **stung**
1 [I,T] if an insect or a plant stings you, it causes a sharp pain and that part of your body swells: *Henry was stung by a bee at the picnic.* **2** [I,T] to make something hurt with a sudden sharp pain for a short time, or to hurt in this way: *The paper cut on my finger really stings.* | *Cigarette smoke stings my eyes.* **3** [T usually passive] if a remark or criticism stings, it makes you feel upset and embarrassed: *Lathan was stung by the senator's harsh criticism.* | [sting sb into (doing) sth] *Her harsh words stung him into action.*

sting² *n.* **1** [C] a wound or mark made when an insect or plant stings you: *The bee sting had left a red mark on my arm.* **2** [singular] a sharp pain in your eyes or skin, caused by being hit, by smoke etc.: *I still felt the sting of her slap on my cheek.* **3** [singular] the bad effects of a bad situation: *I had never felt the sting of discrimination before.* | *Winning the award* **takes the sting out of** (=makes it easier to deal with the bad effects of) *not being in the playoffs.* **4** [C] a situation in which the police catch criminals by pretending to be involved in criminal activity themselves

sting·er /ˈstɪŋɚ/ *n.* [C] the sharp needle-like part of an animal or insect's body that can be pushed through the skin of a person or animal, often leaving poison —see picture at INSECT

sting·ing /ˈstɪŋɪŋ/ *adj.* **a stinging report/letter/rebuke etc.** a report, letter, rebuke etc. that severely and strongly expresses criticism

stinging net·tle /ˈ.. ˌ../ *n.* [C] a wild plant with leaves that sting and leave red marks on the skin

sting·ray /ˈstɪŋreɪ/ *n.* [C] a large fish with a flat body and several sharp points on its back near its tail

stin·gy /ˈstɪndʒi/ *adj.* **stingier, stingiest** INFORMAL not generous, especially with money, when you can easily afford to be: *Residents here have a history of being stingy with their tax dollars.* **2** a stingy amount of something, especially food, is too small to be enough: *I was given a stingy portion of vegetables with rice.* —**stingily** *adv.* —**stinginess** *n.* [U]

[I] **1** to have a strong and very bad smell: *Your shoes stink.* | [+ of] *His apartment stank of stale beer.* | *It stinks of smoke in here.* | *The school's bathrooms* **stink to high heaven** (=stink very much). **2 sth stinks!** SPOKEN **a)** used to say that something is bad or that you do not like it: *Don't eat there – the food stinks!* **b)** used to say that you think something is not fair or legal: *Not getting a scholarship to college really stinks.*

stink sth ↔ **up** INFORMAL *phr. v.* [T] **1** to fill a place with a very bad smell: *Those onions are stinking the whole house up.* **2 stink up the place** to perform badly in a play, game etc.: *Scoring only four points, McClellan really stunk up the place.*

stink² *n.* **1** [C] a very bad smell: [+ of] *the stink of burning rubber* **2 make/raise/cause etc. a stink** to complain very strongly because you are annoyed about something: *Activists have raised a stink about the shipments of nuclear waste.*

stink bomb /ˈ. ./ *n.* [C] a small container that produces an extremely bad smell when it is broken

stink·er /ˈstɪŋkɚ/ *n.* [C] INFORMAL **1** someone who behaves badly, especially a child: *That son of theirs is a little stinker!* **2** a movie, book, sports team etc. that is very bad: *The movie is Brandon's first stinker.*

stink·ing /ˈstɪŋkɪŋ/ *adj.* **1** having a very strong bad smell: *a dump full of stinking garbage* **2** [only before noun] SPOKEN used to emphasize what you are saying when you are angry or do not like something: *I don't want to watch that stinking TV show.* **3 stinking rich** INFORMAL an expression meaning "extremely rich," used especially when you think this is unfair: *Jane's family is stinking rich.* **4 stinking drunk** very drunk: *Clayton got positively stinking drunk.*

stink·y /ˈstɪŋki/ *adj.* **stinkier, stinkiest** INFORMAL smelling very bad; SMELLY: *stinky swamp water*

stint¹ /stɪnt/ *n.* [C usually singular] a limited or particular period of work or effort: [+ as/in/at] *After a three-year stint in the Marines, Walker got a job in marketing.*

---

stint² *v.* [I usually in negatives] to give or use too little of something: [+ on] *Lee's book about Armstrong doesn't stint on the gossip.*

sti·pend /ˈstaɪpɛnd, -pənd/ *n.* [C] a particular amount of money paid regularly to someone such as a priest or student, as a salary or money to live on

stip·ple /ˈstɪpəl/ *v.* [T] to draw or paint a picture or pattern using very short STROKES or spots instead of longer lines —**stippled** *adj.* —**stippling** *n.* [U]

stip·u·late /ˈstɪpyəˌleɪt/ *v.* [T] to say that something must be done, when you are making an agreement or offer: *Laws stipulate the maximum interest rate that banks can charge.* | [stipulate that sth be done] *Gordon's will stipulated that his fortune be given to his two daughters.*

stip·u·la·tion /ˌstɪpyəˈleɪʃən/ *n.* [C,U] something that must be done which is stated as part of an agreement: [+ that] *The agreement included a stipulation that half of the money be spent on housing for lower-income families.*

stir¹ /stɚ/ *v.* **1** [T] to move a liquid or substance around with a spoon or stick in order to mix it together: *Could you stir the spaghetti sauce for me?* | [stir sth with sth] *She stirred her coffee with a spoon.* | [stir sth in/into sth] *Stir in a cup of cooked brown rice to the mixture.* **2** [I] to move slightly or change your position, especially because you are uncomfortable, anxious, or you are about to wake up: *The crowd began to stir as they waited for the band to start.* **3 a)** [T] to make someone have a strong feeling or reaction | **stir memories/emotions etc.** *Finding my old yearbook stirred memories of our summer romance.* | *The Arizona landscape* **stirs the imagination. b)** [I] if a feeling stirs in you, you begin to feel it: *Excitement stirred inside her.* **4** [T] to make someone feel they must do something: [stir sb to do sth] *The incident has stirred students to protest.* **5** [T] to make something move slightly: *A gentle breeze stirred the curtains.*

stir up *phr. v.* [T] **1** [stir sb/sth ↔ up] to deliberately try to cause arguments or problems between people: *His speech really stirred up the crowd.* | *John was always* **stirring up trouble** *in class.* | *Dave's just trying to* **stir things up** *because he's jealous.* **2** [stir sth ↔ up] to make something move around in the air or in water: *The wind had stirred up a powdery red dust that covered everything.*

stir² *n.* **1** [C usually singular] a feeling of excitement or annoyance | **create/cause a stir** *The nude paintings at the library have created quite a stir.* **2** [C usually singular] an act of stirring something **3** [C,U] OLD-FASHIONED, SLANG a prison

stir-cra·zy /ˈ. ˌ../ *adj.* INFORMAL extremely nervous and upset, especially because you feel trapped in a place: *I'm going to* **go stir-crazy** *if I don't get out of this house.*

stir-fry /ˈ. ./ *v.* **stir-fries, stir-fried, stir-frying** [T] to cook something by cutting it into small pieces and cooking it in a small amount of hot oil for a short time: *stir-fried vegetables* —**stir-fry** *n.* [C]

stir·ring /ˈstɚɪŋ, ˈstʌrɪŋ/ *adj.* producing strong feelings or excitement in someone: *a stirring speech* —**stirringly** *adv.*

stir·rings /ˈstɚɪŋz/ *n.* [plural] early signs that something is starting to happen, or that you are beginning to feel a particular emotion: **stirrings of love/doubt/rebellion etc.** *It is a region already unsettled by stirrings of nationalism.*

stir·rup /ˈstɚəp, ˈstɪrəp/ *n.* [C] **1** a ring of metal that hangs from each side of a horse's SADDLE for someone to put their foot in as they ride the horse **2** a U-shaped object that is used for supporting or holding something such as your feet: *the stirrup of a shoeshine stand*

stirrup pants /ˈ.. ˌ./ *n.* [plural] women's pants made of a material that stretches, that have bands at the bottom of the legs that fit under your feet

stitch¹ /stɪtʃ/ *n.*

1 `sewing` [C] in sewing, a stitch is made by the thread going into and out of the cloth one time: *The seam of the shirt was straight and the stitches tight and regular.*

2 `for wound` [C] a piece of special thread that fastens the edges of a wound together: *Sandstrom needed 10 stitches to close a cut on his forehead.*

3 `pain` [C, usually singular] a sharp pain in the side of your body, that you can get by running or laughing very hard: *After jogging about a mile, I suddenly got a stitch in my side.*

4 `knitting` [C] one of the small circles that are formed when you are KNITting, that join together to make a SWEATER etc. —see also **drop a stitch** (DROP¹ (35))

5 `style` [C,U] a particular way of sewing or KNITting that makes a particular pattern: *Purl and plain are the two main stitches in knitting.*

6 not have a stitch on INFORMAL to be wearing no clothes

7 not have a stitch to wear to not have any clothing that is appropriate for a particular occasion

8 a stitch in time (saves nine) SPOKEN used to say that it is better to deal with problems early on than to wait until they get worse

stitch² *v.* [T] to sew two pieces of cloth together, or to sew a decoration onto a piece of cloth: *Mary spent six months stitching our new bedspread.* | **stitch sth onto/across sth** *He was given a baseball jersey with his name stitched across the back.*

stitch sth ↔ **up** *phr. v.* [T] **1** to put stitches in cloth or a wound in order to fasten parts of it together: *She stitched up the cut and left it to heal.* **2** to get a deal or agreement completed satisfactorily so that it cannot be changed: *The deal was stitched up in minutes.*

stitch sth ↔ **together** *phr. v.* [T] **1** to put different things or parts of something together to make one larger thing: *In ten years, they have been able to stitch together a national network of banks.* **2** to get a deal or agreement completed satisfactorily, so that it cannot be changed: *The city council finally stitched together a compromise plan.*

stitch·er·y /'stɪtʃəri/ *n.* [U] NEEDLEWORK

stitch·es /'stɪtʃɪz/ *n.* **in stitches** INFORMAL unable to stop laughing | **keep/have sb in stitches** *Tony kept us in stitches all evening.*

stitch·ing /'stɪtʃɪŋ/ *n.* [U] a line of stitches in a piece of material

St. John's /seɪnt 'dʒɑnz/ the capital city of Antigua and Barbuda

St. Kitts and Ne·vis /seɪnt ˌkɪts ən 'nivɪs/ also **St. Christopher and Nevis** a country consisting of two islands in the Caribbean Sea

St. Law·rence Riv·er, the /seɪnt 'lɔrəns/ a river in North America that flows from Lake Ontario to the Gulf of St. Lawrence and forms part of the border between the U.S. and Canada

St. Lawrence Sea·way, the /. ˌ.. '../ a system of CANALS in North America connecting the St. Lawrence River and all the Great Lakes. It was built by the U.S. and Canada and was opened in 1959.

St. Lou·is /seɪnt 'luɪs/ a city in the U.S. state of Missouri which is a port on the Mississippi River

St. Lu·cia /seɪnt 'luʃə/ a country that is an island in the Caribbean Sea

stoat /stoʊt/ *n.* [C] a small thin animal with brown fur that is similar to a WEASEL, and kills other animals

S W **stock¹** /stɑk/ *n.*

1 `in a store` [C,U] a supply of a particular type of thing that a store has to sell: *We have a huge stock of quality carpets on sale.* | *I'll call to see if our other store has that dress* **in stock** (=available at a particular store). | *I'm sorry, that swimsuit is completely* **out of stock** (=unavailable at a particular store) *in your size.* | *I spent the whole weekend at the store* **taking stock** (=checking and counting the goods in a store).

2 `finance` **a)** [C] one of the equal parts into which the OWNERSHIP of a company is divided, used especially when you are talking about the number of parts or the price of each one —compare SHARE² (4) **b)** [U] the total value of all of a company's stocks

3 `cooking` [C,U] a liquid made by boiling meat or bones and vegetables, which is used to make soups or to add FLAVOR to other dishes: *chicken stock*

4 `amount available` [C] the total amount of something in a particular area that is available to be used: *Cod stocks in the North Atlantic have dropped radically.*

5 `supplies` [C] a supply of something that you keep and can use when you need to: [+ of] *Uncle Gene kept a large stock of food in the cellar.* | *They had reportedly hidden large stocks of chemical weapons.*

6 `animals` [U] farm animals, especially cattle; LIVESTOCK: *Sellew has built his stock to a herd of nearly 100 goats.*

7 take stock (of sth) to think carefully about the things that have happened in a situation in order to decide what to do next: *While in the hospital, Jeremy took stock of his life.*

8 `gun` [C] the part of a gun that you hold or put against your shoulder, usually made of wood

9 the stocks a) a wooden structure in a public place to which criminals were fastened by their feet or hands in past times **b)** a wooden structure in which a ship is held while it is being built

10 `plant` **a)** a plant that you can cut stems off to make new plants grow **b)** a thick part of a stem onto which another plant can be added so that the two plants grow together

11 sb's stock is high/low if someone's stock is high or low, they are very popular or very unpopular: *Simon's stock is high in the network news business.*

12 a stock of jokes/knowledge/words etc. the jokes, knowledge, words etc. that someone knows or has: *John seems to have an inexhaustible stock of funny stories.*

13 be of Scottish/Protestant/good etc. stock to belong to a family that in the past lived in Scotland, were Protestants, were respected etc.

14 `theater` [C] a STOCK COMPANY (2) —see also SUMMER STOCK

15 `clothing` [C] a wide band of cloth that goes around the neck so that the ends hang in front of your chest, worn especially by some priests —see also LAUGHINGSTOCK, **lock, stock, and barrel** (LOCK² (2)), ROLLING STOCK

stock² *v.* [T] **1** if a store stocks a particular product, it keeps a supply of it to be sold: *Do you stock camping equipment?* **2** to provide a supply of something so that it is ready to use: [**stock sth with sth**] *Our refrigerator at college was always stocked with beer.* **3** to put fish in a lake or river: [**stock sth with sth**] *Oak Creek is stocked with trout.* —see also WELL-STOCKED

stock up *phr. v.* [I] to buy a lot of something to use when you need to: [+ **on**] *I have to stock up on snacks for the party.*

stock³ *adj.* **stock excuse/question/remark etc.** an excuse, question etc. that people often say or use, especially when they cannot think of anything more interesting or original

stock·ade¹ /stɑ'keɪd/ *n.* [C usually singular] a wall or fence made of large upright pieces of wood, built to defend a place

stockade² *v.* [T] to put a stockade around a place in order to defend it

stock·breed·er /'stɑkˌbridɚ/ *n.* [C] a farmer who breeds cattle

stock·brok·er /'stɑkˌbroʊkɚ/ *n.* [C] someone whose job is to buy and sell STOCKS, BONDS etc. for other people —**stockbroking** *n.* [U]

stock car /'. ./ *n.* [C] **1** a car that has been made stronger so that it can compete in a race where cars often crash into each other **2** a railroad car used for cattle

stock cer·tif·i·cate /'. .ˌ.../ *n.* [C] an official document that shows that you own STOCK in a company

stock com·pa·ny /'. ˌ.../ *n.* [C] **1** a company whose money is divided into STOCKS so that many people own a small part of it **2** a group of actors who work together doing several different plays

stock ex·change /'. .,./ *n.* [C usually singular] **1** the business of buying STOCKs and SHAREs: *She made a fortune on the stock exchange.* **2** a place where STOCKs and SHAREs are bought and sold

stock·hold·er /'stɑk,hoʊldə/ *n.* [C] someone who owns STOCKs in a business

Stock·holm /'stɑkhoʊlm/ the capital and largest city of Sweden

stock in·dex /'. ,../ *n.* [C] an official and public list of STOCK prices

stock·ing /'stɑkɪŋ/ *n.* [C usually plural] **1** a thin close-fitting piece of clothing that covers a woman's leg and foot —compare PANTYHOSE, TIGHTS **2** OLD-FASHIONED a man's sock **3 in your stockinged/ stocking feet** not wearing any shoes —see also BODY STOCKING, CHRISTMAS STOCKING

stocking cap /'.. .'./ *n.* [C] a type of soft hat that fits close around your head, used to keep you warm

stocking mask /'.. ,./ *n.* [C] a stocking or NYLONS that someone wears over their face, especially when doing something illegal

stock-in-trade /,. . './ *n.* [U] **1** something that is typical of a particular person or thing, especially what they say or do: *Stewart's stock-in-trade was the face-to-face interview.* **2** LITERARY the things you need to do your job: *Vanessa's looks have been her stock-in-trade as an actress.*

stock·man /'stɑkmən/ *n.* [C] a man whose job it is to take care of farm animals

stock mar·ket /'. ,../ *n.* [C usually singular] **1** the STOCK EXCHANGE **2** the average value of STOCKs sold in the STOCK EXCHANGE

stock op·tion /'. ,../ *n.* [C usually plural] STOCK that a company offers to sell an EMPLOYEE at a price that is lower than the usual price

stock·pile¹ /'stɑkpaɪl/ *n.* [C] a large supply of goods, weapons etc. that are kept ready to be used in the future, especially when they may become difficult to obtain: [+ of] *stockpiles of nuclear missiles*

stockpile² *v.* [T] to keep adding to a supply of goods, weapons etc. that you are keeping ready to use if you need them in the future: *Several militant groups are continuing to stockpile illegal weapons.*

stock·pot /'stɑkpɑt/ *n.* [C] a pot in which you make STOCK¹ (3)

stock·room /'stɑkrum/ *n.* [C] a room for storing things in a store or office

stock split /'. ./ *n.* [C] a situation in which the STOCKs in a company are divided into more stocks that are less valuable, but which together are worth the same amount as the original stocks: *a 2-for-1 stock split*

stock-still /,. './ *adv.* not moving at all: *Oscar stood stock-still and listened.*

stock·y /'stɑki/ *adj.* **stockier, stockiest** a stocky person is short and heavy and looks strong: *a blond, stocky boy* —**stockily** *adv.* —**stockiness** *n.* [U]

stock·yard /'stɑkyɑrd/ *n.* [C] a place where cattle, sheep etc. are kept before being taken to a market and sold

stodg·y /'stɑdʒi/ *adj.* **stodgier, stodgiest** **1** a stodgy person is boring and behaves rather formally **2** stodgy writing or organizations are boring, formal, and old-fashioned: *the stodgy banking industry* —**stodginess** *n.* [U]

sto·gie /'stoʊgi/ *n.* [C] INFORMAL a CIGAR, especially a thick cheap one

sto·ic /'stoʊɪk/ *n.* [C] someone who does not show their emotions and does not complain when something bad happens to them

sto·i·cal /'stoʊɪkəl/ also **stoic** *adj.* not complaining or feeling unhappy when bad things happen to you —**stoically** /-kli/ *adv.*

sto·i·cism /'stoʊɪ,sɪzəm/ *n.* [U] patience and calmness when bad things happen to you

stoke /stoʊk/ also **stoke up** *v.* [I,T] **1** to add more coal or wood to a fire used for cooking or heating: *I stoked the furnace for the night.* **2** to cause something

to increase: *Rising oil prices stoked inflation in the 1970s.* | **stoke fear/anger/resentment etc.** *The recent budget cuts have stoked public outrage.*

stoke up *phr. v.* [T **stoke** sth ↔ **up**] to add more coal or wood to a fire: *They keep the old steam locomotive stoked up 24 hours a day.*

stoked /stoʊkt/ *adj.* [not before noun] SPOKEN very excited about something good that is happening and that you did not expect: *I'm stoked about getting a new car.*

stok·er /'stoʊkə/ *n.* [C] someone whose job is to put coal or other FUEL¹ into a FURNACE

stole¹ /stoʊl/ *v.* the past tense of STEAL

stole² *n.* [C] a long straight piece of cloth or fur that a woman wears across her shoulders

sto·len¹ /'stoʊlən/ *v.* the past participle of STEAL

stolen² *adj.* having been taken illegally: *stolen cars*

stol·id /'stɑlɪd/ *adj.* someone who is stolid does not react to situations or seem excited by them when most people would react —**stolidly** *adv.*

stom·ach¹ /'stʌmək/ *n.* [C] **1** the organ inside your body where food begins to be DIGESTed —see pictures at BODY and DIGESTIVE SYSTEM **2** the front part of your body, below your chest: *He turned around and punched Steve in the stomach.* **3 do sth on an empty stomach** to do something when you have not eaten: *You shouldn't take the pills on an empty stomach.* **4 turn sb's stomach** to make someone feel sick or upset: *The pictures of the starving people were enough to turn my stomach.* **5 have no stomach for a fight/ task etc.** to have no desire to do something because you do not like doing it or are frightened to do it —see also **have a strong stomach** (STRONG (25))

stomach² *v.* [T usually in questions and negatives] **1** to be able to accept something, especially something bad; ENDURE: **can/could stomach** *A 26% water rate increase is more than most residents can stomach.* | **hard/difficult to stomach** *Their horrible loss in the Super Bowl has been difficult for many fans to stomach.* **2** to eat something without becoming sick: *I've never been able to stomach seafood.*

stom·ach·ache, stomach ache /'stʌmək,eɪk/ *n.* [C,U] pain in your stomach or near your stomach

stomach pump /'.. ,./ *n.* [C] a machine with a tube that doctors use to suck out the food or liquid inside someone's stomach, especially after they have swallowed poison

stomp /stɑmp, stɔmp/ *v.* [I,T] to walk with heavy steps or to put your foot down very hard, especially because you are angry: *In the middle of the show, the lead singer stomped off the stage.* | [+ on] *Several rioters repeatedly stomped on an American flag.*

stomping ground /'.. ,./ *n.* **sb's stomping ground** a favorite place where someone often goes

stone¹ /stoʊn/ *n.*
1 [piece of rock] [C] a small piece of rock of any shape, found on the ground: *Kids were throwing stones into the water.*
2 [rock] [U] a hard solid mineral substance; rock: *a stone wall* | *Messina is a city built of stone.*
3 [jewelry] [C] a jewel: *The gold ring was set with four precious stones.*
4 [medical] [C] a ball of hard material that can form in organs such as your BLADDER or KIDNEYs
5 a stone's throw (from/away) INFORMAL very close to something: *My parents' house is a stone's throw from Fourth Avenue.*
6 be made of stone also **have a heart of stone** to not show any emotions or pity for someone
7 not be carved/etched in stone used to say an idea or plan could change: *John has several new ideas for the show, but nothing is etched in stone yet.*
—see also FOUNDATION STONE, **kill two birds with one stone** (KILL¹ (12)), **leave no stone unturned** (LEAVE¹ (39)), PAVING STONE, STEPPING STONE, **sticks and stones can/may break my bones** (STICK² (9))

stone² *v.* [T] **1** to throw stones at someone or something: *Rioters blocked roads and stoned vehicles.*

2 stone sb to death to kill someone by throwing stones at them, used as a punishment in past times

Stone /stoʊn/, **Har·lan** /ˈhɑrlən/ (1872–1946) a CHIEF JUSTICE on the U.S. Supreme Court

Stone Age /ˈ. ./ n. a very early time in human history, when only stone was used for making tools, weapons etc. —compare BRONZE AGE, IRON AGE

stone-cold /ˌ. ˈ.◂/ adj. **1** completely cold, in a way that is bad: *Dinner was stone-cold by the time I got home.* **2** if a player on a sports team is stone-cold, they are not able to get any points: *Notre Dame's offense was stone-cold in the second half.* **3** stone-cold sober having drunk no alcohol at all

stoned /stoʊnd/ adj. [not before noun] **1** INFORMAL feeling very excited or extremely relaxed because you have taken an illegal drug **2** OLD-FASHIONED very drunk

stone dead /ˌ. ˈ.◂/ adj. used to emphasize that a person or animal is dead

stone deaf /ˌ. ˈ.◂/ adj. completely unable to hear

stone-faced /ˈ. ./ also **stony-faced** /ˈ.. ./ adj. showing no emotion or friendliness

stone-ground /ˌ. ˈ.◂/ adj. stone-ground flour is made by crushing grain between two MILLSTONES

stone·ma·son /ˈstoʊnˌmeɪsən/ n. [C] someone whose job is cutting stone into pieces to be used in buildings —see also MASON (1)

ston·er /ˈstoʊnər/ n. [C] SLANG someone who smokes MARIJUANA very often

stone·wall /ˈstoʊnwɔl/ v. [I] to delay a discussion, decision etc. by talking a lot and refusing to answer questions

stone·ware /ˈstoʊnwɛr/ n. [U] pots, bowls etc. that are made from a special hard clay

stone·washed /ˈstoʊnwɑʃt/ adj. stonewashed JEANS etc. have been made softer by a washing process in which they are beaten with stones

stone·work /ˈstoʊnwɜrk/ n. [U] the parts of a building that are made of stone, especially when they are used for decoration

ston·y /ˈstoʊni/ adj. stonier, stoniest **1** covered by stones or containing stones: *the stony hillside* **2** without friendliness or pity: *They drove home in stony silence.* | *She looked at him with stony eyes.* **3 fall on stony ground** if a request, suggestion, joke etc. falls on stony ground, it is ignored or people do not like it —**stonily** adv.

stood /stʊd/ v. the past tense and past participle of STAND¹

stooge /studʒ/ n. [C] **1** one of two performers who is the subject of jokes made by the other performer **2** INFORMAL someone who always does what someone else wants them to

stool /stul/ n. [C] **1** a seat without any supporting part for your back or arms: *a bar stool* —see picture at CHAIR¹ **2** TECHNICAL a piece of solid waste from your body

stool·pi·geon /ˈstulˌpɪdʒən/ n. INFORMAL [C] someone, especially a criminal, who helps the police to catch another criminal, usually by giving them information; INFORMER

stoop¹ /stup/ v. [I] **1** also **stoop down** to bend your body forward and down: *We had to stoop to pass through the low entrance.* | *David stooped down to tie his shoes.* **2** to stand with your back and shoulders bent forward

stoop to sth phr. v. [T] to do something, even though you know it is bad or morally wrong, because you think it will help you achieve something: [**stoop to doing sth**] *I am shocked that the magazine would stoop to publishing nude pictures of the couple.* | **stoop to sb's/that level** *You don't have to stoop to that level to be successful.*

stoop² n. **1** [C] a raised area at the door of a house, usually big enough to sit on **2** [singular] if you have a stoop, your shoulders slope forward or seem too round: *Mr. Hamilton was an odd, quiet man who walked with a stoop.*

stooped /stupt/ adj. having a stoop: *a stooped old man*

stoop·ing /ˈstupɪŋ/ adj. stooping shoulders are bent forward or have become too round

stop¹ /stɑp/ v. stopped, stopping

1 not move or continue [I,T] to not move or continue to do something anymore, or to make someone or something do this: *Stop! There's a car coming.* | [**stop sth**] *Apply pressure to stop the bleeding.* | *Stop the car – I think we have a flat tire.* | [**stop doing sth**] *We couldn't stop laughing.* | **stop and look/stare/ listen etc.** *She stopped and looked at the statue.* | *His new truck can* **stop on a dime** (=stop very quickly).

2 prevent [T] to prevent someone from doing something or something from happening: *He wanted to quit college, and no one could stop him.* | [**stop sb (from) doing sth**] *I tried to stop them from fighting.* | *There's nothing to stop you from calling her to say you're sorry.*

3 end [I,T] to end or make something end: *We'll go out when the rain stops.* | **stop sth** *The referee stopped the fight.* | [+ at] *The road stops at the farm.*

4 stop that/it SPOKEN said when you want someone to stop annoying, upsetting, or hurting you or someone else: *Stop it! Don't push me!*

5 pause [I] to pause in an activity, trip etc. in order to do something before continuing: [**stop for sth**] *This looks like a good place to stop for lunch.* | [+ at] *I need to stop at the gas station first.* | [**stop to do sth**] *I stopped to buy bread on the way home.* | **stop to think/consider** *Have you stopped to consider how selfishly you're behaving?*

6 stop at nothing (to do sth) to be ready to do anything, even if it is cruel, dishonest, or illegal, to get what you want: *Johnson would stop at nothing to win an election.*

7 walking/traveling [T] to go to someone and speak to them or make them stop when they are walking or traveling somewhere: *Someone stopped me in the street and asked for directions.* | *I got stopped by a policeman for having a broken headlight.*

8 stop short of (doing) sth to stop before you do one more thing that would be too dangerous, risky etc.: *Shepherd stopped short of calling him a liar.*

9 stop a check also **stop payment (on a check)** to tell your bank to not pay money for a check that you have written to someone

10 stop the presses a) to make a PRINTING PRESS stop working, especially because something very important has happened and you need to add it to the newspaper before it finishes printing **b)** to close a company that prints newspapers, magazines, or books **c)** SPOKEN, HUMOROUS said before telling someone surprising news: *Stop the presses! Lewis is coming back.*

11 stop (dead) in your tracks to suddenly stop, especially because something has frightened or surprised you

stop back phr. v. [I] to go back to a place you have been to earlier: *Can you stop back later? I'm really busy right now.*

stop by phr. v. [I,T] to make a short visit to a place or person, especially while you are going somewhere else: *Could you stop by the store and pick up a roll of film for me?*

stop in phr. v. [I] INFORMAL to make a short visit to a place or person, especially while you are going somewhere else: *You can just stop in and drop the papers off next week.* | [+ at] *I need to stop in at the office for a minute.*

stop off phr. v. [I] to make a short visit to a place while you are going somewhere else: [+ in/at etc.] *I'm going to stop off at the sporting goods store after work.*

stop over phr. v. [I] to stop somewhere and stay a short time before continuing a long trip, especially when traveling by airplane: *The plane stops over in Dubai on the way to India.*

stop sth ↔ **up** phr. v. [T] **1** to block something such as a pipe so that water, smoke etc. cannot go through it: *A big ball of hair had stopped up the drain.* **2** be **stopped up** if your nose or head is stopped up, it is full of thick liquid because you have a cold

stop² n. [C]

1 put a stop to sth to prevent something from continuing or happening: *She decided to put a stop to their relationship.*

2 during trip a time or place when you stop during a trip for a short time: *Our trip to Africa included a stop in the Serengeti.* | *We'll **make a stop** (=stop somewhere while traveling) in Hong Kong before returning home.*

3 come to a stop if a vehicle, an activity etc. comes to a stop, it stops moving or happening: *The elevator finally came to a stop at the 56th floor.*

4 bring sth to a stop to stop something moving or happening: *David brought the truck to a shuddering stop.*

5 roll to a stop if a vehicle with wheels rolls to a stop, it moves forward while slowing down before stopping: *A black-and-white police car rolled to a stop at the corner.*

6 bus/train a place where a bus or train regularly stops for people to get on and off: *I'm getting off at the next stop.*

7 check the action or fact of telling your bank not to pay money for a check that you have written to someone: *I'll have to **put a stop on** that check.*

8 music **a)** a set of pipes on an ORGAN (2) that produce sound **b)** a set of handles that you push in or out in an organ to control the amount of sound it produces

9 consonant TECHNICAL a CONSONANT sound, like /p/ or /k/, made by stopping the flow of air completely and then suddenly letting it out of your mouth —see also **pull out all the stops** at **pull out** (PULL¹)

stop·cock /'stapkak/ n. [C] a VALVE that can be opened or closed with a TAP (=object you turn) to control the flow of a liquid in a pipe

stop·gap /'stapgæp/ n. [C] something or someone that you use for a short time until you can replace it with something better: *The Senate has passed a stop-gap funding measure.*

stop·light /'staplait/ n. [C] also **stoplights** PLURAL a set of colored lights used to control and direct traffic

stop·o·ver /'stap,ouvə/ n. [C] a short stay somewhere between parts of a trip, especially on a long airplane trip: *a two-day stopover in Hong Kong* —see picture at NONSTOP

stop·page /'stapidʒ/ n. **1** [C] a situation in which workers stop working for a short time as a protest: *a one-day work stoppage* **2** [C,U] the act of stopping something from moving or happening: *a stoppage of welfare payments* **3** [C] something that blocks a tube or container: *The plumber cleared the stoppage in the building's sewer line.*

stop·per /'stapə/ n. [C] the thing that you put in the top part of a bottle to close it —**stopper** v. [T]

stopping dis·tance /'.. ,../ n. [C,U] the distance that a driver is supposed to leave between their car and the one in front in order to be able to stop safely

stop press /,. '. ./ n. [singular] late news added to a newspaper after the main part has been printed

stop·watch /'stapwatʃ/ n. [C] a watch used for measuring the exact time it takes to do something, especially to finish a race

stor·age /'storidʒ/ n. [U] **1** the act of keeping or putting something in a special place while it is not being used: *the storage of radioactive material* **2 in storage** if furniture or other goods are in storage, they are being kept in a special place until you need to use them **3 storage space/capacity** the amount of space or room that can be used for storing things: *The car's trunk has a huge storage capacity.* **4** the price you pay for having goods or furniture stored

storage room /'.. ,./ n. [C] a room that is used to store things

store¹ /stor/ n. [C] **1** a place where goods are sold: *a shoe/clothing/grocery etc. store* (=one that sells one type of goods) | *I need to **go to the store** (=go to a store that sells food) for some milk.* —see also CONVENIENCE STORE, DEPARTMENT STORE, DRUGSTORE **2 be in store** if something unexpected such as a surprise or problem is in store, it is going to happen: *Margaret*

had no way of knowing what was in store for her later that year. **3** a supply or large amount of something, especially that you keep to use later: *The book is a store of knowledge about Dickens.* | *[+ of]* *Granny always had a special store of chocolate for us.*

store² v. [T] **1** also **store away** to put things away and keep them until you need them: *All of my old books are stored in boxes in the attic.* **2** to keep facts or information in your brain or a computer: *How much information can you store on your hard drive?* **3 store up trouble/problems etc.** to behave in a way that will cause trouble for you later: *Sarah is storing up problems for herself by lying to him.*

store brand /'. ./ n. [C] a type of goods that are produced for a particular store and have the store's name on them: *store brand cereals*

store de·tec·tive /'. ,../ n. [C] someone who is employed in a large store to watch the customers and to stop them stealing

store·front /'storfrʌnt/ n. [C] **1** the part of a store that faces the street **2 storefront office/church/school etc.** a small office, church etc. in a shopping area

store·house /'storhaus/ n. [C] **1** a storehouse of information/memories etc. something that contains a lot of information etc. **2** OLD-FASHIONED a building where things are stored: WAREHOUSE

store·keep·er /'stor,kipə/ n. [C] someone who owns or manages a store

store·room /'stor-rum/ n. [C] a room where goods are stored

-storied /'storid/ [in adjectives] **1 two-storied/five-storied etc.** having two, five etc. floors: *a six-storied building* **2** [only before noun] LITERARY being the subject of many stories; FAMOUS

stork /stork/ n. [C] a tall white bird with long legs and a long beak

storm¹ /storm/ n. **1** [C] a period of very bad weather when there is a lot of rain or snow, strong winds, and sometimes LIGHTNING: *It was the first big storm we've had all season.* **2** [C usually singular] a situation in which people suddenly express very strong feelings about something that someone has said or done: *Jarrett **stirred up** quite **a storm** with his comments about Marsalis.* | *a storm of protest/abuse/laughter etc.* *University admission policy changes met a storm of student protest.* **3 take sth by storm a)** to be very successful in a particular place: *In 1959, Carol Burnett took Broadway by storm.* **b)** to attack a place using large numbers of people or soldiers to succeed in getting control of it: *General Santa Anna threatened to take the city by storm.* **4 dance/sing/cook etc. up a storm** INFORMAL to do something with all your energy: *After the championship, we partied up a storm.*

storm² v. **1** [T] to suddenly attack and enter a place using a lot of force: *Several dozen rebels stormed the ambassador's residence.* **2** [I always + adv./prep.] to go somewhere in a noisy fast way that shows you are extremely angry: *[+ out of/into/off etc.]* *Sally stormed into his office for an explanation.* **3** [I,T] LITERARY to shout something because you feel extremely angry: *"What difference does it make?" she stormed.*

storm cel·lar /'. ,../ n. [C] a place under a house or under the ground where you can go to be safe during violent storms

storm cloud /'. ./ n. [C] **1** a dark cloud that you see before a storm **2** [usually plural] a sign that something very bad is going to happen: *Storm clouds are gathering over the trade negotiations.*

storm door /,. '. ./ n. [C] a second door that is fitted outside a door to a house to give protection against rain, snow, wind etc.

storm·troop·er /'storm,trupə/ n. [C] a member of a special group of German soldiers in World War II who were trained to be very violent

storm win·dow /,. '.. ./ n. [C] a special window that gives protection against rain, snow, wind etc.

S

storm·y /ˈstɔrmi/ adj. **stormier, stormiest 1** stormy weather, a stormy sky etc. is full of strong winds, heavy rain or snow, and dark clouds: *a stormy winter night* **2** a stormy relationship, meeting etc. is full of strong and often angry feelings: *a stormy meeting* | *Their relationship has been often stormy.*

S W 1 1 **sto·ry** /ˈstɔri/ n. plural **stories** [C]
1 for entertainment a description of an event or how something happened, that is intended to entertain people and may be true or imaginary: *The movie is based on a true story.* | *Don't be frightened, Connie – it's only a story* (=it is imaginary). | [+ **about/of**] *It's a story about friendship and courage.* | *the story of "Snow White"* | **a ghost/love/war etc. story** (=a story about ghosts, love, war etc.) | **tell/read sb a story** *Mommy, will you read me a story?* | *Bedtime stories are an important part of our evening ritual.*
2 news a report in a newspaper or news broadcast about a recent event: *"The Chronicle" ran* (=published) *a three-page story on the flood.* | **a/the cover story** (=the main story in a magazine that is about the picture on the cover) —see also **success story** (SUCCESS (4))
3 events a description of the most important events in someone's life or in the development of something: *the story of dancer Alvin Ailey* —see also LIFE STORY
4 building a floor or level of a building: *a fifth story apartment* | **two-story/three-story etc.** *a ten-story building*
5 movie/play etc. what happens in a movie, play, or book; PLOT[1] (1): *The story doesn't get interesting till midway through.*
6 excuse an excuse or explanation, especially one that you have invented: *When I asked her why she didn't call, she gave me some story about her dog getting sick.*
7 **my/your etc. side of the story** the way that a particular person describes what happened: *I still haven't heard Linda's side of the story.*
8 what people say information that people tell each other, but that may not be true; RUMOR: *There are a lot of wild stories going around.* | *Polly's mother's mother, so the story goes* (=people are saying this), *ran away when she was 15.*

SPOKEN PHRASES

9 **it's a long story** used to tell someone that you do not want to give them all the details that a full answer to their question would need
10 **it's the same story here/there etc.** used to say the same thing is happening in another place: *Aspen received 10 inches of new snow – it's the same story in Denver.*
11 **it's the same old story** used to say that the present bad situation has often happened before: *It's the same old story – too much work and not enough time.*
12 **to make/cut a long story short** used when you want to finish a story quickly: *To make a long story short, I didn't get the job.*
13 **that's not the whole story** used to say that there are more details that people need to know in order to understand the situation
14 **that's the story of my life** used after a disappointing experience to mean that similar disappointing things always seem to happen to you
15 **but that's another story** used when you have mentioned something that you are not going to talk about on this occasion
16 **end of story** used to mean that there is nothing more to say about a particular subject: *I'm not going to lend you any more money, end of story.*
17 a lie a word meaning a "lie," used by or to children: *Have you been telling stories again?*

—see also **cock and bull story** (COCK[1] (3)), **hard luck story** (HARD[1] (21)), SHORT STORY, SOB STORY, -STORIED

sto·ry·book[1] /ˈstɔriˌbʊk/ n. [C] a book of stories for children
storybook[2] adj. **a storybook ending/marriage/**romance etc. an ending, marriage, romance etc. that is so happy or perfect that it is like one in a children's story: *Patterson had sort of a storybook childhood.*

story line /ˈ.. ./ n. [C] the main set of related events in a story; PLOT[1]
sto·ry·tell·er /ˈstɔriˌtɛlə/ n. [C] someone who tells stories, especially to children
stoup /stup/ n. [C] **1** a container for holy water near the entrance to a church **2** a glass or MUG used for drinking in past times
stout[1] /staʊt/ adj. **1** fairly fat and heavy or having a thick body: *She was a stout woman with an Austrian accent.* —see Usage Note at FAT[1] **2** LITERARY strong and thick: *a stout wooden beam* | *the stout walls of Kanazawa Castle* **3** strong and determined: **stout defense/support/resistance** *Chicago used its stout defense to win over Atlanta.* —**stoutly** adv.: *She stoutly denied the rumors.* —**stoutness** n. [U]
stout[2] n. [U] a strong dark beer
stout·heart·ed /ˈstaʊtˌhɑrtɪd/ adj. LITERARY brave and determined
stove[1] /stoʊv/ n. [C] **1** a piece of kitchen equipment on which you cook food in pots and pans, and that contains an OVEN —see picture at KITCHEN **2** a thing used for heating a room or for cooking, which works by burning wood, coal, oil, or gas: *a wood-burning stove* | *a camp stove* **S W 2**
stove[2] v. the past tense and past participle of STAVE[1]
stove·pipe hat /ˌstoʊvpaɪp ˈhæt/ n. [C] a tall black silk hat worn by men in past times
stove top /ˈ. ./ n. [C] the top of a stove where the BURNERS (=the places where the heat comes from) are
stove-top /ˈ. ./ adj. [only before noun] **1** made to be used on top of a STOVE: *a stove-top grill* **2** able to be cooked using only the stove top: *stove-top tuna casserole*
stow /stoʊ/ also **stow** sth ↔ **away** v. [T always + adv./prep.] to put or pack something neatly away in a space until you need it again: *All of our camping equipment is stowed in the attic.*
stow away phr. v. [I] to hide on a ship or airplane in order to travel secretly or without paying: *As a teenager, she once stowed away on a ship bound for Ireland.* —see also STOWAWAY
stow·age /ˈstoʊɪdʒ/ n. [C] space available on a boat for storing things
stow·a·way /ˈstoʊəˌweɪ/ n. [C] someone who hides on a ship or airplane in order to avoid paying or to travel secretly
Stowe /stoʊ/, **Har·ri·et Bee·cher** /ˈhæriɪt ˈbitʃə/ (1811–1896) a U.S. writer famous for her NOVEL "Uncle Tom's Cabin," which influenced many people to oppose SLAVERY
St. Pat·rick's Day /seɪnt ˈpætrɪks ˌdeɪ/ n. [C,U] SAINT PATRICK'S DAY
St. Paul /seɪnt ˈpɔl/ the capital city of the U.S. state of Minnesota
St. Pe·ters·burg /seɪnt ˈpitəzˌbəg/ a city in Russia, on the Baltic Sea, that was the capital of Russia from 1712 to 1918. It was called Leningrad from 1924 until 1991.
strad·dle /ˈstrædl/ v. [T] **1** to sit or stand with your legs on either side of someone or something: *Riders straddled their mountain bikes waiting for the race to begin.* **2** if something straddles a line, road, or river, part of it is on one side and part on the other side: *The forest straddles the U.S.–Mexico border.* **3** to include different areas of activity: *Her job straddled marketing and public relations.*
strafe /streɪf/ v. [T] to attack a place by flying an airplane low over the ground and firing many bullets
strag·gle /ˈstrægəl/ v. [I] **1** if members of a group straggle somewhere, they move at different speeds, so that there are large spaces between them: [+ **in/into/toward etc.**] *Students were beginning to straggle in from lunch.* | [+ **behind**] *Several people straggled behind, looking at the paintings.* **2** to move, grow, or spread out in a messy way in different directions: *Her hair straggled around her face.*

strag·gler /'stræglə/ *n.* [C] someone who is behind the others in a group, especially because they walk more slowly: *Wait for the stragglers to catch up.*

strag·gly /'strægli/ *adj.* **stragglier, straggliest** growing in a messy way and spreading out in different directions: *straggly hair*

straight¹ /streɪt/ *adv.*
1 in a straight line in a straight line or direction: *Terry was so tired he couldn't walk straight.* | [+ ahead/at/down etc.] *He looked straight at McFarlane.* | *She walked straight past me.* | *Carlos always combs his hair straight back.*
2 immediately [+ adj./adv.] immediately or without delay: [+ to/down/back etc.] *Let's get straight down to business.* | *You should have gone straight to the police.* | *I'd planned to go straight home from the barber shop.*
3 one after the other happening one after the other in a series, especially an unusually long series: *It's rained for eight days straight.*
4 see/think if you cannot think or see straight, you cannot think or see clearly: *Harry was so drunk he couldn't see straight.*
5 sit up straight to sit so that your back is upright and not bent: *Sit up straight in your chair and pay attention.*
6 tell/ask sb straight out SPOKEN to tell someone something clearly without trying to hide your meaning: *I asked her straight out if she was lying.*
7 come straight out (and do sth) SPOKEN to tell someone something without waiting: *The boys came straight out and admitted they had stolen the car.*
8 say sth straight to sb's face also tell sb sth straight to sb's face SPOKEN to say something to someone in a very clear and direct way, especially something that will offend or upset them: *I'll tell him straight to his face what I think of him.*
9 straight up SLANG **a)** used to ask someone if they are telling the truth: *This is your second time at this college, straight up?* **b)** used to emphasize that what you are saying is true: *Ben earns $10,000 a month, straight up.*
10 go straight INFORMAL to stop being a criminal and live an honest life: *Tony's been trying to go straight for about six months* —see also **damn straight/right** (DAMN³ (4)), **(straight/right) from the horse's mouth** (HORSE¹ (2))

straight² *adj.*
1 not bending or curving something such as a line or road that is straight goes in one direction and does not bend or curve: *The crash occurred on a straight section of the highway.* | *a straight line* | *She has straight black hair* (=hair without curls).
2 level or upright level, upright, or flat in position or shape: *Is my tie straight?* | *straight teeth*
3 one after another immediately one after another in a series, especially in an unusually long series: *The New York Rangers have won seven straight games.*
4 truthful honest and truthful: *Are you going to be straight with me or not?* | *Jack never gives me a straight answer.* | *Voters need more straight talk from the candidates.*
5 a straight face someone who has a straight face looks serious although they really want to smile or laugh, or even though they are lying or saying something stupid: *With a straight face, he said my work wasn't good enough.* | *She looked so ridiculous it was hard to keep a straight face.*
6 get straight A's/B's etc. to earn the grade "A," "B" etc. in all of your school subjects: *Becky got straight A's all through high school.*
7 alcoholic drinks alcoholic drinks that are straight have no water or ice or any other liquid added: *I like my vodka straight.*
8 sex INFORMAL: SEE HETEROSEXUAL
9 not limited simple and not limited by any conditions; STRAIGHTFORWARD (2): *Did you do it? Just give me a straight yes or no.*
10 completely one type of sth completely one particular type of something: *It's not a straight historical novel.*
11 choice/exchange a straight choice, exchange

etc. involves only two possible choices, exchanges etc.: *How about a straight swap, my "U2" album for this one?*

SPOKEN PHRASES
---

12 get sth straight to understand the facts about a situation and be able to tell them correctly: *The reporter didn't get the details of the story straight.* | *get this/it straight Let me get this straight – you just want lettuce for dinner.*
13 set sb straight (on sth) to make someone understand the facts about a situation: *Alice thought that we were buying dinner for everyone, but Helen set her straight.*
14 set things straight to do something or say something to solve a problem or fix a mistake: *Debra set things straight by paying all the money back.*
15 not owing sb money [not before noun] not owing money to someone or being owed money by someone anymore: *Here's your dollar back – now we're straight.*
16 drugs SLANG not using drugs

—see also **set/ put/keep the record straight** (RECORD¹ (9))

straight³ *n.* **1** [C usually plural] SLANG someone who is sexually attracted to people of the opposite sex **2** the straight and narrow an honest and moral way of living: *The program keeps many of these kids on the straight and narrow.* **3** [C] if you have a straight in a card game, you have been given several cards whose numbers are CONSECUTIVE, for example 2, 3, 4, 5, 6

straight-arm /'. ./ *v.* [T] to STIFF-ARM someone —**straight-arm** *n.* [C]

straight ar·row /ˌ. '../ *n.* [C] INFORMAL someone who never does anything illegal or unusual and exciting

straight·a·way¹ /ˌstreɪtə'weɪ/ *adv.* at once; immediately: *We should discuss the issue of the budget straightaway.*

straight·a·way² /'streɪtəˌweɪ/ *n.* [singular] the straight part of a RACETRACK

straight·edge /'streɪtedʒ/ *n.* [C] a long flat piece of wood, plastic, or metal used for drawing straight lines or checking to see if something is straight

straight·en /'streɪtn/ *v.* **1** [I,T] also **straighten out** to become straight or make something straight: *Try straightening your arm.* | *The road twisted and turned and then straightened out.* **2** [I] also **straighten up** to make your back straight, or to stand up straight after bending down: *I had trouble straightening up after I bent down to pick up the coins.* **3** [T] also **straighten up** to make something neat and clean: *I want to get the house straightened up before everyone gets here.*
  straighten sb/sth ↔ out *phr. v.* [T] **1** to settle a difficult situation by dealing with the things that are causing problems or confusion: *There are a few things that need straightening out between us.* **2** to deal with someone's bad behavior or personal problems: *Five years in the Navy helped straighten him out.*
  straighten up *phr. v.* [I] to begin to behave well after behaving badly: *You'd better straighten up, young lady!*

straight·faced /ˌstreɪt'feɪst◂/ *adj.* not showing by the expression on your face that you are really joking or saying something that is not true: *A straight-faced Soviet newsman described the incident as regrettable.*

straight·for·ward /ˌstreɪt'fɔrwəd◂/ *adj.* **1** honest about your feelings or opinions and not hiding anything: *Wes is a straightforward person.* **2** simple and easy to understand: *The directions to the campsite are fairly straightforward.* —**straightforwardly** *adv.* —**straightforwardness** *n.* [U]

straight·jack·et /'streɪtˌdʒækɪt/ *n.* [C] another spelling of STRAITJACKET

straight-laced /'. ./ *adj.* another spelling of STRAITLACED

straight man /'. ./ n. [C] a male entertainer who works with a COMEDIAN, providing him or her with opportunities to make jokes

straight ra·zor /'. ,../ n. [C] a cutting tool with a straight blade that a man uses to SHAVE, used especially in past times

straight shoot·er /'. ,../ n. [C] INFORMAL an honest person who you can trust

straight tick·et /,. '../ n. [C] a vote in which someone chooses all the CANDIDATEs of a particular political party in the U.S.: *This time I voted a straight ticket.*

straight·way /,streɪt¬'weɪ, 'streɪt¬weɪ/ adv. OLD USE: see STRAIGHTAWAY

strain¹ /streɪn/ n.
1 worry [C,U] worry caused by having to deal with a problem or having to work too hard over a long period of time: *He had trouble handling the strain of raising eight kids.* | *At the time, we were both under a lot of strain.*
2 difficulty [C] a problem or difficulty that is caused when something is used more than is normal or acceptable: *His college loan payments were putting a strain on his finances.*
3 force [U] a force that pulls, stretches, or pushes something: *The rope is capable of bearing a strain of three tons.* | *The beams collapsed under the strain* (=because of the force putting pressure on them).
4 injury [C,U] an injury to a muscle or part of your body caused by using it too much: *eye strain* | *a back strain*
5 plant/disease/animal [C] a breed or type of plant, disease, or animal: [+ of] *a deadly strain of influenza*
6 distrust [C,U] a situation in which two people, groups etc. have stopped being friendly or trusting each other; TENSION: *The strain was beginning to show in their friendship.*
7 the strains of sth LITERARY the sound of music being played: [+ of] *Through the window we could hear the strains of Mozart.*
8 quality [singular] a particular quality that people have: [+ of] *There is a strong strain of nationalism in the country.*

strain² v.
1 part of body [T] to injure a muscle or part of your body by making it work too hard: *James strained his right knee playing football.* | *You'll strain your eyes trying to read in this light.* —compare SPRAIN
2 effort [I,T] to try very hard to do something, using all your physical or mental strength: [strain to do sth] *I strained to remember where I had met him before.* | **strain your ears/eyes** (=try very hard to hear or see) | *Don't strain yourself* (=try too hard) – *we can finish the report tomorrow.*
3 liquid [T] to separate solid things from a liquid by pouring the mixture through something with very small holes in it: *Strain the sauce through a sieve.* —see picture on page 425
4 beyond a limit [T] to force something to be used to a degree that is beyond a normal or acceptable limit: *Repairs to the roof have severely strained the school's budget.*
5 strain relations also **strain sb's friendship/relationship/marriage etc.** to cause problems between people, countries etc.: *The bombing has strained relations between the two communities.*
6 pull/push [I] to pull hard at something or push hard against something: [+ against] *Spectators strained against the barriers to get a closer look.* | [+ at] *The dog barked, straining at his chain.*
7 straining at the leash INFORMAL eager to be allowed to do what you want: *Lasiter was straining at the leash to be put in the game.*
8 strain every nerve to try as hard as possible to do something

strained /streɪnd/ adj. **1** a situation or behavior that is strained makes people feel nervous and uncomfortable, and unable to behave naturally; TENSE: *I* couldn't stand the strained atmosphere at dinner anymore.* **2** showing the effects of worry or too much work: *a strained expression*

strain·er /'streɪnɚ/ n. [C] a kitchen tool for separating solids from liquids: *a tea strainer*

strait /streɪt/ n. [C] also **straits** [plural] a narrow passage of water between two areas of land, usually connecting two large areas of water, for example two oceans: *the Strait of Magellan* —see also **be in dire straits** (DIRE (2))

strait·ened /'streɪtnd/ adj. FORMAL **straitened circumstances** a situation that is difficult because of a lack of money: *Emma did not want him to know of her straitened circumstances.*

strait·jack·et, straightjacket /'streɪt,dʒækɪt/ n. [C] **1** a special piece of clothing that is used to control the movements of someone who is mentally ill and violent **2** something such as a law or set of ideas that puts very strict or unfair limits on someone: *the straitjacket of tradition*

strait-laced, straight-laced /,streɪt'leɪst◄/ adj. having strict, old-fashioned ideas about moral behavior: *a strait-laced Lutheran minister*

Strait of Ma·gel·lan, the /,streɪt əv mə'dʒɛlən/ a narrow area of sea south between Tierra del Fuego and the mainland of South America that connects the Atlantic Ocean with the Pacific Ocean

strand¹ /strænd/ n. [C] **1** a single thin piece of thread, wire, hair etc.: *a strand of silk* **2 a strand of pearls/beads** a single row of PEARLs or BEADs on a string, worn as jewelry **3** one of the parts of a story, problem etc.: *Plato draws all the strands of the argument together at the end.*

strand² v. [T usually passive] to put someone one in a place or situation from which they need help to leave: *Rising river water stranded four teenagers on the island.* | [be stranded in/on/at etc.] *We were stranded in the desert, without water.* | *The airline went out of business, leaving thousands of passengers stranded abroad.*

strange¹ /streɪndʒ/ adj. **1** unusual or surprising, especially in a way that is difficult to explain or understand: *a strange noise* | *Gabby is a strange girl.* | *That's strange. I don't remember that store being there.* | *It's strange that Linda hasn't even called.* | *There's something really strange about their relationship.* **2** someone or something that is strange is not familiar because you have not seen or met them before: *Meryl was lost and all alone in a strange city.* **3 truth/fact etc. is stranger than fiction** used to say that what happens in the real world is often more unusual than what happens in stories **4 feel strange** to feel as if something is slightly wrong, physically or emotionally: *I left the debate feeling strange – I didn't know what to believe.* —strangeness n. [U]

strange² adv. [only after verb] INFORMAL, NONSTANDARD in a way that is different from what is normal: *The dog's been acting strange all week.*

strange·ly /'streɪndʒli/ adv. in a way that is different from what is normal: *After moving into the new house, she began behaving strangely.* | *The whole city was strangely peaceful.* —see also **strangely/oddly/funnily enough** (ENOUGH¹ (2))

strang·er /'streɪndʒɚ/ n. [C] **1** someone whom you do not know: *Carly, don't ever take candy from strangers.* | **a complete/perfect/total stranger** *I can't believe you'd give that kind of information to a total stranger.* **2 be no stranger to sth** to have had a lot of a particular type of experience: *Derek is no stranger to controversy.* **3** someone in a new and unfamiliar place **4 Don't be a stranger!** SPOKEN said when someone is leaving to invite them back to visit you often **5 Hello, stranger!** SPOKEN, HUMOROUS said to greet someone you have not seen for a long time

stran·gle /'stræŋgəl/ v. [T] **1** to kill someone by pressing on their throat with your hands, a rope etc.: *Freitas was strangled with a nylon cord.* **2** to limit or prevent the growth or development of something: *The economy is being strangled by inefficiency and corruption.* —strangler n. [C]

stran·gled /ˈstræŋgəld/ *adj.* **a strangled cry/sound/ gasp etc.** a cry, sound, gasp etc. that is suddenly stopped before it is finished

stran·gle·hold /ˈstræŋgəl,hoold/ *n.* [C] **1** [usually singular] complete control over a situation, organization etc.: [+ **on**] *a four-decade stranglehold on power* | *It's the story of three young black men who break the stranglehold of the inner city.* **2** a strong hold around someone's neck that is meant to stop them from breathing

stran·gu·la·tion /ˌstræŋgyəˈleɪʃən/ *n.* [U] the act of killing someone by strangling them, or the fact of being killed in this way —**strangulate** /ˈstræŋgyə-ˌleɪt/ *v.* [T]

strap¹ /stræp/ *n.* [C] a narrow band of strong material that is used to fasten, hang, or hold onto something: *a bra strap* —see also CHINSTRAP, SHOULDER STRAP —see picture at BAG¹

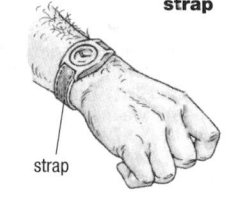

strap

strap

strap² *v.* **strapped, strapping** [T always + adv./ prep.] to fasten something or someone in place with one or more straps: [**strap sth in/on/down etc.**] *Chuck drove away with the Christmas tree strapped to the roof of the car.* | *Are the kids strapped in* (=do they have a belt fastened around them in a car)*?*

strap·less /ˈstræplɪs/ *adj.* **a strapless dress/gown/ top etc.** a dress or shirt that has no straps over your shoulders

strapped /stræpt/ *adj.* **strapped (for cash)** INFORMAL having little or no money at the moment: *Could you lend me $10? I'm a little strapped for cash.*

strap·ping /ˈstræpɪŋ/ *adj.* [only before noun, no comparative] a strapping young man or woman is strong, tall, and looks healthy and active: *a strapping 6-foot 18-year-old*

Stras·berg /ˈstræsbɔg/**, Lee** /li/ (1901–1982) a U.S. teacher of acting and theater DIRECTOR, famous for using and developing the ideas of METHOD ACTING

stra·ta /ˈstreɪtə, ˈstreɪtə/ *n.* **1** [plural] the plural of STRATUM **2** [singular] a word that many people use to mean STRATUM, although some people consider this incorrect

strat·a·gem /ˈstrætədʒəm/ *n.* [C] FORMAL a trick or plan to deceive an enemy or gain an advantage

stra·te·gic /strəˈtidʒɪk/ also **stra·te·gi·cal** /strəˈti-dʒɪkəl/ *adj.* **1** done as part of a plan, especially in a military, business, or political situation: *strategic bombing* | *We need a strategic plan for education in the next century.* **2** useful or right for a particular purpose: *The remote province is in a strategic location on the border with China.* | *a strategic alliance* **3** used in fighting wars: *strategic materials such as iron or steel* | **strategic arms/weapons etc.** (=weapons designed to reach an enemy country from your own) —compare TACTICAL —**strategically** /-kli/ *adv.*

strat·e·gist /ˈstrætədʒɪst/ *n.* [C] someone who is good at planning, especially military movements

strat·e·gy /ˈstrætədʒi/ *n. plural* **strategies 1** [C] a well-planned action or series of actions for achieving an aim: *learning strategies* | [**a strategy to do sth**] *Scientists are looking for cheaper strategies to reduce carbon dioxide.* | [**a strategy for doing sth**] *Is home health care an effective strategy for delivering services?* **2** [U] the skill of planning military movements **3** [U] skillful planning in general: *The company needs to focus on strategy.*

strat·i·fi·ca·tion /ˌstrætəfəˈkeɪʃən/ *n.* [C,U] **1** [+ **of**] the way that a society develops into different social classes **2** the way that different layers of earth, rock etc. develop over time **3** the position that different layers of something have in relation to each other —**stratify** /ˈstrætə,faɪ/ *v.* [I,T]

strat·i·fied /ˈstrætə,faɪd/ *adj.* **1** having different

social classes: *a highly stratified society* **2** having several layers of earth, rock etc.: *stratified rock*

strat·o·sphere /ˈstrætə,sfɪr/ *n.* **1 the stratosphere** the part of the air surrounding the Earth above the TROPOSPHERE, starting at about six miles above the Earth **2** a very high position, level, or amount: *The nation's teenage pregnancy rate is soaring into the stratosphere.* | **the fashion/political/ratings etc. stratosphere** (=the highest position in fashion, politics etc.)

stra·tum /ˈstrætəm, ˈstreɪ-/ *n. plural* **strata** /-tə/ [C] **1** a layer of rock of a particular kind, especially one with different layers above and below it **2** a social class in a society **3** a layer of earth, such as one where tools, bones etc. from an ancient CIVILIZATION are found by digging

Strauss /straʊs/**, Jo·hann** /ˈyoohɑn/ **1 Johann Strauss the elder** (1804–1849) an Austrian musician who wrote CLASSICAL music **2** (1825–1899) an Austrian musician who wrote more than 400 WALTZes

Strauss, Le·vi /ˈlivaɪ/ (1829–1902) a U.S. clothing MANUFACTURER who was the first person to make JEANS and started the clothing company Levi Strauss

Strauss, Rich·ard /ˈrɪkɑrt/ (1864–1949) a German musician who wrote CLASSICAL music

Stra·vin·sky /strəˈvɪnski/**, I·gor** /ˈigɔr/ (1882–1971) a Russian musician who wrote modern CLASSICAL music

straw /strɔ/ *n.* **1 a)** [U] the dried stems of wheat or similar plants that are used for animals to sleep on, and for making things such as baskets, MATS etc.: *a straw hat* **b)** [C] a single dried stem of wheat or a similar plant **2** [C] a thin tube of paper or plastic for sucking a drink from a bottle or cup —see picture at SUCK¹ **3 the last straw** also **the straw that breaks the camel's back** the last problem in a series of problems that finally makes you give up, get angry etc.: *Making me work late on a Friday was the last straw!* **4 be grasping/clutching at straws** to be trying everything you can to succeed, even though the things you are trying are not likely to help or work: *Researchers admit they are grasping at straws with the new treatment.* **5 a straw man** a weak opponent or imaginary argument that can easily be defeated —see also **you can't make bricks without straw** (BRICK¹ (4)), **draw straws** (DRAW¹ (26)), **draw the short straw** (DRAW¹ (27))

straw·ber·ry /ˈstrɔ,beri/ *n. plural* **strawberries** [C] a soft red juicy fruit with small pale seeds on its surface, or the plant that grows this fruit

strawberry blond /ˌ… ˈ./ *adj.* strawberry blond hair is light reddish yellow —**strawberry blond** *n.* [C]

straw-col·ored /ˈ. ,../ *adj.* light yellow

straw poll also **straw vote** /ˈ. ˈ./ *n.* [C] an unofficial test of people's opinions before an election, to see what the result is likely to be

stray¹ /streɪ/ *v.* **strays, strayed, straying** [I] **1** to leave the place where you should be without intending to: [+ **into/onto/from**] *Three of the soldiers strayed into enemy territory.* **2** to begin to deal with a different subject than the main one, without intending to: [+ **into/onto/from**] *Gates says he tries not to stray too far from talking about technology.*

stray² *adj.* [only before noun] **1** a stray animal, such as a dog or cat, is lost or has no home **2** accidentally separated from other things of the same kind: *Four people were killed by stray bullets from the shoot-out.* | *a stray sock*

stray³ *n. plural* **strays** [C] **1** an animal that is lost or has no home **2** INFORMAL someone or something that has become separated from others of the same kind

streak¹ /strik/ *n.* [C] **1** a colored line, especially one that is not straight or has been made accidentally: *Nancy dyes her hair to hide the gray streaks.* **2** a part of someone's character that is different from the rest of their character: *My father has a streak of heroism in him that I admire.* | *a stubborn streak* **3** a period of time during which you continue to be successful or to fail: *a streak of bad luck* | **be on a winning/ losing streak** (=have a period of time when you continue to win or lose) **4 a streak of lightning/fire/ light etc.** a long straight burst of LIGHTNING, fire etc.

streak² *v.* **1** [T usually passive] to cover something with streaks: *The evening sky was streaked red and orange.* | [+ **with**] *By the end of the trip, my shirt was streaked with perspiration.* **2** [I always + adv./prep.] to run or fly somewhere so fast you can hardly be seen: [+ **across/along/down etc.**] *A cat streaked across the top of the wall and was gone.* **3** [I] to run across a public place with no clothes on to shock people

streak·er /'strikɚ/ *n.* [C] someone who runs across a public place with no clothes on to shock people

streak·y /'striki/ *adj.* **1** a streaky sports player or team plays very well for a period of time, and then plays badly for a period of time **2** marked with streaks, or in the form of streaks: *streaky grayish marks*

S W **stream¹** /strim/ *n.* [C] **1** a natural flow of water that
3 moves across the land and is narrower than a river: *a mountain stream* —see also DOWNSTREAM, UPSTREAM **2** a long and almost continuous series of events, people, objects etc.: [+ **of**] *a stream of insults* | *A steady stream of trucks and cars whizzed by.* **3** a flow of water, air, smoke etc., or the direction in which it is flowing: *A stream of air swirled the dust into clouds.* —see also GULF STREAM, JET STREAM **4 go/swim against the stream** to do or think something differently from what people in general do or think: *We try to swim against the stream and publish books that are a little different.* **5 come on stream** TECHNICAL to start producing something such as oil, electricity, goods etc.: *The new plant will come on stream at the end of the year.* —see also BLOODSTREAM, MAINSTREAM¹, STREAM OF CONSCIOUSNESS

stream² *v.* **1** [I always + adv./prep.] to flow quickly and in great amounts: [+ **out/in/onto etc.**] *Lava came streaming from the mountain.* | *Tears streamed down her cheeks.* **2** [I always + adv./prep.] to move in a continuous flow in the same direction: [+ **out/ across/past etc.**] *Crowds began streaming off the parade route and into the parks.* **3** [I always + adv./ prep.] if light streams somewhere, it shines through an opening into a place or onto a surface: [+ **in/ through/from etc.**] *Sunlight was streaming through the open windows.* **4** [I always + adv./prep., usually in progressive] to move freely in a current of wind or water: [+ **in/out/behind etc.**] *Elise ran, her hair streaming out behind her.* **5** [I] to produce a continuous flow of liquid: [+ **with**] *His eyes were streaming with tears.*

stream·er /'strimɚ/ *n.* [C] **1** a long narrow piece of colored paper, used for decoration at special occasions **2** a long narrow flag

stream·line /'strimlaɪn/ *v.* [T] **1** to make something such as a business, organization etc. work more simply and effectively: *We're taking steps to streamline operations and increase productivity.* **2** to form something into a smooth shape so that it moves easily through the air or water —**streamlined** *adj.*: *streamlined cars*

stream of con·scious·ness /ˌ. . '.../ *n.* [U] the expression of thoughts and feelings in writing exactly as they pass through your mind, without the usual ordered structure they have in formal writing

S W **street** /strit/ *n.* [C] **1** a public road in a city or town
1 1 that has houses, stores etc. on one or both sides: *They live on Clay Street.* **2 the street** also **the streets** the busy public parts of a city where there is a lot of activity, excitement, and crime, or where people without homes live: *An estimated 200,000 people are homeless and living on the streets.* **3 the man/woman on the street** also **the man/woman in the street** the average person, who represents the general opinion about things: *What practical effect does this mathematical discovery have on the man in*

the street? **4 a one-way/two-way street** a process that fully involves the opinions and feelings of only one person or group, or of both people or groups: *Marriage is a two-way street.* **5 be back on the street/streets** if a criminal is back on the streets, they have been allowed to leave prison —see also BACKSTREET, **be on easy street** (EASY¹ (14)), STREET SMARTS, **walk the streets** (WALK¹ (14))

USAGE NOTE: STREET

WORD CHOICE: street, road
A **street** is in a town or city, and usually has stores and other buildings beside it: *a street corner* (NOT *"road corner"*). A **road** is usually in the country, but sometimes very wide **streets** are also called **roads**: *the road to Rochester* (NOT *street*).

---

street·car /'stritˌkɑr/ *n.* [C] a type of bus that runs on electricity along metal tracks in the road

street clothes /'. ./ *n.* [plural] ordinary clothes that people wear, rather than uniforms or other special clothes: *a policeman in his street clothes*

street·lamp /'stritlæmp/ *n.* [C] a streetlight

street·light /'stritlaɪt/ *n.* [C] a light at the top of a tall post in the street

street map /'. ./ *n.* [C] a map showing the position and names of all the streets in a town or city

street mu·si·cian /'. .ˌ../ *n.* [C] a musician who performs outdoors in towns to earn money

street peo·ple /'. ˌ../ *n.* [plural] people who have no home and live on the streets

street·scape /'stritskeɪp/ *n.* [C] a view or plan of a street or a group of streets in a city: *a bleak urban streetscape*

street smarts /'. ./ *n.* [U] the ability to deal with difficult situations on the streets of a big city: *I was just a kid from Iowa with no street smarts at all.* —**street-smart** *adj.*: *He's a street-smart ex cab driver from New York.*

street val·ue /'. ˌ../ *n.* [C,U] the price for which a drug can be sold illegally to people: *The cocaine police seized had an estimated street value of $8 million.*

street·walk·er /'stritˌwɔkɚ/ *n.* [C] a PROSTITUTE who stands on the street to attract customers

street·wise /'stritˌwaɪz/ *adj.* smart and experienced enough to deal with difficult situations on the streets of a big city: *a streetwise detective*

strength /strɛŋkθ, strɛnθ/ *n.*
1 physical [U] the physical power and energy that **S W** makes someone strong: *He barely had the strength* **3 2** *to lift the fork.* | *Kim exercises every day to build up her strength.* | *Sarah hugged her brother with all her strength.* —see Usage Note at FORCE¹
2 determination [U] the quality of being brave or determined in dealing with difficult or bad situations: *moral strength* | [**the strength to do sth**] *Your prayers and support have given me the strength to carry on.* | *It takes unusual strength of character* (=strong ability to deal with difficult situations) *to fight against so much opposition.* | *Schuller found an inner strength that helped him through his recovery.* —see also **tower of strength** (TOWER¹ (3))
3 organization/country etc. [U] the political, military, or economic power of an organization, country, or system: [+ **of**] *the strength of the U.S. economy* | *Despite a show of strength* (=an occasion when a country or organization shows how powerful it is) *by police, violence spread to other neighborhoods.*
4 feeling/belief etc. [U] how strong a feeling, belief, or relationship is: [+ **of**] *Never underestimate the strength of a mother's love for her child.* | *She didn't convince me, but I was impressed by the strength of her convictions.*
5 useful quality or ability [C] a particular quality or ability that gives someone or something an advantage: [+ **of**] *What are the strengths of the plan?* | *Managers need to know their colleagues' strengths and weaknesses.*
6 substance/mixture [C,U] how strong a substance or mixture such as an alcoholic drink, medicine, or

cleaning liquid is: **full-strength/half-strength/double-strength etc.** *a maximum-strength pain reliever*

7 money [U] the value of a country's money when compared to other countries' money: [+ **of**] *The strength of the dollar is appealing to foreign investors.*
8 on the strength of sth because of something that persuaded you: *Manuel was hired immediately on the strength of Cassidy's recommendation.*
9 wind/current [U] how strong a wind or current of water is: [+ **of**] *the awesome strength of the river*
10 object [U] how strong an object or structure is, especially its ability to last for a long time without breaking: [+ **of**] *I have doubts about the strength of that beam in the ceiling.*
11 number of people [U] the number of people in a team, army etc.: *If the Latinos turn out in strength* (=in large numbers) *in November, they could make up one fifth of the Texas vote.*
12 color/light [U] how bright a light or color is
13 give me strength SPOKEN used when you are annoyed or angry about something —see also **not know your own strength** (KNOW[1] (22)), **a position of strength** (POSITION[1] (14))

strength·en /ˈstrɛŋkθən, ˈstrɛnθən/ *v.*
1 feeling/belief/relationship [I,T] to become stronger, or make something stronger: *Our friendship has steadily strengthened over the years.* | [**strengthen sth**] *Her encouragement strengthened Chang's resolve to overcome his handicap.*
2 financial situation [I,T] if the financial situation of a country or company strengthens or is strengthened, it improves or is made to improve: *The President's first priority was to strengthen the economy.*
3 body/structure [T] to make something such as your body or a building stronger: *I've started swimming to strengthen my upper body.* | *Metal supports were added to strengthen the outer walls.*
4 money [I,T] to increase in value, or to make money do this: *The dollar has steadily strengthened against the yen in recent weeks.*
5 team/army etc. [T] to make an organization, army etc. more powerful, especially by increasing the number or quality of the people in it: *We're looking for ways to strengthen our sales team.*
6 proof/reason [T] to give support to a reason or an attempt to prove something: *Ali's testimony seems to have strengthened the case for the prosecution.*
7 strengthen sb's hand to make someone more powerful or give them an advantage over an opponent: *Tuesday's election results will strengthen the Prime Minister's hand in the parliament.*
8 wind/current [I] to increase in force: *The wind had strengthened during the night.*

stren·u·ous /ˈstrɛnyuəs/ *adj.* **1** needing great effort or strength: *The doctor advised Ken to avoid strenuous exercise.* **2** active and determined: *Fernandez was approved as director over the strenuous objections of the faculty.* —**strenuously** *adv.*: *Burke argued strenuously against the proposal.*

strep /strɛp/ *n.* [U] **1** strep throat **2** streptococcus
strep throat /ˌ. ˈ./ *n.* [U] an illness in which your throat is very painful
strep·to·coc·cus /ˌstrɛptəˈkɑkəs/ *n. plural* **streptococci** /-ˈkɑksaɪ, -ˈkɑkaɪ/ [C] a type of BACTERIA that causes infections, especially in your throat —**streptococcal** *adj.*
strep·to·my·cin /ˌstrɛptoʊˈmaɪsən, -tə-/ *n.* [U] a strong drug used in medicines to kill BACTERIA

stress¹ /strɛs/ *n.* **1** [C,U] continuous feelings of worry about your work or personal life, that prevent you from relaxing: *My headaches are caused by stress.* | *Single mothers are always under a lot of stress.* | *The stresses and strains of* (=worries related to) *running a company were too much for him.* | *a stress-related* (=caused by stress) *illness* **2** [U] the special attention or importance given to a particular idea, fact, or activity; EMPHASIS: **put/lay stress on sth** *Grandmother put a great deal of stress on the importance of proper behavior.* **3** [C,U] the physical force or pressure on an object: *Exercise puts stress on bones as well as muscles.* **4** [C,U] the degree of force or loudness with which a part of a word is

pronounced or a note in music is played, which makes it sound stronger than other parts or notes —see also ACCENT[1] (3)

stress² *v.* [T] **1** to emphasize a statement, fact, or idea: [**stress that**] *Traffic engineers stress that the plan is only one possible option.* | *In recent interviews, Crawford has stressed the need for more housing downtown.* **2** to emphasize a word or part of a word so that it sounds louder or more forceful: *The word "basket" is stressed on the first syllable.*
stressed /strɛst/ *adj.* **1** [not before noun] so worried and tired that you cannot relax **2** TECHNICAL an object, especially a metal object, that is stressed has had a lot of pressure or force put on it
stressed out, stressed-out /ˌ. ˈ.◂/ *adj.* INFORMAL so worried and tired that you cannot relax: *stressed-out nurses* | *She's got three finals this week, so she's a little stressed out.*
stress frac·ture /ˈ. ˌ../ *n.* [C] a small crack in a bone, caused by repeated pressure on that part of your body
stress·ful /ˈstrɛsfəl/ *adj.* a stressful job, experience, or situation makes you worry a lot: *Keeping the whole thing a secret is obviously very stressful for her.*
stress mark /ˈ. ./ *n.* [C] a mark that shows which part of a word is emphasized the most
stretch¹ /strɛtʃ/ *v.*

1 make sth bigger/looser [I,T] to make something bigger or looser by pulling it, or to become bigger or looser in this way: *A spider's web can stretch considerably without weakening.* | [**stretch sth**] *Where can I buy those things that stretch your shoes?*

stretch

2 body [I,T] to bring your arms, legs, or body to full length: *Carl sat up in bed, yawned, and stretched.*
3 in space [I always + adv./prep.] also **stretch out** to spread out or cover a large area: [+ **to/into/away etc.**] *The flat Texas farmland stretched before us.* | *Headstones, each marking the grave of a soldier, stretched out in all directions.*
4 time/series [I always + adv./prep.,T] to continue over a period of time or in a series, or make something do this: [+ **into/on/over etc.**] *The research program stretched over several years.* | [**stretch sth**] *The Kings have stretched their winning streak to 11 games.*
5 change shape [I not in progressive] if material stretches, it can become bigger or longer when you pull it and then return to its original shape when you stop: *Lycra shorts will stretch to fit you perfectly.*
6 make sth tight [T] to pull something so that it is tight: *Campers stretched string between posts to mark off their sites.*
7 [I,T] food/money if you make an amount of money, food etc. stretch, or it stretches, it continues for a longer time than it usually would: *Sometimes we have to stretch one day's food into two.*
8 stretch sb/sth to the limit to use as much of a supply of something as is available, without having enough for anything else, or to make someone do this: *Working families are already stretched to the limit.*
9 be stretching it INFORMAL to say something that makes something seem more important, bigger etc. than it really is: *He's a good player, but calling him "world class" is stretching it.*
10 stretch the truth/facts to say or write something that is not completely true: *Reporters sometimes stretch the facts to catch a reader's eye.*
11 stretch your legs INFORMAL to go for a walk, especially after sitting for a long time: *A few of the passengers got off the bus to stretch their legs.*

S

12 stretch (sb's) credulity/patience etc. to be almost beyond the limits of what someone can believe, accept etc.: *Her theories about reincarnation stretch credulity.*
13 abilities [T] to make someone use all of their skill, abilities or intelligence: *The game is a lot of fun, and it really stretches the kids.*
14 stretch a/the point to allow something that would not normally be allowed by a rule or limit —**stretchable** *adj.*

stretch out *phr. v.* **1** [I always + adv./prep.] INFORMAL to lie down, usually in order to sleep or rest: *I just want to stretch out for a few minutes.* **2** [T **stretch sth ↔ out**] to put out your hand, foot etc. in order to reach something: *The baby was stretching out his arms, asking to be picked up.* **3** [I,T **stretch sth ↔ out**] if you stretch out a piece of clothing, or it stretches out, it becomes bigger or looser by being worn or pulled: *No, you can't wear my sweater – you'd stretch it out.*

stretch² *n.*
1 length of land/water [C] an area of land or water, especially one that is long and narrow: [+ **of**] *an empty stretch of highway*
2 time [C] a continuous period of time: [+ **of**] *a stretch of three weeks without sunshine* | *Tom would disappear sometimes for four or five days at a stretch.*
3 by any stretch (of the imagination) SPOKEN used to emphasize that a negative statement is true: *Raising children isn't easy by any stretch of the imagination.*
4 sth difficult something that is difficult to do or believe: *Playing a teenager is a bit of a stretch for the 35-year-old actress.*
5 body [C] the action of stretching a part of your body out to its full length, or a particular way of doing this: *I do my stretches the minute I get out of bed.*
6 the home/final stretch a) the last part of a track before the end of a race **b)** the last part of an activity, trip, or process: *We're in the home stretch now – we just have to make sure all the details are taken care of.*
7 material [U] the ability a material has to increase in length or width without tearing: *Washing in hot water can make the fabric lose its stretch.* —see also STRETCHY
8 prison [C usually singular] INFORMAL a period of time spent in prison: *a seven-year stretch*

stretch·er /ˈstrɛtʃɚ/ *n.* [C] a covered frame for carrying someone who is too injured or sick to walk
stretch lim·o /ˌstrɛtʃ ˈlɪmoʊ/ also **stretch limousine** /ˌ. ˈ.../ *n.* [C] a very large comfortable car that has been made longer than usual
stretch mark /ˈ. ./ *n.* [C usually plural] a mark left on a your skin as a result of it stretching too much, especially during PREGNANCY
stretch·y /ˈstrɛtʃi/ *adj.* **stretchier, stretchiest** stretchy material, clothes etc. can stretch when you pull them and then return to their original shape: *a stretchy Spandex tube top*
strew /stru/ *v. past tense* **strewed** *past participle* **strewn** /strun/ or **strewed** [T usually passive] FORMAL **1** to scatter things around a large area: [be **strewn with sth**] *The yard was strewn with garbage.* | [**strew sth around/about/over sth**] *Two million mines had been strewn throughout the country.* **2 be strewn with sth** containing a lot of something: *Serban's work is strewn with symbolism.*
stri·at·ed /ˈstraɪˌeɪtɪd/ *adj.* TECHNICAL having narrow lines or bands of color; STRIPED
stri·a·tion /straɪˈeɪʃən/ *n.* TECHNICAL [C usually plural] one of a number of narrow lines or bands of color; STRIPE
strick·en¹ /ˈstrɪkən/ *adj.* FORMAL very badly affected by trouble, illness etc.: *At last the pilot managed to land his stricken aircraft.* | **drought-stricken/cancer-stricken/tragedy-stricken etc.** *Fires are*

common in this drought-stricken region. —see also GRIEF-STRICKEN, PANIC-STRICKEN, POVERTY-STRICKEN
stricken² *v.* a past participle of STRIKE¹
strict /strɪkt/ *adj.* **1** demanding that rules be obeyed: *a strict teacher* | [+ **about**] *The hospital is quite strict about visiting hours.* | [+ **with**] *Mom and Dad were always very strict with us kids.* **2** a strict order or rule is one that must be obeyed: *Japan has very strict laws against drugs and guns.* | *I'm telling you this in the strictest confidence* (=it must be kept completely secret). **3** [usually before noun] exact and correct, often in a way that seems unreasonable: *The book is not actually "autobiographical" in the strict sense.* **4** a strict Muslim/vegetarian etc. someone who obeys all the rules of a particular religion, belief etc. —**strictness** *n.* [U]
strict·ly /ˈstrɪktli/ *adv.* **1** exactly and completely: *Some people objected, but it was all strictly legal.* **2 strictly speaking** used when you are using words or explaining rules in an exact and correct way: *Strictly speaking, spiders are not insects, although most people think they are.* **3** only for a particular person, thing, or purpose and nothing else: *I play the piano strictly for fun.* **4** in a way that must be obeyed: *Local driving regulations are strictly enforced.*
stric·ture /ˈstrɪktʃɚ/ *n.* [C often plural] FORMAL **1** a rule that strictly limits what you can do: [+ **against/on**] *the Church's strictures on birth control* **2** a severe criticism
stride¹ /straɪd/ *v. past tense* **strode** *past participle* **stridden** /ˈstrɪdn/ [I always + adv./prep.] to walk quickly with long steps: [+ **across/into/down etc.**] *"Thank you," she said coldly, and strode away.*
stride² *n.*
1 walking [C] a long step: *Len was out of the room in two strides.*
2 improvement [C] an improvement in a situation or in the development of something: **make great/major/giant etc. strides** *We've made tremendous strides in reducing crime in the city.*
3 take sth in stride to not allow something to annoy, embarrass, or upset you: *Neil took the criticism in his stride.*
4 pattern of steps [singular] the pattern of your steps, or the way you walk or run: *She'd lost some weight and seemed to move with a quicker stride.*
5 hit your stride to become comfortable with a job so you can do it continuously and well: *He released his first album in 1968, but he never really hit his stride till 10 years later.*
6 break (your) stride a) to begin moving more slowly or to stop when you are running or walking **b)** if you break your stride, or if someone or something breaks it, you allow them to interrupt or annoy you: *He's usually able to deal with anything life sends his way without breaking stride.*
7 knock/throw/keep sb off stride to make someone unable to do something effectively by not allowing them to give all their attention to it: *In an attempt to knock the Democrats off stride, the President offered several proposals to limit the government subsidies.*
8 (match sb) stride for stride also **go stride for stride with sb** to manage to be just as fast, strong, skilled etc. as someone else even if they keep making it harder for you
stri·dent /ˈstraɪdnt/ *adj.* **1** forceful and determined: *strident critics* | *the strident demands of the American media* **2** a strident sound or a voice that is strident is not nice to listen to because it is loud and often high —**stridently** *adv.* —**stridency** *n.* [U]
strife /straɪf/ *n.* [U] FORMAL trouble between two or more people or groups; CONFLICT: *eight years of ethnic strife*
strike¹ /straɪk/ *v. past tense* **struck** *past participle* **struck**
1 hit [I always + adv./prep.,T] FORMAL to hit or knock hard against something: [**strike sb/sth**] *A pebble from the road struck Art in the forehead.* | *The girl was struck by a car as she crossed San Carlos Avenue.*
2 thought/idea [T not in progressive] if a thought, idea, fact etc. strikes you, you think of it, notice it, or realize that it is important, interesting, surprising,

bad etc.: [**it strikes sb that**] *It suddenly struck me that I hadn't spoken to Debbie in months.* | [**be struck by sth**] *We were struck by her patience with all the children.*

3 strike sb as (being) sth to seem to have a particular quality or feature: *Mr. West struck me as a very good businessman.* | *His arguments struck us as completely ridiculous.* | *How does breakfast in bed strike you* (=do you like the idea)? | **strike sb as strange/odd/funny etc.** *Didn't it strike you as odd that they chose Martin?*

4 `stop work` [I] if a group of workers strike, they deliberately stop working for a time because of a disagreement with their company about pay, working conditions etc.: *The flight attendants are threatening to strike.* | [**+ for/against**] *Over 100,000 factory workers are striking for higher wages.*

5 `with your hand` [T] FORMAL to deliberately hit someone or something hard, especially with your hand: *He struck her across the face and broke her nose.* | [**strike sth with**] *Jumping up, he struck the table with his fist.* | *She struck the dog a blow with her umbrella.*

6 `attack` [I] to attack suddenly: *Police fear that the killer will strike again.* | *The snake releases the mouse after striking.* | [**+ at**] *Fighter bombers struck at the presidential palace.*

7 strike a balance (between sth) to give the correct amount of importance or attention to two opposing things: *Eastin is trying to strike a balance between family life and her work.*

8 `sth unpleasant` [I] if something bad strikes, it suddenly happens: *Tragedy struck two days later when Tammy was in a serious car accident.*

9 strike a deal/bargain to agree to do something if someone else does something for you: *Republicans have struck a deal with Democrats on tax cuts.*

10 `disease` FORMAL [T usually passive] *past participle* also **stricken** to make someone become sick: [**be stricken by/with sth**] *He was stricken with polio when he was just two.*

11 strike a cheerful/conciliatory/cautious etc. note also **strike a...tone** to express a particular feeling or attitude: *Davis tried to strike a hopeful note in his speech.*

12 strike a chord to express an opinion or idea that other people agree with or have sympathy with: *Morse's book struck a deep chord with the American Jewish community.*

13 strike a match to make a match burn by hitting it against a hard surface

14 strike gold/oil etc. a) to suddenly find gold, oil etc., especially after you have been looking for it: *Fuller moved to California, hoping to strike gold.* **b)** to become very successful at something and earn a lot of money: *Ford worked as a carpenter before he struck gold as an actor.*

15 `clock` [I,T] when a clock strikes, or it strikes one, three, six etc., its bell sounds one, three, six etc. times to show the time: *The clock had just struck two.* | *The tower bell was beginning to strike the hour* (=strike when it is exactly one o'clock, two o'clock etc.).

16 `lightning` [I,T] when LIGHTNING strikes something, it hits and damages it: *Lightning struck the barn and set it on fire.*

17 strike sb dead if something, especially LIGHTNING, strikes you dead, it hits and kills you very suddenly

18 strike a blow for sb to do something to help an idea, belief, or organization: *We feel we have struck a blow for freedom of speech.*

19 strike a blow to/at/against sth to have a harmful effect on people's behavior, beliefs etc.: *The court has struck another blow to the state's civil rights commission.*

20 be within striking distance (of sth) to be very close to something or very near to achieving something: *Johansson is now within striking distance of winning the tournament.*

21 strike sb/sth from sth FORMAL *past participle* **stricken** to remove a name or a thing from something written: *His testimony was stricken from the record* (=removed from the official court record).

22 strike at the heart of sth to attack or have a strong negative effect on the most important part of something: *The Oklahoma City bombing struck at the heart of America.*

23 `gain advantage` [I] to do something that gives you an advantage or harms your opponent in a fight, competition etc.: *The Cardinals struck first with two touchdowns in the first quarter.*

24 strike it rich to suddenly make a lot of money: *They're hoping to strike it rich in Las Vegas.*

25 `light` [T] to fall on a surface: *Watch what happens when light strikes the prism.*

26 strike terror/fear into sb's heart to make someone feel afraid

27 strike a pose to stand or sit with your body in a particular position: *Eva turned, and struck a pose with her head to one side.*

28 be struck dumb to be unable to speak, usually because you are very surprised —see also DUMB-STRUCK

29 strike while the iron is hot to do something immediately rather than waiting until a later time when you are less likely to succeed

30 `tent/sail/set` [T] to take down a tent, sail, or SET (=structures built for a play): *We struck camp at daybreak.*

31 be struck with horror/terror/awe etc. to suddenly feel very shocked, afraid etc. —see also AWESTRUCK

32 `coins` [T usually passive] to make a coin —see also **hit/strike home** (HOME[2] (5)), STRICKEN[1], STRIKING

strike back *phr. v.* [I] to attack or criticize someone who has attacked or criticized you first: [**+ at**] *Whittle struck back at critics of his educational policies.*

strike down *phr. v.* [T] **1** [**strike sth ↔ down**] if a court strikes down a law, it decides not to allow it: *The Supreme Court struck down a similar law in Louisiana.* **2** [**strike sb ↔ down**] [usually passive] to make someone die or become very sick: *Thousands of people were struck down by the disease.* **3** [**strike sb ↔ down**] LITERARY to hit someone so hard that they fell down

strike on/upon sth *phr. v.* [T] to discover something or have a good idea about something: *In 1514, Werner struck on a way to use the motion of the moon as a location finder.*

strike out *phr. v.*
1 `baseball` [I,T **strike sb ↔ out**] to fail to hit the ball in baseball three times so that you are not allowed to continue trying, or to make someone do this —see also STRIKEOUT
2 strike out on your own to start doing something new or living by yourself, without other people's help: *It feels great to strike out on your own and find a job and a place to live.*
3 `attack` [I] to criticize or attack someone suddenly or violently: [**+ at**] *Depressed men often strike out at their wives and children.*
4 `in a direction` [I always + adv./prep.] to start moving in a particular direction, especially in a determined way: *The travelers left St. Cloud and struck out across the prairie to Albion.*
5 `not succeed` [I] SPOKEN to be unsuccessful at something: *"Did you kiss her?" "No, I struck out."*
6 `word` [T **strike sth ↔ out**] OLD-FASHIONED to draw a line through something written on a piece of paper

strike up *phr. v.* **1 strike up a friendship/conversation/correspondence etc. (with sb)** to start to become friendly with someone, start talking to them etc.: *I struck up a conversation with the taxi driver on the way to the airport.* **2** [I,T] to begin playing a piece of music: *Strike up the band* (=tell it to begin playing), *and let's get this party started.*

strike² *n.* **1** [C,U] a period of time when a group of workers deliberately stop working because of a disagreement about pay, working conditions etc.: *About 500 university workers went on strike Tuesday over wages.* | *In Minsk, factory workers were on strike for a second day today.* | *The leadership called the* *strike* (=asked people to stop working) *to protest dangerous working conditions.* | *Union leaders are calling for* **a general strike** (=one involving most of the workers in the country). | **a machinists'/players' etc. strike** *During the teachers' strike, all the schools were closed.* **2** [C] a military attack, especially by aircraft dropping bombs: [+ **against/on**] *military strikes on specific targets* | *The country is threatening to* **launch** *air strikes against its neighbors.* **3 two/three/several etc. strikes against sb/sth** two, three etc. things that make it extremely difficult for someone or something to be successful: *I was a woman and I was black, so in that company I already had two strikes against me.* **4** [C] an attempt to hit the ball in baseball that fails, or a ball that is thrown to the BATTER in the correct area, but is not hit —compare FOUL[3] (2) **5** [C] a situation in BOWLING in which you knock down all the PINs (=bottle shaped objects) with a ball on your first attempt —see also HUNGER STRIKE, LIGHTNING STRIKE, OIL STRIKE, RENT STRIKE, THREE-STRIKES

strike·bound /'straɪkbaʊnd/ *adj.* unable to move, happen, or work because of a strike: *a strikebound shipyard*

strike·break·er /'straɪkˌbreɪkɚ/ *n.* [C] someone who takes the job of someone who is on strike —compare SCAB (2) —**strikebreaking** *n.* [U]

strike·out /'straɪk-aʊt/ *n.* [C] in baseball, the action of throwing three STRIKES[2] (4) so that the BATTER is not allowed to try to hit the ball anymore —see also **strike out** (STRIKE[1])

strike pay /'. ./ *n.* [U] money paid by a union to workers who are not working because they are on STRIKE

strik·er /'straɪkɚ/ *n.* [C] someone who is not working because they are on STRIKE

strike zone /'. ./ *n.* [C] in baseball, the area over HOME PLATE between the BATTER's knees and the top of the arms, where the ball must be thrown to be considered a STRIKE[2] (4)

strik·ing /'straɪkɪŋ/ *adj.* **1** unusual or interesting enough to be noticed: **a striking contrast/example/parallel etc.** *Douglas has noticed some striking similarities between the two cultures.* **2** someone who is striking is very attractive, often in an unusual way: *a dark man with striking features* —**strikingly** *adv.* —see also **be within striking distance** (STRIKE[1] (20))

Strind·berg /'strɪndbɚg/, **August** (1849–1912) a Swedish writer of plays

s w   **string**[1] /strɪŋ/ *n.*
2 3
1 |thread| [C,U] a strong thread made of several threads twisted together, used for tying or fastening things: *I need a piece of string to tie this package.* | *The pen was hanging from a string on the wall.* **2** |group/series| [C] **a)** a number of similar things or events coming one after another: [+ **of**] *They asked me a string of questions about Gerald and Bob.* **b)** a group of similar things: [+ **of**] *She owns a string of health clubs.* **c)** TECHNICAL a group of letters, words, or numbers, especially in a computer program **3 no strings (attached)** having no special conditions or limits on an agreement, relationship etc.: *Howard's agreed to lend me the money with no strings attached.* **4 a string of pearls/beads/lights etc.** several objects of the same kind connected with a thread, chain etc. **5 the strings** [plural] the part of an ORCHESTRA that consists of stringed instruments, such as VIOLINs **6** |on an instrument| [C] one of the long thin pieces of wire, NYLON etc. that is stretched across a musical instrument and produces sound **7 have sb on a string** INFORMAL to be able to make someone do whatever you want: *Lester claims to have several women on a string.* —see also G-STRING, **pull strings** (PULL[1] (6)), **pull the/sb's strings** (PULL[1] (7)), **hold/control the purse strings** (PURSE[1] (4)), -STRING

string[2] *v.* past tense and past participle **strung** [T] **1** to put things together onto a thread, chain etc.:

Help me string the popcorn to hang on the Christmas tree. **2** [always + adv./prep.] to hang things in a line, high up, especially for decoration: [+ **string sth up/along/across etc.**] *Paper lanterns were strung up across the courtyard.* **3** [usually passive, always + adv./prep.] also **string out** to spread something in a line: *The 200 houses are strung along a narrow 5-mile road.* **4** to put a string or a set of strings onto a musical instrument —see also HIGH-STRUNG

string along *phr. v.* INFORMAL [T] to deceive someone for a long time by making them believe that you will help them, that you love them etc.: *He's never going to marry you – he's just stringing you along.*

string sth ↔ **out** *phr. v.* [T] INFORMAL to make something last longer: *The process could string out the dispute for months.* —see also STRUNG OUT

string sth ↔ **together** *phr. v.* [T] **1** to combine two or more things together to make something that is complete, good, useful etc., especially when you have trouble doing it: *He managed to string together enough financial aid to go to a community college.* | *The Chargers could only string together two first downs in the first half.* **2 string two words/ phrases/ sentences together** to say or write something that makes sense to other people, especially when you have trouble doing it: *He was so drunk he could hardly string two words together.*

string sth/sb ↔ **up** *phr. v.* [T] INFORMAL to kill someone by hanging them

-string /strɪŋ/ [in adjectives] **first-string/second-string/ third-string** relating to or being a member of a sports team with the highest, second highest etc. level of skill: *a first-string quarterback*

string bean /'. ./ *n.* [C] **1** a GREEN BEAN **2** SPOKEN, INFORMAL a very tall thin person

stringed in·stru·ment /ˌ. '../ *n.* [C] a musical instrument, such as a VIOLIN, that produces sound from a set of STRINGS[1] (6)

strin·gent /'strɪndʒənt/ *adj.* **1** a stringent law, rule, standard etc. is very strict and must be obeyed: *stringent anti-noise regulations* **2** stringent economic conditions exist when there is a severe lack of money and strict controls on the supply of money —**stringently** *adv.* —**stringency** *n.* [U]

string·er /'strɪŋɚ/ *n.* [C] **1** someone who regularly sends in news stories to a newspaper, but who is not employed by that newspaper **2 a first-stringer/ second-stringer/third-stringer** one of the players on a sports team who has the highest, second highest etc. level of skill

string tie /ˌ. './ *n.* [C] a narrow piece of cloth worn around your neck and tied in a bow

string·y /'strɪŋi/ *adj.* **stringier, stringiest 1** stringy meat, fruit, or vegetables are full of thin pieces that are difficult to eat: *The chicken was dry and stringy.* **2** stringy hair is very thin and looks like string, especially because it is dirty: *Her stringy black hair kept falling in her eyes.* **3** someone or a part of their body that is stringy is very thin so that their muscles show through their skin: *stringy arms and knobby wrists*

strip[1] /strɪp/ *v.* **stripped, stripping**   **s w**
3
1 |take off clothes| **a)** [I,T] to take off your clothes or take off someone else's clothes: *Tim stripped and climbed into bed.* | [**strip (off) sth**] *Inside the apartment, he stripped off his shirt and pants and sat on the sofa.* | [**strip sb**] *Police say she was stripped and beaten by the men.* | *A tall man approached who was barefoot and* **stripped to the waist** (=not wearing any clothes on the top half of his body). | *I was surprised to see Alison had* **stripped down to** *her swimming suit* (=removed all her clothes except her swimming suit). | *The boys* **stripped naked** (=removed all their clothes) *and jumped in the pond.* **b)** [I] to take off your clothes in a sexually exciting way as entertainment for someone else

2 |remove a layer| [T] to remove something that is covering the surface of something else: [**strip sth off/from sth**] *We need to strip the wallpaper off the walls first.* | [**strip sth of sth**] *The land around the buildings had been stripped of trees.* **3 strip sb of sth** to take away something important

from someone as a punishment, for example their title, property, or power: *The state board stripped Larsen of his psychology license on Tuesday.*
4 **building/car etc.** [T] to remove everything that is inside a building, all the equipment from a car etc. so that it is completely empty: *The apartment had been **stripped bare**.*
5 **damage** to damage or break the GEARS in a machine or the THREADS (=lines) on a screw so that they do not work correctly anymore
6 **bed** [T] to take all the sheets off a bed —see also ASSET STRIPPING
strip sth ↔ **away** *phr. v.* [T] to gradually get rid of habits, customs etc. or their influence: *I wanted to strip away the years of lies and find out the truth.*

strip² *n.* [C] **1** a long narrow piece of paper, cloth etc.: *a strip of bacon* **2** a long narrow area of land: *A strip of sand between the cliffs and the ocean.* **3** a road with a lot of stores, restaurants etc. along it: *the Las Vegas strip* **4** a COMIC STRIP —see also LANDING STRIP

strip club /ˈ. ./ *n.* [C] a place where people go to see performers who take off their clothes to music

stripe /straɪp/ *n.* [C] **1** a line of color, especially one of several lines of color all close together: *a shirt with black and white stripes* —see picture at ZEBRA **2** politicians/musicians/scientists etc. of all stripes INFORMAL used to mean all different types of politicians, musicians etc.: *Politicians of all stripes are praising the deal.* **3** a narrow piece of material worn on the arm of a uniform as a sign of rank: *a sergeant's stripes* —see also **earn your stripes** (EARN (6)), STARS AND STRIPES

striped /straɪpt, ˈstraɪpɪd/ *adj.* having lines or bands of color: *a blue and white striped T-shirt* —see picture at PATTERN¹

strip joint /ˈ. ./ *n.* [C] INFORMAL a strip club

strip·ling /ˈstrɪplɪŋ/ *n.* [C] LITERARY a boy who is almost a young man

strip mall /ˈ. ./ *n.* [C] a row of stores built together, with a large area for parking cars in front of it

strip mine /ˈ. ./ *n.* [C] a very large hole that is made in the ground to remove metal, coal etc. from the earth —**strip-mine** *v.* [I,T] —**strip mining** *n.* [U]

stripped-down /ˌ. ˈ.◂/ *adj.* [only before noun] having only the basic features, with everything special and additional removed: *a stripped-down computer*

strip·per /ˈstrɪpɚ/ *n.* [C] **1** someone, especially a woman, who takes off their clothes in a sexually exciting way in order to entertain people **2** a tool or liquid used to remove something from a surface: *paint stripper*

strip pok·er /ˌ. ˈ../ *n.* [C] a game of POKER (=card game) in which players that lose take off pieces of their clothing

strip search /ˈ. ./ *n.* [C] a process in which you have to remove your clothes so that your body can be checked, usually for hidden drugs —**strip-search** *v.* [T]

strip show /ˈ. ./ *n.* [C] a form of entertainment where people, especially women, take off their clothes in a sexually exciting way

strip·tease /ˈstrɪptiz/ *n.* [C,U] a performance in which someone, especially a woman, takes off their clothes in a sexually exciting way

strive /straɪv/ *v. past tense* **strove** *past participle* **striven** /ˈstrɪvən/ *n.* [I] FORMAL to make a great effort to achieve something: [+ **for**] *We will continue to strive for a better standard of living for all.* | **strive to do** sth *The film studio is striving to improve its public image.*

strobe light /ˈstroʊb laɪt/ also **strobe** *n.* [C] a light that flashes on and off very quickly, often used in places where you can dance

strode /stroʊd/ the past tense of STRIDE

stroke¹ /stroʊk/ *n.* [C]
1 **illness** an occasion when an ARTERY (=tube carrying blood) in your brain suddenly bursts or becomes blocked: *Aspin died suddenly of a stroke.* | **have/suffer a stroke** *Blair's father suffered a stroke that left him unable to speak.*

2 **swimming/rowing** a) one of a set of movements in swimming or rowing in which you move your arms or the OAR forward and then back repeatedly: *With our first paddle strokes, the canoe started moving rapidly down the river.* b) a style of swimming or rowing: *the back stroke*
3 **sports** a movement of the upper part of your body that you use to hit the ball in games such as tennis, GOLF etc.: *a backhand stroke*
4 **a stroke of luck/fortune** something lucky that you did not expect to happen: *In an amazing stroke of luck, a liver donor was found almost immediately.*
5 **pen/brush** a) a single movement of a pen or brush when you are writing or painting: *He paints the pictures with a series of quick strokes.* b) a line made by doing this: *The most complex Chinese character contains 64 strokes.* —see also BRUSH STROKE
6 **a stroke of genius/inspiration etc.** a very good idea about what to do to solve a problem: *It was a stroke of genius to film the movie in Toronto.*
7 **with/at a stroke of the pen** if you do something with a stroke of the pen, you do it by signing a piece of paper: *With a stroke of the pen, the two leaders have cut the number of nuclear weapons in half.*
8 **at the stroke of seven/ten etc.** at exactly seven o'clock, ten o'clock etc.: *The judge stepped into the courtroom at the stroke of nine.*
9 **a bold stroke** something very brave that someone does to achieve something
10 **at a/one stroke** with a single sudden action: *Brian saw a chance of solving all his problems at one stroke.*
11 **hit** an action of hitting someone with something such as a whip or a thin stick: *If we talked back to the teacher, we got two strokes on the palm.*
12 **clock/bell** [C] a single sound made by a clock giving the hours, or by a bell, GONG etc.
13 **a stroke of lightning** a bright flash of LIGHTNING, especially one that hits something —see also **different strokes (for different folks)** (DIFFERENT (4))

stroke² *v.* [T] **1** to move your hand gently over something: *Sandy took the baby in her arms and stroked his cheek.* **2** [T] to hit a ball in tennis, baseball, GOLF etc.: *Gallego stroked the ball over Martinez's head.* **3** [T] to say nice things to someone to make them feel good, especially because you want something from them: *He knew he had to tolerate Haley, stroke him some, and wait for his rage to subside.*

stroll /stroʊl/ *v.* [I,T] to walk somewhere in a slow relaxed way: [+ **along/across/around etc.**] *We strolled through the gardens, admiring the flowers.* | [**stroll** sth] *After dinner I strolled the deserted beach.* —**stroll** *n.* [C]

stroll·er /ˈstroʊlɚ/ *n.* [C] a small chair on wheels in which a small child sits and is pushed along —compare BABY CARRIAGE

stroll·ing /ˈstroʊlɪŋ/ *adj.* [only before noun] a strolling musician plays music while walking among listeners: *a strolling mariachi band*

strong /strɔŋ/ *adj.*
1 **physical** having a lot of physical power so that, for example, you can lift or move heavy things: *strong arms* | *My brother is stronger than I am.*
2 **things** not easily broken or destroyed: *Do you think the ladder is strong enough to support your weight?* | *the strongest adhesive you can buy*
3 **power** having a lot of power or influence: *a strong president* | *America must maintain a strong national defense.*
4 **feelings/opinions** strong emotions, opinions, beliefs etc. are ones that you feel very serious about: *Goldsmith has very strong feelings about protecting the environment.* | *There's **a very strong sense of** ethnic pride in this town.*
5 **argument/reason etc.** likely to persuade other people that something is true or the correct thing to do: *Siegel's conclusions are supported by strong evidence.*
6 **able to deal with difficulty** determined and able

S

to deal with a difficult or upsetting situation: *I don't think she's strong enough to handle the news.*
7 [relationship] a strong relationship, friendship etc. is very loyal and likely to last a long time: *The family felt a strong emotional bond with Edward.* | *strong trade ties between the two nations*
8 [taste/smell] having a taste or smell that you notice easily: *a strong garlic taste* | *The strong smell of beef soup filled the kitchen.*
9 [affect/influence] a strong desire, influence etc. affects you very much: *Degas had a strong influence on Toulouse-Lautrec's work.* | *The temptation to keep a little of the money for himself was very strong.*
10 [likely] likely to succeed or happen: *Midler was considered a strong candidate for the best actress nomination.* | *a strong possibility/probability/chance We feel we have a strong chance of winning in Florida.*
11 50/600/10,000 etc. strong [only after number] used to give the number of people in a crowd or organization: *The staff, now 900 strong, has doubled in three years.*
12 [good at sth] very good at doing something: *Dallas is a stronger team than Pittsburgh, in my opinion.*
13 [alcohol/drugs etc.] having a lot of a substance such as alcohol that gives something its effect: *strong cough syrup* | *This margarita is really strong.*
14 [done well] done very well or skillfully: *We are expecting another strong performance from our investments next year.* | **sb's strong point/suit** (=the thing someone does best)
15 a strong wind/current/tide etc. wind, water etc. that moves with great force
16 be in a strong position to be in a situation where you have power over other people or are likely to get what you want: *At the end of the war, the U.S. was in a strong position to influence the future of Europe.*
17 [money] a strong CURRENCY (=the type of money used in a country) does not easily lose its value compared with other currencies: *The dollar is strong at the moment.*
18 [light/color] bright and easy to see: *The light was not very strong.*
19 be going strong to continue to be active or successful, even after a long time: *The program is 20 years old this month and is still going strong.*
20 [healthy] healthy, especially after you have been sick: *I don't think her heart is very strong.*
21 strong language speech or writing that contains a lot of swearing: *The film contains strong language and violence.*
22 a strong accent the way that someone pronounces words that shows clearly that they come from a particular area or country: *a strong Russian accent*
23 a strong nose/chin etc. a nose, chin etc. that is large and noticeable, especially in an attractive way: *Imelda's strong features reflect her Indian heritage.*
24 sb is the strong, silent type used to say that someone, usually a man, does not say very much but who seems confident, physically strong, and interesting
25 have a strong stomach a) to be able to watch something that shows people bleeding, being hurt etc. without feeling sick or upset: *It's a very violent film. You'll need a strong stomach to sit through it.* **b)** to be able to do something risky without becoming frightened: *You have to have a strong stomach to invest in today's bond market.*
26 strong medicine a way of dealing with a problem that is very severe, but is expected to be effective: *Welfare reform is strong medicine, but it's what the American people want.*
27 a strong verb TECHNICAL a verb that does not add a regular ending in the past tense, but may change a vowel —see also **come on strong/fast** at **come on** (COME¹), STRONGLY

strong-arm /'. ./ *adj.* [only before noun] INFORMAL **strong-arm methods/tactics etc.** methods that use force or violence, especially when this is not necessary —**strong-arm** *v.* [T]

strong·box /'strɔŋbɑks/ *n.* [C] a box, usually made of metal, that can be locked and that valuable things are kept in

strong·hold /'strɔŋhoʊld/ *n.* [C] **1** an area where there is a lot of support for a particular attitude, way of life, political party etc.: *Kentucky is a traditional Democratic stronghold.* **2** an area that is strongly defended by a military group: *a rebel stronghold*

strong·ly /'strɔŋli/ *adv.* **1** if you feel or believe something strongly, you are very sure and serious about it: *We strongly believe that she is innocent.* **2** in a way that is meant to persuade someone to do something: **strongly urge/advise/encourage** *Tourists in poor health are strongly advised not to make the trip.* **3** in a way that is easy to notice: *Harold's suit smelled strongly of mothballs.* ▫ S W 3

strong·man /'strɔŋmæn/ *n.* [C] **1** a man with a lot of political power who uses force to keep that power: *military strongmen* **2** a very strong man who performs at a CIRCUS

strong-mind·ed /,. '..◂/ *adj.* not easily influenced by other people to change what you believe or want: *Adele is an independent strong-minded woman.* —**strong-mindedly** *adv.* —**strong-mindedness** *n.* [U]

strong room /'. ./ *n.* [C] a special room in a bank, shop etc. where valuable objects can be kept safely

strong-willed /,. '..◂/ *adj.* knowing exactly what you want to do and being determined to achieve it, even if other people advise you against it: *the strong-willed party leader*

stron·ti·um /'strɑntiəm/ *n.* [U] *symbol* Sr a soft metal that is one of the chemical ELEMENTS

strop /strɑp/ *n.* [C] a narrow piece of leather used to make RAZORS sharp

strove /stroʊv/ the past tense of STRIVE

struck /strʌk/ the past tense of STRIKE

struc·tur·al /'strʌktʃərəl/ *adj.* relating to the structure of something: *structural damage* | *structural changes in the economy* —**structurally** *adv.*

structural en·gi·neer /,... ..'./ *n.* [C] an engineer skilled in planning the building of large structures such as bridges —**structural engineering** *n.* [U]

struc·tur·al·ism /'strʌktʃərə,lɪzəm/ *n.* [U] a method of studying language, literature, society etc. in which you examine the different parts or ideas in a subject to find a common pattern —**structuralist** *n., adj.*

struc·ture¹ /'strʌktʃɚ/ *n.* **1** [C,U] the way in which the parts of something are connected with each other and form a whole, or the thing that these parts make up: *good sentence structure* | *crystal structures* **2** [C] something that has been built, especially something large such as a building or bridge: *a three-story wooden structure* **3** [C,U] the way in which relationships between people or groups are organized in a society or in an organization: *The membership on the committee reflects Boston's power structure.* **4** [C,U] the condition of having ideas, activities etc. organized and planned: *As I was growing up, Mom gave me structure and a sense of responsibility.* ▫ S W 2

structure² *v.* [T] to arrange the different parts of something into a pattern or system in which each part is connected to the others: *Bidwell still has not decided how to structure the business.*

struc·tured /'strʌktʃɚd/ *adj.* carefully organized, planned, or arranged: *The school day is highly structured* (=very carefully organized). | *a loosely structured* (=planned, but without involving too many details) *program of events*

stru·del /'strudl/ *n.* [C,U] a type of Austrian or German cake, made of PASTRY with fruit inside: *apple strudel*

strug·gle¹ /'strʌgəl/ *v.* [I] **1** to try extremely hard to achieve something, or deal with something, even though it is very difficult: *Johnny is struggling in school.* | [**struggle to do sth**] *I swallowed hard and struggled to keep from crying.* | [**+ with**] *Most of us have struggled with the question of what makes life meaningful.* | [**+ for**] *Since he became manager, Roberts has struggled for respect from his employees.* ▫ S W 2

2 to fight someone who is attacking you or holding you, especially so that you can escape: [+ **with**] *Liz struggled fiercely with her attacker.* **3** if two people struggle, they fight each other for something, especially something one of them is holding: [+ **for**] *The two men struggled for the gun.* **4** to move somewhere with great difficulty: [+ **toward/into** etc.] *Fern struggled up the stairs to her bedroom.*

struggle on *phr. v.* [I] to continue doing something that you find difficult, tiring etc.: *He felt weak but forced himself to struggle on till he reached the house.*

struggle² *n.* **1** [C,U] a long hard fight to get freedom, political rights etc.: [+ **for**] *the nation's struggle for independence* | *When the king died, there was* **a power struggle** *among members of the royal family.* **2** [C,U] a long period of time in which you try to deal with a difficult problem, disease etc.: [+ **with**/ **against**] *Kelly's struggle with cancer* **3** [C] a fight between two people for something, or an attempt by one person to escape from the other: *The suspect died after a violent struggle with police officers.* **4 be a struggle (for sb)** if an activity, job etc. is a struggle for someone, they find it very difficult to do: *Reading is a struggle for Tim.*

strum /strʌm/ *v.* **strummed, strumming** [I,T] to play an instrument such as a GUITAR by moving your fingers up and down across its strings

strum·pet /'strʌmpɪt/ *n.* [C] OLD USE an insulting word meaning a woman who has sex for money

strung /strʌŋ/ the past tense and past participle of STRING²

strung out, strung-out /ˌ. '.◂/ *adj.* INFORMAL **1** strongly affected by drugs and unable to react normally: *strung-out junkies* | [+ **on**] *The kids were all strung out on drugs.* **2** extremely tired and worried: *Mattie's nerves were strung out.*

strut¹ /strʌt/ *v.* **strutted, strutting** [I] **1** to walk proudly with your head high and your chest pushed forward, showing that you think you are important: *Jackson strutted around on stage between songs.* **2 strut your stuff** INFORMAL to show your skill at doing something: *Look at Dave strutting his stuff on the dance floor.*

strut² *n.* **1** [C] a long thin piece of metal or wood used to support a part of a building, the wing of an aircraft etc. **2** [singular] a proud way of walking, with your head high and your chest pushed forward

strych·nine /'strɪknaɪn, -nən, -nin/ *n.* [U] a very poisonous substance sometimes used in small amounts as a medicine

Stu·art /'stuət/ the name of the royal family that ruled Scotland from 1371 to 1603, and ruled Britain from 1603 to 1649 and from 1660 to 1714

stub¹ /stʌb/ *n.* [C] **1** the short part that is left when the rest of something long and thin, such as a cigarette or pencil, has been used: *a cigar stub* **2** the part of a ticket that is returned to you after it has been torn, as proof that you have paid **3** a piece of a check that is left after the main part has been torn off

stub² *v.* **stubbed, stubbing** [T] **stub your toe** to hurt your toe by hitting it against something

stub sth ↔ **out** *phr. v.* [T] to stop a cigarette from burning by pressing the end of it against something

stub·ble /'stʌbəl/ *n.* [U] **1** short stiff hairs that grow on a man's face, a woman's legs etc. when they have not SHAVEd for a period of time **2** short stiff pieces left in the fields after wheat, corn etc. has been cut —**stubbly** *adj.*

stub·born /'stʌbən/ *adj.* **1** determined not to change your mind, even when people think you are being unreasonable: *Your father is so stubborn – he won't listen.* | *Amos has* **a stubborn streak** *(=stubborn part of his character) that makes him very difficult to work with.* | *She's* **as stubborn as a mule** *(=very stubborn).* **2 stubborn opposition/determination/ persistence** etc. very strong and determined opposition, desire to do something etc.: *I couldn't understand his stubborn refusal to see a doctor.* **3** difficult to remove, deal with, or use: *stubborn weeds* —**stubbornly** *adv.* —**stubbornness** *n.* [U]

stub·by /'stʌbi/ *adj.* **stubbier, stubbiest** short and thick or fat: *stubby little fingers*

stuc·co /'stʌkoʊ/ *n.* [U] a type of PLASTER or CEMENT mixture that is used especially to cover the outside walls of houses

stuck¹ /stʌk/ the past tense and past participle of STICK¹

stuck² *adj.* [not before noun] **1** firmly fastened or attached in a particular position and unable to move or be moved: *This drawer is stuck.* | *We would have been here sooner, but we were* **stuck in traffic.** | *The* candy **got stuck** *in my teeth.* | *Somehow he* **got** *his toe* **stuck** *in the drain.* **2** unable to do any more of something that you are working on because it is too difficult: *Can you help me with my homework, Dad? I'm* **stuck.** **3** unable to escape from a boring or difficult situation: [+ **in/at**] *Bob was stuck in meetings all afternoon.* | [+ **with**] *I don't want to get stuck with a bunch of old ladies playing cards.* **4 be stuck with sth** to have something you do not want because you cannot get rid of it: *We're renting the house, so we're stuck with this ugly wallpaper.* **5 be stuck for sth** to be unable to think of something or to find something that you need to have: *Most of what they accused him of was true, and Wyden was stuck for an answer.* **6 be stuck on sb** INFORMAL to be attracted to someone: *Jane's really stuck on the new boy in her class.*

stuck-up /ˌ. '.◂/ *adj.* INFORMAL proud and unfriendly because you think you are better and more important than other people: *I can't stand her – she's so stuck-up.*

stud /stʌd/ *n.* **1** [C] INFORMAL a man who is very sexually attractive **2** [C] a small round EARRING **3** [C] a board that is used to build the frame of a house **4** [U] the use of animals, such as horses, for breeding, or an animal that is used for this: *a stud farm* **5** [C] a round piece of metal that is stuck into a surface for decoration: *a leather jacket with silver studs*

stud·book /'stʌdbʊk/ *n.* [C] a list of names of race horses from which other race horses have been bred

stud·ded /'stʌdɪd/ *adj.* **1** decorated with a lot of studs or small jewels etc.: *studded leather boots* | **jewel-studded/silver-studded/nail-studded** etc. *a diamond-studded watch* **2** covered or filled with a lot of something: [+ **with**] *The island is studded with white sand beaches.* —see also STAR-STUDDED

stu·dent /'studnt/ *n.* [C] **1** someone who is studying at a school, college etc.: *There are only 15 students in each class.* | **law/medical/engineering** etc. **student** *Matt is a first-year medical student at UCSF.* | a **student teacher/nurse** *(=someone who is learning to be a teacher or nurse)* | a **(straight) A/B/C** etc. **student** *(=someone who always earns A's, B's etc. for their school work)* **2 a student of sth** someone who is very interested in a particular subject: *Myles was a profound student of human nature.*

student bod·y /ˌ.. '../ *n.* [C] all of the students in a high school, college, or university, considered as a group

student coun·cil /ˌ.. '../ *n.* [C,U] the group of students at a high school who are elected to represent the students in meetings and who organize school activities

student gov·ern·ment /ˌ.. '../ *n.* [C,U] the group of students in a high school or college who are elected to represent the students in meetings and who organize school activities

student loan /ˌ.. '. / *n.* [C] a method of paying for your education in which college students borrow money from a bank or the government and repay it when they start working

student teach·ing /ˌ.. '../ *n.* [U] the period of time during which students who are learning to be teachers practice teaching in a school

student u·nion /ˌ.. '../ *n.* [C] a building at a college where students go to meet socially, buy books, relax etc.

stud·ied /'stʌdid/ *adj.* a studied way of behaving is

deliberate and often not sincere, because it has been planned carefully: *Richardson's studied informality is quite annoying.*

stu·di·o /'studi,ou/ *n. plural* **studios** [C] **1** a room where television and radio programs are made and broadcast, or where music is recorded: *a recording studio* **2** also **studios** [singular] a movie company or the buildings it owns and uses to make its movies: *Universal Studios* **3 a)** a room where a painter or photographer regularly works **b)** a company that produces pictures or photographs **4** also **studio apartment** a small apartment with one main room **5** a room where dancing or music lessons are given, or that dancers use to practice in

studio au·di·ence /,... '.../ *n.* [C] a group of people who watch and are sometimes involved in a television or radio program while it is being made

stu·di·ous /'studiəs/ *adj.* **1** spending a lot of time studying and reading: *a quiet, studious girl* **2** careful in your work: *Warren's studious attention to detail has made him successful.* —**studiously** *adv.* —**studiousness** *n.* [U]

stud·y¹ /'stʌdi/ *n. plural* **studies**
1 piece of work [C] a piece of work that is done to find out more about a particular subject or problem, and usually includes a written report: [+ of/into] *Rodman did a study of lower-class families in Trinidad.* | *They have begun a study into the causes of climate changes.* | **make/conduct/carry out** etc. **a study** *A study of children's eating habits was carried out in 1976.*
2 subject [U] a particular type of subject that people learn about and study, especially a science: *Paleontology is the study of ancient life.*
3 studies [plural] subjects that people study, especially several related subjects: *I'm thinking of specializing in Chinese studies.* | *How are you doing in your studies?*
4 room [C] a room in a house that is used for work or studying
5 be a study in sth to be a perfect example of something: *Franklin and Eleanor Roosevelt were a study in contrasts.*
6 school work [U] the activity of studying for school, college etc.: *Woodward's busy work schedule left little time for study on her MBA degree.* —see Usage Note at KNOW¹
7 art [C] a small detailed drawing, especially one that is done to prepare for a large painting: *Renoir's studies of small plants and flowers*
8 music [C] a piece of music, usually for piano, that is often intended for practice

study² *v.* **studies, studied, studying 1** [I,T] to spend time reading, going to classes etc. in order to learn about a subject: *I can't study with that music playing all the time.* | **study to be a doctor/lawyer** etc. *Alex is studying to be an engineer.* | **study for an exam/test** etc. *Ellen has to stay home and study for a quiz.* | **study law/business** etc. (=study a subject at college) | *He studied violin under* (=was trained by) *Andor Toth.* **2** [T] to watch and examine something carefully over a period of time in order to find out more about it: *Schultes has spent a lifetime studying hallucinogenic drugs.* | [study how/why/when etc.] *Keith is studying how maternal nutrition affects the birth weight of twins.* **3** [T] to spend a lot of time carefully examining a plan, document, problem etc.: *We spent all afternoon studying the recommendations.* | [study how/why/when etc.] *University officials are studying how to increase minority enrollment.*

study group /'.. ,./ *n.* [C,U] a group of students that meets in order to help each other study for a class at a college, or the time when they do this

study hall /'.. ,./ *n.* [U] a period of time during a school day when a student must go to a particular place to study instead of to a regular class

stuff¹ /stʌf/ *n.*
1 substance [U] INFORMAL a type of substance or material: *That stuff stinks.* | *I've got some sort of sticky stuff on my shoe.*
2 things [U] INFORMAL a number of different things: *They sent me a bunch of stuff about the university.*
3 subject INFORMAL [U] the subject of something such as a book, television program, lesson etc.: *What kind of stuff did they teach you there?*
4 activities [U] INFORMAL all the activities that someone does: *I've got so much stuff to do this weekend.*
5 sb's stuff INFORMAL things that belong to someone: *You can put your stuff over here for now.*
6 do/show your stuff SPOKEN to do what you are good at when everyone wants you to do it: *It's amazing to watch him do his stuff on the basketball court.*
7 the stuff of dreams/fantasy/novels** etc. exactly the kind of thing that dreams, FANTASY, NOVELS etc. consist of: *What Johnson did at the Olympics is the stuff of legend.*
8 character [U] INFORMAL the qualities of someone's character: *Becky's got the right stuff* (=qualities that make her able to deal with difficulties) *for becoming a good doctor.* | *I thought you were made of sterner stuff* (=more determined) – *don't give up.* —see also **hot stuff** (HOT (14)), **kid stuff** (KID¹ (4)), **know your stuff** (KNOW¹ (50)), **strut your stuff** (STRUT¹ (2))

stuff² *v.*
1 push [T always + adv./prep.] to push or put something into a small space, especially in a careless hurried way: [stuff sth into/in/up etc. sth] *She just stuffed all her dirty clothes under the bed.* | [stuff sth with sth] *Dad had stuffed the cigar boxes with old pictures.* | *The trunk was stuffed full of old tires.*
2 fill [T] to fill something with soft material: [stuff sth with sth] *The sleeping bag is stuffed with polyester fibers.*
3 food [T] to fill a chicken, TOMATO etc. with a mixture of bread or rice, onion etc.: *Could you help me stuff these peppers?*
4 dead animal [T] to fill the skin of a dead animal in order to make the animal look alive: *He had the fish stuffed to put on the wall in his office.*
5 stuff yourself also stuff your face INFORMAL to eat so much food that you cannot eat anything else: [+ with] *Dean stuffed his face with pizza.*
6 sb can stuff sth (up their ass) VULGAR used to say very angrily or rudely that you do not want what someone is offering: *You can stuff your money – I don't need your help.*

stuffed /stʌft/ *adj.* [not before noun] completely full, so that you cannot eat any more: *The cake looks great, but I'm stuffed.*

stuffed an·i·mal /,. '.../ *n.* [C] a toy animal made of a cloth like fur and filled with soft material

stuffed shirt /,. '., '. ./ *n.* [C] someone who behaves in a very formal way and thinks they are important: *Marcus was a true intellectual stuffed shirt.*

stuffed-up /,. '.</ *adj.* unable to breathe easily through your nose because you have a cold

stuff·ing /'stʌfɪŋ/ *n.* [U] **1** a mixture of bread, onion, HERBS and other foods, that you put inside a chicken, vegetable etc. before cooking it; DRESSING **2** soft material that is used to fill something such as a CUSHION —see also **knock the stuffing out of sb** (KNOCK¹ (3))

stuff·y /'stʌfi/ *adj.* **stuffier, stuffiest 1** a room or building that is stuffy does not have enough fresh air in it: *It's getting stuffy in here – do you mind if I open the window?* **2** someone who is stuffy is too formal and has old-fashioned ideas —**stuffily** *adv.* —**stuffiness** *n.* [U]

stul·ti·fy·ing /'stʌltə,faɪ-ɪŋ/ *adj.* so boring that you feel as though you are losing your ability to think: *a stultifying corporate environment* —**stultify** *v.* [T] —**stultification** /,stʌltəfə'keɪʃən/ *n.* [U]

stum·ble /'stʌmbəl/ *v.* **1** [I] to hit your foot against something or put your foot down awkwardly while you are walking or running, so that you almost fall: *One runner stumbled, but was able to regain her balance.* | [+ over/on] *He stumbled over the curb as he crossed the street.* **2** [I always + adv./prep.] to walk in an unsteady way and often almost fall:

[+ **in/out/across** etc.] *I stumbled into the kitchen to answer the phone.* **3 stumble on/across/upon etc. sth** to discover something or meet someone when you do not expect to: *We had the good fortune to stumble upon a romantic little cafe.* **4** [I always + adv./prep.] to stop or make a mistake when you are reading to people or speaking: [+ **over/at/through**] *Harrison stumbled through his speech.* **5 stumbling block** a problem or difficulty that prevents you from achieving something: [+ **to**] *My biggest stumbling block to getting in shape is finding the time.* —**stumble** *n.* [C]

stump[1] /stʌmp/ *n.* [C] **1** the bottom part of a tree that is left in the ground after the rest of it has been cut down **2** the short part of someone's leg, arm etc. that remains after the rest of it has been cut off **3** the small useless part of something that remains after most of it has broken off or worn away: *All that was left was a stump of what used to be a statue.*

stump[2] *v.* **1** [T] to ask someone such a difficult question that they are completely unable to think of an answer: *The case has stumped the police for months.* | **get/have sb stumped** *This question'll have them all stumped.* **2** [I,T] to travel around an area, meeting people and making speeches in order to gain political support: *Harkin plans to stump in Illinois this weekend.* **3** [I + **up/along/across**] to walk with heavy steps; STOMP

stump speech /'. ./ *n.* [C] a speech made by a politician while traveling around to get political support

stump·y /'stʌmpi/ *adj.* **stumpier, stumpiest** INFORMAL short and thick in an unattractive way

stun /stʌn/ *v.* **stunned, stunning** [T not in progressive] **1** to surprise or upset someone so much that they do not react immediately: *Howard was stunned when Garrett rejected the offer.* **2** to make someone unconscious for a short time: *The impact of the ball had stunned her.* —see also STUNNING

stung /stʌŋ/ *v.* the past tense and past participle of STING[1]

stun gun /'. ./ *n.* [C] a weapon that produces a very strong electric current and can be used to make animals or people unconscious

stunk /stʌŋk/ *v.* a past tense and the past participle of STINK[1]

stunned /stʌnd/ *adj.* too surprised or shocked to speak: *He looked completely stunned.* | *The audience sat in stunned silence.*

stun·ner /'stʌnɚ/ *n.* [C] **1** something that surprises you, especially a situation or event: *Tuesday's agreement was a stunner.* **2** OLD-FASHIONED someone or something that is very attractive or impressive, especially a woman

stun·ning /'stʌnɪŋ/ *adj.* **1** extremely attractive or beautiful: *the restaurant's stunning decor* | *Ella's stunning photography* **2** very surprising or shocking: *a stunning victory* —**stunningly** *adv.*

stunt[1] /stʌnt/ *n.* **1** [C] a dangerous action that is done to entertain people, especially in a movie: *Lockiear was the first pilot to do aerial stunts for the movies.* **2** [C] something that is done to attract people's attention, especially in advertising or politics: *The hunger strike is thought to be just another political stunt.* —see also **publicity stunt** (PUBLICITY (3)) **3 pull a stunt** to do something that is silly or embarrassing, or that is slightly dangerous: *He says he loves his kids, but when he pulls a stunt like this it makes me wonder.*

stunt[2] *v.* [T] to stop something or someone from growing to their full size or developing correctly: *Slow economic growth stunted corporate profits last quarter.*

stunt man /'. ./ *n.* [C] a man who is employed to take the place of an actor when something dangerous has to be done in a movie

stunt wom·an /'. ,../ *n.* [C] a woman who is employed to take the place of an actress when something dangerous has to be done in a movie

stu·pe·fied /'stupəˌfaɪd/ *adj.* so surprised, tired, or bored that you cannot think clearly: *Foreman looked stupefied by the results of the test.* —**stupefaction** /ˌstupəˈfækʃən/ *n.* [U]

stu·pe·fy·ing /'stupəˌfaɪ-ɪŋ/ *adj.* making you feel extremely surprised, tired, or bored: *The amount of money raised from the event is stupefying.* —**stupefy** *v.* [T]

stu·pen·dous /stuˈpɛndəs/ *adj.* [no comparative] extremely large or impressive: *a stupendous achievement* —**stupendously** *adv.*

stu·pid[1] /'stupɪd/ *adj.* **1** showing a lack of good sense or good judgment: *We did a lot of stupid things in high school.* | *a stupid question* | *It was stupid of me to give her money.* **2** having a low level of intelligence, so that you have difficulty learning or understanding things: *He's so stupid that he couldn't even find New York on the map.* | *She is sometimes naive, but she's not stupid.* **3** SPOKEN something that is stupid makes you annoyed or impatient: *I have to stay late and finish this stupid report.* | *This is stupid – I don't want to play this game anymore.* **4 be stupid with shock/exhaustion/fear etc.** to be unable to think clearly because you are extremely shocked, tired, frightened etc. —**stupidly** *adv.*: *Stupidly, she took their advice.*

stupid[2] *n.* [singular, not with **the**] an insulting way of talking to someone who you think is being stupid: *No, stupid, don't do it like that!*

stu·pid·i·ty /stuˈpɪdəti/ *n. plural* **stupidities 1** [U] the quality of lacking intelligence or good judgment: *Several guys were wounded because of his stupidity.* **2** [C,U] behavior or actions that show a lack of good judgment or intelligence: *The past 41 years have been an endless parade of stupidities.*

stu·por /'stupɚ/ *n.* [C,U] a state in which you cannot think, speak, see, or hear clearly, usually because you have drunk too much alcohol or taken drugs: *He drank himself into a stupor every night.*

stur·dy /'stɚdi/ *adj.* **sturdier, sturdiest 1** an object that is sturdy is strong, well-made, and not easily broken: *a table that was old and sturdy* | *sturdy walking shoes* **2** someone who is sturdy is strong and healthy looking but not thin: *She was a large, sturdy woman in her mid-fifties.* | *a sturdy jaw* **3** determined and not easily persuaded to change your opinions: *They kept up a sturdy opposition to the plan.* —**sturdily** *adv.* —**sturdiness** *n.* [U]

stur·geon /'stɚdʒən/ *n.* [C,U] a large fish, from which CAVIAR is obtained, or the meat of this fish

stut·ter[1] /'stʌtɚ/ *v.* **1** [I,T] to speak with difficulty because you cannot stop yourself from repeating the first CONSONANT of some words: *Other children often teased me because I stuttered.* **2** [I] if something such as a machine stutters, it makes quick exploding noises and does not work smoothly

stutter[2] *n.* [C usually singular] an inability to speak normally because you stutter: *You can't hear Ron's stutter when he sings.*

St. Vin·cent and the Gren·a·dines /seɪnt ˌvɪnsənt ən də 'grɛnədinz/ a country that consists of a group of islands in the Caribbean Sea

sty /staɪ/ *n. plural* **sties** [C] **1** also **stye** an infected place on the edge of your EYELID, which becomes red and swollen **2** a place where pigs are kept; PIGSTY (2)

Styg·i·an /'stɪdʒiən/ *adj.* LITERARY dark and making you feel nervous or afraid: *Stygian caverns*

style[1] /staɪl/ *n.*

1 way of doing/making [C,U] a particular way of doing, designing, or producing something, especially one that is typical of a particular period of time or group of people: *It was built in Colonial style to match the old part of the city.* | [+ **of**] *Hammill's favorite style of cooking? Mexican.* | *Our style of play is difficult for them to cope with.* | **Swedish/new/country etc. style** *Sanders built his house in a Belgian farmhouse style.* | *a southern-style barbecue sandwich*

2 fashion/design [C,U] a particular design or fashion for something such as clothes, hair, furniture etc.: *The women were wearing '50s style housedresses.* | [+ **of**] *They have over two hundred styles of*

wallpaper to choose from. | *Are tight jeans **in style*** (=fashionable) *this year?* | *The room was decorated **with style*** (=in a beautiful and stylish way).
3 way of behaving/working [C] the particular way that someone behaves, works, or deals with other people: [+ **of**] *Neville has a unique style of singing.* | **management/teaching/directing** etc. **style** *I prefer a more informal teaching style.* | *She would never lie like that – **it's not her style*** (=it is not the way she usually behaves). | *I **like your style*** (=approve of the way you do things), *Simpson. I think you'll do well here.* | *I don't think the parachuting weekend is for me – the art class is **more my style*** (=used to say that you prefer something).
4 art/music/film [C,U] the typical way that someone paints, writes music etc., or a typical way of painting etc. from a particular period of time: *Several of her early paintings were done in an expressionistic style.* | *Pollock's style is instantly recognizable.*
5 writing/literature [C,U] the particular way someone uses words to express ideas, tell stories etc., or a way of spelling or using words that is considered correct: *Hundreds of novelists have tried to copy Hemingway's direct style.* | *At this publisher, it isn't style to spell "worshipping" with one "p."* —see also STYLISTIC
6 special quality [U] a confident and attractive quality that makes people admire you, and that is shown in your appearance or the way you do things: *Sue may be hard to work with, but she definitely **has style***. —see also STYLISH
7 in style done in a way that people admire, especially because it is impressive, shows great determination, or involves spending a lot of money: **in great/grand/fine** etc. **style** *Leonora arrived at the ball in grand style.* —see also **cramp sb's style** (CRAMP² (3))
style² v. [T] **1** to design clothing, furniture etc. in a particular way, or to cut someone's hair in a particular way: *The car was styled and engineered by Ford and Mazda.* | *I only let Betty style my hair.* **2 style yourself (as) sth** FORMAL to give yourself a particular title or name, or to behave as if you are a particular type of person: *He styles himself as a tough guy.* —see also SELF-STYLED
styl·ing /'staɪlɪŋ/ also **stylin'** /'staɪlɪn/ adj. SLANG attractive and fashionable; COOL: *If I had a car like his, I'd be stylin'.*
styling brush /'.. ,./ n. [C] a heated brush used, especially by women, to make their hair a particular shape
styl·ings /'staɪlɪŋz/ n. [plural] the way in which someone performs music, jokes etc.: *breathy vocal stylings*
styl·ish /'staɪlɪʃ/ adj. attractive in a fashionable way: *a stylish black suit* —**stylishly** adv. —**stylishness** n. [U]
styl·ist /'staɪlɪst/ n. [C] **1** someone who cuts or arranges people's hair as their job **2** someone who has carefully developed a good style of writing
sty·lis·tic /staɪ'lɪstɪk/ adj. related to the style of a piece of writing or art —**stylistically** /-kli/ adv.
sty·lis·tics /staɪ'lɪstɪks/ n. [U] the study of style in written or spoken language
styl·ized /'staɪə,laɪzd/ adj. drawn, written, or done in a style or way that is not normal or natural: *Lisa performed a stylized version of the classic song "Silent Night."* —**stylize** v. [T]
sty·lus /'staɪləs/ n. **1** the small pointed part of a RECORD PLAYER that touches the record **2** a pointed instrument used in the past for writing on WAX¹ (1)
sty·mie /'staɪmi/ v. [T] INFORMAL to prevent someone from doing what they have planned or want to do; THWART: *The investigation has been stymied by witnesses who refuse to cooperate.*
styp·tic pencil /'stɪptɪk ,pɛnsəl/ n. [C] a type of medicine in the shape of a pencil that is used to stop the bleeding of small cuts, especially cuts from shaving (SHAVE)

Sty·ro·foam /'staɪrə,foum/ n. [U] TRADEMARK a soft light plastic material that prevents heat or cold from passing through it, used especially to make containers: *a Styrofoam cup*
sua·sion /'sweɪʒən/ n. [U] FORMAL: see PERSUASION
suave /swɑv/ adj. a man who is suave is polite, confident, and relaxed: *a suave and sophisticated gentleman* —**suavely** adv. —**suavity** also **suaveness** n. [U]
sub¹ /sʌb/ n. [C] INFORMAL **1** a SUBMARINE **2** a long bread roll split open and filled with meat, cheese etc.; SUBMARINE SANDWICH **3** a SUBSTITUTE in sports such as football **4** a SUBSTITUTE TEACHER
sub² v. **subbed, subbing** INFORMAL [I] to act as a SUBSTITUTE for someone: [+ **for**] *Lassiter was subbed for Ramos in the second half.*
sub- /sʌb/ prefix **1** under or below a particular level or thing: *sub-zero temperatures* (=below zero) | *substandard housing* (=below an acceptable standard) | *a movie with subtitles* **2** part of a bigger whole: *the Indian subcontinent* | *a subdivision of a large city* **3** less important or powerful than the main person or thing: *a subcommittee* **4** almost or nearly: *subtropical heat*
sub·arc·tic /,sʌb'arktɪk, -'artɪk/ adj. near the Arctic Circle, or typical of this area
sub·a·re·a /'sʌb,ɛriə/ n. [C] an area that is part of a larger area
sub·a·tom·ic /,sʌbə'tamɪk◂/ adj. smaller than an atom or existing within an atom
subatomic par·ti·cle /,.... '.../ n. [C] a piece of matter smaller than an atom
sub·com·mit·tee /'sʌbkə,mɪti/ n. [C] a small group formed from a committee to deal with a particular subject in more detail
sub·com·pact /,sʌb'kampækt/ n. [C] a type of very small and inexpensive car
sub·con·scious¹ /,sʌb'kanʃəs/ adj. [no comparative] subconscious feelings, desires etc. are hidden in your mind and you do not know that you have them: *His subconscious male bias clearly shows in the report.* —**subconsciously** adv.
subconscious² n. [singular] the part of your mind that has thoughts and feelings that you do not always realize you have: *These conflicting values waged war in my subconscious.*
sub·con·ti·nent /,sʌb'kantᵊn-ənt, -tənənt/ n. [C] **1** a very large area of land that is part of a CONTINENT **2 the subcontinent** the area of land that includes India, Pakistan, and Bangladesh
sub·con·ti·nen·tal /,sʌbkantᵊn'ɛntl/ adj. relating to a subcontinent
sub·con·tract /,sʌb'kantrækt/ v. [T] also **subcontract sth ↔ out** if a company subcontracts work, they pay other people to do part of their work for them: *They subcontract out the repair and maintenance of their rental car fleet.* —**subcontract** n. [C]
sub·con·trac·tor /,sʌb'kantræktɚ/ n. [C] someone who does part of the work of another person or firm
sub·cul·ture /'sʌb,kʌltʃɚ/ n. [C] a particular group of people within a society and their behavior, beliefs, and activities, often a group that many people disapprove of: *the drug subculture in Detroit*
sub·cu·ta·ne·ous /,sʌbkyu'teɪniəs◂/ adj. TECHNICAL beneath your skin: *subcutaneous fat* —**subcutaneously** adv.
sub·di·vide /,sʌbdə'vaɪd, 'sʌbdə,vaɪd/ v. [T] to divide into smaller parts or groups something that is already divided: *Rocks can be subdivided into types on the basis of texture.*
sub·di·vi·sion /'sʌbdə,vɪʒən/ n. **1** [C] an area of land that has been subdivided for building houses on **2** [C,U] the act of dividing something that has already been divided, or the parts that result from doing this
sub·due /səb'du/ v. [T] **1** to stop a person or group from behaving violently, especially by using force: *Security guards used pepper spray to subdue the man.* **2** FORMAL to take control of a place by defeating the people who live there: *Government forces have managed to subdue the rebels.* **3** FORMAL to prevent your

emotions from being so strong: *He felt the urge to apologize, but then subdued it.*

sub·dued /səb'dud/ *adj.* **1** a person, place, or sound that is subdued is unusually quiet: *Price had seemed rather subdued after the meeting.* **2** an event or business activity that is subdued does not have as much excitement or interest as you would expect: *Inflation remained subdued in September.* **3** subdued lighting, colors etc. are less bright than usual

sub·freez·ing /ˌsʌb'frizɪŋ◂/ *adj.* subfreezing temperatures are below 32°F (0°C)

sub·group /'sʌbgrup/ *n.* [C] a separate, smaller, and sometimes less important part of a group

sub·head·ing /'sʌbˌhɛdɪŋ/ *n.* [C] a short phrase used as a title for a small part within a longer piece of writing

sub·hu·man /ˌsʌb'hyumən◂/ *adj.* **1** behaving or thinking in a very bad way that you would not expect from humans: *He treats women as subhuman creatures, as things.* **2** a subhuman situation or condition is very dirty, crowded, or uncomfortable, or is cruel in some way: *The orphaned children were living in subhuman conditions.*

subj. a written abbreviation for "subject"

sub·ject¹ /'sʌbdʒɪkt/ *n.* [C]
1 thing talked about the thing you are talking about or considering in a conversation, discussion, book, movie etc.: *Truffaut's childhood memories were the subject of his first film.* | *Chris quickly changed the subject* (=started talking about something different) *when I asked him about his grades.* | *Several good books have been written on the subject of personality disorders.* | *"Class Action" is rated "R" for language and adult subject matter.* | **be a subject of debate/discussion/gossip etc.** *Kennedy's death continues to be a subject of debate.* **get/be/stay off the subject** *The discussion got off the subject of art when we started talking about public morality.*
2 school an area of knowledge that you study at a school or college: *History was my favorite subject in school.*
3 test a person or animal that is used in a test or EXPERIMENT, especially a medical or PSYCHOLOGICAL one: *Half of the subjects were given caffeine.*
4 art the thing you are dealing with when you paint a picture, take a photograph etc.: *Monet loved to use gardens as his subjects.*
5 grammar TECHNICAL a noun, noun phrase, or PRONOUN that usually comes before a main verb and represents the person or thing that performs the action of the verb, or about which something is stated. For example, in the sentence "She hit John" the subject is "she," and in "Elephants are big" the subject is "elephants." —compare OBJECT¹ (5)
6 country someone who was born in a country that has a king or queen, or someone who has a right to live there: *a British subject* —compare CITIZEN (2), NATIONAL²

subject² *adj.* **1 subject to sth a)** if you are subject to a set of rules or laws, you must obey them: *When you are in a foreign country, you are subject to its laws.* **b)** dependent on something else: *The agreement is subject to approval by teachers.* **2 subject to change** likely or possible to change: *Availability of sale items is subject to change without notice.* **3** [not before noun] likely to be affected by something, especially something bad: [+ **to**] *Several highways are subject to closing due to snow.* | *Nancy's often subject to self-doubt.* **4** FORMAL [only before noun] a subject country, state, people etc. is strictly governed by another country

sub·ject³ /səb'dʒɛkt/ *v.* [T] FORMAL to force a country or group of people to be ruled by you and control them very strictly

subject sb/sth to sth *phr. v.* [T] to force someone or something to experience something very bad, upsetting, or difficult, especially over a long time: *Many of the prisoners were subjected to severe beatings.*

sub·jec·tion /səb'dʒɛkʃən/ *n.* [U] FORMAL **1 in/into subjection (to sth)** strictly controlled by someone: *They lived in fear and subjection to their father's demands.* **2** the act of forcing a country or group of

people to be ruled by you: *Rome was intent on the subjection of the world.*

sub·jec·tive /səb'dʒɛktɪv/ *adj.* **1** a statement, report, attitude etc. that is subjective is influenced by personal opinion and can therefore be unfair: *Hiring new employees can be very much a subjective process.* —compare OBJECTIVE² (1) **2** [no comparative] existing only in your mind or imagination: *A person's perception of stress is often very subjective.* **3** TECHNICAL related to the subject in grammar —**subjectively** *adv.* —**subjectivity** /ˌsʌbdʒɛk'tɪvəti/ *n.* [U]

subject mat·ter /'.. ˌ../ *n.* [U] what is being talked about in speech or writing, or represented in art: *Griggs became famous for the controversial subject matter of his art.*

sub·ju·gate /'sʌbdʒəˌgeɪt/ *v.* [T] to defeat a person or group and make them obey you: *In 1619, the Dutch subjugated the island of Java.* —**subjugation** /ˌsʌbdʒə'geɪʃən/ *n.* [U]

sub·junc·tive /səb'dʒʌŋktɪv/ *n.* [C] TECHNICAL a verb form or a set of verb forms in grammar, used in some languages to express doubt, wishes, or possibility. For example, in "if I were you," the verb "to be" is in the subjunctive. —compare IMPERATIVE² (2), INDICATIVE² —**subjunctive** *adj.*

sub·lease /'sʌblis/ *n.* [C] an agreement in which someone who rents property from its owner then rents that property to someone else —**sublease** *v.* [I,T]

sub·let /sʌb'lɛt, 'sʌblɛt/ *v.* **sublet, subletting** [I,T] to rent to someone else a property that you rent from its owner —**sublet** /'sʌblɛt/ *n.* [C]

sub·li·mate /'sʌbləˌmeɪt/ *v.* [I,T] FORMAL to use the energy that comes from particular feelings and desires, especially sexual feelings, to do something that you think is better or more acceptable: *Players have to sublimate their egos for the good of the team.*

sub·li·ma·tion /ˌsʌblə'meɪʃən/ *n.* [U] **1** the process of sublimating **2** TECHNICAL the process of changing a solid substance to a gas by heating it and then changing it back to a solid, in order to make it pure

sub·lime¹ /sə'blaɪm/ *adj.* [no comparative] **1** excellent in a way that makes you feel extremely happy: *The almond cake is particularly sublime.* **2** not caring or thinking at all about the result of your actions: *I was amazed at his sublime insensitivity to other people's feelings.* —**sublimely** *adv.* —**sublimeness** *n.* [U] —**sublimity** /sə'blɪməti/ *n.* [U]

sublime² *n.* **1 the sublime** something that has excellent qualities and that makes you feel extremely happy: *In the age of machines, there is little place for the sublime.* **2 from the sublime to the ridiculous** used to say that a serious and important thing or event is being followed by a silly thing or event: *His paintings range from the sublime to the ridiculous.*

sub·lim·i·nal /ˌsʌb'lɪmənl/ *adj.* at a level of your mind that you are not completely conscious of: *Movies are constantly sending young people subliminal messages glorifying violence.*

sub·lin·gual /ˌsʌb'lɪŋgwəl/ *adj.* under your tongue: *The medicine also comes in a sublingual dosage.*

sub·ma·chine gun /ˌsʌbmə'ʃin ˌgʌn/ *n.* [C] a type of MACHINE GUN that is light and easily carried

sub·ma·rine¹ /'sʌbməˌrin, ˌsʌbmə'rin/ *n.* [C] a ship, especially a military one, that can stay under water: *a nuclear submarine*

submarine² *adj.* [only before noun] TECHNICAL growing, used, or existing under the ocean: *submarine mountain ranges*

sub·ma·rin·er /ˌsʌbmə'rinə, ˌsʌb'mærɪnə/ *n.* [C] a sailor who lives and works in a submarine

submarine sand·wich /ˌ... '../ *n.* [C] a SUB¹ (2)

sub·merge /səb'mɝdʒ/ *v.* **1** [I,T] to go under the surface of water, or to put something under water or another liquid: *Sonar was used to locate the submerged plane wreckage.* **2** [I,T] to make yourself very busy doing something, or to be very involved in something or affected by it: *Poindexter and North were both completely submerged in the scandal.* | [**submerge yourself in sth**] *Alice submerged herself in work to try and forget about Tom.* **3** [T] to hide something such as information or feelings: *He could submerge his anger for only so long.* —**submergence** *n.* [U]

sub·merged /səbˈmɜːdʒd/ *adj.* just under the surface of water or another liquid: *submerged icebergs*

sub·mersed /səbˈmɜːst/ *adj.* submersed plants live under the water

sub·mers·i·ble /səbˈmɜːsəbəl/ *n.* [C] a vehicle that can travel under water

sub·mer·sion /səbˈmɜːʒən/ *n.* [U] the activity of going under water, or the state of being completely covered in liquid

sub·mis·sion /səbˈmɪʃən/ *n.* **1** [U] the state of being completely controlled by a person or group, and accepting that you have to obey them: **force/frighten/beat etc. sb into submission** *They often beat the wild horses into submission.* | *In submission to* (=in obedience to) *the church's will, Agnes moved to Bengal.* **2** [C,U] the act of giving a plan, piece of writing etc. to someone in authority for them to consider or approve, or the plan, piece of writing etc. itself: *The deadline for the submission of proposals is May 1st.* **3** [C] LAW a request or suggestion that is given to a judge for them to consider

sub·mis·sive /səbˈmɪsɪv/ *adj.* always willing to obey someone, even if they are not nice to you: *The stereotype that foreign women are submissive is completely false.* —**submissively** *adv.* —**submissiveness** *n.* [U]

sub·mit /səbˈmɪt/ *v.* **submitted, submitting** **1** [T] to give a plan, piece of writing etc. to someone in authority for them to consider or approve: *The agency must submit an annual budget to the board each July.* **2** [I,T] FORMAL to agree to obey a person, group, set of rules etc., or to agree to do something, especially because you have no choice: [+ **to**] *Workers have refused to submit to drug tests.* **3** [T] FORMAL to suggest or say something: *I submit that the jury has been influenced by the publicity in this case.*

sub·nor·mal /ˌsʌbˈnɔːməl◂/ *adj.* less or lower than normal: *subnormal temperatures*

sub·or·bit·al /ˌsʌbˈɔːbɪtl/ *adj.* TECHNICAL making less than one complete ORBIT (=trip around the Earth): *a suborbital space flight*

sub·or·di·nate¹ /səˈbɔːdənɪt/ *n.* [C] someone who has a lower position and less authority than someone else in an organization: *The prospect of being judged by subordinates made some managers very uneasy.*

subordinate² *adj.* [no comparative] less important than something else, or in a lower position with less authority: *Women had a subordinate status in our society.* | [+ **to**] *The CIA Director is subordinate to the Secretary of Defense.* —compare SUBSERVIENT

sub·or·di·nate³ /səˈbɔːdnˌeɪt/ *v.* [T] to put someone or something in a less important position: [**subordinate sth to sb/sth**] *Product research is often subordinated to sales tactics.* —**subordination** /səˌbɔːdnˈeɪʃən/ *n.* [U]

subordinate clause /..ˌ... ˈ./ *n.* [C] a DEPENDENT CLAUSE

sub·orn /səˈbɔːn/ *v.* [T] LAW to persuade someone to tell lies in a court of law or to do something else that is illegal, especially for money —**subornation** /ˌsʌbɔːˈneɪʃən/ *n.* [U]

sub·par /ˌsʌbˈpɑː/ *adj.* below an expected level of quality: *Barkley's performance in last Sunday's game was subpar.*

sub·plot /ˈsʌbplɒt/ *n.* [C] a PLOT (=set of events) that is less important than and separate from the main plot in a story, play etc.

sub·poe·na¹ /səˈpiːnə/ *n.* [C] LAW a written order that you must come to a court of law and be a witness

subpoena² *v. past tense* **subpoenaed** [T] LAW to order someone to come to a court of law and be a witness

sub ro·sa /ˌsʌb ˈrəʊzə/ *adv.* secretly —**sub-rosa** *adj.*

sub·rou·tine /ˈsʌbruːˌtiːn/ *n.* [C] a part of a computer PROGRAM containing a set of instructions for doing a small job that is part of a larger job

sub·scribe /səbˈskraɪb/ *v.* **1** [I] to pay money regularly to have copies of a newspaper or magazine sent to you: [+ **to**] *What newspaper do you subscribe to?* **2** to give money regularly for a service: [+ **to**] *About 60 percent of U.S. households already subscribe to cable TV.* **3** to pay money regularly to be a member of an organization or to help its work: [+ **to**] *For several years now, we've subscribed to the Zoo Fund.* **4** [T] FORMAL to sign your name: *Please subscribe your name to the document.*

    subscribe to sth *phr. v.* [T usually in questions and negatives] if you subscribe to an idea, view etc., you agree with it or support it: *Jacobs does not subscribe to the belief that people are basically good.*

sub·scrib·er /səbˈskraɪbə/ *n.* [C] **1** someone who pays money regularly to receive copies of a newspaper or magazine **2** someone who gives money regularly for a service: *Internet service subscribers* **3** someone who pays money to be part of an organization or to help its work **4** FORMAL someone who signs their name on a document

sub·script /ˈsʌbskrɪpt/ *adj.* [only before noun] written or printed next to and below a number, letter etc. —compare SUPERSCRIPT —**subscript** *n.* [C]

sub·scrip·tion /səbˈskrɪpʃən/ *n.* [C] **1** an amount of money you pay regularly to receive copies of a newspaper or magazine **2** an amount of money you pay regularly to be a member of an organization or to help its work **3** an amount of money you pay regularly for a service

sub·sec·tion /ˈsʌbˌsekʃən/ *n.* [C] a part of a SECTION

sub·se·quent /ˈsʌbsəkwənt/ *adj.* FORMAL coming after or following something else: *Subsequent investigations did not uncover any new evidence.* | [**subsequent to doing sth**] *The soldiers developed leprosy subsequent to* (=after) *leaving the army.* —compare CONSEQUENT

sub·se·quent·ly /ˈsʌbsəˌkwentli, -kwəntli/ *adv.* FORMAL after an event in the past: *New safety guidelines were subsequently adopted.*

sub·ser·vi·ent /səbˈsɜːviənt/ *adj.* **1** DISAPPROVING someone who is subservient is too willing to do what other people want them to do **2** FORMAL less important than something else; SUBORDINATE: [+ **to**] *The regime was subservient to the Soviet Union.* —**subserviently** *adv.* —**subservience** *n.* [U]

sub·set /ˈsʌbset/ *n.* [C] a set that is part of a larger set

sub·side /səbˈsaɪd/ *v.* [I] **1** if a feeling, noise, weather condition etc. subsides, it gradually decreases: *Side effects of the drug tend to subside as time passes.* | *An hour later, the flood waters began to subside.* **2** FORMAL if something such as water, land, or a building subsides, it gradually sinks to a lower level

sub·si·dence /səbˈsaɪdns, ˈsʌbsədəns/ *n.* [C,U] TECHNICAL the process by which land sinks to a lower level, or the state of land or buildings that have sunk: *Is your house insured against subsidence?*

sub·sid·i·ar·y¹ /səbˈsɪdiˌeri/ *n. plural* **subsidiaries** [C] a company that is owned or controlled by another company: *InterHarvest is a subsidiary of United Brands.*

subsidiary² *adj.* relating to, but less important than, the main plan, subject, event etc.: [+ **to**] *The Pacific Fleet's plan was subsidiary to the Navy's overall strategy.*

sub·si·dize /ˈsʌbsəˌdaɪz/ *v.* [T] to pay part of the cost of something so that the buyer can pay less for it: *Many day care facilities are subsidized by the city.* —**subsidized** *adj.*: *subsidized housing for the elderly* —**subsidization** /ˌsʌbsədəˈzeɪʃən/ *n.* [U]

sub·si·dy /ˈsʌbsədi/ *n. plural* **subsidies** [C] money that is paid by a government or organization to make prices lower, support someone who is producing goods etc.: *Congress may cut some subsidies to farmers.*

sub·sist /səbˈsɪst/ v. [I] to stay alive on only small amounts of food or money: [+ **on**] *Many of the soldiers had to subsist on insects and roots.*

sub·sis·tence /səbˈsɪstəns/ n. [U] **1** the condition of having enough food or money to live: *Settlers to the area threatened the bears' subsistence.* **2** a small amount of money or food that is just enough to provide you with the basic things people need to have: *Factory workers were paid a subsistence wage.* | *Most of the villagers live by **subsistence farming** (=growing just enough food to live on).*

subsistence lev·el /.ˈ.. ˌ../ n. [singular,U] a very poor standard of living, in which people can only get the things that are completely necessary for life and nothing more: *Half of the population exists below the subsistence level.*

sub·soil /ˈsʌbsɔɪl/ n. [U] the layer of soil between the surface and the lower layer of hard rock

sub·son·ic /ˌsʌbˈsɑnɪk◄/ adj. slower than the speed of sound: *subsonic aircraft*

sub·spe·cies /ˈsʌbˌspiʃiz, -ˌspisz/ n. [C] a group of similar plants or animals, which is smaller than a SPECIES

S W **sub·stance** /ˈsʌbstəns/ n.
3
1 material [C] a type of solid, liquid, or gas that has particular qualities: *The transportation of flammable substances is tightly regulated.* | *She was arrested for smoking marijuana, an illegal substance.* | *toxic substances*
2 main ideas [singular,U] FORMAL the most important ideas of what someone says or in a piece of writing; ESSENCE: [**the substance of sth**] *No one knows what the substance of their conversation was.* | *It was an entertaining speech, but without much substance* (=without many important or serious ideas). | *In substance, he means that we must work harder.*
3 importance [U] FORMAL the quality of being important, especially because problems are dealt with; SIGNIFICANCE: *matters/issues of substance Both leaders have promised to make progress on matters of substance.*
4 truth [U usually in questions and negatives] FORMAL basic facts that are true: *Brown did not contest the substance of the reports.* | [+ **to**] *There was no substance to the reports of his death.*
5 a man/woman of substance LITERARY a man or woman who has a lot of money and power

substance a·buse /ˈ.. ˌ../ n. [U] the habit of taking too many drugs, so that you are harmed by them —see also DRUG ABUSE

sub·stand·ard /ˌsʌbˈstændəd◄/ adj. not as good as the average, and not acceptable: *substandard medical care* —compare NONSTANDARD, STANDARD²

S W **sub·stan·tial** /səbˈstænʃəl/ adj. **1** large enough in
3
amount, number, or degree to be noticeable or to have an important effect: *A substantial number of houses were damaged by the floods.* | *The refugees face a substantial threat of harm if they are sent home.* **2** large enough to satisfy you: *a substantial salary* | *The breakfast they provide is substantial.* **3** large and strongly made: *a substantial mahogany desk* **4** FORMAL having a lot of influence or power, usually because of wealth: *a very substantial family in the wool trade*

sub·stan·tial·ly /səbˈstænʃəli/ adv. **1** a lot more or a lot less compared to something else: *Attendance at the conference was substantially lower this year.* **2** in an important way or to a great degree: *The first chapter had been changed substantially.*

sub·stan·ti·ate /səbˈstænʃiˌeɪt/ v. [T] FORMAL to prove the truth of something that someone has said, claimed etc.: *No evidence has been found to substantiate the story.* —**substantiation** /səbˌstænʃiˈeɪʃən/ n. [U]

sub·stan·tive¹ /ˈsʌbstəntɪv/ adj. FORMAL, APPROVING **1** substantive talks, changes, agreements etc. involve important problems and help to solve them: *The new regulations are both symbolic and substantive.* **2** substantive ISSUES, arguments, questions etc. are important and deal with real problems: *Reporters are often reluctant to examine substantive political issues.* —**substantively** adv.

substantive² n. [C] TECHNICAL a noun —**substantival** /ˌsʌbstənˈtaɪvəl/ adj.

sub·sta·tion /ˈsʌbˌsteɪʃən/ n. [C] a place where electricity is passed on from the place that produces it into the main system

sub·sti·tute¹ /ˈsʌbstəˌtut/ n. **1** [C] something new or different that you use instead of something else that you used previously: *Egg substitutes cost 20 to 50 percent more than eggs.* | [+ **for**] *Chewing tobacco is not a safe substitute for smoking cigarettes.* **2** [C] someone who does someone else's job for a limited period of time, especially on a sports team or school: *Today we had a substitute in history class.* **3** be no substitute for sth to not have the same good or desirable qualities as something or someone else: *There is no substitute for educated workers with good work habits.*

substitute² v. **1** [T] to use something new or different instead of something else: [**substitute sth for/with sth**] *You can substitute broccoli for spinach in the recipe.* **2** [I,T] to do someone's job until the person who usually does it is able to do it again: [+ **for**] *She often substitutes for absent teachers in their Spanish classes.*

substitute teach·er /ˌ... ˈ../ n. [C] a teacher who teaches a class when the usual teacher is sick

sub·sti·tu·tion /ˌsʌbstəˈtuʃən/ n. [C,U] someone or something that you use instead of the person or thing you would normally use, or the act of using them: *Coach Packard made two substitutions in the second half.*

sub·stra·tum /ˈsʌbˌstreɪtəm, -ˌstræ-/ n. plural **substrata** /-tə/ [C] **1** a layer that lies beneath another layer, especially in the earth: *a substratum of rock* **2** FORMAL a quality that is hidden: *His books have tapped into a deep substratum of human religiosity.*

sub·struc·ture /ˈsʌbˌstrʌktʃə/ n. [C] **1** one of the STRUCTURES¹ (3) within a society or organization that combines with others to form a whole **2** a solid base under the ground that supports a building above the ground

sub·sume /səbˈsum/ v. [T] FORMAL to include someone or something as part of a larger group, rather than considering them as separate: *States subsume many of the responsibilities of governing from the county.* | [**subsume sb/sth under sth**] *The women's athletic department will be subsumed under the men's.*

sub·ten·ant /ˌsʌbˈtɛnənt/ n. [C] someone who lives in or uses an apartment, office etc. and who pays rent to the person who is renting it from the owner —**subtenancy** n. [C,U] —see also SUBLET

sub·tend /səbˈtɛnd/ v. [T] TECHNICAL to be opposite to a particular angle or ARC, and form the limits of it in GEOMETRY

sub·ter·fuge /ˈsʌbtəˌfyudʒ/ n. [C,U] FORMAL a secret trick or slightly dishonest way of doing something, or the use of this: *The ballot issue is a subterfuge designed to confuse voters.*

sub·ter·ra·ne·an /ˌsʌbtəˈreɪniən◄/ adj. beneath the surface of the Earth: *subterranean passages*

sub·text /ˈsʌbtɛkst/ n. [C] a hidden or second meaning in something that someone says or writes: *One subtext of the book is accepting one's ethnic identity.*

sub·ti·tle¹ /ˈsʌbˌtaɪtl/ n. [C] **1** subtitles [plural] the words printed at the bottom of a movie to translate what is being said by the actors, when the movie is in a foreign language: *a French film with English subtitles* **2** a less important title below the main title in a book

subtitle² v. [T usually passive] **1** to print subtitles at the bottom of a movie **2** to give a subtitle to a book

sub·ti·tled /ˈsʌbˌtaɪtld/ adj. having subtitles or a particular subtitle

sub·tle /ˈsʌtl/ adj. **1** not easy to notice or understand unless you pay careful attention: *Some of the more subtle forms of malnutrition are difficult to identify.*

2 a subtle taste or smell is pleasant and delicate: *a subtle hint of almond* **3** a subtle person, plan, method etc. skillfully hides what they really want or intend to do or does it in a very indirect way: *She wasn't ever subtle in giving her opinion.* | *Linda was able to influence her superiors in subtle ways.* **4** very smart about noticing and understanding things; SENSITIVE: *a subtle mind* —**subtly** *adv.*

sub·tle·ty /ˈsʌlti/ *n. plural* **subtleties 1** [U] the quality of being subtle: *At press conferences, he is a master of tact and subtlety.* **2** [C usually plural] a thought, idea, or detail that is important but difficult to notice or understand: [+ **of**] *Some of the subtleties of the language are lost in translation.*

sub·to·tal /ˈsʌbˌtoʊtḷ/ *n.* [C] the total of a set of numbers, especially on a bill, before other numbers are also added to form a complete total: *the subtotal before sales tax is added*

sub·tract /səbˈtrækt/ *v.* [T] to take a number or an amount from something larger: [**subtract sth from sth**] *If you subtract 10 from 30, you get 20.* —compare ADD (4), DEDUCT, MINUS[1] (1)

sub·trac·tion /səbˈtrækʃən/ *n.* [C] the act of subtracting —compare ADDITION (5)

sub·trop·i·cal /ˌsʌbˈtrɑpɪkəl/ *adj.* relating to an area near to a tropical area, or typical of that area: *subtropical climates*

sub·urb /ˈsʌbəb/ *n.* [C] an area away from the center of a town or city, where a lot of people live: [+ **of**] *They live in Lakewood, a suburb of Denver.* | *My family moved to **the suburbs** when I was 10.*

sub·ur·ban /səˈbəbən/ *adj.* **1** relating to a suburb, or in a suburb: *suburban life* | *a suburban shopping center* **2** boring and having very traditional beliefs and interests: *suburban attitudes*

sub·ur·ban·ite /səˈbəbəˌnaɪt/ *n.* [C] someone who lives in a suburb

sub·ur·bi·a /səˈbəbiə/ *n.* [U] **1** suburban areas in general: *Their dream is to own a home in suburbia.* **2** the behavior, opinions, and ways of living that are typical of people who live in a suburb: *middle-class suburbia*

sub·ven·tion /səbˈvɛnʃən/ *n.* [C] FORMAL a gift of money for a special use

sub·ver·sion /səbˈvəʒən/ *n.* [U] secret activities that are intended to encourage people to oppose the government

sub·ver·sive[1] /səbˈvəsɪv/ *adj.* ideas, activities etc. that are subversive are often secret and intended to encourage people to oppose a government, religion etc.: *subversive organizations* —**subversively** *adv.* —**subversiveness** *n.* [U]

subversive[2] *n.* [C] someone who is subversive

sub·vert /səbˈvət/ *v.* [T] FORMAL **1** to try to destroy the power and influence of a government or established system etc.: *Smith was sentenced to 14 years for plotting to subvert the government.* **2** to destroy someone's beliefs or loyalty

sub·way /ˈsʌbweɪ/ *n. plural* **subways** [C] a railroad that runs under the ground, especially used in a city as a form of PUBLIC TRANSPORTATION: *the New York subway system* —see picture on page 1331

sub·ze·ro, subzero /ˌ. ˈ...◂/ *adj.* sub-zero temperatures are below 32°F (0°C)

s w **suc·ceed** /səkˈsid/ *v.*
1 not fail [I] if you succeed, you do what you have tried or wanted to do: *I'm sure you'll succeed if you work hard.* | [**succeed in (doing) sth**] *Officers succeeded in persuading the man to put down his gun.* | *You've **only** succeeded in* (=done the opposite of what you intended to do) *upsetting your mother.*
2 have a good result [I] if something succeeds, it has the result or effect it was intended to have: *Teachers and parents will have to work together for the program to succeed.* | [**succeed in (doing) sth**] *Our advertising campaign has succeeded in attracting more customers.*
3 reach a high position [I] to do well in your job,

especially because you have worked hard at it for a long time: [+ **as**] *Nobody thought he would ever succeed as an artist.* | [+ **in**] *His determination has helped him succeed in the banking industry.*
4 follow sb in a position [I,T] to be the next person to take a position or rank after someone else: [**succeed sb as sth**] *Wolcott will succeed Dr. Johansen as director of the museum.*
5 replace [T] FORMAL to come after and replace something else: *By the early '90s, CDs had succeeded records in popularity.*
6 nothing succeeds like success used to say that success often leads to even greater success

suc·ceed·ing /səkˈsidɪŋ/ *adj.* coming after something else: *She became more well-known with each succeeding novel.*

suc·cess /səkˈsɛs/ *n.* **1** [U] the achievement of something that you have tried to do or wanted to do: *The unprecedented success of Mitchell's work inspired a generation of writers.* | [**success in (doing) sth**] *The program helps people have long-term success in losing weight.* **2** [C] something that has the result or effect that you intended, usually so that it earns a lot of money, is popular etc.: **a great/huge/big etc. success** *The show was a big success.* | *At $3.99, their all-you-can-eat lunch buffet has **proved a resounding success** (=has become successful).* | *If anyone can **make a success out of** the shopping mall, it's Samuel Vincent.* **3** [C] someone who does very well in their job: [+ **in**] *Despite his success in Hollywood, Tartikoff did not enjoy great happiness in life.* | [+ **as**] *Hal was not a great success as a rock singer.* **4 success story** someone or something that becomes successful in spite of difficulties: *Richardson is one of the few success stories from the housing projects.*

suc·cess·ful /səkˈsɛsfəl/ *adj.* **1** having the effect or result you intended: *The surgery was successful.* | [**successful in (doing) sth**] *They have been very successful in marketing their jeans to teenagers.* **2** a successful person earns a lot of money or is very well known and respected: *a successful businessman* | [**successful in (doing) sth**] *She has been successful in the music business.* **3** a successful business, movie etc. makes a lot of money: *For twenty years, he was the head of a successful law firm.* —**successfully** *adv.*

suc·ces·sion /səkˈsɛʃən/ *n.* **1** a succession of sb/sth a number of people or things of the same type that happen or follow one after another: *I heard a succession of loud bangs outside.* **2 in succession** happening one after the other without anything different happening in between: *The U.S. women have won 11 international softball titles **in succession.*** | **in close/quick succession** (=quickly one after the other) **3** [U] the act of taking over an office or position, or the right to be the next to take it: [+ **to**] *Ferdinand was first in line of succession to the throne.* —compare ACCESSION (1)

suc·ces·sive /səkˈsɛsɪv/ *adj.* [only before noun] coming or following one after the other: *The food shortage is a result of three years of successive floods.* —**successively** *adv.*

suc·ces·sor /səkˈsɛsə/ *n.* [C] **1** someone who takes a position previously held by someone else: [+ **as**] *Ms. Barrick will be Sloan's successor as treasurer.* **2** FORMAL a machine, system etc. that exists after another one in a process of development: *The refrigerator was the successor to the ice box.* —opposite PREDECESSOR

suc·cinct /səkˈsɪŋkt, səˈsɪŋkt/ *adj.* APPROVING clearly expressed in a few words: *a succinct description of the Egyptian writing system* —**succinctly** *adv.* —**succinctness** *n.* [U]

suc·cor /ˈsʌkə/ *n.* [U] LITERARY help that is given to someone who is having problems —**succor** *v.* [T]

suc·co·tash /ˈsʌkətæʃ/ *n.* [U] a dish made from corn, beans, and TOMATOes cooked together

suc·cu·bus /ˈsʌkyəbəs/ *n. plural* **succubi** /-baɪ, -bi/ [C] LITERARY a female DEVIL that has sex with a sleeping man —compare INCUBUS

suc·cu·lent /ˈsʌkyələnt/ *adj.* **1** juicy and DELICIOUS: *succulent tropical fruit* **2** TECHNICAL a succulent plant has thick soft leaves or stems that can hold a lot of liquid —**succulence** *n.* [U]

suc·cumb /sə'kʌm/ *v.* [I] FORMAL **1** to stop opposing someone or something that is stronger than you, and allow them to take control [+ **to**] *The country has not yet succumbed to international pressure to stop nuclear testing.* | *I succumbed to temptation and ordered the lemon meringue pie.* **2** if you succumb to an illness, you become very sick or die of it: *Lewis succumbed to cancer in 1985.*

s w **such¹** /sʌtʃ/ *determiner* **1** used to talk about a person, thing etc. that is like the one that has already been mentioned: *Such extreme conditions required thickly insulated clothing.* | *Few such experts know much about Russia's economy.* **2** **such as** used when giving an example of something: *The homeless shelter needs $1,000 a month for supplies such as toilet articles, coffee, and bedding.* | *Cartoon characters such as Mickey Mouse and Snoopy are still popular with youngsters.* **3** **such a kind/tall/nice etc.** used to emphasize how kind, tall, nice etc. someone or something is: *I've never seen such a clean garage.* | *You didn't have to buy me such an expensive present.* | *Eric's such a nice young man.* [+ **(that)**] *I thought he did such a good job that I paid him extra.* **4** **or some such person/thing etc.** a person, thing etc. like the one just mentioned: *There was a ladybug or some such small creature on the window.* **5** **such as it is**, **such as they are etc.** used when you do not think that something is good enough, complete enough, or impressive enough: *Kenen's instructions, such as they were, came directly from the mayor.* **6** **there's no such person/thing etc. as** used to say that a particular person or thing does not exist: *There is no such thing as an escape-proof jail.* **7** **such...as** FORMAL OR LITERARY used to emphasize that there is a small amount of something or that it is of poor quality: *Such food as they gave us was warm and nutritious.*

USAGE NOTE: SUCH

GRAMMAR: such, so
Use **such** and **so** to emphasize a particular quality that a person has. Use **so** before an adjective or adverb: *Janet's so nice!* | *Why does Rick always have to talk so loudly?* If the adjective is before a noun, however, use **such** or **such a**: *Janet and Ted are such nice people.* | *He's such a stupid jerk!*

---

such² *pron.* **1** used to talk about a person, thing etc. that is like the one that has already been mentioned: *Such was the punishment for students who talked in class.* **2** **be such that/as...** FORMAL OR LITERARY used to give a reason or explanation for something: *Brown's influence was such that he was never investigated.* | *The power of the explosion was such as no one had ever seen.* **3** **and such** SPOKEN and people or things like that: *Veggie burgers are made from herbs and such.* **4** **not...as such** SPOKEN not exactly what the word used is usually understood to mean: *The committee doesn't have a plan of action as such.* **5** **such...as** FORMAL those people or things of a particular group or type: *Such of you as wish to leave may do so now.*

such and such, such-and-such /'. . .,./ *pron., determiner* SPOKEN used instead of a particular name of something, especially because it is not important: *Try something like, "I need such-and-such in order to complete the report."*

such·like /'sʌtʃlaɪk/ *pron.* things of that kind: *The U.N. had to borrow from the fund to pay salaries and suchlike.* —**suchlike** *adj.* [only before noun]

s w **suck¹** /sʌk/ *v.* [I,T] **1** **put in mouth** to hold something in your mouth and pull on it with your tongue and lips: *He's eight years old and he still sucks his thumb.* | [+ **on**] *Molly was sitting on the couch sucking on a candy cane.* **2** **pull** to pull someone or something with great power and force to a particular place: [+ **down**/ **into**] *The cause of the crash was several geese getting sucked into the jet's engines.* | [**suck sb/sth under**] *The strong waves threatened to suck us under.*

---

3 **drink/breathe** to take liquid or air into your mouth by making your lips tight and using the muscles of your mouth to pull the liquid or air in: *Miguel put the cigarette to his mouth and sucked in some smoke.* | [+ **at**] *The baby sucked at his mother's breast.*

suck on a straw

4 **suck sb into sth** to make someone become involved in a particular situation, event etc., especially a bad one: *I refuse to let them suck me into their argument.*

5 **sb/sth sucks** SPOKEN, IMPOLITE an expression meaning that something is very bad in quality or that a situation is very bad: *This class sucks.* | [+ **at**] *Diane sucks at tennis.*

6 **suck it up** SPOKEN used to tell someone to do something and stop worrying or complaining about how bad or difficult it is: *Just suck it up and tell her how you feel.*

suck up *phr. v.* [I] INFORMAL, DISAPPROVING to say or do a lot of nice things in order to make someone like you or to get what you want: [**suck up to sb**] *Brad's always sucking up to the teacher.*

suck² *n.* [C] an act of sucking

suck·er¹ /'sʌkɚ/ *n.* [C] **1** INFORMAL someone who is easily deceived, tricked, or persuaded to do something they do not want to do: *I can't believe you sent them money – what a sucker!* **2** **be a sucker for sth** to like something so much that you cannot refuse it: *I'm a sucker for babies.* **3** SPOKEN a thing: *How much did that sucker cost you?* **4** a LOLLIPOP **5** NOT TECHNICAL a part of an insect or of an animal's body that it uses to hold on to or stick to a surface: *Tree frogs have suckers on their feet.* **6** a part of a plant that grows from the root or lower stem of a plant to become a new plant

sucker² *v.*

sucker sb into sth *phr. v.* [T] to persuade someone to do something they do not want to do, especially by tricking them or lying to them: [**sucker sb into doing sth**] *Laurie got suckered into babysitting her little sister.*

sucker punch /'.. ./ *v.* [T] INFORMAL to hit someone very quickly when they do not expect to be hit —**sucker punch** *n.* [singular]

suck·le /'sʌkəl/ *v.* FORMAL **1** [T] to feed a baby or young animal with milk from the breast **2** [I] if a baby or young animal suckles, it sucks milk from a breast —compare BREAST-FEED, NURSE² (3)

suck·ling /'sʌklɪŋ/ *n.* [C] LITERARY a young human or animal still taking milk from its mother's breast

suckling pig /'.. ./ *n.* [C] a young pig still taking milk from its mother, which is often cooked whole and eaten on special occasions

suck·y /'sʌki/ *adj.* SLANG very bad or not fun: *Todd has a really sucky job.*

su·crose /'sukrouz, 'syu-/ *n.* [U] TECHNICAL the most common form of sugar —compare FRUCTOSE, LACTOSE

suc·tion /'sʌkʃən/ *n.* [U] the process of removing air or liquid from a container or space so that another substance can be pulled in, or so that two surfaces stick together: *the suction of the vacuum cleaner*

suction cup /'.. ./ *n.* [C] a small round piece of rubber or plastic that sticks to a surface by suction

suction pump /'.. ./ *n.* [C] a pump that works by removing air from an enclosed space, so that the substance to be pumped is pulled in

Su·dan /su'dæn/ also **the Sudan** a country in northeast Africa, south of Egypt and west of Ethiopia —**Sudanese** /ˌsudn'iz/ *adj.*

sud·den /'sʌdn/ adj. **1** happening, coming, or done quickly or when you do not expect it: *Don't make any sudden moves around the animals.* | *There's been a sudden change of plans.* **2 (all) of a sudden** suddenly: *All of a sudden the lights went out.* —**suddenness** n. [U]

sudden death /ˌ.. '.ˈ/ n. [U] if a game goes into sudden death, it continues after its usual ending time until one player or team gains the lead and wins

Sudden In·fant Death Syn·drome /ˌ.. .. '. ˌ..ˈ/ n. [U] TECHNICAL a situation in which a baby stops breathing and dies while it is sleeping, for no known reason; CRIB DEATH

sud·den·ly /'sʌdnli/ adv. quickly and without warning: *Suddenly there was a knock on the door.* | *Jane suddenly realized she was falling in love with him.*

suds /sʌdz/ n. [plural] **1** the BUBBLES formed on the top of water with soap in it **2** INFORMAL beer —**sudsy** adj.

sue /su/ v. [I,T] **1** to make a legal claim against someone, especially for money, because they have harmed you in some way: *If the builders don't fulfill their side of the contract, we'll sue.* | **sue sb for libel/negligence/malpractice etc.** *Aaron is being sued for fraud.* | **sue sb for $100,000/damages/compensation etc.** *Tonelli was sued for $40,000 by a former employee.* | *At the time, she didn't want to sue for divorce* (=in order to end a marriage). **2 sue for peace** FORMAL if a country or army sues for peace, they ask for peace, especially because there is no other good choice: *They had hoped to force the North to sue for peace.* **3 sue the pants off sb** INFORMAL to take someone to a court of law and sue them for a lot of money

suede /sweɪd/ n. [U] soft leather with a slightly rough surface: *a suede jacket*

su·et /'suɪt/ n. [U] hard fat from around an animal's KIDNEYs, used in cooking

Su·ez, the Gulf of /'suɛz/ an INLET of the Red Sea at its northern end, that is between the main part of northern Egypt and Sinai

Suez Ca·nal, the /ˌ.. .ˈ./ a CANAL in northeast Egypt that connects the Mediterranean Sea to the Gulf of Suez and the Red Sea

suf·fer /'sʌfɚ/ v.
1 pain [I,T] to experience physical or mental pain: *Hardesty suffered severe burns to his face and body.* | *I would hate to see the animals suffer.* | [+ from] *For years, Kevin has suffered from a bad back.*
2 bad situation [I,T] to be in a very bad situation that makes things very difficult for you: *Small businesses have suffered financially during the recession.* | [+ for] *Jones often suffered for his extreme political views.* | *If workers cannot learn to adapt, they will suffer the consequences* (=have something bad happen to them).
3 bad experience [T] if someone suffers a bad or difficult experience, it happens to them: *The Democrats have just suffered a huge defeat in the polls.* | suffer damage/injury/loss *Many of the houses suffered water damage from the flood.*
4 become worse [I] to become worse in quality because a bad situation is affecting something or because no one is taking care of it: *My grades suffered as a result of having to work more hours.*
5 not suffer fools gladly to not be patient with people you think are stupid
6 suffer sb to do sth OLD USE to allow someone to do something

suf·fer·ance /'sʌfərəns/ n. **on (sb's) sufferance** FORMAL if you live or work somewhere on sufferance, you are allowed to do it by someone who would rather you did not do it: *Portugal has always controlled Macau on China's sufferance.*

suf·fer·er /'sʌfərɚ/ n. [C] someone who suffers, especially from a particular illness: *Studies indicate that the treatment has helped headache sufferers.*

suf·fer·ing /'sʌfərɪŋ/ n. [C,U] physical or mental pain and difficulty, or an experience of this: *It is hard to imagine the pain and suffering they went through.*

suf·fice /sə'faɪs/ v. [not in progressive] **1** [I] FORMAL to be enough: *A one-page letter should suffice.* | [**suffice to do sth**] *Analysts doubt that the lay-offs will suffice to make the company profitable again.* **2 suffice (it) to say (that)** used to say that the statement that follows is enough to explain what you mean, even though you could say more: *Suffice it to say that prayer is an important activity in the Synagogue.*

suf·fi·cien·cy /sə'fɪʃənsi/ n. FORMAL **1** [U] the state of being or having enough: *The war has affected the country's economic sufficiency.* **2 a sufficiency of sth** a supply that is enough: *Make sure there a sufficiency of time allowed for the analysis of data.*

suf·fi·cient /sə'fɪʃənt/ adj. [no comparative] FORMAL as much as is needed for a particular purpose; enough: *Proof of sufficient funds is required for entrance into Namibia.* | [**sufficient sth to do sth**] *There is sufficient reason to believe that he is lying.* | [+ for] *The size of the apartment was barely sufficient for a family of four.* —opposite INSUFFICIENT —see also SELF-SUFFICIENT —see Usage Note at ADEQUATE

suf·fix /'sʌfɪks/ n. [C] a letter or letters added to the end of a word to form a new word. For example you can add the suffix "ness" to the word "kind" to form "kindness." —see also AFFIX[2] —compare PREFIX[1] (1)

suf·fo·cate /'sʌfəˌkeɪt/ v. **1** [I,T] to die or make someone die by preventing them from breathing: *They pushed a plastic bag over his head and almost suffocated him.* **2 be suffocating** to feel uncomfortable because there is not enough fresh air: *Can you open a window? I'm suffocating.* **3** [T] to prevent a relationship, plan, business etc. from developing well or being successful: *Their mother suffocated them with overprotective love.* —**suffocation** /ˌsʌfə'keɪʃən/ n. [U]

suf·fo·cat·ed /'sʌfəˌkeɪtɪd/ adj. **feel suffocated** to feel like you are not free or do not have enough space: *I felt suffocated living in the city.*

suf·fra·gan /'sʌfrəgən/ adj. [only before noun] a suffragan BISHOP helps another bishop of higher rank in their work —**suffragan** n. [C]

suf·frage /'sʌfrɪdʒ/ n. [U] the right to vote in national elections

suf·fra·gette /ˌsʌfrə'dʒɛt/ n. [C] a woman who tried to gain the right to vote for women, especially in the early 20th century

suf·fuse /sə'fyuz/ v. [I,T] LITERARY **1** if warmth, color, liquid etc. suffuses something or someone, it covers or spreads through them: *The broad landscape was suffused in golden light.* **2** to spread through all of a situation, group of people, country etc.: *Catholic values suffuse the state's approach to all issues.* —**suffusion** /sə'fyuʒən/ n. [U]

Su·fi /'sufi/ n. [C] a believer in Islam who practices a form of MYSTICISM, trying to come close to God through prayer and MEDITATION —**Sufism** n. [U]

sug·ar[1] /'ʃʊgɚ/ n. **1** [U] a sweet white or brown substance that is obtained from plants and used to make food and drinks sweet: *Do you take sugar in your coffee?* **2** TECHNICAL one of several sweet substances formed in plants —compare GLUCOSE **3** OLD-FASHIONED, SPOKEN used to address someone you like very much

sug·ar[2] v. [T] to add sugar or cover something with sugar

sugar beet /ˈ.. ./ n. [U] a vegetable that grows under the ground, from which sugar is obtained —compare BEET (1)

sug·ar·cane /'ʃʊgɚkeɪn/ n. [U] a tall tropical plant from whose stems sugar is obtained

sugar-coat·ed /ˌ.. '..◂/ adj. **1** made to seem better than something really is: *The movie offers a sugar-coated view of lower middle-class life.* **2** covered with sugar —**sugar-coat** v. [T]

sugar cube /ˈ.. ./ n. [C] a square piece of solid sugar

sugar dad·dy /ˈ.. ˌ../ n. [C] INFORMAL an older man who gives a young woman presents and money in return for having a relationship with her and possibly for sex

sug·ared /'ʃʊgəd/ *adj.* covered in sugar: *sugared cereals*

sug·ar·less /'ʃʊgəlıs/ *adj.* containing no sugar: *sugarless gum*

sugar ma·ple /ˌ.. '../ *n.* [C] a type of MAPLE tree that grows in North America, whose SAP (=liquid from the tree) is used to make MAPLE SYRUP

sug·ar·y /'ʃʊgəri/ *adj.* **1** containing sugar or tasting like sugar: *sugary foods* **2** language, emotions etc. that are sugary are too nice and seem insincere. *He was full of sugary talk about world peace and love.*

sug·gest /səg'dʒɛst, sə'dʒɛst/ *v.* **1** [T] to tell someone your ideas about what they should do, where they should go etc.: *Who suggested this restaurant?* | [**suggest doing sth**] *I suggest talking to a lawyer before you do anything.* | [**suggest (that)**] *Mark's sister just suggested that we go to Mexico this summer.* | [**suggest how/where/what etc.**] *The students can suggest how their work should be displayed.* —see Usage Note at PROPOSE **2** [T] to make someone think that a particular thing is true; INDICATE: *Current data suggests that there could be life on Mars.* | [**suggest (that)**] *The article suggested that Rivas may resign.* **3** [T] to tell someone about something that is appropriate for a particular activity: [**suggest sth for sth**] *This accounting technique is suggested for use in health care programs.* —see Usage Note at RECOMMEND **4 I'm not suggesting** SPOKEN used to say that what you have said is not exactly what you intended to say: *I'm not suggesting that she's stupid or anything.* **5** [T] to make someone think of something that is similar to something else, or help them to imagine it: *He spread his hands to suggest the size of the fish.*

sug·gest·i·ble /səg'dʒɛstəbəl/ *adj.* easily influenced by other people or by things you see and hear: **highly/very suggestible** *At that age, kids are highly suggestible.*

sug·ges·tion /səg'dʒɛstʃən/ *n.* **1** [C] an idea, plan, or possibility that someone mentions: *a list of holiday gift suggestions* | [**suggestion that**] *I rejected his suggestion that I spend another day in the hospital.* | *Can I make a suggestion?* | *Let me know if you have any suggestions.* | *My boss is always open to suggestions* (=willing to listen to ideas). —see Usage Note at PROPOSE **2 suggestion of/that** a sign or possibility of something: *There was also a suggestion of illegal drug use.* | *Chilton denied any suggestion of wrongdoing.* **3** [U] the act of telling someone your idea about what they should do: *At the suggestion of* (=because someone suggested something) *his attorneys, he stopped talking to the press.* **4** [U] an indirect way of making people accept an idea: *Don't underestimate the power of suggestion.* **5 a suggestion of sth** a slight amount or sign of something: *She looked at him with just a suggestion of a smile.*

sug·ges·tive /səg'dʒɛstıv/ *adj.* **1** a remark, behavior etc. that is suggestive makes you think of sex. *His songs are full of suggestive lyrics.* **2** reminding you of something: [+ **of**] *The sounds were suggestive of whales calling to each other.* —**suggestively** *adv.* —**suggestiveness** *n.* [U]

su·i·ci·dal /ˌsuə'saıdl/ *adj.* **1** wanting to kill yourself: *He felt depressed and suicidal.* | *For many years before treatment, Clare had suicidal tendencies* (=behavior that showed she wanted to kill herself). **2** likely to lead to a lot of damage or trouble: *it would be suicidal for the senator to oppose this policy* **3** likely to lead to death: *Mike often went on suicidal bike rides down Main Street.*

su·i·cide /'suə,saıd/ *n.* [C,U] **1** the act of killing yourself: *Some of the terrorists committed suicide to avoid being captured.* —see Usage Note at KILL[1] **2 political/social suicide** something you do that ruins your good position in politics or society

suicide pact /'... ,./ *n.* [C] an arrangement between two or more people to kill themselves at the same time

suicide watch /'... ,./ *n.* [C] a period of time during which a prisoner is guarded carefully to prevent

them from killing themselves: *Webber has been placed under a 24-hour suicide watch.*

suit[1] /sut/ *n.* [C] **1** a set of clothes made of the same material, usually including a JACKET (=short coat) with pants or a skirt: *Vince was dressed in a blue wool suit.* —see also MORNING SUIT **2 jogging/swimming/bathing etc. suit** a piece of clothing or a set of clothes used for running, swimming etc. —see also SWIMSUIT, WET SUIT **3** a problem or complaint that a person or company brings to a court of law to be settled, LAWSUIT: *Larkin has filed suit* (=officially brought the problem to a court of law) *against the corporation.* **4** one of the four types of cards in a set of playing cards **5 sb's strong suit** something that you are good at: *Politeness is not his strong suit.* **6 plead/press your suit** OLD USE to ask a woman to marry you —see also **in your birthday suit** (BIRTHDAY (2)), **follow suit** (FOLLOW (8))

suit[2] *v.* **1** [T] to be acceptable, appropriate, or CONVENIENT for a particular person or in a particular situation: *It takes time to find a college that will suit your child's needs.* | *"Eight o'clock?" "That suits me fine."* (=is completely acceptable for me) **2 well/best/ideally etc. suited** to have the right qualities to do something: *Megan is well suited for library work.* **3** [T not in passive] clothes or colors that suit someone make them look attractive: *That coat really suits Paul.* | *Red suits you.* **4 suit yourself** SPOKEN used to tell someone they can do whatever they want to, even though it annoys you or you think they are not doing the right thing: *"I think I'll just stay home tonight." "Suit yourself."*

suit sth to sb/sth *phr. v.* [T] FORMAL to make something exactly right for something else: *She had the ability to suit her performances to the audience.*

suit·a·bil·i·ty /ˌsutə'bıləti/ *n.* [U] the degree to which something or someone has the right qualities for a particular purpose: [+ **for**] *Critics doubt his suitability as a leader*

suit·a·ble /'sutəbəl/ *adj.* having the right qualities for a particular person, purpose, or situation; appropriate. *Applicants for the position must have suitable work experience* | [+ **for**] *The show is not suitable for young children.* | [**suitable to do sth**] *These driving techniques are more suitable for the terrain and climate.* —opposite UNSUITABLE —**suitableness** *n.* [U]

suit·a·bly /'sutəbli/ *adv.* **1 suitably dressed/prepared/equipped etc.** wearing the right clothes, having the right information, equipment etc. for a particular situation: *It was clear that the team was not suitably prepared for the game.* **2 suitably impressed/amazed/outraged etc.** showing or having the amount of feeling or quality that you would expect in a particular situation: *Bruck is suitably cautious about his future.*

suit·case /'sut,keıs/ *n.* [C] a large bag or box with a handle, used for carrying clothes and possessions when you travel —see picture at CASE[1]

suite /swit/ *n.* [C] **1** a set of expensive rooms in a hotel: *Raymond's staying in a suite on the fifth floor.* **2** a set of rooms or offices in an office building **3** a piece of music made up of several short parts: *the Nutcracker Suite* **4** TECHNICAL a group of related computer PROGRAMS that make a set **5** a set of matching furniture for a room: *a new dining room suite*

suit·ing /'sutıŋ/ *n.* [U] TECHNICAL material used for making suits, especially woven wool

suit·or /'sutə/ *n.* [C] **1** OLD-FASHIONED a man who wants to marry a particular woman **2** someone or a company that is trying to buy or gain control of another company

su·ki·ya·ki /ˌsuki'yɑki/ *n.* [U] a type of Japanese STEW made with meat, vegetables, and TOFU that are cooked together

Suk·koth, Sukkot /'sukəs, su'koʊs/ *n.* [singular] a Jewish holiday in the fall when people remember the time when Jews traveled from Egypt to Israel in ancient times

S

sul·fate /'sʌlfeɪt/ *n.* [C,U] a chemical compound formed from SULFURIC ACID: *copper sulfate*

sul·fide /'sʌlfaɪd/ *n.* [C,U] a mixture of sulfur with another substance

sul·fur /'sʌlfɚ/ *n.* [U] *symbol* S an ELEMENT that is usually in the form of a light yellow powder and is used in drugs, explosives, and industry

sulfur di·ox·ide /,.. .'../ *n.* [U] a poisonous gas that is a cause of air POLLUTION in industrial areas

sul·fu·ric a·cid /sʌl,fyʊrɪk 'æsɪd/ *n.* [U] a powerful acid

sul·fur·ous /'sʌlfərəs, sʌl'fyʊrəs/ *adj.* related to, full of, or used with sulfur

sulk /sʌlk/ *v.* [I] to show that you are annoyed about something by being silent and having an unhappy expression on your face: *You can't sit around sulking all day.* —**sulk** *n.* [C]

sulk·y /'sʌlki/ *adj.* **1** showing that you are sulking: *a sulky frown* **2** sulking, or tending to sulk: *a sulky child* —**sulkily** *adv.* —**sulkiness** *n.* [U]

sul·len /'sʌlən/ *adj.* **1** silently showing anger or a bad mood: *The girl was sullen and uncooperative.* **2** LITERARY dark and not looking nice; GLOOMY: *a sullen gray sky* —**sullenly** *adv.* —**sullenness** *n.* [U]

sul·ly /'sʌli/ *v.* **sullies, sullied, sullying** [T] FORMAL OR LITERARY to spoil or reduce the value of something that was perfect: **sully sb's image/reputation** *The report has sullied the company's reputation for quality work.*

sul·phate /'sʌlfeɪt/ *n.* [C,U] another spelling of SULFATE

sul·phide /'sʌlfaɪd/ *n.* [C,U] another spelling of SULFIDE

sul·phur /'sʌlfɚ/ *n.* [U] another spelling of SULFUR

sul·phu·ric ac·id /sʌl,fyʊrɪk 'æsɪd/ *n.* [U] another spelling of SULFURIC ACID

sul·tan /'sʌlt⁻n/ *n.* [C] a ruler in some Muslim countries

sul·tan·a /sʌl'tænə/ *n.* [C] the wife, mother, or daughter of a sultan

sul·tan·ate /'sʌltə,neɪt/ *n.* [C] **1** a country ruled by a sultan: *the sultanate of Oman* **2** the position of a sultan, or the period of time during which he rules

sul·try /'sʌltri/ *adj.* **sultrier, sultriest 1** weather that is sultry is very hot with no wind, and makes you feel uncomfortable **2** a woman who is sultry makes other people feel strong sexual attraction for her: *a sultry voice* —**sultriness** *n.* [U]

sum¹ /sʌm/ *n.*

1 money [C] an amount of money: [+ of] *Curran purchased the home for a reported sum of $1.1 million.* | **a large/small sum** *One hundred dollars was a large sum in Victorian times.* —see also LUMP SUM, **princely sum/fee/price etc.** (PRINCELY (1))
2 [C] the total produced when you add two or more numbers or things together: [+ of] *The sum of the three angles of a triangle is 180°.*
3 greater/more than the sum of its parts a group of things or people that is greater than the sum of its parts has a quality or effectiveness as a group that you would not expect from looking at each member separately
4 in sum used before a statement that gives the main information about something in a few simple words: *In sum, we need to cut costs.* —see also SUM TOTAL

sum² *v.* **summed, summing**

sum up *phr. v.* **1** [I,T **sum** sth ↔ **up**] to give the main information about a report, speech, TRIAL etc. in a short statement at the end; SUMMARIZE: *To sum up, it is now clear that the spread of AIDS will not be easily stopped.* | *Hill was able to sum up the city's policy in one sentence.* **2 that (about) sums it up** SPOKEN used to say that you have said everything that is important about a subject —see also SUMMATION

Su·me·ri·an /su'mɛriən/ one of the people who lived

in the part of Mesopotamia that is now Iraq from about 3500 B.C. until about 2000 B.C. —**Sumerian** *adj.*

sum·ma cum lau·de /,sʊmə kʊm 'laʊdə, -deɪ/ *adv.* with highest honor; if you GRADUATE summa cum laude, you have achieved the highest level in your college or university degree —compare CUM LAUDE, MAGNA CUM LAUDE

sum·mar·i·ly /sə'mɛrəli/ *adv.* FORMAL immediately, without paying attention to the usual processes, rules etc.: *The previous commander had been summarily dismissed.*

sum·ma·rize /'sʌmə,raɪz/ *v.* [I,T] to make a short statement giving only the main information and not the details of a plan, event, report etc.: *I wrote a letter summarizing the main points we had discussed.*

sum·ma·ry¹ /'sʌməri/ *n.* plural **summaries** [C] a short statement that gives the main information about something, without giving all the details: [+ of] *We've read a summary of his findings.* | *In summary, the title of the book is great, but the rest isn't so good.*

summary² *adj.* [only before noun, no comparative] **1** FORMAL done immediately, without paying attention to the usual processes, rules etc.: *a summary execution* **2** a summary report, statement etc. gives only the main information about something, so that it is shorter than the full report

sum·ma·tion /sə'meɪʃən/ *n.* [C] FORMAL **1** a statement giving the main facts, but not the details of something, especially made by lawyers at the end of a TRIAL in a court of law **2** the total amount or number you get when two or more things are added together

sum·mer¹ /'sʌmɚ/ *n.* **1** [C,U] the season of the year when the sun is hottest and the days are longest, between spring and fall: *the summer of 1972* | *It never rains here in the summer.* | *Do you have any vacation plans this summer?* | **last/next summer** (=the summer before or after this one) | **summer clothes/jobs/sports etc.** (=clothes, jobs, sports etc. that are used or done in the summer) **2** [C usually plural] LITERARY a word that is used to mean year, used when talking about someone's age: *He looked much younger than his 70 summers.* —see also INDIAN SUMMER, SUMMERY

summer² *v.* [I always + adv./prep.] to spend the summer in a particular place: [+ in/at/on etc.] *McKean's family usually summered on the North Shore.*

summer camp /'.. ,./ *n.* [C,U] a place where children can stay during the summer, and take part in various activities

summer home /'.. ,./ *n.* [C] a house that you live in only in the summer

summer house /'.. ,./ *n.* [C] **1** also **summerhouse** a building in a yard or park, where you can sit in warm weather **2** a summer home

summer school /'.. ,./ *n.* [C,U] courses you can take in the summer at a school or college

summer sol·stice /,.. '../ *n.* [singular] the longest day of the year, which in the northern HEMISPHERE (=top half of the Earth) is around June 21

summer stock /'.. ,./ *n.* [U] a group of actors who work together on several plays during the summer, or the plays performed by these actors

sum·mer·time /'sʌmɚ,taɪm/ *n.* [U] the time of the year when it is summer: *Sailing is a great thing to do in the summertime.*

sum·mer·y /'sʌməri/ *adj.* appropriate for summer, or reminding you of the summer: *a light summery dress*

sum·mit /'sʌmɪt/ *n.* [C] **1** a set of important meetings among a group of people, especially the leaders of two or more governments: *a U.S.–Russian summit* | *a national education summit* | **a summit meeting/conference** *A summit meeting with China is likely by the end of the year.* **2** the top of a mountain: *a trip to the summit of Pike's Peak* —see picture on page 428 **3 the summit of sth** FORMAL the greatest amount or highest level of something: *Working with her was the summit of my life's experience.*

sum·mit·ry /'sʌmɪtri/ *n.* [U] FORMAL a situation in which important summit meetings are held: *four days of superpower summitry*

sum·mon /'sʌmən/ *v.* [T] FORMAL **1** to formally order or ask someone to come to a particular place: *Russo saw the fight and summoned the police.* | [**summon sb to sth**] *Republican leaders were summoned to the White House for a brief meeting.* **2** also **summon up** to make a great effort to use your strength, courage, energy etc.: *I finally summoned the courage to ask my father to lend me the car.*

sum·mons /'sʌmənz/ *n. plural* **summonses** [C] an official order to appear somewhere, especially in a court of law: *Pasqua was issued a summons to appear in court the following week.*

su·mo /'sumoʊ/ also **sumo wrest·ling** /,.. '../ *n.* [U] a Japanese form of WRESTLING, done by men who are very fat —**sumo wrestler** *n.* [C]

sump /sʌmp/ *n.* [C] the lowest part of a DRAINAGE system where liquids or wastes remain

sump·tu·ous /'sʌmptʃuəs/ *adj.* very impressive and expensive; LUXURIOUS: *a sumptuous banquet* —**sumptuously** *adv.*: *a sumptuously illustrated book* —**sumptuousness** *n.* [U]

sum to·tal /,. '../ *n.* **the sum total of sth** the whole amount of something, especially when this is less than expected or needed: *My career is important to me, but it is not the sum total of my life.*

sun¹ /sʌn/ *n.* **1 the sun** the large bright yellow circular object that shines in the sky during the day, that gives us light and heat, and around which the Earth moves **2** [U] the heat and light that come from the sun: *That side of the house gets the most sun.* | *I can't sit in the sun anymore – it's too hot.* **3** [C] any star around which PLANETS move: *a distant sun* **4 (every-thing/anything) under the sun** used to emphasize that you are talking about something that includes very large numbers of ideas, things etc.: *They expect us to do everything under the sun!* **5 get/catch some sun** INFORMAL to spend time outside in the sun, especially in order to make your skin brown: *It looks like you got a little sun today.* —see also **make hay while the sun shines** (HAY (2)), **there's nothing new under the sun** (NEW (15))

sun² *v.* **sunned, sunning** [I,T] also **sun yourself** to sit or lie outside while the sun is shining: *We spent a week sunning ourselves on Australian beaches.*

Sun. the written abbreviation of Sunday

sun-baked /'. ./ *adj.* made very hard and dry by the sun: *the sun-baked Moroccan desert*

sun·bathe /'sʌnbeɪð/ *v.* [I] to sit or lie outside in the sun, especially in order to become brown

sun·beam /'sʌnbim/ *n.* [C] a beam of light from the sun that you can see because it is shining through a cloud, window etc.

sun·bed /'sʌnbɛd/ *n.* [C] a metal structure the size of a bed, that you lie on to make your skin brown using light from special lamps —see also SUNLAMP

Sun Belt, Sunbelt /'. ./ *n.* **the Sun Belt** the southern or southwestern parts of the U.S., where the sun shines a lot and the weather is often very warm

sun block, sunblock /'. ./ *n.* [C,U] cream or oil that you rub into your skin, in order to stop the sun's light from burning you

sun·bon·net /'sʌn,bʌnɪt/ *n.* [C] a hat worn in past times by women as protection from the sun

sun·burn /'sʌnbɚn/ *n.* [C,U] a condition of having skin that is red and painful, as a result of spending too much time in the sun —**sunburned** also **sunburnt** *adj.* —compare SUNTAN

sun·burst /'sʌnbɚst/ *n.* [C] a pattern or drawing that looks like the sun with lines coming out from the center

sun·dae /'sʌndi, -deɪ/ *n.* [C] ice cream with sweet sauce poured over it, with nuts, whipped cream etc. on top: *a hot fudge sundae*

Sun·day /'sʌndi, -deɪ/ *written abbreviation* **Sun.** *n. plural* **Sundays** [C,U] the first day of the week, between Saturday and Monday: *Football season starts Sunday.* | *It snowed on Sunday.* | *We had friends over*

last Sunday. | *We're going to go on a picnic* **next Sunday.** | *What are you going to do* **this Sunday** (=the next Sunday coming)? | *I always read the paper* **on Sundays** (=each Sunday). | *Christmas falls* **on a Sunday** *this year.* | **Sunday morning/afternoon/ night etc.** *We're going out to dinner Sunday night.*

USAGE NOTE: SUNDAY

GRAMMAR

On Sunday/Monday/Tuesday etc. is used with the past tense to talk about a particular day in the week that has just passed, or with the present tense to talk about a particular day in the week that is coming: *It rained on Sunday.* | *We are leaving on Sunday.* Only use "the" in front of the name of a day if you are talking about a particular day of a particular week: *Let's meet on the Sunday before Easter.*

Sunday school /'.. ./ *n.* [C,U] a class in a church where children go on Sundays to be taught about the Christian religion

sun deck /'. ./ *n.* [C] a wooden structure like a floor, built next to a house or other building, or on a ship, where people can sit in order to be in the sun

sun·der /'sʌndɚ/ *v.* [T] LITERARY to break something into parts, especially violently —see also ASUNDER

sun·dial /'sʌndaɪl/ *n.* [C] an object used for telling the time, by looking at the position of a shadow made on a stone circle by a pointed piece of metal

sun·down /'sʌndaʊn/ *n.* [U] SUNSET (1): *During Ramadan, the family does not eat or drink before sundown.*

sun·drenched /'. ./ *adj.* a sun-drenched place is one where the sun shines most of the time: *the sun-drenched Mediterranean*

sun·dress /'sʌndrɛs/ *n.* [C] a dress that you wear in hot weather, that does not cover your arms, neck, or shoulders

sun-dried /'. ./ *adj.* [only before noun] sun-dried food has been left in the sun to dry in order to give it a particular taste: *sun-dried tomatoes*

sun·dries /'sʌndriz/ *n.* [plural] FORMAL small objects that are not important enough to be named separately —see also SUNDRY

sun·dry /'sʌndri/ *adj.* [only before noun, no comparative] FORMAL **1** not similar enough to form a group; MISCELLANEOUS: *They manufacture clothing and sundry other products made from hemp.* **2 all and sundry** everyone, not just a few carefully chosen people —see also SUNDRIES, **various and sundry sth** (VARIOUS (2))

sun·fish /'sʌnfɪʃ/ *n. plural* **sunfish** or **sunfishes** [C] an ocean fish that has a large flat circular body

sun·flow·er /'sʌn,flaʊɚ/ *n.* [C] a very tall plant with a large yellow flower and seeds that can be eaten

sung /sʌŋ/ the past participle of SING

sun·glass·es /'sʌn,glæsɪz/ *n.* [plural] dark glasses that you wear to protect your eyes when the sun is very bright

sun god /'. ./ *n.* [C] a god in some ancient religions who represents the sun or has power over it

sun hat /'. ./ *n.* [C] a hat that you wear to protect your head from the sun —see picture at HAT

sunk /sʌŋk/ a past tense and the past participle of SINK¹

sunk·en /'sʌŋkən/ *adj.* **1** [only before noun] having fallen to the bottom of the ocean or a lake: *sunken ships* | *sunken treasure* **2** [only before noun] built or placed at a lower level than the surrounding floor, ground etc.: *a sunken bath* | *a sunken living room* **3 sunken cheeks/eyes** if someone has sunken cheeks or eyes, they look thin, old, or unhealthy

sun·lamp /'sʌnlæmp/ *n.* [C] a lamp that produces a special light used for making your skin brown

sun·less /'sʌnlɪs/ *adj.* LITERARY having no light from the sun: *a sunless prison cell*

sun·light /'sʌnlaɪt/ n. [U] natural light that comes from the sun | **bright/direct sunlight** *This plant needs direct sunlight.*

sun·lit /'sʌn,lɪt/ adj. made brighter by light from the sun: *a sunlit valley*

Sun·na, Sunnah /'sʊnə/ n. **the Sunna** a set of Muslim customs and rules based on the words and acts of Mohammed

Sun·ni /'sʊni/ n. [C] a Muslim who follows one of the two main branches of the Muslim religion —compare SHIITE

sun·ny /'sʌni/ adj. **sunnier, sunniest 1** full of light from the sun: *a sunny afternoon* | *a sunny kitchen* **2** INFORMAL cheerful and happy: *a sunny smile*

sunny-side up /ˌ.. . '. ./ adj., adv. [not before noun] an egg that is cooked sunny-side up is cooked on one side only, and not turned over in the pan

sun porch /'. . / n. [C] a room with large windows and often a glass roof, designed to let in a lot of light

sun·rise /'sʌnraɪz/ n. **1** [U] the time when the sun first appears in the morning: *Sunrise is at 6:10 tomorrow.* **2** [C,U] the part of the sky where the sun first appears in the morning: *We watched the sunrise at Ayers Rock.* | *a beautiful sunrise*

sun·roof /'sʌnruf/ n. [C] **1** a part of the roof of a car that you can open to let in air and light —see picture on page 427 **2** a flat roof of a building where you can sit when the sun is shining

sun·screen /'sʌnskrin/ n. [C,U] a cream or oil that you rub into your skin to stop the sun from burning you for a period of time

sun·set /'sʌnsɛt/ n. **1** [U] the time of day when the sun disappears and night begins: *The park is open from 8 a.m. to sunset.* **2** [C,U] the part of the sky where the sun gradually disappears at the end of the day: *a purple and orange sunset* **3 ride/head/sail** etc. **off into the sunset** HUMOROUS to leave a place or a job without plans of ever coming back because you believe you have finished everything you wanted to do

sun·shade /'sʌnʃeɪd/ n. [C] something that you put in your car window to stop the sun from shining in

sun·shine /'sʌnʃaɪn/ n. [U] **1** a word meaning the light and heat that come from the sun, used when you want to say that this is nice: *We sat outside in the warm spring sunshine.* **2** INFORMAL happiness: *Percy was the only ray of sunshine in her gloomy life.* **3** SPOKEN used to address someone you love, or someone who is making you annoyed: *Good morning, sunshine.* | *Look, sunshine, are you ever going to do anything today?*

sun·spot /'sʌnspat/ n. [C] a small dark area on the sun's surface

sun·stroke /'sʌnstrok/ n. [U] fever, weakness etc. caused by being outside in the sun for too long

sun·tan /'sʌntæn/ n. [C] attractively brown skin which you get when you spend a lot of time in the sun; TAN —**suntanned** adj. —compare SUNBURN

suntan lo·tion /'.. ,../ also **suntan oil** /'.. ,./ n. [C,U] a cream or oil that you rub into your skin to stop the sun from burning you too much

sun-up /'sʌnʌp/ n. [U] INFORMAL: see SUNRISE (1)

sun wor·ship·er /'. ,../ n. [C] **1** INFORMAL someone who likes to lie in the sun to get a suntan **2** someone who considers the sun a god and respects it, prays to it etc.

Sun Yat-Sen /ˌsʊn yat 'sɛn/ (1866–1925) a Chinese political leader who established the National Party in China, and helped to remove the last Manchu emperor from power. He became the first President of the new Republic of China in 1911.

sup /sʌp/ v. [I] OLD USE to eat supper

supe /sup/ n. [C] SPOKEN **1** a SUPERVISOR **2** a SUPERINTENDENT

su·per¹ /'supɚ/ adj. INFORMAL extremely good; WONDERFUL: *"Would you like some lemonade?" "That would be super."* | *You guys really did a super job.* | *"I'll see you at 8." "Super!"*

super² adv. SPOKEN extremely: *Some of the bus drivers are super nice, but most aren't.*

super³ n. [C] SPOKEN a SUPERINTENDENT

super- /supɚ/ prefix **1** larger, greater, stronger etc. than other things or people of the same type: *a super-market* | *a supertanker* (=ship that can carry extremely large loads) | *the Superbowl* (=most important football game) **2** above others, or in a more powerful position than others: *a supervisor* (=who has authority over other people) | *to super-impose one picture on another* (=put it on top of the other)

su·per·a·bun·dance /ˌsupərə'bʌndəns/ n. **a super-abundance of sth** FORMAL more than enough of something —**superabundant** adj.

su·per·an·nu·at·ed /ˌsupɚ'ænyu,eɪtɪd/ adj. FORMAL old, and not useful or not working anymore: *super-annuated computer equipment*

su·perb /sʊ'pɚb/ adj. [no comparative] extremely good; EXCELLENT: *The meal was superb.* | *a superb performance* —**superbly** adv.

Super Bowl /'.. ,./ n. [C usually singular] a football game played once a year to decide which professional team is the best in the U.S.

su·per·charged /'supɚ,tʃɑrdʒd/ adj. **1** a super-charged engine is very powerful because air or FUEL is supplied to it at a higher pressure than normal **2** extremely powerful, strong etc.: *The Skyline Fund attracted interest because of its supercharged performance.*

su·per·cil·i·ous /ˌsupɚ'sɪliəs/ adj. FORMAL behaving as if you think that other people are less important than you: *a supercilious laugh*

su·per·com·put·er /'supɚkəm,pyutɚ/ n. [C] a computer that is more powerful than almost all other computers

su·per·con·duc·tiv·i·ty /ˌsupɚ,kɑndʌk'tɪvəti/ n. [U] TECHNICAL the ability of some substances to allow electricity to flow through them very easily, especially at very low temperatures —**superconductive** /ˌsupɚkən'dʌktɪv/ adj.

su·per·con·duc·tor /'supɚkən,dʌktɚ/ n. [C] TECHNICAL a substance that allows electricity to flow through it very easily, especially at very low temperatures —**superconducting** adj.

su·per·cool /ˌsupɚ'kul/ v. [T usually passive] TECHNICAL to cool a liquid below the temperature at which it would normally freeze, without the liquid becoming solid

super-du·per /ˌsupɚ 'dupɚ/ adj. SPOKEN, INFORMAL extremely good; SUPER: *a super-duper new toy*

su·per·e·go /ˌsupɚ'igoʊ/ n. [C usually singular] TECHNICAL a word meaning your "conscience," used in Freudian PSYCHOLOGY —compare EGO (3), ID

su·per·fi·cial /ˌsupɚ'fɪʃəl/ adj. **1** based on or involving only the features or qualities that you notice first, rather than complete knowledge of the way things really are: *a superficial understanding of physics* | *On a superficial level, the two stories may seem similar.* **2** affecting only the surface of your skin or the outside part of something, and therefore not serious: *Barlow was treated for a superficial gun-shot wound to the leg.* **3** DISAPPROVING someone who is superficial does not think about things that are serious or important; SHALLOW: *All the other girls seemed silly and superficial to Darlene.* **4** not important or not having a big effect: *Debbie kept canceling our dates for superficial reasons.* | *superficial changes in government policies* **5** TECHNICAL existing in or relating to the top layer of something, especially soil, rock etc. —**superficially** adv. —**superficiality** /ˌsupɚfɪʃi'æləti/ n. [U]

su·per·flu·ous /sʊ'pɚfluəs/ adj. FORMAL more than is needed or wanted; UNNECESSARY: *We're cutting out superfluous layers of managers.* —**superfluously** adv. —**superfluousness** n. [U]

Su·per·fund /'supɚ,fʌnd/ n. [singular] a law that provides money from the U.S. government to clean up areas that have been POLLUTED with dangerous substances, but that also allows the government to demand money in a court of law from the companies that made the area dirty

Su·per·glue /'supəglu/ *n.* [U] TRADEMARK a very strong glue that sticks very quickly and is difficult to remove —**superglue** *v.* [T]

su·per·he·ro /'supəˌhɪroʊ/ *n. plural* **superheroes** [C] a character in stories who uses special powers, such as great strength or the ability to fly, to help people

su·per·high·way /ˌsupəˈhaɪweɪ/ *n. plural* **superhighways** [C] FORMAL a very large road on which you can drive fast for long distances —see also INFORMATION SUPERHIGHWAY

su·per·hu·man /ˌsupəˈhyumən◂/ *adj.* much greater than ordinary human powers or abilities: **superhuman strength/power** etc. *It would take a superhuman effort to supervise five little kids.*

su·per·im·pose /ˌsupəɪmˈpoʊz/ *v.* [T] **1** to put one picture, image, or photograph on top of another so that both can be partly seen: [superimpose sth on/onto sth] *Moore has superimposed the head of an animal on a human body.* **2** to combine two systems, ideas, opinions etc. so that one influences the other: [superimpose sth on/onto sth] *Superimposing capitalism on another economic system is apt to cause problems.* —**superimposition** /ˌsupəˌɪmpə'zɪʃən/ *n.* [U]

su·per·in·tend /ˌsupəɪn'tɛnd/ *v.* [T] FORMAL to be in charge of something, and control how it is done —**superintendence** *n.* [U]

su·per·in·tend·ent /ˌsupəɪn'tɛndənt/ *n.* [C] **1** also **superintendent of schools** someone who is in charge of all the schools in a particular area in the U.S. **2** someone who is in charge of an apartment building and is responsible for making repairs in the building **3** someone who is officially in charge of a place, job, activity etc. —see also SIDEWALK SUPERINTENDENT

su·pe·ri·or¹ /sə'pɪriə, su-/ *adj.* [no comparative] **1** better, more powerful, more effective etc. than a similar person or thing, especially one that you are competing against: [+ to] *Today's computers are superior to anything we had ten years ago.* | *They were beaten by the vastly superior naval power of the enemy.* **2** [only before noun] FORMAL of very good quality: *superior craftsmanship* | *a superior academic record* **3** thinking that you are better than other people: *a superior attitude* | *She always acts so superior to everyone else.* **4** having a higher position or rank than someone else: *Are you questioning the orders of a superior officer?* **5** TECHNICAL higher in position; UPPER —see also MOTHER SUPERIOR —compare INFERIOR¹

superior² *n.* [C] someone who has a higher rank or position than you, especially in a job: *It is important to have a good working relationship with **your immediate superior** (=the person in the position directly above yours).* —compare INFERIOR²

Su·pe·ri·or, Lake /sə'pɪriə, su/ the largest of the five Great Lakes on the border between the U.S. and Canada

Superior Court, superior court /.,.. './ *n.* [C,U] a court of law that has more authority than other courts in a particular area

su·pe·ri·or·i·ty /sə,pɪri'orəti, -'ɑr-/ *n.* [U] **1** the quality of being better, more skillful, more powerful etc. than other things: [+ of] *I'm tired of hearing about the superiority of their product.* | [+ over] *The organization has a technical superiority over its rivals.* | [+ in] *U.S. superiority in air power* **2** an attitude that shows you think you are better than other people: **an air/attitude etc. of superiority** *Dina's college degree gives her a sense of superiority over her friends.*

su·per·la·tive¹ /sə'pələtɪv, su-/ *adj.* [no comparative] **1** excellent: *superlative special effects* **2** a superlative adjective or adverb expresses the highest degree of a particular quality. For example, the superlative form of "tall" is "tallest". —compare COMPARATIVE¹ (4)

superlative² *n.* **1 the superlative** the superlative form of an adjective or adverb. For example, "biggest" is the superlative of "big". **2** [C] a word in

this form, used especially when expressing great praise or admiration: *"Ulee's Gold" has earned superlatives from critics wherever it has played.*

su·per·la·tive·ly /sə'pələtɪvli/ *adv.* extremely

su·per·man /'supəˌmæn/ *n. plural* **supermen** /-ˌmɛn/ [C] a man of unusually great ability or strength

su·per·mar·ket /'supəˌmarkɪt/ *n.* [C] a large store where customers can buy many different kinds of food and things for the house

su·per·mod·el /'supəˌmadl/ *n.* [C] an extremely famous fashion MODEL

su·per·mom /'supəˌmam/ *n.* [C usually singular] INFORMAL a mother who takes care of her children, cooks, cleans the house etc., in addition to having a job outside the house, and is admired because of this

su·per·nat·u·ral¹ /ˌsupə'nætʃərəl◂, -tʃrəl◂/ *adj.* impossible to explain by natural causes, and therefore seeming to involve the powers of gods or magic: *supernatural powers* —**supernaturally** *adv.*

supernatural² *n.* **the supernatural** supernatural events, powers, and creatures: *belief in the supernatural*

su·per·no·va /ˌsupə'noʊvə/ *n. plural* **supernovas** or **supernovae** /-vi/ [C] a very large very bright exploding star —compare NOVA

su·per·nu·mer·ar·y /ˌsupə'numəˌrɛri/ *n.* [C] **1** FORMAL someone or something that is additional to the number of people or things that are needed **2** TECHNICAL someone who is in a play, OPERA etc. without speaking, usually as part of a large group of people —**supernumerary** *adj.*

sup·er·pow·er /'supəˌpaʊə/ *n.* [C] a nation that has very great military and political power

su·per·script /'supəˌskrɪpt/ *adj.* [only before noun] written or printed above a number, letter etc. —**superscript** *n.* [C,U] —compare SUBSCRIPT

su·per·sede /ˌsupə'sid/ *v.* [T] if a new idea, product, or method supersedes another one, it becomes used instead because it is more modern or effective or has more authority: *The new deal supersedes the old agreement.*

su·per·son·ic /ˌsupə'sanɪk◂/ *adj.* faster than the speed of sound: *a supersonic jet* —compare SUBSONIC

su·per·star /'supəˌstar/ *n.* [C] an extremely famous performer, especially a musician or movie actor

su·per·sti·tion /ˌsupə'stɪʃən/ *n.* [C,U] DISAPPROVING a belief that some objects or actions are lucky and some are unlucky or cause particular results, based on old ideas of magic: *There is a widely held superstition that garlic protects against evil.*

su·per·sti·tious /ˌsupə'stɪʃəs/ *adj.* DISAPPROVING influenced by the belief that some objects or actions are lucky or unlucky or cause particular results: *My mother is so superstitious she won't step on a crack when we walk down the street.* —**superstitiously** *adv.*

su·per·store /'supəˌstɔr/ *n.* [C] a very large store that sells many different types of product

su·per·struc·ture /'supəˌstrʌktʃə/ *n.* [singular,U] **1** a structure that is built on top of the main part of something such as a ship or building **2** FORMAL a political or social system that is based on a simpler system: *the colonial superstructure of the country*

su·per·tank·er /'supəˌtæŋkə/ *n.* [C] an extremely large ship that can carry large quantities of oil or other liquids

Super Tues·day /ˌ.. '../ *n.* [U] a Tuesday in March during a year in which there is an election for U.S. President, when important PRIMARY ELECTIONS take place in many states

su·per·vise /'supəˌvaɪz/ *v.* [I,T] to be in charge of a process, organization, or group of workers or students etc. and be responsible for making sure that everyone does what they are supposed to do: *Ruff supervises a staff of more than 200 lawyers.*

su·per·vi·sion /ˌsupə'vɪʒən/ *n.* [U] the act of supervising someone or something: *The medicine should only be taken **under** a doctor's **supervision**.*

su·per·vis·or /'supɚˌvaɪzɚ/ n. [C] **1** someone who supervises workers or students **2** someone who is a member of the city, COUNTY etc. government in some parts of the U.S. —**supervisory** /ˌsupɚ'vaɪzɚi/ adj.: *supervisory responsibilities*

su·per·wom·an /'supɚˌwomən/ n. plural **super-women** /-ˌwɪmɪn/ [C] a woman who is very successful in her job and also usually takes care of her children and home

su·pine /su'paɪn, 'supaɪn/ adj. FORMAL **1** lying on your back: *a supine position* —compare PRONE (2) **2** allowing other people to make decisions instead of you in a way that seems very weak: *a supine parliament* —**supinely** adv.

sup·per /'sʌpɚ/ n. [C,U] an informal meal that is eaten in the evening —compare DINNER

supper club /'.. ./ n. [C] a small NIGHTCLUB, where you can eat, drink, dance etc.

sup·per·time /'sʌpɚtaɪm/ n. [U] the time of the evening when people eat supper

sup·plant /sə'plænt/ v. [T] FORMAL to take the place of a person or thing so that they are not used anymore, not in a position of power anymore etc.: *Some would argue that New York has supplanted Paris as the center of new culture.*

sup·ple /'sʌpəl/ adj. **1** leather, skin, wood etc. that is supple is soft and bends easily **2** someone who is supple bends and moves easily and gracefully: *Exercise will help keep your joints and muscles supple.* —**suppleness** n. [U]

sup·ple·ment¹ /'sʌpləmənt/ n. [C] **1** something that you add to something else to improve it or make it complete: *vitamin E supplements* **2** an additional part at the end of a book, or a separate part of a newspaper, magazine etc.: *a Sunday supplement* **3** an amount of money that is added to the price of a service, hotel room etc.

sup·ple·ment² /'sʌpləˌmɛnt/ v. [T always + adv./ prep.] to add something, especially to what you earn or eat, in order to increase it to an acceptable level: [**supplement sth with sth**] *Athletes who train for long periods should supplement their diets with sports drinks.* —**supplementation** /ˌsʌpləmɛn'teɪʃən/ n. [U]

sup·ple·men·ta·ry /ˌsʌplə'mɛntəri/ adj. **1** also **supplemental** provided in addition to what already exists: *supplementary insurance coverage* **2** TECHNICAL two angles that are supplementary add up to 180° —compare COMPLEMENTARY (2)

sup·pli·ant /'sʌpliənt/ n. [C] LITERARY a supplicant —**suppliant** adj.

sup·pli·cant /'sʌplɪkənt/ n. [C] LITERARY someone who asks for something, especially from someone in a position of power or from God

sup·pli·ca·tion /ˌsʌplə'keɪʃən/ n. [C,U] LITERARY the action of asking or praying for help from someone in power or from God: *The man fell to his knees, his arms stretched out **in supplication**.* —**supplicate** /'sʌpliˌkeɪt/ v. [I,T]

sup·pli·er /sə'plaɪɚ/ n. [C] **1** a company that provides a particular product: [+ **of**] *Libya is Italy's largest supplier of oil.* **2** someone who provides someone with something, especially illegal drugs

sup·ply¹ /sə'plaɪ/ n. plural **supplies** **1** [C] an amount of something that is available to be used: *The nation's fuel supplies will not last forever.* | [+ **of**] *All the construction has created a plentiful supply of housing.* **2 supplies** [plural] food, clothes and things necessary for daily life, especially for a group of people over a period of time: *Emergency supplies are being sent to the flooded region.* **3 medical/school/ cleaning etc. supplies** the tools, equipment etc. that are needed for a particular purpose **4 gas/electric- ity/water etc. supply** a system that is used to supply gas, electricity, water etc.: *This valley needs a reli- able water supply.* **5** [C,U] the act or process of pro- viding something: [+ **of**] *Blood clots can stop the supply of blood to the brain, causing a stroke.* **6 a supply ship/ convoy/route etc.** a ship, a group of

trucks, a route etc. used for bringing or storing supplies —see also MONEY SUPPLY, **be in short supply** (SHORT¹ (11))

supply² v. **supplies, supplied, supplying** [T] **1** to provide people with something that they need or want, especially regularly over a long period of time: *Paint for the project was supplied by the city.* | [**supply sb with sth**] *In the 1850s, Stanford started his business by supplying miners with shovels.* | [**supply sth to sb**] *Archer has refused to supply the information to federal investigators.* **2 be well/ poorly/generously supplied with sth** to have a lot of something, a little of something etc.: *The lounge was well supplied with ashtrays.*

supply and de·mand /.,. . .'. ./ n. [U] the relationship between the amount of goods for sale and the amount that people want to buy, especially the way this relationship influences prices

supply line /.'. ./ n. [C usually plural] a road, path etc. along which supplies are brought to someone, especially to an army during a war: *The bombing was designed to **cut off** enemy **supply lines**.*

supply-side ec·o·nom·ics /.'. . .,.,./ n. [U] the idea that if the government reduces taxes, producers will be able to make more goods and this will improve a country's economic situation

sup·port¹ /sə'pɔrt/ v. [T] **1** [agree with sb/sth] to say that you agree with an idea, group, person etc. and want them to succeed: *The changes in the tax code are supported by the Democratic party.* | [**support sb in sth**] *We need to support teachers in their efforts to keep schools drug- free.* | *The U.S. **strongly supports** the trade agree- ment.* **2** [hold sth up] to hold the weight of something, keep it in place, or prevent it from falling: *During the reno- vations, a temporary wall will support the ceiling.* **3** [help sb] to help someone by being nice to them during a difficult time in their life: *My friends and family have all supported me through the divorce.* **4** [provide money to live] to provide enough money for someone to pay for all the things they need: *If she can't support herself, how's she going to support a child?* **5** [give money to sth] to give money to a group, organization or event etc. to encourage it or pay for its costs: *I always support the Girl Scouts by buying a few boxes of cookies.* **6 support a habit** to get and use money to pay for a bad habit, such as taking drugs: *Paul started dealing drugs to support his own cocaine habit.* **7** [prove sth] to show or prove that something is true or correct: *Wang's theory is supported by arche- ological evidence.* **8** [computers] to provide information and material to improve a computer program or system, to make it continue working: *I don't think they support that version of the program anymore.* **9** [land] if land can support people or animals, it is of good enough quality to grow enough food for them to live: *This land isn't fertile enough to support many cattle.* **10** [money/prices] to do something to prevent prices, the value of a country's money etc. from decreasing —**supportable** adj. —see also INSUPPORT- ABLE

support² n. **1** [approval] [U] approval and encouragement for a person, idea, plan etc.: [+ **for**] *There appears to be a lot of support for independence in the territory.* | *Con- gress has **given** its **support to** the military action.* | *A number of people spoke **in support of** the new rule.* | *Thompson has **won the support of** half the party.* | *The mayor is trying to **drum up support for** (=get many people's approval for) the new subway line.* **2** [sympathy/help] [U] sympathetic encouragement and help that you give to someone: *Thanks for all your support – it's been a hard year.* —see also **moral support** (MORAL¹ (3)) **3** [hold sth up] [C,U] something that presses on something else to hold it up or in position, or the result of doing this: *supports for the bridge* | *This sofa has good back support.*

4 [money] [C,U] money that you give a person, group, organization etc. to help pay for their costs: *The GI bill provided **financial support** for soldiers who wanted to get a college education.* —see also CHILD SUPPORT, PRICE SUPPORT

5 [soldiers] [U] help or protection that is given by one group of soldiers to another group who are fighting in a battle: *logistical support* | **air/ground support** (=help or protection that comes from people in aircraft or people on the ground)

6 [computers] —see TECHNICAL SUPPORT

sup·port·er /sə'pɔrtɚ/ *n.* [C] **1** someone who supports a particular person, group, or plan: [+ **of**] *a supporter of abortion rights* | **a strong/firm/staunch etc. supporter** *Cox is one of Carter's biggest supporters.* **2** a JOCKSTRAP

support group /.'. ./ *n.* [C] a group of people who meet to help each other with a particular problem, for example ALCOHOLISM

support hose /.'. ./ *n.* [U] special PANTYHOSE that hold your legs very firmly and help blood move through your legs

sup·port·ing /sə'pɔrtɪŋ/ *adj.* **1 a supporting part/ role/ actor etc.** a small part in a play or movie, or the actor who plays such a part **2 supporting wall/ beam etc.** a wall, piece of wood etc. that supports the weight of something

sup·port·ive /sə'pɔrtɪv/ *adj.* APPROVING giving help or encouragement, especially to someone who is in a difficult situation: *I can always count on Gail to be supportive when things go wrong.* | [+ **of**] *All the team members are very supportive of each other.*

sup·pose /sə'pouz/ *v.* **1 be supposed to do/be sth a)** used to say what someone should or should not do, especially because of rules or what someone in authority has said: *You're not supposed to smoke in the building.* | *We're supposed to check out of the hotel by 11:00.* | *What time are you supposed to be there?* **b)** used to say what is expected or intended to happen, especially when this has failed to happen: *No one was supposed to know about it.* | *Was that supposed to be a joke?* | *"Ultra Velvet" is supposed to perform at the club on Friday.* **c)** used to say that something is believed to be true by many people, although you are not certain: *I didn't really like the book, but the movie is supposed to be very funny.* | *This is supposed to be the best Chinese restaurant in town* | *Mrs. Carver is supposed to have a lot of money.* **2** [T not in progressive] to think that something is probably true, based on what you know: *His government has lasted longer than his enemies supposed.* | [**suppose (that)**] *After all his attention, Mattie supposed he would ask her to marry him.* | *Lefkowitz argues **there is no reason to suppose that** (=it is unlikely that) Cleopatra was black.* **3** [T not in progressive] FORMAL to expect something will happen or imagine something is true and then base something on it; PRESUPPOSE: *The company's plan supposes a steady increase in orders.*

SPOKEN PHRASES

4 I suppose a) used to say you think something is true, although you are uncertain about it: *"The kids will love it, don't you think?" "I suppose."* | [**I suppose (that)**] *I suppose it must be pretty hot in the summer where you come from.* **b)** used when agreeing to let someone do something, especially when you do not really want them to do it: *"Can we come with you?" "Oh, **I suppose so.**"* **c)** used when saying in an angry way that you expect something is true: [**I suppose (that)**] *I suppose you want mine too!* **d)** used to say that you think that something is probably true, although you wish it were not and hope someone will tell you it is not: [**I suppose (that)**] *I suppose I'll have to take this over to Gene's house.* **e)** used when guessing that something is true: *"What is this?" "It's one of Beethoven's violin sonatas, I suppose."* **5 suppose/ supposing** used to ask someone to imagine what would happen if a particular situation existed: *Suppose Bobby really is telling the truth. What then?* **6 what's that supposed to mean?** said when you are annoyed by what someone has just said: *"It sounds like things aren't going too well for you lately." "What's that supposed to mean?"* **7 I**

don't suppose (that) a) used to ask in an indirect way if something is true: *I don't suppose you have any idea where my address book is, do you?* **b)** used to ask for something in a very polite way: *I don't suppose you'd be willing to go get the napkins?* **c)** used to say that you think it is unlikely that something will happen: *I don't suppose the painting will ever be worth a thousand dollars.* **8 do you suppose (that)...?** used to ask someone's opinion about something: *Do you suppose people will ever live on Mars?* **9 who/what/why etc. do you suppose...?** used to ask someone who, what etc. they think did something, is something etc., or to ask them to guess: *And who do you suppose we saw at the restaurant?*

sup·posed /sə'pouzd/ *adj.* [only before noun] claimed by other people to be true or real, although you do not think they are right: *Even the supposed experts are unable to explain what's happening.*

sup·pos·ed·ly /sə'pouzɪdli/ *adv.* used when saying what many people say or believe is true, especially when you disagree with them: [**sentence adverb**] *Anne is coming for a visit in March, supposedly.* | [+ adj./adv.] *How could a supposedly intelligent person make so many stupid mistakes?*

sup·pos·ing /sə'pouzɪŋ/ *conjunction* used when talking about a possible condition or situation, and then imagining the result: *Supposing you fire three or four shots, at least one of them will hit the target.*

sup·po·si·tion /ˌsʌpə'zɪʃən/ *n.* [C,U] something that you think is true even though you are not certain and cannot prove it: *The report will be based on fact, not supposition.* | [**supposition (that)**] *Police are acting on the supposition that she took the money.*

sup·pos·i·to·ry /sə'pɑzəˌtɔri/ *n. plural* **suppositories** [C] a small piece of solid medicine that is placed in someone's RECTUM or VAGINA

sup·pres·sant /sə'prɛsənt/ *n.* **a cough/appetite/pain etc. suppressant** a drug or medicine that makes you cough less, makes you less hungry etc.

sup·press /sə'prɛs/ *v.* [T] **1** to stop people from opposing the government, especially by using force: *For 70 years the Communist government had suppressed all dissent.* **2** to prevent important information or opinions from becoming known, especially by people who have a right to know: *Some evidence had been suppressed by Spira's lawyers.* **3** to prevent something from growing or developing, or from working effectively: *The virus suppresses the body's immune system.* **4** to stop yourself from showing your feelings or from doing an action: **suppress a grin/laugh/burp etc.** *"I grew it myself," he said, trying to suppress a smile.* —**suppressed** *adj.*: *suppressed rage* —**suppressible** *adj.* —**suppression** /sə'prɛʃən/ *n.* [U] —compare REPRESS

sup·pres·sor /sə'prɛsɚ/ *n.* [C] something that prevents something from developing, working effectively, or being noticeable: *a jet engine noise suppressor* —**suppressor** *adj.* [only before noun] TECHNICAL *cancer-suppressor genes*

su·pra·na·tion·al /ˌsuprə'næʃənl/ *adj.* FORMAL involving more than one country, and often having more authority than these countries: *a supranational organization*

su·prem·a·cist /su'prɛməsɪst/ *n.* [C] someone who believes that their own particular group or race is better than any other —see also WHITE SUPREMACIST

su·prem·a·cy /sə'prɛməsi, su-/ *n.* [U] the position in which you are more powerful or advanced than anyone else

su·preme /sə'prim, su-/ *adj.* **1** having the highest position of power, importance, or influence: *the supreme commander of the fleet* | *In the U.S., the automobile **reigns supreme** (=has a position of great importance).* **2** [only before noun] the greatest possible: *Going in after the little girl was a supreme act of courage.* | *They've made **a supreme effort** to repair the damage.* **3 make the supreme sacrifice** to die for your country, for a principle etc.

Supreme Be·ing /ˌ. '../ *n.* [singular] LITERARY God

Supreme Court /ˌ. '../ *n.* **1 the Supreme Court** the court of law with the most authority in the U.S. **2** [C] a court of law in most U.S. states with more authority than all other courts in that state

su·preme·ly /səˈprimli/ *adv.* [+ adj./adv.] extremely, or to the greatest possible degree: *At work, Diane was a supremely confident executive.*

Supt. the written abbreviation of SUPERINTENDENT

sur·cease /ˈsɔˈsis/ *n.* [U + of] LITERARY the act of stopping, or of making something do this —**surcease** *v.* [I,T]

sur·charge /ˈsɔtʃɑrdʒ/ *n.* [C] money that you have to pay in addition to the basic price of something: [+ on] *a 10% surcharge on all imports* —**surcharge** *v.* [T]

sure¹ /ʃʊr, ʃɚ/ *adj.*
1 certain you know sth [not before noun] confident that you know something or that something is true or correct: *I think Leah lives here, but I'm not sure.* | [sure (that)] *I'm sure I had the keys when we left the house.* | *Are you sure you know how to get there?* | [+ of] *No one is really sure of what the policy is.* | [+ about] "Kent said he would be here by 8:30." "Are you sure about that?" | [not sure how/where/when etc.] *She's not sure how she's going to tell him.* | [not sure if/whether] *I'm not sure if I'm pronouncing this name correctly.* | *I'm pretty sure it was John.* —see Usage Note at CERTAINLY
2 certain about your feelings [not before noun] certain about what you feel, want, like etc.: [sure (that)] *Are you sure you really want a divorce?* | [+ of] *Carla says she is very sure of her love for Tony.*
3 make sure a) to find out if something is true or to check that something has been done: *I know I asked you before, but I just wanted to make sure.* | [make sure (that)] *First, make sure that the printer has paper in it.* b) to do something so that you can be certain of the result: [make sure (that)] *I'll walk you home to make sure no one bothers you.* —see Usage Note at INSURE
4 certain to be true certain to be true: *One thing is sure: women voters will play an important role in the next election.* | a sure sign/indication *There are more crickets in the field – a sure sign that fall is coming.*
5 certain to happen/succeed certain to happen, succeed, or have a particular result: [sure to do sth] *Don't talk about Sheryl around Mom – it's sure to upset her.* | *Not having sex is the only sure way to avoid getting pregnant.* | a sure bet/thing (=something that is certain to happen, win, or succeed)
6 for sure a) INFORMAL certainly or definitely: *No one knows for sure how many people are infected.* b) SPOKEN used to emphasize that something is true: *He wasn't using drugs, that's for sure.* | *Aging may not be fun, but one thing's for sure (=this is true and certain): We're all doing it.* c) [C] SLANG used to agree with someone
7 sure of yourself confident in your own abilities and opinions, sometimes in a way that annoys other people: *Go ahead and try, if you're so sure of yourself.*
8 be sure to do sth used to tell someone to remember to do something: *Be sure to read all the directions carefully.*
9 be sure of sth to be confident and certain of having, getting, or keeping something, or to be confident and certain that something will happen: *Despite the criticism, Gray is still sure of his job.* | *For the first time in my life, I wasn't sure of my ability.*
10 sure thing SPOKEN used to agree to something: "*Could you give me that spoon?*" "*Sure thing.*"
11 to be sure used to admit that something is true, before saying something that is the opposite: *It was difficult, to be sure, but somehow we managed to finish the job.*
12 (as) sure as hell SPOKEN used to emphasize a statement: *I'm sure as hell not gonna do it.*
13 a sure footing a) a situation in which your feet are placed firmly so they cannot slide —see also

SURE-FOOTED b) a situation that is calm, and in which there is little danger of failure: *The government is trying to get the economy back on a sure footing.* —**sureness** *n.* [U]

sure² *adv.*
1 sure enough INFORMAL used to say that something did actually happen in the way that you said it would: *Sure enough, Mike managed to get lost.*

<table><tr><td colspan="2">SPOKEN PHRASES</td></tr></table>

2 used to say "yes" used to say "yes" to someone: "*Would you like some iced tea?*" "*Sure.*"
3 used as a reply used as a way of replying to someone when they thank you: "*Thanks for your help, Karen.*" "*Sure.*"
4 used to emphasize sth used to emphasize a statement: *It sure is hot out here.* | "*The turkey looks pretty good, doesn't it?*" "*It sure does.*" | *I sure hope they get there all right.*
5 used before statement used at the beginning of a statement admitting that something is true, especially before adding something very different: *Sure, he's cute, but I'm still not interested.*

sure-fire, surefire /ˌ. '.ˌ/ *adj.* [only before noun] INFORMAL certain to succeed: *a sure-fire winner* | *She says she has a surefire way to make a million dollars in real estate.*

sure-foot·ed, surefooted /ˌ. '.ˌ/ *adj.* able to walk without sliding or falling in a place where it is not easy to do this: *a sure-footed mountain goat*

sure·ly /ˈʃʊrli, ˈʃɚli/ *adv.* **1** [sentence adverb] used to show that you think something must be true, especially when people seem to be disagreeing with you: *Surely Beverly would be willing to help.* | *I thought surely you knew!* **2** OLD-FASHIONED certainly: *Such sinners will surely be punished.* **3** OLD-FASHIONED used to say "yes" to someone or to express agreement with them —see also slowly but surely (SLOWLY (2)) —see Usage Note at CERTAINLY

sur·e·ty /ˈʃʊrəti/ *n. plural* **sureties 1** [C,U] LAW money someone gives to make sure that someone will appear in court **2** [C,U] the condition of being sure about something, or something you are sure about **3** [C] LAW someone who will pay a debt, appear in court etc. if someone else fails to do so

surf

surfboard

surf¹ /sɔf/ *v.* **1** [I,T] to ride on ocean waves standing on a special board **2** surf the Net/Web to use a computer to look through information on the Internet for anything that interests you: *I can easily spend a whole evening surfing the Net.* —**surfer** *n.* [C] —see also SURFING

surf² *n.* [U] **1** the white substance that forms on top of ocean waves as they move toward the shore **2** surf 'n' turf also surf and turf a expression used in some restaurants for a meal of SHELLFISH, usually LOBSTER, and STEAK

sur·face¹ /ˈsɔfəs/ *n.* **1** [C] the outside or top layer of something: *the moon's surface* | [+ of] *the surface of the glass* | *Oil made colorful patterns on the surface of the water.* **2** the surface the qualities someone or something seems to have until you learn more about them: *On the surface he was charming and friendly, but secretly he hated them all.* | **below/beneath/ under the surface** *Anti-American feelings are never far beneath the surface in the region.* | **come/rise to the surface** *There's a dark side of Chuck's personality that sometimes comes to the surface.* **3** [C] an area on a desk, table etc. used for working: *Pour out the flour on a clean work surface.* **4** [C] TECHNICAL one of the sides of an object: *A cube has six surfaces.* —see also **scratch the surface** (SCRATCH¹ (5))

surface² *v.* **1** [I] if information or feelings surface, they become known about or easy to notice: *Rumors about the killings have begun to surface in the press.* **2** if someone or something surfaces, they suddenly appear somewhere, especially after being gone or hidden for a period of time: *Three years later, Toole surfaced again – this time in Cuba.* **3** [I] to rise to the surface of water: *Suddenly one whale surfaced right beside our boat.* **4** [T] to put a surface on a road

surface³ *adj.* [only before noun] **1** appearing to be true or real, but not representing what someone really feels or what something is really like; SUPER-FICIAL: *Beneath the surface calm, she felt insecure like everyone else.* | *a surface resemblance* **2** relating to the part of the Army, Navy etc. that travels by land or on the ocean, rather than by air or UNDERWATER: *the U.S. Navy Reserve Surface Fleet*

surface a·re·a /'.. ,.../ *n.* [C] the area of the outside of an object that can be measured

surface mail /'.. ,./ *n.* [U] the system of sending letters or packages to other countries by trucks, ships etc., rather than by airplanes

surface ten·sion /,.. '../ *n.* [U] the way the MOL-ECULES in the surface of a liquid stick together so that the surface is held together

surface-to-air mis·sile /,.. . . '. / *adj.* a MISSILE that is fired at airplanes from the land or from a ship

surf·board /'sɔrfbɔrd/ *n.* [C] a long piece of plastic, wood etc. that you stand on to ride over ocean waves for fun —see picture at SURF¹

sur·feit /'sɔrfɪt/ *n.* FORMAL **a surfeit of sth** an amount of something that is too large or more than you need: *There is a surfeit of managers in the company.*

surf·ing /'sɔrfɪŋ/ *n.* [U] **1** the activity or sport of riding over the waves on a special board: *When we were in Hawaii we **went surfing** every day.* **2 Web/ Net surfing** the activity of using a computer to look through the Internet for something that interests you —see also CHANNEL SURFING, WINDSURFING

surge¹ /sɔrdʒ/ *v.* [I] **1** [always + adv./prep.] to suddenly move forward very quickly: [+ **forward/ through** etc.] *The crowd of protesters surged out into the streets.* **2** to increase suddenly by a large amount: *Stocks surged Wednesday following positive economic reports.* **3** also **surge up** if a feeling surges or surges up, you begin to feel it very strongly: *A feeling of rage surged up inside him.* **4** [always + adv./prep.] if a large amount of water, electricity etc. surges, it moves very suddenly and powerfully

surge² *n.* [C usually singular] **1** a sudden increase in something such as demand, profit, interest etc.: [+ **of**] *Congress hopes cutting taxes will lead to a surge of economic growth.* | [+ **in**] *a surge in sales of the book* **2** a sudden strong feeling: [+ **of**] *Charles felt a surge of hope.* **3** a sudden powerful movement of a lot of water, electricity etc.: *a power surge* | [+ **of**] *A surge of flood water slammed into the car and shoved it off the road.* **4** a sudden movement of a lot of people: [+ **of**] *The city is preparing for a surge of visitors this summer.*

sur·geon /'sɔrdʒən/ *n.* [C] a doctor who does operations in a hospital —see also DENTAL SURGEON —see Usage Note at DOCTOR¹

Surgeon Gen·e·ral /,.. '.../ *n.* **the Surgeon General** the medical officer with the highest rank in the U.S. Public Health Service or a similar state organization

surge pro·tec·tor also **surge sup·pres·sor** /'. .,../ *n.* [C] a piece of electrical equipment that prevents a sudden large increase in electricity from affecting other equipment, especially computers, connected to it

sur·ger·y /'sɔrdʒəri/ *n. plural* **surgeries 1** [C,U] medical treatment in which a surgeon cuts open your body to repair or remove something inside: *heart surgery* | **have/undergo surgery on sth** *Lopez has undergone three surgeries on his knee in the past two years.* | **major/minor surgery** *Bertelli's heart condition required major surgery.* —see also COSMETIC SURGERY, PLASTIC SURGERY **2** [U] the part of medical science concerned with this type of treatment **3** [C,U] the place where operations are done in a hospital: *Dr. Bremner is in surgery right now.*

sur·gi·cal /'sɔrdʒɪkəl/ *adj.* [only before noun] **1** relating to or used for medical operations: *surgical instruments* | *a surgical procedure* **2** carefully planned to affect only a particular area or part of something, without affecting anything else: *The attack was carried out with surgical precision.* —**surgically** /-kli/ *adv.*: *The tumor was surgically removed.*

surgical strike /,... './ *n.* [C] a carefully planned quick military attack intended to destroy something in a particular place without damaging the surrounding area

Su·ri·nam, Suriname /,surɪ'nɑm/ a country on the northern coast of South America between Guyana and French Guiana —**Surinamese** /,surənə'miz/ *adj.*

sur·ly /'sɔrli/ *adj.* **surlier, surliest** in a bad mood, unfriendly, and often rude: *a staff of surly teenagers* —**surliness** *n.* [U]

sur·mise /sɔr'maɪz/ *v.* [T] FORMAL to guess that something is true using the information you know already: [**surmise (that)**] *I could only surmise from their behavior that he and Lila had met before.* —**surmise** *n.* [C,U]

sur·mount /sɔr'maʊnt/ *v.* [T] FORMAL **1** to succeed in dealing with a problem or difficulty; OVERCOME: *None of the problems are so bad that we can't surmount them.* **2** [usually passive] to be above or on top of something: *The arch is surmounted by a triumphant statue of Columbus.* —**surmountable** *adj.*

sur·name /'sɔrneɪm/ *n.* [C] FORMAL a LAST NAME

sur·pass /sɔr'pæs/ *v.* [T] **1** to be even better or greater than someone or something else: *In 15 years, China will likely surpass the U.S. as the world's largest market.* | **surpass expectations/hopes/ dreams** (=be better than you had expected, hoped etc.) **2 surpass yourself** FORMAL to do something even better than you have ever done before: *Stewart has surpassed himself with his latest novel.*

sur·pass·ing /sɔr'pæsɪŋ/ *adj.* [only before noun] LITERARY much better than that of other people or things: *a young woman of surpassing beauty*

sur·plice /'sɔrplɪs/ *n.* [C] a piece of clothing made of white material worn over other clothes by priests or singers in church

sur·plus¹ /'sɔrplʌs/ *n.* [C,U] **1** an amount of something that is more than what is needed or used: [+ **of**] *There is a slight surplus of oil worldwide.* **2** the amount of money that a country or company has left after it has paid for all the things it needs: *a budget surplus* **3** a TRADE SURPLUS

surplus² *adj.* **1** [only before noun] more than what is needed or used: *surplus grain* | *Anne bought a surplus Army Jeep.* **2 be surplus to needs/requirements etc.** FORMAL to not be necessary anymore

sur·prise¹ /sɔr'praɪz, sə'praɪz/ *n.*
1 **event** [C] an unexpected or unusual event: *Hal! What a surprise to see you here.* | *The school's closing* **came as a surprise to** (=was not expected by) *the whole community.* | *It should* **come as no surprise** (=be expected) *that Stuart has been given the vice president's job.* —see Usage Note at SHOCK²
2 **feeling** [C,U] the feeling you have when something unexpected or unusual happens: *Then –* **much to my surprise** (=in a way that surprised me) – *they offered me the job.* | **in/with surprise** *Gretchen looked up in surprise as Dale walked in.* | **get/have a surprise** *Dan got a nasty surprise when he turned on his computer – all the programs had been erased.*

S

3 catch/take sb by surprise a) to surprise or shock someone by happening in a way that is not expected: *Ernie's kiss took her by surprise.* **b)** to suddenly attack a place or an opponent when they are not ready: *The sudden attack took the government by surprise.*
4 gift/party etc. [C] an unexpected present, trip etc. which you give to someone or organize for them, often on a special occasion: *I've got a little surprise waiting for you at home.*
5 surprise! SPOKEN said when you show someone something that you know will surprise them, or when they arrive at a surprise party for them
6 surprise, surprise INFORMAL used when saying in a joking way that you expected something to happen or be true: *The study showed – surprise, surprise – that coffee makes you more alert.*
7 method [U] the use of methods which are intended to cause surprise: *The element of surprise is a useful tool in making an arrest.*

s w **surprise²** /sə'praɪzd/ *v.* [T] **1** to make someone feel surprised: *It was the tone of his voice that surprised me.* | *The report's conclusions have surprised many analysts.* | [sth does not surprise sb] *Russ's success doesn't surprise me at all.* | [it surprises sb (that)] *It surprised us all that Shannon did so well.* | [it surprises sb to see/find/know etc.] *Would it surprise you to hear that they're talking about getting married?* | *What surprised me the most was that she didn't seem to care.* **2** to find, catch, or attack someone when they are not expecting it, especially when they are doing something they should not be doing: *Police surprised Dyer in the parking lot of the building where he worked.*

surprise³ *adj.* [only before noun] not expected: *a surprise visitor* | **a surprise speech/move/attack etc.** *In a surprise announcement yesterday, the mayor said he would resign.*

s w **sur·prised** /sə'praɪzd/ *adj.* having a feeling of surprise: *I was so surprised when I saw you walk in!* | [+ at/by] *He was surprised at how angry Sabina sounded.* | [surprised (that)] *No one is really surprised that the negotiations failed.* | [surprised to see/hear/learn etc.] *Lucia's friends were surprised to learn she played the guitar.* | **I wouldn't be surprised if** *Jacobs won the tournament* (=I think it is likely this will happen). | **Don't be surprised if** *a lot of people end up losing their jobs* (=this is likely to happen). | **a surprised look/expression** *He smiled at me, noticing the surprised look on my face.*

surprise par·ty /.'. ,../ *n.* [C] a party that is given for someone who does not expect it, at which the guests shout "Surprise!" when that person arrives

sur·pris·ing /sə'praɪzɪŋ/ *adj.* unusual or unexpected: *There are a surprising number of taxis for such a small city.* | [it is surprising (that)] *It's not very surprising that Rose denies taking the money.* | [it is surprising how/what etc.] *It was surprising how much they were able to finish in a month.* | **hardly/scarcely surprising** *Linley's confession is hardly surprising, given all the evidence against her.* —see Usage Note at SHOCK²

sur·pris·ing·ly /sə'praɪzɪŋli/ *adv.* at a time or in a way that is surprising or unexpected: [+ adj./adv.] *It's surprisingly warm this morning.* | [sentence adverb] *Surprisingly, only a few Celtic words were taken into the English language.* | **Not surprisingly**, *Barbara left him when she found out about the affair.*

sur·real /sə'riːl/ *adj.* a situation or experience that is surreal is very strange, like something from a dream: *The party was a surreal mix of punk rockers and men in business suits.*

sur·re·al·ism /sə'riːə,lɪzəm/ *n.* [U] a style of 20th century art or literature in which the artist or writer connects unrelated images and objects in a strange way —**surrealist** *adj.*: *a surrealist painting* —**surrealist** *n.* [C]

sur·re·al·is·tic /sə,riːə'lɪstɪk/ *adj.* **1** seeming very strange because of a combination of many unusual,

unrelated events, images etc. **2** relating to surrealism —**surrealistically** /-kli/ *adv.*

sur·ren·der¹ /sə'rɛndə/ *v.* **1** [I] also **surrender yourself** to say officially that you want to stop fighting because you realize that you cannot win: *All three gunmen had surrendered by the end of the day.* | [surrender to sb] *After 74 days of battle, the army surrendered to the British.* **2** [T] to give your soldiers or land to an enemy after they have beaten you in a battle: [surrender sth/sb to sb] *Cornwallis surrendered his troops to Washington at Yorktown.* **3** [T] to give up something that is important or necessary, often because you feel forced to: *Ventura has agreed to surrender custody of all six of her children.* **4** [T] FORMAL to give something such as a ticket or a PASSPORT to someone in authority: [surrender sth to sb] *The court ordered Bond to surrender his passport to the authorities.*
surrender to sth *phr. v.* [T] to allow yourself to be controlled or influenced by something: *The government claims it will "surrender to the will of the people" and hold elections.*

surrender² *n.* [singular,U] **1** the act of saying officially that you want to stop fighting because you realize that you cannot win: *The allies demanded* **unconditional surrender** (=the act of accepting total defeat). **2** LITERARY the act of allowing yourself to be controlled or influenced by something: [+ to] *a surrender to the forces of evil*

sur·rep·ti·tious·ly /,sɜːəp'tɪʃəsli, ,sʌrəp-/ *adv.* FORMAL secretly, quickly, or quietly, so that other people do not notice: *Two boys were smoking cigarettes surreptitiously behind the bushes.* —**surreptitious** *adj.* —**surreptitiousness** *n.* [U]

sur·rey /'sɜːi, 'sʌri/ *n. plural* **surreys** [C] a light CARRIAGE with two seats, which was pulled by a horse and was used in past times

sur·ro·gate¹ /'sɜːəgɪt, 'sʌrə-/ *adj.* [only before noun] a surrogate person or thing is one that takes the place of someone or something else: *The old couple across the street see us like surrogate grandparents to me.* —see also SURROGATE MOTHER

surrogate² *n.* [C] **1** someone or something that takes the place of someone or something else: *The President's surrogates have been campaigning for him non-stop.* **2** a surrogate mother —**surrogacy** *n.* [U]

surrogate moth·er /,... '../ *n.* [C] a woman who has a baby for another woman who is unable to give birth, and then gives her the baby after it is born —**surrogate motherhood** *n.* [U]

sur·round¹ /sə'raʊnd/ *v.* [T] **1** to be all around someone or something: *She sat in an armchair, surrounded by her 12 cats.* | *Mountains surround the village on three sides.* **2 be surrounded by sb/sth** to have a lot of a particular type of people or things near you: *At work, I'm surrounded by people who don't know what they're doing.* **3** if police or soldiers surround a place, they arrange themselves in positions all the way around it: *We've got the place surrounded. Come out with your hands up.* **4** to be closely related to a situation or event: *A great deal of controversy has surrounded the new drug.* **5 surround yourself with sb/sth** to choose to have certain people or things near you all the time: *Surrounding himself with capable men, Romero worked hard to achieve his goals.* s v

surround² *n.* [C] an area around the edge of something, especially one that is decorated or made of a different material

sur·round·ing /sə'raʊndɪŋ/ *adj.* [only before noun] near or around a particular place: *the surrounding villages* | *Anders spent the afternoon hiking in the surrounding hills.*

sur·round·ings /sə'raʊndɪŋz/ *n.* [plural] the objects, buildings, natural things etc. that are around a person or thing at a particular time: *It took me a few weeks to get used to my new surroundings.* | *The mountaintop provides a spectacular view of Innsbruck and its surroundings.*

surround-sound, surround sound /.'. ./ *n.* [U] a system of four or more SPEAKERS (=pieces of equipment that sound comes out of) used with movies and television so that the sounds from the movie come from all directions —**surround-sound** adj. [only before noun] surround-sound speakers

sur·tax /'sɜtæks/ n. [U] an additional tax, especially on money you earn if it is higher than a particular amount

sur·veil /sə'veɪl/ v. **surveilled, surveilling** [T] SPOKEN, NONSTANDARD to watch a person or place carefully because they may be connected with criminal activities

sur·veil·lance /sə'veɪləns/ n. [U] **1** the act of carefully watching a person or place because they may be connected with criminal activities: *Police said the couple had been* **under surveillance** *for about five days.* | **a surveillance camera/tape etc.** (=equipment used for surveillance) **2** the act of carefully watching the military activities of another country to see what they are planning to do: **a surveillance plane/mission/satellite etc.** *The country refuses to allow U.S. surveillance flights over its territory.*

sur·vey¹ /'sɜveɪ/ n. plural **surveys** [C] **1** a set of questions that you ask a large number of people in order to find out about their opinions or behavior: **conduct/take a survey** *The university is conducting a survey of students' eating habits.* **2** an examination of an area of land in order to make a map of it: *a geological survey* **3** a general description or report about a particular subject or situation: [+ of] *a survey of modern English literature*

sur·vey² /sə'veɪ, 'sɜveɪ/ v. **surveys, surveyed, surveying** [T] **1** to ask a large number of people questions in order to find out their attitudes or opinions: *Southwest Junior High is surveying parents about their children wearing uniforms.* | *Of the 1007 people surveyed, 74% supported the decision.* **2** to look at or consider someone or something carefully, especially in order to form an opinion about them: *Kramer quickly surveyed the competition and decided he had nothing to worry about.* **3** to examine and measure an area of land and record the details on a map

survey course /'.. ,./ n. [C] a college course that gives an introduction to a subject for people who have not studied it before

sur·vey·or /sə'veɪə/ n. [C] someone whose job is to measure and record the details of an area of land

sur·viv·al /sə'vaɪvəl/ n. [U] **1** the state of continuing to live or exist: *Doctors say his chances of survival are not good.* | [+ of] *Rain forest destruction is threatening the cultural survival of the Yanomami people.* | **fight/struggle for survival** (=struggle or work hard in order to continue to exist) **2 survival of the fittest** a situation in which only the strongest and most successful people or things continue to exist

sur·viv·al·ist /sə'vaɪvəlɪst/ n. [C] someone who carefully prepares so that they will survive something bad that they think is going to happen, such as a war, especially by storing food and weapons —**survivalist** adj. —**survivalism** n. [U]

survival kit /.'.. ,./ n. [C] a set of things in a special container that you need to help you stay alive if you get hurt or lost

sur·vive /sə'vaɪv/ v. **1** [I,T] to continue to live after an accident, war, illness etc.: *Only 12 of the 140 passengers survived.* | *Hannah prayed every night that her husband would survive the war.* **2** [I,T] to continue to exist in spite of many difficulties and dangers: *A few pages of the original manuscript still survive.* | *None of our photos survived the fire.* | *Analysts expect the surviving airlines to be stronger than ever.* **3** [I,T] to continue to live normally and not be too upset by your problems: *I'll show everyone I can survive as a single parent.* **4** [T usually passive] to live longer than someone else, usually someone closely related to you: *Virginia is survived by three children and eight grandchildren.* —**survivable** adj. —**survivability** /sə,vaɪvə'bɪləti/ n. [U]

survive on sth phr. v. [T] to continue to live a normal life, even though you have very little money: *She is barely surviving on her monthly Social Security payments.*

sur·vi·vor /sə'vaɪvə/ n. [C] **1** someone or something that still exists in spite of having been almost

destroyed or killed: *There were no survivors among at least 261 people on board.* | **the sole/lone survivor** (=the only person who survives) **2** someone who is still alive when a close relative has died: *Miss Arthur never married and left no survivors.* **3** someone who manages to live their life without being too upset by problems: *Don't worry about Kurt; he's a survivor.*

sus·cep·ti·bil·i·ty /sə,sɛptə'bɪləti/ n. plural **susceptibilities 1** [C,U] the condition of being easily affected or influenced by something: [+ to] *Genetics may play a role in a person's susceptibility to alcohol abuse.* **2 sb's susceptibilities** [plural] someone's feelings that are easily hurt: *The policy has no regard for the susceptibilities of minority groups.*

sus·cep·ti·ble /sə'sɛptəbəl/ adj. **1** likely to suffer from a particular illness or be affected by a particular problem: [+ to] *The only other animal susceptible to polio is the monkey.* **2** easily influenced or affected by something: *a susceptible young boy* | [+ to] *Reporters are often susceptible to personal biases.* **3 susceptible of change/interpretation/analysis etc.** FORMAL able to be changed etc.: *The data is susceptible of different interpretations.*

su·shi /'suʃi/ n. [U] a type of Japanese food consisting of pieces of raw fish eaten with cooked rice

sus·pect¹ /sə'spɛkt/ v. **1** [T not in progressive] to think that someone is probably guilty of a crime: *Although they were in the area on the day of the robbery, no one suspected them.* | **[suspect sb of (doing) sth]** *Two of the bank's managers were suspected of fraud.* | *Burton was suspected of poisoning her husband.* **2** [T not in progressive] to think that something is probably true or likely, especially something bad: **[suspect (that)]** *I suspect it's going to be a pretty difficult day.* | *Inspectors suspected that chemical weapons were hidden somewhere on the site.* | *The Royal Newfoundland Constabulary said police did not* **suspect foul play** (=think that murder was likely) *in Noseworthy's death.* **3** [T not in progressive] to not trust someone, or doubt the truth of something: *We eventually began to suspect his loyalty.*

sus·pect² /'sʌspɛkt/ n. [C] someone who is thought to be guilty of a crime: *Two suspects were arrested today in connection with the robbery.*

suspect³ adj. **1** something that is suspect seems likely to have something wrong with it or may be illegal and should not be trusted, believed, or depended on: *The health benefits of the treatment are suspect.* | *Democrats have returned $1.5 million in suspect contributions.* **2** [only before noun] suspect packages, goods etc. look as if they contain something illegal or dangerous: *Police found the suspect package next to a trash can.*

sus·pect·ed /sə'spɛktɪd/ adj. **1** likely or believed to be something bad, illegal, or dangerous: *Four men were arrested for their suspected roles in the bombing.* **2 a suspected criminal/terrorist/spy etc.** someone the police believe is a criminal, TERRORIST, spy etc.

sus·pend /sə'spɛnd/ v. [T]
1 stop sth to officially stop something from continuing, especially for a short time: *Any store that has had its license suspended for more than 30 days will have to apply for a permit.*
2 from school/job etc. to make someone leave school, a job, or an organization temporarily, especially because they have broken the rules: **[suspend sb (from sth)]** *Knight was suspended from her job for not following safety guidelines.*
3 hang sth to hang something, especially something heavy, from something else: **[suspend sth from sth]** *Two large stainless steel frames were suspended from the ceiling.*
4 TECHNICAL **be suspended in water/air/space etc.** if something is suspended in a liquid or in air, it floats in it without moving much
5 be suspended in time to seem as if no change or progress has happened after a long period of time: *The town seemed suspended in time.*

6 suspend (your) disbelief to forget or allow yourself to forget that something such as a performance, movie etc. is not real or true: *The movie is a lot of fun, once you suspend disbelief.* —see also **suspend/ reserve judgment** (JUDGMENT (3))

suspended an·i·ma·tion /.,.. ..'../ n. [U] **1** a state in which someone's body processes are slowed down to a state almost like death **2** a feeling that you cannot do anything because you have to wait for what happens next

suspended sen·tence /.,.. '../ n. [C] a punishment given by a court in which the criminal will only go to prison if they do something else illegal within a particular period of time: *a two-year suspended sentence*

sus·pend·ers /sə'spɛndəz/ n. [plural] two bands of cloth that go over your shoulders and fasten to your pants to hold them up

sus·pense /sə'spɛns/ n. [U] a feeling of excitement or nervousness when you do not know what will happen next: *It is a classic story of love and suspense.* | **keep/hold sb in suspense** *Don't keep me in suspense – tell me what happened!* | **The suspense is killing me** (=used to say that the suspense is making you too nervous)! —**suspenseful** adj.: *a suspenseful story*

sus·pen·sion /sə'spɛnʃən/ n. **1** [U] the act of officially stopping something from continuing for a period of time: [+ of] *a suspension of military activities* **2** [C] the removal of someone from a team, job, school etc. for a period of time, especially to punish them: *Baker was given a two-week suspension for criticizing the coach.* **3** [U] equipment attached to the wheels of a vehicle which makes riding in the vehicle feel smoother, especially on bad roads **4** [C] TECHNICAL a liquid mixture containing very small pieces of solid material that have not combined with the liquid —compare COLLOID

suspension bridge /.'.. ,./ n. [C] a bridge that is hung from strong steel ropes attached to towers —see picture at BRIDGE[1] —see picture on page 1331

sus·pi·cion /sə'spɪʃən/ n. **1** [C,U] a feeling that someone is probably guilty of a crime or that something is wrong in a situation: [+ of] *Evidence was gathered that confirmed our suspicions of child abuse.* | *His unusual spending habits* **aroused** *the FBI's* **suspicions** (=made them think he was doing something wrong). | *Wheeler was arrested* **on suspicion of** *drunk driving* (=because police thought he was drunk). | *Hudson* **is under suspicion of** *committing the murders* (=police think he murdered someone).| **above/beyond suspicion** (=definitely not guilty of a crime) **2** [U] a feeling that you do not like or trust someone: *New people in our town were regarded* **with suspicion**. **3 I have a (sneaking) suspicion** also **I have my suspicions** to think you know something that is supposed to be secret: *I'm not sure who told you, but I have a sneaking suspicion it might be Brent.* **4 a suspicion of sth** LITERARY a very small amount of something seen, heard, tasted etc.: *Not one of them had a suspicion of fat on their bodies.*

sus·pi·cious /sə'spɪʃəs/ adj. **1** thinking that someone might be guilty of a crime or of doing something wrong, without being sure: *The tone of Danny's voice made Nancy suspicious.* | [+ of/about] *Police became suspicious of them.* **2** likely to be illegal or morally wrong: *Butler has been involved in several suspicious business deals.* | **under/in suspicious circumstances** *The king's father died under suspicious circumstances.* —see also SUSPECT[3] **3** feeling that you do not like or trust someone or something: [+ of] *Many people are suspicious of new technology.*

sus·pi·cious·ly /sə'spɪʃəsli/ adv. **1** in a way that shows you think someone has done something wrong or dishonest: *The soldiers watched us suspiciously.* **2 suspiciously quiet/nice/good/friendly etc.** too quiet, nice, good friendly etc. so that you think something might be wrong or illegal: *Be careful of Internet providers with suspiciously low prices.* | *Our soup*

tasted suspiciously sour. **3 sth looks/ sounds etc. suspiciously like sth** used to say that something looks, sounds etc. very much like something else, especially something worse: *His compliments often sound suspiciously like insults.*

Sus·que·han·nock /,sʌskwə'hænək/ a Native American tribe that formerly lived in the northeastern area of the U.S.

sus·tain /sə'steɪn/ v.
1 make sth continue FORMAL [T] to make something continue over a period of time; MAINTAIN: *More public works construction could help sustain job growth.* | *The program needs sustained government involvement to survive.*
2 food/water [T] to provide enough food, water etc. for people to stay alive: *The planet cannot sustain more than 6 billion people.*
3 sustain damage/injury/defeat etc. FORMAL to be damaged, hurt or defeated: *The driver sustained a severe head injury.*
4 strength [T] to make it possible for someone to stay strong or hopeful: *The thought of getting home was the only thing that sustained me in the hospital.*
5 (objection) sustained LAW used by a judge in a court of law to say that someone was right to object to another person's statement —opposite **(objection) overruled** (OVERRULE (2))
6 weight [T] FORMAL to hold up the weight of something: *The floor cannot sustain the weight of a piano.*
7 idea [T] FORMAL to support or prove an idea, argument etc.

sus·tain·a·ble /sə'steɪnəbəl/ adj. an action or process that is sustainable can continue or last for a long time: *sustainable economic growth*

sus·te·nance /'sʌstənəns/ n. [U] **1** FORMAL food that people, animals, or plants need to stay alive and healthy; NOURISHMENT: *The buffalo were the Plains Indians' main source of sustenance.* **2** LITERARY something that gives you strength or hope

su·ture /'sutʃə/ n. [C,U] the act of sewing a wound together, or a stitch used in this —**suture** v. [T]

SUV n. [C] a SPORT-UTILITY VEHICLE

Su·va /'suvə/ the capital city of Fiji

su·ze·rain·ty /'suzərənti, -reɪn-/ n. [U] the right of a country or leader to rule over another country —**suzerain** n. [singular]

svelte /svɛlt/ adj. someone who is svelte is thin and graceful: *a svelte young woman*

Sven·ga·li /svɛn'gali/ n. [C] a man who has the power to control people's minds and make them behave in a bad way

S.W., SW the written abbreviation of SOUTHWEST

swab[1] /swab/ n. [C] **1** a small piece of material used by a doctor or nurse to clean a wound or put medicine on someone's body: *a cotton swab* **2** a small amount of something that is taken from someone's body using a swab, in order to do a medical test

swab[2] v. **swabbed, swabbing** [T] **1** also **swab down** to clean something, especially the floors of a ship **2** also **swab out** to clean a wound with a piece of material

swad·dle /'swadl/ v. [T] OLD-FASHIONED to wrap a baby tightly to protect it

swaddling clothes /'.. ,./ n. [plural] OLD USE pieces of cloth wrapped around babies to protect them

swag /swæg/ n. **1** [C] a deep fold of material, especially in or above a curtain **2** [U] SLANG the goods stolen when someone is robbed —compare LOOT[2] (1)

swag·ger[1] /'swægə/ v. [I] DISAPPROVING **1** [always + adv./prep.] to walk in a way that shows that you are extremely confident: [+ down/in/out etc.] *J.D. swaggered over to the bar to get a drink.* **2** to talk or behave in a very proud way

swagger[2] n. [singular,U] a way of behaving or walking that is too confident or unusually confident: *Karlson is full of swagger when it comes to talking about his team.*

swain /sweɪn/ n. [C] LITERARY **1** a young man who is in love with a girl **2** a young man from the country

swal·low[1] /'swɑloʊ/ v.

1 food [I,T] to make food or drink go down your throat and to your stomach: *Alice swallowed her iced tea hurriedly.*

2 nervously [I] to make this type of movement with your throat, especially because you are nervous: *She swallowed twice, preparing to tell him the truth.*

3 believe/accept [T] INFORMAL to immediately believe a story, explanation etc. that is not actually true: *The story about his father being rich is hard to swallow* (=difficult to believe).

4 swallow your pride to do something even though it embarrasses you or you feel that you should not have to do: *He'll have to swallow his pride and apologize.* | *I swallowed my pride and did as I was told.*

5 feeling [T] to stop yourself from showing your feelings, especially bad feelings: *Mary tried hard to swallow her anger.* —see also **a bitter pill (to swallow)** (BITTER (7))

swallow sb/sth **up** *phr. v.* [T usually passive] **1** if something such as an amount of money or time is swallowed up by something else, a large amount or all of it is used by something else: *Housing costs swallowed up most of their income.* **2** if something such as a company or a country is swallowed up by a large company, organization etc. it becomes part of it and does not exist on its own anymore **3** to fill or use a lot of space: *Farmland is being swallowed up by new housing developments.*

swal·low[2] n. [C] **1** a small bird with a V-shaped tail and long pointed wings that flies quickly and gracefully **2** an act of making food go down your throat: *Glen took a long swallow of his drink.*

swal·low·tail /'swɑloʊˌteɪl/ n. [C] a black and yellow BUTTERFLY with two long thin parts at the bottom of its wings

swam /swæm/ the past tense of SWIM[1]

swa·mi /'swɑmi/ n. [C] a Hindu religious teacher

swamp[1] /swɑmp, swɔmp/ n. [C,U] a large area of low wet land near a river, where wild plants and trees grow —**swampy** adj.: *swampy ground* —compare BOG[1], MARSH —see picture on page 428

swamp[2] v. [T] **1** [usually passive] to suddenly give someone a lot of work, problems etc. to deal with: **[swamp sb with sth]** *We've been swamped with new orders all week.* **2** to suddenly cover something with a lot of water, especially in a way that causes damage: *The river jumped its banks and swamped hundreds of homes.*

swan /swɑn/ n. [C] a large white bird with a long graceful neck, that lives on rivers and lakes

swan dive /'. ./ n. [C] a DIVE[2] (4) into water, that starts with your arms stretched out from the sides of your body

swank·y /'swæŋki/ adj. **swankier, swankiest** INFORMAL, DISAPPROVING very fashionable, expensive, and designed to make people notice: *a swanky Manhattan jewelry store*

swan song /'. ./ n. [C] the last piece of work or last performance of a poet, painter etc.: *Foreman said his next fight would be his swan song.*

swap[1] /swɑp/ v. **swapped, swapping** [I,T] INFORMAL **1** to exchange something with someone, especially so that each of you gets what you want; TRADE[2]: **[swap sth for sth]** *The government refused to swap prisoners for hostages.* | **[swap sth with sb]** *I swapped hats with Mandy.* | **[swap sth for sth]** *I'll swap you my earrings for yours.* **2 swap places/seats** to let someone sit or stand in your place, so that you can have their place **3 swap stories (with sb)** to tell someone about things that have happened to you and listen to them tell you similar things: *Harvey and I spent the evening swapping travel stories.*

swap[2] n. [C] INFORMAL **1** [usually singular] an exchange of one thing for another: *a swap of arms for hostages* **2** a swap meet

swap meet /'. ./ also **swap** n. [C] an occasion when people meet to buy and sell used goods, or to exchange them

swarm[1] /swɔrm/ n. [C] **1** a large group of insects or other animals which move together, especially BEES: **[+ of]** *a swarm of locusts* **2** a crowd or large number of people: **[+ of]** *Swarms of tourists visit the resort every summer..*

swarm[2] v. [I always + adv./prep.,T] **1** if people swarm somewhere, they go there quickly as a very large crowd: *Reporters swarmed the area outside the courtroom.* | *Hundreds of refugees swarmed across the border.* **2** if insects or other animals swarm, they attack or surround someone or something: *Flies swarmed around him.*

swarm with sb/sth *phr. v.* also **be swarming with** sb/sth to be full of a moving crowd of people or animals: *The downtown area was swarming with police.*

swar·thy /'swɔrði, -θi/ adj. **swarthier, swarthiest** someone who is swarthy has dark skin and often looks slightly dangerous

swash·buck·ling /'swɑʃˌbʌklɪŋ, 'swɔʃ-/ adj. enjoying adventures and fighting, used especially in stories: *a swashbuckling ship captain* —**swashbuckler** n. [C]

swas·ti·ka /'swɑstɪkə/ n. [C] an ancient sign consisting of a cross with each end bent at 90°, the REVERSEd (REVERSE[1] (3)) form of which was used in the 20th century as a sign for the Nazi Party

SWAT /swɑt/ adj. **a SWAT team/unit** a Special Weapons and Tactics team/unit; a specially trained group of police who handle the most dangerous and violent situations

swat /swɑt/ v. **swatted, swatting** [T] to hit an insect to try to kill it —**swat** n. [C]

swatch /swɑtʃ/ n. [C] a piece of cloth that is used as an example of a type of material or its quality

swathe[1] /swɑθ, sweɪð/ also **swath** /swɑθ/ n. [C] FORMAL **1** a long band of cloth or color: *a swathe of beige cloth* **2** any large area of land that is different from the land on either side of it: *The fire had destroyed huge swathes of land.* **3 cut a swathe through sth** if someone or something cuts a swathe through a place, they affect or change it a lot: *Unemployment is cutting a wide swathe through the West.*

swathe[2] v. LITERARY **be swathed in sth** to be dressed, wrapped, or covered in something: *She was swathed in a black leather jacket.*

sway[1] /sweɪ/ v. **sways, swayed, swaying 1** [I,T] to move slowly from one side to another, or make something do this: *The boat swayed from side to side in the storm.* | *Mel swayed her hips in time with the music.* **2** [T] to influence someone who has not yet decided about something so that they change their opinion: *The judge was not swayed by her apology.*

sway[2] n. [U] **1** power to rule or influence people; control: *No one has more sway with Congress than the media.* | **hold/gain sway** (=have or get great power or influence) **2** swinging movement from side to side: *the constant sway of the small aircraft*

sway·backed /'sweɪbækt/ adj. **1** having a back that curves in too much **2** a swaybacked bridge, building etc has a top surface that curves down in the middle

Swa·zi·land /'swɑziˌlænd/ a country in southeast Africa between South Africa and Mozambique —**Swazi** n., adj.

swear /swɛr/ v. past tense **swore** past participle **sworn**

1 offensive language [I] to use offensive language, especially because you are angry: *I've never heard her swear.* | **[swear at sb/sth]** *I'm sorry I swore at you.* | **swear like a sailor/trooper** (=use very offensive language)

2 state the truth [T not in progressive] SPOKEN to emphasize that what you have said is the truth: **[swear (that)]** *Tim swore that he gave me the book yesterday.* | **I swear to God** *I didn't take anything out of your room.* | *She swears up and down* (=used to emphasize something) *the house is worth a hundred and sixty thousand.*

S

3 I could have sworn that... also **I could swear that...** SPOKEN used to say that you were sure about something, but now you are not sure: *I could've sworn that I'd met her before, but she didn't recognize me at all.*

4 serious/official promise [T] to make a very serious promise: [**swear (that)**] *Sam swore that he would always support them.* | [**swear to do sth**] *Do you swear to tell the whole truth?* | *All of us* **swore an oath** *to protect our country as military officers.* | *Bouchard refused to* **swear allegiance to** (=promise to be loyal to) *the queen.*

5 swear sb to secrecy/silence to make someone promise not to tell anyone what you have told them

swear by sth *phr. v.* [T not in progressive] INFORMAL to believe strongly that something is good or effective: *I have a friend who swears by this stuff as a cure for joint pain.*

swear sb ↔ **in** *phr. v.* [T usually passive] **1** to make someone promise publicly to be loyal to a country, official job etc.: [**swear sb in as sth**] *McCrory was sworn in as city manager last March.* **2** to make someone give an official promise in a court of law: *The jury had to be sworn in first.* —see also SWEARING-IN

swear off sth *phr. v.* [T] to promise to stop doing something that is bad for you: *I'm swearing off alcohol after last night!*

swear to sth *phr. v.* **1** [T] to say that something is true, especially in a court of law: *The maid saw her leave at 1:30, and she's willing to swear to it.* **2 not swear to (doing) sth** to be unwilling to say that something is true because you are not sure about it: *I think I parked across the street, but I wouldn't swear to it.*

swearing-in /ˌ. '. './ also **swearing-in cer·e·mo·ny** /ˌ. '. ˌ..../ n. [U] an official ceremony when someone promises publicly to be loyal to a country, do an official job well and honestly etc.: *The swearing-in took place at 12:05 p.m.*

swear word /'. ./ n. [C] a word that is considered to be offensive or shocking by most people

sweat[1] /swɛt/ v.
1 liquid from skin [I] to have liquid coming out through your skin, especially because you are hot or frightened: *It's so hot, you start sweating the minute you walk outside.* | **sweat heavily/profusely** (=sweat a lot) | *You're* **sweating like a pig** (=sweating a lot). | *After working in the field all day, I was* **sweating buckets** (=sweating a lot).
2 work [I] INFORMAL to work hard: *They sweated and saved for ten years to buy a house.* | [+ **over**] *The committee spent months sweating over the new budget.* | *Many people have* **sweated blood** (=worked very hard) *to build up the company.*
3 worry [I] INFORMAL to be anxious, nervous, or worried about something: *Let them sweat – I'll give them a decision tomorrow.* | *We were* **sweating bullets** (=worrying) *until we found out we wouldn't lose our jobs.*
4 don't sweat it SPOKEN used to tell someone not to worry about something: *Don't sweat it – you'll pass the test, no problem.*
5 don't sweat the small stuff SPOKEN used to tell someone not to worry about unimportant things
6 sweat equity the amount of value that something gains as a result of a lot of work: *The volunteer work that parents put into the school system was calculated to be worth $2.2 million in sweat equity.*
7 produce liquid [I] if something such as cheese sweats, liquid from inside appears on its surface

sweat sth **out** *phr. v.* [T] **1** [**sweat** sth ↔ **out**] to get rid of an illness by making yourself sweat a lot: *I was in bed for two days sweating out a fever.* **2** [**sweat** sth **out**] to worry while you wait for something to happen: *He was sweating out the judge's decision.* **3** [**sweat** sth **out**] to continue something until it is finished, even though it is difficult: *Steffes sweated out a win over Johnson.* **4 sweat it out** to do hard physical exercise: *They were sweating it out in*

the gym. **5 sweat sth out of sb** INFORMAL to find out information from someone by asking lots of questions and threatening them: *Finally, they sweated the other names out of him.*

sweat sth ↔ **off** *phr. v.* [T] to lose weight by sweating: *I sweated off a few pounds in the steam room.*

sweat[2] n.
1 liquid on skin [U] liquid that comes out through your skin when you are hot, frightened, or doing exercise: *Sweat poured off his face.*
2 work up a sweat to work very hard so that you are sweating: *Can you bring us a drink? We're working up a sweat out here.*
3 break a sweat to begin to sweat while you are working or exercising hard: *The Lakers were ahead 11 to 2 before they even broke a sweat.*
4 sweats [plural] INFORMAL a SWEAT SUIT or the pants from a sweat suit
5 break into a sweat also **break out in a sweat** INFORMAL to become very frightened, worried, or nervous about something: *As the market share dropped, company executives broke out in a sweat.*
6 no sweat SPOKEN used to say that you can do something easily: *"I'll finish this by tomorrow, no sweat."*
7 a (cold) sweat nervousness or fear that makes you sweat, even though you are not hot: *I woke up from the nightmare in a cold sweat.*
8 have/get the sweats to sweat because you are sick
9 work [singular] hard work, especially when it is boring or difficult
10 the sweat of sb's brow LITERARY the hard effort that someone has made in their work

sweat·band /'swɛtbænd/ n. [C] **1** a narrow band of cloth that you wear around your head or wrist to stop sweat from running down when you are running, playing a sport etc. **2** a narrow piece of cloth that you wear sewn or stuck in the inside of a hat

sweat·er /'swɛtɚ/ n. [C] a piece of warm wool or cotton clothing for the top half of your body, that has long SLEEVES

sweat gland /'. ./ n. [C] a small organ under your skin that produces sweat

sweat pants /'. ./ n. [plural] soft thick pants, worn especially for sports

sweat·shirt /'swɛt-ʃɚt/ n. [C] a piece of thick cotton clothing with long SLEEVES, worn on the top half of your body, especially for playing sports

sweat·shop /'swɛt-ʃɑp/ n. [C] a small business or factory, especially an illegal one, where people work hard in bad conditions for very little money

sweat sock /'. ./ n. [C] a type of sock that you wear when you play sports

sweat suit /'. ./ n. [C] a set of clothes made of thick soft material, worn especially for sports

sweat·y /'swɛti/ adj. **sweatier, sweatiest 1** covered with SWEAT[2]: *sweaty palms* **2** smelling like sweat: *sweaty clothes* **3** a can, glass, or food that is sweaty has drops of liquid on its surface: *a sweaty can of beer* **4** too hot or difficult so that you SWEAT[1]: *a sweaty job*

Swe·den /'swidn/ a country on the PENINSULA of Scandinavia in northern Europe —**Swede** n. [C] —**Swedish** adj., n. [U]

sweep[1] /swip/ v. past tense and past participle **swept**
1 clean sth [T] to clean the floor or ground using a BROOM, or remove dirt, dust etc. by doing this: *I just finished sweeping the kitchen floor.* | [**sweep sth off/out/up etc.**] *Could you sweep the snow off the patio for me?*
2 push sth somewhere [T always + adv./prep.] to move something to a particular place or in a particular direction with a brushing or swinging movement: *Linda swept the coins into her purse.*
3 wind/waves etc. [I always + adv./prep.,T] if winds, waves, storms etc. sweep something somewhere or sweep through, across etc. a place, they move quickly and with a lot of force: *Strong waves swept the boy out into the surf.* | [+ **across/through** etc.] *A series of tornadoes swept through Kansas.*

4 **become popular/common** [I always – adv./prep.,T] if an idea, feeling, or activity sweeps a group of people or sweeps across, over etc. a group, it quickly becomes very popular or commonly used: [+ **across/through** etc.] *Interest in the show is sweeping across the nation.* | **sweep the nation/country/state etc.** *Rumors of his resignation have swept the capital.*

5 **guilt/anger/relief etc. sweeps over sb** if a feeling sweeps over you, you feel it immediately: *As I tried to straighten up, nausea swept over me.*

6 **group** [I always + adv./prep.] if a group of people or animals sweep somewhere, they quickly move there together: [+ **through/along** etc.] *Soldiers swept through the city looking for rebels.*

7 **politics** [I,T] to win an election easily and in an impressive way: *The Democrats had swept the fall elections and were about to take control of the Senate.* | *Herera was swept into office two years ago.* | **sweep to power/victory** *Reformers like Mr. Yakamoto swept to power by promising change.*

8 **sports** [T] to win all of the games in a series of games against a particular team: *Houston swept Orlando to become the NBA Champions.*

9 **sweep sb away/along etc. a)** if a crowd sweeps someone along or away it forces them to move in the same direction it is moving in: *I got swept along by the crowd of commuters.* **b)** if a feeling, idea, or problem sweeps you along or away, you are so involved or interested in it that you forget about other things: *All of Paris was swept away in celebration.*

10 **person** [I always + adv./prep.] if someone sweeps somewhere, they move quickly and confidently, especially because they are impatient or like to look important: [+ **into/through** etc.] *Ms. Chao had a habit of sweeping into class ten minutes late.*

11 **sweep sb off their feet** to make someone feel suddenly and strongly attracted to you in a romantic way: *Donald absolutely swept me off my feet.*

12 **look** [I always + adv./prep.,T] if lights or someone's eyes sweep an area, they move or look quickly around it: [+ **over/across/around** etc.] *Lufkin's eyes swept over the audience.* | *The helicopter's searchlights swept the streets below.*

13 **form a curve** [I always + adv./prep.,T] to form a long curved shape: [+ **down/around** etc.] *A large staircase swept up to the second floor.*

14 **sweep sth under the rug/carpet** to try to keep something a secret, especially something you have done wrong: *The committee cannot deal with sexual harassment by sweeping it under the rug.*

15 **sweep your hair back** if you sweep your hair back, you pull it back from your face, especially so that it stays in that style: [+ **in/into**] *Kerry swept her hair back into a bun.*

sweep sth ↔ **aside** *phr. v.* [T] to refuse to pay attention to something someone says: *Doubts about the drug's safety were swept aside.*

sweep away *phr. v.* **1** [T **sweep** sth ↔ **away**] to completely destroy something or make something disappear: *Half of the town was swept away by the hurricane.* **2** [T **sweep** sb ↔ **away**] to make someone so interested or involved in something that they forget about other things: *We couldn't help being swept away by Bette's enthusiasm.*

sweep up *phr. v.* **1** [I,T **sweep** sth ↔ **up**] to clean a place using a special brush, or to pick up dirt, dust etc. in this way: *Sweep up the dirt as soon as you can.* | *I'll just sweep up before I go.* **2** [T **sweep** sb ↔ **up**] to pick someone up in one quick movement: *Joe swept her up in his arms and kissed her.* **3 sweep your hair up** to pull your hair back away from your face so that it is on top of your head, especially so that it stays in that style

sweep² *n.* [C] **1** a long swinging movement of your arm, a weapon etc.: *The whale swam away with great sweeps of its tail.* **2** [usually singular] a search or attack that moves over a large area: *Police made a sweep of the area to arrest drug dealers.* **3** a series of several games that one team wins against another team: *The Giants completed their four-game sweep of Atlanta.* **4 the sweep of sth a)** a long curved line or area of land: [+ **of**] *the sweep of the hills in the distance* **b)** the quality that an idea, plan, piece of

writing etc. has of considering or affecting many different and important things: *The sweep of the court's decision could affect all car manufacturers.* **5** a CHIMNEY SWEEP —see also **clean sweep** (CLEAN¹ (10))

sweep·er /'swipɚ/ *n.* [C] **1** someone or something that sweeps: *a road sweeper* **2** a SOCCER player who plays in a position behind all of the other defending players on a team

sweep·ing /'swipɪŋ/ *adj.* **1** affecting many things, or making an important difference to things: **sweeping changes/cuts/laws etc.** *The computer industry has undergone sweeping changes.* **2** lacking knowledge or consideration of facts or details: *You're always making **sweeping generalizations** about women drivers.* **3** [only before noun] including a lot of information about a particular subject, especially about events that happened at different times and places: *a sweeping novel* **4 a sweeping view of sth** a view in which you can see for a long way: *a sweeping view of the coast*

sweep·ings /'swipɪŋz/ *n.* [plural] dirt, dust etc. that is left to be swept up

sweeps /swips/ *n.* **sweeps month/period etc.** also **the sweeps** a period of time during the year when TV stations try to find out which shows are the most popular

sweep·stakes /'swipsteɪks/ *n.* [C usually singular] **1** a type of competition in which you have a chance to win a prize if your name is chosen **2** a type of BETting in which the winner gets all of the money risked by everyone who BETS **3** a competition, election, argument etc. in which you cannot guess who will win or get the most advantages: *Three new candidates have declared their intentions to enter the presidential sweepstakes.*

sweet¹ /swit/ *adj.*
1 **taste** having a taste like sugar: *The pie is a little too sweet for me.* | *sweet, juicy peaches* —compare BITTER (4), SOUR¹ (1)

2 **character** kind, gentle, and friendly: *Fran is such a sweet person.* | *It was **sweet of you** to get me a gift.*

3 **children/small things** looking pretty and attractive; CUTE: *Jessica looks so sweet in that hat.*

4 **feelings** making you feel happy and satisfied: *Revenge is sweet.* | *We've lost to them four times, so beating them was really sweet.*

5 **Sweet!** SPOKEN used to say that you think that something is very good: *"I got four tickets to the concert." "Sweet!"*

6 **a sweet deal** a business or financial deal in which you get an advantage, pay a low price etc.: **give/get a sweet deal** *I got a sweet deal on the car.*

7 **do sth in your own sweet time/way** to do something when you want to and in exactly the way that you want to, without caring whether other people approve: *Harris does everything in his own sweet time.*

8 **smell** having a pleasant smell; FRAGRANT: *sweet-smelling flowers*

9 **sound** nice to listen to: *a sweet singing voice*

10 **have a sweet tooth** to like things that taste like sugar: *Danny's always had a sweet tooth.*

11 **be sweet on sb** OLD-FASHIONED to be very attracted to or in love with someone

12 **sweet nothings** things that you say to someone that you have a romantic relationship with: *He whispered sweet nothings in her ear while they danced.*

13 **sweet sixteen** INFORMAL used to describe a girl when she is 16 years old —see also **home sweet home** (HOME¹ (14)), **short and sweet** (SHORT¹ (12)), SWEETNESS —**sweetly** *adv.*

sweet² *n.* **1 sweets** [plural] sweet food or candy: *I don't eat sweets very often.* **2 (my) sweet** OLD-FASHIONED used when speaking to someone you love

sweet-and-sour /ˌ. . '. ˌ/ *adj.* [only before noun] sweet-and-sour food in Chinese cooking has both sweet and sour tastes together: *sweet-and-sour pork*

S

sweet·bread /'switbrɛd/ n. [C] OLD-FASHIONED a small organ from a sheep or young cow, used as food

sweet·corn /'swit¬kɔrn/ n. [U] a type of corn that people eat

sweet·en /'swit¬n/ v. **1** [I,T] to make something sweeter, or become sweeter: *Add just enough sugar to sweeten the fruit slightly.* **2** [T] INFORMAL to make an offer or deal better by giving something more: *Mattel Inc. is expected to sweeten its offer.* | *The company is trying to **sweeten the pot** (=make the offer better) by offering stock options.* **3** [T] LITERARY to make someone kinder, gentler etc.: *Old age had not sweetened her.*

sweetened con·densed milk /ˌ.. .'. ./ n. [U] CONDENSED MILK

sweet·en·er /'swit¬n-ɚ, -nɚ/ n. **1** [C,U] a substance used to make something taste sweeter: *Most "diet" foods are full of artificial sweeteners.* **2** [C] INFORMAL something that you give to someone to persuade them to do something: *These tax cuts are just a pre-election sweetener.*

sweet gum /'. ./ n. [C] a tree with hard wood and groups of seeds like PRICKLY balls, common in North America

s w **sweet·heart** /'swithɑrt/ n. [C] **1** a way of addressing someone you love: *Sweetheart, I've got good news for you.* **2** an informal way of talking to a woman you do not know, which most women find offensive **3** sweetheart deal/arrangement/contract an agreement that is unfair because it gives people who know each other well or who have a lot of influence an unfair advantage: *Members of the council had arranged a sweetheart deal with CTS.* **4** OLD-FASHIONED the person that you love

s w **sweet·ie** /'switi/ n. [C] **1** INFORMAL a way of addressing someone you love **2** something or someone that is small, pretty, and easy to love: *Look at that little dog – isn't he a sweetie!*

sweetie pie /'... ./ n. [C] SPOKEN a way of addressing someone you love

sweet·ness /'switnɪs/ n. [U] **1** how sweet something is **2** be all sweetness and light to be very pleasant and friendly: *The negotiations were not all sweetness and light.*

sweet pea /'. ./ n. **1** [C] a climbing plant with sweet-smelling flowers in various colors **2** [singular] a way of addressing someone you love, used especially when speaking to children

sweet po·ta·to /'. .,../ n. [C] a sweet-tasting vegetable that looks like a red potato and is yellow inside —compare YAM (2)

sweet roll /'. ./ n. [C] a small sweet PASTRY

sweet spot /'. ./ n. [C] **1** the area on a RACKET, BAT, or CLUB that is most effective in hitting a ball **2** INFORMAL a situation or position in which you can be successful

sweet-talk /'. ./ v. [T] INFORMAL to try to persuade someone to do something by talking to them in a nice way: *Don't try to sweet-talk me.* —**sweet talk** n. [U]

sweet-tem·pered /ˌ. '..◂/ adj. having a character that is kind and gentle

sweet wil·liam /ˌswit 'wɪlyəm/ n. [C,U] a plant with sweet-smelling flowers

swell¹ /swɛl/ v. past tense **swelled** past participle **swollen**
1 size [I] also **swell up** to gradually increase in size: *Put some ice on your knee before it swells up.* | *The doors always swell in the winter.*
2 amount/number [I,T] to gradually increase in amount or number, or to make something increase in this way: *The river was swelling rapidly with the constant rain.* | *White-collar workers are swelling the ranks of (=increasing the number of) the opposition party.*
3 swell with pride/anger/confidence etc. to feel very proud, angry, confident etc.: *Cartwright was swelling with pride as he discussed his department's achievements.*
4 shape [I,T] also **swell (sth) out** to get or give something a full round shape: *The wind swelled the sails.*
5 sound [I] LITERARY to become louder: *Music swelled around us.*
6 ocean [I] to move suddenly and powerfully up —see also GROUNDSWELL, **swell the ranks** (RANK¹ (7)), SWOLLEN²

swell² n. **1** [C] a single long wave in the ocean away from the shore: *The ships rolled as much as 45 degrees in the **heavy swells** (=very large swells).* **2** [C usually singular] an increase in sound level, especially in music; CRESCENDO **3** [U] the roundness and fullness of something: *the swell of her breasts* **4** [C] LITERARY a large number or amount of something: *The scandal has produced swells of protest against him.* —see also GROUNDSWELL **5** [C] OLD-FASHIONED a fashionable or important person

swell³ adj. OLD-FASHIONED very good: *You look swell!*

swell·ing /'swɛlɪŋ/ n. **1** [C] an area of your body that has become larger than normal, because of illness or injury: *My doctor examined the swelling on my back.* **2** [U] the condition of having swelled: *Nothing seemed to stop the swelling.*

swel·ter /'swɛltɚ/ v. [I] to feel too hot and uncomfortable: *Farm workers sweltered in the fields.*

swel·ter·ing /'swɛltərɪŋ/ adj. too hot, and making you feel uncomfortable: *the sweltering summer sun*

swept /swɛpt/ the past tense and past participle of SWEEP

swept-back /'. ./ adj. **1** hair that is swept-back is brushed backward from your face **2** swept-back wings on an aircraft form the shape of the letter "V"

swerve

swerve /swɚv/ v. [I] **1** to make a sudden sideways movement while moving forward, especially in order to avoid hitting something: *She swerved to avoid the cyclist.* | *[+ across/off etc.] The truck swerved into a median.* **2** [usually in negatives] FORMAL to change from an idea, course of action, purpose etc.: *[+ from] McLaren would never swerve from the truth.* —**swerve** n. [C]

swift¹ /swɪft/ adj. **1** happening quickly and immediately: *Their victory was swift and decisive.* **2** [only before noun] moving, or able to move, very fast: *a swift runner* **3** be swift to do sth to do something as soon as you can, without any delay: *The U.N. was swift to condemn the attack.* **4** sb is not too swift INFORMAL used to say that someone is not very intelligent when you do not want to say this directly: *Eric's not too swift, is he?* **5** swift of foot LITERARY able to run fast —**swiftly** adv. —**swiftness** n. [U]

swift² n. [C] a small brown bird that has pointed wings, flies very fast, and is similar to a SWALLOW

Swift /swɪft/, **Jon·a·than** /'dʒɑnəθən/ (1667–1745) an Irish writer famous for his book "Gulliver's Travels" who wrote many other SATIRICAL stories and articles

swig /swɪg/ v. **swigged, swigging** [T] INFORMAL to drink something in large mouthfuls, especially from a bottle: *Jack swigged the last of his coffee and left.* —**swig** n. [C] *I took a few swigs of the whiskey.*

swill¹ /swɪl/ v. [T] INFORMAL to drink something in large amounts: *He does nothing but swill beer all day.*

swill² n. [U] food for pigs, mostly made of unwanted pieces of human food

swim¹ /swɪm/ v. past tense **swam** past participle **swum** present participle **swimming 1 a)** [I,T] to move yourself through water using your arms, legs etc., or to cross an area of water by doing this: *I didn't learn to swim until I was ten years old.* | *Let's go swimming this afternoon.* | *Dad swims fifty laps in the pool every morning.* **b)** [T] to use a particular style of movement when you move through water in this way: *I don't like swimming the breaststroke.* **2** [I] **a)** if your head swims, you start to feel confused or DIZZY: *The incense was so sweet and thick that it made my head swim.* **b)** if something you are looking at swims, it seems to move because you feel DIZZY: *The numbers swam before my eyes.* **3 be swimming in sth** to be covered by a lot of liquid: *The only Italian food we'd ever heard about was a bowl of spaghetti swimming in tomato sauce.* **4 swim against the tide/current/stream** to do or say different things from what most people do, because you do not mind being different: *Gordon's ability to swim against the political tide and still win elections is impressive.* —opposite **swim with the tide/current/stream** —see also **sink or swim** (SINK¹ (13))

swim² n. [C] a period of time that you spend swimming: *Let's go for a swim.* —see also **in the swing/swim of things** (SWING² (5))

swim club /'. ./ n. [C] **a)** a place where people can go to swim, take swimming lessons, and where swim teams compete against other clubs **b)** a team from this type of place

swim·mer /'swɪmɚ/ n. [C] **1** someone who swims, especially in competitions: **a good/strong swimmer** (=someone who swims well) **2** someone who is swimming: *On weekends, there's not enough room for all the boats and swimmers.*

swim·ming /'swɪmɪŋ/ n. [U] the sport of swimming: *I've been involved in swimming since I was six.*

swimming cap /'. ./ n. [C] a type of tight-fitting hat that you wear when you swim to keep your hair dry

swimming hole /'. ./ n. [C] INFORMAL a POND (=area of water like a small lake) where you can go swimming

swim·ming·ly /'swɪmɪŋli/ adv. OLD-FASHIONED **go swimmingly** if something you plan goes swimmingly, it happens without problems

swimming pool /'. ,. / n. [C] a structure that has been built and filled with water for people to swim in; POOL¹

swimming suit /'. ./ n. [C] a SWIMSUIT

swimming trunks /'. ./ n. [plural] a piece of clothing like SHORTS, worn by men for swimming

swim·suit /'swɪmsut/ n. [C] a piece of clothing worn for swimming

swim team /'. ./ n. [C] a team that competes in swimming competitions: *the Olympic swim team*

swim·wear /'swɪmwɛr/ n. [U] clothing worn for swimming

swin·dle /'swɪndl/ v. [T] to get money from someone by deceiving them: **[swindle sb out of sth]** *The two men swindled the company out of $130,000.* —**swindle** n. [C]

swine /swaɪn/ n. plural **swine** [C] **1** LITERARY OR OLD USE a pig **2** INFORMAL someone whose behavior is extremely rude or DISGUSTING: *Pay no attention to this swine.* —see also **cast pearls before swine** (CAST¹ (22))

swine·herd /'swaɪnhɚd/ n. [C] OLD USE someone who takes care of pigs

swing¹ /swɪŋ/ v. past tense and past participle **swung 1** [move backward/forward] [I,T] to move backward and forward from a particular point, or to make something do this: *The only sound was the creak of a sign swinging in the wind.* | *The speedometer needle swung wildly back and forth.* | *We began the workout by swinging our arms.*

2 [move in a curve] [I always + adv./prep.,T] to move quickly in a smooth curve, or to make something move like this: *The door swung open slowly.* | *She swung the ax, hitting the log squarely in the middle.* | **[swing sth through/into/around etc. sth]** *Pat swung the bag over his shoulder and left.*

3 [vehicle] [I always + adv./prep.,T always + adv./prep.] if a vehicle or its driver swings in a particular direction, it turns or moves in a curve in that direction: *The car swung north towards the Arizona mountains.* | *The driver swung the Cadillac off the road with a squeal of tires.*

4 [hit sb/sth] [I,T] **a)** to move your arm to try to hit someone: **[swing at sb]** *Wright swung at me and missed.* | *Bennett kicked a leg out, then swung a fist that didn't make contact.* **b)** to move a baseball BAT or GOLF CLUB in order to try to hit the ball: **[swing at sth]** *The pitch was low, and Pinero didn't swing at it.*

5 [emotions/opinions] [I,T] if emotions or opinions swing or something swings them, they change quickly to the opposite of what they were: *His opinions would often swing from one extreme to the other.*

6 [arrange sth] [T] SPOKEN to make arrangements for something to happen, although it takes a lot of effort to do this: *I still have a lot to do, but if I can swing it this weekend, let's play tennis.*

7 [play] [I] to sit on a SWING² (1) and make it move backward and forward by bending your legs: *We used to have contests to see who could swing the highest.*

8 sb swings both ways INFORMAL used to say that someone is BISEXUAL

9 [sex] [I] SLANG to go to parties that are specially arranged so that men and women in COUPLES can have sex with people from other couples: *Do you swing?*

10 swing for sth OLD-FASHIONED to be killed by HANGING as a punishment for a crime —see also **there's not enough room to swing a cat** (ROOM¹ (6)), **the swinging sixties** (SWINGING (2))

swing around phr. v. **1** [I,T **swing sth ↔ around**] to turn around quickly or make something turn around quickly, to face in the opposite direction: *The machine swung around and dumped its load onto the pile.* | *Kendra swung the boat around and headed for the dock.* **2** [I] if a wind swings around, it changes direction suddenly and quickly: *The wind has swung around to the north-east.*

swing by phr. v. [I,T] INFORMAL to visit a place or person for a short time, usually for a particular purpose: *I told Tom I might swing by later.* | **[swing by sth]** *I'll swing by the grocery store on my way home.*

swing² n.

1 [seat with ropes] [C] a seat hanging from ropes or chains, that children sit on and make move forward and backward through the air: *Hannah loves to play on the swings.* —see picture on page 423

2 [movement] [C] a swinging movement with your arm, leg etc., especially made in order hit something: *Apparently a customer took a swing at (=tried to hit) the salesman.*

3 [baseball/golf] [singular] the swinging movement of your arms and body when you hit the ball in baseball or GOLF: *Ed said he could help me with my swing.*

4 [change] [C] a large change, especially in opinions, ideas, or feelings: *There has been a huge swing in public opinion on the issue.* —see also **a mood swing** (MOOD (5))

5 be in the swing/swim of sth also **get into the swing/swim of sth** INFORMAL to be or become fully involved in an activity or situation: *By the third year of law school, I was really in the swing of things academically.*

6 [music] [U] JAZZ music of the 1930s and 1940s, usually played by a big band, or a dance done to this music —see also **in full swing** (FULL¹ (10))

swing·er /'swɪŋɚ/ n. [C] OLD-FASHIONED **1** someone who is very active and fashionable, and goes to many parties, NIGHTCLUBs etc. **2** someone who has sexual relationships with many people

swing·ing /'swɪŋɪŋ/ adj. OLD-FASHIONED **1** exciting, fun, and enjoyable: *a swinging party* **2 the swinging sixties** the years 1960 to 1969, thought of as a time when there was an increase in social and sexual freedom

swinging door /'. ,. / n. [C] a door that can be

pushed open from either side, and swings shut by itself

swing set /'. ./ n. [C] a tall metal frame with SWINGS² (1) hanging from it, for children to play on

swing shift /'. ./ n. [singular] workers who work from 3 or 4 o'clock in the afternoon until 11 or 12 o'clock at night, or the system of working these times

swipe¹ /swaɪp/ v. 1 [T] INFORMAL to steal something: *Someone broke into my car and swiped my stereo.* 2 [I,T] to hit or to try to hit someone or something by swinging your arm very quickly: *Jody swiped me across the face.* | [+ at] *A lineman swiped at Bartkowski's arm as he threw the ball.* 3 [T] to pull a special plastic card through a machine to record information on a computer: *You need to swipe your card to get in the building.*

swipe² n. [C] 1 a public criticism of someone or something in a speech or in writing: *Dole took a swipe at Clinton's foreign policy.* 2 an attempt to hit someone or something: *Jones was arrested for taking a swipe at* (=trying to hit) *one of the policemen.*

swirl¹ /swəl/ v. 1 [I,T] to turn around quickly in a twisting circular movement, or make something do this: *The ice cubes swirled down the drain.* | *Swirl butter into the sauce.* 2 [I] if something such as a story swirls, lots of people hear about it and tell it to other people: *Reports that the company is in trouble continue to swirl.*

swirl² n. [C] 1 a swirling movement: [+ of] *a swirl of dust* 2 a twisting circular pattern: [+ of] *The sheets were covered in bright swirls of color.*

swish /swɪʃ/ v. 1 [I,T] to move or make something move quickly through the air with a smooth quiet sound: *We watched the train swish past the empty platforms.* | *The horse swished its tail.* 2 [T] to move liquid around in your mouth 3 [T] to win points in a basketball game by throwing the ball through the basket in a way that makes a smooth quiet sound: *McCoy swished a three-point shot with four seconds left.* —**swish** n. [singular]

Swiss¹ /swɪs/ adj. coming from or relating to Switzerland

Swiss² n. [plural] **the Swiss** the people of Switzerland

Swiss chard /,. './ n. [U] CHARD

Swiss cheese /,. './ n. [U] a type of cheese with holes in it

Swiss steak /,. './ n. [C,U] a thick flat piece of BEEF covered in flour and cooked in a SAUCE

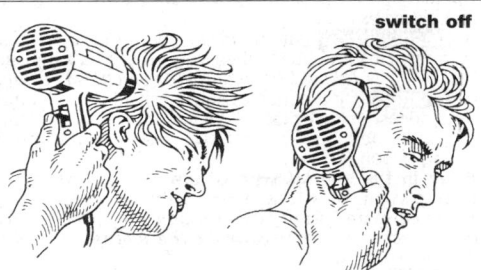

switch off

switch on/turn on   switch off/turn off

switch¹ /swɪtʃ/ v. 1 [I,T] to change from doing or using one thing to doing or using another: [+ to] *Phoenix has switched to plastic pipes in its water system.* | [**switch sth to/from/away etc.**] *The department has switched from film to computerized photographs.* | *Students here often switch between English and Spanish.* | *Webber eventually switched his attention from musicals to movies.* | **switch seats/places/chairs etc.** (=move from one seat, place etc. to another) 2 [T] to replace an object with a similar object, especially secretly or accidentally:

We must have switched umbrellas by mistake. 3 [T] to change the way a machine operates by using a switch or button: [**switch sth to sth**] *Switch the oven to "broil."* 4 [I] to help someone you work with who needs time away from the job by agreeing to work particular hours for them if they do the same for you: [**switch with sb**] *I need to find someone to switch with me on Friday.*

switch off phr. v. 1 [I,T **switch** sth ↔ **off**] if you switch off a machine, electric light, radio etc. or if a machine does this, it turns off: *Switch off the radio before you go to bed.* | *The TV suddenly switched off.* 2 [I] INFORMAL to stop listening or paying attention: *I found myself switching off during the meeting.*

switch on phr. v. [I,T **switch** sth ↔ **on**] if you switch on a machine, electric light, radio etc. or if a machine does this, it turns on: *Every time I switch on the TV, there's another figure skating show.* | *The tape recorder switches on when you begin talking.*

switch over phr. v. 1 [I] to change completely from one method, product etc. to another: [+ **from/to**] *NASA has switched over to a new backup power system.* 2 **switch over to/from sth** to change from one television or radio station to another: *Switch over to Channel 7 – I want to watch the news.* —see Usage Note at OPEN²

switch² n. [C] 1 the part on a light, radio, machine etc. that starts or stops the flow of electricity when you push it up or down: *a light switch* | *Where's the power switch?* | **flip/flick/throw a switch** (=turn on something with a switch) 2 a complete change from one thing to another: *The switch to a free market economy will not be easy.* | *Some of the farms have made a switch from agricultural to dairy production.* 3 **make the switch** [usually passive] to exchange one object for another similar object, especially secretly or accidentally: *The switch was made when the painting was being moved to its new location.* 4 a thin stick of wood that bends easily, used in past times for hitting children as a punishment or for making animals move

switch·back /'swɪtʃbæk/ n. [C] a road that goes up a steep hill in a series of sharp turns, or one of these turns

switch·blade /'swɪtʃbleɪd/ n. [C] a knife with a blade inside the handle which springs out when you press a button

switch·board /'swɪtʃbɔrd/ n. [C] a central system used to connect telephone calls in an office building, hotel etc., or the people who operate the system: *switchboard operators* —see also **jam the switchboard** (JAM¹ (6))

switch·er·oo /,swɪtʃə'ru/ n. [singular] INFORMAL a situation when someone secretly SWITCHes one object for a similar object

switch·hit·ter /'. ,../ n. [C] a baseball player who can hit the ball well from either side of HOME PLATE —**switch-hit** v. [I]

Swit·zer·land /'swɪtsələnd/ a country in western Europe, surrounded by France, Germany, Austria, and Italy —see also SWISS

swiv·el¹ /'swɪvəl/ v. 1 also **swivel sth around** [I,T] to turn around a central point, or make something do this: *The satellite has difficulty swiveling its antenna toward Earth.* 2 also **swivel around** [I] if someone swivels, they turn around quickly: *Kovitsky swiveled around to look at her.*

swivel² n. [C] an object that joins two parts of something in such a way that one or both parts can turn around freely

swivel chair /'.. ./ n. [C] a chair that can turn around to face a different direction without the legs moving —see picture at CHAIR¹

swiz·zle stick /'swɪzəl ,stɪk/ n. [C] a small stick for mixing drinks

swol·len¹ /'swoʊlən/ the past participle of SWELL¹

swollen² adj. 1 a part of your body that is swollen is bigger than usual because of illness or injury: *My knee's still really swollen from the accident.* 2 a river that is swollen has more water in it than usual

swoon /swun/ v. [I] 1 to feel so much excitement, happiness, or admiration that you feel physically weak: [+ **over**] *Everyone from young girls to aged grandmothers swooned over Elvis.* **2** OLD-FASHIONED to become unconscious and fall down; FAINT[2] —**swoon** *n.* [singular]

swoop /swup/ *v.* [I usually + adv./prep.] **1** if a bird or aircraft swoops it moves suddenly and steeply down through the air, especially to attack something: [+ **in/down** etc.] *Suddenly a bat swooped down, just missing my head.* **2** to make a sudden attack or ARREST: [+ **in/on** etc.] *On July 3rd, the FBI swooped in, closing down three illegal factories.* —**swoop** *n.* [C] —see also **at/in one fell swoop** (FELL[3])

swoosh /swuʃ, swuʃ/ *v.* [I] to make a sound by moving quickly through the air —**swoosh** *n.* [C]

sword /sɔrd/ *n.* [C] **1** a weapon with a long pointed blade and a handle, used in past times **2 beat/turn swords into plowshares** to stop fighting or thinking about war and start living peacefully **3 a/the sword of Damocles** the possibility of something bad or dangerous happening at any time: *The treaty hung like a sword of Damocles over French politics.* **4 put sb to the sword** OLD USE to kill someone with a sword —see also **cross swords (with sb)** (CROSS[1] (12))

sword·fish /'sɔrd,fɪʃ/ *n.* [C] a large fish with a very long pointed upper jaw

sword·play /'sɔrdpleɪ/ *n.* [U] the activity of fighting with swords: *There's plenty of action and swordplay in the movie.*

swords·man /'sɔrdzmən/ *n.* [C] someone who fights with a sword, or someone who is skilled in this

swords·man·ship /'sɔrdzmən,ʃɪp/ *n.* [U] skill in fighting with a sword

swore /swɔr/ the past tense of SWEAR

sworn[1] /sworn/ the past participle of SWEAR —see also **I could have sworn that...** (SWEAR (3))

sworn[2] *adj.* **1 sworn statement/testimony/deposition etc.** a statement, TESTIMONY etc. that someone makes after officially promising to tell the truth: *The sworn statements of Mitchell and Cryer were never made public.* **2 sworn enemies** two people or groups of people who will always hate each other **3 sworn duty** something that you have to do because you have promised to do it

swum /swʌm/ the past participle of SWIM[1]

swung /swʌŋ/ the past tense and past participle of SWING[1]

syb·a·rit·ic /,sɪbə'rɪtɪk/ *adj.* wanting or enjoying expensive pleasures and comforts —**sybarite** /'sɪbə,raɪt/ *n.* [C]

syc·a·more /'sɪkə,mɔr/ *n.* [C] an eastern North American tree with broad leaves, or the wood of this tree

syc·o·phant /'sɪkəfənt/ *n.* [C] someone who praises important or powerful people in order to get something from them: *Reese's mistake was to surround himself with sycophants.* —**sycophantic** /,sɪkə'fæntɪk/ *adj.*

Syd·ney /'sɪdni/ the largest city in Australia, which is the capital city of the state of New South Wales

syl·lab·ic /sɪ'læbɪk/ *adj.* of or based on syllables: *a syllabic writing system* | *syllabic sounds*

syl·la·ble /'sɪləbəl/ *n.* [C] a word or part of a word which contains a single vowel sound

syl·la·bus /'sɪləbəs/ *n.* plural **syllabuses** or **syllabi** /-baɪ/ [C] a plan that states exactly what students at a school or college should learn in a particular class —compare CURRICULUM

syl·lo·gism /'sɪlə,dʒɪzəm/ *n.* [C] a statement with three parts, the first two of which prove that the third part is true, for example "all men will die; Socrates is a man; therefore Socrates will die" —**syllogistic** /,sɪlə'dʒɪstɪk/ *adj.*

sylph /sɪlf/ *n.* [C] LITERARY **1** an attractively thin and graceful girl or woman **2** an imaginary female spirit that, according to some stories, lived in the air

sylph·like /'sɪlf,laɪk/ *adj.* LITERARY attractively thin and graceful: *sylphlike models*

syl·van /'sɪlvən/ *adj.* LITERARY in the forest or belonging to the forest

sym- /sɪm/ *prefix* together or with; used instead of SYN- before the letters "b," "m," or "p"

sym·bi·o·sis /,sɪmbi'oʊsɪs, -baɪ-/ *n.* [U] **1** a relationship between people or organizations that depend on each other equally **2** TECHNICAL the relationship between two different living things that depend on each other for particular advantages —**symbiotic** /-'ɑtɪk/ *adj.: a symbiotic relationship*

sym·bol /'sɪmbəl/ *n.* [C] **1** a picture, shape, color etc. that has a particular meaning or represents an idea: *The cross is the most important symbol in Christianity.* | [+ **of**] *A hammer is often used in art as a symbol of authority.* **2** a letter, number, or sign that represents a sound, an amount, a chemical substance etc.: *"H" is the scientific symbol for hydrogen.* **3** someone or something that represents a quality or idea: *Rollins has emerged as a symbol of modern jazz at its finest.* —see also SEX SYMBOL, STATUS SYMBOL

sym·bol·ic /sɪm'bɑlɪk/ also **sym·bol·i·cal** /sɪm'bɑlɪkəl/ *adj.* **1** if an event, speech, action etc. is symbolic, it represents something important, but does not really change anything: *The President's trip to Russia was mostly symbolic.* | *We feel that wearing a red ribbon to support AIDS victims is an important symbolic gesture.* **2** using pictures, shapes, colors etc. to represent ideas or qualities: *a symbolic painting* **3** representing an idea or quality: [+ **of**] *The low test scores are symbolic of how bad our public schools are.* —**symbolically** /-kli/ *adv.*

sym·bol·ism /'sɪmbə,lɪzəm/ *n.* [U] **1** the use of pictures, shapes, colors etc. to represent an idea: *religious symbolism* **2** an idea or quality that something represents: *The symbolism was obvious, as the rebel leader removed bullets from his gun in front of hundreds of cameras.*

sym·bol·ize /'sɪmbə,laɪz/ *v.* [T] if one thing, event etc. symbolizes an idea or quality, it represents the idea or quality: *Wedding rings symbolize a couple's commitment to each other.* | *To people in the community, Hernandez's death symbolizes years of mistreatment by police.* —**symbolization** /,sɪmbələ'zeɪʃən/ *n.* [U]

sym·met·ri·cal /sə'mɛtrɪkəl/ also **sym·met·ric** /sə'mɛtrɪk/ *adj.* a thing or design that is symmetrical has two halves that are exactly the same in shape, size, and arrangement: *The columns on either side of the door were perfectly symmetrical.* —opposite ASYMMETRICAL —**symmetrically** /-kli/ *adv.*

sym·me·try /'sɪmətri/ *n.* [U] **1** the quality of being symmetrical: *We were impressed by the symmetry and the elegance of the city.* **2** the quality that a situation has when two events or actions seem to be balanced or equal in some way: *There was a certain symmetry to coming back to New York, where I started my artistic life all those years ago.*

sym·pa·thet·ic /,sɪmpə'θɛtɪk/ *adj.* **1** willing to listen to someone's problems, or able to understand someone's problems: *Dr. Williams is such a sympathetic person.* | [+ **to/toward**] *I'm sympathetic to parents who are worried about what their children see on television.* | *Taler says she tried to offer the student a sympathetic ear* (=willingness to listen to someone else's problems). **2** [not before noun] willing to give approval and support to an idea or plan: [+ **to/toward**] *Senator Capp is very sympathetic to environmental issues.* **3 a sympathetic figure/character** LITERARY someone in a book, play etc. who most people like —**sympathetically** /-kli/ *adv.*

sym·pa·thize /'sɪmpə,θaɪz/ *v.* [I] **1** to feel sorry for someone because you understand their problems: *I sympathize, but I don't know how to help.* | [+ **with**] *I can sympathize with those who have lost loved ones.* **2** to support someone's ideas or actions: [+ **with**] *The public has sympathized with the firefighters' request for a raise.*

sym·pa·thiz·er /'sɪmpə,θaɪzɚ/ *n.* [C] someone who supports the aims of an organization or political party but does not belong to it: *In the 1940s, my uncle was accused of being a Nazi sympathizer.*

sym·pa·thy /'sɪmpəθi/ *n. plural* **sympathies 1** [U, plural] the feeling of being sorry for someone who is in a bad situation and understanding how they feel: *I'm not asking for sympathy.* | **have/feel sympathy for sb** *Dad has a lot of sympathy for people with drug problems.* | *I have absolutely no sympathy for students who cheat on tests.* | *Many sent handwritten cards offering sympathy to the Cosby family.* | *He's just trying to play on your sympathy* (=make you feel sorry for him in order to gain an advantage) *so you'll give him money.* | **our/my sympathies are with sb** *Our sympathies are with the families of the victims.* | **our/my sympathies go out to sb** *My sympathies go out to the boy's mother.* | *Hollis sent his sympathies* (=sent a message saying how sorry he was) *to the grieving widow.* **2** [U, plural] belief in or support for a plan, idea, or action, especially a political one: *Willard is in sympathy with many Green Party issues.* | **have/express sympathy for** *Sullivan expressed sympathy for the striking federal workers.* | *The majority of people had declared that their sympathies lay with the allied powers.* | **communist/Republican/left-wing etc. sympathies** *Matheson is known for his pro-socialist sympathies.* **3** [U] a feeling that you understand someone because you are similar to them

sym·pho·ny /'sɪmfəni/ *n. plural* **symphonies** [C] **1** a long piece of music usually in four parts, written for an ORCHESTRA: *Tchaikovsky's Symphony No. 6* **2** also **symphony orchestra** a large group of CLASSICAL (2) musicians led by a CONDUCTOR, or the building where they play: *the St. Louis Symphony* | *The symphony is looking for a new conductor.* —**symphonic** /sɪm-'fɑnɪk/ *adj.*

sym·po·si·um /sɪm'pouziəm/ *n. plural* **symposiums** or **symposia** /-ziə/ [C] **1** a formal meeting in which people who know a lot about a particular subject have discussions about it: [+ **on**] *a symposium on women's health* **2** a group of articles on a particular subject collected together in a book

symp·tom /'sɪmptəm/ *n.* [C] **1** a physical condition which shows that you have a particular illness: *The tablets help relieve cold symptoms.* | [+ **of**] *Common symptoms of diabetes are weight loss and fatigue.* **2** a sign that a serious problem exists: [+ **of**] *The disappearance of jobs is a symptom of a deeper socioeconomic change.*

symp·to·mat·ic /,sɪmptə'mætɪk/ *adj.* **1** **be symptomatic of sth** if a situation or type of behavior is symptomatic of something, it shows that a serious problem exists: *Poor grades could be symptomatic of a learning disorder.* **2** TECHNICAL related to medical symptoms —**symptomatically** /-kli/ *adv.*

syn- /sɪn/ *prefix* together; WITH: *a synthesis* (=combining of separate things)

syn·a·gogue /'sɪnə,gɑg/ *n.* [C] a building where Jewish people meet for religious WORSHIP

syn·apse /'sɪnæps, sɪ'næps/ *n.* [C] TECHNICAL the space between two nerve cells in your body, across which information travels to make muscles, GLANDS etc. work

sync, synch /sɪŋk/ *n.* **in sync a)** two or more parts of a machine, process, group etc. that are in sync are well-matched or working well together: *The two mechanisms have to work in sync, otherwise the machine shuts down.* | [+ **with**] *The soundtrack wasn't in sync with the picture, so we left the theater.* **b)** able to understand the way another person or group thinks or behaves: [+ **with**] *The NBA is the sports league most in sync with young lifestyles.* **c)** one idea or thing that is in sync with another is closely related to it: *The group's harsh, industrial-punk sound is in sync with the album's theme of betrayal.* —opposite **out of sync**

syn·chro·nic·i·ty /,sɪŋkrə'nɪsəti/ *n.* [U] the fact of two or more events happening at the same time or place, when these events are believed to be connected in some way

syn·chro·nize /'sɪŋkrə,naɪz/ *v.* **1** [T] to arrange for two or more actions to happen at exactly the same time: *Our company must synchronize production with marketing campaigns.* **2** **synchronize your watches** to make two or more watches or clocks show exactly the same time **3** [I,T] if the sound and action of a movie synchronize or if you synchronize them, they go at exactly the same speed —**synchronization** /,sɪŋkrənə'zeɪʃən/ *n.* [U]

synchronized swim·ming /,... '.. ./ *n.* [U] a sport in which swimmers move in patterns in the water to music

syn·chro·nous /'sɪŋkrənəs/ *adj.* if two or more things are synchronous, they are working or moving together at the same speed

syn·co·pa·tion /,sɪŋkə'peɪʃən/ *n.* [U] a RHYTHM in a line of music in which the BEATS[2] that are usually weak are emphasized —**syncopated** /'sɪŋkə,peɪtɪd/ *adj.*: *syncopated rhythms*

syn·co·pe /'sɪŋkəpi/ *n.* [U] TECHNICAL **1** the loss of consciousness when someone faints **2** a way of making a word shorter by leaving out sounds or letters in the middle of it, for example changing "cannot" to "can't"

syn·di·cate[1] /'sɪndəkɪt/ *n.* [C] a group of people or companies who join together in order to achieve a particular aim: [+ **of**] *a syndicate of banks*

syn·di·cate[2] /'sɪndɪ,keɪt/ *v.* **1** [T usually passive] to arrange for written work, photographs etc. to be sold to a number of different newspapers, magazines etc.: *His column is syndicated throughout America.* **2** [I,T] to form into a syndicate

syn·di·ca·tion /,sɪndɪ'keɪʃən/ *n.* [U] **be in syndication** if a TV show is in syndication, different TV stations pay to show it

syn·drome /'sɪndroʊm/ *n.* [C] **1** TECHNICAL a set of physical or mental problems considered together as a disease: *Herniated disk syndrome is more common in males.* —see also DOWN'S SYNDROME, PREMENSTRUAL SYNDROME, SUDDEN INFANT DEATH SYNDROME **2** a set of qualities, events, or behaviors that is typical of a particular type of problem: *"The underdog syndrome" is a belief that things are beyond your control.*

syn·er·gy /'sɪnədʒi/ *n.* [U] TECHNICAL the additional energy or greater effect that is produced by two or more people combining their energy and ideas

syn·od /'sɪnəd/ *n.* [C] an important meeting of church leaders to make decisions concerning the church

syn·o·nym /'sɪnə,nɪm/ *n.* [C] a word with the same meaning or almost the same meaning as another word in the same language, such as "sad" and "unhappy" —compare ANTONYM

syn·on·y·mous /sɪ'nɑnəməs/ *adj.* **1** a situation, quality, idea etc. that is synonymous with something else is the same or nearly the same as another: [+ **with**] *Nixon's name has become synonymous with political scandal.* **2** two words that are synonymous have the same or nearly the same meaning —**synonymously** *adv.*

syn·op·sis /sɪ'nɑpsɪs/ *n. plural* **synopses** /-siz/ [C] a short description giving the general idea and the most important facts from something longer, for example a book; SUMMARY[1]

syn·tac·tic /sɪn'tæktɪk/ *adj.* TECHNICAL related to syntax: *The two sentences have the same syntactic structure.* —**syntactically** /-kli/ *adv.*

syn·tax /'sɪntæks/ *n.* [U] TECHNICAL **1** the way words are arranged in order to form sentences or phrases, or the rules of grammar which control this —compare MORPHOLOGY (1) **2** the rules that describe how words and phrases are used in a computer language

syn·the·sis /'sɪnθəsɪs/ *n.* **1** [C] something such as a substance or an idea, made by combining different things: [+ **of**] *a synthesis of scientific knowledge and religious faith* **2** [U] the act of combining separate things, ideas etc. into a complete whole: [+ **of**] *synthesis of thyroid hormone in the body* | *The NOAA provides information about water quality problems through synthesis of existing information, techniques, and policies.* **3** [C] the production of the sounds of speech or music by electronic means

syn·the·size /'sɪnθə,saɪz/ *v.* [T] **1** to produce something by combining different things or substances:

The spider can synthesize several different silk proteins. | *DDT is a pesticide that was first synthesized in 1874.* **2** to combine several different ideas, experiences, or information in order to make something new: *It is possible to synthesize all your personal and career needs to find out which career will give you the most satisfaction.*

syn·the·sized /ˈsɪnθəˌsaɪzd/ *adj.* **1** produced by combining different things, especially making something similar to a natural product by combining chemicals: *synthesized hormones* **2** synthesized sounds are produced using a machine such as a synthesizer: *synthesized dance music*

syn·the·siz·er /ˈsɪnθəˌsaɪzɚ/ *n.* [C] an electronic instrument that produces the sounds of various musical instruments —see also SPEECH SYNTHESIZER

syn·thet·ic /sɪnˈθɛtɪk/ *adj.* produced by combining different artificial substances, rather than being naturally produced: *The jacket is made of synthetic materials.* —**synthetically** /-kli/ *adv.*

syn·thet·ics /sɪnˈθɛtɪks/ *n.* [plural] chemical substances that are made to be like natural substances, especially cloth: *In the 1970s, synthetics began taking the place of wool.*

syph·i·lis /ˈsɪfəlɪs/ *n.* [U] a very serious disease that is passed from one person to another during sexual activity

Syr·i·a /ˈsɪriə/ a country in west Asia, south of Turkey and west of Iraq —**Syrian** *n., adj.*

sy·ringe[1] /səˈrɪndʒ/ *n.* [C] an instrument for taking blood from someone's body or putting liquid, drugs etc. into it, consisting of a hollow plastic tube and a needle

syringe[2] *v.* [T] to clean something with a syringe

syr·up /ˈsɚəp, ˈsɪrəp/ *n.* [U] **1** thick sticky liquid made from sugar, eaten on top of or mixed with other foods: *chocolate syrup* | *maple syrup* **2** sweet liquid, especially sugar and water that are combined: *Drain the syrup from the can of peaches.* **3** medicine in the form of a thick sweet liquid: *cough syrup* —see picture at MEDICATION

syr·up·y /ˈsɚəpi, ˈsɪrəpi/ *adj.* **1** thick and sticky like syrup or containing syrup: *syrupy canned fruits* **2** too nice or kind in a way that seems insincere: *a syrupy speech about world peace*

S W **sys·tem** /ˈsɪstəm/ *n.* [C]
1 1
1 related parts a group of related parts that work

together as a whole for a particular purpose: *Florida's public school system* | *a car alarm system* | *the digestive system*

2 method an organized set of ideas, methods, or ways of working: *the U.S. legal system* | [+ **of/for**] *Ben has a unique system for filing documents.*

3 computers a group of computers that are connected to each other: *Our communications software tends to crash the system.* —see also OPERATING SYSTEM

4 sb's system a phrase meaning someone's body, used when you are talking about its medical or physical condition: *I need to get some of the alcohol out of my system before I can even think about another party.*

5 get sth out of your system INFORMAL to get rid of bad or upsetting feelings: *I couldn't get the feelings of guilt out of my system.*

6 the system INFORMAL all of the official rules and powerful groups or organizations that seem to control your life and limit your freedom: *Harris has spent his entire career fighting the system.* | *Gomez tried to beat the system* (=avoid or break the rules) *by moving his money between his bank and investment accounts.*

sys·tem·at·ic /ˌsɪstəˈmætɪk/ *adj.* organized carefully and done thoroughly: *A systematic approach is needed for proper diagnosis.* | *Analysis of the data should have been more systematic.* —**systematically** /-kli/ *adv.*

sys·tem·a·tize /ˈsɪstəməˌtaɪz/ *v.* [T] to put facts, numbers, ideas etc. into a particular order —**systematization** /ˌsɪstəmətəˈzeɪʃən/ *n.* [U]

sys·tem·ic /sɪˈstɛmɪk/ *adj.* TECHNICAL affecting the whole of a system: *Corruption in the police force is systemic.* | *a systemic bacterial infection* —**systemically** /-kli/ *adv.*

systems an·a·lyst /ˈ.. ˌ.../ *n.* [C] someone whose job is to study a company's computer needs and provide them with the appropriate SOFTWARE and equipment —**systems analysis** /ˌ.. ˈ.../ *n.* [U]

system soft·ware /ˈ.. ˌ../ *n.* [U] computer PROGRAMS that make up the OPERATING SYSTEM (=a system that controls the way a computer works) —compare APPLICATION (2)

S

T

T, t /ti/ *plural* **T's, t's** *n.* [C] **1** the 20th letter of the English alphabet **2 to a T** INFORMAL perfectly or exactly: *He matched the description to a T.*

T.A. *n.* [C] the abbreviation of TEACHING ASSISTANT

tab¹ /tæb/ *n.* [C]
1 money you owe **a)** the amount of money that you owe for a meal in a restaurant, drinks in a bar etc.: *Our tab for the meal came to just $48.* | *I'll put it on your tab and you can pay tomorrow.* **b)** an amount of money that someone owes, especially an amount that has gradually become very large: *While they were gone, their son ran up a $40,000 tab in long distance calls.*
2 pick up the tab to pay for something, especially when it is not your responsibility to pay: *Airlines will have to pick up the tab for new safety regulations.*
3 keep (close) tabs on sb/sth INFORMAL to watch someone or something carefully to check what they are doing: *He keeps tabs on everyone in the building.*
4 on a can/box etc. a small piece of metal, plastic, or paper that you pull to open a container
5 small piece of paper/plastic a small piece of paper or plastic you attach to a page, FILE etc. in order to find it easily
6 in typing a TAB KEY
7 drugs SLANG a solid form of the illegal drug LSD: *a tab of acid*

tab² **1** [I] to press the TAB KEY on a computer or TYPE-WRITER to move forward to a particular place on a line of text **2** [T usually passive] to choose someone or something for an activity or AWARD: *Twenty-year-old Tavarez was tabbed to play the leading role.*

Ta·bas·co /tə'bæskou/ also **tabasco sauce** /.'.. ,./ *n.* [U] TRADEMARK a very SPICY red liquid made from CHILIS, used in cooking

tab·by /'tæbi/ *n.* [C] a cat with orange, gray, or brown marks on its fur —**tabby** *adj.*

tab·er·na·cle /'tæbə,nækəl/ *n.* [C] **1** a church or other building used by some Christian groups **2 the tabernacle** the small tent in which the ancient Jews kept their most holy objects **3** a box in which holy bread and wine are kept in Catholic churches

tab key /'. ./ *n.* [C] a button on a computer or TYPE-WRITER that you push, in order to move forward to a particular place on a line of TEXT

ta·ble¹ /'teɪbəl/ *n.*
1 furniture a piece of furniture with a flat top supported by legs: *the dining room table* | *Could you help me set the table* (=put knives, forks etc. on a table before a meal)? | *Gary smiled at both of us as the waiter cleared the table* (=took the empty plates, glasses etc. off a table). | **reserve/book a table** (=ask a restaurant to keep a table available for you) —see also CARD TABLE, COFFEE TABLE, HEAD TABLE
2 list a list of numbers, facts, or information arranged in rows across and down a page: *Table 18 shows the relationship between education and voting practices.* —see also TABLE OF CONTENTS, MULTIPLICA-TION TABLE, TIMES TABLE
3 turn the tables (on sb) to change a situation completely so that someone loses an advantage and you gain one: *Her record speed has turned the tables on Runyan, the defending champion.*
4 at the table when sitting at a table eating a meal: *It's not polite to blow your nose at the table.*
5 on the table an offer, idea etc. that is on the table has been officially suggested and someone is considering it: *Kelly hopes to have a proposal on the table within four months.*
6 under the table INFORMAL money that is paid under the table is paid secretly and illegally: *They*

paid him under the table so he wouldn't have to pay taxes.* | *payments made under the table to local offi-cials* —see also **drink sb under the table** (DRINK¹ (2))

table² *v.* [T] **table a bill/measure/proposal etc.** to leave an offer, idea etc. to be dealt with in the future

tab·leau /'tæblou/ *n. plural* **tableaux** /-blouz/ [C] **1** a place or situation that is like a picture or a scene from a play: *By day the town is a small tableau of white-washed homes.* **2** a group of people who do not speak or move arranged on stage to look like a painting

ta·ble·cloth /'teɪbəl,klɔθ/ *n.* [C] a cloth used for covering a table

table lamp /'.. ,./ *n.* [C] a small lamp that is made to be used on a table

ta·ble·land /'teɪbəl-lænd/ also **tablelands** *n.* [C] TECHNICAL a large area of high flat land; PLATEAU¹

table lin·en /'.. ,../ *n.* [U] all the cloths used during a meal, such as NAPKINS and tablecloths

table man·ners /'.. ,../ *n.* [plural] the way in which someone eats their food, considered according to the usual rules of social behavior about eating

table of con·tents /,.. '../ *n.* [C] a list at the begin-ning of a book that tells you the order and the page numbers of the CHAPTERS

table salt /'.. ./ *n.* [U] salt in the form of extremely small white grains, commonly used for adding taste to food

ta·ble·spoon /'teɪbəl,spun/ *n.* [C] **1 a)** a special spoon used for measuring small amounts in cooking, equal to 3 TEASPOONS or 15 ml **b)** also **tablespoonful** the amount a tablespoon can hold **2** a large spoon commonly used for eating or serving food —see picture at SPOON¹

tab·let /'tæblɪt/ *n.* [C] **1** a small round hard piece of medicine; PILL: *vitamin C tablets* **2** a set of pieces of paper for writing on that are glued together at the top **3** a flat piece of stone or metal with words cut into it

table ten·nis /'.. ,../ *n.* [U] an indoor game played on a table by two or four players who hit a small plastic ball to each other across a net; PING-PONG

ta·ble·top¹, table top /'teɪbəl,tɑp/ *n.* [C] the flat top surface of a table

tabletop², table-top *adj.* [only before noun] done, existing, or kept on a table: *a table-top stereo*

ta·ble·ware /'teɪbəlwɛr/ *n.* [U] the plates, glasses, knives etc. used when eating a meal

table wine /'.. ,./ *n.* [C,U] a fairly cheap wine intended for drinking with meals

tab·loid /'tæblɔɪd/ *n.* [C] a newspaper that has small pages, a lot of photographs, stories about sex, famous people etc., and not much serious news: *Her latest affair was splashed across the cover of the super-market tabloids.* —**tabloid** *adj.*: *the tabloid press*

ta·boo¹ /tə'bu, tæ-/ *adj.* **1** a taboo subject, word, activity etc. is one that people avoid because they think it is extremely offensive or embarrassing: *In the '50s it was taboo for co-workers to date each other.* **2** TECHNICAL too holy or evil to be touched, or used

taboo² *n. plural* **taboos** [C] a religious or social custom which means a particular activity or subject must be avoided: [+ **about/on/against**] *There is a strong taboo against marrying outside the group.*

tab·u·lar /'tæbyələ/ *adj.* arranged in the form of a TABLE (=set of numbers arranged in rows across and down a page)

tab·u·la ra·sa /,tæbyələ 'rɑzə, -sə/ *n.* [C usually sin-gular] LITERARY your mind in its original state, before you have learned anything

tab·u·late /'tæbyə,leɪt/ *v.* [T] to arrange figures or information together in a set or a list so that they can be easily compared —**tabulation** /,tæbyə'leɪʃən/ *n.* [U]

ta·chom·e·ter /tæ'kɑmətə/ *n.* [C] a piece of equip-ment used to measure the speed at which the engine of a vehicle turns

tac·it /'tæsɪt/ *adj.* **tacit agreement, approval, support** etc. is given without actually being spoken or officially agreed to: *Roh's remarks indicated a tacit*

acceptance of the high-level talks. —**tacitly** *adv.*
—**tacitness** *n.* [U]

tac·i·turn /'tæsə,tɔ·n/ *adj.* speaking very little, so that you seem unfriendly: *It was unlike her to be so taciturn.* —**taciturnly** *adv.* —**taciturnity** /,tæsə'tɔ·nəti/ *n.* [U]

tack¹ /tæk/ *n.*
1 way of doing sth a method that you use to achieve something: *If that doesn't work, we'll try a different tack.*
2 pin [C] a short pin with a large round flat top, for attaching notices to boards, walls etc.; THUMBTACK
3 nail [C] a small nail with a sharp point and flat top
4 ship **a)** [C,U] the direction of a sailing ship, based on the direction of the wind and the position of its sails **b)** [C] the action of changing the direction of a sailing boat, or the distance it travels between these changes: *a long tack into the bay*
5 sewing [C] a long loose stitch used for fastening pieces of cloth together before SEWING them
6 horses [U] all the equipment you need for horse riding

tack² *v.* **1** [T always + adv./prep.] to attach something to a wall, board etc. using a TACK¹ (3): [**tack sth up**] *Supporters tacked up brightly colored posters around the city.* | [**tack sth to sth**] *The handwritten note was tacked to the wall.* **2** [I] to change the course of a sailing ship so that the wind blows against its sails from the opposite direction **3** [T] to fasten pieces of cloth together with long loose stitches, before SEWING them

tack sth ↔ **on** *phr. v.* [T] INFORMAL to add something to something that already exists or is complete, especially in a way that seems badly planned: *Senators managed to tack on an additional 15 amendments.* | [**tack sth on/onto sth**] *Valencia kept tacking bedrooms onto the house to make room for all the children.*

tack·le¹ /'tækəl/ *v.* **1** [T] to make a determined effort to deal with a difficult problem: *A task force was formed to tackle Charlestown's rising crime rate.* **2** [I,T] to force someone to the ground so that they stop running, especially in a game such as football or RUGBY: *I didn't know if he had the ball or not, so I just tackled him.* **3** [I,T] to try to take the ball away from an opponent in a game such as SOCCER

tack·le² *n.* **1 a)** [C] the act of stopping an opponent by forcing them to the ground, especially in football or RUGBY **b)** the act of trying to take the ball from an opponent in a game such as SOCCER **2** [C] a player in football who stops other players by tackling them or preventing them from moving forward **3** [U] the equipment used in some sports, especially fishing **4** [C,U] ropes and PULLEYs (=wheels) used for lifting heavy things, moving a ship's sails etc.

tack·y /'tæki/ *adj.* **tackier, tackiest 1** showing that you do not have good judgment about what is fashionable, socially acceptable etc.: *I think it's kind of tacky to give her a present that someone else gave you.* **2** cheap looking and of very bad quality: *tacky souvenirs* **3** slightly sticky: *The paint's still a little tacky.* —**tackily** *adv.* —**tackiness** *n.* [U]

ta·co /'takou, 'tæ-/ *n. plural* **tacos** [C] a type of Mexican food made from a fried (FRY) corn TORTILLA that is folded and filled with meat, beans etc.

tact /tækt/ *n.* [U] the ability to be polite and careful about what you say or do so that you do not upset or embarrass other people: *Teresa's skills as an editor and her tact with sensitive authors were respected within the department.*

tact·ful /'tæktfəl/ *adj.* careful not to say or do anything that will upset or embarrass other people: *Can you help me think of a tactful way to ask her to stop calling?* —opposite TACTLESS —**tactfully** *adv.*

tac·tic /'tæktɪk/ *n.* **1** [C] a method that you use to achieve something: *We may have to use more aggressive tactics to get rid of him.* | *Republicans accuse Democrats of using delaying tactics (=something you do in order to give yourself more time) to prevent a final vote on the bill.* **2 tactics** [plural] the way in which military forces are arranged in order

to win a battle, or the science of arranging them —see also SCARE TACTICS

tac·ti·cal /'tæktɪkəl/ *adj.* **1 a tactical weapon/missile/aircraft etc.** a weapon, airplane etc. that is only used over short distances to support military forces: *tactical nuclear weapons* —compare STRATEGIC (3) **2** relating to what you do to achieve what you want at a later time, especially in a game or large plan: *They have agreed to close the business as a tactical move to avoid public criticism.* | *a tactical advantage* | **a tactical error/mistake/blunder** (=a mistake that will harm your plans later) **3** relating to the way military forces are organized in order to win battles: *a tactical army unit* —**tactically** /-kli/ *adv.*

tac·ti·cian /tæk'tɪʃən/ *n.* [C] someone who is very good at TACTICS

tac·tile /'tæktl/ *adj.* **1** relating to your sense of touch: *a tactile sensation* **2** wanting to touch things or be touched often: *a tactile animal*

tact·less /'tæktlɪs/ *adj.* likely to upset or embarrass someone without intending to: *a tactless comment* —opposite TACTFUL —**tactlessly** *adv.* —**tactlessness** *n.* [U]

tad /tæd/ *n.* SPOKEN, OLD-FASHIONED **a tad** a small amount, or to a small degree: *He seems a tad confused on the subject.*

tad·pole /'tædpoʊl/ *n.* [C] a small creature that has a long tail, lives in water, and grows into a FROG or TOAD

Tae-Bo /,taɪ 'boʊ/ *n.* [U] a type of exercise that combines dancing, kicking, and quick hand movements

tae·kwon do /taɪ 'kwɑn doʊ/ *n.* [U] a style of fighting from Korea in which you kick, hit with your hands etc.

taf·fe·ta /'tæfətə/ *n.* [U] a shiny stiff cloth made from silk or NYLON

taf·fy /'tæfi/ *n. plural* **taffies** [C,U] a type of soft CHEWY candy

Taft /tæft/, **William** (1857–1930) the 27th President of the U.S.

tag¹ /tæg/ *n.*
1 piece of paper/plastic [C] a small piece of paper, plastic etc. attached to something to show what it is, who owns it, what it costs etc.: *Do we have to wear these name tags?* | *I can't find a price tag on it anywhere.* —see also DOG TAG
2 game [U] a children's game in which one player chases and tries to touch the others
3 description INFORMAL a word or phrase which is used to describe a person, group, or thing, but which is often unfair or not correct; LABEL: *I don't blame her for hating the tag "ex-girlfriend."*
4 on a car tags [plural] INFORMAL the LICENSE PLATE on a car: *a car with out-of-state tags*
5 on a string [C] a metal or plastic point at the end of a piece of string or SHOELACE that prevents it from splitting
6 name/symbol [C] SLANG someone's name or symbol that they paint illegally on a wall, vehicle etc. —see also PHONE TAG, TAG QUESTION

tag² *v.* **tagged, tagging** [T] **1** to fasten a tag onto something: *Each bird was tagged and released into the wild.* **2** to give someone or something a name or title, or think of them in a particular way that is difficult to change: *His teammates have tagged him with a second nickname.* | [**be tagged (as) stupid/a failure etc.**] *Gray refuses to be tagged a racist.* **3** to touch someone you are chasing in a game, especially to touch someone with the ball in baseball: *Reyes tagged Thompson out at home plate.* —see picture at BASEBALL **4 Tag! (You're it!)** SPOKEN said in a children's game when a player manages to touch someone they are chasing

tag along *phr. v.* [I] INFORMAL to go somewhere with someone, although you are not wanted or needed: *When my husband goes on a business trip, I usually tag along.*

tag sth ↔ **on** *phr. v.* [T] to add something to something that already exists or is complete, especially in a way that looks badly planned: *As punishment the judge tagged on 60 more days to her sentence.*

tag·a·long /'. .,./ *n.* [C] INFORMAL someone who goes somewhere with someone else, especially when they are not wanted —**tag-along** /'tægə,lɔŋ/ *adj.* [only before noun]

tag·ging /'tægɪŋ/ *n.* [U] SLANG the illegal activity of painting your name or sign on a wall, a vehicle etc.

ta·glia·tel·le /,tælyə'tɛli, ,tɑ-/ *n.* [U] a type of PASTA that is cut in very long thin flat pieces

tag line /'. ./ *n.* [C] a sentence or phrase in an advertisement or advertising song that is the most important or easiest to remember

tag ques·tion /'. ,../ *n.* [C] TECHNICAL a question that is formed by adding a phrase such as "can't we?," "wouldn't he?," or "is it?" to a sentence

tag sale /'. ./ *n.* [C] a sale of used things that someone does not want anymore, or a sale at which the normal prices for things have been reduced

Ta·hi·ti /tə'hiti/ an island in French Polynesia, in the Pacific Ocean, which is governed by France —**Tahitian** /tə'hiʃən/ *n.*, *adj.*

Ta·hoe, Lake /'tɑhou/ a large lake in the southwestern U.S. on the border between the states of Nevada and California

tai chi /,tai 'tʃi/ *n.* [U] a Chinese form of physical exercise that trains your mind and body in balance and control

s w **tail¹** /teɪl/ *n.* [C]
2 **1** animal the movable part at the back of an animal's body: *Taffy always wags her tail when I come home.* | **white-tailed/black-tailed/long-tailed/ring-tailed etc.** (=having a tail that is white, black, long etc.) —see picture on page 429
2 aircraft the back part of an aircraft
3 shirt the bottom part of your shirt at the back, that you put inside your pants
4 back part [usually singular] the back part of something, or something that is connected to the back of something, especially something that is moving away from you: *the tail of a comet*
5 tails [plural] INFORMAL a man's suit coat with two long parts that hang down the back, worn to formal events
6 tails [U] SPOKEN said when you are TOSSing a coin (=throwing it up in the air to decide which of two things you will do or choose), to talk about the side of the coin that does not have a picture of someone's head on it: *Which do you want, heads or tails?*
7 the tail end of sth the last part of an event, situation, or period of time: *We're just at the tail end of the rainy season now.*
8 be on sb's tail also **ride sb's tail** to follow another car too closely
9 turn tail INFORMAL to run away because you are too frightened to fight or attack
10 follow [C] INFORMAL someone who is employed to watch and follow someone, especially a criminal: *He put a tail on his wife.*
11 with your tail between your legs embarrassed or unhappy because you have failed or been defeated
12 it's (a case of) the tail wagging the dog INFORMAL used to say that an unimportant thing is wrongly controlling a situation
13 chase tail VULGAR, SLANG to try to get a woman or girl to have sex with you —see also **work your butt/tail/ass off** (WORK¹ (13))

tail² *v.* [T] INFORMAL to follow someone and watch what they do, where they go etc.: *He claims police have been tailing him for several months.*
tail off *phr. v.* [I] to become gradually smaller or weaker, sometimes stopping completely: *Her movie career tailed off in the '60s.*

tail·back /'teɪlbæk/ *n.* [C] the player who is the farthest back from the front line in football, and who often runs with the ball

tail·bone /'teɪlboun/ *n.* [C] the bone at the very bottom of your back —see picture at SKELETON

tail·coat /'teɪlkout/ *n.* [C] a coat worn by men to formal events such as weddings, that is short at the front and divides into two long pieces at the back

tailgate

tail·gate¹ /'teɪlgeɪt/ *n.* [C] **1** a door at the back of a truck or car that opens out and down **2** a tailgate party

tailgate² *v.* [I,T] to drive too closely behind another vehicle —**tailgater** *n.* [C]

tailgate par·ty /'.. ,../ *n.* [C] a party before a football game where people eat and drink in the PARKING LOT of the place where the game is played

tail·light /'teɪl-laɪt/ *n.* [C] one of the two red lights at the back of a vehicle —see picture on page 427

tai·lor¹ /'teɪlə/ *n.* [C] someone whose job is to make clothes, especially men's clothes, that are measured to fit each customer perfectly

tailor² *v.* [T] to make something so that it is exactly right for someone's particular needs: [**tailor sth to sb/sth**] *Treatment is tailored to the needs of each patient.* | [**tailor sth for sb**] *We tailored the part specifically for her.*

tai·lored /'teɪlərd/ *adj.* **1** a piece of clothing that is tailored is made to fit very well **2** made to fit a particular need or situation: *carefully tailored legislation*

tai·lor·ing /'teɪlərɪŋ/ *n.* [U] the work of making clothes or the style in which they are made

tailor-made /,.. '. ./ *adj.* exactly right or appropriate for someone or something: [**+ for**] *The job's tailor-made for you.*

tail·pipe /'teɪlpaɪp/ *n.* [C] the pipe on the back of a car, truck etc. that gases from the engine come out of —compare EXHAUST PIPE

tail·spin /'teɪlspɪn/ *n.* [C] **1 in/into a tailspin** in or into a situation with many big problems that you cannot control, so that the situation becomes worse and worse: *Raising interest rates could send the economy into a tailspin.* **2** an uncontrolled fall of an airplane through the air, in which the back of the airplane spins in a wider circle than the front

tail wind, tailwind /'. ./ *n.* [C] a wind blowing in the same direction that a vehicle is traveling

taint¹ /teɪnt/ *v.* [T usually passive] **1** if something bad taints a situation or person that it is connected with, it makes the person or situation seem bad or less desirable: *Baker argues that his trial was tainted by negative publicity.* **2** to ruin something by adding an unwanted substance to it: *It appeared the water supply had been tainted with a deadly toxin.*

taint² *n.* [singular] the appearance of being related to something shameful or terrible: [**+ of**] *The city has suffered for many years under the taint of corruption.*

taint·ed /'teɪntɪd/ *adj.* **1** a tainted substance, especially food or drink, is not safe because it is spoiled or contains poison: *a tainted blood supply* **2** affected or influenced by something illegal, dishonest, or morally wrong: *a tainted witness*

Tai·pei /,tai'pei/ the capital and largest city of Taiwan

Tai·wan /,tai'wɑn/ an island near the southeast coast of China, which was formerly called Formosa —**Taiwanese** /,taiwɑ'niz/ *adj.*

Ta·ji·kistan /tɑˈdʒɪkɪˌstɑn, -ˌstæn/ a country in central Asia, between Uzbekistan and China, formerly part of the Soviet Union —**Tajik** *n., adj.*

take off

He took his coat off.

The plane took off.

S W
1 1

take¹ /teɪk/ *v. past tense* **took** *past participle* **taken**
1 **move sth/help sb** [T] to move something from one place to another, or help someone go from one place to another: *Take an umbrella, just in case it rains.* | *I think her mother's already taken her home.* | [take sb/sth to sth] *Could you take these old clothes to the church for me?* | *He needs someone to take him to the hospital.* | [take sb sth] *We should take your grandma some of these flowers.* | [take sb/sth with you] *Don't forget to take your passport with you.*
2 **do sth** [T] used with some nouns to say that you do the actions relating to the noun: *Hurry up. I need to take a shower too.* | *Would you like to take a walk around the block?* | *Take a deep breath and start over.* | *The new rules take effect January 1.* | **take a test/exam** *I'm going to ask if I can take the test early.*
3 **time** [T] to need or use a particular amount of time to do something or for something to happen: *The whole process takes two hours.* | [take sb 10 minutes/3 hours etc. (to do sth)] *It takes me about 20 minutes to get to work.* | *What took you so long?*
4 **accept/get** to accept something, or get something for yourself: *He should have taken that job.* | *Do you take American Express?* | *Take some more candy if you want.* | *Did he take your advice?* | *Jim took all the credit, even though he hadn't done much of the work.*
5 **study** [T] to study a particular subject: *Are you taking French again this semester?* *Steve took piano for years.*
6 **remove sth** [T always + adv./prep.] to remove something from a particular place: [take sth off/out/away etc.] *I wish he would take that old picture off the wall.* | *Can you take the turkey out of the oven for me?*
7 **need** [T] to need a particular quality, amount of money, amount of effort etc. in order for you to achieve something or make something happen: *Telling the truth in this case took a lot of courage.* | [it takes sth to do sth] *It will take nearly $650,000 to restore the house.*
8 **photograph** to use a camera or similar piece of equipment to make a picture: [+ of] *Excuse me. Could you take a picture of us?* | *I think we'd better take an X-ray.*
9 **steal/borrow** [T] to steal something or borrow something without someone's permission: *The burglars took just about everything.* | *Did you take my pen again?*
10 **hold/put** [T] to reach for something and then hold it or put it somewhere: *Let me take your coats.* | *He took her hand and led her into the living room.*
11 **get control** [T] to get possession or control of something: *Rebel forces have taken the capital.* | **take control/charge** *It is unlikely Democrats will take control of Congress this year.*
12 **accept sth bad/annoying** [T] INFORMAL to accept a bad situation or someone's bad or annoying behavior without becoming upset: *I can't take much more of this stress.* | *You didn't just sit there and take it, did you?* | *When she starts talking about how smart her kids are, it's a little* **hard to take**.
13 **machine/vehicle** [T] if a machine, vehicle etc. takes a particular type of gasoline, BATTERY etc., you have to use that in it: *What kind of gas does your car take?*
14 **medicine/drug** [T] to take a drug into your body: *You really need to take something for that cough.* | *They say he used to* **take drugs** (=take illegal drugs).
15 **taxi/bus/train/road etc.** [T] to use a taxi, bus, train etc. to go somewhere, or to travel using a particular road: *Take the 21 bus to get to my place.*
16 **take sth seriously/lightly/personally etc.** to consider someone or something in a particular way: *I can't take his suggestions very seriously.*
17 **write** [T] to write down information that you have just been given: *It might be a good idea to take notes during the lecture.* | *He's not here right now. Can I take a message?*
18 **test/measure sth** [T] to test or measure something: *Hold still while I take your temperature.*
19 **take a left/right** to turn left or right while driving a vehicle: *When you get to State Street, take a right.*
20 **emotion/attitude** [T] used with some nouns that represent emotions or attitudes, to say that someone has or feels that emotion or attitude: *Dad* **takes an interest** *in everything we do.* | *Howard* **took pity** *on the man and gave him some food.* | *I* **take offense at** (=feel offended by) *what he said.*
21 **take sth well/badly/hard** to react well or badly when you find out that something has happened or is true: *She didn't take the news very well.*

T

SPOKEN PHRASES

22 **I take it (that)** used to say that based on something you have noticed, you think something else is likely to be true: *I take it you two have already met.*
23 **take sb/sth (for example)** said when you want to give an example of something you have just been talking about: *Not everyone is doing so well. Take Sheryl, for example – she's still looking for a job.*
24 **take it or leave it** used to say that what you have offered will not change: *I'll give you $15 – take it or leave it.*
25 **take it from me** used to persuade someone that what you are saying is true: *Take it from me – it's the best sushi restaurant in town.*
26 **take a hike** INFORMAL used to tell someone to go away in an impolite way: *If you don't like it, you can take a hike.*
27 **what do you take me for?** used to say that you would never do something that someone has suggested you might do: *I'm not going to do it alone. What do you take me for – a fool?*
28 **it takes all kinds (to make a world)** said when you think what someone is doing, likes etc. is very strange
29 **take it outside** to go outside to continue an argument or fight

30 **suffer sth** [T] to experience something bad because you cannot avoid it: *Employees are being forced to take a 5% pay cut.*
31 **be taken with/by sb/sth** to be attracted by a particular idea, plan, or person: *The men were taken with her beauty.*
32 **take it upon yourself to do sth** to decide to do something without permission or approval: *Judy just took it upon herself to make the arrangements.*
33 **not take sth lying down** to refuse to accept being treated badly: *We're not going to take this attack lying down – we intend to fight back.*

34 food/drinks [T not in progressive] to use something such as salt, sugar, milk etc. in your food or drinks: *Do you take sugar in your coffee?*
35 size [T] to wear a particular size of clothes or shoes: *What size shoe do you take?*
36 use a word meaning to use something, used when giving instructions: *Take one tortilla and top with cheese, tomatoes, and beans.*
37 have space/strength for [T not in progressive or passive] to have only enough space or strength to contain or support a particular amount of something, or a particular number of things: *The shelf won't take any more books.*
38 numbers [T] also **take away** to subtract one number from another number: [take sth from sth] *Take four from nine and what do you get?*
39 take ill/sick also be taken ill OLD-FASHIONED to suddenly become sick: *Shortly after that, Harding took sick and died.*
40 sex [T] LITERARY if a man takes a woman, he has sex with her
41 take a bend/fence/corner etc. [T] to try to get over or around something in a particular way: *You're driving too fast to take that curve.*
42 sth works [I] if a DYE (=coloring substance) or INJECTION (=medicine) takes, it is successful —see also **take care** (CARE² (4)), **take part** (PART¹ (5)), **take place** (PLACE¹ (5)), **point taken** (POINT¹ (21)), **have what it takes** (WHAT¹ (17))—see Usage Note at BRING

take aback *phr. v.* [T] **be taken aback** to be very surprised about something: *I think he was a little taken aback by my response.*

take after sb *phr. v.* [T not in progressive] to look or behave like an older relative: *Everyone says I take after my mother.*

take sb/sth **apart** *phr. v.* [T] **1** to separate something into pieces; DISMANTLE: *He had to take the whole engine apart before he found the problem.* **2** to beat someone very easily in a game or sport

take away from sth *phr. v.* [T] to spoil the good effect or success of something; DETRACT: *Knowing too much ahead of time can take away from the enjoyment of going to a movie.*

take back *phr. v.* [T] **1** [take sth ↔ back] to admit that you were wrong to say something: **take it/that back** *All right, I'm sorry. I take it back.* **2** [take sth ↔ back] to take something you have bought back to a shop because it does not fit, is not what you wanted etc.: *If the shirt doesn't fit, take it back.* **3** sth takes sb back used to say that something makes someone remember a time in the past: *Boy, that song really takes me back.* **4** [take sb back] to be willing to start a romantic relationship again with someone after ending it: *After all the things I said, I don't think she'd ever take me back.*

take sth ↔ **down** *phr. v.* [T] **1** to remove something from its place, especially by separating it into pieces: *When are you going to take down your Christmas tree?* **2** to write something on a piece of paper in order to remember it or have a record of it: *Let me take down your name and number.*

take in *phr. v.*
1 money [T take sth ↔ in] to collect or earn an amount of money: *How much did you take in at the garage sale?*
2 understand/remember sth [take sth ↔ in] to understand and remember new facts and information: *I needed a minute to take in what Carter had told me.*
3 car/equipment etc. [T take sth ↔ in] to bring something to a place in order to have it repaired: *The car's still making that noise – I'm going to have to take it in again.*
4 person [T take sb ↔ in] to let someone stay in your house or a shelter, especially because they have nowhere else to stay: *Brett's always taking in stray animals.*
5 be taken in to be completely deceived by someone: [+ by] *You have to be pretty dumb to be taken in by an offer like that.*
6 clothes [T take sth ↔ in] to make a piece of

clothing narrower so that it fits you —opposite **let** sth **out** (LET)
7 movie/play etc. [T take in sth] OLD-FASHIONED to go to see something such as a movie, play etc.

take off *phr. v.*
1 remove sth [T take sth ↔ off] to remove something, especially a piece of clothing: *Could you take off your shoes before you come in?* | [take sth off sth] *You'd better be careful, or she'll take your name off the guest list.* —opposite **put** sth **on** (PUT)
2 aircraft/space vehicle [I] to rise into the air at the beginning of a flight: *What time did the plane finally take off?*
3 leave a place [I] INFORMAL to leave somewhere suddenly, especially without telling anyone: *Ken took off about an hour ago.*
4 work [T take sth ↔ off] also **take off work** to not go to work for a period of time: *I'm taking Friday off to go to the dentist.*
5 take off weight/take off 5 pounds etc. to become thinner and lighter: *My Aunt took off 12 pounds and she's thrilled.*
6 success [I] to suddenly start being successful: *His record business took off after World War II.* —see also TAKEOFF

take on *phr. v.* [T] **1** [take sb/sth ↔ on] to compete or fight against someone or something: *Tonight the 49ers take on the Raiders in Los Angeles.* **2** [take on sth] to begin to have a different quality or appearance: *His voice took on a deeper tone as he began the prayer.* **3** [take sth ↔ on] to start doing some difficult work or to start being responsible for something important: *If you agree to take on this project, it'll mean a lot of extra work.* **4** [take sb on] to start to employ someone: *We've taken on three new employees this month.*

take out *phr. v.* [T] **1** [take sb out] to take someone to a restaurant, theater, club etc. and pay for their meal or entertainment: *I'm taking Melinda out for dinner tonight.* **2** [take sth ↔ out] to arrange to get something officially, especially from a bank, insurance company, or a court of law: *Carmela's taken out ads in all the local papers.* | *We decided to take out a 30-year-mortgage.* **3** sth takes it out of sb used to say that something makes someone feel very tired: *These days, even raking leaves really takes it out of me!* **4** [take sb/sth ↔ out] INFORMAL to kill someone, or destroy something: *The bombing took out the entire village.* —see also TAKEOUT

take sth **out on** sb *phr. v.* [T] to treat someone badly because you are feeling angry, tired etc.: *Don't take it out on me! It's not my fault.*

take over *phr. v.* [I,T] to take control of something: *Jack is supposed to take over for Carmen while she's on maternity leave.* | [take sth ↔ over] *Sometimes I think he wants to take over the world.* —see also TAKEOVER

take to sth *phr. v.* [T not in passive] **1** [take to sb/sth] to start to like someone or something: *We took to each other right away.* **2** take to the streets/highways etc. to go out into the streets for a particular purpose, usually to protest something: *Thousands of people took to the streets after the government declared the elections void.* **3** [take to sth] to start doing something regularly or as a habit: *After his business failed, he took to drink (=started drinking alcohol regularly).* | [take to doing sth] *Lately he's taken to staying up till the middle of the night.* **4** take to something like a duck to water to learn how to do something very easily or to quickly change your behavior and attitudes to match a new situation: *She's taken to her new position like a duck to water.*
5 take to your bed OLD-FASHIONED to go to your bed and stay there, especially because you are sick

take up *phr. v.* [T]
1 space/time [take up sth] if something takes up a particular amount of time or space it fills or uses it: *I don't go to the gym – it takes up too much time.* | *Our new car takes up the whole garage.* | [be taken up with sth] *The first week of the trial was taken up with jury selection.*
2 activity/subject [take up sth] to become interested in a particular activity or subject and spend time doing it: *Now she wants to take up boxing.*

3 **idea/suggestion/subject** [take sth ↔ up] to begin discussing or considering something: *This chapter takes up the subject of geologic structures.*

4 **offer** [take sth ↔ up] to accept an offer or CHALLENGE that someone has made: *We must take up the challenge of confronting crime in our neighborhoods.*

5 **job/responsibility** [take up sth] to start a new job or have a new responsibility: *He moved overseas with his family to take up the bank position.*

6 **take up residence** to start living somewhere

7 **position** [take up sth] to put yourself in a particular position ready for something to happen, or so that you can see better: *The runners took up their positions on the starting line.*

8 **floor/carpet etc.** [take sth ↔ up] to remove something that is attached to the floor: *They had to take up the carpet to fix the pipes.*

9 **clothes** [take sth ↔ up] to reduce the length of a skirt or pair of pants

10 **continue an activity** [take sth ↔ up] to continue a story or activity that someone else started, or that you have started but had to stop

11 **take up arms** LITERARY to fight a battle using weapons

take sb **up on** sth *phr. v.* [T] to accept an invitation that someone has made: *I might just take you up on that offer of lunch.*

take up with *phr. v.* **1** [T take sth ↔ up with sb] to discuss something with someone, especially a complaint or problem: *You can take it up with your mother when she gets home.* **2** [T take up with sb] OLD-FASHIONED to begin a friendship or a romantic relationship, especially with someone you should not have a relationship with: *I bet she wishes now she'd never taken up with Sam.*

S W ⬚ 3

take² *n.* [C] **1** the act of filming a scene for a movie or television program: *We had to do twelve takes to get this particular scene right.* **2** INFORMAL [usually singular] the amount of money earned by a store or business in a particular period of time **3** sb's **take on** sth INFORMAL someone's opinion about a situation or idea: *Let's hear your take on what just happened.* **4** **be on the take** INFORMAL to be receiving money for doing things that are wrong or illegal **5** [usually singular] the number of fish or animals caught at one particular time

take·down /'teɪkdaʊn/ *n.* [C] **1** a movement in WRESTLING in which you put your opponent on his back on the ground: *Jackson scored four points on a takedown to secure the win.* **2** an act of causing someone to lose their position of power or taking them away by the police

take-home pay /ˌ.. ˈ., ˈ. ˌ./ *n.* [U] the amount of money that you receive from your job after taxes etc. have been taken out

tak·en /'teɪkən/ the past participle of TAKE¹

take·off /'teɪk-ɔf/ *n.* **1** [C,U] the time when an airplane or ROCKET rises into the air —compare LIFT-OFF **2** [C] an amusing performance that copies a show, movie, or the way someone behaves: *The show is a take-off on the movie "It's a Wonderful Life."* **3** [C] the act of leaving the ground as you make a jump —see also **take off** (TAKE¹)

take·out, take-out /'teɪk-aʊt/ *n.* [C,U] a meal that you buy at a restaurant to eat at home or somewhere else: *Let's get Chinese takeout tonight.* —**takeout** *adj.*: *a fast food takeout restaurant*

take·o·ver /'teɪkˌoʊvɚ/ *n.* [C] **1** the act of getting control of a company by buying most of the STOCK in it: [+ of] *The Exon-Florio Act allows the President to block foreign takeovers of U.S. firms.* —see also **hostile takeover/bid/buyout** (HOSTILE (4)) **2** an act of getting control of a country or political organization, especially by using force: [+ of] *the military takeover of the government*

tak·er /'teɪkɚ/ *n.* **1** [C] someone who accepts or buys something that is offered: *There have been no takers for the multi-million-dollar property.* **2** **a risk-taker/ test-taker/hostage-taker etc.** someone who takes risks, tests etc. **3** [C] someone who cares only about themselves: *Tommy is a giver, not a taker.*

talc /tælk/ *n.* [U] **1** talcum powder **2** a soft smooth

---

mineral that feels like soap and is used for making paints, plastics, etc.

tal·cum pow·der /'tælkəm ˌpaʊdɚ/ *n.* [U] a fine powder which you put on your skin after washing to make it dry or smell nice

tale /teɪl/ *n.* [C] **1** a story of imaginary, usually exciting, events: [+ of] *a charming tale of knights and dragons* **2** a spoken description of an event or situation, often one containing strong emotions or one that is not completely true: *The guys sat around telling tales of fishing in Canada.* | *Bankers are used to hearing tales of woe from would-be borrowers.* **3** **live/survive to tell the tale** to still be alive after a dangerous or frightening event: *Miraculously, Szwajger lived to tell the tale of her imprisonment.* —see also FAIRY TALE, **old wives' tale** (OLD (27)), **tall tale** (TALL (4)), TATTLETALE

S W ⬚ 2

tal·ent /'tælənt/ *n.* **1** [C,U] a special natural ability or skill: *You need talent and hard work to be a tennis player.* | *Woods was chosen to play the cop because of his acting talent.* | [+ for] *Gary has a talent for making people laugh.* | **a man/woman of many talents** (=someone who has the ability to do several things very well) | **talent contest/show/competition** (=a competition in which people show how well they can sing, dance, tell jokes etc.) **2** [C,U] a person or people with a special natural ability or skill: *The NBA is even searching grade schools for talent.* | *As a singer, she's a great talent.* —see Usage Note at ABILITY

S W ⬚ 3

tal·ent·ed /'tæləntɪd/ *adj.* having a very good natural ability or skill in a particular activity: *a talented journalist*

talent scout /'.. ./ *n.* [C] someone whose job is to find young people who are good at a sport or activity

tal·is·man /'tælɪsmən, -lɪz-/ *n.* [C] an object that is believed to have magic powers of protection

talk¹ /tɔk/ *v.*
1 **conversation** [I] to say things to someone, especially in a conversation: *In high school, we often got in trouble for talking in class.* | [+ to/with] *I haven't talked to Gene in years.* | [+ about] *Let's talk not about the accident.* | *Once Lou gets talking* (=starts having a conversation), *you know you're going to be there a while.* | *Sandy talks about herself* (=tells other people about details of her life) *all the time.* —see Usage Note at SAY¹
2 **discuss** [I] to discuss something with someone, especially an important or serious subject: *We need to talk right now.* | [+ about/of] *Jenny and I have talked about getting married some day.* | [+ to/with] *I'd like to talk with you in private.* | **talk sports/ business/politics etc.** *I don't feel like talking business right now.*
3 **talk shop** INFORMAL to talk about things that are connected with your work, especially at a social event, in a way that other people find boring: *Are you two going to talk shop all night?*
4 **speech** [I] to give a speech: [+ on/about] *Prof. Simmons will talk on the benefits of genetic research.*
5 **say words** [I] to produce words in a language: *Jerrod's only one year old and he's already starting to talk.* | *Is this one of those birds that can talk?*
6 **secret information** [I] to give someone important secret information because they force you to: *Even after three days of interrogation, Maskell refused to talk.*

T

S W ⬚ 1

SPOKEN PHRASES

7 **what are you talking about?** **a)** used when the person you are talking to has just said something stupid or annoying, or used to say that you disagree with what they have said: *What are you talking about? – Ron has lots of money.* **b)** used to ask someone what their conversation is about
8 **know what you are talking about** to know a lot about a particular subject: *Look, I know what I'm talking about because I was there when it happened.* | *Wayne, you don't know what the hell you're talking about.*

9 talk about rich/funny/stupid etc. used to emphasize that the person or thing you are talking about is very rich, funny, stupid etc.: *Talk about nasty! I could hardly eat a bite of that meatloaf.*

10 now you're talking used when you think someone's suggestion is a very good idea: *"Why don't we go to the lake this weekend?" "Now you're talking!"*

11 look who's talking also **you can talk** used to tell someone they should not criticize someone else because they are just as bad: *"You need to get more exercise." "Look who's talking!"*

12 we're/you're talking sth used to tell someone what will be necessary in order to do or get what they are asking you about: *For a new set of tires, you're talking $250.*

13 I'm talking to you! used when you are angry because the person you are talking to is not paying attention to you: *Hey! I'm talking to you! Look at me!*

14 talk sb's ear off to talk too much to someone

15 sth is like talking to a brick wall used to say that it is difficult and annoying to try to speak with someone because they do not react: *Talking to Ray is just like talking to a brick wall.*

16 people will talk also **people are talking** used to emphasize that people will think you are doing something bad: *If we are seen going out together, people will talk.*

17 be talking out (of) your ass SLANG to talk as if you know about something, when in fact you do not

18 talk your way out of sth INFORMAL to escape from a bad or embarrassing situation by giving explanations, excuses etc.: *How did Cindy talk her way out of getting a speeding ticket?*

19 talk to yourself to say things out loud, which are not directed at another person: *"What did you say?" "Nothing, I was just talking to myself."*

20 talk tough INFORMAL to tell people very strongly what you want from them: *Both sides are talking tough, and a strike appears likely.*

21 talk dirty INFORMAL to talk in a sexual way to someone in order to make them feel sexually excited

22 talk trash INFORMAL to say impolite or offensive things to or about someone, especially to opponents in a sports competition: *Both teams talk trash on the basketball court.*

23 not be talking INFORMAL if two people are not talking they refuse to talk to each other because they have argued: *Pat and Alan are still not talking.*

24 talk (some) sense into sb INFORMAL to persuade someone to behave in a sensible way: *Someone needs to talk sense into Rob before he gets hurt.*

25 talk sense INFORMAL to give sensible opinions about things: *I just want our politicians to talk sense for a change.*

26 talk the talk to say the things that people expect or think are necessary in a particular situation: *Mayor Brown has always been able to talk the talk of the common man.* —compare **walk the walk** (WALK[1] (13))

27 talk a blue streak INFORMAL to talk very quickly, without stopping

28 talk turkey INFORMAL to talk seriously about important things, especially in order to agree on something: *They said they would be willing to talk turkey at $125 per shipment.*

talk back *phr. v.* [I] to answer someone rudely after they have criticized you or told you to do something: [+ to] *Kenny got in trouble for talking back to his teacher.*

talk sb/sth ↔ **down** *phr. v.* [T] **1** to give instructions on a radio to a PILOT so that they can bring an aircraft to the ground safely **2** to persuade someone to come down from a high place when they are threatening to jump and kill themselves

talk down to sb *phr. v.* [T] to talk to someone as if they were stupid when in fact they are not; PATRONIZE

talk sb **into** sth *phr. v.* [T] to persuade someone to do something: *She didn't want to come, but I talked her into it.* | [**talk sb into doing sth**] *Linda finally talked me into buying a new car.*

talk sth ↔ **out** *phr. v.* [T] INFORMAL to talk about a problem in order to solve it: *There are still a lot of details that we need to talk out.*

talk sb **out of** sth *phr. v.* [T] to persuade someone not to do something: *Eric was thinking about quitting school, but I talked him out of it.* | [**talk sb out of doing sth**] *Don't let anyone talk you out of going to the doctor.*

talk sth ↔ **over** *phr. v.* [T] to discuss a problem or situation with someone before you decide what to do: *Don't worry; we have plenty of time to talk it over.* | [+ **with**] *I'm going to have to talk it over with Dale first.*

talk sb/sth **through** *phr. v.* [T] **1** [**talk** sth ↔ **through**] to discuss all of something so that you are sure you understand it: *The course teaches couples to talk their problems through.* **2** [**talk sb through** sth] to give someone instructions on how to do something by giving them a little information at a time: *Get a specialist to talk you through the installation of the software.*

talk[2] *n.*
1 conversation [C] a conversation: [+ **about**] *We had a long talk about the future of our relationship.* | *Listen, John, you're going to have to* **have a talk with** *Marty.*

2 speech [C] a speech or LECTURE: [+ **on/about**] *a series of talks on linguistics* | *Last week, Nora* **gave a talk** *at the University of Minnesota.*

3 news [U] news that is not official or not completely true: *There's* **talk of** *more factory closures in the area.* | **sth is just/only talk** *At this point, building a new sports complex is just talk.*

4 talks [plural] formally organized discussions between governments, organizations etc.: *Talks broke down over how the city's money could be used.* | *peace talks*

5 type of conversation [U] a particular type of conversation or way of talking: *It's so annoying to see two adults talk* **baby talk** *(=talking like a baby) to each other.* | **girl/guy/football etc. talk** *We're just talking guy talk.*

6 be all talk (and/but no action) SPOKEN to always be talking about what you have done or what you are going to do without ever actually doing anything

7 be the talk of the town/company etc. to be the person or thing that everyone is talking about because they are very interested, excited, shocked etc.: *The trial has been the talk of the campus.* —see also SMALL TALK, SWEET-TALK

talk·a·tive /ˈtɔkətɪv/ *adj.* liking to talk a lot —**talkativeness** *n.* [U]

talk·er /ˈtɔkɚ/ *n.* [C] INFORMAL someone who talks a lot or talks in a particular way: *Will's a fast talker.*

talk·ie /ˈtɔki/ *n.* [C] OLD-FASHIONED a movie with sounds and words

talk·ing book /ˌ.. ˈ./ *n.* [C] a book that has been recorded for blind people to listen to

talking head /ˌ.. ˈ./ *n.* [C] INFORMAL someone on television who talks directly to the camera, for example when reading the news

talk·ing-to /ˈ.. ./ *n.* **give sb a talking-to** INFORMAL to talk to someone angrily because you are annoyed about something they have done: *You need to give her a good talking-to about her lying.*

talk ra·di·o /ˌ. ˈ.../ *n.* [U] a type of radio program in which listeners call the radio station to give their opinions or to discuss a subject

talk show /ˈ. ./ *n.* [C] a television or radio show on which people talk about their lives and are asked questions

talk·y /ˈtɔki/ *adj.* INFORMAL talking too much about things that are not important: *The play is terribly talky and slow.*

tall /tɔl/ *adj.* **1** a person, building, tree etc. that is tall has a greater than average height: *Do you need to be tall to play basketball well?* | *First, we need to find a nice tall tree.* —see picture at HIGH[1] **2** measuring a particular distance from bottom to top: *Lorna is a little taller than her husband.* | *How tall is the Eiffel Tower?* | **3 feet/two meters etc. tall** *Tammy is only five feet tall.* **3 be a tall order** INFORMAL if a request or piece of work is a tall order, it will be almost impossible for you to do: *Finding extra time to read to their kids is a tall order for busy parents.* **4 tall tale** a story that is difficult to believe, because it makes events seem more exciting, dangerous etc. than they really were **5 a tall drink of water** OLD-FASHIONED, HUMOROUS someone, especially a woman, who is very tall —**tallness** *n.* [U] —see also **stand tall** (STAND¹ (26)), **walk tall** (WALK¹ (11)) and see Usage Note at HIGH¹

Tal·la·has·see /ˌtæləˈhæsi/ the capital city of the U.S. state of Florida

tall·boy /ˈtɔlbɔɪ/ *n.* [C] a can of beer that holds 16 OUNCES

Tal·linn /ˈtɑlɪn/ the capital and largest city of Estonia

tal·low /ˈtæloʊ/ *n.* [U] hard animal fat used for making CANDLES

tal·ly¹ /ˈtæli/ *n. plural* **tallies** [C] a record of how much you have spent, won, obtained etc. so far: *The final tally was 11 ships sunk, and over 20 enemy planes destroyed.* | *Keep a tally of how many cars enter the lot each hour.*

tally² *v.* **tallies, tallied, tallying 1** also **tally up** [T] to calculate the total number of points won, things done etc.: *Absentee ballots were tallied three days after the election.* **2** [I] if numbers or statements tally, they match each other exactly: [+ **with**] *Lilly says things that don't always tally with the truth.*

Tal·mud /ˈtɑlmʊd, ˈtælməd/ *n.* **the Talmud** the collection of writings that make up Jewish law about religious and non-religious life —**Talmudic** /tɑlˈmudɪk/ *adj.*

tal·on /ˈtælən/ *n.* [C] a sharp powerful curved nail on the feet of some birds that catch animals for food —see picture on page 429

ta·ma·le /təˈmɑli/ *n.* [C] a SPICY Mexican dish made of meat and PEPPERS wrapped in DOUGH made from corn, then in corn HUSKS, and then cooked in steam

tam·a·rind /ˈtæmərənd/ *n.* [C] a tropical tree, or the fruit of this tree

tam·bou·rine /ˌtæmbəˈrin/ *n.* [C] a circular musical instrument with small pieces of metal around the edge that make a sound when you shake it

tame¹ /teɪm/ *adj.* **1** an animal that is tame is not wild anymore because it has been trained to live with people **2** boring or unexciting: *The '70s series now seem tame by today's standards.* —**tamely** *adv.* —**tameness** *n.* [U]

tame² *v.* [T] **1** to train a wild animal to obey you and not to attack people —compare DOMESTICATE **2** to reduce the power or strength of something and prevent it from causing trouble: *Statistics show that rent control laws haven't tamed inflation.*

ta·mox·i·fen /təˈmɑksəfən/ *n.* [U] a drug that is used to treat breast CANCER

tamp /tæmp/ *v.* [T always + adv./prep.] also **tamp down** to press or push something down by lightly hitting it several times: *Before you start laying the bricks, tamp down the soil underneath.*

Tam·pa /ˈtæmpə/ a city, port, and holiday RESORT in the U.S. state of Florida

Tam·pax /ˈtæmpæks/ *n.* [U] TRADEMARK the name of a common type of TAMPON

tam·per /ˈtæmpər/ *v.*

tamper with sth *phr. v.* [T] to touch something or make changes to it without permission, especially in order to deliberately damage it: *Police revealed that the telephone line had been tampered with.*

tamper-proof /ˈ.. ./ *adj.* a package or container that is tamper-proof is made in a way that prevents someone from opening it before it is sold

tamper-re·sis·tant /ˈ.. ˌ../ also **tamper-ev·i·dent** /ˈ.. ˌ../ *adj.* a package or container that is tamper-resistant is made so that you can see if someone has opened it before it is sold in stores

tam·pon /ˈtæmpɑn/ *n.* [C] a tube-shaped mass of cotton or similar material that a woman puts inside her VAGINA during her PERIOD (=monthly flow of blood)

tan¹ /tæn/ *adj.* **1** having a pale yellowish brown color

2 having darker skin after spending time in the sun: *Shannon's face is really tan.*

tan² *n.* **1** [U] a light yellowish-brown color **2** [C] the brown color that someone with pale skin gets after they have been in the sun; SUNTAN: *Monica got a nice tan during her trip.* **3** [C] TECHNICAL an abbreviation of TANGENT (3)

tan³ *v.* **tanned, tanning 1** [I] if you tan, your skin becomes darker because you spend time in the sun: *I don't tan well – I just get red.* **2** [T] if the sun tans you, it makes your skin become darker **3** [T] to make animal skin into leather by treating it with a type of acid —see also **have/tan sb's hide** (HIDE² (2))

tan·dem /ˈtændəm/ *n.* [C] **1 in tandem** doing something together or at the same time as someone or something else: *The music and computer graphics for the movie were developed in tandem.* | [+ **with**] *The word processor is designed to work in tandem with the spreadsheet program.* **2** two people who work well together: *The tandem of Mitchell and Bookman combined for three touchdowns.* **3** also **tandem bicycle** a bicycle built for two riders sitting one behind the other

tan·door·i /tænˈdʊri/ *adj.* tandoori chicken, lamb, etc. is an Indian dish that has been cooked in a large closed clay pot

Ta·ney /ˈtɔni/**, Rog·er** /ˈrɑdʒər/ (1777–1864) a CHIEF JUSTICE on the U.S. Supreme Court

tang /tæŋ/ *n.* [singular] a strong, slightly sour, taste or smell: *The lemon added a nice tang to the sauce.* —**tangy** *adj.*: *tangy barbecue sauce*

Tan·gan·yi·ka, Lake /ˌtæŋgənˈyikə/ a large lake in central Africa between the Democratic Republic of Congo and Tanzania

tan·ge·lo /ˈtændʒəloʊ/ *n.* [C] a fruit that is a CROSS (=mixture) between a TANGERINE and a GRAPEFRUIT

tan·gent /ˈtændʒənt/ *n.* [C] **1 go off on a tangent** INFORMAL to suddenly start thinking or talking about a completely new and different subject: *Let's stay with the topic and not go off on a tangent.* **2** TECHNICAL a straight line that touches the outside of a curve but does not cut across it **3** TECHNICAL a number relating to an angle in a RIGHT TRIANGLE that is calculated by dividing the length of the side across from the angle by the length of the side next to it —compare COTANGENT

tan·gen·tial /tænˈdʒɛnʃəl/ *adj.* FORMAL tangential information, remarks etc. are only related to a particular subject in an indirect way: *Even the tangential characters are wittily drawn.* —**tangentially** *adv.*: *Ferrara's speech was only tangentially related to the conference theme.*

tan·ger·ine /ˌtændʒəˈrin/ *n.* [C] a small sweet fruit like an orange with a skin that comes off easily

tan·gi·ble /ˈtændʒəbəl/ *adj.* **1 tangible proof/results/evidence etc.** proof, results etc. that are easy to see so that there is no doubt: *We won't see any tangible benefits from the new system before next year.* —opposite INTANGIBLE **2** FORMAL able to be seen and touched: *tangible personal property* —**tangibly** *adv.* —**tangibility** /ˌtændʒəˈbɪləti/ *n.* [U]

tan·gle¹ /ˈtæŋgəl/ *n.* [C] **1** a twisted mass of something such as hair or thread: *It takes forever to comb the tangles out of my hair.* | **a tangle of branches/weeds/threads etc.** *The floor was a tangle of electrical cords.* **2** a confused situation: [+ **of**] *a tangle of bureaucratic and legal obstacles* **3** an argument or fight: [+ **with**] *I did not want to be in a tangle with the press.*

tangle² *v.* **1** [I] to fight or argue with someone: *Seikaly and Kitchner tangled for several minutes before the referees separated them.* **2** [I,T] also **tangle up** to become twisted together or make something become twisted together in a messy way: *My hair tangles easily.*

tangle with sb *phr. v.* [T] INFORMAL to argue or fight with someone: *Steve has repeatedly tangled with his manager over his ethnic jokes.*

T

T

tan·gled /ˈtæŋgəld/ also **tangled up** adj. **1** twisted together in a messy way: *The phone cord is all tangled up.* **2** complicated or consisting of many confusing parts: *the country's tangled politics* **3 a tangled web (of sth)** a situation that is very complicated or consists of many confusing parts: *The court focused its attention on his tangled web of illegal business deals.*

tan·go¹ /ˈtæŋgoʊ/ n. plural **tangos** [C] a lively dance from South America, or a piece of music for this dance

tango² v. [I] **1** to dance the tango **2 it takes two to tango** SPOKEN used to say that if a problem involves two people, then both people are equally responsible

tank¹ /tæŋk/ n. [C] **1** a large container for storing liquid or gas: *The hot water tank is leaking.* | *I've been thinking about buying a fish tank* (=a tank that fish are kept in). | *Some water must have gotten into the gas tank.* **2** also **tankful** the amount of liquid or gas held in a tank: [+ of] *When I left the house, the car only had a half tank of gas.* **3** a heavy military vehicle that has a large gun and runs on two metal belts that go around its wheels **4** a large artificial pool for storing water —see also SEPTIC TANK, THINK TANK

tank² v. [I] SLANG to decrease quickly or be very unsuccessful: *Car buying tanked as Saturn's first car rolled off the assembly line.*

tank up phr. v. [I] **1** INFORMAL to put gasoline in your car so that the tank is full **2** SLANG to drink a lot of alcohol, especially beer: [+ on] *The guys had tanked up on cheap beer before the game.*

tan·kard /ˈtæŋkəd/ n. [C] a large metal cup, usually with a handle and lid, used for drinking beer

tanked up /ˌ. ˈ. ◂/ also **tanked** adj. [not before noun] SLANG drunk: *Bill gets violent when he's tanked up.*

tank·er /ˈtæŋkə/ n. [C] a vehicle or ship specially built to carry large quantities of gas or liquid, especially oil —see also OIL TANKER

tank top /ˈ. ./ n. [C] a shirt with a wide round opening for your neck and no SLEEVES

tanned /tænd/ adj. having a darker skin color because you have been in the sun

tan·ner /ˈtænə/ n. [C] someone whose job is to make animal skin into leather by TANning

tan·ner·y /ˈtænəri/ n. [C] a place where animal skin is made into leather by TANning

tan·nin /ˈtænɪn/ also **tan·nic ac·id** /ˌtænɪk ˈæsɪd/ n. [U] an acid used in preparing leather, making ink etc.

tanning bed /ˈ.. ./ n. [C] a piece of equipment shaped like a box with special lights inside, that you lie in to make your skin darker

tan·ta·lize /ˈtæntlˌaɪz/ v. [T] to show or promise something that someone really wants, but then not allow them to have it

tan·ta·liz·ing /ˈtæntlˌaɪzɪŋ/ adj. making you feel a strong desire to have something that you cannot have: *The tantalizing smell of barbecue was in the air.* —**tantalizingly** adv.: *The Raiders came tantalizingly close to beating the Broncos.*

tan·ta·mount /ˈtæntəˌmaʊnt/ adj. **be tantamount to sth** if an action, suggestion, plan etc. is tantamount to something, it is almost the same thing as that thing or is very likely to result in it: *Journalists argued that the law was tantamount to censorship.*

tan·trum /ˈtæntrəm/ also **temper tantrum** n. [C] a sudden moment of unreasonable anger and annoyance: **throw/have a tantrum** *Rachel threw a tantrum when we didn't get her an ice cream cone.*

Tan·za·ni·a /ˌtænzəˈniə/ a country in east Africa between Kenya and Mozambique —**Tanzanian** n., adj.

Tao /taʊ, daʊ/ n. [U] the natural force that unites all things in the universe, according to Taoism

Tao Chi /ˌdaʊ ˈtʃi, ˌtaʊ-/ (1630–1714) a Chinese PAINTER who was one of the greatest artists of the Qing dynasty

Tao·ism /ˈtaʊɪzəm, ˈdaʊ-/ n. [U] a way of thought developed in ancient China, based on the writings of Lao Tzu, emphasizing a natural and simple way of life

tap¹ /tæp/ n.
1 water/gas [C] a piece of equipment for controlling the flow of water, gas etc. from a pipe or container: *She gave Mike a drink of water from the tap.* —compare FAUCET —see also TAP WATER
2 on tap a) beer that is on tap comes from a BARREL, rather than from a bottle or can **b)** INFORMAL something that is on tap is ready to use when you need it: *Plenty of good food will be on tap for the Memorial Day celebration.*
3 hit [C] an act of hitting something lightly, especially to get someone's attention: [+ at/on] *Rita felt a tap on her shoulder.*
4 sound [C] a sound of something hitting something else lightly: *There was a tap at the door.*
5 telephone [C] an act of secretly listening to someone's telephone, using electronic equipment: *The FBI had put a tap on Mitchell's phone line.*
6 barrel [C] a specially shaped object used for letting liquid out of a BARREL, especially beer
7 dancing also **tap dancing** [U] dancing in which you wear special shoes with pieces of metal on the bottom which make a loud sharp sound on the floor
8 taps [U] a song or tune played on the BUGLE at night in an army camp, and at military funerals

tap² v. **tapped, tapping**
1 hand or foot [I,T] to hit your fingers or foot lightly against something, especially to get someone's attention or without thinking about it: *The whole crowd was clapping and tapping their feet to the music.* | [+ on] *I went up and tapped on the window.* | **tap sth on/against etc.** *Ted nervously tapped his fingers on the desk.* | **tap sb on the arm/shoulder etc.** *One of the students tapped Mia on the shoulder.* —compare KNOCK¹ (1)
2 energy/money also **tap into** [T] to use or take what is needed from something such as an energy supply or amount of money: *To continue the research project, the university plans to tap funds primarily from private foundations.*
3 ideas [T] also **tap into** to make as much use as possible of the ideas, experience, knowledge etc. that a group of people has: *The rain forest theme products tap into consumer interest in the environment.*
4 telephone [T] to listen secretly to someone's telephone by using a special piece of electronic equipment: *Investigators had tapped the drug dealer's phone line.*
5 choose sb [T] to choose someone to do something, especially to have an important job: *Williams is expected to be tapped as the new director of operations.*
6 tree [T] to get liquid from the TRUNK of a tree by making a hole in it

tap sth ↔ in phr. v. to hit or kick a ball into a hole or GOAL from a short distance away, in sports such as GOLF or SOCCER

tap sb/sth ↔ out phr. v. [T] **1** to hit something lightly, especially with your fingers or foot, to make a sound: *He tapped out various beats on the bottom of the bucket.* **2** to write something with a TYPEWRITER or computer: *Wright spent all day in his office tapping out his novel.* **3** INFORMAL to use all of the money or energy that someone or something has: *Our ski trip to Colorado tapped me out.* —see also TAPPED OUT

tap·as /ˈtæpəs, -pæs/ n. [U] small dishes of food eaten as part of the first course of a Spanish meal

tap danc·ing /ˈ. ˌ../ n. [U] dancing in which you wear special shoes with pieces of metal on the bottom, which make a sharp sound —**tap-dance** v. [I] —**tap dancer** n. [C]

tape¹ /teɪp/ n.
1 recording **a)** [U] narrow plastic material covered with a special MAGNETIC substance, on which sounds, pictures, or computer information can be recorded and played: *I don't like the sound of my voice on tape* (=recorded on tape). **b)** [C] a special plastic box containing a length of tape that sound

can be recorded on; CASSETTE: *Now that I have a CD player, I don't listen to my tapes anymore.* | [+ of] *I'd like a tape of the concert.* **c)** [C] a special plastic box containing a length of tape that sound and pictures can be recorded on; VIDEOTAPE: *Bring me a blank tape* (=with nothing recorded on it) *if you want me to record the movie for you.*
2 sticky material [U] narrow length of sticky material used to stick things together —see also MASKING TAPE, SCOTCH TAPE
3 the tape a string stretched out across the finishing line in a race and broken by the winner
4 for measuring a TAPE MEASURE
5 thin piece of material [C,U] a long thin piece of material used in sewing, tying things together etc. —see also RED TAPE

tape² *v.* **1** also **tape-record** [I,T] to record sound or pictures onto a TAPE¹ (1): *Do you mind if I tape this interview?* **2** [T] to stick something onto something else using TAPE¹ (2): **[tape sth to sth]** *Why is this envelope taped to the refrigerator?* **3** also **tape up** [T] to fasten a package, box etc. with TAPE¹ (2): *They've got this taped up so well I can't get it open.* **4** also **tape up** [T usually passive] to tie a BANDAGE firmly around an injured part of someone's body: *Wilkins came out of the game to get his knee taped up.*

tape deck /'. ./ *n.* [C] the part of a TAPE RECORDER that winds the tape, and records and plays back sound, used as part of a system

tape drive /'. ./ *n.* [C] a small machine attached to a computer that passes information from a computer to a tape or from a tape to a computer

tape meas·ure /'. ,../ *n.* [C] a long narrow band of cloth or steel, marked with inches, centimeters etc. which is used for measuring things

tape play·er /'. ,../ *n.* [C] a piece of electrical equipment that can play back sound on TAPE

ta·per¹ /'teɪpɚ/ *v.* [I,T] also **taper off** to become gradually narrower toward one end: *The jeans taper towards the ankle.*
taper off *phr. v.* [I] to decrease gradually: *Showers from the storm are expected to taper off later tonight.* —**tapering** *adj.*: *long tapering fingers* —see also TAPERED

ta·per² *n.* [C] **1** [usually singular] a gradual decrease in the width of a long object **2** a very thin CANDLE **3** a piece of string covered in WAX, used for lighting lamps and CANDLES

tape-re·cord /'. ,../ *v.* [T] to record sound using a tape recorder

tape re·cord·er /'. ,../ *n.* [C] a piece of electrical equipment that can record sound on TAPE and play it back

tape re·cord·ing /'. ,../ *n.* [C] something that has been recorded with a tape recorder: *The court heard secretly obtained tape recordings of the meeting.*

ta·pered /'teɪpɚd/ *adj.* having a shape that gets narrower toward one end: *tapered candles*

tap·es·try /'tæpɪstri/ *n. plural* **tapestries** [C,U] heavy cloth or a large piece of cloth on which colored threads are woven to produce a picture, pattern etc.

tape·worm /'teɪpwɚm/ *n.* [C] a long flat PARASITE that lives in the BOWELs of humans and other animals

tap·i·o·ca /ˌtæpiˈoʊkə/ *n.* [U] small hard white grains made from the crushed dried roots of CASSAVA, or a DESSERT made of tapioca

ta·pir /'teɪpɚ/ *n.* [C] an animal like a pig with thick legs, a short tail, and long nose, that lives in tropical America and Southeast Asia

tapped out /ˌ. '.◂/ *adj.* INFORMAL not having any more of something, especially money: *We can't give any more – we're all tapped out.*

tap·root /'tæprut/ *n.* [C] the main root of a plant, that grows straight down and produces smaller side roots

tap wa·ter /'. ,../ *n.* [U] water that comes out of a FAUCET, rather than a bottle

taq·ue·ri·a /ˌtækəˈriə/ *n.* [C] an informal Mexican restaurant, especially in the southwest U.S.

tar¹ /tɑr/ *n.* [U] **1** a black substance, thick and sticky when hot but hard when cold, used especially for

making road surfaces —see also COAL TAR **2** a sticky substance that is formed by burning tobacco: **high/low/medium tar** *high tar cigarettes*

tar² *v.* **tarred, tarring** [T] **1** to cover a surface with tar **2** to spoil the good opinion that people have about someone: *Kleider has been tarred by recent business scandals.* **3 be/get tarred with the same brush** to be blamed along with someone else for their faults or crimes **4 tar and feather sb a)** to cover someone in tar and feathers, done as a cruel punishment in past times **b)** to criticize or punish someone very severely and publicly: *If our boss had heard the song, the whole team would have been tarred and feathered.*

Ta·ra·hu·ma·ra /ˌtɑrəhuˈmɑrə/ a Native American tribe from northern Mexico

tar·an·tel·la /ˌtærənˈtɛlə/ *n.* [C] a fast Italian dance, or the music for this dance

ta·ran·tu·la /təˈræntʃələ/ *n.* [C] a large poisonous SPIDER from Southern Europe and tropical America

Ta·ra·wa /təˈrɑwə, ˈtærəˌwɑ/ the capital city of Kiribati

tar·dy /'tɑrdi/ *adj.* FORMAL **1** done or doing something later than it should have been done: *We apologize for our tardy response to your letter.* **2** arriving late, especially for a class at school: *He was never tardy or absent the whole semester.* **3** acting or moving slowly; SLUGGISH —**tardily** *adv.* —**tardiness** *n.* [U]

tar·get¹ /'tɑrgɪt/ *n.* [C]
1 object of attack an object, person, or place that is deliberately chosen to be attacked: [+ for/of] *Fort Sumter was the target of the first shot fired in the Civil War.* | *Poor women were easy targets for sexual abuse.*
2 an aim a result, such as a total, an amount, or a time, which you aim to achieve; GOAL: *The company will reach its target of 12% growth this year.* | *Our year-end results were right on target* (=where we hoped they would be). | *Dealers are under pressure to meet* (=achieve) *sales targets.*
3 object of an action the person or place that is most directly affected by an action, especially a negative one: [+ of] *The cable TV company has been a frequent target of criticism from the community.* | *The area is a prime target* (=very likely target) *for redevelopment.*
4 shooting something that you practice shooting at, especially a round board with circles on it: *The area is used by the army for target practice.*
5 target group/area/audience etc. a limited group, area etc. that something such as a plan or idea is aimed at: *Our target market for the day camp is the Hispanic community.* —see also TARGET LANGUAGE

target² *v.* [T] **1** to make something have an effect on a limited group or area: **[target sth at/on sb/sth]** *The ad campaign has been targeted at adults who smoke.* **2** to aim something at someone or something: **target sth at/on sb/sth** *The missiles are targeted at several key military sites.* **3** to choose a particular person or place to do something to, especially to attack them: **[target sb/sth for sth]** *Guerrilla groups targeted Menendez for assassination.*

target lan·guage /'.. ,../ *n.* [C usually singular] TECHNICAL the language that something such as a document is going to be translated into —compare SOURCE LANGUAGE

Tar Heel /'. ./ *n.* [C] an informal name for someone who comes from North Carolina

tar·iff /'tærɪf/ *n.* [C] a tax on goods coming into a country or going out of a country: [+ on] *Some representatives recommended higher tariffs on imported goods.*

Tar·king·ton /'tɑrkɪntən/, **Booth** /buθ/ (1869–1946) a U.S. writer of NOVELs

tar·mac /'tɑrmæk/ *n.* **1** [U] a mixture of TAR and very small stones, used for making the surface of roads **2 the tarmac** an area covered with tarmac, especially where airplanes take off or land: *Three hours later, the plane was still sitting on the tarmac.*

tar·nish[1] /ˈtɑrnɪʃ/ v. **1** [T] if an event or fact tarnishes someone's REPUTATION, record, image etc., it makes it worse: *Neighbors' testimony tarnished Wilson's image as a loving mother.* **2** [I,T] if metals such as silver, COPPER, or BRASS tarnish, or if something tarnishes them, they become dull and lose their color: *The brass is nice, but it will tarnish really easily.* —**tarnished** *adj.*: *tarnished silverware*

tarnish[2] *n.* [singular,U] **1** loss of color or brightness on metal **2** a worsening of someone's REPUTATION, record, image etc.

ta·ro /ˈtɑroʊ/ *n.* [U] a tropical plant grown for its thick root which is boiled and eaten

tar·ot /ˈtæroʊ/ *n.* [singular,U] a set of 78 cards with pictures on them, used for telling what might happen to someone in the future

tarp /tɑrp/ also **tar·pau·lin** /tɑrˈpɔlɪn/ *n.* [C,U] a cloth that water cannot go through, used for protecting things from the rain

tar·pa·per /ˈtɑrˌpeɪpɚ/ *n.* [U] thick paper that has been covered in TAR, used in covering houses or roofs

tar·ra·gon /ˈtærəgɑn, -gən/ *n.* [U] the leaves of a small plant, used in cooking to give food a special taste

tar·ry[1] /ˈtæri/ *v.* **tarries, tarried, tarrying** [I] LITERARY **1** to stay in a place, especially when you should leave **2** to delay or be slow in going somewhere

tar·ry[2] /ˈtɑri/ *adj.* covered with TAR (=a thick black liquid)

tar·sus /ˈtɑrsəs/ *n.* [C] TECHNICAL your ANKLE or one of the seven small bones in your ankle —**tarsal** *adj.*

tart[1] /tɑrt/ *adj.* **1** food that is tart has a slightly sour taste: *a tart green apple* **2 tart reply/remark etc.** a reply, remark etc. that is sharp and not nice —**tartly** *adv.*: *"Isn't that interesting?" Clarke said tartly.* —**tartness** *n.* [U]

tart[2] *n.* **1** [C,U] a small PIE, usually containing fruit **2** [C] INFORMAL an insulting word for a woman whose appearance or behavior makes you think that she is too willing to have sex **3** [C] OLD-FASHIONED, INFORMAL a PROSTITUTE

tart[3] *v.*

tart up *phr. v.* INFORMAL **1 tart yourself up** OFTEN HUMOROUS if a woman tarts herself up, she tries to make herself look attractive, by putting on jewelry, MAKEUP etc. **2** [T **tart sth ↔ up**] to try to make something more attractive by decorating it, often in a way that other people think looks cheap or ugly: *The textbooks have been tarted up with cartoons, colored type, and lots of pictures.*

tar·tan /ˈtɑrt[n]/ *n.* [C,U] a traditional Scottish pattern of colored squares and crossed lines, or cloth, especially wool cloth, with this pattern —**tartan** *adj.*

Tar·tar /ˈtɑrtɚ/ *n.* [C] **1** a member of the groups of people from Central Asia that attacked Western Asia and Eastern Europe in the Middle Ages **2** a TATAR —**Tartar** *adj.*

tar·tar /ˈtɑrtɚ/ *n.* **1** [U] a hard yellowish substance that forms on your teeth and can damage them **2** [U] TECHNICAL a reddish-brown substance that forms on the inside of wine BARRELS —see also CREAM OF TARTAR

tartar sauce /ˈ.. ˌ./ *n.* [U] a cold white SAUCE often eaten with fish, made from eggs, oil, PICKLES, CAPERS etc.

tart·y /ˈtɑrti/ *adj.* INFORMAL wearing or looking like the type of clothes that people think a PROSTITUTE would wear

Tash·kent /tæʃˈkɛnt, tɑʃ-/ the capital city of Uzbekistan

task /tæsk/ *n.* [C] **1** a piece of work that must be done, especially one that is difficult or that must be done regularly: *Many older people need help with daily tasks like dressing and eating.* | [+ of] *After the floods, we were faced with the task of repairing the damage.* | *New workers will be shown how to*

perform *routine* **tasks** *first.* **2** a piece of work that is difficult but very important: *Our main task is to improve the economy.* **3 take someone to task** to tell someone that you strongly disapprove of something they have done

task force /ˈ. ./ *n.* [C] **1** a group formed for a short time to deal with a particular problem: *a government task force on urban education* **2** a military force sent to a place for a special purpose

task·mas·ter /ˈtæskˌmæstɚ/ *n.* someone who forces people to work very hard or use a lot of effort: **a hard/stern/tough taskmaster** *Our high school coach was a tough taskmaster.*

Tas·ma·ni·a /tæzˈmeɪniə/ a large island near the southeast coast of Australia, which is one of the states of Australia —**Tasmanian** *n., adj.*

tas·sel /ˈtæsəl/ *n.* [C] a mass of threads tied together into a round ball at one end and hung as a decoration on clothes, curtains etc. —**tasseled** *adj.*

taste[1] /teɪst/ *n.*

1 food [singular,U] the special feeling that is produced by a particular food or drink when you put it in your mouth: *The flour gives a faintly sweet taste to the crust.* | [+ of] *Noriko doesn't like the taste of American coffee.* —compare FLAVOR[1] (1)

2 judgment [U] someone's judgment about what is good or appropriate when they choose clothes, music, art etc.: *No one with any taste would buy a painting like that.* | *Rubin has shown* **good taste in** *the roles she has chosen to play.*

3 sth you like [C,U] the type of thing that you tend to like or like to do: *The resort caters to people with expensive tastes.* | [+ **for**] *A rafting trip through the Grand Canyon will satisfy your taste for adventure.* | [+ **in**] *Nick admits he has a bizarre taste in clothing.* | *She had the whole house redecorated* **to** *her* **taste**.

4 small amount of food [C usually singular] a small amount of food or drink that you put in your mouth to try it: *Can I have a taste of your sundae?*

5 experience [C usually singular] a small example or short experience of something, especially something that you want more of: [+ **of**] *I parked my car and started walking to get a taste of Chinatown.* | *Begley got his* **first taste** *of fame on the 1970s television show.*

6 be (in) good/bad/poor taste to be appropriate or inappropriate for a particular occasion: *I thought Craig's joke was in pretty poor taste.*

7 leave a bad/bitter/sour taste in sb's mouth to make someone feel angry or upset as a result of something bad: *Being laid off with so little notice left a bad taste in my mouth.*

8 with tongue [U] the sense by which you know one food from another: *Smoking can damage your sense of taste.*

9 to taste a phrase meaning as much as is needed to make something taste the way you like, used in instructions for cooking: *Add salt and pepper to taste.* —see also **there's no accounting for taste** (ACCOUNT[2] (5)), **an acquired taste** (ACQUIRE (4))

taste[2] *v.* **1** [linking verb] to have a particular type of taste: *The cake tastes pretty good to me.* | *I don't like cranberries – they just kind of sour.* | [**taste like sth**] *I've never had rabbit, but they say it tastes like chicken.* | **sweet-tasting/strong-tasting etc.** (=having a sweet, strong etc. taste) **2** [T] to put a small amount of food or drink into your mouth to see what it is like: *Taste your eggs before you put salt on them.* | *Did you taste the salsa?* **3** [T not in progressive] to experience the taste of food or drink: *I can't taste anything with this cold.* **4 taste fame/freedom etc.** to have a short experience of something that you want more of: *Once the people have tasted freedom, they are unlikely to give it up.* **5 sth tastes like dishwater** INFORMAL used to say that a drink such as tea or coffee tastes bad because it is too weak

---

USAGE NOTE: TASTE

WORD CHOICE: taste, try, sample
You can use **taste** to mean to eat or drink a little of something just in order to find out its flavor: *Have you tasted the ice cream yet?* But **taste** is much more often

used in other meanings, where you experience the taste of something: *I can really taste the garlic on the pizza.*| *This wine tastes good* (NOT *"This wine is very good taste."*). Usually people use the word **try** to mean to eat or drink something deliberately to see if they like it – not just what it tastes like, but also how it feels, how it smells etc.: *Let me try some of that dip.* You can also use **sample** to mean to try just a little food or drink: *You'll have a chance to sample all the cheeses of the region.*

taste bud /'. ./ *n.* [C usually plural] one of the small parts of the surface of your tongue which can tell the difference between foods according to their taste

taste·ful /'teɪstfəl/ *adj.* made, decorated, or chosen with good TASTE[1] (2): *Williams says the love scenes in the movie are "tasteful."* —**tastefully** *adv.*: *a tastefully furnished apartment* —**tastefulness** *n.* [U] —compare TASTY

taste·less /'teɪstlɪs/ *adj.* **1** offensive or inappropriate for a particular situation: *a tasteless TV talk show* | *tasteless jokes* **2** food or drink that is tasteless is not good, because it has no particular taste: *The salad was limp and tasteless.* **3** made, decorated, or chosen with bad TASTE[1] (2): *gaudy and tasteless designs* —**tastelessly** *adv.* —**tastelessness** *n.* [U]

tast·er /'teɪstɚ/ *n.* [C] someone whose job is to test the quality of foods, wines etc. by tasting them: *a wine taster*

tast·ing /'teɪstɪŋ/ *n.* [C,U] an event that is organized so that you can try different foods or drinks to see if you like them, or the activity of doing this: *a wine and cheese tasting*

tast·y /'teɪsti/ *adj.* **tastier, tastiest 1** tasty food has a good taste: *These cookies are very tasty.* —compare TASTEFUL **2** INFORMAL tasty news, GOSSIP etc. is especially interesting and is often related to sex or surprising behavior —**tastiness** *n.* [U]

tat /tæt/ *n.* [U] —see TIT FOR TAT

ta·ta·mi /tɑ'tami, tə-/ *n.* [U] woven pieces of straw used as a covering for a floor in a house, especially in Japan —**tatami** *adj.*: *tatami mats*

Ta·tar /'tɑtɚ/ *n.* **1** [C] a member of a group of people who live in parts of Russia, Ukraine, and Central Asia **2** [U] one of the languages of these people —**Tatar** *adj.*

ta·ter /'teɪtɚ/ *n.* [C] SPOKEN a potato

Tater Tots, tater tots /'.. ,./ *n.* [plural] TRADEMARK potatoes that are cut into small pieces, made into balls, frozen, and then fried (FRY) or baked

tat·tered /'tætɚd/ *adj.* **1** clothes, books etc. that are tattered are old and torn: *She was poorly dressed in a tattered knit sweater.* **2** dressed in old torn clothes

tat·ters /'tætɚz/ *n.* [plural] **1** clothing or pieces of cloth that are old and torn **2 in tatters a)** a plan, POLICY etc. that is in tatters is ruined or badly damaged: *After the war, the country's economy was in tatters.* **b)** clothes that are in tatters are old and torn

tat·ting /'tætɪŋ/ *n.* [U] a type of LACE that you make by hand, or the process of making it

tat·tle /'tætl/ *v.* [I] **1** if a child tattles, they tell a parent or teacher that another child has done something bad: [+ on] *Robert is always tattling on me for things I didn't do.* **2** OLD-FASHIONED to talk about small unimportant things, or about other people's private affairs; GOSSIP —**tattling** *n.* [U] —**tattler** *n.* [C]

tat·tle·tale /'tætl,teɪl/ *n.* [C] a word meaning someone who tattles, used by or to children

tat·too[1] /tæ'tu/ *n.* plural **tattoos 1** [C] a picture or message that is permanently marked on your skin with a needle and ink: *a tattoo of a lion* **2** [singular] a rapid continuous beating of drums, especially played as a military signal, or a sound like this **3** [C] a signal played on a drum or BUGLE (=type of horn) to tell soldiers to go to bed at night

tattoo[2] *v.* [T] **1** to make a permanent picture or message on someone's skin with a needle and ink **2** to mark someone in this way —**tattooed** *adj.*: *a heavily tattooed arm*

tattoo art·ist /.'. ,../ also **tat·too·ist** /tæ'tuɪst/ *n.* [C] someone whose job is tattooing

tattoo par·lor /.'. ,.., '.. ,../ *n.* [C] a building where you go to get a tattoo

tat·ty /'tæti/ *adj.* **tattier, tattiest** INFORMAL looking old and dirty, or in a bad condition; SHABBY: *a tatty old hat*

taught /tɔt/ the past tense and past participle of TEACH

taunt[1] /tɔnt, tɑnt/ *v.* [T] to try to make someone angry or upset by saying things that are not nice, or by laughing at their faults or failures: *The older boys taunted Chris and called him a girl.* —**taunting** *adj.* —**tauntingly** *adv.*

taunt[2] *n.* [C often plural] a remark or joke intended to make someone angry or upset: *He wears a bike helmet – even though it brings taunts from his peers.*

taupe /toup/ *n.* [U] a brownish, gray color —**taupe** *adj.*

Tau·rus /'tɔrəs/ *n.* **1** [U] the second sign of the ZODIAC, represented by a BULL, and believed to affect the character and life of people born between April 20 and May 20 **2** [C] someone who was born between April 20 and May 20: *Lisa's a Taurus.*

taut /tɔt/ *adj.* **1** stretched tight: *He asked a student to hold a rubber band taut between her hands.* | *taut stomach muscles* **2** showing signs of worry or anxiety: *Catherine looked upset, her face taut.* **3** not using more words or time than necessary to tell a story: *His new film is a taut suspenseful thriller.*

tau·tol·o·gy /tɔ'tɑlədʒi/ *n.* plural **tautologies** [C,U] TECHNICAL a statement in which you say the same thing twice using different words when you do not need to, for example, "He sat alone by himself." —**tautological** /,tɔtə'lɑdʒɪkəl/ *adj.* —**tautologically** /-kli/ *adv.* —compare REDUNDANT (1)

tav·ern /'tævɚn/ *n.* [C] a place where alcoholic drinks can be bought and drunk; BAR

taw·dry /'tɔdri/ *adj.* **1** behaving in a way that you should be ashamed of, or showing this quality: *a tawdry scandal* **2** cheaply and badly made: *tawdry jewelry* —**tawdriness** *n.* [U]

taw·ny /'tɔni/ *adj.* brownish yellow in color: *a lion's tawny fur*

tax[1] /tæks/ *n.* **1** [C,U] an amount of money that you must pay to the government according to your income, property, goods etc. that is used to pay for public services: *The city will have to raise taxes to pay for the roads.* | [+ on] *Farrell was accused of failing to pay taxes on his 1996 income.* | **The tax burden** (=amount of taxes all people must pay) *is not shared equally in this state.* | **before-tax/after-tax** *The company reported an after-tax profit of $1.2 million.* **2** [singular] FORMAL something that uses a lot of your strength, PATIENCE etc. —see also CAPITAL GAINS TAX, **corporation tax** (CORPORATION (2)), INCOME TAX, PROPERTY TAX, SALES TAX

tax[2] *v.* [T] **1 a)** to charge a tax on a product, income, property etc.: *Company profits are currently taxed at 34%.* | *Gasoline is heavily taxed in Europe.* **b)** to charge someone a tax for their income, property etc.: *The rich are supposed to be taxed at a higher rate than the poor.* **2 tax sb's patience/strength etc.** FORMAL to use almost all of someone's patience, strength etc.: *Recent events have taxed the nation's strength.* —**taxable** *adj.*: *taxable income* —see also TAXING

tax·a·tion /tæk'seɪʃən/ *n.* [U] the system or process of charging taxes, or the money paid for taxes: *How do I protect my investments from taxation?*

tax a·void·ance /'. .,../ *n.* [U] legal ways of paying less tax —compare TAX EVASION

tax brack·et /'. ,../ *n.* [C] a particular range of income levels on which the same rate of tax is paid

tax break /'. ./ *n.* [C] a special reduction in taxes that the government allows for a particular purpose or group of people: *a tax break for small business owners*

tax col·lec·tor /'. .,../ *n.* [C] someone who works for the government and makes sure that people pay their taxes

tax cut /'. ./ *n.* [C] an official decision by the government to charge people less tax on what they earn

tax-de·duct·i·ble, tax deductible /,. .'...ᐠ/ *adj.* tax-deductible costs can be subtracted from your total income before you calculate how much tax you owe: *Contributions to the charity are completely tax deductible.*

tax-de·ferred /,. .'.ᐠ/ *adj.* not taxed until a later time: *tax-deferred savings*

tax dodge /'. ./ *n.* [C] INFORMAL a way of paying less tax, which may be legal or illegal —**tax dodger** *n.* [C]

tax e·va·sion /'. .,./ *n.* [U] the crime of paying too little tax, or paying no tax at all

tax-ex·empt /,. .'.ᐠ/ *adj.* not taxed, or not having to pay tax: *tax-exempt savings* | *a tax-exempt charity*

tax ex·ile /'. ,../ *n.* [C] someone who moves to another country in order to avoid paying high taxes in their own country

tax-free /,. '.ᐠ/ *adj.* not taxed: *tax-free winnings*

tax ha·ven /'. ,../ *n.* [C] a place where people go to live in order to avoid paying high taxes in their own countries

tax·i[1] /'tæksi/ *n. plural* **taxis** [C] a car with a driver that you pay to take you somewhere; CAB: *Let's just hail a taxi* (=wave or shout at a taxi to make it stop).

taxi[2] *v.* **taxis** or **taxies, taxied, taxiing** [I] if an airplane taxis, it moves slowly along the ground before taking off or after landing

tax·i·cab /'tæksikæb/ *n.* [C] a taxi

tax·i·der·mist /'tæksə,dɚmɪst/ *n.* [C] someone whose job is taxidermy

tax·i·der·my /'tæksə,dɚmi/ *n.* [U] the art of specially preparing the skins of dead animals, birds, or fish, and then filling them with a special material so that they look as though they are alive

tax·ing /'tæksɪŋ/ *adj.* needing a lot of effort; DEMANDING: *It is an extremely physically taxing competition.*

tax in·spec·tor /'. .,../ *n.* [C] someone who works for the government, deciding how much tax a person or company should pay

taxi stand /'.. ,./ *n.* [C] a place where taxis wait for customers

tax·i·way /'tæksi,weɪ/ *n.* [C] the hard surface like a road that an airplane drives on to get from the airport to the RUNWAY

tax·man /'tæksmæn/ *n.* [C] **1** a TAX COLLECTOR or tax inspector **2 the taxman** INFORMAL the government department that collects taxes

TAXOL, taxol /'tæksɔl/ *n.* [U] TRADEMARK a drug made from the outer surface of a tree, that is used to treat CANCER of the ovaries (OVARY)

tax·on·o·my /tæk'sɑnəmi/ *n. plural* **taxonomies** [C,U] the process or result of organizing things such as plants or animals into different groups or sets that show their natural relationships

tax·pay·er /'tæks,peɪɚ/ *n.* [C] a person or organization that pays tax

tax re·lief /'. .,./ *n.* [U] a reduction in the amount of tax you have to pay, especially as a result of a change in a law

tax re·turn /'. .,./ *n.* [C] the form on which you calculate your taxes and which you must send to the government

tax shel·ter /'. ,../ *n.* [C] a plan or method that allows you to legally avoid paying taxes

tax year /'. ./ *n.* [C] the period of 12 months in which your income is calculated for paying taxes

Tay·lor /'teɪlɚ/, **Zach·a·ry** /'zækəri/ (1784–1850) the 12th President of the U.S.

TB *n.* **1** [U] tuberculosis; a serious infectious disease that affects your lungs and other parts of your body **2** [C] the written abbreviation of TAILBACK

TBA To Be Announced; used to say that a piece of information will be decided or given at a later time: *game time TBA*

T-ball /'ti bɔl/ *n.* [U] TRADEMARK an easy form of baseball for young children in which you hit the ball off a special stick

Tbi·li·si /təbə'lisi/ the capital and largest city of Georgia

T-bill /'ti bɪl/ *n.* [C] the abbreviation of TREASURY BILL

T-bone steak /,ti boun 'steɪk/ also **T-bone** *n.* [C] a thinly cut piece of BEEF that has a T-shaped bone in it

tbs., tbsp. *n.* [C] the written abbreviation of TABLESPOON: *1 tbs. sugar*

T cell, T-cell /'ti sɛl/ *n.* [C] a type of WHITE BLOOD CELL that helps the body fight disease

Tchai·kov·sky /tʃaɪ'kɔfski/, **Pe·ter Il·yich** /'pitɚ 'ɪlɪtʃ/ (1840–1893) a Russian musician who wrote CLASSICAL music

TDD *n.* [C,U] telecommunications device for the deaf; a piece of equipment that makes it possible for people who are unable to hear to use the telephone by typing (TYPE[2] (2)) the words they want to say

TE *n.* [C] the written abbreviation of TIGHT END

tea /ti/ *n.* **1** [U] a hot brown drink made by pouring boiling water onto the dried leaves from a particular bush: *How about a cup of tea?* —see also ICED TEA **2 mint/chamomile/herbal etc. tea** a hot drink made by pouring boiling water onto the leaves or flowers of a particular plant, sometimes used as a medicine **3** [U] the dried leaves of a particular Asian bush, used for making tea: *tea plantations* **4 (not) for all the tea in China** OLD-FASHIONED, INFORMAL used to say that you would refuse to do something, whatever happened: *I wouldn't marry her for all the tea in China.* —see also **not be your cup of tea** (CUP[1] (9)) ⬜ S W 1 3

tea·bag /'tibæg/ *n.* [C] a small paper bag with tea leaves inside, used for making tea

teach /titʃ/ *v. past tense and past participle* **taught** ⬜ S W 1 1
1 ‖school/college etc.‖ [I,T] to give lessons at a school, college, or university: *Russell has been teaching in Japan for almost ten years.* | *I teach 18- to 21-year-olds.* | [**teach sth to sb**] *Volunteers were sent to teach reading to inner-city children.* | [**teach sb about sth**] *We need to do more to teach teenagers about AIDS.* | **teach English/mathematics/history etc.** *Do you know who's teaching biology this semester?* | **teach school/college etc.** *She teaches third grade in Little Rock.*
2 ‖show sb how‖ [T] to show someone how to do something: [**teach sb (how) to do sth**] *My mother taught me how to drive.* | *Eli's teaching me to play chess.* | [**teach sb sth**] *Can you teach me one of your card tricks?*
3 ‖change sb's ideas‖ [T] to show or tell someone how they should behave or what they should think: [**teach sb to do sth**] *Parents need to teach their children to share.* | [**teach sb sth**] *No one ever taught him the difference between right and wrong.*
4 ‖experience shows sth‖ [T] if an experience or situation teaches you something, it helps you to understand something about life: [**teach sb sth**] *Camp teaches kids a lot about nature.* | [**teach sb to do sth**] *Playing sports has taught me never to give up.*
5 that'll teach you! SPOKEN used when something bad has just happened to someone, especially because they ignored your warning: **that'll teach you to do sth** *That'll teach you to park in a loading zone.*
6 teach sb a lesson INFORMAL to make someone avoid doing something bad or unwise again: *They say they beat Scott up to teach him a lesson.*
7 you can't teach an old dog new tricks used to say that older people often do not want to change or cannot change the way they do things —see Usage Note at LEARN

USAGE NOTE: TEACH

WORD CHOICE: teach, instruct, tutor, train, educate
Teach is the general word for helping a person or group of people to learn something: *He teaches math at the high school.*| *Who taught you how to sew?* If you **instruct** someone, you teach them, especially in a practical way and about a practical skill: *Patients can be*

instructed in how to perform the tests at home. You **tutor** someone when they need help learning a particular subject outside the ordinary educational system: *I need someone to tutor me in French.* You can **train** a person or group of people, especially in the particular skills and knowledge they need to do a job: *It will take at least a month to train the new assistant.* You can also **train** an animal: *The dogs are trained to attack any stranger that comes near.* **Educate** means to teach people over a long period of time, in all kinds of knowledge (not just school subjects): *It will be very difficult to educate our children without decent school buildings.| We need to educate the public about the dangers of drugs.*

Teach /tiʧ/, **Ed·ward** /ˈɛdwəd/ also **Blackbeard** (died 1718) a British PIRATE

teach·er /ˈtiʧə/ *n.* [C] someone whose job is to teach: *Mrs. Sherwood was my first-grade teacher.* | **history/ English/chemistry etc. teacher** *Mel wants to be a French teacher when she finishes college.*

teacher's pet /ˌ.. ˈ./ *n.* [C] INFORMAL a child who everyone thinks is the teacher's favorite student and is therefore disliked by the other students

teach-in /ˈ. ./ *n.* [C] a situation in which people protest a political or social problem by coming together to give information about it and discuss it: *Students held a teach-in to protest the war.*

teach·ing /ˈtiʧɪŋ/ *n.* [U] **1** the work or profession of a teacher: *Ann's planning to go into teaching after she graduates from college.* | *I did my **student teaching** (=period of teaching done while training to be a teacher) in a small town in Indiana.* **2** also **teachings** [plural] the moral, religious, or political ideas spread by a particular person or group: *the teachings of Confucius*

teaching as·sist·ant /ˈ.. ˌ.ˌ./ *n.* [C] a GRADUATE student at a university who teaches classes

teaching hos·pi·tal /ˈ.. ˌ.ˌ./ *n.* [C] a hospital where medical students receive practical training from experienced doctors

tea co·zy /ˈ. ˌ.ˌ./ *n.* [C] a thick cover that you put over a TEAPOT to keep the tea hot

tea·cup /ˈtikʌp/ *n.* [C] a cup that you serve tea in

tea gar·den /ˈ. ˌ.ˌ./ *n.* [C] a public garden where people can buy and drink tea

tea·house /ˈtihaʊs/ *n.* [C] a special building in China or Japan where tea is served, often as part of a ceremony

teak /tik/ *n.* **1** [U] a very hard yellowish-brown wood that is used for making ships and good-quality furniture **2** [C] the South Asian tree that this wood comes from

tea ket·tle, teakettle /ˈ. ˌ.ˌ./ *n.* [C] a metal container with a handle and a SPOUT that is used for boiling water

teal /til/ *n.* **1** [U] a greenish blue color **2** [C] a small wild duck —**teal** *adj.*

tea leaves /ˈ. ./ *n.* **1** [plural] the small finely cut pieces of leaves used for making tea **2 read the tea leaves** to look at tea leaves in the bottom of a cup to try to find out what will happen in the future

team¹ /tim/ *n.* [C] **1** a group of people who play a game or sport together against another group: *a football team.* | *I really want to **play for** the Olympic hockey team.* | *How long have you been **on the** basketball team?* | *Scott didn't **make** the soccer team* (=be chosen for the team) *this year.* **2** a group of people who have been chosen to work together to do a particular job: [+ of] *She will be represented by a team of the nation's best lawyers.* **3** two or more animals that are used to pull a vehicle

team² *v.*

team up *phr. v.* [I] to join with someone in order to work on something: [+ with] *The university is teaming up with a school in England for the research project.*

team·mate /ˈtim-meɪt/ *n.* [C] someone who plays on the same team as you

team play·er /ˌ. ˈ.ˌ./ *n.* [C] INFORMAL someone who works well with other people so the whole group is successful

team spir·it /ˌ. ˈ.ˌ./ *n.* [U] willingness to work with other people as part of a team

team·ster /ˈtimstə/ *n.* [C] someone who controlled pairs or groups of animals that pulled vehicles in past times

Team·sters, the /ˈtimstəz/ a large U.S. UNION, mainly for people who drive trucks

team·work /ˈtimwək/ *n.* [U] the ability of a group of people to work well together

tea par·ty /ˈ. ˌ.ˌ./ *n.* [C] **1** a small party in the afternoon at which tea, cake etc. is served **2 be no tea party** INFORMAL to be very difficult or not nice to do

tea·pot /ˈtipɑt/ *n.* [C] a container for making and serving tea, which has a handle and a SPOUT —see also **a tempest in a teapot** (TEMPEST (2))

tear¹ /tɪr/ *n.* [C] a drop of salty liquid that flows from your eye when you are crying: *Is that a tear on your face?* | *tear-stained cheeks* | *Things were so bad at work, I would often come home **in tears** (=crying). | When you see a grown man **burst into tears** (=suddenly start crying), you know something is wrong. | In court Burg **broke down in tears** (=started crying) while reading the statement. | **Fighting back tears** (=trying very hard not to cry), she kissed her son goodbye. | I could tell you stories that would **bring tears to your eyes** (=make you almost cry). | He's a tough director who can easily **reduce** actors **to tears** (=make someone cry, especially by being unkind to them). | We're not **shedding** any **tears** (=crying because we are sad) over his resignation. | **tears of joy/anger/sadness etc.** Tears of gratitude shone in his eyes. | **be close to tears/be on the verge of tears** (=be almost crying)* —see also **crocodile tears** (CROCODILE (3))

tear² /tɛr/ *v. past tense* **tore** *past participle* **torn**

tear up

1 paper/cloth **a)** [T] to damage something such as paper or cloth by pulling it too hard or letting it touch something sharp: *How did you tear your pocket?* | *Don't tear pages out of the book.* | *I tore a hole in my new blouse.* | *Celia grabbed the envelope and tore it open.* **b)** [I] if paper or cloth tears, a hole appears in it, or it splits, because it has been pulled too hard or has touched something sharp: *Careful – the paper is very old and tears easily.*

2 remove sth [T always + adv./prep.] to pull something violently from the place where it is attached or held: [**tear sth from/away/off etc.**] *After tearing the gold chain off the victim's neck, the mugger ran away.* | *The impact tore loose the rear engine of the plane.*

3 move quickly [I always + adv./prep.] to move somewhere very quickly, especially in a dangerous or careless way: [+ **away/up/past etc.**] *Would you kids stop tearing around the house?*

4 tear sb/sth to shreds/pieces a) to tear something into very small pieces: *Male Siamese fighting fish will tear each other's fins to shreds.* **b)** to criticize someone or something very severely: *In the end the prosecutor's case was torn to shreds by Russell's lawyer.*

5 muscle [T] to damage a muscle or LIGAMENT (=a strong band connected to your muscles)

6 tear sb limb from limb to attack someone in a very violent way, or tear their body apart: *Garcia's opponents are angry enough to tear him limb from limb.* —see also **tear/pull your hair out** (HAIR (5)), **tear/rip sb's heart out** (HEART (10)), **TORN²**

tear sb/sth **apart** *phr. v.* [T] **1** to break something into many small pieces, especially in a violent way: *Two tornadoes tore apart airplanes at the small airport.* **2** to make an organization, group etc. start having problems: *Disagreement over the minister is tearing our church apart.* **3** to make someone feel extremely unhappy or upset: *It would tear me apart to see one of my kids suffer like that.* **4** to make a close relationship between two or more people end in a sad way, especially by making one person move away: *War tore the family apart.* **5** to criticize someone very strongly: *My Dad didn't like him and just tore him apart.*

tear at sb/sth *phr. v.* [T] to pull violently at someone or something: *The children were screaming and tearing at each other's hair.*

tear sb ↔ **away** *phr. v.* [T] **1 tear yourself away** to leave a place or stop doing something when you do not really want to: [+ **from**] *We're going to a movie if she ever tears herself away from that computer.* **2** to persuade or force someone to leave a place or stop doing something, when they do not want to leave

tear sth ↔ **down** *phr. v.* [T] to knock down a large building or part of a building: *They're finally tearing down that old house on State Street.*

tear into sb/sth *phr. v.* [T not in passive] **1** to attack someone, especially by hitting them very hard: *The Steelers tore into the Patriots, winning 37–20.* **2** to start doing something with a lot of energy: *"This looks great!" Jen said, tearing into her dinner.* **3** to criticize someone very strongly, especially unfairly: *Then Bob started tearing into her for spending money.*

tear sth ↔ **off** *phr. v.* to remove your clothes as quickly as you can: *Kelly tore off his shirt and jumped in the pool.*

tear sb/sth ↔ **up** *phr. v.* [T] **1** [**tear** sth ↔ **up**] to destroy a piece of paper or cloth by tearing it into small pieces: *Tear up the check before you throw it away.* **2** [**tear** sth ↔ **up**] to break the surface of a street or area of land into small pieces and make it rough: *People couldn't get there because the streets were torn up.* **3** [**tear** sb **up**] to make someone feel extremely unhappy or upset: *When I hear people criticize the food we serve, it just tears me up.* **4** [**tear** sth ↔ **up**] to damage or ruin a place, especially by behaving violently: *Kari tore up the apartment looking for her keys.* **5 tear up an agreement/contract etc.** to suddenly decide to stop being restricted by a contract etc.

tear³ /tɛr/ *n.* [C] a hole in a piece of cloth, paper etc. where it has been torn —see also **wear and tear** (WEAR² (4))

tear⁴ /tɪr/ *v.* [I] if your eyes tear, they produce tears because it is cold, you are sick etc.

tear up *phr. v.* [I] to almost start crying: *Ed teared up when he talked about his father.*

tear·drop /'tɪrdrɑp/ *n.* [C] **1** a single drop of salty liquid from your eye **2** a shape that is pointed at one end and wide and round at the other end

tear·ful /'tɪrfəl/ *adj.* crying a little, or almost crying: *a tearful goodbye* —**tearfully** *adv.*

tear gas /'tɪr gæs/ *n.* [U] a gas that stings your eyes, used by the police to control crowds —**teargas** *v.* [T]

tear·jerk·er /'tɪr,dʒɜrkɚ/ *n.* [C] INFORMAL a movie, book, story etc. that makes you feel very sad

tea·room /'tirum/ *n.* [C] a restaurant where tea and small meals are served

S W 2 **tease¹** /tiz/ *v.* **1** [I,T] to make jokes and laugh at someone in order to have fun by embarrassing them, either in a friendly way or in an unkind way: *I didn't mean to make you mad; I was only teasing.* | *Brad was one of the kids who used to tease me at school.* | [**tease** sb **about** sth] *If I were you, I wouldn't tease Gerri about her hair.* **2** [T] to deliberately annoy an animal: *The dog's going to bite you if you don't stop teasing it.* **3** [I,T] to deliberately make someone sexually excited without intending to have sex with them: *Donna's only interested in teasing guys.* **4** [T] to comb your hair in the opposite direction of which it grows, so that it looks thicker

tease sth ↔ **out** *phr. v.* **1** to succeed in finding information, the meaning of something etc., even though this is difficult and may take a long time: *Scientists could tease out clues as to how the Earth began.* **2** to gently loosen or straighten hairs or threads that are stuck together: *She teased out the knots in her hair.* **3 tease sth out of sb** to persuade someone to tell you something that they do not want to tell you

tease² *n.* [C] INFORMAL **1** DISAPPROVING someone who deliberately makes another person sexually excited, but has no intention of having sex: *Erin's such a big tease.* **2** someone who enjoys making jokes at people, and embarrassing them, especially in a friendly way **3** an act of teasing someone, or something that teases them: *The movie preview should be a tease of what is to follow.* —see also STRIPTEASE

teas·er /'tizɚ/ *n.* [C] INFORMAL **1** a very difficult question that you have to think about very hard —see also BRAINTEASER **2** a TEASE²

tea ser·vice /'. ,../ *n.* [C] a matching set of cups, plates, pot etc., used for serving tea

tea·spoon /'tispun/ *n.* [C] **1** a small spoon commonly S W used for eating and for mixing sugar into tea, coffee 3 etc. —see picture at SPOON¹ **2 a)** a special spoon used for measuring small amounts in cooking, equal to ¹/₃ of a TABLESPOON or 5 ml **b)** also **tea·spoon·ful** /'tispunful/ the amount a teaspoon can hold

teat /tɪt, tit/ *n.* [C] one of the small parts on a female animal's body that her babies suck milk from

tech /tɛk/ *n.* [C] a short form of "technical," used especially in the name of a TECHNICAL COLLEGE

tech·ie /'tɛki/ *n.* [C] INFORMAL someone who knows a lot about computers and electronic equipment and is very skillful at using and repairing them —**techie** *adj.* [only before noun] *techie toys*

tech·ni·cal /'tɛknɪkəl/ *adj.*

1 industry/science relating to practical knowl- S W edge, skills, or methods, especially in industrial or 3 scientific work: *No one here has the technical knowledge to fix the copier.* | *technical experts* | *technical training* —see Usage Note at TECHNIQUE

2 details involving small details and needing a lot of attention and special knowledge or skill: *Jurors must deal with many technical legal questions.* | *Many books on furniture making are too technical or require artistic skills.*

3 language using words in a special way that is difficult for most people to understand because it is connected with one particular subject: *The technical term for a heart attack is an "infarction."*

4 technical problem/difficulty a problem involving the way an engine or system works: *The space probe's launch was delayed due to a technical problem.*

5 according to rules according to the exact details in a set of rules: *a technical foul*

6 in music/art etc. relating to the special skill of doing something difficult, especially in music, art, sports etc.: *As a quarterback, Elway has excellent technical skills.*

technical col·lege /'... ,../ *n.* [C] a college where students study subjects that involve making, building, or repairing things, such as cars, houses, or electronic equipment —compare JUNIOR COLLEGE, COMMUNITY COLLEGE

tech·ni·cal·i·ty /,tɛknɪ'kæləṭi/ *n. plural* **technicalities** [C] a small detail in a system, a law, or a set of rules, especially one that needs special knowledge to understand: *Unless you're an experienced musician, you wouldn't be able to explain the technicalities of the music.* | *A legal technicality delayed the scheduled start of the trial.* | *Walls won the fishing tournament on a technicality* (=only because of a technicality).

tech·ni·cally /'tɛknɪkli/ *adv.* **1** [sentence adverb] S W according to the exact details of rules, laws etc.: 3 *Technically, you are responsible if someone gets injured on your property.* **2** [+ adj./adv.] showing the special skills relating to a particular activity: *Bob is technically the best golfer on the team.* **3 technically possible/impossible/difficult etc.** possible, impossible etc. using the scientific knowledge that is available now: *In the future, it will be technically possible to live on the moon.*

technical school /'... ,.'/ *n.* [C] a TECHNICAL COLLEGE

technical sup·port /,... .'./ also **tech support** *n.* [U] help or information that you receive to improve a computer program or system, make it continue working, or use it correctly

tech·ni·cian /tɛk'nɪʃən/ *n.* [C] **1** a skilled scientific or industrial worker: *a dental technician* **2** someone who is very good at the skills of a particular sport, art etc.: *Stewart has become a real technician as an offensive guard.*

Tech·ni·col·or /'tɛknə,kʌlɚ/ *n.* [U] TRADEMARK a method of making color movies that produces very clear bright colors

tech·ni·col·or /'tɛknə,kʌlɚ/ *adj.* [only before noun] having many very bright colors, usually too bright: *Sam's technicolor jacket*

s w **tech·nique** /tɛk'nik/ *n.* **1** [C] a special skill or way of **2** doing something, especially one that has to be **3** learned: *Doctors are developing a painless technique to give shots.* **2** [U] the level of skill or the set of skills that someone has: *the artist's impressive style and technique*

USAGE NOTE: TECHNIQUE

WORD CHOICE: technique, technology, technical, high-tech

The noun **technique** [C] is a specific way of doing something, usually involving some skill: *We want our teachers to learn the latest teaching techniques.* **Technology** is a noun that means the scientific knowledge which is used for practical purposes such as making machines, electronic equipment etc.: *The technology (NOT "the technique") to make photographs did not exist in the 16th century.| Space research has produced major advances in computer technology (NOT "computer technique").* **Technical** is an adjective and means detailed practical knowledge of something involving science, technology, or machines: *Her job requires a lot of technical training* (NOT "technique training"). **High-tech** is also an adjective. It is short for *high technology* (NOT "high technique" or "high technical") and is used about things that use the most modern technology.

---

tech·no /'tɛknoʊ/ *n.* [U] a type of popular electronic dance music with a fast strong beat

techno- /tɛknə/ *prefix* relating to TECHNOLOGY: *technophobia* (=dislike and fear of computers, machines etc.) | *techno-literacy* (=skill in using computers or other equipment)

tech·noc·ra·cy /tɛk'nɑkrəsi/ *n.* [C,U] a social system in which people with a lot of scientific or technical knowledge have a lot of power

tech·no·crat /'tɛknəkræt/ *n.* [C] a highly skilled scientist who has a lot of power in industry or government

tech·no·log·i·cal /,tɛknə'lɑdʒɪkəl/ *adj.* relating to technology: **technological advances/improvements/innovations etc.** *Prices have been going down, as a result of technological progress.*

tech·no·log·i·cal·ly /,tɛknə'lɑdʒɪkli/ *adv.* in a way that is related to technology: *technologically advanced products* | [sentence adverb] *Technologically, transportation and communication costs have fallen dramatically.*

tech·nol·o·gist /tɛk'nɑlədʒɪst/ *n.* [C] someone who works in a job using equipment that needs special knowledge of technology: *an X-ray technologist*

s w **tech·nol·o·gy** /tɛk'nɑlədʒi/ *n. plural* **technolo-**
1 **gies 1** [C,U] knowledge about scientific or indus-
3 trial methods, or the use of these methods: *laser technology* | *environmentally safe technologies for pest control* —see Usage Note at TECHNIQUE **2** [U] machinery and equipment used or developed as a result of this knowledge: *We use cutting-edge technology to insure product quality.*

tech·no·phobe /'tɛknəfoʊb/ *n.* [C] INFORMAL someone who does not like modern machines, such as computers —**technophobia** /,tɛknə'foʊbiə/ *n.* [U]

tech sup·port /,. .'./ *n.* [U] INFORMAL: see TECHNICAL SUPPORT

tec·ton·ic /tɛk'tɑnɪk/ *adj.* relating to PLATE TECTONICS

tec·ton·ics /tɛk'tɑnɪks/ *n.* [U] PLATE TECTONICS

Te·cum·seh /tə'kʌmsə/ (?1768–1813) a Shawnee chief, famous for trying to unite the Native American tribes in North America so that together they could fight against white people to keep their land

ted·dy /'tɛdi/ *n. plural* **teddies** [C] **1** a teddy bear **2** a piece of clothing for women, intended to be worn in bed or under other clothes, consisting of PANTIES and a top with thin STRAPS over the shoulders, all in one piece

teddy bear /'.. ,./ *n.* [C] a soft toy in the shape of a bear

te·di·ous /'tidiəs/ *adj.* boring, tiring, and continuing for a long time: *a tedious lecture* —**tediously** *adv.* —**tedium** /'tidiəm/ *n.* [U] *I couldn't handle the tedium of work in the factory.* —**tediousness** *n.* [U]

tee¹ /ti/ *n.* [C] **1** a small object, used in GOLF to hold the ball above the ground before you hit it **2** a flat raised area of ground from which you hit the ball in a game of GOLF

tee²
    tee off *phr. v.* **1** [I] to hit the ball off the tee in a game of GOLF **2** [T **tee** sb **off**] INFORMAL to make someone angry: *I think my comment about Mike's hair really teed him off.*

tee-ball /'. ./ *n.* [U] another spelling of T-BALL

teed off /,. './ *adj.* [not before noun] INFORMAL annoyed or angry

teem /tim/ *v.* [I]
    teem with sth *phr. v.* [T] to be full of people, animals etc.: *Local lakes are teeming with bass this spring.*

teem·ing /'timɪŋ/ *adj.* full of people, animals, etc. that are all moving around: **teeming city/streets/market etc.** *the teeming township of Katlehong*

teen¹ /tin/ *adj.* INFORMAL [only before noun] relating to or involving teenagers, or done by teenagers: *teen actresses* | *teen smoking*

teen² *n.* **1** [C usually plural] a teenager: *Marijuana use by teens doubled between 1992 and 1995.* **2 sb's teens** the period of your life when you are between 13 and 19 years old: *Lisa was in her teens when she started her singing career.*

teen·age /'tineɪdʒ/ also **teen·aged** /'tineɪdʒd/ *adj.* [only before noun] aged between 13 and 19, or relating to someone of that age: *my teenage daughter*

teen·ag·er /'ti,neɪdʒɚ/ *n.* [C] someone who is **s w** between 13 and 19 years old —see Usage Note at **3** CHILD

tee·ny /'tini/ also **teen·sy** /'tinzi/ *adj.* INFORMAL very small; TINY

teen·y·bop·per /'tini,bɑpɚ/ *n.* [C] OLD-FASHIONED a young person, especially a girl, between the ages of about 9 and 14, who is very interested in popular music, teenage fashions etc.

teeny wee·ny /,tini 'wini/ also **teen·sy ween·sy** /,tinzi 'winzi/ *adj.* INFORMAL a word meaning "very small," used especially by or to children

tee·pee /'tipi/ *n.* [C] another spelling of TEPEE

tee shirt /'. ./ *n.* [C] another spelling of T-SHIRT

tee·ter /'titɚ/ *v.* [I] **1** to stand or move in an unsteady way as if you are going to fall: [+on/along/across etc.] *Stacks of books teetered on his desk.* **2 be teetering on the brink/edge of sth** to be very close to an extreme and dangerous situation: *The country is teetering on the brink of a massive financial crisis.*

teeter-tot·ter /'.. ,../ *n.* [C] a large toy like a board on which two children sit, one at each end; SEESAW¹

teeth /tiθ/ *n.* the plural of TOOTH

teethe /tið/ *v.* [I] **be teething** if a baby is teething, its first teeth are growing —**teething** *n.* [U]

teething pains /'.. ,./ also **teething prob·lems** /'.. ,../ *n.* [plural] small problems that a company, product, system etc. has at the beginning: *There will* *always be a few teething pains associated with new technology.*

tee·to·tal·er /ˈtiˌtoʊt̬lɚ/ *n.* [C] someone who never drinks alcohol

TEFL /ˈtɛfəl/ *n.* [U] the teaching of English as a foreign language —compare TESOL

Tef·lon /ˈtɛflɑn/ *n.* TRADEMARK a type of plastic that things will not stick to, often used on the inside surfaces of cooking pans

Te·gu·ci·gal·pa /təˌɡusɪˈɡælpə/ the capital and largest city of Honduras

Teh·ran, Teheran /tɛˈrɑn, -ˈræn/ the capital and largest city of Iran

tel. the written abbreviation of telephone number

Tel A·viv /ˌtɛl əˈviv/ the second largest city of Israel, which is on the coast of the Mediterranean Sea

tele- /tɛlə/ *prefix* **1** at or over a long distance; FAR: *a telescope* | *telecommunications* **2** by or for television: *a teleplay* | *telegenic* (=attractive when seen on television)

tel·e·cast /ˈtɛləkæst/ *n.* [C] a broadcast on television —**telecast** *v.* [T]

tel·e·com /ˈtɛləkɑm/ *n.* [U] the abbreviation of TELECOMMUNICATIONS: *the telecom industry*

S W
3 **tel·e·com·mu·ni·ca·tions** /ˌtɛləkəˌmyunəˈkeɪʃənz/ *n.* [U,plural] also **telecommunication** [U] the process or business of sending and receiving messages by telephone, radio, television etc.: *public telecommunications networks*

tel·e·com·mut·er /ˈtɛləkəˌmyut̬ɚ/ *n.* [C] an EMPLOYEE who works at home using computers, FAX machines, telephones etc. to communicate with people at work —**telecommute** *v.* [I] —**telecommuting** *n.* [U]

tel·e·con·ference[1] /ˈtɛləˌkɑnfrəns/ *n.* [C] a business meeting in which people in different places communicate by telephone, radio, television etc. —**teleconferencing** *n.* [U] *video teleconferencing equipment*

teleconference[2] *v.* [I] to have a meeting with people who are not in the same place as you, and be able to see and talk to them by using special VIDEO equipment or computers and telephone lines

tel·e·gen·ic /ˌtɛləˈdʒɛnɪk/ *adj.* attractive when seen on television: *a telegenic political candidate*

tel·e·gram /ˈtɛləˌɡræm/ *n.* [C] a message sent by telegraph

tel·e·graph[1] /ˈtɛləˌɡræf/ *n.* **1** [U] an old-fashioned method of sending messages using radio or electrical signals, in which short and long signals are used to form letters of the alphabet **2** [C] a piece of equipment that receives or sends messages in this way —**telegraphic** /ˌtɛləˈɡræfɪk/ *adj.* —**telegraphically** /-kli/ *adv.*

telegraph[2] *v.* **1** [I,T] to send a message by telegraph: *Barrett telegraphed the owner to see if he would sell the property.* **2** [T] to let people clearly see what you intend to do without saying anything: *Hills' main weakness as quarterback is that he telegraphs his passes.*

te·leg·ra·pher /təˈlɛɡrəfɚ/ *n.* [C] someone whose job is to send and receive messages by telegraph

te·leg·ra·phy /təˈlɛɡrəfi/ *n.* [U] TECHNICAL the process of sending messages by TELEGRAPH[1]

tel·e·ki·ne·sis /ˌtɛləkɪˈnisɪs, -kaɪ-/ *n.* [U] the ability to move physical objects using only the power of your mind —**telekinetic** /ˌtɛləkɪˈnɛt̬ɪk/ *adj.*: *telekinetic powers*

Te·le·mann /ˈtɛləmɑn/, **Ge·org** /ˈɡeɪɔrɡ/ (1681–1767) a German musician who wrote CLASSICAL music

tel·e·mar·ket·ing /ˌtɛləˈmɑrkət̬ɪŋ/ *n.* [U] a method of selling things in which you call people on the telephone and ask if they want to buy something —**telemarketer** *n.* [C]

te·lem·e·try /təˈlɛmətri/ *n.* [U] TECHNICAL the use of special scientific equipment to measure something and send the results somewhere by radio

te·le·ol·o·gy /ˌtili'ɑlədʒi, ˌtɛ-/ *n.* [U] the belief that all natural things and events were specially planned for a particular purpose —**teleological** /ˌtiliə'lɑdʒɪkəl, ˌtɛ-/ *adj.*

tel·e·path·ic /ˌtɛlə'pæθɪk/ *adj.* **1** having a mysterious ability to know what other people are thinking: *How did he know that? He must be telepathic.* **2** relating to or sent by telepathy: *telepathic messages*

te·lep·a·thy /tə'lɛpəθi/ *n.* [U] the communication of thoughts directly from one person's mind to someone else's without speaking, writing, or signs

tel·e·phone[1] /ˈtɛlə,foʊn/ *n.* **1** [C] a piece of equipment that you use to speak to someone in another place; PHONE: *Is that my telephone ringing?* | *a cordless telephone* | *a telephone conversation* | *Reservations can be made by telephone.* | *I was on the telephone* (=using the telephone) *when Dave came in.* | *Do you know your neighbor's telephone number?* | *Roberts did not return telephone calls* (=call the person who called first) *yesterday.* **2** [C] the part of a telephone that you hold close to your ear and mouth; RECEIVER: *Fran hung up the telephone and looked out the window.* —**telephonic** /ˌtɛlə'fɑnɪk/ *adj.* **S W**
2 2

USAGE NOTE: TELEPHONE

WORD CHOICE: telephone, phone, call, give sb a call
The noun **phone** is more common in spoken English than **telephone**: *You can use the phone in the kitchen.* **Telephone** and **phone** can also be used as verbs, but they are not used very much in American English. **Call** and **give sb a call** are the most common ways to say this, especially in speech: *I have to call Mom tonight.* | *Give me a call when you get home.*

---

telephone[2] *v.* [I,T] FORMAL to speak to someone by telephone; call: *At 4:45 a.m., neighbors telephoned police to report a man firing shots.*

telephone book /'... ,./ *n.* [C] a PHONE BOOK

telephone booth /'... ,./ *n.* [C] a PHONE BOOTH

telephone di·rec·to·ry /'... ,...,./ *n.* [C] a PHONE BOOK

telephone ex·change /'... .,./ *n.* [C] a central building or office where telephone calls are connected to other telephones

telephone pole /'... ,./ *n.* [C] a tall wooden pole that supports telephone wires

telephone tag /'... ,./ *n.* [U] PHONE TAG

te·leph·o·ny /tə'lɛfəni/ *n.* [U] TECHNICAL computer HARDWARE and SOFTWARE that allow a computer to make and receive telephone calls

tel·e·pho·to lens /ˌtɛlə,foʊtoʊ 'lɛnz/ *n.* [C] a special camera LENS (2) used for taking clear photographs of things that are far away

tel·e·play /ˈtɛlə,pleɪ/ *n.* [C] a story written for a television program or movie

tel·e·print·er /ˈtɛlə,prɪnt̬ɚ/ *n.* [C] a TELETYPE

Tel·e·Promp·Ter, teleprompter /ˈtɛlə,prɑmptɚ/ *n.* [C] TRADEMARK a machine from which someone speaking on television reads the words of their speech, shown on a screen

tel·e·scope[1] /ˈtɛlə,skoʊp/ *n.* [C] a piece of scientific equipment shaped like a tube, used for making distant objects such as stars and PLANETS look larger and closer —see also RADIO TELESCOPE

telescope[2] *v.* **1** [T usually passive] to make a process or set of events seem to happen in a shorter time: *The play's three acts are admirably telescoped into a 2¹/₂-hour program.* **2** [I,T] if something telescopes or you telescope it, it becomes longer or shorter by sliding parts over each other: *The steering wheel can be tilted up and down and telescoped in and out.*

tel·e·scop·ic /ˌtɛlə'skɑpɪk/ *adj.* **1** also **telescoping** made of parts that slide over each other so that the whole thing can be made longer or shorter: *a tripod with telescopic legs* **2** relating to a telescope or made by using a telescope: *a telescopic picture of Mars* | *The rifle comes with a telescopic sight.*

tel·e·thon /ˈtɛlə,θɑn/ *n.* [C] a special television program in which famous people provide entertainment and ask people to give money to a CHARITY

Tel·e·type /'tɛlətaɪp/ n. [C] **1** TRADEMARK a machine used for writing TELEX messages that you are sending, and for printing messages received; a TELEPRINTER **2** a message that is sent or received by this machine

tel·e·type·writ·er /,tɛlə'taɪpraɪtɚ/ n. [C] a Teletype

tel·e·van·gel·ist /,tɛlə'vændʒəlɪst/ n. [C] a Christian minister who regularly talks about Christianity on television —**televangelism** n. [U]

tel·e·vise /'tɛlə,vaɪz/ v. [T] to broadcast something on television: WGN will televise 30 Chicago Bulls games this season. | the first televised presidential debate

tel·e·vi·sion /'tɛlə,vɪʒən/ n. **1** [C] also **television set** FORMAL a piece of electronic equipment shaped like a box with a screen, on which you can watch programs; TV: a 36-inch television **2** [U] the programs broadcast in this way; TV: Frank *watches television* all the time. | **television program/show/commercial etc.** Tammy's favorite television series is "Friends." **3 on television** broadcast or being broadcast on television: What's on television tonight? **4** [U] the business or activity of making and broadcasting programs on television: Blair has spent his entire career *in television*. | **television producer/reporter/cameraman etc.** Jenner works as a television sports commentator.

tel·ex /'tɛlɛks/ n. **1** [U] the system of sending messages from one business to another on the telephone network, by SATELLITE (1) etc. **2** [C] a message sent in this way —**telex** v. [I,T]

tell /tɛl/ v. past tense and past participle **told**
1 say/information [T] to give someone facts or information about something: **[tell sb (that)]** Tell Teresa I said hi. | I wish someone had told me that the meeting was canceled. | **[tell sb sth]** Tell me your phone number again. | **tell sb who/why/what etc.** She wouldn't tell me why she was angry. | **[tell sb about sth]** Did you tell Jennifer about the party? | **tell a story/joke/secret etc.** Patrick tells lies all the time. | For once, I think he's *telling the truth*. —see Usage Note at SAY[1]
2 recognize the signs [I,T not in progressive] to know something or be able to recognize something because of certain signs that show this: **[tell (that)]** I could tell Darren was really nervous. | **can/could tell** Yes, I do dye my hair. How can you tell? | **tell when/how etc.** They did such a good job, I wasn't even able to tell where the hole had been. | **tell by/from sth** I can tell by the way he talks that he's from the South. | **hard/difficult/impossible etc. to tell** It's hard to tell what Kay's thinking sometimes. | **there's no telling what/how/whether etc.** There's no telling what Bree would do if Nick divorced her.
3 what sb should do [T] to say that someone must do something: **[tell sb to do sth]** Mom told me to take out the trash before I leave. | **[tell sb (that)]** Denise was told she had to work overtime tonight. | **tell sb what/how etc.** Stop trying to tell me what to do all the time. | *Do as you're told* (=obey me) *and don't ask questions.*
4 recognize difference [T not in progressive] to be able to see how one person or thing is different from another: **[tell sb and sb apart]** Adults had the hardest time telling Mike and his brother apart. | **[tell sth from sth]** Most experts can tell an expensive diamond from a cheap one. | It's fairly easy to *tell the difference* between good coffee and bad coffee.
5 warn [T usually in past tense] to warn someone that something bad might happen: **[tell sb (that)]** Alan told Marge she shouldn't walk around alone at night. | **[tell sb to do sth]** I was told to watch out for purse thieves at the market.
6 be a sign of sth [T not in progressive or passive] to give information in ways other than talking which helps you know or understand more about a situation: **[tell sb (that)]** The red light tells you it's recording. | **[tell sb what/why etc.]** The timer will tell you when the rice is finished cooking. | **[tell sb about sth]** Studying of meteorites can tell us about the origins of the universe.
7 tell yourself to remind yourself of the facts of a situation because it is difficult to accept or because it worries you: I kept telling myself that it wasn't my fault.

8 bad behavior [I] INFORMAL to tell someone in authority about something wrong that someone has done: If you don't give back my pen, I'm going to tell. | **[+ on]** I was afraid my little sister would tell on us.
9 affect [I not in progressive] to have an effect on someone, especially a harmful one: His years in the army certainly tell in his attitude to his work. | **[+ on]** I think the strain was beginning to tell on her. —see also TELLING
10 tell time to be able to know what time it is by looking at a clock

SPOKEN PHRASES

11 (I'll) tell you what used when you are suggesting or offering something: I'll tell you what, I'll pay for the movie if you drive.
12 I tell you also **I'm telling you, let me tell you** used to emphasize that what you are saying is true, even though it may be difficult to believe: I tell you, Stan's in a really bad mood.
13 (I) told you (so) used when you have warned someone about a possible danger that has now happened and they have ignored your warning
14 to tell (you) the truth used to emphasize that you are being very honest: To tell you the truth, I can't stand Sandy's cooking.
15 tell me used before asking a question: Tell me, do you think this dress matches theses shoes? | So tell me – what're you doing in Argentina?
16 I'll tell you something/one thing/another thing also **let me tell you something/one thing/another thing** used to make someone pay attention to what you are going to say: Let me tell you something – if I catch you kids smoking, you'll be grounded for a whole year at least.
17 I couldn't tell you used to tell someone that you do not know the answer to their question: "Is it going to rain tomorrow?" "I couldn't tell you."
18 I can't tell you a) used to say that something is a secret, so you cannot answer their question: "So is Maggie really pregnant?" "I can't tell you." **b)** used to say that you cannot express your feelings or describe something well: I can't tell you how grateful I am for your help.
19 I'm not telling (you) used to say that you refuse to tell someone something
20 don't tell me used to interrupt someone because you know what they are going to say or because you want to guess: "We finally made it here." "Don't tell me – you couldn't find your keys." | Don't tell me we're out of milk!
21 sb tells me (that) used to say what someone has told you: Debbie tells me you're looking for a new job.
22 there's no telling what/how etc. used to say that it is impossible to know what has happened or what will happen next: There's no telling how he'll react to the news.
23 to hear sb tell it used to say that someone is gave their opinion of an event, which may not be completely true or correct: To hear Betsy tell it, you'd think we burned the house down.
24 you're telling me used to emphasize that you already know and agree with something that someone has just said: "Wow, it's really hard working outside all day." "You're telling me!"
25 tell me about it used to say that you already know how bad something is, especially because you have experienced it yourself: "I'm totally sick of my boss." "Yeah, tell me about it."
26 you never can tell also **you can never tell** used to say that you cannot be certain about what will happen in the future: "One day they might get married and have kids." "You never can tell."
27 tell sb where to get off SLANG to tell someone angrily that you are not interested in them, what they want etc.: "Did you give him the money?" "No, I told him where to get off."
28 tell me another one used when you do not believe what someone has told you

—see also **all told** (ALL[2] (16))

tell sb/sth **apart** phr. v. [T not in progressive] I've never been able to tell the twins apart.

tell sb/sth **from** sb/sth phr. v. [T not in progressive] to be able to correctly IDENTIFY two people or things, even though they are very similar: The paintings were so good I couldn't tell the copy from the original.

tell of sb/sth phr. v. [T] LITERARY to describe the details of an event or person: Chavez often told of his mother's kindness to strangers.

tell sb ↔ **off** phr. v. [T] to talk angrily to someone because they have done something wrong: Pat, hardly a shy woman, regularly told her husband off in public.

Tell /tɛl/, **William** a Swiss FOLK HERO of the 14th century, who opposed the Austrians who ruled Switzerland

tell·er /'tɛlə/ n. [C] **1** someone whose job is to receive and pay out money in a bank **2** someone who counts votes

Tel·ler /'tɛlə/, **Ed·ward** /'ɛdwəd/ (1908–) a U.S. scientist, born in Hungary, who worked on the development of the ATOM BOMB and HYDROGEN BOMB

tell·ing /'tɛlɪŋ/ adj. **1** having a great or important effect; SIGNIFICANT: The case will have a telling impact on the automotive industry. **2** showing the true character or nature or someone or something, often without being intended: **telling detail/remark/sign etc.** In his most telling remark, Greenspan said that inflation was "too high to ignore." —**tellingly** adv.

tell·tale /'tɛlteɪl/ adj. **telltale signs/marks etc.** signs etc. that clearly show something bad or that is supposed to be secret: There was a telltale trace of alcohol on the captain's breath.

tem·blor /'tɛmblə, -blɔr/ n. [C] FORMAL an EARTHQUAKE

te·mer·i·ty /tə'mɛrəti/ n. [U] **have the temerity to do sth** FORMAL to do or say something that is annoying to someone because they think you are not showing them respect: Klein attacks anyone who has the temerity to disagree with his "ethics."

temp¹ /tɛmp/ n. [C] an office worker who is only employed for a short period of time

temp² v. [I] to work as a temp: Carol's temping until she can find another job.

tem·per¹ /'tɛmpə/ n.
1 tendency to be angry [C,U] a tendency to become angry suddenly: Jill needs to learn to control her temper. | According to Nathan, Robin **has** quite **a temper**. | **Tempers flared** (=people became angry) during the protest. | **a bad/quick/violent etc. temper** I would argue with him too much – he's got a short temper.
2 **lose your temper** to suddenly become so angry that you cannot control yourself: As the argument escalated, Faison lost his temper completely.
3 [singular,U] an uncontrolled feeling of anger that continues for a short time: I left the meeting in **a bad temper**. | In **a fit of temper** (=a quick expression of anger), she smashed the vase against the wall.
4 **keep your temper** to stay calm when it would be easy to get angry
5 attitude [singular] FORMAL the general attitude that people have in a particular place at one time; mood: [+ of] Gandhi knew the temper of the country and saw the necessity for action. —see also BAD-TEMPERED, EVEN-TEMPERED, ILL-TEMPERED, TEMPERED

tem·per² v. [T] **1** FORMAL to make something difficult or bad more acceptable or nicer: [temper sth with sth] Eventually, Williams taught himself to temper anger with humor. **2** to make metal as hard as is needed by heating it and then putting it in cold water —see also TEMPERED

tem·per·a /'tɛmpərə/ n. **1** [U] a type of paint used for painting pictures and signs, which contains a thick liquid such as egg **2** [C] a picture painted with tempera paint

tem·per·a·ment /'tɛmprəmənt/ n. [C,U] the emotional part of someone's character, especially how

likely they are to be happy, angry etc.: Pete has a calm, quiet temperament.

tem·per·a·men·tal /ˌtɛmprə'mɛntl/ adj. **1** likely to suddenly become upset, excited, or angry: our temperamental housekeeper **2** a machine, system etc. that is temperamental does not always work correctly: The concert was good, despite a temperamental sound system. **3** relating to the emotional part of someone's character: Mike and Louis are temperamental opposites. —**temperamentally** adv.

tem·per·ance /'tɛmprəns/ n. [U] **1** OLD-FASHIONED the practice of never drinking alcohol for moral or religious reasons **2** FORMAL sensible control of the things you say and do, especially the amount of alcohol you drink

tem·per·ate /'tɛmprɪt/ adj. **1** **temperate climate/region/area etc.** a type of weather or a part of the world that is never very hot or very cold **2** FORMAL behavior that is temperate is calm and sensible —see also INTEMPERATE

tem·per·ate zone /'.. ˌ./ n. [C] one of the two parts of the Earth that are north and south of the TROPICS

tem·per·a·ture /'tɛmprətʃə/ n. **1** [C,U] a measure of how hot or cold a place or thing is: It was sunny, but the temperature was well below zero. | A rapid **change in temperature** could kill a fish. | The exhibit room has to be kept at **a constant temperature**. | **high/low temperature** The low temperature tomorrow will be in the 40s. | **a rise/fall etc. in temperature** Next week we should expect a fall in temperatures. | **the temperature rises/goes up** (=it gets warmer) | **the temperature falls/drops/goes down** (=it gets colder) —see also ROOM TEMPERATURE **2** sb's **temperature** the temperature of your body, especially used as a measure of whether you are sick or not: The nurse **took** (=measured) **my temperature**. **3** **have a temperature** also **be running a temperature** to have a body temperature that is higher than normal, especially because you are sick

tem·pered /'tɛmpəd/ adj. tempered metal has been made hard by heating it and then putting it in cold water: tempered steel —see also TEMPER²

-tempered /tɛmpəd/ [in adjectives] **good-tempered/foul-tempered/quiet-tempered etc.** usually in a good, bad etc. mood: Matt's a witty, sweet-tempered person.

temper tan·trum /'.. ˌ../ n. [C] a TANTRUM

tem·pest /'tɛmpɪst/ n. **1** [C] LITERARY a violent storm **2** **a tempest in a teapot** an unimportant matter that a lot of people become upset about: Haley dismissed the lawsuit as a tempest in a teapot.

tem·pes·tu·ous /tɛm'pɛstʃuəs/ adj. **1** FORMAL a tempestuous relationship or period of time involves a lot of difficulty and strong emotions **2** LITERARY a tempestuous ocean or wind is very rough and violent; STORMY —**tempestuously** adv. —**tempestuousness** n. [U]

tem·plate /'tɛmpleɪt/ n. [C] **1** a thin sheet of plastic or metal in a special shape or pattern used to help cut other materials in a similar shape **2** TECHNICAL a computer document containing some basic information that you use as a model for writing other documents, such as business letters, envelopes etc.

tem·ple /'tɛmpəl/ n. [C] **1** a building where people go to WORSHIP, in the Jewish, Hindu, Buddhist, Sikh, and Mormon religions **2** [usually plural] one of the two fairly flat areas on each side of your FOREHEAD

tem·po /'tɛmpoʊ/ n. plural **tempos** [C] **1** the speed at which music is played or should be played **2** the speed at which something happens; PACE: From the start, Dallas controlled the tempo of the game.

tem·po·ral /'tɛmpərəl/ adj. FORMAL **1** relating to or limited by time: Our physical bodies are just a temporal, passing reality. **2** relating to practical instead of religious affairs: The Emperor was both a temporal and a spiritual ruler.

temporal lobe /ˌ... './ n. [C] TECHNICAL one of the two lower parts of the brain at either side

tem·po·rar·y /'tɛmpəˌrɛri/ adj. **1** continuing for only a limited period of time: France has agreed to a temporary suspension of military activities.

2 intended to be used for only a limited period of time: *temporary housing* —opposite PERMANENT[1] —**temporarily** /ˌtɛmpəˈrɛrəli/ *adv.: The elevator will be temporarily out of order.* —**temporariness** *n.* [U]

tem·po·rize /ˈtɛmpəˌraɪz/ *v.* [I] FORMAL to delay or avoid making a decision in order to gain time

tempt /tɛmpt/ *v.* [T] **1** to try to persuade someone to do something by making it seem attractive: [**tempt sb to do sth**] *The Knicks are hoping a huge salary bonus will tempt Riley to return as head coach.* | [**tempt sb into doing sth**] *Dantley thinks his new recipes will tempt his customers into trying rabbit.* **2 be tempted to do sth** to make someone want to have or do something, even though they know they really should not: *It's so nice outside that I'm tempted to forget work and go to the lake.* **3 tempt fate a)** to do something that involves unnecessary risk and may cause serious problems: *Fire officials said developers are tempting fate by building deep into the scenic canyons.* **b)** to say too confidently that something will have a good result, that there will be no problems etc., when it is likely that there will be problems

temp·ta·tion /tɛmpˈteɪʃən/ *n.* **1** [C,U] a strong desire to have or do something even though you know you should not: [**temptation to do sth**] *There's a great temptation to blame others for your situation.* | *Try to **resist the temptation** (=not do something, even though you want to) to snack between meals.* | *Rick **gave in to the temptation** (=did something although he knew he should not) to steal the watch.* **2** [C,U] something that makes you want to have or do something, even though you know you should not: *Selling alcohol at truck stops is an unnecessary temptation for drivers.*

tempt·ing /ˈtɛmptɪŋ/ *adj.* something that is tempting seems very good and you would like to have it or do it: *a tempting job offer* | *Their soups are also very tempting.* | [**tempting to do sth**] *It's tempting to believe that Don would never lie.* —**temptingly** *adv.*

tempt·ress /ˈtɛmptrɪs/ *n.* [C] OLD-FASHIONED a woman who makes a man want to have sex with her

tem·pu·ra /ˈtɛmpərə, tɛmˈpʊrə/ *n.* [U] a Japanese dish of vegetables and SEAFOOD covered in BATTER and cooked in hot oil

tem·pus fu·git /ˌtɛmpəs ˈfyudʒɪt/ LITERARY a phrase meaning "time flies"; used to say that time passes very quickly

ten[1] /tɛn/ *number* **1** 10 **2** 10 o'clock: *My appointment's at ten.* **3 ten to one** INFORMAL used to say that something is very likely: *Ten to one Marsha will be late.* —see also TENTH[1]

ten[2] *n.* [C] **1** a piece of paper money worth $10: *Do you have two tens for a twenty?* **2 a ten** INFORMAL used to give a perfect SCORE in sports, or humorously to praise someone or something: *I'd give the service at P & J's Deli a ten.*

ten·a·ble /ˈtɛnəbəl/ *adj.* FORMAL a belief, argument etc. that is tenable is reasonable and can be defended successfully —opposite UNTENABLE

te·na·cious /təˈneɪʃəs/ *adj.* determined to do something and unwilling to stop trying even when the situation becomes difficult —**tenaciously** *adv.* —**tenaciousness** or —**tenacity** /təˈnæsəti/ *n.* [U]

ten·an·cy /ˈtɛnənsi/ *n.* FORMAL **1** [C] the period of time that someone rents a house, land etc.: *After a five-year tenancy, we were ready to move out.* **2** [C,U] the right to use a house, land etc.: *Property held in joint tenancy automatically passes to the surviving spouse after the death of the other.*

ten·ant /ˈtɛnənt/ *n.* [C] someone who lives in a house, room etc. and pays rent to the person who owns it

tenant farm·er /ˌ.. ˈ../ *n.* [C] someone who farms land that is rented from someone else

tend /tɛnd/ *v.* **1 tend to do sth** to often do a particular thing, especially something that is bad or annoying, and to be likely to do it again: *Bill tends to talk too much when he's nervous.* | *It tends to rain a lot during the winter.* **2** also **tend to** [T] to take care of someone or something: *Mom was usually busy tending to my younger sisters.* | *Jose was outside tending*

the garden when the fire broke out. **3 tend bar** to work as a BARTENDER: *Scott tended bar part-time while going to college.* **4 tend toward sth** to have a particular quality or feature more than others: *The guest rooms tend toward a country look with lots of antiques.* **5** [I always + adv./prep.] FORMAL to move or develop in a particular direction: [+ **upward/downward**] *Interest rates are tending upward.*

tend·en·cy /ˈtɛndənsi/ *n. plural* **tendencies** [C] **1** a PROBABILITY that you will develop, think, or behave in a certain way: [**a tendency to do sth**] *Her tendency to react quickly made her successful in politics.* | *The M16 assault rifle **has a tendency** to jam.* | [+ **toward**] *Jeff works with children who have tendencies toward aggression.* | [+ **for**] *A teenager's tendency for acne problems could be genetic.* **2** a general change or development in a particular direction: [**a tendency (for sb) to do sth**] *There is an increasing tendency for women to have children later in life.* | [+ **toward**] *The survey found a growing tendency toward greater student activism.* **3 artistic/alcoholic etc. tendencies** particular skills, weaknesses, or desires that make someone behave in a particular way: *For years, Kurt kept his suicidal tendencies a secret.*

ten·den·tious /tɛnˈdɛnʃəs/ *adj.* FORMAL a tendentious speech, remark, book etc. expresses a strong opinion that is intended to influence people —**tendentiousness** *n.* [U]

ten·der[1] /ˈtɛndə/ *adj.*
1 food easy to cut and eat, especially because of being well cooked: *The sirloin was moist and tender on the inside.* —opposite TOUGH[1] (4)
2 gentle gentle and careful in a way that shows love: *They gave each other a tender kiss.* | *a tender, caring woman*
3 part of your body a tender part of your body is painful if someone touches it: *Your mouth will be tender for a few days after the operation.*
4 easily damaged easily damaged: *tender blossoms*
5 tender loving care sympathetic treatment and a lot of attention: *Mom gave us kids a lot of tender loving care.*
6 tender age HUMOROUS OR LITERARY the time when you are young or do not have much experience: *Wayne began working in the family store **at the tender age of five**.* —**tenderly** *adv.* —**tenderness** *n.* [U]

tender[2] *v.* [T] **1** [T] FORMAL to give someone something, especially in business: [**tender sth to sb**] *About 66% of NCR shares have been tendered to the phone company.* | *The California Angels have **tendered an offer** to Bobby Bonilla.* | *Minton **tendered her resignation** (=officially said that she was going to leave her job) on Friday.* **2** [T] OLD-FASHIONED to give money as a payment

tender[3] *n.* [C] **1** a small boat that takes people or supplies between the shore and a larger boat **2** OLD-FASHIONED part of a steam train used for carrying coal and water for the train —see also BARTENDER, LEGAL TENDER, TENDER OFFER

ten·der·foot /ˈtɛndəfʊt/ *n.* [C] INFORMAL someone who does not have much experience at doing something

tender-heart·ed /ˌ.. ˈ../ *adj.* very kind and gentle —**tender-heartedly** *adv.* —**tender-heartedness** *n.* [U]

ten·der·ize /ˈtɛndəˌraɪz/ *v.* [T] to make meat softer and easier to eat by preparing it in a special way

ten·der·iz·er /ˈtɛndəˌraɪzə/ *n.* [C,U] a substance that is put onto raw meat to make it softer and easier to eat after it is cooked

ten·der·loin /ˈtɛndəlɔɪn/ *n.* [U] meat that is soft and easy to eat, cut from each side of the BACKBONE of cows or pigs: *broiled beef tenderloin*

tender of·fer /ˈ.. ˌ../ *n.* [C] TECHNICAL a formal statement of the price you would charge for doing a job or providing goods or services

ten·di·ni·tis /ˌtɛndəˈnaɪtɪs/ *n.* [U] continual pain in a tendon because of an injury

ten·don /ˈtɛndən/ *n.* [C] a thick strong string-like part of your body that connects a muscle to a bone

ten·dril /ˈtɛndrəl/ *n.* [C] **1** a thin leafless curling stem by which a climbing plant fastens itself to a support **2** LITERARY a thin curling piece of hair

ten·e·ment /ˈtɛnəmənt/ *n.* [C] a large building divided into apartments, especially in the poorer areas of a city

ten·et /ˈtɛnɪt/ *n.* [C] a principle or belief, especially one that is part of a larger system of beliefs: *Individualism is **a basic tenet of** Western culture.*

ten·fold /ˈtɛnfoʊld/ *adj. adv.* FORMAL ten times as much or as many of something: *Traffic across the border has increased tenfold.*

ten-gal·lon hat /ˌ.. ˈ./ *n.* [C] A tall hat made of soft material with a wide BRIM, worn especially by COWBOYS

Ten·nes·see /ˌtɛnəˈsiː/ *written abbreviation* **TN** a state in the southeastern U.S.

ten·nies /ˈtɛniz/ *n.* [plural] SPOKEN: see TENNIS SHOES

S W | **ten·nis** /ˈtɛnɪs/ *n.* [U] a game for two people or two pairs of people who use RACKETS to hit a small soft ball backward and forward over a net

tennis brace·let /ˈ.. ˌ../ *n.* [C] a type of BRACELET (=band worn around the wrist) which is made of many small valuable stones, such as DIAMONDS, which are connected together in a row

tennis court /ˈ.. ˌ./ *n.* [C] the four-sided area that you play tennis on

tennis el·bow /ˌ.. ˈ../ *n.* [U] a medical problem in which your elbow becomes very painful after you have bent it too often

tennis shoe /ˈ.. ˌ./ *n.* [C] a light shoe used for sports, with a rubber surface on the bottom —see picture at SHOE[1]

Ten·ny·son /ˈtɛnɪsən/**, Al·fred** /ˈælfrɪd/ **Alfred, Lord Tennyson** (1809–1892) an English poet

ten·on /ˈtɛnən/ *n.* [C] an end of a piece of wood, that has been cut to fit exactly into a MORTISE in order to form a strong joint

ten·or /ˈtɛnɚ/ *n.* **1 a)** [C] a man with a singing voice that can reach the range of notes just below the lowest woman's voice **b)** [U] the part of a piece of music this person sings: *He used to sing tenor in the church choir.* **c)** [C] a musical instrument with the same range of notes as the singer **2 the tenor of sth** FORMAL **a)** the general way in which an event or process takes place; TONE: *The tenor of yesterday's talks was relatively good-natured.* **b)** the general meaning of something written or spoken, or the general attitude expressed in it; TONE: *It's the racist tenor of the court's ruling that disturbs me the most.* —**tenor** *adj.*: *a tenor saxophone*

S W | **tense[1]** /tɛns/ *adj.* **1** feeling very nervous and worried because of something bad that might happen: *Williams looked a little tense before the game.* | **tense moment/atmosphere/situation** etc. *Nine months of tense negotiations finally ended in a deal.* **2** unable to relax your body or part of your body because your muscles feel tight: *I can feel you're really tense in your lower back.* | *tense muscles* —**tensely** *adv.* —**tenseness** *n.* [U] —see also TENSION

tense[2] *v.* [I,T] also **tense up** to make your muscles tight and stiff, or to become tight and stiff: *He put his arm around me, and I tensed up.* | *Neal tensed slightly as the plane took off.*

tense[3] *n.* [C,U] any of the forms of a verb that show an action or state in the past, present, or future time. "I study" is in the present tense, "I studied" is in the past tense, and "I will study" is in the future tense.

tensed up /ˌ. ˈ.◂/ *adj.* [not before noun] INFORMAL feeling so nervous or worried that you cannot relax: *Brian got so tensed up he could hardly speak.*

ten·sile /ˈtɛnsəl/ *adj.* able to be stretched: *high-tensile Egyptian cotton*

tensile strength /ˈ.. ˌ./ *n.* [U] TECHNICAL the ability of materials such as steel, CONCRETE, and cloth to bear pressure or weight

ten·sion /ˈtɛnʃən/ *n.* S W

1 no trust [C,U] the feeling that exists when people or countries do not trust each other and may suddenly attack each other or start arguing: *Tension in the region has grown due to recent bombings.* | *racial tension* | [+ **between**] *The conflict is typical of the tension between developers and residents.*

2 nervous feeling [U] a nervous worried feeling that makes it impossible for you to relax: *The room was filled with tension as students waited for the test to begin.*

3 different influences [C,U] a situation in which different needs, forces, or influences work in different directions and make the situation difficult: [+ **between**] *Dan struggled to reduce the tension between work and family life.*

4 tightness [U] tightness or stiffness in a wire, rope, muscle etc.: *Often a hot bath will help relieve **muscle tension**.* | [+ **on**] *There a lot of tension on the wire.*

5 force [U] the amount of force that stretches something: *The rope can take up to 300 pounds of tension.*

ten-speed /ˈ. ./ *n.* [C] a bicycle with ten GEARS

tent /tɛnt/ *n.* [C] **1** a shelter consisting of a sheet of cloth supported by poles and ropes, used for camping or at an outdoor party or FESTIVAL: *We can **pitch our tent** (=put our tent up) over there.* —see also OXYGEN TENT **2** OFTEN HUMOROUS a very loose-fitting dress or BLOUSE

S W

ten·ta·cle /ˈtɛntəkəl/ *n.* [C] **1** one of the long thin parts of a sea creature such as an OCTOPUS which it uses for holding things —see picture at OCTOPUS **2 tentacles** [plural] the bad or harmful influence or effects that something has on something or someone else: *Agents thought they would find a terrorist network with tentacles extending nationwide.*

ten·ta·tive /ˈtɛntətɪv/ *adj.* **1** not definite or certain, because you may want to change your mind: *Workers have reached a tentative agreement with management.* **2** done without confidence: *Evan's writing is very tentative.* —**tentatively** *adv.*: *Our meeting is tentatively scheduled for 2 p.m. Monday.* —**tentativeness** *n.* [U]

ten·ter·hooks /ˈtɛntɚhʊks/ *n.* **be on tenterhooks** to feel worried or excited because you are waiting for something: *Waiting for the outcome of the trial has kept the community on tenterhooks.*

tenth[1] /tɛnθ/ *adj.* 10th; next after the ninth: *October is the tenth month.*

tenth[2] *pron.* **the tenth** the 10th thing in a series: *Let's have dinner on the tenth* (=the 10th day of the month).

tenth[3] *n.* [C] 1/10; one of ten equal parts: *A tenth of a mile* | **one-tenth/two-tenths/three-tenths** etc. *Charities employ about one-tenth of the nation's workforce.*

ten·u·ous /ˈtɛnyuəs/ *adj.* **1** if a situation or relationship is tenuous, it is uncertain and likely to change: *For now, the band's travel plans are tenuous.* | **a tenuous link/relationship/situation** etc. *Rebel soldiers continue to maintain tenuous control of the capital.* **2** LITERARY very thin and easily broken —**tenuously** *adv.* —**tenuousness** *n.* [C]

ten·ure /ˈtɛnyɚ/ *n.* [U] **1** the right to stay permanently in a teaching job: *If a professor doesn't get tenure after ten years, he probably never will.* **2** FORMAL the period of time when someone has an important job: *Under Richardson's tenure as commander, the Navy grew dramatically.* **3** LAW the legal right to live in a house or use a piece of land for a period of time

ten·ured /ˈtɛnyɚd/ *adj.* **1** a tenured teacher, PROFESSOR etc. has gained the right to stay permanently in a teaching job **2** a tenured position at a school, college, or university is one from which a teacher or PROFESSOR cannot be dismissed in most situations

tenure-track /ˈ.. ˌ./ *adj.* [only before noun] a tenure-track teaching position at a college or university is one which can lead to the person in that position getting tenure in the future

Ten·zing Nor·gay /ˌtɛnzɪŋ ˈnɔːrgeɪ/ (1914–1986) a Nepalese mountain climber and guide. He and Sir Edmund Hillary were the first people to reach the top of Mount Everest.

te·pee /ˈtipi/ *n.* [C] a round tent with a pointed top, used by some Native Americans

tep·id /ˈtɛpɪd/ *adj.* **1** a feeling, reaction etc. that is tepid shows a lack of excitement or interest: *Keizer could only offer tepid praise for Hanshaw's work.* **2** tepid liquid is slightly warm, especially in a way that does not seem nice: *tepid coffee* —**tepid·ly** *adv.* —**tepidness** *n.* [U] —see also LUKEWARM

te·qui·la /təˈkilə/ *n.* [C,U] a strong alcoholic drink made in Mexico from the AGAVE plant

ter·a·byte /ˈtɛrəˌbaɪt/ *n.* [C] a unit for measuring the amount of information a computer can store or use, equal to about a TRILLION BYTES

ter·cen·ten·a·ry /ˌtɜːrsɛnˈtɛnəri, tɜːrˈsɛntⁿnˌɛri/ *n.* [C] the day or year exactly 300 years after a particular event

Te·re·sa, Mother /təˈrisə/ MOTHER TERESA

Te·resh·ko·va /ˌtɛrɪʃˈkoʊvə/, **Val·en·ti·na** /ˌvælənˈtinə/ (1937–) a Russian ASTRONAUT who was the first woman in space

ter·i·ya·ki /ˌtɛriˈyaki/ *n.* [U] a Japanese dish containing meat which has been kept in a liquid mixture before cooking, to give it a special taste —**teriyaki** *adj.*: *teriyaki chicken*

term¹ /tɜːrm/ *n.* [C]
1 word/expression [C] a word or expression that has a particular meaning, especially one that concerns a particular subject: *"Limited English Proficient" is a term used for students who can speak some English.* | *Harris used the term "crisis" to describe the company's financial situation* | **a medical/legal/scientific etc. term** *"Sub rosa" is the legal term for a secret agreement.*
2 in financial/artistic/psychological etc. terms if you describe or consider something in financial, artistic etc. terms, you are mainly interested in the financial, artistic etc. side of it: *In business terms, the war was a good risk.* | *These accidents have cost £18.2 billion in dollar terms alone.*
3 in terms of sth if you explain or judge something in terms of a particular fact or event, you are only interested in its relation to that fact or event: *Kmart is the nation's second-largest retailer in terms of sales volume.* | *In terms of quality ingredients, this is the best ice cream you can buy.*
4 come to terms with sth to accept a bad situation or event and not feel upset or angry about it anymore: *It took years for Rob to come to terms with his mother's death.*
5 come to terms with sb/sth to accept the conditions of a contract: *On Sunday, Smith came to terms with the Dallas Cowboys.*
6 think/talk in terms of doing sth SPOKEN to consider or discuss doing something, especially in a particular way: *We've got to think in terms of expanding the agency's services.*
7 in the long/short/near etc. term also **over the long/short/near etc. term** considered over a period from now until a long, short etc. time in the future: *Cutting staff may reduce costs in the short term.* —see also LONG-TERM, SHORT-TERM
8 on equal terms having the same advantages, rights, or abilities as anyone else: [+ **with**] *Women are demanding to compete for jobs on equal terms with men.*
9 in real terms a change of a price or cost in real terms has been calculated to include the effects of other changes such as INFLATION: *In real terms, U.S. foreign aid has dropped by 30%.*
10 be on speaking terms to be able to talk to someone and have a friendly relationship with them, especially after an argument: *Ditka and Anderson are not on speaking terms these days.*
11 be on good/bad terms to have a friendly relationship or bad relationship with someone: [+ **with**] *Tim's still on good terms with his ex-wife.*

12 prison/jail term a period of time that someone must spend in prison: *Reynolds could get a prison term of up to 85 years.*
13 time doing a job [C] a period of time for which someone is elected to an important government job: **term of/in office** *Mayor Johnson announced that he would not seek another term of office.*
14 school/college [C] one of the periods that the school or college year is divided into: **summer/fall/winter/spring term** *Medical schools accepted 16,205 new students for the fall term.* —see also MIDTERM² (1) —compare SEMESTER
15 in no uncertain terms in a clear and usually angry way: *We were told in no uncertain terms that we were not welcome at their house.*
16 conditions terms [plural] the conditions of an agreement, contract, legal document etc.: *According to the terms of the contract, Shehan can buy the entire company in three years.* | **good/easy/bad terms** *Idris said he could use his contacts to obtain good terms for oil purchases.*
17 business [C] the period of time that a contract, LOAN¹ (1) etc. continues for: *Officials now are trying to extend the term of the loan by two years.*
18 in glowing terms if you describe something in glowing terms, you show that you admire something very much: *The two men speak in glowing terms of their friendship.*
19 in sb's terms according to one person's set of opinions: *In Wallace's terms, self-respect is the willingness to form relationships with others.*
20 on your (own) terms according to the conditions that you want or ask for: *Owens lived life on his own terms.*
21 terms of reference the agreed limits of what an official committee or report has been asked to study: *Both sides have to agree on the terms of reference before there can be a trade deal.*
22 a term of endearment/respect/abuse etc. a word or expression used to say you love someone, to show respect for someone etc.: *In Japanese, "san" is a term of respect similar to "Mr." or "Mrs." in English.*
23 having a baby [U] TECHNICAL the end of the period of time when a woman is PREGNANT: *Carrie's medical condition will make it hard to **carry** the baby **to term** (=keep the baby until the normal time for it to be born).*
24 number/sign [C] TECHNICAL one of the numbers or signs used in a mathematical calculation —see also **a contradiction in terms** (CONTRADICTION (3))

term² *v.* [T] **1** to use a particular word or expression to name or describe something: *Seifert termed his relationship with Walsh as "good."* | *Lukens apologized for what he termed "a dumb mistake."* | [**be termed sth**] *Herrera's failure to take sides in the argument could hardly be termed weakness.* **2 be termed out of office** to have to leave a political position because the law says someone can be in that position for only a particular number of years: *Senator Jansen will be termed out of office next year.*

ter·mi·nal¹ /ˈtɜːmənəl/ *adj.* **1** a terminal illness cannot be cured, and causes death: *terminal cancer* **2 terminal decline/decay** the state of becoming worse and worse, and never getting better **3 terminal boredom** HUMOROUS the feeling of being extremely bored **4** [only before noun] TECHNICAL existing at the end of something: *terminal buds* —**terminally** *adv.*: *terminally ill patients*

terminal² *n.* [C] **1** a large building where people wait to get onto airplanes, buses, or ships, or where goods are loaded: *A free shuttle bus runs between the airport terminal and the train station.* **2** a piece of computer equipment consisting of at least a KEYBOARD and a screen, that you use for putting in or taking out information from a large computer **3** one of the points at which you can connect wires in an electrical CIRCUIT

terminal a·dapt·er /ˈ... ... ./ *n.* [C] TECHNICAL a piece of electronic equipment that allows information from one computer to be sent along special ISDN telephone lines to another computer

ter·mi·nate /'tɚmə‚neɪt/ v. **1** [I,T] FORMAL if something terminates, or if you terminate it, it ends: *The company had the right to terminate his employment at any time.* **2** [T] INFORMAL to kill someone

ter·mi·na·tion /‚tɚmə'neɪʃən/ n. **1** [C,U] FORMAL the act of ending something, or the end of something: *the termination of nuclear weapons tests* **2** [C] TECHNICAL a medical operation to end the life of a developing child before it is born; ABORTION

ter·mi·nol·o·gy /‚tɚmə'nɑlədʒi/ n. plural terminologies [C,U] the technical words or expressions that are used in a particular subject: *medical terminology* —**terminological** /‚tɚmənə'lɑdʒɪkəl◂/ adj.

ter·mi·nus /'tɚmənəs/ n. [C] the station or stop at the end of a train line or bus service

ter·mite /'tɚmaɪt/ n. [C] an insect that eats and destroys wood from trees and buildings

term lim·it /'. ‚../ also **term lim·i·ta·tion** /'. ..‚../ n. [C] a particular number of years that the law allows someone to stay in a particular political position

term pa·per /'. ‚../ n. [C] a long piece of written work by a school or college student, as the most important piece of work in a course

tern /tɚn/ n. [C] a black and white sea bird that has long wings and a tail with two points

ter·na·ry /'tɚnəri/ adj. TECHNICAL consisting of three parts —compare BINARY

Ter·ra /'tɛrə/ the Roman name for the goddess Gaea

ter·race /'tɛrɪs/ n. [C] **1** a flat outdoor area next to a building or on a roof, where you can sit outside to eat, relax etc. **2** a flat area cut out of a slope, usually one in a series that rise up the slope, that is often used to grow crops

ter·raced /'tɛrɪst/ adj. [only before noun] a terraced field, slope, garden etc. has been cut into a series of flat areas along the side of the slope: *terraced rice fields*

ter·ra cot·ta, terracotta /‚tɛrə'kɑtə◂/ n. [U] **1** hard reddish-brown baked CLAY: *terracotta roof tiles* **2** a reddish-brown color

terra fir·ma /‚tɛrə 'fɚmə/ n. [U] USUALLY HUMOROUS land, rather than water or air: *We were glad to be back on terra firma again.*

ter·rain /tə'reɪn/ n. [C,U] a particular type of land: *rocky terrain*

ter·ra·pin /'tɛrəpən/ n. [C] a small TURTLE (=animal with four legs and a hard shell) that lives in water in warm areas

ter·rar·i·um /tə'rɛriəm/ n. [C] a large glass container that you grow plants in as a decoration

ter·res·tri·al /tə'rɛstriəl/ adj. TECHNICAL **1** relating to the Earth, rather than the moon or other PLANETS —see also EXTRATERRESTRIAL[2] **2** living on or relating to land rather than water —**terrestrially** adv.

ter·ri·ble /'tɛrəbəl/ adj. **1** extremely severe in a way that causes harm or damage: *a terrible accident* | *We're worried that something terrible might have happened to Greg.* **2** extremely bad; AWFUL: *The movie was terrible.* | *I have a terrible headache.* **3** the **terrible twos** INFORMAL the period of time when a child is two years old and difficult to deal with **4** making you feel afraid or shocked: *There was a terrible noise and the roof caved in.*

ter·ri·bly /'tɛrəbli/ adv. **1** [+ adj./adv.] very; extremely: *I'm terribly sorry if I mispronounced your name.* | *John's not terribly interested in school.* **2** very badly: *The team played terribly.*

ter·ri·er /'tɛriɚ/ n. [C] a small active type of dog that was originally used for hunting

ter·rif·ic /tə'rɪfɪk/ adj. **1** very good, especially in a way that makes you feel happy and excited: *That's a terrific idea.* | *Your dress looks terrific!* **2** very large in size or degree: *a terrific crisis*

ter·rif·i·cal·ly /tə'rɪfɪkli/ adv. **1** [+ adj./adv.] very; extremely: *Living in New York can be terrifically*

expensive. **2** very well: *The movie's main character, Ricky, is terrifically played by Mark Benton.*

ter·ri·fied /'tɛrə‚faɪd/ adj. very frightened: *a terrified old woman* | [+ **of**] *The children were terrified of the dog.* | [+ **at**] *They were terrified at the thought of getting caught.* | [**terrified (that)**] *Cheri went to a neighbor's, terrified that her ex-husband was following her.*

ter·ri·fy /'tɛrə‚faɪ/ v. terrifies, terrified, terrifying [T] to make someone extremely afraid: *Speaking in public terrifies me.*

ter·ri·fy·ing /'tɛrə‚faɪ-ɪŋ/ adj. extremely frightening: *Spending a night in jail was a terrifying experience.* —**terrifyingly** adv.

ter·rine /tə'rin, tɛ-/ n. [C,U] a food made of cooked meat, fish, or fruit formed into a LOAF shape and served cold, or the dish this is served in

ter·ri·to·ri·al /‚tɛrə'tɔriəl/ adj. **1** [no comparative] relating to land that is owned or controlled by a particular country: *a territorial dispute* **2** TECHNICAL territorial animals or people closely guard the area of land that they consider to be their own —**territoriality** /‚tɛrətɔri'æləti/ n. [U]

territorial wa·ters /‚..‚... '../ n. [plural] the ocean near a country's coast, which that country has legal control over

ter·ri·to·ry /'tɛrə‚tɔri/ n. plural territories

1 ▐government land▌ [C,U] land that is owned or controlled by a particular government, ruler, or military force: *We crossed the river into enemy territory.*

2 ▐type of land▌ [U] land of a particular type: *Chile is a country filled with unexplored territory.*

3 ▐not a state▌ [C] land that belongs to a country, but is not a state, PROVINCE etc.: *U.S. territories and possessions*

4 ▐experience▌ [U] a particular area of experience or knowledge: *We are in uncharted territory* (=an area that we do not yet know about) *with the new drug.*

5 ▐animal/group▌ [C,U] the area that an animal, person, or group considers to be their own and will defend against others: *The antelope will control and defend its territory.*

6 **come/go with the territory** to be a natural and accepted part of a particular job, situation, place etc.: *I expected the criticism – it comes with the territory when you're a public figure.*

7 ▐business▌ [C,U] an area of business, especially in selling, for which someone is responsible: *a sales territory*

ter·ror /'tɛrɚ/ n. **1** [U] a feeling of extreme fear: *A feeling of terror gripped us as we listened to his story.* | *The children were under the bed, screaming in terror.* | *We lived in terror of waking Dad when he was napping.* | *a moment of sheer terror* (=complete terror) **2** [U] violent action for political purposes; TERRORISM: *The resistance movement started a campaign of terror.* **3** [C] an event or situation that makes people feel extremely frightened, especially because they think they may die: *He barely survived the terror of the river rapids.* **4** [C] INFORMAL a very annoying person, especially a child: *That Johnson kid's a real terror!* **5** **hold no terrors for sb** FORMAL to not frighten or worry someone: *Death held no terrors for me.* —see also **a holy terror** (HOLY (4)), **reign of terror** (REIGN[1] (3)), **strike terror/fear into sb's heart** (STRIKE[1] (26))

ter·ror·ism /'tɛrə‚rɪzəm/ n. [U] the use of violence such as bombing, shooting, or KIDNAPPING to obtain political demands: *The party has renounced terrorism as a political tool.*

ter·ror·ist /'tɛrərɪst/ n. [C] someone who uses violence such as bombing, shooting etc. to obtain political demands —**terrorist** adj. [only before noun] *a terrorist attack* —compare GUERRILLA

ter·ror·ize /'tɛrə‚raɪz/ v. [T] to deliberately frighten people by threatening to harm them, especially so they will do what you want: *Drug dealers have been terrorizing the neighborhood.*

ter·ry·cloth /'tɛri‚klɔθ/ also **ter·ry** /'tɛri/ n. [U] a type of thick cotton cloth with uncut threads on both sides, used to make TOWELS etc.

terse /tɜːs/ *adj.* a terse reply, message etc. uses very few words and often shows that you are annoyed: *The White House issued a terse statement saying the President would not comment on the allegations.* —**tersely** *adv.*: *"Thank you for your time," he said tersely.* —**terseness** *n.* [U]

ter·ti·ar·y /'tɜːʃi,eri, -ʃəri/ *adj.* TECHNICAL third in place, degree, or order

TESL /'tɛsl/ *n.* [U] the teaching of English as a second language

Tes·la /'tɛslə/, **Nik·o·la** /'nɪkələ/ (1856–1943) a U.S. scientist, born in Croatia, who discovered how to produce ALTERNATING CURRENT and made other important developments in electricity and radio

TESOL /'tisɔl/ *n.* [U] the teaching of English to speakers of other languages

tes·sel·la·tion /,tɛsə'leɪʃən/ *n.* [C] TECHNICAL a pattern made of repeating shapes and colors that fit together

test¹ /tɛst/ *n.* [C] **1** a set of questions, exercises, or practical activities to measure someone's skill, ability, or knowledge: *How did you do on the spelling test?* | **[+ on]** *We have a test on irregular verbs tomorrow.* | *Why didn't you have to take the test?* | *Teachers are under pressure to improve test scores.* | **pass/fail a test** *I didn't pass my driving test the first time.* **2 a)** a short medical examination on a part of your body, or to find out what is wrong with you: *a hearing test* | *I'm still waiting for my test results from the hospital.* | **run/do a test** *They've run all kinds of tests on her, but they still don't know what's wrong.* **b)** equipment for carrying out a medical test: *a home pregnancy test* **3** a situation in which the qualities of someone or something are clearly shown: *a test of character/strength/skill etc. It looks as though the meeting will be a test of wills.* **4 a) put sb/sth to the test** to force someone or something into a situation that is so difficult that it shows what the limits of their strength or skills are: *Kathy's students are putting her patience to the test.* | *The war is putting some of the military's expensive new technology to the test.* **5** a process used to find out whether equipment works correctly, or whether something contains a particular substance: *nuclear weapons tests* | **[+ for]** *Bottled water must pass tests for lead and other chemicals.* | *test site/equipment/procedure NASA improved its test procedures for the external tanks.* **6** something that is used as a standard to judge or examine something else: *A good test of any Chinese restaurant is its sweet and sour soup.* —see also BREATH TEST, MEANS TEST, **stand the test of time** (STAND¹ (28)), TEST CASE

test² *v.*

1 medical **a)** [T] to give someone a short medical examination on a part of their body, or to find out what is wrong with them: *I need to get my eyes tested.* | **[test sb for sth]** *Have you been tested for HIV?* **b)** to get a particular result when a medical test is done on you: *test positive/negative Grissom tested positive for steroids.*

2 exam **a)** [T] to measure someone's skill, ability, or knowledge, using a test: **[test sb on sth]** *Which chapters are you going to test us on?* | *This section tests your mathematical skills.* **b) test well/badly/poorly** to perform well or badly on a test: *I don't test very well.*

3 machine/product [T] to try using something to see if it works in the correct way: *The store began testing the coupon machines last May.* | **[test sth on sb/sth]** *Marr decided to test the vaccine on herself.*

4 show how good/strong [T] to show how good or strong someone's or something's qualities are, especially by putting them in a difficult situation: *The next six months will test your powers of leadership.* | *Sharon decided to test the truth of their story by doing a little investigating of her own.*

5 find out [T] to examine something in order to find out something about it: **[test sth for sth]** *Paint in old apartments should be tested for lead.*

6 test the waters to check people's reaction to a plan before you decide to do anything: *Wilder is testing the waters for a presidential run.* —see also **just testing** (JUST¹ (31)), **tried and tested** (TRIED²)

tes·ta·ment /'tɛstəmənt/ *n.* [C] FORMAL **1 a testament to sth** something that shows or proves something else very clearly: *The movie's success is a testament to the power of advertising.* **2** OLD-FASHIONED a WILL² (2) —see also NEW TESTAMENT, OLD TESTAMENT

test ban /'. ./ *n.* [C] an agreement between countries to stop testing NUCLEAR WEAPONS

test case /'. ./ *n.* [C] a legal case that establishes a particular principle and is then used as a standard which other similar cases can be judged against

test drive /'. ./ *n.* [C] an occasion when you drive a car to see if it works well or if you like it so that you can decide if you want to buy it —**test-drive** *v.* [T]

test·er /'tɛstə/ *n.* [C] **1** a person or piece of equipment that tests something **2** a small bottle of PERFUME, COLOGNE etc., in a store, for customers to try

test-fly, test fly /'. ./ *v.* [T] to fly an aircraft to see if it operates in the correct way

tes·ti·cle /'tɛstɪkəl/ *n.* [C] one of the two round organs that produce SPERM in a male, that are enclosed in a bag of skin below the PENIS —**testicular** *adj.*

tes·ti·fy /'tɛstə,faɪ/ *v.* **testifies, testified, testifying 1** [I,T] to make a formal statement of what is true, especially in a court of law: *Mr. Molto has agreed to testify at the trial.* | **[for/against]** *She shouldn't be required to testify against her own daughter.* | **[+ about]** *Taft will be called to testify about what he saw.* | **[testify that]** *Several neighbors testified that they heard a strange noise that night.* **2** [I,T] FORMAL to be a clear sign that something is true: **[+ to]** *The company's experience testifies to the difficulties of opening a business in a foreign country.* **3** [I] to stand up and tell people about how God has helped you in your life

tes·ti·mo·ni·al /,tɛstə'moʊniəl/ *n.* [C] **1** something that is said or given to someone to show thanks, praise, or admiration, especially in front of other people: *Ed stood and gave a testimonial to (=said nice things about) his mother.* **2** a formal written statement describing someone's character and abilities **3** a favorable statement someone makes about a product, used especially in advertising to encourage other people to buy and use that product

tes·ti·mo·ny /'tɛstə,moʊni/ *n. plural* **testimonies** [C, U] **1** a formal statement that something is true, such as the one a WITNESS makes in a court of law: *The grand jury today heard testimony from numerous witnesses.* | *In his testimony, he denied that his company had ignored the safety procedures.* **2** a fact or situation that shows or proves something very clearly: **[+ to/of]** *War is a testimony to our lack of humanity.*

testing ground /'.. ,./ *n.* [C] **1** a place where machines, cars etc. are tried to see if they work **2** a situation, place, or problem in which you can try new ideas and methods to see if they work: *Latin America has become a testing ground for new business ideas.*

tes·tis /'tɛstəs/ *n. plural* **testes** /-tiz/ [C] TECHNICAL a TESTICLE

test mar·ket /'. ,../ *n.* [C] a small area where a new product is sold to find out how people like it before it is sold everywhere else —**test-market** *v.* [T] *The new beer will be test-marketed in San Diego.*

tes·tos·ter·one /tɛ'stɑstə,roʊn/ *n.* [U] the HORMONE (=type of chemical substance) in males that gives them their male qualities

test pat·tern /'. ,../ *n.* [C] a pattern or picture that is shown on television when there are no programs

test pi·lot /'. ,../ *n.* [C] a pilot who flies new aircraft in order to test them

test run /'. ./ *n.* [C] an occasion when you try doing something or using something to make sure everything works before you really need to use it: *The generator failed three times during its test run.*

test tube /'. . ./ *n.* [C] a small glass container with a long narrow shape and a round bottom, used in science

test-tube ba·by /,. . . '../ *n.* [C] NOT TECHNICAL a baby that started to develop from an egg removed from a woman's body, that was then put back inside the woman to continue developing

tes·ty /'tɛsti/ *adj.* **testier, testiest** impatient and easily annoyed: *By the end of the day everyone was getting a little testy.* —**testily** *adv.*: *"What do you mean by that?" Alice asked testily.* —**testiness** *n.* [U]

tet·a·nus /'tɛt⁻n-əs, -nəs/ *n.* [U] a serious illness caused by BACTERIA that enter your body through cuts and wounds and make your muscles, especially your jaw, become stiff

tête-à-tête¹ /,teɪt ə 'teɪt, ,tɛt ə 'tɛt/ *n.* [C] a private conversation between two people: *The two leaders emerged from their tête-à-tête late in the afternoon.*

tête-à-tête² *adv.* [only after verb] if two people meet, speak, or eat tête-à-tête, they are together in private

teth·er¹ /'tɛðɚ/ *n.* [C] **1** a rope or chain that something, especially an animal, is tied to so that it can only move around within a limited area **2 be at the end of your tether** to be so worried, tired etc., that you feel you cannot deal with a difficult or upsetting situation

tether² *v.* [T + to] to tie something, especially an animal, to a post so that it can only move around within a limited area

Te·ton Range, the /'titɑn/ also **the Tetons** a RANGE of mountains in the northwestern U.S. that is part of the Rocky Mountains and is in the states of Idaho and Wyoming

tetra- /tɛtrə/ *prefix* having four of something: *a tetrahedron*

tet·ra·cy·cline /,tɛtrə'saɪklin/ *n.* [U] a type of ANTIBIOTIC (=medicine)

tet·ra·he·dron /,tɛtrə'hidrən/ *n.* [C] a solid shape with four sides that are shaped like TRIANGLES

Teu·ton /'tut⁻n/ a member of one of the ancient German tribes of northwestern Europe

Teu·ton·ic /tu'tɑnɪk/ *adj.* **1** relating to the ancient Germanic peoples of northwestern Europe: *Teutonic mythology* **2** HUMOROUS having qualities that are thought to be typical of German people: *Teutonic efficiency*

Tex·as /'tɛksəs/ a large state in the southern U.S., on the border of Mexico —**Texan** *n., adj.*

Texas toast /'.. ,./ *n.* [U] a type of TOAST (=heated bread) that is very large and thick

Tex-Mex /,tɛks 'mɛks‹/ *adj.* INFORMAL relating to the music, cooking etc. of Mexican-American people in Texas, or the Southwest in general: *a Tex-Mex restaurant*

text /tɛkst/ *n.* **1** [U] the writing in a book, magazine etc. rather than the pictures or notes, or any written material: *The word processor automatically divides your text into pages.* **2** [C] a book or other piece of writing that is related to learning or intended for study: *religious texts* **3** a textbook: *a chemistry text* **4 the text of sth** the exact words of a speech, article etc.: *Printed here is the full text of the senator's resignation speech.* **5** [C] a short piece from the Bible that someone reads and talks about

text·book¹ /'tɛkstbʊk/ *n.* [C] a book that contains information about a subject that people study: *a biology textbook*

textbook² *adj.* [only before noun] done or happening exactly as something should be done or as it should happen: *McCourtney's case is a textbook example of the problems that working mothers face.*

tex·tile /'tɛkstaɪl/ *n.* **1** [C] a word used mainly in business for woven material that is made in large quantities: *Their main exports are textiles, especially silk and cotton.* | **textile industry/market etc.** *a textile manufacturer* **2 textiles** [plural] the industry that makes cloth

tex·tu·al /'tɛkstʃuəl, -tʃəl/ *adj.* relating to the way that a book, magazine etc. is written: *a detailed textual analysis of the stories*

tex·ture /'tɛkstʃɚ/ *n.* [C,U] **1** the way a surface, substance, or material feels when you touch it, and how smooth or rough it looks: *a smooth, silky texture* | *the grainy texture of the film* | *The beer has a creamy texture.* **2** LITERARY the way the different parts are combined in a piece of writing, music, art etc. in order to affect you in a particular way: *The actors work hard to recreate the texture of Brooklyn in the '30s.* —**textural** *adj.* —**texturally** *adv.* —see also -TEXTURED

tex·tured /'tɛkstʃɚd/ *adj.* **1** having a surface that is not smooth: *textured stockings* **2** having many different parts that are combined to produce a particular effect: *richly textured storytelling*

-textured /tɛkstʃɚd/ [in adjectives] **coarse-textured/smooth-textured/fine-textured etc.** having a particular type of texture: *eggs with fine-textured shells*

textured vege·ta·ble pro·tein /,.. ,... '../ *n.* [U] a substance made from beans, that can be used in cooking instead of meat

TGIF *interjection* thank God it's Friday; used to say that you are glad the WORKWEEK is almost finished

-th /θ/ *suffix* **1** forms ORDINAL numbers, except with 1, 2, and 3: *the 17th of June* | *a fifth of the total* —see also -ND, -RD, -ST **2** OLD USE OR BIBLICAL another form of the SUFFIX -ETH: *he doth* (=does)

Thack·er·ay /'θækəri/, **Wil·liam Make·peace** /'wɪljəm 'meɪkpis/ (1811–1863) a British writer of NOVELS

Thad·de·us /'θædiəs/ in the Bible, one of the 12 APOSTLES, also called Jude

Thai·land /'taɪlænd/ a country in southeast Asia, north of Malaysia and east of Myanmar. Before 1949, Thailand was called Siam. —**Thai** *n., adj.*

thal·a·mus /'θæləməs/ *n.* [C] TECHNICAL the middle part of your brain that is used to organize the information from your eyes, ears etc.

tha·lid·o·mide, Thalidomide /θə'lɪdə,maɪd/ *n.* [U] a drug given to people to make them calm, used in the past until it was discovered that it harmed the development of the arms and legs of unborn babies

thal·li·um /'θæliəm/ *n.* [U] *symbol* Tl a soft metal ELEMENT (=basic substance) that is very poisonous

Thames, the /tɛmz/ a river in England that flows from the west through London

than¹ /ðən, ðɛn; *strong* ðæn/ *conjunction* **1** used when comparing two different things, amounts, situations etc. to introduce the second thing: *You carry it – you're stronger than I am.* | *It's a nice car, but it costs more than we want to pay.* **2 would rather/sooner... than...** used to say that you prefer one thing to another: *I think I'd rather stay home than go to the party.* **3 no sooner...than...** used to say that something had just happened when something else happened: *No sooner was one fire under control than another one had begun.* —see also **other than** (OTHER¹ (7)), **rather than** (RATHER (1))

USAGE NOTE: THAN

GRAMMAR: as, then

In spoken and informal English, many people use object pronouns such as "me," "him" etc. after **than**: *Doris is older than me.* Many teachers think this is incorrect. They say that the form of the pronoun that follows **than** should depend on whether it is the subject or object of a verb (even when the verb is not there): *Doris is older than I* (=than I am).| *The news upset my wife more than me* (=than it upset me). In informal speech, we often use object pronouns such as **me, her, him** etc. before words like "as," "than," and "be" when making comparisons: *He's a lot older than her.| You got the same grade as me.* In written or formal English, it is better to use subject pronouns such as **I, she, he** etc.: *The other players are as good as he.| My daughter is more beautiful than I.*

---

than² *prep.* **1** used when comparing two different

things to introduce the second thing: *My brother is easier to get along with than my sister.* | *She says she feels a little better than yesterday.* **2 more/less/fewer etc. than** used when comparing two different amounts, numbers etc. to introduce the second amount or number: *It's hard to concentrate like that for more than a half an hour.* | *If it costs more than $60, I won't buy it.* **3** used with some words such as "else" or "other" to mean "except" or "besides": *Moreno talks about little else than his desire to fly.*

thang /θæŋ/ *n.* [C usually singular] SPOKEN, SLANG a humorous way of saying "thing": *We're just doing the study thang here.*

^{S W}
thank /θæŋk/ *v.* [T] **1** to tell someone that you are pleased and grateful for something they have done, or to be polite about it: *I haven't had a chance to thank him yet.* | [thank sb for (doing) sth] *Did you thank Aunt Edith for the present?* | *Padma thanked me several times for coming.* **2 have sb to thank (for sth)** used when saying who is responsible for something helpful or, humorously, who is responsible for something unhelpful: *In accepting this honor, I have many people to thank.* | *It looks like we have Sheila to thank for this little mix-up.*

SPOKEN PHRASES

3 thank God/goodness/heavens said to show that you are very glad about something: *Thank God the semester's almost over!* | [+ for] *Thank heavens for e-mail! I don't know what I'd do without it.* **4 thank your lucky stars** used to tell someone that they are very lucky, especially because they have avoided a bad or dangerous situation: *Thank your lucky stars the boy wasn't seriously hurt.* **5 you'll thank me** used to tell someone not to be annoyed with you for doing or saying something, because it will be helpful to them later: *You'll thank me for this one day, Laura.* **6 I'll thank you to do sth** FORMAL used to tell someone in an angry way not to do something because it is annoying you: *I'll thank you to mind your own business.*

—see also THANK YOU

thank·ful /ˈθæŋkfəl/ *adj.* [not before noun] grateful and glad about something that has happened, especially because without it the situation would be much worse: [+ for] *We really have a lot to be thankful for.* | [thankful (that)] *She was relieved and thankful that her son was safe.* | [thankful to do sth] *I was never so thankful to see a friendly face.* —**thankfulness** *n.* [U]

thank·ful·ly /ˈθæŋkfəli/ *adv.* **1** [sentence adverb] used to say that you are glad that something has happened, especially because a difficult situation has ended or been avoided: *Thankfully, my children are grown and able to support themselves.* **2** feeling grateful and glad about something, especially because a difficult situation has ended or been avoided: *We came in and collapsed thankfully onto our beds.*

thank·less /ˈθæŋklɪs/ *adj.* **1** a thankless job is difficult and you do not get any praise for doing it: **thankless role/task/work** *Edna was tired of her thankless role as wife and mother.* **2** LITERARY a thankless person is not grateful: *a thankless child*

^{S W}
thanks¹ /θæŋks/ *interjection* INFORMAL **1** used to tell someone that you are grateful for something they have given you or done for you; thank you: *Could you hold the door for me? Thanks.* | [thanks for (doing) sth] *It was good to talk to you. Thanks for calling.* | *Thanks for dinner – that was good.* **2 thanks a lot a)** used to tell someone that you are very grateful for something they have given you or done for you: *Thanks a lot for the ride.* **b)** used when you are annoyed about something and do not really mean thank you at all: *"I forgot to bring your money." "Well, thanks a lot!"* **3** used as a polite way of accepting something that someone has offered you: *"Do you want another cup of coffee?" "Oh, thanks."* **4 no, thanks** used to say politely that you do not want something: *"Do you want to dance?" "No, thanks. I'm kind of tired."* **5** used when politely answering someone's question about you: *"Hi, Bill,*

how are you?" "Fine, thanks." **6 thanks a bunch** INFORMAL an expression meaning "thank you very much," used especially as a joke when you are not grateful at all **7 thanks for nothing** used to tell someone in an angry or humorous way that they have not helped you

thanks² *n.* [plural] **1** the things you say or do to show that you are grateful to someone: *She received a personal letter of thanks from the President.* **2 thanks to sb a)** used to say that someone or something has been very helpful or useful: *Dietrich rose to international stardom, thanks to the Viennese director von Sternberg.* **b)** used to thank someone for doing something very helpful or useful: *Many thanks to Lapin for writing this interesting and informative article.* **c)** used to say, angrily or humorously that someone has caused a problem: *It was supposed to be a surprise, but thanks to your big mouth she knows all about it now.* **3 thanks to sth** used to say that something good is caused by something else: *Some ski resorts opened early, thanks to a late-October snowstorm.* **4 no thanks to sb/sth** SPOKEN an expression meaning "in spite of," used when someone or something should have helped you but did not: *Everyone got out safely, no thanks to the smoke alarm – its batteries were dead.*

Thanks·giv·ing /ˌθæŋksˈgɪvɪŋ/ *n.* **1** [C,U] also **Thanksgiving Day** /ˈ.. ˌ./ a holiday in the U.S. and Canada when families have a large meal together to celebrate and be thankful for food, health, families etc., celebrated in November in the U.S. and in October in Canada **2** [U] the period of time just before and after this day: *Where are you going for Thanksgiving?*

thanks·giv·ing /ˌθæŋksˈgɪvɪŋ/ *n.* [C,U] an expression of thanks to God

thank you /ˈ. ./ *interjection* **1** used to tell someone that you are grateful for something they have given you or done for you: *"Here, Mommy. This is for you!" "Thank you, dear."* | [thank you for (doing) sth] *Thank you for helping me with my homework.* | *Dear Grandma, Thank you very much for the birthday card and money.* **2** used as a polite way of saying that you would like something that someone has offered: *"Can I give you a ride home?" "Oh, thank you."* **3 no, thank you** used to say politely that you do not want something: *"Would you like some more coffee?" "No, thank you, I'm fine."* **4** used when politely answering someone's question about you: *"How are you feeling today?" "Much better, thank you."* **5** used at the end of a sentence when telling someone firmly that you do not want their help or advice and are slightly annoyed by it: *I can do it myself, thank you!*

thank-you² /ˈ. ./ *n.* [C] **1** something you say or do in order to thank someone: *She baked them a dozen cookies as a thank-you.* **2 a thank-you letter/note/card etc.** a short letter, note etc. in which you thank someone

Tharp /θɑrp/, **Twy·la** /ˈtwaɪlə/ (1941–) a U.S. dancer and CHOREOGRAPHER of modern dance and BALLET

^{S W}
that¹ /ðæt/ *pron.* **1** *plural* **those** used to talk about a person, thing, idea etc. that has already been mentioned or is already known about: *She's really funny – that's why I like her so much.* | *"Here's a picture of Kelly and me." "Oh, that's cute."* | *I'm not sure why she'd want to marry a man like that.* | *"Can I borrow your white gloves?" "I'm not sure where I put those."* | *"I have to go," she said, and* **with that** (=after doing that) *she hung up the phone.* **2** *plural* **those** used to talk about the person or thing that is farther from you in time, distance etc. than someone or something else: *Is that my pen?* | *Our tomatoes never get as big as those.* | *That's Jeff over by the fountain.* **3** /ðət/ used after a noun as a RELATIVE PRONOUN like "who," "whom," or "which" to introduce a CLAUSE: *What's the name of the girl that works at Costco?* | *Josh is the one that she used to live with.* | *There are lots of things that I need to buy before the trip.* —see

Usage Notes at WHICH and WHO **4** /ðət/ **the year/time etc. that...** the year, the time etc. when something happened: *I'll never forget the day that she was born.* **5** /ðət/ used to introduce a CLAUSE after a SUPERLATIVE: *Trina's the nicest person that I've ever met.* | *It's the most expensive movie that was ever made.* **6** plural **those** FORMAL used when talking about a particular person, thing, or group, especially one which is a particular type or kind: *There are those who still insist the world is flat.* | [+ of] *His own experience is different from that of his friends.* **7 that is (to say)** used to correct a statement or give more exact information about something: *One solution would be to change the shape of the TV screen – that is, to make it wider.*

SPOKEN PHRASES

8 that's it a) said when what you have mentioned is all of something or the end of something: *It rains till late February or early March, and that's it.* **b)** also **that does it** said when you are angry about a situation and you do not want it to continue: *OK, that's it. If you're not going to try, I'm not going to help you.* **c)** said in order to tell someone that they are doing something correctly: *Slowly... slowly... Yeah, that's it.* **9 that's that** said when something is completely finished or when a decision will not be changed: *We're offering $2700, and that's that* **10 that's life/men/politics etc.** used to say that something is typical of a particular situation, group of people etc.: *I guess I made a mistake, but hey, that's life.* **11 that's all there is to it** said to emphasize that something is simple to do, explain etc.: *You're going to have to do it on your own, Travis. That's all there is to it.* **12 at that** said to give more information about something mentioned before: *She's pregnant and having twins at that!*

—compare THIS²

USAGE NOTE: THAT

GRAMMAR
In informal speech or writing, **that** is often not used at the beginning of clauses that follow a verb, noun, or adjective, especially when the subject of the main clause and the *that* clause are the same: *He says he's going to come next week* (instead of: *He says that he...*).| *I was sick – that's the reason I didn't come* (instead of: *...the reason that I...*).| *I'm sorry I can't help you.* (instead of: *I'm sorry that I...*) In more formal speech and writing, **that** is used more often: *Authorities suspect that one man died in the fire.*| *New research shows that reading to children from birth improves intellectual development.*

that² /ðæt/ *determiner plural* **those 1** used before a noun or PRONOUN to talk about the person or thing that is farther away in distance, time etc. than someone or something else: *No, I wanted that one over there.* | *That last test was a lot easier than this one.* | *Look at those men in that car. What on earth are they doing?* **2** used before a noun or PRONOUN to talk about a person, thing, idea etc. that has already been mentioned or is already known about: *When are you going to give me that money you owe me?* | *He met Bobby Jones on Monday of that week.* | *What did you do with those sandwiches?* | *I saw that woman again today.* —compare THIS¹

that³ /ðət; *strong* ðæt/ *conjunction* **1** used after verbs, nouns, and adjectives to introduce a CLAUSE which gives more information, a reason, an explanation etc.: *Joe said that his girlfriend is coming to visit.* | *Are you sure that they live on Park Lane?* | *I can't believe that she told you.* | *I think Vic feels threatened by the fact that I'm smarter than he is.* **2 a) so big/ tall etc. that...** very big, very tall etc. with the result that something happens or someone does something: *I was so scared that I almost wet my pants.* **b) such a big man/such a tall house etc. that...** a very big man, a very tall house etc. with the result that something happens or someone does something: *It was such a bad snowstorm that they shut the airport down.* **3** FORMAL in order that, or so that something may happen or someone may do something: *We pray that he may recover soon.* **4** FORMAL used at the beginning of a CLAUSE, so that it can be used as a noun or, for example, the subject of a sentence: *That he talked about it to reporters surprises me.* **5** LITERARY used when you wish that something would happen, that you could do something etc.: *Oh, that Glenda were alive to see this.* —see also **so (that)** (SO² (4))

that⁴ /ðæt/ *adv.* [+ adj./adv.] **1 that long/many/big etc.** SPOKEN used to say how long, how many etc., especially because you are showing the size, number etc. with your hands or because the person you are talking to knows it already: *Does grass really grow that fast?* | *He's about that tall with brown hair.* **2 not that much/long/big etc.** SPOKEN not very much, long etc.: *Let's get another beer – it's not that late.* | *The show isn't all that funny.*

thatch /θætʃ/ *n.* **1** [C,U] STRAW, leaves, or REEDs used to make a roof, or a roof made of this **2** [singular] HUMOROUS a thick messy pile of hair on someone's head

thatched /θætʃt/ *adj.* made with dried STRAW, REEDs leaves etc.: *a thatched roof* —**thatch** *v.* [I,T]

Thatch·er /'θætʃər/, **Mar·garet** /'mɑrgrɪt/ (1925–) a British politician who was the UK's first woman Prime Minister, from 1979 until 1990

thaw¹ /θɔ/ *v.* **1** [I,T] also **thaw out** if ice or snow thaws or is thawed, it becomes warmer and turns into water: *When the lakes start to thaw, it's dangerous to go skating.* **2** also **thaw out** [I,T] to let frozen food unfreeze until it is ready to cook: *Put the chicken in the microwave to thaw it out.* **3** [I] to become friendlier and less serious: *As the Cold War thawed, defense budgets shrank.*

thaw² *n.* **1** [C] an improvement in relations between two countries after a period of opposition: *the thaw in East-West tensions* **2** [singular] a period of warm weather during which snow and ice melt: *the spring thaw*

the¹ /ðə, *before a vowel* ði; *strong* ði/ *determiner* **1** used to refer to, talk about, or show a particular thing or person when everyone knows which thing or person you are talking about, or because only one such person or thing exists: *Well, here's one shoe, but where's the other one?* | *Don't stay out in the sun too long.* | *I'm going to the store – do you want anything?* | *Where is the lowest point on Earth?* | *That's the guy I was telling you about.* | *Be sure to ask the doctor about that spot.* —compare A (1) **2** used as part of some names and titles: *the United States* | *the Pacific Ocean* | *Peter the Great* | *The Dunbars* (=the whole Dunbar family) *are planning to move.* **3** used to talk about or show something that everyone knows because it happens in nature or is a part of daily life: *We'll have to finish this in the morning.* | *I don't mind the heat – it's the humidity that bothers me.* | *Annette's been complaining about the traffic keeping her awake at night.* **4** used before an adjective to make it into a noun when you are talking about or showing all the people who that adjective describes: *a school for the deaf* | *She devoted her life to helping the poor.* | *The English and the French have a long history of conflict.* **5** used before a singular noun to make it general: *Jefferson chose the bald eagle as our nation's symbol.* | *The computer has changed the way people work.* **6** used before the names of musical instruments when talking about the activity of playing them: *How long have you played the cello?* | *Can anybody here play the piano?* **7** used to talk about or show a part of the body or to something that belongs to someone: *She kissed him right on the lips* (=his lips). | *How's the arm* (=your arm)? | *The car* (=our car) *broke down again today.* **8** used to talk about or show a period of time, especially one that continues ten or a hundred years: *the sexual revolution of the sixties* (=the 1960s) | *Hill traveled to Oregon by covered wagon in the late 1800s.* | *Veterans gathered to remember the war years.* **9 by the yard/by the dozen/by the**

handful etc. used before the names of measurements when describing how something is calculated, sold, or used: *This cloth is sold by the yard* (=it is measured in yards in order to calculate its price). | *We get paid by the hour.* **10** used before a plural noun to talk about or show a particular kind of thing: *How late are the stores open tonight?* | *The winters here are a lot milder than in the Midwest.* **11** used before an adjective to make it into a noun when you are talking about or showing a situation that that adjective describes: *I'm afraid you're asking for the impossible.* | **border/verge on the sth** *His version of events borders on the absurd.* **12** used before a noun, especially in negative sentences to show an amount or degree needed for a particular purpose: *I don't have the time to answer all these questions.* | *Steve didn't even have the common decency to let me know he wasn't coming.* **13** used before the name of a thing that represents a particular activity: *He's let the bottle* (=drinking alcohol) *ruin his life.* | *Ever since the accident she's been afraid to get behind the wheel* (=drive a car). **14** used before talking about or showing a particular date: *the third of October* | *Could we meet again on the twelfth?* **15 the flu/the measles/the mumps etc.** used before the names of certain not very serious illnesses: *I got the chicken pox from my brother.*

SPOKEN PHRASES

16 said with strong pronunciation before a noun to show that it is the best, most famous etc. person or thing of its kind: *"I saw Robin Williams in the grocery store yesterday." "The Robin Williams?"* | *They say it's the big movie of the year.* **17** said before a word that describes someone or something when you are angry, JEALOUS, surprised etc.: *He forgot to buy toilet paper again, the idiot.* | *I can't get this carton open, the stupid thing.* **18** used in certain phrases that express anger, surprise etc. *So I figured, What the heck? I might as well try.*

USAGE NOTE: THE

GRAMMAR
Do not use **the** with uncountable or plural nouns when you are using the general sense of the noun: *My favorite food is ice cream.* | *Glen really likes dogs.* Use **the** with uncountable or plural nouns when you mean a particular thing or a particular group of things: *The ice cream we bought yesterday tastes funny.* | *Did you see the dogs in that window?* Use **the** if you are mentioning specific things that are already known to the reader or listener: *I'm sorry. I gave the dress to Maggie* (=the dress that I just told you about or that you know about). Also use **the** before a noun that is followed by a phrase that says more specifically what type of thing you mean: *The life of an artist is not always easy.* | *This is the best steak I've ever eaten.* DO NOT use **the** in the following situations (unless there is extra information that tells specifically which thing you are talking about): 1. With many times of day and night and names of days, months etc., especially after **at**, **by**, and **on**: *at noon* | *We'll be there by dawn.* | *on Tuesday* (but: *during the night* | *Let's have dinner on the Tuesday after next.*) 2. When you are talking about meals, especially after **at**, **before**, **during**, **after**, **for**, and the verb **have**: *We'll do it after dinner.* | *What's for lunch?* | *We had breakfast in bed.* (but: *The dinner we had at Marcia's house was delicious.*) 3. In many fixed expressions such as: *by car/bus etc.* | *at school/college etc.* | *to bed/jail/church etc.* | *arm in arm* | *from beginning to end* 4. With names of languages and most diseases: *She speaks Norwegian.* | *My father has cancer.* 5. With most names of streets, places, countries, mountains, people, businesses etc.: *Pine Street* | *I'm flying into O'Hare airport.* | *South Korea* | *Florida* | *Mount Fuji* | *Let's eat at Burger King.* However, some such names always contain **the**, especially the names of countries that are plural or contain the words "state" or "republic": *Russ is staying at the Hilton.* | *the United States* | *the Czech Republic.* Also use **the** before the names of rivers, oceans, and groups of mountains: *the Mississippi* | *the Indian Ocean* | *the Himalayas.*

the² *adv.* **1** used in comparisons to show that two things happen together: *The more I read, the less I seem to understand.* | *"When do you want this done?" "The sooner the better."* **2** used in front of the SUPERLATIVE form of adjectives and adverbs to emphasize that something is as big, good etc. as it is possible to be: *Frieda likes you the best.* | *Tevis usually finishes the fastest.* **3** used in comparisons to show that someone or something has more or less of a particular quality than before: *They replaced the painting with a copy and the public was none the wiser* (=not knowing more about something than before, or not realizing what has happened). | **the better/the worse** *America will be the better for these changes.*

the- /θi/ *prefix* another form of the PREFIX THEO-

the·a·ter, theatre /ˈθiətɚ/ *n.* **1** [C] a building or place with a stage where plays are performed: *an open-air theater* | *the Orpheum Theater* **2** [U] **a)** the work of acting in, writing, or organizing plays: *I'm taking a theater class at the community college.* | *Reed began his career in the theater in 1957.* **b)** plays as a form of entertainment: *Elizabethan theater* | *People know what they want, and they want good theater* (=plays of high quality). **3** [C] a building where movies are shown **4** [C] a large area where a war is being fought: *the Pacific theater during World War II* **5** [C] a special room in a hospital where people can watch a medical operation being done

the·a·ter·go·er /ˈθiətɚˌgoʊɚ/ *n.* [C] someone who regularly watches plays at the theater

theater-in-the-round /ˌ.... . './ *n.* [U] the performance of a play on a central stage with the people watching sitting in a circle around it

the·a·tre /ˈθiətɚ/ *n.* another spelling of THEATER

the·at·ri·cal /θiˈætrɪkəl/ *adj.* **1** relating to the performing of plays: *a theatrical troupe* | *theatrical skills* **2** relating to movies that are shown in theaters rather than on television: *The movie was intended for theatrical release* (=to be shown in theaters). **3** behaving in a loud or very noticeable way that is intended to get people's attention: *He was speaking in a stupid theatrical accent.* —**theatrically** /-kli/ *adv.*

the·at·ri·cals /θiˈætrɪkəlz/ *n.* [plural] performances of plays: *amateur theatricals*

the·at·rics /θiˈætrɪks/ *n.* [plural] behavior that is very loud or noticeable and intended to get people's attention: *The jurors laughed at McKittrick's theatrics, but the judge did not find them so amusing.*

thee /θi/ *pron.* OLD USE the OBJECT form of THOU; YOU

theft /θɛft/ *n.* **1** [U] the crime of stealing: *Pushard was arrested and charged with auto theft.* **2** [C] an act of stealing something: *Most of the thefts occurred during the weekend.* | [+ of] *the theft of $200 from the office*

their /ðɚ; strong ðɛr/ *possessive adj.* [possessive form of "they"] **1** belonging to or relating to the people, animals, or things that have been mentioned or are known about: *Bill and his wife and their two boys are coming for dinner.* | *I love koala bears – their faces are so cute.* **2** used to avoid saying "his" or "her" after words like "anyone," "no one," "everyone" etc.: *Everyone has their own room.* —compare HIS¹ and see Usage Note at HIS¹

USAGE NOTE: THEIR

GRAMMAR: they, them, themselves, their, theirs
In spoken and informal English, it is very common for people to use **they**, **them**, **themselves**, **their**, or **theirs** to talk about a singular noun or a singular pronoun such as "anyone" or "everyone." This is especially common when it is not clear whether they are speaking about men or women or both: *If a student needs help, I am always happy to talk to them.* | *Someone left their umbrella in the closet.* Many teachers do not approve of using these pronouns in this way. They suggest using "he or she," "him or her," "his or her," etc.: *Someone left his or her umbrella in the closet.*

S W **theirs** /ðɛrz/ *possessive pron.* [possessive form of
3 "they"] **1** the thing or things belonging to or relating to the people or things that have been mentioned
or are known about: *When our washing machine
broke, our neighbors let us use theirs.* | *Our report
was better than theirs.* **2** used to avoid saying "his"
or "hers" after words like "anyone," "no one,"
"everyone" etc.: *Okay, get your coats. Does everyone
have theirs?* —compare HIS²

the·ism /ˈθiɪzəm/ *n.* [U] TECHNICAL **1** belief in the
existence of one God **2** belief in the existence of a
god or gods —**theistic** /θiˈɪstɪk/ *adj.* —**theistically**
/-kli/ *adv.*

S W **them¹** /ðəm, əm; *strong* ðɛm/ *pron.* **1** the object form
1 1 of "they": *Careful with those dishes. Don't break
them.* | *They looked a little tired when I saw them last
week.* **2** used to avoid saying "him" or "her" after
words like "anyone," "no one," "everyone" etc.: *If
anyone calls, tell them I'll be back around 5.* —see
Usage Note at THEIR

them² /ðɛm/ *determiner* SPOKEN, NONSTANDARD those: *I
couldn't understand all them big words.*

the·mat·ic /θiˈmætɪk/ *adj.* relating to a particular
theme, or organized according to themes: *a thematic
travel guide*

S W **theme** /θim/ *n.* [C] **1** a main subject or idea in a
3 2 piece of writing, speech, movie etc.: *The conference's
theme is education and training.* **2** a particular style:
The master bedroom is decorated in a Victorian theme.
3 also **theme music/song** music or a song that is
often played during a movie or musical play or at
the beginning and end of a television or radio program: *I really like the theme song to the "Mary Tyler
Moore Show."* **4** a short simple tune that is repeated
and developed in a piece of music: *Freia's theme in
Wagner's opera* **5** OLD-FASHIONED a short piece of
writing on a particular subject that you do for
school: *a two-page theme on pollution* —see also
-THEMED

-themed /θimd/ [in adjectives] **holiday-themed/gay-
themed/Civil-War themed etc.** having a particular
style or relating to a particular group of people:
*Galder is a spokeswoman for the rock 'n' roll-themed
club.*

theme park /ˈ. ./ *n.* [C] a type of park where you can
have fun riding on big machines such as a ROLLER
COASTER or a FERRIS WHEEL, but where the whole park
is based on one subject such as space travel or water

theme par·ty /ˈ. ˌ../ *n.* [C] a party where everyone
has to dress in a particular way relating to a particular subject

S W **them·selves** /ðəmˈsɛlvz, ðɛm-/ *pron.* **1** the REFLEX-
1 1 IVE form of "they": *Those guys only talk about them-
selves.* | *Do you think they killed themselves?* **2** the
strong form of "they," used to emphasize the subject
or object of a sentence: *Why don't they just do it themselves?* **3** also **themself** SPOKEN used to avoid saying
"himself" or "herself" after words like "everyone,"
"anyone," "no one" etc.: *Everyone I know who has
tried it has hurt themselves somehow.* **4** in **themselves** also **in and of themselves** considered without other related ideas or situations: *The carvings
are works of art in themselves, even disregarding their
religious significance.* **5 (all) by themselves a)** alone:
*They are both old enough to go to the pool by them-
selves.* **b)** without help from anyone else: *I'm hoping
these spots will go away by themselves.* **6 (all) to
themselves** if people have something to themselves,
they do not have to share it with anyone: *They had
the whole beach to themselves.* —see Usage Note at
THEIR

S W **then¹** /ðɛn/ *adv.* **1** after something has happened;
1 1 NEXT: *First Sue was a teacher. Then she was an artist.
Who knows what she'll do next!* | *I finished cleaning
and then I took a little nap.* **2** at a particular time in
the past or future: *I wish I knew then what I know
now.* | *It was then that Jan realized he had lied to
her.* | *They're sending the results next week, so I won't
know anything until then.* | *We moved to Phoenix in*

'78, and from then on (=starting at that time) *we've
lived in this house.* | *We need to become a lot more
united. Only then will we have power.* | *Olga turned
out the light and closed her eyes.* *Just then the door
opened.* | *Even back then* (=a long time ago when
things were different) *I didn't like to stay out all
night.* | *If we washed the dishes, then and only then
would she allow us to go out and play with the other
children.* **3** SPOKEN used to show that what you are
saying is related in some way to what has been said
before: *"He said he'd call if he got lost." "Then you
don't need to worry about it."* | *So, then, why did you
move to Alabama?* | *"Friday's no good." "Then how
about Saturday?"* **4** used to say that if one thing is
true, another thing is also true or should be the correct result: *"We're supposed to be there at 7." "Then
we'd better leave right away."* | *If you're going to say
things like that, then you'd better have some evidence.* **5 but then (again)** ESPECIALLY SPOKEN used to
say that although something is true something else
is also true which makes the first thing seem less
important: *I don't think she liked my present, but then
again it could just be my imagination.* **6** used to add
something to what you have just said: *We have to
invite your parents and my parents, and then there's
your brother.* **7** so that something happens or so
that someone does something: *Don't make eye contact
– then they won't ask for money.* **8 then and there**
also **there and then** immediately: *If I come across a
mistake, I fix it right then and there.* —see also
(every) now and then (NOW¹ (22))

then² *adj.* **the then-president/then-director/then-** **S W**
21-year-old etc. the president, director etc. at a 2
particular time in the past: *In 1950, it cost the then-
enormous price of $7,500 to construct the machine.*

thence /ðɛns/ *adv.* LITERARY **1** from there: *We traveled to Cape Town, and thence to India via Madagascar.* **2** for that reason

thence·forth /ˈðɛnsˌfɔrθ, ˌðɛnsˈfɔrθ/ *adv.* LITERARY
starting from that time

theo- /θiə/ *prefix* relating to God or gods: *theology*
(=study of religion)

the·oc·ra·cy /θiˈɑkrəsi/ *n.* [C] a social system or state
controlled by religious leaders —**theocratic**
/ˌθiəˈkrætɪk◂/ *adj.*: *a theocratic Islamic country*

the·o·lo·gian /ˌθiəˈloʊdʒən/ *n.* [C] someone who has
studied theology

theological sem·i·nar·y /ˌ.....ˈ..../ *n.* [C] a college
for training people to become church ministers,
priests, or RABBIS

the·ol·o·gy /θiˈɑlədʒi/ *n. plural* **theologies 1** [U] the
study of religion and religious ideas and beliefs: *He
studied theology at college.* **2** [C,U] a particular
system of religious beliefs and ideas: *According to
Muslim theology there is only one God.* —**theological**
/ˌθiəˈlɑdʒɪkəl◂/ *adj.*: *theological traditions* —**theolog-
ically** /-kli/ *adv.*

the·oph·yl·line /θiˈɑfələn/ *n.* [U] a drug like CAFFEINE
that is used to treat heart and breathing problems

the·o·rem /ˈθiərəm, ˈθɪrəm/ *n.* [C] TECHNICAL a statement, especially in mathematics, that you can prove
by reasoning

the·o·ret·i·cal /ˌθiəˈrɛtɪkəl/ also **the·o·ret·ic** /ˌθiəˈrɛtɪk/
adj. **1** relating to the study of scientific ideas rather
than with practical uses of science or practical experience: *theoretical research* —compare PRACTICAL (1)
2 a theoretical situation or condition could exist but
does not really exist: *There is a theoretical chance of
infection, but it is not very likely.*

the·o·ret·i·cal·ly /ˌθiəˈrɛtɪkli/ *adv.* **1** [sentence
adverb] used to say what is supposed to be true in a
particular situation, especially when the opposite is
true: *Theoretically, the department exists to help
people, but it often seems otherwise.* **2** according to a
scientific idea that has not been proven to be true in
a practical way: *It is theoretically possible to identify
a person from just one tooth if the tooth is unusual.*

the·o·rist /ˈθiərɪst/ also **the·o·re·ti·cian** /ˌθiərəˈtɪʃən/
n. [C] someone who develops ideas within a particular subject that explain why particular things
happen or are true: *a leading feminist theorist*

the·o·rize /ˈθiəˌraɪz/ v. [I,T] to think of a possible explanation for an event or fact: [+ **about/on**] *Jenkins said she didn't want to theorize about what is killing the birds.* | [**theorize (that)**] *Police theorize that the two men were working together.*

the·o·ry /ˈθiəri, ˈθɪri/ n. plural **theories** 1 [C] an idea or set of ideas that is intended to explain something about life or the world, especially one that has not yet been proven to be true: [+ **of**] *Einstein's theory of relativity* | [**theory that**] *New evidence supports the theory that the dinosaurs were wiped out by an asteroid.* 2 [C] an idea that someone thinks is true but for which they have no proof: [**theory that**] *I have a theory that it only rains when I wash my car.* 3 [U] the general principles or ideas of a subject, especially a scientific subject: *Freudian theory has had a great influence on psychology.* | *music theory* 4 **in theory** something that is true in theory is supposed to be true, but may not be true: *In theory, more competition means lower prices for consumers.* —compare **in practice** (PRACTICE¹ (3))

ther·a·peu·tic /ˌθɛrəˈpyutɪk/ cdj. 1 relating to the treatment or cure of disease: *therapeutic drugs* | *The treatment has little therapeutic value.* 2 making you feel calm and relaxed: *I find swimming very therapeutic.* —**therapeutically** /-kli/ adv.

ther·a·peu·tics /ˌθɛrəˈpyutɪks/ n. [U] TECHNICAL the part of medical science concerned with the treatment and cure of illness

ther·a·pist /ˈθɛrəpɪst/ n. [C] someone who has been trained to give a particular form of treatment for mental or physical illness: *a sex therapist*

ther·a·py /ˈθɛrəpi/ n. plural **therapies** [C,U] 1 the treatment of an illness or injury over a fairly long period of time, especially using drugs or operations: *A full recovery will require years of physical therapy.* 2 the treatment or examination of someone's mental problems by talking to them for a long time about their feelings: *Julie's been in therapy for two years.* —see also OCCUPATIONAL THERAPY, PHYSICAL THERAPY, SPEECH THERAPY

there¹ /ðɛr/ pron. **there is/are/exists/remain etc.** used to say that something exists or happens: *Is there any milk left?* | *There are a few things I'd like to talk to you about.* | *There must be a reason she's acting like this.* | *Suddenly there was a popping noise and a flash of light.* | *There remains a good deal of controversy over the agreement.* | *There seem to be so many squirrels this year.*

USAGE NOTE: THERE

GRAMMAR
When **there** is the subject of the sentence, the form of the verb depends on whether the noun that follows it is singular or plural. If the noun is singular, the verb is singular; if the noun is plural, the verb is plural: *There are two Vietnamese students in my class.*| *There's a letter for you in the kitchen.* In informal spoken English, many people use **there's** before a plural noun: *There's two cookies left in the package.* This should not be used in formal writing, however.

---

there² adv. 1 in or to a particular place that is not where you are or near you: *Australia? No, I've never been there.* | *Are you just going to sit there or are you going to help?* | *What made you decide to move there?* | [**out/in/under etc. there**] *"Have you tried looking for your shoes under the bed?" "Yes, I've already looked under there."* | *Don't worry. We'll get there* (=arrive) *before the stores close.* | *"Carmen's now living in Thailand." "How long has she been over there?"* 2 at a particular point in time, in a story etc.: *Don't stop there! Tell me the rest!* 3 if something is there, it exists: *You don't have to eat all the candy just because it's there.* 4 **be there (for sb)** to be ready to help someone or be kind to them when they have problems: *My parents were always there for me when I was growing up.* 5 used to say which statement, idea, or reason you agree with, want to say more about etc.: *"Of course the military bases will have to be closed." "I'm not sure I agree with you there."* 6 **there and back** the distance, cost etc.

there and back is the total distance or cost of the trip to a place, added to the distance or cost of the return: *It only takes four hours, there and back.* 7 **sb/sth is there to do sth** used to say what someone or something's duty or purpose is: *Police are there to make sure everyone obeys the laws.*

SPOKEN PHRASES

8 **there is sth** also **there it is a)** said to make someone look or pay attention to something: *There's the statue I was telling you about.* **b)** said when you have found something you were looking for: *"Where are my slippers?" "There they are, under the couch."* 9 **there (you go) a)** also **there you are** said when giving something to someone or when you have done something for someone: *Do you need a tissue, Mr. Phillips? There you go.* **b)** used in order to tell someone that they have done something correctly or understood something: *Can you turn just a little to the left? There you go.* **c)** also **there you have it** said when someone has just said something that you expected or that seems to explain a situation: *"I can't do everything I used to, but I am almost 50." "Well, there you go."* 10 **there you go a)** used to say that something that has happened cannot be changed or was what you expected: *Well, there you go, he really did go to Harvard.* 11 **there he/she etc. is** said when someone you have been waiting for arrives, or when you find someone you have been looking for: *There you are! What took you so long?* 12 **there he/she etc. goes again** said when someone starts saying or doing something again that you do not approve of: *There she goes again complaining about money.* 13 **there goes sth** used to show your disappointment when something does not happen the way you want it to or when it changes what you were doing: *Well, there goes my chance to a raise.* | *Look at all that food – there goes my diet!* 14 **there goes sb/sth** also **there he/she/it etc. goes a)** said when you see someone or something moving past you or away from you: *Look, there goes a fire engine.* **b)** said when you lose something such as money or an opportunity: *There go our chances of winning the championship.* 15 **hi/hello/hey there** said when greeting someone, especially when you have just noticed them: *Hi there. You must be Liane.* 16 **sb's not all there** a phrase used to describe someone who is not very intelligent and seems slightly crazy, used when you want to avoid saying this directly 17 **that book there/those shoes there etc.** said when showing or pointing to where something is: *Can you hand me that towel there?*

—see also **then and there** (THEN¹ (8)) —compare HERE¹

there³ interjection 1 used to express success or satisfaction, especially when you have finished something: *There! I figured it out* 2 **there, there** used to comfort someone who is upset: *There, there. It's not the end of the world.*

there·a·bouts /ˌðɛrəˈbaʊts, ˈðɛrəˌbaʊts/ adv. near a particular time, place, number etc., but not exactly: *The women were all 50 or thereabouts.*

there·af·ter /ðɛrˈæftɚ/ adv. FORMAL after a particular event or time; AFTERWARD: *Halfon was born in Marseilles, but shortly thereafter his family moved to an island off Tunisia.*

there·by /ðɛrˈbaɪ, ˈðɛrbaɪ/ adv. FORMAL with the result that something else happens: *He redesigned the process, thereby saving the company thousands of dollars.*

there·fore /ˈðɛrfɔr/ adv. FORMAL as a result of something that has just been mentioned: *It was clear Lucy was unhappy. Therefore, it comes as no surprise she has decided to resign.* —see Usage Note at THUS

there·in /ðɛrˈɪn/ adv. FORMAL 1 **therein lies sth** used to say that something is caused by or comes from a particular situation: *The treaty was imposed by force, and therein lay the cause of its ineffectiveness.* 2 in that place, or in that piece of writing: *Kramer was* *interviewed for the book and is quoted therein.* —compare HEREIN

there·of /ðɛr'ʌv/ *adv.* FORMAL concerning something that has just been mentioned: *The company's success, or its lack thereof, depends on the quality of its product.*

there·on /ðɛr'ɔn/ *adv.* FORMAL **1** on the thing that has just been mentioned **2** THEREUPON

there·to /ðɛr'tu/ *adv.* FORMAL **1** to something that has just been mentioned **2** concerning an agreement or piece of writing that has just been mentioned

there·to·fore /'ðɛrtə,fɔr/ *adv.* FORMAL before or until a particular time

there·un·der /ðɛr'ʌndə/ *adv.* FORMAL **1** under something that has just been mentioned **2** according to a document, law, or part of an agreement that has just been mentioned

there·up·on /'ðɛrə,pɑn, ,ðɛrə'pɑn/ *adv.* FORMAL **1** immediately after something else has happened, and usually as a result of it; then: *Thereupon the whole audience stood up and began cheering.* **2** concerning a subject that has just been mentioned

therm /θɚm/ *n.* [C] a measurement of heat equal to 100,000 BTUs

therm- /θɚm/ *prefix* another spelling of THERMO-, used before some vowels

ther·mal¹ /'θɚməl/ *adj.* [only before noun] **1** relating to or caused by heat: *thermal energy* | *thermal radiation* **2** thermal clothing is made from special material to keep you warm in very cold weather: *thermal underwear* **3** thermal water is heated naturally under the earth: *thermal springs*

thermal² *n.* [C] **1** a rising current of warm air **2 thermals** INFORMAL special warm clothing, especially underwear

ther·mi·on·ics /,θɚrmi'ɑnɪks/ *n.* [U] TECHNICAL the part of science that deals with the flow of ELECTRONS from heated metal

thermo- /θɚrmou, -mə/ *prefix* TECHNICAL relating to heat: *a thermostat* (=for controlling temperature) —see also THERM-

ther·mo·dy·nam·ics /,θɚrmoudaɪ'næmɪks/ *n.* [U] the science that deals with the relationship between heat and other forms of energy —**thermodynamic** *adj.*

ther·mom·e·ter /θɚ'mɑmətɚ/ *n.* [C] a piece of equipment that measures the temperature of the air, of your body etc.

ther·mo·nu·cle·ar /,θɚrmou'nukliə/ *adj.* thermonuclear weapons use a NUCLEAR reaction, involving the splitting of atoms, to produce very high temperatures and a very powerful explosion

ther·mo·plas·tic /,θɚrmə'plæstɪk◂/ *n.* [C,U] TECHNICAL a plastic that is soft and bendable when heated but hard when cold

Ther·mos, thermos /'θɚrməs/ TRADEMARK *n.* [C] a special container that is designed to keep drinks hot or cold

ther·mo·stat /'θɚrmə,stæt/ *n.* [C] an instrument used for keeping a room or a machine at a particular temperature —see picture at ENGINE

the·sau·rus /θɪ'sɔrəs/ *n. plural* **thesauruses** or **thesauri** /-raɪ/ [C] a book in which words are put into groups with other words that have similar meanings

S W
1
these /ðiz/ *determiner, pron.* the plural of THIS

the·sis /'θisɪs/ *n. plural* **theses** /-siz/ [C] **1** a long piece of writing about a particular subject that you do as part of an advanced university degree, such as a MASTER'S DEGREE: [+ **on**] *Keller wrote his master's thesis on Swedish choral music.* **2** FORMAL an idea or statement that tries to explain why something happens: *The book seems to have no central thesis.*

thesis state·ment /,.. '../ *n.* [C] the statement in a piece of writing that gives the main idea or the writer's opinion

thes·pi·an /'θɛspiən/ *n.* [C] FORMAL OR HUMOROUS an actor —**thespian** *adj.*

Thes·sa·lo·ni·ans /,θɛsə'louniənz/ **1 Thessalonians, 2 Thessalonians** two books in the New Testament of the Christian Bible

they /ðeɪ/ *pron.* [used as the subject of a verb] **1** used to talk about two or more people or things that have been mentioned already or that the person you are talking to already knows about: *Sara and Michael said they won't be able to come.* | *They sell the best coffee in town.* **2** a particular group or organization, or the people involved in it: *"Naranjas" is what they call oranges in Spain.* | *Where are they going to build the new highway?* **3 they say/think etc.** SPOKEN used to say what people in general think, believe, are saying etc.: *They say it's safer to fly than to drive.* **4** used to avoid saying "he" or "she" after words like "anyone," "no one," "everyone" etc.: *You can tell if someone is really interested in buying a car by the questions they ask.* —see Usage Note at THEIR

S W
1 1

they'd /ðeɪd/ **1** the short form of "they had": *They said they'd already seen it.* **2** the short form of "they would": *Come with me. I'm sure they'd all like to see you.*

they'll /ðeɪl, ðɛl/ the short form of "they will": *They'll be here tomorrow around noon.*

they're /ðɚ; strong ðɛr/ the short form of "they are": *They're spending Christmas in Florida.*

they've /ðeɪv/ the short form of "they have," when "have" is an AUXILIARY VERB: *They've lived there about three years, haven't they?*

thi·a·min, thi·a·mine /'θaɪəmən/ *n.* [U] a natural chemical in some foods, that you need in order to prevent particular illnesses

thick¹ /θɪk/ *adj.*

1 not thin measuring a large distance or a larger distance than usual, between two opposite surfaces or sides: *a thick layer of frosting* | *If you want a thicker blanket, there are more here in the closet.* | [+ **with**] *Roads are thick with ice and driving is hazardous.* —opposite THIN¹

2 2 feet thick/12 inches thick etc. used to describe the exact measurement between two opposite sides or surfaces of something: *The brick wall is about 16 inches thick.*

3 liquid not solid, but moving or flowing slowly: *Is this gravy thick enough?* | *thick spaghetti sauce* —opposite THIN¹

4 smoke/cloud etc. filling the air, and difficult to see through or breathe in: *Thick clouds of black smoke went up from the oil fires.* | *a thick blanket of fog* | [+ **with**] *The room was thick with cigarette smoke.* —opposite THIN¹

5 hair/fur etc. forming a deep soft covering: *You have such thick, beautiful hair.* —opposite THIN¹

6 trees/bushes etc. growing very close together, or having a lot of leaves, so there is not much space in between: *In the hills, all the houses are surrounded by thick brush.* | *a thick forest* —opposite THIN¹

7 way of speaking clearly belonging to a particular place or part of the country: **a thick Irish/Southern/Russian etc. accent** *"Why now?" he asked in a thick German accent.*

8 voice not as clear or as high as usual because someone is angry, confused etc. about something: *Bill's voice was thick and gruff.* | [+ **with**] *Her voice was thick with emotion as she read the letter out loud.*

9 be (as) thick as thieves if two people are as thick as thieves, they are very friendly with each other and seem to share a lot of secrets

10 be thick with sb OLD-FASHIONED to be very friendly with someone —**thickly** *adv.* —see also **have thick/thin skin** (SKIN¹ (6)), THICKNESS, THICK-SKINNED

thick² *adv.* **1** if you spread, cut etc. something thick, you spread or cut it in a way that produces a thick layer or piece: *Slice the cheese a little thicker.* **2 thick and fast** arriving or happening very frequently, in large numbers or amounts: *Rumors flew thick and fast that the government would close the newspaper.* —see also **lay it on thick** at **lay on** (LAY¹)

thick³ *n.* **1 in the thick of sth** in the busiest, most active, most dangerous etc. part of a situation: *Williams was wounded in the thick of the battle.*

S W
3 3

2 through thick and thin in spite of any difficulties or problems: *I'm so grateful to Barb – she's supported me through thick and thin.*

thick·en /ˈθɪkən/ v. [I,T] to become thick, or make something thick: *The fog was beginning to thicken.* | [**thicken sth with sth**] *You can thicken the soup slightly with flour.* —see also **the plot thickens** (PLOT¹ (3))

thick·en·er /ˈθɪkənɚ/ also **thick·en·ing** /ˈθɪkənɪŋ/ n. [C,U] a substance used to thicken a liquid

thick·et /ˈθɪkɪt/ n. [C] a group of bushes and small trees

thick-head·ed /ˌ. ˈ...◂/ adj. INFORMAL extremely stupid: *He's so thick-headed he can't understand the simplest instructions.*

thick·ness /ˈθɪknɪs/ n. **1** [C,U] how thick something is: *Flatten the meat to about ⅟₈-inch thickness.* **2** [C] a layer of something: *Wrap the spices in a double thickness of cloth.*

thick·set /ˌθɪkˈsɛt◂/ adj. having a wide strong body: *a short thickset man*

thick-skinned /ˈ. .◂/ adj. not easily offended by other people's criticism or insults: *You don't become a major newspaper columnist without being thick-skinned.*

thief /θif/ n. plural **thieves** /θivz/ [C] someone who steals things, especially without using violence: *a car thief* | *Thieves took a marble statue from the church sometime last night.* —compare BURGLAR, ROBBER —see also **be (as) thick as thieves** (THICK¹ (9))

USAGE NOTE: THIEF

WORD CHOICE: thief, shoplifter, pickpocket, mugger, burglar, robber
All of these words mean "someone who takes things that do not belong to them." A **thief** is a general word for someone who steals. Someone who takes things from stores without paying for them is a **shoplifter**. Someone who takes things from the pockets of other people on the street, on a bus etc. is a **pickpocket**. A **mugger** is someone who uses violence when taking things from people, usually in a public place. A **burglar** takes things from houses, usually at night. A **robber** takes money from banks, people etc. and often uses violence.

---

thiev·er·y /ˈθivəri/ also **thieving** n. [U] FORMAL the practice of stealing things

thiev·ing /ˈθivɪŋ/ adj. [only before noun] involved in the practice of stealing things from other people: *He's just another lying, thieving politician.*

thiev·ish /ˈθivɪʃ/ adj. LITERARY like a thief

thigh /θaɪ/ n. [C] **1** the top part of your leg, between your knee and your HIP —see picture at BODY **2** the top part of a bird's leg, used as food: *chicken thighs*

thigh·bone /ˈθaɪboʊn/ n. [C] NOT TECHNICAL the bone in your thigh —see picture at SKELETON

thim·ble /ˈθɪmbəl/ n. [C] a small metal or plastic cap used to protect your finger when you are sewing

thim·ble·ful /ˈθɪmbəlfʊl/ n. [C + of] INFORMAL a very small quantity of liquid

Thim·pu /ˈθɪmbu/ the capital city of Bhutan

_{S W}
_{2 2}
thin¹ /θɪn/ adj. **thinner, thinnest**
1 [**not thick**] measuring a small distance or a smaller distance than usual between two opposite sides or surfaces: *a thin gold chain* | *My curtains are too thin to keep the sun out.* | *The TV screen is coated with a thin film of dust.* | *Cut the meat in* ***paper-thin*** (=very thin) *slices.* —opposite THICK¹

2 [**not fat**] having little fat on your body: *He's tall and thin and wears glasses.* | *I wish my legs were thinner.* —opposite FAT¹

3 [**air**] air that is thin is more difficult to breathe than usual because it has less OXYGEN in it: *The air is so thin up here I can hardly breathe.*

4 [**smoke/mist/fog**] smoke, mist, or FOG that is thin is easy to see through: *The sun quickly burned away the thin layer of fog.* —opposite THICK¹

5 [**hair/plants**] hairs or plants that are thin have

spaces between them: *a thin, straggly beard* | *thin vegetation* | *His hair's getting thin on top.* —opposite THICK¹

6 [**liquid**] a liquid that is thin flows very easily because it has a lot of water in it: *thin broth* —opposite THICK¹

7 [**voice/sound**] a thin voice or sound is high and weak, and is not nice to listen to: *"What do you want?" gasped Helen in a thin, frightened voice.*

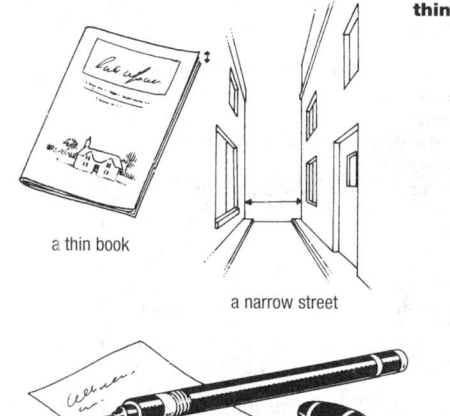

a thin book

a narrow street

a fine point

8 a thin margin/majority etc. a very small number or amount of something: *Engle beat Blanchard by **a razor-thin margin*** (=a very small number of votes) *in the race for governor.*

9 [**excuse/argument/explanation**] a thin excuse, argument, or explanation is not good or detailed enough to persuade you that it is true: *That's a pretty thin excuse – he could have gotten there if he'd really wanted to.*

10 [**business**] thin trading is a situation in which people are not buying or selling very much at a STOCK EXCHANGE —opposite HEAVY¹

11 [**information/description**] a piece of information or a description that is thin is not detailed enough to be useful or effective: [+ **on**] *The report is very thin on information and material to back up his claims.*

12 be (skating) on thin ice to be in a situation in which you are likely to upset someone or cause trouble: *You're skating on thin ice, showing up late for work every day.*

13 disappear/vanish into thin air to disappear or vanish completely in a mysterious way —**thinness** n. [U] —see also THINLY and see Usage Note at NARROW

USAGE NOTE: THIN

WORD CHOICE: thin, slim, slender, skinny, underweight, emaciated
Thin is a general word that describes people who do not have much fat on their bodies: *She used to be a lot thinner.* If someone is thin in a way that is attractive, you can also use **slim** or **slender**: *How do you keep so slim?* | *long slender legs.* **Skinny** is an informal word that means that someone is too thin: *Who's the skinny kid with glasses in the front row?* **Underweight** means that someone does not weigh enough, and is often used by doctors or by people who are worried about their weight: *Seven months into her pregnancy, Brenda was still 15 pounds underweight.* **Emaciated** means that someone is extremely thin in a way that is dangerous to their health: *an emaciated survivor of the prison camp*

---

thin² v. **thinned, thinning 1** [I] also **thin out** if a crowd thins or thins out, the people gradually leave so there are fewer of them: *The small group of pro-testers thinned out by midnight.* **2** [I,T] to make something thinner, or to become thinner: *Add a little oil to thin the mixture.* | *Zhao's hair has thinned and turned gray.* **3 thin the ranks** if something thins the ranks of a group of people, there are less of them as a result of it: *Higher prices have thinned the ranks of prospective home owners.* **4** also **thin out** [T] to make more room for plants to grow by removing the weaker ones: *They went through the fields to thin the sugar beets.* **5 thin the herd** to kill some animals in a group so that there are not so many of them —see also THINNING

thin³ *adv.* so as to be thin: *Don't cut the bread so thin.*

thine¹ /ðaɪn/ *possessive pron.* OLD USE yours

thine² *possessive adj.* OLD USE a word meaning "your," used before a word beginning with a vowel or "h"

thing /θɪŋ/ *n.*

SW 11

1 idea/action/feeling/fact [C] anything that you can think of as a single ITEM, for example an idea, an action, a feeling, or a fact: *The first thing I'm going to do when I get home is take a nap.* | *I have better things to do with my time.* | *What kind of thing do you think would help?* | **do the right/decent/hon-orable etc. thing** *He did the decent thing by giving back the money.*

2 object [C] an object: *What does this thing do?* | *There were all kinds of things in the attic.* | *I don't have a thing to wear!*

3 situation things [plural] life in general and the way it is affecting people: *How are things going at work?* | *Things can get pretty dangerous out in the woods.*

4 objects things [plural] what you own or what are carrying: *You can put your things over there for now.*

5 the last thing sb wants/expects/needs etc. something that someone does not want, expect etc. at all: *Money is the last thing Margaret cares about right now.*

6 there is no such thing (as sth) used to emphasize that something does not really exist or happen: *Lin-guistically, there is no such thing as a good language or a bad one.*

7 first thing (in sth) at the beginning of a day, morn-ing, afternoon etc., before anything else: *Let's talk about the report first thing in the morning.*

8 among other things used when you are giving one fact, reason, effect etc. but want to suggest that there are many others: *Among other things, Bradley talked about his days as a senator.*

9 poor/lovely/funny (little) etc. thing a person or animal that is unlucky, attractive, funny etc.: *Poor thing looks like it hasn't eaten in days.*

10 do your own thing INFORMAL to do something in the way that you like instead of copying other people or following strict rules: *We don't talk much anymore – we're both too busy doing our own thing.*

11 be a thing of the past to not exist or happen anymore: *Life-long employment with a single company is a thing of the past.*

12 make things easy/difficult/hard etc. to deliber-ately make it easy, difficult etc. for someone to do something: [+ **for**] *John's drinking made things hard for his family.*

13 all things considered having considered all the facts about something: *All things considered, it's the wrong time for us to start our own business.*

14 not know/feel/see etc. a thing to know, feel etc. nothing: *Turn on the light – I can't see a thing in here.*

15 the (latest) thing INFORMAL the thing that is pop-ular or fashionable at the moment: *Twenty years ago, "Pong" was the latest thing in video games.*

16 have a thing about sb/sth INFORMAL to have very strong and often unreasonable bad feelings about someone or something: *Judith has a thing about people chewing gum.*

17 make a big thing out of sth to make something seem more important than it really is, by getting

angry, excited etc.: *Hank didn't want to make a big thing out of his surgery.*

18 be onto a good thing INFORMAL to be in a situa-tion that is very helpful, comfortable, or profitable for you: *When he first invested in the company, he knew he was onto a good thing.*

19 be all things to all men/people to behave in a way that makes everyone like you, because you do what they need you to do: *I finally realized I could not be all things to all people.*

20 the shape of things to come the way in which events, situations etc. will probably happen or develop in the future: *A business approach to educa-tion could be the shape of things to come.*

21 in all things in every situation: *In all things, he was very practical.*

22 the thing is used when explaining a problem or the reason for something: *The thing is, I'm allergic to seafood.*

23 for one thing used to give one reason for some-thing: *We can't invite everyone – for one thing, it would cost too much.*

24 it is a good thing (that) used to say that it is lucky or good that something has happened: *It's a good thing I brought my umbrella.*

25 and things used to mean "and other things," without giving more examples: *We talked about babies and things all afternoon.*

26 thing to do something that someone does: *The best thing to do is to book your flight early.*

27 thing to say something that someone says; remark: *That was a really nice thing to say to your sister.*

28 (it's) just one of those things used to say that something that has happened is not someone's fault or could not have been avoided: *When you play basketball, you accept that injuries are just one of those things.*

29 it's one of those things (that) used to say that something is included in a particular type of group: *I think it's one of those things people don't like to admit they watch on TV.*

30 it's (just) one thing after another used to say that a lot of bad or unlucky things keep happening to you: *Train strikes, computer problems, illness – it's just one thing after another!*

31 that (is the) kind/type/sort of thing used to mean other things of the same type, without giving more examples: *That's the sort of thing that only crazy people do.*

32 of all things used to show that you are surprised or shocked by something that someone has done or said: *Jones left his job and became, of all things, a priest.*

33 the thing with sb/sth used to say what the prob-lem with someone or something is: *The thing with Josh is that he likes everything planned out first.*

34 just the thing also **the very thing** exactly the thing that you want or that is necessary: *That's just the thing I was looking for.*

35 one thing led to another used when explaining the way in which something happened, without giving many details: *We were drinking and talking and one thing led to another.*

36 things are not right used to say that there are problems with a relationship or situation: *I had a feeling that things were not right with Larry.*

37 have (got) a thing for sb to like someone or a type of person very much: *He has a thing for blondes.*

38 it's one thing to..., (but) it's another thing to..., used to say that doing one thing is very different from doing another thing: *It's one thing to not put someone on life support, but it's another thing to take them off it after they're on it.*

39 (do/try) the...thing used to talk about an activity and everything that is involved with it: *Rick's doing the starving artist thing right now.*

thing·a·ma·jig /ˈθɪŋəməˌdʒɪg/ also **thing·a·ma·bob** /ˈθɪŋəməˌbɑb/, **thingy** *n.* [C] SPOKEN used when you cannot remember or do not know the name of the thing you want to mention: *What's this silver thinga-majig used for?*

thing·y /ˈθɪŋi/ *n. plural* **thingies** [C] SPOKEN used when you cannot remember or do not know the name of the thing you want to mention: *Hand me that thingy over there, will you?*

think /θɪŋk/ *v. past tense and past participle* **thought**
1 opinion/belief [T] to have an opinion or belief about something: [**think (that)**] *What do you think we should do?* | *I always thought soccer was boring.* | [**+ of/about**] *What do you think of my new office?*
2 use your mind [I] to use your mind to solve problems, decide something etc.: *You really should think before you say anything.* | *Be quiet, I'm thinking.* | [**+ about/of**] *She couldn't think about anything else but going home.*
3 words/ideas in your mind [T] to have words or ideas in your mind, without telling them to anyone: *"He looks upset," Camilla thought.* | *"I don't care what they think," she thought to herself.*
4 **think of/about doing sth** to consider the possibility of doing something: *I've often thought about starting my own business.*
5 **think twice (before doing sth)** to think very carefully before deciding to do something, because you know about the dangers or problems: *Employers think twice about hiring someone who has done time in jail.*
6 **think again** to think of a new idea or plan because you realize that the first one is wrong: *If you thought running a restaurant was easy, think again.*
7 **think nothing of (doing sth)** to do something easily or without complaining, even though other people would find it difficult: *Clyde thought nothing of driving a thousand miles a day.*
8 **not think much of sb/sth** to think that someone or something is bad, useless etc.: *I don't think much of that new restaurant.*
9 **think better of it** to not do something that you had planned to do, because you realize that it is not a good idea: *She felt like slapping him in the face, but thought better of it.*
10 **think for yourself** to have ideas and thoughts of your own rather than believing what other people say: *I try to encourage my students to think for themselves.*
11 **think out loud** also **think aloud** to say what you are thinking, without talking to anyone in particular: *Oh, sorry; I guess I was thinking out loud.*
12 **think a lot of sb/sth** also **think highly of sb/sth** to admire or respect someone: *Johnson has always thought highly of her writing ability.*
13 **think big** INFORMAL to plan to do things that are difficult, but will be very impressive, make a lot of profit etc.: *By investing over $1.2 million, Levin and his partner are thinking big.*
14 **think positively/positive** to believe that you are going to be successful or that a situation is going to have a good result: *If you want to lose weight, you need to start by thinking positively*
15 **think on your feet** to answer questions or think of ideas quickly, without preparing before: *He can think on his feet quicker than anyone I've ever met.*
16 **think less/badly of sb (for doing sth)** to respect someone less than you did before: *Nobody thought less of him for showing his emotions.*
17 **think the best/worst of sb** to consider someone's actions in a way that makes them seem as good as possible or as bad as possible: *Ellie's the type of person that always thinks the best of people.*
18 **think outside the box** to think of new, different, or unusual ways of doing something, especially in business

SPOKEN PHRASES

19 I think used when you are saying that you believe something is true, although you are not sure: *I think you're right.* | *I think he used to be an accountant.*
20 I thought (that) a) used when you are saying what you thought or believed was true, although you were not sure: *I thought the dishwasher was broken, did you get it fixed?* **b)** used when you are politely suggesting something to do: *I thought we could go to the lake this weekend.*
21 I think I'll do sth used when saying what you

will probably do: *I think I'll leave the rest of this work for tomorrow.*
22 I think so used when answering a question, to say that you believe something is true: *"Is Matt coming to the party?" "I think so."*
23 I would think used when you are saying that you believe something is probably true: *I would think that she would get tired of cleaning up the house every day.*
24 I can't think who/where/what... used to say that you cannot remember or understand something: *I can't think why she would say that.*
25 do you think (that)...? a) used when you are asking someone politely to do something for you: *Do you think you could give me a ride to work tomorrow?* **b)** used to ask someone's opinion: *Do you think its too late to call her?*
26 who/what etc. do you think? a) used to ask someone's opinion: *What do you think? Do these shoes look good with this dress?* | *How do you think the test went?* **b)** used when asking someone angrily about something: *Who do you think you are, talking to me like that?* | *Where do you think you're going?*
27 come to think of it used when you are adding something more to what you have said, because you have just remembered it or realized it: *Actually, come to think of it, I've never been formally introduced to her.*
28 who would have thought (that)...? used to say that something is very surprising: *Who would have thought those two would end up getting married?*
29 just think used to ask someone to imagine or consider something: *Just think, in a couple of hours we'll be eating lunch in Paris.* | [**+ of**] *Just think of all the things you could buy with a million dollars.*
30 when you think about it used to say that you realize something when you consider a fact or subject: *When you think about it, most of what he says doesn't make sense.*
31 you would think (that) also **you would have thought (that)** used to say that you expect something to be true, although it is not: *You would think somebody who could sing that well would take better care of their voice.*
32 I wasn't thinking used as a way of saying you are sorry because you have upset someone: *Sorry, I wasn't thinking. Do you want a cup too?*
33 think the world of sb to like or love someone very much: *Sonya thinks the world of you.*
34 if you think..., you've got another think coming! used to tell someone that if they think someone is going to do something, they are wrong: *If they think it's going to be an easy game, they've got another think coming!*
35 to think (that)...! used to show that you are very surprised or upset about something: *To think that they're making money off poor people is just outrageous.*
36 not think to do sth to not remember to do something: *I didn't even think to ask about him about how Christal's doing.*
37 That's what you/they etc. think! used to say that you strongly disagree with someone: *"You'll never get into medical school." "That's what you think!"*
38 I think not FORMAL used to strongly say that you believe something is not true or that you disagree with someone
39 I thought as much used to say that you are not surprised by what you have just found out: *"Andy failed his driving test." "I thought as much when I saw his face."*
40 think nothing of it OLD-FASHIONED used when someone has thanked you for doing something, to say politely that you did not mind doing it

think back *phr. v.* [I] to think about things that happened in the past: [**+ on/to**] *When I think back on that day, I can barely recall how she looked.*
think of sb/sth *phr. v.* [T] **1** to produce a new idea, name, suggestion etc. by thinking: *I can't think of any other way to do this.* | *They're still trying to*

T

think of a name for the baby. **2** to remember a name or fact: *Jay couldn't think of the name of that movie either.* **3** to behave in a way that shows that you want to treat other people well: *Hannah's very good about thinking of others.* **4 only think of yourself** to only do what you want or what is good for you: *Dave only thinks of himself.*

think sth ↔ **out** *phr. v.* [T] to think about something carefully, considering all the possible problems, results etc.: *The arguments had not been thought out very carefully.*

think sth ↔ **over** *phr. v.* [T] to think about something carefully: *Why don't you think it over for a while, and give me a call.*

think sth ↔ **through** *phr. v.* [T] to think carefully about the possible results of doing something: *You should seriously think it through before you get married.*

think sth ↔ **up** *phr. v.* [T] to produce a new idea, name etc. by thinking hard about something: *Who thinks up the stories for these stupid TV shows?*

think·a·ble /ˈθɪŋkəbəl/ *adj.* [not before noun] able to be thought about or considered; possible: *It would not have been thinkable to criticize a Soviet leader before these changes came about.*

think·er /ˈθɪŋkɚ/ *n.* [C] **1** someone who is famous for their important work in a subject such as science or PHILOSOPHY: *thinkers such as Sartre and Camus* **2 an independent/positive/free etc. thinker** someone who thinks in a particular way

think·ing¹ /ˈθɪŋkɪŋ/ *n.* [U] **1** your opinion about something or your attitude toward it: **negative/ positive thinking** *Don's negative thinking has affected the whole department.* | **To my way of thinking** (=in my opinion), *giving free needles to drug users is morally wrong.* **2 put on your thinking cap** INFORMAL to think seriously about a problem, in order to try and solve it

thinking² *adj.* [only before noun] a thinking person is intelligent and tries to think carefully about important subjects

think tank /ˈ. ./ *n.* [C] a committee of people with experience in a particular subject, that an organization or government establishes to produce ideas and give advice: *The Cato Institute is a conservative think tank.*

thin·ly /ˈθɪnli/ *adv.* **1** in a way that has a very small distance between two sides or two flat surfaces: *thinly sliced carrots* **2** scattered or spread over a large area, with a lot of space in between: *Sow the radish seeds thinly.* | **thinly populated/settled** etc. *Although the Baltic region is quite a large area, most of it is thinly populated.* **3 thinly disguised/veiled/ concealed** etc. easy to see or understand what something really is or who someone really is: *a thinly veiled threat* **4 thinly staffed** a thinly staffed business or office does not have enough people to do all of the work that needs to be done **5** not being bought or sold quickly on the STOCK EXCHANGE: *thinly traded stocks*

thin·ner /ˈθɪnɚ/ *n.* [U] a liquid such as TURPENTINE that you add to paint to make it less thick

thin·ning /ˈθɪnɪŋ/ *adj.* someone with thinning hair is losing their hair, so that in the future they will become BALD

thin-skinned /ˈ. ./ *adj.* too easily offended or upset by criticism

third¹ /θɚd/ *adj.* **1** 3rd; next after the second: *This is her third marriage.* **2 (the) third time's the charm** SPOKEN used when you have failed to do something twice and hope to be successful the third time **3 give sb the third degree** INFORMAL to ask someone a lot of questions in order to get information from them: *Look, I was out with friends – you don't have to get me the third degree.* **4 feel like a third wheel** INFORMAL to feel that the two people you are with do not want you to be there: *After Susan met Michael, I felt a little like a third wheel.*

third² *pron.* **the third** the 3rd thing in a series: *Is your birthday on the 3rd (=the 3rd day of the month)?*

third³ *n.* [C] ¹/₃: one of three equal parts: *Divide the sandwich into thirds.* | *A third of these types of jobs were held by women.* | **one-third/two-thirds** *Two-thirds of the profits are given to various charities.*

third base /ˌ. ˈ./ *n.* [singular] the third place that a player must touch before they can earn a point in baseball

third class /ˌ. ˈ.◂/ *n.* [U] **1** a cheap class of mail in the U.S., usually used for sending advertisements —compare FIRST CLASS, SECOND CLASS **2** OLD USE the cheapest and least comfortable part of a train or ship —**third-class** *adj., adv.: Send the package third-class.*

third-de·gree burn /ˌ. .ˌ. ˈ./ *n.* [C usually plural] the most serious kind of burn, that goes right through your skin

third par·ty /ˌ. ˈ..◂/ *n.* [C] **1** LAW someone who is not one of the two main people involved in an agreement or legal case, but who is affected by it or involved in some way: *Both companies will meet with a neutral third party to resolve the disagreement.* **2** a political group whose CANDIDATEs oppose the main political parties, especially in a country like the U.S. that only has two main political parties —**third-party** *adj.*

third per·son /ˌ. ˈ..◂/ *n.* TECHNICAL **1 the third person** a form of a verb or PRONOUN that is used for showing the person, thing, or group that is being mentioned. For example, "he," "she," "it," and "they" are pronouns in the third person, and "he/ she/it is" is the third person singular form of the verb "to be." **2 in the third person** a story in the third person is told as the experience of someone else, using the pronouns "he," "she," or "they" —compare FIRST PERSON, SECOND PERSON

third-rate /ˌ. ˈ.◂/ *adj.* of very bad quality: *a third-rate business school*

Third World /ˌ. ˈ.◂/ *n.* **the Third World** the poorer countries of the world that are not industrially developed —**Third World** *adj.: Third World economies*

thirst¹ /θɚst/ *n.* **1** [singular] the feeling of wanting or needing a drink: *After exercising, fruit juices are excellent because they quench your thirst* (=get rid of your thirst). | *Walking around downtown, we really worked up a thirst* (=do work or exercise that makes you thirsty). **2** [U] the state of not having enough to drink: *Many of them died of thirst.* **3 a thirst for knowledge/power/education etc.** LITERARY a strong desire for knowledge, power etc.: *"Off the Beaten Path" is especially appealing to travelers with a thirst for adventure.*

thirst² *v.* [I] OLD USE to be thirsty

thirst for/after sth *phr. v.* [T] LITERARY to want something very much: *She thirsted for the affection she was denied as a child.*

thirst·y /ˈθɚsti/ *adj.* **thirstier, thirstiest 1** needing to drink or feeling that you want a drink: *Are you thirsty?* **2 thirsty for knowledge/power** LITERARY having a strong desire for knowledge etc. **3** LITERARY OR INFORMAL fields or plants that are thirsty need water —**thirstily** *adv.*

thir·teen /ˌθɚˈtin◂/ *number* 13

thir·teenth¹ /ˌθɚˈtinθ◂/ *adj.* 13th; next after the twelfth: *the thirteenth century*

thirteenth² *pron.* **the thirteenth** the 13th thing in a series: *Let's have dinner on the thirteenth* (=the 13th day of the month).

thir·ti·eth¹ /ˈθɚtiɪθ/ *adj.* 30th; next after the twenty-ninth: *It's our thirtieth anniversary next week.*

thirtieth² *pron.* **the thirtieth** the 30th thing in a series: *Let's have dinner on the thirtieth* (=the 30th day of the month).

thir·ty /ˈθɚti/ *number* **1** 30 **2 the thirties** also **the '30s** the years from 1930 to 1939 **3 sb's thirties** the time when someone is 30 to 39 years old: **in your early/mid/late thirties** *I'd like to have a family when I'm in my early thirties.* **4 in the thirties** if the temperature is in the thirties, it is between 30° and 39° FAHRENHEIT: **in the high/low thirties** *It was cold – it was in the high thirties all week.*

thir·ty-some·thing /ˈθɚti.sʌmθɪŋ/ *adj.* INFORMAL if

someone is thirtysomething, they are in their thirties, and are usually well-educated and have a good job, plenty of money etc.: *Over in the corner was a group of well-dressed thirtysomething women.* —**thirtysomethings** *n.* [plural]

this[1] /ðɪs/ *determiner plural* **these 1** used when talking about someone or something that is closer in time, distance etc. than someone or something else: *The band plans to go on tour this year.* | *Steve's going to Miami this Thursday.* | *Are all of these clothes dirty?* **2** used to talk about a person, thing, idea etc. that has already been mentioned or that the person you are talking to already knows about: *In this chapter of the book, we look at a number of new economic theories.* | *Add this mixture to the cranberry sauce.*

SPOKEN PHRASES

3 used in conversation to mean a particular person or thing, especially when you do not know their name: *Then this girl came up and kissed him on the lips.* | *When am I going to meet this boyfriend of yours?* **4 (right) this minute/second** immediately: *You don't have to give me your answer right this minute.* **5 what's (all) this...?** used to ask what is happening, what someone's problem is etc.: *What's all this yelling about?*

---

this[2] *pron. plural* **these 1** used to talk about a person, thing, idea etc. that has already been mentioned or that the person you are talking to knows about already: *This is hopeless – I can't get the machine to work.* | *Anyone who thinks this is a good baseball team is crazy.* | *These are all very expensive cities to live in.* **2** used when talking about someone or something that is closer in time, distance etc. than someone or something else: *Here, try this – it might help your headache.* | *These are just some of my vacation pictures.* **3 a)** INFORMAL used to introduce someone to someone else: *Sam, this is my sister, Liz.* **b)** used when you have answered the telephone and you want to give your name: *Hi, Barry – this is Mark.* **4** a particular time: *I thought he would have been back before this.* **5 this, that, and the other** also **this and that** SPOKEN various different things, subjects etc.: *"What have you been doing lately?" "Oh, this, that, and the other."*

this[3] *adv.* [+ adj./adv.] **this big/many etc.** SPOKEN used to say how big or how many, especially because you are showing the size, number etc. with your hand: **this big/tall/wide etc.** *Dana's about this tall and has brown hair.* | **this much/many** *He only opened the door about this much.*

this·tle /ˈθɪsəl/ *n.* [C,U] a wild plant with long pointed leaves and purple or white furry flowers

thith·er /ˈθɪðɚ/ *adv.* OLD USE in that direction

tho' /ðoʊ/ *adv.* a short form of "though"

Thom·as /ˈtɑməs/**, Dy·lan** /ˈdɪlən/ (1914–1953) a Welsh poet and writer

Thomas, Saint in the Bible, one of the 12 APOSTLES, who did not believe the news that Jesus was alive again after he had been killed

Thomas à Kem·pis /ˌtɑməs ə ˈkɛmpɪs/ —see KEMPIS, THOMAS A

thong /θɔŋ, θɑŋ/ *n.* **1 thongs** [plural] a type of shoe that covers the bottom of your foot, with a STRAP that goes between your toes to hold it on your foot as you walk —see picture at SHOE[1] **2** [C] a pair of underwear or the bottom half of a BIKINI that has a single string instead of the back part **3** [C] a long thin piece of leather used to fasten something or as part of a whip

Thor /θɔr/ in Norse MYTHOLOGY, the god of THUNDER and the strongest of the gods

tho·rax /ˈθɔræks/ *n. plural* **thoraxes** or **thoraces** /-rəsiz/ [C] **1** TECHNICAL the part of your body between your neck and the DIAPHRAGM (=area above your stomach) **2** the part of an insect's body between its head and its ABDOMEN —see picture at INSECT —**thoracic** /θəˈræsɪk/ *adj.*

Tho·reau /θəˈroʊ/**, Hen·ry Da·vid** /ˈhɛnri ˈdeɪvɪd/ (1817–1862) a U.S. writer and PHILOSOPHER best known for his simple life in the countryside, and for his

ideas about refusing to obey unfair laws, which influenced Gandhi and Martin Luther King, Jr.

thorn /θɔrn/ *n.* **1** [C] a sharp point that grows on the stem of a plant such as a rose —see picture at ROSE[1] **2 a thorn in your side** someone or something that annoys you or causes problems for a long period of time: *The anti-smoking campaign remains a thorn in the tobacco industry's side.*

thorn·y /ˈθɔrni/ *adj.* **thornier, thorniest 1 a thorny question/problem/point etc.** a question, problem etc. that is complicated and difficult: *These are some of the thorny issues pastors face as they work with abusive families.* **2** a thorny bush, plant etc. has thorns —**thorniness** *n.* [U]

thor·ough /ˈθɚoʊ, ˈθʌroʊ/ *adj.* **1** including every possible detail: *Building inspectors should have a thorough knowledge of construction materials.* | *The report was thorough and detailed.* **2** careful to do things correctly, so that you avoid mistakes: *Researchers have to be very thorough to make sure lab results are accurate.* | *a thorough investigation* **3 a thorough pest/nuisance/mess** used to emphasize the bad qualities of someone or something —see also THOROUGHLY —**thoroughness** *n.* [U]

thor·ough·bred /ˈθɚəˌbrɛd, ˈθɚoʊ-, ˈθʌr-/ *n.* [C] **1** a horse that has parents of the same very good breed **2** someone who naturally does something to a very high standard: *John Henry, a Football Hall of Fame thoroughbred*

thor·ough·fare /ˈθɚəˌfɛr, ˈθɚoʊ-, ˈθʌr-/ *n.* [C] the main road through a place such as a city or town: *The Visitor's Center is located on Bay Street, the town's main thoroughfare.*

thor·ough·go·ing /ˌθʌrəˈgoʊɪŋ◂/ *adj.* [only before noun] **1** very thorough and careful: *a thoroughgoing investigation of the case* **2** [only before noun] a thoroughgoing action or quality is complete or total: *The tutoring program is a thoroughgoing success.*

thor·ough·ly /ˈθɚoʊli/ *adv.* **1** completely: *Eating only thoroughly cooked foods will reduce your risk of illness.* | *I was thoroughly confused.* **2** carefully, so that nothing is forgotten: *The body was thoroughly examined by physicians.* | *Thoroughly wash all surfaces which have come into contact with raw meat.*

Thorpe /θɔrp/**, Jim** /dʒɪm/ (1888–1953) a U.S. ATHLETE famous for winning GOLD MEDALS in the Olympics in 1912

those /ðoʊz/ *determiner, pron.* the plural of THAT

thou /ðaʊ/ *pron.* OLD USE a word meaning "you," used as the subject of a sentence —see also HOLIER-THAN-THOU

though[1] /ðoʊ/ *conjunction* **1** used to introduce a statement that makes the other main statement seem surprising or unlikely: *Though she was no more than twenty-two, she was already a highly successful businesswoman.* **2** used to add a fact or opinion that makes what you have just said seem less serious, less important etc.: *I guess he'd been drinking, though I wasn't completely sure of that.* **3 as though** in a way that suggests that something is true or not true, or that something is possible but you are not sure about it: *Bill looked as though he wanted to say something.* —see also ALTHOUGH, **even though** (EVEN[1] (3))

though[2] *adv.* [sentence adverb] SPOKEN used at the end of a sentence to add a fact or opinion that makes what you have just said seem less important, or to add a very different fact or opinion: *George did say one nice thing, though.*

thought[1] /θɔt/ *v.* the past tense and past participle of THINK

thought[2] *n.*
1 sth you think about [C] something that you think of, remember, or realize; idea: *News of the crash dominated his thoughts.* | **[the thought (that)]** *The thought that she might not see him again was too much to bear.* | **[+ of]** *Even the thought of* (=used when a thought produces strong emotions) *flying*

scares me. | I've just **had a thought** (=suddenly thought of something) – why don't we invite Judith? | "You should ask her out to dinner sometime." "**The thought had crossed my mind** (=used to say that you have thought about something before)."

2 `act of thinking` [U] the act of thinking: Greg seemed **deep in thought** (=thinking so much that he did not notice anything) when I walked in. | These studies help us to understand the **thought processes** (=way people's minds work) of children.

3 `careful consideration` [U] careful and serious consideration: Writing a good essay requires a lot of thought and effort. | You should **give** some **thought to** (=think carefully about) going to art school.

4 `suggestion` [C] a suggestion or opinion about something: [+ on] The interview included Cosby's thoughts on young people today.

5 `caring about sth` [C,U] a feeling of worrying or caring about something: Michael never gave any thought to others. | You are **always in my thoughts** (=used to tell someone that you think about them and care about them a lot).

6 `intention` [C,U] the intention or hope of doing something: [+ of] I had no thought of gaining any personal advantage.

7 **sb's thoughts turn to sb/sth** if your thoughts turn to someone or something, you start to think about them: Our thoughts turn to all those who will not be with their families this Christmas.

8 `way of thinking` [U] a way of thinking that is typical of a particular group, period of history etc.: ancient Greek thought

SPOKEN PHRASES

9 **that's a thought** used to say that someone has made a good suggestion: "You could always take the class next semester." "That's a thought."

10 **(it's) just a thought** used to say that what you have just said is only a suggestion and you have not thought about it very much: We could sell the car – just a thought.

11 **don't give it another thought** used to tell someone politely not to worry after they have told you they are sorry: "I'm really sorry about that." "Don't give it another thought."

12 **it's the thought that counts** used to say that someone's actions are very kind even if they have only done something small or unimportant

—see also **perish the thought** (PERISH (3)), **school of thought** (SCHOOL¹ (8)), **have second thoughts (about sth)** (SECOND¹ (5)), **on second thought** (SECOND¹ (6)), **not give sth a second thought** (SECOND¹ (7)), **without a second thought** (SECOND¹ (8)), **train of thought** (TRAIN¹ (2))

thought·ful /ˈθɔtfəl/ adj. **1** always thinking of the things you can do to make people happy or comfortable: Paula's such a thoughtful girl. | [+ of] It was really thoughtful of you to remember my birthday. **2** well planned or thought about a lot: thoughtful analysis **3** serious and quiet because you are thinking a lot: a thoughtful expression —**thoughtfully** adv. —**thoughtfulness** n. [U]

thought·less /ˈθɔtlɪs/ adj. forgetting about the needs and feelings of other people because you are thinking about what you want: the thoughtless use of nuclear technology | [it is thoughtless of sb to do sth] It was thoughtless of him to not send her flowers. —**thoughtlessly** adv. —**thoughtlessness** n.

thought-out /ˌ. ˈ.◂/ adj. **carefully/well/badly etc. thought-out** planned and organized carefully, well etc.: a well thought-out argument

thought-pro·vok·ing /ˈ. .ˌ../ adj. making you think a lot: The film had a thought-provoking message.

thou·sand /ˈθaʊzənd/ number **1** 1000 **2 thousands** a lot: [+ of] We've receive thousands of letters from fans. —see Usage Note at HUNDRED¹

thou·sandth¹ /ˈθaʊzəndθ/ adj. 1000th

thousandth² pron. **the thousandth** the 1000th thing in a series

thousandth³ n. [C] ¹/₁₀₀₀; one of one thousand equal parts

thrall /θrɔl/ n. **in sb's/sth's thrall** also **in thrall to sb/sth** LITERARY controlled or strongly influenced by someone or something: We have a Congress that is in thrall to the gun lobby.

thrall·dom, **thraldom** /ˈθrɔldəm/ n. [U] LITERARY the state of being a slave; SLAVERY

thrash¹ /θræʃ/ v. **1** [I always + adv./prep.] to move or make something move from side to side in a violent or uncontrolled way: [+ around] He started thrashing around when police tried to arrest him. **2** [T] INFORMAL to defeat someone very easily in a game: The Gators soundly thrashed San Jose State. **3** [T] to beat someone violently in order to punish them

thrash sth ↔ **out** phr. v. [T] to discuss a problem thoroughly with someone until you find an answer: The board of supervisors thrashed out a plan to save the business.

thrash² n. **1** [singular] a violent movement from side to side **2** [U] INFORMAL a type of ROCK music with very loud fast electric GUITAR playing

thrash·ing /ˈθræʃɪŋ/ n. [C] **1 give/get a thrashing** to beat someone or be beaten violently as a punishment: Uncle Hal often gave us a thrashing for no reason. **2** an easy defeat in a game

thread¹ /θrɛd/ n.

1 `for sewing` [C,U] a long thin string of cotton, silk etc. used to SEW or weave cloth: a spool of white thread

2 `connection` [C] an idea, feeling, or feature that forms the connection between the different parts of an explanation, story, group of people etc.: A strong thread of spirituality runs through L'Engle's books. | The **common thread** among these groups is a hate for government.

3 pick up the threads (of sb's life) to begin something again after a long period, especially a relationship or way of life: After the war, Richard found it hard to pick up the threads of his life.

4 `small amount` [C usually singular] a small amount of a quality: I tried to hold on to a thread of decency and courage.

5 `line` LITERARY [C] a long thin line of something such as light, smoke etc.

6 `on a screw` [C] a continuous raised line of metal that winds around the curved surface of a screw

7 threads [plural] OLD-FASHIONED clothes —see also **hang by a thread** (HANG¹ (11))

thread² v. [T] **1** to put a thread or string through a hole: The hole is big so that children can **thread the needle** (=push a thread through the hole in a needle). **2** to put a film, TAPE etc. correctly through parts of a camera, PROJECTOR, or TAPE RECORDER **3** to connect objects by pushing a string through a hole in them: Thread the beads on a string and make a necklace. **4 thread your way through/into etc.** to move through a place by carefully going around things that are blocking your way: We threaded our way through the crowd.

thread·bare /ˈθrɛdbɛr/ adj. [no comparative] **1** clothes, CARPETS etc. that are threadbare are very thin and in bad condition because they have been used a lot: his threadbare cotton shirt **2 threadbare excuse/argument/joke etc.** an excuse etc. that is not effective anymore because it has been used too much

threat /θrɛt/ n. **1** [C,U] a statement that you will cause someone pain, unhappiness, or trouble, especially if they do not do something you want: Your threats don't scare me! | [+ of] the threat of physical punishment | On several occasions, she had **made threats** to her ex-husband. | It was just **an empty threat** (=a threat to do something that you will not really do). | Soldiers were **under threat of** (=threatened with) death if they did not fight. | **a death/bomb etc. threat** The bank has received several bomb threats this year. **2** [C usually singular] the possibility that something very bad will happen: [+ of] the threat of rioting **3** [C usually singular] someone or something that is regarded as a possible danger: [+ to] Drilling for oil poses a threat to wildlife in the area.

S W
2

threat·en /ˈθrɛt̚n/ v. **1** [T] to say that you will cause someone pain, worry, or trouble if they do not do what you want: [threaten to do sth] *He threatened to punch me in the mouth.* | [threaten sb with sth] *Many of them were threatened with losing their job.* | [threaten sb] *Don't you threaten me!* | [threaten sth] *The unions are threatening a one-day strike.* **2** [T] to be likely to harm or destroy something: *Pollution is threatening the marine life in the bay.* **3** [I,T] if something threatens to cause a bad situation, it seems likely that it will cause it: [threaten sb/sth with sth] *Large areas of the jungle are now threatened with destruction.* | [threaten to do sth] *Lack of funding threatens to close down the museum.*

threat·en·ing /ˈθrɛt̚n-ɪŋ/ adj. **1** talking or behaving in a way that is intended to threaten someone: *Avoid sudden or threatening movements around the birds.* **2** making threats: *threatening telephone calls* —**threateningly** adv.

three¹ /θri/ number **1** 3 **2** 3 o'clock: *Let's meet at three by the library.* —see also THIRD¹

three² n. [C] INFORMAL a set or group of three people or things: *Students were grouped in threes around each desk.*

three-cor·nered /ˌ. ˈ..◂/ adj. **1** having three corners **2 three-cornered contest/fight** a competition that involves three people or groups

three-D, 3-D /ˌθri ˈdi/ adj. a three-D movie or picture is made so that it appears to be three-dimensional —**three-D** —**3-D** n. [U] *a film in 3-D*

three-di·men·sion·al /ˌ. .ˈ...◂/ adj. **1** having or seeming to have length, depth, and height: *a three-dimensional drawing* **2** a three-dimensional character in a book, movie etc., seems like a real person

three·fold /ˈθrifoʊld/ adj. three times as much or as many —**threefold** adv.

three-leg·ged race /ˌθri lɛgɪd ˈreɪs/ n. [C] a race in which two people run together, with one person's right leg tied to the other person's left leg

three-peat /ˈθripit/ n. [C] INFORMAL the action of winning a sports competition three times, one after the other

three-piece suit /ˌ. . ˈ./ n. [C] a suit that consists of a JACKET, VEST, and pants made from the same material

three-ply /ˈ. ./ adj. three-ply wood, YARN, TISSUE (1) etc. consists of three layers or threads

three-point·er, 3-pointer /ˌ. ˈ../ n. [C] a SHOT in basketball from outside a particular line, so that if the ball goes in the basket, the team receives three points

three-point turn /ˌ. . ˈ./ n. [C] a way of turning your car so that it faces the opposite way, by driving forward, backward, and then forward again while turning

three-quar·ter /ˌ. ˈ..◂/ adj. [only before noun] three quarters of the full size, length etc. of something: *a three-quarter moon* | **three-quarter-length/three-quarter-size etc.** *a three-quarter-size piano*

three-quar·ters /ˌ. ˈ../ n. [plural] an amount equal to three of the four equal parts that make up a whole: [+ of] *Our presentation should take about three-quarters of an hour.*

three-ring cir·cus /ˌ. . ˈ../ n. **1** [singular] INFORMAL a place or situation that is confusing because there is too much activity: *The contract negotiations have turned into a three-ring circus.* **2** [C usually singular] a CIRCUS that has three areas in which people or animals perform at the same time

three R's /θri ˈarz/ n. **the three R's** INFORMAL reading, writing, and ARITHMETIC (=working with numbers), considered as the basic things that children must learn

three·score /ˈθriskɔr/ number OLD USE 60 —see also SCORE¹ (8)

three·some /ˈθrisəm/ n. [C usually singular] INFORMAL a group of three people or things

three-star /ˈ. ./ adj. a three-star hotel, restaurant etc. is officially judged to be of a good standard

three-strikes /ˈ. ./ adj. [only before noun] also

three-strikes-and-you're-out a three-strikes law puts people in prison for a long time if they are guilty of three serious crimes, without any chance of getting out of prison early

three-wheel·er /ˌ. ˈ..◂/ n. [C] a vehicle that has three wheels, especially a MOTORCYCLE, TRICYCLE, or special WHEELCHAIR

thren·o·dy /ˈθrɛnədi/ n. plural **threnodies** [C] LITERARY a funeral song for someone who has died

thresh /θrɛʃ/ v. [I,T] to separate the grain from the rest of corn, wheat etc., by beating it with a special tool or machine —**thresher** n. [C]

threshing ma·chine /ˈ.. .ˌ./ n. [C] a machine used for separating the grain from the rest of corn, wheat etc.

thresh·old /ˈθrɛʃhoʊld, -ʃoʊld/ n. [C] **1** the entrance to a room or building, or the area of floor at the entrance **2** the level at which something starts to happen, becomes something, or has an effect: *Eighty percent was the threshold for approval of the plan.* | **have a high/low pain threshold** (=be able or not be able to suffer a lot of pain before you react) **3 on the threshold of sth** at the beginning of a new and important event or development: *The region seems to be on the threshold of war.*

threw /θru/ v. the past tense of THROW¹

thrice /θraɪs/ adv. OLD USE three times

thrift /θrɪft/ n. [U] OLD-FASHIONED wise and careful use of money, so that none is wasted —see also SPEND-THRIFT

thrift shop /ˈ. ./ n. [C] a store that sells used goods, especially clothes, often in order to earn money for a CHARITY

thrift·y /ˈθrɪfti/ adj. **thriftier, thriftiest** using money carefully and wisely: *Cutting taxes on savings may persuade Americans to be more thrifty.* —**thriftily** adv. —**thriftiness** n. [U]

thrill¹ /θrɪl/ n. **1** [C] a sudden strong feeling of excitement and pleasure, or the thing that makes you feel this: *Winning the gold medal was a thrill.* | **[the thrill of (doing) sth]** *Kendrick talked about the thrill of attending a White House dinner.* | *Mr. Samuels still gets a thrill out of teaching science.* | *Bundy often stole candy bars for the thrill of it* (=for excitement and not for any serious reason). **2 thrills and chills** also **thrills and spills** the excitement and danger involved in an activity, especially a sport —see also **cheap thrill** (CHEAP¹ (10))

thrill² v. [T] to make someone feel excited and happy: *It thrills me to know that our organization has helped change lives.*

thrill to sth phr. v. [T] to make someone feel excited and happy: *In the 1960s, the American public thrilled to the idea of space exploration.*

thrilled /θrɪld/ adj. [not before noun] very excited, happy, and pleased: *He says he's thrilled to be working full-time again.* | **be thrilled to pieces/bits** (=be very thrilled)

thrill·er /ˈθrɪlɚ/ n. [C] a book or movie that tells an exciting story about murder, crime, or spies (SPY)

thrill·ing /ˈθrɪlɪŋ/ adj. interesting and exciting: *a thrilling end to the story* —**thrillingly** adv.

thrive /θraɪv/ v. past tense **thrived** or **throve** [I] FORMAL to become very successful or very strong and healthy: *Most herbs need direct sun all day in order to thrive.* | *Wineries have thrived in the town for more than a century.*

thrive on sth phr. v. [T] to enjoy or be successful in conditions that other people, businesses etc. find difficult or unfavorable: *Some people seem to thrive on the pressure of working under a deadline.*

thriv·ing /ˈθraɪvɪŋ/ adj. a thriving company, business etc. is very successful: *the country's thriving oil industry*

throat /θroʊt/ n. [C] **1** the passage from the back of your mouth to the top of the tubes that go down to your lungs and stomach: *Does your throat hurt?*

2 the front of your neck: *The attacker grabbed Siegel by the throat and refused to let go.* **3 clear your throat** to make a noise in your throat, especially before you speak or in order to get someone's attention **4 force/ram sth down sb's throat** INFORMAL to force someone to accept or listen to your ideas and opinions: *I don't like people forcing their politics down my throat.* **5 be at each other's throats** if two people are at each other's throats, they are fighting or arguing: *Lisa and Nicole were at each other's throats the whole trip.* **6 cut your own throat** to behave in a way that is certain to harm you, especially because you are too proud or angry: *You would be cutting your own throat by refusing to accept their generous offer.* —see also **bring a lump to sb's throat** (LUMP¹ (3)), **have a frog in your throat** (FROG (2)), **jump down sb's throat** (JUMP¹ (7)), **stick in your throat** (STICK¹ (7))

throat·y /ˈθroʊti/ *adj.* **throatier, throatiest** making a low rough sound when you speak or sing: *"Be quiet," she said in a throaty voice.* —**throatily** *adv.* —**throatiness** *n.* [C,U]

throb¹ /θrɑb/ *v.* **throbbed, throbbing** [I] **1** if a part of your body throbs, you get a regular feeling of pain in it: *Every morning I wake up with a throbbing headache.* **2** if music or a machine throbs, it makes a sound with a strong regular beat: *throbbing samba music* **3** if your heart throbs, it beats faster or more strongly than usual

throb² *n.* [C] a low strong regular beat or sensation: *the throb of her beating heart* —see also HEARTTHROB

throes /θroʊz/ *n.* [plural] **in the throes of sth** in the middle of a very difficult situation: *At the time, Liberia was still in the throes of a civil war.* —see also DEATH THROES

throm·bo·sis /θrɑmˈboʊsɪs/ *n.* [C,U] TECHNICAL a serious medical problem caused by a CLOT² forming in your blood, especially in your heart

throne /θroʊn/ *n.* **1 the throne a)** the position and power of being a king or queen: *By 2002, the Queen will have been **on the throne** (=ruling as king or queen) for fifty years.* | **ascend/assume the throne** (=become king or queen) **2** [C] INFORMAL a toilet **2** [C] a special chair used by a king or queen at important ceremonies

throng¹ /θrɔŋ, θrɑŋ/ *n.* [C] LITERARY a large group of people in one place; crowd: *The throng greeted Sutter with cheers and applause.* | [+ of] *a throng of reporters*

throng² *v.* **1** [I always + adv./prep., T] if people throng a place, they go there in large numbers: *Student protesters thronged the plaza outside the administration building.* | [+ to] *Mourners thronged to his tomb.* **2 be thronged with sb** if a place is thronged with people, it is very crowded with them: *Yosemite was thronged with tourists.*

throt·tle¹ /ˈθrɑtl/ *v.* [T] **1** to hold someone's throat very tightly so that they cannot breathe; STRANGLE **2** to make it difficult or impossible for something to succeed: *The government is attempting to throttle the uprising before it spreads.*

throttle back *phr. v.* [I,T **throttle** sth ↔ **back**] to reduce the amount of gasoline or oil flowing into an engine, in order to reduce speed

throttle² *n.* [C] TECHNICAL **1** a piece of equipment that controls the amount of gasoline, oil etc. going into a vehicle's engine: *As I went into the turn, I eased back on the throttle* (=pulled the throttle back to slow down). | *When the planes take off, they are **on full throttle** (=the throttle is open completely, so that a lot of fuel is going to the engine).* **2 full throttle** as fast or as much as possible: *The Bear's offense ran full-throttle* (=ran very fast). | *A statewide search for Jones' replacement is **at full throttle*** (=is being done as quickly as possible).

through¹ /θru/ *prep.* **1** entering something such as a door, passage, tube, or hole at one end or side and leaving it at the other: *The two men fled through the back door and escaped from police.* | *Rabbits got into the backyard through a hole in the fence.* | *As the water passes through the filter, dirt is taken out.* **2** going into an area, group etc. and moving across it or within it: *Rescue workers searched through the wreckage for survivors.* | *Over the weekend, we took a leisurely drive through the countryside.* **3** if you see something or someone through glass, a window etc., you are on one side of the glass, window etc. and they are on the other: *We could barely see the cars in front of us through the fog.* | *Through the kitchen window, I saw the mailman walking up to the house.* **4** passing a place where you are supposed to stop: *The driver had gone straight through the traffic lights and hit an oncoming car.* | *Fill out this form before you pass through customs.* **5** cutting, breaking, or making a hole from one side of something to the other: *Workers had to cut a hole through the ceiling to install the heating system.* | *The bullet had passed through his right arm.* **6** during and to the end of a period of time: *It will be several months before your newborn sleeps through the night.* | *We've got enough food to last us through the winter.* **7** if you get through a difficult situation or experience, you deal with it successfully: *Janet needed a lot of support to make it through the death of her husband.* **8 look/search/go etc. through** to do something from beginning to end and include all parts of it: *Our lawyers are going through each part of the contract.* **9** because of someone or something: *It was through sheer laziness that we didn't get our flight booked on time.* **10 go through sth** to use a lot of something: *Robin goes through at least two packs of gum a day.* **11** using a particular person, organization etc. to help you achieve something: *He bought the tickets through a friend at the stadium.* **12 May through June/Wednesday through Friday etc.** from May until June, from Wednesday until Friday etc.: *The store is open Monday through Saturday.* **13** if you go through a country or area, you travel across it: *Visitors traveling through this part of Asia should remain in constant contact with their embassy.* **14** if a law passes through Congress or another group that makes laws, it is agreed and accepted as a law: *The bill's passage through Congress was not a smooth one.* —see also THRU

through² *adv.* **1** from one end or side of something to the other: *Excuse me, could you let me through?* | [+ **to**] *Something is preventing the gas from flowing through to the engine.* **2 read/think/talk etc. sth through** to read, think etc. about something very carefully from beginning to end: *Make sure you talk it through with your wife before you decide.* **3 through and through** if someone is a particular type of person through and through, they are completely that type of person: *Lofgren is a politician through and through.* —see also **come through** (COME¹), **get through** (GET), **go through** (GO¹), **pull through** (PULL¹), **put through** (PUT), **sail through** (SAIL¹)

through³ *adj.* **1 be through (with sb/sth)** INFORMAL **a)** to have finished doing something, using something etc.: *I need to use the computer when you're through.* | *Newman's broken leg means he is through for the season* (=he cannot play anymore). **b)** to not be having a romantic relationship with someone anymore: *As much as I hate to admit it, I think we're through.* **2 a through train/road/street** a train or road by which you can reach a place, without having to use other trains or roads

through·out¹ /θruˈaʊt/ *prep.* **1** in every part of a particular area, place etc.: *Outbreaks of cholera have been reported throughout the country.* **2** during all of a particular period, from the beginning to the end: *Stories of love and adventure were popular throughout the Middle Ages.*

throughout² *adv.* [usually at the end of a sentence] **1** in every part of a particular area, place etc.: *The handwriting of the letter was very difficult to read throughout.* **2** during all of a particular period, from the beginning to the end: *He managed to remain calm throughout.*

through·put /ˈθruːpʊt/ *n.* [U] the amount of work, materials etc. that can be dealt with in a particular period of time: *Tosco oil refinery plans on increasing throughput by 20 percent.*

through·way /ˈθruːweɪ/ *n.* [C] a THRUWAY

throve /θroʊv/ *v.* OLD-FASHIONED the past tense of THRIVE

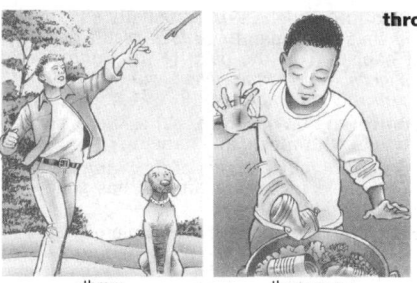

throw

throw   throw away

s w **throw**[1] /θroʊ/ *v.* past **threw** *past participle* **thrown**

1 throw a ball/stone etc. [I,T] to make an object such as a ball move quickly from you through the air by moving your arm quickly and letting go of the object: *She's only three, and she can throw pretty accurately.* | [throw sth at/to/toward etc.] *Someone threw a bottle at him.* | [throw sb sth] *Could you throw me an apple?*

2 put sth carelessly [T always + adv./prep.] to put something somewhere quickly and carelessly: [throw sth on/onto/down etc.] *I quickly threw my clothes into a bag and left.*

3 push roughly [T always + adv./prep.] to push someone or something roughly in a particular direction or into a particular position: **throw a door/window open** *James threw the door open and ran into the house.* | *Police* **threw** *the attacker* **to the ground.**

4 make sb fall [T] **a)** to make your opponent fall to the ground in WRESTLING or JUDO **b)** if a horse throws its rider it makes them fall onto the ground

5 throw yourself at/on/into/down etc. to move or jump somewhere suddenly and with a lot of force: *He threw himself onto the bench.*

6 move hands/head etc. [T always + adv./prep.] to suddenly and quickly move your hands, arms, head etc. into a new position: [throw sth back/up/around etc.] *J.D. laughed loudly, throwing her head back.*

7 throw sb into prison/jail to suddenly put someone in prison: *Taylor was thrown into prison for attempted murder.*

8 throw sb out of work/office etc. to suddenly take away someone's job or position of authority: *More than 500 employees were thrown out of work.*

9 throw sb into confusion/chaos/disarray etc. to suddenly make a group of people very confused and uncertain about what they should do: *The new computer system has thrown the office into chaos.*

10 confuse/shock [T] to confuse or shock someone, especially by suddenly saying something: *Mora was* **completely thrown** *by news of their engagement.* | *His death* **threw** *her* **for a loop** (=confused and shocked her).

11 throw suspicion/doubt on sth also **throw sth into question** to make people think that someone is probably guilty or that something may not be true: *New evidence has thrown doubt on Pollard's innocence.*

12 throw (sb) a look/glance/smile etc. to quickly look at someone with a particular expression that shows how you are feeling: *Hanson threw a mean look at her.*

13 throw a fit/tantrum to react in a very angry way: *Rogers threw a fit when he didn't get the sales account.*

14 throw a switch/handle/lever to make a large machine or piece of electrical equipment start or stop working by moving a SWITCH[2] (1)

15 throw a party to organize a party and invite people: *The German club is throwing a party this Friday night.*

16 throw yourself into sth to start doing an activity eagerly and using a lot of time and effort: *Since her husband died, she's thrown herself into her work.*

17 throw dice also **throw a four/five etc.** to roll DICE or to get a particular number by rolling DICE: *I need to throw a five to win.*

18 throw money at sb/sth INFORMAL to try to solve a problem by spending a lot of money, but without really thinking carefully about the problem: *Congress thinks they can just throw money at the problem and it will go away.*

19 throw your weight around to use your position of authority to tell people what to do in an unreasonable way: *The commission has a reputation for throwing its weight around.*

20 throw your weight behind sb/sth to publicly support a plan, person etc. and use your power to make sure they succeed: *Bahlman is throwing his weight behind the cultural center proposal.*

21 throw yourself at sb INFORMAL to try very hard to make someone like or notice you, because you want to have a sexual relationship with them: *Could you believe how Diana threw herself at Eric?*

22 throw light/shadows/rays to make light, shadows etc. fall on a particular place: *Huge office buildings threw long shadows across the courtyard.*

23 throw cold water on sth to say that a plan, suggestion etc. is unlikely to succeed, or to prevent a plan from succeeding: *Quackenbush threw cold water on the prospects of a pay raise.*

24 throw money down the drain also **throw good money after bad** to waste money by spending it on something that has already failed or that is of bad quality

25 throw the book at sb INFORMAL to punish someone as severely as possible, or to CHARGE someone with as many offenses as possible in a court of law: *Judge Smith threw the book at Flynn, fining him $1.6 million and giving him six years in prison.*

26 throw caution to the wind to ignore the risks and deliberately behave in a way that may cause trouble or problems: *Throwing caution to the wind, Sandy quit her job and moved to L.A. to become an actress.*

27 throw a game/match/fight etc. to deliberately lose a fight or sports game that you could have won

28 throw the baby out with the bath water DISAPPROVING to get rid of the good parts of a system, organization etc. as well as the bad parts, when you are changing it in order to try and make it better

29 throw sth (back) in sb's face also **throw sth back at sb** to remind someone of something they have done or said in order to embarrass them: *It was no fun having my own words thrown back at me by my kids.*

30 throw a punch/a left/a right etc. to try to hit someone with your hand in a fight

31 throw your hat into the ring to officially announce that you will compete or take part in something

32 throw questions/remarks/comments (at sb) to ask a lot of questions or suddenly say something: *About 80 journalists gathered for the opportunity to throw questions at Newman.*

33 throw your voice to use a special trick to make your voice seem to be coming from a different place than the place where you are standing

34 be thrown back on sth to be forced to have to depend on your own skills, knowledge etc.: *For first time in his life, he was being thrown back on the his own resources.*

35 pot [T] to make a clay object such as a bowl, using a POTTER'S WHEEL —see also **shed/throw light on sth** (LIGHT[1] (11))

throw sth ↔ **away** *phr. v.* [T] **1** to get rid of something that you do not want or need: *If it's broken, go ahead and throw it away.* **2** to lose or waste something good that you have, for example a skill or an opportunity: *Jones later realized he had thrown away his best chance at becoming a professional golfer.*

T

throw back sth *phr. v.* [T] INFORMAL to drink something very quickly: *Ted threw back three shots of whiskey before we even ordered dinner.*

throw in *phr. v.* [T] **1** [**throw** sth ↔ **in**] to add something to what you are selling, without increasing the price: *When we bought the car, the dealer threw in the floor mats.* **2 throw in the towel** INFORMAL to stop doing something because you cannot succeed: *After three months of campaigning for President, Wilson has thrown in the towel.* **3** [**throw** sth ↔ **in**] if you throw in a remark, you say it suddenly without thinking carefully

throw off *phr. v.* [T] **1** [**throw** sth ↔ **off**] to take off a piece of clothing in a quick careless way: *She threw off her jacket as she came in.* **2** [**throw** sb/sth ↔ **off**] to get free from something that has been limiting your freedom: *In 1648, Ukrainian Cossacks threw off their Polish rulers.* **3 throw sb off the scent/trail** to escape from someone or something that is chasing you: *Haskell attempted to throw police off his trail by dressing as a woman.* **4** [**throw** sth ↔ **off**] to produce large amounts of heat, light, RADIATION etc.: *The factory still throws off lots of pollution.* **5** [**throw** sth ↔ **off**] if you throw off a slight illness such as a COLD, you succeed in getting better fairly quickly

throw sth ↔ **on** *phr. v.* [T] to put on a piece of clothing quickly and carelessly: *I threw on some jeans and a T-shirt and headed out the door.*

throw sth ↔ **open** *phr. v.* [T] **1** to allow people to go into a place that is usually kept private: *The Getty Center will throw open its doors to the public July 8th.* **2** to allow anyone to take part in a competition or a discussion

throw out *phr. v.* [T] **1** [**throw** sth ↔ **out**] to get rid of something that you do not want or need, especially when you are cleaning a place: *My wife made me throw out my old tennis shoes.* **2** [**throw** sb ↔ **out**] to make someone leave a place, school, organization etc. quickly, especially because they have been behaving badly or made you angry: *His drug habit got him thrown out of his apartment.* **3** [**throw** sth ↔ **out**] if Congress, a court, or another official or political organization throws out a plan or suggestion, they refuse to accept it and make it legal, especially after voting: *Simon's case was thrown out of court.* **4 throw out an idea** to suggest an idea: *I just want to throw out this idea for discussion.*

throw together *phr. v.* [T] **1** [**throw** sth ↔ **together**] to make something quickly and not very carefully: *Our report was thrown together this morning.* **2** [**throw** sb ↔ **together**] if a situation throws people together, it makes them meet and know each other when they normally would not: *The program throws together children of different ages in the same classes.*

throw up *phr. v.* **1** [I,T **throw** sth ↔ **up**] to bring food or drink up from your stomach out through your mouth because you are sick or drunk; VOMIT[1]: *The smell almost made me throw up.* **2** [T **throw** sth ↔ **up**] to build something quickly: *Fences were thrown up along the border to keep illegal immigrants out.* **3** [T **throw** sth ↔ **up**] to show pictures or words on a screen: *My computer often throws up a error message when I try to print.* **4** [T **throw** sth ↔ **up**] if a vehicle throws up dirt, water etc., it makes it go up in the air

throw[2] *n.* [C] **1** an act of throwing something such as a ball: *Martinez made a nice throw to third base for the last out.* **2** the distance which something is thrown: *Lundgren won the discus competition with a throw of 130 yards.* **3** the result of throwing something in a game such as DARTS or DICE

throw·a·way[1] /'θroʊə,weɪ/ *adj.* [usually before noun] **1 throwaway line/comment/remark etc.** a short remark etc. that is said quickly and without careful thought: *Too much has been made of what was, in fact, a throwaway line by Danforth.* **2** something that has been produced cheaply so that it can be thrown away after it has been used; DISPOSABLE **3 a/the throwaway society** used to show disapproval when talking about

modern societies in which products are not made to last a long time **4 a throwaway song** a song that is not very good or will only be popular for a short time

throwaway[2] *n.* [C] **1** something that is thrown away after it has been used **2** a song that is not very good or will be popular for only a short time

throw·back /'θroʊbæk/ *n.* [C usually singular] something that is similar to or is a result of something that happened in the past: [+ **to**] *Hanoi remains a throwback to a time when cities were built for humans, not automobiles.*

throw·down /'θroʊdaʊn/ *n.* [C] SLANG a party, especially one with music and dancing

throw-in /'. ./ *n.* [C] the act of throwing the ball back onto the field in SOCCER, after it has gone over the line at the side of the field

thrown /θroʊn/ *v.* the past participle of THROW

throw rug /'. ./ *n.* [C] a small RUG (=cloth or wool covering for a floor)

thru /θru/ *prep.* NONSTANDARD a short form of "through": *The store is open Monday thru Saturday.* —**thru** *adj., adv.* —see also DRIVE-THROUGH

thrum /θrʌm/ *v.* **thrummed, thrumming** [I,T] to make a low sound like something beating or shaking: *The engine thrummed as we drove through the countryside.*

thrush /θrʌʃ/ *n.* **1** [C] a brown bird with spots on its front **2** [U] an infectious disease that affects the mouth

thrust[1] /θrʌst/ *v. past tense and past participle* **thrust** [T] **1** to push something somewhere with a sudden or violent movement: [**thrust** sth **into/back/forward** etc.] *Toby thrust the gift into her arms.* **2 have sth thrust upon/on you** to be forced to accept something that you did not expect or want: *Fame had been thrust upon Gooden at too early an age.* **3 thrust sb into sth** to put someone in a difficult or unusual situation very quickly: *Saving the child's life has thrust Collins into the media spotlight.* **4** [I + **at**] to make a sudden movement forward with a sword or knife

thrust[2] *n.* **1** [C usually singular] the main meaning or most important part of what someone says or does: [+ **of**] *The main thrust of their work is to help kids finish high school.* **2** [C] a sudden strong movement that pushes forward: *With a thrust of its fins, the shark moved through the water.* **3** [U] TECHNICAL the force of an engine that pushes something such as an airplane forward: *The new jet engines that will deliver more thrust at top speeds.*

thru·way, throughway /'θruweɪ/ *n. plural* **thruways** [C] a wide road for fast traffic that you pay to use

Thu. *n.* a written abbreviation of Thursday

thud[1] /θʌd/ *n.* [C] the low sound made by a heavy object hitting something else: *She landed on the floor with a thud.*

thud[2] *v.* **thudded, thudding** [I] to hit or fall onto something with a low sound

thug /θʌg/ *n.* [C] a violent man or boy —**thuggery** *n.* [U]

thumb[1] /θʌm/ *n.* [C] **1** the part of your hand that is shaped like a thick short finger and helps you to hold things **2** the part of a GLOVE that fits over your thumb **3 be all thumbs** INFORMAL to be unable to do things neatly and carefully with your hands: *Gary's all thumbs when it comes to fixing anything.* **4 give sth the thumbs up/down** also **get the thumbs up/down from sb** INFORMAL to show that you approve or disapprove of something: *The movie has gotten the thumbs up from the public.* **5 be under sb's thumb** to be so strongly influenced by someone that they control you completely: *Meg's really got Darren under her thumb.* —see also **have a green thumb** (GREEN[1] (7)), **stick out like a sore thumb** at **stick out** (STICK[1]), **rule of thumb** (RULE[1] (6))

thumb[2] *v.* **1 thumb a ride** INFORMAL to persuade a driver of a passing car to stop and take you somewhere, by putting your hand out with your thumb raised; HITCHHIKE **2 thumb your nose at sb/sth** to show that you do not respect rules, laws, someone's opinion etc.: *This is yet another example of Republicans thumbing their nose at the poor.*

thumb through sth *phr. v* [I,T] to look through a book, magazine etc. quickly: *He thumbed through his guidebook to show me a map of northern Italy.*

thumb in·dex /'. ,../ *n.* [C] a series of U-shaped cuts in the edge of a large book, usually showing the letters of the alphabet, that help you find the part you want

thumb·nail[1] /'θʌmneɪl/ *n.* [C] the NAIL on your thumb

thumbnail[2] *adj.* a thumbnail sketch/description a short description giving only the main facts about something

thumb·print /'θʌmprɪnt/ *n.* [C] a mark made by the pattern of lines at the end of your thumb —see also FINGERPRINT[1]

thumb·screw /'θʌmskru/ *n.* [C] an instrument used in past times to punish or TORTURE people by crushing their thumbs

thumb·tack /'θʌmtæk/ *n.* [C] a short pin with a broad flat top, used especially for putting a piece of paper on a wall —see picture at NAIL[1]

thump[1] /θʌmp/ *v.* **1** [I always + adv./prep., T] to make a dull sound by beating or falling against a surface: *The dog's tail continued to thump the rug.* | [+ against/on/into] *My head thumped against the floor.* **2** [T] INFORMAL to hit someone or something with your closed hand or with your KNUCKLES: *Thump the watermelon to see if it's ripe.* **3** [I] if your heart thumps, it beats very quickly because you are frightened or excited **4** [T] INFORMAL to be defeated in a game: *Last night, the Dodgers were thumped at home by the Giants.*

thump[2] *n.* **1** [C] the dull sound that is made when something hits a surface: *Jimmy heard a thump, followed by the slamming of the front gate.* **2 give sb a thump on the back/head etc.** to hit someone on the back, head etc. with your closed hand or with your KNUCKLES

thump·ing[1] /'θʌmpɪŋ/ *n.* [C] INFORMAL the act of defeating someone in a game: *Houston's 10–3 thumping of the Atlanta Braves was their best game of the season.* —see also **chest-thumping/chest-pounding** (CHEST (5))

thumping[2] *adj.* thumping music has a very low-sounding RHYTHM that you can feel: *the band's thumping Salsa beat*

thun·der[1] /'θʌndə/ *n.* **1** [U] the loud noise that you hear during a storm, usually after a flash of LIGHTNING: *The storm brought strong winds, **thunder and lightning**.* | *A **clap of thunder** (=one sudden noise of thunder) boomed overhead.* | *Off in the distance, we heard **rolling thunder** (=a noise of thunder that continues for a short time).* **2** [singular] a loud deep noise like thunder: *Outside my window was the constant thunder of delivery trucks.* —see also **steal sb's thunder** (STEAL[1] (8))

thunder[2] *v.* **1** if it thunders, there is a loud noise in the sky, usually after a flash of LIGHTNING: *Did you hear it thunder just now?* **2** [I always + adv./prep.] to move in a way that makes a very loud noise: *Fighter jets thundered across the sky.* **3** [T] to shout loudly and angrily: *"Be quiet!" Miguel thundered.*

thun·der·bolt /'θʌndə,boʊlt/ *n.* [C] **1** a flash of LIGHTNING that hits something and a noise of thunder together **2** a sudden event or piece of news that shocks you **3** an imaginary weapon of thunder and LIGHTNING, used by the gods to punish people

thun·der·clap /'θʌndə,klæp/ *n.* [C] a single loud noise of thunder

thun·der·cloud /'θʌndə,klaʊd/ *n.* [C] a large dark cloud that you see before or during a storm

thun·der·head /'θʌndə,hɛd/ *n.* [C] a thundercloud

thun·der·ous /'θʌndərəs/ *adj.* extremely loud: *a thunderous bang* —**thunderously** *adv.*

thun·der·show·er /'θʌndə,ʃaʊə/ *n.* [C] a short thundershower: *Thundershowers are likely in the afternoon.*

thun·der·storm /'θʌndə,stɔrm/ *n.* [C] a storm with THUNDER and LIGHTNING: *Around 3 p.m. the dark clouds of the thunderstorm rolled in.* —see picture on page 1333

thun·der·struck /'θʌndə,strʌk/ *adj.* [not before noun] extremely surprised or shocked: *I was thunderstruck to find out he had been lying the whole time.*

thunder thighs /'.. ,./ *n.* [plural] INFORMAL, HUMOROUS an impolite word used when someone's THIGHS (=the upper part of your legs) are very big and fat, or used for someone who has fat legs

thun·der·y /'θʌndəri/ *adj.* thundery weather is the type of weather that comes before a thunderstorm

thunk /θʌŋk/ *v.* **1 who'd have thunk it?** NONSTANDARD, HUMOROUS used to say that something is surprising or unexpected **2** [I,T] to make a dull sound by beating or falling against a surface

Thur·ber /'θɜbə/, **James** (1894–1961) a U.S. humorous writer and CARTOONIST

Thurs·day /'θɜzdi, -deɪ/ *written abbreviation* **Thu., Thur.,** or **Thurs.** *n.* [C,U] the fifth day of the week, between Wednesday and Friday: *I tried to call you Thursday.* | *Andy's leaving for Chicago on Thursday.* | *I wasn't home last Thursday.* | *I made my dentist appointment for next Thursday at 10:00 am.* | *I'm going to do my laundry this Thursday (=the next Thursday that is coming).* | *We go jogging together on Thursdays (=each Thursday).* | *Thanksgiving is always on a Thursday.* | *Thursday morning/afternoon/night etc. Let's go out to dinner Thursday night.* —see Usage Note at SUNDAY

thus /ðʌs/ *adv.* FORMAL **1** [sentence adverb] as a result of something that you have just mentioned: *The houses were used for soldiers. Thus, the structures survived the Civil War.* **2** also **thusly** in this manner or way: *The product was delivered on time, and we have thus fulfilled our promise.* | *Doucet sums it up thusly: "To me, Cajun music really is the heart of our culture."* **3 thus far** until now: *Robinson thus far has been able to keep his promises to the voters.*

USAGE NOTE: THUS

WORD CHOICE: thus, so, therefore, consequently, for this reason, as a result

Thus is formal and is used almost always in writing: *A nitrogen molecule contains a total of 14 protons and 14 neutrons. Thus, it has a "molecular weight" of 28.* In spoken English, you usually use **so**: *The smell of paint can give you a headache, so (NOT "thus") it's a good idea to keep the windows open.* In formal speech as well as in writing, **therefore, consequently, for this reason,** and **as a result** may be used: *Money market accounts are not insured, and therefore are considered more risky than passbook accounts.* | *In the past three years, change at the plant has occurred often. Consequently, employee morale has suffered.*

---

thwack /θwæk/ *v.* [T] to hit someone or something making a short loud sound —**thwack** *n.* [C]

thwart[1] /θwɔrt/ *v.* [T] FORMAL to prevent something from succeeding or prevent someone from doing what they are trying to do: *Efforts to clean up the oil spill have been thwarted by storms.*

thwart[2] *n.* [C] TECHNICAL a seat fastened across a ROWBOAT

thy /ðaɪ/ *possessive adj.* OLD USE your

thyme /taɪm/ *n.* [U] a plant used for giving food a special taste

thy·mus /'θaɪməs/ also **thymus gland** /,.. './ *n.* [C] a very small organ at the top of your chest that helps produce T CELLS

thy·roid /'θaɪrɔɪd/ also **thyroid gland** /,.. './ *n.* [C] an organ in your neck that produces HORMONES (=substances) that affect the way you develop and behave

thy·self /ðaɪ'sɛlf/ *pron.* OLD USE yourself

ti /ti/ *n.* [singular] the seventh note in a musical SCALE according to the SOL-FA system

ti·a·ra /ti'arə, ti'ɛrə/ *n.* [C] a piece of jewelry like a small CROWN, that a woman wears on her head on formal occasions

Ti·ber, the /'taɪbə/ a river in central Italy that flows south and through the city of Rome to the Mediterranean Sea

Ti·bet /tɪˈbɛt/ a large area of southwest China which has been an independent country for much of its history but which came under Chinese control in 1951 —**Tibetan** n., adj.

tib·i·a /ˈtɪbiə/ n. plural **tibiae** /-bi-i/ or **tibias** [C] TECHNICAL a bone in the front of the lower part of your leg —see picture at SKELETON

tic /tɪk/ n. [C] a sudden uncontrolled movement of a muscle in your face, usually because of a nervous illness

tick[1] /tɪk/ n. **1** [C] the short repeated sound that a clock or watch makes every second, or a series of these sounds **2** [C] a very small creature like an insect that lives on the skin of other animals and sucks their blood **3** [C] a small change in the amount or value of something, especially in the price of a STOCK in a company

tick[2] v. **1** [I] if a clock or watch ticks, it makes a short sound every second **2 what makes sb tick** INFORMAL the thoughts, desires, opinions etc. that give someone their character or make them behave in a particular way: Nobody can figure out what makes him tick.

tick away phr. v. **1** [I] also **tick by** if time ticks away or by, it passes, especially when you are waiting for something to happen: Belinda stared at the clock as the morning ticked away. **2** [T **tick sth ↔ away**] if a clock or watch ticks away the hours, minutes etc., it shows them as they pass

tick off phr. v. [T] **1** [**tick sb ↔ off**] INFORMAL to annoy someone: Her attitude is really ticking me off. **2** [**tick sth ↔ off**] to tell someone a list of things, especially when you touch a different finger as you tell each thing on the list: Carville stood and began ticking off points on his fingers.

ticked off /ˌ. ˈ.ˌ/ adj. [not before noun] angry or annoyed: Mark's ticked off with me for some reason.

tick·er /ˈtɪkɚ/ n. [C] **1** a special machine that prints or shows the prices of company STOCKs as they go up and down **2** INFORMAL your heart

ticker tape /ˈ.. ˌ./ n. [U] long narrow paper on which information is printed by a ticker

ticker-tape pa·rade /ˌ.. .. .ˈ., ˈ.. ˌ. .ˌ/ n. [C] an occasion when someone important or famous walks or drives through a city and pieces of paper are thrown from high buildings to welcome them or celebrate something they have done

tick·et[1] /ˈtɪkɪt/ n. [C]
1 movie/bus/plane etc. a printed piece of paper that shows that you have paid to do something, for example enter a theater, travel on a bus or airplane etc.: [+ to] tickets to the concert | They got round-trip tickets (=tickets for travel from one place to another and back again) to Miami for $297. | Isn't it more expensive to buy one-way tickets (=tickets for travel in one direction)? —see also SEASON TICKET
2 driving offense an official printed note ordering you to pay money because you have done something illegal, especially while driving or parking your car: a parking ticket
3 election [usually singular] a list of the people supported by a particular political party in an election: He ran unsuccessfully for governor on the Republican ticket.
4 in stores a piece of paper attached to something in a store that shows its price, size etc.; TAG
5 a ticket to success/happiness/fame etc. a way of becoming successful, happy etc.: Michael thought an MBA from Stanford would be an instant ticket to success.
6 be (just) the ticket OLD-FASHIONED to be exactly what is needed —see also MEAL TICKET

ticket[2] v. [T] **1** to give someone a ticket for parking their car in the wrong place, driving too fast etc.: Sanders was ticketed for speeding. **2** to choose or mark someone or something for a particular use, purpose, job etc.: [**ticket sb/sth for sth**] Three of the

army bases have been ticketed for closure. **3** to attach a small piece of paper onto something to show its price, size etc.; TAG

ticket a·gen·cy /ˈ.. ˌ..../ n. [C] a company that sells tickets for sports events or entertainment such as concerts or plays

ticket booth /ˈ.. ˌ./ n. [C] a very small building or room where you can buy tickets to sports events or entertainment such as movies or concerts

tick·et·ed /ˈtɪkɪtɪd/ adj. **a ticketed passenger** someone who already has a ticket for an airplane, train etc.: Only ticketed passengers are allowed beyond this point.

tick·et·ing /ˈtɪkɪtɪŋ/ n. [U] the process or system of selling or printing tickets for airplanes, trains, concerts etc.: Most airlines are using electronic ticketing now.

ticket of·fice /ˈ.. ˌ../ n. [C] an office or place in a building that sells tickets for entertainment, sports events, airplanes etc. —compare BOX OFFICE

ticket win·dow /ˈ.. ˌ../ n. [C] a small window in a building or wall where you can buy tickets to sports events, for entertainment, for a train etc.

tick·ing /ˈtɪkɪŋ/ n. [U] a thick strong cotton cloth used for making MATTRESS and PILLOW covers

tick·le[1] /ˈtɪkəl/ v. **1** [T] to move your fingers lightly over someone's body in order to make them laugh: Stop tickling me! **2** [I,T] if something touching your body tickles you, it makes you want to rub your body because it is uncomfortable: Your beard tickles. **3** [T] INFORMAL if a situation, remark etc. tickles you, it amuses or pleases you: Dick will be tickled pink (=very pleased) to see you. **4 tickle sb's fancy** OLD-FASHIONED if something tickles your fancy, it seems interesting and makes you want to do it **5 tickle the ivories** OLD-FASHIONED to play the piano

tickle[2] n. [C] a feeling in your throat that makes you want to cough: I've had this tickle in my throat for over a week.

tick·lish /ˈtɪklɪʃ/ adj. **1** someone who is ticklish is sensitive to being tickled: I didn't know you were so ticklish. **2** INFORMAL a ticklish situation or problem must be dealt with very carefully, especially because you may offend or upset people: Then we were faced with the ticklish issue of who would pay for the meal. —**ticklishness** n. [U]

tick-tock /ˈtɪk ˌtɑk, ˌtɪk ˈtɑk/ interjection the sound that a large clock makes when it TICKS

tick·y-tack·y /ˈtɪki ˌtæki/ adj. INFORMAL ticky-tacky houses, buildings etc. are made of material that is cheap and of low quality —**ticky-tacky** n. [U]

tic-tac-toe, tick-tack-toe /ˌtɪk tæk ˈtoʊ/ n. [U] a children's game in which two players draw X's and O's in a pattern of nine squares, trying to get three in a row

tid·al /ˈtaɪdl/ adj. relating to the regular rising and falling of the ocean: tidal currents

tidal wave /ˈ.. ˌ./ n. [C] **1** an extremely large ocean wave that flows over the land and destroys things **2** a very large amount of a particular kind of feeling or activity happening at one time: [+ of] There has been a tidal wave of unemployment in the region.

tid·bit /ˈtɪdˌbɪt/ n. [C] **1** a small piece of food that tastes good **2** a small piece of interesting information, news etc.: tidbits of gossip

tid·dly·winks /ˈtɪdliwɪŋks/ n. [U] a children's game in which you try to make small round pieces of plastic jump into a cup by pressing one edge with a larger piece

tide[1] /taɪd/ n. **1** [C,U] the regular rising and lowering of the level of the ocean: Driftwood on the beach was brought in by the tide. | **the tide is in/out** (=the ocean is at a high or low level) —see also HIGH TIDE, LOW TIDE **2** [C usually singular] the way in which events, opinions etc. are developing: The tide of public opinion has turned against the war (=people's opinions have changed so that they no longer approve of it). | Parents seem to be swimming against the tide (=opposing what most people think) by protesting sex on TV. | The government has been unable to stem the tide of violence in the south (=prevent it from developing and getting worse). **3** [C] a current of water caused by the tide: *Strong tides make swimming dangerous.* **4** [singular] a large number of people or things moving along together: *It is unclear who will pay for the tide of refugees flowing into the country.*

tide²

tide sb over *phr. v.* [T] if food, money etc. tides you over, it is enough to last until you are able to get some more: *Can you lend me $50 to tide me over till the end of the month?*

tide pool /'. ./ *n.* [C] a small area of water left among rocks by the ocean when the tide goes out

tide·wa·ter /'taɪd,wɔtə/ *n.* **1** [U] water that flows onto the land when the tide rises to a very high level **2** [U] water in the parts of rivers that are affected by tides **3** [C] an area of land at or near the ocean coast

tid·ings /'taɪdɪŋz/ *n.* [plural] OLD USE news: **good/glad tidings** (=good news)

ti·dy¹ /'taɪdi/ *adj.* **tidier, tidiest 1** a tidy room, house, desk etc. is neatly arranged with everything in the right place: *Zola always keeps her kitchen **neat and tidy**.* **2 a tidy sum/profit** INFORMAL a large amount of money: *In 1899, the mansion cost the tidy sum of $350,000.* **3** someone who is tidy keeps their house, clothes etc. neat and clean —**tidily** *adv.* —**tidiness** *n.* [U]

tidy² also **tidy up** *v.* **tidies, tidied, tidying** [I,T] to make a place look neat: *I was tidying up my desk when the phone rang.*

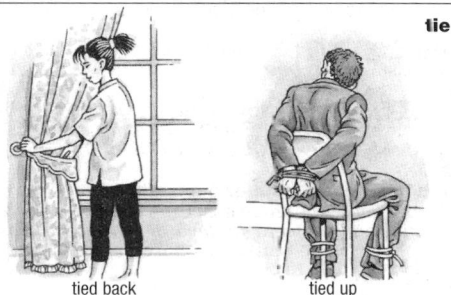

tie

tied back | tied up

1 `string/rope` **a)** [T] to fasten one thing to another with a piece of string, rope etc. using a knot or BOW²: [**tie sth to/behind/onto etc. sth**] *Paul took off the sweater and tied it around his waist.* | [**tie sb to sth**] *He says the men tied him to a tree and beat him up.* | **tie sb's hands/feet** (=tie them together) **b)** [T] also **tie up** to fasten a piece of string, rope etc. around something using a knot or BOW², in order to keep it closed or keep all its parts together: [**tie sth with sth**] *The flowers were tied with a red ribbon.* | *I wore my suit and **tied back my hair** (=fastened my hair behind my head).* **c)** [T] to make a knot in a piece of string, rope etc., for example to fasten shoes or other clothes: *Daddy, can you tie my shoe?* | **tie a knot/bow** *We learned how to tie knots in the Boy Scouts.* **d)** [I] to be fastened using pieces of string, RIBBON etc. in a knot or BOW²: *The dress ties at the back.*
2 `game/competition` [I] also **be tied** if two players, teams etc. tie or are tied in a game or competition, they have an equal number of points: [**+ with**] *The Saints were tied with Atlanta for the division lead.* | [**+ for**] *Near the end of the tournament, three teams are tied for second place.*
3 be tied to sth a) to be related to something or dependent on it: *At least 20% of their pay was tied to performance.* **b)** to be unable to leave the situation, place, job etc. that you are in: *That's why I never married – I didn't want to be tied to the kitchen sink.* **c)** to like something that you have very much and not want to lose it or leave it: *Some people are very tied to their pets.*
4 tie the knot INFORMAL to get married
5 tie yourself (up) in knots INFORMAL to become very upset because you are worried, nervous, or confused: *Sharon has tied herself up in knots worrying about her job.*

6 tie one on INFORMAL to get drunk —see also **sb's hands are tied** (HAND¹ (25))

tie sb down *phr. v.* [T] to stop someone from being free to do the things they want to do: [**+ to**] *Ken doesn't want to be tied down to any one woman.*

tie in *phr. v.* [I] **1** if one idea or statement ties in with another one, it helps to prove the same thing: [**+ with**] *Marsden's conclusions tie in with our theory perfectly.* **2** to happen at the same time as something else, or be closely related in some way to something else: [**+ with/to**] *The company will produce a number of items to tie in with the team's 25th anniversary.*

tie up *phr. v.*
1 `person` [T **tie sb ↔ up**] to tie someone's arms, legs etc. so that they cannot move: *We had to tie him up so he wouldn't escape.*
2 `object` [T **tie sth ↔ up**] to fasten something together by using string or rope tied in a bow or knot: *I put the cake in the box and tied it up with a red and white string.*
3 be tied up to be so busy that you cannot do anything else: *"May I speak to Professor Smithers?" "I'm sorry. He's tied up at the moment."*
4 `traffic/phone/court of law etc.` [T **tie sth ↔ up**] to block a system or use it so much that other people cannot use it or it does not work effectively: *Protesters tied up traffic on Highway 12 for three hours today.* | *Don't tie up the phone lines making personal calls.*
5 `money` [T **tie sth ↔ up**] if you tie your money up in something, it is all being used for that thing and you cannot use it for anything else: [**tie sth up in sth**] *Most of our money is tied up in real estate.*
6 tie sb/sth up in court to keep someone or something involved in a CASE in a court of law for a long time without ever deciding anything: *The case has been tied up in federal court since 1996.*
7 be tied up with sth to be very closely related to something: *Christianity in Africa is tied up with its colonial past.*
8 tie up loose ends to do the things that are necessary in order to finish a piece of work: *There are still a few loose ends to tie up before we have an agreement.*
9 `arrangements` [T **tie sth ↔ up**] to finish arranging all the details of something such as an agreement or a plan
10 `boat` [I] to tie a boat to something: *We tied up alongside a barge.*

tie² *n.* [C] **1** a long narrow piece of cloth that you wear around your neck, tied in a special knot in front —see also BLACK-TIE, BOW TIE **2** a relationship between two people, groups, or countries: *He apparently has **close ties** to several leading Democrats.* **3** a piece of string, wire etc. used to fasten or close something such as a bag **4** [usually singular] the result of a game, competition, or election in which two or more people get the same number of points, votes etc.: *The game **ended in a tie**.* **5** a heavy piece of wood or metal supporting a railroad track **sw 22**

tie-break·er /'. ./ also **tie·break** /'taɪbreɪk/ *n.* [C] an additional question, point, or game that decides the winner when two people or teams have the same number of points in a competition

tie clip also **tie clasp** /'. ./ *n.* [C] a special piece of bent metal used for keeping a man's TIE fastened to his shirt or as a decoration

tie-dye /'. ./ *v.* [T] to tie string around parts of a piece of material and color it with DYE (=colored liquid) in order to make a special pattern —**tie-dye, tie-dyed** *adj.: a tie-dye T-shirt* —**tie-dye** *n.* [U]

tie-in /'. ./ *n.* [C] a product such as a record, book, or toy that is related to a movie, television show etc.

tier /tɪr/ *n.* [C] **1** one of several rows or layers of something, especially seats, that rise one behind another **2** one of several levels in an organization or system: *The strong economy has done little for workers at the lowest tier.* **3 two-tier/three-tier etc.** also **two-tiered/three-tiered etc.** having two, three etc. layers: *a three-tiered wedding cake*

T

Ti·er·ra del Fue·go /tiˌɛrə dɛl ˈfweɪɡoʊ/ a group of islands near the south coast of South America, which belong to Chile and Argentina

tie tack also **tie pin** /ˈ. ./ n. [C] a special pin used for keeping a man's TIE fastened to his shirt or as a decoration

tie-up /ˈ. ./ n. [C] INFORMAL **1** a situation in which traffic is prevented from moving, or in which there is a problem that prevents a system or plan from working: *frustrating traffic tie-ups* **2** an agreement to become business partners: [+ **with/between**] *There has been talk about Fiat's possible tie-up with Chrysler.* —see also **tie up** (TIE[1])

tiff /tɪf/ n. [C] a slight argument between people who know each other well: *He had a tiff with his wife.*

Tif·fa·ny /ˈtɪfəni/**, Lou·is** /ˈluɪs/ (1848–1933) a U.S. PAINTER and glassmaker, famous for designing glass objects in the ART NOUVEAU style

ti·ger /ˈtaɪɡɚ/ n. [C] a large strong animal that is orange with black lines on its body and is a member of the cat family —see also **paper tiger** (PAPER[2] (4))

S W
3 3
tight[1] /taɪt/ adj.
1 clothes fitting a part of your body very closely, especially in a way that is uncomfortable: *a tight skirt* | *This jacket is too tight.* —see also SKIN-TIGHT, TIGHT-FITTING
2 pulled/stretched string, wire, cloth etc. that is tight has been pulled or stretched firmly so that it is straight or cannot move: *She tied the rope around the post and pulled it tight.*
3 a tight hold/grip a) a firm hold on something **b)** also **a tight rein** a situation in which someone controls someone or something very strictly: *The new business manager has a tight hold on the budget.* | *Wherever she is, her husband keeps a tight rein on her.*
4 strictly controlled controlled very strictly and firmly: *The treaty would place tight limits on weapons testing.* | *Security at the conference was extremely tight.*
5 money INFORMAL **a)** if money is tight, you do not have enough of it: *Money has been really tight because we had major car problems.* **b)** someone who is tight is not generous and tries very hard to avoid spending money: *Ken hasn't always been so tight with money.* —see also TIGHT-FISTED
6 firmly attached/fastened something such as a screw or lid that is tight is firmly fastened and is difficult to move: *Make sure the lid is tight enough so that it won't leak.*
7 time if time is tight, it is difficult for you to do everything you need to do in the time available: *My schedule is very tight right now, but I'll try to fit you in.* | *a tight deadline*
8 jobs/products etc. a tight market is a situation in which not many jobs, products etc. are available: *Companies have had to raise salaries in this tight labor market* (=one in which few workers are available).
9 run a tight ship to manage a company, organization etc. very effectively by having strict rules
10 little space if space is tight, there is just barely enough space to fit something into a place: **a tight squeeze/fit** *Three adults in the back seat would be a tight squeeze.*
11 close relationship a tight group of people, countries etc. have a close relationship with each other and are closely connected with each other
12 in a tight spot/situation/corner INFORMAL in a difficult situation: *Even when she's in a tight spot, Lynne always believes that things will get better.*
13 close together placed or standing very close together: *The planes approached in a tight grouping.*
14 chest/stomach etc. feeling painful, stiff, or uncomfortable because you are sick or worried: *My chest was tight with tension.*
15 smile/expression/voice etc. showing that you are annoyed or upset: *Her mother gave a tight, forced smile.* —see also TIGHT-LIPPED

16 turn/bend if a turn, bend, corner etc. is tight, it is very curved so that it turns very quickly to another direction: *We made a tight right turn onto Blossom Hill Avenue.*
17 play/performance performed very exactly, with no unnecessary pauses: *a tight, well-rehearsed production*
18 game/competition a tight game, competition etc. is one in which the teams, competitors etc. all play well and it is not easy to win: *They eventually won the tight game in the fourth quarter.*
19 drunk [not before noun] OLD-FASHIONED, INFORMAL drunk —see also AIRTIGHT, WATERTIGHT —**tightly** adj.: *Cover the pan tightly with foil.* —**tightness** n. [U]

tight[2] adv. very firmly or closely: *Her eyes were shut tight as she screamed.* | **Hold tight** *and don't let go of my hand.* —see also **sit tight** (SIT (5)), **sleep tight** (SLEEP[1] (4))

S W
2

tight ass /ˈ. ./ n. [C] INFORMAL, DISAPPROVING an insulting word for someone you think is too worried about embarrassing themselves and will not try anything unusual or exciting —**tight-assed** adj.

tight·en /ˈtaɪtn/ also **tighten up** v.
1 close/fasten [T] to close or fasten something firmly by turning it: *I need to tighten the screw on my glasses.* | *Tighten up the lid on that juice before you put it away.*
2 rope/string etc. [I,T] if you tighten a rope, wire etc., or if it tightens, it is stretched or pulled so that it becomes tight: *When you tighten guitar strings, the note gets higher.* | *The rope tightened and Steve was pulled off balance.*
3 make sth fit [T] to make something fit as closely as possible: *She bent down and tightened the muzzle on the dog.*
4 body to become stiff or make a part of your body become stiff: *Tighten your stomach muscles and hold for three seconds.* | *Judy's lips tightened in a thin smile.*
5 tighten your hold/grip on sth a) to control a place or situation more strictly: *Torture increased as the military tightened its hold on the country.* **b)** to hold someone or something more firmly: *Sam tightened his grip on my arm as he tried to apologize.*
6 rule/law etc. [T] to make a rule, law, or system more strict or effective: *The bill would tighten existing gun-control regulations.* | [**tighten up on sth**] *Green wants teachers to tighten up on student attendance.*
7 tighten your belt INFORMAL to spend less money than you usually spend: *Colleges have tightened their belts and are giving fewer scholarships than before.*
8 tighten the screws on sb INFORMAL to force someone to do something by threatening them —see also **put/tighten the screws on sb** (SCREW[1] (3))

tight end /ˌ. ˈ./ n. [C] a player who begins playing at one of the ends of the front line in football, and often blocks opposing players or catches the ball

tight-fist·ed /ˌ. ˈ../ adj. INFORMAL not generous with money; STINGY —**tight-fistedness** n. [U]

tight-fit·ting /ˌ. ˈ../ adj. fitting very closely or tightly: *tight-fitting jeans*

tight·ie whit·ies /ˌtaɪti ˈwaɪtiz/ n. [plural] SLANG a word for white JOCKEY SHORTS, used by people who consider them unfashionable

tight-knit /ˌ. ˈ./ adj. [only before noun] a tight-knit group of people are closely connected with each other: *Filipinos have established a tight-knit community in the city.*

tight-lipped /ˌtaɪt ˈlɪpt/ adj. **1** unwilling to talk about something: *Authorities have been extremely tight-lipped about the investigation.* **2** with your lips tightly pressed together because you are angry: *He stared at her, tight-lipped.*

tight·rope /ˈtaɪtroʊp/ n. [C] **1** a rope or wire high above the ground that someone walks along in a CIRCUS **2 walk a tightrope** to be in a difficult situation in which you must be careful about what you say or do

tights /taɪts/ n. [plural] a piece of clothing that girls or women wear, that tightly fits over their legs and feet and goes up to their waist, and that is colored and thick enough that you cannot see through it —compare PANTYHOSE

tight-wad /'taɪt‑wɑd/ n. [C] INFORMAL someone who hates to spend or give money

ti-gress /'taɪgrɪs/ n. [C] a female tiger

Ti-gris, the /'taɪgrɪs/ a river in southwest Asia that flows through Turkey and Iraq

tike /taɪk/ n. [C] another spelling of TYKE

'til /tɪl/ a short form of TILL¹

til-de /'tɪldə/ n. [C] a mark (~) placed over the letter "n" in Spanish to show that it is pronounced /nj/

tile¹ /taɪl/ n. **1** [C] a flat square piece of baked clay or other material, used for covering walls, floors etc.: *bathroom tiles* **2** [C] a thin curved piece of baked clay used for covering roofs

tile² v. [T] to cover a roof, floor etc. with tiles —**tiled** adj.: *a red-tiled floor* —**tiler** n. [C]

til-ing /'taɪlɪŋ/ n. [U] a set of tiles used to cover a roof, floor etc.

till¹ /tɪl, tl/ prep., conjunction until: *Kate didn't walk till she was 18 months old.* | *I have to work till eight tonight.*

till² /tɪl/ v. [T] to prepare land for growing crops, especially by cutting it and turning it over: *The townspeople tilled the soil and produced most everything they ate.*

till³ n. [C] **1 the till** money in the till is money that a company or organization has: *The campaign has more than $3.3 million in the till.* **2** OLD-FASHIONED a CASH REGISTER

till-age /'tɪlɪdʒ/ n. [U] the activity of preparing land for growing crops

til-ler /'tɪlɚ/ n. [C] **1** a long handle fastened to the RUDDER (=part that controls the direction) of a boat **2** a person or machine that tills land

tilt¹ /tɪlt/ v. **1** [I,T] to move or make something move into a position where one side is higher than the other: *Tilt the pan so that the sauce covers the bottom.* **2** [T] to move your head or chin up or to the side: *Carl tilted his head and looked sideways at her.* **3** [T] if an opinion or situation tilts or something tilts it, it changes so that people prefer one person, belief etc.: *This new evidence may tilt the balance of opinion in his favor.*

tilt at sb phr. v. [T] **1 tilt at windmills** to try to do something that is considered impossible: *Manning admits he was tilting at windmills in trying to change the nation's prison system.* **2** OLD USE to move quickly on a horse toward someone, in order to attack them with a LANCE

tilt² n. **1 (at) full tilt** as fast as possible: *Our factories are running at full tilt.* **2** [C] a situation in which someone prefers one person, belief etc., or in which one person, belief etc. has an advantage: *We're seeing a tilt in the balance of military power.* **3** [C,U] a movement or position in which one side of something is higher than the other: *a questioning tilt of the head*

tim-ber /'tɪmbɚ/ n. **1** [U] trees that are cut down and used for building or making things **2** [C] a wooden beam, especially one that forms part of the main structure of a house **3 timber!** SPOKEN used to warn people that a tree being cut down is about to fall —see also HALF-TIMBERED

tim-ber-land /'tɪmbɚ‚lænd/ n. [C U] an area of land that is covered by trees, especially ones that will be used for wood

tim-ber-line /'tɪmbɚ‚laɪn/ n. TECHNICAL **a)** the timberline the height above SEA LEVEL above which trees will not grow **b)** the northern or southern limit in the world beyond which trees will not grow

tim-bre /'tæmbɚ/ n. [C,U] the quality of the sound made by a particular instrument or voice

tim-brel /'tɪmbrəl/ n. [C] OLD USE a TAMBOURINE

Tim-buk-tu /‚tɪmbʌk'tu/ n. [singular, not with the] INFORMAL a place that is a long way from a town or any interesting place

time¹ /taɪm/ n.

1 minutes/hours etc. [U] something that is measured in minutes, hours, years etc. using clocks:

Drugs can alter our understanding of time and space. | *Time passes slowly when you've got nothing to do.* | *I guess he'll learn as time goes by.*

2 on the clock [singular,U] a particular point in time shown on a clock in hours and minutes: *What time is it?* | *Excuse me – do you have the time* (=used to ask someone politely what time it is)*?* | *Susie's just learning to tell time* (=know what time it is by looking at the clock)*.* | *Honey, look at the time* (=used to say it is later than you thought it was)*! We've got to go.*

3 occasion [C] an occasion when something happens or someone does something: *That was the only time Hoffman visited Dallas.* | *Tell Bud "hello" for me next time you see him.* | *I'm not going to help you this time – you'll have to do it yourself.* | *I remember one time* (=once) *she came dressed in a leather miniskirt.* | *Smoking is not permitted at any time.* | **the first/second/last etc. time** *Was that the last time you saw him?* | **every/each time** *Every time I see him he's with a different woman.*

4 period of time [singular] a period during which something happens or someone does something: *I didn't really enjoy my time in Boston.* | *Becky's been looking for a good used car for a long time.* | *Scientists have known for some time* (=for a fairly long time) *that nicotine is addictive.* | *I was thinking about you the whole time* (=continuously during the period of time) *I was gone.* | **a long time ago/some time ago** *Friday's meeting was planned some time ago and can't be changed now.*

5 most of the time very often or almost always: *Most of the time he's a really nice guy, but sometimes he can be really nasty.*

6 when sth happens [C,U] the particular minute, hour, day etc. when something happens or someone does something: *What time did Scott leave?* | *Police asked Harry where he was at the time of the robbery.* | *Karl and I were hired at the same time.* | *By the time they got him to the hospital, he was already dead.* | **opening/closing time** (=the time when a store, bar etc. opens or closes) | **arrival/departure time** (=the time when a train, airplane etc. arrives or leaves) | **lunch/dinner/break etc. time** *I hate it when the phone rings at dinner time.* | **this time tomorrow/yesterday etc.** *This time next week I'll be lying on a beach in Mexico.*

7 time needed [C,U] the amount of time that it takes you to do something: *How much time do you think they'll need to paint the house?* | *It takes a long time to copy all the pages.* | **travel/commute/flight time** *Travel time between the two cities is about two hours.*

8 time available [U] the amount of time that is available for you to do something: *Time is running out in the hostage crisis.* | *I really don't have time for a serious relationship right now.* | *Most teachers don't have the time to design their own materials.* | *There's still time if you want to get another drink.* | *I seem to spend most of my time on the phone.* | *Stop wasting time – we need to get this finished.* | *Nomi's excellent experience means we won't lose precious time training her.*

9 make/find time to arrange your plans in order to have enough time to do something: *I never seem to find time to go to the gym.*

10 it's time used to say when something should be done, should happen, or is expected to happen: [+ for] *It's almost time for bed, girls.* | [it's time to do sth] *Come on everybody. It's time to start cleaning up.* | [it's time sb did sth] *It's time Armstrong told the truth about what he knows.*

11 on time arriving or happening at the correct time or the time that was arranged: *McCoy did not show up on time for the trial.* | *Mr. Frank ended the meeting right on time.*

12 in time a) early or soon enough to do something: [+ for] *Will you be back in time for dinner?* | [in time to do sth] *I should be back in time to watch the show.* | *We got to the theater just in time* (=with very little extra time)*.* **b)** after a certain period of time, especially after a gradual process of change and development: *In time I think she'll realize how foolish she's been.*

13 ahead of time before something else happens, or earlier than is expected or necessary: *Pat always gets everything ready ahead of time so she can relax when guests arrive.*

14 appropriate time [C,U] an appropriate or convenient time for something to happen or someone to do something: *Now is not the time to discuss this.* | **a good/bad time** *I think this is a good time to take a break.* | **the right/wrong time** *Making a noise at the wrong time could put everyone in danger.*

15 three/four/ten etc. times used to say how often something happens: *He's seen "Star Wars" at least 20 times.* | *How many times have you been to Hawaii?* | *Sometimes Peggy calls three times a day.*

16 all the time continuously or very often: *Gabrielle talks about her kids all the time.*

17 one/three/ten etc. at a time separately, or in groups of three, ten etc. together at the same time: *Add the eggs to the batter one at a time.* | *I could only read a few pages of the manual at a time.*

18 five/ten/many etc. times... used to say how much bigger, better etc. one thing is than another: *The tower is three times taller than anything else in the city.* | *This stationery costs three times as much as it used to.*

19 nine times out of ten/99 times out of 100 used to say that something is almost always true or almost always happens: *Nine times out of ten stories like that are made up.*

20 from time to time sometimes, but not regularly or very often: *The two still talk on the phone from time to time.*

21 when the time comes when something that you expect to happen actually happens, or when something becomes necessary: *We'll decide how to tell her when the time comes.*

22 at the/that time at a particular moment or period in the past, especially when the situation is very different now: *It seemed like a good idea at the time.* | *At that time, Carlson was only 14 years old.*

23 for the time being for a short period of time from now, but not permanently: *Bob's keeping his car in our garage for the time being.*

24 take your time a) to do something slowly or carefully without hurrying: *Just take your time and think about what you're saying and you'll be fine.* **b)** to do something more slowly than seems reasonable: *The bus is taking its sweet time getting here.*

25 experience [C] a good time, bad time, difficult time, etc. is a period or part of your life when you have good, bad, difficult etc. experiences: *I spent some of the happiest times of my life in Germany.* | **have a good/great/fantastic etc. time** *Did you have a good time at the party?* | **good/bad/hard etc. times** *The bad times help you appreciate the good times even more.*

26 history [C] also **times** [plural] a particular period in history: [**the time of sb/sth**] *Marlowe wrote plays at about the time of Shakespeare.* | *Gibson is remembered as one of the most significant athletes of our time* (=of the present period in history). | **Roman/Greek/medieval etc. times** *Celts lived in this region in ancient times.*

27 in no time (at all) also **in less than no time** very quickly or soon, especially in a way that is surprising: *The men promised them they could double their money in no time.*

28 in part of the world [U] the time in one particular part of the world, or the time used in one particular area: *Eastern Standard Time* | *Welcome to Las Vegas, where the local time is 2:30 p.m.*

29 at times sometimes but not usually: *At times Jean deeply regretted not having children.*

SPOKEN PHRASES

30 half the time if something happens half the time, especially something annoying, it happens fairly often: *Half the time I don't even know where he is.*

31 it's about time said when you are annoyed because you think something should have happened earlier: *"Joey's home." "Well, it's about time."*

32 (sb's) time is up used to say that someone has to stop doing something, because they have done it for long enough: *Time's up! Turn in your tests.*

33 there's no time like the present used to say that now is a good time to do something: *"I should probably wash the car." "Well, there's no time like the present."*

34 be out of time an expression used on television and radio programs when saying that there is no more time left: *It looks like we're out of time, but we'll be back again tomorrow with Anne Rice.*

35 time was (when) INFORMAL used to say that there was a time when something good used to happen that does not happen anymore: *Time was when you could buy a new car for less than $500.*

36 that time of the month the time when a woman has her PERIOD[1] (4)

37 in a race [C] the amount of time taken by a runner, swimmer etc. in a race: *What's his best time in the 100 meters?*

38 a time of (the) year/day etc. a particular period or moment during a year, day etc.: *At this time of year we expected it to be a little warmer here.*

39 in time to sth if you do something in time to a piece of music, you do it using the same RHYTHM and speed as the music: *I listened to the car radio, tapping on the steering wheel in time to the music.*

40 music [U] the number of BEATS in each BAR in a piece of music: *Waltzes are usually in three-four time.* | **beat/keep time** (=move your hand or play an instrument at the same speed as a piece of music)

41 do time INFORMAL to spend a period of time in prison: *Hyland did hard time* (=spent time in a very strict prison) *for armed robbery 25 years ago.*

42 at all times used especially in official notices or announcements to say what always happens or should always happen: *Many books recommend carrying your passport with you at all times.*

43 have all the time in the world used to say that you have as much time as you want in which to do something: *You don't have to rush – we have all the time in the world.*

44 time after time also **time and (time) again** happening often over a long period, especially in a way that is annoying: *We've seen management make the same mistakes time and again.*

45 at this time FORMAL at this particular moment: *It would be difficult at this time to explain all the new regulations.*

46 at one time at some time in the past but not now: *At one time forests covered about 20% of Lebanon.*

47 for a time for a fairly short time, until something happens to change the situation: *For a time both countries followed the terms of the treaty.*

48 for any length of time for more than just a short time: *They will not be able to survive in the desert for any length of time.*

49 for hours/months etc. at a time for a period that continues for several hours, months etc.: *Dad would be gone for six days at a time and never tell us where he'd been.*

50 have the time of your life to have a very enjoyable time: *The kids had the time of their lives at the waterslide.*

51 behind the times people, ideas, or organizations that are behind the times are old-fashioned and do not know or understand what is happening now: *The company's marketing plan is a little behind the times.*

52 be ahead of your time someone who is ahead of their time uses the newest ideas and methods, which are later used by many other people: *Eisenhower was ahead of his time in trying to improve U.S.–Soviet relations.*

53 be ahead of its time a machine, system, idea etc. that is ahead of its time is a more modern or advanced than other similar things: *Hyde Park was a school way ahead of its time.*

54 at no time did/should etc. sb do sth also **at no time was sb** used to say strongly that something never happened or should never happen: *At no time were the prisoners mistreated.*

55 (only) time will tell used to say that it will become clear after a period of time whether or not something is true, right etc. at some time in the future: *Only time will tell if this agreement will bring a lasting peace.*

56 the time is ripe (for sth) used to say that the conditions are now right or favorable for something to happen: *Amato thinks the time is ripe for educational reform.*

57 time is money used to say that wasting time or delaying something costs money

58 it's (just/only) a matter/question of time used to say that something will definitely happen at some time in the future, but you do not know when: *It's just a matter of time before he quits or gets fired.*

59 over time if something happens over time, it happens gradually during a long period: *Images that people have of themselves change over time.*

60 time flies (when you're having fun) INFORMAL used to say that time seems to pass quickly when you are having a good time

61 there's no time to lose used to say that you must do something quickly because there is very little time

62 make good time if you make good time on a trip, you travel quickly, especially more quickly than you expected: *Once we got on the freeway, we made good time.*

63 before sb's time a) something that is before someone's time happened before they were born, before they started working or living somewhere etc.: *"Did you ever see Babe Ruth play?" "No, he was long before my time."* **b)** if you do something before your time, you do it before the time when most people usually do it in their lives: *I don't want to turn into a grumpy old man before my time.*

64 time heals all wounds used to say that things you are worried or upset about will gradually disappear as time passes

65 keep time if a clock or watch keeps time, it works correctly: **keep good/perfect etc. time** *My watch keeps perfect time.*

66 on sb's own time if you do work or studying on your own time, you do it outside normal school or work hours: *Bob rearranged the office on his own time.*

67 with time also **given time** after a certain period of time, especially after a gradual process of change and development: *I guess things will improve with time.*

68 not have (much) time for sb/sth also **have no time for sb/sth** INFORMAL to dislike and not want to waste your time on someone or something: *She's always complaining – I don't have time for people like that.*

69 time is of the essence FORMAL used to say that it is important that something be done quickly

70 race/work/battle etc. against time to try to do something even though you have very little time

71 with time to spare sooner than expected or necessary: *She arrived at the hospital with little time to spare.*

72 in sb's time during someone's life: *I've met some rude women in my time, but she's the worst.*

73 the best/biggest etc.... of all time the best, biggest etc. of a particular kind of person or thing that has ever existed: *the most successful movie of all time*

74 time is on sb's side used to say that someone is young enough to be able to wait before doing something or until something happens

75 sb's time is up also **sb's time is drawing near** used to say that someone is going to die soon

76 in sb's own good time INFORMAL when someone is ready: *The old system allowed people to pay their taxes in their own good time.*

77 all in good time used to tell someone to be patient because something they are waiting for will definitely happen, and probably fairly soon

78 not give sb the time of day to refuse to pay any attention to someone, in an impolite way: *After what she did to you, I wouldn't even give her the time of day!*

79 from time out of mind LITERARY for as long as you can remember

80 since/from time immemorial from a very long time in the past: *The Pathan tribesman have lived in the Khyber Pass since time immemorial.* —see also **at the best of times** (BEST³ (12)), **bide your time** (BIDE (1)), BIG-TIME, **the fullness of time** (FULLNESS (3)), FULL-TIME, HALFTIME, **it is high time sb did sth** (HIGH¹ (16)), **kill time** (KILL¹ (5)), **mark time** (MARK¹ (10)), **move with the times** (MOVE¹ (20)), **in the nick of time** (NICK¹ (1)), **for old times' sake** (OLD (25)), **once upon a time** (ONCE¹ (11)), PART-TIME, **pass the time of day (with sb)** (PASS¹ (11)), **play for time** (PLAY¹ (19)), **at the same time** (SAME¹ (2)), **be a sign of the times** (SIGN¹ (6)), **a stitch in time (saves nine)** (STITCH¹ (8)), **have a whale of a time** (WHALE¹ (2))

time² *v.* [T] **1** [usually passive] to do something or arrange for something to happen at a particular time: [**time sth to do sth**] *They timed the fireworks to go off between flights landing at the airport.* | *Geiger's speech was **timed to coincide with** (=planned to happen at the same time as) the governors' conference.* **2** to measure how fast someone or something is going, how long it takes to do something etc.: *I'm going to run to the corner and back – time me.* | [**time sb/sth at**] *Radar guns timed Hershiser's pitches at around 90 miles per hour.* **3** to hit, throw etc. a ball in a game at a particular moment: *Walker timed the pass perfectly.* —see also ILL-TIMED, MISTIME, WELL-TIMED

time out *phr. v.* [I] if a computer is timed out, it stops using a particular computer PROGRAM because the computer user has not done any work for a particular period of time

time and a half /ˌ. . . './ *n.* [U] one and a half times the normal rate of pay: *We get time and a half for overtime.*

time and mo·tion stud·y /ˌ. . '.. ˌ../ *n.* [C] a study of working methods to find out how effective they are

time bomb /'. ./ *n.* [C] **1** a situation that is likely to become a very serious problem: *With the rise in teenage HIV infection rates, we are sitting on a time bomb.* **2** a bomb that is set to explode at a particular time

time cap·sule /'. ˌ../ *n.* [C] a container that is filled with objects from a particular time, so that people in the future will know what life was like then

time card /'. ./ *n.* [C] a piece of stiff paper on which the hours you have worked are recorded by a time clock

time clock /'. ./ *n.* [C] a special clock that records the exact time when someone arrives at and leaves work

time-con·sum·ing /'. .ˌ../ *adj.* taking a long time to do: *Filling out the paperwork is a time-consuming process.*

time frame /'. ./ *n.* [C] the period of time during which you expect or agree that something will happen or be done.: *We're unlikely to finish the project within the two-year time frame.*

time-hon·ored /'. ../ *adj.* a time-honored method, custom etc. is one that has existed for a long time: *The afternoon nap is a time-honored tradition in many cultures.*

time·keep·er /'taɪm,kipəʳ/ *n.* [C] someone who officially records the times taken to do something, especially at a sports event —**timekeeping** *n.* [U]

time lag also **time lapse** /'. ./ *n.* [C] the period of time between two related events: *There is always a long time lag between a proposal and any concrete results.*

time-lapse /'. ./ *adj.* time-lapse photography involves taking many pictures of something over a long period of time, and then showing these pictures together so that you can clearly see the changes in a very slow process

time·less /'taɪmlɪs/ *adj.* **1** remaining beautiful, attractive etc. and not becoming old-fashioned:

Origami is the timeless Japanese art of paper folding. **2** LITERARY continuing forever: *the timeless universe* —**timelessly** *adv.* —**timelessness** *n.* [U]

time lim·it /'. ,../ *n.* [C] the longest time that you are allowed to do something in: *You have a 50-minute time limit for the test.*

time·line /'taimlain/ *n.* [C] **1** a plan for when things will happen or how much time you expect something to take: *We need some kind of timeline for when you want this finished.* **2** a line next to which you write different events to show the order in which they happened

time·ly /'taimli/ *adj.* **timelier, timeliest** done or happening when expected or at exactly the right time: *a piece of timely advice* | **in a timely manner/fashion** *Failure to make payments in a timely manner may lead to penalties.*

time ma·chine /'. .,./ *n.* [C] an imaginary machine in which people can travel backward or forward in time

time off /,. './ *n.* [U] **1** time when you are officially allowed not to be at work or studying: **take/have/get time off** *I need to take some time off and get some rest.* **2 time off for good behavior** time that you do not have to spend in prison because you have behaved well while you are there

time out /,. './ *n.* **1 take time out** INFORMAL to rest or do something different from your usual job or activities **2** [C] a short break during a sports game when the teams can rest, get instructions from their COACH etc. **3** [C] a time when a child must stop what they are doing, sit alone, and be quiet as a punishment for something they have done **4** [C] an occasion when a computer stops using a particular computer PROGRAM because the computer user has not done any work for a particular period of time

time·piece /'taimpis/ *n.* [C] OLD USE a clock or watch

tim·er /'taimɚ/ *n.* [C] **1** an instrument that you use to measure time, when you are doing something such as cooking: *Did you set the timer?* —see also EGG TIMER **2 a part-timer/full-timer** someone who works part or all of a normal working week

S W 2 **times** /taimz/ *prep.* multiplied by: *Two times two equals four* (=2 x 2 = 4).

time·sav·ing /'. ,../ *adj.* designed to reduce the time usually needed to do something: *time-saving techniques* —**timesaver** *n.* [C]

time·serv·er /'taim,sɚvɚ/ *n.* [C] INFORMAL someone who does the least amount of work possible —**time-serving** *adj., n.* [U]

time·share /'taimʃɛr/ *n.* [C] a vacation home that you buy with other people so that you can each spend a period of time there every year —**timeshare** *adj.*

time-shar·ing /'. ,../ *n.* [U] **1** the practice of owning a timeshare **2** TECHNICAL a situation in which one computer is used by many people at different TERMINALs at the same time —**time-sharing** *adj.*

time sheet /'. ./ *n.* [C] a piece of paper on which the hours you have worked are written or printed

time sig·nal /'. ,../ *n.* [C] a sound on the radio that shows the exact time

time sig·na·ture /'. ,.../ *n.* [C] two numbers at the beginning of a line of music that tell you how many BEATS[2] (2) there are in a MEASURE[1] (13)

times ta·ble /,. './ *n.* [C usually plural] SPOKEN a MULTIPLICATION TABLE

time switch /'. ./ *n.* [C] an electronic control that can be set to start or stop a machine at a particular time

time·ta·ble /'taim,teibəl/ *n.* [C] **1** a plan of events and activities, with their dates and times; SCHEDULE: *Officials have set no* **timetable** *for deciding on a security plan.* **2** a list of the times at which buses, trains, airplanes etc. arrive and leave; SCHEDULE

time tri·al /'. ,../ *n.* [C] a practice race to decide who will take part in an important race and what order they will start in

time warp /'. ./ *n.* [C] **1 be (caught/stuck) in a time warp** to have not changed even though everyone or everything else has: *The sleepy little town seems to be caught in a time warp.* **2** an imaginary situation in which the past or future becomes the present

time-worn /'. ./ *adj.* something time-worn is old and has been used a lot: *time-worn phrases*

time zone /'. ./ *n.* [C] one of the 24 areas that the world is divided into, each of which has its own time

tim·id /'timid/ *adj.* not having courage or confidence: *a timid child* | *The nation's newspapers are usually timid in criticizing the military.* —**timidly** *adv.* —**timidity** /tə'midəti/ *n.* [U]

tim·ing /'taimiŋ/ *n.* [U] **1** a word meaning the time, day etc. when someone does something or something happens, especially when you are considering how appropriate this is: **good/bad/perfect etc. timing** *Perfect timing! I was just going to call you.* **2** the way in which electricity is sent to the SPARK PLUGs in a car engine

tim·or·ous /'timərəs/ *adj.* FORMAL lacking confidence and easily frightened: *She was no helpless, timorous female.* —**timorously** *adv.*

Tim·o·thy /'timəθi/ **1 Timothy, 2 Timothy** two books in the New Testament of the Christian Bible

tim·pa·ni /'timpəni/ *n.* [U] a set of KETTLEDRUMs

tim·pa·nist /'timpənist/ *n.* [C] someone who plays the timpani

tin[1] /tin/ *n.* **1** [U] *symbol* Sn a soft white metal that is an ELEMENT and is often used to cover and protect iron and steel: *A machine separates the tin from paper and plastic in the trash.* **2** [C] a metal container with a lid in which food can be stored: *a tin of Christmas cookies* **3** [C] a metal container in which food is cooked; PAN: *a muffin tin* **4** [C] BRITISH a CAN[2] (1)

tin[2] *adj.* **1** made of tin: *a tin cup* **2 have a tin ear** INFORMAL to be unable to hear the difference between musical notes

tinc·ture /'tiŋktʃɚ/ *n.* [C,U] **1** [+ of] TECHNICAL a medical substance mixed with alcohol **2** a substance that is used to DYE (=change the color of) something, or the color it makes

tin·der /'tindɚ/ *n.* [U] dry material that burns easily and can be used for lighting fires

tin·der·box /'tindɚ,baks/ *n.* **1** [C usually singular] a place or situation that is dangerous and where there could suddenly be a lot of fighting or problems: *The refugee camps are a tinderbox waiting to catch fire.* **2** [C] a box containing things needed to make a fire, used in past times

tinder-dry, tinder dry /,. '.◂/ *adj.* extremely dry and likely to burn very easily: *After two years of drought, the forest is tinder dry.*

tine /tain/ *n.* [C] a pointed part of something that has several points, for example on a fork —compare PRONG (1)

tin·foil /'tinfɔil/ *n.* [U] thin shiny metal that bends like paper and is used for covering food

ting /tiŋ/ *n.* [C] a high clear ringing sound: *the ting of a bell* —**ting** *v.* [I,T]

ting-a-ling /,tiŋ ə 'liŋ/ *n.* [C] INFORMAL the high clear ringing sound that is made by a small bell

tinge[1] /tindʒ/ *n.* [C] a very small amount of a color, emotion, or quality: [+ of] *She had a tinge of sadness in her voice.*

tinge[2] *v.* [T + with] to give something a small amount of a particular color, emotion, or quality

tinged /tindʒd/ *adj.* showing a small amount of a color, emotion, or quality: [+ with] *The autumn leaves are tinged with gold.* | **lemon-tinged/blue-tinged/jazz-tinged etc.** *They danced all night to the Scottish-tinged music.*

tin·gle /'tiŋgəl/ *v.* [I] if a part of your body tingles, you feel a slight stinging feeling, especially on your skin: [+ with] *My skin was tingling with a strange sense of excitement.* —**tingle** *n.* [C] —**tingling** *n.* [C] —**tingly** *adj.*

tin·ker[1] /'tiŋkɚ/ *v.* [I] to make small changes to something in order to repair it or make it work better:

[+ **with**] *Congress has spent months tinkering with the new tax legislation.*

tinker[2] *n.* [C] **1** someone who travels from place to place selling things or repairing metal pots, pans etc., especially in past times **2 not give a tinker's damn** SPOKEN, INFORMAL to not care about something at all **3 not be worth a tinker's damn/dam** SPOKEN, INFORMAL to not be worth anything at all

tin·kle[1] /'tɪŋkəl/ *n.* [C usually singular] **1** a light ringing sound: [+ **of**] *the tinkle of Christmas bells* **2** [U] an expression meaning URINE (=liquid waste from your body), used especially by or to children: *Do you have to go tinkle?*

tinkle[2] *v.* [I,T] **1** to make light ringing sounds or to make something do this: *Bells tinkled as she opened the door.* **2** a word meaning to URINATE (=pass liquid waste from your body), used especially by and to children

tinned /tɪnd/ *adj.* tinned food is sold in a can and can be kept for a long time before it is opened; CANNED

tin·ni·tus /'tɪnɪtəs, tə'naɪtəs/ *n.* [U] TECHNICAL an illness in which you hear noises, especially ringing, in your ears

tin·ny /'tɪni/ *adj.* **tinnier, tinniest 1** a tinny sound is high, weak, and not nice to listen to, and sounds like it is coming out of something made of metal: *The recording of the concert was very tinny.* **2** a tinny metal object is badly or cheaply made

Tin Pan Al·ley /ˌ. ˌ. '. ./ *n.* [U] INFORMAL the people who produce popular music and their way of life, used especially about the music business in the early part of the 20th century in the U.S.

tin·plate /ˌtɪn'pleɪt/ *n.* [U] very thin sheets of iron or steel covered with TIN

tin·pot /ˌ. '. ./ *adj.* [only before noun] a tin-pot person, organization etc. is not very important, although they think that they are: *a tin-pot dictator*

tin·sel /'tɪnsəl/ *n.* [U] **1** thin strings of shiny paper used as decorations, especially at Christmas **2** something that seems attractive but is not valuable or important: *Not everything about the job was flash and tinsel.*

tin shears /'. ./ *n.* [plural] heavy scissors for cutting metal

tint[1] /tɪnt/ *n.* [C] **1** a light shade or small amount of a particular color: *Petal colors include every tint between white and pink.* **2** artificial color, used to slightly change the color of your hair

tint[2] *v.* [T] to give something, especially your hair, a slightly different artificial color

tint·ed /'tɪntɪd/ *adj.* [only before noun] tinted glass is colored, rather than completely transparent

T-in·ter·sec·tion /'ti ˌɪntəsɛkʃən/ *n.* [C] a place where two roads meet and form the shape of the letter T

tin·tin·nab·u·la·tion /ˌtɪntənæbyə'leɪʃən/ *n.* [C,U] LITERARY the sound of bells

Tin·to·ret·to /ˌtɪntə'rɛtoʊ/ (1518–1594) an Italian painter famous for his religious paintings and his PORTRAITS

ti·ny /'taɪni/ *adj.* **tinier, tiniest** extremely small: *Inflation increased a tiny 0.2% in November.* | *a tiny little baby*

-tion /ʃən/ *suffix* [in nouns] another form of the SUFFIX -ION

tip[1] /tɪp/ *n.*
1 end [C] the end of something, especially something pointed: [+ **of**] *There was a smudge of flour on the tip of Toni's nose.* | *They live on the southern tip of the island.* —see also FINGERTIP
2 money [C] a small amount of additional money that you give to someone, such as a WAITER or a taxi driver: *a 15% tip* | *Did you leave a tip?*
3 advice [C] a helpful piece of advice: [+ **on**] *The pamphlet offers several tips on how to find a job.*
4 on the tip of your tongue if a word, name etc. is on the tip of your tongue, you know it but cannot remember it
5 secret information a secret warning or piece of information, especially to police about illegal activities: *Acting on a tip, police went to the motel and arrested Upton.*

6 the tip of the iceberg a small sign of a problem that is much larger: *Investigators say the irregular campaign contributions may be just the tip of the iceberg.*
7 horse race [C] INFORMAL special information about which horse will win a race

tip[2] *v.* **tipped, tipping**
1 fall [I,T] also **tip (sth ↔) over** to fall or turn over, or make something do this: *A gust of wind tipped the truck over.* | *The canoe tipped and we fell in the water.*
2 money [I,T] to give an additional amount of money to someone such as a WAITER or taxi driver: *How much should I tip the driver?*
3 lean [I,T] to lean at an angle instead of being level or straight, or to make something do this: *Don't tip the chair back so far.*
4 tip the balance/scales to give a slight but important advantage to someone or something: *Your support tipped the balance in our favor.*
5 likely to succeed [T usually passive] to say who you think is most likely to be successful at something: [**tip sb/sth to do sth**] *Hashimoto was tipped to become the country's next prime minister.*
6 gold-tipped/steel-tipped/rubber-tipped etc. having a tip that is made of or covered with gold, steel etc.: *felt-tipped pens*
7 tip the scales at 150/180/200 etc. pounds to weigh a particular amount before a BOXING or WRESTLING match: *Briggs tipped the scales at 227 pounds.*
8 pour [T] to pour something from one place or container into another: [**tip sth out/into/onto etc.**] *Cook 30 more seconds and then tip the crepe onto a serving plate.*
9 cover **be tipped with sth** to have one end covered in something: *The swordfish's sword is tipped with poison.*
10 secret information to give someone such as the police a secret warning or piece of information, especially about illegal activities; TIP OFF: *Investigators were tipped to watch for two men driving a horse van.*
11 tip your hand to allow someone to know your true plans or intentions after keeping them secret, especially when you do not intend to do this: *Faris has not tipped his hand concerning the board's recommendation.*
12 tip your hat to sb INFORMAL to show that you think someone is very good, helpful, successful etc.

tip sb ↔ off *phr. v.* [T] **1** to give someone such as the police a secret warning or piece of information, especially about illegal activities: [**tip sb off to sth**] *Informants tipped police off to Carillo's whereabouts.* **2** to show that something that you do not expect to be true is true: *There was nothing to tip me off that something was wrong.*

ti·pi /'tipi/ *n.* [C] another spelling of TEEPEE

tip-off /'. ./ *n.* [C] **1** INFORMAL something that shows you that something that you do not expect to be true is true: *The fact he hasn't called should be a tip-off that he's not interested.* **2** the beginning of a basketball game, when the ball is thrown into the air and two players jump up to try to gain control of it: *Tip-off is at 7:30 tonight in the Coliseum.* **3** INFORMAL a warning that something is going to happen, especially a warning to the police about illegal activities

tip·per /'tɪpə/ *n.* INFORMAL **a good/bad/big etc. tipper** someone who gives large, small etc. TIPS to WAITERS, taxi drivers etc. for their services: *He's a very generous tipper.*

tip·pler /'tɪplə/ *n.* [C] INFORMAL someone who drinks alcohol —**tipple** /'tɪpəl/ *v.* [I,T]

tip·py·toes /'tɪpitoʊz/ *n.* [plural] **on (my) tippytoes** a phrase meaning on tiptoe, used especially by children or when speaking to them

tip·ster /'tɪpstə/ *n.* [C] someone who gives secret information about a crime, about which horse is likely to win a race etc.

tip·sy /'tɪpsi/ *adj.* **tipsier, tipsiest** INFORMAL slightly drunk —**tipsily** *adv.* —**tipsiness** *n.* [U]

T

tip·toe[1] /ˈtɪptoʊ/ n. **on tiptoe(s)** if you stand or walk on tiptoe you stand or walk on your toes, in order to make yourself taller or in order to walk very quietly: *I had to stand on tiptoe to kiss him.*

tiptoe[2] v. [I] to walk quietly and carefully on your toes: [+ across/down etc.] *Emily tiptoed over to the window and looked outside.*

tip-top /ˌ. ˈ. ◂/ adj. INFORMAL excellent: **in tip-top condition/shape** *The car's in tip-top condition.*

ti·rade /ˈtaɪreɪd/ n. [C] a long angry speech criticizing someone or something: *Hahn is known for his tirades against immigrants.*

Ti·ra·na /tɪˈrɑnə/ the capital and largest city of Albania

tire[1] /taɪɚ/ n. [C] a thick round piece of rubber that fits around the wheel of a car, bicycle etc.: *I had a flat tire* (=all the air went out of it) *on the way home.* —see pictures at BICYCLE[1] and on page 427

tire[2] v. **1** [I,T] to start to feel tired or make someone feel tired: *I felt as if I could run all day without tiring.* **2 tire of sb/sth** to become bored with someone or something: *They began their affair in April, but he quickly tired of her.* **3 never tire of doing sth** to enjoy doing something again and again, especially in a way that annoys other people: *He never tires of talking about the good old days.*

tire sb ↔ **out** phr. v. [T] to make someone very tired: *All that walking really tired me out.*

tired /taɪɚd/ adj. **1** feeling that you want to sleep or rest: *I'm so tired!* | *the tired parents of newborns* **2 tired out** very tired, especially after a lot of hard work, traveling etc. **3** bored with something because it is not interesting anymore, or has become annoying: [**tired of doing sth**] *I'm tired of hearing about her new car.* | [+ **of**] *I'm getting tired of my hair – I think I'll get it cut.* **4 a tired (old) subject/joke etc.** a subject, joke etc. that is boring because it is too familiar —**tiredness** n. [U] —**tiredly** adv. —see also DOG-TIRED, **be sick (and tired) of sth** (SICK[1] (4))

tire·less /ˈtaɪɚlɪs/ adj. working very hard in a determined way without stopping: *Lynch's tireless efforts to help the homeless will not be forgotten.* —**tirelessly** adv.

tire·some /ˈtaɪɚsəm/ adj. making you feel annoyed, bored, or impatient: *Awards shows can get awfully tiresome.*

tir·ing /ˈtaɪərɪŋ/ adj. making you feel that you want to sleep or rest: *Working full time can be extremely tiring.*

'tis /tɪz/ POETIC a short form of "it is"

tis·sue /ˈtɪʃu/ n. **1** [C] a piece of soft thin paper, used especially for blowing your nose on: *a box of tissues* **2** [U] also **tissue paper** light thin paper used for wrapping, packing etc. **3** [U] the material forming animal or plant cells: **plant/lung/brain etc. tissue** *When you exercise you replace fat tissue with denser muscle tissue.* **4 a tissue of lies** a story or account that is completely untrue

tit /tɪt/ n. [C] **1** VULGAR a woman's breast **2** INFORMAL a TEAT

ti·tan, Titan /ˈtaɪt⁼n/ n. [C] a very strong or important person; GIANT: *a titan of the Hollywood film industry*

ti·tan·ic /taɪˈtænɪk/ adj. very big, strong, impressive etc.: *a titanic struggle between the forces of good and evil*

ti·ta·ni·um /taɪˈteɪniəm/ n. [U] symbol **Ti** a strong, light, and very expensive metal that is an ELEMENT

Ti·tans, the /ˈtaɪt⁼nz/ in Greek MYTHOLOGY, the first gods who ruled the universe who were thought of as GIANTs

tit for tat /ˌ. . ˈ. ◂/ n. [U] INFORMAL something bad that you do to someone because they have done something bad to you —**tit-for-tat** adj. [only before noun] *tit-for-tat insults*

tithe /taɪð/ n. [C usually plural] **1** a particular amount, usually 10% of income, that members of some Christian churches are expected to give to the church **2** a tax paid to the church, in past times —**tithe** v. [I]

Ti·tian /ˈtɪʃən/ (1477–1576) an Italian painter admired for his use of color

ti·tian /ˈtɪʃən/ n. [C] LITERARY a brownish-orange color —**titian** adj.: *titian hair*

Ti·ti·ca·ca, Lake /ˌtɪtɪˈkɑkə/ the largest lake in South America, in the Andes mountains between Bolivia and Peru

tit·il·late /ˈtɪtlˌeɪt/ v. [T] if a picture or a story titillates someone, it makes them feel excited or interested, especially in a sexual way: *The sex scandal is titillating the American public.* —**titillating** adj. —**titillation** /ˌtɪtlˈeɪʃən/ n. [U]

ti·tle /ˈtaɪtl/ n. **1** [C] the name given to a particular book, painting, play etc.: *"Confrontation on the Job" is the title of the workshop.* **2** [C] a book, VIDEOTAPE etc. that you can buy: *By Christmas, the publisher expects to have 25 titles available.* **3** [C] **a)** a name such as "Sir" or "Professor" or abbreviations such as "Mrs." or "Dr." that are used before someone's name to show their rank or profession, whether they are married etc. **b)** a name that describes someone's job or position: *Lewis's official title is "temporary co-chairman."* **4** [singular,U] TECHNICAL the legal right to own something: [+ **to**] *He holds title to dozens of buildings in the city.* **5** [C] the position of being the winner of an important sports competition: *Tyson won the WBA title in 1987.* —see also TITLIST

ti·tled /ˈtaɪtld/ adj. having a title such as "lord," "DUKE," "EARL" etc. because of being a member of the NOBILITY

title deed /ˈ.. ˌ./ n. [C] a piece of paper giving legal proof that someone owns a particular property

title hold·er /ˈ.. ˌ../ n. [C] **1** a person or team that is the winner of an important sports competition **2** someone who owns a title deed

title page /ˈ.. ˌ./ n. [C] the page at the front of a book that shows the book's name, writer etc.

title role /ˌ.. ˈ./ n. [C] the main acting part in a play or movie, when it is the same as the name of the play

title track /ˌ.. ˈ./ n. [C] the song on a CD, CASSETTE etc. that has the same name as the whole CD or cassette

ti·tlist /ˈtaɪtl-ɪst/ n. [C] someone who has won a TITLE in an important sports competition

tit·ter /ˈtɪtɚ/ v. [I] to laugh quietly in a high voice, especially because you are nervous or embarrassed: *At the word "breast," some of the class tittered.* —**titter** n. [C]

tit·tle-tat·tle /ˈtɪtl ˌtætl/ n. [U] unimportant conversation about other people and what they are doing; GOSSIP

tit·ty /ˈtɪti/ n. plural **titties** [C] SLANG a woman's breast

tit·u·lar /ˈtɪtʃələ/ adj. [only before noun] **a titular head/leader/monarch etc.** someone who is the official leader or ruler of a country but who does not have real power or authority

Ti·tus /ˈtaɪtəs/ a book in the New Testament of the Christian Bible

Ti·wa /ˈtiwə/ a Native American tribe from the southern area of the U.S.

tiz·zy /ˈtɪzi/ also **tizz** /tɪz/ n. [singular] INFORMAL **in a tizzy** feeling worried, nervous, and confused: *Her mother was in a tizzy over Liz's divorce.*

TLC n. [U] INFORMAL tender loving care; kindness and love that you show to make them feel better and happier

Tlin·git /ˈtlɪŋgɪt/ n. a Native American tribe who live in Alaska —**Tlingit** adj.

TM[1] a written abbreviation of TRADEMARK

TM[2] an abbreviation of TRANSCENDENTAL MEDITATION

TN the written abbreviation of Tennessee

TNT n. [U] a powerful explosive

to[1] /tə, before a vowel tʊ; strong tu/ [used before a verb to show that it is the infinitive, but not before "can," "could," "may," "might," "will," "would," "shall," "should," "must," or "ought." The following senses show the patterns in which "to" is used.] **1** used after some verbs: *We tried to tell her, but she would not listen.* | *You can drive today if you want to.* | *The manager finally asked them to leave.* **2** used after "how," "where," "who," "whom," "whose," "which," "when," "what," or "whether": *My father still doesn't know how to set the VCR.* | *Melinda is always telling people what to do.* | *Tell me when to stop.* **3** used after some nouns: *It is his third attempt to climb the mountain.* | *If you get a chance to see the play, you should.* | *I don't see any reason to be nice to her.* **4** used after some adjectives: *That's very easy to say.* | *She said she'd be happy to write me a letter of recommendation.* | *I'm sorry to keep bothering you.* **5** used to show the purpose of an action: *We're getting up early tomorrow to fly to Memphis.* | *I borrowed money to buy my car.* | *You should leave now to avoid the traffic.* **6** used after "too" and an adjective: *It's too cold to go out.* | *I've been too lazy to write any letters.* **7** used after an adjective and "enough": *Are you tall enough to reach that jar for me?* | *He's not old enough yet to chew gum.* **8** used to talk about or show or to emphasize a particular verb: *"To look for" is a phrasal verb.* | *Their plan is to tear down the warehouse and put up an apartment building.* **9** used to introduce a statement: *To be honest, I'm not sure I want to go.* | *Dinner was a disaster, to put it bluntly.* | *To begin with, let's look at Chapter 3.* **10** used after "there is" and a noun: *There's nothing to do around here.* | *There are some shirts to iron in the bedroom if you're not busy.* **11 bride/husband/parent etc. to be** someone who will soon be married, soon be a parent etc.

to² /tu/ *prep.* **1** toward or in the direction of a place or person: *Where can I catch the bus to the airport?* | *Throw the ball to me.* | *We're planning a trip to Egypt.* **2** in order to be in a particular place or area: *He's going to Tokyo on a business trip.* | *Do you want to go to Mika's wedding with me?* | *What time do the kids normally go to bed?* **3** in order to be in a particular situation, or in a particular physical or mental state: *She sang the baby to sleep.* | *They say she starved herself to death.* | *After an hour outside, my hands had turned to ice.* **4** used to show the person or thing to which actions or words are directed or to whom things belong: *Who is that letter addressed to?* | *He doesn't even say "Hi" to me anymore.* | *The quilt belonged to my grandmother.* **5** in a direction from a particular person or thing: *Mt. Eddy is directly to the west of Mt. Shasta.* | *Nathan, you sit here to my right.* **6** reaching as far as a particular thing: *Jason's hair is down to his shoulders now.* **7** used to show the person or thing that is affected by an action or situation: *Why are you always so mean to me?* | *The coal mine is a pollution threat to the park.* | *What did you do to the radio? I can't make it work.* **8** in a position in which two things are touching: *There's some gum stuck to the bottom of my shoe.* | *They spent the evening dancing* **cheek to cheek.** **9** facing something or in front of it: *He turned his back to me and walked away.* | *Bob and I sat* **face to face** *across the table.* **10** starting with one thing or in one place and ending with or in another: *A to Z* | *Zoe can count to ten in four languages.* | *From here to the city will take you about 30 minutes.* | *She read the novel from beginning to end.* **11** fitting or being a part of a machine or piece of equipment: *Do you have the keys to the house?* **12** used when comparing two numbers, things etc.: *The Falcons won the game 27 to 0.* **13** used to show

that there is a certain amount of time before an event or before a particular time: *It's just a week to the wedding – how do you feel?* | *"What time is it?" "Ten to five."* (=ten minutes before 5:00) **14** used to show how things affect, concern, or influence someone, especially after verbs such as "seem," "feel," or "sound": *It seems to me that we should just buy a new TV.* | *To some people, death is not such a frightening thought.* **15** according to a particular feeling or attitude: *Jerry's never been married to my knowledge* (=according to what I know). | *To Gordon's way of thinking, cooking was women's work.* | *to sb's liking/taste etc. The food was not really to our liking.* **16 to sb's surprise/annoyance/delight etc.** in a way that makes someone feel a particular emotion: *Much to her surprise, Becky found that she actually liked sushi.* | *Simon agreed to sing one more song, to everyone's delight.* **17** forming something or being one of the separate parts that makes something up: *You can get 130 yen to the dollar right now.* | *There are sixteen ounces to a pound.* **18** used between two numbers when you try to guess an exact number: *The recipe makes about 20 to 24 cookies.* | *Contreras was driving at 80 to 90 miles per hour.* **19** used when saying what the chances of something happening are or when giving the ODDS for a BET, and usually written with the symbol (–): *100–1 odds* | *I'll bet you 50 to one he doesn't show up.*

to³ /tu/ *adv.* if you push a door to, or something moves a door to, it closes: *The wind blew the door to.* —see also **come to** (COME¹), TO AND FRO¹

toad /toud/ *n.* [C] a small animal that looks like a large FROG but is brown and lives mostly on land

toad·stool /'toudstul/ *n.* [C] a wild plant like a MUSH-ROOM, that can be poisonous

toad·y¹ /'toudi/ *n. plural* **toadies** [C] INFORMAL, DISAPPROVING someone who pretends to like an important person and does whatever that person wants, especially in order to gain an advantage in the future —**toadyism** *n.* [U]

toady² *v.* **toadies, toadied, toadying** [I] to pretend to like an important person or do whatever they want, so that they will help you: [+ **to**] *Some politicians have been accused of toadying to the NRA.*

to and fro¹ /,tu ən 'frou/ *adv.* if someone or something moves to and fro, they move in one direction and then back again: *A monkey ran to and fro.* —**to-and-fro** *adj.*

to and fro² *n.* [U] INFORMAL continuous movement of people or things from place to place

toast¹ /toust/ *n.* **1** [U] a piece of bread that has been put near heat so that it turns brown on both sides and is not soft anymore: *toast with butter and jam* —see also FRENCH TOAST, MELBA TOAST, TEXAS TOAST **2** [C] an occasion when you ask everyone who is present to drink something in order to thank someone, wish someone luck etc.: *I'd like to* **propose a toast** (=ask people to drink a toast) *to the bride and groom.* **3 be the toast of Broadway/Hollywood etc.** to be very popular and praised by many people for something you have done in a particular field of work: *Josephine Baker was the toast of Paris in the 1920s.* **4 warm as toast** comfortably warm: *The kerosene stove kept the room warm as toast.*

toast² *v.* [T] **1** to drink a glass of wine, etc. to thank someone, wish someone luck etc.: *Let's toast Edward for a job well done.* **2** to make bread or other food brown by placing it close to heat: *Lightly toast the nuts.* **3** to sit near a fire to make yourself warm

toast·er /'toustɚ/ *n.* [C] a machine you use for toasting bread —see picture at KITCHEN

toast·mas·ter /'toust,mæstɚ/ *n.* [C] someone who introduces the speakers at a formal occasion such as a BANQUET (=large formal meal)

toast·mis·tress /'toust,mɪstrɪs/ *n.* [C] a woman who introduces the speakers at a formal occasion such as a BANQUET (=large formal meal)

toast·y /'tousti/ *adj.* **toastier, toastiest** INFORMAL warm and comfortable: *It was warm and toasty under the blanket.*

to·bac·co /təˈbækoʊ/ *n.* [U] the dried brown leaves that are smoked in cigarettes, pipes etc.

to·bac·co·nist /təˈbækənɪst/ *n.* [C] someone who has a special store that sells tobacco, cigarettes etc., or the store itself

To·bit /ˈtoʊbɪt/ a book in the Apocrypha of the Protestant Bible

to·bog·gan¹ /təˈbɑgən/ *n.* [C] a light wooden board with a curved front, used for sliding down hills covered in snow

toboggan² *v.* [I] to slide down a hill on a toboggan —**tobogganing** *n.* [U]

toc·ca·ta /təˈkɑtə/ *n.* [C] a piece of music, usually for piano or organ, that is played very quickly

Tocque·ville /ˈtoʊkvɪl/**, A·lex·is de** /əˈlɛksɪs də/ (1805–1859) a French writer and politician who traveled in the U.S. and wrote a book which examined the strengths and weaknesses of the American system of government

toc·sin /ˈtɑksən/ *n.* [C] LITERARY a signal of danger that is made by ringing a bell

to·day¹ /təˈdeɪ/ *adv.* **1** on the day that is happening now: *What did you do today?* | *Today she and Charlie are driving to the beach.* **2** at the present time: *Kids today just don't understand the value of money.*

today² *n.* [U] **1** the day that is happening now: *Today is Friday.* | *Have you heard today's news?* **2** the present period of time: *By today's standards, his ideas seem very old-fashioned.* | *The music industry of today is very different from the one in the 1950s.*

tod·dle /ˈtɑdl/ *v.* [I] if a small child toddles, it walks with short unsteady steps: *He is just now beginning to toddle around the house.*

tod·dler /ˈtɑdlɚ/ *n.* [C] a very young child who is just learning to walk —see Usage Note at CHILD

tod·dy /ˈtɑdi/ *n.* —see HOT TODDY

to-do /tə ˈdu/ *n.* [singular] INFORMAL a lot of excitement about something, especially when it is not necessary: *It caused quite a to-do when a mistake was made in the Labor Department statistics.*

to-do list /. ˈ. ./ *n.* [C] a list of things that someone is planning to do

toe¹ /toʊ/ *n.* [C] **1** one of the five movable parts at the end of your foot: *I hurt my big toe* (=the largest of your toes) *kicking the door.* | *We stood on our toes* (=stood on the ends of our toes) *to get a better view of the parade.* —see also **stub your toe** (STUB²) and see picture at BODY **2** the part of a shoe or sock that covers the front part of your foot **3 step on sb's toes** to offend someone, especially by becoming involved in something that they are responsible for: *I told Tony I didn't want to step on his toes.* **4 keep sb on their toes** to make sure that someone is ready for anything that might happen: *With a test every Friday, she keeps her students on their toes.* **5 make sb's toes curl** to make someone feel very embarrassed or uncomfortable about something **6 touch your toes** to bend down so that your hands touch your toes —see also **from head to toe** (HEAD¹ (7)), TIPTOE¹, -TOED

toe² *v.* [T] **toe the line** to do what other people in a job or organization say you should do, whether you agree with them or not: *Catholic politicians have been pressured to toe the line on issues such as abortion.*

toe·cap /ˈtoʊkæp/ *n.* [C] a piece of metal or leather that covers the front part of a shoe

-toed /toʊd/ [in adjectives] **1 steel-toed/square-toed/pointy-toed etc.** a steel-toed etc. shoe has a toe made of steel, shaped like a square etc. —see also OPEN-TOED **2 three-toed/long-toed/five-toed etc.** having three toes, long toes etc., especially used to describe animals: *a long-toed salamander*

TOEFL /ˈtoʊfəl/ *n.* [singular] TRADEMARK Test of English as a Foreign Language; a test that students

can take that shows how good their English is, when English is not their first language

toe·hold /ˈtoʊhoʊld/ *n.* **1** [singular] your first involvement in a particular activity, from which you can develop and become stronger: *Minorities say they've gotten a small toehold in broadcasting.* **2** [C] a small hole in a rock where you can put your foot when you are climbing

TOEIC /ˈtoʊɪk/ *n.* [singular] TRADEMARK Test of English for International Communication; a test that students can take that shows how good their English is, when English is not their first language

toe·nail /ˈtoʊneɪl/ *n.* [C] the hard part that covers the top of each of your toes

toe-to-toe /ˌ. . ˈ.◂/ *adv.* **go/stand/fight toe-to-toe (with sb)** to argue or fight with someone in a way that shows you will not stop: *Anyone willing to stand toe-to-toe with King must be admired.* —**toe-to-toe** *adj.*

tof·fee /ˈtɔfi, ˈtɑfi/ *n.* [C,U] a sticky sweet brown substance that you can eat, made by boiling sugar, water, and butter together, or a piece of this substance

to·fu /ˈtoʊfu/ *n.* [U] a soft white food like cheese, that is made from SOY BEANS

tog /tɑg, tɔg/ *n.* **1 togs** [plural] INFORMAL clothes **2** [C] TECHNICAL a unit for measuring the warmth of QUILTS etc.

to·ga /ˈtoʊgə/ *n.* [C] a long loose piece of clothing worn by people in ancient Rome

to·geth·er¹ /təˈgɛðɚ/ *adv.*
1 make one thing if you put two or more things together, you join them so that they form a single subject or group: *I glued the vase back together.* | *Now add the numbers together to get the subtotal.* | [+ with] *Mix the meat sauce together with the cooked rice.*
2 with each other if two or more people are together or do something together, they are with each other or do something with each other: *The two leaders chatted together for fifty-four minutes.* | *They lived together during college.*
3 in one place if you keep, collect etc. things together, you keep or collect them all in one place: *She keeps all the important documents together in one file.*
4 close/packed/crowded etc. together if people or objects are close together, packed together etc., they are placed very near to each other: *Stacks of books were crowded together in the corner.*
5 against each other if you rub, touch etc. things together, you rub or touch them against each other: *They banged their heads together trying to catch the ball.*
6 in agreement if people are together, come together etc., they are or become united and work with each other: *I hope both countries can come together on this issue.*
7 at the same time at the same time: *I mailed both packages together.* | *All together now!* (=used to tell a group of people to do something at the same time)
8 together with sth in addition to something else, or happening at the same time as something else: *For short stays, the exit visa is issued together with the entry visa.*
9 without stopping OLD USE without interruption: *It rained for four days together.* —see also **get your act together** (ACT¹ (4)), **hold together** (HOLD¹), **piece sth together** (PIECE²), **pull together** (PULL¹), **put sth together** (PUT)

together² *adj.* SPOKEN someone who is together always thinks clearly and does things in a very sensible organized way: *Jane is such a together person.*

to·geth·er·ness /təˈgɛðɚnɪs/ *n.* [U] the feeling you have when you are part of a group of people who have a close relationship with each other: *Our family has a strong sense of togetherness.*

tog·gle /ˈtɑgəl/ *n.* [C] **1** a small piece of wood or plastic that is used as a button on coats, bags etc. —see picture at FASTENER **2** something on a computer that lets you change from one operation to another

toggle switch /'.. ,./ n. [C] TECHNICAL a small part on a machine that is used to turn electricity on and off by moving it up or down

To·go /'tougou/ a country in west Africa between Benin and Ghana —**Togolese** /,touga'liz/ adj.

toil[1] /tɔɪl/ v. [I always + adv./prep.] **1** also **toil away** to work very hard for a long period of time: *My immigrant parents toiled night and day to make a living.* **2** to move slowly and with great effort: [+ up/ through/against etc.] *They toiled up the long hill in snowshoes.*

toil[2] n. [U] FORMAL **1** hard difficult work done over a long time: *a life of toil* **2 the toils of sth** LITERARY if you are caught in the toils of a bad feeling or situation, you are trapped by it

toi·let /'tɔɪlɪt/ n. **1** [C] a large bowl that you sit on to get rid of waste liquid or solid waste from your body: *Someone forgot to flush the toilet* (=make water go through the toilet to clean it). **2 go to the toilet** to pass waste liquid or solid waste from your body —see also **go to the bathroom** (BATHROOM (3)) **3** FORMAL: see TOILETTE

USAGE NOTE: TOILET

POLITENESS: toilet
We do not use the word **toilet** to talk about a room that has a toilet in it. Use **bathroom** for the room in a house that contains a toilet. Use **restroom**, **lavatory**, **ladies' room**, or **men's room** to talk about a room in a public place that has one or more toilets.

---

toilet pa·per /'.. ,../ n. [U] soft thin paper used for cleaning yourself after you have used the toilet

toi·let·ries /'tɔɪlətriz/ n. [plural] things such as soap and TOOTHPASTE that are used for washing yourself

toi·lette /twɑ'lɛt/ n. [U] FORMAL the act of washing and dressing yourself

toilet train·ing /'.. ,../ n. [U] the act of teaching a child to use a toilet; POTTY TRAINING —**toilet-train** v. [T] —**toilet-trained** adj.

toilet wa·ter /'.. ,../ n. [U] a type of PERFUME (=pleasant smelling liquid) that does not have a very strong smell

toke[1] /touk/ n. [C] SLANG **1** the action of taking the smoke of a MARIJUANA cigarette into your lungs: *Mike took a long heavy toke and closed his eyes.* **2** a MARIJUANA cigarette; JOINT[2] (3)

toke[2] v. [I,T] SLANG to smoke a MARIJUANA cigarette: *She lit the joint and toked.*

to·ken[1] /'toukən/ n. [C] **1** a round piece of metal that you use instead of money in some machines: *a subway token* (=a token used to pay to ride the subway) **2** FORMAL something that represents a feeling, fact, event etc.: *a token of your gratitude/ respect/appreciation etc. Please accept this gift as a small token of our appreciation.* —see also **by the same token** (SAME[1] (6))

token[2] adj. [only before noun] **1** a token action, change etc. is small and not very important: *Arafat won the presidency, with only token opposition.* **2 token black/woman/minority etc.** someone who is included in a group to make people believe that the group is trying to be fair and include all types of people, when this is not really true **3** done as a first sign that an agreement, promise etc. will be kept and that more will be done later: *Both sides agreed to a few token compromises.*

to·ken·ism /'touka,nizəm/ n. [U] actions that are intended to make people think that an organization deals fairly with people or problems when in fact it does not: *They worry that the job-sharing experiment may be tokenism rather than a real attempt at change in the way working mothers are treated.*

To·ky·o /'touki,ou/ the capital and largest city of Japan

told /tould/ v. the past tense and past participle of TELL

tol·er·a·ble /'tɑlərəbəl/ adj. **1** a situation that is tolerable is not very good, but you are able to accept it: *Most traffic jams are tolerable, lasting only 5 minutes*

or so. **2** difficult or painful, and barely acceptable: *The taste of the medicine is bitter but tolerable.*

tol·er·a·bly /'tɑlərəbli/ adv. [+ adj./adv.] fairly, but not very much: *The test produces tolerably accurate results.*

tol·er·ance /'tɑlərəns/ n. **1** [U] willingness to allow people to do, say, or believe what they want without criticizing them: *racial tolerance* | [+ of/toward/ for] *Gordon shows little tolerance for people with different views.* **2** [C,U] the degree to which someone can suffer pain, difficulty etc. without being harmed or damaged: [+ of/to] *Chris has a very low tolerance to alcohol.* **3** [C,U] TECHNICAL the amount by which the size, weight etc. of something can change without causing problems

tol·er·ant /'tɑlərənt/ adj. **1** allowing people to do, say, or believe what they want without punishing or criticizing them: *a tolerant community* | [+ of] *Officers will be tolerant of peaceful demonstrations.* **2** not being harmed or damaged by problems, a lack of something, or too much of something: *Many of these plants are drought tolerant.*

tol·er·ate /'tɑlə,reɪt/ v. [T] **1** to allow people to do, say, or believe something without criticizing or punishing them: *Drug dealers will not be tolerated in this community.* **2** to accept something bad or difficult, even though you do not like it: *Mom tolerated Dad's smoking.* **3** FORMAL if you tolerate a particular medicine, it does not have a bad effect on your body: *The medication is well tolerated by most patients.*

tol·er·a·tion /,tɑlə'reɪʃən/ n. [U] willingness to allow people to do say, or believe what they want without being punished or criticized: *religious toleration*

toll[1] /toul/ n. [C] **1** [usually singular] the number of people killed or injured in a particular accident, by a particular illness etc.: *The death toll of the plane crash has risen to 118.* **2 take its toll (on sb/sth)** to have a very bad effect on something or someone over a long period of time: *The pressure to tour is beginning to take its toll on the band.* **3** the money you have to pay to use a particular road, bridge etc. **4** the sound of a large bell ringing slowly

toll[2] v. [I,T] if a large bell tolls, or you toll it, it keeps ringing slowly, especially to show that someone has died

toll·booth /'toulbuθ/ n. [C] a place where you pay to drive on a road, bridge etc.

toll·bridge /'.. ./ n. [C] a bridge that you pay to drive across

toll call /'.. ./ n. [C] a telephone call that you must pay for —compare TOLL-FREE

toll-free /,. '. ./ adj. a toll-free telephone number does not cost you anything when you call it: *Call this toll-free number for details!* —**toll-free** adv.

toll·gate /'toulgeɪt/ n. [C] a gate across a road, at which you have to pay money before you can drive any further

toll pla·za /'. ,../ n. [C] an area on a HIGHWAY that is wider than the rest, where you stop to pay to use the road

toll road /'. ./ n. [C] a road that you pay to use

toll·way /'toulweɪ/ n. plural **tollways** a large long road that you pay to use

Tol·stoy /'toulstɔɪ/, **Count Le·o** /'liou/ (1828–1910) a Russian writer of NOVELS

Tol·tec /'toultɛk/ one of the tribes who lived in southern Mexico from the 10th century to the 12th century

tom /tɑm/ n. [C] INFORMAL a TOMCAT

tom·a·hawk /'tɑmə,hɔk/ n. [C] a light AX used by Native Americans

to·ma·to /tə'meɪtou/ n. plural **tomatoes** [C] a round soft red fruit eaten raw or cooked as a vegetable —see picture at VEGETABLE

tomb /tum/ n. [C] a grave, especially a large one above the ground: *the tomb of Saint Francis*

tom·boy /'tɑmbɔɪ/ n. [C] a girl who likes playing the same games as boys: *She was a joking, teasing tomboy.*

tomb·stone /'tumstoʊn/ *n.* [C] a stone that is put on a grave and shows the dead person's name, dates of birth and death etc.; HEADSTONE

tom·cat /'tɑmkæt/ *n.* [C] a male cat

tome /toʊm/ *n.* [C] LITERARY OR HUMOROUS a large heavy book: *It's the latest tome from Tom Clancy.*

tom·fool /ˌtɑmˈfuːl‹/ *adj.* [only before noun] OLD-FASHIONED very silly or stupid: *That was a tomfool thing to do!*

tom·fool·er·y /ˌtɑmˈfuːləri/ *n.* [U] silly behavior

tom·my gun /'tɑmi ˌgʌn/ *n.* [C] OLD-FASHIONED, INFORMAL a gun that can fire many bullets very quickly

to·mor·row[1] /təˈmɑroʊ, -ˈmɔr-/ *adv.* on or during the day after today: *We're playing tennis tomorrow.* | **tomorrow morning/afternoon/night/evening** *He'll be in town tomorrow afternoon.*

tomorrow[2] *n.* **1** [U] the day after today: *I'll see you at tomorrow's meeting.* **2** the future, especially the near future: *The worker of tomorrow will need to be better educated.* **3 do sth like there's no tomorrow** to do something very quickly and often carelessly: *Ben drives like there's no tomorrow.*

tom-tom /'. ./ *n.* [C] a long narrow drum you play with your hands

ton /tʌn/ *n.* [C] **1** *plural* **tons** or **ton** a unit for measuring weight, equal to 2000 pounds or 907.2 kilos in the U.S. **2 tons of sth** INFORMAL a lot of something: *They must be making tons of money.* **3 weigh a ton** INFORMAL to be very heavy: *Your bag weighs a ton!* **4 hit sb like a ton of bricks** INFORMAL to have a strong emotional effect on someone: *The news of her accident hit me like a ton of bricks.* **5 come down on sb like a ton of bricks** INFORMAL to get very angry with someone about something they have done

to·nal /'toʊnl/ *adj.* [no comparative] **1** relating to tones of color or sound: *The exaggerated tonal contrasts Manet used added drama to his paintings.* **2** TECHNICAL a piece of music that is tonal is based on a particular KEY[1] (4) —opposite ATONAL

to·nal·i·ty /toʊˈnæləti/ *n.* [C,U] TECHNICAL the sound of a piece of music that depends on the KEY[1] (4) of the music and the way in which the tunes and harmonies (HARMONY (1)) are combined

tone[1] /toʊn/ *n.*

1 | voice | [C] [plural] the way your voice sounds that shows how you are feeling or what you mean: *His tone was hesitant.* | *I don't like your tone of voice.* (=used when you think someone is being rude to you because of the way their voice sounds)

2 | writing/activity | [singular,U] the general feeling or attitude expressed in a piece of writing, an activity etc.: *The tone of the play is very moralistic.* | *Although liberal in tone, the 1787 Constitution did not abolish slavery.* | *Jordan's 25 points in the first quarter set the tone* (=established the general attitude or feeling) *for the game.*

3 | sound | [C,U] the quality of a sound, especially the sound of a musical instrument or someone's voice: *Tony's guitar has a nice tone.* | **deep-toned/even-toned/shrill-toned** etc. *a nasal-toned Brooklyn voice*

4 | color | [C] one of the many types of a particular color, each slightly darker, lighter, brighter etc. than the next; SHADE: *A lighter tone of yellow would look better in the kitchen.* —see also TWO-TONE

5 | electronic sound | [C] a sound made by electronic equipment, such as a telephone: *Please leave a message after the tone.* —see also DIAL TONE

6 | body | [U] TECHNICAL how firm and strong your muscles, skin etc. are: *Swimming improves your muscle tone.*

7 | music | [C] TECHNICAL the difference in PITCH[1] (3) between two musical notes that are separated by one KEY[1] (4) on the piano

8 | voice level | [C] TECHNICAL the PITCH[1] (3) of someone's voice as they speak

9 | socially acceptable | [U] the degree to which something is considered polite, interesting, socially acceptable etc. | **lower/raise the tone** *That horrible building lowers the whole tone of the neighborhood.*

tone[2] *v.* [T] to improve the strength and firmness of your skin, muscles etc.: *It cleanses and tones your skin.*

tone sth ↔ down *phr. v.* [T] **1** to reduce the effect of something such as a speech or piece of writing, so that people will not be offended: *McEnroe has tried to tone down his bad-boy image in recent years.* **2** to make a color less bright

tone sth/sb ↔ up *phr. v.* [T] to make your body or part of your body feel healthier and stronger: *Aerobics really tones up your muscles.*

tone-deaf /'. ./ *adj.* unable to hear the difference between musical notes

tone lan·guage /'. ˌ../ *n.* [C] TECHNICAL a language such as Chinese, in which the way a sound goes up or down affects the meaning of the word

tone·less /'toʊnləs/ *adj.* a toneless voice does not express any feelings: *The chairman's voice was firm but toneless.* —**tonelessly** *adv.*

tone po·em /'. ˌ../ *n.* [C] a piece of music written to represent an idea, scene, or story

ton·er /'toʊnɚ/ *n.* [U] **1** a type of ink used in computer PRINTERS, PHOTOCOPIERS etc. **2** a liquid that you put on your face to make your skin feel good

Ton·ga /'tɑngə/ a country consisting of about 170 small islands in the southwest Pacific Ocean —**Tongan** /'tɑngən, 'tɑŋən/ *n., adj.*

tongs /tɑŋz, tɔŋz/ *n.* [plural] a tool that is U- or V-shaped, so that you can press the open ends together to pick things up

tongue /tʌŋ/ *n.*

1 | mouth | [C] the soft movable part inside your mouth that you use for tasting and speaking: *The computer, for disabled people, is operated using your tongue.* | *Rianne stuck her tongue out* (=put her tongue outside her mouth as a rude gesture) *at him.*

2 **have a sharp/silver/eloquent etc. tongue** also **sharp-tongued/silver-tongued/rough-tongued** etc. if you have a sharp, silver etc. tongue, or if you are sharp-tongued etc., you speak in a way that shows your anger, shows that you are able to express your ideas well etc.: *Virginia has quite a sharp tongue.*

3 slip of the tongue a mistake in something you say: *In an apparent slip of the tongue, Ms. Bianchi referred to Omaha as Oklahoma.*

4 bite your tongue to stop yourself from saying something because it is better not to: *When he said he was the best on the team, I just bit my tongue.* | **bite your tongue!** (=used to tell someone angrily that they should not say the type of thing they have just said)

5 | language | [C] LITERARY a language: *Russian is not a tongue I speak.* —see also MOTHER TONGUE, **native tongue** (NATIVE[1] (3))

6 | shoe | the part of a shoe that lies on top of your foot, under the part where you tie it —see picture at SHOE[1]

7 watch your tongue! SPOKEN used to tell someone that they should not have said something rude

8 with tongue in cheek if you say something with tongue in cheek, you say it as a joke: *"I'm a big-city guy," he said with tongue in cheek.* —see also TONGUE-IN-CHEEK

9 roll/trips off sb's tongue if a name, phrase etc. rolls or trips off your tongue, it is easy or pleasant to say: *Answers rolled off her tongue during the press conference.*

10 | food | [U] the tongue of a cow or sheep, cooked and eaten as food

11 speak in tongues to speak using strange words as part of a religious experience: *Hearing people in the church speak in tongues fascinated me.*

12 tongues wagging INFORMAL used to mean that people are talking about someone in a way that is not nice: *Thurmond set tongues wagging again in 1968 when he married a woman 20 years younger than him.*

13 | shape | [C] LITERARY something that has a long thin shape: [+ of] *the thirsty tongues of tree roots*

14 loosen sb's tongue if something such as alcohol loosens your tongue, it makes you talk a lot: *The wine loosened his tongue.*

15 find your tongue to speak after being silent because you were afraid or shy: *When she came into the room, I had trouble finding my tongue.*

16 hold your tongue! OLD-FASHIONED, SPOKEN used to tell someone angrily to stop speaking

17 keep a civil tongue in your head OLD-FASHIONED, SPOKEN used when you think someone should speak politely

18 a tongue and groove joint TECHNICAL a type of connection between two pieces of wood —see also **Cat got your tongue?** (CAT[1] (7)), **speak with forked tongue** (FORKED (2)), **on the tip of your tongue** (TIP[1] (4))

tongue de·pres·sor /'. .,../ *n.* [C] a little flat piece of wood a doctor uses to hold down your tongue while examining your throat

tongue-in-cheek /,. . './ *adj.* a tongue-in-cheek remark, COMMENT etc. is said or done as a joke: *a tongue-in-cheek rock video* —**tongue-in-cheek** *adv.*

tongue-lash·ing /'. ,../ *n.* [C] an angry criticism of someone: *She gave the clerk a tongue-lashing for giving her the wrong change.*

tongue-tied /'. ./ *adj.* unable to speak easily to other people, especially because you feel embarrassed: *He often sounds tongue-tied in interviews.*

tongue twist·er /'. ,../ *n.* [C] a word or phrase that is difficult to say quickly and correctly, for example "she sells sea shells by the sea shore"

ton·ic[1] /'tɑnɪk/ *n.* **1** [C,U] also **tonic water** a clear bitter tasting drink that is mixed with alcoholic drinks such as GIN or VODKA: *I'll have a gin and tonic.* **2** [C usually singular] something that improves someone or something's health, strength, or confidence: *Humor was the tonic that brought Reeves out of his depression.* **3** [C] OLD-FASHIONED a type of liquid medicine, especially one that is designed to give you more energy or strength when you feel tired: *an herbal tonic* **4** [C usually singular] TECHNICAL the first note in a musical SCALE[1] (9)

tonic[2] *adj.* [only before noun] FORMAL improving something or making someone feel healthier and stronger: *It has had a tonic effect on stock prices.*

to·night[1] /tə'naɪt/ *adv.* on or during the night of today: *Let's go to a movie tonight.*

tonight[2] *n.* [U] the night of today: *Did you listen to tonight's weather report?*

ton·nage /'tʌnɪdʒ/ *n.* [C,U] **1** the size of a ship or the amount of goods it can carry, shown in TONS **2** the total number of TONS that something weighs

tons /tʌnz/ *adv.* INFORMAL very much: *Ricky is tons better looking than his brother.* —see also **tons of sth** (TON (3))

ton·sil /'tɑnsəl/ *n.* [C] one of two small round pieces of flesh at the sides of the throat near the back of the tongue: *The doctor said I had to have my tonsils out* (=have my tonsils removed by a doctor).

ton·sil·lec·to·my /,tɑnsə'lɛktəmi/ *n. plural* **tonsillectomies** [C] a medical operation in which one or both tonsils are removed

ton·sil·li·tis /,tɑnsə'laɪtɪs/ *n.* [U] a serious infection of the tonsils

ton·so·ri·al /tɑn'sɔriəl/ *adj.* HUMOROUS relating to the cutting or styling (STYLE[2]) of hair

ton·sure /'tɑnʃɚ/ *n.* [C,U] the act of removing a circle of hair from the top of your head to show that you are a MONK, or the part of your head that has had the hair removed in this way —**tonsured** *adj.*

ton·y /'touni/ *adj.* **tonier, toniest** INFORMAL fashionable, expensive, and having a lot of style: *a tony resort hotel*

too /tu/ *adv.* **1** [+ adj./adv.] more than is needed, wanted, or possible, or more than is reasonable: *It's too early to go to dinner now.* | **too much/little/many etc. sth** *You put too much salt on the casserole.* | **too tall/old etc. for** *The hat is too small for me.* | **too old/hot/big to do sth** *It's too cold to go outside.* | **much/far/way etc. too** *New York's way too expensive.* **2** [at the end of a sentence or clause]

also: *Thursday is Vivian's birthday too.* | *I love you, too.* —compare EITHER[4] **3** [+ adj./adv.] very: *I wasn't able to get too much sleep last night.* | *It won't be too long before dinnertime.* **4 all too/only too** used to say that something is very easy to do, happens very often etc., when it should not: *Violent behavior is all too common in our society.* **5 I am/he is/you are etc. too** INFORMAL used to emphasize that you disagree with what someone has said: *"I'm not good enough to be a professional actor." "You are too!"* **6 too little, too late** used to say that someone did not do enough to prevent something bad from happening: *A 3 percent funding increase is too little, too late to save the tutoring program.* **7** used to emphasize that you are angry or surprised, or that you agree with something: *"Seth finally got a job." "It's about time too."* —see also **too bad** (BAD[1] (15)) and see Usage Note at ALSO

took /tʊk/ *v.* the past tense of TAKE

tool[1] /tul/ *n.* [C] **1** something such as a hammer that you hold in your hand and use to make or repair things: *a carpenter's tools* —see picture on page 1534 and Usage Note at MACHINE[1] **2** something such as a piece of equipment or a skill that is useful for doing your job: *The Internet has been an effective tool for advertising.* | *Drugs, weapons, and hidden cameras are tools of the trade for undercover agents.* **3** someone who is used unfairly by someone else: [+ of] *Many see the senator as a tool of the auto industry.* **4** TABOO, SLANG a PENIS (=the male sex organ)   S W 2 2

tool[2] *v.* [I] INFORMAL to drive along a street, especially for fun: [+ around/along/down] *Gary Cooper used to tool around town in his green Bentley.*

tool up *phr. v.* [I,T **tool sth ↔ up**] to prepare a factory for production by providing the necessary tools and machinery: *Airplane factories were able to tool up quickly for expanded production when the war began.*

tool box /'. ./ *n.* [C] a special box that holds tools

tooled /tuld/ *adj.* tooled leather has been decorated using a special tool that presses designs into the leather

tool kit /'. ./ *n.* [C] a set of various tools

tool shed /'. ./ *n.* [C] a small building outside, where tools are kept

toon /tun/ *n.* [C] INFORMAL a short form of CARTOON (1)

too·nie, twoonie /'tuni/ *n.* [C] CANADIAN, INFORMAL a Canadian two-dollar coin

toot[1] /tut/ *v.* [I,T] **1** if you toot a horn, especially a car horn, or if it toots, it makes a short high sound: *A passing riverboat tooted its horn.* **2 toot your own horn** INFORMAL to tell other people about the good things you have done: *I don't want to toot my own horn, but nobody else has worked as hard as I have.* **3** INFORMAL to make air come out of your BOWELS; FART

toot[2] *n.* [C] a short high sound, made especially by a car horn

tooth /tuθ/ *n. plural* **teeth** /tiθ/ [C]
1 in mouth one of the hard white objects in your mouth that you use to bite and CHEW your food: *Brush your teeth twice a day.* | *The baby's cutting a tooth* (=growing a new tooth). | *The dog, a Rottweiler sank his teeth into* (=bit into) *the little girl's arm.*
2 on a tool etc. one of the pointed parts that sticks out from the edge of a comb, SAW, COG (1) etc.
3 fight tooth and nail to try with a lot of effort or determination to do something: *We had to fight tooth and nail to get the government to admit they were wrong.*
4 get/sink your teeth into sth INFORMAL to start to do something with eagerness and energy: *It's the kind of project I can really sink my teeth into.*
5 in the teeth of sth a) despite opposition or danger from something: *In the teeth of enormous social sanctions, women are making their own sexual choices.* **b)** experiencing bad weather: *The state is in the teeth of the worst snowstorm in a decade.*

T

6 set sb's teeth on edge if a sound, taste etc. sets your teeth on edge, it makes you feel physically uncomfortable: *His high-pitched squeaky voice set my teeth on edge.*
7 have teeth, give sth teeth if a law, REGULATION etc. has teeth, or if you give it teeth, it has the power to force people to obey it: *Critics of the law say it has no teeth and will not prevent violent crime.* —see also **cut your teeth on sth** (CUT¹ (32)), **a kick in the teeth** (KICK² (3)), **lie through your teeth** (LIE² (3)), **by the skin of your teeth** (SKIN¹ (5)), **have a sweet tooth** (SWEET¹ (10)), -TOOTHED

tooth·ache /ˈtuθeɪk/ *n.* [C,U] a pain in a tooth

tooth·brush /ˈtuθbrʌʃ/ *n.* [C] a small brush for cleaning your teeth —see picture at BRUSH¹

-toothed /tuθt/ [in adjectives] **sharp-toothed/saw-toothed/fine-toothed etc.** having sharp parts that stick out from the edge, parts like the edge of a SAW etc.: *saw-toothed mountain peaks* | *a fine-toothed comb* (=a comb with a lot of thin teeth set very close together)

tooth fair·y /ˈ. ,../ *n.* **the tooth fairy** an imaginary person that children believe comes into their BEDROOM to take the teeth that have come out of their mouth, and leaves them money for each tooth

tooth·less /ˈtuθlɪs/ *adj.* **1** having no teeth: *a toothless old man* **2** a law that is toothless has no power to make someone obey it: *Congress has passed several toothless gun control laws.*

tooth·paste /ˈtuθpeɪst/ *n.* [U] a substance used to clean your teeth

tooth·pick /ˈtuθ,pɪk/ *n.* [C] a very small pointed stick for removing pieces of food that are stuck between your teeth

tooth pow·der /ˈ. ,../ *n.* [U] a special powder used to clean your teeth

tooth·some /ˈtuθsəm/ *adj.* HUMOROUS tasting good; DELICIOUS: *toothsome chocolates*

tooth·y /ˈtuθi/ *adj.* **toothy smile/grin** a smile in which you show a lot of teeth

too·tle /ˈtutl/ *v.* [I] **1** to play an instrument such as a FLUTE, especially without producing any particular tune **2** OLD-FASHIONED to move slowly in a car

toots /tuts/ also **toot·sie** /ˈtutsi/ *n.* [C] SPOKEN, OLD-FASHIONED a way of talking to a woman, sometimes considered offensive: *Hey toots! How're you doing?*

toot·sies /ˈtutsiz/ *n.* [plural] INFORMAL a word meaning "toes," used especially by or to children

top¹ /tɑp/ *n.* [C]   SW 1 1
1 ‖the highest part‖ the highest part of something: *The elevator will take you all the way to the top.* | [the top of sth] *I could feel the sun on the top of my head.* | [at the top (of sth)] *At the top of the page, the teacher had written my grade.* | *Denise stood at the top of the stairs.* | *They had put his shoes at the very top* (=the highest part) *of the flag pole.* | **tree-top/ roof-top/hill-top etc.** *a beautiful hill-top chapel* —opposite BOTTOM¹
2 ‖upper surface‖ the flat upper surface of an object: *We got the Christmas tree home by tying it to the top of the car.* | *Boyd nervously tapped his pencil on the table top.*
3 ‖best position‖ **the top** the best, most successful, or most important position in an organization, company, group etc.: *She became a CEO at 37, making it to the top quicker than anyone imagined.* | [+ of] *Stong's intellect and drive helped him reach the top of his profession.* | **(at) the top of the class/division etc.** *Martins graduated at the top of his class.* —opposite BOTTOM¹ —see also TOP-OF-THE-LINE
4 ‖cover‖ something that you put on a pen, bottle etc. to close it, especially something that you push or turn: *Put the top back on the bottle when you're finished.*
5 ‖clothes‖ a piece of clothing that you wear on the upper part of your body: *The skirt comes with a matching top.* —see also **halter top** (HALTER (1)), TANK TOP
6 on top a) on the highest point or surface of something: *Sprinkle some Parmesan on top and grill.* | *You left your coffee on top of the car.* | *You*

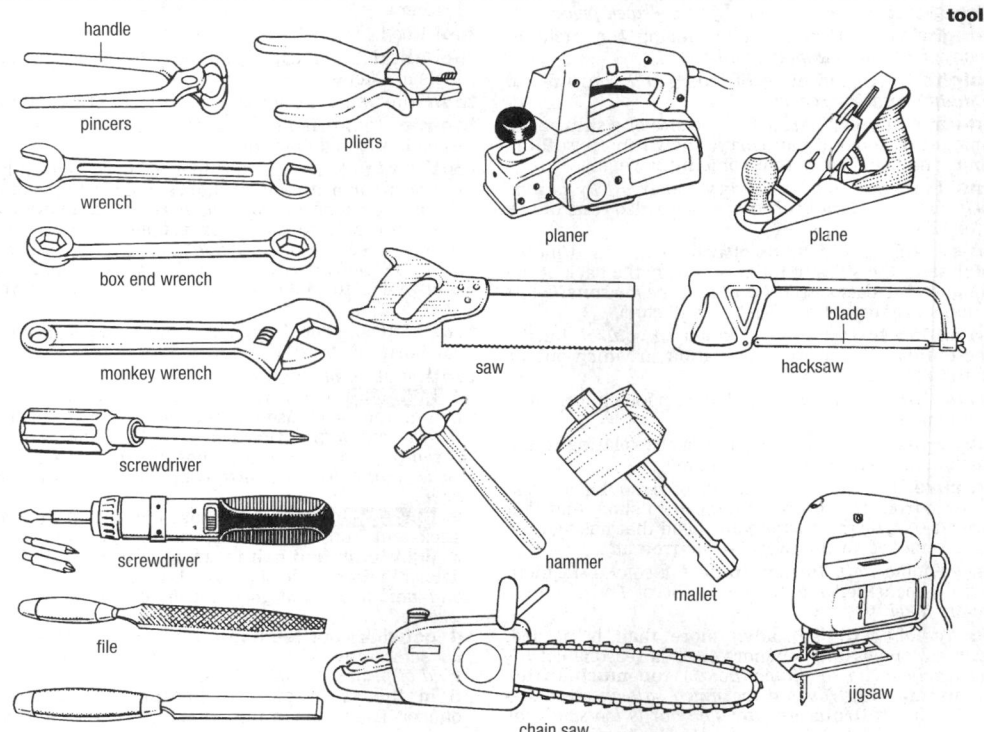

tools

handle

pincers

pliers

wrench

planer

plane

box end wrench

saw

blade

hacksaw

monkey wrench

screwdriver

screwdriver

hammer

mallet

file

jigsaw

chain saw

chisel

shouldn't have put the egg cartons **on top of each other.** —opposite UNDERNEATH **b)** in the most successful or important position in business, a game etc.: *Dallas was on top by 15 points at halftime.* **c)** on the highest part of your head: *My hair's too long on top.*

7 on top of sb/sth a) if someone or something is on top of you, they have moved very close to where you are: *FBI agents were on top of them before they could react.* **b)** if something bad happens to you on top of something else, it happens when you have other problems: *On top of losing my job, my car broke down.* **c)** in complete control of a job, situation etc.: *Nathan always stays on top of his studies.*

8 come out on top to win a difficult struggle or argument, especially one that has continued for a long time: *Usually the team with the most talent comes out on top.*

9 get on top of sth to work hard to gain control of a job, situation etc.: *Local police have failed to get on top of the gang situation.*

10 be (at the) top of the list/agenda something that is at the top of the list will be dealt with or discussed first: *Improving education is at the top of the mayor's agenda.*

11 on top of the world INFORMAL extremely happy: *After winning the batting title, Bagwell appeared to be on top of the world.*

12 (from) top to bottom if something is done from top to bottom, it is done very thoroughly: *The university's admission system was changed from top to bottom.* | *Police searched his apartment top to bottom.*

13 off the top of your head INFORMAL if you answer a question or provide information off the top of your head, you do it immediately without checking the facts: *"Do you remember her name?" "Not off the top of my head."*

14 sing/shout/yell etc. at the top of your voice also **sing/shout/yell etc. at the top of your lungs** to sing, shout etc. as loudly as you possibly can

15 plant [C] the part of a fruit or vegetable where it was attached to the plant, or the leaves of a plant whose root you can eat: *Cut the pineapples lengthwise, without removing the tops.*

16 from the top SPOKEN an expression meaning "from the beginning," used especially when practicing a play, acting a movie etc. *All right. Once more from the top. Action!*

17 tops SPOKEN used after a number to say that it is the highest possible amount of money you will get or pay: *It'll cost $15 tops.*

18 toy a child's toy that spins around on its point when the child twists it

19 be (the) top OLD-FASHIONED, INFORMAL to be the best

S W
3 3
top² *adj.* [only before noun]

1 highest in the highest place or position: *My keys are in the top drawer.* | *You have some peanut butter on your top lip.* | *the top left-hand corner of the page* —opposite BOTTOM²

2 most successful the most important or successful: *Sue is in the top 10% of her class.* | *Carlson is our top salesman.* —opposite BOTTOM²

3 best best or most successful: *top quality beef*

4 top speed the fastest speed a vehicle can move at: *The ferry's top speed is 25 mph.*

5 the top brass INFORMAL people in positions of high rank, especially in the army, navy etc.

6 top dog INFORMAL the person in the highest or most important position, especially after a struggle or effort

7 top copy a piece of written material that is produced first and from which copies have been or can be made.

8 high social class OLD-FASHIONED, INFORMAL from the highest social class

top³ *v.* **topped, topping** [T]

1 be higher to be higher or more than something: *U.S. wine exports have already topped $51 million this year.*

2 be topped by/with sth if something, especially a piece of clothing, a mountain, or a building, is topped by something else, it has that thing on its top: *The hotel is topped by the revolving View Restaurant.* | *The fence is topped with razor wire.*

3 be topped with sth to have something on the top: *The toasted garlic bread was topped with fresh tomato and basil.* —see also TOPPING

4 top the list/charts/agenda etc. to come first in a list or in an order of things: *Libraries topped the list of good public services.* —see also CHART-TOPPING

5 top an offer/bid etc. to offer more money than someone else: *Dutton topped their bid and bought the firm for $2.7 billion.*

6 be better to be better or greater than something else: *The appearance of Comet Hale-Bopp topped that of Comet Hyakutake.*

7 top that SPOKEN used to tell someone to do something better, say something funnier etc. than you have: *I work 90 hours a week – top that!*

8 to top it all (off) SPOKEN in addition to other bad things that have happened to you: *And to top it all off, I wrecked my car.*

9 reach the top LITERARY if you top a slope, hill, or mountain, you reach the top of it: *After two days of climbing, we finally topped the peak.*

top sth ↔ off *phr. v.* [T] **1** to complete something successfully by doing a last action or adding a last detail: *We topped off a perfect day by watching the sun set on the river.* **2** to fill a partly empty container with liquid: *Let me top off your drink.*

top out *phr. v.* [I] if something such as a price that is increasing tops out, it reaches its highest point and stops rising: *Real estate prices seem to have topped out.*

top sth ↔ up *phr. v.* [T] to fill a partly empty container with liquid: *I had him top up the fluid levels in the car.*

top 40 /ˌtɑp ˈfɔrți/ *n.* **1 the Top 40** the list of 40 most popular songs in the U.S. during a particular week: *Palmer's "Addicted to Love" hit the Top 40 in 1986.* **2** [U] POP MUSIC: *I like top 40 better than hard rock.* —**Top-40** *adj.*: *a Top-40 song*

to·paz /ˈtoupæz/ *n.* [C,U] a transparent yellow jewel or the mineral that it is cut from

top-class /ˌ. ˈ.◂/ *adj.* being the best, most skillful etc.: *Berkeley needed to pay higher salaries to attract top-class faculty.* | *top-class hotels*

top·coat /ˈtɑpkout/ *n.* **1** [C,U] the last layer of paint that is put on a surface **2** [C] OLD-FASHIONED a warm long coat

top-down /ˌ. ˈ.◂/ *adj.* **1 a top-down business/company/corporation etc.** a top-down business, company etc. is one in which all the ideas and decisions for running the business come from people in the highest positions **2** a top-down plan or way of thinking is one in which you start with a general idea of what you want and then add the details later

top-drawer /ˌ. ˈ.◂/ *adj.* INFORMAL of the highest quality or social class: *top-drawer antiques*

top dress·ing /ˈ. ˌ../ *n.* [C,U] TECHNICAL a layer of FERTILIZER that is spread over land

to·pee, topi /touˈpi, ˈtoupi/ *n.* [C] a hard hat for protecting your head in tropical SUNSHINE

To·pe·ka /təˈpikə/ the capital city of the U.S. state of Kansas

top-flight /ˌ. ˈ.◂/ *adj.* most successful, skillful, or important: *top-flight attorneys*

top gear /ˌ. ˈ./ *n.* [U] the highest GEAR of a car, bus etc.: *Engine noise is not a problem once it's in top gear.*

top-gross·ing /ˈ. ˌ../ *adj.* a top-grossing movie earns more money than any other movie at a particular time

top hat /ˈ. ˌ./ *n.* [C] a man's tall black or gray hat, now worn only on very formal occasions, such as a wedding —see picture at HAT

top-heav·y /ˈ. ˌ../ *adj.* **1** too heavy at the top and therefore likely to fall over **2** an organization that is top heavy has too many managers compared to the number of ordinary workers: *the school district's top-heavy administration*

to·pi /ˈtoupi, ˈtoupi/ *n.* [C] another spelling of TOPEE

to·pi·ar·y /'toʊpiˌɛri/ *n*. [U] trees and bushes cut into the shapes of birds, animals etc., or the art of cutting them in this way

top·ic /'tɑpɪk/ *n*. [C] a subject that people talk or write about: [+ **of**] *Griggs addressed the topic of sex education in schools.* | *Pedestrian safety has long been* **a hot topic** (=a topic people are very interested in now) *in the city.* | *Their divorce has been the main topic of conversation around here.*

top·i·cal /'tɑpɪkəl/ *adj*. **1** a story, subject, problem etc. that is topical is interesting because it deals with something that is important at the present time: *He is known for recording topical songs about social issues.* **2** relating to the top part or surface of something: *a topical anesthetic* (=a drug that is put on the skin) —**topically** /-kli/ *adv*. —**topicality** /ˌtɑpɪˈkæləti/ *n*. [U]

topic sen·tence /ˌ.. '../ *n*. [C] the sentence in a PARAGRAPH that states the main idea you are writing about

top·knot /'tɑpnɑt/ *n*. [C] hair that is tied together on the top of your head, or feathers that stick up on the top of a bird's head

top·less /'tɑplɪs/ *adj*. a woman who is topless is not wearing any clothes on the upper part of her body, so that her breasts are uncovered: **a topless bar/ show** (=one in which the women serving or performing are topless)

top-lev·el /ˌ. '..◂/ *adj*. [only before noun] involving the most powerful people in a country, organization etc.: *Munitz needs to fill some top-level positions within the university's staff.*

top·most /'tɑpmoʊst/ *adj*. [only before noun] the topmost part of something is its highest part: *the topmost row of seats*

top-notch /ˌ. '.◂/ *adj*. INFORMAL having the highest quality or standard: *top-notch scientists*

top-of-the-line /ˌ. . . '.◂/ *adj*. the best or most expensive of a group of things: *top-of-the-line computers*

to·pog·ra·phy /təˈpɑgrəfi/ *n*. [U] **1** the shape of an area of land, including its hills, valleys etc.: [+ **of**] *the mountainous topography of the county* **2** the science of describing an area of land, or making maps of it **3** the state of the different features of a society or country, such as the state of its CULTURE, ECONOMY etc.: *Latin America's religious topography is changing rapidly.* —**topographer** *n*. [C] —**topographical** /ˌtɑpəˈgræfɪkəl◂/ *adj*.

to·pol·o·gy /təˈpɑlədʒi, tɑ-/ *n*. [C] TECHNICAL the way in which a computer network is arranged

top·per /'tɑpɚ/ *n*. [C] INFORMAL a TOP HAT

top·ping /'tɑpɪŋ/ *n*. [C,U] something you put on top of food to make it look nicer or taste better: *vanilla ice cream with a chocolate topping*

top·ple /'tɑpəl/ *v*. **1** [T] to take power away from a leader or government, especially by force; OVERTHROW: *Political corruption threatens to topple the regime.* **2** [I,T] to become unsteady and then fall over, or to make something do this: *High winds toppled several telephone poles.* | [+ **over/to/backward** etc.] *The magazines toppled to the floor.*

top-ranked /ˌ. '.◂/ *adj*. considered by most people to be the best, especially at a particular sport: *the world's top-ranked golfer*

top-rank·ing /ˌ. '..◂/ *adj*. most powerful and important within an organization: *top-ranking diplomats*

top-rat·ed /ˌ. '..◂/ *adj*. INFORMAL very popular with the public: *a top-rated TV show*

top round /ˌ. '.◂/ *n*. [U] high quality BEEF cut from the upper leg of the cow

tops /tɑps/ *adj*. [not before noun] OLD-FASHIONED if someone or something is tops, they are the best: *Mussey was tops among international-fund managers.*

top-se·cret /ˌ. '..◂/ *adj*. top-secret documents or information must be kept completely secret: *top-secret government reports*

top·side /'tɑpsaɪd/ *adv*. toward or onto the DECK (=upper surface) of a boat or ship

top·soil /'tɑpsɔɪl/ *n*. [U] the upper level of soil, in which most plants have their roots

top·spin /'tɑpˌspɪn/ *n*. [U] the turning movement of a ball that has been hit or thrown in such a way that it spins forward: *Sampras put a lot of topspin on that serve.*

top·sy-tur·vy /ˌtɑpsi ˈtɚvi◂/ *adj*. INFORMAL **1** in a state of complete disorder or confusion: *Molly's topsy-turvy bedroom was heaped with toys, clothes, magazines, and books.* **2** having some very good parts and some very bad parts: *Ball can look back on a topsy-turvy two years as mayor.* **3** with the top part on the bottom, and the bottom part on the top; UPSIDE DOWN

toque /toʊk/ also **tuque** /tuk/ *n*. [C] CANADIAN a STOCKING CAP

To·rah /'tɔrə/ *n*. **the Torah** all the writings and teachings concerned with Judaism, especially the first five books of the Jewish Bible

torch[1] /tɔrtʃ/ *n*. [C] a long stick with burning material at one end that produces light: *the Olympic torch* —see also **carry a torch for sb** (CARRY[1] (29)), **carry the torch of sth** (CARRY[1] (30)), **pass the torch to sb** (PASS[1] (19))

torch[2] *v*. [T] INFORMAL to deliberately make a building start to burn: *Thibault was caught torching the restaurant.*

torch·light /'tɔrtʃlaɪt/ *n*. [U] the light produced by burning torches

torch song /'. ./ *n*. [C] a sad song about love that has ended or about loving someone who does not love you

tore /tɔr/ *v*. the past tense of TEAR[2]

tor·ment[1] /'tɔrmɛnt/ *n*. **1** [U] severe mental or physical suffering, often continuing for a long time: *The book's theme of incest and sexual torment was largely autobiographical.* **2** [C] someone or something that makes you suffer

tor·ment[2] /tɔrˈmɛnt, ˈtɔrmɛnt/ *v*. [T] **1** to make someone suffer a lot, especially so that they feel guilty or very unhappy: *Jealousy, fear, and suspicion tormented Harriet.* **2** to deliberately treat someone cruelly by annoying them or hurting them: *My older sister loved to torment me.* —**tormentor** *n*. [C]

torn[1] /tɔrn/ *v*. the past participle of TEAR[2]

torn[2] *adj*. **1** **be torn between sth and sth** to be unable to decide between two people or things, because you want both: *I'm torn between getting a new car and going on vacation.* **2** **be torn by sth** **a)** if a country or family is torn by an argument, war etc., it is very badly affected by it: *The nation is still torn by war and riots.* **b)** to feel very worried, guilty, anxious etc. because you are affected by a strong emotion or feeling that you think you should not have: *I was torn by my feelings of loyalty to him* (=I felt loyal to him, but I knew that he had done something wrong).

tor·na·do /tɔrˈneɪdoʊ/ *n*. plural **tornadoes** or **tornados** [C] an extremely violent storm consisting of air that spins very quickly and causes a lot of damage —compare HURRICANE, CYCLONE —see picture on page 1333

To·ron·to /təˈrɑntoʊ/ the capital and largest city of the Canadian PROVINCE of Ontario

tor·pe·do[1] /tɔrˈpidoʊ/ *n*. plural **torpedoes** [C] a long narrow weapon that is fired under the surface of the ocean and explodes when it hits something

torpedo[2] *v*. [T] **1** to attack or destroy a ship with a torpedo: *The Dutch ship was torpedoed by an enemy submarine in March of 1942.* **2** to stop something such as a plan from succeeding: *The CEO torpedoed the deal in its final hours.*

tor·pid /'tɔrpəd/ *adj*. FORMAL not active because you are lazy or sleepy, or making you feel like this: *By 1976, the union had become torpid, old, and bureaucratic.* —**torpidly** *adv*.

tor·por /'tɔrpɚ/ *n*. [singular,U] FORMAL a state of being not active because you are lazy or sleepy: *He had* *sunk into an intellectual torpor.* —**torpidity** /tɔr-ˈpɪdəti/ *n.* [U]

torque /tɔrk/ *n.* [U] TECHNICAL the force or power that makes something turn around a central point, especially in an engine

Tor·que·ma·da /ˌtɔrkəˈmɑdə/, **Tom·ás de** /touˈmɑs deɪ/ (1420–1498) a Spanish Christian leader who started the Spanish Inquisition, the Catholic organization that punished people whose religious beliefs were considered unacceptable

tor·rent /ˈtɔrənt, ˈtɑr-/ *n.* [C] **1** a large amount of water moving very rapidly and strongly in a particular direction: *Heavy rains had turned the small stream into a torrent.* **2 a torrent of abuse/criticism/protest etc.** a lot of insults, criticism etc. that someone suddenly receives: *The proposal received a torrent of criticism.*

tor·ren·tial /tɔˈrɛnʃəl, tə-/ *adj.* **torrential rain** very heavy rain

tor·rid /ˈtɔrɪd, ˈtɑr-/ *adj.* **1** involving strong emotions, especially of sexual love: *a torrid love affair* **2** increasing or happening very quickly: *Economies in these regions are growing at a torrid pace.* **3** LITERARY torrid weather is very hot: *the torrid heat of noon*

tor·sion /ˈtɔrʃən/ *n.* [U] TECHNICAL the twisting of a piece of metal

tor·so /ˈtɔrsoʊ/ *n.* [C] **1** your body, not including your head, arms, or legs: *He had burns over much of his torso.* **2** a STATUE of a torso

tort /tɔrt/ *n.* [C] LAW an action that is wrong but not criminal and can be dealt with in a CIVIL (3) court of law

torte /tɔrt/ *n.* [C,U] a type of cake made with a lot of eggs and very little flour: *chocolate torte*

tor·til·la /tɔrˈtiyə/ *n.* [C] a piece of thin flat bread made from corn or wheat flour, eaten in Mexican cooking

tor·toise /ˈtɔrtəs/ *n.* [C] a slow-moving land animal that can pull its head and legs into the hard round shell that covers its body —compare TURTLE

tor·toise·shell /ˈtɔrtəsˌʃɛl/ *n.* **1** [U] hard shiny brown and white material made from the shell of a tortoise: *a tortoiseshell brush* **2** [U] plastic material that looks like tortoiseshell: *tortoiseshell glasses* **3** [C] a cat that has yellow, brown, and black marks on its fur

tor·tu·ous /ˈtɔrtʃuəs/ *adj.* **1** a tortuous path, stream, road etc. has a lot of bends in it and is therefore difficult to travel along: *a tortuous mountain trail* **2** complicated and long and therefore confusing: *It took six months of tortuous negotiations to reach an agreement.* —**tortuously** *adv.* —**tortuousness** *n.*

tor·ture¹ /ˈtɔrtʃɚ/ *n.* **1** [U] an act of deliberately hurting someone in order to force them to tell you something, to punish them, or to be cruel: *The militias have been known to use torture to get people to confess.* **2** [C,U] severe physical or mental suffering: *What torture parent's lectures are for children!*

torture² *v.* [T] **1** to deliberately hurt someone to force them to give you information, to punish them, or to be cruel: *Several of the prisoners confirmed that they had been tortured.* **2** if a feeling or knowledge tortures you, it makes you suffer mentally: *He is still tortured by memories of the attack.* —**torturer** *n.* [C]

tor·tured /ˈtɔrtʃɚd/ *adj.* **1** full of pain: *a tortured look* **2** too long, difficult, or complicated: *the tortured logic of his argument*

tor·tur·ous /ˈtɔrtʃərəs/ *adj.* **1** too long, slow, or difficult: *my torturous summer language class* **2** causing pain: *torturous memories*

To·ry /ˈtɔri/ *n.* [C] INFORMAL **1** a member of the Progressive Conservative Party in Canada **2** a member of the Conservative Party in Great Britain

toss¹ /tɔs/ *v.*

1 throw [T] to throw something, especially something light, without much force: [**toss sth into/down/on etc.**] *I tossed the suitcase into the backseat.* | [**toss sth (over) to sb**] *Now toss the ball over to Steve.* | [**toss sb sth**] *Toss me a pillow.*

2 throw away [T] also **toss out** to get rid of something you do not want: *The hot dog tasted funny, so I tossed it.*

3 move [I,T] to move and turn around continuously in a violent or uncontrolled way, or make something do this: *The kite was being tossed by the wind.* | *I tossed and turned* (=kept changing my position in bed because I could not sleep) *all night trying to think of a solution.*

4 toss your head/hair to move your head back suddenly, often with a shaking movement: *The girl tossed her hair and twisted in her chair.*

5 in cooking [T] to cover food in a liquid by moving it around in the liquid: *Pour the marinade over the mushrooms and toss them lightly.*

6 toss the salad to mix the different parts of a SALAD

7 a coin [I,T] to make a coin go up and spin in the air, and then catch it to see which side is on top, used as a way of deciding something; FLIP¹

8 toss your cookies SPOKEN INFORMAL to VOMIT¹

toss sth ↔ **back** *phr. v.* [T] INFORMAL to drink something quickly: *He and some of his buddies had been tossing back beers all day.*

toss sth ↔ **in** *phr. v.* [T] INFORMAL to include something with something else: *Make your own gift pack, with wines, cheeses, and nuts, and toss in a fancy corkscrew.*

toss off *phr. v.* [T] INFORMAL **1** [**toss** sth ↔ **off**] to say or write something quickly without much effort: *She could toss off facts and figures convincingly.* **2** [**toss** sb **off**] to make someone leave a place or group, especially because of bad behavior: *She was tossed off the team for not turning up to practices.*

toss out *phr. v.* [T] INFORMAL **1** [**toss** sth ↔ **out**] to get rid of something you do not want: *All of my old baseball cards got tossed out when we moved.* **2** [**toss** sb **out**] to make someone leave a place, especially because of bad behavior: *Kurt got tossed out of the club for trying to start a fight.*

toss² *n.* [C] **1** also **coin toss** the act of throwing a coin in the air to decide something, especially to make a choice at the beginning of a game or race: **win/lose the (coin) toss** *The Raiders won the coin toss and had the first chance to score.* **2** a sudden backward movement of your head, so that your hair moves: *With a toss of her head, she walked out of the room.* **3** the act of gently throwing something: *George faked a toss to Kaufman, and ran in for a touchdown.*

tossed /tɔst/ *adj.* **a tossed (green) salad** a SALAD that is made by mixing together different types of food such as LETTUCE, TOMATOEs etc.

toss-up /ˈ. ./ *n.* [singular] INFORMAL **be a toss-up** used when you do not know which of two things will happen, or which of two things to choose: *It's a toss-up as to who will be picked the player of the year.*

tot¹ /tɑt/ *n.* [C] INFORMAL a very small child

tot² *v.* **totted, totting**

tot sth ↔ **up** *phr. v.* [T] INFORMAL to add together numbers or amounts of money in order to find the total: *Louis totted up the scores to see who was winning.*

to·tal¹ /ˈtoʊtl/ *adj.* **1** [only before noun] complete, and affecting or including everything: *The company was in total chaos before Richards arrived.* | *Roller skis provide an excellent total body workout.* **2 total number/amount/cost etc.** the number, amount etc. of all the numbers in a group added together: *Total manufacturing exports were $8.9 billion.*

total² *n.* [C] the final number or amount of things, people etc. when everything has been counted: *If you add 30 and 45 the total is 75.* | [+ **of**] *A total of thirty neighborhood meetings were conducted to discuss the issue.* | *In total, over 250 employees completed the safety training.* —see also **grand total** (GRAND¹ (2)), SUM TOTAL

total³ *v.* **1** [linking verb] to reach a particular total: *Contributions totaled $28,000.* **2** [T] INFORMAL to damage a car so badly that it cannot be repaired: *The truck was totaled, but no one was hurt.*

total sth ↔ **up** *phr. v.* [T] to find the total number or total amount of something by adding: *We'll have the results totaled up by the end of the week.*

to·tal·i·tar·i·an /toʊˌtæləˈtɛriən/ *adj.* based on a political system in which ordinary people have no power and are completely controlled by the government: *a totalitarian government* —**totalitarianism** *n.* [U]

to·tal·i·ty /toʊˈtæləti/ *n.* [U] FORMAL **1** the whole of something: *Cranston's political career should be judged on the totality of his accomplishments.* | *It's essential that we look at the problem in its totality* (=as a complete thing). **2** a total amount

S W
1
3
to·tal·ly¹ /ˈtoʊtl-i/ *adv.* completely: *Los Angeles is totally different from New York.* | *All of the ice had totally melted.* | *I agree totally.*

totally² *interjection* SLANG used to say that you agree with what someone has said: *"This is such a cool song." "Yeah, totally."*

Total Qual·i·ty Man·age·ment /ˌ.. ˈ... ...../ *abbreviation* **TQM** *n.* [singular] a system for making sure that each department in an organization works in the most effective way and that the goods or services it produces are of the best quality

tote /toʊt/ *v.* [T] INFORMAL also **tote around** to carry something, especially regularly: *My job was to tote their golf bags and wash their cars.*

tote bag /ˈ. ./ *n.* [C] a large bag for carrying things —see picture at BAG¹

to·tem /ˈtoʊtəm/ *n.* [C] a figure made to look like an animal, plant etc. that is believed to have a special SPIRITUAL relationship with a particular Native American TRIBE

totem pole /ˈ.. ˌ./ *n.* [C] **1** a tall wooden pole with one or more totems cut or painted on it, made by the Native Americans of northwest North America **2 low man on the totem pole** someone of low rank in an organization or business

to·to /ˈtoʊtoʊ/ —see IN TOTO

tot·ter /ˈtɑtɚ/ *v.* [I] **1** to walk or move in an unsteady way from side to side as if you are going to fall over: *She tottered into the room in red high-heeled shoes.* **2** if a political system or organization totters, it becomes less strong and is likely to stop working: *The country's welfare system is tottering toward collapse.* **3** if something such as a building totters, it moves and looks as if it is going to fall over —**tottering** *adj.*: *a tottering foot bridge*

tou·can /ˈtukæn, -kɑn/ *n.* [C] a tropical American bird with bright feathers and a very large beak

S W
1
2
touch¹ /tʌtʃ/ *v.*

1 feel [T] to put your finger, hand etc. on something or someone: *Don't touch that – the paint is still wet.* | *Wash your hands thoroughly after touching raw meat.* | *He gently touched her hand and smiled.*

2 no space between [I,T] if two things are touching, they reach each other so that there is no space between them: *Make sure the wires do not touch.* | [touch sth] *Don't let the flag touch the ground.*

3 not touch sth a) to not use or handle something: *Curt doesn't let anyone touch his golf clubs.* | *Don't touch that button* (=used to warn someone not to handle or touch something because it is dangerous or not allowed)! **b)** to not eat or drink something: *What's wrong? You've haven't touched your dinner.* | *James never touches the stuff* (=does not drink alcohol). **c)** to not do any work on or give any time to something that needs work or attention: *There's a stack of mail on his desk that hasn't been touched.*

4 not touch sb to not hit someone or hurt them physically: *Hardin claimed he never touched the man.*

5 touch a nerve to mention a subject that makes someone feel upset or angry: *Your comment about his mom really touched a nerve.*

6 make sb feel emotions [T] to affect someone's emotions, especially by making them feel pity or sympathy: *Their insults and criticism never seemed to touch him.* | *The pictures touched everyone present.* —see also TOUCHED

7 deal with sth [T] to deal with or become involved with a particular matter, situation, or problem: *He was the only lawyer who would touch the case.*

8 be touched by sth to be affected by something: *Many had come from nations touched by famine or civil war.*

9 touch base (with sb on sth) to talk for a short time with someone in order to discuss something or give them information: *I'm calling to touch base with you on the Simons proposal.*

10 wouldn't touch sth/sb with a ten-foot pole SPOKEN used to say that something is bad in some way and you do not want to get involved with it: *Most politicians wouldn't touch the issue of abortion with a ten-foot pole.*

11 have an effect on sb/sth [T] to have an effect on someone or something, especially by changing or influencing them: *Every business Gibbons touches becomes successful.*

12 expression [T] if an expression such as a smile touches your face, your face has that expression for a short time: *A slight grin touched his face when he was told the news.*

13 nothing/no one can touch sth also **there is nothing/no one that can touch sth** used to say that nothing or no one is as good as something or someone: *Nothing can touch the experience of skydiving.*

14 relate to [T] to concern a particular subject, situation, or problem: *Though the question touched a new vein, Nelson answered promptly.*

15 touch bottom to reach the ground at the bottom of the ocean, a river etc.: *The lake was too deep for their long poles to touch bottom.*

touch down *phr. v.* [I] if an aircraft or space vehicle touches down, it goes down to the ground: *Their flight is scheduled to touch down at 4 p.m.*

touch sth ↔ **off** *phr. v.* [T] to cause a difficult situation or violent events to begin: *The incident which touched off the crisis was a relatively minor one.*

touch on/upon sth *phr. v.* [T] to mention or deal with a particular subject for a short period of time when talking or writing: *Many other psychological issues are touched upon in the book.*

touch sth ↔ **up** *phr. v.* [T] to improve something by changing it or adding to it slightly: *She quickly touched up her lipstick.*

touch² *n.*

S W
2
2
1 act of touching [C usually singular] the action of putting your finger, hand etc. on someone or something, either deliberately or not deliberately: *He felt a touch on his shoulder and saw it was Mrs. Lyden.*

2 get in touch to write or speak to someone on the telephone in order to tell them something: [+ with] *You can get in touch with me at the office if necessary.*

3 keep/stay in touch to speak or write to someone when you cannot see them as often as you used to: [+ with] *She makes an effort to keep in touch with friends from her hometown.*

4 be in touch to speak to someone, especially on the telephone, or to write to someone about something: [+ with] *Fisher has not been in touch with our office regarding the decision.*

5 lose touch to not speak or write to someone anymore, because they do not live near you, work with you etc.: [+ with] *After he moved to Utah, I lost touch with Jason.*

6 put sb in touch with sb to give someone the name, address, or telephone number of a person or organization they need: *Gary put me in touch with a good lawyer.*

7 with/at the touch of a button used to emphasize that you can do something easily by pressing a button: *With the touch of a button, the satellite dish can be turned.*

8 a touch of sth a very small amount of something: *All this room needs is a touch of paint.* | *I think I've got a touch of the flu.*

9 sense [U] the sense that you use to discover what something feels like, by putting your hand or another part of your body on it: *The car's control buttons are impossible to distinguish by touch.* | *My forehead was hot to the touch.*

10 be/keep/stay in touch with sth to have or get the latest information, knowledge, and understanding about a subject: *Use the Internet to keep in touch with the latest sports news.*

11 lose touch with sth also **be out of touch with sth** to not have the correct information or a good understanding about a subject anymore: *The citizens' group was out of touch with residents' wishes.*

12 detail/addition [C] a small detail that improves or completes something: *The ice caves added a nice touch to what could have been a typical roller coaster.* | **finishing touch/touches** *The chef is putting the finishing touches on the cake.*

13 way of doing sth [C] a particular way of doing something: *Great service and a friendly staff give the hotel a personal touch.*

14 ability to do sth your ability to do something: *Reid has a good touch for shooting the ball.* | *Judging from his latest novel, Goldman hasn't lost his touch.*

15 get in touch with sth to realize and understand something, especially your feelings or someone else's: *I'm finally able to get in touch with who I am.*

16 feel sb/sth [C usually singular] the way that someone or something feels and the effect they have on your body: *The soft touch of a clean cotton shirt was comforting.*

17 a touch cold/strange/unfair etc. slightly cold, strange etc.: *I was feeling a touch annoyed with her.* —see also **the common touch** (COMMON[1] (11)), **the midas touch** (MIDAS TOUCH), a **soft touch** (SOFT (13))

touch-and-go /ˌ. . '.◂/ *adj.* INFORMAL in a touch-and-go situation, there is a serious risk that something bad could happen: *It'll be touch-and-go for the first three days after the operation.*

touch-down /'tʌtʃdaʊn/ *n.* [C] **1** an act of moving the ball across the opposing team's GOAL LINE in football **2** the moment at which an airplane or SPACECRAFT comes down and touches the ground

tou-ché /tuˈʃeɪ/ *interjection* used when you want to emphasize in a humorous way that someone has made a very good point against you during an argument

touched /tʌtʃt/ *adj.* [not before noun] **1** feeling happy and grateful because of what someone has done for you: [+ by] *I was really touched by the invitation.* | **[touched that]** *Jane was touched that you came to visit her.* —see also TOUCH[1] (6) **2** OLD-FASHIONED, INFORMAL slightly strange in your behavior

touch foot·ball /ˌ. '../ *n.* [U] a type of football in which you touch the person with the ball instead of tackling (TACKLE[1] (2)) them

touch·ing[1] /'tʌtʃɪŋ/ *adj.* affecting your emotions, especially making you feel pity, sympathy, sadness etc.: *Fox gave a touching tribute to his late father.* —**touchingly** *adv.* —see also TOUCH[1] (6)

touching[2] *prep.* FORMAL concerning: *Feingold will give evidence touching on the current case.*

touch-line /'tʌtʃlaɪn/ *n.* [C] a line along each of the two longer sides of a sports field, especially in SOCCER

touch screen /'. ./ *n.* [C] a special computer screen that you touch with your finger or a special electronic pen in order to choose something from the screen that you want the computer to do

touch·stone /'tʌtʃstoʊn/ *n.* [C] something used as a test or standard: [+ of] *Motherhood is seen as a touchstone of female identity.*

Touch-Tone phone, touch-tone phone /ˌ. '. ./ *n.* [C] TRADEMARK a telephone that produces different sounds when different numbers are pushed

touch-type /'. ./ *v.* [I] to be able to use a TYPEWRITER or computer KEYBOARD without having to look at the letters while you are using it

touch-up /'. ./ *n.* [C] a small improvement you make to something by changing it or adding to it slightly

touch·y /'tʌtʃi/ *adj.* **touchier, touchiest 1** easily becoming offended or annoyed: *He's a little touchy about how you pronounce his name.* **2 touchy subject/question etc.** a subject, question etc. that needs to be dealt with very carefully: *The presence of U.S. troops there has been a touchy issue for years.* —**touchily** *adv.* —**touchiness** *n.* [U]

---

touchy-feel·y /ˌ.. '../ *adj.* DISAPPROVING too concerned with feelings and emotions, rather than with facts or action: *a touchy-feely drama*

tough[1] /tʌf/ *adj.*   S W / 1 / 2

1 difficult difficult to do or deal with, and needing a lot of effort and determination: *Being the new kid at school is always tough.* | *The investigators asked a lot of tough questions.* | *It was a tough call* (=difficult decision), *but we had to cancel the fair because of the weather.*

2 strong people very determined and able to deal with or live through difficult or severe conditions: *Geri's a tough lady.* | **a tough cookie/customer/nut** (=someone who is very determined to do what they want) —see also **as tough/hard as nails** (NAIL[1] (4))

3 strict very strict or determined: [+ on/with] *Mom was always very tough with us kids.* | *Jordan has promised to get tough on* (=deal with them in a strict way) *drugs.* | *The President is taking a tough line on* (=being very strict about) *trade issues.*

4 food difficult to cut or eat: *The meat was tough and stringy.* —opposite TENDER[1] (1)

5 strong thing not easily broken or made weaker: *The box is made of tough durable plastic.*

6 not sorry SPOKEN also **tough luck, tough shit** VULGAR said when you do not have any sympathy for someone's problems: *She didn't tell us she was coming, so if this screws up her plans that's just tough.*

7 tough luck also **tough break** SPOKEN said when you feel sympathy for someone's problems: *Oh, you can't come tomorrow? Tough luck.*

8 not gentle likely to behave violently and having no gentle qualities: *Everyone thinks Jack is a tough guy, but he's really very sweet.*

9 violent area a tough part of a town has a lot of crime or violence: *a tough neighborhood*

10 unfortunate unfortunate in a way that seems unfair, and causing you problems: [+ on] *Losing his job was tough on him.*

11 tough love love and strictness at the same time —**toughly** *adv.* —**toughness** *n.* [U]

tough[2] *v.*

tough sth ↔ out *phr. v.* [T] INFORMAL to manage to stay in a difficult situation by being determined: *We weren't used to the cold winters, but we toughed it out.*

tough[3] *adv.* INFORMAL in a way that shows that you are determined or strong: *The team plays tough when it has to.* —see also **talk tough** (TALK[1] (20))

tough[4] *n.* [C] OLD-FASHIONED someone who often behaves in a violent way

tough·en /'tʌfən/ *v.* [I,T] also **toughen up** to become tougher or make someone or something tougher: *The state is toughening its anti-smoking laws.*

tough·ie /'tʌfi/ *n.* [C] SPOKEN **1** a difficult question, problem, situation etc.: *"Who are your role models?" "That's a toughie. I'm not really sure."* **2** someone who is very strict, or not strict at all

Tou·louse-Lau·trec /tʊˌluz looˈtrɛk/, **Hen·ri de** /ɑnˈri də/ (1864–1901) a French PAINTER famous for his pictures of PROSTITUTEs, dancers, actors etc. and his theater POSTERS

tou·pee, toupée /tuˈpeɪ/ [C] a small artificial piece of hair that some men wear over a place on their heads where the hair does not grow anymore

tour[1] /tʊr/ *n.* [C]   S W / 2 / 2   **1** a trip for pleasure, during which you visit several different towns, areas etc.: *a bicycle tour* | [+ of] *a four-month tour of South America* —see also PACKAGE TOUR **2** a short trip through a place to see it: [+ of/through/around] *They took us on a tour of the campus.* **3** a planned trip made by musicians, a sports team, a politician etc. in order to perform, play, speak etc. in several places: [+ of] *The musical is making a year-long tour of the U.S. and Canada.* | *Jennings is on tour promoting his new children's book.* | *The last leg of its Asian tour* (=the last part of its tour) *will take the band to Tokyo.* **4** a period during which you go to live somewhere, usually abroad, to do your job, especially military work:

  T

a three-year tour in Germany with the Army —see also TOUR OF DUTY **5 tour of inspection** an official visit to a place, institution, group etc. in order to check its quality or performance

tour² v. [I,T] to visit somewhere on a tour: Sosa toured the world with an Afro-Cuban jazz band.

tour de force /ˌtʊr də ˈfɔrs/ n. [singular] something that is done very skillfully and successfully, in a way that seems impressive to people: Hartman's new novel is a literary tour de force.

tour·ism /ˈtʊrɪzəm/ n. [U] the business of providing things for people to do, places for them to stay etc. while they are on vacation: Tourism is an important part of Egypt's economy.

tour·ist /ˈtʊrɪst/ n. [C] someone who is traveling or visiting a place for pleasure

tourist at·trac·tion /ˈ.. .,../ n. [C] a place or event that a lot of tourists go to: The Grand Canyon is Arizona's biggest tourist attraction.

tourist class /ˈ.. ,./ n. [U] the cheapest standard of traveling conditions on an airplane, ship etc.

tourist of·fice /ˈ.. ,../ also **tourist in·for·ma·tion of·fice** /ˌ.. ..'.. ,../ n. [C] an office that gives information to tourists in an area

tourist town /ˈ.. ,./ n. [C] a town that tourists visit

tourist trap /ˈ.. ,./ n. [C] a place that many tourists visit, but where drinks, hotels etc. are more expensive

tour·ist·y /ˈtʊrɪsti/ adj. INFORMAL, DISAPPROVING **1** a place that is touristy is full of tourists and the things that attract tourists: Niagara Falls is too touristy for me. **2** a touristy activity is typical of the things that tourists do: Of course we did all the touristy things while we were in Washington.

tour·na·ment /ˈtʊrnəmənt, ˈtɔr-/ n. [C] **1 a tennis/chess/basketball etc. tournament** a competition in which players compete against each other in a series of games until there is one winner **2** a competition to show courage and fighting skill between soldiers in the Middle Ages

tour·ney /ˈtʊrni, ˈtɔr-/ n. [C] INFORMAL a TOURNAMENT (1)

tour·ni·quet /ˈtʊrnɪkɪt, ˈtɔr-/ n. [C] a band of cloth that is twisted tightly around an injured arm or leg to stop it from bleeding

tour of du·ty /ˌ.. ˈ../ n. plural **tours of duty** [C] a period of time when you are working in a particular place or job, especially abroad while you are in the military

tour op·er·a·tor /ˈ. ,..../ n. [C] a company that arranges travel TOURS

tour·ti·ère /ˌtʊrtiˈɛr/ n. [C] a type of meat PIE eaten in Canada

tou·sle /ˈtaʊzəl, -səl/ v. [T] to make someone's hair look messy

tou·sled /ˈtaʊzəld/ adj. tousled hair or a tousled appearance looks messy: Beth smoothed her tousled hair.

tout¹ /taʊt/ v. **1** [T] to praise something or someone in order to persuade people that they are important or valuable: Chef Foley was one of the first to tout Midwestern cuisine. | [be touted as sth] Marijuana has been touted as a useful treatment for glaucoma. **2** [I,T] to try to persuade people to buy goods or services you are offering: Slick ads tout everything from beauty products to electronic gadgets. **3** [I,T] to give someone information about a horse in a race

tout² n. [C] someone who tries to sell goods or services to people passing on the street in a determined or annoying way

tow¹ /toʊ/ v. [T] to pull a vehicle or ship along behind another vehicle, using a rope or chain: [tow sth away] When I came back the car had been towed away. —see picture on page 1504

tow² n. **1 in tow** INFORMAL following closely behind someone or something: Hannah arrived with her four kids in tow. **2** [C] an act of pulling a vehicle behind another vehicle, using a rope or chain **3 take sth in**

tow to connect a rope or a chain to a vehicle or ship so that it can be towed

to·ward /tɔrd, təˈwɔrd/ also **towards** prep. **1** moving, looking, or pointing in a particular direction: Sheila was coming toward us across the parking lot. | All the windows face towards the river. **2** a feeling, attitude etc. toward someone or something is how you feel or what you think about them: I was surprised by Carolyn's anger toward her mother. **3** if you do something toward something, you do it in order to achieve it: Both sides appear to be working toward an agreement. **4** near or just before a particular time: We left toward the middle of the afternoon. **5** money put, saved, or given toward something is used to pay for it: Half of the money will be put toward the fight against AIDS. **6** near a particular place: He lives somewhere over toward the coast.

tow·a·way zone /ˈtoʊəweɪ ˌzoʊn/ n. [C] an area where cars are not allowed to park, and from which they can be taken away by the police

tow·boat /ˈtoʊboʊt/ n. [C] a TUG² (1)

tow·el /ˈtaʊəl/ n. [C] a piece of cloth that you use for drying your skin or for drying things such as dishes: a bath towel —see also PAPER TOWEL, **throw in the towel** at **throw in** (THROW¹)

towel² v.
  towel off phr. v. [I,T **towel** sth ↔ **off**] to dry yourself or something else using a towel: Paula climbed out of the pool and toweled off.

towel bar /ˈ.. ,./ n. [C] a TOWEL RACK

tow·el·ette /ˌtaʊəˈlɛt/ n. [C] a small piece of soft wet paper that you use to clean your hands or face

tow·el·ing /ˈtaʊəlɪŋ/ n. [U] thick soft cloth, used especially for making TOWELS or BATHROBES

towel rack also **towel rail** /ˈ.. ,./ n. [C] a bar or frame on which TOWELS can be hung, especially in a BATHROOM

tow·er¹ /ˈtaʊər/ n. [C] **1** a tall narrow building either built on its own or forming part of a castle, church etc.: a clock tower **2** a tall structure, often made of metal, used for signaling, broadcasting etc.: radio towers **3 tower of strength** someone who gives you a lot of help, sympathy, and support when you are in trouble: My mother has been a tower of strength. —see also COOLING TOWER, **ivory tower** (IVORY (3)), WATER TOWER

tower over

Gary is the tallest on the team, towering over all his teammates.

tower² *v.* [I] **1** to be much taller than the people or things around you: [+ over/above] *Mrs. Liepa towers over her husband.* **2** to be much better than any other person or organization that does the same thing as you: [+ over/above] *Edwards towered above other religious thinkers of his day.*

tow·er·ing /ˈtaʊərɪŋ/ *adj.* [only before noun] **1** very tall: *towering redwood trees* **2** much better than other people of the same kind: *a towering figure in Supreme Court history* **3 in a towering rage** very angry

tower mod·el /ˈ.. ˌ../ *n.* [C] a computer in the shape of a tall box

tow·head /ˈtoʊhɛd/ *n.* [C] someone with very light-colored, almost white, hair —**towheaded** *adj.*

tow·line /ˈtoʊlaɪn/ *n.* [C] a rope or chain used for pulling vehicles

town /taʊn/ *n.*
1 ❚place❚ [C] an area with houses, stores, offices etc. where people live and work that is smaller than a city: *He grew up in a small town.* | *a town of about 35,000 people*
2 ❚where you live❚ [U] the town or city where you live: *I'll be out of town for about a week.* | *Let's get together while you're in town.* | *Do we have any visitors today from out of town* (=from a different town)? | *The Cubs are coming to town Friday.*
3 ❚main center❚ [U] the business or shopping center of a town: *I need to go into town to do a little shopping.* —see also DOWNTOWN
4 go to town (on sth) INFORMAL to do something in a very eager or thorough way: *Sandy went to town on the displays.*
5 on the town INFORMAL going to restaurants, bars, theaters etc. for entertainment in the evening: *Frank is taking me out for a night on the town.*
6 ❚people❚ [singular] all the people who live in a particular town: *Just about the whole town showed up at the funeral.* —see also GHOST TOWN, **paint the town (red)** (PAINT² (6))

town cen·ter /ˌ. ˈ../ *n.* [C] the main business area in the center of a town; DOWNTOWN

town clerk /ˌ. ˈ./ *n.* [C] an official who keeps records for a town

town coun·cil /ˌ. ˈ../ *n.* [C] a group of elected officials who are responsible for governing a town and making its laws

town cri·er /ˌ. ˈ../ *n.* [C] someone employed in past times to walk around the streets of a town, shouting news, warnings etc.

town hall /ˌ. ˈ./ *n.* [C] a public building used for a town's local government

town·house, town house /ˈtaʊnhaʊs/ *n.* [C] **1** also **townhome** a house in a row of houses that share one or more walls **2** a house in a town or city, especially a fashionable one in a central area

town·ie /ˈtaʊni/ *n.* [C] INFORMAL someone who lives in a town, especially a town that other people often visit

town meet·ing /ˌ. ˈ../ also **town hall meet·ing** /ˌ. . ˈ../ *n.* [C] **1** a meeting at which the people who live in a town discuss subjects or problems that affect their town **2** a large discussion in which many different people can express their opinions, especially one using television, radio, or telephones: *a nationwide town meeting on crime*

town plan·ning /ˌ. ˈ../ *n.* [U] the study of the way towns work, so that roads, houses, services etc. can be provided as effectively as possible

town·ship /ˈtaʊnʃɪp/ *n.* [C] **1** a town in Canada or the U.S. that has some local government **2** a part of a U.S. COUNTY that has some local government **3** a town in South Africa where Black citizens live: *the black township of Soweto*

towns·peo·ple /ˈtaʊnzˌpipəl/ also **towns·folk** /ˈtaʊnz foʊk/ *n.* [plural] all the people who live in a particular town

tow·path /ˈtoʊpæθ/ *n.* [C] a path along the side of a CANAL or river, used especially in past times by horses pulling boats

tow rope /ˈ. ./ *n.* [C] a TOWLINE

tow truck /ˈ. ./ *n.* [C] a strong truck that is used to pull cars behind it

tox·e·mi·a /tɑkˈsimiə/ *n.* [U] a medical condition in which your blood contains poisons

tox·ic /ˈtɑksɪk/ *adj.* poisonous, or containing poison: *toxic chemicals* —**toxicity** /tɑkˈsɪsəti/ *n.* [U]

tox·i·col·o·gy /ˌtɑksɪˈkɑlədʒi/ *n.* [U] the science and medical study of poisons and their effects

toxic shock syn·drome /ˌ.. ˈ. ˌ../ *n.* [U] also **toxic shock** a serious illness that causes a high temperature and is thought to be related to the use of TAMPONS

toxic waste /ˌ.. ˈ./ *n.* [C,U] waste products from industry that are harmful to people, animals, or the environment

tox·in /ˈtɑksɪn/ *n.* [C] a poisonous substance, especially one that is produced by BACTERIA and causes a particular disease

toy¹ /tɔɪ/ *n. plural* **toys** [C] **1** an object for children to play with: *Did you get any new toys for your birthday?* | *toy boat/car/truck etc. The kids were fighting with toy guns and plastic swords.* **2** an object that you buy because it gives you pleasure and enjoyment: *The red Porsche is his latest toy.* ❙S W 2 3❙

toy² *v.* **toys, toyed, toying**
toy with *phr. v.* [T] **1** [toy with sth] to think about an idea or possibility, usually for a short time and not very seriously: *The new owners briefly toyed with the idea of selling the building.* **2** [toy with sth] to move and touch an object, often while you are thinking about something else: *Rodrigues toyed with a pen as he spoke.* **3** [toy with sb/sth] to treat someone in a way that shows you do not respect them or are trying to control them, especially by making them think you like or love them when you do not: *The kidnappers are toying with the emotions of the families involved.*

toy³ *adj.* [only before noun] a toy animal or dog is a type of dog that is specially bred to be very small

toy boy /ˈ. ./ *n.* [C] INFORMAL a young man who is having a sexual relationship with an older woman

toy·mak·er /ˈtɔɪˌmeɪkɚ/ *n.* [C] a person or a company that makes toys

TQM /n.* [U] the abbreviation of TOTAL QUALITY MANAGEMENT

trace¹ /treɪs/ *v.*
1 ❚origins❚ [I,T usually passive] to find the origins of something in a place, time, or action, or have origins there: *The tradition traces back to medieval Spain.* | [trace sth (back) to sth] *The success of the company can be traced to good marketing.*
2 ❚history/development❚ [T] to study or describe the history, development, or progress of something: *Students will trace the development of labor unions in the U.S.*
3 ❚copy❚ [T] to copy a drawing, map etc. by putting a piece of paper over it and then drawing the lines you can see through it: *"Did you draw this yourself?" "No, I traced it."*
4 ❚find sb/sth❚ [T] to find someone or something that has disappeared by searching for them carefully: *Police are still trying to trace the missing child.*
5 ❚draw❚ [T] to draw real or imaginary lines on the surface of something, usually with your finger or toe [trace sth on/in/across] *Jen traced her name in the sand.*
6 ❚telephone❚ [T] to find out where a telephone call is coming from by using special electronic equipment: *Keep him on the line so we can trace the call.* —**traceable** *adj.*

trace² *n.*
1 ❚small amount❚ [C] a very small amount of a quality, emotion, substance etc. that is difficult to see or notice: [+ of] *a trace of poison* | *Rosenfeld speaks English with no trace of an accent.*
2 ❚sign of sth❚ [C,U] a small sign that shows that someone or something was present or existed:

T

Stewart checked all the hospitals in the area but found *no trace of* his brother. | Cook the chicken until it has lost *all trace of* pink. | **disappear/ vanish/sink without a trace** (=disappear completely, without leaving any sign of what happened) **3** telephone [C] TECHNICAL a search to find out where a telephone call came from, using special electronic equipment: [+ on] *Could the police have put a trace on the call that fast?* **4** recorded information [C] the mark or pattern made on a SCREEN or on paper by a machine that is recording an electrical signal: *This trace shows the heartbeat.* **5 kick over the traces** to stop following the rules of a social group and do what you want **6** cart/carriage [C] one of the two pieces of leather, rope etc. by which a CART or carriage is fastened to the animal that is pulling it

trace el·e·ment /ˌ. ˈ.../ *n.* [C] TECHNICAL **1** a chemical ELEMENT that your body needs a very small amount of to live **2** a chemical ELEMENT that only exists in small amounts on Earth

trac·er /ˈtreɪsɚ/ *n.* [C] a bullet that leaves a line of smoke or flame behind it

trac·er·y /ˈtreɪsəri/ *n.* [C,U] **1** TECHNICAL the curving and crossing lines of stone in the upper parts of Gothic church windows **2** LITERARY an attractive pattern of lines that cross each other

tra·che·a /ˈtreɪkiə/ *n.* [C] TECHNICAL the tube that takes air from your throat to your lungs

tra·che·ot·o·my /ˌtreɪkiˈɑtəmi/ *n.* [C] TECHNICAL an operation to cut a hole in someone's throat so that they can breathe

trac·ing /ˈtreɪsɪŋ/ *n.* [C] a copy of a map, drawing etc. made by tracing (TRACE[1] (3)) it

tracing pa·per /ˈ.. ˌ../ *n.* [U] strong transparent paper used for tracing (TRACE[1] (3))

track[1] /træk/ *n.*
1 keep track of sb/sth to pay attention to someone or something so that you know where they are or what is happening to them: *When you work in a busy office, keeping track of documents can be very difficult.* —opposite **lose track of sb/sth**
2 be on the right track to be doing or thinking things that are likely to make you succeed: *Over half the country thinks the economy is on the right track.* —opposite **be on the wrong track**
3 on track a) in a situation that is likely to lead to success: *Adams has announced a complete reorganization to get the company on track.* | **be/get/stay on track** *We want to make sure our relations with Russia stay on track.* **b)** dealing with the same subject that was being discussed, without changing to something new: **keep/stay on track** *The talks have stayed on track.*
4 off track a) in a situation that is likely to lead to failure: *Sixty percent of those polled said the country has gone off track.* **b)** dealing with a new subject rather than the main one which was being discussed: *That's an interesting point, Katherine, but let's not get off track.*
5 for racing [C] a circular road around which runners, cars, horses etc. race, which often has a specially prepared surface
6 sports [U] **a)** the sport that involves running on a track: *He ran track in high school.* **b)** all the sports that involve running races, jumping, and throwing things: *Are you going to go out for track* (=join the school's track team) *this spring?*
7 music/song [C] one of the songs or pieces of music on a record, CASSETTE, or CD: *I really like the first two tracks on this album.*
8 marks on ground tracks [plural] the marks left on the ground by a moving person, animal, or vehicle, which are usually in a line: *tire tracks* | *Coyote tracks are similar to dog tracks.*
9 railroad [C] the two metal lines along which trains travel: *train tracks*
10 school a group or set of classes for a particular

group of students based on their abilities: *college-track classes* (=classes that prepare you for college)
11 direction [C] the direction or line taken by something as it moves: [+ of] *the track of the asteroid through space*
12 path/road [C] a narrow path or road with a rough uneven surface, especially one made by people or animals frequently moving through the same place: *A narrow track leads from the road to the cabins.*
13 make tracks INFORMAL to leave somewhere quickly, or hurry when going somewhere: *When the doors open, customers make tracks for the sale items.*
14 cover/hide your tracks to be careful not to leave any signs that could let people know where you have been or what you have done, because you want to keep it a secret: *Mozer covered his tracks by changing records of the illegal sales.*
15 be on the track of sb/sth to hunt or search for someone or something: *Police are on the track of a gang that has robbed five mini-marts in the last month.*
16 on a vehicle [C] a metal band over the wheels of a vehicle such as a BULLDOZER or TANK, that allows it to move over uneven ground
17 for recording [C] a BAND[1] on a TAPE on which music or information can be recorded: *an eight-track tape*
18 drugs tracks [plural] SLANG the marks that are left on the skin of someone who takes drugs such as HEROIN using a needle —see also **off the beaten track/path** (BEATEN (2)), ONE-TRACK MIND, **stop (dead) in your tracks** (STOP[1] (11)), **be from the wrong side of the tracks** (WRONG[1] (11))

track[2] *v.*
1 search [T] to search for a person or animal by following the marks they leave behind, their smell etc.: *Berstein was still in Florida tracking the four Miami men.*
2 [T] behavior/development to record or study the behavior or development of someone or something over time: *The progress of each student is tracked by computer.*
3 aircraft/ship [T] to follow the movements of an aircraft or ship by using RADAR
4 mark [T] to leave behind marks of something such as mud or dirt when you walk, especially in a line: *Which of you boys tracked mud all over the kitchen floor?*
5 camera [I + in/out] to move a movie or television camera away from or toward a scene in order to follow the action that you are recording
6 school [T] to put students in groups or classes according to their ability or needs
track sb/sth ↔ **down** *phr. v.* [T] to find someone or something that is difficult to find by searching or asking questions in several different places: *I had to make a few phone calls, but I finally tracked him down.*

track and field /ˌ. . ˈ./ *n.* [U] the sports that involve running races, jumping, and throwing things

track·ball /ˈtrækbɔl/ *n.* [C] a small ball connected to a computer, that you turn in order to move the CURSOR

track·er /ˈtrækɚ/ *n.* [C] **1** someone who follows and finds other people, especially criminals **2** a person or machine that follows the movement of something else: *a star tracker* **3** a person, computer etc. that records or studies the behavior or development of someone or something: *a financial investment tracker*

track event /ˈ. ˌ./ *n.* [C] a running race

track·ing /ˈtrækɪŋ/ *n.* [U] **1** the system on a VCR that keeps the picture from a VIDEOTAPE clear on the screen **2** the system of putting students in groups or classes according to their abilities and needs

tracking sta·tion /ˈ.. ˌ../ *n.* [C] a place from which objects moving in space, such as SATELLITEs and ROCKETs, can be recognized and followed

track light·ing /ˈ. ˌ../ *n.* [U] a system of LIGHTING in which electric lights are attached in a row to a metal bar on the ceiling or a wall

track meet /ˈ. ./ *n.* [C] a sports event consisting of competitions in running, jumping etc.

track rec·ord /ˈ. ˌ../ *n.* [C] the facts that are known about the past successes and failures of a company, product, or person: *Make sure you invest in firms with solid track records* (=good ones).

tract /trækt/ *n.* [C] **1 the digestive/reproductive/urinary etc. tract** a system of connected organs in your body that have one main purpose, such as DIGESTING food etc. **2** a large area of land: *There are large tracts of vacant land near the river.* **3** a short piece of writing, especially about a moral or religious subject: *Bible tracts*

trac·ta·ble /'træktəbəl/ *adj.* FORMAL easy to control or deal with: *The country's economic problems are less tractable than first thought.* —opposite INTRACTABLE —**tractability** /ˌtræktə'bɪləti/ *n.* [U]

tract house also **tract home** /'. ./ *n.* [C] a house that is similar in style to the other houses that are built on the same large piece of land —**tract housing** *n.* [U]

trac·tion /'trækʃən/ *n.* [U] **1** the force that prevents something such as a wheel from sliding on a surface: *Rubber soles give the shoes better traction.* **2** the process of treating a broken bone with special medical equipment that pulls it: *He was in traction for weeks after the accident.* **3** the type of power needed to make a vehicle move, or to pull a heavy load

trac·tor /'træktər/ *n.* [C] **1** a strong vehicle with large wheels, used for pulling farm machinery **2** a type of big truck that pulls TRAILERS to carry goods

tractor-trail·er /ˌ.. '../ *n.* [C] a large vehicle consisting of a tractor that pulls one or two TRAILERS (=large boxes on wheels), used for carrying goods

S W 1 **trade**¹ /treɪd/ *n.* **1** [U] the activity of buying, selling, or exchanging goods within a country or between countries: *New agreements will increase trade between the two countries.* | [+ in] *the trade in precious metals* | **the arms/drug/slave etc. trade** (=the buying and selling of weapons, drugs etc.) —see also BALANCE OF TRADE, FREE TRADE, SLAVE TRADE **2 the hotel/banking/tourist etc. trade** the business done by or involving hotels, banks etc.: *The whole town lives off the tourist trade.* **3** [C] a particular job, especially one needing special skill with your hands: *She enrolled in the tech school to learn a trade.* | *My grandfather was a plumber by trade* (=that was his job). —see Usage Note at JOE **4** [C] an exchange of something you have for something someone else has: *The rebels want to make a trade – two of their prisoners for one of the government's.* **5 the trade** a particular kind of business, and the people who are involved in it: *These companies are known in the trade as "service bureaus."* —see also JACK-OF-ALL-TRADES, **ply your trade** (PLY¹ (1)), STOCK-IN-TRADE

S W 1 **trade**² *v.* **1** [I,T] to buy and sell goods, services etc.: [+ with] *The U.S. has not traded with the country since the early '90s.* **2** [I,T] to exchange something you have for something someone else has: *"What do you have for lunch, a peanut butter sandwich?" "Want to trade?"* | **[trade sth (with sb)]** *Sometimes I wouldn't mind trading jobs with her.* | **[trade sth for sth]** *Some guy wanted to trade his Pete Rose baseball card for my Nolan Ryan.* | **[trade sb (sth for sth)]** *I'll trade you this pie for that cheesecake.* **3 a)** [T usually passive] TECHNICAL to buy or sell something on the STOCK EXCHANGE: *Over a million shares were traded during the day.* **b)** [I] TECHNICAL if STOCKS trade, they are bought and sold on the STOCK EXCHANGE **4 trade insults/blows etc. (with sb)** if two people trade insults, blows etc., or if one person trades insults etc. with someone else, the two people insult each other, hit each other etc. during an argument or fight

trade down *phr. v.* [I,T trade sth ↔ down] to sell something such as a car or house in order to buy one that costs less

trade sth ↔ in *phr. v.* [T] to give something such as a car to the person you are buying a new one from, so that you pay less: *Are they going to trade in the BMW?* —see also TRADE-IN

trade off *phr. v.* **1** [I] if two or more people trade off, they each do something sometimes so that they share the work fairly: *"Who gets up with the baby at night?" "Sharon and I have been trading off."* **2** [T trade sth ↔ off] to balance one situation or quality

---

against another, in order to produce an acceptable result: *We have to trade off the risks of the investment with its possible benefits.* —see also TRADE-OFF

trade on/upon sth *phr. v.* [T] to use a situation or someone's kindness in order to get an advantage for yourself: *She traded on her father's name to get her job.*

trade up *phr. v.* [I,T trade sth ↔ up] to sell something such as a car or house so you can buy a better car or house: [+ to] *Computer makers expect people to trade up to faster, more powerful models.*

trade def·i·cit /'. ..../ also **trade gap** *n.* [C] the amount by which the value of what a country buys from other countries is more than the value of what it sells to them

trade dis·count /'. ../ *n.* [C] a special reduction in the price of goods sold to people who are going to sell the goods in their own store or business

trade fair /'. ./ *n.* [C] a large event when several companies show their goods or services in one place, to try to sell them

trade gap /'. ./ *n.* [C] TRADE DEFICIT

trade-in /'. ./ *n.* [C] a used object, often a car, that you give to the seller to reduce the price of the new one that you are buying: *Your old car isn't going to be worth much as a trade-in.* | **trade-in price/value** *The trade-in value of the car is roughly $3000.*

trade jour·nal /'. ..../ *n.* [C] a magazine that is written for and bought by people in a particular business and not people in general

trade·mark /'treɪdmɑrk/ *n.* [C] **1** a special name, sign, or word that is marked on a product to show that it is made by a particular company **2** a particular way of behaving, dressing etc. by which someone or something can be easily recognized: *Large hats became Abzug's trademark.*

trade name /'. ./ *n.* [C] a name given to a particular product, that helps you recognize it from other similar products; BRAND NAME

trade-off /'. ./ *n.* [C] an acceptable balance between two opposing things: *Inflation is often a trade-off for healthy economic growth.*

trad·er /'treɪdər/ *n.* [C] someone who buys and sells goods S W 2

trade route /'. ./ *n.* [C] a way across land or the ocean often used by traders' vehicles, ships etc.

trade school /'. ./ *n.* [C] a school where people go in order to learn a particular TRADE¹ (3)

trade se·cret /'. ..../ *n.* [C] **1** a piece of secret information about a particular business, that is only known by the people who work there: *There are strict laws against revealing trade secrets.* **2** INFORMAL a piece of information about how to do or make something, that you do not want other people to know: *"What's the recipe?" "Sorry, that's a trade secret."*

trades·man /'treɪdzmən/ *n.* [C] someone who works at a job or TRADE that involves skill with their hands

trades·peo·ple /'treɪdzˌpipəl/ *n.* [plural] people who work at a job or TRADE that involves skill with their hands

trade sur·plus /ˌ. '../ *n.* [C] TECHNICAL the amount by which the value of the goods that a country sells to other countries is more than the value of what it buys from them

trade un·ion /'. ..../ *n.* [C] a LABOR UNION —**trade unionist** *n.* [C]

trade wind /'. ./ *n.* [C] a tropical wind that blows continuously toward the EQUATOR from either the northeast or the southeast

trad·ing /'treɪdɪŋ/ *n.* [C] the activity of buying and selling something on the STOCK EXCHANGE: **heavy/light trading** (=a lot of trading or a little trading)

trading part·ner /'.. ..../ *n.* [C] a country that buys your goods and sells their goods to you

trading post /'.. ./ *n.* [C] a place where people can buy and exchange goods in an area that is far away from cities or towns, especially in the U.S. or Canada in past times

trading stamp /ˌ.. './ n. [C] a small stamp that a store gives you every time you spend a particular amount of money, which you can collect and use to get other goods, done especially in past times

s w **tra·di·tion** /trəˈdɪʃən/ n. **1** [C] a belief, custom, or way of doing something that has existed for a long time: *Indian spiritual traditions* | *a family tradition* | [+ **of**] *There is a long tradition of conflict between the two countries.* | [**a tradition that**] *It's a tradition that the groom should not see the bride before the wedding.* **2** [U] beliefs or customs like this in general: *There is a lot of tradition connected to this school.* | *By tradition, the youngest child reads the questions.* | *The Emperor broke with tradition* (=stopped doing things the way they had always been done) *and became involved in political affairs.* **3** (be) in the tradition of sb/sth to have the same features as something that has been made or done in the past: *His latest movie is in the tradition of 1950s horror movies.* **4** [C] a way of thinking about something, especially a religion, or a group of people who think in this way: *They come from very different Christian traditions.* —see Usage Note at HABIT

s w **tra·di·tion·al** /trəˈdɪʃənəl/ adj. **1** relating to the traditions of a country or group of people: *Kumar gave the traditional Hindu greeting.* | *Having turkey is traditional at Thanksgiving.* **2** following ideas and methods that have existed for a long time rather than doing anything new or different; CONVENTIONAL: *traditional ideas about education* —**traditionally** adv.

tra·di·tion·al·ism /trəˈdɪʃənlˌɪzəm/ n. [U] belief in the importance of traditions and customs

tra·di·tion·al·ist /trəˈdɪʃənl-ɪst/ n. [C] someone who respects TRADITION and does not like change —**traditionalist** adj.

tra·duce /trəˈdus/ v. [T] FORMAL to deliberately say things about someone or something that are not true or nice

s w **traf·fic¹** /ˈtræfɪk/ n. [U] **1** the vehicles moving along a road or street: *There's been a lot more traffic around here since they opened the mall.* | *light/heavy traffic* (=a small or large amount of traffic) **2** the movement of aircraft, ships, trains etc. from one place to another: *air traffic control* **3** FORMAL the movement of people or goods by aircraft, ships, or trains: [+ **of**] *The increased traffic of crude oil in the gulf means a higher risk of oil spills.* **4** the secret buying and selling of illegal goods: [+ **in**] *illegal traffic in marijuana*

traffic² v. **trafficked, trafficking** [I,T] to buy and sell illegal goods: [+ **in**] *Hughes admits that his company trafficked in stolen documents.*

traffic cir·cle /ˈ.. ˌ../ n. [C] a circular area of road that cars must drive around, where three or more roads join

traffic cone /ˈ.. ˌ./ n. [C] a plastic object in the shape of a CONE that is put on the road to show where repairs are being done

traffic cop /ˈ.. ˌ./ n. [C] INFORMAL **1** a police officer who stands in the road and directs traffic **2** a police officer who stops drivers who drive in an illegal way

traffic court /ˈ.. ˌ./ n. [C] a court of law that deals with people who have done something illegal while driving

traffic is·land /ˈ.. ˌ../ n. [C] a raised area in the middle of the road, that separates the two sides of the road or where people can wait for traffic to pass before crossing

traffic jam /ˈ.. ˌ./ n. [C] a long line of vehicles that cannot move along the road, or that can only move very slowly: *We were stuck in a traffic jam on the freeway for two hours.*

traf·fick·er /ˈtræfɪkɚ/ n. [C] someone who buys and sells illegal goods, especially drugs

traf·fick·ing /ˈtræfɪkɪŋ/ n. [U] the buying and selling of illegal goods, especially drugs: *drug trafficking*

traffic lights /ˈ.. ˌ./ n. [C] a set of lights at a place where roads meet, that control the traffic by means of red, yellow, and green lights

traffic school /ˈ.. ˌ./ n. [C] a class that teaches you about driving laws, that you can go to instead of paying money for something you have done wrong while driving

traffic sig·nal /ˈ.. ˌ../ n. [C] traffic lights

tra·ge·di·an /trəˈdʒidiən/ n. [C] FORMAL an actor or writer of tragedy

trag·e·dy /ˈtrædʒədi/ n. plural **tragedies** **1** [C,U] a very sad event that shocks people because it involves death: *Tragedy struck the family when their two-year old son died of leukemia.* **2** [C] INFORMAL something that seems very sad and unnecessary because something will be wasted, lost, or harmed: *The real tragedy is that the city will no longer have an orchestra.* **3 a)** [C] a serious play or book that ends sadly, especially with the death of the main character: *Shakespeare's tragedies* **b)** [U] this style of writing: *Oedipus is one of the most famous characters in Greek tragedy.*

trag·ic /ˈtrædʒɪk/ adj. **1** a tragic event or situation makes you feel very sad, especially because it involves death: *Both sisters died in a tragic car accident.* **2** [only before noun] relating to tragedy in books, movies, or plays: *a great tragic actor* | *The film portrays Nixon as a tragic hero* (=the main character in a tragedy). **3 a tragic flaw** a weakness in the character of the main person in a tragedy that causes their own problems and usually death: *Jealousy is Othello's tragic flaw.*

trag·i·cal·ly /ˈtrædʒɪkli/ adv. in a very sad or unfortunate way, especially one involving death: *The marriage ended tragically when Norman caught her with another man.* | [+ adj./adv.] *The number of patients with access to the drugs is tragically low.*

trag·i·com·e·dy /ˌtrædʒɪˈkɑmədi/ n. plural **tragicomedies** [C,U] a play or a story that is both sad and funny —**tragicomic** /ˌtrædʒɪˈkɑmɪk◂/ adj.

trail¹ /treɪl/ v. **1** [I,T] also **trail behind** to be losing in a game, competition, or election: *Nelson is trailing in the polls.* | [**trail (sb) by sth**] *The Suns trail the Spurs by two games in the playoffs.* **2** [I,T always + adv./prep.] if something trails behind you, or if you trail it behind you, it gets pulled behind you as you move along: [+ **across/in/through**] *One mitten on a string trailed along behind her.* | [**trail sth in/on/through sth**] *I moved around the kitchen trailing the phone cord behind me.* **3** [I always + adv./prep.] to follow a short distance behind someone or go somewhere after other people, especially in a slow or bored way: [+ **along/behind/around**] *I trailed along behind them to make sure they got there all right.* **4** [T] to follow a person or animal or look for signs of the direction they are moving in, in order to try catch them: *Police have been trailing the gang for several days.* —see also TRAILER

trail away/off phr. v. [I] if someone's voice or a sound trails away or off, it becomes gradually quieter and then stops: *Jerry's voice trailed off before he finished the thought.*

trail² n. [C] **1** a rough path across open country or **s w** through a forest: *This trail leads to the lighthouse.* —see picture on page 428 **2 a trail of blood/clues/destruction etc.** a series of marks or signs left by someone or something that is moving: *She walked to her room, leaving a trail of wet footprints.* **3 be on the trail of sb/sth** to be following or looking for someone or something that is difficult to find or catch: *Cutler and Johnson are on the trail of the killer.* | *Recruiters are hot on the trail of the young basketball star* (=they are watching him closely because they want him to join their team). **4 while the trail is still hot** if you chase someone while the trail is still hot, you follow them soon after they have left **5** the marks or smell left by a person or animal, by which they can be hunted or followed: *The dogs followed the trail of the dying animal.* **6 a trail of broken hearts/a trail of unpaid bills etc.** a series of unhappy people or bad situations all caused by the same person: *As her career advanced, she left behind* a trail of damaged friendships. —see also **blaze a trail** (BLAZE[1] (4)), **paper trail** (PAPER[2] (3))

trail·blaz·er /ˈtreɪlˌbleɪzɚ/ n. [C] someone who is the first to do something, or who first discovers or develops new methods of doing something: *a political trailblazer* —**trail-blazing** *adj.*

trail·er /ˈtreɪlɚ/ n. [C] **1** a vehicle that can be pulled behind a car, used for living and sleeping in during a vacation **2** an advertisement for a new movie or television show, usually consisting of small scenes taken from it **3** a vehicle that can be pulled behind another vehicle, used for carrying something such as a boat or large piece of equipment **4** a vehicle like a large box on wheels, that is pulled by a truck and is used for carrying goods

trailer park also **trailer court** /ˈ.. ˌ./ n. [C] an area where trailers are parked and used as people's homes

trailer trash /ˈ.. ˌ./ n. [U] INFORMAL, OFFENSIVE poor people who live in trailer parks, who are considered by the person speaking to have no good qualities

trail·head /ˈtreɪlhɛd/ n. [C] the beginning of a TRAIL[2]

Trail of Tears, the /ˌ. . ˈ./ the path that the Cherokees traveled in the fall and winter of 1838 to 1839 when the U.S. government forced them to move away from their homes in the southeastern area of the U.S. to RESERVATIONs west of the Mississippi River. The journey was extremely long, cold, and difficult and about 4000 Cherokees died.

train¹ /treɪn/ n. [C]
1 railroad a set of connected railroad cars pulled by an engine along a railroad: [+ to] *an overnight train to Vienna* | *Traveling by train is not so convenient in America.*
2 train of thought a related series of thoughts developing in your mind: *I'm sorry. I've lost my train of thought* (=I've forgotten what I was planning to say).
3 people/animals/vehicles a long line of moving people, animals, or vehicles: *a wagon train*
4 dress a part of a long dress that spreads out over the ground behind the person who is wearing it: *a wedding dress with a long train*
5 bring sth in its train FORMAL if an action or event brings something in its train, that thing happens as a result of it: *The rapid growth of the cities brings in its train huge health and crime problems.*
6 a train of sth a series of related events, actions etc.: *The demonstration started a train of events that led to Cordova's resignation.*

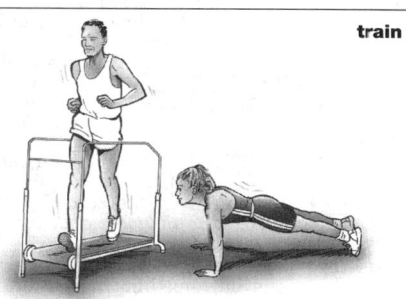

train

train² v. **1** [I,T] to teach someone or be taught the skills of a particular job or activity: [+ as] *Before I trained as a teacher, I wanted to be a journalist.* | [train to do sth] *Will is training to become a certified counselor.* | [train sb in sth] *The report could only be understood by someone who is trained in chemistry.* **2** [T] to teach an animal to do something or to behave correctly: *Hamilton trains and sells horses.* | [train sth to do sth] *The dogs have been trained to attack intruders.* **3** [I,T] to prepare for a sports event by exercising and practicing, or to make someone do this: [+ for] *I started training for this race in September.* **4** [T] to aim a gun, camera etc. at someone or something: [train sth on/at] *TV stations trained their cameras on the governor.* **5** [T] to make a plant grow in a particular direction by bending, cutting, or tying it —**trained** *adj.*: *a highly trained professional* —**trainable** *adj.* —see also TRAINING —see Usage Note at TEACH

train·bear·er /ˈtreɪnˌbɛrɚ/ n. [C] someone who holds the train of a dress, especially at a wedding

train·ee /treɪˈni/ n. [C] someone who is being trained for a job | **a management/police/nurse etc. trainee** *He was hired as a sales trainee in 1960.*

train·er /ˈtreɪnɚ/ n. [C] someone who trains people or animals for sports, work etc.

train·ing /ˈtreɪnɪŋ/ n. **1** [singular,U] the process of teaching or being taught skills for a particular job or activity: *a training manual* | [+ in] *We received training in several different teaching methods.* **2** [U] special physical exercises that you do to stay healthy or prepare for a sporting event: *Weight training has built up his upper body.* | *David's in training for the marathon.* —see also SPRING TRAINING

training camp /ˈ.. ˌ./ n. [C] a place where sports teams go to practice playing their sport and live for a short time

train·load /ˈtreɪnloʊd/ n. [C] the number or amount of things or people that fill a train

train set /ˈ. ./ n. [C] a toy train with railroad tracks

train sta·tion /ˈ. ˌ./ n. [C] the place where trains stop for passengers to get on and off

traipse /treɪps/ v. [I always + adv./prep., T] INFORMAL to walk somewhere slowly, without a clear direction: [+ up/down/around etc.] *I spent all day traipsing through town looking for Leif's uncle's house.*

trait /treɪt/ n. [C] FORMAL a particular quality in someone's character; CHARACTERISTIC: *Does Bryce have any bad traits?* | *a genetic trait*

trai·tor /ˈtreɪtɚ/ n. [C] someone who is not loyal to their country, friends etc.: [+ to] *a traitor to the country*

trai·tor·ous /ˈtreɪtərəs/ adj. LITERARY not loyal to your country, friends etc. —**traitorously** adv.

tra·jec·to·ry /trəˈdʒɛktəri/ n. plural **trajectories** [C] TECHNICAL the curved path of an object that is fired or thrown through the air

tram /træm/ also **tram·car** /ˈtræmkɑr/ n. [C] **1** a vehicle that hangs from a CABLE, used to take people to the top of mountains; CABLE CAR **2** a vehicle that has several cars connected together to carry a lot of people: *a tram tour of Universal Studios*

tram·mel /ˈtræməl/ v. [T] FORMAL to limit or prevent the free movement, activity, or development of someone or something

tram·mels /ˈtræməlz/ n. [plural] FORMAL something that limits or prevents free movement, activity, or development: *He has rejected the trammels of a career he hates.* —see also UNTRAMMELED

tramp¹ /træmp/ n. [C] **1** DISAPPROVING an insulting word for a woman who has too many sexual partners **2** someone who has no home or job and moves from place to place, often asking for food or money **3** the tramp of sth the sound of heavy walking: *the steady tramp of soldiers' boots on the road* **4** a long or difficult walk

tramp² v. [I always + adv./prep., T] to walk around or through somewhere with firm or heavy steps: [+ across/over/up etc.] *Crowds of tourists tramped across the fields.*

tram·ple /ˈtræmpəl/ v. [I always + adv./prep., T] **1** to step heavily on something so that you crush it with your feet: *Kids chasing balls have trampled the flower beds.* | *Two people were trampled to death in the riot.* **2** to behave in a way that shows that you do not care about someone's rights, hopes, ideas etc.: [+ on] *Opponents say the law tramples on the right to free speech.*

tram·po·line /ˌtræmpəˈlin, ˈtræmpəˌlin/ n. [C] a piece of equipment that you jump up and down on as a sport, made of a sheet of material tightly stretched across a metal frame —**trampoline** v. [I] —**trampolining** n. [U]

tramp steam·er /ˈ. ˈ../ n. [C] a ship that carries goods from place to place when someone pays for it to do so, but not on a regular basis

trance /træns/ *n.* [C] **1** a state in which you behave as if you were asleep, but you are still able to hear and understand what is said to you: *a hypnotic trance* **2** a situation in which you are thinking about something so much that you do not notice what is happening around you: *Gee! You were really in a trance. Didn't you hear me at all?*

tran·quil /ˈtræŋkwəl/ *adj.* pleasantly calm, quiet, and peaceful: *a tranquil mountain community* —**tranquilly** *adv.* —**tranquility** /træŋˈkwɪləti/ *n.* [U]

tran·quil·ize /ˈtræŋkwəˌlaɪz/ *v.* [T] to make a person or animal calm or unconscious by using a drug

tran·quil·iz·er /ˈtræŋkwəˌlaɪzə/ *n.* [C] a drug that makes a person or animal calm or unconscious, often used to make someone less nervous or anxious

trans- /træns, trænz/ *prefix* **1** on or to the far side of something: *transatlantic flights* | *the trans-Siberian railroad* **2** from one place or thing to another: *public transportation* (=that takes you from one place to another) | *We'll transfer the money to your account* (=move it into your account from another one). **3** used to show that something changes: *a complete transformation* (=change in appearance or character) | *the transmutation of metal into gold*

trans·act /trænˈzækt/ *v.* [I,T] FORMAL to do business: *Most deals are transacted over the phone.*

trans·ac·tion /trænˈzækʃən/ *n.* FORMAL **1** [C] a business deal: *real estate transactions* **2 transactions** [plural] discussions or business that take place at a meeting, or a written record of these **3** [U] the process of doing business: *All meetings for the transaction of business are open to the public.*

trans·at·lan·tic /ˌtrænzətˈlæntɪk/ *adj.* [only before noun] **1** crossing the Atlantic Ocean: *transatlantic flights* **2** involving countries on both sides of the Atlantic Ocean: *a transatlantic organization* **3** on the other side of the Atlantic Ocean: *a transatlantic ally*

trans·cei·ver /trænˈsivə/ *n.* [C] a radio that can both send and receive messages

trans·cend /trænˈsɛnd/ *v.* [T] FORMAL to go above or beyond the limits of something: *The beauty of her songs transcend words and language.*

tran·scen·dent /trænˈsɛndənt/ *adj.* FORMAL going far beyond ordinary limits: *The Olympics are a transcendent event.* —**transcendence** *n.* [U]

tran·scen·den·tal /ˌtrænsɛnˈdɛntl/ *adj.* existing above or beyond human knowledge, understanding, and experience: *transcendental harmony*

tran·scen·den·tal·ism /ˌtrænsɛnˈdɛntlˌɪzəm/ *n.* [U] the belief that knowledge can be obtained by studying thought and not necessarily by practical experience —**transcendentalist** *n.* [C]

transcendental med·i·ta·tion /ˌ..,.. ˈ../ *n.* [U] a method of becoming calm by repeating special words in your mind

trans·con·ti·nen·tal /ˌtrænskɑntənˈɛntl, ˌtrænz-/ *adj.* [only before noun] crossing a CONTINENT: *a transcontinental railroad*

tran·scribe /trænˈskraɪb/ *v.* [T] FORMAL **1** to write down something exactly as it was said: *The phone conversations were transcribed and sent to the FBI.* **2** to write an exact copy of something: *Secretaries were busy transcribing medical records.* **3** TECHNICAL to represent speech sounds with special PHONETIC letters **4** to arrange a piece of music for a different instrument or voice: *Fleck has transcribed Bach for the banjo.* **5** to copy recorded music, computer information, speech etc. from one system to another, for example from TAPE to CD **6** [+ into] FORMAL to change a piece of writing into a different writing system or language

tran·script /ˈtrænˌskrɪpt/ *n.* [C] **1** an exact written or printed copy of something: [+ of] *A transcript of Clay's testimony was released to the press.* **2** an official college document that shows a list of a student's classes and the results they received

tran·scrip·tion /trænˈskrɪpʃən/ *n.* **1** [U] the act or process of transcribing something: *Pronunciation is shown by a system of phonetic transcription.* **2** [C] an exact written or printed copy of something; transcript

trans·duc·er /trænzˈdusə/ *n.* [C] TECHNICAL a small piece of electronic equipment that changes one form of energy to another

tran·sect /trænˈsɛkt/ *v.* [T] FORMAL to divide something by cutting across it

tran·sept /ˈtrænsɛpt/ *n.* [C] one of the two parts of a large church that are built out from the main area of the church to form a cross shape

trans·fer¹ /ˈtrænsfə, trænsˈfə/ *v.* **transferred, transferring**

1 person [I,T] to move from one place, school, job etc. to another, or to make someone do this, especially within the same organization: [+ to] *Halfway through the first year, he transferred to Berkeley.* | [**transfer sb (from sth) to sth**] *Davis is being transferred from New York to Houston next month.*
2 thing/activity [T] FORMAL to move something from one place or position to another: [**transfer sth (from sth) to sth**] *Remove the roast from the oven and transfer it to a platter.*
3 money [T] to move money from the control of one account or institution to another: *I need to transfer some money from my savings account to my checking account.*
4 skill/idea/quality [I,T] if a skill, idea, or quality transfers from one situation to another, or if you transfer it, it is used in the new situation: *Ideas that work in one school often don't transfer well to another.*
5 transfer power/responsibility/control to officially give power etc. to another person or organization: [+ to] *Republicans want to transfer more power back to the states.*
6 phone to connect the telephone call of someone who has called you to someone else's telephone so that that person can speak to them: *Hold one moment while I transfer your call.*
7 property [T] LAW to officially give property or money to someone else: *The assets were transferred into his wife's name.*
8 bus/airplane [I] to change from one bus, airplane etc. to another during a trip: *If you take the bus, you'll have to transfer twice.*
9 transfer your affection/loyalty etc. to change from loving or supporting one person to loving or supporting a different one: [+ to] *He quickly transferred his loyalty from the old government to the new.*
10 recorded information [T] to copy recorded information, music etc. from one system to another, for example from TAPE to CD: *Transfer the files onto floppy disk.*
11 picture/pattern [I,T] if a pattern, design etc. transfers from one surface to another, or if you transfer it, it appears on the second surface: *The design is transferred to the loom and woven into the carpet.* —**transferable** *adj.*

trans·fer² /ˈtrænsfə/ *n.* **1 a)** [C,U] the process by which someone or something moves or is moved from one place, situation, job etc. to another: *a job transfer* | *Most of the bills are paid by electronic transfer.* **b)** [C] someone or something that has been moved in this way **2 transfer of power** a process by which the control of a country is taken from one person or group and given to another: *the smooth transfer of power in Hong Kong* **3** [C] **a)** a ticket that allows a passenger to change from one bus, train etc. to another without paying more money **b)** the action of changing from one bus, airplane etc. to continue a trip **4** [C] a drawing, pattern etc. that can be printed onto a surface by pressing it against that surface

trans·fer·ence /ˈtrænsfərəns, trænsˈfɛrəns/ *n.* [U] **1** TECHNICAL in PSYCHOLOGY, the process by which your feelings or desires concerning one person become connected to another person instead **2** FORMAL a process by which someone or something is moved from one place, position, job etc. to another

trans·fig·ure /trænsˈfɪgyə/ *v.* [T] LITERARY to change

the way someone or something looks, especially so that they become more beautiful: *The woman's face was transfigured with joy.* —**transfiguration** /ˌtræns-ˌfɪɡjəˈreɪʃən/ *n.* [C,U]

trans·fix /trænsˈfɪks/ *v.* [T] **1** to make someone unable to move because they are very surprised, shocked, frightened etc.: *The sight of the fire transfixed the passersby.* **2** LITERARY to make a hole through someone or something with a sharp pointed weapon

trans·fixed /trænsˈfɪkst/ *adj.* [not before noun] unable to move because you are very surprised, interested, shocked, frightened etc.: *Her brilliant speech kept the students transfixed.*

S W
3
trans·form /trænsˈfɔrm/ *v.* [T] to completely change the appearance, form, or character of something or someone: *Increased population has transformed the landscape.* | [transform sb/sth into sth] *Using a computer, a photograph can easily be transformed into a greeting card.* —**transformable** *adj.*

trans·for·ma·tion /ˌtrænsfəˈmeɪʃən/ *n.* [U] a complete change in someone or something: [a transformation from sth to sth] *Will Rogers lived through the transformation from silent films to talking pictures.*

trans·form·er /trænsˈfɔrmə/ *n.* [C] a piece of equipment for changing electricity from one VOLTAGE to another

trans·fu·sion /trænsˈfjuʒən/ *n.* [C,U] **1** the process of putting blood from one person into another person's body: *She received three blood transfusions before the bleeding stopped.* **2** the process of giving something important or necessary such as money to a group or organization that needs it: *The mayor has promised a transfusion of $8 million in redevelopment funds.* —**transfuse** /trænsˈfjuz/ *v.* [T]

trans·gen·der /trænzˈdʒɛndə/ *adj.* also **trans·gendered** /trænzˈdʒɛndəd/ a transgender person wants to be or look like a member of the opposite sex, especially by having a medical operation —**transgender** *n.* [C] —**transgenderism** *n.* [U]

trans·gen·ic /trænzˈdʒɛnɪk/ *adj.* TECHNICAL having GENES from a different type of animal or plant: *transgenic mice*

trans·gress /trænzˈɡrɛs/ *v.* [I,T] FORMAL to do something that is against the rules of social behavior or against a moral principle: *The terms of the treaty were transgressed almost immediately.* —**transgressor** *n.* [C] —**transgression** /trænzˈɡrɛʃən/ *n.* [C,U]

tran·sient¹ /ˈtrænʒənt/ *adj.* FORMAL **1** passing quickly through a place or staying there for only a short time: *Phoenix has a very transient population.* **2** continuing only for a short time: *transient pleasures* —**transience, transiency** *n.* [U]

transient² *n.* [C] someone who has no home and moves around from place to place

tran·sis·tor /trænˈzɪstə/ *n.* [C] **1** a small piece of electronic equipment in radios, televisions etc. that controls the flow of electricity **2** a transistor radio

tran·sis·tor·ize /trænˈzɪstəˌraɪz/ *v.* [T] TECHNICAL to put transistors into something so that it can be made smaller

transistor ra·di·o /.ˌ.. ˈ.../ *n.* [C] a small radio that has transistors in it instead of VALVES

tran·sit /ˈtrænzɪt/ *n.* **1** [U] the action or process of moving through a place or from one place to another, or of moving people or products this way: *The shipment was lost in transit* (=in the process of being moved). **2** a system for doing this: *The museum can be reached using public transit.* **3** [C,U] TECHNICAL the movement of a PLANET or moon in front of a larger object in space, such as the sun

transit camp /ˈ.. ˌ./ *n.* [C] a place where REFUGEES stay before moving to somewhere more permanent

S W
3 3
tran·si·tion /trænˈzɪʃən/ *n.* [C,U] **1** FORMAL the act or process of changing from one form or state to another: *The program helps families who are making the transition from welfare to work.* | *Uzbekistan is a country in transition.* **2** TECHNICAL a phrase or sentence in a piece of writing or speech that connects two different ideas smoothly: *You need a better transition between the second and third paragraphs.*

tran·si·tion·al /trænˈzɪʃənl/ *adj.* **1** relating to a period of change from one form or condition to another: **a transitional stage/period** etc. *Schmidt expects this to be a transitional year for the company.* **2 a transitional government** a government that is temporary during a period of change **3 a transitional word/phrase** etc. a word, phrase etc. that connects two different ideas in a piece of writing or speech —**transitionally** *adv.*

tran·si·tive /ˈtrænsətɪv, -zə-/ *adj.* TECHNICAL a transitive verb must have an object. For example, in the sentence "Sue hates spinach," "hate" is transitive. Transitive verbs are marked [T] in this dictionary —compare INTRANSITIVE —**transitive** *n.* [C] —**transitively** *adv.* —**transitivity** /ˌtrænsəˈtɪvəti/ *n.* [U]

transit lounge /ˈ.. ˌ./ *n.* [C] an area in an airport where passengers can wait

tran·si·to·ry /ˈtrænzəˌtɔri/ *adj.* continuing or existing for only a short time: *the transitory nature of young love*

transit vi·sa /ˈ.. ˌ../ *n.* [C] a VISA (=special document) that allows someone to pass through one country on their way to another

S W
2
3
trans·late /ˈtrænzleɪt, ˌtrænzˈleɪt/ *v.*
1 change languages [I,T] to change speech or writing into another language: *No one else spoke French, so I had to translate.* | [translate sth (from sth) into sth] *Later the book was translated into Spanish.* —compare INTERPRET (1)
2 happen as result **translate into sth** also **be translated into sth** if one thing translates into another, the second thing happens as a result of the first: *It remains to be seen if increased demand will translate into more jobs.*
3 have same meaning **translate into/to sth** to have the same meaning or be the same amount as something else: *A 16% raise translates to an extra $700 a month.*
4 be understood to be easily understood by someone who speaks a different language: *Hollywood has to produce movies that translate easily into any language.*
5 change forms [T] to change something from one form to another: [translate sth into sth] *Marey had the photographs translated into sculpture.*
6 use in new situation [I,T] to be used in a new situation, or to make something do this: [+ to] *Many business ideas translate very well to government.* —**translatable** *adj.*

S W
3
trans·la·tion /trænzˈleɪʃən, træns-/ *n.* **1** [C,U] the act of translating something, or something that has been translated: *a new translation of the Bible* | [+ from] *"It goes without saying" is a direct translation from French.* | *I don't like reading poetry in translation.* | *His message is too important to be lost in translation* (=no longer effective or understood when translated). **2** [U] FORMAL the process of changing something into a different form, or using it in a new situation: *the translation of beliefs into actions*

trans·la·tor /ˈtrænzˌleɪtə/ *n.* [C] someone who changes speech or writing into a different language —compare INTERPRETER

trans·lit·er·ate /trænzˈlɪtəˌreɪt, træns-/ *v.* [T] to write a word, sentence etc. in the alphabet of a different language or writing system —**transliteration** /trænzˌlɪtəˈreɪʃən/ *n.* [C,U]

trans·lu·cent /trænzˈlusənt/ *adj.* not transparent, but clear enough to allow light to pass through: *translucent paper* —**translucence** *n.* [U] —compare OPAQUE, TRANSPARENT

trans·mi·gra·tion /ˌtrænzmaɪˈɡreɪʃən/ *n.* [U] TECHNICAL the time when the soul passes into another body after death, according to some religions —**transmigrate** /trænzˈmaɪɡreɪt/ *v.* [I]

trans·mis·si·ble /trænzˈmɪsəbəl/ *adj.* FORMAL able to be passed from one person to another: *a transmissible disease*

trans·mis·sion /trænzˈmɪʃən/ *n.* **1** [U] the process of sending out of electrical signals, messages etc., by

T

radio or similar equipment: *Because of transmission difficulties, we have not received today's stock prices.* **2** [C] FORMAL something that is broadcast on television, radio etc. **3** [C,U] the part of a vehicle that takes power from the engine to the wheels: *My car has an automatic transmission.* **4** [U] FORMAL the process of sending or passing something from one person, place, or thing to another: *the sexual transmission of AIDS*

trans·mit /trænz'mɪt/ *v.* **transmitted, transmitting** **1** [I,T] to send out electric signals, messages etc. by radio or other similar equipment; broadcast: *The U.S. Open will be transmitted live via satellite.* **2** [T] to send or pass something from one person, place, or thing to another: *Cultural values are transmitted from parent to child.* | *Malaria is transmitted to humans by mosquitoes.* —see also SEXUALLY TRANSMITTED DISEASE **3** [T] TECHNICAL if an object or substance transmits sound or light, it allows sound or light to travel through or along it —**transmittal** *n.* [U]

trans·mit·ter /trænz'mɪtɚ, 'trænz,mɪtɚ/ *n.* [C] equipment that sends out radio or television signals

trans·mog·ri·fy /trænz'mɑgrəfaɪ/ *v.* **transmogrifies, transmogrified, transmogrifying** FORMAL OR HUMOROUS to change the shape or character of something completely, as if by magic: *Love had transmogrified him into a romantic idiot.*

trans·mute /trænz'myut/ *v.* [T] FORMAL to change one substance or type of thing into another: *Sienra's paintings show humans transmuting into animals.* —**transmutable** *adj.* —**transmutation** /,trænzmyu'teɪʃən/ *n.* [C,U]

trans·na·tio·nal /trænz'næʃənl/ *adj.* involving more than one country, or existing in more than one country: *transnational corporations*

trans·o·ce·an·ic /trænz,ouʃi'ænɪk/ *adj.* [only before noun] crossing an ocean, or involving countries on both sides of an ocean: *a transoceanic voyage*

tran·som /'trænsəm/ *n.* [C] **1** a small window over a door or over a larger window **2** a bar of wood above a door, separating the door from a window above it **3** a bar of wood or stone across a window, dividing the window into two parts

trans·par·en·cy /træns'pærənsi, -'per-/ *n. plural* **transparencies** **1** [C] a sheet of plastic through which light can be shone to show a picture or writing on a large screen **2** [U] the quality of glass, plastic etc. that makes it possible for you to see through it

trans·par·ent /træns'pærənt/ *adj.* **1** something that is transparent allows light to pass through it, so that you can see things through it: *The plastic is transparent.* | *a thin transparent fabric* —compare OPAQUE, TRANSLUCENT **2** a transparent lie, excuse etc. does not deceive people **3** FORMAL speech or writing that is transparent is clear and easy to understand —**transparently** *adv.*

tran·spi·ra·tion /,trænspə'reɪʃən/ *n.* [U] TECHNICAL the process of transpiring (TRANSPIRE (3))

tran·spire /træn'spaɪɚ/ *v.* **1** [T] FORMAL to happen: *I was surprised at what transpired.* **2 it transpires that** FORMAL if it transpires that something is true, people find out that it is true: *If it transpires that he is guilty, he will almost certainly lose everyone's support.* **3** [I,T] TECHNICAL when a plant transpires, it gives off water from its surface

trans·plant¹ /træns'plænt/ *v.* [T] **1** to move a plant from one place and plant it in another: *You need to transplant that cactus.* **2** to move an organ, piece of skin etc. from one person's body to another: *His kidney was transplanted in his daughter.* **3** to move something or someone from one place to another: *The club looks like a little bit of Las Vegas transplanted in Texas.* —**transplanted** *adj.* [only before noun] *a transplanted Midwesterner in Los Angeles* —**transplantation** /,trænsplæn'teɪʃən/ *n.* [U]

trans·plant² /'trænsplænt/ *n.* **1** [C,U] the operation of transplanting an organ, piece of skin etc., or the

organ itself: *a liver transplant* **2** [C] INFORMAL someone or something that has moved from one place to another: *a New York transplant to California* —compare IMPLANT²

trans·po·lar /træns'poulɚ/ *adj.* [only before noun] across the area around the North or South Pole

tran·spond·er /træn'spɑndɚ/ *n.* [C] TECHNICAL a piece of radio or RADAR equipment that sends out a particular signal when it receives a signal telling it to do this

trans·port¹ /træns'pɔrt, 'trænspɔrt/ *v.* [T] **1** to take goods, people etc. from one place to another in a vehicle: [**transport sb/sth to sth**] *The women were transported to a nearby hospital for treatment.* **2 be transported back/to etc. sth** to imagine that you are in another place or time because of something that you see or hear: *Seeing her again, I was transported back to the day we met.* **3** to send a criminal to a distant country as a punishment in past times **4 be transported (by/with sth)** LITERARY to feel very strong emotions of pleasure, happiness etc.: *He was transported by the beauty of the music* —**transportable** *adj.*

trans·port² /'trænspɔrt/ *n.* **1** [U] the process or business of taking goods, information etc. from one place to another: [+ **of**] *Construction will require the transport of over 500 tons of dirt.* **2** [U] TRANSPORTATION (1) **3** [C] a ship or aircraft for carrying soldiers or supplies **4 be in a transport of delight/joy etc.** LITERARY to be feeling very strong emotions of pleasure, happiness etc.

trans·por·ta·tion /,trænspɚ'teɪʃən/ *n.* [U] **1** a system for carrying passengers or goods from one place to another: *I get so tired of taking public transportation.* | **a mode/means/method of transportation** *Bicycles were a popular mode of transportation after the war.* **2** the process or business of taking goods from one place to another: [+ **of**] *the transportation of stolen property* **3** OLD USE the punishment of sending a criminal to a distant country

trans·port·er /træn'spɔrtɚ, 'træns,pɔrtɚ/ *n.* [C] a large truck, airplane etc. that can carry one or more other vehicles or many people

transport plane /'.. ,./ *n.* [C] an airplane that is used especially for carrying military equipment or soldiers

transport ship /'.. ,./ *n.* [C] a ship used especially for carrying soldiers

trans·pose /træns'pouz/ *v.* [T] TECHNICAL **1** FORMAL to change the order or position of two or more things: *I had transposed the last two digits of her phone number.* **2** to write or perform a piece of music in a musical KEY that is different from the one that it was first written in —**transposition** /,trænspə'zɪʃən/ *n.* [C,U]

trans·sex·u·al /trænz'sɛkʃuəl/ *n.* [C] someone who wants to be or look like a member of the opposite sex, especially by having a medical operation —**transsexual** *adj.* —**transsexualism** *n.* [U]

trans·ship·ment /træn'ʃɪpmənt/ *n.* [C,U] the process or action of moving goods from one ship, airplane, truck etc. to another so that they can be delivered —**transship** *v.* [I,T]

tran·sub·stan·ti·a·tion /,trænsəb,stænʃi'eɪʃən/ *n.* [U] TECHNICAL the belief of some Christians that the bread and wine in the MASS (=a religious ceremony) become the actual body and blood of Jesus Christ —compare CONSUBSTANTIATION

trans·verse /,trænz'vɚs◂/ *adj.* TECHNICAL lying or placed across something: *a transverse beam*

trans·ves·tite /trænz'vɛstaɪt/ *n.* [C] someone who enjoys dressing like a person of the opposite sex —**transvestite** *adj.* —**transvestism** *n.* [U]

trap¹ /træp/ *n.* [C]
1 for animals a piece of equipment for catching animals: *Have you set traps to catch the squirrels?* —see also MOUSETRAP
2 smart trick a trick that is used to catch someone or to make them do or say something that they did not intend to: *She was completely unaware of the*

*trap he had **laid** for her with his question.* | **fall/ walk into a trap** *Hopefully, the thief will fall right into our trap.*

3 `bad situation` a bad or difficult situation that is difficult to escape from: *It's all too easy to get **caught in the trap of** working too much.*

4 fall into the trap of doing sth to do something that is easy or seems good at the time but is not sensible or wise: *Don't fall into the trap of arguing with employees in front of others.* —opposite **avoid the trap of doing sth**

5 `pipe` the part of a pipe from a SINK, toilet etc. that is bent to hold water and stop gases from passing through

6 keep your trap shut SPOKEN to not say anything about things that are secret: *Tell him to keep his trap shut and let me ask the questions.*

7 shut your trap! SPOKEN used to tell someone rudely and angrily to stop talking

8 `door` a TRAPDOOR

9 `sports` a SAND TRAP

10 `vehicle` a light vehicle with two wheels, pulled by a horse —see also BOOBY TRAP, DEATH TRAP, SPEED TRAP, TRAPSHOOTING

trap² *v.* [T]
1 `in a dangerous place` [usually passive] to prevent someone from escaping from a dangerous place: *Workers were trapped in the ship's engine room by the fire.*

2 `catch sb` to catch someone by forcing them into a place from which they cannot escape: *Police have the man trapped inside the bar.*

3 be/feel trapped to be in a bad situation from which you cannot escape: *At 31, Peggy feels trapped in a boring job.*

4 `trick sb` to trick someone so that you make them do or say something that they did not intend to: [**trap sb into (doing) sth**] *Anthony says she trapped him into marriage before he was ready.*

5 `gas/water etc.` to prevent something such as water, dirt, heat etc. from escaping or spreading: *Greenhouse gases trap heat in the Earth's atmosphere.*

6 `animal` to catch an animal or bird using a trap

trap·door /ˌtræp dɔr/ *n.* [C] a small door that covers an opening in a roof or floor

tra·peze /træˈpiz/ *n.* [C] a short bar hanging from two ropes high above the ground, used by ACROBATS

tra·pe·zi·um /trəˈpiziəm/ *n.* [C] TECHNICAL a shape with four sides, none of which are parallel

tra·pe·zi·us /trəˈpiziəs/ *n.* [C] TECHNICAL also **trapezius mus·cle** /.ˈ... ˌ../ one of the two large TRIANGLE-shaped muscles in your back

trap·e·zoid /ˈtræpəzɔɪd/ *n.* [C] TECHNICAL a shape with four sides, of which only two are parallel

trap·per /ˈtræpɚ/ *n.* [C] someone who traps wild animals, especially for their fur

trap·pings /ˈtræpɪŋz/ *n.* [plural] things such as clothes, possessions etc. that show someone's rank, success, or position: [**+ of**] *He never got used to the trappings of fame.*

Trap·pist /ˈtræpɪst/ *n.* [C] a member of a Catholic religious society whose members never speak

trap·shoot·ing, trap shooting /ˈtræpˌʃutɪŋ/ *n.* [U] the sport of shooting at special clay objects fired into the air

trash¹ /træʃ/ *n.* [U] **1** waste material that will be thrown away, usually considered together with the container or bag holding it; GARBAGE: *Will someone **take out the trash** (=take it outside the house)?* | *Just put it **in the trash**.* **2** INFORMAL something that is of very poor quality: *How can you read that trash?* **3 on the trash heap (of sth)** not used or respected anymore: *One banner said that the party belonged "on the trash heap of history."* **4** INFORMAL, OFFENSIVE people who are considered by the person speaking to have no good qualities **5 one man's trash is another man's treasure** used to say that different people like different things or consider things differently —see also **talk trash** (TALK¹ (22)), WHITE TRASH

trash² *v.* [T] **1** to criticize someone or something severely: *Some of the people he trashed on the show are planning to sue.* **2** INFORMAL to destroy something

completely, either deliberately or by using it too much: *The team celebrated their victory by trashing their hotel rooms.*

trash bag /'. ./ *n.* [C] a large plastic bag for holding waste material

trash bin /'. ./ *n.* [C] a large trash can

trash can /'. ./ *n.* [C] a large container, usually with a lid, used to hold waste material; GARBAGE CAN —compare WASTEBASKET, DUMPSTER and see picture at KITCHEN

trash com·pac·tor /'. .ˌ../ *n.* [C] a machine that presses waste material together into a very small mass

trashed /træʃt/ *adj.* SPOKEN **1** very drunk: *I was so trashed I don't remember anything.* **2** completely destroyed: *The place was trashed.*

trash·talk /ˈtræʃ-tɔk/ *n.* [U] INFORMAL things you say about someone else that are not nice —compare **talk trash** (TALK¹ (22))

trash·y /ˈtræʃi/ *adj.* **trashier, trashiest 1** of extremely bad quality, and often about sex: *trashy novels* **2** behaving in a way that is morally unacceptable, especially involving sex —**trashiness** *n.* [U]

trat·to·ri·a /ˌtrætəˈriə/ *n.* [C] a restaurant that serves Italian food

trau·ma /ˈtrɔmə, ˈtraumə/ *n.* **1** [C] a very bad and upsetting experience: *A trauma such as a fire can upset a child for months.* **2** [U] a mental state of extreme shock caused by a very frightening or bad experience: *She has not recovered from **the emotional trauma** of the rape.* **3** [C,U] TECHNICAL injury: *a head trauma*

trau·mat·ic /trəˈmætɪk, trɔ-/ *adj.* a traumatic experience is so shocking and upsetting that it affects you for a long time: *My parents' divorce was very traumatic for me.* —**traumatically** /-kli/ *adv.*

trau·ma·tize /ˈtrɔməˌtaɪz, ˈtrau-/ *v.* [T usually passive] to shock someone so badly that they are unable to do things normally: *These children have been traumatized by the violence in their home.* —**traumatized** *adj.*

trav·ail /trəˈveɪl, ˈtræveɪl/ *n.* [U] LITERARY **1** also **travails** [plural] difficult and bad situations or experiences, or very tiring work: [**+ of**] *the travails of old age* **2 in travail** a woman who is in travail is feeling the pain of giving birth

trav·el¹ /ˈtrævəl/ *v.*
1 `trip` **a)** [I] to go from one place to another, or to several places, especially distant ones: *Helena really likes to travel.* | [**+ to/through/around etc.**] *Fitzsimmons traveled to Germany to learn about their education system.* | *During a year of research, they **traveled widely** (=went to many different places) in the U.S.* | *We always **travel light** (=without taking many possessions).* | **travel by train/car etc.** *After the meeting, the President traveled by helicopter to Camp David.* **b) travel the world/country** to go to most parts of the world or most parts of a particular country

2 `news` [I] to be passed quickly from one person or place to another: *News travels fast in a small town like this.*

3 `distance/speed` [I,T] to go a particular distance or at a particular speed: *We traveled 2251 miles in 11 days.* | [**+ at**] *Police say the car was traveling at about 80 miles per hour.*

4 well-traveled a) also **widely traveled** having traveled to many different countries: *Beck's parents were well-educated, well-traveled people.* **b)** having been traveled on by many people: *a well-traveled trade route*

5 `light/sound` [I] to move at a particular speed or in a particular direction: *Light travels faster than sound.*

6 `food/wine` **travel well** to remain in good condition when taken long distances

7 `basketball` [I] to take more than three steps while you are holding the ball in basketball

8 for business [I] to go from place to place to sell and take orders for your company's products: [+ **for**] *Villalon spends much of his time traveling for Dior.*

USAGE NOTE: TRAVEL

WORD CHOICE: travel, traveling, travels, trip, journey, voyage

The nouns **travel** and **traveling** are usually used about the general activity of going from one place to another, especially for long distances and long periods of time: *We were exhausted after four months of train travel.* | *I haven't really done much traveling.* If someone moves from place to place over a period of time, you talk about **sb's travels**: *Tell us more about your travels in Asia, Doug.* A **trip** is the time spent and distance traveled in going from one place to another: *I'm going to make a quick trip to the library. Do you want to come along?* | *They're taking a trip to Sweden this summer.* **Journey** is a formal word for a trip that is very long or difficult: *a journey across the desert.* **Voyage** is used mainly in stories to talk about traveling by ship or in a spacecraft. You can **take**, **make**, or **go on** a **trip**, **journey**, or **voyage**, but you cannot use these verbs with **travel**.

S W
2
3
travel² *n.* [U] **1** the act or activity of traveling: *The State Department has advised against travel in the region.* **2 travels** [plural] trips to places that are far away: *Her travels have taken her all over China and the Far East.* **3 travel clock/iron/hair dryer etc.** a clock, iron etc. designed to be used when you are traveling

travel a·gen·cy /'.. ,.../ *n. plural* **travel agencies** [C] an office or company that makes travel arrangements and organizes vacations for people

travel a·gent /'.. ,../ *n.* [C] someone who owns or works in a travel agency

travel bu·reau /'.. ,../ *n.* [C] a TRAVEL AGENCY

trav·el·er /'trævələ/ *n.* [C] someone who is on a trip or someone who travels often: *Travelers to remote areas should boil water before drinking.*

traveler's check /'... ,./ *n.* [C] a special check that can be exchanged for the money of a foreign country

trav·el·ing¹ /'trævəlɪŋ/ *n.* [U] **1** the act or activity of going from one place to another, especially places that are far away: *After retiring, we'll do some traveling.* **2** taking more than three steps while holding the ball in basketball: *Miller was called for traveling.*

traveling² *adj.* **1 traveling expenses** money that is used to pay for TRANSPORTATION while someone is on a trip for their company **2 a traveling companion** someone you are on a trip with **3 a traveling musician/show/circus etc.** a musician, show etc. that goes from place to place in order to work or perform

traveling sales·man /,... '../ *n.* [C] someone who goes from place to place, selling their company's products

trav·el·ler /'trævələ/ *n.* the British and Canadian spelling of TRAVELER

trav·e·logue, travelog /'trævə,lɔg, -,lɒg/ *n.* [C] a movie, television program, or speech that describes travel in a particular country, or that describes a particular person's travels

tra·verse¹ /trə'vəs/ *v.* [T] FORMAL to move across, over, or through something: *An estimated 250,000 cars traverse the bridge daily.*

trav·erse² /'trævəs/ *n.* [C] TECHNICAL a sideways movement across a very steep slope, used in mountain climbing

trav·es·ty /'trævɪsti/ *n. plural* **travesties** [C] an extremely bad example of something, especially one in which the opposite result should have happened: *It would have been **a travesty of justice** to not punish them.*

trawl¹ /trɔl/ *v.* [I,T] **1** to fish by DRAGging a special wide net behind a boat: *Shrimp boats can trawl continuously for hours at a time.* **2** to search through a lot of information, lists etc. in order to find out information: [+ **through**] *Haley trawled through public records to piece together his family's history.*

trawl² *n.* [C] **1** a wide net that is pulled along the bottom of the ocean to catch fish **2** a TRAWL LINE **3** an act of searching through a lot of documents, lists etc. in order to find something: [+ **through**] *The FBI should have taken another trawl through their files.*

trawl·er /'trɔlə/ *n.* [C] a fishing boat that trawls

trawl line /'. ./ *n.* [C] a long fishing line to which many smaller lines are fastened

tray /treɪ/ *n. plural* **trays** [C] a flat piece of plastic, metal, or wood, with raised edges, used for carrying things such as plates, food etc.: *The tray was heavy with food and drinks.* —see also BAKING TRAY

S W
3

treach·er·ous /'trɛtʃərəs/ *adj.* **1** someone who is treacherous cannot be trusted because they are not loyal and secretly intend to harm you: *Her stepmother was a treacherous, selfish woman.* **2** ground, roads, weather conditions etc. that are treacherous are particularly dangerous because you cannot see the dangers very easily: *They traveled on horseback over treacherous Himalayan footpaths.* —**treacherously** *adv.*

treach·er·y /'trɛtʃəri/ *n.* **1** [U] actions that are not loyal to someone who trusts you, especially when these actions help that person's enemies: *Selling military secrets is an unforgivable act of treachery.* **2** [C usually plural] a disloyal action against someone who trusts you

trea·cle /'trikəl/ *n.* [U] a way of expressing love and emotions that seems silly or insincere: *It is a socially conscious film that does not turn into treacle.*

tread¹ /trɛd/ *v. past tense* **trod** *past participle* **trodden** **1 tread carefully/warily/cautiously etc.** to be very careful about what you say or do in a difficult situation: *I was treading cautiously, as I didn't want to risk offending our best client.* **2 tread water** *past tense and past participle* **treaded a)** to stay floating upright in deep water by moving your legs as if you are riding a bicycle **b)** to make no progress in a particular situation, especially because you are waiting for something to happen **3** [I always + adv./prep., T] OLD-FASHIONED to walk or step on something: *We trod carefully over the icy cobblestones.* **4 tread the boards** HUMOROUS to work as an actor

tread² *n.* **1** [C,U] the pattern of lines on the part of a tire that touches the road **2** [C] TECHNICAL the part of a stair that you put your foot on **3** [singular] OLD-FASHIONED the particular sound that someone makes when they walk

tread·le /'trɛdl/ *n.* [C] a flat piece of metal or wood that you move with your foot to turn a wheel in a machine

tread·mill /'trɛdmɪl/ *n.* **1** a piece of exercise equipment that has a large belt around a set of wheels, that moves when you walk or run on it: *He ran two miles on the treadmill.* **2** [singular] work or a way of life that seems very boring because you always have to do the same things **3** [C] a MILL¹ worked in the past by prisoners walking on steps attached to a very large wheel

treadmill test /'.. ,./ *n.* [C] a medical test in which you walk on a treadmill while electronic machines record how well your heart is working

treas. *n.* **1** the written abbreviation of TREASURY **2** the written abbreviation of TREASURER

trea·son /'trizən/ *n.* [U] the crime of being disloyal to your country or its government, especially by helping its enemies or trying to remove the government using violence: *Norris was sentenced to 20 years for treason.* | [+ **against**] *He was wrongly accused of treason against the U.S. government.* | *Any criticism of the emperor was treated like **high treason** (=treason against a government or leader).*

trea·son·a·ble /'trizənəbəl/ also **trea·son·ous** /'trizənəs/ *adj.* a treasonable offense can be punished as treason: *treasonable actions*

treas·ure¹ /'trɛʒə/ *n.* **1** [U] a collection of valuable things such as gold, silver, jewels etc.: **buried/ sunken treasure** (=treasure that is under the ground or in the ocean) **2** [C] a very valuable and important object such as a painting or ancient document: *Your old furniture could be a treasure to a* growing number of collectors. **3** [C usually singular] someone who is very useful or important to you: *A husband that cooks and cleans is a real treasure.* —see also **One man's trash is another man's treasure** (TRASH[1] (5))

treasure[2] *v.* [T] to treat something as being very special, important, or valuable: *I treasure the watch my grandfather gave me.* —**treasured** *adj.: a treasured possession*

treasure chest /'.. ,./ *n.* [C] a box that holds treasure

treasure hunt /'.. ,./ *n.* [C] a game in which you have to find something that has been hidden by answering questions that are left in different places

treas·ur·er /'treʒərə/ *n.* [C] someone who is in charge of the money for an organization, club etc.

treasure trove /'treʒə ,troʊv/ *n.* [C] **1** a collection of valuable or interesting things or information: *Angkor is a treasure trove of history, culture and art.* **2** valuable objects, coins etc. that are found where they have been hidden or buried and that do not have an owner

treas·ur·y /'treʒəri/ *n. plural* **treasuries 1 the Treasury (Department)** a government department that controls the money that the country collects and spends **2** [C] a place where money or valuable objects are kept in a castle, church, PALACE etc.

Treasury bill /'... ,./ *abbreviation* **T-bill** *n.* [C] TECHNICAL a special piece of paper that the U.S. government sells for less money than it is worth later, as a way of borrowing money: *a three-month Treasury bill with a 4% interest rate*

Treasury bond /'... ,./ *abbreviation* **T-bond** *n.* [C] TECHNICAL a BOND sold by the U.S. government, that is worth its full amount in ten years or longer

treasury note /'... ,./ *n.* [C] an official document from the U.S. government saying that it will repay money it has borrowed with INTEREST between one and ten years' time

treat[1] /trit/ *v.* [T] **1** [always + adv./prep.] to behave toward someone in a particular way: [**treat sb like/ as sth**] *Mom still treats us like children.* | *Debbie was always treated as one of the boys.* | **badly treated/ well treated** *The prisoners were well treated by their guards.* | **treat sb with respect/contempt/kindness etc.** *Williams was careful to treat his employees with respect.* | **treat sb like dirt/a dog** (=treat someone unkindly and without respect) **2** [always + adv./ prep.] to deal with, discuss, or react to something in a particular way: [**treat sth as sth**] *Authorities are treating every bomb threat as real.* | *She treats everything I say as some kind of joke.* | **treat sth seriously/carefully/favorably etc.** *Russell urged the university to treat campus security seriously.* **3** to try to cure an illness or injury by using drugs, hospital care, operations etc.: *Some sleep problems can be temporarily treated with sleeping pills.* **4** to buy something special for someone that you know they will enjoy, or to do something special with someone: [**treat sb to sth**] *Guests were treated to wine and caviar at the reception.* | *Once a year, I treat myself to a ski trip.* **5** to put a special substance on something or use a chemical process in order to protect, clean, or preserve it: *In remote areas, make sure your drinking water has been treated.* —see also TRICK OR TREAT

treat with sb/sth *phr. v.* [T] FORMAL to try to reach an official agreement with someone: *U.S. representatives proceeded to treat with the Sioux tribe regarding land rights.*

treat of sth *phr. v.* [T] FORMAL if a book, article etc. treats of something, it is about that subject

treat[2] *n.* **1** [C] something special that you give someone or do for them because you know they will enjoy it: *Many women think of facials as a treat.* **2** [C usually singular] an event that gives you a lot of pleasure, especially if it is unexpected: *Listening to trombonist Slide Hampton is a treat.* **3** [C] a special food that tastes good, especially one that you do not eat very often: *The cafe serves a surprising assortment of healthy gourmet treats.* **4 my treat** SPOKEN used to tell someone that you will pay for something

such as a meal for them: *Let's go out for dinner – my treat this time.*

treat·a·ble /'tritəbəl/ *adj.* a treatable illness or injury can be helped with drugs or an operation

trea·tise /'tritəs/ *n.* [C] a serious book or article about a particular subject: [+ **on**] *a treatise on drugs and youth*

treat·ment /'tritmənt/ *n.* **1** [C,U] a method that is intended to cure an injury or illness: [+ **of/for**] *Chemotherapy is the most common treatment of cancer.* | **get/receive treatment** *His wife urged him to get treatment for his depression.* | *Michael has responded well to treatment* (=got better when he was treated). **2** [U] a particular way of behaving toward someone or of dealing with them: [+ **of**] *Civil rights groups have complained about the harsh treatment of prisoners.* | **special/preferential treatment** (=when one person is treated differently than another) **3** [C,U] a particular way of dealing with or talking about a subject: *Many historians were stunned by the book's inaccurate treatment of the battle.* **4** [U] a process by which something is cleaned, protected etc.: *the treatment of polluted rivers*

trea·ty /'triti/ *n. plural* **treaties** [C] a formal agreement between two or more countries or governments, or the document of this agreement: *The Soviet Union and the U.S. signed a treaty reducing long-range missiles.*

tre·ble[1] /'trebəl/ *adj. adv.* FORMAL three times as big, as much, or as many as something else

treble[2] *v.* [I,T] to become three times as big in amount, size, or number, or to make something increase in this way: *Sales are expected to treble in the next two years.*

treble[3] *n.* **1** [U] the upper half of the whole range of musical notes —compare BASS[1] (3) **2** [C] a boy with a high singing voice —**treble** *adj., adv.: a clear treble voice*

treble clef /,.. './ *n.* [C] TECHNICAL a sign (𝄞) at the beginning of a line of written music which shows that the note written on the bottom line of the STAVE is an E above MIDDLE C

tree /tri/ *n.* [C] **1** a very tall plant that has a wooden trunk, branches, and leaves, and lives for many years: *It's a beautiful park, with a pond and large trees.* **2** a drawing that shows how several things are related to each other by having lines that connect things —see also CHRISTMAS TREE, FAMILY TREE, **money doesn't grow on trees** (MONEY (19))

tree fern /'. ./ *n.* [C] a large tropical FERN

tree·house /'trihaʊs/ *n.* [C] a wooden structure for children to play in, built in the branches of a tree

tree-hug·ger /'. ../ *n.* [C] INFORMAL, DISAPPROVING someone who is concerned about the environment in a way that is sometimes not reasonable: *It's not just tree-huggers who are concerned about air quality.* —**tree-hugging** *adj.* [only before noun] *tree-hugging environmentalists*

tree·less /'trilɪs/ *adj.* a treeless area has no trees in it

tree line /'. ./ *n.* [singular] the TIMBERLINE

tree-lined /'. ./ *adj.* a tree-lined street has trees on both sides

tree sur·ger·y /'. ,.../ *n.* [U] the treatment of damaged trees, especially by cutting off branches

tree·top /'tritɑp/ *n.* [C usually plural] the branches at the top of a tree: *A cool breeze rustled the treetops.*

tree-trunk /'. ./ *n.* [C] the thick central part of a tree

tre·foil /'trifɔɪl, 'trɛ-/ *n.* [C] **1** a type of small plant that has leaves that divide into three parts **2** a pattern of these shapes of these leaves

trek[1] /trɛk/ *v.* **trekked, trekking** [I always + adv./ prep.] **1** to make a long and difficult trip, especially on foot: *Hunters can't trek deep into snowy woods.* **2** to walk a long way, especially in the mountains, as an adventure: [+ **in/across** etc.] *He dreamed of trekking in the Himalayan foothills.*

trek[2] *n.* [C] **1** a long and difficult trip, made especially on foot: *The exhibit will display pictures from his trek across Siberia.* **2** INFORMAL a distance that seems long when you walk it: *It was quite a trek to the grocery store.*

trel·lis /'trɛlɪs/ *n.* [C] a frame made of long narrow pieces of wood that cross each other, used to support climbing plants

trem·ble /'trɛmbəl/ *v.* [I] **1** to shake slightly in a way that you cannot control, especially because you are upset or frightened: *Ginna's whole body trembled as she spoke about her son's death.* | **tremble with anger/fear/rage etc.** *Her hands trembled with fear.* **2** to shake slightly: *The ground beneath them trembled as the trucks rolled past.* **3** if your voice trembles, it sounds nervous and unsteady **4** to be worried or frightened about something: **I tremble to think (that)** *I trembled to think he might have been murdered.* —**tremble** *n.* [C] —**trembly** *adj.*

tre·men·dous /trɪ'mɛndəs/ *adj.* **1** very big, fast, powerful etc.: *The tremendous force of the tornado wiped out the town.* | *The progress that has been made in microelectronics is tremendous.* **2** excellent: *Shandon is a tremendous athlete.*

trem·o·lo /'trɛməloʊ/ *n.* [C] rapidly repeated musical notes

trem·or /'trɛmɚ/ *n.* [C] **1** a small EARTHQUAKE in which the ground shakes slightly **2** a slight shaking movement that you cannot control, especially because you are sick, weak, or upset: *The medication can cause hair loss, tremors, and increased weight.*

trem·u·lous /'trɛmyələs/ *adj.* LITERARY shaking slightly, especially because you are nervous: *a tremulous voice* —**tremulously** *adv.*

trench /trɛntʃ/ *n.* [C] **1** a long narrow hole dug into the surface of the ground: *Workers dug a trench for gas lines.* **2** TECHNICAL a long narrow valley in the ground beneath the ocean: *the Puerto Rico Trench* **3** [C usually plural] a deep trench dug in the ground as a protection for soldiers: *the fighting men in the trenches of France* **4 the trenches** the place or situation where most of the work or action in an activity takes place: *Tobias spent 35 years in the trenches of the feminist movement.*

tren·chant /'trɛntʃənt/ *adj.* expressed very strongly, effectively, and directly, without worrying about offending people: *Brown's article contains trenchant social criticism.* —**trenchantly** *adv.* —**trenchancy** *n.* [U]

trench coat /'. ./ *n.* [C] a long RAINCOAT with a belt

trench mouth /'. ./ *n.* [U] an infection of the mouth and throat

trench war·fare /ˌ. '../ *n.* [U] a method of fighting in which soldiers from opposing armies try to keep safe in TRENCHes across the BATTLEFIELD from each other

trend¹ /trɛnd/ *n.* [C] **1** a general tendency in the way a situation is changing or developing: *If current trends continue, tourism in the state will increase by 10%.* | [+ **in**] *The agency monitors trends in drug use among teenagers.* | [+ **toward**] *There is a recent trend toward more parental involvement in schools.* | *Davis is hoping to* **reverse the trend** (=make a trend go in the opposite direction) *of rising taxes.* **2 set the trend** to start doing something that other people copy: *Larger corporations are setting the trend for better maternity benefits.* —see also TRENDSETTER

trend² *v.* [I always + adv./prep.] to show a general tendency in the way a situation is changing or developing: [+ **upward/downward/lower etc.**] *Prices of new homes are trending upward.*

trend·set·ter /'trɛndˌsɛtɚ/ *n.* [C] someone who starts a new fashion or makes it popular —**trendsetting** *adj.*

trend·spot·ter /'. ˌ../ *n.* [C] someone who notices and reports on new fashions, activities that people are starting to do, or the way a situation is developing

trend·y /'trɛndi/ *adj.* **trendier, trendiest** influenced by the most fashionable styles and ideas: *a trendy*

New York night club —**trendily** *adv.* —**trendiness** *n.* [U]

Tren·ton /'trɛntⁿn/ the capital city of the U.S. state of New Jersey

tre·pan /trɪ'pæn/ *v.* [T] to cut a round piece of bone out of your SKULL (=bone in your head) as part of a medical operation

trep·i·da·tion /ˌtrɛpə'deɪʃən/ *n.* [U] a feeling of anxiety or fear about something that is going to happen: *The students,* **with** *some* **trepidation***, asked about violence at the prison.*

tres·pass¹ /'trɛspæs/ *v.* [I + **on**] **1** to go onto someone's private land without their permission **2** OLD USE to do something wrong; SIN —**trespasser** *n.* [C]

trespass on sth *phr. v.* [T] FORMAL to do something that you should not do or are not allowed to do: *Navy officers who trespass on the authority of their superiors are usually severely punished.*

tres·pass² *n.* **1** [C,U] LAW the offense of trespassing **2** [C] BIBLICAL something you have done that is morally wrong; SIN

tres·pass·ing /'trɛspæsɪŋ, -pəsɪŋ/ *n.* [U] the offense of going onto someone's land without their permission

tress·es /'trɛsɪz/ *n.* [plural] LITERARY a woman's beautiful long hair

tres·tle /'trɛsəl/ *n.* [C] **1** an A-shaped frame used as one of the supports for a table, shelf, or bridge **2** also **trestle bridge** a bridge with this kind of a frame supporting it

trestle ta·ble /'.. ˌ../ *n.* [C] a table made of a long board supported on trestles

Tre·vi·no /trə'vinoʊ/**, Lee** /li/ (1939–) a U.S. GOLFer

trey /treɪ/ *n.* [C] INFORMAL **1** an action of throwing a basketball through the HOOP that is worth three points **2** a playing card or the side of a DIE² (2) or DOMINO with three marks on it

tri- /traɪ/ *prefix* three: *trilingual* (=speaking three languages) | *a triangle* (=shape with three sides) —see also BI-, DI-

tri·ad /'traɪæd/ *n.* [C] **1** a Chinese secret criminal group **2** a group of three people or things that are related or similar to each other

tri·age /tri'ɑʒ, 'triɑʒ/ *n.* [U] TECHNICAL the method of deciding who receives medical treatment first, according to how seriously someone is injured

tri·al /'traɪəl/ *n.*

1 |court| [C,U] a legal process in which a court of law examines a case to decide whether someone is guilty of a crime: *a murder trial* | *Warner will* **stand trial on** (=be judged in a court of law concerning) *charges of insurance fraud.* | *Both men* **are on trial for** (=are being judged in a court of law concerning) *bank robbery.* | **go/come to trial** (=begin being judged in a court of law) —see also SHOW TRIAL

2 |test| [C,U] a process of testing to find out whether something works effectively and is safe: *The drug is being evaluated in clinical trials.*

3 |try sb/sth| [C,U] a short period during which you use something or employ someone to find out whether they are satisfactory for a particular purpose or job: *Smith was hired* **on a** six-month **trial basis.** | *There is* **a trial period** *of one month during which you can return the car for a full refund.*

4 by/through trial and error if you do something by trial and error, you test many different methods of doing something in order to find the best: *They learned to farm the land through trial and error.*

5 |difficulty| [C usually plural] something that is difficult to deal with, and that is worrying or annoying: *People in Russia are exhausted by the daily trials of living.* | **be a trial (to/for sb)** *Learning to live with blindness was a major trial for the young girl.* | *Jones endured the* **trials and tribulations** *of being a single mother.*

6 |sports| **trials** [plural] a sports competition that tests a player's ability: *Metcalf placed fifth in the long jump in the 1988* **Olympic Trials** (=competition to decide who will go to the Olympics).

trial bal·loon /ˌ.. .'./ *n.* [C] something that you do or say in order to see whether other people will accept something or not: *Senator Lott is **floating trial balloons** to test public opinion on the bill.*

trial run /ˌ.. ˈ./ *n.* [C] an occasion when you test a new method or system to see if it works well: *The airline's new check-in system will be given a trial run this weekend.*

tri·an·gle /ˈtraɪˌæŋgəl/ *n.* [C] **1** a flat shape with three straight sides and three angles —see picture at SHAPE¹ **2** something that is shaped like a triangle: *His nose was a small triangle on his wide face.* **3** a musical instrument made of metal bent in the shape of a triangle, that you hit to make a ringing sound **4** a flat plastic object with three sides that has one angle of 90° and is used for drawing angles —see also LOVE TRIANGLE

tri·an·gu·lar /traɪˈæŋgyələ/ *adj.* **1** shaped like a triangle **2** involving three people or teams: *a triangular relationship*

tri·an·gu·la·tion /traɪˌæŋgyəˈleɪʃən/ *n.* [U] a method of finding your position by measuring the lines and angles of a triangle on a map

tri·ath·lete /traɪˈæθlit/ *n.* [C] someone who takes part in triathlons

tri·ath·lon /traɪˈæθlɑn, -lən/ *n.* [C] a sports competition in which competitors run, swim, and ride a bicycle for long distances

trib·al /ˈtraɪbəl/ *adj.* relating to a tribe or tribes: *tribal councils | tribal warfare*

trib·al·ism /ˈtraɪbəˌlɪzəm/ *n.* [U] **1** the state of being organized into tribes **2** behavior and attitudes that are based on strong loyalty to your tribe

S W
tribe /traɪb/ *n.* [C] **1** a social group consisting of people of the same race who have the same beliefs, customs, language etc., and usually live in one particular area ruled by a chief: *Western Australian tribes* —see RACE¹ (2) and see Usage Note at RACE¹ **2** a group of related animals or plants: *There is a tribe of beetles that specializes in feeding on bitter plants.* **3** HUMOROUS a large family: *We were only expecting Jack and his wife, but the whole tribe turned up.*

tribes·man /ˈtraɪbzmən/ *n.* [C] a man who is a member of a tribe

tribes·wom·an /ˈtraɪbzˌwʊmən/ *n.* [C] a woman who is a member of a tribe

trib·u·la·tion /ˌtrɪbyəˈleɪʃən/ *n.* [C,U] FORMAL serious trouble or a serious problem: *the tribulations of his personal life* —compare TRIAL (5)

tri·bu·nal /traɪˈbyunl, trɪ-/ *n.* [C] a type of court that is given official authority to deal with a particular situation or problem: *the Nuremberg war-crimes tribunal*

trib·une /ˈtrɪbyun, trɪˈbyun/ *n.* [C] an official in ancient Rome who was elected by the ordinary people to protect their rights

tri·bu·tar·y¹ /ˈtrɪbyəˌteri/ *n. plural* **tributaries** [C] a stream or river that flows into a larger river

tributary² *adj.* FORMAL having a duty to pay TRIBUTE (3)

trib·ute /ˈtrɪbyut/ *n.* **1** [C,U] something that you say, do, or give in order to express your respect or admiration for someone: *The song was sung as **a tribute to** his late grandfather. | Friends **paid tribute to** Herrera's courage* (=praised and admired publicly). **2 be a tribute to sb/sth** to be a clear sign of the good qualities that someone or something has: *Her home is a tribute to Rococo-era decor.* **3** [C,U] a payment of goods or money by one ruler or country to a more powerful one

trice /traɪs/ *n.* **in a trice** LITERARY very quickly

tri·ceps /ˈtraɪsɛps/ *n.* [C] the large muscle at the back of your upper arm

S W
trick¹ /trɪk/ *n.* [C]

1 deceive sb something you do in order to deceive someone: *The pregnancy was just a trick to get him to marry her. | Pretending he doesn't remember is an old trick of his.*
2 joke something you do to surprise someone and to make other people laugh: *It's a tradition for Sun employees to **play tricks on** each other for April Fool's Day.*

3 magic a skillful set of actions that seem like magic, done to entertain people: *For my final trick, I will make this elephant disappear.*
4 smart method a way of doing something that works very well: *In college, I learned a trick to remember names. | Being a master gardener isn't just knowing **the tricks of the trade*** (=methods used in a particular job).
5 do the trick SPOKEN if something does the trick, it solves a problem or provides what is needed to get a good result: *The second surgery on my knee seemed to do the trick.*
6 a dirty/rotten/mean trick an unkind or unfair thing to do: *Bomb threats and other dirty tricks kept many voters at home.*
7 use every trick in the book to use every method that you know, even dishonest ones, to achieve what you want: *Vicki used every trick in the book to get Patty fired.*
8 be up to sb's old tricks INFORMAL to be doing the same dishonest things that you have often done before: *It appears Larkin and his law firm are up to their old tricks.*
9 cards [C] the cards played or won in one part of a game of cards: *He won the first three tricks easily.*
10 teach/show sb a trick or two INFORMAL used to say that someone knows more than someone else or can do something better than them: *Experienced teachers can teach new teachers a trick or two.*
11 never miss a trick SPOKEN to always know exactly what is happening even if it does not concern you: *Mrs. White knew we hadn't studied – she never misses a trick.*
12 sex [C] someone who pays a PROSTITUTE to have sex
13 turn a trick SLANG to have sex with someone for money
14 how's tricks? OLD-FASHIONED, SPOKEN used to greet someone in a friendly way: *Hello Bill! How's tricks?* —see also CONFIDENCE TRICK, HAT TRICK, **play a joke/trick on sb** (PLAY¹ (12)), **you can't teach an old dog new tricks** (TEACH (7))

trick² *v.* [T] to deceive someone in order to get something from them or to make them do something: *You tricked me! |* [**trick sb into doing sth**] *She was tricked into signing the paper. |* [**trick sb out of sth**] *Winston had tricked the elderly couple out of $5000.*

trick³ *adj.* **1 trick photography** photography that changes the way things really look **2 a trick question** a question that seems easy to answer but has a hidden difficulty **3 a trick knee/ankle/shoulder etc.** a joint that is weak and can suddenly cause you problems

trick·er·y /ˈtrɪkəri/ *n.* [U] the use of tricks to deceive or cheat people

trick·le¹ /ˈtrɪkəl/ *v.* [I always + adv./prep.] **1** if liquid trickles somewhere, it flows slowly in drops or in a thin stream: [+ **down/into/out**] *Blood trickled down the side of her head.* **2** if people, vehicles, goods etc. trickle somewhere, they move there slowly in small groups or amounts: [+ **in/into/away**] *The first few fans started to trickle into the stadium.*

trickle² *n.* **1** [C] a thin slow flow of liquid: *A trickle of juice ran down his chin.* **2** [singular] a movement of people, vehicles, goods etc. into a place in very small numbers or amounts: *Ice on the roads reduced the morning rush hour traffic to a trickle.*

trickle-down ef·fect /ˌ.. ˌ. ./ *n.* [singular] a belief that additional wealth gained by the richest people in society will have a good economic effect on the lives of everyone because they will put the money into businesses, INVESTMENTS etc.

trick or treat /ˌ.. ˈ./ *v.* **1** the words that children say when they go trick or treating, in order to say that they will play a trick on someone if they are not given a TREAT (=piece of candy) **2 go trick or treating** if children go trick or treating, they dress in COSTUMES and go from house to house on HALLOWEEN saying "trick or treat" in order to get candy

trick·ster /ˈtrɪkstɚ/ n. [C] someone who deceives or cheats people

trick·y /ˈtrɪki/ adj. **trickier, trickiest** 1 a tricky situation or job is difficult to deal with or do because it is very complicated and full of problems: *Getting everyone to use the new technology will be tricky.* 2 a tricky person is likely to deceive you; CRAFTY —**trickiness** n. [U] —**trickily** adv.

tri·col·or /ˈtraɪˌkʌlɚ/ n. [C] a flag with three equal bands of different colors, especially the national flags of France and Ireland

tri·cy·cle /ˈtraɪsɪkəl/ n. [C] a bicycle with three wheels, especially one for young children

tri·dent /ˈtraɪdnt/ n. [C] 1 a weapon with three points that looks like a large fork 2 **Trident missile/submarine** a type of NUCLEAR weapon, or the SUBMARINE that shoots it

tried¹ /traɪd/ v. the past tense and past participle of TRY¹

tried² adj. **tried and tested** also **tried and true** a tried and tested method has been used successfully many times: *tried and tested research methods*

tri·en·ni·al /traɪˈɛniəl/ adj. happening every three years

tri·fle¹ /ˈtraɪfəl/ n. 1 **a trifle tired/nervous/sleepy etc.** FORMAL slightly tired, nervous etc.: *He seemed a trifle irritated.* 2 [C] OLD-FASHIONED something unimportant or not valuable: *Buying a house is no trifle for middle class families.* 3 [C,U] a cold sweet DESSERT that consists of layers of cake, fruit, JELL-O, CUSTARD, and cream

trifle² v.
trifle with sb/sth phr. v. [T] to treat someone or something without enough respect or seriousness: *John Mitchell was not someone to be trifled with.*

tri·fling /ˈtraɪflɪŋ/ adj. unimportant or of little value: *a trifling matter* | *a trifling sum of money*

tri·fo·cals /ˈtraɪˌfoʊkəlz/ n. [plural] special glasses in which the upper part of the LENS is made for seeing things that are far away, the lower part is made for reading, and the middle part is for seeing things in between —compare BIFOCALS

trig /trɪg/ n. [U] 1 SPOKEN the short form for TRIGONOMETRY 2 also **trig.** the written abbreviation of TRIGONOMETRY

trig·ger¹ /ˈtrɪgɚ/ n. [C] 1 the part of a gun that you press with your finger to fire it: **pull/squeeze the trigger** *Jackson is convinced Ray pulled the trigger.* 2 **be the trigger (for sth)** to be the thing that quickly causes a serious problem: *Illegal banking practices were the trigger for the financial crisis.* —see also HAIR-TRIGGER¹, **whatever trips your trigger** (WHATEVER¹ (8))

trigger² also **trigger off** v. [T] to make something happen very quickly, especially a series of violent events: *The incident could trigger a civil war.* | **trigger a feeling/memory** (=make you suddenly feel or remember something)

trigger-hap·py /ˈ.. ˌ../ adj. INFORMAL much too willing to shoot at people: *trigger-happy soldiers*

trigger man /ˈ.. ˌ./ n. [C] the person who shoots someone, especially a criminal who does this

trig·o·nom·e·try /ˌtrɪgəˈnɑmətri/ n. [U] the part of mathematics that is concerned with the relationship between the angles and sides of TRIANGLEs —**trigonometrical** /ˌtrɪgənəˈmɛtrɪkəl/ adj.

trike /traɪk/ n. [C] INFORMAL a TRICYCLE

tri·lat·er·al /ˌtraɪˈlætərəl/ adj. involving or including three groups or countries: *a trilateral agreement*

tril·by /ˈtrɪlbi/ n. [C] a man's soft FELT² hat

tri·lin·gual /ˌtraɪˈlɪŋgwəl/ adj. able to speak or use three languages

trill¹ /trɪl/ v. [I,T] 1 to sing or play a musical instrument with repeated short high notes: *A mockingbird trilled from atop a telephone pole.* 2 to say something in a pleasant high cheerful voice: *"Have a nice time, darling," she trilled.*

trill² n. [C] 1 TECHNICAL a musical sound made by quickly going up and down several times between two notes a HALF TONE apart 2 a sound like this, especially one made by a bird 3 TECHNICAL a speech sound produced by quickly moving the end of your tongue against the top part of your mouth when you pronounce the sound /r/

tril·lion /ˈtrɪlyən/ number quantifier 1 1,000,000,000,000 2 also **trillions** INFORMAL a very large number of something

tri·lo·bite /ˈtraɪləˌbaɪt/ n. [C] a small simple sea creature that lived millions of years ago and is now a FOSSIL

tril·o·gy /ˈtrɪlədʒi/ n. plural **trilogies** [C] a group of three related plays, books, movies etc. about the same characters: *Coppola was also the director of "The Godfather" trilogy.*

trim¹ /trɪm/ v. **trimmed, trimming** [T] 1 to make something look neater by cutting small pieces off it: *I need to trim my mustache.* | *We trimmed the bushes in front of the house.* 2 to remove parts of a plan in order to reduce its cost: *Congress plans to trim $200 million from the Pentagon budget.* 3 [usually passive] to decorate something, especially the edges of clothes, by putting something on it: [**trim sth with sth**] *Her black dress was trimmed with blue ribbon.* | *Three weeks before Christmas we get together and **trim the tree** (=decorate the Christmas tree).* 4 to move the sails of a boat into a position that makes the boat go faster
trim sth ↔ **off** phr. v. [T] to cut small pieces off something, especially so that it looks neater: *Wash the cauliflower, and trim off the green leaves.*

trim² adj. 1 thin, attractive, and healthy looking: *Walking to work helps her keep trim.* | *a trim, neatly dressed young man* 2 neat and well taken care of: *a trim suburban yard*

trim³ n. 1 [C usually singular] an act of cutting something to make it look neater: *I'm going to the barbershop to get a trim.* 2 [singular,U] decoration on a car, piece of clothing etc., that goes along the length of it: *Borough Hall was a brick building with white trim.* 3 [U] the degree to which an aircraft is level in relation to the horizon

tri·ma·ran /ˈtraɪməˌræn/ n. [C] a sailing boat that has three separate but connected parts that float on the water

tri·mes·ter /ˈtraɪmɛstɚ, traɪˈmɛstɚ/ n. [C] 1 one of the three-month periods of a PREGNANCY 2 one of three periods of equal length that the year is divided into in some schools —see also TERM¹ (14)

trim·mer /ˈtrɪmɚ/ n. [C] a machine for cutting the edges of HEDGEs, LAWNs etc.

trim·mings /ˈtrɪmɪŋz/ n. [plural] 1 **all the trimmings** all the other types of food that are traditionally served with the main dish of a meal: *We had a Thanksgiving meal with all the trimmings.* 2 the small pieces that have been cut off something larger: *tree trimmings* 3 pieces of material used to decorate clothes: *She wore a blue velvet gown with black trimmings.*

Trin·i·dad and To·ba·go /ˌtrɪnɪdæd ən təˈbeɪgoʊ/ a country in the south Caribbean Sea, close to the coast of Venezuela, and consisting of the islands of Trinidad and Tobago —**Trinidadian** /ˌtrɪnɪˈdædiən/ n., adj.

trin·i·ty /ˈtrɪnəti/ n. plural **trinities** 1 **the Trinity** the union of Father, Son, and Holy Spirit in one God, according to the Christian religion 2 [C] LITERARY a group of three people or things

trin·ket /ˈtrɪŋkɪt/ n. [C] a piece of jewelry or a small pretty object that is not worth much money: *One shelf displayed trinkets from each country she had visited.*

tri·o /ˈtrioʊ/ n. plural **trios** [C] 1 a group of three people or three related things: [+ **of**] *an interesting trio of poems* 2 a group of three singers or musicians who perform together 3 a piece of music for three performers —compare DUET, QUARTET

trip¹ /trɪp/ n. [C] 1 an occasion when you travel from one place to another; JOURNEY: *How was your trip?* | [+ **to**] *Let's **take a trip** to Mexico.* | *They're going on* *a trip to Canada this summer.* | *There was so much stuff we had to* **make three trips** *to carry it all in.* | **business/school/skiing** etc. **trip** *a business trip to Japan* —see Usage Note at TRAVEL¹ **2** [usually singular] SLANG a person or experience that is amusing and very different from normal: *You're a trip.* **3** SLANG the experiences someone has while their mind is affected by a drug such as LSD: *a bad trip* **4** an act of falling as a result of hitting something with your foot —see also ROUND TRIP

trip

trip² *v.*

1 fall [I] to hit something with your foot while you are walking or running so that you fall or almost fall: *I tripped as I got out of the car.* | [+ over/on] *He almost tripped over the dog.* | *Dana tripped on her bathrobe and fell forward.*

2 make sb fall [T] also **trip sb up** to make someone fall by putting your foot in front of them when they are moving: *Gretzky was tripped by O'Donnell near the goal.*

3 **trip a switch/wire** to accidentally make an electrical system operate by moving part of it: *She tripped her own car alarm when she opened the trunk.*

4 **trip off the tongue** to be easy to say or pronounce: *His name, "Roberto Carlos," just trips off the tongue.*

5 walk/dance [I always + adv./prep.] LITERARY to walk or run with quick light steps as if you are dancing: **trip along/over/down** etc. *She watched her two kids tripping down the sidewalk.*

6 **sb is tripping** SLANG used to say that you think someone is not thinking clearly or being reasonable: *Ken's tripping if he thinks I'm going to lend him $500.*

7 drug [I] also **trip out** SLANG to experience the effects of an illegal drug such as LSD

8 **trip the light fantastic** OLD-FASHIONED to dance —see also **whatever trips your trigger** (WHATEVER¹ (8))

trip on sb/sth *phr. v.* [T] SLANG to enjoy someone or something and think about how unusual they are: *I was tripping on her bright red army boots.*

trip up *phr. v.* **1** [T **trip** sb **up**] to trick someone into making a mistake: *The questions look simple, but they're designed to trip you up.* **2** [T **trip** sb **up**] to make someone fall by putting your foot in front of them when they are walking **3** [I] to make a mistake [+ over] *Many people get tripped up over the new tax laws.*

trip out *phr. v.* [I,T **trip** sb **out**] SLANG if you trip out or someone or something trips you out, you enjoy something and think about how unusual they are: *I started saying some things in Russian and she totally tripped out.*

tri·par·tite /traɪˈpɑrtaɪt/ *adj.* FORMAL **1** **tripartite agreement/alliance** etc. involving three groups or nations **2** having three parts: *a tripartite political system*

tripe /traɪp/ *n.* [U] **1** INFORMAL something that has been said or written which is stupid or not true: *I don't waste my time watching the tripe that's on TV.* **2** the stomach of a cow or pig used for food

tri·ple¹ /ˈtrɪpəl/ *adj.* [only before noun] **1** having three parts or involving three people or groups: *a triple-layer chocolate cake* | *a triple jump in ice skating* **2** **triple digits** a number that is at least 100 but less than 1000: *The Lakers scored in triple digits for the fifth time this month.* **3** **a triple play** three OUTS⁴ (2) at one time in baseball

triple² *v.* [I,T] to become three times as much or as

many, or to make something do this: *The population of the valley has tripled in the past 20 years.* | [triple sth] *We want to triple our profits by next year.*

triple³ *n.* [C] **1** a hit of the ball in BASEBALL that allows the BATTER¹ (2) to reach the third BASE² (9) **2** three turns of your body in the same direction in sports such as ICE SKATING, GYMNASTICS etc.

Triple A /ˌtrɪpəl ˈeɪ/ *n.* SPOKEN: see AAA

triple jump /ˈ.. ˌ./ *n.* **the triple jump** an ATHLETICS event in which you try to jump as far as you can by jumping first with one foot, then onto the other foot, and finally with both feet together

tri·plet /ˈtrɪplɪt/ *n.* [C] **1** one of three children born at the same time to the same mother **2** [C] TECHNICAL three musical notes or BEATS² (2) which are played together or quickly one after the other

tri·plex /ˈtraɪplɛks, ˈtrɪ-/ *n.* [C] **1** a house which has three separate floors or parts that different people live in —compare DUPLEX **2** a movie theater with three separate movie screens

trip·li·cate /ˈtrɪpləkɪt/ *n.* **in triplicate** if a document is written in triplicate, there are three copies of it

tri·pod /ˈtraɪpɑd/ *n.* [C] an object with three legs, used to support a camera, TELESCOPE etc.

Trip·ol·i /ˈtrɪpəli/ the capital and largest city of Libya

trip·tych /ˈtrɪptɪk/ *n.* [C] TECHNICAL a picture, especially a religious one, painted on three pieces of wood that are joined together

trip·wire /ˈtrɪpˌwaɪɚ/ *n.* [C] a wire stretched across the ground as part of a trap

tri·reme /ˈtraɪrim/ *n.* [C] an ancient WARSHIP with three rows of OARS on each side

tri·sect /ˈtraɪsɛkt, traɪˈsɛkt/ *v.* [T] TECHNICAL to divide a line, angle etc. into three equal parts

tri·state /ˈtraɪsteɪt/ *adj.* related to a group of three states in the U.S.

trite /traɪt/ *adj.* a trite remark, idea etc. has been used so often that it seems boring and not sincere: *The movie's dialogue is trite and uninspired.* —**triteness** *n.* [U]

tri·umph¹ /ˈtraɪəmf/ *n.* [C] **1** an important victory or success, especially after a difficult struggle: *Mary's final triumph was to see both of her boys go to college.* | [+ over] *The dam represents man's triumph over nature.* **2** a feeling of pleasure and satisfaction that you get from victory or success: *a cry of triumph* **3** a very successful example of something: [+ of] *The compromise is a triumph of cooperation between the city and developers.*

triumph² *v.* [I] to gain a victory or success, especially after a difficult struggle: [+ over] *Nathan triumphed over his learning disability to become a surgeon.*

tri·um·phal /traɪˈʌmfəl/ *adj.* [only before noun] done or made in order to celebrate a triumph: *The general was given a triumphal parade up Broadway.*

tri·umph·al·ism /traɪˈʌmfəˌlɪzəm/ *n.* [U] the feeling of being too proud about a victory and too pleased about your opponent's defeat

tri·um·phant /traɪˈʌmfənt/ *adj.* **1** having gained a victory or success: *the triumphant women's gymnastics team* **2** expressing pleasure and pride because of your victory or success: *a triumphant grin* —**triumphantly** *adv.*

tri·um·vi·rate /traɪˈʌmvərət/ *n.* [C] FORMAL a group of three very powerful people who share control over something

triv·et /ˈtrɪvət/ *n.* [C] **1** an object placed under a hot pot or dish to protect the surface of a table, which is usually made of metal or wood **2** an object for holding a pot over a fire

triv·i·a /ˈtrɪviə/ *n.* [U] **1** detailed facts about past events, famous people, sports etc., often used in games **2** unimportant or useless details: *News programs tend to focus on trivia at the expense of serious issues.*

triv·i·al /ˈtrɪviəl/ *adj.* unimportant or of little value: *She often loses her temper over trivial matters.* —**trivially** *adv.*

T

triv·i·al·i·ty /ˌtrɪvi'æləti/ n. plural **trivialities 1** [U] the fact of being not important or serious at all **2** [C] something that is not important at all: *The mayor is too concerned with such trivialities as the size of his office.*

triv·i·al·ize /'trɪviə,laɪz/ v. [T] to make an important subject seem less important than it really is: *The media also has trivialized the peace movement and its leaders.* —**trivialization** /ˌtrɪviələ'zeɪʃən/ n. [U]

tro·chee /'troʊki/ n. [C] TECHNICAL a unit in poetry consisting of one strong or long beat followed by one weak or short beat, as in "father"

trod /trɑd/ v. the past tense of TREAD[1]

trod·den /'trɑdn/ v. the past participle of TREAD[1]

trog·lo·dyte /'trɑglə,daɪt/ n. [C] someone living in a CAVE, especially in very ancient times

troi·ka /'trɔɪkə/ n. [C] **1** a group of three people working together, especially in government **2** a Russian carriage pulled by three horses side by side

Tro·jan /'troʊdʒən/ one of the people that lived in the ancient city of Troy, whose war with the Greeks is described by the Greek poet Homer

Trojan Horse /ˌ... './ n. [C] **sb/sth is (like) a Trojan Horse** if someone or something is a Trojan Horse, they are being used to hide someone's true purpose or intention: *The bill is a Trojan Horse designed to weaken the union's power.*

troll /troʊl/ n. [C] an imaginary creature in ancient Scandinavian stories, like a very large or very small ugly person

trol·ley /'trɑli/ n. plural **trolleys** [C] **1** also **trolley car** an electric vehicle for carrying passengers which moves along the street on metal tracks **2** a TROLLEYBUS **3** the part of an electric vehicle that connects it to the electric wires above

trol·ley·bus /'trɑli,bʌs/ n. [C] a bus that gets its power from electric wires above the street

trol·lop /'trɑləp/ n. [C] OLD-FASHIONED OR HUMOROUS **1** an insulting word for a sexually immoral woman **2** an insulting word for a very messy woman

Trol·lope /'trɑləp/**, An·tho·ny** /'ænθəni/ (1815–1882) an English writer of NOVELS

trom·bone /trɑm'boʊn/ n. [C] a large musical instrument made of metal that you blow into, and which has a long tube that you slide in and out to change the notes

trom·bon·ist /trɑm'boʊnɪst/ n. [C] a musician who plays a trombone

tromp /trɑmp, trɔmp/ v. [I always + adv./prep.] to walk around or through somewhere with firm, heavy steps: *We tromped a mile through the snow to get home*

SW1 **troop**[1] /trup/ n. **1 troops** [plural] soldiers, especially in organized groups: *The President is sending three hundred troops to the area.* **2 troop movements/ concentrations** movements or gatherings of troops **3** [C] a group of boy or girl SCOUTS led by an adult **4** [C] a group of soldiers, especially on horses or in TANKS **5** [C] a group of people or wild animals, especially when they are moving —compare TROUPE

troop[2] v. [I always + adv./prep.] to move together in a group: [+ into/along/out etc.] *The team trooped out of the clubhouse and onto the field.*

troop car·ri·er /'. ,.../ n. [C] a ship, aircraft, or vehicle used for carrying soldiers

troop·er /'trupɚ/ n. **1** [C] the lowest ranking soldier in the part of the army that uses TANKS or horses **2** [C] also **state trooper** a member of a state police force in the U.S. **3 sb's a (real) trooper** SPOKEN used to say that someone is able to deal well with a difficult situation, especially because they continue to try to do something despite the difficulties **4 swear like a trooper** to swear a lot

troop·ship /'trup,ʃɪp/ n. [C] a ship used for carrying a large number of soldiers

trope /troʊp/ n. [C] TECHNICAL a FIGURE OF SPEECH

tro·phy /'troʊfi/ n. plural **trophies** [C] **1** a prize for winning a race or other competition, especially a silver cup or a PLAQUE: *the NCAA championship trophy* **2** something that you keep to show that you have been successful in something, especially in war or hunting: *He kept the antlers as a trophy.* **3 trophy wife** a young, beautiful woman who is married to a rich and successful man: *The resort was full of doctors and lawyers with their trophy wives.*

trop·ic /'trɑpɪk/ n. **1 the tropics** [plural] the hottest part of the world, which is between the two tropics **2** [C] one of the two imaginary lines around the world, either the Tropic of Cancer which is $23\frac{1}{2}°$ north of the EQUATOR, or the Tropic of Capricorn which is $23\frac{1}{2}°$ south of the EQUATOR

trop·i·cal /'trɑpɪkəl/ adj. **1** coming from or existing in the hottest parts of the world: *tropical birds* **2 tropical medicine** the study of diseases that are common in tropical countries **3** weather that is tropical is very hot and wet: *the tropical summer of Cuba*

tro·po·sphere /'troʊpə,sfɪr, 'trɑ-/ n. **the troposphere** the lowest part of the ATMOSPHERE

trot[1] /trɑt/ v. **trotted, trotting 1** [I] if a horse trots, it moves fairly quickly, with each front leg moving at the same time as the opposite back leg **2** [I always + adv./prep.] **a)** to run fairly slowly, taking short steps: *He locked the door and trotted down the stairs to my car.* **b)** SPOKEN to walk or go somewhere: *I'm going to trot over to the post office.*

trot sth ↔ out phr. v. [T] INFORMAL **1** to give opinions, excuses, reasons etc. that you have used too often to seem sincere: *The drugs industry will trot out its usual defense to explain the high prices.* **2** to show or present something you want other people to see or notice: *Morgan trotted out a few songs from her new album.*

trot[2] n. **1** [singular] the movement of a horse at trotting speed: *With a click, the horse started into a trot.* **2** [singular] a fairly slow way of running, in which you take short steps: *As soon as we saw the ice-cream truck, we broke into a trot* (=increase your speed to a trot). **3 the trots** [plural] INFORMAL, HUMOROUS: see DIARRHEA **4** [C] a ride on a horse at trotting speed **5** a CRIB NOTE

troth /trɑθ, trɔθ, troʊθ/ n. OLD USE **1 by my troth** used when expressing an opinion strongly **2 in troth** truly; INDEED

Trot·sky /'trɑtski/**, Le·on** /'liɑn/ (1879–1940) a Russian political leader, born in the Ukraine, who had an important part in the Russian Revolution of 1917

Trot·sky·ite /'trɑtski,aɪt/ also **Trot·sky·ist** /'trɑtski- ɪst/ n. [C] someone who believes in the political ideas of Leon Trotsky, especially that the working class should take control of the state —**Trotskyite** adj.

trou·ba·dour /'trubə,dɔr/ n. [C] a type of singer and poet who traveled around the PALACES and castles of southern Europe in the 12th and 13th centuries

SW11 **trou·ble**[1] /'trʌbəl/ n.
1 problems [C,U] problems that make something difficult, make you change your plans, make you worry etc.: *The U.S. is responsible for its own troubles.* | [+ with] *We've been having trouble with our teenage son.* | [**trouble doing sth**] *I have trouble staying awake in class.* | **What's the trouble?** (=used to ask someone what is causing a particular problem)

2 doing sth wrong [U] a situation in which someone in authority is angry with you or is likely to punish you: *Joseph often got into trouble for not doing his homework.* | *My brother's in trouble with the police again.* | *I just told him the truth – I didn't mean to get you into trouble* (=put someone into a situation in which they are likely to be punished). | **be in (serious/deep/big) trouble** *If Dad finds out that you've been smoking, you'll be in big trouble.*

3 difficult situation [U] a difficult or dangerous situation: *We ran into trouble installing the water heater.* | *The pilots got into trouble when they lost radio contact with the airport.* | *Our new network software has been causing us a lot of trouble.*

4 effort [U] an amount of effort and time that is needed to do something, especially when it is inconvenient for you to do it: *I don't want to put you to*

any **trouble** (=make someone use a lot of time and effort). | *Only 20% of the people* **took the trouble to vote** (=make a special effort to do something). | *She* **went to a lot of trouble** (=used a lot of time and effort) *organizing the picnic for everyone.* | *Using my credit card* **saves me the trouble of** (=makes it unnecessary for me to do something) *getting cash at the bank.* | *Taking the train is* **more trouble than it's worth** (=used to say that something takes too much time and effort to do).
5 |machine/system| [U] something that is wrong with a machine, vehicle, or system: *engine trouble* | [+ with] *We're having trouble with our oven.*
6 |health| [U] a problem that you have with your health, especially one that is painful: [+ with] *Grandma has had trouble with her heart.* | *heart/ stomach/skin etc. trouble Murayama was taken to hospital with stomach trouble.*
7 |argument/violence| [C,U] a situation in which people argue or fight with each other: *When they walked by, I knew there was going to be trouble.* | *The troubles are far from over.* | **cause/make trouble** (=deliberately start an argument or fight)

SPOKEN PHRASES

8 the trouble with sb/sth used when explaining what is not satisfactory about someone or something: *The trouble with you is that you don't listen.*
9 the trouble is... used when explaining why something is impossible or difficult: *The trouble is they're all jealous of me.*
10 be asking for trouble to take risks or do something stupid that is likely to cause problems: *Walking around downtown late at night is just asking for trouble.*
11 it's no trouble (at all) used to say that you are very willing to do something because it is not inconvenient for you: *"Thanks for helping me move." "It's no trouble at all."*
12 have trouble with sth to disagree with something, especially because it is against your MORALS or principles: *I have trouble with the idea of casual sex.*
13 sb's no trouble if a child is no trouble, they do not annoy or worry you: *You can leave the children with me. They're no trouble.*
14 sb's (nothing but) trouble used to say that someone often does bad things

---

USAGE NOTE: TROUBLE

WORD CHOICE: trouble, problem
Trouble and **problem** are very similar in meaning. However, **trouble** usually refers to several problems that someone or something is causing you, especially when this makes you worried or annoyed. **Trouble** is usually uncountable: *Bill's having trouble with his math homework.* | *She has trouble getting to work on time.* A **problem** is a bad situation that must be dealt with because it is harmful or inconvenient for you. Also, **problems** can be counted: *Teenage crime is a big problem.* | *The new traffic system is causing problems for everyone.*

---

trouble² *v.* **1** [T] if a problem troubles you, it makes you feel worried: *Many workers said they were troubled by the lack of safety procedures.* **2 sorry to trouble you** also **may/could I trouble you (for sth)?** SPOKEN, FORMAL used when politely asking someone to do something for you or give you something: *Sorry to trouble you, but could I borrow your pen?* **3** [T] if a medical problem troubles you, it causes you pain or makes you suffer: *Stephen's been troubled with an earache all week.* **4** [T] FORMAL to ask someone to do something for you when it is inconvenient for them: *He often troubled the neighbors to take care of his dog.*

trou·bled /'trʌbəld/ *adj.* **1** feeling worried or anxious: *She had a troubled look on her face.* **2** having many problems: *Greg had a troubled childhood.*

trouble-free /,.. '.◂/ *adj.* causing no difficulty or worry

trou·ble·mak·er /'trʌbəl,meɪkɚ/ *n.* [C] someone who deliberately causes problems, especially someone who complains or argues with people: *Some of the*

tenants are troublemakers who break the rules of the condominiums.

trou·ble·shoot·er /'trʌbəl,ʃutɚ/ *n.* [C] someone who is employed by a company to solve difficult or serious problems

trou·ble·shoot·ing /'trʌbəl,ʃutɪŋ/ *n.* [U] the act of trying to solve difficult or serious problems

trou·ble·some /'trʌbəlsəm/ *adj.* causing you trouble or worry over a long period of time: *troublesome rumors*

trouble spot /'.. ,./ *n.* [C] a place where trouble often happens, especially war or violence: *The area around 5th and Baker Streets has a history of being a trouble spot.*

trough /trɔf/ *n.* [C] **1** a long narrow open container that holds water or food for animals **2** the hollow area between two waves in the ocean or between two hills **3** a short period when prices are low, when there is not much activity etc. in something that is continuously measured over a longer period: *the peaks and troughs of economic cycles* **4** TECHNICAL a long area of fairly low pressure between two areas of high pressure on a weather map

trounce /traʊns/ *v.* [T] to defeat someone by a large amount: *It's Washington's worst loss since Detroit trounced them 38–6.*

troupe /trup/ *n.* [C] a group of singers, actors, dancers etc. who perform together

troup·er /'trupɚ/ *n.* [C] **1** INFORMAL someone who has a lot of experience of work in the entertainment business **2** someone who works hard and keeps trying, even when the situation is difficult: *Eric was a real trouper, helping his mother when he could.*

trou·sers /'traʊzɚz/ *n.* [plural] a piece of clothing that covers the lower half of your body and that has a separate part for each leg; PANTS (1) —**trouser** *adj.* [only before noun]

trous·seau /'trusoʊ, tru'soʊ/ *n.* [C] OLD-FASHIONED the personal possessions that a woman brings with her when she marries

trout /traʊt/ *n. plural* **trout** [C,U] a common river fish or the meat of this fish

trove /troʊv/ *n.* [C] a TREASURE TROVE

trow·el /'traʊəl/ *n.* [C] **1** a garden tool like a very small SHOVEL **2** a small tool with a flat blade, used for spreading CEMENT on bricks etc.

troy ounce /,trɔɪ 'aʊns/ *n.* [C] a small unit of troy weight that is equal to 31.1 grams: *Platinum sells for about $460 per troy ounce.*

troy weight /'trɔɪ weɪt/ *n.* [U] a system of measuring weight, especially used for weighing gold, silver, GEMs etc.

tru·an·cy /'truənsi/ *n.* [U] the practice of deliberately staying away from school without permission

tru·ant /'truənt/ *adj.* a student who is truant stays away from school without permission: *Nick was truant 7 days this month.* —**truant** *n.* [C]

truce /trus/ *n.* [C] an agreement between enemies to stop fighting or arguing for a short time, or the period for which this is arranged: *Both sides agreed on a truce during New Year celebrations.* | **call/ declare a truce** (=announce a truce) —compare ARMISTICE, CEASE-FIRE

truck¹ /trʌk/ *n.* **1** [C,U] a large road vehicle used by companies to carry goods or pull heavy things: *a garbage truck* | *Most of their package deliveries are made by truck.* **2** [C] a vehicle the size of a car, that has a large open part at the back that is used for carrying things; PICK-UP: *You can borrow my truck to go to the store.* **3 have no truck with sb/sth** to completely avoid dealing with someone or becoming involved in an activity: *Katz didn't have any truck with the radical politics of the late 1960s.* **4** [C] a simple piece of equipment consisting of something flat that is attached to wheels, used especially to move heavy things

truck² *v.* **1** [T] also **truck in** to take something

T

S W
1
2

somewhere by truck: *Some Texas ranchers are having hay trucked in from Colorado.* **2** [I always + adv./prep.] SPOKEN to go, move, or travel quickly: [+ **along/down/over etc.**] *I trucked over to Holt's house to watch the game.* **3 get trucking** SPOKEN to leave a place: *I guess it's time to get trucking.*

truck driv·er /'. ,../ *n.* [C] someone whose job is to drive a big truck that carries goods

truck·er /'trʌkə/ *n.* [C] INFORMAL a truck driver

truck farm /'. ./ *n.* [C] a small farm for growing vegetables and fruit for sale

truck·ing /'trʌkɪŋ/ *n.* **1** [U] the business of taking goods from place to place by road **2 keep on trucking** SPOKEN a phrase used to encourage someone to continue what they are doing, used especially in the 1970s

truck·load /'trʌkloʊd/ *n.* [C] the amount that fills a truck

truck stop /'. ./ *n.* [C] a cheap place to eat on a main road, used mainly by TRUCK DRIVERS

truc·u·lent /'trʌkyələnt/ *adj.* easily made angry and always willing to argue with people: *The National Assembly was being truculent over the budget proposals.* —**truculently** *adv.* —**truculence** *n.* [U]

trudge[1] /trʌdʒ/ *v.* [I always + adv./prep.] to walk with slow heavy steps, especially because you are tired: **trudge home/along/through etc.** *I had to trudge up four flights of stairs to my hotel room.*

trudge[2] *n.* [C usually singular] a long tiring walk

true[1] /tru/ *adj.*
1 not false based on facts, and not imagined or invented: *Everything I've said is true.* | *The movie is based on a true story.* | [be true of sb/sth] *The text is poorly written, which is true of many textbooks.* | [be true (that)] *Is it true that you spent time in jail?* | *Answer the following questions* **true or false.** —opposite FALSE (1)
2 the true value/seriousness/nature etc. the real value, seriousness etc. of something rather than what seems at first to be correct: *They had tried to conceal the true nature of their business dealings.*
3 sb's true feelings/beliefs/motives etc. your true feelings, beliefs, opinions etc. are the ones that you really have and not the ones that you pretend to have: *It was hard to read Alvin's true feelings.*
4 having all the right qualities strong or complete, and having all the qualities something should have: *True courage is facing danger when you are afraid.* | *Even the U.S. is not really a true democracy.*
5 come true if wishes, dreams etc. come true, they happen in the way that someone has said or hoped that they would: *After 21 years, Carl's dream of owning a home came true.* —see also **a dream come true** (DREAM[1] (3))
6 loyal faithful and loyal to someone, whatever happens: [+ **to**] *Johnson was always true to the Democratic party.*
7 a true friend/believer/sportsman etc. someone who behaves in the way that a good friend, believer etc. should behave: *Bob is my one true friend.*
8 admitting sth SPOKEN used when you are admitting that one thing is correct, when you want to say that something else is also correct: *True, my family was wealthy, but my parents taught me to work hard.*
9 sb's (one) true love the person that someone loves the most in a romantic way: *Adrienne was his one true love.*
10 true to form used to say that someone is behaving in the bad way that you expect them to: *True to form, Jimmy did not show up for his court date.*
11 true to sb's word/promise doing exactly what you have promised to do: *True to her word, Susan paid back every cent she owed us.*
12 be true to sb's principles/beliefs etc. to behave according to the principles that you claim to believe in: *Scott felt he couldn't be true to his principles if he became a politician.*
13 true mammal/fish/plant etc. having all the qualities of a particular type of object, animal, plant

etc., according to an exact description of it: *Despite its appearance, the whale is a true mammal.*
14 straight/level [not before noun] TECHNICAL built, placed, or formed in a way that is perfectly flat, straight, correct etc.: *The table top doesn't look completely true.*
15 sb's aim is true if your aim is true, you hit the thing that you were throwing or shooting at —see also **be too good to be true** (GOOD[1] (50)), **show your true colors** (SHOW[1] (16)), TRULY, TRUTH

true[2] *adv.* **1** in an exact straight line: *The arrow flew straight and true to its target.* **2** OLD USE in a truthful way **3** TECHNICAL if a type of animal breeds true, the young animals are exactly like their parents —see also **not ring true** (RING[2] (5))

true[3] *n.* **out of true** not completely straight, level, or balanced: *The doorway was out of true.*

true-blue /ˌ. '.◂/ *adj.* completely loyal to a person or idea: *a true-blue friend*

true-false also **true/false** /ˌ. '.◂/ *adj.* **1 a true-false question** a statement on a test which you have to decide is true or false **2 a true-false test/exam/quiz etc.** a test that contains true-false questions

true-life /ˌ. '.◂/ *adj.* [only before noun] based on real facts and not invented: *a true-life horror story* —compare TRUE-TO-LIFE

true north /ˌ. './ *n.* [U] north as it appears on maps, calculated as a line through the center of the Earth rather than by using the MAGNETIC POLE

true-to-life /ˌ. . '.◂/ *adj.* a book, play, description etc. that is true-to-life seems like something that could happen in real life; REALISTIC —compare TRUE-TO-LIFE

truf·fle /'trʌfəl/ *n.* [C] **1** a soft creamy candy made with chocolate **2** a black or light brown FUNGUS that grows under the ground, and is a very expensive food

tru·ism /'truɪzəm/ *n.* [C] a statement that is clearly true, so that there is no need to say it: *It is a truism that you get what you pay for.*

tru·ly /'truli/ *adv.* [+ adj./adv.] **1** used to emphasize that the way you are describing something is really true: *Getting accepted into Yale is truly an accomplishment.* | *It was a truly embarrassing moment.* **2** in an exact or correct way: *No adult twins are truly identical.* **3 really and truly** also **really truly** SPOKEN used to emphasize that something is definitely true: *I really truly love you.* —see also **yours truly** (YOURS (3))

Tru·man /'trumən/, **Har·ry S** /ˈhæri ɛs/ (1884–1972) the 33rd President of the U.S.

Trum·bull /'trʌmbəl/, **John** (1756–1843) a U.S. PAINTER famous for his paintings of scenes from the American Revolutionary War

trump[1] /trʌmp/ *n.* [C] **1** also **trump card** a card from the SUIT (=one of the four types of cards in a set) that has been chosen to have a higher value than the other suits in a particular game **2** the SUIT chosen to have a higher value than the other suits in a particular game: *Spades are trump.* **3 your trump card** something that gives you a big advantage in a particular situation, that you can use after keeping it secret for some time: *The trade agreement was always Bush's trump card in the discussions.*

trump[2] *v.* [T] **1** to play a trump that beats someone else's card in a game **2** to do something better than someone else, so that you gain an advantage: *Benckiser trumped Green's bid to buy the company.*
trump sth ↔ up *phr. v.* [T] to use false information to make someone seem guilty of a crime: *Keller claims authorities trumped up a sexual assault charge against him.* —see also TRUMPED-UP

trumped-up /ˌ. '.◂/ *adj.* **trumped-up charges/evidence/allegations etc.** false information that has been used to make someone seem guilty of a crime: *Nathan was imprisoned on trumped-up corruption charges.*

trump·er·y /'trʌmpəri/ *adj.* OLD USE not valuable

trum·pet[1] /'trʌmpɪt/ *n.* **1** [C] a musical instrument that you blow into, which consists of a curved metal tube that is wide at the end and three buttons to change the note **2** [singular] the loud noise that an ELEPHANT makes

trumpet[2] *v.* **1** [T] to tell everyone about something that you are proud of, in an annoying way: *Wald has often trumpeted his role in developing the vaccine.* **2** [I] if an ELEPHANT trumpets, it makes a loud noise

trun·cate /'trʌŋkeɪt/ *v.* [T] FORMAL to make something shorter —**truncation** /trʌŋ'keɪʃən/ *n.* [J]

trun·cat·ed /'trʌŋˌkeɪtɪd/ *adj.* made shorter than before, or shorter than usual

trun·cheon /'trʌnʃən/ *n.* [C] a short thick stick that police officers carry as a weapon; NIGHTSTICK

trun·dle /'trʌndl/ *v.* [I always + adv./prep., T] **1** to move slowly along on wheels, or to make something do this by pushing or pulling it: *Mothers trundled their children down the sidewalk in strollers.* **2** [I always + adv./prep.] to move or walk slowly: *A steady stream of shoppers trundled from store to store.*

trundle sb ↔ **off to** *phr. v.* [T] to send someone somewhere, even if they do not want to go: *The little kids are then trundled off to bed.*

trundle bed /'.. ˌ./ *n.* [C] a low bed on wheels that you can slide under a larger bed

S W / 3 — **trunk** /trʌŋk/ *n.* [C] **1** the thick central wooden stem of a tree —see picture at OAK **2** the part at the back of a car where you can put bags, tools etc. **3** the very long nose of an ELEPHANT —see picture at MAMMOTH[2] **4** TECHNICAL the main part of your body, not including your head, arms, or legs **5 trunks** [plural] also **swim/swimming trunks** short pants that end above the knee, worn by men for swimming **6** a very large box made of wood or metal, in which clothes, books etc. are stored or packed for travel —see picture at CASE[1]

truss[1] /trʌs/ *v.* [T] **1** also **truss up** to tie someone's arms, legs etc. very firmly with rope so that they cannot move: *They trussed up their victim and left him for dead.* **2** to prepare a chicken, duck etc. for cooking by tying its legs and wings together

truss[2] *n.* [C] **1** a special belt worn to support a HERNIA (=medical problem that affects the muscles below your stomach) **2** a frame supporting a roof or bridge

S W / 3 — **trust**[1] /trʌst/ *n.*
1 belief [U] a strong belief in the honesty, goodness etc. of someone or something: *Their partnership is based on trust and cooperation.* | *The company has put its trust in Stover to manage the factory.* | *I never thought I would ever betray his trust* (=do something that shows someone should not have trusted you).
2 financial arrangement [C,U] an arrangement by which someone has legal control of your money or property, especially until you are old enough to use it: *The money has been set aside in a trust.* | **hold/put/place sth in trust** *Their inheritance will be held in trust until the children are 18.* —see also TRUST FUND
3 organization [C usually singular] an organization or group that has control over money that will be used to help someone else: *a charitable trust*
4 a position of trust a job or position in which you have been given the responsibility of making important decisions: *McWilliams was in a position of trust as a church leader.*
5 companies [C] a group of companies that illegally work together to reduce competition and to control prices: *anti-trust laws*
6 take sth on trust to believe that something is true without having any proof: *I just had to take it on trust that he would deliver the money.*

S W / 2 2 **trust**[2] *v.* [T]
1 believe sb is honest to believe that someone is honest and will not harm you, cheat you etc.: *I never trusted him.* | [trust sb to do sth] *Managers must trust their employees to get the job done.* | **trust sb completely/implicitly** *His mother is the only person he trusts implicitly.* —opposite DISTRUST[2]
2 depend on sth to believe that something is true or will happen, or to depend on: *You can trust the quality of the meat they sell.* | [trust sth to do sth] *I wouldn't trust the ladder to support my weight.*
3 trust sb's judgment to think that someone is likely to make the right decisions: *Alfred had trusted Roy's judgment in business matters.*

4 trust sb with sth to believe that someone would be careful with something valuable or dangerous if you gave it to them: *They trusted him with their lives.*
5 trust sth to luck/chance/fate etc. to hope that things will happen in the way that you want, especially because you think there is nothing else you can do: *Organizing a business shouldn't be trusted to chance – get professional advice.*
6 I wouldn't trust sb any farther than I can throw him/her SPOKEN used to say that you do not trust someone very much
7 I trust (that) SPOKEN, FORMAL used to say politely that you hope something is true: *I trust that you will seriously consider my offer.* —see also TRUSTING

trust in sb/sth *phr. v.* [T] FORMAL to believe in someone or something and to depend on them to do something: *The Pilgrims trusted in God to provide food.*

trust com·pa·ny /'. ˌ.../ *n.* [C] a TRUST[1] (3)

trust·ee /trʌ'sti/ *n.* [C] **1** someone who has control of money or property that is in a TRUST[1] (2) for someone else **2** a member of a group that controls the money of a company, college, or other organization

trus·tee·ship /trʌ'stiʃɪp/ *n.* **1** [C,U] the job of being a trustee **2** [U] the position of having the authority to govern an area, which is given by the United Nations to a country or countries

trust·ful /'trʌstfəl/ *adj.* ready to trust other people —**trustfully** *adv.* —**trustfulness** *n.* [U]

trust fund /'. ./ *n.* [C] money belonging to someone that is controlled for them by a trustee

trust·ing /'trʌstɪŋ/ *adj.* willing to believe that other people are good and honest: *Elderly people are often taken advantage of because they are too trusting.*

trust·wor·thy /'trʌstˌwɜˈði/ *adj.* someone who is trustworthy can be trusted and depended on —**trustworthiness** *n.* [U]

trust·y[1] /'trʌsti/ *adj.* [only before noun] OLD USE OR HUMOROUS a trusty weapon, vehicle, animal etc. is one that you have had for a long time and can depend on: *I quickly started typing on my trusty Macintosh.*

trust·y[2] *n.* [C] a prisoner who prison officials have given special jobs or rights, because they behave in a way that can be trusted

truth /truθ/ *n.*
S W / 2 1
1 the truth the true facts about something, as opposed to what is not true, is imagined, or is guessed: *I didn't steal the money and that's the truth.* | [+ about] *At first, Soviet leaders hid the truth about the accident at Chernobyl.* | *We weren't absolutely certain he was telling the truth.* | *The American public is eager to get to the truth* (=find out what really happened) *of the scandal.* | *The truth of the matter is that I plan to retire June 1.*
2 being true [U] the state or quality of being true: *There is no truth to the rumors about him being arrested.* | *There wasn't a grain of truth* (=a small amount of truth) *in Uncle Hal's story.*
3 important ideas [C usually plural] FORMAL an important fact or idea that is accepted as being true: *One of the basic truths about human beings is that we want our lives to have meaning.*
4 in truth in fact; really: *In truth, the two brothers really did care for each other.*
5 (if the) truth be known/told used when telling someone the real facts about a situation, or your real opinion: *Truth be told, I really hate going camping.*
6 nothing could be further from the truth used to say that something is definitely not true: *They say he is a spy, but nothing could be further from the truth.*
7 to tell (you) the truth SPOKEN used when giving your personal opinion or admitting something: *I'm not sure how he did it, to tell you the truth.*
8 the truth hurts SPOKEN used to say that it is sometimes difficult or embarrassing to hear someone tell you something that is true
9 the truth will out OLD-FASHIONED used to say that even if you try to stop people from knowing something, they will find out in the end —see also **the**

gospel truth (GOSPEL (4)), HALF-TRUTH, **the moment of truth** (MOMENT (9)), **truth/fact is stranger than fiction** (STRANGE¹ (3))

truth·ful /ˈtruθfəl/ *adj.* **1** someone who is truthful does not usually tell lies: *I think she is a truthful and moral person.* **2** a truthful statement gives the true facts about something —**truthfully** *adv.* —**truthfulness** *n.* [U]

truth se·rum /ˈ. ˌ../ *n.* [C,U] a drug that is supposed to make people tell the truth

try¹ /traɪ/ *v.* tries, tried, trying

1 attempt [I,T] to attempt to do or get something: *Tim may not be good at math, but at least he tries.* | *Harriet picked up the ball and tried a shot at the basket.* | [**try to do sth**] *She tried to forget about what had happened.* | [**try and do sth**] *You have to try and eat, or you won't get better.* | *I try and try, but I can't lose weight.* | **try your best/hardest** *I'll try my best to finish the work for this evening.* | **try hard/desperately** *Juanita tried hard not to laugh as he danced faster and faster.*

2 test/use [T] to do or use something for a short while to discover if it is appropriate, good, or enjoyable: *Running is really good exercise – you should try it.* | [**try doing sth**] *"My plant is dying." "Have you tried putting it in a sunnier room?"* | [**try sth on sb/sth**] *Scientists are trying the new drugs on rats.* | **try something new/different** (=do or use something that is different from what you usually do or use)

3 see if sth opens/works [T] to attempt to open a door, window etc. to see if it is locked, or to attempt to use a machine, piece of equipment etc. to see if it works: *We tried the doors, but they were all locked.* | *I'll go try the phone upstairs.*

4 food/drink [T] to taste food or a drink to find out if you like it: *Would you like to try some of my soup?* —see Usage Note at TASTE¹

5 try to find sb/sth [I,T] to go to a place or person, or call them, in order to find something or someone: *Nadine tried six stores before she found the book Sam wanted.* | *I'm sorry, but Ms. Bouvier is out of the office. Could you try again later.*

6 law [T usually passive] to examine and judge a legal case, or someone who is thought to be guilty of a crime in a court of law: [**try sb for sth**] *Ray was never tried for murder of the women.*

7 try sb's patience/temper/nerves etc. to make someone feel impatient, angry, nervous etc.: *This salesman is beginning to try my patience.*

8 try as sb might used to say that someone tried as hard as possible to do something but was unsuccessful: *Try as I might, I just couldn't find the source of the quotation I remembered.*

9 try your hand at sth to try a new activity in order to see whether it interests you or whether you are good at it: *Diane has always wanted to try her hand at acting.*

10 try your luck to try to achieve something or get something you want, usually by taking a risk: *Stern says he wants to try his luck as a candidate for mayor.*

11 not for want/lack of trying used to say that if someone does not achieve something, it is because of some other reason, because they have tried very hard to do it: *Even if Kara doesn't find a job, it won't be for lack of trying.*

12 sb couldn't do sth if they tried SPOKEN used to say that someone does not have the skill or ability to do something: *Joe couldn't hit a baseball if he tried.*

try for sth *phr. v.* [T] to try and get something you really want such as a job, prize, or a chance to study somewhere: *Anna is one of 12 students at her school trying for the international diploma.*

try sth ↔ **on** *phr. v.* [T] **1** to put on a piece of clothing to see if it fits you or if it looks good on you: *Go try on the sweater and see if it fits.* **2 try sth on for size a)** to put on a piece of clothing to see if it fits **b)** INFORMAL to consider something to see if it is appropriate for you or your situation: *Tell the school board to try this idea on for size: we could hold classes on buses.*

try out *phr. v.* **1** [T **try** sth ↔ **out**] to test something such as a method or a piece of equipment to see if it is effective or works well: *Jamie could hardly wait to try out his new bike.* **2** [T **try** sth ↔ **out**] to practice a skill in order to improve it: [**try sth out on sb/sth**] *I tried out my new accent on a girl in the coffee shop.* **3** [I] to try to be chosen as a member of a team, for a part in a play etc.: [+ **for**] *There were 120 kids who tried out for the 40 spots on the team.*

try² *n. plural* **tries** [C] **1** an attempt to do something: *She didn't manage to break the record, but it was a good try.* | *After several tries, Lou finally reached Sylvia at her office phone number.* | *"Do you think it will help?" "It's worth a try."* **2 give sth a try** to try using, doing, tasting etc. something to see if it is appropriate or successful: *If you like rice, I recommend you give this dish a try.* | *I've never cut someone else's hair, but I'll give it a try.* —see also **give sth the (old) college try** (COLLEGE (5))

try·ing /ˈtraɪ-ɪŋ/ *adj.* annoying or difficult in a way that makes you feel tired, impatient etc.: *The experience has been very trying for us.*

try·out /ˈtraɪ-aʊt/ *n.* [C] **1** a time when people who want to be on a sports team, activity etc. are tested, so that the best can be chosen: *baseball tryouts* **2** a period of time during which a play, TV show etc. is shown to find out if people like it

tryst /trɪst/ *n.* [C] **1** a meeting between lovers in a secret place or at a secret time: *secret hotel trysts* **2** a place where lovers meet secretly

tsar /zar, tsar/ *n.* another spelling of CZAR

tsa·ri·na /zɑˈrinə, tsɑ-/ *n.* another spelling of CZARINA

tsar·ism /ˈzɑrɪzəm, ˈtsɑ-/ *n.* another spelling of CZARISM —**tsarist** *n.* [C] —**tsarist** *adj.*

tset·se fly, tzet·ze fly /ˈtɛtsi ˌflaɪ, ˈtsɛtsi-/ *n.* [C] an African fly that sucks the blood of people and animals and spreads serious diseases

T-shirt, tee-shirt /ˈti ʃərt/ *n.* [C] a soft shirt, usually made of cotton, that stretches easily and has short SLEEVES and no collar

Tsi·mshi·an /ˈtʃɪmʃiən, ˈtsɪm-/ a Native American tribe from western Canada and Alaska

tsk tsk *interjection* a sound made by touching your tongue to the top of your mouth and drawing it backward, used to show disapproval

tsp. the written abbreviation of TEASPOON: *1 tsp. vanilla extract*

T-square /ˈti skwɛr/ *n.* [C] a large T-shaped piece of wood or plastic used to draw exact plans or pictures

tsu·na·mi /tsʊˈnami/ *n.* [C] a TIDAL WAVE

Tu. a written abbreviation of Tuesday

tub /tʌb/ *n.* [C] **1** a large container in which you sit to wash yourself; BATHTUB: *I'm going to go get in the tub.* **2** an open container that is usually round, and whose sides are usually shorter than the width of its base: *a tub of popcorn* | *a plastic tub full of dirty dishes* **3** also **tubful** the amount of liquid, food etc. that a tub can contain **4** INFORMAL someone who is short and fat: *Big Lil was a tub of a woman.* —see also HOT TUB

tu·ba /ˈtubə/ *n.* [C] a large musical instrument that consists of a curved metal tube with a wide opening that points straight up, that you play by blowing into it, and that produces very low sounds

tub·by /ˈtʌbi/ *adj.* **tubbier, tubbiest** INFORMAL short and fat, with a round stomach —see Usage Note at FAT¹

tube¹ /tub/ *n.*

1 pipe for liquid [C] a round pipe made of metal, glass, rubber etc., especially for liquids or gases to go through —see also INNER TUBE, TEST TUBE

2 container [C] a narrow container made of plastic or soft metal and closed at one end, that you press between your fingers in order to push out the soft substance that is inside: *a tube of toothpaste* —see picture at CONTAINER

3 in your body [C] a tube-shaped part inside your body: *Fallopian tubes*

4 go down the tubes INFORMAL if a situation goes down the tubes, it becomes ruined or spoiled: *The whole experiment could go down the tubes.*

5 [television] **the tube** SPOKEN television: *Let's see what's on the tube tonight.*
6 [electrical equipment] [C] also **picture tube** the part of a television that causes the picture to appear
7 have your tubes tied if a woman has her tubes tied, she has a medical operation on her FALLOPIAN TUBES so that she will not be able to have babies

tube² *v.* [I] to float on a river on a large INNER TUBE for fun —see also TUBING (2)

tu·ber /ˈtubɚ/ *n.* [C] **1** TECHNICAL a round swollen part on the stem of some plants, such as the potato, that grows below the ground and from which new plants grow **2** HUMOROUS a potato —**tuberous** *adj.*

tu·ber·cu·lo·sis /tʊˌbɚkyəˈloʊsɪs/ *n.* [U] a serious infectious disease that affects many parts of your body, especially your lungs; TB —**tubercular** /tʊˈbɚkyələ/ *adj.*

tube sock /ˈ. ./ *n.* [C] a sock, especially a white one, that is long and straight and has no special place for your heel

tube top /ˈ. ./ *n.* [C] a piece of women's clothing that goes around your chest and back to cover your breasts, but does not cover your shoulders or stomach

tub·ing /ˈtubɪŋ/ *n.* [U] **1** tubes in general, especially when connected together into a system: *rubber tubing* **2** the activity of floating on a river on a large INNER TUBE

Tub·man /ˈtʌbmən/, **Har·ri·et** /ˈhæriɪt/ (?1820–1913) an African-American woman who was born a SLAVE, famous for helping many slaves to escape from their owners

Harriet Tubman

tub-thump·ing /ˈ. ˌ. ./ *adj.* [only before noun] INFORMAL trying to persuade people about your opinions in a loud and forceful way: *He's running for Congress as an old-fashioned tub-thumping liberal.* —**tub-thumping** *n.* [U] —**tub-thumper** *n.* [C]

tu·bu·lar /ˈtubyələ/ *adj.* made of tubes or in the form of a tube: *tubular steel structure*

tuck¹ /tʌk/ *v.* [T] **1** [always + adv./prep.] to push the edge of a piece of cloth or paper into something so that it looks neater or stays in place: **tuck sth in/into/under** *Tuck your shirt in!* **2** [always + adv./prep.] to put something into a small space, especially in order to protect or hide it: [**tuck sth behind/under/into sth**] *She tucked the bottle under her jacket and walked out of the store.* | *Aidan sat with his knees tucked under his chin.* **3** to put a TUCK (=a special fold) in a piece of clothing

tuck sth ↔ away *phr. v.* [T] **1 be tucked away a)** if a place is tucked away, it is in a quiet area: *The campground is tucked away in a valley.* **b)** if someone or something is tucked away, they are hidden or difficult to find: *Nell's private letters were tucked away in a box in the attic.* **2** to store something, such as money or information, in a safe place: *I tucked the idea away in the back of my mind for future thought.*

tuck sb/sth ↔ **in** *phr. v.* [T] **1** to make a child comfortable in bed by arranging the sheets around them: *I'll come up and tuck you in in a minute.* **2** to move a part of your body in so that it does not stick out so much: *Stand up slowly, keeping your chin tucked in.*

tuck² *n.* **1** [C] a narrow flat fold of cloth sewn into a piece of clothing for decoration or to give it a special shape **2** [C] a small medical operation done to make your face or stomach look flatter and younger: *Rivers has had a face-lift and a tummy tuck* (=an operation to make her stomach flatter).

tuck·er /ˈtʌkɚ/ *v.*

tucker sb **out** *phr. v.* [T usually passive] INFORMAL to make someone very tired: *By the end of the day I was all tuckered out.*

Tuc·son /ˈtusɑn/ a city in the U.S. state of Arizona

'tude /tud/ *n.* [C,U] HUMOROUS a style, behavior etc. that shows you have the confidence to do unusual and exciting things without caring what other people think; attitude: *Atlanta is definitely a city with 'tude.*

-tude /tud/ *suffix* [in nouns] the state of having a particular quality: *disquietude* (=anxiety) —see also -ITUDE

Tu·dor /ˈtudɚ/ *adj.* relating to the period in English history between 1485 and 1603: **Tudor houses/architecture etc.** (=built in the style used in the Tudor period)

Tues·day /ˈtuzdi, -deɪ/ *written abbreviation* **Tue.** or **Tues.** *n.* [C,U] the third day of the week, between Monday and Wednesday: *The report is due Tuesday.* | *Do you want to see that new movie with me on Tuesday?* | *Rachel had a barbecue last Tuesday.* | *We have tickets to the Packers game next Tuesday.* | *I'm taking my driving test this Tuesday* (=the next Tuesday that is coming). | *I try to clean the house on Tuesdays* (=each Tuesday). | *My birthday is on a Tuesday this year.* | **Tuesday morning/afternoon/night etc.** *Sam and I went out for lunch Tuesday afternoon.* —see Usage Note at SUNDAY

tuft /tʌft/ *n.* [C] a mass of hair, feathers, grass etc. growing or held closely together at their base: [+ of] *A tiny tuft of red hair poked out from under her scarf.*

tuft·ed /ˈtʌftɪd/ *adj.* **1** a tufted chair, SOFA etc. has buttons on its surface which are stitched through soft material under the surface **2** having a tuft or tufts: *The old man's ears were tufted with white hair.*

tug¹ /tʌg/ *v.* **tugged, tugging** [I,T] **1** also **tug at** to pull with one or more short quick pulls: *"Come on," Alice said, tugging at his hand.* **2 tug at sb's heart/heartstrings** to make someone feel sympathy for someone or something: *The sight of the puppies in the cages tugged at the women's hearts.*

tug² *n.* [C] **1** also **tugboat** a small strong boat used for pulling or guiding ships into a port, up a river etc. **2** [usually singular] a sudden strong pull: *I seized the door handle and gave it a good tug.* **3** something that influences your thoughts or feelings and makes you want to do something, be with someone, or go somewhere: *If you were in the crowd, you couldn't fail to feel an emotional tug.*

tug-of-war /ˌ. . ˈ./ *n.* **1** [singular,U] a test of strength in which two teams pull opposite ends of a rope against each other **2** [singular] a situation in which two people or groups try very hard to get or keep the same thing: *The children are trapped in an emotional tug-of-war between their parents.*

tu·i·tion /tuˈɪʃən/ *n.* [U] **1** the money you pay for being taught at a school or college: *Tuition is $2,800 per year.* **2** the act of teaching, especially in small groups

tu·lip /ˈtulɪp/ *n.* [C] a brightly colored flower that is shaped like a cup and grows from a BULB in the spring

tulle /tul/ *n.* [U] a thin soft silk or NYLON material like a net

tum·ble¹ /ˈtʌmbəl/ *v.* [I] **1** [always + adv./prep.] to fall down quickly and suddenly, especially with a rolling movement: [+ over/backward/down etc.] *Huge rocks tumbled down the mountainside.* **2** [always + adv./prep.] to move in an uncontrolled way: [+ into/through etc.] *A line of tourists tumbled off the bus.* **3** if prices or figures tumble, they go down suddenly and by a large amount: *On October 19, 1987, the stock market tumbled 508 points.* **4 come tumbling down a)** if a building or structure comes tumbling down, it falls suddenly to the ground **b)** if an organization, system etc. comes tumbling down, it suddenly stops working completely because of many problems: *Soon her marriage came tumbling down.* **5** [always + adv./prep.] if someone's hair tumbles down, it is long and thick and has curls: *Grace's blonde hair tumbled down her back.* **6** to do
TUMBLING

T

tumble² *n.* [C] a fall, especially from a high place: *That's quite a tumble you took.* —see also ROUGH-AND-TUMBLE

tum·ble·down /'tʌmbəldaʊn/ *adj.* [only before noun] **tumbledown building/house/cottage etc.** a building, house etc. that is old and beginning to fall down: *a tumbledown cabin by the lake*

tumble-dry /'.. .,./ *v.* **tumble-dries, tumble-dried, tumble-drying** [T] to dry clothes in a DRYER (=machine that uses hot air to dry them after they have been washed)

tum·bler /'tʌmblə/ *n.* [C] **1** a drinking glass with a flat bottom and no handle **2** OLD-FASHIONED someone who performs special movements such as doing FLIPS (=a jump in which you turn over completely in the air); ACROBAT

tum·ble·weed /'tʌmbəlwid/ *n.* [C,U] a plant that grows in the desert areas of North America and is blown from place to place by the wind

tum·bling /'tʌmblɪŋ/ *n.* [U] a sport similar to GYMNASTICS but with all the exercises done on the floor

tu·mes·cent /tu'mɛsənt/ *adj.* TECHNICAL swollen or swelling —**tumescence** *n.* [U]

tum·my /'tʌmi/ *n. plural* **tummies** [C] a word for STOMACH, used especially by or to children: *Mommy, my tummy hurts.*

tu·mor /'tumə/ *a* mass of diseased cells in your body that have divided and increased too quickly: *a brain tumor* | **a malignant/benign tumor** (=dangerous/harmless tumor) —**tumorous** *adj.*

tu·mult /'tumʌlt/ *n.* [C,U] FORMAL **1** a confused, noisy, and excited situation, often caused by a large crowd: *She could simply not be heard in the tumult.* **2** a state of mental confusion caused by strong emotions such as anger, sadness etc.: *Sheila confessed that she spends most of her time in a tumult of anger and disbelief.*

tu·mul·tu·ous /tu'mʌltʃuəs/ *adj.* **1** full of activity, confusion, or violence: *1961 was a tumultuous year for Alvin.* **2** very loud: *tumultuous applause* —**tumultuously** *adv.*

tu·na /'tunə/ *n. plural* **tuna** or **tunas** **1** [C] a large ocean fish caught for food **2** [U] also **tunafish** the flesh of this fish, usually sold cooked in cans

tun·dra /'tʌndrə/ *n.* [C,U] the large flat areas of land in the north of Russia, Canada etc., where it is very cold and there are no trees

tune¹ /tun/ *n.* **1 a)** [C] a series of musical notes that are played or sung and are nice to listen to: *an old familiar tune* | *The gospel song is sung **to the tune of** "Danny Boy."* **b)** [C] INFORMAL a song, or pieces of music in general: *Turn on the radio – let's hear some tunes.* **2 be in tune with sb/sth** to be able to realize, understand, or agree with what someone else thinks or wants: *He sees himself as a political outsider who is in tune with the American voters.* —opposite **be out of tune with sb/sth 3 in tune** playing or singing the correct musical note: *A trained singer knows when her voice is in tune.* **4 out of tune** playing or singing higher or lower than the correct musical note: *The guitar was badly out of tune.* **5 to the tune of $1000/$50 million etc.** INFORMAL used to emphasize how large an amount of money is: *The factory has been renovated to the tune of $350 million.* —see also **carry a tune** (CARRY¹ (25)), **sb can't carry a tune in a bucket** (CARRY¹ (26)), **change your tune** (CHANGE¹ (12)), **dance to sb's tune** (DANCE¹ (5)), SHOW TUNE

tune² *v.* [T] **1** to make a radio or television receive broadcasts from a particular place: *The television was tuned to a rerun of "M.A.S.H."* **2** to make a musical instrument play at the right PITCH² (7): *Someone's coming tomorrow to tune the piano.* **3** to make small changes to an engine so that it works better: *If the engine needs to be tuned, Dad can do it.* **4 stay tuned a)** SPOKEN said on TV or radio stations to tell people not to change to a different station: *Stay tuned for more on this late-breaking story.* **b)** INFORMAL used

to tell people to keep paying attention to see how a situation develops: *Could the same thing happen in the stock market this year? Stay tuned.* **5 finely tuned sense/perception/balance etc.** a very careful and skillful way of judging something, understanding situations etc.: *finely tuned political instincts*

tune in *phr. v.* [I] **1** to watch or listen to a program on television or the radio: [+ **to**] *Tune in to 91.3 FM for the best music in the city.* **2** also **be tuned in**to realize or understand what is happening or what other people are thinking: [+ **to**] *I suddenly tuned in to what she was trying to say.*

tune out *phr. v.* [I,T] INFORMAL to ignore or stop listening to someone or something: *If the story becomes too complicated, a small child will tune out.* | [**tune sb/sth ↔ out**] *Liz didn't like what we were talking about, so she tuned us out.*

tune up *phr. v.* **1** [T **tune sth ↔ up**] to repair and clean a car's engine **2** [I] when musicians tune up, they prepare their instruments to play at the same PITCH² (7) as each other **3** [T **tune sth ↔ up**] to make a musical instrument play at the right PITCH² (7)

tune·ful /'tunfəl/ *adj.* FORMAL nice to listen to: *tuneful melodies*

tune·less /'tunlɪs/ *adj.* not having a pleasant tune: *a tuneless rendition of the song* —**tunelessly** *adv.*

tun·er /'tunə/ *n.* [C] **1** the part of a television or radio that you can change to receive different stations **2** a PIANO TUNER

tune·smith /'tunsmɪθ/ *n.* [C] FORMAL someone who writes songs

tune-up /'. ./ *n.* [C] the process of making small changes to an engine so that it works as well as possible

tung·sten /'tʌŋstən/ *n.* [U] *symbol* **W** a hard metal that is an ELEMENT and is used in LIGHT BULBs and in making steel

tu·nic /'tunɪk/ *n.* [C] a long loose shirt

tuning fork /'.. ,./ *n.* [C] a small U-shaped metal instrument that makes a particular musical note when you hit it

tuning peg /'.. ,./ *n.* [C] a wooden screw used to make the strings on a VIOLIN, GUITAR etc. tighter

Tu·nis /'tunɪs/ the capital and largest city of Tunisia

Tu·ni·sia /tu'niʒə/ a country in northwest Africa, between Libya and Algeria —**Tunisian** *n., adj.*

tun·nel¹ /'tʌnl/ *n.* [C] **1** a passage that has been dug under the ground, through a mountain etc. for people, cars, or trains to go through **2** a passage under the ground that animals have dug to live in

tunnel² *v.* [I always + adv./prep., T] to dig a long passage under the ground: [+ **under/through etc. sth**] *Rescuers tunneled toward the men trapped in the mine.* | *The prisoners spent a year secretly **tunneling their way** (=moving somewhere by digging a passage) to freedom.*

tunnel vi·sion /'.. ,../ *n.* [U] **1** the tendency to only think about one part of something such as a problem or plan, instead of considering all the parts of it: *Calipari certainly has tunnel vision where profits are concerned.* **2** a condition in which someone's eyes are damaged so that they can only see things that are straight ahead

Tun·ney /'tʌni/, **Gene** /dʒin/ (1897–1978) a U.S. BOXER who was world CHAMPION in 1926–1928

Tup·per·ware /'tʌpə,wɛr/ *n.* [U] TRADEMARK a type of plastic container that closes very tightly and is used to store food

Tupperware par·ty /'... ,../ *n.* [C] a party at which people, especially women, get together at someone's house to buy TUPPERWARE food containers

tuque /tuk/ *n.* [C] a TOQUE

tur·ban /'tɜbən/ *n.* [C] a long piece of cloth that you wind tightly around your head, worn by men in parts of North Africa and Southern Asia and sometimes by women as a fashion

tur·bid /'tɜbɪd/ *adj.* FORMAL turbid water or liquid is dirty and muddy —**turbidity** /tə'bɪdəţi/ *n.* [U]

tur·bine /'tɜbaɪn, -bɪn/ *n.* [C] an engine or motor in which the pressure of a liquid or gas moves a special wheel around —see also GAS TURBINE, WIND TURBINE

tur·bo /'tɜːboʊ/ *n. plural* **turbos** [C] **1** a TURBOCHARGER **2** a car with a turbocharger: *an Audi Turbo Diesel*

tur·bo·charge /'tɜːboʊˌtʃɑːrdʒ/ *v.* [T usually passive] **1** to put a TURBOCHARGER in an engine: *a turbocharged 2.3-liter, five-cylinder engine* **2** INFORMAL to make something much stronger or more powerful: *a turbocharged PC*

tur·bo·charg·er /'tɜːboʊˌtʃɑːrdʒɚ/ *n.* [C] a system that makes a vehicle more powerful by using a turbine to force air and gasoline into the engine under increased pressure

tur·bo·jet /'tɜːboʊˌdʒɛt/ *n.* [C] **1** a powerful engine that makes something, especially an aircraft, move forward, by forcing out hot air and gases at the back **2** an aircraft that gets power from this type of engine

tur·bo·prop /'tɜːboʊˌprɑːp/ *n* [C] **1** a TURBINE engine that drives a PROPELLER **2** an aircraft that gets power from this type of engine

tur·bu·lence /'tɜːbyələns/ *n.* [U] **1** a political or emotional situation that is very confused: *Political turbulence is spreading throughout the country.* **2** irregular and violent movements of air or water that are caused by the wind: *The plane encountered severe turbulence during the flight.*

tur·bu·lent /'tɜːbyələnt/ *adj.* **1** a turbulent situation or period of time is one in which there are a lot of sudden changes and often wars or violence: *a turbulent relationship* | *Jason grew up in the South during the turbulent years of the 1960s.* **2** turbulent air or water moves around a lot because of the wind: *the turbulent white sea* **3** turbulent crowds or people are noisy and violent

turd /tɜːd/ *n.* [C] VULGAR **1** a piece of the solid waste material passed from the body **2** OFFENSIVE an annoying or unkind person: *You stupid little turd!*

tu·reen /tʊ'riːn/ *n.* [C] a large dish with a lid, used for serving soup or vegetables

turf /tɜːf/ *n.* [U] **1** a surface that is made up of soil and a thick covering of grass, or an artificial substance made to look like this: *Injuries are more common on artificial turf than on grass.* **2** INFORMAL an area that you think of as being your own: *They are determined to defend their turf against any outsiders.* | **a turf war/battle** (=a fight or argument over the area or things you think belong to you) **3** the track on which horses race —see also ASTROTURF. **surf 'n' turf** (SURF² (2))

Tur·ge·nev /tɜː'geɪnjəf/**, I·van** /'aɪvən/ (1818–1883) a Russian writer of NOVELs, short stories, and plays

tur·gid /'tɜːdʒɪd/ *adj.* FORMAL **1** turgid writing or speech is boring and difficult to understand: *turgid technical manuals* **2** full and swollen with liquid or air —**turgidly** *adv.* —**turgidity** /tɜː'dʒɪdəti/ *n.* [U]

Tur·key /'tɜːki/ a country which is mainly in west Asia but partly in southeast Europe, between the Mediterranean Sea and the Black Sea —**Turk** *n.* [C] —**Turkish** *adj.*

tur·key /'tɜːki/ *n. plural* **turkeys 1** [C] a bird that looks like a large chicken and is often eaten at Christmas and at Thanksgiving **2** [U] the meat from a turkey eaten as food: *roast turkey* **3** INFORMAL an unsuccessful movie or play **4** [C] INFORMAL someone who is silly or stupid —see also COLD TURKEY, **talk turkey** (TALK¹ (28))

turkey bast·er /'.. ,../ *n.* [C] a large plastic tube with a hollow rubber part at one end that you use for putting liquid on a TURKEY while it is cooking

turkey shoot /'... . *n.* [C usually singular] a competition or fight in which one person or side is much stronger and defeats the other very easily

Turkish bath /,.. './ *n.* [C] a treatment to help you relax, that involves sitting in a very hot steamy room

Turkish cof·fee /,.. '../ *n.* [C,U] very strong black coffee that you drink in small cups with sugar

Turkish de·light /,.. .'./ *n.* [U] a type of candy made from GELATIN that is cut into pieces and covered in sugar or chocolate

Turk·men·i·stan /tɜːk'mɛnɪˌstɑːn, -ˌstæn/ a country in central Asia between Iran and Uzbekistan, formerly part of the Soviet Union —**Turkmen** /'tɜːkmɛn, -mən/ *n., adj.*

tur·mer·ic /'tɜːmərɪk, 'tuː-/ *n.* [U] yellow powder used to give a special color or taste to food

tur·moil /'tɜːmɔɪl/ *n.* [U,singular] a state of confusion, excitement, and trouble: *Most of the country is in economic and social turmoil.*

turn¹ /tɜːn/ *v.*

1 your body [I] to move your body so that you are looking in a different direction: *She turned and looked Seth straight in the eyes.* | [+ **around/ away/ to** etc.] *Turn around and show me the back of the dress.* | *Kurt finally turned to Frank and spoke.* | [**turn to do sth**] *As she turned to go, Carly saw the package in the corner.* | *Without a word, he turned on his heel* (=turned away suddenly) *and left the room.*

2 object [I,T] to move something so that it is pointing or aiming in a different direction: *Turn the plant so it's facing the sun.* | [**turn sth around/over** etc.] *She turns the bowls upside down to keep the dust out.* | *Come and help me turn the mattress over.*

3 direction **a)** [I,T] to go in a new direction when you are walking, driving etc., or to make the vehicle you are using do this: [+ **into/off/left/right** etc.] *Turn left at the next light.* | *We turned left onto West Glen Road.* | [**turn sth around/into** etc.] *If you two don't stop fighting, I'll turn the car around and we'll go home.* **b)** [I] to curve in a particular direction: *The road turns sharply at the top of the hill.*

4 move around central point [I,T] to move around a central point, or make something move in this way: *The wheels turned slowly at first, but then began to pick up speed.* | [**turn sth**] *I knocked on the door and then turned the knob.*

5 age [linking verb] if someone turns a particular age, they become that age: *Simmons will turn 32 in August.*

6 color **a)** [linking verb] to become a different color: *Heat the peas briefly till they turn bright green.* | *The sky turned a pale orange as the sun began to set.* **b)** [T] to make something become a different color: *I got a perm that turned my hair green.*

7 skin color [linking verb] if a person turns a particular color, their skin looks that color because they feel sick, embarrassed etc.: *I felt myself turn red with embarrassment.* | *Thomas gasped for breath and started turning blue.*

8 gray/white hair [linking verb] if your hair turns gray or white, it becomes that color because you are getting older: *She was only 34 and already she was turning gray!*

9 turn a/the corner a) to pass around a corner when you are walking, driving etc.: *As Karo turned the corner he saw the girl heading toward him.* **b)** to start to improve after a period of being in a bad condition: *The team has turned a corner and is starting to play better.*

10 turn nasty/grim/sour etc. to change to a worse condition or attitude, especially suddenly: *The protest turned violent by late afternoon.*

11 page [T] if you turn a page in a book, you move it so that you can read the next page —see also **turn to** (TURN¹)

12 turn your back (on sb/sth) a) to refuse to help, support, or be involved with someone or something: *He would never turn his back on a fellow veteran.* | *Many immigrants turn their back on the old ways.* **b)** to turn so that your back is pointing toward someone or something: *He turned his back on Shauna and walked to the window.*

13 turn a profit to make a profit: *The company is not expected to turn a profit for two years.*

14 weather [linking verb] to change, especially becoming cold or worse: *The weather turned cold and it started to rain.*

15 attention/thoughts etc. **a)** [T] to direct your attention, your thoughts, a conversation etc. from one person, thing, or subject to another: *Charles turned his gaze upward to admire the ceiling.* | *Then Black made a comment that turned the conversation in another direction.* | **turn your attention/ thoughts/efforts etc. to sth** *Many investors have turned their attention to opportunities abroad.* **b)** [I] to be directed in this way: *Joe found his thoughts turning to his days on the college football team.*

16 turn sth inside out a) to pull a piece of clothing, bag etc. so that the inside is facing out: *Turn the pants inside out before you wash them.* **b)** also **turn sth upside down** to search everywhere for something, in a way that makes a place very messy: *I've turned the house upside down looking for that book!* **c)** also **turn sth upside down** or **turn sth on its head** to do something that makes an organization, a set of rules, a way of understanding something etc. change completely: *Lukens' theories have turned the financial world upside down.*

17 time [linking verb] if it has turned a particular time, that time has just passed: *"What time is it?" "It just turned 3:00."*

18 injury [T] if you turn your ANKLE, you twist it in a way that injures it

19 an actor-turned-politician/a housewife-turned-author etc. someone who has done one job and then does something completely different

20 turn the tide (of sth) to change the progress or development of something and make it go in the opposite direction: *Their decisive victory turned the tide of the war in North Africa.*

21 turn a phrase to say or write something in a clever, interesting, funny etc. way

22 turn (people's) heads if something turns people's heads, they are surprised by it: *Wilkins has turned some heads by claiming to be the best football player ever.*

23 turn sb's head OLD-FASHIONED to be attractive in a romantic or sexual way to a particular person: *So it seems some young woman has finally turned Steve's head.*

24 making bread [T always + adv./prep.] also **turn out** to pour DOUGH from a container: *Turn the dough out onto a lightly floured board.*

25 dirt [T] to break up land to prepare it for growing crops or for building something —see also **turn a blind eye** (BLIND¹ (2)), **turn the other cheek** (CHEEK (4)), **turn a deaf ear** (DEAF (4)), **sb would turn/roll over in their grave** (GRAVE¹ (2)), **turn your hand to sth** (HAND¹ (35)), **turn your nose up (at sth)** (NOSE¹ (5)), **turn sb's stomach** (STOMACH¹ (4)), **turn the tables (on sb)** (TABLE¹ (3)), **turn tail** (TAIL¹ (9)) —see Usage Notes at BECOME and OPEN¹

turn sb **against** sb/sth *phr. v.* [T] to make someone decide not to like someone anymore or not to agree with something anymore: *Brenda even tried to turn my sister against me.*

turn around *phr. v.* **1** [T **turn** sth ↔ **around**] to manage an unsuccessful business so well that it becomes successful again: *Jones is asking for patience as he tries to turn the company around.* **2 turn around and do sth** SPOKEN to do or say something that is unexpected or seems unfair or unreasonable: *He says he loves me and then turns around and asks me for $500.* **3 every time sb turns around...** SPOKEN very often or all the time: *It seems like every time I turn around my manager is checking up on me.* **4** [T **turn** sth ↔ **around**] to complete the process of making a product or providing a service: *We can turn around 500 units by next week.*

turn away *phr. v.* **1** [T **turn** sb ↔ **away**] to refuse to let someone into a place such as a theater or restaurant because there is no more space: *We waited in line for an hour, only to be turned away at the door.* **2** [I,T **turn** sth ↔ **away**] to refuse to give someone sympathy, help, or support: [+ **from**] *Lots of my friends have turned away from me since I got sick.* | *We never turn patients away, even if they don't have money.*

turn back *phr. v.* **1** [I] to go in the opposite direction: *It's getting late – maybe we should turn back.*

2 [T **turn** sb ↔ **back**] to tell someone to go in the opposite direction, often because there is danger ahead: *The marchers were turned back by police as they neared the presidential palace.* **3 turn back the clock a)** to do something the way it was done at an earlier time or make things like they were before, especially when that is worse than the way things are now: *This bill turns back the clock on women's rights.* **b)** if you want to turn back the clock, you wish you had the chance to do something again so you could do it better: *I wish I had the power to turn back the clock and undo the past.*

turn sb/sth ↔ **down** *phr. v.* [T] **1** to make a machine such as an OVEN, radio etc. produce less heat, sound etc.: *Could you turn down the air conditioning? It's too cold in here.* **2** to refuse an offer, request, or invitation: *His application to med school was turned down.* | *She was so convincing, I couldn't turn her down.* —see Usage Note at REFUSE¹

turn in *phr. v.* **1** [T **turn** sth ↔ **in**] to give back something you have borrowed or rented to a person in authority, or give them something you have found: *We have to turn the bikes in by 6:00.* | [**turn sth in to sb**] *My wallet was turned in to the police two days after it was stolen.* **2** [T **turn** sth ↔ **in**] to give a piece of work to a teacher, your BOSS etc.: *If you don't turn in the assignment, you won't pass.* **3** [T **turn** sb ↔ **in**] to tell the police who or where a criminal is: *Winkler drove to the station and turned himself in.* **4** [I] INFORMAL to go to bed: *Well, I think I'll turn in. I've got to get up early.*

turn into sth *phr. v.* [T] **1** to become something different, or make someone or something do this: *Shelly was 18 and turning into an adult.* | *These growths could turn into cancer.* | [**turn sb/sth into sth**] *Stein turned the garage into an artist's studio.* **2** to change by magic from one thing into another, or make something do this: *The wall of thorns suddenly turned into a wall of big beautiful flowers.* | [**turn sb/sth into sth**] *With a wave of her hand, the witch turned him into a frog.* **3 days turned into weeks/months turned into years etc.** used to say that time passed slowly while you waited for something to happen: *Months turned into years without a new album from the group.* **4** if one season turns into another season, it changes gradually from one to the next

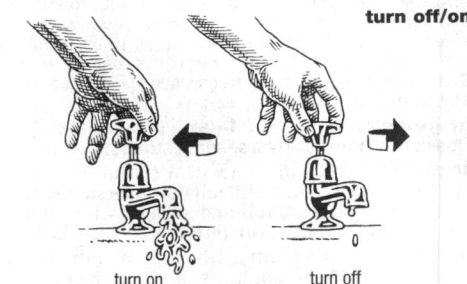

turn off/on

turn on   turn off

turn off *phr. v.* **1** [T **turn** sth ↔ **off**] to make a machine or piece of electrical equipment such as a television, car, light etc. stop operating by pushing a button, turning a key etc.: *Don't forget to turn off the lights when you leave.* | *Could we turn the TV off while we eat?* **2** [T **turn** sth ↔ **off**] to stop the supply of water, gas etc. from flowing by turning a handle as far as possible: *I can't turn the water off.* **3** [I,T] to leave one road, especially a large one, and drive along another one: [**turn off at/near etc. sth**] *A few miles down the road, we turned off at the park.* | [**turn off sth**] *The car drove west on the highway and turned off on a gravel road.* —see also TURN-OFF (1) **4** [T **turn** sb ↔ **off**] to do something that makes someone decide they do not like someone or something: *I was really turned off by the salesman's attitude.* —see also TURN-OFF (2) **5** [T **turn** sb ↔ **off**] to do something that makes someone feel that they are not attracted to you in a sexual way: *Something about me seems to turn women off.* —see also TURN-OFF (2)

turn on *phr. v.* [T]

1 electrical equipment [**turn** sth ↔ **on**] to make

a machine or piece of electrical equipment such as a car, television, light etc. start operating by pushing a button, turning a key etc.: *Peter always turns on all the lights when he comes home.* | *It's so hot – why don't you turn the fan on?*

2 water/gas [**turn** sth ↔ **on**] to make the supply of water, gas etc. start flowing from something by turning a handle: *You turn on the faucet and only rusty water comes out.*

3 attack [**turn on** sb] to suddenly attack someone or treat them badly, using physical violence or cruel words: *Without warning, Franny turned on him, kicking and screaming*

4 depend [**turn on** sth] if a situation, event, or argument turns on a particular thing or idea, it depends on that thing in order to work: *The trial turned on one key issue: Did Mason know about the plan?*

5 sexual [**turn** sb **on**] to make someone feel sexually excited —see also TURN-ON

6 interest [**turn** sb **on**] to make someone become interested in a product, idea etc.: [+ **to**] *Reading "Scientific American" really turned me on to biology.*

7 weapon [**turn** sth **on** sb/sth] to use a weapon, your anger etc. against someone or something: *Cranwell killed six people before turning the gun on himself.*

turn out *phr. v.* **1** [linking verb] to happen in a particular way, or to have a particular result, especially one that you did not expect: *Don't worry – I'm sure it will all turn out fine.* | *The car turned out to be more expensive than we thought.* | *It turns out that Nancy didn't want to come anyway.* | *As it turned out, they were both right.* **2** [T **turn** sth ↔ **out**] if you turn out a light, you stop the flow of electricity to it by pushing a button, pulling a string etc.: *Did you turn out the light in the bathroom?* **3** [I] if people turn out for an event, they gather together to see it happen: *Over 3,000 fans turned out to support the team.* | [+ **for**] *How many people turned out for the parade?* —see also TURNOUT **4** [T **turn** sth ↔ **out**] to produce or make something: *The factory turns out 300 units a day.* **5** [T **turn** sb ↔ **out**] to force someone to leave a place, especially their home: *If the man is found guilty, his family will be turned out on the street.* **6** well/beautifully/badly etc. **turned out** to be dressed in good, beautiful etc. clothes: *Tyler looked trim and well turned out in a new dark suit.*

turn over *phr. v.* **1** [T **turn** sth ↔ **over**] to give someone the right to own something, or the responsibility for something such as a plan, business, piece of property etc.: [+ **to**] *Local police have turned the case over to the FBI.* | *Russia turned Alaska over to the U.S. in 1867.* **2** [T **turn** sb ↔ **over**] to bring a criminal to the police or other official organization: [+ **to**] *Mr. Cruz was so upset by his son's drug use that he turned him over to the authorities.* **3** [I] if an engine turns over, it starts to work **4 turn over a new leaf** to decide to change the way you behave and become a better person **5 turn sth over in your mind** to think about something carefully, considering all the possibilities: *I kept turning the idea over in my mind.* **6** [**turn over** sth] if a business turns over a particular amount of money, it makes that amount in a particular period of time

turn to sb/sth *phr. v.* [T] **1** to try to get help, advice, or sympathy from someone or by doing something: *Whenever I have problems, I always turn to God.* | *After Roy could no longer work as a sailor, he turned to writing.* **2** to look at a particular page in a book: *Turn to page 655 for more information on this subject.* **3** FORMAL to change to a different form, condition, or attitude, especially a worse one, or to make someone or something do this: *The rain has turned to snow in the mountains.* | *My frustration quickly turned to anger.* | [**turn** sb/sth **to** sth] *Cooking the mushrooms too long will turn them to mush.* **4** to begin discussing a new subject: *Turning to education, the Senator described his plans for English-only classes.*

turn up *phr. v.* **1** [T **turn** sth ↔ **up**] to make a machine such as an OVEN, radio etc. produce more heat, sound etc.: *If you're cold, I can turn the heat up.* | *Turn up the radio!* **2** [I] to suddenly appear

after having been lost or searched for: *Don't worry about the necklace. It'll turn up sooner or later.* **3** [I] to arrive at a place: *Stan's mom turned up in a miniskirt.* **4** [I] if an opportunity or situation turns up, it happens, especially when you are not expecting it: *I'm ready to take any job that turns up.* **5** [T **turn** sth ↔ **up**] to find something by thoroughly searching for it: *The investigation turned up no evidence to support Wood's claims.*

turn upon sb *phr. v.* [T] FORMAL to suddenly attack someone or treat them badly, using physical violence or cruel words

turn² *n.*

1 chance to do sth the time when it is your chance, duty, or right to do something that a group of people are doing one after another: [**sb's turn to do sth**] *Whose turn is it to wash the dog?* | *It's your turn. Roll the dice.*

2 take turns if two or more people take turns doing work or playing a game, they each do it one after the other in order to share work or play fairly: *You'll have to take turns on the swing.* | [**take turns doing sth**] *We take turns cooking dinner.*

3 in turn a) as a result of something: *Working outside can mean too much sun exposure, which in turn can lead to skin cancer.* **b)** one after the other, especially in a particular order: *The President spoke to each of us at the table in turn.*

4 change direction [C] a change in the direction you are moving: **make a left/right turn** *Make a left turn at the light.*

5 act of turning sth [C] the act of turning something completely around a central point: *Tighten the screw another two or three turns.*

6 road [C] the place where one road goes in a different direction from another: *Take the first turn on your right.*

7 the turn of the century the time when one century ends and a new one begins: *There were about 500,000 cafés in Paris at the turn of the last century* (=in 1900). —see also TURN-OF-THE-CENTURY

8 take a turn for the worse/better to suddenly become worse or better: *The country's financial crisis has taken a turn for the worse.*

9 turn of events a change in what is happening, especially an unusual one: *For the drought-stricken region, the rains are being seen as a welcome turn of events.*

10 a turn of phrase a) a particular way of saying something: *"Peanuts" is a rather odd turn of phrase for what may be millions of dollars.* **b)** the ability to say things in a clever or funny way: *Catledge has a folksy turn of phrase and a gift for storytelling.*

11 at every turn if something happens at every turn, it happens again and again: *Government officials demanded bribes from us at every turn.*

12 speak/talk out of turn to say something you should not say in a particular situation, especially because you do not have enough authority to say it: *I hope I'm not speaking out of turn, but I don't think this is the best way to proceed.*

13 by turns LITERARY if someone shows different feelings or qualities by turns, they change from one to another: *She had been by turns confused, angry, and finally jealous.*

14 do sb a good turn OLD-FASHIONED to do something that is helpful for someone

15 turn of mind LITERARY the way that someone usually thinks or feels: *He is a very intelligent man with a scientific turn of mind.*

16 one good turn deserves another used to say that if someone does something nice for you, you should do something nice for them to thank them

17 give sb a turn OLD-FASHIONED to frighten someone

turn·a·bout /ˈtɜrnəbaʊt/ *n.* **1** [C usually singular] a complete change in someone's opinions or ideas: *a surprising turnabout in church policy* **2 turnabout is fair play** used to say that because someone else has done something to you, you can do it to them too

turn·a·round /'tənə,raʊnd/ *n.* **1** [C usually singular] a complete change from a bad situation to a good one: *Jenkins is confident the company will make a major turnaround this year.* **2** [C,U] the time it takes to receive something, deal with it and send it back, especially on an airplane, ship etc.: *Their products are good, but their turnaround time is slow.* —see also **turn around** (TURN¹) **3** [usually singular] a TURNABOUT (1)

turn·coat /'tənkoʊt/ *n.* [C] someone who stops supporting a political party or group and joins the opposing side: *a mafia turncoat*

turn·er /'tənə/ *n.* [C] something, especially a piece of kitchen equipment, used to turn things over: *a pancake turner*

Tur·ner /'tənə/, **J.M.W.** (1775–1851) a British PAINTER, famous for his WATERCOLORS

turning cir·cle /'.. ,../ *n.* [C] the smallest space in which a vehicle can drive around in a circle

turning point /'.. ,./ *n.* [C] the time when an important change starts, especially one that improves the situation: *The fall of the Berlin Wall marked a turning point in East-West relations.*

tur·nip /'tənɪp/ *n.* [C] a large round pale yellow or white vegetable that grows under the ground, or the plant that produces it

turn·key¹ /'tənki/ *adj.* [only before noun] ready to be used immediately: *The software is not a turnkey system that can be simply loaded and run.*

turnkey² *n. plural* **turnkeys** [C] OLD USE a prison guard

turn-off /'. ./ *n.* **1** [C] a smaller road that leads off a main road: *I think that was the turn-off for the campground.* **2** [usually singular] INFORMAL something that you lose interest in something, especially sex: *Hair on a guy's back is a real turn-off.* —see also **turn off** (TURN¹)

turn-of-the-cen·tu·ry /,. . . '../ *adj.* [only before noun] existing or happening at the around the beginning of a century, especially the beginning of the 20th century: *Turn-of-the-century New Orleans was a fascinating mix of cultures.*

turn-on /'. ./ *n.* [C usually singular] INFORMAL something that makes you feel excited, especially sexually: *Her voice is a total turn-on.* —see also **turn on** (TURN¹)

turn·out /'tənaʊt/ *n.* [C] **1** [usually singular] the number of people who go to a party, meeting, or other organized event: *These shows are always popular, and we're expecting a big turnout.* **2** [usually singular] the number of people who vote in an election: **a high/low turnout** *This election had the lowest voter turnout since 1824.* —see also **turn out** (TURN¹) **3** a place at the side of a narrow road where cars can wait to let others pass

turn·o·ver /'tən,oʊvə/ *n.* **1** [singular,U] the rate at which people leave an organization and are replaced by others: *We're doing everything we can to reduce staff turnover.* **2** [singular, U] the rate at which a particular type of goods is sold, or the amount of business done: *Quick turnover is good for cash flow.* **3** [C] a small PIE made with a piece of DOUGH that has been folded over fruit, meat, or vegetables: *an apple turnover* **4** [C] a situation in a football or basketball game in which something happens so that one team loses the ball and the other team gets control of it

turn·pike /'tənpaɪk/ *n.* [C] a large road for fast traffic that drivers have to pay to use: *the New Jersey Turnpike*

turn sig·nal /'. ,../ *n.* [C] one of the lights on a car that flash to show which way the car is turning —see picture on page 427

turn·stile /'tənstaɪl/ *n.* [C] a small gate that spins around and only lets one person at a time go through an entrance

turn·ta·ble /'tən,teɪbəl/ *n.* [C] **1** the round flat surface on a RECORD PLAYER that you put records on **2** a round surface that turns around, for example on a table or in a MICROWAVE OVEN **3** a large round flat surface on which railroad engines are turned around

tur·pen·tine /'təpən,taɪn/ *n.* [U] a type of oil used for making paint more liquid or removing it from clothes, brushes etc.

tur·pi·tude /'təpətud/ *n.* [U] LITERARY evil: *a crime of moral turpitude*

tur·quoise /'təkwɔɪz, -kɔɪz/ *n.* [U] **1** a valuable greenish-blue stone, or a jewel that is made from this **2** a greenish-blue color —**turquoise** *adj.*

tur·ret /'təɪt, 'tʌrɪt/ *n.* [C] **1** a small tower on a large building, especially a CASTLE **2** the place on a TANK (=army vehicle) *from which guns are fired* —**turreted** *adj.*

tur·tle /'tətl/ *n.* [C] **1** an animal that has a soft body covered by a hard shell **2** **turn turtle** if a ship or boat turns turtle, it turns upside down

tur·tle·dove /'tətl,dʌv/ *n.* [C] a type of bird that makes a pleasant soft sound and is sometimes used to represent love

tur·tle·neck /'tətl,nɛk/ *n.* [C] **1** a type of SWEATER or shirt with a high close-fitting collar that covers most of your neck **2** a high close-fitting collar on a SWEATER or shirt

turtleneck

a turtleneck sweater

Tus·ca·ro·ra /,tʌskə'rɔrə/ a Native American tribe from the southeastern area of the U.S.

tush /tʊʃ/ *n.* [C] INFORMAL the part of your body that you sit on

tusk /tʌsk/ *n.* [C] one of a pair of very long pointed teeth, that stick out of the mouth of animals such as ELEPHANTs —see picture at MAMMOTH²

tus·sle¹ /'tʌsəl/ *n.* [C] INFORMAL a struggle or fight using a lot of energy: *The two women got into a violent tussle in which Joan was thrown to the ground.* | *a tussle for control of the party*

tussle² *v.* [I + with] INFORMAL to fight or struggle without using any weapons, by pulling or pushing someone rather than hitting them: *Shea tussled with the doorman when he was not allowed in the club.*

tus·sock /'tʌsək/ *n.* [C] LITERARY a small thick mass of grass

Tu·tan·kha·men, Tutankhamon /,tutaŋ'kamən/ also **King Tut** (14th century B.C.) an Egyptian PHARAOH (=ruler) whose TOMB and the valuable things in it were discovered in 1922

tu·te·lage /'tutəlɪdʒ/ *n.* [U] FORMAL **1** the state or period of being taught or taken care of by someone: *Marcelle began her artistic career **under the tutelage of** (=being taught by) her father.* **2** regular teaching over many years or months **3** responsibility for someone's education, actions, or property

turnstile

tu·tor¹ /'tutə/ *n.* [C] someone who teaches one student or a small group, and is paid directly by them: *a math tutor* —see Usage Note at TEACH

tutor[2] *v.* [T] to teach someone as a tutor: [**tutor sb in sth**] *Lydia tutors kids in French during the summer.*

tu·to·ri·al /tuˈtɔriəl/ *n.* [C] **1** a computer program that is designed to teach you another program without help from someone else **2** a period of teaching and discussion with a tutor: *a psychology tutorial* —**tutorial** *adj.*

tut·ti frut·ti /ˌtuti ˈfruti/ *n.* [U] a type of ICE CREAM that has very small pieces of fruit and nuts in it

tut-tut[1] /ˌtʌt ˈtʌt/ *interjection* a sound made by touching the top of the mouth with the tongue twice, in order to show disapproval

tut-tut[2] *v.* [I] to express disapproval, especially by saying "tut-tut": *In 1924, The Times tut-tutted about the crossword puzzle craze sweeping America*

tu·tu /ˈtutu/ *n.* [C] a short skirt made of many folds of stiff material worn by BALLET dancers

Tu·va·lu /tuˈvɑlu/ a country in the southern Pacific Ocean, east of the Solomon Islands, made up of nine CORAL islands —**Tuvaluan** *n.*, *adj.*

tux /tʌks/ *n.* [C] INFORMAL a tuxedo

tux·e·do /tʌkˈsidoʊ/ *n. plural* **tuxedos** [C] **1** a type of man's suit, usually black, that is worn on formal occasions **2** the JACKET that is a part of this suit

TV *n. plural* **TVs** or **TV's** [C,U] television: *Rob's going to be on TV tonight.* | *TV show/station/star etc. We still have time to watch the TV news.* —see picture on page 426

TV-14 /ˌti vi fɔrˈtin/ *adj.* used to show that a television show is not appropriate for children under the age of 14

TV din·ner /ˌ. ˈ../ *n.* [C] a meal that is sold already prepared and frozen, so that you just need to heat it before eating

TV-G *adj.* used to show that a television show is appropriate for people of all ages, including children

TV-M *adj.* used to show that a television show is not appropriate for people under the age of 17

TVP /n.* [U] the abbreviation of TEXTURED VEGETABLE PROTEIN

TV-PG *adj.* used to show that a television show may include parts that are not appropriate for young children to see

TV-Y *adj.* used to show that a television show is appropriate for children

TV-Y7 /ˌti vi waɪ ˈsɛvən/ *adj.* used to show that a television show is not appropriate for children under the age of 7

twad·dle /ˈtwɑdl/ *n.* [U] INFORMAL something that someone has said or written that you think is stupid; NONSENSE: *I don't believe in all this twaddle about fate.*

twain /tweɪn/ *prep.* **1** OLD USE two **2** **(East is East and West is West and) never the twain shall meet** FORMAL OR HUMOROUS used to say that two things or people are so different that they can never exist together or agree

Twain /tweɪn/**, Mark** (1835–1910) a U.S. writer famous for his NOVELS. His real name was Samuel Longhorne Clemens.

Mark Twain

twang /twæŋ/ *n.* [C usually singular] **1** a quality in the way someone speaks, produced when the air used to speak passes through their nose as well as their mouth: *a high-pitched Midwestern twang* **2** a quick ringing sound like the one made by pulling a very tight wire and then suddenly letting it go —**twang** *v.* [I,T]

'twas /twɒz/ POETIC a short form of "it was": *'Twas the night before Christmas.*

twat /twɑt/ *n.* [C] TABOO a word for the female sex organ, also used as an insulting word for someone you are angry with

tweak /twik/ *v.* [T] **1** to suddenly pull or twist something: *Matthew tweaked her nose and laughed.* **2** to make small changes to something to improve it: *Maybe you should tweak a few sentences before you send the report.* —**tweak** *n.* [C usually singular]

tweed /twid/ *n.* **1** [U] rough wool cloth woven from threads of different colors, used mostly to make JACKETS, suits, and coats **2** **tweeds** [plural] a suit of clothes made from tweed

tweed·y /ˈtwidi/ *adj.* **1** wearing tweed clothes or acting in a way that is thought to be typical of college PROFESSORS, writers etc.: *tweedy academics* **2** made of tweed or like tweed

'tween /twin/ *prep.* POETIC a short form of "between": *'tween heaven and earth*

tweet /twit/ *v.* [I] to make the short high sound of a small bird —**tweet** *n.* [C]

tweet·er /ˈtwitɚ/ *n.* [C] a SPEAKER (=piece of equipment) through which the higher sounds from a radio, STEREO etc. come —compare WOOFER

tweez·ers /ˈtwizɚz/ *n.* [plural] a small tool that has two narrow pieces of metal joined at one end, used to pull or move very small objects: *a pair of tweezers*

twelfth[1] /twɛlfθ/ *adj.* 12th; next after the eleventh: *December is the twelfth month.*

twelfth[2] *pron.* **the twelfth** the 12th thing in a series: *Let's have dinner on the twelfth* (=the 12th day of the month).

twelfth[3] *n.* [C] $\frac{1}{12}$; one of twelve equal parts

twelve /twɛlv/ *number* **1** 12 **2** 12 o'clock: *We usually eat lunch at about twelve.*

Twelve Step also **12-step** /ˈ. ./ *adj.* TRADEMARK **a Twelve Step program** a method of helping people stop drinking alcohol, using drugs etc., developed by Alcoholics Anonymous

twen·ti·eth[1] /ˈtwɛntiɪθ/ *adj.* 20th; next after the nineteenth: *the twentieth century*

twentieth[2] *pron.* **the twentieth** the 20th thing in a series: *Let's have dinner on the twentieth* (=the 20th day of the month).

twen·ty[1] /ˈtwɛnti/ *number* **1** 20 **2** **the twenties** also **the '20s** the years from 1920 through 1929 **3** **sb's twenties** the time when someone is 20 to 29 years old: **be in your early/mid/late twenties** *I'd say he's in his late twenties.* **4** **in the twenties** if the temperature is in the twenties, it is between 20° and 29° FAHRENHEIT: **in the high/low twenties** *The temperature was in the low twenties the whole week.*

twenty[2] *n. plural* **twenties** [C] a piece of paper money worth $20: *Sorry, I don't have anything smaller than a twenty.*

twenty-four sev·en also **24/7** /ˌ.. ˌ. ˈ../ *adv.* SLANG twenty-four hours a day, seven days a week; all the time: *He listens to the radio 24/7.*

twenty-one /ˌ.. ˈ.◂/ *n.* [U] a card game, usually played for money; BLACKJACK

twen·ty·some·thing /ˈtwɛntiˌsʌmθɪŋ/ *adj.* [only before noun] between the ages of 20 and 29: *a twentysomething lawyer* —**twentysomething** *n.* [C usually singular plural]

twenty-twenty also **20/20** /ˌ.. ˈ..◂/ *adj.* **1** **20/20 vision** the ability to see things normally, without needing glasses **2** **20/20 hindsight** also **hindsight is 20/20** used to say that it is easy to know what you should have done in a situation after it has happened, but you did not know what to do earlier

twenty-two also **.22** /ˌ.. ˈ.◂/ *n.* [C] a gun that fires small bullets, used for hunting small animals

twerp /twɚp/ *n.* [C] SPOKEN a small person who you think is stupid or annoying

twice[1] /twaɪs/ *adv.* **1** two times: *I've only met him twice.* **2** two times more, bigger, better etc. than something else: *The image is twice as sharp as ordinary TV.* —see also **once bitten, twice shy** (ONCE[1] (15)), **once or twice** (ONCE[1] (12)), **think twice** (THINK (5))

twice² *determiner* two times more, bigger, better etc. than something else: *Heinemann's plane was the first to go twice the speed of sound*

twid·dle /'twɪdl/ *v.* **1 twiddle your thumbs** INFORMAL **a)** to do nothing while you are waiting for something to happen **b)** to join your fingers together and move your thumbs in a circle around each other, because you are bored **2** [T] also **twiddle with** to move or turn something around with your fingers many times, especially because you are bored —**twiddle** *n.* [C]

twig /twɪg/ *n.* [C] a small very thin stem of wood that grows from a branch on a tree —**twiggy** *adj.* —see picture at OAK

twi·light /'twaɪlaɪt/ *n.* [U] **1** the small amount of light in the sky as the day ends: *She could barely make out the figure of a man in the twilight.* **2** the time when day is just starting to become night: *We stayed outside till twilight.* **3** the period just before the end of the most active part of someone's life or the end of an important period of time: [+ of] *the twilight of the Victorian age | She's looking for something meaningful to do in her twilight years* (=the last years of her life). **4 twilight world** LITERARY a strange situation involving mystery, deceit etc.: *the twilight world of New York punk clubs*

twi·lit /'twaɪlɪt/ *adj.* LITERARY lit by twilight: *the twilit gray of the sea*

twill /twɪl/ *n.* [U] strong cloth woven to produce parallel sloping lines across its surface: *cotton twill pants*

twin¹ /twɪn/ *n.* [C] one of two children born at the same time to the same mother: *They look enough like each other to be twins.* —see also IDENTICAL TWIN, FRATERNAL TWIN, SIAMESE TWIN

twin² *adj.* [only before noun] **1 twin sister/brother/daughters etc.** someone who is a twin: *Did you know Gordie has a twin sister?* **2** like something else and considered with it as a pair: *the twin cities of Minneapolis and St. Paul | twin towers* **3 twin problems/goals etc.** two problems, goals etc. that happen at the same time and are related to each other: *the twin problems of poverty and unemployment*

twin³ *v.* [T usually passive] to form a relationship between two places, people, or ideas, or make other people think that this relationship exists: [**twin sb/sth with sb/sth**] *Dole has been twinned in the history books with his old rival Bush.*

twin bed /ˌ. './ *n.* [C] a bed for one person —see picture at BED¹

Twin Cit·ies, the /ˌ. '../ the cities of Minneapolis and St. Paul in the U.S. state of Minnesota

twine¹ /twaɪn/ *n.* [U] strong string made by twisting together two or more threads or strings

twine² *v.* [I,T] to wind or twist around something else, or to make something do this: [**twine sth around sth**] *Rochelle sat and twined the scarf around her fingers.* | [+ around] *A dark green ivy plant twined around the pole.*

twin-en·gine also **twin-engined** /ˌ. '..ˌ/ *adj.* a twin-engine aircraft has two engines

twinge /twɪndʒ/ *n.* [C] **1** a sudden feeling of slight pain: *Johnson felt a twinge on the inside of his right leg.* **2 a twinge of guilt/fear/jealousy etc.** a sudden slight feeling of guilt, fear etc.: *For an instant Bedford felt a twinge of sympathy for him.*

twin·kle¹ /'twɪŋkəl/ *v.* [I] **1** if a star or light twinkles, it shines in the dark, quickly changing from bright to faint: *The lights of the town twinkled beyond the desert.* **2** if someone's eyes twinkle, they have a cheerful expression: [+ with] *"I'd love to meet him,"* Christine said, her eyes twinkling with delight.

twinkle² *n.* [C usually singular] **1 a twinkle in your eye** an expression in your eyes that shows you are happy or amused: *Jake walked into the room with a twinkle in his eye.* **2** a small bright shining light that becomes brighter and then fainter **3 when you were just a twinkle in your father's eye** before you were born

twin·kling /'twɪŋklɪŋ/ *n.* **1 in the twinkling of an eye** LITERARY also **in a twinkling** very quickly **2** [U] the act of shining with a small light that becomes brighter and then fainter

twin-size also **twin-sized** /ˌ. '.ˌ/ *adj.* relating to a TWIN BED: *twin-size sheets*

twirl /twɜrl/ *v.* [I,T] to turn around and around, or make someone or something do this: *Elaine twirled across the dance floor.* | *Do you know how to twirl a baton?* | [**twirl sb/sth around**] *He lifted Carrie off her feet and twirled her around.* —**twirl** *n.* [C] —**twirly** *adj.*

twist¹ /twɪst/ *v.*

1 bend [T] to bend or turn something, such as wire, hair, or cloth, several times with your hands, especially in order to make something or to tie it to something: *Wrap the paper around the candy and twist the ends shut.* | [**twist sth into/around etc. sth**] *The silkmaker twists threads together into strands of raw silk.*

2 move [I,T] to turn a part of your body around, or change your position by turning: *Max twisted around to see who had entered the room.*

3 turn [T] to turn something using your hand: [**twist sth off**] *These bottle caps aren't so easy to twist off.* —see picture on page 424

4 road/river [I] if a road, river etc. twists, it changes direction in a series of curves: *The road twisted back and forth up the side of the mountain.*

5 twist your wrist/ankle/knee etc. to hurt a joint in your body by pulling or turning it too suddenly while you are moving

6 words [T] to change the true or intended meaning of a statement, especially in order to get some advantage for yourself; DISTORT: *He's always trying to twist my words and make me look bad.*

7 twist sb's arm a) INFORMAL to persuade someone to do something they do not want to do: *We had to twist her arm to get her to come.* **b)** to bend someone's arm up behind their back in order to hurt them

8 leave sb twisting in the wind to fail to make a definite decision about something important that will affect someone: *It's unfair to leave the diplomatic nominees twisting in the wind like this.*

9 twist and turn a) if a path, road, stream etc. twists and turns, it has a lot of bends in it **b)** if a person or animal twists and turns, they make twisting movements

10 dance to dance the TWIST² (6)

11 twist my arm! SPOKEN, HUMOROUS used to accept an invitation, a drink etc. —see also **twist/wrap sb around your little finger** (FINGER¹ (9)), **twist/turn the knife** (KNIFE¹ (5))

twist² *n.* [C]

1 unexpected an unexpected feature or change in a situation or series of events: *This was Sunday afternoon football with a twist – the players were women.* | *It's getting hard to follow the twists and turns of the investigation.* | **a twist of fate/fortune/irony** *Getting the role was a strange twist of fate.*

2 shape a shape made by twisting something, such as paper, rope, or hair: *Lorna wears her hair in a twist.* | [+ of] *a twist of tobacco*

3 movement a twisting action or movement: *The diamond sparkled with each twist of the chain.*

4 bend a bend in a river or road

5 drink a small piece of the PEEL (=skin) of a CITRUS fruit that is put in a drink, or the juice that you SQUEEZE from it: *a martini with a twist* | [+ of] *a twist of lemon*

6 dance **the twist** a popular fast dance from the 1960s, in which you twist your body from side to side —see also TWISTY

twist·ed /'twɪstɪd/ *adj.* **1** also **twisted up** something twisted has been bent in many directions or turned many times, so that it has lost its original shape: *the twisted wreckage of the plane* **2** seeming to enjoy things that are cruel or shocking, in a way that is not normal, or showing this quality: *I think she does love me in some twisted way.* | *a twisted mind*

twist·er /'twɪstər/ *n.* [C] INFORMAL a TORNADO

twist tie /'. ./ *n.* [C] a small piece of wire covered with paper or plastic that can be twisted around the top of a plastic bag to keep it closed

twist·y /ˈtwɪsti/ adj. INFORMAL **1** having a lot of twists or bends: *a twisty road* **2** having a lot of unexpected developments: *a novel with a twisty plot*

twit[1] /twɪt/ n. [C] INFORMAL a stupid or silly person

twit[2] v. **twitted, twitting** [T] to laugh at someone or try to make them look silly or stupid: *Kearns twitted the chairman for the committee's lack of progress.*

twitch[1] /twɪtʃ/ v. **1** [I,T] if a part of someone's body twitches or if they twitch it, it makes a small, sudden, uncontrolled movement: *Greg's always twitching – it makes me nervous.* | [twitch sth] *Look at how the cat is twitching her tail.* **2** [T] to move something quickly and suddenly: *Sarah twitched the reins, and we moved off.*

twitch[2] n. [C] **1** a quick movement of a muscle that you cannot control: *a nervous twitch* **2** a sudden quick movement

twitch·y /ˈtwɪtʃi/ adj. **twitchier, twitchiest 1** behaving in a nervous way because you are anxious about something: *a twitchy mood* **2** repeatedly making sudden small movements: *twitchy legs*

twit·ter[1] /ˈtwɪtə/ v. [I] **1** if a bird twitters, it makes a lot of short high sounds **2** if a woman twitters, she talks very quickly and nervously in a high voice

twitter[2] n. **1** [C] the short high sounds that birds make **2 be in a twitter** to be excited and nervous —see also ATWITTER

twixt /twɪkst/ prep. OLD USE between

two /tu/ number **1 2** two o'clock: *We're supposed to be there at two.* **3 sb's two cents (worth)** INFORMAL someone's opinion or what they want to say about a subject: *We all got a chance to **put in our two cents** on the topic.* **4 put two and two together** to guess the meaning of something you have heard or seen: *When we found the money and the drugs in his room, it was easy to put two and two together.* **5 two bits** OLD-FASHIONED, INFORMAL twenty-five CENTS, or a coin that is worth this amount of money

SPOKEN PHRASES

6 two's company, three's a crowd used to say that it is better to leave two people alone to spend time with each other **7 that makes two of us** used to tell someone that you are in the same situation and feel the same way: *"I'd like to work in Hawaii." "Yeah, that makes two of us."* **8 two can play at that game** used to tell someone that they will not have an advantage over you by doing something because you can do it too **9 for two cents, I'd...** used when you are describing angrily what you would like to do to change a situation: *For two cents I'd take the kids and leave tomorrow.*

—see also **be two of a kind** (KIND[1] (7)), **be of two minds about sth** (MIND[1] (35)), **it takes two to tango** (TANGO[2] (2)), **no two ways about it** (WAY[1] (51))

two-bit /ˈ. ./ adj. [only before noun] INFORMAL not good or important at all: *What do you think I am, some two-bit crook?*

two-by-four /ˈ. . ,./ n. [C] a long piece of wood that is two inches thick and four inches wide

two-di·men·sion·al /,. .ˈ.../ adj. **1** flat: *a two-dimensional drawing* **2** a two-dimensional character in a book, play etc. does not seem like a real person

two-edged /,. ˈ. / adj. **a two-edged sword** something that has as many bad results as good ones: *The policy is a two-edged sword – it saves money but angers staff.*

two-faced /,. ˈ. / adj. INFORMAL changing what you say according to who you are talking to, in a way that is insincere and not nice: *Barb is the most two-faced woman I've ever met.*

two·fer /ˈtufə/ n. [C] INFORMAL a situation or arrangement in which you receive two things, but you only have to pay for one

two-fist·ed /,. ˈ.../ adj. [only before noun] **1** doing something with a lot of energy and determination, or done in this way: *a two-fisted labor organizer* | *a two-fisted attack* **2** TWO-HANDED (1)

two·fold /ˈtufoʊld/ adj. **1** having two important parts: *The answer to the question is twofold.* **2** [only before noun] two times as much or as many of

something: *a twofold increase in the genetic mutations* —**twofold** adv.

two-four /,. ˈ. / n. [C] CANADIAN, INFORMAL twenty-four bottles of beer sold together in a box

two-hand·ed /,. ˈ...◂/ adj. **1** done using both hands: *Seles' powerful two-handed backhand* **2** a two-handed tool is used by two people together

twoo·nie /ˈtuni/ n. [C] TOONIE

two per·cent milk /,. .. ˈ./ n. [U] milk that has had cream removed so that two PERCENT of what remains is fat —compare ONE PERCENT MILK, SKIM MILK, WHOLE MILK

two-piece /,. ˈ.◂/ adj. [only before noun] a two-piece suit consists of a matching JACKET and pants

two-ply /ˈ. ,./ adj. consisting of two threads or layers: *two-ply yarn* | *two-ply toilet paper*

two-seat·er /,. ˈ.◂/ n. [C] a car, aircraft etc. with seats for two people

two-sid·ed /,. ˈ...◂/ adj. **1** having two different parts: *a two-sided issue* **2** having two specially prepared sides: *two-sided adhesive tape* —see also ONE-SIDED, MANY-SIDED

two·some /ˈtusəm/ n. [C usually singular] **1** two people who work together or spend a lot of time together: *Ulrich and Fonda play a lovestruck twosome.* **2** a game of GOLF for two people

two-step /ˈ. ./ n. **a) the two-step** a dance with long sliding steps, or the music for this type of dance **b)** a type of quick COUNTRY AND WESTERN dance

two-stroke /ˈ. ./ adj. a two-stroke engine is one in which there is a single up-and-down movement of a PISTON

two-time /ˈ. ./ v. [T] INFORMAL to have a secret relationship with someone who is not your regular partner: *It turns out Ryan was two-timing Jeannie with her best friend.* —**two-timer** n. [C]

two-tone /,. ˈ.◂/ adj. two-tone furniture, clothes etc. are made of material in two colors: *two-tone shoes*

two-way /,. ˈ.◂/ adj. **1** moving or allowing movement in both directions: *two-way traffic* | *two-way trade* **2** a two-way radio both sends and receives messages

two-way mir·ror /,. .. ˈ./ n. [C] glass that looks like a mirror from one side, but that you can see through from the other side

two-way street /,. . ˈ./ n. [C usually singular] INFORMAL a situation that depends on two people working well together: *Education is a two-way street.*

TX the written abbreviation of Texas

-ty /ti/ suffix [in nouns] the state of having a particular quality, or something that has that quality: *certainty* (=being certain) —see also -ITY

ty·coon /taɪˈkun/ n. [C] someone who is successful in business or industry and has a lot of money and power: *a Greek shipping tycoon*

ty·ing /ˈtaɪ-ɪŋ/ the present participle of TIE

tyke /taɪk/ n. [C] INFORMAL a small child

Ty·ler /ˈtaɪlə/, **John** (1790–1862) the tenth President of the U.S.

type[1] /taɪp/ n. **1** [C] a group of people or things that have similar features or qualities: *Hutchins has been writing novels of this type for years.* | *Rosa has trouble finding cosmetics for her skin type.* | [+ of] *What type of movies do you like?* **2** [C] someone with particular qualities or interests: *The second woman was a grandmotherly type.* | *the artistic type* | [the type to do sth] *Walter was not the type to kill someone.* **3 sb's type** the kind of person someone is sexually attracted to: *He wasn't really my type.* | *What is your type?* **4** [U] printed letters: *bold type* **5** [C,U] a small block with a raised letter on it that is used in printing, or a set of these —see also BLOOD TYPE

type[2] v. **1** [T] to print a document on a piece of paper using a TYPEWRITER: *These letters still need to be typed.* **2** [I] to write using a TYPEWRITER or a computer: *I don't know how to type.* **3** [T] TECHNICAL to find out what type a plant, disease etc. is

written using a typewriter: *I've got a lot of typing to do today.*

typing pool /'.. ./ *n.* [C] a group of typists in a large office who type letters for other people, especially in past times

typ·ist /'taɪpɪst/ *n.* [C] **1** a secretary whose main job is to TYPE letters **2 a good/bad/fast/slow etc. typist** someone who writes using a TYPEWRITER or computer in a particular way: *I'm not a very good typist.*

ty·po /'taɪpoʊ/ *n. plural* **typos** [C] a small mistake in the way something has been TYPED² (2) or printed: *This report is full of typos.*

ty·pog·ra·pher /taɪ'pɑgrəfɚ/ *n.* [C] **1** someone who designs TYPEFACES **2** a COMPOSITOR

ty·po·graph·i·cal /ˌtaɪpə'græfɪkəl/ also **ty·po·graph·ic** /ˌtaɪpə'græfɪk/ *adj.* relating to typography —**typographically** /-kli/ *adv.*

ty·pog·ra·phy /taɪ'pɑgrəfi/ *n.* [U] **1** the work of preparing written material for printing **2** the arrangement, style, and appearance of printed words

ty·pol·o·gy /taɪ'pɑlədʒi/ *n.* [U] the study or system of dividing a large group into smaller groups according similar features or qualities: *language typology* —**typological** /ˌtaɪpə'lɑdʒɪkəl/ *adj.*

ty·ran·ni·cal /tɪ'rænɪkəl/ *adj.* **1** behaving in a cruel and unfair way toward someone you have power over: *a tyrannical boss* **2** tyrannical rules, laws etc. are based on a system in which a single ruler uses their power unfairly: *a tyrannical regime*

tyr·an·nize /'tɪrəˌnaɪz/ *v.* [T] to use power over someone in a cruel or unfair way: *The household was tyrannized by a brutal father.*

ty·ran·no·saur·us /təˌrænə'sɔrəs/ also **tyranno-saurus rex** /təˌrænəsɔrəs 'rɛks/ *n.* [C] a very large flesh-eating DINOSAUR

tyr·an·nous /'tɪrənəs/ *adj.* OLD-FASHIONED: see TYRAN-NICAL

tyr·an·ny /'tɪrəni/ *n. plural* **tyrannies 1** [C,U] gov-ernment by one person or a small group that has gained power unfairly and uses it in a cruel way **2** [U] unfair and strict control over someone: *parental tyranny* **3 the tyranny of fashion/the clock** etc. the way that fashion, time etc. limits people's freedom to do things the way they want to do **4** [C often plural] a cruel or unfair action that limits someone's freedom: *He was eager to tell everyone of his father's tyrannies.*

ty·rant /'taɪrənt/ *n.* [C] **1** a ruler who has complete power and uses it in a cruel and unfair way: *The Romanian tyrant Ceauçescu was overthrown in 1989.* **2** someone who uses their power or influence over other people unfairly or cruelly: *Little Kyle is an absolute tyrant in the family.*

tyre /taɪɚ/ *n.* [C] the British spelling of TIRE

ty·ro /'taɪroʊ/ *n. plural* **tyros** [C] FORMAL someone who is only beginning to learn something

Ty·son /'taɪsən/**, Mike** /maɪk/ (1966–) a U.S. BOXER

tzar /zɑr, tsɑr/ *n.* [C] another spelling of CZAR —**tzarist** *adj.*

tza·ri·na /zɑ'rinə, tsɑ-/ *n.* [C] another spelling of CZARINA

tzar·is·m /'zɑˌrɪzəm,'tsɑ-/ *n.* [U] another spelling of CZARISM

tze·tze fly /'tɛtsi flaɪ, 'tsɛtsi-/ *n.* [C] another spelling of TSETSE FLY

Type A /ˌtaɪp 'eɪ / *adj.* relating to the qualities or behavior of the type of people who are often deter-mined, angry, or impatient: **Type A personality/ behavior** *People with Type A personalities are at a higher risk for heart attacks.* —compare TYPE B

Type B /ˌtaɪp 'bi/ *adj.* relating to the qualities or behavior of the type of people who are usually relaxed, friendly, and patient —compare TYPE A

type·cast /'taɪpkæst/ *v.* [T usually passive] **1** to always give an actor the same type of character to play: *I don't want to get typecast as a comedy actress.* **2** to think of someone only in a particular way, or only give them a particular type of job, activity etc. to do, because you think it is appropriate for their character —**typecasting** *n.* [U]

type·face /'taɪpfeɪs/ *n.* [C] a group of letters, num-bers etc. of the same style and size, used in printing

type·script /'taɪpˌskrɪpt/ *n.* [C] a copy of a document, made using a TYPEWRITER

type·set·ter /'taɪpˌsɛtɚ/ *n.* [C] a person or machine that arranges the letters, words etc. on a page or screen for printing

type·set·ting /'taɪpˌsɛtɪŋ/ *n.* [U] the job or activity of arranging TYPE¹ (4) for printing —**typeset** *v.* [T]

type·writ·er /'taɪpˌraɪtɚ/ *n.* [C] a machine with keys that you press to print letters of the alphabet onto paper

type·writ·ten /'taɪpˌrɪtⁿn/ *adj.* written using a type-writer: *a typewritten letter*

ty·phoid /'taɪfɔɪd/ also **typhoid fe·ver** /ˌ.. '../ *n.* [U] a serious infectious disease that is caused by dirty food or water

ty·phoon /taɪ'fun/ *n.* [C] a very violent storm in tropical areas in which the wind moves in circles

ty·phus /'taɪfəs/ *n.* [U] a serious infectious disease carried by insects that live on the bodies of people and animals

typ·i·cal /'tɪpɪkəl/ *adj.* **1** having the usual features or qualities of a particular group or thing: *Kim's a typ-ical teenager – she doesn't want anything to do with her parents.* | [+ **of**] *This painting is fairly typical of his early work.* **2** behaving or happening in the usual way: [+ **of**] *It's typical of Craig not to notice my new dress.* **3 typical!** SPOKEN used to show that you are annoyed when something bad happens again or someone does something bad again: *What? Amber didn't show up again? Typical.*

typ·i·cal·ly /'tɪpɪkli/ *adv.* **1** [sentence adverb] in the way that a particular type of thing usually happens: *We typically have between 35,000 and 45,000 people at the conference.* | *Typically, half a pound per person should be enough.* **2** [+ adj./adv.] in a way that a person or group is generally believed to behave, or a type of thing is believed to be: *It's typically American to serve all the food for a meal at the same time.*

typ·i·fy /'tɪpəˌfaɪ/ *v.* **typifies, typified, typifying** [T not in progressive] **1** to be a typical example of something: *Phyllis typifies suburban housewives.* **2** to be a typical part or feature of something: *Confidence in the future used to typify the Republican party.*

typ·ing /'taɪpɪŋ/ *n.* [U] the activity of using a TYPEWRITER to write something, or something that is

U

U, u /yu/ *n. plural* **U's, u's** [C] the 21st letter of the English alphabet

U., U an abbreviation of "university"

UAW United Automobile, Aerospace, and Agricultural Implement Workers; a UNION in the U.S.

u·biq·ui·tous /yu'bıkwətəs/ *adj.* FORMAL seeming to be everywhere: *Plastic containers are ubiquitous nowadays.* —**ubiquitously** *adv.* —**ubiquity** *n.* [U]

U-boat /'yu boʊt/ *n.* [C] a German SUBMARINE, especially one that was used in World War II

ud·der /'ʌdə/ *n.* [C] the part of a female cow, goat etc. that hangs down near its back legs and that produces milk

UFO *n.* [C] Unidentified Flying Object; a strange object in the sky, sometimes thought to be a SPACESHIP from another world

UFW —see UNITED FARM WORKERS

U·gan·da /yu'gændə, -'gɑn-/ a country in central Africa, east of the Democratic Republic of Congo and west of Kenya —**Ugandan** *n., adj.*

ugh /ʌg, ʌk, ʌh/ *interjection* used to show strong dislike: *I saw her haircut. Ugh!*

ug·ly /'ʌgli/ *adj.* **uglier, ugliest 1** extremely unattractive, and not nice to look at: *That's a really ugly picture of me.* | *An ugly chair* | *Her cousin's* **ugly as sin** (=very ugly). **2** extremely bad or violent, and making you feel frightened or upset: *They're in an ugly fight over who will get the children.* **3 an ugly duckling** someone who is less attractive, skillful etc. than other people when they are young, but who becomes beautiful and successful later —**ugliness** *n.* [U] —see also **sth rears its ugly head** (REAR³ (4))

uh /ʌ/ *interjection* said when you are thinking about what you are going to say: *Jimmy's from, uh, Texas.*

UHF *n.* [U] Ultra-High Frequency; a range of radio WAVEs between 300 and 3000 MEGAHERTZ, used also for television —compare VHF

uh huh /n'hn, m'hm, ə'hʌ/ *interjection* INFORMAL a sound that you make to mean "yes" or to show that you understand something: *"Is that you in the picture?" "Uh huh."* —opposite UH-UH

uh oh /'ʌ ˌʔoʊ/ *interjection* INFORMAL said when you have made a mistake or have realized that something bad has happened: *Uh oh, I think I locked my keys in the car.*

uh-uh /'ʌ ʌ, 'n n/ *interjection* INFORMAL a sound that you make to say "no": *"You didn't get hurt?" "Uh-uh."* —opposite UH HUH

U-ie /'yui/ *n.* [C] SPOKEN a U-TURN (1): **pull/do a U-ie** *I can't believe you actually pulled a U-ie on Main Street.*

U.K. *n.* the abbreviation of United Kingdom

u·ke·le·le /ˌyukə'leıli/ *n.* [C] a musical instrument with four strings, like a small GUITAR

U·kraine /yu'kreın, 'yukreın/ a country in eastern Europe, between Poland and Russia. It was formerly part of the Soviet Union and is now a member of the CIS. —**Ukrainian** /yu'kreıniən/ *n., adj.*

U·laan·baa·tar /ˌulɑn'bɑtɑr/ the capital city of Mongolia, formerly called Ulan Bator

-ular /'yələ/ *suffix* [in adjectives] relating to something, or shaped like something: *muscular* (=relating to the muscles) | *circular* (=shaped like a circle) —see also -AR (1)

ul·cer /'ʌlsə/ *n.* [C] a sore area on your skin or inside your body that may BLEED or produce poisonous substances: *a stomach ulcer* —**ulcerous** *adj.*

ul·cer·ate /'ʌlsəˌreıt/ *v.* [I,T] to form an ulcer, or become covered with ulcers —**ulcerated** *adj.* —**ulceration** /ˌʌlsə'reıʃən/ *n.* [U]

-ule /yul, yʊl/ *suffix* [in nouns] TECHNICAL a small type of something: *a granule* (=small grain)

ul·na /'ʌlnə/ *n.* [C] TECHNICAL the inner bone of your lower arm, on the side opposite to your thumb —see picture at SKELETON

ul·te·ri·or /ʌl'tıriə/ *adj.* **an ulterior motive/purpose/reason etc.** a reason for doing something that you deliberately hide in order to get an advantage for yourself: *He just being nice. I don't think he has any* **ulterior motives.**

ul·ti·mate¹ /'ʌltəmıt/ *adj.* [only before noun] **1** an ultimate aim, purpose etc. is the final and most important one: *The ultimate goal of the military was to restore the democratic government.* **2** better, bigger, worse etc. than all other objects of the same kind: *"The Rolling Stones" is the ultimate rock and roll band.* **3** an ultimate decision, responsibility etc. is one that you cannot pass on to someone else: *Ultimate responsibility lies with the President.*

ultimate² *n.* **the ultimate in stupidity/comfort/technology etc.** something that shows the highest possible level of stupidity, comfort etc.: *Prada called the fashion designs "the ultimate in bad taste."*

ultimate fris·bee /ˌ... '../ *n.* [U] a sport like football that is played with a FRISBEE rather than a ball

ul·ti·mate·ly /'ʌltəmıtli/ *adv.* after everything or everyone else has been done or considered: [sentence adverb] *Ultimately, you'll have to decide for yourself.*

ul·ti·ma·tum /ˌʌltə'meıtəm/ *n.* [C] a threat saying that if someone does not do what you want by a particular time, you will do something to punish them: *After seven years she gave him an ultimatum: either stop drinking or move out.*

ultra- /ʌltrə/ *prefix* **1** TECHNICAL above and beyond something in a range: *ultraviolet light* (=beyond the range of colors you can see) —compare INFRA- **2** extremely: *an ultramodern building*

ul·tra·con·ser·va·tive /ˌʌltrəkən'səvətıv/ *adj.* DISAPPROVING extremely opposed to changes in politics, religion, morality etc.: *an ultraconservative Republican* —**ultraconservative** *n.* [C]

ultra-high fre·quen·cy /ˌ... '.../ *n.* [U] UHF

ul·tra·light /'ʌltrəˌlaıt/ *n.* [C] a very small light aircraft you fly in for fun —**ultralight** *adj.* [only before noun]

ul·tra·ma·rine /ˌʌltrəmə'rin◂/ *n.* [C,U] a very bright blue color —**ultramarine** *adj.*

ul·tra·mod·ern /ˌʌltrə'mɑdən◂/ *adj.* extremely modern in style or design: *ultramodern furniture*

ul·tra·son·ic /ˌʌltrə'sɑnık◂/ *adj.* ultrasonic sound waves are too high for humans to hear

ul·tra·sound /'ʌltrəˌsaʊnd/ *n.* **1** [U] sound that is too high for humans to hear, and is often used in medical processes **2** [C] a medical process using this type of sound that produces an image of something inside your body, especially a baby

ul·tra·vi·o·let /ˌʌltrə'vaıəlıt◂/ *adj.* **1** ultraviolet light is beyond the purple end of the range of colors that people can see **2** [only before noun] an ultraviolet lamp, treatment etc. uses this light to treat skin diseases or make your skin darker

ul·u·late /'ʌlyəˌleıt/ *v.* [I] to make a long high sound with your voice to show strong emotions —**ululation** /ˌʌlyə'leıʃən/ *n.* [C,U]

U·lys·ses /yu'lısiz/ the Roman name for the HERO Odysseus

um /m/ *interjection* INFORMAL used when you are thinking about what to say next: *So, um, I guess I'll be back around 9.*

U·ma·til·la /ˌyumə'tılə/ a Native American tribe from the northwestern area of the U.S.

um·ber /'ʌmbə/ *n.* [C,U] a brown color like earth —**umber** *adj.*

um·bil·i·cal cord /ʌm'bılıkəl ˌkɔrd/ *n.* [C] a long narrow tube of flesh that joins an unborn baby to its mother

um·bil·i·cus /ʌm'bılıkəs/ *n.* [C] TECHNICAL **1** the part of an umbilical cord that is left attached to a baby after it is born **2** your NAVEL

um·brage /ˈʌmbrɪdʒ/ *n.* **take umbrage (at sth)** to be offended by something that someone has done or said: *Maynard angrily took umbrage at Campbell's remarks.*

um·brel·la /ʌmˈbrelə/ *n.*
[C] **1** a circular folding frame covered with cloth or plastic that you hold above your head when it is raining —compare PARA-SOL **2** also **umbrella orga-nization / group / agency** an organization that has many smaller groups **3** also **umbrella term/ word** a word whose mean-ing includes many differ-ent types of a particular thing **4** the protection given by a powerful coun-try or army, a weapons system etc.: *These countries have prospered under the U.S. military umbrella.*

umbrella

um·laut /ˈumlaut, ˈom-/ *n.* [C] a sign (¨) written over a German vowel to show how it is pronounced

ump /ʌmp/ *n.* [C] SPOKEN an umpire

um·pire[1] /ˈʌmpaɪɚ/ *n.* [C] the person who makes sure that the players obey the rules in sports such as baseball and tennis —compare REFEREE[1] —see picture at BASEBALL —see Usage Note at REFEREE[1]

umpire[2] *v.* [I,T] to be the umpire for a game or competition

ump·teenth /ˈʌmptinθ, ˌʌmˈtinθ/ *adj.* INFORMAL a word used when you do not know the specific number of something in a series, but you want to emphasize that the number is very large: *They're showing "The Wizard of Oz" for the umpteenth time.* —**umpteen** *quantifier*

U.N., UN *n.* **the U.N.** the United Nations; an inter-national organization that tries to find peaceful solutions to world problems

un- /ʌn/ *prefix* **1** [in adjectives and adverbs] used to show an opposite state or a negative; not: *unfair* | *unhappy* | *unfortunately* **2** [especially in verbs] used to show an opposite action: *to undress* (=take your clothes off) | *Have you unpacked yet* (=taken your clothes out of your suitcase)?

USAGE NOTE: UN-

WORD FORMATION
Un- is the most frequent negative prefix in English and is used in many common words. It can also be added to adjectives, adverbs, and verbs to make new negative and opposite words. Because of this, there are many more "un-" words than those that appear in this dictionary. The words that are shown here either are very common or have a special meaning besides just the negative or opposite of the meaning of the main part of the word.

---

sw **un·a·bashed** /ˌʌnəˈbæʃt◂/ *adj.* not ashamed or embarrassed, especially when doing something unusual or rude: *Tyler is an unabashed fan of Holly-wood glamour.* | *unabashed enthusiasm*

un·a·bat·ed /ˌʌnəˈbeɪtɪd/ *adj.* continuing without becoming any weaker or less violent: *The noises of the late evening traffic* **continued unabated.** | *unabated expansion*

sw **un·a·ble** /ʌnˈeɪbəl/ *adj.* [not before noun] not able to
2 do something: [**unable to do sth**] *Ben was unable to get out of bed for four days.*

un·a·bridged /ˌʌnəˈbrɪdʒd◂/ *adj.* a piece of writing, speech etc. that is unabridged is in its full form with-out being made shorter: *an unabridged dictionary*

un·ac·cept·a·ble /ˌʌnəkˈsɛptəbəl◂/ *adj.* something that is unacceptable is so wrong or bad that you think it should not be allowed: *McCartney's response is totally unacceptable.* | *unacceptable behavior* —**unacceptably** *adv.*

un·ac·com·pa·nied /ˌʌnəˈkʌmpənid◂/ *adj.* **1** some-one who is unaccompanied has no one with them: *Unaccompanied children are not allowed on the premises.* **2** unaccompanied bags/luggage etc. bags, SUITCASEs etc. that are sent on an airplane, train etc. without their owner **3** an unaccompanied singer or musician sings or plays alone

un·ac·count·a·ble /ˌʌnəˈkaʊntəbəl◂/ *adj.* FORMAL **1** very surprising and difficult to explain: *For some unaccountable reason he was sure I would be success-ful.* **2** not having to explain your actions or deci-sions to anyone else: *unaccountable federal agency officials* —**unaccountably** *adv.*

un·ac·count·ed·for, unaccounted-for /ˌʌnəˈkaʊn-tɪd fɔr/ *adj.* something or someone that is unac-counted for cannot be found or their absence cannot be explained: *Fifteen people are still unaccounted for after the fire.*

un·ac·cus·tomed /ˌʌnəˈkʌstəmd◂/ *adj.* FORMAL **1** unaccustomed to sth not familiar or comfortable with something because it does not happen often: *They were unaccustomed to seeing Richard in casual clothes.* **2** [only before noun] not usual, typical, or familiar: *unaccustomed speed and decisiveness* **3** unaccustomed as I am (to sth) SPOKEN, FORMAL used in a speech to say that something you are doing is not usual or familiar

un·ac·knowl·edged /ˌʌnəkˈnɑlɪdʒd◂/ *adj.* **1** ignored, or not noticed or accepted: *unacknowledged anger* **2** not generally or publicly praised, rewarded, or thanked, even though this is deserved: *Women's work in the home tends to be both unpaid and unacknowledged.*

un·a·dorned /ˌʌnəˈdɔrnd◂/ *adj.* not having any unnecessary or special features or decorations: *an unadorned dress*

un·a·dul·ter·at·ed /ˌʌnəˈdʌltəˌreɪtɪd/ *adj.* **1** [only before noun] complete or total: *What unadulterated nonsense!* **2** not mixed with other less pure substances

un·af·fect·ed /ˌʌnəˈfɛktɪd/ *adj.* **1** not changed or influenced by something: [+ by] *Salmon were unaf-fected by the poison.* **2** APPROVING natural in the way you behave: *He sounds completely unaffected in interviews.* —**unaffectedly** *adv.*

un·aid·ed /ʌnˈeɪdɪd/ *adj.* without help: *Jerry cannot stand up unaided.* | *Venus is easily seen* **with the unaided eye** (=without using special instruments).

un·al·ien·a·ble /ʌnˈeɪliənəbəl, -lyə-/ *adj.* FORMAL: see INALIENABLE

un·al·loyed /ˌʌnəˈlɔɪd◂/ *adj.* LITERARY not mixed with anything else: *an unalloyed victory*

un·al·ter·a·ble /ʌnˈɔltərəbəl/ *adj.* FORMAL not possi-ble to change: *an unalterable fact* —**unalterably** *adv.*

un·am·big·u·ous /ˌʌnæmˈbɪgyuəs◂/ *adj.* a statement, instruction etc. that is unambiguous is clear and easy to understand because it can only mean one thing: *an unambiguous message* —**unambiguously** *adv.*

un·A·mer·i·can /ˌʌn əˈmɛrɪkən◂/ *adj.* **1** not loyal to generally accepted American customs and ways of thinking: *This kind of censorship is un-American.* **2** un-American activities political activity believed to be harmful to the U.S.

u·na·nim·i·ty /ˌyunəˈnɪməti/ *n.* [U] FORMAL a state or situation of complete agreement among a group of people

u·nan·i·mous /yuˈnænəməs/ *adj.* **1** a unanimous decision, statement, vote etc. is one that everyone agrees with **2** agreeing completely about something: *Parents have been unanimous in supporting the after-school program.* —**unanimously** *adv.*

un·an·nounced /ˌʌnəˈnaʊnst◂/ *adj.* happening without anyone expecting or knowing about it: *an unannounced visit*

un·an·swer·a·ble /ʌnˈænsərəbəl/ *adj.* **1** an un-answerable question is one that seems to have no possible answer or solution **2** FORMAL definitely true and therefore impossible to argue against: *unanswerable criminal charges*

un·an·swered /ˌʌnˈænsəd◂/ adj. an unanswered question, letter, telephone etc. has not been answered

un·a·pol·o·get·ic /ˌʌnəˌpaləˈdʒɛtɪk◂/ adj. not feeling or saying you are sorry for something you have done: [+ about/for] *Hallinan remains unapologetic about his remarks.*

un·ap·peal·ing /ˌʌnəˈpilɪŋ◂/ adj. not pleasant or attractive: *The fish was an unappealing shade of gray.*

un·armed /ˌʌnˈɑrmd◂/ adj. not carrying any weapons: *Soldiers killed 17 unarmed civilians.*

un·a·shamed /ˌʌnəˈʃeɪmd◂/ adj. not feeling embarrassed or ashamed about something that people might disapprove of: *Sue seems completely unashamed and relaxed about sex.* —**unashamedly** /ˌʌnəˈʃeɪmɪdli/ adv.

un·asked /ˌʌnˈæskt◂/ adj. an unasked question is not asked, often because people are embarrassed by it

un·as·sail·able /ˌʌnəˈseɪləbəl◂/ adj. FORMAL not able to be criticized, attacked, or made weaker: *unassailable logic*

un·as·sist·ed /ˌʌnəˈsɪstɪd◂/ adj. without help: *The patient cannot breathe unassisted.*

un·as·sum·ing /ˌʌnəˈsumɪŋ◂/ adj. showing no desire to be noticed or given special treatment; MODEST: *a hard-working, unassuming father of four*

un·at·tached /ˌʌnəˈtætʃt◂/ adj. **1** not involved in a romantic relationship; SINGLE: *Are there any unattached straight men in this city?* **2** not connected or fastened to anything: *an unattached garage*

un·at·tain·a·ble /ˌʌnəˈteɪnəbəl◂/ adj. impossible to achieve: *an unattainable goal*

un·at·tend·ed /ˌʌnəˈtɛndɪd◂/ adj. left alone without anyone being responsible: *unattended luggage* | *The parents are accused of **leaving** the children **unattended** for days at a time.*

un·at·trac·tive /ˌʌnəˈtræktɪv◂/ adj. **1** not attractive, pretty, or pleasant to look at: *He was physically unattractive.* **2** not good or desirable: *Reducing city services and raising taxes are both unattractive alternatives.* —**unattractively** adv.

un·au·thor·ized /ʌnˈɔθəˌraɪzd/ adj. without official approval or permission: *Her biography of Sinatra was unauthorized.* | *This area is closed to all unauthorized persons.*

un·a·vail·a·ble /ˌʌnəˈveɪləbəl◂/ adj. [not before noun] **1** not able to be obtained: *Many common medicines are unavailable in the country.* **2** not able or willing to meet someone: *School officials were **unavailable for comment** (=not willing to speak to reporters).*

un·a·vail·ing /ˌʌnəˈveɪlɪŋ◂/ adj. FORMAL not successful or effective: *unavailing efforts*

un·a·void·a·ble /ˌʌnəˈvɔɪdəbəl◂/ adj. impossible to prevent: *The accident was really unavoidable.* —**unavoidably** adv.

un·a·ware /ˌʌnəˈwɛr◂/ adj. [not before noun] not noticing or realizing what is happening: [+ of] *Mike seems unaware of the trouble he's causing.* | [unaware that] *Until that moment, I was unaware that I was holding the knife.* —**unawareness** n. [U]

un·a·wares /ˌʌnəˈwɛrz◂/ adv. **1 take/catch sb unawares** to happen or to do something to someone when they are not expecting it or are prepared for it: *I was caught unawares by his kiss.* **2** LITERARY without noticing: *Tommy and Don stood in the corner, chatting unawares.*

un·bal·anced /ˌʌnˈbælənst◂/ adj. **1** someone who is unbalanced seems slightly crazy **2** an unbalanced report, argument etc. is unfair because it emphasizes one opinion too much **3 an unbalanced budget** a situation in which a government plans to spend more money than is available **4** an unbalanced situation or relationship is one in which one part, group, or person has more influence, power etc. than the other —**unbalance** v. [T]

un·bear·a·ble /ʌnˈbɛrəbəl◂/ adj. too bad, painful, or annoying for you to deal with; INTOLERABLE: *The smell in the streets was almost unbearable.* —**unbearably** adj.: *an unbearably hot day*

un·beat·a·ble /ʌnˈbitəbəl◂/ adj. **1** something that is unbeatable is the best of its kind: *unbeatable prices* **2** an unbeatable team, player etc. cannot be defeated

un·beat·en /ˌʌnˈbitn◂/ adj. an unbeaten player, team etc. has not been defeated: *The Oilers extended their **unbeaten streak** to four games.*

un·be·com·ing /ˌʌnbɪˈkʌmɪŋ◂/ adj. **1** behavior that is unbecoming is shocking or not appropriate: *Snyder was charged with **conduct unbecoming** (=behavior that is not appropriate for) an officer.* **2** OLD-FASHIONED unbecoming clothes do not make you look attractive

un·be·knownst /ˌʌnbɪˈnoʊnst/ also **un·be·known** /-ˈnoʊn/ [sentence adverb] **unbeknownst to sb** without that person knowing about it: *Unbeknownst to his family, Ken had been driving a taxi for a year.*

un·be·lief /ˌʌnbəˈlif/ n. [U] FORMAL a lack of belief or a refusal to believe in a religious faith —compare DISBELIEF

un·be·liev·a·ble /ˌʌnbɪˈlivəbəl◂/ adj. **1** extremely surprising, especially in a good way: *He has unbelievable talent.* **2** very difficult to believe and therefore probably not true: *I find it unbelievable that Mr. Carvey has no memory of that day.* —**unbelievably** adv.: *unbelievably lucky*

un·be·liev·er /ˌʌnbəˈlivə/ n. [C] someone who does not believe in a particular religion —**unbelieving** adj.

un·bend /ʌnˈbɛnd/ v. **1** [I,T] to become straight or make something straight **2** [I] to relax and start behaving in a less formal way: *She unbent enough to ask us in for something to eat.*

un·bend·ing /ʌnˈbɛndɪŋ/ adj. not willing to change your opinions, decisions etc.: *an unbending determination*

un·bi·ased /ˌʌnˈbaɪəst◂/ adj. able to make a fair judgment, especially because you are not influenced by your own or other people's opinions: *All the publicity is making it hard to find an unbiased jury.*

un·bid·den /ˌʌnˈbɪdn◂/ adj. LITERARY not having been asked for, expected, or invited

un·blem·ished /ˌʌnˈblɛmɪʃt◂/ adj. **1** not spoiled by any mistake or bad behavior: *an unblemished safety record* **2** not spoiled by any mark: *unblemished skin*

un·blink·ing /ˌʌnˈblɪŋkɪŋ◂/ adj. LITERARY **1** looking at something continuously without BLINKing: *a steady, unblinking gaze* **2** considering or showing all the details of something without avoiding the bad parts: *The film offers an unblinking look at life in the prisons.*

un·born /ˌʌnˈbɔrn◂/ adj. [only before noun] not yet born: *an unborn child*

un·bound·ed /ˌʌn baʊndɪd◂/ adj. FORMAL extreme or without any limit: *unbounded curiosity*

un·bowed /ʌnˈbaʊd/ adj. LITERARY not willing to accept defeat

un·break·a·ble /ˌʌnˈbreɪkəbəl◂/ adj. **1** not able to be broken: *an unbreakable bottle* **2** an unbreakable rule, agreement etc. must be obeyed

un·bridge·a·ble /ˌʌnˈbrɪdʒəbəl◂/ adj. unbridgeable differences between two people, groups, or ideas are too big to be gotten rid of: *an **unbridgeable gap/ gulf/chasm** etc. There is a seemingly unbridgeable gap between the two main parties.*

un·bri·dled /ˌʌnˈbraɪdld◂/ adj. LITERARY not controlled and often too extreme or violent: *unbridled passion*

un·bro·ken /ˌʌnˈbroʊkən◂/ adj. **1** continuing without being broken or interrupted: *an unbroken silence* | *The horizon is flat, unbroken by even a tree.* **2** not broken: *unbroken egg yolks*

un·buck·le /ʌnˈbʌkəl/ v. [T] to unfasten the BUCKLE on something

un·bur·den /ʌnˈbɜrdn/ v. [T] **1 unburden yourself** to tell someone your problems, secrets etc. so that you feel better: [+ to] *With regret and relief, he unburdened himself to her.* **2** LITERARY to take a heavy load, a large responsibility etc. away from someone or something

un·but·ton /ʌnˈbʌt⁻n/ v. [T] to unfasten a piece of clothing that is fastened with buttons: *He pulled down his necktie and unbuttoned his shirt.*

un·called for, uncalled-for /ʌnˈkɔld fɔr/ adj. INFORMAL behavior or remarks that are uncalled for are unfair or inappropriate: *That comment was totally uncalled for.*

un·can·ny /ʌnˈkæni/ adj. **uncannier, uncanniest** very strange and difficult to explain: *He has an uncanny ability to guess what you're thinking.* —**uncannily** adv.

un·cared for, uncared-for /ʌnˈkɛrd fɔr/ adj. not taken care of, or not taken care of in the right way: *The yard was dirty and uncared for.*

un·ceas·ing /ʌnˈsisɪŋ/ adj. never stopping: *an unceasing battle against racial discrimination* —**unceasingly** adv.

un·cer·e·mo·ni·ous·ly /ʌnˌsɛrəˈmouniəsli/ adv. without paying any attention to politeness or good MANNERS: *Himes was unceremoniously kicked out of the club.* —**unceremonious** adj. —**unceremonious·ness** n. [U]

un·cer·tain /ʌnˈsət⁻n/ adj. **1** not sure, or feeling doubt: [+ about] *I was uncertain about who I should call.* | [**uncertain if/whether/what/who etc.**] *Nelson looked up, uncertain whether he should continue.* **2** not clear, definite, or decided: *A spokesman said the governor's travel plans were still uncertain.* | *They were worried about their son's uncertain future.* **3** **in no uncertain terms** if you tell someone something in no uncertain terms, you tell them very clearly without trying to be polite: *They let us know in no uncertain terms that we were not welcome.* **4** if someone walks in an uncertain way, they seem as though they might fall: *She took a few uncertain steps forward.* —**uncertainly** adv.

un·cer·tain·ty /ʌnˈsət⁻nti/ n. plural **uncertainties** **1** [U] the quality of not being sure or of feeling doubt about what will happen: *There is a great deal of uncertainty about the future of the company.* **2** [C] something that you are not sure about: *Life is full of uncertainties and problems.*

un·chal·lenged /ʌnˈtʃæləndʒd/ adj. **1** accepted and believed by everyone and not doubted: *Willem's theories did not go unchallenged for very long.* **2** someone who goes somewhere unchallenged is not stopped and asked who they are or what they are doing **3** not having an opponent in a competition: *an unchallenged candidate for city supervisor*

un·changed /ʌnˈtʃeɪndʒd/ adj. not having changed: *Sales have remained unchanged for the past year.*

un·chang·ing /ʌnˈtʃeɪndʒɪŋ/ adj. always staying the same: *an unchanging truth*

un·char·ac·ter·is·tic /ʌnˌkærɪktəˈrɪstɪk/ adj. not typical of someone or something and therefore surprising: [+ of] *It's uncharacteristic of Margaret to get so angry.* —**uncharacteristically** /-kli/ adv.

un·char·i·ta·ble /ʌnˈtʃærɪt̬əbəl/ adj. not kind or fair in the way you judge people: *uncharitable thoughts*

un·chart·ed /ʌnˈtʃɑrt̬ɪd/ adj. LITERARY **1** not marked on any maps: *an uncharted island* **2** **uncharted waters/territory/terrain** a situation or activity that no one has never experienced or tried before: *We're moving into uncharted territory with the new project.*

un·checked /ʌnˈtʃɛkt/ adj. **1** an unchecked activity, disease etc. develops and gets worse because it is not controlled or stopped: *The severity of the financial crisis, if left unchecked, will only worsen over time.* **2** not tested for quality, safety etc.

un·claimed /ʌnˈkleɪmd/ adj. unclaimed money, land, LUGGAGE etc. is money, land etc. that no one has demanded or said belongs to them: *The unclaimed prize money will be given to charity.*

un·cle /ˈʌŋkəl/ n. [C] **1** the brother of your mother or father, or the husband of your AUNT: *Uncle Roscoe* **2** used as a name or title for a man who is a close

friend of your parents **3** **say uncle** SPOKEN used by children to tell someone to admit they have been defeated —see also **I'll be a monkey's uncle** (MONKEY¹ (6))

un·clean /ˌʌnˈklin/ adj. **1** dirty: *unclean eating utensils* **2** BIBLICAL morally or SPIRITUALly bad: *an unclean spirit* **3** unclean food, animals etc. are those that must not be eaten, touched etc. in a particular religion

un·clear /ˌʌnˈklɪr/ adj. **1** difficult to understand or be sure about, so that there is doubt or confusion: *The causes of the disease are unclear.* | [**it is unclear whether/who/what etc.**] *It is still unclear why he bought the gun in the first place.* **2** not understanding something clearly: [+ about] *If you're unclear about the answers, ask more questions.*

Uncle Sam /ˌʌŋkəl ˈsæm/ n. [singular] INFORMAL the U.S., or the U.S. government, sometimes represented by the figure of a man with a white BEARD and tall hat

Uncle Tom /ˌʌŋkəl ˈtɑm/ n. [C] DISAPPROVING an African-American person who is too friendly or respectful to white people

un·clog /ʌnˈklɑg/ v. **unclogged, unclogging** [T] to clear a tube, pipe, road etc. that has become blocked, so that it works correctly again: *Doctors are using lasers to unclog blocked arteries.*

un·clothed /ʌnˈkloʊðd/ adj. FORMAL not wearing clothes or not covered by clothes; NAKED

un·clut·tered /ˌʌnˈklʌt̬əd/ adj. APPROVING an uncluttered space, room, pattern etc. is not covered or filled with too many things that make it look messy: *an uncluttered house*

un·coil /ʌnˈkɔɪl/ v. [I,T] if you uncoil something, or if it uncoils, it stretches out straight, after being wound around in a circle

un·com·fort·a·ble /ʌnˈkʌmftəbəl, ʌnˈkʌmfət̬əbəl/ adj. **1** not feeling physically comfortable, or not making you feel comfortable: *cheap uncomfortable shoes* | *You look uncomfortable. Why don't you sit over here?* **2** unable to relax because you are embarrassed or worried: *an uncomfortable silence* | *I feel uncomfortable talking about Gayle when she isn't here.* —**uncomfortably** adv.

un·com·mit·ted /ˌʌnkəˈmɪt̬ɪd/ adj. not having decided or promised to support a particular group, political belief etc.: *uncommitted voters*

un·com·mon /ʌnˈkɑmən/ adj. rare or unusual: *Violent crimes against the elderly are fortunately very uncommon.* | [**it is not uncommon for sb/sth to do sth**] *It is not uncommon for Barrett to write 15 or 18 drafts of a book.*

un·com·mon·ly /ʌnˈkɑmənli/ adv. [+ adj./adv.] FORMAL very or especially: *an uncommonly beautiful woman*

un·com·plain·ing /ˌʌnkəmˈpleɪnɪŋ/ adj. willing to accept a difficult or bad situation without complaining: *an obedient, uncomplaining servant* —**uncomplainingly** adv.

un·com·pli·cat·ed /ʌnˈkɑmpləˌkeɪt̬ɪd/ adj. APPROVING easy to understand without a lot of hidden problems: *My dad was an uncomplicated man.* | *an uncomplicated life* | *an uncomplicated registration process*

un·com·pre·hend·ing /ˌʌnkɑmprɪˈhɛndɪŋ/ adj. not understanding what is happening: *She gave me a helpless uncomprehending look.* —**uncomprehendingly** adv.

un·com·pro·mis·ing /ʌnˈkɑmprəˌmaɪzɪŋ/ adj. unwilling to change your opinions or intentions: *The group has taken an uncompromising position on environmental issues.* —**uncompromisingly** adv.

un·con·cern /ˌʌnkənˈsən/ n. [U] an attitude of not caring about something that other people worry about: *We were shocked by their apparent unconcern for their own safety.*

un·con·cerned /ˌʌnkənˈsənd/ adj. **1** not anxious or worried about something: [+ about] *The man seemed unconcerned about his wife's health.* **2** not interested in a particular aim or activity: [+ with] *These competitive women are unconcerned with motherhood.* —**unconcernedly** /-nɪdli/ adv.

un·con·di·tion·al /ˌʌnkənˈdɪʃənəl/ adj. not limited by or depending on any conditions: *The release of all political prisoners must be unconditional.* | *Dogs provide us with **unconditional love**.* —**unconditionally** adv.

un·con·firmed /ˌʌnkənˈfɚmd/ adj. **unconfirmed report/story/rumor etc.** a report, story etc. that has not been proved or supported by official information: *There were unconfirmed reports yesterday that the president might attend.*

un·con·nect·ed /ˌʌnkəˈnɛktɪd/ adj. not related to or involved with something else: [+ **to/with**] *Wolf's work is completely unconnected to the current study.*

un·con·scion·a·ble /ʌnˈkɑnʃənəbəl/ adj. FORMAL morally wrong or unacceptable: *I think a "not guilty" verdict in this case would be unconscionable.* —**unconscionably** adv.

un·con·scious[1] /ˌʌnˈkɑnʃəs/ adj. **1** unable to see, move, feel etc. in the normal way because you are not conscious: *Billy was unconscious for two days after the accident.* | **knock/beat sb unconscious** *She fell off the bike and was knocked unconscious.* **2** relating to or coming from the part of your mind in which there are thoughts and feelings that you do not realize you have: *the unconscious mind* | *unconscious desires* —compare SUBCONSCIOUS[1] **3 be unconscious of sth** to not realize the effect of something, especially something you have said or done: *Barb seemed quite unconscious of the attention her dress was attracting.* —**unconsciously** adv. —**unconsciousness** n. [U]

unconscious[2] n. **the/sb's unconscious** the part of your mind in which there are thoughts and feelings that you do not realize you have; SUBCONSCIOUS

un·con·sti·tu·tion·al /ˌʌnkɑnstəˈtuʃənl/ adj. not allowed by the CONSTITUTION (=set of rules or principles by which a country or organization is governed): *Organized prayer in public schools is unconstitutional.* —**unconstitutionality** /ˌʌnkɑnstətuʃəˈnæləti/ n. [U]

un·con·test·ed /ˌʌnkənˈtɛstɪd/ adj. **1** an uncontested action or statement is one which no one opposes or disagrees with **2** an uncontested election is one in which only one person wants to be elected

un·con·trol·la·ble /ˌʌnkənˈtroʊləbəl/ adj. **1** uncontrollable emotions, types of behavior, or situations are ones that you cannot control or stop: *We could hear her uncontrollable weeping down the hall.* **2** someone who is uncontrollable behaves badly and will not obey anyone —**uncontrollably** adv.

un·con·trolled /ˌʌnkənˈtroʊld/ adj. **1** uncontrolled emotions, behavior, or activities continue because no one stops or controls them: *uncontrolled violence* **2** without rules or laws: *uncontrolled capitalism*

un·con·ven·tion·al /ˌʌnkənˈvɛnʃənəl/ adj. very different from the way people usually behave, think, dress etc.: *unconventional religious beliefs*

un·con·vinced /ˌʌnkənˈvɪnst/ adj. [not before noun] not certain that something is true: *They say the new highway will be good for the town, but I'm unconvinced.*

un·cool /ˌʌnˈkul/ adj. [not before noun] INFORMAL, DISAPPROVING not fashionable, attractive, or relaxed: *My parents are so uncool!*

un·co·op·er·a·tive /ˌʌnkoʊˈɑprətɪv/ adj. not willing to work with or help someone: *Police say the boyfriend of the missing woman has been uncooperative.*

un·co·or·di·nat·ed /ˌʌnkoʊˈɔrdnˌeɪtɪd/ adj. **1** someone who is uncoordinated is not good at physical activities because they cannot control their movements effectively: *I was always too uncoordinated to be good at tennis.* **2** an uncoordinated plan or operation is not well organized, so that the different parts of it do not work together effectively

un·cork /ʌnˈkɔrk/ v. [T] to open a bottle by removing its CORK

un·count·a·ble /ʌnˈkaʊntəbəl/ adj. **1** too many to be counted: *The region has suffered uncountable tragedies.* **2** an uncountable noun has no plural form and means something which cannot be counted or considered either singular or plural, for example

"milk" or "happiness." In this dictionary uncountable nouns are marked [U]. —compare COUNTABLE

un·count·ed /ˌʌnˈkaʊntɪd/ adj. **1** very large in number or amount: *Thompson appeared in 18 movies and uncounted TV shows.* **2** not counted

un·count noun /ˌʌnkaʊnt ˈnaʊn/ n. [C] TECHNICAL an uncountable noun —compare COUNT NOUN

un·couth /ʌnˈkuθ/ adj. DISAPPROVING behaving and speaking in a way that is impolite or socially unacceptable: *The city's elite viewed her as an uncouth farm girl.*

un·cov·er /ʌnˈkʌvɚ/ v. [T] **1** to discover something that has been kept secret: *A search of their luggage uncovered two pistols.* **2** to remove the cover from something

un·crit·i·cal /ʌnˈkrɪtɪkəl/ adj. unable or unwilling to see faults or problems in someone or something: *an uncritical attitude toward new technologies* —**uncritically** /-kli/ adv.

un·crowned /ˌʌnˈkraʊnd/ adj. **the uncrowned king/queen etc. of sth** the person who is thought to be the best or most famous in a particular activity: *Bausch is the uncrowned empress of modern dance theater.*

unc·tu·ous /ˈʌŋktʃəs/ adj. FORMAL **1** DISAPPROVING too friendly or interested, or praising people too much in a way that does not seem completely sincere: *Dave is genuinely friendly without being unctuous.* **2** containing a lot of oil or fat: *unctuous food*

un·curl /ʌnˈkɚl/ v. [I,T] to stretch out straight from a curled position, or to make something do this

un·cut /ˌʌnˈkʌt/ adj. **1** an uncut movie, book etc. has not been made shorter, for example by having violent or sexual scenes removed: *the uncut version of the interview* **2** not having been cut: *uncut hair* **3** an uncut forest has not had its trees cut down and removed **4** an uncut jewel has not yet been cut into a particular shape: *uncut diamonds*

un·dat·ed /ˌʌnˈdeɪtɪd/ adj. an undated letter, article, photograph etc. does not have the date written on it

un·daunt·ed /ˌʌnˈdɔntɪd, -ˈdɑn-/ adj. not afraid of continuing to try to do something in spite of difficulties or danger: *undaunted courage* | [+ **by**] *Undaunted by previous defeats, Baker said he is ready to win the election.*

un·de·cid·ed /ˌʌndɪˈsaɪdɪd/ adj. **1** not having made a decision about something important: *undecided voters* | [+ **about/on**] *We are still undecided about buying a house.* **2** an undecided game or competition has no definite winner —**undecidedly** adv.

un·de·clared /ˌʌndɪˈklɛrd/ adj. not officially announced or called something: *an undeclared war*

un·de·fined /ˌʌndɪˈfaɪnd/ adj. not clear or made definite: *Some of my job duties are still undefined.*

un·de·mon·stra·tive /ˌʌndɪˈmɑnstrətɪv/ adj. not showing your feelings of love or friendliness, especially by not touching or kissing people

un·de·ni·a·ble /ˌʌndɪˈnaɪəbəl/ adj. definitely true or certain: *Her popularity among teenagers is undeniable.* —**undeniably** adv.

un·der[1] /ˈʌndɚ/ prep. **1** directly below something, or covered by it: *He has a small scar under his nose.* | *I could see something glittering under the water.* —opposite OVER[1] (1) —see picture at BELOW[1] **2** moving to a position below something, or to a position on the other side of something by passing below it: *"Where's the cat?" "She crawled under the couch."* | *The ship sailed under the Golden Gate Bridge on its way into the Pacific.* **3** less than a particular number, amount, age, or price: *What can I buy for under ten dollars?* | *Selling alcohol to anyone under age 21 is a crime.* **4** controlled by a particular leader, government, system etc.: *Under Schaefer's leadership, the downtown area has been rebuilt.* **5 under construction/discussion/attack etc.** in the process of being CONSTRUCTed, discussed etc.: *Three sites are under consideration for the new factory.* | *Goodell has come under attack for his recent remarks.*

6 affected by a particular condition, influence, or situation: *I've been under a lot of stress lately.* | *He was arrested for driving under the influence of alcohol.* **7 under sb's control/influence/thumb etc.** controlled or influenced by someone: *Those who came under John's spell did anything he asked.* **8** if you are under someone at your job, you have a lower position than they do, and they help to direct your work: *He's been working under Amato for six months.* —opposite OVER¹ (10) **9** according to a particular agreement, law etc.: *The organization is tax exempt under section 501 of the tax code.* **10 be under anesthesia/sedation/treatment etc.** to be treated by a doctor using a particular drug or method: *Daniels is under treatment at a psychiatric hospital.* **11** if you write or do something under another name, you do it using a name that is not your real name: *Krentz writes historical romances under the name Amanda Quick.* **12** in a particular part of a list, book, system etc. where you can find information: *The information is filed under the child's last name.* —see also **be under the impression (that)** (IMPRESSION (2))

USAGE NOTE: UNDER

WORD CHOICE: under, underneath, below, beneath
Under is the most common word used to talk about one thing being placed or moving directly under another, or being covered by it: *He reached under the bed and pulled out a box.* **Underneath** is often used instead of **under** to emphasize the idea of covering, touching, or hiding: *The girls wear shorts underneath their cheerleading skirts.* | *The money had been buried somewhere underneath the theater floor.* You use **under** to talk about something that is covered by something that is also all around it, but you would not use **underneath** so often in this way: *Sea lions can travel much faster underwater.* **Beneath** can also be used in all these ways, but is a little old-fashioned or literary: *They strolled hand in hand beneath the summer moon.* **Below** suggests that one thing is in a lower position than another, although it may not be directly under it: *From the cliffs we could barely see the people in the valley below us.*

U

under² *adv.* **1** in or to a place that is below something or covered by it: *He dived into the water and stayed under for five minutes.* **2** less in age, number, amount etc. than the age, number etc. mentioned: *Children twelve and under must be accompanied by an adult.* **3** in or into an UNCONSCIOUS condition because a doctor has given you DRUGS before SURGERY —see also **put sb out** (PUT)

under- /ˈʌndɚ/ *prefix* **1** less of an action or quality than is appropriate, needed, or desired: *underdevelopment* | *undercooked meat* **2** going under something: *an underpass* (=road that goes under another road) **3** inside or beneath other things: *underwear*

un·der·a·chiev·er /ˌʌndərəˈtʃivɚ/ *n.* [C] someone who does not do as well as they could if they worked harder, especially at school —compare OVERACHIEVER —**underachieve** *v.* [I] —**underachievement** *n.* [U]

un·der·age /ˌʌndɚˈeɪdʒ◂/ *adj.* too young to legally buy alcohol, drive a car, vote etc., or being done by someone who is too young: *underage drinking*

un·der·arm¹ /ˈʌndɚˌɑrm/ *adj.* [only before noun] relating to or used on your ARMPITS: *underarm deodorant*

underarm² *n.* [C] your ARMPIT

un·der·bel·ly /ˈʌndɚˌbɛli/ *n. plural* **underbellies** [C] LITERARY **1** the weakest or most easily damaged part of a country, plan etc.: *Democrats are attacking the soft underbelly of the Republican Party.* **2** the bottom side of something such as a ship or an airplane **3** the soft stomach or bottom side of an animal

un·der·brush /ˈʌndɚbrʌʃ/ *n.* [U] bushes, small trees etc. growing under and around larger trees in a forest; UNDERGROWTH

un·der·cap·i·tal·ized /ˌʌndɚˈkæpɪtlˌaɪzd/ *adj.* if a business is undercapitalized, it does not have enough money to operate effectively —**undercapitalize** *v.* [T usually passive]

un·der·car·riage /ˈʌndɚˌkærɪdʒ/ *n.* [C] the wheels of an aircraft, car etc. and the structure that holds them

und·er·charge /ˌʌndɚˈtʃɑrdʒ/ *v.* [I,T] to charge too little or less than the correct amount of money for something —opposite OVERCHARGE

un·der·class /ˈʌndɚˌklæs/ *n.* [singular] the lowest social class, consisting of people who are very poor and who are not likely to be able to improve their situation: *an urban underclass* —compare LOWER CLASS, MIDDLE CLASS, UPPER CLASS

un·der·class·man /ˌʌndɚˈklæsmən/ *n.* [C] a student in the first two years of high school or college

un·der·clothes /ˈʌndɚˌkloʊðz, -ˌkloʊz/ also **un·der·clo·thing** /ˈʌndɚˌkloʊðɪŋ/ *n.* [plural] UNDERWEAR

un·der·coat /ˈʌndɚˌkoʊt/ *n.* [C] a layer of paint that you put onto a surface before you put the final layer on

un·der·count /ˌʌndɚˈkaʊnt/ *v.* [T] to make a mistake of counting less than all of a group of people or things, especially in an official situation: *Native Americans are severely undercounted in unemployment figures.* —**undercount** *n.* [C]

un·der·cov·er /ˌʌndɚˈkʌvɚ◂/ *adj., adv.* working or done secretly, in order to catch criminals or find out information: *an undercover investigation* | *Police went undercover to buy the drugs.*

un·der·cur·rent /ˈʌndɚˌkɚənt, -ˌkʌr-/ *n.* [C] **1** a feeling, especially of anger or dissatisfaction, that people do not express openly: [+ of] *There's a strong undercurrent of racism in this town.* **2** a hidden and often dangerous current of water that flows under the surface of the ocean or a river

un·der·cut /ˌʌndɚˈkʌt, ˈʌndɚˌkʌt/ *v.* [T] **1** to make someone's work, plans etc. not be successful or effective: *These stories, if true, would greatly undercut Thomas's credibility.* **2** to sell something more cheaply than someone else: *The store sells its own brand of jeans, undercutting the prices of better-known brands.*

un·der·de·vel·oped /ˌʌndɚdɪˈvɛləpt◂/ *adj.* **1** an underdeveloped country/region etc. a country, REGION etc. that is poor and where there is not much modern industry —compare **a developing country/nation** (DEVELOPING (2)) **2** not having grown or developed as much as is usual or necessary: *The baby weighed only 1.4 pounds and had underdeveloped lungs.*

un·der·dog /ˈʌndɚˌdɔg/ *n.* [C] **1** a person or team in a competition that is expected to lose **2** a person, country etc. that is weak and is always treated badly

un·der·done /ˌʌndɚˈdʌn◂/ *adj.* meat that is underdone is not completely cooked —compare OVERDONE

un·der·dressed /ˌʌndɚˈdrɛst◂/ *adj.* wearing clothes that are too informal for a particular occasion

un·der·em·ployed /ˌʌndɚɪmˈplɔɪd◂/ *adj.* working in a job where you cannot use all your skills or where there is not enough work for you to do

un·der·es·ti·mate¹ /ˌʌndɚˈɛstəˌmeɪt/ *v.* **1** [I,T] to think that something is smaller, cheaper, less important etc. than it really is: *People often underestimate the importance of training.* **2** [T] to think that someone is not as good, smart, or skillful as they really are: *I wouldn't underestimate her if I were you – she's smarter than you think.*

un·der·es·ti·mate² /ˌʌndɚˈɛstəmɪt/ *n.* [C] a guessed amount or number that is too low

un·der·ex·pose /ˌʌndɚɪkˈspoʊz/ *v.* [T] to not let enough light reach the film when you are taking a photograph —opposite OVEREXPOSE

un·der·fed /ˌʌndɚˈfɛd/ *adj.* not given enough food to eat

un·der·foot /ˌʌndɚˈfʊt/ *adv.* **1** under your feet where you are walking: *The pine needles were soft underfoot.* **2** if children, animals etc. are underfoot, they are in a position that prevents you from walking freely: *How can I get anything done with all these* kids *underfoot*? **3 trample/crush/grind** etc. sb/sth **underfoot a)** to crush someone or something on the ground by stepping heavily on them **b)** to completely destroy someone or something

un·der·fund /ˌʌndəˈfʌnd/ *v.* [T usually passive] to not provide a program, organization etc. with enough money: *The childcare program is seriously underfunded.* —**underfunding** *n.* [U]

un·der·gar·ment /ˈʌndəˌgɑrmənt/ *n.* [C] OLD-FASHIONED a piece of underwear

un·der·go /ˌʌndəˈgou/ *v. past tense* **underwent** *past participle* **undergone** /-ˈgɔn/ [T not in passive] if you undergo a change, a bad experience etc., it happens to you or is done to you: *In March he underwent surgery for the cancer.* | *The computer industry has undergone some major changes over the past 15 years.*

un·der·grad·u·ate /ˌʌndəˈgrædʒuɪt/ *n.* [C] a student in the first four years of college, who is working for their first degree —**undergraduate** *adj.* [only before noun] *an undergraduate degree* —compare GRADUATE[1]

un·der·ground[1] /ˈʌndəˌgraund/ *adj.* **1** below the surface of the earth: *The office's parking garage is underground.* | *underground nuclear testing* **2** [only before noun] an underground group, organization etc. is secret and illegal: *an underground terrorist organization* **3** underground music, literature, art etc. is not officially approved and usually seems strange or slightly shocking: *an underground newspaper*

underground[2] *adv.* **1** under the earth's surface: *The insect spends most of its life underground, eating roots and stems.* **2** **go underground** to start doing something secretly, or hide in a secret place: *Denkins went underground to escape police.*

underground[3] *n.* **1 the underground** an illegal group working secretly against the rulers of a country **2** [singular] BRITISH a railroad system under the ground; SUBWAY

un·der·growth /ˈʌndəˌgrouθ/ *n.* [U] bushes, small trees, and other plants growing around and under bigger trees: *Something rustled in the undergrowth.*

un·der·hand /ˈʌndəˌhænd/ *adv.* if you throw a ball underhand, you throw it without moving your arm above your shoulder —opposite OVERHAND

un·der·hand·ed /ˌʌndəˈhændɪd/ *adj.* dishonest and done secretly: *an underhanded mayoral campaign* —**underhandedly** *adv.* —**underhandedness** *n.* [U]

un·der·lie /ˌʌndəˈlaɪ/ *v. past tense* **underlay** /-ˈleɪ/ *past participle* **underlain** /-ˈleɪn/ [T] FORMAL **1** to be a very basic part of something, or the real cause of or reason for something: *Social problems and poverty underlie much of the crime in today's big cities.* **2** to exist at a lower level or in a lower layer than something else: *The soil is underlain by hard clay.*

un·der·line /ˈʌndəˌlaɪn, ˌʌndəˈlaɪn/ *v.* [T] **1** to draw a line under a word to show that it is important or because it is the name of a book, movie, play etc. **2** to show that something is important: *The recent shootings underline the need for more security.*

un·der·ling /ˈʌndəlɪŋ/ *n.* [C] an insulting word for someone who has a low rank

un·der·ly·ing /ˈʌndəˌlaɪ-ɪŋ/ *adj.* [only before noun] very basic or important, but not easily noticed: *an underlying concern* | **an underlying reason/cause/assumption** etc. *Their underlying goal was to get control of the organization's money.*

un·der·manned /ˌʌndəˈmænd/ *adj.* not having enough workers

un·der·mine /ˈʌndəˌmaɪn, ˌʌndəˈmaɪn/ *v.* [T] **1** to gradually make someone or something less strong or effective: *Unfair criticism can undermine employees' self-confidence.* | *Losing the witness will seriously undermine the government's case against Jones.* **2** to gradually take away the earth from under something

un·der·neath /ˌʌndəˈniθ/ *adv. prep.* **1** directly under or below another object, used especially when one thing is covering or hiding another: *The stream actually runs underneath the building.* | *There's a picture with a short article underneath.* —see Usage Note at UNDER[1] **2** if someone is nice, shy, frightened

etc. underneath, they really are nice, shy etc. even though their behavior shows a different character: *She seems aggressive, but underneath she's pretty shy.* | **Underneath it all**, *he knew Peg really cared about him.*

un·der·nour·ished /ˌʌndəˈnɔrɪʃt, -ˈnʌrɪʃt/ *adj.* unhealthy and weak because you have not had enough food: *undernourished children* —**undernourishment** *n.* [U]

un·der·paid /ˌʌndəˈpeɪd/ *adj.* earning less money than you deserve for your work: *State employees are generally overworked and underpaid.*

un·der·pants /ˈʌndəˌpænts/ *n.* [plural] a short piece of underwear worn on the lower part of the body

un·der·pass /ˈʌndəˌpæs/ *n.* [C] a road or path that goes under another road or a railroad

un·der·pay /ˌʌndəˈpeɪ/ *v. past tense and past participle* **underpaid** /-ˈpeɪd/ **1** [T] to pay someone too little for their work **2** [I,T] to pay less money for something than you should, especially your taxes

un·der·per·form /ˌʌndəpəˈfɔrm/ *v.* [I,T] if a business, INVESTMENT etc. underperforms, it earns you less money than expected or than other possible investments would have —**underperformance** *n.* [U]

un·der·pin /ˈʌndəˌpɪn/ *v.* **underpinned, underpinning** [T] **1** to give strength or support to something and help it succeed: *These two scientific discoveries have underpinned modern agriculture.* **2** to put a solid piece of metal under something such as a wall in order to make it stronger —**underpinning** *n.* [C,U] *the underpinnings of the nation's economy*

un·der·play /ˌʌndəˈpleɪ/ *v.* **underplays, underplayed, underplaying** [T] **1** to make something seem less important or exciting than it really is: *She has a way of underplaying her achievements.* —opposite OVERPLAY **2 underplay your hand** to discuss something with someone without telling them everything about your plans, abilities etc.

un·der·priv·i·leged /ˌʌndəˈprɪvlɪdʒd/ *adj.* very poor, with worse living conditions, educational opportunities etc. than most people in society: *underprivileged youth*

un·der·rat·ed /ˌʌndəˈreɪtɪd/ *adj.* someone or something that is underrated is not believed to be as good, important etc. as they really are: *Richmond is the most underrated player on the team.* —opposite OVERRATED —**underrate** *v.* [T]

un·der·rep·re·sent·ed /ˌʌndəˌrɛprɪˈzɛntɪd/ *adj.* an underrepresented group of people has fewer members in a particular organization, in a particular job etc. than you would expect there to be, according to the size of the group in general: *Blacks and Latinos are significantly underrepresented on the campus.* —**underrepresentation** /ˌʌndəˌrɛprɪzənˈteɪʃən/ *n.* [U]

un·der·score /ˈʌndəˌskɔr/ *v.* [T] **1** to emphasize something so that people pay attention to it: *The report underscores the importance of childhood immunizations.* **2** to draw a line under a word or phrase to show that it is important; UNDERLINE

un·der·sea /ˌʌndəˈsi/ *adj.* [only before noun] happening or existing below the surface of the ocean: *undersea exploration*

un·der·sec·re·tar·y /ˌʌndəˈsɛkrəˌtɛri/ *n. plural* **undersecretaries** [C] a very important official in a government department who is one position in rank below the SECRETARY

un·der·sell /ˌʌndəˈsɛl/ *v. past tense and past participle* **undersold** /-ˈsould/ [T] **1** to sell goods at a lower price than someone else: *Our prices are the lowest. We will not be undersold!* **2** to make other people think that someone or something is less good, effective, skillful etc. than they really are

un·der·served, under-served /ˌʌndəˈsəvd/ *adj.* not getting enough care and help, especially from the government: *the underserved areas of the state*

un·der·shirt /'ʌndɚˌʃɚt/ *n.* [C] a piece of underwear with or without arms, worn under a shirt

un·der·shorts /'ʌndɚˌʃɔrts/ *n.* [plural] UNDERPANTS for men or boys

un·der·side /'ʌndɚˌsaɪd/ *n.* **the underside (of sth) a)** the bottom side or surface of something **b)** the part of something that contains its bad features, which are usually hidden: *The book gives a glimpse of the city's seamy underside* (=the bad parts of the city).

un·der·signed /'ʌndɚˌsaɪnd/ *n.* FORMAL **the undersigned** the person or people who have signed a piece of writing, used especially in formal letters —**undersigned** *adj.* [only before noun]

un·der·sized /ˌʌndɚ'saɪzd◂/ also **un·der·size** /-'saɪz◂/ *adj.* smaller than usual, or too small: *undersized clothes*

un·der·staffed /ˌʌndɚ'stæft◂/ *adj.* not having enough workers, or fewer workers than usual: *The cafeteria is a little understaffed.* —opposite OVER-STAFFED

s w **un·der·stand** /ˌʌndɚ'stænd/ *v.* past tense and past participle **understood** [not in progressive]
1 meaning [I,T] to know the meaning of what someone is telling you, or the language that they speak: *Unfortunately she doesn't understand English.* | *I'm sorry. I still don't understand. Can you say it slower?* | *Let me see if I **understand** you **correctly**.*
2 fact/idea [I,T] to know how or why a situation, event, process etc. happens or what it is like, especially through learning or experience: *Sondra doesn't understand football at all.* | [**understand how/why/where etc.**] *You don't need to understand how computers work to be able to use them.* | *Researchers still do not **fully understand** what causes the disease.*
3 person/feelings [I,T] to know how someone feels, and why they behave the way they do: *How can I make you understand?* | [**understand sb/sth**] *I understand her anger, but I still don't think that makes it right.* | *Larry is the only one who really understands Myra.* | [**understand how/what etc.**] *I think I understand how you feel.* —see also UNDERSTANDING²
4 I understand (that) SPOKEN, FORMAL used to say that someone has told you that something is true: *I understand you invited Mrs. Struthers.*
5 make yourself understood to make what you say clear to other people, especially when speaking a foreign language: *I often have trouble making myself understood in Japanese.*
6 be understood (that) FORMAL if something is understood, everyone knows it or has agreed to it and there is no need to discuss it: *From childhood, it was understood your parents would choose your husband.*
7 understand sth to be/mean sth to accept something as having a particular meaning, quality etc.: *We understood his lack of response to mean "no."*
8 do you understand (me)? SPOKEN used when you are telling someone what they should or should not do, especially when you are angry with them: *Never speak to me like that again! Do you understand?* —see also **give sb to understand/believe that** (GIVE¹ (44))

un·der·stand·a·ble /ˌʌndɚ'stændəbəl/ *adj.* **1** understandable behavior, reactions etc. seem normal and reasonable because of the situation you are in: *Although I don't approve of his actions, I think they are understandable.* **2** able to be understood; COMPREHENSIBLE —**understandably** /-bli/ *adv.*: *They were understandably upset by the news.*

s w **un·der·stand·ing¹** /ˌʌndɚ'stændɪŋ/ *n.* **1** [C usually singular] a private, unofficial agreement: *Eventually they **came to an understanding** about Luke's role in the company.* | *We said he could stay with us **on the understanding that** it would just be temporary.* **2** [singular,U] knowledge about something, based on learning or experience: [+ **of**] *Reese spent time with the native people to **gain a** better **understanding** of the country.* **3** [singular,U] sympathy toward someone's character and behavior: *Mutual understanding is*

important in all relationships. **4 sb's understanding (of sth)** the way in which someone judges the meaning of something: *My understanding is that none of us are required to attend.* | *What's your understanding of the letter?* **5** [U] the ability to know and learn; INTELLIGENCE —see Usage Note at COMPREHENSION

understanding² *adj.* sympathetic and kind about other people's problems: *Matt is a very understanding guy.*

un·der·state /ˌʌndɚ'steɪt/ *v.* [T] to describe something in a way that makes it seem less important than it really is: *Even these shocking statistics understate the seriousness of the situation.* —opposite OVER-STATE

un·der·stat·ed /ˌʌndɚ'steɪtɪd/ *adj.* APPROVING not too strong, colorful, big etc., in a way that is pleasing: *understated elegance*

un·der·state·ment /ˌʌndɚ'steɪt'mənt/ *n.* **1** [C] a statement that is not strong enough to express how good, bad, impressive etc. something really is: *To say I was surprised would be an understatement.* **2** [U] a way of describing things as being less good, bad, important etc. than they really are

un·der·stood /ˌʌndɚ'stʊd/ *v.* the past tense and past participle of UNDERSTAND

un·der·stud·y /'ʌndɚˌstʌdi/ *n. plural* **understudies** [C] an actor who learns a part in a play so that they can perform it if the usual actor cannot —**understudy** *v.* [T]

un·der·take /ˌʌndɚ'teɪk/ *v.* past tense **undertook** /-'tʊk/ past participle **undertaken** /-'teɪkən/ FORMAL **1** [T] to accept that you are responsible for a piece of work, and start to do it: *Two new studies have been undertaken to determine the effects of the chemicals.* **2 undertake to do sth** to promise or agree to do something: *Each country undertakes to negotiate in good faith.*

un·der·tak·er /'ʌndɚˌteɪkɚ/ *n.* [C] OLD-FASHIONED someone whose job is to arrange funerals; FUNERAL DIRECTOR

un·der·tak·ing /'ʌndɚˌteɪkɪŋ/ *n.* **1** [C usually singular] an important job, piece of work, or activity, especially a difficult one: *Building the dam will be a major undertaking.* **2** [U] the business of an undertaker **3** [C] FORMAL a promise to do something

un·der·tone /'ʌndɚˌtoʊn/ *n.* **1** a feeling or quality that is not directly expressed but can still be recognized: [+ **of**] *There was an undertone of excitement among the passengers.* **2** [C] a quiet voice or sound —compare OVERTONE

un·der·tow /'ʌndɚˌtoʊ/ *n.* [singular] the water current under the surface that pulls back toward the ocean when a wave comes onto the shore

un·der·used /ˌʌndɚ'yuzd◂/ *adj.* something that is underused is not used as much as it could be: *an underused office*

un·der·u·til·ized /ˌʌndɚ'yutl̩ˌaɪzd◂/ *adj.* something that is underutilized is not used as effectively as it could be: *underutilized computer equipment*

un·der·val·ue /ˌʌndɚ'vælyu/ *v.* [T] to think that someone or something is less important or valuable than they really are: *She felt that the company undervalued her work.* —**undervalued** *adj.*

un·der·wa·ter /ˌʌndɚ'wɔtɚ/ *adj.* [only before noun] below the surface of an area of water, or able to be used there: *underwater plants* —**underwater** *adv.*

underwater

un·der·way, under way /ˌʌndɚ'weɪ/ *adj., adv.* [not before noun] **1** already started: *Plans are underway to build a new stadium in the city.* | *The 13th annual Blues Festival **gets underway** (=starts happening) today.* **2** something such as a boat or train that is underway is moving

swimming underwater

un·der·wear /ˈʌndəˌwɛr/ n. [U] clothes that you wear next to your body under your other clothes

un·der·weight /ˌʌndəˈweɪt◂/ adj. weighing less than is expected or usual: *a premature, underweight baby* —opposite OVERWEIGHT —see Usage Note at THIN[1]

un·der·went /ˌʌndəˈwɛnt/ v. the past tense of UNDERGO

un·der·whelm /ˌʌndəˈwɛlm/ v. [T] HUMOROUS to not seem very impressive to someone —**underwhelmed** adj. —**underwhelming** adj. —compare OVERWHELM

un·der·wire bra /ˌʌndəwaɪə ˈbrɑ/ n. [C] a BRA with wires sewn into it to help support a woman's breasts

un·der·world /ˈʌndəˌwɜld/ n. **the underworld a)** the criminals in a particular place and the criminal activities they are involved in **b)** the place where the spirits of the dead are believed to live, especially in ancient Greek stories

un·der·write /ˈʌndəˌraɪt, ˌʌndəˈraɪt/ v. past tense **underwrote** /-ˈroʊt/ past participle **underwritten** /-ˈrɪtˈn/ [T] **1** FORMAL to support an activity, business plan etc. with money, so that you are financially responsible for it: *The project is underwritten by a National Science Foundation grant.* **2** TECHNICAL to be responsible for an insurance agreement

un·der·writ·er /ˈʌndəˌraɪtə/ n. [C] someone who makes insurance contracts

un·de·served /ˌʌndɪˈzɜvd◂/ adj. undeserved criticism, praise etc. is unfair because you do not deserve it: *Lamarck has an undeserved reputation as a loser.*

un·de·sir·a·ble /ˌʌndɪˈzaɪrəbəl◂/ adj. FORMAL something or someone that is undesirable is not welcome or wanted because they may affect a situation or person in a bad way: *Rent control laws can have a number of undesirable effects.*

un·de·sir·a·bles /ˌʌndɪˈzaɪrəbəlz/ n. [plural] people who are considered to be immoral, criminal, or socially unacceptable

un·de·tect·a·ble /ˌʌndɪˈtɛktəbəl/ adj. not large or strong enough to be noticed: *Drugs have reduced the virus to undetectable levels.*

un·de·tec·ted /ˌʌndɪˈtɛktɪd◂/ adj. not seen or noticed: *How could the bomb go through the X-ray machine undetected?*

un·de·ter·mined /ˌʌndɪˈtɜmɪnd◂/ adj. not known, decided, or calculated: *Negotiations will begin on an undetermined date, no later than April 1.*

un·de·terred /ˌʌndɪˈtɜd/ adj. not persuaded to stop doing something by something bad that has happened or what someone has said: [+ by] *Barkeley, undeterred by injury, continues to play.*

un·de·vel·oped /ˌʌndɪˈvɛləpt◂/ adj. undeveloped land has not been built on or used for a particular purpose: *undeveloped beachfront property* —compare UNDERDEVELOPED

un·did /ʌnˈdɪd/ v. the past tense of UNDO

un·dies /ˈʌndiz/ n. [plural] SPOKEN underwear

un·di·lut·ed /ˌʌndɪˈlutɪd◂/ adj. **1** LITERARY an undiluted feeling or quality is very strong and is not mixed with other feelings or qualities: *undiluted hate* **2** an undiluted mixture has not been made weaker by adding water

un·di·min·ished /ˌʌndɪˈmɪnɪʃt◂/ adj. not weaker or less important than before: *After more than 20 years, the power and attraction of "Star Wars" remains undiminished.*

un·dis·ci·plined /ʌnˈdɪsɪplɪnd/ adj. not controlled, or not obeying appropriate rules or limits: *undisciplined spending*

un·dis·closed /ˌʌndɪsˈkloʊzd◂/ adj. undisclosed information has not been made available to people in general: *The Denver TV station bought the videotape for an undisclosed sum.*

un·dis·guised /ˌʌndɪsˈgaɪzd◂/ adj. clearly shown and not hidden: *undisguised contempt*

un·dis·put·ed /ˌʌndɪˈspyutɪd◂/ adj. **1** accepted by everyone: **the undisputed leader/master/champion etc.** *In 1927 Stalin became the undisputed leader of the Soviet Union.* **2** known to be definitely true, and not argued about: *undisputed facts* | [**undisputed**

that] *It is undisputed that the two were involved in a two-year relationship.*

un·dis·tin·guished /ˌʌndɪˈstɪŋgwɪʃt◂/ adj. not having any special features, qualities, or marks, or not having done anything important or noticeable: *undistinguished brick apartment buildings* | *an undistinguished politician*

un·dis·turbed /ˌʌndɪˈstɜbd◂/ adj. not interrupted, moved, or changed: *The tomb was left undisturbed for over 800 years.*

un·di·vid·ed /ˌʌndɪˈvaɪdɪd◂/ adj. **1 undivided attention/support/loyalty etc.** complete attention, support etc.: *I'll give the matter my undivided attention.* **2** not separated into smaller parts or groups

un·do /ʌnˈdu/ v. past tense **undid** past participle **undone** [T] **1** to unfasten something that is tied or wrapped: *She carefully undid the ribbons and opened the scroll.* **2** to try to remove the bad effects of something you have done: *I wish it was possible to undo what I've done.* **3** to make someone fail, not have any hope etc.: *Stelling was eventually undone by his political mistakes.*

un·doc·u·ment·ed /ʌnˈdɑkyəˌmɛntɪd/ adj. **1** an **undocumented alien/worker/immigrant etc.** someone who is living or working in a country without official permission **2** undocumented information, claims etc. have not been officially recorded or shown to be true

un·do·ing /ʌnˈduɪŋ/ n. **sb's undoing** a situation in which someone fails: *In the end, Cohen's refusal to listen to others was his undoing.*

un·done /ʌnˈdʌn/ adj. [not before noun] **1** not fastened: *One of your buttons is coming undone.* **2** not finished or completed: *He decided he couldn't leave the job undone.* **3** OLD USE destroyed and without hope

un·doubt·ed·ly /ʌnˈdaʊtɪdli/ adv. [sentence adverb] used to emphasize that something is definitely true: *This course of action will undoubtedly lead to war.* —**undoubted** adj.: *His courage is undoubted.*

un·dreamed of, undreamed-of /ʌnˈdrimd ʌv/ much more or much better than you could imagine: *These technological advances were undreamed of even 20 years ago.* | *undreamed-of luxury*

un·dress[1] /ʌnˈdrɛs/ v. [I,T] to take your clothes off, or take someone else's clothes off: *Duane undressed and got under the blanket.*

undress[2] n. [U] FORMAL a state in which you are wearing few or no clothes: *The dancers walked around backstage in various stages of undress.*

un·dressed /ʌnˈdrɛst/ adj. **1** [not before noun] not wearing any clothes: *Haley refused to get undressed* (=take her clothes off) *in front of the doctor.* **2** an undressed wound has not been covered to protect it

un·due /ˌʌnˈdu/ adj. [only before noun] FORMAL more than is reasonable, appropriate, or necessary: *The safety policy will protect workers and the public from undue risk.*

un·du·lat·ing /ˈʌndʒəˌleɪtɪŋ/ adj. [only before noun] FORMAL moving or shaped like waves that are rising and falling: *the undulating motion of a snake* | *We drove through undulating farmland.* —**undulate** v. [I] —**undulation** /ˌʌndʒəˈleɪʃən/ n. [C,U]

un·du·ly /ʌnˈduli/ adv. FORMAL much more than necessary or appropriate, or much too extreme: *The Senator has been unduly influenced by a few wealthy contributors.*

un·dy·ing /ʌnˈdaɪ-ɪŋ◂/ adj. [only before noun] continuing forever: *undying love*

un·earned /ʌnˈɜnd◂/ adj. **1 unearned income** money that you receive from something other than working, for example from INVESTMENTS **2** not deserved: *unearned sympathy*

un·earth /ʌnˈɜθ/ v. [T] **1** to find out the truth about something: *The surprising story was unearthed by reporters at the "Post."* **2** to find something after searching for it, especially something that has been buried in the ground: *I unearthed this old picture of him from a box in the basement.*

un·earth·ly /ʌn'ɜːθli/ *adj.* very strange and unnatural: *The cabin was surrounded by an unearthly green light.* —**unearthliness** *n.* [U]

un·ease /ʌn'iːz/ *n.* [U] a feeling of nervousness and anxiety that makes you not able to relax: *There is a growing sense of unease in the financial world about the industry's future.*

un·eas·y /ˌʌn'iːzi/ *adj.* **uneasier, uneasiest 1** nervous, anxious, and unable to relax because you think something bad might happen: [+ **about**] *She felt a little uneasy about being alone in the room with Todd.* —see Usage Note at NERVOUS **2** an uneasy period of time is one when people have agreed to stop fighting or arguing, but which is not really calm: *An uneasy truce has been declared in the bloody two-year conflict.* **3** not comfortable, peaceful, or relaxed: *an uneasy relationship* | *She eventually fell into an uneasy sleep.* —**uneasily** *adv.* —**uneasiness** *n.* [U]

un·ed·u·cat·ed /ʌn'ɛdʒəˌkeɪtɪd/ *adj.* not educated to the usual level: *uneducated farmworkers*

un·e·lec·ted /ˌʌni'lɛktɪd/ *adj.* having an important government position although you were not elected: *the British Parliament's unelected House of Lords*

un·e·mo·tion·al /ˌʌni'moʊʃənl/ *adj.* not showing your feelings: *a cold, unemotional voice*

un·em·ployed[1] /ˌʌnɪm'plɔɪd/ *adj.* without a job: *an unemployed steel worker*

unemployed[2] *n.* **the unemployed** [plural] people who have no job: *The bill would extend benefits to the long-term unemployed* (=people who have not had a job for a long time).

un·em·ploy·ment /ˌʌnɪm'plɔɪmənt/ *n.* [U] **1** also **unemployment rate** the number of people in a country who do not have a job: *National unemployment is only 6%.* | **low/high unemployment** (=a small number or a large number of people without jobs) **2** the fact of having no job: *Closure of the plant will mean unemployment for 500 workers.* **3** money paid regularly by the government to people who have no job: *He's been on unemployment for three months.*

unemployment ben·e·fits /..'.. ,..../ *n.* [plural] money paid regularly by the government to people who do not have a job

unemployment com·pen·sa·tion /..'.. ..,../ *n.* [U] unemployment benefits

unemployment line /..'.. ,./ *n.* [C] **1** also **the unemployment line** people without jobs, in general: *In February, about 450,000 people lost their jobs and joined the unemployment line.* **2** the line that people without jobs must stand in to get their unemployment benefits

un·en·cum·bered /ˌʌnɪn'kʌmbəd/ *adj.* not restricted or slowed down by problems, rules etc.: [+ **by**] *Let us move into the future unencumbered by the mistakes of the past.*

un·end·ing /ʌn'ɛndɪŋ/ *adj.* something that is unending, especially something that is bad or tiring, seems as if it will continue forever: *an unending series of interruptions*

un·en·vi·a·ble /ʌn'ɛnviəbəl/ *adj.* difficult and unpleasant: *The President is in an unenviable position.* | *Lee had the unenviable task of reorganizing the department.*

un·e·qual /ʌn'iːkwəl/ *adj.* **1** unfairly treating different people or groups in different ways: *unequal educational opportunities* | *the unequal distribution of power* **2** not the same in size, number, value, rank etc. **3 be unequal to the task/job etc.** to not have enough strength, ability etc. to do something —**unequally** *adv.*

un·e·qualed, unequalled /ʌn'iːkwəld/ *adj.* better than any other: *The scenery is unequaled.*

un·e·quiv·o·cal /ˌʌni'kwɪvəkəl/ *adj.* FORMAL completely clear and without any possibility of doubt: *His* answer was an unequivocal "No." —**unequivocally** /-kli/ *adv.*

un·er·ring /ʌn'ɜːrɪŋ, ʌn'ər-ɪŋ/ *adj.* always exactly right: *He danced with an unerring sense of rhythm.* —**unerringly** *adv.*

UNESCO /ju'nɛskoʊ/ United Nations Educational, Scientific and Cultural Organization; a part of the U.N., based in Paris, which is concerned especially with providing help for poorer countries with education and science

un·eth·i·cal /ʌn'ɛθɪkəl/ *adj.* not obeying rules of moral behavior, especially those concerning a profession: *It would be unethical for me to reveal anything my client has discussed with me.* —**unethically** /-kli/ *adv.*

un·e·ven /ʌn'iːvən/ *adj.* **1** not smooth, flat, or level: *The driveway was uneven, with cracks running through it.* **2** good in some parts and bad in others: *The library's record collection is of uneven quality.* **3** not equal or equally balanced: *an uneven income distribution* **4** not regular: *We listened to the uneven rhythm of the wind's roar.* —**unevenly** *adv.* —**unevenness** *n.* [U]

un·e·vent·ful /ˌʌni'vɛntfəl/ *adj.* with nothing exciting or unusual happening: *Our trip up to New England was uneventful.* —**uneventfully** *adv.* —**uneventfulness** *n.* [U]

un·ex·cit·ing /ˌʌnɪk'saɪtɪŋ/ *adj.* ordinary and slightly boring: *The food was adequate but unexciting.*

un·ex·cused /ˌʌnɪk'skjuːzd/ *adj.* **an unexcused absence** an occasion when you are away from school or work without permission

un·ex·pect·ed /ˌʌnɪk'spɛktɪd/ *adj.* surprising because of not being expected: *He greeted me with unexpected warmth.* —**unexpectedness** *n.* [U]

un·ex·pect·ed·ly /ˌʌnɪk'spɛktɪdli/ *adv.* in a way or at a time that you did not expect: *Les died unexpectedly of a stroke.*

un·ex·plained /ˌʌnɪk'spleɪnd/ *adj.* not understood or made clear: *The death of his first wife remains unexplained.* | *He wants to move to Georgia for some unexplained reason.*

un·ex·pur·gat·ed /ʌn'ɛkspəˌgeɪtɪd/ *adj.* an unexpurgated book, play etc. is complete and has not had parts that might offend people removed

un·fail·ing /ʌn'feɪlɪŋ/ *adj.* always there, even in times of difficulty or trouble: *I'd like to thank you all for your unfailing love and support.* —**unfailingly** *adv.*

un·fair /ˌʌn'fɛr/ *adj.* not right or fair, especially by not giving an equal opportunity to everyone: *an unfair advantage* | *U.S. industries want to protect themselves from unfair foreign competition.* | [+ **to**] *The welfare system is unfair to both taxpayers and recipients.* | [**it is unfair (of sb) to do sth**] *It's unfair to give it to John and not to me.* —**unfairly** *adv.* —**unfairness** *n.* [U]

un·faith·ful /ʌn'feɪθfəl/ *adj.* **1** someone who is unfaithful has sex with someone who is not their wife, husband, or usual partner: [+ **to**] *Nell was shocked to discover her father had been unfaithful to her mother.* **2** not loyal to a principle, person etc. —**unfaithfully** *adv.* —**unfaithfulness** *n.* [U]

un·fal·ter·ing /ʌn'fɔːltərɪŋ/ *adj.* FORMAL strong, determined, and not becoming weaker: *unfaltering loyalty* —**unfalteringly** *adv.*

un·fa·mil·iar /ˌʌnfə'mɪljə/ *adj.* not known to you: *an unfamiliar name* | [+ **with**] *We were unfamiliar with the neighborhood.* | [+ **to**] *Everything in the house seemed unfamiliar to him.* —**unfamiliarity** /ˌʌnfəˌmɪli'ærəti/ *n.*

un·fash·ion·a·ble /ʌn'fæʃənəbəl/ *adj.* not popular or fashionable at the present time: *unfashionable clothes* | *Smoking has become very unfashionable.*

un·fas·ten /ˌʌn'fæsən/ *v.* [T] to disconnect or untie something such as a button, belt, rope etc.: *Do not unfasten your safety belt until the plane has stopped.*

un·fath·om·a·ble /ʌn'fæðəməbəl/ *adj.* LITERARY too strange or mysterious to be understood: *the unfathomable mysteries of human nature* —**unfathomably** *adv.*

un·fa·vor·a·ble /ʌnˈfeɪvərəbəl/ *adj.* **1** unfavorable conditions, situations etc. are not as good as they should be or usually are: *It's unfavorable weather for sailing.* **2** expressing disapproval: *According to the poll, 58% of the public have an unfavorable opinion of him.* —**unfavorably** *adv.*

un·fazed /ʌnˈfeɪzd/ *adj.* not confused or shocked by a difficult situation or something bad that has happened: [+ **by**] *Newton seemed unfazed by the warning.*

un·feel·ing /ʌnˈfilɪŋ/ *adj.* not sympathetic toward other people's feelings: *an unfeeling government bureaucracy*

un·fet·tered /ʌnˈfɛtəd/ *adj.* FORMAL not restricted by laws or rules: *an unfettered market economy*

unf·illed /ˌʌnˈfɪld/ *adj.* **1 an unfilled order** a request by a customer for a product that has not been sent **2** an unfilled job, position etc. is available but no one has been found for it yet

un·fin·ished /ˌʌnˈfɪnɪʃt/ *adj.* **1** not completed: *She looked away, leaving her sentence unfinished.* **2 unfinished business** something that needs to be done or dealt with that you have not yet done

un·fit /ʌnˈfɪt/ *adj.* **1** not good enough to do something or to be used for a particular purpose: *an unfit mother* | [+ **for**] *Brown is unfit for public office.* | [**unfit to do sth**] *The disease has left her medically unfit to fly.* | **unfit for human habitation/consumption** (=not good enough for someone to live in or to eat) **2** not in a good physical condition

un·flag·ging /ʌnˈflægɪŋ/ *adj.* continuing strongly, and never becoming tired or weak: *Her unflagging ambition more than made up for her lack of education.* —**unflaggingly** *adv.*

un·flap·pa·ble /ʌnˈflæpəbəl/ *adj.* INFORMAL having the ability to stay calm and not get upset, even in difficult situations: *A good radio-host must be unflappable.* —**unflappably** *adv.*

un·flat·ter·ing /ʌnˈflætərɪŋ/ *adj.* making someone look or seem bad or unattractive: *an unflattering photograph* | *An unflattering article about her appeared on the front page of the tabloids.*

un·flinch·ing /ʌnˈflɪntʃɪŋ/ *adj.* not changing or becoming weaker, even in a very difficult or dangerous situation: *an unflinching description of human suffering* —**unflinchingly** *adv.*

un·fo·cused, unfocussed /ʌnˈfoukəst/ *adj.* **1** not dealing with or paying attention to the important ideas, causes etc.: *So far the protest movement has been unorganized and unfocused.* **2** if someone's eyes are unfocused, their eyes are open but they are not looking at anything

un·fold /ʌnˈfould/ *v.* [I,T] **1** if a story, plan etc. unfolds, it becomes clearer as you hear or learn more about it: *As the story unfolds, our image of Claudia changes.* **2** to open something that was folded: *Miss Male nervously folded and unfolded her napkin as she spoke.*

un·fore·seen /ˌʌnfɔrˈsin, -fə-/ *adj.* an unforeseen situation is one that you did not expect to happen: *These actions may have unforeseen consequences.*

un·for·get·ta·ble /ˌʌnfəˈɡɛtəbəl/ *adj.* an unforgettable experience, sight etc. affects you so strongly that you will never forget it, especially because it is particularly good or beautiful: *It was an unforgettable evening.* —**unforgettably** *adv.*

un·for·giv·a·ble /ˌʌnfəˈɡɪvəbəl/ *adj.* an unforgivable action is so bad or cruel that you cannot forgive the person who did it: *His betrayal was unforgivable.* | **an unforgivable sin/act/crime** *Refusing to help was, in my opinion, an unforgivable act.* —**unforgivably** *adv.*

un·for·giv·ing /ˌʌnfəˈɡɪvɪŋ/ *adj.* someone who is unforgiving does not forgive people easily

un·formed /ˌʌnˈfɔrmd/ *adj.* not yet completely developed: *His new company is still unformed and unnamed.*

un·for·tu·nate¹ /ʌnˈfɔrtʃənɪt/ *adj.* **1** someone who is unfortunate has something bad happen to them: *When we entered the room, the teacher was yelling at some unfortunate student.* **2** an unfortunate situation, condition, quality etc. is one that you wish were different: *an unfortunate marriage* | *He has an unfortunate habit of repeating himself.* | **It's unfortunate that** *so few people seem willing to help.* **3** happening because of bad luck: *an unfortunate accident* **4** FORMAL unfortunate behavior, remarks etc. are not appropriate and make people feel embarrassed or offended: *an unfortunate choice of words*

unfortunate² *n.* [C] LITERARY someone who has no money, home, job etc.: *a poor unfortunate*

un·for·tu·nate·ly /ʌnˈfɔrtʃənɪtli/ *adv.* [sentence adverb] used when you are mentioning a fact that you wish were not true: *Unfortunately, I've already made plans for that weekend.*

un·found·ed /ˌʌnˈfaundɪd/ *adj.* unfounded statements, feelings, opinions etc. are wrong because they are not based on true facts: *Suspicions of a government cover-up are entirely unfounded.*

un·friend·ly /ʌnˈfrɛndli/ *adj.* **unfriendlier, unfriendliest 1** not kind or friendly: *an unfriendly expression* | *He wasn't actually unfriendly, but I still didn't feel comfortable.* **2** having a bad or harmful effect on someone: [+ **to**] *We have created cities that are unfriendly to pedestrians.* **3** an unfriendly government, power, nation etc. is one that opposes yours

un·frock /ʌnˈfrɑk/ *v.* [T usually passive] to DEFROCK someone —**unfrocked** *adj.*

un·ful·filled /ˌʌnfʊlˈfɪld/ *adj.* **1** an unfulfilled wish, desire, hope etc. has not been achieved: *The people are tired of unfulfilled promises.* **2** someone who is unfulfilled feels they could be achieving more in their job, relationship etc.: *Nick felt dissatisfied and unfulfilled with his work.*

un·fund·ed /ˌʌnˈfʌndɪd/ *adj.* **1** an unfunded PROJECT has not been given the money it needs to work **2 an unfunded mandate** something that the U.S. government demands the states do although they do not give them money to do it

un·fun·ny /ʌnˈfʌni/ *adj.* INFORMAL, DISAPPROVING an unfunny joke or action is not amusing, although it is intended to be

un·furl /ʌnˈfəl/ *v.* [T] to unroll and open a flag, sail etc.

un·fur·nished /ˌʌnˈfənɪʃt/ *adj.* an unfurnished room, house etc. has no furniture in it

un·gain·ly /ʌnˈɡeɪnli/ *adj.* moving in a way that does not look graceful: *I felt old, fat, and ungainly.*

un·glued /ʌnˈɡlud/ *adj.* **come unglued** INFORMAL **a)** if a plan, situation etc. comes unglued, it stops working well: *When his parents got divorced, his whole world came unglued.* **b)** to become extremely upset or angry about something: *If someone talked to me like that, I would just come unglued.*

un·god·ly /ʌnˈɡɑdli/ *adj.* **1** [only before noun] INFORMAL an ungodly time or noise is unreasonable and annoying: *Why did you wake me up at such an ungodly hour?* **2** LITERARY showing a lack of respect for God

un·gov·ern·a·ble /ʌnˈɡʌvənəbəl/ *adj.* **1** a country or area that is ungovernable is one in which the people cannot be controlled by the government, the police etc. **2** FORMAL feelings or types of behavior that are ungovernable are impossible to control

un·gra·cious /ʌnˈɡreɪʃəs/ *adj.* not polite or friendly: *an ungracious loser* —**ungraciously** *adv.*

un·grate·ful /ʌnˈɡreɪtfəl/ *adj.* not expressing thanks for something that someone has given to you or done for you: *I don't mean to sound ungrateful, but I really don't need any help.* —**ungratefully** *adv.* —**ungratefulness** *n.* [U]

un·guard·ed /ˌʌnˈɡɑrdɪd/ *adj.* **1 an unguarded moment** a time when you are not paying attention to what you are doing or saying: *In an unguarded moment, he admitted taking the file.* **2** not guarded or protected by anyone: *an unguarded border* **3** an unguarded remark, statement etc. is one that you make carelessly without thinking of the possible effects

U

un·guent /'ʌŋgwənt/ n. [C] LITERARY an oily substance used on your skin; OINTMENT

un·hand /ʌn'hænd/ v. [T] OLD USE to stop holding someone you have caught

un·hap·pi·ly /ʌn'hæpəli/ adv. **1** in a way that shows you are not happy: *"I don't know," Bill answered unhappily.* **2** [sentence adverb] OLD-FASHIONED used when you are mentioning a fact that you wish were not true; UNFORTUNATELY: *Unhappily, she was not able to complete the class.*

un·hap·py /ʌn'hæpi/ adj. **unhappier, unhappiest** **1** not happy: *Arlene has had an unhappy life.* **2** feeling worried or annoyed because you do not like what is happening in a situation: [+ with] *We were all unhappy with the quality of the service.* | [+ about] *Dennis is unhappy about having to work on a Saturday.* **3** FORMAL an unhappy remark, situation etc. is not appropriate, lucky, or desirable —**unhappily** adv. —**unhappiness** n. [U]

un·harmed /ʌn'hɑrmd/ adj. [not before noun] not hurt or harmed: *The hostages were released unharmed.*

un·health·y /ʌn'hɛlθi/ adj. **unhealthier, unhealthiest** **1** likely to make you sick: *Eating all that junk food is really unhealthy.* **2** not normal or natural and likely to be harmful: *an unhealthy relationship* | *an unhealthy interest/obsession/fear etc. Ben is showing an unhealthy interest in guns.* **3** not physically healthy: *an unhealthy baby* **4** unhealthy skin, hair etc. shows that you are sick or not healthy: *an unhealthy pale complexion* —**unhealthily** adv. —**unhealthiness** n. [U]

un·heard /ˌʌn'hɔd/ adj. **go/be unheard** to not be heard or listened to: *His suggestions went largely unheard.*

unheard of, unheard-of /.ˈ. ./ adj. something that is unheard of is so unusual that it has not happened or been known before: *In 1927 the Times paid him the unheard-of sum of $125,000 for the story.*

un·heed·ed /ʌn'hidɪd/ adj. LITERARY noticed but not listened to, accepted, or believed: *The report's detailed recommendations have all gone unheeded.*

un·help·ful /ʌn'hɛlpfəl/ adj. not willing or able to help in a situation and sometimes making it worse: *The customs officials were impatient, rude, and unhelpful.* —**unhelpfully** adv. —**unhelpfulness** n. [U]

un·her·ald·ed /ʌn'hɛrəldɪd/ adj. FORMAL something or someone that is unheralded is not known about by very many people, and is sometimes not considered very good or important when it really is: *an unheralded accomplishment*

un·hinge /ʌn'hɪndʒ/ v. [T] **1** to make someone become very upset or mentally ill: *The stress of the job has unhinged many workers.* **2** to disconnect something or take it off its HINGEs —**unhinged** adj.

un·hip /ˌʌn'hɪp◂/ adj. SLANG unfashionable

un·ho·ly /ʌn'houli/ adj. [no comparative] **1** an **unholy alliance** an unusual agreement between two people or organizations who would not normally work together, usually for a bad purpose **2** [only before noun] INFORMAL unreasonable and annoying: *What are you making such an unholy fuss about?* **3** not holy, or not respecting what is holy

un·hook /ʌn'hʊk/ v. [T] to unfasten or remove something from hook: *Can you unhook this necklace for me?*

un·hoped-for /ʌn'hoʊpt fɔr/ adj. much better than had been expected: *unhoped-for success*

un·hur·ried /ʌn'hɔid, -'hʌrid/ adj. done slowly and calmly: *He preferred the unhurried pace of a small town.* —**unhurriedly** adv.

un·hurt /ʌn'hɔt/ adj. [not before noun] not hurt: *The driver of the car was unhurt.*

uni- /yuni/ prefix one: *unidirectional* (=going only in one direction)

u·ni·cam·eral /ˌyuni'kæmrəl/ adj. [only before noun] a unicameral LEGISLATURE (=law-making institution) consists of only one part —compare BICAMERAL

UNICEF /'yuniˌsɛf/ n. United Nations International Children's Fund; an organization that helps children in the world suffering from disease, HUNGER etc.

u·ni·corn /'yuniˌkɔrn/ n. [C] an imaginary animal like a white horse with a long straight horn growing on its head

u·ni·cy·cle /'yuniˌsaɪkəl/ n. [C] a vehicle that is like a bicycle but has only one wheel

un·i·den·ti·fied /ˌʌni'dɛntəˌfaɪd, ˌʌnaɪ-/ adj. an unidentified person or thing is one that you do not recognize, do not know the name of etc.: *Three of the victims remain unidentified.*

u·ni·fi·ca·tion /ˌyunəfə'keɪʃən/ n. [U] the act of combining two or more groups, countries etc. to make a single group or country: *the unification of Germany*

u·ni·form¹ /'yunəˌfɔrm/ n. [C,U] **1** a particular type of clothing worn by all the members of a group or organization, such as the police, the army etc.: *a school uniform* **2** in uniform **a)** wearing a uniform **b)** someone in uniform is a member of the Army, Navy etc.

uniform² adj. being the same in all its parts or among all its members: *Grade A eggs must be of uniform size.* —**uniformly** adv.

u·ni·formed /'yunəˌfɔrmd/ adj. wearing a uniform: *a uniformed guard*

u·ni·for·mi·ty /ˌyunə'fɔrməti/ n. [U] the quality of being or looking the same as all other members of a group: *There seems to be no uniformity among the various systems.*

u·ni·fy /'yunəˌfaɪ/ v. **unifies, unified, unifying** **1** [I,T] if you unify two or more groups, the parts of a country etc., or they unify, they are combined to make a single unit: *Strong support for the war has unified the nation.* **2** [T] to combine different ideas, styles etc. to make a new idea, style etc.: *His music unifies traditional and modern themes.* —**unified** adj.

u·ni·lat·er·al /ˌyunə'lætərəl/ adj. FORMAL **1** a unilateral action or decision is done by only one of the groups involved in a situation: *a unilateral ban on landmines* **2** unilateral disarmament the process of a country getting rid of its own NUCLEAR weapons without waiting for other countries to do the same —compare BILATERAL, MULTILATERAL —**unilateralism** n. —**unilaterally** adv.

un·i·mag·i·na·ble /ˌʌni'mædʒənəbəl/ adj. not possible to imagine: *almost unimaginable pain* —**unimaginably** adv.

un·i·mag·i·na·tive /ˌʌni'mædʒənətɪv◂/ adj. **1** lacking the ability to think of new or unusual ideas **2** too ordinary and boring: *unimaginative architecture* **3** an unimaginative solution to a problem does not work very well because it does not involve any new or intelligent ideas: *unimaginative social reform*

un·i·mag·ined /ˌʌni'mædʒɪnd◂/ adj. [usually before noun] so good, large, great etc. that it may be difficult to believe: *a place of unimagined beauty*

un·im·paired /ˌʌnɪm'pɛrd◂/ adj. not damaged or made weak: *A stroke left Ed unable to speak, but his mind was completely unimpaired.*

un·im·peach·a·ble /ˌʌnɪm'pitʃəbəl◂/ adj. FORMAL so good or definite that criticism or doubt is impossible: *unimpeachable statistical proof* —**unimpeachably** adv.

un·im·ped·ed /ˌʌnɪm'pidɪd◂/ adj. happening or moving without being stopped or having difficulty: *unimpeded traffic flow*

un·im·por·tant /ˌʌnɪm'pɔrtnt◂/ adj. not important, and not worth considering: *Employees' opinions were often treated as unimportant.*

un·im·pressed /ˌʌnɪm'prɛst/ adj. not thinking that someone or something is good, interesting, unusual etc.: [+ with/by] *Board members were unimpressed with the plan.*

un·im·pres·sive /ˌʌnɪm'prɛsɪv◂/ adj. not as good, large, important, skillful etc. as expected or necessary: *unimpressive test results*

un·in·cor·po·rat·ed /ˌʌnɪn'kɔrpəˌreɪtɪd◂/ adj. an

unincorporated area of land has not officially become part of a city or town

un·in·formed /ˌʌnɪnˈfɔrmd/ *adj.* not having enough knowledge or information: *Many immigrants are uninformed about U.S. tax laws.*

un·in·hab·it·a·ble /ˌʌnɪnˈhæbɪtəbəl/ *adj.* **1** an uninhabitable place is impossible to live in **2** an uninhabitable house or apartment is too dirty, cold etc. to live in

un·in·hab·it·ed /ˌʌnɪnˈhæbɪtɪd/ *adj.* an uninhabited place does not have anyone living there: *an uninhabited island*

un·in·hib·it·ed /ˌʌnɪnˈhɪbɪtɪd/ *adj.* confident or relaxed enough to do or say what you want to: *uninhibited curiosity* —**uninhibitedly** *adv.*

un·in·i·ti·at·ed /ˌʌnɪˈnɪʃiˌeɪtɪd/ *n.* **the uninitiated** [plural] people who do not have special knowledge or experience of something: *The sport of kayaking can seem frightening to the uninitiated.* —**uninitiated** *adj.*

un·in·spired /ˌʌnɪnˈspaɪəd/ *adj.* not showing any imagination: *an uninspired performance*

un·in·spir·ing /ˌʌnɪnˈspaɪrɪŋ/ *adj.* not interesting or exciting at all: *Thul was an uninspiring speaker.*

un·in·stall /ˌʌnɪnˈstɔl/ *v.* [T] to completely remove a piece of SOFTWARE from a computer, often using a special program

un·in·sured /ˌʌnɪnˈʃʊrd/ *adj.* not having INSURANCE: *We provide free medical care for uninsured children.* —**the uninsured** *n.* [plural]

un·in·tel·li·gi·ble /ˌʌnɪnˈtɛlədʒəbəl/ *adj.* impossible to understand: *a series of unintelligible syllables* —**unintelligibly** *adv.*

un·in·tend·ed /ˌʌnɪnˈtɛndɪd/ *adj.* FORMAL not planned or expected: *unintended consequences of the new law* | *unintended pregnancies*

un·in·ten·tion·al /ˌʌnɪnˈtɛnʃənl/ *adj.* not said or done deliberately: *Defense attorneys claimed the shooting was unintentional.* —**unintentionally** *adv.*

un·in·ter·est·ed /ʌnˈɪntrɪstɪd, -ˈɪntərəs-/ *adj.* not interested: [+ in] *Older workers are generally uninterested in computers.* —compare DISINTERESTED

un·in·ter·rupt·ed /ˌʌnɪntəˈrʌptɪd/ *adj.* continuous: *uninterrupted coverage of the press conference* —**uninterruptedly** *adv.*

un·in·vit·ed /ˌʌnɪnˈvaɪtɪd/ *adj.* not wanted or asked for: *uninvited guests*

un·in·vit·ing /ˌʌnɪnˈvaɪtɪŋ/ *adj.* an uninviting place seems unattractive or not nice: *The old part of the city is tiny and uninviting.*

un·ion /ˈyunyən/ *n.* **1** [C] also **labor union** an organization formed by workers to protect their rights: *the National Farmers' Union* | *union members* **2** [singular,U] FORMAL the act of joining two or more things together, or the state of being joined together: [+ with] *Some militants favor independence for Kashmir or union with Pakistan.* | *a mystical union with God* | [+ of] *A lecture discussing the union of art and medical science is set for 4 p.m. today.* **3** [singular,U] a group of countries or states with the same national government: *Alaska and Hawaii both joined the union (=the U.S.) in 1959.* | *the Soviet Union* **4 the Union** used in the past to talk about the U.S., especially the northern states, during the Civil War: *soldiers who fought for the Union* **5** [C,U] FORMAL marriage **6** [C,U] FORMAL the activity of having sex, or an occasion when this happens

un·ion·ism /ˈyunyəˌnɪzəm/ *n.* [U] belief in the principles of UNIONS (1) —**unionist** *n.* [C]

un·ion·ize /ˈyunyəˌnaɪz/ *v.* [I,T] if workers unionize or are unionized, they become members of a UNION (1) —**unionization** /ˌyunyənəˈzeɪʃən/ *n.* [U]

Union Jack /ˈ.. ./ *n.* **the Union Jack** the national flag of the U.K.

union la·bel /ˈ.. ,../ *n.* [C] a piece of paper or other material attached to a product which tells you that the product was made by people belonging to a union

union stew·ard /ˈ.. ,../ *n.* [C] a SHOP STEWARD

union suit /ˈ.. ,/ *n.* [C] a piece of underwear that covers the whole body, with long legs and long SLEEVES

u·nique /yuˈnik/ *adj.* **1** unusually good and special: *Joan has a unique talent for languages.* | *a unique business opportunity* **2** [no comparative] being the only one of its kind: *Every person is unique.* **3 unique to sb/sth** existing only in a particular place or in relation to a particular person or people: *Of course, the issues discussed here are not unique to the U.S.* —**uniqueness** *n.* [U]

USAGE NOTE: UNIQUE

GRAMMAR

Although you will often hear people say that someone or something is *very unique, more unique, the most unique* etc. to mean that it is special or unusual, some teachers consider this usage incorrect.

---

u·nique·ly /yuˈnikli/ *adv.* **1** in a way that is unusually good and special: *Mr. Lake is uniquely qualified for the position of CEO.* | *Alexandre was a uniquely talented figure.* **2** in a way that is typical of a particular place or group of people, and that does not exist anywhere else: **uniquely American/French/Japanese** etc. *a uniquely American festival* **3** in a way that is different from anything else: *NC operates 13 uniquely equipped aircraft.*

u·ni·sex /ˈyunəˌsɛks/ *adj.* intended for both men and women: *unisex clothing*

u·ni·son /ˈyunəsən/ *n.* **1 in unison a)** if people speak or do something in unison, they say the same words at the same time or do the same thing at the same time: *"Good morning!" the kids replied in unison.* **b)** if two groups, governments etc. do something in unison, they do it together because they agree with each other: *Management and workers must act in unison to compete with foreign business.* **2** [C,U] a way of singing, playing music, or dancing in which everyone plays or sings the same tune or dances the same way at the same time

u·nit /ˈyunɪt/ *n.* [C]
1 group a group of people working together as part of the structure of a larger group, organization, company etc.: *Garrett is part of an elite military unit.* | *HSBC Futures Inc. is a unit of Hong Kong Shanghai Bank.* | *Some police units were stationed nearby.*
2 measuring an amount or quantity of something used as a standard of measurement: *Milk costs less per unit when purchased in gallon containers.* | [+ of] *The watt is a unit of electrical power.*
3 part a thing, person, or group that is regarded as one single whole part of something larger: *The basic social unit in ancient Germanic tribes was the clan.*
4 part of a book one of the numbered parts into which a TEXTBOOK (=a book used in schools) is divided
5 product a single complete product made by a company: *The Presario 1410 monitor, a 14-inch unit, will sell for $399.* —see also UNIT COST, UNIT PRICE
6 part of a machine a piece of equipment which is part of a larger machine: **control/filter/cooling etc. unit** *The cooling unit should be replaced.*
7 apartment one of the parts or areas that a large building is divided into: *a twenty-four-unit apartment building*
8 school/college the measurement of the amount of work that a student has done to complete their studies: *How many units do you need to graduate?*
9 furniture a piece of furniture, especially one that can be attached to others of the same type: **an office/storage etc. unit** (=a piece of furniture designed for the kitchen, office etc.)
10 number TECHNICAL the smallest whole number; the number 1

U·ni·tar·i·an /ˌyunəˈtɛriən/ *n.* a member of a Christian religious group that does not believe in the Trinity —**Unitarian** *adj.*

u·ni·tar·y /ˈyunəˌtɛri/ *adj.* FORMAL relating to or existing as a single unit: *Both authors' work has been combined into a unitary whole.*

unit cost /'.. ,./ n. [C] the amount of money that it costs to produce one of a particular product —compare UNIT PRICE

u·nite /yu'naɪt/ v. **1** [I,T] to join together with other people, organizations to achieve something: *We are united by a common language and culture.* | [+ in/against/behind] *Republicans should unite behind their candidate to win the election.* | [unite to do sth] *In 1960, the regions united to form the Somali Republic.* **2 be united (in marriage/matrimony)** FORMAL if two people are united, they become married in a ceremony

u·nit·ed /yu'naɪtɪd/ adj. **1** joined or closely connected by feelings, GOALs etc.: *a united Europe* | [+ in/with/against etc.] *The community is united in its commitment to quality education.* **2** involving or done by everyone: *Nations of the world must present a united front against terrorists.* —**unitedly** adv.

United Ar·ab Em·ir·ates, the /yu,naɪtɪd ,ærəb 'ɛmərɪts/ a country in the Middle East, between Qatar and Oman, consisting of seven small EMIRATES including Abu Dhabi and Dubai

United Farm Work·ers /.,.. '. ,./ a UNION in the U.S. for people who work on farms, especially poor MIGRANT workers who pick fruit and vegetables at many different farms

United King·dom, the /.,.. '. ,./ a country in northwest Europe, officially called the United Kingdom of Great Britain and Northern Ireland, consisting of England, Wales, Scotland, and Northern Ireland

United Na·tions /.,.. '. ,./ n. **the United Nations** an international organization that tries to find peaceful solutions to world problems

United States of A·mer·i·ca, the /.,.. .. .. '...,/ also **the United States, the U.S., the U.S.A.** a country in North America, made up of 50 states, the District of Columbia, and several territories

United Way, the /.,.. './ a CHARITY organization in the U.S. which collects money from the public, and then divides this money to give to many different charities

unit price /'.. ,./ n. [C] the price that is charged for each single thing or quantity that is sold —compare UNIT COST

unit pric·ing /'.. ,./ n. [U] a method of setting the price of a product based on what it costs to produce it

u·ni·ty /'yunəti/ n. plural **unities 1** [U] agreement between a group of people or countries in which they work together for a particular purpose: *The team suffers from a lack of unity.* | *economic unity* **2** [U] the quality of being complete: *His essays often lack unity.* **3** [C] TECHNICAL one of three related principles in DRAMA that say that the action in a play should consist of a single set of related events which take place in one place on one day

Univ. n. a written abbreviation of "university"

u·ni·ver·sal /,yunə'vɚsəl/ adj. **1** involving or affecting all the members of a group, or used by them: *free universal healthcare* | *a universal language* **2** understood by or affecting to everyone or every place in the world: *Popular culture seems to have universal appeal.* **3** true or appropriate in every situation: *a universal truth* —**universally** adv. —**universality** /,yunəvɚ'sæləti/ n. [U]

universal joint /..'.. ,./ n. [C] a part in a machine, at the point where two other parts join together, that can turn in all directions

Universal Prod·uct Code /,.... '.. ,./ abbreviation **UPC** n. [C] a BAR CODE

u·ni·verse /'yunə,vɚs/ n. [singular] **1 the universe** all space, including all the stars and PLANETs **2 be the center of sb's universe** to be the most important person or thing to someone **3** a person's life, including all of the people, places, and ideas which affects them: *Archer accepted his wealth as part of the structure of his universe.*

u·ni·ver·si·ty /,yunə'vɚsəti/ n. plural **universities** [C] an educational institution at the highest level, where you can study for a BACHELOR'S DEGREE, a MASTER'S DEGREE, or a DOCTORATE, and where people also do RESEARCH —compare COLLEGE (1)

UNIX /'yunɪks/ n. [U] TRADEMARK a type of computer OPERATING SYSTEM used mainly in business, industry, and universities

un·just /,ʌn'dʒʌst◂/ adj. FORMAL not fair or reasonable: *unjust punishment* —**unjustly** adv.

un·jus·ti·fi·a·ble /ʌn,dʒʌstə'faɪəbəl/ adj. completely wrong and unacceptable: *unjustifiable delays* —**unjustifiably** adv.

un·jus·ti·fied /ʌn'dʒʌstə,faɪd/ adj. not having an acceptable explanation or reason: *unjustified federal spending*

un·kempt /,ʌn'kɛmpt◂/ adj. looking messy because of not being taken care of: *an unkempt beard*

un·kind /,ʌn'kaɪnd◂/ adj. FORMAL cruel or not nice: *They had said a lot of unkind things.* —**unkindly** adv. —**unkindness** n. [U]

un·know·ing /ʌn'noʊɪŋ/ adj. [only before noun] FORMAL not realizing what you are doing or what is happening; UNAWARE: *Incompetent doctors could seriously injure their unknowing patients.* —**unknowingly** adv.

un·known¹ /,ʌn'noʊn◂/ adj. adv. **1** not known about: *For some unknown reason, Fred quit his job and moved to Alaska.* | *The year of Gabor's birth is unknown.* **2 unknown to sb** without someone knowing: *Unknown to his family, Ron was suffering from a brain infection.* **3** not famous: *an unknown artist* **4 be an unknown quantity** if someone or something is an unknown quantity, you do not know what their abilities are or how they are likely to behave

unknown² n. **1** [C] someone who is not famous: *After 30 years in show business, Butler is still an unknown.* **2** [C] something that is not known: *The long-term effects of the drug are still an unknown.* **3 the unknown a)** a place that is not known about or that has not been visited by humans: *The astronauts began their journey into the unknown.* **b)** things that you do not know or understand: *a fear of the unknown*

un·law·ful /ʌn'lɔfəl/ adj. FORMAL not legal: *unlawful activities* —**unlawfully** adv.

un·lead·ed /,ʌn'lɛdɪd◂/ adj. unleaded gasoline does not contain any LEAD³ (1) —**unleaded** n. [U] *Ben's car only takes unleaded.* —compare REGULAR² (2)

un·learn /ʌn'lɚn/ v. [T] INFORMAL to deliberately forget something you have learned, in order to change the way you do something: *It's difficult to unlearn bad driving habits.*

un·leash /ʌn'liʃ/ v. [T] **1** to suddenly let a strong force, feeling etc. have its full effect: *Lefevre's comments unleashed a wave of protest in Paris.* **2** to let a dog run free after it has been held on a LEASH¹ (1)

un·leav·ened /,ʌn'lɛvənd◂/ adj. unleavened bread is flat because it is not made with YEAST

un·less /ən'lɛs, ʌn-/ conjunction used when one thing will only happen or be true as long as another thing happens or is true: *Don't call me at the office unless it's absolutely necessary.* | *Unless you are a military fan, the Pentagon tour isn't very exciting.*

USAGE NOTE: UNLESS

WORD CHOICE: unless, if...not
Use **if...not** about something that did not happen or that you know is not true: *She would have died if the doctors hadn't operated immediately* (=but they did). | *If Troy weren't so stupid* (=but he is stupid) *he would understand.* Do not use **unless** in this way. Use **unless** about something that *could* happen if something else does not happen or is not done, or if something *could* be true: *Unless the doctors operate immediately, she'll die.* | *She'll die unless the doctors operate immediately* (=the doctors have not operated yet, and may or may not do so). | *Unless he's a complete idiot, he'll understand* (=he may or may not be a complete idiot). **Unless** and **if...not** can both be used to say that what you will

do depends on something else happening: *Unless Brad comes soon, I'm going without him.* | *If Brad doesn't come soon, I'm going without him.*

un·let·tered /ʌnˈlɛt̬ɚd/ *adj.* LITERARY unable to read, or uneducated

un·li·censed /ˌʌnˈlaɪsənst/ *adj.* without a LICENSE (=official document that gives you permission to do or have something): *unlicensed guns* | *unlicensed drivers*

un·like¹ /ˌʌnˈlaɪk◂/ *prep.* **1** completely different from a particular person or thing: *Ashley was unlike any woman I have ever known.* **2** not typical of something or someone at all: *It's unlike Greg to be late.*

unlike² *adj.* LITERARY not alike; different: *Fanny argues that her temper and Henry's are too unlike to get married.*

un·like·ly /ˌʌnˈlaɪkli◂/ *adj.* **1** not likely to happen: [unlikely to do sth] *The quality of education is unlikely to improve.* | **It's unlikely that** *we'll be able to get reservations for tonight.* **2** not likely to be true: *an unlikely story* **3 an unlikely pair** two people who do something together, but who seem so different from each other that it seems strange that they could get along

un·lim·it·ed /ˌʌnˈlɪmɪt̬ɪd◂/ *adj.* **1** without any limit: *unlimited access to information* **2** very large in amount: *an unlimited variety of cookies*

un·list·ed /ˌʌnˈlɪstɪd◂/ *adj.* **1** not in the list of numbers in the telephone DIRECTORY: *an unlisted phone number* **2** not shown on an official STOCK EXCHANGE list

un·lit /ˌʌnˈlɪt◂/ *adj.* dark because there are no lights: *an unlit parking lot*

unload

The kids unloaded the groceries from the car.

un·load /ʌnˈloʊd/ *v.*
1 vehicle/ship **a)** [T] to remove a load from a vehicle, ship etc.: *Could you unload the dishwasher?* | *Paul's job was mainly unloading cartons and stacking them.* | [unload sth from sth] *I need some help unloading the sofa from the truck.* **b)** [I,T] if a vehicle, ship etc. unloads, the goods that it carries are removed from it: *The ship is unloading at the dock right now.*
2 get rid of [T] INFORMAL **a)** to get rid of something illegal or not very good by selling it quickly: *Investors continued to unload technology stocks Thursday.* **b)** to get rid of work or responsibility by giving it to someone else: [unload sth on/onto sb] *Ben has a habit of unloading his work on others.*
3 criticize [I,T] to express strong feelings, especially anger, to someone when you are extremely upset: *Koch unloaded his concerns over dinner one night.* | [unload (sth) on sb] *When he got back to the office, Green unloaded on his staff.*
4 camera to remove the film from a camera
5 gun [I,T] to remove the bullets or SHELLS¹ (3) from a gun

un·lock /ʌnˈlɑk/ *v.* [T] **1** to unfasten the lock on a door, box etc. **2 unlock the secrets/mysteries of sth** to discover the most important facts about something: *Scientists succeeded in unlocking the secrets to polio's cause.*

un·loose /ʌnˈlus/ *v.* [T] LITERARY to untie or unfasten something: *Ezra unloosed the rope and pulled it in.*

un·loved /ˌʌnˈlʌvd◂/ *adj.* not loved by anyone

un·luck·y /ˌʌnˈlʌki◂/ *adj.* **unluckier, unluckiest**
1 having bad luck: *Chicago was unlucky to lose in the final minute of the game.* | *He's been especially unlucky in love* (=having bad luck in romantic relationships). **2** causing bad luck: *Some people think that black cats are unlucky.* **3** happening as a result of bad luck: *an unlucky accident* —**unluckily** *adv.*

un·made /ˌʌnˈmeɪd◂/ *adj.* an unmade bed is not neat because the sheets, BLANKETS etc. have not been arranged since someone slept in it

un·man·age·a·ble /ˌʌnˈmænɪdʒəbəl◂/ *adj.* difficult to control or deal with

un·man·ly /ˌʌnˈmænli◂/ *adj.* not thought to be appropriate for or typical of a man

un·manned /ˌʌnˈmænd◂/ *adj.* a machine, vehicle etc. that is unmanned does not have a person operating or controlling it

un·marked /ˌʌnˈmɑrkt◂/ *adj.* something that is unmarked has no words or signs on it to show where or what it is: *an unmarked grave* | *an unmarked police car*

un·mar·ried /ˌʌnˈmærid◂/ *adj.* not married: *unmarried mothers*

un·mask /ʌnˈmæsk/ *v.* [T] to make known the hidden truth about someone: *The CIA succeeded in unmasking the spy who sold military secrets.*

un·matched /ˌʌnˈmætʃt◂/ *adj.* LITERARY better than any other: *The hotel's top-floor lounge offers unmatched views of the city.*

un·me·di·at·ed /ʌnˈmidiˌeɪt̬ɪd/ *adj.* direct, without any other influence in between: *Television offers ordinary citizens an unmediated view of the world.*

un·men·tion·a·ble /ˌʌnˈmɛnʃənəbəl◂/ *adj.* too bad or embarrassing to talk about

un·men·tion·a·bles /ˌʌnˈmɛnʃənəbəlz/ *n.* [plural] OLD-FASHIONED OR HUMOROUS underwear

un·met /ˌʌnˈmɛt◂/ *adj.* unmet needs, demands, desires etc. have not been dealt with or achieved: *unmet expectations*

un·mis·tak·a·ble /ˌʌnmɪˈsteɪkəbəl◂/ *adj.* familiar and easy to recognize: *He spoke with an unmistakable Russian accent.* —**unmistakably** *adv.*

un·mit·i·gat·ed /ʌnˈmɪt̬əˌɡeɪt̬ɪd/ *adj.* [only before noun] **an unmitigated disaster/failure/pleasure etc.** something that is completely bad or good

un·mo·lest·ed /ˌʌnməˈlɛstɪd◂/ *adj.* FORMAL without being annoyed or interrupted: [do sth unmolested] *Residents just want to be able to walk around town unmolested.*

un·moved /ˌʌnˈmuvd◂/ *adj.* [not before noun] feeling no pity, sympathy, or sadness, especially in a situation where most people would feel this: *Walter seemed unmoved by the tragedy.*

un·named /ˌʌnˈneɪmd◂/ *adj.* an unnamed person, place, or thing is one whose name is not known publicly: *An unnamed source claimed that the company had gang associations.*

un·nat·u·ral /ʌnˈnætʃərəl/ *adj.* **1** different from what you would normally expect: *It was very cold, which seemed unnatural for late spring.* **2** seeming false, or not real or natural: *Father Gannon's laugh seemed forced and unnatural.* **3** different from normal human behavior in a way that seems morally wrong: *unnatural sexual practices* **4** different from anything produced by nature: *unnatural colors* —**unnaturally** *adv.*

un·nec·es·sar·y /ʌnˈnɛsəˌsɛri/ *adj.* **1** not needed, or more than is needed: *We can't afford any unnecessary delays.* **2** an unnecessary remark or action is or unreasonable or not nice —**unnecessarily** /ˌʌnˈnɛsəˈsɛrɪli/ *adv.*: *The instructions are unnecessarily complicated.*

un·need·ed /ʌnˈnidɪd/ *adj.* not necessary: *About 200 unneeded weather stations are scheduled to be closed.*

un·nerve /ʌnˈnɝv/ v. [T] to upset or frighten someone so that they lose their confidence or their ability to think clearly: *Peggy's strange smile unnerved me slightly.* —**unnerving** adj.: *Brenda has an unnerving habit of staring at you when you're talking.*

un·no·ticed /ʌnˈnoʊtɪst/ adj. adv. without being noticed: **go/pass unnoticed** *Teenage gambling often goes unnoticed.*

un·num·bered /ˌʌnˈnʌmbɚd◂/ adj. **1** not having a number: *stacks of unnumbered U.S. currency* **2** LITERARY too many to be counted

un·ob·served /ˌʌnəbˈzɝvd/ adj., adv. not noticed: *Mr. Fong was able to enter the building unobserved.*

un·ob·struct·ed /ˌʌnəbˈstrʌktɪd◂/ adj. not blocked by anything: *an unobstructed view of the lake*

un·ob·tru·sive /ˌʌnəbˈtrusɪv/ adj. not attracting your attention, and not easily noticeable: *The sprinkler heads are unobtrusive, almost invisible against the ceiling.* —**unobtrusively** adv.

un·oc·cu·pied /ʌnˈɑkyəˌpaɪd/ adj. **1** a seat, house, room etc. that is unoccupied has no one in it **2** an unoccupied country or area is not controlled by the enemy during a war: *The family fled to unoccupied France.*

un·of·fi·cial /ˌʌnəˈfɪʃəl◂/ adj. **1** without formal approval and permission from the organization or person in authority: *"Take Me Home, Country Road" became West Virginia's unofficial state song.* **2** not made publicly known as part of an official plan: *Feinstein emphasized that the trip was "an unofficial mission."* —**unofficially** adv.

un·o·pened /ʌnˈoʊpənd/ adj. an unopened package, letter etc. has not been opened yet: *The letter was returned to us unopened.*

un·op·posed /ˌʌnəˈpoʊzd◂/ adj., adv. without any opponent or opposition, especially in an election: *Corbin ran unopposed for mayor.*

un·or·gan·ized /ʌnˈɔrgəˌnaɪzd/ adj. **1** DISORGANIZED **2** people who are unorganized do not have an organization, UNION, group etc. to help or support them

un·or·tho·dox /ʌnˈɔrθəˌdɑks/ adj. unorthodox beliefs or methods are different from what is usual or accepted by most people: *an unorthodox management approach*

un·pack /ʌnˈpæk/ v. **1** [I,T] to take everything out of a box or SUITCASE **2** [T] TECHNICAL to change information in a computer so that it can be read or used

un·paid /ˌʌnˈpeɪd◂/ adj. **1** an unpaid bill or debt has not been paid **2** done without receiving payment: *an unpaid internship*

un·pal·at·a·ble /ʌnˈpælətəbəl/ adj. FORMAL **1** an unpalatable fact or idea is very bad and difficult to accept: *Senator Long tends to avoid unpalatable social issues.* **2** unpalatable food tastes bad

un·par·al·leled /ʌnˈpærəˌlɛld/ adj. FORMAL greater or better than all others: *a period of unparalleled economic prosperity*

un·par·don·a·ble /ʌnˈpɑrdn-əbəl/ adj. FORMAL unpardonable behavior is completely unacceptable —**unpardonably** adv.

un·paved /ˌʌnˈpeɪvd◂/ adj. an unpaved road does not have a hard surface

un·peeled /ˌʌnˈpild◂/ adj. unpeeled fruit or vegetables still have their skin on them

un·per·turbed /ˌʌnpɚˈtɝbd◂/ adj. not worried, annoyed, or upset, even though something bad has happened

un·planned /ˌʌnˈplænd◂/ adj. not planned or expected: *an unplanned pregnancy*

un·pleas·ant /ʌnˈplɛzənt/ adj. **1** not pleasant or enjoyable: *an unpleasant odor* **2** not nice or friendly: *Gabby had never seen two girls be so unpleasant to their mother.* —**unpleasantly** adv.

un·pleas·ant·ness /ʌnˈplɛzəntnɪs/ n. [U] FORMAL trouble or arguments

un·plug /ʌnˈplʌg/ v. **unplugged, unplugging** [T] to disconnect a piece of electrical equipment by taking its PLUG out of an OUTLET

un·plugged /ʌnˈplʌgd/ adj., adv. if a group of musicians performs unplugged, they perform without electric instruments

un·plumbed /ˌʌnˈplʌmd◂/ adj. **the unplumbed depths of sth** something that is not known about because it has never been examined or EXPLOREd

un·pol·ished /ʌnˈpɑlɪʃt/ adj. **1** having a surface that is rough or not shiny because of not being polished **2** not skillful, graceful, or having good MANNERS: *McRae is an unpolished campaigner and public speaker.*

un·pop·u·lar /ʌnˈpɑpyələ/ adj. not liked by most people: *an unpopular decision* —**unpopularity** /ˌʌnpɑpyəˈlærəţi/ n. [U]

un·prec·e·dent·ed /ʌnˈprɛsəˌdɛnţɪd/ adj. never having happened before, or never having happened so much: *unprecedented success*

un·pre·dict·a·ble /ˌʌnprɪˈdɪktəbəl◂/ adj. **1** something that is unpredictable changes a lot, so that it is impossible to know what will happen: *unpredictable weather* **2** someone who is unpredictable tends to change their behavior or ideas suddenly, so that you never know what they are going to do or think

un·pre·pared /ˌʌnprɪˈpɛrd◂/ adj. not ready to deal with something: [+ **for**] *Many high school graduates are unprepared for the workplace.* | [**unprepared to do sth**] *The ferry was unprepared to handle a disaster.*

un·pre·pos·sess·ing /ˌʌnpripəˈzɛsɪŋ/ adj. FORMAL not very attractive or noticeable

un·pre·ten·tious /ˌʌnprɪˈtɛnʃəs◂/ adj. APPROVING not trying to seem better, more important etc. than you really are: *an unpretentious, well-written comedy*

un·prin·ci·pled /ʌnˈprɪnsəpld/ adj. FORMAL not caring about whether what you do is morally right; UNSCRUPULOUS

un·print·a·ble /ʌnˈprɪntəbəl/ adj. words that are unprintable are very offensive or shocking

un·pro·duc·tive /ˌʌnprəˈdʌktɪv◂/ adj. not producing any good results: *It was a very unproductive meeting.*

un·pro·fes·sion·al /ˌʌnprəˈfɛʃənl◂/ adj. not following the standards for behavior that are expected in a particular profession or activity: *Johnson was fired for unprofessional conduct.* —**unprofessionally** adv.

un·prof·it·a·ble /ʌnˈprɑfɪţəbəl/ adj. **1** making no profit: *unprofitable state-owned enterprises* **2** LITERARY bringing no advantage or gain

un·prom·is·ing /ʌnˈprɑməsɪŋ/ adj. not likely to be good or successful: *At that time, the outlook for peace was unpromising.*

un·pro·nounce·a·ble /ˌʌnprəˈnaʊnsəbəl◂/ adj. an unpronounceable word or name is very difficult to say

un·pro·tect·ed /ˌʌnprəˈtɛktɪd◂/ adj. **1** **unprotected sex** sex without a CONDOM, which could allow sexual diseases such as AIDS to be passed on **2** someone or something that is unprotected could be hurt or damaged

un·prov·en /ˌʌnˈpruvən◂/ adj. not tested, and not shown to be definitely true: *unproven medical treatments*

un·pro·voked /ˌʌnprəˈvoʊkt◂/ adj. unprovoked anger, attacks etc. are directed at someone who has not done anything to deserve them

un·pub·lished /ʌnˈpʌblɪʃt/ adj. an unpublished book, speech, report etc. has not been published and so is not widely available: *Nabokov may have left behind some unpublished manuscripts.*

un·pun·ished /ʌnˈpʌnɪʃt/ adj. **go unpunished** to not be punished for something you have done, when someone else thinks you deserve to be punished: *Before 1870, a husband could legally go unpunished for beating his wife.*

un·qual·i·fied /ʌnˈkwɑləˌfaɪd/ adj. **1** not having the right knowledge, experience, or education to do something: *unqualified teachers* | [**be/feel unqualified to do sth**] *Jones thinks Marshall is unqualified to manage the department.* **2** unqualified success/praise/disaster etc. used to emphasize that a situation or quality is one that is completely good or bad: *The experiment had been an unqualified failure.*

un·quench·a·ble /ʌnˈkwɛntʃəbəl/ *adj.* FORMAL an unquenchable desire is one that is impossible to get rid of or satisfy: **unquenchable spirit/interest/ enthusiasm** etc. *the seemingly unquenchable Japanese thirst (=desire) for Western art*

un·ques·tion·a·ble /ʌnˈkwɛstʃənəbəl/ *adj.* impossible to doubt; certain: *Glenn is a man of unquestionable integrity.* —**unquestionably** *adv.*

un·ques·tioned /ʌnˈkwɛstʃənd/ *adj.* something that is unquestioned is accepted or believed by everyone: *Ogden's work ethic is unquestioned.*

un·ques·tion·ing /ʌnˈkwɛstʃənɪŋ/ *adj.* an unquestioning faith, attitude etc. is very certain and without doubts: *their unquestioning obedience* —**unquestioningly** *adv.*

un·qui·et /ʌnˈkwaɪət/ *adj.* LITERARY tending to make you feel nervous: *unquiet dreams*

un·quote /ˈʌnkwoʊt/ *adv.* —see **quote...unquote** (QUOTE[1] (4))

un·rat·ed /ʌnˈreɪtɪd/ *adj.* an unrated movie has not been given a letter from the system which shows whether or not it is appropriate for children

un·rav·el /ʌnˈrævəl/ *v.* **1** [T] to understand or explain something that is very complicated: *Scientists have not yet unraveled every detail of how genes work.* **2** [I] if a plan, agreement, relationship etc. unravels, it fails or stops working well: *After three years, their partnership began to unravel.* **3** [I,T] if you unravel threads or if they unravel, they become separated

un·read /ʌnˈrɛd/ *adj.* not yet read: *There was a pile of unread mail on his desk.*

un·read·a·ble /ʌnˈridəbəl/ *adj.* **1** an unreadable book or piece of writing is difficult to read because it is boring or complicated **2** unreadable writing is so messy that you cannot read it; ILLEGIBLE

un·real /ʌnˈril/ *adj.* **1** not related to real things that happen: *Battle scenes in the movie seemed entirely unreal.* **2** [not before noun] an experience, situation etc. that is unreal seems so strange that you think you must be imagining or dreaming it: *What we see on the news seems increasingly unreal to me.* **3** SPOKEN very exciting; excellent: *Our trip to Disneyland was totally unreal.* —**unreality** /ˌʌnriˈæləti/ *n.* [U]

un·re·al·is·tic /ˌʌnriəˈlɪstɪk/ *adj.* unrealistic ideas, hopes etc. are not based on facts: *unrealistic cost estimates* | *It is unrealistic to expect criminals to just turn in their weapons.* | *I think Nick's being unrealistic about how much money he'll make.* —**unrealistically** /-kli/ *adv.*

un·re·al·ized /ʌnˈriəˌlaɪzd/ *adj.* **1** not achieved: *unrealized hopes* **2** TECHNICAL unrealized profits, losses etc. have not been changed into a form that can be used as money

un·rea·son·a·ble /ʌnˈrizənəbəl/ *adj.* **1** an unreasonable belief, request, action etc. is wrong or unfair: *unreasonable expectations* | *It is not unreasonable to (=it seems sensible to) assume that 70% of energy needs can be met by gas and coal.* **2** unreasonable prices, costs etc. are too high **3** behaving in an unfair, bad, or stupid way: *Now he's just being unreasonable.* —**unreasonably** *adv.*: *an unreasonably large amount of money*

un·rea·son·ing /ʌnˈrizənɪŋ/ *adj.* FORMAL an unreasoning feeling is one that is not based on fact or reason: *unreasoning anger*

un·rec·og·niz·a·ble /ˌʌnrɛkəgˈnaɪzəbəl/ *adj.* someone or something that is unrecognizable has changed or been damaged so much that you do not recognize them —**unrecognizably** *adv.*

un·rec·og·nized /ʌnˈrɛkəgˌnaɪzd/ *adj.* **1** not noticed or not thought to be important: *Many minor disease outbreaks often go unrecognized.* **2** someone who is unrecognized for something they have done has not received the admiration or respect they deserve

un·re·con·struct·ed /ˌʌnrikənˈstrʌktɪd/ *adj.* OLD-FASHIONED not changing your ideas, even though many people think they are not modern or useful anymore: *a group of unreconstructed Stalinists*

un·re·cord·ed /ˌʌnrɪˈkɔrdɪd/ *adj.* not written down or recorded: *Throughout history, countless good deeds have gone unrecorded.*

un·re·cov·er·a·ble /ˌʌnrɪˈkʌvərəbəl/ *adj.* unrecoverable debts, losses etc. are ones that are impossible to get back

un·reel /ʌnˈril/ *v.* **1** [I,T] to unwind or make something unwind from around an object: *Wagner's safety line unreeled behind him.* **2** [I] if a story, movie etc. unreels, it is told or shown to you: *Miller has created a film that unreels like a slick TV commercial.*

un·re·fined /ˌʌnrɪˈfaɪnd/ *adj.* **1** an unrefined substance has not been separated from the other substances that it is combined with in its natural form: *unrefined sugar* **2** FORMAL not polite or educated

un·reg·is·tered /ʌnˈrɛdʒɪstərd/ *adj.* not recorded on an official list, especially when this is illegal or not allowed: *an unregistered gun* | *unregistered stocks and bonds* | *unregistered voters* (=who cannot vote because they are not on the official list)

un·reg·u·lat·ed /ʌnˈrɛgyəˌleɪtɪd/ *adj.* unregulated businesses, industries etc. are not controlled by the government and are free to do what they want —compare DEREGULATE

un·re·lat·ed /ˌʌnrɪˈleɪtɪd/ *adj.* **1** not connected or related to each other in any way: *The police think that the two incidents are unrelated.* **2** people who are unrelated are not members of the same family

un·re·lent·ing /ˌʌnrɪˈlɛntɪŋ/ *adj.* FORMAL a bad situation that is unrelenting continues for a long time without stopping: *Everyone at the office works at an unrelenting pace.* | *unrelenting headaches* —see also RELENTLESS

un·re·li·a·ble /ˌʌnrɪˈlaɪəbəl/ *adj.* **1** unable to be trusted or depended on: *Local telephone service is unreliable.* | *an unreliable witness* **2 unreliable narrator** TECHNICAL a character in some books who tells the story, but whose opinions influence the way he or she tells the story

un·re·lieved /ˌʌnrɪˈlivd/ *adj.* a bad situation that is unrelieved continues for a long time because nothing happens to change it: *The people have suffered decades of unrelieved poverty.*

un·re·mark·a·ble /ˌʌnrɪˈmɑrkəbəl/ *adj.* FORMAL not especially beautiful, interesting, or impressive: *She had a pale and unremarkable face.*

un·re·mit·ting /ˌʌnrɪˈmɪtɪŋ/ *adj.* FORMAL continuing for a long time and unlikely to stop: *The group faced unremitting hostility from the FBI.* —**unremittingly** *adv.*

un·re·peat·a·ble /ˌʌnrɪˈpitəbəl/ *adj.* **1** something that someone says that is unrepeatable is too impolite or offensive for you to want to say it again **2** unable to be done again

un·re·pent·ant /ˌʌnrɪˈpɛntˀnt/ *adj.* not feeling ashamed of behavior or beliefs that other people think are wrong: *an unrepentant racist*

un·re·port·ed /ˌʌnrɪˈpɔrtɪd/ *adj.* not told to the public or to anyone in authority: *Injuries from domestic violence often go unreported.*

un·rep·re·sent·a·tive /ˌʌnrɛprɪˈzɛntətɪv/ *adj.* not typical of a group: *These workers are unrepresentative of the general population.*

un·re·quit·ed /ˌʌnrɪˈkwaɪtɪd/ *adj.* **unrequited love** romantic love that you feel for someone, but that they do not feel for you

un·re·served /ˌʌnrɪˈzərvd/ *adj.* complete and without any doubts or limits: *unreserved enthusiasm* —**unreservedly** /ˌʌnrɪˈzərvɪdli/ *adv.*: *Daschle was unreservedly positive about the future.*

un·re·solved /ˌʌnrɪˈzɑlvd/ *adj.* an unresolved problem or question has not been answered or solved: *unresolved safety issues*

un·re·spon·sive /ˌʌnrɪˈspɑnsɪv/ *adj.* **1** not reacting to something or affected by it: [+ **to**] *Her infection had become totally unresponsive to medication.* **2** not reacting to what people say to you: [+ **to**] *Board members have been very unresponsive to our suggestions.*

un·rest /ʌnˈrɛst/ *n.* [U] a social or political situation in which people protest or behave violently: *Shortages in*

food have added to the growing unrest in the capitol. |
social/civil/political etc. **unrest** *Due to recent civil unrest, avoid travel in the northwest.*

un·re·strained /ˌʌnrɪ'streɪnd◂/ *adj.* not controlled or limited: *unrestrained population growth* —**unre-strainedly** /ˌʌnrɪ'streɪnɪdli/ *adv.*

un·re·strict·ed /ˌʌnrɪ'strɪktɪd◂/ *adj.* not limited by anyone or anything: *Under the new plan, people would have unrestricted choice of doctors.*

un·ripe /ˌʌn'raɪp/ also **un·rip·ened** /ʌn'raɪpənd/ *adj.* unripe fruit, grain etc. is not fully developed or ready to be eaten: *unripe bananas*

un·ri·valed /ʌn'raɪvəld/ *adj.* FORMAL better than any other: *the unrivaled beauty of St. Barts' white sand beaches*

un·roll /ʌn'roʊl/ *v.* [I,T] to open something that was curled into the shape of a ball or tube, and make it flat, or to become opened in this way: *We unrolled our sleeping bags and went to sleep.*

un·ruf·fled /ʌn'rʌfəld/ *adj.* APPROVING calm and not upset by a difficult situation: *After two hours of intense questioning, he remained unruffled.*

un·ru·ly /ʌn'ruli/ *adj.* **1** behaving in an uncontrolled or violent way: *unruly children* **2** unruly hair is not neat, and is difficult to comb or brush —**unruliness** *n.* [U]

un·sad·dle /ʌn'sædl/ *v.* [T] to remove the SADDLE (=leather seat) from a horse

un·safe /ʌn'seɪf◂/ *adj.* **1** dangerous, or likely to cause harm or damage: *unsafe products* **2** **unsafe sex** sex without a CONDOM, which could allow sexual diseases such as AIDS to be passed on

un·said /ʌn'sɛd/ *adj.* **be left unsaid** if something is left unsaid, you do not say it although you might be thinking it: *Some things are **better left unsaid** (=it is better not to mention them).*

un·san·i·tar·y /ʌn'sænəˌtɛri/ *adj.* very dirty and likely to cause disease: *unsanitary conditions*

un·sat·is·fac·to·ry /ʌnˌsætɪs'fæktəri/ *adj.* not good enough, or not acceptable: *an unsatisfactory explanation*

un·sat·is·fied /ʌn'sætɪsˌfaɪd/ *adj.* not pleased because you want more of something or you want something to be better: *unsatisfied consumers* —**unsatisfying** *adj.*: *an unsatisfying explanation* —compare DISSATISFIED

un·sa·vor·y /ʌn'seɪvəri/ *adj.* bad or morally unacceptable: *The train station was full of **unsavory characters** (=dirty, dishonest, or dangerous people).*

un·scathed /ʌn'skeɪðd/ *adj.* [not before noun] not hurt by a bad or dangerous situation: *Few retailers were left unscathed by the recession.*

un·sched·uled /ˌʌn'skɛdʒʊld◂/ *adj.* not planned or expected: *Bad weather forced the pilots to make an unscheduled landing.*

un·sci·en·tif·ic /ˌʌnsaɪən'tɪfɪk◂/ *adj.* not following usual scientific methods or systems: *An unscientific poll of my friends revealed that no one knew who the lieutenant governor was.*

un·scram·ble /ʌn'skræmbəl/ *v.* [T] to change a television SIGNAL or a message that has been sent in CODE so that it can be seen or read

un·screw /ʌn'skru/ *v.* [T] **1** to open or unfasten something by twisting it **2** to take the screws out of something

un·script·ed /ˌʌn'skrɪptɪd◂/ *adj.* an unscripted broadcast, speech etc. is not written or planned before it is actually made

un·scru·pu·lous /ʌn'skrupyələs/ *adj.* behaving in an unfair or dishonest way: *unscrupulous lawyers* —**unscrupulously** *adv.* —**unscrupulousness** *n.* [U]

un·seal /ʌn'sil/ *v.* [T] **1** to make something available to be seen or known to everyone, especially legal documents: *FBI interview transcripts were unsealed Friday in U.S. District Court.* **2** to open a container that has been tightly closed

un·sealed /ˌʌn'sild◂/ *adj.* **1** an unsealed envelope,

box etc. is not tightly closed or stuck together, so that things can be put into it or taken out **2** unsealed legal documents are available to be seen or made public

un·sea·son·a·bly /ʌn'sizənəbli/ *adj.* **unseasonably warm/cold/dry** etc. unusually warm, cold etc. for the time of year —**unseasonable** *adj.*

un·seat /ʌn'sit/ *v.* [T] **1** to remove someone from a position of power or strength: *In November, Sweeney failed to unseat Congressman Jim Kolbe.* **2** if a horse unseats someone, it throws them off its back

un·se·cured /ˌʌnsɪ'kyʊrd◂/ *adj.* **1** an unsecured LOAN or debt is one which does not make you promise to give the bank something you own if you cannot pay it back **2** not locked, guarded, or safe from attack

un·seed·ed /ˌʌn'sidɪd◂/ *adj.* not chosen as a SEED (=someone with a numbered rank in a competition), especially in a tennis competition

un·see·ing /ˌʌn'siɪŋ/ *adj.* LITERARY not noticing anything even though your eyes are open: *He turned to me, his eyes open yet unseeing.* —**unseeingly** *adv.*

un·seem·ly /ʌn'simli/ *adj.* FORMAL unseemly behavior is not polite or appropriate for a particular occasion: *It was considered unseemly for women to smoke.* —**unseemliness** *n.* [U]

un·seen /ˌʌn'sin◂/ *adj.* FORMAL not noticed or seen: *The grizzly bear is a species unseen in our state since 1906.* —see also **sight unseen** (SIGHT¹ (11))

un·self·ish /ʌn'sɛlfɪʃ/ *adj.* caring about other people and willing to help them instead of trying to get some advantage for yourself —**unselfishly** *adv.* —**unselfishness** *n.* [U]

Un·ser /'ʌnzɚ/, **Al** /æl/ (1939–) a U.S. race car driver

Unser, Bob·by /'bɑbi/ (1934–) a U.S. race car driver

un·set·tle /ʌn'sɛtl/ *v.* [T] to make someone feel slightly upset or nervous: *His silence unsettled me.* —**unsettling** *adj.*

un·set·tled /ˌʌn'sɛtld◂/ *adj.*
1 situation making people feel uncertain about what will happen: *unsettled financial markets*
2 argument or disagreement still continuing without reaching any agreement: *The issue of pay raises remains unsettled.*
3 land an unsettled area of land does not have any people living on it
4 stomach making you feel uncomfortable and a little sick: *The bus ride made my stomach feel unsettled.*
5 feeling slightly worried, upset, or nervous
6 weather changing a lot in a short period of time

un·shak·a·ble, unshakeable /ʌn'ʃeɪkəbəl/ *adj.* unshakable faith, beliefs etc. are very strong and cannot be destroyed or changed

un·shav·en /ʌn'ʃeɪvən/ *adj.* a man who is unshaven has short hairs growing on his face because he has not SHAVEd

un·sight·ly /ʌn'saɪtli/ *adj.* FORMAL not nice to look at; ugly: *an unsightly skin disease* | *unsightly stains* —**unsightliness** *n.* [U]

unscrew

He tried to unscrew the lid.

un·signed /ˌʌn'saɪnd◂/ *adj.* **1** an unsigned sports player or musician has not yet signed a contract to play for a sports team or record music for a company **2** an unsigned document or letter has not been signed with someone's name

un·skilled /ˌʌnˈskɪld◂/ adj. **1** an unskilled worker has not been trained for a particular type of job: *unskilled labor* (=people who have had no special training) **2** unskilled work, jobs etc. do not need people with special skills

un·smil·ing /ˌʌnˈsmaɪlɪŋ/ adj. LITERARY looking serious and often slightly angry or unhappy: *She stared at the camera, stiff and unsmiling.*

un·so·cia·ble /ˌʌnˈsoʊʃəbəl/ adj. not friendly and not liking to be with people or to go to social events

un·sold /ˌʌnˈsoʊld◂/ adj. something that is unsold is for sale and has not yet been sold: *Over 3000 tickets remained unsold three days before the concert.*

un·so·lic·it·ed /ˌʌnsəˈlɪsɪtɪd/ adj. unsolicited advice, offers, opinions etc. have not been asked for by the person who receives them and are usually not wanted

un·solved /ˌʌnˈsɑlvd◂/ adj. a problem, mystery, or crime that is unsolved has never been solved

un·so·phis·ti·cat·ed /ˌʌnsəˈfɪstəˌkeɪtɪd/ adj. **1** having little knowledge or experience of something, especially modern fashionable things, and showing this by the way you talk or behave: *There are a lot of unsophisticated investors in the market nowadays.* **2** unsophisticated tools, methods, processes etc. are simple, without many of the features of more modern ones: *an unsophisticated pipe bomb*

un·sound /ˌʌnˈsaʊnd◂/ adj. **1** unsound arguments, methods etc. are not based on fact or reason: *unsound banking practices* **2** an unsound building or structure is in bad condition **3** FORMAL someone with an unsound body or mind is sick or mentally ill

un·spar·ing /ʌnˈspɛrɪŋ/ adj. showing your true feelings or opinions, even if this hurts someone's feelings: [+ in] *Advani was unsparing in his criticism of the Congress.*

un·speak·a·ble /ʌnˈspikəbəl/ adj. **1** unspeakable actions or people are extremely bad: *unspeakable crimes* **2** LITERARY unspeakable feelings are so extreme that it is impossible to describe them: *unspeakable loneliness* —**unspeakably** adv.

un·spe·ci·fied /ʌnˈspɛsəˌfaɪd/ adj. not known, or not made publicly known: *The terrorists were given an unspecified amount of money to free the hostages.*

un·spoiled /ˌʌnˈspɔɪld◂/ adj. APPROVING **1** an unspoiled place has not been changed for a long time, especially by new roads, buildings etc. **2** someone who is unspoiled continues to be a good person, despite the good or bad things that have happened to them: *She remained unspoiled by her success.*

un·spo·ken /ʌnˈspoʊkən/ adj. **1** an unspoken agreement, rule etc. has not been discussed, but is understood by everyone in a particular group: *We had an unspoken agreement not to ask personal questions.* **2** not said for other people to hear: *unspoken thoughts*

un·sports·man·like /ʌnˈspɔrtsmənˌlaɪk/ adj. not behaving in a fair, honest, or polite way when competing in sports: *unsportsmanlike conduct/behavior* *Johnson was ejected from the game for unsportsmanlike conduct.*

un·sta·ble /ʌnˈsteɪbəl/ adj. **1** dangerous and likely to fall over because not balanced or well supported **2** likely to change suddenly and perhaps become worse: *an unstable economy* **3** someone who is unstable changes very suddenly so that you do not know how they will react or behave **4** an unstable chemical substance is likely to separate into simpler substances

un·stat·ed /ʌnˈsteɪtɪd/ adj. not specifically mentioned or said: *The unstated assumption here is that the time is not right for using force.*

un·stead·y /ʌnˈstɛdi/ adj. **1** shaking or moving in an uncontrolled way, or likely to move or shake: *My hand felt unsteady as I signed the paper.* | *an unsteady table* **2** a relationship, agreement etc. that is unsteady could end or change at any time: *an unsteady peace* | *unsteady work* **3** showing that you are nervous or not confident: *I gave her an unsteady smile.*

un·stint·ing /ʌnˈstɪntɪŋ/ adj. unstinting support, help, agreement etc. is complete and given willingly —**unstintingly** adv.

un·stop·pa·ble /ʌnˈstɑpəbəl/ adj. unable to be stopped: *Favre was unstoppable in last night's game.*

un·stressed /ˌʌnˈstrɛst◂/ adj. an unstressed word or part of a word is pronounced with less force than other ones

un·struc·tured /ˌʌnˈstrʌktʃəd/ adj. unstructured time, activities, or methods are not organized in a complete or detailed way

un·stuck /ˌʌnˈstʌk◂/ adj. **come unstuck a)** if something comes unstuck, it becomes separated from the thing that it was stuck to **b)** INFORMAL if a situation comes unstuck, it becomes more uncertain and likely to become worse

un·sub·stan·ti·at·ed /ˌʌnsəbˈstænʃiˌeɪtɪd/ adj. not proven or shown to be true: *unsubstantiated reports*

un·suc·cess·ful /ˌʌnsəkˈsɛsfəl◂/ adj. not having a successful result or achieving what was intended: *Their attempts to crush the revolt were unsuccessful.* | *unsuccessful negotiations* | *an unsuccessful artist* —**unsuccessfully** adv.: *Dukakis ran unsuccessfully for President in 1988.*

un·suit·a·ble /ʌnˈsutəbəl/ adj. not having the right qualities for a particular person, purpose, or situation: [+ for] *Half the planes were judged unsuitable for combat.*

un·sul·lied /ʌnˈsʌlid/ adj. LITERARY not spoiled or made ugly by anything

un·sung /ˌʌnˈsʌŋ◂/ adj. not praised or famous for something you have done, although you deserve to be: *Public defenders are the* **unsung heroes** *of the legal system.*

un·sure /ˌʌnˈʃʊr◂/ adj. **1** not certain about something or about what you have to do: [+ of/about] *Police were unsure of the motive for the attack.* **2** unsure of yourself not having enough confidence: *Chris seemed nervous and unsure of herself.*

un·sur·passed /ˌʌnsəˈpæst◂/ adj. better than all others of a particular type: *As warriors, the Huns were unsurpassed.*

un·sur·pris·ing /ˌʌnsəˈpraɪzɪŋ◂/ adj. not making you feel surprised —**unsurprisingly** adv. [sentence adverb] *Unsurprisingly, wealthier investors were more optimistic about their future retirement income.*

un·sus·pect·ing /ˌʌnsəˈspɛktɪŋ◂/ adj. not knowing that something bad is about to happen: *unsuspecting victims*

un·sus·tain·a·ble /ˌʌnsəˈsteɪnəbəl/ adj. not able to continue for very long: *unsustainable economic growth*

un·swayed /ʌnˈsweɪd/ adj. [not before noun] not changing your opinion, even though someone is trying to make you do so

un·sweet·ened /ˌʌnˈswitˈnd◂/ adj. without sugar added: *unsweetened chocolate*

un·swerv·ing /ʌnˈswɜvɪŋ/ adj. an unswerving belief, attitude etc. is one that is very strong and never changes: **unswerving loyalty/devotion/support** etc. *Castro's unswerving devotion to socialism*

un·sym·pa·thet·ic /ˌʌnsɪmpəˈθɛtɪk/ adj. not willing to understand or support someone else's ideas, problems, plans etc.: *an unsympathetic boss* | [+ to/toward] *Fonti was entirely unsympathetic to Glen's concerns.*

un·taint·ed /ʌnˈteɪntɪd/ adj. not affected or influenced by something bad: [+ by] *After 28 years in parliament, Chuan is still untainted by corruption.*

un·tamed /ˌʌnˈteɪmd◂/ adj. **1** an untamed animal has not been trained to live or work with people; wild **2** an untamed area of land is still in its natural state and has not been developed by people

un·tan·gle /ʌnˈtæŋgəl/ v. [T] **1** to separate pieces of string etc. that are twisted together **2** to make something less complicated

un·tapped /ˌʌnˈtæpt◂/ adj. untapped supplies, markets, TALENT etc. are available but have not yet been used

U

un·ten·a·ble /ʌnˈtɛnəbəl/ adj. FORMAL **1** an untenable situation has become so difficult that it is impossible to continue: *Government restrictions have put the business in an untenable position.* **2** an untenable suggestion, argument etc. is impossible to defend against criticism

un·test·ed /ʌnˈtɛstɪd/ adj. **1** an untested person, idea, method etc. has not been used in a particular situation, so you do not know whether they are good enough: *A "flat" tax is still an untested concept.* | *untested leadership* **2** untested products, drugs etc. have not been given any scientific tests to see if they work well or are safe to use

un·think·a·ble /ʌnˈθɪŋkəbəl/ adj. impossible to accept or imagine: *The idea of a world without music is unthinkable.*

un·think·ing /ʌnˈθɪŋkɪŋ/ adj. not thinking about the effects of something you say or do —**unthinkingly** adv.

un·ti·dy /ʌnˈtaɪdi/ adj. FORMAL messy

un·tie /ʌnˈtaɪ/ v. [T] to take the knots out of something or undo something that has been tied —**untied** adj.: *He often walked around with his shoelaces untied.*

un·til /ənˈtɪl, ʌn-/ prep., conjunction used to say that something stops happening or someone stops doing something at a particular time or when something else happens: *The meeting lasted until 6:30.* | *It wasn't until I got home that I realized I'd lost my wallet.* | **Up until** *last year, they didn't even own a car.*

un·time·ly /ʌnˈtaɪmli/ adj. **1** an untimely death/end etc. a death, end etc. that is much earlier than usual or expected **2** OLD-FASHIONED not appropriate or good for a particular occasion or time: *an untimely injury* —**untimeliness** n. [U]

un·tir·ing /ʌnˈtaɪərɪŋ/ adj. APPROVING never stopping while working hard or trying to do something: *Gonzales has been an untiring fighter for democracy.* —**untiringly** adv.

un·ti·tled /ʌnˈtaɪtld/ adj. an untitled work of art, song etc. has not been given a title

un·to /ˈʌntu/ prep. OLD USE to: *Thanks be unto God.*

un·told /ˌʌnˈtoʊld/ adj. [only before noun] **1** used to emphasize that an amount or quantity is very large, especially when the exact number or size is not known: *Untold numbers of innocent people died in the prisons.* **2** used to emphasize how bad something is: *The floods have caused* **untold misery** *to hundreds of homeowners.*

un·touch·a·ble /ʌnˈtʌtʃəbəl/ adj. **1** someone who is untouchable is in such a strong position that they cannot be beaten, affected, or punished in any way: *As sheriff of the county, Weber thought he was untouchable.* **2** belonging to the lowest social group, especially in the Hindu CASTE system —**untouchable** n. [C]

un·touched /ˌʌnˈtʌtʃt/ adj. **1** not affected or damaged by someone or something: [+ **by**] *Most residents found their homes untouched by floods.* **2** not touched, moved, eaten, etc.: *Most valuables were left untouched, but file cabinets had been emptied and searched.*

un·to·ward /ˌʌnˈtɔrd/ adj. FORMAL unexpected, unusual, or not wanted: **anything/nothing untoward** *Paul went back to work as if nothing untoward had happened.*

un·trained /ˌʌnˈtreɪnd/ adj. **1** not trained to do something: *Their army is made up mostly of untrained volunteers.* **2 to the untrained eye/ear etc.** when someone who does not have special knowledge or experience looks at something, listens to it etc.: *To the untrained eye, the two stones look almost the same.*

un·tram·meled /ʌnˈtræməld/ adj. FORMAL without any limits

un·treat·ed /ˌʌnˈtritɪd/ adj. **1** an untreated illness or injury has not had medical treatment **2** harmful substances that are untreated have not been made safe: *untreated drinking water*

un·tried /ˌʌnˈtraɪd/ adj. **1** not having any experience of doing a particular job: *At the time, Richards was an unknown, untried movie director.* **2** not yet tested to see whether it is successful: *an untried strategy*

un·true /ˌʌnˈtru/ adj. **1** a statement that is untrue does not give the right facts; false **2 be untrue to sb** LITERARY to deceive someone, especially by not being faithful to them in a relationship

un·trust·wor·thy /ʌnˈtrʌstˌwɚði/ adj. someone who is untrustworthy cannot be trusted, especially because you think they are dishonest

un·truth /ʌnˈtruθ, ˈʌntruθ/ n. [C] FORMAL a word meaning a "lie," used because you want to avoid saying this directly

un·truth·ful /ʌnˈtruθfəl/ adj. dishonest or not true —**untruthfully** adv.

un·tucked /ʌnˈtʌkt/ adj. the bottom edge of an untucked shirt is hanging loose, instead of being inside someone's pants

u·num /ˈunəm/ —see E PLURIBUS UNUM

un·used¹ /ˌʌnˈyuzd/ adj. not being used, or never used: *an unused office* | *unused ammunition*

un·used² /ʌnˈyust/ adj. unused to (doing) sth not experienced in dealing with something: *I was unused to the heavy city traffic.* | *He was a man who was unused to sitting still.*

un·su·al /ʌnˈyuʒuəl, -ʒəl/ adj. different from what is usual or ordinary: *a very unusual flavor* | *It's unusual for Dave to be late.* | **It's not unusual to** (=it is fairly common to) *spend $10,000 fixing up a car.*

un·u·su·al·ly /ʌnˈyuʒuəli, -ʒəli/ adv. **unusually hot/difficult/quiet etc.** more hot, difficult etc. than is usual

un·ut·ter·a·ble /ʌnˈʌtərəbəl/ adj. LITERARY an unutterable feeling is too extreme to be expressed in words —**unutterably** adv.

un·var·nished /ˌʌnˈvɑrnɪʃt/ adj. **1** [only before noun] plain and without additional description: *the unvarnished truth* **2** without any VARNISH (=a transparent substance like paint, used to protect the surface of wood)

un·veil /ʌnˈveɪl/ v. [T] **1** to show or tell people something that was previously kept secret: *The city unveiled plans for a $1.7 billion airport.* **2** to remove the cover from something such as a work of art, especially as part of a formal ceremony —**unveiling** n. [C,U]

un·voiced /ˌʌnˈvɔɪst/ adj. TECHNICAL unvoiced CONSONANTS are produced without moving the VOCAL CORDS; for example /d/ and /g/ are VOICED consonants, and /t/ and /k/ are unvoiced

un·want·ed /ˌʌnˈwɑntɪd, -ˈwɑn-, -ˈwɔn-/ adj. not wanted or needed: *an unwanted pregnancy*

un·war·rant·ed /ʌnˈwɔrəntɪd, -ˈwɑr-/ adj. done without good reason, and therefore annoying: *unwarranted criticism*

un·war·y /ʌnˈwɛri/ adj. not knowing about possible problems or dangers, and therefore easily harmed or deceived

un·washed /ˌʌnˈwɑʃt/ adj. **1** needing to be washed; dirty: *unwashed dishes* **2 the great unwashed** HUMOROUS poor uneducated people

un·wav·er·ing /ʌnˈweɪvərɪŋ/ adj. unwavering beliefs, feelings, decisions etc. are strong and do not change: *Miller is unwavering in her support of the governor.*

un·wed /ˌʌnˈwɛd/ adj. an unwed mother or father was not married when their baby was born

un·wel·come /ʌnˈwɛlkəm/ adj. **1** something that is unwelcome is not wanted, especially because it might cause embarrassment or problems: *unwelcome advice* **2** unwelcome guests, visitors etc. are people that you do not want in your home

un·well /ʌnˈwɛl/ adj. [not before noun] FORMAL sick, especially for a short time

un·wield·y /ʌnˈwildi/ adj. **1** an unwieldy object is big, heavy, and difficult to carry or use **2** an unwieldy system, argument, or plan is difficult to control or manage because it is too complicated —**unwieldiness** *n.* [U]

un·will·ing /ʌnˈwɪlɪŋ/ *adj.* **1** [not before noun] not wanting to do something, and refusing to do it: [**unwilling to do sth**] *So far the landlord has been unwilling to lower our rent.* **2** [only before noun] not wanting to do something, but doing it: *unwilling participants* —**unwillingly** *adv.* —**unwillingness** *n.* [U]

un·wind /ʌnˈwaɪnd/ *v.* past tense and past participle **unwound** **1** [I] to relax and stop feeling anxious: *Reading helps me unwind.* **2** I,T] to undo something that has been wrapped around something else, or to be undone in this way

un·wise /ˌʌnˈwaɪz◂/ *adj.* not based on good sense and experience: *I think it would be unwise to borrow more money.* —**unwisely** *adv.*

un·wit·ting·ly /ʌnˈwɪtɪŋli/ *adv.* in a way that shows you do not know or realize something: *Laura unwittingly threw away the winning lottery ticket.* —**unwitting** *adj.* [only before noun] *an unwitting victim*

un·world·ly /ʌnˈwɜrldli/ *adj.* **1** not interested in money or possessions **2** not having a lot of experience of complicated things in life; NAIVE

un·wor·thy /ʌnˈwɜrði/ *adj.* **1** not good enough to deserve respect, admiration etc.: *Baker feels that he is unworthy to receive such a great award.* **2** be **unworthy of sth** to not deserve to be thought about or treated in a particular way: [+ **of**] *She married a man who was unworthy of her love and devotion.*

un·wound /ʌnˈwaʊnd/ the past tense and past participle of UNWIND

un·wrap /ʌnˈræp/ *v.* **unwrapped, unwrapping** [T] to remove the paper, plastic etc. from around something: *Bill finished his sandwich and unwrapped a candy bar.*

un·writ·ten /ˌʌnˈrɪtⁿ◂/ *adj.* known about and understood by everyone but not formally written down: **an unwritten rule/law** *There is an unwritten social rule against kissing in public.*

un·yield·ing /ʌnˈyildɪŋ/ *adj.* **1** strict and not willing to change or accept change, even though other people want this: *Even his supporters admit that he is selfish and unyielding.* **2** LITERARY something that is unyielding is hard and not comfortable: *the unyielding mountainous terrain*

un·zip /ʌnˈzɪp/ *v.* **unzipped, unzipping** [T] **1** to open the ZIPPER on a piece of clothing, bag etc. **2** to make a computer FILE its normal size again in order to use it, after it has been made to take up less space —see also ZIP FILE

up¹ /ʌp/ *adv.* **1** toward a higher position from the floor, ground, or bottom of something: *Put the picture higher up on the wall.* | *Darryl climbed up onto the roof.* **2** at or in a high position: *"Where is Alex?" "He's up in his room."* | *The helicopter hovered up above us.* **3** into an upright or raised position: *Everyone stood up for the national anthem.* | *Larry's hair was sticking straight up.* **4** in or toward the north: *We're driving up to Chicago for the conference.* | *My cousins live up north.* **5** toward someone so that you are near, or in the place where they are: *He came right up and asked my name.* | *I walked up to the counter and demanded my money back.* **6** increasing in loudness, strength, level of activity etc.: *Turn up the radio.* | *Violent crime went up by 9% last year.* **7** so as to be completely finished or used so that there is nothing left: *Who ate up all the chips?* | *The closet's completely filled up with all Mia's old clothes.* **8** so as to be in small pieces or divided into equal parts: *We'll split the money up evenly.* | *Why did you tear up the letter?* **9** so as to be firmly fastened, covered, or joined: *The men tied the store clerk up and took the money.* | *Let's cover up the machinery just in case it rains.* **10** so as to be brought or gathered together: *Let's just add up these figures quickly.* | *I picked up as many of the beads as I could find.* **11** if a surface or part of something is a particular way up, it is on top: *Make sure this side of the box is facing up.* | *Put the playing cards **right side up** on the table.* **12** so as to receive attention: *Elaine brought up the issue of childcare.* **13** above

and including a certain amount or level: *Power was lost **from** the tenth floor **up**.* | *The movie is appropriate for children twelve and* **up. 14 up and down a)** higher and lower: *We all **jumped up and down** (=jumped repeatedly) for joy.* **b)** first in one direction, then in the opposite direction, again and again: *I want you kids to stop running up and down in the hall.* —see also **look sb up and down** (LOOK¹ (23)) **15 up to sth a)** up to and including a certain amount or level: *Our car can hold up to five people.* **b)** also **up until sth** if something happens up to a certain time, date etc., it happens until that time: *She continued to care for her father up to the time of his death.*

up² *adj.* **1** [not before noun] not in bed: *Are the kids still up?* **2** [not before noun] if a number, level, or amount is up, it is higher than before: [+ **by**] *Interest rates are up by 1%.* | [+ **on**] *Profits are up on last year.* **3** [not before noun] INFORMAL if a period of time is up, it is finished: *I'll give you a signal when the ten minutes are up.* **4 up to sb** depending on someone and what they decide to do: *I'll leave the final decision up to Lloyd.* | *"Which sofa should we get?" "**It's up to you.**"* **5 up to sth a)** doing something secret or something that you should not be doing: *I have a feeling that Jo's up to something.* | *I think Ken's **up to no good** (=doing something wrong or illegal).* **b)** [in negatives and questions] smart, good, or well enough for a particular purpose or in order to do something: *Since the operation, Sue hasn't been up to playing tennis (=has not felt well enough to play).* **c)** if something is up to a particular standard, it is good enough to reach that standard: *This new CD is not up to the group's usual standard.* **6 up for sth** available or intended for a particular purpose: *The house is up for sale.* | *Even the most personal subjects were up for discussion.* **7 up and running** if a new system or process is up and running, it is working well: *Our new factory in Belize is finally up and running.* **8** [not before noun] if a computer system is up, it is working —opposite DOWN² (3) **9 be up against sth/sb** to have to deal with a difficult situation or fight an opponent: *Hugh is up against some stiff competition in the 100-meter dash.* **10** [only before noun] moving or directed to a higher position: *the up escalator* | *Press the up arrow key.* **11 up to your ears/eyes/neck in sth** INFORMAL deeply involved in a difficult or illegal situation: *Rona and Hank are up to their ears in debt (=they owe a lot of money).*

SPOKEN PHRASES

12 be up on sth to know a lot about something: *Conrad's really up on his geography, isn't he?* **13 be up for sth** to be interested in doing something or willing to do something: *Is anybody up for a game of tennis?* **14 bring/get sb up to speed** to tell someone the latest information about something: *Bill, I want you to bring Peter up to speed on the project.* **15** if something is up, someone is feeling unhappy because they have problems, or there is something wrong in a situation: *I could tell by the look on Joan's face that something was up.* —see also **what's up?** (WHAT¹ (18)), **what's up with sb/sth?** (WHAT¹ (19)) **16 be up and about** to be well enough to walk around and have a normal life after you have been in bed because of an illness or accident: *It's good to see you up and about again.* **17 What have you been up to (lately)?** used to ask someone what they have been doing since the last time you saw them **18 be up to here (with sb/sth)** to be very upset and angry because of a particular person or situation: *I'm up to here with your lying.* **19** [not before noun] said by restaurant workers when food or a drink is ready to be eaten or drunk: *Table three, you're order's up.*

up³ *prep.* **1** toward or in a higher place: *Go up the stairs and turn right.* | *I laughed so hard that the water went up my nose.* **2** toward or at the top or far end of something: *I'll go up the road to ask for directions.* **3** if you sail or go up a river, you go toward its SOURCE: *We spent five days sailing up the Mississippi River.* **4 up yours!** VULGAR used to insult someone when they have done or said something that annoys you: *"Hey, when're you going to learn to bat?" "Up yours, Wilkie!"*

up⁴ *n.* **1 ups and downs** the mixture of good and bad experiences that happen in any situation or relationship: *We had a lot of ups and downs in our marriage.* **2 be on the up and up** SPOKEN if a person or business is on the up and up, they are honest and do things legally

up⁵ *v.* **upped, upping** **1** [T] INFORMAL to increase the amount or level of something: *They upped their offer by 5%.* **2 up and...** SPOKEN if you up and do something, you suddenly start to do something different or surprising: *Without saying another word, he **up and left**.*

up- /ʌp/ *prefix* **1** [in verbs] to make something greater, higher, or better: *to upgrade a software program* (=make it do more things and work better) **2** [in adverbs and adjectives] at or toward the top or beginning of something: *climbing uphill | sailing upriver* (=nearer to where the river starts) **3** [in verbs] to take something from its place or turn it upside down: *an uprooted tree* **4** [in adjectives and adverbs] at or toward the higher or better part of something: *an upscale grocery store* (=attracting richer people) —compare DOWN-

up-and-com·er /ˌ. . '../ *n.* [C] INFORMAL someone or something that is likely to be successful: *an up-and-comer in the computer industry*

up-and-com·ing /ˌ. . '.◂/ *adj.* [only before noun] likely to be successful or popular: *an up-and-coming Broadway actor*

up·beat /ˌʌp'bit◂/ *adj.* happy and confident that good things will happen: *For all the trouble she's been through, Anna is remarkably upbeat. | an upbeat report* —opposite DOWNBEAT¹

up·braid /ʌp'breɪd/ *v.* [T] FORMAL to tell someone angrily that they have done something wrong

up·bring·ing /'ʌpˌbrɪŋɪŋ/ *n.* [singular,U] the care and training that parents give their children when they are growing up: *Our grandmother took charge of our religious upbringing.*

UPC *n.* [C] the abbreviation of UNIVERSAL PRODUCT CODE

up·chuck /'ʌp-tʃʌk/ *v.* [I] INFORMAL to VOMIT¹

up·com·ing /'ʌpˌkʌmɪŋ/ *adj.* [only before noun] happening soon: *my upcoming exams*

up·coun·try /ˌʌp'kʌntri◂/ *adj.* OLD-FASHIONED from an area of land without many people or towns, especially in the middle of a country

up·date¹ /'ʌpdeɪt, ˌʌp'deɪt/ *v.* [T] **1** to add the most recent information to something: *The immigration information booklet is updated yearly.* **2** to make something more modern in the way it looks or operates: *The award-winning film updates a Tolstoy tale about Russian soldiers.* **3** SPOKEN to tell someone the most recent information about something: [**update sb on sth**] *So, I just thought I'd update you on the negotiations.*

up·date² /'ʌpdeɪt/ *n.* [C] the most recent news about something: [+ **on**] *For an update on road conditions, contact the highway department.*

Up·dike /'ʌpdaɪk/**, John** (1932–) a U.S. writer famous for his NOVELs

up·draft /'ʌpdræft/ *n.* [C] **1** an UPWARD movement of air **2** a situation in which prices, STOCKs etc. go up, or when business becomes better —opposite DOWN-DRAFT

up·end /ʌp'ɛnd/ *v.* [T] to push something over, especially so that it is upside down

up·front /ʌp'frʌnt/ *adj.* [not before noun] behaving or talking in a direct and honest way: *You need to be upfront with Val about your past.* —see also **up front** (FRONT¹ (10))

up·grade /'ʌpgreɪd/ *v.* **1** [I,T] to make a machine, a computer, or a piece of SOFTWARE better

and able to do more things **2** [I,T] to give someone or be given a better seat on an airplane than the one originally paid for **3 upgrade your skills** to learn new things about how to do a particular job **4** [T] to change the official description of something such as a someone's medical condition to a better one: [**upgrade sb to sth**] *Winnie has been upgraded to stable condition.* **5** [T] to give someone a more important job —**upgrade** /'ʌpgreɪd/ *n.* [C] —opposite DOWNGRADE¹

up·heav·al /ʌp'hivəl, 'ʌpˌhivəl/ *n.* [C,U] **1** a very big change that often causes problems: *political upheaval* **2** a very strong movement UPWARD, especially of the earth

up·hill¹ /ˌʌp'hɪl◂/ *adj.* **1** toward the top of a hill —opposite DOWNHILL² (1) **2 an uphill battle/struggle/fight etc.** something that is very difficult to do and needs a lot of effort

uphill² *adv.* toward the top of a hill: *The water had to be pumped uphill.* —opposite DOWNHILL¹

up·hold /ʌp'hoʊld/ *v.* past tense and past participle **upheld** /-'hɛld/ [T] **1** if a court upholds a decision made by another court, it states that the decision was correct: *A federal court has upheld legislative term limits in Maine.* **2** to defend or support a law, system, or principle so that it is not made weaker: *They want to uphold traditional family values.* —**upholder** *n.* [C]

up·hol·ster /ə'poʊlstɚ, ʌp'hoʊl-/ *v.* [T] to cover a chair etc. with material —**upholstered** *adj.* —**upholsterer** *n.* [C]

up·hol·ster·y /ə'poʊlstəri/ *n.* [U] **1** material used to cover chairs etc. **2** the process of covering chairs etc. with material

up·keep /'ʌpkip/ *n.* [U + **of**] the care needed to keep something in good condition

up·lands /'ʌpləndz/ *n.* PLURAL the parts of a country that are away from the ocean and are higher than other areas —**upland** *adj.*: *upland forests*

up·lift¹ /'ʌplɪft/ *n.* [U] a sudden happy feeling

up·lift² /ʌp'lɪft/ *v.* [T] FORMAL **1** to make someone feel happier **2** to make something higher

up·lift·ed /ʌp'lɪftɪd/ *adj.* **1** feeling happier **2** LITERARY raised up

up·lift·ing /ˌʌp'lɪftɪŋ◂/ *adj.* making you feel more cheerful

up·load /'ʌploʊd/ *v.* [I,T] if information, a program etc. uploads, or if you upload it, you move it from a computer to a larger computer system that is connected to it —compare DOWNLOAD

up·mar·ket /ˌʌp'markət◂/ *adj.* UPSCALE —opposite DOWNMARKET

up·on /ə'pan, ə'pɔn/ *prep.* FORMAL on: *A dark cloud descended upon the valley. | Her friends look upon her with envy.* —see also **once upon a time** (ONCE¹ (11)), **take it upon yourself to do sth** (TAKE¹ (32))

up·per¹ /'ʌpɚ/ *adj.* [only before noun] **1** in a higher position than something else: *His upper arms were like tree trunks. | the upper lip* **2** near or at the top of something: *An investment firm occupies the upper floors of the building. | The recommended upper limit* (=highest limit) *of calories from fat in your diet is about 600.* **3 have/gain the upper hand** to have more power than someone else, so that you are able to control a situation: *Police have gained the upper hand over the drug dealers in the area.* **4** more important than other parts or ranks in an organization, system etc.: *upper-income consumers | the upper echelons* (=the most important and most senior members) *of corporate management* **5** farther from the ocean or farther north than other parts of an area: *the upper reaches of the Mekong River* —opposite LOWER¹ —see also **keep a stiff upper lip** (STIFF¹ (9))

upper² *n.* [C] **1** the top part of a shoe that covers your foot: *leather uppers* **2** SLANG an illegal drug that gives you a lot of energy; AMPHETAMINE

upper case /ˌ.. '.◂/ *n.* [U] letters written in capitals (A, B, C) rather than in small form (a, b, c) —**upper-case** *adj.* —opposite LOWER CASE

upper class /ˌ.. '.◂/ n. [C] **the upper class** the group of people who belong to the highest social class —compare LOWER CLASS, MIDDLE CLASS, WORKING CLASS —**upper-class** adj.

up·per·class·man /ˌʌpɚˈklæsmən/ n. [C] a student in the last two years at a school or college —compare UNDERCLASSMAN

upper crust /ˌ.. '.◂/ n. [singular] INFORMAL the group of people who belong to the highest social class —**upper-crust** adj.

up·per·cut /ˈʌpɚˌkʌt/ n. [C] an act of hitting someone in which you swing your hand up into their chin

upper house /ˌ.. './ n. [C usually singular] the smaller of two elected groups of government officials, that make laws usually less REPRESENTATIVE[1] and made up of more experienced officials than the larger group —compare LOWER HOUSE

up·per·most /ˈʌpɚˌmoʊst/ adj. **1 be uppermost in your mind** if something is uppermost in your mind, you think about it a lot because it is very important to you: *Succeeding in her career was uppermost in her mind.* **2** [usually before noun] higher than anything else: *Place the pizza on the uppermost oven rack.* **3** [usually before noun] more important than anything else: *The children's safety should be your uppermost concern.*

up·pi·ty /ˈʌpəti/ adj. INFORMAL, DISAPPROVING behaving as if you are more important than you really are, or not showing someone enough respect: *uppity kids*

up·raised /ˌʌpˈreɪzd◂/ adj. LITERARY raised or lifted up: *She held a torch in her upraised hand.*

up·right[1] /ˈʌp-raɪt/ adv. **1** with your back straight: *After my back surgery, it took a while before I could walk upright.* | **sit/stand (bolt) upright** *Andy stood upright when he heard the noise.* **2** if something is pulled, held etc. upright, it is put into a position in which it is standing straight up

upright[2] adj. **1** standing straight up **2** always behaving in an honest way: *a brave, upright man* —**uprightness** n. [U]

upright[3] n. [C] **1** a long piece of wood or metal that stands straight up and supports something **2** an upright piano

upright pi·an·o /ˌ.. .'../ n. [C] a tall piano with strings that are set in an up and down direction —compare GRAND PIANO

up·ris·ing /ˈʌpˌraɪzɪŋ/ n. [C] an occasion when a group of people use violence to try to change the rules, laws etc. in an institution or country

up·riv·er /ʌpˈrɪvɚ/ adv. toward the place where a river begins —opposite DOWNRIVER

up·roar /ˈʌp-rɔr/ n. [singular,U] a lot of noise or angry protest about something: *The court's decision set off an uproar among religious activists.*

up·roar·i·ous /ʌpˈrɔriəs/ adj. very noisy, because a lot of people are laughing or shouting —**uproariously** adv.

up·root /ʌpˈrut/ v. [T] **1** to pull a plant and its roots out of the ground **2** to make someone leave their home for a new place, especially when this is difficult or upsetting: *In 1854, my grandfather decided to uproot his family and move to Los Angeles.*

up·scale /ˌʌpˈskeɪl◂/ adj. made for or relating to people from a high social class who have a lot of money: *an upscale department store* —opposite DOWNSCALE[1]

up·set[1] /ˌʌpˈsɛt/ v. past tense and past participle **upset** [T]
1 make unhappy to make someone feel unhappy or worried: *I'm sorry – I didn't mean to upset you.*
2 upset sb's stomach to make someone feel sick in their stomach: *Spicy food upsets my stomach.*
3 defeat to defeat someone who is who is expected to win a game or competition: *France upset Brazil in the World Cup final.*
4 cause problems to change a plan or situation in a way that causes problems: *Recent bank failures threaten to upset the entire world economy.*

5 push sth over to push something over without intending to: *She was careful not to upset the bottle of nail polish on the bed.*
6 upset the apple cart OLD-FASHIONED to completely spoil someone's plans

up·set[2] /ˈʌpsɛt/ n. [C] an occasion when a person or team that is not expected to win beats a stronger opponent in a competition, election etc.: *Stephanie White led Purdue to an upset over No. 4-ranked Stanford.*

up·set[3] /ˌʌpˈsɛt/ adj. **1** [not before noun] unhappy and worried because something bad or disappointing has happened: [+ **about/over**] *What are you upset about?* | [**upset that**] *Marcy was upset that she was invited.* **2 an upset stomach** an illness that affects the stomach and makes you feel sick

up·set·ting /ʌpˈsɛtɪŋ/ adj. making you feel unhappy and worried: *upsetting news*

up·shot /ˈʌpʃɑt/ n. **the upshot (of sth)** the final result of a situation: *The upshot of the new system was more delay and expense for travelers.*

up·side[1] /ˈʌpsaɪd/ n. [singular] the positive part of a situation that is generally bad: [+ **of**] *The upside of the whole thing is that we got a free trip to Jamaica.* —opposite DOWNSIDE

upside[2] prep. **upside the head/face etc.** SPOKEN, NONSTANDARD on the side of someone's head etc.

upside down

inside out

backward

upside down

upside down[1] /ˌ.. '.◂/ adv. with the top at the bottom and the bottom at the top: *You're holding the book upside down.* —opposite **right side up** (RIGHT[1] (11)) —see also **turn sth upside down** (TURN[1] (16))

upside down[2] adj. **1** in a position with the top at the bottom and the bottom at the top: *an upside down U shape* **2** messy or not organized: *Evans described EFI as a "crazy, upside-down world."*

up·stage[1] /ʌpˈsteɪdʒ/ v. [T] to do something that takes people's attention away from someone else who is more important: *Jake was furious when Marley and Jamie upstaged him at his own wedding.*

up·stage[2] /ˌʌpˈsteɪdʒ◂/ adv. toward the back of the stage in a theater —**upstage** adj.

up·stairs[1] /ˌʌpˈstɛrz◂/ adv. toward or on an upper floor in a building: *Lucy came rushing upstairs after her sister.* | *My office is upstairs on the right.* —compare

DOWNSTAIRS —**upstairs** adj.: an upstairs bedroom —see also **kick sb upstairs** (KICK¹ (10))

up·stairs² n. **1 the upstairs** one or all of the upper floors in a building **2 sb does not have much upstairs** SPOKEN used to say that someone is not very intelligent **3 the man upstairs** SPOKEN God

up·stand·ing /ˌʌpˈstændɪŋ/ adj. FORMAL honest and responsible: an upstanding citizen

up·start /ˈʌpstɑrt/ n. [C] someone or an organization that becomes successful very quickly, and is not liked by other people or companies because of their success —**upstart** adj.: a young upstart lawyer

up·state /ˌʌpˈsteɪt◂/ adj. [only before noun] in the northern part of a particular state: upstate New York —**upstate** adv. —compare DOWNSTATE

up·stream /ˌʌpˈstrim◂/ adv. along a river, in the opposite direction from the way the water is flowing —**upstream** adj. —opposite DOWNSTREAM

up·surge /ˈʌpsɚdʒ/ n. [C] **1** a sudden increase: [+ in] In recent years, there has been an upsurge in terrorist activity. **2** a sudden strong feeling: [+ of] She felt an unexpected upsurge of jealousy.

up·swing /ˈʌpswɪŋ/ n. [C] an improvement or increase in the level of something: [+ in] an upswing in business | The airline's earnings are now **on the upswing**. —opposite DOWNSWING

up·take /ˈʌpteɪk/ n. **1 be slow/quick on the uptake** INFORMAL to be slow or fast at learning or understanding things **2** [C,U] TECHNICAL the rate at which a substance is taken into a system, machine etc.: The disease limits the uptake of water and nutrients into the tree.

up·tem·po /ˌ. ˈ..◂/ adj. moving or happening at a fast rate: up-tempo gospel songs —**up-tempo** adv.

up·tick /ˈʌptɪk/ n. [C] UPSWING: [+ in] We have had an uptick in sales this year.

up·tight /ˌʌpˈtaɪt◂/ adj. **1** INFORMAL having strict, traditional opinions and seeming unable to relax **2** behaving in an angry way because you are feeling nervous and worried: I just try not to get too uptight about anything.

up-to-date /ˌ. . ˈ.◂/ adj. **1** including all the newest information: up-to-date travel information | **keep/ bring sb up-to-date** (=give someone all the newest information about something) | **keep/bring sth up-to-date** (=add all the newest information about something to a list, document etc.) **2** modern or fashionable: a more up-to-date hairstyle —see Usage Note at NEW

up-to-the-min·ute /ˌ. . . ˈ.◂/ adj. [only before noun] **1** including all the newest information: up-to-the-minute financial information **2** very modern or fashionable

up·town /ˌʌpˈtaʊn◂/ adv. in or toward the northern areas of a city —**uptown** adj.: an uptown bar —**uptown** /ˈʌptaʊn/ n. [U] —compare DOWNTOWN, MIDTOWN

up·trend /ˈʌptrɛnd/ n. [C] a period of time when business or economic activity increases —opposite UPTREND

up·turn /ˈʌptɚn/ n. [C] an increase in the level of something: [+ in] an upturn in profits —opposite DOWNTURN

up·turned /ˈʌptɚnd, ˌʌpˈtɚnd/ adj. **1** curving up at the end: an upturned nose **2** turned upside down: an upturned flowerpot

up·ward¹ /ˈʌpwɚd/ also **upwards** adv. **1** moving or pointing toward a higher position: He pointed upward with his left hand. —opposite DOWNWARD¹ **2** increasing to a higher level: Stock prices have moved upward. **3** more than a particular amount, time etc.: The ships can carry a cargo of three hundred tons and upward. | Good lawyers can bill clients at rates **upward of** $250 per hour.

upward² adj. [only before noun] **1** increasing to a higher level: an upward trend in gasoline prices **2** moving or pointing toward a higher position: an upward movement of the hand —opposite DOWNWARD²

upwardly mo·bile /ˌ... ˈ../ adj. moving up through the social classes and becoming richer —**upward mobility** /ˌ.. ˈ.../ n. [U]

U·ral River, the /ˈyʊrəl/ a river in eastern Europe that flows from the Ural Mountains in Russia through Kazakstan to the Caspian Sea

U·rals, the /ˈyʊrəlz/ also **the Ural Mountains** a range of mountains that runs from the north to the south of Russia and is often considered to mark the border between Europe and Asia

u·ra·ni·um /yʊˈreɪniəm/ n. [U] symbol **U** a heavy white metal that is an ELEMENT, is RADIOACTIVE, and is used to produce NUCLEAR power and weapons

U·ra·nus /yʊˈreɪnəs, ˈyʊrənəs/ **1** the PLANET that is the seventh in order from the Sun **2** in Greek MYTHOLOGY, the god of heaven and the first ruler of the universe

ur·ban /ˈɚbən/ adj. [only before noun] **1** relating to a city, or to cities in general: urban unemployment | the urban population —opposite RURAL **2** urban blight problems that make part of a city ugly and hard to live in: It is the minority groups who are living in the worst conditions of urban blight and official neglect.

ur·bane /ɚˈbeɪn/ adj. behaving in a relaxed and confident way in social situations —**urbanely** adv. —**urbanity** /ɚˈbænəti/ n. [U]

Ur·ban II /ˌɚbən ðə ˈsɛkənd/ (?1042–1099) the POPE who encouraged the First Crusade

ur·ban·ize /ˈɚbəˌnaɪz/ v. [T usually passive] **1** to build houses, cities etc. in the COUNTRYSIDE: urbanized areas **2** if someone is urbanized, they become more typical of people who live in cities, rather than being like people who live in the COUNTRYSIDE: the newly urbanized Northeastern middle class —**urbanization** /ˌɚbənəˈzeɪʃən/ n. [U]

urban leg·end /ˌ... ˈ../ also **urban myth** /ˌ.. ˈ./ n. [C] a well-known story that many people believe, about an unusual or terrible event that is claimed to have happened to an ordinary person

urban re·new·al /ˌ.. .ˈ../ n. [U] the process of improving poor city areas by building new houses, stores etc.

urban sprawl /ˌ.. ˈ./ n. [U] the spread of city buildings and houses into an area that was COUNTRYSIDE

ur·chin /ˈɚtʃɪn/ n. [C] OLD-FASHIONED a small dirty messy child —see also SEA URCHIN

Ur·du /ˈʊrdu, ˈɚdu/ n. [U] the official language of Pakistan, also used in India

-ure /yɚ/ suffix [in nouns] used to make nouns that show actions or results: failure (=act of failing) | a mixture (=what you get when you mix things)

u·re·thra /yʊˈriθrə/ n. [C] the tube through which URINE flows from your BLADDER, and also through which the SEMEN of males flows

urge¹ /ɚdʒ/ v. [T] **1** to strongly suggest that someone do something: Herrera urged patience in the negotiations. | [urge sb to do sth] Katy's family urged her to find another job. | [urge that] Graft urged that the city use the money for new playgrounds. | [urge sth on/upon sb] During summer vacation, Mrs. White regularly urged books on me. **2** [always + adv./prep.] LITERARY to make someone or something move by shouting, pushing them etc.: [+ into/forward] Daniel urged the horses forward with a whip.

urge sb ↔ on phr. v. [T] to encourage a person or animal to work harder, go faster etc.: Urged on by fans, Johnson danced in celebration with his teammates.

urge² n. [C] a strong wish or need: sexual urges | [an/the urge to do sth] I resisted the urge to slap his face.

ur·gent /ˈɚdʒənt/ adj. **1** very important and needing to be dealt with immediately: urgent news | One hostage was **in urgent need of** medical attention. **2** FORMAL done or said in a way that shows that you want something to be dealt with immediately: an urgent whisper —**urgency** n. [U] a matter of great urgency —**urgently** adv.

urgh /ɚ/ interjection said when you feel a sudden pain or are using a lot of effort to do something

u·ric /ˈyʊrɪk/ adj. TECHNICAL relating to URINE

u·ri·nal /ˈyʊrənəl/ n. [C] a type of toilet for men, that is fastened onto the wall

u·ri·nar·y /ˈyʊrəˌnɛri/ adj. TECHNICAL connected with urine or the parts of your body through which urine passes

u·ri·nate /ˈyʊrəˌneɪt/ v. [I] FORMAL to make urine flow out of your body —**urination** /ˌyʊrəˈneɪʃən/ n. [U]

u·rine /ˈyʊrɪn/ n. [U] the yellow liquid waste that comes out of your body from your BLADDER

URL n. [C] TECHNICAL Uniform Resource Locator; a series of abbreviations, signs, and letters that act as an address where you can find a document on the Internet

urn /ərn/ n. [C] **1** a decorated container, especially one that is used for holding the ASHes of a dead body **2** a metal container that holds a large amount of tea or coffee

u·rol·o·gist /yʊˈrɑlədʒɪst/ n. [C] a doctor who treats conditions relating to the URINARY system and men's sexual organs —**urology** n. [U] —**urological** / yʊrə-ˈlɑdʒɪkəl/ adj.

Ur·su·line /ˈ-əˌlɪn, -laɪn/ a member of a group of Catholic NUNS

U·ru·guay /ˈyʊrəˌgwaɪ/ a country in South America, between Argentina and Brazil —**Uruguayan** / yʊrə-ˈgwaɪən/ n., adj.

U.S., US n. the U.S. the United States of America —**U.S.** also **US** adj.: the U.S. Navy

us /əs; strong ʌs/ pron. the object form of "we": Do you want to go with us to the fair? | Kate told us she was getting a new car.

U.S.A., USA n. the U.S.A. the United States of America

us·a·ble /ˈyuzəbəl/ adj. something that is usable is in an appropriate condition to be used

USAF the abbreviation of the United States Air Force

us·age /ˈyusɪdʒ/ n. **1** [C,U] the way that words are used in a language: a book on modern English usage **2** [U] the way in which something is used, or the amount of it that is used: Gas usage fell by almost 14 percent.

USDA n. [singular] United States Department of Agriculture; an official government organization that sets standards for food quality and makes sure that places where food is produced or PACKAGEd are clean and the food is safe to eat

use¹ /yuz/ v.

1 |use sth| [T] if you use a particular tool, method, service, ability etc., you do something with that tool, by means of that method etc., for a particular purpose: Can I use your pen? | Carla often doesn't use good judgment in selecting boyfriends. | [use sth for doing sth] We only use the car for driving in the city. | [use sth as sth] I use the dining-room table as a desk. | The officer is accused of using excessive force (=using violent methods) during the arrest.

2 |amount of sth| [T] to take something from a supply of food, gas, money etc. with the result that there is less left: Standard washing machines use about 40 gallons of water.

3 |use a person| to make someone do something for you in order to get something you want: Can't you see Tad's just using you? | [use sb to do sth] Smugglers use innocent people to carry drugs through customs.

4 |an advantage| [T] to take advantage of a situation: [use sth to do sth] Some people think he used his political influence to get the contract.

5 sb/sth could use sth SPOKEN **a)** if you say you could use something, you mean you would really like to have it: You look like you could use some sleep. **b)** if you say something could use something, you mean it needs it: The house could use another coat of paint.

6 |word| [T] to say or write a particular word or phrase: I try not to use bad language around the kids.

7 |product| [T] to buy a particular product regularly: What brand of toothpaste do you use?

8 |drugs| [I,T] to regularly take illegal drugs

9 |name| [T] to call yourself by a name that is not

yours in order to keep your real name secret: Martens uses her stage name when she travels.

use up

Sally used up all the toothpaste.

use sth ↔ **up** phr. v. [T] to use all of something, so there is none left: Who used up the ketchup?

use² /yus/ n. **1** [C] a way in which something can be used, or a purpose for which it can be used: A pastry brush has a variety of uses in the kitchen. **2** [U] the act of using something, or the amount that is used: [+ of] The military has agreed to allow public use of the land. | Increased use of fertilizers has led to water pollution. **3 make use of sth** to use something that is available in order to achieve something or get an advantage for yourself: It's a shame that teachers don't make use of the new computer lab. | I have to learn to **make better use of** my time. **4 put sth to (good) use** to use knowledge, skills etc. for a particular purpose: I'd like a job where I could put my degree in languages to good use. **5** [U] the ability or right to use something: [+ of] Joe's given me the use of his office till he gets back. | He lost the use of both legs as a result of the accident. **6 be (of) no use** to be completely useless: Our computers are not use – they're just too slow to run the program. | [be (of) no use to sb] Now that I've quit law school, the books are of no use to me.

> ### SPOKEN PHRASES
>
> **7 it's no use doing sth** used to tell someone not to do something because it will have no effect: It's no use complaining – you just need to take the test again later. **8 it's no use!** used to say that you are going to stop doing something because you do not think it will be successful: Oh, it's no use! I can't fix it. **9 what's the use (of sth)?** used to say that something seems to be a waste of time: What's the use of having a window in your office if you can't open it? **10 sth has its uses** HUMOROUS used to say that something can sometimes be useful, even though it may not seem that way: Being stubborn can have its uses.

11 be of use to be useful: Were my directions of any use? **12 be in use** a machine, place etc. that is in use is being used: All of the washing machines are in use. **13 for the use of sb** provided for a particular person or group of people to use: The board room is for the use of company executives only. **14 come into use** also **bring sth into use** to start being used, or to start using something: Tanning beds came into use around 1979. **15 go/be out of use** a machine, place etc. that goes out of use or is out of use, stops being used, or is not being used **16 have no use for sb/sth** to have no respect for someone or something: My company has no use for workers who are not motivated. **17** [C] one of the meanings of a word, or the way that a particular word is used

used¹ /yust/ adj. **be/get used to (doing) sth** to have experienced something, so that it does not seem surprising, difficult, strange etc. anymore: Zach's not used to such spicy food. | I still haven't **gotten used to** working nights. —see Usage Note at USED TO

used² /yuzd/ adj. **1** used cars/clothes/books etc. cars, clothes etc. that have already had an owner; SECOND HAND **2** dirty or not in good condition anymore, as a result of use: used tissues | a used syringe

S W
1 1

used to /'yustə; *final or before a vowel* 'yustu/ *modal verb* **1 sb/sth used to (do sth)** if something used to happen, it happened regularly or all the time in the past, but does not happen now: *Janie used to go to my high school.* | *Freight trains used to come right through the middle of town.* | *"Do you play golf?" "No, but I used to."* **2 sb/sth used to be sth** used to say they something was true in the past, but now is not true anymore: *You used to be so shy.* | *There used to be a grocery store over there.*

USAGE NOTE: USED TO

WORD CHOICE: used to/be used to/get used to
We use **used to** before a verb to talk about something that someone did regularly in the past: *Marianne used to play the piano every day, but she hardly ever plays now.* Use **be used to** and **get used to** to talk about being or becoming more comfortable with a situation or activity, so that it does not seem strange or difficult anymore: *Tina's used to getting up at 5:30.* | *I can't get used to the climate here.*

S W
2
3

use·ful /'yusfəl/ *adj.* helping you to do or get what you want: *Investigators have not found any useful clues in the case.* | [+ **to**] *They are working to develop technology that is useful to farmers.* | [+ **for**] *The book contains general information useful for travel in Africa.* | *Matt, **make yourself useful** and help me with the dishes.* | *Such techniques might **prove useful** in detecting breast cancer.* —see also **come in useful/handy** at **come in** (COME[1]) —**usefully** *adv.*

use·ful·ness /'yusfəlnɪs/ *n.* [U] the state of being useful: *The test's usefulness in measuring intelligence is limited.* —see also **outlive your usefulness** (OUTLIVE (3))

use·less /'yuslɪs/ *adj.* **1** not useful or effective in any way: *Without electricity, the radio's useless.* | *a useless piece of information* | [+ **for**] *The sewing machine is useless for heavy fabric.* | [**it is useless to do sth**] *It was useless to discuss the finances any further.* **2** INFORMAL unable or unwilling to do anything well: *As a secretary, she was useless.* —**uselessly** *adv.* —**uselessness** *n.* [U]

U

Use·net /'yuznɛt/ *n.* [singular] the computer BULLETIN BOARD SYSTEM that is available on the Internet

S W
2

us·er /'yuzɚ/ *n.* [C] **1** someone or something that uses a product, service etc.: *library users* | *a computer user* **2** INFORMAL someone who regularly takes illegal drugs —see also END USER

user fee /'.. ,./ *n.* [C] **1** a tax that someone must pay in addition to the price of certain services, products etc.: *airport user fees* **2** an amount of money someone pays for using an ONLINE SERVICE

user-friend·ly /,.. '..◂/ *adj.* easy to use or operate: *user-friendly software* —**user-friendliness** *n.* [U]

ush·er[1] /'ʌʃɚ/ *n.* [C] someone who guides people to their seats at a theater, wedding etc.

usher[2] *v.* [T] to help someone to get from one place to another, especially by guiding them: [**usher sb into/ to etc.**] *Security guards ushered the man out of the theater.*

usher sth ↔ in *phr. v.* [T] to be the start of something new: *The Industrial Revolution ushered in an era of rapid social change.*

USIA United States Information Agency; a government department which sends representatives to other countries to provide information about the United States

USMC the abbreviation of the United States Marine Corps

USN the abbreviation of the United States Navy

USO United Services Organizations; an organization that helps members of the U.S. military

U.S. of A. /,yu ɛs əv 'eɪ/ *n.* **the (good ol') U.S. of A.** SPOKEN, HUMOROUS the United States of America

USP *n.* [C] Unique Selling Proposition; a feature of a product that makes it different from other similar products, and therefore more attractive to people who might buy it

USS, U.S.S. the abbreviation of United States Ship, used at the beginning of a military ship's name: *the USS Nimitz*

S W
2
3

u·su·al /'yuʒuəl, -ʒəl/ *adj.* **1** the same as what happens most of the time or in most situations: *I'll meet you at the usual time.* | *The usual adult dose is 600 mg daily.* | **better/more/worse etc. than usual** *Recently, John's been working later than usual.* **2 as usual** in the way that happens or exists most of the time: *Dorothy arrived late as usual.* **3 the usual** SPOKEN the drink or food that you usually have, especially at a bar or restaurant: *I'll have the usual, Frank.* —see also **business as usual** (BUSINESS (12))

S W
1 1

u·su·al·ly /'yuʒuəli, -ʒəli/ *adv.* used when describing what happens on most occasions or in most situations: *Janet usually wears jeans to work.* | *It's not usually this cold in April.* | *Usually, I'll just get a sandwich for lunch.*

u·su·rer /'yuʒərɚ/ *n.* [C] LITERARY someone who lends money to people and makes them pay too high a rate of INTEREST[1] (3)

u·su·ri·ous /yu'ʒʊriəs/ *adj.* LITERARY a usurious price or rate of INTEREST[1] (3) is unfairly high

u·surp /yu'sɚp/ *v.* [T] FORMAL to take someone else's power, position, job etc. when you do not have the right to: *He accused Congress of trying usurp the authority of the President.* —**usurper** *n.* [C] —**usurpation** /,yusɚ'peɪʃən/ *n.* [U]

u·su·ry /'yuʒəri/ *n.* [U] FORMAL the practice of lending money to people, especially making them pay unfairly high rates of INTEREST[1] (3)

UT the written abbreviation of Utah

U·tah /'yutɑ/ *written abbreviation* **UT** a state in the western U.S.

Ute /yut/ *n.* a Native American tribe from the western region of the U.S.

u·ten·sil /yu'tɛnsəl/ *n.* [C] a tool or object with a particular use, especially in cooking: *kitchen utensils*

u·ter·us /'yuṭərəs/ *n. plural* **uteri** /-raɪ/ or **uteruses** [C] the organ in a woman's or female MAMMAL's body where babies develop —**uterine** /'yuṭəraɪn, -rən/ *adj.*

u·til·i·tar·i·an /yu,tɪlə'tɛriən/ *adj.* **1** FORMAL useful and practical rather than being used for decoration: *utilitarian clothes* **2** TECHNICAL based on a belief in utilitarianism

u·til·i·tar·i·an·ism /yu,tɪlə'tɛriə,nɪzəm/ *n.* [U] TECHNICAL the belief that an action is good if it helps the greatest possible number of people

S W

u·til·i·ty /yu'tɪləṭi/ *n. plural* **utilities 1** [usually plural] a service such as gas or electricity provided for people to use: *Does your rent include utilities?* **2** [U] FORMAL the amount of usefulness that something has

utility pole /.'... ,./ *n.* [C] a tall wooden pole that supports telephone and electric wires

utility room /.'... ,./ *n.* [C] a room in a house where the washing machine, FREEZER, cleaning equipment etc. are kept

u·til·ize /'yutḷ,aɪz/ *v.* [T] FORMAL to use something for a particular purpose: *The old fire station could be utilized as a theater.* —**utilizable** *adj.* —**utilization** /,yutḷ-ə'zeɪʃən/ *n.* [U]

ut·most[1] /'ʌt⌐moʊst/ *adj.* **the utmost importance/ respect/care etc.** the greatest possible importance, respect etc.: *I have the utmost respect for his research.*

utmost[2] *n.* **1 do your utmost** to try as hard as you can to achieve something: *Kimball said he would do his utmost to achieve a peaceful solution.* **2 the utmost** the most that can be done: *The murders deserve to be punished to the utmost.*

u·to·pi·a /yu'toʊpiə/ *n.* [C,U] an imaginary perfect world where everyone is happy —**utopian** *adj.* —compare DYSTOPIA

ut·ter[1] /'ʌṭɚ/ *adj.* [only before noun] **utter failure/ darkness/nonsense etc.** a complete failure, darkness etc.: *We sat there in utter silence.* | *All of your talk about quitting school is utter nonsense.*

utter² *v.* [T] FORMAL **1** to say things: *No one had ever heard Thomas utter an unkind word.* **2** to make a sound with your voice, especially with difficulty: *The wounded prisoner uttered a groan.*

ut·ter·ance /ˈʌtərəns/ *n.* **1** [C] FORMAL something that someone says: *Dozens of reporters are always nearby to record his every step and utterance.* **2 give utterance to sth** LITERARY to express something in words

ut·ter·ly /ˈʌtəli/ *adv.* completely or totally: [+ adj./ adv.] *Her comments about men are utterly ridiculous.*

U-turn /ˈyu tən/ *n.* [C] **1** a turn that you make in a car, on a bicycle etc., so that you go back in the direction you came from: **make/do a U-turn** *I did a U-turn and headed back home.* **2** a complete change of ideas, plans etc.: **make/do a U-turn** *Mitterrand made a decisive U-turn in 1983 and cut government spending.*

UV an abbreviation of ULTRAVIOLET

u·vu·la /ˈyuvyələ/ *n.* [C] a small soft piece of flesh which hangs down from the top of your mouth at the back

Uz·bek·i·stan /ʊzˈbɛkɪˌstɑn, -ˌstæn/ a country in central Asia between Turkmenistan and Kazakhstan, that was formerly part of the Soviet Union —**Uzbek** /ˈʊzbɛk/ *n., adj.*

U·zi /ˈuzi/ *n.* [C] a type of MACHINE GUN

U

V

V, v /viː/ *n. plural* **V's, v's** [C] the 22nd letter of the English alphabet

V /viː/ **1** the number 5 in the system of ROMAN NUMERALS **2** used to show that a television show contains violent scenes **3** [usually singular] something that has a shape like the letter V: *Ducks flew overhead in a V.*

v. 1 a written abbreviation of VERSUS, used especially when talking about the names of legal TRIALS: *Roe v. Wade* —see also VS. **2** the written abbreviation of "verb" **3** the abbreviation of VERSE (4)

VA the written abbreviation of Virginia

vac /væk/ *n.* [C] a VACUUM CLEANER

va·can·cy /ˈveɪkənsi/ *n. plural* **vacancies 1** [C,U] a room or building that is not being used and is available for someone to stay in, or the situation in which a room or building like this is available: *The hotel had hung out its "No vacancy" sign.* **2** [C] a job that is available for someone to start doing: *There are still two vacancies on the school board.*

va·cant /ˈveɪkənt/ *adj.* **1** a vacant seat, room etc. is empty and available for someone to use: *Half of the apartments in the building are vacant.* | *There were several vacant lots* (=empty, unused areas of land in a city) *downtown.* **2** FORMAL a vacant job or position in an organization is available for someone to start doing **3 a vacant expression/smile/stare etc.** an expression that shows that someone is not thinking about anything: *He gazed at me with vacant eyes.* —**vacantly** *adv.*: *Loretta smiled vacantly at the others in the room.*

va·cate /ˈveɪkeɪt/ *v.* [T] FORMAL **1** to leave a job or position so that it is available for someone else to do: *Clay will vacate the position on June 19.* **2** to leave a seat, room etc. so that someone else can use it: *Renters have refused to vacate the building.*

s w **va·ca·tion¹** /veɪˈkeɪʃən, və-/ *n.* **1** [C,U] time spent not working or at school, especially when you take a trip: *Don's on vacation this week.* | *How did you spend your **summer vacation?*** | *We're **taking a two-week vacation** to Mexico.* **2** [U] the number of days, weeks etc. that you are allowed not to work at your job, while still getting paid: *How much vacation do you get at your new job?*

USAGE NOTE: VACATION

WORD CHOICE: vacation, break, holiday, leave
Use **vacation** to talk about the time people spend away from school or work: *Where are you going on vacation this summer?* Use **break** to talk about a time that you stop working in order to rest, or about a short vacation from school: *I'm getting really tired – let's take a break.* | *We're going skiing over spring break.* Use **holiday** to talk about a day when no one officially has to go to work or school, or a special religious day: *Christmas is my favorite holiday.* Use **leave** to talk about time when you are allowed not to work for a special reason: *Gretchen hasn't taken a day of sick leave in ten years.*

---

vacation² *v.* [I] to go somewhere for a vacation: [+ in/at] *The two met while vacationing in Hawaii.*

va·ca·tion·er /veɪˈkeɪʃənɚ/ *n.* [C] someone who has gone somewhere for a vacation

vac·ci·nate /ˈvæksəˌneɪt/ *v.* [T] to protect someone from a disease by giving them a vaccine: [**vaccinate sb against sth**] *All children should be vaccinated against measles.* —compare IMMUNIZE, INOCULATE

vac·ci·na·tion /ˌvæksəˈneɪʃən/ *n.* [C,U] the act of INJECTING a vaccine into someone's body to prevent disease, or the practice of doing this: *yellow fever and cholera vaccinations* | *international vaccination programs*

vac·cine /vækˈsin/ *n.* [C,U] a substance which contains a weak form of the BACTERIA or VIRUS that causes a disease and is used to protect people from that disease: *a hepatitis vaccine*

vac·il·late /ˈvæsəˌleɪt/ *v.* [I] to continue to change your opinions, ideas, behavior etc.; WAVER: [+**between**] *Eve vacillates between love and anger for the father who abandoned her.* —**vacillation** /ˌvæsəˈleɪʃən/ *n.* [C,U]

va·cu·i·ty /væˈkyuəti, və-/ *n.* [U] FORMAL a lack of intelligent, interesting, or serious thought

vac·u·ous /ˈvækyuəs/ *adj.* FORMAL showing no intelligence or having no useful purpose: *vacuous cocktail-party conversation* —**vacuously** *adv.* —**vacuousness** *n.* [U]

vac·uum¹ /ˈvækyum/ *n.* **1** [C] a vacuum cleaner **2** [C] a space that is completely empty of all gas, especially one from which all the air has been taken away **3** [singular] a situation in which someone or something is missing or gone: **a power/political/moral etc. vacuum** *Rice's resignation has left a huge power vacuum at the company.* **4 in a vacuum** completely separately from other people or things and with no connection with them: *These laws were not made in a vacuum.*

vacuum² *v.* [I,T] to clean using a vacuum cleaner

vacuum clean·er /ˈ.. ˌ../ *n.* [C] a machine that cleans floors by sucking up the dirt from them

vacuum-packed /ˈ.. ˌ./ *adj.* vacuum-packed food is in a container from which most of the air has been removed, so that the food will stay fresh for longer

vacuum tube /ˈ... ˌ./ *n.* [C] a closed glass tube, used to control the flow of electricity in old radios, televisions etc.

Va·duz /fɑˈduts/ *the capital city of Liechtenstein*

vag·a·bond /ˈvægəˌbɑnd/ *n.* [C] LITERARY someone who has no home but travels from place to place —compare VAGRANT

va·ga·ry /ˈveɪgəri/ *n. plural* **vagaries** [C usually plural] FORMAL unusual or unexpected events, changes, ideas etc.: [+ **of**] *the vagaries of U.S. policy toward Asia*

va·gi·na /vəˈdʒaɪnə/ *n.* [C] the passage between a woman's outer sexual organs and her UTERUS —**vaginal** *adj.*

va·gran·cy /ˈveɪgrənsi/ *n.* [U] the criminal offense of living on the street and BEGGING from people

va·grant /ˈveɪgrənt/ *n.* [C] FORMAL someone who has no home or work, especially someone who BEGS

vague /veɪg/ *adj.* **1** unclear because someone does not give enough details or does not say exactly what they mean: *vague promises of support* | [+ **about**] *Johann was a little vague about where he was going.* **2 have a vague idea/feeling/recollection etc.** to think that something might be true or that you remember something, although you cannot be sure: *Larry had the vague feeling he'd done something embarrassing the night before.* **3** not having a clear shape or form: *There were vague shapes of hills in the distance.* | *a vague smile* —**vagueness** *n.* [U]

vague·ly /ˈveɪgli/ *adv.* **1** slightly: *Her face is vaguely familiar.* | *I found the whole situation vaguely upsetting.* **2** not clearly: *His statement was very vaguely worded.* **3** in a way that shows you are not thinking about what you are doing: *Audrey smiled vaguely at the ceiling.*

vain /veɪn/ *adj.* **1** DISAPPROVING someone who is vain is too proud of their good looks, abilities, or position: *Men can be just as vain as women.* **2 in vain a)** without success in spite of your efforts: *Workers tried in vain to keep the building from collapsing.* **b)** without purpose or without positive results: *If people don't learn from this, then his suffering and death were in vain.* **3 a vain attempt/hope/effort etc.** an attempt, hope etc. that fails to achieve the result you wanted: *Jordan made funny faces in a vain attempt to cheer her up.* —**vainly** *adv.*: *He tried vainly to explain his actions.* —see also **take the name of the Lord in vain** (NAME¹ (11)), VANITY

vain·glo·ri·ous /veɪnˈglɔriəs/ *adj.* LITERARY too proud of your own abilities, importance etc. —**vaingloriously** *adv.* —**vainglory** *n.* [U]

val·ance /ˈvæləns/ n. [C] **1** a narrow piece of cloth that hangs from the edge of a shelf or from the frame of a bed to the floor **2** a narrow piece of cloth above a window, covering the bar that the curtains hang on

vale /veɪl/ n. [C] LITERARY **1** a broad low valley **2** this/ **the vale of tears** an expression used to mean the difficulties of life

val·e·dic·to·ri·an /ˌvælədɪkˈtɔriən/ n. [C] the student who has received the best grades all the way through high school, and usually makes a speech at the GRADUATION ceremony

val·e·dic·to·ry /ˌvæləˈdɪktəri/ n. [C] FORMAL a speech or statement in which you say goodbye when you are leaving a school, job etc., especially on a formal occasion —**valedictory** adj.: a valedictory speech

va·lence /ˈveɪləns/ also **va·len·cy** /ˈveɪlənsi/ n. [C] TECHNICAL a measure of the ability of atoms to combine together to form compounds

val·en·tine /ˈvæ],ntaɪn/ n. [C] **1** a card you send to someone on Valentine's Day **2** be my valentine written in a card on Valentine's Day to tell someone that you love them

Valentine's Day /ˈ... ,./ n. [C,U] February 14; a day when people give cards, candy, or flowers to people they love

Va·lé·ry /ˌvæləˈri/, **Paul** (1871–1945) a French poet

val·et /væˈleɪ, ˈvæleɪ/ n. [C] **1** also **valet parker** someone who parks your car for you at a hotel or restaurant **2** a male servant who takes care of a man's clothes, serves his meals etc. **3** someone who cleans the clothes of people staying in a hotel, on a ship etc.

valet park·ing also **valet serv·ice** /ˌ.. '../ n. [U] the service of having someone else park your car for you at a restaurant, hotel etc.

Val·hal·la /vælˈhælə/ in Norse MYTHOLOGY, a place in the Norse heaven, to which the souls of those who died bravely in battle are taken by the VALKYRIES

val·iant /ˈvælyənt/ adj. very brave, especially in a difficult situation: Despite valiant efforts, firemen were unable to save the house.

val·id /ˈvælɪd/ adj. **1** a valid ticket, document, or agreement can be used legally or is officially acceptable, especially until a particular time or according to particular rules: a valid driver's license | The tourist visa is valid for three months. **2** a valid reason, comparison etc. is based on what is true or sensible, and so should be accepted or treated in a serious way: They had some valid concerns about the safety of the airplane.

val·i·date /ˈvælə,deɪt/ v. [T] **1** FORMAL to prove that something is true or correct, or to make a document or agreement officially and legally acceptable: The Supreme Court has validated the lower court's interpretation of the law. —see also INVALIDATE **2** to make someone feel that their ideas and feelings are respected and considered seriously: Talking with people who think like you helps validate your feelings. **3** if a business validates the piece of paper you receive when you park in a PARKING GARAGE, it puts a special mark on it showing that it will pay the parking costs —**validation** /ˌvælɔˈdeɪʃən/ n. [C,U]

validated park·ing /ˈ.... ,./ n. [U] the system in which a business pays the cost of PARKING for people who use their business

va·lid·i·ty /vɔˈlɪdəti/ n. [U] **1** the state of being real, true, or based on facts: [+ of] Educators are challenging the validity of the tests. **2** the condition of being legally or officially acceptable

va·lise /vɔˈlis, -ˈliz/ n. [C] OLD-FASHIONED a small SUITCASE

Val·i·um /ˈvæliəm/ n. [U] TRADEMARK a drug to make people feel calmer and less anxious

Val·kyr·ie /vælˈkɪri/ n. in Norse MYTHOLOGY, one of Odin's female servants, who ride their horses into battles and take the souls of dead soldiers to Valhalla

Val·let·ta /vɔˈlɛtə/ the capital city of Malta

val·ley /ˈvæli/ n. plural **valleys** [C] an area of lower land between two lines of hills or mountains, usually

with a river flowing through it: the Mississippi River valley

Valley Forge /ˌvæli ˈfɔrdʒ/ a place in the U.S. state of Pennsylvania where George Washington's soldiers stayed during the winter of 1777–78 in the American Revolutionary War. Many men died because of the cold and lack of food.

Va·lois /vælˈwɑ/ the name of a family of French kings who ruled from 1328 to 1589

val·or /ˈvælɔr/ n. [U] LITERARY great courage, especially in war —**valorous** adj. —see also **discretion is the better part of valor** (DISCRETION (4))

val·ua·ble /ˈvælyəbəl, -yuəbəl/ adj. **1** worth a lot of money: a valuable piece of farmland **2** valuable help, information etc. is very useful because it helps you to do something: I think we've all learned a valuable lesson today. **3** important because there is only a limited amount available: Valuable time was wasted correcting Dan's mistakes. —compare INVALUABLE

val·ua·bles /ˈvælyəbəlz/ n. [plural] things that you own that are worth a lot of money, such as jewelry, cameras etc.: Please do not leave money or valuables in the lockers.

val·ua·tion /ˌvælyuˈeɪʃən/ n. [C,U] a judgment about how much something is worth, how effective or useful a particular idea or plan will be etc.: The company's market valuation is now at $2.1 billion.

val·ue¹ /ˈvælyu/ n.
1 money a) [C,U] the amount of money that something is worth, or the qualities that something has that make it worth the money that it costs: Real estate values continue to rise. | increase/decrease etc. in value The French franc has fallen in value against the dollar in recent weeks. | The only item of value (=worth a lot of money) was a small bronze statue. | value for your dollar/money Students today want more value for their dollar. —see also MARKET VALUE, STREET VALUE b) [C] used in advertising to mean a price that is lower than usual: Check out the values this week at Price Chopper. | This three-CD collection is a really good value at $25. —see Usage Note at WORTH²
2 importance [U] the importance or usefulness of something: Fiber has no calories or nutritional value. | The locket has great sentimental value (=importance because it was a gift, it reminds you of someone etc.). | of great/little value His research has been of little practical value.
3 values [plural] your principles about what is right and wrong, or your ideas about what is important in life: shared cultural values
4 math [C] TECHNICAL a mathematical quantity shown by a letter of the alphabet or sign: If K equals 3, what is the value of X?
5 shock/curiosity/novelty etc. value a good or interesting quality something has because it is surprising, different, new etc.: Every once in a while I shave my head for shock value. —see also FACE VALUE, FAMILY VALUES

value² v. [T] **1** to think that something is important to you: He valued Lucille's honesty. **2** [usually passive] to decide how much money something is worth, by comparing it with similar things: [value sth at sth] The estate has been valued at $3.7 million. —**valued** adj.: Arnold remains a valued friend.

value-add·ed /ˌ.. '../ adj. TECHNICAL relating to the increase in value of a product or service at each stage of its production: a value-added industrial process

value-added re·sell·er /ˌ... ... ˈ.../ abbreviation VAR n. [C] a person or company who sells goods after combining them with other goods or services, especially computers

value-added tax /ˌ... .. ˈ./ abbreviation VAT n. [C,U] a tax added to the price of goods and services based on their increase in value at each stage of production

V

value judg·ment /ˈ.. ˌ../ *n.* a decision or judgment about how good something is, based on opinions not facts: *I'm not going to make a value judgment about her lifestyle.*

val·ue·less /ˈvælyulɪs/ *adj.* worth no money or very little money: *valueless currency*

valve /vælv/ *n.* [C] **1** a part of a tube or pipe that opens and shuts like a door to control the flow of liquid, gas, air etc. passing through it: *heart valves* —see picture at BICYCLE[1] **2** the part on a TRUMPET or similar musical instrument that you press to change the sound of the note —see also BIVALVE, SAFETY VALVE

va·moose /væˈmus, vɔ-/ *v.* [I] OLD-FASHIONED to leave a place, especially in a hurry

vamp[1] /væmp/ *n.* [C] OLD-FASHIONED a woman who uses her sexual attractiveness to make men do things for her

vamp[2] *v.* [I] to behave in a sexy way that you think will make people pay attention to you

vam·pire /ˈvæmpaɪɚ/ *n.* [C] a dead person that is believed to suck people's blood by biting their necks

vampire bat /ˈ.. ˌ./ *n.* [C] a South American BAT that sucks the blood of other animals

S W **van** /væn/ *n.* [C] **1** a truck for carrying goods with an 2 enclosed back: *a moving van* **2** a large box-like car that can carry a lot of people

Van Bu·ren /væn ˈbyʊrən/, **Mar·tin** /ˈmɑrt͟n/ (1782–1862) the eighth President of the U.S. and Vice President under Andrew Jackson

Van·cou·ver /vænˈkuvɚ/ **1** the third largest city in Canada, which is in the PROVINCE of British Columbia **2** an island near the southwest coast of Canada

Van·dal /ˈvændl/ one of the Germanic people related to the Goths who moved from Germany into Gaul, Spain, and North Africa, and attacked Rome, in the fifth century A.D.

van·dal /ˈvændl/ *n.* [C] someone who deliberately damages things, especially public property

van·dal·ism /ˈvændlˌɪzəm/ *n.* [U] the crime of deliberately damaging things, especially public property

van·dal·ize /ˈvændlˌaɪz/ *v.* [T] to damage or destroy things deliberately, especially public property: *Most of the public phones have been vandalized.*

Van·der·bilt /ˈvændɚˌbɪlt/, **Cor·ne·li·us** /kɔrˈniliəs/ (1794–1877) a U.S. INDUSTRIALIST who became extremely rich by building steamships and railways in the 19th century

V

Van Dyck /væn ˈdaɪk/, **Sir An·tho·ny** /ˈænθəni/ (1599–1641) a Flemish PAINTER

vane /veɪn/ *n.* [C] A flat surface or blade that is moved by wind or water to produce power to drive a machine —see also WEATHER VANE

Van Gogh /væn ˈgoʊ, ˈgɑf/, **Vin·cent** /ˈvɪnsənt/ (1853–1890) a Dutch PAINTER famous for his paintings using bright colors and thick lines of paint in circular patterns

van·guard /ˈvæŋgɑrd/ *n.* **the vanguard a)** the most advanced group or position in the development of an idea, a change etc.: **in/at the vanguard (of sth)** *Poland put itself at the vanguard of Eastern Europe's democratic revolution.* **b)** the leading position at the front of an army or group of ships moving into battle, or the soldiers who are in this position

va·nil·la[1] /vəˈnɪlə/ *n.* [U] a substance used to give a special taste to ICE CREAM, cakes etc., made from the beans of a tropical plant

vanilla[2] *adj.* **1** having the taste of vanilla: *vanilla ice cream* **2** also **plain-vanilla** plain, ordinary, or uninteresting: *The company produces inexpensive plain-vanilla computer chips.*

van·ish /ˈvænɪʃ/ *v.* [I] **1** to disappear suddenly, especially in a way that cannot easily be explained: *Before she could scream, the man had vanished into the night.* | *Earhart vanished without a trace* (=disappeared so that no sign remained) *on July 2, 1937.* —see also **disappear/vanish into thin air** (THIN[1]

(13)) **2** to stop existing, especially suddenly: *Statistics show that Santa Clara's farmland is vanishing.* **3 a vanishing act** INFORMAL a situation in which someone or something disappears suddenly in a way that is not expected or explained

van·ish·ing point /ˈ... ˌ./ *n.* **the vanishing point** TECHNICAL the point in the distance, especially on a picture, where parallel lines seem to meet

van·i·ty /ˈvænəti/ *n.* [U] **1** too much PRIDE in yourself, so that you are always thinking about yourself and your appearance: *Her vanity kept her from getting a hearing aid.* **2** a DRESSING TABLE **3 the vanity of sth** LITERARY the lack of importance of something compared to other things that are much more important

vanity case /ˈ... ˌ./ *n.* [C] a small box or bag with a handle used by a woman for carrying MAKEUP, a mirror etc.

vanity plate /ˈ... ˌ./ *n.* [C] a car LICENSE PLATE that has a combination of numbers or letters chosen by the owner, so that they spell a word that relates to or describes the owner

vanity press /ˈ... ˌ./ also **vanity pub·lish·er** /ˈ... ˌ../ *n.* [C usually singular] a company that writers pay to print their books

van·quish /ˈvæŋkwɪʃ/ *v.* [T] LITERARY to defeat someone or something completely

van·tage point /ˈvæntɪdʒ ˌpɔɪnt/ also **vantage** *n.* [C] **1** a good position from which you can see something: *We enjoyed the lights of Los Angeles from a vantage point high above the city.* **2** a way of thinking about things that comes from your own particular situation or experiences; POINT OF VIEW: *From Burke's vantage point, there is a lot to be unhappy about.*

Van·u·a·tu /ˌvænuˈɑtu, ˌvænwɑˈtu/ a country in the southwest Pacific Ocean, east of Australia, made up of many VOLCANIC islands

vap·id /ˈvæpɪd/ *adj.* FORMAL lacking intelligence, interest, or imagination: *a vapid TV announcer* —**vapidly** *adv.* —**vapidness** *n.* [U] —**vapidity** /vəˈpɪdəti/ *n.* [U]

va·por /ˈveɪpɚ/ *n.* **1** [C,U] a mass of very small drops of a liquid which float in the air, for example because the liquid has been heated: *water vapor* **2 the vapors** OLD USE a condition when you suddenly feel as if you might FAINT —**vaporous** *adj.*

va·por·ize /ˈveɪpəˌraɪz/ *v.* [I,T] to change into a vapor, or to make something do this: *The fire was so hot that water from the fire hoses vaporized.* —**vaporization** /ˌveɪpərəˈzeɪʃən/ *n.* [U]

va·por·izer /ˈveɪpəˌraɪzɚ/ *n.* [C] a machine that heats water to make steam for people to breathe when they are sick

vapor trail /ˈ.. ˌ./ *n.* [C] the white line that is left in the sky by an airplane

VAR *n.* [C] the abbreviation of VALUE-ADDED RESELLER

var·i·a·ble[1] /ˈvɛriəbəl, ˈvær-/ *adj.* **1** likely to change often: *Expect variable cloudiness and fog tomorrow.* **2** sometimes good and sometimes bad: *Medical insurance coverage in foreign countries is highly variable.* **3** able to be changed: *The drill has variable speeds.* —**variably** *adv.* —**variability** /ˌvɛriəˈbɪləti/ *n.* [U]

variable[2] *n.* [C] **1** something that may be different in different situations, so that you cannot be sure what will happen: *There are too many variables to predict who will win the war.* **2** TECHNICAL a mathematical quantity which can represent several different amounts —compare CONSTANT[2]

var·i·ance /ˈvɛriəns, ˈvær-/ *n.* **1 be at variance (with sb/sth)** FORMAL if two people or things are at variance with each other, they do not agree or are very different: *Her current statement is at variance with what she said July 10.* **2** [C,U] FORMAL the amount by which two or more things are different or by which they change: *a price variance of 5%* **3** [C] LAW the official permission to do something different from what is normally allowed: *The church requested a variance to expand its parking lot.*

var·i·ant /ˈvɛriənt, ˈvær-/ *n.* [C] something that is slightly different from the usual form of something: [+ **of**] *Floyd is a variant of the name Lloyd.* | *the*

Japanese variant of capitalism —**variant** *adj.*: *a variant strain of the disease*

var·i·a·tion /ˌvɛriˈeɪʃən, ˌvær-/ *n.* **1** [C,U] a difference between similar things, or a change from the usual amount or form of something: *There is a great deal of variation among the responses.* | [+ **in**] *slight variations in Mercury's orbit* **2** [C] something that is done in a way that is different from the way it is usually done: *Chase offers a colorful variation on the traditional cookbook theme.* **3** [C] one of a set of short pieces of music, each based on the same simple tune: *Bach's Goldberg variations*

var·i·cose veins /ˌværəkoʊs ˈveɪnz/ *n.* [plural] a medical condition in which the VEINS in your leg become swollen and painful

var·ied /ˈvɛrid, ˈvær-/ *adj.* consisting of or including many different kinds of things or people, especially in a way that seems interesting: *a varied diet* | *The rhythm of the poem is varied.*

var·i·e·gat·ed /ˈvɛriˌgeɪtɪd, ˈvær-/ *adj.* **1** a variegated plant, leaf etc. has different colored marks on it: *variegated holly* **2** FORMAL consisting of a lot of different types of things

s w **va·ri·e·ty** /vəˈraɪəti/ *n. plural* **varieties 1 a variety of sth** a lot of things of the same type that are different from each other in some way: *For a variety of reasons, our team will not be participating.* | *The T-shirts are available in a wide variety of colors.* **2** [C] a type of something, such as a plant or animal, that is different from others in the same group: [+ **of**] *There are about 7000 known varieties of apples.* **3** [U] the different types of things within a group, the differences in a set of actions etc. that make it interesting: *I really like the variety the store has to offer.* | *Add variety to your menu with a vegetable puree.* **4 sb/sth of the...variety** HUMOROUS a particular type of person or thing: *Mata Hari was a dancer of the exotic variety.* **5 variety is the spice of life** used to say that doing a lot of different things, meeting different people etc. is what makes life interesting

variety show /.'... ,./ *n.* [C] a television or radio program or a performance that consists of many different shorter performances, especially musical and humorous ones

variety store /.'... ,./ *n.* [C] a store that sells many different kinds of goods, often at low prices

s w **var·i·ous** /ˈvɛriəs, ˈvær-/ *adj.* [usually before noun] **1** several different: *Long held various positions at the company before becoming President.* **2 various and sundry sth** many different types of something: *Various and sundry rumors about his sex life have been going around.*

var·i·ous·ly /ˈvɛriəsli/ *adv.* in many different ways: **variously described/estimated etc.** *His age has been variously reported as 19 and 22.*

var·mint /ˈvɑrmənt/ *n.* [C] OLD-FASHIONED, SPOKEN **1** a small wild animal, such as a rabbit, that causes a lot of trouble **2** an annoying person

var·nish[1] /ˈvɑrnɪʃ/ *n.* [C,U] a clear liquid that is painted onto things, especially things made of wood, to protect them, or the hard shiny surface produced by this

varnish[2] *v.* [T] to cover something with varnish —see also UNVARNISHED

var·si·ty /ˈvɑrsəti/ *n.* [C,U] the main team that represents a university, college, or school in a sport: *the varsity football team* —compare JV

s w **var·y** /ˈvɛri, ˈværi/ *v.* **varied**, **varying 1** [I] if several things of the same type vary, they are all different from each other: *Test scores vary from school to school.* | [+ **in**] *Tickets vary in price from $8 to $15.* | *The programs have had varying degrees of success.* | **vary greatly/considerably/enormously** *Young children vary enormously in their social abilities.* **2** [I] to change often: *The price of seafood varies according to the season.* | *"How often do you play tennis?" "Oh, it varies."* **3** [T] to regularly change what you do or the way that you do it: *Warhol often varied the colors slightly from one print to the next.* —see also VARIED

vas·cu·lar /ˈvæskyələr/ *adj.* TECHNICAL relating to the tubes through which liquids flow in the bodies of animals or in plants: *vascular tissue*

vase /veɪs, veɪz, vɑz/ *n.* [C] a container used to put flowers in or for decoration

va·sec·to·my /vəˈsɛktəmi/ *n. plural* **vasectomies** [C,U] a medical operation to cut the small tube through which a man's SPERM passes so that he is unable to produce children

Vas·e·line /ˈvæsəˌlin, ˌvæsəˈlin/ *n.* [U] TRADEMARK a soft clear substance used for various medical and other purposes

vas·sal /ˈvæsəl/ *n.* [C] **1** a man in the Middle Ages who was given land to live on by a LORD in return for promising to work or fight for him **2** FORMAL a country that is controlled by another country: *a vassal state*

vast /væst/ *adj.* **1** extremely large: *a vast improvement* | *the vast expanse of the desert* | *Vast numbers of people showed up to help.* **2 the vast majority (of sth)** used when you want to emphasize that something is true about almost all of a group of people or things: *The vast majority of the immigrants have settled in the inner cities.* —**vastness** *n.* [U]

s w

vast·ly /ˈvæstli/ *adv.* very much: *vastly different opinions*

VAT /ˌvi eɪ ˈti, væt/ *n.* [C,U] VALUE-ADDED TAX

vat /væt/ *n.* [C] a very large container for storing liquids in

Vat·i·can /ˈvætɪkən/ *n.* **the Vatican a)** the large PALACE in Rome where the Pope lives **b)** the government of the Pope: *the Vatican's policies on birth control*

Vatican City, the /ˌ... '../ an independent state with Italy, in the city of Rome, which contains the Vatican

vaude·ville /ˈvɔdvɪl, ˈvɑ-/ *n.* [U] a type of theater entertainment, popular from the 1880s to the 1950s, in which there were many short performances of different kinds, including singing, dancing, jokes etc.

Vaughan /vɔn/**, Sa·rah** /ˈsærə/ (1924–1990) a JAZZ singer

Vaughan Wil·liams /ˌ. '../**, Ralph** /reɪf/ (1872–1958) a British musician who wrote CLASSICAL music

vault[1] /vɔlt/ *n.* [C] **1** a room with thick walls and a strong door where money, jewels etc. are kept to prevent them from being stolen or damaged: *a bank vault* **2** a room where people from the same family are buried, often under the floor of a church **3** a jump over something —see also POLE VAULT **4** a roof or ceiling that consists of several ARCHes that are joined together, especially in a church

vault[2] *v.* **1** [I] to move quickly from a lower rank or level to a higher one: [+ **from/to**] *On Sunday Michigan vaulted from No. 4 to the nation's top team.* **2** [T] also **vault over** to jump over something in one movement, using your hands or a pole to help you: *Stephan vaulted over the table and grabbed Gil by the throat.* —**vaulter** *n.* [C]

vault·ed /ˈvɔltɪd/ *adj.* **a vaulted roof/ceiling etc.** a roof, ceiling etc. that consists of several ARCHes which are joined together

vault·ing[1] /ˈvɔltɪŋ/ *n.* [U] **1** ARCHes in a roof **2** the POLE VAULT

vaulting[2] *adj.* **vaulting ambition** LITERARY the desire to achieve as much as possible

vaunt·ed /ˈvɔntɪd, ˈvɑn-/ *adj.* a vaunted achievement, plan, quality etc. is one that people say is very good, important etc., especially with too much pride: *The country's vaunted educational system is not as good as once thought.*

V-chip /ˈvi tʃɪp/ *n.* [C] an electronic CHIP in a television that allows parents to prevent their children from watching programs that are violent or have sex in them

VCR *n.* [C] video cassette recorder; a machine which is used to record television programs or to play VIDEOTAPES

V

VD *n.* [U] OLD-FASHIONED venereal disease; a disease that is passed from one person to another during sex; STD

VDT *n.* [C] TECHNICAL video display terminal; a machine like a television that shows the information from a computer; MONITOR

've /v, əv/ *v.* the short form of "have": *We've started looking through the report.*

veal /vil/ *n.* [U] meat from a CALF (=a young cow)

Veb·len /'vɛblən/, **Thor·stein** /'θɔrstaɪn/ (1857–1929) a U.S. ECONOMIST who wrote books about the way society is organized

vec·tor /'vɛktɚ/ *n.* [C] TECHNICAL **1** a quantity that has a direction as well as a size, usually represented by an ARROW **2** TECHNICAL an insect or small animal that carries disease from one person or animal to another

Ve·da /'veɪdə/ *n.* [C] any of the oldest writings of the Hindu religion

vee·jay /'vidʒeɪ/ *n.* [C] a VJ

veep /vip/ *n.* [C] SPOKEN a VICE PRESIDENT

veer /vɪr/ *v.* [I] **1** [always + adv./prep.] to change direction suddenly: [+ **off/away/across** etc.] *He apparently fell asleep and veered into the oncoming traffic.* | *The storm moved toward the coast before veering out to sea.* **2** [always + adv./prep.] to change suddenly to a very different belief, opinion, or subject: [+ **toward/from** etc.] *Clark never veered from his opinions about Samantha's death.*

veg /vɛdʒ/ also **veg out** *v.* **vegges, vegged, vegging** [I] SPOKEN to relax by doing something that needs very little effort: *We were just vegging out in front of the TV.*

Ve·ga /'veɪgə/, **Lo·pe de** /'loʊpeɪ də/ (1562–1635) a Spanish writer of plays

veg·an /'vigən, 'veɪ-, 'vɛdʒən/ *n.* [C] someone who does not eat meat, fish, eggs, cheese, and milk —**vegan** *adj.*

vege·ta·ble /'vɛdʒtəbəl/ *n.* [C] **1** a plant such as a bean, CARROT, or potato which is eaten raw or cooked: *Make sure to eat plenty of **green vegetables**.* —compare FRUIT[1] **2** INFORMAL, OFFENSIVE someone who cannot think or move because their brain has been damaged in an accident

veg·e·tar·i·an /ˌvɛdʒə'tɛriən/ *n.* [C] someone who eats only vegetables, bread, fruit, eggs etc. and does not eat meat and fish —**vegetarian** *adj.*: *a vegetarian restaurant* —compare VEGAN

veg·e·tar·i·an·ism /ˌvɛdʒə'tɛriəˌnɪzəm/ *n.* [U] the practice of not eating meat or fish

veg·e·tate /'vɛdʒəˌteɪt/ *v.* [I] to not do anything and feel bored because there is nothing interesting for you to do: *When I retired I didn't want to just vegetate.*

veg·e·ta·tion /ˌvɛdʒə'teɪʃən/ *n.* [U] plants in general, especially in one particular area: *They made their way through the thick vegetation in the valley.*

veg·e·ta·tive /'vɛdʒəˌteɪtɪv/ *adj.* **1 a vegetative state** NOT TECHNICAL a condition in which you cannot think or move because your brain has been damaged in an accident **2** relating to plants: *vegetative growth*

veg·gie[1] /'vɛdʒi/ *n.* [C usually plural] INFORMAL a vegetable

veggie[2] *adj.* INFORMAL **a veggie burger/sandwich/burrito** etc. a HAMBURGER, SANDWICH etc. that is made using vegetables or grain, rather than meat

ve·he·ment /'viəmənt/ *adj.* showing very strong feelings or opinions: *Lincoln was a vehement opponent of slavery.* —**vehemently** *adv.*: *Hoff vehemently denies the accusations.* —**vehemence** *n.* [U]

ve·hi·cle /'viɪkəl/ *n.* [C] FORMAL **1** a thing such as a car, bus etc. that is used for carrying people or things from one place to another: *a motor vehicle* **2** something that you use in order to achieve something or as a way of spreading your ideas, expressing your opinions etc.: [+ **for**] *Drawing, like writing, can be a vehicle for exploring your feelings.*

ve·hic·u·lar /vi'hɪkyələ/ *adj.* FORMAL relating to road vehicles: *vehicular traffic*

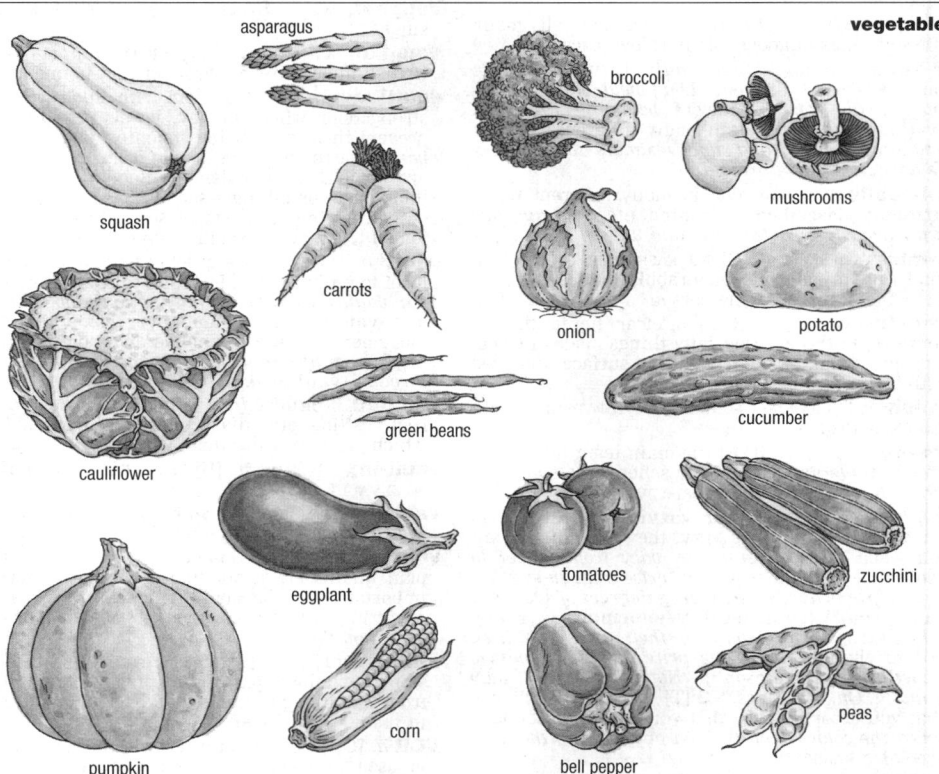

vegetables

asparagus

broccoli

mushrooms

squash

carrots

onion

potato

cauliflower

green beans

cucumber

eggplant

tomatoes

zucchini

pumpkin

corn

bell pepper

peas

V

veil¹ /veɪl/ n. [C] **1** a thin piece of material worn by women to cover their faces at formal occasions such as weddings, or for religious reasons **2 a veil of secrecy/deceit/silence etc.** something that stops you knowing the full truth about a situation: *It is time to lift the veil of secrecy surrounding the murders.* **3 a veil of smoke/clouds etc.** a thin layer of smoke, clouds etc. that covers something so that you cannot see it clearly **4 the veil** the system in Islamic countries in which women must keep their faces covered in public places

veil² v. [T] **1** to cover someone or something with a veil or other cloth: *The women were veiled from head to foot.* **2 be veiled in mystery/secrecy** if something is veiled in mystery or secrecy, very little is known about it and it seems mysterious

veiled /veɪld/ adj. **a veiled threat/attempt/hint etc.** a threat, attempt etc. that is not said or done directly, and is barely hidden by more acceptable words or actions: *The promoters were willing to put aside their thinly veiled racism in order to sell tickets.*

vein /veɪn/ n. **1** [C] one of the tubes through which blood flows toward your heart from other parts of your body —compare ARTERY (1) **2** [C] **a)** one of the thin lines on a leaf or on the wing of an insect **b)** one of the thin lines on a piece of wood, cheese, MARBLE (=type of stone) etc. **3** [C] a thin layer of a valuable metal or mineral which is contained in rock: *a vein of gold* **4** [singular] a particular style or way of doing something, especially when speaking or writing about something: *They can't continue in the same vein because they aren't making any money.* | **in a serious/similar/philosophical etc. vein** *This play treats the same subject in a more humorous vein.* **5 a vein of humor/malice etc.** an amount of a particular quality: *There's a rich vein of* (=a large amount of) *creativity that runs through this town.*

veined /veɪnd/ adj. having a pattern of thin lines on its surface that looks like veins: *blue-veined cheese*

ve·lar /ˈvilər/ adj. TECHNICAL a velar CONSONANT such as /k/ or /g/ is pronounced with the back of your tongue close to the soft part at the top of your mouth —**velar** n. [C]

Ve·las·quez /vəˈlæskɪs, -ˈlæ-/, **Di·e·go Ro·drig·uez de Sil·va y** /diˈeɪgou rəˈdriɡɛs də ˈsɪlvə i/ (1599–1660) a Spanish PAINTER famous for his pictures of the Spanish royal family

Vel·cro /ˈvɛlkrou/ n. [U] TRADEMARK a material used for fastening clothes, which is made from two special pieces of cloth with different surfaces that stick to each other —see picture at FASTENER

veldt, veld /vɛlt/ n. **the veldt** the high flat area of land in South Africa that is covered in grass and has few trees

vel·lum /ˈvɛləm/ n. [U] a material used for making book covers, and in the past for writing on, made from the skins of young cows, sheep, or goats

ve·loc·i·pede /vəˈlɑsəˌpid/ n. [C] a type of bicycle, used in former times

ve·loc·i·ty /vəˈlɑsəti/ n. plural **velocities 1** [C,U] TECHNICAL the speed at which something moves in a particular direction: *the velocity of electrons* **2** [U] FORMAL a high speed —see also ESCAPE VELOCITY

vel·o·drome /ˈvɛləˌdroum/ n. [C] a circular track for bicycle racing

ve·lour /vəˈlʊr/ n. [U] heavy cloth which has a soft surface like velvet

vel·vet /ˈvɛlvɪt/ n. [U] cloth with a soft surface on one side which is used for making clothes, curtains etc.

vel·vet·een /ˌvɛlvəˈtin/ n. [U] cheap material which looks like velvet

vel·vet·y /ˈvɛlvɪti/ adj. looking, feeling, tasting or sounding smooth and soft: *a deep velvety voice*

ve·nal /ˈvinl/ adj. FORMAL using power in a dishonest or unfair way and accepting money as a reward for doing this: *a venal tyrant* —**venality** /viˈnæləti/ n. [U] —compare VENIAL

vend /vɛnd/ v. [T] FORMAL OR LAW to sell something

vend·er /ˈvɛndər/ n. [C] another spelling of vendor

ven·det·ta /vɛnˈdɛtə/ n. [C] **1** an effort to harm a

person or group because you feel very angry about something that they did to you in the past: [+ against] *They've started a political vendetta against me because I told the truth.* **2** a serious argument that has continued for a long time between two people or groups, so that they try to harm each other

vending ma·chine /ˈ.. ..,./ n. [C] a machine that you can get cigarettes, candy, drinks etc. from by putting in a coin

ven·dor /ˈvɛndər/ n. [C] **1** someone who sells things, especially on the street: *a hot-dog vendor* | *Mr. Chang started out working as a street vendor*. **2** a company that sells a particular product, especially to or for another company: *a computer vendor*

ve·neer¹ /vəˈnɪr/ n. **1** [C,U] a thin layer of good quality wood which covers the outside of a piece of furniture which is made of a cheaper material: *walnut veneer* **2** [singular] FORMAL behavior or a quality that hides someone's real character or feelings or the way something really is: [+ of] *a thin veneer of modesty*

ve·neer² v. [T + with/in] to cover something with a veneer

ven·er·a·ble /ˈvɛnərəbəl/ adj. **1** FORMAL OR HUMOROUS a venerable person or thing is very old and respected because of their age, experience, historical importance etc.: *a venerable New York City law firm* **2** FORMAL also **Venerable** considered very holy or important in a particular religion

ven·er·ate /ˈvɛnəˌreɪt/ v. [T] FORMAL to treat someone or something with great respect, especially because they are old or connected with the past: *Ataturk died in 1938, but he is still widely venerated in Turkey.* —**veneration** /ˌvɛnəˈreɪʃən/ n. [U]

ve·ne·re·al dis·ease /vəˈnɪriəl dɪˈziz/ n. [C,U] VD

Ve·ne·tian /vəˈniʃən/ adj. relating to or coming from Venice —**Venetian** n. [C]

Venetian blind /. ...,. ˈ./ n. [C] a set of long flat bars of plastic or metal which can be raised or lowered to cover a window

Ven·e·zue·la /ˌvɛnəˈzweɪlə/ a country in the north of South America, east of Colombia and west of Brazil —**Venezuelan** n., adj.

venge·ance /ˈvɛndʒəns/ n. **1** [U] the act of doing something violent or harmful that you do to someone in order to punish them for harming you, your family etc.: *Thousands have joined the rebels, seeking vengeance against the government.* **2 with a vengeance** more completely or with more energy than is expected or normal: *The storm struck the Carolina coast with a vengeance.* —compare AVENGE, REVENGE¹

venge·ful /ˈvɛndʒfəl/ adj. LITERARY very eager to punish someone: *a vengeful God* —**vengefully** adv.

ve·ni·al /ˈviniəl/ adj. FORMAL a venial fault, mistake etc. is not very serious and can therefore be forgiven: *a venial sin* —compare VENAL

ven·i·son /ˈvɛnəsən/ n. [U] the meat of a DEER

Venn di·a·gram /ˈvɛn ˌdaɪəgræm/ n. [C] a picture that shows the relationship between a number of things by using circles that OVERLAP each other

ven·om /ˈvɛnəm/ n. [U] **1** a liquid poison that some snakes, insects etc. produce and that they use when biting or stinging another animal or insect **2** extreme anger or hatred: *Suzanne reacted with angry venom.*

ven·om·ous /ˈvɛnəməs/ adj. **1** a venomous snake, insect etc. produces poison to attack its enemies **2** full of extreme hatred or anger: *a venomous debate over health care* —**venomously** adv.

ve·nous /ˈvinəs/ adj. TECHNICAL relating to the VEINS (=tubes that carry the blood) in your body

vent¹ /vɛnt/ n. [C] **1** a hole or pipe through which gases, smoke, liquid etc. can enter or escape from an enclosed space or a container: *an air vent* **2 give vent to sth** FORMAL to do something to express a strong feeling, especially of anger: *Gary grew*

V

impatient and finally gave vent to his anger. **3** TECH-NICAL a narrow straight opening at the bottom of a JACKET or coat, at the sides or back **4** TECHNICAL the small hole through which small animals, birds, fish, and snakes get rid of waste matter from their bodies

vent² *v.* **1** [I,T] INFORMAL to do or say something to express your feelings, especially anger, often in a way that is unfair: *Thanks for letting me vent a little.* | *He called up a friend in Chicago to vent his spleen* (=express his anger). **2** [T] to allow gases, smoke, liquid etc. to escape from an enclosed space or a container, or to make the container able to do this —**venting** *n.* [U]

ven·ti·late /'vɛntḷˌeɪt/ *v.* [T] **1** to let fresh air into a room, building etc.: *Ventilate your house when painting.* **2** FORMAL to express your opinions or feelings about something: *Doctrinal issues were never ventilated.* —**ventilation** /ˌvɛntəˈleɪʃən/ *n.* [U] *a ventilation system*

ven·ti·lat·ed /'vɛntḷˌeɪtɪd/ *adj.* **1** a ventilated room or space has fresh air passing through it: **well-venti-lated/poorly ventilated etc.** *Make sure the attic is well-ventilated.* **2** something that is ventilated has holes cut in it to allow air to pass in and out: *ventilated shoes*

ven·ti·la·tor /'vɛntḷˌeɪtɚ/ *n.* [C] **1** a piece of equipment that pumps air into and out of someone's lungs when they cannot breathe without help; RESPIRA-TOR **2** a thing designed to let fresh air into a room, building etc.

ven·tral /'vɛntrəl/ *adj.* [only before noun] TECHNICAL relating to the stomach of an animal or fish —com-pare DORSAL

ven·tri·cle /'vɛntrɪkəl/ *n.* [C] TECHNICAL **1** one of the two spaces in the bottom of your heart from which blood is pumped out into your body —compare AURICLE **2** a small hollow place in your brain or in an organ

ven·tril·o·quist /vɛnˈtrɪləˌkwɪst/ *n.* [C] someone who can speak without moving their lips and makes the sound seem to come from a DUMMY (=figure of a person or animal), usually as part of a performance —**ventriloquism** *n.* [U]

sw **ven·ture¹** /'vɛntʃɚ/ *n.* [C] a new business activity that involves taking risks: *a real-estate venture* —see also JOINT VENTURE

venture² *v.* FORMAL **1** [I always + adv./prep.] to risk going somewhere when it could be dangerous: [+ out/through/into etc.] *I take my dog with me when I venture out at night.* **2** [T] to say something although you are not sure of it, or are afraid of how someone may react to it: *If I may venture an opin-ion, I'd say the plan needs more thought.* | **venture to say/ask/claim etc.** *I couldn't even venture to guess how much money he makes.* **3 nothing ven-tured, nothing gained** used to say that you cannot achieve anything unless you take a risk **4** [T] to take the risk of losing something; GAMBLE

venture cap·i·tal /ˌ.. ˈ.../ *n.* [U] money that is lent to someone so that they can start a new business

ven·ture·some /'vɛntʃɚsəm/ *adj.* LITERARY **1** always ready to take risks: *a venturesome spirit* **2** a ven-turesome action involves taking risks

ven·ue /'vɛnyu/ *n.* [C] a place or a building where people go for an arranged event or activity: *a 2500 seat concert venue*

Ve·nus /'vinəs/ *n.* **1** the PLANET that is second in order from the Sun **2** the Roman name for the goddess Aphrodite

Venus fly·trap /ˌvinəs 'flaɪtræp/ *n.* [C] a plant that catches and eats insects

ve·rac·i·ty /vəˈræsəti/ *n.* [U] FORMAL the quality of being true or of telling the truth —**veracious** /vəˈreɪʃəs/ *adj.*

ve·ran·da, verandah /vəˈrændə/ *n.* [C] an open area with a floor and usually a roof that is built on the side of a house on the ground floor

verb /vɚb/ *n.* [C] a word or group of words that is used to describe an action, experience, or state, for example "see," "be," "put on," or "may" —see also AUXILIARY VERB, PHRASAL VERB

ver·bal /'vɚbəl/ *adj.* **1** spoken, rather than written: *verbal communication* —compare NONVERBAL **2** relat-ing to words, or using words: *verbal skill* | *verbal abuse* **3** relating to a verb —**verbally** *adv.*

ver·bal·ize /'vɚbəˌlaɪz/ *v.* [I,T] FORMAL to express something in words: *Encourage your children to ver-balize their feelings.*

verbal noun /ˌ.. ˈ./ TECHNICAL *n.* [C] a GERUND

ver·ba·tim /vɚˈbeɪtɪm/ *adj. adv.* repeating the actual words that were spoken or written: *a verbatim quote* | *She recited the speech verbatim.*

ver·bi·age /'vɚbi-ɪdʒ/ *n.* [U] FORMAL too many unnec-essary words in speech or writing: *Cut out the excess verbiage.*

ver·bose /vɚˈboʊs/ *adj.* FORMAL talking too much, or using or containing too many words: *a verbose television sportscaster* —**verbosity** /vɚˈbɑsəti/ *n.* [U] —compare VERBAL

ver·bo·ten /vɚˈboʊtⁿn, fɚ-/ *adj.* HUMOROUS not allowed; FORBIDDEN: *Smoking in the workplace is now strictly verboten.*

ver·dant /'vɚdənt/ *adj.* LITERARY verdant land is cov-ered with freshly growing green grass and plants: *verdant hills*

Ver·di /'vɛrdi/, **Giu·sep·pe** /dʒuˈsɛpi/ (1813–1901) an Italian musician who wrote OPERAs

ver·dict /'vɚdɪkt/ *n.* [C] **1** an official decision made by a JURY in a court of law about whether someone is guilty or not guilty of a crime: *a guilty verdict* | *The jury reached a verdict after four days of delib-eration.* | **return/deliver/render a verdict** (=give a verdict) **2** an official decision or opinion made by a person or group that has authority: *The Ethics Com-mittee will deliver its verdict next week.* **3** INFORMAL an opinion or decision about something: [+ on] *What's your verdict on the movie?*

ver·di·gris /'vɚdəˌgri, -ˌgris/ *n.* [U] a greenish-blue substance that forms a thin layer on COPPER or BRASS when they are kept in wet conditions

ver·dure /'vɚdʒɚ, -dyɚ/ *n.* [U] LITERARY the bright green color of grass, plants, trees etc., or the plants themselves

verge¹ /vɚdʒ/ *n.* [C] **be on the verge of (doing) sth** to be about to do something: *on the verge of divorce* | *He seemed on the verge of making a great business deal.*

verge² *v.*

verge on sth *phr. v.* [T] to be very close to an extreme or harmful state or condition: *Her eyes were closed, and her heavy breathing verged on snoring.* | **verge on the impossible/ridiculous etc.** *Sometimes his beliefs verge on the fanatical.*

ver·i·fi·ca·tion /ˌvɛrəfəˈkeɪʃən/ *n.* [U] proof that something is real, true, legal, or allowed, or the act of checking this: [+ of] *Both sides have agreed to international verification of the cease-fire.*

ver·i·fy /'vɛrəˌfaɪ/ *v.* **verified, verifying** [T] **1** to find out if a fact, statement etc. is correct or true; CHECK: *Accountants are working to verify the figures.* | **[verify sth with sb]** *If you doubt the information, you can verify it with Ms. Sherwood.* | **[verify that]** *Could you call to verify that our names are still on the list?* **2** to state that something is true; CONFIRM: *The prisoner's statement was verified by several witnesses.* —**verifiable** /ˌvɛrəˈfaɪəbəl/ *adj.*

ver·i·ly /'vɛrəli/ *adv.* BIBLICAL truly

ver·i·si·mil·i·tude /ˌvɛrəsəˈmɪləˌtud/ *n.* [U] FORMAL the quality of a piece of art, a performance etc. that makes it seem like something real

ver·i·ta·ble /'vɛrətəbəl/ *adj.* FORMAL a word used to emphasize a comparison that you think is correct: *The male bird is a veritable rainbow of colors.* —**ver-itably** *adv.*

ver·i·ty /'vɛrəti/ *n. plural* **verities** [C usually plural] FORMAL an important principle or fact about life, the world etc., that is true in all situations: *one of the eternal verities of life*

Ver·laine /vɚˈleɪn, -ˈlɛn/, **Paul** (1844–1896) a French poet

Ver·meer /vɚˈmɪr/, **Jan** /yɑn/ (1632–1675) a Dutch PAINTER famous for his pictures of ordinary scenes from daily life

ver·mi·cel·li /ˌvɚməˈtʃɛli, -ˈsɛli/ *n.* [U] a type of PASTA that is in the shape of long thin strings

ver·mil·lion /vɚˈmɪlyən/ *n.* [U] a very bright red color —**vermillion** *adj.*

ver·min /ˈvɚmɪn/ *n.* [plural] **1** small animals or insects that are harmful or difficult to control —compare PEST **2** people who cause strong feelings of DISGUST or hate: *Vermin like that should never be allowed near children.* —**verminous** *adj.*

Ver·mont /vɚˈmɑnt/ *written abbreviation* **VT** a state in the northeastern U.S.

ver·mouth /vɚˈmuθ/ *n.* [U] an alcoholic drink made from wine that has strong-tasting substances added to it

ver·nac·u·lar /vɚˈnækyəlɚ/ *n.* [C usually singular] the language or DIALECT spoken in a country or area, especially when it is not the official language —**vernacular** *adj.*

ver·nal /ˈvɚnl/ *adj.* [only before noun] LITERARY OR TECHNICAL relating to the spring season

Verne /vɚn/, **Jules** /dʒulz/ (1828–1905) a French writer of SCIENCE FICTION

ver·sa /ˈvɚsə/ —see VICE VERSA

ver·sa·tile /ˈvɚsətl/ *adj.* APPROVING **1** good at doing a lot of different things and able to learn new skills quickly and easily: *a versatile athlete* **2** having many different uses: *Few foods are as versatile as cheese.* —**versatility** /ˌvɚsəˈtɪləti/ *n.* [U]

verse /vɚs/ *n.* **1** [C] a set of lines that forms one part of a song: *I only know the words to the first verse.* —compare CHORUS¹ (1) **2** [U] words arranged in the form of poetry: *The entire play is written in verse.* —compare PROSE —see also BLANK VERSE, FREE VERSE **3** [C] a set of lines of poetry that forms one part of a poem, and that usually has a pattern that is repeated in the other parts **4** [C] one of the numbered groups of sentences that make up each CHAPTER of a book of the Bible —see also **give/quote chapter and verse** (CHAPTER (5))

versed /vɚst/ *adj.* **be versed in sth** to know a lot about a subject, or to be skillful at doing something; WELL-VERSED: [+ in] *The judges are all highly versed in Islamic law.*

ver·si·fi·ca·tion /ˌvɚsəfəˈkeɪʃən/ *n.* [U] TECHNICAL the particular pattern that a poem is written in

S W ②②
ver·sion /ˈvɚʒən/ *n.* [C] **1** a copy of something that is slightly different from other forms of it: [+ of] *The CD contains instrumental jazz versions of Gershwin classics.* | *a simpler/earlier/later etc. version of sth This was written with an older version of Word-Perfect.* **2** a description of an event given by one person, especially when it is compared with someone else's description of the same thing: [+ of] *I'm not sure I believe Bobby's version of the story.* **3** a translation of a book, poem, or other piece of writing: [+ of] *the King James Version of the Bible* | *The Spanish version of the journal appears one week after the English version.*

ver·so /ˈvɚsoʊ/ *n.* [C] TECHNICAL a page on the LEFT-HAND side of a book —**verso** *adj.* —compare RECTO

S W ②
ver·sus /ˈvɚsəs/ *prep.* **1** used when comparing the advantages of two different things, ideas etc.: *The story revolves around the classic theme of love versus duty.* | *She will earn $2,500 per month under the new plan, versus $2,400 under the old one.* **2** *written abbreviation* **vs.** or **v.** used to show that two people or teams are against each other in a game or court case: *the Broncos versus New England* | *the Supreme Court decision in Brown versus the Board of Education*

ver·te·bra /ˈvɚtəbrə/ *n. plural* **vertebrae** /-breɪ, -bri/ [C] one of the small hollow bones down the middle of your back —**vertebral** *adj.*

ver·te·brate /ˈvɚtəbrət, -ˌbreɪt/ *n.* [C] a living creature that has a BACKBONE (2) —**vertebrate** *adj.* —compare INVERTEBRATE

ver·tex /ˈvɚtɛks/ *n. plural* **vertices** /-təsiz/ or **vertexes** [C + of] TECHNICAL **1** the angle opposite the base of a shape such as a PYRAMID, CONE, TRIANGLE etc. **2** the point where the two lines of an angle meet **3** the highest point of something

ver·ti·cal¹ /ˈvɚtɪkəl/ *adj.*
1 pointing straight up and down in a line and forming an angle of 90 degrees with the ground or with another straight line: *vertical stripes* | *a terrifying vertical drop of 3,500 feet* **2** having a structure in which there are top, middle, and bottom levels: *a vertical management arrangement* **3** TECHNICAL involving all the different stages of a product or service, from producing it to selling it: *vertical integration of the industry* —**vertically** /-kli/ *adv.* —compare HORIZONTAL¹

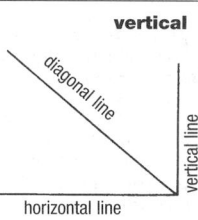

vertical
diagonal line
vertical line
horizontal line

vertical² *n.* **the vertical** the direction or position of something that is vertical

ver·tig·i·nous /vɚˈtɪdʒənəs/ *adj.* FORMAL **1** making you feel DIZZY and sick: *a vertiginous 400 foot drop* **2** feeling DIZZY and sick

ver·ti·go /ˈvɚtɪˌgoʊ/ *n.* [U] a sick DIZZY feeling, often caused by looking down from a very high place or by too much movement around you

verve /vɚv/ *n.* [U] the quality of being cheerful and excited which is shown in the way someone does something: *Pat has a remarkable verve for life.*

S W ①①
ve·ry¹ /ˈvɛri/ *adv.* **1** [+ adj./adv.] used to emphasize an adjective or adverb or to add force to an expression: *It's very cold outside.* | *Sid gets embarrassed very easily.* | *There is a very real possibility that two stores will have to be closed.* | *The two brothers died on the very same day.* **2** [+ adj.] used to emphasize SUPERLATIVE adjectives: *Carter went to the very best schools.* **3 not very a)** only slightly: *The freezer's not very cold – is it broken?* **b)** used before a quality to mean exactly the opposite of that quality: *She wasn't very happy* (=she was angry) *when I told her you weren't coming.* **4 sb's very own (sth)** used to emphasize the fact that something belongs to one particular person and to no one else: *I finally have my very own bedroom.* **5 very much** a lot, or to a great degree: *I haven't read very much of the book yet.* | *I know Glenn would like very much to be here today.* **6 very well/good** SPOKEN, FORMAL said when you understand and accept what someone has said, especially when you are not happy about it: *"The shipment should be here tomorrow." "Very well, I'll come back then."* **7 sb can't very well do sth** SPOKEN used to say that it would not be appropriate or possible for someone to do something: *I already invited them! I can't very well ask them not to come now.* **8 very much so** SPOKEN used to emphasize that you mean "yes" or "to a great degree": *"Were you surprised?" "Very much so."*

V

USAGE NOTE: VERY

GRAMMAR
Do not use **very** to emphasize adjectives or adverbs that already have strong meanings, such as "starving," "huge," "terrible" etc.: *By the time I got home I was exhausted* (NOT *"very exhausted"*). Do not use **very** before phrases that begin with "in," "on," "at" etc. In formal English, you can use **very much** instead: *His life is very much in danger* (NOT *"very in danger"*).

S W ②②
very² *adj.* **1 the/this/that very...** used to emphasize a noun: *He died in this very room.* | *We have to leave this very minute* (=now). | *The very idea that Dawn could become a famous actress is ridiculous.* | *Then she went and did the very thing I had asked her not to.* | *Abby was disgusted by the very thought of* (=just thinking about) *touching him.* **2 the very top/back/beginning etc.** used to emphasize an

extreme point in time or position in space: *We stayed till the very end of the parade.* | *The keys were in the very bottom of my purse.* —see Usage Note at ALMOST

very high fre·quen·cy /ˌ... ˈ.../ *n.* [U] VHF

very low fre·quen·cy /ˌ... ˈ.../ *n.* [U] TECHNICAL: see VLF

ves·pers /ˈvɛspɚz/ *n.* [U] the evening service in some types of Christian churches

Ves·puc·ci /vɛˈsputʃi/, **A·mer·i·go** /əˈmɛrɪˌgoʊ/ (1451–1512) an Italian sailor and EXPLORER who sailed to the Caribbean Sea and South America and discovered the place where the Amazon River flows into the ocean, and after whom America was named

ves·sel /ˈvɛsəl/ *n.* [C] **1** FORMAL a ship or large boat: *a sailing vessel* **2** OLD USE OR FORMAL a container for holding liquids **3** TECHNICAL a tube that carries blood through your body, such as a VEIN, or that carries liquid through a plant

vest[1] /vɛst/ *n.* [C] **1** a piece of clothing without SLEEVES that has buttons down the front and is worn over a shirt, often under a JACKET as part of a suit **2** a SWEATER without SLEEVES **3** a piece of special clothing without SLEEVES that is worn to protect your body: *a bulletproof vest*

vest[2] *v.* [T usually passive] FORMAL to give someone the official or legal right to use power, property etc.: **[vest sth in sb]** *The power to grant pardons is vested in the president alone.* | **[vest sb with sth]** *The agency is vested with the authority to regulate working conditions.*

Ves·ta /ˈvɛstə/ the Roman name for the goddess Hestia

vest·ed /ˈvɛstɪd/ *adj.* **1 a vested interest** if you have a vested interest in something happening, you have a strong reason for wanting it to happen because you will get an advantage from it: *We all have a vested interest in making this peace process work.* **2 vested interests** the groups of people who have a vested interest in something: *Powerful vested interests are keeping American products out of that market.* **3** vested rights, property etc. belong to you and cannot be taken away **4** having full rights to use or keep money or property: *After three years in the pension plan, you become fully vested.* **5** wearing a vest

ves·ti·bule /ˈvɛstəˌbyul/ *n.* [C] FORMAL **1** a wide passage or small room inside the front door of a public building **2** the enclosed passage at each end of a railroad car that connects it with the next car

ves·tige /ˈvɛstɪdʒ/ *n.* [C] FORMAL **1** a small part or amount of something that still remains when most of it does not exist anymore: *The new laws get rid of* ***the last vestiges of*** *Communist rule.* **2** the smallest possible amount of a quality or feeling: [+ **of**] *Marks was not shown even a vestige of pity.*

ves·tig·i·al /vɛˈstɪdʒiəl, -dʒəl/ *adj.* **1** FORMAL remaining as a sign that something existed after most of it has disappeared: *vestigial remnants of Western influence in the city* **2** TECHNICAL a vestigial body part on an animal has almost disappeared, because that type of animal does not use it anymore: *Some snakes have vestigial legs.*

vest·ment /ˈvɛstmənt/ *n.* [C usually plural] a piece of clothing worn by priests during church services

vest-pock·et /ˌ. ˈ../ *adj.* [only before noun] **1** using only a small amount of space: *a vest-pocket park* **2** made to fit inside a VEST pocket: *a vest-pocket notebook*

ves·try /ˈvɛstri/ *n.* [C] a small room in a church where the priest and CHOIR change into their vestments and where holy plates, cups etc. are stored

Ve·su·vi·us /vəˈsuviəs/ also **Mount Vesuvius** a VOLCANO in southeast Italy

vet[1] /vɛt/ *n.* [C] INFORMAL **1** a VETERINARIAN **2** a VETERAN[1]: *a Vietnam vet*

vet[2] *v.* [T] **1** to check someone's past activities, relationships etc. in order to make sure they are the right person for a particular job, especially one that involves dealing with secret information: *Tanner*

had already been vetted and confirmed for his job at the CIA. **2** to check a report or speech carefully to make sure it is acceptable

vet·er·an[1] /ˈvɛtərən/ *n.* [C] **1** someone who has been a soldier, sailor etc. in a war: *Gulf War veterans* **2** someone who has had a lot of experience of a particular activity: *a 12-year classroom veteran* | [+ **of**] *a veteran of the 1960s civil rights battles*

veteran[2] *adj.* [only before noun] having a lot of experience in a particular activity: *a veteran journalist* | *a 28-year veteran congressman*

Veterans Day /ˈ... ˌ./ *n.* [C,U] a holiday on November 11 during which people show special respect to people who fought in a war as soldiers, SAILORS etc.

Veterans of For·eign Wars /ˌ... ˌ.. ˈ./ VFW

vet·er·i·nar·i·an /ˌvɛtərəˈnɛriən, ˌvɛtrə-, ˌvɛtˈnɛr-/ *n.* [C] someone who is trained to give medical care and treatment to sick animals; VET

vet·er·i·nar·y /ˈvɛtərəˌnɛri, ˈvɛtrə-/ *adj.* [only before noun] TECHNICAL relating to the medical care and treatment of sick animals: *veterinary medicine*

ve·to[1] /ˈvitoʊ/ *v.* **vetoed, vetoing** [T] **1** to officially refuse to allow something to happen, especially something that other people or organizations have agreed: *The governor vetoed another version of the bill last fall.* **2** to refuse to accept a particular plan or suggestion: *Jenny wanted to invite all her friends, but I quickly vetoed that idea.*

veto[2] *n.* plural **vetoes** [C,U] a refusal to give official permission for something, or the right to refuse to give such permission: *Congress has voted to* ***override*** *the President's* ***veto on*** (=change his decision to give permission for) *the labor bill.*

vex /vɛks/ *v.* [T] OLD-FASHIONED to make someone feel annoyed or worried —see also VEXED, VEXING

vex·a·tion /vɛkˈseɪʃən/ *n.* **1** [U] FORMAL the feeling of being worried or annoyed by something **2** [C] OLD-FASHIONED something that worries or annoys you

vex·a·tious /vɛkˈseɪʃəs/ *adj.* OLD-FASHIONED making you feel annoyed or worried

vexed /vɛkst/ *adj.* **1** OLD-FASHIONED [+ **at/with**] annoyed or worried **2 a vexed question/issue** a complicated problem that has caused a lot of arguments and is difficult to solve: *No politician wants to discuss the vexed issue of paying for tax cuts.*

vex·ing /ˈvɛksɪŋ/ *adj.* making you feel annoyed or worried: *Few problems are as vexing as welfare reform.*

V-for·ma·tion /ˈvi fɔrˌmeɪʃən/ *n.* [C] if birds or airplanes fly in a V-formation, they form the shape of the letter V as they fly

VFW Veterans of Foreign Wars; a U.S. organization for former soldiers who have fought in wars abroad

VGA *n.* [singular] video graphics array; a standard of GRAPHICS (=pictures and letters) on a computer screen that has many different colors and is of a high quality

VHF *n.* [U] very high frequency; a range of radio WAVES between 30 and 300 MEGAHERTZ, used also for television —compare UHF

VHS *n.* [U] TRADEMARK the type of VIDEOTAPE used by most people in the U.S.

vi·a /ˈvaɪə, ˈviə/ *prep.* **1** traveling through a place on the way to another place: *We flew to Bali via Singapore.* **2** using a particular person, machine etc. to send something: *Do not send the application via fax.*

vi·a·ble /ˈvaɪəbəl/ *adj.* **1** a viable plan or system can work successfully: *Everyone's criticizing the plan, but no one is offering* ***a viable alternative.*** | **economically/commercially/politically etc. viable** *There are still doubts whether the electric car is commercially viable.* **2** TECHNICAL able to continue to live or to develop into a living thing —**viability** /ˌvaɪəˈbɪləti/ *n.* [U] *the viability of the treaty*

vi·a·duct /ˈvaɪəˌdʌkt/ *n.* [C] a long high bridge across a valley that has a road or railroad track on it

Vi·ag·ra /vaɪˈægrə/ *n.* [U] TRADEMARK a drug that helps men have ERECTIONS (1)

vi·al /ˈvaɪəl/ *n.* [C] a small bottle, especially for liquid medicines: *a vial of pure cinnamon oil*

vi·ands /ˈvaɪəndz/ *n.* [plural] OLD USE food

V

vibe /vaɪb/ *n.* INFORMAL **1** [C usually plural] the feelings that a particular person, group, or situation seems to produce and that you react to: **good/bad/strange etc. vibes** *I'm getting weird vibes from this guy – I think maybe he's lying to us.* **2 vibes** INFORMAL a vibraphone

vi·brant /'vaɪbrənt/ *adj.* **1** exciting and full of activity and energy: *Hong Kong is a vibrant, fascinating city.* **2** a vibrant color or light is bright and strong: *vibrant fall colors* —**vibrancy** *n.* [U] —**vibrantly** *adv.*

vi·bra·phone /'vaɪbrəˌfoʊn/ *n.* [C] a musical instrument that consists of metal bars that you hit to produce a sound —**vibraphonist** *n.* [C]

vi·brate /'vaɪbreɪt/ *v.* [I,T] to shake or make something shake continuously with small fast movements: *Strings vibrate more quickly if they are short and thin.*

vi·bra·tion /vaɪ'breɪʃən/ *n.* [C,U] **1** a continuous slight shaking movement: *the vibrations of the ship's engine* **2** [C usually plural] a VIBE (1)

vib·ra·to /vɪ'brɑtoʊ, vaɪ-/ *n.* [U] a way of singing or playing a musical note so that it goes up and down very slightly in PITCH

vi·bra·tor /'vaɪbreɪtɚ/ *n.* [C] a piece of electrical equipment that produces a small shaking movement, used especially in MASSAGE or to get sexual pleasure

vic·ar /'vɪkɚ/ *n.* [C] **1** a Catholic priest who represents a BISHOP or the Pope **2** an Episcopal priest who is in charge of a CHAPEL **3** a priest in the official Church of England who is in charge of a church in a particular area

vic·ar·age /'vɪkərɪdʒ/ *n.* [C] a house where a vicar lives

vi·car·i·ous /vaɪ'kɛriəs/ *adj.* [only before noun] experienced by watching, hearing, or reading about someone else doing something, rather than by doing it yourself: **vicarious pleasure/satisfaction/excitement etc.** *I got a vicarious thrill listening to his stories.* —**vicariously** *adv.*: *Many viewers live vicariously through the show.*

vice¹ /vaɪs/ *adj.* **a vice principal/chairman/mayor etc.** a person next in official rank below someone in a position of authority, who can represent them or act instead of them

vice² *n.* **1** [U] criminal activities that involve sex, drugs, GAMBLING etc. **2** [C] a bad habit: *Smoking is one of his few vices.* **3** [C] a bad or immoral quality in someone's character —opposite VIRTUE **4** [C] another spelling of VISE

vice ad·mi·ral /ˌ. '...ˌ/ *n.* [C] a high rank in the navy, or someone who has this rank

vice chan·cel·lor /ˌ. '...ˌ/ *n.* [C] someone who is in charge of a particular part of some universities: *the vice chancellor for student affairs*

vice pres·i·dent /ˌ. '...ˌ/ *n.* [C] **1** the person who is next in rank to the President of a country and who is responsible for the President's duties if he or she is unable to do them **2** someone who is responsible for a particular part of a company: *the vice president of human resources*

vice·roy /'vaɪsrɔɪ/ *n.* [C] a man who was sent by the king or queen to rule another country in past times

vice squad /'. ./ *n.* [C usually singular] the part of the police force that deals with crimes involving sex, drugs, GAMBLING etc.

vi·ce ver·sa /ˌvaɪs 'vɚsə, ˌvaɪsə-/ *adv.* used to mean the opposite of a situation you have just described: *There's a bag for you and a box for Tom, or vice versa.*

vi·cin·i·ty /və'sɪnəti/ *n.* **in the vicinity (of sth)** FORMAL **a)** in the area around a particular place: *Smith says she was attacked in the vicinity of the bus station.* **b)** close to a particular amount or measurement: *The meteorites are somewhere in the vicinity of 4.5 billion years old.*

vi·cious /'vɪʃəs/ *adj.* **1** violent and dangerous, and likely to hurt someone: *a vicious killer* | *vicious dogs* | *a vicious crime* **2** cruelly and deliberately trying to hurt someone's feelings or make their character seem bad: *John gets pretty vicious when he's drunk.* | **a vicious attack/campaign/rumor etc.**

Sands has become the target of vicious rumors about her personal life. **3** very strong or severe: *a vicious headache* —**viciously** *adv.*: *The dog growled viciously.* —**viciousness** *n.* [U]

vicious cir·cle also **vicious cy·cle** /ˌ.. '../ *n.* [singular] a situation in which one problem causes another problem that then causes the first problem again, so that the whole process continues to be repeated: *Abused children often grow up to abuse their own children – it's a vicious circle.*

vi·cis·si·tudes /və'sɪsəˌtudz/ *n.* [plural] the continuous changes and problems that affect a situation or someone's life: **[+ of]** *the vicissitudes of married life*

Vicks·burg /'vɪksbɚg/ a city in the U.S. state of Mississippi, where an important battle was fought during the American Civil War

vic·tim /'vɪktɪm/ *n.* [C] **1** someone who has been attacked, robbed, or murdered: *It is all too common to blame the victim in rape cases.* | **a crime/rape/murder etc. victim** *Most homicide victims are under 30.* **2** someone who suffers because they are affected by a bad situation or by an illness: *a victim of circumstance* | **a famine/earthquake/flood etc. victim** *Flood victims spent the night in local shelters.* | **a polio/cholera/AIDS etc. victim** *The drug helps ovarian cancer victims live longer.* **3** something that is badly affected or destroyed by a situation or action: *In the late '70s, steel mills fell victim to* (=became a victim of) *foreign competition and changes in the industry.* **4 be a victim of its own success** to be badly affected by some unexpected results of being very successful: *The helpline is a victim of its own success with so many people calling that no one can get through.* —see also FASHION VICTIM

vic·tim·ize /'vɪktəˌmaɪz/ *v.* [T] to deliberately treat someone unfairly: *Brown feels he has been victimized by the press.* —**victimization** /ˌvɪktəmə'zeɪʃən/ *n.* [U]

vic·tor /'vɪktɚ/ *n.* [C] **1** FORMAL the winner of a battle, game, competition etc. **2 to the victor go/belong the spoils** used to say that the person or group that wins a competition, war etc. gets power, valuable things etc.

Vic·to·ri·a /vɪk'tɔriə/ **1** the capital city of the Canadian PROVINCE of British Columbia **2** a state in southeast Australia **3** the capital city of the Seychelles

Victoria, Lake the largest lake in Africa, which is surrounded by Uganda, Tanzania, and Kenya

Victoria, Queen (1819–1901) the British queen from 1837 until her death, who also had the title "Empress of India"

Victoria Falls /.,... './ a very large WATERFALL on the Zambezi River between Zimbabwe and Zambia in southern Africa

Vic·to·ri·an¹ /vɪk'tɔriən/ *adj.* **1** relating to or coming from the period from 1837 to 1901 when Victoria was Queen of England: *Victorian architecture* **2** having the strict moral attitudes typical of the society of this period

Victorian² *n.* [C] **1** a house built in the Victorian style **2** an English person living in the period when Queen Victoria ruled

vic·to·ri·ous /vɪk'tɔriəs/ *adj.* having won a victory: *a victorious candidate* | *We were confident that the Allies would emerge victorious* (=finally win). —**victoriously** *adv.*

vic·to·ry /'vɪktəri/ *n. plural* **victories** [C,U] **1** the success you achieve by winning a battle, game, race etc.: **[+ over/against]** *the Raiders' 35–17 victory over St. Louis* | *Brock has won a major victory in court.* | *Mitterrand led the Socialist Party to victory in 1981.* | *The Senate vote is a resounding victory* (=a very clear and important victory) *for civil rights.* —opposite DEFEAT¹ (1) **2 a victory for common sense** a solution to a problem or argument that is the most sensible or fair one: *The Senator called the gun control measure a victory for common sense.* —see also PYRRHIC VICTORY

V

vict·uals /ˈvɪtlz/ n. [plural] OLD USE food and drink

vi·cu·ña, vicuna /vɪˈkunyə, -nə/ n. **1** [C] a large South American animal related to the LLAMA, from which soft wool is obtained **2** [U] the cloth made from this wool

vid·e·o¹ /ˈvɪdioʊ/ n. plural **videos 1** [C,U] a copy of a movie, television program, etc. recorded on VIDEO-TAPE: *Let's rent a video tonight.* | *the video store* | *Do they have any of the 1950s sitcoms on video?* **2** [C] a short movie or VIDEOTAPE that contains a particular piece of popular music, and is shown as entertainment; MUSIC VIDEO **3** [U] the process of recording and showing television programs, movies, real events etc. using video equipment: *Communication has changed greatly in the age of video.*

video² adj. [only before noun] relating to or used in the process of recording and broadcasting sound and pictures on VIDEOTAPE: *video equipment* —compare AUDIO

video ar·cade /ˈ... .ˌ./ n. [C] a public place where there are a lot of VIDEO GAMES that you play by putting money in the machines

video cam·era /ˈ... .ˌ./ n. [C] a special camera that can be used to film events using VIDEOTAPE

vid·e·o·cas·sette /ˌvɪdioʊkəˈsɛt/ n. [C] a VIDEOTAPE

videocassette re·cord·er /ˌ....ˈ. .ˌ./ n. [C] a VCR

video con·fer·en·cing /ˌ... ˈ.../ n. [U] a system that allows people to communicate with each other by sending pictures and sounds electronically

vid·e·o·disk, videodisc, video disk/disc /ˈvɪdioʊ-ˌdɪsk/ n. [C] a round flat piece of plastic from which movies can be played and watched on a television —compare DVD

video dis·play ter·mi·nal /ˌ... ˈ. .ˌ../ n. [C] a VDT

video game /ˈ... .ˌ/ n. [C] a game in which you press electronic controls to move images on a screen

vid·e·og·ra·pher /ˌvɪdiˈɑgrəfər/ n. [C] FORMAL someone who records events using a VIDEO CAMERA —**videography** n. [U]

video jock·ey /ˈ... .ˌ./ n. [C] a VJ

vid·e·o·phone /ˈvɪdioʊˌfoʊn/ n. [C] a type of telephone that allows you to see the person you are talking to on a machine like a television

video re·cord·er /ˈ... .ˌ../ n. [C] a VCR —see picture on page 426

vid·e·o·tape¹ /ˈvɪdioʊˌteɪp/ n. [C,U] a long narrow band of MAGNETIC material in a flat plastic container, on which movies, television program etc. can be recorded

videotape² v. [T] to record a television program, movie, event etc. on a videotape: *Will you videotape tonight's game for me?*

vie /vaɪ/ v. **vied, vying** [I] to compete very hard with someone in order to get something: [+ for] *The state champions will vie for the national title.* | **[vie with sb to do sth]** *Students are vying with each other to see who can sell the most tickets.*

Vi·en·na /viˈɛnə/ the capital and largest city of Austria —**Viennese** /ˌviəˈniz/ n., adj.

Vien·tiane /ˌvyɛnˈtyɑn/ the capital and largest city of Laos

Viet·nam /ˌvyɛtˈnɑm, -ˈnæm/ a country in southeast Asia, south of China and east of Laos and Cambodia —**Vietnamese** /ˌvyɛtnəˈmiz/ adj.

Viet·nam War, the /ˌ... ˈ./ a long CIVIL WAR between the Communist forces of North Vietnam and the non-Communist forces of South Vietnam, which began in 1954 and ended when South Vietnam was finally defeated in 1975, and Vietnam was united again as one country. Between 1965 and 1973, U.S. soldiers fought in Vietnam to support the army of South Vietnam.

view¹ /vyu/ n.

1 opinion [C] what you think or believe about something: [+ on/about] *Baxter now shares his wife's views on gun control.* | *In my view* (=I believe), *Reagan was one of our greatest presidents.* | *Another*

supervisor *expressed the view that* abortion should be kept legal. | *We have always taken the view that* (=had the opinion that) *we should do as much as we can.* —see also POINT OF VIEW

2 way of considering [C usually singular] a way of considering or understanding something: [+ of] *Forty-nine percent of Californians have a favorable view of the state lottery.* | *James always did have a rather romantic view of life.* | *In his new book, Blake gives us **a clear view of** (=a definite and specific idea about) what the war was like.* | *Management **takes a dim view of** (=disapproves of) union organizing efforts.* | *an inside/insider's view of sth* (=a way of understanding something based on someone's experience in an organization, group etc.)

3 sight [singular,U] what you are able to see, or the possibility of seeing it: *How is the view from the balcony?* | *Lois slowed down as the ocean **came into view*** (=began to be seen). | *Kim and Rob started fighting **in full view of** the guests* (=where they could clearly see it happening). | *He left the brandy sitting out **in plain view*** (=where it could be easily seen) *on the counter.* | *A gigantic neon sign outside the window **blocked** our view of the mountains.* | *have a good/bad/wonderful etc. view (of sb/sth) We had a really good view of the whole stage from where we were sitting.* —see also BIRD'S-EYE VIEW

4 scenery [C] the whole area, especially a beautiful place, that you can see from somewhere: *a spectacular view across the valley*

5 picture [C] a photograph or picture showing a beautiful or interesting place: [+ of] *The book of postcards contains 12 different views of the cathedral.*

6 on view paintings, photographs etc. that are on view are in a public place where people can go to look at them: *The Russian jewels are currently on view at the Corcoran Gallery of Art.*

7 in view of sth FORMAL used to introduce the reason for a decision, action, or situation: *In view of all that has happened, Conklin is expected to resign.*

8 with a view to (doing) sth because you are planning to do something in the future: *They've torn down the old buildings with a view to renovating the whole neighborhood.*

view² v. **1** [T always + adv./prep.] to consider someone or something in a particular way: *If it is viewed from an environmental perspective, the factory's closing is a good thing.* | **[view sth as sth]** *The group views alcoholism as a physical, mental, and spiritual disease.* | **view sth with caution/enthusiasm/horror etc.** *Townspeople viewed the newcomers with suspicion.* **2** [T] FORMAL to look at something, especially because you are interested: **[view sth from sth]** *The figures carved in the mountain can only be viewed from a helicopter.* **3** [I,T] FORMAL to watch a television show, movie etc.: *After viewing the film, we felt we had a better understanding of the conflict.* **4** view a house/apartment/property etc. to go to see the inside of a house, apartment etc. that you are interested in buying

view·er /ˈvyuər/ n. [C] **1** someone who watches television: *The network is trying to attract younger viewers.* —compare LISTENER (1) **2** a small box with a light in it used to look at SLIDES (=color photographs on special film)

view·er·ship /ˈvyuərˌʃɪp/ n. [U] all the people who watch a particular television show, considered together as a group

view·find·er /ˈvyuˌfaɪndər/ n. [C] the small square of glass on a camera that you look through to see exactly what you are photographing —see picture at CAMERA

view·ing /ˈvyuɪŋ/ n. [C] **1** an occasion when you see or watch something: *The movie is still fascinating even after repeated viewings.* **2** the time before a funeral when friends and relatives meet to remember the dead person and look at the body; WAKE

view·point /ˈvyupɔɪnt/ n. [C] **1** a particular way of thinking about a problem or subject: *From his viewpoint, he had done nothing wrong.* | *a different/historical/religious etc. viewpoint I'm more tolerant of other cultural viewpoints than I used to be.* **2** a place from which you can see something

vig·il /ˈvɪdʒəl/ n. [C,U] **1** a silent political protest in which people gather outside, especially during the night: *Demonstrators held a candlelight vigil at the site of the bombing.* **2** a period of time, especially during the night, when you stay awake in order to pray or remain with someone who is sick: *Rice has been keeping a bedside vigil since his wife became sick.*

vig·i·lance /ˈvɪdʒələns/ n. [U] careful attention that you give to what is happening, so that you will notice any danger or illegal activity: *Keeping the food supply safe requires constant vigilance.*

vig·i·lant /ˈvɪdʒələnt/ adj. giving careful attention to what is happening, so that you will notice any danger or illegal activity: *Travelers in foreign countries are reminded to be vigilant at all times.* —**vigilantly** adv.

vig·i·lan·te /ˌvɪdʒəˈlænti/ n. [C] someone who illegally catches and punishes criminals, usually because they think the police are ineffective —**vigilantism** n. [U]

vi·gnette /vɪˈnyɛt/ n. [C] FORMAL **1** a short description in a book or play showing the typical features of a person or situation **2** a small drawing or pattern placed at the beginning of a book or CHAPTER

vig·or /ˈvɪgɚ/ n. [U] physical and mental energy and determination: *"Hello, Tom!" she called out with unusual vigor.*

vig·or·ous /ˈvɪgərəs/ adj. **1** using a lot of energy and strength or determination: *a vigorous opponent of gun control* | *Your dog needs at least 20 minutes of vigorous exercise every day.* | *Williams' question started a vigorous debate among board members.* **2** strong and very healthy: *At 80, Peck was still vigorous and living in Paris.*

vig·or·ous·ly /ˈvɪgərəsli/ adv. done with a lot of energy and strength or determination: *Zedillo vigorously defended his public record.* | *Stir the mixture vigorously until it is smooth.*

Vi·king /ˈvaɪkɪŋ/ n. [C] a member of the group of Scandinavian people in the 8th to 11th centuries who sailed in ships to attack areas along the coasts of northern and western Europe

vile /vaɪl/ adj. **1** INFORMAL very bad or disgusting: *vile language* | *The Vietnam era is a vile period in American history.* **2** evil or immoral: *a vile act of betrayal* —**vilely** adv. —**vileness** n. [U]

vil·i·fy /ˈvɪləˌfaɪ/ v. **vilifies, vilified, vilifying** [T] FORMAL to say bad things about someone, especially things that are not true, in order to influence other people against them: *Stevens has been vilified by his opponents in the press.* —**vilification** /ˌvɪləfəˈkeɪʃən/ n. [C,U]

vil·la /ˈvɪlə/ n. [C] a big country house

SW² **vil·lage** /ˈvɪlɪdʒ/ n. [C] **1** a very small town in the country outside the U.S. and Canada **2 the village** the people who live in a village: *The entire village was invited to the banquet.* **3** an official description of certain small towns in the U.S., used in legal or official documents —**villager** n.

village id·i·ot /ˌ.. ˈ.../ n. [C] someone considered to be very stupid by many people in their town, NEIGHBORHOOD etc.

vil·lain /ˈvɪlən/ n. [C] **1** the main bad character in a movie, play, or story **2 the villain (of the piece)** the person or thing that is blamed for causing all the trouble in a particular situation: *The mayor appears to be the villain of the piece.* | *Energy prices were clearly the villain in the overall rise in inflation.* **3** INFORMAL a bad person or criminal

vil·lain·ous /ˈvɪlənəs/ adj. LITERARY evil or criminal: *a villainous attack* | *Lucas plays the part of his villainous aunt.*

vil·lain·y /ˈvɪləni/ n. [U] LITERARY evil or criminal behavior

-ville /vɪl, vəl/ suffix **1** used in the names of places to mean "city or town": *Jacksonville, Florida* **2** HUMOROUS used with adjectives or nouns + "s" to show that a person, place, or thing has a particular quality or condition: *Her party was really dullsville* (=very boring). | *The guy's totally weirdsville* (=very strange).

Vil·ni·us /ˈvɪlniəs/ the capital and largest city of Lithuania

vim /vɪm/ n. [U] OLD-FASHIONED energy: *She was full of vim and vigor.*

vin·ai·grette /ˌvɪnɪˈgrɛt/ n. [U] a mixture of oil, VINEGAR, salt, and pepper that you put on a SALAD

Vin·cent de Paul, Saint /ˌvɪnsɪnt də ˈpɔl/ (?1581–1660) a French priest who started two groups of Catholics that do CHARITY work

vin·di·cate /ˈvɪndəˌkeɪt/ v. [T usually passive] FORMAL **1** to prove that someone who was blamed for something is in fact not guilty: *The charges are false, and we are sure we will be vindicated in court.* **2** to prove that someone or something is right or true; JUSTIFY: *Several tests have fully vindicated Einstein's theory.* —**vindication** /ˌvɪndəˈkeɪʃən/ n. [singular,U] *Fox says the award is a vindication of her husband's work.*

vin·dic·tive /vɪnˈdɪktɪv/ adj. deliberately cruel and unfair toward someone you believe has harmed you, in a way that seems unreasonable to others: *After the divorce Joan's ex-husband became increasingly vindictive.* —**vindictively** adv. —**vindictiveness** n. [U]

vine /vaɪn/ n. [C] **1** a plant that grows long thin stems that attach themselves to other plants, trees, buildings etc. **2** a GRAPEVINE

vin·e·gar /ˈvɪnɪgɚ/ n. [U] a sour-tasting liquid made from wine that is used to improve the taste of food or to preserve it —**vinegary** adj.

vine·yard /ˈvɪnyɚd/ n. [C] a piece of land where GRAPEVINES are grown in order to produce wine

vi·no /ˈvinoʊ/ n. [U] SPOKEN wine

Vin·son, Fred·er·ick /ˈvɪnsən/, /ˈfrɛdrɪk/ (1890–1953) a CHIEF JUSTICE on the U.S. Supreme Court

vin·tage¹ /ˈvɪntɪdʒ/ adj. [only before noun] **1** vintage wine is good quality wine made in a particular year **2** old, and showing high quality: *vintage cars* **3** showing all the best or most typical qualities of something: *The latest film has a vintage Disney charm.* **4 a vintage year a)** a year when a good quality wine was produced **b)** a year when something of very good quality was produced: *This was not a vintage year for new music.*

vintage² n. **1** [C] a particular year or place in which a wine is made, or the wine that was produced then **2 of recent vintage** FORMAL having happened or started not very long ago: *Most restrictive abortion laws in the U.S. are of relatively recent vintage.*

vint·ner /ˈvɪntnɚ/ n. FORMAL [C] someone who buys and sells wines

vi·nyl /ˈvaɪnl/ n. [U] **1** a type of strong plastic: *a vinyl chair* | *a vinyl tablecloth* **2** a word for records that are played on a RECORD PLAYER, used when comparing them to CDs or TAPES: *This album is no longer available on vinyl.*

vi·o·la /viˈoʊlə/ n. [C] a musical instrument like a VIOLIN but larger and with a lower sound

SW³ **vi·o·late** /ˈvaɪəˌleɪt/ v. [T] **1** to disobey or do something against an official agreement, law, principle etc.: *Protesters argue that their arrest violated their right to free speech.* | *Borden's actions violated a court order to stay away from his ex-wife.* **2 violate sb's privacy** to do something rude that makes someone else's life less private: *Nearly 80% of those asked feel the media violates people's privacy.* **3** LITERARY to force a woman to have sex; RAPE **4** FORMAL to break open a grave, or force your way into a holy place without showing any respect: *Vandals had violated the graveyard.*

vi·o·la·tion /ˌvaɪəˈleɪʃən/ n. [C,U] **1** an action that breaks a law, agreement, principle etc.: *human rights violations* | [+ of] *The military maneuvers are a clear violation of the treaty.* | *The bar was built in violation of city codes.* **2** FORMAL an action that causes harm or damage by treating someone or their possessions without respect: [+ of] *He regarded the burglary as a violation of his home.*

V

vi·o·lat·or /ˈvaɪəˌleɪtɚ/ *n.* [C] someone who has done something illegal

S W **vi·o·lence** /ˈvaɪələns/ *n.* [U] **1** behavior that is intended to hurt other people physically: *Police said violence in the city was continuing into the night.* | *There is too much sex and violence shown on television.* | *Police suspect Tang's killing was a random act of violence.* | *Shea had long been a victim of domestic violence* (=violence between family members or people who live together). | *Neither side wants to resort to violence* (=use violence when nothing else is effective). **2** extreme force: *the tremendous violence of a tornado* **3** LITERARY an angry way of speaking or reacting: *"Leave me alone,"* she hissed with sudden violence. **4 do violence to sth** FORMAL to spoil something: *Excluding one-third of the population does violence to the principles of democracy.*

S W **vi·o·lent** /ˈvaɪələnt/ *adj.* **1** involving actions that are intended to injure or kill people, by hitting them, shooting them etc.: *Violent crime has decreased in the last decade.* | *a violent overthrow of the government* | *The campus protests quickly turned violent* (=became violent) *on Tuesday.* | *The riots ended in the violent deaths of three teenagers.* **2** someone who is violent is likely to attack, hurt, or kill other people: *violent street gangs* | *The man suddenly turned violent* (=became violent) *and began smashing chairs.* **3 a violent movie/play/show etc.** a movie, play etc. that contains a lot of violence **4 a violent storm/explosion/earthquake etc.** a storm, explosion etc. that happens with a lot of force **5** violent feelings or reactions are strong and very difficult to control: *Joe has a violent temper.* | *a violent coughing fit*

vi·o·lent·ly /ˈvaɪələntli/ *adv.* **1** in a way that involves violence: *Several women have been violently attacked in the subway.* **2** with a lot of force in a way that is very difficult to control: *I was trembling less violently, but my teeth still chattered.* **3** with a lot of energy or emotion, especially angry: *When she heard they had gotten engaged, Jenny protested violently.*

vi·o·let /ˈvaɪəlɪt/ *n.* **1** [C] a plant with small dark purple flowers, or sometimes white or yellow ones —see also SHRINKING VIOLET **2** [U] a bluish-purple color —**violet** *adj.*

vi·o·lin /ˌvaɪəˈlɪn/ *n.* [C] the smallest instrument in the group of wooden musical instruments that are played by pulling a BOW (=special stick) across its four strings —**violinist** *n.* [C]

VIP *n.* [C] very important person; someone who is very famous or powerful and is treated with special care and respect: *They treated us like VIPs.*

vi·per /ˈvaɪpɚ/ *n.* [C] **1** a small poisonous snake **2** LITERARY someone who behaves in a nasty way and harms other people

vi·ra·go /vəˈragoʊ/ *n.* [C] LITERARY an angry woman with a loud voice

vi·ral /ˈvaɪrəl/ *adj.* relating to or caused by a VIRUS: *viral pneumonia*

Vir·gil, Vergil /ˈvɝdʒəl/ (70–19 B.C.) an ancient Roman poet

vir·gin¹ /ˈvɝdʒɪn/ *n.* [C] **1** someone who has never had sex, especially a girl or young woman **2 the (Blessed) Virgin**, also **the Virgin Mary** a name for Mary, the mother of Jesus Christ, used especially by Catholics **3** SPOKEN, HUMOROUS someone who has never done a particular activity: *This is the first model computer virgins can operate as soon as it lands on their desks.* **4 virgin territory** something new that you are experiencing for the first time: *Until the end of The Civil War, North America was virgin territory for British tourists.*

virgin² *adj.* [only before noun] **1 virgin land/snow/ soil etc.** land, snow etc. that is still in its natural state and has not been used or changed by people: *The owl lives in old trees in virgin forests.* **2** without sexual experience: *a virgin bride* **3** a virgin drink normally contains alcohol but has been made without any: *a virgin piña colada* **4 virgin olive oil** EXTRA VIRGIN OLIVE OIL **5** not having done, heard, or seen something before: *He was eager to try out his jokes on a virgin audience.*

vir·gin·al /ˈvɝdʒɪnəl/ *adj.* like a virgin

virgin birth /ˌ.. ˈ./ *n.* **the virgin birth** the birth of Jesus Christ, which Christians believe was caused by God, not by sex between a man and a woman

Vir·gin·ia /vɚˈdʒɪnyə/ *written abbreviation* **VA** a state on the east coast of the U.S.

Virginia creep·er /.ˌ.. ˈ../ *n.* [C,U] a garden plant that grows up walls and has large leaves that turn deep red in the fall

Virgin Is·lands, the /ˌvɝdʒɪn ˈaɪləndz/ a group of about 100 small islands in the east Caribbean Sea, some of which are ruled by the U.S.

vir·gin·i·ty /vɚˈdʒɪnəti/ *n.* [U] the condition of never having had sex: *I was 18 when I lost my virginity* (=had sex for the first time). —compare CHASTITY

Vir·go /ˈvɝgoʊ/ *n.* **1** [U] the sixth sign of the ZODIAC, represented by a young woman, and believed to affect the character and life of people born between August 23 and September 22 **2** [C] someone who was born between August 23 and September 22: *Kim is a Virgo.*

vir·ile /ˈvɪrəl/ *adj.* APPROVING having or showing traditionally male qualities such as strength, courage, and sexual attractiveness

vi·ril·i·ty /vəˈrɪləti/ *n.* [U] **1** the typically male quality of being strong, brave, and full of energy, in a way that is sexually attractive **2** the ability of a man to have sex or make a woman PREGNANT; POTENCY

vi·rol·o·gy /vaɪˈrɑlədʒi/ *n.* [U] the scientific study of VIRUSes or of the diseases caused by them

vir·tu·al /ˈvɝtʃuəl/ *adj.* [only before noun] **1** so nearly having or being a particular quality, condition, position etc. that any difference is unimportant: *Children were forced to work as virtual slaves in the factories.* | *The two countries are locked in a virtual state of war.* | *Buying a week's worth of groceries for this family in one trip is a virtual impossibility.* **2** relating to something that is made, done, seen etc. on a computer, rather than in the real world: *The website allows you to take a virtual tour of the campus.*

vir·tu·al·ly /ˈvɝtʃuəli, -tʃəli/ *adv.* **1** almost: *Virtually* **S W** *everyone expects Monica to succeed.* | *He was virtually unknown before running for office.* **2** done on a computer, rather than in the real world: *virtually published on the Internet*

virtual re·al·i·ty /ˌ... .ˈ.../ *n.* [U] an environment produced by a computer that looks and seems real to the person experiencing it

vir·tue /ˈvɝtʃu/ *n.* **1** [U] FORMAL moral goodness of character and behavior: *Women have often been used as symbols of virtue and nobility.* —opposite VICE² **2** [C] a particular good quality in someone's character: *Among their many virtues, they are always direct and honest.* | *heroic virtues* **3** [C,U] an advantage that makes something better or more useful than something else: [+ of] *Adam Smith believed strongly in the virtues of free trade.* **4 by virtue of sth** FORMAL by means of, or as a result of something: *I am Claire's aunt by virtue of marriage.* **5 preach/extol/ tout etc. the virtues of sth** to talk about how good or important something is and try to persuade other people about this: *Johnson is now preaching the virtues of self-control.* **6 make a virtue of necessity/ troubles etc.** to pretend that you are doing something because you want to do it, when actually it is something that you must do

vir·tu·os·i·ty /ˌvɝtʃuˈɑsəti/ *n.* [U] FORMAL a very high degree of skill in performing: *the guitarist's amazing technical virtuosity*

vir·tu·o·so /ˌvɝtʃuˈoʊsoʊ/ *n. plural* **virtuosos** [C] someone who is a very skillful performer, especially in music —**virtuoso** *adj.* [only before noun] *a virtuoso performance*

vir·tu·ous /ˈvɝtʃuəs/ *adj.* **1** FORMAL behaving in a very honest and moral way: *The story repeats the theme of the unfaithful husband and virtuous wife.*

2 OLD-FASHIONED not willing to have sex, at least until you are married —**virtuously** *adv.*

vir·u·lent /ˈvɪrələnt, ˈvɪryə-/ *adj.* **1** a poison, disease etc. that is virulent is very dangerous and affects people very quickly: *a more virulent strain of HIV* **2** FORMAL, DISAPPROVING full of hatred for something, or expressing this in a strong way: *virulent anti-Semitism* | *a virulent critic of the United Nations* —**virulence** *n.* [U] *the virulence of breast cancer* —**virulently** *adv.*

vi·rus /ˈvaɪrəs/ *n.* **1** [C] a very small living thing that causes infectious illnesses: *the common cold virus* —compare BACTERIA **2** [C] the illness caused by a virus: *There's a virus going around – four people in my office were sick last week.* **3** [C,U] a set of instructions secretly put into a computer or computer program, that can destroy information stored there and possibly the equipment itself

vi·sa /ˈvizə/ *n.* [C] an official mark put on your PASSPORT by the representative of a foreign country, that gives you permission to enter, pass through, stay in, or leave that country: *work/exit/entry etc. visa* *A tourist visa is good for three months.*

vis·age /ˈvɪzɪdʒ/ *n.* [C] LITERARY a face

vis-à-vis /ˌvizəˈvi/ *prep.* FORMAL in relation to or in comparison with something or someone: *Kennedy was in a weak position vis-à-vis Congress.*

vis·cer·a /ˈvɪsərə/ *n.* [plural] TECHNICAL the large organs inside your body, such as your heart, lungs, and stomach

vis·cer·al /ˈvɪsərəl/ *adj.* **1** LITERARY relating to or resulting from strong feelings rather than careful thought: *We've seen a strong visceral reaction to the flag-burning issue.* **2** TECHNICAL relating to the viscera

vis·cous /ˈvɪskəs/ *adj.* TECHNICAL a viscous liquid is thick and sticky and does not flow easily —**viscosity** /vɪˈskɑsəţi/ *n.* [U]

vise /vaɪs/ *n.* [C] a tool that holds an object firmly so that you can work on it using both your hands

vise·like, **vise-like** /ˈvaɪslaɪk/ *adj.* **a viselike grip** a very firm hold

vis·i·bil·i·ty /ˌvɪzəˈbɪləţi/ *n.* [U] **1** the distance it is possible to see, especially when this is affected by weather conditions: *Planes must have at least a half-mile of visibility to land.* | **good/poor/low visibility** *The search for survivors was abandoned because of poor visibility.* **2** the situation of being noticed by people in general: *The article in the paper meant good visibility for the company.* | *As head of the Red Cross, she has* **high visibility**. **3** the fact of being easy to be seen

vis·i·ble /ˈvɪzəbəl/ *adj.* **1** something that is visible can be seen: *The stars were barely visible that night.* **2** an effect that is visible is strong enough to be noticed: *The results of the housing policy are clearly visible.* | *She showed no* **visible signs of** *regret.* **3** someone who is visible is in a situation in which many people can notice them: *Black performers have become much more visible on Broadway.* —opposite INVISIBLE

vis·i·bly /ˈvɪzəbli/ *adv.* in a way that is easy to see or notice: *He was visibly upset by the loss.*

Vis·i·goth /ˈvɪzəˌgɑθ/ *n.* one of a tribe of Goths that settled in France and Spain in the fourth century A.D.

vi·sion /ˈvɪʒən/ *n.* **1** [U] your ability to see: *As Martha grew older, her vision began to fail.* | **sb's field/line of vision** (=the area someone is able to see without turning their head) —see also **twenty-twenty vision** (TWENTY-TWENTY) **2** [C] an idea of what you think something should be like: *[+ of] Simmons is willing to do anything to achieve his vision of social justice.* **3** [C] something that you seem to see, especially in a dream, as part of a powerful religious experience: *She says that an angel appeared to her* **in a vision**. | *I suddenly* **had a vision** *of the car spinning out of control and sliding off the road.* **4** [U] the knowledge and imagination that are needed in planning for the future with a clear purpose: *We need a leader with vision and strong principles* **5 a vision (of beauty/loveliness etc.)** LITERARY a woman who is very beautiful

vi·sion·ar·y[1] /ˈvɪʒəˌnɛri/ *adj.* **1** having clear ideas of what the world should be like in the future: *Under his visionary leadership, the city prospered.* **2** existing only in someone's mind and unlikely to ever exist in the real world

visionary[2] *n. plural* **visionaries** [C] **1** someone who has clear ideas and strong feelings about the way something should be in the future **2** a holy person who has VISIONS (3)

vis·it[1] /ˈvɪzɪt/ *v.* **1** [I,T] to go and spend time in a place or with someone, especially for pleasure or interest: *We've got some friends visiting from out of town this weekend.* | *Eric went to Seattle to visit his cousins.* | *Which cities did you visit in Spain?* | *[+ in] He first met her in a club when she was visiting in Miami.* | *I was really pleased that they* **came to visit** *me.* **2** [T] to go to a place as part of your official job, especially to examine it: *The inspection team visited the plant twice in October.* **3** [T] to use a WEBSITE on the Internet **4** [I] INFORMAL to talk socially with someone: *[+ with] Why don't you kids play outside while the adults visit with each other?* **5** [T] FORMAL to go to see a doctor, lawyer etc. in order to get treatment or advice: *You should visit the dentist twice a year.*

visit sth on sb/sth *phr. v.* [T] BIBLICAL OR LITERARY to do something to punish someone or show them that you are angry: *God's wrath will be visited on sinners.*

USAGE NOTE: VISIT

WORD CHOICE: visit, go to, go/come to see
Visit is a slightly formal word. You might write: *We visited the Grand Canyon*, or *I visited my mother*. But in spoken English, you usually say that you **go to** a place, especially when the place is not unusual or special, or **go/come to see** (or **go/come and see**) a place or a person: *We went to a really good restaurant last night.* | *When are you going to come and see me?*

---

visit[2] *n.* [C] **1** an occasion when someone goes to spend time in a place or goes to see a person: *[+ to] a visit to London* | *[+ from] Liz is expecting a visit from her brother, Frank.* | *Lang will accompany the President* **on a visit** *to Rome.* | *I decided to* **pay** *him* **a visit** *at his office.* **2** INFORMAL an occasion when you talk socially with someone, or the time you spend doing this: *Polly and I had a nice long visit.* **3** an occasion when you see a doctor, lawyer etc. for treatment or advice —see also HOME VISIT

vis·it·a·tion /ˌvɪzəˈteɪʃən/ *n.* **1** [C] FORMAL an official visit to a place or a person, especially to see a dead body after someone has died: *Visitation at the funeral home is from 2 to 8 p.m. on Monday.* **2** [C,U] LAW an occasion when a parent is allowed to spend time with their children when the children live with the other parent after a DIVORCE, or the right to do this: *visitation rights* **3** [C] LITERARY an event that is believed to be God's punishment for something: *[+ of] visitations of plague, famine, and war* **4** [C] an occasion when God or a spirit is believed to appear to someone on earth

visiting hours /ˈ... ˌ./ *n.* [plural] the period of time when you can visit people who are in the hospital

visiting nurse /ˌ... ˈ./ *n.* [C] a nurse who comes to people's homes to treat them

visiting pro·fes·sor /ˌ... .ˈ../ *n.* [C] a university teacher who has come from another university to teach for a period of time

vis·i·tor /ˈvɪzəţɚ/ *n.* [C] someone who comes to visit a place or a person: *Doug, I think you have a visitor.* | *[+ to] Rina is a frequent visitor to the city.*

vi·sor /ˈvaɪzɚ/ *n.* [C] **1** the curved part of a cap that sticks out in front above your eyes **2** the part of a HELMET (=protective hard hat) that can be lowered to protect your face **3** a flat piece of material above the front window inside a car that can be pulled down to keep the sun out of your eyes; **4** a curved piece of plastic that you wear on your head so that it sticks

V

out above your eyes and protects them from the sun

vis·ta /ˈvɪstə/ n. [C] **1** LITERARY a view of a large area of beautiful SCENERY, especially one seen by looking between rows of trees, buildings etc.: *a spectacular mountain vista* **2** the possibility of new experiences, ideas, events etc.: *Exchange programs open up new vistas for students.*

vis·u·al /ˈvɪʒuəl, ˈvɪʒəl/ adj. [usually before noun] relating to seeing: *Artists translate their ideas into visual images.* | *a powerful visual impact* —see also VISUALLY

visual aid /ˌ... ˈ./ n. [C] something such as a map, picture, film etc. that helps people understand, learn, or remember information

visual arts /ˌ... ˈ./ n. [plural] art such as painting, SCULPTURE, etc. that you look at, as opposed to literature or music that you read or hear

vis·u·al·ize /ˈvɪʒuəˌlaɪz/ v. [T] to form a picture of someone or something in your mind; IMAGINE: *I tried to visualize the house as he described it.* | [**visualize sb doing sth**] *She visualized him getting angry when she told him about the damage.* | [**visualize how/what etc.**] *It's hard to visualize how these tiles will look in our bathroom.* —**visualization** /ˌvɪʒuələˈzeɪʃən/ n. [U]

vi·su·al·ly /ˈvɪʒuəli, ˈvɪʒəli/ adv. **1** in appearance: *The chair should be visually attractive as well as comfortable.* **2 visually impaired/handicapped** unable to see normally: *She teaches visually impaired children.* **3** in a way that involves the eyes: *Babies are still developing visually when they are born.*

s w **vi·tal** /ˈvaɪtl/ adj. **1** extremely important and necessary for something to succeed or exist: *Schools are a vital part of American neighborhoods.* | [+ **to**] *We view this partnership as vital to achieving our goals.* | [+ **for**] *Regular exercise is vital for your health.* | [**it is vital that**] *It is vital that the document be neat and clearly worded.* | *Code-breaking played a vital role in winning the war.* | *The drug problem is of vital importance to both our countries.* **2** full of energy in a way that is exciting and attractive: *Rodgers and Hart's music still sounds as fresh and vital as the day it was written.* | *a strong, vital man* **3** [only before noun] necessary in order to keep you alive: *the body's vital processes*

vi·tal·i·ty /vaɪˈtæləti/ n. [U] **1** great energy and cheerfulness: *There is an attractive vitality to John.* **2** the ability of an organization, country etc. to continue working effectively: *Maintaining the state's economic vitality is an important issue in this fall's election.*

vi·tal·ize /ˈvaɪtlˌaɪz/ v. [T] to make something more active, or make it have more energy

vi·tal·ly /ˈvaɪtl-i/ adv. in a very important or necessary way: *Terrorism is an issue that vitally affects the security of the United States.* | *It is vitally important that you follow the directions exactly.*

vital or·gan /ˌ... ˈ../ n. [C] a part of your body that is necessary to keep you alive, such as your heart and lungs

vi·tals /ˈvaɪtlz/ n. [plural] OLD USE your vital organs

vital signs /ˌ... ˈ./ n. [plural] things that you can measure to find out whether a person's health is in danger, such as their breathing, body temperature, and how fast their heart is beating

vital sta·tis·tics /ˌ... .ˈ../ n. [plural] **1** figures or facts concerning birth, death, marriage etc., especially within a population **2** INFORMAL important information or facts about someone or something such as height, address, cost etc.

s w **vi·ta·min** /ˈvaɪtəmɪn/ n. [C] **1** a chemical substance found in food that is necessary for good health: *vitamin A/B/C etc. Does vitamin C really help prevent colds?* **2** a PILL containing vitamins

vi·ti·ate /ˈvɪʃiˌeɪt/ v. [T] FORMAL to make something less effective or spoil it: *Changes at this point may actually vitiate the entire system.* —**vitiation** /ˌvɪʃiˈeɪʃən/ n. [U]

vit·i·cul·ture /ˈvɪtəˌkʌltʃɚ/ n. [U] the study or practice of growing GRAPES for making wine

vit·re·ous /ˈvɪtriəs/ adj. FORMAL made of or looking like glass

vit·ri·ol /ˈvɪtriəl/ n. [U] **1** LITERARY very cruel and angry remarks that are intended to hurt someone's feelings **2** OLD-FASHIONED: see SULFURIC ACID

vit·ri·ol·ic /ˌvɪtriˈɑlɪk/ adj. FORMAL vitriolic language, writing etc. is very cruel and angry and intended to hurt someone's feelings: *She attacked him in a vitriolic seven-page letter to the newspaper.* —**vitriolically** /-kli/ adv.

vi·tro /ˈvitroʊ/ —see IN VITRO FERTILIZATION

vit·tles /ˈvɪtlz/ n. [plural] OLD-FASHIONED, INFORMAL food

vi·tu·per·a·tion /vaɪˌtupəˈreɪʃən, vɪ-/ n. [U] FORMAL angry and cruel criticism: *The speeches were full of vituperation and slander.* —**vituperative** /vaɪˈtupərˌətɪv, -ˌreɪtɪv/ adj.

vi·va /ˈvivə/ interjection used to show that you approve of or support someone or something and want them to continue to exist or be successful: *Viva Mandela!*

vi·va·ce /vɪˈvɑtʃeɪ, -tʃi/ adj., adv. played or sung quickly and with energy

vi·va·cious /vɪˈveɪʃəs, vaɪ-/ adj. someone, especially a woman, who is vivacious has a lot of energy and a happy attractive manner: *a vivacious and outgoing personality* —**vivaciousness** n. [U] —**vivacity** /vɪˈvæsəti/ n. [U]

Vi·val·di, An·to·ni·o /vɪˈvɑldi, ænˈtoʊnioʊ/ (1678–1741) an Italian musician who wrote CLASSICAL music

viv·id /ˈvɪvɪd/ adj. **1** vivid memories, dreams, descriptions etc. are so clear that they seem real: *Include details to make your story as vivid as possible.* **2 a vivid imagination** an ability to imagine unlikely situations very clearly **3** vivid colors or patterns are very bright: *a vivid red cape* —**vividness** n. [U]

viv·id·ly /ˈvɪvɪdli/ adv. **1** in a way that is so clear that memories, dreams, descriptions etc. seem real: *I recall what he said vividly.* **2** brightly: *a vividly colored gown*

viv·i·sec·tion /ˌvɪvəˈsɛkʃən/ n. [U] the practice of cutting open the bodies of living animals to do medical or scientific tests on them —**vivisectionist** n. [C]

vix·en /ˈvɪksən/ n. [C] **1** LITERARY a woman who is cruel or not nice **2** a female FOX —**vixenish** adj.

viz. /vɪz/ adv. FORMAL used to introduce specific details or a list of examples that make your meaning clearer; NAMELY

vi·zier /vəˈzɪr/ n. [C] an important politician in certain Muslim countries in the past

VJ n. [C] video jockey; someone who introduces music VIDEOS on television

VLF n. [U] TECHNICAL very low frequency; a range of radio waves between 3 and 30 KILOHERTZ

V-neck /ˈvi nɛk/ n. [C] an opening for the neck in a piece of clothing shaped like the letter V —**V-necked** adj.: *a V-necked sweater*

vo·cab /ˈvoʊkæb/ n. [U] INFORMAL: see VOCABULARY

s w **vo·cab·u·lar·y** /voʊˈkæbyəˌlɛri, və-/ n. plural **vocabularies**
1 words you know [C,U] all the words that someone knows, learns, or uses: *Naomi has been using flash cards to increase her vocabulary.* | **sb's active/passive vocabulary** (=the words someone can use, or the words they understand)
2 special words [C,U] the words that are typically used when talking about a particular subject: *Most technical jobs use a specialized vocabulary.*
3 words in a language [C] all the words in a particular language: *English has the largest vocabulary of any language.*
4 skills/features [C,U] the special skills or features that are typical of a particular subject: [+ **of**] *Mingus' sense of sound and feeling for rhythm expanded the vocabulary of jazz.*
5 list of words [C] a list of words with explanations of their meanings, often in a book for learning a language
6 failure/guilt/compromise etc. is not in sb's

vocabulary used to say that someone never thinks of accepting failure, never feels guilty etc.: *"Compromise" is not a word in her vocabulary – for her, competition is everything.*

vo·cal[1] /ˈvoʊkəl/ *adj.* **1** expressing strong opinions publicly, especially about things with which you disagree: *a vocal critic of the government* | *[+ about] Mr. Syron has been very vocal about improving the organization.* **2** [only before noun] relating to the voice: *vocal music* —**vocally** *adv.*

vocal[2] *n.* [C usually plural] the part of a piece of music that is sung rather than played on an instrument: *The album features Jim Boquist on vocals.*

vocal cords, vocal chords /ˈ.. ./ *n.* [plural] thin pieces of muscle in your throat that produce sounds when you speak

vo·cal·ist /ˈvoʊkəlɪst/ *n.* [C] someone who sings popular songs, especially with a band —compare INSTRUMENTALIST

vo·cal·ize /ˈvoʊkəˌlaɪz/ *v.* **1** [T] to express a feeling or opinion by speaking: *Getz vocalized what everyone else at the meeting was thinking.* **2** [I,T] TECHNICAL to make a sound using the vocal cords —**vocalization** /ˌvoʊkələˈzeɪʃən/ *n.* [C,U]

vo·ca·tion /voʊˈkeɪʃən/ *n.* [C,U] **1 a)** the feeling that the purpose of your life is to do a particular job, especially because it allows you to help other people **b)** the particular job itself: *At 17, she found her vocation as a writer.* —see Usage Note at JOB **2** a strong belief that you have been chosen by God to be a priest or a NUN; CALLING: **a vocation for the priesthood**

vo·ca·tion·al /voʊˈkeɪʃənl/ *adj.* **vocational training/ guidance/education etc.** training, advice etc. relating to the skills you need to do a particular job

vocational school /.ˈ.... ,. / *n.* [C] a school that teaches students the skills that they will need for particular jobs, especially ones in which they will use their hands such as MECHANICS or CARPENTRY

voc·a·tive /ˈvɑkətɪv/ *n.* [C] TECHNICAL a particular form of a noun in certain languages, used when speaking or writing to someone. For example in the sentence, "Sue, have you seen my hat?", the name "Sue" is a vocative. —**vocative** *adj.*

vo·cif·er·ous /voʊˈsɪfərəs/ *adj.* FORMAL **1** expressing your opinions loudly and strongly: *a vociferous opponent of the plan* **2** vociferous opinions, wishes etc. are loudly and strongly expressed: *vociferous demands* —**vociferously** *adv.*

vod·ka /ˈvɑdkə/ *n.* [U] a strong clear alcoholic drink from Russia or Poland

vogue /voʊg/ *n.* [C usually singular,U] if there is a vogue for something, it is popular or fashionable for a period of time: *[+ for] "The Castle of Otranto" began the vogue for Gothic romance novels.* | *Untanned skin is back in vogue for the first time since the 1920s.*

voice[1] /vɔɪs/ *n.*

1 speaking [C,U] the sounds that you make when you speak, or the ability to make these sounds: *I thought I heard voices outside.* | *Kent's at home today – he has a cold and he's lost his voice* (=he cannot speak). | *Don't you raise your voice* (=speak louder, especially in an angry way) *at me.* | *Keep your voice down* (=speak more quietly) *– we don't want to wake everyone up.* | *I liked Ben's relaxed tone of voice* (=the quality of his voice which expresses his attitude). | *Nancy took a deep breath and shouted at the top of her voice* (=as loud as she could). | *A small voice* (=a shy and quiet voice) *in the back of the room said "No."* | *lower/drop your voice* (=speak more quietly) | *a loud/deep/soft etc. voice Angie has a really low voice for a woman.* | *angry/ excited/worried etc. voice From downstairs came angry voices, arguing over whose turn it was to cook dinner.* | *in a normal/loud/surprised etc. voice "I can't wait!" Tim said in an excited voice.* | *sb's voice cracks/breaks As he spoke of the accident, his voice broke and tears came to his eyes.*

2 singing **a)** [C,U] the quality of sound you produce when you sing: *He has a beautiful tenor voice.* | *Brandy was in good voice* (=singing well) *the night*

of the concert. **b)** [C] a person singing: *The piece was written for six voices and piano.*

3 opinion **a)** [singular,U] the right or ability to express an opinion, to vote, or to influence decisions: *Shouldn't parents have a voice in deciding how their children are educated?* | *Lippmann gave voice to* (=expressed openly) *the concerns of the community.* **b)** [C] an opinion or wish that is expressed: *The government needs to listen to the voice of middle-class Americans.* | *You can make your voice heard* (=express your opinion so that people notice it) *at the meeting tonight.* | *Since the new ESL program was introduced, there has been only one dissenting voice* (=person expressing disagreement). | *In a news conference, Brown added his voice to* (=expressed his support for) *the criticism of the President's plan.*

4 representative [singular] a person, organization, newspaper etc. that expresses the opinions or wishes of a group of people: *"Wired" magazine quickly became the voice of the computer-generation.*

5 the voice of reason/sanity/experience etc. opinions or ideas that are reasonable, sensible, based on experience etc., or someone with these ideas: *Green has been the voice of reason throughout the crisis.*

6 the active/passive voice TECHNICAL the form of a verb that shows whether the subject of a sentence does an action or has an action done to it —see also **find your voice** (FIND[1] (21)), **sb's inner voice** (INNER (5)), **speak with one voice** (SPEAK (11)), -VOICED

voice[2] *v.* [T] **1** to tell people your opinions or feelings about a particular subject: **voice opinions/ doubts/complaints etc.** *He voiced several objections to the plan.* **2** TECHNICAL to produce a sound with a movement of the VOCAL CORDS as well as the breath

voice box /ˈ. ./ *n.* [C] NOT TECHNICAL the part of your throat that you use to produce sounds when you speak; LARYNX

voiced /vɔɪst/ *adj.* TECHNICAL voiced sounds are made using the VOCAL CORDS. For example /d/ and /g/ are voiced consonants.

-voiced /vɔɪst/ [in adjectives] **deep-voiced/squeaky-voiced/husky-voiced etc.** having a voice that is deep, very high etc.: *a sweet-voiced girl*

voice·less /ˈvɔɪslɪs/ *adj.* **1** a voiceless group of people does not have any political power, and their opinions are not listened to or respected: *the voiceless immigrant community* **2** TECHNICAL voiceless sounds are made without using the VOCAL CORDS; UNVOICED. For example /p/ and /k/ are voiceless consonants.

voice mail /ˈ. ./ *n.* [U] a system in which people can leave recorded messages for someone who does not answer their telephone

voice-o·ver /ˈ. ,../ *n.* [C] an explanation or remarks that are spoken in a television advertisement or movie by someone who cannot be seen

voice print /ˈ. ./ *n.* [C] someone's voice, recorded on a machine, which can be used to check whether that person is allowed to enter a place, use a computer system etc. by matching their voice to the recording

void[1] /vɔɪd/ *n.* [C usually singular] **1** a feeling of great sadness and emptiness that you have when someone you love dies, when something is taken from you etc.: *After losing his job, Molly began eating to fill the void* (=put something in the place of something she no longer has) *in her life.* **2** a completely empty area of space: *She looked over the cliff into the void.* **3** a situation in which something important or interesting is needed or wanted but does not exist: *The amusement park will fill a void* (=give them something they were lacking) *in this town, which has little entertainment for children.*

void[2] *adj.* **1** LAW a contract or official agreement that is void is not legal and has no effect; NULL AND VOID: *The court ruled the state law was unconstitutional and void.* **2 be void of sth** FORMAL completely empty or lacking something: *Her eyes were void of all expression.*

void[3] *v.* [T] **1** LAW to make a contract or agreement have no legal effect: *The ruling party voided elections*

V

in 14 cities. **2 void the bladder/bowels** FORMAL to pass waste liquid or solid matter from your body

voi·là /vwɑˈlɑ/ *interjection* used when suddenly showing or telling someone something surprising: *Add a veil, and voilà! the dress becomes a wedding gown.*

voile /vɔɪl/ *n.* [U] a very light almost transparent cloth made of cotton, wool, or silk

vol. the written abbreviation for VOLUME

vol·a·tile /ˈvɑlət̬l/ *adj.* **1** a volatile situation is likely to change suddenly and without much warning: *People are afraid to change jobs in today's volatile economy.* **2** someone who is volatile can suddenly become angry or violent **3** a volatile liquid or substance changes easily into a gas —**volatility** /ˌvɑləˈtɪlət̬i/ *n.* [U]

vol·can·ic /vɑlˈkænɪk, vɔl-/ *adj.* **1** relating to or caused by a volcano: *volcanic ash* —see picture on page 1330 **2** happening or reacting suddenly and violently: *a volcanic temper*

vol·ca·no /vɑlˈkeɪnoʊ/ *n.* *plural* **volcanoes** or **volcanos** [C] a mountain with a large hole at the top, through which hot rocks and ash sometimes rise into the air from inside the earth

volcano

vole /voʊl/ *n.* [C] a small animal like a mouse with a short tail that lives in fields and woods and near rivers

Vol·ga, the /ˈvɑlgə, ˈvoʊlgə/ a river in Russia that flows into the Caspian Sea and is the longest river in Europe

vo·li·tion /vəˈlɪʃən, voʊ-/ *n.* [U] FORMAL **1 of your own volition** because you want to do something, not because you are forced to do it: *Deena left the company of her own volition.* **2** the power to choose or decide something, or the action of doing this

vol·ley¹ /ˈvɑli/ *n.* *plural* **volleys** [C] **1** a large number of bullets, ARROWs, rocks etc. shot or thrown through the air at the same time: [+ of] *a volley of gunfire* **2** a lot of questions, insults, attacks etc. that are all said or made at the same time: [+ of] *a volley of accusations* | *a volley of blows* **3** a hit in TENNIS, a kick in SOCCER etc. when the player hits or kicks the ball before it touches the ground

vol·ley² *v.* **volleys, volleyed, volleying 1** [I,T] to hit or kick a ball before it touches the ground, especially in TENNIS or SOCCER **2** [I] if a large number of guns volley, they are all fired at the same time

vol·ley·ball /ˈvɑliˌbɔl/ *n.* **1** [U] a game in which two teams use their hands to hit a ball over a high net **2** [C] the ball used in this game

volt /voʊlt/ *n.* [C] TECHNICAL a unit for measuring the force of an electric current

Vol·ta /ˈvoʊltə/, **Al·es·san·dro** /ˌælɪˈsændroʊ/ (1745–1827) an Italian scientist who did important work on electricity and invented the first electric BATTERY

Vol·ta, the /ˈvoʊltə/ a river in West Africa that flows south through Ghana to the Atlantic Ocean

volt·age /ˈvoʊltɪdʒ/ *n.* [C,U] TECHNICAL electrical force measured in volts: *low-voltage electrical current* —see also HIGH-VOLTAGE

Vol·taire /voʊlˈtɛr, vɔl-/ (1694–1778) a French writer and PHILOSOPHER who was one of the leaders of the Enlightenment

volt·me·ter /ˈvoʊltˌmit̬ɚ/ *n.* [C] an instrument for measuring voltage

vol·u·ble /ˈvɑlyəbəl/ *adj.* FORMAL **1** talking a lot: *a voluble and witty man* **2** a voluble speech, explanation etc. uses a lot of words and is spoken quickly —**volubly** *adv.* —**volubility** /ˌvɑlyəˈbɪlət̬i/ *n.* [U]

vol·ume /ˈvɑlyəm, -yum/ *n.* **1** [U] the amount of

the volume on the stereo turned up all the way. **2** [C,U] the total amount of something, especially when it is large or increasing: *sales volume* | [+ of] *a large volume of mail* | *The volume of trade between the two regions continues to grow.* **3** [C] **a)** a book that is part of a set or one into which a very long book is divided: *The period from 1940 to 1949 is in Volume 9.* | *a 13-volume report* **b)** FORMAL any book: *a volume of poetry* **4** [C,U] the amount of space that a substance or object contains or fills: *The unit is equal to the volume of a container measuring 8 by 8 by 20 feet.* —see also **sth speaks volumes** (SPEAK (7))

vo·lu·mi·nous /vəˈlumənəs/ *adj.* FORMAL **1** voluminous books, documents etc. are very long and contain a lot of detail: *The voluminous report was sent to Congress.* **2** a voluminous piece of clothing is very large and loose: *a voluminous fiesta skirt* **3** a voluminous container is very large and can hold a lot of things: *a voluminous suitcase*

vol·un·ta·rism /ˈvɑləntəˌrɪzəm/ *n.* [U] VOLUNTEERISM

vol·un·tar·y¹ /ˈvɑlənˌtɛri/ *adj.* **1** done willingly, without being forced or without being paid: *voluntary cooperation* | *Participation in the program is strictly voluntary.* | *These soldiers joined the Army **on a voluntary basis** (=without being forced).* | **voluntary work/service etc.** (=work that someone does without expecting to be paid) —compare COMPULSORY **2 a voluntary organization/group/institution etc.** an organization, group etc. that is organized or supported by people who give their money, services etc. because they want to, without expecting payment **3 a voluntary worker/helper/assistant etc.** someone who works without expecting or receiving payment **4** TECHNICAL voluntary movements of your body are controlled by you —opposite INVOLUNTARY —**voluntarily** /ˌvɑlənˈtɛrəli/ *adv.*: *She wasn't fired – she left voluntarily.*

voluntary² *n.* [C] a piece of music, usually for the ORGAN, written to be played in church

vol·un·teer¹ /ˌvɑlənˈtɪr/ *n.* [C] **1** someone who does something without being paid, or who is willing to offer to help someone: *Most of the relief work was done by volunteers.* | *I need someone to rake the yard. Any volunteers?* | *a volunteer fire department* **2** someone who offers to join the army, navy, or air force

volunteer² *v.* **1** [I,T] to offer to do something without expecting any reward, often something that other people do not want to do: **[volunteer to do sth]** *Helen volunteered to have Thanksgiving at her house this year.* | [+ **for**] *Gage has volunteered for guard duty.* | **volunteer your services/time/skills etc.** *Private boat owners volunteered their services to the rescue workers.* **2** [T] to tell someone something without being asked: *Michael volunteered the information before I had a chance to ask.* **3** [I] to offer to join the army, navy, or air force: *Andy didn't wait to be drafted – he volunteered.* **4 volunteer sb for sth** to say that someone else will do a job even though they may not want to: *"Did they find someone to watch the kids?" "I volunteered Dad for it."*

vol·un·teer·ism /ˌvɑlənˈtɪrɪzəm/ *n.* [U] the principle of working to support schools, organizations etc. and help other people without expecting payment

vo·lup·tu·ar·y /vəˈlʌptʃuˌɛri/ *n.* [C] LITERARY someone who enjoys physical, especially sexual, pleasure and owning expensive things

vo·lup·tu·ous /vəˈlʌptʃuəs/ *adj.* **1** a woman who is voluptuous has large breasts and a soft curved body, and is considered sexually attractive **2** LITERARY something that is voluptuous gives you pleasure because it looks, smells, or tastes good: *the voluptuous exotic feel of the Orient* —**voluptuously** *adv.* —**voluptuousness** *n.* [U]

vom·it¹ /ˈvɑmɪt/ *v.* [I,T] to bring food or drink up from your stomach out through your mouth, because you are sick

vomit² *n.* [U] food or other substances that come up from your stomach and through your mouth when you vomit

von Bingen /fɑn ˈbɪŋən/, **Hil·de·gaard** /ˈhɪldəˌgɑrd/ (1098–1179) a German musician who wrote CLASSICAL music

Von Braun /fɑn ˈbraʊn/, **Wern·her** /ˈvɛnɚ/ (1912-1977) a ROCKET engineer who was born in Germany and developed the V-2 flying bomb for the Nazis. After World War II he went to the U.S. and worked for NASA on the Apollo Program to send a SPACE-CRAFT to the moon.

voo·doo /ˈvudu/ n. [U] magical beliefs and practices used as a form of religion, especially in parts of Africa, Latin America, and the Caribbean —**voodoo·ism** n. [U]

voodoo doll /ˈ.. ˌ./ n. [C] a doll that looks like a particular person that some people believe you can stick pins in, burn etc. in order to hurt that person

vo·ra·cious /vəˈreɪʃəs, vɔ-/ adj. [usually before noun] **1** eating or wanting large quantities of food: *Caterpillars are voracious leaf-eaters.* | *Kids can have voracious appetites.* **2** extremely eager to read books, gain knowledge etc.: *a voracious reader* —**voraciously** adv. —**voraciousness** n. [U] —**voracity** /vəˈræsəti/ n. [U]

vor·tex /ˈvɔrtɛks/ n. plural **vortexes** or **vortices** /-təsiz/ [C] LITERARY **1** a large area of wind or water that spins rapidly and pulls things into its center **2** [usually singular] a situation that has a powerful effect on people's lives and that influences their behavior, even if they did not intend it to: [+ of] *His statements helped calm the vortex of emotions surrounding the case.*

vo·ta·ry /ˈvoʊtəri/ n. [C] FORMAL someone who is a strong believer of a particular religion, or a strong supporter of a particular leader

vote¹ /voʊt/ v.
1 ■choice choice [I,T] to show by marking a paper, raising your hand etc. which person you want to elect or whether you support a particular plan: *Greg says he has never voted.* | [+ for/against] *Who did you vote for in the last election?* | *Only Stevens voted against the measure.* | [+ on] *If we can't agree, we'll have to vote on it.* | [vote to do sth] *Union members voted to accept management's offer.* | **vote Democrat/Republican/Socialist etc.** *My father always votes Republican.*
2 vote sb into power/office/Congress etc. to elect someone to a position of power by voting: *Later that year, his district voted him back into Congress.* —opposite **vote sb out of power/office/Congress etc.**
3 ■title/prize title/prize [T] to choose someone or something for a particular title or prize by voting for them: [vote sb/sth sth] *Wolf's program was just voted the best show on television.*
4 ■money money [T] to agree to provide money for a particular purpose as a result of voting: *The Board of Supervisors has refused to vote more money for the project.*
5 I vote... SPOKEN said to show that you prefer one choice or possible action: [I vote (that)] *I vote that we go to the movies.* | [+ for] *"What do you want to eat?" "I vote for Mexican."*
6 vote with your feet to show that you do not support a decision or action by leaving a place or organization: *Women are voting with their feet and leaving the party in large numbers.*
7 vote with your pocketbook a) also **vote your pocketbook** to vote for someone or something that you think will help you have the most money: *People generally vote their pocketbooks against new taxes.* **b)** also **vote with your dollars** to show your support for someone or something by the way you spend your money: *Readers vote with their pocketbooks every day when they choose a newspaper.*
vote sth ↔ down phr. v. [T] to defeat a plan, law etc. by voting against it: *The amendment to cancel the space station was voted down 289-121.*
vote sb ↔ in phr. v. [T] to elect someone by voting: *A new chairman was voted in last week.*
vote sb ↔ out phr. v. [T] to remove someone from a position of power by voting: *If they don't keep their promises, we'll just vote them out.*

vote² n. [People]
1 ■choice choice [C] a choice or decision that you make by voting in an election or meeting: *Do you think my vote really makes a difference?* | *All the votes were counted before 6 o'clock.* | [+ for/against] *There were*

402 votes for Williams, and 372 against. | *Kerry ended the interview to **cast a vote** in the Senate.*
2 ■election election [C usually singular] an act of voting, when a group of people vote in order to decide or choose something: *The three proposals will be **put to a vote** next week.* | *They **took a vote**, and it was unanimous.*
3 ■result result [singular] the result of a vote: *Both sides expect a close vote.* | *The motion was passed **by a vote of 215 to 84**.*
4 the vote a) the total number of votes made in an election or the total number of people who vote: *Davis won the election with 57% of the vote.* | **the African-American/Irish/Jewish etc. vote** (=all the votes of African-Americans, Irish people etc.) **b)** the right to vote in political elections: *American women got the vote in 1920.*
5 sb/sth gets my vote SPOKEN used to say that you are ready to support someone or something: *Barkeley gets my vote for sexiest man of the decade.*

vote-get·ter /ˈ.. ˌ../ n. [C] INFORMAL someone who is voted for in an election: *Pfeifer was **the top vote-getter** in last year's election.*

vote of con·fi·dence /ˌ. . ˈ.../ n. [C] **1** a formal process in which people vote in order to show that they support someone or something, especially a government **2** something that you do or say that shows you support someone or something: *Analysts view new investment as a vote of confidence in the nation's economic future.*

vote of no con·fi·dence, vote of no-confidence /ˌ. . . . ˈ.../ n. [C] **1** a formal process in which people vote in order to show that they do not support someone or something, especially a government **2** something that you do or say that shows that you do not support someone or something

vot·er /ˈvoʊtɚ/ n. [C] someone who votes or has the right to vote, especially in a political election: *Only 40% of eligible voters participated in the last election.*

voting booth /ˈ.. ˌ./ n. [C] an enclosed place where you can vote secretly

voting ma·chine /ˈ.. ˌ./ n. [C] a machine that records votes as they are made

vo·tive /ˈvoʊtɪv/ adj. [only before noun] given or done because of a promise made to God or to a SAINT: *votive offerings*

votive can·dle /ˈ.. ˌ../ n. [C] a small CANDLE, often used for religious purposes

vouch /vaʊtʃ/ v.
vouch for sb/sth phr. v. [T] **1** to say that you firmly believe that something is true or good because of your experience or knowledge of it: *If Dr. Sheldon vouches for it, it must be true.* **2** to say that you believe that someone will behave well and that you will be responsible for their behavior, actions etc.: *Don't worry about Andy – I'll vouch for him.*

vouch·er /ˈvaʊtʃɚ/ n. [C] **1** a type of ticket that can be used instead of money for a particular purpose: *a travel voucher* **2** an official statement or RECEIPT that is given to someone to prove that their accounts are correct or that money has been paid

vouch·safe /vaʊtʃˈseɪf/ v. [I + for,T] **1** to offer, give, or tell someone something in a way that shows you trust them **2** to make it certain that something will be safe

vow¹ /vaʊ/ n. [C] **1** a serious promise: *Jim **made a vow that** he would find his wife's killer.* | **keep/break a vow** (=do or not do what you promised) **2** a religious promise that you will do something for God, the Church etc.: **take a vow of silence/chastity/poverty etc.** (=to promise that you will not speak, have sex etc.) **3 vows a)** also **marriage/wedding vows** the promises you make during a wedding ceremony: *Ron and Rhea **exchanged vows** in front of more than 100 friends on Saturday.* **b)** the promises someone makes when they become a Catholic priest, NUN etc.: *None of the women were pressured to join the Order or **take vows**.*

vow² /v./ [T] **1** to make a serious promise to yourself or someone else: [**vow to do sth**] *Supporters have vowed to continue the protest until Adams is released.* | [**vow (that)**] *I vowed that I would never drink again.* **2** FORMAL to make a religious promise that you will do something for God, the church etc.

vow·el /'vauəl/ *n.* [C] **1** one of the speech sounds that you make by letting your breath flow out without closing any part of your mouth or throat **2** a letter of the alphabet used to represent a vowel. In English the vowels are a, e, i, o, u, and sometimes y.

vox pop·u·li /,vɑks 'pɑpyəlaɪ, -'pɑpyəli/ *n.* FORMAL **the vox populi** the opinions of ordinary people

voy·age¹ /'vɔɪ-ɪdʒ/ *n.* [C] a long trip in a ship or a space vehicle: *The voyage from England to India used to take six months.*

voyage² *v.* [I] LITERARY to make a long trip in a ship or a space vehicle —see Usage Note at TRAVEL¹

voy·ag·er /'vɔɪ-ɪdʒɚ/ *n.* [C] LITERARY someone who makes long and often dangerous trips in a ship

voy·eur /vɔɪ'ɚ/ *n.* [C] **1** someone who gets sexual pleasure from secretly watching other people's sexual activities **2** someone who enjoys watching other people's private behavior or suffering —**voyeurism** *n.* [U] —**voyeuristic** /,vɔɪə'rɪstɪk◂/ *adj.*

VP, V.P. *n.* [C] INFORMAL a VICE PRESIDENT

VR *n.* [U] an abbreviation of VIRTUAL REALITY

vs. a written abbreviation of VERSUS, used especially in sports competitions: *UCLA vs. Miami*

V-shaped /'vi ʃeɪpt/ *adj.* having the shape like the letter V: *a V-shaped formation* —**V-shape** *n.* [C]

V-sign /'vi saɪn/ *n.* [C] a sign meaning "peace" or "victory" made by holding up the first two fingers of your hand

VT the written abbreviation of Vermont

Vul·can /'vʌlkən/ the Roman name for the god Hephaestus

vul·ca·nize /'vʌlkə,naɪz/ *v.* [T] to make rubber stronger using a special chemical treatment —**vulcanization** /,vʌlkənə'zeɪʃən/ *n.* [U]

vul·gar /'vʌlgɚ/ *adj.* **1** dealing with or talking about sex and body wastes in a way people think is disgusting and not socially acceptable: *vulgar language* | *Norman was a vulgar, ignorant man.* **2** not showing good judgment about what is attractive or appropriate: *a vulgar display of wealth* **3** FORMAL relating to ordinary people or the way they speak —**vulgarly** *adv.*

vul·gar·ism /'vʌlgə,rɪzəm/ *n.* [C] a VULGARITY (2)

vul·gar·i·ty /vʌl'gærəti/ *n. plural* **vulgarities 1** [U] the state or quality of being vulgar **2** [C usually plural] vulgar remarks, jokes etc.

vul·gar·ize /'vʌlgə,raɪz/ *v.* [T] FORMAL to spoil the quality or lower the standard of something that is good —**vulgarization** /,vʌlgərə'zeɪʃən/ *n.* [U]

Vul·gate /'vʌlgeɪt, -gət/ *n.* **the Vulgate** the Latin Bible commonly used in the Catholic church

vul·ner·a·ble /'vʌlnərəbəl/ *adj.* **1** someone who is vulnerable is easily harmed or hurt emotionally, physically, or morally: *I've been feeling very vulnerable since we broke up.* | [+ to] *Girls in their early teens are particularly vulnerable to negative influences.* **2** a place, thing, or idea that is vulnerable is easy to attack, damage etc.: *The bridge is extremely vulnerable.* | [+ to] *Inconsistencies in the theory make it vulnerable to criticism.* —opposite INVULNERABLE —**vulnerably** *adv.* —**vulnerability** /,vʌlnərə'bɪləti/ *n.* [C,U] *the area's vulnerability to flooding*

vul·ture /'vʌltʃɚ/ *n.* [C] **1** a large bird that eats dead animals **2** someone who uses other people's troubles for their own advantage

vul·va /'vʌlvə/ *n.* [C] TECHNICAL the outer part of a woman's sexual organs

vy·ing /'vaɪ-ɪŋ/ the present participle of VIE

V

W

W, w /'dʌbəlyu, -bəyu/ *n. plural* **W's, w's** [C] **1** the 23rd letter of the English alphabet **2** the written abbreviation of "west" or "western" **3** the written abbreviation of WATT

w/ a written abbreviation of "with," used especially when writing notes quickly —see also w/o

WA a written abbreviation of Washington

Wac, WAC /wæk/ *n.* [C] a member of the Women's Army Corps, especially during World War II

wack /wæk/ *adj.* SLANG: see WHACKED (3)

wack·o /'wækou/ *n. plural* **wackos** [C] INFORMAL someone who is crazy or strange

wack·y /'wæki/ *adj.* **wackier, wackiest 1** INFORMAL silly in an exciting or amusing way **2 wacky weed** SLANG: see MARIJUANA —**wackiness** *n.* [U]

wad[1] /wɑd/ *n.* [C] **1** a thick pile of paper or pieces of thin material: *a wad of dollar bills* **2** a thick soft mass of material that has been pressed together: *a wad of bubble gum* **3** a piece of tobacco that you hold in your mouth and chew —see also **shoot your wad** (SHOOT[1] (18)), TIGHTWAD

wad[2] *v.*

wad sth ↔ up *phr. v.* [T] to press something such as a piece of paper or cloth into a small tight ball

wad·ding /'wɑdɪŋ/ *n.* [U] soft material used for packing or to protect a wound

wad·dle /'wɑdl/ *v.* [I] to walk with short steps, swinging from one side to another like a duck: [+ **up/along/around etc.**] *The old lady waddled over to the stove to make me some tea.* —**waddle** *n.* [singular]

wade /weid/ *v.* [I always + adv./prep.,T] to walk through water that is not deep: [+ **through/across/into etc.**] *One of the bears waded into the river to fish.*

The dog wagged its tail.

wade in *phr. v.* [I] INFORMAL to interrupt someone or become involved in something in an annoying way: *I wish you wouldn't always wade in with your opinion.*

wade through sth *phr. v.* [T] to read or deal with a lot of boring papers or written work: *Employers do not have time to wade through a thirty-page resume.*

wad·ers /'weidərz/ *n.* [plural] high rubber boots that you wear for walking in water, especially when you are fishing or hunting

wad·ing bird /'.. ,./ *n.* [C] a bird that has long legs and a long neck and walks around in water to find its food

wad·ing pool /'weidɪŋ pul/ *n.* [C] a small pool filled with water that is not very deep, for small children to play in

wa·fer /'weifər/ *n.* [C] **1** a very thin CRACKER (1) **2** a thin round piece of bread used by some churches in the Christian religious ceremony of COMMUNION (1)

wafer-thin /,.. '. ◂/ *adj.* **1** extremely thin: *wafer-thin slices of cucumber* **2** a wafer-thin amount of something is extremely small: *Profits on each individual computer are wafer-thin.*

waf·fle[1] /'wɑfəl/ *n.* [C] a thin flat bread, marked with a pattern of deep squares, and usually eaten for breakfast

waffle[2] *v.* [I] INFORMAL to talk or write, often using a lot of words, but without making any decisions or without answering a question: [+ **on/about/over**] *For months, the mayor has waffled on the issue of improving public transportation.*

waffle i·ron /'.. ,../ *n.* [C] a piece of kitchen equipment used to cook waffles

---

waft /wɑft, wæft/ *v.* [I always + adv./prep.] **1** if a smell, wind, or smoke wafts somewhere, it moves gently through the air: [+ **up/along/off etc.**] *The smell of incense wafted through the theater.* **2** if music wafts somewhere, you hear it there and it is pleasant and not very loud: [+ **across/through/from etc.**] *Chamber music wafts through the bar area.*

wag[1] /wæg/ *v.* [I,T] **1** if a dog wags its tail or if its tail wags, the dog moves its tail repeatedly from one side to the other **2** to shake your finger or head repeatedly, especially to show disapproval: *He wagged his finger at Leroy.* —see also **it's (a case of) the tail wagging the dog** (TAIL[1] (12)), **tongues wagging** (TONGUE (12))

wag

wag[2] *n.* **1** [C] someone who says amusing things **2** [C usually singular] a wagging movement

wage[1] /weidʒ/ *n.* [singular] **1** also **wages** [plural] money you earn that is paid according to the number of hours, days, or weeks that you work: *Steve makes a decent wage as a civil engineer.* | *In general, computer jobs pay good wages.* | *Last year, pilots received a wage increase of 5%.* | **an hourly/daily/weekly wage** *She earns an hourly wage of $12.* | **wage levels/rates** (=fixed amounts of money paid for particular jobs) —see also MINIMUM WAGE —compare SALARY **2 a living wage** money you earn that is enough to pay for the basic things that you need to live **3 a wage freeze** an action taken by a company, government etc. to stop wages from being increased **4 a wage claim** the amount of money demanded by workers as an increase in wages —see Usage Note at PAY[2]

wage[2] *v.* [T] to be actively involved in a war, struggle, or fight against someone or something: [**wage (a) war on/against**] *Rebels have waged a 12-year war against the government.* | **wage a campaign/struggle/fight etc.** *The group has waged a letter-writing campaign to get Harris released from prison.*

wage earn·er, wage-earner /'. ,../ *n.* [C] **1** someone in a family who earns money for the rest of the family: *Jim is the family's main wage earner.* **2** someone who works for wages, often someone who works in a factory, builds things etc.

wa·ger[1] /'weidʒər/ *v.* [T] OLD-FASHIONED **1** to agree to risk money on the result of something such as a race or game: [**wager sth on sb/sth**] *He wagered fifty dollars on Dallas to win the Super Bowl.* **2 I'll wager** SPOKEN used to say that you are so sure that something is true that you are willing to risk money on it: *I'll wager that boy's never worked in his life!* —compare BET[1] (1)

wager[2] *n.* [C] an agreement in which you win or lose money according to the result of something such as a race; BET[2] (1)

wag·gle /'wægəl/ *v.* [I,T] to WIGGLE —**waggle** *n.* [C]

Wag·ner, Rich·ard /'vɑgnər, 'rɪkɑrt/ (1813–1883) a German musician who is most famous for writing long OPERAS based on German MYTHOLOGY —**Wagnerian** /vɑg'nɪriən/ *adj.*

wag·on /'wægən/ *n.* [C] **1** a strong vehicle with four wheels, used for carrying heavy loads and usually pulled by horses **2** INFORMAL a STATION WAGON **3 be on the wagon** INFORMAL to not drink alcohol anymore **4 fall off the wagon** INFORMAL to start drinking alcohol again after you have decided to stop —see also PADDY WAGON

wagon train /'.. ,./ *n.* [C] a long line of wagons and horses used by the people who moved to the West of America in the 19th century

waif /weif/ *n.* [C] someone, especially a child, who is pale and thin and looks as if they do not have a home

W

wail /weɪl/ v. **1** [I,T] to say something in a loud, sad, and complaining way: *"The world is coming to an end!" the woman wailed.* **2** [I] to cry out with a long, high sound, especially because you are very sad or in pain: *People were wailing on the streets.* **3** [I] to make a long, high sound, or to sing this way —**wail** *n.* [C] *the wail of police sirens* —**wailing** *n.* [singular,U]

wain·scot /'weɪnskət, -skoʊt, -skɑt/ also **wain·scot·ing** /'weɪnskətɪŋ/ n. [C,U] wood that is put on the bottom part of a wall inside a house or office, as a decoration —**wainscoted** *adj.*

waist /weɪst/ n. [C] **1** the part in the middle of your body, just above the HIPS: *The dress emphasized her tiny waist.* | **from the waist up/down** *Lota was paralyzed from the waist down.* | *The guy stood there, stripped to the waist* (=not wearing any clothes on the top half of his body). —see picture at BODY **2** the part of a piece of clothing that goes around this part of your body **3** TECHNICAL the middle part of a ship —see also -WAISTED

waist·band /'weɪstbænd/ n. [C] the part of a skirt, pair of pants etc. that fastens around your waist

waist·coat /'weskət, 'weɪstkoʊt/ n. [C] a VEST¹ (1)

waist-deep /ˌ. '.ᵗ/ adj. adv. deep enough to reach your waist: *The water was waist-deep.*

-waisted /'weɪstɪd/ [in adjectives] **slim-waisted/narrow-waisted/thick-waisted etc.** having a thin, thick etc. waist

waist-high /ˌ. '.ᵗ/ adj., adv. high enough to reach your waist: *a waist-high fence*

waist·line /'weɪstlaɪn/ n. [C] **1** the area around your waist, especially used to judge how fat or thin you are: *a trim waistline* **2** the part of a piece of clothing that fits around your waist

wait¹ /weɪt/ v.

1 delay/not start sth [I] to not do something or go somewhere until something else happens, someone arrives etc.: *Hurry up! Everyone's waiting.* | [+ for] *I've been waiting for 30 minutes.* | *Wait right here until I come back.* | [wait to do sth] *Are you waiting to use the phone?* | *I'm sorry to have kept you waiting* (=made you wait, especially because I arrived late or was busy doing something else).

2 expect sth to happen [I] to expect something to happen that has not happened yet: *"Have you heard about the job?" "No, I'm still waiting."* | [wait for sth] *I'm still waiting for my test results.* | [wait for sth to happen] *We're waiting for the prices to go down before we buy a computer.* | [wait for sb to do sth] *Mom's still waiting for Dad to repaint the house.*

3 wait tables to have the job of serving food to people at their table in a restaurant: *I spent the summer waiting tables.*

SPOKEN PHRASES

4 wait a minute/second/moment etc. a) used to stop someone for a short time when they are leaving or starting to do something: *Wait a moment, I've got to get my books.* **b)** used to interrupt someone, especially because you do not agree with what they are saying: *Wait a minute, I've already paid you for it.* **c)** used when you suddenly remember or notice something: *Wait a minute, I think that's her house over there.*

5 I can't wait also **I can hardly wait a)** used when you feel excited and impatient about something that is going to happen soon: *We're going to Australia on Saturday – I can't wait!* | [sb can't wait to do sth] *I can't wait to tell Gloria the good news.* | [+ for] *I can't wait for my vacation.* **b)** HUMOROUS used to say that something seems likely to be very boring: *A lecture on transformational grammar? I can hardly wait.*

6 sth can/can't wait used to say that something is very urgent or is not urgent: *Go home – the report can wait until tomorrow.*

7 wait and see used to say that someone should be patient because they will find out about something

later: *I don't know what his decision will be – we'll have to wait and see.*

8 wait until/till used when you are excited about telling or showing someone something: *Wait till you see Gaby's new house!*

9 sth is (well) worth waiting for used to say that something is very good, even though it takes a long time to come: *Tuesday night's Boston-Chicago game was worth waiting for.*

10 what are you waiting for? used to tell someone to do something immediately: *What are you waiting for? Ask her out on a date.*

11 what are we waiting for? used to say in a cheerful way that you think everyone should start doing something immediately: *What are we waiting for? Let's go eat.*

12 wait your turn used to tell someone to stay calm and wait until it is their turn to do something, instead of trying to move ahead of other people

13 (just) you wait used to tell someone that you are sure something will happen: *It'll be a huge success, just you wait.*

14 be waiting INFORMAL if something is waiting for you, it is ready for you to use, get etc.: *The report was typed up and waiting when they came back from coffee.*

15 be waiting in the wings to be ready to do something if it is necessary or if an appropriate time comes: *Young, a talented quarterback, was waiting in the wings for the day when Montana couldn't play.*

16 (play) a/the waiting game to deliberately do nothing and wait to see what other people do, in order to get an advantage for yourself

wait around *phr. v.* [I] to stay in the same place and do nothing while you are waiting for something to happen, someone to arrive etc.: *I waited around for 20 minutes and she never showed up.*

wait on sb/sth *phr. v.* [T] **1** to serve food to someone at their table, especially in a restaurant **2** to wait for a particular event, piece of information etc., especially before doing something or making a decision: *I'm waiting on a phone call from our sales rep.* **3 wait on sb hand and foot** to do everything for someone while they do nothing: *Oliver expects us to wait on him hand and foot.*

wait sth ↔ **out** *phr. v.* [T] if you wait out an event or period or time, especially a bad one, you wait for it to finish: *We spent the night at the airport, waiting out the snow storm.*

wait up *phr. v.* [I] **1** to wait for someone to return before you go to bed: [+ for] *Don't wait up for me – I'll be very late.* **2 Wait up!** SPOKEN used to tell someone to stop, so that you can talk to them or go with them

---

USAGE NOTE: WAIT

WORD CHOICE: wait, expect, await
If you **wait for** someone to come or for something to happen, you delay doing something or change what you are doing until they come or until it happens. Often you do not do other things because you are **waiting:** *I'm waiting for Judy to call.* | *I'm waiting to use that machine.* If you **expect** someone or something, you are sure that the person will come or that the event will happen, but you do not necessarily change what you are doing now because of this: *I can't talk very long – I'm expecting guests at 8 p.m.* | *She's expecting a letter from my boyfriend.* **Await** is a very formal word for **wait for.**
GRAMMAR
You **wait for** someone or something (NOT *"wait them"* or *"wait it"*). But you **await** something (NOT *"await for it"*).

---

wait² n. [C] a period of time in which you wait for something to happen, someone to arrive etc.: *There is often a one-hour wait to see a doctor.* —see also **lie in wait (for sb/sth)** (LIE¹ (7))

Waite /weɪt/, **Mor·ri·son** /'mɔrəsən/ (1816–1888) a CHIEF JUSTICE on the U.S. Supreme Court

wait·er /'weɪtɚ/ n. [C] a man who serves food and drinks to the people at the tables in a restaurant

wait·ing list /'.. ,./ n. [C] a list of people who have asked for something but who must wait before they can have it: *I heard there's a waiting list to get into the school.*

waiting room /'.. ,./ n. [C] a room for people to wait in, for example to see a doctor, take a train etc.

wait·ress /'weitris/ n. [C] a woman who serves food and drink to people at the tables in a restaurant

wait·staff /'weitstæf/ n. [U] all the waiters and waitresses that work at a restaurant

waive /weiv/ v. [T] to state officially that a right, rule etc. can be ignored, because at this time it is not useful or important: *She waived her right to a lawyer.*

waiv·er /'weivɚ/ n. [C] TECHNICAL an official written statement saying that a right, claim etc. can be waived

wake¹ /weik/ v. past tense **woke** past participle **woken** [I,T] also **wake up** to stop sleeping, or to make someone stop sleeping: *Dad said he woke up at five this morning.* | *Try not to wake the baby if you go in the bedroom.*

wake up phr. v. [I,T] **1** to start to listen or pay attention to something: *Wake up! I'm trying to tell you something important.* **2 wake up and smell the coffee** SPOKEN used to tell someone to recognize the truth or reality of a situation

wake (up) to phr. v. [T] **1** to start to realize and understand a danger, an idea etc.: *You have to wake up to the fact that alcohol is killing you.* **2** to experience something as you are waking up: *Nancy woke to the sound of birds outside her window.*

wake² n. [C] **1 in the wake of sth** if something, especially something bad, happens in the wake of an event, it happens afterward and usually as a result of it: *In the wake of Thailand's economic troubles, Malaysia's currency also sank.* **2 in sb's/sth's wake** behind or after someone or something has moved quickly away: *The tornado left hundreds of damaged homes in its wake.* **3** the track or path made behind a boat, car etc. as it moves along **4** the time before a funeral when friends and relatives meet to remember the dead person

Wake At·oll /,weik 'ætɒl/ also **Wake Is·land** /,. '../ a U.S. TERRITORY that is an island in the western Pacific Ocean

wake·ful /'weikfəl/ adj. **1 a)** unable to sleep: *She had been up most of the night with a wakeful baby.* **b)** a wakeful period of time is one when you cannot sleep **2** FORMAL always watching and ready to do whatever is necessary —**wakefulness** n. [U]

wak·en /'weikən/ v. [I,T] FORMAL to wake, or to wake someone: *He wasn't sure if he should waken his mother.* | *Agnes would often waken at the slightest sound.*

wake-up call /'. . ,./ n. [C] **1** a telephone call that someone makes to you, especially at a hotel, to wake you up in the morning **2** an experience or event which shocks you and makes you realize that something bad is happening and that changes must be made: *The latest report on increased drug use is a wake-up call for America.*

wak·ing /'weikiŋ/ adj. **waking hours/life/day etc.** all the time when you are awake: *Children spend almost half their waking hours in school.*

Wal·dorf sal·ad /,woldorf 'sæləd/ n. [C] a mixture of small pieces of apples, CELERY, nuts, and MAYONNAISE

Wales /weilz/ a country in the United Kingdom, west of England

Wa·le·sa /vɑ'lɛnsɑ/, **Lech** /lɛk/ (1943–) the President of Poland from 1990 to 1995

walk¹ /wɔk/ v.

1 move along [I] to move along by putting one foot in front of the other: *I'll bet we walked at least three miles.* | [+ **to/along/around** etc.] *Turn left and walk up the hill.* | *We spent the day walking around the city.* | **walk back/home** *It's late – are you sure you want to walk back by yourself?* | **walk up/over to** *Jane walked over to him and asked the time.*

2 area/distance [T] to walk in order to get somewhere, across a particular area or distance: *I normally walk the six blocks to the office.*

3 walk the dog to take a dog outside so that it can walk, run, play etc.

4 walk to a place with sb [T] to walk somewhere with someone, especially to make sure that they are safe: *It's late – I'll walk you home.* | *Schools are urging parents to walk their children to school.* | *Ted said he'd walk me to my car.*

5 walk free also **walk** INFORMAL to leave a court of law without being punished or sent to prison: *Ferguson walked free after the charges were dropped.* | *If more evidence isn't found, Harris will walk.*

6 walk it SPOKEN to go somewhere by walking: *If the last bus has gone, we'll have to walk it.*

7 baseball [I,T] if a PITCHER walks a BATTER or if the batter walks, the pitcher throws the ball four times outside the area he is aiming at, so that the batter is allowed to go to the first of the four BASES: *Pitchers intentionally walked McCovery 260 times.*

8 be walking on eggshells/eggs to be treating someone very carefully because they easily become very angry or very upset: *Everyone was walking on eggshells at the office.*

9 heavy object [T] to move a heavy object slowly by moving first one side and then the other: *Let's try walking the refrigerator over to the wall.*

10 walking pace the speed that you normally walk at

11 walk tall to be proud and confident because you know that you have not done anything wrong

12 be walking on air to feel extremely happy: *On my first day, I earned $190, and I was walking on air.*

13 walk the walk to do the things that people expect or think are necessary in a particular situation: *People are motivated by leaders who actually walk the walk.* —compare **talk the talk** (TALK¹ (26))

14 walk the streets OLD-FASHIONED an expression meaning to be a PROSTITUTE

15 walk the plank a phrase meaning to be forced to walk along a board laid over the side of the ship until you fall off into the ocean, used especially in relation to PIRATES

walk away phr. v. [I] **1** to leave a situation to do something else, especially to leave a bad situation rather than staying and trying to make it better: [+ **from**] *She walked away from a successful career in pop music to have a family.* **2** to come out of an accident or very bad situation without being harmed: *Amazingly, Darcy walked away without a scratch.*

walk away with sth phr. v. [T] to win something easily or in way that surprises everyone: *Nicholson walked away with the award for Best Actor.*

walk in phr. v. [I,T] to enter a building or room, especially in an unexpected way without being invited: *Don't just walk in without knocking first.* | *As soon as I walked in the door, she started yelling at me.* | *At the clinic, patients can walk in off the street* (=visit someone such as a doctor without having previously arranged to see them) *and get help.*

walk in on sb phr. v. [T] to go into a place and interrupt someone who you did not expect to be there: *I walked in on Joe and Susan kissing in his office*

walk into sth phr. v. [T] **1** to hit an object accidentally as you are walking along: **walk straight/right** etc. **into sth** *He walked straight into the edge of the door.* **2** if you walk into a bad situation, you become involved in it without intending to **3** to make yourself look stupid when you could easily have avoided it if you had been more careful: **walk straight/right into** *I guess I walked right into that joke.*

walk off phr. v. **1** [I] to leave someone by walking away from them, especially in a rude or angry way: *He took his books and walked off without saying goodbye.* **2** [T] if you walk off an injury or a bad feeling, you walk for a little while to try to make it go away: *I twisted my ankle – I'm going to try to walk it off.* **3 walk off dinner/a meal etc.** to walk outside for a little while so that your stomach feels less full **4 walk off (the/your job)** to stop working as a protest: *Without new contracts, mine workers will*

W

walk off their jobs Thursday. **5 walk sb's legs off** SPOKEN to make someone tired by making them walk too far

walk off with sth *phr. v.* [T] to take, win, or steal something: *Somebody walked off with my jacket.* | *The Soviet team walked off with the most Olympic gold medals.*

walk over sb *phr. v.* [T] to treat someone badly by always making them do what you want them to do: *Greg lets his older sister walk all over him.*

walk out *phr. v.* [I] **1** to go outside: [+ into] *Jerri and I walked out into the backyard.* **2** to leave a place suddenly, especially because you disapprove of something: *Fred walked out of the party when someone started smoking a joint.* **3** to stop working as a protest: *Workers are threatening to walk out if an agreement is not reached.*

walk out on *phr. v.* [T] **1** [walk out on sb] to leave your husband, wife etc. suddenly: *When she was three months pregnant, Pete walked out on her.* **2** [walk out on sth] to stop doing something you have agreed to do or that you are responsible for: *Several investors have walked out of the project.*

walk sth ↔ **through** *phr. v.* [T] practice something: *Let's walk through scene two to see how long it takes.*

walk sb **through** sth *phr. v.* [T] to give someone careful instructions as they do something: *I need someone to walk me through the software installation.*

walk² *n.* **1** [C] a trip that you make by walking, especially for exercise or enjoyment: *It's a long walk. Maybe we should get the bus.* | *From here to the bus station is a five-minute walk.* | *Why don't we take the kids for a walk?* | *Let's go for a walk.* | *I'm going to take a walk at lunchtime.* | [walk to/through/across etc.] *The walk across the bridge is wonderful.* **2** [C] a particular path or ROUTE that you walk, especially through an attractive or interesting area: *There are some particularly interesting walks to the north of the city.* **3** [singular,U] the way someone walks: *He has a funny walk.* —see also WALK OF LIFE

walk·a·thon /ˈwɔkəˌθɑn/ *n.* [C] an occasion when a lot of people go for a long walk, especially in order to earn money for a CHARITY

walk·a·way /ˈwɔkəweɪ/ *n.* [C] INFORMAL an easy victory

walk·er /ˈwɔkɚ/ *n.* [C] **1** someone who walks for pleasure or exercise: *On most weekdays, you can see dozens of elderly walkers in the mall.* **2 a fast/slow etc. walker** someone who walks fast, slowly etc. **3** a metal frame with wheels that old or sick people use to help them walk **4** a frame on wheels that supports a baby so that it can use its legs to move around before it is able to walk

walk·ie-talk·ie /ˌwɔki ˈtɔki/ *n.* [C] a small radio that you can carry and use to speak to other people who have the same type of radio

walk-in /ˈ. ./ *adj.* [only before noun] big enough for a person to walk inside: *a walk-in closet*

walk·ing¹ /ˈwɔkɪŋ/ *n.* [U] **1** the activity of going for walks: *I like to go walking in the woods just to breathe the fresh air.* **2** the sport of walking long distances as fast as you can without actually running

walking² *adj.* [only before noun] **1 walking shoes/boots** shoes or boots that are strong and comfortable, because they are intended for walking long distances **2 a walking tour** a TOUR in which you walk around to see interesting parts of a city, town etc. **3 a walking dictionary/encyclopedia** HUMOROUS someone who knows a lot, and always has the information that you want **4 a walking disaster (area)** HUMOROUS someone who always drops things, has accidents, makes mistakes etc.

walking pa·pers /ˈ.. ˌ../ *n.* [plural] **give sb their walking papers** to tell someone that they must leave a place or a job

walking stick /ˈ.. ˌ./ *n.* [C] **1** a stick that is used to support someone, especially an old person, while they walk **2** an insect with a long thin body that looks similar to a small stick

Walk·man /ˈwɔkmən/ *n.* [C] TRADEMARK a small CASSETTE DECK with HEADPHONES, that you carry with you so that you can listen to music; PERSONAL STEREO

walk of life /ˌ.. ˈ./ *n.* [C] the position in society someone has, especially the type of job they have: **from every walk of life/from all walks of life** *People from all walks of life took part in the celebration.*

walk-on /ˈ. ./ *n.* [C] **1** someone who plays for a college sports team without having been given a sports SCHOLARSHIP **2 a)** also **walk-on part** a small acting part with no words to say in a play or movie **b)** an actor who has a part like this

walk·out /ˈwɔk-aʊt/ *n.* [C] an occasion when people stop working or leave somewhere as a protest: *Students have staged several walkouts in protest of tuition increases.* —see also **walk out** (WALK¹)

walk·o·ver /ˈwɔkˌoʊvɚ/ *n.* [C] INFORMAL a very easy victory —see also **walk over** (WALK¹)

walk-up /ˈ. ./ *n.* [C] INFORMAL **1** a tall apartment building that does not have an ELEVATOR **2** an apartment, office etc. in a building like this

walk·way /ˈwɔk-weɪ/ *n. plural* **walkways** [C] an outside path, sometimes above the ground, built to connect two parts of a building or two buildings: *a covered walkway*

wall¹ /wɔl/ *n.*

1 in a building [C] one of the sides of a room or building: *We should hang the picture on this wall over here.*

2 around an area [C] an upright structure with flat sides that is made of stone or brick, that divides one area from another: *A brick wall surrounds the building.*

3 tube/container [C] the side of something hollow, such as a pipe or tube: *The walls of the blood vessels had been damaged.*

4 wall of fire/water etc. a tall mass of something such as fire or water, that prevents anything getting through: *A wall of fire was advancing through the forest.*

5 wall of silence a situation in which no one will tell you what you want to know: *The police investigation was met with a wall of silence.*

6 drive sb up the wall SPOKEN to annoy someone very much: *Her music is driving me up the wall.*

7 climb the walls INFORMAL to feel extremely anxious and impatient, especially because something annoys you: *After spending three hours in a car with Katie, I was climbing the walls.*

8 push/drive/send sb to the wall INFORMAL if someone pushes or drives someone to the wall, they make things very difficult for them: *Consumers are pushing retailers to the wall by demanding lower prices.*

9 go to the wall a) if a company goes to the wall, it fails, especially because of financial difficulties **b)** INFORMAL if someone goes to the wall for someone or to do something, they do everything that is possible to help someone or to achieve something: *He's not a candidate that Democrats would go to the wall for.*

10 these four walls SPOKEN the room that you are in, especially considered as a private place: *I don't want anything that I have said repeated outside these four walls.*

11 the walls have ears used to warn people to be careful what they say, because other people, especially enemies, could be listening

12 hit the wall INFORMAL if someone hits the wall, they reach the point when they are the most physically tired when doing a sport —see also **have your back to the wall** (BACK² (13)), **bang your head against/on a (brick) wall** (BANG¹ (5)), **nail sb to the wall/cross** (NAIL² (4)), OFF-THE-WALL, **sth is like talking to a brick wall** (TALK¹ (15)), **the handwriting is on the wall** (HANDWRITING (2))

wall² *v.*

wall sth ↔ **in** *phr. v.* [T] to surround an open area with walls: *They decided to wall the garden in.*

wall off *phr. v.* [T] **1** [wall sth ↔ off] to keep one area or room separate from another, by building a wall: *The back half of the museum was walled off for renovation.* **2** [wall sb/sth ↔ off] to completely separate someone or something from someone or something else: *The child began to wall himself off from family and friends.*

wall sth ↔ **up** *phr. v.* [T] to fill in a DOORWAY, window etc. with bricks or stone: *The church's entrance has been walled up for over a century.*

wal·la·by /'wɑləbi/ *n. plural* **wallabies** [C] an Australian animal that looks like a small KANGAROO

wall·board /'wɔlbɔrd/ *n.* [C] a type of board made of sheets of paper over GYPSUM, that is used to make walls inside a building

wall·chart /'wɔltʃɑrt/ *n.* [C] a large piece of paper with information on it that is put on a wall

wall cov·er·ing /'. ,.../ *n.* [C] material such as paper or cloth that is used to cover walls: *red damask silk wall coverings*

walled /wɔld/ *adj.* [only before noun] **a walled garden/city/town etc.** a garden, city etc. that has a wall around it

wal·let /'wɑlɪt, 'wɔ-/ *n.* [C] a small flat folding case that you carry in your pocket, for holding paper money etc. —compare PURSE¹ (1)

wall·eye /'wɔlaɪ/ also **walleyed pike** /,.. '.../ *n.* [C,U] a type of FRESHWATER fish that has large eyes on opposite sides of its head

wall-eyed /,. '.‹/ *adj.* having one or both eyes that seem to point to the side, rather than straight forward

wall·flow·er /'wɔl,flaʊər/ *n.* [C] **1** INFORMAL someone at a party, dance etc. who is not asked to dance or take part in the activities **2** a sweet-smelling garden plant with yellow and red flowers

wal·lop¹ /'wɑləp/ *v.* [T] INFORMAL to hit someone or something very hard

wallop² *n.* [C] INFORMAL a hard hit, especially with your hand

wal·lop·ing¹ /'wɑləpɪŋ/ *n.* SPOKEN **give sb/get a walloping** to hit someone repeatedly as a punishment

walloping² *adj.* [only before noun] SPOKEN very big: *walloping steaks*

wal·low¹ /'wɑloʊ/ *v.* [I] **1 wallow in self-pity/despair/defeat etc.** DISAPPROVING to seem to enjoy being sad, upset etc., especially because you get sympathy from other people: *Stop wallowing in self-pity, and do something positive.* **2** if an animal wallows, it rolls around in mud, water etc. for pleasure: *pigs wallowing in the mud*

wallow² *n.* [C] a place where animals go to wallow, especially in mud

wall paint·ing /'. ,../ *n.* [C] a picture that has been painted directly onto a wall, especially a FRESCO

wall·pa·per¹ /'wɔl,peɪpər/ *n.* [C,U] **1** paper that you stick onto the walls of a room in order to decorate it **2** the picture on the screen of your computer, behind the FILES you are using

wallpaper² *v.* [T] to put wallpaper onto the walls of a room

Wall Street /'. ./ *n.* **1** a street in New York City, where the American STOCK EXCHANGE is **2** the American STOCK EXCHANGE, or the people who work there: *Wall Street expects high earnings from industrial stocks.* —see picture on page 1328

wall-to-wall /,. . '.‹/ *adj.* **1** [only before noun] covering the whole floor: *wall-to-wall carpeting* **2** INFORMAL filling all the space or time available, especially in a way you do not like: *a room of wall-to-wall children*

wal·nut /'wɔlnʌt/ *n.* **1** [C] a slightly bitter nut with a large light brown shell: *coffee and walnut cake* **2** [C] also **walnut tree** a tree that produces this type of nut **3** [U] the wood from a walnut tree, often used to make furniture

wal·rus /'wɔlrəs, 'wɑl-/ *n.* [C] a large sea animal with two long TUSKs coming out from the sides of its mouth

waltz¹ /wɔlts/ *n.* [C] **1** a fairly slow dance with RHYTHM consisting of patterns of three beats: *Viennese waltzes* **2** a piece of music intended for this type of dance: *a Strauss waltz*

waltz² *v.* **1** [I,T] to dance a waltz **2** [I always + adv./prep.] INFORMAL to walk somewhere calmly and

confidently: [**waltz in/into etc.**] *You can't just waltz in here and start ordering people around.*

waltz off with sth *phr. v.* [T] INFORMAL to take something without permission or without realizing you have done this: *Someone just waltzed off with my pen again.*

waltz through sth *phr. v.* [T] INFORMAL **waltz through a test/game/exam etc.** to pass a test, win a game etc. without any difficulty: *Utah is expected to waltz through the playoffs.*

Wam·pa·no·ag /,wɑmpə'noʊæg/ a Native American tribe from the northeastern U.S.

wam·pum /'wɑmpəm/ *n.* [U] **1** shells put into strings, belts etc., used in past times as money by Native Americans **2** INFORMAL money

wan /wɑn/ *adj.* LITERARY looking pale, weak, or tired: *Angela looked wan and tired.* —**wanly** *adv.*

wand /wɑnd/ *n.* [C] **1** a thin stick you hold in your hand to do magic tricks **2** a tool that looks like a thin stick: *a mascara wand*

wan·der /'wɑndər/ *v.* **1** [I,T] to move slowly across or around an area, without a clear direction or purpose: *With their parents at work, the kids are left to wander the streets.* | [**wander in/through/around etc.**] *The nightclub closed and people started wandering out to the parking lot.* **2** also **wander off** [I] to move away from where you are supposed to stay: *She may have wandered off and become lost.* **3** [I] to start to talk about something not related to the main subject that you were talking about before: [**+ from/off**] *Professor Cartmel often wandered from the subject.* **4 sb's mind wanders** also **sb's thoughts wander a)** if your mind, thoughts etc. wander, you stop paying attention to something and think about something else, especially because you are bored or worried: *I'm sorry, my mind was wandering. What did you say?* | [**+ to**] *My thoughts wandered to my childhood in Florida.* **b)** used to say that someone has become unable to think clearly, especially because they are old **5** [I] if a road or a river wanders somewhere, it does not go straight but in curves: [**+ through/across/along**] *A wooden fence wanders along the edge of the farm.* —**wanderer** *n.* [C]

wan·der·ings /'wɑndərɪŋz/ *n.* [plural] LITERARY trips to many different places, where you do not stay for very long: *Ruess financed his wanderings through Asia by selling his paintings.*

wan·der·lust /'wɑndər,lʌst/ *n.* [singular,U] a strong desire to travel to different places

wane¹ /weɪn/ *v.* [I] **1** if something such as power, influence, or a feeling wanes, it gradually becomes less strong or less important: *When girls hit adolescence, their self-confidence begins to wane.* **2** when the moon wanes, you gradually see less of it —compare **wax and wane** (WAX² (5))

wane² *n.* **on the wane** becoming smaller, weaker, or less important: *Gonzales' power was on the wane.*

wan·gle /'wæŋgəl/ *v.* [T] INFORMAL to get something or arrange for something to happen, by persuading or tricking someone: [**wangle sth (out of sb)**] *Tanner managed to wangle a pay raise out of him.* | *Somehow he wangled his way out of* (=got out of a difficult or bad situation) *the meeting.* —**wangle** *n.* [singular]

wan·na /'wʌnə, 'wɑnə/ a short form of "want to" or "want a," used in writing to show how people sound when they speak: *Do you wanna go to a movie tonight?*

wan·na·be /'wʌnəbi/ *n.* [C] INFORMAL someone who wants to be like someone famous or have money and power: *Kohler is a 17-year-old rapper wannabe from Montana.* —**wannabe** *adj.* —compare WOULD-BE

want¹ /wʌnt, wɑnt, wɔnt/ *v.* [not usually in progressive]

1 [desire/need] [T] to have a desire or need for something: *I want some coffee.* | *Do you just want clothes for your birthday?* | [**want to do sth**] *Adam* *wants to go see a movie.* | [**want sb to do sth**] *I don't want my boss to know that I'm looking for another job.* | [**want sth done**] *Mr. Bernstein wants that letter typed today.* | **What do you want with** (=why do you want) *a hammer?* —see Usage Note at WISH¹

2 want sth from/of sb to desire someone to do something: *I'm not exactly sure what my supervisor wants from me.*

3 want in/out INFORMAL **a)** to want to go in to or out of a place: *The cat wants out.* **b)** to want to take part in a plan or to want to stop being involved: *We definitely want in on the deal.*

4 lack [I,T] FORMAL to suffer because you do not have something: *In many poorer countries, people still want basic food and shelter.*

5 sex [T] VULGAR if you want someone, you want to have sex with them

SPOKEN PHRASES

6 want...? used when offering something to someone: *Want to go fishing?*

7 what do you want? used to ask, often in a slightly rude way, what someone wants you to give them, do for them etc.: *What do you want now? I'm busy.*

8 who wants...? a) used when offering something to a group of people: *Who wants ice cream?* **b)** used to say that you do not like something, do not think that it is worth doing etc.: *I wasn't invited, but who wants to listen her stories all night anyway?*

9 if you want used to make a suggestion, or to say that you will do something that someone else has suggested: *I can go to the store for you if you want.*

10 I don't want to sound/be..., but... used to be polite when you are going to tell someone something that may upset them: *I don't want to sound rude, but I think you've had too much to drink.*

11 ask for sb [T] to ask for someone to come and talk to you, or to come to a particular place: *He wants you in his office right away.*

12 I want (you to do) sth used to tell someone to do something, especially to show that you are serious or angry: *I want an explanation right now.*

13 should [T] ought or should: [**want to do sth**] *You really want to get your brakes checked as soon as possible.*

14 what I want used to explain or say exactly what it is that you want: *What I want is a large house in the country.*

15 all I want used to say that you only want something simple or small, and you think it is fair to ask for it: *All I want is some peace and quiet around here.*

16 I just wanted to say/know etc. used to politely say something, ask about something etc.: *I just wanted to make sure we're still meeting at 8 p.m.*

17 it's/that's just what I (always) wanted used to say that you like a present you have just been given very much

18 (do) you want a piece of me? SPOKEN used to ask someone if they want to fight with you

—see also **waste not, want not** (WASTE² (5))

want for sth *phr. v.* [T] OLD-FASHIONED to not have something that you need: *At least I can say that my kids never wanted for anything.*

want² *n.*

1 lack [C,U] FORMAL something that you need but do not have: *The expansion of the bus system satisfies a want in the community.* | *The building is in want of repair.*

2 for want of a better word/term/phrase etc. used to say that there is no exact word to describe what you are talking about, and to give a new word or phrase instead: *For want of a better expression, I'll call these activities "good religion."*

3 for want of sth used to say that the lack of something has caused a particular situation, especially a bad situation: *My uncle lies ill for want of better medical care.*

4 not for want of trying/asking etc. used to say that even though something did not happen or succeed, it was not because you did not try hard enough, ask

enough etc.: *We didn't get permission, but it wasn't for want of asking.*

5 for want of anything better (to do) if you do something for want of anything better, you do it only because there is nothing else you want to do

6 not enough food/money etc. [U] FORMAL a situation in which people do not have enough food, money, clothes etc.: *People need to have freedom from want.*

want ad /'. ./ *n.* [C] a CLASSIFIED AD

want·ed /'wɑntɪd/ *adj.* **1** [usually not before noun] someone who is wanted is being looked for by the police: [**+ for**] *Larson is wanted for bank robbery.* **2** [not before noun] needed or desired: *Mr. Bendiger, you're wanted on the telephone.* —opposite UNWANTED **3** someone, especially a child, who is wanted is loved and cared for: *I never felt wanted by my parents.* —opposite UNWANTED

want·ing /'wɑntɪŋ/ *adj.* [not before noun] FORMAL not as good as or not of as high a standard as you think someone or something should be: [**+ in**] *Our evaluation shows the teacher wanting in several skill areas.* | *Medical facilities in the country have been found wanting.*

wan·ton /'wɑntⁿn, 'wɔn-/ *adj.* **1** wanton cruelty, destruction etc. deliberately harms someone or damages something for no reason: *the wanton killing of civilians* **2** OLD-FASHIONED a wanton woman is considered immoral because she has sex with a lot of men **3** FORMAL uncontrolled: *wanton jungle growth* —**wantonly** *adv.*

wap·i·ti /'wɑpəti/ *n. plural* **wapiti** or **wapitis** [C] an ELK

war /wɔr/ *n.* **1** [C,U] fighting between two or more countries or between opposing groups within a country, involving large numbers of soldiers and weapons: *the Spanish-American War* | [**+ between**] *The war between the north and the south was particularly brutal.* | *Congress is not interested in* **fighting a war** *with our allies.* | **War broke out** (=war began) *in September of 1939.* | **be at war (with/against)** *In 1793, England was at war with France.* | *Britain had already* **declared war on** (=announced publicly and officially that they were going to fight a war against) *Germany.* | **go to war (with/against)** (=start to fight a war with another country) | **wage war (on/against)** (=start and continue a war, especially for a long period) | **a nuclear/guerrilla/ground etc. war** (=a war fought with a particular kind of weapon, in a particular kind of way, or in a particular place) **2** [C,U] a struggle over a long period of time to control something harmful: [**+ against/on**] *the city's war on hunger* **3** [C,U] a situation in which a person or group is fighting for power, influence, or control: *Gas stations in the city are involved in a price war.* **4 This means war!** SPOKEN, HUMOROUS used to say that you are ready to argue or fight about something —see also CIVIL WAR, COLD WAR, PRICE WAR, PRISONER OF WAR, WAR OF ATTRITION, WAR OF NERVES, WAR OF WORDS, WARRING

War be·tween the States, the /,. .... './ another name for the U.S. CIVIL WAR

war·ble /'wɔrbəl/ *v.* [I,T] **1** HUMOROUS to sing **2** to sing with a high continuous but rapidly changing sound, the way a bird does —**warble** *n.* [singular]

war·bler /'wɔrblɚ/ *n.* [C] **1** a bird that can make musical sounds **2** HUMOROUS a singer, especially one who does not sing very well

war bon·net, warbonnet /'. ,../ *n.* [C] a type of Native American hat decorated with feathers

war bride /'. ./ *n.* [C] a woman who marries a foreign soldier who is in her country because there is a war

war cab·i·net /'. ,.../ *n.* [C] a group of important politicians who meet to make decisions for a government during a war

war chest /'. ./ *n.* [C] **1** INFORMAL the money that a group, politician, or business has available to spend on an election, advertising etc. **2** INFORMAL the money that a government has available to spend on war

war crime /'. ./ *n.* [C] an illegal and cruel act done during a war —**war criminal** *n.* [C]

war cry /ˈ. ./ n. plural **war cries** [C] a shout used by people fighting in a battle to show their courage and frighten the enemy —see also BATTLE CRY

ward[1] /wɔrd/ n. [C] **1** an area in a hospital where people who need medical treatment stay: **the maternity/psychiatric/pediatric etc. ward** (=the ward for women who are having babies, for people who are mentally ill, for children etc.) **2** LAW someone, especially a child, who is under the legal protection of another person or of a law court: *At the age of five, Jason became a ward of the state.* **3** one of the small areas that a city has been divided into for the purpose of local elections

ward[2] v.

ward sth ↔ **off** phr. v. [T] to do something to protect yourself from something such as an illness, danger, attack etc.: *To ward off sharks, lanterns are hung near the surface of the water.*

-ward /wəd/ suffix [in adjectives and adverbs] toward a particular direction or place: *a homeward journey* | *Move forward, please.* | *a downward movement*

Ward /wɔrd/, **A. Mont·gom·ery** /eɪ mɒntˈɡʌmri/ (1844–1913) a U.S. businessman who was the first person to sell goods by MAIL ORDER and started the Montgomery Ward mail order company

war dance /ˈ. ./ n. [C] a dance performed by tribes in preparation for battle or to celebrate a victory

war·den /ˈwɔrdn/ n. [C] **1** the person in charge of a prison **2** an official whose job is to make sure that rules are obeyed —see also GAME WARDEN

ward heel·er /ˈ. ˌ../ n. [C] INFORMAL someone who works in a particular area for a POLITICAL MACHINE

war·drobe /ˈwɔrdroub/ n. **1** [C] the clothes that someone has: *His wardrobe consists almost entirely of black T-shirts and pants.* **2** [C] a piece of furniture like a large cupboard that you hang clothes in **3** [U] a department in a theater, television company etc. that deals with the clothes worn by actors: *Judy works in wardrobe.* | **a wardrobe master/mistress** (=man or woman who is in charge of this department)

ward·room /ˈwɔrdrum/ n. [C] the space in a ship, especially a WARSHIP, where the officers live and eat, except for the CAPTAIN

-wards /wədz/ suffix [in adverbs] another spelling of -WARD, used only in adverbs: *traveling northwards* | *moving backwards*

-ware /wɛr/ suffix [in U nouns] **1** things made of a particular material, especially for use in the home: *glassware* (=glass bowls, glasses etc.) | *silverware* (=silver knives, forks, spoons etc.) **2** things used in a particular place for the preparation or serving of food: *ovenware* (=dishes for use in the OVEN) | *tableware* (=plates, glasses, knives, etc.) **3** things used in operating a computer: *software* (=computer programs) | *hardware* (=computer equipment)

war ef·fort /ˈ. ˌ../ n. **the war effort** things that all the people in a country do to help when that country is at war

ware·house /ˈwɛrhaʊs/ n. [C] a large building for storing large quantities of goods

warehouse store also **warehouse club** /ˈ.. ˌ./ n. [C] a type of store that sells things in large amounts, so that you can buy them at a lower price than at normal stores

ware·hous·ing /ˈwɛrˌhaʊzɪŋ/ n. [U] the process of storing large quantities of things, especially in a warehouse, so that they can be sold or used at a later time: *We are concerned about the rising cost of warehousing.*

wares /wɛrz/ n. [plural] things that are for sale, usually not in a store: *Along the sidewalk were artists displaying their wares.*

war·fare /ˈwɔrfɛr/ n. [U] **1** a word meaning the activity of fighting in a war, used especially when talking about particular methods of fighting: **nuclear/chemical/trench etc. warfare** *Chemical warfare has been banned by the Geneva Convention.* | *Guerrilla warfare* (=warfare by small groups of fighters) *continued despite increased American military assistance.* **2** a continuous argument between groups,

countries etc. in which they try to gain an advantage over each other: **political/economic/information etc. warfare** (=warfare using politics, economics etc. instead of weapons) —see also **psychological warfare** (PSYCHOLOGICAL (3))

war game /ˈ. ./ n. [C] **1** an activity in which soldiers fight an imaginary battle in order to test military plans **2** a game played by adults in which models of soldiers, guns, horses etc. are moved around a table

war·head /ˈwɔrhed/ n. [C] the explosive part at the front of a MISSILE (1)

War·hol /ˈwɔrhɔl/, **An·dy** /ˈændi/ (1926–1987) a U.S. artist who is famous for his pictures in the POP ART style and who also made movies

war·horse /ˈwɔrhɔs/ n. [C] **1** INFORMAL a soldier or politician who has been in their job a long time, and enjoys dealing with all the difficulties involved in it **2** a horse used in battle

war·like /ˈwɔrlaɪk/ adj. **1** liking war and being skillful in it: *a warlike nation* **2** threatening war or attack: *warlike behavior*

war·lock /ˈwɔrlɑk/ n. [C] a man who has magical powers, especially evil powers

war·lord /ˈwɔrlɔrd/ n. [C] a military leader, especially an unofficial one who is fighting against a government or king

warm[1] /wɔrm/ adj.

1 `slightly hot` slightly hot, especially in a pleasant way: *a warm bath* | *I hope we get some warmer weather soon.* | *I've put your dinner in the oven to keep it warm* (=stop it from becoming cold).

2 `feel warm` feeling slightly hot, or making you feel this way: *Are you warm enough?* | **keep/stay warm** (=wear enough clothes not to feel cold)

3 `clothes/buildings` clothes or buildings that are warm can keep in heat or keep out cold: *I need to buy a warm pair of boots for camping.*

4 `friendly` friendly in a way that makes you feel comfortable: *He gave Gabrielle a warm hug.* | *She certainly gave you a warm welcome.*

5 `color` colors that are warm are red, yellow, orange, and similar colors

6 `correct` used especially in games to say that someone is near to guessing the correct answer or finding a hidden object: *You're getting warmer.* —opposite COLD[1] (13)

7 warm scent/trail a smell or path that has been made recently, which a hunter can easily follow

8 the warm fuzzies INFORMAL good, pleasant feelings: *The new "Garfield" cartoon gives me the warm fuzzies.*

9 `angry/excited` fairly angry or excited: *The atmosphere in the meeting grew warm.*

10 as warm as toast OLD-FASHIONED pleasantly warm —**warmness** n. [U] —compare WARMTH

warm[2] v. also **warm up** [I,T] to make someone or something warm or warmer, or to become warm or warmer: *Serve in warmed tortillas, with salsa.* | [+ **in/by/on**] *The balloon rises as the helium gas warmed in the sun.*

warm to sb/sth phr. v. [T] **1** to begin to like someone you have just met: *He usually doesn't warm to people very fast.* **2** to become more eager, interested, or excited about something: *She eventually warmed to the idea of putting her son in daycare.*

warm up phr. v. **1** [I,T **warm** sb/sth ↔ **up**] to become warm or to make someone or something warm: *A nice bowl of soup will warm you up.* | *I'll just warm up some leftovers for lunch.* **2** [I] to do gentle physical exercises to prepare your body for sports, dancing, singing etc.: *The women's basketball team were warming up for the game.* **3** [I,T **warm** sth ↔ **up**] if you warm up a machine or engine or it warms up, it becomes ready to work correctly: *It takes a few minutes for the copier to warm up.* **4** [I,T **warm** sth ↔ **up**] if a party, election etc. warms up, it starts to become enjoyable or interesting, especially because more is happening: *The race for governor is beginning to warm up.* **5** [I,T **warm** sb ↔ **up**] to become cheerful, eager, and excited, or to make someone feel this way: *He warmed up the audience by telling them a few jokes.* —see also **like death warmed over** (DEATH (11))

warm up to sb/sth *phr. v.* to warm to (WARM²) someone or something

warm-blood·ed /ˌ. '..◂ / *adj.* animals that are warm-blooded have a body temperature that remains fairly high whether the temperature around them is hot or cold —compare COLD-BLOODED

warmed o·ver /ˌ. '..◂ / *adj.* **1** food that is warmed over has been cooked before and then heated again for eating **2** an idea or argument that is warmed over has been used before and is not interesting or useful anymore: *Dukakis offered Democrats a warmed-over New Deal liberalism.* —see also **like death warmed over** (DEATH (11))

war me·mo·ri·al /ˈ. .ˌ.../ *n.* [C] a MONUMENT (1) put up to remind people of soldiers etc. who were killed in a war

warm front /ˈ. ./ *n.* [C] TECHNICAL the front edge of a mass of warm air that is moving toward a place —compare COLD FRONT

warm-heart·ed /ˌ. '..◂ / *adj.* friendly, kind, and always willing to help: *a warm-hearted old man* —compare COLD-HEARTED —**warm-heartedly** *adv.* —**warm-heartedness** *n.* [U]

warm·ing /ˈwɔrmɪŋ/ *n.* [singular] **1** an increase in the temperature of something: *Scientists predict a gradual warming of the Earth caused by pollution.* —see also GLOBAL WARMING **2** a situation in which a relationship becomes more friendly: *Lately, there has been a warming in U.S.-Chinese relations.*

warming pan /ˈ.. ˌ./ *n.* [C] a metal container with a long handle, used in past times to hold hot coals for warming beds

warming trend /ˈ.. ˌ./ *n.* [C] a period of time when the weather becomes warmer in a particular area

warm·ly /ˈwɔrmli/ *adv.* **1** in a friendly way: *We were warmly welcomed by the villagers.* **2** in a way that makes something or someone warm: *Make sure the children are dressed warmly* (=so they do not become cold). **3** eagerly: *I sprang to my feet. "I am your man," I declared warmly.*

war·mon·ger /ˈwɔrˌmʌŋgɚ, -ˌmaŋ-/ *n.* [C] someone, especially a politician, who is eager to start a war to achieve an aim —**warmongering** *adj.* —**warmongering** *n.* [U]

warmth /wɔrmθ/ *n.* [U] **1** a feeling of being warm: *the warmth of the fire* **2** friendliness and happiness: *Fonda speaks of his father with great warmth.*

warm-up /ˈ. ./ *n.* [C] **1** a set of gentle exercises you do to prepare your body for sports, dancing, singing etc.: *Bozek did the warm-up but sat out the game due to an injured back.* **2** a set of clothes you wear when you are doing these exercises: *Players wearing Kansas warm-ups were on the field.* | *a warm-up jacket*

W

warn /wɔrn/ *v.* [I,T] to tell someone that something bad or dangerous may happen, so that they can avoid it or prevent it: [**warn sb about sth**] *She warned me about the broken chair.* | [**warn (sb) of sth**] *You were warned of the risks involved.* | [**warn sb not to do sth**] *He warned patients not to stop using the drug without talking to their doctors.* | [**warn sb (that)**] *Be warned that the photos contain graphic violent images.*

warn sb **against** sth *phr. v.* [T] to advise someone not to do something, because it may have dangerous or bad results: *Her financial adviser warned her against such a risky investment.* | [**warn sb against doing sth**] *Tourist are being warned against walking alone at night.*

warn sb ↔ **off** *phr. v.* [T] **1** to tell someone to go away or not come near something, using threats: *A sign was posted to warn off trespassers.* **2** to advise someone to go away or not do something: [**warn sb off doing sth**] *Two girls tried to warn the men off going any further.*

War·ner /ˈwɔrnɚ/, **Har·ry Mor·ris** /ˈhæri ˈmɔrɪs/ (1881–1958) a U.S. movie PRODUCER who started the Warner Brothers movie company with his brothers Albert, Samuel, Louis, and Jack

warn·ing /ˈwɔrnɪŋ/ *n.* **1** [C,U] something, especially a statement, that tells you that something bad, annoying, or dangerous might happen: *You should always read the warnings on the back of medicine bottles.* | [**+ against**] *Due to political unrest, there is a warning against travel to the region.* | [**+ of**] *Satellite images provide advance warning of military movement.* | [**a warning to sb**] *The court issued a warning to the owner to make repairs immediately.* | *The weather service has* **issued a** *thunder storm* **warning.** | *This type of heart disease kills otherwise healthy people* **without warning.** **2** [C] a statement telling someone that if they continue to behave in an unsatisfactory way, they will be punished: *This is your last warning – leave or I'll call the police.* **3 warning sign/signal** something that shows or tells you that something bad will happen in the future: *This brochure describes the* **early warning signs** *of asthma.* **4 give fair warning** to tell someone about something long enough before it happens that they have time to get ready

war of at·tri·tion /ˌ. . .'../ *n.* [C] a struggle in which you harm your opponent in a lot of small ways, so that they become gradually weaker

war of nerves /ˌ. . './ *n.* [C] an attempt to make an enemy worried, and to destroy their courage by threatening them, spreading false information etc.

war of words /ˌ. . './ *n.* [C] a public argument between politicians, countries, organizations etc.

warp¹ /wɔrp/ *v.* **1** [I,T] to become bent or twisted, or to make something do this: *The hot sun had warped the wooden fence.* —see picture on page 424 **2** [T] to have a bad effect on someone so that they think strangely about things: *Those violent video games must have warped your mind.* —see also WARPED

warp² *n.* **1** [singular] a part of something that is not straight or in the right shape **2 the warp** TECHNICAL the threads used in weaving cloth that go from the top to the bottom —compare WEFT —see also TIME WARP, WARP SPEED

war paint /ˈ. ./ *n.* [U] **1** paint that some tribes put on their bodies and faces before going to war **2** HUMOROUS: see MAKEUP (1)

war·path /ˈwɔrpæθ/ *n.* INFORMAL **be on the warpath** to be angry and looking for someone to argue with or punish

warped /wɔrpt/ *adj.* **1** someone who is warped has ideas or thoughts that most people think are bad or strange: *a warped mind* | *You really* **have a warped sense of humor** (=think strange and disgusting things are funny). **2** something that is warped is bent or twisted so that it is not in the correct shape: *The window frames are warped.*

war·plane /ˈwɔrpleɪn/ *n.* [C] an airplane designed to be used in a war

warp speed /ˈ. ./ *n.* [U] an extremely fast speed: *Judge Clark's ruling allowed the trial to proceed at* **warp speed.**

war·rant¹ /ˈwɔrənt, ˈwɑ-/ *n.* **1** [C] written permission from a court of law allowing the police to take a particular action: [**+ for**] *The court issued a warrant for his arrest.* —see also DEATH WARRANT, SEARCH WARRANT **2** [U] FORMAL good enough reason for doing something; JUSTIFICATION —see also UNWARRANTED

warrant² *v.* **1** [T] to be a good enough reason for something: *Any plan that could reduce costs warrants serious consideration.* **2** [I,T] OLD-FASHIONED used to say that you are sure about something: *I'll warrant we won't see him again.*

warrant of·fi·cer /ˈ.. ˌ.../ *n.* [C] a middle rank in the Army, Navy, Air Force, or Marines, or someone who has this rank

war·ran·ty /ˈwɔrənti, ˈwɑ-/ *n.* plural **warranties** [C] a written promise that a company makes to replace or repair a product if it breaks or does not work correctly: [**+ against**] *The water heater comes with a 10-year warranty against defects.* | *If the car is still*

under warranty (=protected by a warranty), they will replace the part free of charge. —compare GUARANTEE² (2)

war·ren /ˈwɔrən, ˈwɑ-/ n. [C] **1** the place under the ground where rabbits live **2** a place with so many streets, rooms etc. that it is difficult to find your way through it: [+ of] a warren of cubicles

War·ren /ˈwɔrən, ˈwɑ-/, **Earl** /ɚl/ (1891–1974) a CHIEF JUSTICE on the U.S. Supreme Court

Warren, Rob·ert Penn /ˈrɑbɚt pɛn/ (1905–1989) a U.S. poet and writer of NOVELS

war·ring /ˈwɔrɪŋ/ adj. [only before noun] at war or fighting each other: **warring factions/countries/sides etc.** (=groups of people fighting each other)

war·ri·or /ˈwɔriɚ, ˈwɑ-/ n. [C] a soldier or man experienced in fighting, especially in past times —see also WEEKEND WARRIOR

War·saw /ˈwɔrsɔ/ the capital and largest city of Poland

war·ship /ˈwɔrʃɪp/ n. [C] a ship with guns that is used in a war

wart /wɔrt/ n. **1** [C] a small hard raised spot on someone's skin, caused by a VIRUS **2 warts and all** INFORMAL including all the faults or bad things: The biography is an in-depth look at Jefferson's life, warts and all. —**warty** adj.

wart·hog /ˈwɔrthɑg, -hɔg/ n. [C] an African wild pig with long TUSKS that stick out of the side of its mouth

war·time /ˈwɔrtaɪm/ n. [U] a period of time when a nation is fighting a war: **in/during wartime** Subway passages were used as bomb shelters during wartime. —**wartime** adj.: the country's wartime economy —opposite PEACETIME

war-torn /ˈ. ./ adj. [only before noun] a war-torn country, city etc. is being destroyed by war, especially war between opposing groups from the same country

war wid·ow /ˈ. .../ n. [C] a woman whose husband has been killed in a war

war·y /ˈwɛri/ adj. **warier, wariest** careful because you think something might be dangerous or harmful: **[be wary of (doing) sth]** Congress is wary of becoming too dependent on foreign oil. —**wariness** n. [U] —**warily** adv.

war zone /ˈ. ./ n. [C] an area where a war is being fought

was /wəz; strong wʌz, wɑz/ v. the first and third person singular of the past tense of BE

Wa·satch Range, the /ˈwɑsætʃ/ a RANGE of mountains in the northwestern U.S. that is part of the Rocky Mountains and runs from the state of Idaho to the state of Utah

S W
1 |
| 3
wash¹ /wɑʃ, wɔʃ/ v.
1 ‖wash something‖ [T] to clean something using water and usually soap: Wash your face and brush your teeth. | My jeans need to be washed. | It's your turn to **wash the dishes**.
2 ‖wash body‖ [I] to clean your body, especially your hands or face, with water and soap: I just need to wash before dinner.
3 ‖flow‖ [I always + adv./prep.,T always + adv./prep.] if a liquid or something carried by a liquid washes or is washed somewhere, it flows there: [+ against/away etc.] The waves washed against the shore. | **[wash sth away/against/down etc.]** Floods had washed away the topsoil.
4 sth doesn't/won't wash SPOKEN used to say that you do not believe or accept someone's explanation, reason, attitude etc.: John's bad attitude just doesn't wash around here.
5 wash your hands of sth to refuse to be responsible for something anymore: Dunbar has already washed his hands of the project.
6 wash sb's mouth out (with soap) also **sb needs their mouth washed out (with soap)** SPOKEN used when someone has just sworn or said something offensive, to tell them they should not have spoken that way: If I had ever said that, Mom would have washed my mouth out with soap.
7 wash well to be easy to clean using soap and water: Silk doesn't wash well. —see also **wash your dirty laundry/linen in public** (DIRTY¹ (8))

wash sth ↔ down phr. v. [T] **1** to drink something to help you swallow food or medicine: How about a beer to wash down your burger? | **[wash down sth with sth]** I washed down the pills with a glass of water. **2** to clean something large using a lot of water: Can you wash down the driveway?
wash off phr. v. **1** [T **wash sth ↔ off**] to clean dirt, dust etc. from the surface of something with water **2** [I] if a substance washes off, you can remove it from the surface of something by washing: Don't worry, the paint will wash off.
wash out phr. v. **1** [T **wash sth ↔ out**] to wash something quickly to get rid of the dirt in it: Wash out the cups and leave them in the sink. **2** [T **wash sth ↔ out**] if rain or a storm washes out a road, path etc. or if a road, path etc. is washed out, the water damages or destroys the road, path etc. so that you cannot travel on it: Hurricane Opal washed out the road to the mainland last year. **3** [I] if a substance washes out, you can remove it from a material by washing it: Grass stains don't wash out easily. **4 be washed out** if an event is washed out, it cannot continue because of rain: The parade was washed out by heavy thunderstorms. —see also WASHED-OUT, WASHOUT
wash over sb phr. v. [T] if a feeling washes over you, you suddenly feel it very strongly: As I read the report, a sense of dread washed over me.
wash up phr. v. **1** [I] to clean part of your body, especially your hands and face: I need to wash up before dinner. **2** [I always + adv./prep.,T usually passive] if something washes up or if waves wash it up, it comes in to the shore: [+ on/along] Tons of wreckage from the ship have washed up on the beach. | **[wash sth ↔ up]** Balls of heavy oil are being washed up along the shoreline. WASHED-UP

USAGE NOTE: WASH

GRAMMAR: wash yourself
Do not use the expression **wash yourself** unless you want to talk about someone's ability to take a shower or bath by themselves: She got so sick that she couldn't even wash herself.

---

wash² n.
S W
| 3
1 ‖clothes‖ [singular,U] clothes that need to be washed, are being washed, or have just been washed: I have to **do the wash** (=wash dirty clothes) tonight. | I think she's outside **hanging out the wash** (=putting it on the CLOTHESLINE). | Your black pants are **in the wash**.
2 ‖act of cleaning‖ [C] an act of cleaning something using soap and water: The floor needs a wash.
3 it'll all come out in the wash SPOKEN used to tell someone not to worry about a problem because it will be solved in the future: If what you say is true, it'll all come out in the wash.
4 a/the wash of sth a) the movement or sound made by flowing water, or something that is like this: I could feel the wash of the surf around my feet. **b)** a sudden feeling: A wash of confusion came over me.
5 sth is a wash SPOKEN used to say that an activity, event, situation etc. was not very successful, but was not a failure either: So far, the plan has been a wash in terms of jobs gained or lost.
6 ‖river‖ also **dry wash** [C] a river in a desert that has no water in it most of the time
7 ‖boat/plane‖ [singular,U] the movement of water caused by a passing boat or the movement of air caused by an airplane
8 ‖skin‖ [C] a liquid used to clean your skin: an antibacterial face wash
9 ‖color‖ [C] a very thin transparent layer of paint, color, or light
10 ‖area of land‖ [singular] an area of land that is sometimes covered by the ocean

Wash. a written abbreviation of Washington

wash·a·ble /ˈwɑʃəbəl/ adj. **1** something that is washable can be washed without being damaged: Is the jacket washable? | The blouse has the look and

W

*feel of silk, and is **machine washable**. 2 paint, ink etc. that is washable will come out of cloth when you wash it*

wash-and-wear /ˌ. . '.ˈ./ *adj.* wash-and-wear clothes do not need to be IRONed

wash·ba·sin /'wɑʃˌbeɪsən/ *n.* [C] a container like a small SINK used for washing your hands and face

wash·board /'wɑʃbɔrd/ *n.* [C] **1** a piece of metal with a slightly rough surface, used in past times for rubbing clothes on when you are washing them **2 a washboard stomach** someone's stomach on which you can see all the muscles clearly

wash·bowl /'wɑʃboʊl/ *n.* [C] a washbasin

wash·cloth /'wɑʃklɔθ/ *n.* [C] a small square cloth used for washing your hands and face

wash·day /'wɑʃdeɪ/ *n.* [C,U] OLD-FASHIONED the day each week when you wash your clothes, sheets etc.

washed-out /ˌ. '.ˈ./ *adj.* **1** not brightly colored anymore, especially as a result of being washed many times or left in a strong light too long: *The photograph looks kind of washed-out.* **2** feeling weak and looking unhealthy because you are very tired: *Mr. Field always looked washed-out.* —see also **wash out** (WASH¹)

washed-up /ˌ. '.ˈ./ *adj.* if a person or an organization is washed-up, they will never be successful again: *a washed-up rock band* —see also **wash up** (WASH¹)

wash·er /'wɑʃɚ/ *n.* [C] **1** INFORMAL a WASHING MACHINE **2** a thin flat ring of plastic, metal, rubber etc. that is put over a BOLT before the NUT (2) is put on in order to make the bolt fit tighter, or that is put between two pipes to make them fit more tightly together

washer-dry·er /ˌ.. '../ also **washer-dryer u·nit** /ˌ.. '.. ,./ *n.* [C] two machines sold as a set, with one that washes clothes and one that dries them

washing day /'.. ˌ./ *n.* [C] WASHDAY

washing ma·chine /'.. ˌ.,./ *n.* [C] a machine for washing clothes

Wash·ing·ton /'wɑʃɪŋtən/ **1** WASHINGTON, D.C. **2** also **Washington State** *written abbreviation* **WA** a state in the northwestern U.S.

Washington, Book·er T. /'bʊkɚ ti/ (1856–1915) an African-American teacher who started the Tuskegee Institute, one of the first U.S. colleges for African-Americans

Washington, D.C. /ˌwɑʃɪŋtən di 'si/ the capital city of the U.S., which is in the District of Columbia, a special area that governs itself and is not contained in any of the 50 states

Washington, George (1732–1799) the first President of the U.S., who had been commander of the COLONIAL armies during the American Revolutionary War, and the leader of the Constitutional Convention

Washington, Mar·tha /'mɑrθə/ (1731–1802) the wife of George Washington, and the FIRST LADY of the U.S. from 1789 to 1797

Washington, Mount a mountain in the northeastern U.S. that is the highest of the White Mountains and is in the state of New Hampshire

Wash·oe /'wɑʃoʊ/ a Native American tribe from the western area of the U.S.

wash·out, wash out /'wɑʃ-aʊt/ *n.* [C] INFORMAL **1** a failure: *The picnic was a total washout – nobody turned up!* **2** a place where heavy rain has washed away a lot of soil, pieces of a road etc. from a place, or an occasion when this happens: *Parts of Highway 40 remain closed due to mudslides and washouts.* —see also **wash out** (WASH¹)

wash·room /'wɑʃrum/ *n.* [C] a word meaning a room where you use the toilet, used to avoid saying this directly

wash·stand /'wɑʃstænd/ *n.* [C] a table in a BEDROOM used in past times for holding the things needed for washing your face

wash·tub /'wɑʃtʌb/ *n.* [C] a large round container, that you wash clothes in

was·n't /'wʌzənt, 'wɑzənt/ *v.* the short form of "was not": *Claire wasn't at school today.*

WASP /wɑsp/ *n.* [C] White Anglo-Saxon Protestant; an American whose family was originally from northern Europe and who is therefore considered to be part of the most powerful group in society —**WASPy** *adj.: a very WASPy family*

wasp /wɑsp, wɔsp/ *n.* [C] a thin black and yellow flying insect that can sting you

wasp·ish /'wɑspɪʃ/ *adj.* in a bad mood and saying cruel things: *a waspish old woman*

was·sail /'wɑseɪl/ *v.* OLD USE to enjoy yourself eating and drinking at Christmas —**wassail** *n.* [U]

wast /wəst, wɑst/ *v.* **thou wast** OLD USE you were

wast·age /'weɪstɪdʒ/ *n.* [singular,U] FORMAL the loss or destruction of something, especially in a way that is not useful or reasonable, or the amount that is lost or destroyed

waste¹ /weɪst/ *n.*

1 bad use [singular,U] the use of something, for example money or skills, in a way that is not effective, useful, or sensible, or an occasion when you use more of something than you should: *The committee will study the issue of waste in state spending.* | [+ *of*] *Working as a secretary is a waste of your talent.*

2 be a waste of time/money/effort etc. to be not worth the time, money etc. that you use because there is little or no result: *Buying a used truck is a waste of money.*

3 go to waste if something goes to waste, it is not used after it has been prepared or done: *Don't let this food go to waste.*

4 unwanted materials [U] unwanted materials or substances that are left after you have used something: *It's a good idea to recycle household waste.* | **industrial/chemical/nuclear etc. waste** *Finding ways to safely dispose of nuclear waste has not been easy.*

5 sb is a waste of space SPOKEN used to say that someone has no good qualities

6 land [C usually plural] ESPECIALLY LITERARY a large empty or useless area of land: *the icy wastes of Antarctica* —see also WASTELAND

waste² *v.*

1 not use sth effectively [T] to not use money, time, energy etc. in a way that is effective, useful, or sensible, or to use more of it than you should: *Letting the water run while you brush your teeth wastes water.* | [**waste sth on sb/sth**] *I can't believe you wasted $500 on a new dress!*

2 waste no time (in) doing sth to do something as quickly as you can because it will help you: *Peter wasted no time finding himself another girlfriend.*

3 be wasted on sb if something is wasted on someone, they do not understand it or think it is worth considering: *The irony of the situation was not wasted on me.*

4 be wasted in sth if someone is wasted in a job, they are not using all of their abilities: *Garofalo's comic talent is wasted in the movie.*

5 waste not, want not used to say that if you use what you have carefully, you will not be left with nothing later

6 kill sb [T] SLANG to kill someone or defeat them: *One of the men threatened to waste the bank teller if he didn't get the money.*

7 because of illness [T] if an illness wastes someone, they become thinner and weaker —see also **don't waste your breath** (BREATH (4)), WASTED (3), WASTING

waste away *phr. v.* [I] to gradually become thinner and weaker, usually because you are sick

waste³ *adj.* [usually before noun] **1** waste materials, substances etc. are unwanted because the good part of them has been removed **2** used for holding or carrying away materials and substances that are not wanted anymore: *a sewage waste pipe* | *a waste tank* —see also **lay waste (to sth)** (LAY¹ (8)), WASTELAND

waste·bas·ket /'weɪstˌbæskɪt/ *n.* [C] a small container, usually indoors, into which you put paper or other things that you want to get rid of —see picture at BASKET

wast·ed /'weɪstɪd/ *adj.* **1 a wasted trip/phone call/opportunity etc.** an action that is unsuccessful because it has no helpful result: *Jeff had hoped to meet with the director, but it was a wasted trip.* **2** SLANG very drunk or affected by drugs **3** very tired and weak-looking

waste dis·pos·al /'. .,../ *n.* [U] the process or system of getting rid of unwanted materials or substances

waste·ful /'weɪstfəl/ *adj.* using too much of something or wasting it: *That's so wasteful to throw away a clean sheet of paper.* —**wastefully** *adv.* —**wastefulness** *n.* [U]

waste·land /'weɪstlænd/ *n.* [C,U] **1** land that is empty, ugly, and not used for anything: *a barren desert wasteland* **2** DISAPPROVING a situation in which nothing is good or attractive: *Saturday morning television is still the vast wasteland it was 10 years ago.*

waste pa·per /'. ,../ *n.* [U] paper that has been thrown away, especially because it has already been used

waste·pa·per bas·ket /'weɪstˌpeɪpɚ ˌbæskɪt/ *n.* [C] a WASTEBASKET

waste prod·uct /'. ,../ *n.* [C] something useless, such as GARBAGE or gas, that is produced in a process that produces something useful: *Kidneys separate water and waste products from the blood.*

wast·er /'weɪstɚ/ *n.* [C] **a time-waster/energy-waster/money-waster etc.** someone or something that uses up too much time, energy, money etc.: *Being lost on the Internet can be a big time-waster.*

waste·wa·ter /'weɪstˌwɔtɚ/ *n.* [U] water that has been used and contains waste products

wast·ing /'weɪstɪŋ/ *n.* [U] a wasting disease or illness makes someone gradually become thinner and weaker

wast·rel /'weɪstrəl/ *n.* [C] LITERARY someone who wastes their time, money etc.

watch¹ /wɑtʃ, wɔtʃ/ *v.*
1 ■**look at** [I,T] to look at and pay attention to something that is happening or moving: *"Do you want to play too?" "No, thanks. I'll just watch."* | *Ed likes to go to the park and watch the pigeons.* | *All she does is sit around and watch TV.* | [watch sb do/doing sth] *Spectators watched police struggle with the man.* | [watch what/how/when etc.] *Watch what happens when I add water* —see Usage Note at SEE¹
2 ■**be careful** [T] to be careful about something, or about how you use or do something: *Watch your fingers – I'm closing the door.* | [watch what/how/where etc.] *Watch where you're going! You almost knocked me over.* | *I really should be watching my weight* (=being careful not to become fat).
3 ■**take care of** [T] to take care of someone or something so that nothing bad happens to them: *Who can I get to watch the kids tonight?*
4 ■**secretly** [T] to secretly watch a person or place: *I feel like I'm being watched.*
5 watch the clock INFORMAL to keep checking what time it is because you are doing something that you do not want to be doing
6 watch your back INFORMAL to be careful and pay attention to what is happening around you so that your opponents cannot attack you or defeat you: *He may be prime minister for now, but he still needs to watch his back.*
7 watch the world go by to spend time looking at what is happening around you: *In this little village you can still sit in the town café and watch the world go by.*
8 watch this space INFORMAL an expression used especially in newspapers to tell people to wait because things are going to develop further

SPOKEN PHRASES

9 watch out! also **watch it! a)** used to tell someone to be more careful, especially in a dangerous situation: *Watch out! There's a car coming.* **b)** used to threaten someone: *You'd better watch it when Dad's around.*
10 watch this! also **just watch!** used to tell someone to watch you while you do something surprising

or exciting: *Okay, watch this! I'm going to make the egg disappear.*
11 watch your step a) used to warn someone to be careful, especially about making someone angry: *You'd better watch your step if you want to keep your job.* **b)** used to tell someone to be careful when they are walking
12 watch your mouth/language! used to tell someone to stop using words that offend you or that could offend other people: *You'd better watch your mouth, young man!*
13 watch yourself! used to warn someone to be careful not to hurt themselves, get into danger etc.

watch for sth *phr. v.* [T] to look for something, so that you are ready to deal with it: *Soldiers guarded the camp, watching for any signs of intruders.*
watch out for sth/sb *phr. v.* [T] **1** to be careful with someone or something that might hurt you or cause problems for you: *Watch out for this branch.* | *Watch out for the guy downstairs – he's a little strange.* **2** to protect someone or something, so that nothing bad happens: *Larry's older sisters watched out for him.*
watch over sb/sth *phr. v.* [T] to guard or take care of someone or something: *The older children watched over the younger ones.*

watch² *n.*
1 ■**clock** [C] a small clock that you wear on your wrist or carry in your pocket: *He held the watch to his ear to see if it was working.*
2 keep a (close) watch on sb/sth to check a person, place, or situation carefully so that you always know what is happening and are ready to deal with it: *The government is keeping a close watch on the group's activities.*
3 keep watch (over sb/sth) to continue looking around an area in order to warn people of any danger: *Dan kept watch over the others as they slept.*
4 keep a watch (out) for sb/sth to look carefully in order to try and find someone or something, while you are doing other things: *Walking through the sewers, Joe keeps a watch out for rats.*
5 be on the watch (for sb/sth) to be looking and waiting for something that might happen or someone you might see: *I'm always on the watch for new ideas.*
6 on sb's watch INFORMAL during the time that someone is responsible for a government, organization etc.: *Barry said again that none of the incidents had happened on his watch.*
7 ■**people** [C] a group of people employed to guard or protect someone or something
8 ■**guarding sth** [C,U] a period of the day or night when a group of people must look carefully for any signs of danger or attack: **be on watch** *Who's on watch tonight?* —see also NEIGHBORHOOD WATCH, SUICIDE WATCH

watch·band /'wɑtʃbænd/ *n.* [C] a piece of leather or metal for fastening your watch to your wrist

watch·dog /'wɑtʃdɔg/ *n.* [C] **1** a committee or person whose job is to make sure that companies do not do anything illegal or harmful: *a consumer watchdog* **2** a dog used for guarding property

watch·er /'wɑtʃɚ/ *n.* **1 a market-watcher/trend-watcher/industry-watcher etc.** someone who pays a lot of attention to a particular business, activity, or organization and reports on the changes **2 a bird-watcher/whale-watcher etc.** someone who spends their free time watching birds, WHALES etc. because they find them interesting **3** [C] someone who watches something, especially instead of doing something: *Parade watchers strained to get a better look.* —**watching** *n.* [U]

watch·ful /'wɑtʃfəl/ *adj.* careful to notice what is happening, in case anything bad happens: *To guarantee the safety of your children in the water, make sure that a watchful adult is on hand at all times.* | *The Reichardt farm is run under the watchful eye of Jim Reichardt.* —**watchfulness** *n.* [U] —**watchfully** *adv.*

W

watch·mak·er /'wɑtʃˌmeɪkə/ n. [C] someone who makes or repairs watches and clocks

watch·man /'wɑtʃmən/ n. [C] OLD-FASHIONED someone whose job is to guard a building or place; SECURITY GUARD: *He works as the building's night watchman.*

watch·tow·er /'wɑtʃˌtaʊə/ n. [C] a high tower used for guarding a place, from which you can see things that are happening

watch·word /'wɑtʃwəd/ n. [singular] a word or phrase that explains what people should do in a particular situation: *The new watchword in the campaign is "balance."*

s w **wa·ter**[1] /'wɔtə, 'wɑ-/ n. [U]

1 liquid the clear colorless liquid that falls as rain, forms lakes and rivers, and is necessary for life to exist: *I'd just like a glass of water, please.* | *The Environmental Protection Agency sets* **drinking water** *standards in the United States.* | **seawater/bathwater/rainwater** etc. (=a particular type of water) —see also FRESHWATER, SALTWATER[1]

2 supply the supply of water that comes to homes, factories etc. through pipes: *All rooms have hot and cold* **running water** (=water that flows out of pipes). | *I can't believe our water bill is so high.* | *The city is facing* **a serious water shortage** *because of the drought* (=a situation when there is not much water available).

3 area of water **a)** an area of water such as a lake, river etc.: *Come swimming! The water's great!* | *The island has no airport and can only be reached* **by water** (=by boat). **b)** the surface of a lake, river etc.: *There's something floating on the water.* | *We were at least 50 feet* **under water**. —see also UNDERWATER

4 waters [plural] **a)** the water in a particular lake, river etc.: *the icy waters of the Atlantic* **b)** an area of the ocean near or belonging to a particular country: *Molly's parents live near the coastal waters of Maine* **c)** water containing minerals from a natural spring: *She's gone to a resort in Florida to* **take the waters** (=drink the waters because you think it is good for your health).

5 turbulent/murky/unknown etc. waters a situation that is dangerous and difficult to control: *Authorities censored newspapers, trying to keep control in choppy political waters.*

6 be water under the bridge SPOKEN to be in the past and not worth worrying about: *I never figured out why she stopped talking to me, but that's water under the bridge.*

7 water on the brain/knee etc. liquid that collects around the brain, knee etc. as the result of a disease

8 be (like) water off a duck's back INFORMAL if advice, warnings, or rude remarks are like water off a duck's back to someone, they have no effect on them

9 woman when a PREGNANT woman's water breaks, liquid flows out of her body just before the baby is ready to be born

10 high/low water the highest or lowest level of the ocean and some rivers; TIDE

11 pass/make water OLD-FASHIONED, FORMAL to URINATE —see also **in deep water** (DEEP[1] (10)), **feel like a fish out of water** (FISH[1] (3)), **keep your head above water** (HEAD[1] (8)), HEAVY WATER, **not hold water** (HOLD[1] (33)), **be in hot water** (HOT (26)), **muddy the waters** (MUDDY[2] (2)), **pour cold water over/on sth** (POUR (6)), **still waters run deep** (STILL[1] (4)), **take to something like a duck to water** at **take to sth** (TAKE[1]), **test the waters** (TEST[2] (6)), **tread water** (TREAD[1] (2))

s w **water**[2] v. **1** [T] to pour water on an area of land, a plant etc., especially in order to make things grow: *Could you water my plants while I'm gone?* **2** if your eyes water, TEARS come out of them because of cold weather, pain etc.: *Chopping onions always makes my eyes water.* —see also MOUTH-WATERING, **make your mouth water** (MOUTH[1] (8)) **3** [T usually passive] TECHNICAL if an area is watered by a river, the river flows through it and provides it with water: *The plain is watered by the Tigris and Euphrates rivers.* **4** [T] to give an animal water to drink

water sth down phr. v. [T usually passive] **1** to make a statement, report etc. less forceful by removing parts that may offend people: *The ruling party has done all it can to water down the reforms.* —see also WATERED-DOWN **2** to add water to a liquid, especially for dishonest reasons; DILUTE: *This whiskey's been watered down.*

wa·ter·bed /'wɔtəˌbɛd/ n. [C] a bed made of rubber and filled with water

water bird /'.. ˌ./ n. [C] a bird that swims or walks in water

wa·ter·borne /'wɔtəˌbɔrn/ adj. waterborne diseases are spread or carried by water

water bot·tle /'.. ˌ./ n. [C] **1** a bottle used for carrying drinking water **2** a HOT-WATER BOTTLE

water boy /'.. ˌ./ n. [C] a boy who provides the players on a sports team with water

water buf·fa·lo /'.. ˌ..ˌ/ n. [C] a large black animal like a cow with long horns, used for pulling vehicles and farm equipment in Asia

water bug /'.. ˌ./ n. [C] an insect that lives in or on water

water can·non /'.. ˌ../ n. [C] a machine that sends out water at high pressure, used by police to control crowds of people

water chest·nut /'.. ˌ../ n. [C] a white fruit like a nut from a plant grown in water, used in Chinese cooking

water clos·et /'.. ˌ../ n. [C] OLD-FASHIONED a toilet

wa·ter·col·or /'wɔtəˌkʌlə/ n. **1** [C usually plural,U] paint that you mix with water and use for painting pictures **2** [C] a picture painted with watercolors: *Emma paints watercolors for children's books.*

water cool·er /'.. ˌ../ n. **1** [C] a piece of equipment that holds a lot of water for drinking and keeps it cold, used especially in offices **2** [singular] the place or situation in an office in which workers talk about other people in the office, their lives outside the office etc.: *water cooler gossip*

wa·ter·course /'wɔtəˌkɔrs/ n. [C] **1** a passage with water flowing through it, that can be natural or built **2** a flow of water such as a river or UNDERGROUND stream

wa·ter·cress /'wɔtəˌkrɛs/ n. [U] a small plant with strong tasting green leaves that grows in water

watered-down /ˌ.. '.◄/ adj. **1** a watered-down statement, plan etc. is much weaker and less effective than a previous statement, plan etc.: *The House approved a watered-down version of the bill in November.* **2** a watered-down drink, especially an alcoholic drink, has had water added to it, especially in order to cheat people —see also **water sth down** (WATER[2])

watered silk /ˌ.. './ n. [U] a type of silk that looks as if it is covered with shiny waves

wa·ter·fall /'wɔtəˌfɔl/ n. [C] water that falls straight down over a cliff or big rock —see picture on page 428

water foun·tain /'.. ˌ../ n. [C] a DRINKING FOUNTAIN

wa·ter·fowl /'wɔtəˌfaʊl/ n. plural **waterfowl** [C,U] a bird that swims in water, such as a duck, GOOSE etc.

wa·ter·front /'wɔtəˌfrʌnt/ n. [C usually singular] a part of a town or an area of land that is next to the ocean, a river etc.: *They've opened a new restaurant on the waterfront.*

water gun /'.. ˌ./ n. [C] a WATER PISTOL

water heat·er /'.. ˌ../ n. [C] a piece of equipment in a house that heats and holds water to be used for baths, washing dishes etc.

wa·ter·hole /'wɔtəˌhoʊl/ n. [C] a watering hole

watering can /'... ˌ./ n. [C] a container with a long tube on the front, used for pouring water on garden plants

watering hole /'... ˌ./ n. [C] **1** INFORMAL a bar or other place where people go to drink alcohol **2** a small area of water in a dry country, where wild animals go to drink

water jump /'.. ˌ./ n. [C] an area of water that horses or runners have to jump over during a race or competition

water lil·y /'.. ,../ n. plural **water lilies** [C] a plant that floats on the surface of water and has large flowers, which are often white or pink

wa·ter·line /'wɔtə‚laɪn/ n. **the waterline a)** the level that water reaches on the side of a ship **b)** the edge or highest level of an area of water, or the mark the water leaves on the ground a wall etc.

wa·ter·logged /'wɔtə‚lɒgd, -‚lɑgd/ adj. waterlogged areas, land or objects are so wet they cannot hold any more water, usually because of a flood: *The National Guard went in yesterday to help waterlogged communities in Louisiana.*

Wa·ter·loo /‚wɔtə'lu/ n. **sb's Waterloo** a situation in which someone who has been very successful, famous etc. fails

water main /'.. ‚./ n. [C] a large pipe under the ground that carries the public supply of water to houses and other buildings

wa·ter·mark /'wɔtə‚mɑrk/ n. [C] **1** a design that is put into paper and can only be seen when you hold it up to the light: *There is a watermark on this $50 bill.* **2 the high/low watermark a)** a line showing the highest or lowest levels of the ocean or a river **b)** a period of great success or failure: *tae high watermark of U.S. power*

wa·ter·mel·on /'wɔtə‚melən/ n. [C,U] a large round fruit with hard green skin, juicy red flesh, and a lot of black seeds —see picture at FRUIT[1]

water me·ter /'.. ‚../ n. [C] a piece of equipment that measures how much water passes through a pipe

water mill /'.. ‚./ n. [C] a MILL that has a big wheel that is turned by the flow of water

water moc·ca·sin /'.. ‚../ n. [C] a poisonous North American snake that lives in water

water pipe /'.. ‚./ n. [C] a pipe used for smoking tobacco, that consists of a long tube and a container of water

water pis·tol /'.. ‚../ n. [C] a toy gun that shoots water

water po·lo /'.. ‚../ n. [U] a game played by two teams of seven swimmers with a ball

water pow·er /'.. ‚../ n. [U] power obtained from moving water, used to produce electricity or to make a machine work

wa·ter·proof /'wɔtə‚pruf/ adj. **1** waterproof clothing or material does not allow water to go through it: *a waterproof tent* —see picture at CLOTHES **2** substances such as ink, MAKEUP, or SUNSCREEN that are waterproof do not come off or spread when they get wet

water rat /'.. ‚./ n. [C] a small animal like a large mouse that lives in holes near water and can swim

water-re·pel·lent /'.. ‚../ adj. cloth or clothes that are water-repellent are specially treated with chemicals so that water runs off them —**water repellent** n. [C,U]

water-re·sis·tant, water resistant /'.. ‚../ adj. something that is water-resistant does not allow water to go through easily, but does not keep all water out: *The watch is water resistant, but not waterproof.*

wa·ter·shed /'wɔtə‚ʃed/ n. [C] **1** an event or period when important changes or improvements happen in history or in someone's life: [+ in] *The fall of the Berlin Wall was a watershed in modern European history.* | **a watershed year/event/moment etc.** *Passage of the law in 1936 was a watershed event.* —compare TURNING POINT **2** the high land separating two river systems

wa·ter·side /'wɔtə‚saɪd/ n. [singular] the edge of a lake, river etc. —**waterside** adj.

water-ski·ing, water skiing /'.. ‚../ n. [U] a sport in which you SKI over water while being pulled by a boat: *Do you want to go water-skiing?* —**water-ski** v. [I] —**water-skier** n. [C] —**water ski** n. [C]

water soft·en·er /'.. ‚../ n. **1** [U] a chemical used for removing unwanted minerals from water **2** [C] a piece of equipment used to do this

water-sol·u·ble /'.. ‚../ adj. a water-soluble substance becomes part of a liquid when mixed with water

water sports /'.. ‚./ n. [plural] sports played on or in water

wa·ter·spout /'wɔtə‚spaʊt/ n. [C] **1** a type of storm over the sea in which a violent circular wind pulls water into a tall twisting mass —compare TORNADO **2** a pipe that lets rain water flow off a building onto the ground

water sup·ply /'.. ‚../ n. [U] the water provided for a building or area, or the system of lakes, pipes etc. through which it flows

water ta·ble /'.. ‚../ n. [C] the level below the surface of the ground where there is water

wa·ter·tight /'wɔtə‚taɪt/ adj. **1** something that is watertight does not allow water to pass through it: *a watertight compartment* **2 a watertight plan/explanation/argument etc.** a plan, explanation etc. that is so carefully made or done that there is no chance of mistakes or problems: *Police can't do anything, he's got a watertight alibi.* —compare AIRTIGHT

water tow·er /'.. ‚../ n. [C] a very tall structure supporting a large container into which water is pumped in order to supply water to surrounding buildings

water va·por /'.. ‚../ n. [U] water in the form of gas in the air

wa·ter·way /'wɔtə‚weɪ/ n. [C] a river or CANAL that boats travel on

water wheel /'.. ‚./ n. [C] a wheel that is turned by water as part of a machine or system

wa·ter·wings /'wɔtə‚wɪŋz/ n. [plural] two bags filled with air that you put on your arms when you are learning to swim

wa·ter·works /'wɔtə‚wɜrks/ n. [plural] **1** the system of pipes and artificial lakes used to clean and store water before it is supplied to a town **2 turn on the waterworks** INFORMAL to start crying in order to get someone's sympathy

wa·ter·y /'wɔtəri/ adj. **1** watery food or drink contains too much water and does not taste good: *Nicole got a cup of watery coffee from the machine downstairs.* **2** full of water: *Ragweed causes runny noses and watery eyes.* **3** weak and difficult to see or hear: *a watery green light* **4 a watery grave** LITERARY if someone goes to a watery grave, they DROWN

WATS /wɒts/ n. [singular] Wide Area Telephone Service; a telephone service that allows a company or organization to make and receive as many telephone calls, especially long-distance calls, as they want each month for a particular price

Wat·son /'wɒtsən/, **James** (1928–) a U.S. scientist who, together with Francis Crick, discovered the structure of DNA

watt /wɒt/ n. [C] a measure of electrical power: *a 60-watt light bulb*

Watt /wɒt/, **James** (1736–1819) a British engineer who made important improvements to the STEAM ENGINE

W

watt·age /'wɒtɪdʒ/ n. [singular,U] the power of a piece of electrical equipment measured in watts

wat·tle /'wɒtl/ n. [U] **1** a material used for making fences consisting of small sticks on a frame of rods **2** a piece of loose flesh that grows from the head or neck of some birds such as a TURKEY

wave[1] /weɪv/ v.

1 hand [I,T] to move your hand or arm from side to side in order to greet someone or attract their attention: *Nelson was waving from the upstairs window.* | [+ to/at] *Who are you waving at?* | [**wave sth around**] *The driver was waving his arms around, demanding more money.*

2 signal [T always + adv./prep.] to show someone where to go by waving your hand in that direction: [**wave sb through/on/away etc.**] *Gabby waved her gently in the direction of the dining room.*

3 wave goodbye (to sb) to say goodbye to someone by waving to them.: *Arlene's family waved goodbye to us as we drove away.*

S W
3 3

4 make sth move [T] to hold something and move it from side to side: *"Get out of here!" he shouted, waving his gun.* | [wave sth under/around/at etc.] *Burt kept waving the newspaper in my face.*

5 move smoothly [I,T] to move smoothly up and down, or from side to side: *The flag waved proudly in the breeze.*

6 hair [I] if hair waves, it grows in loose curls

7 be like waving a red flag in front of a bull used to say that doing or saying something will definitely make someone angry: *Legally, the proposal can be accepted without a vote, and that is like waving a red flag in front of a bull to taxpayer groups.*

8 wave goodbye to sth INFORMAL to be forced to accept that something you want will not happen: *Well, we can wave goodbye to first place now.*

wave sth ↔ away also wave sth ↔ aside *phr. v.* [T] to refuse to pay attention to an idea, a question, help etc. because you do not think it is important, especially by waving your hand: *Fred stood slowly, waving away everyone's help.*

wave sb/sth ↔ down *phr. v.* [T] to signal to the driver of a car to stop by waving your arm at them

wave off *phr. v.* [T] **1** [wave sb ↔ off] to show someone that you want them to go away by waving your hand: *Myrtle closed her eyes and waved us off.* **2** [wave sb ↔ off] to wave goodbye to someone as they leave **3** [wave sth ↔ off] to refuse to pay attention to an idea, a question, help etc. because you do not think it is important, especially by waving your hand: *Pamela quickly waved off the criticism.*

s w
z 2
wave² *n.*

1 ocean [C] a line of raised water that moves across the surface of the ocean: *Ten-foot waves crashed against the shore.* —see picture on page 428

2 sudden increase [C] a sudden increase in a particular type of behavior or activity: [+ of] *There was another wave of applause as Adams stepped up to the podium.* | *A crime wave has been sweeping downtown Milwaukee.* | *New infections are beginning a slow but steady rise in the second wave (=the appearance again and growth) of the epidemic.* —see also HEAT WAVE

3 group of people/things [C] a large number of people or things arriving somewhere at the same time: [+ of] *The U.S. has always adjusted to each new wave of immigrants.*

4 feeling [C] a sudden strong feeling that spreads over someone or from one person to another: [+ of] *A wave of nausea crept over me as he described the procedure.*

5 your hand [C usually singular] a movement of your hand or arm from side to side: *Leona dismissed the servants with a wave of the hand.*

6 in waves if something happens in waves, a short period of activity is followed by a pause: *The pain swept over him in waves.*

7 soldiers [C] a group of soldiers, aircraft etc. that attack together: [+ of] *At 6:00 the first wave of bombers were sent out from the carrier.*

8 light/sound [C] the form in which some types of energy such as light and sound move: *radio waves* —see also LONG WAVE, MEDIUM WAVE, SHORTWAVE

9 the wave of the future something modern that is expected to replace something else or an old way of doing something: *In the 1950s everyone believed that nuclear energy was the wave of the future.*

10 hair [C] a part of your hair that curls slightly: *Kelly's hair has a natural wave to it.*

11 make waves INFORMAL to cause problems: *Lora can do what ever she wants at work as long as she doesn't make waves.*

12 the wave a situation in which people in a large group, especially at sports events, stand up and sit down quickly one after another, so that it looks like a wave is moving across the group: *Come on. Let's do the wave.*

wave·band /ˈweɪvbænd/ *n.* [C] a set of sound waves of similar length which are used to broadcast radio programs

wave·length /ˈweɪvleŋkθ/ *n.* [C] **1** the size of a radio wave used to broadcast a radio signal **2** the distance between two waves of energy such as sound or light **3** be on the same wavelength INFORMAL to have the same opinions and feelings as someone else: *Luckily, everyone working on the project is on the same wavelength.* —opposite be on a different wavelength

wa·ver /ˈweɪvɚ/ *v.* [I] **1** to be or become weak and uncertain: *Sue's gaze did not waver as she watched Pat leave.* | *Jessica's faith in her husband never wavered.* **2** to not make a decision because you have doubts: [+ between] *Wallace says he is wavering between the two proposals.* **3** to move in an unsteady way first in one direction then in another: *I lay still, watching the moonlight waver on the wall.*

wav·y /ˈweɪvi/ *adj.* wavier, waviest **1** wavy hair grows in loose curls **2** a wavy line or edge has smooth curves in it —waviness *n.* [U]

wax¹ /wæks/ *n.* [U] **1** a solid material made out of fats or oils used to make CANDLEs, polish etc.: *We put a layer of wax down on the floor.* —see picture at CANDLE **2** a natural sticky substance in your ears —see also BEESWAX

wax² *v.* **1** [T] to put a thin layer of wax on a floor, table, car etc. in order to polish it **2** wax eloquent/philosophical/poetic etc. LITERARY to talk about someone or something in an eager, thoughtful way: *Ken's father would often wax eloquent about the importance of rewarding work.* **3** [T] to put a thin layer of wax on your arms, legs etc. and then pull it off in order to remove hairs **4** [I] when the moon waxes, it grows larger **5** wax and wane LITERARY to increase and then decrease

wax bean /ˈ. ./ *n.* [C] a type of yellowish STRING BEAN

wax·en /ˈwæksən/ *adj.* LITERARY **1** someone who has waxen skin looks very pale and unhealthy: *a waxen complexion* **2** made of or covered in wax

wax mu·se·um /ˈ. .,../ also **wax·works** /ˈwæks-wɚks/ *n.* [C] a place where you pay to see models of famous people made of wax

wax pa·per also **waxed paper** /ˈ. ,.., ,. ˈ../ *n.* [U] paper with a thin layer of WAX on it, used to wrap food

wax·work /ˈwækswɚk/ *n.* [C] a model of a person made of WAX

wax·y /ˈwæksi/ *adj.* waxier, waxiest **1** looking or feeling like WAX: *a waxy coating on the leaves* **2** made of or covered in WAX —waxiness *n.* [U]

way¹ /weɪ/ *n. plural* ways

s w
1 1
1 method [C] a method of doing something: *You can put the model together in several different ways.* | [a way of doing sth] *We have no way of knowing whether she got the message.* | [a way to do sth] *No one knows the best way to raise children.* | *The Internet is the easiest way to go about making travel plans.* | the right/wrong way *Here, let me show you - you're not doing it the right way.*

2 manner [C] a manner in which something happens or is done, especially when there are several possible ones: *Look at the way he's dressed!* | *The argument was a terrible way to end a wonderful week.* | *Emma wondered if he thought of her in the same way that she thought of him.* | in a strange/friendly/nasty etc. way *Marge kept staring at him in a funny way.*

3 road/direction [C usually singular] a road, path, direction etc. that you must follow to get to a particular place: *Which way should we go?* | *Jill's office is that way.* | [+ to/from] *Could you tell me the quickest way to the library from here?* | *I hope you know the way because I don't.* | *They got on the wrong trail and lost their way.* | *A teenage boy offered to show us the way to Dutton's farm.* | a way in/out/across etc. *We kept looking for a way down to the beach, but we couldn't find one.* —see also find your way (FIND¹ (9))

4 feature of a situation [C] a feature of a situation, idea, plan etc. that you are considering in order to decide how true a statement is: *In some ways, she thought she might like being married again.* | *Tamara was his equal in every way.* | *Gray's comments should in no way be considered official policy.*

5 in a way used to say that something is partly true, or to make a statement weaker: *In a way, I'm a little surprised he accepted the offer.*

6 distance [singular] also **ways** INFORMAL a distance, especially a long one: *Ottumwa? That's quite a ways from here, isn't it?* | *We still have a long way to go.* | *I didn't come all this way to listen to you criticize me.* | **all the way down/across/through etc.** *Let's see if we can run all the way back.*

7 (in) one way or another used to say that something will happen in somehow, or be done by some means, although you do not know how: *One way or another, Roberts will pay for what he's done.*

8 one way or the other used to talk about two choices or possibilities that have just been mentioned: *The doctors haven't given me information one way or the other.*

9 a way out (of sth) a possible method of solving a problem or difficult situation: *There seems to be no way out of the current economic crisis.* —see also **take the easy way out** (EASY¹ (5))

10 a way around sth a possible method of avoiding dealing with a difficult problem or situation: *There's no way around it: The bank's president is involved in illegal activities.* —see also **know your way around** (KNOW¹ (9))

11 in the/sb's way if someone or something is in your way, you cannot pass them or can pass them only with difficulty: *I tried to go into the parking lot, but there was a big dump truck in the way.* | *I'm sorry – am I in your way? I can move.*

12 stand/get in the way of sth to prevent someone from doing something, or prevent something from happening: *He won't let anything get in the way of spending time with his family.* —see also **stand in sb's way** (STAND¹ (38))

13 push/talk etc. your way [always + adv./prep.] to do or say something in order to move or progress to a new place or position, especially in a forceful way: [+ **into/through/onto etc.**] *"Money can't buy your way into heaven," said Graham.* | *A middle-aged shopper elbowed her way into the first waiting cab.*

14 out of the way a) also **out of sb's way** in or to a position that is not blocking a road, someone's path etc.: *Workers were unable to push the car out of the way.* | *Get out of my way.* **b)** a place that is out of the way is fairly far from any town —see also OUT-OF-THE-WAY **c)** if you get something out of the way, especially something difficult or bad, you deal with it so that you can do something else: *Good. Now that's out of the way, we can start working.*

15 keep/stay out of sb's way to avoid someone: *When Mark gets in one of these moods, it's best to keep out of his way.*

16 on the/sb's way while traveling from one place to another: [+ **to**] *I ran out of gas on the way to the airport.* | **on sb's way home/downtown/out etc.** *I've got to pick up some milk on my way home.*

17 be on sb's way to live, exist, or be done in the direction that someone is going: *I can pick you up in the morning – you're on my way.* —opposite **be out of sb's way**

18 be on the/your way to be moving toward a particular place: *Carla's already on her way here.* | *I'm on my way.* | [+ **to**] *The fleet is on its way to the Coral Sea.*

19 be on the/your way out to be rapidly becoming less popular, important, powerful etc.: *Platform shoes are on the way out.*

20 sth is on its/the way used to say that something is going to happen soon.: *Forecasters say warmer weather is on the way.* —see also **have a baby on the way** (BABY¹ (8))

21 in more ways than one INFORMAL used to say that there are several reasons without mentioning them all: *Trees are extremely important to humans in more ways than one.*

22 behavior [C] the particular style of behaving of a person or group of people: [+ **about**] *Amelia has a quiet deliberate way about her.* | *The President told several short stories, as is his way.* | **change/mend your ways** (=stop your bad behavior)

23 get/have your (own) way to do what you want to, even though someone else wants something

different: *Monica's so spoiled – she always gets her own way.*

24 have a way with sb/sth to have a special ability to deal well with someone or something: *David seemed to have a way with children.* | *Marla really has a way with words* (=the ability to express ideas and opinions well)

25 have a (long) way to go to need to develop or change a lot in order to reach a particular standard: *Despite the progress in recent months, we still have a long way to go.*

26 that/this way a) used to talk about a fact or idea that was just mentioned, or that you are about to mention: *He never got mad at me. He was wonderful that way.* **b)** used when telling the results of an action or situation that was just mentioned: *I hope he transfers to another school. That way, I wouldn't have to see him anymore.*

27 by way of sth FORMAL **a)** as a form of something, or instead of something: *"She asked for it," Kyle said by way of explanation.* **b)** if you travel by way of a place, you go through it: *We flew to Europe by way of Iceland.* **c)** using a particular method: *Bacteria communicate with each other by way of chemical messages.*

28 in sb's own way a) using a method that is different from what other people are using: *Each woman dealt with her grief in her own way.* **b)** used when you want to say that someone really thinks, feels, or does something, although other people might think that they do not: *I suppose she probably loves me in her own way.*

29 go your (own) way to do what you want to do, make your own decisions etc.

30 to sb's way of thinking used before giving someone's opinion: *To my way of thinking, success comes more from hard work than from natural ability*

31 time [singular] also **ways** [plural] a length of time, especially a long one: *The two events were a long way apart.* —see also **go back a long way** at **go back** (GO¹)

32 along the way a) while traveling from one place to another: *I'd like to do a little exploring along the way.* **b)** while developing from one situation or part of your life to another: *Louise has made quite a number of enemies along the way.*

33 nothing/little/much etc. in the way of sth also **nothing/little/much etc. by way of sth** INFORMAL the particular amount or type of something: *The city doesn't offer much in the way of hotels.*

34 have your way with sb a) OLD-FASHIONED OR HUMOROUS to persuade someone to love you or have sex with you **b)** to easily defeat an enemy: *Florida should not have had its way with the Braves, but it did.*

35 ways and means special methods for doing something, especially when this involves deciding how to pay for something: *Atkins has promised to find ways and means to strengthen the economy.*

36 split sth two/three etc. ways also **divide sth two/three etc. ways** to divide something into two, three etc. equal parts: *If we split the hundred dollars five ways, it's only $20 apiece.*

37 way around a particular order or position that something should be in: *Which way around does this skirt go?* —see also **the other way around** (OTHER¹ (8))

SPOKEN PHRASES

38 no way! a) used to say that you do not believe something or are very surprised by it: *"It costs $37 per person." "No way!"* **b)** used to say that you will definitely not do something: *"Can I borrow your VCR for a week?" "No way!"* | *You think I'm going to help you paint your house? No way, José* (=used to emphasize that you will not do something).

39 way to go! a) used to tell someone that they have done something very well, or achieved something special **b)** used, especially as a joke, when someone has done something silly or stupid: *Way to go, Kim! Now we'll have to start all over again.*

W

40 the way things are (going) used to say that because of the present situation you expect another situation to develop, especially a bad one: *The way things are right now, I don't think we'll be able to afford the trip.*
41 if I had my way used before telling someone how you think something should be done: *If I had my way, there'd be a baseball game every day of the year.*
42 the way I see it used to give your opinion about something: *The way I see it, it was a fair trade.*
43 have it your (own) way! used to tell someone in an annoyed way that you will allow them to have or do what they want
44 that's (just) the way sth is/goes used to say that a particular situation cannot be changed: *If you want it typed, it's going to cost you. That's the way it is.*
45 that's (just) the way sb is used to say that someone has particular qualities that will not change: *Sometimes Tim needs to be alone. That's just the way he is.*
46 not in any way, shape, or form also **in no way, shape, or form** used to emphasize that a statement is not true and could not possibly be true: *I am not responsible for his actions in any way, shape, or form.*
47 the way sb likes sth the particular condition, quality, or situation that someone prefers: *The chicken was nice and crispy – just the way I like it.*
48 have a way of doing sth to usually happen or behave in a particular way: *Don't worry too much. These problems usually have a way of working out.*
49 that's the way used to tell someone that they are doing something correctly or well, especially when you are showing them how: *Now bring your foot gently off the clutch – that's the way.*
50 be with sb all the way to agree with someone completely: *I applaud their efforts, and I'm with them all the way.*
51 no two ways about it used to say that something is definitely true, especially something you might want to avoid: *We're just going to have to try to get along. No two ways about it.*
52 that's no way to do sth used to tell someone that they should not be doing something in a particular manner: *That's no way to speak to your father!*
53 there's more than one way to skin a cat used to say that there is more than one possible method of doing something
54 way out! SLANG an expression meaning that something is very good or exciting, used especially in the 1970s

—see also AMERICAN WAY, **you can't have it both ways** (BOTH[1] (2)), **by the way** (BY[1] (11)), **come sb's way** (COME[1] (23)), **either way** (EITHER[2] (3)), **see the error of your ways** (ERROR (3)), **find your way** (FIND[1] (9)), **go the way of all flesh** (FLESH[1] (9)), **give way** (GIVE[1]), **go out of your way to do sth** (GO[1] (21)), HALFWAY, **lead the way** (LEAD[1] (11)), **make your way** (MAKE[1] (11)), **make way (for sb/sth)** (MAKE[1] (12)), ONE-WAY, **pay your way** (PAY[1] (14)), RIGHT OF WAY, **see your way (clear) to do sth** (SEE[1] (18)), **talk your way out of sth** (TALK[1] (18)), TWO-WAY, UNDERWAY, **work your way over/out/back etc.** (WORK[1] (10))

USAGE NOTE: WAY

WORD CHOICE: on the way/in the way
Use **on the way** to talk about something you do while you are going somewhere, or a place that you will pass as you go there: *I'll get some milk on the way home.* | *Jenna's house is on the way to the mall.* Use **in the way** to say that something is preventing you from getting to the place where you are going: *I can't get my car out of the garage because Dave's motorcycle is in the way.*

---

s w way[2] *adv.* [+ adj./adv.] INFORMAL **1** by a great distance, or by a large degree: [**way ahead/behind/out etc.**] *Let's go some other time – it's way across town.* | *Way off in the distance, we could see the lights of the city.* | [**way above/below/over etc.**] *It is way past your bedtime!* | *Guess again – you're way off* (=very

far from being correct). | *They first met way back* (=a long time ago) *in 1970.* | **way heavier/smarter/bigger etc.** *Tickets were way more expensive than I thought.* **2** SLANG very: *I think she's way cool, man.*

way·bill /ˈweɪbɪl/ *n.* [C] TECHNICAL a document sent with goods that says where the goods are to be delivered, how much they are worth, and how much they weigh, used especially with goods being sent by ship, train, airplane etc.

way·far·er /ˈweɪˌfɛrɚ/ *n.* [C] LITERARY a traveler who walks from one place to another —**wayfaring** *adj.* [only before noun]

way·lay /ˈweɪleɪ/ *v.* **waylaid, waylaying** [T] to stop someone when they are trying to go some place, especially so that you can talk to them, or so that you can rob or attack them: *Thousands of passengers were waylaid by the airline strike.*

way of life /ˌ. . ˈ./ *n. plural* **ways of life** [C] **1** the way someone lives, or the way people in a society usually live: *Tribe elders want to protect their traditional way of life.* | **the American/British/Amish etc. way of life** (=the life typical of Americans, British people etc.) **2** a job or interest that is so important that it affects everything you do: *Nursing isn't just a job; it's a whole way of life.*

way-out /ˌ. ˈ.◂/ *adj.* INFORMAL very modern, and unusual or strange: *I like some jazz, but not the way-out stuff.*

-ways /weɪz/ *suffix* [in adverbs] in a particular direction: *leaning sideways* (=to the side)

way·side /ˈweɪsaɪd/ *n.* [singular] LITERARY the side of a road or path —see also **fall by the wayside** (FALL[1] (30))

way sta·tion /ˈ. ˌ../ *n.* [C] a place to stop between the main stations on a of a path, railroad etc.

way·ward /ˈweɪwɚd/ *adj.* behaving in a way that is not considered right or appropriate: *wayward youth*

wa·zoo /wɑˈzu/ *n.* [C] SPOKEN **up/out the wazoo** in a large amount, or to a great degree: *That winter we had snow up the wazoo.*

WC *n.* [C] OLD-FASHIONED water closet; a TOILET or BATHROOM

we /wi/ *pron.* [used as the subject of a verb] **1** the person who is speaking and one or more people: *We're looking forward to seeing you on Sunday.* | *What should we* (=you and I) *do tonight, Sean?* | *Can we* (=I and the others) *have some cake, Mom?* **2** people in general: *We still know very little about what causes the disease.* | *We all grew up believing that our parents were perfect.* **3** used by a writer or a speaker to mean you (the reader or listener) and them: *As we saw in Chapter 4, slavery was not the only cause of the Civil War.* **4** used especially to children and people who are sick to mean "you": *We don't hit other people, do we, Tommy?* **5** FORMAL used by a king or queen in official language to mean "I": *We are not amused.*

weak /wik/ *adj.* **weaker, weakest**
1 physically not physically strong: *Betty was too weak to get out of bed.* | [+ **with**] *We were all weak with hunger.* | **weak heart/bladder/eyes etc.** (=parts of your body that do not work properly)
2 character easily influenced by other people because you cannot make decisions by yourself: *Unfortunately, our leader was a weak and indecisive man.*
3 not skilled not having much ability or skill in a particular activity or subject: *Martin is a weak swimmer.* | [+ **in/at**] *I'm kind of weak in algebra.*
4 leaders/countries/organizations etc. not having much power or influence: *Recent elections have left Christian Democrats weak.*
5 argument/explanation/story etc. not having the power to persuade or interest people: *a weak excuse* | *The actors are good, but the plot is weak.*
6 industry/company etc. not successful financially: *weak sales of men's clothing* | *The dollar was weaker on Monday.*
7 buildings/objects unable to support a lot of weight: *Be careful – that ladder looks a little weak.*
8 drink/liquid containing a lot of water or having little taste: *Do you like your tea strong or weak?*

9 light/sound difficult to see or hear: *a weak radio signal*
10 the weak people or animals who are not strong and who do not have much power compared to others: *The tribes were continually at war, and the stronger drove out the weak.*
11 a weak point/spot a part of something or of someone's character that can easily be attacked or criticized: [+ in] *Hill has identified several weak spots in Richardson's record.*
12 weak in the knees INFORMAL not feeling strong or well, especially because you have had a sudden surprise or because you have seen someone you love: *His Spanish accent made her go weak in the knees.*
13 a weak smile a slight smile, especially because you are not very happy
14 a weak chin/jaw a weak chin or jaw is not very well developed and people often think it suggests a weak character
15 in a weak moment at a time when you can be persuaded more easily than usual: *In a weak moment, I told him I'd help organize the party.* —compare **a moment of weakness** (MOMENT (10))
16 the weaker sex OLD-FASHIONED an expression meaning "women," now considered offensive
17 a weak verb TECHNICAL a verb that forms the past tense and past participle in a regular way
18 weak consonant/syllable a CONSONANT or SYLLABLE that is not emphasized

weak·en /'wikən/ *v.* [I,T] **1** to make someone or something less powerful or less important, or to become less powerful: *Some parents are worried that public education weakens the family's influence.* **2** to make someone lose their physical strength, or to become physically weak: *Hartman was weakened by flu, but still managed to play.* **3** to make a building, structure etc. less strong and less able to support a lot of weight, or to become less strong and less able to support a lot of weight: *The explosion severely weakened the foundations of the house.* **4** to make someone less determined, or to become less determined: **weaken sb's determination/resolve** *These terrorist bombings have not weakened our resolve to remain in the region.* **5** if a particular country's money or a company's STOCK prices weaken or are weakened, their value is reduced —**weakening** *n.* [U]

weak-kneed /'. ./ *adj.* INFORMAL **1** lacking courage and unable to make your own decisions: *a weak-kneed coward* **2** not feeling strong or well, especially because you have had a sudden surprise or because you have seen someone you love —see also **weak in the knees** (WEAK (12))

weak·ling /'wik-lɪŋ/ *n.* [C] someone who is not physically strong

weak·ly /'wikli/ *adv.* without much force or energy: *The border is weakly defended.*

weak·ness /'wiknɪs/ *n.*
1 body [U] the state of being physically weak: *muscle weakness*
2 fault [C] a fault in someone's character or in a system, organization, design etc.: *The plan has strengths and weaknesses.* | *Frank's biggest weakness is his lack of tolerance.* | *The car has some serious structural weaknesses.*
3 lack of power [U] lack of power and influence: *the weakness of the country's law-making body*
4 character [U] lack of determination shown in someone's behavior: *Compromising might be seen as a sign of weakness.*
5 money [U] the condition of not being worth a lot of money: *the weakness of the yen against the dollar*
6 a weakness for sth if you have a weakness for something, you like it very much even though it may not be good for you: *Lisa has a weakness for handsome young men.*

weak-willed /ˌ. '.‹ / *adj.* unable to make decisions easily or do what you intend to do

weal /wil/ *n.* [C] a red swollen mark on the skin where someone has been hit

wealth /wɛlθ/ *n.* **1** [U] a large amount of money and possessions: *The country's wealth comes from*

its oil. —opposite POVERTY **2 a wealth of experience/knowledge/resources etc.** a large number or amount of experience, knowledge etc.: *The report contains a wealth of information about Tahiti.*

wealth·y¹ /'wɛlθi/ *adj.* **wealthier, wealthiest** **1** having a lot of money, possessions etc.: *Joan comes from a wealthy family* **2 the wealthy** people who have a lot of money, possessions etc.

wean /win/ *v.* **1 wean sb from/off sth** to make someone gradually stop doing something you disapprove of: *Cities have been told to wean themselves from dependence on federal aid.* **2** [I,T] to gradually stop feeding a baby or young animal on its mother's milk and start giving it ordinary food: *Some infants are weaned at six months.*
wean sb on sth *phr. v.* [T usually passive] INFORMAL to be influenced by something from a very early age.: *Boz Scaggs was weaned on the music of the '50s.*

weap·on /'wɛpən/ *n.* [C] **1** something that you use to fight with, such as a knife, bomb, or gun: *Police are still looking for the murder weapon.* | *It is important that we control the spread of **weapons of mass destruction** (=weapons that can kill many people at one time).* **2** a type of behavior, knowledge of a particular subject etc. that you can use against someone when you are in a difficult situation: *Community rejection of gangs is a powerful weapon against them.* —see also **secret weapon** (SECRET¹ (2))

weap·on·ry /'wɛpənri/ *n.* [U] a word meaning "weapons," used especially when talking about particular types of weapons: *nuclear weaponry*

wear¹ /wɛr/ *v. past tense* **wore** *past participle* **worn**
1 on your body [T] to have something such as clothes, shoes, or jewelry on your body: *Do you think I can wear these shoes with this dress?* | *Neither person in the car was **wearing a seatbelt**.* | **wear blue/black/red etc.** *I rarely wear bright colors.* | **wear sth to a party/dance/interview etc.** *What should I wear to the wedding?* —see picture at DRESS¹ —see Usage Note at DRESS¹
2 hair [T] to have your hair or BEARD in a particular style or shape: *Rosa was wearing her hair in a long braid down her back.*
3 damage [I,T] to become thinner, weaker etc. after continuous use, or to make something do this: *The cushions on this chair are starting to wear a little.* | **wear a hole/groove/rut etc.** *You've worn a hole in the seat of your pants.*
4 expression [T] to have a particular expression on your face: **wear a frown/grin/scowl etc.** *Jill wore a phony smile, pretending to have a good time.*
5 wear well a) to remain in good condition without becoming broken or damaged after a period of time: *Brass wears as well as steel in most hinges.* **b)** if something wears well, it continues to be interesting even after you have heard or seen it many times: *Pavement's album from 1991 still wears well.*
6 sth wears thin a) if something wears thin, you are bored with it because it is not interesting anymore, or has become annoying: *His little jokes were starting to wear thin.* **b)** if your patience wears thin, you have very little left: *My patience with Jean is wearing thin.*
7 sb wears sth well a) used to say that someone looks good in a particular piece of clothing **b)** used to say that someone looks good or works effectively in a particular situation: *The twins wore the strain well.*
8 wear your heart on your sleeve INFORMAL to show your true feelings openly
9 wear the pants INFORMAL to be the person in a family who makes the decisions.: *Don't forget – I wear the pants around here.* —**wearable** *adj.*
wear away *phr. v.* [I,T] to gradually become damaged or thinner or weaker by being used, rubbed etc., or to make something do this: [wear sth ↔ away] *Constant rubbing is wearing away the features on the statue's face.*
wear down *phr. v.* **1** [T wear sb ↔ down] to make someone physically weaker or less determined: *After*

W

an hour of begging, I wore him down enough to give me one more chance. **2** [I,T] to gradually become smaller or make something smaller, for example by rubbing it a lot or using it a lot: *Mountains are slowly worn down by wind and rain.*

wear off *phr. v.* [I] if pain or the effect of something wears off, it gradually stops: *The effects of the anesthetic were starting to wear off.*

wear on *phr. v.* **1** [I] if time wears on, it passes very slowly, especially when you are waiting for something to happen: *As the evening wore on, I grew less and less interested in the conversation.* **2** [T **wear on** sb] to gradually make someone feel tired or annoyed: *The constant travel was beginning to wear on the players.*

wear out *phr. v.* [I,T] **1** to become weak, broken, or useless, or to make something do this by using it a lot or for a long time: *After years of running, his knees started to wear out.* | [**wear** sth ↔ **out**] *The kids have worn out the carpet in the living room.* **2** to make someone feel extremely tired; EXHAUST: [**wear** sb ↔ **out**] *Working two jobs can really wear you out.* | *I thought I'd just let him scream and wear himself out.* **3 wear out your welcome** to stay with someone longer than they want you to —see also WORN OUT

wear[2] *n.* [U] **1** damage caused by continuous use over a long period: *After five years, the stadium is beginning to show signs of wear.* **2** the amount of use an object, piece of clothing etc. has had, or the use you can expect to get from it: *This type of sofa can take a lot of wear.* | *I've gotten a lot of wear out of these jeans.* **3 casual/evening/children's etc. wear** the clothes worn for a particular occasion or activity, or by a particular group of people: *Men were dressed in formal wear and top hats.* —see also FOOTWEAR, MENSWEAR, SPORTSWEAR **4 wear and tear** the amount of damage you expect to be caused to furniture, cars, equipment etc. when they are used for a long period of time: *The washer should last for ten years allowing for normal wear and tear.* —see also **the worse for (the) wear** (WORSE[2] (4))

wear·er /ˈwɛrɚ/ *n.* [C] someone who wears a particular type of clothing, jewelry, etc.: *Bicycle helmets offer wearers protection against serious head injury.*

wear·ing /ˈwɛrɪŋ/ *adj.* **1** making you feel tired or annoyed: *The constant arguments at home are very wearing.* **2** gradually making something weaker or less effective: [+ **on**] *The new process is less wearing on the equipment.*

wea·ri·some /ˈwɪrisəm/ *adj.* FORMAL making you feel bored, tired, or annoyed: *a wearisome bus ride*

wea·ry[1] /ˈwɪri/ *adj.* **wearier, weariest 1** very tired, especially because you have been doing something for a long time: *I was so weary, I fell asleep as soon as I lay down.* | [+ **of**] *Jo had grown weary of explaining why she was a vegetarian.* **2** very tiring —**wearily** *adv.* —**weariness** *n.* [U]

weary[2] *v.* **wearies, wearied, wearying** [I,T] FORMAL to become very tired, or make someone very tired: *Kerry's constant need for attention wearies me.* | [**weary of doing** sth] *He never wearied of telling me how he'd won the championship.*

wea·sel[1] /ˈwizəl/ *n.* [C] **1** a small thin furry animal that kills and eats rats and birds **2** INFORMAL someone who has been disloyal to you or has deceived you

weasel[2] *v.*

weasel out *phr. v.* [I] INFORMAL to avoid doing something you should do by using dishonest excuses or lies: [+ **of**] *Fife is now in court trying to weasel out of $25 million in debts.*

weasel word /ˈ.. ./ *n.* [C usually plural] INFORMAL a word used instead of another word because it is less direct, honest, or clear

weath·er[1] /ˈwɛðɚ/ *n.* **1** [singular,U] the temperature and other conditions such as sun, rain, and wind: *What's the weather like today?* | **hot/wet/cold etc. weather** *We've had some cold weather lately.* **2 the**

weather INFORMAL the description of what the weather will be like in the near future, on radio, television, in newspapers etc.: *I just want to hear the weather, and then we can turn it off.* **3 weather permitting** if the weather is good enough: *The game starts at 7 tomorrow, weather permitting.* **4 under the weather** INFORMAL slightly sick: *Louise looked a little under the weather when I saw her.* **5 keep a weather eye on sth** to watch a situation carefully so that you notice anything unusual or bad —see also ALL-WEATHER

weather[2] *v.* **1** [T] to come through a very difficult situation safely: *The police department has weathered the storm of criticism after the incident.* **2** [I,T usually passive] if rock, wood etc. weathers, or if wind, sun, rain etc. weathers them, they change color or shape over a period of time —see also WEATHERED, WEATHERING

weather bal·loon /ˈ.. ,./ *n.* [C] a large BALLOON that is sent into the air with special equipment to collect information about the weather

weather-beat·en /ˈ.. ,../ *adj.* weather-beaten buildings, skin, clothing etc. look old and damaged because they have been outside in bad weather: *a weather-beaten table*

weather bu·reau /ˈ.. ,../ *n.* [C] a place where information about the weather is collected and where reports are produced

weath·er·cock /ˈwɛðɚkɑk/ *n.* [C] a WEATHER VANE in the shape of a ROOSTER

weath·ered /ˈwɛðɚd/ *adj.* weathered wood, stone, skin etc. has changed shape or color over a period of time because of the wind, rain, sun etc.: *I could see laughter and wisdom in Akio's weathered face.*

weather fore·cast /ˈ.. ,../ *n.* [C] a report saying what the weather is expected to be like in the near future

weather fore·cast·er /ˈ.. ,.../ *n.* [C] someone on television or radio who tells you what the weather will be like

weath·er·ing /ˈwɛðərɪŋ/ *n.* [U] the effect of the wind, rain etc. on earth and stone over time

weath·er·ize /ˈwɛðəˌraɪz/ *v.* [T] to protect a building against cold weather by putting in INSULATION, making windows fit tightly etc. —**weatherization** /ˌwɛðərəˈzeɪʃən/ *n.* [U]

weath·er·man /ˈwɛðɚˌmæn/ *n.* [C] a male weather forecaster

weather map /ˈ.. ./ *n.* [C] a map that shows what the weather is like in a particular place at a particular time

weather pat·tern /ˈ.. ,../ *n.* [C] the way the weather usually is or changes over a long period of time in a particular area

weath·er·proof /ˈwɛðɚˌpruf/ *adj.* weatherproof clothing or material can keep out wind and rain —**weatherproof** *v.* [T]

weather re·port /ˈ.. ,./ *n.* [C] a report saying what the weather has been like and how it might change

weather sta·tion /ˈ.. ,../ *n.* [C] a place or building used for studying and recording weather conditions

weather strip·ping /ˈ.. ,../ *n.* [U] thin pieces of plastic or other material put along the edge of a door or window to keep out cold air —**weather strip** *v.* [I,T]

weather vane /ˈ.. ./ *n.* [C] a metal thing fastened to the top of a building that blows around to show the direction the wind is coming from

weave[1] /wiv/ *v.* *past tense* **wove** *past participle* **woven 1** [I,T] to make threads into cloth by crossing them under and over each other in a way, or to make cloth in this way: *Only a few of the Navajo women still weave full time.* **2** [T] to make something by twisting pieces of something together: *Visitors to the center can weave a white oak basket.* **3** [T] to put many different ideas, subjects, stories etc. together and connect them smoothly: *Shakespeare wove several smaller stories together into a unified whole.* **4** *past tense and past participle* **weaved** [I always + adv./prep.,T always + adv./prep.] to move somewhere by turning and changing direction a lot: [+ **through/across etc.**] *The car was weaving in and* *out of traffic at speeds of up to 85 miles per hour.* | *Miles* **weaved his way** *through the crowded room.* —**weaving** *n.* [U]

weave² *n.* [C] **1** the way in which a material is woven, and the pattern formed by this: *a fine weave* **2** INFORMAL a HAIR WEAVE

weav·er /ˈwivə/ *n.* [C] someone whose job is to weave cloth

web /wɛb/ *n.* [C] **1 the Web** the system on the Internet that allows you to find and use information that is held on computers all over the world **2** a net of thin threads made by a SPIDER to catch insects: *A spider had **spun** its **web*** (=made its web) *across the door.* —see also COBWEB —see picture at SPIDER **3 a web of sth** a closely related set of things that can be very complicated: *Jordan found himself caught in his own web of lies.* **4** a piece of skin that connects the toes of ducks and some other birds, and helps them to swim well

webbed /wɛbd/ *adj.* webbed feet or toes have skin between the toes

web·bing /ˈwɛbɪŋ/ *n.* [U] **1** strong woven material in narrow bands, used for supporting seats, holding things etc. **2** pieces of skin between fingers or toes

We·ber /ˈveɪbə/, **Max** /mæks/ (1864–1920) a German ACADEMIC and writer whose ideas are important as the beginning of modern sociology

web-foot·ed /ˌ. ˈ../ *adj.* having toes that are connected by pieces of skin

web·mas·ter /ˈwɛbˌmæstə/ *n.* [C] someone who organizes a WEBSITE and keeps it working

web page, Web page /ˈ. ./ *n.* [C] a part of a WEBSITE

web·site, web site /ˈwɛbsaɪt/ *n.* [C] a place on the Internet where you can find information about a variety of subjects, including people, products and organizations

Web·ster /ˈwɛbstə/, **Daniel** (1782–1852) a U.S. politician famous for his skill at public speaking

Webster, Noah /ˈnoʊə/ (1758–1843) an American LEXICOGRAPHER (=someone who writes dictionaries) famous for his American dictionaries and for setting rules for American spelling which were different from British spelling rules

web-toed /ˌ. ˈ./ *adj.* WEB-FOOTED

we'd /wid/ **1** the short form of "we had": *We'd both eaten already.* **2** the short form of "we would": *We'd rather stay.*

wed /wɛd/ *v.* past tense and past participle **wedded** or **wed, wedding** [I,T not in progressive] **1** a word meaning "to marry," used especially in literature or newspapers: *They were wed at the church where they met in 1920.* **2 be wedded to sth** to be unable or unwilling to change a particular idea or way of doing things: *This is a big problem, and we're not wedded to any one solution*

Wed. a written abbreviation of Wednesday

wed·ded /ˈwɛdɪd/ *adj.* **1** sb's (lawful) **wedded husband/wife/spouse** FORMAL someone's legal husband or wife **2 wedded bliss** HUMOROUS the happiness that comes when you are married

wed·ding /ˈwɛdɪŋ/ *n.* [C] **1** a ceremony at which two people become married, especially one with a religious service: *a wedding present/reception/cake etc. We got that silver tray as a wedding present.* **2 (hear) wedding bells** SPOKEN used to say that you think it is likely that two people will get married: *He's out with Leslie again – I think I hear wedding bells.*

wedding band /ˈ.. ./ *n.* [C] a WEDDING RING

wedding chap·el /ˈ.. ../ *n.* [C] a small building like a church, used for wedding ceremonies

wedding dress also **wedding gown** /ˈ.. ./ *n.* [C] a long white dress worn at a traditional wedding

wedding par·ty /ˈ.. ../ *n.* **the wedding party** all the people who are officially involved in someone's wedding, and who usually wear special clothes

wedding ring /ˈ.. ./ *n.* [C] a ring worn on your left hand to show that you are married, which is given to you on your wedding day

wedding vows /ˈ.. ./ *n.* [plural] the promises you

make during a wedding ceremony: **exchange/break wedding vows** *Tammy and John exchanged their wedding vows in front of family and friends.*

wedge¹ /wɛdʒ/ *n.* [C] **1** a piece of wood, metal etc. that has one thick edge and one pointed edge and is used especially for keeping a door open or for splitting wood **2** a piece of food shaped like this: *lemon wedges* | *a wedge of pie* —see also **drive a wedge between sb/sth** (DRIVE¹ (15))

wedge² *v.* **1** [T always + adv./prep.] to force something firmly into a narrow space: [**wedge sth behind/under/in etc.**] *They have three desks wedged into that tiny office.* | *Somehow she got her head wedged between the bars of the railing.* **2 wedge sth open/shut** to put something under a door, window etc. to make it stay open or shut

wedg·ie /ˈwɛdʒi/ *n.* [C] SLANG the situation of having your underwear pulled too tightly between your BUTTOCKS (=parts of your body you sit on), or the action of pulling someone's underwear into this position as a joke

wed·lock /ˈwɛdlɑk/ *n.* [U] OLD USE the state of being married —see also **be born out of wedlock** (BORN (1))

Wednes·day /ˈwɛnzdi, -deɪ/ *written abbreviation* **Wed.** *n.* [C,U] the fourth day of the week, between Tuesday and Thursday: *Jane comes home Wednesday.* | *The staff meeting is **on Wednesday**.* | *I didn't go to work **last Wednesday**.* | *I'll be in California **next Wednesday**.* | *My yoga class starts **this Wednesday** (=the next Wednesday that is coming).* | *We usually go out for a beer after work **on Wednesdays** (=each Wednesday).* | *Kelly died **on a Wednesday**.* | *Wednesday morning/afternoon/night etc. Do you feel like getting together Wednesday evening around 8:00?* —see Usage Note at SUNDAY

wee¹ /wi/ *adj.* [usually before noun] **1 the wee (small) hours** the early hours of the morning, just after MIDNIGHT: *The recording session extended into the wee hours.* **2 a wee bit** INFORMAL to a small degree: *Don't you think her behavior is just a wee bit bizarre?* **3** OLD-FASHIONED very small: *a wee girl* —see also PEEWEE

wee² *v.* [I] SPOKEN a word meaning "to pass water from your body," used by or to children; URINATE —**wee** *n.* [singular,U]

weed¹ /wid/ *n.* **1** [C] a wild plant growing where it is not wanted, that prevents crops or garden flowers from growing as they should: *Dorothea bent down and pulled weeds out of the garden.* —see also SEAWEED **2** [U] SLANG: see MARIJUANA **3 the weed** OLD-FASHIONED cigarettes or tobacco —see also **grow like a weed** (GROW (1))

weed² *v.* [I,T] to remove unwanted plants from a garden or other place

weed sb/sth ↔ out *phr. v.* [T] to get rid of people or things that are not very good: *Unsuitable recruits were soon weeded out.*

weed·kil·ler /ˈwidˌkɪlə/ *n.* [C,U] poison used to kill unwanted plants

weed whack·er /ˈ. ˌ../ *n.* [C] a piece of equipment with a long straight handle and a blade or a piece of strong string that turns around very fast, that is used for cutting weeds and small areas of grass

weed·y /ˈwidi/ *adj.* **weedier, weediest** INFORMAL **1** full of weeds, or like a weed: *a weedy lawn* **2** tall, thin, and weak: *a weedy young man*

week /wik/ *n.* [C] **1** a period of seven days and nights, beginning Sunday and ending Saturday: *The class meets once a week.* | *Greg just started working here **this week**.* | **last/next week** (=the week before or after this one) **2** any period of seven days and nights: *It would probably take a week to hike that far.* | **In a week** (=seven days after today) *you'll be a married woman!* | **a week from today/tomorrow/Monday etc.** *Are you free a week from Friday?* **3** the part of the week when you go to work, usually from Monday to Friday; WORKWEEK: *a 40-hour week* | *I*

W

don't go out much during the week. **4 week after week** also **week in, week out** SPOKEN continuously for many weeks: *We keep practicing the same dance steps week in, week out.*

week·day /'wikdeɪ/ *n. plural* **weekdays** [C] any day of the week except Saturday and Sunday

week·end¹ /'wikɛnd/ *n.* [C] **1** Saturday and Sunday (and sometimes also Friday evening), especially when considered as time when you do not work: *What are you planning to do this weekend?* | *Over the weekend* (=during the weekend) *we went to visit my wife's parents.* | *Robert also works a part-time job on weekends to make ends meet.* | *Rich spent the weekend learning how to use his new computer.* | *last/next weekend* (=the weekend before or after this one) **2** *a three-day/four-day weekend* three or four days, including Saturday and Sunday, during which you do not have to work: *The 4th of July is on Friday this year, so we get a three-day weekend.* **3** a vacation from Friday evening until Sunday evening: *You've won a weekend for two in Chicago!* —see also **a long weekend** (LONG¹ (7))

weekend² *v.* [I always + adv./prep.] to spend the weekend somewhere

week·end·er /'wik,ɛndə/ *n.* [C] someone who spends time in a place only at weekends

weekend war·ri·or /'.. ,.../ *n.* [C] INFORMAL **1** someone who works during the week, but does activities outside during the weekend that take a lot of energy, such as HIKING, camping etc. **2** someone who is in the National Guard or in the Army, Navy etc. RESERVE

week·long /,wik'lɔŋ◂/ *adj.* [only before noun] continuing for a week: *a weeklong music festival*

week·ly¹ /'wikli/ *adj.* **1** happening or done every week: *weekly ballet lessons* **2** relating to a single week: *Weekly rates at the hotel start at $627.* —**weekly** *adv.*

weekly² *n. plural* **weeklies** [C] a magazine that appears once a week: *a popular news weekly*

week·night /'wiknaɪt/ *n.* [C] any night except Saturday or Sunday

wee·nie /'wini/ *n.* [C] INFORMAL **1** a type of SAUSAGE; WIENER: *a weenie roast* **2** a word meaning someone who is weak, afraid, or stupid, used especially by children

ween·sy /'winsi/ *adj.* SPOKEN a word meaning something that is extremely small or a very small amount of something, used especially by children —see also TEENY WEENY

weep /wip/ *v. past tense and past participle* **wept** **1** [I,T] FORMAL OR LITERARY to cry, especially because you feel very sad: *Jesus wept.* | *At the trial, she wept bitterly* (=cried loudly). —see Usage Note at CRY¹ **2** [I] if a wound weeps, liquid comes out of it —**weep** *n.* [singular]

W **weep·ie** /'wipi/ *n.* [C] a book or movie that tries to make people cry

weeping wil·low /'.. ,../ *n.* [C] a tree with branches that hang down toward the ground

weep·y /'wipi/ *adj.* **weepier, weepiest** INFORMAL tending to cry a lot or looking like you will cry: *Her eyes were red and weepy.*

wee·vil /'wivəl/ *n.* [C] a small insect that destroys plants, grain etc. by eating them

wee-wee /'. ./ *v.* [I] SPOKEN a word meaning "to pass water from your body," used by or to children; URINATE —**wee-wee** *n.* [U]

weft /wɛft/ *n.* **the weft** TECHNICAL the threads in a piece of cloth that are woven across the threads that go from top to bottom —compare WARP² (2)

weigh /weɪ/ *v.*
1 be a particular weight [linking verb] to have a particular weight: *Some of their players weigh over 300 pounds.* | *How much do you weigh?*
2 measure the weight [T] to use a machine to find out what something or someone weighs: *Dieters shouldn't weigh themselves too often.*

3 **weigh a ton** to be very heavy: *Your suitcase weighs a ton!*
4 consider/compare [T] to consider something carefully so that you can make a decision about it: *I haven't had time to weigh all of my options.* | [**weigh sth against sth**] *We have to weigh the costs of the new system against the benefits it will bring.*
5 **weigh your words** to think very carefully about what you say because you do not want to say the wrong thing
6 influence [I always + adv./prep.] FORMAL to influence a result or decision: [+ **with**] *Greg's opinion usually weighs strongly with our supervisor.* | *The new data weighed in favor of the effectiveness of drug treatment.* | *The brutal nature of the crime weighed against Smith being released early.*
7 **weigh anchor** to raise an ANCHOR and sail away

weigh down

The hotel porter was weighed down by the luggage.

weigh sb/sth ↔ **down** *phr. v.* [I always + adv./prep.,T usually passive] **1** to make someone or something bend or feel heavy under a load: [+ **with/by**] *Weigh down the garbage can lids with stones to discourage raccoons.* **2** to make it difficult for something to progress or improve: [+ **by/with**] *Catholic schools are not weighted down by bureaucracy.* **3** to feel worried about a problem or difficulty: [+ **with/by**] *His conscience was weighed down with guilt.*

weigh in *phr. v.* [I] **1** to have your weight tested before taking part in a fight, other sport, or a horse race: [+ **at**] *Williams weighed in at 235 pounds.* —see also WEIGH-IN **2** **weigh in (with sth)** INFORMAL to add a remark to a discussion or an argument: *Each member weighed in with their own opinion.*

weigh on sb/sth *phr. v.* [T] to make someone worried or give them problems: *Boyd's arguments weighed on her mind.* | *The possibility of being laid off weighed heavily on them.*

weigh sth ↔ **out** *phr. v.* [T] to measure an amount of something by weight: *The clerk quickly weighed out a half pound of shrimp.*

weigh-in /'. ./ *n.* [C usually singular] a check on the weight of a BOXER or a JOCKEY before a fight or a horse race —see also **weigh in** (WEIGH)

weight¹ /weɪt/ *n.*
1 what sb/sth weighs [C,U] how heavy someone or something is when measured by a particular system: *My height is six feet, and my weight is 173 pounds.* | [+ **of**] *The cable is strong enough to hold the weight of an elephant.*
2 how fat [U] how heavy and especially how fat someone is: *She's always worried about her weight.* | *I think I've put on weight* (=gotten fatter) *lately.* | *Have you lost weight* (=gotten thinner)? | *Exercise and watch your weight* (=be careful about what you eat so that you do not get fat). | *For years, Gerry's had a weight problem* (=been too fat). —see also OVERWEIGHT, UNDERWEIGHT
3 heaviness [U] the fact of being heavy: *The weight of the water makes the tub sink slightly.* | *Some buildings collapsed under the weight of the ash from the volcano.*
4 heavy thing [C] something that is heavy: *My job requires lifting heavy weights such as TVs and refrigerators.*
5 for exercise [C] a piece of metal that weighs a certain amount and is lifted by people who want bigger muscles or who are competing in lifting competitions —see also WEIGHTLIFTING

6 **responsibility/worry** [C] something that causes you a lot of worry: [+ of] *Since he was 18, he's had the full weight of raising his younger brothers.*

7 a weight off your mind something that solves a problem and makes you feel happier: *Selling the house was a great weight off my mind.*

8 **importance** [U] the value, influence, or importance that something has when you are forming a judgment or opinion: *The weight of evidence against her led to her conviction.* | *Harry's opinion doesn't carry much weight* (=have influence) *around here.* | *New findings have added weight to the theory that there is life on other planets.* | *I don't attach too much weight to the rumors* (=I do not think that they are true or important).

9 **for measuring quantities** [C] a piece of metal weighing a particular amount that is used to measure what something else weighs by balancing it in a SCALE

10 **system** [C,U] a system of standard measures of weight: *metric weight* | *weights and measures*

11 throw your weight around INFORMAL to use your position of authority to tell people what to do in a way that is unreasonable and not nice

12 throw your weight behind sb to use all your power and influence to support someone: *The mayor has thrown his weight behind the new stadium deal.*

13 weight of numbers the combined strength, influence etc. of a large group: *They are likely to win this battle through sheer weight of numbers.*

14 take the weight off your feet SPOKEN used to tell someone to sit down: *Come in, take the weight off your feet.*

15 **science** [C,U] TECHNICAL the amount of force with which an object is pulled down by GRAVITY (1) —see also DEAD WEIGHT, **pull your weight** (PULL¹ (8)), -WEIGHT

weight² *v.* [T] also **weight down** to add something heavy to something or put a weight on it, especially in order to keep it in place: *fishing lines weighted with lead*

-weight /weɪt/ [in adjectives] **summer-weight/winter-weight** a piece of clothing that is summer-weight or winter-weight is made of material that is appropriate for summer or winter

weight·ed /ˈweɪtɪd/ *adj.* [not before noun] producing conditions that are favorable or unfavorable to a particular person or group: [+ toward/against] *The voting system is weighted against the smaller parties.* | *His policies are heavily weighted in favor of Muslims.*

weight·less /ˈweɪtlɪs/ *adj.* having no weight, especially when you are floating in space or water —**weightlessly** *adv.* —**weightlessness** *n.* [U]

weight·lift·ing /ˈweɪtˌlɪftɪŋ/ *n.* [U] **1** the sport of lifting special WEIGHTS attached to ends of a bar **2** also **weight training** the activity of lifting special weights as a form of exercise —**weightlifter** *n.* [C]

weight·y /ˈweɪti/ *adj.* **weightier, weightiest** **1** important and serious: *Before deciding on any weighty matter, he consults his staff.* **2** ESPECIALLY LITERARY heavy

weir /wɪr, wɛr/ *n.* [C] **1** a low structure built across a river or stream to control the flow of water **2** a wooden fence built across a stream to make a pool where you can catch fish

weird /wɪrd/ *adj.* INFORMAL unusual and very strange: *He has some weird ideas about things.* | *Robin's boyfriend is kind of weird.* —**weirdly** *adv.* —**weirdness** *n.* [U]

weird·o /ˈwɪrdoʊ/ *n.* plural **weirdos** [C] INFORMAL someone who behaves strangely, wears unusual clothes etc.: *There's always a bunch of weirdos around the train station.*

welch /wɛltʃ/ *v.* [I] to not do something you have promised to do for someone, such as not paying them money: [+ on] *I'll make sure Bill doesn't welch on the bet.*

wel·come¹ /ˈwɛlkəm/ *interjection* **1** an expression of greeting to a guest or someone who has just arrived: [+ to] *Welcome to New York!* | *Welcome home* (=used when someone has been away and returns

home! | *Welcome back* (=used when someone has been away and returns to a place) – *it's good to see you again.* **2 welcome to the club** SPOKEN used to make someone feel better when they are in a bad situation, by telling them you are in that situation too

welcome² *adj.* **1** someone who is welcome is gladly accepted in a place: *I don't think I'm welcome there anymore.* | [+ at] *You're welcome at my house anytime.* | *They did their best to make me feel welcome* (=make me feel that they were pleased I had come). **2** something that is welcome is pleasant and enjoyable, especially because it is just what you need or want: *The trip to Mexico will be a welcome break from work.*

SPOKEN PHRASES

3 you're welcome a polite way of replying to someone who has just thanked you for something: *"Thank you for your help." "You're welcome."* **4 be welcome to do sth** used to invite someone to do something if they would like to: *You're welcome to borrow my bike.* **5 be welcome to sth** used to say that someone can have something if they want it, because you certainly do not want it: *If you're still hungry, you're welcome to another sandwich.*

---

welcome³ *n.* [C] **1** a greeting you give to someone when they arrive: *The team was given a warm welcome* (=greeted in a very friendly way) *when they returned to Chicago.* | *Rodney received a hero's welcome* (=a very excited friendly welcome to someone who has done something good) *in his hometown.* **2 a hero's welcome** a very excited friendly welcome to someone who has done something good: *Havel received a hero's welcome at the White House.* **3 overstay/outstay your welcome** FORMAL to stay at someone's house longer than they want you to —compare **wear out your welcome** at WEAR OUT (WEAR¹)

welcome⁴ *v.* [T] **1** to say hello in a friendly way to someone who has just arrived: *Jill was busy welcoming the guests.* **2** to accept an idea, suggestion etc. happily: *Many citizens welcomed Smith's resignation from office.* | *I welcome the challenge with open arms* (=very happily). **3 welcome sb with open arms** to be very glad that someone has come: *Her family welcomed me with open arms.*

welcome wag·on /ˈ.. ˌ../ *n.* [C] someone who welcomes someone who has just arrived in a new place, or something that is done to make someone feel welcome: *City leaders have rolled out the welcome wagon for several new businesses.*

wel·com·ing /ˈwɛlkəmɪŋ/ *adj.* making you feel happy and relaxed: *a welcoming smile* | *The room was bright and welcoming.* | **a welcoming committee/party** (=group of people who welcome someone)

weld¹ /wɛld/ *v.* **1** [I,T] to join metals by melting them and pressing them together when they are hot, or to be joined in this way **2** [T always + adv./prep.] to join or unite people into a single, strong group: *A person of vision was needed to weld the various political factions together.* —compare FORGE¹ (4), SOLDER²

weld² *n.* [C] a joint that is made by welding two pieces of metal

weld·er /ˈwɛldə/ *n.* [C] someone whose job is to weld things

wel·fare /ˈwɛlfɛr/ *n.* [U] **1** money paid by the government to people who are very poor, do not have jobs, are sick etc.: *Most of the people in this neighborhood are on welfare.* **2** health, comfort, and happiness; WELL-BEING: *We are very concerned about the welfare of U.S. citizens abroad.* —compare BENEFIT¹ (1), SOCIAL SECURITY

welfare state /ˈ.. ˌ./ *n.* **1 the welfare state** the system by which the government provides money, free medical care etc. for people who are old, do not have jobs, are sick etc. **2** [C] a country with such a system

we'll /wɪl; *strong* wil/ the short form of "we will" or "we shall": *We'll leave about eight.*

well[1] /wɛl/ *adv.* comparative **better** *superlative* **best**
1 satisfactorily in a successful or satisfactory way: *We didn't win, but at least we played well.* | *Dad does not hear very well anymore.* | **fairly/moderately/pretty well** *The condos sold fairly well.* | *I hope that your presentation **goes well*** (=happens in the way you planned or hoped).
2 do well a) if someone who has been sick or injured is doing well, they are becoming healthy again: *The operation was successful and the patient is doing well.* **b)** to be successful, especially in work or business: [+ **in**] *I heard Liz is doing well in her new job.*
3 thoroughly in a thorough way: *Before you open it, shake the bottle well.*
4 as well as in addition to something else: *My son has asthma as well as allergies.* | [**as well as doing sth**] *The organization encourages members to meet on a regular basis, as well as providing them with financial support.*
5 as well in addition to something or someone else: *Did Joe go as well?* —see Usage Note at ALSO
6 may/might/could well do sth also **may/might/could well be sth** used to say that something is likely to happen or is likely to be true: *If he doesn't stop, he could well find himself in jail.* | *We may well be broke by the end of the month.*
7 may/might/could (just) as well do sth a) INFORMAL used when you do not particularly want to do something but you decide to do it: *I might as well eat the last little piece.* **b)** used to mean that another course of action would have an equally good result: *You may as well buy the chair here since it costs the same as in the other place.*
8 be well on the/your way to (doing) sth to have almost finished changing from one state or situation to another, especially a better one: *We are well on the way to reaching our sales targets.* | *Cindy is well on her way to recovery.*
9 well before/behind/down etc. a long way or a long time before, behind etc.: *It was well after midnight when he got home.* | *I finished the test well before the time limit.*
10 well pleased/aware etc. very pleased, AWARE etc.: *I'm well aware of how hard you've worked on this project.* | *It's **well worth** taking the time to stretch before you jog.*
11 know full well to know or realize something very well: *You know full well what I mean.*
12 speak/think well of sb to talk about someone in an approving way or to have a favorable opinion of them: *Uncle Brian always thought well of you.*
13 well done!/well played! etc. used to praise someone when you think they have done something very well
14 as well sb might/may FORMAL used to say that there is a good reason for someone's feelings or reactions: *Marilyn looked guilty when she saw me, as well she might.*
15 be well up on sth INFORMAL to know a lot about a particular subject: *Foster's well up on the latest marketing data.*
16 well and truly completely: *I went out and got well and truly drunk.*
17 do well by sb INFORMAL to treat someone generously —see Usage Note at GOOD

well[2] *interjection*
1 emphasizing sth used before a statement or question to emphasize it: *Well, I think you should wait for a better offer.* | ***Well then** call and tell him so.*
2 pausing used to pause or give yourself time to think before saying something: *This needs to be copied, and, well, I don't have time to do it.* | *Well, let's see now, I could book you in for an appointment next Thursday.* | ***Well, I mean** you shouldn't just take things without asking.*
3 accepting a situation also **oh well** used to show that you accept a situation even though you feel disappointed or annoyed about it: *Well, I suppose this*

room will be big enough for the meeting. | *Oh well, at least we have a place to stay tonight.*
4 showing surprise also **well, well (,well)** used to express surprise or amusement: *Well, you look really good in a suit and tie.* | *Well, well, well, I didn't think I'd see you here, Sue.*
5 showing anger used to express anger or disapproval: *Well, you'd think at least she might have phoned to say she wasn't coming!* | **well honestly/well really** *Well really, she didn't have to be so rude to me.*
6 final remark used to show that you are about to finish speaking or stop doing an activity: *Well, that's all for today, I'll see you all tomorrow.*
7 expressing doubt used to express doubt or the fact that you are not sure about something: *Well, I don't think she's the best person for the job.*
8 agreeing **very well** used to show that you agree with or accept a suggestion, invitation etc.: *Very well, you can go to Emily's house, but be back by 7 p.m.*
9 continuing a story used to connect two parts of a story that you are telling people, especially in order to make it seem more interesting: *You know the guy I was telling you about? Well, he dropped out of school.*
10 demanding an explanation **Well?** used to demand an explanation or answer when you are angry with someone: *You were out past 3 a.m.! Well?*

well[3] *adj.* comparative **better** *superlative* **best**
1 healthy: *Ellen hasn't been very well lately.* | *I should be better by this weekend.* | **look/feel well** *What's wrong? Don't you feel well?* | *I hope you **get well soon*** (=used to say that you hope someone soon feels better). **2 all is well/all is not well** FORMAL used to say that a situation is satisfactory or not satisfactory: *All is not well at the office.* **3 all's well that ends well** used after a situation has ended in a satisfactory way

SPOKEN PHRASES

4 it is just as well (that) used to say that things have happened in a way that is fortunate or desirable: *It's just as well I took the train today – I heard the traffic was really bad.* **5 it's/that's all very well...** used to say that you think something is good in one way, but is not really satisfactory or acceptable in others, even if someone else thinks it is: *It's all very well to read books by non-Western authors, but don't discard Shakespeare and Chaucer.* **6 that's/it's (all) well and good** used to say that you accept or approve of one part of a situation or thing but not of another part: *That's well and good from a business standpoint, but not from a tax standpoint.* **7 it might be as well** used to give someone advice or make a helpful suggestion: *It might be as well to leave him on his own for a few hours.*

well[4] *n.* [C] **1** a deep hole in the ground from which people take water **2** an OIL WELL **3** an enclosed space in a building which goes straight up and down and surrounds an ELEVATOR, stairs etc. —see also STAIRWELL

well[5] *v.* [I always + adv./prep.] **1** if liquids well or well up, they start to flow: [+ **up/in/inside**] *As he spoke, his eyes welled up.* | *Tears welled in her eyes.* **2** if feelings well or well up, they start to get stronger: [+ **up/in/inside**] *Rage and helplessness welled inside him.*

well-ad·just·ed /ˌ. .ˈ...◂/ *adj.* emotionally healthy and able to deal well with the problems of life

well-ad·vised, **well advised** /ˌ. .ˈ.◂/ *adj.* **sb would be well-advised to do sth** used when you are strongly advising someone to do something that will help them avoid trouble: *High school students interested in technical fields would be well-advised to take physics.*

well-ap·point·ed /ˌ. .ˈ...◂/ *adj.* FORMAL a well-appointed house, hotel etc. has very good furniture and equipment

well-ba·by /ˌ. ˈ../ *adj.* [only before noun] relating to or providing medical care and advice for babies who are not sick, to make sure that they stay healthy:

well-baby program/care/check-up etc. *The hospital provides free transportation for well-baby check-ups.*

well·bal·anced /ˌ. '.◂/ *adj.* **1** a well-balanced meal or DIET contains all the things you need to keep you healthy **2** a well-balanced person is sensible and is not controlled by strong emotions; STABLE[1] (2)

well·be·haved /ˌ. .'.◂/ *adj.* behaving in a polite or socially acceptable way: *a well-behaved child* | *The crowd was noisy but well-behaved.*

well·be·ing /ˌ. '../ *n.* [U] a feeling of being comfortable, healthy, and happy: [+ of] *We hope to improve the health and well-being of poor children.* | *physical/social/economic etc.* **well-being** *Divorce has a strong effect on people's psychological well-being.* | *Being fully employed can do wonders for your sense of well-being* (=a feeling of being satisfied with your life).

well·born /ˌ. '.◂/ *adj.* born into a rich or UPPER CLASS family

well·bred /ˌ. '.◂/ *adj.* someone who is well-bred is very polite and behaves or speaks as if they come from a family of high social class

well·brought·up /ˌ. . '.◂/ *adj.* a child who is well-brought-up has been taught to be polite and to behave well

well·built /ˌ. '.◂/ *adj.* **1** someone who is well-built is big and strong **2** something that is well-built has been made to work well and exist or continue a long time: *a well-built car*

well·cho·sen /ˌ. '.◂/ *adj.* carefully chosen: *a well-chosen cast* | *I had a few **well-chosen words*** (=words appropriate for the situation, especially angry or offensive ones) *for the driver who pulled out in front of me.*

well·con·nect·ed /ˌ. '.◂/ *adj.* knowing or being related to powerful and socially important people

well·de·fined /ˌ. .'.◂/ *adj.* very clear and easy to understand, recognize, or see: *well-defined muscles* | *well-defined rules*

well·dis·posed /ˌ. .'.◂/ *adj.* feeling friendly toward a person or positive about an idea or plan: [+ to/toward] *The country is not well-disposed toward democracy.*

well·doc·u·ment·ed /ˌ. '....◂/ *adj.* well-documented events, behavior, information etc. definitely exist and people have written a lot about them: *The role of body weight in affecting blood pressure is well-documented.*

well·done /ˌ. '.◂/ *adj.* food that is well-done, especially meat, has been cooked thoroughly —compare MEDIUM[1] (2), RARE (2) —see also **well done!/well played! etc.** (WELL[1] (13))

well·dressed /ˌ. '.◂/ *adj.* wearing attractive, fashionable, and usually expensive clothes

well·earned /ˌ. '.◂/ *adj.* something that is well-earned is something you deserve because you have worked hard: *The city has a well-earned reputation for cleanliness.*

well·ed·u·cat·ed /ˌ. '....◂/ *adj.* a well-educated person has studied at good schools, especially at a good college: *Most of their customers are well-educated.*

well·en·dowed /ˌ. .'.◂/ *adj.* INFORMAL OR HUMOROUS **1** a woman who is well-endowed has large breasts **2** a man who is well-endowed has a large PENIS (=sex organ)

Welles /welz/**, Or·son** /'ɔrsən/ (1915–1985) a U.S. actor, movie DIRECTOR, PRODUCER, and writer

well·es·tab·lished /ˌ. .'.◂/ *adj.* established for a long time and respected: *a well-established photographer* | *The training program is now well-established.*

well·fed /ˌ. '.◂/ *adj.* regularly eating plenty of good healthy food, especially if this has made you a little fat: *well-fed cattle*

well·found·ed /ˌ. '.◂/ *adj.* WELL-GROUNDED (2)

well·groomed /ˌ. '.◂/ *adj.* having a very neat, clean appearance: *A well-groomed young couple sat at the table next to ours.*

well·ground·ed /ˌ. '.◂/ *adj.* **1** well-grounded in sth

fully trained in an activity or skill: *Irwin is well-grounded in both engineering and robotics.* **2** a belief, feeling etc. that is well-grounded is based on facts or good judgment: *well-grounded suspicions*

well·head /'welhed/ *n.* [C] **1** the top part of an OIL WELL where the oil is pumped out **2 the wellhead price/cost/rate etc.** the WHOLESALE price of oil

well·heeled /ˌ. '.◂/ *adj.* INFORMAL rich and usually of a high social class

well·hung /ˌ. '.◂/ *adj.* INFORMAL OR HUMOROUS having a large PENIS (=male sex organ)

well·in·formed /ˌ. .'.◂/ *adj.* knowing a lot about a particular subject or about many subjects: [+ on/about] *Stacy is well-informed on international politics.*

Wel·ling·ton /'welɪŋtən/ the capital city of New Zealand, on the North Island

Wellington, Duke of —see DUKE OF WELLINGTON, THE

well·in·ten·tioned /ˌ. .'...◂/ *adj.* trying to be helpful, but failing or actually making things worse: *Even the most well-intentioned doctors can forget to suggest routine tests.*

well·kept /ˌ. '.◂/ *adj.* **1** a well-kept building or garden is very well cared for and looks neat and clean **2** a well-kept secret is known only to a few people

well·knit /ˌ. '.◂/ *adj.* having several parts or features joined together in a way that works well: *a well-knit orchestra*

well·known /ˌ. '.◂/ *adj.* known by a lot of people: *It's a well-known fact that smoking can cause lung cancer.* | [+ for] *The town is well-known for growing watermelons.* —see Usage Note at FAMOUS[1]

well·made, well made /ˌ. '.◂/ *adj.* well-made furniture, clothes etc. are skillfully made and are of high quality: *a well-made car* | *The shirts are plain, but well made.*

well·man·nered /ˌ. '...◂/ *adj.* polite and having very good MANNERS: *Julio is a clean-cut, well-mannered 15-year-old boy.* —opposite ILL-MANNERED —see also MILD-MANNERED

well·mean·ing /ˌ. '.◂/ *adj.* intending or intended to be helpful, but not succeeding: *It was a well-meaning effort to help the poor.* —see also **he/she means well** (MEAN[1] (16))

well·meant /ˌ. '.◂/ *adj.* something you say or do that is well-meant is intended to be helpful, but does not have the result you intended: *well-meant advice* —see also **he/she means well** (MEAN[1] (16))

well·ness /'welnɪs/ *n.* [U] the state of being healthy: *Many colleges have established **wellness programs*** (=programs to help people stay healthy) *for their students.*

well·nigh /'. ./ *adv.* OLD-FASHIONED almost, but not completely: *It is **well-nigh impossible** to get a taxi in this part of town.*

well·off /ˌ. '.◂/ *adj.* having more money than many other people, or enough money to have a good standard of living: *Stella's family is well-off.* —compare BADLY-OFF, BAD-OFF, BETTER OFF

well·oiled /ˌ. '.◂/ *adj.* **1 a well-oiled machine** an organization or system that works very well **2** INFORMAL drunk

well·or·dered /ˌ. '...◂/ *adj.* arranged or planned in a very organized or neat way: *Tables were set up in well-ordered rows.*

well·paid /ˌ. '.◂/ *adj.* providing or receiving good pay: *well-paid managers*

well·pre·served /ˌ. .'.◂/ *adj.* HUMOROUS someone who is well-preserved still looks fairly young although they are getting old

well·read /ˌwel 'red◂/ *adj.* having read many books and knowing a lot about different subjects

well·round·ed /ˌ. '.◂/ *adj.* **1** someone who is well-rounded has had a wide variety of experiences in life or is able to do many different things: *The Twins are a well-rounded ball club.* | *We encourage the kids to*

W

be well-rounded. **2** well-rounded education or experience of life is complete and gives you knowledge of a wide variety of subjects: *At Cornell University, she received a well-rounded education.* **3** including many different abilities, parts etc., so that something or someone seems complete: *a well-rounded character* | *The museum displays a well-rounded selection of paintings and sculptures.* **4** a woman who is well-rounded has a pleasantly curved figure

Wells /wɛlz/, **H.G.** /eɪtʃ dʒi/ (1866–1946) a British writer of NOVELs and political ESSAYs, known for his SCIENCE FICTION

well-spo·ken /ˌ. ˈ..◂/ *adj.* speaking in a clear and polite way, and in a way that is socially approved of

well·spring /ˈwɛlsprɪŋ/ *n.* [C] LITERARY **1** a large amount of something: [+ of] *Her campaign to free the hostages has generated a wellspring of public support.* **2** the situation or place from which something begins: [+ of] *Poverty and hopelessness are so often the wellspring of crime.*

well-stocked /ˌ. ˈ.◂/ *adj.* having a large supply and a variety of things: *a well-stocked refrigerator*

well-thought-of /ˌ. ˈ. .◂/ *adj.* liked and admired by other people: *As a financial officer, Gilford is well-thought-of on Wall Street.*

well-thought-out /ˌ. . ˈ.◂/ *adj.* carefully and thoroughly planned: *a well-thought-out training program*

well-thumbed /ˌ. ˈ.◂/ *adj.* a well-thumbed book, magazine etc. has been used a lot: *a well-thumbed Bible*

well-timed /ˌ. ˈ.◂/ *adj.* said or done at the most appropriate moment: *Wyse's movement into the software market appears to be well-timed.*

well-to-do¹ /ˌ. . ˈ.◂/ *adj.* rich and with a high social position: *a well-to-do young woman* | *a well-to-do suburb*

well-to-do² *n.* the well-to-do people who are rich

well-turned /ˌ. ˈ.◂/ *adj.* a well-turned phrase or sentence is carefully expressed

well-turned-out /ˌ. . ˈ.◂/ *adj.* someone who is well-turned-out wears fashionable clothes and looks attractive

well-versed /ˌ. ˈ.◂/ *adj.* [not before noun] knowing a lot about something: [+ in/on] *Mr. Chang is well-versed in economic policy.*

well-wish·er /ˈ. ˌ../ *n.* [C] someone who does something to show that they admire someone and want them to succeed, be healthy etc.: *The family has received thousands of letters from well-wishers.*

well-wom·an /ˌ. ˈ../ *adj.* [only before noun] relating to or providing medical care for women who are not sick, to make sure that they stay healthy: *a well-woman program at the hospital*

well-worn /ˌ. ˈ.◂/ *adj.* **1** worn or used a lot for a long period of time: *a well-worn pair of slippers* **2** a well-worn argument, phrase etc. has been repeated so often that it is not interesting or effective anymore: *well-worn excuses*

Welsh /wɛlʃ/ *n.* **1** [U] the original language of Wales **2** the Welsh people from Wales —**Welsh** *adj.*

welsh /wɛlʃ/ *v.* [I + on] INFORMAL to WELCH

welt /wɛlt/ *n.* [C] **1** a raised place on someone's skin where they have been hit or stung **2** a piece of leather around the edge of a shoe, to which the top and bottom of the shoe are stitched

wel·ter /ˈwɛltɚ/ *n.* a welter of sth a large and confusing number of different details, emotions etc.: *Construction of the hospital has been halted by a welter of lawsuits.*

wel·ter·weight /ˈwɛltɚˌweɪt/ *n.* [C] a BOXER who is heavier than a LIGHTWEIGHT but lighter than a MIDDLE-WEIGHT

Wel·ty /ˈwɛlti/, **Eu·dor·a** /juˈdɔrə/ (1909–2001) a U.S. writer of NOVELs and short stories (SHORT STORY)

wench /wɛntʃ/ *n.* [C] OLD USE OR HUMOROUS a girl or young woman, especially a servant

wend /wɛnd/ *v.* **wend your way** LITERARY to move or travel slowly from one place to another: *We watched the train wend its way through the mountain pass.*

went /wɛnt/ *v.* the past tense of GO

wept /wɛpt/ *v.* the past tense and past participle of WEEP

we're /wɪr/ the short form of "we are": *We're going to Disneyland!*

were /wɚ/ *v.* the past tense of BE

weren't /wɚnt, ˈwɚənt/ the short form of "were not": *Paula and Thea weren't working that night.*

were·wolf /ˈwɛrwʊlf/ *n.* [C] a person who, in some stories, sometimes changes into a WOLF

wert /wɚt/ *v.* thou wert OLD USE you were

Wes·ley /ˈwɛsli, ˈwɛz-/, **John** (1703–1791) an English religious leader who started a new type of church in the Christian religion called Methodism

west¹, **West** /wɛst/ *written abbreviation* **W.** *n.* [singular,U] **1** the direction opposite from which the sun rises, that is on the right of someone facing north: *Which way is west?* | *I-95 coming from the west* goes all the way to the east coast. | *We live three miles to the west of the park.* **2** the west the western part of a country, state etc.: *The farmers in the west have been struggling due to the recent drought.* **3** the West a) the western part of the world and the people that live there, especially Western Europe and North America b) the part of the U.S. that is west of the Mississippi River: *David grew up in New York, but he moved to the West as soon as he graduated.* —compare MIDWEST **4** out West in or to the west of a particular country, state etc., especially the western part of the U.S.: *The first time I got to ride a horse was out West.* —compare back East (EAST¹ (4))

west² *adj.* **1** *written abbreviation* **W.** in, to, or facing the west: *We drove down the west coast of the U.S.* | [+ of] *70 miles west of Flagstaff* **2** a west wind comes from the west

west³ *adv.* toward the west: *Go west on I-80 toward Denver* | *The window faces west.*

west·bound /ˈwɛstbaʊnd/ *adj., adv.* traveling or leading toward the west: *westbound traffic* | *The car was driving westbound on Route 66.*

West Coast /ˌ. ˈ.◂/ *n.* the West Coast the part of the U.S. that is next to the Pacific Ocean

west·er·ly /ˈwɛstɚli/ *adj.* **1** toward or in the west: *The storm is moving in a westerly direction.* **2** a westerly wind comes from the west

west·ern¹, **Western** /ˈwɛstɚn/ *adj.* **1** from or relating to the west part of the world or of a country: *In western Iowa, there's not a whole lot to do.* **2** relating to ideas or ways of doing things that come from Europe and the Americas: *Western philosophies*

western² *n.* [C] a movie about life in the 19th century in the American West

West·ern·er /ˈwɛstɚnɚ/ *n.* [C] **1** someone who lives in or comes from the western part of the world **2** someone who lives in or comes from the western part of the U.S.

Western Eu·rope /ˌ.. ˈ../ *n.* [singular, not with the] the western part of Europe or the countries in it, especially the ones that did not have COMMUNIST governments, such as France and the Netherlands —compare CENTRAL EUROPE, EASTERN EUROPE

Western Hem·i·sphere /ˌ.. ˈ.../ *n.* the Western Hemisphere the half of the Earth that includes the Americas and the Caribbean

west·ern·ize /ˈwɛstɚˌnaɪz/ *v.* [T] to bring customs, business methods etc. that are typical of Europe and the U.S. to other countries —**westernization** /ˌwɛstɚnəˈzeɪʃən/ *n.* [U]

west·ern·ized /ˈwɛstɚˌnaɪzd/ *adj.* copying the customs, behavior etc. typical of the U.S. or Europe

western med·i·cine /ˌ.. ˈ.../ *n.* [U] the type of medical treatment that is standard in the WEST¹ (3) —compare ALTERNATIVE MEDICINE

west·ern·most /ˈwɛstɚnˌmoʊst/ *adj.* furthest west: *the westernmost island of South America*

W

Western Sa·mo·a /ˌwɛstən səˈmoʊə/ a country that consists of a group of islands in the southern Pacific Ocean

West In·dies /wɛst ˈɪndiz/ **the West Indies** the islands in the Caribbean Sea —**West Indian** adj.

West·ing·house /ˈwɛstɪŋˌhaʊs/, **George** (1846–1914) a U.S. engineer who made many improvements to trains and railroads

Wes·ton /ˈwɛstən/, **Ed·ward** /ˈɛdwəd/ (1886–1958) a U.S. PHOTOGRAPHER

West Point /ˌ. ˈ./ the usual name for the United States Military Academy, at West Point in New York, which is the oldest military college in the U.S.

West Vir·gin·ia /ˌwɛst vəˈdʒɪnyə/ written abbreviation **W.V.** a state in the eastern central U.S.

west·ward /ˈwɛstwəd/ adv. also **westwards** toward the west: We drove westward through the night. —**westward** adj.

wet¹ /wɛt/ adj. **wetter, wettest 1** covered in or full of water or another liquid: a wet towel | Be careful, the floor is still wet. | [+ with] His face was wet with sweat. | I don't want to get my shoes wet. | **soaking/sopping/dripping wet** (=extremely wet) **2** not yet dry: Don't touch the wall – the paint's still wet. **3** if the weather is wet, it is raining **4 wet behind the ears** INFORMAL very young and without much experience of life **5 sb is all wet** INFORMAL to be completely wrong —**wetness** n. [U]

wet² v. past tense **wet** or **wetted** [T] **1** to make something wet: Wet your hair and apply the shampoo. **2** to make yourself, your clothes, or your bed wet because you pass liquid waste from your body by accident: I nearly wet myself I was so scared. | Sean wet his bed again. **3 wet your whistle** OLD-FASHIONED to have an alcoholic drink

wet·back /ˈwɛtˌbæk/ n. [C] TABOO someone from Mexico who has come to the U.S. illegally. Do not use this word.

wet bar /ˈ. ./ n. [C] a small bar with a SINK and equipment for making alcoholic drinks, in a house, hotel room etc.

wet blan·ket /ˌ. ˈ../ n. [C] INFORMAL someone who tries to spoil other people's fun

wet dream /ˈ. ./ n. [C] VULGAR a sexually exciting dream that a man has that results in an ORGASM

wet·land /ˈwɛtlənd, -lænd/ n. [U] also **wetlands** [plural] an area of land that is usually wet, such as a MARSH or SWAMP —see also GRASSLAND, WOODLAND

wet nurse /ˈ. ./ n. [C] a woman who is employed to give her breast milk to another woman's baby, especially in past times

wet suit /ˈ. ./ n. [C] a piece of clothing, usually made of rubber, that swimmers, SURFERS etc. wear to keep warm in the ocean, a lake etc.

wetting a·gent /ˈ.. ˌ../ n. [C] a chemical substance which, when spread on a solid surface, makes it hold liquid

wetting so·lu·tion /ˈ.. .ˌ. / n. [C,U] a liquid used for storing CONTACT LENSes in, or for making them more comfortable to wear

wet wil·lie /ˌ. ˈ../ n. [C] SLANG the action of putting a wet finger in someone's ear as a joke

we've /wiv/ the short form of "we have": We've tried that already.

whack¹ /wæk/ v. [T] INFORMAL **1** to hit someone or something hard: Apparently someone whacked the side of my car with their door. **2** to kill someone, especially someone who is involved in crime, as a punishment for something they have done

    whack off phr. v. [I] SLANG to MASTURBATE

whack² n. [C] SPOKEN **1** the act of hitting something hard or the noise this makes: She gave my hand a whack with a ruler. | Singleton took a whack at (=tried to hit) Miller's head. **2 out of whack** if a system, machine etc. is out of whack, the parts are not working together correctly: The printer is out of whack again. **3 take a whack at sth** to try to do something: The lawn mower won't start? Here, let me take a whack at it. **4 in one whack** all on one occasion: Steve lost $500 in one whack.

whacked /wækt/ adj. [not before noun] INFORMAL **1 whacked out** behaving strangely, especially because of having too much alcohol or drugs **2** also **whacked out** very tired **3** also **wack** SLANG a whacked situation is very strange, especially in an unacceptable way: Everyone was running around naked. It was totally whacked.

whale¹ /weɪl/ n. [C] **1** a very large animal that lives in the ocean, breathes through a hole in the top of its head, and looks like a fish, but is actually a MAMMAL **2 have a whale of a time** OLD-FASHIONED to enjoy yourself very much

whale² v. **whale into/on sb/sth** to start hitting someone or something

whale·bone /ˈweɪlboʊn/ n. [U] a hard substance taken from the upper jaw of whales, used in past times for making women's clothes stiff

whal·er /ˈweɪlə/ n. [C] **1** someone who hunts whales **2** a boat used for hunting whales

whal·ing /ˈweɪlɪŋ/ n. [U] the activity of hunting whales

wham¹ /wæm/ interjection **1** used to describe the sound of something suddenly hitting something else very hard: I moved slightly, and wham, the bear hit me again. **2** used to express the idea that something very unexpected suddenly happens: Life is going along nicely and then, wham, you lose your job.

wham² n. [C] the sound made when something is hit very hard

wham·my /ˈwæmi/ n. [C] **put the whammy on sb** to use magic powers to make someone have bad luck —see also DOUBLE WHAMMY

wharf /wɔrf/ n. plural **wharves** /wɔrvz/ or **wharfs** [C] a structure that is built out into the water so that boats can stop next to it; PIER

Whar·ton /ˈwɔrtn/, **E·dith** /ˈidɪθ/ (1862–1937) a U.S. writer of NOVELS

whas·sup /ˌwʌsˈʌp/ interjection SLANG —see **what's up** (WHAT¹ (18))

what¹ /wət; strong wʌt, wɑt/ determiner, pron.

1 questions about sb/sth used when asking questions about a thing or person that you do not know anything about: What are you doing? | What did you say? | What kind of dog is that? | "What do you do for a living?" "I'm a doctor."

2 used in order to talk about things or information, especially in questions that are not direct: Let me see what you've got in the box. | I'm not sure what I can do to help you. | They're discussing what to do next. | She gave him what money she had (=all the money she had, although she did not have much).

3 what? a) used to ask someone to repeat something they have just said because you did not hear it very well: "Could you pass me the salt?" "What?" | "I went to the store and bought some new shoes." "You went to the store and what?" **b)** used during conversations when you have heard someone talking to you and want to tell them to continue: "Mike!" "What?" "Could help me with something?" **c)** used to show that you are surprised by what someone has said: "I think the car's out of gas." "What?"

4 very good/bad etc. used at the beginning of a sentence to show that you think someone or something is very good, very bad etc.: What a mean thing to say! | What nice weather we're having!

5 what about...? SPOKEN **a)** used to make a suggestion: What about Czechoslovakia? I'd like to see Prague. | What about doing What about going to a movie this evening? **b)** used to introduce a new person or thing into a conversation: What about Patrick? What's he doing nowadays? | We've chosen the food, now, what about the wine?

6 I/I'll tell you what used to make an offer or suggestion: I tell you what, I'll make you dinner if you drive me to the store.

7 guess what! used before telling someone some

exciting or surprising news: *Guess what! I got an "A" on my biology exam.*

8 what (...) for ? a) why?: *"She's decided to work part-time." "What for?"* **b)** used to ask what purpose something has: *What's this tool for?*

9 what's what what a situation is really like as opposed to what people believe it is like, or what they try and make you believe: *I keep my ears open and I know what's what around the office.*

10 what the hell/devil/blazes...? also **what in God's/heaven's name...?** used to ask in an extremely angry or surprised way what is happening, what someone is doing etc.: *What the hell are you doing? | What in heaven's name will she think of next?*

11 what the hell used to say that you have decided to do something even though it is very expensive, difficult etc.: *"Do you want to go dancing tonight?" "Sure, what the hell."*

12 ...or what? used to show that you are impatient when asking a question, or because you think there is only one possible answer to the question: *Do you want to be a member of the club, or what?*

13 so what? used to say that you do not care about something or to tell someone angrily that something does not concern them: *"Don't go in there, he's sleeping." "So what?"*

14 you what? used to show that you are surprised: *"I got the job!" "You what?"*

15 what if... a) used to make a suggestion: *What if we move the sofa over here? Would that look better?* **b)** used to ask what will happen in a situation, usually if a bad or frightening situation happens first: *What if it rains tomorrow? Will we still have soccer practice?*

16 ...and what have you used at the end of a list of things to mean other things of a similar kind: *The shelves were crammed with books, documents, and what have you.*

17 have what it takes to have the right qualities or skills in order to succeed: *Elaine has what it takes to make acting her career.*

18 what's up? used to say hello to someone, especially someone you know well: *"Hey Chris, what's up?" "Not much."* —compare WHASSUP

19 what's up with sb/sth? used to ask someone what is wrong or what is happening: *[+ with] What's up with this printer? It was working yesterday.*

20 what's up with that? used to say that you do not understand a situation or think it is unreasonable: *The college is raising tuition by 20% – What's up with that?*

21 what's with sth used to ask the reason for something: *What's with the all the sad faces?*

22 what's with sb used to ask why a person or group of people who are behaving strangely: *What's with Nathan? He looks upset.*

23 what of it? used to say that you do not care about something or to tell someone angrily that something does not concern them: *I know he really doesn't love me, but what of it?*

24 emphasis used at the beginning of a statement to emphasize what you are going to say: *What I need is a nice hot bath.*

25 what's it to you used to tell someone angrily that something does not concern them: *That's right, I didn't pass the test, what's it to you?*

26 (and) what's more used when adding something to what you have already said, especially when it is exciting or interesting: *These detergents are environmentally friendly; what's more, they're relatively cheap.*

27 now what? used to ask what is going to happen next, what you should do etc.

what² *adv.* **1** used especially in questions to ask to what degree or in what way something matters: *We may be a little late, but what does it matter? | What do you care (=why are you concerned) if I buy a motorcycle?* **2** SPOKEN used to give yourself time to think before guessing a number or amount: *You're*

looking at, what, about $4000 for a decent second-hand car. **3 what with sth** SPOKEN used to introduce a list of reasons that have made something happen or have made someone feel a particular way: *They've been under a lot of stress, what with Joe losing his job and all.*

what·cha·ma·call·it /ˈwʌtʃəməˌkɔlɪt/ *n.* [C] SPOKEN a word you use when you cannot remember the name of something: *The guy was wearing one of those whatchamacallits on his head.*

what·ev·er¹ /wətˈɛvə/ *determiner, pron.*

1 wanted/needed etc. any or all of the things that are wanted, needed, or possible: *David will do whatever she asks him. | Help yourself to whatever you want.*

2 not important used to say that it is not important what happens, what you do etc. because it does not change the situation: *Whatever I do, it's never good enough for him.*

SPOKEN PHRASES

3 don't know the name of sb/sth used to say that you do not know the exact meaning of something, or the exact name of someone or something: *Whatever it is that she cooked, it doesn't taste very good. | We could get SDD or whatever they call it.*

4 ...or whatever used after naming things on a list to mean other things of the same kind: *Then you do tricep kicks, push backs, or whatever. | Bring waterproof clothing, boots, or whatever else you might need.*

5 whatever you do used to emphasize that you do not want someone to do something: *Whatever you do, don't tell Judy that I spent so much money.*

6 don't care used as a reply to tell someone that something does not matter, or that you do not care or are not interested when they ask or tell you something: *"Do you want sausage or pepperoni on your pizza?" "Whatever."*

7 whatever you say/think/want used to tell someone that you agree with them or will do what they want, often when you do not really agree or want to do it: *"You need to check the oil in your car regularly." "Whatever you say."*

8 whatever floats your boat also **whatever trips your trigger** HUMOROUS used when someone has just mentioned something unusual that they like or enjoy doing, but you do not like it yourself: *"And then we put on wigs and high heels and walked around downtown." "Well, whatever floats your boat, I guess."*

9 surprised OLD-FASHIONED used to show that you are angry or surprised when making a statement or asking a question: *Whatever do you mean by that? | "Peter wants to join the circus." "Whatever next (=used to show surprise, especially when someone keeps doing surprising things)!"*

whatever² *adv.* used to emphasize a negative statement: *She gave no sign whatever of what she was thinking.*

whatever³ *adj.* **1** of any possible type: *I'll take whatever help I can get.* **2** of some type that you are not sure about: *Ellen's refusing to come, for whatever reason.*

what-for /ˌ. ˈ./ *n.* **give sb what-for** SPOKEN to complain to someone in a loud and angry way

what-if /ˈ. ., .ˈ./ *n.* [C usually plural] INFORMAL something that could happen in the future or could have happened in the past: *If I thought about all of the what-ifs in my life, I would go crazy.*

what·not /ˈwʌtˈnɑt/ *n.* **1 and whatnot** SPOKEN an expression used at the end of a list of things when you do not want to give the names of everything: *You can put all of your paper, pencils, and whatnot in this drawer.* **2** [C] a piece of furniture with shelves, used especially in the 19th century to show small pretty objects

what's-her-face, whatsherface /ˈwʌtsɚˌfeɪs/ *pron.* SPOKEN what's-her-name

what's-her-name, whatshername /ˈwʌtsɚˌneɪm/ *pron.* SPOKEN used to talk about a woman or girl when you have forgotten her name: *Have you seen what's-her-name lately?*

what's-his-face, whatshisface /ˈwʌtsɪzˌfeɪs/ *pron.* SPOKEN what's-his-name

what's-his-name, whatshisname /ˈwʌtsɪz neɪm/ *pron.* SPOKEN used to talk about a man or boy when you have forgotten his name: *Is she still dating what's-his-name?*

whats·it /ˈwʌtsɪt/ *n.* [C] SPOKEN a word you use when you cannot think of what something is called: *The curtains were green with little whatsits along the edge.*

what·so·ev·er /ˌwʌtsoʊˈɛvɚ/ *adv.* used to emphasize a negative statement: *I have no reason whatsoever to doubt what he says.*

wheat /wit/ *n.* [U] **1** the grain that is used to make flour and such foods as bread **2** the plant that this grain grows on: *a field of wheat* **3 separate the wheat from the chaff** to choose the good and useful things or people and get rid of the others
SW 3

wheat·germ /ˈwitdʒɚm/ *n.* [U] the center of a grain of wheat

whee /wi/ *interjection* used by children to express happiness or excitement

whee·dle /ˈwidl/ *v.* [I,T] to persuade someone to do something by saying pleasant things that you do not really mean: [**wheedle sb into doing sth**] *I kept after him, and finally wheedled him into doing it.* | [**wheedle sth from/out of sb**] *Wexler tried to wheedle the information out of him.*

wheel¹ /wil/ *n.* [C]
SW 2 3
1 on a vehicle one of the round things under a car, bus, bicycle etc. that turns and allows it to move **2** for turning the piece of equipment in the shape of a wheel that you turn to make a car, ship etc. move in a particular direction; STEERING WHEEL: *The driver either fell asleep at the wheel or was run off the road.* | *Joey wouldn't let her behind the wheel* (=drive) *of his new car.* | *My son took the wheel* (=drove instead of someone else) *as we headed for Abilene.* **3** in machine a flat round part in a machine that turns around when the machine operates: *a gear wheel* **4** on wheels with wheels on the bottom: *a table on wheels* **5** wheels also set of wheels SPOKEN a car: *Nice wheels!* **6** big wheel INFORMAL an important person **7** wheeled having wheels: *wheeled containers* | *three-wheeled/six-wheeled etc. three-wheeled roller skis*

wheel² *v.* **1** [T always – adv./prep.] **a)** to move someone or something that is in or on an object with wheels, such as a WHEELCHAIR or a CART: *They then wheeled me into the operating room.* **b)** to push something that has wheels: *wheel sth down/into/across etc. sth*] *She slowly wheeled her shopping cart over to the checkout stand.* **2** [I] if birds or airplanes wheel, they fly around in circles **3** [I] to turn around suddenly: [+ around] *She wheeled around and started yelling at us.* **4 wheel and deal** to do a lot of complicated and sometimes slightly dishonest deals, especially in politics or business

wheel sb/sth ↔ **out** *phr. v.* [T] INFORMAL to publicly show someone or something: *This weekend Hollywood will begin to wheel out its big summer movies.*

wheel·bar·row /ˈwilˌbæroʊ/ *n.* [C] a small CART that you use outdoors to carry things, that has one wheel in the front and two long handles

wheel·base /ˈwilbeɪs/ *n.* [C] TECHNICAL the distance between the front and back AXLES of a vehicle

wheel·chair /ˈwilˌtʃɛr/ *n.* [C] a chair with wheels, used by people who cannot walk —see picture at CHAIR¹

wheeler-deal·er /ˌ.. ˈ../ *n.* [C] someone who does a lot of complicated, often dishonest deals, especially in business or politics

wheel·house /ˈwilhaʊs/ *n.* [C] the place on a ship where the CAPTAIN stands at the WHEEL¹ (2)

wheel·ie /ˈwili/ *n.* [C] **do/pop a wheelie** INFORMAL to balance on the back wheel of a bicycle or MOTORCYCLE that you are riding

wheeling and deal·ing /ˌ... ˈ../ *n.* [U] the activity of making a lot of complicated and sometimes dishonest deals, especially in business or politics

wheel·wright /ˈwilraɪt/ *n.* [C] someone who made and repaired the wooden wheels of vehicles pulled by horses in past times

wheeze¹ /wiz/ *v.* [I] to breathe with difficulty, making a whistling sound in your throat and chest: *People with asthma may start to wheeze.*

wheeze² *n.* [C] **1** the act or sound of wheezing **2** an old joke that no one thinks is funny anymore

wheez·y /ˈwizi/ *adj.* **wheezier, wheeziest** wheezing or making a wheezing sound

whelk /wɛlk/ *n.* [C] a small sea animal that has a shell and can be eaten

whelp¹ /wɛlp/ *n.* [C] a young animal, especially a dog or lion

whelp² *v.* [I] OLD-FASHIONED if a dog or lion whelps, it gives birth

when¹ /wɛn/ *adv.* at what time: *When are you going to the store?* | *When did she notice it was missing?*
SW 1 1

when² *conjunction* **1** at the time that: *I hated green beans when I was a little boy.* | *When you come to Baker Street, turn right.* | *The handle broke when he tried to open the door.* **2** used in order to show what happens in a particular situation: *When you think about it, you'll realize I'm right.* **3** even though or in spite of the fact that something is true: *Why do you want a new job when you have such a good one already?* **4 when all is said and done** used after an explanation or story to give the most important facts about it or to state your opinion about it: *When all is said and done, people will remember him as a great man.*
SW 1 1

when³ *pron.* **1 since when** used in questions to mean since what time: *Since when did you smoke cigarettes?* **2 the day/time/afternoon when** the day, time etc. on or at which: *That's the day when Leigh is coming.*

whence /wɛns/ *adv., pron.* OLD USE from where: *Whence came this man?* —compare WHITHER (2)

when·ev·er /wɛnˈɛvɚ, wən-/ *adv. conjunction* **1** every time that a particular thing happens: *Kent always blames me whenever anything goes wrong.* **2** at any time: *I'd like to see you whenever it's convenient.* **3** SPOKEN used when it does not matter what time something happens, or when you do not know the exact time something happens: *"I can bring you the books this afternoon." "Whenever."*
SW 1 3

where /wɛr/ *adv., conjunction* **1** at, to, or from a particular place or position: *Where do you live?* | *I asked Lucy where she was going.* | *Do you know where my glasses are?* —see Usage Note at POSITION² **2** in, toward, or from a particular situation, story etc.: *Now where was I? Oh yes, I was telling you about taking mother to the airport.* | *Where do you want to be in ten years?* **3** used at the beginning of a sentence in which the second part of the sentence expresses the opposite or something different from the first part: *Gail saw a scared and lonely woman where others only saw a cruel, demanding boss.*
SW 1 1

where·a·bouts¹ /ˈwɛrəˌbaʊts, ˌwɛrəˈbaʊts/ *adv.* SPOKEN used to ask in what general area something or someone is: *Whereabouts did you grow up?*

where·a·bouts² /ˈwɛrəbaʊts/ *n.* [U] the place or area where someone or something is: *The whereabouts of the painting is still a mystery.* | *None of his friends know his whereabouts.*

where·as /wɛrˈəz; strong wɛrˈæz/ *conjunction* **1** used to say that although something is true of one thing, it is not true of another: *A bowl of instant oatmeal costs about $.15, whereas regular oatmeal costs only $.05 per bowl.* **2** LAW used at the beginning of an official document to mean because of a particular fact
SW 3

where·at /wɛrˈæt/ *conjunction* FORMAL **1** used when something happens immediately after something

W

else, or as a result of something happening **2** at a particular place; where

where·by /wɛrˈbaɪ/ *adv.* FORMAL by means of which or according to which: *The mall created a frequent-shopper plan whereby customers earn discounts.*

where·fore /ˈwɛrfɔr/ *adv. conjunction* OLD USE **1** used to ask why something has happened **2** for that reason —see also **the why(s) and wherefore(s)** (WHY³)

where·in /wɛrˈɪn/ *adv., conjunction* FORMAL in which place or part: *Bastian hosts a talk show wherein he interviews local celebrities.*

where·of /wɛrˈʌv/ *adv., conjunction* OLD USE of which: *The houses whereof I speak are theirs.*

where·on /wɛrˈɔn/ *adv., conjunction* OLD USE on which

where·so·ev·er /ˈwɛrsoʊˌɛvɚ/ *adv., conjunction* LITERARY another word for WHEREVER

where·to /wɛrˈtu, ˈwɛrtu/ *adv., conjunction* OLD USE to which place

where·u·pon /ˌwɛrəˈpɑn, ˈwɛrəˌpɑn/ *conjunction* used when something happens immediately after something else, or as a result of something happening: *The rioters headed downtown, whereupon they attacked city hall.*

SW 3 **wher·ev·er** /wɛrˈɛvɚ/ *adv.* **1** to or at whatever place, position, or situation: *You can sit wherever you want.* **2 wherever possible** when it is possible to do something: *Wherever possible, get the best medical insurance available.* **3** used at the beginning of a question to show surprise: *Wherever did you get that idea?* **4 wherever that may be** also **wherever that is** used to say that you do not know where a place or town is or have never heard of it: *Rita lives in Horwich now, wherever that may be.*

where·with·al /ˈwɛrwɪðˌɔl, -wɪθ-/ *n.* **the wherewithal to do sth** the money you need in order to do something: *His family didn't have the wherewithal to send him to college.*

whet /wɛt/ *v.* [T] **1 whet sb's appetite (for sth)** if an experience whets your appetite for something, it increases your desire for it: *To whet your appetite for a trip to Santa Fe, here is a list of our favorite sights.* **2** LITERARY to make the edge of a blade sharp

SW 11 **wheth·er** /ˈwɛðɚ/ *conjunction* **1** used when talking about a choice you have to make or about two different possibilities: *He asked me whether I wanted to play golf this afternoon.* | *I can't tell whether or not the teacher likes me.* **2** used to say that something definitely will or will not happen whatever the situation is: *I'm sure we'll see each other again soon, whether here or in New York.* | *Whether you like it or not, I'm taking you to the doctor.*

USAGE NOTE: WHETHER

GRAMMAR
Whether and **if** are often used in similar contexts. However, **whether** is usually used together in sentences with the word **or**, especially at the beginning of a sentence. People say: *Whether you see Jamie or not, call me later.* | *If you see Jamie, call me.* **If** can usually be used instead of **whether** with clauses following some verbs and adjectives: *Sam wasn't sure if he could come* (NOT *"whether could he come"*). But you use **whether** (NOT **if**) before infinitives: *The question is whether to go or stay.* **Whether** is also used after prepositions: *It depends on whether he's ready or not*, and after nouns: *It's your decision whether you go or stay.*

whet·stone /ˈwɛtstoʊn/ *n.* [C] a stone used to make the blade of cutting tools sharp

SW 3 **whew** /hwyu, hwu/ *interjection* used when you are surprised, very hot, or feeling glad that something bad did not happen: *Whew, it's hot outside.*

whey /weɪ/ *n.* [U] the watery liquid that is left after the solid part has been removed from sour milk, when making cheese

SW 11 **which** /wɪtʃ/ *determiner, pron.* **1** used to ask or state

what people or things you mean when a choice has to be made: *Which coat do you like best?* | *Both desserts look good – I can't decide which to order.* **2** used to show what specific thing or things you mean: *This is the book which I told you about.* **3** used in order to add more information about something, or about the first part of a sentence, used especially in written language after a COMMA: *This is better than my old apartment, which was always so cold.* | *She may have missed the train, in which case* (=because of this) *she won't arrive for another hour.* **4 which is which** used to say that you cannot tell the difference between two very similar people or things: *They look so much alike it's difficult to tell which is which.*

USAGE NOTE: WHICH

FORMALITY: which, that
When you are giving more specific information about a particular thing, **that** is used more often than **which** in informal English: *I often visit the farmers' market which/that is held near my house.* In informal or spoken English, you can often leave out **that** or **which**. For example, it is more common to say: *Did you get the things you wanted?* rather than *Did you get the things that/which you wanted?* You would more usually say: *the club (that) he belonged to.* In relative clauses that add information but do not restrict the meaning of what comes before the clause, you usually use **which**, especially after a comma: *Dave's always really rude, which is why people tend to avoid him.*

which·ev·er /wɪtʃˈɛvɚ/ *determiner, pron.* **1** used to say that it does not matter what thing you choose, what you do etc. because it does not change the situation: *You'll get the same result whichever method you use.* **2** used to talk about a specific thing, method etc.: *I'll use whichever remedy the vet recommends.*

whiff /wɪf/ *n.* [C] **1** a very slight smell of something: [+ of] *a whiff of smoke* | **get/catch a whiff of sth** *From the doorway, I got a whiff of freshly baked bread.* **2 a whiff of danger/adventure/freedom etc.** a slight sign that something dangerous, exciting etc. might happen or is happening: *There would be an investigation if there is even a whiff of discrimination.*

whif·fle ball /ˈwɪfəl ˌbɔl/ *n.* [C,U] another spelling of WIFFLE BALL

Whig /wɪg/ *n.* [C] **1** a member of an American political party in the 19th century who opposed the Democratic Party **2** a supporter of the war against England during the American Revolution

SW 11 **while¹** /waɪl/ *conjunction* **1** during the time that something is happening: *I read the book while I was on the plane.* | *Someone broke into her house while she was on vacation.* **2** used to emphasize the difference between two situations, activities etc.: *Schools in the north tend to better equipped, while schools in the south are relatively poor.* **3** used to show that you partly agree with or accept something, but not completely: *While teaching standards could be raised, more funding would also help.* **4** in spite of the fact that; though: *While she is a likable girl, she can be extremely difficult to work with.* **5 while you're at it** SPOKEN used to tell someone to do something while they are doing something else, because it would be easier to do both things at the same time: *Mail these letters for me and get me some stamps while you're at it.*

SW 11 **while²** *n.* **1 a while** a period of time, especially a short one: *Can you wait a while?* | **For a while,** *I worked in the Sales Department.* | **a short/little while** *I'm going to the store – I'll be back in a little while.* | *It's been quite a while* (=a fairly long time) *since I played baseball.* | *Frank left for work a while ago* (=a fairly long time ago). —compare AWHILE **2 all the while** during a particular period of time: *All the while I was in college, Joan was traveling.* —see also **every once in a while** (ONCE¹ (3)), **sth is worth your while** (WORTH¹ (5))

while³ *v.* **while away the hours/evening/days etc.** to spend time in a pleasant and lazy way: *I whiled away the days on the beach.*

W

whim /wɪm/ *n.* [C] a sudden feeling that you would like to do something or have something, especially when there is no particularly important or good reason: *She decided to make the trip on a whim* (=because of a whim). | *Building permits are issued or revoked at the whim of corrupt government officials.* | *Parents shouldn't cater to their child's every whim* (=they shouldn't give their child everything he or she wants).

whim·per¹ /ˈwɪmpə/ *v.* [I] to make low crying sounds, or to speak in this way: *I found the puppy whimpering next to the front door.*

whimper² *n.* [C] **1 with a whimper** if something ends with a whimper, it does not end in an exciting way: *The Cold War ended with a whimper, not a bang.* **2** a low crying sound **3 with nary/hardly/barely a whimper** also **without a whimper** if something happens or ends without a whimper, no one protests about it: *When women are sick, they keep going, without a whimper.*

whim·si·cal /ˈwɪmzɪkəl/ *adj.* unusual or strange and often amusing: *Miller is known for her whimsical paintings.* —**whimsically** /-kli/ *adv.*

whim·sy /ˈwɪmzi/ *n. plural* **whimsies 1** [U] unusual, strange, and often amusing: *Karla Hour's designs combine style and whimsy.* **2** [C] a strange idea or desire that does not seem to have any sensible purpose

whine /waɪn/ *v.* [I] **1** to complain in a sad, annoying voice about something: *Stop whining, or you won't get any candy.* | [+ **about**] *I have to listen her whine all day about her boyfriend* **2** to make a long high sound because you are in pain or unhappy: *The dog's whining for food.* **3** if a machine whines, it makes a continuous high sound —**whine** *n.* [C] *the whine of the plane's engine* —**whiner** *n.* [C]

whin·ny /ˈwɪni/ *v.* **whinnies, whinnied, whinnying** [I] if a horse whinnies, it NEIGHs (=makes the sound that a horse makes) quietly —**whinny** *n.* [C]

whin·y /ˈwaɪni/ *adj.* **whinier, whiniest** someone who is whiny, whines a lot or is whining

whip¹ /wɪp/ *v.* **whipped, whipping 1** [T] to hit someone with a whip **2** [I always + adv./prep.,T always + adv./prep.] to move quickly and violently, or to make something do this: [+ **across/around/past** etc.] *We stood on the platform as the train whipped past us.* | [**whip sth around**] *Sarah whipped the car around to get the parking spot.* **3** [T always + adv./prep.] to move or remove something with a quick sudden movement: [**whip sth ↔ away/off/out** etc.] *He whipped out a gun.* **4** [T] also **whip up** to mix cream or the clear part of an egg very quickly, until it becomes stiff —compare BEAT¹ (3), WHISK¹ **5** [T] to defeat a team, opponent etc. very badly: *Top-ranked Duke whipped the Harvard team, 118–65.* **6 whip sb/sth into shape** INFORMAL to make someone or something better, so that they reach the necessary standard

whip through sth *phr. v.* [T] INFORMAL to finish something such as a job very quickly: *She whipped through the test in less than an hour.*

whip up *phr. v.* [T] **1** [**whip** sth ↔ **up**] to quickly make something to eat: *I'll whip up some lunch for us.* **2** [**whip** sb/sth ↔ **up**] to deliberately try to make people feel or react strongly: **whip up support/anger/enthusiasm** etc. *Democrats are trying to whip up public support for the bill. Sanders really knows how to whip up a crowd.*

whip² *n.* **1** [C] a long thin piece of rope or leather with a handle, that you swing and hit with in order to make animals move or punish people **2** [C] a member of the U.S. Congress or the British PARLIAMENT who is responsible for making sure that the members of their party attend and vote —see also **crack the whip** (CRACK¹ (7))

whip·cord /ˈwɪpkɔrd/ *n.* [U] **1** a strong type of CORD (3) **2** a strong wool material

whip·lash /ˈwɪplæʃ/ *n.* [C,U] a neck injury caused when your head moves forward and back again suddenly and violently, especially in a car accident

whipped /wɪpt/ *adj.* someone, especially a man, who is whipped likes someone very much and will do anything to make that person happy

whipped cream /ˌ. ˈ./ *n.* [U] cream that has been beaten until it is thick, eaten on sweet foods such as PIES

whip·per·snap·per /ˈwɪpəˌsnæpə/ *n.* [C] OLD-FASHIONED a young person who is too confident and does not show enough respect to older people

whip·pet /ˈwɪpɪt/ *n.* [C] a small thin racing dog like a GREYHOUND

whip·ping /ˈwɪpɪŋ/ *n.* [C usually singular] a punishment given to someone by whipping them

whipping boy /ˈ.. ˌ./ *n.* [C, usually singular] someone or something that is blamed for someone else's mistakes; SCAPEGOAT

whipping cream /ˈ.. ˌ./ *n.* [U] a type of cream that becomes very stiff when you beat it

whip·poor·will /ˈwɪpəˌwɪl/ *n.* [C] a small North American bird that makes a noise that sounds like its name

whip·saw¹ /ˈwɪpsɔ/ *v.* **1** [T] if two or more things whipsaw an economy, company etc., they happen at the same time to make it weaker: *Political and currency troubles have whipsawed stock prices.* | [**whipsaw sth between sth**] *These programs seem to whipsaw the economy between inflation and recession.* **2** [I,T] INFORMAL if the price of something whipsaws or is whipsawed, it rises and falls repeatedly: *The shares have whipsawed a lot in recent months.* **3** [T] to strongly persuade someone to do something, especially by using threats: [**whipsaw sb into doing sth**] *Simpson claims city officials whipsawed her into selling the property.* **4** [I,T] to cut something, especially a tree, with a whipsaw

whipsaw² *n.* [C] a large tool that has a flat blade with a row of sharp points and a handle on each end, used for cutting wood by two people at once

whir /wɜ/ *v.* [I] another spelling of WHIRR

whirl¹ /wɜl/ *v.* **1** [I,T] to spin around very quickly, or to make something do this: *The room began to whirl before my eyes.* | [+ **around/toward** etc.] *Dozens of dancers whirled around the stage.* | [**whirl sth around/away** etc.] *The wind kicked up and started whirling the leaves around.* **2** [I] if your head is whirling, your mind is full of thoughts and ideas, and you feel very confused or excited

whirl² *n.* [C usually singular] **1 give sth a whirl** INFORMAL to try something that you are not sure you are going to like or be able to do: *Why don't you give golf a whirl?* **2** [singular] a lot of activity of a particular kind: *The recent whirl of legal problems has left him little time for his family.* **3 be in a whirl** to feel very excited or confused about something **4** a spinning movement, or the shape of a substance that is spinning: *a whirl of dust*

whirl·i·gig /ˈwɜliˌgɪg/ *n.* [C] a toy that spins

whirling der·vish /ˌ.. ˈ../ *n.* [C] a DERVISH

whirl·pool /ˈwɜlpul/ *n.* [C] **1** a powerful current of water that spins around and can pull things down into it **2** a large bathtub that makes hot water move in strong currents around your body

whirl·wind /ˈwɜlˌwɪnd/ *n.* [C] **1** an extremely strong wind that moves quickly with a circular motion, causing a lot of damage **2 a whirlwind romance/tour** etc. something that happens much more quickly than usual **3 a whirlwind of activity/emotions** etc. a situation in which you experience a lot of different activities or emotions one after another

whirl·y·bird /ˈwɜliˌbɜd/ *n.* [C] INFORMAL a HELICOPTER

whirr /wɜ/ *v.* **whirred, whirring** [I] to make a fairly quiet spinning sound, like the sound of a bird or insect moving its wings very fast: *The hard drive whirred as I copied the files.* —**whirr** *n.* [C usually singular]

whisk¹ /wɪsk/ *v.* [T] to mix liquid or soft things very quickly so that air is mixed in, especially with a fork or a whisk —see picture on page 425

whisk sb/sth ↔ **away** *phr. v.* [T] **1** to take someone quickly away from a place: *Security guards came and*

whisked the man away. **2** to take or remove something very quickly: *He whisked the letter away before I could read it.*

whisk sb **off** *phr. v.* [T] to take someone quickly away from a place

whisk² *n.* [C] **1** a small kitchen tool made of curved pieces of wire, used for beating eggs, cream etc. **2** [usually singular] a quick light sweeping movement: [+ of] *a whisk of the cow's tail*

whisk broom /'. ./ *n.* [C] a small stiff BROOM used especially for brushing clothes

whisk·er /'wɪskɚ/ *n.* [C] **1** [usually plural] one of the long, stiff hairs that grow near the mouth of a cat, mouse etc. —see picture on page 429 **2** [usually plural] one of the hairs that grow on a man's face **3** win/lose **by a whisker** INFORMAL to win or lose by a very small amount: *Davidson won the election by a whisker.* **4** come within a whisker of (doing) sth to almost succeed or fail at doing something

whis·key, whisky /'wɪski/ *n. plural* whiskeys or whiskies [C,U] a strong alcoholic drink made from grain, or a glass of this drink

s w **whis·per¹** /'wɪspɚ/ *v.* **1** [I,T] to speak or say something very quietly, using your breath rather than your voice: *Those two always sit in the back of the room and whisper.* | [whisper sth to sb] *James leaned over to whisper something to Michael.* | *"I love you," she whispered in his ear.* **2** [T] to say or suggest something privately or secretly: [whisper that] *Some people were whispering that Miss Moore was a communist.*

whisper² *n.* [C] **1** the very quiet voice you use when you are whispering: *"Well, that's finally over," I said in a whisper.* **2** a piece of news or information that has not been officially announced; RUMOR: [+ that] *We've been hearing whispers that Dylan might not make the Olympic team.* **3** the whisper of wind/snow/silk etc. LITERARY a low soft sound made by wind, snow etc. **4** LITERARY a whisper of sth an amount of a quality or substance that is almost too small to notice: *He had just a whisper of a mustache.*

whispering cam·paign /'... .,./ *n.* [C] a situation in which someone privately spreads criticism about another person in order to make people have a bad opinion of them

whist /wɪst/ *n.* [U] a card game for four players in two pairs, in which each pair tries to win the most TRICKS

s w **whis·tle¹** /'wɪsəl/ *v.*

1 high sound [I,T] to make a high or musical sound by blowing air out through your lips: *Fans yelled and whistled when the band came on stage.* | [whistle at/to sb] *I hate it when men whistle at me!* | *whistle a song/tune Tony quietly whistled a tune to himself.*

2 go/move fast [I always + adv./prep.] to move quickly with a whistling sound: *A bullet whistled past his left cheek.*

3 steam/wind etc. [I] to make a high sound when air or steam is forced through a small hole: *The kettle was whistling on the stove.*

4 be whistled for sth if a player is whistled for something during a sports game, the REFEREE blows into a whistle to show they have done something wrong: *Fleming was whistled for two fouls during the first quarter of the game.*

5 bird [I] to make a high, often musical sound

6 be whistling in the dark INFORMAL to be trying to show that you are brave when you are afraid, or that you know about something when you do not: *I'm just whistling in the dark on this one – I could really use some help.*

7 whistle past the graveyard to try to show that you are brave when you are afraid

8 sb's not just whistling Dixie also sb ain't just whistling Dixie SPOKEN **a)** used to emphasize that what someone says is definitely true: *"That man is trouble!" "You ain't just whistling Dixie."*

9 whistle in the wind to do or say something that has no real effect

whistle² *n.* [C] **1** a small object that produces a high whistling sound when you blow into it: *The lifeguard blew his whistle.* **2** a piece of equipment on a train or boat that makes a high noise when air is forced through it **3** a high sound made by blowing a whistle, by blowing air out through your lips, or when air or steam is forced through a small opening —see also WOLF WHISTLE **4** the sound of something moving quickly through the air: *Ashley heard the whistle of the ax as it swung by.*

whistle-blow·er /'.. ,../ *n.* [C] someone who tells people in authority or the public about dishonest or illegal practices in business, government etc. —**whistle-blowing** *n.* [U] —see also **blow the whistle on sb** (BLOW¹ (9))

Whis·tler /'wɪslɚ/, **James Mc·Neill** /dʒeɪmz mək'nil/ (1834–1903) a U.S. PAINTER famous for his ideas about the COMPOSITION of pictures and the use of color

whistle-stop /'.. ,./ *n.* [C] **1** a whistle-stop speech/tour/trip a short speech that a politician makes while visiting a small town, or a trip during which a politician makes these speeches many times **2** a small town, especially one where, in the past, trains only stopped if there were passengers who wanted to get on or off

whit /wɪt/ *n.* not a whit not at all, or no amount at all: *The patients' needs don't seem to matter a whit to the hospital.*

s w **white¹** /waɪt/ *adj.* **1** having the color of milk, salt, or snow: *white daisies* **2 a)** belonging to the race of people with pale skin who originally come from Europe **b)** relating to or used by white people: *a white neighborhood* **3** looking pale, because of illness, strong emotion etc.: *Are you OK? You're white as a sheet* (=extremely pale). | white with anger/fear etc. *The man turned white with anger.* **4** white wine is a pale yellow **5** a white Christmas/Thanksgiving etc. a Christmas, Thanksgiving etc. when there is snow —**whiteness** *n.* [U]

white² *n.*

1 color [U] the color of milk, salt, or snow

2 people [C] also **White** someone who belongs to the race of people with pale skin who were originally from Europe: *Whites make up 60% of the student population.*

3 wine [C,U] wine that is pale yellow in color: *a nice bottle of white* | *Californian whites are selling well.*

4 eye [C] the white part of your eye

5 egg [C,U] the part of an egg that surrounds the YOLK (=yellow part) and becomes white when cooked

6 whites [plural] **a)** white clothes, sheets etc., which are separated from dark colored clothes when they are washed **b)** white clothes that are worn for some sports, such as TENNIS

white³ *v.*

white sth **out** *phr. v.* [T] to cover something written on paper, especially a mistake, with a special white liquid so that it cannot be seen anymore

White /waɪt/, **E.B.** /i bi/ (1899–1985) a U.S. writer famous for his ESSAYS and his books for children

White, Ed·ward /'ɛdwɚd/ (1845–1921) a CHIEF JUSTICE on the U.S. Supreme Court

white blood cell /,. '. ./ *n.* [C] one of the cells in your blood which fights against infection —compare RED BLOOD CELL

white·board /'waɪtbɔrd/ *n.* [C] a large board with a white smooth surface that you can write on, used in rooms where classes are taught —compare BLACK-BOARD —see picture at BOARD¹

white bread /,. './ *n.* [U] bread that is made with white flour

white-bread /,. '.◂/ *adj.* INFORMAL relating to white people who have traditional values and who are often considered boring: *a white-bread suburban town*

white·caps /'waɪtkæps/ *n.* [plural] waves in the ocean or on a lake that are white at the top

white-col·lar /,. '..◂/ *adj.* **1** relating to jobs in offices, banks etc., as opposed to jobs working in factories, building things etc.: *a white-collar worker*

2 white-collar crime crimes involving white-collar workers, for example when someone secretly steals money from the organization they work for —compare BLUE-COLLAR, PINK-COLLAR

white cor·pus·cle /ˌ. '.../ n. [C] a WHITE BLOOD CELL

white dwarf /ˌ. './ n. [C] TECHNICAL a hot star near the end of its life, that is more solid but less bright than the sun —compare RED GIANT

white el·e·phant /ˌ. '.../ n. [C] something that is completely useless, although it may have cost a lot of money: *The dam has become something of a white elephant.*

white·fish /'waɪtfɪʃ/ n. [C,U] a type of white or silvery fish that lives in lakes or rivers, or the meat of this fish

white flag /ˌ. './ n. [C] something that shows that you accept that you have failed or been defeated: **wave/ raise/show etc. the white flag** *If things are starting to go well, why raise the white flag?*

white flight /ˌ. './ n. [U] the situation in which white people move away from an area or send their children to private schools to avoid being around people who are not white

white flour /ˌ. './ n. [U] wheat flour from which the BRAN (=outer layer) and WHEATGERM (=inside seed) have been removed —compare WHOLE WHEAT

white·fly /'waɪtflaɪ/ n. *plural* **whiteflies** [C] a type of insect with long wings that damages plants

white·head /'waɪthɛd/ n. [C] a PIMPLE that is white on the surface —compare BLACKHEAD

white heat /ˌ. './ n. [U] the very high temperature at which a metal turns white

white-hot /ˌ. '.‹/ adj. **1** white-hot metal is so hot that it shines white **2** involving a lot of activity or strong feelings: *white-hot anger*

White House /ˈ. ./ n. **1** [singular] the President of the U.S. and the people who advise him: *a Democratic White House* **2 the White House** the official home in Washington, D.C., of the President of the U.S.

white knight /ˌ. './ n. [C] a person or company that puts money into a business in order to save it from being controlled by another company

white-knuck·le /ˌ. '.‹/ adj. making you very worried, nervous, or afraid: *a white-knuckle flight*

white-knuck·led /ˌ. '.‹/ adj. worried, nervous, or afraid: *white-knuckled drivers*

white lie /ˌ. './ n. [C] INFORMAL a small lie that you tell someone, especially in order to avoid hurting their feelings: *What's the harm of a white lie if it will make her feel better?*

white light·ning /ˌ. '../ n [U] MOONSHINE (=illegal strong alcohol)

white mag·ic /ˌ. '../ n. [U] magic used for good purposes —compare BLACK MAGIC

white meat /ˈ. ./ n. [U] the pale-colored meat from the breast, wings etc. of a cooked chicken, TURKEY, or other bird —compare DARK MEAT, RED MEAT

White Mountains, the /ˈ. ,../ a part of the northern Appalachians that is in the U.S. state of New Hampshire

whit·en /'waɪtn/ v. [I,T] to become more white, or to make something do this: *This stuff is supposed to whiten your teeth.*

whit·en·er /'waɪtn-ɚ/ n. [C,U] a substance used to make something more white

white noise /ˌ. './ n. [U] noise coming from a radio or television which is turned on but not TUNEd to any station

white·out /'waɪtaʊt/ n. [C] weather conditions in which there is so much cloud or snow that you cannot see anything —see also WITE-OUT

white pa·ges /ˈ. ,../ n. **the white pages** also **the White Pages** the white part of a telephone DIRECTORY with the names, addresses, and telephone numbers of people with telephones —compare YELLOW PAGES

white pa·per /ˌ. '../ n. [C] an official report on a particular subject, especially one that is written by a company or government

white pep·per /ˌ. '../ n. [U] a white powder made

from the crushed inside of a PEPPERCORN which gives a slightly SPICY taste to food

white sale /'. ./ n. [C] a period when a store sells sheets, TOWELS etc. for a lower price

white sauce /ˌ. './ n. [C,U] a thick white liquid made from flour, milk, and butter which can be eaten with meat and vegetables

white sla·ve·ry /ˌ. '.../ n. [U] OLD-FASHIONED the practice or business of taking girls to a foreign country and forcing them to be PROSTITUTEs

white su·prem·a·cist /ˌ. '.../ n. [C] someone who believes that white people are better than other races —**white supremacy** n. [U]

white-tailed deer /ˌ. . './ n. [C] a common North American DEER with a tail that is white on the bottom side

white-tie /ˌ. '.‹/ adj. a white-tie social occasion is a very formal one at which the men wear white BOW TIES and TAILS —compare BLACK-TIE

white trash /ˌ. './ n. [U] INFORMAL an insulting expression meaning white people who are poor and uneducated

white·wall /'waɪtwɔl/ n. [C] a car tire that has a wide white band on its side

white·wash¹ /'waɪtˌwɑʃ/ v. [T] **1** to cover something with whitewash: *Protesters whitewashed the offensive billboards.* **2** to hide the true facts about a serious accident or illegal action: *Investigators are accused of whitewashing the governor's record.*

whitewash² n. **1** [C,U] a report or examination of events that hides the true facts about something, so that the person who is responsible will not be punished **2** [U] a white liquid mixture used especially for painting walls

white·wa·ter, white water /'waɪt ˌwɔtɚ/ n. [U] a part of a river that looks white because the water is running very quickly over rocks: *whitewater rafting* —see picture on page 1332

whit·ey /'waɪti/ n. [C,U] TABOO used by African-Americans and other MINORITY groups to mean a white person or white people in general. Do not use this word.

whith·er /'wɪðɚ/ adv. **1** FORMAL a word used to ask if something will exist, or how it will develop, in the future: *Whither NATO?* **2** OLD USE a word meaning "to which place"; WHERE

whit·ing /'waɪtɪŋ/ n. [C] a black and silver fish that lives in the ocean and can be eaten

whit·ish /'waɪtɪʃ/ adj. almost white in color

Whit·man /'wɪtˈmən/, **Walt** /wɔlt/ (1819–1892) a U.S. writer known for his poetry about the beauty of nature and the value of freedom

Whit·ney /'wɪtni/, **E·li** /'ilaɪ/ (1765–1825) the U.S. inventor of the COTTON GIN —see picture on page 1329

Whitney, Mount a mountain in the Sierra Nevada that is the highest mountain in the CONTINENTAL U.S.

Whit·sun /'wɪtsən/ n. [C,U] also **Whit Sun·day** /ˌ. '../ PENTECOST

Whit·ti·er /'wɪtiɚ/, **John Green·leaf** /dʒɑn 'grinlif/ (1807–1892) a U.S. poet

whit·tle /'wɪtl/ v. [I,T] **1** also **whittle down** to gradually make something smaller by taking parts away: *The list of candidates has been whittled down from 61 to 12.* **2** to cut a piece of wood into a particular shape by cutting off small pieces with a small knife

whittle away *phr. v.* [I,T] to gradually reduce the amount or value of something, especially something that you think should not be reduced: [+ **at**] *Congress is whittling away at our freedom of speech.* | [**whittle** sth ↔ **away**] *Centralizing measures have whittled away the powers of local government.*

whiz¹ /wɪz/ v. **whizzed, whizzing** [I always + adv./ prep.] **1** INFORMAL to move very quickly, often making a sound like something rushing through the air: [+ **by/around/past** etc.] *She stood by the side of the road watching the cars whiz by.* **2** to do something very quickly: *We whizzed through the chapter* *so fast, I didn't understand a thing.* **3** SLANG to URINATE —see also GEE-WHIZ

whiz[2] *n.* **1** [C] *plural* **whizzes** INFORMAL someone who is very fast, intelligent, or skilled in a particular activity: *Darryl is a whiz on the computer.* **2 take a whiz** SLANG to URINATE

whiz·bang /ˈwɪzˌbæŋ/ *n.* [C] INFORMAL something that is noticed a lot because it is very good, loud, or fast: [+ of] *a whizbang of a stereo*

whiz kid /ˈwɪzkɪd/ *n.* [C] INFORMAL a young person who is very skilled or successful at something: *Grant is a marketing whiz kid.*

WHO —see WORLD HEALTH ORGANIZATION, THE

who /hu/ *pron.* **1** used in questions to ask which person or people: *Who was that on the phone?* | *Who wants another beer?* **2** used especially after a noun to give information about which person or people you are talking about: *The talk was given by a man who used to live in Russia.* | *Oh, now I know who he is!* | *When I go to those family reunions, I can never remember* **who's who** (=the names of people or their relationships to each other). **3** used especially in written language after a COMMA, to add more information about a person or people: *Ron, who usually doesn't drink alcohol, had two beers.* **4 who is sb to do sth?** SPOKEN used to say that someone does not have the right or the authority to say or do something: *Who are you to tell me what to do?* **5 sth is a who's who of sth** used to say that something includes all the important people within a particular organization or group: *The list of artists she has appeared with reads like a who's who of rhythm and blues.*

USAGE NOTE: WHO

WORD CHOICE: who, whom, that
In informal English, you can use **who** as an object, especially in questions: *Who did they end up hiring?* | *Who are you talking about?* In very formal English, it is considered better to use **whom**: *Whom did you see there?* Immediately after a preposition, it is more common to use **whom**, but this still sounds fairly formal: *To whom are you sending that letter?* It is much more natural to say: *Who are you sending that letter to?* In informal or spoken English, it is also very common to use **that** instead of **who** when it is the subject of a relative clause: *I hate people that don't know when to leave.* You can also use **that**, or nothing at all, instead of **whom** when it is the object of a relative clause: *He's the guy that I was talking about.* | *Are you sure she's the one you saw?*

---

whoa /woʊ, hwoʊ, hoʊ/ *interjection* **1** used to tell someone to become calmer or to do something more slowly: *Whoa! Calm down, dude.* **2** said to show that you are surprised or that you think something is impressive: *Whoa. That's a lot of money.* **3** used to tell a horse to stop

who·dun·it /huˈdʌnɪt/ *n.* [C] INFORMAL a book, movie etc. about a murder, in which you do not find out who killed the person until the end

who·ev·er /huˈɛvɚ/ *pron.* **1** used to say that it does not matter who does something, is in a particular place etc.: *Give these clothes to whoever needs them.* | *I'll get the number from Mary or Gloria* **or whoever**. **2** used to talk about a specific person or people, although you do not know who they are: *Whoever is responsible for this will be punished.* **3 whoever sb is** used to say that you do not know who someone is: *You're wife is a lucky woman, whoever she is.* **4** used at the beginning of a question to show surprise or anger: *Whoever could be calling at this time of night?*

whole[1] /hoʊl/ *adj.*
1 all of something; ENTIRE: *It took a whole day to get the computers running again.* | *She drank a whole bottle of wine.* | *Ricky just talked about his kids* **the whole time**. | **The whole thing** (=everything about a situation) *really irritates me.* | the whole school/

country/town etc. (=all the people in a school, country etc.)
2 a whole variety/series/range etc. (of sth) used to emphasize that there are a lot of different things of a similar type: *In my job I come into contact with a whole range of people.*
3 not divided complete and not divided or broken into parts: *Place a whole onion inside the chicken.*
4 the whole point (of sth) an expression used to emphasize that one thing is the reason that something else happens: *The whole point of coming here was to visit the cathedral.*
5 in the whole (wide) world an expression meaning "anywhere" or "at all," used to emphasize a statement: *You're my best friend in the whole wide world!*
6 the whole nine yards SPOKEN including everything that is typical of or possible in an activity, situation, set of things etc.: *We're going to hike there, sleep outside, cook our food on the campfire – the whole nine yards.*
7 go (the) whole hog INFORMAL to do something as completely or as well as you can, without any limits: *We decided to go whole hog and stay at the Hilton.*
8 a whole 'nother sth SPOKEN, NONSTANDARD **a)** used to emphasize that there is another complete thing of the same type as the thing you were talking about: *There's a whole 'nother package in the cupboard.* **b)** used to say that something is completely different from what you have been talking about or from what you are used to: *Texas is like a whole 'nother country for me.* —see also **a whole new ball game** (BALL GAME (2)), **the whole enchilada** (ENCHILADA (3)), **the whole shebang** (SHEBANG), WHOLLY —**wholeness** *n.* [U]

whole[2] *n.* **1 as a whole** used to say that all the parts of something are being considered together: *The U.S. population, as a whole, is very mobile compared to other countries.* **2 the whole of sth** all of something, especially something that is not a physical object: *The religious movement of the late 1500s affected the whole of Europe.* **3 on the whole** used to say that something is generally true: *On the whole, he seems like an intelligent, likable person.* **4** [C usually singular] something that consists of a number of parts, but is considered as a single unit: *Two halves make a whole.*

whole food /ˈ. ./ *n.* [C,U] food that is considered healthy because it is in a simple natural form

whole·heart·ed /ˌhoʊlˈhɑrtɪd◂/ *adj.* involving all your feelings, interest etc.: **wholehearted support/approval/effort etc.** *The people have given their wholehearted support to the war effort.* —**wholeheartedly** *adv.*: *The others joined in wholeheartedly.*

whole milk /ˌ. ˈ./ *n.* [U] milk that has not had any fat removed —compare ONE PERCENT MILK, TWO PERCENT MILK

whole note /ˈ. ./ *n.* [C] TECHNICAL a musical note which continues for as long as two HALF NOTEs —see picture at MUSIC

whole num·ber /ˌ. ˈ../ *n.* [C] a number such as 0, 1, 2 etc. that is not a FRACTION

whole·sale[1] /ˈhoʊlseɪl/ *n.* [U] the business of selling goods in large quantities to other businesses —compare RETAIL[1]

whole·sale[2] *adj.* **1** relating to the business of selling goods in large quantities to other businesses: *wholesale prices* **2** [only before noun] affecting almost everything or everyone, and often done without any concern for the results: *What we need is a wholesale restructuring of the process.* —**wholesale** *adv.*: *I can get it for you wholesale.*

whole·sal·er /ˈhoʊlˌseɪlɚ/ *n.* [C] a person or a company that sells goods wholesale

whole·some /ˈhoʊlsəm/ *adj.* **1** likely to make you healthy: *well-balanced wholesome meals* **2** considered to have a good moral effect: *wholesome family life* —**wholesomeness** *n.* [U]

whole wheat /ˌ. ˈ.◂/ *adj.* whole wheat flour or bread is made using every part of the WHEAT grain, including the outer layer

who'll /hul/ the short form of "who will": *You never know who'll show up.*

whol·ly /'hoʊli/ *adv.* FORMAL completely: *a wholly satisfactory solution* | *She still did not wholly trust her instincts.*

whom /hum/ *pron.* the object form of "who," used especially in formal speech or writing: *I spent two hours talking to Kaz, whom I'd met only once before.* | *She had three lovers, none of whom knew about the others.* —see Usage Note at WHO

whom·ev·er /hu'mɛvɚ/ *pron.* FORMAL used to say that it does not matter who receives something or has something done to them: *You can invite whomever you want.*

whomp /wɑmp, wɔmp/ *v.* [T] SPOKEN **1** to hit someone very hard with your hand closed **2** to defeat another team easily

whoop /hup, wup/ *v.* [I] **1** to shout loudly and happily **2 whoop it up** INFORMAL to enjoy yourself very much, especially in a large group: *Drunken fans whooped it up in the streets.* **3 whoop sb's ass** SLANG to hurt someone badly by hitting them, or to defeat someone completely in a competition —**whoop** *n.* [C] *excited whoops and cheers*

whoop-de-do¹ /ˌwup di 'du, ˌhup-/ *interjection* used to show that you do not think something that someone has told you is as exciting or impressive as they think it is: *"He says he'll give me a $20 raise." "Well, whoop-de-do."*

whoop-de-do² *n.* [C] SPOKEN a noisy party or celebration

whoop·ee¹ /'wʊpi, 'wu-/ *interjection* said when you are very happy about something: *Whoopee! I won!*

whoopee² *n.* **make whoopee** OLD-FASHIONED to have sex

whoopee cush·ion /'.. ˌ../ *n.* [C] a rubber CUSHION filled with air that makes a noise like a FART when you sit on it

whoop·ing cough /'hupɪŋ kɔf, 'wup-/ *n.* [U] an infectious disease, especially affecting children, that makes them cough and have difficulty breathing

whoops /wʊps/ *interjection* **1** said when you have fallen, dropped something, or made a small mistake: *Whoops, sorry. Did I hurt your hand?* **2 whoops-a-daisy** said when someone, usually a child, falls down

whoosh /wʊʃ, wuʃ/ *v.* [I always + adv./prep.] to move very fast with a soft rushing sound: *Cars whooshed by.* —**whoosh** *n.* [C usually singular] *a whoosh of flame*

whop /wɑp/ *v.* [T] INFORMAL: see WHUP

whop·per /'wɑpɚ/ *n.* [C] INFORMAL **1** a big lie: *She tells one whopper after another.* **2** something unusually big: *This storm's going to be a whopper.*

whop·ping /'wɑpɪŋ/ *adj.* [only before noun] INFORMAL very large: *a whopping 28% increase*

who're /'huɚ, hur/ the short form of "who are": *Who're they?*

whore /hɔr/ *n.* [C] OFFENSIVE **1** a woman who has sex for money; PROSTITUTE **2** an insulting word for a woman who has many sexual partners

whore·house /'hɔrhaʊs/ *n.* [C] INFORMAL, IMPOLITE a place where men can pay to have sex with women

whor·ing /'hɔrɪŋ/ *n.* [U] OLD-FASHIONED, IMPOLITE the activity of having sex with a PROSTITUTE

whorl /wɔrl/ *n.* [C] **1** a pattern made of a line that curls out in circles that get bigger and bigger **2** a circular pattern of leaves or flowers on a stem

who's /huz/ **1** the short form of "who is": *Who's going to take her home?* **2** the short form of "who has," when "has" is an AUXILIARY VERB: *I need to find someone who's finished the assignment.*

whose¹ /huz/ *possessive adj., possessive pron.* used to ask which person or people a particular thing belongs to: *Whose car is he driving?* | *Whose is this?*

whose² *pron.* used to show the relationship between a person or thing and something that belongs to that person or thing: *He held a small child whose face I couldn't see.* | *Solar energy is an idea whose time has come.*

who·so·ev·er /ˌhusoʊ'ɛvɚ/ *pron.* OLD USE: see WHO-EVER (2)

who've /huv/ the short form of "who have": *We're sharing a room with two girls who've been traveling for six months.*

whup /wʌp/ *v.* [T] SPOKEN **1** to defeat someone easily in a sport or fight: *I'm gonna whup your ass* (=defeat you very easily). **2** to hit someone and hurt them very badly, for example by using a belt to hit them

why¹ /waɪ/ *adv. conjunction* **1** for what reason: *Why do you want to go to Louisville?* | *I don't understand why I have to type this.*

SPOKEN PHRASES

2 why not? a) used to ask the reason something does not happen or is not true: *"I just can't do it." "Why not?"* **b)** used to show that you agree with a suggestion or idea: *"Maybe we could drive over to the beach today." "Yeah, why not."* **3 why doesn't sb do sth?** also **why not do sth?** used to make a suggestion: *Why don't you give me your number, and I'll call you.* | *Why not have the picnic in Glendale?* **4 why (in) the hell...?** used to ask in a very angry way why something has happened: *Why the hell won't he leave me alone?* **5 why sb?** used to ask why something has been done, given etc. to someone and not to a different person: *Why me? Why can't someone else drive you?* **6 why on earth...?** used to ask in a surprised way why something has happened: *Why on earth would she save all those cards?* **7 why, oh why...?** used to show that you are very sorry about something you did: *Why, oh why didn't we use traveler's checks?*

why² *interjection* OLD-FASHIONED **1** said to show that you are slightly surprised or annoyed: *Why, look who's here!* **2** said when the next sentence has an important idea in it: *And I thought to myself, why, I can do that.*

why³ *n.* **the why(s) and wherefore(s)** the reasons or explanations for something: *They're happy to live without understanding the whys or wherefores of their existence.*

why'd /waɪd/ the short form of "why did": *Why'd you do that?*

WI the written abbreviation of Wisconsin

Wic·ca /'wɪkə/ *n.* [U] a religion related to WITCHCRAFT that involves respect for nature —**Wiccan** *adj.* —**Wiccan** *n.* [C]

wick /wɪk/ *n.* [C] **1** the piece of thread in a CANDLE that burns when you light it —see picture at CANDLE **2** a long piece of material in an oil lamp that sucks up oil so that the lamp can burn

wick·ed¹ /'wɪkɪd/ *adj.* **1** behaving in a way that is morally wrong; EVIL: *a wicked witch* **2** INFORMAL behaving badly in a way that is amusing: *She gave him a wicked smile.* **3** SLANG very good: *That's a wicked bike!* —**wickedly** *adv.* —**wickedness** *n.* [U]

wicked² *adv.* [+ adj./adv.] SLANG very: *I'm wicked thirsty.*

wick·er¹ /'wɪkɚ/ *adj.* [only before noun] made from thin dried tree branches woven together: *a wicker chair*

wicker² *n.* [U] thin dried tree branches that are woven together to make furniture, BASKETS etc.

wick·et /'wɪkɪt/ *n.* [C] **1** a small window or hole in a wall, especially one at which you can buy tickets **2** a curved wire under which you hit your ball in the game of CROQUET

wide¹ /waɪd/ *adj.*

1 distance a) measuring a large distance from one side to the other: *a wide necktie* | *The river is very wide.* | *Wreckage was spread across a wide area.* —opposite NARROW¹ **b)** measuring a particular distance from one side to the other: *How wide is the door?* | *five feet/two miles/three inches etc. wide The desk is four feet long and 2 feet wide.*

2 variety including or involving a large variety of different people, things, or situations: *wide experience in government and business* | **a wide range/variety/selection etc. (of sth)** *The center offers a wide range of services to low-income families.*

3 in many places [usually before noun] happening among many people or in many places: *Coles gained wide publicity after predicting the earthquake.*
4 a wide difference/gap/variation etc. a large and noticeable difference: *Funding schools in this way will lead to wide differences in educational opportunities.*
5 the wider issues/view/context etc. the more general features of a situation, rather than the specific details: *We have to consider the student protests in a wider context.*
6 eyes LITERARY wide eyes are fully open, especially when someone is very surprised, excited, or frightened: *Her eyes grew wide in anticipation.*
7 ball/bullet etc. not hitting the point you were aiming at: [+ of] *The throw was wide of first base.*
8 give sb/sth a wide berth to avoid someone or something: *Sandie's been giving her a wide berth since the argument.*
9 the (big) wide world SPOKEN places outside the small familiar place where you live —see also **be wide of the mark** (MARK[2] (6)), **in the whole (wide) world** (WHOLE[1] (5)), WIDELY, WIDTH

USAGE NOTE: WIDE

WORD CHOICE: wide, broad, big, large
Wide is the most usual word to describe something that measures a long distance from one side to another: *a wide road/lake/doorway/entrance/staircase.* You also use **wide** to express how much something measures from side to side: *The gap was only a few inches wide.* **Broad** is often used about parts of the body: *broad shoulders/hips* | *a broad nose/forehead.* **Broad** often suggests that something is wide in a good or attractive way: *a broad driveway leading up to the mansion.* Sometimes you may need to think whether you really mean **wide** or **broad**, or just **big** or **large** (=wide in all directions): *a wide carpet/field* or *a large carpet/field.*

---

wide[2] *adv.* **1 wide open/awake/apart** completely open, awake, or apart: *The door was wide open when we got here.* | *It was 3 a.m., but I was wide awake.* | *He sat with his legs wide apart.* —see also WIDE-OPEN **2** opening or spreading as much as possible: **open/spread sth wide** *Spiro spread his arms wide in a welcoming gesture.* **3** not hitting the point you were aiming at: *Wilton hit the ball high and wide.*

-wide /waɪd/ *suffix* [in adjectives] used with nouns that are places or organizations to mean "affecting all the people in that place or organization": *statewide elections* | *a company-wide picnic*

wide-an·gle lens /ˌ. .. ˈ./ *n.* [C] a camera LENS that lets you take photographs with a wider view than normal

wide·bod·y /ˈwaɪdˌbɑdi/ *adj.* [only before noun] a widebody airplane is wider than other airplanes and holds many people —**widebody** *n.* [C]

wide-eyed /ˈ. ./ *adj.* **1** having your eyes wide open, especially because you are surprised or frightened: *wide-eyed wonder* | *Ralph lay awake in the dark, wide-eyed.* **2** too willing to believe, accept, or admire things because you do not have much experience of life; NAIVE: *a wide-eyed idealist*

wide·ly /ˈwaɪdli/ *adv.* **1** in a lot of different places or by a lot of people: *Copies of the report have been made widely available.* | *At one time it was widely believed that the sun revolved around the Earth.* **2 vary/differ widely** to be different by a large degree: *Different brands of tuna can vary widely in price.*

wid·en /ˈwaɪdn/ *v.* [I,T] **1** to become wider, or make something wider: *When are they going to widen the road?* **2** to become larger in degree or range, or make something do this: *Maryland widened its lead to 14 points.* **3** [I] if your eyes widen, they open more, especially because you are surprised or frightened —opposite NARROW[2]

wide-o·pen, wide open /ˌ. ˈ.◂/ *adj.* **1** a wide-open area does not have any objects, buildings, etc. in it: *wide-open spaces* **2** wide-open eyes or mouths are

completely open: **eyes/mouth wide-open** *Kerry stared, her mouth wide-open.* **3** a competition, election etc. that is wide open can be won by anyone: *The presidential race is still wide open.*

wide-rang·ing /ˌ. ˈ..◂/ *adj.* including a wide variety of subjects, things, or people: *a wide-ranging investigation* | *Her criticism was wide-ranging and sometimes contradictory.*

wide re·ceiv·er /ˌ. .ˈ../ *n.* [C] a player in football who starts in a position at the end of the line of players, far from the others, and who catches the ball

wide·scale, wide-scale /ˈwaɪdˌskeɪl◂/ *adj.* involving a large number of things, people etc.: *wide-scale outbreaks of violence*

wide·spread /ˌwaɪdˈsprɛd◂/ *adj.* existing or happening in many places or situations, or among many people: *the widespread use of computers*

widg·et /ˈwɪdʒɪt/ *n.* [C] **1** INFORMAL a word used to represent an imaginary product that a company might produce, used especially in business classes: *Imagine your company sells 240 widgets a month.* **2** SPOKEN a small piece of equipment that you do not know the name for

wid·ow[1] /ˈwɪdoʊ/ *n.* [C] **1** a woman whose husband has died and who has not married again **2 a football/golf/hunting etc. widow** HUMOROUS a woman whose husband spends all his free time watching football, playing GOLF etc.

widow[2] *v.* **be widowed** to become a widow or widower: *Carla was widowed very young.* —**widowed** *adj.*: *John's widowed mother*

wid·ow·er /ˈwɪdoʊɚ/ *n.* [C] a man whose wife has died and who has not married again

wid·ow·hood /ˈwɪdoʊˌhʊd/ *n.* [U] the time when you are a widow

widow's peak /ˈ.. ˌ./ *n.* [C] the edge of someone's hair that forms the shape of a "V" at the top of their face

width /wɪdθ, wɪtθ/ *n.* **1** [C,U] the distance from one side of something to the other, or the measurement of this: *Paolo saw him across the width of the church.* | *The slits are about 1 mm in width.* —compare BREADTH (1), LENGTH (1) **2** [U] the quality or fact of being wide: *I was surprised by the width of his shoulders.* **3** [C] a piece of a material that has been measured and cut

wield /wild/ *v.* [T] **1 wield power/influence/authority etc.** to have a lot of power, influence etc., and be ready to use it: *Central banks wield enormous power in today's global economy.* **2** to hold a weapon or tool that you are going to use: *The man moved toward them, wielding a stick.*

wie·ner /ˈwinɚ, ˈwini/ *n.* [C] **1** a type of SAUSAGE **2** SPOKEN someone who is silly or stupid **3** SPOKEN a word used by children meaning a PENIS

wiener dog /ˈ.. ˌ./ *n.* [C] SPOKEN a DACHSHUND

wie·nie /ˈwini/ *n.* [C] INFORMAL another spelling of WEENIE

wife /waɪf/ *n. plural* **wives** /waɪvz/ [C] the woman that a man is married to: *Have you met my wife, Doris?*

wife·ly /ˈwaɪfli/ *adj.* OLD-FASHIONED relating to qualities or behavior that is considered to be typical of a good wife

Wif·fle ball /ˈwɪfəl ˌbɔl/ *n.* [C,U] TRADEMARK a plastic baseball with holes it, or the game that is played with this

wig[1] /wɪg/ *n.* [C] a covering of hair that you wear on your head, either because you have no hair or want to cover your hair: *a blond wig* —compare TOUPEE

wig[2] *v.*
wig out *phr. v.* [I,T **wig sb ↔ out**] SLANG to become very anxious, upset, or afraid, or make someone do this: *I'm wigging out about going to public school.*

wig·gle /ˈwɪgəl/ *v.* [I,T] to move with small movements from side to side or up and down, or make something move like this: *Can you wiggle your ears?* —**wiggle** *n.* [C]

wig·gly /ˈwɪgli/ *adj.* INFORMAL a wiggly line is one that has small curves in it; WAVY

wig·wam /ˈwɪgwɑm/ *n.* [C] a structure with a round roof used as a house by some Native American tribes in the past

S W
2 2

wild¹ /waɪld/ *adj.*

1 plants/animals living in a natural state, not changed or controlled by humans: *a wild rose* | *wild horses* —opposite DOMESTICATED

2 emotions showing strong uncontrolled emotions, especially anger, happiness, or excitement: *wild laughter* | *[+ with] Stone's eyes were wild with rage.*

3 behavior behaving in an uncontrolled, sometimes violent way: *Jed was really wild in high school.*

4 go wild a) to suddenly become very noisy and active because you are excited or angry: *When Jordan's picture flashed on the screen, the crowd went wild.* **b)** if something that is usually controlled or planned goes wild, it happens or works in an unexpected or uncontrolled way: *The stock market went wild today.*

5 unusual SPOKEN exciting, interesting, unusual, or strange: *a wild party* | *"It turns out she went to college with my sister." "That's wild."*

6 be wild about sb/sth to be very interested in or excited about someone or something: *I'm not wild about driving in the snow.*

7 without careful thought done or said without much thought or care, or without knowing all the facts: *wild accusations* | *I'm going to take **a wild guess** and say you're 42.*

8 not sensible wild ideas, plans etc. are not sensible or are not based on fact: *Where do you get these wild ideas?*

9 a throw not controlled or going where you were aiming: *a wild pitch*

10 beyond sb's wildest dreams beyond anything someone imagined or hoped for: *The business has succeeded beyond our wildest dreams.*

11 not/never in sb's wildest dreams used to say that you did not expect or imagine that something would happen, especially after it has happened: *Never in my wildest dreams did I expect to win the race.*

12 colors/patterns bright, unusual, and noticeable: *a wild Hawaiian shirt*

13 weather violent and strong: *wild winds*

14 wild and woolly exciting and dangerous or complicated: *the wild and woolly world of Russian politics*

15 card games a card that is wild can be used to represent any other card in a game —see also WILD CARD (3)

16 get/have a wild hair (up your ass) VULGAR to suddenly have a strong need to do something that seems strange to other people

17 do the wild thing SLANG to have sex —**wildness** *n.* [U] —see also **sow your wild oats** (SOW¹ (3)), WILDLY

wild² *adv.* **1 run wild** to behave in an uncontrolled way because there are no rules or people to control you: *Pam just lets her kids run wild.* **2 grow wild** if plants grow wild, they are not planted or controlled by people

wild³ *n.* **1 in the wild** in natural and free conditions, not kept or controlled by humans: *Most of the animals we treat would not survive in the wild.* **2 the wilds of Africa/Alaska/Borneo etc.** areas where there are no towns and not many people live

wild boar /ˌ. ˈ./ *n.* [C] a large wild pig with long hair

wild card /ˈ. ./ *n.* [C] **1** someone or something that may affect a situation, but in a way that you do not know and cannot guess: *China remains a wild card in the negotiations.* **2** a sports team that must win additional games to be allowed to play in an important competition, especially in football and baseball **3** a playing card that can represent any other card **4** TECHNICAL a sign that can represent any letter or set of letters in some computer commands

wild·cat¹ /ˈwaɪldkæt/ *n.* [C] a type of large cat that lives in mountains, forests etc.

wildcat² *v.* [I] to look for oil in a place where no one has found any yet —**wildcatter** *n.* [C]

wildcat strike /ˌ.. ˈ./ *n.* [C] an occasion when people suddenly and stop working in an unofficial way in order to protest something

Wilde /waɪld/**, Os·car** /ˈɑskɚ/ (1854–1900) an Irish writer of poems, stories, and humorous plays, famous for his WIT in conversation

wil·de·beest /ˈwɪldəˌbist/ *n.* [C] a large southern African animal with a tail and curved horns; GNU

Wild·er /ˈwaɪldɚ/**, Bil·ly** /ˈbɪli/ (1906–) a U.S. movie DIRECTOR, who was born in Austria

Wilder, Thorn·ton /ˈθɔrnt‿n/ (1897–1975) a U.S. writer of plays and NOVELS

wil·der·ness /ˈwɪldɚnɪs/ *n.* [C usually singular] **1** a large area of land that has never been built on or changed by humans **2 in the (political) wilderness** away from the center of political power or activity: *The Labor party spent its time in the political wilderness changing its radical image.*

wilderness a·re·a /ˈ... ˌ.../ *n.* [C] an area of public land in the U.S. where no buildings or roads are allowed to be built

Wilderness Road, the /ˌ... ˈ./ a way to reach the Ohio River by traveling from Virginia across the Appalachians that was discovered by Daniel Boone in 1775 and used by many people who wanted to settle in the Midwest

Wilderness So·ci·e·ty, the /ˈ... ˌ.../ an organization that works to protect the environment and wild animals, birds etc.

wild-eyed /ˌ. ˈ.◂/ *adj.* **1** having a crazy look in your eyes **2** extremely determined in a way that is slightly frightening: *a wild-eyed radical*

wild·fire /ˈwaɪldˌfaɪɚ/ *n.* [C,U] a fire that moves quickly and cannot be controlled —see **spread like wildfire** (SPREAD¹ (3))

wild·flow·er /ˈwaɪldˌflaʊɚ/ *n.* [C] a flower that no one has planted, but that grows naturally

wild·fowl /ˈwaɪldfaʊl/ *n.* [plural] birds, especially ones that live near water

wild goose chase /ˌ. ˈ. ˌ./ *n.* [C] a situation in which you waste a lot of time looking for something that cannot be found: *Investigators have been **on a wild goose chase**, looking for a woman who may already be dead.*

wild·lands /ˈwaɪldlændz/ *n.* [plural] an area of land that has never been developed or farmed —**wildland** *adj.* [only before noun] *wildland fires*

wild·life /ˈwaɪldlaɪf/ *n.* [U] animals and plants living in natural conditions, not kept by people: *The park has an abundance of wildlife.*

wild·ly /ˈwaɪldli/ *adv.* **1** in a way that is not calm or controlled: *The audience cheered wildly.* **2** extremely: *The band Sierra Maestra is wildly popular in Cuba.*

wild rice /ˌ. ˈ./ *n.* [U] the seed of a type of grass that grows in parts of North America and China that can be cooked and eaten

Wild West /ˌ. ˈ.◂/ *n.* **the Wild West** the western part of the U.S. in the 19th century before the government and laws were strong

wile /waɪl/ *v.* another spelling of WHILE³

wiles /waɪlz/ *n.* [plural] things you say or tricks you use to persuade someone to do what you want: *He somehow managed to resist all my **feminine wiles**.*

wil·ful /ˈwɪlfəl/ *adj.* another spelling of WILLFUL

Wil·helm I /ˌvɪlhɛlm ðə ˈfɚst/ (1797–1888) the king of Germany when Bismarck joined all the separate German states together to form one country

Wilhelm II /ˌvɪlhɛlm ðə ˈsɛkənd/ also **Kaiser Wilhelm** (1859–1941) the king of Germany during World War I

wi·li·ness /ˈwaɪlinɪs/ *n.* [U] the quality of being WILY

will¹ /wəl, əl, l; *strong* wɪl/ *modal verb short form* **'ll** *negative short form* **won't** **1** used to make the future tense: *The conference will be held in San Antonio.* | *What time will you get here?* | *I'll call her tonight.* **2** used to show that someone is willing or

W

S W
1 1

ready to do something: *Who'll help me put the groceries away?* | *The baby won't eat anything.* | *Dr. Weir will see you now.* **3** used to ask someone to do something: *Will you stir the soup while I go downstairs?* **4** used to give the result in CONDITIONAL sentences when the condition is in the present tense: *If Jeff loses his job, we'll have to move.* **5** used like "can" to show what is possible: *This car will seat five people comfortably.* **6** used to say what always happens in a particular situation or what is generally true: *Accidents will happen.*

SPOKEN PHRASES

7 used to order or tell someone angrily to do something: *Will you two please stop fighting!* **8** used to offer something to someone or to invite them to do something: *Will you have some more tea?* **9** used like "must" to show what you think is likely to be true: *That'll be Ron now.* **10** used to describe someone's habits, especially when you find them strange or annoying: *Nancy will keep talking unless you tell her to shut up.*

USAGE NOTE: WILL

WORD CHOICE: will, be going to
Use **will** when you talk about future plans that you make at the time you are speaking: *"Oops. I spilled my juice." "I'll go get a paper towel."* Use **be going to** when you have made the plans earlier: *I'm going to go to the library later. Do you want to come along?* When you talk about what you think will happen in the future, you can use **will** or **be going to**. However, you usually use **be going to** when something in the present situation makes it very clear what will happen next, and **will** when you are not so sure: *Craig's going to be in big trouble when Mom finds out.* | *Marie will probably show up an hour late again.*

S W
2
will[2] /wɪl/ *n.*

1 determination [C,U] determination to do something that you have decided to do, even if this is difficult: *Even as a baby, Joseph had a strong will.* | **the will to live/fight/succeed etc.** *It seems that Edith just lost the will to live.* | **a battle/clash/test/contest of wills** (=a situation in which two people who both have strong wills oppose each other) —see also FREE WILL, STRONG-WILLED, WEAK-WILLED
2 legal document [C] a legal document that says who you want your money and property to be given to after you die: *Have you made a will yet?* | *Her father left her the entire estate in his will.*
3 what sb wants [singular] what someone wants to happen in a particular situation: *I guess it's just God's will.* | *Anna was forced to marry him against her will.* | *I don't think the church has the right to impose its will on the rest of us* (=make us do what it wants).
4 at will whenever you want, and in whatever way you want: *He can't just hire and fire people at will, can he?*
5 where there's a will there's a way SPOKEN used to say that if you really want to do something, you will find a way to succeed
6 have a will of iron to have an extremely strong and determined character

will[3] *v.* **1** [T] to try to make something happen by thinking about it very hard: [**will sb/sth to do sth**] *I have willed myself to stop thinking about him.* **2 if you will a)** FORMAL used when choosing a word to describe something, which you think the person listening may not agree with, approve of, believe in etc.: *She possessed all sorts of secret wisdom, or magic, if you will.* **b)** SPOKEN, FORMAL used to ask someone politely to think about something, especially a particular situation: *Imagine, if you will, a frightened seven-year-old child.* **3** [T] to officially give something that you own to someone else after you die: [**will sth to sb**] *Reid willed all his shares in the company to his wife.* **4 do what you will** also **do what he/she/it will etc.** FORMAL to do whatever you

want: *Students can do what they will with their science education.* **5** [I,T] OLD USE to want something to happen

Wil·lard /'wɪlɚd/, **Em·ma** /'ɛmə/ (1787–1870) a U.S. educator who started the first school in the U.S. that educated women to a level high enough for them to enter college

will call /'. ./ *n.* [U] the place, especially at a theater, where you can get the tickets you have already ordered

will·ful /'wɪlfəl/ *adj.* **1** continuing to do what you want, even after you have been told to stop: *a willful child* **2 willful damage/misconduct/neglect etc.** FORMAL OR LAW deliberate damage, bad behavior etc., when you know that what you are doing is wrong —**willfully** *adv.* —**willfullness** *n.* [U]

Wil·liam I /ˌwɪlyəm ðə 'fɚst/ **William the Conqueror** (1027–1087) the king of England from 1066 to 1087, who became England's first Norman king after defeating the Saxon King Harold

Wil·liams /'wɪlyəmz/, **Hank** /hæŋk/ (1923–1953) a U.S. singer and writer of COUNTRY AND WESTERN music

Williams, Ted /tɛd/ (1918–) a U.S. baseball player known for his skill as a BATTER

Williams, Wil·liam Car·los /'wɪlyəm 'kɑrloʊs/ (1883–1963) a U.S. poet

wil·lie /'wɪli/ *n.* **1 the willies** SPOKEN a nervous or frightened feeling: *All this talk about dead people is giving me the willies.* **2** [C] SLANG a PENIS —see also WET WILLIE

will·ing /'wɪlɪŋ/ *adj.* **1 be willing (to do sth)** to be happy and ready to do something, or to be able to be persuaded to do something: *How much are they willing to pay?* | *I'm perfectly willing to wait here.* **2 a willing helper/worker etc.** someone who is eager to help, work etc. and does not have to be persuaded —opposite UNWILLING —**willingness** *n.* [U] —see also **God willing** (GOD (17))

S W
2 2

will·ing·ly /'wɪlɪŋli/ *adv.* without needing to be forced or persuaded, because you want to do something: *Davis willingly accepted the terms of the contract.*

will-o'-the-wisp /ˌ. . . './ *n.* [C usually singular] someone that you can never completely depend on, or something that you can never achieve

wil·low /'wɪloʊ/ *n.* [C,U] a type of tree that has long thin branches and grows near water, or the wood from this tree

wil·low·y /'wɪloʊi/ *adj.* someone, especially a woman, who is willowy is tall, thin, and graceful: *Tania was tall and willowy with topaz eyes.*

will·pow·er /'wɪl,paʊɚ/ *n.* [U] the ability to control your mind and body in order to achieve something that you want to do: *Losing weight is largely a matter of willpower.*

Wills (Moody) /wɪlz, 'mudi/, **Hel·en** /'hɛlən/ (1905–1998) a U.S. tennis player, famous as the best woman player of the 1920s and 1930s

wil·ly-nil·ly /ˌwɪli 'nɪli/ *adv.* **1** without planning, clear organization, or control: *Cable companies are accused of raising prices willy-nilly.* **2** if something happens willy-nilly, it happens whether you want it to or not: *Today's church is being forced willy-nilly to deal with today's social problems.*

Wil·son /'wɪlsən/, **Au·gust** /'ɔgəst/ (1945–) an African-American writer of plays

Wilson, Ed·mund /'ɛdmənd/ (1895–1972) a U.S. writer famous especially for his work as a CRITIC of literature

Wilson, Wood·row /'wʊdroʊ/ (1856–1924) the 28th President of the U.S.

wilt[1] /wɪlt/ *v.* [I] **1** if a plant or flower wilts, it bends over because it is too dry or old **2** to feel weak, tired, or upset, especially because you are too hot: *I'm starting to wilt – can we go home?*

wilt[2] *v.* OLD USE **thou wilt** used to say "you will" when speaking to one person

wil·y /'waɪli/ *adj.* **wilier, wiliest** good at getting what you want, especially by tricking people in a clever way: *a wily businessman* —**wiliness** *n.* [U]

wimp[1] /wɪmp/ *n.* [C] INFORMAL **1** someone who has a

W

weak character and is too afraid to do something difficult: *Don't be such a wimp.* **2** a man who is thin and physically weak —**wimpy** —**wimpish** *adj.*

wimp² *v.*

wimp out *phr. v.* [I] SPOKEN to not do something that you intended to do, because you do not feel brave enough, strong enough etc.: *Tyler was supposed to go skydiving with us but he wimped out.*

wim·ple /'wɪmpəl/ *n.* [C] a piece of cloth that a NUN wears over her head

win¹ /wɪn/ *v.* past tense and past participle **won** present participle **winning**

1 competition/race [I,T] to be the best or first in a competition, game, election etc.: *Who do you think is going to win?* | [+ **at**] *I never win at tennis.* | [**win sth**] *The Dodgers really need to win this game.* | *Jackson is expected to win hands down* (=win very easily). | *win by 10 points/40 votes etc. Harris won by 358 votes.*

2 prize [T] to earn a prize in a competition or game: *Milburn won a gold medal in the 1972 Olympics.* | *How much money did she win?*

3 get/achieve [T] to get or achieve something that you want because of your efforts or abilities: [**win sb sth**] *Those tactics will win them any votes.* | **win sb's approval/trust/love etc.** *Donahue has won the respect of his fellow workers.*

4 **win sb's heart** to make someone love you: *In the end, he won the princess's heart.*

5 **win the day** to finally be successful in a discussion, argument, or competition, or to make it possible for someone to do this: *Defiance feels good, but it won't win the day.*

SPOKEN PHRASES

6 **you win** used to agree to what someone wants after you have tried to persuade them to do or think something else: *OK, you win – we'll go to the movies.*

7 **sb can't win** used to say that there is no satisfactory way of dealing with a particular situation: *First they say I'm overqualified – then they say I'm underqualified. I just can't win.*

8 **you can't win 'em all** used to show sympathy when someone has had a disappointing experience

—see also WINNABLE, WINNER, WINNING

win sb/sth ↔ **back** *phr. v.* [T] to succeed in getting back something or someone that you had before: *How can I win back her trust?*

win out *phr. v.* [I] to finally defeat or be considered more important than everyone or everything else, in spite of problems: [+ **over**] *Style wins out over substance too often in Hollywood movies.*

win sb ↔ **over** *phr. v.* [T] to get someone's support or friendship by persuading them or being nice to them: *The President was unable to win over Senate leaders, who vowed to fight the bill.* —see Usage Note at GAIN

USAGE NOTE: WIN

WORD CHOICE: win, beat, defeat
You **win** a game, race, competition, election etc.: *The Tigers won the championship!* But you **beat** another person or team: *We beat their team by ten points* **Defeat** is a more formal word for **beat**: *Mondale was defeated in the 1984 election.*

win² *n.* [C] a success or victory, especially in sports: *The Broncos opened the season with 12 wins in their first 13 games.* | [+ **over**] *Florida's 14–11 win over Cleveland* —see also NO-WIN SITUATION

wince /wɪns/ *v.* [I] to react to something by looking upset or moving slightly, especially because you are in pain or embarrassed: *When he laughed, he winced with pain.* | [+ **at**] *I still wince at the memory of dancing with Josh.* —**wince** *n.* [singular]

winch¹ /wɪntʃ/ *n.* [C] a machine with a rope or chain for lifting heavy objects

winch² *v.* [T always + adv./prep.] to lift something or someone up using a winch

wind¹ /wɪnd/ *n.*

1 air [C,U] the air outside when it moves with a lot of force: *a 30-mile-an-hour wind* | *An icy wind blew through the open door.* | *Dolly's hat was blown off by a sudden gust of wind.* | *Toward late afternoon, a strong wind came up* (=it started blowing). | *The wind picked up* (=it began to blow more strongly) *and dust began to swirl.* | *Let's wait till the wind dies down* (=it starts blowing less strongly). | **blow/sway/flap etc. in the wind** *She stood on the hill, her hair blowing in the wind.* | **a strong/high wind** *The forecast is for strong winds and heavy rain.* | **a gentle/soft/light wind** *Clear skies and light winds helped cleanup workers today.* | **a bitter/chill/biting wind** (=a very cold wind) | **east/west/north/south wind** (=wind coming from the east etc.) —see also HEADWIND

2 **get/catch wind of sth** INFORMAL to hear or find out about something secret or private, especially if you learn it accidentally or in an unofficial way: *Other scientists soon got wind of Goldstine's project.*

3 **take the wind out of sb's sails** INFORMAL to make someone lose their confidence, especially by saying or doing something unexpected: *Last night's defeat has taken some of the wind out of the team's sails.*

4 **see which way the wind is blowing** to find out what the situation is before you do something or make a decision

5 **sth is in the wind** used to say that something is happening or going to happen, but not many people know what it is: *If there was talk of a merger in the wind, I'm sure we'd hear about it.*

6 **the winds of change/freedom/opinion etc.** events and changes that have started to happen and will have important effects, and that cannot be stopped: *The winds of democratic reform are sweeping across the country.*

7 **the winds** [plural] also **the wind section** the part of an ORCHESTRA that consists of WIND INSTRUMENTS

8 **have the wind at your back a)** to be walking, moving etc. in the same direction as the wind **b)** to be in a favorable situation that helps you succeed

9 breathe [U] your ability to breathe without difficulty

10 talk [U] INFORMAL useless talk that does not mean anything —see also **break wind** (BREAK¹ (45)), **knock the wind out of sb** (KNOCK¹ (3)), **second wind** (SECOND¹ (12)), WINDED, WINDPIPE, WINDY

wind² /waɪnd/ *v.* past tense and past participle **wound**
1 [I always + adv./prep.,T always + adv./prep.] to turn or twist something repeatedly, especially around something else: [**wind sth around sth**] *Delia wound a piece of string around the box to keep it shut.* | [+ **around**] *The snakes wound slowly around her arms.* **2** also **wind up** [T] to turn something such as a handle or part of a machine around and around, especially in order to make something move or start working: *I hate watches that you have to wind.* | *She wound up the little car and let it go.* —see also WINDUP² **3** [I always + adv./prep.] also **wind its way** if a road, track, river etc. winds, it has many smooth bends and is usually very long: [+ **across/through/around etc.**] *The narrow road winds its way up to the top of Peaked Hill* —see also WINDING **4** to make a CASSETTE TAPE or VIDEOTAPE go backward or forward in order to hear or see what is on a different part of it —see also REWIND —**wind** *n.* [C] —compare UNWIND (2)

wind down *phr. v.* [I,T **wind** sth ↔ **down**] to gradually become slower, less active etc., or to make an activity do this: *The party started winding down after midnight.*

wind up *phr. v.* **1** [linking verb] INFORMAL to do something, go somewhere, become involved in something etc., without intending or wanting to: [+ **with/in/at etc.**] *Patterson eventually wound up in jail.* | [**wind up doing sth**] *The company could wind up paying more that $50 million in losses.* | **wind up drunk/dead/sick etc.** *Tucker wound up homeless a year and a half ago.* —see also WOUND UP **2** [I,T **wind** sth ↔ **up**] to end an activity, meeting etc.: *Let's see if we can wind this up by 7.* —see also WINDUP¹

wind·bag /ˈwɪndbæg/ *n.* [C] INFORMAL someone who talks too much and says nothing important

wind·blown, wind-blown /ˈwɪndbloʊn/ *adj.* a wind-blown place or object is blown by the wind, or has been blown by it: *windblown hair*

wind·break /ˈwɪndbreɪk/ *n.* [C] a fence, line of trees, or wall that is intended to protect a place from the wind

wind break·er /ˈwɪndˌbreɪkɚ/ *n.* [C] a type of coat that is made specially to keep the wind out

wind·burn /ˈwɪndbɚn/ *n.* [C,U] the condition of having sore red skin because you were in the wind too long

wind·chill fac·tor /ˈwɪndtʃɪl ˌfæktɚ/ also **windchill** *n.* [U] the combination of cold weather and strong winds that makes the temperature seem colder

wind chime /ˈwɪnd tʃaɪm/ *n.* [C] long thin pieces of metal or glass hanging together in a group that make musical sounds when the wind blows

wind·ed /ˈwɪndɪd/ *adj.* unable to breathe easily, because you have been running or you have been hit in the stomach: *Climbing the hill left him winded.* —see also LONG-WINDED

wind·fall /ˈwɪndfɔl/ *n.* [C] **1** an amount of money that you get unexpectedly: *The merger could mean a $2.2 billion windfall for shareholders.* | **a windfall gain/profit etc.** (=a profit that you did not expect to make) **2** a piece of fruit that has fallen off a tree

Wind·hoek /ˈvɪnthʊk/ the capital and largest city of Namibia

wind·ing /ˈwaɪndɪŋ/ *adj.* having a twisting turning shape: *a winding creek* —see also WIND[2] (3)

winding sheet /ˈwaɪndɪŋ ʃit/ *n.* [C] OLD USE a SHROUD[1] (1)

wind in·stru·ment /ˈwɪnd ˌɪnstrəmənt/ *n.* [C] a musical instrument that you play by blowing through it, such as a CLARINET

wind·jam·mer /ˈwɪndˌdʒæmɚ/ *n.* [C] a large sailing ship of the type that was used for trade in the 19th century

wind·lass /ˈwɪndləs/ *n.* [C] a machine for pulling or lifting heavy objects

wind·mill /ˈwɪndˌmɪl/ *n.* [C] a building or structure with parts that turn around in the wind, used for producing electrical power or crushing grain

s w
1 1

win·dow /ˈwɪndoʊ/ *n.* [C] **1** an opening in the wall of a building, car etc., covered with glass, that lets in light and can usually be opened to let in air: *Could you open a window?* | *Suddenly a strange face appeared in the window* (=on the other side of the window). —see picture on page 423 **2** one of the separate areas on a computer screen where different processes or PROGRAMS are working **3** also **window of opportunity** a short period of time that is available for a particular activity: *Early in the history of the planet, the climate conditions opened a window of opportunity that allowed life to form.* **4 go out the window** INFORMAL to disappear completely, or not have any effect anymore: *If the court were to say Congress cannot expand constitutional rights, 130 years of law would go right out the window.*

window box /ˈ.. ./ *n.* [C] a long narrow box in which you can grow plants outside your window

window clean·er /ˈ.. ./ *n.* **1** [C] a WINDOW WASHER **2** [U] a liquid used to clean windows

window dress·er /ˈ.. ./ *n.* [C] someone whose job is to arrange goods attractively in store windows

window dress·ing /ˈ.. ./ *n.* [U] **1** something that is done to give people a favorable idea about your plans or activities, and to hide the true situation: *Critics say that the organization's call to include more minorities is just window dressing.* **2** the art of arranging goods in a shop window so that they look attractive to customers

win·dow·pane /ˈwɪndoʊˌpeɪn/ *n.* [U] a single whole piece of glass in a window

window seat /ˈ.. ˌ./ *n.* [C] **1** a seat next to the window on a bus, airplane etc. **2** a seat built directly below a window

window shade /ˈ.. ˌ./ *n.* [C] a SHADE[1] (4)

window shop·ping /ˈ.. ˌ./ *n.* [U] the activity of looking at goods in store windows without intending to buy them —**window-shop** *v.* [I] —**window shopper** *n.* [C]

win·dow·sill /ˈwɪndoʊˌsɪl/ *n.* [C] a shelf that is attached to the bottom of a window —see picture on page 423

window wash·er /ˈ.. ˌ./ *n.* [C] someone whose job is to clean windows

wind·pipe /ˈwɪndpaɪp/ *n.* [C] NOT TECHNICAL the tube through which air passes from your mouth to your lungs

wind·screen /ˈwɪndskrin/ *n.* [C] BRITISH a WINDSHIELD

wind shear /ˈ. ./ *n.* [U] TECHNICAL a sudden change in the direction and speed of wind, which can make airplanes crash to the ground

wind·shield /ˈwɪndʃild/ *n.* [C] the large piece of glass or plastic, that you look through when driving a car, bus, MOTORCYCLE etc. —see picture on page 427

windshield wip·er /ˈ.. ˌ./ *n.* [C] a long thin piece of metal with a rubber edge that moves across a windshield to remove rain —see picture on page 427

wind·sock /ˈwɪndsɑk/ *n.* [C] a tube of material fastened to a pole at airports to show the direction of the wind

Wind·sor /ˈwɪnzɚ/ the name of the present British royal family

wind·storm /ˈwɪndstɔrm/ *n.* [C] a period of bad weather when there are winds but not much rain

wind·surf·ing /ˈwɪndˌsɚfɪŋ/ *n.* [U] the sport of sailing across water by standing on a board and holding on to a large sail —**windsurfer** *n.* [C] —**windsurf** *v.* [I]

wind·swept /ˈwɪndswɛpt/ *adj.* **1** a windswept place is often windy because there are not many trees or buildings to protect it: *the windswept Montana plains* **2** windswept hair, clothes etc. have been blown around by the wind

wind tun·nel /ˈ. ˌ./ *n.* [C] a large enclosed passage where models of aircraft are tested by forcing air past them

wind tur·bine /ˈwɪnd ˌtɚbaɪn, -bɪn/ *n.* [C] a modern WINDMILL for providing electrical power

wind-up[1], wind-up /ˈwaɪndʌp/ *n.* [C] **1** a series of actions that are intended to complete a process, meeting etc.: *The President made a statement at the windup of the summit in Helsinki.* **2** a series of movements a baseball PITCHER goes through before throwing the ball

windup[2], wind-up *adj.* [only before noun] a wind-up toy, clock etc. has a small KNOB on it that you twist in order to make it work

wind·ward /ˈwɪndwɚd/ *adj. adv.* **1** toward the direction from which the wind is blowing **2** pointing toward the wind: *the windward side of the island* —opposite LEEWARD

Wind·ward Is·lands, the /ˌwɪndwɚd ˈaɪləndz/ a group of islands in the Caribbean Sea that includes Martinique, Grenada and St. Lucia

wind-whipped /ˈ. ./ *adj.* a wind-whipped place or thing is blown very hard by the wind: *a wind-whipped fire*

wind·y /ˈwɪndi/ *adj.* **windier, windiest 1** with a lot of wind blowing: *It's too cold and windy for hiking.* **2** getting a lot of wind: *a windy street* **3** windy talk is full of words that sound impressive but do not mean much: *windy rhetoric* —**windiness** *n.* [U]

wine[1] /waɪn/ *n.* [C,U] **1** an alcoholic drink made from GRAPES, or a particular type of this drink: *a glass of wine* | *a new Australian wine* **2** an alcoholic drink made from another fruit or plant: *elderberry wine* **3 wine, women, and song** OLD-FASHIONED used, especially by men, to talk about time spent drinking lots of alcohol and enjoying yourself

s w
1 2

wine[2] *v.* [T] **wine and dine sb** to entertain someone well with a meal, wine etc.: *Companies spend millions wining and dining their clients.*

wine bar /'. ./ *n.* [C] a place that serves mainly wine and light meals

wine cel·lar /'. ,../ *n.* [C] **1** a cool room, usually under the ground, where people keep their wine **2** a collection of wine

wine cool·er /'. ,../ *n.* [C] **1** a drink made with wine, fruit juice, and water **2** a special container that you put a bottle of wine into to make it cool

wine·glass /'waɪnglæs/ *n.* [C] a glass for wine with a base, a thin upright part, and a bowl-shaped top —see picture at GLASS

wine·mak·ing /'waɪn,meɪkɪŋ/ *n.* [U] the skill or business of making wine —**winemaker** *n.* [C]

win·er·y /'waɪnəri/ *n. plural* **wineries** [C] a place where wine is made and stored

wine tast·ing /'. ,../ *n.* [C,U] the activity or skill of tasting different types of wine to find out which is good, or an occasion when this happens —**wine taster** *n.* [C]

wine vin·e·gar /,. '.../ *n.* [U] a type of VINEGAR made from sour wine, used in cooking

wing¹ /wɪŋ/ *n.* [C]

1 birds/insects **a)** one of the parts of a bird's or insect's body that it uses for flying: *butterfly wings* | *The children laughed as the parrot flapped its wings* (=moved them up and down). **b)** the meat on the wing bone of a chicken, duck etc.: *spicy chicken wings* —see picture on page 429

2 plane one of the large flat parts that stick out from the side of an airplane and help to keep it in the air

3 building one of the parts of a large building, especially one that sticks out from the main part: *the south wing of the Capitol* | *a new children's wing at the hospital*

4 politics a group within a political party or similar organization, whose members share particular opinions and aims, especially when these are different from those of most people in the organization: *the most conservative wing of the Republican Party* —see also LEFT WING (1), RIGHT WING (1)

5 take sb under your wing to give help and protection, especially to someone younger or less experienced: *Murphy took the young reporter under his wing.*

6 (waiting) in the wings ready to take action or ready to be used when the time is right: *There's no one waiting in the wings who can take over if Gibson resigns.*

7 the wings [plural] the parts at either side of a stage where the actors are hidden from people watching the play

8 take wing LITERARY **a)** if an idea or plan takes wing, it starts developing quickly and successfully **b)** to fly away

9 be on the wing LITERARY if a bird is on the wing, it is flying

10 sports **a)** the far left or right part of the field or playing area in games like HOCKEY or SOCCER **b)** the position of someone who plays in this area

11 get your wings to pass the necessary flying examinations and become a pilot —see also **spread your wings** (SPREAD¹ (15))

wing² *v.* **1 wing it** INFORMAL to do something without planning or preparation: *I don't have time to write a speech, so I'm just going to wing it.* **2** [I always + adv./prep.] LITERARY to fly: *We watched pelicans winging down the coastline.* **3** [T] INFORMAL to wound a person or bird in the arm or wing, especially with a gun shot

wing chair /'. ./ *n.* [C] a comfortable chair that has a high back and pieces pointing forward on each side

wing col·lar /'. ,../ *n.* [C] a type of shirt collar for men that is worn with very formal clothes

wing·ding /'wɪŋdɪŋ/ *n.* [C] OLD-FASHIONED, INFORMAL a party

winged /wɪŋd/ *adj.* having wings: *winged insects*

wing·er /'wɪŋə/ *n.* [C] **1 a right-winger/left-winger** someone who belongs to the RIGHT WING or LEFT WING of a political group **2** someone who plays on a WING¹ (10a)

wing nut /'. ./ *n.* [C] a NUT (2) for fastening things, which has sides that stick out to make it easier to turn

wing·span /'wɪŋspæn/ also **wing·spread** /'wɪŋsprɛd/ *n.* [C] the distance from the end of one wing of a bird, an airplane etc. to the other end of the other

wing·tip /'wɪŋtɪp/ *n.* [C] **1** a type of man's shoe with a pattern of small holes on the toe —see picture at SHOE **2** the point at the end of a bird's or an airplane's wing

wink¹ /wɪŋk/ *v.* **1** [I,T] to close and open one eye quickly, usually to communicate amusement or a secret message: [+ at] *I swear she just winked at me and smiled.* **2** [I] to shine with a light that flashes on and off: *Christmas lights were winking in the tree.*

wink at sth *phr. v.* [T] to pretend not to notice something bad or illegal, in a way that suggests you approve of it: *Authorities have been winking at the health code violations for years.*

wink² *n.* **1** [C] a quick action of opening and closing of your eye, usually as a signal to someone else: *"How are you girls?" Tom asked with a wink.* **2 not sleep a wink** also **not get a wink of sleep** to not be able to sleep at all: *Peter didn't sleep a wink that night.* —see also **forty winks** (FORTY (5)), **quick as a wink** (QUICK¹ (13))

win·less /'wɪnlɪs/ *adj.* not having won any games: *a winless team*

win·na·ble /'wɪnəbəl/ *adj.* a winnable game, CONTEST, election etc. can be won: *a winnable law case*

Win·ne·ba·go /,wɪnə'beɪgoʊ/ a Native American tribe from the Great Lakes area of the U.S.

win·ner /'wɪnə/ *n.* [C] **1** someone who wins a competition, game, election etc.: *a Grammy winner* | [+ of] *the winner of the PGA tour* —see picture at RACE¹ **2** INFORMAL someone or something that is likely to be very successful: *I'm not very good at picking winners in the stock market.* **3 the big/real winner** the person or group that gains the most advantages in a situation: *The real winners in the airline price war are the consumers.*

winner's cir·cle /'.. ,../ *n.* **the winner's circle a)** an area at a RACETRACK where a horse and its rider are taken after winning a race **b)** INFORMAL the state of having won a CONTEST or a race

win·ning /'wɪnɪŋ/ *adj.* [only before noun] **1 a winning score/strategy/combination etc.** a SCORE, plan etc. that makes you win something or be successful: *Greene had a winning time of 9.86 seconds.* **2 a winning team/quarterback/coach etc.** a team, player etc. that wins many games: *Everyone likes to coach a winning team.* **3 a winning record/season/streak etc.** a period of time during which you win more games, competitions etc. than you lose **4 a winning smile/personality etc.** an attractive smile, way of behaving etc. that makes people like you —see also PRIZE-WINNING

win·ning·est /'wɪnɪŋɪst/ *adj.* SLANG the winningest team/pitcher/coach etc. (in sth) used in sports writing to describe the team, player etc. that has won the most games: *Smith became the winningest coach in college basketball history.*

win·nings /'wɪnɪŋz/ *n.* [plural] money that you win in a game or by GAMBLING: *lottery winnings*

win·now /'wɪnoʊ/ *v.* **1** [I,T] also **winnow down** to become smaller, or to make a list, group, or quantity do this, by getting rid of the parts that you do not need or want: *Adams has winnowed the list of contestants to 12.* **2** [I,T] to separate the CHAFF (=outer part) from grain

winnow sth ↔ **out** *phr. v.* [T] to get rid of the parts of something that you do not need or want: *The test winnows out the unskilled applicants from the skilled.*

win·o /'waɪnoʊ/ *n. plural* **winos** [C] INFORMAL someone who drinks a lot of cheap alcohol and lives on the streets

win·some /'wɪnsəm/ *adj.* LITERARY pleasant and attractive, especially in a simple, direct way: *a winsome smile*

win·ter[1] /'wɪntɚ/ *n.* [C,U] the season between fall and spring when the weather is coldest: *Does it snow here much* **in the winter**? | *We might go to Mexico* **this winter**. | **last winter/next winter** (=the winter before or after this one) | **winter coat/shoes/gloves etc.** (=clothes that are designed for cold weather)

winter[2] *v.* [I always + adv./prep.] to spend the winter somewhere

win·ter·green /'wɪntɚˌgrin/ *n.* [U] an EVERGREEN plant with pleasant smelling leaves, or the oil made from them

winter home /ˌ.. './ *n.* [C] a house you live in only in the winter —compare SUMMER HOME

win·ter·ize /'wɪntɚˌraɪz/ *v.* [T] to prepare your car, house etc. for winter conditions

winter sol·stice /ˌ.. '../ *n.* [singular] the shortest day of the year, which in the NORTHERN HEMISPHERE (=top half of the earth) is around December 22nd

winter sports /ˌ.. './ *n.* [plural] sports that take place on snow or ice

win·ter·time /'wɪntɚˌtaɪm/ *n.* [U] the time of year when it is winter

win·try /'wɪntri/ also **win·ter·y** /'wɪntəri/ *adj.* like winter, or typical of winter, especially because it is cold: *a wintry February morning*

win-win sit·u·a·tion /ˌ. ˌ. ..'../ *n.* [U] a situation that will end well for everyone involved in it —compare NO-WIN SITUATION

wipe

windshield wipers

wiping the table

wipe[1] /waɪp/ *v.*

1 clean/rub [T] also **wipe off** **a)** to rub a surface with a cloth in order to remove dirt, liquid etc.: *Ask the waitress to wipe off the table.* | *Bill* **wiped his eyes** (=wiped the tears from his face) *and apologized.* **b)** to clean something by rubbing it against a surface: *Wipe your feet before you come in.*

2 remove dirt [T always + adv./prep.] to remove liquid, dirt, or marks by wiping: [**wipe sth off/from etc.**] *Let me wipe that mustard off your cheek.*

3 **wipe the slate clean** to decide to forget about mistakes or arguments that happened in the past: *It would be nice if we could wipe the slate clean and start over.*

4 **wipe the smile/grin off sb's face** INFORMAL to make someone less pleased or satisfied, especially because they are annoying you: *I'd like to wipe that stupid grin off your face.*

5 **wipe the floor with sb** INFORMAL to defeat someone completely in a competition or argument

6 **wipe sth off the face of the earth** also **wipe sth off the map** to destroy something completely so that it does not exist anymore: *Heavy bombing virtually wiped the city off the map.*

7 **wipe sth out of your mind** to forget an unhappy or upsetting experience

wipe sth ↔ **away** *phr. v.* [T] to do something that completely ruins something or makes it stop existing: *With one speech, he wiped away his entire political future.*

wipe sth ↔ **down** *phr. v.* [T] to completely clean a surface using a wet cloth

wipe out *phr. v.* **1** [T **wipe** sb/sth ↔ **out**] to destroy, kill, remove, or get rid of someone or something

completely: *In 20 years the native culture will be wiped out.* **2** [T **wipe** sb ↔ **out**] INFORMAL to make you feel extremely tired: *Standing on my feet all day really wipes me out.* —see also WIPED OUT **3** [I] SPOKEN to fall or hit another object when driving a car, bicycle etc.: *Scott wiped out on his bike.* **4** [T **wipe** sb ↔ **out**] to make someone lose all of their money: *Another crop disaster could wipe these farmers out.*

wipe sth ↔ **up** *phr. v.* [T] to remove liquid from a surface using a cloth: *Quick. Get something to wipe up the milk.*

wipe[2] *n.* [C] **1** a wiping movement with a cloth **2** a special piece of wet material that you use to clean something and then throw away: *antiseptic wipes* **3** **ass/butt wipe** VULGAR, SLANG someone you do not like or are angry with

wiped out /ˌ. './ *adj.* [not before noun] SPOKEN extremely tired; EXHAUSTED: *I was wiped out last night.*

wip·er /'waɪpɚ/ *n.* [C] a WINDSHIELD WIPER

wire[1] /waɪɚ/ *n.*
1 thin metal [U] thin metal in the form of a thread: *The cable is made of many twisted strands of wire.*
2 piece of wire [C] a piece of metal like this, used especially for carrying electrical currents: *a telephone wire*
3 **under the wire** if something is done under the wire, it is done just before it must be finished: *They got the proposal in just under the wire.*
4 **get your wires crossed** to become confused about what someone is saying because you think they are talking about something else: *We got our wires crossed and I waited for an hour in the wrong place.*
5 recording equipment [C] a piece of electronic recording equipment, usually worn secretly on someone's clothes
6 message [C] a TELEGRAM
7 news [U] an electronic system, used by some news organizations, for sending news stories to many different places at once: *wire reports* | *This story just came* **over the wire**. —see also CHICKEN WIRE, **go/come/be down to the wire** (DOWN[1] (14)), LIVE WIRE, WIRE SERVICE, WIRY

wire[2] *v.* [T]
1 electricity/phones etc. also **wire** sth ↔ **up a)** to put the wires for an electrical, telephone, computer etc. system into a house or building: *The electrician is coming to wire the house tomorrow.* **b)** to connect electrical equipment to the electrical system using wires: *Bud wired the CD player up to the cigarette lighter in his car.*
2 fasten to fasten two or more things together using wire: *Tracy had to have her jaw wired shut.*
3 money to send money electronically: *Could you wire me $50?*
4 message to send a TELEGRAM to someone
5 recording equipment to attach a secret piece of recording equipment to a person or a room —see also WIRING

wire cut·ters /'. ˌ../ *n.* [plural] a special tool like very strong scissors, used for cutting wire

wired /waɪɚd/ *adj.* **1** SPOKEN feeling very active, excited, and awake: *I was so wired I couldn't sleep.* **2** **be wired for sth** to have the necessary wires and connections for an electrical system to work: *All the rooms are wired for cable TV.* **3** SLANG connected to and able to use the Internet —see also HARD-WIRED

wire-haired /'. ./ *adj.* a wire-haired dog has fur that is stiff not soft: *a wire-haired terrier*

wire·less[1] /'waɪɚlɪs/ *adj.* relating to a system of communication that uses radio, not wires

wireless[2] *n.* [C,U] OLD-FASHIONED a radio

wire-rimmed also **wire-rim** /'. ˌ./ *adj.* wire-rimmed GLASSES have a thin piece of metal like wire around the part that you look through

wire serv·ice /'. ˌ../ *n.* [C] a business that collects news stories and sends them to newspapers, radio stations etc. electronically

wire·tap /'waɪɚˌtæp/ *n.* [C] an action of secretly listening to other people's telephone conversations, by attaching something to the wires of their telephone —**wiretap** *v.* [T] —**wiretapping** *n.* [U]

wire trans·fer /'. ,../ *n.* [C] an action of sending money from one bank to another electronically

wir·ing /'waɪərɪŋ/ *n.* [singular] **1** the network of wires that form the electrical system in a building, vehicle, or piece of equipment: *faulty wiring* **2** a length of wire that is used for making a network for electricity: *copper wiring*

wir·y /'waɪəri/ *adj.* **1** someone who is wiry is thin but has strong muscles **2** wiry hair is stiff and curly

Wis·con·sin /wɪs'kɑnsɪn/ *written abbreviation* WI a state in the Midwestern area of the U.S.

wis·dom /'wɪzdəm/ *n.* [U] **1** good judgment and the ability to make wise decisions: *an old man's wisdom* | *Citizens groups are* **questioning the wisdom of** *building an entirely new subway system.* **2** knowledge gained over a long period of time through learning or experience: *the collected wisdom of many centuries* **3** *in sb's (infinite) wisdom* used to say in a joking way that you do not understand why someone, especially someone in authority, has decided to do something: *The board, in its infinite wisdom, has decided to give Waters back his job.* —see also **(the) conventional wisdom** (CONVENTIONAL (3))

Wisdom of Sol·o·mon /ˌwɪzdəm əv 'sɑləmən/ a book in the Apocrypha of the Protestant Bible

wisdom tooth /'.. ,./ *n.* [C] one of the four large teeth at the back of your mouth that do not grow until you are an adult

wise¹ /waɪz/ *adj.*
1 decision/idea etc. wise decisions and judgments are based on intelligent thinking and experience: *Buying good health insurance was a wise decision.* | [be wise to do sth] *It's wise to start saving money now for your retirement.*
2 person someone who is wise makes good decisions, gives good advice etc., especially because they have a lot of experience in life: *a wise old man* | *As a manager, Sanford* **was wise in the ways of** (=knew a lot about) *company politics.*
3 *sb is none the wiser* INFORMAL **a)** also *no one is the wiser* used to say that no one will find out about something bad someone has done: *They had taken his wallet, but he was none the wiser till the men were long gone.* **b)** used to say that you do not understand something, even after it has been explained: *Charlie explained how the system works, but I'm still none the wiser.*
4 *wise guy* INFORMAL someone who says or does annoying things, especially to make themselves seem smarter than other people: *All right wise guy, I don't need to hear any more jokes out of you!* —compare WISEGUY
5 *be wise to sb/sth* INFORMAL to realize that someone is being dishonest: *Experienced teachers are wise to all the methods of cheating used by students.* —**wisely** *adv.*: *I try to use my time wisely.* —see also WISDOM, STREETWISE

wise² *v.*
wise up *phr. v.* INFORMAL [I] to realize the truth about a bad situation and start behaving differently because of it: *One of these days you better wise up and stop smoking.* | [wise up to sth] *Consumers need to wise up to the effect advertising has on them.*

-wise /waɪz/ *suffix* **1** *pricewise/timewise etc.* also *price-wise/time-wise etc.* INFORMAL used to talk about how a situation changes or is affected in relation to prices, time etc.: *Price-wise it's not expensive, but the quality could be better.* | *Security wise they've made a lot of improvements.* **2** *crosswise/length-wise etc.* in a direction across something, along the length of something etc.: *Cut each tomato crosswise into six slices.* —see also CLOCKWISE, COUNTERCLOCK-WISE

Wise /waɪz/, **I·saac May·er** /'aɪzɪk 'maɪə/ (1819–1900) a U.S. religious leader who united Reform Jewish groups in the U.S.

wise·a·cre /'waɪzˌeɪkə/ *n.* [C] OLD-FASHIONED someone who says or does annoying things, especially to make themselves seem smarter than other people

wise·crack /'waɪzkræk/ *n.* [C] a clever funny remark or reply —**wisecrack** *v.* [I] —**wisecracking** *adj.*: *a wisecracking talk show host*

wise·guy /'waɪzgaɪ/ *n. plural* **wiseguys** [C] INFORMAL someone who is involved in the MAFIA —compare **wise guy** (WISE¹ (4))

wish¹ /wɪʃ/ *v.*
1 hope for sth [T] to hope that something is true, will happen, or that you could do something, even if what you hope for is unlikely or impossible: *I wish I didn't have to go to school.* | *Afterward, Violet wished she hadn't said anything.* | [wish (that)] *I wish I could play the piano like that!* | *I wish I could remember* (=said when you are trying to remember) *his name.*
2 formal [I,T] FORMAL used in formal situations to say that you want to do something: [wish to do sth] *I wish to report a robbery.* | *The police wish to question him about the fire.* | *If you wish, you can substitute chicken breasts for the veal.*
3 happiness/luck etc. [T] to say that you hope someone will have good luck, a happy life etc.: [wish sb sth] *She called to wish me a happy birthday.* | *Wish me luck!* | *They* **wished me well** (=said that they hope that good things will happen to me) *in my new job.*

> ### SPOKEN PHRASES
>
> **4** *I wish sb would do sth* SPOKEN used to say that you want someone to stop doing something that annoys you: *I wish you'd hurry!* | *I wish she'd shut up!*
> **5** *I/you wish!* SPOKEN used to say that something is not true, but you wish it was: *"I think he really likes you." "I wish!"*
> **6** *you wish!* SPOKEN used to tell someone that what they want to happen or be true will definitely not happen or become true: *"I'm going to be a millionaire one day." "You wish!"*
> **7** *wouldn't wish sth on/upon sb* SPOKEN used to say that you do not like something you have to do, and you would not want anyone else to have to do it: *James says he wouldn't wish a military career on anyone.*

wish for sth *phr. v.* [T] to want something to happen or want to have something, especially when it seems unlikely or impossible: *When I was little, I used to wish for an older sister.*
wish sth ↔ **away** *phr. v.* [T] to want something bad or difficult to disappear, without doing anything about it: *You can't just wish your problems away, you know!*

> ### USAGE NOTE: WISH
>
> **WORD CHOICE: wish, want**
> In sentences where both can be used, **wish** sounds much more formal than **want**. In a conversation, you might say: *I want to go the store.* In a formal letter, you might write: *I wish to express my dissatisfaction with your service.*

wish² *n.* [C] **1** a desire to do something, have something, or have something happen: [the wishes of sb] *It's important to respect the wishes of the patient.* | [sb's wish to do sth] *Ken finally got his wish to live in the country.* | *Pete Carril* **got his wish** – *his team won his last game as head coach.* | *Her* **wish** *to travel the world* **came true** (=she got what she wanted, especially in a surprising and unexpected way). | *sb's last/dying wish* (=something that you say you want just before you die) | *sb's wish is granted/fulfilled* (=someone gets what they want) **2** *against sb's wishes* if you do something against someone's wishes, you do it even though you know they do not want you to: *He became a dancer against the wishes of his family.* **3** *have no wish to do sth* FORMAL used to emphasize that you do not want or intend to do something: *I have no wish to offend anybody.* **4** a silent request for something to happen as if by magic: *Close your eyes and* **make a wish**. **5** *your wish is my command* HUMOROUS used to say that you will do whatever someone asks you to do —see also **best wishes** (BEST¹ (4))

wish·bone /'wɪʃboʊn/ n. [C] the breast bone from a cooked chicken etc., which two people pull apart to decide whose wish will come true

wish·ful think·ing /ˌwɪʃfəl 'θɪŋkɪŋ/ n. [U] the wish to have something or have something happen that is impossible to get or that will not happen

wish·ing well /'.. ˌ./ n. [C] a WELL⁴ or pool of water that people throw coins into while making a wish

wish list /'. ./ n. [C] INFORMAL all the things that you want in a particular situation: *Also on the governor's wish list is more funding for schools.*

wish·y-wash·y /'wɪʃ ˌwɑʃi, -ˌwɔʃi/ adj. DISAPPROVING **1** a wishy-washy person does not have firm or clear ideas and seems unable to decide what they want: *Brown has been criticized for being wishy-washy on political reform.* **2** colors that are wishy-washy are pale and unexciting, not bright

wisp /wɪsp/ n. [C] **1 a wisp of hair/hay/grass etc.** a thin piece of hair etc. that is separate from the rest: *Wisps of light brown hair poked out from her braids.* **2 a wisp of smoke/steam/incense etc.** a small thin line of smoke, steam etc. that rises up —see also WILL-O'-THE-WISP —**wispy** adj.

wis·ter·i·a /wɪ'stɪriə/ n. [C,U] a climbing plant with purple or white flowers

wist·ful /'wɪstfəl/ adj. feeling a little sad, especially because you are thinking of something that you would like but cannot have: *"I wish life was always like this," she said with a wistful sigh.* —**wistfully** adv. —**wistfulness** n. [U]

wit /wɪt/ n. **1** [U] the ability to say things that are clever and amusing: *People love him for his wit and charm.* | *Kelly is a soft-spoken politician known for his **quick wit** (=ability to quickly think of intelligent and amusing things to say).* **2** [C] someone who has this ability: *Oscar Wilde was a famous wit.* **3 wits** [plural] your ability to think quickly and make the right decisions: *You have to rely on your wits to be successful in business.* | **keep/have your wits about you** (=be ready to think quickly and do what is necessary in a difficult situation) **4 scare/frighten sb out of their wits** INFORMAL to frighten someone very much: *The dogs scared her out of her wits.* **5 be at your wits' end** to be very upset because you have not been able to solve a problem even though you have tried very hard: *I'm at my wits' end trying to fix this computer.* **6 collect/gather your wits** make yourself think about what you are going to do next after you have been surprised by something: *Before I could gather my wits, he pushed me down again.* **7 have the wit to do sth** to be intelligent enough to know the right thing to do: *Thankfully, Reid had the wit to see what was wrong with the plan.* **8 to wit** LITERARY used to make what you just said clear by giving an example —see also **a battle of wits** (BATTLE¹ (7)), HALF-WIT, **live by your wits** (LIVE¹ (6)), OUTWIT, QUICK-WITTED, WITLESS, WITTY

witch /wɪtʃ/ n. [C] **1** a woman who is supposed to have magic powers, especially to do bad things **2** INFORMAL an insulting word for a woman who is old or not nice —see also BEWITCHED

witch·craft /'wɪtʃkræft/ n. [U] the use of magic to make things happen

witch-doc·tor /'. ˌ../ n. [C] a man who is believed to have magic powers and the ability to cure people of diseases, especially in some parts of Africa

witch-ha·zel /'. ˌ../ n. [C,U] a substance used for treating small wounds on the skin, or the tree that produces it

witch-hunt /'. ./ n. [C] a deliberate attempt, often based on false information, to find and punish people in a society or organization whose opinions are considered wrong or dangerous: *The investigation is just another political witch-hunt.*

witching hour /'.. ˌ./ n. **the witching hour** LITERARY the time in the middle of the night, usually midnight, when strange or magic things are believed to happen

Wite-out /'waɪtaʊt/ n. [U] TRADEMARK white liquid that is used to cover mistakes in writing, typing (TYPE) etc.

with /wɪθ, wɪð/ prep. **1** together in the same place or at the same time: *She went out to lunch with Jimmy.* | *I always wear these shoes with this dress.* **2** having, possessing, or showing a particular thing, quality, or feeling: *a book with a green cover* | *Molly beamed with pride as her son received the prize.* **3** including: *The meal comes with fries and a drink.* **4** using something, or by means of something: *Stop eating with your fingers.* | *You can fix it with a screwdriver.* **5** used to show the idea of filling, covering, or containing something: *The truffles are made with the finest Belgian chocolate.* | *Workers filled the hole with cement.* **6** concerning, or in the case of: *What's wrong with the radio?* | *He's in love with you.* **7** against or opposing someone: *I'm tired of you two arguing with each other.* **8** in the same direction as someone or something: *It's easier to run with the wind.* —opposite AGAINST (6) **9** at the same time or rate as something else: *The wine improves with age.* **10** supporting or liking someone or something: *I agree with what you said.* **11** used when comparing two things or considering the relationship between them: *Compared with other schools, the salaries here are very low.* **12** used to introduce a particular situation that is happening, and show how it affects something: *With the kids at school, I have more time for my hobbies.* **13 be with sb** INFORMAL **a)** supporting someone by agreeing with what they say or do: *I'm with Harry all the way on this one.* **b)** to understand someone's explanation about something: *Go ahead and continue the story – I'm with you.* **14** used in some expressions to show that one person or thing separates from another: *Joan doesn't want to **part with** the money.* | *The ceremony is a complete **break with** tradition.* **15** SPOKEN used in some phrases to express a strong wish or command: *Down with racism!* **16 (and) with that** used to say that something happens immediately after something else: *"I have to go. I'll call you in New York," and with that she hung up.*

with·al /wɪð'ɔl, wɪθ-/ adv. OLD USE besides; together with this

with·draw /wɪθ'drɔ, wɪð-/ v. past tense **withdrew** /-'dru/ past participle **withdrawn** /-'drɔn/
1 ▸money◂ [T] to take money out of a bank account: **[withdraw sth from sth]** *I need to withdraw some money from my checking account.*
2 ▸take sth away◂ [T] to remove something or take it back, often because of an official decision: *The developers withdrew their request to build on the land.* | **[withdraw sth from sth]** *Franks has withdrawn his name from consideration for the job.* | *The drug has been **withdrawn from the market** (=stores have stopped selling it) for further tests.*
3 withdraw a remark/accusation/statement to say that a remark that you made earlier was untrue or unfair: *Miller later withdrew his statement that Jones stole any money.*
4 ▸from activity/organization◂ [I,T] to stop taking part in an activity, belonging to an organization etc., or to make someone stop doing this: **[+ from]** *A knee injury forced Joyner to withdraw from the tournament.* | *City officials want to withdraw from the Metropolitan Transit Authority.* | **[withdraw sth/ sb from sth]** *Several parents have withdrawn their children from the school.*
5 ▸stop communicating◂ [I] to become quieter, less friendly, and more concerned about your own thoughts: **[+ from/into]** *Ralph has withdrawn from other kids in the class.*
6 ▸leave a place◂ **a)** [I,T] if an army withdraws or is withdrawn, it leaves a place, especially in order to avoid defeat **b)** [I] FORMAL to leave a place, especially in order to be alone or go somewhere quiet: **[+ from/into]** *He bowed and withdrew from the room.*

with·draw·al /wɪθ'drɔəl/ n.
1 ▸money◂ [C,U] the act of taking money from a bank account, or the amount you take out: *I would like to **make a withdrawal** from my savings account.*

2 army [C,U] the act of moving an army, weapons etc. away from the area where they were fighting: [+ of/from] *The Navy is considering a withdrawal of ships from the area.*

3 of a support/service etc. [U] the act of ending or taking away something such as support, an offer, or a service: [+ of] *a withdrawal of government aid*

4 activity/organization [U] when someone stops being part of an activity or organization: [+ from] *Management's withdrawal from the negotiations greatly disturbs us.*

5 drugs [U] the period after you have given up a drug that you were dependent on, and the mental and physical effects that this process involves: *At this stage, a patient will begin to experience with-drawal symptoms* (=painful or bad effects caused by withdrawal).

6 statement [U] the act of saying that something you previously said was untrue or unfair: [+ of] *the withdrawal of all allegations*

with·drawn /wɪθˈdrɔn/ *adj.* very shy and quiet and concerned only about your own thoughts

with·drew /wɪθˈdru/ the past tense of withdraw

with·er /ˈwɪðɚ/ also **wither away** *v.* [I,T] if plants wither they become drier and smaller and start to die

with·ered /ˈwɪðɚd/ *adj.* **1** a withered plant has become drier and smaller and is dead or dying **2** a withered person looks thin and weak and old **3** a withered arm or leg has not developed correctly and is thin and weak

with·er·ing /ˈwɪðərɪŋ/ *adj.* **a withering look/remark etc.** a look, remark etc. that makes someone feel stupid, embarrassed, or lose confidence: *Morse put together a withering critique of the news media.* —**witheringly** *adv.*

with·ers /ˈwɪðɚz/ *n.* [plural] the highest part of a horse's back, above its shoulders

with·hold /wɪθˈhoʊld, wɪð-/ *v. past tense and past participle* **withheld** [T] **1** to refuse to let someone have something, especially until something else is done: [withhold sth from sb] *The hospital is accused of withholding treatment from people who could not afford to pay.* **2 withhold facts/evidence/information** to refuse to give facts, evidence etc.: *The report confirms that Johnson withheld important evidence.*

withholding tax /.'.. ,./ *n.* [C,U] money that is taken out of your pay as tax

with·in /wɪðˈɪn, wɪθ-/ *adv., prep.* **1 a)** before a certain period of time has passed: *They are supposed to finish the bridge within two years.* **b)** during a certain period of time: *Her car has been broken into three times within a month.* | **within the space of a year/month etc.** *Within the space of five days, the fire destroyed over 4000 acres.* **2** inside a certain area and not beyond it: *Hunting is not permitted within the park.* *Cigarette advertising is not allowed within 1000 feet of* (=in an area that is less than 1000 feet from) *schools.* **3** inside a society, organization, or group of people: *There have been a lot of changes within the department since I joined.* **4** according to particular limits or rules: *Within the terms of the agreement, Delta will buy 50 new aircraft.* | *The machine is not being operated within safety guidelines.* **5 within sight/earshot etc.** if someone or something is within sight, earshot etc. you can see or hear them **6 within reach a)** if something you want to achieve is within reach, it is possible to do it: *The dream of owning a house is not within reach for many Americans.* **b)** near enough to be picked up or touched when you stretch out your hand: *I always have my cellular phone within reach.* **c)** near, so that people can get there without difficulty: *Lake Tahoe is easily within reach of Bay Area residents.*

with-it, with it /'. ./ *adj.* **1** feeling full of energy and able to understand things easily: *I'm sorry I'm not very with-it today – could you repeat that?* **2** fashionable and modern in the way that you dress, think etc.: *When it comes to music, dad's not very with-it.*

with·out /wɪðˈaʊt, wɪθ-/ *adv., prep.* **1** lacking something, especially something that is basic or necessary: *After the storm, we were without electricity for five days.* | *I don't think grandpa could survive*

without his cigars. —see also **do without** (DO²) **2** not doing or having something, or not showing a particular feeling, especially when it is considered normal or polite: *He had gone out without his parents' permission.* | **[without doing sth]** *For fifty years, she did her job without complaining.* | **Without wanting to,** *I had betrayed my closest friend.* **3 without so much as...** used to talk about something you think someone should have done: *Without so much as a simple thank-you, she took the money I offered.* **4** not being with someone, or not having them to help you, especially someone you like or need: *I don't know what I would do without Lisa.* **5** used to show that something bad did not happen: *This time Clark finished the race without falling.* | *Marin played the first piece without a hitch* (=without any mistakes). **6** OLD USE outside

with·stand /wɪθˈstænd, wɪð-/ *v. past tense and past participle* **withstood** [T] **1** to be strong enough to remain unharmed by something such as great heat or cold great pressure etc.: *The bridge is built to withstand an earthquake of 8.3 magnitude.* **2** to defend yourself successfully against people who attack, criticize, or oppose you: *Owens has withstood many attacks on his leadership.* **3 withstand the test of time** to still be important, effective etc. after a long time: *Newton's theories that have withstood the test of time.*

wit·less /ˈwɪtlɪs/ *adj.* **1 scare sb witless** to make someone very frightened **2** not very intelligent or sensible; silly —**witlessly** *adv.* —**witlessness** *n.* [U]

wit·ness¹ /ˈwɪtnɪs/ *n.* **1** [C] someone who sees a crime or an accident and can describe what happened: *Police have appealed for witnesses to come forward.* | **[+ to]** *One witness to the accident said that the driver appeared to be drunk.* **2** [C] someone in a court of law who tells what they saw or what they know about a crime: *The witness was asked to identify the robber in the courtroom.* **3** [C] someone who is present when an official paper is signed, and who signs it too, to prove that they saw it happen: **[+ to]** *His brother was a witness to the will.* **4 be witness to sth** FORMAL to be present when something happens, and watch it happening: *We have been witness to the rapid transformation of the neighborhood.* **5** [C,U] a public statement of Christian beliefs, or someone who does this —see also **bear witness to sth** (BEAR¹ (18))

witness² *v.*

1 see sth happen [T] to see something happen, especially a crime or accident: *Several residents claim to have witnessed the attack.*

2 experience sth [T] to experience important events or changes: *Priests have witnessed an increase in religious intolerance.*

3 time/place [T] if a time or place witnesses an event, the event happens during that time or in that place: *Recent years have witnessed the collapse of the steel industry.*

4 official document [T] to be present when someone signs an official document, and sign it yourself to show this: *It is not legal unless the pastor witnesses the marriage license.*

5 ..., as witnessed by... also **witness...** used to give an example that proves something you have just mentioned: *There are alternative ways to teach children, as witnessed by Rosemont Elementary's program.* | *Bad economic times can result in political dictatorships. Witness Germany in the 1930s.*

6 Christian beliefs [I] to speak publicly about your Christian beliefs

witness to sth *phr. v.* [T] FORMAL to formally state that something is true or happened: *Her principal was called to witness to her good character.*

witness stand /.. ,./ *n.* [C] the place in a court of law where a witness answers questions

Witt·gen·stein /ˈvɪtgənˌʃtaɪn/, **Lud·wig** /ˈlʊdvɪg/ (1889–1951) an Austrian PHILOSOPHER who studied the relationship between language and the physical world

W

wit·ti·cism /ˈwɪtəˌsɪzəm/ *n.* [C] a clever amusing remark

wit·ty /ˈwɪti/ *adj.* **wittier, wittiest** using words in a clever and amusing way: *a witty speaker* | *witty remarks* —**wittily** *adv.* —**wittiness** *n.* [U]

wives /waɪvz/ the plural of WIFE

wiz /wɪz/ *n.* [C] INFORMAL a wizard

wiz·ard /ˈwɪzəd/ *n.* [C] **1** someone who is very good at something: [+ at/with] *Gail is a wizard with numbers.* | **a computer/guitar/financial** etc. **wizard** *Ken has a reputation for being the local dance floor wizard.* **2** a man who is believed to have magic powers

wiz·ard·ry /ˈwɪzədri/ *n.* [U] impressive ability to do something or an impressive achievement: *Many credit the company's success to Neuheisel's organizational wizardry.*

wiz·ened /ˈwɪzənd/ *adj.* a wizened person is small and thin and has skin with a lot of lines and WRINKLES: *a wizened face* | *The wizened doctor slowly pressed three fingers against the artery in my wrist.*

wk. the written abbreviation of "week"

wkly. the written abbreviation of "weekly"

w/o the written abbreviation of "without," especially used when writing notes quickly —see also W/

wob·ble /ˈwɑbəl/ *v.* [I] **1** to move in an unsteady way from side to side: *The whole washing machine began to wobble.* **2** [always + adv./prep.] to go in a particular direction, moving in an unsteady way from side to side: [+ off/along/across etc.] *The old lady wobbled over to the window.* **3** to be unsure whether to do something: *The President appeared to wobble over sending the troops in.* —**wobble** *n.* [C]

wob·bly /ˈwɑbli/ *adj.* **1** moving in an unsteady way from side to side: *a wobbly chair* **2** INFORMAL feeling weak and unable to keep your balance: *As I stood up, I began to feel a little wobbly.* **3** a wobbly voice is weak and goes up and down in TONE, especially when you feel frightened or upset

woe /woʊ/ *n.* **1 woes** [plural] the problems and troubles affecting someone: *They tend to blame all of Africa's woes on colonialism.* **2** [U] LITERARY great sadness **3 woe is me** OLD USE OR HUMOROUS used to say that you are unhappy or that life is difficult for you **4 woe to sb** LITERARY used to warn someone that there will be trouble if they do something: *Woe to the man who steals from widows and orphans.*

woe·be·gone /ˈwoʊbɪˌgɔn, -ˌgɑn/ *adj.* looking very sad or in bad condition: *a woebegone expression* | *the woebegone coal industry*

woe·ful /ˈwoʊfəl/ *adj.* **1** used to emphasize that something is very bad: *the woeful state of the economy* | *a woeful lack of imagination* **2** LITERARY very sad: *a woeful cry of frustration* —**woefully** *adv.*: *woefully inadequate facilities*

wok /wɑk/ *n.* [C] a wide pan shaped like a bowl, used in Chinese cooking —see picture at PAN[1]

woke /woʊk/ the past tense of WAKE[1]

wo·ken /ˈwoʊkən/ the past participle of WAKE[1]

wolf[1] /wʊlf/ *n.* plural **wolves** [C] **1** a wild animal that looks like a large dog and lives and hunts in groups: *a pack of wolves* **2 a wolf in sheep's clothing** someone who seems to be friendly but is in fact dishonest, not nice etc. —**wolfish** *adj.*: *a wolfish grin* —see also **cry wolf** (CRY[1] (8)), LONE WOLF

wolf[2] also **wolf down** *v.* [T] INFORMAL to eat something very quickly, swallowing it in big pieces

Wolfe /wʊlf/**, Tom** /tɑm/ (1931–) a U.S. JOURNALIST famous for writing about American society and for his NOVELS

wolf·hound /ˈwʊlfhaʊnd/ *n.* [C] an extremely large dog which used to be trained to hunt wolves

wolf whis·tle /ˈ. ˌ../ *n.* [C] a way of whistling that men sometimes use to show that they think a woman is attractive —**wolf-whistle** *v.* [I]

Woll·stone·craft /ˈwʊlstənˌkræft/**, Mary** (1759–1797)

a British writer who is regarded as one of the first FEMINISTS

wol·ver·ine /ˌwʊlvəˈrin/ *n.* [C] a short strong-looking animal with dark fur that is similar to a WEASEL

wolves /wʊlvz/ the plural of WOLF

wom·an /ˈwʊmən/ *n.* plural **women** /ˈwɪmɪn/
1 female [C] an adult female person: *Who was the dark-haired woman you were talking to?* | *married women* | *women's clothes*
2 any woman [singular] women in general: *What can a woman do when she can't trust her best friend?*
3 a businesswoman/congresswoman etc. a woman who has a particular type of job: *a meeting of local businesswomen* —see also CHAIRWOMAN, SPOKESWOMAN
4 be your own woman to make your own decisions and be in charge of your own life, without depending on anyone else
5 the other woman INFORMAL the woman that a man is having a sexual relationship with, even though he is married to or already in a relationship with someone else: *I couldn't believe it when the other woman turned out to be my next-door neighbor.*
6 sb's old woman SPOKEN an expression for someone's wife or GIRLFRIEND, which many women think is offensive
7 a woman of the night also **a woman of easy virtue** OLD-FASHIONED a PROSTITUTE —see also **make an honest woman (out) of sb** (HONEST (5)), **wine, women, and song** (WINE[1] (3)), **a man/ woman of the world** (WORLD[1] (20))

wom·an·hood /ˈwʊmənˌhʊd/ *n.* [U] **1** the state of being a woman, not a man or a girl **2** FORMAL women in general —compare MANHOOD

wom·an·ish /ˈwʊmənɪʃ/ *adj.* looking or behaving in a way that is typical of women

wom·an·iz·er /ˈwʊməˌnaɪzə/ *n.* [C] DISAPPROVING a man who has sexual relationships with many different women —**womanize** *v.* [I] —**womanizing** *n.* [U]

wom·an·kind /ˈwʊmənˌkaɪnd/ *n.* [U] women considered together as a group —compare MANKIND

wom·an·ly /ˈwʊmənli/ *adj.* APPROVING behaving, dressing etc. in a way that is thought to be typical of or appropriate for a woman: *She had a very womanly figure.* —**womanliness** *n.* [U]

woman-to-woman /ˌ.. '..◂/ *adj. adv.* if two women have a woman-to-woman talk or they talk woman-to-woman, they discuss something in an honest, open way

womb /wum/ *n.* [C] the part of a female's body where her baby grows before it is born

wom·bat /ˈwɑmbæt/ *n.* [C] an Australian animal like a small bear whose babies live in a pocket of skin on its body

wom·en /ˈwɪmɪn/ the plural of WOMAN

wom·en·folk /ˈwɪmɪnˌfoʊk/ *n.* [plural] OLD-FASHIONED all the women in a particular family or society

women's lib /ˌ.. './ also **women's lib·e·ra·tion** /ˌ.. ..'../ *n.* [U] the expression, used in the 1960s and 1970s, for all the ideas, actions, and politics related to giving women the same rights and opportunities as men —**women's libber** *n.* [C]

women's move·ment /ˈ.. ˌ../ *n.* **the women's movement** all the women who are involved in the aim of improving the social, economic, and political position of women and of ending sexual DISCRIMINATION

women's rights /ˌ.. './ *n.* [plural] the rights of women to have and do everything that men have and do, especially those rights given by special laws

women's room /ˈ.. ˌ./ *n.* [C] a public REST ROOM for women

women's shel·ter /ˈ.. ˌ../ *n.* [C] a place where women and their children can go to escape being physically hurt by their husband, partner etc.

won[1] /wʌn/ the past tense and past participle of WIN[1]

won[2] /wɑn/ *n.* [C] the standard unit of money used in Korea

won·der[1] /ˈwʌndə/ *v.* [I,T] **1** to think about something that you are not sure about and try to guess what is true, what will happen etc.: **wonder who/ what/how** etc. *I wonder where Joe is now.* | **wonder if/whether/why** *Have you ever wondered why she looks so sad all the time?* | *He's been leaving work early a lot – it makes you wonder, doesn't it?* **2 I was wondering if/whether** a) SPOKEN used to politely ask someone to help you: *I was wondering if you could babysit tomorrow night.* **b)** used to ask someone if they would like to do something: *We were wondering if you'd like to come with us.* **3 I wonder if/whether** SPOKEN used to ask politely for something: *I wonder if you could help me.* **4** [I,T] to have doubts about whether something is good, true, normal etc.: **[+ about]** *You have to wonder about a guy who can spend all that money on comic books.* | **wonder if/ whether** *I've been wondering if I installed the program in the right place.*

wonder[2] *n.* **1 a)** [U] a feeling of surprise and admiration for something very beautiful or new to you: **[+ with]** *We listened with wonder to our father's stories.* **b)** [C] something that makes you feel surprise and admiration: *technological wonders* | *the Seven Wonders of the World* **2 (it's) no/small/little wonder** SPOKEN used to say that you are not surprised by something: *You haven't changed the oil? No wonder the car doesn't run.* **3 it's a wonder (that)** SPOKEN used to say that something is very surprising: *It's a wonder no one got hurt.* **4 do/work wonders** to be very effective in solving a problem: *A long weekend away from work will do wonders for your peace of mind.* **5 wonders will never cease!** SPOKEN, HUMOROUS used to show you are surprised and pleased about something **6 sb is a wonder** OLD-FASHIONED used to say that someone is good at doing difficult things

wonder[3] *adj.* [only before noun] very good and effective: *a new wonder drug*

won·der·ful /'wʌndəfəl/ *adj.* **1** making you feel very happy: *We had a wonderful time in Spain.* **2** making you admire someone or something very much: *You're lucky you have such wonderful kids.* —**wonderfully** *adv.*

won·der·ing·ly /'wʌndərɪŋi/ *adv.* in a way that shows admiration, surprise and pleasure: *She stared at him wonderingly.*

won·der·land /'wʌndə,lænd/ *n.* [U] an imaginary place in stories that is full of wonderful things

won·der·ment /'wʌndəmənt/ *n.* [U] LITERARY a feeling of pleasant surprise or admiration

won·drous /'wʌndrəs/ *adj.* LITERARY good or impressive in a surprising way

wonk /wɑŋk, wɔŋk/ *n.* [C] INFORMAL someone who works hard and is very serious: *These are issues that would only entertain* **policy wonks** (=people interested in details of government).

won't /woʊnt/ *v.* the short form of "will not": *I won't eat my peas.*

wont[1] /wɔnt, woʊnt/ *adj.* LITERARY **sb is wont to do sth** used to say that someone usually does something: *She called me by my full name – William Bryce – as she was wont to do when she was really angry.*

wont[2] *n.* LITERARY **as is sb's wont** used to say that it is someone's habit to do something: *As was his wont, Churchill drank scotch with water, but no ice.*

wont·ed /'wɔntɪd/ *adj.* [only before noun] LITERARY usual

woo /wu/ *v.* [T] **1** to try to persuade someone to buy something from you, do something for you, work for you etc.: *Colleges have been aggressively wooing the top African-American and Hispanic students.* **2** OLD-FASHIONED to try to persuade a woman to love you and marry you —**wooer** *n.* [C]

wood /wʊd/ *n.* **1** [C,U] the material that trees are made of: *I'm going out to get some wood for the fire.* | *The blocks are made of wood.* | **soft/hard wood** *All of the furniture here is made from carefully selected hard woods.* —see also WOODEN **2 the woods** [plural] an area of land covered with trees: *We went for a walk in the woods after lunch.* **3** [singular] POETIC a small area of land covered with trees **4 not be out of the woods yet** INFORMAL used to say that there are likely to be more difficulties before things improve:

It looks like we might make a profit, but we're not out of the woods yet. **5** [C] one of a set of four GOLF CLUBS with wooden heads

Wood /wʊd/, **Grant** /grænt/ (1892–1942) a U.S. PAINTER

wood al·co·hol /'.. '.../ *n.* [U] METHANOL: see METHANOL

wood·block /'wʊdblɑk/ *n.* [C] **1** a piece of wood with a shape cut on it, used for printing **2** a block of wood used in making a floor

wood·carv·ing /'wʊd,kɑrvɪŋ/ *n.* [C,U] the process of shaping wood with special tools, or a piece of art produced in this way

wood·chuck /'wʊdtʃʌk/ *n.* [C] a GROUNDHOG

wood·craft /'wʊdkræft/ *n.* [U] the practical knowledge of woods and forests

wood·cut /'wʊdkʌt/ *n.* [C] **1** a picture that you make by pressing a shaped piece of wood covered with a coloring substance onto paper **2** a WOODBLOCK (1)

wood·cut·ter /'wʊd,kʌtə/ *n.* [C] LITERARY someone whose job is to cut down trees in a forest

wood·ed /'wʊdɪd/ *adj.* covered with trees: *densely wooded hills*

wood·en /'wʊdn/ *adj.* **1** made of wood: *a wooden box* **2** not showing enough expression, emotion, or movement, especially when speaking or performing in public: *Dr. Harvey usually seems very wooden during his lectures.* —**woodenly** *adv.* —**woodenness** *n.* [U]

wooden·head·ed /,.. '...' / *adj.* INFORMAL stupid and slow to understand things

wooden spoon /,.. './ *n.* [C] a large spoon made of wood that is used in cooking —see picture at SPOON[1]

wood·land /'wʊdlənd, -lænd/ *n.* [U] also **woodlands** [plural] land that is covered with trees —see also GRASSLAND, WETLAND

wood·peck·er /'wʊd,pɛkə/ *n.* [C] a bird with a long beak that it uses to make holes in trees

wood·pile /'wʊdpaɪl/ *n.* [C] a pile of wood to be burned in a fire

wood pulp /'. ./ *n.* [U] wood crushed into a soft mass, used for making paper

wood·shed /'wʊdʃɛd/ *n.* [C] a place for storing wood that is to be used for burning

woods·man /'wʊdzmən/ *n. plural* **woodsmen** /-mən/ [C] someone who knows a lot about the woods, especially about living in the woods

woods·y /'wʊdzi/ *adj.* INFORMAL **1** having a lot of trees: *a woodsy subdivision* **2** relating to the woods: *The sauce gives the beef a woodsy taste.*

wood·wind /'wʊd,wɪnd/ also **the woodwinds** *n.* [C,U] the group of musical instruments that you play by blowing and pressing KEYS[1] (3) —**woodwind** *adj.*

wood·work /'wʊdwək/ *n.* [U] **1** the parts of a house or room that are made of wood: *The interior woodwork had been stripped bare.* **2 come/crawl out of the woodwork** if someone or something, often someone you do not like, comes out of the woodwork, they suddenly appear where you have not noticed or seen them before: *After winning the Oscar he was quoted as saying, "All the bad producers crawl out of the woodwork and send you their terrible scripts."* **3 fade/blend into the woodwork** if someone fades or blends into the woodwork, people do not notice them anymore: *The skipper turned out to be a quiet figure intent on blending into the woodwork.* **4** also **wood·working** the skill or activity of making wooden objects

wood·worm /'wʊdwəm/ *n.* [C] **1** a small insect that makes holes in wood **2** [U] the damage that is caused to wood by this creature

wood·y[1] /'wʊdi/ *adj.* **1** a plant that is woody has a stem like wood **2** feeling, smelling, looking etc. like wood

woody[2] *n.* [singular] HUMOROUS, SLANG an ERECTION (1)

woof[1] /wʊf/ *interjection* a word used for describing the sound a dog makes —**woof** *v.* [I] INFORMAL

woof[2] /wʊf, wuf/ *n.* [C] WEFT

woof·er /'wʊfə/ *n.* [C] a LOUDSPEAKER that produces deep sounds —compare TWEETER

W

wool /wʊl/ n. [U] **1** the soft thick hair that sheep and some goats have on their body **2** material made from wool: *Is this coat wool?* | **a wool jacket/carpet/blanket** etc. *a pure wool skirt* **3** thread made from wool, used for KNITting clothes **4 pull the wool over sb's eyes** to deceive someone by not telling the truth —see also DYED-IN-THE-WOOL, STEEL WOOL

wool·en, woollen /ˈwʊlən/ adj. [only before noun] made of wool: *woolen mittens*

wool·ens, woollens /ˈwʊlənz/ n. [plural] clothes made from wool, especially wool that has been KNITted

Woolf /wʊlf/, **Vir·gin·ia** /vəˈdʒɪnyə/ (1882–1941) a British writer

wool·len /ˈwʊlən/ adj. the British and Canadian spelling of WOOLEN

woolly, wooly /ˈwʊli/ adj. feeling or looking like wool: *He had gray, woolly hair.* —see also **wild and woolly** (WILD¹ (14))

woolly-head·ed also **woolly-mind·ed** /ˌ.. ˈ..ˌ/ adj. not able to think clearly, or not showing clear thinking: *woolly-headed ideals*

Wool·worth /ˈwʊlwəθ/, **Frank** (1852–1919) a U.S. businessman who started the F.W. Woolworth Company, opening many stores in the U.S. and other countries and selling goods for five or ten cents

woo·zy /ˈwuzi/ adj. INFORMAL feeling weak and unsteady; DIZZY: *When I stood up, I felt a little woozy.*

wop /wɑp/ n. [C] TABOO an Italian person. Do not use this word.

word¹ /wəd/ n.

1 language [C] the smallest unit of language that people can understand if it is said or written on its own: *In 500 words or less, write down why you want the scholarship.* | *I don't know all the words to the song.* | *In your own words, tell us what the novel is about.* | *The German word for poison is "Gift."*

2 word for word a) in exactly the same words: *The newspaper printed his speech more or less word for word.* **b)** also **word by word** if you translate a piece of writing from a foreign language word for word, you translate the meaning of each single word rather than the meaning of a whole phrase or sentence

3 news [singular,U] a piece of news or a message: *There's been no word from Susan since July.* | *Word has it that* (=people are saying that) *Judy's going to be promoted soon.* | *Word has already gotten out* (=people have heard) *about the factory closures.* | **send/bring word** (=send or bring a message) | **spread/pass the word** (=tell other people the news)

4 in other words used to introduce a simpler explanation or description of something you have said: *"Well, Randy's not quite ready to make a decision yet." "So, in other words, we have to wait, right?"*

5 not believe/hear/understand a word used to emphasize that you do not believe, cannot hear etc. what someone says or writes: *Don't believe a word he says.* | *I can't hear a word you're saying.*

6 not say/breathe a word INFORMAL to not say anything about something to anyone because it is a secret: *Don't worry, I won't say a word about it.*

7 have a word (with sb) to talk to someone privately and quickly, especially because you are angry with them: *Could I have a word with you after the meeting?*

8 a word of advice/warning etc. also **a few words of advice/warning** etc. a short talk for a particular purpose: *I tried to give her a few words of encouragement before she went on stage, but it all sounded wrong.*

9 take my word for it SPOKEN used to say that someone should accept what you say as true: *Take my word for it – she's really funny.*

10 promise **my/his/your** etc. **word** a sincere promise: *I gave her my word* (=promised her) *that I wouldn't tell anyone.* | *Be careful, Curt often doesn't keep his word* (=do what he has promised). | *Jack's as good as his word* (=does exactly what he has

promised to do). | **a man of his word/a woman of her word** (=a man or woman who does what they have promised to do)

11 take sb at their word to believe what someone has said, even though it is possible that they do not mean it: *I said, "Come and visit me sometime," and I guess she took me at my word.*

12 exchange words (with sb) a) also **have words (with sb)** an expression meaning "to argue with someone," used when you want to avoid saying this directly: *The two of them had words during the party.* **b)** usually **exchange a few words** to talk to someone for a short time: *The captain came into the cabin and exchanged a few words with the crew.*

13 the last/final word a) the power to decide whether or how to do something: *The final word rests with the board.* | **have the last/final word** *My boss has the final word on hiring staff.* **b)** the last statement or speech in a discussion or argument: **have the last/final word** *I'm not going to let you have the final word this time.*

14 an order [C usually singular] an order to do something: *On the word "go" I want you to start running.* | *Unless he gives the word, his generals will not act.*

15 put in a (good) word for sb to praise someone or suggest them for a particular job: *I'll put in a good word for you with the management.*

16 not get a word in edgewise/edgeways INFORMAL to not get a chance to speak: *Once Terry starts talking, it's difficult to get a word in edgeways.*

17 in so many words in a clear direct way: *In so many words, she told me that I don't have any talent.* | *"Did he say we got the contract?" "Not in so many words."*

18 in a word used to introduce and emphasize a very simple answer or explanation: *The band were, in a word, sloppy.* | *"Did you have a good vacation?" "In a word, no."*

19 from the word go INFORMAL from the beginning: *We've been best friends from the word go.*

20 find the words to choose the words that express your feelings or ideas clearly: *Barstow couldn't find the words to describe how she felt.*

21 take the words (right) out of sb's mouth if someone takes the words out of your mouth, they have just said what you were going to say

22 put words into sb's mouth to suggest falsely that someone has said a particular thing: *Stop putting words into my mouth – I never said I disliked the job.*

23 by word of mouth if information or news comes to you by word of mouth, someone tells you instead of you reading about it or seeing an advertisement: *At first, people learn about the band by word of mouth.*

24 the Word (of God) the religious teachings in the Bible

25 never have a good word to say about sb to never praise someone, even if they do something well

26 sth is the last word in comfort/luxury/elegance etc. used to say that something is the most comfortable, LUXURIOUS etc. thing of its type: *Her clothes were always the last word in modesty.*

27 sth is too stupid/funny/ridiculous etc. **for words** INFORMAL used to say that something is very stupid, funny etc.

28 word! SLANG used to say that you understand or agree with what someone has just said

29 tired/angry/happy etc. **isn't the word for it** used to say you are extremely tired, angry etc.

30 words fail me used to say that you are so surprised, angry, or shocked that you do not know what to say

31 (Upon) my word! OLD-FASHIONED, SPOKEN used to say you are very surprised because something unusual has happened —see also **eat your words** (EAT (3)), FOUR-LETTER WORD, **(you) mark my words!** (MARK¹ (11)), **not mince words** (MINCE (2)), **a play on words** (PLAY² (8)), **say the word** (SAY¹ (31))

word² v. [T] to use words that are carefully chosen in order to express something: *Let me word the question a little differently.*

word·ed /ˈwɔ·dɪd/ *adj.* **carefully/clearly/strongly** etc. **worded** using words that express an idea carefully, clearly etc.: *In a strongly worded statement, the group threatened to sue the newspaper.*

word·ing /ˈwɔ·dɪŋ/ *n.* [U] the words and phrases used to express something: *I'm not happy with the wording of the article.*

word·less /ˈwɔ·dlɪs/ *adj.* without words; silent *They stood there in wordless amazement.*

word-play /ˈ. ./ *n.* [U] making jokes by using words in a clever way

word pro·cess·or /ˈ. ˌ.../ *n.* [C] a computer PROGRAM or a small computer that you use for writing letters, reports etc. —**word processing** *n.* [U]

word·smith /ˈwɔ·dsmɪθ/ *n.* [C] someone who is very skillful at using language —**wordsmith** *v.* [I,T] —**wordsmithing** *n.* [U]

Words·worth /ˈwɔ·dzwɔ·θ/, **William** (1770–1850) a British Romantic poet whose poems are mainly about the beauty of nature

word·y /ˈwɔ·di/ *adj.* using too many formal words: *a wordy explanation* —**wordily** *adv.* —**wordiness** *n.* [U]

wore /wɔr/ the past tense of WEAR¹

s w
1 1

work¹ /wɔ·k/ *v.*

1 [do a job your are paid for] [I] to do a job that you are paid for: *Frank's been working here for 32 years.* | [+ for] *I think Linda works for a law firm.* | **work as a secretary/builder** etc. *She works as a management consultant for a design company.*

2 [do things at a job] [I,T] to do the activities and duties that are part of your job: *I have to work on Saturday too.* | [+ with] *Jerry will be working with me on the project.* | **work weekends/nights/days** etc. *Dave often works long hours.* | *I'm tired of working ten-hour days.*

3 [activity] [I] to do an activity which needs time and effort, especially one that you want to do or that needs to be done: *Sue's been working all week to get the house clean for our guests.* | [+ on] *Peter's in the kitchen working on his model airplanes.* | [+ at] *I need to work at shooting the ball.*

4 [try to achieve sth] [I] to try continuously and patiently to achieve a particular thing [+ for] *Trainor spent a lifetime working for equal rights.* | [**work to do sth**] *We worked hard to persuade the French to attend the meeting.* | *They have worked tirelessly* (=worked hard) *to make living conditions better.*

5 [study] [I] to study a subject by reading books, doing exercises etc., especially in college: *You've worked really hard this semester.*

6 [machine/equipment] [I] if a machine or piece of equipment works, it does what it is supposed to do: *Does the TV work?* | *The repairman finally got the heater working* (=made it work) *again.*

7 [method/plan etc.] [I] if a method, plan, or system works, it produces the results you want: *The crime-prevention law sounds good, but will it work?* | *Surgery usually works well in correcting conditions like this.*

8 [art/literature] [I] if a painting, movie, piece of writing etc. works, it is successful because it has the effect on you that the painter, writer etc. intended: *The contrast between the two characters works well in the movie.*

9 [have an effect] [I always + adv./prep.] if something such as a fact, situation, or system works in particular way, it has a particular effect on someone or something: *Your experience in doing this kind of job should work in your favor* (=help you be successful). | *Tax laws tend to work against* (=make things difficult for) *small businesses.*

10 **work your way over/out/back etc.** **a)** if you work your way somewhere, you go there slowly and with great effort: *It took us three hours to work our way back to the parking lot.* **b)** to use a lot of effort during a long period of time to become successful: *He started in the mailroom and worked his way to the top of the company.*

11 **work your way through school/college** to do a job while you are in college because you need the money to help pay for it: *Galman worked her way through college as a waitress.*

12 [machine/equipment] [T] to make a complicated machine or piece of equipment do what it is supposed to do: *I have no idea how to work these new phones.*

13 **work your butt/tail/ass off** to work very hard: *I've been working my butt off since I walked in the door.*

14 **work it/things so that...** to make arrangements for something to happen, especially by acting in a clever or skillful way: *We tried to work it so that we could all go together.*

15 **(sth) works for me/her/him** etc. used to say that something is acceptable to someone: *"Do you want to meet at 8:00?" "Works for me."*

16 **work it!** SLANG used to encourage someone to dance or move with a lot of energy: *Get out there on the floor and work it, girl!*

17 [move into a place/position] [I always + adv./prep., T always + adv./prep.] to move into a particular state or position very gradually, either in a series of small movements or after a long time: *It'll take some time to work the door frame back into place.* | *Somehow the bolt had worked its way loose.*

18 [area] [T] to travel around a particular area as part of your job, especially in order to sell something: *Markowitz works the Tri-State area.*

19 [use a material/substance] [I] to use a particular material or substance in order to make something such as a picture, design, jewelry etc.: [+ in/with] *I prefer to work in watercolors.*

20 [cut/shape sth] [T] if you work a material such as metal, leather, or clay, you cut, sew, or shape it in order to make something

21 **work sb (hard)** [T] to make someone use a lot of time or effort when doing a job or activity: *The coach has been working us really hard this week.*

22 [part of your body] **a)** [T] if you work a muscle or part of your body, you do an exercise to make it stronger **b)** [I,T] if a part of your body works or you work it, it moves with a lot of effort: *Robert worked his face into something like a smile.*

23 [mind/brain] [I] if your mind or brain is working, you are thinking or trying to solve a problem: *I could see Brian's brain start working overtime* (=thinking very hard) *as soon as I mentioned the deal.*

24 **work like magic** also **work like a charm** if a plan, method, or trick works like magic or like a charm, it happens in exactly the way you planned it to happen

25 **work wonders (on/with sth)** to be effective in dealing with a difficult problem or situation in a way that surprises you: *This herbal tea works wonders on headaches.*

26 **work yourself into a frenzy/rage etc.** to make yourself become very excited, angry etc.: *Jay usually works himself into a frenzy over deadlines.*

27 **work your fingers to the bone** INFORMAL to work very hard

28 **work the door** to take tickets from people as they enter a theater, club, etc.

29 [calculate] [T] to calculate the answer to a mathematical problem

30 [land/soil] [T] if you work the land or the soil, you do all the work necessary to grow crops on it

31 [mine] [T] to remove a substance such as coal, gold etc. from under the ground

work in *phr. v.* **1** [T **work** sth ↔ **in**] to include something you want to say or do while you are doing or saying something else: *Nowadays they're very clever about working in advertisements in movies.* | [**work sth into sth**] *The minister will try and work a visit to hospital into his schedule.* **2** [T **work** sb **in**] SPOKEN to arrange meet someone even though you are very busy: *My schedule's pretty full, but I think I can work you in at 4 p.m.* **3** [T **work** sth ↔ **in**] to add

W

one substance to another and mix them together in a very thorough way: [**work sth into sth**] *Work the butter into the flour with your fingers.*

work off *phr. v.* **1** [T **work** sth ↔ **off**] to try to get rid of a feeling such as anger, disappointment, or embarrassment, especially by not being nice to other people or by behaving violently: *Jogging helps me work off frustration from work.* **2** [T **work off** sth] to pay for something you have done wrong or for something you have broken by doing a job for free: *He's working off the window he broke by mowing my lawn.*

work on *phr. v.* **1** [T **work on** sth] to spend time making, improving, or repairing something: *As a team, we still need to work on free throws.* **2** [T **work on** sb] INFORMAL to try continuously to influence someone or persuade them to do something: [**work on sb to do sth**] *She still working on me to take her to the opera.*

work out *phr. v.*
1 plan [T **work** sth ↔ **out**] to think carefully about how you are going to do something and plan a good way of doing it: *Have you worked out the schedule for next month?* | **work out what/where/how** etc. *She's still trying to work out how we'll pay for a new car.* | *It sounds like you have it all worked out* (=have already planned how you are going to do something).
2 calculate [T **work** sth ↔ **out**] to calculate an answer, amount, price, or value: *I still have to work out a budget for next year.* | **work out how much/many** etc. *We'll have to work out how much food we'll need for the party.*
3 get better [I,T **work** sth **out**] if a problem or complicated situation works out, it gradually gets better or gets solved: *It's too bad that the deal didn't work out.* | *The situation should work itself out* (=become better without any help).
4 happen [I] if a situation works out in a particular way, it happens in that way: *Things didn't work out like we'd planned.* | **work out well/badly** *I hope your new job works out well.*
5 understand [T **work** sth ↔ **out**] to think about something and manage to understand it: *It took me a while to work out their relationship with each other.* | [**work sth out for yourself**] *I can't tell you what happened – work it out for yourself.*
6 cost sth **works out to/at** sth if something works out to a particular amount, you calculate that it costs that amount: *Your total works out to $32.50.*
7 exercise [I] to make your body healthy and strong, especially by doing a program of exercises: *How often do you work out?*
8 be worked out if a mine is worked out, all the coal, gold etc. has been removed from it

work sb **over** *phr. v.* [T] INFORMAL to hit someone hard and repeatedly all over their body: *They really worked him over.*

work up *phr. v.* **1 work up enthusiasm/interest/courage etc.** to become enthusiastic, interested etc., or to make others feel this way: *It's been difficult to work up any public interest in the project.* **2 work up an appetite/thirst/sweat** to become hungry, THIRSTY etc., especially by doing physical exercise: *There's nothing like skiing to work up an appetite.* **3** [T **work** sb ↔ **up**] to make someone very angry, excited, or upset about something: *He has a gift for working up the crowd with his speeches.* | [**work yourself up**] *You don't have to work yourself up over this.* —see also WORKED UP **4** [T **work** sth ↔ **up**] to develop and improve something such as a piece of writing: *I'd like for you to work up a detailed summary of our meeting.*

work up to sth *phr. v.* [T] to gradually prepare yourself to do something difficult: *I'm working up to running two miles a day.*

work with sb *phr. v.* [T] to do a job that involves trying to help a group of people with a particular problem: *Larry works with the poor to help them get jobs.* —see Usage Note at JOB

1 [U] a job you are paid to do or an activity that you do regularly to earn money: *We usually start work at 8 o'clock.* | *How do you like your work?* | *There isn't a lot of work at this time of the year.* | *Jean's been out of work* (=has not had a job) *for six months.* | *I'm sure you'll find work soon.* | *Anne left college a year ago and she's still looking for work.* | *I'll meet you after work* (=at the end of a day of work) *at Purdy's.* | *In my line of work* (=the kind of work I do), *you tend to meet all kinds of interesting people.* | *Walter returned to work* (=started work again) *two months after the accident.*
2 place [U] a place where you do your job, which is not your home: *Could I ride with you to work tomorrow?* | *I usually leave work around 5 p.m.* | *She's still at work. I'll ask her to call you when she gets home.*
3 duties [U] the duties and activities that are part of your job: *What kind of work are you looking for?* | *A large part of the work we do involves using computers.* | **secretarial/legal etc. work** *Lately I've been doing a lot of volunteer work* (=work that you do for free).
4 result [U] something that you produce as a result of doing your job or doing an activity: *We're very pleased with the work you've done so far.* | *This report really is an excellent piece of work.*
5 useful activity [U] the act of doing something that needs to be done or that you want to do, or the time and effort needed to do it: *I can see you've done a lot of work in the garden.* | *It's time for everyone to get down to work* (=start doing work).
6 study [U] study or RESEARCH, especially for a particular purpose: [+ **on/in**] *In 1867, Hauron published a work on color photography.* | *Markowitz did his postgraduate work in Sociology.*
7 book/painting/music [C] something such as a book, play, painting, or piece of music produced by a writer, painter, or musician: *The museum is full of Picasso's works.*
8 at work a) doing your job or a particular activity: *Danger! Men at work.* **b)** having a particular influence or effect: *It's great seeing his diplomatic skills at work.*
9 nice/good work SPOKEN used to praise someone for doing something well: *Nice work! The project looks good.*
10 sth is in the works INFORMAL used to say that something is being planned, developed etc.: *A surprise birthday party for Matt is in the works.*
11 the (whole) works SPOKEN used when you are buying something that has many parts or choices, to choose everything that is available: *I'd like a hot dog with ketchup, onions … the works.*
12 you have your work cut out (for you) INFORMAL used to say that it will be very difficult for you to do something: *Payne has his work cut out for him in turning the business around.*
13 it's all in a day's work SPOKEN used to say that you do not mind doing something even though it will give you more work than usual.
14 work clothes/boots etc. work clothes, boots are designed for people to work in, rather than to look attractive
15 work practices/conditions the ways of working or the conditions in which people in a particular company work, including safety, health, rights, and duties: *Work conditions at construction sites need to be safer.*
16 work hours the time you spend working at your job
17 iron/gas/cement etc. works a building or group of buildings where a particular type of goods are produced in large quantities or where an industrial process happens: *The brick works closed last year.* —see also PUBLIC WORKS
18 machine **the works** the moving parts of a machine
19 force [U] TECHNICAL force multiplied by distance —see also **do sb's dirty work** (DIRTY¹ (7)), **make short work of sth** (SHORT¹ (15)), WORKING²

work·a·ble /ˈwɔːkəbəl/ *adj.* **1** a workable system, idea etc. can be used in a practical and effective way:

a workable and safe solution **2** a substance that is workable can be shaped with your hands: *workable clay*

work·a·day /'wəkə,deɪ/ *adj.* [only before noun] ordinary and not interesting: *Terry deals with the workaday details of running a store.*

work·a·hol·ic /,wəkə'hɒlɪk/ *n.* [C] INFORMAL someone who is always working, and does not have time for anything else

work·bench /'wəkbentʃ/ *n.* [C] a strong table with a hard surface for working on things with tools

work·book /'wəkbʊk/ *n.* [C] a school book containing questions and exercises

work·day /'wəkdeɪ/ *n. plural* **workdays** [C] **1** the amount of time that you spend working in a day: *a 10-hour workday* **2** a day when people usually work, especially one that is not a holiday, Saturday, or Sunday: *It'll take four workdays to process the application.*

worked up /,. '. / *adj.* [not before noun] **be/get worked up** INFORMAL very upset or excited about something: *Why are you so worked up? It's not that important.* | [+ about/over] *You're getting all worked up over nothing.* —see also **work up** (WORK¹)

work·er /'wəkə/ *n.* [C] **1** one of the people who works for an organization, business etc. and is below the level of a manager: **a factory/farm/office etc. worker** (=someone who works in a factory, on a farm etc.) | **a skilled/unskilled worker** (=someone who has or does not have special skills) **2 rescue/campaign etc. worker** someone who works to achieve a particular purpose: *Three civil rights workers were taken into the Mississippi forest and murdered.* **3** someone who works very well or quickly: *We need more workers around here.* | **a good/hard/quick etc. worker** *Mike's always been a hard worker.* **4 the workers** people who belong to the WORKING CLASS: *the workers' revolution* —see also SOCIAL WORKER

workers' com·pen·sa·tion /,.. ..'.. / also **worker's comp** /,.. '. / SPOKEN *n.* [U] money that a company must pay to a worker who is injured or becomes sick as a result of their job

work eth·ic /'. ,.. / *n.* [singular,U] a belief in working hard, or the willingness to work hard: *Employers are looking to hire people with a good work ethic.*

work ex·pe·ri·ence /'. .,... / *n.* the experience you have had of working in a particular type of job: *She's well qualified but has no relevant work experience.*

work·fare /'wəkfɛr/ *n.* [U] a system that makes it necessary for unemployed people to work before they are given money for food, rent etc. by the government —compare WELFARE

work·force /'wəkfɔrs/ *n.* [singular] all the people who work in a particular country, industry, or factory: *a workforce of 3500 employees*

work haz·ard /'. ,.. / *n.* [C] something that could be dangerous to people who work in a particular place

work·horse /'wəkhɔrs/ *n.* [C] **1** someone who does most of the work, especially when it is hard or boring: *Cunningham is the team's defensive workhorse.* **2** a machine or vehicle that can be used to do a lot of work: *The Boeing 707 used to be the workhorse of air travel.*

work·house /'wəkhaʊs/ *n.* [C] a building in the past where poor people were sent to live because they could not pay their debts

work·ing¹ /'wəkɪŋ/ *adj.* [only before noun]
1 having a job **a)** having a job that you are paid for: *a working mother* **b)** having a job that needs physical ability rather than INTELLECTUAL ability: *an ordinary working man*
2 working practices/conditions the ways of working or the conditions in which people in a particular company work, including safety, health, rights, and duties: *The factory is being investigated for illegal working practices.*
3 working hours the period of time during the day when you are doing your job
4 a working knowledge of sth enough knowledge of a system, foreign language etc. to be able to use it,

although your knowledge is limited: *Andy has a good working knowledge of accounting practices.*
5 a working relationship the relationship between people or groups who work together, especially people who work well together: *We developed a working relationship with the university's engineering department.* | **a strong/good/close working relationship** *McCurry said that the White House had a good working relationship with the Senate committee.*
6 be in working order to be working correctly and not broken: **be in good/perfect working order** *My typewriter is still in good working order.*
7 a working definition/theory a definition or theory that is not complete in every detail, but is good enough for you to use when you are studying something or starting a job
8 a working breakfast/lunch/dinner etc. a breakfast, lunch etc. which is also a business meeting
9 a working model a model that has parts that move
10 working parts the parts of a machine that move and operate the machine

working² *n.* **1** [singular] also **workings** the way something such as a system, piece of equipment, or organization works: [+ of] *Grigg's book gives us insight into the workings of the Pentagon.* | *Her skills were essential to the smooth working of the business.* **2** [C usually plural] a mine or part of a mine where soil has been dug out in order to remove metals or stone

working cap·i·tal /,.. '... / *n.* [U] the money that is available to be used for the costs of a business —see also VENTURE CAPITAL

working class /'.. ,. / *n.* **the working class** the group of people in society who traditionally do physical work and do not have much money or power —**working-class** *adj.*: *a working-class neighborhood* —compare LOWER CLASS, MIDDLE CLASS, UPPER CLASS

working day /'.. ,. / *n.* [C] a WORKDAY

working girl /'.. ,. / *n.* [C] OLD-FASHIONED **1** a word for a woman who has sex for money, used when you want to avoid saying this directly **2** a young woman who has a paid job

working group /'.. ,. / *n.* [C] a committee that is established to examine a particular situation or problem and suggest ways of dealing with it

working life /'.. ,. / *n.* [C] the part of your adult life when you work: *McKenzie has spent most of her working life at the FBI.*

working pap·ers /'.. ,.. / *n.* [plural] an official document that you need in the U.S. in order to get a job if you are young or were born in a different country

working par·ty /'.. ,.. / *n.* [C] a WORKING GROUP

working poor /,.. '. / *n.* **the working poor** [plural] the people who have jobs, but barely earn enough money to live on

working stiff /,.. '. / *n.* [C] INFORMAL an ordinary person who works in order to earn enough money to live and usually has a boring job

work·load /'wəkloʊd/ *n.* [C] the amount of work that a person or machine is expected to do: *We hired another secretary to handle the increased workload.*

work·man /'wəkmən/ *n. plural* **workmen** /-mən/ [C] someone who does physical work such as building, repairing things etc.

work·man·like /'wəkmən,laɪk/ *adj.* done or made skillfully, but often in an uninteresting way: *a workmanlike campaign*

work·man·ship /'wəkmən,ʃɪp/ *n.* [U] skill in making things, especially in a way that makes them look good

workmen's com·pen·sa·tion /,.. ..'.. / also **workmen's comp** /,.. '. / *n.* [U] WORKERS' COMPENSATION

work of art /,.. '. / *n. plural* **works of art** [C] **1** a painting, SCULPTURE etc. of very high quality **2** HUMOROUS something that is very attractive and skillfully made: *His stomach muscles are a work of art.*

work·out /'wɜːk-aʊt/ *n.* [C] a period of physical exercise, especially as training for a sport —see also **work out** (WORK¹)

work per·mit /'. ˌ../ *n.* [C] an official document from a foreign government that gives you permission to work in that country

work·place /'wɜːkpleɪs/ *n.* [C] the room, building etc. where you work: *How do you keep your personal problems out of the workplace?*

work re·lease /'. ˌ./ *n.* [U] a situation in which a prisoner is allowed to work outside of prison: *Hudson now is* **on work release** *six days a week.*

work·room /'wɜːkrum/ *n.* [C] a room that you work in, especially where you make things

work·sheet /'wɜːkʃit/ *n.* [C] a piece of paper with questions, exercises etc. for students

s w
2
work·shop /'wɜːkʃɑp/ *n.* [C] **1** a room or building where tools and machines are used for making or repairing things **2** a meeting at which people try to improve their skills by discussing their experiences and doing practical exercises: *a theater workshop for high school students*

work·site /'wɜːksaɪt/ *n.* [C] a place where people work, especially outside

work·sta·tion /'wɜːkˌsteɪʃən/ *n.* [C] the part of an office where you work, where your desk, computer etc. are

work-stud·y /'. ˌ../ *n.* [U] work that a student does on a college or university CAMPUS in order to earn money to pay for their education

work·up /'wɜːkʌp/ *n.* [C] a series of tests used to find out if someone is physically or mentally healthy: *a full medical workup*

work·week /'wɜːkwik/ *n.* [C] the total amount of time that you spend working during a week: *a 40-hour workweek*

s w
1 1
world¹ /wɜːld/ *n.*

1 our planet/all people **the world** the PLANET we live on, and all the people, cities, and countries on it; EARTH: *the world's oldest tree* | *At that time China was the most powerful country* **in the world**. | *People from* **all over the world** *want to learn English.*

2 society [singular] the society that we live in and the kind of life we have: *We thought we could change the world then.* | *Parents want a better world for their children.*

3 **in the world** used to emphasize a statement you are making: *I felt like the luckiest guy in the world.* | *Nothing* **in the world** *can make up for the loss of a mother.* | **what/who/where/how etc. in the world...?** *What in the world are you talking about?*

4 area of activity/work [C usually singular] a particular area of activity or work, and the people who are involved in it: *the fast-paced business world* | [+ **of**] *the world of fashion*

5 group of countries [singular] a particular group of countries or part of the world: *the Western world* | *Our public schools are among the worst in the developed world.* —see also THIRD WORLD

6 period in history [singular] a particular period in history and the society and people of that time: *the world of the Anglo-Saxons* | *Heron's book was widely copied in the ancient world.*

7 **the animal/plant/insect world** animals, plants etc. considered as a group of living things with their own particular way of living or behaving

8 type of place/situation [C usually singular] a particular type of place or situation: [+ **of**] *Truong found himself living in a world of poverty and uncertainty.*

9 sb's life [C] the life a particular person or group of people lives, especially the things they do and the people they know: *Alvin's world was full of dance and music.*

10 **the world over** in every country or area of the world; EVERYWHERE: *Fireflies have delighted people the world over for thousands of years.*

11 place like the earth [C] a PLANET in another part of the universe where other things may live: *strange creatures from another world*

12 **a world of sb's own** also **sb's own (little) world** INFORMAL a situation or way of thinking in which someone does not seem to notice what is happening around them and is more concerned with their own thoughts: *I tried to talk to Ed about it, but he was off in his own little world.*

13 **do sb a world of good** INFORMAL to make someone feel much better: *A week by the ocean will do you a world of good.*

14 **a world of difference** a very large difference between two things: *There's a world of difference between owning a gun and using it.*

15 **be worlds apart** also **be a world apart** people, opinions, or situations that are worlds apart are so completely different that there is almost nothing about them that is similar: [+ **from**] *Nicholson is worlds apart from the old director.*

16 **give the world sth** to produce or invent something that affects many people: *Walton is the man who gave the world linoleum.*

17 **be out of this world** INFORMAL something that is out of this world is so good, enjoyable etc., it is unlike anything else you have ever experienced: *The apple fritters were out of this world.*

18 **not for the world** if someone would not do a particular thing for the world, they would never do it whatever happened: *I wouldn't hurt Amy for the world.*

19 **think (that) the world owes you a living** INFORMAL to be unwilling to work in order to get things, and expect them to be provided for you

20 **a man/woman of the world** someone who has had many experiences, knows how to behave, and is not easily shocked

21 **come into the/this world** LITERARY to be born

22 **depart/leave this world** LITERARY to die

23 **the Fidel Castros/John Lennons etc. of this world** SPOKEN used when making a general remark about a particular kind of person: *The Einsteins and Edisons of this world, the late developers, need encouragement.*

24 **for all the world like...** also **for all the world as if...** LITERARY exactly like, or exactly as if: *The man looked and sounded for all the world like Elvis Presley.*

25 **for (all) the world to see** also **for the whole world to see** available for everyone to see or know: *Nixon's failings were finally exposed for all the world to see.*

26 **the world is sb's oyster** used to tell someone that there is no limit to the opportunities that they have: *If you've got a good education, the world is your oyster.*

27 not religious **the world** the way of life most people live, rather than a SPIRITUAL way of life: *John renounced the world when he became a monk.*

28 **workers/women/people etc. of the world** used when talking to all workers, women etc. in a speech, book etc.

29 **the world to come** also **the next world** LITERARY the place where people's souls are believed to go after they die —see also NEW WORLD, OLD WORLD —see Usage Note at EARTH

world² *adj.* [only before noun] existing in, involving, or affecting the whole world: *The Denver Broncos have won the world championship.* | *The present conflict is a threat to world peace.*

world beat /'. ./ *n.* [U] WORLD MUSIC

world-beat·er /'. ˌ../ *n.* [C] someone or something that is the best at a particular activity: *UCLA's football team looks like a world-beater this season.* —**world-beating** *adj.*

world-class /ˌ. '.ˌ/ *adj.* among the best in the world: *a world-class orchestra*

world-fa·mous /ˌ. '.ˌ/ *adj.* known about by people all over the world: *a world-famous gymnast*

World Health Or·gan·i·za·tion, the /ˌ. '. ...ˌ../ an international organization that is part of the UN and helps countries to improve their people's health by giving medicines and providing information

world·ly /'wɜːldli/ *adj.* [only before noun] **1** sb's **worldly goods/possessions** the things that someone

W

owns: *A nearby shopping cart holds all of his worldly possessions.* **2** having a lot of experience and knowledge about people and life: *Marilyn is a worldly New Yorker in her 60s.* **3** relating to ordinary daily life, rather than SPIRITUAL or religious ideas: *Members of the church tried to isolate themselves from worldly influences.* —**worldliness** n. [U]

worldly-wise /'.. ,./ adj. having a lot of experience and knowledge about life so that you are not easily shocked or deceived

world mu·sic /,. '../ n. [U] a type of music that combines traditional styles of music from around the world with modern popular styles

world pow·er /,. '../ n. [C] a country that has a lot of power and influence in many parts of the world

world rec·ord /,. '../ n. [C] the fastest speed, longest distance, highest or lowest level etc. that has ever been achieved or reached in the world, especially in sports: *Reynolds is the former world record holder in the 400 meters.* —**world-record** adj. [only before noun] *a world-record time*

World Se·ries /,. '../ n. the World Series the last series of baseball games that is played each year in order to decide the best professional team in the U.S. and Canada

World Trade Or·gan·i·za·tion, the /,. '. . .,./ an international organization that deals with the rules of trade between different nations and encourages them to trade fairly

world·view, world view /,wəld'vyu/ n. [C usually singular] the way in which someone understands the world, which includes their beliefs and attitudes

World War I /,wəld wɔr 'wʌn/ also **the First World War** (1914–1918) a war fought in Europe between France, the U.K. and its EMPIRE, Russia, and the U.S. on one side (known together as "the Allies"), and Germany, Austria-Hungary, and Turkey on the other side.

World War II /,wəld wɔr 'tu/ also **the Second World War** (1939–1945) a war involving almost every major country in the world. On one side were the Allies (including the U.K., France, and Poland, and after 1941 the U.S. and the Soviet Union) and on the other side the Axis (including Germany, Japan, and Italy).

world-wear·y /'. ,../ adj. feeling that life is not interesting or exciting anymore: *world-weary soldiers*

world·wide /,wəld'waid◂/ adj., adv. everywhere in the world: *a worldwide economic crisis* | *Many credit cards can be used worldwide.*

World Wide Web /,. ,. './ written abbreviation **WWW** n. the WEB (1)

worm¹ /wəm/ n. **1** [C] a long thin creature with no bones and no legs, especially one that lives in soil **2** [C] INFORMAL someone who you do not like or respect **3 worms** [plural] PARASITES (=small creatures that eat your food or your blood) that live in a person's or animal's body: *The vet said Ginger has worms.* **4** the worm turns LITERARY used to say that someone who is normally quiet and OBEDIENT has changed and has become strong and active —see also **a (whole) can of worms** (CAN² (5))

worm² v. [T] **1 worm your way into sb's life/heart/confidence etc.** to gradually make someone love or trust you, especially by being dishonest: *Once again, Liz wormed her way into the Brady family's affections.* **2 worm your way out of (doing) sth** to avoid doing something that you have been asked to do by making an excuse that is dishonest: *Somehow Ben wormed his way out of mowing the lawn.* **3 worm your way into/through etc.** to move through a small place or a crowd slowly, carefully, or with difficulty: *Rescue workers wormed their way down the mine shaft.* **4** to give an animal medicine in order to remove PARASITES that live inside it

worm sth out of sb phr. v. [T] to get information from someone who does not want to give it: *I hoped that Faustino wouldn't worm my new address out of my friends.*

worm-eat·en /'. ,../ adj. **1** worm-eaten wood or fruit has holes in it because it has been eaten by worms **2** old and damaged

worm·hole /'wəmhoul/ n. [C] a hole in a piece of wood etc. made by a type of WORM

worm·wood /'wəmwud/ n. [U] a plant with a bitter taste, used in making some types of alcohol

worm·y /'wəmi/ adj. full of worms: *a wormy apple*

worn¹ /wɔrn/ the past participle of WEAR

worn² adj. **1** a worn object is old and damaged: *Paula handed me several worn dollar bills.* **2** someone who looks worn seems tired: *Lying on the hospital bed, Pete looked worn and fragile.*

worn out, worn-out /,. '.◂/ adj. **1** very tired because you have been working hard: *I'm worn out.* **2** too old or damaged to be used: *an old, worn-out pair of pants*

wor·ried /'wəid, 'wʌrid/ adj. **1** unhappy because you keep thinking about a problem, or are anxious about something: *What's wrong? You look worried.* | [+ about] *You shouldn't be so worried about your weight.* | [worried (that)] *Dana's worried that we'll be late again.* | **a worried expression/look/frown etc.** *"I think he's in trouble," she said in a worried voice.* | *When you didn't call, I started getting worried.* | *Where on earth have you been? I was worried sick (=extremely worried)!* **2 you had me worried** SPOKEN used to say that someone made you feel confused or anxious because you did not correctly understand what they said, or did not realize that is was a joke: *You really had me worried – I thought you didn't like the present.* —**worriedly** adv. —see Usage Note at NERVOUS

wor·ri·er /'wəiə/ n. [C] someone who often worries about things: *Stop being such a worrier.*

wor·ri·some /'wəisəm/ adj. FORMAL making you anxious: *The political situation in the region is particularly worrisome.*

wor·ry¹ /'wəi, 'wʌri/ v. worries, worried, worrying **1** be anxious [I] to be anxious or unhappy about something so that you think about it a lot: [+ about] *Fran worries too much about the way she looks.* | [+ over] *Dad worries over the slightest thing.* | [worry (that)] *All of us worry that the office will close next year.* **2 don't worry** SPOKEN **a)** used when you are trying to make someone feel less anxious: *Don't worry; I'll lend you money if you need it.* **b)** used to tell someone that they do not need to do something: *Don't worry – I'll do the laundry this time.* | [+ about] *Don't worry about filing those invoices right now.* **3** make sb anxious [T] to make someone feel anxious about something: *The rise in housing costs worries most young families.* | [worry sb that] *It worries me that Christina hasn't found a job yet.* | *You shouldn't worry yourself so much – everything will be fine.* **4 (there is) nothing to worry about** SPOKEN used to tell someone that something is not as serious or difficult as they think: *There's nothing to worry about – I made all the reservations.* **5 have enough to worry about** SPOKEN used to say that someone already has a lot of problems or is very busy: *Stop arguing with me – I have enough to worry about.* **6** annoy [T] OLD-FASHIONED to annoy someone: **worry sb with sth** *Stop worrying your grandfather with all those questions.*

worry² n. plural **worries 1** [C] a problem that you are anxious about or are not sure how to deal with: *financial worries* | [+ about] *Doctors still have a few worries about the effectiveness of the treatment.* | [+ to/for] *Money was always a big worry for us.* | *Not having money for a car was the least of his worries* (=used to say that he had more important things to worry about). **2** [U] the feeling of being anxious about something: *We were all sick with worry when we heard about the accident.*

worry beads /'.. ,./ n. [plural] small stones or wooden balls on a string that you move and turn in order to keep yourself calm

W

wor·ry·ing /ˈwɔ-i-ɪŋ/ *adj.* making you feel anxious: *a worrying rise in crime* | **a worrying time/week/year etc.** *The dry weather has made this a worrying year for many farmers.*

wor·ry·wart /ˈwɔi,wɔrt/ *n.* [C] SPOKEN someone who worries all the time about everything

S W
1
3

worse¹ /wɔ˞s/ *adj.* **1** [the comparative of bad] not as good as someone or something else, or more unpleasant or of a lower standard: *The damage to the house is worse than I expected.* | *Catalog sales were much worse than last year.* | *Their relationship has gotten worse in the last few months.* | **make matters/things/it worse** *I tried to help, but I think I made things worse.* —opposite BETTER¹ **2** sicker than before or in a condition that is not as good as before: *If the symptoms get worse, take two of these tablets.* | *My knee feels worse than it did yesterday.* **3 worse off a)** having less money than before or than someone else; poorer: *There are many families worse off than we are.* **b)** in a worse situation than before or than someone else: *Without Bryant playing quarterback, the team is worse off.* **4 it/things could be worse** SPOKEN used to say that a bad situation is not as bad as it could be: *Things could be worse – at least you're not living on the street.* **5 there's nothing worse than...** SPOKEN used to say that you are very annoyed at something bad that often happens: *There's nothing worse than getting stuck in traffic downtown.* **6 sb can/could do worse than do sth** SPOKEN used to say that you think it is a good idea if someone does a particular thing: *Young film directors could do worse than study Morris' films.* —see also **go from bad to worse** (BAD¹ (22))

> **USAGE NOTE: WORSE**
>
> **GRAMMAR: worse, worst**
> **More** and **most** are not used together with **worse** or **worst**: *Math is my worst subject* (NOT *"my most worse/most worst subject"*). | *The situation is much worse than it was last week* (NOT *"much more worse"*). Some people think that **worse** should not be used as an adverb meaning "in a worse way." However, many people use it this way in spoken English: *I hope the team doesn't play any worse next week.*

worse² *n.* **1** [U] something that is not as good as something else: *This movie was bad, but I've seen worse.* **2 if worse comes to worst** also **if worst comes to worst** if the situation develops in the worst possible way: *If worse comes to worst, I can always get my old job back.* **3 take a turn for the worse** to change and become worse: *Stock prices have taken a turn for the worse.* **4 the worse for (the) wear** INFORMAL in poor condition, or very tired: *After celebrating, some of the players were a little worse for the wear.* | *Apparently none the worse for wear* (=still in good condition), *Young returned to practice Wednesday.* —compare BETTER³ —see also **none the worse/better etc.** (NONE² (1))

S W
2

worse³ *adv.* [comparative of badly] **1** in a more severe or serious way than before: *My foot hurts even worse today.* **2** to a lower standard or quality, or less successfully: *No one sings worse than I do.*

wors·en /ˈwɔ˞sən/ *v.* [I,T] to become worse or make something worse: *Relations between the two countries have steadily worsened.* | *worsening economic conditions*

wor·ship¹ /ˈwɔ˞ʃɪp/ *v.* **worshiped, worshiping** also **worshipped, worshipping 1** [I,T] to show respect and love for God or a god, especially by praying in a church, TEMPLE etc. **2** [T] to admire and love someone very much: *Kevin practically worships his older brother.* **3 worship the ground sb walks on** to admire or love someone so much that you cannot see their faults —**worshiper, worshipper** *n.* [C]

worship² *n.* [U] **1** the activity of praying and singing etc. in order to show respect and love for God or a god: **a house/place of worship** (=a church, temple etc.) **2** a strong feeling of respect and love

for God or a god: *Helping the poor is a form of true worship to God.* **3** a strong feeling of love or admiration for someone or something, especially so that you cannot see their faults —see also HERO WORSHIP

wor·ship·ful /ˈwɔ˞ʃɪpfəl/ *adj.* LITERARY showing respect or admiration for God, admiration for, or something

worst¹ /wɔ˞st/ *adj.* [the superlative of bad] **1** [only before noun] worse than anything else of the same kind or worse than at any time before: *I was always the worst student in the class.* | *This is the worst musical I've ever been to.* | *Mike's so boring, and worst of all he never stops talking.* **2 worst-case scenario** a description of the worst possible way a situation could develop: *Assuming a full house of 42,000 spectators, the worst-case scenario is that 75% would arrive by car.* **3 sb is his/her own worst enemy** used to say that someone's behavior is so stupid or thoughtless that it harms them or stops them from becoming successful —see Usage Note at WORSE¹

S W
2 2

worst² *n.* **1 the worst** the person, thing, situation, state, part etc. that is worse than all others of the same kind or worse than at any time before: *Most of the girls were pretty mean, but Sabrina was the worst.* | *As for the storm,* **the worst of it** (=the worst part of it) *is over.* | **expect/fear the worst** (=expect the situation to have the worst possible result) **2 at (the) worst** if things are as bad as they can be: *Many drivers feel their job is unpleasant at best, and dangerous at worst.* **3 at sb's/sth's worst** as bad as someone or something can be: *You haven't seen Tina at her worst.* **4 if worst comes to worst** —see WORSE² (2) **5 let sb/sth do their worst** used to say that you are not worried by the power of someone or something to harm you: *Let summer heat and humidity do their worst while the TV networks try to lure us indoors.*

worst³ *adv.* [the superlative of badly] most badly: *It was the worst written book I've ever read.* | *Chris is the worst-dressed man in the office.*

worst·ed¹ /ˈwʊstɪd, ˈwɔ˞s-/ *adj.* worsted wool is made from long FIBERS twisted together

worsted² *n.* [U] a type of wool cloth

worth¹ /wɔ˞θ/ *prep.* **1 be worth** to have a value in money: *How much is the ring worth?* | **sth is worth $10/$50 etc.** *The vase is worth $3500.* | *My stamp collection is definitely* **worth a lot.** | *If the dolls are not in their original package, they're* **not worth anything.** | *Haring's paintings are now* **worth a fortune** (=extremely valuable). **2 be worth millions/billions** also **be worth a fortune** INFORMAL to be extremely rich: *Jenkins is a venture capitalist worth billions.* **3 sth is worth doing/reading/finding etc.** to be something that will be useful and helpful if you do, read etc. something: *It's the only TV show worth watching.* | *It's well worth getting there an hour early, if you want a good seat.* **4 it's worth sth** used to say that someone should give the time or money needed to do something, because they will gain something useful: **it's worth your time/effort** *It's worth your effort to climb the stairs to the top of the overlook.* | *Let a lawyer look at the contract first –* **it's worth it.** **5 sth is worth your while** used to say that you should give the time or money needed to do something, because you will gain something useful: *Taking a computer class would be* **well worth your while.** | *It's* **worth your while to** *go and ask the teacher for help.*

S W
1
2

> **SPOKEN PHRASES**
>
> **6 for what it's worth** used to say that you are not sure of the value or usefulness of what you are saying: *For what it's worth, I think you did a fine job.* **7 make it worth sb's while** to offer someone money or something if they agree to do something for you, especially something dishonest: *I'll make sure they approve your application if you make it* **worth my while.** **8 sb can't do sth worth a damn/darn** used to say that someone is not able to do something well at all: *I can't spell worth a darn.* **9 not be worth a damn/darn** to not have even a little value: *None of Ed's ideas are worth a damn.*

W

10 worth his/her salt doing their job well or deserving respect: *A cop worth his salt wouldn't take a bribe.* **11 for all sb is worth** with as much effort as possible: *Tom pulled at the rope for all he was worth.* **12 be worth its/his/her weight in gold** to be very useful or valuable: *A good employee like Meg Jones is worth her weight in gold.*

USAGE NOTE: WORTH

WORD CHOICE: worth, value
Worth as a noun means the same as **value**, but **worth** sounds old-fashioned or literary: *the value of life* (NOT "the *worth* of life"). In an old story you might read: *a pearl of great worth.*

---

worth² *n.* **1** [U] value and importance, or value in money: *What's the current worth of the company?* | [+ of] *I spent about $5 worth of quarters playing video games.* | *Scaife's net worth* (=amount of money and property he owns) *was estimated at $800 million.* **2 ten minutes'/a week's etc. worth of sth** something that takes ten minutes or a week to happen, do, or use: *The batteries have an hour's worth of energy left in them.* | *There's about a week's worth of work left.*

worth·less /ˈwɚθlɪs/ *adj.* **1** having no value, importance, or use: *a completely worthless exercise* **2** a worthless person has no good qualities or useful skills —**worthlessly** *adv.* —**worthlessness** *n.* [U]

worth·while /ˌwɚθˈwaɪl/ *adj.* something worthwhile deserves the time, effort, or money you give to it: *Programs like this one get kids involved in worthwhile activities.*

wor·thy¹ /ˈwɚði/ *adj.* **worthier, worthiest 1 be worthy of (sb's) admiration/contempt etc.** to deserve to be thought about or treated in a particular way: [+ of] *Jenny's proposal is certainly worthy of consideration.* **2** FORMAL a worthy person, plan etc. deserves respect or admiration because they have good qualities: *a worthy opponent* **3** having many good qualities, but not very interesting or exciting: *Brodkey's book is worthy bedtime reading.* **4 I'm/We're not worthy!** SPOKEN, HUMOROUS used to say that you consider it a great honor to be with someone because they are much more famous, TALENTED etc. than you are, and you are feeling very strong emotions because of this

worthy² *n. plural* **worthies** [C usually plural] FORMAL someone who is important and should be respected: *Rutledge definitely has a place among other American worthies.*

Wo·tan /ˈvoʊtɑn/ the German name for the Norse god Odin

would /wəd, əd, d; *strong* wʊd/ *modal verb negative short form* **wouldn't 1** used instead of "will" to describe what someone has said, asked etc.: *Andy said he would give me a ride home.* **2** used in CONDITIONAL sentences that use past tense verbs, especially in order to show what is likely or possible: *Dad would be really mad if he knew we borrowed his car.* **3** used to describe what someone used to do a lot or what used to happen a lot: *We would often go for long walks in the park.* **4 would rather** used to say that you would prefer to do or have one thing rather than another thing: *I would rather stay home tonight.* **5 would you...?** **a)** used to express a polite request: *Would you shut the window, please?* **b)** used to express a polite offer or invitation: *Would you like to stay and watch a movie?* **6** used to show disapproval when talking about someone's annoying habits or behavior: *You would go and spoil it, you jerk!* **7 I would...** SPOKEN used to tell someone what you think they should do in a particular situation: *I would apologize immediately.* **8** used before verbs that express what you think, feel, or suppose, to make your opinion or feeling less definite: *The total cost, I would guess, might be $100 per person.* **9 would that...** LITERARY used to express a strong wish or desire: *Would that we had seen her before she died.*

would-be /ˈ. ./ *adj.* **a would-be actor/thief etc.** someone who hopes to have a particular job or intends to do a particular thing

---

would·n't /ˈwʊdnt/ *v.* the short form of "would not": *He wouldn't say what was wrong.*

wouldst /wʊdst/ OLD USE the second person singular of "would"

would've /ˈwʊdəv/ *v.* the short form of "would have": *I would've helped you if I'd known.*

wound¹ /waʊnd/ the past tense and past participle of WIND²

wound² /wund/ *n.* [C] **1** an injury, especially a cut or hole made in your skin by a weapon such as a knife or a bullet: *gunshot wounds* | *The security guard was lucky that it was only a flesh wound* (=slight injury to the skin). —see Usage Note at DAMAGE¹ **2** a feeling of emotional or mental pain that you get when someone says or does something that is not nice to you: *The war left many veterans with deep emotional wounds.* —see also **lick your wounds** (LICK¹ (5)), **open old wounds** (OPEN² (21)), **rub salt into a wound** (RUB¹ (8))

wound³ /wund/ *v.* [T] **1** to injure someone, especially by making a cut or hole in their skin using a knife, gun etc.: *Police managed to wound one of the hijackers.* | **be fatally/mortally wounded** (=to be wounded so badly that you will die) **2** to make someone feel unhappy or upset: *a wounding remark*

wound·ed /ˈwundɪd/ *adj.* **1** injured by a weapon such as a gun or knife: *a wounded soldier* **2** very upset because of something that someone has said or done: *wounded pride* **3 the wounded** people who have been injured, especially in a war

Wound·ed Knee, the Battle of /ˌwundɪd ˈni/ the last important battle between the U.S. army and the Native Americans, which took place at Wounded Knee Creek in South Dakota in 1890. U.S. soldiers killed almost 200 Sioux people, including women and children.

wound up /ˌwaʊnd ˈʌp/ *adj.* [not before noun] anxious, worried, or excited: *I was too wound up to sleep.*

wove /woʊv/ the past tense of WEAVE¹

wo·ven /ˈwoʊvən/ the past participle of WEAVE¹

wow¹ /waʊ/ *interjection* INFORMAL used when you think something is impressive or surprising: *Wow! That's a great car!*

wow² *v.* [T] INFORMAL to make people admire you very much: *After 17 years, the band continues to wow audiences.*

WP the abbreviation of WORD PROCESSOR

wpm /ˌdʌbəlju pi ˈɛm/ the abbreviation of "words per minute"

wrack /ræk/ *v.* **1 be wracked by/with sth a)** to make someone suffer great mental or physical pain: *Spencer was wracked by guilt for having left his wife.* —see also NERVE-RACKING **b)** to suffer with a particular problem: *This part of the world is continually wracked by terrorism and violence.* **2** another spelling of RACK²

wraith /reɪθ/ *n.* [C] LITERARY a GHOST, especially of someone who has just died

Wrang·ell, Mount /ˈræŋɡəl/ a high mountain that is one of the Wrangell Mountains in southern Alaska

Wrangell Moun·tains /ˈ.. ˌ../ a RANGE of mountains in southern Alaska

wran·gle¹ /ˈræŋɡəl/ *n.* [C] a long and complicated argument: *wrangles over the budget*

wrangle² *v.* **1** [I] to argue with someone angrily for a long time **2** [T] to gather together cows or horses from a large area

wran·gler /ˈræŋɡlɚ/ *n.* [C] INFORMAL a COWBOY

wrap¹ /ræp/ *v.* **wrapped, wrapping** [T] **1** to wind or fold cloth, paper etc. around something: **[wrap sth around sth/sb]** *Rita wrapped the scarf around her neck.* | **[wrap sth/sb in sth]** *Wrap these plates in newspaper and put them in the box.* **2** if you wrap your arms, legs, fingers etc. around something, you use them to hold it: **[wrap sth around sb/sth]** *David wrapped his arms lovingly around Meg and* *gave her a kiss.* —see also **twist/wrap sb around your little finger** (FINGER¹ (9))

wrap up *phr. v.* **1** [T **wrap** sth ↔ **up**] to completely cover something by folding paper, cloth etc. around it: *We need to wrap the presents up before Neil comes.* **2** [T **wrap** sth ↔ **up**] to finish or complete a job, meeting etc.: *Both companies hope to wrap up the deal by Friday.* **3** [I] to put on warm clothes: **wrap up warm/well** *Make sure you wrap up warm – it's freezing outside.* **4 be wrapped up in your children/work etc.** to give so much of your attention to your children, your work etc. that you do not have time for anything else

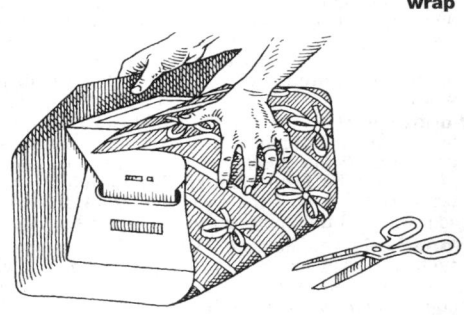

wrap

She wrapped the present.

wrap² *n.* **1** [U] thin transparent plastic used to cover food **2** [C] a piece of cloth that you wear around your shoulders to keep you warm: *The women wore evening gowns and light summer wraps.* **3 keep sth under wraps** to keep something secret **4** [C] a type of SANDWICH made with thin bread which is rolled around meat, vegetables etc. **5** [singular] the end of a day's filming: *OK everybody, it's a wrap!*

wrap·a·round /'ræpə,raʊnd/ *adj.* **1 wraparound skirt/ sunglasses etc.** a wraparound skirt, sunglasses etc. fit closely around your body, head etc. **2 wraparound deck/porch** a PLATFORM built onto more than one side of a house, where you can sit and relax outside

wrap·per /'ræpɚ/ *n.* [C] the piece of paper or plastic that covers something when it is sold: *a candy wrapper*

wrap·ping /'ræpɪŋ/ *n.* [C,U] cloth, paper, or plastic that is wrapped around something to protect it

wrapping pa·per /'.. ,../ *n.* [U] colored paper that you use for wrapping presents

wrap-up /'. ./ *n.* [C usually singular] INFORMAL a short report at the end of something, giving the main points again: *Now on to Dan O'Brien with a wrap-up of today's NFL games.*

wrath /ræθ/ *n.* [U] FORMAL extreme anger: *the king's wrath* —**wrathful** *adj.* —**wrathfully** *adv.*

wreak /rik/ *v. past tense and past participle* **wreaked** also **wrought wreak havoc/revenge/damage etc.** to cause a lot of damage, problems, and suffering: *Hurricane Mitch wreaked havoc along the eastern coast.*

wreath /riθ/ *n.* [C] **1** a circle made from leaves or flowers that you hang on your door at Christmas or put on a grave **2** a circle made from leaves that was given to someone in past times for them to wear on their head as an honor

wreathe /rið/ *v.* LITERARY **1 be wreathed in sth** to be surrounded by or covered in something: *Lydia's face appeared to be wreathed in curls.* **2 be wreathed in smiles** to look very happy: *The next day, Emily came to work wreathed in smiles.*

wreck¹ /rɛk/ *v.* [T] **1** to completely spoil or destroy something such as a plan, relationship, or opportunity: *The two years in prison wrecked Jarvis' marriage.* **2** to damage something so badly that it

cannot be repaired: *The bank robbers wrecked Stan's car trying to get away from police.*

wreck² *n.* [C] **1** something such as a car, ship, or airplane that has been damaged very badly, especially in an accident: *Investigators are searching the wreck for clues as to why the plane crashed.* **2** [usually singular] INFORMAL someone who is very nervous, tired, or unhealthy: *Mom looked like a complete wreck after the wedding.* | *I was a **nervous wreck** waiting for you to call.* **3** an accident involving cars or other vehicles: *Ten people were injured in the wreck.* **4** INFORMAL something, especially a car, that is in a very bad condition: *It's embarrassing to be seen driving that old wreck.*

wreck·age /'rɛkɪdʒ/ *n.* [U] **1** the parts of something such as an airplane, ship, or building that are left after it has been destroyed in an accident: *Crews have worked all week clearing away the wreckage.* **2** the destruction of someone's relationships, hopes, plans etc.

wreck·er /'rɛkɚ/ *n.* [C] **1** a vehicle used to move damaged cars or other vehicles **2** someone who destroys a relationship, plan, opportunity etc.: *a **home wrecker** (=someone who destroys someone else's marriage)*

wrecking ball /'.. ,./ *n.* [C] a heavy metal ball attached to a chain or CABLE which is used to knock down buildings or other structures

wrecking crew /'.. ,./ *n.* [C] a group of people whose job is to tear down buildings or other structures

wrecking yard /'.. ,./ *n.* [C] a place where pieces of destroyed buildings, cars etc. are brought

wren /rɛn/ *n.* [C] a very small brown bird

Wren /rɛn/**, Christopher** (1632–1723) a British architect

wrench¹ /rɛntʃ/ *v.* **1** [T always + adv./prep.] to use your strength to pull yourself away from someone who is holding you: [**wrench yourself away/free etc.**] *He tried to grab one of Lorna's arms, but she wrenched herself away.* **2** [T always + adv./prep.] LITERARY to take someone away from somewhere without their permission: *In 1943, the army wrenched the boy's father from him.* **3** [T] to twist a joint in your body suddenly and painfully: *Brian wrenched his back trying to carry a heavy box.* **4** [I,T always + adv./prep.] to twist and pull something from its position using force, or to be moved in this way: *The boat wrenched and banked severely to the right.* | [**wrench sth away/free/off etc.**] *Flood waters even wrenched houses off their foundations.*

wrench² *n.* **1** [C] **a)** a metal tool with a round end that fits over and turns NUTS (2) and BOLTS **b)** also **monkey wrench** a tool that you can use to hold or turn NUTS (2) and BOLTS of different sizes —see picture at TOOL¹ **2 throw a (monkey) wrench in sth** to do something that will cause problems or spoil what someone else is planning **3** [singular] a strong feeling of sadness or other strong emotion: *As she told me the bad news, I felt a wrench in my stomach.* **4** [C usually singular] a twisting movement that pulls something violently: *One wrench of your back could cause permanent damage.*

wrench·ing /'rɛntʃɪŋ/ *adj.* a wrenching situation, story, movie etc. is extremely difficult to deal with because it makes you feel strong emotions: *a wrenching drama* | **gut-wrenching/heart-wrenching** *It was a gut-wrenching decision to leave college.*

wrest /rɛst/ *v.* [T always + adv./prep.] FORMAL **1** to take power or influence away from someone, especially when this is difficult: *The Democrats failed in wresting control of Congress from the Republicans.* **2** to pull something away from someone violently: *A security guard managed to wrest the gun from the man.*

wres·tle /'rɛsəl/ *v.* [I,T] **1** to fight someone by holding onto them and pulling or pushing them: [+ **with**] *You boys stop wrestling with each other!* | *The attacker was **wrestled to the ground** (=pushed down to the ground and held) by three men.* **2** to have difficulty controlling or holding something that is very large, heavy, or difficult to use: [+ **with**] *Several passengers were wrestling with their luggage.*

W

wrestle with sth *phr. v.* [T] to try to deal with or find a solution to a difficult problem: *The city council has been wrestling with the housing issue for almost a year.*

wres·tler /ˈrɛslə/ *n.* [C] someone who wrestles as a sport

wres·tling /ˈrɛslɪŋ/ *n.* [U] a sport in which two people fight by holding onto and pushing each other and trying to make each other fall to the ground: *a wrestling match* —compare PROFESSIONAL WRESTLING

wretch /rɛtʃ/ *n.* [C] **1** someone you are annoyed or angry with: *That miserable little wretch would lie to anyone.* **2** someone you feel sorry for: *What would happen to this poor wretch when we let her go?* **3** LITERARY an evil person

wretch·ed /ˈrɛtʃɪd/ *adj.* LITERARY **1** extremely bad or of very poor quality: *wretched poverty* | *the wretched state of American television* **2** very unhappy or sick: *a lonely and wretched old man* **3 wretched excess** behavior that people think is too extreme and immoral, especially because it involves activities such as spending a lot of money, drinking alcohol, having sex etc.: *Many residents were suffering from the wretched excesses of New Year's Eve parties.* —**wretchedly** *adv.* —**wretchedness** *n.* [U]

wrig·gle /ˈrɪgəl/ *v.* **1** [I] to twist from side to side with small quick movements: [+ **under/through/into** etc.] *I forgot my key, so I wriggled in through an open window.* | *The worm wriggled off my hook.* **2** [T] to make part of your body move this way: *He wriggled his fingers in his pockets.* —**wriggly** *adj.*

wriggle out of sth *phr. v.* [T] to avoid doing something by making excuses: *Once again, Douglas wriggled out of making a final decision.*

-wright /raɪt/ *suffix* [in nouns] someone who makes a particular thing: *a playwright* (=someone who writes plays) | *a wheelwright* (=someone who makes wheels)

Wright /raɪt/, **Frank Lloyd** /fræŋk lɔɪd/ (1869–1959) a U.S. ARCHITECT, generally regarded as one of the most important architects of the 20th century

Wright, Richard (1908–1960) an African-American writer of NOVELS

Wright Broth·ers, the /ˈ. ˌ../ two U.S. brothers, Orville Wright (1871–1948) and Wilbur Wright (1867–1912), who built and flew the world's first plane in 1903 —see picture on page 1329

Wrig·ley /ˈrɪgli/, **William** (1861–1932) a U.S. businessman who made CHEWING GUM and started the Wrigley company

wring /rɪŋ/ *v. past tense and past participle* **wrung** [T] **1** also **wring out** to tightly twist a wet cloth or wet clothes in order to force out the water: *Sally wrung out the socks and hung them on the towel rack.* **2 wring your hands** to rub and twist your hands together because you are worried and upset: *"I don't know what else to do," Dan said, wringing his hands.* —see also HAND-WRINGING **3 I'll wring sb's neck** SPOKEN said when you want to punish someone because they did something that has made you angry: *When Dean gets home, I'm going to wring his neck.* **4 wring sth's neck** to kill something such as a chicken by twisting its neck

wring sth ↔ **out** *phr. v.* [T] to succeed in getting or achieving something, when this seems almost impossible or there seems to be nothing left: *Video stores hope to wring a few more dollars out of these titles by selling them.* —see also WRUNG-OUT

wring·er /ˈrɪŋə/ *n.* [C] **1 go through the wringer** also **put sb through the wringer** INFORMAL to have a difficult, upsetting experience, or to make someone have a difficult experience: *His ex-wife really put Barry through the wringer.* **2** a machine with two ROLLERS that press the water from washed clothes when you turn a handle

wring·ing /ˈrɪŋɪŋ/ *adj.* **wringing wet** extremely wet: *Your clothes are wringing wet.*

wrin·kle¹ /ˈrɪŋkəl/ *n.* [C] **1** a line on your face or skin that you get when you are old **2** a small messy fold in a piece of clothing or paper: *My skirt's full of wrinkles.* **3 iron out the wrinkles (in sth)** to solve the small problems in something —**wrinkly** *adj.*

wrinkle² *v.* **1** [I,T] if you wrinkle a piece of clothing or if it wrinkles, it gets small messy folds in it: *My blue jacket wrinkles too easily.* **2 wrinkle your nose/eyes/brow etc.** to move part of your face so that there are wrinkles on or around it

wrin·kled /ˈrɪŋkəld/ *adj.* skin, cloth, or paper that is wrinkled has lines or small folds in it

wrist /rɪst/ *n.* [C] **1** the joint between your hand and the lower part of your arm —see picture at BODY **2 it's all in the wrist** SPOKEN, HUMOROUS used as a reply to someone who has praised you for something that you did skillfully with your hands

wrist·band /ˈrɪstbænd/ *n.* [C] **1** a band worn around your wrist to keep your hand dry, especially when you are playing sports **2** a band worn around your wrist, for example in a hospital —compare BRACELET

wrist·watch /ˈrɪstwɑtʃ/ *n.* [C] a watch that you wear on your wrist

writ¹ /rɪt/ *n.* [C] a document from a court that orders someone to do or not to do something —see also HOLY WRIT

writ² *adj.* **writ large** [only after noun] FORMAL in a clear and strong form: *Anderson views the United Nations as a democracy writ large.*

write /raɪt/ *v. past tense* **wrote** *past participle* **written** **1 book/article etc. a)** [I,T] to produce a new book, poem song etc.: *The book was written by Daniel Defoe.* | [+ **about**] *Your assignment is to write about your summer vacation.* | **well/badly written** *It's very well written play.* **b)** [I] to be a writer of books, plays, articles etc., especially as a job: *"How long have you been writing?" "About six years."* | [+ **on**] *LeBrun often writes on women's issues.* **2 letter** [I,T] to write a letter to someone: [**write** sb] *Chris hasn't written me for a long time.* | [+ **to**] *I'm going to write to the manager about this.* | [**write that**] *Uncle Brian wrote that he'll come visit on the 26th.* | **write sb a letter/card/postcard etc.** *I wrote Sheila several letters, but she didn't reply.* **3 words a)** [I,T] to form letters or numbers with a pen or pencil: *I learned to write when I was in first grade.* | *The menu is written on a board behind the counter.* **b)** [I] if a pen or pencil writes, it works correctly: *Which one of these pens still writes?* **4 check/document etc.** [T] also **write** sth ↔ **out** to write information on a check, form etc.: *I don't have any cash – could I write you a check?* **5 have sth written all over your face** also **be written all over your face** to show very clearly what you are feeling or thinking: *He had guilt written all over his face.* | *I know you're lying, Tyrell – it's written all over your stupid face.* **6 nothing to write home about** INFORMAL not especially good or special: *Jim and Marcia's new house is nothing to write home about.* **7 sb wrote the book on sth** SPOKEN used to say that someone knows a lot about a subject: *Cheryl wrote the book on being irresponsible.* **8 (that's) all she wrote** SPOKEN used to say that something is completely finished

write away for sth *phr. v.* [T] to write to a company for something that has been advertised: *In sixth grade, Len secretly wrote away for a special diet he'd seen in some magazine.*

write back *phr. v.* [I,T **write** sb **back**] to answer someone's letter by sending them a letter: *I hope she writes back soon.*

write sth ↔ **down** *phr. v.* [T] to write information, ideas etc. on a piece of paper in order to remember them: *Next time, write the message down before you forget.* | *Did you write down his number?*

write in *phr. v.* **1** [I] to write to an organization asking them for information or giving an opinion: *Many viewers wrote in to complain about the show.* **2** [T **write** sb ↔ **in**] to add someone's name to your BALLOT in order to vote for them, when they are not on the official list of CANDIDATEs in a particular election —see also WRITE-IN

write sth **into** sth *phr. v.* [T] to include something such as a rule or condition in a document, agreement etc.: *Time for training was written into the schedule.*

write off *phr. v.* **1** [T write sb/sth ↔ off] to decide that someone or something is useless, unimportant, or a failure: [+ as] *Most coaches wrote Nate off as being too short to play football.* **2** [T write sth ↔ off] to officially say that someone does not have to pay a debt, or to reduce the official value of something you own: *As part of the deal, all their debts were written off.* —see also WRITE-OFF **3** [I] to write to a company, school, organization etc. asking them to send you information about their products, programs etc.: [+ for] *I wrote off for some information about the college.*

write sb/sth ↔ **out** *phr. v.* [T] **1** to write a list, report etc. including all the necessary details: *Could you write out the procedures for ordering new equipment?* **2** to write information on a check or a form: *Write the check out for $235.* **3** to remove one of the characters from a regular television or radio program

write sth/sb ↔ **up** *phr. v.* [T] **1** to write a report, article etc. using notes that you made earlier: *McGraw went back to his office and immediately wrote up an agreement.* **2** [usually passive] to write your opinion about a new book, play, or product for a newspaper, magazine etc.: *Millie's Diner got written up in Details magazine and is now more famous than ever.* —see also WRITE-UP **3** to make an official written report of a crime or something wrong that someone has done: *My supervisor came and saw me smoking, so I got written up for that.*

write-in /'. ./ *n.* [C] a vote you give to someone by writing their name on your BALLOT

write-off /'. ./ *n.* [C] **1** an official agreement that someone does not have to pay a debt **2** an official reduction from an amount or from the value of something, especially used for calculating how much tax someone owes: *The President proposed a tax write-off of $1500 in college tuition expenses.*

writ·er /'raɪtə/ *n.* [C] someone who writes books, stories etc., especially as a job: *a science-fiction writer* | [+ on] *a well-known writer on religion* | [+ of] *a writer of romance novels*

writer's block /'.. ,./ *n.* [U] the problem that a writer sometimes has of not being able to think of new ideas

writer's cramp /'.. ,./ *n.* [U] a feeling of stiffness in your hand that you get after writing for a long time

write-up /'. ./ *n.* [C] a written opinion about a new book, play, or product in a newspaper, magazine etc.: *Morris' play got a really good write-up in the press.*

writhe /raɪð/ *v.* [I] **1** to twist your body from side to side violently, especially because you are suffering pain: **writhe in pain/agony** *One patient writhed in pain after being given a shot.* **2 writhe with anger/hate/shame etc.** LITERARY to feel anger, hate etc. in a very strong way

writ·ing /'raɪtɪŋ/ *n.* **1** [U] words that have been written or printed: *The writing on the label is too small for me to read.* **2 in writing** if you put something in writing, it is official proof of an agreement, promise etc.: **get/put sth in writing** *I want these guarantees put in writing.* **3** [U] books, poems etc. in general, especially those by a particular writer or about a particular subject: *Sherman produced his best writing back in the 1960s.* **4 writings** [plural] the books, stories etc. that a particular person has written: *Plato's writings* **5** [U] the activity of writing books, stories etc.: *In 1991, Richardson retired from politics and took up writing as a career.* **6** [U] the particular way that someone writes with a pen or pencil; HANDWRITING: *Your writing is very neat.* **7 the writing is on the wall** also **see/read the writing on the wall** used to say that it seems very likely that something will not exist much longer or that someone will fail: *The writing is on the wall for old manufacturing industries.*

writing desk /'.. ,./ *n.* [C] a desk with special places for pens, paper etc.

writing pa·per /'.. ,./ *n.* [U] good quality paper that you use for writing letters

writ·ten[1] /'rɪtⁿn/ the past participle of WRITE

written[2] *adj.* [only before noun] **1** recorded in writing: **a written agreement/reply etc.** *Along with your written request, send a check for $12 for postage and handling.* **2 a written test/exam** a test in which you have to write the answers **3 the written word** FORMAL writing as a way of expressing ideas, emotions etc., as opposed to speaking: *Millions of illiterate Americans do not have access to the written word.*

wrong[1] /rɒŋ/ *adj.*

1 not correct saying, believing, or depending on something that is not correct: *The schedule must be wrong.* | **be wrong to think/say** *I was wrong to think that I couldn't trust you.*

2 not the right one not the one that you intended or the one that you should use: *Myrna accidentally took the wrong medicine.* | *The letter was delivered to the wrong address.* | *No, there's no Bruce here – you have* **the wrong number** (=used to say that someone has telephoned the wrong person by mistake).

3 not appropriate not appropriate for a particular purpose, situation, or person: *These shoes are the wrong size.* | [+ for] *This is the wrong paint for the outside of the house.*

4 not moral not morally right or acceptable: *Mom always told us that stealing was wrong.* | [it is wrong (of sb) to do sth] *It was wrong of you to lie to Julia about your past.* | *It is wrong that people like Rick get promoted.* —opposite RIGHT[1] (10)

5 get on the wrong side of sb to do something that gives someone a bad opinion of you, so that they do not like or respect you in the future

6 get/be on the wrong side of the law to get into or be in trouble with the police

7 get off on the wrong foot to start a job, relationship etc. badly by making a mistake that annoys people

8 take sth the wrong way to be offended by a remark because you have understood it differently than someone meant it

9 be in the wrong place at the wrong time to get involved in trouble without intending to: *Kambule claims he was just a bystander when the shooting occurred, a kid in the wrong place at the wrong time.*

10 be on the wrong track to have the wrong idea about a situation so that you are unlikely to get the result you want

11 be from the wrong side of the tracks INFORMAL to be from a poor part of a city or a poor part of society

12 be on the wrong side of thirty/forty etc. HUMOROUS to be older than thirty etc.

SPOKEN PHRASES

13 what's wrong? a) used to ask someone what problem they have, why they are unhappy etc.: *What's wrong? You look so sad.* **b)** used to ask why something does not work: [+ with] *What's wrong with your car?* **c)** used to say that you think something is good, fair etc., and you do not understand why other people think it is not: [+ with] *What's wrong with wearing blue socks with a black suit?*

14 there's something wrong used to say that there is a fault or problem with something: *I think there's something wrong. My drink tastes funny.* | [+ with] *There's something wrong with the phone, the line's dead.* | *Dave has something wrong with his foot.*

15 there's nothing wrong a) used to say that something does not have any faults or problems: *Don't worry; there's nothing wrong.* | [+ with] *There's nothing wrong with your TV. The station had a power outage.* **b)** used to say that you do not think that something is bad or immoral: [+ with] *There's nothing wrong with making lots of money as long as you don't cheat people.*

16 correct me if I'm wrong, but... used as a polite way of saying that you think what you are going to say is correct: *Correct me if I'm wrong, but aren't you in charge of ordering supplies?*

W

USAGE NOTE: WRONG

COLLOCATION/GRAMMAR

Many meanings of **wrong** only belong in particular phrases or structures that cannot be changed. For example, if someone's health is bad, you can say something **is wrong with** them but NOT "They are wrong" (which means "not correct"). You can **do something wrong** (=not in the correct way) but NOT "do a wrong thing" (though you can **do the wrong thing**). If you **do something wrong,** that does not mean there is something **wrong with** you: *He was mad at me, but I hadn't done anything wrong.* Note the expression **there was nothing wrong with me** (=I was not sick or injured). **Wrong** used before a noun usually means "not correct," "not correctly chosen," or "not suitable": *the wrong answer/key/furniture.* You would also say: *I can't find what is wrong* (NOT "I can't find the wrong thing") if you mean that something is not working. **Wrong** also means "morally wrong," and is used in this way: *What you did was completely wrong* (NOT "You did wrong things/action"). Sometimes **bad** is a better word to use.

wrong² *adv.* **1** not in the correct way: *They spelled my name wrong on the envelope.* | *You idiot, Todd – you did it all wrong.* **2 go wrong a)** to make a mistake during a process so that you do not get the right result: *Follow these instructions and you won't go wrong* (=you are sure to succeed). **b)** to do something that makes a plan, relationship etc. fail: *As far the contract was concerned, I don't know where I went wrong.* **c)** to stop working correctly: [+ **with**] *Something's gone wrong with my watch.* **3 get sth wrong** to make a mistake in the way you write, judge, or understand something: *You must have gotten the directions wrong.* | **get/have it all wrong** (=understand a situation in completely the wrong way) **4 don't get me wrong** SPOKEN used when you think someone may understand your remarks in the wrong way, or be offended by them: *Don't get me wrong – I like Jenny, but she can be a little bossy.* **5 you can't go wrong (with sth)** SPOKEN used to say that a particular object or plan will always be appropriate, satisfactory, or work well: *You can't go wrong with a dark gray suit.*

wrong³ *n.* **1** [U] behavior that is not morally right: *Benjy's too young to know right from wrong.* **2** [C] an action, judgment, or situation that is unfair: *Punishment for the wrongs of the regime still needs to be addressed.* | *Lerner believes in the power of the press to help right society's wrongs* (=bring justice to an unfair situation). **3 sb can do no wrong** used to say that someone is considered perfect, especially when some people do not agree with this: *As far as Fanny was concerned, Nicky could do no wrong.* **4 be in the wrong** FORMAL to make a mistake or deserve the blame for something: *Hardin publicly admitted he had been in the wrong.* **5 do sb wrong** HUMOROUS to treat someone badly and unfairly: *Most of Peggy's songs are about men who've done her wrong.* **6 two wrongs don't make a right** SPOKEN used to say that doing something bad will not make another bad situation right or fair

wrong⁴ *v.* [T] FORMAL to treat or judge someone unfairly: *Both athletes felt they had been wronged by the committee's decision.*

wrong·do·er /'rɔŋ,duɚ/ *n.* someone who does something bad or illegal —**wrongdoing** *n.* [C,U]

wrong·ful /'rɔŋfəl/ *adj.* **1 wrongful arrest/termination/dismissal etc.** a wrongful arrest etc. is unfair or illegal because the person affected by it has done nothing wrong: *This law would protect employees against wrongful termination.* **2 wrongful death** LAW used in law to mean that someone's death was caused by someone else doing something illegal —**wrongfully** *adv.*

wrong·head·ed /,rɔŋ'hɛdɪd◂/ *adj.* DISAPPROVING based on or influenced by wrong ideas that you are not willing to change —**wrongheadedly** *adv.*

wrong·ly /'rɔŋli/ *adv.* **1** not correctly or in a way that is not based on facts: *Perrin had wrongly assumed that he would not get caught.* | *Matthew was wrongly diagnosed as having a brain tumor.* **2** in a way that is unfair or immoral: **wrongly accused/convicted/imprisoned etc.** *Franklin was wrongly accused of murdering a cop.* —see also **rightly or wrongly** (RIGHTLY (2))

wrote /rout/ the past tense of WRITE

wrought /rɔt/ **1** the past tense and past participle of WREAK **2** LITERARY OR OLD USE a past participle of WORK: *Robeson's voice was described as "the finest instrument wrought by Nature."*

wrought i·ron /,. '..◂/ *n.* [U] long thin pieces of iron formed into shapes to make gates, fences etc.

wrought-up /,. '.◂/ *adj.* very nervous and excited

wrung /rʌŋ/ the past tense and past participle of WRING

wrung-out /,. '.◂/ *adj.* INFORMAL feeling very weak and tired: *You'll be awfully wrung-out in the morning.*

wry /raɪ/ *adj.* [only before noun] showing in a humorous way that you are not pleased with something: *a wry smile* —**wryly** *adv.*

wt. the written abbreviation of "weight"

WTO —see WORLD TRADE ORGANIZATION, THE

wun·der·kind /'vʊndɚ,kɪnt, 'wʌndɚ,kɪnd/ *n.* [C] a young person who is very successful

wurst /wɚst/ *n.* [U] a type of SAUSAGE

wuss /wʊs/ *n.* [C] SPOKEN someone who you think is weak or lacks courage

WV a written abbreviation of West Virginia

W.Va. a written abbreviation of West Virginia

WWI the abbreviation of World War I

WWII the abbreviation of World War II

WWW *n.* [singular] the written abbreviation of World Wide Web

WY a written abbreviation of Wyoming

Wyc·liffe /'wɪklɪf/, **John** (?1328–1384) an English religious leader who criticized the power of the Catholic Church, and started the translation of the Bible into English

Wy·eth /'waɪəθ/, **An·drew** /'ændru/ (1917–) a U.S. PAINTER

Wyo. a written abbreviation of Wyoming

Wy·o·ming /waɪ'oumɪŋ/ *written abbreviation* **WY** a state in the western U.S.

WYSIWYG /'wɪzi,wɪg/ *n.* [U] What You See Is What You Get; a word used to mean that something appears on a computer screen in exactly the same way as it will look when it is printed

wy·vern /'waɪvɚn/ *n.* [C] an imaginary animal that has two legs and wings and looks like a DRAGON

W

X, x /ɛks/ *n. plural* **X's, x's** [C] **1** the 24th letter of the English alphabet **2** the number 10 in the system of ROMAN NUMERALS **3** a letter used in mathematics to represent an unknown quantity or value that can be calculated: *If 3x=6, then x=2.* **4** a mark used on school work to show that a written answer is wrong **5** a mark used to show that you have chosen something on an official piece of paper, for example when voting **6** a mark used instead of a SIGNATURE by someone who cannot write **7** a mark used to show a kiss, especially at the end of a letter: *Love, Cindy XXOXX* **8** a letter that was used in past times to show that no one under the age of 17 could see a particular movie. It is now used only in an unofficial way for movies that contain a lot of sex. —compare NC-17 **9** a letter used instead of someone or something's real name, because you want to keep it secret, you do not know it, or you are not talking about a specific person or thing: *Suppose Mrs. X wants to make a donation. How can she be sure how her money will be used?* **10 X number of sth** used to say that there are a certain number of people or things, when the exact number is not important: *We can't just keep adding to the project because we only have X number of days to finish it.* —see also GENERATION X

X[1] /ɛks/ *n.* [U] SLANG: see ECSTASY (=an illegal drug)

X[2] *v.*

X sth ↔ **out** *phr. v.* [T] SPOKEN to mark or remove a mistake in a piece of writing using an X; CROSS OUT

Xa·vi·er /ˈzeɪviə/, **St. Fran·cis** /seɪnt ˈfrænsɪs/ (1506–1552) a Spanish Christian priest who traveled to India, southeast Asia, and Japan as a MISSIONARY and who helped to start the religious ORDER of Jesuits

x-ax·is /ˈɛks ˌæksɪs/ *n.* [singular] the line that goes from left to right at the bottom of a GRAPH, by which the positions of points on the graph are measured —compare Y-AXIS

X-chro·mo·some /ˈɛks ˌkrooməˌsoom, -ˌzoom/ *n.* [C] a type of CHROMOSOME that exists in pairs in female cells, and with a Y CHROMOSOME in male cells

xe·non /ˈzinɑn, ˈzɛ-/ *n.* [U] *symbol* **Xe** a rare gas that is one of the chemical ELEMENTS

Xe·noph·a·nes /zɪˈnɑfəˌniz/ (?560–?478 B.C.) a Greek PHILOSOPHER

xen·o·pho·bi·a /ˌzɛnəˈfoobiə, ˌzi-/ *n.* [U] extreme fear or hatred of people from other countries —**xenophobe** /ˈzɛnəˌfoob/ *n.* [C] —**xenophobic** /ˌzɛnəˈfoobɪk/ *adj.*

xe·rog·ra·phy /zɪˈrɑɡrəfi/ *n.* [U] TECHNICAL a way of making copies of papers by using an electric machine which makes a special black powder stick onto paper to form words, pictures etc. —**xerographic** /ˌzɪrəˈɡræfɪk/ *adj.*

Xer·ox, xerox /ˈzɪrɑks, ˈzi-/ *n.* [C] TRADEMARK a copy of a piece of paper with writing or printing on it, made using a special machine; PHOTOCOPY: *We had kept Xeroxes of all the records.* —**Xerox** *v.* [I,T] *Bernstein had Xeroxed notes from reporters at the scene.*

XL the written abbreviation of "EXTRA large," used especially on clothing

X·mas /ˈkrɪsməs, ˈɛksməs/ *n.* [U] INFORMAL a short way of writing the word CHRISTMAS, which some Christians think is offensive

X-rated /ˈɛks ˌreɪtɪd/ *adj.* something that is X-rated is not considered appropriate for children and young people because it contains sex, violence, or offensive words: **X-rated movies/magazines/bookstores** etc. *Two X-rated videos were found in a trash barrel behind the O'Briens' home.*

X-ray[1] /ˈɛks reɪ/ *n. plural* **X-rays** [C] **1** [usually plural] a beam of RADIATION (1) that can go through solid objects and is often used for photographing the inside of the body **2** a photograph of part of the inside of the body, which shows the bones and some organs: *We'll have to take some X-rays to make sure there are no broken bones.* | *a chest X-ray* **3** a medical examination that uses X-rays: *Kemp was taken to the hospital for X-rays of his arm.*

X-ray[2] *v.* **X-rays, X-rayed, X-raying** [T] to photograph the inside of something, especially someone's body, using X-rays: *Jack went to his doctor, who X-rayed the toe.* | *All bags are X-rayed before being put on the planes.*

XS the written abbreviation of "EXTRA small," used especially on clothing

XXX used in an unofficial way to show that a movie, magazine etc. contains a lot of sex

xy·lo·phone /ˈzaɪləˌfoon/ *n.* [C] a musical instrument which consists of a set of wooden bars of different lengths that you hit with a special stick

Y

Y, y /waɪ/ *plural* **Y's, y's** **1** the 25th letter of the English alphabet **2 the Y** INFORMAL the YMCA or the YWCA

-y¹, -ey /i/ *suffix* [in adjectives] **1** full of something, or covered with something: *sugary desserts* (=full of sugar) | *dirty hands* (=covered with dirt) | *a hairy chest* (=covered with hair) **2** having a quality or feeling, or tending to do something: *a messy room* | *a sleepy baby* (=who feels tired) | *curly hair* (=that always curls) | *a plant with droopy leaves* (=that hang down low) **3** like something, or typical of something: *his long, horsey face* (=he looks like a horse) *a cold wintry day* (=typical of winter) —**ily** /əli/ *suffix* [in adverbs] —**iness** /-inis/ *suffix* [in nouns]

-y² *suffix* [in nouns] **1** used to make a word or name less formal, and often to show that you care about someone: *Where's little Johnny?* | *my daddy* (=my father) | *What a nice doggy!* —see also **-IE 2** used to make nouns from some verbs to show an action: *excessive flattery* (=things you say to someone that are too nice) | *an inquiry* (=the act of asking questions formally or officially)

Y2K /ˌwaɪ tu 'keɪ/ *n.* [singular, not with **the**] the abbreviation of "Year 2000," used especially when talking about the possible computer problems caused by the date changing to 2000

ya /yʌ/ *pron.* SPOKEN, INFORMAL you: *See ya later.*

yacht /yɑt/ *n.* [C] a large expensive boat, used for racing or traveling for pleasure

yacht·ing /'yɑtɪŋ/ *n.* [U] the activity of traveling or racing in a yacht

yack /yæk/ *v.* [I + about] another spelling of YAK²

ya·da ya·da ya·da, yadda yadda yadda /ˌyɑdə ˌyɑdə 'yɑdə/ SPOKEN said when you do not want to give a lot of detailed information, because it is boring or because the person you are talking to already knows it: *I started talking to her and – yada yada yada – it turns out she's from New York too.*

ya·hoo¹ /'yɑhu/ *n.* [C] someone who is rough, noisy, and stupid

ya·hoo² /yɑ'hu/ *interjection* shouted when you are very happy or excited about something

Yah·weh /'yɑweɪ/ *n.* [singular, not with **the**] a Hebrew name for God

yak¹ /yæk/ *n.* [C] an animal of central Asia that looks like a cow with long hair

yak² *v.* **yakked, yakking** [I + about] INFORMAL to talk continuously about things that are not very serious

y'all /yɔl/ *pron.* SPOKEN a word meaning "you" or "all of you," used mainly in the southeastern U.S.: *I'm going home now. See y'all later.* —compare **(you) those) guys** (GUY (2))

yam /yæm/ *n.* [C] **1** a SWEET POTATO **2** a tropical plant grown for its large root, which is eaten as a vegetable

yam·mer /'yæmə/ *v.* [I] to talk continuously, in an annoying way: *Television critics are always yammering about how unreal most shows are.*

Yam·ous·sou·kro /ˌyɑmə'sukroʊ/ the capital city of the Ivory Coast

yang /yæŋ/ *n.* [U] the male principle in Chinese PHILOSOPHY which is active, light, positive, and which combines with YIN (=the female principle) to influence everything in the world

Yan·gon /ˌyɑn'goʊn/ the capital and largest city of Myanmar

Yang·tze, the /ˌyæŋ'si/ another name for the Chang river in China

Yank /yæŋk/ *n.* [C] INFORMAL an impolite word meaning an American, used by some British people

yank /yæŋk/ *v.* [I,T] INFORMAL to suddenly pull something quickly and with force: [+ on] *Jamal grabbed my hair and yanked on it.* | [yank sth **out/back/open etc.**] *I yanked my arm away from Tom's grip.*

Yan·kee /'yæŋki/ *n.* [C] **1** a word meaning someone born in or living in the northern states of the U.S., sometimes used in an insulting way by people from the southern U.S. **2** a word meaning an American, often used in an insulting way by people outside the U.S. **3** someone from New England **4 Yankee ingenuity** the ability that Americans are supposed to have to think of new ideas and interesting ways to solve problems

Ya·oun·dé /ˌyɑun'deɪ/ the capital city of Cameroon

yap¹ /yæp/ *v.* **yapped, yapping** [I] **1** if a small dog yaps, it makes short loud sounds in an excited way **2** to talk in a noisy way without saying anything very important or serious: *Some guy was yapping on his cell phone behind us.*

yap² *n.* [C] **1** the short loud sound that a small dog makes **2** SLANG someone's mouth: *I just wish Rob would keep his yap shut.*

Ya·qui /'yɑki/ a Native American tribe from northwest Mexico

yard /yɑrd/ *n.* [C] **1** the land around a house, usually covered with grass: *The ball landed in the neighbors' yard.* | **the front/back yard** *There's a "for sale" sign in Kyle's front yard.* —see also BACKYARD —compare GARDEN (1), LAWN (1) **2** *written abbreviation* **yd.** a unit for measuring length and distance, equal to 3 feet or 0.91 meters **3** an enclosed area next to a building or group of buildings, used for a special purpose, activity, or business: *a prison exercise yard* | *The ship will be moved to the Philadelphia Naval Yard next year.* —see also **the whole nine yards** (WHOLE¹ (6))

yard·age /'yɑrdɪdʒ/ *n.* **1** [U] the number of yards that a team or player moves forward in a game of football **2** [C,U] the size of something measured in yards or square yards: *smaller yardages of fabric*

yard·bird /'yɑrdbəd/ *n.* [C] OLD-FASHIONED, SLANG **1** someone who is in prison, especially for a long time **2** someone who has a low rank in the army and has outdoor duties

yard sale /'. ./ *n.* [C] a sale of used clothes and things from someone's house, that takes place in their YARD —compare GARAGE SALE

yard sign /'. ./ *n.* [C] a sign that you put in front of your house before an election to say which person or political party you support

yard·stick /'yɑrdˌstɪk/ *n.* [C] **1** something that you compare another thing with, in order to judge how good or successful they are: [+ of] *Is profit the only yardstick of success?* **2** a special stick that you use for measuring things, that is exactly one YARD (2) long and is marked in inches

yard·work /'yɑrdwək/ *n.* [U] work that you do outdoors to make your YARD look nice, such as cutting the grass, removing WEEDS, planting flowers etc.

Yar·en /'yɑrɛn/ the capital city of Nauru

yar·mul·ke /'yɑməkə, 'yɑrmələkə/ *n.* [C] a small circular cap worn by some Jewish men

yarn /yɑrn/ *n.* **1** [U] long thick thread made of cotton or wool, which is used to KNIT things **2** [C] a story of adventures, travels etc., made more exciting and interesting by adding things that never really happened

yash·mak /'yæʃmæk/ *n.* [C] a piece of cloth that Muslim women wear across their faces in public

Ya·va·pai /'yɑvɑˌpaɪ/ a Native American tribe from the southwestern area of the U.S.

yaw /yɔ/ *v.* [I] TECHNICAL if a ship, aircraft etc. yaws, it turns away from the correct direction it should be traveling in —**yaw** *n.* [C,U]

yawl /yɔl/ *n.* [C] a type of boat with one main MAST (=pole) and sails, and another small mast and sail close to the back

yawn¹ /yɔn/ *v.* [I] **1** to open your mouth wide and breathe in deeply, usually because you are tired or bored: *Fred stood up, yawned and stretched.* **2 a yawning gap/hole/chasm etc.** a very large hole or space, or a very large difference in people's attitudes, opinions etc.: *Rarely has the yawning gap between the two parties been so clear.*

yawn² *n.* **1** [C] an act of yawning: *Kay shook her head and **stifled a yawn** (=tried to stop yawning).* **2** [singular] INFORMAL someone or something that is boring: *The party was a big yawn.*

y-axis /'waɪ ˌæksɪs/ *n.* [singular] the line that goes up and down along the left side of a GRAPH, by which the positions of points on the graph are measured —compare X-AXIS

Y chro·mo·some /'waɪ ˌkroʊmə,soʊm, -,zoʊm/ *n.* [C] the part of a GENE that makes someone a male instead of a female —compare X CHROMOSOME

yd. the written abbreviation of YARD² or yards

ye¹ /yi, yə/ *pron.* BIBLICAL OR OLD USE a word meaning "you": *Ye shall not steal.*

ye² /yi/ *determiner* a word meaning "the," used especially in the names of stores to make them seem old and attractive: *Ye Olde Antique Shoppe*

yea¹ /yeɪ/ *adv.* OLD USE yes —opposite NAY¹ (2)

yea² *n.* [C] a YES² —opposite NAY²

Yea·ger /'yeɪgɚ/, **Charles (Chuck)** /tʃɑrlz tʃʌk/ (1923–) a U.S. pilot who was the first man to fly faster than the speed of sound

S W
1 1
yeah /yɛə/ *adv.* SPOKEN, INFORMAL yes

S W
1 1
year /yɪr/ *n.* [C]

1 `12 months` a period of about 365 days or 12 months, measured from any particular time: *I moved here two years ago.* | *Jackie has worked here for several years.* | *Jared is 15 years old.* | *a four-year-old child* | *a three-year business plan* —see also FISCAL YEAR

2 `January through December` a period of 365 or 366 days divided into 12 months, beginning on January 1 and ending on December 31; CALENDAR YEAR: *The lease expires at the end of the year.* | *the year 2002*

3 **years** a very long period of time: *It's been years since I heard that joke.* | **in/for years** *I haven't been there for years.* | *It was the first time in years I had seen Kathy smiling.*

4 `usual time for sth` a period of time, about equal to or shorter than a year, that is the usual time for something to happen: **academic/school year** (=the time when schools, colleges etc. normally have classes, usually from September through May or early June in the U.S.)

5 **all year round** during the whole year: *It's warm enough to swim all year round.* —see also YEAR-ROUND

6 **year after year** continuously for many years: *The same birds returned to that tree year after year.*

7 **year by year** as each year passes: *Year by year, things are getting worse.*

8 **not/never in a million years** SPOKEN used to say that you think something is extremely unlikely: *Never in a million years did I think we'd lose.*

9 **childhood/school/war etc. years** a particular period of time in someone's life or in history: *They've been friends since their college years.* | *the drought years of the 1930s*

10 `Earth going around sun` TECHNICAL a measure of time equal to 365¼ days, which is the amount of time it takes for the Earth to travel once around the sun —see also **be getting on (in years)** at GET ON (GET), YEARLY

year-book /'yɪrbʊk/ *n.* [C] a book printed once a year, especially by a school or college, with information and pictures about what happened there in the past year

year-end /ˌ. '.◂/ *n.* [U] the period of time at the end of a year: *Executives hope to raise share prices 4% by year-end.* —**year-end** *adj.* [only before noun] *a year-end report*

year·ling /'yɪrlɪŋ/ *n.* [C] an animal, especially a young horse, between one and two years old

year·long /ˌyɪr'lɔŋ◂/ *adj.* [only before noun] continuing for a year, or all through the year: *a yearlong study of the housing problem*

year·ly /'yɪrli/ *adj. adv.,* happening or appearing every year or once a year: *Investments are reviewed yearly.* |

yearn /yɚn/ *v.* [I] LITERARY to have a strong desire for something, especially something that is difficult or impossible to get: **[+ for]** *Hannah yearned for a child.* | **[yearn to do sth]** *Bud had yearned to be a pilot since he was young.*

yearn·ing /'yɚnɪŋ/ *n.* [C,U] LITERARY a strong desire or feeling of wanting something: **[+ for]** *This yearning for freedom is not going to disappear overnight.* | **[yearning to do sth]** *Gail had a yearning to be loved.*

year-round /ˌ. '.◂/ *adj.* [only before noun] happening or done during the whole year: *Several high schools have switched to year-round schedules.* —**year-round** *adv.*: *Someone will be available year-round to help.*

yeast /yist/ *n.* [U] a substance that is used for producing alcohol in beer and wine, and for making bread rise —**yeasty** *adj.*

yeast in·fec·tion /'. .,./ *n.* [C] an infectious condition that affects the VAGINA in women

Yeats /yeɪts/, **W.B.** /'dʌbəlyu bi/ (1865–1939) an Irish writer of poems and plays

yecch /yʌk/ *interjection* SLANG used to say that you think something is very disgusting; YUCK

yell¹ /yɛl/ *v.* **1** also **yell out** [I,T] to shout or say something very loudly, especially because you are frightened, angry, or excited: *Tim counted to three, then yelled "Go!".* | **[+ at]** *Don't yell at me like that!* **2** [I] SPOKEN to ask for help: *If you need me, just yell.*

S W
2 3

yell² *n.* [C] **1** a loud shout: **a yell of delight/triumph/warning etc.** *Dayton's remark was met by yells of protest.* **2** special words or phrases that students and CHEERLEADERS shout together to show support for their school, college etc.

yel·low¹ /'yɛloʊ/ *adj.* **1** having the color of butter or the middle part of an egg **2** TABOO used to describe the skin color of people from parts of Asia. Do not use this word. **3** ALSO **yellow-bellied** INFORMAL not brave; COWARDLY —**yellow** *n.* [U]

S W
2 2

yellow² *v.* [I,T] to become yellow, or make something become yellow: *The paper had yellowed with age.*

yellow card /'.. ,./ *n.* [C] a yellow card held up by a SOCCER REFEREE to show that a player has done something wrong

yellow fe·ver /ˌ.. '../ *n.* [C] a dangerous tropical disease in which your skin turns slightly yellow

yel·low·ish /'yɛloʊɪʃ/ *adj.* having a slight yellow color: *The fish is dark green on top, with yellowish sides.*

yellow jack·et, yellowjacket /'.. ,../ *n.* [C] a type of WASP (=flying insect) with a yellow and black body, that can sting you

yellow pag·es /ˌ.. '../ *n.* **the yellow pages** also **the Yellow Pages** the name of a book that contains the telephone numbers of businesses and organizations in an area, arranged according to the type of business they do —compare WHITE PAGES

yellow per·il /ˌ.. '../ *n.* [singular] TABOO, OLD-FASHIONED the possibility that people from China and eastern Asia could take control of the whole world, which some people in the U.S. and Europe in the 1940s and 1950s believed would happen. Do not use this phrase.

Yellow Riv·er, the /ˌ.. '../ a river in northern China

Yellowstone National Park

Yel·low·stone Na·tion·al Park /ˌyɛloʊstoʊn ˌnæʃənl 'pɑrk/ a large national park, mostly in the

Y

state of Wyoming, known for its HOT SPRINGS and GEYSERS

yelp /yɛlp/ v. [I] to make a short sharp high cry because of excitement, pain etc.: *The dog, still yelping, was circling the girls.* —**yelp** n. [C] *Sandy let out a yelp.*

Yelt·sin /'yɛltsɪn/, **Bor·is** /'bɔrɪs/ (1931–) a Russian politician who was President of Russia from 1991 to 1999

Yem·en /'yɛmən/ a country in southwest Asia south of Saudi Arabia —**Yemeni** n., adj.

yen /yɛn/ n. plural **yen 1** [C] the standard unit of money in Japan **2** [singular] a strong desire: [+ **to/for**] *He suddenly had a yen to see his old girlfriend.*

yeo·man /'youmən/ n. plural **yeomen** /-mən/ [C] an officer in the U.S. Navy who often works in an office

yep /yɛp/ adv. INFORMAL yes

yer /yɚ/ possessive adj. NONSTANDARD used in writing as an informal way of saying "your"

Ye·re·van /ˌyɛrə'van/ the capital and largest city of Armenia

yes¹ /yɛs/ adv. SPOKEN

1 | positive answer | used as an answer to say that something is true, that you agree, that you want something, or that you are willing to do something: *"Is that real gold?" "Yes, it is."* | *"It was a great show." "Yes, it was."* | *"Would you like some more cake?" "Yes – thanks."* | *"Can you give me a hand here?" "Yes, just a second."* —opposite NO¹ (1)

2 | giving permission | used as an answer to give permission: *"Can I have a glass of water?" "Yes, of course."* | *Let's go ask Dad. I'm sure he'll say yes.*

3 | answer negative question | used as an answer to a question or statement containing a negative, to say that the opposite is true: *"Sarah isn't very smart, is she?" "Yes, she is (=in fact, she is smart) !"* | *"Mom, there's no more cereal." "Yes, there is – it's in the cupboard."*

4 yes, but... used to show politely that you do not agree with part of what someone has said: *"There are still a lot of problems with Jeff's proposal." "Yes, but it's the best one we have."*

5 used to show that you have heard a request, call, command etc.: *"Mike?" "Yes?"* | *Yes, sir, how can I help you?*

6 yes and no used to show that there is not one clear answer to a question: *"Were you surprised?" "Well, yes and no. I knew they were planning something, but I wasn't sure what."*

USAGE NOTE: YES

WORD CHOICE

In spoken English, **yes** is used mainly in fairly formal situations. In more informal speech, we use many different answers instead of **yes**. Some of these are **yeah**, **yep**, **okay**, **uh-huh**, and **sure**.

---

yes² n. [C] a vote, voter, or reply that agrees with an idea, plan, law etc.: *There were a total of five yeses and three noes.* —compare AYE

ye·shi·va, ye·sh·ivah /yə'ʃivə/ n. a school for Jewish students, where they can train to become RABBIS (=religious leaders)

yes-man /'. ./ n. plural **yes-men** [C] someone who always agrees with and obeys their employer, leader, etc. in order to gain some advantage

yes/no ques·tion /ˌ. '. ˌ./ also **yes-and-no question, yes-or-no question** /ˌ. '. ˌ./ n. [C] a question to which you can only answer "yes" or "no"

yes·sir /'yɛsɚ/ adv. a way of writing how someone says "yes, sir"

yes·ter·day¹ /'yɛstɚdi, -ˌdeɪ/ adv. on or during the day before today: *What did you do yesterday?* | *The day before yesterday was Monday.* | *He left yesterday afternoon.* —see also **I wasn't born yesterday** (BORN (9))

yesterday² n. [U] **1** the day before today: *Burns' proposal was accepted at yesterday's meeting.* **2** the recent past: *The events of yesterday cannot fully explain the world of today.* **3 yesterday's news**

information that is old and not interesting anymore: *By then the scandal was already yesterday's news.*

yes·ter·year /'yɛstɚˌyɪr/ n. **of yesteryear** LITERARY from a time in the past: *The magnificent big boats of yesteryear have virtually vanished.*

yet¹ /yɛt/ adv. **1** [in questions or negatives] until now, or until a particular time: *Have they said anything about the money yet?* | *Did Steve call you yet?* | *The potatoes aren't quite ready yet.* —see usage note at JUST¹ **2 not yet** an expression meaning "not now" or "still not," used especially in the answer to questions: *"Is supper ready?" "No, not yet."* **3** in addition to what you have already gotten, done etc.; STILL: **yet more/bigger/later** etc. *California could face yet more financial difficulties.* | *This is **yet another** reason to be cautious.* | *The opening of the Fourth Avenue nightclub appears to have been delayed **yet again** (=one more time after many others).* —see usage note at STILL¹ **4 the biggest/worst/most etc. (sth) yet** used to say that something is the biggest, worst etc. of its kind that has existed up to now: *This could turn out to be our costliest mistake yet.* | *Martinson's latest novel looks like her best yet.* **5 as (of) yet** [in questions or negatives] SPOKEN until or before now: *There are no details available as of yet.* | *As yet, no starting date has been set.* **6** FORMAL at some time in the future, in spite of the way that things seem now: *We may win yet.* **7 sb has yet to do sth** FORMAL used to say that someone still has not done something, or that something still has not happened: *The bank has yet to respond to a letter we sent in January.*

yet² conjunction **1** used to introduce a statement that is surprising after what you have just said: *They charge incredibly high prices, yet customers keep coming back for more.* | *Some battered women live in fear of their husbands, and yet are terrified to leave.* **2** but, or in spite of something: *It's an inexpensive yet effective solution to our problem.*

ye·ti /'yɛti/ n. [C] an ABOMINABLE SNOWMAN

yew /yu/ n. [C,U] a tree with dark green leaves and red berries, or the wood of this tree

yid /yɪd/ n. [C] TABOO a Jewish person. Do not use this word.

Yid·dish /'yɪdɪʃ/ n. [U] a language based on German used by older Jewish people, especially those who are from eastern Europe

yield¹ /yild/ v.
1 | result | [T] to produce a result, answer, or a piece of information: *A search of Mann's home yielded a pair of bloody gloves.*
2 | crops/profits | [T] to produce crops, profits etc.: *Each of these fields could yield billions of barrels of oil.* | *Government securities have traditionally yielded less than stocks.* | **high-yielding/low-yielding** (=producing a large or small amount of something such as crops)
3 | agree unwillingly | [I,T] to allow yourself to be forced or persuaded to do something or stop having something: *The military has promised to yield power after legislators draw up a new constitution.* | [+ **to**] *Wilson refused to yield to requests to raise salaries.* | **yield to pressure/emotion/temptation etc.** *Further action may be necessary if the leaders do not yield to diplomatic pressure.*
4 | traffic | [I] to allow other cars, people etc. to go first: [+ **to**] *Yield to traffic on the right.*
5 | move/bend/break | [I] to move, bend, or break because of physical force or pressure: *Ideally, the surface should yield slightly under pressure.*
6 | change | [I] if one thing yields to another thing, it is replaced by the new thing: [+ **to**] *Laughter quickly yielded to amazement as the show went on.*

yield sth ↔ **up** phr. v. [T] LITERARY to show or give someone something that has been hidden for a long time or is very difficult to obtain: *Darden's detective work yielded up some surprising discoveries.*

yield² n. [C] the amount of profits, crops etc. that something produces: *investments with high yields*

yield·ing /'yildɪŋ/ *adj.* a surface that is yielding is soft and will move or bend when you press it

yikes /yaɪks/ *interjection* said when something frightens you or shocks you

yin /yɪn/ *n.* [U] the female principle in Chinese PHILOSOPHY which is inactive, dark, and negative, and which combines with YANG (=the male principle) to influence everything in the world

ying yang /'yɪŋ yæŋ/ *n.* **have sth up the ying yang** SPOKEN, HUMOROUS to have a very large amount or number of something: *James has college loans up the ying yang.*

yip /yɪp/ *v.* **yipping, yipped** [I] if a dog yips, it makes short loud sounds because it is afraid or excited

yip·pee /'yɪpi/ *interjection* said when you are very pleased or excited about something

YMCA *n.* **the YMCA** Young Men's Christian Association; an organization in many countries that provides places to stay and sports activities for young men —compare YWCA

yo /yoʊ/ *interjection* SLANG used to greet someone, to get their attention, or as a reply when someone says your name: *Yo, dude! How's it going?* | *"Darren?" "Yo!"*

yo·del[1] /'yoʊdl/ *v.* [I,T] to sing while changing between your natural voice and a very high voice, traditionally done in the mountains of countries such as Switzerland and Austria —**yodeler** *n.* [C]

yodel[2] *n.* [C] a song or sound made by yodeling

yo·ga /'yoʊgə/ *n.* [U] **1** a system of exercises that help you control your mind and body in order to relax **2** a Hindu PHILOSOPHY in which you learn exercises to control your mind and body in order to try to become closer to God

yoga

yo·ghurt /'yoʊgət/ *n.* [U] another spelling of YOGURT

yo·gi /'yoʊgi/ *n.* [C] someone who is very good at yoga and has a lot of knowledge about it, and who often teaches it to other people

yo·gurt /'yoʊgət/ *n.* [U] a smooth thick food made from milk with a slightly sour taste, often mixed with fruit

yoke[1] /yoʊk/ *n.* [C] **1** a wooden bar used for keeping two animals, especially cattle, together in order to pull heavy loads **2** a frame that goes across someone's shoulders so that they can carry two equal loads which hang from the frame **3 the yoke of sth** LITERARY something that restricts your freedom, making life difficult: *They longed to break free from the yoke of Communism.* **4** a part of a skirt or shirt just below the waist or collar, from which the main piece of material hangs in folds

yoke[2] *v.* [T + **together/to**] **1** to put a yoke on two animals **2** LITERARY to connect two ideas or people together in people's minds: *Beauty is forever yoked to youth in our culture.*

yo·kel /'yoʊkəl/ *n.* [C] HUMOROUS someone who comes from the country, seems stupid, and does not know much about modern life, ideas etc.

yolk /yoʊk/ *n.* [C,U] the yellow part in the center of an egg —compare EGG WHITE

Yom Kip·pur /ˌyɑm ˈkɪpə, ˌyoʊm kɪˈpʊr/ *n.* [C,U] a Jewish religious holiday on which people do not eat, ~~but~~ pray to be forgiven for the things they have done

~~yan~~/ *determiner* OLD USE: see YONDER[1] —see also ~~er~~ and thither/yon (HITHER (1))

~~der~~[1] /'yandə/ *adv., determiner* OLD USE OR INFOR-

MAL a fairly long distance away: *yonder hills* | *There's some old fellow who lives over yonder.*

yonder[2] *n.* **the wild blue yonder** LITERARY the sky

yoo-hoo /'yu hu/ *interjection* INFORMAL used to attract someone's attention when they are far away from you

yore /yɔr/ *n.* **of yore** LITERARY happening a long time ago

York·shire ter·ri·er /ˌyɔrkʃə ˈtɛriə/ *n.* [C] a type of dog that is very small and has long brown hair

Yo·sem·i·te Na·tion·al Park /yoʊˌsɛməti ˌnæʃənl ˈpɑrk/ a NATIONAL PARK in the state of California in the southwestern U.S., known for its beautiful lakes, WATERFALLS, and large REDWOOD trees

you /yə, yʊ; *strong* yu/ *pron.* [used as a subject or an object] **1** the person or people someone is speaking or writing to: *Hi, Kelly. How are you?* | *I can take all of you in my car.* | *Did Rob give the money to you?* | *I told you this would happen.* | *Only you can make this decision.* **2** people in general: *You have to be careful with people you don't know.* | *You can never be sure what Emily is thinking.* **3** used with nouns or phrases when you are talking to or calling someone: *You boys had better be home by 11:00.* | *You jerk!* | *Hey, you in the blue shirt!* **4 you and yours** LITERARY you and the members of your family: *We wish you and yours a very merry Christmas.*

you'd /yəd, yʊd; *strong* yud/ **1** the short form of "you had": *If you'd been more careful, this wouldn't have happened.* **2** the short form of "you would": *You'd be better off without him.*

you-know-what /ˌ. . '. ./ *pron.* SPOKEN, INFORMAL used to talk about something without mentioning its name, especially so other people will not understand you: *There's some you-know-what in the fridge.*

you-know-who /ˌ. . '. ./ *pron.* SPOKEN, INFORMAL used to talk about someone without mentioning their name, so that other people will not understand you: *Did you see what you-know-who was wearing?*

you'll /yəl, yʊl; *strong* yul/ the short form of "you will": *You'll feel better soon.*

young[1] /yʌŋ/ *adj.*
1 person/animal/plant at an early stage of life or development: *Sometimes I forget you're younger than I am.* | *You're too young to get married.* | *There was a young pine tree in the back yard.* | *He's a perfectly respectable young man.* —opposite OLD
2 idea/organization etc. not having existed for a long time: *At that time, America was still a young nation.* —opposite OLD
3 young lady/man SPOKEN used to speak to a girl or boy when you are angry with them: *Now, you listen to me, young man!*
4 appearance seeming or looking younger than you are; YOUTHFUL: *In just a week, you can have younger, smoother skin.*
5 young blood young people with new ideas: *It's about time we got some young blood in this company.*
6 young at heart APPROVING thinking and behaving as if you were young, even though you are old: *Arthur's 96, but he's still young at heart.*
7 65/82/97 etc. years young SPOKEN used to give the age of an old person who seems or feels much younger: *Next week, Aunt Bessie will be 84 years young.*
8 for young people designed or meant for young people: *I'm looking for something in a younger style.*

young[2] *n.* [plural] **1 the young** young people in general: *Certain drugs have a special appeal to the young.* **2** a group of young animals that belong to a particular mother or type of animal: *The lioness fought to protect her young.*

Young /yʌŋ/, **Brig·ham** /'brɪgəm/ (1801–1877) a U.S. leader of the Mormon religion, who led 5000 Mormons to Utah where they built Salt Lake City

Young, Cy /saɪ/ (1867–1955) a U.S. baseball player known for his skill as a PITCHER

young·er /'yʌŋgə/ *adj.* **sb the Younger** OLD-FASHIONED someone famous who lived in past times and had the same name as their mother or father: *Pliny the Younger* —compare ELDER[1], JR.

young·ster /'jʌŋstɚ/ *n.* [C] OLD-FASHIONED a child or young person

your /jɚ; *strong* jɔr/ *possessive adj.* [possessive form of "you"] **1** belonging to or relating to the person or people someone is speaking to: *Could you move your car?* | *That's your problem* | *If you're not careful, you'll break your neck.* | *Is that your brother over there?* **2** belonging to any person in general: *If you are facing north, east is on your right.* **3** SPOKEN used when mentioning something that is a good example of a particular type of thing or quality: *It was just your basic, ordinary hotel room – nothing special.* | *Well, you've got your waffles, your omelets, your pancakes, or whatever else you want here.*

you're /jɚ; *strong* jɔr/ the short form of "you are": *You're five years old now.*

yours /jʊrz, jɔrz/ *possessive pron.* [possessive form of "you"] **1** the thing or things belonging to or relating to the person or people someone is speaking to: *This is our room, and yours* (=your room) *is just across the hall.* | *Is Maria a friend of yours?* **2 be yours for the asking** if something important, desirable etc. is yours for the asking, you can easily get it by just asking someone for it: *There's plenty of grant money available – it's practically yours for the asking.* **3 yours truly a)** INFORMAL, HUMOROUS used to mean "I," "me," or " MYSELF ": *Members of the judging panel included yours truly.* **b)** also **sincerely yours** or **yours sincerely** used at the end of a business letter, before the SIGNATURE of the person who wrote it —see also **up yours!** (UP³ (4)), **you and yours** (YOU (4))

your·self /jɚˈsɛlf/ *pron. plural* **yourselves** /-ˈsɛlvz/ **1** the REFLEXIVE form of "you": *You'll hurt yourself if you're not careful.* | *You can make yourself a cup of coffee.* **2** the strong form of "you," used to emphasize the subject or object of a sentence: *It must be true – you told me so yourself.* | *If you want something done right, you'd better do it yourself.* **3** NONSTANDARD used instead of "you" to make what you are saying sound more important: *This is the perfect suit for a businessman such as yourself, sir.* **4 (all) by yourself a)** alone: *You can't go home by yourself in the dark.* **b)** without help from anyone else: *Do you think you can move the couch by yourself?* —see Usage Note at ALONE **5 not feel/look/seem like yourself** to not feel or behave in the way you usually do because you are nervous, upset, or sick: *Are you sure you're OK? You just don't look like yourself today.* **6 have sth (all) to yourself** if you have something to yourself, you do not have to share it with anyone else: *Do you feel like you don't have any time to yourself?* —see also DO-IT-YOURSELF, **keep sth to yourself** at keep to KEEP¹

youse /juz/ *pron.* SPOKEN, NONSTANDARD a word meaning "you," used when talking to more than one person: *Shut up, both of youse!*

youth /juθ/ *n. plural* **youths** /juðs, juðz/ **1** [U] the period of time when someone is young, especially the period when someone is a TEENAGER: *Moss knew that not all the dreams of his youth* (=from the time when he was young) *would come true.* | *Many of these people had used drugs in their youth* (=when they were young). **2** [C] a word meaning a TEENAGE boy, used especially in newspapers: *Horton teaches at a school for troubled youths in San Diego.* **3** [U] young people in general: *a church youth group* **4** [U] the quality or state of being young: *Society seems obsessed with youth and wealth.* —see also FOUNTAIN OF YOUTH —see Usage Note at CHILD

youth cul·ture /'. ,../ *n.* [U] the interests and activities of young people, especially the popular music, movies etc. which they enjoy

youth·ful /'juθfəl/ *adj.* **1** typical of young people, or seeming young: *They still have much of their youthful idealism.* | *She has managed to maintain her youthful appearance.* **2** young: *The photo, dated 1944, shows a smiling, youthful Burgos.* —**youthfully** *adv.* —**youthfulness** *n.* [U]

youth hos·tel /'. ,../ *n.* [C] an inexpensive hotel for young people

you've /jɚv, jʊv; *strong* juv/ the short form of "you have," used when "have" is an AUXILIARY VERB: *Now*

you've broken it.

yow /jaʊ/ *interjection* said when you feel sudden pain: *Yow! That's hot!*

yowl /jaʊl/ *v.* [I] to make a long loud cry, especially because you are sad or in pain: *Kip kept yowling and cursing in the kitchen.* —**yowl** *n.* [C]

yo-yo /'joʊjoʊ/ *n. plural* **yo-yos** [C] **1** a toy made of two connected circular parts that go up and down a string that you hold in your hand, as you lift your hand up and down **2** INFORMAL a stupid person **3 yo-yo dieting** the habit of losing weight quickly and then gaining it back again and again over a long period of time

yr. *plural* **yrs.** the written abbreviation of "year"

yu·an /jʊˈɑn, ˈjuən/ *n. plural* **yuan** [C] the standard unit of money in China

Yu·ca·tán /ˌjukəˈtɑn/ **the Yucatán Peninsula** a large PENINSULA in central America, between the Gulf of Mexico and the Caribbean Sea, which consists of Belize, north Guatemala, and part of Mexico

yuc·ca /'jʌkə/ *n.* [C] a desert plant with long pointed leaves on a thick straight stem

yuck /jʌk/ *interjection* used to show that you think something tastes bad or is very disgusting: *Oh, yuck! I hate mayonnaise.*

yuck·y /'jʌki/ *adj.* INFORMAL extremely disgusting, tasting very bad etc.: *Jake didn't watch the yucky parts where Kull kisses girls.*

Yu·go·sla·vi·a /ˌjugəˈslɑviə/ a former country in southeast Europe, made up of six REPUBLICS: Slovenia, Croatia, Bosnia-Herzegovina, Macedonia, Serbia, and Montenegro. Serbia and Montenegro are now know as the Federal Republic of Yugoslavia and the other republics are all separate independent countries —**Yugoslav** /'jugə,slɑv/ also **Yugoslavian** /ˌjugəˈslɑviən/ *n., adj.*

yuk¹ /jʌk/ *interjection* another spelling of YUCK

yuk² *v.* **yukked, yukking yuk it up** HUMOROUS to tell a lot of jokes and behave in a funny way: *She was yukking it up during a guest appearance on Letterman's late-night show.*

Yu·kon, the /'jukɑn/ **1** a TERRITORY in northwest Canada **2** a river in the northeast of North America, flowing from the Yukon area in Canada, through Alaska, and into the Pacific Ocean

yuks /jʌks/ *n.* [plural] HUMOROUS jokes or laughs, especially in a television program or COMEDY show: *Green's live show includes plenty of political yuks.*

Yule /jul/ *n.* OLD USE Christmas

yule log /'. ./ *n.* [C] a long round piece of wood that some people burn on the evening before Christmas

Yule·tide /'julta ɪd/ *n.* [U] LITERARY Christmas

yum /jʌm/ *interjection* INFORMAL said when you think something tastes very good: *Ooh, garlic bread – yum!*

Yu·ma /'jumə/ a Native American tribe from the southwestern U.S.

yum·my /'jʌmi/ *adj.* **yummier, yummiest** INFORMAL tasting very good

yup /jʌp/ *adv.* INFORMAL yes

Yu·pik /'jupɪk/ a Native American tribe from western Alaska and Siberia

yup·pie /'jʌpi/ *n.* [C] someone who only seems to be interested in having a professional job, earning a lot of money, and buying expensive things

yup·pi·fy /'jʌpə,faɪ/ *v.* **yuppified, yuppifying** [T usually passive] HUMOROUS to make someone or something appropriate for or attractive to yuppies: *The restaurant's yuppified interior was done in colors like teal and mauve.*

Yu·rok /'jurɑk/ a Native American tribe from the southwestern U.S.

YWCA *n.* **the YWCA** Young Women's Christian Association; an organization in many countries that provides places to stay and sports activities for young women —compare YMCA

Z

Z, z /zi/ *plural* **Z's, z's** **1** the 26th and last letter of the English alphabet **2 catch/get some Z's** INFORMAL to sleep

za·ba·glio·ne /ˌzabəlˈyooni/ *n.* [U] a thick sweet food made from eggs, sugar, and wine that have been beaten together

zaf·tig /ˈzɑftɪg/ *adj.* HUMOROUS a zaftig woman is slightly fat, with large breasts

Za·greb /ˈzɑgrɛb/ the capital and largest city of Croatia

Za·ïre /ˈzaɪ-ɪr/ the former name of the Democratic Republic of Congo

Za·ïre, the another name for the Congo river in central Africa

Zam·be·zi, the /zæmˈbizi/ a large river in south central Africa

Zam·bi·a /ˈzæmbiə/ a country in south central Africa, north of Zimbabwe and south of the Democratic Republic of Congo —**Zambian** *n., adj.*

za·ny /ˈzeɪni/ *adj.* **zanier, zaniest** crazy or unusual, in a way that is funny and exciting: *a zany new TV comedy*

zap /zæp/ *v.* **zapped, zapping** **1** [T] to attack or destroy something quickly, especially using a beam of electricity: *Doctors have tried zapping tumors with high-voltage radiation.* **2** [T] INFORMAL to cook something in a MICROWAVE OVEN **3** [I,T] to change the CHANNEL on a television by using a REMOTE CONTROL: *Dave just sat there, zapping through all 70-plus channels.* **4** [T] to send information quickly from one computer to another: *Computers identify threats and zap the results back to U.S. pilots in the war zone.*

Za·pa·ta /zɑˈpɑtə/, **E·mi·lia·no** /ˌeɪmiˈlyɑnoʊ/ (1879–1919) a Mexican military leader, who led an army of native Mexicans against the government in an attempt to get back land that had been taken away from them

zap·per /ˈzæpɚ/ *n.* [C] INFORMAL **1** a piece of electrical equipment that attracts and kills insects **2** a television REMOTE CONTROL

zeal /zil/ *n.* [U] eagerness to do something, especially to achieve a particular religious or political aim: *In their zeal to catch drug dealers, police have ignored citizens' basic civil rights.*

zeal·ot /ˈzɛlət/ *n.* [C] someone who has extremely strong beliefs, especially religious or political beliefs, and is too eager to make other people share them: *anti-government zealots* —**zealotry** *n.* [U]

zeal·ous /ˈzɛləs/ *adj.* extremely interested in and excited about something that you believe in very strongly, and behaving in a way that shows this: *zealous political activists* —**zealously** *adv.* —**zealousness** *n.* [U]

ze·bra /ˈzibrə/ *n.* [C] an animal that looks like a horse, but has black and white lines all over its body

ze·bu /ˈzibu/ *n.* [C] an animal from Asia and eastern Africa that looks a little like a cow, but has a large HUMP (=raised part) on its back

Zeb·u·lon /ˈzɛbyələn/ in ⌐ Bible, the head of one ⌐ 12 tribes of Israel

⌐a·ri·ah /ˌzɛkəˈraɪə/ a ⌐ in the Old Testament ⌐ne Christian Bible

zebra

zed /zed/ *n.* [C] SPOKEN the letter "Z" in Canadian and British English, used to show how it is pronounced

zeit·geist /ˈzaɪtgaɪst, ˈtsaɪ-/ *n.* [singular] the general spirit or feeling of a period in history, as shown by people's ideas and beliefs at the time

Zen /zɛn/ also **Zen Bud·dhism** /ˌ. ˈ.../ *n.* [U] a type of Buddhism that emphasizes MEDITATION rather than faith or reading religious books

ze·nith /ˈzinɪθ/ *n.* [C usually singular] **1** the most successful point in the development of something: *Wilson's career reached its zenith in 1978.* **2** TECHNICAL the highest point that is reached by the sun or the moon in the sky —opposite NADIR

Zeph·a·ni·ah /ˌzɛfəˈnaɪə/ a book in the Old Testament of the Protestant Bible

zeph·yr /ˈzɛfɚ/ *n.* [C] LITERARY a soft gentle wind

zep·pe·lin /ˈzɛpəlɪn/ *n.* [C] a German AIRSHIP used in World War I

ze·ro[1] /ˈzɪroʊ, ˈzɪroʊ/ *number plural* **zeros** or **zeroes** **1** 0 **2** the point between + and - on a scale for measuring something, or the lowest point on a scale that shows how much there is left of something: *The pressure gauge was almost down to zero.* | **above/below zero** *Temperatures could drop to five degrees below zero* (=-5° Fahrenheit) *tonight.* **3** INFORMAL the lowest possible amount or level of something: *Iowa's chances of winning are virtually zero.* | *I started with absolutely zero knowledge about computers.* **4 zero growth/inflation/gravity etc.** no growth, INFLATION etc. at all: *zero population growth* | *Over 10 inches of snow fell in blizzard conditions with near zero visibility.* —see also ABSOLUTE ZERO, GROUND ZERO, ZERO TOLERANCE

ze·ro[2] *v.* **zeroes, zeroed, zeroing**
zero in on sb/sth *phr. v.* [T] **1** to direct all your attention toward a particular person or thing: *Police sorted through thousands of clues before they zeroed in on Moore and Thompson.* **2** to aim a gun toward something or someone

ze·ro[3] *n. plural* **zeros** or **zeroes** [C] INFORMAL someone who is considered stupid or unimportant: *We're just zeroes to them.*

zero-cou·pon bond /ˌ.. ˈ. ˌ./ *n.* [C] a type of BOND[1] (2) that does not pay any INTEREST[1] (3) until it is paid back or sold

zero hour /ˈ.. ˌ./ *n.* [singular, not with **the**] the time when a military operation or an important event is planned to begin

zero-sum game /ˌ.. ˌ. ˈ. / *n.* [singular] a situation in which any advantage or success that one person or side gains must be followed by an equal loss by the other person or side: *Job loss is not a zero-sum game, where they win and we lose.*

zero tol·e·rance /ˌ.. ˈ.../ *n.* [U] a way of dealing with crime in which every person who breaks the law, even in a very small way, is punished as severely as possible: *The school board has a policy of zero tolerance for students caught with drugs.*

zest /zɛst/ *n.* **1** [singular,U] eager interest and enjoyment: [+ for] *Francis has brought style and a real zest for life to the Valley.* **2** [singular,U] the quality of being exciting and interesting: *Their CD captures the sparkle and zest of their live performances.* **3** [U] the outer skin of an orange or LEMON, used in cooking —**zestful** *adj.* —**zestfully** *adv.*

Zeus /zus/ in Greek MYTHOLOGY; the king of the gods, and ruler of the universe

Zhou En·lai /ˌdʒoʊ ɛnˈlaɪ/ (1898–1976) a Chinese politician who was Foreign Minister and Prime Minister of China

zig·zag[1] /ˈzɪgzæg/ *n.* [C] a pattern that looks like a line of z's connected together: *The male moth flies in a zigzag pattern.* —see picture at PATTERN[1]

zig·zag[2] *v.* **zigzagged, zigzagging** [I] to move forward in sharp angles, first to the left and then to the right etc.: *The workmen's stairway zigzagged to the top of the scaffolding.*

zilch /zɪltʃ/ *n.* [U] INFORMAL nothing at all: *We have gotten absolutely zilch in return.*

zil·lion /ˈzɪlyən/ *n.* [C] INFORMAL an extremely large

number of something: [+ **of**] *There were zillions of mosquitoes in the woods.*

Zim·ba·bwe /zɪmˈbɑbweɪ/ a country in south central Africa, south of Zambia and north of South Africa —**Zimbabwean** *n., adj.*

zinc /zɪŋk/ *n.* [U] *symbol* **Zn** a bluish-white metal that is an ELEMENT and is used to make BRASS and to cover and protect objects made of iron

zine, 'zine /zin/ *n.* [C] a small magazine, usually about popular CULTURE, that is written and printed by people who are not professional writers

zin·fan·del, Zinfandel /ˈzɪnfənˌdɛl/ *n.* [U] a type of dry red or white wine from California

zing¹ /zɪŋ/ *n.* [U] INFORMAL an exciting quality such as energy, a good taste etc.: *A little chili pepper will add some zing to the sauce.* —**zingy** *adj.*

zing² *v.* [I always + adv./prep.] INFORMAL to move quickly, making a whistling noise: [+ **past/off etc.**] *Neighbors reported pellets and BBs zinging by their heads in their own backyards.*

zing·er /ˈzɪŋə/ *n.* [C] a short insulting but humorous remark

zin·nia /ˈzɪnyə/ *n.* [C] a garden plant with large brightly colored flowers

Zi·on /ˈzaɪən/ **1** a name given to Israel or to an imagined land where the Jewish people could live in peace, after many centuries of not having a land of their own. **2** in the Old Testament of the Bible, another name for Jerusalem

Zi·on·ism /ˈzaɪəˌnɪzəm/ *n.* [U] support for the establishment and development of a nation for the Jews in Israel —**Zionist** *n.* [C]

SW **zip**¹ /zɪp/ *n.* INFORMAL **1** [U] an exciting quality or a lot of energy: *A spoonful of mustard will give the dish some zip.* **2** [U] zero, or nothing: *The Braves lost, three–zip.* | *Sue ordered tickets for three shows, but got zip.* **3** [C usually singular] a ZIP code

zip² *v.* **zipped, zipping 1** [I always + adv./prep ,T] to open or close something using a zipper: *She was wearing a top that zipped at the neck.* | [**zip sth**] *Could you zip my dress?* | [**zip sb in/inside**] *We were all zipped inside our sleeping bags.* | *zip sth open/closed Olsen zipped the bag shut.* **2** [I always + adv./prep.] to do something or go somewhere very quickly: [+ **through/past/down etc.**] *A few cars zipped by.* **3 zip your lip** SPOKEN, INFORMAL used to tell someone not to say anything about something, or to tell them to be quiet

zip up *phr. v.* **1** [T **zip sth ↔ up**] to fasten something such as a piece of clothing using a zipper: *Harry zipped the bag back up and replaced the lock.* —opposite UNZIP **2** [I,T **zip sth ↔ up**] to close the zipper on a piece of clothing that someone else is wearing: *You'd better zip up before we go outside.*

ZIP code, zip code /ˈzɪp koʊd/ *n.* [C] a number that you write at the end of the address on an envelope to help the post office deliver the mail more quickly

ZIP file also **zipped file** /ˈ. ./ *n.* [C] TECHNICAL a computer FILE that has been made smaller so that it is easier to store and move —see also UNZIP (2)

zip gun /ˈ. ./ *n.* [C] a small gun that someone has made himself or herself, used especially by criminals

Zip·loc bag TRADEMARK, **zip-lock bag** /ˈzɪplɑk ˈbæg/ *n.* [C] a small transparent plastic bag that you can store food or other small things in, with a part at the top like a zipper that you press to close the bag tightly

zip·per /ˈzɪpə/ *n.* [C] an object with two lines of small metal or plastic pieces that slide together to fasten a piece of clothing, a bag etc. —see picture at FASTENER

zip·po /ˈzɪpoʊ/ *n.* [U] SPOKEN zero; NOTHING

zip·py /ˈzɪpi/ *adj.* having a lot of energy or moving quickly: *a zippy little car*

zir·co·ni·a /zəˈkoʊniə/ —see CUBIC ZIRCONIA

zit /zɪt/ *n.* [C] INFORMAL a PIMPLE

zith·er /ˈzɪðə/ *n.* [C] a musical instrument from Eastern Europe which you play by pulling its wire strings with your fingers

zlo·ty /ˈzlɑti, ˈzlɔ–/ *n. plural* **zlotys** [C] the standard unit of money used in Poland

zo·di·ac /ˈzoʊdiˌæk/ *n.* **the zodiac** an imaginary area through which the sun, moon, and PLANETS appear to travel, which some people believe influences our lives: *Virgo is the sixth sign of the zodiac.* —**zodiacal** *adj.* —see also ASTROLOGY, HOROSCOPE

Zo·la /ˈzoʊlə/, **Em·ile** /eɪˈmil/ (1840–1902) a French writer of NOVELS

zom·bie /ˈzɑmbi/ *n.* [C] **1** INFORMAL someone who moves very slowly and does not seem to be thinking about what they are doing, especially because they are very tired **2** a dead person whose body is made to move by magic, according to some African and Caribbean religions

zon·al /ˈzoʊnl/ *adj.* [only before noun] TECHNICAL relating to zones, or arranged in zones: *the zonal limits of the treaty* —**zonally** *adv.*

zone¹ /zoʊn/ *n.* [C] **1** a part of an area that is used for **SW** a particular purpose or has a special quality: *This is a no-parking zone.* | *The government has set up a special economic zone in the south for private enterprises.* | **a war/battle/combat zone** *Burda won the medals for serving in a combat zone.* **2 be in the zone** SLANG to be playing a sport very well without needing to think about it: *I was in the zone – I didn't see anything but the ball.* —see also **a buffer zone** (BUFFER¹ (3)), END ZONE, TIME ZONE

zone² *v.* **1** [T usually passive] to officially divide an area into zones for different purposes, or to say officially that a particular area must be used for a particular purpose: *Abrams's land is currently zoned for residential use.* **2** also **zone out** [I] SLANG to stop paying attention and just look in front of you without thinking for a period of time, because you are bored or because you have taken drugs: *What? Oh, sorry – I was just zoning out there for a minute.*

zoned /zoʊnd/ also **zoned out** /ˌ. ˈ./ *adj.* [not before noun] SLANG unable to think clearly and quickly, especially because you are tired or have taken drugs

zon·ing /ˈzoʊnɪŋ/ *n.* [U] an official system of choosing areas to be used for particular purposes, such as building houses or stores

zonk /zɑŋk/ also **zonk out** *v.* SLANG **1** [I] to fall asleep quickly and completely: *We got home and just zonked out on the couch.* **2** [I,T] to act strangely or become unconscious by taking drugs, or to make someone do this

zonked /zɑŋkt/ also **zonked out** /ˌ. ˈ./ *adj.* [not before noun] SLANG **1** under the influence of illegal drugs: *I could tell they were both zonked last night.* **2** extremely tired or completely asleep

zoo /zu/ *n. plural* **zoos** [C] **1** a place, usually in a **SW** city, where many kinds of animals are kept so that people can go to look at them **2** INFORMAL a place that is very loud, DISORGANIZED, and full of people: *The grocery store was a real zoo today.*

zoo·keep·er /ˈ. ˌ../ *n.* [C] someone who takes care of animals in a zoo

zoological gar·den /ˌ...ˌ... ˈ../ *n.* [C] FORMAL a zoo

zo·ol·o·gist /zoʊˈɑlədʒɪst/ *n.* [C] a scientist who studies animals and their behavior

zo·ol·o·gy /zoʊˈɑlədʒi/ *n.* [U] the scientific study of animals and their behavior —**zoological** /ˌzoʊəˈlɑdʒɪkəl/ *adj.*

zoom¹ /zum/ *v.* [I always + adv./prep.] INFORMAL **1** to go somewhere quickly, often making a lot of noise, or to do something very quickly: [+ **past/through/off etc.**] *The car was zooming down residential streets at 90 miles an hour.* | *The reader zooms through the story, hoping for a satisfactory conclusion.* **2** to increase suddenly and quickly: [+ **up/to**] *ITT shares zoomed to $58.50 in late trading.*

zoom in *phr. v.* [I] if a camera zooms in, the size of the object in a picture appears to get larger: [+ **on**] *The camera zoomed in on the child's face.*

zoom out *phr. v.* [I + **from**] if a camera zooms out, the size of the object in a picture appears to get smaller

Z

zoom lens /'. ./ *n.* [C] a camera LENS that can change from a distant to a close view —see picture at CAMERA

zoot suit /'zut sut/ *n.* [C] a man's suit that consists of wide pants and a long JACKET with wide shoulders, worn especially in the 1940s

Zor·o·as·ter /'zɔrou,æstɚ/ **Zar·a·thus·tra** /,zɛrə-'θustrə/ (?628–?553 B.C.) a Persian religious leader who started a new religion called Zoroastrianism

Zor·o·as·tri·an·ism /,zɔrou'æstriə,nɪzəm/ *n.* [U] an ancient religion from Persia, which includes a belief in a struggle between good and evil in the universe —**Zoroastrian** *n.* [C] —**Zoroastrian** *adj.*

zuc·chi·ni /zu'kini/ *n. plural* **zucchini** or **zucchinis** [C] a long green vegetable with dark green skin —see picture at VEGETABLE

Zu·lu /'zulu/ *n. plural* **Zulu** or **Zulus** [C] a member of a large tribe of people who live in South Africa —**Zulu** *adj.*

zwie·back /'zwaɪbæk, 'zwi-/ *n.* [U] a type of hard dry bread, often given to babies

zy·de·co /'zaɪdə,kou/ *n.* [U] a type of Cajun music that is popular in southern Louisiana and combines the styles of French and Caribbean music and the BLUES

zy·gote /'zaɪgout/ *n.* [C] TECHNICAL a cell that is formed when a female's egg cell is FERTILIZEd

Zzz used in writing, especially in CARTOONS, to show that someone is sleeping

Z

Numbers

How numbers are spoken

Numbers over 20

21 twenty-one

22 twenty-two

32 thirty-two

99 ninety-nine

Numbers over 100

101 a/one hundred (and) one

121 a/one hundred twenty-one

200 two hundred

232 two hundred thirty-two

999 nine hundred ninety-nine

Numbers over 1000

1001 a/one thousand (and) one

1121 one thousand one hundred twenty-one

2000 two thousand

2232 two thousand two hundred thirty-two

9999 nine thousand nine hundred ninety-nine

Ordinal numbers

20th twentieth

21st twenty-first

25th twenty-fifth

90th ninetieth

99th ninety-ninth

100th hundredth

101st a/one hundred (and) first

225th two hundred twenty-fifth

Years

1624 sixteen twenty-four

1903 nineteen-oh-three

1997 nineteen ninety-seven

2000 two thousand

2004 twenty-oh-four

What numbers represent

Numbers are often used on their own to show:

Price *It cost eight seventy-five* (=8 dollars and 75 cents: $8.75).

Time *We left at two twenty-five* (=25 minutes after 2 o'clock).

Age *She's forty-six* (=46 years old). | *He's in his sixties* (=between 60 and 69 years old).

Size *This shirt is a twelve* (=size 12).

Temperature *The temperature fell to minus fourteen* (=−14°). | *The temperature was in the mid-thirties* (=about 34–36°).

The score in a game *The Braves were ahead four to two* (=4–2).

Something marked with the stated number *She played two nines and an eight* (=playing cards marked with these numbers). | *I only have a twenty* (=a piece of paper money worth $20).

A set or group of the stated number *The teacher divided us into fours* (=groups of 4).

Numbers and grammar

Numbers can be used as:

Determiners *Five people were hurt in the accident.* | *the three largest companies in the U.S.* | *several hundred cars*

Pronouns *We invited a lot of people but only twelve came/only twelve of them came.* | *Do exercise five on page nine.*

Nouns *Six can be divided by two and three.* | *I got a seventy-five on the biology test.*

Weights and measures

U.S. customary system

Units of length

1 inch	= 2.54 cm	
12 inches	= 1 foot	= 0.3048 m
3 feet	= 1 yard	= 0.9144 m
1,760 yards or 5,280 feet	= 1 mile	= 1.609 km
2,025 yards or 6,076 feet	= 1 nautical mile	= 1.852 km

Units of weight

1 ounce	= 28.35 g	
16 ounces	= 1 pound	= 0.4536 kg
2,000 pounds	= 1 ton	= 907.18 kg
2,240 pounds	= 1 long ton	= 1,016.0 kg

Units of volume (liquid)

1 fluid ounce	= 29.574 ml	
8 fluid ounces	= 1 cup	= 0.2366 l
16 fluid ounces	= 1 pint	= 0.4732 l
2 pints	= 1 quart	= 0.9463 l
4 quarts	= 1 gallon	= 3.7853 l

Units of volume (dry measure)

1 peck	= 8,809.5 cm³	
4 pecks	= 1 bushel	= 35,239 cm³

Units of area

1 square inch	= 645.16 mm²
144 square inches	= 1 square foot = 0.0929 m²
9 square feet	= 1 square yard = 0.8361 m²
4840 square yards	= 1 acre = 4047 m²
640 acres	= 1 square mile = 259 ha

Units of temperature

degrees Fahrenheit	$= (°C \times 9/5) + 32$
degrees Celsius	$= (°F - 32) \times 5/9$

Metric system

Units of length

1 millimeter	= 0.03937 inch	
10 mm	= 1 centimeter	= 0.3937 inch
100 cm	= 1 meter	= 39.37 inches
1,000 m	= 1 kilometer	= 0.6214 mile

Units of weight

1 milligram	= 0.000035 ounce	
1,000 mg	= 1 gram	= 0.035 ounce
1,000 g	= 1 kilogram	= 2.205 pounds
1,000 kg	= 1 metric ton	= 2,205 pounds

Units of volume

1 milliliter	= 0.03 fluid ounce	
1,000 ml	= 1 liter	= 1.06 quarts

Units of area

1 square centimeter	= 0.1550 square inch
10,000 cm²	= 1 square meter = 1.196 square yards
10,000 m²	= 1 hectare = 2.471 acres

Word formation

In English there are many word beginnings (prefixes) and word endings (suffixes) that can be added to a word to change its meaning or its part of speech. The most common ones are shown here, with examples of how they are used in the process of word formation. Many more are listed in the dictionary.

Verb formation

The endings -**ize** and -**ify** can be added to many nouns and adjectives to form verbs, like this:

legal		legalize
modern	**-ize**	modernize
popular		popularize
scandal		scandalize

Elvis Presley helped to make rock 'n' roll more **popular**. *He* **popularized** *rock 'n' roll.*

beauty		beautify
pure	**-ify**	purify
simple		simplify
solid		solidify

These tablets make the water **pure**. *They* **purify** *the water.*

Adverb formation

The ending -**ly** can be added to most adjectives to form adverbs, like this:

easy		easily
main	**-ly**	mainly
quick		quickly
stupid		stupidy

His behavior was **stupid**. *He behaved* **stupidly**.

Noun formation

The endings -**er**, -**ment**, and -**ation** can be added to many verbs to form nouns, like this:

drive		driver
fasten	**-er**	fastener
open		opener
teach		teacher

John **drives** *a bus. He is a bus* **driver**.
A can **opener** *is a tool for* **opening** *cans.*

amaze		amazement
develop	**-ment**	development
pay		payment
retire		retirement

Children **develop** *very quickly. Their* **development** *is very quick.*

admire		admiration
associate	**-ation**	association
examine		examination
organize		organization

The doctor **examined** *me carefully. She gave me a careful* **examination**.

The endings -**ty**, -**ity**, and -**ness** can be added to many adjectives to form nouns, like this:

cruel		cruelty
odd	**-ty**	oddity
pure	**-ity**	purity
stupid		stupidity

Don't be so **cruel**. *I hate* **cruelty**.

dark		darkness
deaf	**-ness**	deafness
happy		happiness
kind		kindness

It was very **dark**. *The* **darkness** *made it impossible to see.*

Adjective formation

The endings -**y**, -**ic**, -**ical**, -**ful**, and -**less** can be added to many nouns to form adjectives, like this:

bush		bushy
dirt	**-y**	dirty
hair		hairy
smell		smelly

There was a bad **smell** *in the room. The room was very* **smelly**.

algebra		algebraic
atom	**-ic**	atomic
biology	**-ical**	biological
mythology		mythological

Her work involves research in **biology**. *She does* **biological** *research.*

pain		painful
hope	**-ful**	hopeful
care		careful

His broken leg caused him a lot of **pain**. *It was very* **painful**.

pain		painless
hope	**-less**	hopeless
care		careless

The operation didn't cause her any **pain**. *It was* **painless**.

The ending **-able** can be added to many verbs to form adjectives, like this:

wash		washable
love	**-able**	lovable
debate		debatable
break		breakable

*You can **wash** this coat. It's **washable**.*

Opposites

The following prefixes can be used in front of many words to produce an opposite meaning. Note, however, that the words formed in this way are not always EXACT opposites, and may have a slightly different meaning.

un-	happy	unhappy
	fortunate	unfortunate
	wind	unwind
	block	unblock

*I'm not very **happy**. In fact, I'm very **unhappy**.*

in-	efficient	inefficient
im-	possible	impossible
il-	literate	illiterate
ir-	regular	irregular

*It's just not **possible** to do that; it's totally **impossible**.*

dis-	agree	disagree
	approve	disapprove
	honest	dishonest

*I don't **agree** with everything you said. I **disagree** with the last part.*

de-	centralize	decentralize
	increase	decrease
	ascend	descend
	inflate	deflate

Increase means to make or become larger in amount or number. **Decrease** means to make or become smaller in amount or number.

non-	sense	nonsense
	alcoholic	nonalcoholic
	violent	nonviolent
	conformist	nonconformist

*Children are not allowed to have **alcoholic** drinks. There are **nonalcoholic** beverages available for them.*

The verb "be"

Present

		questions	*negatives*
I	I am, I'm	am I?	I am not, I'm not, aren't I?
you	you are, you're	are you?	you are not, you're not, you aren't
she/he/it	she is, he's	is she/he/it?	it is not, he's not, she isn't
we/they	we are, they're	are we/they?	we are not, they're not, we aren't

present participle: being

Past

		questions	*negatives*
I	I was	was I?	I was not, I wasn't
you	you were	were you?	you were not, you weren't,
she/he/it	he was	was she/he/it?	she was not, it wasn't
we/they	we were	were we/they?	they were not, we weren't

past participle: been

Irregular verbs

verb	past tense	past participle
abide	abided, abode	abided
alight	alighted, alit	alighted, alit
arise	arose	arisen
awake	awoke	awoken
babysit	babysat	babysat
be	(see Table)	
bear	bore	borne
beat	beat	beaten
become	became	become
befall	befell	befallen
befit	befitted	befitted
beget	begot, begat	begotten
begin	began	begun
behold	beheld	beheld
bend	bent	bent
beseech	beseeched, besought	beseeched, besought
beset	beset	beset
bespeak	bespoke	bespoken
bestride	bestrode	bestridden
bet	bet	bet
betake	betook	betaken
bethink	bethought	bethought
bid[2]	bid	bid
bind	bound	bound
bite	bit	bitten
bleed	bled	bled
blow	blew	blown
bottle-feed	bottle-fed	bottle-fed
break	broke	broken
breastfeed	breastfed	breastfed
breed	bred	bred
bring	brought	brought
broadcast	broadcast	broadcast
browbeat	browbeat	browbeaten
build	built	built
burn	burned, burnt	burned, burnt
burst	burst	burst
buy	bought	bought
can	(see dictionary entry)	
cast	cast	cast
catch	caught	caught
choose	chose	chosen
cleave	cleaved, clove, cleft	cleaved, cloven, cleft
cling	clung	clung
come	came	come
cost[2]	cost	cost
could	(see dictionary entry)	
creep	crept	crept
cut	cut	cut
deal	dealt /dɛlt/	dealt
dig	dug	dug
dive	dived, dove	dived
do	did	done
draw	drew	drawn
dream	dreamed, dreamt	dreamed, dreamt
drink	drank	drunk
drive	drove	driven
dwell	dwelled, dwelt	dwelled, dwelt

verb	past tense	past participle
eat	ate	eaten
fall	fell	fallen
feed	fed	fed
feel	felt	felt
fight	fought	fought
find	found	found
fit	fit, fitted	fit, fitted
flee	fled	fled
fling	flung	flung
fly	flew	flown
forbear	forbore	forborne
forbid	forbade, forbid	forbidden
force-feed	force-fed	force-fed
forecast	forecast	forecast
foresee	foresaw	foreseen
foretell	foretold	foretold
forget	forgot	forgotten
forgive	forgave	forgiven
forgo	forwent	forgone
freeze	froze	frozen
gainsay	gainsaid	gainsaid
get	got	gotten
gird	girded, girt	girded, girt
give	gave	given
go	went	gone
grind	ground	ground
grow	grew	grown
hamstring	hamstrung	hamstrung
hang[1]	hung	hung
have	had	had
hear	heard	heard
heave	heaved, hove	heaved, hove
hew	hewed	hewn, hewed
hide	hid	hidden, hid
hit	hit	hit
hold	held	held
hurt	hurt	hurt
input	inputted, input	inputted, input
inset	inset	inset
interbreed	interbred	interbred
interweave	interwove	interwoven
keep	kept	kept
kneel	**knelt, kneeled**	**knelt, kneeled**
knit	knit, knitted	knit, knitted
know	knew	known
lay	laid	laid
lead	led	led
leap	leaped, leapt	leaped, leapt
leave	left	left
lend	lent	lent
let	let	let
lie	lay	lain
light	lit, lighted	lit, lighted
lose	lost	lost
make	made	made
may	(see dictionary entry)	
mean	meant	meant
meet	met	met
might	(see dictionary entry)	
miscast	miscast	miscast
mishear	misheard	misheard

verb	past tense	past participle
mislay	mislaid	mislaid
mislead	misled	misled
misread	misread /ˌmɪsˈrɛd/	misread /ˌmɪsˈrɛd/
misspend	misspent	misspent
mistake	mistook	mistaken
misunderstand	misunderstood	misunderstood
mow	mowed	mown, mowed
offset	offset	offset
outbid	outbid	outbid
outdo	outdid	outdone
outgrow	outgrew	outgrown
outride	outrode	outridden
outrun	outran	outrun
outsell	outsold	outsold
outshine	outshone	outshone
outshoot	outshot	outshot
outspend	outspent	outspent
overcome	overcame	overcome
overdo	overdid	overdone
overeat	overate	overeaten
overhang	overhung	overhung
overhear	overheard	overheard
overlay	overlaid	overlaid
overpay	overpaid	overpaid
override	overrode	overridden
overrun	overran	overrun
oversee	oversaw	overseen
oversell	oversold	oversold
overshoot	overshot	overshot
oversleep	overslept	overslept
overspend	overspent	overspent
overtake	overtook	overtaken
overthrow	overthrew	overthrown
partake	partook	partaken
pay	paid	paid
plead	pleaded, pled	pleaded, pled
proofread	proofread /ˈpruːfrɛd/	proofread /ˈpruːfrɛd/
prove	proved	proved, proven
put	put	put
quit	quit	quit
read	read /rɛd/	read /rɛd/
rebuild	rebuilt	rebuilt
recast	recast	recast
redo	redid	redone
relay[3]	relaid	relaid
remake	remade	remade
rend	rent	rent
repay	repaid	repaid
rerun	reran	rerun
resell	resold	resold
reset	reset	reset
retell	retold	retold
rethink	rethought	rethought
rewind	rewound	rewound
rewrite	rewrote	rewritten
rid	rid	rid
ride	rode	ridden
ring	rang	rung
rise	rose	risen
run	ran	run
saw	sawed	sawed, sawn

verb	past tense	past participle
say	said	said
see	saw	seen
seek	sought	sought
sell	sold	sold
send	sent	sent
set	set	set
sew	sewed	sewn, sewed
shake	shook	shaken
shall	(see dictionary entry)	
shear	sheared	shorn, sheared
shed	shed	shed
shine[1]	shone	shone
shit	shit, shat	shit, shat
shoe	shod	shod
shoot	shot	shot
should	(see dictionary entry)	
show	showed	shown
shrink	shrank, shrunk	shrunk
shut	shut	shut
sight-read	sight-read /ˈsaɪtrɛd/	sight-read /ˈsaɪtrɛd/
simulcast	simulcast	simulcast
sing	sang	sung
sink	sank, sunk	sunk
sit	sat	sat
slay	slew	slain
sleep	slept	slept
slide	slid	slid
sling	slung	slung
slink	slunk	slunk
slit	slit	slit
smite	smote	smitten
sneak	sneaked, snuck	sneaked, snuck
sow	sowed	sowed, sown
speak	spoke	spoken
speed	sped, speeded	sped, speeded
spill	spilled, spilt	spilled, spilt
spin	spun	spun
spit	spit, spat	spit, spat
split	split	split
spoon-feed	spoon-fed	spoon-fed
spotlight	spotlighted, spotlit	spotlighted, spotlit
spread	spread	spread
spring	sprang, sprung	sprung
stand	stood	stood
steal	stole	stolen
stick	stuck	stuck
sting	stung	stung
stink	stank	stunk
strew	strewed	strewn, strewed
stride	strode	stridden
strike	struck	struck
string	strung	strung
strive	strove	striven
swear	swore	sworn
sweep	swept	swept
swell	swelled	swollen
swim	swam	swum
swing	swung	swung
take	took	taken
teach	taught	taught
tear	tore	torn

verb	past tense	past participle
tell	told	told
think	thought	thought
thrive	thrived, throve	thrived
throw	threw	thrown
thrust	thrust	thrust
tread	trod	trodden
unbend	unbent	unbent
unbind	unbound	unbound
undergo	underwent	undergone
underlie	underlay	underlain
underpay	underpaid	underpaid
undersell	undersold	undersold
understand	understood	understood
undertake	undertook	undertaken
underwrite	underwrote	underwritten
undo	undid	undone
unwind	unwound	unwound
uphold	upheld	upheld
upset	upset	upset
wake	woke	woken
waylay	waylaid	waylaid
wear	wore	worn
weave	wove	woven
wed	wedded, wed	wedded, wed
weep	wept	wept
wet	wet, wetted	wet, wetted
will	(see dictionary entry)	
win	won	won
wind /waɪnd/	wound	wound
withdraw	withdrew	withdrawn
withhold	withheld	withheld
withstand	withstood	withstood
would	(see dictionary entry)	
wreak	wreaked, wrought	wreaked, wrought
wring	wrung	wrung
write	wrote	written

Words used in the definitions in this dictionary

All the definitions in this dictionary have been written using the words on this list. If a definition includes a word that is not on the list, that word is shown in SMALL CAPITAL LETTERS.

The Defining Vocabulary has been carefully chosen after a thorough study of all the well-known frequency lists of English words. Furthermore, only the most common and "central" meanings of the words on the list have actually been used in definitions. We have also used a special computer program that checks every entry to make sure that words from outside the Defining Vocabulary do not appear in definitions.

Restrictions on parts of speech

For some words on the list, a label such as *n.* or *adj.* is shown. This means that this particular word is used in definitions only in the part of speech shown. So **anger**, for example, is used only as a noun and not as a verb. But if no word class is shown for a word, it can be used in any of its usual parts of speech: **answer**, for example, is used in definitions both as a noun and as a verb.

Compound words

Definitions occasionally include compound words formed from words in the Defining Vocabulary, but this is only done if the meaning is completely clear. For example, the word **businessman** (formed from **business** and **man**) is used in some definitions.

Prefixes and suffixes

The main list is followed by a list of common prefixes and suffixes. These can be added to words on the main list to form derived words, provided the meaning is completely clear. For example, the word **nervousness** (formed by adding **-ness** to **nervous**) is used in some definitions.

Phrasal verbs

Phrasal verbs formed by combining words in the Defining Vocabulary (for example, **put up with**) are NOT used in definitions in the dictionary, except in a very small number of cases where the phrasal verb is extremely common and there is no common equivalent. So, for example, **give up** (as in **give up smoking**) and **take off** (as in **the plane took off**) are occasionally used.

Proper nouns

The Defining Vocabulary does not include the names of actual places, nationalities, religions, and so on, which are occasionally mentioned in definitions.

A

a
abbreviation
ability
able
about
above adv., prep.
abroad
absence
absent adj.
accept
acceptable
accident
according (to)
account n.
achieve
acid
across
act
action n.
active adj.
activity
actor, actress
actual
actually
add
addition
address
adjective
admiration
admire
admit
adult
advanced
advantage
adventure n.
adverb
advertise
advertisement
advice
advise
affair
affect v.
afford
afraid
after adv., conj., prep.
afternoon
afterward(s)
again
against
age n.
ago
agree
agreement
ahead
aim
air n.
airplane
airport

alcohol
alive
all adv., pron., determiner
allow
almost
alone
along
alphabet
already
also
although
always
among
amount n.
amuse
amusement
amusing adj.
an
ancient adj.
and
anger n.
angle n.
angry
animal
announce
announcement
annoy
another
answer
anxiety
anxious
any
anymore
anyone
anything
anywhere
apart
apartment
appear
appearance
apple
appropriate
approval
approve
area
argue
argument
arm
army
around
arrange
arrangement
arrival
arrive
art
article
artificial
artist
as
ash

ashamed
ask
asleep
association
at
atom
attach
attack
attempt
attend
attention
attitude
attract
attractive
authority
available
average adj., n.
avoid
awake adj.
away adv.
awkward

B

baby
back adj., adv., n.
background
backward(s) adv.
bad adj.
bag n.
bake
balance
ball n.
band n.
bank n.
bar n.
barely
base n., v.
baseball
basic
basket
basketball
bath n.
bathtub
battle n.
be
beach
beak
beam n.
bean
bear
beard n.
beat n., v.
beautiful
beauty
because
become
bed n.
beer
before

begin
beginning
behave
behavior
behind adv., prep.
belief
believe
bell
belong
below adv., prep.
belt n.
bend
beneath
berry
beside
besides
best adj., adv., n.
better adj., adv.
between
beyond adj., adv.
bicycle n.
big adj.
bill n.
bird
birth
bite
bitter adj.
black adj., n.
blade
blame
bleed
blind
block
blood n.
blow
blue
board n.
boat n.
body
boil
bomb
bone n.
book n.
boot n.
border
bored
boring
born
borrow
both
bottle n.
bottom n.
bowl n.
box n.
boy
brain n.
branch
brave adj.
bread
break v.

breakfast n.
breast n.
breath
breathe
breed
brick n.
bridge n.
bright adj.
bring
broad adj.
broadcast
brother
brown adj., n.
brush
bucket n.
build v.
building
bullet
bunch n.
burn
burst
bury
bus n.
bush n.
business
busy
but conj.
butter n.
button n.
buy v.
by

C

cake n.
calculate
call
calm adj.
camera
camp n., v.
can n., v.
candy
cap n.
capital n.
car
card n.
care
careful
careless
carriage
carry
case n.
castle n.
cat
catch v.
cattle
cause
ceiling
celebrate
cell
cent

center n.
centimeter
central
century
ceremony
certain adj.,
    determiner
chain
chair n.
chance n.
change
character
charge
chase v.
cheap
cheat v.
check n., v.
cheek n.
cheerful
cheese
chemical
chemistry
chest
chew
chicken n.
chief
child
children
chin
chocolate
choice n.
choose
church n.
cigarette
circle n.
circular adj.
citizen
city
claim
class n.
clay
clean adv., v.
clear adj., v.
clerk
clever
cliff
climb v.
clock n.
close adj., adv.,
    v.
cloth
clothes
clothing
cloud n.
club n.
coal
coast n.
coat n.
coffee
coin n.
cold adj., n.

collar n.
collect v.
college
color
comb
combination
combine v.
come
comfort
comfortable
command
committee
common adj.
communicate
communication
company
compare
comparison
compete
competition
competitor
complain
complaint
complete
completely
complicated
compound n.
computer
concern v.
concerning
concert
condition n.
confidence
confident
confuse
connect
connection
conscious
consider
consist
container
continue
continuous
contract n.
control
convenient
conversation
cook n., v.
cookie
cool
copy
corn
corner n.
correct adj.
cost
cotton
cough
could
council
country n.
courage

course n.
court n.
cover
cow n.
crack n., v.
crash n., v.
crazy
cream n.
creature
crime
criminal
criticism
criticize
crop n.
cross n., v.
crowd n.
cruel
crush v.
cry
cup n.
cupboard
cure
curl
current n.
curtain n.
curve
customer
cut

D

daily adj., adv.
damage
dance
danger
dangerous
dark
date n.
daughter
day
dead adj.
deal n.
deal with
death
debt
decay
deceit
deceive
decide
decision
decorate
decoration
decrease
deep adj.
defeat
defense
defend
definite
degree
delay
deliberate

delicate
deliver
demand
department
depend
dependent
depth
describe
description
desert n.
deserve
design
desirable
desire
desk
despite
destroy
destruction
detail n.
determination
determined
develop
dictionary
die v.
difference
different
difficult
difficulty
dig v.
dinner
dip v.
direct
direction
dirt
dirty adj.
disappoint
discover
discovery
discuss
discussion
disease n.
disgusting
dish n.
dismiss
distance n.
distant
divide v.
do v.
doctor n.
document n.
dog n.
dollar
door
double adj., v.
doubt
down adv., prep.
draw v.
drawer
dream
dress n., v.
drink

drive n., v.
drop
drug n.
drum n.
drunk adj.
dry
duck n.
dull adj.
during
dust n.
duty

E

each
eager
ear
early
earn
earth n.
east
eastern
easy adj.
eat
economic
edge n.
educate
educated
education
effect n.
effective
effort
egg n.
eight
eighth
either
elbow n.
elect v.
election
electric
electricity
electronic
else
embarrass
emotion
emphasize
employ v.
employer
employment
empty adj., v.
enclose
encourage
end
enemy
energy
engine
engineer n.
enjoy
enjoyable
enjoyment
enough

enter
entertain
entertainment
entrance *n.*
envelope
environment
equal *adj., n., v.*
equipment
escape
especially
establish
even *adj., adv.*
evening
event
ever
every
everyone
everything
everywhere
evil
exact *adj.*
exactly
examination
examine
example
excellent
except *conj., prep.*
exchange
excite
exciting
excuse
exercise
exist
existence
expect
expensive
experience
explain
explanation
explode
explosion
explosive
express *v.*
expression
extreme
eye

F

face
fact
factory
fail *v.*
failure
faint *adj., v.*
fair *adj.*
fairly
faith
faithful
fall

false *adj.*
family
family
famous
far
farm
farmer
farther
farthest
fashion *n.*
fashionable
fast *adj., adv.*
fasten
fat
father *n.*
fault *n.*
favorable
favorite *adj.*
fear *n.*
feather *n.*
feature
feed *v.*
feel *v.*
feeling(s)
female
fence *n.*
fever
few
field *n.*
fierce
fifth
fight
figure *n.*
fill *v.*
film *v.* (and *n.* for camera)
final *adj.*
finally
financial
find *v.*
find out
fine *adj.*
finger *n.*
finish
fire
firm *adj., n.*
first *adv., determiner*
fish
fit *adj., v.*
five
fix *v.*
flag *n.*
flame *n.*
flash *n., v.*
flat *adj.*
flesh
flight
float *v.*
flood
floor *n.*

flour *n.*
flow
flower *n.*
fly *n., v.*
fold
follow
food
foot *n.*
football
for *prep.*
forbid
force *n., v.*
foreign
forest
forever
forget
forgive
fork *n.*
form *n., v.*
formal
former
fortunate
forward(s) *adv.*
four(th)
frame *n.*
free
freedom
freeze *v.*
frequent *adj.*
fresh
friend
friendly
frighten
frightening
from
front *adj., n.*
fruit *n.*
full *adj.*
fun
funeral
funny
fur *n.*
furniture
further *adj., adv.*
future

G

gain *v.*
gallon
game *n.*
garage *n.*
garden
gas *n.*
gasoline
gate *n.*
gather *v.*
general
generally
generous
gentle

get
gift
girl
give *v.*
glad
glass *adj., n.*
glue
go *v.*
goat
god, God
gold
good
goodbye
goods
govern
government
graceful
grade
gradual
grain
gram
grammar
grand *adj.*
grandfather
grandmother
grandparent
grass *n.*
grateful
grave *n.*
gray *adj., n.*
great *adj.*
green
greet
greeting
ground *n.*
group *n.*
grow
growth
guard *v.*
guess *v.*
guest *n.*
guide
guilty
gun *n.*

H

habit
hair
half
hall
hammer *n.*
hand *n.*
handle
hang *v.*
happen *v.*
happy
hard
hardly
harm
harmful

hat
hate *v.*
hatred
have
he *adj.*
head *n.*
health
healthy
hear
heart
heat
heaven
heavy *adj.*
heel
height
hello
help
helpful
her(s)
here
herself
hide *v.*
high *adj., adv.*
high school
hill
him
himself
his
historical
history
hit *v.*
hold
hole
holiday
hollow *adj.*
holy
home *adv., n.*
honest
honor *n.*
hook *n.*
hope
hopeful
horn
horse *n.*
hospital
hot *adj.*
hotel
hour
house *n.*
how *adv.*
human
humorous
humor
hundred(th)
hungry
hunt *v.*
hurry
hurt *v.*
husband *n.*

I

ice n.
idea
if
ignore
ill adj.
illegal
illness
image
imaginary
imagination
imagine
immediate
immediately
importance
important
impressive
improve
improvement
in adv., prep.
inch
include
including
income
increase
independent
indoor(s)
industrial
industry
infect
infection
infectious
influence
inform
information
injure
injury
ink n.
inner
insect
inside
instead
institution
instruction
instrument
insult v.
insurance
insure
intelligent
intelligence
intend
intention
interest
interesting
international adj.
   interrupt
into
introduce
introduction
invent

invitation
invite
involve
inward(s)
iron adj., n.
island
it pron.
its
itself

J

jaw n.
jewel
jewelry
job
join
joint
joke
judge
judgment
juice
jump
just adv.
justice

K

keep v.
key n.
kick
kill v.
kilogram
kilometer
kind
king
kiss
kitchen
knee n.
kneel
knife n.
knock
knot
know v.
knowledge

L

lack
lady
lake
lamb
lamp
land
language
large
last adv.,
   determiner
late
lately
laugh

laughter
law
lawyer
lay v.
layer n.
lazy n.
lead/led v.
leaf n.
lean v.
learn
least
leather
leave v.
left
leg n.
legal
lend
length
less
lesson
let v.
let go of
let out
letter
level adj., n.
library
lid
lie
lie down
life
lift
light
like prep., v.
likely
limit
line n.
lion
lip
liquid
list n.
listen v.
literature
liter
little
live v.
load
loaf n.
local adj.
lock
lonely
long adj., adv.
look
look for
loose adj.
lose
loss
lot
loud
love
low adj.
lower v.

loyal
loyalty
luck n.
lucky
lung

M

machine n.
machinery
magazine
magic
mail
main adj.
make v.
make into
make up
male
man n.
manage
manager
manner
many
map n.
march
mark
market n.
marriage
married
marry
mass n.
match
material n.
mathematics
matter
may v.
me
meal
mean v.
meaning n.
means
measure
meat
medical adj.
medicine
meet v.
meeting
melt
member
memory
mental
mention v.
mess
message
messy
metal n.
meter
method
middle adj., n.
might v.
mile

military adj.
milk
million(th)
mind
mine n., pron.
mineral
minister n.
minute n.
mirror n.
miss v.
mist n.
mistake
mix v.
mixture
model n.
modern adj.
moment
money
monkey n.
month
monthly
mood
moon n.
moral adj.
more
morning
most
mother n.
motor adj., n.
mountain
mouse
mouth n.
move v.
movement
movie
much
mud
multiply
murder
muscle n.
music
musician
must v.
my
mysterious
mystery

N

nail
name
narrow adj.
nasty
nation
national adj.
natural
nature
navy
near adj., adv.,
   prep.
nearly

neat
necessary
neck
need
needle n.
negative
neither
nerve n.
nervous
nest n.
net n.
network n.
never
new
news
newspaper
next adj., adv.
nice
night
nine
ninth
no adv.,
    determiner
noise n.
none pron.
nonsense
no one
nor
normal
north
northern
nose n.
not
note
nothing
notice
noun
now
nowhere
number n.
nurse
nut

O

obey
object n.
obtain
occasion n.
ocean
o'clock
odd
of
off adv., prep.
offense
offend
offensive adj.
offer
office
officer
official

often
oil n
old
old-fashioned
on adv., prep.
once adv.
one
onion
only
onto
open adj., v.
operate
operation
opinion
opponent
opportunity
oppose
as opposed to
opposite
opposition
or
orange
order
ordinary
organ
organize
organization
origin
original
other
ought
our(s)
out adj., adv.
outdoor(s)
outer
outside
over adv., prep.
owe
own determiner
owner
oxygen

P

pack v.
package
page n.
pain n.
painful
paint
painting
pair n.
pale adj.
pan n.
pants
paper n.
parallel adj., n.
parent n.
park
part n.
particular adj.

partly
partner n.
party n.
pass v.
passage
passenger
past
path
patience
patient adj.
pattern n.
pause
pay
payment
peace
peaceful
pen n.
pencil n.
people n.
pepper n.
per
perfect adj.
perform
performance
perhaps
period n.
permanent
permission
person
personal
persuade
pet n.
photograph
phrase n.
physical adj.
piano n.
pick v.
pick up
picture n.
piece n.
pig n.
pile n.
pilot n.
pin
pink adj., n.
pipe n.
pity
place
plain adj., n.
plan
plane n.
plant
plastic
plate n.
play
pleasant
please
pleased
pleasure n.
plenty pron.
plural

pocket n.
poem
poet
poetry
point
pointed
poison
poisonous
pole n.
police n.
polish
polite
political
politician
politics
pool n.
poor
popular
population
port n.
position n.
positive
possess
possession
possible adj.
possibly
possibility
post
pot n.
potato
pound n.
pour
powder n.
power n.
powerful
practical
practice
praise
pray
prayer
prefer
preparation
prepare
present adj., n.
preserve v.
president
press v.
pressure n.
pretend
pretty adj.
prevent
previous
previously
price n.
priest
prince
principle
print
prison
prisoner
private adj.

prize n.
probably adv.
problem
process n.
produce v.
product
production
profession
profit n.
program
progress n.
promise
pronounce
pronunciation
proof n.
property
proposal
protect
protection
protective
protest
proud
prove
provide
public adj.
publicly
pull
pump
punish
punishment
pure
purple
purpose n.
push
put

Q

quality
quantity
quarrel
quarter n.
queen n.
question
quick adj.
quiet adj., n.

R

rabbit n.
race
radio n.
railroad
rain
raise v.
range n.
rank n.
rapid adj.
rare
rat n.
rate n.

rather
raw
reach
react
reaction
read *v.*
ready *adj.*
real
realize
really
reason
reasonable
receive
recent
recently
recognize
record *n., v.*
red
reduce
reduction
refusal
refuse *v.*
regard *v.*
regular *adj.*
related
relative
relation
relationship
relax
religion
religious
remain
remark *n.*
remember
remind
remove *v.*
rent
repair
repeat *v.*
reply
report
represent
representative *n.*
request *n.*
respect
responsible
rest
restaurant
restrict
result
return *n., v.*
reward
rice
rich
rid
ride
right *adj., adv., n.*
ring
ripe
rise
risk

river
road
rob
rock *n.*
roll *v.*
romantic *adj* .
roof *n.*
room *n.*
root *n.*
rope *n.*
rose
rough *adj.*
round *adj.*
row *n., v.*
royal *adj.*
rub *v.*
rubber
rude
ruin *v.*
rule
ruler
run
rush *v.*

S

sad
safe *adj.*
safety
sail
salary
sale
salt *n.*
same
sand *n.*
satisfaction
satisfactory
satisfy
save *v.*
say *v.*
scale *n.*
scatter *v.*
scene
school *n.*
science
scientific
scientist
scissors
screen *n.*
screw
sea
search
season *n.*
seat
second *adv., n.,*
    determiner
secrecy
secret
secretary
see *v.*
seed *n.*

seem
seize
sell *v.*
send
sensation
sense *n.*
sensible
sensitive
sentence *n.*
separate *adv., v.*
series
serious
seriously
servant
serve
service *n.*
set *n., v.*
settle *v.*
seven(th)
several
severe
sew
sex *n.*
sexual
shade
shadow *n.*
shake
shall
shame *n.*
shape
share
sharp *adj.*
she
sheep
sheet
shelf
shell *n.*
shelter
shine *v.*
shiny
ship *n.*
shirt
shock *n., v.*
shoe *n.*
shoot *v.*
shop
shore *n.*
short *adj.*
shot *n.*
should
shoulder *n.*
shout
show *n., v.*
shut
shy
sick *adj.*
sickness
side
sideways
sight *n.*
sign

signal
silence *n.*
silent
silk
silly *adj.*
silver
similar
similarity
simple
since
sincere
sing
single *adj.*
singular
sink *v.*
sister
sit
situation
six(th)
size *n.*
skill
skillful
skin *n.*
skirt *n.*
sky *n.*
slave *n.*
sleep
slide *v.*
slight *adj.*
slip *v.*
slippery
slope
slow
small
smart
smell
smile
smoke
smooth *adj.*
snake *n.*
snow
so
soap *n.*
social *adj.*
society
sock *n.*
soft
soil *n.*
soldier *n.*
solid
solution
solve
some *pron.,*
    determiner
somehow
someone
something
sometimes
somewhere
son
song

soon
sore *adj.*
sorrow *n.*
sorry
sort *n.*
soul
sound *n., v.*
soup
sour *adj.*
south
southern
space *n.*
spade
speak
special *adj.*
specific
speech
speed *n.*
spell *v.*
spend
spin *v.*
spirit *n.*
split *v.*
spoil *v.*
spoon *n.*
sport(s) *n.*
spot *n.*
spread *v.*
spring
square *adj., n.*
stage *n.*
stair
stamp
stand *v.*
standard
star *n.*
start
state
statement
station *n.*
stay
steady *adj.*
steal *v.*
steam *n.*
steel *n.*
steep *adj.*
stem *n.*
step
stick
sticky
stiff *adj.*
still *adj., adv.*
sting
stitch
stomach *n.*
stone *n.*
stop
store
storm *n.*
story
straight *adj., adv.*

strange
stranger
stream *n.*
street
strength
stretch *v.*
strict
strike *v.*
string *n.*
strong
structure *n.*
struggle
student
study
stupid
style *n.*
subject *n.*
substance
subtract
succeed
success
successful
such
suck *v.*
sudden
suffer
sugar *n.*
suggest
suit
suitcase
suitable
sum *n.*
summer *n.*
sun *n.*
supper
supply *n., v.*
support
suppose
sure *adj.*
surface *n.*
surprise
surround *v.*
swallow *v.*
swear
sweep *v.*
sweet
swell *v.*
swim
swing
sword
sympathetic
sympathy
system

T _____

table *n.*
tail *n.*
take *v.*
take care of
talk

tall
taste
tax
taxi *n.*
tea
teach
team *n.*
tear *v., n.*
technical
telephone
television
tell
temperature
temporary
ten(th)
tend
tendency
tennis
tense *n.*
tent
terrible
terror
test
than
thank
that *conj., pron.,*
   determiner
the
theater
their(s)
them
then *adv.*
there
therefore
these
they
thick *adj.*
thief
thin *adj.*
thing
think *v.*
third
this *pron.,*
   determiner
thorough
those
though
thought
thousand(th)
thread *n.*
threat
threaten
three
throat
through *adv.,*
   prep.
throw
thumb *n.*
ticket *n.*
tie
tiger

tight *adj.*
time *n.*
tire *n.*
tired
tiring
title
to
tobacco
today
toe *n.*
together
toilet
tomorrow
tongue
tonight
too
tool *n.*
tooth
top *adj., n.*
total *adj., n.*
touch
tourist
toward
tower *n.*
town
toy *n.*
track
trade *n.*
tradition
traditional
traffic *n.*
train
training
translate
transparent
trap
travel
treat *v.*
treatment
tree
tribe
trick *n., v.*
trip *n.*
tropical
trouble
truck *n.*
true *adj.*
trunk
truth
trust
try *v.*
tube
tune *n.*
turn
twice
twist
two
type *n.*
typical

U _____

ugly
uncle
under *prep.*
understand
underwear
undo
uniform *n.*
union
unit
unite
universe
university
unless
until
up *adj., adv.,*
   prep.
upper *adj.*
upright *adj., adv.*
upset *v., adj.*
upside down
upstairs *adj.,*
   adv.
urgent
us
use
useful
useless
usual

V _____

vacation
valley
valuable *adj.*
value *n.*
variety
various
vegetable
vehicle
verb
very *adv.*
victory
view *n.*
violence
violent
visit
voice *n.*
vote
vowel

W _____

waist
wait *v.*
wake *v.*
walk
wall *n.*
wander
want *v.*

war *n.*
warm *adj., v.*
warmth
warn
warning
wash
waste
watch
water
wave
way
we
weak
wealth
weapon
wear *v.*
weather *n.*
weave *v.*
wedding
week
weekly *adj., adv.*
weigh
weight *n.*
welcome
well *adj., adv., n.*
west
western *adj.*
wet *adj.*
what *determiner,*
   pron.
whatever
wheat
wheel *n.*
when *adv., conj.*
whenever
where
whether
which
whichever
while *conj.*
whip
whisper
whistle
white
who
whole
whose
why
wide *adj., adv.*
width
wife
wild *adj., adv.*
will
willing
win *v.*
wind *n., v.*
window
wine *n.*
wing *n.*
winter *n.*
wire *n.*

			Y	young
wise *adj.*	wooden	worth		your(s)
wisdom	wool	would		yourself
wish	word *n.*	wound	yard	
with	work	wrap *v.*	year	**Z**
within *prep.*	world	wrist	yearly	
without *prep.*	worm *n.*	write	yellow *adj., n.*	zero
witness *n.*	worry	wrong *adj.,*	yesterday	
woman	worse	*adv., n.*	yet	
wood	worst		you	

Prefixes and suffixes that can be used with words in the Defining Vocabulary

-able	-ed	-ical	ir-	-less	re-
-al	-ence	im-	-ish	-ly	self
-ance	-er	in-	-ity	-ment	-th
-ation	-ful	-ing	-ive	-ness	un-
dis	-ic	-ion	-ize	non-	-y

This dictionary shows pronunciations used by speakers of the most common American English dialects. Sometimes more than one pronunciation is shown. For example, many Americans say the first vowel in *data* as /eɪ/, while many others say this vowel as /æ/. We show *data* as /'deɪtə,'dætə/. This means that both pronunciations are possible and are commonly used by educated speakers. We have not, however, shown all American dialects and all possible pronunciations. For example, *news* is shown only as /nuz/ even though a few Americans might pronounce this word as /nyuz/. The vowels /ɔ/ and /ɑ/ are both shown, but many speakers do not use the sound /ɔ/. These speakers say /ɑ/ in place of /ɔ/, so that *caught* and *cot* are both said as /kɑt/.

Use of the hyphen

When more than one pronunciation is given for a word, we usually show only the part of the pronunciation that is different from the first pronunciation, replacing the parts that are the same with a hyphen: **economics** /ˌɛkə'namɪks, ˌi-/. The hyphen is also used for showing the division between syllables when this might not be clear: **boyish** /'bɔɪ-ɪʃ/, **drawing** /'drɔ-ɪŋ/, **clockwise** /'klɑk-waɪz/.

Symbols

The symbols used in this dictionary are based on the symbols of the International Phonetic Alphabet (IPA) with a few changes. The symbol /y/, which is closer to English spelling than the /j/ used in the IPA, is used for the first sound in *you* /yu/. Other changes are described in the paragraph **American English Sounds**.

Foreign words

English pronunciations have been shown for foreign words, even though some speakers may use a pronunciation closer to that of the original language.

Abbreviations

No pronunciations are shown for most abbreviations. This is either because they are not spoken (and are defined as "written abbreviations"), or because they are pronounced by saying the names of the letters, with main stress on the last letter and secondary stress on the first: **VCR** /ˌvi si 'ɑr/. Pronunciations have been shown where an abbreviation is spoken like an ordinary word: **RAM** /ræm/.

Words that are forms of main words

A form of a main word that is a different part of speech may come at the end of the entry for that word. If the related word is pronounced by saying the main word and adding an ending, no separate pronunciation is given. If the addition of the ending causes a change in the pronunciation of the main word, the pronunciation for the related word is given. For example: **impossible** /ɪm'pasəbəl/, **impossibility** /ɪmˌpasə'bɪləti/.

There are some pronunciation changes that we do not show at these entries, because they follow regular patterns: (1) When a *-ly* or *-er* ending is added to a main word ending in /-bəl/, /-kəl/, /-pəl/, /-gəl/, or /-dəl/, the /ə/ is usually omitted. For example, **audible** is shown as /'ɔdəbəl/. When *-ly* is added to it, it becomes **audibly** /'ɔdəbli/. This difference is not shown. (2) When *-ly* or *-ity* is added to words ending in *-y* /i/, the /i/ becomes /ə/: **angry** /'æŋgri/ becomes **angrily** /'æŋgrəli/. This is not shown.

Stress

In English words of two or more syllables, at least one syllable is said with more force than the others. The sign /'/ is put before the syllable with the most force. We say it has *main stress*: **person** /'pɚsən/, **percent** /pɚ'sɛnt/. Some words also have a stress on another syllable that is less strong than the main stress. We call this *secondary stress*, and the sign /ˌ/ is placed before such a syllable: **personality** /ˌpɚsə'næləti/, **personify** /pɚ'sanəˌfaɪ/. Secondary stress is not usually shown in the second syllable of a two-syllable word, unless it is necessary to show that the second syllable must not be shortened, as in **starlit** /'starˌlɪt/ compared to **starlet** /'starlɪt/.

Unstressed vowels

/ə/ and /ɪ/ Many unstressed syllables in American English are pronounced with a very short unclear vowel. This vowel is shown as /ə/ or /ɪ/; however, there is very little difference between them in normal connected speech. For example, the word *affect* /əˈfɛkt/ and *effect* /ɪˈfɛkt/ usually sound the same. The word *rabbit* is shown as /ˈræbɪt/, but it may also be pronounced /ˈræbət/.

/ə/ and /ʌ/ These sounds are very similar. The symbol /ə/ is used in unstressed syllables, and /ʌ/, which is longer, is used in stressed and secondary stressed syllables. When people speak more quickly, secondary stressed syllables become unstressed so that /ʌ/ may be pronounced as /ə/. For example, *difficult* /ˈdɪfɪˌkʌlt/ and *coconut* /ˈkoʊkəˌnʌt/ may be pronounced as /ˈdɪfɪkəlt/ and /ˈkoʊkənət/. Only the pronunciation with /ʌ/ is shown.

Compound words with a space or hyphen

Many compounds are written with either a space or a hyphen between the parts. When all parts of the compound appear in the dictionary as separate main words, the full pronunciation of the compound is not shown. Only its stress pattern is given. Each syllable is represented by a dot /./, and the stress marks are put before the dots that represent the syllables with stress. For example: **bus stop** /ˈ. ./, **town hall** /ˌ. ˈ./.

Sometimes a compound contains a main word with an ending. If the main word is in the dictionary and the ending is a common one, only a stress pattern is shown. For example: **washing machine** /ˈ.. ˌ.ˌ./. *Washing* is not a main word in the Dictionary, but *wash* is; so only a stress pattern is shown because *-ing* is a common

ending. But if any part is not a main word, the full pronunciation is given: **helter-skelter** /ˌhɛltɚ ˌskɛltɚ/.

Stress shift

A number of compounds may have a shift in stress when they are used before some nouns. For example, the compound **plate glass** would have the pattern /ˌ. ˈ./ when spoken by itself or in a sentence like *The window was made of plate glass*. But the phrase *plate glass window* would usually have the pattern /ˌ.. ˈ../. The mark /◄/ shows this. For example: **plate glass** /ˌ. ˈ.◄/. Stress shift can also happen with some single words: **artificial** /ˌɑrtəˈfɪʃəl◄/, **independent** /ˌɪndɪˈpɛndənt◄/.

Syllabic consonants

The sounds /n/ and /l/ can be *syllabic*. That is, they can themselves form a syllable, especially when they are at the end of a word (and follow particular consonants, especially /t/ and /d/). For example, in **sudden** /ˈsʌdn/ the /n/ is syllabic; there is no vowel between the /d/ and the /n/, so no vowel is shown. In the middle of a word, a hyphen or stress mark after /n/ or /l/ shows that it is syllabic: **botanist** /ˈbɑtⁿnɪst/ and **catalog** /ˈkætlˌɔg/ are three-syllable words.

The sound *r* can be either a consonant, /r/, or a vowel, /ɚ/. When /ɚ/ is followed by an unstressed vowel, it may be pronounced as a sequence of two vowels, /ɚ/ plus the following vowel, or as /ə/ followed by a syllable beginning with /r/. For example, the word *coloring* may be pronounced as /ˈkʌlərɪŋ/ instead of /ˈkʌlərɪŋ/. Only the pronunciation /ˈkʌlərɪŋ/ is shown.

Pronunciation table

Vowels

Symbol	Keyword
i	beat, feed
ɪ	bit, did
eɪ	date, paid
ɛ	bet, bed
æ	bat, bad
ɑ	box, odd, father
ɔ	bought, dog
oʊ	boat, road
ʊ	book, good
u	boot, food, student
ʌ	but, mud, mother
ə	banana, among
ɚ	shirt, murder
aɪ	bite, cry, buy, eye
aʊ	about, how
ɔɪ	voice, boy
ɪr	beer
ɛr	bare
ɑr	bar
ɔr	door
ʊr	tour

/t/	means that /t/ may be dropped
/d/	means that /d/ may be dropped
/ˈ/	shows main stress
/ˌ/	shows secondary stress
/ˏ/	shows stress shift

Consonants

Symbol	Keyword
p	pack, happy
b	back, rubber
t	tie
d	die
k	came, key, quick
g	game, guest
tʃ	church, nature, watch
dʒ	judge, general, major
f	fan, photograph
v	van
θ	thing, breath
ð	then, breathe
s	sip, city, psychology
z	zip, please, goes
ʃ	ship, machine, station, special, discussion
ʒ	measure, vision
h	hot, who
m	men, some
n	sun, know, pneumonia
ŋ	sung, ringing
w	wet, white
l	light, long
r	right, wrong
y	yes, use, music
t̪	butter, bottle
t˥	button

American English Sounds

/t̪/, /t˥/, /t/, /d/, and /nʃ/

/t̪/ The /t/ in *tap* or *sat* is a voiceless sound. Many Americans, however, use a voiced sound like a quick /d/ for the *t* in words like *latter, party,* and *little*. The *t* in these words, shown in this dictionary as /t̪/, sounds like the *d* in *ladder, hardy,* and *middle*. This sound usually occurs between vowels (especially before an unstressed vowel), between *r* and a vowel, or before a syllabic /l/.

/t˥/ This symbol means that many speakers pronounce a *glottal stop* in place of or together with /t/. A glottal stop is the sound in the middle of the expression *uh oh*. For example, in the words **button** /ˈbʌt˥n̩/ and **football** /ˌfʊt˥bɔl/, the *t* does not sound the same as in the word *ton* /tʌn/; it sounds like a short period of silence. The glottal stop usually occurs before a syllabic /n/ or a consonant that begins the next syllable.

/t/ and /d/ These symbols mean that these consonants may be either pronounced or left out. For example, the *t* in **restless** /ˈrɛstlɪs/ and the *d* in **grandfather** /ˈgrænd ˌfɑðɚ/ are usually dropped in normal connected speech, even though it is considered more correct in slow, careful speech to pronounce the *t* and *d* in these words.

/nʃ/ Many speakers pronounce the sequence /nʃ/as/ntʃ/. For example, **attention** /əˈtɛnʃən/, **conscious** /ˈkɑnʃəs/ may also be pronounced as /əˈtɛntʃən/, /ˈkɑntʃəs/. Only the pronunciation with /nʃ/ is shown.

The TOEFL® and TOEIC® tests are widely used to evaluate the English proficiency of people whose native language is not English.

Scores on the TOEFL test are required for purposes of admission by more than 2,400 colleges and universities in the United States and Canada and by institutions in other countries where English is the language of instruction. Government agencies, scholarship programs, and licensing/certification agencies also use TOEFL scores to evaluate English proficiency.

ISBN
0-13-040895-6 (with answer key)
0-13-040902-2 (without answer key)

ISBN
0-201-87791-0

The TOEIC test is taken by more than 1.4 million candidates every year. TOEIC test results are becoming the internationally recognized standard for candidates in all types of business.

The following pages give a step-by-step outline of the TOEIC and TOEFL tests. These pages are taken from two Longman books, which provide extensive practice to prepare fully for the tests.

Contents for TOEFL® and TOEIC®

Overview of the Test

The TOEFL® test is a test to measure the level of English proficiency of nonnative speakers of English. It is required primarily by English-language colleges and universities. Additionally, institutions such as government agencies, businesses, or scholarship programs may require this test. The TOEFL test currently exists in both a paper format and a computer format.

The paper format

The paper format of the TOEFL test has the following sections.

- **Listening Comprehension**: To demonstrate their ability to understand spoken English, examinees must listen to various types of passages on a tape recording and respond to multiple choice questions about the passages.
- **Structure and Written Expression**: To demonstrate their ability to recognize grammatically correct English, examinees must either choose the correct way to complete sentences or find errors in sentences.
- **Reading Comprehension**: To demonstrate their ability to understand written English, examinees must answer multiple choice questions about the ideas and the meanings of words in reading passages.
- **Test of Written English (TWE)**: To demonstrate their ability to produce correct, organized, and meaningful English, examinees must write an essay on a given topic in thirty minutes. The Test of Written English (TWE) is not given with every administration of the paper TOEFL test. The following chart outlines the probable format of a paper TOEFL test. (It should be noted that on certain occasions a longer version of the paper TOEFL test is given.)

The following chart outlines the probable format of a paper TOEFL test:

Listening Comprehension		
	50 questions	35 minutes
Structure and Written Expression		
	40 questions	25 minutes
Reading Comprehension		
	50 questions	55 minutes
Test of Written English (TWE)		
	1 essay question	30 minutes

The computer format

The computer format of the TOEFL test has the following sections.

- **Listening**: To demonstrate their ability to understand spoken English, examinees must first listen to passages on headphones as they see pictures on a computer screen and then answer various types of questions about the passages that they just heard.
- **Structure**: To demonstrate their ability to recognize grammatically correct English, examinees must look at sentences on a computer screen and either choose the correct way to complete the sentences or identify errors in the sentences.
- **Reading**: To demonstrate their ability to understand written English, examinees must read passages on a computer screen and answer various types of questions about the ideas and meanings of words in the passages.
- **Writing**: To demonstrate their ability to produce meaningful, organized, and correct English, examinees must write an essay on a given topic in thirty minutes, either on the computer or by hand.

The following chart outlines the probable format of a computer TOEFL test:

Listening	30–50 questions	40–60 minutes
Structure	20–25 questions	15–20 minutes
Reading	44–60 questions	70–90 minutes
Writing	1 essay question	30 minutes

TOEFL scores

The paper TOEFL test is scored on a scale of 217 to 677 points, while the computer TOEFL test is scored on a scale of 0 to 300 points. There is no passing score on the TOEFL test, but various institutions have their own TOEFL score requirements. You must find out from each institution what TOEFL score is required.

The following chart shows how the scores on the computer TOEFL test and the paper TOEFL test are related:

Paper TOEFL Test	Computer TOEFL Test
677	300
650	280
600	250
550	213
500	173
450	133
400	97
350	63
300	40

riting is scored on a scale of 1 to 6 on both the paper TOEFL test and the computer TOEFL test. However, the score of the writing test is handled differently on the paper test and on the computer test. On the paper test, the writing is not included in the overall TOEFL score. On the computer test, the writing score is included in the overall TOEFL score.

Additional information

Additional information is available in the

TOEFL® Information Bulletin. This bulletin can be ordered free of charge by sending a request to the following address:

TOEFL Services
Educational Testing Service
P.O. Box 6151
Princeton, NJ 08541-6151 USA

Information about the TOEFL test can also be obtained at the TOEFL® website at http://www.toefl.org.

Listening

Listening is tested in the first section on both the paper TOEFL test and the computer TOEFL test. This section consists of a number of different types of listening passages, each followed by one or more questions. The paper and the computer listening sections are **similar** in the following ways:

- *some of the passages*
- *some of the language skills*

The paper and the computer listening sections are **different** in the following ways:

- *some of the passages*
- *some of the language skills*
- *the use of visuals*
- *the number of questions*
- *the amount of time*
- *the control of time between questions*
- *the procedures and strategies*

You will need to determine which version of the TOEFL test you will be taking and will need to prepare accordingly.

Listening on the Paper TOEFL Test

On the paper TOEFL test, the first section is called Listening Comprehension. This section consists of fifty questions (though some tests may be longer). You will listen to recorded

materials and respond to multiple choice questions about the material. You must listen carefully because you will hear the tape one time only and the material on the tape is not written in your test book.

Three types of passages appear in the Listening Comprehension section of the paper TOEFL test:

- *short dialogues*
- *long conversations*
- *long talks*

Short dialogues are found in Part A, long conversations are found in Part B, and long talks are found in Part C.

Short Dialogues on the Paper TOEFL Test

Short dialogues are two-line dialogues between two speakers, each followed by a multiple choice question. You will listen to each short dialogue and question on the tape and then choose the best answer to each question from the four choices in your test book. The thirty short dialogues and thirty questions about them make up Part A of the paper TOEFL test.

Here is an example of a short dialogue from the paper TOEFL test. The dialogue is followed by a multiple choice question that asks about the meaning of an expression used in the dialogue.

Example from the Paper TOEFL Test

On the recording, you hear:

(man)   *This physics course couldn't be any harder.*
(woman)   *I'll say!*
(narrator) *What does the woman mean?*

In your test book, you read:

(A) She has something to say to the man.
(B) She doesn't think the physics course is hard.
(C) She agrees with the man.
(D) She'd like to discuss the physics course.

In the dialogue, when the woman says *I'll say,* she is showing that she *agrees* with what the man just said. Answer (C) is therefore the best answer to this question.

Long Conversations on the Paper

TOEFL Test

Long Conversations are 60–90 second conversations on casual topics between students, each followed by a number of multiple choice questions. You will listen to each long conversation and each of the questions that accompany it on the tape and then choose the best answer to each question from the four choices in your test book. The

two conversations and the seven to nine questions that accompany them make up Part B of the paper TOEFL test.

Look at an example of a long conversation from the paper TOEFL test. This long conversation is accompanied by four multiple choice questions.

Example from the Paper TOEFL Test

On the recording, you hear:

(narrator)	**Questions 1 through 4.** *Listen to a conversation between a professor and a student.*
(man)	*Hello, Professor Denton. Are you free for a moment? Could I have a word with you?*
(woman)	*Come on in, Michael. Of course I have some time. These are my office hours, and this is the right time for you to come and ask questions. Now, how can I help you?*
(man)	*Well, I have a quick question for you about the homework assignment for tomorrow. I thought the assignment was to answer the first three questions at the top of page 67 in the text, but when I looked, there weren't any questions there. I'm confused.*
(woman)	*The assignment was to answer the first three questions at the top of page 76, not 67.*
(man)	*Oh, now I understand. I'm glad I came in to check. Thanks for your help.*
(woman)	*No problem. See you tomorrow.*

After you listen to the long conversation on the tape, you hear the first question and choose the best answer to this multiple choice question from the four answer choices in the test booklet.

---

1. On the recording you hear: *Who is the man?*

    In your test book, you read:
- (A) A professor.
- (B) An office worker.
- (C) Professor Denton's assistant.
- (D) A student.

This question asks you to determine who the man is. Since the man opens the conversation with *Professor Denton* and he asks about the page number of an *assignment for tomorrow,* he is probably a student. The best answer to this question is therefore answer (D).

Twelve seconds after you hear the first question, the second question is played. You must choose the best answer to this multiple choice question from the four answer choices in the test book.

2. On the recording, you hear:

When does the man come to see Professor Denton?

In your test book, you read:

(A) During regular class hours.
(B) Just before class time.
(C) As soon as class is finished.
(D) During office hours.

This question asks about when the man comes to see the professor. The professor says that *these are my office hours,* so the best answer to this question is answer (D).

Twelve seconds after you hear the second question, the third question is played. You must choose the best answer to this multiple choice question from the four answer choices in the test book.

3. On the recording, you hear:

When does the man come to see Professor Denton?

In your test book, you read:

(A) To turn in an assignment.
(B) To ask a question.
(C) To pick up a completed test.
(D) To explain why he did not attend class.

This question asks why the man comes to see the professor. Since the man says *I have a quick question for you,* the best answer to this question is answer (B).

Twelve seconds after you hear the third question, the fourth question is played. You must choose the best answer to this multiple choice question from the four answer choices in the test book.

4. On the recording, you hear:

What incorrect information did the man have?

In your test book, you read:

(A) The date the assignment was due.
(B) The page number of the assignment.
(C) The length of the assignment.
(D) The numbers of the assignment questions.

The fourth question asks what incorrect information the man had. The man thought that the assignment was *on page 67* and *not on page 76,* so he was mistaken about the page number of the assignment. The best answer to this question is therefore answer (B).

Long Talks on the Paper TOEFL Test

Long Talks are 60–90 second talks about school life or on academic subjects, each followed by a number of multiple choice questions. You will listen to each lecture and each of the questions that accompany it on the tape and then choose the best answer to each question from the four choices in your test book. The three lectures and the 11–13 questions that accompany them make up Part C of the paper TOEFL test.

Look at an example of a long talk from the paper TOEFL test. This long talk is accompanied by four multiple choice questions.

Example from the Paper TOEFL Test

On the recording you hear:

(narrator)   **Questions 1 through 4.** *Listen to a talk about the settlement of America.*

(woman)   *The settling of the vast farmlands in central North America was delayed at least partly because of an error by one man. In the early nineteenth century, Lieutenant Zebulon Pike of the U.S. Army was sent out to explore and chart the huge expanses of land in the center of the continent. When he returned from his explorations, he wrote a report in which he erroneously stated that the vast plains in the central part of the continent were desertlike, comparable to the Sahara in Africa. In reality, however, these vast plains contained some of the most fertile farmland in the world. Because of Pike's mistake, the maps of the day depicted the central part of what is today the United States as a vast desert rather than the excellent and available farmland that it was. This mistaken belief about the nature of those lands caused settlers to avoid the central plains for years.*

After you listen to the long conversation on the tape, you hear the first question and choose the best answer to this multiple choice question from the four answer choices in the test booklet.

---

1. On the recording you hear: *What is the topic of this talk?*

     In your test book, you read:
     (A) Zebulon Pike's career.
     (B) A mistake that influenced the settlement of America.
     (C) A report for the army.
     (D) The farmlands.

This question asks about the topic of the talk. The topic of the talk is found in the first sentence of the talk: *The settling of the vast farmlands in central North America was delayed at least partly because of an error by one man.* Therefore, the best answer to the question is (B).

Twelve seconds after you hear the first question, the second question is played. You must choose the best answer to this multiple choice question from the four answer choices in the test book.

---

2. On the recording, you hear: *How did Pike describe the area that he explored?*

     In your test book, you read:
     (A) As a desert.
     (B) As usable for army purposes.
     (C) As located in the Sahara.
     (D) As available for farmland.

The second question is a detail question that asks how Pike described this area. It is stated in the talk that Pike wrote *a report in which he erroneously stated that the vast plains in the central part of the continent were desertlike... .* The best answer to this question is therefore answer (A).

Twelve seconds after you hear the second question, the third question is played. You must choose the best answer to this multiple choice question from the four answer choices in the test book.

3. On the recording, you hear:

   In your test book, you read:

   What was this area really like?

   (A) It was a vast desert.
   (B) It was covered with farms.
   (C) It was excellent farmland.
   (D) It was similar to the Sahara.

The third question is an additional detail question that asks what the area was really like. Because the talk indicates that *in reality these vast plains contained some of the most fertile farmland in the world,* the best answer to this question is (C).

Twelve seconds after you hear the third question, the fourth question is played. You must choose the best answer to this multiple choice question from the four answer choices in the test book.

4. On the recording, you hear:

   In your test book, you read:

   This talk would probably be given in which of the following courses?

   (A) Agricultural Science.
   (B) American History.
   (C) Geology of the United States.
   (D) Military Science.

The fourth question is an inference question. It asks in which course this lecture would probably be given. The word *probably* indicates to you that the question is not answered directly in the talk. You must draw a conclusion from the information in the talk to answer this question. Because this talk refers to *the early nineteenth century* and discusses *the settling of the vast farmlands in central North America,* it would probably be given in an American History course. The best answer to this question is therefore answer (B).

Listening on the Computer TOEFL Test

On the computer TOEFL test, the first section is called the Listening section. This section consists of 30–50 questions. In this section, you will listen to recorded material, look at visual cues, and respond to various types of questions about the material. You must listen carefully because you will hear the recorded material one time only and the recorded material does not appear on the computer screen.

Four types of passages may appear in the Listening section of the computer TOEFL test:

- *short dialogues*
- *casual conversations*
- *academic discussions*
- *academic lectures*

Part A on the computer TOEFL test consists of only short dialogues, while Part B consists of a mixture of casual conversations, academic discussions, and academic lectures. The

Listening section of the computer TOEFL test is computer adaptive. This means that the difficulty of the questions that you see is determined by how well you answer the questions. The section begins with a medium-level question, and the questions that follow will get easier or harder depending on whether or not you answer the questions correctly.

Short Dialogues on the Computer TOEFL Test

Short dialogues consist of two to four-line dialogues between two speakers. Each dialogue is accompanied by a context-setting visual and is followed by one multiple choice question. You will listen to each short dialogue as you see a context-setting visual on the screen. Then you will listen to a question as you see the question and four answer choices on the screen. The 11–17 short dialogues and questions about them make up Part A of the Listening section of the computer TOEFL test.

Example from the Computer TOEFL Test

You see on the computer screen:

You hear:

(woman)   *Do you want to leave now for the concert or wait until later?*

(man)   *Let's leave now. I'd prefer to get there a bit early.*

After the dialogue is complete, the question and answer choices appear on the computer screen as the narrator states the question. This question is a regular multiple choice question that asks what the man means.

You see on the computer screen:

> **Listening**
>
> What does the man mean?
>
> ○ He doesn't want to go to the concert.
> ○ He would prefer to leave later.
> ○ He wants to leave the concert early.
> ○ He wants to go immediately.

You hear:

(narrator)   *WHAT DOES THE MAN MEAN?*

In the dialogue, the man says *let's leave now.* This means that *he wants to go immediately.* The last answer is therefore the best answer to this question.

Casual Conversations on the Computer
TOEFL Test

Casual Conversations consist of five to seven-line conversations on casual topics between students. Each conversation is accompanied by a context-setting visual and is followed by two or three multiple choice questions. You will listen to each casual conversation as you see a context-setting visual on the screen. Then, you will listen to each question as you see the question and the four answer choices on the screen. The two to four conversations and the questions that accompany them are found in Part B on the computer TOEFL test.

Example from the Computer TOEFL Test

You see on the computer screen:

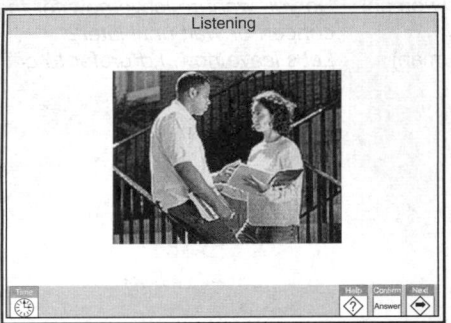

You hear:

(woman) *Look at this syllabus. It's really jam-packed.*

(man) *It lists several chapters per week in the text that we have to get through. Each week, there are two chapters and sometimes three.*

(woman) *And look. Sometimes, there are also supplementary readings in addition to the textbook chapters.*

(man) *I don't know how I'm going to get through all this reading and prepare for the exams, too.*

(woman) *My goodness, there are three unit exams spread throughout the course and then an overall final exam.*

(man) *This course is going to take up an awful lot of my time.*

After the conversation is complete, the first question and answer choices appear on the computer screen as the narrator states the question. This question is a regular multiple choice question that asks about the weekly reading assignments.

You see on the computer screen:

> **Listening**
>
> What are the weekly reading assignments like in this course?
>
> ○ Only textbook chapters
> ○ At least two chapters
> ○ Two or three supplementary readings
> ○ No more than two textbook chapters

You hear:

(narrator) *WHAT ARE THE WEEKLY READING ASSIGNMENTS LIKE IN THIS COURSE?*

The man states in the dialogue that *there are... several chapters per week... two chapters and sometimes three,* and the woman states that *...sometimes there are also supplementary readings.* Because there are *at least two chapters every week,* the second answer is the best answer to this question.

After you have finished with this question, another question and answer choices appear on the computer screen as the narrator states the question. This question asks about the total number of exams.

You see on the computer screen:

> **Listening**
>
> How many total exams are there in this course?
>
> ○ One
> ○ Two
> ○ Three
> ○ Four

You hear:

(narrator) *HOW MANY TOTAL EXAMS ARE THERE IN THIS COURSE?*

The woman states that... *there are three unit exams spread throughout the course and then an overall final exam.* Because there are three unit exams and one overall final exam, the total number of exams is four. The last answer is therefore the best answer to this question.

Academic Discussions on the Computer

TOEFL Test

Academic Discussions consist of 120–150 second discussions on academic topics by two to five speakers. Each discussion is accompanied by a number of context-setting and content visuals and is followed by three to six questions of varying types. You will listen to each academic discussion as you see a series of context-setting and content visuals on the screen. Then you will listen to each question as you see the various types of questions and answers on the screen. The one or two academic discussions and the questions that accompany them are found in Part B on the computer TOEFL test.

A variety of types of questions are possible in this part of the test. Some of these types of questions may follow a discussion:

- a multiple choice question with one correct answer
- a multiple choice question with two correct answers
- a matching question
- an ordering question
- a question with four graphic answer choices
- a question and a graphic with four letters marked

The following example of a discussion shows each of these types of questions. (On the actual computer TOEFL test, you will probably not see all of these types of questions accompanying one discussion.)

Example from the Computer TOEFL Test

You see on the computer screen:

> **Listening**
>
> **History:**
>
> **The Statue of Liberty**

You hear:

(narrator) *LISTEN TO A GROUP OF STUDENTS DISCUSSING INFORMATION FROM A HISTORY CLASS. THE DISCUSSION IS ON THE HISTORY OF THE STATUE OF LIBERTY.*

(man 1) **❶** *First, let's review the historical background of the Statue of Liberty.*

(woman) *Good idea. There's going to be a quiz on Friday, and that's one of the topics on Friday's quiz.*

(man 2) *The Statue of Liberty is on an island in upper New York Bay. What was the name of the island?*

(man 1) *The island used to be known as Bedloe's Island because a man named Isaac Bedloe had owned the island in the seventeenth century. The name was officially changed to Liberty Island in 1956.*

(woman) *In the early nineteenth century, a military fort was built on the island to defend New York against military attack. The fort was named Fort Wood, in honor of military hero Eleazar Wood.*

(man 2) *So the island was named Bedloe's Island, and the fort on the island was named Fort Wood?*

(woman) *Exactly. The fort is a star-shaped construction in the middle of the island. The pedestal of the statue was constructed to rise out of the middle of the star-shaped Fort Wood.* **❷** *You can see this in the picture in our textbook.*

(man) *I believe that the Statue of Liberty was a gift to the American people from the French. The idea for a joint French-American monument to celebrate liberty was proposed, and an organization was established to raise funds and oversee the project.*

(woman) *The statue itself was a gift from the French, but the project was more of a joint French-American project. A total of $400,000 was donated by the French people to build the statue, and the American people raised the funds to build the pedestal on which it stands.*

(man 2) *And it was a French sculptor who designed the statue? Who was he?*

(man 1) *French sculptor Frederic Auguste Bartholdi designed the statue and also oversaw its construction. Did you know that he designed the face of the statue to look like his mother?*

(woman) *No, I didn't. That's interesting. The Statue of Liberty has the face of Bartholdi's mother.*

Listening

(man 1) ❸ *When was the statue constructed?*

(man 2) *Construction on the statue began in 1875 in Paris. Bartholdi had wanted to have the statue completed for the United States' 1876 centennial celebration, but this turned out to be impossible.*

(woman) *But by the time of the centennial celebration in 1876, the right hand and torch had been completed. This part of the statue was sent to the United States for display at centennial celebrations in Philadelphia and New York. Then, at the end of the centennial celebration, this part of the statue was returned to Paris.*

(man 2) *And when did the statue finally get delivered?*

(woman) *The completed statue was not delivered to the United States until eight years later.*

(man 1) *Prior to the arrival of the complete statue in the United States, it was necessary to build a pedestal for the statue. The Americans were responsible for constructing the pedestal the statue stands on.*

(man 2) *What are we supposed to know about the pedestal?*

(man 1) *American architect Richard Hunt designed the pedestal. The pedestal was built in the middle of the star-shaped Fort Wood. Because of financial problems, it was barely ready for the arrival of the French-built statue in 1884.*

(man 2) *So the statue was built in France? How did it get to the United States?*

(woman) *The statue had to be taken apart and packed in hundreds of crates in order to be shipped to the United States.*

(man 1) *Bartholdi's statue arrived in the United States in its packing crates, and it took a year of work to re-assemble the statue on the pedestal that Hunt had designed.*

(woman) *I think we've covered that topic enough. Now let's move on to another topic.*

After the discussion is complete, the first question and answer choices appear on the computer screen as the narrator states the question. This question is a regular multiple choice question that asks what the students are preparing for.

You see on the computer screen:

You hear:

(narrator) *WHAT ARE THE STUDENTS PREPARING FOR?*

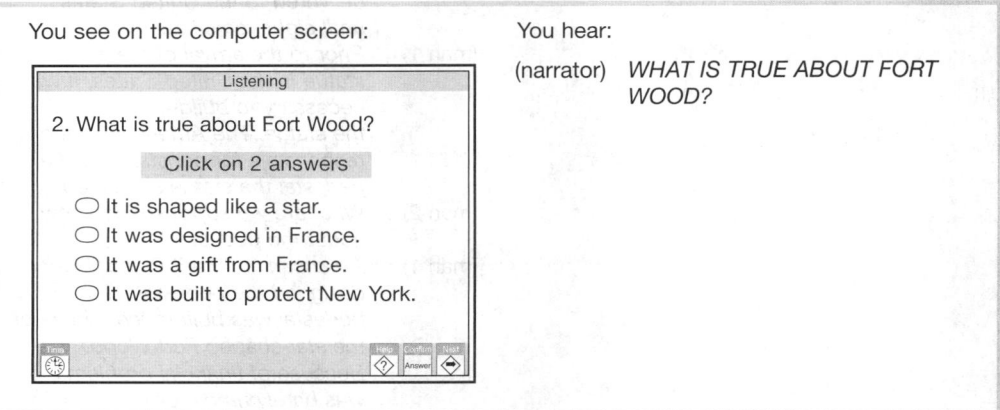

Listening

1. What are the students preparing for?

○ A quiz
○ A class discussion
○ A presentation
○ A final exam

In the discussion, the woman mentions *a quiz on Friday.* You should click on the first answer because the first answer is the best answer to this question.

When you have finished with this question, another question and answer choices appear on the computer screen as the narrator states the question. This question is an example of a multiple choice question with two possible answers.

You see on the computer screen:

You hear:

(narrator) *WHAT IS TRUE ABOUT FORT WOOD?*

Listening

2. What is true about Fort Wood?

Click on 2 answers

○ It is shaped like a star.
○ It was designed in France.
○ It was a gift from France.
○ It was built to protect New York.

In the discussion, the woman says that *the fort was built on the island to defend New York against military attack* and that *the fort is a star shaped construction.* This means that the fort *is shaped like a star* and that it *was built to protect New York.* The first and last answers are therefore the best answers to this question.

After you have finished with the second question, a third question and answer choices appear on the computer screen as the narrator states the question. This question is a matching question about what each person did.

You see on the computer screen:

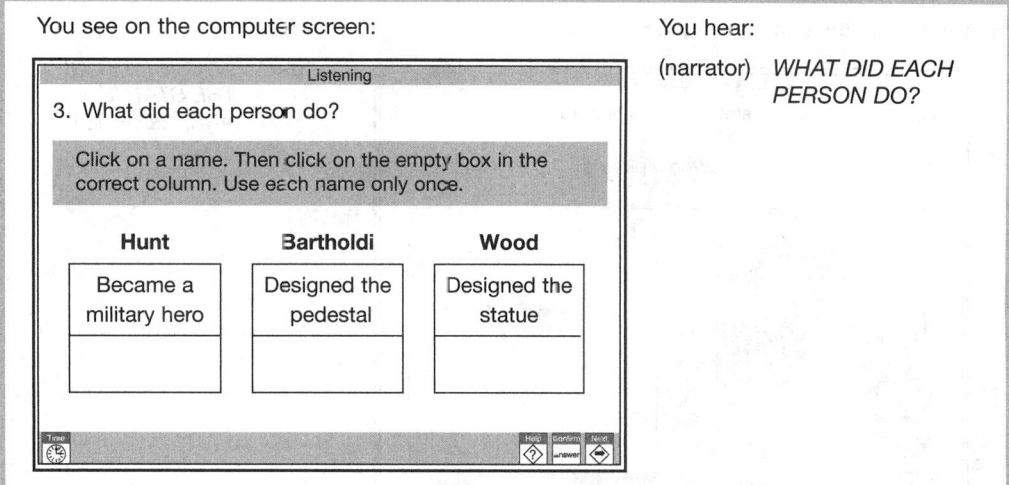

You hear:

(narrator) *WHAT DID EACH PERSON DO?*

In the discussion, the woman mentions *military hero Eleazar Wood,* so Wood became a military hero. The first man mentions that *French sculptor Frederic Auguste Bartholdi designed the statue,* so Bartholdi designed the statue. The first man later mentions that *American architect Richard Hunt designed the pedestal,* so Hunt designed the pedestal.

After you have finished the third question, a fourth question and answer choices appear on the computer screen as the narrator states the question. This question is an ordering question about a historical series of events.

You see on the computer screen:

Listening
4. The professor explains a series of events. Put the events in order.
Click on a sentence. Then click on the space where it belongs. Use each sentence only once.

The American centennial took place.
The construction of the statue was begun.
The statue was completely assembled in New York.
Part of the statue was returned to Paris.

1 [   ]
2 [   ]
3 [   ]
4 [   ]

You hear:

(narrator) *THE PROFESSOR EXPLAINS A SERIES OF EVENTS. PUT THE EVENTS IN ORDER.*

In the passage, it is stated that *construction of the statue began in 1875,* that *the centennial celebration was in 1876,* that *at the end of the celebration this part of the statue was returned to Paris,* that *the arrival of the French-built statue was in 1884,* and that *it took a year of work to reassemble the statue.* From this, it can be determined that first the construction of the statue was begun, then the American centennial took place, then part of the statue was returned to Paris, and finally the statue was completely assembled in New York.

After you have finished the fourth question, a fifth question and answer choices appear on the computer screen as the narrator states the question. This question asks you to click on one of four pictures to indicate which part of the statue arrived first from France.

You see on the computer screen:

You hear:

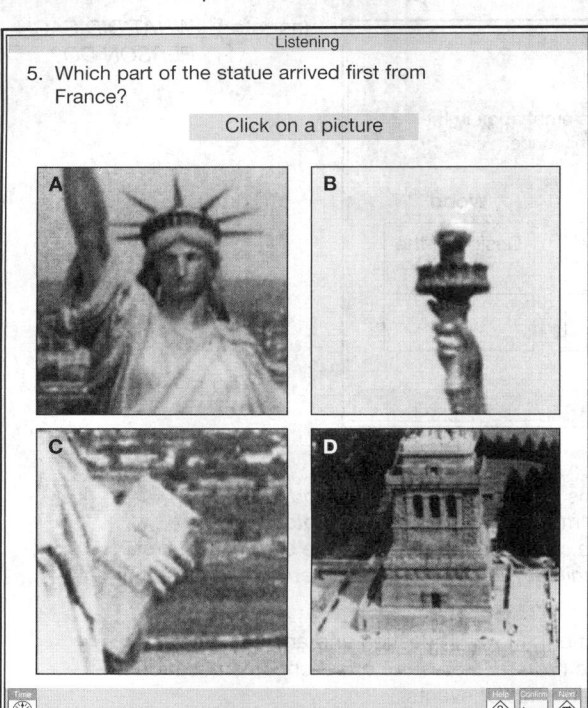

(narrator) *WHICH PART OF THE STATUE ARRIVED FIRST FROM FRANCE?*

In the discussion, the woman says that *by the time of the centennial celebration in 1876, the right hand and torch had been completed* and that *this part of the statue was sent to the United States for display.* From this it can be inferred that the right hand torch arrived first from France. Answer B, which shows the torch, is therefore the best answer to this question.

After you have finished the fifth question, a sixth question and answer choices appear on the computer screen as the narrator states the question. This question asks you to click on one of four letters on a map to identify the island that used to be called Bedloe's.

You see on the computer screen:

You hear:

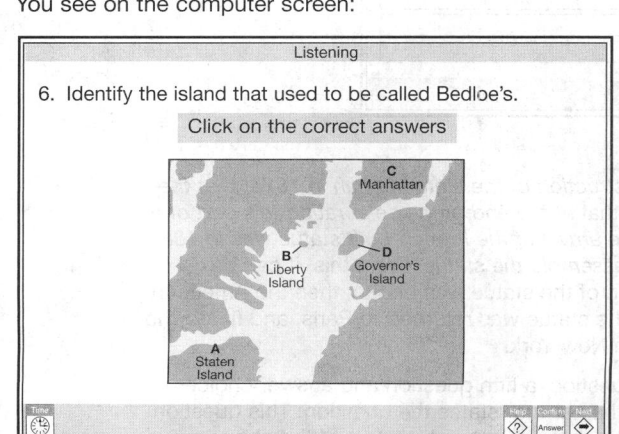

(narrator)   *IDENTIFY THE ISLAND THAT USED TO BE CALLED BEDLOE'S.*

In the discussion, the first man states that *the island used to be known as Bedloe's Island* and that *the name was officially changed to Liberty Island.* From this, it can be determined that Liberty Island used to be called Bedloe's Island. Answer B is therefore the best answer to this question.

Academic Lectures on the Computer

TOEFL Test

Academic Lectures consist of 120–150 second lectures on academic topics by university professors. Each lecture is accompanied by a number of context-setting and content visuals and is followed by three to six questions of varying types. You will listen to each academic lecture as you see a series of context-setting and content visuals on the screen. Then you will listen to each question as you see the various types of questions and answers on the screen. The two to four academic lectures and the questions that accompany them are found in Part B on the computer TOEFL test.

A variety of types of questions are possible in this part of the test. Some of these types of questions may follow a lecture:

- *a multiple choice question with one correct answer*
- *a multiple choice question with two correct answers*
- *a matching question*
- *an ordering question*
- *a question with four graphic answer choices*
- *a question and a graphic with four letters marked*

The following example of a lecture shows each of these types of questions. (On the actual computer TOEFL test, you will probably not see all of these types of questions accompanying one lecture.)

Example from the Computer TOEFL Test

You see on the computer screen:

You hear:

LISTEN TO A LECTURE IN A BIOLOGY CLASS. THE PROFESSOR IS TALKING ABOUT FOOD CHAINS.

❶ *A food chain refers to the process in nature by which animals are fed by other animals and plants. All animals are ultimately dependent on plants for food: some animals eat plants directly, while other animals eat animals that eat plants. In this way, food chains develop.*

Listening

②

SIMPLE FOOD CHAIN
* a producer
* a primary producer
* a secondary producer

A simple food chain consists of one producer, one primary consumer, and one secondary consumer. **②** Look at this diagram of a simple food chain. In such a food chain, a producer is always a plant, and that plant is eaten by a primary consumer, which is a plant-eating animal called a herbivore. The primary consumer is eaten by a secondary consumer, a meat-eating animal called a carnivore. An example of a simple food chain would start with grass, which is eaten by a rabbit, which is then eaten by a fox.

A more complicated food chain can have more than one secondary consumer, or carnivore. In this type of food chain, one meat-eating carnivore devours the plant-eating herbivore, and another meat-eating carnivore devours the first meat-eating carnivore.

Listening

③

③ Look at this example of a more complicated food chain. This example begins with grasses, which are eaten by the plant-eating antelope. At the next stage of the food chain, the antelope is eaten by the carnivorous lion, which then can be devoured by a second carnivore in the food chain, such as a vulture. There cannot be more than one producer in a complicated food chain because one plant does not eat another, and there cannot be more than one primary consumer because one plant-eating animal does not eat another plant-eating animal. However, a food chain can have a number of secondary consumers, carnivores that feast on lower animals in the food chain.

A further complication to some food chains is that one animal can enter the food chain at various stages. This means that one animal can enter a food chain as either a primary consumer, a herbivore, or as a secondary consumer, a carnivore. **④** Now we will look at an example of a food chain in which one of the animals enters the food chain twice. This food chain begins with grasses which can be eaten by the plant-eating rabbit. A baboon can be part of this food chain as either a primary or a secondary consumer. As a primary consumer, it feeds on the grasses, and as a secondary consumer, it feeds on the rabbit. A leopard can also be part of this food chain as a secondary consumer that feeds on the baboon.

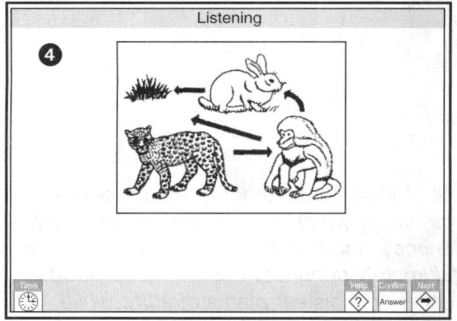

Listening

④

After the discussion is complete, the first question and answer choices appear on the computer screen as the narrator states the question. This question is a regular multiple choice question that asks about a simple food chain.

You see on the computer screen: You hear:

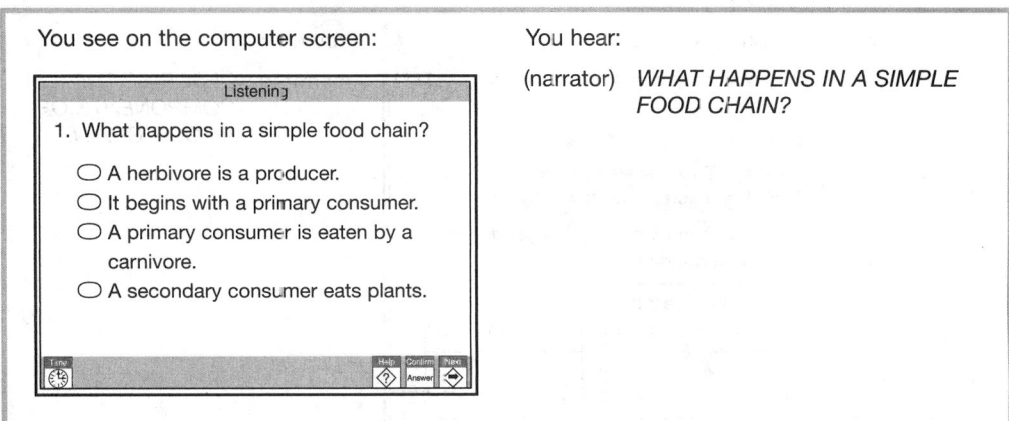

(narrator)   *WHAT HAPPENS IN A SIMPLE FOOD CHAIN?*

In the lecture, the professor states that *the primary consumer is eaten by a secondary consumer, a meat-eating animal called a carnivore*. This means that *a primary consumer is eaten by a carnivore*. The third answer is therefore the best answer to the question.

After you have finished the first question, another question and answer choices appear on the computer screen as the narrator states the question. This question is a multiple choice question with two correct answers.

You see on the computer screen: You hear:

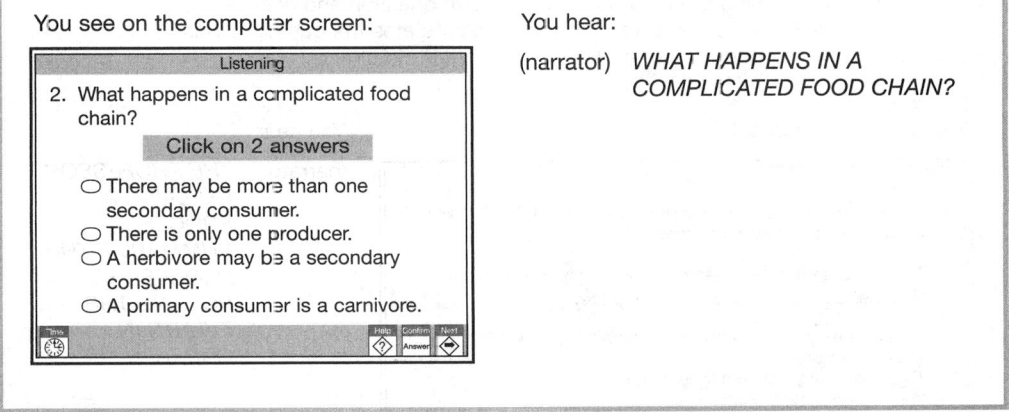

(narrator)   *WHAT HAPPENS IN A COMPLICATED FOOD CHAIN?*

This question asks about a complicated food chain. In the lecture, the professor states that *a more complicated food chain can have more than one secondary consumer* and that *there cannot be more than one producer in a complicated food chain*. This means that *there may be more than one secondary consumer* and that *there is only one producer*. The first and second answers are therefore the best answers to this question.

After you have finished the second question, a third question and answer choices appear on the computer screen as the narrator states the question. This question is a matching question about the components of a food chain.

You see on the computer screen:

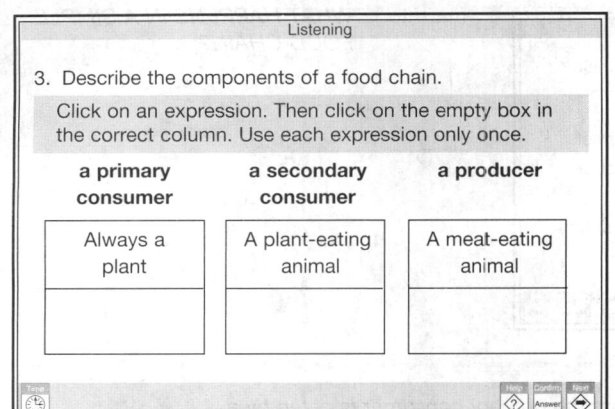

You hear:

(narrator) *DESCRIBE THE COMPONENTS OF A FOOD CHAIN.*

In the lecture, the professor states that *a producer is always a plant..., a primary consumer... is a plant-eating animal...,* and *a secondary consumer is a meat-eating animal. A producer* therefore matches up with *always a plant, a primary consumer* matches up with *a plant-eating animal,* and *a secondary consumer* matches up with *a meat-eating animal.*

After you have finished with the third question, a fourth question and answer choices appear on the computer screen as the narrator states the question. This question is an ordering question about the process of a food chain.

You see on the computer screen:

> **Listening**
>
> 4. The professor explains a process. Summarize the process by putting the events in order.
>
> Click on a sentence. Then click on the space where it belongs. Use each sentence only once.
>
> A carnivore eats a primary consumer.
> A producer grows.
> One secondary consumer eats another.
> A herbivore eats a plant.
>
> 1 _____
> 2 _____
> 3 _____
> 4 _____

You hear:

(narrator) *THE PROFESSOR EXPLAINS A PROCESS. SUMMARIZE THE PROCESS BY PUTTING THE EVENTS IN ORDER.*

In the lecture, the professor states that *a producer is always a plant,* and that a *plant is eaten by a primary consumer, which is a plant-eating animal called a herbivore,* and that *the primary consumer is eaten by a secondary consumer; a meat-eating animal called a carnivore.* The professor later explains that *in a more complicated food chain..., another meat-eating carnivore devours the first meat-eating carnivore.* From this it can be determined that first a producer grows, then a herbivore eats a plant, then a carnivore eats a primary consumer, and finally one secondary consumer eats another.

After you have finished the fourth question, a fifth question and answer choices appear on the computer screen as the narrator states the question. This question asks you to click on one of four pictures to indicate which one could be a herbivore.

You see on the computer screen:

You hear:

(narrator) *WHICH ONE OF THESE IS MOST LIKELY A HERBIVORE?*

In the lecture, the professor states that *a plant-eating animal is called a herbivore.* From this, it can be inferred that the most likely herbivore in the four pictures is the rabbit. The rabbit in answer B is therefore the best answer to this question.

After you have finished the fifth question, the sixth question and answer choices appear on the computer screen as the narrator states the question. This question asks you to click on one of four letters in a diagram to identify the producer.

You see on the computer screen:

You hear:

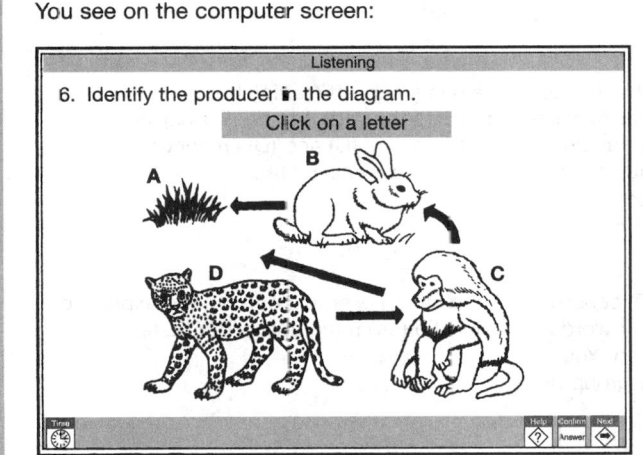

(narrator) *IDENTIFY THE PRODUCER IN THE DIAGRAM.*

In the lecture, the professor states that *a producer is always a plant.* From this, you can determine that the plant in answer A is the producer. Answer A is therefore the best answer to this question.

Structure

Structure is tested in the second section on both the paper TOEFL test and the computer TOEFL test. This section consists of a number of multiple choice questions that test your knowledge of the structure of English sentences and error recognition questions that test your knowledge of correct written expression. The paper and the computer structure sections are **similar** in the following ways:

- *the types of questions*
- *the language skills tested*

The paper and the computer structure sections are **different** in the following ways:

- *the number of questions*
- *the amount of time*
- *the ordering of the questions*
- *the strategies*
- *the scoring*

You will need to determine which version of the TOEFL test (paper or computer) you will be taking and will need to prepare accordingly.

Structure on the Paper TOEFL Test

On the paper TOEFL test, the second section is called Structure and Written Expression. This section consists of forty questions (though some tests may be longer). You have twenty-five minutes to complete the forty questions in this section.

There are two types of questions in the Structure and Written Expression section of the paper TOEFL test:

- *structure questions*
- *written expression questions*

The questions on the paper test are presented in linear order. The fifteen structure questions (1–15) progress from easy to difficult. The twenty-five written expression questions (16-40) also progress from easy to difficult. Your score in this section is based on your answers to these forty questions.

Structure Questions on the Paper TOEFL Test

Structure (questions 1–15) consists of fifteen sentences in which part of each sentence has been replaced with a blank. Each sentence is followed by four answer choices. You must choose the answer that completes the sentence in a grammatically correct way.

Look at an example of a structure question from the paper TOEFL test.

Example from the Paper TOEFL Test

A camel _____ 30 gallons of water in ten minutes.

(A) can drink
(B) it can drink
(C) a large drink of
(D) with a drink of

In this example, you should notice that the sentence has a subject *(camel)* but needs a verb. Answer (A) is the correct answer because it contains the verb *can drink.* Answer (B) is incorrect because it has the extra subject *it,* and answers (C) and (D) are incorrect because they do not have verbs. You should therefore choose answer (A).

Written Expression Questions on the Paper TOEFL Test

Written Expression (questions 16–40) consists of twenty-five sentences in which four words or groups of words have been underlined. You must choose the underlined word or group of words that is not correct.

Look at an example of a written expression question from the paper TOEFL test.

Example from the Computer TOEFL Test

A nerve <u>is</u> <u>actually</u> many nerve <u>fiber</u> <u>bound</u> together.
          A   B   C   D

In this example, you should notice that the plural quantifier *many* is accompanied by the singular noun *fiber*. *Many* should be accompanied by the plural noun *fibers*. You should choose answer (C) because answer (C) is not correct.

Structure on the Computer TOEFL Test

On the computer TOEFL test, the second section is called the Structure section. This section consists of twenty to twenty-five questions. You have fifteen to twenty minutes to complete the questions in this section.

There are two types of questions in the Structure section of the computer TOEFL test:

- structure
- written expression

The Structure section of the computer TOEFL test is computer adaptive. This means that the difficulty of the questions that you see is determined by how well you answer the questions. The section begins with a medium-level question, and the questions that follow will get easier or harder depending on whether or not you answer the questions correctly. Your answers to these questions count as only half of your structure score; the other half of your structure score comes from your answer to the writing question.

Structure Questions on the Computer TOEFL Test

Structure questions consist of sentences in which part of each sentence has been replaced with a blank. Each sentence is followed by four answer choices. You must choose the answer that completes the sentence in a grammatically correct way.

Look at an example of a structure question from the computer TOEFL test.

Example from the Computer TOEFL Test

_____ , a firefighting specialist from Texas, has dealt with numerous major fires worldwide.

○ Red Adair is
○ For Read Adair
○ Red Adair
○ In Red Adair's life

In this example, you should notice that the sentence has a verb *has dealt* but needs a subject. The comma in front of the verb indicates that *specialist* is an appositive and is not the subject. The third answer is the best answer because it contains the subject *Red Adair*. The first answer has an extra verb, and the second and fourth answers contain prepositional phrases, so these answers are incorrect.

Written Expression Questions on the Paper TOEFL Test

Written Expression questions consist of sentences in which four words or groups of words have been underlined. You must choose the underlined word or group of words that is not correct. These two types of questions are intermixed in this section of the test. Look at an example of a written expression question from the computer TOEFL test.

Example from the Computer TOEFL Test

Venus <u>emits</u> very <u>intense</u> radio waves of <u>thermally</u> <u>origin</u>.

In this example, you should notice that the adverb *thermally* is used to describe the noun *origin*. The adjective *thermal* should be used to describe the noun. *Thermally* is the best answer to this question because *thermally* is not correct.

Reading

Reading is tested in the third section on both the paper TOEFL test and the computer TOEFL test. This section consists of reading passages followed by a number of questions. The paper and the computer reading sections are **similar** in the following ways:

- *the types of passages*
- *the language skills tested*
- *the ordering of the questions*

The paper and the computer reading sections are **different** in the following ways:

- *the types of questions*
- *the number of questions*
- *the amount of time*
- *the strategies and procedures*

You will need to determine which version of the TOEFL test (paper or computer) you will be taking and will need to prepare accordingly.

Reading on the Paper TOEFL Test

On the paper TOEFL test, the third section is called Reading Comprehension. This section consists of five passages and fifty questions (although some tests may be longer). You have fifty-five minutes to complete the fifty questions in this section.

There is only one type of question in the Reading Comprehension section of the paper TOEFL test:

- *multiple choice questions*

Now look at a reading passage from the paper TOEFL test, followed by a number of multiple choice questions.

Example from the Paper TOEFL Test

      Obsidian is a distinctive type of igneous rock that forms as a result of the melting of deep crustal granite rocks into magma. Because of the speed at which the magma cools, crystallization does not occur, and a solid, shiny volcanic glass-like rock results. Most commonly a solid shiny black in color, obsidian can also take on a golden or silvery sheen or be striped in a rainbow of hues.

      Obsidian is generally found in small outcrops, though large masses of it can be found in a few notable locations. Two such sites are the giant Valles Caldera in New Mexico, where the obsidian flows are hundreds of feet thick, and the Glass Buttes in Oregon, which are composed entirely of obsidian.

      Because of its properties, obsidian was prized in many ancient cultures. Obsidian is easily worked into shapes with razor sharp edges even sharper than the edges formed from flint and was thus used in the production of simple hunting weapons. It can also be polished to an extremely high luster and was thus held in a high regard in a number of cultures as a semi-precious stone in jewelry and other embellishments.

Line (5) (10) (15)

Look at the first question, which is a multiple choice question that asks about a direct detail from the passage.

1. What is stated in the passage about obsidian?

    (A) It results from rapidly cooling magma.
    (B) It is crystalline.
    (C) It is a sedimentary rock.
    (D) It has a dull finish.

To answer this question, you should find the part of the passage that states that *because of the speed at which the magma cools, crystallization does not occur, and a solid shiny volcanic glass-like rock results.* From this, it can be determined that obsidian *results from rapidly cooling magma,* and that it is not crystalline, that it is a volcanic rather than sedimentary rock, and that it has a shiny finish rather than a dull finish. Answer (A) is therefore the best answer to this question.

Now, look at the second question, which is a multiple choice question that asks about a vocabulary word from the passage.

> 2. The word "sites" in line 8 is closest in meaning to
>
>   (A) pieces
>   (B) layers
>   (C) places
>   (D) distances

To answer this question, you should find the word *sites* in line 8 in the passage and read the context around it. The passage mentions *a few notable locations* and *two such sites.* From this context, you can determine that *sites* is close in meaning to *locations,* or *places.* Answer (C) is therefore the best answer to this question.

Now, look at the third question, which is a multiple choice question that asks you to infer an indirect detail from the passage.

> 3. It can be inferred from the passage that obsidian would least likely have been used to make
>
>   (A) a spear
>   (B) an arrowhead
>   (C) a ring
>   (D) a belt

The passage states that *obsidian was used in the production of weapons* and that *it was held in high regard in a number of cultures as a semi-precious stone in jewelry.* From this, it can be inferred that obsidian would likely have been used to make a *spear* or an *arrowhead,* which are types of weapons, or a *ring,* which is a type of jewelry, and that obsidian, which is a rock, would have been least likely to have been used to make a *belt,* which is an article of clothing. Answer (D) is therefore the best answer to this question.

Now, look at the fourth question, which is a multiple-choice question that asks where in the passage a piece of information can be found.

> 4. Where in the passage does the author discuss the variety of colors in which obsidian is found?
>
>   (A) Lines 1–2
>   (B) Lines 4–6
>   (C) Lines 7–8
>   (D) Lines 15–17

To answer this question, you should skim each of the line numbers in the answer choices for information about the *colors* of obsidian. Lines 4–6 mention that obsidian is *black in color,* that it can *take on a golden or silvery sheen,* and that is can be *striped in a rainbow of hues.* This sentence clearly discusses the *colors* of obsidian, so answer (B) is the best answer to this question.

Reading on the Computer TOEFL Test

On the computer TOEFL test, the third section is called the Reading section. This section consists of four to five passages and forty-four to sixty questions. You have seventy to ninety minutes to complete the questions in this section. There are three types of questions in the Reading section of the computer TOEFL test:

- *multiple choice questions*
- *click-on questions*
- *insertion questions*

The questions in the reading section of the computer test are presented in linear order. The passages progress from easy to difficult, and the questions are presented in the order in which they appear in the passage.

Now, look at an example of a passage from a computer TOEFL test, followed by the various types of questions that appear in the reading section of the computer test. The first question is a multiple choice question about a stated detail from the passage.

Example from the Computer TOEFL Test

Amelia Bloomer (1818–1894) was an important writer and crusader for women's rights in the 19th century. Married to a newspaper editor, she started her own journal, *Lily*, in 1849 to espouse her ideas on rights for women. While she was effective in her work in a number of areas of women's rights, she is best known today for her attempts to improve the style of women's clothing.

Women's fashions in the middle of the 19th century were impractical, uncomfortable, and occasionally unhealthy. The preferred silhouette was a tiny waist flaring out into a wide, wide skirt. This minuscule waist was achieved through corsets; a woman was wrapped in a heavily-boned corset, and the laces of the corset were tightly laced, pulled, and secured to the point where her breathing was inhibited and damage to her ribs was possible. The flared out skirts were created with hoop skirts and petticoats.

Amelia introduced a style of clothing for women that was considerably more practical but also proved quite scandalous. Her outfit consisted of a knee-length tunic with a flared skirt over a very wide-legged pant that was cinched at the ankle. Even though the tunic came down to the knee and the legs were completely hidden beneath the voluminous folds of the pants, society was shocked by an outfit that acknowledged women's legs.

1. It is stated in the passage that Amelia Bloomer

   ○ lived in the 18th century
   ○ kept a private journal
   ○ did not believe in women's suffrage
   ○ tried to effect a change in women's clothing

To answer this question, you should look at the part of the passage at the end of paragraph 1 that mentions Amelia's *attempts to improve the style of women's clothing.* From this, it can be determined that Amelia *tried to effect a change in women's fashions,* so the last answer is the best answer to this question.

After you finish the first question, a second question appears on the computer screen. This question is a click-on-a-sentence question that asks you to find where a specific piece of information can be found in paragraph 1. For this question, you should look at paragraph 1.

Amelia Bloomer (1818–1894) was an important writer and crusader for women's rights in the 19th century. Married to a newspaper editor, she started her own journal, *Lily,* in 1849 to espouse her ideas on rights for women. While she was effective in her work in a number of areas of women's rights, she is best known today for her attempts to improve the style of women's clothing.

2. Click on the sentence in paragraph 1 that indicates what job Amelia's husband held.

To answer this question, you should look at the second sentence of paragraph 1, which states that Amelia was *married to a newspaper editor.* From this, it can be determined that Amelia's husband held the position of newspaper editor. The second sentence of paragraph 1 is therefore the best answer this question.

After you finish the second question, the third question appears on the computer screen. This question is a click-on-a-word question that asks you to find a vocabulary word in paragraph 2 with a similar meaning.

Women's fashions in the middle of the 19th century were impractical, uncomfortable, and occasionally unhealthy. The preferred silhouette was a **tiny** waist flaring out into a wide, wide skirt. This minuscule waist was achieved through corsets; a woman was wrapped in a heavily-boned corset, and the laces of the corset were tightly laced, pulled, and secured to the point where her breathing was inhibited and damage to her ribs was possible. The flared out skirts were created with hoop skirts and petticoats.

3. Look at the word **tiny** in paragraph 2. Click on another word or phrase in paragraph 2 that is close in meaning to **tiny**.

To answer this question, you should see the phrase *a tiny waist* in paragraph 2, and you should notice the context around it. You should notice the phrase in the following sentence that mentions *this minuscule waist.* From this context, you can determine that *minuscule* is close in meaning to *tiny,* so you should click on the word *minuscule* to answer this question.

After you finish the third question, the fourth question appears on the computer screen. This question is an insertion question in which you must add a piece of information to paragraph 2.

Women's fashions in the middle of the 19th century were impractical, uncomfortable, and occasionally unhealthy. **6A** The preferred silhouette was a tiny waist flaring out into a wide, wide skirt. **6B** This minuscule waist was achieved through corsets; a woman was wrapped in a heavily-bored corset, and the laces of the corset were tightly laced, pulled, and secured to the point where her breathing was inhibited and damage to her ribs was possible. **6C** The flared out skirts were created with hoop skirts and petticoats. **6D**

4. The following sentence could be added to paragraph 2.

These petticoats were sometimes stiffened with horsehair to make them hold their shape.

Where would it best fit into that paragraph? Click on the square (■) to add the sentence to the paragraph.

To answer this question, you should study the sentence to be inserted and should look at the context around each of the insertion boxes in paragraph 2. Because the last sentence of the paragraph ends with *petticoats* and the sentence to be inserted begins with *these petticoats,* the sentence should be inserted after the last sentence of the paragraph. Answer **6D** is therefore the best answer to this question.

After you finish the fourth question, the fifth question appears on the computer screen. This question is a click-on-a-paragraph question that asks you to indicate which paragraph discusses a certain topic.

Amelia Bloomer (1818–1894) was an important writer and crusader for women's rights in the 19th century…

....

Women's fashions in the middle of the 19th century were impractical, uncomfortable, and occasionally unhealthy…

....

Amelia introduced a style of clothing for women that was considerably more practical but also proved quite scandalous

....

5. Click on the paragraph that describes the style of clothing that women commonly wore during Amelia's lifetime.

To answer this question, you should look at the question, which asks about the paragraph that describes *the style of clothing that women commonly wore,* and you should look at the first line of each paragraph to see which paragraph discusses this idea. The first sentence of paragraph 2 indicates that paragraph 2 discusses *women's fashions in the middle of the 19th century.* From this, you can determine that paragraph 2 is the best answer to this question.

Writing

Writing sometimes appears on the paper TOEFL test and always appears on the computer TOEFL test. On both forms of the test, writing consists of an essay question which must be answered by the test-taker in thirty minutes. The paper and the computer writing sections are **similar** in the following ways:

- the type of question
- the amount of time
- the way the writing is scored

The paper and the computer writing sections are **different** in the following ways:

- the frequency with which writing is tested
- the place where writing appears on the test
- the method for writing an answer
- the computation of the writing score in the overall score

Writing on the Paper TOEFL Test

On the paper TOEFL test, the writing section is called the Test of Written English (TWE). The TWE is given at the beginning of the TOEFL test, before the Listening Comprehension, Structure and Written Expression, and Reading sections. On the TWE, you are given a specific topic, and you are asked to write an answer to the question. You have thirty minutes to write your answer on a lined sheet of paper.

The TWE only appears on some of the paper TOEFL tests. The dates when the TWE will be given are published in the Bulletin of Information for TOEFL, TWE, and TSE. You should check the bulletin when you apply for the paper TOEFL test to determine whether or not the TWE will be given on the date when you will take the test.

Writing on the Computer TOEFL Test

On the computer TOEFL test, the fourth section is called the Writing section. The Writing section appears every time that the computer TOEFL test is given. In this section, you are given a specific topic, and you are asked to write an answer to the question. You have thirty minutes either to type your answer on the computer or to write your answer on a lined sheet of paper. You should type your answer on the computer only if you are comfortable working on a computer; if you decide to write your answer by hand, then be sure to write neatly.

The Writing Questions

The writing questions on both the paper TOEFL test and the computer TOEFL test ask you to take a position on an issue and support your position. The following are some sample writing questions of the types found on the TOEFL test:

Examples from the Paper TOEFL Test
and the Computer TOEFL Test

1. What is the most important characteristic in a good teacher? Support your response with reasons and examples.

2. Some people prefer to spend a lot of time alone, while other prefer to spend as much time as possible with others. Which type of person are you? Give examples and details to support your response.

3. Do you agree or disagree with the following statement?

    Haste makes waste.

    Use specific examples to support your response.

The Writing Score

The writing score on both the paper TOEFL test and the computer TOEFL test is determined in the same way: the writing is given a score from 1 to 6, where 1 is the lowest score and 6 is the highest score. The following table outlines what each of these scores means:

Writing Scores

6. The writer has very strong organizational, structural, and grammatical skills.

5. The writer has good organizational, structural, and grammatical skills. However, the essay contains some errors.

4. The writer has adequate organizational, structural, and grammatical skills. The essay contains a number of errors.

3. The writer shows evidence of organization, structural, and grammatical skills that still need to be improved.

2. The writer shows a minimal ability to convey ideas in written English.

1. The writer is not capable of conveying ideas in written English.

There is a major difference between the paper and the computer tests in how this writing score of 1 to 6 relates to the overall score. On the paper TOEFL test, the writing score is completely separate from the overall TOEFL score; you will receive a score of 1 to 6 on the TWE, and this will not count as part of the overall score. On the computer TOEFL test, however, the writing score counts as one-half of the score in the Structure section.

About the TOEIC® Test

Overview of the Test

The TOEIC® (Test of English for International Communication) is a multiple-choice test developed by the Educational Testing Service of Princeton, New Jersey, for nonnative speakers of English who use English in nonacademic situations, such as international business, trade, industry, and diplomacy. The TOEIC test measures your listening and reading comprehension by testing your understanding of basic English grammar. The vocabulary of the test attempts to be international and avoids the use of idioms or other culture-based phrases. It does, however, use English in many different contexts.

The TOEIC test consists of a Listening Comprehension section in four parts and a Reading section in three parts.

SECTION	QUESTIONS	TIME
LISTENING COMPREHENSION		45 minutes
Part I	20	
Part II	30	
Part III	30	
Part IV	20	
READING		1 hour 15 minutes
Part V	40	
Part VI	20	
Part VII	40	

Listening Comprehension Section

Part I: Picture

In this part of the test, you will be shown twenty pictures. You will hear four short statements about each picture. You must choose which statement best describes what you see in the picture. These statements will be spoken only once; they will not be repeated. These statements will not be written in your test book.

Example

In your test book, you will see:

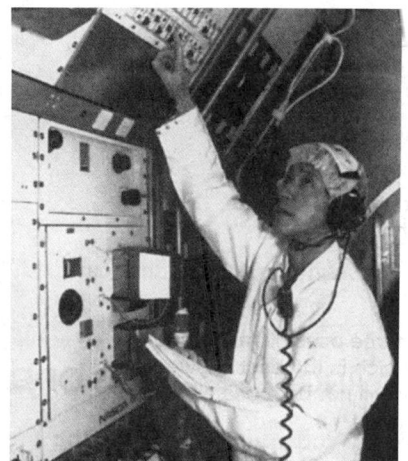

You will hear:

(A) The conductor is raising his baton.
(B) The musician is recording his experiences.
(C) The scientist is signaling for a cab.
(D) The technician is reaching for the controls.

On your answer sheet, you will see:

   (A) (B) (C) (D)

When you listen to the statements, it is important to listen carefully. The statements must match the context of the photograph. Let's analyze the answer choices.

Answer choice (A): *The conductor is raising his baton.*

The person in the photograph could be an orchestra conductor or a train conductor even though the clothing is not appropriate to either profession. The person is raising something, but it is his hand, not a baton.

Do not be confused by one word which is right (*raise*) and miss the whole context of the picture.

Answer choice (B): *The musician is recording his experiences.*

The person in the photograph could be a musician; he is wearing headphones and there is a microphone attached to the headphones. However, the clothes are not the kind musicians might wear. Further, the context of the picture does not look like a recording studio.

Do not be confused by words that can be seen in the photo but are related to other contexts.

The word *experiences* has a similar sound to the word experiments. The person in the photo could be recording (making notes on) some scientific experiment, but that is not what the statement says. The statement tries to confuse you with similar sounding words.

Do not be confused by words that have similar sounds.

Answer choice (C): *The scientist is signaling for a cab.*

The person is wearing protective clothing and the surroundings seem like a scientific laboratory. We can assume that the person might be a scientist.
He is raising his hand, but he is not signaling anything—especially not a taxicab—in this context.

Do not be confused by statements that are partially true.

Answer choice (D): *The technician is reaching for the controls.*

Like a scientist performing experiments, technicians often must wear protective clothing. The instrument panel in front of the technician is covered with control switches. The technician is raising his hand to adjust the controls. Statement (D) most closely describes an aspect of the picture. Therefore, you should mark the oval (D) on your answer sheet.

Strategies

Look at the picture and tell yourself quickly what is represented. Make up a sentence that summarizes what you see. Then listen to the four statements. One of the statements will probably be close to the sentence you made up.

As you listen to the statements, do not be confused by

● words that sound similar to words in the photo
● words that are in the photo but are used out of context
● words that are related to the photo but are not in the photo

Part II: Question–Response

In this part of the test, you will hear twenty questions and three possible answers for each question. You must listen carefully to determine which is the best answer. The questions and answers will be spoken only once; they will not be repeated.

Example

In your test book, you will see:

Mark your answer on your answer sheet.

On your answer sheet, you will see:

You will hear:

What time will he arrive?

You will also hear:

(A) *My mother will be late.*
(B) *About ten o'clock.*
(C) *My watch needs repairing.*

You must listen to every word in the question and three answer choices very carefully. Let's analyze the answer choices.

Answer choice (A): *My mother will be late.*

In this answer choice, the tense *will be* is correct and the time marker *late* is appropriate. However, *my mother* is not a good match for the masculine pronoun *he*. You must listen carefully to catch the difference between *she* and *he*. They are similar sounds.

Be careful of similar sounding words.

Answer choice (B): *About ten o'clock.*

Our question *What time will he arrive?* suggests that our answer will be a time marker (*yesterday, at five o'clock, soon, next year,* etc.). We must decide next if the tense is past, present, or future. In this instance, the question is in the future tense. What will happen in the future? Someone will *arrive.* Who will arrive? *He.* The answer choice contains everything you need to answer the question: one simple time marker. Answer choice (B) most closely answers the question. Therefore, you should mark the oval (B) on your answer sheet.

Answer choice (C): *My watch needs repairing.*

If you heard only the word *time* in the question, you may have assumed that the question was *What time is it?* Consequently, any choice with a time marker might work. The answer choice tries to get you to make a semantic association between time and watch.

Be careful of similar sounding words.

Strategies

Look at the question and determine what kind of question it is. There are two types of questions: a *yes/no* question and a *wh* question. If the question begins with an auxiliary (*will, is, are, can, would, do, did, does*), the answer will probably be a *yes* or *no* statement. Answers may not always begin with *yes* or *no*; sometimes the *yes* or *no* is assumed. But if the question begins with a *wh* word (*who, what, when, where, why, how*) the answer will provide information.

Part III: Short Conversations

In this part of the test, you will hear thirty short conversations between two people. A question about each conversation and four answer choices are written in your test book.

Example

You will hear:

Man: *Would you keep this for me until I get back?*
Woman: *I'm leaving in half an hour, so be fast.*
Man: *It's 4 now. I'll be back in 10 minutes.*

In your test book, you will see:

What time will the woman leave?

(A) 4:00.
(B) 4:10.
(C) 4:30.
(D) 10:00.

On your answer sheet, you will see:

   Ⓓ

Let's analyze the answer choices.

Answer choice (A): *4:00.*

The man says that it is *4:00* now. But that is not when the woman is leaving.

Pay attention to the context.

Answer choice (B): *4:10.*

The man will return at *4:10*, but the woman will leave at 4:30.

Pay attention to the context.

Answer choice (C): *4:30.*

This particular conversation example requires not only that you listen for facts, but that you do a small calculation to arrive at the correct answer. The woman says she is leaving in half an hour and the man tells her it is 4 o'clock. Consequently, the woman is leaving at 4:30. Answer choice (C) most closely answers the question. Therefore, you should mark the oval (C) on your answer sheet.

Answer choice (D): *10:00.*

The number *10* refers to minutes, not the hour.

Be careful of semantic associations.

Strategies

The strategies for Part III are identical to those for Parts I and II. You must listen to the conversation carefully to answer the question.

The conversation could be on any topic. If you can predict the topic before you hear the conversation, it will help you understand the details of the conversation. Reading the question in the textbook before you hear the conversation will help you predict the topic.

In the question *What time will the woman leave?* the key words are *time*, *woman*, and *will leave*. When you listen to the conversation, you should listen for references to a *woman leaving in the future*. You should also listen for the numbers you see in the answer choices: 4 (*4 hours, 4 o'clock*); 30 (*4:30, half past 4, 30 minutes from now, in 30 minutes*); and 10 (*in 10 minutes, 10 past 4, 4:10, etc.*). By listening for the key words (*time, woman, will leave*) and some of the numbers (*4,10*), you will be able to focus your listening.

Part IV: Short Talks

In this part of the test, you will hear forty short talks: an announcement, a talk about a meeting, a weather report, etc. Questions about each talk and the four answer choices are written in the test book. There will be two to four questions about each talk.

Example

You will hear:

All eastbound trains will be delayed until further notice because of flooding on the tracks west of the city. Commuters are urged not to use the trains this morning. Extra buses will be in service shortly.

In your test book, you will see:

What is the problem?

(A) There are not enough buses.
(B) Committees won't use public transportation.
(C) The trains only run east.
(D) The train tracks are covered with water.

On your answer sheet, you will see:

Let's analyze the answer choices.

Answer choice (A): *There are not enough buses.*

The problem concerns trains, not buses. Buses are on the way to rescue stranded commuters.

Pay attention to the context.

Answer choice (B): *Committees won't use public transportation.*

Commuter trains are public transportation, but the talk does not mention committees. Committee does sound similar to commuters.

Be careful of similar sounds.

Answer choice (C): *The trains only run east.*

The trains probably run both east and west (*eastbound trains* and *tracks west of the city*), but whether they do or do not is not the problem.

Pay attention to the context.

Answer choice (D): *The train tracks are covered with water.*

Tracks that are covered with water are *flooded tracks*. Answer choice (D) most closely answers the question. Therefore, you should mark the oval (D) on your answer sheet.

Strategies

The strategies for listening to a short talk are very similar to the strategies for listening to a conversation. You must first focus your attention by reading the questions and the answer choices.

In the example on the preceding page the question indicates there is a problem, and the answer choices suggest the problem is concerned with transportation (key words: *buses, public transportation, trains, east, tracks*). Other key words imply a potential problem (*not enough, won't use, only run east, covered with water*).

⊔u should try to identify the problem that concerns transportation when you hear this short talk. There will be two or more questions about the talk, so you should use the two or three questions that follow in your test booklet to help you make predictions about the talk.

Reading Section

Part V: Incomplete Sentences

This part tests your ability to select a word or phrase that will best complete the sentence. There are forty incomplete sentences in this part. Your knowledge of vocabulary as well as your knowledge of grammar are measured. You must know the appropriate grammar rules and also be able to understand the context of the sentence in order to select the correct answer.

Example

In your test book, you will see:

The _____ dignitaries were shown the plant.

(A) visitors
(B) visitation
(C) visit
(D) visiting

On your answer sheet, you will see:

Ⓐ Ⓑ Ⓒ Ⓓ

Let's analyze the answer choices.

Answer choice (A): *visitors*

Visitors is a plural noun. An adjective is needed between *the* and *dignitaries*.

Answer choice (B): *visitation*

Visitation is a noun.

Answer choice (C): *visit*

Visit could be a noun or a verb.

Answer choice (D): *visiting*

Visiting is the participle form of the verb *visit* and is used here as an adjective. Answer choice (D) is the most appropriate word. Therefore, you should mark the oval (D) on your answer sheet.

Strategies

You can best prepare yourself for this part of the test by analyzing the *Incorrect* sentences. You should pay close attention to what might cause a potential error:

● An incorrect two-word verb is used (turn *in/on/off/down/up*).
  INCORRECT   [Turn *in* the volume.]
  CORRECT   Turn *down* the volume.

● An incorrect form or tense follows a causative verb.
  INCORRECT   [We made *it to happen*.]
  CORRECT   We made *it happen*.